RECORD COLLECTOR

RARE RECORD PRICE GUIDE 2008

PUBLISHED BY
RECORD COL
THE WORLD'S LI
COLLECTORS OF ~~RABILIA~~

EDITOR
Ian Shirley

EDITOR IN CHIEF
Alan Lewis

ADDITIONAL RESEARCH
Jake Kennedy
Jason Draper
Tim Jones

DESIGNER
Ian Gray

PRODUCTION MANAGER
Val Cutts

PRODUCTION ASSISTANT
Simon Oliver

PUBLISHER
Andy McDuff

Published in the United Kingdom 2006 by
Diamond Publishing Ltd. Room 101, 140 Wales Farm Road, London W3 6UG

Founded by Sean O'Mahony in 1987.

Printed in England ISBN No. 0 9532601 5 1

CONTENTS

THE ULTIMATE COLLECTOR'S GUIDE

Welcome to the eighth edition of the *Rare Record Price Guide*, the largest and most comprehensive book of its kind. Like its predecessors, this volume has been compiled by the expert research team of *Record Collector*, the world's leading magazine in the field.

The goal of this book is simple: to list and value every collectable pop and rock record issued in the UK since 1950. As regular readers will already know, the *Rare Record Price Guide* doesn't just include vinyl singles, EPs and LPs, although they are still very heavily featured. It also provides information about every other way in which recorded music has been sold to the public over the last 50 years or more, from the brittle 78rpm shellac singles of the 1950s, to the latest permutations of digital sound on compact discs and beyond. The only format we don't cover is digital downloads!

Musically, the coverage is equally diverse and thorough. Although the majority of items listed in this book could be at least vaguely described as 'rock' or 'pop', every aspect of music-making outside the specialist classical field is featured in these pages. For over 30 years, record collecting itself has expanded enormously, both in terms of the number of people taking part and the types of music that they are interested in.

Rest assured that no matter how obscure your tastes, you'll find the most sought-after items here — whether your particular obsession is 50s rockabilly, 60s MOR, 70s jazz-funk, 80s post-punk, hip-hop, reggae, Northern soul, British jazz or today's indie bands. If it's collectable, and it was released in the UK, then you'll find it in the *Rare Record Price Guide*.

WHO SAYS HOW MUCH IT'S WORTH?

The question we're always asked about the prices listed in this book is how we calculate them. The answer is a mix of our 27 years of experience in the field; our ongoing research into the latest prices at record fairs and shops, and in sales both via mail order and online; and the invaluable help of a dedicated and extremely knowledgeable team of consultants and experts, who themselves regularly buy and sell items in their specialist areas.

THE ROLLING STONES

4

As we always say, however, there is no *fixed* price for a second-hand record, no matter how rare it is. There are still bargains to be found out there, while in other situations — like a feverishly competitive online auction — particularly sought-after items can fetch prices way above their 'book' value. The price of a rare record is purely determined by what people are prepared to pay for it.

That said, our close scrutiny of the collecting market since the start of the 1980s allows us to make the best possible judgement about the records in this book. Prices may vary from one part of the country to another, or depending whether a disc is being sold in a shop, via an advert in *Record Collector*, at a major international fair, or on internet sites like GEMM and eBay. But we believe that the values we list are the most accurate and realistic you'll find anywhere.

The other important point, which can't be repeated often enough, is that anyone selling records to a professional dealer can't expect to raise more than 50% of the prices listed here, except in very unusual cases. It doesn't matter whether you're selling rock'n'roll or jewellery, the same basic mark-up applies right across the collecting field, to cover the dealer's costs and profit margin. If you're selling directly to another collector, however, you can obviously hope to obtain the prices we list — though please remember that all the values in this book are for records in absolutely perfect (or 'Mint') condition. To find out what you should be paying or charging, for a record in less than perfect condition, check the Ready Reckoner printed at the back of this book.

MARC BOLAN

ACROSS THE AGES

Although many of the most valuable items listed in the *Rare Record Price Guide* date back to the 1950s and 1960s, don't be fooled into thinking that record collecting is all about the distant past. As you turn the pages, you'll find plenty of releases from the 21st century as well as the 20th — the latest collectables by major artists, for example, alongside limited edition singles by hot indie bands, and other rarities which were on sale one day and then became fiendishly hard to track down the next.

Check the details of those brand-new collectables, and you'll get some idea which of tomorrow's releases are likely to be sought-after in the future. But there are some things you can't predict — like the identity of the next rock band, rap artist or collectable music pioneer slaving away in his or her bedroom studio who will emerge from obscurity, and become international superstars. It is their first self financed limited edition single or EP released on a small Indie label that will be worth money in the future. Also, don't forget that virtually every record listed in this book, even the one worth several thousand pounds, was once available for a few pounds, or even pence. For all those thousands of releases which have already become collector's items, however, the *Rare Record Price Guide* tells you what they are, what they look like, and how much they're going to cost.

HOW TO USE THE GUIDE

PRICING YOUR RECORDS

Although the *Rare Record Price Guide 2008* contains a comprehensive listing of collectable UK releases, it does NOT list all the recordings made by the artists we've included. More detailed discographies of important artists can be found every month in *Record Collector* magazine.

MINIMUM VALUES FOR INCLUSION

ONLY THOSE RELEASES WHICH ARE CURRENTLY SOLD AT THE MINIMUM VALUES LISTED BELOW HAVE BEEN INCLUDED.
Any other releases obviously sell for less than these prices.

7" SINGLES, MAXI-SINGLES, CASSETTE SINGLES,
    DOUBLE PACKS & FLEXIDISCS...£5
78s £6
10" SINGLES £7
EPs, 12" SINGLES, CASSETTE EPs AND CD SINGLES £8
LPs...£12
DOUBLE-LPs £15
CD ALBUMS £18

NOTE: EPs from the 1950s and 1960s usually sold at around twice the retail price of a 7" single. But most so-called EPs released since 1976 actually retailed at the same price as 7" singles. These records have been included in the Guide if they are worth £5 or more.

CURRENT MINT VALUES

The prices listed in this book are for the original issues of records, cassettes and CDs in MINT condition. Bear in mind that most records which turn up from the 1950s, 60s and even the early 1970s are NOT in Mint condition and their value will be affected accordingly. To find out the value of any item which is in less than Mint condition, consult our Grading System on page 1404 and the Ready Reckoner on page 1505.

ALPHABETICAL ORDER

The artists in this Guide are listed in alphabetical order, from A to Z. After the alphabetical listings, there is a section of Various Artists compilation releases, divided into several sections covering singles and 50s & 60s EPs, 70s, 80s & 90s EPs, LPs, film soundtrack LPs, original cast recordings from theatrical shows and library music.

The alphabetical order within the Guide has been determined by the first letter of a group name or an artist's surname. The word 'The' has not been taken into account when placing artists in alphabetical order; for instance, 'The Beatles' are listed under 'B', rather than 'T'.

The order follows the usual alphabetical principle of 'reading through' an artist's name or title, so that (for example) 'Peter Gabriel' is listed before 'Gabriel's Angels', and 'Generation X' is listed before 'Gen X'. Names and titles which include numbers appear as if the number was spelt out in full; e.g. the band '2.3' are listed as if their name was 'Two.Three'.

6

CHRONOLOGICAL ORDER

Within each artist entry, records are listed in chronological order of release. Singles (including 7", 10", 12", CD, cassette, and double packs) are listed first; then EPs; and finally LPs (including cassette and CD albums).

In the case of long entries, different formats of releases have also been grouped together under separate headers to make them easier to find.

PACKAGING AND INSERTS

All prices refer to records with all their original packaging and inserts (where applicable) intact. Wherever possible, we have provided details of inserts and special items of packaging for each entry — pointing out gatefold sleeves, lyric sheets and other bonus items like posters, for example.

Any record with some or all of these additional items missing will obviously be worth less than the values listed here. The level of depreciation depends on the missing items: in some cases, the value of an album can be dramatically reduced without its collectable insert (as in the case of the Who's *The Who Sell Out* LP, for example), while in others, it is the record itself that is desirable, and the insert is only of secondary importance (as with the Picadilly Line LP, *The Huge World Of Emily Small*).

DOUBLE PRICES: PICTURE SLEEVES

Since 1978, all U.K. 7", 10" and 12" singles have usually been issued in picture sleeves. Before 1978, however, picture covers were definitely the exception rather than the rule.

All those singles which originally appeared in a picture sleeve are listed with the abbreviation '(p/s)'. Where the picture sleeve was only available with the first batch of singles, there are two prices listed: the first refers to the record with its picture sleeve, the second without. If only one price is listed, then the single has to have its picture sleeve intact and in Mint condition to qualify for this value.

Most singles from the 1950s, 1960s and early 1970s were issued in 'company' sleeves, carrying the name and logo of the label which issued the record. Unless a picture sleeve is indicated, the prices listed in this guide are for singles with their company sleeves intact and, like the records themselves, in Mint condition. Most collectors are not too concerned about company sleeves — although in isolated cases (like the cult 60s label Planet), the company sleeves can be harder to find than the records themselves.

Company sleeves don't usually have much effect on a record's value. For example, an original Creation single from 1966, valued at £40, may only be worth £30 without its Planet company sleeve. At the other extreme, no doo-wop collector is going to be bothered if a copy of a rarity like The Penguins' Earth Angel, valued at £1,800+, comes in a plain sleeve, or indeed, no sleeve at all — what matters here is that the record is in Mint condition.

DOUBLE PRICES: FREEBIES & INSERTS

Two prices have been listed for those items which were available in more than one form. 'Freebie' singles given away with newspapers and magazines have two values: the first for the record with the publication, the second for the disc itself. Records which were issued only briefly with an insert, like a poster or lyric sheet, are often priced both with and without the extra packaging.

DOUBLE PRICES: CHANGES IN DESIGN

Two or more prices have been given for records which were released more than once with the same catalogue number, but in slightly different form — with a change of label colour or sleeve design (for instance, the substitution of triangular centres by round centres on late 1950s singles), or the manufacture of more recent singles in a variety of different coloured vinyls.

These variations of packaging and presentation can make an enormous difference to the value of a record, which is why we have documented them here. They help collectors identify the first pressing or edition of each release, which is almost always more sought-after than later issues of the same record. One notable example is the first edition of the Beatles' *Please Please Me* LP, which featured the black-and-gold Parlophone label for a few weeks, before the introduction of the more modern-looking yellow-and-black label. Black-and-gold copies of the stereo version of this LP are worth £2,500, as against £150 for the first yellow-and-black edition issued a few weeks later.

Occasionally, second pressings can be worth more than the originals, as is the case with early Shadows and Cliff Richard singles. Green label copies of these 45s sold in their millions, while later re-pressings on black labels are much scarcer. So always check which pressing of any record you are buying before parting with your money.

MONO AND STEREO

In the case of EPs and LPs from the 1950s and 1960s, mono and stereo releases often have different values — and different catalogue numbers. Both prices are listed, together with the separate catalogue numbers for the two versions of each release (mono first, then stereo). Where the mono and stereo editions are worth the same amount, only one price has been listed.

The last few years have seen a polarisation in the prices between mono and stereo pressings — increasingly so for those late mono releases from 1968 to 1970, when the single-channelled format was being phased out in favour of the twin-tracked stereo. Similarly, early stereo copies should prove to be sound investments.

UK RELEASES AND EXPORT ISSUES

Only U.K. releases are included in the *Rare Record Price Guide*, not overseas issues. The exceptions to this rule are a handful of folk releases and U2 singles, all from the Irish Republic, which were heavily imported into Britain, but not officially issued here. The other exceptions are 'Export Releases'. These were manufactured in the UK in the 1950s and 1960s by companies like EMI and Decca for distribution to countries which didn't have their own pressing plants. Because they were pressed in very small quantities, and then distributed to the furthest corners of the globe, export records by artists like the Beatles and the Rolling Stones are often worth many times the values of similar items pressed for the UK.

UK RELEASES PRESSED OVERSEAS

Although the great majority of the records we've listed were manufactured in the UK, not all UK releases were made in this country — or vice versa. For example, a large proportion of the Rolling Stones' US singles on the London label in the 1960s were actually manufactured in Britain. More recently, many British releases by major labels — notably Warners — have been made in Europe, and sent in identical form to Britain and many other countries. In these cases, the record sleeves often carry many different catalogue numbers, to cater for every country where the records are being distributed.

The problem of identifying the country where a particular record has been issued has grown more difficult with the advent of CDs. In these cases, it is the packaging that helps you identify the origin of a particular CD, rather than the disc itself.

78rpm RELEASES

The common misconception about 78s is that they are more valuable than 7" singles. In fact, the opposite is true in most cases, as far more 78s were sold in the 1950s than 45rpm 7" singles.

The last batches of 78s issued from 1958 to 1960 are the main exception to this rule (see Eddie Cochran's entry, for example). As these were often only available in small quantities (as the public switched to 45s), or even by special order, they can prove to be much harder to find than their 45rpm equivalents.

All these collectable 78s from the 1950s are included in this edition of the *Rare Record Price Guide* although in many cases we have now condensed 78 rpm prices into the entry for the 45rpm release that shares the same catalogue number. So, the 45rpm entry for Chubby Checker's 1959 song The Class/Schooldays, Oh, Schooldays will have (78 rpm = £20) after the song title but before the price.

COMMERCIAL RELEASES, NOT PROMOS

In general, this Guide only includes records which were manufactured for commercial release, or for distribution in some way to the public — as a freebie with a magazine, for example.

Promotional records, demos, acetates and test pressings have not usually been included, apart from exceptional cases where these items actually reached the public, or where (as with artists like the pre-Iron Maiden act, Urchin) one promo single has become so famous among collectors that it would have been misleading for it not to be mentioned. The major exceptions to this rule are artists like the Beatles, and modern artists like The Pet Shop Boys, Kylie Minogue and Madonna whose promos - often with extended hard to find remixes - are sometimes more valuable than their commercial releases and highly sought after by their fans. Also, although we have included some CD-R promo releases in this guide the value of these items usually fluctuate wildly upwards before release and then fall alarmingly once the official album or single is in the shops. Some collectors do want them - especially completists - but we should state that the sale of watermarked and numbered CD-R's is illegal.

Full details of the values of non-commercial rarities like promos, demos, acetates and test pressings can be found in the articles and discographies in *Record Collector* every month.

IMPORTANT NOTE

Ian.shirley@Metropolis.co.uk

THE HISTORY OF THE RARE RECORD PRICE GUIDE

RECORD COLLECTOR MAGAZINE

Record Collector was first published in 1979, and the magazine quickly established itself as the bible of pop and rock history. When the magazine was born, record collecting was a small, rather disorganised business, which wasn't making much effort to encourage new people to get involved.

From the start, *Record Collector* set out to provide the information that collectors needed, whether they'd been buying and selling records for years, or were just starting to build up a collection. There were two vital things they wanted to know: what records had been released by their favourite artists, and how much were they worth?

Every issue of *Record Collector* has provided complete discographies (lists of record releases, complete with full catalogue numbers, release dates and current Mint values) for an amazing variety of performers, from pre-rock stars like Frank Sinatra to the latest chart-bound arrivals and cult indie bands, via every imaginable style and genre along the way. Our in-depth features have provided the essential information to help readers get the most out of their music — by explaining the history of the artists and the records.

THE CHANGING FACE OF THE RARE RECORD PRICE GUIDE

In 1987, we published our first price guide — a slim volume which was designed as a quick and easy reference source to records by around 2000 important artists.

That was only the beginning, though. We soon began work on the first edition of the book you're holding. Published in late 1992, the first *Rare Record Price Guide* filled 960 pages and listed 60,000 rare and collectable records.

The response to that book was tremendous, but we quickly realised that the collecting market was changing so fast that we couldn't rest on our laurels. Every year, thousands of new records reach the shops, in a bewildering variety of formats — everything from 7" singles and cassettes to expensive multi-CD boxed sets.

A small but sizeable proportion of these new releases became instant collector's items. Over the last 20 years, it's been common for record companies to issue special limited editions — anything from a few hundred to a few thousand copies — which sell out in a few days. The most sought-after of these records can triple or quadruple their value within a few months.

At the same time, interest in vinyl from the past continues to grow. As collectors track down all the records they want in a particular genre, they start to broaden their horizons. As a result, obscure items from the 50s, 60s, 70s and 80s become much-wanted treasures on the collectors' market — and their prices rise to reflect the new demand.

That's why we published a second edition, a year later, which grew to 1152 pages, with 70,000 records listed. And this was expanded again for the 1995 edition (over 75,000 entries and 1252 pages) and 1997/98 edition

(85,000 entries and 1440 pages), to take in all the latest collectable release The Millennium Edition ran to 1504 pages; another two years on, the *Rare Record Price Guide 2002* was bigger than ever, the 2004 edition was 1536 pages and the RRPG 2006 1504 pages. Now you're holding the latest edition, covering more than 50 years - and including colour images for the first time.

THE BIRTH OF COLLECTING

When the collecting scene was in its infancy in the 1970s, the market was focused on particular artists or genres. All the early attention was concentrated on 1950s rock'n'roll, and 1960s beat music. In addition, major artists like the Beatles, the Rolling Stones, Elvis Presley and David Bowie began to attract specialist collectors. But the whole collecting scene blossomed during the 1980s and it's now true to say that there aren't any musical styles which *aren't* collectable. Folk, jazz, techno, hip-hop, blues, heavy metal, punk, psychedelia, progressive rock, film soundtracks, soul, funk, reggae, disco, mainstream rock and pop, even classical — each genre boasts its share of in-demand rarities.

LIMITED EDITIONS

In the late 1970s, the arrival of punk spawned scores of new, independent record labels, which had fresh views about the way to market their releases. It became common for singles to appear in picture sleeves, as they had done overseas since the 1960s.

Records also began to appear on coloured vinyl or as picture discs, in an attempt to attract more buyers. Never slow to cash in on a marketing trend, the major record companies soon joined in. By the early 1980s, they were issuing a bewildering variety of editions of the same record in slightly different formats.

This sudden change in marketing techniques helped to trigger an entirely new development on the collecting scene. For the first time, records were becoming instant collector's items. A limited-edition single could be released one week, and sell for twice its retail price a fortnight later.

That opened the floodgates. No longer were 1950s and 1960s records the only things you'd find in the collector's shops. Now, it was open season, for anything and everything from Tubby Hayes to U2.

COMPACT DISCS

The arrival of CDs in the mid-1980s was greeted with doom and gloom in some quarters. But extensive remastering and reissue programs on CD have helped to increase the market for old vinyl releases.

If you grew up in the 1960s, you probably remember that it was difficult to find records that had been hits only a few years earlier. Now, you can go into most record stores and buy compilations and original albums with bonus tracks from every era of music history. For thousands of collectors, however, owning the music on CD isn't enough — and they track down the original releases of music made and released before they were born.

The CD is now well established as a collectable format —particularly for promotional items, limited edition singles, and some original 80's albums which have yet to be remastered. Although under growing pressure from digital downloading, the CD remains the dominant format on which music is released and bought worldwide.

STATE OF THE MARKET

BOB DYLAN

Since the last edition of the *Rare Record Price Guide* there have been seismic changes in the landscape of record collecting. Broadband is now in over nine million homes in the UK and more dealers and record collectors are buying, selling and trading online.

Although we were cautious in the last guide, we believe that this can only be good for long term record collecting. True, we still hear horror stories, with records offered for sale in Mint condition when they are far from it, and items being 'bid up' to fetch a higher price by unscrupulous sellers. But the internet has also connected buyers not only across the UK but internationally. Therefore a Near Mint copy of The Small Faces debut album or a VG copy of Lee 'Scratch' Perry's *Prince In The Black* might attract bids not only from Birmingham, Exeter and Edinburgh but America and Japan as well.

Online bidding has affected prices. It seems that every week a rare UK pressing sells for a new record price. In 2006 an original framed 'golden handshake' A&M copy of the Sex Pistols 7" single *Anarchy In The UK* fetched over £12,000, a copy of XTC's withdrawn Science Friction reached £3,000 while a Tubby Hayes EP on the Tempo label (1955) sold for £165. As with all eBay prices, this does not set the new guide price for these records – far from it – but does demonstrate that at the top end of the market rare records are now seen as investments or vinyl antiques. What's more interesting about sites like eBay, GEMM and Popsike is the other end of the market, where Very Good or Good copies of 7" singles that might have previously sold for £15 or albums that may have sold for £20 can now be snapped up for £5, £12 or even less. This is in large part due to a glut of vinyl coming onto the market as people realise that there is money to be made by clearing out their garages and attics and selling old records online. Of course, the condition of these records varies enormously with many sellers seeing only the 'Mint' price when consulting the RRPG, rather than pricing according to grading. Although we still believe that one of the best ways to buy rare records is face to face from a known specialist, there is no doubt that when it comes to buying and selling, the internet is now an essential tool for both collectors and many established dealers. Internet trading is also helping to solve some Loch Ness vinyl mysteries. It appears that there were no copies of the 1967 Jimi Hendrix album *Are You Experienced* pressed up and released in stereo. If there were, surely one would have turned up for sale on eBay by now? Maybe one will, but until that moment it has been removed from the 2008 edition of the Guide.

As well as online trading, downloading is now part and parcel of the music business. In May 2006 Gnarls Barkley's Crazy single became the first to top the UK charts based on internet download sales alone. New albums ranging from The Flaming Lips *At War With The Mystics* to the Dirty Pretty Things debut *Waterloo To Anywhere*, are not only available on vinyl and CD but sold as downloads as well. This is a double-edged sword for record companies as the format affected most by the broadband download boom is the CD. Sales of CD singles have dropped as more and more people choose to download their favourite chart songs by artists like Madonna and Coldplay. Sales of CD albums are also slowing and high street music retailers face stiff competition as web traders like Amazon, and even supermarkets like Tesco (responsible now for nearly 10 per cent of UK sales), regularly sell new chart albums for as little as £8.99. Thus HMV and Virgin seem to constantly market classic back catalogue albums from £1.99 upwards to clear inventory. Whilst this is good for music fans who can now snap up Iggy Pop's *Raw Power*, Miles Davis' *Kind Of Blue* or Ray Charles' *Live At Newport* for a song, the falling price of CDs has impacted the collectable nature of the CD album as a format.

Whatever the state of CD sales, the use of portable MP3 players has rekindled interest in music. Albums or individual songs are either played on the dominant Apple iPod or a new generation of mobile phones. Listeners download from the internet, import their CD collection - or indeed vinyl collection - hit the shuffle button and listen to songs unfettered by genre and prejudice. Thus as well as the old, a new generation are discovering afresh music by artists as diverse as Jimi Hendrix, The Who, Prince Buster, Bob Marley, The Sex Pistols, James Brown, Peggy Lee and Johnny Cash. Even folk singers like Vashti Bunyan are part of the MP3 playlist. Not only did Bunyan record a new album for the hip Fat Cat label in 2005 but the song Just Another Diamond Day was used in a TV advert for a mobile phone company in 2006. Despite being reissued on CD, her 1970 debut album of the same name remains highly collectable and is now worth £600 in Mint condition.

There has been much debate as to whether the Guide should downgrade its rating system so that the top rated price is for Near Mint or Excellent rather than Mint. We have decided to retain our present rating system because the records listed in this guide are what many serious record collector want to own: which is a Mint copy of a single, EP or album. For anything less than Mint the ready reckoner should be used to determine value. Although established dealers and collectors are aware of our grading system, we would like to stress the importance of correct grading to any new online traders - and charity shop managers - using this book. In mint condition a copy of Bobby Bland's 1961 *Two Steps From The Blues* LP is worth £150, but if the condition is Excellent, then it's £120; and if that falls to Good then it's £75 and so on...

Despite the trend towards increased downloading there continues to be firm interest in collecting music that is both new and old. The sensational rise

ARCTIC MONKEYS

of the Arctic Monkeys has even outstripped that of Franz Ferdinand, and copies of their 2005 limited edition debut EP on vinyl and CD on the Bang Bang label are worth £50 each. Although sales of CD singles has fallen (from 38 million to 20 million) sales of 7" singles has more than doubled in the last two years from 761,000 in 2003 to 1,877,000 in 2005. There is now a distinct trend for artists and record labels to release limited edition 7" singles and then to follow them with a download release. The second single by Folktronica (or is it Nu-Folk?) pioneers Tunng - The Maypole Song - was limited to 100 copies on the Static Caravan label in 2005, and is now worth in excess of £60. Indie bands from Kaiser Chiefs to British Sea Power sell limited edition 7" singles at concerts or through their own official websites and they find a ready market among devoted fans and collectors alike. Record companies also play the vinyl collectors card, with The Raconteurs' debut single being released on a 7" limited to 1000 worldwide and the vinyl edition of Dirty Pretty Things' debut album coming with an exclusive 7" bonus single. So, the vinyl single remains alive, kicking and as collectable as ever!

As for the general market, with 2008 ushering in the 60th anniversary of the vinyl 12" LP, whatever the impact of the internet, blue chip artists continue to command high prices and attract new collectors. UK pressings of The Beatles, The Rolling Stones, Pink Floyd, Sex Pistols, Smiths, U2, Madonna, Pet Shop Boys, Kylie Minogue, Led Zeppelin, Queen and many others attract international interest and command - in most cases - high prices. As for genres, progressive rock, punk, classic rock'n'roll, psychedelia, folk, blues, jazz and soul remain collectable, as do classic labels like Harvest, Island, Blue Horizon, Vertigo, Motown, London and even Factory.

At present, there is huge interest in UK reggae singles. This is not only fuelled by the internet but the fact that UK pressings are - usually - of significantly better quality than their Jamaican counterparts, and thus it's lot easier to identify first pressings and there are complete, numbered label catalogues to collect. Mint copies are fetching - in some cases – very high prices as reggae records have usually seen a lot of action on record decks and may have their centres pressed out or handwriting on labels so that original owners could identify their records after they were played at a house parties in the 60s and 70s. As well as the Island, Blue Beat, Crab, Rio, Punch, Banana, Bamboo, Coxsone, Trojan and Pama labels, late 70s imprints like Adrian Sherwood's Hit Run or the Palmer Brothers Negus Roots have become hugely collectable as, at time of release, very few copies found their way outside the UK. There is also a growing interest in 80s reggae with lovers, UK 'digi-dub' and tunes from the Shaka scene attracting interest. Of course, as with all genres there are bootlegs around as well as official re-presses. For instance there are more Studio One sleeves than there are albums and some re-presses – even today - come in original UK sleeves, for example the Carlton & His Shoes album. So when buying records – of any genre - please make sure to check album and sleeve: something that can only be done face to face with a known dealer rather than an internet trade!

BOB MARLEY

For this edition of the guide we have taken a good hard look at all of the prices. Some have gone up, stayed the same or gone down. Some albums, singles, EPs and even artists have been deleted as their records fall below the entry level for collectables. We have taken market factors into account when pricing but have not followed eBay prices through the roof or into the basement. Also, we have taken the bull by the horns and re-valued rare Northern Soul singles. No doubt some readers will say that some of the prices are too high and others will say that they are not high enough! We have also included new listings for some of the rarest Hip-Hop records issued in the UK as this is an important and growing area of collecting; as is rare Funk. Also, in the wake of his *Chronicles* publication, and with renewed interest in the music of Bob Dylan we have updated his entry and even experimented with the traditional format by listing his collectable singles, EPs and albums by pressing rather than year. Let us know what you think.

We have also added many more collectable records across genres from reggae to folk as well as new and collectable bands and artists who have emerged in the last two years. In addition, there are now four colour sections so that readers can now see some of the UK's more rare and collectable records as well as records that are not worth hundreds of pounds but have cracking sleeves! We have concentrated mainly upon what might be termed the 'classic period' for record collectors of the 50's, 60's and 70's as many of these artists, labels and sleeves are not usually seen on internet web sites. Fans of contemporary collectable bands like Depeche Mode, The Cure, The Pet Shop Boys and U2 should not be aggrieved as there are a vast number of websites that contain full discographies of these bands with many pictures of their rare records.

Finally, with both collectors and members of the public buying and selling records on the internet seven days a week, we feel that the *Rare Record Price Guide* is now more important than ever. Not only does it enable buyers and sellers (old and new) to discover that the guide price for a Mint copy of the highly sought-after demo of Pink Floyd's Arnold Layne in its promo picture sleeve is £1500 but that a copy of Brenda Lee's 1961 single You Can Depend On Me on Brunswick is worth £7!

USING THE GUIDE
A BRIEF SUMMARY

ALL PRICES REFER TO RECORDS AND PACKAGING IN MINT CONDITION

(See pages 1404/1405 for Grading System and Ready Reckoner)

ARTISTS AND GROUPS are listed in alphabetical order.

Numerical names (e.g. 2.3) are listed as if the numbers are spelt in full (i.e. Two.Three).

ALL RECORDS LISTED ARE
U.K. COMMERCIAL RELEASES

with the following exceptions:

(1) Records pressed in the U.K. for export overseas.

(2) Important demo or promo releases.

(3) Records or flexidiscs included as freebies with magazines, books and other records.

In general, promo and demo editions are not included, except when these records contain unique material and/or packaging, or are by major collectable artists.

EACH ENTRY includes:

SINGLES (7" 45s & cassettes) valued at £5 or more

78s and 10" singles valued at £6 or more

EPs, 12" singles & CD singles valued at £8 or more

LPs valued at £12 or more

DOUBLE-LPs valued at £15 or more

CD ALBUMS valued at £18 or more

Records worth less than these prices have not been included.

WITHIN EACH ENTRY, records are listed in chronological

order of release, within each of the following categories (where applicable): 78s, SINGLES, EPs, LPs, CDs, PROMOS. The exceptions are major artists like the Beatles, the Rolling Stones and Elvis Presley, where the entry is further divided into originals, reissues and label variations.

Where TWO PRICES are listed for a single item, they refer to

(a) the record with and without a special insert or piece of packaging

(b) mono and stereo editions of EPs and LPs

(c) versions of the same record with different artwork, vinyl colour, etc.

ACKNOWLEDGEMENTS

CONSULTANTS Kingley Abbot, Keith Bainton, Neil Baylis, Mark Barry (Reckless), Greg Brooks, Nick Brown (Intoxica) Mike Cambridge, Chas Chandler, Jeremy Collingwood, Peter Croxson, Michael De Koningh, Jason Draper, John Esplen, John Fisher, Joe Geesin, Chris Giles (father and son), Kevin Goulding, Paul Green (Sounds Original), Sam Hobden, Dizzy Holmes, Dudley Jaynes, Jake Kennedy, John Manship, Bob Mayhead, Alan McCormick, Joel McIver, Des McMahon, Mark Morris, Richard Morton-Jack, Pete Nash, Pol O' Maoleoin, Alan Ould, Ray Platt, Simon Robinson, Chris Savory, Hans Seegers, Bas Sharp, Barry Smith, Bob Solly, Jonny Trunk, Peter Vickers, Martin Webb, Deke Wheeler, Barry Winton, Eric White (Out Of Time).

THANKS ALSO to Billy Albert, Marc Arscott, Mike Atherton, Ian Bainton, Tony Barton, Paul Bird, Marco Bonacchi, Simon Berkovitch, Jason Crowle, Herve Denoyelle, Ingo Eitelbach, Dave Emlen, Chris Flynn, Oliver Fritsch, Brendan Glover, Andre Helling, Tim Jones, Dave Lewis, Eddie Lock, Billy McLennan, Mike Murphy, Daz Peet, Elle Richardson, Matt Phillips, Eddie Pillar, Debbie Smith, Paul Stevens, J. Walton, Jamie Ward, Martin Webb, Steve Webb.

FINALLY, SPECIAL THANKS to previous editors, contributors and the vast numbers of fanzines, websites and fan clubs whose hard work and expertise has helped - and continues - to make the Guide what it is today.

DEDICATED to the memory of Jack Kane (1965-2005) who edited the three previous volumes of this book.

QUEEN

IMPORTANT TERMS
USED IN THIS GUIDE

acetate	one-off disc cut by hand in a mastering studio, used for demonstration purposes
adaptor	plastic outer disc clipped onto 3" CDs to make them compatible with 5" CD players
art sleeve	pictorial cover using graphics rather than photographs or drawings
artwork	original design for sleeves or labels
audiophile pressing	high quality pressing for hi-fi enthusiasts
blister pack	shaped outer PVC packaging, usually for 3" CDs
bonus disc	disc given away free with another disc
bootleg	illegal pressing of material
box set	records or CDs in presentation case
budget release	pressing which retailed below full-price
catalogue number	manufacturer's reference number on record labels and sleeves
CD-R	one-off CD, digital equivalent of acetate
CD-ROM	audio/visual computer-compatible CD
CD Video	5" CD containing several audio tracks and (usually) one video track; now obsolete
company sleeve	standard non-picture sleeve for singles, printed with name or logo of label
counterfeit	illegal reproduction of official release (a.k.a. pirates)
DAT	digital audio tape
deleted	no longer commercially available
demo	record issued for demonstration purposes; not commercially available
die-cut sleeve	sleeve with circular hole cut in the centre
digipak	gatefold CD sleeve with plastic inner tray
DJ-only	record issued for radio airplay only
double groove	record with two grooves pressed concentrically on same side
double pack	two singles issued together as one package
DVDAC	digital versatile disc Audio
DVD	digital versatile disc
8-track cartridge	1970s tape format, popular for in-car entertainment; now obsolete
EP	extended play disc, with four or more tracks, usually in a picture sleeve
EPK	electronic press kit; i.e. short promo-only documentary available on video
envelope p/s	large mailing-type cover with envelope-style foldover flap
etched disc	one-sided vinyl record with laser-etched graphics (e.g. group's signatures) on other side
export issue	record or CD pressed in the UK for sale exclusively overseas
factory custom pressing	unofficial record pressed after hours (usually on coloured vinyl) at official pressing plant
flexidisc	thin, flexible record, usually issued free with magazine, etc.
flipback sleeve	LP or EP cover glued together with card flaps from the front folded over onto the back
foldaround/foldout/ foldover sleeve	sleeve which opens out as a poster, etc.
freebie	record given away free of charge
gatefold sleeve	double-size sleeve opening out like a book
import	record or CD pressed abroad but sold in the UK
inlay	printed paper booklet with CD packaging
inner sleeve	protective sleeve inside main cover
insert	loose item included as part of a record's packaging, e.g. postcard, poster, lyric sheet, etc.
interview album	spoken word record, often used as promo

jewel case	standard clear plastic case for cassettes and CDs
jukebox centre	plastic centre inserted into record with large centre hole
jukebox issue	record issued exclusively to jukebox franchise holders
laminated sleeve	cover with high-gloss plastic coating
large centre hole	1.5 inch (3.8 cm) hole in singles
long box	tall, rectangular outer card packaging for CDs
LP	long playing vinyl record; standard album format superseded by CDs
matrix number	master tape number, scratched into the 'land' or run-off groove area; sometimes also found on the record label
maxi-single	early 70s term for an EP, featuring more than two tracks, often in a picture sleeve
megamix	medley of different tracks, often linked by dance beats
mid-price release	record which retails at a discount
mispressing	record or CD pressed with incorrect material
mono	one-channelled playback system
numbered (no'd)	individually numbered, limited edition release
obi	sealed paper strip wrapped around sleeve of disc; originated in Japan where obis were printed with Japanese translations of foreign titles
one-sided	vinyl record which plays on one side only
picture disc	novelty record made by sealing a picture within clear vinyl
picture sleeve	pictorial paper or card sleeve, used specifically for one particular record
plain sleeve	single sleeve without special printing or artwork
premium	record available via a special offer with another product — e.g. food or drink
press kit	information pack with photos and biography, used by record companies to promote new releases
private pressing	record issued and distributed by private individuals rather than a company
promo	promotional record or item sent out to the media for publicity purposes
push-out centre	centre of a single connected to the rest of the disc at 3 or 4 points, so it can be pushed out for use on jukeboxes, etc.
quadrophonic	1970s four-channelled playback system, now obsolete
reel-to-reel tape	1960s tape format, superseded by cassette
reissue	re-release of a deleted disc
remix	different version of existing track created by rearranging its component parts
removeable/ replaceable centre	centre which can be removed from a record without damage and later replaced (not to be confused with jukebox or 'spider' centres)
re-pressing	a second run of a record or CD which hasn't been deleted
run-off groove	groove between end of playing surface and record label
sampler	compilation showcasing an artist or label
sealed/shrinkwrapped	machine-wrapped in cellophane
shaped disc	any non-circular record
shellac	brittle material used for 78s
slipcase	small card cover used for some CDs and cassette singles
solid centre	centre of record which cannot be removed, as on LPs
stickered sleeve	sleeve with sticker as an integral part of its packaging
stereo	two-channelled playback system
test pressing	manufacturer's sample record, pressed for quality control
tri-centre	push-out triangular centre on some 1950s singles/EPs
tri-fold	triple fold-out sleeve
uncut picture disc	shaped disc not yet trimmed to proper shape
unissued/unreleased	disc not made commercially available; may or may not have been pressed
vinyl	material from which records are made
warp	buckle in vinyl caused by heat
white label	usually blank, perhaps printed or handwritten labels, often for promo purposes; term also used for demo, promo or test pressing
withdrawn	record deliberately removed from sale by its manufacturer

21

ABBREVIATIONS
USED IN THIS GUIDE

act . . . . actually	mag. . . . . magazine
alt. . . . . alternative	no. . . . . number
b&w . . . . black and white	no'd . . . . numbered
cass. . . . . cassette	p/s. . . . . picture sleeve
cat. no. . . . . catalogue number	pic disc . . . . picture disc
CD . . . . compact disc	pt(s) . . . . part(s)
co. . . . . company	sl. . . . . sleeve
d/pack. . . . . double pack	st. . . . . stereo
dble. . . . . double	stkr . . . . sticker
diff. . . . . different	t/p . . . . test pressing
edn.. . . . . edition	vers. . . . . version
EP. . . . . extended-play record	vol. . . . . volume
ext. . . . . extended	w/ . . . . with
flexi . . . . flexidisc	w/l . . . . white label
g/f(old) . . . . gatefold sleeve	2-CD . . . . double CD
inst. . . . . instrumental	2-LP . . . . double LP
intl. . . . . international	2 x 45 . . . . . two 45rpm singles
LP . . . . . . long-playing record	3-LP. . . . . triple LP
m/s. . . . . mono/stereo	78 . . . . 78rpm single

IMPORTANT RECORD COMPANY ABBREVIATIONS

Amalgam	Amalgamated
B. Banquet	Beggars Banquet
B'full/Brains.	Bucketfull Of Brains
Col	Columbia
Elek	Elektra
Font.	Fontana
L.T.T. Slaughter	Lambs To The Slaughter
M. For Nations.	Music For Nations
MFP	Music For Pleasure
M. Minor	Major Minor
Parl	Parlophone
PSI.	Phil Spector International
Pye Intl.	Pye International
R. Digest	Readers Digest
Regal Zono	Regal Zonophone
R. Stones	Rolling Stones
S'side.	Stateside
St. Tones.	Street Tones
Sweet Folk & C.	Sweet Folk And Country
T. Motown	Tamla Motown
UA.	United Artists
W. Bros	Warner Brothers
WRC	World Record Club

MINT VALUE £

AARDVARK
70	Deram Nova SDN 17	AARDVARK (LP)	80

(see also Home)

A—AUSTR
70	Holy Ground HG 113	A—AUSTR — MUSICS FROM HOLY GROUND (LP, with booklet, 99 only)	250+
89	Magic Mixture MM 1	A—AUSTR (LP, reissue, 425 only)	30
95	Holyground 010101LP	A—AUSTR (LP, second reissue, foldover gatefold sleeve)	20

(see also Bill Nelson)

ABACUS
74	York YR 207	Indian Dancer/Be That Way	6
72	Polydor 2371 215	ABACUS (LP)	45

A BAND CALLED DORIS
(see under Doris)

ABBA
73	Epic EPC 1793	Ring Ring/Rock'N'Roll Band (yellow label)	50
74	Epic EPC 2452	Ring Ring (second version)/Rock'N'Roll Band (yellow label)	5
74	Epic EPC 2848	So Long/I've Been Waiting For You (yellow label)	15
79	Epic EPC 7499	Voulez Vous/Angel Eyes (red or yellow vinyl, p/s)	600
79	Epic EPC 8088	I Have A Dream/Take A Chance On Me (live) (gatefold p/s]	12
80	Epic EPC 12-8835	The Winner Takes It All/Elaine (12", gatefold pop-up p/s)	30
81	Epic EPCA 11-1740	One Of Us/Should I Laugh Or Cry (picture disc)	15
82	Epic EPCA 11-2971	Under Attack/You Owe Me One (picture disc)	30
82	Epic EPCA 2618	GREATEST ORIGINAL HITS (EP)	12
82	Epic EPCA 2618	GREATEST ORIGINAL HITS (EP, cassette)	10
83	Epic A 3894	Thank You For The Music/Our Last Summer (poster p/s)	15
83	Epic WA 3894	Thank You For The Music/Our Last Summer (shaped picture disc)	25
84	Kelloggs KELL 1	I Have A Dream/SHAKIN' STEVENS: Oh Julie ('Rice Krispies' premium)	8
84	Epic ABBA 26	ANNIVERSARY BOXED SET (26 x blue vinyl 7", numbered, 2,000 only)	375
84	Epic ABBA 26	ANNIVERSARY BOXED SET (26 x black vinyl 7")	100
86	Readers Digest (no cat. no.)	The Best Of Abba (flexidisc sampler)	5
93	Polydor 859 085-2	MORE ABBA GOLD (4-track CD, promo only)	50
94	Polydor 853 891-2	DREAM WORLD (CD, 4-track sampler, promo only)	75
99	No label ABBA 1	MAMMA MIA (4-track CD)	15
99	Polydor 563 286-2	ABBA Singles Collection 1974-1982 (29 CD singles in card sleeves & 1-track CD picture disc, with booklet, in silver tin, 20,000 only)	80
74	Epic EPC 80179	WATERLOO (LP, yellow label)	12
75	Epic EPC 80835	ABBA (LP, yellow label)	12
76	Epic EPC 69218	GREATEST HITS (LP, gatefold sleeve, yellow label, some with "Fernando" sticker)	12
78	Epic EPC 86052	THE ALBUM (LP, gatefold with sticker)	12
79	Epic EPC 11-86086	VOULEZ VOUS (LP, picture disc)	50
80	Epic EPC 86123	GRACIAS POR LA MUSICA (LP)	12
80	Epic ABBOX 1	SUPER TROUPER (LP, box set with book & poster)	50
83	Epic ABBOX 11-2/ ABBA-11-10	THE SINGLES — THE FIRST TEN YEARS (2-LP, picture discs, with poster, ticket & booklet in box)	60
83	Epic CDEPC 10022	SUPER TROUPER (CD, original issue)	20
83	Epic CDEPC 10032	THE VISITORS (CD, original issue)	20
84	St. Michael 1361/5704	THE HIT COLLECTION (cassette, with 64-page book *Their Story*, available via Marks & Spencer)	40
86	R. Digest GABA-A-112	THE BEST OF ABBA (5-LP box set)	20
86	R. Digest GABC-C-112	THE BEST OF ABBA (5-cassette box set)	20
99	Polar Music Int. ABBA.INT	THE INTERVIEW ... (CD, 12-page booklet with unique artwork)	20

(see also Hep Stars, Hootenanny Singers, Agnetha Faltskog, Frida, Northern Lights)

BILLY ABBOTT & JEWELS
63	Cameo Parkway P 874	Groovy Baby/Come On And Dance With Me	28

ABERFELDY
04	Fierce Panda RTRAD183	Vegetarian Restaurant/What You Do (ltd 7")	20

A.B.H.
78	Music Bank BECK 694	Geoffrey/Colt 45 Rock (no p/s)	20

SHIRLEY ABICAIR
56	Parlophone MSP 6224	Willie Can/Happy Trails	10
57	Parlophone R 4347	Bimini/Where The Sun Always Shines (with Humphrey Lyttleton)	10
64	Piccadilly 7N 35364	I Will Be There/Am I Losing You	20
66	Pye 7N 17119	Flowers Never Bend With The Rainfall/I Know	6
67	Pye 7N 17389	So Goes Love/Carnival	6
57	Parlophone GEP 8612	FAIR DINKUM (EP)	8

MICK ABRAHAMS (BAND)
71	Chrysalis ILPS 9147	(A MUSICAL EVENING WITH) THE MICK ABRAHAMS BAND (LP, g/fold sleeve)	20
72	Chrysalis CHR 1005	AT LAST (LP, circular foldout sleeve)	35
75	SRT SRTM 73313	HAVE FUN LEARNING THE GUITAR WITH MICK ABRAHAMS (LP, solo, initally with typed insert)	25/16

(see also Blodwyn Pig, Jethro Tull, Mighty Flyers)

ABRASIVE WHEELS
81	Abrasive ABW 1	Army Song/Juvenile/So Low (p/s)	10
82	Riot City RIOT 4	VICIOUS CIRCLE (EP, p/s)	8
82	Riot City RIOT 9	Army Song/Juvenile/So Slow (p/s, reissue, red vinyl)	8
82	Riot City RIOT 16	Burn The Schools/Urban Rebels/Burn 'Em Down (p/s)	8
82	Riot City CITY 001	WHEN THE PUNKS GO MARCHING IN (LP)	25
84	Clay CLAY 9	BLACK LEATHER GIRL (LP)	15

MIKE ABSALOM
60s	Sportsdisc ILP 1081	THE MIGHTY ABSALOM SINGS BATHROOM BLUES (LP)	20
69	Saydisc SDL 162	SAVE THE LAST GHERKIN FOR ME (LP)	75
71	Vertigo 6360 053	MIKE ABSALOM (LP, swirl label, poster sleeve)	125
72	Philips 6308 131	HECTOR AND OTHER PECCADILLOS (LP)	35

ABSOLUTE
85	Reset 7REST 5	TV Glare/At The Third Stroke (p/s)	15
85	Reset 12 REST 5	TV Glare/At The Third Stroke (12", p/s)	25
87	Reset 7REST 8	Can't You See/Love In My Heart (release cancelled)	85

(see also Erasure)

ABSOLUTE ELSEWHERE
76	Warner Bros K 16697	Earthbound/Gold Of The Gods (p/s)	5
76	Warner Bros K 56192	IN SEARCH OF THE ANCIENT GODS (LP, with booklet)	20

(see also Bill Bruford)

ABSOLUTELY FABULOUS
94	Parlophone CDR 6382	Absolutely Fabulous (7" Mix)/(Our Tribe Tongue-In-Cheek Mix)/ Absolutely Dubious/This Wheel's On Fire (CD, card sleeve withdrawn)	15

(see also Pet Shop Boys)

ABYSSINIAN BAPTIST CHOIR
63	Philips 847095 BY	ABYSSINIAN BAPTIST CHOIR (LP)	30

ABYSSINIANS
73	Harry J. HJ 6652	Yim Mas Gan/JOHN CROW GENERATION: Crank Shaft	18
75	Grounation GR 2029	Love Comes And Goes/(Version)	6
76	Tropical S'tracks TST 109	African Race/Satta A Massagana	8
78	Different HAVED 7	Sat A Masagana/I & I (12")	30
79	Different HAVE 18	Declaration Of Rights/African Race	8
77	Different GETL 100	FORWARD ON TO ZION (LP)	30
78	Virgin Front Line FL1019	ARISE (LP, with lyric sheet)	18

ACADEMY
69	Morgan Bluetown BTS 2	Rachel's Dream/Munching The Candy (as Academy featuring Polly Perkins)	20
69	Morgan Bluetown BT 001	POP-LORE ACCORDING TO THE ACADEMY (LP)	120

(see also Polly Perkins)

ACCELERA DECK
90s	Endorphin ENDORLP 0001	NARCOTIC BEATS (2-LP, green vinyl)	20

ACCELERATORS
81	Spiv ACCEL EP	POPGUNS AND GREEN LANTERNS (12" EP)	10

ACCENT
67	Decca F 12679	Red Sky At Night/Wind Of Change	250

(see also Rick Hayward)

ACCENTS
59	Coral Q 72351	Wiggle, Wiggle/Dreamin' And Schemin' (78 rpm = £20)	40

ACCIDENT
84	Flicknife SHARP 016	A CLOCKWORK LEGION (LP)	20

(see also Major Accident)

ACCIDENTS
80	H. Line 'n' Sinker HOOK 1	Blood Spattered With Guitars/Curtains For You (p/s)	25
80	Hook Line 'n' Sinker	KISS ME ON THE APOCALYPSE (LP, unreleased; test pressings only, some supposedly with proof sleeves)	100/50
90's	Detour DRLP04	KISS ME ON THE APOCALYPSE (LP)	15

ACCIDENTS ON THE EAST LANCS.
80	Roach RR 1	The Back End Of Nowhere/Rat Race (p/s)	75
80	Roach SPLIFF 001	We Want It Legalised/Tell Me What You Want (no p/s)	75

ACCOLADE
70	Columbia DB 8688	Natural Day/Prelude To A Dawn	8
70	Columbia SCX 6405	ACCOLADE (LP)	25
72	Regal Zono. SLRZ 1024	ACCOLADE 2 (LP)	35

(see also Gordon Giltrap, Wizz Jones, Pauline Filby, Don Partridge)

ACCURSED
80s	Wrek 'Em ACC 3	Going Down (p/s)	8
83	Wrek 'Em ACC 1	AGGRESSIVE PUNK (LP)	20

AC/DC
76	Atlantic K 10745	It's A Long Way To The Top (If You Wanna Rock'N'Roll)/ Can I Sit Next To You, Girl? (no p/s)	15
76	Atlantic K 10805	Jailbreak/Fling Thing (original issue with running times on label, dark label, heavy print, no p/s)	20
76	Atlantic K 10860	High Voltage/Live Wire (some in p/s)	90/15
77	Atlantic K 10899	Dirty Deeds Done Dirt Cheap/Big Balls/The Jack (maxi-single, 'schoolboy' p/s)	45
77	Atlantic K 11018	Let There Be Rock (edit)/Problem Child (initially with small label lettering & 3.06 timing, no p/s)	10/5

AC/DC

78	Atlantic K 11142	Rock'N'Roll Damnation/Sin City (initially with small label lettering & 3.05 timing, no p/s)	7
78	Atlantic K 11142T	Rock'N'Roll Damnation/Sin City (12", p/s)	20
78	Atlantic K 11207	Whole Lotta Rosie (live)/Hell Ain't A Bad Place To Be (live) (dark labels; later reissued with lighter labels; no p/s)	8/6
78	Atlantic K 11207T	Whole Lotta Rosie (live)/Hell Ain't A Bad Place To Be (live) (12", no p/s)	20
79	Atlantic K 11321	Highway To Hell/If You Want Blood (You've Got It) ('1979' on p/s)	8
79	Atlantic K 11406	Girl's Got Rhythm/Get It Hot (p/s, initially without 'Elephant Head' motif)	12/8
79	Atlantic K 11406E	Girl's Got Rhythm/If You Want Blood (You've Got It)/Hell Ain't A Bad Place To Be (live)/Rock'N'Roll Damnation (EP, gatefold envelope p/s)	10
80	Atlantic K 11435	Touch Too Much/Live Wire (live)/Shot Down In Flames (live) (p/s)	7
80	Atlantic K 11435	Touch Too Much/Live Wire (live)/Shot Down In Flames (live) (p/s, misprinted back-to-front)	10
80	Atlantic K 10805	Jailbreak/Fling Thing (reissue, light label, fine print; initially without 'Elephant Head' motif on p/s)	18/12
80	Atlantic K 11018	Let There Be Rock (edit)/Problem Child (reissue, no p/s, large label lettering)	6
80	Atlantic K 11142	Rock'N'Roll Damnation/Sin City (reissue, initially without 'Elephant Head' motif on p/s)	10
80	Atlantic K 11321	Highway To Hell/If You Want Blood (You've Got It) (reissue, '1980' on p/s)	6
80	Atlantic HM 1	High Voltage/Live Wire (reissue, p/s)	5
80	Atlantic HM 2	Dirty Deeds Done Dirt Cheap/Big Balls/The Jack (reissue, p/s)	5
80	Atlantic HM 3	It's A Long Way To The Top (If You Wanna Rock'N'Roll)/Can I Sit Next To You? (p/s, reissue)	5
80	Atlantic HM 4	Whole Lotta Rosie (live)/Hell Ain't A Bad Place To Be (live) (p/s, reissue)	5
80	Atlantic K 11600	You Shook Me All Night Long/Have A Drink With Me (p/s)	7
80	Atlantic K 11600	You Shook Me All Night Long/Have A Drink With Me (p/s, mispressing, A-side plays "Shake A Leg")	100
80	Atlantic K 11630	Rock'N'Roll Ain't Noise Pollution/Hell's Bells (some with large production credit on p/s)	each 5
80	Atlantic K 11630T	Rock'N'Roll Ain't Noise Pollution/Hell's Bells (12", p/s, with badge)	12/8
82	Atlantic K 11706	Let's Get It Up/Back In Black (live) (p/s)	5
82	Atlantic K 11706T	Let's Get It Up/Back In Black (live)/TNT (12", p/s)	10
82	Atlantic K 11721	For Those About To Rock (We Salute You)/Let There Be Rock (live) (p/s)	5
82	Atlantic K 11721	For Those About To Rock (We Salute You)/Let There Be Rock (live) (p/s, mispressing, B-side actually has 'Gloria' by Laura Branigan)	5
82	Atlantic K 11721T	For Those About To Rock (We Salute You)/Let There Be Rock (ext'd live) (12", p/s)	10
82	Atlantic SAM 143	For Those About To Rock (We Salute You)/C.O.D. (12", p/s, promo only)	65
83	Atlantic A 9774P	Guns For Hire/Landslide (logo-shaped picture disc)	20
84	Atlantic A 9651	Nervous Shakedown/Rock'N'Roll Ain't Noise Pollution (live) (p/s; some with silver labels)	each 5
84	Atlantic A 9651C	Nervous Shakedown/Rock'N'Roll Ain't Noise Pollution (live)/Sin City (live)/This House Is On Fire (live) (cassette)	6
84	Atlantic A 9651P	Nervous Shakedown/Rock'N'Roll Ain't Noise Pollution (live) (shaped picture disc)	20
84	Atlantic A 9651T	Nervous Shakedown/Rock'N'Roll Ain't Noise Pollution (live)/Sin City (live)/This House Is On Fire (live) (12", p/s)	8
85	Atlantic A 9532W	Danger/Back In Business (poster p/s)	5
85	Atlantic A 9532P	Danger/Back In Business (fly-shaped picture disc)	20
86	Atlantic A 9474C	Shake Your Foundations/Stand Up ('calendar' poster p/s)	7
86	Atlantic A 9474P	Shake Your Foundations/Stand Up (Angus-shaped picture disc)	15
86	Atlantic A 9474T	Shake Your Foundations/Stand Up/Jailbreak (live) (12", p/s)	8
86	Atlantic A 9425P	Who Made Who/Guns For Hire (live) (shaped picture disc)	18
86	Atlantic A 9425TW	Who Made Who (remix)/Guns For Hire (live) (12", some with stickered p/s & poster)	15/8
86	Atlantic A 9377P	You Shook Me All Night Long/She's Got Balls (live) (shaped picture disc)	15
88	Atlantic A 9136TP	Heatseeker/Go Zone/Snake Eye (12", picture disc)	12
88	Atlantic A 9136TW	Heatseeker/Go Zone/Snake Eye (12", gatefold p/s)	8
88	Atlantic A 9098TP	That's The Way I Wanna Rock'N'Roll/Kissin' Dynamite/Borrowed Time (12", picture disc)	10
88	Atlantic A 9098CD	That's The Way I Wanna Rock'N'Roll/Kissin' Dynamite/Shoot To Thrill/Whole Lotta Rosie (3" CD with adaptor, 5" case)	10
90	Atco B 8907P	Thunderstruck/Fire Your Guns (10", picture disc)	8
90	Atco SAM 693	Thunderstruck/Mistress For Christmas/Moneytalks/Fire Your Guns (12", red vinyl with insert, promo only)	18
90	Atco B 8886P	Moneytalks/Mistress For Christmas/Borrowed Time (12", picture disc w/ insert)	8
91	Atco 8830X	Are You Ready/Got You By The Balls (numbered p/s, with patch)	5
91	Atco 8830W	Are You Ready/Got You By The Balls (numbered 'satchel' p/s)	5
92	Atco SAM 1089	Highway To Hell (live) (4.57)/Highway To Hell (live) (3.58) (12", with insert, no p/s, promo only)	10
92	Atco SAM 1127	Dirty Deeds Done Cheap (live)/Shoot To Thrill (live) (12", with 2 tracks by Screaming Jets; no p/s, promo only)	12
95	East West 3BALLCD	Hail Caesar/Hard As A Rock/Ballbreaker (CD, no'd hologram p/s, promo only)	25
95	East West A 4368X	Hard As A Rock/Caught With Your Pants Down (yellow vinyl, numbered p/s)	5
76	Atlantic K 50257	HIGH VOLTAGE (LP, 'cartoon' sleeve)	15
77	Atlantic K 50366	LET THERE BE ROCK (LP, with Shorewood Packaging-printed sleeve)	12
77	Atlantic K 50366	LET THERE BE ROCK (LP, mispressing, both sides play Side 1)	200
79	Atlantic K 50628	HIGHWAY TO HELL (LP, test pressing in alternative "live" proof sleeve)	300+
81	Atlantic SAM 155	JAPAN TOUR ' 81 (LP, picture disc, promo only, clear or black rim)	120/100
81	Atlantic 60149	BOX SET (3-LP, including "High Voltage", "Dirty Deeds Done Cheap" & Powerage, promo 7" & poster; export issue)	35
91	Atco WX 364P	THE RAZOR'S EDGE (LP, picture disc with inlay card)	12
95	East West SAM 1693	BALLBREAKERS (CD, promo only compilation)	30

(see also Geordie, A II Z, Home)

ACE

71	Decca F13216	Speed Freak/Ace Of Spades	6

BUDDY ACE
68	Action ACT 4504	Got To Get Myself Together/Darling Depend On Me	20
64	Vocalion VEP 1-70164	BUDDY ACE (EP)	100

CHARLIE ACE
70	High Note HS 051	Creation (Version)/GAYTONES: Creation (Version Three)	15
70	Punch PH 49	Silver And Gold/PHILL PRATT ALLSTARS: Bump And Bore	12
70	Punch PH 53	Book Of Books/WINSTON HARRIS: Musical Dove	12
70	Punch PH 62	Love I Madly/Especially For You (A-side by Charley & Lloyd)	12
70	Punch PH 67	Do Something/MAYTONES: Run Babylon	12
71	G.G. GG 4507	Ontarius Version/G.G. ALL STARS: Ontarius Version 2	10
71	G.G. GG 4518	Do Something/MAYTONES: Groove Me	10
71	Upsetter US 359	The Creeper/UPSETTERS: The Creeper (Version)	18
71	Smash SMA 2325	Need No Whip/Grine Grine	10

(see also Charles, Paulette & Gee, Gaytones, Phil Pratt Allstars, Maytones, G.G. Allstars, Upsetters, Gaby Wilton & Charlie Ace)

JOHNNY ACE
61	Vogue V 9180	Pledging My Love/Anymore	80
61	Vocalion V 9180	Pledging My Love/Anymore (reissue)	25
62	Vogue VE 1-70150	JOHNNY ACE (EP)	100
61	Vocalion VA 160177	THE MEMORIAL ALBUM (LP)	150+

RICHARD ACE (& SOUND DIMENSIONS)
67	Coxsone CS 7031	Don't Let The Sun Catch You Crying/VICEROYS: Magadown	42
67	Studio One SO 2022	I Need You/SOUL VENDORS: Cool Shade	40
69	Studio One SO 2072	More Reggae (with Sound Dimensions)/GLADIATORS: Hello Carol	35
69	Trojan TR 654	Hang 'Em High (with Sound Dimensions)/BLACK & GEORGE: Candy Lady	18
70	Sugar SU 104	Sound Of The Reggae/Got To Build A Wall	10

(see also Viceroys, Soul Vendors, Gladiators, Ken Boothe)

ACEN
92	Production House PNT 042	Trip II the moon (part 1) / Obsessed (12", die-cut p/s)	12
92	Production House PNT 042 R	Trip II the moon (part 2, the darkside) / The life and crimes of a ruffneck (12", die-cut p/s)	12
92	Production House PNT 042 RX	Trip II the moon (part 3, kaleidoscopiklimax) / Obsessed (part 2, pictures of silence) (12", die-cut p/s)	12
92	Production House PNT 034	Close your eyes (XXX mix) / Close your eyes (vitamin 'E' mix) (12")	10

A CERTAIN RATIO
79	Factory FAC 5	All Night Party/The Thin Boys (p/s, 5,000 only, 1,000 with sticker stating "ltd. edition on poor quality vinyl")	10/8
80	Factory FAC 22	Blown Away/Flight/And Then Again (12", p/s, with inner sleeve)	8
81	Factory FAC 52	Waterline/Funaezekea (12", p/s)	8
82	Factory FAC 62-7	Knife Slits Water/Tumba Rumba (p/s)	6
82	Factory FAC 62T	Knife Slits Water/Kether — Hot Knives Mix-In Special (12", p/s)	8
83	Factory FAC 72-7	I Need Someone Tonite (edit)/Don't You Worry 'Bout A Thing (edit) (promo)	8
84	Factory FAC 112P	Life's A Scream (edit)/There's Only This (edit) (promo pack including 7", photo & biography in custom ACR envelope)	10
82	Factory FACT 65	I'D LIKE TO SEE YOU AGAIN (LP)	20
85	private label	A CERTAIN RATIO LIVE IN AMERICA (cassette, sold at gigs)	12

(see also Sir Horatio)

ACES
63	Parlophone R 5094	Wait Until Tomorrow/The Last One	18
64	Parlophone R 5108	I Count The Tears/But Say It Isn't So	15

ACES
81	Etc ETC 01	One Way Street/Why Should It Be Mine (p/s)	20

(see also Menace)

ACHES & PAINS
66	Page One POF 008	There's No Other Like Your Mother/Again And Again	15

ACHILLES & HIS HEELS
61	Fontana H 340	Brigitte Bardot/Acapulco	10

ACHOR
76	Cedar CEDAR 1	END OF MY DAY (LP)	60
78	Dove Tail DOVE 54	HOSANNA TO THE SON OF DAVID (LP)	30

(see also Wine Of Lebanon, Valley Of Achor)

ACID GALLERY
69	CBS 4608	Dance Around The Maypole/Right Toe Blues	80

(see also Christie, Epics, Carl Wayne & Vikings, Roy Wood, Outer Limits)

ACID MOTHERS TEMPLE
00	Staticresonance 2	MONSTER OF THE UNIVERSE (Monster Of The Universe/Wholly Weary Flashback//Surfin' Paris-Texas/Midnight Mountain Dew (EP, 2 x 7", p/s, sold on tour, 500 only)	20
01	Staticresonance 1	ABSOLUTELY FREAKOUT, ZAP YOUR MIND (LP, 1000 only)	20

DAVID ACKLES
68	Elektra EKSN 45039	La Route A Chicago/Down River	7
69	Elektra EKSN 45054	Laissez Faire/Blue Ribbons	7
70	Elektra EKSN 45079	Subway To The Country/That's No Reason To Cry	7
68	Elektra EKL 4022	DAVID ACKLES (LP, orange label, also stereo EKS 74022)	30
70	Elektra EKS 74060	SUBWAY TO THE COUNTRY (LP, orange label)	20
72	Elektra K 42112	AMERICAN GOTHIC (LP)	15
73	CBS 32466	FIVE AND DIME (LP)	15

MINT VALUE £

BARBARA ACKLIN

68	MCA MU 1038	Love Makes A Woman/Come And See Me Baby	12
69	MCA MU 1071	Am I The Same Girl/Be By My Side.	10
69	MCA MU 1102	Love Makes A Woman/Come And See Me Baby (reissue)	8
69	MCA MU 1103	Am I The Same Girl/Be By My Side (reissue).	8
69	MCA MUP(S) 366	LOVE MAKES A WOMAN (LP)	30
71	MCA MUPS 410	SEVEN DAYS OF NIGHT (LP).	30
71	MCA MUPS 416	SOMEBODY ELSE'S ARMS (LP)	30
75	Capitol E-ST 11377	A PLACE IN THE SUN (LP).	15

(see also Gene Chandler & Barbara Acklin)

ACME ATTRACTIONS

80	A Trax KICK 007	Anyway (p/s)	100
81	Orchid OR1	Eve Of Destruction/It's OK (p/s, with Bonnie Parker)	20

SEPH ACRE & PETS

58	Pye International 7N 25001	You Are My Love/Rock And Roll Cha Cha (78 rpm, N 25001 = £10)	15

(see also Pets)

ACT

67	Columbia DB 8179	Cobbled Streets/One Heart	40
67	Columbia DB 8261	Here Come Those Tears Again/Without You	30
68	Columbia DB 8331	Just A Little Bit/The Remedies Of Doctor Brohnicoy	60

ACT

87	ZTT 12 XACT 28	Snobbery And Decay (Naked Civil Remix)/Strong Poison/Theme From Snobbery And Decay (12", gatefold p/s, with poster)	8
87	ZTT CID 28	Emotional Highlights From Snobbery And Decay: Snobbery And Decay (Extended For Stephanie Beecham)/I'd Be Surprisingly Good For You/Poison/(Theme From) Snobbery And Decay (CD, gatefold card sleeve)	20
87	ZTT CT 01	Snobbery And Decay (Moonlighting Mix)/Instant 1/Instant 2 (12" promo, plain black die-cut sleeve)	15
87	ZTT VIMM 1	Absolutely Immune 2/Bloodrush/States Of Logic (12", p/s)	30
88	ZTT CD IMM 2	I Can't Escape From You (Love And Hate)/Heaven Knows I'm Miserable Now/Dear Life/I Can't Escape From You (CD).	15
88	ZTT BET 1	Chance/Winner '88 (p/s, withdrawn)	50
88	ZTT BETT 1	Chance (12 To 1 Mix)/Winner '88/Chance (We Give You Another Chance) (12", p/s, withdrawn)	80+
88	ZTT BETCD 1	Chance (12 To 1 Mix)/Winner '88/Chance (We Give You Another Chance) (CD, existence unconfirmed)	
88	ZTT ZQCD 1	LAUGHTER, TEARS AND RAGE (CD).	30

(see also Propaganda, Claudia Brücken, Glenn Gregory & Claudia Brücken, Thomas Leer)

ACRYLIC TONES

90's Detour DR010	Girl/Theme From.../Rainbow Song (p/s).	6

ACTION

65	Parlophone R 5354	Land Of 1000 Dances/In My Lonely Room	70
66	Parlophone R 5410	I'll Keep On Holding On/Hey Sah-Lo-Ney	75
66	Parlophone R 5474	Baby You've Got It/Since I Lost My Baby	75
67	Parlophone R 5572	Never Ever/Twenty Fourth Hour	75
67	Parlophone R 5610	Shadows And Reflections/Something Has Hit Me.	80
67	Parlophone R 5410	Shadows And Reflections/Something Has Hit Me (p/s for export to Holland)	150
81	Edsel E 5001	I'll Keep On Holding On/Wasn't It You? (p/s)	10
81	Edsel E 5002	Since I Lost My Baby/Never Ever/Wasn't It You (p/s)	10
82	Edsel E 5003	Shadows And Reflections/Something Has Hit Me (p/s)	10
84	Edsel E 5008	Hey Sah-Lo-Ney/Come On, Come With Me (p/s)	10
80	Edsel ED 101	THE ULTIMATE ACTION (LP, with inner sleeve).	20
85	Dojo DOJO LP 3	ACTION SPEAK LOUDER THAN. . . (mini-LP)	20

(see also Boys, Sandra Barry & Boys, Mighty Baby, Reg King, Stone's Masonry)

ACTION PACT

82	Fallout FALL 003	Suicide Bag/Stanwell/Blue Blood (p/s)	10
83	Fallout FALL 010	People/Times Must Change/Sixties Flix (p/s).	10
83	Fallout FALL 019	Question Of Choice/Hook Line & Sinker (p/s)	10
81	Subversive ANARCHO 1	HEATHROW TOUCHDOWN (EP, 1 side by Dead Man's Shadow).	20

ACTION PAINTING

90	Sarah SARAH 028	These Things Happen/Boy Meets World (wraparound p/s, with insert)	10

ACTRESS

69	CBS 4016	It's What You Give/Good Job With Prospects	80

ROY ACUFF & SMOKY MOUNTAIN BOYS

57	Brunswick 05635	I Like Mountain Music/It's Hard To Love (And Not To Be In Love)	15
57	Brunswick 05635	I Like Mountain Music/It's Hard To Love (And Not To Be In Love) (78)	8
65	Capitol T 2276	THE VOICE OF COUNTRY MUSIC (LP)	12
65	Hickory LPM 101	ONCE MORE (LP)	12
65	Hickory LPM 117	HAND CLAPPING GOSPEL SONGS (LP)	12
66	Hickory LPM 125	GREAT TRAIN SONGS (LP)	12
68	London HAB 8361	SINGS FAMOUS OPRY FAVOURITES (LP)	12

ADAM & THE ANTS

78	Decca F 13803	Young Parisians/Lady (some in p/s, original with paper labels).	10/7
79	Do It DUN 8	Xerox/Whip In My Valise (p/s, mispressed b-side 'Physical').	5
81	Lyntone LYN 9285	A.N.T.S. (1-sided blue flexidisc with Flexipop magazine issue 4)	8
82	Do It DUNX 20	Friends/Kick/Physical (picture disc)	5
79	Do It RIDE 3	DIRK WEARS WHITE SOX (LP)	18

(see also Adam Ant, Maneaters, Models)

ADAM, MIKE & TIM
64	Decca F 12040	Little Baby/You're The Reason Why	5
65	Decca F 12112	That's How I Feel/It's All Too True	5
65	Decca F 12221	Little Pictures/Summer's Here Again	5
66	Columbia DB 7836	Flowers On The Wall/Give That Girl A Break	7
66	Columbia DB 7902	A Most Peculiar Man/Wedding Day	7

(see also Mike Sedgewick)

ADAMO
64	Columbia DB 7273	Another Love Affair/Make Tonite Last Forever	5
65	Columbia DB 7329	She Was An Angel/The Stars Will Shine (Vous Permettez Monsiuer)	5

ALICIA ADAMS
61	Capitol CL 15195	Love Bandit/Oom Dooby Doom Lovey Dovey Sh' Boom	15

ARTHUR K. ADAMS
68	Blue Horizon 57-3136	She Drives Me Out Of My Mind/Gimme Some Of Your Lovin'	25

BILLY ADAMS
60	Capitol CL 15107	Count Every Star/Peggy's Party	30

BILLY ADAMS
69	London HL 10258	I Need Your Love/Why Don't You Believe Me	8

CLIFF ADAMS ORCHESTRA
60	Pye International 7N 25056	The Lonely Man Theme/Trigger Happy	7

DANNY ADAMS & CHALLENGERS
64	Philips BF 1346	Bye Bye Baby, Bye Bye/I'm So Proud Of You	10

DERROLL ADAMS
72	Village Thing VTS 17	FEELIN' FINE (LP, with inner sleeve)	20

EDITH ADAMS
55	Brunswick 05406	Ohio (with Rosalind Russell)/A Little Bit In Love	12

EVE ADAMS
61	Qualition PSP 7131	Kookie Talk/My Love Dear	6

FAYE ADAMS
56	London HLU 8339	I'll Be True/Happiness To My Soul (78 rpm = £60)	500

GAYLE ADAMS
82	Epic A 2167	Baby I Need Your Loving/Don't Jump To Conclusions	30

GLADSTON ADAMS
69	Trojan TR 659	Dollars And Cents/TOMMY McCOOK: Popcorn Reggay	20

(see also Gladstone Anderson)

GLEN ADAMS
67	Island WI 3072	Silent Lover/I Remember	30
67	Island WI 3083	She (actually titled "I'm Shocking")/SONNY BURKE: Some Other Time	30
67	Island WI 3099	Grab A Girl/DELROY WILSON: This Heart Of Mine	25
67	Island WI 3100	Hold Down Miss Winey/VINCENT GORDON: Sounds And Soul	38
67	Island WI 3106	That New Girl/UNIQUES: Speak No Evil	25
67	Island WI 3120	She's So Fine/ROY SHIRLEY: Girlie	35
68	Blue Cat BS 126	She Is Leaving/UNIQUES: Girls Like Dirt	18
68	Trojan TR 621	Rent Too High/Every Time	8
68	Collins Downbeat CR 006	Cool Cool Rocksteady (act. D. Tony Lee)/OWEN GRAY: Girl I Will Be Leaving	55
68	Duke DU 58	My Girl/GLADIATORS: You Were To Be	10
68	Bullet BU 414	Cat Woman/PETER TOUCH: Selassie Serenade (B-side actually by Peter Tosh)	15
68	Collins Downbeat CR 010	King Sized/I'm Gonna Take You Back (B-side actually by Owen Gray)	40
68	Giant GN 33	Lonely Girl/ROY SHIRLEY: Warming Up The Scene	20
69	Amalgamated AMG 837	She's So Fine/ERNEST WILSON: Private Number	15
69	Crab CRAB 21	Mighty Organ/ERNEST WILSON: Just Once	20
70	Gas GAS 141	Leaving On A Jet Plane/REGGAE BOYS: Phrases	12
71	Big BG 321	Weary Version 3/TONY BREVETT: Hills And Valleys	14
71	Explosion EX 2048	Never Fall In Love/JET SCENE: Jet 747	8

(see also Glen Amams, Reggae Boys, Roy Shirley, Maxie & Glen, Delroy Wilson, Derrick Morgan, Ernest Wilson, Owen Gray)

JOHNNY ADAMS (& GONDOLIERS)
59	Top Rank JAR 192	Come On/Nowhere To Go (as Johnny Adams & Gondoliers)	15
69	Polydor 56775	Reconsider Me/If I Could See You One More Time	8
72	Atlantic K 10245	I Wish It Would Rain/You're A Lady	8

JONI ADAMS
65	Columbia DB7604	Go With Her/Who Am I?	10

JUNE ADAMS
66	King KG 1038	River Keep Movin'/Heavenly Father	25

MARIE ADAMS
59	Capitol CL 14963	A Fool In Love/What Do You Want To Make Those Eyes At Me For	40

(see also Johnny Otis)

PAUL & LINDA ADAMS
75	S. Folk & Country SFA 27	FAR OVER THE FELL (LP)	18

RAY ADAMS
62	Decca F 11507	Venus In Blue Jeans/He's Got My Sympathy	7
62	Pye 7N 15481	Gypsy/Brother Bill	5

RITCHIE ADAMS
60	London HLU 9200	Back To School/Don't Go My Love, Don't Go	28

Rush ADAMS

RUSH ADAMS
54	Parlophone MSP 6101	I'm Sorry Dear/No One To Cry To 8
55	Parlophone CMSP 33	Then I'll Be Happy/Arizona (with Ace Dooley & Son) (export issue)............. 8
56	MGM SP 1162	Love Plays The Strings Of My Banjo/Kiss! Kiss! Kiss!...................... 8
56	MGM SP 1176	The Birds And The Bees (with Loulie Jean Norman)/My Buddy's Girl 8

(see also David Rose)

RYAN ADAMS
	Lost Highway LC 00268 172	
	259-7	Nuclear/Song For Keith (limited edition, numbered p/s) 12

WOODROW ADAMS
65	Blue Horizon BH 1001	Baby You Just Don't Know/Wine Head Woman (99 copies only) 200

ADAM'S APPLES
77	Brunswick BR 42	Don't Take It Out On This World/Don't You Want To Take Me Home........... 20

AD CONSPIRACY
79	Diamond	AD CONSPIRACY (LP) 25

CANNONBALL ADDERLEY
61	Riverside 45414	Things Are Getting Better/Sidewalks Of New York 10
67	Capitol CL 15489	Mercy Mercy Mercy/Games 10
62	Riverside RLP 12-311	THE CANNONBALL ADDERLEY QUINTET IN SAN FRANCISCO (LP).......... 15
62	Riverside RLP 12-318	WORK SONG (LP, actually by Nat Adderley) 18
63	Riverside 10691R RIF	Tengo Tango/Brother John Dix 15
65	Fontana FJL 107	WOW! (LP) 12
65	Fontana FJL 117	WHAM! (LP) 12
68	Capitol ST 2987	ACCENT ON AFRICA (LP) 12
67	Capitol T2617	WHY AM I TREATED SO BAD? (LP) 20

(see also Nancy Wilson, Miles Davis, John Coltrane)

ADDICTS
64	Decca F 11902	That's My Girl/Here She Comes... 40

JOHN ADDISON
64	United Artists UP 1053	The Girl With Green Eyes/Love Theme From "Tom Jones"................... 5

ADDIX
79	Zig Zag ZZ 22002	Too Blind To See/(No Such Thing As A) Bad Boy (p/s)..................... 15

ADDRISSI BROTHERS
59	London HL 8922	Cherrystone/Lilies Grow High (some copies have tri-centre) (78 rpm = £25) 40
59	London HL 8973	Un Jarro/Saving My Kisses (78 rpm = £20) 25
59	Columbia DB 4370	Back To The Old Salt Mine/It's Love 25

BOBBY ADENO
66	Vocalion V 9279	The Hands Of Time/It's A Sad World (£40+ for demo)....................... 40

ADICTS
81	Dining Out TUX 1	LUNCH WITH THE ADICTS (EP, with insert & screen-printed p/s).............. 30
82	Fall Out FALL 002	Viva La Revolution/Steamroller (p/s)..................................... 10
82	Razor RZS 101	Chinese Takeaway/You'll Never Walk Alone (p/s) 7
83	Razor RZS 104	Bad Boy/Shake, Rattle, Bang Your Head (p/s) 10
83	Razor RZLP 104	Bad Boy/Shake, Rattle, Bang Your Head (shaped picture disc)............... 12
81	Dwed SMT 008	SONGS OF PRAISE (LP).. 18
81	Fall Out FALL LP 006	SONGS OF PRAISE (LP, reissue, yellow vinyl, 2,000 only) 18
81	Fall Out FALL LP 006P	SONGS OF PRAISE (LP, reissue, picture disc) 18
82	Razor RAZ 2	SOUND OF MUSIC (LP) 18
85	Razor RAZ15	SMART ALEX (LP)... 15
87	Fall Out FALLLP021	THIS IS YOUR LIFE (LP).. 18

BETH ADLAM with BUZZ & BOYS
60	Starlite ST45 024	Seventeen/I'll Walk Into The Sea....................................... 15

LARRY ADLER
56	Columbia SCM 5217	Rififi/Malaguena... 12
57	HMV POP 405	Weeping Willows/Theme On Four Notes 12

PETER ADLER
64	Decca 12394	I'm Gonna Turn My Life Around/But I Was Cool 30

ADLIBS (U.K.)
65	Fontana TF 584	Neighbour Neighbour/Lovely Ladies 45

AD-LIBS (U.S.)
66	Red Bird RB 10-102	The Boy From New York City/Kicked Around............................. 40
69	Deep Soul DS 9102	Giving Up/Appreciation 25
75	Contempo CS 9029	The Boy From New York City/Johnny My Boy............................. 20
79	Inferno HEAT 1	New York In The Dark/The Boy From New York City (p/s, coloured vinyl)........ 8

ADMIRALS
65	Fontana TF 597	Promised Land/Palisades Park 40

AD NAUSEUM
83	Flicknife FLS 12	BRAINSTORM (EP, p/s)... 12

A.D. 1984
79	Voyage VOY 005	The Russians Are Coming/New Moon Falling (p/s)......................... 12
81	Grand Prix GP 003	The Clockwork Generation/Melody In The Key Of Time (p/s) 10

ADVENTURES
61	Philips BBL 7548	CAN'T STOP TWISTIN' (LP) 30

ADVENTURERS
60	Capitol CL 15108	Trail Blazer/Rip Van Winkle 40

ADVERTISING
77	EMI EMI 2710	Lipstick/Lonely Guys (p/s)	5
77	EMI EMI 2754	Stolen Love/Suspender Fun (p/s)	5
78	EMI EMC 3253	ADVERTISING JINGLES (LP, with inner sleeve)	12

(see also Secret Affair, Innocents, Simon Boswell)

ANTHONY ADVERSE
| 86 | él GPO 13 | Our Fairy Tale/Eine Symphonie Des Grauens (p/s) | 10 |
| 87 | él GPO 29 | Imperial Violets/Fountain (p/s) | 5 |

ADVERTS
77	Stiff BUY 13	One Chord Wonders/Quickstep (p/s, 1st pressing with push-out centre)	15
77	Stiff BUY 13	One Chord Wonders/Quickstep (p/s, re-pressing with solid centre)	6
77	Anchor ANC 1043	Gary Gilmore's Eyes/Bored Teenagers (p/s)	7
77	Anchor ANC 1047	Safety In Numbers/We Who Wait (p/s)	5
78	Bright BR 1	No Time To Be 21/New Day Dawning (p/s)	8
78	RCA PB 5128	Television's Over/Back From The Dead (p/s)	6
79	RCA 5160	My Place/New Church (p/s)	8
83	Bright BULB 1	Gary Gilmore's Eyes/We Who Wait/New Day Dawning (p/s)	10
78	Bright BRL 201	CROSSING THE RED SEA WITH THE ADVERTS (LP, red vinyl, 5,000 only)	18
81	Butt/Bright ALSO 002	CROSSING THE RED SEA WITH THE ADVERTS (LP, reissue, red vinyl)	15

AEROPLANE
| 71 | RPM 357 | Sweet Sweet Suzie/Of Tomorrow | 20 |

AEROSMITH
73	CBS 1898	Dream On/Somebody	12
76	CBS 4000	Dream On/Somebody (reissue)	5
76	CBS 4452	Last Child/Combination	5
77	CBS 4878	Walk This Way/Uncle Salty	5
77	CBS S AR 2	Draw The Line/Bright, Light, Fright (p/s)	8
78	CBS 6584	Come Together/Kings And Queens	5
80	CBS 8220	Remember (Walking In The Sand)/Bone To Bone (p/s)	5
87	Geffen GEF 29TP	Dude (Looks Like A Lady)/Simoriah/Once Is Enough (12", picture disc)	12
88	Geffen GEF 34TP	Angel/Girl Keeps Coming Apart (12", picture disc)	10
88	Geffen GEF 34CD	Angel (A.O.R. Remix)/Angel/Girl Keeps Coming Apart/	
		Dude (Looks Like A Lady) (3" CD, with adaptor in 5" case)	8
89	Geffen GEF 63TP	Love In An Elevator/Young Lust/Ain't Enough (10", picture disc)	8
89	Geffen GEF 63CD	Love In An Elevator (Edit)/Ain't Enough/Young Lust (3" CD, gatefold p/s)	8
89	Geffen GEF 68P	Janie's Got A Gun/Voodoo Medicine Man (shaped picture disc)	12
89	Geffen GEF 68CD	Janie's Got A Gun/Rag Doll (Live!)/Voodoo Medicine Man (3" CD, gatefold p/s)	8
90	Geffen GEF 72P	Dude (Looks Like A Lady)/Monkey On My Back (shaped picture disc)	12
90	Geffen GEF 72CD	Dude (Looks Like A Lady) (Extended Rockin' Dude)/	
		Love In An Elevator (live)/Walk This Way (live) (CD)	8
90	Geffen GEF 76CD	Rag Doll/Mama Kin (live)/Dream On (live) (CD)	8
89	CBS 4607038	GREATEST HITS (LP, 'European Tour' picture disc)	12
93	Geffen GFST 56	Cryin'/Walk On Down/I'm Down (12", white vinyl)	8
97	Columbia 664075 7	Falling In Love/Fall Together (picture disc, numbered sleeve)	5

(see also Run DMC, Flame)

AEROVONS
| 69 | Parlophone R 5790 | The Train/A Song For Jane | 40 |
| 69 | Parlophone R 5804 | World Of You/Say Georgia | 85 |

A FAIR SET
| 65 | Decca F 12168 | Honey And Wine/Runaround | 12 |

AFEX
| 67 | King KG 1058 | She Got The Time/I Never Knew Love Was Like This | 100 |

AFFINITY
| 70 | Vertigo 6059 007 | I Wonder If I Care As Much/Three Sisters | 20 |
| 70 | Vertigo 6360 004 | AFFINITY (LP, gatefold sleeve, swirl label) | 150 |

(see also Linda Hoyle, Jeff Beck Group, Queen, Ice)

AFFLICTED
81	Bonk AFF 1	I'm Afflicted/Be Aware (rubber-stamped white labels,	
		p/s, some with insert)	40/12
82	Bonk AFF 2	All Right Boy/Who Can Tell (some with p/s, stamped white labels)	40/10
82	Bonk AFF 4	Afflicted (untitled single in stamped striped bag)	20
82	Bonk AFF 3	THE AFFLICTED MAN'S MUSICAL BAG (LP, stamped white label	
		in stamped bag sleeve)	15
82	Bonk AFF 6	HIGH SPEED AND THE AFFLICTED MAN — GET STONED (LP)	12

AFGHAN WHIGS
93	Blast First BFF P89	Gentlemen/Mr Superlove	6
93	Blast First BFF P95	Debonair/My Curse/Ready (gatefold p/s)	6
93	Blast First BFF P96	What Jail Is Like/Revenge	6
94	Blast First BFFP 95T	Debonair/My Curse/Little Girl Blue/Ready (12", with poster)	8

AFI
| 99 | Nitro ADELINE 002 | A FIRE INSIDE EP (ps, insert) | 10 |

A FLOCK OF SEAGULLS
85	Jive AFOS 1	COLLECTION (10 x 7" pack)	18
85	Jive AFLOCK 1	COLLECTION (10 x 12" pack)	20
83	Jive HOPX 201	A FLOCK OF SEAGULLS (LP, picture disc)	12

AFRICAN
| 72 | Sioux SI 006 | Cock Mouth Kill Cock/ERROL T.: I Need To Know | 10 |

AFRICAN BEAVERS
| 65 | RCA RCA 1447 | Find My Baby/Jungle Fever | 20 |

MINT VALUE £

AFRICAN BROTHER
77	Mainline ML 1	Gimme Gimmie African Love/PURE ROOTS: Dub	6

AFRICAN MESSENGERS
64	Page One P04043	Highlife Picadilly/Blues For The Messengers	7

AFRICAN MUSIC MACHINE
72	Mojo 2092 046	Black Water Gold (Pearl)/Making Nassau Fruit Drink	12
73	Contempo CR 13	Tropical/The Girl In France	12
73	Contempo CR 25	Never Name A Baby/Dapp	10
74	Contempo CS 2025	Mr Brown/Camel Time	8

AFRICAN PRINCESS
81	Jah Shaka Shaka 809	Jah Jah Children Cry/Jah Jah Dub (12")	35

AFRIQUE
73	Pye International 7N 25616	Soul Makossa/Hot Mud	10
74	Mainstream MSL 1018	SOUL MAKOSSA (LP)	15

AFRO
71	Punch PH 89	Lonely World/ALTON ELLIS ALL STARS: Put It On	8

AFRO AKINO
74	Afrodesia 1001	Hwe Anna/Maria	10

AFRO DIMENSIONS
72	Ackee 535	Dance With Me/Lonely Nights	15

AFRO ENCHANTERS
63	Island WI 071	Peace And Love/Wayward African	15

AFTERMATH
87	Moshroom MOSH 2001	DON'T CHEER ME UP (LP)	12

AFROTONES
69	Trojan TR 655	Things I Love/ERIC FATTER: Since You've Been Gone	10
69	Duke DU 19	Freedom Sound/BOYS: Easy Sound	12
69	High Note HS 023	All For One/BELTONES: Broken Heart	10

(see also Delroy Wilson)

AFTER DARK
81	After Dark AD 001	Evil Woman/Johnny/Lucy (p/s)	80
83	Lazer PROMO 1	Deathbringer/Call Of The Wild (picture disc, promo only)	50
83	Lazer PROMO 1	Deathbringer/Call Of The Wild (white label test pressing)	100

AFTER TEA
68	Ace Of Clubs SCL-R 1251	AFTER TEA (LP)	50

(see also Ray Fenwick)

AFTER THE FIRE
80	Epic EPC 8394	Love Will Always Make You Cry/Every Mother's Son (p/s, withdrawn)	5
75	Rapid RR 001	SIGNS OF CHANGE (LP, with insert)	35+
80	Epic EPC 84545	80-F (LP, with original mix, unreleased, only on cassette with white labels)	12
82	Epic EPC 85135	BATTERIES NOT INCLUDED (LP, withdrawn version with different sleeve)	12

(see also Narnia, Waiting For The Sun)

AFX
(see under Aphex Twin)

AGENT BLUE
03	Fierce Panda NING 134 CD	SNOWHILL EP (500 only, p/s)	8

AGENT ORANGE
92	Dog Tag AO 001	Sounds Flakey To Me (Jungle Mix)/Only You Have The Bass/ Sounds Flakey To Me (Original Mix) (12")	30

AGENTS
79	Grapevine GRP 142	Trouble/The Love I Hold	15

AGGRESSORS
70	Pye 17889	Whisky And Soda/Soul Of The Jungle	15

AGGROVATORS
70	Jackpot JP 751	Sex Machine/You Left Me And Gone (both act. by Dave Barker & Aggrovators)	25
70	Smash SMA 2302	Big Red Ball Parts 1 & 2 (A-side actually "Big Red Bumble" by Lloyd Tyrell; B-side actually "Big Bumble Version" by Lloyd & Devon)	15
71	Smash SMA 2312	One More Bottle Of Beer/Beer Version	6
73	Smash SMA 2339	Straight To Jackson Head/You Are My Angel	12
73	Downtown DT 500	Dreadlocks Man/Rasta Wants Peace (both actually by Rasta Twins)	10
77	Third World TWS 900	MEETS THE REVOLUTIONARIES (LP)	18

(see also Dave Barker, Dennis Alcapone, Jerry Lewis [Jamaica], Delroy Wilson, John Holt, Alton Ellis, Cornell Campbell)

AGINCOURT
70	Merlin HF 3	FLY AWAY (LP, with insert)	450+

(see also Friends, Ithaca, Alice Through The Looking Glass, Tomorrow Come Someday BBC Radiophonic Workshop/Peter Howell)

AGNES STRANGE
75	Birdsnest BN 1	Give Yourself A Chance/Clever Fool	8
77	Baal BDN 38048	Can't Make Up My Mind/Johnny B. Goode	8
75	Birdsnest BRL 9000	STRANGE FLAVOUR (LP)	80+

AGONY BAG
80	Monza MON 2	Rabies Is A Killer/Never Never Never (p/s)	10

(see also Pesky Gee, Black Widow)

AGORA
94	Z Records ZEDD 010	LATIN CONNECTION EP (12")	10

AGROS
71	Punch PH 56	What Do You Fall In Love For/SLICKERS: Too Much	20

AGROVATORS
73	Downtown DT500	Dreadlocks Man/Rasta Want Peace.	10
76	Groundnation GROL 507	RASTA DUB '76 (LP)	25
78	Live & Love LAP 04	JAMMIES IN A LION STYLE DUB (LP)	35
78	Third World TWS 939	KAYA DUB (LP)	25

AGROVATORS AND THE REVOLUTIONARIES
77	Third World TWS 900	THE AGROVATORS MEET THE REVOLUTIONARIES AT CHANNEL ONE (LP)	40
78	Burning Sounds BS 1028	GUERILLA DUB (LP)	45

A GUY CALLED GERALD
88	Rham RX 8804	Voodoo Ray/Escape/Rhapsody In Acid/Blow Your House Down (12", p/s)	12
92	Juice Box JBOX 001	Digital bad boy/Let it move you/A storm is coming/Could you understand? (12", tracks 1and 4 vocals by MC Tunes)	10
92	Juice Box JBOX 003	Cops/The trak/28 gun bad boy / Paranoia (12")	25
92	Juice Box JBOX 004	Ses makes you wise/Sunshine / King of the jungle/Boase up (12")	15
92	Juice Box JBOX 005	The musical magical midi machine/Let it go/Like a drug/Free Africa (12")	15
93	Juice Box JBOX 009	Too fucked to dance/Darker than I should be/Anything v2.1 / is is the right time (12")	12
93	Juice Box JBOX 014	The Glok track/Gerald's bassline/Ease the pressure/Take me (12")	8
94	Juice Box JBOX 019	Darker than I should be (Ladies mix) / Gloc (Remix) (12")	8

A-HA
84	Warner Bros W 9146	Take On Me/And You Tell Me (silver/blue p/s)	30
84	Warner Bros W 9146T	Take On Me (Extended)/And You Tell Me/Stop And Make Your Mind Up (12", silver/blue p/s, some with poster & stickers)	100/50
85	Warner Bros W 9006T	Take On Me/Love Is The Reason (12", black & white p/s)	8
85	Warner Bros W 9006	Take On Me/Love Is The Reason (reissue, colour p/s with gatefold booklet)	5
86	Lyntone	The Sun Always Shines On T.V. (U.S. Remix) (square picture flexidisc with No. 1 magazine)	8
86	Warner Bros W 8736P	Train Of Thought (Remix)/And You Tell Me (train-shaped picture disc)	12
86	Warner Bros W 8663TP	Hunting High And Low (Extended)/Hunting High And Low (Remix)/ The Blue Sky (Demo) (12", picture disc)	8
86	Warner Bros W 8500TP	Cry Wolf (Extended)/Cry Wolf (7" Version)/Maybe Maybe (12", picture disc)	8
87	Warner Bros W 8405TP	Manhattan Skyline (Extended Remix)/Manhattan Skyline (LP Version)/ We're Looking For The Whales (12", picture disc)	8
87	Warner Bros W 8305TP	The Living Daylights (Extended)/(7" Remix)/(Instrumental) (12", picture disc)	10
88	Warner Bros W 7936TP	Stay On These Roads (Extended Remix)/Soft Rains Of April (Original Mix) (12", picture disc)	10
88	Warner Bros W 7936CD	Stay On These Roads (Extended Remix)/Soft Rains Of April (Original Mix)/ Take On Me/Cry Wolf (3" CD with adaptor in 5" case)	8
88	Warner Bros W 7840TP	The Blood That Moves The Body (Extended)/The Blood That Moves The Body (LP Version)/There's Never A Forever Thing (12", picture disc)	10
88	Warner Bros W 7749WW	Touchy!/Hurry Home ('liquid' poster p/s)	8
88	Warner Bros W 7749CD	Touchy! (Go-Go Mix)/Hurry Home/Hunting High And Low (3" CD, 5" case)	8
88	Warner Bros W 7636TP	You're The One (12" Remix)/You're The One (Instrumental)/ Out Of The Blue Comes Green (12", picture disc)	8

(see also Phenomena)

AHAB
82	Chicken Jazz JAZZ 5	Party Girl/Don't Give Up On Us (p/s)	6

(see also Another Pretty Face, Waterboys)

AHAB & WAILERS
63	Pye 7N 15553	Cleopatra's Needle/Neb's Tune	10

AIM
94	Detour DR 018	Call Your Name/Out On The Streets (p/s,1,000 only, 100 on blue vinyl)	8/6

ALYN AINSWORTH
59	Parlophone R 4533	Bedtime For Drums/The Cobbler's Song (with His Orchestra) (78)	10

AIR
71	Atlantic 2400 148	AIR (LP)	25

AIR
98	Source V 2848	MOON SAFARI (LP)	12

AIR LIQUIDE
94	Smile/Profile SM 9008	ROBOT WARS EP (10", picture disc)	10

AIR SUPPLY
80	Arista Arist 362	All Out Of Love/Old Habits Die Hard	6

AIRTO
71	Buddah 2318 040	SEEDS TO THE GROUND — THE NATURAL SOUNDS OF AIRTO (LP)	18
73	CTI CTI 18	FINGERS (LP)	18
74	CTI CTI 21	IN CONCERT (LP, with Deodato)	18
74	CTI CTI 23	VIRGIN LAND (LP)	18

(see also Deodato)

BOBBY AITKEN (& CARIBBEATS)
62	Island WI 028	Baby Baby (actually with Patsy)/Lonely Boy	18
62	Blue Beat BB 93	Never Never (South Virginia)/Isabella (as Bobby Aitken & Buster's Group)	18
63	Blue Beat BB 146	Don't Leave Me/Mom And Dad (as Bobby Aitken & Tinse)	18
63	Rio R 14	I've Told You/Please Go Back	18
63	Rio R 15	It Takes A Friend/LAUREL AITKEN: Sunshine	18

Bobby AITKEN

64	Rio R 34	Rolling Stone/LESTER STERLING'S GROUP: Man About Town 40
64	Rio R 40	Garden Of Eden/Whiplash 20
64	Rio R 50	Little Girl/Together 10
65	Rio R 52	Rain Came Tumbling Down/SHENLEY & LUNAN: Something Is On Your Mind. . . 15
65	Rio R 64	Mr Judge/BINZ: Times Have Changed 18
65	Black Swan WI 441	Jerico/LESTER STERLING: Lunch Time.. 25
66	Ska Beat JB 252	Thunderball/ORIGINATORS: Chelip Chelip 60
67	Doctor Bird DB 1071	Keep On Pushing/You Won't Regret It 30
67	Doctor Bird DB 1072	Let Them Have A Home/Temptation (with Caribbeats)...................... 30
67	Doctor Bird DB 1077	Sweets For My Sweet/How Sweet It Is (with Caribbeats) 20
67	Island WI 3028	Kiss Bam Bam/CYNTHIA RICHARDS: How Could I........................... 70
67	Giant GN 11	What A Fool/Curfew (with Caribbeats) 25

(see also Caribbeats, Laurel Aitken, Frank Cosmo, Lloyd & Glen)

LAUREL AITKEN (& BLUE BEATS)

59	Kalypso XX 15	Sweet Chariot/Nebuchnezer... 10
59	Kalypso XX 16	Aitken's Boogie/Cherrie... 12
60	Kalypso XX 19	Baba Kill Me Goat/Tribute To Collie Smith............................ 10
60	Starlite ST45 011	Boogie In My Bones/Little Sheila 20
60	Starlite ST45 014	Honey Girl (with Caribs)/Drinkin' Whisky (with Bluebeats) 15
60	Melodisc M 1570	Mary Lee/Lonesome Lover (with Bluebeats) 10
60	Blue Beat B 1	Boogie Rock/Heavenly Angel (white label) 40
60	Blue Beat BB 1	Boogie Rock/Heavenly Angel (blue label) 15
60	Blue Beat BB 10	Jeannie Is Back/If It's Money You Need 10
60	Blue Beat BB 14	Judgment Day/Yea Yea Baby.. 10
60	Blue Beat BB 22	Railroad Track/Tell Me Darling.. 10
60	Blue Beat BB 25	More Whisky/LLOYD CLARKE: Parapinto Boogie..................... 10
61	Starlite ST45 034	Love Me Baby/Stars Were Made 15
61	Blue Beat BB 40	Bartender/Mash Potato Boogie 10
61	Blue Beat BB 52	Bouncing Woman/Nursery Rhyme Boogie (with Blue Beats) 20
61	Blue Beat BB 70	Mighty Redeemer/Please Don't Leave Me 8
62	Blue Beat BB 84	Brother David/Back To New Orleans (with Blue Beats) 8
62	Blue Beat BB 109	Lucille/I Love You More Everyday....................................... 8
62	Blue Beat BB 120	Sixty Days And Sixty Nights/Going To Kansas City 30
62	Blue Beat BB 142	Jenny Jenny/Weary Wanderer (with Bandits and Ruddy & Sketto). 12
62	Dice CC 1	Mabel/You Got Me Rocking (with Hyacinth)......................... 10
63	Dice CC 13	Sweet Jamaica/Bossa Nova Hop....................................... 10
63	Blue Beat BB 164	Zion/Swing Low Sweet Chariot 12
63	Blue Beat BB 194	Little Girl/Daniel Saw The Stone 12
63	Duke DK 1002	Low Down Dirty Girl/Pink Lane Shuffle 20
63	Island WI 092	I Shall Remove/We Got To Move 15
63	Island WI 095	What A Weeping/Zion City Wall 15
63	Island WI 099	In My Soul/One More River To Cross 10
63	Rio R 11	Adam & Eve/BOBBY AITKEN: Devil Woman 12
63	Rio R 12	Mary/Hometown.. 8
63	Rio R 13	Bad Minded Woman/Life 8
63	Rio R 17	Devil Or Angel/Fire 12
63	Rio R 18	Freedom Train/Peace Perfect Peace................................. 12
64	Rio R 35	Rock Of Ages/The Mule 12
64	Rio R 36	Leave Me Standing/Bagaboo (Bug-A-Boo)........................... 15
64	Rio R 37	John Saw Them Coming/Jericho 8
64	R&B JB 167	Yes Indeed/You Can't Stop Me From Loving You 12
64	R&B JB 170	Pick Up Your Bundle And Go/Let My People Go 12
64	R&B JB 171	Bachelor Life/You Was Up 10
64	Columbia DB 7280	Be Mine/Don't Stay Out Late 8
64	Blue Beat BB 249	This Great Day/I May Never See My Baby 12
64	J.N.A.C. 1	West Indian Cricket Test/3 Cheers For Worrell 10
64	Black Swan WI 401	Lion Of Judah/Remember My Darling (B-side with Cynthia Richards).......... 15
64	Black Swan WI 411	The Saint/Go Gal Go... 15
64	Dice CC 28	Jamaica/I Don't Want No More 10
65	Dice CC 31	We Shall Overcome/You Left Me Standing............................ 10
65	Rio R 53	Mary Don't You Weep/I Believe 12
65	Rio R 54	Mary Lou/Jump And Shout 12
65	Rio R 56	One More Time/Ring Don't Mean A Thing 12
65	Rio R 60	Come And Get It/Lonely Nights 18
65	Rio R 65	Let's Be Lovers/I Need You 12
65	Island WI 198	Boogie In My Bones/Little Sheila 12
65	Island WI 252	How Can I Forget You/Weeping And Crying (white label, existence unconfirmed)
66	Blue Beat BB 340	Clementine/Bongo Jerk 15
66	Blue Beat BB 369	Shame And Scandal/Coconut Woman 12
66	Ska Beat JB 232	Jamboree/Looking For My Baby .... 45+
66	Ska Beat JB 236	Propaganda/Shake 20
66	Ska Beat JB 239	Green Banana/Darling 20
66	Rio R 91	How Can I Forget You/I've Been Weeping And Crying 10
66	Rio R 92	Baby Don't Do It/That Girl 10
66	Rio R 97	We Shall Overcome/Street Of Glory 10
66	Rio R 99	Clap Your Hands/Revival 10
66	Rainbow RAI 101	Don't Break Your Promises/Last Night (with Soulmen) 15
66	Rainbow RAI 106	Voodoo Woman/Bewildered And Blue (B-side with Carols)........ 15
67	Rainbow RAI 111	Sweet Precious Love/I Want To Love You Forever (with Carols)... 15
67	Columbia Blue Beat DB 102	Rock Steady/Blowin' In The Wind 8
67	Columbia Blue Beat DB 106	I'm Still In Love With You Girl/Blue Rhythm.............. 8
67	Fab FAB 5	Never You Hurt/I Need You (as Laurel Aitken & Soulmen) 8
68	Fab FAB 45	For Sentimental Reasons/Last Waltz (as Laurel Aitken & Rainbows)........... 8
68	Doctor Bird DB 1160	Mr Lee/Birmingham Girl 20
68	Doctor Bird DB 1161	La La La (Means I Love You)/DETOURS: Sunnyside.............. 15

MINT VALUE £

69	Doctor Bird DB 1187	Fire In Your Wire/Quando Quando	12
69	Doctor Bird DB 1190	Rice And Peas/CLASSICS: Worried Over Me	20
69	Doctor Bird DB 1196	Reggae Prayer/Deliverance Will Come	20
69	Doctor Bird/J.J. DB 1197	The Rise And Fall (Of Laurel)/If You're Not Black	20
69	Doctor Bird DB 1202	Haile Haile (The Lion)/SEVEN LETTERS: Call Collect	25
69	Doctor Bird DB 1203	Carolina/Kingston Town	20
69	Junior JR 105	Think Me No Know/RECO: Trombone Man	10
69	Nu Beat NB 024	Woppi King/Mr Soul	10
69	Nu Beat NB 025	Suffering Still (with Girlie)/Reggae '69	10
69	Nu Beat NB 032	Haile Selassie/Blues Dance	10
69	Nu Beat NB 033	Lawd Doctor (with Girlie)/Big Fight In Hell Stadium	10
69	Nu Beat NB 035	Run Powell Run/RICO RODRIGUEZ: A Message To You	15
69	Nu Beat NB 039	Save The Last Dance/Walk Right Back	8
69	Nu Beat NB 040	Don't Be Cruel/John B	8
69	Nu Beat NB 043	Shoo Be Doo/Babylon Gone	12
69	Nu Beat NB 044	Landlords And Tenants/Everybody Sufferin'	10
69	Nu Beat NB 045	Jesse James/Freedom	12
69	Nu Beat NB 046	Pussy Price Gone Up/Gimme Back Me Dollar	10
69	Nu Beat NB 047	Skinhead Train/Kent People	20
70	Nu Beat NB 048	Skinhead Invasion/Benwood Dick (unissued, blank white label demos only)	25
70	Nu Beat NB 048	Mr Popcorn/GRUVY BEATS: Share Your Popcorn	12
70	Nu Beat NB 049	I've Got Your Love/GRUVY BEATS: Blue Mink	8
70	Nu Beat NB 050	Scandal In Brixton Market/Soul Grinder (both sides with Girlie)	10
70	New Beat NB 054	Nobody But Me/Baby Please Don't Go	8
70	New Beat NB 056	I'll Never Love Any Girl/The Best I Can	8
70	New Beat NB 057	Reggae Popcorn/Take Me Back	8
70	New Beat NB 063	Baby I Need Your Loving/Think It Over	8
70	New Beat NB 065	Sex Machine/Since You Left	8
70	New Beat NB 072	Pachanga/Version	8
70	Ackee ACK 104	Pussy Got Thirteen Life/Single Man	10
70	Ackee ACK 106	Sin Pon You/Everynight	10
70	Bamboo BAM 16	Moon Rock/Cut Up Munno	20
70	Pama PM 818	Mary's Boy Child/RUPIE EDWARDS ALLSTARS: Version	6
70	Pama Supreme PS 300	Why Can't I Touch You/Can't Turn Your Back On Me	6
71	Trojan TR 7826	It's Too Late/AITKEN'S BAND: Slow Rock	7
71	New Beat NB 078	True Love/The Best I Can	6
71	New Beat NB 089	I Can't Stop Loving You/El Paso	6
71	Black Swan BW 1408	If It's Hell Below/Just A Little Bit Of Love	25
72	Big Shot BI 605	Take Me In Your Arms/Two-Timing Woman	6
72	Camel CA 90	Africa Arise/GI GINGRI: Holy Mount Zion	6
72	Columbia DB 8914	Pretty Face In The Market Place/Come Back To My Lonely World	6
75	Camel CA 2007	La Vien Rose/Spanish Eyes	10
75	Punch PU 121	Fattie Bum Bum/Fattie Bum Bum	5
80	I-Spy SEE 4	Big Fat Man/It's Too Late (as Laurel Aitken & Unitone)	6
80	I-Spy SEE 6	Rudi Got Married/Honey Come Back To Me	8
66	Rio LR 1	SKA WITH LAUREL (LP)	120
67	Doctor Bird DLM 5012	SAYS FIRE (LP)	90
69	Pama PSP 1012	THE HIGH PRIEST OF REGGAE (LP)	70
69	Pama ECO 8	SCANDAL IN BRIXTON MARKET (LP, with Girlie)	60
69	J.J.	RISE AND FALL (LP)	90
73	Count Shelly CSLP1	MORIA SOPHIA (LP)	25

(see also Laurel & Owen, Girlie, King Horror, Lorenzo, Ruts, Bobby Aitken, Classics, Beresford Ricketts, Duke Reid, Tommy McCook)

A-JAES
| 64 | Oak RGJ 132 | I'm Leaving You/Kansas City | 1,000 |

AKA & CHARLATANS
| 78 | Vanity VANE 1 | Heroes Are Losers/Lady Of The Night/Perhaps One Day (12", various screen-printed die-cut p/s) | 12 |

JEWEL AKENS
65	London HLN 9954	The Birds And The Bees/Tic Tac Toe	8
65	London HLN 9969	Georgie Porgie/Around The Corner	7
66	Ember EMB S 219	Dancin' Jenny/A Wee Bit More of Your Lovin'	12
65	London HA-N 8234	THE BIRDS AND THE BEES (LP)	40

AK 47
| 81 | Output ORR 202 | Stop! Dance!/Autobiography/Hilversum-Ao (p/s) | 5 |

(see also AK Process, File Under Pop)

JAN AKKERMAN
73	Harvest HAR 5069	Blue Boy/Minstrel-Farmers Dance	6
74	Atlantic K 10427	House Of The King/Javeh	5
78	Atlantic K 11014	Crackers/Wings Of Strings (no p/s)	5
78	Atlantic K 11131	Crackers/Angel Watch (no p/s)	5

(see also Hunters [Holland], Brainbox, Focus)

AK PROCESS
| 79 | Output OPQ 101 | Electronic Music: After All Love/Post Town (p/s, white labels) | 6 |

(see also AK 47)

AKRYLYKZ
80	Double R RED 2	Spyderman/Smart Boy (p/s)	7
80	Polydor POSP 128	Spyderman/Smart Boy (reissue, p/s)	5
80	Polydor 2059 253	J.D./Ska'd For Life (p/s)	6

ROLANDO AL
(see under Roland Alphonso)

AL & VIBRATORS
67	Doctor Bird DB 1085	Move Up/Lone Lover.	22
69	High Note HS 005	Check Up/I'll Come Back	15
69	High Note HS 007	Move Up Calypso/PATSY: Fire In Your Wire	12

(see also Vibrators, Patsy Todd, Lord Power)

ALABAMA JUG BAND
55	Brunswick OE 9161	ALABAMA JUG BAND (EP)	10

STEVE ALAIMO
62	Pye International 7N 25161	My Friends/Going Back To Marty	10
63	Pye International 7N 25174	Every Day I Have To Cry Little Girl	30
63	Pye International 7N 25199	It's A Long Long Way To Happiness/A Lifetime Of Loneliness	10
66	HMV POP 1531	So Much Love/Truer Than True	20
68	Atlantic 588 227	Watching The Trains Go By/Thank You For The Sunshine Days.	10

ALARM
81	White Cross W 3/4	Unsafe Buildings/Up For Murder (gatefold p/s)	25
82	Illegal ILS 0032	Marching On/Across The Border/Lie Of The Land (p/s)	8
83	I.R.S. PFPC 1023	68 Guns Parts 1 & 2 (p/s, with free cassette: The Stand/Across The Border/ Marching On/Lie Of The Land/For Freedom (all live) [CS 70504])	6
84	I.R.S. IRS 103	The Deceiver/Reason 41 (p/s, clear vinyl)	5
84	I.R.S. IRS 103	The Deceiver/Reason 41 (p/s, mispress on mustard vinyl)	45
84	I.R.S. IRSD 103/103A	The Deceiver/Reason 41//Lie Of The Land/Legal Matter (double pack, g/fold p/s)	6
80s	Lyntone	Twp/Swnllyd (red vinyl flexidisc, with tour magazine)	8

(see also Seventeen)

ALBA
77	Rubber RUB 021	ALBA (LP)	12

DAMON ALBARN
03	Honest Johns HJP10	DEMOCRAZY (2x10" white vinyl, picture disc)	20
03	Honest Johns HJP20	A Rappy Song (Remix)/Original Version (12")	8

(see also Blur, Gorillaz)

BILLY ALBERT "THE KID"
56	Vogue Coral Q 72214	Black Jack/The Golden Touch	15

EDDIE ALBERT
55	London HL 8136	I'm In Favour Of Friendship/Come Pretty Little Girl (78 rpm = £10)	30
56	London HLU 8241	Little Child (Daddy Dear) (with Sondra Lee)/Jenny Kissed Me (78 rpm = £10)	30

MEL ALBERT
59	Top Rank JAR 178	Sugar Plum/Never Let Me Go (78 rpm = £15)	18

ALBERTO & RICARDO
64	RCA RCA 1376	Love's Made A Fool Of You/I'll Do It To You	8

ALBERTO Y LOST TRIOS PARANOIAS
76	Big T BIG 541	Dread Jaws/De Version.	6
77	Stiff LAST 2	SNUFF ROCK (EP, p/s)	8
78	Logo GO(D) 323	DEAD MEAT EP (double pack, gatefold p/s)	8
82	New Hormones ORG 30	Cruisin' With Santa/Unfunny Art-School Parody Band (p/s)	7
76	Transatlantic TRA 316	ALBERTO Y LOST TRIOS PARANOIAS (LP, with insert).	12
77	Transatlantic TRA 349	ITALIANS FROM OUTER SPACE (LP)	15
78	Logo LOGO 1009	SKITE (LP)	12

(see also Mothmen, Charlie Parkas)

ALBION BAND
76	Harvest HAR 5113	Hopping Down In Kent/Merry Sherwood Rangers (as Albion Dance Band)	5
77	Harvest HAR 5128	The Postman's Knock/La Sexte Estample Real (as Albion Dance Band)	5
78	Harvest HAR 5156	Poor Old Horse/Ragged Heroes (p/s)	5
79	Harvest HAR 5175	Pain And Paradise/Lay Me Low (p/s)	6

(see also Shirley Collins, Fairport Convention, Keith Dewhurst & Albion Band)

MICHAEL ALBUQUERQUE
69	United Artists UP 35037	Better Men Than Me/Burn Burn Burn	6
70	United Artists UP 35098	Roll Him Over/Blind Man	6

(see also Michael D'Albuquerque, E.L.O.)

ALCO
(see under Threads Of Life)

DENNIS ALCAPONE
70	Explosion EX 2039	Revelation Version/Marka Version.	15
70	Supreme SUP 214	You Must Believe Me (with Niney)/RUPIE EDWARDS ALLSTARS: Funk The Funk	12
70	Big Shot BI 565	Shades Of Hudson/Spanish Amigo.	20
71	Treasure Isle TI 7069	The Great Woggie/TOMMY McCOOK & SUPERSONICS: Buttercup Version	22
71	Banana BA 328	Duppy Serenade (as Innkeeper)/Sunshine Version	18
71	Banana BA 341	(Love Me) Forever Version/I Don't Want To See You Cry	18
71	Upsetter US 373	Well Dread/UPSETTERS: Dread Version.	12
71	Upsetter US 377	Alpha And Omega/JUNIOR BYLES: Beat Down Babylon	15
71	Duke DU 125	Medley Version/Version Two	10
71	Prince Buster PB 8	Sons Of Zion/ANSELL COLLINS: Short Circuit	12
71	Prince Buster PB 12	Let It Roll (with Max Romeo)/ANSELL COLLINS: Clear Blue (w/l demos only)	15
71	Jackpot JP 773	Jumping Jack (with John Holt)/AGGROVATORS: King Of The Track	8
71	Jackpot JP 775	Togetherness (Black & White) (with John Holt)/DELROY WILSON: Live Good	8
71	Jackpot JP 776	Tell It Like It Is/Come Along	8
71	Dynamic DYN 421	Horse And Buggy/ROLAND ALPHONSO & DENZIL LAING: Buggy And Horse	12
71	Dynamic DYN 422	Ripe Cherry/INNER CIRCLE: Red Cherry	10
71	Dynamic DYN 427	Alcapones Guns Don't Bark/Alcapones Guns Don't Bark Version	20
71	Camel CA 74	This A Butter/PHIL PRATT ALLSTARS: Version.	12
71	Tropical AL 003	False Prophet/MAX ROMEO: Rude Medley	12

72	Tropical AL 019	Worldwide Love (with Twinkle Brothers)/CARL MASTERS: Gable Up 12
72	Ackee ACK 146	Power Version/BLUESBLASTERS: Martie (B-side actually titled "Margie")...... 18
72	Prince Buster PB 24	Giant/PRINCE BUSTER: Science.. 20
72	Upsetter US 381	Wonderman (with Dave Barker, actually by Dave Barker)/
		Place Called Africa (with Dave Barker & Junior Byles) 20
72	Upsetter US 388	Master Key/UPSETTERS: Keyhole 20
72	Grape GR 3035	Rasta Dub/UPSETTERS: Rasta Version 20
72	Attack ATT 8027	Fine Style/WINSTON SCOTLAND: On The Track......................... 15
72	Duke DU 131	The Sky's The Limit/HUDSON'S ALLSTARS: Limit Version 12
72	Duke DU 147	Get In The Groove (with Dennis Brown)/DYNAMITES: Version 12
72	Techniques TE 918	Look Into Yourself/TECHNIQUES ALLSTARS: Yourself Version 15
72	Green Door GD 4041	Rub Up A Daughter/TONY'S ALLSTARS: Daughter Version................. 15
72	Bullet BU 509	Dub Up A Daughter/PRINCE TONY'S ALL STARS: Version 18
72	Tropical 19	World Wide Love/Gable Up (recorded with TWINKLE BROS/CARL MASTERS) .. 12
73	Downtown DT 508	You Don't Say/TONY'S ALLSTARS: Version 12
73	Treasure Isle TI 7074	Wake Up Jamaica/Version (with Tommy McCook) 18
73	Jackpot JP 808	Cassius Clay/SLIM SMITH: Love And Affection......................... 18
73	Bread BR 1121	Musical Liquidator/Lorna Banana (B-side with Prince Jazzbo) 18
73	G.G. GG 4538	Musical Alphabet/BUCKLEY ALLSTARS: Things Gonna Change
		(B-side actually by Maytones) 12
73	Pyramid PYR 7008	Belch It Off/Jack Horner.. 10
74	Harry J HJ 6666	Sorry Harry/Party Time.. 8
76	Ethnic Fight EF 001	Pressure In A Babylon/ETHNIC FIGHT BAND: Pressure Dub 6
71	Trojan TBL 187	GUNS DON'T ARGUE (LP).. 30
73	Magnet MGT 001	KING OF THE TRACK (LP).. 30
74	Attack ATLP 1005	BELCH IT OFF (LP)... 15
75	Live And Love LALP 104	DREAD CAPONE (LP)... 40
77	Third World TWS 801	SIX MILLION DOLLAR MAN (LP) 15
77	Third World TWS 911	INVESTIGATOR ROCK (LP) 15

(see also El Paso, Dennis & Lizzy, Mad Roy, D. Smith, Wailing Souls, Innkeepers, GG Allstars,
Stranger Cole, Lizzy & Dennis, Lee)

CRAIG ALDEN
60	London HLW 9224	Crazy Little Horn/Goggle-Eye'd...................................... 10

STEVE ALDO (& CHALLENGERS)
64	Decca F 12041	Can I Get A Witness/Baby What You Want Me To Do (with Challengers)....... 100
66	Parlophone R 5432	Everybody Has To Cry/You're Absolutely Right (solo) 150

RONNIE ALDRICH
54	Decca F 10248	Coach Call Boogie/Donegal Cradle Song................................ 15
54	Decca F 10274	Wolf On The Prowl/Mudhopper.. 15
55	Decca F 10494	Ko Ko Mo (I Love You So)/Rock Love (with Squads) (78 rpm = £6) 20
55	Decca F 10544	Rock Candy/Boom, Boom Boomerang (with Squads) (78 rpm = £6).......... 12
55	Decca F 10564	Rhythm 'N Blues/Where Ya Gone, Baby? (with Squads) (78 rpm = £6) 15
57	Columbia DB 3882	Right Now, Right Now/Rock And Roll Boogie (with Squadronaires)
		(78 rpm = £6) 25
57	Columbia DB 3945	Crazy Bear/The Big Band Beat (with Squadronaires) 12
69	Decca F 12909	Ride My See-Saw/Romance On The North Sea (with London Festival Orch.) 8

(see also Squadronaires, Joan Regan)

URIE ALDRIDGE
71	Harry J. HJ 6634	Set Me Free/LLOYD WILLIS: Free Version 5

(see also John Holt)

ALEANNA
78	Inchrecronin INC 7421	ALEANNA (LP)... 35

AKI ALEONG (& HIS LICORICE TWISTERS)
61	Reprise R 20021	Trade Winds, Trade Winds/Without Your Love 5
61	Reprise R 6011	TWISTIN' THE HITS (LP)... 20

DON ALESSI
66	Salvo SLO 5521 LP	GUITAR SPECTACULAR! (LP) 15

ALETHIONS
70s	Myrrh Gold MYR 1002	R.S.V.P. (LP) 20
70s	Myrrh Gold MST 6506	ONE WAY (LP) 20

ARTHUR ALEXANDER
62	London HLD 9523	You Better Move On/A Shot Of Rhythm And Blues........................ 45
63	London HLD 9566	Where Have You Been/Soldier Of Love 35
63	London HLD 9641	Anna/I Hang My Head And Cry 40
63	London HLD 9667	Go Home Girl/You're The Reason 30
64	London HLD 9899	Black Night/Ole John Amos.. 20
66	London HLU 10023	(Baby) For You/The Other Woman..................................... 30
76	Buddah BDS 439	Everyday I Have To Cry/Everybody Needs Somebody To Love............... 20
63	London RE-D 1364	ALEXANDER THE GREAT (EP) 100
63	London RE-D 1401	ARTHUR ALEXANDER (EP) 100
62	London HA-D 2457	YOU BETTER MOVE ON (LP).. 150

GOLDIE ALEXANDER
81	Project 1	Go Back/Show Me Your Love 20

JEFF ALEXANDER & HIS ORCHESTRA
58	London HA-P 2130	ALFRED HITCHCOCK PRESENTS — MUSIC TO BE MURDERED BY
		(LP, also stereo SH-P 6012).................................... 48/38

LUCIEN ALEXANDER
67	Polydor 56205	Baby, You've Been On My Mind/Play Along (Miss R) 20

MINT VALUE £

TEXAS ALEXANDER
61	Fontana 467 136TE	TREASURES OF NORTH AMERICAN NEGRO MUSIC VOLUME 7 (EP) 15

LLOYD ALEXANDER REAL ESTATE
68	President PT 157	Gonna Live Again/Watcha Gonna Do 40

LOREZ ALEXANDER
61	Pye NJL 35	SING NO SAD SONGS FOR ME (LP) 12

LOREZ ALEXANDRIA
60	Parlophone PMD 1062	LOREZ SINGS PREZ (LP) 25

ALFALFA
77	EMI EMC 3213	ALFALFA (LP, with inner sleeve) 12

IBRAHAM ALFA
97	Mosquito MSQ 09	METHODS OF SIGNAL ANALYSIS (12") 10
98	Mosquito MSQ 011	PROCESSEN EP (12") 8
99	Mosquito MSQ 015	DECODE YOURSELF EP (12") 8

ALFI & HARRY
56	London HLU 8242	Trouble With Harry/A Little Beauty (triangular centre, gold lettering on label) . . . 35
57	London HLU 8494	Closing Time/Safari (78 rpm = £10) 10
	(see also David Seville)	

ALFIE
01	Regal (no cat. no.)	Zoom (p/s, 1-track square coloured vinyl, 300 only) 60
01	Twisted Nerve TN 033	You Make No Bones/Don't Be Blue (p/s) 6
00	Twisted Nerve TN 011	ALFIE EP: Sure And Simple Time/Ooze A Lullaby/Check The Weight (10") 25
00	Twisted Nerve TN 016	BOOKENDS: James's Dream (Parts 1 & 2)/Talking Song (gatefold p/s) 10
00	Twisted Nerve	BOOKENDS EP (10") 15

CLEM ALFORD
74	Columbia SCX 6571	MIRROR IMAGE — THE ELECTRONIC SITAR OF CLEM ALFORD (LP) 45
75	KPM KPM 1183	INDIA (LP, music library issue, side 2 only) 15
	(see also Sagram, Magic Carpet)	

SANDRA ALFRED
58	Oriole CB 1408	Rocket And Roll/Six Day Rock (78 rpm = £30) 75
	(see also Sandra Barry, Slack Alice)	

ALFRED & MELMOTH
68	Island WI 3130	I Want Someone/ALFRED BROWN: One Scotch One Bourbon One Beer 15

AUGUSTO ALGUERO & HIS ORCHESTRA
71	Polydor 2489 034	LAUGH! LAUGH! (LP) 20

LYNN ALICE
76	K&B KB 5520	(You Keep Me) Hanging On/(You Keep Me) Hanging On 7

ALICE IN CHAINS
92	Columbia 658 888-7	Would?/Man In The Box (picture disc, numbered, PVC sleeve) 10
92	Columbia 658 888-6	Would?/Man In The Box/Brother/Right Turn
		(12", green vinyl, no'd die-cut slv.) 12
93	Columbia 659 090-6	Them Bones/We Die Young/Got Me Wrong/Am I Inside (12", no'd, blue vinyl) . . . 15
93	Columbia 659 365-7	Angry Chair/I Know Somethin' About You (snakeskin wallet sleeve) 10
93	Columbia 659 751-7	Down In A Hole/Rooster (picture disc) 10
93	Columbia 659 751-6	Down In A Hole/A Little Bitter/Rooster/Love Hate Love (12", die cut p/s) 8
93	Columbia 659 751-2	Down In A Hole/Version/What The Hell Have I/Rooster (CD) 8
95	Columbia 662 623-7	Grind/Nutshell (green vinyl, numbered card) 10
96	Columbia 662893-7	Heaven beside you / Would? (live) (white vinyl, foldover p/s
		in stickered PVC sleeve) 5
91	Columbia 467201-1	FACELIFT (LP) 15
92	Columbia 472330-1	DIRT (LP) 15
94	Columbia 475713-1	JAR OF FLIES / SAP (LP, yellow vinyl with blue vinyl,
		1-sided, etched 12" EP) 25
95	Columbia 481114-1	ALICE IN CHAINS (double LP, gatefold sleeve, inners) 20

ALICE ISLAND BAND
74	Warren WAR 341	SPLENDID ISOLATION (LP, with insert) 150

ALICE THROUGH THE LOOKING GLASS
69	H&F Recording/SNP	ALICE THROUGH THE LOOKING GLASS (LP, private pressing,
	(no cat. no.)	handmade sleeve, actually by Peter Howell & John Ferdinando) 300
97	Tenth Planet TP 032	ALICE THROUGH THE LOOKING GLASS (LP, reissue, no'd, 1,000 only) 12
	(see also Ithaca, Friends, Agincourt, Tomorrow Come Someday, BBC Radiophonic Workshop/Peter Howell)	

ALIEN KULTURE
81	RAR LRAR 1	Asian Youth/Culture Crossover (p/s) 40

ALIEN SEX FIEND
83	Anagram ANA 11	Ignore The Machine/The Gurl At The End Of My Gun (p/s) 5
84	Anagram ANA 18	R.I.P./New Christian Music (cream & black p/s & red vinyl or
		b&w poster p/s) 6/7
84	Anagram 10 ANA 18	R.I.P./New Christian Music/Crazee (10", p/s) 7
84	Anagram 11 ANA 25	E.S.T. (Trip To The Moon)/Boneshaker Baby/I Am A Product (live)
		(11", PVC sleeve with insert) 8
90	Windsong 02	ASF BOX (box set, export issue, 4,000 only, with 3 coloured vinyl singles
		[12", 11" & 10"], poster, T-shirt & imitation dog turd) 25
	(see also Demon Preacher, Demons)	

(Dr.) ALIMANTADO
70s	Sun & Star ST 003	Best Dress Chicken/She Wreng-Ep. 10
77	Greensleeves GRE 002	Born for a purpose/Reason for living (with the Rebels) 6
78	Virgin VOLE 1	Slavery let I go/Find the one (12") 8

MINT VALUE £

78	Greensleeves GRE 5	Still alive/Life all over (with the Rebels)	6
78	Greensleeves GRE 13	Best dressed chicken in town/Can't conquer Natty Dreadlocks	6
79	Greensleeves GRED 10	Born for a purpose / Reason for living/Still alive/Life all over (12", with the Rebels)	20
79	Greensleeves GRED 17	Sitting in the park / Skanking in the park (12", with the Rebels)	10
80	Isda SUS 11	It cold in a Babylon/Version (12")	8
78	Greensleeves GREL 1	BEST DRESSED CHICKEN IN TOWN (LP)	15

ALIVE 'N KICKING
70 Roulette RO 517 — Tighter, Tighter/Sunday Morning ... 6

ALKALINE TRIO
02	B-Unique BUN 013-7	Private eye / Private eye (original) (picture disc, stickered PVC sleeve)	10
03	Universal 9809024	We've had enough / Blue in the face (live) (picture disc, stickered PVC sleeve)	8
03	Universal 9811507	All on black / This could be love (acoustic SBN session) (picture disc)	8

ALKATRAZ
76 Rockfield UAS 30001 — DOING A MOONLIGHT (LP) ... 15

ALL ABOUT EVE
85	Eden EDEN 1	D For Desire/Don't Follow Me (12", p/s)	20
86	Eden EDEN 2	In The Clouds/End Of The Day/Love Leads Nowhere (12", p/s, some with poster)	12/10
87	Eden EVENX 3	Our Summer (extended)/Lady Moonlight/Shelter From The Rain (12", p/s)	8

(see also Ghost Dance, Gene Loves Jezebel)

ALLAM
73 Fab FAB 190 — Hide & Seek/Version (actually by Allen & Mr. Lonely) ... 8

JOHNNIE ALLAN
74 Oval 1001 — Promised Land/SHELTON DUNAWAY: Betty And Dupree ... 8

STEVE ALLAN
79 Creole CR 164 — Together We Are Beautiful/All Mine ... 5

(see also Alan Carvell, Carvells, Five Sapphires, Al Southern)

ALL DAY
73 private pressing — YORK POP MUSIC PROJECT (LP) ... 200

BARRY ALLDIS
63 Decca F11642 — Like Lazy/Go Get It ... 6

ANNISTEEN ALLEN
| 55 | Capitol CL 14264 | Fujiyama Mama/Wheels Of Love (78 rpm = £25) | 220 |
| 57 | Brunswick 05639 | Don't Nobody Move/The Money Tree (78 rpm = £12) | 40 |

BARBARA ALLEN
59 Felsted AF 115 — Tommy's Song/Never Let Me Go (78 rpm = £12) ... 12

BOBBY ALLEN (& COMMANCHES)
62	Fontana 267252 TF	Your Cheatin' Heart/I'll Forget About You	8
63	Fontana TF 401	Here Comes The Bride/Nothing's Impossible	8
64	Fontana TF 429	Half As Much As You/So In Love With You (with Commanches)	8

(see also Commanches)

CLAY ALLEN
62	Starlite ST45 086	This Time It's Really Goodbye/Broken Home	10
63	Starlite ST45 096	I Can't Stop The Blues From Moving/You've Got The Cleanest Mind	10
63	Starlite ST45 106	Crazy Crazy World/Just A Stone's Throw Away	10

DAEVID ALLEN
75	Virgin VS 123	Fred The Fish/It's The Time Of Your Life (p/s, promo only)	10
79	Charly CY 51056	Much Too Old/I Am A Freud (with New York Gong, p/s with insert)	6
83	Charly CY 2101	ALIEN IN NEW YORK (12" EP)	8
75	Caroline C 1512	BANANA MOON (LP)	20
76	Virgin V 5024	GOOD MORNING! (LP, by Daevid Allen & Euterpe)	12
81	Shanghai HAI 201	THE DEATH OF ROCK AND OTHER ENTRANCES (mini-LP, with poster)	12

(see also Gong, Planet Gong, Soft Machine)

DAVE ALLEN
69 Philips BF 1748 — The Good Earth/A Way Of Life ... 10

DEAN ALLEN
58 London HLM 8698 — Rock Me To Sleep/Ooh-Ooh Baby Baby (78 rpm = £20) ... 40

HENRY 'RED' ALLEN
66 CBS BPG 62400 — FEELING GOOD (LP) ... 15

JEFF ALLEN
57 HMV JO 477 — That'll Be The Day/Guilty Mind (export issue) ... 38

JERRY ALLEN & HIS TRIO
| 54 | Decca F 10248 | S'Posin'/When I Needed You Most | 6 |
| 55 | Decca F 10443 | Kind/Delaunay's Dilemma | 7 |

LEE ALLEN (& HIS BAND)
58	HMV POP 452	Walkin' With Mr. Lee/Promenade (78 rpm = £25)	35
59	Top Rank JAR 265	Cat Walk/Creole Alley	12
59	Top Rank JKR 8020	WALKIN' WITH MR LEE (EP)	42
62	Ember ELR 3312	MOOD MUSIC LIBRARY (LP, uncredited library issue, generic sleeve)	55

(see also Huey 'Piano' Smith & Clowns)

MINT VALUE £

MAURICE ALLEN
58   Pye 7N 15128   Ooh Baby/Rockhearted (78 rpm = £10)..28

MERV ALLEN & JIMMY JOHNSTON SHOWBAND
67   Emerald HD1080   A Pub With No Beer/Going Won't Be Easy....................................6

PATRICK ALLEN
77   Kab KB 5540   Groovy Feeling/Instrumental..6

PETER ALLEN
77   A&M AMLH 63706   IT IS TIME FOR (2xLP)..30

RED ALLEN
62   Longhorn BLH 0005   Trouble Round My Door/Beautiful Brown Eyes.............................10

REX ALLEN
54   Brunswick 05341   This Ole House/They Were Doin' The Mambo (with Tex Williams)..........18
57   Brunswick 05675   The Little White Horses/Drango...10
57   Brunswick 05677   Wringle Wrangle/Westward Ho The Wagons................................10
57   Brunswick 05699   Flower Of San Antone/Money, Marbles And Chalk.........................10
59   Top Rank JAR 188   One More Sunrise (Morgen)/The Little Old Church In The Valley (78 rpm = £15)..6
62   Mercury AMT 1191   Don't Go Near The Indians/Touched So Deeply............................6
57   Brunswick OE 9317   WESTWARD HO THE WAGONS (EP)...15
64   Mercury 10011MCE   COUNTRY AND WESTERN ACES (EP)...15
     (see also Tex Williams, Patti Page)

STEVE ALLEN (& HIS ORCHESTRA)
56   Vogue Coral Q 72118   The Ballad Of Davy Crockett/Very Square Dance.........................12
58   Vogue Coral Q 72310   Pretend You Don't See Her/But I Haven't Got Him (78 rpm = £10).........5
58   London HL 8742   Almost In Your Arms (Love Song From "Houseboat")/Hula Hoop.............5
58   London HL 8742   Almost In Your Arms (Love Song From "Houseboat")/Hula Hoop (78).......15
     (see also George Cates)

TONY ALLEN
62   Philips BBE 12522   Time To Swing (EP)...10

VERNON ALLEN
64   R&B JB 169   Fari Come/Babylon..100

(Vernon) ALLEN & (Milton) HAMILTON
66   Blue Beat BB 348   It Is I/Baby What's More...12
66   Blue Beat BB 353   You're The Angel/Someone Like You......................................12

WOODY ALLEN
64   Colpix PX 775   Spot Floyd/The Bullet...5
65   Colpix PXL 488   WOODY ALLEN VOLUME 2 (LP)..18
65   Colpix PXL 518   WOODY ALLEN (LP)...18

DAVE ALLENBY
69   RCA 1865   Where Has All The Love Gone/Somewhere In The World.....................6

ALLENS
75   Mowest MW 3029   High Tide/California Music..8

ALLEY CATS
59   Vogue V 9155   Last Night/Snap-Crackle And Pop (78 rpm = £50+)........................30

BOBBY ALLISON
64   Solar SRP 103   You've Got Everything/Change Your Mind.................................18

GENE ALLISON
58   London HLU 8605   Hey, Hey, I Love You/You Can Make It If You Try (78 rpm = £50+)...........110

JERRY ALLISON & CRICKETS
65   Liberty LIB 10196   Now Hear This/Everybody's Got A Little Problem.........................18
     (see also Crickets, Ivan)

LUTHER ALLISON
71   Delmark DS 625   LOVE ME MAMA (LP, blue label)..15

LYNN ALLISON
57   Columbia DB 3867   Mama From The Train (A Kiss, A Kiss)/Song Of The Sparrow................8
57   Columbia DB 3906   If Only/The Sky...8

MOSE ALLISON
61   Fontana H 292   Baby Please Don't Go/Deed I Do...35
64   Columbia DB 7330   I Love The Life I Live/Life Is Suicide.................................10
59   Esquire EP 214   PARCHMAN FARM (EP)...30
59   Esquire EP 221   BACK COUNTRY SUITE (EP)..20
60   Esquire EP 224   BLUEBERRY HILL (EP)..20
61   Esquire EP 231   THAT MAN MOSE AGAIN (EP)...20
64   Columbia SEG 8353   ALLISON SINGS THE BLUES (EP)...20
59   Esquire 32-051   BACK COUNTRY SUITE (LP)..35
59   Esquire 32-071   LOCAL COLOUR (LP)..35
59   Esquire 32-083   YOUNG MAN MOSE (LP)..35
60   Esquire 32-094   CREEK BANK (LP)..35
61   Esquire 32-131   AUTUMN SONG (LP)...35
62   Esquire 32-171   RAMBLIN' WITH MOSE (LP)..35
63   London HA-K 8083   SWINGIN' MACHINE (LP, as Mose Allison Jazz Group).....................20
64   Columbia SX 6058   V-8 FORD (LP)..20
64   Stateside SL 10106   MOSE ALLISON SINGS (LP)..15
66   Atlantic 587/588 007   MOSE ALIVE (LP)..15
66   CBS Realm RM(S) 52318   I LOVE THE LIFE I LIVE (LP)..15
66   Atlantic 587/588 031   WILD MAN ON THE LOOSE (LP)...10
67   Transatlantic PR 7189   AUTUMN SONG (LP)...10

MINT VALUE £

68	Transatlantic PR 7279	MOSE ALLISON (LP)	10
72	Atlantic 2400 205	WESTERN MAN (LP)	15
72	Prestige PR 24002	MOSE ALLISON (2-LP)	15
73	Atlantic K 40460	MOSE IN YOUR EAR (LP)	15

ALLISONS (U.K.)
61	Fontana H 294	Are You Sure/There's One Thing More (as Allisons [Bob & John])	8
61	Fontana H 304	Words/Blue Tears	10
61	Fontana H 336	What A Mess!/Lorraine (some in p/s)	15/5
61	Fontana H 362	Lesson In Love/Oh, My Love	10
62	Fontana 267 231TF	Sweet And Lovely/Sugar Love	7
62	Fontana 267 255TF	I'll Cross My Fingers/You Should Be Sorry	7
61	Fontana TFE 17339	THE ALLISONS (EP)	25
61	Fontana TFL 5135	ARE YOU SURE (LP, also stereo STFL 558)	30/35

ALLISONS (U.S.)
64	Stateside SS 289	Surfer Street/Money (vocal: Darlene Love)	30

(see also Blossoms, Darlene Love)

ALLMAN BROTHERS BAND
73	Capricorn/Sound For Industry SFI 165	Ramblin' Man/MARSHALL TUCKER BAND: Take The Highway (flexidisc free with *Rolling Stone* magazine)	8/5
69	Atco 228 033	THE ALLMAN BROTHERS BAND (LP)	30
71	Atco 2400 032	IDLEWILD SOUTH (LP)	20

(see also Duane Allman, Gregg Allman, Duane & Gregg Allman, Allman Joys, Hourglass)

DUANE ALLMAN
72	Capricorn K 67502	AN ANTHOLOGY (2-LP)	15

(see also Allman Brothers, Duane & Gregg Allman)

DUANE & GREGG ALLMAN
73	Polydor 2310 235	DUANE & GREGG ALLMAN (LP)	15

(see also Allman Brothers, Duane Allman, Gregg Allman)

GREGG ALLMAN
73	Capricorn K 47508/CP0116	LAID BACK (LP)	15

(see also Allman Brothers, Duane & Gregg Allman)

ALLMAN JOYS
73	Mercury 6398 005	ALLMAN JOYS (LP)	16

ALL NIGHT BAND
79	Contact CON 5	Lovely Ladies/It's My Life	25

TOMMY ALLSUP
65	London HA-U 8218	BUDDY HOLLY SONG BOOK (LP)	45

TONY ALMERICO'S DIXIELAND JAMBOREE ALLSTARS
55	London RE-P 1019	DIXIELAND (EP, reissued as RE-D 1019)	15/12

JOHNNY ALMOND MUSIC MACHINE
69	Deram DM 266	Solar Level/To R.K.	20
69	Deram DML/SML 1043	PATENT PENDING (LP)	40
70	Deram SML 1057	HOLLYWOOD BLUES (LP)	45

(see also Alan Price Set, Zoot Money, Paul Williams Set, John Mayall & Bluesbreakers, Mark-Almond, Jon Mark)

MARC ALMOND
SINGLES
84	Some Bizzare BZS 2310	The Boy Who Came Back (Extended)/Joey Demento (Extended) (10", p/s)	12
84	Some Bizzare BZS 2410	You Have (Ext.)/Black Mountain Blues/Split Lip (Ext.) (10", p/s, with lyric sheet)	10
84	Some Bizzare BZS 2412	You Have (Long Version)/Joey Demento/Split Lip (Long Version) (12", p/s)	8
84	Some Bizzare BZS 2510	Tenderness Is A Weakness (Extended)/Love For Sale/Pink Shack Blues (live)/The Heel (live) (10", p/s, with lyric insert)	12
86	Some Bizzare GLOWY 2-10	A Woman's Story/The Heel/A Salty Dog/The Plague/The Little White Cloud That Cried/For One Moment/Just Good Friends (10", picture disc, stickered PVC sl.)	8
86	Some Bizzare GLOW 3-13	Ruby Red (Re-recorded Extended Dance Mix)/(Instrumental)/I'm Sick Of You Tasting Of Somebody Else (12", stickered p/s; some mispressed with same track repeated on Side 1)	15/12
87	Some Bizzare GLOWD 4	Melancholy Rose/Gyp The Blood//Pirate Jenny/Surabaya Johnny (double pack, gatefold p/s)	6
87	Some Bizzare GLOW 4-12	Melancholy Rose/Gyp The Blood/A World Full Of People/Black Lullaby (12", p/s with postcard)	8
88	Parlophone RX 6186	Tears Run Rings/Everything I Wanted Love To Be (box set with booklet, cards & badge)	5
89	Parlophone RX 6201	Something's Gotten Hold Of My Heart (with "Special Guest Star Gene Pitney")/Something's Gotten Hold Of My Heart (numbered box set with booklet, 2 cards & badge & sticker)	8
89	Parlophone PSR 500	Kept Boy (etched B-side, no p/s, cancelled freebie intended for "The Stars We Are")	20
90	Parlophone 12RPD 6252	The Desperate Hours/The Gambler (12", picture disc)	8
91	WEA Y 2633TP	My Hand Over My Heart/Deadly Serenade (12", picture disc)	8
91	Mercury SOFCP 1	Say Hello Wave Goodbye '91/Numbers (Original Version)/Torch (Original Extended Version) (CD, picture disc)	10
91	Mercury SOFCD 2	Tainted Love (Original 7" Version)/Where The Heart Is (Remix)/Tainted Love (Remixed By Mendelsohn) (CD in leather wallet, various colours)	10
92	WEA YZ 638T	Extract From Trois Chanson De Bilitis/The Days Of Pearly Spencer/Dancing In A Golden Cage/Dancing In A Golden Cage (Reflection In A Golden Eye) (12", withdrawn, 300 only)	12
92	WEA YZ 638CDX	Extract From "Trois Chanson De Bilitis"/The Days Of Pearly Spencer/Dancing In A Golden Cage (CD, no'd holographic disc in metallic card p/s)	8
84	Gutter Hearts GH 1	BITE BACK + BLUES (fan club-only LP, credited to "Raoul & The Ruined")	30

Marc ALMOND

| 95 | EMI CDMATBOX 1 | TREASURE BOX 1 (2-CD, box set) | 20 |
| 97 | Some Bizzare SBZCD 022 | VIOLENT SILENCE/FLESH VOLCANO (CD, withdrawn) | 20 |

FLEXIDISCS & FREEBIES

82	Lyntone LYN 12505	Discipline (as 'Marc Almond & Friends', pink flexidisc with *Flexipop* issue 23. Friends are Throbbing Gristle)	20/15
84	Gutter Hearts LYN 14210	My Death (fan club flexidisc)	12
86	MM Vinyl Conflict 1	Oily Black Limousine (col. vinyl, b/w 3 songs by others, free with *Melody Maker*)	6
86	(no label or cat. no.)	Your Aura (live) (fan club flexidisc)	10
89	Offbeat 1	Tears Run Rings (La Magia Dance Mix) (3" CD, with *Offbeat* magazine)	10
92	(no label or cat. no.)	Christmas In Vegas (fan club flexidisc)	5
95	(no label or cat. no.)	When I Was A Young Man (fan club cassette)	10

(see also Soft Cell, Marc & Mambas, Burmoe Brothers, Vicious Pink Phenomena, Flesh Volcano, Annie Hogan, Sally Timms, Gene Pitney)

ALMOND LETTUCE

| 68 | Columbia DB 8442 | The Tree Dog Song/To Henry With Hope | 6 |
| 69 | Philips BF 1764 | Magic Circle/Twenty Weary Miles | 20 |

ALMOND MARZIPAN

| 70 | Trend TNT 53 | Open Up Your Heart/Summer Love | 12 |
| 70 | Trend TNT 55 | Marie Take A Chance/I'll Forget You | 6 |

ALONE AGAIN OR

| 84 | All One ALG 1 | Drum The Beat (In My Soul)/Smartie Edit (p/s) | 10 |

(see also Shamen)

HERB ALPERT (& TIJUANA BRASS)

64	Stateside SS 286	Mexican Drummer Man/The Great Manolette	5
67	Pye International 7N 25419	Casino Royale (From The Film)/The Wall Street Rag (unissued)	
68	A&M AMS 700	Casino Royale (From The Film)/The Wall Street Rag (p/s)	10
69	A&M AMS 755	Without Her/Sandbox (p/s)	5
70	A&M AMS 810	Jerusalem/Strike Up The Band	5

ALPHASTONE

| 90s | Enraptured RAPTLP 18 | ELASTICATED WAVEBAND (LP, clear vinyl, 100 only) | 15 |
| 90s | Enraptured RAPTLP 33 | LIFE IS A MOTORWAY EP (2 x 12", gatefold sleeve, limited issue) | 10 |

CARLTON ALPHONSO

| 67 | Pama PM 700 | Where In This World/Peace Makers | 20 |
| 69 | Grape GR 3000 | Belittle Me/Keep Your Love | 12 |

CLYDE ALPHONSO

| 69 | Studio One SO 2076 | Good Enough/Let The Music Play | 25 |

ORVILLE ALPHONSO

| 65 | Caribou CRC 1 | Belly Lick/Inspiration | 10 |

PANCHO ALPHONSO AND THE REVOLUTIONARIES

| 78 | Trojan TRLS 165 | NEVER GET TO ZION (LP) | 18 |

ROLAND ALPHONSO (alias ROLAND AL)

61	Blue Beat BB 58	Blackberry Brandy/ALVIN & CECIL: Marjorie	35
62	Blue Beat BB 112	Four Corners Of The World (with Alley Cats)/SHINERS: Romantic Shuffle	45
64	R&B JB 161	Mr President/The MAYTALS: A Man Who Knows	25
64	R&B JB 164	Crime Wave/MAYTALS: Hello Honey	40
65	Island WI 217	El Pussy Cat/LORD BRYNNER: Tiger In Your Tank	30
65	Ska Beat JB 210	Nimble Foot/ANDY & JOEY: Love Is Stronger	50
65	Ska Beat JB 216	Nuclear Weapon (with Baba Brooks)/STRANGER COLE: Love Thy Neighbour	50
65	Rio R 5804	Jazz Ska/HYACINTH: Oh Gee	40
66	Blue Beat BB 356	Just A Closer Walk/Jericho Train	70
66	Island WI 259	James Bond/LEE PERRY: Just Keep It Up	90
66	Doctor Bird DB 1010	From Russia With Love/Cleopatra (with Soul Brothers)	80
66	Doctor Bird DB 1011	Sufferer's Choice (with Soul Brothers)/SOULETTES: I Want To Be	50
66	Doctor Bird DB 1013	WAILERS: Rude Boy/ROLANDO AL & SOUL BROTHERS: Ringo's Theme (This Boy)	75
66	Doctor Bird DB 1017	Sugar And Spice/Get Out Of My Life (with Soul Brothers)	40
66	Doctor Bird DB 1020	Phoenix City (with Soul Brothers)/DEACONS: Men Alone	20
66	Doctor Bird DB 1023	Doctor Ring-A-Ding/FREDDIE & HEARTACHES: Here Is My Heart	80
66	Doctor Bird DB 1035	I Love You/Song Of Love	20
66	Doctor Bird DB 1039	WAILERS: Rasta Put It On/ROLAND AL & SOUL BROTHERS: Ska With Ringo	100
66	Ska Beat JB 231	Rinky Dink (So Good) (with Studio One Orchestra)/SCRATCH & DYNAMITES: Deacon Johnson	50
67	Pyramid PYR 6003	Middle East/Wise Man	30
67	Pyramid PYR 6004	El Torro/007 (Shanty Town)	10
67	Pyramid PYR 6005	Women Of The World (& Beverley's Allstars)/SPANISHTONIANS: Kisses	20
67	Pyramid PYR 6006	On The Move (& Beverley's Allstars)/DESMOND DEKKER & ACES: It's A Shame	12
67	Pyramid PYR 6007	Jungle Bit (& Beverley's Allstars)/NORMAN GRANT: Somebody Please Help Me	15
67	Pyramid PYR 6008	The Cat/DESMOND DEKKER & ACES: Rudy Got Soul	30
67	Pyramid PYR 6009	Guantanamera Ska (& Beverley's Allstars)/SPANISHTONIANS: Suffer Me Not	30
67	Pyramid PYR 6011	Nothing For Nothing/DESMOND DEKKER & ACES: Rude Boy Train	25
67	Pyramid PYR 6018	Sock It To Me (& Beverley's Allstars)/SPANISHTONIANS: Rudie Gets Plenty	30
68	Pyramid PYR 6022	Whiter Shade Of Pale/On The Move	10
68	Pyramid PYR 6030	Dreamland/MAYTALS: 54-46, That's My Number	20
68	Pyramid PYR 6043	Stream Of Life/MAYTALS: Struggle	60
68	Coxsone CS 7077	Reggae In The Grass/ROY RICHARDS: Get Smart	45
69	Gas GAS 112	A Thousand Tons Of Megaton (actually by Derrick Morgan)/Musical Resurrection	20
70	Punch PH 39	Roll On (& Upsetters)/CARL DAWKINS: True Love	15

| 71 | Banana BA 340 | Mellow Mood (Way To My Heart)/MAYTALS: Marching On | 20 |
| 68 | Hi Note BSLP 5001 | ABC ROCK STEADY (with the Originals Orchestra) | 75 |

(see also Eric Morris, Bob Marley/Wailers, Prince Buster, Hopeton Lewis, Joe White, Johnny Melody; Monty & Roy; Derrick Morgan, Niney, Jackie Opel; Owen & Leon; Kentrick Patrick, Duke Reid; Roy & Millie; Slickers, Lou Sparkles, Jack Sparrow, Austin Faithful, Clancy Eccles, Charmers, Denny & Wilson, Dennis Alcapone, Ken Boothe, Larry Marshall)

ALPINES
| 68 | Double D DD 110 | Get Ready/CARIBBEATS: Come Back Charlie | 20 |

ALQUIN
| 73 | Polydor 2480 152 | MARKS (LP) | 12 |

RITA ALSTON
| 70 | Trojan TR 7751 | Popcorn Funky Reggae/NAT COLE: My Love | 10 |
| 70 | Trojan TR 7752 | All Kinds Of Everything/CARL LEVEY: Instrumental Version | 6 |

(see also Rita, Nat Cole)

SHIRLEY ALSTON
| 75 | London HLA 10506 | I'd Rather Not Be Loving You/Can't Stop Singin' (Bout The Boy I Love) | 6 |
| 75 | London SHA 8491 | WITH A LITTLE HELP FROM MY FRIENDS (LP) | 20 |

(see also Shirelles)

ALTECS
| 61 | London HLU 9387 | Easy/Recess | 15 |

(see also The Black Dog)

ALTERNATIVE TV
77	Sniffing Glue SG 75 RPS	Love Lies Limp (1-sided flexidisc with *Sniffing Glue* fanzine issue 12)	20/5
77	Deptford Fun City DFC 02	How Much Longer/You Bastard (p/s)	7
77	Deptford Fun City DFC 02	How Much Longer/You Bastard (p/s, labelled 'alternate versions')	7
78	Deptford Fun City DFC 04	Life After Life/Life After Dub (p/s)	5
78	Deptford Fun City DFC 06	Life/Love Lies Limp (p/s)	5
78	Deptford Fun City DFC 07	Action Time Vision/Another Coke (live p/s)	6
79	Deptford Fun City DFC 10	The Force Is Blind/Lost In Room (Vibing Up The Senile Man) (p/s, last track uncredited)	5
78	Deptford Fun City DLP 01	THE IMAGE HAS CRACKED (LP)	15
78	Deptford Fun City DLP 02	WHAT YOU SEE IS ... WHAT YOU ARE (LP, 1 side by Here & Now)	12
78	Deptford Fun City DLP 03	VIBING UP THE SENILE MAN (PART ONE) (LP)	12
79	Crystal CLP 01	LIVE AT THE RAT CLUB '77 (authorised bootleg) (LP)	12
80	Deptford Fun City DLP 05	ACTION TIME VISION (LP, with inner sleeve)	12
80	Weird Noise WEIRD 001	SCARS ON SUNDAY (shared C60 cassette, 1 side by Good Missionaries)	15
80	Conventional CON 14	AN YE AS WELL (cassette, shared with Good Missionaries)	15

(see also Mark Perry, Good Missionaries, The Door & The Window, Reflections, Jools Holland, Alex Fergusson, Rat & Whale)

ALTERNATORS
| 78 | Energy NRG 001 | No Answers/The Kid Don't Know (no p/s) | 70 |

ALTERNOMEN UNLIMITED
| 79 | Object OM 06 | Facade/Connections (p/s) | 5 |

(see also Spherical Objects)

ALTHEA & DONNA
77	Lightning LIG 506	Uptown Top Ranking/Calico Suit	6
77	Lightning 12LIG 506	Uptown Top Ranking/Calico Suit (12")	8
78	Virgin Front Line FL 1012	UPTOWN TOP RANKING (LP)	15

ALTON (Ellis) & EDDY
| 60 | Blue Beat BB 17 | Muriel/CLUE J. & HIS BLUES BLASTERS: Silky | 12 |
| 62 | Island WI 009 | My Love Divine/Let Me Dream | 15 |

(see also Alton Ellis)

ALTON & FLAMES
(see under Alton Ellis)

ALVARO
| 77 | Squeaky Shoes SSRM 1 | DRINKING MY OWN SPERM (LP) | 15 |

(see also 101'ers)

ALVIN'S HEARTBEATS
| 74 | Magnet MAG 24 | Chilli Willi/Chilli Willi (Part 2) | 5 |

ALVYN
| 69 | Morgan Bluetown MR 18S | You've Gotta Have An Image/Mind The Gap | 7 |

AMALGAM
| 69 | Transatlantic TRA 196 | A PRAYER FOR PEACE (LP) | 40 |
| 73 | A Records A 002 | PLAY BLACKWELL & HIGGINS (LP) | 22 |

GLEN AMAMS
| 69 | Escort ES 804 | Rich In Love/WOODPECKERS: Zumbelly | 15 |

(see also Glen Adams)

A MAN CALLED ADAM
| 90s | Acid Jazz JAZID 15T | Earthly Powers/Techno Powers (12", p/s) | 12 |

(see also Leftfield)

AMAZIAH
| 74 | Sunrise SR 001 | STRAIGHT TALKER (LP, private pressing with insert) | 120 |

AMAZING BLONDEL
72	Island WIP 6153	Alleluia (Cantus Firmus To Counterpoint)/Safety In God Alone	5
70	Bell SBLL 131	THE AMAZING BLONDEL AND A FEW FACES (LP)	85+
70	Island ILPS 9136	EVENSONG (LP, gatefold sleeve)	20
71	Island ILPS 9156	FANTASIA LINDUM (LP, with inner lyric sleeve)	18

72	Island ILPS 9205	ENGLAND (LP, gatefold sleeve)	18
73	Island ILPS 9257	BLONDEL (LP, gatefold sleeve)	15

(see also Dimples, Gospel Garden)

AMAZING DANCING BAND
68	Verve VS 567	Deep Blue Train/Simon Smith & His Amazing Dancing Bear	25
67	Verve SVLP 9214	AMAZING DANCING BAND (LP)	25

AMAZING FRIENDLY APPLE
69	Decca F 12887	Water Woman/Magician	100

AMAZING SPACE FROGS
79	Ribbett RIB 1	THE DIRTY HABITS EP	300

AMBASSADOR 277
88	El GPUT37	Pop Up Man/Malediction (10" p/s)	15

AMBERGRIS
70	Paramount SPFL 262	AMBERGRIS (LP)	15

AMBER SQUAD
80	Sound Of Leicester ST 1	(I Can't) Put My Finger On You/Tell You A Lie (p/s)	55
80	Dead Good DEAD 17	Can We Go Dancing?/You Should See (What I Do To You In My Dreams) (p/s)	35

AMBOY DUKES (U.K.)
66	Polydor 56149	Turn Back To Me/I Never Complain About You	5
67	Polydor 56172	All I Need/Doing The Best I Can	5
67	Polydor 56190	High Life In Whitley Wood (Parts 1 & 2)	5
68	Polydor 56228	Judy In Disguise/Who's Foolin' Who	15
68	Polydor 56243	Simon Says/The Marquis	10
68	Polydor 56281	He Came To See Me Yesterday/Easy Going Me	5

(AMERICAN) AMBOY DUKES
68	Fontana TF 971	Let's Go Get Stoned/It's Not True	18
67	Fontana (S)TL 5468	THE AMBOY DUKES (LP)	80
69	London HA-T/SH-T 8378	JOURNEY TO THE CENTER OF THE MIND (LP, as American Amboy Dukes)	32
69	London HA-T/SH-T 8392	MIGRATION (LP, as American Amboy Dukes)	32
74	Discreet DS 2203	TOOTH, FANG AND CLAW (LP)	20

(see also Ted Nugent)

AMBROSE & HIS ORCHESTRA
56	MGM SP 1151	Lilacs In The Rain/Deep Purple	6

AMANDA AMBROSE
63	RCA Victor RD 7605	THE AMAZING AMANDA AMBROSE (LP)	15

SAMMY AMBROSE
65	Stateside SS 385	This Diamond Ring/Bad Night	150
65	Stateside SS 399	Monkey See Monkey Do/Welcome To Dreamsville	250

AMBROSE SLADE
69	Fontana TF 1015	Genesis/Roach Daddy	220
69	Fontana STL 5492	BEGINNINGS (LP, laminated sleeve, black label with silver print; beware of counterfeits with matt sleeve & black & white label)	240
75	Contour 6870 678	BEGINNINGS OF SLADE (LP, reissue, different cover & running order, withdrawn)	40

(see also Slade, 'N Betweens)

AMBROSIA
75	20th Century BT 434	AMBROSIA (LP)	15
76	20th Century BT 519	SOMEWHERE I'VE NEVER TRAVELLED (LP, with inner sleeve)	15

AMBULANCE LTD
04	TVT Records SHAG024	HEAVY LIFTING EP (7" p/s)	8

AMEBIX
82	Spiderleg SDL 6	Who's The Enemy/Carnage/No Gods No Masters (p/s)	20
83	Spiderleg SDL 10	Winter/Beginning Of The End (p/s)	18

LOLA AMECHE
53	Oriole CB 1143	Rock The Joint/Don't Let The Stars Get In Your Eyes (78)	15
53	Oriole CB 1172	The Knockin' Song/So Far So Good (78)	10

AMEN
99	Road Runner RR 21315	COMA AMERICA EP	6

AMEN CORNER
67	Deram DM 136	Gin House Blues/I Know (early copies entitled "Gin House" on label)	10
67	Deram DM 151	The World Of Broken Hearts/Nema	6
68	Deram DM 172	Bend Me Shape Me/Satisnek The Job's Worth	6
68	Deram DM 197	High In The Sky/Run, Run, Run	6
69	Deram DM 228	The World Of Broken Hearts/Gin House Blues	6
69	Immediate IM 073	(If Paradise Is) Half As Nice/Hey Hey Girl	6
69	Immediate IM 081	Hello Susie/Evil Man's Gonna Win	8
69	Immediate IM 084	Get Back/Farewell To The Real Magnificent Seven	10
69	Immediate AS 3	So Fine (promo only 'single sampler' for IMSP 023)	20
68	Deram DML/SML 1021	ROUND AMEN CORNER (LP)	28
69	Immediate IMSP 023	THE NATIONAL WELSH COAST LIVE EXPLOSION COMPANY (LP, g/fold sl.)	20
69	Immediate IMSP 028	FAREWELL TO THE REAL MAGNIFICENT SEVEN (LP, gatefold sleeve)	15

(see also Andy Fairweather-Low, Fairweather, Mayfield's Mule, Judas Jump)

AMERICAN BREED
67	CBS 2888	Step Out Of Your Mind/The Same Old Thing	12
67	CBS 2972	Step Out Of Your Mind/The Same Old Thing (reissue)	6
68	Stateside SS 2078	Bend Me Shape Me/Mindrocker	8

68	Dot DOT 101	Green Light/Don't It Make You Cry	15
68	Dot DOT 106	Ready, Willing And Able/Take Me If You Want Me	7
67	Dot DOLP 255	AMERICAN BREED (LP)	25
68	Dot (S)LPD 502	BEND ME, SHAPE ME (LP)	25
68	Dot (S)LPD 507	NO WAY TO TREAT A LADY (LP, soundtrack)	20
68	Dot (S)LPD 518	PUMPKIN, POWDER, SCARLET AND GREEN (LP)	15
69	Dot (S)LPD 526	THE LONELY SIDE OF THE CITY (LP)	12

AMERICAN GYPSY

71	CBS 7027	Gypsy Queen Pt 1/Dead & Gone	6
75	BTM SBT 101	Angel Eyes/Lady Eleanor	10
75	BTM BTM 1001	AMERICAN GYPSY (LP)	40

(AMERICAN) POETS

66	London HLC 10037	She Blew A Good Thing/Out To Lunch (as American Poets)	150
71	United Artists UP 35308	She Blew A Good Thing/Out To Lunch (reissue, as Poets)	15

AMERICAN SPRING

72	United Artists UP 35376	Good Time/Sweet Mountain	10
72	United Artists UP 35421	Mama Said/Tennessee Waltz	10
73	CBS CBS 1590	Shyin' Away/Falling In Love	12
72	United Artists UAG 29363	AMERICAN SPRING (LP)	40

(see also Beach Boys, Honeys)

AMERICAN YOUTH CHOIR

71	Polydor 2066 013	Together We Can Make It/Keep Your Fine Self Near Me	50

EDDIE AMES

57	HMV POP 311	The Bean Song/I'd Give You The World	8
67	RCA 1577	My Cup Runneth Over/Climb Every Mountain (as Ed Ames)	7

NANCY AMES

66	Columbia DB 7809	Friends And Lovers Forever/I've Got A Lot Of Love	20
66	Columbia DB 8039	Cry Softly/I Don't Want To Talk About It	50

AMES BROTHERS

53	HMV 7M 153	You, You, You/My Life, My Love, My Happiness	15
54	HMV 7M 179	I Can't Believe That You're In Love/Boogie Woogie Maxine	28
54	HMV 7M 209	The Man With The Banjo/Man, Man, Is For The Woman Made	10
54	HMV 7M 253	Hopelessly/One More Time	10
55	HMV 7M 281	The Naughty Lady Of Shady Lane/Addio	15
55	HMV 7M 310	Sweet Brown-Eyed Baby/Sympathetic Eyes	10
55	HMV 7M 322	Wrong Again/Merci Beaucoup	10
55	HMV 7M 331	So Will I/My Bonnie Lassie	10
56	HMV 7M 410	My Love, Your Love/If You Wanna See Mamie Tonight	10
56	HMV 7MC 46	If You Wanna See Mamie Tonight/It Only Hurts For A Little While (export issue)	10
56	RCA RCA 1015	Rocking Shoes/Tammy (78 rpm = £6)	12
57	RCA RCA 1021	So Little Time/Melodie D'Amour	10
58	RCA RCA 1049	In Love/A Very Precious Love	10
58	RCA RCA 1091	No One But You (In My Heart)/Pussy Cat	10
59	RCA RCA 1104	Red River Rose/When The Summer Comes	10
59	RCA RCA 1118	(Yes, I Need) Only Your Love/Dancin' In The Streets	10
59	RCA RCA 1135	Someone To Come To/Mason-Dixon Line (78 rpm = £8)	10
57	HMV 7EG 8237	EXACTLY LIKE YOU (EP)	10
59	RCA RCX 1047	BEST OF THE AMES BROTHERS (EP)	10
56	Coral LVA 9071	THE SOUNDS OF CHRISTMAS HARMONY (LP)	15

AMITY

76	Red Rag RRR 001	AMITY (LP)	120

AMM

66	Incus EP 1	AT THE ROUNDHOUSE (EP)	165
67	Elektra EUKS 7256	AMM MUSIC (LP)	120+

(see also Eddie Provost Band)

ALBERT AMMONS

52	Vogue V 2109	Boogie Woogie Stomp/Boogie Woogie Blues (78)	6
54	Vogue V 2201	Chicago In Mind (with Meade 'Lux' Lewis)/Two And Few (78)	8
54	Vogue V 2213	Bass Goin' Crazy/Suitcase Blues (78)	8
55	Vogue EPV 1071	ALBERT AMMONS (EP)	35
57	Brunswick OE 9325	BOOGIE WOOGIE STOMP (EP)	35
54	Mercury MG 25012	ALBERT AMMONS (10" LP)	40
62	Storyville SLP 184	BOOGIE WOOGIE TRIO (LP)	25

(see also [Big] Joe Turner)

ALBERT AMMONS & PETE JOHNSON

55	HMV DLP 1011	EIGHT TO THE BAR (10" LP)	30

ALBERT AMMONS, PETE JOHNSON & MEADE 'LUX' LEWIS

55	Columbia SEG 7528	SHOUT FOR JOY (EP)	15
63	Riverside RLP 12-106	GIANTS OF BOOGIE WOOGIE (LP)	15

(see also Pete Johnson, Meade 'Lux' Lewis)

GENE AMMONS (BAND)

60	Starlite ST45 017	Echo Chamber Blues/Ammons' Boogie	50
63	Starlite ST45 097	Anna/Cae' Cae'	12
62	Esquire EP 249	BOSSA NOVA BY THE BOSS (EP)	12
59	Esquire 32-047	HI FI JAM SESSION (LP)	22
59	Esquire 32-077	FUNKY (LP)	22
60	Esquire 32-097	JAMMIN' WITH GENE (LP)	22
62	Esquire 32-147	BLUE GENE (LP)	22
63	Esquire 32-177	BOSS TENOR (LP)	22

Gene AMMONS

63	Esquire 32-178	BAD! BOSSA NOVA (LP)	35
72	Prestige PR 24021	JUG & DODO (LP, with Dodo Marmarosa)	15
73	Prestige PR 10019	YOU TALK THAT TALK (LP)	15

AMON DÜÜL II
70	Liberty LBF 15355	Archangel's Thunderbird/Burning Sister	35
69	Liberty LBS 83279	PHALLUS DEI (LP)	60
70	Liberty LSP 101/LBS 83359	YETI (2-LP, gatefold sleeve)	35
71	United Artists UAD 60003/4	DANCE OF THE LEMMINGS (2-LP, gatefold sleeve)	35
72	Sunset SLS 50257	PHALLUS DEI (LP, reissue)	15
72	United Artists UAG 23927	CARNIVAL IN BABYLON (LP, gatefold sleeve)	25
72	United Artists UAG 29406	WOLF CITY (LP, gatefold sleeve)	20
73	United Artists USP 102	LIVE IN LONDON (LP)	15
73	United Artists UAS 29504	VIVE LA TRANCE (LP, with inner sleeve)	15

(see also Utopia)

AMORPHOUS ANDROGYNOUS
| 93 | Quigley LPEBV 1 | TALES OF EPHIDRINA (LP) | 18 |
| 93 | Quigley CDEBV 1 | TALES OF EPHIDRINA (CD) | 18 |

(see also Future Sound Of London)

ADAM AMOS & NOEL ROCKS
| 60s | Celtic Music CM 011 | CASUAL ON THE BALCONY (LP) | 25 |
| 60s | Celtic Music CM 026 | ADAM AMOS & NOEL ROCKS (LP) | 20 |

TORI AMOS
91	East West YZ 618T	ME AND A GUN EP (12")	15
91	East West YZ 618CD	ME AND A GUN EP (CD)	15
91	East West YZ 618	Silent All These Years/Me And A Gun (p/s)	5
91	East West YZ 618T	Silent All These Years/Upside Down/Me And A Gun/Thoughts (12", p/s)	10
91	East West YZ 618CD	Silent All These Years/Upside Down/Me And A Gun/Thoughts (CD)	10
92	East West A 7531T	China/Sugar/Flying Dutchman/Humpty Dumpty (12", p/s)	10
92	East West A 7531CD	China/Sugar/Flying Dutchman/Humpty Dumpty (CD)	10
92	East West A 7504	Winter/The Pool (p/s)	5
92	East West A 7479CDX	CRUCIFY LIVE EP (CD, box set, with art prints, some sealed)	15+/12+
92	East West A 7433	Silent All These Years/Ode To The Banana King Part 1 (p/s)	5
92	East West A 7433CDX	Silent All These Years/Ode To The Banana King Part 1/Song For Eric/Happy Phantom (CD, digipak)	18
94	East West A 7281CDX	Cornflake Girl/A Case Of You/If 6 Were 9/Strange Fruit (CD, digipak)	15
94	East West A 7251	God/God (Acapella vocal and rain mix) (picture disc)	6
98	East West AT 0045C	Raspberry Swirl (Lip Gloss Version)/(Sticky Extended Vocal Mix)/(Scarlet Spectrum Feels) (CD, withdrawn)	12
99	Atlantic AT 0077CD2	GLORY OF THE 80s EP (CD, part 2 of 2-CD set, mispressing, plays CD-1 tracks)	12
97	East West PROP 100	BOYS FOR PELE (CD, promo, card sleeve)	30

AMOS & SARA
| 81 | (private release) | THE PRIVATE WORLD OF AMOS (cassette) | 10 |
| 82 | It's War Boys £9 | Go Home Soldier/Enough Is Enough/Surveillance O.H.M.S. (12", screenprint p/s) | 10 |

(see also Homosexuals)

AMP
| 90s | Enraptured RAPTLP 16 | PASSÉ*PRÉSENT (2-LP, 1 disc audiophile vinyl, 1 blue vinyl, numbered) | 20 |

AMPHETAMEANIES
| 99 | F&J Records SHAG024 | Last Night/Suzie The Muppet Ltd (7" p/s 600 pressed) | 8 |
(see also Belle and Sebastian, Franz Ferdinand))

CURTIS AMY
61	Vogue LA12287	GROOVIN' BLUE (LP, with Frank Butler)	15
60s	Fontana 688136ZL	KATANGA (LP)	15
60s	Vogue	THE BLUE MESSAGE (LP, with Paul Bryant)	15
60s	Vogue	MEETIN' HERE (LP, with Paul Bryant)	15

ANAL FLEAS
| 82 | Rectal FLEA 45 | Psych/Over the Edge/Landlord/Go Down (p/s, with insert) | 80 |

ANAN
| 68 | Pye 7N 17571 | Haze Woman/I Wonder Where My Sister's Gone | 50 |
| 68 | Pye 7N 17642 | Madena/Standing Still | 25 |

PETER ANATHAN
| 66 | Fontana TF 705 | You Can't Stop Me Loving You/Feel I'm Falling | 15 |

ANATHEMA
| 94 | Peaceville CC 6 | We Are The Bible (purple vinyl) | 25 |

ANCIENT GREASE
| 71 | Mercury 6338 033 | WOMAN AND CHILDREN FIRST (LP) | 40+ |
(see also Eyes Of Blue, Big Sleep, Man, Gary Pickford-Hopkins)

AND ALSO THE TREES
83	Reflex (no cat. no.)	AND ALSO THE TREES (EP, cassette only)	20
84	Reflex RE 3	The Secret Sea/Secrecy (p/s)	8
84	Reflex 12 RE 6	The Secret Sea/Secrecy/There Were No Bounds/The Tease The Tear/Midnight Garden/Wallpaper Dying (12", p/s)	10
84	Reflex FS 9	Shantell/Wallpaper Dying (p/s)	8
84	Reflex LEX 1	AND ALSO THE TREES (LP)	20

ERIC ANDERSEN
| 65 | Fontana TFL 6061 | TODAY IS THE HIGHWAY (LP) | 30 |
| 68 | Fontana STFL 6068 | 'BOUT CHANGES AND THINGS TAKE 2 (LP) | 16 |

BILL ANDERSON
63	Brunswick 05887	Still/You Made It Easy	10

CARLEEN ANDERSON
90s	Circa YR12	DUSKY SAPPHO EP (12", p/s)	15

CAROL ANDERSON
79	Grapevine GRP 133	Sad Girl/I'll Get Off At the Next Stop	8

ERNESTINE ANDERSON
59	Mercury AMT 1035	Be Mine/I Don't See Me In Your Eyes Any More	5
59	Mercury AMT 1073	My Love Will Last/Call Me Darling	5
60	Mercury AMT 1082	There Are Such Times/You, You, You	5
60	Mercury AMT 1103	A Kiss To Build A Dream On/Come On, Baby, Let's Go	10
61	Mercury AMT 1137	A Lover's Question/That's All I Want From You	15
64	Sue WI 309	Keep An Eye On Love/Continental Mind	100
65	Stateside SS 455	Somebody Told You/How Many Times	10
65	Mercury MF 912	Jerk & Twine/You Can't Buy Love	10
60	Mercury ZEP 10057	RUNNING WILD (EP)	10
60	Mercury ZEP 10089	WELCOME TO THE CLUB (EP)	10
61	Mercury ZEP 10105	AZURE-TE (EP)	10
61	Mercury ZEP 10124	JUST A SWINGIN' (EP)	10
64	Mercury 10007 MCE	ERNESTINE ANDERSON (EP)	10
58	Pye Nixa NPT 19025	BY SPECIAL REQUEST (LP)	10
59	Mercury MMC 14016	RUNNIN' WILD (LP)	20
60	Mercury MMC 14037	THE FASCINATING ERNESTINE (LP)	15
61	Mercury MMC 14062	MOANIN' (LP)	20
64	Sue ILP 911	THE NEW SOUND OF ERNESTINE ANDERSON (LP, unissued)	150
67	Columbia S(C)X 6145	ERNESTINE ANDERSON (LP)	15

GLADSTONE ANDERSON (& FOLLOWERS)
69	Blue Cat BS 172	Judas/The World Come To An End (with Followers)	20
74	Ashanti ASH 413	It May Sound Silly/Gladdy's Workshop	6
73	Ashanti SHAN 103	IT MAY SOUND SILLY (LP)	15

(see also Stranger & Gladdy, Tommy McCook)

IAN (A.) ANDERSON
71	Village Thing VTSX 1002	One More Chance/Policeman's Ball	12
69	Saydisc EP SD 134	ALMOST THE COUNTRY BLUES (EP, with Elliot Jackson)	30
68	Saydisc Matchbox SDM 159	THE INVERTED WORLD (LP, with Mike Cooper)	45
69	Liberty LBS 83242E	STEREO DEATH BREAKDOWN (LP, as Ian Anderson Country Blues Band)	40
70	Fontana STL 5542	BOOK OF CHANGES (LP)	30
70	Village Thing VTS 3	ROYAL YORK CRESCENT (LP)	15
72	Village Thing VTS 9	A VULTURE IS NOT A BIRD YOU CAN TRUST (LP)	15
72	Village Thing VTS 18	SINGER SLEEPS ON AS BLAZE RAGES (LP)	12

(see also Mike Cooper, Anderson Jones Jackson)

JON ANDERSON
76	Atlantic K 10840	Flight Of The Moorglade/To The Runner	5
80	Atlantic K 11619	Some Are Born/Days (p/s)	5

(see also Hans Christian, Warriors, Yes, Mike Oldfield, Jon & Vangelis)

KIP ANDERSON
67	President PT 163	You'll Lose A Good Thing/I'm Out Of Love	15

LEROY ANDERSON
55	Brunswick 05485	Forgotten Dreams/The Last Rose Of Summer	6

MILLER ANDERSON
71	Deram DM 337	Bright City/Another Time, Another Place	10
71	Deram SDL 3	BRIGHT CITY (LP)	35

(see also Voice, At Last The 1958 Rock'n'Roll Show, Keef Hartley Band, Hemlock, Dog Soldier, Lyn Dobson)

MOIRA ANDERSON
69	Decca F 12989	The Holy City/Ave Maria	6

REUBEN ANDERSON
66	Doctor Bird DB 1045	Christmas Time Again/DESMOND TUCKER: Oh Holy Night	25

SONNY ANDERSON
60	London HLP 9036	Lonely Lonely Train/Yes, I'm Gonna Love You	80

UDELL T. ANDERSON
69	Direction 58-4212	Love Ain't Love/Funky Walk	8
69	Direction 58-4459	Keep On Loving Me/Rainmaker	8

VICKI ANDERSON
71	Mojo 2001 150	Super Good/Super Good (Version)	15
73	Mojo 2093 005	I'm Too Tough For Mr Big Stuff/Sound Funky	15
74	Mojo 2093 028	Don't Throw Your Love In The Garbage Can/Land Of Milk And Honey/	
		BOBBY BYRD: Sayin' It And Doin' It Are Two Different Things	15

(see also Bobby Byrd, James Brown)

ANDERSON, HARLEY & BATT
88	Epic PEEPS 1	Whatever You Believe/Whatever You Believe (live) (p/s)	10
88	Epic PEEPS 12P 1	Whatever You Believe (live)/Whatever You Believe/	
		Deep Is My Yearning (12", p/s)	10

(see also Steve Harley, Mike Batt)

ANDERSON, JONES, JACKSON
68	Saydisc 33 SD 125	ANDERSON, JONES, JACKSON (EP)	25

(see also Ian A. Anderson, Al Jones)

ANDERSON'S ALLSTARS
68	Blue Cat BS 133	Intensified Girls/Jump And Shout	40

MINT VALUE £

BARBARA ANDREWS
70 Escort ERT 838   Lonesome Feeling/RAINY BOP: Hop Scotch 20

BARRY ANDREWS
80 Virgin VS 378   Rossmore Road (NW1)/Win A Night Out With A Well Known Paranoiac (p/s) 5
(see also XTC, Shriekback, Robert Fripp)

CATHERINE ANDREWS
80 Cat Tracks PURR LP 2   FRUITS (LP, with lyric sheet & poster sleeve) 55
(see also Gordon Giltrap, Inner City Unit)

CHRIS ANDREWS
66 Decca F 22365   Something On My Mind/I'll Do The Best I Can 10
66 Decca F 22404   Whatcha Gonna Do Now?/Lady Oh Lady 5
66 Decca F 22472   Stop That Girl/I'd Be Far Better Off Without You 6
66 Decca F 22521   That's What She Said/Write It Down 5
67 Decca F 22597   I'll Walk To You/They've All Got Their Eyes On You 5
67 Decca F 22668   Hold On/Easy 30
68 Pye 7N 17617   The Man With The Red Balloon/Keep Your Mind On The Right Side 5
69 Pye 7N 17727   Pretty Belinda/Maker Of Mistakes 5
70 Pye 7N 17958   Yo Yo/Hey Babe 5
(see also Chris Ravel & Ravers)

DAVE ANDREWS & SUGAR
68 Jewel JL 04   I'm On My Way/Beatin' Of My Heart 60

ERNIE ANDREWS
60 Vogue V 9166   'Round Midnight/Lover Come Back To Me 12
65 Capitol CL 15407   Where Were You/What Do I See In The Girl 20
76 Capitol CL 15873   Fine Young Girl/Then I'll Know 10

HARVEY ANDREWS
72 Cube BUG 20   In The Darkness/Soldier 5
72 Cube BUG 26   Learning The Game/Don't Know The Time 5
65 Transatlantic TRAEP 133   HARVEY ANDREWS (EP) 20
75 Transatlantic BIG 525   (I'm Resigning) From Today/Darby And Joan (with Graham Cooper) . . 5
70 Decca Nova SDN 9   PLACES AND FACES (LP) 35
72 Cube HIFLY 10   WRITER OF SONGS (LP, with lyric insert) 15
73 Fly HIFLY 15   FRIENDS OF MINE (LP, gatefold sleeve) 15

INEZ ANDREWS & ANDREWETTES
65 Vogue EDVP 1283   INEZ ANDREWS & ANDREWETTES (EP) 45

JOHN ANDREWS & LONELY ONES
66 Parlophone R 5455   A Rose Growing In The Ruins/It's Just Love 80

LEE ANDREWS (& HEARTS)
57 London HL 7031   Teardrops/Girl Around The Corner (solo, export issue) 300
58 London HLM 8546   Teardrops/Girl Around The Corner (solo) (78 rpm = £70) 300
58 London HLU 8661   Try The Impossible/Nobody's Home (as Lee Andrews & Hearts) (78 rpm = £70). 500

PATTY ANDREWS
55 Capitol CL 14324   Without Love/Where To My Love? 12
55 Capitol CL 14374   Suddenly There's A Valley/Booga Da Woog 12
(see also Bing Crosby, Jimmy Durante)

TIM ANDREWS
67 Parlophone R 5656   Sad Simon Lives Again/You Won't Be Seeing Me Anymore 7
68 Parlophone R 5695   Your Tea Is Strong/(Something About) Suburbia 7
70 Parlophone R 5824   Tiny Goddess/Josephine 6
(see also Fleur De Lys, Rupert's People)

TIM ANDREWS & PAUL KORDA
68 Parlophone R 5714   Smile If You Want To/Makin' Love To Him 5
68 Parlophone R 5746   Angel Face/Waiter Get Me A Drink 5
69 Parlophone R 5769   How Many Hearts Must Be Broken/Discovery 5
(see also Paul Korda)

ANDREWS SISTERS
57 Capitol CL 14705   Rum And Coca-Cola/No, Baby 10
57 Capitol CL 14807   I'm Goin' Home/By His Word 10
60 Capitol CL 15170   Rum And Coca-Cola/I'll Be With You In Apple Blossom Time 6
57 Capitol LCT 6132   IN HI-FI (LP) 15

ANDROIDS OF MU
80 Fuck Off FLP 001   BLOOD ROBOTS (LP) 12

ANDROMEDA
69 RCA RCA 1854   Go Your Way/Keep Out 'Cos I'm Dying 22
69 RCA SF 8031   ANDROMEDA (LP) 170
90 Reflection MM 06   SEVEN, LONELY STREET (LP, numbered & signed, 500 only) 15
95 Kissing Spell KSLP 9497   LIVE 1967 (LP) 12
(see Attack, Five Day Week Straw People, Hard Stuff, Atomic Rooster, John Du Cann, Fuzzy Duck)

AND THE NATIVE HIPSTERS
79 Heater Volume HVR 003   There Goes Concorde Again.../Stands, Still The Building.../
                                  I Wanna Be Around (several different coloured photocopied foldaround
                                  sleeves with insert in polythene bag) . . . . each 8
82 Illuminated/Glass HIP 1   TENDERLY HURT ME (Poor Prince/Hang Ten/Tenderly Hurt Me/Stuck)
                                  (12" EP, p/s) 12

ANDWELLA('S DREAM)
69 CBS 4301   Sunday/Midday Sun (as Andwella's Dream) 38
69 CBS 4469   Mrs. Man/Felix (as Andwella's Dream) 60
69 CBS 4634   Mr. Sunshine/Shades Of Grey (as Andwella's Dream) 40

70	Reflection RS 1	Every Little Minute/Michael Fitzhenry (as Andwella)	5
70	Reflection RS 3	Hold Onto Your Mind/Shadow Of The Night (as Andwella)	8
71	Reflection RS 6	People's People/Are You Ready (as Andwella)	7
69	CBS 63673	LOVE AND POETRY (LP, as Andwella's Dream)	350
70	Reflection REFL 10	WORLD'S END (LP, as Andwella, with poster)	35
71	Reflection REF 1010	PEOPLE'S PEOPLE (LP, as Andwella)	35

(see also David Lewis, David Baxter)

BOB ANDY

67	Island WI 3040	I've Got To Get Back Home/SONNY BURKE: Rudy Girl	40
68	Studio One SO 2063	Too Experienced/Let Them Stay	40
68	Coxsone CS 7074	Born A Man/MARCIA GRIFFITHS: Mark My Word	40
69	Doctor Bird DB 1183	The Way I Feel/ETHIOPIANS: Long Time Now	45
69	Studio One SO 2075	I'm Going Home/SOUND DIMENSION: Straight Flush	40
70	Harry J. HJ 6612	Peace Of Mine/Weep	10
71	Trojan TR 7809	Green Green Valley/Peace Of Mind	6
71	Trojan TR 7821	One Woman/You Don't Know (B-side actually "Save Me Version" by Bob Andy Band)	6
71	Trojan TR 7840	One Woman/You Don't Know	6
71	London HLJ 7127	Games People Play/GAYLETTES: Son Of A Preacher Man (export issue)	10
72	Sioux SI 019	Baby I Need Your Loving/CIRCLES: Mammy Blue	6
72	Sioux SI 020	Everyday People/HONG GANG: Smoking Wild	6
72	Green Door GD 4047	Life/HARRY J. ALL STARS: Version	10
73	Green Door GD 4059	You Don't Know/The Border Song	18
73	Horse HOSS 31	One Woman/Second Hand Love	6
75	Fab FAB 241	Feeling Soul/SOUND DIMENSION: Part 2	12

(see also Bob & Marcia, Larry & Alvin)

HORACE ANDY

72	Count Shelley 2	Cha Cha Children/Version	8
72	Attack ATT 8026	Feel Good All Over/PHIL PRATT ALLSTARS: Feel Good (Version)	6
73	Bread BR 1170	Don't Try To Use Me/Goddess Of Love	8
73	Randy's RAN 533	Don't Think About Me (with Earl Flute)/DINO PERKINS: Skin Him Alive	20
74	Ackee ACK 530	Til/IMPACT ALLSTARS: Version	6
75	Fab FAB 260	Oh Lord Why Lord/SOUND DIMENSION: Part 2	10
75	Morpheus MOR 1010	Got To Get You	6
77	Serious Business SB 02	Rock To Sleep/Version	25
79	Sufferer's Height SUFF 005	Purple Ranking/The Return Of Jammy's Hi-Fi (Round One)/TREVOR RANKING: Whip Them Jah Jah (12")	30
72	Trojan TBL 197	YOU ARE MY ANGEL (LP)	25

(see also Jon Cuno, Big Youth)

HORACE ANDY & FREDDIE McKAY

| 75 | Treble 7 | Talking Love/Dub | 8 |

PATRICK ANDY

| 78 | Grove Music GMDM 3 | Woman, Woman, Woman/TOMMY MCCOOK: Lamb's Bread (12") | 30 |

ANDY & BEY SISTERS

| 59 | Fontana H 174 | Pretty Baby/Sweeter Than Sweet (78 rpm = £20) | 10 |
| 59 | Fontana H 197 | Scoubidou/Don't Get Around Much Anymore (78 rpm = £20) | 10 |

ANDY & CLYDE

65	Rio R 62	Never Be A Slave/Magic Is Love	12
65	Rio R 69	I'm So Lonesome/WINSTON STEWART: Day After Day	12
65	Rio R 71	We All Have To Part/UPSETTERS: Scandalizing	12

ANDY & JOEY

62	Island WI 056	Have You Ever/Cross My Heart	12
64	Port-O-Jam PJ 4009	I Want To Know/My Love Has Gone	30
64	Ska Beat JB 162	You're Wondering Now/You'll Never (copies also exist on R&B label)	15

(see also Roland Alphonso)

ANGEL

| 74 | Cube BUG 51 | Little Boy Blue/Tragedy Queen | 10 |

ANGEL

77	Casablanca CBC 104	Magic Touch/Big Boy	12
76	Casablanca CBC 4007	ANGEL (LP, with insert)	22
76	Casablanca CBC 4010	HELLUVA BAND (LP)	18

JOHNNY ANGEL

60	Parlophone R 4642	Chinese Butterfly/My Very Good Friend The Milkman	12
60	Parlophone R 4679	Too Young To Go Steady/You're Thrilling	12
61	Parlophone R 4750	What Happens To Love/Luna Luna Luna Lu	12
61	Parlophone R 4795	Trocadero-Double-Nine-One-O/Web Of Love	12
62	Parlophone R 4874	Look, Look Little Angel/Jenny From Missouri	12
62	Parlophone R 4948	Better Luck Next Time/The Power Of You	10
63	Parlophone R 5026	A Touch Of Venus/The Two Together	10

MARIAN ANGEL

65	Columbia DB 7537	It's Gonna Be Alright/Tomorrow's Fool	18
65	Columbia DB 7705	You Can't Buy My Love/One Way Only	12
66	CBS 202391	Little Bit Of Sunshine/All The Time In The World	6

ANGELA & HER FANS

| 66 | Pye 7N 17108 | Love Ya Illya/I Know You | 25 |

(see also Alma Cogan)

ANGELETTES

| 72 | Decca F 13284 | Don't Let Him Touch You/Rainy Day | 6 |

MINT VALUE £

ANGELIC UPSTARTS

78	Dead IS/AU/1024	Murder Of Liddle Towers/Police Oppression (p/s, 1,000 only)	50
78	Rough Trade RT/SW 001	Murder Of Liddle Towers/Police Oppression (reissue, p/s)	5
79	Warner Bros K 17354	I'm An Upstart/Leave Me Alone (green vinyl, no p/s)	5
79	Warner Bros K 17354T	I'm An Upstart/Leave Me Alone (12", p/s)	8
79	Warner Bros K 17426C	Teenage Warning/The Young Ones (red vinyl, no p/s)	5
80	Warner Bros SPZ 2	I'm An Upstart/Never 'Ad Nothin' (cassette single)	6
80	Zonophone Z 7	Last Night Another Soldier/The Man Who Came In From The Beano (p/s)	5
81	Zonophone Z 12	England/Stick's Diary (p/s)	12
83	Anagram ANA 12	The Burglar (p/s, unissued)	
85	Gas GM 3010	Brighton Bomb/Thin Red Line/Soldier (12", banned 'Maggie Thatcher' p/s)	15
79	Warner Bros K 56717	TEENAGE WARNING (LP)	12
80	Warner Bros K 56806	WE GOTTA GET OUT OF THIS PLACE (LP)	12
81	Zonophone ZEM 102	LIVE (LP, some with free live flexidisc: We're Gonna Take The World/ Leave Me Alone/The Young Ones/White Riot [no cat. no.])	15/10
83	Anagram GRAM 007	ANGEL DUST (LP)	12
85	Gas GLP 4012	THE POWER OF THE PRESS (LP)	12
85	Razor RAZM 32	LIVE IN YUGOSLAVIA (LP)	15
85	Anagram GRAM004	REASONS WHY (LP, with inner sleeve)	12

ANGELINA

65	Fontana TF 648	I Just Don't Know How/Wishing My Life Away	5

BOBBY ANGELO & TUXEDOS

61	HMV POP 892	Baby Sitting/Skinny Lizzie	30
61	HMV POP 982	Don't Stop/I Gotta Have You	45

(see also Innocents [UK], End)

JERRY ANGELO

59	Parlophone R 4548	Crush Me/Mary Lou	15
59	Parlophone R 4561	If You Change Your Mind/I Love You My Love (78 rpm = £12)	15
60	Parlophone R 4656	Maria Elena/Old Man River	12
62	Palette PG 9031	Lonely Hill/Make Her Mine	12
62	Palette PG 9034	Innocent Angel/The Boy Who Walks Alone	12

MICHAEL ANGELO & HIS ORCHESTRA

61	Columbia DB 4705	Rocco's Theme/Spinneree	12
62	Columbia DB 4800	Tears/The Roman Spring Of Mrs Stone	15

(see also John Barry)

MAYA ANGELOU

57	London HA-U 2062	MISS CALYPSO (LP)	30

ANGEL PAVEMENT

69	Fontana TF 1059	Baby You've Gotta Stay/Green Mello Hill	18
70	Fontana TF 1072	Tell Me What I've Got To Do/When Will I See June Again	20

(see also Fortes Mentum, Pussy)

ANGELS

62	Pye International 7N 25150	Everybody Loves A Lover/Blow Joe	12
63	Mercury AMT 1211	My Boyfriend's Back/Now	20
63	Mercury AMT 1215	I Adore Him/Thank You And Goodnight	15
64	Philips BF 1312	Wow Wow Wee/Snowflakes And Teardrops	10

(see also Beach-Nuts)

ANGEL WITCH

80	EMI EMI 5064	Sweet Danger/Flight Nineteen (p/s)	10
80	EMI 12EMI 5064	Sweet Danger/Flight Nineteen/Hades Paradise (12", p/s)	25
80	Bronze BRO 108	Angel Witch/Gorgon (p/s)	8
81	Bronze BRO 121	Loser/Suffer/Dr Phibes (p/s)	10
85	Killerwatt KIL 3001	Goodbye/Reawakening (no p/s)	6
80	Bronze BRON 532	ANGELWITCH (LP)	15
85	Killerwatt KILP 4001	SCREAMIN' N' BLEEDIN' (LP)	20

ANGIE

79	Stiff BUY 51	Peppermint Lump/ANGIE'S ORCHESTRA: Breakfast In Naples (p/s)	6

(see also Pete Townshend)

ANGLIANS

67	CBS 202489	A Friend Of Mine/Daytime Lover	25

(see also Moving Finger)

ANGLOS

65	Brit WI 004	Incense/You're Fooling Me	50
65	Fontana TF 589	Incense/You're Fooling Me (reissue)	25
67	Sue WI 4033	Incense/You're Fooling Me (unissued)	
69	Island WIP 6061	Incense/You're Fooling Me (2nd reissue)	10

(see also Spencer Davis Group, Stevie Winwood)

ANGRY YOUNG MEN

59	Fontana H 187	Big Daddy/Ciribiribin (78 rpm = £20)	10

ANIMAL MAGNET

81	EMI 12 EMI 5240	Welcome To The Monkey House/Game Over Player 1 (12")	8

ANIMALS

64	Columbia DB 7247	Baby Let Me Take You Home/Gonna Send You Back To Walker	12
64	Columbia DB 7301	The House Of The Rising Sun/Talkin' 'Bout You	7
64	Columbia DB 7354	I'm Crying/Take It Easy	7
65	Columbia DB 7445	Don't Let Me Be Misunderstood/Club-A-Go Go (standard issue, matrix: '2N')	6
65	Columbia DB 7445	Don't Let Me Be Misunderstood/Club-A-Go Go (mispressing, with 'demo' version of A-side, matrix: '1N')	20
65	Columbia DB 7539	Bring It On Home To Me/For Miss Caulker	7

65	Columbia DB 7639	We've Gotta Get Out Of This Place/I Can't Believe It 7
65	Columbia DB 7741	It's My Life/I'm Going To Change The World 8
66	Decca F 12332	Inside Looking Out/Outcast 15
66	Decca F 12407	Don't Bring Me Down/Cheating 15
82	Rak RRP 1	The House Of The Rising Sun/Don't Let Me Be Misunderstood/I'm Crying (picture disc) 5
63	Graphic Sound ALO 10867	I JUST WANNA MAKE LOVE TO YOU (12" EP, 1-sided, 99 only, as Alan Price Rhythm & Blues Group or as Animals, private pressing, blank white cover, typed label) 475
64	Columbia SEG 8374	THE ANIMALS IS HERE (EP) 20
65	Columbia SEG 8400	THE ANIMALS (EP) 30
65	Columbia SEG 8439	THE ANIMALS NO. 2 (EP) 35
65	Columbia SEG 8452	THE ANIMALS ARE BACK (EP) 30
65	Decca DFE 8643	IN THE BEGINNING THERE WAS EARLY ANIMALS (EP, reissue of Graphic Sound EP) 40
66	Columbia SEG 8499	ANIMAL TRACKS (EP) 35
64	Columbia 33SX 1669	THE ANIMALS (LP) 50
64	EMI Regal SREG 1104	THE ANIMALS (LP, export issue) 30
65	Columbia 33SX 1708	ANIMAL TRACKS (LP) 55
65	Columbia TA-SX 1708	ANIMAL TRACKS (reel-to-reel tape) 20
66	Columbia SX 6035	THE MOST OF THE ANIMALS (LP) 30
66	Columbia TA-SX 6035	THE MOST OF THE ANIMALS (reel-to-reel tape) 15
66	Decca LK 4797	ANIMALISMS (LP) 45
76	DJM DJSL 069	IN CONCERT FROM NEWCASTLE (LP) 12
77	Barn 2314104	BEFORE WE WERE RUDELY INTERRUPTED (LP) 12

(see also Eric Burdon & Animals, Alan Price, Danny McCullough)

ANIMALS & MEN
| 80 | Strange Days DAYS 1 | The Terraplane Fixation/Shell Shock (p/s) .... 5 |
| 80 | TW HIT 101 | Don't Misbehave In The New Age/Machines (p/s) .... 5 |

ANIMATED EGG
| 69 | Marble Arch MAL 890 | ANIMATED EGG (LP) .... 25 |

ANITA & TH' SO AND SO'S
| 62 | RCA RCA 1278 | Joey Baby/Rinky Tinky Rhythm. .... 5 |

PAUL ANKA
57	Columbia DB 3980	Diana/Don't Gamble With Love (mauve label) 10
57	Columbia DB 3980	Diana/Don't Gamble With Love (re-pressings on green or black label) 18
57	Columbia DB 4022	I Love You, Baby/Tell Me That You Love Me (mauve or green label) 6
58	Columbia DB 4063	You Are My Destiny/When I Stop Loving You (mauve or green label) 6
58	Columbia DB 4110	Crazy Love/Let The Bells Keep Ringing (mauve or green label) (78 rpm = £8) 6
58	Columbia DB 4172	Midnight/Verboten! (Forbidden) (78 rpm = £8) 6
58	Columbia DB 4199	Just Young/So It's Goodbye (78 rpm = £8) 6
59	Columbia DB 4241	(All Of A Sudden) My Heart Sings/That's Love (78 rpm = £8). 5
59	Columbia DB 4286	I Miss You So/Late Last Night (78 rpm = £12) 5
59	Columbia DB 4324	Lonely Boy/Your Love (78 rpm = £12). 6
59	Columbia DB 4355	Put Your Head On My Shoulder/Don't Ever Leave Me (78 rpm = £12). 5
60	Columbia DB 4390	It's Time To Cry/Something Has Changed Me (78 rpm = £15) 5
60	Columbia DB 4434	Puppy Love/Adam And Eve 8
60	Columbia DB 4472	My Home Town/Waiting For You 5
60	Columbia DB 4504	Hello Young Lovers/I Love You In The Same Old Way 5
60	Columbia DB 4524	Summer's Gone/I'd Have To Share 5
61	Columbia DB 4582	The Story Of My Love/Don't Say You're Sorry. 5
61	Columbia DB 4629	Tonight My Love, Tonight/I'm Just A Fool Anyway 5
61	Columbia DB 4669	I Talked To You (On The Telephone)/Dance On Little Girl. 5
61	Columbia DB 4702	Cinderella/Kissin' On The Phone. 5
62	Columbia DB 4772	The Bells At My Wedding/Loveland 5
62	RCA RCA 1276	Love Me Warm And Tender/I'd Like To Know 5
62	RCA RCA 1318	Eso Beso/Give Me Back My Heart. 5
63	RCA RCA 1340	Remember Diana/At Night (p/s) 10
65	RCA RCA 1434	To Wait For Love/Behind My Smile (some in p/s). 8/5
67	RCA RCA 1567	I Don't Wanna Catch Him Round You Anymore/Sunrise, Sunset 5
68	RCA RCA 1676	Can't Get You Out Of My Mind/When We Get There 40

EPs
57	Columbia SEG 7747	DIANA (EP). 25
58	Columbia SEG 7801	ANKA AGAIN (EP). 20
59	Columbia SEG 7890	SING SING SING (EP) 20
60	Columbia SEG 7985	SINGS SONGS FROM 'GIRLS' TOWN' AND OTHER SUCCESSES (EP). 25
64	RCA RCX 7127	FLY ME TO THE MOON (EP). 15
64	RCA RCX 7152	FOUR GOLDEN HITS (EP) 15
64	RCA RCX 7170	SYLVIE (EP) 15

LPs
58	Columbia 33SX 1092	PAUL ANKA (LP, green label) 40
59	Columbia 33SX 1196	MY HEART SINGS (LP) 25
60	Columbia 33SX 1268	ANKA SWINGS FOR YOUNG LOVERS (LP) 25
60	Columbia 33SX 1282	PAUL ANKA SINGS HIS BIG 15 (LP) 20
60	Columbia 33SX 1287	IT'S CHRISTMAS EVERYWHERE (LP). 35
61	Columbia 33SX 1395	PAUL ANKA SINGS HIS BIG 15 VOL. 2 (LP) 18
62	Columbia 33SX 1432	PAUL ANKA SINGS HIS BIG 15 VOL. 3 (LP) 18
62	RCA RD 27257/SF 5129	YOUNG ALIVE AND IN LOVE (LP, mono/stereo; add £5 with photo insert) 15/20
62	RCA RD/SF 7533	LET'S SIT THIS ONE OUT (LP, mono/stereo) 15/20
63	RCA RD/SF 7547	OUR MAN AROUND THE WORLD (LP, mono/stereo) 15/20
63	RCA RD/SF 7573	ANKA'S 21 GOLDEN HITS (LP, mono/stereo) 15/20

Paul ANKA

63	RCA RD/SF 7613	SONGS I WISH I'D WRITTEN (LP, mono/stereo)	15/20
64	RCA RD 7700	EXCITEMENT ON PARK AVENUE — LIVE AT THE WALDORF ASTORIA (LP)	20
68	RCA RD/SF 7956	TIMELESS (LP)	15

(see also Micki Marlo & Paul Anka, Neil Sedaka)

ANNALISE
| 99 | Boss Tunage BOSTAGE 701 | Signposts And Alleyways/Empire Builder (p/s, 1-sided green vinyl with free CD, numbered, 250 copies only) | 10 |

ANNETTE (& AFTERBEATS)
59	Top Rank JAR 137	Lonely Guitar/Wild Willie (78 rpm = £20)	18
59	Top Rank JAR 233	First Name Initial/My Heart Became Of Age (with Afterbeats)	15
60	Top Rank JAR 343	It Took Dreams/O Dio Mio	10
60	Pye International 7N 25061	Pineapple Princess/Luan Cha Cha Cha (with Afterbeats)	10
64	HMV POP 1272	Muscle Beach Party/I Dream About Frankie	30
64	HMV POP 1322	Scrambled Egghead/Merlin Jones	12
65	HMV POP 1447	The Monkey's Uncle (with The Beach Boys)/How Will I Know My Love	35
59	Gala 45XP 1046	TALL PAUL (EP)	18
64	HMV CLP 1782	ANNETTE'S BEACH PARTY (LP)	30
60s	Buena Vista BV 3305	DANCE ANNETTE (LP)	25

ANNETTE & KEYMEN
| 64 | King KG 1006 | Look Who's Blue/How Can I Tell Him | 5 |

ANNIS
| 79 | GTO GT 266 | Don't Play Your Games/After Me | 30 |

ANNIVERSARY
| 78 | Aerco AERE 102 | GIVE ME A SMILE (EP) | 20 |

ANN-MARGRET
61	RCA RCA 1245	I Just Don't Understand/I Don't Hurt Anymore	10
61	RCA RCA 1267	It Do Me So Good/Gimme Love	8
64	RCA RCA 1396	Man's Favourite Sport/Hey Little Star	8
64	RCA RCX 7148	THE VIVACIOUS ONE (EP)	35
62	RCA RD 27239/SF 5116	AND HERE SHE IS (LP, mono/stereo)	20/30
62	RCA Victor RD/SF 7503	ON THE WAY UP (LP, mono/stereo)	20/30
63	RCA Victor RD/SF 7580	BYE BYE BIRDIE (LP, mono/stereo)	15/20
64	RCA Victor RD/SF 7632	BEAUTY AND THE BEARD (LP, mono/stereo, with Al Hirt)	15/20
64	RCA Victor RD/SF 7649	BACHELORS' PARADISE (LP, mono/stereo)	30/40
64	RCA Victor RD/SF 7591	ANNE MARGRET' (LP, mono/stereo)	30/40

(see also Al Hirt)

ANNO DOMINI
| 71 | Deram SML-R 1085 | ON THIS NEW DAY (LP) | 150 |

ANONYMOUSLY YOURS
69	Trojan TR 680	Get Back/ERNIE SMITH: Not For Sale	12
69	Trojan TR 681	It's Your Thing/'69 (B-side actually by Wallace Wilson)	15
69	Duke DU 40	Organism/Itch	12

ANOREXIA
| 80 | Slim SJP 812 | Rapist In The Park/I'm A Square/Pets | 35 |

ANOTHER PRETTY FACE
79	New Pleasures Z1	All The Boys Love Carrie/That's Not Enough (green & white foldout p/s)	10
79	New Pleasures Z1	All The Boys Love Carrie/That's Not Enough (red & white p/s)	7
80	Virgin VS 320	Whatever Happened To The West?/Goodbye 1970's (p/s)	6
80	Chicken Jazz JAZZ 1	Only Heroes Live Forever/Heaven Gets Closer Everyday (poster p/s)	10
81	Chicken Jazz JAZZ 2	I'M SORRY THAT I BEAT YOU, I'M SORRY THAT I SCREAMED, FOR A MOMENT THERE I REALLY LOST CONTROL (8-track cassette, some with fanzine; add £5 if also with badge)	40/25

(Some copies of the above cassette exist with tracks from the DNV single taped onto the end; see under DNV)

| 81 | Chicken Jazz JAZZ 3 | Soul To Soul/A Woman's Place/God On The Screen (foldout p/s) | 12 |

(see also DNV, Funhouse, Waterboys, Ahab)

ANOTHER SUNNY DAY
88	Sarah SARAH 003	Anorak City (5¾" flexidisc free with *Are You Scared To Get Happy* fanzine [SARAH 004], 1,500 only)	30/15
88	Sarah SARAH 007	I'm In Love With A Girl Who Doesn't Know I Exist/Things Will Be Nice/The Centre Of My Little World (14" x 10" foldout poster p/s)	25
89	Caff CAFF 7	Genetic Engineering/Kilburn Towers (p/s, with inner)	30

BRETT ANSELL
| 62 | Oriole CB 1701 | That's Where Lonesome Lives/The Door Is Open | 15 |
| 62 | Oriole CB 1725 | Rosalita/The Outsider | 20 |

ANSELL (Collins) & ELAINE
| 72 | Camel CA 98 | Presenting Cheater/RON WILSON: Official Trombone | 15 |

MARK ANSLEY
| 70 | Mother MOT 2 | 909/Venus | 10 |

ANSWERS
| 66 | Columbia DB 7847 | It's Just A Fear/You've Gotta Believe Me | 150 |
| 66 | Columbia DB 7953 | That's What You're Doing To Me/Got A Letter From My Baby | 50 |

(see also Misunderstood, High Tide)

ADAM ANT
82	CBS A 2367	Goody Two Shoes/Red Scab (p/s, credited to 'Adam & the Ants')	5
83	CBS KELL 3	Puss 'N' Boots/BONNIE TYLER: Total Eclipse Of The Heart (Kellogg's Rice Crispies freebie)	5
85	CBS A 6367	Vive Le Rock/Greta X (p/s, mispressing, both sides play Vive Le Rock)	6

85	CBS CD 26583	VIVE LE ROCK (CD, with extra track "Human Bondage Den")	45
04	NV CDEP 10	SAVE THE GORILLA EP: Save The Gorilla/Jungle Rock/Monkey Man/Monkey Man/Stranded In The Jungle (CD, batch destroyed, 2 copies only)	40

(see also Adam & The Ants, Maneaters)

ANTEEEKS
66 Philips BF 1471   I Don't Want You/Ball And Chain . . . . 175+

PAUL ANTELL
65 Pye International 7N 25329   The Times They Are A-Changin'/Yesterday And Tomorrow 12

ANTHILL MOB
93	Anthill ANT 2T	Antology/Black rushin'/The hooded claw (tango mix) (12")	30
96	Confetti COEP 01	Promise of.../Was she ever mine?/So in love/Got to do it (12")	25
96	Confetti COEP 02	Feel the groove/ANTHILL MOB FEATURING P. PITSTOP - Do you know?/P. PITSTOP -I know how to love! (12")	25
97	Confetti COEP 05	Why (inside the rise)/Things just started (12")	30
97	Confetti COEP 06	Cloudy day/Agitator (12")	25
97	Confetti CODP 01	Missing/Player/X2C/Flava/Sound/Cuts (2 x 12")	40
97	Love Peace & Unity LOVE 03	Burning (the original mix) (10" picture disc, 500 only, same track both sides)	35
97	Love Peace & Unity LOVE 04	A SPECIAL COLLECTION OF ENCHANTED RHYTHMS (double LP)	40

BILLIE ANTHONY
54	Columbia SCM 5143	This Ole House/Oh, What A Dream	15
54	Columbia SCM 5155	Teach Me Tonight/Don't Let The Kiddygeddin	12
55	Columbia SCM 5164	Butterscotch Hop/No More	12
55	Columbia SCM 5174	Tweedlee Dee/Shake The Hand Of A Stranger	25
55	Columbia SCM 5184	Something's Gotta Give/Boom Boom Boomerang	7
55	Columbia SCM 5191	The Banjo's Back In Town (with Big Ben Banjo Band)/Ten Little Kisses	7
55	Columbia SCM 5210	Bring Me A Bluebird/The Old Pi-anna Rag	7
57	Columbia DB 3874	I Dreamed/The Charge Of The Light Brigade (B-side with ex-R.S.M. Brittain)	7
57	Columbia DB 3935	Rock-A-Billy/A Needle And Thread	18
57	Columbia DB 3970	One/It's Fun Finding Out About London (with Big Ben Banjo Band)	7
57	Columbia DB 4021	Love And Kisses/Everybody's Buddy	7
58	Columbia DB 4141	You/Careful, Careful (Handle Me With Care)	7

(see also Big Ben Banjo Band)

DAVE ANTHONY'S MOODS
66 Parlophone R 5438   New Directions/Give It A Chance 50
(see also David Anthony)

DAVID ANTHONY
68 Island WI 3148   All Night/Out Of My Mind 40
(see also Dave Anthony's Moods)

JIM ANTHONY
72 Satril SAT 4   Sasha/White Rose 6

LITTLE JOHN ANTHONY
60 Ember EMB 3302   TEENAGE DANCE PARTY (LP) 20

MARC ANTHONY
63 Stateside SS 210   Let's All Cheer Again/Why Do I Love You 12

MARK ANTHONY & JETS
70 Unity UN 565   More Balls/TONY KING: Bum Ball (Chapter II) 7

RAY ANTHONY
55	Capitol CL 14205	I Don't Hurt Anymore/Woman's World	5
55	Capitol CL 14243	Juke Box Special/Heat Wave (78 rpm = £6)	10
55	Capitol CL 14275	Baby You/Happy Hornblowers (with Dick Stabile Orchestra)	5
55	Capitol CL 14306	Sluefoot/Something's Gotta Give	5
55	Capitol CL 14321	Learnin' The Blues/Mmmm Mamie	5
55	Capitol CL 14345	Pete Kelly's Blues/DC-7	5
55	Capitol CL 14354	Hernando's Hideaway/The Bunny Hop	10
56	Capitol CL 14525	Flip-Flop/Hurricane Anthony	10
56	Capitol CL 14553	Cry Me A River/Bullfighter's Lament	5
56	Capitol CL 14567	Rockin' Through Dixie/Madeira	5
56	Capitol CL 14588	The Sleep Walker/Braziliera (Mexican Storm Song)	5
56	Capitol CL 14648	I Love You, Samantha/I Am In Love	5
56	Capitol CL 14670	Love Is Just Around The Corner/Dancing Lovers	5
57	Capitol CL 14689	Rock Around The Rock Pile/The Girl Can't Help It (78 rpm = £20)	40
57	Capitol CL 14703	Plymouth Rock/Calypso Dance	10
57	Capitol CL 14740	The Incredible Shrinking Man/This Could Be The Night	5
57	Capitol CL 14752	The Lonely Trumpet/Cello-phane	5
57	Capitol CL 14769	The Bunny Hop/The Hokey Pokey	10
57	Capitol CL 14775	Drive-In/Show Me The Way To Go Home	5
58	Capitol CL 14929	Peter Gunn/Tango For Two (Mmm Shall We Dance?)	12
59	Capitol CL 15019	The Bunny Hop Rock/Walkin' To Mother's	10
57	Capitol EAP 1-823	THE GIRL CAN'T HELP IT (EP)	45
57	Capitol EAP 1-958	ROCK AND ROLL WITH RAY ANTHONY (EP)	40
57	Capitol EAP 1008	THE LONGEST WALK (EP)	10
53	Capitol LC 6570	RAY ANTHONY'S ORCHESTRA (10" LP)	12
53	Capitol LC 6615	SWEET AND LOVELY (10" LP)	12
53	Capitol LC 6617	HOUSE PARTY (10" LP)	12
54	Capitol LC 6653	I REMEMBER GLENN MILLER (10" LP)	12
55	Capitol LC 6692	ARTHUR MURRAY SWING FOXTROTS (10" LP)	12
57	Capitol LC 6809	STANDARDS (LP)	12

(see also Gordon MacRae & Ray Anthony)

RAYBURN ANTHONY
60 London HLS 9167   Who's Gonna Shoe Your Pretty Little Feet/There's No Tomorrow 35

MINT VALUE £

VAL ANTHONY
53	Columbia SCM 5079	Walk With The Wind/No Tears, No Regrets	10
54	Columbia SCM 5103	The Heart Of A Fool/The Portuguese Fishermen	10

ANTHONY & IMPERIALS
(see under Little Anthony & Imperials)

ANTHRAX (U.K.)
83	Small Wonder SMALL 27	THEY'VE GOT IT ALL WRONG (EP, p/s)	6
83	Crass 221984/9	CAPITALISM IS CANNIBALISM (EP, foldout p/s)	5

ANTHRAX (U.S.)
86	Island 12ISP 285	Madhouse/Air/God Save The Queen (12", picture disc)	15
86	Island 12IS 285	Madhouse/Air/God Save The Queen (12", p/s with patch)	10
87	Megaforce MRS 05(P)	Armed And Dangerous (12" EP, import, some as picture disc)	15/10
87	Island LAWP 1	I Am The Law/Bud E. Luvbomb And Satan's Lounge Band (picture disc)	10
87	Island ISX 316	I Am The Law (live)/Bud E. Luvbomb And Satan's Lounge Band/Madhouse (live) (red vinyl, p/s)	12
87	Island 12IS 316	I Am The Law/Bud E. Luvbomb And Satan's Lounge Band (12", poster p/s)	18
87	Island ISP 325	Indians/Sabbath Bloody Sabbath (picture disc with sticker)	8
87	Island IS 325	Indians/Sabbath Bloody Sabbath (p/s, orange vinyl)	6
87	Island IS 325	Indians/Sabbath Bloody Sabbath (p/s, orange vinyl, mispress)	8
87	Island 12IS 325	Indians/Sabbath Bloody Sabbath/Taint (12", poster p/s)	8
87	Island 12ISP 325	Indians/Sabbath Bloody Sabbath/Taint (12", picture disc)	8
87	Island ISP 338	I'm The Man/Caught In A Mosh (logo-shaped picture disc)	8
88	Island CIDP 379	Make Me Laugh/Friggin' In The Riggin'/Anti-Social (live) (CD, 7" 'pyramid' card pack)	10
89	Island CIDX 409	Anti-Social/Parasite/Le Sects (3" CD)	10
90	Island ISP 476	Got The Time/Who Put This Together (picture disc)	6
86	Music For Nations MFN62P	SPREADING THE DISEASE (LP, picture disc)	18
87	Music For Nations MFN14P	FISTFUL OF METAL (LP, picture disc)	18
87	Island PILPS 9865	AMONG THE LIVING (LP, picture disc)	20

ANTI ESTABLISHMENT
80	Charnel House CADAV 1	1980/Mechanical Man (p/s)	10
82	Glass GLASS 022	Future Girl/No Trust (p/s)	5
83	Glass GLASS 023	Anti Men/Misunderstood (p/s)	5

ANTI NOWHERE LEAGUE
81	WXYZ ABCD1	Streets Of London (1-sided test pressing)	35
82	WXYZ ABCD 1	So What/Streets Of London (p/s, withdrawn)	8
82	WXYZ ABCD 2	I Hate … People/Let's Break The Law (p/s)	6
82	WXYZ ABCD 4	Woman/Rocker (picture disc)	6
87	GWR A1	Crime/Working For The Company (Unreleased Test Pressing)	20
82	WXYZ LMNOP1	WE ARE…THE LEAGUE (LP)	15

ANTI PASTI
90	Dose DOSE1	FORE SORE POINTS (EP, 500 only)	18
80	Rondelet ROUND 2	FORE SORE POINTS (EP, re-issue)	15
81	Rondelet ABOUT 5	LAST CALL (LP)	12

ANTI SOCIAL
77	Dynamite DRO 1	Traffic Lights/Teacher Teacher (no p/s)	500

ANTI SOCIAL
82	Lightbeat SOCIAL 1	MADE IN ENGLAND (EP)	20
82	Beat The System BTS 2	Battle Scarred Skinheads/Sewer Rat/Official Hooligan (p/s)	12
82	Beat The System FIT 2	Too Many People/Let's Have Some (p/s)	5
82	Lightbeat (no cat. no.)	THE NEW PUNKS EP (cassette)	12

ANTI SYSTEM
83	Paragon/Pax PAX 11	DEFENCE OF THE REALM (EP)	10

ANTOINE
66	Vogue VRS 7009	Les Elucubrations D'Antoine/J'ai Oublié La Nuit	10
66	Vogue VRS 7017	Before The Good Thing/Elephants Looking At Me	6
66	Vogue VRS 7022	Ma Fete Forraine/Only These Few Snowflakes	6
68	Vogue VRS 7028	La Tramontana/Io Voglie Andaré In Guerra	6
69	Vogue VRS 7031	The Football Match/Where Did Everyone Go To	6
68	Vogue VRL 3032	ANTOINE (LP)	30

ANTOINETTE
64	Decca F 11820	Jenny Let Him Go/Please Don't Hurt Me Anymore	15
64	Piccadilly 7N 35201	There He Goes (The Boy I Love)/Little Things Mean A Lot	15
65	Piccadilly 7N 35223	Thank You For Loving Me/If You Really Love Me	15
65	Piccadilly 7N 35252	Our House/What's A-Happening To Me	5
66	Piccadilly 7N 35293	Why Don't I Run Away From You/There's No-One In The Whole Wide World	30
66	Piccadilly 7N 35310	Lullaby Of Love/I'm For You	25

(see also Toni Daly)

REY ANTON
62	Oriole CB 1771	Hey Good Looking/Mary Lou	12
63	Oriole CB 1811	Peppermint Man/Can't Say More Than That (with Batons)	12
63	Oriole CB 1843	How Long Can This Last/If You Don't Want Me Now	20
64	Parlophone R 5132	You Can't Judge A Book By The Cover/It's Cold Outside (with Peppermint Men)	30
64	Parlophone R 5172	Heard It All Before/I Want You (with Peppermint Men)	15
65	Parlophone R 5245	Wishbone/Kingsway (with Peppermint Men)	20
65	Parlophone R 5274	Girl You Don't Know Me/Don't Treat Me Bad (with Peppermint Men)	25
65	Parlophone R 5310	Nothing Comes Easy/Breakout (with Peppermint Men)	18
65	Parlophone R 5358	Premeditation/Now That It's Over (with Pro Form)	35

| 66 | Parlophone R 5420 | Don't You Worry Boy/Hold It Babe (with Pro Formula) | 15 |
| 66 | Parlophone R 5487 | Things Get Better/Newsboy (with Pro Form) | 15 |

TERRY ANTON
| 65 | Pye 7N 15857 | Leave A Little Love/Don't Say Goodbye | 8 |

DAVE ANTONY
| 68 | Mercury MF 1031 | Race With The Wind/Hide And Seek | 25 |

(see also Dave Anthony['s Moods])

MARK ANTONY & AVENGERS
| 60s | Malconi MCD LP 17 | MARK ANTONY & THE AVENGERS (LP, private pressing, plain sleeve) | 100+ |

ANTS
| 63 | Parlophone R 5082 | Christmas Star/Wandering | 10 |

ANVIL FLUTES & CAPRICORN VOICES
| 68 | Deram DM 208 | April Showers/Jolie Gendarme | 6 |
| 68 | Deram DML/SML 1026 | SOMETHING NEW IS COMING (LP) | 15 |

ANY TROUBLE
| 84 | EMI AMLS 2401203 | WRONG SIDE OF THE RACE (2-LP) | 18 |

APACHE INDIAN & TIM DOGG
| 94 | Island 12IS586 | Make Way For The Indian (12") | 8 |

APARTMENT
| 80 | Heartbeat PULSE 7 | The Car/Winter (p/s) | 20 |

APEX RHYTHM & BLUES ALLSTARS
| 59 | John Lever AP 100 | Yorkshire Relish/Caravan | 40+ |
| 60s | John Lever JLEP 1 | APEX RHYTHM & BLUES ALLSTARS (EP, no p/s) | 350+ |

(see also Ian Hunter)

APHEX TWIN
91	Mighty Force 01	ANALOGUE BUBBLEBATH VOL. 1 (12", with Schizophrenia, 4-track, label on 1 side only)	25
91	Rabbit City CUT 001	ANALOGUE BUBBLEBATH VOL. 1 (12" EP)	40
91	Rabbit City 009	Analogue Bubblebath Vol. 2 (Didgeridoo 'Aboriginal' Mix) (12", 1-sided, white label, 500 only)	40
92	Outer Rhythm/R+S RSUK	DIDGERIDOO (12", 4-track in stickered sleeve)	15
92	Outer Rhythm/R+S RSUK	DIDGERIDOO (CD EP)	85
92	R&S/Apollo AMBLP 39	SELECTED AMBIENT WORKS 85-92 (2-LP)	25
93	Rabbit City CUT 002	ANALOGUE BUBBLEBATH VOL. 2 (12" EP, 1-sided, 500 only)	50
93	Rephlex CAT 008	ANALOGUE BUBBLEBATH VOL. 3 (12" EP, paper bag sleeve)	15
93	Warp WAP 39R	ON — REMIXES (12" EP)	20
93	Warp WAP 39	ON (12" EP)	15
93	Warp WAPCDR 39	ON — REMIXES (CD single)	12
93	Warp WAPCD 39	ON (CD single)	8
93	Rephlex CAT 008	ANALOGUE BUBBLEBATH VOL. 3 (CD EP, bubble wrap sleeve)	18
93	Warp WAP 60	VENTOLIN EP (2 x 12")	15
93	Warp WAP 60R	VENTOLIN EP — REMIXES (2 x 12")	20
94	Rephlex CATCD 019	ANALOGUE BUBBLEBATH 4 (CD single)	20
94	Warp WAPCDR 60	VENTOLIN EP REMIXES (CD single)	12
	Warp WAPCD 60	VENTOLIN EP (CD single)	8
94	Warp WARPLP 21	SELECTED AMBIENT WORKS VOL. 2 (3-LP, brown vinyl, gatefold sleeve, numbered limited edition)	30
94	Rephlex CAT 019	ANALOGUE BUBBLEBATH VOL. 4 (12", 4-track, p/s)	8
	Warp WAP 63	Icct Hedral/Donkey Rhubarb (12")	15
	Warp WAP 78	GIRL/BOY EP (12")	12
96	Warp WAP CD 78	GIRL/BOY EP (CD)	8
95	Warp WAP 67	HANGABLE AUTOBULB I EP (12" EP, plain sleeve, 1,000 only)	40
95	Warp WAP 69	HANGABLE AUTOBULB II EP (12" EP, plain sleeve, 1,000 only)	30
97	Warp WAP 94P	Come To Daddy/Pappy Mix//Little Lord Fauntleroy Mix/Mummy Mix (2 x 12")	15
97	Warp WAP 94P	Come To Daddy/Pappy & Fauntleroy Mix/Flim Mix/Bucephalus Mix (12")	10
97	Warp WAPCD 94	COME TO DADDY (CD single)	8
97	Warp WAPCDR 94	COME TO DADDY REMIXED (To Cure A Weakling/Contour Regard) (CD single)	10
97	Rephlex CAT 00897	ANALOGUE BUBBLEBATH VOL 3.1 (12" only, 4 different tracks)	8
99	Warp WAP 105	Window Licker/Nannou (12")	8
99	Warp WAPCD 105	Window Licker (CD)	5
01	no label 01 DRUKS	Cock 10 (Delco Freedom Mix)/54 Cymru Beats (Argonaut Mix)	5
94	Warp WARPLP 21	SELECTED AMBIENT WORKS VOL. 2 (3-LP, brown vinyl, gatefold sleeve, numbered limited edition)	30
94	Warp WARPLP 21	SELECTED AMBIENT WORKS VOL. 2 (3-LP, brown vinyl, gatefold sleeve, numbered limited edition)	30
95	Warp WARPLP 30	I CARE BECAUSE YOU DO (2-LP)	20
96	Warp WARLP 43	RICHARD D. JAMES (LP)	15
01	Warp WARLP	DRUKQS (4-LP)	25

(see also Caustic Window, Polygon Window, Q-Chastic, Kosmic Kommando)

APHRODITE'S CHILD
68	Mercury MF 1039	Rain & Tears/Don't Try To Catch A River	15
69	Mercury MF 1079	End Of The World/You Always Stand In My Way	10
69	Polydor 56769	I Want To Live/Magic Mirror	12
69	Polydor 56785	Let Me Love, Let Me Live/Marie Jolie	5
70	Polydor 56791	It's Five O'Clock/Funky Mary	5
72	Vertigo 6032 900	Break/Babylon	10
68	Mercury SMCL 20140	END OF THE WORLD/RAIN AND TEARS (LP)	30

MINT VALUE £

69	Mercury 138 351	IT'S FIVE O'CLOCK	30
72	Vertigo 6673 001	666 — THE APOCALYPSE OF JOHN (2-LP, swirl labels, black cover)	150
77	Vertigo 6641 581	666 (2-LP, reissue, as Aphrodite's Child with Demis Roussos & Vangelis, different sleeve, 'spaceship' labels)	15

(see also Vangelis, Forminx)

APOLLOS
60	Mercury AMT 1096	Rockin' Horses/Just Dreaming	10

APOLLO XI
91	Wau! Mr. Modo APOLLO 11	Peace (In The Middle East) (7" Mix 2)/Peace (Sea Of Tranquility Mix)/Peace (Is This Really The Orb? Mix) (12")	10

(see also Orb)

APOSTOLIC INTERVENTION
67	Immediate IM 043	(Tell Me) Have You Ever Seen Me/Madame Garcia	200+

(see also Small Faces, Humble Pie)

APPALACHIANS
63	HMV POP 1158	Bony Moronie/It Takes A Man	10
65	Mercury MF 930	Look Away/My Broken Heart	5

APPALOOSA
94	Recoil RCL 003	UNPLUGGED EP (12", 3-track, die-cut sleeve)	15

(see also Global Communications)

DAVE APPELL (& APPLEJACKS)
55	Brunswick 05396	Smarter/My Heart Will Wait For You (as Dave Appell & Applejacks) (78 rpm = £8)	20
57	Columbia DB 3894	Country Dance/Applejack (as Dave Appell & Applejacks) (78 rpm = £10)	20
62	Columbia DB 4763	Happy Jose/Noivous (as Dave Appell & Orchestra)	5

(see also Applejacks [U.S.], John Zacherle)

APPLE
68	Page One POF 101	Let's Take A Trip Down The Rhine/Buffalo Billy Can	75
68	Page One POF 110	Doctor Rock/The Other Side	100
69	Page One POLS 016	AN APPLE A DAY (LP, some with 'apple' insert)	600/500

APPLEJACKS (U.K.)
64	Decca F 11833	Tell Me When/Baby Jane	8
64	Decca F 11916	Like Dreamers Do/Everybody Fall Down	8
64	Decca F 11981	Three Little Words/You're The One For Me	5
65	Decca F 12050	Chim Chim Chiree/It's Not A Game Anymore (export, unissued)	20
65	Decca F 12106	It's Not A Game Anymore/Bye Bye Girl	5
65	Decca F 12216	I Go To Sleep/Make Up Or Break Up	18
65	Decca F 12301	I'm Through/We Gotta Get Together	5
67	CBS 202615	You've Been Cheating/Love Was In My Eyes	20
64	Decca LK 4635	THE APPLEJACKS (LP)	100+

APPLEJACKS (U.S.)
58	London HLU 8753	Mexican Hat Rock/Stop, Stop Red Light (78 rpm = £12)	12
58	London HL 7063	Mexican Hat Rock/Stop, Stop Red Light (export issue)	12
59	London HLU 8806	Rocka-Conga/Am I Blue (78 rpm = £22)	15
60	Top Rank JAR 273	Circle Dance/Love Scene	8

(see also Dave Appell)

APPLETREE THEATRE
68	Verve (S)VLP 6018	PLAYBACK (LP)	35

CHARLIE APPLEWHITE
54	Brunswick 05358	No One But You/Parade	5
55	Brunswick 05411	Prize Of Gold/Mister Publisher (Have I Got A Song For You)	5
55	Brunswick 05416	Blue Star — The Medic Theme/A Prayer Was Born	18

APPLIANCE
90s	Enraptured RAPT 1020	TIME AND SPACE EP: Number Three Channel Is Clear/King Of The Flight Simulator/In The Event Of Just Looking/Ursa Major (10", p/s)	8

APPOLINAIRES
80s	Two Tone 20 TT	Feelings Gone/Feelings Back (paper labels)	10

APRIL SHOWERS
84	Chrysalis CHS 122787	Abandon Ship/Everytime We Say Goodbye (12", p/s)	100

APRIL WINE
72	Pye 7N 45163	Bad Side Of The Moon/Believe In Me	6
73	Pye 7N 45624	Weeping Widow/Just Like That	6

AQUARIAN AGE
68	Parlophone R 5700	10,000 Words In A Cardboard Box/Good Wizard Meets Naughty Wizard	150

(see also Twink, Tomorrow, Clem Cattini Ork, Nicky Hopkins)

AQUARIANS
71	Ackee ACK 135	Circy Cap/Circy Version	12
71	Ackee ACK 137	Rebel/Invasion Version	35

(see also Augustus Pablo, Herman)

AQUATONES
58	London HLO 8631	You/She's The One For Me (78 rpm = £10)	45

AQUILA
70	RCA SF 8126	THE AQUILA SUITE (LP, gatefold sleeve)	60

(see also Patrick Campbell-Lyons)

ARABIS
69	Doctor Bird DB 1204	Jump High Jump Low/TONY SHABAZZ: Stool Pigeon	18

ARABS
78	Hit Run APLP 9002	CRY TUFF — DUB ENCOUNTER CHAPTER 1	55

(see also Prince Far I)

ARAB STRAP
96	Chemikal Underground CHEM 007	The First Big Weekend/Gilded (700 only)	20
	Chemikal Underground CHEM 017	Hey! Fever/Girls Of Summer (p/s)	10
98	Too Many Cooks BROTH 001	Live: Packs Of Three/Blood	18
99	Go! Beat STRAP PRO	Sampler (CD, promo, 4-track, card sleeve)	12
98	Chemikal U'nd CHEM 021	PHILOPHOBIA (2-LP)	18
99	Go! Beat 547387	MAD FOR SADNESS (LP, 1000 only)	15
99	Go! Beat 547387 2	MAD FOR SADNESS (CD, 3000 only)	18
02	Private Pressing	QUIET VIOLENCE (LP)	45

ARANBEE POP SYMPHONY ORCHESTRA
66	Immediate IMLP/IMSP 003	TODAY'S POP SYMPHONY (LP)	100

(see also Andrew Oldham Orchestra, Keith Richard[s])

ARC
71	Decca SKL-R 5077	ARC . . . AT THIS (LP)	50

(see also Heavy Jelly, Skip Bifferty, Bell & Arc)

ARC
80	Orchrist ORC 1	Tribute (To Mike Hailwood) (p/s)	60

ARCADE FIRE
03	Private Pressing	ARCADE FIRE DEMO EP (CD, p/s Known as Us Kids Now)	35
05	Rough Trade RTRADS225	Neighbourhood #2/My Buddy (p/s)	7
05	Rough Trade RTRADS232	Neighbourhood #2/My Buddy (luminous vinyl, p/s)	7
05	Rough Trade RTRADSX232	Neighbourhood#3 (live) (p/s)	7

ARCADIA
85	EMI 12 NSR 1	Election Day (Consensus Mix)/Election Day (7" Version)/ She's Moody And Grey She's Mean And She's Restless (12", promo in foil sleeve, some sealed)	20/15
85	EMI 12 NSRA 1	Election Day (Cryptic Cut No Voice Mix)/Election Day (7" Mix)/ Election Day (Consensus Mix) (12", p/s)	10
85	EMI 12 NSRX 1	Election Day (The Fact And Story Mix) (12", 1-sided, white label, plain black black sleeve, promo only)	40

(see also Duran Duran)

ARCADIUM
69	Middle Earth MDS 102	Sing My Song/Riding Alone	150
69	Middle Earth MDLS 302	BREATHE AWHILE (LP)	300

(see also 'Middle Earth Sampler' in Various Artists)

ARCHIES
69	RCA RD/SF 8073	SUGAR SUGAR (LP)	12

ARCTIC MONKEYS
05	Bang Bang BANGB 71	Fake Tales Of San Francisco/From The Ritz To The Rubble (500 only, p/s)	50
05	Bank Bang BANGBCD	Fake Tales Of San Francisco/From The Ritz To The Rubble (CD, 1000 only)	50
05	Domino RUG 213	I Bet You Look Good On The Dancefloor/Bigger Boys And Stolen Sweethearts (p/s)	7

TONI ARDEN
55	HMV 7M 314	Beware/I'll Step Aside	6
57	Brunswick 05645	Little By Little/Without Love (There Is Nothing)	15
57	Brunswick 05679	My Empty Heart/Like A Baby	15
58	Brunswick 05745	Padre/All At Once	6

NEIL ARDLEY
65	Decca SKL 4690	WESTERN UNION (LP)	120
70	Columbia SCX 6414	GREEK VARIATIONS (LP, with Ian Carr & Don Rendell)	200
72	Regal Zono. SLRZ 1028	A SYMPHONY OF AMARANTHS (LP)	175
74	Argo ZDA 164/5	WILL POWER (2-LP, with Ian Carr, Stan Tracey & Mike Gibbs)	125
75	Gull GULP 1018	KALEIDOSCOPE OF RAINBOWS (LP)	40
78	Decca TXS-R 133	HARMONY OF THE SPHERES (LP, featuring John Martyn)	20

(see also Ian Carr, Don Rendell, New Jazz Orchestra, Michael Gibbs)

COLIN AREETY
72	Deram DM 360	To Give All Your Love Away/Poco Joe	5
72	Deram DM 370	Holy Cow/I Can't Do It For You	5
73	Deram DM 383	(If Loving You Is Wrong) I Don't Want To Be Right/One Night Affair	10

ARENA TWINS
59	London HL 7071	Mama, Care Mama/Little Pig (export issue)	20

ARGENT
71	Epic S EPC 5423	Celebration/Kingdom	5
71	Epic S EPC 9135	Hold Your Head Up/Closer To Heaven/Keep On Rollin' (p/s)	5
72	Epic S EPC 8115	Tragedy/Rejoice.	5
73	Epic S EPC 1628	It's Only Money (Part 2)/Candle On The River	5
73	Epic S EPC 1243	God Gave Rock'N'Roll To You/Christmas For The Free	5
70	CBS 63781	ARGENT (LP)	30
71	Epic EPC 64190	RING OF HANDS (LP)	20
72	Epic EPC 64962	ALL TOGETHER NOW (LP, with booklet)	15
74	Epic EQ 32195/Q 65475	IN DEEP (LP, quadrophonic)	20

MINT VALUE £

74	Epic EPC 88063	ENCORE (2-LP)	15
74	Epic EPC 65924	NEXUS (LP, yellow label, with insert)	12
75	Epic EPC 80691	CIRCUS (LP, yellow label with insert)	12

(see also Zombies, Unit 4 + 2, Roulettes, John Verity Band, Phoenix)

ARGONAUTS
85	Lyntone LYN 18249/50	Apeman/Under My Thumb (signed white label, no p/s)	10

(see also Madness)

ARGOSY
69	DJM DJS 214	Mr. Boyd/Imagine	80

ARGUS
84	ABS SRT 4KS258	Holocaust/The Widow (title sleeve)	250

(see also People Like Us)

ARISTOCRATS
64	Oriole CB 1928	Girl With The Laughing Eyes/I Picked You	8

ARIZONA BOYS' CHOIR
56	Columbia SCM 5215	Ballad Of Davy Crockett/Blue Shadows On The Trail	10

ARIZONA SWAMP COMPANY
70	Parlophone R 5841	Train Keeps Rollin'/Tennessee Woman	30

(see also Nashville Teens)

ARKADE
70	Stateside SS 8053	Sing Out The Love/Susan	5
71	Probe PRO 521	Morning Of Our Lives/Rhythm Of The People	5

DEE ARLEN
59	Philips PB 950	Stay/Why Should We Wait Any Longer (78 rpm = £10)	10

STEVE ARLEN
58	Melodisc M 1458	That's Love/Easy 'N' Free (78 rpm = £6)	10
60	HMV POP 835	Suddenly I'm In Love/Happy Days	5

DEKE ARLON (& OFFBEATS)
64	HMV POP 1340	I Need You/I Must Go And Tell Her	20
64	Columbia DB 7194	I'm Just A Boy/Can't Make Up My Mind	40
65	Columbia DB 7487	If I Didn't Have A Dime/Gotta Little Girl	10
65	Columbia DB 7753	Little Piece Of Paper/I've Been Away (solo)	10
66	Columbia DB 7841	Hard Times For Young Lovers/Little Boy (solo)	15

ARMADA ORCHESTRA/ULTRAFUNK
76	Contempo CX13	For The Love Of Money/Sting Your Jaws (Part 1) (12")	30

ARMAGEDDON
75	A&M AMLH 64513	ARMAGEDDON (LP, with inner sleeve)	22

(see also Keith Relf, Steamhammer)

KAY ARMEN
55	MGM SP 1146	He/Suddenly There's A Valley	5
58	Brunswick 05729	Ha! Ha! Ha! (Chella Lla!)/Till	5

ARMENIAN JAZZ QUARTET
57	London HLR 8454	Pretty Girl/Harem Dance	15

RUSSELL ARMS
57	London HLB 8406	Cinco Robles (Five Oaks)/The World Is Made Of Lisa (gold/silver label)	25/14
57	London HLB 8406	Cinco Robles (Five Oaks)/The World Is Made Of Lisa (78)	8
57	London HL 7018	Cinco Robles (Five Oaks)/The World Is Made Of Lisa (export issue)	12

ARMS & LEGS
76	MAM MAM 140	Janice/She'll Surprise You	8
76	MAM MAM 147	Heat Of The Night/Good Times	8
77	MAM MAM 156	Is There Any More Wine/She'll Surprise You	8

(see also Joe Jackson)

FRANKIE ARMSTRONG (& FRIENDS)
79	Action Against Corrie RRFA 001	We Must Choose/RED RINSE: A Woman's Right To Choose (private pressing)	30
72	Topic 12TS 216	LOVELY ON THE WATER (LP)	15
75	Topic 12TS 273	SONGS AND BALLADS (LP)	15

(see also A.L. Lloyd)

JACK ARMSTRONG
57	Beltona SEP 43	NORTHUMBRIAN PIPE MUSIC (EP)	12
74	Saydisc SDL 252	CELEBRATED MINSTREL (LP)	15

LORNA ARMSTRONG
74	Ackee 535	Dance With Me/Lonely Nights	15

LOUIS ARMSTRONG
SINGLES
50	Brunswick 04627	Life Is So Peculiar/You Rascal You (with Louis Jordan) (78)	6
53	Columbia SCM 5061	King Of The Zulus/Lonesome Blues	7
54	Columbia SCM 5118	Chicago Breakdown/Twelfth Street Rag	7
54	Columbia SCM 5142	I'm Not Rough/Put 'Em Down Blues	7
54	Brunswick 05303	Basin Street Blues (Parts 1 & 2)	7
54	Brunswick 05332	Skokiaan (Parts 1 & 2)	7
54	Brunswick 05347	Muskrat Ramble/Someday You'll Be Sorry (B-side with Commanders)	7
55	Brunswick 05364	Trees/Spooks	7
55	Brunswick 05400	Ko Ko Mo (I Love You So)/Struttin' With Some Barbecue (with Gary Crosby)	12
55	Brunswick 05460	Pretty Little Missy/Bye And Bye	5
55	Brunswick 05505	Christmas Night In Harlem/Christmas In New Orleans	5

MINT VALUE £

56	Brunswick 05574	Easy Street/Lazybones (with Gary Crosby)	5
56	Capitol CL 14643	Now You Has Jazz (with Bing Crosby)/High Society Calypso	5
57	Brunswick 05649	This Younger Generation/In Pursuit Of Happiness	5
58	Brunswick 05772	The Mardi Gras March/I Love Jazz	5
59	MGM MGM 1035	The Beat Generation/Someday You'll Be Sorry	5
59	Philips PB 967	Mack The Knife/The Faithful Hussar (78 rpm = £15)	5
59	Pye International 7N 25043	The Formula For Love (with Nina & Frederick)/Struttin' With Some Barbecue (with Velma Middleton)	5
60	Philips JAZ 108	Mahogany Hall Blues Stomp/On The Sunny Side Of The Street (p/s)	5
60	Philips JAZ 112	Way Down Yonder In New Orleans/Do You Know What It Means To Miss (p/s)	5
60	MGM MGM 1107	Muskrat Ramble/Dardanella	5
61	HMV POP 954	Battle Royal Parts 1 & 2	5
68	Stateside SS 2116	The Sunshine Of Love/Hellzapoppin'	5
69	United Artists UP 35059	We Have All The Time In The World/Pretty Little Missy	40
69	United Artists UA 3172	We Have All The Time In The World/Pretty Little Missy (reissue, p/s)	35
55	Brunswick OE 9035	PRESENTING LOUIS ARMSTRONG AND THE MILLS BROTHERS (EP)	10

LPs

51	Brunswick LA 8528	LOUIS ARMSTRONG CLASSICS (10")	15
51	Brunswick LA 8534	JAZZ CONCERT (10")	15
52	Brunswick LA 8537	NEW ORLEANS DAYS (10")	15
52	Brunswick LAT 8017	SATCHMO AT SYMPHONY HALL	15
52	Brunswick LAT 8018	SATCHMO AT SYMPHONY HALL	15
52	Brunswick LAT 8019	SATCHMO AT PASADENA	15
53	Brunswick LA 8597	LOUIS ARMSTRONG JAZZ — CLASSICS (10")	15
53	London AL 3501	PLAYS THE BLUES (10")	25
53	Columbia 33S 1007	JAZZIN' WITH ARMSTRONG (10")	15
53	HMV DLP 1015	NEW YORK TOWN HALL CONCERT 1947 (10")	15
54	Columbia 33SX 1029	LOUIS ARMSTRONG AND HIS HOT FIVE	15
54	HMV DLP 1036	LAUGHIN' LOUIS (10")	15
54	Columbia 33S 1041	LOUIS ARMSTRONG AND HIS HOT SEVEN (10")	15
54	Brunswick LA 8679	SATCHMO SERENADES (10")	15
54	Brunswick LA 8681	LOUIS ARMSTRONG AND THE MILLS BROTHERS (10")	15
54	Brunswick LA 8691	BASIN STREET BLUES (10")	15
55	Columbia 33S 1058	RENDEZVOUS AT THE SUNSET CAFE (10")	15
55	Columbia 33S 1069	LOUIS ARMSTRONG (10")	15
55	HMV DLP 1105	SATCHMO SESSION (10")	15
55	Philips BBL 7017	SATCHMO PLAYS W.C. HANDY	12
55	Philips BBL 7046	LOUIS ARMSTRONG AND EARL HINES	12
55	Brunswick LA 8698	LOUIS' HOT FIVES AND SEVENS (10")	18
55	Brunswick LA 8700	BLUEBERRY HILL (10")	18
56	Philips BBL 7064	SATCH PLAYS FATS	12
56	Philips BBL 7091	AMBASSADOR SATCH	12
56	Brunswick LAT 8084	LOUIS ARMSTRONG AT THE CRESCENDO VOL. 1	12
56	Brunswick LAT 8085	LOUIS ARMSTRONG AT THE CRESCENDO VOL. 2	12
57	Philips BBL 7134	LOUIS ARMSTRONG STORY VOL. 1	12
57	Philips BBL 7189	LOUIS ARMSTRONG STORY VOL. 2	12
57	Brunswick LAT 8210	LOUIS AND THE ANGELS	12
57	Brunswick LAT 8211	SATCHMO — A MUSICAL AUTOBIOGRAPHY	12
57	Brunswick LAT 8212	SATCHMO — A MUSICAL AUTOBIOGRAPHY	12
57	Brunswick LAT 8213	SATCHMO — A MUSICAL AUTOBIOGRAPHY	12
57	Brunswick LAT 8214	SATCHMO — A MUSICAL AUTOBIOGRAPHY	12
58	Philips BBL 7202	LOUIS ARMSTRONG STORY VOL. 3 (with Earl Hines)	12
58	Fontana TFR 6003	LOUIS ARMSTRONG AND HIS HOT FIVE (10")	15
70	Philips 6369 401	FEATURING LEON THOMAS & HIS FRIENDS	12

(see also Danny Kaye, Ella Fitzgerald & Louis Armstrong, Nina & Frederick, Bing Crosby, Earl 'Fatha' Hines, Red Onion Jazz Babies)

B.J. ARNAU

72	Mojo 2092 028	I Want To Go Back There Again/I Love You	8
72	Polydor 2058 238	The Big Hurt/Hey Brenda	10
73	RCA RCA 2365	Live And Let Die/In One Night	5

(see also Brenda Arnau)

BRENDA ARNAU

| 68 | United Artists UP 2244 | Gonna Spread Love/Christian | 5 |
| 68 | United Artists UP 2265 | Yesterday I Heard The Rain/Where Do You Go | 7 |

GINNY ARNELL

60	Brunswick 05836	Carnival/We	15
63	MGM MGM 1217	Dumb Head/How Many Times Can One Heart Break	30
63	MGM MGM 1243	I Wish I Knew What Dress To Wear/He's My Little Devil	20
65	MGM MGM 1270	Just Like A Boy/Portrait Of A Fool	30
65	MGM MGM 1283	Little Bit Of Love/B-I-I-I-Why	20

CHICO ARNEZ (& HIS LATIN AMERICAN ORCHESTRA)

59	Pye N 15196	Yashmak/Ain't She Sweet (78) (45 rpm 7" = £20)	30
69	Columbia DB 8642	Hippy Parade/Tina	10
68	Columbia SCX6265	FROM CHICO...WITH LOVE (LP)	15

CALVIN ARNOLD

| 68 | MGM MGM 1378 | Funky Way/Snatchin' Back | 10 |
| 68 | MGM MGM 1449 | Mama In Law/Mini Skirt | 10 |

EDDY ARNOLD

53	HMV MH 178	Moonlight And Roses/I'm Gonna Lock My Heart (& Throw Away The Key) (78, export issue)	7
54	HMV 7MC 10	Prayer/Robe Of Calvary (export issue)	30
54	HMV 7MC 16	Free Home Demonstrations/If I Never Get To Heaven (export issue)	15
54	HMV 7MC 19	Second Fling/My Everything (export issue)	15

54	HMV 7MC 22	Hep Cat Baby/This Is The Thanks I Get (For Loving You) (export issue)	30
55	HMV 7MC 32	In Time/Two Kinds Of Love (export issue)	15
55	HMV 7M 339	I Walked Alone Last Night/The Richest Man (In The World)	1
57	RCA RCA 1008	Gonna Find Me A Bluebird/Little Bit	1
57	RCA RCA 1017	Scarlet Ribbons/Bayou Baby (A Cajun Lullaby)	1
58	RCA RCA 1057	Little Miss Sunbeam/My Darling, My Darling	1
59	RCA RCA 1138	Tennessee Stud/What's The Good (Of All This Love) (78 rpm = £10)	1
60	RCA RCA 1212	Just Out Of Reach/Before This Day Ends	8
54	HMV 7EG 8020	EDDY ARNOLD (EP)	1
55	HMV 7EG 8080	CHAPEL ON THE HILL (EP)	1
59	RCA Camden CDN 133	EDDY ARNOLD (LP)	18

KOKOMO ARNOLD
69	Saydisc Matchbox SDR 163	KOKOMO ARNOLD (LP)	30

MALCOLM ARNOLD
58	Philips BBE 12194	BRIDGE ON THE RIVER KWAI (EP)	12
62	Decca DFE 8507	THE LION (EP)	12

PAUL ARNOLD
67	Pye 7N 17317	Somewhere In A Rainbow/Got A Feeling	7
68	Pye 7N 17473	Bon Soir Dame/Don't Leave	8
	(see also Overlanders)		

P.P. ARNOLD
66	Immediate IM 040	Everything's Gonna Be Alright/Life Is But Nothin'	150
67	Immediate IM 047	The First Cut Is The Deepest/Speak To Me	20
67	Immediate IM 055	The Time Has Come/If You See What I Mean	15
68	Immediate IM 061	(If You Think You're) Groovy/Though It Hurts Me Badly	15
68	Immediate IM 067	Angel Of The Morning/Life Is But Nothin'	10
69	Immediate IM 079	The First Cut Is The Deepest/The Time Has Come	8
69	Polydor 56350	Bury Me Down The River/Give A Hand, Take A Hand	8
70	Polydor 2058 061	Likely Piece Of Work/May The Winds Blow	8
80	Virgin/NEMS SV 103	Angel Of The Morning/Everything's Gonna Be Alright/The First Cut Is The Deepest/Groovy/The Time Has Come (doublepack, gatefold p/s)	15
70s	Immediate IM 109	First Cut Is The Deepest/King Of Kings (re-issue)	15
67	Immediate IMLP/IMSP 011	THE FIRST LADY OF IMMEDIATE (LP, withdrawn)	500+
68	Immediate IMSP 017	KAFUNTA (LP, gatefold sleeve)	70
	(see also Ikettes, Nice, Small Faces, Spectrum, P.P. & Primes)		

P.P. ARNOLD & THE JEFF WAYNE SINGERS
60s	Pepsi Lyntone 2498	We've Got Pepsi (1-sided with Pepsi Company sleeve)	15

AROVANE
99	City Centre Offices BLOCK 1	Occer (plain black sleeve, with inserts, 850 only)	20

ARRIVAL
69	Decca F 12986	Friends/Don't Turn His Love Away	6
71	CBS S 7617	Family Tree/Part Of My Dream	10
70	Decca SKL 5055	ARRIVAL (LP)	20

ARRIVALS
69	Pye 7N 17761	Scooby Doo/She's About A Mover	20

ARROWS (U.K.)
69	Pye 7N 17756	Mercy/See Saw	5

ARROWS (U.S.)
65	Capitol CL 15386	Apache '65/Blue Guitar	20

ARSENAL 1ST TEAM SQUAD
71	Pye 7N 46067	Good Old Arsenal/The Boys From Highbury (some in p/s)	15/5

ARS NOVA
68	Elektra EKSN 45029	Zoroaster/Pavan For My Lady	12
68	Elektra EKSN 45034	Fields Of People/Song To The City	12
68	Elektra EKS 74020	ARS NOVA (LP, orange label, gatefold sleeve)	35
69	Atlantic 588 196	SUNSHINE AND SHADOWS (LP)	25

ART
67	Island WIP 6019	What's That Sound (For What It's Worth)/Rome Take Away Three	25
69	Island WIP 6048	Room With A View/SPOOKY TOOTH: Nobody There At All (promo only)	40
75	Island WIP 6224	What's That Sound (For What It's Worth)/Flying Anchors	7
67	Island ILP 967	SUPERNATURAL FAIRY TALES (LP, pink label, laminated sleeve)	150
75	Island ILP 967	SUPERNATURAL FAIRY TALES (LP, reissue, matt sleeve, 'palm tree' label)	30
	(see also V.I.P.'s, Baron With His Pounding Piano, Spooky Tooth, Luther Grosvenor, Hapshash & Coloured Coat)		

ART ATTACKS
78	Albatross TIT 1	I'm A Dalek/Neutron Bomb (p/s)	20
79	Fresh FRESH 3	First And Last: Punk Rock Stars/Rat City/First And Last (p/s)	18
	(see also Monochrome Set, Tagmemics, Kray Cherubs)		

ART BEARS
81	Recommended RE 6622	CODA TO MAN AND BOY (EP, live, 1-sided clear vinyl, silk-screened p/s, 1,750 only, 500 signed & numbered for subscribers)	12/18
78	Recommended REC 2188	HOPES AND FEARS (LP, gatefold sleeve with poster & booklet)	12
79	Recommended REC 0618	WINTER SONGS (LP, with booklet)	12
81	Recommended RE 6622	THE WORLD AS IT IS TODAY (LP, 45rpm, with booklet)	12
	(see also Henry Cow, Slapp Happy)		

ARTERY
79	Limited Edition TAKE 1	Mother Moon/Pretends/Heinz (p/s)	10
80	Aardvark STEAL 3	Unbalanced/The Slide (p/s, some with EP [Perhaps/Turtle/Toytown/Heinz])	8/6

81	Aardvark AARD 5	Cars In Motion/Life And Death (p/s)	6
81	Armageddon AS 026	Afterwards/Into The Garden (p/s)	6
82	Red Flame RFM 4	OCEANS (LP, with insert)	12

(see also Mission)

DAVE & TONI ARTHUR

70	Trailer LER 1	Bushes And Briars/Lazio Feher	6
67	Transatlantic TRA 154	MORNING STANDS ON TIPTOE (LP)	50
69	Topic 12T 190	THE LARK IN THE MORNING (LP, blue label)	40
71	Trailer LER 2017	HEARKEN TO THE WITCHES' RUNE (LP, red label)	35

ARTISTICS

66	Coral Q 72488	I'm Gonna Miss You/Hope We Have	40
67	Coral Q 72492	Girl I Need You/I'm Glad I Met You	50
70	MCA MU 1117	I'm Gonna Miss You/Hope We Have (reissue)	10
76	Brunswick BR 39	I'm Gonna Miss You/GENE CHANDLER: There Was A Time	15
66	Columbia	GET MY HANDS ON SOME LOVIN' (LP, unconfirmed existence)	250+

ART MOVEMENT

68	Decca F 12768	I Love Being In Love With You/The Game Of Love	12
68	Decca F 12836	Loving Touch/Happy Song	6
69	Columbia DB 8602	Yes Sir . . . No Sir/Sally Goes Round The Moon	5
70	Columbia DB 8651	For As Long As You Need Me/Nice 'n' Easy	5
70	Columbia DB 8697	The Sooner I Get To You/Morning Girl	5

ART NOUVEAUX

| 64 | Fontana TF 483 | Extra Terrestrial Visitations/The Way To Play It | 22 |

ART OBJECTS

80	Heartbeat PULSE 10	Showing Off To Impress The Girls/Our Silver Sister (live) (p/s)	15
81	Fried Egg EGG 007	Hard Objects/Bibliotheque/Fit Of Pique (p/s)	12
81	Heartbeat HB 5	BAGPIPE MUSIC (LP)	20

ART OF NOISE

83	ZTT ZTIS 100	INTO BATTLE WITH THE ART OF NOISE (12" EP)	8
84	ZTT P ZTPS 01	Close (To The Edit)/A Time To Hear (Who's Listening) (picture disc)	5
84	ZTT 12 P ZTPS 01	Edited/A Time To Clear (It Up) (12", picture disc)	8
85	ZTT 12 ZTPS 1	CLOSE TO THE EDIT (12", stamped green label, unreleased)	8
85	ZTT P ZTPS 02	Moments In Love/Beatbox (tortoise-shaped picture disc)	6
91	China CHINX 23	Art Of Love/(Ambience Of Love Mix) (12", some in p/s)	15/8

ART SCIENCE TECHNOLOGY

| 90 | Debut DEBTX 3100 | A.S.T./Esus Flow (2 mixes) (12", p/s) | 12 |

(see also Future Sound Of London, Stakker)

ARTWOODS

64	Decca F 12015	Sweet Mary/If I Ever Get My Hands On You	60
65	Decca F 12091	Oh My Love/Big City	40
65	Decca F 12206	Goodbye Sisters/She Knows What To Do	40
66	Decca F 12384	I Take What I Want/I'm Looking For A Saxophonist Doubling French Horn Wearing Size 37 Boots	50
66	Decca F 12465	I Feel Good/Molly Anderson's Cookery Book	50
67	Parlophone R 5590	What Shall I Do/In The Deep End	150
66	Decca DFE 8654	JAZZ IN JEANS (EP)	300+
66	Decca LK 4830	ART GALLERY (LP)	275+
70	Decca Eclipse ECM 2025	ART GALLERY (LP, reissue in different sleeve, also stereo [ECS 2025])	25
73	Spark SRLM 2006	THE ARTWOODS (LP)	30

(see also St. Valentine's Day Massacre, Keef Hartley Band, Jon Lord, Dog Soldier, Lucas & Mike Cotton Sound)

ARZACHEL

| 69 | Evolution Z 1003 | ARZACHEL (LP) | 300 |

(see also Egg, Steve Hillage, Khan, Hatfield & the North, National Health, Gong)

A.S.A.P.

(see under Adrian Smith & Project)

ASGARD

72	Threshold TH 10	Friends/Children Of A New Born Age	6
73	Threshold TH 15	In The Realm Of Asgard/Town Cryer	6
72	Threshold THS 6	IN THE REALM OF ASGARD (LP, gatefold sleeve)	45

ASH

94	La La Land LA LA 001	Jack Names The Planets/Don't Know (wraparound p/s in poly bag, 5,000 only)	15
94	Infectious INFECT 13S	Petrol/The Little Pond/A Message From Oscar Wilde And Patrick The Brewer (p/s, 500 only)	12
94	Infectious INFECT 16S	Uncle Pat/Different Today (p/s, 1,000 only)	12
95	Infectious INFECT 21J	Kung Fu/Day Of The Triffids (p/s, 'Japanese' wraparound no'd p/s in poly bag)	8
95	Infectious INFECT 21S	Kung Fu (mispressed, 1-sided only, p/s)	6
95	Infectious INFECT 21C	Kung Fu/Kung Fu (red vinyl promo)	8
95	Infectious INFECT 27C	Angel Interceptor/Angel Interceptor (blue vinyl, promo only, hand-stamped p/s)	7
95	Infectious INFECT 27J	Angel Interceptor/Girl From Mars (jukebox issue)	7
95	Fantastic Plastic FP 004	Get Ready/Zero Zero Zero (red vinyl, 1,000 only)	7
95	Infectious INFECT 24S	Girl From Mars/Astral (Conversations With Toulouse Lautrec)/Cantina Band (p/s)	10
95	Infectious INFECT 27S	Angel Interceptor/5 A.M. Eternal/Give Me Some Truth (ltd. Ed., numbered p/s)	6
94	Infectious INFECT 14LP	TRAILER (LP, with yellow vinyl 7", Silver Surfer/Jazz '59 [INFECT 14S])	18

IRVING ASHBY & HIS COMBO

| 58 | London HLP 8578 | Big Guitar/Motatin' (78 rpm = £18) | 30 |

MINT VALUE £

JOHNNY ASHCROFT
59	Felsted AF 118	A Pub With No Beer/Bouquet For The Bride (78 rpm = £10)	5
60	HMV POP 759	Little Boy Lost/My Love Is A River	8

PEGGY ASHCROFT & MARTIN BEST
70s	Argo ZSW 532	SENSE AND NONSENSE (LP)	40

ASHFORD & SIMPSON
78	Warner Brothers 12K 17096	Don't Cost You Nothing/Let Love Use Me (12")	15
78	Warner Brothers 12K 17237	It Seems To Hang On (12")	12

(see also Valerie Simpson)

ASHKAN
70	Decca Nova (S)DN-R 1	IN FROM THE COLD (LP)	60

TYRONE ASHLEY
76	Pye 7N 25704	Feet Start Moving/Moving On	5
76	Tomorrow 10	Nothing Short Of A Miracle/(Instrumental Version)	10

MICKEY ASHMAN
60	Pye Jazz NJL 25	TAKING THE MICKEY (LP)	40
61	Pye Jazz NJL 29	THROUGH DARKEST ASHMAN (LP)	60

VIC ASH QUARTET
56	Tempo A 135	Blue Lou/Doxy	8
56	Tempo A 137	Early Morning/Just One Of Those Things	8
55	Jazz Today JTE 100	SESSION FOR FOUR (EP)	35
56	Nixa NJE 1002	HOAGY (EP)	15
56	Nixa NJE 1032	VIC ASH & FOUR (EP)	25
56	Columbia SEG 7634	CLARINET VIRTUOSO (EP)	15
56	Tempo EXA 44	MODERN JAZZ SCENE (EP)	15

(see also Maxine Sullivan, Jazz Five)

BUD ASHTON (& HIS GROUP)
60	Embassy WB 409	Because They're Young/Apache (78) (45 rpm 7" = £5)	8
60	Embassy WB 422	Kommotion/STEVE STANNARD: Rockin' Goose (78)	8

(see also Typhoons, Jaybirds)

GARY ASHTON
68	Pye 7N 17494	Springtime Of Our Years/His Lordship	5

TONY ASHTON
72	Purple PUR 109	Celebration/Sloeback	5

(see also Green Bullfrog)

(TONY) ASHTON & (JON) LORD
74	Purple PUR 121	We're Gonna Make It/Band Of The Salvation Army Band	7
74	Oyster OYR 101	TONY ASHTON: The Resurrection Shuffle/Ballad Of Mr Giver	6
74	Purple TPS 3507	FIRST OF THE BIG BANDS (LP)	15

(see also Tony Ashton, Ashton Gardner & Dyke, Paice Ashton & Lord, Jon Lord, Deep Purple)

ASHTON, GARDNER & DYKE
69	Polydor 56306	Maiden Voyage/See The Sun In My Eyes	60
70	Polydor 583 081	ASHTON, GARDNER & DYKE (LP)	15
71	Capitol E-ST 563	THE WORST OF ASHTON, GARDNER AND DYKE (LP)	15
72	Capitol EA-ST 22862	WHAT A BLOODY LONG DAY IT'S BEEN (LP)	15

(see also Ashton & Lord, Remo Four, Creation, Birds, Mike Hurst & Method, Badger, Medicine Head, Family)

ASIA
82	Geffen GEFA 2228	Only Time Will Tell/Ride Easy (picture disc)	10
82	Geffen WA 3580	Don't Cry/True Colours (blue or green logo-shaped picture disc)	12/10
92	IRS 951.959	AQUA (LP, gatefold sleeve)	12

(see also Yes, Emerson Lake & Palmer, Steve Howe)

ED ASKEW
69	Fontana	ED ASKEW (LP)	50

ASLAN
76	Profile GMOR 006	PAWS FOR THOUGHT (LP)	120
77	Profile GMOR 144	SECOND HELPINGS (LP)	125

SVEND ASMUSSEN
54	Philips PB 343	Sh-Boom/Do, Do, Do, Do, Do, Do It Again (78)	12

MONICA ASPELUND
77	RCA PB 9044	Lapponia/La-La, Sing A Song	8

ASPECTS
98	Hombre MEX 007	2012 (EP)	25
99	Hombre MEX 010	REVENGE OF THE NERDS (EP)	15

RON ASPERY
72	Blakey BLP5989	BACK DOOR (LP)	50

ASPHALT RIBBONS
88	Tigerlily LILY 002	PASSION, COOLNESS, INDIFFERENCE (12", p/s)	30
89	In Tape IT 063	THE ORCHARD EP (p/s)	25
89	In Tape ITTI 063	THE ORCHARD EP (12", p/s + T-Shirt inset)	30/35
89	In Tape ITTI 063	THE ORCHARD EP (12", 200 pressed at 48rpm and withdrawn)	30
89	In Tape IT 068	Good Love/Long Lost Uncle/The Day I Turned Bad (p/s)	35
89	In Tape ITTI 068	Good Love/Long Lost Uncle/The Day I Turned Bad (12", p/s)	20
89	In Tape IT 6545 1	Over Again/EVA: Unquenchable (p/s, promo only)	15
91	ETT 101-1	OLD HORSE (LP)	30
91	ETT 101-2	OLD HORSE (CD)	40

(see also Tindersticks)

MARY ASQUITH

78	Mother Earth MUM 1204	CLOSING TIME (LP)	30

ASSAGAI

71	Vertigo 6059 034	Telephone Girl/I'll Wait For You	10
71	Vertigo 6360 030	ASSAGAI (LP, gatefold sleeve, swirl label)	45
72	Philips 6308 079	ZIMBABWE (LP)	40
72	Contour 2870 394	ASSAGAI (LP)	20
70s	Sounds Superb SPR 90054	AFRO ROCK (LP) (Same as Vertigo 6360030)	15

ASSOCIATES

79	Double Hip DHR 1	Boys Keep Swinging/Mona Property Girl (no p/s, 500 only)	70
79	MCA MCA 537	Boys Keep Swinging/Mona Property Girl (no p/s, demos more common, £25)	35
80	Fiction FICS 11	The Affectionate Punch/You Were Young (p/s)	5
81	Fiction FICSX 13	A/Would I ... Bounce Back (p/s)	5
81	RSO RSO 78	Kites/A Girl Named Property (p/s, band on A-side credited as "39 Lyon St.")	5
81	RSO RSOX 78	Kites/A Girl Named Property (12", p/s, A-side credited as "39 Lyon St.")	8
82	Lyntone LYN 11649	Even Dogs In The Wild (clear 1-sided flexi free with *Flexipop* mag, issue 20)	8
82	Lyntone LYN 11649	Even Dogs In The Wild (one-sided hard vinyl test pressing)	30
82	Beggars Banquet BEG 86	Tell Me Easter's On Friday/Straw Towels (unreleased, white labels only)	25
84	WEA YZ 16T	Waiting For The Loveboat (Extended Version)/(John Peel Session Version)/Schampout (Extended Version) (12", stickered p/s)	8
85	WEA YZ 28P	Breakfast/Breakfast Alone (picture disc, stickered PVC sleeve)	5
85	Sounds/WEA CRACKER 1	CHRISTMAS CRACKER 45 (cassette, includes "Breakfast [live at Ronnie Scott's", free with *Sounds*)	5
85	WEA YX 47TE	Take Me To The Girl/Perhaps/God Bless The Child (live)/Even Dogs In The Wild (live)/The Boy That Santa Claus Forgot (live) (10", p/s)	10
88	WEA YZ 310 TX	Heart Of Glass (The Temperament Mix)/Heart Of Glass/Her Only Wish/Heaven's Blue (12", 3-D p/s, shrinkwrapped with 3-D glasses)	10
88	WEA YZ 310CD	Heart Of Glass/Her Only Wish/Breakfast/Those First Impressions (3" CD in 5" case, with adaptor)	15
88	WEA YZ 329B	Country Boy/Just Can't Say Goodbye (12" Mix)/Take Me To The Girl/Heart Of Glass (Dub Mix) (33rpm, p/s, unissued)	
88	WEA YZ 329T	Country Boy/Heart Of Glass (Dub Mix)/Just Can't Say Goodbye (12" Mix) (12", p/s, unissued, white labels only)	100
88	WEA YZ 329CD	Country Boy/Just Can't Say Goodbye (12" Mix)/Take Me To The Girl/Heart Of Glass (Dub Mix) (3" CD with adaptor in jewel case, unissued)	100
89	Strange Fruit SFPSC 075	PEEL SESSIONS: It's Better This Way/Nude Spoons/Me, Myself And The Tragic Story/A Matter Of Gender/Ulcragyceptemol (cassette)	5
90	Circa YRTB 46	Fever (Album Version)/Green Tambourine/Groovin' With Mr. Bloe (12", p/s, with 2 prints)	8
90	Circa YRTB 46	Fever (Single Version)/Green Tambourine/Groovin' With Mr. Bloe (12", p/s, with different B-sides, unreleased, handwritten white label, test pressings only)	15
90	Circa YRCDT 46	Fever (Single Version)/Groovin' With Mr. Bloe/Fever In The Shadows (CD)	15
90	Circa YRTX 49	Fire To Ice/The Glamour Chase/Green Tambourine/Groovin' With Mr. Bloe (10", p/s)	7
90	Circa YRCD 49	FIRE TO ICE EP (CD, card p/s, with inner sleeve)	18
90	Circa YRCD 56	JUST CAN'T SAY GOODBYE EP (CD, slimline jewel case)	18
90	WEA YZ 534	POPERETTA EP: Waiting For The Loveboat (Slight Return)/Club Country Club (p/s)	5
90	WEA YZ 534C	POPERETTA EP: Waiting For The Loveboat (Slight Return)/Club Country Club (cassette)	5
90	WEA YZ 534T	POPERETTA EP: Waiting For The Loveboat (Extended Voyage)/Club Country Club/Club Country Club (Time Unlimited)/Waiting For The Loveboat (Slight Return) (12", p/s)	10
90	WEA YZ 534CD	POPERETTA EP: Waiting For The Loveboat (Slight Return)/Club Country Club/Waiting For The Loveboat (Extended Voyage)/Club Country Club (Time Unlimited) (CD)	10
91	Circa YRTPR 56	Just Can't Say Goodbye (Extended Mix)/(Club Mix) (12", unreleased, white label test pressing, label credits "I Never Can Say Goodbye")	10
90	Circa BILLY 1	WILD AND LONELY (12" sampler, p/s)	8
90	Circa BILLYC 1	WILD AND LONELY (cassette sampler, card sleeve)	10
90	Circa BILLYCD 1	WILD AND LONELY (CD sampler, printed PVC sleeve)	12
93	Amnesty Intl. DSAPC 71	Amnesty International (picture disc, PVC sleeve, Billy MacKenzie features on photograph but not on recording, promo only)	15
90	Circa CIRCD 11	WILD AND LONELY (CD)	30
82	Beggars Banquet BEGA 43	FOURTH DRAWER DOWN (LP, gatefold sleeve with poster, label also credits SITU 2)	15
82	WEA 240 005-4 (WX 24C)	SULK (cassette, includes U.S. edition, U.K. edition, extra tracks & exclusive remixes)	12
88	WEA WX 222C	THE GLAMOUR CHASE (unreleased, advance cassette only; with extra track Take Me To The Girl)	40
88	WEA 244 619-2	THE GLAMOUR CHASE (CD, with extra track Take Me To The Girl, unissued)	
88	WEA K 240 005-2	SULK (CD)	18

(see also Billy MacKenzie, Jih)

ASSOCIATION

66	London HLT 10054	Along Comes Mary/Your Own Love	10
66	London HLT 10074	Cherish/Don't Blame It On Me	8
66	London HLT 10098	Pandora's Golden Heebie Jeebies/Standing Still	18
67	London HLT 10118	No Fair At All/Looking Glass	8
67	London HLT 10140	Windy/Sometime	10
67	London HLT 10157	Never My Love/Requiem For The Masses	10
68	Warner Bros WB 7163	Everything That Touches You/We Love Us	6
68	Warner Bros WB 7195	Time For Livin'/Birthday Morning	6
68	Warner Bros WB 7229	Six Man Band/Like Always	6

MINT VALUE £

69	Warner Bros WB 7267	Goodbye Columbus/The Time It Is Today	8
69	Warner Bros WB 7119	Windy/Never My Love	7
70	Warner Bros WB 7372	Just About The Same/Look At Me, Look At You	6
67	London HA-T 8305	AND THEN . . . ALONG COMES THE ASSOCIATION (LP)	40
67	London HA-T 8313	RENAISSANCE (LP)	30
67	London HA-T/SH-T 8342	INSIGHT OUT (LP)	30
68	Warner Bros W(S) 1733	BIRTHDAY (LP)	25
69	Warner Bros W(S) 1767	GREATEST HITS (LP)	25
69	Warner Bros W(S) 1786	GOODBYE COLUMBUS (LP, soundtrack)	25
69	Warner Bros W(S) 1800	THE ASSOCIATION (LP)	25

FRED ASTAIRE

57	HMV POP 337	Funny Face/AUDREY HEPBURN: How Long Has This Been Going On	7
57	MGM MGM 964	The Ritz Roll And Rock/JANIS PAIGE: Satin And Silk (78 rpm = £8)	10
57	MGM EP 601	SHOES WITH WINGS ON (EP)	10
56	Philips BBL 7052	THE BEST OF FRED ASTAIRE (LP)	20

(see also Judy Garland, Bing Crosby)

ASTRA NOVA ORCHESTRA

74	Alaska ALA 26	Ev'ry Little Beat Of Your Heart/Soul Sleeper	35

ASTERIX

70	Decca F 13075	Everybody/If I Could Fly	30

EDWIN/TED ASTLEY (ORCHESTRA)

63	Oriole CB 1880	The World Ten Times Over/Soho	20
65	RCA RCA 1492	Danger Man Theme/Saint Theme	40
66	Decca F 12389	The Baron/Drop Head (as Ted Astley)	30

ANN ASTON

74	Pye 7N 45403	I Can't Stop Myself From Loving You Babe/Freedom Train	6

ASTON & YEN

66	Doctor Bird DB 1064	Skillamy/BABA BROOKS & BAND: Party Time	20

ASTON HALL

80	Tamebeat TAME 001	The Daily Sun/Popular People (p/s)	8

ASTORS

65	Atlantic AT 4037	Candy/I Found Out	60
69	Atlantic 584 245	Candy/I Found Out (reissue)	22

ASTRAL NAVIGATIONS

71	Holyground HG 114/ NSR 172	ASTRAL NAVIGATIONS (LP, actually by Lightyears Away & Thundermother, poster cover & booklet, 250 copies only, some numbered)	300
89	Magic Mixture MM 2	ASTRAL NAVIGATIONS (LP, reissue with booklet, 425 copies only)	35
90s	Holyground HBG 122/1 CD	ASTRAL NAVIGATIONS (CD)	18

(see also Bill Nelson, David John & Mood)

ASTRONAUTS (U.K.)

79	Bugle BLAST 1	THE ASTRONAUTS EP (All Night Party/Back Soon/ Everything Stops The Baby/Survivors) (p/s)	12
80	Bugle BLAST 5	PRANKSTERS IN REVOLT (EP)	10
81	Bugle GENIUS 001	PETER PAN HITS THE SUBURBS (LP)	40
82	Bugle GENIUS 002	IT'S ALL DONE BY MIRRORS (LP)	30
86	All The Madmen MAD 5	IT'S ALL DONE BY MIRRORS (LP, reissue)	12

(see also Restricted Hours, Syndicate)

ASTRONAUTS

63	RCA Victor RCA 1349	Baja/Kuk	18
63	RCA Victor RD 7662	ORBIT KAMPUS (LP)	48

ASTRONAUTS

66	Hala Gala HG 9	Before You Leave/Syncopate	5
67	Island WI 3065	Before You Leave/Syncopate (reissue)	8

A SUDDEN SWAY

(see under Sudden Sway)

ASWAD

76	Island WIP 6312	Back to Africa/Africa	8
76	Island WIP 6338	Three Babylon/Ire woman	8
78	Grove Music GMDM 9	It's not our wish (that we should fight)/Stranger	20
80	Grove Music 12WIP 6575	Rainbow culture/Covenant (dub)	15
81	Grove Music 12WIP 6693	Babylon/Behold	15
81	Grove Music IPR 2037	Warrior charge/Dub charge (12")	20
79	Grove Music GMLP 6	HULET (LP)	20

ASYLUM CHOIR

68	Mercury SMCL 21041	A LOOK INSIDE THE ASYLUM CHOIR (LP)	20

(see also Leon Russell)

ATACAMA

71	Charisma CAS 1039	ATACAMA (LP)	20
72	Charisma CAS 1060	THE SUN BURNS UP ABOVE (LP)	20

ATHENIANS

64	ESC ESC 1	You Tell Me/Little Queenie (custom sleeve)	50
64	Waverley SLP 532	I've Got Love If You Want It/I'm A Lover Not A Fighter (some in p/s)	140/75
65	Waverley SLP 533	Thinking Of Your Love/Mercy Mercy (some in custom sleeve)	60/30

GLENN ATHENS & TROJANS

65	Spot 7E 1018	GLENN ATHENS & TROJANS (EP)	375+

ATHLETE
00s	Regal REG 72	Westside/Dungeness/One Of Those Days (p/s, with stencil, 1,000 only)	12
00s	Regal REG 72CD	Westside/Dungeness/One Of Those Days (CD, card sleeve, 1,000 only)	12

PETE ATKIN
70	Philips 6006 050	Be Careful When They Offer You The Moon/Master Of The Revels	5
70	Fontana 6309 011	BEWARE THE BEAUTIFUL STRANGER (LP)	15
71	Philips 6308 070	DRIVING THROUGH MYTHICAL AMERICA (LP)	12
73	RCA SF 8336	A KING AT NIGHTFALL (LP)	12

BENNY ATKINS
60	Mercury AMT 1113	Lipstick On Your Lips/I'm Following You	20

CHET ATKINS
59	RCA Victor RCA 1153	Boo Boo Stick Beat/Django's Castle (78 rpm = £15)	10
60	RCA Victor RCA 1174	Teensville/One Mint Julep (78 rpm = £25)	10
60	RCA Victor RCA 1209	The Dark At The Top Of The Stairs Theme/Hocus Pocus	5
64	RCA Victor RCA 1382	Susie Q/Windy & Warm	5
65	RCA Victor RCA 1441	Cloudy And Cool/Travelin'	5
65	RCA Victor RCA 1464	Yakety Axe/Letter Edged In Black	6
66	RCA Victor RCA 1515	From Nashville With Love/Rhythm Guitar	5
63	RCA Victor RCX 7118	GUITAR GENIUS (EP)	20
60	RCA Victor RD 27168	TEENSVILLE (LP)	20
60	RCA Victor RD 27194	THE OTHER CHET ATKINS (LP)	15
60	RCA Victor RD 27214	CHET ATKINS' WORKSHOP (LP)	15
62	RCA Victor RD 7507	GENIUS WITH CHET ATKINS (LP)	15
62	RCA Victor RD 7519	CARIBBEAN GUITAR (LP)	15
63	RCA Victor RD/SF 7529	OUR MAN IN NASHVILLE (LP, mono/stereo)	15/20
63	RCA Victor RD 7557	TRAVELIN' (LP)	15
63	RCA Victor RD/SF 7602	TEENSCENE (LP, mono/stereo)	15/20
63	RCA Victor RD/SF 7647	PROGRESSIVE PICKING (LP, mono/stereo)	15/20
63	RCA Victor RD 7664	BEST OF CHET ATKINS (LP)	12
64	RCA Victor RD 7691	REMINISCING (LP, with Hank Snow)	12
65	RCA Victor RD 7710	MY FAVOURITE GUITARS (LP)	12
65	RCA Victor RD 7763	MORE OF THAT GUITAR COUNTRY (LP)	12
66	RCA Victor RD/SF 7813	CHET ATKINS PICKS ON THE BEATLES (LP, mono/stereo)	12
67	RCA Victor RD 7838	FROM NASHVILLE WITH LOVE (LP)	12
67	RCA Victor RD 7882	IT'S A GUITAR WORLD (LP)	12
68	RCA Victor RD/SF 7934	SOLO FLIGHTS (LP)	12

(see also Country Hams, Hank Snow, Mark Knopfler)

ATLANTIC BRIDGE
71	Dawn DNX 2507	I Can't Lie To You/Hilary Dickson/Childhood Room (p/s)	7
70	Dawn DNLS 3014	ATLANTIC BRIDGE (LP, gatefold sleeve)	20

ATLANTICS
64	Windsor WPS 129	Don't Say No/Send Him To Me	20

ATLANTICS
64	Oriole CB-1963	Bombora/Greensleeves	18

ATLANTIS
73	Vertigo 6360 609	ATLANTIS (LP, swirl label)	15

ATLAS
78	Emerging WIL 001	AGAINST ALL THE ODDS (LP, private pressing)	25

AT LAST THE 1958 ROCK & ROLL SHOW
68	CBS 3349	I Can't Drive/Working On The Railroad	30

(see also Ian Hunter, Mott The Hoople, Freddie 'Fingers' Lee, Miller Anderson, Charles Woolfe)

ATMOSFEAR
79	Elite DAZZ 1	Dancing In Outer Space/Dancing In Outer Space (Version) (12")	20
79	MCA 12 MCA 543	Dancing In Outer Space/Dancing In Outer Space (Version) (12", co. sleeve)	15
80	Elite DAZZ 2	Motivation/Extract (12", p/s)	10
79	Elite DAZZ 4	Journey To The Powerline (Remix)/LEVEL 42: Sandstorm (12", w/l promo)	100
83	Elite DAZZ 23	What Do We Do? (Club Mix)/What Do We Do?/Xtra Special (12", p/s)	8
84	Elite DAZZ 31	When Tonight Is Over/(versions) (12")	10
84	Elite DAZZ 35	Telepathy/(versions) (12")	10
81	MCA MCF 3110	ENTRANCE (LP)	15
84	Elite ATM 33-1	FIRST/FOURMOST (mini-LP)	15

(see also Level 42)

ATMOSPHERES
59	London HLW 8977	Kabalo/The Fickle Chicken (78 rpm = £18)	30
60	London HLW 9091	Telegraph/Caravan	30

ATOMIC ROOSTER
70	B&C CB 121	Friday The 13th/Banstead (initial copies in p/s)	15/8
72	Dawn DNS 1027	Stand By Me/Never To Lose	6
72	Dawn DNS 1029	Save Me/Close Your Eyes	6
74	Decca FR 13503	Tell Your Story (Sing Your Song)/O.D. (as Vincent Crane's Atomic Rooster)	8
80	EMI EMI 5084	Do You Know Who's Looking For You/Throw Your Life Away (p/s)	6
80	EMI 12EMI 5084	Do You Know Who's Looking For You (Ext.)/Throw Your Life Away (12", p/s)	10
81	Polydor POSP 334	Play It Again/Start To Live (p/s)	5
81	Polydor POSPX 334	Play It Again/Start To Live/Devil's Answer (live) (12", p/s)	5
82	Polydor POSP 408	End Of The Day/Living Underground (p/s)	5
82	Polydor POSPX 408	End Of The Day/Living Underground/Tomorrow Night (live) (12", p/s)	8
70	B&C CAS 1010	ATOMIC ROOSTER (LP)	32
70	B&C CAS 1026	DEATH WALKS BEHIND YOU (LP, gatefold sleeve)	30
71	Pegasus PEG 1	IN HEARING OF ATOMIC ROOSTER (LP, gatefold sleeve)	22
72	Dawn DNLS 3038	MADE IN ENGLAND (LP, limited 'denim' cover)	35

ATOMIC ROOSTER

73	Dawn DNLS 3038	MADE IN ENGLAND (LP, re-pressing, standard cover) 20
73	Dawn DNLS 3049	NICE'N'GREASY (LP) 35
80	EMI EMC3341	ATOMIC ROOSTER (LP) 12

(see also Crane/Farlowe, Chris Farlowe, Crazy World Of Arthur Brown, Hard Stuff, Leaf Hound, Andromeda, John Du Cann)

ATOMS
79	Rinka R 23	Max Bygraves Killed My Mother/Beatles Jacket (colour silk-screened p/s in poly bag with inserts) 10

ATORIE
89	Conscious CON001	It's My Time/Peace Of Mind (12") 20

A II Z
81	Polydor POSP 243	No Fun After Midnight/Treason (no p/s) 12
81	Polydor POSPX 243	No Fun After Midnight/Treason/Valhalla's Force (12", p/s, red vinyl) 18
81	Polydor POSP 314	I'm The One Who Loves You/Ringside Seat (p/s) 15
80	Polydor 2383 587	THE WITCH OF BERKELEY — LIVE (LP, initially sealed with sew-on patch) .. 25/20

(see also AC/DC)

ATTACK (U.K.)
67	Decca F 12550	Try It/We Don't Know 150
67	Decca F 12578	Any More Than I Do/Hi-Ho Silver Lining 40
67	Decca F 12631	Created By Clive/Colour Of My Mind 60
67	Decca F 12631	Created By Clive/Colour Of My Mind (p/s for export to Holland) 150
68	Decca F 12725	Neville Thumbcatch/Lady Orange Peel 90
72	Decca F 13353	Hi-Ho Silver Lining/Any More Than I Do (reissue, unissued)
90	Reflection MM 08	MAGIC IN THE AIR (LP) 15

(see also Andromeda, Five Day Week Straw People, Nice)

ATTACK (U.S.)
67	Philips BF 1585	Washington Square/Please Phil Spector 18

ATTAK
82	No Future OI 17	Today's Generation: Murder In The Subway/Future Dreams (p/s) 8
83	No Future PUNK 6	ZOMBIES (LP) 15

ATTEMPTED MOUSTACHE
78	Skeleton SKL 003	Superman/No Way Out (folded p/s) 8

AT THE GATES
94	Peaceville CC7	Gardens Of Grief (yellow vinyl) 12

ATTICA BLUES
95	Mo' Wax MW 038	BLUEPRINT (12" EP) 15
97	Mo' Wax MW 38	Blueprint/Until Next Time/Lonesome Child (12") 8
97	Mo' Wax MWCD 38	Blueprint/Until Next Time/Lonesome Child (CD, card sleeve) 10
97	Mo' Wax MW 38R	Blueprint/(Mixes) (12") 15

ATTRACTION
66	Columbia DB 7936	Stupid Girl/Please Tell Me 60
66	Columbia DB 8010	Party Line/She's A Girl 120

ATTRITION
81	Sound For Industry SFI 671/A.R.R. 002	Fear/Devoid (flexidisc, p/s, some with *Adventures In Reality* fanzine, issue 5) 10/5
85	Third Mind TMS 04	Shrinkwrap/Pendulum Turns (12", p/s with insert) 10
84	Uniton Recordings 1984-1	MONKEY IN A BIN (12" EP, poster p/s, split with tracks by Schamanen Circel) .. 12
87	Hamster HAM 18	DEATH HOUSE (mini-LP) 12
87	Hamster HAM 18	DEATH HOUSE (cassette) 12

ATTRIX
78	Attrix RB 01	Lost Lenore/Hard Times (p/s, stamped white labels) 15
81	Scoff DT 011	Procession/11th Hour (p/s) 10

WINIFRED ATWELL
55	Decca F 10448	Song Of The Sea/The Black Mask Waltz 8
55	Decca F 10476	Big Ben Boogie/Winnie's Waltzing Rag 10
55	Decca F 10496	17th Century Boogie/Stranger In Paradise 7
55	Decca F 10634	"Let's Have A Ding-Dong" Medley 7
56	Decca F 10681	Poor People Of Paris (Poor John)/Piano Tuners Boogie 12
56	Decca F 10727	Port-Au-Prince/Startime 7
56	Decca F 10762	Left Bank (C'est A Hambourg)/Rampart Street Rock 7
56	Decca F 10785	Bumble Boogie/St. Louis Blues 10
56	Decca F 10796	Make It A Party (medley, both sides) 7
57	Decca F 10852	Let's Rock 'N' Roll (medley, both sides) 7
57	Decca F 10886	Spaceship Boogie/Jane Street (78 rpm = £6) 10
55	Decca DFE 6099	BOOGIE WITH WINIFRED ATWELL (EP) 10

AUBREY SMALL
72	Polydor 2058 204	Loser/Oh What A Day It's Been 15
71	Polydor 2383 048	AUBREY SMALL (LP, with insert) 60

(see also Sons Of Man)

AUDIENCE
71	Charisma CB 126	Belladonna Moonshine/The Big Spell 6
71	Charisma CB 141	Indian Summer/It Brings A Tear/Priestess (some in p/s) 8/5
71	Charisma CB 156	You're Not Smiling/Eye To Eye 5
72	Charisma CB 185	Stand By The Door/Thunder And Lightnin' 5
72	Charisma CB 196	Raviole/Hard Cruel World 5
69	Polydor 583 065	AUDIENCE (LP) 100
70	Charisma CAS 1012	FRIEND'S FRIEND'S FRIEND (LP) 30
71	Charisma CAS 1032	THE HOUSE ON THE HILL (LP, gatefold sleeve with lyric inner sleeve) 20
72	Charisma CAS 1054	LUNCH (LP, gatefold sleeve) 15

(see also Howard Werth & Moonbeams)

MIKE AUDSLEY
72	Sonet SNTF 641	DARK AND DEVIL WATERS (LP, with insert)	30
74	Sonet SNTF 659	STORYBOARD (LP)	20

AUDREY
69	Downtown DT 414	Love Me Tonight/BROTHER DAN ALLSTARS: Show Them Amigo	12
69	Downtown DT 418	Lover's Concerto/BROTHER DAN ALLSTARS: Along Came Roy	12
69	Downtown DT 436	You'll Lose A Good Thing/DESMOND RILEY: If I Had Wings	10
70	Downtown DT 452	Sweeter Than Sugar/The Way You Move	10
70	Downtown DT 454	Oh I Was Wrong/Let's Try It Again (B-side with Dandy)	10
70	Downtown DT 457	Someday We'll Be Together/MUSIC DOCTORS: Sunset Rock	12
70	Downtown DT 463	How Glad I Am/DANDY & AUDREY: I'm So Glad	8
70	Trend 6099 006	Getting Ready For A Heartache/M Y O B: Leave Me Alone	10

(see also Dandy)

AUDREY
81	Jah Skaka 826	English Girl/African Queen (12")	12

BRIAN AUGER (&) TRINITY
65	Columbia DB 7590	Fool Killer/Let's Do It Tonight (as Brian Auger Trinity)	70
65	Columbia DB 7715	Green Onions '65/Kiko (as Brian Auger Trinity)	60
67	Columbia DB 8163	Tiger/Oh Baby, Won't You Come Back Home To Croydon, Where Everybody Beedle's And Bo's (solo)	45
67	Marmalade 598 003	Red Beans And Rice Pts 1 & 2	35
68	Marmalade 598 006	I Don't Know Where You Are/A Kind Of Love In (with Julie Driscoll, unissued in favour of This Wheel's On Fire)	
69	Marmalade 598 015	What You Gonna Do/Bumpin' On Sunset	20
70	RCA RCA 1947	I Want To Take You Higher/Just Me Just You	10
71	Polydor 2058 119	This Wheel's On Fire/Road To Cairo (as Brian Auger & Julie Driscoll)	6
71	Polydor 2058 133	Marie's Wedding/Tomorrow City (as Brian Auger's Oblivion Express)	6
73	CBS 1444	Inner City Blues/Light Of The Path (as Brian Auger's Oblivion Express)	10
74	CBS 2309	Straight Ahead/Change	6
68	Marmalade 608 004	DON'T SEND ME NO FLOWERS (LP, with Jimmy Page & Sonny Boy Williamson)	60
69	Marmalade 607/608 003	DEFINITELY WHAT! (LP)	45
69	Polydor 2334 004	THE BEST OF BRIAN AUGER, JULIE DRISCOLL & THE TRINITY (LP)	15
70	RCA SF 8101	BEFOUR (LP)	25
71	RCA SF 8170	OBLIVION EXPRESS (LP)	20
71	Polydor 2383 062	BETTER LAND (LP)	20
72	Polydor 2383 104	SECOND WIND (LP, as Brian Auger's Oblivion Express)	20
73	CBS 65625	CLOSER TO IT (LP)	18
74	CBS 80058	STRAIGHT AHEAD (LP)	15

(see also Julie Driscoll Brian Auger & Trinity, Shotgun Express, Jimmy Page, Sonny Boy Williamson)

AU GO-GO SINGERS
65	Columbia DB 7493	San Francisco Bay Blues/Pink Polemoniums	10
64	Columbia 33SX 1696	THEY CALL US AU GO-GO SINGERS (LP)	50

(see also Buffalo Springfield, Stephen Stills, Poco)

AUM
69	London HA-K/SH-K 8401	BLUESVIBES (LP)	30

CLIFF AUNGIER
68	Polydor 56250	Time/Fisherboy	30
68	RCA RCA 1730	My Love And I/Abigail	10
69	Pye 7N 17753	Lady From Baltimore/Back On The Road Again	10

(see also Royd Rivers & Cliff Aungier)

AUNTIEPUS
79	Septic AUNT 1	Half-Way To Venezuela/Marmalade Freak (p/s)	6

(see also Damned)

AU PAIRS
81	Human HUMAN 1	PLAYING WITH A DIFFERENT SEX (LP)	12
82	Kamera KAM 010	SENSE AND SENSUALITY (LP, with insert)	12
83	AKA AKA 6	LIVE IN BERLIN (LP)	12

AURORA
83	Aurora RAM 9	I'll Be Your Fantasy/If I Really Knew Her (no p/s)	60

BURNER-LEE AUSTIN
73	Mojo 2093 027	Gimme Your Hand/Real Woman	6

PATTI AUSTIN
69	United Artists UP 35018	The Family Tree/Magical Boy	10
70	United Artists UP 35097	Your Love Made The Difference In Me/It's Easier To Laugh Than Cry	8
71	CBS 7180	Are We Ready For Love/Now That I Know What Loneliness Is	30
74	Probe PRO 608	Music To My Heart/Love 'Em And Leave 'Em Kind Of Love	15

PETER AUSTIN
68	Caltone TONE 125	Your Love/Time Is Getting Harder	30
75	Terminal 108	When You Are Near/Dub	7

(see also Little Freddy, Mr. Foundation)

REG AUSTIN
65	Pye 7N 15885	My Saddest Day/I'll Find Her	60

SIL AUSTIN
57	Mercury MT 132	Slow Walk/Wildwood (78)	15
58	Mercury MT 189	Fall Out/Green Blazer (78)	15
58	Mercury 7MT 220	Don't You Just Know It/Rainstorm (78 rpm = £20)	15
58	Mercury 7MT 225	Hey, Eula/The Last Time (78 rpm = £20)	10
58	Mercury MEP 9540	THE BAND WITH THE BEAT (EP)	50

Sil AUSTIN

| 58 | Mercury MEP 9541 | GO SIL GO (EP) | 50 |
| 58 | Mercury MPL 6534 | SLOW WALK ROCK (LP) | 60 |

AUSTRALIAN PLAYBOYS
| 67 | Immediate IM 054 | Black Sheep R.I.P./Sad | 1000 |

(see also Procession)

AUTECHRE
91	Hardcore HARD 003	Cavity Job/Accelera 1 + 2 (12", 1,000 only)	40
94	Warp 10WAP 11	BASSCADET REMIXES (3 x 10" p/s in box)	15
93	Warp LP 17LTD	INCUNABULA (2-LP set, silver vinyl)	35

(see also Gescom)

AUTOGRAPHS
| 78 | RAK RAK 281 | While I'm Still Young/Fabulous (p/s) | 15 |

AUTOMATIC DLAMINI
87	D For Drum DLAM 2	I Don't Know You But... /I've Never Seen That Colour Anywhere Before (p/s, with insert)	5
87	Idea IDEA 009	Me And My Conscience (p/s)	5
87	Idea IDEAT 009	Me And My Conscience (12", p/s)	8
87	Idea IDEALP 001	THE D IS FOR DRUM (LP)	12
92	Big Intl. BOT 04	FROM A DIVA TO A DIVER (LP, also CD BOT 04CD)	12/20

(see also P.J. Harvey)

AUTOMATICS
| 78 | Island WIP 6433 | Wakin' With The Radio On/Watch Her Now (unissued) | |
| 78 | Island WIP 6439 | When Tanks Roll Over Poland Again/Watch Her Now (p/s) | 10 |

AUTOPSY
| 89 | Peaceville VILE 12 | SEVERED SURVIVAL (LP, picture disc) | 20 |
| 91 | Peaceville VILE 25 | MENTAL FUNERAL (LP, picture disc) | 20 |

GENE AUTRY
| 59 | London HLU 9001 | Nine Little Reindeer/Buon Natale (78 rpm = £8) | 5 |
| 66 | Realm RM 52319 | THE BEST OF GENE AUTRY (LP) | 12 |

AUTUMN VINE
| 70 | Evolution E 2447 | He Ain't No Superman/Maxi Baby | 6 |

AVALANCHE
| 71 | Parlophone R 5890 | Finding My Way Home/Rabbits | 40 |

(see also Norman Haines Band)

FRANKIE AVALON
58	HMV POP 453	Dede Dinah/Ooh-La-La (78 rpm = £25)	30
58	London HL 8636	You Excite Me/Darlin' (78 rpm = £35)	40
58	HMV POP 517	Ginger Bread/Blue Betty (78 rpm = £35)	25
59	HMV POP 569	I'll Wait For You/What Little Girl? (78 rpm = £30)	25
59	HMV POP 603	Venus/I'm Broke (78 rpm = £25+)	15
59	HMV POP 636	Bobby Sox To Stockings/A Boy Without A Girl (78 rpm = £30+)	15
59	HMV POP 658	Just Ask Your Heart/Two Fools (78 rpm = £30+)	15
60	HMV POP 688	Why/Swinging On A Rainbow (78 rpm = £35+)	5
60	HMV POP 727	Don't Throw Away All Those Teardrops/Talk, Talk, Talk	6
60	HMV POP 742	The Faithful Kind/Gee Whizz — Whilikins — Golly Gee	10
60	HMV POP 766	Where Are You/Tuxedo Junction	10
60	HMV POP 794	Togetherness/Don't Let Love Pass Me By	6
60	HMV POP 816	Green Leaves Of Summer/Here's To The Ladies	6
58	HMV 7EG 8471	FRANKIE AVALON (EP)	32
58	HMV 7EG 8482	FRANKIE AVALON NO. 2 (EP)	32
58	HMV 7EG 8507	FRANKIE AVALON NO. 3 (EP)	32
60	HMV 7EG 8632	SONGS OF THE ALAMO (EP)	22
59	HMV CLP 1346	SWINGIN' ON A RAINBOW (LP)	32
60	HMV CLP 1423	SUMMER SCENE (LP)	32
60	HMV CLP 1440/CSD 1358	YOUNG AND IN LOVE (LP, mono/stereo)	25/35
64	United Artists ULP 1078	MUSCLE BEACH PARTY (LP)	50

AVALONS
| 66 | Island WI 263 | Everyday/I Love You | 15 |

AVANT-GARDE
| 68 | CBS 3704 | Naturally Stoned/Honey And Gall | 7 |

AVANT GARDENER(S)
| 77 | Virgin VEP 1003 | GOTTA TURN BACK (EP) | 6 |
| 80 | Appaloosa AP 013 | DIG IT (LP) | 12 |

AVAVA
| 91 | A5 AVA 5555 | AVAVA (LP, 500 only) | 12 |

AVENGER
| 83 | Neat NEAT 31 | Too Wild To Tame/On The Rocks (p/s) | 5 |
| 85 | Neat NEAT 1026 | KILLER ELITE (LP, with lyric insert) | 15 |

AVENGERS
| 68 | Parlophone R 5661 | Everyone's Gonna Wonder/Take My Hand | 20 |

(see also Vanity Fair)

HARVEY AVERNE BARRIO BAND
| 90s | Acid Jazz JAZID 93 | THE HARVEY AVERNE BARRIO BAND (LP) | 12 |

AVO-8
| 80 | Stroppo STROP 1 | Gone Wrong/Target One/No Hesitation (p/s) | 10 |

ALAN AVON & TOY SHOP

70	Concord CON 005	These Are The Reasons/Night To Remember	200

(see also Hedgehoppers Anonymous)

VALERIE AVON

67	Columbia DB 8201	He Knows I Love Him Too Much/To Be Let	20

(see also Avons)

AVON CITIES' JAZZ BAND

56	Tempo A 151	Shim-Me Sha-Me Wabble/Hawaiian War Chant	8
60	Tempo A 169	Upper Set/American Patrol	8
56	Tempo LAP 10	AVON CITIES JAZZ BAND (LP)	40+
58	Tempo TAP 18	AVON CITIES JAZZ (LP, with Ray Bush)	40+
60s	Eclipse ECS 2175	BRISTOL FASHION (LP)	12

(see also Ray Bush)

AVONS

59	Columbia DB 4363	Seven Little Girls Sitting In The Back Seat/Alone At Eight (78 rpm = £20)	6
60	Columbia DB 4413	Pickin' Petals/We Fell In Love	7
60	Columbia DB 4461	We're Only Young Once/I Keep Dreaming	7
60	Columbia DB 4522	Four Little Heels/This Was Meant To Be	5
61	Columbia DB 4569	Rubber Ball/Cool And Cosy	5
61	Columbia DB 4700	Skin Divin'/Little Bo Peep	5
62	Columbia DB 4280	Tonight I Cannot Sleep/Gotta Go	6
62	Columbia DB 4899	A Wonderful Dream/Tonight You Belong To Me	7
63	Decca F 11588	Hey Paula/I Wanna Do It	6
63	Decca F 11641	Love Should Be True/All About You	5
64	Fontana TF 442	I Am The Girl/Once Upon A Summer's Day	5

(see also Valerie Avon, Avon Sisters)

AVON SISTERS

59	Columbia DB 4236	Jerri-Lee (I Love Him So)/Baby-O (78 rpm = £25)	15

AWAY FROM THE SAND

70s	Beaujangle DB 0003	AWAY FROM THE SAND (LP)	30

(see also Bev Pegg, Dave Cartwright, Brindley Brae)

AXEGRINDER

89	Peaceville VILE 7	RISE OF THE SERPENT MEN (LP)	20

DAVID AXELROD

68	Capitol ST 2982	SONGS OF INNOCENCE (LP)	40
73	MCA MCF 2664	THE AUCTION (LP)	40

AXIS

80	Metal Minded ISAX 1047	Lady/Messiah (p/s)	6
81	Axis	When You Hold Me	8
81	Neat NEAT 13	You Got It/One Step Ahead (p/s)	5

HOYT AXTON

64	Stateside SL 10082	GREENBACK DOLLAR (LP)	25
64	Stateside SL 10096	THUNDER 'N' LIGHTNIN' (LP)	25
66	London HA-F/SH-F 8276	THE BEST OF HOYT AXTON (LP)	22

KEVIN AYERS (& WHOLE WORLD)

70	Harvest HAR 5011	Singing A Song In The Morning/Eleanor's Cake Which Ate Her	10
70	Harvest HAR 5027	Butterfly Dance/Puis-Je? (with Whole World)	12
71	Harvest HAR 5042	Stranger In Blue Suede Shoes/Stars (with Whole World)	10
72	Harvest HAR 5064	Oh! Wot A Dream/Connie On A Rubber Band	10
73	Harvest HAR 5071	Caribbean Moon/Take Me To Tahiti (some in p/s)	20/5
74	Island WIP 6194	The Up Song/Everybody's Sometimes & Some People's All The Time Blues	6
74	Island WIP 6201	After The Show/Thank You Very Much	6
75	Harvest HAR 5100	Caribbean Moon/Take Me To Tahiti	6
76	Island WIP 6271	Falling In Love Again/Everyone Knows The Song	6
76	Harvest HAR 5107	Stranger In Blue Suede Shoes/Fake Mexican Tourist Blues (possibly some in p/s)	20/5
76	Harvest HAR 5109	Caribbean Moon/Take Me To Tahiti (reissue, some in different p/s)	20/5
77	Harvest HAR 5124	Star/The Owl	6
80	Harvest HAR 5198	Money, Money, Money/Stranger In Blue Suede Shoes (p/s)	6
83	Charly/Celluloid CYZ 7107	My Speeding Heart/Champagne & Valium (p/s)	10
86	Illuminated LEV 71	Stepping Out/Only Heaven Knows (no p/s)	15
70	Harvest SHVL 763	JOY OF A TOY (LP, gatefold sleeve, 1st pressing with no EMI box)	60
70	Harvest SHSP 4005	SHOOTING AT THE MOON (LP, with Whole World)	40
72	Harvest SHVL 800	WHATEVERSHEBRINGSWESING (LP, gatefold sleeve)	20
73	Harvest SHVL 807	BANANAMOUR (LP, gatefold sleeve, some with booklet)	60/20
74	Island ILPS 9263	THE CONFESSIONS OF DR. DREAM AND OTHER STORIES (LP, with inner)	15
75	Island ILPS 9322	SWEET DECEIVER (LP, with inner sleeve)	12
75	Harvest SHDW 407	JOY OF A TOY/SHOOTING AT THE MOON (2-LP, reissue, gatefold sleeve)	15
76	Harvest SHSP 2005	ODD DITTIES (LP)	12
76	Harvest SHSP 4057	YES WE HAVE NO MAÑANAS (LP, with inner sleeve)	12
78	Harvest SHSP 4085	RAINBOW TAKEAWAY (LP)	15
86	Illuminated AMA 25	AS CLOSE AS YOU THINK (LP)	25
92	Permanent PERM LP 5	STILL LIFE WITH GUITAR (LP)	15

(see also Soft Machine, Lady June, Lol Coxhill, David Bedford, Mike Oldfield, Bridget St. John)

J AYRES

77	Hawkeye HE 004	Pretty Looks/THE REVOLUTIONARIES – Ugly	6

AYERS, CALE, NICO & ENO

74	Island ILPS 9291	JUNE 1ST, 1974 (LP)	15

(see also Kevin Ayers, John Cale, Nico, Brian Eno)

Roy AYERS

ROY AYERS (UBIQUITY)

76	Polydor 2066 671	Evolution/Mystique Voyage (as Roy Ayers' Ubiquity)	8
77	Polydor 2066 842	Running Away/Cincinnati Growl (as Roy Ayers' Ubiquity)	8
78	Polydor 2066 896	Freaky Dee Jay/You Came Into My Life	5
78	Polydor AYERS 12	Get On Up Get On Down/And Don't Say No (12")	10
79	Polydor POSP 53	Fever/Is It Too Late To Try	5
79	Polydor POSPX 53	Fever/Is It Too Late To Try (12")	10
80	Polydor STEPX 9	Don't Stop The Feeling (12")	10
80	Polydor POSP 135	Running Away/Can't You See Me	5
80	Polydor POSPX 135	Running Away/Can't You See Me (12")	12
80	Polydor POSPX 186	Sometimes, Believe In Yourself (12")	8
83	Polydor UM 1T	Silver Vibrations/Fast Money (12")	8
87	Urban URBX 6	Can't You See Me/Love Will Bring Us Back Together/Sweet Tears (12", p/s)	8
83	Polydor Super 2391 256	VIBRATIONS (LP)	20
83	Uno Melodic UMLP 2	DRIVIN' ON UP (LP)	15

(see also Jack Wilson Quartet)

ALBERT AYLER

64	Transatlantic TRA 130	SPIRITS (LP)	40
64	Fontana Jazz SFJL 925	GHOSTS (LP)	40
64	Fontana Jazz STJL 927	MY NAME IS (LP)	40
65	Fontana 933 SFJL	SPIRITUAL UNITY (LP)	40
65	Fontana SFJL 925	GHOSTS (LP, reissue)	30
65	Fontana Jazz SFJL 927	MY NAME IS (LP, reissue)	30
67	Polydor 2383089	WITCHES & DEVILS (LP)	25
68	Impulse IMPL 8022	NEW GRASS (LP, gatefold sleeve)	25
69	Impulse SIPL 519	NEW GRASS (LP, reissue, single sleeve)	20
69	Sonet SNTF 604	FIRST RECORDINGS (LP)	15
70s	Freedom 40101 FLP	WITCHES & DEVILS (LP, reissue)	15
70s	Freedom 41000 FLP	VIBRATIONS (LP)	15

AYRSHIRE FOLK

74	Deroy	AYRSHIRE FOLK (LP, private pressing)	55

AYSHEA

65	Fontana TF 627	Eeny Meeny/Peep My Love	12
68	Polydor 56276	Celebration Of The Year/Only Love Can Save Me Now	40
69	Polydor 56302	Another Night/Taking The Sun From My Eyes	12
70	Polydor 2001 029	Mr White's White Flying Machine/Ship Of The Line	10
70	Polydor 2058 074	Who's Gonna Rescue Jesus/The Flowers Are Mine	6
71	MAM MAM 59	Old Fashioned Love Song/Family Of A Man	6
73	Harvest HAR 5073	Farewell/The Best Years Of My Life	10
74	DJM DJS 339	Another Without You Day/Moonbeam	5
70	Polydor 2384 026	AYSHEA (LP)	35
74	DJM DJLPS 445	LIFT OFF WITH AYSHEA (LP)	15

(see also Ayshea Brough)

AZTEC CAMERA

81	Postcard 81-3	Just Like Gold/We Could Send Letters (die-cut sleeve, some with card)	18/10
81	Postcard 81-8	Mattress Of Wire/Lost Outside The Tunnel (p/s)	15
82	Rough Trade RT 112	Pillar To Post/Queen's Tattoos (p/s)	5
82	Rough Trade RT 112P	Pillar To Post/Queen's Tattoos (picture disc)	8
83	Rainhill ACFC 1	Oblivious (Langer/Winstanley Remix)/Oblivious (Colin Fairley Remix) (fan club issue, no p/s)	20

(see also French Impressionists)

AZUSA PLANE

96	Enraptured RAPT 4506	untitled/GRIMBLE GRUMBLE: untitled (some on blue vinyl)	10/6

(B)

IKE B & CRYSTALS

68	Island WI 3151	Try A Little Merriness/Patricia	25

B's

70s	private pressing	IN YOUR BONNET (LP)	35

MARK B & BLADE

00	Wordplay WORD005T	Ya Don't See The Signs (12")	8

(see also Blade)

MEHER BABA

70	Univ. Spiritual League 1	HAPPY BIRTHDAY (LP, with booklet and lyric sheet, 6 Pete Townshend tracks, 100 only)	110
70	Univ. Spiritual League 2	I AM (LP, with inserts, features 5 Pete Townshend tracks)	65
76	Univ. Spiritual League 3	WITH LOVE (LP, features 3 Pete Townshend tracks)	55
70s	MBO MBO 1	STAR OF THE SILENT SCREEN . . . MEHER BABA (LP, reissue of Happy Birthday without inserts)	20
70s	MBO MBO 2	I AM (LP, reissue, without inserts)	20

(see also Pete Townshend)

78   Rare Record Price Guide 2008

BABE RUTH

71	Decca F13234	Rupert's Magic Feather/Flood	7
71	Capitol CL 15869	Elusive/Say No More	8
72	Harvest HAR 5087	Wells Fargo/Theme From A Few Dollars More	5
75	Harvest HAR 5090	Private Number/Somebody's Nobody	5
72	Harvest SHSP 4022	FIRST BASE (LP)	30
73	Harvest SHVL 812	AMAR CABALLERO (LP)	12
75	Harvest SHSP 4038	BABE RUTH (LP)	12

(see also Jenny Haan, Bernie Marsden, Wild Turkey)

BABES IN TOYLAND

92	Strange Fruit SFPMA 211	PEEL SESSIONS EP (10", numbered, 4000 copies)	7
95	WEA WO 291TEX	Sweet 69/SFW (numbered p/s)	5

ALICE BABS

63	Fontana TF 409	After You've Gone/St. Louis Blues Twist	8
64	Oriole CB1955	Drip Drop/Droppen Drip Och Droppen Drapp	8

MONTY BABSON

59	London HLJ 8877	All Night Long/The Things Money Cannot Buy (78 rpm = £8)	8
60	London HAJ 2212	ALL NIGHT LONG (LP)	18

BABY BIRD

96	Echo ECS 026	You're Gorgeous/Bebe Limonade (p/s, gold vinyl)	7
96	Echo ECS 031	Candy Girl/Farmer (picture disc)	6
97	Echo ECS 033	Cornershop/Death Of A Neighbourhood (picture disc)	6
95	Baby Bird LP 1	IF I WAS BORN A MAN (LP, 500 only)	14
95	Baby Bird LP 2	BAD SHAVE (LP, 500 only)	14

BABY DOLLS

60	Warner Bros WB 16	Quiet!/Hey, Baby!	10
65	Columbia DB 7432	The Bell That Wouldn't Jingle/We're No Angels	7

BABY HUEY

71	Buddah 2365 001	LIVING LEGEND — THE BABY HUEY STORY (LP)	50

BABY JANE & ROCKABYES

63	United Artists UP 1010	How Much Is That Doggie In The Window/My Boy John	12

BABY LEMONADE

87	Sha La La 003	The Jiffy Neckware Creation/BACHELOR PAD: Girl Of Your Dreams (flexidisc, p/s, with *Are You Scared To Be Happy* fanzine)	10/6
87	Narodnik NRK 004	The Secret Goldfish/Real World (p/s)	8

BABYLON

69	Polydor 56356	Into The Promised Land/Nobody's Fault But Mine (some in p/s)	35/20

(see also Carole Grimes)

BABYSHAMBLES

04	Amelia's	What Katie Did (Demo) (1,000 numbered copies of clear flexi, with *Annelise's Magazine*. With/without magazine)	65/35
04	High Society HS7IN011	Babyshambles/At The Flophouse (p/s, 1000 only)	45
04	High Society HSCDS003	Babyshambles/At The Flophouse (CD, 1,000 only)	45
04	Rough Trade RTRADS201	Killamanjiro/The Man Who Came To Stay (Limited edition, p/s)	8
05	Rough Trade RTRADLP240	DOWN IN ALBION (2xLP with side 4 etched)	15

(see also Libertines, Wolfman)

BABY SUNSHINE

75	Deroy DER 1301	BABY SUNSHINE (LP, with insert)	75

(see also Fairy's Moke)

BACCA

73	Grape GR 3048	George Foreman/Version	6

BURT BACHARACH

65	London HLR 9958	Don't Go Breaking My Heart/24 Hours From Tulsa	7
65	London HLR 9968	Trains And Boats And Planes/Wives And Lovers	7
65	London HLR 9983	What's New Pussycat/My Little Red Book (B-side with Tony Middleton)	32
65	London HLR 9958	24 Hours From Tulsa/Don't Go Breaking My Heart	8
69	A&M AMS 702	Bond Street/Alfie	15
65	London HAR/SHR 8233	HIT MAKER! (LP, 1st pressing, plum/blue label, mono/stereo)	12
67	RCA Victor RD/SF 7874	CASINO ROYALE (LP, soundtrack, mono/stereo)	50/60
67	A&M AMLS 908	REACH OUT (LP, with flipback sleeve)	15
68	A&M AMLS 938	MAKE IT EASY ON YOURSELF (LP)	12

(see also Tony Middleton, Breakaways)

BACHDENKEL

77	Initial IRL 001	LEMMINGS (LP, some with bonus EP)	25/15
77	Initial IRL 002	STALINGRAD (LP, numbered)	15

JOHNNY BACHELOR

60	London HLN 9074	Mumbles/Arabella Jean	100

BACHELORS (U.K.)

58	Parlophone R 4454	Platter Party/Love Is A Two Way Street (78 rpm = £8)	35
59	Parlophone R 4547	Please Don't Touch/Ding Dong	30
60	Decca F 11300	Lovin' Babe/Why Can't It Be Me	20

BACHELORS (Ireland)

67	Decca F22689	Learn To Live Without You/3 O'Clock Flamingo Street	6
72	Decca F 13248	Diamonds Are Forever/Where There's A Heartache	5

BACH TWO BACH

71	Mushroom 100 MR 10	BACH TWO BACH (LP)	18

MINT VALUE £

BACK ALLEY CHOIR
72	York SYK 517	Smile Born Of Courtesy/Why Are You Here	40
73	York FYK 406	BACK ALLEY CHOIR (LP, 500 only)	260

BACKBEAT PHILHARMONIC
61	Top Rank JAR 576	Rock And Roll Symphony Parts 1 & 2	10

BACK DOOR
72	Blakey BLP 5989	BACK DOOR (LP, sold at gigs)	40
73	Warner Bros K 46231	BACK DOOR (LP)	12
76	Warner Bros K 56243	ACTIVATE (LP)	12

MIRIAM BACKHOUSE
77	Mother Earth MUM 1203	GYPSY WITHOUT A ROAD (LP)	110

BACK PORCH MAJORITY
65	Columbia DB 7627	Ramblin' Man/Good Time Joe	6

BACKSEAT ROMEOS
80	Future Earth FER 007	Zero Ambition/In The Night (p/s)	35

BACK STREET BAND
69	Ember EMBS 277	This Ain't The Road/Daybreak (p/s)	10/5

BACK TO ZERO
79	Fiction FICS 004	Your Side Of Heaven/Back To Back	10

JIM BACKUS
58	London HLJ 8674	Delicious (The Laughing Song)/I Need A Vacation	10

BACKWORLD
01	World Serpent H7 004	A Vagrant Thought/The Tide (picture disc, no p/s)	5
02	World Serpent H7 006	Hands Of Ash/Melody (p/s)	5

BACKYARD BABIES
98	MVG SAM 3024	TOTAL 05 (CD sampler, card sleeve)	15
98	Coalition COLA 046	Look At You/Powderhead/Can't Find The Door/Wireless Mind (gatefold p/s)	8
98	Coalition COLA 051	Bombed (Out Of My Mind)/Rocker (featuring Michael Monroe) (yellow vinyl, fully-autographed numbered gatefold p/s, 2000 only)	15
99	Coalition COLA 073	Babylon (featuring Wildhearted Ginger)/Stars (red vinyl, foldover p/s & insert in poly bag, 1000 copies sold at gigs only)	15
99	Coalition COLA073DDJ	Babylon (featuring Wildhearted Ginger) (CD, pic-stickered PVC wallet, promo only)	15
99	Coalition COLA 073 TJ	Babylon (Infinite Mass Remix, feat. Wildhearted Ginger) (12" w/label, promo only)	15

(see also Hanoi Rocks, Super$hit666, Wildhearts)

BACKYARD HEAVIES
73	Action ACT 4616	Just Keep On Truckin'/Never Can Say Goodbye	25

GAR BACON
58	Felsted AF 107	Mary Jane/Chains Of Love (78 rpm = £40)	30
59	Fontana H 196	Marshal, Marshal/Too Young To Love (78 rpm = £40)	30

BACON FAT
70	Blue Horizon 57-3171	Nobody But You/Small's On 53rd	18
70	Blue Horizon 57-3181	Evil/Blues Feeling	18
70	Blue Horizon 7-63858	GREASE ONE FOR ME (LP)	50
71	Blue Horizon 2431 001	TOUGH DUDE (LP)	90

(see also Dirty Blues Band, George 'Harmonica' Smith)

BAD ACTORS
80	Sophist. Noise SONO 1	Strange Love/Energy Society (p/s)	6
80	Plastic Speech	Love Song/Are They Hostile (p/s)	5

BAD BOYS
64	Piccadilly 7N 35208	The Owl And The Pussycat/That's What'll Do	15

BAD BRAINS
82	Alt. Tentacles VIRUS 13	I Luv Jah/Sailin' On/Big Takeover (12", p/s)	8
83	Food For Thought YUMT101	I And I Survive (An' T'ing)/Destroy Babylon (12", insert, p/s)	20

BADFINGER
70	Apple APPLE 20	Come And Get It/Rock Of All Ages (p/s)	10
70	Apple APPLE 31	No Matter What/Better Days (p/s)	18
71	Apple APPLE 35	Name Of The Game/Suitcase (unreleased)	
72	Apple APPLE 40	Day After Day/Sweet Tuesday Morning (p/s)	15
72	Apple APPLE 42	Baby Blue/Flying (unreleased in U.K.)	
74	Apple APPLE 49	Apple Of My Eye/Blind Owl	25
70	Apple SAPCOR 12	MAGIC CHRISTIAN MUSIC (LP)	50
70	Apple SAPCOR 16	NO DICE (LP, gatefold sleeve)	55
72	Apple SAPCOR 19	STRAIGHT UP (LP)	50
73	Warner Bros K 56023	BADFINGER (LP, with insert)	30
74	Apple SAPCOR 27	ASS (LP, with inner sleeve)	40
74	Warner Bros K 56076	WISH YOU WERE HERE (LP, withdrawn)	70+
91	Apple SAPCOR 12	MAGIC CHRISTIAN MUSIC (LP, reissue, gatefold sleeve with bonus 12" [SAPCOR 121])	25
92	Apple SAPCOR 16	NO DICE (LP, reissue, gatefold sleeve with bonus 12" [SAPCOR 161])	25
93	Apple SAPCOR 19	STRAIGHT UP (LP, reissue, gatefold sleeve with bonus 12" [SAPCOR 191])	25
95	Apple SAPCOR 28	COME AND GET IT — THE BEST OF BADFINGER (2-LP, gatefold sleeve)	30

(see also Iveys, Masterminds, Gary Walker & Rain, Natural Gas, Blue Goose)

BADGE
81	Metal Minded MM 2	Silver Woman/Something I've Lost (p/s)	25

BADGER

74	Epic EPC 2326	White Lady/Don't Pull The Trigger	5
73	Atlantic K 40473	ONE LIVE BADGER (LP, gatefold pop-up sleeve)	22
74	Epic EPC 80009	WHITE LADY (LP)	12

(see also Ashton Gardner & Dyke, Jackie Lomax)

BADLY DRAWN BOY

98	Twisted Nerve TNXL001	Roadmovie/My Friend Cubilas (feat. Doves) (die-cut sleeve, with insert)	8
90s	Twisted Nerve (no cat. no.)	I Love You All (one-track musical box, 150 only)	100
01	Twisted Nerve TNXL 011	Donna And Blitzen (p/s, one-sided, 800 only)	8
97	Twisted Nerve TN 001	EP1 (EP, 500 only)	80
98	Twisted Nerve TN 002	EP2: I Love You All/The Treeclimber/I Love You All (I Loop You All Andy Votel Mix)/Thinking Of You (EP, 1,000 only)	60
98	Twisted Nerve XL TN 001T	EP3 (EP, 1,000 only)	10
99	Twisted Nerve TNXL 002R	IT CAME FROM THE GROUND (10" EP, orange vinyl, card sleeve, 500 only)	8
00	Twisted Nerve TNXL 004T	Another Pearl/Another Pearl (The Broadcast Remix) (10" p/s)	6
00	Twisted Nerve TNXLCD 133	THE HOUR OF THE BEWILDERBEAST (LP, 1st pressing, withdrawn, with version of Magic In The Air with the line "Love Is Contagious", and Woody Allen on sleeve)	15

(see also Doves)

BAD COMPANY

(Drum'n'bass, not the rock group!)

98	BC Recordings BCR 001	The Nine/The Bridge (company p/s)	15
99	BC Recordings BCR 002	THE FEAR EP: 4 Days/Refuge/The Fear/Jellyfish (2 x 12", p/s)	8
01	BC Recordings BCRUKEP 001	BOOK OF THE BAD VOL. 1 EP: The Voice/Numbers/Spider/Believe (2 x 12", p/s)	10
01	BC Recordings BCRUKEP 002	BOOK OF THE BAD VOL. 2 EP: Dogs On The Moon/Grunge/Ladies Of Spain/ The Running Man (2 x 12", p/s)	10
01	BC Recordings BCRUKEP 003	BOOK OF THE BAD VOL. 3 EP: Mindgames/Rodeo/Miami flashback/ Storyteller (2 x 12", p/s)	10
00	BC Recordings BCRLP 001	INSIDE THE MACHINE (LP, 5 discs)	35

BAD NEWS

87	EMI EM 24X	Bohemian Rhapsody/Life With Brian (scratch'n'sniff p/s)	5
87	EMI EMP 24	Bohemian Rhapsody/Life With Brian (p/s, with sew-on patch)	6
87	EMI 12EM 24	Bohemian Rhapsody/Pretty Woman/Life With Brian (12", standard p/s)	8
87	EMI 12EM 24X	Bohemian Rhapsody/Pretty Woman/Life With Brian (12", scratch'n'sniff p/s)	8
87	EMI EMG 36	Cashing In On Christmas/Bad News (Christmas card pack)	5
87	EMI 12EM 36	Cashing In On Christmas (Let's Bank Mix)/Bad News/Cashing In On Christmas (12", p/s)	8

(see also Brian May)

BAD RELIGION

95	Columbia 661143-0	21st Century (Digital Boy)/American Jesus (live)/No Control (live)/ We're Only Gonna Die (live) (10" picture disc)	10

BAD TASTE

88	Newgate SRT8KS 1554	Rockin' Girl (p/s, some with insert)	30/10

JOAN BAEZ

65	Fontana TF 564	We Shall Overcome/Don't Think Twice It's All Right	6
65	Fontana TF 587	There But For Fortune/Plaisir D'Amour	6
66	Fontana TF 727	Pack Up Your Sorrows/Swallow Song	6
65	Fontana TF 604	It's All Over Now Baby Blue/Daddy You've Been On My Mind	6
65	Fontana TF 639	Farewell Angelina/Queen Of Hearts	5
66	Vanguard VA 2	Love Minus Zero/Love Is Just A Four-Letter Word	5
60	Fontana TFE 18005	JOAN BAEZ SINGS SILVER DAGGER & OTHER SONGS (EP)	10
63	Fontana TFE 18007	DON'T THINK TWICE (EP)	30
63	Fontana TE 18012	WITH GOD ON OUR SIDE (EP)	15
60	Fontana (S)TFL 6002	JOAN BAEZ (LP)	12
61	Fontana (S)TFL 6025	JOAN BAEZ 2 (LP)	12
62	Fontana (S)TFL 6035	IN CONCERT 2 (LP)	12
64	Fontana (S)TFL 6043	JOAN BAEZ 5 (LP)	12

(see also Earl Scruggs, Bob Dylan)

DOC BAGBY

58	Fontana H 106	Dumplin's/Sylvia's Calling (78)	15

BURR BAILEY (& SIX SHOOTERS)

63	Decca F 11686	San Francisco Bay/Like A Bird Without Feathers (with Six Shooters)	30
64	Decca F 11846	Chahawki/You Made Me Cry	60

CLIVE BAILEY & RICO'S GROUP

62	Blue Beat BB 92	Evening Train/Going Home	12

DEREK BAILEY

70s	Incus INCUS 2	SOLO GUITAR (LP)	100
70s	Incus INCUS 2R	SOLO GUITAR (LP)	100
74	Incus INCUS 12	LOT 74 (LP)	60
80	Incus INCUS 40	AIDA (LP)	30
85	Incus INCUS 48	NOTES (LP)	30
04	Organ Of Corti	TAPS (LP, 220gm vinyl, limited issue)	15

(see also Tony Oxley, Springboard, Steve Lacy & Derek Bailey, Anthony Braxton & Derek Bailey, Jamie Muir & Derek Bailey)

DEREK BAILEY & EVAN PARKER

75	Incus INCUS 16	THE LONDON CONCERT (LP)	40
85	Incus INCUS 50	COMPATIBLES (LP)	40

(see also Evan Parker)

Derek BAILEY & Han BENNINK

DEREK BAILEY & HAN BENNINK
| 72 | Incus INCUS 9 | SELECTIONS FROM LIVE PERFORMANCES AT VERITY'S PLACE (LP) | 60 |
| 76 | Incus INCUS 25 | COMPANY 3 (LP) | 50 |

DEREK BAILEY & TONY COE
| 79 | Incus INCUS 34 | TIME (LP) | 50 |

DEREK BAILEY & TRISTAN HONSINGER
| 76 | Incus INCUS 20 | DUO (LP) | 50 |

DEREK BAILEY, ANTHONY BRAXTON & EVAN PARKER
| 76 | Incus INCUS 23 | COMPANY 2 (LP) | 30 |

DEREK BAILEY, BARRY GUY & PAUL RUTHERFORD
| 70 | Incus INCUS 3/4 | ISKRA 1903 (LP) | 60 |

(see also Barry Guy)¶

DEREK BAILEY, EVAN PARKER & HAN BENNINK
| 70 | Incus INCUS 1 | THE TOPOGRAPHY OF THE LUNGS (LP) | 60 |

DEREK BAILEY, HUGH DAVIES, JAMIE MUIR, EVAN PARKER
| 70s | Incus INCUS 17 | THE MUSIC IMPROVISATION COMPANY 1968-1971 (LP) | 30 |

MILDRED BAILEY
| 57 | Parlophone GEP 8600 | MILDRED BAILEY AND HER ALLEY CATS (EP) | 10 |
| 54 | Brunswick LA 8692 | THE ROCKIN' CHAIR LADY (10" LP) | 15 |

PEARL BAILEY
56	London HLN 8354	That Certain Feeling/Hit The Road To Dreamland	10
56	London REU 1104	THAT CERTAIN FEELING (EP)	10
62	Columbia SX 1447	HAPPY SOUNDS (LP, with Louis Bellson)	12

RICKY BAILEY
| 76 | Kub KB 5525 | Proud Man/Proud Man | 6 |

ROY BAILEY (U.K.)
71	Trailer LER 3021	ROY BAILEY (LP)	15
76	Fuse AC 262	NEW BELL AWAKE (LP)	12
82	Fuse CF 382	HARD TIMES (LP, with insert)	12

(see also Leon Rosselson)

ROY BAILEY (Jamaica)
| 72 | Duke DU 146 | Run Away Child/Wedding March | 7 |

ZEDDIE BAILEY
| 73 | Grape GR 3037 | Babylon Gone/TONY KING: Speak No Evil | 7 |

ALY BAIN & MIKE WHELLANS
| 70s | Trailer LER 2022 | ALY BAIN & MIKE WHELLANS (LP) | 15 |

BOB BAIN & HIS MUSIC
| 58 | Capitol CL 14912 | Wagon Wheels/Strollin' Home | 5 |
| 58 | Capitol T965 | ROCKIN' ROLLIN' AND STROLLIN' (LP) | 45 |

ARTHUR BAIRD SKIFFLE GROUP
| 56 | Beltona BL 2669 | Union Train/Union Maid (78 rpm = £20) | 35 |

BAJA MARIMBA BAND
| 63 | London HL 9828 | Comin' In The Back Door/December Child | 5 |

CHET BAKER (QUARTET)
56	Vogue V 2377	My Funny Valentine/But Not For Me	5
56	Vogue V 2381	Just Friends/Daybreak	5
56	Vogue V 2232	Winter Wonderland/This Time The Dream's On Me	5
56	Vogue V 2309	Long Ago And Far Away/Bea's Flat	5
54	Vogue LDE 045	CHET BAKER QUARTET (10" LP)	35
55	Philips BBL 7022	CHET BAKER AND STRINGS (LP)	25
55	Vogue LDE 116	CHET BAKER QUARTET (10" LP)	25
56	Vogue LAE 12018	CHET BAKER SINGS (LP)	25
56	Vogue LDE 159	CHET BAKER SEXTET (10" LP)	30
56	Vogue LDE 163	CHET BAKER ENSEMBLE (10" LP)	25
56	Vogue LDE 182	CHET BAKER SINGS (10" LP)	25
56	Felsted PDL 85008	CHET BAKER QUARTET VOL. 1 (LP)	30
56	Felsted PDL 85013	CHET BAKER QUARTET VOL. 2 (LP)	20
57	Felsted PDL 85036	I GET CHET (LP, as Chet Baker & His Combo)	20
57	Vogue LAE 12044	CHET BAKER QUARTET AT ANN ARBOR (LP)	25
57	Vogue LAE 12076	CHET BAKER AND HIS CREW (LP, mono)	25
58	Vogue LAE 12109	CHET BAKER — PHIL'S BLUES (LP)	25
59	Vogue SEA 5005	CHET BAKER AND HIS CREW (LP, stereo)	20
59	Vogue LAE 12164	CHET BAKER SINGS (LP)	20
59	Vogue LAE 12183	CHET BAKER AND ART PEPPER SEXTET — PLAYBOYS! (LP)	20

(see also Art Pepper, Russ Freeman & Chet Baker Quartet, Gerry Mulligan)

DESMOND BAKER & CLAREDONIANS
| 66 | Island WI 295 | Rude Boy Gonna Jail/SHARKS: Don't Fool Me | 25 |

(see also Claredonians)

ERNEST BAKER
| 00 | Grapevine 2000 110 | Alone Again/Do It With Feeling | 10 |

GINGER BAKER('S AIRFORCE)
70	Polydor 56380	Man Of Constant Sorrow/Doin' It	5
71	Polydor 2058 107	Atunde! (We Are Here)/Part 2 (as Ginger Baker Drum Choir)	5
70	Polydor 2662 001	GINGER BAKER'S AIRFORCE (2-LP, gatefold sleeve)	30

82 Rare Record Price Guide 2008

MINT VALUE £

| 70 | Polydor 2383 029 | AIRFORCE II (LP, gatefold sleeve, with insert) | 20 |
| 72 | Polydor 2383 133 | STRATAVARIOUS (LP) | 20 |

(see also Graham Bond Organisation, Cream, Blind Faith, Fela Ransome-Kuti [& Africa '70], Harold McNair, Griffin, Denny Laine)

GLEN BAKER
| 85 | The Stand THE STAND 3 | BRIEF ENCOUNTER (LP) | 20 |

(see also Enid)

JEANETTE BAKER
| 59 | Vogue Pop V 9143 | Everything Reminds Me Of You/JEANETTE & DECKY: Crazy With You | 250+ |
| 59 | Vogue Pop V 9143 | Everything Reminds Me Of You/JEANETTE & DECKY: Crazy With You (78) | 85 |

KENNY BAKER
53	Parlophone MSP 6019	Round About Midnight/Afternoon In Paris	5
53	Parlophone MSP 6057	Hayfoot, Strawfoot/The Continental	5
54	Parlophone MSP 6062	Trumpet Fantasy/Melancholy Baby	5
54	Parlophone MSP 6082	That's My Desire/Stompin' At The Savoy	5
54	Parlophone MSP 6114	I Speak To The Stars/Wanted	5
54	Parlophone MSP 6121	Peg O' My Heart/The Other Side	6
56	Pye Nixa N 15059	Blues I Love To Sing/Baker's Dozen (as Kenny Baker Dozen) (78)	8
55	Jazz Today JTL 1	OPERATION JAM SESSION (10" LP, with The Jazz Today Unit)	30
55	Jazz Today JTL 4	KENNY BAKER QUARTET/AFTER HOURS GROUP (10" LP)	20
55	Jazz Today JTL 5	TRIBUTE TO BENNY CARTER (10" LP, with The Jazz Today Unit, one side by Bertie King Jazz Group)	15
57	Pye Nixa NJL 10	PRESENTS THE HALF DOZEN (LP)	20
57	Pye Nixa NJT 517	BAKER PLAYS McHUGH (LP)	15
59	Columbia 33S1140	BLOWIN' UP A STORM (LP)	25
75	77 77S56	BAKER'S JAM (LP)	15

LAVERN BAKER (& GLIDERS)
55	Columbia SCM 5172	Tweedle Dee/Tomorrow Night (with Gliders) (78 rpm, DB 3591 = £45)	450
55	London HLA 8199	Play It Fair/That Old Lucky Sun (with Gliders) (78 rpm = £30)	315
56	London HLE 8260	My Happiness Forever (with Gliders)/Get Up! Get Up! (You Sleepy Head)	325
56	London HLE 8260	My Happiness Forever (with Gliders)/Get Up! Get Up! (You Sleepy Head) (78)	30
57	Columbia DB 3879	Jim Dandy/Tra La La (with Gliders) (78 rpm = £22)	350
57	London HLE 8396	I Can't Love You Enough/Still (78 rpm = £25)	150
57	London HLE 8442	Game Of Love/Jim Dandy Got Married (78 rpm = £22)	250
57	London HLE 8524	Humpty Dumpty Heart/Love Me Right (78 rpm = £25)	150
58	London HLE 8638	Learning To Love/Substitute (78 rpm = £20)	100
58	London HLE 8672	Whipper Snapper/Harbour Lights (78 rpm = £20)	100
59	London HLE 8790	I Cried A Tear/St. Louis Blues (78 rpm = £20)	50
59	London HLE 8871	I Waited Too Long/You're Teasing Me (78 rpm = £20)	30
59	London HLE 8945	So High So Low/If You Love Me (I Won't Care) (78 rpm = £25)	30
60	London HLE 9023	Tiny Tim/For Love Of You	40
60	London HLE 9252	Bumble Bee/My Turn Will Come	30
61	London HLE 9300	You're The Boss/I'll Never Be Free (with Jimmy Ricks)	40
61	London HLK 9343	Saved/Don Juan	30
61	London HLK 9468	Hey, Memphis/Voodoo Voodoo	55
63	London HLK 9649	See See Rider/The Story Of My Love (I Had A Dream)	25
65	Atlantic AET 6009	THE BEST OF LAVERN BAKER (EP)	85
58	London HA-E 2107	ROCK 'N' ROLL WITH LAVERN BAKER (LP)	500
58	London Jazz LTZK 15139	SINGS BESSIE SMITH (LP)	75+
61	London HA-K 2422	SAVED (LP)	90+
63	London HA-K 8074	SEE SEE RIDER (LP)	70+
64	Atlantic ATL 5002	THE BEST OF LAVERN BAKER (LP, plum label)	70+
68	Atlantic 587/588 133	SEE SEE RIDER (LP, reissue)	20

MICKEY BAKER
| 70 | Major Minor SMLP 67 | IN BLUNDERLAND (LP) | 22 |

(see also Mighty Flea)

SALLY BAKER
| 70s | Old Dog PUP 1 | IN THE SPOTLIGHT (LP) | 30 |

SAM BAKER
| 68 | Monument MON 1009 | I Believe In You/I'm Number One | 15 |

TWO-TON BAKER
| 55 | London HL 8121 | Clink, Clank (In My Piggy Bank)/Mr. Froggie (Went A Courtin') (78 rpm = £12) | 40 |

VICKY BAKER
| 64 | London HLU 9856 | No More Foolish Stories/Darling Say The Word | 15 |

YVONNE BAKER
| 77 | London HLU 10553 | You Didn't Say A Word/BOBBY PARIS: Night Owl | 30 |

(see also Sensations, Bobby Paris)

BAKER-GURVITZ ARMY
| 75 | Mountain TOP 4 | The Gambler/Time | 5 |
| 74 | Vertigo 9103 201 | BAKER-GURVITZ ARMY (LP) | 15 |

(see also Ginger Baker, Three Man Army, Parrish & Gurvitz, Gun)

BAKERLOO
| 69 | Harvest HAR 5004 | Driving Backwards/Once Upon A Time | 25 |
| 69 | Harvest SHVL 762 | BAKERLOO (LP) | 150 |

(see also May Blitz)

BAKER STREET PHILHARMONIC
| 71 | Pye International 7N 25540 | The Last One/Theme From 'Love Story' | 6 |
| 70 | Pye Intl. NSPL 28131 | BY THE LIGHT OF THE MOON (LP) | 20 |

(see also Mike Vickers)

MINT VALUE £

BAKER TWINS
| | | | |
64 Pye 7N 15628 — He's No Good/Words Written On Water 20

BALANCE
81 Portrait PRTA 1477 — Breaking Away/It's So Strange 8
73 Incus INCUS 11 — BALANCE (LP)....................................... 70
73 private pressing — IN FOR THE COUNT (LP) 22
81 Portrait — BALANCE (LP, reissue) 15
82 Portrait — IN FOR THE COUNT (LP, reissue) 12

BALDHEAD GROWLER
67 Jump Up JU 531 — Sausage/Bingo Woman 8

CHRIS BALDO
68 Vogue VRS 7029 — Living For Your Love/Arretez – Vous A Saint Michel..................... 15

LONG JOHN BALDRY
64 United Artists UP 1056 — Up Above My Head (I Hear Music In The Air)/You'll Be Mine (with Rod Stewart)............................. 50
65 United Artists UP 1078 — I'm On To You Baby/Goodbye Baby 15
65 United Artists UP 1107 — How Long Will It Last/House Next Door 40
66 United Artists UP 1124 — Unseen Hands/Turn On Your Lovelight 15
66 United Artists UP 1136 — The Drifter/Only A Fool Breaks His Own Heart 50
66 United Artists UP 1158 — Cuckoo/Bring My Baby Back To Me 25
67 United Artists UP 1204 — Only A Fool Breaks His Own Heart/Let Him Go (And Let Me Love You)... 20
67 Pye 7N 17385 — Let The Heartaches Begin/Annabella (Who Flies To Me When She's Lonely) 5
68 Pye 7N 17455 — Hold Back The Daybreak/Since I Lost You Baby....................... 5
68 Pye 7N 17563 — Mexico (Underneath The Sun In)/We're Together 5
68 Pye 7N 17593 — When The Sun Comes Shining Thru'/Wise To The Ways Of The World 5
69 Pye 7N 17664 — It's Too Late Now/Long And Lonely Nights 5
69 Pye 7N 17815 — Wait For Me/Don't Pity Me 5
70 Pye 7N 17921 — Setting The Tail Of A Fox On Fire/Well I Did 5
70 Pye 7N 45007 — When The World Is Over/Where Are My Eyes? 5
71 Warner Bros K 16105 — Rock Me When He's Gone/Flying (as John Baldry)............... 5
72 Warner Bros K 16175 — Iko Iko/Mother Ain't Dead (with Rod Stewart) 5
72 Warner Bros K 16217 — Everything Stops For Tea/Hambone 5
65 United Artists UEP 1013 — LONG JOHN'S BLUES (EP, with Hoochie Coochie Men) 70
64 United Artists ULP 1081 — LONG JOHN'S BLUES (LP, with Hoochie Coochie Men) 100
66 United Artists (S)ULP 1146 — LOOKING AT LONG JOHN (LP) 45
67 Pye N(S)PL 18208 — LET THE HEARTACHES BEGIN (LP)........................... 20
68 Pye N(S)PL 18228 — LET THERE BE LONG JOHN (LP, unissued)
69 Pye N(S)PL 18306 — WAIT FOR ME (LP) 20
(see also Rod Stewart, Alexis Korner, Bluesology)

THOR BALDURSSON
67 Decca F12653 — Tin Soldier/Painter............................... 15

KEITH BALFOUR
69 Studio One SO 2079 — Dreaming/Tired Of Waiting........................... 18

BALIL
93 Rising High RSN 72 — Parasignt/Island/Rosary Pilots/Avidya (12")..................... 8
95 Pure Plastic PP 005 — Nine Open/ RUE EAST: Endless Filters (12") 8

CANNON BALL (Carl Bryan) & JOHNNY MELODY (Moore)
69 Big Shot BI 518 — Parapinto/Cool Hand Luke........................... 20

KENNY BALL & HIS (JAZZ) BAND
59 Collector JDN 101 — Waterloo/Wabash Cannonball 10
60 Pye 7N 15272 — Teddy Bears' Picnic/Waltzing Matilda 10
67 Pye 7N 17348 — When I'm Sixty Four/Goodnight Irene....................... 5
59 Jazz Collector JEN 2 — KENNY BALL & HIS BAND (EP)....................... 15
59 Tempo EXA 83 — KENNY BALL JAZZ BAND (EP)....................... 15
60 Pye NJE 1086 — KENNY BALL PLAYS (EP) 10
60 Pye Jazz NJL 24 — INVITATION TO THE BALL (LP)....................... 20
61 Pye Jazz NJL 28 — KENNY BALL AND HIS JAZZMEN (LP)....................... 15
62 Pye Jazz NJL 42 — THE KENNY BALL SHOW (LP, as Kenny Ball & His Jazzmen)............. 15
64 Pye Jazz NJL 54 — TRIBUTE TO TOKYO (LP)....................... 20
(see also Gary Miller)

BALLADEERS
59 Columbia DB 4364 — Tom Gets The Last Laugh/Morning Star...................... 5

DAVE BALLANTYNE
66 Columbia DB 7807 — I Can't Express It/Ginger Eyes......................... 5
66 Columbia DB 7896 — Love Around The World/Wonder Full Of Women.................... 5
(see also Just Plain Jones, Esprit De Corps)

FLORENCE BALLARD
68 Stateside SS 2113 — It Doesn't Matter How I Say It (It's What I Say That Matters)/Goin' Out Of My Head................... 50
(see also Supremes)

HANK BALLARD (& MIDNIGHTERS)
59 Parlophone R 4558 — The Twist/Kansas City 50
60 Parlophone R 4682 — Finger Poppin' Time/I Love You, I Love You So-o-o 45
60 Parlophone R 4688 — The Twist/Teardrops On Your Letter 38
60 Parlophone R 4707 — Let's Go, Let's Go, Let's Go/If You'd Forgive Me................ 40
61 Parlophone R 4728 — The Hoochie Coochie Coo/LITTLE WILLIE JOHN: Walk Slow 40
61 Parlophone R 4762 — Let's Go Again/Deep Blue Sea...................... 55
61 Parlophone R 4771 — The Continental Walk/What Is This I See 30
72 Mojo 2093 010 — Annie Had A Baby/Teardrops On Your Letter................... 10

80s	Urban	From The Loveside/FOSTER SYLVERS: Misdemeanor	10
61	Parlophone PMC 1158	SPOTLIGHT ON HANK BALLARD (LP)	100+
63	London HA 8101	THE JUMPIN' HANK BALLARD (LP)	110

(see also Midnighters)

KAYE BALLARD
| 55 | Brunswick 05376 | Triumph Of Love/Where Were You Last Night? | 10 |
| 55 | Brunswick 05436 | Don't You Tell Pa/In Love And Out Again | 10 |

RUSS BALLARD
74	Epic S EPC 3122	Loose Women/Danger Zone Part 1	6
78	Epic S EPC 6316	Treat Her Right/What Does It Take	5
85	EMI EA 185	Voices/Living Without You (p/s)	5

(see also Argent, Roulettes)

BALLOON BUSTERS
| 69 | Pye 7N 17748 | Alcock And Brown/Bluer Than Blue | 5 |

BALLOON FARM
| 68 | London HLP 10185 | A Question Of Temperature/Hurtin' For Your Love | 75 |

BALLS
| 71 | Wizard WIZ 101 | Fight For My Country/Janie Slow Down | 25 |

(see also Denny Laine, Lemon Tree, Trevor Burton, Uglys, Wizzard)

LORI BALMER
| 68 | Polydor 56293 | Treacle Brown/Four Faces West | 12 |

BALTIMORE & OHIO MARCHING BAND
| 67 | Stateside SS 2045 | Lapland/Condition Red (DJ copy = £175) | 100 |
| 68 | Stateside (S)SL 10231 | LAPLAND (LP) | 30 |

BAMA WINDS
| 69 | Island ILPS 9096 | WINDY (LP) | 25 |

BAMBIS
| 64 | Oriole CB 1965 | Not Wrong/Handle With Care | 40 |
| 65 | CBS 201778 | Baby Blue/If This Is Love | 40 |

BAMBOO SHOOT
| 68 | Columbia DB 8370 | The Fox Has Gone To Ground/There And Back Again Lane | 250 |

BAMBOOS OF JAMAICA
| 70 | Pye Intl. 7N 25515 | Reggae Man/Candy | 5 |

BANANA BUNCH
| 71 | DJM DJS 252 | Tra-La-La Song/Season Of The Rain | 5 |

(see also Nite People)

BANANAMEN
| 83 | Big Beat NS 88 | The Crusher/Love Me/Surfin' Bird (p/s) | 5 |

BANANARAMA
81	Demon D 1010	Aie A Mwana/Dubwana (p/s)	5
81	Deram DMX 446	Aie A Mwana (Extended)/Dubwana (Extended) (12", p/s)	8
83	London NANX 6	Robert De Niro's Waiting/Push (3 x 12", coloured vinyl with different labels)	8
86	London NANDP 11	More Than Physical (Alternate Mix)/Scarlett/Venus/White Train (double pack, gatefold p/s)	5
85	London NANPD 9	Do Not Disturb (Keren, Sarah or Siobhan-shaped picture disc) . each 8
86	London NANPD 10	Venus/White Train (picture disc)	8
86	London NANA 11	More Than Physical/Scarlet (poster p/s)	5
86	London NANE 12	TRICK OF THE NIGHT EP (gatefold p/s)	8
88	London NANXR 14	Love In The First Degree (Eurobeat Style)/Mr. Sleaze (Rare Groove Remix) (12", p/s)	8
88	London NANB 17	Love, Truth & Honesty/Strike It Rich (box set with 4 postcards & poster)	8
88	London NANCD 18 (CD)	Nathan Jones (Extended Version)/Venus (Extended Version)/Once In A Lifetime	14

BANBARRA
| 76 | United Artists UP 36113 | Shack Up Parts 1 & 2 | 10 |
| 85 | Stateside 12STATES 1 | Shack Up (Extended)/Shack Up (Part 1)/Shack Up (Part II) (12" p/s) | 10 |

BANCO DE GAIA
| 95 | Bark L 011 S | LAST TRAIN TO LHASA (4-LP, limited edition) | 18 |

THE BAND
68	Capitol CL 15559	The Weight/I Shall Be Released	8
69	Capitol CL 15613	Up On Cripple Creek/The Night They Drove Old Dixie Down	8
69	Capitol CL 15737	Rag Mama Rag/The Unfaithful Servant	6
73	Capitol CL 15767	Ain't Got No Home/Get Up Jake	5
78	Warner Bros K 17187	Theme From The Last Waltz/Out Of The Blue	5
68	Capitol (S)T 2955	MUSIC FROM BIG PINK (LP, black/rainbow label)	20

(see also Levon & The Hawks, Bob Dylan, Ronnie Hawkins, Robbie Robertson)

BAND AID
| 85 | Mercury FEEDP 1 | Do They Know It's Christmas?/Feed The World (shaped picture disc) | 5 |

BANDITS
02	Centro Del Banco 7176-47	The Warning/Free Me Rain (stickered die-cut sleeve, 500 only)	15
02	Centro Del Banco 7176-6	Once Upon A Time/On My Way (stickered die-cut sleeve, 750)	12
00s	Centro Del Banco (no cat. no.)	The Warning Dub/Guns Of Brixton (Live [The Bandits V The Mad Professor]) (12", p/s, 1000 only)	12

MINT VALUE £

BAND OF ANGELS
64	United Artists UP 1049	Not True As Yet/Me	25
64	United Artists UP 1066	Gonna Make A Woman Of You/She'll Never Be You	25
66	Piccadilly 7N 35279	Leave It To Me/Too Late My Love	25
66	Piccadilly 7N 35292	Invitation/Cheat And Lie	40

(see also Mike D'Abo)

BAND OF MERCY & SALVATION
69	Duke DU 20	Suffering Stink/BOB MELODY: The Break (B-side actually by Winston Francis)	10

BANDOGGS
78	Transatlantic LTRA 504	BANDOGGS (LP)	12

(see also Peter & Chris Coe)

BANDWAGON
(see under Johnny Johnson & Bandwagon)

BANDY LEGS
74	WWW WWS 01	Ride Ride/Don't Play Games	20
76	Jet JET 783	Bet You Can't Dance/Circles	20

(see also Quartz)

ED BANGER
78	Rabid TOSH 106	Kinnel Tommy/Baby Was A Baby (p/s)	7
78	EMI International INT 570	Kinnel Tommy/Baby Was A Baby (reissue, numbered p/s)	7
81	Spiv DIV 1	I've Just Had My Car Nicked/P.C. Plod/Sponge (p/s, with photo insert)	8
83	Cloud Nine CNS 01	Poor People/Vicars In The Dark (p/s)	7

(see also Nosebleeds, Slaughter & The Dogs)

BANGOR FLYING CIRCUS
70	Stateside-Dunhill SSL 5022	BANGOR FLYING CIRCUS (LP)	20

BESSIE BANKS
64	Red Bird BC 106	Go Now/Sounds Like My Baby	70
67	Verve VS 563	I Can't Make It (Without You Baby)/Need You	80
68	Soul City SC 105	Go Now/Sounds Like My Baby (reissue)	25
75	Contempo CS 2070	Baby You Sure Know How To Get To Me/Try To Leave Me If You Can	25

DARRELL BANKS
66	London HL 10070	Open The Door To Your Heart/Our Love (Is In The Pocket) (demo only)	850
66	Stateside SS 536	Open The Door To Your Heart/Our Love (Is In The Pocket) (1st/2nd pressings)	50/30
67	Atlantic 5841 120	Angel Baby (Don't You Ever Leave Me)/Look Into The Eyes Of A Fool	60
69	Stax STAX 124	Just Because Your Love Is Gone/I'm The One Who Loves You	150
77	Atlantic K 10879	Angel Baby (Don't You Ever Leave Me)/Look Into The Eyes Of A Fool (reissue)	10
69	Stax SXATS 1011	HERE TO STAY (LP)	70

HOMER BANKS
66	Liberty LIB 12028	A Lot Of Love/Fighting To Win	30
67	Liberty LIB 12047	60 Minutes Of Your Love/Do You Know What	30
67	Liberty LIB 12060	Hooked By Love/Lady Of Stone	40
68	Minit MLF 11004	Round The Clock Lover Man/Foolish Hearts Break Fast	15
68	Minit MLF 11007	60 Minutes Of Your Love/A Lot Of Love	20
69	Minit MLF 11015	Me Or Your Mama/I Know You Know I Know You Know	15
70	Liberty LBF 15392	60 Minutes Of Your Love/I Know You Know I Know You Know	10
72	United Artists UP 35360	Hooked By Love/Lady Of Stone (reissue)	10

LARRY BANKS
67	Stateside SS 579	I Don't Wanna Do It/I'm Coming Home	50

LLOYD BANKS
66	Reaction 591 008	We'll Meet Again/Look Out Girl	18

DR. MURRAY BANKS
60	Viva MB104	THE DRAMA OF SEX (LP)	18

PETER BANKS
73	Sovereign SNVA 7256	PETER BANKS (LP, gatefold sleeve)	18

(see also Syndicats, Syn, Neat Change, Yes, Flash, Jan Akkerman, Phil Collins, Steve Hackett)

ROSIE BANKS
76	Tamla Motown TMG 1037	Darling Baby/Whole New Thing	10

(see also Sly & Family Stone)

BANNED
77	Can't Eat EAT 1 UP	Little Girl/CPGJ's (stamped white labels, some in handmade p/s)	50/12

BANSHEES
64	Columbia DB 7361	I Got A Woman/Don't Say Goodnight And Mean Goodbye	40
65	Columbia DB 7530	Big Buildin'/Mockingbird	25
65	Columbia DB 7752	I'm Gonna Keep On Loving You/Yes Indeed	20

(NB: this group does not include Bryan Ferry)

BARBARA & BRENDA
68	Direction 58-3799	Never Love A Robin/Sally's Party	25

BARBARA & WINSTON
64	Island WI 418	The Dream/I Love You	18

BARBARA ANN
65	Piccadilly 7N 35221	You've Lost That Loving Feeling/Till The Summer Time	20
65	Piccadilly 7N 35244	Black Is The Colour Of My True Love's Hair/Since You've Loved Me	5

BARBARIANS
65	Stateside SS 449	Are You A Boy Or Are You A Girl/Take It Or Leave It	25
66	Stateside SS 497	Moulty/I'll Keep On Seeing You	30

BARBECUE BOB
67	Kokomo K 1002	GEORGIA BLUES NO. 1 (LP, 99 copies only)	100

JOHN HENRY BARBEE
65	Storyville 670 171	PORTRAITS IN BLUES VOLUME 9 (LP)	20

CHRIS BARBER('S JAZZ BAND)
SINGLES
51	Esquire 12-013	Oh, Didn't He Ramble/CRANE RIVER JAZZ BAND: Eh La Bas! (78)	12
52	Tempo A101	Camp Meeting Blues/Stomp Off, Let's Go (78)	8
52	Tempo A 102	When Erastmus Plays His Old Kazoo/Misty Morning (78)	8
54	Decca F 10417	Chimes Blues/Merrydown Rag	5
54	Columbia SCMC 10	White Christmas/On A Christmas Day (with Lonnie Donegan, export issue)(78 = £8)	25
55	Decca F 10492	Bobby Shafto/The Martinique	10
55	Decca F 10666	It's Tight Like That/All The Girls Go Crazy About The Way I Walk	10
56	Decca FJ 10724	The World Is Waiting For The Sunrise/St. Louis Blues	8
56	Decca FJ 10790	I Never Knew Just What A Girl Could Do/Storyville Blues	8
56	Tempo A 116	Precious Lord, Lead Me On (with Lonnie Donegan)/Tiger Rag (78 rpm = £6)	12
56	Tempo A 132	Saratoga Swing/Ice Cream (78 rpm = £6)	8
57	Tempo A 160	Ice Cream/Down By The Riverside (78 rpm =£6)	8

EPs
55	Columbia SEG 7568	PLAYS SPIRITUALS	8
55	Columbia SEG 7586	BARBER GOES TO TOWN WITH ELLINGTON	8
55	Tempo EXA 6	CHRIS BARBER'S NEW ORLEANS JAZZ BAND	8
55	Tempo EXA 22	CHRIS BARBER'S JAZZ BAND	8
55	Decca DFE 6238	JAZZ AT THE ROYAL FESTIVAL HALL	8
55	Decca DFE 6252	CHRIS BARBER AT THE ROYAL FESTIVAL HALL	8
56	Decca DFE 6344	CHRIS BARBER AT THE ROYAL FESTIVAL HALL NO. 2	8
56	Decca DFE 6382	BARBER'S BEST	8
56	Jazz Today JTE 103	PLUS/MINUS 1	12
56	Pye Jazz NJE 1013	PLUS/MINUS 1 (reissue)	8
56	Pye Jazz NJE 1007	CHRIS BARBER SPECIAL	10
57	Pye Jazz NJE 1039	CHRIS BARBER IN CONCERT PT. 1	10
57	Pye Jazz NJE 1040	CHRIS BARBER IN CONCERT PT. 2	10
57	Decca DFE 6463	NEW ORLEANS BLUES	10
58	Pye Jazz NJE 1068	CHRIS BARBER JAZZ PARADE VOL. 1	10
58	Pye Jazz NJE 1073	CHRIS BARBER JAZZ PARADE VOL. 2	10
59	Esquire EP 206	CHRIS BARBER NOT IN HI FI (with Washboard Wonders)	10
59	Columbia SEG 7980	BANDBOX VOL. 1 (also stereo ESG 7789)	10
60	Pye Jazz NJE 1084	CHRIS BARBER JAZZ PARADE VOL. 8	10
60	Columbia SEG 7994	BANDBOX VOL. 1 No. 2 (also stereo ESG 7801)	10
60	Columbia SEG 8030	EXTRACTS FROM BARBER IN BERLIN (with Ottilie Patterson, also stereo ESG 7821)	10
61	Columbia SEG 8081	PAT (with Pat Halcox, also stereo ESG 7846)	10
61	Columbia SEG 8110	INTRODUCING IAN (with Ian Wheeler)	12
62	Columbia SEG 8182	INTERNATIONAL VOL. 2 PT. 1 – BARBER IN COPENHAGEN	10
62	Columbia SEG 8214	BARBER'S BLUES BOOK VOL. 1	10
63	Columbia SEG 8224	IN BARBER'S CHAIR	10

LPs
54	Decca LF 1198	NEW ORLEANS JOYS (10", with Lonnie Donegan's Skiffle Group)	30
55	Nixa Jazz Today NJL 1	ECHOES OF HARLEM (with Ottilie Patterson)	30
55	Jazz Today JTL 3	CHRIS BARBER PLAYS VOL. 1 (10")	25
56	Nixa Jazz Today NJT 500	CHRIS BARBER PLAYS VOL. 1 (10", reissue)	20
56	Nixa Jazz Today NJT 502	CHRIS BARBER PLAYS VOL. 2 (10")	20
57	Nixa Jazz Today NJT 505	CHRIS BARBER PLAYS VOL. 3 (10")	20
57	Nixa Jazz Today NJT 508	CHRIS BARBER PLAYS VOL. 4 (10")	20
57	Columbia 33S 1112	JAZZ SACRED AND SECULAR (10", with Lonnie Donegan)	30
57	Nixa Jazz Today NJL 6	CHRIS BARBER IN CONCERT (with Ottilie Patterson)	20
58	Pye Nixa Jazz NJL 15	CHRIS BARBER IN CONCERT VOL. 2 (with Ottilie Patterson)	20
58	Pye Nixa Jazz NJL 17	CHRIS BARBER IN CONCERT VOL. 3 (with Ottilie Patterson)	20
58	Decca LK 4246	BARBER'S BEST	20
59	Columbia 33SX 1158	BAND BOX VOL. 1	22
59	Columbia 33SX 1189	BARBER IN BERLIN VOL. 1 (with Ottilie Patterson)	30
59	Columbia 33SX	BARBER IN BERLIN VOL. 2 (with Ottilie Patterson)	30
60	Columbia 33SX 1245	BAND BOX VOL. 2 – ELITE SYNCOPATIONS (stereo SCX 3319) each	20
60	Ace Of Clubs ACL 1037	THE BEST OF CHRIS BARBER (with Ottilie Patterson & Lonnie Donegan)	15
61	Columbia 33SX 1274	BARBER IN COPENHAGEN (also stereo SCX 3342) each	20
61	Columbia 33SX 1321	CHRIS BARBER'S AMERICAN JAZZ BAND (also stereo SCX 3376) each	20
61	Columbia 33SX 1333	BLUES BOOK (with Ottilie Patterson, also stereo SCX 3384) each	20
61	Columbia 33SX 1346	AT THE LONDON PALLADIUM (also stereo [SCX 3392]) each	30
61	Columbia 33SX 1401	BEST YET!	20
65	Columbia 33SX 1657	GOOD MORNIN' BLUES	20
65	Decca LK 4742	FOLK BARBER STYLE (mono)	20
65	Phase 4 Stereo PFS 4070	FOLK BARBER STYLE (as Chris Barber & His Jazz Band)	20
71	Polydor 2683 001	GET ROLLING	15

(see also Ottilie Patterson, Lonnie Donegan, Sonny Terry & Brownie McGhee,
Kenneth Washington & Chris Barber, Dickie Bishop & Sidekicks)

CHRIS BARBER'S SKIFFLE GROUP
51	Esquire 10-180	Everybody Loves My Baby/Whoop It Up (with Washboard Wonders) (78)	10
58	Pye Jazz 7NJ 2014	Doin' My Time/Where Could I Go? (with Johnny Duncan)	10
58	Pye Jazz 7NJ 2017	Can't You Line 'Em/Gipsy Dave (with Dickie Bishop)	10
57	Pye Jazz NJE 1025	CHRIS BARBER SKIFFLE GROUP (EP)	10

(see also Lonnie Donegan, Johnny Duncan & Blue Grass Boys)

Chris BARBER & HIS BAND

CHRIS BARBER AND HIS BAND
67	Marmalade 598 005	Catcall/Mercy Mercy Mercy	40
69	Marmalade 558 013	Battersea Rain Dance/Sleepy Joe	12
69	Marmalade 608 009	BATTERSEA RAIN DANCE (LP, as Chris Barber & His Band)	30
69	Polydor 2384 020	BATTERSEA RAIN DANCE (LP) (2nd Pressing)	40

CHRIS BARBER SOUL BAND
65	Columbia DB 7461	Finishing Straight/Morning Train	12

(see also Louis Jordan & Chris Barber)

FRANK BARBER FIVE
62	Ember JBS 709	Flyover/Golden Shadows	6

(see also Frank & Barbarians)

DAVE BARBOUR & HIS ORCHESTRA
59	Oriole CB 1507	Tough/Bu Bam (78 rpm = £8)	9

EDDIE BARCLAY & HIS ORCHESTRA
57	Felsted ESD 3041	JAMES DEAN — MUSIC FROM HIS FILMS (EP)	20

EDDIE BARCLAY & QUINCY JONES
58	Felsted PDL 85056	EDDIE AND QUINCY (LP)	20

RUE BARCLAY & PEGGY DUNCAN
54	London HL 8033	Tongue Tied Boy/River Of Tears	35

BARCLAY JAMES HARVEST
68	Parlophone R 5693	Early Morning/Mr. Sunshine	30
69	Harvest HAR 5003	Brother Thrush/Poor Wages	15
70	Harvest HAR 5025	Taking Some Time On/The Iron Maiden	15
71	Harvest HAR 5034	Mocking Bird/Vanessa Simmons	10
72	Harvest HAR 5051	I'm Over You/Child Of Man	10
72	Harvest HAR 5058	Thank You/Medicine Man	10
73	Harvest HAR 5068	Rock And Roll Woman/The Joker (BJH logo p/s)	12
74	Polydor 2058 474	Poor Boy Blues/Crazy City	7
74	Polydor (matrix: SH 1041/2)	Negative Earth/RARE BIRD: Diamonds (33rpm flexidisc free with *Sounds*)	10/6
75	Harvest HAR 5094	Mocking Bird/Galadriel	5
91	Swallowtail SWALLOW 2	Too Much On Your Plate (fan club flexi)	10
70	Harvest SHVL 770	BARCLAY JAMES HARVEST (LP)	18
71	Harvest SHVL 788	ONCE AGAIN (LP)	12
71	Harvest SHVL 794	BARCLAY JAMES HARVEST AND OTHER SHORT STORIES (LP)	12
72	Harvest Q4SHVL 788	ONCE AGAIN (LP, quadrophonic)	18
73	Harvest SHSP 4023	BABY JAMES HARVEST (LP)	12

(see also Bombadil, John Lees, Woolly Wolstenholme)

PETER BARDENS
70	Transatlantic TRA 222	THE ANSWER (LP)	30
71	Transatlantic TRA 243	PETER BARDENS (LP, gatefold sleeve)	30
76	Transatlantic TRASAM 36	VINTAGE '69 (LP, featuring Peter Green, some on clear vinyl)	15

(see also Cheynes, Peter B's, Shotgun Express, Them, Village, Camel, Steve Tilston)

BRIGITTE BARDOT
66	Vogue VRS 7018	Mister Sun/Gang Gang (some in p/s)	100+/30
68	Pye International 7N 25450	Harley-Davidson/Contact (some in p/s)	100/30
63	Philips BL 7561	BRIGITTE BARDOT (LP)	100

BARDS
68	Capitol CL 15536	The Owl And The Pussycat/Light Of Love	30

BOBBY BARE
60	Top Rank JAR 310	I'm Hanging Up My Rifle/That's Where I Want To Be	10
62	RCA RCA 1302	Shame On Me/Above And Beyond	6
63	RCA RCA 1352	Detroit City/Heart Of Ice	6
63	RCA RCA 1366	500 Miles Away From Home/It All Depends On Linda	6
64	RCA RCA 1387	Miller's Cave/Jeannie's Last Kiss	6
64	RCA RCX 7139	DETROIT CITY (EP)	15
66	RCA RD 7783	CONSTANT SORROW (LP)	12

(see also Bill Parsons, Skeeter Davis & Bobby Bare)

BAREFOOT BLUES BAND
70	Beacon BEA 163	Can't You See/Sunday Morning Barefoot Blues	15
72	Deram DM 353	The Spirit Of Joe Hill/I Believe In Music	8
73	Deram DM 372	Getting Better All The Time/Half Of Me	6

MINOUCHE BARELLI
67	CBS 2806	Boum Badaboum/Let Me Take You	20

MARK BARKAN
67	Stateside SS 2064	A Great Day For The Clown/Pity The Woman	20

BAR-KAYS
67	Stax 601 014	Soul Finger/Knucklehead	15
68	Stax 601 036	A Hard Day's Night/I Want Someone	10
69	Atlantic 584 244	Soul Finger/Knucklehead (reissue)	8
69	Stax STAX 135	Midnight Cowboy/A.J. The House Fly	5
70	Stax STAX 146	Sing And Dance/I Thank You	5
69	Atco 228 030	SOUL FINGER (LP)	30
69	Stax SXATS 1009	GOTTA GROOVE (LP)	25
71	Stax 2362 003	BLACK ROCK (LP)	20
73	Stax 2325 087	DO YOU SEE WHAT I SEE? (LP)	15
76	Stax STX 1033	COLD BLOODED (LP)	20

(see also Otis Redding)

BUTCH BARKER
75	Creole CR 113	The Joker/Juicie Brucie	8

DAVE BARKER
70	Duke DU 74	Funkey Reggae/TOMMY McCOOK & SUPERSONICS: I Love You My Baby (B-side actually by Versatiles)	30
70	Punch PH 20	Prisoner Of Love/BUSTY & UPSETTERS: Soul Juice	25
70	Punch PH 22	You Betray Me/Will You Still Love Me Tomorrow?	20
70	Punch PH 25	Shocks Of Mighty Parts 1 & 2	15
70	Punch PH 42	Reggae Meeting/MARTIN ALL STARS: Soul Bone	20
70	Jackpot JP 736	The Fastest Man Alive/NORMAN GRANT: Bloodshot Eyes	15
70	Jackpot JP 742	Wet Version/I Got To Get Away	15
70	Jackpot JP 745	Girl Of My Dreams/On Broadway	40
70	High Note HS 049	She Want It/FIRST GENERATION: Give Him Up	15
70	Randy's RAN 503	October/RANDY'S ALLSTARS: Time Out	12
70	Unity UN 567	Blessed Are The Meek (with Slim Smith)/JEFF BARNES & UNIQUES: The People's Voice	15
70	Upsetter US 331	Shocks Of Mighty/Set Me Free (with Upsetters)	15
70	Upsetter US 344	Some Sympathy/UNTOUCHABLES: Tender Love	20
70	Upsetter US 347	Sound Underground/Don't Let The Sun Catch You Crying	20
71	Upsetter US 358	Shocks '71/HURRICANES: You've Got To Be Mine	20
71	Upsetter US 362	Groove Me/UPSETTERS: Screwdriver	15
71	Upsetter US 364	What A Confusion/UPSETTERS: Confusion — Version 2	25
71	Ackee ACK 113	Johnny Dollar/Version	15
71	Ackee ACK 119	Life Of A Millionaire/Version	12
71	Trojan TR 7851	Sex Machine/You Left Me And Gone (both sides with Aggrovators)	20
71	Punch PH 69	What A Confusion/BOB MARLEY: Small Axe	45
71	Supreme SUP 228	Double Heavy/Johnny Dollar	18
71	Downtown DT 482	Only The Strong Survive/Only The Strong — Version	12
72	Jackpot JP 803	You'll Be Sorry/Green Grow The Lilacs	8
72	Big Shot BI 614	Are You Sure/I Don't Know Why (B-side actually by Sensations)	6
72	Fab FAB 25	Green Grow The Lilacs/JIMMY RILEY: Keep An Eye (On Your Closest Friend) (white label)	12
76	Trojan TRL 127	PRISONER OF LOVE (LP)	45

(see also Glen & Dave, Dave & Ansell Collins, Bobby & Dave, Aggrovators, David Crooks, Dennis Alcapone, Don Drummond, Owen Gary, Lizzy & Dennis, Bob Marley, Lester Sterling, Busty Brown)

RONNIE BARKER
78	EMI EMI 2768	Going Straight/String Bean Queen	10
78	BBC RESL 60	But First The News/Night Night (With Ronnie Corbett)	6
78	Alaska ALA 2015	Pismonunciation/The Vicar of St. Cain and Abel	6

(see also Two Ronnies)

TIM BARKER & THE CARLISLE UNITED SINGERS
74	Keswick KES 001	Looking Good/We're Carlisle United/Going On	5

BARLASTON DOWN
60s	Decca 13321	Mean Woman Mambo/Part 2	10

BARLEY BREE
67	Piccadilly 7N 35393	Sometime In The Morning/Save Your Love	15

BARNABY RUDGE
68	CBS 3262	Joe, Organ & Co./Railway Jim	6

(see also Will Malone)

BARNEY J. BARNES & INTRO.
67	Decca F 12662	It Must Be Love/Can't Stand The Pain	10

BARNES/ADAMS
60s	Lyntone LYN 1021	When It Comes To The Crunch (It's Smiths Time)/Rhythm And Crunch (flexi, p/s)	25/15

BENNY BARNES
60	Mercury AMT 1094	Token Of Love/That-A-Boy Willie	20

DENA BARNES
80	Grapevine GRP 141	If You Ever Walked Out Of My Life/Who Am I	25

JEFF BARNES
70	Jackpot JP 735	Get In The Groove/JOHN HOLT: A Little Tear	12
70	Unity UN 568	1,000 Tons Of Version/Wake The Nation (B-side with Hugh Roy)	20
70	Pama PM 802	Jeff Barnes Thing/LENNOX BROWN: Lover's Mood	12
71	Smash SMA 2313	Wake The Nation (with Hugh Roy)/1,000 Tons Of Version	12

(see also Hugh Roy, Dave Barker, Darker Shade Of Blue, Delroy Wilson)

J.J. BARNES
67	Polydor 56722	Day Tripper/Deeper In Love	30
69	Stax STAX 130	Baby Please Come Back Home/Easy Living	25
73	Tamla Motown TMG 870	Real Humdinger/Please Let Me In/I Ain't Gonna Do It	10
74	Contempo CS 2009	To An Early Grave/To An Early Grave (Instrumental Version)	5
75	Contempo CLP 520	THE GROOVESVILLE MASTERS (LP)	15
77	Contempo CLP 604	SARA SMILE (LP)	20

J.J. BARNES/STEVE MANCHA
69	Stax SXATS 1012	RARE STAMPS (LP)	75

LLOYD BARNES
64	Blue Beat BB 235	Time Is Hard/BUSTER'S ALLSTARS: Reincarnation	30

MINT VALUE £

RICHARD BARNES
68	Columbia DB 8436	Woman, Woman/The Princess And The Soldier	5
68	Columbia DB 8507	Look Away/Mr In Between	5
70	Philips BF 1840	Take To The Mountains/But It's Now I Need Your Love	6
70	Philips 630 8027	RICHARD BARNES (LP)	15

(see also Quiet Five)

SIDNEY BARNES
76	Charly CYS 1007	I Hurt On The Other Side/Good Lovin'	20

ERIC BARNET(T)
68	Gas GAS 100	The Horse (actually by Theo Beckford & Group)/Action Line (actually by Versatiles)	12
69	Gas GAS 106	Te Ta Toe (act. by Theo Beckford & Group)/MILTON BOOTHE: Lonely And Blue	12
69	Crab CRAB 37	Quaker City/Double Up (both actually by Theo Beckford & Group)	12
70	Gas GAS 130	Pink Shark/Swing Free (both actually by Theo Beckford & Group)	10
70	Gas GAS 147	Bumper To Bumper/Fat Turkey (both actually by Theo Beckford & Group)	18

(see also Theo[philus] Beckford)

BARRY BARNETT
58	HMV POP 487	The Book Of Love/All I Have To Do Is Dream	12
58	HMV POP 511	When/Secretly	10
58	HMV POP 521	My Lucky Love/Too Young To Love	10
58	HMV POP 532	Susie Darlin'/Just A Dream (78 rpm = £8)	12
59	HMV POP 579	The Diary/Only A Memory (78 rpm = £10)	10
59	HMV POP 627	Cuckoo Girl/I'll String Along With You	10
66	Mercury MF 945	How Can You Explain/If There Wasn't Any You	7

BARNSTORMERS SPASM BAND
58	Parlophone R 4416	Whistling Rufus/Won't You Come Home, Bill Bailey? (78 rpm = £15)	10
59	Tempo A 168	Stormin' The Barn/That's All There Is (There Ain't No More) (78 rpm = £15)	10

(see also Original Barnstormers Spasm Band)

H.B. BARNUM
61	Fontana H 299	Lost Love/Hallelujah	15
65	Capitol CL 15391	The Record (Baby I Love You)/I'm A Man	60
76	Capitol CL 15851	Heartbreaker/Searchin' For My Soul	10
79	Capitol CL 16067	Heartbreaker/BOBBY PARIS: I Walked Away	10
64	RCA Victor RCX 7147	THE GREAT H.B. BARNUM (EP)	200
62	RCA Victor RD/SF 7500	THE BIG VOICE OF BARNUM . . . H.B., THAT IS (LP, mono/stereo)	15
63	RCA Victor RD/SF 7543	EVERYBODY LOVES H.B. (LP, mono/stereo)	15

(see also Robins)

CARL BARON & CHEETAHS
63	Columbia DB 7162	This Is Only The Beginning/Beg Borrow Or Steal	15

RIKKY BARON
60	Parlophone R 4706	Angry Young Man/My Lonely Heart	10
63	Parlophone R 4754	Everybody/You're Breaking My Heart	10

BARON WITH HIS POUNDING PIANO
65	Sue WI 398	Is A Blue Bird Blue/In The Mood	40

(see also V.I.P.'s)

BARONS (U.S.)
57	London HLP 8391	Don't Walk Out/Once In A Lifetime (78 rpm = £210)	1,500
71	Jay Boy BOY 45	No More Baby Love/Society Don't Let Us Down	10

BARONS (U.K.)
61	Oriole CB 1608	Cossack/Summertime	20
61	Oriole CB 1620	Samurai/Whirlwind	20

BARRABAS
76	Atlantic K 10716	Checkmate/Four Seasons Woman	8

BARRACUDAS
79	Cells CELLOUT 1	I Want My Woody Back/Subway Surfin' (p/s)	20+
80	Zonophone Z 5	Summer Fun/Chevy Baby (p/s, with/without stickers)	18/8
80	Zonophone Z 8	His Last Summer/Barracuda Waver/Surfers Are Back (p/s)	6
80	Zonophone Z 11	(I Wish It Could Be) 1965 Again/Rendezvous (p/s)	5
81	Zonophone Z 17	I Can't Pretend/The KGB (Made A Man Out Of Me) (p/s)	5
80	Zonophone ZONO 103	DROP OUT WITH THE BARRACUDAS (LP)	15

DICKIE BARRETT
58	MGM MGM 976	Smoke Gets In Your Eyes/Remember Me (78 rpm = £8)	65

JOE BARRETT
55	Brunswick 05432	I'm Sincere/Why Did You Break My Heart?	10

RICHARD BARRETT & CHANTELS
59	HMV POP 609	Come Softly To Me/Walking Through Dreamland	25

(see also Chantels)

RITCHIE BARRETT
62	London HLK 9552	Some Other Guy/Tricky Dicky	75

'SWEET EMMA' BARRETT
60s	Riverside RLP 364	THE BELL GAL AND HER DIXIELAND BOYS (LP)	15

SYD BARRETT
69	Harvest HAR 5009	Octopus/Golden Hair	120
69	Harvest HAR 5009	Octopus/Golden Hair (Promo with mispelt 'Barratt' and release date 14.11.69)	200
88	Strange Fruit SFPS 043	THE PEEL SESSIONS (12", EP, initially with metallic sleeve)	15/12
88	Strange Fruit SFPSCD 043	THE PEEL SESSIONS (CD EP)	10
70	Harvest SHVL 765	THE MADCAP LAUGHS (LP, laminated or matt gatefold sleeve)	35/25

70	Harvest SHSP 4007	BARRETT (LP, laminated or textured flipback sleeve) 40/25
70s	Harvest SHSP 4007	BARRETT (LP, textured non-flipback sleeve) 15
74	Harvest SHDW 404	SYD BARRETT (2-LP, reissue of "Madcap" & "Barrett", gatefold sleeve) 18
88	Harvest SHSP 4126	OPEL (LP, gatefold sleeve) 12
93	EMI SYD BOX 1	CRAZY DIAMOND (3-CD box set, with booklet) 20
97	Harvest 7423 855663 18	THE MADCAP LAUGHS (LP, 180gm reissue, heavy quality sleeve) 15
97	Harvest 7423 821450 11	BARRETT (LP, 180gm reissue, heavy quality sleeve) 15
99	Harvest SVLP 153	OPEL (2-LP, 180gm reissue, heavy quality sleeve) 18
99	Simply Vinyl SVLP 153	OPEL (LP 180gm reissue, heavy quality gatefold sleeve) 18
00	Simply Vinyl SVLP 281	BARRETT (LP, 180gm reissue, heavy quality gatefold sleeve) 18
00	Simply Vinyl SVLP 289	THE MADCAP LAUGHS (LP, 180gm reissue, heavy quality gatefold sleeve) 18

(see also Pink Floyd)

WILD WILLY BARRETT
77	Logo GO 105	Return Of Kong/Nice To Know You're My Friend (p/s) 5
79	Polydor 2059 067	Let's Play Schools/I Did It Otway (p/s) 5
86	Galvanised DIP 1	ORGANIC BONDAGE (LP, with Stephen Two Names; in wooden sleeve) 15

(see also John Otway/Wild Willy Barrett)

RAY BARRETT
69	Fontana STF 5487	NO TROUBLE NOW (LP) 12

RAY BARRETTO
63	Columbia DB 7051	El Watusi/Ritmo Sabroso 30
65	Columbia DB 7684	El Watusi/Swingin' Shepherd Blues 20
69	London HL 10262	Acid/Mercy Mercy Baby 30
67	Island ILP 946	EL WATUSI (LP) 50
69	London HA/SH 8383	ACID (LP) 50

BARRIER
68	Eyemark EMS 1013	Georgie Brown/Dawn Breaks Through (some in handmade p/s) 450/250
68	Philips BF 1692	The Tide Is Turning/Place In Your Heart 8
68	Philips BF 1731	Spot The Lights/Uh 45

BARRINO BROTHERS
72	Invictus INV 523	I Shall Not Be Moved/When Love Was A Child 25

BARRON KNIGHTS
62	Fontana H 368	Let's Face It/Never Miss A Chance 12
63	Columbia DB 7108	Jo-Anne/That's My Girl 8
64	Columbia DB 7188	Comin' Home Baby/Peanut Butter. 8
64	Columbia DB 7317	Call Up The Groups Medley (both sides) 8
64	Columbia DB 7375	Come To The Dance/Choose Me Tonight 5
64	Columbia DB 7427	The House Of Johann Strauss/She's The One 5
65	Columbia DB 7698	It Was A Very Good Year/Worry And Wonder. 6
66	Columbia DB 7884	Round The World Rhythm & Blues/Where There's A Will 6
66	Columbia DB 7933	Doing What She's Not Supposed To Do/Every Night 6
66	Columbia DB 8071	Under New Management Medley (both sides) 5
67	Columbia DB 8161	Lazy Fat People/In The Night. 5
67	Columbia DB 8280	Here Come The Bees/It's A Sin 5
68	Columbia DB 8423	I Never Will Marry/Cold In My Nose. 5
68	Columbia DB 8485	An Olympic Record/An Olympic Record 5
69	Columbia DB 8612	Love And The World Loves With You/Along Come Those Summer Days 5
69	Columbia DB 8679	Traces/Awake. 5

BARROW POETS
68	Fontana TF 939	Letter In A Bottle (Music Sleepy Lagoon)/Dynamite Barbee (Music Barbee Song) 5
67	Barrow BR 1	AT THE PRINTER'S DEVIL (EP, private pressing) 25
63	Argo PLP 1072	PRESENT AN ENTERTAINMENT OF POETRY AND MUSIC (LP) 25
68	Fontana 6857 003	FINEST FOLK (LP). 18
70	RCA SF 8110	JOKER (LP) 18
72	Argo ZSW 508	OUTPATIENTS (LP) 20
72	Argo ZSW 511	MAGIC EGG (LP). 20

AL BARRY
70	Duke DU 81	Ooh Wee/Hold It Baby. 5
70	Doctor Bird DB 1502	Morning Sun/MARKONIANS: Over And Over. 10
71	Creole 1005	Down We Go/It Pays To Do Good 6

(see also Desmond Dekker & Aces)

DAVE BARRY & SARA BERNER
56	London HLU 8324	Out Of This World With Flying Saucers Parts 1 & 2 (78 rpm = £10) 45

GENE BARRY
65	Pye 7N 15873	I'll Remember You/I've Got Your Number) 5

JOE BARRY
61	Mercury AMT 1149	I'm A Fool To Care/I Got A Feeling 20
68	Stateside SS 2127	I Started Loving You Again/California Bound 18
62	Mercury ZEP 10130	A FOOL TO CARE (EP) 125

JOHN BARRY (SEVEN)
SINGLES
57	Parlophone R 4363	Zip Zip/Three Little Fishes (as John Barry & The Seven) (78 rpm = £15) 80
58	Parlophone R 4394	Every Which Way/You've Gotta Way (as John Barry Seven) (78 rpm = £15) 50
58	Parlophone R 4418	Big Guitar/Rodeo (as John Barry Seven) (78 rpm = £15) 40
58	Parlophone R 4453	Pancho/Hideaway (as John Barry Seven) (78 rpm = £15). 15
58	Parlophone R 4488	Farrago/Bee's Knees (as John Barry Seven) (78 rpm = £15) 15
59	Parlophone R 4530	Long John/Snap 'n' Whistle (as John Barry Seven) (78 rpm = £15) 15
59	Parlophone R 4560	Little John/For Pete's Sake (as John Barry Seven) (78 rpm = £15) 15
59	Parlophone R 4582	Twelfth Street Rag/Christella (as John Barry Seven) 15

John BARRY

60	Columbia DB 4414	Hit And Miss/Rockin' Already (as John Barry Seven)	10
60	Columbia DB 4446	Beat For Beatniks/Big Fella (as John Barry Orchestra)	10
60	Columbia DB 4480	Blueberry Hill/Never Let Go (as John Barry Orchestra)	10
60	Columbia DB 4505	Walk Don't Run/I'm Movin' On (as John Barry Seven)	7
60	Columbia DB 4554	Black Stockings/Get Lost Jack Frost (as John Barry Seven)	7
61	Columbia DB 4598	The Magnificent Seven/Skid Row (as John Barry Seven)	7
61	Columbia DB 4659	The Menace/Rodeo (as John Barry Orchestra)	6
61	Columbia DB 4699	Starfire/A Matter Of Who (as John Barry Seven)	6
61	Columbia DB 4746	Watch Your Step/Twist It (as John Barry Seven)	6
62	Columbia DB 4806	Cutty Sark/Lost Patrol (as John Barry Seven & Orchestra)	6
62	Columbia DB 4898	The James Bond Theme/The Blacksmith Blues (with Orchestra) (green or black labels)	8
62	Columbia DB 4941	The Lolly Theme/March Of The Mandarins (as John Barry Seven & Orchestra)	6
63	Columbia DB 7003	The Human Jungle/Onward, Christian Spacemen (some in p/s)	18/5
63	Ember EMB S 178	Kinky/Fancy Dance	8
63	Ember EMB S 181	007/From Russia With Love (some in p/s)	18/5
63	Ember EMB S 183	Elizabeth/The London Theme	5
63	Ember EMB S 185	Zulu Stamp/Monkey Feathers (mauve/grey or red/yellow label; some in p/s)	20/5
63	Lyntone LYN 378	Theme Music From The Ingersoll Trendsetters TV Commercial (flexidisc; some with 8-page A4 promo booklet)	35/20
64	Columbia DB 7414	Twenty-Four Hours Ago/Seven Faces	10
64	United Artists UP 1060	Seance On A Wet Afternoon/Oublie Ça.	10
64	United Artists UP 1068	Goldfinger/Troubador	10
64	Stateside SS 296	Barney's Blues/Theme From The Film, *Man In The Middle* (No More)	12
65	CBS 201747	A Man Alone (*Ipcress File* Theme)/Barbara's Theme	10
65	CBS 201822	The Syndicate/What A Question	10
66	CBS 202390	Vendetta/The Danny Scipio Theme	5
66	CBS Special WB 730	James Bond Theme/RAY CONNIFF: Love Is Blue (p/s)	5
67	CBS 202451	Wednesday's Child (*Quiller Memorandum*)/Sleep Well My Darling	10
67	CBS 2825	You Only Live Twice/The Girl With The Sun In Her Hair	10
67	Ember EMB S 243	007/The Loneliness Of Autumn (some in p/s)	15/7
69	CBS 3935	The Lion In Winter Parts 1 & 2.	10
69	CBS 4468	Midnight Cowboy/Fun City.	10
69	CBS 4680	On Her Majesty's Secret Service/We Have All The Time In The World	10
70	Probe PRO 518	The Last Valley/Main Title Theme	5
71	CBS 7469	Theme From *The Persuaders*/The Girl With The Sun In Her Hair	5
72	Polydor 2058 216	This Way Mary/Diamonds Are Forever	10
72	Polydor 2058 275	The Adventurer/Follow Follow.	10
80	United Artists UP 634	Midnight Cowboy/Fun City (p/s)	5

EPs

58	Parlophone GEP 8737	THE BIG BEAT (as John Barry Seven)	40
61	Columbia SEG 8069	THE JOHN BARRY SOUND (as John Barry Seven)	20
62	Columbia SEG 8138	BEAT GIRL (as John Barry Seven, with Adam Faith)	40
63	Columbia SEG 8255	JOHN BARRY THEME SUCCESSES	20
63	United Artists UEP 1011	FROM RUSSIA WITH LOVE (soundtrack)	25
64	Ember EMB EP 4544	LONELINESS OF AUTUMN.	20
64	United Artists UEP 1012	GOLDFINGER (soundtrack)	25
65	Ember EMB EP 4551	JAMES BOND IS BACK	25
65	United Artists UEP 1015	THUNDERBALL: Thunderball/Death Of Fiona/Bond Below Disco Volante/ Mr Kiss Kiss Bang Bang (soundtrack)	25
67	CBS WEP 1126	THEMES FROM JAMES BOND FILMS (mail order via Carr's Sport biscuits)	15
67	CBS WEP 1129	BIG THEMES FROM THE BIG SCREEN (mail order via Wall's)	10
67	CBS WEP 1131	GREAT SCREEN THEMES (mail order via Lyon's Bakery)	10

LPs

60	Columbia 33SX 1225	BEAT GIRL (soundtrack, with Adam Faith)	50
61	Columbia 33SX 1358	STRINGBEAT (also stereo SCX 3401)	30/40
63	United Artists (S)ULP 1052	FROM RUSSIA WITH LOVE (soundtrack, mono/stereo)	30/40
63	Colpix PXL 459	ELIZABETH TAYLOR IN LONDON (mono/stereo)	40/50
64	Ember NR 5012	ZULU (soundtrack, yellow/orange label, flipback sleeve)	25
64	Stateside S(S)L 10087	MAN IN THE MIDDLE (soundtrack, with Lionel Bart)	30
64	United Artists (S)ULP 1076	GOLDFINGER (soundtrack, mono/stereo)	22/28
65	Ember NR 5025	JOHN BARRY PLAYS 007.	30
65	Ember NR 56088	FOUR IN THE MORNING (soundtrack, mono/stereo)	30/40
65	CBS BPG 62598	PASSION FLOWER HOTEL (original cast, mono only)	30
65	CBS BPG 62530	THE IPCRESS FILE (soundtrack, mono only)	50
65	United Artists ULP 1104	THE KNACK (AND HOW TO GET IT) (soundtrack)	30
65	United Artists (S)ULP 1110	THUNDERBALL (soundtrack, mono/stereo).	22
65	Fontana (S)TL 55021	KING RAT (soundtrack)	20
66	Fontana STL 5387	THE WRONG BOX (soundtrack, release cancelled)	
66	CBS (S)BPG 62402	THE GREAT MOVIE SOUNDS OF JOHN BARRY	15
66	Ember NR 5032	JOHN BARRY MEETS CHAD & JEREMY	15
66	CBS (S)BPG 62665	THE CHASE (soundtrack, mono/stereo)	30/40
66	CBS (S)BPG 62869	THE QUILLER MEMORANDUM (soundtrack, mono/stereo)	20/25
66	MGM MGM-C 8010	BORN FREE (soundtrack, featuring Matt Monro, 1st pressing)	20
67	CBS 63038	JOHN BARRY CONDUCTS HIS GREATEST MOVIE HITS	12
67	United Artists (S)ULP 1168	THE WHISPERERS (soundtrack)	30
67	United Artists (S)ULP 1171	YOU ONLY LIVE TWICE (soundtrack)	20
67	United Artists LAS 29021	THE BEST OF BOND (mono)	15
68	Stateside S(S)L 10263	DEADFALL (soundtrack, Shirley Bassey on 1 track)	35
69	United Artists UAS 29020	ON HER MAJESTY'S SECRET SERVICE (soundtrack, foldout sleeve)	40
69	United Artists UAS 29021	THE BEST OF BOND (stereo reissue)	15
69	CBS 70049	THE LION IN WINTER (soundtrack)	20
69	MCA MUPS 360	BOOM! (soundtrack, with Georgie Fame)	80
70	CBS 63952	READY WHEN YOU ARE, JB	15
71	CBS 64816	THE PERSUADERS (TV soundtrack)	15

71	United Artists UAS 29216	DIAMONDS ARE FOREVER (soundtrack)..................................... 20
71	Probe SPB 1027	THE LAST VALLEY (soundtrack, some with insert)..................... 35/30
71	MCA MUPS 441	MARY QUEEN OF SCOTS (soundtrack)................................... 25
72	Ember SE 8008	JOHN BARRY REVISITED (foldout sleeve, initially in 'nude' gatefold sleeve).. 25/20
72	Warner Bros K 56009	ALICE'S ADVENTURES IN WONDERLAND (soundtrack, gatefold sleeve)....... 15
72	CBS 64816	FILM THEMES FROM JOHN BARRY...................................... 15
72	United Artists UAD 60027/8	THE JAMES BOND COLLECTION (2-LP, with booklet)...................... 25
73	Polydor 2383 156	THE CONCERT JOHN BARRY... 18
74	United Artists UAS 29671	THE MAN WITH THE GOLDEN GUN (soundtrack)........................ 15
74	Polydor 2383 300	PLAY IT AGAIN.. 18
74	Phase 4 Stereo PFS 4339	THE DAY OF THE LOCUST (soundtrack)................................ 12
76	CBS 22014	THE MUSIC OF JOHN BARRY (2-LP)................................... 22
76	Polydor 2383 405	AMERICANS.. 22
76	Reprise K 54090	KING KONG (soundtrack, with poster)................................ 15
79	EMI MUTM 21	THE BEST OF JOHN BARRY 7 & ORCHESTRA............................. 12
79	United Artists UAG 30247	MOONRAKER (soundtrack)... 12
79	Pickwick SHM 3017	THE BLACK HOLE (soundtrack)....................................... 12
83	A&R FILM 001	HIGH ROAD TO CHINA (soundtrack).................................. 15
83	A&M 394 967-2	OCTOPUSSY (CD, soundtrack, withdrawn).............................. 75
92	EMI CD BOND 007	THE BEST OF JAMES BOND 30th ANNIVERSARY COLLECTION (2-CD, limited ed.)... 40

(see also Alan Bown, Chad & Jeremy, Adam Faith, Elizabeth Taylor, Desmond Lane, Johnny Pearson, Tony Bennett, Jim Lowe, Lyn Paul, Russ Conway, Lance Fortune, Alan Haven, Countdowns, Johnny De Little, Marion Ryan, Dick Kallman)

KAY BARRY
| 65 | Embassy WB 674 | Terry/Girl Don't Come.. 6 |

(see also Bud Ashton)

LEN BARRY
65	Cameo Parkway P 969	Hearts Are Trump/Little White House................................. 20
65	Brunswick 05942	1-2-3/Bullseye.. 10
66	Brunswick 05949	Like A Baby/Happiness... 10
66	Brunswick 05955	Somewhere/It's A Crying Shame..................................... 10
66	Brunswick 05962	It's That Time Of The Year/Happily Ever After......................... 10
66	Brunswick 05966	I Struck It Rich/Love Is.. 15
67	RCA RCA 1588	The Moving Finger Writes/Our Love.................................. 20
68	Bell BLL 1022	4-5-6 Now I'm Alone/Funky Night................................... 5
71	Now! NOW 1003	Now I'm Alone/Funky Night....................................... 8
72	MCA MU 1172	1-2-3/You Baby... 8
73	Paramount PARA 3031	Heaven And Earth/I'm Marching To The Music......................... 15
73	Paramount PARA 3039	It's Time To Fall In Love/Touching, Holding, Feeling..................... 5
66	Cameo Parkway CPE 556	HAVIN' A GOOD TIME (EP)... 30
65	Brunswick LAT 8637	1-2-3 (LP).. 25
66	Cameo Parkway C 1082	LEN BARRY AND THE DOVELLS (LP).................................. 25
69	Bulldog BDL 1013	MORE FROM THE 1-2-3 MAN (LP)................................... 20
69	RCA Intl. INTS 1027	MY KIND OF SOUL (LP).. 20

(see also Dovells, Electric Indian)

MARGARET BARRY (& MICHAEL GORMAN)
| 58 | Topic 10T 6 | STREET SONGS AND FIDDLE TUNES OF IRELAND (10" LP, mid-blue label, later buff/black or dark blue/silver labels)..................... 15 |

SANDRA BARRY (& THE BOYS)
64	Decca F 11851	Really Gonna Shake/When We Get Married (as Sandra Barry & Boys)........ 40
65	Pye 7N 15753	The End Of The Line/We Were Lovers................................ 15
65	Pye 7N 15840	Question/You Can Take It From Me.................................. 15
66	Pye 7N 17102	Stop! Thief/I Won't Try To Change Your Mind......................... 20

(see also Boys, Sandra Alfred, Slack Alice)

BARRY & THE TAMERLANES
63	Warner Bros WB 116	I Wonder What She's Doing Tonight/Don't Go......................... 35
64	Warner Bros WB 124	Roberta/Butterfly.. 20
64	Warner Bros WM 8145	I WONDER WHAT SHE'S DOING TONIGHT (LP)........................ 75

(see also Barry De Vorzon)

BARRY & TONY
| 65 | Decca F 12224 | Lost Love/Make It Or Break It...................................... 5 |

(see also Brothers Grimm)

BARRY SISTERS (U.S.)
56	London HLA 8248	Cha Cha Joe/Baby Come A Little Closer (78 rpm = £10)................. 50
56	London HLA 8304	Till You Come Back To Me/Intrigue (78 rpm = £10)..................... 50
56	Columbia DB 3843	Sing Me A Sentimental Love Song/The Italian Theme.................... 10
58	Columbia DB 4215	I Hear Bells/I Get Up Ev'ry Morning................................. 8
60	Columbia DB 4562	Misty/Why Don't You Do Right?..................................... 8
60	Columbia 33SX 1309	SIDE BY SIDE (LP).. 20

(see also Three Barry Sisters)

CHRIS BARTLEY
67	Cameo Parkway P 101	The Sweetest Thing This Side Of Heaven/Love Me Baby................. 75
68	Bell BLL 1031	I Found A Goodie/Be Mine Forever.................................. 25
75	Right On RO 105	I See Your Name/I See Your Name (Instrumental)...................... 10
86	Move MIS 4	Baby I'm For Real/I've Found A Goodie/Truer Words Were Never Spoken/ The Sweetest Thing This Side Of Heaven (12", p/s)..................... 15

BARTOK
| 82 | On ON 1 | Insanity/I Am The Bomb (p/s)...................................... 8 |

(see also Jah Wobble)

MINT VALUE £

RIA BARTOK
64	Columbia DB 7362	See If I Care/I Don't Wanna Leave You	6

EILEEN BARTON
55	Vogue Coral Q 72060	The Year We Fell In Love/I Don't Want To Mambo Polka	15
55	Vogue Coral Q 72075	Fujiyama Mama/I'd've Baked A Cake (78 rpm = £8)	100
56	Vogue Coral Q 72122	Cry Me A River/Come Home (78 rpm = £8)	25
56	Vogue Coral Q 72148	Teenage Heart/My Social Hot Dog (78 rpm = £10)	20
56	Vogue Coral Q 72205	Spring It Was/I Have To Tell You (78 rpm = £10)	10
57	Vogue Coral Q 72250	Too Close For Comfort/Here I Am In Love Again.	10
57	Vogue Coral Q 72270	Without Love/The Scene Of The Crime (78 rpm = £10).	10

ROD BARTON (& THE LINCOLNAIRES)
62	Salvo SLO 1812	Dear Old San Francisco/NERVOUS NORVOUS: Does A Chinese Chicken Have A Pigtail	60

BASEMENT
03	Deltasonic DLT 009	Medicine Day/Stuck On The Street (At Minus Ten) (numbered p/s, 1000 only)	7
03	Deltasonic DLTCDC009	Medicine Day/Stuck On The Street (At Minus Ten) (CD, 1,000 only)	8

BASEMENT 5
80	Island ILPS9641	1965-80 (LP, with inner, poster and embossed sleeve)	18

BASHERS
76	Virgin VS 154	The Womble Bashers/Womble Bashers Wock	20
	(see also Mike McGear)		

BASHFUL ALLEY
82	Ellie Jay BA 001	Running Blind/My, My, My (p/s, black-and-white or black-and-yellow sleeve)	50
82	Graffiti BA 001	Running Blind/My, My, My (p/s, reissue)	35

BASIC BLACK AND PEARL
75	Bus Stop BUS 1030	There'll Come A Time, There'll Come A Day/Right On Baby	6

COUNT BASIE & HIS ORCHESTRA
67	Coral Q 72497	Green Onions/Hang On Sloopy	18
68	MCA MCA 1014	For Your Precious Love/Uptight (with Jackie Wilson).	8
68	Decca AD 1008	For Your Precious Love/Uptight (with Jackie Wilson, export issue)	16
53	Brunswick LA 8589	BASIE'S BEST (10" LP)	15
53	Mercury MG 25015	KANSAS CITY 7/LESTER YOUNG QUARTET (LP, 1 side each)	15
54	Oriole/Mercury MG 25015	COUNT BASIE/LESTER YOUNG (10" LP, 1 side each)	15
55	Columbia 33S 1054	THE COUNT (10" LP)	15
55	Philips BBR 8036	THE OLD AND THE NEW COUNT (10" LP)	15
55	Columbia Clef 33C 9010	THE COUNT BASIE SEXTET (10" LP)	15
61	Columbia SX 1332	STRING ALONG WITH BASIE (LP)	15
65	Verve VLP/SVLP 9082	BASIELAND (LP)	15
66	United Artists (S)ULP 1127	BASIE MEETS BOND (LP)	18
	(see also Joe Williams, Jackie Wilson, Tony Bennett, Lester Young, Ella Fitzgerald)		

BASIES
67	Coxsone CS 7030	River Jordan/SOUL VENDORS: Swing Easy	35

BASKIN & COPPERFIELD
70	Decca F 13053	The Long And Winding Road/Beautiful Blue Eyes	6

BILLY BASS
69	Pama PM 761	I Need Your Love So Bad/I'm Coming To	30

FONTELLA BASS
65	Chess CRS 8007	Don't Mess Up A Good Thing (with Bobby McClure)/OLIVER SAIN: Jerk Loose.	30
65	Chess CRS 8007	Don't Mess Up A Good Thing/Baby What You Want Me To Do (different B-side, existence unconfirmed)	40
65	Chess CRS 8023	Rescue Me/Soul Of The Man	18
66	Chess CRS 8027	Recovery/Leave It In The Hands Of Love	20
66	Chess CRS 8032	I Can't Rest/Surrender	25
66	Chess CRS 8042	Safe And Sound/You'll Never Know	20
69	Chess CRS 8090	Rescue Me/I Can't Rest	15
69	Chess CRS 8023	Rescue Me/Soul Of The Man (reissue)	8
72	Mojo 2092 032	Who You Gonna Blame/Hold On This Time	5
72	Mojo 2092 045	I Want Everyone To Know/I Need To Be Loved	5
66	Chess CRE 6015	FONTELLA'S HITS (EP)	40
66	Chess CRE 6020	I CAN'T REST (EP)	40
66	Chess CRE 6025	FONTELLA BASS AND BOBBY McCLURE (EP).	50
66	Chess CRL 4517	THE NEW LOOK (LP)	40
72	Mojo 2916 018	FREE (LP).	20
	(see also Bobby McClure)		

SHIRLEY BASSEY
SINGLES
57	Philips JK 1006	The Banana Boat Song/Tra La La (jukebox issue)	15
57	Philips JK 1018	If I Had A Needle And Thread/Tonight My Heart She Is Crying (jukebox issue).	15
57	Philips JK 1034	Puh-leeze! Mister Brown/Take My Love, Take My Love (jukebox issue).	15
58	Philips PB 845	As I Love You/Hands Across The Sea	6
58	Philips PB 860	Kiss Me, Honey Honey, Kiss Me/There's Never Been A Night (78 rpm = £8)	6
59	Philips PB 917	Love For Sale/Crazy Rhythm (78 rpm = £15)	6
59	Philips PB 919	My Funny Valentine/How About You? (78 rpm = £15)	6
59	Philips PB 975	Night And Day/The Gypsy In My Soul (78 rpm = £25)	7
61	Philips BF 1091	Birth Of The Blues/The Careless Love Blues.	5
64	Columbia DB 7360	Goldfinger/Strange How Love Can Be	5
66	United Artists UP 1134	Don't Take The Lovers From The World/Takeaway	20
67	United Artists UP 1192	Big Spender/Dangerous Game	5
68	United Artists UP 2254	To Give/My Love Has Two Faces.	5

MINT VALUE £

71	United Artists UP 35293	Diamonds Are Forever/Pieces Of Dreams	5
58	Philips BBR 8130	BORN TO SING THE BLUES (10" LP)	15
60	Columbia 33SX 1286	SHIRLEY (also stereo SCX 3352)	each 12
62	Columbia 33SX 1454	LET'S FACE THE MUSIC (also stereo SCX 3454)	each 12

(see also Yello, Nelson Riddle Orchestra, John Barry)

BASSIX
| 90 | Champion CHAMP 12 | CLOSE ENCOUNTERS (12", p/s) | 12 |

BAS-SHEVA
| 55 | Capitol CL 14218 | Flame Of Love/I Just Wanna Be Your Loving Baby | 10 |

JOE BATAAN
75	RCA RCA 2457	Latin Strut/Peace, Friendship And Solidarity	15
75	RCA RCA 2553	The Bottle/When You're Down	15
69	London HA/SH 8386	RIOT! (LP)	50

JUNE BATEMAN
| 64 | Sue WI 347 | I Don't Wanna/NOBLE 'THIN MAN' WATTS & HIS BAND: Noble's Theme | 50 |

COLLIN BATES TRIO
| 68 | Fontana SFJL 913 | BREW (LP) | 100 |

JON BATES
| 65 | CBS 202818 | Where Were You Last Night/If Anything Goes Wrong | 5 |

MARTYN BATES
| 82 | Cherry Red TRED 38 | LETTERS WRITTEN (10" EP) | 10 |
| 80s | Ambivalent Scale | IMAGINATION FEELS LIKE POISON (CD, with book, 500 only) | 20 |

(see also Eyeless In Gaza)

BATMAN THEME
| 88 | Bam Caruso NRIC 107 | Batman Theme/Batman Theme (Instrumental Mix) (p/s) | 12 |

(see also Jan & Dean)

STIV BATORS
| 79 | London/Bomp HLZ 10575 | It's Cold Outside/The Last Year (p/s) | 15 |

(see also Dead Boys, Lords Of The New Church, Wanderers)

BATS
64	Columbia DB 7429	Accept It/Lovers Lie Sleeping	20
66	Decca F 22534	Listen To My Heart/Stop Don't Do It	30
67	Decca F 22568	You Will Now, Won't You?/You Look Good Together	20
67	Decca F 22616	Hard To Get Up In The Morning/Take Me As I Am	20

MIKE BATT
68	Liberty LBF 15093	Mister Poem/Fading Yellow	18
68	Liberty LBF 15122	I See Wonderful Things In You/Mary Goes Round	10
69	Liberty LBF 15210	Your Mother Should Know/Suddenly	10

(see also Hapshash & Coloured Coat, Anderson Harley & Batt)

BATTERED ORNAMENTS
| 70 | Harvest HAR 5013 | Goodbye We Loved You (Madly)/CHRIS SPEDDING: Rock'n'Roll Band | 20 |
| 69 | Harvest SHVL 758 | MANTLE-PIECE (LP) | 125 |

(see also Pete Brown & His Battered Ornaments, Chris Spedding, People Band)

SKIP BATTIN
| 72 | Signpost SGP 756 | Central Park/St. Louis Browns | 6 |
| 72 | Signpost SG 4255 | SKIP (LP) | 22 |

(see also Skip & Flip, Byrds, Flying Burrito Brothers, Evergreen Blueshoes)

BATTLE
| 05 | Fierce Panda NING169CD | Isabelle/Feel The Same (CD, p/s) | 7 |
| 05 | Transgressive TRANS009B | Demons/Damascus (3" CD, 1000 copies) | 10 |

JEAN BATTLE
| 72 | Mojo 2027 010 | Love Making/When A Woman Loves A Man | 10 |

BATTLEAXE
| 82 | Guardian GRC 132 | Burn This Town/Battleaxe (no p/s) | 22 |

BAUHAUS
79	Small Wonder TEENY 2	Bela Lugosi's Dead/Boys/Dark Entries (12", p/s, black vinyl, later white vinyl)	7/15
88	Small Wonder TEENY 2P	Bela Lugosi's Dead/Boys/Dark Entries (12", reissue, picture disc)	10
88	Small Wonder TEENY 2CD	Bela Lugosi's Dead/Boys/Dark Entries (CD, no'd reissue, 2,000 only)	10
89	Small Wonder TEENY 2	Bela Lugosi's Dead/Boys/Dark Entries (12", reissue, green or blue vinyl, p/s)	12/10
91	Small Wonder TEENY 2	Bela Lugosi's Dead/Boys/Dark Entries (12", reissue, pink, clear or purple vinyl, in corresponding coloured p/s)	each 10
80	Axis AXIS 3	Dark Entries/Untitled (brown label, p/s)	18
80	Axis AD 3	Dark Entries/Untitled (blue label, p/s)	8
80	4AD BEG 37	Dark Entries/Untitled (p/s, blue 4AD labels, lists BEG 37 on sleeve)	10
80	Beggars Banquet BEG 37	Dark Entries/Untitled (p/s, red Beggars Banquet labels)	10
82	Beggars Banquet AD 3	Dark Entries/Untitled (reissue, 'nudes' label, no contact address on p/s)	7
80	4AD AD 7	Terror Couple Kill Colonel/Scopes/Terror Couple Kill Colonel II (p/s)	5
80	4AD AD 7	Terror Couple Kill Colonel/Scopes/Terror Couple Kill Colonel II (version) (mispressed with 'rejected' version of third track, p/s)	25
80	4AD AD 17	Telegram Sam/Crowds (p/s)	5
81	Beggars Banquet BEG 54	Kick In The Eye/Satori (p/s)	5
81	Beggars Banquet BEG 54T	Kick In The Eye/Satori (12", white label in stamped plain sleeve)	8
81	Beggars Banquet BEG 59	The Passion Of Lovers/David J: Peter Murphy: Kevin Haskins: Daniel Ash (p/s, with lyric insert)	5
82	Beggars Banquet BEG 74	Kick In The Eye/Harry/Earwax (p/s)	5

BAUHAUS

MINT VALUE £

82	Beggars Banquet BEG 74T	Kick In The Eye/Poison Pen/Harry/Earwax (12" mispressing, p/s, matrix: A1) . . . 30
82	Beggars Banquet BEG 79	Spirit/Terror Couple Kill Colonel (live) (p/s, with Beggars labels) 5
82	Beggars Banquet BEG 79	Spirit/Terror Couple Kill Colonel (live) (p/s, mispressed, A-side plays Gary Numan's We Take Mystery [To Bed]) 10
82	Beggars Banquet BEG 79P	Spirit/Terror Couple Kill Colonel (live) (picture disc in printed PVC sleeve) 8
82	Beggars Banquet BEG 83	Ziggy Stardust/Third Uncle ('Bauhaus' label with p/s, or Beggars label, no p/s) . . 5
82	Beggars Banquet BEG 83T	Ziggy Stardust/Party Of The First Part/Third Uncle/Waiting For The Man (12", p/s, with stickered poster p/s) 10
82	Lyntone LYN 12106	A God In An Alcove (Early Version) (blue flexidisc with *Flexipop*, issue 23) . . . 12/7
82	Lyntone LYN 12106	A God In An Alcove (Early Version) (hard vinyl test pressing) 30
83	Lyntone LYN 13777/8	The Sanity Assassin/Spirit In The Sky (fan club freebie, 320 only). 250
84	Beggars Banquet BEG 91P	She's In Parties/Departure (picture disc in PVC sleeve). 8
88	Beggars Banquet BBP 4CD	THE SINGLES 1981-1983 (CD EP) 10
82	Beggars Banquet BEGA 38	PRESS THE EJECT AND GIVE ME THE TAPE (LP, with bonus 45 Satori In Paris [BH 1] & poster) 12
82	Beggars Banquet BEGA 42	THE SKY'S GONE OUT (LP, with bonus LP, PRESS THE EJECT AND GIVE ME THE TAPE [BEGA 38] & inner sleeves) 12
83	B. Banquet BEGA 45P	BURNING FROM THE INSIDE (LP, picture disc) 12
85	Beggars Banquet BEGA 64	1979-1983 (LP, with numbered inserts) 12
88	B. Banquet BAUCD BOX 1	1979-1983 (2-CD, boxed set with book & badge, numbered, 2,000 only, export issue) 30

(see also Sinister Ducks, Tones On Tail, David J., Love & Rockets)

ART BAXTER
56	Philips PB 652	Jingle Rock/Rock And Roll Rag (78) 15
57	Philips PB 666	Don't Knock The Rock/Rock Rock Rock (78). 15
57	Philips BBR 8107	ROCK YOU SINNERS (10" LP) 250

DAVID BAXTER
| 70 | Reflection REFL 9 | GOODBYE DAVE (LP) . . . . 30 |

(see also David Lewis)

JEAN BAXTER
| 58 | Parlophone R 4470 | Ich Liebe Dich (I Love You)/The Only One For Me . . . . 7 |

LES BAXTER & HIS ORCHESTRA
54	Capitol CL 14166	I Love Paris/Manhattan 10
55	Capitol CL 14217	When You're In Love/Romantic Rio 10
55	Capitol CL 14237	Cherry Pink And Apple Blossom White/Play Me Hearts And Flowers 10
55	Capitol CL 14239	Earth Angel/Happy Baby (as Les Baxter & Bombers). 20
55	Capitol CL 14257	I Ain't Mad At You (with Bombers)/Blue Mirage. 10
55	Capitol CL 14257	Unchained Melody/Blue Star (The Medic Theme) 12
55	Capitol CL 14344	Wake The Town And Tell The World/I'll Never Stop Loving You 10
59	Capitol T/ST 1248	WILD GUITARS (LP) 15
60	Capitol (S)T 1355	TEEN DRUMS (LP) 18

(see also Leonard Pennario)

RONNIE BAXTER
| 60 | Top Rank JAR 293 | I Finally Found You/Is It Because? . . . . 6 |

BAYTOWN SINGERS
| 60s | Decca 1005 | Walking Down The Line/Lord. . . . . 10 |

B.B. BLUNDER
71	United Artists UP 35203	Sticky Living/Rocky Yagbatee Yagbag 6
71	United Artists UP 35204	Little Boy/10,000 Miles 6
71	United Artists UAG 29156	WORKERS' PLAYTIME (LP) 20

(see also Reg King & B.B. Blunder, Action, Julie Driscoll Brian Auger & Trinity, Kevin Westlake, Mark Charig)

BBC RADIOPHONIC WORKSHOP/PETER HOWELL
64	Decca F 11837	Doctor Who/BRENDA & JOHNNY: This Can't Be Love (unboxed Decca logo) . . . 20
72	Decca F 11837	Doctor Who/BRENDA & JOHNNY: This Can't Be Love (reissue, boxed logo) 8
73	BBC RESL 11	Doctor Who/Reg (blue/white label, credits 'Delia Derbyshire', 'TARDIS' p/s) . . . 10/6
76	BBC RESL 11	Doctor Who/Reg (reissue, no p/s, silver label) 6
78	BBC RESL 11	Doctor Who/Reg (2nd reissue, in 'TARDIS' p/s, blue label, white rim) 6
80	PRT RESL 80	Doctor Who/The Astronauts ('Tom Baker' p/s, as 'Peter Howell & BBC Radiophonic Workshop') 8
82	PRT RESL 80	Doctor Who/The Astronauts (reissue, 'Peter Davison' p/s) 8
84	PRT RESL 80	Doctor Who/The Astronauts (2nd reissue, 'Colin Baker' p/s) 5
72	BBC REC 93S	TEST CARD MUSIC (LP). 12
78	BBC REC 316	DOCTOR WHO SOUND EFFECTS No. 19 (LP) 12

(see also Dr. Who, Jon Pertwee, Ray Cathode, Radiophonic Workshop, Ithaca, Alice Through The Looking Glass, Agincourt, Blossom Toes)

BBC RADIOPHONIC WORKSHOP
| 73 | BBC RED 93 S | FOURTH DIMENSION (LP) . . . . 15 |
| 70s | BBC REC 25 M | BBC RADIOPHONIC MUSIC — WORK BY DELIA DERBYSHIRE (LP) . . . . 20 |

BEA & DEE
| 59 | Capitol CL 15066 | Jerry/Wishing Time . . . . 10 |

BEACH BOYS
SINGLES
62	Capitol CL 15273	Surfin' Safari/409. 40
63	Capitol CL 15285	Ten Little Indians/County Fair 80
63	Capitol CL 15305	Surfin' USA/Shut Down. 20
64	Capitol CL 15339	Fun, Fun, Fun/Why Do Fools Fall In Love 30
64	Capitol CL 15350	I Get Around/Don't Worry Baby. 10
64	Capitol CL 15361	When I Grow Up (To Be A Man)/She Knows Me Too Well 10
65	Capitol CL 15370	Dance, Dance, Dance/The Warmth Of The Sun 10
65	Capitol CL 15384	All Summer Long/Do You Wanna Dance 9

MINT VALUE £

65	Capitol CL 15392	Help Me Rhonda/Kiss Me Baby	9
65	Capitol CL 15409	California Girls/Let Him Run Wild	9
65	Capitol CL 15425	The Little Girl I Once Knew/There's No Other (Like My Baby)	10
66	Capitol CL 15432	Barbara Ann/Girl Don't Tell Me	9
66	Capitol CL 15441	Sloop John B/You're So Good To Me	9
66	Capitol CL 15459	God Only Knows/Wouldn't It Be Nice	9
66	Capitol CL 15475	Good Vibrations/Wendy	9
67	Capitol CL 15502	Then I Kissed Her/Mountain Of Love	8
67	Capitol CL 15510	Heroes And Villains/You're Welcome	8
67	Capitol CL 15521	Wild Honey/Wind Chimes	8
68	Capitol CL 15527	Darlin'/Country Air	6
68	Capitol CL 15545	Friends/Little Bird	6
68	Capitol CL 15554	Do It Again/Wake The World	6
68	Capitol CL 15572	Bluebirds Over The Mountain/Never Learn Not To Love	6
69	Capitol CL 15598	Break Away/Celebrate The News	6
70	Capitol CL 15640	Cottonfields/The Nearest Faraway Place (black label)	6
70	Stateside SS 2181	Tears In The Morning/It's About Time	6
71	Stateside SS 2190	Long Promised Road/Deirdre	6
71	Stateside SS 2194	Don't Go Near The Water/Student Demonstration Time (demos in p/s £20)	6
72	Reprise K 14173	You Need A Mess Of Help To Stand Alone/Cuddle Up (p/s)	10
72	Capitol CMS 1	Wouldn't It Be Nice/Fun Fun Fun/California Girls (printed sleeve)	6
72	Capitol CMS 2	Barbara Ann/Dance Dance Dance/You're So Good To Me (printed sleeve)	6
74	Reprise K 14346	California Saga: California/Sail On Sailor/Marcella/I'm The Pied Piper (printed sleeve)	5
76	Reprise K 14411	Child Of Winter/Susie Cincinnati (withdrawn)	125+
76	Reprise K 14440	Rock And Roll Music/The T.M. Song (p/s)	5
76	Capitol PSR 402	Good Vibrations/Interview With Carl Wilson (promo only)	10
77	Reprise K 14481	Mona/Rock And Roll Music/Sail On Sailor/Marcella (p/s)	5
77	Capitol CL 15954	Little Saint Nick/Little Saint Nick (Instr.)/Santa Claus Is Coming To Town	7
78	Capitol CL 15969	Little Deuce Coupe/SUNRAYS: I Live For The Sun/SUPERSTOCKS: Hot Rod High (p/s)	5
79	Caribou 12-7204	Here Comes The Night/(Disco Version)/Baby Blue (12", p/s, blue vinyl)	10
79	Capitol BBP 26	SINGLES COLLECTION (26 x 7" box set)	50

EPs

63	Capitol EAP 1-20540	SURFIN' USA	30
64	Capitol EAP 1-20603	FUN, FUN, FUN	30
64	Capitol 5267	FOUR BY THE BEACH BOYS	25
64	Capitol EAP 4-2198	BEACH BOYS CONCERT	25
64	Capitol EAP 1-20781	THE BEACH BOYS HITS	18
67	Capitol EAP 6-2458	GOD ONLY KNOWS	20
77	EMI PSR 402	20 GOLDEN GREATS ALL YOU NEED TO KNOW (promo, white sleeve)	35

LPs

62	Capitol T 1808	SURFIN' SAFARI (mono only)	40
63	Capitol (S)T 1890	SURFIN' USA (mono/stereo)	30/40
63	Capitol (S)T 1981	SURFER GIRL (mono/stereo)	25/35
63	Capitol (S)T 1998	LITTLE DEUCE COUPE (mono/stereo)	22/30
63	Capitol (S)T 2027	SHUT DOWN VOLUME 2 (mono/stereo)	22/30
64	Capitol (S)T 2164	THE BEACH BOYS' CHRISTMAS ALBUM (mono/stereo)	30/25
64	Capitol (S)T 2198	BEACH BOYS CONCERT (mono/stereo)	20/25
64	Capitol (S)T 2110	ALL SUMMER LONG (mono/stereo)	20/25
65	Capitol (S)T 2398	BEACH BOYS' PARTY! (mono/stereo)	20/25
65	Capitol (S)T 2269	BEACH BOYS TODAY! (mono/stereo)	20/25
65	Capitol (S)T 2354	SUMMER DAYS (AND SUMMER NIGHTS!!) (mono/stereo)	20/25
66	Capitol (S)T 2458	PET SOUNDS	35
66	Capitol (S)T 20856	THE BEST OF THE BEACH BOYS	12
67	Capitol (S)T 1981	SURFER GIRL (reissue, non-flipback sleeve)	12
67	Capitol (S)T 20956	THE BEST OF THE BEACH BOYS VOL. 2	12
67	Capitol (S)T 9001	SMILEY SMILE	20
68	Capitol (S)T 2859	WILD HONEY (mono/stereo)	25/18
68	Capitol (S)T 2895	FRIENDS (mono/stereo)	30/18
69	Capitol (S)T 21142	THE BEST OF THE BEACH BOYS VOL. 3 (mono/stereo)	15/12
69	Capitol E-T/E-ST 133	20/20 (mono/stereo, gatefold sleeve)	22/18

(The above LPs were originally issued with flipback sleeves & rainbow-rim black labels; later orange or yellow label copies are worth half-to-two-thirds the value.)

70	Stateside SSLA 8251	SUNFLOWER (gatefold sleeve)	22
71	Stateside SSL 10313	SURF'S UP (textured sleeve, some with gatefold insert)	20/15
73	Reprise/Brother K 54008	HOLLAND (with insert & bonus EP "Mount Vernon And Fairway" [K 54008/7] in p/s)	35
73	Reprise/Brother K 54008	HOLLAND	12
77	EMI EMTV 1	20 GOLDEN GREATS (blue vinyl)	12
78	Brother K 54102	M.I.U. ALBUM (with inner sleeve)	12
79	Caribou CRB 11-86081	L.A. (LIGHT ALBUM) (picture disc)	15
70s	Capitol ST 2458	PET SOUNDS (reissue, green or orange label)	12
81	WRC SM 651-657	THE CAPITOL YEARS (7-LP box set)	35

(see also Brian Wilson, Dennis Wilson, Bruce Johnston, Legendary Masked Surfers, American Spring, Annette, Flame, Flames, California Music, Rutles, Moon, Murry Wilson, Mike Love, Survivors)•

BEACHCOMBER

70	Parlophone R 5850	Surfin' Soul/Nothing To Say	7

BEACHCOMBERS

63	Columbia DB 7124	Mad Goose/You Can't Sit Down	30
64	Columbia DB 7200	Night Train/The Keel Row	32

(the above singles do not feature Keith Moon)

MINT VALUE £

BEACH-NUTS
65	London HL 9988	Out In The Sun (Hey-O)/Someday Soon	25

(see also Angels, Strangeloves)

BEACON STREET UNION
68	MGM MGM 1416	Blue Suede Shoes/Four Hundred And Five	30
68	MGM MGM-C(S) 8069	THE EYES OF THE BEACON STREET UNION (LP)	35

GEORGE BEAN
63	Decca F 11762	Secret Love/Lonely Weekends	25
64	Decca F 11808	Will You Be My Lover Tonight?/It Should Be You	10
64	Decca F 11922	A Sad Story/Er Um Er	10
65	Decca F 12228	She Belongs To Me/Why Must They Criticise? (as George Bean & Runners)	12
67	CBS 2801	The Candy Shop Is Closed/Smile From Sequin	15
68	CBS 3374	Bring Back Lovin'/Floatin'	25

(see also Trifle, Bean & Loopy's Lot)

BEAN & LOOPY'S LOT
66	Parlophone R 5458	A Stitch In Time/Haywire	25

(see also Alan Bown Set)

BEANO
74	Deram DM 424	Candy Baby/Rock And Roll (Gonna Save Your Soul)	5
75	Deram DM 427	Little Cinderella/Bye And Bye	5

BEANS
62	Starlite ST45 071	Jumping Beans/Salute To Fitz	10
62	Starlite ST45 076	Hey Janey/Crazy Dog	10

BEAR
68	Verve FTS 3059	GREETINGS CHILDREN OF PARADISE (LP)	35

DEAN BEARD & CREW CATS
57	London HLE 8463	Rakin' And Scrapin'/On My Mind Again (78 rpm = £35)	300

BEARS
79	Good Vibrations Intl. GVI 1	Insane/Decisions (p/s)	25
79	Waldo's JS 001	On Me/Wot's Up Mate (p/s, various designs, with insert)	18

BEARZ
80	Axis AXIS 2	She's My Girl/Girls Will Do (p/s)	20
84	Occult OCC 1	Darwin/Julie (p/s)	12

BEAS
68	Pama PM 744	Dr. Goldfoot And His Bikini Machine/Where Do I Go From You	30

BEASTIE BOYS
86	Def Jam A 7055	Hold It, Now Hit It/Acapulco (p/s)	6
86	Def Jam TA 7055	Hold It, Now Hit It/Acapulco (12", p/s)	10
86	Def Jam 650 114 7	She's On It/Slow'n'Low (p/s with 3 badges)	8
86	Def Jam 650 114 6	She's On It/Slow'n'Low/Hold On, Now Hit It (12", p/s)	10
87	Def Jam 650 169 7	It's The New Style/Paul Revere (p/s)	6
87	Def Jam 650 169 6	It's The New Style/It's The New Style (Instrumental)/Paul Revere/Paul Revere (Instrumental) (12", p/s)	8
87	Def Jam 650 418 7	(You Gotta) Fight For Your Right (To Party)/Time To Get Ill (p/s)	6
87	Def Jam 650 418 6	(You Gotta) Fight For Your Right (To Party)/Time To Get Ill (12", p/s)	10
87	Def Jam BEASTP 1	No Sleep Till Brooklyn/Posse In Effect (plane-shaped picture disc)	10
87	Def Jam BEASTT 1	No Sleep Till Brooklyn/Posse In Effect (12", p/s)	10
87	Def Jam BEASTP 3	Girls/She's Crafty (poster p/s)	8
87	Def Jam BEASTQ 3	Girls/She's Crafty (logo shaped picture disc)	10
92	Capitol CDCL 665	Jimmy James (Single Version)/The Blue Nun/Jimmy James (Original Original Version)/Drinkin' Wine (CD, slimline jewel case)	18
92	Capitol 12CLS 665	Frozen Metal Head/Jimmy James (Single Version)/So What'cha Want (All The Way Live Freestyle Version)/Jimmy James (Original Original Version)/Drinkin' Wine (12", white p/s)	10
92	Capitol CDCLS 665	Frozen Metal Head/Jimmy James (Single Version)/So What'cha Want (All The Way Live Freestyle Version)/Jimmy James (Original Original Version)/Drinkin' Wine (CD)	18
94	Capitol CL 716	Get It Together/Sabotage/Dope Little Song (green vinyl, p/s)	8
94	Capitol 7243 8 8173476	Sure Shot/Mullet Head/Sure Shot (Caldato Mix) (red vinyl, p/s)	8
82	Rat Cage MOTR 21	POLLY WOG STEW (EP)	12
82	Rat Cage MOTR 21	POLLY WOG STEW (12" EP)	14
86	Rat Cage MOR 26	COOKY PUSS EP: Cooky Puss/Bonus Batter/Beastie Revolution/Cookie Puss (Censored Version) (p/s)	6
88	Rat Cage MOTR 21T	POLLY WOG STEW (12" EP, reissue)	12
92	Capitol CDCL 653	PASS THE MIC (Netty's Girl/Something's Got To Give/Pass The Mic [Pt. 2, Skills To Pay The Bills]) (CD, slimline jewel case)	14
95	Grand Royal GR 026	AGLIO E OLIO (CD EP, card sleeve)	12
87	Def Jam 450 062 1	LICENSED TO ILL (LP, with poster)	15

(see also Money Mark)

BEAT
79	2-Tone TT 6	Tears Of A Clown/Ranking Full Stop (paper label, company sleeve)	5
80	Go-Feet FEET 1217	Can't Get Used To Losing You (1983 Remix Version)/Mirror In The Bathroom/Spar Wid Me (12", p/s)	8
80	Go-Feet BEAT 001	JUST CAN'T STOP IT (LP, with inner)	12

(see also Fine Young Cannibals)

NICKY BEAT & THE BEATNICKS
78	Rigid IS BEAT 1033	I Can Hear Voices/Split Second Love/Starstruck (p/s)	10

BEAT BOYS
63	Decca F 11730	That's My Plan/Third Time Lucky	30

(see also Rats)

BEAT BROTHERS
63   Polydor NH 52185   Nick Nack Hully Gully/Lantern Hully Gully................................ 40
(see also Tony Sheridan & Beat Brothers, Bobby Patrick Big Six)

BEAT CHICS
64   Decca F 12016   Skinny Minnie/Now I Know 30

BEATHOVEN
88   CBS 651 626-7   Socrates/Socrates (withdrawn) 30

THE BEATLES
SINGLES
*(Original Parlophone Beatles singles came in a variety of company sleeves, which are referred to here as "Type X", etc.,
and are depicted in the illustrations on pages 1400 - 1403. When a sleeve is not specified, details are unknown.)*

1962
*(with "The Parlophone Co. Ltd." in upper-lower case & "Recording first published 1962" label text, without "Sold in UK ...";
all issues before 1967 have push-out centres)*

FIRST PRESSING
Parlophone 45-R 4949   Love Me Do/P.S. I Love You (red label, 'Ringo on drums & no tambourine' version;
                             with or without "Made In Great Britain" credit; in sleeve Type A, B, or C) 80
(note: the 1982 red label re-pressing of Love Me Do includes the word "mono" & "Produced by George Martin" on the label)

1963
*(with "The Parlophone Co. Ltd." in either upper-lower or upper case & "Recording first published 1963" label text,
without "Sold in UK ...")*

FIRST PRESSINGS
Parlophone 45-R 4983   Please Please Me/Ask Me Why (red label; with or without "Made In Great Britain"
                             credit; in sleeve Type A, B or C) 120
Parlophone R 5015   From Me To You/Thank You Girl (in Type 1 sleeve) 8
Parlophone R 5055   She Loves You/I'll Get You (in Type 1 sleeve)............................. 8
Parlophone R 5084   I Want To Hold Your Hand/This Boy (with "The Parlophone Co. Ltd"
                             in upper-case only; in Type 1 sleeve) 8

KNOWN SECOND PRESSINGS
Parlophone R 4949   Love Me Do/P.S. I Love You (black label, with
                             "The Parlophone Co. Ltd" in upper-lower case, matrix suffixed
                             with '1N' indicating 'Ringo on drums & no tambourine' version)................. 100
Parlophone 45-R 4983   Please Please Me/Ask Me Why (black label, with "The Parlophone Co. Ltd"
                             in upper-lower case, with "45" prefix)................................... 10

KNOWN THIRD PRESSING
Parlophone R 4983   Please Please Me/Ask Me Why (black label, with "The Parlophone Co. Ltd"
                             in upper-lower case, without "45" prefix)................................ 15

1964
FIRST PRESSINGS
*(with "The Parlophone Co. Ltd." in either upper-lower, or upper case, "Recording first published 1964" &
"Sold in UK ..." label text)*
Parlophone R 5114   Can't Buy Me Love/You Can't Do That (with "The Parlophone Co. Ltd"
                             in upper case; in Type 1 sleeve).. 8
Parlophone R 5160   A Hard Day's Night/Things We Said Today (Type 1B sleeve) 8
Parlophone R 5200   I Feel Fine/She's A Woman (with "The Parlophone Co. Ltd" in upper case;
                             in Type 1B sleeve)... 8

KNOWN THIRD PRESSING
Parlophone R 4949   Love Me Do/P.S. I Love You (black label, with "The Parlophone Co. Ltd"
                             in upper case, matrix suffixed with 1N' indicating
                             'Ringo on drums & no tambourine' version) 50

KNOWN FOURTH PRESSING
Parlophone R 4983   Please Please Me/Ask Me Why (with "The Parlophone Co. Ltd" in upper case)..... 15

1965
FIRST PRESSINGS
(with "The Parlophone Co. Ltd." in upper case, & "Sold in UK ..." label text)
Parlophone DP 562   If I Fell/Tell Me Why (domestic pressing of export issue; in Type 1B sleeve)........ 35
Parlophone R 5265   Ticket To Ride/Yes It Is (in Type 2 sleeve) 8
Parlophone R 5305   Help!/I'm Down (in Type 2 sleeve)...................................... 8
Parlophone R 5389   We Can Work It Out/Day Tripper (in Type 3 sleeve) 10

KNOWN SECOND PRESSINGS
(with "The Gramophone Co. Ltd" in upper case, & "Sold in UK ..." label text)
Parlophone R 5305   Help!/I'm Down 8
Parlophone R 5389   We Can Work It Out/Day Tripper 8

1966
(with "The Gramophone Co. Ltd" in upper case, & "Sold in UK ..." label text)
FIRST PRESSINGS
Parlophone R 5452   Paperback Writer/Rain (in Type 4 or 5 sleeve).......................... 8
Parlophone R 5493   Yellow Submarine/Eleanor Rigby (in Type 5 or 6 sleeve)................. 8

1967
*(all the pressings listed below have push-out or solid centres, with "The Gramophone Co. Ltd"
in upper case & "Sold in UK ..." label text)*
FIRST PRESSINGS
Parlophone R 5570   Strawberry Fields Forever/Penny Lane (250,000 only in p/s) 50
Parlophone R 5655   Hello, Goodbye/I Am The Walrus (company sleeve, with "7/- to 50/- " on reverse) ... 8

KNOWN SECOND PRESSINGS
Parlophone R 5452   Paperback Writer/Rain (solid centre only) 8
Parlophone R 5493   Yellow Submarine/Eleanor Rigby (solid centre only) 8
Parlophone R 5570   Strawberry Fields Forever/Penny Lane (in Type 5, 6 or 7 sleeve)............... 8
Parlophone R 5620   All You Need Is Love/Baby You're A Rich Man (with reference to "Live World
                             Television Transmission"; most in Type 8 sleeve)........................ 8

THE BEATLES

1968
FIRST PRESSINGS
Parlophone R 5675   Lady Madonna/The Inner Light (with Fan Club insert; sleeve with
"7/- to 50/-" on reverse)..45
(all Apple pressings except for early issues of "Let It Be" come in black, glossy "Apple" sleeves)
Apple R 5722   Hey Jude/Revolution...10
KNOWN SECOND PRESSINGS
Parlophone R 5675   Lady Madonna/The Inner Light (no insert) 8
Parlophone R 5084   I Want To Hold Your Hand/This Boy (solid centre) 25

1969
FIRST PRESSINGS
Apple R 5777   Get Back/Don't Let Me Down (as "The Beatles with Billy Preston") 10
Apple R 5786   Ballad Of John And Yoko/Old Brown Shoe 10
Apple R 5814   Something/Come Together (without "Sold in UK..." label text) 12
KNOWN SECOND PRESSINGS
(without "Sold in UK ..." label text)
Apple R 5722   Hey Jude/Revolution...8
Apple R 5777   Get Back/Don't Let Me Down (as "The Beatles with Billy Preston") 8
Apple R 5786   Ballad Of John And Yoko/Old Brown Shoe 8
KNOWN THIRD PRESSING
Parlophone R 5305   Help!/I'm Down (with "The Parlophone Co. Ltd" label text)....................10
(later 1970s Parlophone copies of Beatles singles with EMI boxed logos are of nominal value.
add £10 to the value for any singles with a red & white "Factory Sample Not For Sale" sticker)

1970
FIRST PRESSING
Apple R 5833   Let It Be/You Know My Name (Look Up The Number)
(scratched-out B-side matrix: APPLES 1002, p/s) 25
KNOWN SECOND PRESSING
Apple R 5833   Let It Be/You Know My Name (Look Up The Number)
(scratched-out B-side matrix: APPLES 1002, no p/s).......................8
KNOWN THIRD PRESSING
Apple R 5833   Let It Be/You Know My Name (Look Up The Number)
B-side matrix: 7YCE 21408, no p/s).................................5

EXPORT SINGLES
64	Parlophone DP 562	If I Fell/Tell Me Why (without "Sold in UK..." label text)................	40
65	Parlophone DP 563	Yesterday/Dizzy Miss Lizzy	75
66	Parlophone DP 564	Michelle/Drive My Car.......................................	150
68	Parlophone DP 570	Hey Jude/Revolution (with or without Swedish p/s)	40/50
70	Parlophone P-R 5833	Let It Be/You Know My Name (Look Up The Number) (no p/s).........	80

("Let It Be" was pressed with "Parlophone" label text on one side & "Gramophone" on the other)
70	Apple P-R 5833	Let It Be/You Know My Name (Look Up The Number) (no p/s)	100

FAN CLUB FLEXIDISCS
63	Lyntone LYN 492	The Beatles' Christmas Record (gatefold p/s)......................	75
64	Lyntone LYN 757	Another Beatles Christmas Record (p/s, with gatefold newsletter insert)	35
65	Lyntone LYN 948	The Beatles' Third Christmas Record (p/s, with gatefold newsletter insert)	40
66	Lyntone LYN 1145	Pantomime: Everywhere It's Christmas (p/s, with 7" x 7" newsletter insert)	50
67	Lyntone LYN 1360	Christmas Time (Is Here Again) (p/s, with 7" x 7" newsletter insert)...........	60
68	Lyntone LYN 1743/4	The Beatles' Sixth Christmas Record (p/s, some with 'Superpix' sales insert) ...	50/55
69	Lyntone LYN 1970/1-IL	The Beatles' Seventh Christmas Record	
		(p/s, some with 2 x foolscap fan club newsletters)	50/55

(fan club flexidiscs are worth around £10 less without newsletters, and a third of the listed values without picture sleeves)

DEMO SINGLES
62	Parlophone 45-R 4949	Love Me Do/P.S. I Love You (McCartney misspelt "McArtney", 250 only)........	2,500
63	Parlophone 45-R 4983	Please Please Me/Ask Me Why......................................	1,250
63	Parlophone (45-)R 5015	From Me To You/Thank You Girl (with or without '45-' prefix)	each 600
63	Parlophone R 5055	She Loves You/I'll Get You..	600
63	Parlophone R 5084	I Want To Hold Your Hand/This Boy	600
64	Parlophone R 5114	Can't Buy Me Love/You Can't Do That	600
64	Parlophone R 5160	A Hard Day's Night/Things We Said Today (red "A" on both sides)...........	600
64	Parlophone R 5200	I Feel Fine/She's A Woman (existence unconfirmed)	
65	Parlophone R 5265	Ticket To Ride/Yes It Is...	500
65	Parlophone R 5305	Help!/I'm Down (existence unconfirmed)	
65	Parlophone R 5389	We Can Work It Out/Day Tripper (red "A" on both sides)	500
66	Parlophone R 5452	Paperback Writer/Rain	500
66	Parlophone R 5493	Yellow Submarine/Eleanor Rigby (existence unconfirmed)	

(the above demos have white labels with a red "A" on the A-side, unless otherwise stated)
67	Parlophone R 5570	Strawberry Fields Forever/Penny Lane (existence unconfirmed)	
67	Parlophone R 5620	All You Need Is Love/Baby You're A Rich Man	400
67	Parlophone R 5655	Hello, Goodbye/I Am The Walrus....................................	400
68	Parlophone R 5675	Lady Madonna/The Inner Light	400
69	Parlophone R 5814	Something/Come Together..	800

(the above 5 demos have green labels with a white "A" on the A-side.
Demos with centres missing are worth half the listed values)
68	Apple (no cat. no.)	Hey Jude/Revolution (green & white Apple 'custom' label, handwritten details)	350
69	Apple R 5777	Get Back/Don't Let Me Down (green and white Apple 'custom' label test pressing,	
		typed details)..	350
69	Parlophone R 5786	Ballad Of John And Yoko/Old Brown Shoe (existence unconfirmed)	
70	Parlophone R 5833	Let It Be/You Know My Name (Look Up The Number) (existence unconfirmed)	
76	Parlophone R 6013	Yesterday/I Should Have Known Better (green generic p/s)	25
76	Parlophone R 6016	Back In The U.S.S.R./Twist And Shout (green generic p/s)	25
78	Parlophone R 6022	Sgt. Pepper's Lonely Hearts Club Band/With A Little Help From My Friends/	
		A Day In The Life (p/s)..	25

(the last three demos listed above have silver/black paper labels with a silver "A")

UNIQUE PROMO SINGLES

68	Apple (no cat. no.)	**OUR FIRST FOUR** (4 x 7" in presentation pack, including Hey Jude [R 5722] & Those Were The Days by Mary Hopkin [APPLE 2], Sour Milk Sea by Jackie Lomax [APPLE 3] & Thingumybob by Black Dyke Mills Band [APPLE 4]; each mounted in PVC pocket on printed dayglo card insert, in 10" x 12" card or scarcer plastic outer box)	750/1,000
76	EMI SPSR 401	**Medley Of Songs For "Rock'n'Roll Music"** (excerpts)	250

80s & 90s SINGLES: REISSUES & PICTURE DISCS

82	Parlophone R 4949	**Love Me Do/P.S. I Love You** (p/s, red label reissue, with "mono" notice & publishing miscredited to "Ardmore & Beechwood")	5
82	Parlophone RP 4949	**Love Me Do/P.S. I Love You** (picture disc, with/without publishing miscredit)	15/10
82	Parlophone 12R 4949	**Love Me Do/P.S. I Love You/Love Me Do** (Original Single Version) (12", p/s)	8
83	Parlophone RP 4983	**Please Please Me/Ask Me Why** (picture disc)	8
83	Parlophone RP 5015	**From Me To You/Thank You Girl** (picture disc, some with "Souvenir From Abbey Road Studios" sticker on sleeve)	15/8
83	Parlophone RP 5055	**She Loves You/I'll Get You** (picture disc)	15
83	Parlophone RP 5084	**I Want To Hold Your Hand/This Boy** (picture disc)	8
84	Parlophone RP 5114	**Can't Buy Me Love/You Can't Do That** (picture disc)	8
84	Parlophone RP 5160	**A Hard Day's Night/Things We Said Today** (picture disc)	15
84	Parlophone RP 5200	**I Feel Fine/She's A Woman** (picture disc)	8
85	Parlophone RP 5265	**Ticket To Ride/Yes It Is** (picture disc)	8
85	Parlophone RP 5305	**Help!/I'm Down** (picture disc)	8
85	Parlophone RP 5389	**We Can Work It Out/Day Tripper** (picture disc)	8
86	Parlophone RP 5452	**Paperback Writer/Rain** (picture disc)	10
86	Parlophone RP 5493	**Yellow Submarine/Eleanor Rigby** (picture disc)	10
87	Parlophone RP 5570	**Strawberry Fields Forever/Penny Lane** (picture disc, later with slightly larger picture on disc)	each 10
87	Parlophone RP 5620	**All You Need Is Love/Baby You're A Rich Man** (picture disc)	10
87	Parlophone 12R 5620	**All You Need Is Love/Baby You're A Rich Man** (12", p/s)	8
87	Parlophone RP 5655	**Hello, Goodbye/I Am The Walrus** (picture disc)	8
88	Parlophone RP 5675	**Lady Madonna/The Inner Light** (picture disc, with "Past Masters" insert)	8
88	Apple RP 5722	**Hey Jude/Revolution** (picture disc, with "Apple" insert)	8
88	Apple 12R 5722	**Hey Jude/Revolution** (12", p/s)	10
88	Apple 12RP 5722	**Hey Jude/Revolution** (12", picture disc with "Apple" insert)	10
89	Apple RP 5777	**Get Back/Don't Let Me Down** (with Billy Preston, picture disc, with "20th Anniversary" insert)	8
89	Apple RP 5786	**Ballad Of John And Yoko/Old Brown Shoe** (picture disc, with "20th Anniversary" insert)	8
89	Apple RP 5814	**Something/Come Together** (picture disc, with "20th Anniversary" insert)	8
90	Apple RP 5833	**Let It Be/You Know My Name (Look Up The Number)** (picture disc, with "20th Anniversary" insert)	8

(all the picture discs listed above were issued in PVC sleeves)

SINGLES BOX SETS

76	Parlophone/Apple BS 24	**THE BEATLES' SINGLES COLLECTION 1962-1970** (24 x 7", each in green p/s, green & white stickered box set)	25
76	Parlophone/Apple/ World Record Club	**THE BEATLES' COLLECTION** (24 x 7", mail-order black box set; later copies with Sgt. Pepper's Lonely Hearts Club Band [R 6022])	25
78	Parlophone/Apple BSC 1	**THE BEATLES' SINGLES COLLECTION** (26 x 7", blue box set, with insert; some copies include mispressing of Get Back [Apple R 5777])	35
82	Parlophone/Apple BSCP 1	**THE BEATLES' SINGLES COLLECTION** (27 x 7" blue box set, with bonus picture disc Love Me Do [RP 4949], export issue)	40
82	Parlophone/Apple BSCP 1	**THE BEATLES' SINGLES COLLECTION** (27 x 7" blue box set, with mispressed picture disc Love Me Do/Love Me Do [RP 4949], export issue)	40
89	Parlophone/Apple CDBSC 1	**THE BEATLES' SINGLES COLLECTION** (22 x 3" CD single box set)	40

EPs: 1963

(unless otherwise indicated, all 60s EPs have push-out centres & laminated, flipback sleeves, with "The Parlophone Co. Ltd." & "Recording first published 1963" label text, but without "Sold in UK ...")

FIRST PRESSINGS

Parlophone GEP 8882	**TWIST AND SHOUT**	15
Parlophone GEP 8880	**THE BEATLES' HITS** (without "Recording first published 1963" label text)	15
Parlophone GEP 8883	**THE BEATLES (No. 1)**	15

KNOWN SECOND PRESSING

Parlophone GEP 8880	**THE BEATLES' HITS**	15

EPs: 1964

(with "The Parlophone Co. Ltd.", "Recording first published 1964" & "Sold in UK ..." label text)

FIRST PRESSINGS

Parlophone GEP 8891	**ALL MY LOVING** (without "Sold in UK..." label text)	15
Parlophone GEP 8899	**GOLDEN DISCS** (unreleased, 2 x 1-sided test pressings [matrices: 7TCE-1N & 7TCE-1N] & 1 set of label proofs only; price does not include labels)	2,000
Parlophone GEP 8913	**LONG TALL SALLY**	15
Parlophone GEP 8920	**EXTRACTS FROM THE FILM A HARD DAY'S NIGHT**	15
Parlophone GEP 8924	**EXTRACTS FROM THE ALBUM A HARD DAY'S NIGHT**	25

KNOWN SECOND PRESSING

Parlophone GEP 8882	**TWIST AND SHOUT**	15
Parlophone GEP 8891	**ALL MY LOVING**	15

EPs: 1965

(with "The Parlophone Co. Ltd.", & "Sold in UK ..." label text)

FIRST PRESSINGS

Parlophone GEP 8931	**BEATLES FOR SALE**	20
Parlophone GEP 8938	**BEATLES FOR SALE (No. 2)**	30

(with "The Gramophone Co. Ltd.", & "Sold in UK ..." label text)

THE BEATLES

KNOWN SECOND PRESSING
(with "The Gramophone Co. Ltd.", & "Sold in UK ..." label text)
Parlophone GEP 8883   THE BEATLES (No. 1)... 15

KNOWN THIRD PRESSING
Parlophone GEP 8880   THE BEATLES' HITS... 15
Parlophone GEP 8882   TWIST AND SHOUT... 15

EPs: 1966
(with "The Gramophone Co. Ltd.", & "Sold in UK ..." label text)
FIRST PRESSINGS
Parlophone GEP 8948   YESTERDAY... 60
Parlophone GEP 8952   NOWHERE MAN 80

KNOWN SECOND PRESSING
Parlophone GEP 8946   THE BEATLES' MILLION SELLERS (with "Million Sellers" label text) 20

EPs: 1967
(with "The Gramophone Co. Ltd.", & "Sold in UK ..." label text)
FIRST PRESSING
Parlophone MMT-1   MAGICAL MYSTERY TOUR (2-EP, gatefold sleeve, with booklet
    & blue lyric sheet; push-out or solid centre; mono) 30
Parlophone SMMT-1   MAGICAL MYSTERY TOUR (2-EP, gatefold sleeve, with booklet & blue lyric sheet;
    stereo).. 35

KNOWN SECOND PRESSINGS
Parlophone GEP 8931   BEATLES FOR SALE (with "The Parlophone Co. Ltd" label text; solid centre) 15
Parlophone GEP 8952   NOWHERE MAN (solid centre) 25
(the above titles with "The Gramophone Co. Ltd.", & label text, but without "Sold in UK..." are 70s re-pressings, and are worth half the listed values. Later copies with "EMI" label text & varnished sleeves are worth approximately one-third of the listed values)

EPs: REISSUES & BOX SET
73   Parlophone SMMT-1   MAGICAL MYSTERY TOUR (2-EP, gatefold sleeve, stereo only, with booklet &
    yellow lyric sheet) 10
81   Parlophone BEP 14   THE BEATLES EP COLLECTION (14-EP box set, with bonus stereo EP [SGE 1])... 30

LPs: 1963
(with "The Parlophone Co. Ltd." label text but without "Sold in UK ...")
FIRST PRESSINGS
Parlophone PMC 1202   PLEASE PLEASE ME (black & gold label, with "Dick James Mus. Co."
    publishing credit for Please Please Me, I Saw Her Standing There, Misery,
    Do You Want To Know A Secret & There's A Place; E. J. Day sleeve; mono) 600
Parlophone PCS 3042   PLEASE PLEASE ME (black & gold label, with "Dick James Mus. Co."
    publishing credit for Please Please Me, I Saw Her Standing There, Misery,
    Do You Want To Know A Secret & There's A Place; E. J. Day sleeve; stereo) 2,500
Parlophone PMC 1206   WITH THE BEATLES (black & yellow label, with "Recording first published",
    & "Jobete" publishing credit for Money; G & L or E. J. Day sleeve,
    with large "mono" on front cover; mono)................................. 70
Parlophone PCS 3045   WITH THE BEATLES (black & yellow label, with "Recording first published",
    & "Jobete" publishing credit for Money; G & L or E. J. Day sleeve,
    with large "stereo" on front cover; stereo)................................ 150
(above pressings have polythene-lined "Use Emitex" die-cut inner sleeves)

SECOND PRESSINGS
(with "The Parlophone Co. Ltd." label text but without "Sold in UK ...")
Parlophone PMC 1202   PLEASE PLEASE ME (black & gold label, with "Northern Songs" publishing
    credit for "Please Please Me", I Saw Her Standing There, Misery,
    Do You Want To Know A Secret & There's A Place; E. J. Day sleeve; mono) 600
Parlophone PCS 3042   PLEASE PLEASE ME (black & gold label, with "Northern Songs" publishing
    credit for Please Please Me, I Saw Her Standing There, Misery,
    Do You Want To Know A Secret & There's A Place; E. J. Day sleeve; stereo) 2,500
Parlophone PMC 1206   WITH THE BEATLES (black & yellow label, with "Recording first published",
    & "Dominion, Belinda" publishing credit for Money; G & L or E. J. Day sleeve,
    with large "mono" on front cover; mono)................................. 40
Parlophone PCS 3045   WITH THE BEATLES (black & yellow label, with "Recording first published",
    & "Dominion, Belinda" publishing credit for Money; G & L or E. J. Day sleeve,
    with large "stereo" on front cover; stereo)................................ 100

THIRD PRESSINGS
(with "The Parlophone Co. Ltd." label text but without "Recording first published 1963" & "Sold in UK ...")
Parlophone PMC 1202   PLEASE PLEASE ME (with large "mono" on front cover; E. J. Day sleeve; mono) ... 90
Parlophone PCS 3042   PLEASE PLEASE ME (with large "stereo" on front cover;
    E. J. Day sleeve; stereo)... 150

FOURTH PRESSINGS
(with "The Parlophone Co. Ltd." & "Recording first published 1963", label text but without "Sold in UK ...")
Parlophone PMC 1202   PLEASE PLEASE ME (G & L or E. J. Day sleeve, with large "mono"
    on front cover; mono) 40
Parlophone PCS 3042   PLEASE PLEASE ME (G & L or E. J. Day sleeve, with large "stereo"
    on front cover; stereo)... 120

LPs: 1964
FIRST PRESSINGS
(with "The Parlophone Co. Ltd.", "Recording first published 1964" & "Sold in UK ..." label text)
Parlophone PMC 1230   A HARD DAY'S NIGHT (G & L or E. J. Day sleeve, mid-sized "mono"
    on front cover; mono) 40
Parlophone PCS 3058   A HARD DAY'S NIGHT (G & L sleeve, mid-sized "stereo"
    on front cover; stereo)... 100
Parlophone PMC 1240   BEATLES FOR SALE (G & L gatefold sleeve, with outline "mono"
    on front cover; mono) 40
Parlophone PCS 3062   BEATLES FOR SALE (G & L gatefold sleeve, with outline "stereo"
    on front cover; stereo)... 80

FIFTH PRESSINGS
(with "The Parlophone Co. Ltd.", "Recording first published 1963" & "Sold in UK ..." label text)

Parlophone PMC 1202	**PLEASE PLEASE ME** (G & L sleeve, with large "mono" on front cover; mono)	30
Parlophone PCS 3042	**PLEASE PLEASE ME** (G & L sleeve, with large "stereo" on front cover; stereo)	60

LPs: 1965
FIRST PRESSINGS
(with "The Gramophone Co. Ltd.", & "Sold in UK ..." label text)

Parlophone PMC 1255	**HELP!** (G & L sleeve, with outline "mono" on front cover; mono)	40
Parlophone PCS 3071	**HELP!** (G & L sleeve, with outline "stereo" on front cover; stereo)	70
Parlophone PMC 1267	**RUBBER SOUL** ('loud' cut matrix: [XEX 579-1], G & L or E. J. Day sleeve; mono)	80
Parlophone PCS 3075	**RUBBER SOUL** (G & L or E. J. Day sleeve; stereo)	75

SECOND PRESSINGS
(with "The Gramophone Co. Ltd.", & "Sold in UK ..." label text)

Parlophone PMC 1230	**A HARD DAY'S NIGHT** (small "mono" on front cover; mono)	30
Parlophone PCS 3058	**A HARD DAY'S NIGHT** (small "stereo" on front cover; stereo)	40
Parlophone PCS 3062	**BEATLES FOR SALE** (outline "stereo" on front gatefold sleeve; stereo)	40
Parlophone PMC 1267	**RUBBER SOUL** (matrix: [XEX 579-4 or 5]; mono)	45

THIRD PRESSINGS
(with "The Gramophone Co. Ltd..", & "Sold in UK ..." label text)

Parlophone PCS 3045	**WITH THE BEATLES** (small "stereo" on front cover; stereo)	40

SIXTH PRESSINGS
(with "The Gramophone Co. Ltd.", & "Sold in UK ..." label text)

Parlophone PMC 1202	**PLEASE PLEASE ME** (mono, with small "mono" on front cover)	30
Parlophone PCS 3042	**PLEASE PLEASE ME** (stereo, with small "stereo" on front cover)	40

(above pressings come with tracing-paper-lined ,"Use Emitex" die-cut inner sleeves)

LPs: 1966
FIRST PRESSINGS
(with "The Gramophone Co. Ltd.", & "Sold in UK ..." label text)

Parlophone PCS 7009	**REVOLVER** (G & L or E. J. Day sleeve; stereo)	80
Parlophone PMC 7016	**A COLLECTION OF BEATLES OLDIES** (G & L or E. J. Day sleeve; mono)	50
Parlophone PCS 7016	**A COLLECTION OF BEATLES OLDIES** (G & L or E. J. Day sleeve; stereo)	60

SECOND PRESSINGS
(with "The Gramophone Co. Ltd.", & "Sold in UK ..." label text)

Parlophone PMC 1255	**HELP!** (G & L sleeve; mono, with small solid black "mono" on front cover)	30
Parlophone PCS 3071	**HELP!** (G & L sleeve; stereo, with small solid black "stereo" on front cover)	45
Parlophone PMC 7009	**REVOLVER** (G & L or E. J. Day sleeve; mono)	60

(above pressings come with plain white or sepia "LP advertising" inner sleeves)

LPs: 1967
FIRST PRESSINGS
(with "The Gramophone Co. Ltd.", & " Sold in UK ..." label text)

Parlophone PMC 7027	**SGT. PEPPER'S LONELY HEARTS CLUB BAND** (G & L laminated gatefold sleeve, with red & white inner & cut-out insert; mono)	60
Parlophone PCS 7027	**SGT. PEPPER'S LONELY HEARTS CLUB BAND** (G & L laminated gatefold sleeve, with red & white inner & cut-out insert; stereo)	70

LPs: 1968
FIRST PRESSINGS
(with top-opening G & L gatefold sleeve, black inners, poster & 4 colour prints. Dark green label with "Sold in UK ..." text)

Apple PMC/PCS 7067/8	**THE BEATLES** (mono or stereo, numbered below 0000010)	5,000-8,000+
Apple PMC/PCS 7067/8	**THE BEATLES** (mono or stereo, numbered between 0000011 & 0001000)	1,000+
Apple PMC/PCS 7067/8	**THE BEATLES** (mono or stereo, numbered between 0001001 & 0010000)	500
Apple PMC 7067/8	**THE BEATLES** (mono, numbered above 0010000)	180
Apple PCS 7067/8	**THE BEATLES** (stereo, numbered above 0010000)	120

1969
FIRST PRESSINGS
(with G & L sleeve & black inners. Dark green label with& "Sold in UK ..." text)

Apple PMC 7070	**YELLOW SUBMARINE** (with red lines above & below rear sleevenote; mono)	175
Apple PCS 7070	**YELLOW SUBMARINE** (with red lines above & below rear sleevenote; stereo)	60
Apple PCS 7080	**GET BACK** (LP, unreleased; acetates only)	
Apple PCS 7088	**ABBEY ROAD** (black or plain white inner sleeve, with Apple logo aligned to Side 1 track listing on rear sleeve; with "Her Majesty" credit on label)	30

SECOND PRESSINGS
(with G & L sleeve. Label text with "The Gramophone Co. Ltd." but without "Sold in UK ...")

Parlophone PCS 3075	**RUBBER SOUL** (some with E. J. Day sleeve; stereo)	35
Parlophone PCS 7009	**REVOLVER** (stereo)	35
Parlophone PMC 7016	**A COLLECTION OF BEATLES OLDIES** (mono)	40
Parlophone PCS 7016	**A COLLECTION OF BEATLES OLDIES** (stereo)	35
Parlophone PCS 7027	**SGT. PEPPER'S LONELY HEARTS CLUB BAND** (gatefold sleeve, with white inner & cut-out insert; stereo)	35

(above pressings come with plain white or sepia "LP advertising" inner sleeves with G & L sleeve, black inners. Label text without "Sold in UK ...")

Apple PCS 7067/8	**THE BEATLES** (top-opening, numbered g/fold sl., poster & 4 colour prints; stereo)	35
Apple PCS 7070	**YELLOW SUBMARINE** (with red lines above & below rear sleevenote; stereo)	35

THIRD PRESSINGS
(with G & L sleeve. Label text with "The Gramophone Co. Ltd." but without "Sold in UK ...")

Parlophone PMC 1230	**A HARD DAY'S NIGHT** (small "mono" on front cover; mono)	35
Parlophone PCS 3058	**A HARD DAY'S NIGHT** (small "stereo" on front cover; stereo)	35
Parlophone PCS 3062	**BEATLES FOR SALE** (gatefold sleeve; stereo)	35
Parlophone PMC 1255	**HELP!** (small solid black "mono" on front cover; mono)	35
Parlophone PCS 3071	**HELP!** (small solid black "stereo" on front cover; stereo)	35

THE BEATLES

Parlophone PMC 1267	RUBBER SOUL (mono)	40
Parlophone PMC 7009	REVOLVER (mono)	40
Parlophone PMC 7027	SGT. PEPPER'S LONELY HEARTS CLUB BAND (laminated gatefold sleeve, & cut-out insert; mono)	45

(above pressings come with plain white or sepia "LP advertising" inner sleeves)

FOURTH PRESSINGS

(with G & L sleeve. Label text with "The Gramophone Co. Ltd." but without "Sold in UK ...")

Parlophone PCS 3045	WITH THE BEATLES (small "stereo" on front cover; stereo)	40

(above pressings have plain white or sepia "LP advertising" inner sleeves)

SEVENTH PRESSINGS

(with G & L sleeve & sepia "LP advertising" inner. Label has "The Gramophone Co. Ltd." but no "Sold in UK ...")

Parlophone PMC 1202	PLEASE PLEASE ME (small "mono" on front cover; mono)	45
Parlophone PCS 3042	PLEASE PLEASE ME (small "stereo" on front cover; stereo)	40

*(Please Please Me, With The Beatles, A Hard Day's Night, Help!, Rubber Soul, Revolver, A Collection Of Beatles Oldies & Yellow Submarine were originally issued with **flipback** sleeves. Beatles For Sale, Sgt. Pepper's Lonely Hearts Club Band & The Beatles have visible flaps inside gatefold sleeves. Abbey Road has internal flaps)*

LPs: 1970
FIRST PRESSINGS

(with G & L sleeve & dark green label)

Apple PXS 1	LET IT BE (box set, dark green label red Apple logo on rear sleeve & white inner, with Get Back book housed in black card tray ['PXS 1' not listed on package])	175
Apple/Lyntone LYN 2154	FROM THEN TO YOU (The Beatles' Christmas Album)	

EXPORT LPs: ORIGINALS

(with yellow/black labels, unless otherwise stated)

65	Parlophone CPCS 101	SOMETHING NEW (1st pressing, with "Parlophone Co. Ltd." label text)	500
65	Parlophone CPCS 101	SOMETHING NEW (2nd pressing, with "Gramophone Co. Ltd." label text)	350
66	Parlophone CPCS 103	THE BEATLES' SECOND ALBUM	400
66	Parlophone CPCS 104	BEATLES VI	400
68	Parlophone P-PCS 7067/8	THE BEATLES (2-LP, numbered, top opening 'mono' gatefold sleeve with "stereo" sticker & black inners, poster & 4 colour prints)	800
69	Odeon PPCS 7070	YELLOW SUBMARINE (Odeon sticker on rear of Apple sleeve)	1,500
69	Parlophone P-PCS 7088	ABBEY ROAD (Parlophone sticker on rear of Apple sleeve)	800
70	Parlophone P-PCS 7096	LET IT BE	800
70	Parlophone CPCS 106	HEY JUDE (silver/black label, one EMI boxed logo, laminated sleeve)	400

EXPORT LPs: REISSUES

(with silver/black labels, unless otherwise stated)

69	Parlophone CPCS 101	SOMETHING NEW (one EMI boxed logo)	200
69	Parlophone CPCS 103	THE BEATLES' SECOND ALBUM (one EMI boxed logo)	200
69	Parlophone CPCS 104	BEATLES VI (one EMI boxed logo)	200
69	Parlophone P-PCS 7088	ABBEY ROAD (Parlophone sticker on rear of Apple sleeve; one EMI boxed logo)	250
69	Apple CPCS 106	HEY JUDE (2nd reissue, dark green label)	100
70	Parlophone P-PCS 7096	LET IT BE (one EMI boxed logo)	250
70	Parl./Apple (P-)PCS 7096	LET IT BE (2nd reissue, Apple label [PCS 7096] in Parlophone sleeve)	35
70	Parlophone CPCS 103	THE BEATLES' SECOND ALBUM (2nd reissue, two EMI boxed logos)	150
70s	Parl./Apple (P-)CPCS 106	HEY JUDE (Apple label [CPCS 106] in Parlophone sleeve [P-CPSC 106])	50
73	Apple CPCS 106	HEY JUDE (3rd reissue, light green label)	25
78	Parlophone PCTC 255	MAGICAL MYSTERY TOUR (transparent yellow vinyl)	40
78	Apple PCS 7067/8	THE BEATLES (2-LP, white vinyl, gatefold sleeve)	50
78	Apple PCS 7088	ABBEY ROAD (green vinyl)	30
78	Apple PCS 7096	LET IT BE (white vinyl)	30

LPs: 1969 RE-PRESSINGS

*(with laminated flipback sleeves & silver/black labels with **one** boxed EMI logo)*

69	Parlophone PMC 1202	PLEASE PLEASE ME (mono)	35
69	Parlophone PCS 3042	PLEASE PLEASE ME (stereo)	15
69	Parlophone PCS 3045	WITH THE BEATLES (stereo only)	15
69	Parlophone PCS 3058	A HARD DAY'S NIGHT (stereo only)	15
69	Parlophone PCS 3062	BEATLES FOR SALE (gatefold sleeve, stereo only)	15
69	Parlophone PMC 1255	HELP! (mono)	75
69	Parlophone PCS 3071	HELP! (stereo)	15
69	Parlophone PCS 3075	RUBBER SOUL (stereo only)	15
69	Parlophone PCS 7009	REVOLVER (stereo only)	15
69	Parlophone PCS 7016	A COLLECTION OF BEATLES OLDIES (stereo only)	15
69	Parlophone PMC 7027	SGT. PEPPER'S LONELY HEARTS CLUB BAND (laminated gatefold sleeve, with cut-out insert, mono)	40
69	Parlophone PCS 7027	SGT. PEPPER'S LONELY HEARTS CLUB BAND (laminated gatefold sleeve, with cut-out insert, stereo)	15
73	Apple PCS 7067/8	THE BEATLES (2-LP, un-numbered, laminated, side-opening gatefold sleeve, with poster & 4 soft card colour prints, stereo only)	20

LPs: 1980s RE-PRESSINGS

(lightweight vinyl with yellow/black labels listing "mono", unless otherwise stated)

82	Parlophone PMC 1202	PLEASE PLEASE ME (mono)	12
82	Parlophone PMC 1206	WITH THE BEATLES (mono)	12
82	Parlophone PMC 1230	A HARD DAY'S NIGHT (mono)	12
82	Parlophone PMC 1240	BEATLES FOR SALE (gatefold sleeve, mono)	12
82	Parlophone PMC 1255	HELP! (mono)	12
82	Parlophone PMC 1267	RUBBER SOUL (mono)	12
82	Parlophone PMC 7009	REVOLVER (mono)	12
82	Parlophone PMC 7027	SGT. PEPPER'S LONELY HEARTS CLUB BAND (gatefold sleeve with cut-out inserts, mono)	12
82	Apple PMC 7067/8	THE BEATLES (2-LP, un-numbered, side-opening gatefold sleeve, with poster & 4 prints, light green Apple label; mono)	15
82	Apple PMC 7070	YELLOW SUBMARINE (light green Apple label; mono)	12

LPs: RETROSPECTIVES

76	Parlophone PCTC 255	MAGICAL MYSTERY TOUR (gatefold sleeve with 24-page stapled insert)	18
78	Apple PCSPR 717	THE BEATLES 1962-1966 (2-LP, red vinyl, gatefold stickered sleeve with lyric inners; without sticker £10)	15
78	Apple PCSPB 718	THE BEATLES 1967-1970 (2-LP, blue vinyl, gatefold stickered sleeve with lyric inners; without sticker £10)	15
79	Parlophone PCS 7184	HEY JUDE (black/silver label with two boxed EMI logos)	12
82	Parlophone EMTVS 34	THE BEATLES' GREATEST HITS (2-LP, unreleased)	
82	Parlophone PCS 7218	REEL MUSIC (with inner & 12-page insert)	12
88	HMV BPM 1	PAST MASTERS VOLUME 1 & 2 (2-LP, gatefold sleeve)	12
94	Apple PCSP 726	LIVE AT THE BBC (2-LP, gatefold sleeve, with inners)	12
99	Apple 521 4811	YELLOW SUBMARINE SONGTRACK (gatefold stickered sleeve)	12
99	Apple 521 4811	YELLOW SUBMARINE SONGTRACK (yellow vinyl, gatefold stickered sleeve)	12

REEL-TO-REEL TAPES: ORIGINALS

69	Apple DTA-PMC 7067/8	THE BEATLES (5" spool, mono)	40
69	Apple DTD-PCS 7067/8	THE BEATLES (5" spool, stereo)	25
70	Apple TA-PMC 7088	ABBEY ROAD (mono)	60
70	Apple TD-PCS 7088	ABBEY ROAD (stereo)	25
70	Apple TA-PMC 7096	LET IT BE (mono)	70
70	Apple TD-PCS 7096	LET IT BE (stereo)	25

(unless otherwise stated, the above issues were on 4" spools with printed leaders, and were housed in jewel cases with inlays)

REEL-TO-REEL TAPES: REISSUES

(issued on 4" spools with printed leaders, and housed in jewel cases with inlays)

68	Parlophone TA-PMC 1202	PLEASE PLEASE ME (mono)	12
68	Parlophone TD-PCS 3042	PLEASE PLEASE ME (stereo)	12
68	Parlophone TA-PMC 1206	WITH THE BEATLES (mono)	12
68	Parlophone TD-PCS 3045	WITH THE BEATLES (stereo)	12
68	Parlophone TA-PMC 1230	A HARD DAY'S NIGHT (mono)	12
68	Parlophone TD-PCS 3058	A HARD DAY'S NIGHT (stereo)	12
68	Parlophone TA-PMC 1240	BEATLES FOR SALE (mono)	12
68	Parlophone TD-PCS 3062	BEATLES FOR SALE (stereo)	12
68	Parlophone TA-PMC 1255	HELP! (mono)	12
68	Parlophone TD-PCS 3071	HELP! (stereo)	12
68	Parlophone TA-PMC 1267	RUBBER SOUL (mono)	12
68	Parlophone TD-PCS 3075	RUBBER SOUL (stereo)	12
68	Parlophone TA-PMC 7009	REVOLVER (mono)	12
68	Parlophone TD-PCS 7009	REVOLVER (stereo)	12
68	Parlophone TA-PMC 7016	A COLLECTION OF BEATLES OLDIES (mono)	12
68	Parlophone TD-PCS 7016	A COLLECTION OF BEATLES OLDIES (stereo)	12
68	Parlophone TA-PMC 7027	SGT. PEPPER'S LONELY HEARTS CLUB BAND (mono)	12
68	Parlophone TD-PCS 7027	SGT. PEPPER'S LONELY HEARTS CLUB BAND (stereo)	12

ALBUM BOX SETS

78	Parlophone BC 13	THE BEATLES COLLECTION (13 x LP, stereo, some with poster)	60
82	Parlophone BMC 10	THE BEATLES MONO COLLECTION (10 x LP, red box)	275

CD ALBUMS & BOX SETS

87	HMV BEACD 25/1	PLEASE PLEASE ME/WITH THE BEATLES/A HARD DAY'S NIGHT/ BEATLES FOR SALE (4 x CD, numbered 12" black box set with *Book Of Beatles Lists* paperback book)	80
87	HMV BEACD 25/2	HELP!/RUBBER SOUL/REVOLVER (3 x CD, numbered 12" red box set with insert & reprint of *Beatles Book Monthly*, issue 12)	40
87	HMV BEACD 25/3	SGT. PEPPER'S LONELY HEARTS CLUB BAND (CD, numbered 12" box set with booklet & badge)	20
87	HMV BEACD 25/4	THE BEATLES (2-CD, numbered 12" box set with booklet & badge)	25
87	HMV BEACD 25/5	YELLOW SUBMARINE (CD, numbered 12" box set with insert, cut-outs & badge)	25
87	HMV BEACD 25/6	MAGICAL MYSTERY TOUR (CD, numbered 12" box set with booklet, poster & badge)	25
87	HMV BEACD 25/7	ABBEY ROAD (CD, numbered 12" box set with 2 posters, booklet & badge)	15
87	HMV BEACD 25/8	LET IT BE (CD, numbered 12" box set with booklet & badge)	15

POLYDOR RECORDINGS

SINGLES

(with push-out centres & orange labels, unless otherwise stated)

62	Polydor NH 66833	My Bonnie/The Saints (When The Saints Go Marching In) (as Tony Sheridan & The Beatles; 1st pressing, 'broad' title & "Made In England" label text)	50
63	Polydor NH 66833	My Bonnie/The Saints (When The Saints Go Marching In) (as Tony Sheridan & The Beatles; 2nd pressing, push-out or solid centre, 'narrow' title & "Made In England" label text)	40
64	Polydor NH 52906	Sweet Georgia Brown/Nobody's Child (German import only, unissued in U.K.)	
64	Polydor NH 52275	Cry For A Shadow (A-side credited to 'Beatles')/ TONY SHERIDAN & THE BEATLES: Why (Can't You Love Me Again) ('scroll' label, with "Made In England" text)	35
64	Polydor NH 52317	Ain't She Sweet (A-side as 'The Beatles', vocal: John Lennon')/If You Love Me, Baby (B-side credited to 'The Beatles with Tony Sheridan, vocal'; 1st pressing, 'scroll' label with "Made In England" text)	40
64	Polydor NH 52317	Ain't She Sweet/If You Love Me, Baby (2nd pressing, red label, with "Made In England" text)	15

EPs

64	Polydor EPH 21 610	TONY SHERIDAN WITH THE BEATLES (1st pressing, German import in U.K. p/s, orange 'scroll' label; Why songwriting credit as 'Sheridan' or 'Sheridan-Crompton')	50
64	Polydor EPH 21 610	TONY SHERIDAN WITH THE BEATLES (2nd pressing, German import in U.K. p/s, red label; Why songwriting credit as 'Sheridan' or 'Sheridan-Crompton')	25

THE BEATLES

LPs

64	Polydor Hi-Fi 46 432	THE BEATLES' FIRST (purple/black sleeve, Germany only, unissued in U.K.)
67	Polydor Special 236 201	THE BEATLES' FIRST (as Tony Sheridan & The Beatles, 1st pressing, without 'stereo' on label or sleeve, 'pop art' sleeve)............................. 35
67	Polydor Special 236 201	THE BEATLES' FIRST (later pressings with 'stereo' on label & sleeve, minor label variations, 'pop art' sleeve).................................... 25

CONTRACT PRESSINGS

(Records pressed by non-EMI companies on contract, owing to overwhelming demand; Decca contract pressings have no stamper letters (G or D) positioned at 3 o'clock to the matrix number; the centre has a ridge 3mm from the perimeter. Pye pressings have no stamper letters (G or D) at 3 o'clock to the matrix number; the centre has no ridge, and is finished with rough edges. Pye pressings are thicker and heavier than EMI and Decca pressings.)

SINGLES

63	Parlophone R 5055	She Loves You/I'll Get You (Decca pressing)............................... 25
63	Parlophone R 5084	I Want To Hold Your Hand/This Boy (Decca pressing)..................... 25
63	Parlophone R 5084	I Want To Hold Your Hand/This Boy (Pye pressing)....................... 25
64	Parlophone R 5114	Can't Buy Me Love/You Can't Do That (Pye pressing)................... 25
64	Parlophone R 5200	I Feel Fine/She's A Woman (Decca pressing) 25
64	Parlophone R 5200	I Feel Fine/She's A Woman (Pye pressing) 25
65	Parlophone R 5305	Help!/I'm Down (Decca pressing) 35
67	Parlophone R 5655	Hello Goodbye/I Am The Walrus (Decca pressing)....................... 30
68	Apple R 5722	Hey Jude/Revolution (Decca pressing) 35
68	Apple R 5722	Hey Jude/Revolution (Philips pressing, three-pronged push-out centre) 80
68	Apple R 5722	Hey Jude/Revolution (Pye pressing) 35

LPs

(Decca contract pressings have no stamper letters (G or D) positioned at 3 o'clock to the matrix number; the label has a circular impression 15mm from the outer edge. Pye pressings are a dark, translucent red when held up to a strong light.)

63	Parlophone PMC 1202	PLEASE PLEASE ME (Decca pressing) 150
63	Parlophone PMC 1206	WITH THE BEATLES (Decca pressing)............................. 100
63	Parlophone PMC 1206	WITH THE BEATLES (Pye pressing).............................. 200
68	Parlophone P-PCS 7067/8	THE BEATLES (export issue, yellow & black labels, Decca pressing)........... 3,000
69	Parlophone P-PCS 7088	ABBEY ROAD (export issue, yellow & black labels, Decca pressing) 2,000
69	Parlophone P-PCS 7099	ABBEY ROAD (export issue, silver & black labels, Decca pressing) 600
70s	Apple PCSP 717	THE BEATLES 1962-1966 (2-LP, gatefold sleeve with lyric inners, Pye pressing) 75
84	Parlophone/ Nimbus PCS 7027	SGT. PEPPER'S LONELY HEARTS CLUB BAND (mail-order only, from *Practical Hi-Fi Magazine*, Nimbus pressing).................... 400

FRENCH PRESSINGS

SINGLE

67	Parlophone R 5655	Hello Goodbye/I Am The Walrus (Pathé Marconi pressing) 35

LPs

(Parlophone label LPs have 'Made in France' on EMI rim copy. Apple label LPs have 'Made in France by Pathé Marconi EMI' rim copy. All discs are in British-printed sleeves bearing 'Made in France' stickers.)

73	Parlophone PCS 3042	PLEASE PLEASE ME 15
73	Parlophone PCS 3045	WITH THE BEATLES 15
73	Parlophone PCS 3058	A HARD DAY'S NIGHT 15
73	Parlophone PCS 3062	BEATLES FOR SALE (gatefold sleeve)............................. 15
73	Parlophone PCS 3071	HELP! 12
73	Parlophone PCS 3075	RUBBER SOUL 12
73	Parlophone PCS 7009	REVOLVER... 12
73	Parlophone PCS 7016	A COLLECTION OF BEATLES OLDIES.............................. 12
73	Parlophone PCS 7027	SGT. PEPPER'S LONELY HEARTS CLUB BAND (gatefold sleeve with cut-out insert, some copies with banded vinyl) 12
73	Apple PCS 7067/8	THE BEATLES (2-LP, un-numbered, laminated, side-opening gatefold sleeve, with four colour prints & poster) 20
73	Apple PCS 7070	YELLOW SUBMARINE 12
73	Apple PCS 7088	ABBEY ROAD (some copies with banded vinyl) 12
73	Apple PCS 7096	LET IT BE... 12
73	Apple PCSP 717	THE BEATLES 1962-1966 (2-LP, gatefold sleeve with lyric inners) 15
73	Apple PCSP 718	THE BEATLES 1967-1970 (2-LP, gatefold sleeve with lyric inners) 15

MISPRINTS & MISPRESSINGS

SINGLES

63	Parlophone R 4983	Please Please Me/Ask Me Why (A-side actually plays 'Quiet Morning' by the Brian Fahey Orchestra).. 50
67	Parlophone R 5620	All You Need Is Love/Baby You're A Rich Man (with no reference to "Live World Television Transmission") 75

EPs

64	Parlophone GEP 8882	TWIST AND SHOUT (label error: Do You Want A Know A Secret) 25
65	Parlophone GEP 8946	THE BEATLES' MILLION SELLERS (label error: "Beatles Golden Discs") 20

LPs

64	Parlophone PCS 3062	BEATLES FOR SALE (label error: I'm A Losser)....................... 250
65	Parlophone CPCS 101	SOMETHING NEW (export issue, label error: "Sold in UK") 550
65	Parlophone PCS 3075	RUBBER SOUL (label error: Norweigian Wood)...................... 250
66	Parlophone CPCS 106	BEATLES VI (export issue, label error: "Sold in UK") 550
66	Parlophone PMC 7009	REVOLVER (copies with side 2 matrix no.: XEX 606-1 have 'Remix 11' of Tomorrow Never Knows, G & L or E. J. Day sleeve; mono only)................. 300
67	Parlophone PMC 7027	SGT. PEPPER'S LONELY HEARTS CLUB BAND (label omits A Day In The Life credit; G & L laminated gatefold sleeve, with plain white inner & insert,; mono only) 275
68	Apple PCS 7067/8	THE BEATLES (label error: Rocky Racoon) 200
69	Parlophone PMC 7027	SGT. PEPPER'S LONELY HEARTS CLUB BAND (mono; matrix YEX 637/8; plays stereo) 400
69	Apple CPCS 106	HEY JUDE (label error: Revolutions) 350
69	Apple PCS 7088	ABBEY ROAD (Apple logo misaligned to Side 1 track listing on rear sleeve; with or without "Her Majesty" credit on label; black or plain white inner sleeve) 75

69	Apple PCS 7088	ABBEY ROAD (label omits "Her Majesty").	40
99	Parlophone PCS 3075	RUBBER SOUL (label error: pressed on Apple)	125

(see also John Lennon, Paul McCartney/Wings, George Harrison, Ringo Starr, Pete Best Four, Quarry Men, Tony Sheridan, George Martin, Billy Preston, Yoko Ono)

BEATMEN
64	Pye 7N 15659	You Can't Sit Down/Come On Pretty Baby	20
65	Pye 7N 15792	Now The Sun Has Gone/Please Believe	12

BEAT MERCHANTS
64	Columbia DB 7367	Pretty Face/Messin' With The Man	50
65	Columbia DB 7492	So Fine/She Said Yeah	50

BEAT SIX
64	Decca F 12011	Bernadine/The River And I	15

(see also Guys)

BEATSTALKERS
65	Decca F 12259	Ev'rybody's Talking 'Bout My Baby/Mr. Disappointed	35
66	Decca F 12352	Left Right Left/You'd Better Get A Better Hold On	35
66	Decca F 12460	A Love Like Yours/Base Line	28
67	CBS 2732	My One Chance To Make It/Ain't No Soul (Left In These Old Shoes)	45
67	CBS 3105	Silver Treetop School For Boys/Sugar Coated Man	40
68	CBS 3557	Rain Coloured Roses/Everything Is For You	30
69	CBS 3936	When I'm Five/Little Boy	30

PAUL BEATTIE
57	Parlophone R 4385	I'm Comin' Home/Nothing So Strange	40
58	Parlophone R 4429	Me, Please Me/Wanderlust	10
58	Parlophone R 4468	A House, A Car, And A Wedding Ring/Banana	20
68	Parlophone R 4664	Slick Chick/The Big Bounce	30

E.C. BEATTY
59	Felsted AF 127	Ski King/I'm A Lucky Man (78 rpm = £10)	40

BEAU
69	Dandelion S 4403	1917 Revolution/Sleeping Town	7
69	Dandelion S 63751	BEAU (LP)	40
71	Dandelion DAN 8006	CREATION (LP, with The Way We Live)	30

(see also Way We Live)

BEAU BRUMMELS
65	Pye International 7N 25293	Laugh, Laugh/Still In Love With You Baby	12
65	Pye International 7N 25306	Just A Little/They'll Make You Cry	10
65	Pye International 7N 25318	You Tell Me Why/I Want You	10
65	Pye International 7N 25333	Don't Talk To Strangers/In Good Time	10
66	Pye International 7N 25342	Good Time Music/Sad Little Girl (unissued)	
65	Pye International NPL 28062	INTRODUCING THE BEAU BRUMMELS (LP, mono only)	50

BEAU-MARKS
60	Top Rank JAR 377	Clap Your Hands/Daddy Said	40

(see also Del-Tones, Milton De Lugg Orchestra)

JIMMY BEAUMONT
66	London HLZ 10059	You Got Too Much Going For You/I Never Loved Her Anyway	125

BEAVER & KRAUSE
72	Warner Bros K 46130	GANDHARVA (LP)	15
72	Warner Bros K 46184	ALL GOOD MEN (LP)	15

BEAVERS
58	Capitol CL 14909	Road To Happiness/Low As I Can Be	10

JACKIE BEAVERS
75	Buddah BDS 423	Mr Bump Man/Somebody Help The Bigger Man	10
76	Jay Boy BOY 102	Trying To Get Back To You Girl/Trying To Get Back To You Girl (Version)	15

BEAZERS
64	Decca F 11827	The Blue Beat/I Wanna Shout	38

(see also Chris Farlowe, Little Joe Cook)

BE-BOP DELUXE
73	Smile LAFS 001	Teenage Archangel/Jets At Dawn (mono, 1,000 only)	25
74	Harvest HAR 5081	Jet Silver (And The Dolls Of Venus)/Third Floor Heaven	6
75	Harvest HAR 5091	Between The Worlds/Lights (withdrawn)	40+
75	Harvest HAR 5098	Maid In Heaven/Lights	5
76	Harvest HAR 5110	Kiss Of The Light/FUNKY PHASER & HIS UNEARTHLY MERCHANDISE: Shine	5
77	Harvest SHVL 816	LIVE! IN THE AIR AGE (LP, with bonus EP "Live! In The Air Age" [PSR 412])	12

(see also Bill Nelson)

BE-BOP PRESERVATION SOCIETY
71	Dawn DNLS 3027	THE BE-BOP PRESERVATION SOCIETY (LP, gatefold sleeve with insert)	30

GILBERT BECAUD
59	HMV POP 574	The Day The Rains Came/Les Marches De Provence (78 rpm = £8)	7

SIDNEY BECHET
50	Melodisc 1103	Some Of These Days/Black & Blue (78)	7
50	Melodisc 1105	I Told You Once, I Told You Twice/Georgia (78)	7
51	Decca C 16169	King Porter Stomp/DUTCH SWING COLLEGE: Dutch King College Blues (78)	8
54	Vogue V 2391	Royal Garden Blues/Mon Homme	8
58	Vogue V 2394	Theme From The "Threepenny Opera"/Army Song	10
59	Vogue V 9141	Petit Fleur/Dans La Rue D'Antibes (78 rpm = £8)	15
59	Vogue V 9157	Le Marchand de Poissons/Si Tu Vois Ma Mere (78 rpm = £6)	5
60	Philips JAZ 110	My Woman's Blues/What A Dream (p/s)	5

MINT VALUE £

55	Melodisc EPM 7-51	SIDNEY BECHET WITH HUMPHREY LYTTELTON'S BAND (EP)	20
56	Melodisc EPM 7-62	BECHET/SPANIER BIG FOUR (EP, with Mugsy Spanier)	10
56	Melodisc EPM 7-68	BECHET-SPANIER IN NEW YORK, BECHET-LYTTELTON IN LONDON (EP)	10
64	Melodisc MLP 12-148	REQUIEM A BECHET (LP)	20

(see also Humphrey Lyttelton, Mezz Mezzrow)

BECHET-SPANIER BIG FOUR
| 50 | Melodisc 8001 | Four Or Five Times/China Boy (12" 78) | 8 |

BECK
94	Geffen GFS 67	Loser/Alcohol/Fume (p/s)	10
94	Geffen GFSJB 67	Loser/Loser (jukebox issue, no p/s)	10
94	Geffen GFSTD 67	Loser/Totally Confused/Corvette Bummer/MTV Makes Me Want To Smoke Crack (Lounge Act Version) (CD)	8
94	Geffen GFS 73	Pay No Mind (Snoozer)/Special People (withdrawn)	60
94	Geffen GFST 73 (Sunchild)	Pay No Mind (Snoozer)/Special People/Trouble All My Days/Super Golden (12", p/s, withdrawn – at least 100 pressed up)	50
94	Geffen GFST 73	Pay No Mind (Snoozer)/Special People/Trouble All My Days/ Super Golden (Sunchild) (CD – blue image on CD)	15
94	Geffen GED 21911	Pay No Mind (Snoozer)/Special People/Trouble All My Days/ Super Golden (Sunchild) (CD – pink image on CD)	15
94	Geffen GED 21939	Beercan/Got No Mind/Asskizz Powergrudge (Payback! '94)/Spanking Room/ Loser (Pseudo-Muzak) (unlisted track) (CD)	15
94	Geffen GFS 19235	Beercan/Spanking Room (p/s, 1500 copies)	30
96	Geffen GFST 22156	Where It's At/Where It's At (Remix By Mario C. & Mickey P.)/Bonus Beats/ Where It's At (Remix by U.N.K.L.E) (12" p/s)	8
96	Geffen GFS 22183	Devil's Haircut/Lloyd Price Express (Remix By John King) (p/s)	7
96	Geffen GFS 22205	The New Pollution/Electric Music And The Summer People (p/s)	7
97	Geffen GFS 22253	Sissyneck/Feather In Your Cap (p/s)	7
97	Select SELECT 12	Clock/The Little Drum Machine Boy/Totally Confused (with/without *Select* mag)	8/6
97	Geffen GFSTD 22276	Jack-Ass (Butch Vlg Mix)/Jack-Ass (Lowrider Mix By Butch Vlg)/Burro/Strange Invitation/Devil Got My Woman/Brother (CD, card p/s)	8
97	Geffen GFS 22276 Ass(Lowrider	Jack-Ass (Butch Vig Mix)/Strange Invitation/Devil Got My Woman/Jack- Mix By Butch Vig) Burro Brother (Double 7" gatefold some have Butch Vig Mix with no Lowrider Mix	7
97	Geffen GFS 22293	Deadweight (Edit)/Erase The Sun (p/s)	5
98	Geffen GFS 22365	Tropicalia (LP Version)/Halo Of Gold (p/s)	5
99	Geffen 497182-7	Sexxlaws/Salt In The Wound (picture disc, stickered p/s)	7
00	Geffen 497312-7	Mixed Bizness/(Dirty Bixin Mizness Remix) (gatefold p/s – 1,500 copies)	7
97	Geffen GFSTD 22205	New Pollution/Electric Music And The Summer People (p/s)	8
96	Geffen GED 24908	ODELAY (CD, with bonus track Diskobox & unlisted track Clock)	18
04	Interscope BECK 2	A BRIEF OVERVIEW (Promo-only 13-track GUERO sampler, (CD, in jewel case)	15

GORDON BECK (QUARTET)
68	Morgan MJ 1	GYROSCOPE (LP)	300
69	M. Minor MMLP/SMLP 21	EXPERIMENTS WITH POPS (LP, as Gordon Beck Quartet)	125
69	M. Minor MMLP/SMLP 22	HALF A JAZZ SIXPENCE (LP)	100
69	Major Minor SMLP 88	DR. DOOLITTLE LOVES JAZZ (LP)	40
72	Dire FO 341	BECK-MATTHEWSON-HUMAIR TRIO (LP)	30

(see also Seven Ages Of Man)

JEFF BECK
67	Columbia DB 8151	Hi-Ho Silver Lining/Beck's Bolero	10
67	Columbia DB 8227	Tallyman/Rock My Plimsoul	10
68	Columbia DB 8359	Love Is Blue (L'Amour Est Bleu)/I've Been Drinking	10
69	Columbia DB 8590	Plinth (Water Down The Drain)/Hangman's Knee (unissued)	
72	Epic EPC 7720	Got The Feeling/Situation	8
75	Epic EPC 3334	She's A Woman/It Doesn't Really Matter	10
80	Epic EPC 8806	The Final Peace/Space Boogie	8
80	Epic EPCA 1009	The Final Peace/Scatter Brain/Too Much To Lose/Led Boots (12", p/s)	10
82	Rak RRP 3	Hi Ho Silver Lining/Beck's Bolero/Rock My Plimsoul (picture disc)	6
68	Columbia S(C)X 6293	TRUTH (LP, 1st pressing, blue/black labels, mono/stereo)	60/40
69	Columbia S(C)X 6351	BECK-OLA (LP, 1st pressing, blue/black labels, mono/stereo)	40/28
69	Columbia SCX 6293	TRUTH (LP, 2nd pressing, silver/black labels, mono/stereo)	15
69	Columbia SCX 6351	BECK-OLA (LP, 2nd pressing, silver/black labels, mono/stereo)	12
72	Epic EPC 64619	ROUGH AND READY (LP, yellow label)	18
72	Epic EPC 64899	JEFF BECK GROUP (LP, yellow label)	20
72	Epic EQ 30973	ROUGH AND READY (LP, quadrophonic)	22
74	CBS EQ 31331	JEFF BECK GROUP (LP, quadrophonic)	25

(see also Yardbirds, Beck Bogert Appice, Donovan, Rod Stewart, Cozy Powell, Honeydrippers, Buddy Guy with Jeff Beck)

BECK, BOGERT & APPICE
73	Epic S EPC 1251	Black Cat Moan/Livin' Alone	6
73	CBS EPC 22001	BECK, BOGERT & APPICE (LP)	15
75	CBS EQ 32140/Q 65455	BECK, BOGERT & APPICE (LP, quadrophonic)	20

(see also Jeff Beck, Vanilla Fudge, Cactus)

HAROLD BECKETT
71	Philips 6308 026	FLARE UP (LP)	130
72	RCA SF 8225	WARM SMILES (LP)	80
73	RCA SF 8264	THEME FOR FEGA (LP)	25
75	Cadillac SGC 1004	JOY UNLIMITED (LP)	20
76	Ogun OG 800	MEMORIES OF BACARES (LP, as Harry Beckett's Joy Unlimited)	15
70s	Ogun OG 020	GOT IT MADE (LP, as Harry Beckett's Joy Unlimited)	12

(see also Graham Collier, Galliard, Ninesense)

STUART BECKETT
60s	Sherwood SRS 1001	Kariline/Breakthrough.	30

JENNY BECKETT
65	Parlophone R 5373	My Love And I/Lock Away Your Love	7

(KEE)LYN BECKFORD
68	Island WI 3144	Combination/Hey Little Girl	20
69	Jackpot JP 707	Kiss Me Quick/MRS. MILLER: Feel It	12
69	Big Shot BI 521	Suzie Wong (as K. Beckford)/SWINGING KINGS: Deebo	25
71	G.G. GG 4514	Groove Me/Groove Version (as Keeling Beckford)	12

THEO(PHILUS) BECKFORD
61	Blue Beat BB 33	Jack And Jill Shuffle/Little Lady (as Theophilus Beckford & Clue J. & His Blues Blasters)	12
61	Blue Beat BB 50	Georgie And The Old Shoe/That's Me (as Theo Beckford & City Slickers)	12
62	Blue Beat BB 87	Walking Down King Street/The Clock (B-side actually by Sir D's Group)	12
62	Blue Beat BB 132	Bringing In The Sheep (song actually Bringing In The Sheaves)/Run Away	12
62	Island WI 026	I Don't Want You (actually by King Edward's All Stars)/Seven Long Years	15
63	Island WI 106	Daphney/Boller Man	10
64	Blue Beat BB 250	She's Gone/Old Flame (as Cotheo Beckford, B-side act. by Frederick Hibbert)	15
64	Blue Beat BB 257	Don't Worry To Cry/Love Me Or Leave Me (as Theophilus Beckford, B-side actually by Lloyd Clarke)	12
64	Blue Beat BB 287	On Your Knees/Now You're Gone (with Yvonne Harrison)	15
65	Blue Beat BB 303	Dig The Dig (as Basil Gabbidon)/Don't Let Me Cry No More	15
65	Black Swan WI 452	Take Your Time/STRANGER COLE: Happy-Go-Lucky.	20
65	Island WI 238	Trench Town People/PIONEERS: Sometime	25
65	Island WI 243	You Are The One Girl/Grudgeful People.	20
65	Island WI 246	If Life Was A Thing/L. CLARKE: Parro Saw The Light (B-side actually Pharaoh Saw The Light by Lloyd Clarke)	12
65	Island WI 248	What A Whoe/Bajan Girl.	20
68	Nu Beat NB 009	Easy Snappin'/ERIC MORRIS: My Lonely Days.	15
69	Crab CRAB 25	Brother Ram Goat (as T. Beckford)/STARLIGHTS: What A Condition.	20

(see also Eric Barnet[t], Maytals, Clue J & His Bluesblasters)

BOB BECKHAM
59	Brunswick 05808	Just As Much As Ever/Your Sweet Love	10
60	Brunswick 05822	Crazy Arms/Beloved	15
60	Brunswick 05835	Mais Oui/Only The Broken Hearted.	5
60	Brunswick 05837	Nothing Is Forever/Two Wrongs Don't Make A Right (78 rpm = £15)	5

GERRY BECKLES
61	Oriole CB 1906	No Love For Johnnie/Come Back Running	6

BEDASSE & CHIN'S CALYPSO QUINTET
55	Kalypso C 1003	Industrial Fair/Samson & Delilah	25
56	Kalypso C 1008	Big Bog & Teacher/Red Tomato	10
58	Kalypso XX 01	Walk & Talk/Night Food	15

DAVID BEDFORD
70	Argo ZRG 638	MUSIC FOR ALBION MOONLIGHT (LP, 1 side by Elizabeth Lutyens)	25
72	Dandelion 2310 165	NURSE'S SONG WITH ELEPHANTS (LP, gatefold sleeve)	25

(see also Coxhill/Bedford Trio, Kevin Ayers & Whole World, Mike Oldfield)

BEDLAM
73	Chrysalis CFB 1	I Believe In You/Whiskey And Wine.	8
73	Chrysalis CHR 1048	BEDLAM (LP).	25

(see also Cozy Powell, Ace Kefford Stand, Big Bertha)

BEDROCKS
68	Columbia DB 8516	Ob-La-Di, Ob-La-Da/Lucy	5

EDWIN BEE
68	Decca F 12781	I've Been Loving You/Call For My Baby	12

MOLLY BEE
57	London HLD 8400	Since I Met You, Baby/I'll Be Waiting For You (78 rpm = £15)	40
58	Capitol CL 14849	Going Steady (With A Dream)/Magic Mirror.	10
58	Capitol CL 14880	Don't Look Back/Please Don't Talk About Me When I'm Gone	7
58	Capitol CL 14949	After You've Gone/Five Points Of A Star	7
65	MGM MGM 1280	Single Girl Again/Keep It A Secret.	10

BEE BEE CEE
77	Rel RE 48-S	You Gotta Know Girl/We Ain't Listening (p/s, 2,000 only)	70

JOHNNY BEECHER
63	Warner Bros WB89	Sax Fifth Avenue/Jack Sax The City	10

BEEFEATERS
64	Pye International 7N 25277	Please Let Me Love You/Don't Be Long	120
70	Elektra 2101 007	Please Let Me Love You/Don't Be Long (reissue)	30

(see also Byrds)

BEE GEES
67	Polydor 56727	Spicks And Specks/I Am The World	12
67	Polydor 56161	New York Mining Disaster 1941/I Can't See Nobody	7
67	Polydor 56178	To Love Somebody/Close Another Door	6
67	Polydor 56192	Massachusetts/Barker Of The U.F.O.	6
67	Polydor 56220	World/Sir Geoffrey Saved The World	5
68	Polydor 56229	Words/Sinking Ships	5
68	Polydor 56242	Jumbo/The Singer Sang His Song	5
68	Polydor 56273	I've Gotta Get A Message To You/Kitty Can	5
69	Polydor 56304	Odessa Parts 1 & 2 (unissued)	

BEE GEES

69	Polydor 56304	First Of May/Lamplight	5
69	Polydor 56331	Tomorrow Tomorrow/Sun In The Morning	5
69	Polydor 56343	Don't Forget To Remember/The Lord	5
70	Polydor 56377	I.O.I.O./Sweetheart.	5
70	Polydor 2001 104	Lonely Days/Man For All Seasons	5
71	Polydor 2058 115	How Can You Mend A Broken Heart/Country Woman.	5
77	RSO 2090224	Children Of The World/Boogie Child.	5
67	Polydor 582/583 012	BEE GEES FIRST (LP)	5
68	Polydor 582/583 020	HORIZONTAL (LP).	25
68	Polydor 236 221	RARE PRECIOUS AND BEAUTIFUL (LP)	20
68	Polydor 236 513	RARE PRECIOUS AND BEAUTIFUL VOL. 2 (LP)	20
68	Polydor 582/583 036	IDEA (LP)	20
69	Polydor 236 556	RARE PRECIOUS AND BEAUTIFUL VOL. 3 (LP)	20
69	Polydor 582 049/050	ODESSA (2-LP, felt cover)	40
70	Polydor 2383 010	CUCUMBER CASTLE (LP)	18
70	Polydor 2310 069	TWO YEARS ON (LP)	18
71	Polydor 2383 052	TRAFALGAR (LP)	18
72	Polydor 2383 139	TO WHOM IT MAY CONCERN (LP)	15

(see also Barry Gibb, Robin Gibb, Maurice Gibb, Humpy Bong, Fut)

BEEKEEPERS
81	Rundown ACE 40	PLATFORM FIVE EP	10

MARK BEER
81	My China TAO 001	DUST ON THE ROAD (LP)	15

BEES (UK)
01	We Love You ARMOUR 120	YOU GOT TO LEAVE EP (p/s, 500 only)	8

BEES UK)
67	Blue Beat BB 386	Jesse James Rides Again/The Girl In My Dreams.	18
68	Columbia Blue Beat DB 111	The Prisoner From Alcatraz/The Ska's The Limit	12

BEES MAKE HONEY
73	EMI EMI 2078	Knee Trembler/Caldonia.	5
72	EMI EMC 3013	MUSIC EVERY NIGHT (LP)	20

BILLY BEETHOVEN
75	DJM DJS 10377	Dreams (Out In The Forest)/We're Free	100

(see also Graham Bonnet)

BEEZ
79	Edible SNACK 001	Easy/Vagrant (gatefold p/s)	65
78	Edible SNACK 002	THE BEEZ EP: Do The Suicide (no p/s)	65

B.E.F. (British Electric Foundation)
91	Ten TEN 386	Free (Edit)/Secret Life Of Arabia (stickered p/s, as B.E.F. featuring Billy MacKenzie, unissued, 200 copies only)	50
80	Virgin V 2888	MUSIC FOR STOWAWAYS (cassette)	12
80	Virgin V 2888	MUSIC FOR STOWAWAYS (LP, unissued, white label test pressing with press release)	30
81	Virgin BEF 1	MUSIC FOR LISTENING TO (LP, export issue).	12
82	Virgin VV 2219	MUSIC OF QUALITY & DISTINCTION VOL. 1 (5 x 7" box set & insert)	12

(see also Heaven 17, Billy MacKenzie)

SI BEGG
97	Mosquito MSQ 010	WORKING ON THE FRONT LINE EP (12")	20
00	Mosquito MSQ 016	BAD DOO DOO (mini-LP)	15

SI BEGG MEETS NEIL LANDSTRUMM
01	Mosquito MSQ 017	TOKYO ASSASSIN (12" EP)	10

BEGGARS FARM
84	White Rabbit WR 1001	THE DEPTH OF A DREAM (LP)	25

BEGGARS HILL
76	Moonshine MS 60	BEGGARS HILL (LP, private pressing)	150

BEGGARS OPERA
70	Vertigo 6059 026	Sarabande/Think	18
72	Vertigo 6059 060	Hobo/Pathfinder	12
73	Vertigo 6059 088	Two Timing Woman/Lady Of Hell Fire	8
74	Vertigo 6059 105	Classical Gas/Sweet Blossom Woman	6
70	Vertigo 6360 018	ACT ONE (LP, swirl label, gatefold sleeve).	35
71	Vertigo 6360 054	WATERS OF CHANGE (LP, swirl label, gatefold sleeve)	45
72	Vertigo 6360 073	PATHFINDER (LP, swirl label, foldout poster cover)	40
73	Vertigo 6360 090	GET YOUR DOG OFF ME! (LP, 'spaceship' label)	15

BEGINNING OF THE END
71	Atlantic 2091 097	Funky Nassau Parts 1 & 2 (initially red label)	15/10
71	Atlantic K 40304	FUNKY NASSAU (LP, gatefold sleeve)	40

BRENDAN BEHAN
60	HMV 7EG 8491	THE HOSTAGE (EP)	15
60	Argo RG 239	THE HOSTAGE (LP)	15

DOMINIC BEHAN
59	Decca F 11147	The Bells Of Hell/The Captains And The Kings (78 rpm = £8)	5
60	Topic STOP 115	The Patriot Game/Erin Go Brath (p/s).	5
64	Piccadilly 7N 35172	Liverpool Lou/Love Is Where You Find It	5
65	Piccadilly 7N 35238	Arkle/Lonely Days.	6
68	Major Minor MM 575	Wormwood Scrubs/Rifles Of The IRA.	8
58	Collector JEL 3	SONGS OF THE STREETS (EP).	18
60	Topic 12T 35	DOWN BY THE LIFFEYSIDE – IRISH STREET BALLADS (LP)	18

61	Topic 12T 44	EASTER WEEK AND AFTER — SONGS OF "THE TROUBLES" (LP)	18
66	Pye NPL 18134	IRELAND SINGS (LP)	15
69	Marble Arch MAL 1123	ARKLE (LP)	20

(see also Ewan MacColl)

BIX BEIDERBECKE & HIS GANG
60	Philips JAZ 116	Since My Best Gal Turned Me Down/At The Jazz Band Ball	5
55	Columbia SEG 7523	BIX BEIDERBECKE AND HIS ORCHESTRA (EP)	12
56	Columbia SEG 7577	BIX BEIDERBECKE (EP)	12
55	Columbia 33SL 1035	THE GREAT BIX (10" LP)	25

(HARRY) BELAFONTE
54	HMV 7M 202	Hold 'Em Joe/Suzanne (Every Night When The Sun Goes Down)	7
54	HMV 7M 224	I'm Just A Country Boy/Pretty As A Rainbow	7
55	Capitol CL 14312	Close Your Eyes/I Still Get A Thrill (Thinking Of You)	7
57	HMV POP 308	Banana Boat Song (Day-O)/Jamaica Farewell	7
57	HMV POP 339	Mama Looka Boo Boo/Don't Ever Love Me	7
57	HMV POP 360	Scarlet Ribbons (For Her Hair)/Hold 'Em Joe	7
57	RCA RCA 1007	Island In The Sun/Coconut Woman	5
58	RCA RCA 1033	Judy Drowned/Lucy's Door	5
58	RCA RCA 1035	Lead Man Holler/Haiti Cherie	5
59	RCA RCA 1116	Darlin' Cora/Turn Around (78 rpm = £6)	5
59	RCA RCA 1125	Fifteen/Round The Bay Of Mexico (78 rpm = £8)	5
61	RCA RCA 1247	Hole In The Bucket (with Odetta)/Chickens	6
57	HMV DLP 1147	THE VERSATILE MR. BELAFONTE (10" LP)	20
57	HMV CLP 1122	MARK TWAIN AND OTHER FOLK FAVOURITES (LP)	18
57	RCA RC 24005	BELAFONTE SINGS OF THE CARIBBEAN (10" LP)	20
59	RCA RD 27129	PORGY AND BESS (LP, with Lena Horne)	15
59	RCA SF 5050	BELAFONTE AT CARNEGIE HALL (LP, stereo)	12

(see also Lena Horne)

BELBORN
01	World Serpent WS7 005	Seelenruhe/Phoenix (picture disc)	5

BEL CANTOS
65	R&B MRB 5003	Feel Aw Right Parts 1 & 2	25

BELFAST GYPSIES
66	Island WI 3007	Gloria's Dream/Secret Police	50
77	Sonet SNTF 738	THEM BELFAST GYPSIES (LP)	25

(see also Them, Jackie McAuley, Freaks Of Nature)

ED 'TEX' BELIN
63	Starlite STEP 39	ED 'TEX' BELIN (EP)	12

ALEXANDER BELL
67	CBS 2977	Alexander Bell Believes/Hymn ... With Love	10

ARCHIE BELL & THE DRELLS
68	Atlantic 584 185	Tighten Up/Dog Eat Dog	15
68	Atlantic 584 217	I Can't Stop Dancing/You're Such A Beautiful Child	12
71	Atlantic 2091 156	Tighten Up/I Can't Stop Dancing/(There's Gonna Be A) Showdown	8
72	Atlantic K 10210	Here I Go Again/A World Without Music	8
73	Atlantic K 10263	There's Gonna Be A Showdown/Tighten Up	6
76	Portrait TA 7254	Don't Let Love Get You Down/Where Will You Go When The Party's Over/The Soul City Walk (12")	8
76	Philly int. 4803	Where Will You GO When The Music's Over?/Part 2	10
68	Atlantic	TIGHTEN UP (LP)	50
72	Atlantic K 40454	HERE I GO AGAIN (LP)	20

BELINDA BELL
73	Columbia DB 8995	If Only You Believe/Stone Valley	5
73	Columbia SCXA 9255	STONE VALLEY (LP, gatefold sleeve)	16
73	One Up OU 2009	MUSIC OF W. GULGOWSKI (LP)	12

BENNY BELL & BLOCK BUSTERS
57	Parlophone R 4372	The Sack Dress/Dr. Jazz	10

CAREY BELL
60s	Delmark DS 622	CAREY BELL'S BLUES HARP (LP)	12

CHARLES BELL & CONTEMPORARY JAZZ QUARTET
63	London HA-K/SH-K 8095	ANOTHER DIMENSION (LP)	25

ERIC BELL BAND
81	Hobo HOS 016	Lonely Man/Anyone Seen My Baby (p/s)	30

(see also Thin Lizzy, Noel Redding Band)

FREDDIE BELL & BELLBOYS
56	Mercury MT 122	Giddy-Up-A Ding Dong/I Said It And I'm Glad (78)	10
57	Mercury MT 141	Hucklebuck/Rompin' And Stompin' (78)	12
57	Mercury MT 146	Teach You To Rock/Take The First Train Out Of Town (78)	12
57	Mercury MT 149	Big Bad Wolf/Rockin' The Polonaise (78)	15
57	Mercury MT 159	Rockin' Is My Business/You're Gonna Be Sorry (78)	20
56	Mercury MEP 9508	ROCK WITH THE BELL BOYS (EP)	35
57	Mercury MEP 9512	ROCK WITH THE BELL BOYS VOL. 2 (EP)	60

FREDRICK BELL
68	Nu Beat NB 004	Rocksteady Cool/CARLTON ALPHONSO: I Have Changed	20

GARY BELL
67	CBS 202234	Is This What I Get For Loving You?/To Keep You	15
67	CBS 2646	Anyway That You Want Me/Leave It To Me	10

MINT VALUE £

GRAHAM BELL
66	Polydor 56067	How Can I Say I Don't Love You/If You're Gonna Go	10
72	Charisma CB 201	Too Many People/Before You're A Man	5
73	Charisma CB 209	You Need A 60 Minute Man/The Whole Town Wants You Hung	5
75	Charisma CB 250	You Need A 60 Minute Man/That's The Way It Is	5

(see also Heavy Jelly, Griffin, Every Which Way, Skip Bifferty, Bell & Arc)

MADELINE BELL
63	HMV POP 1215	I Long For Your Love/Because You Didn't Care	10
64	Columbia DB 7257	You Don't Love Me No More/Don't Cross Over To My Side Of The Street	20
65	Columbia DB 7512	Daytime/Don't Cry My Heart	10
65	Philips BF 1448	What The World Needs Now Is Love/I Can't Wait To See My Baby's Face	20
66	Philips BF 1501	Don't Come Running To Me/I Got Carried Away	20
66	Philips BF 1526	One Step At A Time/You Won't See Me	10
67	Philips BF 1611	Picture Me Gone/Go Ahead On	40
68	Philips BF 1656	I'm Gonna Make You Love Me/I'm Gonna Leave You	10
68	Philips BF 1688	Thinkin'/Don't Give Your Love Away	5
68	Philips BF 1726	Hold It/What Am I Supposed To Do?	5
69	Philips BF 1799	We're So Much In Love/How Much Do I Love You	5
71	Philips 6006 082	If You Didn't Hear Me The First Time/You Walked Away	5
67	Philips (S)BL 7818	BELLS A POPPIN' (LP)	40
68	Philips SBL 7865	DOIN' THINGS (LP)	35
75	Pye NSPL 18483	THIS IS ONE GIRL	18

(see also Seven Ages Of Man, Underground, Ian Green [Revelation])

PADDIE BELL
65	Parlophone R5361	Everytime/The Rose And The Thorn	7

SIMON BELL
78	Pye 7N 46050	Givin' It Plenty/Love Like Lightning	8

WILLIAM BELL
67	Atlantic 584 076	Never Like This Before/Soldier's Goodbye	10
69	Atlantic 584 259	Everyday Will Be Like A Holiday/Ain't Got No Girl	8
67	Stax 601 019	Eloise (Hang On In There)/One Plus One	8
68	Stax 601 038	A Tribute To A King/Every Man Oughta Have A Woman	8
69	Stax STAX 110	I Forgot To Be Your Lover/Bring The Curtain Down	8
69	Stax STAX 121	My Whole World Is Falling Down/All God's Children Got Soul	25
69	Stax STAX 128	Happy/Johnny I Love You	40
69	Atco 228 003	A TRIBUTE TO A KING (LP)	30
69	Stax SXATS 1016	BOUND TO HAPPEN (LP)	20
71	Stax 2362 009	WOW . . . WILLIAM BELL (LP)	20
72	Stax 2362 027	PHASES OF REALITY (LP)	25

(see also Judy Clay & William Bell)

BELLA & ME
67	Columbia DB 8243	Whatever Happened To The Seven Day Week/Help Me Break This Habit	12

GEORGE BELLAMY
65	Parlophone R 5282	Where I'm Bound/How Could I Ever	25
72	Chapter One CH 167	Maman/Come To The Party	7

(see also Tornados)

PETER BELLAMY
68	Argo	MAINLY NORFOLK (LP)	25
69	Xtra XTRA 1075	FAIR ENGLAND'S SHORE (LP)	35
69	Topic 12T 200	THE FOX JUMPS OVER THE PARSON'S GATE (LP, blue label)	20
70	Argo ZFB 11	OAK, ASH AND THORN (LP)	25
72	Argo ZFB 37	WON'T YOU GO MY WAY (LP)	20
72	Argo ZFB 81	MERLIN'S ISLE OF GRAMARYE (LP)	20
74	Trailer LER 2089	TELL IT LIKE IT IS (LP)	15
83	Fellside FE 032	PETER BELLAMY WITH FRIENDS: KEEP ON KIPLING (LP)	12

(see also Young Tradition)

BELL & ARC
71	Charisma CB 170	She Belongs To Me/Dawn	6
71	Charisma CAS 1053	BELL & ARC (LP, gatefold sleeve)	25

(see also Skip Bifferty, Arc, Every Which Way, Graham Bell)

BELL BROTHERS
68	Action ACT 4510	Tell Him No/Throw Away The Key	15

BELLE & SEBASTIAN
97	Jeepster JPR 7001	Dog On Wheels/The State I Am In (p/s, 1,000 only)	8
97	Jeepster JPR 7003	A Century Of Fakers/Le Pastie De La Bourgeoisie (p/s)	8
96	Elektric Honey EHRLP 5	TIGERMILK (LP, 1,000 only)	100

(see also Amphetameanies)

BELLES
70	President PT 311	Don't Pretend/Words Can't Explain	20

BELLFIELD
73	Downtown DT 514	Sugar Plum/Sugar Plum Dub	6

BELL NOTES
59	Top Rank JAR 102	I've Had It/Be Mine (78 rpm = £15)	15
59	Top Rank JAR 147	Old Spanish Town/She Went That-A-Way (78 rpm = £15)	12
59	Top Rank JAR 201	That's Right/Betty Dear	20

BELLS OF JOY
55	Vogue V 2357	I'm Gonna Press On/How Sweet It Is (78)	10

BELL SOUNDS
59	HMV POP 685	Marching Guitars/Chloe	8

LOUIS BELLSON (ALL STARS/QUINTET/BAND/OCTET)
53	Capitol LC 6568	JUST JAZZ (LP)	15
57	Columbia Clef C 9040	DRUMORAMA (10" LP)	15
58	Columbia Clef CX 10142	AT THE FLAMINGO (LP)	15
59	HMV CLP 1343	THE BRILLIANT BELLSON SOUND (LP)	15
61	Columbia SCX 3418	AROUND THE WORLD IN PERCUSSION (LP)	15
66	HMV CLP/CSD 3558	THUNDERBIRD (LP)	15
70	Pye NSPL 18349	LOUIE IN LONDON (LP, as Louie Bellson)	15
72	Parlophone PCS 7151	CONVERSATIONS (LP)	15

(see also Duke Ellington)

BELL-TONES
62	Columbia DB 4848	Selina/Did You Ever See A Dream Walking?	10

TONY BELLUS
59	London HL 8933	Robbin' The Cradle/Valentine Girl (78 rpm = £20)	50

BELLY
92	4AD AD 2018	Gepetto/Sexy S (p/s, with 2 postcards, 2,000 only)	6
93	4AD AD 3001	Feed The Tree/Dream On Me (p/s, with 2 postcards)	6
95	4AD CADD 5004CD	KING (CD, with A5 book pack)	18

(see also Throwing Muses)

BELMONTS
61	Pye International 7N 25094	Tell Me Why/Smoke From Your Cigarette	45
62	Stateside SS 128	Come On Little Angel/How About Me?	30

(see also Dion & Belmonts)

BELOVED
86	Flim Flam HARP 2	A Hundred Words (Radio Mix)/Slow Drowning (freebie)	5
86	Flim Flam HARP 3	This Means War/If Only (p/s)	5
87	Flim Flam HARP 5T	HAPPY NOW: A Kiss Goodbye/If Pennies Came/Righteous Me (12", p/s)	8
87	Flim Flam HARP 7ET	Forever Dancing/Forever Dancing (Remix)/Surprise Me (12", p/s)	8
88	WEA YZ 311T	Loving Feeling (Feeling Lovely Mix)/Acid Love (Love & Ecstasy Mix) (12", p/s)	8

BELT & BRACES ROADSHOW BAND
75	Belt & Braces Roadshow	BELT & BRACES ROADSHOW BAND (LP, with lyric sheet)	15

BELTONES
68	Trojan TR 628	No More Heartaches/I'll Follow You	18
69	Duke DU 17	Home Without You/Why Pretend	6
69	High Note HS 017	Mary Mary/Going Away	8
69	High Note HS 023	A Broken Heart/AFROTONES: All For One	10
72	Ackee ACK 150	Wrapped Up In Love/SOUND DIMENSION: Pasero	10

(see Bop & Beltones, Trevor Shield)

JOHN BELTRAN
96	Peacefrog PF 049	TEN DAYS OF BLUE (2-LP)	18

JESSE BELVIN
59	RCA RCA 1119	Guess Who/Funny (78 rpm = £8)	20

BEN
71	Vertigo 6360 052	BEN (LP, gatefold sleeve, swirl label)	350

PAT BENATAR
79	Chrysalis CHS 2373	If You Think You Know How To Love Me/So Sincere (p/s)	5
80	Chrysalis CHS 2403	We Live For Love/I Need A Lover (p/s)	5
81	Chrysalis CHSP 2529	Fire And Ice/Hard To Believe (picture disc)	5
83	Chrysalis CHSP 2662	Shadows Of The Night/The Victim (shaped picture disc)	5
84	Chrysalis CHSP 2747	Love Is A Battlefield/Hell Is For Children (live) (picture disc)	5
85	Chrysalis PATP 2	Shadows Of The Night/Hit Me With Your Best Shot (shaped pic disc & plinth)	5

STEVE BENBOW
65	Columbia DB 7691	The Gallows Pole/I Can't Tell	5
68	L'gue Against Cruel Sports	Tattered Doll (mail-order only)	6
59	Collector	STEVE BENBOW AND THE FOLK FOUR (EP)	12
62	HMV CLP 1603	STEVE BENBOW SINGS (LP)	18
63	HMV CLP 1687	I TRAVEL THE WORLD (LP)	15
67	Decca LK/SKL 4881	OF SITUATIONS AND PREDICAMENTS (LP)	15

RALF BENDIX & LITTLE ELIZABETH
65	Columbia DB 7774	Sag Mir Deine Sorgen/Baby Sittin' Boogie	8

BENNY BENGIMAN
81	Negus Roots NERT 010	Health And Sorrow/Love A Dub Song	25

BENNY BENNETT
50s	Seeco LDS 024	BENNY BENNETT AND HIS ORCHESTRA (LP)	15

BOBBY BENNETT (U.K.)
67	CBS 202511	Just Say Goodbye/She Believes In Me	6
68	Columbia DB 8435	All My Life Is You/To Give (The Reason I Live)	6
69	Columbia DB 8532	Music Mother Made/You're Ready Now	40

BOBBY BENNETT (U.S.)
69	London HL 10274	Big New York/Baby, Try Me	15

BOYD BENNETT & HIS ROCKETS (WITH BIG MOE)
SINGLES
55	Parlophone MSP 6161	Everlovin'/Boogie At Midnight (with Big Moe) (78 rpm = £40)	340
55	Parlophone MSP 6180	Seventeen/Little Ole You-All (as Boyd Bennett & His Rockets) (78 rpm = £25)	275
56	Parlophone MSP 6203	My Boy — Flat Top/Banjo Rock And Roll (with Big Moe) (78 rpm = £25)	350
56	Parlophone MSP 6233	Blue Suede Shoes/Oo-Oo-Oo (with Big Moe) (78 rpm = £25)	300

Boyd BENNETT & HIS ROCKETS

56	Parlophone R 4214	The Groovy Age/Hit That Jive, Jack	
		(as Big Moe with Boyd Bennett & His Rockets) (78 rpm = £25)	300
56	Parlophone R 4252	The Most/Rockin' Up A Storm (as Boyd Bennett & His Rockets) (78 rpm = £25+) . .	300
58	Parlophone R 4423	Click Clack/Move (as Boyd Bennett & His Rockets) (78 rpm = £30+)	275
59	Mercury AMT 1031	Tear It Up/Tight Tights (as Big Moe & His Orchestra) (78 rpm = £35+)	100

(see also Moon Mullican)

BRIAN BENNETT

67	Columbia DB 8294	Canvas/Slippery Jim De Grize	20
74	Fontana 6007 040	Chase Side Shoot-Up/Pegasus	20
76	DJM DJS 10714	Thunderbolt/Clearing Skies (promos in p/s)	12/5
77	DJM DJS 10756	Saturday Night Special/Farewell To A Friend (promos in p/s)	12/5
77	DJM DJS 10791	The Girls Back Home/Jonty Jump (as the Brian Bennett Band)	10
78	DJM DJS 10843	Pendulum Force/Ocean Glide	5
82	DJM DJS 10981	Top Of The World/Soul Ice	8
67	Columbia S(C)X 6144	CHANGE OF DIRECTION (LP)	50
69	Col. Studio Two TWO 268	THE ILLUSTRATED LONDON NOISE (LP)	60
77	DJM DJF 20499	ROCK DREAMS (LP, as the Brian Bennett Band)	18
78	DJM DJF 20532	VOYAGE (LP)	20

(see also Shadows, Thunder Company, Wasp, Marty Wilde, Krewcats, Collage, Alan Skidmore, Big Jim Sullivan, Heat Exchange, Julian [Scott])

BRUCE BENNETT

71	Big BG 311	If You Don't Mind/Lenore (both actually by Dobby Dobson)	7

CAROLE BENNETT

56	Capitol CL 14652	The Little Magician/I Was Your Only Love	5
57	Capitol CL 14692	Play The Music/Miser's Gold	15
57	Capitol CL 14725	Haunted Lover/Let The Chips Fall (Where They May)	25

CLIFF BENNETT

69	Parlophone R 5792	Memphis Streets/But I'm Wrong	

CLIFF BENNETT & REBEL ROUSERS

61	Parlophone R 4793	You've Got What I Like/I'm In Love With You	40
61	Parlophone R 4836	That's What I Said/When I Get Paid	35
62	Parlophone R 4895	Poor Joe/Hurtin' Inside (Twist)	35
63	Parlophone R 5046	Everybody Loves A Lover/My Old Stand-By	20
63	Parlophone R 5080	You Really Got A Hold On Me/Alright	15
63	Parlophone DP 560	Poor Joe/Hurtin' Inside (Twist) (export issue, black label)	15
63	Parlophone DP 561	When I Get Paid/That's What I Said (export issue, black label)	20
64	Parlophone R 5119	Got My Mojo Working/Beautiful Dreamer	15
64	Parlophone R 5173	One Way Love/Slow Down	7
65	Parlophone R 5229	I'll Take You Home/Do You Love Him?	10
65	Parlophone R 5259	Three Rooms Of Running Water/If Only You'd Reply	25
65	Parlophone R 5317	I Have Cried My Last Tear/As Long As She Looks Like You	7
66	Parlophone R 5406	You Can't Love 'Em All/Need Your Loving Tonight	7
66	Parlophone R 5466	Eyes For You/Hold On I'm Coming	10
66	Parlophone R 5489	Got To Get You Into My Life/Baby Each Day	8
66	Parlophone R 5534	Never Knew Lovin' Could Be So Doggone Good/Don't Help Me Out	6
67	Parlophone R 5565	I'm Sorry/I'll Take Good Care Of You	6
67	Parlophone R 5598	I'll Be There/Use Me	6
63	Parlophone DP 560	Poor Joe/Hurtin' Inside (Twist) (export issue, black label)	20
64	Parlophone DP 561	When I Get Paid/That's What I Said (export issue, black label)	20
65	Parlophone GEP 8923	CLIFF BENNETT AND THE REBEL ROUSERS (EP)	40
65	Parlophone GEP 8936	TRY IT BABY (EP)	35
66	Parlophone GEP 8955	WE'RE GONNA MAKE IT (EP)	50
64	Parlophone PMC 1242	CLIFF BENNETT AND THE REBEL ROUSERS (LP, yellow/black label)	50
66	EMI Regal REG 1039	CLIFF BENNETT (LP, export issue)	25
67	Parlophone PMC/PCS 7017	GOT TO GET YOU INTO OUR LIFE (LP, yellow/black label)	40

CLIFF BENNETT BAND

68	Parlophone R 5666	Take Your Time/House Of A Thousand Dolls	7
68	Parlophone R 5691	You're Breaking Me Up (And I'm Wasting Away)/I Hear Her Voice	12
68	Parlophone R 5711	Lonely Weekends/Good Times	8
68	Parlophone R 5728	One More Heartache/Nobody Runs Forever	15
68	Parlophone R 5749	Back In The USSR/This Man	10
68	Parlophone PMC/PCS 7054	BRANCHES OUT (LP, yellow/black label)	32

CLIFF BENNETT'S REBELLION

71	CBS 7231	Amos Moses/Movin' And Travelin' On	5
71	CBS 64487	CLIFF BENNETT'S REBELLION (LP)	15

(see also Charles Hodges, Rebel Rousers, Toefat, Screaming Lord Sutch & Savages)

DICKIE BENNETT

55	Decca F 10595	There, But For The Grace Of God Go I/Stars Shine In Your Eyes	10
56	Decca F 10697	Dungaree Doll/Can't We Be Partners (After The Dance)	15
56	Decca F 10782	You Don't Know Me/Cry Upon My Shoulder	10

DUSTER BENNETT

68	Blue Horizon 57-3141	It's A Man Down There/Things Are Changing	20
69	Blue Horizon 57-3148	Raining In My Heart/Jumpin' For Joy	15
69	Blue Horizon 57-3154	Bright Lights, Big City/Fresh Country Jam (with His House Band)	20
69	Blue Horizon 57-3164	I'm Gonna Wind Up Endin' Up Or I'm Gonna End Up Windin' Up With You/	
		Rock Of Ages, Cleft For Me	15
70	Blue Horizon 57-3173	I Chose To Sing The Blues/If You Could Hang Your Washing	
		Like You Hang Your Lines	10
70	Blue Horizon 57-3179	Act Nice And Gentle/I Want You To Love Me	10
74	Rak RAK 177	Comin' Home/Pretty Little Thing	15
68	Blue Horizon 7-63208	SMILING LIKE I'M HAPPY (LP, with His House Band, i.e. Fleetwood Mac)	65
69	Blue Horizon 7-63221	BRIGHT LIGHTS... (LP, gatefold sleeve)	80

70	Blue Horizon 7-63868	12 DB's (LP)	45

(see also Fleetwood Mac)

JOE BENNETT & SPARKLETONES
57	HMV POP 399	Black Slacks/Boppin' Rock Boogie (78 rpm = £35)	150
58	HMV POP 445	Rocket/Penny Loafers And Bobby Socks (78 rpm = £45)	175+

JO JO BENNETT
67	Doctor Bird DB 1097	The Lecture/Cantelope Rock (with Fugitives)	40
67	Doctor Bird DB 1116	Rocksteady/Real Gone Loser (with Fugitives)	50
70	Explosion EX 2029	Groovy Jo Jo/Ten Steps To Soul (both actually with Mudie's All Stars)	25
70	Trojan TR 7774	Leaving Rome/In The Nude (both with Mudie's All Stars)	12
71	Moodisc MU 3514	Snowbird/MUDIE'S ALLSTARS: Change The Tide	10
71	Moodisc HME 108	Poison Ivy/MUDIE'S ALLSTARS: Ivy Poison	8
70	Trojan TBL 133	GROOVY JO JO (LP, with Mudie's Allstars)	45

(see also Fugitives, I Roy)

KIM BENNETT
55	Decca F 10449	Softly Softly/ROLAND SHAW ORCHESTRA: Trumpeter's Lullaby	7
55	Decca F 10460	Melody Of Love/Ding Dong	7
55	Decca F 10599	The Kentuckian Song/Overnight	6
56	Decca F 10706	No, Not Much/You Can't Keep Running	6

(see also Roland Shaw)

LEE BENNETT & SUNLINERS
64	Decca F 12024	Poor Bachelor Boy/Fool, Fool, Fool	5

RAY BENNETT
62	Decca F 11550	Go Away Little Girl/Twistin' To The Blues	6
62	Decca DFE 8516	INTRODUCING RAY BENNETT (EP)	40

ROY BENNETT
68	Blue Cat BS 146	I Dangerous/DEE SET: I Know A Place	25

RUDI BENNETT
68	Decca F 12741	I'm So Proud/WHISTLING JACK SMITH: Havah Nagilah	6

(see also Whistling Jack Smith)

TONY BENNETT
53	Columbia SCM 5048	Congratulations To Someone/Take Me	10
54	Columbia 39745	Here In My Heart/I'm Lost Again	10
57	Philips JK 1008	Whatever Lola Wants/Heart (jukebox issue)	20
59	Philips PB 1079	Till/Ask Anyone In Love	5
53	Columbia B 2620	TONY BENNETT SPOTLITE (EP)	10
54	Columbia B 2079	TONY BENNETT (EP)	10
55	Philips BBE 12009	TONY BENNETT (EP)	10
57	Columbia B 2582	ONE FOR MY BABY (EP)	10
58	Philips BBE 12223	TONY BENNETT — PHILIPS TV SERIES (EP)	10
60	Philips BBE 12338	HOMETOWN, MY HOMETOWN (EP)	10
55	Philips BBR 8051	CLOUD 7 (10" LP)	20
56	Philips BBR 8089	THE VOICE OF YOUR CHOICE (10" LP)	20
57	Philips BBL 7138	TONY BENNETT SHOWCASE (LP)	15
57	Philips BBL 7219	THE BEAT OF MY HEART (LP)	15
58	Philips BBL 7219	LONG AGO AND FAR AWAY (LP)	15
60	Philips BBL 7308	IN PERSON! (LP, with Count Basie Orch., with fake audience noise, mono)	15
60	Philips SBBL 542	IN PERSON! (LP, with Count Basie Orch., with fake audience noise, stereo)	15
60	Philips BBL 7413	TO MY WONDERFUL ONE (LP)	15
60	Philips BBL 7452	ALONE TOGETHER (LP)	15
61	Philips BBL 7455	SINGS A STRING OF HAROLD ARLEN (LP, also stereo SBBL 609)	15
61	Philips BBL 7479	TONY SINGS FOR TWO (LP)	15
61	Philips BBL 7495	MY HEART SINGS (LP)	15

(see also Count Basie, John Barry)

VAL BENNETT
68	Island WI 3113	Jumping With Mr. Lee/ROY SHIRLEY: Keep Your Eyes On The Road	45
68	Island WI 3146	The Russians Are Coming (Take Five)/LESTER STERLING: Sir Lee's Whip	80
68	Trojan TR 611	Spanish Harlem/ROY SHIRLEY: If I Did Know	15
69	Trojan TR 640	Baby Baby/Barbara	20
69	Crab CRAB 6	Reggae City/CANNON KING: Mellow Trumpet (B-side actually by Carl 'King Cannon Ball' Bryan)	15
69	Camel CA 24	Midnight Spin/SOUL CATS: Money Money	15

(see also Roy Shirley, Max Romeo, Derrick Morgan, Clancy Eccles, Harry J Allstars, George A Penny, Lloyd Terrell, Uniques, Versatiles)

JOHNNY BENNINGS & HIS RHYTHM & BLUES BAND
54	Esquire 10-376	Third Degree Blues/Timber (78)	25

BENNY & TINA
69	Mercury MF 1133	This Love Is Real/Over My Dead Body	10

BARRY BENSON
66	Parlophone R 5446	Stay A Little While/That's For Sure	30
66	Parlophone R 5484	Not A One Girl Guy/Sunshine Child	5
66	Parlophone R 5544	Always Waitin'/My Friend And I	5
67	Parlophone R 5578	Cousin Jane/Meet Jacqueline	5
67	Page One POF 034	I Can't Wait/Oh No	7

BOBBY BENSON & HIS COMBO
58	Philips PB 854	Taxi Driver, I Don't Care/Gentleman Bobby	10

GARY BENSON
66	Pye 7N 17032	This Man's Got No Luck/I'm So Tired	7
70	Penny Farthing PEN 727	Holly/Oak Tree	6

George BENSON

MINT VALUE £

GEORGE BENSON (QUARTET)
66	CBS (S)BPG 62817	IT'S UPTOWN (LP, as George Benson Quartet)	15
67	CBS (S)BPG 62971	THE GEORGE BENSON COOKBOOK (LP)	15

MARIE BENSON & THE LONDONAIRES
55	Decca F 10452	Mambo Italiano/Mobile	10
55	Philips PB 528	Sooty/Mr. Dumpling (78)	6
57	Philips PB 711	The Jukebox Is Broken/One (78)	6

MICHAEL BENTINE
62	Parlophone PMC 1179	IT'S A SQUARE WORLD (LP, also stereo PCS 3031)	18
62	Parlophone 4927	Football Results/The Astronauts	10
67	RCA Victor RD 7885	SQUARE BASHING (LP)	15
(see also Goons)			

BRIAN BENTLEY & THE BACHELORS
60	Philips PB 1085	Wishing Well/Please Make Up Your Mind	20
60	Philips PB 1086	First Flight East/Sunday Break	5
62	Salvo SLO 1813	Caramba/Nellie Dean (99 copies only)	20

JAY BENTLEY & THE JET SET
64	Vocalion VN 9230	Watusi '64/I'll Get You	10

BENTLEY BROTHERS
59	Top Rank JAR 208	Ma (She's Making Eyes At Me)/Yes, We Have No Bananas	5

BROOK BENTON
58	RCA RCA 1044	A Million Miles From Nowhere/Devoted (78 rpm = £12)	25
58	Mercury AMT 1014	It's Just A Matter Of Time/Hurtin' Inside (78 rpm = £12)	5
59	Mercury AMT 1043	Endlessly/So Close (78 rpm = £10)	5
59	Mercury AMT 1061	Thank You Pretty Baby/With All Of My Heart	10
59	Mercury AMT 1068	So Many Ways/I Want You Forever	7
60	Mercury AMT 1097	The Ties That Bind/Hither And Thither And Yon	5
60	Mercury AMT 1109	Kiddio/The Same One	10
60	Mercury AMT 1121	Fools Rush In/Somebody You'll Want Me To Want You	7
61	Mercury AMT 1134	For My Baby/Think Twice	5
61	Mercury AMT 1148	The Boll Weevil Song/Your Eyes	6
61	Mercury AMT 1157	Frankie And Johnny/It's Just A House Without You	7
61	Mercury AMT 1168	Revenge/Really Really	5
62	Mercury AMT 1172	Walk On The Wild Side/Somewhere In The Used To Be	10
62	Mercury AMT 1178	Hit Record/Thanks To The Fool	10
62	Mercury AMT 1187	Lie To Me/The Touch Of Your Hand	5
62	Mercury AMT 1194	Hotel Happiness/Still Waters Run Deep	6
62	Mercury AMT 1203	I Got What I Wanted/Dearer Than Life	5
63	Mercury AMT 1208	My True Confession/Tender Years	5
63	Mercury AMT 1212	Two Tickets To Paradise/Don't Hate Me	10
63	Mercury AMT 1217	Baby You Got It Made/Stop Foolin' (with Damita Jo)	10
64	Mercury MF 806	Going Going Gone/After Midnight	5
64	Mercury MF 822	Too Late To Turn Back Now/Another Cup Of Coffee	5
64	Mercury MF 828	A House Is Not A Home/Come On Back	5
64	Mercury MF 842	Do It Right/Please, Please Make It Easy	5
68	Atlantic 584 222	Do Your Own Thing/I Just Don't Know What To Do With Myself	5
69	Atlantic 584 266	Touch 'Em With Love/She Knows What To Do For Me	5
69	Atlantic 584 267	Nothing Can Take The Place Of You/Woman Without Love	5
58	RCA RCX 169	BROOK BENTON (EP, tri centre)	40
58	Fontana TFE 17151	BROOK BENTON AT HIS BEST (EP)	22
59	Mercury ZEP 10023	THE CARESSING VOICE OF BROOK BENTON (EP)	15
60	Mercury ZEP 10046	MAKE A DATE WITH BROOK BENTON (EP)	15
60	Mercury ZEP 10076	I'M IN THE MOOD FOR LOVE (EP)	15
60	Mercury ZEP 10091	WHEN I FALL IN LOVE (EP, also stereo [SEZ 19009])	10/12
61	Mercury ZEP 10107	WHEN YOU'RE IN LOVE (EP, also stereo [SEZ 19019])	10/12
61	Mercury ZEP 10125	SO WARM (EP, also stereo [SEZ 19024])	10/12
58	Mercury MMC 14015	IT'S JUST A MATTER OF TIME (LP)	20
59	Mercury MMC 14022	ENDLESSLY (LP)	20
60	Mercury MMC 14042	I LOVE YOU IN SO MANY WAYS (LP)	20
60	Mercury MMC 14060	SONGS I LOVE TO SING (LP, also stereo [CMS 18041])	16/20
61	Mercury MMC 14090	THE BOLL WEEVIL SONG (LP, also stereo [CMS 18060])	16/20
61	Mercury MMC 14108	THERE GOES THAT SONG AGAIN (LP, also stereo [CMS 18068])	16/20
62	Mercury MMC 14124	GOLDEN HITS (LP)	15
62	Mercury 20024 MCL	BORN TO SING THE BLUES (LP)	15
63	Mercury 20040 MCL	IT'S JUST A MATTER OF TIME (LP)	15

BROOK BENTON & DINAH WASHINGTON
60	Mercury AMT 1083	Baby (You've Got What It Takes)/I Do	25
60	Mercury AMT 1099	A Rockin' Good Way/I Believe	15
69	Mercury MF 1100	A Rockin' Good Way/I Do	5
61	Mercury ZEP 10120	A ROCKING GOOD WAY (EP, also stereo SEZ 19022)	25
64	Mercury 20069 MCL	THE TWO OF US (LP)	25

STEVE BERESFORD
75	Incus INCUS 15	TEATIME (LP)	50

BERETS
70	Avant Garde AVS 116	THE MASS FOR PEACE (LP, with insert)	25

INGRID BERGMAN
56	Brunswick OE 9252	THE PIED PIPER OF HAMELIN (EP, tri-centre)	10

BERKELEY KITES
68	Polydor 56742	Hang Up City/Mary-Go-Round	8
69	Polydor 56770	Alice In Wonderland/What Goes Up Must Come Down	8

JUSTIN BERKOVI
97	Mosquito MSQ 07	CROUTON EP (12").. 8

MILTON BERLE
56	Vogue Coral Q 72197	In The Middle Of The House/Buffalo............................... 10

BERLIN RITZ
80	Big Muff BM 001	Crazy Nights/You're Where I Belong (no p/s)...................... 50

BERMUDAS
64	London HLN 9894	Donnie/Chu Sen Ling.. 20

BERNADETTE
67	Rim RIM 2	Come Kiss Me Love/Let Me Do The Talking........................ 15
68	Philips 1725	Toys, Toys, Toys/Kiss And Run Away.............................. 6

KENNY BERNARD (& WRANGLERS)
65	Pye 7N 15920	The Tracker/You Gotta Give (with Wranglers)..................... 20
66	Pye 7N 17131	Nothing Can Change This Love/What Love Brings.................. 75
67	Pye 7N 17233	Ain't No Soul (Left In These Old Shoes)/Hey Woman.............. 50
67	CBS 2936	Somebody/Pity My Feet... 100
68	CBS 3860	Victim Of Perfume And Lace/A Change Is Gonna Come 20

(see also Kenny & Wranglers, Wranglers, Cat's Pyjamas)

KENNY BERNARD
70s	Pye Disco Demand DDS 2004	What Love Brings/LEON YOUNG STRINGS: Glad All Over (company sleeve)..... 8

ROD BERNARD
59	London HLM 8849	This Should Go On Forever/Pardon, Mr. Gordon (78 rpm = £18)... 30
59	Mercury AMT 1070	One More Chance/Shedding Teardrops Over You................. 15

BERNIE & BUZZ BAND
68	Decca F 22829	The House That Jack Built/PETE KELLY'S SOULUTION: Midnight Confessions (export issue)............................ 18
68	Deram DM 181	When Something's Wrong With My Baby/Don't Knock It.......... 35

(see also Pete Kelly's Soulution)

ELMER BERNSTEIN
56	Brunswick 05544	Clark Street Parts 1 & 2 (gold or silver print on label)..................... 10/5
63	MGM MGM 1238	Rat Race/Saints & Sinners....................................... 20
66	United Artists UP 1163	The Magnificent Seven/Return Of The Seven 10
60	Capitol EAP1 1287	STACCATO (EP)... 10
56	Brunswick LAT 8101	THE MAN WITH THE GOLDEN ARM (LP, soundtrack) 25
57	Brunswick LAT 8195	SWEET SMELL OF SUCCESS (LP, soundtrack)................... 25
57	London HA-P 2076	MEN IN WAR (LP, soundtrack) 75
58	London HA-D 2074/5	THE TEN COMMANDMENTS (2-LP, soundtrack) 40
58	London HA-D 2111	DESIRE UNDER THE ELMS (LP, soundtrack)..................... 25
58	London HA-T 2125	GOD'S LITTLE ACRE (LP, soundtrack)............................ 30
58	Capitol LCT 6165	KINGS GO FORTH (LP, soundtrack)............................... 15
59	Capitol LCT 6180	SOME CAME RUNNING (LP, soundtrack)......................... 25
62	MGM MGM-C 891	WALK ON THE WILD SIDE (LP, soundtrack) 20
63	MGM MGM-C 934	TO KILL A MOCKINGBIRD (LP, soundtrack)....................... 15
63	United Artists ULP 1041	THE GREAT ESCAPE (LP, soundtrack, mono/stereo).............. 20
64	MGM MGM-C 984	THE CARPETBAGGERS (LP, soundtrack) 15
64	London HA-A/SH-A 8219	THE CARPETBAGGERS (LP, soundtrack) 15
65	CBS (S)BPG 62558	THE SONS OF KATIE ELDER (LP, soundtrack, feat. Johnny Cash) 30/40
65	United Artists SULP 1106	THE HALLELUJAH TRAIL (LP, soundtrack) 15
66	United Artists (S)ULP 1140	CAST A GIANT SHADOW (LP, soundtrack, feat. Vince Hill) 15
67	United Artists (S)ULP 1156	RETURN OF THE SEVEN (LP, soundtrack)......................... 15
67	RCA Victor RD 7792	THE SILENCERS (LP, soundtrack, feat. Vikki Carr) 45
67	Fontana TL 5306	BABY, THE RAIN MUST FALL (LP, soundtrack).................... 40
68	United Artists (S)ULP 1190	THE SCALPHUNTERS (LP, soundtrack)............................ 15
69	Paramount SPFL 254	WHERE'S JACK? (LP, soundtrack, feat. Mary Hopkin)............ 12
70	Capitol E-ST 263	TRUE GRIT (LP, soundtrack, feat. Glen Campbell) 20
74	Philips 9299 225	GOLD (LP, soundtrack)... 15

CHUCK BERRY

78s
56	London HLU 8275	Down Bound Train/No Money Down (gold label)................... 70
57	London HLN 8375	You Can't Catch Me/Havana Moon (gold label) 40
57	London HLU 8428	Roll Over Beethoven/Drifting Heart 40
57	Columbia DB 3951	School Day (Ring! Ring! Goes The Bell)/Deep Feeling 30
57	London HLM 8531	Rock And Roll Music/Blue Feeling 45
58	London HLM 8585	Sweet Little Sixteen/Reelin' And Rockin'......................... 35
58	London HLM 8629	Johnny B. Goode/Around And Around 40
58	London HL 8677	Beautiful Delilah/Vacation Time 45
58	London HL 7055	Carol/Hey Pedro (export single) 50
58	London HL 8712	Carol/Hey Pedro 40
58	London HLM 8767	Sweet Little Rock And Roller/Jo Jo Gunne .... 45+
59	London HLM 8853	Almost Grown/Little Queenie .... 75+
59	London HLM 8921	Back In The U.S.A./Memphis, Tennessee......................... 75+

SINGLES
56	London HLU 8275	No Money Down/Down Bound Train (silver lettering on label, triangular or round centre) 400/250
57	London HLN 8375	You Can't Catch Me/Havana Moon (gold lettering on label, later silver) 325/165
57	London HLU 8428	Roll Over Beethoven/Drifting Heart 100
57	Columbia DB 3951	School Day (Ring! Ring! Goes The Bell)/Blue Feeling 100
57	London HLM 8531	Rock And Roll Music/Blue Feeling 100
58	London HLM 8585	Sweet Little Sixteen/Reelin' And Rockin' 40
58	London HLM 8629	Johnny B. Goode/Around And Around............................ 40
58	London HL 8677	Beautiful Delilah/Vacation Time................................. 50

Chuck BERRY

58	London HL 8712	Carol/Hey Pedro	50
58	London HL 7055	Carol/Hey Pedro (export issue)	40
58	London HLM 8767	Sweet Little Rock And Roller/Jo Jo Gunne	30
59	London HLM 8853	Almost Grown/Little Queenie	30
59	London HLM 8921	Back In The U.S.A./Memphis, Tennessee	25

(The above London 45s were originally issued with triangular centres;
later silver top label/round centre pressings are worth half to two-thirds these values.)

60	London HLM 9069	Let It Rock/Too Pooped To Pop	25
60	London HLM 9159	Bye Bye Johnny/Mad Lad	25
61	Pye International 7N 25100	I'm Talkin' 'Bout You/Little Star (blue label, later red/yellow)	25/10
63	Pye International 7N 25209	Go Go Go/Come On	10
63	Pye International 7N 25218	Memphis, Tennessee/Let It Rock	10
63	Pye International 7N 25228	Run Rudolph Run/Johnny B. Goode	10
64	Pye International 7N 25236	Nadine (Is It You?)/O Rangutang	10
64	Pye International 7N 25242	No Particular Place To Go/Liverpool Drive	10
64	Pye International 7N 25257	You Never Can Tell/Brenda Lee	10
64	Pye International 7N 25271	Little Marie/Go Bobby Soxer	10
65	Pye International 7N 25285	The Promised Land/The Things I Used To Do	10
65	Chess CRS 8006	I Got A Booking/Lonely School Days	10
65	Chess CRS 8012	Dear Dad/My Little Lovelight	10
65	Chess CRS 8022	It Wasn't Me/It's My Own Business	10
66	Chess CRS 8037	Ramona Say Yes/Lonely School Days	10
66	Mercury MF 958	Club Nitty Gritty/Laugh And Cry	10
67	Mercury MF 994	Back To Memphis/I Do Really Love You	10
68	Mercury MF 1057	St. Louis To Frisco/Ma Dear	10
69	Mercury MF 1102	Back To Memphis/Roll Over Beethoven	10
68	Chess CRS 8075	Johnny B. Goode/Sweet Little Sixteen	5
69	Chess CRS 8089	No Particular Place To Go/It Wasn't Me	5
72	Chess 6145 007	Rock And Roll Music/Johnny B. Goode/School Days	5
73	Chess 6145 020	Reelin' And Rockin' (Live)/I Will Not Let You Go	5
73	Chess 6145 027	South Of The Border (Live)/Bio	5
75	Chess 6145 038	Shake Rattle And Roll/I'm Just A Name	5
79	Atlantic K 11354	Oh What A Thrill/California	5

EPs

56	London REU 1053	RHYTHM AND BLUES WITH CHUCK BERRY (maroon/gold label, tri-centre)	175
56	London REU 1053	RHYTHM AND BLUES WITH CHUCK BERRY (later pressing, maroon/silver label, round centre)	60
60	London REM 1188	REELIN' AND ROCKIN' (maroon or gold label, tri or round centre)	220/125
63	Pye Intl. NEP 44011	CHUCK BERRY	22
63	Pye Intl. NEP 44013	THIS IS CHUCK BERRY	22
63	Pye Intl. NEP 44018	THE BEST OF CHUCK BERRY	22
64	Pye Intl. NEP 44028	CHUCK BERRY HITS	22
64	Pye Intl. NEP 44033	BLUE MOOD	22
65	Chess CRE 6002	THE PROMISED LAND	32
65	Chess CRE 6005	COME ON	32
66	Chess CRE 6012	I GOT A BOOKING	32
66	Chess CRE 6016	YOU CAME A LONG WAY FROM ST. LOUIS	40

LPs

58	London HA-M 2132	ONE DOZEN BERRYS	150
62	Pye Intl. NPL 28019	NEW JUKE BOX HITS	45
63	Pye Intl. NPL 28024	CHUCK BERRY	25
63	Pye Intl. NPL 28027	CHUCK BERRY ON STAGE	25
63	Pye Intl. NPL 28028	MORE CHUCK BERRY	25
64	Pye Intl. NPL 28031	THE LATEST AND THE GREATEST	25
64	Pye Intl. NPL 28039	YOU NEVER CAN TELL	25
65	Chess CRL 4005	CHUCK BERRY IN LONDON	22
65	Chess CRL 4506	FRESH BERRYS	22
66	Golden Guinea GGL 0352	CHUCK BERRY (reissue of NPL 28024)	15
66	Chess CRL 4548	CHUCK BERRY'S GREATEST HITS	15
67	Mercury 20110 (S)MCL	CHUCK BERRY IN MEMPHIS	15
67	Mercury 20112 (S)MCL	LIVE AT THE FILLMORE AUDITORIUM — SAN FRANCISCO	15
69	Mercury 20162 (S)MCL	CONCERTO IN B. GOODE	15
72	Chess 6310 113	BACK HOME	15
72	Chess 6310 115	SAN FRANCISCO DUES	15
72	Chess 6310 122	THE LONDON CHUCK BERRY SESSIONS	15
72	Philips Int. 6619 008	ST. LOUIE TO FRISCO TO MEMPHIS (2-LP)	20
72	Chess 6641 018	GOLDEN DECADE (2-LP, gatefold sleeve)	15

CHUCK BERRY/BO DIDDLEY

63	Pye Intl. NEP 44009	CHUCK AND BO (EP)	20
63	Pye Intl. NEP 44012	CHUCK AND BO, VOL. 2 (EP)	20
64	Pye Intl. NEP 44017	CHUCK AND BO, VOL. 3 (EP)	25
73	Chess 6145 012	BIG DADDIES (EP)	30
64	Pye Intl. NPL 28047	TWO GREAT GUITARS (LP, mono)	40

(see also Bo Diddley)

DAVE BERRY (& THE CRUISERS)

63	Decca F 11734	Memphis Tennessee/Tossin' & Turnin' (with Cruisers)	10
63	Decca F 11803	My Baby Left Me/Hoochie Coochie Man (B-side with Cruisers)	10
64	Decca F 11876	Baby It's You/Sweet And Lovely	7
64	Decca F 11937	The Crying Game/Don't Gimme No Lip Child	5
64	Decca F 12020	One Heart Between Two/You're Gonna Need Somebody	10
65	Decca F 12103	Little Things/I've Got A Tiger By The Tail	10
65	Decca F 12188	This Strange Effect/Now	10
65	Decca F 12258	I'm Gonna Take You There/Just Don't Know	7
66	Decca F 12337	If You Wait For Love/Hidden	7

MINT VALUE £

66	Decca F 12435	Mama/Walk, Walk, Talk, Talk	10
66	Decca F 12513	Picture Me Gone/Ann	20
67	Decca F 12579	Stranger/Stick By The Book	7
67	Decca F 12651	Forever/And I Have Learned To Dream	10
68	Decca F 12739	Just As Much As Ever/I Got A Feeling	8
68	Decca F 12771	(Do I Figure) In Your Life/Latisha	15
69	Decca F 12905	Oh What A Life (by Dave Berry & Sponge)/Huma Luma	8
70	Decca F 12999	Change Our Minds/Long Walk To D.C.	8
70	Decca F 13080	Chaplin House/Trees	8
72	CBS 7780	Movin' On (Turn Around)/Don't Bring Me Down	7
88	Flagstaff 002	Out Of Time/Serenade To Alice (p/s, 200 only)	8
64	Decca DFE 8601	DAVE BERRY (EP)	25
65	Decca DFE 8625	CAN I GET IT FROM YOU (EP)	30
64	Decca LK 4653	DAVE BERRY (LP)	30
66	Ace Of Clubs ACL 1218	ONE DOZEN BERRIES (LP, also stereo SCL 1218)	20
66	Decca LK 4823	THE SPECIAL SOUND OF DAVE BERRY (LP)	20
68	Decca LK/SKL 4932	DAVE BERRY '68 (LP)	35

(see also Cruisers)

LEN & BARBARA BERRY
| 60s | Greenwich Village GVR 229 | THE PORTWAY PEDDLERS (LP) | 25 |

MIKE BERRY (& THE OUTLAWS)
61	Decca F 11314	Will You Love Me Tomorrow/My Baby Doll (with The Outlaws)	30
61	HMV POP 912	Tribute To Buddy Holly/What's The Matter (with The Outlaws)	12
62	HMV POP 979	It's Just A Matter Of Time/Little Boy Blue	
		(backing group miscredited as Admirals, actually The Outlaws)	10
62	HMV POP 1042	Every Little Kiss/How Many Times	20
62	HMV POP 1105	Don't You Think It's Time/Loneliness (with The Outlaws) (blue or black label)	7/5
63	HMV POP 1142	My Little Baby/You'll Do It, You'll Fall In Love	10
63	HMV POP 1194	It Really Doesn't Matter/Try A Little Bit Harder	18
64	HMV POP 1257	This Little Girl/On My Mind	20
64	HMV POP 1284	Lovesick/Letter Of Love	10
64	HMV POP 1314	Who Will It Be/Talk (with Innocents)	12
64	HMV POP 1362	Two Lovers/Don't Try To Stand In My Way	10
65	HMV POP 1449	That's All I Ever Wanted From You/She Didn't Care	12
65	HMV POP 1494	It Comes And Goes/Gonna Fall In Love	5
66	HMV POP 1530	Warm Baby/Just Thought I'd 'Phone	10
67	Polydor 56182	Raining In My Heart/Eyes	6
72	York SYK 516	Going Down To Virginia/Love Her	10
72	York SYK 530	Drift Away/Keep Your Eyes On The Road	6
63	HMV 7EG 8793	IT'S TIME FOR MIKE BERRY (EP, with Outlaws)	30
63	HMV 7EG 8808	A TRIBUTE TO BUDDY HOLLY (EP)	30
72	York FYK 409	AMBUSH (LP)	20
72	York FYK409	DRIFT AWAY (LP)	20

(see also Outlaws, Le Roys, Shepperton Flames, Innocents [U.K], UK Jones)

RICHARD BERRY & PHARAOHS
| 64 | Ember EMB EP 4527 | RHYTHM AND BLUES VOL. 3 (EP) | 200 |

BERRY STREET STATION
| 75 | Crystal CR 7024 | Chocolate Sugar/All I Want Is You | 30 |

BERTY B AND DILLINJA
| 95 | Lionheart BERT1 | Lionheart/Art Of Control (12") | 10 |

ADAM BEST
| 70 | Fontana SFL 13209 | WALL OF SOUND (LP) | 15 |

JON BEST
| 65 | Decca F 12077 | Young Boy Blues/Living Without Love | 15 |

PETE BEST FOUR
| 64 | Decca F 11929 | I'm Gonna Knock On Your Door/Why Did I Fall In Love With You? | 65 |

(see also Beatles, Lee Curtis & All Stars)

BETA BAND
97	Regal REG 16	CHAMPION VERSIONS EP: Dry The Rain/I Know/B+A/Dog's Got A Bone (12", p/s, 1,000 only)	60
98	Regal REG 18	THE PATTY PATTY SOUND EP: Inner Meet Me/The House/The Monolith/She's The One (2 x 12", p/s, 1,000 only)	25
98	Regal REG 18	THE PATTY PATTY SOUND EP: Inner Meet Me/The House/The Monolith/She's The One (CD, card slipcase)	22

SIR JOHN BETJEMAN
| 75 | Charisma CAS 1096 | LATE FLOWERING LOVE (LP, with Jim Parker) | 12 |

BETTERDAYS
65	Polydor BM 56024	Don't Want That/Here 'Tis	150+
91	N.T.B. 001	HOWL OF THE STREETS (EP, numbered p/s)	5
92	N.T.B. 1002	DOWN ON THE WATERFRONT (EP, numbered p/s)	5

HAROLD BETTERS
| 65 | Sue WI 378 | Do Anything You Wanna (Parts 1 & 2) | 40 |

BEVERLEY
| 66 | Deram DM 101 | Happy New Year/Where The Good Times Are | 20 |
| 67 | Deram DM 137 | Museum/DENNY CORDELL ENSEMBLE: A Quick One For Sanity | 20 |

(see also John & Beverley Martyn, Levee Breakers)

BEVERLEY SISTERS
| 55 | Decca F 10539 | I Remember Mama/I've Been Thinking | 8 |
| 55 | Decca F 10603 | Humming Bird/Have You Ever Been Lonely? | 5 |

BEVERLEY SISTERS

MINT VALUE £

55	Decca F 10641	My Heart Goes A-Sailing/Teddy Bear	5
56	Decca F 10705	Willie Can/I've Started Courtin'	5
56	Decca F 10729	Rickshaw Boy/You Ought To Have A Wife	5
56	Decca F 10770	Born To Be With You/It's Easy	8
56	Decca F 10813	Come Home To My Arms/Doodle-Doo-Doo	5
57	Decca F 10832	I Dreamed/Mama From The Train (A Kiss, A Kiss)	5
57	Decca F 10853	Greensleeves/I'll See You In My Dreams	5
57	Decca F 10893	Mr. Wonderful/Blow The Wind Southerly	5
57	Decca F 10909	Bye, Bye Love/It's Illegal, It's Immoral, Or It Makes You Fat	5
57	Decca F 10943	Riding Down From Bangor/The Young Cavaliero	6
58	Decca F 10971	Long Black Nylons/Without You	18
56	Columbia SEG 7602	THREE'S COMPANY (EP)	10
56	Decca DFE 6307	THE BEVERLEY SISTERS (EP)	12
57	Decca DFE 6401	THE BEVERLEY SISTERS NO. 2 (EP)	12
57	Decca DFE 6402	THE BEVERLEY SISTERS NO. 3 (EP)	12
58	Decca DFE 6512	THE BEVERLEY SISTERS NO. 4 (EP)	12
60	Decca DFE 6611	THE BEVS FOR CHRISTMAS (EP)	12
55	Philips BBR 8052	A DATE WITH THE BEVS (10" LP)	30

BEVERLEY'S ALLSTARS
65	Black Swan WI 449	Go Home/THEO BECKFORD: Ungrateful People	25
69	Trojan TR 683	Double Shot/Gimme Gimme Gal (B-side act. "Banana Water" by Mellotones)	15
70	Trojan TR 7729	Moon Dust/Fat Cat (both sides actually by Ansell Collins)	20

(see also Clarendonians, Gaylads, Ken Boothe, Glen Brown, Desmond Dekker, Bob Marley, Maytals, Melodians, Derrick Morgan, Pioneers, Rockstones, Bruce Ruffin, Delroy Wilson)

FRANK BEVERLY & BUTLERS
79	Inferno HEAT 4	If That's What You Wanted/Love (Your Pain Goes Deep) (some with p/s)	10/8

BEVERLY HILLBILLIES
66	Starlite GRK 602	THE FABULOUS BEVERLY HILLBILLIES (LP)	20

BEVERLY HILLS BLUES BAND
76	Warner Bros K 16752	Just Because/If I Can Just Get Through Tonight	10

(see also Four Seasons)

BEVIS FROND
88	Freakbeat/Lyntone	African Violets/THE STEPPES: History Hates No Man (flexidisc free with *Freakbeat* fanzine)	8/6
88	Bucketfull/Brains BOB 21	High In A Flat/DREAM SYNDICATE: Blind Willie McTell (free with *Bucketfull Of Brains* issue 27, 33rpm, yellow die-cut sleeve)	12/10
90	Clawfist PIS 1	Sexorcist/WALKINGSEEDS: Reflection In A Tall Mirror (p/s, mail-order only)	5
87	Woronzow WOO 3	MIASMA (LP)	12
87	Woronzow WOO 4	INNER MARSHLAND (LP)	8
87	Woronzow WOO 5 1/2	BEVIS THROUGH THE LOOKING GLASS – THE GREAT MAGNET DISASTER (2-LP, 500 only, originals all signed, with booklet; counterfeits unsigned)	50
88	Woronzow WOO 8	TRIPTYCH (LP)	12
90	Woronzow WOO 13	MAGIC EYE (LP, featuring Twink, 200 only)	12
91	Woronzow WOO 16	NEW RIVER HEAD (2-LP, 1st 500 with EP & insert)	18/12
92	Woronzow WOO 18	LONDON STONE (LP)	12
92	Woronzow WOO 26	SUPERSEEDER (2-LP)	15
93	Woronzow WOO 22	SPRAWL (2-LP, gatefold sleeve, with insert)	15
97	Woronzow WOO 406	NORTH CIRCULAR (3-LP, with insert, 750 only, signed & numbered)	25

(see also Von Trap Family, Room 13)

PAUL BEVOIR
85	Dance Network WORK 2	THE HAPPIEST DAYS OF YOUR LIFE (LP)	12

(see also Jetset)

RODNEY BEWES
69	Revolution REV 1003	Remember When/Dear Mother Love Albert	15
70	Revolution Pop REVP 1001	Dear Mother Love Albert/Meter Maid	15

(see also Highly Likely)

B-52's
79	Island WIP 6527	6060-842/Hero Worship (p/s)	5
80	Island PWIP 6551	Planet Claire/There's A Moon In The Sky (Called The Moon) (picture disc)	5
80	Island WIP 6579	Give Me Back My Man/Give Me Back My Man (Version) (p/s, mispressed, B-side plays Strobe Light)	8
80	Island WIP 6685	Strobe Light/Dirty Back Road (in blue/black plastic bag)	8
86	Island BFTR/BFTL/BFTP 1	Rock Lobster/Planet Claire (set of 3 x 10" x 7" picture discs ['rock'/'lobster'/'planet'], each with same tracks, in printed PVC folder)	12
90	Reprise W 9917P	Love Shack/Planet Claire (live)/Rock Lobster (live) (picture disc, promo only)	10
79	Island ILPS 9580	THE B-52's (LP, with bonus single Rock Lobster/52 Girls [PSR 438])	15
80	Island ILPS 9622	WILD PLANET (LP, in plastic bag with badge)	15

MAURICIO BIANCHI
81	Sterile SR 2	SYMPATHY FOR A GENOCIDE (LP, 200 only)	70

GENE BIANCO GROUP
53	London L 1209	Limehouse Boogie/Harpin' Boogie (78)	12
60	Vogue V 9167	Alarm Clock Rock/Harp Rock Boogie	30

BIBBY
65	Blue Beat BB 289	Rub It Down/Wicked Man (actually by Harris Seaton)	22

(see also B.B. Seaton, Horace Seaton)

BIDDU
67	Regal Zonophone RZ 3002	Daughter Of Love/Look Out Here I Come	7
69	Polydor 56323	Started Me Thinking/Where In The World	6
73	DJM DJS 284	What's Wrong With England/Kids Never Harm Anybody At All	6

BIFF BANG POW!
84	Creation CRE 003	Fifty Years Of Fun/Then When I Scream (foldaround sprayed p/s in poly bag)...	35
84	Creation CRE 007	There Must Be A Better Life/The Chocolate Elephant Man (foldaround p/s in poly bag)...	35
90	Caff CAFF 13	Sleep/TIMES: Extase (p/s, with insert)...	20
89	Creation CRELP 046	THE ACID HOUSE ALBUM (LP, hand-sprayed sleeve)...	12

(see also Laughing Apple, Times)

BIFFY CLYRO
00	Electric Honey HER 013 CD	Thekidswhopoptodaywillrocktomorrow (CD, 1000 only)...	80
01	Beggars Banquet BBQ 352	27/Instruction/Breathe Her (CD)...	10
01	Beggars Banquet BBQ 335CD	Justboy/Being Gabriel/Unsubtle (CD)...	10
02	Beggars Banquet BBQ 361	Joy.Discovery. Invention/Toys Toys Toys Choke/Toys Toys Toys/All The Way Down Chapter 2 (p/s)...	8
03	Beggars Banquet BBQLP233	THE VERTIGO OF BLISS (LP)...	12
04	Beggars Banquet BBQLP238	INFINITY LAND (LP)...	12

BIG AMONGST SHEEP
83	Rock Solid RSS 01	ASTROPOP (12" EP, p/s)...	12
82	Rock Solid RSR 2001	TERMINAL VELOCITY (LP)...	60

(see also Inner City Unit, Silverwing)

BIG BARON
60	Top Rank JAR 404	Swinging Bells (Oberon Jump)/Romance...	15

BIG BERTHA featuring ACE KEFFORD
69	Atlantic 584 298	This World's An Apple/Gravy Booby Jamm...	25

(see also Cozy Powell, Ace Kefford Stand, Bedlam, Youngblood)

BIG BLACK
87	Blast First BFFP 24	He's A Whore/The Model (p/s)...	5
85	Homestead HMS 007	RACER-X (12" EP, with insert)...	8
87	Blast First BFFP 14T	HEADACHE (12" p/s, 1,000 only, free 45, Heartbeat/Things To Do Today/I Can't Believe)...	10
87	NOT 2 (BUT 1)	SOUND OF IMPACT (LP, matt sleeve, no'd up to 1,000, with 8-page booklet)...	30
87	NOT 2 (BUT 1)	SOUND OF IMPACT (LP, laminated sleeve, numbered from 1,001-1,500, with 8-page booklet)...	20
87	NOT 2 (BUT 1)	SOUND OF IMPACT (LP, unnumbered, with 8-page booklet)...	10
92	Touch & Go TG 81	PIGPILE (LP, boxed set with video & T-shirt with insert)...	30

(see also Rapeman)

BIG BOB
59	Top Rank JAR 185	Your Line Was Busy/What Am I...	60

BIG BOPPER
58	Mercury AMT 1002	Chantilly Lace/The Purple People Eater Meets The Witchdoctor (78 rpm = £40)...	20
59	Mercury AMT 1017	Big Bopper's Wedding/Little Red Riding Hood (78 rpm = £55)...	30
59	Mercury AMT 1046	It's The Truth, Ruth/That's What I Am Talking About...	40
59	Mercury ZEP 10004	THE BIG BOPPER (EP)...	200
59	Mercury ZEP 10027	PINK PETTICOATS (EP)...	300
58	Mercury MMC 14008	CHANTILLY LACE (LP)...	200
74	Contour 6870 531	CHANTILLY LACE (LP)...	12

BIG BORIS
72	RCA RCA 2197	Big Country/Devil's Drive...	10

BIG BOSS MAN
01	Blow Up BU017	Sea Groove/Sea Groove (Version)...	20

BIG BOY PETE
68	Camp 602 005	Cold Turkey/My Love Is Like A Spaceship...	90
96	Tenth Planet TP 026	HOMAGE TO CATATONIA (LP)...	18

(see also Miller, Pete Miller)

BIG BROTHER & HOLDING COMPANY
67	Fontana TF 881	Bye Bye Baby/All Is Loneliness...	18
68	CBS 3683	Piece Of My Heart/Turtle Blues (some in p/s)...	20/7
68	London HLT 10226	Down On Me/Call On Me...	10
67	Fontana (S)TL 5457	BIG BROTHER & THE HOLDING COMPANY (LP, with Janis Joplin, mono/stereo)...	45/35
68	CBS (S)63392	CHEAP THRILLS (LP, with Janis Joplin, laminated single sleeve, mono/stereo)...	60/30
69	London HA-T/SH-T 8377	BIG BROTHER & THE HOLDING COMPANY (LP, reissue, mono/stereo)...	15
71	CBS S 64118	BE A BROTHER (LP)...	20

(see also Janis Joplin, Nick Gravenites)

BIG CARROT
73	EMI EMI 2047	Blackjack/Squint Eye Mangle...	35

(see also Marc Bolan/T. Rex)

BIG COUNTRY
84	Mercury COUNT 5-5	Wonderland/Giant//Lost Patrol (Live – parts 1 & 2) (2 x 7")...	10
84	Mercury MERD 185	Where The Rose Is Sown/Belief In The Small Man//Wonderland (Live)/In A Big Country (Live)/Auld Lang Syne (Live) (2 x 7")...	10

(see also Skids)

BIG DAVE (Cavanaugh) & HIS ORCHESTRA
54	Capitol CL 14195	Loosely With Feeling/The Cat From Coos Bay (triangular centre)...	20
55	Capitol CL 14245	Rock And Roll Party/Your Kind Of Love (triangular centre) (78 rpm = £8)...	35

BIG FLAME
84	Laughing Gun PLAQUE 001	Sink/The Illness/Sometimes (p/s, with insert)...	10

MINT VALUE £

BARRY BIGGS
70	Dynamic DYN 401	Got To Be Mellow/Love Grows	8
75	Dynamic DYN 101	Walk All Day/Play All Night.	6
76	Dynamic DYN 118	Sideshow/I'll Be Back	5
76	Dynamic DYLP 3005	MR. BIGGS (LP)	12

(see also Bob & Marcia)

BIG IN JAPAN
77	Eric's ERICS 0001	Big In Japan/CHUDDIE NUDDIES: Do The Chud (p/s)	10
78	Zoo CAGE 1	FROM Y TO Z AND NEVER AGAIN (EP, foldout p/s)	15

(see also Pink Industry/Military, Holly, Holly Johnson, Yachts, Bill Drummond, Creatures, Siouxsie & Banshees, Lightning Raiders)

BIG JOE (Joseph Spalding)
73	Chanan Jah 1003	Natty Love/Musical Air Raid.	8
74	Dip DL 5007	Selassie Skank/Version	15
74	Dip DL 5008	Weed Specialist/CHERRY & DUB MASTER: Rub A Daughter	12
74	Dip DL 5027	Hog In A Me Minty/Sweet Melody	12
75	Fab FAB 243	American Pum Pum/Tape White Wash	8
79	Tribesman TM 013	Respect Jah Word (with Rodney)/The Profit Says (12")	20
77	Live & Love LAP001	KEEP ROCKING AND SWINGING (LP)	35
78	Trojan TRLS 152	AFRICAN PRINCESS (LP).	30

BIG LUCKY, BIG AMOS & DONALD HINES
72	London SHU 8425	RIVER TOWN BLUES (LP)	25

BIG MAYBELLE
57	London HLC 8447	I Don't Want To Cry/All Of Me (78 rpm = £20)	50
59	London HLC 8854	Baby, Won't You Please Come Home/Say It Isn't So (78 rpm = £18).	30
65	London HL 9941	Careless Love/My Mother's Eyes	25
67	CBS 2735	Turn The World Around The Other Way/I Can't Wait Any Longer	70
67	CBS 2926	Mama (He Treats Your Daughter Mean)/Keep That Man	40
68	Direction 58-3312	Quittin' Time/I Can't Wait Any Longer.	40
67	CBS 62999	THE PURE SOUL OF BIG MAYBELLE (LP).	75

BIG MOE with BOYD BENNETT & ROCKETS
(see under Boyd Bennett)

BIG MOOSE (Walker)
60s	Python PKM 01	Ramblin' Woman/Puppy Howl Blues.	40

BIG NOISE
90s	President PCOM 1111	BIG NOISE (CD).	18

(see also Gary Numan)

BIGROUP
70s	Peer Intl. Library PIL 009	BIG HAMMER (LP, library disc)	120

BIG ROY
76	Rockers 6	In The Desert/Natty Judge	6

BIG SLEEP
71	Pegasus PEG 4	BLUEBELL WOOD (LP, gatefold sleeve).	60

(see also Eyes Of Blue, Ancient Grease, Gentle Giant, Man, Ritchie Francis, Gary Pickford-Hopkins)

BIG SPENDERS
70	Gemini GMS 008	If It Feels Good, Do It/Why Don't Ya Tend To Your Business	12
70	Gemini GMS 010	Who's Making Love/Cum Ba Ye.	10

BIG STAR
78	Stax STAX 504	September Gurls/Mod Lang	7
78	Aura AUS 103	Kizza Me/Dream Lover (p/s)	7
78	Aura AUS 107	Jesus Christ/Big Black Car	7
78	Stax SXSP 302	RADIO CITY/BIG STAR (2-LP)	30
78	Aura AUL 703	THIRD ALBUM (LP)	12

(see also Alex Chilton, Box Tops)

BIG THREE (U.K.)
63	Decca F 11614	Some Other Guy/Let True Love Begin	15
63	Decca F 11689	By The Way/Cavern Stomp	7
63	Decca F 11752	I'm With You/Peanut Butter	12
64	Decca F 11927	If You Ever Change Your Mind/You've Got To Keep Her Under Hand	15
73	Polydor 2058 343	Some Other Guy/Let It Rock/If You Gotta Make A Fool Of Somebody	7
63	Decca DFE 8552	AT THE CAVERN (EP)	20
73	Polydor 2383 199	RESURRECTION (LP)	18

(see also Escorts, Paddy Klaus & Gibson, Johnny Gustafson, Faron's Flamingos, Johnny & John)

BIG THREE (U.S.)
68	Roulette RCP 5002	THE BIG THREE FEATURING MAMA CASS (LP)	30

(see also Mama Cass [Elliot], Mamas & Papas)

BIG YOUTH
72	Blue Beat BB 424	Chi Chi Run/JOHN HOLT: OK Fred	25
73	Downtown DT 497	Dock Of The Bay/CRYSTALITES: Bass And Drums (Version)	20
73	Gayfeet CS 206	Medicine Doctor/Facts Of Life	15
73	Prince Buster PB 46	Chi Chi Run/Drums And Bass (Version)	12
73	Prince Buster PB 48	Leggo Beast/Leave Your Skeng.	12
73	Prince Buster PB 50	Cain And Abel/Cain And Abel (Version)	20
73	Grape GR 3040	Foreman Versus Frazier/Foreman Versus Frazier Round Two	18
73	Grape GR 3044	JA To UK/JA To UK (Version).	12
73	Grape GR 3051	Opportunity Rock/Double Attack.	12
73	Grape GR 3061	Concrete Jungle/Screaming Tonight.	12
73	Green Door GD 4051	Cool Breeze/CRYSTALITES: Windstorm.	20
73	Summit SUM 8542	A So We Say (with Dennis Brown)/WINSTON SCOTLAND: Scarface	8

74	Harry J. HJ 6682	Ride On Ride On/Wild Goose Chase (both with Dennis Brown)	8
75	Attack ATT 8104	Mammy Hot And Daddy Cold/GROOVEMASTERS: Some Like It Dread	8
75	Dip DL 5097	Big Youth Dread/Another Version	10
75	Lucky DL 5103	Natty Warning/Version	8
75	Klik KLP 9001	Dread Locks Dread	15
76	Lucky LY 6001	Get Up Stand Up/Version (with Dennis Brown)	8
72	Fab MS 8	CHI CHI RUN (LP)	45
73	Trojan TRLS 61	SCREAMING TARGET (LP, orange & white label)	20
75	Klik KLP9001	DREAD LOCKS DREAD (LP)	15
76	Trojan TRLS 123	NATTY CULTURAL DREAD (LP)	15
76	Trojan TRLS 137	HIT THE ROAD JACK (LP)	12
78	Virgin Front Line FL1011	ISIAH, FIRST PROPHET OF OLD (LP)	18

(see also Upsetters, Keith Hudson)

BIG YOUTH & KEITH HUDSON
| 73 | Pyramid PYR 7055 | Can You Keep A Secret/HORACE ANDY & EARL FLUTE: Peter And Judas | 25 |

(see also Keith Hudson)

BIKINIS
| 58 | Columbia DB 4149 | Bikini/Boogie Rock And Roll (78 rpm = £10) | 25 |

(Mr.) ACKER BILK (& HIS PARAMOUNT JAZZ BAND)
60	Melodisc 1547	Goodnight Sweet Prince/East Coast Trot	10
62	Columbia SEG 8178	BAND OF THIEVES (EP)	10
58	77 LEU 12/1	ACKER'S EARLY DAYS (LP)	15
58	Pye Nixa NJT 513	ACKER BILK REQUESTS (10" LP)	18
59	Columbia 33S 1141	THE NOBLE ART OF ACKER BILK (10" LP)	15
60	Pye NJL 22	THE MR ACKER BILK OMNIBUS (LP)	15
60	Columbia 33SX 1205	SEVEN AGES OF ACKER (LP)	18
60	Columbia 33SX 1248	ACKER (LP)	18
60	Society SOC 908	MY EARLY DAYS (LP)	15
61	Columbia 33SX 1348	LANDSDOWNE FOLIO (LP)	15
62	Columbia 33SX 1456	BEAU JAZZ (LP)	15
63	Columbia 33SX 1525	CALL ME MISTER (LP)	15
65	Columbia 33SX 1747	ACK'S BACK (LP)	15
67	Columbia S(C)X 6241	THE VERITABLE MR BILK (LP)	15

(see also Michael London)

BILL & COO
| 75 | Bradley's BRAD 7513 | Smoochy Smoochy/Always I Love You | 7 |

(see also Twinkle)

BILLIE & EDDIE
| 59 | Top Rank JAR 249 | The King Is Coming Back/Come Back, Baby | 30 |

BILLION DOLLAR BABIES
| 77 | Polydor 2391 273 | BATTLE AXES (LP) | 12 |

(see also Alice Cooper)

BILLY & ESSENTIALS
| 63 | London HLW 9657 | Over The Weekend/Maybe You'll Be There | 50 |

BILLY & LILLIE (& Billy Ford & Thunderbirds)
58	London HLU 8564	La Dee Dah/BILLY FORD'S THUNDERBIRDS: The Monster (78 rpm = £18)	35
58	London HLU 8630	Creepin', Crawlin', Cryin'/Happiness (with Billy Ford & Thunderbirds) (78 rpm £30)	40
58	London HLU 8689	The Greasy Spoon/Hangin' On To You (with Billy Ford & Thunderbirds) (78 rpm = £20)	30
59	London HLU 8795	I Promise You/Lucky Ladybug (78 rpm = £30)	30
59	Top Rank JAR 157	Bells, Bells, Bells/Honeymoonin' (as Billie & Lillie) (78 rpm = £15)	10

BIM & BAM
70	Crab CRAB 48	The Pill (with Clover)/TOMMY McCOOK: Spring Fever	15
70	Crab CRAB 49	Immigrant Plight (w/ Clover)/PETER AUSTIN & HORTENSE: Bang Shangalang	15
73	Gayfeet GS 201	Fatty/Landlord	10

BIM, BAM & CLOVER
| 70 | Trojan TR 7754 | Party Time Parts 1 & 2 | 8 |

UMBERTO BINDI
| 60 | Oriole CB 1577 | Il Nostro Concerto/Un Giorno Un Mese Un Anno | 5 |

BINGO
| 73 | Polydor 2066 365 | We Can't Get Enough/Mumblin' Man | 10 |

SONNY BINNS (& RUDIES)
69	Downtown DT 420	The Untouchables/Lazy Boy	15
69	Downtown DT 424	Wheels/Night Train	12
70	Escort ES 818	Boss A Moon (as S. Binns)/BUNNY LEE ALLSTARS: Brotherly Love	35

(see also Rudies)

TONY BINNS
| 71 | Explosion EX 2044 | Love I Madly/Musical Shower | 10 |
| 71 | Explosion EX 2046 | Humpty Dumpty/Got To Get A Message | 8 |

BIONIC BOOGIE
(see under Gregg Diamond)

BIOTA
| 85 | Recommended DYS 12 & 13 | RACKABONES (LP, with inserts) | 40 |

STANLEY & JEFFREY BIRD
| 60 | HMV POP 702 | Johnny At The Crossheads/Betty, Betty (Go Steady With Me) | 12 |

MINT VALUE £

BIRD LEGS & PAULINE
66 Sue WI 4014   Spring/In So Many Ways 20

BIRDS
64 Decca F 12031   You're On My Mind/You Don't Love Me (You Don't Care).................. 100
65 Decca F 12140   Leaving Here/Next In Line .... 75+
65 Decca F 12257   No Good Without You Baby/How Can It Be .... 75+
85 Demon WEST 901   THESE BIRDS ARE DANGEROUS (LP).. 20
(see also Birds Birds, Ron Wood, Faces, Creation, Ashton Gardner & Dyke)

BIRDS & BRASS
70 Rediffusion ZS 57   SOUNDSATIONAL (LP) 15
74 Rediffusion 0100 171   ... ARE BACK (LP)... 20

BIRDS BIRDS
66 Reaction 591 005   Say Those Magic Words/Daddy Daddy.................................... 500+
(see also Birds, Gods)

BIRDS OF A FEATHER
69 Page One POF 156   Blacksmith Blues/Sing My Song And Pray 10
70 Page One POF 179   All God's Children Got Soul/Get It Together 7
72 Jam JAM 23   You Know Me Better/Summer Has Gone 6
72 DJM DJS 243   Thank You/Baby Don't You Bring Me Down 6
70 Page One POLS 027   BIRDS OF A FEATHER (LP) 50
(see also Chanters, Chanter Sisters)

JANE BIRKIN & SERGE GAINSBOURG
69 Fontana TF 1042   Je T'Aime, Moi Non Plus/Jane B (initially with p/s) 10/6
69 Major Minor MM 645   Je T'Aime, Moi Non Plus/Jane B (reissue)............................... 5
72 Philips 6009 201   La Decadanse/Les Langues De Chat 8
74 Antic K 11511   Je T'Aime, Moi Non Plus/Jane B (2nd reissue, 'nude' p/s).............. 7
69 Fontana STL 5493   JANE BIRKIN AND SERGE GAINSBOURG (LP)................................. 40

BIRMINGHAM
71 Grosvenor GRS 1011   BIRMINGHAM (LP) 100
(see also Dave Peace Quartet)

BIRTH CONTROL
71 Charisma CAS 1036   BIRTH CONTROL (LP) 20

BIRTHDAY PARTY
80 4AD AD 12   The Friend Catcher/Waving My Arms/Cat Man (p/s) 8
81 4AD AD 111   Release The Bats/Blast Off (p/s)...................................... 8
81 4AD AD 114   Mr. Clarinet/Happy Birthday (p/s) 8
81 (no cat. no.)   Mr. Clarinet/Missing Link (sold at gigs only) 50
82 Masterbag BAG 005   Dead Joe (flexidisc free with *Masterbag* magazine issue 15) 8/6
(see also Nick Cave & Bad Seeds, Roland S. Howard & Lydia Lunch)

DICKIE BISHOP & THE SIDEKICKS
57 Decca F 10869   Cumberland Gap/No Other Baby... 18
57 Decca F 10959   The Prisoner's Song/Please Remember Me................................ 10
58 Decca F 10981   Skip To My Lou/No Other Baby 10
58 Decca F 11028   They Can't Take That Away From Me/Jumpin' Judy 15
(see also Chris Barber's Skiffle Group)

TOMMY BISHOP'S RICOCHETS
65 Decca F 12238   I Should Have Known/On The Other Hand................................. 15
(see also Rock 'n' Roll Revival Show)

BISHOPS
(see under Count Bishops)

BITCH
79 Hurricane FIRE 5   Big City/Wild Kids (p/s) 20

BITCH
81 Rutland RX 101   First Bite/Maggie (some with p/s & promo insert) 15/20

BITCHES SIN
81 Neat NEAT 09   Always Ready For Love/Sign Of The Times (p/s) 8
83 Quiet QT 001   No More Chances/Overnight/Ice Angels (12", p/s) 25
83 Terminal TCAS 21   OUT OF MY MIND (EP, cassette, 6-track) 8
82 Heavy Metal HMRLP 4   PREDATOR (LP, textured sleeve) 18

BITCH MAGNET
91 Caff CAFF 14   Sadie/Ducks And Drakes (p/s, with insert)............................. 8

BITTER SUITE
75 Bus Stop BUS 1023   How Married Are You Marianne/Love Is A Friend Of Mine 8

BITSTREAM
City Centre Offices   Crab Nebula (plain sleeve with inserts, 1000 only)................... 12
BLOCK 015

BIZ
93 Warp WARP LP 9   ELECTRO SOMA (LP, orange vinyl) 12

BIZET BOYS
89 Parlophone RIDE 1   Ride 'Em Cowboy/Ride 'Em Cowboy (Speechless) (p/s) 5
89 Parlophone 12RIDE 1   Ride 'Em Cowboy (A Classic Mix)/Ride 'Em Cowboy (Opera House Mix)/
                           Ride 'Em Cowboy (3 M's Much More Mix) (12", p/s) 10
(see also Sigue Sigue Sputnik)

BJÖRK

93	One Little Indian BJDJ 101	One Day (Endorphin Mix)/(Springs Eternal Mix) (10", die-cut sleeve, promo only, 2,000 copies)	12
93	One Little Indian BJDJ 102	Violently Happy (12" Mix)/(Basso Hitto Dubo) (10", die-cut sleeve, promo only, 2,000 copies)	14
93	One Little Indian BJDJ 103	Come To Me (Black Dog Productions)/Anchor Song (Black Dog Productions) (10", die-cut sleeve, promo only, 2,000 copies)	12
93	One Little Indian BJDJ 104	Human Behaviour (The Underworld Dub 1)/(The Underworld Dub 2) (10", die-cut sleeve, promo only, 1,000 copies)	25
93	One Little Indian 112TP 12P	Human Behaviour (Speedy J. Close To Human Mix)/(Dom T. Mix)/ (Bassheads Edit) (12", promo only)	8
93	One Little Indian 112TP 12DJ	Human Behaviour (The Underworld Mix)/(The Underworld Dub) (12", promo only)	10
93	One Little Indian BJDJ 123	One Day (Adrenalin — Far Removed) (12", 1-sided, promo only, 1,000 copies)	25
93	O. L. Indian BJDJ 124/125	BIG TIME SENSUALITY (12" EP, double pack, promo only, 500 copies)	12
93	O. L. Indian BJDJ 124/125g	BIG TIME SENSUALITY (12" EP, double pack, promo only, 1,000 copies)	18
95	One L. Indian 162 TP12P	ARMY OF ME (12" EP, remix double pack, single p/s, promo copies)	8
95	One L. Indian 162 TP12GM	ARMY OF ME (Graham Massey Mix) (12", white label, no p/s, promo only)	8
96	O. Little Indian 193TP12DM	Enjoy/Possibly Maybe (12", 1,000 only, numbered p/s)	18
96	O. Little Indian 193TP12TD	POSSIBLY MAYBE (12" EP, 1,000 only, numbered p/s)	12
97	O. L. Indian TPLP 81	JOGA (12" triple-pack, inner sleeves, p/s)	12
97	O. L. Indian 20 TP7 BOX	JOGA (CD box set, 3 x CD singles & 1-track video, 3,000 only)	35
97	O. L. Indian 20 TP7 BOX 212	BACHELORETTE (CD box set, 3 x CD singles & 1-track video, 3,000 only)	25
93	One Little Indian TPLP 31L	DEBUT (LP, 5,000 with 16-page lyric booklet)	18/10
94	One Little Indian 152TP 7	THE BEST MIXES FROM THE ALBUM DEBUT FOR THOSE PEOPLE WHO DON'T BUY WHITE LABELS (mini-LP)	12
95	One L. Indian TPLP 51L	POST (LP, pink vinyl, with inner sleeve)	18
95	One L. Indian TPLP 51CDX	POST (CD, digipak w/poster & lyric book, some copies in PVC purse)	18/15
97	One L. Indian TPLP71	HOMOGENIC (Some with set of 4 postcards)	15
00	One L. Indian TPLP151	SELMA SONGS (LP)	14
01	One L. Indian TPLP101	VERSPERTINE (2 x LP, gatefold with poster)	18
02	One L. Indian	GREATEST HITS & FAMILY TREE (Promo boxed set with 6xCD, video and photos)	50
02	One L. Indian TPLP365CD	GREATEST HITS & FAMILY TREE (CDx6 boxed set)	40
03	One L. Indian TPLP355CDBOX	LIVEBOX (CD x 4, DVD)	25
04	One L. Indian TPLP358	MEDULLA (2 x LP)	15
	(see also Sugarcubes, Kukl)		

BJÖRK vs FUNKSTÖRUNG

98	Fat Cat 12FAT 022	All Is Full Of Love (FunkstÖrung Remix)/The Shit (12", custom stamped sleeve)	12

BLACK

81	Rox ROX 17	Human Features/Electric Church (p/s)	10

BILL BLACK'S COMBO

59	Felsted AF 129	Smokie Parts 1 & 2 (78 rpm = £30)	20
60	London HLU 9090	White Silver Sands/The Wheel	12
60	London HLU 9156	Josephine/Dry Bones	15
60	London HLU 9212	Don't Be Cruel/Rollin'	10
61	London HLU 9267	Blue Tango/Willie	10
61	London HLU 9306	Hearts Of Stone/Royal Blue	10
61	London HLU 9383	Ole Buttermilk Sky/Yogi	10
61	London HLU 9436	Movin'/Honky Train	12
61	London HLU 9479	Twist-Her/My Girl Josephine	10
62	London HLU 9594	So What/Blues For The Red Boy	22
62	London HLU 9645	Joey's Song/Hot Taco	10
63	London HLU 9721	Do It — Rat Now/Little Jasper	10
63	London HLU 9788	Monkey-Shine/Long Gone	10
64	London HLU 9855	Comin' On/Soft Winds	10
64	London HLU 9903	Tequila/Raunchy	10
64	London HLU 9925	Little Queenie/Boo-Ray	30
68	London HLU 10216	Turn On Your Love Light/Ribbon Of Darkness	5
60	London REU 1277	BILL BLACK'S COMBO (EP)	40
63	London REU 1369	THE UNTOUCHABLE SOUND OF BILL BLACK (EP)	40
62	London HA-U 2310	SOLID AND RAUNCHY (LP)	35
62	London HA-U 2427	LET'S TWIST (LP, also stereo SAH-U 6222)	25/30
62	London HA-U 2433	MOVIN' (LP)	25
63	London HA-U 8080	THE UNTOUCHABLE SOUND OF BILL BLACK (LP)	25
63	London HA-U 8113	GREATEST HITS (LP)	20
64	London HA-U 8187	PLAYS CHUCK BERRY (LP)	25
68	London HA-U/SH-U 8367	BILL BLACK'S BEAT GOES ON (LP)	15
69	London HA-U/SH-U 8373	TURN ON YOUR LOVE LIGHT (LP)	15
69	London HA-U/SH-U 8389	SOULIN' THE BLUES (LP)	15
	(see also Elvis Presley)		

CILLA BLACK

64	Parlophone GEP 8901	ANYONE WHO HAD A HEART (EP)	8
64	Parlophone GEP 8916	IT'S FOR YOU (EP)	10
66	Parlophone GEP 8954	CILLA'S HITS (EP)	10
67	Parlophone GEP 8967	TIME FOR CILLA (EP)	20
65	Parlophone PCS 3063	CILLA (LP, stereo, yellow/black label)	12
68	Parlophone PCS 7041	SHER-OO! (LP, stereo, yellow/black label)	12
68	Parlophone PMC/PCS 7065	THE BEST OF CILLA BLACK (mono/stereo, yellow/black label)	12

'FLIP' BLACK & BOYS UPSTAIRS

59	Capitol CL 15037	For You My Lover/Tell Her Mister Moon	8

MINT VALUE £

FRANK BLACK
93	4AD CADD 3004	FRANK BLACK (LP, die-cut screen-printed sleeve, with lyric inner)	12

(see also Pixies)

JEANNE BLACK
60	Capitol CL 15131	He'll Have To Stay/JEANNE & JANIE: Under Your Spell Again	8
60	Capitol CL 12456	Lisa/ JEANNE & JANIE: Journey of Love	10

(see also Janie, Jeanne & Janie)

MATT BLACK & THE DOODLEBUGS
76	Punk BCS 0005	Punky Xmas/Nightmare (no p/s)	15

BLACK ABBOTTS
70	Chapter One CH 123	She Looked Away/I Don't Mind	7
71	Evolution E 3001	How About Me/Everybody Needs A Little Sunshine	7
71	Evolution E 3004	Love Is Alive/The Painter	25

BLACK ACE
61	XX MIN 701	BLACK ACE (EP)	25
62	Heritage HLP 1006	BLACK ACE (LP, 99 copies only)	100

BLACK ANGELS
84	Gull GULP 1041	KICKDOWN (LP)	12

BLACK AXE
80	Metal MELT 1	Highway Rider/Red Lights (some in p/s)	15/6

BLACKBEARD
80	More Cut RDC 2002	I WAH DUB (LP)	20

BLACK BEATLES
70	Pama PM 804	Reggae And Shout/LENOX BROWN: The Green Hornet	8

BLACKBIRDS
68	Saga OPP 3	No Destination/Space (company sleeve, possibly promo only)	25
68	Saga FID 2113	NO DESTINATION (LP)	30

BLACK BLOOD
76	Bradleys 1002	Rasteferai/Ewohe Dance	6

BLACK, BROWN & BEIGE
72	Regal Zonophone RZ 3051	We Are The Champions/What Is A Man	5

BRYAN BLACKBURN AND PETER REEVE
61	Fontana SEBL 636	AT THE BLUE ANGEL (LP)	15

BLACKBYRDS
74	Fantasy FTC 113	Do It Fluid/Summer Love	8
75	Fantasy FTC 114	Walking In Rhythm/Baby	6
75	Fantasy FTC 117	I Need You/All I Ask	6
76	Fantasy FTC 122	Rock Creek Park/Flying High	8
76	Fantasy FTC 129	Happy Music/Love So Fine	6
85	Streetwave SWAVE 3	Rock Creek Park/Walking In Rhythm (12")	12
75	Fantasy FT 9444	BLACKBYRDS (LP)	20
75	Fantasy FT 522	FLYING START (LP)	15
76	Fantasy FTA 3003	CITY LIFE (LP)	15
77	Fantasy FT 534	ACTION (LP)	15
79	Fantasy FT 555	NIGHT GROOVES — THE BEST OF THE BLACKBYRDS (LP)	15

(see also Donald Byrd)

BLACK CAT BONES
70	Decca Nova SDN 15	BARBED WIRE SANDWICH (LP)	80

(see also Leaf Hound, Brian Short, Free, Foghat)

BLACK COUNTRY THREE
66	Transatlantic TRA 140	BLACK COUNTRY THREE (LP)	50
66	W.F.C. WS 100	BLACK COUNTRY SONGS (EP)	250

(see also Jon Raven)

BLACK COUNTRY THREE
66	W.F.C. WS 100	BLACK COUNTRY SONGS (EP)	250

(see also Jon Raven)

BLACK DOG
91	GPR GENP(X) 2	PARALLEL EP (12", p/s)	22
92	Black Dog Prods BDP 001	VIRTUAL EP (12", p/s)	125
92	Black Dog Prods BDP 002	AGE OF SLACK (12", p/s)	75
92	Black Dog Prods BDP 003	BLACK DOG EP (12", p/s, 500 only)	100
92	GPR GENP(X) 3	VIR 2 L (12", custom sleeve)	60
92	GPR GENP(X) 9	VANTOOL EP (12", custom sleeve)	50
93	GPR GENP(X) 17	COST II (12", custom sleeve)	15
93	Rising High RSN 046	BLACK DOG PRODUCTIONS (12", 4-track, p/s)	25
91	GPR GPR 004	PARALLEL SQUELCH (LP)	30
92	GPR GPRLP 1	TEMPLE OF TRANSPARENT BALLS (2-LP, some with poster)	22/20
93	GPR GPRCD 1	TEMPLE OF TRANSPARENT BALLS (CD)	20
95	GPR GPRLP 15	PARALLEL (2-LP)	35
95	GPR GPRCD 15	PARALLEL (CD)	30
95	Warp PUPLP 1	SPANNERS (2-LP)	30
95	Warp WAP LP 8LTD	BYTES (LP, bronze vinyl)	40

(see also Alter Ego, Plaid, Repeat, Unexplored Beats, Shiva)

BLACK DYKE MILLS BAND
68	Apple APPLE 4	Thingumybob/Yellow Submarine	50

BLACK DYNAMITES
60	Top Rank JAR 319	Brush Those Tears/Lonely Cissy	30

BLACK EASTER
82 Illuminated KILL 13   READY TO ROCK (EP, p/s) 5

BLACK FLAG
81 Alt. Tentacles VIRUS 9   Six Pack/I've Heard It All Before/American Waste (p/s) 12
84 SST SST 12001   Family Man/I Won't Stick Any Of You Unless And Until I Can
     Stick All Of You (12", p/s) 10

J.D. BLACKFOOT
71 Mercury 6338 031   THE ULTIMATE PROPHECY (LP) 75

BLACKFOOT SUE
73 Jam JAL 104   NOTHING TO HIDE (LP) 20
75 DJM DJLPS 455   GUN RUNNING (LP, withdrawn) 45

BLACK IVORY
74 Kwanza 19500   What Goes Around/Comes Around 10

BLACKJACK
80 Polydor POSP 76   Without Your Love/Heart Of Mine (p/s) 20
79 Polydor 2391 411   BLACKJACK (LP) 20
80 Polydor   WORLDS APART (LP) 12
(see also Michael Bolotin, Michael Bolton)

BLACKJACKS
63 Pye 7N 15586   Woo Hoo/Red Dragon 15
(see also Pat Harris & Blackjacks)

BLACK KNIGHTS
65 Columbia DB 7443   I Gotta Woman/Angel Of Love 25

HONOR BLACKMAN
68 CBS 3896   Before Today/I'll Always Be Loving You (some in p/s) 30/15
64 Decca LK/SKL 4642   EVERYTHING I'VE GOT (LP, mono/stereo) 40
(see also Patrick MacNee & Honor Blackman)

PAUL BLACKMAN
79 Daddy Kool DKR 123   Earth, Wind & Fire/A. Pablo: Ras-Menlik Congo (12") 25

RITCHIE BLACKMORE (ORCHESTRA)
65 Oriole CB 314   Getaway/Little Brown Jug (Spelt "Richie" on label) 350
(see also Outlaws, Neil Christian & Crusaders, Deep Purple, [Ritchie Blackmore's] Rainbow, Rally Rounders, Green Bullfrog, Rock Aid Armenia)

BLACK NASTY
80 Grapevine GRP 140   Cut Your Motor Off/Keep On Stepping 8

BLACK OAK ARKANSAS
75 Atlantic K 10621   Fancy Nancy/Keep On 7
71 Atlantic 2400 180   BLACK OAK ARKANSAS (LP) 12

BLACK RIDERS
85 Plastic Head GILP 555   CHOSEN FEW (LP) 15

BLACK ROSE
82 Teesbeat TB 5   Sucker For Your Love/No Point Runnin' (some in p/s) 125/35
83 Bullet BOLT 3   BLACK ROSE (12" EP) 8
83 Bullet BOLT 6   WE'RE GONNA ROCK YOU (12" EP) 8
84 Bullet BOLT 9   Boys Will Be Boys/Liar (p/s, some with patch) 35
85 Neat NEAT 4812   Nightmare/Need A Lot Of Lovin'/Rock Me Hard (12", p/s) 8
84 Bullet BULP 3   BOYS WILL BE BOYS (LP) 12

BLACK SABBATH
70 Fontana TF 1067   Evil Woman/Wicked World 90
70 Vertigo V2   Evil Woman/Wicked World (reissue, Vertigo 'swirl' sleeve) 20
70 Vertigo 6059 010   Paranoid/The Wizard (Vertigo 'swirl' sleeve) 20
72 Vertigo 6059 061   Tomorrow's Dream/Laguna Sunrise (Vertigo 'swirl' sleeve) 18
72 Phonogram DJ 005   Children Of The Grave/STATUS QUO: Roadhouse Blues
     (100 promo copies only) 400
73 WWA WWS 002   Sabbath Bloody Sabbath/Changes (company sleeve) 8
75 NEMS 6165 300   Am I Going Insane? (Radio)/Hole In The Sky (no p/s) 10
78 Vertigo SAB 001   Never Say Die/She's Gone (p/s) 7
78 Vertigo SAB 002   Hard Road/Symptom Of The Universe (purple or black vinyl) .... each 6
80 Vertigo SAB 412   Die Young/Heaven And Hell (extended live) (12", p/s) 8
81 Vertigo SAB 512   Mob Rules/Die Young (live) (12", p/s) 10
82 Vertigo SABP 6   Turn Up The Night/Lonely Is The Word (picture disc) 5
82 Vertigo SABP 612   Turn Up The Night/Lonely Is The Word (12", picture disc) 8
86 Vertigo SABDJ 12   In For The Kill/Turn To Stone/Heart Like A Wheel (12", promo only) 15
87 Vertigo SABAF 1   4 SONGS FROM THE ETERNAL IDOL (12", p/s, promo only) 15
89 I.R.S. EIRS CB 107   Headless Cross (Edit)/Cloak And Dagger (signed label,
     stickered PVC sleeve) 6
89 I.R.S. EIRSPD 115   Devil And Daughter (1-sided picture disc) 5
89 I.R.S. EIRSB 115   Devil And Daughter (box set, 1-sided disc with stencil, insert & 2 postcards) 8
92 I.R.S. EIRSDJ 180   Master Of Insanity (edit)/Time Machine/Neon Knights (live)/TV Crimes (live)/
     Die (live)/Children Of The Sea (live) (CD, no p/s, promo only) 12
70 Vertigo VO 6   BLACK SABBATH (LP, 1st pressing, with black gatefold sleeve and
     lyric printed on cross; swirl label) 50-60
70 Vertigo VO 6   BLACK SABBATH (LP, 2nd pressing, with white gatefold sleeve and Dunbar
     credit for 'Warning'; swirl label, some with laminated sleeve) 30/200
70 Vertigo 6360 011   PARANOID (LP, gatefold sleeve, swirl label) 35
71 Vertigo 6360 050   MASTER OF REALITY (LP in box cover, swirl label, some with poster) 75/25
72 Vertigo 6360 071   BLACK SABBATH VOL. 4 (LP, gatefold sleeve with booklet,
     initially with swirl label, later with 'spaceship' label) 200/15
85 Nems BSBLP 001   THE SABBATH COLLECTION (7-LP box set) 50

BLACK SABBATH

88	Castle BSBCD 001	THE BLACK SABBATH CD COLLECTION (6-CD box set with badge & book, numbered, 3,000 only)	40
89	I.R.S. EIRSAPD 1002	HEADLESS CROSS (LP, picture disc, with bonus track Cloak And Dagger)	18
90	I.R.S. EIRSACV 1038	TYR (LP, picture disc with sticker insert & 2 bonus live tracks)	18

(see also Ozzy Osborne, Dio, Elf, Cozy Powell, Quartz, Phenomena, Rock Aid Armenia)

BLACK SLATE
78	Ted TCDD 008	Sticks Man (12")	40+
78	Slate KG 008	Live Up To Love/Jah In The Ghetto (12")	10

BLACK SWAN
71	Ember EMBS 303	Echoes And Rainbows/Belong Belong (some with p/s)	15/8

BLACKTHORN
77	WHM 1921	BLACKTHORN (LP)	60
78	WHM 1923	BLACKTHORN II (LP)	100

BLACK TWANG
95	Sound Of Money SNM005	Queen's Head (12")	8
95	Sound Of MoneySNM004	What's Going On?/Everyday News (12")	35
95	Sound Of MoneySNM005	Queen's Head/Mr Jam Promota (12")	30
96	Sound Of MoneySNM007	Real Estate (12")	20
96	Sound Of MoneyANTI T3	Dettwork South East/Don't Let Dem Fool You (12")	30

BLACK UHURU
77	Third World TWDIS 009	Natural Mystic/Sorry For The Man (12")	20
79	Warrior WAR 140	Bad Girl/African Love/PRINCE HAMMER - Yogi Bear (12")	15
79	DEB DEB 034	Rent Man/Rent Board/ALTON ELLIS - La La Means I Love You/Version (12")	15
79	DEB DEB 036	Wood For My Fire/EARL CUNNINGHAM/JAH THOMAS - Words Of The Father (12")	15
79	D-Roy DDR 09	Plastic Smile/Guess Who's Coming To Dinner (12")	25
80	Island 12WIP 6626	Sinsemilla (discomix)/Guess Who's Coming To Dinner (Discomix) (12")	10
77	Third World TWS 925	LOVE CRISIS (LP, as Black Sounds Uhro)	35
79	D-Roy DRLP 1003	SHOWCASE (LP)	25

(See also Don Carlos)

BLACK VELVET
71	Mams MAM 47	Make It Better/Tropicana	15
72	Pye NSPL 18392	PEOPLE OF THE WORLD	18
73	Seven Sun SUNLP1	CAN YOU FEEL IT?	75

CHARLES BLACKWELL ORCHESTRA
61	HMV POP 977	Taboo/Midnight In Luxembourg	15
62	Columbia DB 4839	Supercar/Persian Theme	18
62	Columbia DB 4919	Freight Train/Death Valley	10
60	Triumph TRY 4000	THOSE PLUCKING STRINGS (LP, unreleased, test pressings only)	500+

(Joe Meek fans, please note Those Plucking Strings was finally released on CD in 2006)

OTIS BLACKWELL
58	London HLE 8616	Make Ready For Love/When You're Around (78 rpm = £25)	45

RORY BLACKWELL & HIS BLACKJACKS
57	Parlophone R 4326	Bye Bye Love/Such A Shame (78 rpm = £18)	30
78	Ellie Jay EJR 604	THE 2 SIDES OF RORY BLACKWELL (LP)	12

SCRAPPER BLACKWELL
67	Collector JEN 7	SCRAPPER BLACKWELL (EP)	10
63	'77' LA 12/4	BLUES BEFORE SUNRISE (LP)	45
60s	Xtra XTRA 5011	MR SCRAPPER'S BLUES (LP)	22

BLACKWELLS (U.K.)
65	Columbia DB 7442	Why Don't You Love Me/All I Want Is Your Love	30

BLACKWELLS (U.S.)
60	London HLW 9135	Unchained Melody/Mansion On The Hill	15
61	London HLW 9334	Love Or Money/Big Daddy And The Cat	15

BLACK 2
70	CBS 5031	Come To The Sabbat/Way To Power	20
71	CBS 7596	Wish You Would/Accident	12
70	CBS 63948	SACRIFICE (LP, gatefold sleeve)	20
70	CBS 64133	BLACK WIDOW II (LP)	20
72	CBS 64562	BLACK WIDOW III (LP, with inner)	20

(see also Pesky Gee, Agony Bag)

BLACK RADICAL/SIR NOVA
88	Bass Inc B1001 500	B Boys Be Wise/We Outta Here (12")	25

BLACK RADICAL MKII
89	2 The Bone LYN2304	Monsoon/B Boys B Wisell (12")	12
90	Mango 12 MNG 764	Rippin' Up The Industry (12")	8
91	Mango 12 MNG 782DJ	Sign Of The Beast (12" grey vinyl)	12

BLADE
89	Raw Bass 1202	Lyrical Maniac/The Comin' Is Near/We're Going Independent (12")	25
89	691 Influential BLADE1203	Mind Of An Ordinary Citizen/ Forward (12")	25
91	691 Influential BLADE1204	Rough It Up/Whatcha Waitin' For?/You Better Get Yours (12")	20
93	691 Influential BLADE1206	Clear The Way/They Ain't Shit To Me (12", white vinyl)	50
94	Sound Of Money SOM 01	Queens Head (12")	15
96	691 Influential SURV 1	Survival Of The Hardest Working (12")	20
97	Bomb 2006	Rhyme Bomb/The Way It Has To Be (12")	12
92	691 Influential BLADE1205	SURVIVAL OF THE HARDEST WORKING (LP)	25
93	691 Influential BLADE1202	THE LION GOES FROM STRENGTH TO STRENGTH (LP)	35
95	691 Influential BLADE 1208	PLANNED AND EXECUTED (LP)	15

(see also Mark B and Blade)

The Beatles' debut demo, limited to 250 copies, Mint copies are extremely hard to locate. Note the mis-spelt 'McArtney'.

The Beatles' debut single as it originally appeared in the shops. Note that this record features the so-called 'beach stripe' Company sleeve.

Released at the same time as the above, some versions featured 'Made in Gt. Britain' and some omitted this credit, such as this example.

The Beatles' second demo, this near to Mint version was the final demo disc to include the defunct '45' prefix.

Note that 'B' sides did not feature the distinctive red 'A', so that DJs would not mistakenly play the wrong side of the disc.

This record again may be found with or without the 'Made in Gt. Britain' credit. This has been supplied in the 'triangular design' Company sleeve.

Initial copies were pressed using the Black & Gold label. First issues featured 'Dick James' publishing label details on four 'Lennon/McCartney' tracks that should have been attributed to 'Northern Songs'.

Second pressings featured corrected publishing details and it is believed that fewer copies of this version exists than the 'Dick James' version.

Initial copies released on Friday 26th April, five weeks after mono pressing. Around 900 pressed, making album extremely rare. Like the mono album there are 'Dick James' and 'Northern Songs' versions.

First issue on the newly designed black and silver Parlophone single label. EMI used this re-pressing to reset the copy, deleting the '45' prefix on the catalogue number.

Given to members of the Fan Club for Christmas 1963. Around 30,000 pressed up, making this earliest Christmas disc the hardest to locate. There are known counterfeit copies of sleeve.

These 'flexi – discs' were manufactured by Lyntone and had fairly poor sound quality. Surviving discs are generally in poor condition. Even the best have loud background noise.

Demo copies of EMI records were issued in 'Top Pop' bags. Demo's from Love Me Do until A Hard Day's Night would have featured a blue, yellow or red bag.

Due to demand, sometimes EMI had to 'contract out' orders. This example pressed by Decca in New Malden, Surrey. The ridged, dinked centre is not characteristic of EMI manufactured singles.

Released on 10th July 1964, The Beatles' second single of 1964 and the seventh since they signed with Parlophone. This demo version is highly desirable.

It is not known why this side of the disc features the large red 'A'. From contemporary documentation, the track was not marketed as a double 'A' side.

First Beatles' records manufactured in UK for release in export territories. Copies of If I Fell also exist with the central remark 'Sold in the UK, subject to resale price conditions'.

This copy of Beatles For Sale pressed after 1965 features label error I'm A Losser. Some copies credit 'Northern Ssongs' for the title 'Eight Day's A Week' on side 2.

This label uses incorrect spelling Norweigian Wood instead of Norwegian. Very few copies found their way into the public domain, making this the hardest of all label misprints to find.

Extremely rare Parlophone export single. Both tracks from *Rubber Soul* album, Michelle backed with Drive My Car. Label copy from the sleeve has been used, giving lead and backing singers

Released on 8th July 1966, the majority of fans having previously purchased the tracks featured on *Rubber Soul* gave this EP a miss. Now the rarest of The Beatles' EPs.

Side 1 label of the rarely seen *Nowhere Man* EP. Side 2 songs consisted of Michelle and You Won't See Me.

This was the first bespoke sleeve to feature on a UK Beatles' record. Printed on same stock as standard Company sleeves, these were flimsy and few survive in Excellent condition.

Initial copies of the single failed to include the credit '(Recorded during 'Live' World Television Transmission)'.

This mono pressing omits the song credit for A Day In The Life. It probably originates from 1968, as no known examples have surfaced in the red psychedelic inner sleeve.

Hi-Fi Magazine marketed a specially mastered and pressed version of *Sgt. Pepper* manufactured by quality classical label Nimbus. The release was exclusive, making Mint copies highly desirable.

At beginning of the 70s, EMI combined mono and stereo catalogue numbers on the rear of this sleeve. Shortly after, PMC 7027 Mono versions were deleted and only stereo sleeves were used.

Sgt. Pepper is one of three mono LP Beatles titles pressed using the black/silver 1 x EMI box label, circa 1970. Reference YEX 637 indicates stereo pressing plates were used.

Sleeves for mono/stereo versions identical, except for printed catalogue number on rear. 'Beatles' design alleged to contain secret telephone number '834 1735' reported to connect callers to a Beatle aide.

Front cover of 1967 Christmas flexi attributed to Julian Lennon, John Lennon and Ringo Starr. Printed on lighter weight cardboard than previous flexis. Many have not survived in Mint condition.

By 1968, Fan Club membership had fallen from its peak in 1964 & 1965, so membership application form was included in initial copies of Lady Madonna, released 15th March 1968.

Side 1 label for the Parlophone export version of *The Beatles* PCS 7067/8, aka *The White Album*. The additional 'P' in the prefix is for 'Parlophone'.

Rarest Beatles' export long-player. Odeon was the label used for The Beatles' release in Portugal, so it would appear that EMI produced a small batch of LP's and exported them.

At time of release, Apple had not produced 'Demonstration Record' labels. White label was stickered by Apple Custom Recording labels. Factory white label covers anti-slip grooves of 'dinked' example.

Something, released from the *Abbey Road* LP, used a Parlophone demonstration label. It remains a very collectable demo that is relatively hard to locate.

Given to reviewers, important retail accounts and staff members, this stickered 'Factory Sample' is stamped '28th October 1969', possibly the date it was to be despatched, 2 days prior to release.

Rare Record Price Guide 2008

Extremely rare export LP. EMI had already begun releasing product on the black/silver 1 x EMI box design. The sight of this label quickens the pulse of labelologists.

So rarely seen, here is Side 2 of this export long-player.

EMI overstickered the 'misplaced' Apple logo sleeve with this gold foil 'Parlophone Trade Mark of The Gramophone Co. Ltd'. Misplaced Apple logo visible at the left-hand side.

More numerous than the black and yellow versions, this is an example of the second issue on the black & silver 1 x EMI box Parlophone label.

Released on 6th March 1970, and final Beatles original single until Free As A Bird in 1995. Picture sleeve printed on good quality board and available on initial run of singles.

Release of this single in 1970 would indicate that the Apple trade-mark had still not been cleared in some territories. Therefore, it was necessary to release this single on Parlophone.

Why these even exist is a mystery. Identical to the UK definitive issue with the addition of a 'P' included in the catalogue number.

After 1966, EMI test pressings were manufactured on plain white labels. Very few copies pressed. As with singles, Apple received pre-production copies and applied typed acetate Apple Custom Recording labels.

Released on black & silver 1 x EMI box, these LPs (unlike *Abbey Road*) had PPCS 7096 catalogue numbered sleeve printed on spine and Parlophone logo reproduced on back cover.

UK export issue of Hey Jude released on Parlophone for territories where Apple label could not be used. Track 3 lists PAPER BACK WRITER (sic) as three words, not two.

Note that in addition to the erroneous space between 'Paper' and 'Back', the final track Revolution has become 'Revolutions'.

Who says that Ringo Starr's records are not worth money? This 1972 'Ringo' or 'Robin' 1-sided interview 7" single is worth £2,000.

ANDY BLADE
80	SMS SMS 001	Break The News/Girl With The Goods (p/s)	10

(see also Eater)

BLADES
80	Energy NRG 3	Hot For You/The Reunion	
		(p/s; Irish with paper labels; later UK with plastic labels, in plastic sleeve)	20/15
81	Energy NRG 5	Ghost Of A Chance/Real Emotion	
		(p/s; Irish with paper labels; UK with plastic labels, in plastic sleeve)	20/12
84	Reekus RKS 013	The Last Man In Europe (p/s)	12
85	Reekus RKS 15	Those Were The Days (p/s)	10
85	Reekus RKSY 15	Those Were The Days (picture disc)	12
86	Reekus RKS 017	Downmarket/Truth Don't Hurt (as Blades with Paul Cleary)	10
84	Reekus RKLP 1	THE LAST MAN IN EUROPE (LP)	20
86	Reekus RKLP 3	RAY TOWN REVISITED (LP)	20

(see also Partisans)

BLADES OF GRASS
67	Stateside SS 2040	Happy/That's What A Boy Likes	10
68	Stateside SS 2101	Charlie And Fred/You Won't Find That Girl	8

BLAH BLAH BLAH
79	Absurd ABSURD 1	In The Army/Why Diddle? (p/s)	5
80s	Lyntone LYN 17627	Heavenly View/ST. VITUS DANCE: Meet Mohammed	
	Good Vibes H 002	(1-sided 33rpm flexidisc with *Helden* fanzine)	6/5
81	Some Bizzare	BLAH BLAH BLAH (LP, unreleased, stickered sleeve,	
		white label test pressings only)	40

HAL BLAINE (& YOUNG COUGARS)
64	RCA RCA 1379	Gear Stripper/Challenger II (with Young Cougars)	20
64	RCA RD/SF 7624	DEUCES, T'S, ROADSTERS AND DRUMS (LP, mono/stereo)	44/55

VIVIAN BLAINE
53	Brunswick 05137	A Bushell And A Peck/My Time Today/Take Back Your Mink (78)	20
54	Parlophone MSP 6070	Changing Partners/Lonely	10

BLAIR
79	Miracle M4	Night Life/Virgo Princess (12")	40

BEVERLEY BLAIR
58	Mercury 7MT 209	With Love We Live/Tony	20

HENRY BLAIR
50s	Capitol EAP 1-3003	SPARKY'S MAGIC PIANO (EP)	10

SALLY BLAIR
58	MGM MGM 1000	Whatever Lola Wants (Lola Gets)/Daddy (78 rpm = £8)	25

GARRY BLAKE
66	Columbia DB 7885	Strawberries And Cream/Look Out Now!	5
66	Columbia DB 7977	Wait Until Dark/Jungle Juice	5
66	Columbia DB 8074	The Danny Scipio Theme/Celebration Day	5

KARL BLAKE
80	Daark Inc. 1	TANK DEATH (C-60 cassette)	12
81	Daark Inc. 2	THE NEW POLLUTION (C-60 cassette)	12
83	Glass GLASS 013	THE PREHENSILE TAPES (LP)	12
92	Tak Tak Tak TAK 07	MANDIBLES (cassette, 500 only)	12

(see also Lemon Kittens, Shock Headed Peters, Underneath, Gland Shrouds, Fur Fur, Sol Invictus)

KEITH BLAKE
68	Blue Cat BS 102	Musically/I'm Moving On	35

(see also Overtakers, Uniques)

TIM BLAKE
78	Barclay Towers BAR 711	Generator Laserbeam/Woodland Voice (p/s)	8
78	Barclay Towers CLAY 7005	BLAKE'S NEW JERUSALEM (LP)	15

(see also Gong, Hawkwind)

WINSTON BLAKE & M-SQUAD
71	Green Door GD 4003	Carrol Street/ANSELL COLLINS & M-SQUAD: Carol St. Version	12

ART BLAKEY JAZZ MESSENGERS
60	Fontana TFE 17257	BLUES MARCH (EP)	8
61	Fontana TFE 17337	I REMEMBER CLIFFORD (EP)	8
61	Fontana TFE 17364	ARE YOU REAL (EP, with Lee Morgan & Benny Golson)	8
61	Fontana TFL 5116	OLYMPIA CONCERT (LP)	15
62	HMV CLP 1532	ART BLAKEY JAZZ MESSENGERS (LP, also stereo CSD 1423)	each 15
62	Fontana TFL 5184	DANGEROUS FRIENDSHIPS (LP, soundtrack)	18
63	United Artists (S)ULP 1017	THREE BLIND MICE (LP, mono/stereo)	each 15
64	Riverside RLP 438	CARAVAN (LP)	15
64	HMV CLP 1760	A JAZZ MESSAGE (LP)	15
64	Riverside RLP 464	UGETSU (LP)	30
65	Limelight (S)LML 4000	'S MAKE IT (LP)	12
66	Limelight (S)LML 4012	SOUL FINGER (LP)	12
66	Limelight (S)LML 4021	BUTTERCORN LADY (LP)	12
67	Limelight (S)LML 4023	HOLD ON, I'M COMIN' (LP)	12
67	Atlantic 590 009	BLUE MONK (LP, with Thelonious Monk)	15

(see also Annie Ross)

ART BLAKEY/MILES DAVIS
66	Fontana FJL 135	L'ASCENSEUR POUR L'ECHAFAUD/FEMME DISPARAISSANTE	
		(LP, soundtrack, 1 side each)	50

(see also Thelonious Monk, Miles Davis)

MEL BLANC
56	Capitol Junior CJ 104	Bugs Bunny & Aladdin's Lamp parts 1 & 2 (78, with p/s)	7
56	Capitol Junior CJ 107	Bugs Bunny & The Pirate parts 1 & 2 (78, with p/s)	7
56	Capitol Junior CJ 108	Bugs Bunny & The Grow-Small Juice parts 1 & 2 (78, with p/s)	7
56	Capitol Junior CJ 109	Woody Woodpecker Meets Davy Crockett/Davy Crockett (78)	7
56	Capitol Junior CJ 110	Pied Piper Pussy Cat (Parts 1 & 2) (78)	7
56	Capitol Junior CJ 117	Tweety Pie Pts 1 & 2 (78)	7
58	Capitol CL 14950	I Taut I Taw A Puddy Cat/K-K-K-Katy	7
60	Warner Bros WB 26	Tweety's Twistmas Twouble/I Keep Hearing Those Bells	7

BURT BLANCA
60	Zodiac ZR 004	Texas Rider/Shamash	20

BLANCMANGE
80	Blaah Music MFT-1	IRENE AND MAVIS (EP, gatefold p/s)	25
82	Lyntone LYN 1183/84	Living On The Ceiling/Sad Day (excerpt)/PASSAGE: Born Every Minute (33rpm black flexidisc free with *Melody Maker* magazine)	6/5
82	London SHPD 8552	HAPPY FAMILIES (LP, picture disc)	12
84	London SHPD 8554	MANGE TOUT (LP, picture disc)	12
85	London 820 301-2	BELIEVE YOU ME (CD)	20

BILLY BLAND
60	London HL 9096	Let The Little Girl Dance/Sweet Thing	20
71	Atlantic 2091 130	Let The Little Girl Dance/Chicken Hop	10

BOBBY BLAND
61	Vogue V 9178	Cry Cry Cry/I've Been Wrong So Long	30
61	Vogue V 9182	Lead Me On/Hold Me Tenderly	30
61	Vogue V 9188	Don't Cry No More/St. James Infirmary	30
62	Vogue V 9190	You're The One (That I Need)/Turn On Your Love Light	30
62	Vogue V 9192	Blue Moon/Who Will The Next Fool Be?	40
64	Vocalion VP 9222	Ain't Nothing You Can Do/Honey Child	30
64	Vocalion VP 9229	After It's Too Late/Share Your Love With Me	30
65	Vocalion VP 9232	Yield Not To Temptation/How Does A Cheating Woman Feel?	30
65	Vocalion VP 9251	These Hands (Small But Mighty)/Today	30
66	Vocalion VP 9262	I'm Too Far Gone (To Turn Around)/ If You Could Read My Mind	25
66	Vocalion VP 9273	Good Time Charlie/Good Time Charlie (Working His Groove Bag)	40
68	Sue WI 4044	That Did It/A Touch Of The Blues	40
69	Action ACT 4524	Rockin' In The Same Old Boat/Wouldn't You Rather Have Me?	28
69	Action ACT 4538	Gotta Get To Know You/Baby I'm On My Way	25
69	Action ACT 4548	Share Your Love With Me/Honey Child	20
69	Action ACT 4553	Chains Of Love/Ask Me 'Bout Nothing But The Blues	20
74	ABC ABC 4014	Ain't No Love In The Heart Of The City/Twenty Four Hours	10
75	ABC ABC 4030	I Wouldn't Treat A Dog (The Way You Treat Me)/ I Ain't Gonna Be The First To Cry	8
77	ABC ABC 4186	The Soul Of A Man/If I Weren't A Gambler	8
63	Vocalion VEP 170153	YIELD NOT INTO TEMPTATION (EP)	75
64	Vocalion VEP 170157	BOBBY BLAND (EP)	75
60	Vogue VA 160183	TWO STEPS FROM THE BLUES (LP)	150
61	Vocalion VA 160183	TWO STEPS FROM THE BLUES (LP)	100
61	Vogue/Vocalion VAP 8027	AIN'T NOTHING YOU CAN DO (LP)	75
61	Vogue VAP 160183	TWO STEPS FROM THE BLUES (LP)	25
64	Vocalion VAP 8027	AIN'T NOTHING YOU CAN DO (LP)	40
63	Vogue/Vocalion VAP 8034	CALL ON ME/ THAT'S THE WAY LOVE IS (LP)	75
64	Vocalion VAP 8034	CALL ON ME/ THAT'S THE WAY LOVE IS (LP)	40
60s	Vogue VAP 8034	CALL ON ME/THAT'S THE WAY LOVE IS (LP, later issue)	45
66	Vocalion VAP 8041	HERE'S THE MAN (LP)	75
68	Island ILP 974	A TOUCH OF THE BLUES (LP)	60
69	Action ACLP 6006	A PIECE OF GOLD (LP)	40
74	Polydor 2383 257	BLUES FOR MR. CRUMP (LP, with tracks by Junior Parker & Howlin' Wolf)	20

B,L&G
71	Birds Nest BN 3	Live In The Mountains/Janie Slow Down	10

(see also Trevor Burton, Denny Laine, Steve Gibbons)

MARCIE BLANE
62	London HLU 9599	Bobby's Girl/A Time To Dream	25
63	London HLU 9673	What Does A Girl Do/How Can I Tell Him	25
63	London HLU 9744	Little Miss Fool/Ragtime Sound	25
63	London HLU 9787	You Gave My Number To Billy/Told You So	25
63	London REU 1393	MARCIE BLANE (EP)	140

BLANKS
79	Void SRTS/79/CUS/560	The Northern Ripper/Understand (p/s)	60

(see also Destructors)

BLARNEY SISTERS
67	GO AJ11407	The Greatest Blessing/Golden Band	15

BLAZE
99	Slip And Slide SLIP 99	Wishing You Were Here/(mixes) (2x12")	18

BLAZER, BLAZER
78	Logo GO 362	Cecil B. Devine/Warsaw/Six O'Clock In The Morning (p/s)	10

BLAZERS
58	Fontana TFR 6010	ROCK AND ROLL (10" LP)	100

BLAZING SONS
83	Cool Ghoul COOL 002	Chant Down The National Front/N.F. Dub (no p/s)	10

(see also Phantom)

BLEACH BOYS
78	Tramp THF 002	Chloroform/You've Got Nothing (no p/s, 1,000 only)	60
85	Zombie International ZOMBO 103010	Stocking-Clad Nazi Death Squad Bitches/Death Before Disco/ Gimme That Neutron Taste (12", p/s)	25

BLEAK HOUSE
80s	Buzzard BUZZ 1	Rainbow Warrior/Isandlhwana/Inquisition (some in p/s)	100/30
82	Buzzard BUZZ 2	LIONS IN WINTER (Chase The Wind/No Reply/Down To Zero/ Flight Of The Salamander) (EP, p/s with insert)	90

BLEECHERS
69	Trojan TR 679	Ease Up/You're Gonna Feel It	12
69	Upsetter US 314	Come Into My Parlour/MELOTONES: Dry Up Your Tears	15
70	Col. Blue Beat DB 118	Send Me The Pillow (That You Dream On)/Adam And Eve	8
71	Duke DU 118	Put It Good/J.J. ALLSTARS: Good Good Version	10

(see also Busty Brown, Upsetters)

PETER BLEGVAD
80	Recommended RRA 5.75	Alcohol (p/s, 1-sided, other side etched)	5

(see also Slapp Happy)

BLENDELLS
64	Reprise RS 20291	La La La La La La/Huggies Bunnies	25
64	Reprise RS 20340	Dance With Me/Get Your Baby	25

CARLA BLEY
72	JCOA JT 4001	ESCALATOR OVER THE HILL (3-LP, with Paul Haines & Jack Bruce)	25
74	Watt WATT 1	TROPIC APPETITES (LP)	15

(see also Jazz Composers Orchestra, Michael Mantler, Jack Bruce)

PAUL BLEY TRIO
69	Fontana SFJL 929	TOUCHING (LP)	40

(see also Bley-Peacock Synthesizer Show, Annette Peacock)

ARCHIE BLEYER & HIS ORCHESTRA
54	London HL 8035	Amber/Julie's Jump (78 rpm = £6)	25
54	London HL 8111	The Naughty Lady Of Shady Lane/While The Vesper Bells Were Ringing (78 rpm = £6)	25
55	London HLA 8176	Hernando's Hideaway/S'il Vous Plait	20
56	London HLA 8243	Nothin' To Do/JANET BLEYER: 'Cause You're My Lover (78 rpm = £6)	15
56	London HLA 8263	Bridge Of Happiness/You Tell Me Your Dream, I'll Tell You Mine (78 rpm = £6)	15

BLEY-PEACOCK SYNTHESIZER SHOW
72	Polydor 2425 043	REVENGE (LP)	50

(see also Annette Peacock, Paul Bley)

BLIND BLAKE
50	Tempo R 23	Hey Hey Daddy Blues/Brownskin Mama Blues (78)	12
50	Tempo R 40	Southern Rag/CC Pill Blues (78)	12
54	Jazz Collector L 97	Hot Potatoes/Southbound Rag (78)	12
58	Ristic LP 18	THE LEGENDARY BLIND BLAKE (10" LP)	70
50s	Jazz Collector JLP 2001	THE LEGENDARY BLIND BLAKE (10" LP, reissue)	20
67	Riverside RLP 8804	BLUES IN CHICAGO (LP)	30
60s	Whoopee 101	BLIND BLAKE 1927-30 (LP)	15

(see also Paramount Allstars)

BLIND BLAKE/CHARLIE JACKSON
50s	Heritage HLP 1011	BLIND BLAKE AND CHARLIE JACKSON (LP, 99 only)	100+

BLIND BLAKE/RAMBLIN' THOMAS
59	Jazz Collector JEL 4	THE MALE BLUES VOLUME 3 (EP)	10

BLIND FAITH
69	Island (no cat. no.)	Change Of Address From June 23rd 1969 (promo issue, 500 only)	200+
69	Polydor 583 059	BLIND FAITH (LP, gatefold sleeve)	25

(see also Stevie Winwood, Ginger Baker, Eric Clapton)

BLIND FURY
85	Roadrunner RR 9814	OUT OF REACH (LP)	12

BLINKERS
69	Pye 7N 17752	Original Sin/Dreams Secondhand	80

BLINKY & EDWIN STARR
69	Tamla Motown TMG 720	Oh How Happy/Ooo Baby Baby (unissued, demos only)	250
70	Tamla Motown TMG 748	Oh How Happy/Ooo Baby Baby	10
70	T. Motown (S)TML 11131	JUST WE TWO (LP, as Edwin Starr & Blinky)	25

(see also Edwin Starr)

BLISS
69	Chapter One CH 107	Courtyards In Castile/Lifetime	20

MELVIN BLISS
77	Contempo CS 2013	Reward/Synthetic Substitution	30

BLITZ
81	No Future OI 1	ALL OUT ATTACK (EP, rubber-stamped labels, 500 only)	25
81	No Future OI 1	ALL OUT ATTACK (EP, reissue, white labels, later printed labels)	15/10
82	No Future OI 6	Never Surrender/Razor In The Night (p/s)	12
82	No Future OI 16	Warriors/Youth (p/s)	12
82	No Future PUNK 1	VOICE OF A GENERATION (LP, with inner sleeve)	22

(see also Rose Of Victory)

BLITZ BOYS
80	Told You So TYS 001	Eddy's New Shoes/Eddie's Friend/She Told My Friends (foldover p/s)	100

BLITZKRIEG
81	Neat NEAT 10	Buried Alive/Blitzkrieg (p/s)	60
91	Roadrunner R 09302	10 YEARS OF BLITZKRIEG (EP)	10
85	Neat NEAT 1023	A TIME OF CHANGES (LP)	40

BLITZKRIEG
82	No Future OI 8	LEST WE FORGET (EP)	18

BLITZKRIEG BOP
77	Mortonsound MTN 3172/3	Let's Go/Nine Till Five/Bugger Off (p/s, 500 only)	55
77	Lightning GTL 504	Let's Go (re-recorded)/Life Is Just A So-So/Mental Case (p/s)	15
78	Lightning GTL 543	U.F.O./Bobby Joe (p/s)	20

BLIZZARD
71	CBS CBS 7238	Baby Blue/Mama, The Sparrow And The Tree	5

BLOATED TOADS
79	Shattered SHAT 4	Why/Essential In Some Form/Happy Home/Yankee TV Victim (p/s, with insert)	5

BLOC PARTY
04	Trash Aesthetics TA701	She's Hearing Voices/The Marshals Are Dead/The Answer (p/s clear vinyl, 500 only)	70
04	Moshi Moshi MOSHI10	Banquet/Staying Fat (p/s, 500 only)	15
04	Moshi Moshi MOSH110CD	Banquet/Staying Fat (p/s, 2000 only)	12
04	Wichita WEBB067S	Little Thoughts/Storm and Stress (Blue vinyl, p/s)	12
05	Wichita WEBB088S	The Pioneers/The Pioneers (Bloc Party vs Mystery Jets) (numbered pic disc)	7
05	Wichita WEBB075LP	SILENT ALARM (LP)	12
05	Wichita WEBB075PD	SILENT ALARM (LP, picture disc)	20
05	Wichita WEBB090LP	SILENT ALARM REMIXED (2xLP)	13

BLODWYN PIG
69	Island WIP 6059	Dear Jill/Sweet Caroline	10
69	Island WIP 6069	Walk On The Water/Summer Day	10
70	Chrysalis WIP 6078	Same Old Story/Slow Down	10
89	private release	A TASTE OF THINGS TO COME (cassette, 50 only, sold at gigs)	25
69	Island ILPS 9101	AHEAD RINGS OUT (LP, gatefold sleeve, pink or 'pink rim palm tree' label)	25/12
70	Chrysalis ILPS 9122	GETTING TO THIS (LP, gatefold sleeve)	25

(see also Mick Abrahams, Jethro Tull)

BLOND
69	Fontana TF 1040	(I Will Bring You) Flowers In The Morning/I Wake Up And Call	15
69	Fontana STL 5515	THE LILAC YEARS (LP, gatefold sleeve)	150

(see also Tages)

BLONDE ON BLONDE
69	Pye 7N 17637	All Day All Night/Country Life	60
70	Ember EMB S 279	Castles In The Sky/Circles (some in p/s)	20/12
72	Ember EMB S 316	Sad Song For An Easy Lady/Happy Families	6
79	Pye YN 46189	Whole Lotta Love/Make Me Smile	6
69	Pye NSPL 18288	CONTRASTS (LP, gatefold sleeve)	70
70	Ember NR 5049	RE-BIRTH (LP, gatefold sleeve)	40
71	Ember NR 5058	REFLECTIONS ON A LIFE (LP, gatefold sleeve)	40
70s	Ember LP 7005	BLONDE ON BLONDE (LP, unissued, test pressings only)	100+

BLONDIE
77	Private Stock PVT 90	X Offender/In The Sun (unissued, promos or stock copies, no p/s)	750+
77	Private Stock PVT 105	In The Flesh/X Offender (no p/s)	20
77	Chrysalis CHS 2180	Rip Her To Shreds/In The Flesh/X Offender (p/s)	8
77	Chrysalis CHS 2180-12	Rip Her To Shreds/In The Flesh/X Offender (12", green labels, '75p' p/s)	8
78	Chrysalis CHS 2204	Denis (Denee)/Contact In Red Square (red p/s)	5
78	Chrysalis CHS 2242	Picture This/Fade Away (And Radiate) (p/s, yellow vinyl)	5
78	Chrysalis CHE 2266	Hanging On The Telephone/Will Anything Happen (p/s, export issue)	5
78	Chrysalis CHE 2275	Heart Of Glass/Rifle Range (p/s, export issue with "pain in the ass" lyrics)	8
80	Flexi FLX 146	Speaking From The Studio (Blondie Fan Club flexidisc)	15
82	Lyntone LYN 10840/1	Yuletown Throwdown (Rapture) (with Freddie)/BRATTLES: The Christmas Song/SNUKY TATE: Santa's Agent (33rpm blue or orange vinyl flexi with *Flexipop* issue 15)	8/5
89	Chrysalis CHSP 12 3342	Call Me (Remix)/Backfired (Remix)/Call Me (1989) (12", picture disc)	8
98	EMI 12 ATOM 150	ATOMIC 98 (Remixes) (12", p/s, withdrawn)	15
98	EMI CD ATOM 150	ATOMIC 98 (Remixes) (CD, withdrawn)	18
76	Private Stock PVLP 1017	BLONDIE (LP)	18
82	Chrysalis PCDL 1384	THE HUNTER (LP, picture disc)	15
89	Chrysalis CHR 1658	THE 12" MIXES (2-LP)	15
89	Chrysalis CCD 1658	THE 12" MIXES (CD)	18
95	Chrysalis CD CHR 6105	BEAUTIFUL – THE REMIX ALBUM (CD)	18
98	Chysalis 4949962	ATOMIC (CD)	18

(see also Debbie Harry, New York Blondes, Wind In The Willows, Rodney & Brunettes)

BLOOBLO
73	Contour 2870338	REGGAE PARTY TIME (LP)	12
76	Feelgood FG1	CHAKA (LP)	12

BLOOD
83	No Future OI 22	Megalomania/Calling The Shots/Parasite In Paradise (p/s)	15
83	Noise NOY 1	Stark Raving Normal/Mesrine (p/s)	10
82	Noise NOYZLP 1	FALSE GESTURES FOR A DEVIOUS PUBLIC (LP)	20
85	Conquest QUEST 3	SE PARARE NEX (LP)	15
89	Link Classics CLINK 5	FALSE GESTURES FOR A DEVIOUS PUBLIC (LP, reissue, red vinyl)	15

BLOODROCK
71	Capitol CL 15670	D.O.A./Children's Heritage	5
71	Capitol E-ST 491	BLOODROCK 2 (LP)	12
71	Capitol E-ST 765	BLOODROCK 3 (LP)	12

BOBBY BLOOD
70	Polydor 2058 051	Montego Bay/Try A Little Harder	5

BLOOD SISTERS
79	Sound City SCD 002	Ring My Bell/Dub (12")	15
79	Sound City SCD 004	What About Me/I'd Rather Go Blind (12")	15

BLOOD, SWEAT & TEARS
68	CBS 3563	I Can't Quit Her/House In The Country	15
69	CBS 4116	You've Made Me So Very Happy/The Blues, Part 2	5
69	CBS 4220	Spinning Wheel/More And More	5
68	CBS 63296	CHILD IS THE FATHER TO THE MAN (LP)	20

(see also Al Kooper, David Clayton-Thomas)

ROGER BLOOM'S HAMMER
67	CBS 202654	Out Of The Blue/Life's A Gamble	12
67	CBS 2848	Polly Pan/Fifteen Degree Temperature Rise	6

MIKE BLOOMFIELD
69	CBS 63652	IT'S NOT KILLING ME (LP)	20

(see also Barry Goldberg Reunion, Stephen Stills, K.G.B.)

MIKE BLOOMFIELD & AL KOOPER
69	CBS 4094	The Weight/59th Street Bridge Song	10
69	CBS 66216	THE LIVE ADVENTURES OF MIKE BLOOMFIELD AND AL KOOPER (2-LP)	20

(see also Al Kooper, Paul Butterfield Blues Band, Electric Flag)

BLOSSOMS
58	Capitol CL 14833	Move On/He Promised Me	50
58	Capitol CL 14856	Little Louie/Have Faith In Me	40
58	Capitol CL 14947	No Other Love/Baby Daddy-O	40
68	MGM MGM 1435	Tweedle Dee/You Got Me Hummin'	20
71	Pama PM 814	Stand By/Soul And Inspiration	20
73	Mojo 2027 013	Touchdown/It's All Up To You	8

(see also Darlene Love, Allisons [U.S.])

BLOSSOM TOES
67	Marmalade 598 002	What On Earth/Mrs Murphy's Budgerigar/Look At Me I'm You (some in p/s)	70/30
68	Marmalade 598 009	I'll Be Your Baby Tonight/Love Is	30
68	Marmalade 598 012	Postcard/Everyone's Leaving Me Now	30
69	Marmalade 598 014	Peace Loving Man/Up Above My Hobby Horse's Head	30
69	Marmalade 598 022	New Day/Love Bomb (unissued, existence unconfirmed)	
67	Marmalade 607/608 001	WE ARE EVER SO CLEAN (LP)	80+
69	Marmalade 608 010	IF ONLY FOR A MOMENT (LP)	100+

(see also B.B. Blunder, Stud, Kevin Westlake)

MICHAEL BLOUNT
70	CBS 7022	Sometimes/Angelina Baby	5
72	York SYK 519	Beautiful Morning/Feathered Cloud	5
72	York SYK 28	Tackle And Sack/Pretty Face	5
72	York SKY 535	Rosie/Trombone Man	5
71	CBS 64230	PATCHWORK (LP)	18
72	York FYK 401	SOUVENIRS (LP)	15
73	York FYK 414	FANTASIES (LP)	15

BLOW MONKEYS
82	Parasol PAR 1	Live Today Love Tomorrow/In Cold Blood (no p/s)	6
87	RCA MONKX 6	(Celebrate) The Day After You (Election Mix)/It's Not Unusual (live)/Beautiful Child/The Smile On Her Face (Sweet Murder) (10", with Curtis Mayfield, withdrawn 'Thatcher' p/s, 'General Election Party Edition')	10

(see also Curtis Mayfield)

BLOWZABELLA
70s	Special Delivery SPD 1028	VANILLA (LP)	30
70s	Plant Life PLR 051	IN COLOUR (LP)	20

BLUE
73	RSO 2090 109	Red Light Song/Look Around	6
73	RSO 2090 114	Little Jody/The Way Things Are	6
73	RSO 2394 105	BLUE (LP)	15

(see also Poets)

BABBITY BLUE
65	Decca F 12053	Don't Make Me (Fall In Love With You)/I Remembered How To Cry	10
65	Decca F 12149	Don't Hurt Me/Question	10

BOBBY BLUE
70	Duke DU 86	Going In Circles (actually by Lloyd Charmers)/Doggone Right (actually by Bobby Davis)	8

DAVID BLUE
67	Elektra EKL 4003	DAVID BLUE (LP, red label)	30
72	Asylum SYL 9001	STORIES (LP)	15
73	Asylum SYL 9009	NICE BABY AND THE ANGEL (LP)	15
75	Asylum SYL 9025	COMIN' BACK FOR MORE (LP)	12
76	Asylum K 53056	CUPID'S ARROW (LP)	12

MINT VALUE £

PAMELA BLUE
63   Decca F 11761   My Friend Bobby/Hey There Stranger................................... 85

TIMOTHY BLUE
68   Spark SRL 1014   The Room At The Top Of The Stairs/She Won't See The Light 15

BLUE ACES
64   Pye 7N 15672   Land Of Love/Love Song Of The Waterfall............................. 7
64   Pye 7N 15713   I Beat You To It/I Just Can't Help Loving You 7
65   Pye 7N 15821   Ain't What You Say/You Don't Care 12
65   Columbia DB 7755   Tell Me What You're Gonna Do/All I Want............................ 100
66   Columbia DB 7954   That's All Right/Talk About My Baby............................... 125
   (see also Riot Squad)

BLUE & FERRIS
68   Blue Cat BS 147   You Stole My Money/Tell Me The Reason.............................. 40

BLUE ANGEL
80   Polydor POSP 212   I'm Gonna Be Strong/Anna Blue (no p/s)............................. 6
81   Polydor POSP 241   I Had A Love/Can't Blame Me....................................... 6
84   Polydor POSP 212   I'm Gonna Be Strong/Anna Blue (p/s, reissue) 10
80   Polydor 2391 486   BLUE ANGEL (LP)... 30
   (see also Cyndi Lauper)

BLUE ARSED FLY
95   Ferox FER 012   IN THE BAG EP (12")... 15
96   Mosquito MSQ 04   BLUE ARSED FLY EP (12")... 20
   (see also Christian Vogel, Neil Landstrumm)

BLUE BEARD
71   Ember EMB S 302   Country Man/Sly Willy (some in p/s) 20/10
71   Ember LT 7004   BLUE BEARD (LP, unreleased, test pressings only)................... 200

BLUEBEATS
64   Ember EMB EP 4525   THE FABULOUS BLUEBEATS VOL. 1 (EP)................................. 50
64   Ember EMB EP 4526   THE FABULOUS BLUEBEATS VOL. 2 (EP)................................. 50

BLUE BEATS
60   Blue Beat 45/BB 20   Baby What You Done Me Wrong/Go Pretty Baby Go 10

BLUEBEATERS
64   Piccadilly 7N 35181   Little David/Ain't Got A Care 10
64   Piccadilly 7N 35191   Early In The Morning/There I Go................................... 7

BLUEBELLS
82   London LON(F) 14/   Forevermore/Aim In Life (p/s, with free 33rpm clear vinyl flexidisc
     Lyntone LYN 12361   Everybody's Somebody's Fool)...................................... 6

BLUE-BELLES
62   HMV POP 1029   I Sold My Heart To The Junkman/Itty Bitty Twist.................... 30

BLUEBERRIES
65   Mercury MF 894   It's Gonna Work Out Fine/Please Don't Let Me Know.................. 30

BLUE BLOOD
70   Sonet SNTF 615   BLUE BLOOD (LP) 25

BLUE BLUDD
87   Blud Donor no cat. No.   LIQUOR 'N' POKER (EP)... 20

BLUE CHEER
68   Philips BF 1646   Summertime Blues/Out Of Focus 20
68   Philips BF 1684   Just A Little Bit/Gypsy Ball 12
68   Philips BF 1711   Feathers From Your Tree/Sun Cycle 12
69   Philips BF 1778   West Coast Child Of Sunshine/When It All Gets Old 12
71   Philips 6051 010   Pilot/Babaji... 10
68   Philips (S)BL 7839   VINCEBUS ERUPTUM (LP, mono/stereo)............................. 50/30
68   Philips SBL 7860   OUTSIDEINSIDE (LP, gatefold sleeve)............................... 40
69   Philips SBL 7896   NEW! IMPROVED! (LP).. 30
69   Philips 6336 001   BLUE CHEER (LP).. 35
71   Philips 6336 004   B.C. #5 THE ORIGINAL HUMAN BEING (LP)............................ 40
   (see also Leigh Stephens, Group B)

BLUE CHIPS
65   Pye 7N 15970   I'm On The Right Side/You're Good To Me........................... 30
66   Pye 7N 17111   Some Kind Of Lovin'/I Know A Boy 45
66   Pye 7N 17155   Tell Her/Good Lovin' Never Hurt 30

BLUE DIAMONDS
60   Decca F 21292   Ramona/All Of Me 7
60   Decca DFE 6675   I'M FOREVER BLOWING BUBBLES (EP).................................. 15

BLUE EPITAPH
74   Holyground HG 117   ODE (LP, 99 copies only).. 225+
91   Holyground HG 117   ODE (LP, reissue, folded gatefold sleeve) 18
   (see also Magus)

BLUE EYES
91   Union Hall001   Pick Up The Mic On A Soul Tip/The Law (12")....................... 30

BLUE FLAMES
63   R&B JB 114   J.A. Blues/Orange Street 40
63   R&B JB 126   Stop Right Here/Rik's Tune 40
   (see also Georgie Fame & Blue Flames)

BLUE GOOSE
75	Anchor ANC 1015	Loretta/Call On Me	5
75	Anchor ANCL 2005	BLUE GOOSE (LP)	12

(see also Badfinger, Curtis Knight & Zeus, Motörhead)

BLUE JEANS
69	Columbia DB 8555	Hey Mrs. Housewife/Sandfly	35

(see also Swinging Blue Jeans, Ray Ennis & Blue Jeans)

BLUE MAGIC
74	Atlantic K 10494	Sideshow/Just Don't Want To Be Lonely	5
75	Atlantic K 10553	Three Ring Circus/Spell	5

(see also Margie Joseph)

BLUE MAXI
70	Major Minor MM 705	Here Comes Summer/Famous Last Words	6

(see also Jean-Jacques Burnel & Dave Greenfield)

BLUE MEN
60	Triumph RGXST 5000	I HEAR A NEW WORLD (PART ONE) (EP)	300+
60	Triumph RGXST 5001	I HEAR A NEW WORLD (PART TWO) (EP, only sleeves exist)	sleeve 25
60	Triumph TRX ST 9000	I HEAR A NEW WORLD (LP, unreleased, white label demos only)	800+

(see also Joe Meek, Peter Jay & Blue Men, Rodd-Ken & Cavaliers)

BLUE MINK
74	EMI EMC3021	FRUITY (LP)	12

BLUE MITCHELL
73	Mainstream MSL 1015	THE LAST TANGO = BLUES	25

BLUE MOUNTAIN BOYS
63	Oriole CB 1774	Drop Me Gently/One Small Photograph Of You	5

BLUE MOVIES
79	ROK ROK 9	Mary Jane/THE NOISE: Criminal (company sleeve)	15

BLUE NILE
81	RSO RSO 84	I Love This Life/The Second Act (p/s)	25
84	Linn LKS 1	Stay/Saddle The Horses (white p/s)	8
84	Linn LKS 1-12	Stay/Saddle The Horses (12", white p/s)	12
84	Linn LKS 1	Stay (Remix)/Saddle The Horses (p/s)	5
84	Linn LKSD 1	Stay (Remix)/Saddle The Horses//Tinsel Town In The Rain/Heatwave (Instrumental) (p/s, double pack)	8
84	Linn LKS 1-12	Stay (Extended Remix)/Saddle The Horses (12", p/s)	8
84	Linn LKS 2	Tinsel Town In The Rain/Heatwave (Instrumental) (p/s)	5
84	Linn LKS 2-12	Tinsel Town In The Rain (Extended)/Regret/Heatwave (Instrumental) (12", p/s)	8
89	Linn LKYCD 4	Headlights On The Parade (CD, collector's pack)	8
80s	Linn	flexidisc (demonstration disc)	20

BLUENOTES
60	Top Rank JAR 291	I Don't Know What It Is/You Can't Get Away From Love	10

BLUE ORCHIDS
81	Rough Trade RT 065	Disney Boys/The Flood (p/s)	5
81	Rough Trade RT 067	Work/The House That Faded Out (p/s)	5
82	Rough Trade RT 117T	AGENTS OF CHANGE (12" EP, in carrier bag)	8
84	Rough Trade ROUGH 37	GREATEST HITS (LP)	12

(see also Nosebleeds, Fall)

BLUE ÖYSTER CULT
76	CBS 4483	(Don't Fear) The Reaper/R U Ready 2 Rock	5
76	CBS 4483	(Don't Fear) The Reaper/Tattoo Vampire (promo with different B-side)	10
78	CBS 5689	Going Through The Motions/Searching For The Celine	5
78	CBS 12-6333	(Don't Fear) The Reaper (12")	8
79	CBS 7763	Mirrors/Lonely Teardrops (clear vinyl)	5
81	CBS A 1453	Burnin' For You/Heavy Metal (p/s)	5
73	CBS 64904	BLUE ÖYSTER CULT (LP)	12

BLUE PHANTOM
72	Kaleidoscope KAL 101	DISTORTIONS (LP)	70

BLUE RIDGE RANGERS
73	Fantasy FTC 105	Hearts Of Stone/Somewhere Listening For My Name	6
73	Fantasy FTC 110	You Don't Own Me/Back In The Hills	6
73	Fantasy FT 511	BLUE RIDGE RANGERS (LP)	18

(see also John Fogerty, Creedence Clearwater Revival)

BLUE RONDOS
64	Pye 7N 15734	Little Baby/Baby I Go For You	40
65	Pye 7N 15833	Don't Want Your Lovin' No More/What Can I Do	50

BLUES BAND
80	Blues Band BBBP 101	OFFICIAL BOOTLEG ALBUM (LP, numbered, with autographs, 3000 only)	20

(see also Paul Jones, McGuinness-Flint, Manfred Mann)

BLUES BENDERS
66	Rio R93	Girl Next Door/Leave Me Out	25

BLUESBREAKERS
(see under John Mayall & Bluesbreakers)

BLUES BUSTERS
63	Blue Beat BB 73	There's Always Sunshine/You Had It All Wrong	20
59	Limbo XL101	Little Vilma/ Early One Morning	20
61	Starlite ST45 031	The Spiritual/ Lost My Baby	20
61	Blue Beat BB55	Donna/ You're Driving Me Crazy	15

MINT VALUE £

62	Blue Beat BB73	There's Always Sunshine/ You Had It Wrong	12
62	Starlite ST45 072	Your Love/ You Send Me Crazy	20
62	Island WI-023	Behold/ Oh Baby	20
62	Blue Beat BB102	Tell Me Why/ I've Done You Wrong	15
65	Island WI-214	How Sweet It Is/ I Had A Dream	25
65	Island WI-219	Wide Awake In A Dream (actually by Philip James solo)/ MAYTALS: Tell Me The Reason	100
65	Island WI-222	Wings Of A Dove/ BYRON LEE & DRAGONAIRES: Dan Is The Man	25
66	Doctor Bird DB1030	I've Been Trying/ Pretty Girls	25
67	Doctor Bird DB 1078	There's Always Sunshine/ Lovers' Reward	25
71	Dynamic DYN408	Each One Teach One/ Thinking Of You	5
71	Jay Boy BOY 44	I Can't Stop/Inspired To Love You	10
71	Trojan TR7819	Thinking Of You/ Version	5
65	Island ILP-923	BEHOLD!	60
67	Docto Bird DLM5008	BEST OF THE BLUES BUSTERS	50
78	Sarge LP1001	TRUTH	12
78	Sarge LP1003	TRIBUTE TO SAM COOKE	18

BLUES BY FIVE
64	Decca F 12029	Boom Boom/I Cried	60

BLUES COUNCIL
65	Parlophone R 5264	Baby Don't Look Down/What Will I Do	100

BLUES 5
64	Studio 36 (no cat. no.)	Hey Baby/When You're In Love	130

BLUES IMAGE
70	Atlantic 2091 009	Ride Captain Ride/Pay My Dues	5
71	Atlantic 2400 120	RED, WHITE AND BLUES IMAGE (LP)	12

BLUES INCORPORATED
(see under Alexis Korner)

BLUES MAGOOS
66	Mercury MF 954	(We Ain't Got) Nothin' Yet/Gotta Get Away	25
67	Fontana TF 848	One By One/Love Seems Doomed	15
71	Probe PRO 522	Can't Get Enough Of You/Sea Breeze Express	5
66	Fontana (S)TL 5402	BLUES MAGOOS (LP, mono/stereo)	50/45
71	Probe SPB 1024	GULF COAST BOUND (LP)	12

BLUES MASTERS
63	Island WI 078	5 O'Clock Whistle/African Blood (both sides actually by Baba Brooks)	30

BLUESOLOGY
65	Fontana TF 594	Come Back Baby/Time's Getting Tougher Than Tough	250
66	Fontana TF 668	Mister Frantic/Everyday (I Have The Blues)	300

(see also Stu Brown & Bluesology, Elton John, Long John Baldry, Elton Dean, Mark Charig)

BLUES PROJECT
67	Verve Forecast VS 1505	I Can't Keep From Crying/The Way My Baby Walks	35
67	Verve (S)VLP 6004	PROJECTIONS (LP)	20

(see also Al Kooper, Tommy Flanders, Seatrain)

BLUE STARS
65	Decca F 12303	Please Be A Little Kind/I Can Take It	200

BLUE STEAM
78	Rip Off RIP 5	Lizard King/Cortina Cowboys (p/s)	10

BLUE SYSTEM
90	RCA PB 43733	Magic Symphony/Magic Symphony (Power Edit) (p/s)	8
90	RCA PT 43734	Magic Symphony (Power Mix)/Magic Symphony (Fun Mix)/ Magic Symphony (7" Mix) (12", p/s)	12
90	RCA PD 43734	Magic Symphony (7" Mix)/Magic Symphony (Fun Mix)/ Magic Symphony (Power Mix) (CD)	25

BLUETONES
95	Superior Quality TONE 001	Slight Return/The Fountainhead (blue vinyl, plain white sleeve in stickered polythene bag, 2,000 only, sold by mail-order & at gigs, some numbered)	18/12
95	Superior Quality TONE 001	Slight Return/The Fountainhead (red vinyl, foldover p/s in poly bag, 1,000 only, export issue to Japan)	18
96	Superior Qual. BLUE 003X	Slight Return/Don't Stand Me Down (red vinyl, export issue to Japan with Japanese text on rear of p/s)	22
98	A&M BLUEV008	RETURN TO THE LAST CHANCE SALOON (LP)	12

BLUE VELVET BAND
69	Warner Bros WS 1802	SWEET MOMENTS WITH THE BLUE VELVET BAND (LP, gatefold sleeve)	15

BLUEWATER FOLK
70s	Folk Heritage	BLUEWATER FOLK (LP)	60
70s	Moonraker MOO 1	BUGS, BLACK PUDDINGS AND CLOGS (LP, with insert)	12
70s	Moonraker MOO 2	A LANCASHIRE LIFE (LP, with insert)	12

BLUE YOGURT
70	Penny Farthing PEN 732	Lydia/Umbrella Man	6

COLIN BLUNSTONE
71	Epic EPC 7095	Mary, Won't You Warm My Bed/I Hope I Didn't Say Too Much Last Night	5
71	Epic EPC 7520	Caroline Goodbye/Though You Are Far Away	5
72	Epic EPC 7765	Say You Don't Mind/Let Me Come Closer (p/s)	7
72	Epic EPC 8434	I Don't Believe In Miracles/I've Always Had You	5
73	Epic EPC 1197	How Could We Dare To Be Wrong?/Time's Runnin' Out	5

73	Epic EPC 1775	Wonderful/Beginning 6
74	Epic EPC 2413	It's Magical/Summersong. 6
71	Epic EPC 64557	ONE YEAR (LP, textured sleeve) 15
72	Epic EPC 65278	ENNISMORE (LP, textured sleeve). 15
74	Epic EPC 65805	JOURNEY (LP). 12

(see also Zombies, Neil MacArthur, Mitchell-Coe Mysteries)

BLUNT INSTRUMENT
| 78 | Diesel DCL 01 | No Excuse/Interrogation (p/s) . . . . 5 |

BLUR
90	Food FOOD 26	She's So High (Edit)/I Know (7" p/s) 6
90	Food 12FOOD 26	She's So High (Definitive)/Sing/I Know (Extended) (12", p/s). 12
90	Food CDFOOD 26	She's So High/I Know (Extended)/Down (CD) 20
91	Food FOOD 29	There's No Other Way/Inertia (7" p/s) 5
91	Food 12FOOD 29	There's No Other Way (Extended)/Inertia/Mr. Briggs/I'm All Over (12", p/s). . . 20
91	Food 12 FOODX 29	There's No Other Way (The Blur Remix)/Won't Do It/
		Day Upon Day (live) (12", p/s lists '12 FOODDX 29'). 30
91	Food CDFOOD 29	There's No Other Way/Inertia/Mr. Briggs/I'm All Over (CD) 20
91	Food FOOD 31	Bang/Luminous (7" p/s) 5
91	Food 12FOOD 31	Bang (Extended)/Explain/Luminous/Uncle Love (12", p/s). 10
91	Food CDFOOD 31	Bang/Explain/Luminous/Beserk (CD) 20
91	Food 12BLUR 4	High Cool (Easy Listening Mix)/Bad Day (Leisurely Mix)
		(12", blue & gold company sleeve, promo, 1,000 only) 15
92	Food FOOD 37	Popscene/Mace (7" p/s) 8
92	Food TCFOOD 37	Popscene/Mace (cassette) 5
92	Food 12FOOD 37	Popscene/I'm Fine/Mace/Garden Central (12", p/s) 18
92	Food CDFOOD 37	Popscene/Mace/Badgeman Brown (CD). 20
92	Food BLUR 6	The Wassailing Song (1-sided 7" gig freebie, no p/s, 500 only) 100
92	Food TCFOOD 40	For Tomorrow/Into Another/Hanging Over (cassette) 5
92	Food 12FOOD 40	For Tomorrow (Visit To Primrose Hill Extended)/Into Another/
		Hanging Over/Peach (12", p/s). 18
92	Food CDFOOD 40	For Tomorrow (Visit To Primrose Hill Extended)/Peach/Bone Bag
		(CD, double jewel case) 20
92	Food CDSFOOD 40	For Tomorrow (Single Version)/When The Cows Come Home/
		Beachcoma/For Tomorrow (Acoustic Version) (CD) 20
93	Food FOODS 45	Chemical World/Maggie May (7" red vinyl, paper labels, p/s) 5
93	Food 12FOOD 45	Chemical World/Es Schmecht/Young And Lovely/My Ark
		(12", p/s with print) 15
93	Food CDFOODS 45	Chemical World (Reworked)/Never Clever (live)/Pressure On Julian (live)/
		Come Together (live) (CD, double jewel case). 12
93	Food CDFOOD 45	Chemical World/Young And Lovely/Es Schmecht/My Ark (CD) 10
93	Food FOODS 46	Sunday Sunday/Tell Me, Tell Me (B-side as "Blur featuring Seymour")
		(yellow vinyl 7", p/s) 6
93	Food 12FOODS 46	Sunday Sunday/Long Legged/Mixed Up
		(B-sides as "Blur featuring Seymour") (12", p/s with print) 8
93	Food CDFOOD 46	Sunday Sunday/Dizzy/Fried/Shimmer (CD, final 3 tracks as B-sides as
		"Blur featuring Seymour"). 12
93	Food CDFOODX 46	THE SUNDAY SUNDAY POPULAR COMMUNITY SONG CD:
		Sunday Sunday/Daisy Bell/Let's All Go Down The Strand (CD) 10
94	Food FOODS 47	Girls And Boys/Magpie/People In Europe (7" p/s, numbered) 5
94	Food CDFOOD 47	Girls And Boys/People In Europe/Peter Panic (CD, slimline jewel case) 8
94	Food CDFOODS 47	Girls And Boys/Magpie/Anniversary Waltz (CD, digipak) 6
94	Food CDFOOD 50	To The End/Girls And Boys (Pet Shop Boys 7" Remix)/Girls And Boys
		(Pet Shop Boys 12" Remix) (CD, slimline jewel case) 10
94	Food CDFOOD 53	Parklife/Beard/To The End (French Version) (CD, slimline jewel case) 5
96	Fan Club DEATH 1	Death Of A Party (demo) (CD, 1-track, card p/s, fan club issue, 3250 only) 25
97	Fan Club LOVE 001	I Love Her (CD, card p/s, fan club issue, 3,500 only) 25
02	no label no cat. no.	(red label, bearing Arabic writing which translates as "Don't bomb when you
		are the bomb"; large centre hole; 1,000 7" were pressed,
		but many were blown up). 50
91	Food FOODLP 6	LEISURE (LP). 15
93	Food FOODLP 9	MODERN LIFE IS RUBBISH (LP). 15
94	Food FOODLP 10	PARKLIFE (LP). 20
95	Food FOODLP 14	THE GREAT ESCAPE (LP) 15

PROMOS
90	Food 12BLUR1	She's So High/I Know (Extended) (12" in company die cut sleeve) 6
90		Bad Day/Bad Day (version) (white label) 30
91	Food 12FOODDJ 29	There's No Other Way (Extended)/(Blur Remix) (12" in company die cut sleeve) . . 6
91	Food 12FOODDJ 31	Bang (Edited)/Bang (Unedited) (12" die cut company sleeve). 6
92	Food 12BLUR5	Popscene (1-sided promo 12" in die cut company sleeve. 1000 only) 20
93	Food 12FOODDJ 40	For Tomorrow (Visit to Primrole Hill extended version/Into Another/
		Hanging Over (12" in company die cut sleeve) 15
94	Food CD5 BET BET BET	Girls and Boys/Jubilee/Trouble In The Message Centre/Lot 105 (Live CD promo
		produced for Mark Radcliffe show). 20
95	Food CDFOODDJ 59	This Is A Low (CD, promo only, plain card sleeve with set of 4 stamps) . . . 15
95	Food 12FOODDJ 63	Country House (12", promo only, 1-sided, die-cut p/s). 10
95	Food 12FOODDJ 69	The Universal/Entertain Me (The Live It! Remix)
		(12", promo only, die-cut p/s). 10
95	Food LH 69	The Universal/Entertain Me (Live It! Remix) (DJ promo) 5
97	Food 12BLURDJ 7	On Your Own (Crouch End Broadway Mix) (12", 1-sided, promo only) 20
97	Food CDIN 106	BLURB (CD, interview, promo only) 15
97	Food CDFOODDJ 109	Death Of A Party (7" Remix)/(Well Blurred Remix)/(Billy Whiskers Mix)/
		(Album Version) (CD, promo only, card p/s) 8
99	Food CD FOOD DJ 117	Tender (LP version)/(radio edit) (CD, silver foil pack, promo only) 8
99	Food FOOD CDJX 29	13 (CD in duffelbag with folder, photos, ski-hat and biography, promo only) . . . 80
99	Food 10FOODDJ 117	Tender (10" promo, plays inside to out, foil sealed) 12

99	Food No Cat No	15ON13 (Interview CD, p/s) 20
00	Food CDFOODDJ 135	Music Is My Radar (Edit) (CD, p/s) 6
00	Food 10FOODDJ 135	Music Is My Radar (12" one-sided w/10" cat. No., white die cut sleeve, stamped label) 10
03	Parlophone THINK1	THINK TANK (CD Promo in card wallet with unique Banksy artwork) 8
03	Parlophone THINK3	Crazy Beat/Brothers And Sister/Moroccan Peoples Revolutionary Bowls Club/ Gene By Gene (12" sampler, white die cut sleeve, stamped labels) 10
03	Parlophone THINK4	THINK TANK INTERVIEW CD (CD in promo p/s, track by track 52 min interview). 15

(see also Graham Coxon, Gorillaz, Damon Albarn)

BLURT

80	Test Pressing TP 1	My Mother Was A Friend Of An Enemy Of The People/Get (p/s) 5
81	Armageddon AS 013	The Fish Needs A Bike/This Is My Royal Wedding Souvenir (p/s). 5

BLUSH

79	Venal Vinyl PMB 117	Everyday/Before We Came Together (no p/s, 200 only) 150

HENRY BLYTHE

56	Oriole MG 20009	AN INVESTIGATION INTO REINCARNATION (LP) 15

JIMMY BLYTHE

54	London AL 3527	SOUTH SIDE BLUE PIANO (10" LP) 25
54	London AL 3529	SOUTH SIDE CHICAGO JAZZ (10" LP) 25

ENID BLYTON

53	HMV BD 1297	Noddy & Big Ears Go Shopping/Noddy Builds His House (78, picture label) 10
53	HMV BD 1298	Noddy At The Police Court/Noddy Lets The Animals Out Of The Ark (78, picture label). 10
53	HMV BD 1299	Noddy's Adventures With His Car/Noddy Is Naughty (78, picture label) 10
57	HMV 7EG 8260	NODDY STORIES (EP) 15

B-MOVIE

80	Dead Good DEAD 9	TAKE THREE (EP) 20
80	Dead Good BIG DEAD 12	NOWHERE GIRL (12" EP, with insert, 800 only) 20
81	Lyntone LYN 10410	Remembrance Day/SOFT CELL: Metro Mr X (red or green flexidisc with *Flexipop* magazine, issue 12) 12/6
81	Deram DM 443	Marilyn Dreams/Film Music (Part 1) (p/s) 5
81	Deram DMX 443	Marilyn Dreams/Film Music (Part 1) (12", p/s) 8
88	Wax 12 WAX 3	Nowhere Girl/Remembrance Day (12", p/s, 250 on orange vinyl, numbered) 10
88	Wax 12 WAX 3	Nowhere Girl/Remembrance Day (12", p/s, pink or black vinyl, numbered) 10/7
88	Wax 12 WAX 4	Polar Opposites/Taxi Driver (12", clear vinyl or picture disc). .... each 8
88	Wax CD WAX 4	Polar Opposites/Taxi Driver (CD). 15
88	Wax WAXLP 1P	THE DEAD GOOD TAPES (LP, picture disc). 18
88	Wax WAXCD 1	THE DEAD GOOD TAPES (CD) 18
91	Dead Good GOOD 3	REMEMBRANCE DAYS (LP, with 7" "The Fool"/"Swinging Lights" [CHEAP 1]) .. 12

BMX BANDITS

86	53rd & 3rd AGARR 3	Sad?/E102 (p/s, with comic). 10
86	53rd & 3rd AGARR 312	Sad?/E102/The Cat From Outer Space (live)/Strawberry Sunday (live)/ Groovy Good Luck Friend (live) (12", p/s) 10
87	53rd & 3rd AGARR 6	What A Wonderful World/The Day Before Tomorrow (p/s) 6
87	53rd & 3rd AGARR 612	What A Wonderful World/The Day Before Tomorrow/ Johnny Alucard/Sad?/Sandy's Wallet (12", p/s). 8
92	Sunflower SUN 006	GORDON KEEN & HIS BMX BANDITS EP (p/s, red vinyl). 8

(see also Soup Dragons, Boy Hairdressers, Teenage Fanclub, Vaselines)

EDDIE BO

73	Action ACT 4609	Check Your Bucket Parts 1 & 2 30

BO & PEEP

64	Decca F 11968	Young Love/The Rise Of The Brighton Surf. 45

(see also Andrew Oldham Orchestra)

BOARDS OF CANADA

94	Music 70 THS 012	HOOPER'S BAY (12" or cassette EP). 100/25
96	Skam SKA 008	Hi Scores/Turquoise Hexagon Sun/Nlagon/June 9th/ See Ya Later/Everything You Do Is A Balloon (12", p/s) 10
98	Skam KMAS 1	Aquarius/Chinook (p/s, with insert, 500 only) 30
05	Skam Ska 008	Hi Scores (12" reissue in brail embossed sleeve). 10
95	Music 70 BOARD 1	2ISM (LP or cassette, 100 copies only of each) 400/100
02	Warp	GEOGADDI (LP, blue vinly test pressing - etched – 10 only). .... 200+

BOARDWALKERS

60s	own label J.C. 1	A Miracle/Any Man's Girl 200

(see also Warren Davis)

BOATMEN

70s	Sweet Folk SFA 018	STRAIGHT FROM THE TUNNEL'S MOUTH (LP). 35

BOBALOUIS

81	WEA K18441	Not A Second Chance/City Boys. 25

BOB (Relf) & EARL (Nelson)

65	Sue WI 374	Harlem Shuffle/I'll Keep Running Back. 20
65	Sue WI 393	Baby I'm Satisfied/The Sissy 40
67	Sue WI 4030	Don't Ever Leave Me/Fancy Free 40
69	Island WI 6053	Harlem Shuffle/I'll Keep Running Back (reissue) 10
69	B&C CB 102	Dancin' Everywhere/Baby It's Over 10
69	Warner Bros WB 6059	Everybody Jerk/He's A Playbrother 10
70	Uni UN 519	Pickin' Up Love's Vibrations/Uh, Uh, Naw Naw Naw 15
72	Jay Boy BOY 72	I Can't Get Away/I'll Keep Running Back. 10
72	Jay Boy BOY 73	My Little Girl/His & Her Shuffle (as Bob & Earl Band) 10
73	Contempo C 4	Harlem Shuffle/Harlem Shuffle (Instrumental Version) 5

67	Sue ILP 951	HARLEM SHUFFLE (LP)	125
69	Joy JOYS 199	TOGETHER (LP)	15
69	B&C BCB 1	BOB AND EARL (LP)	20
71	Jay Boy JSX 2004	HARLEM SHUFFLE (LP)	20

(see also Bob Relf, Jackie Lee, Earl Nelson, Hollywood Flames)

BOB & JERRY
| 58 | Pye International 7N 25003 | Ghost Satellite/Nothin' (78 rpm = £18) | 20 |
| 61 | Philips PB 1205 | Dreamy Eyes/We're The Guys | 6 |

BOB (Andy) & MARCIA (Griffiths)
70	Bamboo BAM 40	Really Together/BOB ANDY: Desperate Lover	18
70	Harry J. HJ 6605	Young, Gifted And Black/JAY BOYS: Young, Gifted & Black (Instrumental)	6
70	Escort ES 824	Young, Gifted And Black/BARRINGTON BIGGS: My Cheri Amour	12
71	Trojan TR 7818	Pied Piper/Save Me	5
72	Trojan TR 7854	But I Do/I Don't Care	5
70	Trojan TBL 122	YOUNG, GIFTED & BLACK (LP)	20
72	Trojan TRLS 26	PIED PIPER (LP)	15

(see also Bob Andy, Marcia Griffiths)

BOB (ANDY) & TIE (TYRONE EVANS)
| 69 | Coxsone CS 7086 | I Don't Care/LASCELLES PERKINS: Little Green Apples | 38 |

BOB(B)ETTES
57	London HLE 8477	Mr. Lee/Look At The Stars (78 rpm = £30)	95
58	London HLE 8597	Come-A Come-A/Speedy (78 rpm = £22)	75
60	London HLE 9173	I Shot Mr. Lee/Untrue Love	50
60	London HLE 9248	Have Mercy Baby/Dance With Me Georgie	40
60	Pye International 7N 25060	I Shot Mr. Lee/Billy (as Bobettes)	30
72	Action ACT 4603	That's A Bad Thing To Know/All In Your Mind	20

BOBBIE & VERA
| 69 | Decca F 12897 | I Know That He Knows/City Of Dreams | 5 |

BOBBSEY TWINS
| 57 | London HLA 8474 | A Change Of Heart/Part-Time Gal (78 rpm = £12) | 40 |

BOBBY & BETTY
| 70s | Happy House C20 | BOBBY AND BETTY GO TO THE MOON (LP) | 20 |

BOBBY & DAVE
| 71 | Ackee ACK 116 | Build My World Around You/LIZZY & TONY BOP: Sammy Version | 15 |

(see also Dave Barker, Lizzy & Dennis)

BOBBY & JIM
| 58 | Capitol CL 14877 | Carry My Books/A Lover Can Tell | 10 |

BOBBY & LAURIE
| 66 | Parlophone R 5480 | Hitch Hiker/You'll Come 'Round | 15 |

BOBBY & MIDNITES
| 84 | CBS 26046 | WHERE THE BEAT MEETS THE STREET (LP) | 25 |

(see also Bob Weir, Grateful Dead)

BOBBY (ELLIS) & TOMMY (McCOOK)
| 74 | Attack ATLP 1004 | GREEN MANGO (LP) | 25 |

BOBCATS
| 67 | Pye 7N 17242 | Can't See For Looking/Let Me Get By | 15 |

BOBO MR. SOUL
| 73 | London HLU 10418 | Hitch Hiking To Heartbreak/She's My Woman | 15 |

WILLIE BOBO
| 66 | Verve SVLP9134 | ELATION (LP) | 20 |
| 71 | A&M AMLS 68034 | DO WHAT YOU WANT TO DO (LP) | 25 |

FRIDA BOCCARA
| 69 | Philips BF 1765 | Through The Eyes Of A Child/So Fair | 15 |

BOCKY & VISIONS
| 65 | Atlantic AT 4049 | I Go Crazy/Good Good Lovin' | 40 |

BODAST
| 81 | Cherry Red BRED 12 | THE BODAST TAPES FEATURING STEVE HOWE (LP) | 12 |

(see also Steve Howe, Tomorrow)

BODGER'S MATE
| 78 | Cottage COT 521 | BRIGHTER THAN USUAL (LP) | 25 |

BODIES
| 79 | Waldo's HS 007 | Art Nouveau/Machinery (poster p/s, 5 different colours) | 5 |

BODKIN
| 72 | West CSA 104 | BODKIN (LP, private pressing in posthumously-designed sleeve) | 300+ |

BODY
| 81 | Recession | THE BODY ALBUM (LP, private pressing with booklet) | 60 |

BODY AND SOUL
| 70 | Penny Farthing PEN 720 | Here Comes That Feeling/Go Back To School | 10 |

BODYSNATCHERS
| 80 | 2-Tone CHS TT 9 | Let's Do Rocksteady/Ruder Than You (paper label, company PVC sleeve) | 6 |
| 80 | 2-Tone CHS TT 12 | Easy Life/Too Experienced (paper label, company PVC sleeve) | 6 |

BOEING DUVEEN & BEAUTIFUL SOUP
| 68 | Parlophone R 5696 | Jabberwock/Which Dreamed It (demos with p/s) | 200/100 |

MINT VALUE £

BOFFALONGO
70	United Artists UP 35144	Dancing In The Moonlight/Endless Questions.	7
71	United Artists UAG 29130	BEYOND YOUR HEAD (LP)	22

DIRK BOGARDE
65	Fontana TF 615	Darling/MOVIE SOUNDS: Pavanne For Diane	10
60	Decca LK 4373	LYRICS FOR LOVERS (LP)	22

BOGDON
81	Black Label GB 3	Oh Eddie/Reet Petite (p/s)	10
81	Brilliant HIT 1	Who Do You Think You Are?/Take Me Back (p/s)	10

(see also Whitesnake, Bernie Marsden)

BOGIES
64	private press (no cat. no.)	THE BOGIES ON CAMPUS (LP)	200
64	private press (no cat. no.)	BYE BYE BOGIES (LP)	200

ERIC BOGLE
70s	Autogram ALLP 211	LIVE IN PERSON (LP)	28
81	Plant Life PLR 033	PLAIN AND SIMPLE (LP)	15
83	Plant Life PLR 046	SCRAPS OF PAPER (LP)	15
85	Topic 12TS 437	WHEN THE WIND BLOWS (LP)	15
88	Plant Life PLR 042	NOW I'M EASY (LP)	15

LEE BOGLE
71	Black Swan BW 1406	Tomorrow's Dreams/SWANS: Hot Pants Reggae	8

HAMILTON BOHANNON
75	Brunswick BR 16	South African Man/Have A Good Day	5
78	Mercury 6167 700	Let's Start The Dance/I Wonder Why	5
78	Mercury 9199 830	Let's Start The Dance/I Wonder Why (12")	10
79	London HLX10582	Let's Start The Dance Again/Version (12")	10
83	Compleat CTL1	Let's Start The Dance III/Instrumental (12")	12
75	Brunswick BRLS 3013	SOUTH AFRICAN MAN (LP)	12
75	Brunswick BRLS 3014	INSIDES OUT (LP)	12

HOUSTON BOINES
66	Blue Horizon 45 BH 1006	Superintendent Blues/Monkey Motion (99 copies only)	150

(Ike Turner on piano)

BOLA 1
95	Skam SKA 5	Forcasa 3/Krak Jakomo/Metalurg 2/Ballom (12", custom sleeve)	40

MARC BOLAN
65	Decca F 12288	The Wizard/Beyond The Rising Sun (some as "Marc Bölan"; demos £300)	450
66	Decca F 12413	The Third Degree/San Francisco Poet (demos £325)	500
66	Parlophone R 5539	Hippy Gumbo/Misfit (demos £400)	700
72	Track 2094 013	Jasper C. Debussy/Hippy Gumbo/The Perfumed Garden Of Gulliver Smith (p/s, withdrawn) (white label £50)	65
81	Rarn MBFS 001C	Sing Me A Song/Endless Sleep (Extended Version)/The Lilac Hand Of Menthol Dan (12", no p/s, clear vinyl, handwritten labels)	10
81	Rarn MBFS 001P	Sing Me A Song/Endless Sleep (Extended Version)/The Lilac Hand Of Menthol Dan (12" picture disc, misprinted with black rim; also white rim)	15/7
81	Rarn MBFS 001P	Sing Me A Song/Endless Sleep (Extended Version)/The Lilac Hand Of Menthol Dan (12", picture disc misprinted back-to-front)	15
81	Cherry Red CHERRY 29	You Scare Me To Death/The Perfumed Garden Of Gulliver Smith (initial copies with bronze label, glossy p/s & free flexidisc [Lyntone LYN 10086])	10
81	Cherry Red CHERRY 29	You Scare Me To Death/The Perfumed Garden Of Gulliver Smith (later pressing with silver label/matt p/s)	5
81	Cherry Red CHERRY 32	Cat Black/Jasper C. Debussy (p/s)	5
82	Cherry Red CHERRY 39	The Wizard/Beyond The Rising Sun/Rings Of Fortune (p/s)	5
72	Track 2406 101	HARD ON LOVE (LP, unreleased, white label test pressing, 2 copies only)	800
72	Track 2406 009	HARD ON LOVE (LP, unrel, 2-sided EMIdisc acetate with "swearing intro")	2250
74	Track 2410 201	THE BEGINNING OF DOVES (LP)	20
81	Cherry Red PERED 20	YOU SCARE ME TO DEATH (LP, picture disc)	12
81	Cherry Red ERED 20	YOU SCARE ME TO DEATH (LP, gatefold sleeve; early copies with booklet stapled into sleeve; later copies with loose booklet) each	12
89	Media Motion MEDIA 2	THE BEGINNING OF DOVES (LP, reissue, 750 only, withdrawn)	20

(see also Marc Bolan/T. Rex, Marc Bolan & Gloria Jones, Toby Tyler, John's Children, Big Carrot, Dib Cochran & The Earwigs)

MARC BOLAN & GLORIA JONES
77	EMI EMI 2572	To Know You Is To Love You/City Port	15

(see also Gloria Jones)

MARC BOLAN/T. REX
SINGLES
70	Octopus OCTO 1	Ride A White Swan/Summertime Blues/Jewel (unreleased, handwritten white label, 2/3 test pressings only)	2,500+
70	Fly BUG 1	Ride A White Swan/Is It Love/Summertime Blues (p/s, purple labels, later with mustard labels)	20/7
71	Fly	Hot Love/Woodland Rock/King Of The Mountain Cometh (IBC Sound Recordings Studios acetate)	280
71	Fly BUG 6	Hot Love/Woodland Rock/King Of The Mountain Cometh (mustard labels, later with 'fly' design)	10/5
71	Fly BUG 10	Get It On/There Was A Time/Raw Ramp (p/s, black label with silver 'fly' logo)	20
70s	Fly BUG 10	Get It On/There Was A Time/Raw Ramp (p/s, black label with white 'fly' or later silver 'fly' text) each	6
71	Fly GRUB 1	Electric Warrior Preview Single: Jeepster/Life's A Gas (gig freebie, originally in pink envelope sleeve, later standard paper sleeve)	200/145+

MINT VALUE £

71	Fly BUG 16	Jeepster/Life's A Gas (white 'fly' label, or scarce issue w/out 'GRUB 1A' ref.) . . . 5/4
72	EMI T REX 101	Telegram Sam/Cadillac/Baby Strange 6
72	Magni Fly ECHO 102	One Inch Rock/The Woodland Bop/The Throat Of Winter (unreleased, rejected 1-sided test pressing for B-side of Debora/One Inch Rock, stamped white label) 150
72	Magni Fly ECHO 102	Debora/One Inch Rock/The Woodland Bop/Seal Of Seasons (p/s) 6
72	EMI MARC X	Metal Guru (rejected 1-sided test pressing with Marc's annotation 'bad cut') . . . 300
72	EMI MARC 1	Metal Guru/Thunderwing/Lady 6
72	EMI MARC 2	Children Of The Revolution/Jitterbug Love/Sunken Rags 6
72	EMI MARC 3	Solid Gold Easy Action/(5th Dimension track) (mispressing) 15
72	EMI MARC 3	Solid Gold Easy Action/(Partridge Family track) (mispressing) 15
72	EMI SPRS 346	Chariot Choogle/The Slider (promo only, 'T. Rex' picture label or white label) 425/375
72	Lyntone	Christmas Time/Wanna Spend My Christmas With You/ Christmas/Everybody Knows It's Christmas (fan club flexi, some with letter in brown envelope) 45/30
73	EMI MARC 5	The Groover/Midnight 6
73	EMI MARC 6	Truck On (Tyke)/Sitting Here 6
74	EMI MARC 7	Teenage Dream/Satisfaction Pony (credited to 'Marc Bolan & T. Rex' or 'Marc Bolan') 6/5
74	EMI MARC 8	Light Of Love/Explosive Mouth 6
74	EMI MARC 9	Zip Gun Boogie/Space Boss 6
75	EMI MARC 10	New York City/Chrome Sitar. 6
75	EMI MARC 11	Dreamy Lady/Do You Wanna Dance?/Dock Of The Bay (as T. Rex Disco Party) . . . 6
75	EMI MARC 12	Christmas Bop/Telegram Sam/Metal Guru (unreleased, A- & B-side paper labels exist, 2 sets only) . . . . labels 1,250
76	EMI MARC 13	London Boys/Solid Baby 6
76	Cube BUG 66	Hot Love/Get It On 6
76	EMI MARC 14	I Love To Boogie/Baby Boomerang 8
76	EMI MARC 15	Laser Love/Life's An Elevator 8
77	EMI MARC 16	The Soul Of My Suit/All Alone 8
77	EMI MARC 17	Dandy In The Underworld/Groove A Little/Tame My Tiger (p/s) 10
77	EMI MARC 18	Celebrate Summer/Ride My Wheels (p/s) 10
78	EMI MARC 19	Crimson Moon/Jason B. Sad (p/s). 10
77	Cube ANT 1	BOLAN'S BEST PLUS ONE (EP, p/s). 8
77	Cube ANT 2	Hot Love/Raw Ramp/Lean Woman Blues (p/s, misprinted Raw Amp, sleeve credits 'Bolan', label credits 'T.Rex') 8
78	Cube BINT 1	Steve Dixon Interview (free with initial copies of compilation LP [HIFLD 1]). 8
79	Cube ANTS 001	Life's A Gas/Find A Little Wood/Once Upon The Seas Of Abyssinia/ Blessed Wild Apple Girl (12", p/s) 14
81	Cube/Dakota	Christmas Jingle/Sailors Of The Highway (MBFS fan club flexidisc) 6
82	Marc ABOLAN 2	THE CHILDREN OF RARN (10" EP, p/s, 33rpm, gatefold sleeve with 12-page lyric book) 25
82	Marc SBOLAN 13	Mellow Love/Foxy Box/Lunacy's Back (p/s, blue vinyl, as Marc Bolan) 8
82	Rarn MBFS RAP 2	Deep Summer/Oh Baby/One Inch Rock (unreleased version) (12", p/s, blue vinyl) 10
83	Marc SBOLAN 12EP	CHRISTMAS BOP EP (12", p/s, OMBFS only, extra tracks: acoustic versions of King Of The Rumbling Spires & Savage Beethoven) 10
83	Marc SBOLAN 14PD	Think Zinc/Till Dawn/Magical Moon (picture disc). 5
84	Marc On Wax SPS 1	Mister Motion (1-sided, from Child Of The Revolution — 14 Greats LP, p/s) 8
84	Cube BUG 99	Sailor Of The Highway/Do You Remember (7" in plain black sleeve) 15
84	Cube HBUG 99	RARE MAGIC (12" EP) 12
85	Cambra MAIN 1	(Whatever Happened To The) Teenage Dream (Ext.)/Solid Gold Segue (picture disc free with "Mainman" LP) 8
85	Marc PTANX 1	Megarex 1/Megarex 1 (shaped picture disc, with free plinth). 8
87	Marc MARCX 1	Children Of The Revolution (remix)/The Slider (remix)/Tear For The High Star (tribute by Dave Ash-B) (shaped picture disc). 8
94	Edsel MBPROMO 1	T. REX (CD, picture disc, 4-track sampler, tri-fold digipak, promo only) 20
97	Edsel MARC 20-50	20th Century Boy/Carsmile Smith & The Old One/ All My Love/Dandy In The Underworld (CD, gig freebie) 20
01	Thunderwing TPLCDS 1	TPL SAMPLER (CD, 7-track sampler, promo only) 15

LPs

70	Fly HIFLY 2	T. REX (semi-gatefold sleeve) 20
71	Fly HIFLY 6	ELECTRIC WARRIOR (unreleased version with Jeepster on side 2, 1 test pressing copy only, with Marc's annotations on white sleeve). 700
71	Fly HIFLY 6	ELECTRIC WARRIOR (with poster & inner sleeve; some with stickered sleeve) . 25
72	Fly HIFLY 8	BOLAN BOOGIE (1-sided test pressing with The Visit instead of Jewel). 375
72	Fly HIFLY 8	BOLAN BOOGIE 12
72	EMI BLN 5001	THE SLIDER (with lyric inner sleeve) 20
73	EMI BLN 5002	TANX (with poster & inner sleeve) 20
73	EMI BLN 5003	GREAT HITS (with poster) 12
74	EMI BNLA 7751	ZINC ALLOY AND THE HIDDEN RIDERS OF TOMORROW (with 3-way numbered promo fold-out sleeve & inner, given as competition prize with letter from *Pink* or *Mirabelle* magazines, 1,000 or 1,500 only. First 25 signed by Bolan = £300+) 250
74	EMI BNLA 7751	ZINC ALLOY AND THE HIDDEN RIDERS OF TOMORROW (with 3-way promo fold-out sleeve & inner, without letter; numbered or un-numbered copies) 250/200
74	EMI BNLA 7751	ZINC ALLOY AND THE HIDDEN RIDERS OF TOMORROW (commercial gatefold sleeve with lyric inner sleeve) 18
75	EMI BNLA 7752	BOLAN'S ZIP GUN (diamond-cut sleeve & inner sleeve) 20
76	EMI BLNA 5004	FUTURISTIC DRAGON (with lyric inner sleeve). 15
77	EMI BLNA 5005	DANDY IN THE UNDERWORLD (with round-cut sleeve & lyric inner sleeve) 15
78	Cube HIFLD 1	MARC: THE WORDS AND MUSIC OF MARC BOLAN 1947-1977 (2-LP, gatefold sleeve, with free single [BINT 1]). 22

81	Marc ABOLAN 1P	T. REX IN CONCERT (picture disc, 2 designs)	15
82	Cube/Dakota ICSX 1004	ACROSS THE AIRWAVES (picture disc)	10
82	Marc ABOLAN 3P	ELECTRIC WARRIOR (picture disc)	10
84	Marc ABOLAN 5	T. REXTASY (with 12" Jam (live)/	
		Elemental Child (live) [ABOLAN 5F], Official Fanclub only)	15
86	Marc On Wax WARRIOR 1/4	HISTORY OF T. REX (4-LP, numbered picture disc set,	
		some with free fanclub T-shirt)	45/35

(see also Marc Bolan, Tyrannosaurus Rex, Dib Cochran & the Earwigs, John's Children, Big Carrot)

FRANCY BOLAND
69	Polydor 583054	FRANCY BOLAND LIVE AT RONNIE SCOTT'S VOL. 1 (LP, with Kenny Clark)	20
69	Polydor 583055	FRANCY BOLAND LIVE AT RONNIE SCOTT'S VOL. 2 (LP, with Kenny Clark)	20
75	Freedom FLP40176	PAPILLON NOIR (LP)	20

TOMMY BOLIN
76	Nemperor K 10730/NE 4	The Grind/Homeward Strut	10
75	Atlantic K 50208	TEASER (LP, some stickered)	18/15
76	CBS S 81612	PRIVATE EYES (LP)	12

(see also James Gang, Deep Purple)

SIMON BOLIVAR ORCHESTRA
| 56 | London HLG 8245 | Meringue Holiday/Shy (78 rpm = £6) | 20 |

BOLLARD
| 72 | Satril SAT 1 | I Need Your Love/Sunshine In The Morning | 6 |

BOLLARDS
| 70s | Bumkin Records | BOLLARDS (LP) | 15 |

MICHAEL BOLOTIN
| 75 | RCA SF 8451 | MICHAEL BOLOTIN (LP) | 15 |

(see also Blackjack, Michael Bolton)

BOLT THROWER
| 89 | Earache MOSH 13 | REALM OF CHAOS (LP, picture disc) | 15 |

BOMBADIL
| 72 | Harvest HAR 5056 | Breathless/When The City Sleeps (p/s) | 10 |
| 75 | Harvest HAR 5095 | Breathless/When The City Sleeps (p/s, reissue) | 6 |

(see also Barclay James Harvest)

BOMBAY DUCKS
80	Complete Control CON 1	Sympathy For The Devil/1-0-6-9 (p/s)	10
80s	United Dairies UD 05	DANCE MUSIC (LP)	18
80s	Eraserhead C-60	ANYONE CAN BE ENO (cassette)	12
80s	Eraserhead C-30	A RETROSPECTIVE LOOK AT THE BOMBAY DUCKS (cassette with mask)	12

BOMB THE BASS
| 87 | Misteron DOOD121 | Beat Dis (12") | 8 |

ELI BONAPARTE
| 71 | Decca F 13202 | it's Your Love/Sometime You'll Find | 6 |

BON-BONS
| 55 | London HL 8139 | That's The Way Love Goes/Make My Dreams Come True (78 rpm = £12) | 60 |
| 56 | London HLU 8262 | Circle/Frog On A Log (78 rpm = £10) | 60 |

BOBBY BOND
| 61 | Pye International 7N 25081 | You're A Livin' Doll/Sweet Love | 10 |
| 69 | Warner Bros WB 7292 | One More Mile, One More Town/If You're Leaving Me | 5 |

BRIGITTE BOND
| 64 | Blue Beat BB 212 | Oh Yeah Baby/Blue Beat Baby | 40 |

GRAHAM BOND (ORGANISATION)
64	Decca F 11909	Long Tall Shorty/Long Legged Baby (as Graham Bond Organization)	50
65	Columbia DB 7471	Wade In The Water/Tammy (as Graham Bond Organisation)	48
65	Columbia DB 7528	Tell Me (I'm Gonna Love Again)/Love Come Shining Through	
		(as Graham Bond Organisation)	45
65	Columbia DB 7647	Lease On Love/My Heart's In Little Pieces (as Graham Bond Organisation)	35
66	Columbia DB 7838	St James Infirmary/Soul Tango (as Graham Bond Organisation)	35
67	Page One POF 014	You've Gotta Have Love Babe/I Love You	55
70	Warner Bros WB 8004	Walking In The Park/Springtime In The City (solo)	15
71	Vertigo 6059 042	Twelve Gates To The City/Water Water (as Graham Bond with Magick)	10
65	Columbia 33SX 1711	THE SOUND OF '65 (LP, 1st pressing, with '33SX' on blue/black label)	180
65	Columbia 33SX 1750	THERE'S A BOND BETWEEN US	
		(LP, 1st pressing, with '33SX' on blue/black label)	180
66	Columbia SX 1711	THE SOUND OF '65 (LP, 2nd pressing, with 'SX' on blue/black label)	110
66	Columbia SX 1750	THERE'S A BOND BETWEEN US	
		(LP, 2nd pressing, with 'SX' on blue/black label)	110
69	Columbia SX 1711	THE SOUND OF '65 (LP, 3rd pressing, with boxed logo on silver/black label)	60
69	Columbia SX 1750	THERE'S A BOND BETWEEN US	
		(LP, 3rd pressing, with boxed logo on blue/black label)	60

(N.B., all of the above LPs have '33SX' on the sleeve, but only the 1st pressings have '33SX' on the label)

71	Warner Bros WS 3001	SOLID BOND (2-LP)	40
71	Vertigo 6360 021	HOLY MAGICK (LP, gatefold sleeve, swirl label,	
		as Graham Bond & Magick)	30
71	Vertigo 6360 042	WE PUT OUR MAGICK ON YOU (LP, gatefold sleeve, swirl label,	
		as Graham Bond With Magick)	45
72	Philips 6382 010	BOND IN AMERICA (2-LP, solo [individual discs: 6499 200/1])	28
72	Philips 6382 010	THIS IS GRAHAM BOND (LP, solo)	20

(see also Jack Bruce, Dick Heckstall-Smith, Ginger Baker, Duffy Power, Who, Don Rendell, Steve York's Camelo Pardalis)

MINT VALUE £

GRAHAM BOND & PETE BROWN
| 71 | Greenwich GSS 104 | Lost Tribe/Macumbe/Milk Is Turning Sour In My Shoes (maxi-single) | 25 |
| 72 | Chapter One CHSR 813 | TWO HEADS ARE BETTER THAN ONE (LP) | 80 |

(see also Pete Brown)

ISABEL BOND
68	Major Minor MM 565	Cry/When A Woman Loves A Man (some in p/s)	20/5
69	Major Minor MM 627	Don't Forget About Me/You'll Never Get The Chance Again	10
68	Major Minor MMLP 28	THE HEART AND SOUL OF ISABEL BOND (LP)	25

JACKI BOND
65	Columbia DB 7719	My Sister's Boy/Now I Know	15
66	Strike JH 302	Tell Him To Go Away/Don't You Worry	15
66	Strike JH 320	He Say/Why Can't I Love Him	40

JANE BOND & UNDERCOVER MEN
| 86 | Dreamworld BIG DREAM 1 | POLITICALLY CORRECT (LP) | 12 |

JOHNNY BOND
60	London HLU 9189	Hot Rod Jalopy/Five-Minute Love Affair	25
60	London HL 7100	Hot Rod Lincoln/Five-Minute Love Affair (export issue)	20
65	London HLB 9957	Ten Little Bottles/Eleven More Months And Ten More Days (B-side with Cowboy Copas)	10
62	Stateside SL 10008	THAT WILD, WICKED BUT WONDERFUL WEST (LP)	20
63	London HA-B 8098	LIVE IT UP (LP, as Johnny Bond & His Friends On Stage)	20
65	London HA-B 8228	THE SONGS THAT MADE HIM FAMOUS (LP)	25
66	London HA-B 8272	FAMOUS HOT RODDERS I HAVE KNOWN (LP)	20
67	London HA-B 8269	THE MAN WHO COMES AROUND (LP)	15
67	London HA-B 8316	THE BRANDED STOCK (LP)	15

JOHNNY BOND'S RED RIVER VALLEY BOYS
| 51 | Columbia DB 2844 | Love Song In 32 Bars/CHAMP BUTLER: Dear, Dear, Dear (78) | 10 |

(see also Champ Butler)

JOYCE BOND
67	Airborne NBP 0011	It's Alright/Mrs. Soul	50
66	Island WI 3019	Tell Me What It's All About/Tell Me Right Now	50
67	Island WIP 6010	Do The Teasy/Sugar	15
67	Island WIP 6018	This Train/Not So With Me	15
68	Island WIP 6051	Ob-La-Di, Ob-La-Da/Robin Hood Rides Again	8
68	Pama PM 718	Back To School/They Wish	8
69	Pama PM 771	Mr. Pitiful/Let's Get Married (as Joyce Bond & Little John)	10
70	Upfront UPF 5	Wind Of Change/First In Line	7
71	Trojan TR 7837	Help Me Make It Through The Night/Reconsider Our Love	8
68	Island ILP 968	SOUL AND SKA (LP, mono only)	90
72	Windmill WMD 121	SOUL OF CHANGE (LP)	20

LOUIS BOND
| 74 | Cooltempo 2005 | Tell Me When/Instrumental | 15 |

MARGARET BOND
55	Decca F 10506	You'll Always Be My Lifetime Sweetheart/Where Is The One For Me	5
55	Decca F 10555	My Love's A Gentle Man/Mirror, Mirror	5
55	Decca F 10632	There's Always A First Time/Dancing In My Socks	10
57	Parlophone R 4283	Your Love Is My Love/Goodnight My Love, Pleasant Dreams	5
57	Parlophone R 4312	The Wind In The Willow/Young And In Love	5

OLIVER BOND
| 66 | Parlophone R 5476 | I Saw You All Alone/Let Me Love You | 15 |

(see also Oliver Bone)

TONY BOND
| 66 | Decca SKL 4776 | PRESENTING TONY BOND (LP) | 20 |

(see also Kestrels)

RONNIE BOND
| 69 | Page One POF 123 | Anything For You/Carolyn | 35 |

(see also Troggs)

(GARY) 'U.S.' BONDS
60	Top Rank JAR 527	New Orleans/Please Forgive Me (as U.S. Bonds)	25
61	Top Rank JAR 566	Not Me/Give Me One More Chance (as U.S. Bonds)	10
61	Top Rank JAR 575	Quarter To Three/Time Ole Story (as U.S. Bonds)	8
61	Top Rank JAR 581	School Is Out/One Million Tears	10
61	Top Rank JAR 595	School Is In/Trip To The Moon	10
62	Top Rank JAR 602	Dear Lady Twist/Havin' So Much Fun	15
62	Top Rank JAR 615	Twist Twist Senora/Food Of Love	15
62	Stateside SS 111	Seven Day Weekend/Gettin' A Groove	15
62	Stateside SS 125	Copy Cat/I'll Change That Too	15
63	Stateside SS 144	Mixed Up Faculty/I Dig This Station	15
63	Stateside SS 179	Where Did That Naughty Little Girl Go?/Do The Limbo With Me	15
63	Stateside SS 219	What A Dream/I Don't Wanta Wait	15
64	Stateside SS 271	New Orleans/Quarter To Three	15
64	Stateside SS 308	My Sweet Baby Rose/Ella Is Yella	10
67	Stateside SS 2025	Send Her To Me/Workin' For My Baby	20
75	London HLA 10485	Grandma's Washboard Band/Believing You	7
61	Top Rank 35/114	DANCE 'TIL QUARTER TO THREE WITH U.S. BONDS (LP)	50
62	Stateside SL 10001	TWIST UP CALYPSO (LP)	30
63	Stateside SL 10037	THE GREATEST HITS OF GARY (U.S.) BONDS (LP)	30

OLIVER BONE & SOUNDS MAXIMUM
| 66 | Parlophone R 5527 | Knock On Wood/Jugger Tea | 20 |

(see also Oliver Bond)

BROTHER BONES & HIS SHADOWS

BROTHER BONES & HIS SHADOWS
60	Oriole CB 1030	Sweet Georgia Brown/Margie 5

BONGO HERMAN (Davis)
70	Songbird SB 1018	True Grit/True Grit Version 2 (both credited with Les Crystalites but actually with Les & Crystalites) 20
71	Songbird SB 1060	BONGO HERMAN & LES BUNNY: Know For I/CRYSTALITES: Version (B-side actually titled 'Know Fari') 15
71	Songbird SB 1066	BONGO HERMAN & LES & BUNNY: Salaam (Peace)/CRYSTALITES: Scraper.... 12
72	Big BG 332	Eternal Drums/ERROL DUNKLEY: Darling Ooh Wee (both actually by Hugh Roy Junior) 15
72	Green Door GD 4049	African Breakfast/BONGO HERMAN & LES AND BUNNY: Chairman Of The Board 15
72	Songbird SB 1069	We Are Praying/CRYSTALITES: Version 10

BONGO LES & HERMAN
71	Songbird SB 1050	Home Sweet Home/Hail I 12

(see also Heptones, Scotty, Meditators)

BON JOVI
84	Vertigo VER 11	She Don't Know Me/Breakout (p/s) 22
84	Vertigo VERX 11	She Don't Know Me/Breakout (12", p/s) 30
84	Vertigo VER 14	Runaway/Breakout (live) (p/s) 22
84	Vertigo VERX 14	Runaway/Breakout (live)/Runaway (live) (12", p/s) 30
85	Vertigo VER 19	In And Out Of Love/Roulette (live) (p/s) 10
85	Vertigo VERP 19	In And Out Of Love/Roulette (live) (picture disc) 35
85	Vertigo VERX 19	In And Out Of Love/Roulette (live)/Shot Through The Heart (live) (12", p/s) ... 15
85	Vertigo VER 22	The Hardest Part Is The Night/Always Run To You (p/s) 12
85	Vertigo VERDP 22	The Hardest Part Is The Night/Always Run To You//Tokyo Road (live)/ Shot Through The Heart (live) (double pack, gatefold p/s) 18
85	Vertigo VERX 22	The Hardest Part Is The Night/Always Run To You/Tokyo Road (live) (12", p/s) .. 18
85	Vertigo VERXR 22	Red Hot And Two Parts Live: The Hardest Part Is The Night/ Tokyo Road (live)/In And Out Of Love (live) (12", p/s, red vinyl) 30
86	Vertigo VERP 26	You Give Love A Bad Name/Let It Rock (10", shaped picture disc) 30
86	Vertigo VERX 26	You Give Love A Bad Name/Let It Rock/Borderline (12", p/s with poster) 12
86	Vertigo VERXR 26	You Give Love A Bad Name/Let It Rock/ The Hardest Part Is The Night (live)/Burning For Love (live) (12", p/s, blue vinyl) 18
86	Vertigo VERPA 28	Livin' On A Prayer/Wild In The Streets (p/s, with patch) 10
86	Vertigo VERP 28	Livin' On A Prayer/Wild In The Streets (picture disc) 18
86	Vertigo VERXR 28	Livin' On A Prayer/Wild In The Streets/Edge Of A Broken Heart (12", green vinyl, p/s) 12
86	Vertigo VERXG 28	Livin' On A Prayer/Wild In The Streets/Only Lonely (live)/ Runaway (live) (12", gatefold p/s) 18
88	Mercury 080 042-2	Livin' On A Prayer/Let It Rock/Wild In The Streets (CD Video) 20
87	Vertigo JOVS 1	Wanted Dead Or Alive/Shot Through The Heart (p/s, with metal stickers) 8
87	Vertigo JOVPB 112	Wanted Dead Or Alive/Shot Through The Heart/Social Disease (12", poster p/s) 18
87	Vertigo JOVR 112	Wanted Dead Or Alive/Shot Through The Heart/Social Disease/ Get Ready (live) (12", p/s, silver vinyl) 15
87	Vertigo JOVCD 1	Wanted Dead Or Alive (Full Version)/(Radio Edit)/(Acoustic) (CD, promo only) .. 30
87	Vertigo JOVR 212	Never Say Goodbye/Raise Your Hands/Wanted Dead Or Alive (Acoustic Version) (12", yellow vinyl, PVC sleeve) 12
87	Vertigo	Never Say Goodbye (CD video) 25
87	Vertigo	Wanted Dead Or Alive (CD video) 25
87	Vertigo 080 042-2	Livin' On A Prayer/Borderline/Let It Rock/Wild In The Streets (CD video) 25
88	Vertigo JOVS 3	Bad Medicine/99 In The Shade (fold-out photofile p/s) 12
88	Vertigo JOVCD 3	Bad Medicine/Lay Your Hands On Me/99 In The Shade (CD, card sleeve) 12
88	Vertigo JOVS 4	Born To Be My Baby/Love For Sale (gold 'calendar' card envelope pack) 8
88	Vertigo JOVR 412	Born To Be My Baby/Love For Sale/Wanted Dead Or Alive (live) (12", gatefold p/s) 8
88	Vertigo JOVP 412	Born To Be My Baby/Love For Sale/Wanted Dead Or Alive (live) (12", picture disc) 12
88	Vertigo JOVCD 4	Born To Be My Baby/Love For Sale/Runaway/Livin' On A Prayer (CD) 12
89	Vertigo JOVPB 5	I'll Be There For You/Homebound Train (p/s, with poster) 12
89	Vertigo JOVCD 5	I'll Be There For You/Homebound Train/Borderline/Edge Of A Broken Heart (CD, card sleeve) 12
89	Vertigo JOVS 661	Lay Your Hands On Me/Bad Medicine (live) (red vinyl, stickered PVC sleeve) 6
89	Vertigo JOVS 662	Lay Your Hands On Me/Bad Medicine (live) (white vinyl, stickered PVC sleeve). . 6
89	Vertigo JOVS 663	Lay Your Hands On Me/Bad Medicine (live) (blue vinyl, stickered PVC sleeve) ... 7
89	Vertigo JOVS 661-663	Lay Your Hands On Me/Bad Medicine (live) (3 x 7", red, blue or white vinyl, paper box set) 22
89	Vertigo JOVP 610	Lay Your Hands On Me/Bad Medicine (live)/Blood On Blood (10", picture disc with insert) 10
89	Vertigo JOVCD 6	Lay Your Hands On Me/You Give Love A Bad Name/Let It Rock (CD) 12
89	Vertigo JOVR 712	Living In Sin/Love Is War/The Boys Are Back In Town (12", white vinyl with stickered card insert) 12
89	Vertigo JOVCD 7	Living In Sin/Love Is War/Ride Cowboy Ride/Stick To Your Guns (CD, box set).. 18
92	Vertigo JOVCD 8	Keep The Faith/I Wish Everyday Could Be Like Christmas/ Little Bit Of Soul (CD, digipak) 10
92	Vertigo JOVLH 9	Bed Of Roses/Bed Of Roses (jukebox issue, no p/s) 6
92	Vertigo JOVCD 9	Bed Of Roses/Lay Your Hands On Me (live)/Tokyo Road (live)/ I'll Be There For You (CD, slimline jewel case) 10
93	Vertigo JOVMB 10	In These Arms/Bed Of Roses (Acoustic) (cassette, pull-apart outer card slipcase with tour pass) 6
93	Vertigo JOVD 11	Sleep When I'm Dead/Blaze Of Glory/You Give Love A Bad Name/ Bad Medicine (CD, digipak) 10
94	Vertigo JOVBX 13	Dry County/Stranger In This Town (live)/Blood Money (live) (gold CD, digipak).. 8
94	Vertigo JOVJB 14	Always (edit)/Always (jukebox issue, no p/s) 6

94	Vertigo JOVCD 14	ALWAYS (CD EP, digipak)... 12
94	Vertigo JOVJB 15	Someday I'll Be Saturday Night/Always (live) (jukebox issue, no p/s).......... 7
94	Vertigo JOVP 15	Someday I'll Be Saturday Night (picture disc, with insert)...................... 5
94	Vertigo JOVDD 15	Someday I'll Be Saturday Night/Good Guys Don't Always Wear White/
		Someday I'll Be Saturday Night (live) (CD, in red circular tin)................. 8
94	Vertigo JOVJB 16	Please Come Home For Christmas/Back Door Santa (jukebox issue, no p/s)..... 6
94	Vertigo JOVP 16	Please Come Home For Christmas/Back Door Santa (picture disc)............... 7
88	Vertigo VERHP 38	SLIPPERY WHEN WET (LP, picture disc with poster)........................... 15
88	Vertigo VERHP 62	NEW JERSEY (LP, picture disc, stickered PVC sleeve)......................... 15
89	Vertigo JOVI 1989	ESSENTIAL (CD, 8-track sampler, promo only)............................... 25

JON BON JOVI
90	Vertigo JBJ 212	Miracle/Dyin' Ain't Much Of A Livin'/Interview With Jon Bon Jovi
		(12", p/s, with poster & numbered sticker)................................. 15
90	Vertigo JBJP 212	Miracle/Dyin' Ain't Much Of A Livin'/Going Back (live)
		(12", picture disc with insert)... 18

JUKE BOY BONNER
69	Blue Horizon 57-3163	Runnin' Shoes/Jackin' In My Plans... 30
60s	Jan & Dil JR 451	MORE DOWN HOME BLUES (EP)... 30
68	Flyright LP 3501	THE ONE MAN TRIO (LP)... 30
69	Liberty LBS 83319	THINGS AIN'T RIGHT (LP).. 35

GRAHAM BONNET
72	RCA RCA 2230	Rare Specimen/Whisper In The Night.. 8
73	RCA RCA 2380	Trying To Say Goodbye/Castles In The Air................................... 5
74	DJM DJS 328	Back Row In The Stalls/Ghost Writer In My Eye.............................. 5
77	Ring O' 2017 105	It's All Over Now, Baby Blue/Heroes On My Picture Wall (company sleeve)...... 6
77	Ring O' 2017 106	Danny/Rock Island Line (company sleeve, some in promo p/s)............... 10/5
77	Ring O' 2017 110	Goodnight And Goodmorning/Wino Song (company sleeve).................... 5
78	Ring O' 2017 114/POSP 2	Warm Ride/10/12 Observation (company sleeve)............................ 5
78	Ring O' POSP 002	Warm Ride/10/12 Observation (12", company sleeve)....................... 8
81	Lyntone LYN 10138/9	Night Games/POLECATS: We Say Yeah/THIN LIZZY: Song For Jimmy/WAY
		OF THE WEST: Monkey Love (orange flexi with Flexipop mag, issue 10)..... 12/8
81	Vertigo VER 4	That's The Way That It Is/Don't Tell Me To Go (p/s)......................... 6
77	Ring O' 2320 103	GRAHAM BONNET (LP, with inner sleeve).................................. 18
	(see also Marbles, Rainbow, Cozy Powell, Forcefield, Fut, Michael Schenker Group, Jon Lord)	

GRAHAM BONNEY
65	Columbia DB 7773	My Little World Is All Blue/Why Can't We Be Friends......................... 10
66	Columbia DB 7843	Super Girl/Hill Of Lovin'.. 15
66	Columbia DB 7934	Baby's Gone/Later Tonight.. 15
66	Columbia DB 8005	No One Knows/Mixed Up Baby Girl... 12
67	Columbia DB 8111	Thank You Baby/Briony.. 5
67	Columbia DB 8142	Happy Together/That Bad Day.. 5
67	Columbia DB 8283	Papa Joe/My Jenny... 5
68	Columbia DB 8338	By The Way I Love You/Devil's Child.. 5
68	Columbia DB 8382	I'll Be Your Baby Tonight/Back From Baltimore.............................. 5
68	Columbia DB 8464	Frenzy/Something I've Got To Tell You....................................... 5
69	Columbia DB 8531	Get Ready/Fly Me High Lorelei... 15
69	Columbia DB 8592	Leanda Angeline/Mixing The Wine.. 8
70	Columbia DB 8648	Sign On The Dotted Line/Words We Said.................................... 25
70	Columbia DB 8687	When Evelyn Was Mine/Sunny Has Gone.................................... 10
66	Columbia SX 6052	SUPER GIRL (LP)... 40
	(see also Riot Squad)	

BONNIE & SKITTO
| 63 | Island WI 122 | Get Ready (actually by Vikings [alias Maytals])/ |
| | | DON DRUMMOND: The Rocket... 30 |

BONNIE & TREASURES
| 65 | London HLU 9998 | Home Of The Brave/Our Song.. 55 |

BONO & GAVIN FRIDAY
94	Island CID 593	In The Name Of The Father (7" Edit)/(12" Remix)/(12" Beats Mix)/
		(LP Instrumental) (CD).. 18
94	Island 12IS593	In The Name Of The Father (7" Edit)/(12" Remix)/(12" Beats Mix)/
		(LP Instrumental) (12" single).. 12
94	Island IS593	In The Name Of The Father/Eden (Gavin Friday) (7" p/s).................... 8
	(see also U2, Clannad & Bono, The Passengers, Virgin Prunes)	

BONZO DOG (DOO-DAH) BAND
66	Parlophone R 5430	My Brother Makes The Noises For The Talkies/
		I'm Gonna Bring A Watermelon To My Gal Tonight.......................... 30
66	Parlophone R 5499	Alley Oop/Button Up Your Overcoat.. 25
67	Liberty LBF 15040	Equestrian Statue/The Intro And The Outro................................. 10
68	Liberty LBF 15144	Urban Spaceman/Canyons Of Your Mind
		(initially with spoken intro to A-side)................................... 10/5
69	Liberty LBF 15201	Mr. Apollo/Ready Mades... 12
69	Liberty LBF 15273	I Want To Be With You/We Were Wrong..................................... 12
70	Liberty LBF 15314	You Done My Brain In/Mr. Slater's Parrot................................... 12
74	United Artists UP 35662	Mr. Slater's Parrot/Noises For The Leg..................................... 7
92	China WOK 2021	No Matter Who You Vote For The Government Always Gets In/
		NEIL INNES: Them (promo only)... 7
67	Liberty LBL/LBS 83056	GORILLA (LP, some with booklet)....................................... 35/20
67	Sunset SLS 50160	GORILLA (LP).. 12
68	Liberty LBL/LBS 83158E	THE DOUGHNUT IN GRANNY'S GREENHOUSE
		(LP, gatefold sleeve, some with booklet)................................ 40/25
68	Sunset SLS 50210	THE DOUGHNUT IN GRANNY'S GREENHOUSE (LP, single sleeve)........... 12
69	Liberty LBS 83257	TADPOLES (LP, die-cut sleeve, some with insert)........................ 40/25

BONZO DOG (DOO-DAH) BAND

69	Liberty LBS 83290	KEYNSHAM (LP, gatefold sleeve)	40
69	Sunset SLS 50375	KEYNSHAM (LP, single sleeve)	12
69	Sunset SLS 50350	I'M THE URBAN SPACEMAN (LP)	12
72	United Artists UAS 29288	LET'S MAKE UP AND BE FRIENDLY (LP)	18
74	United Artists UAD 60071/2	THE HISTORY OF THE BONZOS (2-LP, gatefold sleeve with booklet)	30

(see also Vivian Stanshall, Neil Innes, Grimms, Roger Ruskin Spear, Topo D. Bill, New Vaudeville Band)

BETTY BOO
79	Grapevine GRP 125	Say It Isn't So/Say It Isn't So (Instrumental)	15

BOOGALOOS
69	President PT 253	Rule Britannia/Love Is Blind	6

BOOGIE MAN ORCHESTRA
76	Cooltempo 2082	Lady Lady Lady/Instrumental	8

JAMES BOOKER
61	Vogue V 9177	Cool Turkey/Gonzo	30
63	Vocalion VEP 170154	GONZO (EP)	75

BOOKER T. & THE M.G.s
62	London HLK 9595	Green Onions/Behave Yourself	25
63	London HLK 9670	Jelly Bread/Aw' Mercy	15
63	London HLK 9784	Chinese Checkers/Plum Nellie	15
65	Atlantic AT 4033	Boot-Leg/Outrage	10
66	Atlantic AT 4063	Be My Lady/Red Beans And Rice	15
66	Atlantic 584 044	My Sweet Potato/Booker Loo	15
66	Atlantic 584 060	Jingle Bells/Winter Wonderland	10
67	Atlantic 584 088	Green Onions/Boot-Leg	10
67	Stax 601 009	Hip Hug Her/Summertime (initially dark blue label; later light blue)	15/10
67	Stax 601 018	Groovin'/Slim Jenkins' Place	8
67	Stax 601 026	Chinese Checkers/Plum Nellie (reissue)	8
68	Stax STAX 102	Soul Limbo/Heads Or Tails	6
69	Stax STAX 119	Time Is Tight/Hang 'Em High	6
69	Stax STAX 127	Soul Clap '69/Mrs. Robinson	6
69	Stax STAX 136	The Horse/Slum Baby	6
71	Stax 2025 026	Melting Pot/Kinda Easy Like	10
72	Stax 2025 074	Jamaica This Morning (as the MGs)/Fuquawi	6
63	London REK 1367	R&B WITH BOOKER T (EP)	40
64	Atlantic AET 6002	R&B WITH BOOKER T VOL. 2 (EP)	40
64	London HA-K 8182	GREEN ONIONS (LP)	55
65	Atlantic ATL 5027	SOUL DRESSING (LP)	50
66	Atlantic 587/588 033	GREEN ONIONS (LP, reissue)	15
67	Atlantic 587 047	SOUL DRESSING (LP, reissue)	15
67	Stax 589 002	AND NOW! (LP)	20
68	Stax 589 013	SOUL CHRISTMAS (LP)	15
68	Stax 230 002/231 002	DOIN' OUR THING (LP)	20
68	Stax (S)XATS 1001	SOUL LIMBO (LP)	20
69	Atco 228 004	GET READY (LP)	15
69	Stax (S)XATS 1005	UPTIGHT (LP, soundtrack, with Judy Clay)	18
69	Stax (S)XATS 1015	THE BOOKER T. SET (LP)	15
69	Atco 228 015	THE BEST OF BOOKER T. AND THE M.G.s (LP)	15
70	Stax SXATS 1031	McLEMORE AVENUE (LP)	18
71	Stax 2325 030	MELTING POT (LP)	15

(see also Mar-Keys, Steve Cropper, Albert King, Judy Clay)

BOOKER T (Jamaica)
76	Ethnic Fight 2	Eleanor/Version	8

BOOMERANGS
64	Fontana TF 507	Rockin' Robin/Don't Let Her Be Your Baby	28
65	Fontana TF 555	Another Tear Falls/Fun Fun Fun	15

BOOMERANGS
66	Pye 7N 17049	Dream World/Upgraded	12

PAT BOONE
SINGLES
55	London HLD 8172	Ain't That A Shame/Tennessee Saturday Night	40
55	London HLD 8197	At My Front Door/No Arms Can Ever Hold You	25
56	London HLD 8233	Gee Whittakers/Take The Time	25
56	London HLD 8253	I'll Be Home/Tutti Frutti	25
56	London HLD 8291	Long Tall Sally/Just As Long As I'm With You	40
56	London HLD 8303	I Almost Lost My Mind/I'm In Love With You	15
56	London HLD 8316	Two Hearts, Two Kisses/Rich In Love	15
56	London HLD 8346	Friendly Persuasion (Thee I Love)/Chains Of Love	15

(The above 45s were originally issued with gold lettering labels; later silver lettering copies are worth half these values.)

57	London HLD 8370	Don't Forbid Me/Anastasia	10
57	London HLD 8404	Why Baby Why/I'm Just Waiting For You	15
57	London HLD 8445	Love Letters In The Sand/Bernadine	10
57	London HLD 8479	Remember You're Mine/There's A Goldmine In The Sky	10
57	London HLD 8512	April Love/When The Swallows Come Back To Capistrano	10
57	London HLD 8520	White Christmas/Jingle Bells	5
58	London HLD 8574	A Wonderful Time Up There/It's Too Soon To Know	5
58	London HLD 8640	Sugar Moon/Cherie, I Love You	5
58	London HLD 8675	If Dreams Came True/That's How Much I Love You	5
58	London HLD 8739	Gee, But It's Lonely/For My Good Fortune	5
59	London HLD 8775	I'll Remember Tonight/The Mardi Gras March (78 rpm = £7)	5
59	London HLD 8824	There's Good Rockin' Tonight/With The Wind And The Rain In Your Hair (78 rpm £7)	15

MINT VALUE £

59	London HLD 8855	For A Penny/Wang Dang Taffy-Apple Tango (78 rpm = £8)	5
59	London HLD 8910	Rock Boll Weevil/Twixt Twelve And Twenty (78 rpm = £8)	5
59	London HLD 8974	A Fool's Hall Of Fame/Brightest Wishing Star (78 rpm = £8)	10

(The above 45s were originally issued with triangular centres; later round centre copies are worth two-thirds these values.)

60	London HLD 9029	Beyond The Sunset/The Faithful Heart (78 rpm = £10)	5
60	London HLD 9067	(Welcome) New Lovers/Words (78 rpm = £15)	5
60	London HLD 9138	Walking The Floor Over You/Spring Rain	5
60	London HLD 9184	Delia Gone/Candy Sweet (78 rpm = £25)	5
64	Dot DS 16658	Beach Girl/Little Honda	10

EXPORT SINGLES

56	London HL 7007	I'll Be Home/Tutti Frutti	25
56	London HL 7010	Long Tall Sally/Just As Long As I'm With You	25
56	London HL 7012	I Almost Lost My Mind/I'm In Love With You	10
56	London HL 7015	Friendly Persuasion (Thee I Love)/Chains Of Love	10
57	London HL 7019	Love Letters In The Sand/Bernadine	10
58	London HL 7033	A Wonderful Time Up There/It's Too Soon To Know	10
58	London HL 7041	Sugar Moon/Cherie, I Love You	10
58	London HL 7051	If Dreams Came True/That's How Much I Love You	10
58	London HL 7059	Gee, But It's Lonely/For My Good Fortune	10
59	London HL 7070	With The Wind And The Rain In Your Hair/There's Good Rocking Tonight	10
59	London SLD 4002	For A Penny/Wang Dang Taffy-Apple Tango (both tracks stereo)	30
61	London HLD 7112	Moody River/The Exodus Song	10
63	London HL 7118	Send Me The Pillow You Dream On/(You've Got) Personality	20
63	London HL 7121	Mexican Joe/In The Room	20

EPs

56	London RE-D 1063	PAT BOONE SINGS THE HITS	20
57	London RE-D 1069	PAT 'ON MIKE'	10
57	London RE-D 1086	PAT BOONE SINGS THE HITS NO. 2	20
57	London RE-D 1109	FOUR BY PAT	10
58	London RE-D 1112	PAT BOONE SINGS THE HITS NO. 3	20
58	London RE-D 1132	PAT PART ONE	10
58	London RE-D 1133	PAT PART TWO	10
58	London RE-D 1139	PAT'S VOICE (export issue)	10
58	London RE-D 1166	SINGS IRVING BERLIN	10
59	London RE-D 1244	JOURNEY TO THE CENTRE OF THE EARTH	10
61	London RE-D 1294	ALL HANDS ON DECK	10
62	London RE-D 1335	PAT BOONE'S LATEST AND GREATEST NO. 2	10
63	London RE-D 1384	ALWAYS YOU AND ME	10

LPs

57	London HA-D 2024	PAT'S BIG HITS	25
57	London HA-D 2030	HOWDY!	15
57	London HA-D 2049	PAT!	15
58	London HA-D 2078	APRIL LOVE (soundtrack, with Shirley Jones & Lionel Newman Orchestra)	15
58	London HA-D 2082	SINGS IRVING BERLIN (also stereo SAH-D 6038)	12/15
58	London HA-D 2098	PAT'S BIG HITS, VOL. 2	15
58	London HA-D 2127	STARDUST (also stereo SAH-D 6001)	12/15
59	London HA-D 2144	YES INDEED! (also stereo SAH-D 6010)	12/15
59	London HA-D 2161	PAT SINGS (stereo edition SAH-D 6013 unissued)	12/15
60	London HA-D 2204	TENDERLY (also stereo SAH-D 6053)	12/15
60	London HA-D 2210	SIDE BY SIDE (with Shirley Boone, also stereo SAH-D 6057)	12/15
60	London HA-D 2265	MOONGLOW (also stereo SAH-D 6085)	12/15
61	London HA-D 2305	THIS AND THAT	12/15
61	London HA-D 2354	THE GREAT GREAT GREAT PAT BOONE (also stereo SAH-D 6155)	12/15
61	London HA-D 2382	MOODY RIVER (also stereo SAH-D 6182)	12/15
62	London HA-D 2452	I'LL SEE YOU IN MY DREAMS (also stereo SAH-D 6240)	12/15
62	London HA-D/SH-D 8031	PAT BOONE'S GOLDEN HITS (mono/stereo)	12/15
63	London HA-D/SH-D 8053	I LOVE YOU TRULY (with Shirley Boone, mono/stereo)	12/15
63	London HA-D/SH-D 8073	DAYS OF WINE AND ROSES (mono/stereo)	12/15
63	London HA-D/SH-D 8109	SINGS ... GUESS WHO? (mono/stereo)	35/40
65	Dot (D)DLP 3594	BOSS BEAT	15

(see also Fontane Sisters)

ANTHONY BOOTH

69	Tangerine DP 0008	Till Death Do Us Part/September Days	7

BARRY BOOTH

68	Pye NPL 18216	DIVERSIONS! (LP)	18

(see also Monty Python)

KEN BOOTHE

66	Island WI 3020	The Train Is Coming/This Is Me	40
66	Island WI 3035	I Don't Want To See You Cry/Baby I Need You (B-side actually by Wailers)	90
66	Ska Beat JB 248	You're No Good/SOULETTES: Don't Care What The People Say	60
67	Doctor Bird DB 1110	Say You/LYN TAITT & JETS: Smokey Places	50
67	Coxsone CS 7006	Lonely Teardrops/Oowee Baby	25
67	Coxsone CS 7020	Home Home Home/SOUL BROTHERS: Windell	60
67	Caltone TONE 107	The One I Love/You Left The Water Running	75
67	Studio One SO 2000	Feel Good/Mustang Sally	35
67	Studio One SO 2012	Puppet On A String/ROLAND ALPHONSO: Look Away	20
67	Studio One SO 2014	Fatty Fatty (actually Heptones)/Mother Word (actually by Delroy Wilson)	20
67	Studio One SO 2026	Why Did You Leave (actually by Leroy Sibbles)/Don't Try To Reach Me (actually by Gaylads)	30
68	Studio One SO 2039	When I Fall In Love/HEPTONES: Christmas Time	30
68	Studio One SO 2041	The Girl I Left Behind/TERMITES: My Last Love	25
68	Studio One SO 2053	Tomorrow/Movin' Away	35
68	Fab FAB 63	I Remember Someone/Can't You See?	85

68	Coxsone CS 7041	Everybody Knows/GAYLADS: I'm Free.	30
69	Coxsone CS 7094	Sherry/I've Got You	22
69	Studio One SO 2073	You're On My Mind/RICHARD ACE & SOUND DIMENSIONS: Love To Cherish	30
69	High Note HS 003	Lady With The Starlight/LESLIE BUTLER & COUNT OSSIE: Gay Drums	25
69	Bamboo BAM 4	Pleading/SOUND DIMENSION: Call 1143	50
69	Bamboo BAM 8	Be Yourself/SOUND DIMENSION: Rathid	20
70	Trojan TR 7716	Why, Baby Why/Keep My Love From Fading	7
70	Trojan TR 7756	Freedom Street/BEVERLEY'S ALLSTARS: Freedom Version.	8
70	Trojan TR 7772	It's Gonna Take A Miracle/Now I Know	10
70	Trojan TR 7780	Drums Of Freedom/BEVERLEY'S ALLSTARS: Version.	8
70	Gas GAS 169	Give To Me/Why.	8
70	Jackpot JP 748	You Left The Water Running/PHIL PRATT ALL STARS: Cut Throat	12
70	Punch PH 30	Artibella/PRATT ALLSTARS: Version Of Artibella	15
70	Punch PH 33	Morning/Morning (Version)	8
71	Punch PH 70	Stop Your Crying/CONSCIOUS MINDS: Suffering Through The Nation	10
71	Banana BA 352	Original Six (Parts 1 & 2)	15
71	Summit SUM 8518	I Wish It Could Be Peaceful Again/BEVERLEY'S ALLSTARS: Peaceful Version	8
71	Summit SUM 8519	Your Feeling And Mine/BEVERLEY'S ALLSTARS: Your Feeling Version	8
71	Big Shot BI 590	So Nice/So Nice Version.	8
71	Green Door GD 4002	Medley Version/Medley Version 2	8
71	Dynamic DYN 411	Hallelujah/Trying To Reach	8
72	Dynamic DYN 453	Tears From My Eyes/CONSCIOUS MINDS: Tears From My Eyes Version	5
72	Pama Supreme PS 369	Look What You've Done/LLOYD CHARMERS: Look What You've Done Version.	8
73	Trojan TR 7893	Is It Because I'm Black/Black, Gold And Green.	12
73	Green Door GD 4053	Silver Words/Rasta God Version.	8
73	Mirto 100	Is It Because I'm Black?/Just Like A Shelter	15
74	Trojan TR 7920	Everything I Own/Drum Song	5
74	Trojan TR 7944	Crying Over You/Now You Can See Me Again	5
75	Fab FAB 270	Thinking/Moving Away	20
67	Studio One SOL 9001	MR. ROCK STEADY (LP)	200
73	Trojan TRLS 58	BLACK, GOLD AND GREEN (LP).	35
74	Trojan TRLS 83	LETS GET IT ON (LP)	12

(see also Stranger & Ken, Keith Hudson, Gaylads, Richard Ace, Lloyd & Ken)

BOOTLES
| 64 | Vocalion VN 9216 | I'll Let You Hold My Hand/Never Till Now | 20 |

BOOTS
68	CBS 3550	Even The Bad Times Are Good/The Animal In Me.	20
68	CBS 3833	Keep Your Lovelight Burning/Give Me One More Chance	25
70	Youngblood YB 1018	You Better Run/A To D	30

DAVE BOOTS
| 60s | Solent SM 013 | GREEN SATIN AND GOLD (LP) | 110 |

BOOTSY'S RUBBER BAND
77	Warner Bros K 16964T	Pinocchio Theory/Psychoticbumpschool/What's A Telephone (12").	10
78	Warner Bros K 17196T	Bootzilla/Hollywood Squares (12", p/s)	10
76	Warner Bros K 56200	STRETCHIN' OUT IN BOOTSY'S RUBBER BAND (LP)	15
77	Warner Bros K 56302	AHH... THE NAME IS BOOTSY, BABY! (LP, gatefold sleeve)	15
78	Warner Bros K 56424	BOOTSY? PLAYER OF THE YEAR (LP, gatefold sleeve)	12
79	Warner Bros K 56615	THE BOOT IS MADE FOR FONK-N (LP, with inner sleeve).	12
81	Warner Bros K 56998	THE ONE GIVETH, THE COUNT TAKETH AWAY (LP)	12

(see also Parliament, Funkadelic)

BOOVER BOYS
| 70 | Torpedo TOR 22 | A.G.G.R.O/Sha La La La Lee | 30 |

RANNY BOP
| 70 | Gas GAS 155 | Pipe Dream/Suck Suck | 10 |

BOP & BELTONES
| 67 | Coxsone CS 7012 | Treat Me Good/PETER TOUCH & WAILERS: Dancing Time (B-side actually also by Bop & Beltones). | 40 |

(see also Beltones, Soul Vendors, Jackie Mittoo)

VICTOR BORGE
| 51 | Columbia DC 536 | Phonetic Punctuation parts 1 & 2 (78, export issue). | 6 |

BILLY BORLYNN
| 60 | Philips PB 1031 | Baby Listens/Liebelei | 7 |
| 60 | Philips PB 1057 | Every Step Of The Way/It Takes Time | 7 |

BORN B.C.
| 82 | Xcentric Noise FIRST 1 | THE POWER & THE PRIVILEGE (EP) | 8 |

BOSS
| 86 | Power House (no cat. no.) | One Good Reason/Wake Up Children (p/s, with lyric sheet) | 6 |

BOSS ATTACK
| 71 | Fab FAB 187 | Hell-EI/TEARDROPS: Let Me Be Free | 15 |

BOSS COMBO
| 62 | Coral LVA 9205 | GOLDEN ROCK AND ROLL INSTRUMENTALS (LP) | 25 |

BOSS GUITARS
| 65 | London HA-R/SH-R 8237 | PLAY THE WINNERS (LP). | 25 |

EARL BOSTIC (ORCHESTRA)
SINGLES
54	Parlophone MSP 6075	Off Shore/What! No Pearls	15
54	Parlophone MSP 6089	Deep Purple/Smoke Rings	15
54	Parlophone MSP 6105	Melancholy Serenade/Don't You Do It	15

54	Parlophone MSP 6110	Jungle Drums/Danube Waves	15
54	Parlophone MSP 6119	Mambolino/Blue Skies	15
54	Parlophone MSP 6131	These Foolish Things/Mambostic	15
54	Parlophone CMSP 8	Cherokee/The Song Is Ended (export issue)	20
55	Parlophone MSP 6162	Melody Of Love/Sweet Lorraine	15
56	Vogue V 2145	Flamingo/Sleep	15
56	Vogue V 2148	Moonglow/Ain't Misbehaving	15
56	Parlophone R 4208	The Bo-Do Rock (with Bill Doggett)/Mean To Me	20
56	Parlophone R 4232	For All We Know/Beyond The Blue Horizon	10
57	Parlophone R 4263	I Hear A Rhapsody/Harlem Nocturne	10
57	Parlophone R 4278	Bubbins Rock/Indiana (with Bill Doggett)	15
57	Parlophone R 4305	Avalon/Too Fine For Crying (B-side with Bill Jones)	10
57	Parlophone R 4370	Temptation/September Song	10
58	Parlophone R 4460	Over The Waves Rock/Twilight Time	10
59	Parlophone DP 553	Barcarolle/My Reverie (export single)	15
62	Ember JBS 708	Tuxedo Junction/Air Mail Special	15
66	Island WI 271	Honeymoon Night/PATSY COLE: Disappointed Bride	15

EPs

54	Parlophone GEP 8506	FLAMINGO	15
55	Parlophone GEP 8513	LINGER AWHILE	15
55	Parlophone GEP 8520	EARL BOSTIC AND HIS ALTO SAX	15
55	Vogue EPV 1010	EARL BOSTIC	25
56	Vogue EPV 1111	VELVET SUNSET	15
56	Parlophone GEP 8539	WRAP IT UP	15
56	Parlophone GEP 8548	EARL'S IMAGINATION	10
56	Parlophone GEP 8565	ALTO SAX AND MAMBO STRINGS	10
56	Parlophone GEP 8571	MUSIC A LA BOSTIC NO. 1	10
56	Parlophone GEP 8574	MUSIC A LA BOSTIC NO. 2	10
57	Parlophone GEP 8603	MUSIC A LA BOSTIC NO. 3	10
57	Parlophone GEP 8637	BOSTIC IN HARLEM	10
58	Parlophone GEP 8701	BOSTIC BEAT	25
58	Parlophone GEP 8741	ROCKING WITH BOSTIC	25
58	Parlophone GEP 8754	ALTO MAGIC	10
50s	Parlophone CGEP 1	EARL BOSTIC (export issue)	10
50s	Parlophone CGEP 10	EARL BOSTIC (export issue)	10

10" LPs

54	Vogue LDE 100	EARL BOSTIC AND HIS ORCHESTRA	30
54	Parlophone PMD 1016	EARL BOSTIC AND HIS ALTO SAX	30
56	Parlophone PMD 1040	EARL BOSTIC AND HIS ALTO SAX NO. 2	30
58	Parlophone PMD 1054	BOSTIC MEETS DOGGETT (with Bill Doggett)	30
58	Parlophone PMD 1068	BOSTIC ROCKS	30
59	Parlophone PMD 1071	BOSTIC SHOWCASE OF SWINGING DANCE HITS	25
59	Parlophone PMD 1074	SWEET TUNES OF THE FANTASTIC FIFTIES	30
59	Parlophone PMD 1115	SWEET TUNES OF THE ROARIN' TWENTIES	20
59	Parlophone PMD 1117	SWEET TUNES OF THE SWINGIN' THIRTIES	20
59	Parlophone PMD 1119	SWEET TUNES OF THE SENTIMENTAL FORTIES	20
60	Parlophone PMC 1125	PLAYS THE HIT TUNES OF THE BIG BROADWAY SHOWS (12" LP)	20

(see also Bill Doggett, Sonny Carter)

BOSTON

78	Epic 12 6653	Don't Look Back/The Journey (12", p/s)	8
79	Epic EPC 7888	Don't Look Back/More Than A Feeling/Smokin' (p/s)	5
76	Epic EPC 81611	BOSTON (LP)	12
76	Epic EPCH 81611	BOSTON (LP, audiophile pressing)	15
76	Epic EPC 81611	BOSTON (LP, picture disc)	15
78	Epic E 9945050	DON'T LOOK BACK (LP, picture disc)	12
86	MCA MCGP 6017	THIRD STAGE (LP, picture disc)	18
94	MCA MCGP	WALK ON (LP, picture disc)	18

BOSTON CRABS

65	Columbia DB 7586	Down In Mexico/Who?	18
65	Columbia DB 7679	As Long As I Have You/Alley Oop	18
66	Columbia DB 7830	Gin House/You Didn't Have To Be So Nice	15

BOSTON DEXTERS

64	Contemporary CR 101	Matchbox/La Bamba	200
64	Contemporary CR 102	You've Been Talking About Me/Nothing's Gonna Change Me	125
64	Contemporary CR 103	What Kind Of Girl Are You/I've Got Troubles Of My Own	125
65	Columbia DB 7498	I Believe To My Soul/I've Got Something To Tell You	50
65	Columbia DB 7641	Try Hard/No More Tears	45

(see also Buzz, Tam White)

BO STREET RUNNERS

64	Decca F 11986	Bo Street Runner/Tell Me	30
65	Columbia DB 7488	Tell Me What You're Gonna Do/And I Do Just What I Want	75
65	Columbia DB 7640	Baby Never Say Goodbye/Get Out Of My Way	50
66	Columbia DB 7901	Drive My Car/So Very Woman (featuring Mike [Too Much] Patto)	75
64	Oak RGJ 131	BO STREET RUNNERS (EP, 49 copies only)	1,500+

(see also [Mike] Patto, Timebox, Chicago Line, Cheynes, Fleetwood Mac)

CONNIE BOSWELL

| 54 | Brunswick 05319 | T-E-N-N-E-S-S-E-E (Spells …)/If I Give My Heart To You | 10 |
| 55 | Brunswick 05397 | How Important Can It Be?/Fill My Heart With Happiness | 10 |

ERIC BOSWELL

| 70 | Gayfeet GS 204 | Little Donkey (actually by Lou & Maxine)/
Hope And Joy (actually by Lou Sparkes) | 5 |

(see also Lou Sparkes)

EVE BOSWELL

53	Parlophone MSP 6006	Sugar Bush/Moon Above Malaya (China Nights)	30
55	Parlophone MSP 6158	Ready, Willing And Able/Pam-Poo-Dey	18
55	Parlophone MSP 6160	The Heart You Break (May Be Your Own)/Tika Tika Tok	18
56	Parlophone MSP 6208	Young And Foolish/Where You Are	18
56	Parlophone MSP 6220	It's Almost Tomorrow/Cookie	18
56	Parlophone MSP 6250	Saries Marias/Come Back My Love	18
56	Parlophone R 4230	True Love/Where In The World Is Billy?	15
57	Parlophone R 4275	Rock Bobbin' Boats/Tra La La	18
57	Parlophone R 4299	Chantez, Chantez/She Said (Aunt Magnolia)	10
57	Parlophone R 4328	With All My Heart/Sugar Candy	10
57	Parlophone R 4341	The Gypsy In My Soul/Stop Whistlin' Wolf	10
57	Parlophone R 4362	Swedish Polka (Chickadee)/Tell My Love	7
58	Parlophone R 4401	(I Love You) For Sentimental Reasons/Bobby	7
58	Parlophone R 4414	I Do/Love Me Again	12
58	Parlophone R 4455	Left Right Out Of Your Heart/Voom-Ba-Voom	7
58	Parlophone R 4479	More Than Ever (Come Prima)/I Know Why	7
58	Parlophone R 4492	Christmas Lullaby/The Christmas Tree	10
59	Parlophone R 4517	If I Had A Talking Picture Of You/Piccaninny	6
59	Parlophone R 4544	Wimoweh Cha Cha/Boegoeberg Se Dam	6
59	Parlophone R 4555	Once Again/You Are Never Far Away From Me	6
60	Parlophone R 4618	Misty/Turnabout Heart	6
69	Morgan MRS 19	This Is My Love/Lonely In A Crowd	6
76	EMI EMI 2517	Sugar Bush '76/This Time	6
57	Parlophone GEP 8601	THE ENCHANTING EVE (EP)	18
58	Parlophone GEP 8690	EVE BOSWELL'S SHOWCASE (EP)	18
58	Parlophone GEP 8717	EVE BOSWELL'S SHOWCASE NO. 2 (EP)	18
56	Parlophone PMD 1039	SUGAR AND SPICE (10" LP)	60
57	Parlophone PMC 1038	SENTIMENTAL EVE (LP)	45
59	Parlophone PMC 1105	FOLLOWING THE SUN AROUND (LP)	40

SIMON BOSWELL

75	Transatlantic TRA 307	MIND PARASITES (LP)	15

(see also Advertising)

BOTHY BAND

70	Polydor 2383 417	OLD HAG YOU HAVE KILLED ME (LP)	12

PERRY BOTKIN

60	Brunswick 05838	The Executioner Theme/Waltz Of The Hunter	5

(see also Charles Boyer)

BOULEVARD

79	Chopper CHOP 5D	MAGIC MAN (12", red vinyl, no p/s)	10
81	Boulevard VARD 1	Dawn Raid/Take It Or Leave It (p/s)	50

DENNIS BOVELL

81	Fontana 6381047	BRAIN DAMAGE (LP)	15

BOW BELLS

65	Polydor 56030	Not To Be Taken/I'll Try Not To Hold It Against You	5
66	Parlophone R 5520	Belinda/When You're In	5

(see also Nola York)

DENNIS BOWELL

78	Tempus TEMLP 001	STRICTLY DUBWISE (LP)	40
78	Ballistic LBR 1031	STRICTLY DUBWISE (LP)	15

(see also Matumbi, Rama)

JIMMY BOWEN

57	Columbia DB 3915	I'm Stickin' With You/Ever Lovin' Fingers (78 rpm = £18)	90
57	Columbia DB 3984	Warm Up To Me, Baby/I Trusted You (78 rpm = £15)	60
57	Columbia DB 4027	Cross Over/It's Shameful (78 rpm = £18)	30
58	Columbia DB 4184	The Two Step/By The Light Of The Silvery Moon (78 rpm = £20)	25
65	Reprise RS 23043	The Eagle (demos & some issues list "The Golden Eagle")/Spanish Cricket	35
67	Reprise RS 20592	Raunchy (with Chorus & Orchestra)/It's Such A Pretty World Today (wth Singers)	5
58	Columbia SEG 7757	MEET JIMMY BOWEN (EP)	125
58	Columbia SEG 7793	MEET JIMMY BOWEN NO. 2 (EP)	125

BEN BOWERS

55	Columbia SCM 5192	The Kentuckian Song/The Man From Laramie	10
56	Columbia SCM 5260	To You, My Love/I'm Still A King To You	10
57	Parlophone R 4317	Country Boy (with His Royal Jamaicans)/	
		Rum And Coconut Water (Rum And Coca-Cola) (78 rpm = £6)	6
59	Pye N 15175	Naughty Little Flea/Donkey City (78)	6
57	Pye Jazz NJE 1001	BIG BEN BLUES (EP, with His Bluesicians)	10

DAVID BOWIE

SINGLES

66	Pye 7N 17020	Can't Help Thinking About Me/And I Say To Myself (with Lower Third)	175
66	Pye 7N 17079	Do Anything You Say/Good Morning Girl	200
66	Pye 7N 17157	I Dig Everything/I'm Not Losing Sleep	200
66	Deram DM 107	Rubber Band/The London Boys	180
67	Deram DM 123	The Laughing Gnome/The Gospel According To Tony Day	
		(with inverted matrix number on label)	70
67	Deram DM 135	Love You Till Tuesday/Did You Ever Have A Dream	200
69	Philips BF 1801	Space Oddity/Wild Eyed Boy From Freecloud (unreleased p/s,	
		only 2 or 3 copies known to exist)	3,000+
69	Philips BF 1801	Space Oddity/Wild Eyed Boy From Freecloud (mono; stereo 45s unconfirmed)	170
70	Mercury MF 1135	The Prettiest Star/Conversation Piece	170
70	Mercury 6052 026	Memory Of A Free Festival Parts 1 & 2	170

71	Mercury 6052 049	Holy Holy/Black Country Rock	180
72	RCA RCA 2160	Changes/Andy Warhol	8
72	RCA RCA 2199	Starman/Suffragette City (some in p/s)	100/6
72	RCA RCA 2263	John, I'm Only Dancing/Hang Onto Yourself (original pressing with slow 'acoustic guitar' version; later pressings have faster version with sax, £4)	6
72	Pye 7NX 8002	Do Anything You Say/I Dig Everything/I Can't Help Thinking About Me/I'm Not Losing Sleep (p/s)	20
72	RCA RCA 2302	The Jean Genie/Ziggy Stardust	6
73	RCA RCA 2352	Drive-In Saturday/Round And Round	6
73	RCA RCA 2316	Life On Mars?/The Man Who Sold The World (some in p/s)	35/5
73	Deram DM 123	The Laughing Gnome/The Gospel According To Tony Day (reissue, matrix number correct way up on label)	6
74	RCA RCA 2424	Sorrow/Amsterdam	6
74	RCA LPBO 5009	Rebel Rebel/Queen Bitch	6
74	RCA LPBO 5021	Rock'N'Roll Suicide/Quicksand	6
74	RCA APBO 0293	Diamond Dogs/Holy Holy	6
74	RCA/Mainman/	Bowie's Greatest Hits (excerpts from Knock On Wood/	
	Lyntone LYN 2929	Space Oddity/The Man Who Sold The World/Life On Mars?/Starman/Jean Genie/Sorrow/Diamond Dogs) (33rpm 1-sided flexidisc with Record Mirror/Popswop magazine)	20/8
74	RCA RCA 2466	Knock On Wood/Panic In Detroit	6
75	RCA RCA 2523	Young Americans/Suffragette City	6
75	Decca F 13579	The London Boys/Love You Till Tuesday	12
75	Decca F 13579	The London Boys/Love You Till Tuesday (Demo)	200
75	RCA RCA 2579	Fame/Right	6
75	RCA RCA 2593	Space Oddity/Changes/Velvet Goldmine (p/s)	12
76	RCA RCA 2726	Suffragette City/Stay (p/s)	18
77	RCA PB 0905	Sound And Vision/A New Career In A New Town	6
77	RCA PB 1017	Be My Wife/Speed Of Life	6
77	RCA PB 1121	'Heroes'/V-2 Schneider	6
78	RCA PB 1190	Beauty And The Beast/Sense Of Doubt (some with p/s)	6/10
79	RCA BOW 2	Boys Keep Swinging/Fantastic Voyage (p/s)	6
79	RCA BOW 3	DJ/Repetition (p/s, some on green vinyl)	22/6
79	RCA BOW 4	John, I'm Only Dancing (Again)/John, I'm Only Dancing (p/s)	6
79	RCA BOW 12-4	John, I'm Only Dancing (Again) (Extended)/John, I'm Only Dancing (12", p/s)	10
80	RCA BOW 5	Alabama Song/Space Oddity (poster p/s)	6
80	RCA BOW 6	Ashes To Ashes/Move On (with 3 different p/s & 4 different sheets of 9 stamps)	6
81	RCA BOW 8	Scary Monsters/Because You're Young (p/s)	6
81	RCA BOWC 8	Scary Monsters/Because You're Young (cassette, card sleeve)	10
81	RCA BOW 9	Up The Hill Backwards/Crystal Japan (p/s)	6
81	RCA BOWC 9	Up The Hill Backwards/Crystal Japan (cassette, card sleeve)	10
82	RCA BOW 11	IN BERTHOLT BRECHT'S BAAL (EP, foldout p/s)	8
82	RCA BOW 100	FASHIONS (10 x 7" picture discs in plastic wallet [BOWP 101-110], each £4)	45
82	RCA BOWT 12	Peace On Earth/Little Drummer Boy/Fantastic Voyage (12", p/s, picture labels, with Bing Crosby)	8
83	EMI America 45-TCEA 152	Let's Dance/Cat People (cassette)	6
83	EMI America EAP 157	China Girl/Shake It (picture disc)	10
83	EMI America 12 EA 158	Modern Love/Modern Love (Live) (12", p/s with poster)	12
84	EMI America EA 187	Tonight/Tumble And Twirl (poster p/s)	6
85	EMI America EAP 195	Loving The Alien (Remixed Version)/Don't Look Down (Remixed Version) (shaped picture disc)	15
85	EMI America 12 EAG 195	Loving The Alien (Extended Dance Mix)/Don't Look Down (Extended Dub Mix)/Loving The Alien (Extended Dub Mix) (12", gatefold p/s with poster)	10
86	Virgin VSS 838	Absolute Beginners/Absolute Beginners (Dub Mix) (square picture disc)	12
86	EMI America EAP 216	Underground (Edited Version)/Underground (Instrumental) (shaped picture disc)	15
86	Virgin VSS 906	When The Wind Blows/When The Wind Blows (Instrumental) (shaped pic disc)	15
87	EMI America 12 EAX 230	Day-In Day-Out (Remix)/(Extended Dub Mix)/Julie (12", stickered black p/s)	8
87	EMI America EAP 237	Time Will Crawl (Single Version)/Girls (Single Edit) (poster p/s)	8
87	EMI America 12 EAX 237	Time Will Crawl (Dance Crew Mix)/(Dub)/Girls (Japanese Version) (12", p/s)	8
87	EMI America EAP 239	Never Let Me Down/'87 And Cry (picture disc)	8
88	Virgin CDT 20	Absolute Beginners (Full Length Version)/(Dub Mix) (3" CD, card sleeve)	15
88	PRT PYX 6001	I'm Not Losing Sleep/I Dig Everything/Can't Help Thinking/Do Anything You Say (picture disc)	12
90	EMI USA CD FAME 90	FAME 90 (Remixes) (CD)	12
93	BMG Arista 136977	Jump They Say (Radio Edit)/Pallas Athena (Don't Stop Praying Mix) (jukebox issue, no p/s)	8
93	Arista 13942-2	Jump They Say (7" Version)/Pallas Athena (Don't Stop Praying Mix) (CD, double jewel case with booklet)	10
93	BMG Arista 177057	Buddha Of Suburbia/Dead Against It (p/s)	8
93	BMG Arista 18168-2	Buddha Of Suburbia/Dead Against It (CD, holographic disc)	10
97	RCA 307031	The Heart's Filthy Lesson (Alternative Mix)/(Bowie Mix)/(Rubber Mix)/(Simple Text Mix)/(Filthy Mix) (12", picture disc)	10
95	RCA 329407	Strangers When We Meet (Edit)/The Man Who Sold The World (live) (green vinyl, stickered card p/s)	8
95	RCA 353847	Hallo Spaceboy (Remix)/The Heart's Filthy Lesson (Radio Edit) (pink vinyl, stickered card p/s)	8
97	RCA 7432 1475841	Dead Man Walking/Hous/Vigor Mortis/Paradox (plain sleeve, stickered)	8
97	RCA 512347	Seven Years In Tibet (Edit)/Seven Years In Tibet (Mandarin Version) (p/s, clear vinyl)	8
97	RCA 39741-1	Telling Lies (Paradox Mix)/Telling Lies (Feelgood & Adam F Mix) (12", p/s)	8
99	Virgin VSP 1767	Survive/Seven (live) (picture disc)	10

David BOWIE

LPs

67	Deram DML/SML 1007	DAVID BOWIE (mono/stereo)	250/280
69	Philips SBL 7912	DAVID BOWIE (gatefold sleeve).	350
70	Decca PA 58	THE WORLD OF DAVID BOWIE (mono)	22
72	Decca SPA 58	THE WORLD OF DAVID BOWIE (stereo, 'curly hair' cover)	10
71	Mercury 6338 041	THE MAN WHO SOLD THE WORLD (with 'dress' cover)	350
71	Mercury 6338 041	THE MAN WHO SOLD THE WORLD (cassette, with 'dress' cover)	50
71	RCA SF 8244	HUNKY DORY (orange label with lyric sheet)	10
72	RCA SF 8287	THE RISE AND FALL OF ZIGGY STARDUST AND THE SPIDERS FROM MARS (orange label with lyric inner sleeve)	15
72	RCA LSP 4813	SPACE ODDITY (reissue of SBL 7912 in different sleeve, orange label with lyric inner sleeve & poster).	22
72	RCA LSP 4816	THE MAN WHO SOLD THE WORLD (orange label with inner sleeve & poster)	15
73	RCA RS 1001	ALADDIN SANE (orange label, gatefold sleeve & lyric inner sleeve, some with fan club membership card)	18/10
74	RCA APL 1-0576	DIAMOND DOGS (orange label, gatefold sleeve)	10
74	RCA APL 2-0771	DAVID LIVE (2-LP, gatefold sleeve, orange label, photos on inners)	12
76	RCA APLI 1327	STATION TO STATION (with original colour proof sleeve)	500+
76	RCA RS 1055	CHANGESONEBOWIE (with 'sax' version of John I'm Only Dancing)	20
78	RCA PL 02913	STAGE (2-LP, gatefold sleeve, some yellow vinyl)	20/10
77	RCA INTS 5065	LOW (red vinyl, semi-official 'factory custom pressing')	500+
80	RCA BOW LP 2	SCARY MONSTERS (AND SUPER CREEPS) (purple vinyl, semi-official 'factory custom pressing').	600+
80	K-Tel NE 1111	THE BEST OF BOWIE (with incorrect tracklisting)	12
81	RCA BL 43606	CHRISTIANE F. WIR KINDER VOM BAHNOF ZOO (soundtrack)	12
83	EMI America AMLP 3029	LET'S DANCE (picture disc)	12
84	RCA BOPIC 1	ALADDIN SANE (picture disc with numbered insert)	18
84	RCA BOPIC 2	HUNKY DORY (picture disc with numbered insert).	18
84	RCA BOPIC 3	ZIGGY STARDUST (picture disc with numbered insert)	18
84	RCA BOPIC 4	PIN-UPS (picture disc with numbered insert)	18
84	RCA BOPIC 5	DIAMOND DOGS (picture disc with numbered insert)	18
94	MAINMAN GYLP 002	SANTA MONICA LIVE '72 (2xLP, gatefold sleeve)	30
95	RCA 307021	EXCERPTS FROM OUTSIDE (with 12" booklet & lyric sheet)	18
97	RCA 44949	EARTHLING (gatefold sleeve)	18

CDs

84	Deram 800 087-2	DAVID BOWIE (withdrawn with white title).	60
84	RCA PD 89002	STAGE (2-CD, withdrawn)	40
84	RCA PD 84234	LODGER (withdrawn)	20
84	RCA PD 83856	LOW (withdrawn).	20
84	RCA PD 83857	'HEROES' (withdrawn)	20
85	RCA PD 84623	HUNKY DORY (withdrawn)	20
85	RCA PD 84654	THE MAN WHO SOLD THE WORLD (withdrawn).	25
85	RCA PD 84702	THE RISE AND FALL OF ZIGGY STARDUST AND THE SPIDERS FROM MARS (withdrawn)	20
85	RCA PD 84813	SPACE ODDITY (withdrawn)	25
85	RCA PD 84653	PIN-UPS (withdrawn)	20
85	RCA PD 83890	ALADDIN SANE (withdrawn)	20
85	RCA PD 80998	YOUNG AMERICANS (withdrawn).	20
85	RCA PD 81327	STATION TO STATION (withdrawn)	25
85	RCA PD 81732	CHANGESONEBOWIE (withdrawn)	35
85	RCA PD 83856	LOW (withdrawn).	25
85	RCA PD 83889	DIAMOND DOGS (withdrawn)	25
86	RCA PD 82743	PETER AND THE WOLF (withdrawn)	20
85	RCA PD 83647	SCARY MONSTERS (AND SUPER CREEPS) (withdrawn)	20
84	RCA PD 84202	CHANGESTWOBOWIE (withdrawn)	30
84	RCA PD 94792	GOLDEN YEARS (withdrawn)	30
84	RCA PD 84919	FAME AND FASHION (ALL TIME GREATEST HITS) (withdrawn)	50
93	EMI BOWIE 1	SELECTIONS FROM THE SINGLES COLLECTION 10-track sampler,card p/s, promo only)	20
93	Arista 17822-2	THE BUDDHA OF SUBURBIA (special edition in clear plastic case, with novel)	22
93	BBC MMCD 0072	BBC SESSIONS 1969-1972 (CD, picture disc, promo-only, withdrawn)	200
99	Virgin CDVX 2900	'hours...' (hologram sleeve)	22

PROMOS

77	RCA BOW-1E	From The New Album LOW (excerpts from Speed Of Life, Breaking Glass, What In The World, Sound And Vision, Be My Wife & A New Career In A New Town; demo only).	450+
83	RCA LIFETIMES 1	LIFETIMES (LP, promo, numbered, with insert)	35
90	BMG BOW 908	SO FAR (CD, 8-track sampler for Sound & Vision box set)	35
91	Rykodisc VRCD 0142	BOWIE / ENO: IT'S TIME TO LISTEN (CD, 9-track sampler from Ryko reissues; includes "Sound + Vision", Be My Wife, Some Are, Heroes, Joe The Lion, Abdulmajid, "DJ", Boys Keep Swinging, Look Back In Anger)	22
93	BMG MEAT 1	Pallas Athena (12", white label, no p/s, includes two exclusive Meat Beat Manifesto remixes)	45
93	Back To Basics HOME 1	Night Flights/(B-side by Moodswings) (12")	20
95	RCA HALLO 2	Hallo Spaceboy (12" Remix) (12", 1-sided, no p/s)	20
95	BMG SOLO 1	EXCLUSIVE TOUR CD: Strangers When We Meet/MORRISSEY: The Boy Racer (Outside Tour CD)	80
95	RCA OUT 1	The Heart's Filthy Lesson (12", 1-sided promo)	10
96	RCA SPACE 2	Hallo Spaceboy (12" Remix) (1-sided 12", some copies listed as RCA HALLO 2, no p/s)	30
96	RCA SPACE 3	Hallo Spaceboy (Double Click Mix)/Hallo Spaceboy (Instrumental)/ Hallo Spaceboy (Lost In Space Mix) (12", no p/s)	60
99	Virgin CDVDJ 2900	'hours...' (CD, card sleeve)	22

| 99 | EMI CDLRL 015 | ALBUM SAMPLER (CD, 17-track sampler, promo only) | 25 |
| 99 | EMI QUEENWL 28 | Under Pressure (Remixes) (with Queen) (12", white label, unreleased mix, promo only) | 70 |

(see also Davie Jones & King Bees, Davy Jones & Lower Third, Manish Boys, Arnold Corns, Spiders From Mars, Mick Ronson, Queen, Tao Jones Index, Bing Crosby)

BOWMAN-HYDE PLAYERS
| 61 | Ember EMB S 141 | I Like A Little Honey/Teenage Kiss | 10 |
| 61 | Parlophone PMC 1155 | SING ME A SOUVENIR (LP) | 20 |

ALAN BOWN (SET)
65	Pye 7N 15934	Can't Let Her Go/I'm The One	20
66	Pye 7N 17084	Baby Don't Push Me/Everything's Gonna Be Alright	20
66	Pye 7N 17148	Headline News/Mister Pleasure	50
66	Pye 7N 17192	Emergency 999/Settle Down	60
67	Pye 7N 17256	Gonna Fix You Good (Everytime You're Bad)/I Really Really Care	45
67	Music Factory CUB 1	We Can Help You/Magic Handkerchief (as the Alan Bown!)	12
67	MGM MGM 1355	Toyland/Technicolour Dream	8
68	MGM MGM 1387	Story Book/Little Lesley	20
69	Deram DM 259	Still As Stone/Wrong Idea	10
69	Deram DM 278	Gypsy Girl/All I Can	6
70	Island WIP 6091	Pyramid/Crash Landing	5
75	CBS 3721	Rockford Files/I Don't Know	6
68	Music Factory CUB LM/LS 1	OUTWARD BOWN (LP)	50
69	Deram DML/SML 1049	THE ALAN BOWN! (LP)	40
70	Island ILPS 9131	LISTEN (LP)	25

(see also Robert Palmer, John Barry Seven, Bronco, Jonesy)

ALAN BOWN SET/JIMMY JAMES & VAGABONDS
| 68 | Pye N(S)PL 18156 | LONDON SWINGS — LIVE AT THE MARQUEE CLUB (LP, 1 side each) | 50 |

(see also Jimmy James & Vagabonds)

ANDREW BOWN
| 70 | Parlophone R 5856 | Tarot (Theme From 'Ace Of Wands')/Lulli Rides Again | 80 |

(see also Andy Bown)

BOWWOWWOW
| 80 | Wow 1 | Louis Quatorze/Fools Rush In (Promo DJ copy) | 8 |
| 80 | PSLP323 | C30C60C90 GO! (1-sided test pressing) | 25 |

ANDY BOWN
79	EMI EMI 2906	Another Shipwreck/Another Night With You	6
79	EMI EMI 2943	Good Advice/One More Chance	5
81	EMI EMI 5245	Say It Was Magic/One Forward Two Back Again (in p/s)	10
82	EMI EMI 5312	Marianne/One Forward Two Back Again	5
82	EMI EMI 5372	Help Me/Marianne (p/s)	5
72	Mercury 6310 002	GONE TO MY HEAD (LP)	12
73	GM GML 1001	SWEET WILLIAM (LP)	12
77	EMI EMC 3176	COME BACK ROMANCE, ALL IS FORGIVEN (LP, with inner sleeve)	12

(see also Andrew Bown, Herd, Judas Jump, Status Quo, Rossi & Frost, Storyteller)

DAVID BOX
| 64 | London HLU 9874 | If You Can't Say Something Nice/Sweet Sweet Day | 20 |
| 64 | London HLU 9924 | Little Lonely Summer Girl/No One Will Ever Know | 20 |

(see also Crickets)

BOX CAR RACER
| 00s | MCA MCS 40290 | I Feel So/Cat Like Thief (picture disc) | 8 |

(see also Blink 182)

BOXER
| 75 | Virgin V 2049 | BELOW THE BELT (LP, with uncensored full-frontal back cover) | 15 |
| 76 | Virgin V 2073 | BLOODLETTING (LP, withdrawn) | 80 |

(see also Patto, Timebox)

BOX TOPS
67	Stateside SS 2044	The Letter/Happy Times	15
67	Stateside SS 2070	Neon Rainbow/She Knows How	15
68	Bell BLL 1001	Cry Like A Baby/The Door You Closed To Me	8
68	Bell BLL 1017	Choo Choo Train/Fields Of Clover	6
68	Bell BLL 1035	I Met Her In Church/People Gonna Talk	6
69	Bell BLL 1045	Sandman/Sweet Cream Ladies, Forward March	6
69	Bell BLL 1063	I Shall Be Released/I Must Be The Devil	6
69	Bell BLL 1068	Soul Deep/The Happy Song	8
69	Bell BLL 1084	Turn On A Dream/Together	6
70	Bell BLL 1097	You Keep Tightening Up On Me/Come On Honey	6
73	London HLU 10402	Sugar Creek Woman/It's All Over	6
68	Stateside (S)SL 10218	THE LETTER/NEON RAINBOW (LP)	30
68	Bell MBLL/SBLL 105	CRY LIKE A BABY (LP)	25
69	Bell MBLL/SBLL 108	NON-STOP (LP)	20
69	Bell SBLL 120	DIMENSIONS (LP)	20
70	Bell MBLL/SBLL 129	SUPER HITS (LP)	15
70	Bell BELLS 149	BOX TOPS (LP)	15

(see also Big Star, Alex Chilton)

EL BOY
| 57 | Columbia DB 3927 | Jack, Jack, Jack/Tonight My Heart She Is Crying | 5 |

DENNY BOYCE & HIS ORCHESTRA/RHYTHM
| 57 | Oriole CB 1358 | One Man Went To Rock/Thunderstorm (78) | 6 |
| 58 | Oriole CB 1458 | Bad Boy/When Your Hair Has Turned To Silver | 10 |

MINT VALUE £

TOMMY BOYCE
65	MGM MGM 1287	Pretty Thing/I Don't Have To Worry 'Bout You	10

TOMMY BOYCE & BOBBY HART
67	A&M AMS 705	Out And About/My Little Chickadee	5
67	A&M AMS 710	Sometimes She's A Little Girl/Love Every Day	5
68	A&M AMS 714	I Wonder What She's Doing Tonight?/Ambushers	5
68	A&M AMS 722	Goodbye Baby/Where Angels Go Trouble Follows	5
68	A&M AMS 729	Alice Long (You're Still My Favourite Girlfriend)/P.O. Box 9847	5
67	A&M AML 907	TEST PATTERNS (LP)	15

(see also Monkees, Tommy Boyce)

EDDIE BOYD
66	Blue Horizon 45 BH 1009	It's So Miserable To Be Alone/Empty Arms	150
67	Blue Horizon 57-3137	The Big Boat/Sent For You Yesterday (with Fleetwood Mac)	30
62	Esquire EP 247	BOYD'S BLUES (EP, as Eddie Boyd Blues Combo)	70
65	Fontana SFJL 905	FIVE LONG YEARS (LP)	50
67	Decca LK/SKL 4872	EDDIE BOYD AND HIS BLUES BAND FEATURING PETER GREEN (LP)	125
68	Blue Horizon 7-63202	7936 SOUTH RHODES (LP, with Fleetwood Mac)	85
68	Storyville SLP 4054	IN CONCERT (LP)	30

(see also Fleetwood Mac)

EDDIE BOYD/BUDDY GUY
66	Chess CRE 6009	WITH THE BLUES (EP, 2 tracks each)	30

(see also Buddy Guy)

FRANKLYN BOYD
57	Nestles NR 01	Bye, Bye Love (78, 1-sided card flexi)	10
57	Nestles NR 05	Teddy Bear (78, 1-sided card flexi)	10

JIMMY BOYD
53	Columbia SCM 5072	I Saw Mommy Kissing Santa Claus/Little Train A-Chuggin' In My Heart	40

WILLIAM BOYD
56	Capitol Junior CJ 100	Hopalong Cassidy & The Mail Train Robbery parts 1 & 2 (78, with p/s)	10
56	Capitol Junior CJ 103	Hopalong Cassidy & The Big Ranch Fire parts 1 & 2 (78, with p/s)	10

CHARLES BOYER
65	London HAT 8268	WHERE DOES LOVE GO (LP)	15

BOY FRIDAY
70	Downtown 470	Girl/Version Girl	12

BOYFRIENDS
78	United Artists UP 36424	I'm In Love Today/Saturday Night (p/s)	10
78	United Artists UP 36442	Jenny/Don't Ask Me To Explain (p/s)	10
78	United Artists UP 36478	Last Bus Home/Romance (p/s)	10

(see also Vibrators)

BOYFRIENDS
82	Plastic PRES 001	Boyfriend/Give A Little, Take A Little (p/s)	40

BOY GEORGE
87	Virgin CDEP 9	To Be Reborn/Where Are You Now? (CD, gatefold card p/s)	10
88	Virgin BOY 105-12	Live My Life/Live My Life (Klub Mix)/Live My Life (12" Club Remix) (12", poster sleeve)	8
88	Virgin BOYT 106	No Clause 28 (Space Face Full Remix)/(Space Face Full Dub)/ (Full Version) (3" CD, in 5" slimline jewel case, with adaptor)	10
88	Virgin BOYCD 106	No Clause 28 (5" CD)	8
89	Virgin BOYCD 107	Don't Cry/Leave In Love/Don't Cry (Full Version)/A Boy Called Alice (3" CD)	10
89	Virgin BOYCD 108	Don't Take My Mind On A Trip/I Go Where I Go/Girlfriend/ What Becomes Of The Broken Hearted (3" CD, card p/s)	10
98	More Protein PROT 112	Sad (Mixes)/Butterfly (Mixes)	10
98	More Protein (no cat. no.)	Open House With Boy George & Family (CD-ROM, available at selected concerts)	25
98	Back Door BDCD 01	THE UNRECOUPABLE ONE MAN BANDIT (CD, 1st issue)	18

(see also Culture Club, Jesus Loves You)

BOY HAIRDRESSERS
88	53rd & 3rd AGARR T12	Golden Showers/Tidalwave/The Assumption As An Elevator (12", p/s)	25

(see also Teenage Fanclub, BMX Bandits, Clouds)

BOY KRAZY
91	Polydor PZCD 158	That's What Love Can Do (Extended Version)/One Thing Leads To Another/ That's What Love Can Do (7" version) (CD, p/s)	10
91	Polydor 828 403-2	BOY KRAZY (CD)	20

BILLY BOYLE
62	Decca F 11503	My Baby's Crazy 'Bout Elvis/Held For Questioning	30
63	Decca F 11709	I'm Coming Home/Sunday's Child	15
63	Columbia DB 7111	Lovers Hill/She's New To You	7
63	Columbia DB 7127	Hootin' In The Kitchen/Lover's Hill	7
64	Columbia DB 7294	Walk, Walk, Walkin'/My Baby Tonight (with Le Roys)	10
70	UPC UPC112	Lookin' For Love/Pisces Man	10

(see also Le Roys)

A. BOYNE
70	Punch PH 36	Oh My Darling (actually Audley Rollins)/DENNIS SMITH: Ball Of Confusion	10

BOYS (Jamaica)
69	Duke DU 19	Easy Sound/AFROTONES: Freedom Sound	15

(see also Harry J. Allstars)

BOYS (U.K.)
63	Parlophone R 5027	Polaris/Jumpin'	20

BOYS (U.K.)
64	Pye 7N 15726	It Ain't Fair/I Want You	100

(see also Sandra Barry & Boys, Action)

BOYS (U.K.)
77	NEMS NES 102	I Don't Care/Soda Pressing (p/s)	15
77	NEMS NES 111	First Time/Whatcha Gonna Do/Turning Grey (p/s)	15
78	NEMS NES 116	Brickfield Nights/Teacher's Pet (p/s)	10
79	Safari SAFE 21	Kamikaze/Bad Days (p/s, some with booklet)	7/5
80	Safari SAFE 23	Terminal Love/I Love Me (p/s)	5
80	Safari SAFE 27	You Better Move On/Schoolgirls (p/s)	5
80	Safari SAFE 31	Weekend/Cool (p/s)	5
80	Safari SAFE 33	Let It Rain/Lucy (p/s)	6
77	NEMS NES 6001	THE BOYS (LP)	15
78	NEMS NEL 6015	ALTERNATIVE CHARTBUSTERS (LP, with inner sleeve)	15
79	Safari 1-2 BOYS	TO HELL WITH THE BOYS (LP, with songbook & stickered sleeve)	12

(see also Yobs, Rowdies, Hollywood Brats)

BOYS (U.K.)
88	private pressing	Happy Days/Standard Avenue/Learn How To Dance (p/s)	8

(see also Ocean Colour Scene)

BOYS BLUE
65	HMV POP 1427	You Got What I Want/Take A Heart	40

(see also Jeff Elroy & Boys Blue)

BOYS OF THE LOUGH
73	Trailer LER 2086	THE BOYS OF THE LOUGH (LP)	15
74	Trailer LER 2090	SECOND ALBUM (LP)	15
75	Transatlantic TRA 296	RECORDED LIVE (LP)	12

BOYS WONDER
87	Sire W 8195	Shine On Me/Stop It (p/s)	5
87	Sire W 8293	What Now, Earthman?/Ten Million Ton Headache (p/s)	5
88	Boys Wonder BW 1	Goodbye Jimmy Dean/Hot Rod (p/s)	5
90	Flat OUTS 001	Eat Me, Drink Me/Harley Davidson (p/s)	5
89	Flat OUTA 002	RADIO WONDER (LP)	12

BOZ
66	Columbia DB 7832	You're Just The Kind Of Girl I Want/Isn't That So	10
66	Columbia DB 7889	Meeting Time/No (Ah) Body Knows The Blues	10
66	Columbia DB 7941	Pinocchio/Stay As You Are	8
66	Columbia DB 7972	The Baby Song/Carry On Screaming	8
68	Columbia DB 8406	I Shall Be Released/Down In The Flood	7
68	Columbia DB 8468	Light My Fire/Back Against The Wall	10

(see also King Crimson)

JANET BRACE
55	Brunswick 05272	Teach Me Tonight/My Old Familiar Heartache	10

BRACKEN
79	Look LKLP 6438	PRINCE OF THE NORTHLANDS (LP, private pressing, with insert)	85

PROF. ALEX BRADFORD
63	London REU 1357	TOO CLOSE TO HEAVEN (EP)	22
63	Stateside SL 10047	ONE STEP (LP)	25

(see also Bradford Singers)

BOBBY BRADFORD
73	Emanem 302	LOVE'S DREAM (LP)	30

BRADFORD SINGERS
62	Stateside SL 10026	BLACK NATIVITY (LP)	20
64	Stateside SL 10083	ANGEL ON VACATION (LP)	20

(see also Prof. Alex Bradford)

GEORGE BRADLEY & HIS BAND
65	HMV POP 1459	Breakout/Vendetta	12

JAN BRADLEY
63	Pye International 7N 25182	Mama Didn't Lie/Lovers Like Me	50

MARTIN BRADLEY
80	Greenwich Village GVR 205	TIME CAN'T STAND STILL (LP)	15

OWEN BRADLEY (ORCHESTRA/QUINTET)
56	Brunswick 05528	Theme From The Threepenny Opera/Lights Of Vienna (with Orchestra)	6
57	Brunswick 05700	White Silver Sands/Midnight Blues (as Owen Bradley Quintet)	7
58	Brunswick 05736	Big Guitar/Sentimental Dream (as Owen Bradley Quintet) (78 rpm = £10)	20
60	Brunswick LAT 8327	THE BIG GUITAR (LP)	30

BRADLEY STRYDER
92	Rephlex CAT 001	BRADLEY'S BEAT (12" EP, logo sleeve)	20
96	Rephlex CAT 020	BRADLEY'S ROBOT (12" EP, poster p/s)	10

DON BRADSHAW-LEATHER
72	Distance DIST 101	DISTANCE BETWEEN US (2-LP, gatefold sleeve, private pressing)	50

(supposedly by Robert John Godfrey)

BUDDY BRADSHAW
59	Capitol CL 15036	Nothing You Can Say/Tonight I Walk Alone	15

(see also Owen Gray)

SONNY BRADSHAW (& YOUNG JAMAICA)
61	Duke DK 1003	Yellow Birds/Festival Jump Up	15
71	Big Shot BI 576	Wig Wam/Peace And Love (as Sonny Bradshaw & Young Jamaica)	12

TINY BRADSHAW & HIS ORCHESTRA

52	Vogue V 2146	Breaking Up The House/Walk That Mess (78)	10
54	Parlophone CMSP 3	South Of The Orient/Later (export issue)	20
54	Parlophone MSP 6118	The Gypsy/Spider Web (78 rpm Parlophone R 3894 = £6)	15
55	Parlophone DP 418	Bradshaw Boogie/Walkin' The Chalk Line (78, export issue)	10
55	Parlophone DP 427	Choice/Light (78, export issue)	6
55	Parlophone MSP 6145	Overflow/Don't Worry 'Bout Me (78 rpm Parlophone R3959 = £10)	20
54	Parlophone GEP 8507	TRAIN KEPT A ROLLING (EP)	50
56	Parlophone GEP 8552	POMPTON TURNPIKE (EP)	28
55	Parlophone CGEP 2	TINY BRADSHAW (export EP)	25

TINY BRADSHAW ORCHESTRA/WYNONIE HARRIS

70	Polydor 623 273	KINGS OF RHYTHM AND BLUES (LP, 1 side each)	20
	(see also Wynonie Harris)		

BOB BRADY & CONCHORDS

68	Bell BLL 1025	Everybody's Goin' To The Love-In/It's Been A Long Time Between Kisses	25
70	Bell BLL 1114	Everybody's Goin' To The Love-In/It's Been A Long Time Between Kisses (reissue)	15

MAJELLA BRADY

65	Rex R11015	Light In My Window/Girl	8

PHIL BRADY & RANCHERS

65	Rex R 11011	Little Rose/Just One More Time	6
	(see also Ranchers)		

PHIL BRADY & THE RANCH SET

67	Go AJ 11406	Lonesome For You/Please Come Back	30

VICTOR BRADY

70	Polydor	BROWN RAIN (LP)	22

BRADY BUNCH

73	Paramount SPFL 284	MEET THE BRADY BUNCH (LP)	15

AL 'TNT' BRAGGS

66	Vocalion VP 9278	Earthquake/How Long (Do You Hold On)	30
68	Action ACT 4506	Earthquake/How Long (Do You Hold On) (reissue)	15
69	Action ACT 4526	I'm A Good Man/I Like What You Do To Me	20
65	Vocalion VEP 170163	AL 'TNT' BRAGGS (EP)	90

ERNEL BRAHAM

66	Rio R 79	Musical Fight/EDWARDS ALLSTARS: Pipeline	30
	(see also Kent Walker)		

ROY BRAHAM

64	R&B 166	Believe Me/Red Sea	30

BRAIN

67	Parlophone R 5595	Nightmares In Red/Kick The Donkey	70
87	Bam Caruso OPRA 63	Nightmares In Red/SRC: Black Sheep (jukebox edition, die-cut company sleeve)	10
	(see also Giles Giles & Fripp, Trendsetters Ltd, League Of Gentlemen)		

BRAINBOX

69	Parlophone R 5775	Woman's Gone/Down Man	12
70	Parlophone R 5842	So Helpless/To You	8
70	Parlophone PCS 7094	BRAINBOX (LP)	60
	(see also Jan Akkerman, Hunters, Focus)		

BRAINCHILD

70	A&M AMS 805	Cage/Autobiography	6
70	A&M AMLS 979	HEALING OF THE LUNATIC OWL (LP)	45

BRAINIAC 5

80	Roach RR 5002	Working/Feel (p/s)	10
78	Roach RREP 5001	MUSHY DOUBT (EP, 33rpm, p/s)	10

BRAINSTORM

79	Miracle M5	Lovin' Is Really My Game/Stormin' (12", no p/s)	40

BRAINTAX

92	Low LifeLow 2	FAT HEAD (EP)	50
97	Low LifeLow 4	Future Years (EP	30
99	Low LifeLow 9	The Travel Show (EP)	18
00	Low LifeLow 11	Hardworking/Escuchame/First Joint(12")	10
01	Low LifeLow 14	Don't Drag Me In/Biro Funk (12")	8
01	Low LifeLow 15	BIRO FUNK (LP)	12

BRAKES

80	Magnet MAGL	FOR WHY YOU KICKA MY DONKEY? (LP)	15

WILFRED BRAMBELL

63	Parlophone R 5058	Secondhand/Ragtime Ragabone Man	15
71	CBS 7062	The Decimal Song/Time Marches On	8

WILFRED BRAMBELL & HARRY H. CORBETT

63	Pye 7N 15588	Steptoe And Son At Buckingham Palace (Parts 1 & 2, some in p/s)	8
63	Pye NEP 24169	THE FACTS OF LIFE (EP)	10
63	Pye NEP 24180	THE WAGES OF SIN (EP)	10
65	Pye NPL 18135	LOVE AND HAROLD STEPTOE (LP)	12
66	Pye NPL 18153	GEMS FROM THE STEPTOE SCRAP HEAP (LP)	12

DELANEY BRAMLETT
64	Vocalion VP 9227	Heartbreak Hotel/You Never Looked Sweeter	15
65	Vocalion VP 9237	Liverpool Lou/You Have No Choice	30

(see also Delaney & Bonnie, King Curtis with Delaney & Friends)

BRAM STOKER
72	Windmill WMD 117	HEAVY ROCK SPECTACULAR (LP)	25

BILL BRAMWELL
58	Starlite ST45 004	My Old Man/Shoutin' In That Amen Corner	10
60	Decca F 11309	Candid Camera Theme/Frederika	5

BRAN
74	Sain 1038M	AIL DDECHRA (LP)	65
76	Sain 1070M	HEDFAN (LP)	65
78	Sain 1120M	GWRACH Y HOS (LP, with inner sleeve)	65

BRAND
64	Piccadilly 7N 35216	I'm A Lover Not A Fighter/Zulu Stomp	100

BRAND NEW HEAVIES
91	Acid Jazz JAZID 39P	Never Stop (12", company sleeve, withdrawn)	30
92	Acid Jazz JAZID 23	THE BRAND NEW HEAVIES (LP)	12

BILL BRANDON
73	Mercury 6052 186	I Am Free Of Your Love/(Take Another Little) Piece Of My Heart	12

JOHNNY BRANDON
55	Polygon P1131	Tomorrow/High As A Mountain (78)	8
56	Parlophone MSP 6238	Rock-A-Bye Baby/Lonely Lips	50
56	Parlophone R 4207	Shim Sham Shuffle/I Didn't Know	50
56	Decca F 10778	Glendora/Song For A Summer Night	20
57	Decca F 10858	Nothing Is Too Good For You/A Sort-Of-A-Feeling	15
59	Top Rank JAR 241	Santa Claus Jnr./I Heard A Bluebird Sing	10
55	Pye NEP 24003	JOHNNY BRANDON HITS (EP)	20

KIRK BRANDON & PACK OF LIES
87	SS SS1N2/SS2N1	KIRK BRANDON AND THE PACK OF LIES (EP)	7

(see also Theatre Of Hate, Spear Of Destiny, Senate, Pack)

TONY BRANDON
68	MGM MGM 1401	Candy Kisses/Get Going Baby	5

VERN BRANDON
62	Decca F 11472	Let Me Be The One/Gotta Know The Reason (Jimmy Page on guitar!)	25

BRAND X
79	Charisma CB 340	Soho/Dance Of The Illegal Aliens (no p/s)	5
79	Charisma CB 340-12	Soho/Dance Of The Illegal Aliens/Noddy Goes To Sweden/Pool Room Blues (12", p/s)	8
76	Charisma CAS 1117	UNORTHODOX BEHAVIOUR (LP)	20

(see also Phil Collins)

BRANDY BOYS
65	Columbia DB 7507	Gale Winds/Don't Come Knocking At My Door	10

BRANDY WINE BRIDGE
77	Cottage COT 311	THE GREY LADY (LP)	28
78	Cottage COT 321	AN ENGLISH MEADOW (LP, hand-drawn sleeve with insert)	28

BRANDY WINE SINGERS
63	Columbia DB 7156	Funny Face/Will It Last	7
68	President PT 204	Mandy/Two Little Boys	6

JOHNNY BRANTLEY'S ALL STARS
58	London HLU 8606	The Place/Pot Luck (78 rpm = £12)	25

BRASS ALLEY
(see under Various Artists EPs)

ANDRÉ BRASSEUR
65	Pye International 7N 25332	Early Bird Satellite/Special 230	10
67	CBS 202557	The Kid/Holiday	25
71	CBS 2557	The Kid/Holiday (reissue)	10
66	CBS 62858	TASTY (LP)	20

BRASS INCORPORATED
71	Philips 6303 025	BRASS MONKEY (LP)	30

BRASS MONKEY
70	Pye International 7N 25520	At The Sign Of The Swinging Cymbal/Just Like That	15

BRASS TACKS
68	Big T BIG 110	I'll Keep On Holding On/Let The Sunshine In	35
68	Big T BIG 114	Maxwell Ferguson/Sunshine After The Rain	100

BRATZ
80	A Famous Record AFR 1	The Bratz Are Coming/Coast To Coast/Everyone Wants To Be Elvis (p/s)	6

BOB BRAUN
62	Brunswick 05875	Till Death Do Us Part/So It Goes	5

RICHARD BRAUTIGAN
69	Zapple ZAPPLE 03	LISTENING TO RICHARD BRAUTIGAN (LP, unreleased, acetates exist)	750+

MINT VALUE £

BRAVERY
04	Polydor 9868862	Unconditional/No Brakes/Out Of Line (12" p/s)	25
04	Polydor 9868861	Unconditional/No Brakes/Out Of Line	25
05	Loog LOGO009	Live – An Honest Mistake/Unconditonal (p/s)	6

CEDRIC BRAVO
65	Ska Beat JB 229	Merry Christmas/Sugar Baby	20

LOS BRAVOS
66	Decca F 22419	Black Is Black/I Want A Name	6
66	Decca F 22484	I Don't Care/Don't Be Left Out In The Cold	6
66	Decca F 22529	Going Nowhere/Brand New Baby	20
67	Decca F 22615	I'm All Ears/You'll Never Get The Chances Again	7
67	Decca F 22682	Like Nobody Else/Wearing A Smile	7
68	Decca F 22765	Bring A Little Lovin'/Make It Last	15
69	Decca F 22853	Save Me, Save Me/Baby I Love You Because I Need You	7
70	Decca F 13064	People Talking Around/Every Dog Has His Night	5
66	Decca LK 4822	BLACK IS BLACK (LP)	35
68	Decca LK/SKL 4905	LOS BRAVOS (LP)	30
	(see also Mike Kennedy)		

ANTHONY BRAXTON & DEREK BAILEY
73	Emanem 601	DUO (2-LP)	30
84	Incus INCUS 43	ROYAL VOLUME 1 (LP)	20
	(see also Derek Bailey)		

PRISCILLA BRAZIER
74	Dovetail DOVE 9	PRISCILLA BRAZIER (LP)	40
76	Key KL 038	SOMETHING BEAUTIFUL (LP)	35

BREAD
69	Elektra EKSN 45071	London Bridge/Dismal Day	6
70	Elektra 210 010	Making It With You/Why Do You Keep Me Waiting	5
69	Elektra EKS 74044	BREAD (LP)	15
	(see also David Gates, Pleasure Fair)		

BREAD & BEER BAND
69	Decca F 12891	Dick Barton Theme (The Devil's Gallop)/Breakdown Blues	75
72	Decca F 13354	Dick Barton Theme (The Devil's Gallop)/Breakdown Blues (reissue)	40
69	Rubbish (no cat. no.)	THE BREAD AND BEER BAND (LP, 1 copy known to exist)	2,000+
	(see also Elton John, Caleb)		

BREAD, LOVE & DREAMS
69	Decca F 12958	Virgin Kiss/Switch Out The Sun	18
69	Decca LK/SKL 5008	BREAD, LOVE AND DREAMS (LP)	85
70	Decca LK/SKL 5048	THE STRANGE TALE OF CAPTAIN SHANNON AND THE HUNCHBACK FROM GIGHA (LP)	85
71	Decca SKL 5081	AMARYLLIS (LP)	300
	(see also Human Beast)		

BREAKAWAYS
62	Pye 7N 15471	He's A Rebel/Wishing Star	15
63	Pye 7N 15585	That Boy Of Mine/Here She Comes	15
64	Pye 7N 15618	That's How It Goes/He Doesn't Love Me	20
65	Pye 7N 15973	Danny Boy/Your Kind Of Love	12
67	CBS 2833	Sacred Love/Don't Be A Baby	10
68	MCA MU 1018	Santo Domingo/So In Love Are We	12
	(see also Vernons Girls, Burt Bacharach Orchestra, Mike Patto, Ken Cope, Sharades, De Laine Sisters)		

BREAKDOWN
77	MCP 001	MEET ME ON THE HIGHWAY (LP, private pressing with insert)	25

BREAKING THE ILLUSION
92	Lowlife LOW 1	WHERE WILL IT END? (EP, 12" p/s)	25

BREAKTHRU'
68	Mercury MF 1066	Ice Cream Tree/Julius Caesar	25

BREAKWATER
86	Arista ARIST 12674	Say You Love Me Girl/Work It Out (12", p/s)	12

PATRICIA BREDIN
59	Top Rank JAR 257	Till The Right Times Comes/I Live To Love You	5

JIMMY BREEDLOVE
57	London HLE 8490	Over Somebody Else's Shoulder/That's My Baby (78 rpm = £50)	120
62	Pye International 7N 25121	You're Following Me/Fabulous	40
75	Pye Disco Demand DDS 110	I Can't Help Loving You/I Saw You	10
	(see also Cues)		

BOBBY BREEN
62	Fontana 373	When The Lights Go Out/Everybody Twist	20

BUDDY BREGMAN & HIS ORCHESTRA
56	HMV 7MC 40	Theme From "Picnic"/Riviera (export issue)	5

JACQUES BREL
68	Fontana SFJL 967	A L'OLYMPIA (LP)	12

BRELLO CABAL
67	CBS 3214	Margarine Flavoured Pineapple Chunk/Follow That	10
	(see also Anita Harris)		

BEVERLEY BREMERS
72	Wand WN 18	Get Smart Girl/Don't Say You Don't Remember	15
72	Wand WN 28	We're Free/Colours Of Love	5
72	Wand WN 34	I'll Make You Music/I Made A Man Out Of You Jimmy	5

BRENDA & THE TABULATIONS
67	London HL 10127	Dry Your Eyes/The Wash	28
67	London HL 10174	When You're Gone/Hey Boy	25
68	Direction 58-3678	Baby You're So Right For Me/To The One I Love	10
69	Action ACT 4541	That's In The Past/I Can't Get Over Her	40
70	London HL 10325	A Child No One Wanted/'Scuse Uz Y'all	10
71	CBS 7279	Right On The Tip of My Tongue/Always And Forever	10
73	Epic EPC 1361	One Girl Too Late/The Magic Of Your Love	10
69	Action ACLP 6003	DRY YOUR EYES (LP)	50

BRENDON
76	Magnet MAG 80	Gimme Some/Changing My Life Won't Do	6

BUDDY BRENNAN QUARTET
60	London HLU 9049	Big River/The Chase	10

ROSE BRENNAN
55	HMV 7M 299	Ding Dong/Sincerely	15
55	HMV 7M 328	Wake The Town And Tell The People/Ten Little Kisses	15
56	HMV 7M 360	You Are My Love/My Dublin Bay	8
56	HMV 7M 383	Band Of Gold/My Believing Heart	8
57	HMV POP 302	Without Love (There Is Nothing)/Tra La La	10
59	Top Rank JAR 152	Johnny Let Me Go/My Summer Diary (78 rpm = £10	7
61	Philips PB 1193	Tall Dark Stranger/This Girl With The Wistful Eyes	5

WALTER BRENNAN
60	London HLD 9148	Dutchman's Gold/Back To The Farm	8
62	Liberty LIB 55436	Old Rivers/Epic Ride Of John H Glenn	6
62	Liberty LIB 55477	Houdini/The Old Kelly Place	5
63	Liberty LIB 55508	Mama Sang A Song/Who Will Take Gramma	5
64	Liberty LBY 1249	GUNFIGHT AT THE OK CORRAL (LP)	25

BERNIE BRENT'S COMBO
60s	Honey Hit TB 4501	BERNIE BRENT'S COMBO (EP)	5

FRANKIE BRENT
57	Pye N 15102	Rockin' Shoes/I Ain't Never Gonna Do You No Good (78)	10
57	Pye N 15103	Be My Girl/Rang Dang Doo (78)	10

TONY BRENT
58	Columbia SEG 7824	TONY CALLS THE TUNE (EP)	20
58	Columbia SEG 7869	TIME FOR TONY (EP)	20
59	Columbia SEG 8019	OFF STAGE (EP)	20
59	Columbia SEG 8040	OFF STAGE NO. 2 (EP)	20
58	Columbia 33S 1125	OFF STAGE (10" LP)	25
60	Columbia 33SX 1200	TONY TAKES FIVE (LP, also stereo SCX 3288)	20/22
60s	Columbia 33SX 5001	TONY'S BIG HITS (LP)	28

(see also Coronets)

TONY BRENT & JULIE DAWN
53	Columbia SCM 5029	Ding Dong Boogie/When Are We Gonna Get Married?	15

(see also Julie Dawn)

BRENT FORD & THE NYLONS
78	Brumbeat	19th Nervous Breakdown/Big Rock Candy Mountain (handmade foldout p/s)	50

BRENTWOOD ROAD ALLSTARS
70	Bamboo BAM 23	Love At First Sight/MAYTALS: Life Could Be A Dream	25
70	Bamboo BAM 25	Soul Shake/Moon Ride	25

GERRY BRERETON
53	Parlophone MSP 6056	From Here To Eternity/If You've Never Been In Love	12
54	Parlophone MSP 6081	The Book/Somewhere Someone (Is Saying A Prayer)	6
55	Columbia SCM 5195	A Million Helping Hands/Fair Sets The Wind For Love	5

(see also Eddie Calvert)

BERNARD BRESSLAW
58	HMV POP 522	Mad Passionate Love/You Need Feet	5
59	HMV POP 599	Charlie Brown/The Teenager's Lament (78 rpm = £8)	5
59	HMV POP 669	Ivy Will Cling/I Found A Hole (78 rpm = £15)	5
59	HMV 7EG 8439	I ONLY ARSKED (EP)	10

PAUL BRETT('S SAGE)
70	Pye 7N 17974	Three D Mona Lisa/Mediterranean Lazy Heat Wave	7
71	Dawn DNX 2508	Reason For Your Askin'/Everlasting Butterfly/Savannah Ladies/	
		To Everyman (Freedom) (p/s)	10
71	Dawn DNS 1010	Goodbye Forever/Good Old Fashioned Funky Kind Of Music	6
72	Dawn DNS 1021	Dahlia/Cottage Made For Two	6
73	Bradley's BRAD 301	Mr. Custer/Good Times, Hard Times	6
73	Bradley's BRAD 305	Summer Driftin'/Clocks (p/s)	7
70	Pye NSPL 18347	PAUL BRETT SAGE (LP)	22
71	Dawn DNLS 3021	JUBILATION FOUNDRY (LP, gatefold sleeve, as Paul Brett's Sage)	18
72	Dawn DNLS 3032	SCHIZOPHRENIA (LP, foldout sleeve, as Paul Brett's Sage)	25
73	Bradley's BRADL 1001	PAUL BRETT (LP, envelope sleeve with inner)	18
73	Bradley's BRADL 1004	CLOCKS (LP)	18
75	PF private pressing	PHOENIX FUTURE (LP, 500 only)	20
70s	private pressing	MUSIC MANIFOLD (LP, library issue)	25

(see also Elmer Gantry's Velvet Opera, Fire)

MINT VALUE £

STEVE BRETT & MAVERICKS
65	Columbia DB 7470	Wishing/Anything That's Part Of You	85
65	Columbia DB 7581	Sad, Lonely And Blue/Candy	125
65	Columbia DB 7794	Sugar Shack/Chains On My Heart	100

(see also 'N Betweens, Slade)

TONY BREVETT
71	Supreme SUP 224	Don't Get Weary/BREVETT ALLSTARS: Version	15
74	Dip DL 5028	You Don't Love Me/Version	7

(see also Melodians, Glen Adams)

BREW
60s	Oak LONDON	Crossroads/Play Your Tune (acetate, unreleased, handwritten labels)	150

(see also Camel)

TERESA BREWER
54	Vogue Coral Q 2011	Skinny Minnie (Fishtail)/I Had Someone Else Before I Had You (78 rpm = £5)	20
54	Vogue Coral Q 2029	Au Revoir/Danger Signs (78 rpm = £5)	20
55	Vogue Coral Q 72043	Let Me Go, Lover (with Lancers)/Baby, Baby, Baby	20
55	Vogue Coral Q 72065	How Important Can It Be?/What More Is There To Say?	15
55	Vogue Coral Q 72066	Tweedlee Dee/Rock Love (78 rpm = £5)	25
55	Vogue Coral Q 72077	Pledging My Love/I Gotta Go Get My Baby	20
55	Vogue Coral Q 72083	You're Telling Our Secret/Time	15
55	Vogue Coral Q 72098	The Banjo's Back In Town/How To Be Very, Very Popular	10
56	Vogue Coral Q 72130	A Good Man Is Hard To Find/It's Siesta Time	10
56	Vogue Coral Q 72139	Rememb'ring/My Sweetie Went Away	10
56	Vogue Coral Q 72146	A Tear Fell/Bo Weevil	10
56	Vogue Coral Q 72172	A Sweet Old-Fashioned Girl/Goodbye, John	10
56	Vogue Coral Q 72199	Keep Your Cotton Pickin' Paddies Offa My Heart/ So Doggone Lonely	10
56	Vogue Coral Q 72213	Crazy With Love/The Moon Is On Fire	10
57	Vogue Coral Q 72224	Nora Malone/When I Leave The World Behind	10
57	Vogue Coral Q 72239	I'm Drowning My Sorrows/How Lonely Can One Be	10
57	Vogue Coral Q 72251	Empty Arms/The Ricky-Tick Song	10
57	Vogue Coral Q 72278	Lula Rock-A-Hula/Teardrops In My Heart (78 rpm = £8)	15
57	Vogue Coral Q 72292	You Send Me/Born To Love (78 rpm = £8)	15
58	Coral Q 72301	Careless Caresses/Mutual Admiration Society (78 rpm = £8)	10
58	Coral Q 72320	Saturday Dance/I Think The World Of You (78 rpm = £8)	10
58	Coral Q 72336	Pickle Up A Doodle/The Rain Falls On Ev'rybody (78 rpm = £8)	10
58	Coral Q 72340	The Hula Hoop Song/So Shy (78 rpm = £8)	10
58	Coral Q 72349	I Like Christmas/Jingle Bell Rock (78 rpm = £8)	10
58	Coral Q 72354	Satellite/The One Rose (That's Left In My Heart) (78 rpm = £8)	10
59	Coral Q 72364	Heavenly Lover/Fair Weather Sweetheart (78 rpm = £10)	10
59	Coral Q 72375	Bye Bye Baby Goodbye/Chain Of Friendship (78 rpm = £10)	15
59	Coral Q 72383	Bill Bailey, Won't You Please Come Home/Mexicali Rose (78 rpm =£10)	5
60	Coral Q 72386	Peace Of Mind/Venetian Sunset	5
60	Coral Q 72396	How Do You Know It's Love/If There Are Stars In My Eyes	5
60	Coral Q 72405	Anymore/That Piano Man	5
60	Coral Q 72418	Have You Ever Been Lonely/When Do You Love Me	5
60	Coral Q 72447	Pretty Lookin' Boy/Your Cheatin' Heart	5

EPs
50s	London BEP 6039	TERESA BREWER WITH THE ALL STARS (export issue)	20
50s	London BEP 6041	TERESA BREWER WITH JACK PLEIS AND THE ALL STARS (export issue)	20
59	Coral FEP 2013	HULA HOOP TIME WITH TERESA BREWER	20
59	Coral FEP 2036	WHEN YOUR LOVER HAS GONE PART 1	20
59	Coral FEP 2037	WHEN YOUR LOVER HAS GONE PART 2	20
59	Coral FEP 2038	WHEN YOUR LOVER HAS GONE PART 3	20
60	Coral FEP 2047	TERESA BREWER AND THE DIXIELAND BAND PART 1	20
60	Coral FEP 2048	TERESA BREWER AND THE DIXIELAND BAND PART 2	20
60	Coral FEP 2061	HOW DO YOU KNOW IT'S LOVE	20

LPs
51	London H-APB 1006	SHOWCASE (10")	30
57	Coral LVA 9020	MUSIC! MUSIC! MUSIC!	30
58	Coral LVA 9075	FOR TEENAGERS IN LOVE	25
58	Coral LVA 9091	AT CHRISTMAS TIME	25
59	Coral LVA 9095	TIME FOR TERESA BREWER	20
59	Coral LVA 9100	WHEN YOUR LOVER HAS GONE (also stereo SVL 3003)	20
59	Coral LVA 9107	TERESA BREWER AND THE DIXIELAND BAND	20
60	Coral LVA 9129	RIDIN' HIGH	20
60	Coral LVA 9131	MY GOLDEN FAVOURITES	20
60	Coral LVA 9138	NAUGHTY NAUGHTY NAUGHTY	20
61	Coral LVA 9145	SONGS EVERYBODY KNOWS	20
62	Coral LVA 9152	ALOHA FROM TERESA	20
62	Coral LVA 9204	DON'T MESS AROUND WITH TESS	20

(see also Snooky Lanson)

BREWER & SHIPLEY
71	Kama Sutra 2013 015	One Toke Over The Line/People Love Each Other	5
70	Kama Sutra 2361 001	TARKIO ROAD (LP)	15
71	Kama Sutra 2361 005	WEEDS (LP)	15
72	Kama Sutra 2319 021	SHAKE OFF THE DEMON (LP)	12

BREWER'S DROOP
72	RCA RCA 2216	Sweet Thing/Heart Of Stone/It Ain't The Meat — It's The Motion (p/s)	6
72	RCA SF 8301	OPENING TIME (LP)	20

BRIAR
82	Happy Face MM 142	Rainbow (To The Skies)/Crying In The Rain (p/s)	15
87	PRT BRIAR 1	Edge Of A Broken Heart/Don't Forget Me When You're On Your Own (p/s)	5

87	PRT BRIART 1	Edge Of A Broken Heart/Don't Forget Me When You're On Your Own (shaped picture disc, some with headband)	15/10
87	PRT BRIARP 1	Edge Of A Broken Heart/La Bamba/ Don't Forget Me When You're On Your Own (shaped picture disc)	8
87	UK UKPT 003	Frankie (12", p/s)	8
89	Shotgun Charlie SCR 1	Gimme All You Got/Stop Me Foolin' Around (with p/s)	8
92	Shotgun Charlie SCR 2	All She Wants/To My Door (p/s)	5
85	Heavy Metal HMRLP 41	TOO YOUNG (LP, with 7" & poster)	12
87	UK UKALP 002	CROWN OF THORNS (LP)	15

BRIDES OF FUNKENSTEIN
| 78 | Atlantic K 50545 | FUNK OR WALK (LP) | 15 |
| | *(see also Parliament, Funkadelic)* | | |

BOBBY BRIDGER
70	Beacon BEA 149	The World Is Turning On/Why Do I Love You	6
70	Beacon BEA 159	Sugar Shaker/You're In Love	15
	(see also Errol Sobers)		

DEE DEE BRIDGEWATER
| 80 | Elektra K12 490 | Lonely Disco Dancer/One In A Million Guy (12", no p/s) | 12 |

MARC BRIERLEY
68	CBS 3857	Hold On, Hold On, The Garden Sure Looks Good Spread On The Floor/ Autograph Of Time	8
69	CBS 4191	Stay A Little Longer Merry Ann/Flaxen Hair	7
69	CBS 4632	Lady Of The Light/Sunny Weather	7
70	CBS 5266	Be My Brother/If You Took The Bandage Off	6
60s	Transatlantic TRAEP 147	MARC BRIERLEY (EP)	50+
67	CBS 63478	WELCOME TO THE CITADEL (LP)	180
69	CBS 63835	HELLO (LP)	80

ANNE BRIGGS
63	Topic TOP 94	THE HAZARDS OF LOVE (EP, with leaflet)	160
71	Topic 12TS 207	ANNE BRIGGS (LP)	150
71	CBS 64612	THE TIME HAS COME (LP)	115
	(see also A.L. Lloyd)		

BILLY BRIGGS
| 51 | Columbia DB 2938 | Chew Tobacco Rag (No. 2)/Alarm Clock Boogie (78) | 6 |

DUGGIE BRIGGS
| 78 | It IT 3 | Punk Rockin' Granny/I'm A Flasher (p/s) | 12 |
| 78 | It ITEP 5 | THE DUGGIE BRIGGS FLASHES ON IT AGAIN (EP) | 18 |

LILLIAN BRIGGS
| 55 | Philips PB 522 | I Want You To Be My Baby/Give Me A Band And My Baby (78) | 6 |
| 60 | Coral Q 72408 | Not A Soul (Blanket Roll Blues)/Smile For The People | 5 |

ANNE BRIGHT
| 69 | Columbia DB 8587 | Concerning Love/Sneakin' Up On You | 20 |

GREG BRIGHT
| 69 | private pressing | ROOM BY GREG (LP) | 200 |

LEN BRIGHT COMBO
| 86 | Empire LEN 1 | Someone Must've Nailed Us Together/Mona (p/s) | 6 |
| | *(see also Wreckless Eric, Milkshakes)* | | |

BRIGHTER
| 89 | Sarah SARAH 019 | Around The World In 80 Days (p/s, with inserts) | 8 |

BRIGHTON HORNS
| 66 | Stateside SS 526 | Surf Dell'amore/High Midnight | 10 |

BRIGHTWATER
| 70s | Myrrh MYR 1030 | A BAND FOR ALL SEASONS (LP) | 20 |

BRILLIANT CORNERS
84	SS20 SS21	She's Got Fever/Black Water (red or pink p/s)	15/30
84	SS20 SS22	Big Hip/Tangled Up In Blue (p/s)	10
88	McQueen MCQ2T	Why Do You Have To Go Out With Him?/Shangri La (12" p/s)	10
88	McQueen MCQLP	SOMEBODY UP THERE LIKES ME (LP, with inner)	15

BRIMSTONE
| 71 | Deram DM 322 | Keyhole Jake/The Monkey Song | 6 |
| 71 | Decca DF 13222 | If Ever You See Me/Work Out | 5 |

LOS BRINCOS
| 67 | Page One POF 023 | Lola/Passport (1st 5,000 in p/s) | 35/10 |
| 67 | Page One POF 031 | Nobody Wants You Now/Train | 60 |

BRINDLEY BRAE
| 70s | Harmony DB 0002 | VILLAGE MUSIC (LP, private pressing with insert) | 35 |
| | *(see also Bev Pegg, Away From The Sand)* | | |

BRINSLEY SCHWARZ
70	United Artists UP 35118	Shining Brightly/What Do You Suggest	6
71	Liberty LBY 15419	Country Girl/Funk Angel	8
72	United Artists UP 35312	Country Girl/Funk Angel (reissue)	6
73	United Artists UP 35588	Speedo/I Worry	5
74	United Artists UP 35642	I've Cried My Last Tear/Bringdown	5
74	United Artists UP 35700	(What's So Funny 'Bout) Peace, Love And Understanding/ Ever Since You're Gone	6
75	United Artists UP 35768	Everybody/I Like You, I Don't Love You	6

BRINSLEY SCHWARZ

75	United Artists UP 35812	There's A Cloud In My Heart/I Got The Real Thing	6
70	United Artists UAS 29111	BRINSLEY SCHWARZ (LP, gatefold sleeve)	25
70	Liberty LBG 83427	DESPITE IT ALL (LP, gatefold sleeve)	25
72	United Artists UAS 29217	SILVER PISTOL (LP, with poster)	25
72	United Artists UAS 29374	NERVOUS ON THE ROAD (LP)	18
73	United Artists UAS 29489	PLEASE DON'T EVER CHANGE (LP)	25
74	United Artists UAS 29641	THE NEW FAVOURITES OF BRINSLEY SCHWARZ (LP)	15

(see also Kippington Lodge, Hitters, Knees, Limelight, Nick Lowe, Ernie Graham, Rumour, Chilli Willi & Red Hot Peppers, Ducks Deluxe)

LLOYD BRISCO
64	Rio R42	Fabulous Eyes/What You See	18
64	Island WI 187	Jonah The Master/Mr. Cleveland	20

BRITISH ELECTRIC FOUNDATION
(see under B.E.F.)

BRITISH SEA POWER
01	Golden Chariot BSP 01	Fear Of Drowning/A Wooden Horse (CD, 500 only)	30
01	Rough Trade RTRADE S032	Remember Me/A Lovely Day Tomorrow (p/s, 500 only)	10
	Rough Trade RTRADE SCD048	The Lonely/Spirit Of St. Louis (CD)	10
02	Rough Trade RTRADES 069	Childhood Memories/Favours In The Beetroot Fields (p/s, 1000 only)	8
03	Rough Trade RTRADE S092	Carrion/Apologies To Insect Life (handdrawn, textured sleeve, 1264 only)	12
03	Rough Trade RTRADES 125	Remember Me/The Scottish Wildlife Experience (handdrawn sleeve 2003 copies)	18
04	Rough Trade RTRADESCD179	A Lovely Day Tomorrow/Zitra Buke Krasney Den/Fakir (CD limited edition, 1942 copies)	10
05	None	Thirteen Ways To Disappear (CD-R sent to first 13 buyers from BSP web shop)	12
05	Rough Trade RTRADS302	Remember Me/I Am A Cider Drinker (7" limited edition, 1,966 copies)	12

(see also The Wurzels)

BRITISH LIONS
78	Vertigo 6059 192	One More Chance To Run/Booster (p/s)	5
78	Vertigo 6059 201	International Heroes/Eat The Rich	5
78	Vertigo 9102 019	BRITISH LIONS (LP, with inner sleeve)	12

(see also Mott The Hoople, Medicine Head)

BRITISH WALKERS
65	Pye International 7N 25298	I Found You/Diddley Daddy	30

BRITT
66	Piccadilly 7N 35273	You Really Have Started Something/Leave My Baby Alone	20

(see also Britt Ekland)

MAY BRITT
59	Top Rank JAR 230	Falling In Love Again/Lola-Lola	8

TINA BRITT
65	London HLC 9974	The Real Thing/Teardrops Fell	50

BUDDY BRITTEN & REGENTS
62	Piccadilly 7N 35075	My Pride, My Joy/Long Gone Baby	15
62	Decca F 11435	Don't Spread It Around/The Beat Of My Heart	15
63	Oriole CB 1827	If You Gotta Make A Fool Of Somebody/Money	15
63	Oriole CB 1839	Hey There/I'll Cry No More	15
63	Oriole CB 1859	My Resistance Is Low/When I See You Smile	15
63	Oriole CB 1889	Money/Sorrow Tomorrow	20
64	Oriole CB 1911	I Guess I'm In The Way/Zip-A-Dee-Doo-Dah	20
65	Piccadilly 7N 35241	She's About A Mover/Since You've Gone	15
65	Piccadilly 7N 35257	Right Now/Jailer Bring Me Water	7

(see also Regents)

CHRIS BRITTON
69	Page One POLS 022	AS I AM (LP)	300

(see also Troggs)

TERRY BRITTEN
69	Columbia DB8580	2000 Weeks/Bargain Day	18

BRIXTON MARKET
69	Beacon SBEAB 8	BLACK FUNK (LP)	15

BROADCAST
96	Wurlitzer Jukebox WJ 6	Accidentals/We've Got Time (p/s, some with sticker)	20/12
96	Duophonic DS 45-14	Living Room/Phantom (wraparound p/s, 1,500 only)	20
96	Duophonic DS 45-16	THE BOOK LOVERS EP (12", p/s, 2,000)	15
96	Duophonic DS 45-CD 16	THE BOOK LOVERS EP (CD, 2,500 only)	12
96	Warp	WORK AND NON-WORK (LP, promo-only, die-cut sleeve)	15

BROADSIDE
71	Lincolnshire Ass. LA 4	THE GIPSY'S WEDDING DAY (10" LP)	55
73	Topic 12TS 228	THE MOON SHONE BRIGHT (As The Broadside From Grimsby) (LP, blue label)	40
75	Guildhall GHS 5	SONGS FROM THE STOCKS (LP)	80
75	Guildhall GHS 12	DRIVE THE DARK AWAY (LP)	55

DAVE BROCK
83	Flicknife FLS 024	Social Alliance/Raping Robots In The Street (p/s)	5
83	Flicknife FLS 024P	Social Alliance/Raping Robots In The Street (picture disc)	8
84	Flicknife SHARP 018	EARTHED TO THE GROUND (LP)	12
88	Flicknife SHARP 042	AGENT OF CHAOS (LP)	12

(see also Dr. Technical & Machines, Hawkwind)

NORAH BROCKSTEDT
60	Top Rank JAR 353	Big Boy/Tell Me No Lies	5

PETER BROGGS
79	Hit Run HITDD 13	Higher Field Marshall (Feat. Prince Far I)/I And I A The Chosen One/PRINCE FAR I & BRIGADIER JAM DOWN : Loved By Everyone (12")	40
80	Cha Cha CHAD 25	Never Forget Jah/CORNWALL CAMPBELL : Rainbow (12")	30

BROKEN BONES
85	Fall Out FALL 020	Decapitated/Problem/Liquidated Brains (p/s)	5
85	Fall Out FALL 034P	Seeing Through My Eyes/The Point Of Agony/It's Like (picture disc)	5
85	Fall Out FALL 10034	Seeing Through My Eyes/The Point Of Agony/It's Like/Decapitated/Part 2/ Death Is Imminent (10", p/s)	7
83	Fall Out FALL LP 028	BROKEN BONES (LP)	15
84	Stoned Spliff 1	LIVE AT THE 100 CLUB (LP)	20

BROKEN GLASS
75	Capitol E-ST 11510	BROKEN GLASS (LP)	18

JOHN BROMLEY
68	Polydor 56224	What A Woman Does/My My	8
68	Polydor 56287	And The Feeling Goes/Sweet Little Princess	5
69	Polydor 56305	Melody Fayre/Sugar Love	40
69	Polydor 56340	Hold Me Woman/Weather Man	5
69	Atlantic 584 289	Kick A Tin Can/Wonderland Avenue U.S.A.	20
69	Polydor 583 048	SING (LP)	40

(see also Fleur De Lys, Three People)

BRONCO
70	Island ILPS 9124	COUNTRY HOME (LP, gatefold sleeve, pink or 'pink rim palm tree' label)	30/15
71	Island ILPS 9161	ACE OF SUNLIGHT (LP, gatefold sleeve, 'pink rim palm tree' label)	18
73	Polydor 2383 215	SMOKIN' MIXTURE (LP)	15

(see also Alan Bown Set)

BRONX CHEER
70	Parlophone R 5865	Drive My Car/Foxtrot	8
71	Dawn DNX 2512	Barrelhouse Player/Surprising Find/Whether Or Not/Party For One (p/s)	5
72	Dawn DNS 1019	Hold On To Me/Late Date	6
72	Dawn DNLS 3004	GREATEST HITS VOLUME 3 (LP, gatefold sleeve)	18

BRONZ
84	Bronze BRO 178	Send Down An Angel/Tiger (p/s)	5
84	Bronze BROX 178	Send Down An Angel/Tiger/Stranded (12", p/s)	8
80s	Lyntone LYN 14383	Taken By Storm (flexidisc)	5

MICHAEL BROOK
92	4AD TAD 2011	LIVE AT THE AQUARIUM (CD, digipak)	18

PATTI BROOK (& DIAMONDS)
60	Pye 7N 15300	Since You've Been Gone/That's The Way It's Gonna Be (as Patti Brook & Diamonds)	5
61	Pye 7N 15339	When The Red Red Robin/Look What You've Done To Me	5
62	Pye 7N 15422	I Love You, I Need You/Unloved, Unwanted	7

TONY BROOK & BREAKERS
64	Columbia DB 7279	Meanie Genie/Ooh Poo Pah Doo (some in p/s)	160/110
65	Columbia DB 7444	Love Dances On/I Won't Hurt You	12

BROOK BROTHERS
60	Top Rank JAR 349	Green Fields/How Will It End?	10
60	Top Rank JAR 409	Please Help Me, I'm Falling/When Will I Be Loved	10
60	Pye 7N 15298	Say The Word/Everything But Love	10
61	Pye 7N 15333	Warpaint/Sometimes	7
61	Pye 7N 15352	Little Bitty Heart/Tell Her	7
61	Pye 7N 15369	Ain't Gonna Wash For A Week/One Last Kiss	10
61	Pye 7N 15387	Married/I Love Girls	10
62	Pye 7N 15409	He's Old Enough To Know Better/Win Or Lose	8
62	Pye 7N 15415	Too Scared/Tell Tale	8
62	Pye 7N 15441	Just Another Fool/Double Trouble	8
62	Pye 7N 15453	Welcome Home Baby/So Long	8
62	Pye 7N 15463	I Can't Make Up My Mind/Town Girl	8
63	Pye 7N 15498	Trouble Is My Middle Name/Let The Good Times Roll	8
63	Pye 7N 15527	I'm Not Jimmy/Side By Side (with RBQ)	7
63	Pye 7N 15570	Crosswords/Whistle To The Wind	7
61	Pye NEP 24140	BROOK BROTHERS HIT PARADE (EP)	25
61	Pye NEP 24148	BROOK BROTHERS HIT PARADE VOLUME 2 (EP)	25
62	Pye NEP 24155	BROOK BROTHERS (EP)	20
61	Pye NPL 18067	BROOK BROTHERS (LP)	40

(see also Brooks)

BROOKLYN
80	Rondelet ROUND 3	I Wanna Be A Detective (p/s)	30
81	Rondelet ROUND 6	Hollywood/Late Again (p/s)	15
80	Rondelet ABOUT 3	YOU NEVER KNOW WHAT YOU'LL FIND (LP)	30

BROOKLYN BRIDGE
68	Pye International 7N 25473	From My Window I Can See/Little Red Boat By The River	7
69	Buddah 201 029	The Worst That Could Happen/Your Kite, My Kite	8
70	Buddah 2011 010	Free As The Wind/He's Not A Happy Man	6
70	Buddah 2011 034	Down By The River/Look Again	6

(see also Johnny Maestro)

MINT VALUE £

BROOKS
64	Decca F 11868	Once In A While/Poor Poor Plan	10

(see also Brook Brothers)

BABA BROOKS
63	Island WI 078	5 O'Clock Whistle/African Blood (by Blues Masters)	40
63	Island WI 096	Bank To Bank (Parts 1 & 2)	40
63	Island WI 127	Three Blind Mice/BILLY & BOBBY: We Ain't Got Nothing	30
63	R&B JB 125	Water Melon Man/STRANGER COLE: Things Come To Those Who Wait	40
64	Black Swan WI 137	Portrait Of My Love/STRANGER COLE: Goodbye Peggy	20
64	Black Swan WI 412	Jelly Beans/ERIC MORRIS: Sampson	30
64	Black Swan WI 414	Key To The City/ERIC MORRIS: Solomon Grundie	40
64	Black Swan WI 434	Spider/Melody Jamboree	30
64	Black Swan WI 438	Cork Foot/HERSANG COMBO: B.B.C. Channel 2	30
65	Black Swan WI 442	Musical Workshop/DUKE WHITE: Be Wise	30
65	Black Swan WI 444	Bus Strike/DUKE WHITE: Sow Good Seeds	25
65	Black Swan WI 451	Ethiopia/ARCHIBALD TROTT: Promised Land	35
65	Black Swan WI 466	Baby Elephant Walk/DON DRUMMOND: Don's Special	30
65	Ska Beat JB 189	Dr. Decker/OWEN & LEON SILVERA : Woman	15
65	Ska Beat JB 220	One Eyed Giant (with His Band)/DYNAMITES: Walk Out On Me	30
65	Island WI 229	Guns Fever/DOTTY & BONNIE: Don't Do It	45
65	Island WI 233	Independent Ska/STRANGER & CLAUDETTE: Seven Days	30
65	Island WI 235	Duck Soup/ZODIACS: Renegade	80+
65	Island WI 239	Vitamin A/ALTON ELLIS: Dance Crasher	50
65	Island WI 241	Teenage Ska/ALTON ELLIS: You Are Not To Blame	40
65	Rio R 061	Shenk I Sheck (& Band)/SHENLEY & HIACYNTH: Set Me Free	40
66	Doctor Bird DB 1042	The Clock (& Band)/LYN TAITT & COMETS & SILVERTONES: Raindrops	40
66	Doctor Bird DB 1046	Jam Session (with His Band)/CONQUERORS: What A Agony	40
67	Ska Beat JB 268	One Eyed Giant (with His Band)/DYNAMITES: Walk Out On Me (reissue)	20

(see also Blues Masters, Eric Brooks, Stranger & Patsy, Riots, Joey Smith, Saints, Richard Brothers, Derrick Morgan, Lord Tanamo, Lord Brisco, Hippy Boys, Roy Panton, Higgs & Wilson, Vinley Gayle, Joe White, Stranger & Patsy)

CHUCK BROOKS
69	Soul City SC 116	Black Sheep/I've Got To Get Myself Together	25

D. BROOKS
70	Big BG 304	Oh Me Oh My (actually Every Time by Hi-Tals)/ANSEL COLLINS: Staccato (actually Every Time Version by Rupie Edwards Allstars)	12

DALE BROOKS
65	King KG 1025	Army Green/Reminds Me Of You	10
66	Stateside SS 553	I Wanna Be Your Girl/Like Other Girls Do	30

DONNIE BROOKS
60	London HLN 9168	Mission Bell/Do It For Me (78 rpm = £35)	15
60	London HLN 9253	Doll House/Round Robin	10
61	London HLN 9361	That's Why/Memphis	10
62	London HLN 9572	Oh, You Beautiful Doll/Just A Bystander	10
61	London HA-N 2391	THE HAPPIEST DONNIE BROOKS (LP)	40

ELKIE BROOKS
64	Decca F 11928	Something's Got A Hold On Me/Hello Stranger	25
64	Decca F 11983	Nothing Left To Do But Cry/Strange Though It Seems	20
65	Decca F 12061	The Way You Do The Things You Do/Blue Tonight	20
65	HMV POP 1431	He's Gotta Love Me/When You Appear	25
65	HMV POP 1480	All My Life/Can't Stop Thinking Of You	15
66	HMV POP 1512	Baby Let Me Love You/Stop The Music	15
69	NEMS 56-4136	Come September/If You Should Go	5
74	Island WIP 6187	Rescue Me/Sweet Nuthin's	5
74	Chrysalis CHS 2069	Sacrifice/ALICE COOPER: I'm Flash (p/s, unissued, promo only)	35

(see also Dada, Vinegar Joe, Steve York's Camelo Pardalis, Elki & Owen)

HADDA BROOKS
50	London L 684	I Hadn't Anyone 'Till You/Hadda's Boogie (78)	6

MIKE BROOKS
79	Hit Run HIT DD 9	Love Is Like A Password/Feeling Of Reggae (12")	15
79	Hit Run HIT DD 23	Long Long Time/Dub In Time (12")	20

NORMAN BROOKS & G-BOYS
54	London L 1166	Hello Sunshine/You're My Baby	30
54	London L 1202	Somebody Wonderful/You Shouldn't Have Kissed Me The First Time	30
54	London L 1228	A Sky-Blue Shirt And A Rainbow Tie/This Waltz With You	32
54	London HL 8015	I'm Kinda Crazy/I'd Like To Be In Your Shoes, Baby	32
54	London HL 8041	I Can't Give You Anything But Love (solo)/GO-BOYS: Johnny's Tune (78 rpm = £6)	32
54	London HL 8051	Candy Moon/My 3-D Sweetie	32
55	London HL 8115	Back In Circulation/Lou Lou Louisiana	32
54	London RE-P 1004	PRESENTING NORMAN BROOKS VOLUME 1 (EP)	40
55	London RE-P 1021	BABY MINE (EP)	40

PAM BROOKS
70	Big BG 307	Oh Me Oh My/ANSELL COLLINS: Staccato	18

BROOKS & JERRY
68	Direction 58-3267	I Got What It Takes Parts 1 & 2	15

MARK BROOM
95	Ferox FER 017	SHUFFLE THIS (12" EP)	8

BIG BILL BROONZY/CHICAGO BILL

51	Vogue V 2068	Back Water Blues/Lonesome Road Blues (78)	15
51	Vogue V 2073	In The Evenin'/Low Land Blues (78)	15
51	Vogue V 2074	John Henry/Blues In 1890 (78)	15
51	Vogue V 2075	Big Bill Blues/Hey Hey Baby (78)	15
51	Vogue V 2076	House Rent Stomp/The Moppin' Blues (78)	15
51	Vogue V 2077	Black, Brown And White/Feelin' Low Down (78)	15
52	Vogue V 2078	Make My Getaway/What I Used To Do (78)	15
52	Melodisc 1191	Keep Your Hands Off Her/Stump Blues (78, as Chicago Bill)	15
52	Melodisc 1203	Five Foot Seven/Plough Hand Blues (78, as Chicago Bill)	15
50s	private pressing	Keep Your Hand On Your Heart/T For Texas (78)	25
56	Pye Jazz NJ 2012	When Do I Get To Be Called A Man/Mindin' My Own Business (78)	15
57	Pye Jazz NJ 2016	Southbound Train/It Feels So Good (78)	10
58	Vogue V 2351	Guitar Shuffle/When Did You Leave Heaven	10
61	Storyville A 44053	Midnight Special/Black Brown And White	10
55	Vogue EPV 1024	HEY BUD BLUES (EP)	20
56	Vogue EPV 1074	SINGS THE BLUES (EP)	20
56	Vogue EPV 1107	GUITAR SHUFFLE (EP)	20
56	Pye Jazz NJE 1005	MISSISSIPPI BLUES VOLUME 1 (EP)	15
56	Pye Jazz NJE 1015	MISSISSIPPI BLUES VOLUME 2 (EP)	15
56	Melodisc EPM7 65	KEEP YOUR HANDS OFF (EP)	15
57	Pye Jazz NJE 1047	SOUTHERN SAGA (EP)	15
57	Columbia SEG 7674	BIG BILL BROONZY SINGS THE BLUES (EP)	15
57	Tempo EXA 61	BILL BAILEY WON'T YOU PLEASE COME HOME (EP)	15
58	Columbia SEG 7790	BIG BILL BROONZY SINGS THE BLUES NO. 2 (EP)	15
60	Mercury ZEP 10065	WALKIN' DOWN A LONESOME ROAD (EP)	15
60	Mercury ZEP 10093	HOLLERIN' BLUES (EP)	22
60s	Mercury/Emearcy MMB 12003	THE BLUES (LP)	20
62	Storyville SEP 383	BLUES ANTHOLOGY VOLUME 3 (EP)	12
64	Mercury 10003 MCE	BLUES-GOSPEL-SPIRITUAL (EP)	15
57	Vogue LAE 12009	BIG BILL BLUES (LP)	38
57	Philips BBL 7113	BIG BILL BROONZY (LP)	40
58	Vogue LAE 12063	THE BLUES (LP)	40
58	Pye Nixa Jazz NJL 16	TRIBUTE TO BIG BILL (LP)	35
59	Tempo TAP 23	AN EVENING WITH BIG BILL BROONZY (LP)	38
61	HMV CLP 1544	LAST SESSION PART 1 (LP)	20
62	HMV CLP 1551	LAST SESSION PART 2 (LP)	20
62	HMV CLP 1562	LAST SESSION PART 3 (LP)	20
65	Storyville SLP 143	AN EVENING WITH BROONZY (LP)	15
65	Fontana 688 206ZL	TROUBLE IN MIND (LP)	22
66	Mercury 20044 MCL	REMEMBERING BROONZY — THE GREATEST MINSTREL OF THE AUTHENTIC BLUES (LP)	15
66	Storyville SLP 188	BLUES IN EUROPE (LP)	15
67	Storyville 670 154	PORTRAITS IN BLUES VOLUME 2 (LP)	22
69	CBS Realm 52648	BIG BILL'S BLUES (LP)	15
69	Xtra XTRA 1093	SINGS COUNTRY BLUES (LP)	15

(see also Chicago Bill)

BIG BILL BROONZY & PETE SEEGER

64	Xtra XTRA 1006	IN CONCERT (LP)	25
66	Verve Folkways VLP 5006	IN CONCERT (LP, reissue, also stereo SVLP 506)	each 15

(see also Pete Seeger)

BIG BILL BROONZY/SONNY BOY WILLIAMSON

65	RCA Victor RD 7685	BIG BILL AND SONNY BOY (LP)	65

(see also Sonny Boy Williamson [I])

BIG BILL BROONZY, SONNY TERRY & BROWNIE McGHEE

64	Xtra XTRA 1004	BIG BILL BROONZY/SONNY TERRY/BROWNIE McGHEE (LP)	35

(see also Sonny Terry & Brownie McGhee, Washboard Sam)

BROTH

71	Mercury 6338 032	BROTH (LP)	28

BROTHER

89	4th & Broadway 12BRW139	Beyond The 16th Parallel (12")	12

BROTHER BARON

70s	Fab FAB 281	Your Love/Your Love Version	6

BROTHER BUNG

68	Avenue BEV 1054	BLUES CRUSADE (EP)	20

(see also Bob Pearce, Fresh)

BROTHER DAN ALLSTARS

68	Trojan TR 601	Donkey Returns/Tribute To Sir K.B.	15
68	Trojan TR 602	Eastern Organ/JIVERS: Our Love Will Last	25
68	Trojan TR 603	Hold Pon Them/OWEN GRAY: Answer Me	12
68	Trojan TR 607	Read Up/Gallop	12
68	Trojan TR 608	Another Saturday Night/Bee's Knees	10
68	Trojan TBL 101	LET'S CATCH THE BEAT (LP)	45
69	Trojan TRL 1	FOLLOW THAT DONKEY (LP)	32

(see also Audrey, Pooch Jackson)

BROTHER D & THE COLLECTIVE EFFORT

80	Island IPR 2005	How We Gonna Make The Black Nation Rise (12")	10

BROTHERHOOD

69	Philips BF 1766	Paper Man/Give It To Me Now	10

BROTHERHOOD
91	Bite It BITE1	Descendants Of The Holocaust	20
92	Bite It BITE1	Way Of The Wise (12")	10
93	Bite It BITE1	XXXIII (EP)	10

BROTHERHOOD OF BREATH
74	Ogun OG 100	LIVE AT WILLISAU (LP, with Chris McGregor)	20

(see also Chris McGregor's Brotherhood Of Breath, Mark Charig)

BROTHERHOOD OF MAN
69	Deram DM 276	Love One Another/A Little Bit Of Heaven	6
70	Deram DM 317	This Boy/You Can Depend On Me	5
71	Deram DM 327	Reach Out Your Hand/Better Tomorrow	15
74	Dawn DNS 1055	When Love Catches Up With You/How Can You Love (p/s)	6
70	Deram SML 1066	UNITED WE STAND (LP)	20
72	Deram SML 1089	BROTHERHOOD OF MAN (LP)	12
75	dawn DNLS 3063	GOOD THINGS HAPPENING (LP)	12

(see also Sue & Sunny, Sue & Sunshine, Stockingtops)

BROTHERS
67	London HLU 10158	Love Story/The Girl's Alright	5

BROTHERS
75	People PEO 118	In The Pocket/Everybody Loves A Winner	5
75	People PLEO 25	DISCO SOUL (LP)	15

BROTHERS & SISTERS (U.K.)
68	private pressing	ARE WATCHING YOU (LP)	110

BROTHERS & SISTERS (U.S.)
69	CBS 4583	Mighty Quinn/Chimes Of Freedom	5
69	CBS 63746	DYLAN'S GOSPEL (LP)	20

BROTHERS FOUR
60	Philips PB 1009	Greenfields/East Virginia	5
60	Philips PB 1072	Beautiful Brown Eyes/The Green Leaves Of Summer	5

BROTHERS GRIMM
65	Decca F 12224	Lost Love/Make It Or Break It	8
66	Ember EMB 222	A Man Needs Love/Looky Looky	60

(see also Barry & Tony)

BROTHERS KANE
66	Decca F 12448	Walking In The Sand/Won't You Stay Long	10

(see also Sarstedt Brothers, Peter Lincoln, Peter Sarstedt, Clive Sands, Wes Sands, Eden Kane)

BROTHERS TWO
68	Action ACT 4513	Here I Am, In Love Again/I'm Tired Of You Baby	25

BROTHERS WILLIAM
65	Parlophone R 5293	Linda Jane Blues/Honey Love	8

AYSHEA BROUGH
71	RCA RCA 2105	Master Jack/Both Sides Now	7

(see also Ayshea)

PETER BROUGH & ARCHIE ANDREWS
53	HMV BD 1306	The Little Fir Tree/I Saw Mommy Kissing Santa Claus (78, picture label)	15

EDGAR BROUGHTON BAND
69	Harvest HAR 5001	Evil/Death Of An Electric Citizen	10
70	Harvest HAR 5015	Out Demons Out/Momma's Reward	7
70	Harvest HAR 5021	Up Yours!/Officer Dan	8
70	Harvest HAR 5032	Apache Drop Out/Freedom	7
71	Harvest HAR 5040	Hotel Room/Call Me A Liar	8
72	Harvest HAR 5049	Gone Blue/Someone/Mr. Crosby	8
69	Harvest SHVL 757	WASA WASA (LP, gatefold sleeve)	35
70	Harvest SHVL 772	SING BROTHER SING (LP, gatefold sleeve, with lyric insert)	40
71	Harvest SHVL 791	THE EDGAR BROUGHTON BAND (LP, gatefold sleeve)	40
72	Harvest SHTC 252	IN SIDE OUT (LP, gatefold sleeve with lyric sheet)	40
73	Harvest SHVL 810	OORA (LP, wraparound card sleeve in clear artwork plastic bag)	35

AL BROWN (Jamaica)
71	Banana BA 360	No Soul Today/RUFFIANS: Where Did I Go Wrong (B-side actually Bang Shang Alang by Peter Austin & Hortense Ellis)	25
71	Fab FAB 186	Ain't Got No Soul/TEARDROPS: I Got A Feeling	20

AL BROWN'S TUNETOPPERS (U.S.)
60	Top Rank JAR 374	The Madison/Mo' Madison	6

(CRAZY WORLD OF) ARTHUR BROWN
65	Lyntone LYN 770/1	You Don't Know (as Arthur Brown & Diamonds)/DIAMONDS: You'll Be Mine (Reading University Rag Week flexidisc)	60
67	Track 604 008	Devil's Grip/Give Him A Flower	12
68	Track 604 022	Fire!/Rest Cure (push-out or large centre)	6/5
68	Track 604 026	Nightmare/What's Happening (some copies list "Music Man" as B-side)	6
74	Gull GULS 4	Gypsies/Dance	5
75	Gull GULS 13	We Gotta Get Out Of This Place/Here I Am	5
77	Gull SIXPACK 4	SIX-PACK/SIX TRACK (EP, picture disc, die-cut sleeve with stand, 5,000 only)	6
68	Track 612 005/613 005	THE CRAZY WORLD OF ARTHUR BROWN (LP, mono/stereo)	40/30
77	Gull GUD 2003/4	THE LOST EARS (2-LP, gatefold sleeve, as Arthur Brown's Kingdom Come)	25
88	Reckless 2 RECK	STRANGELANDS (LP, unreleased)	

(see also Kingdom Come, Nick Greenwood, Atomic Rooster, Crane/Farlowe)

BARRY BROWN

79	Justice JUDIS 126	Big Big Politician/No Wicked Shall Enter (12")	30
79	Sufferer's Heights SUFF 003	I Love Sweet Jah Jah/RANKING JOE : Youthman Promotion (12")	25
80	Attack TACK 17	Mr. CID/SCIENTIST AND ROOTS RADICAL BAND: King Tubby's Rockers (12")	30
80	Attack TACK 21	Separation/Scientist In A Fine Style (12")	40+
80	Justice JUDIS 135	We Can't Live Like This/From Creation I Man Free (12")	40
81	Greensleeves GRED 68	Give Israel Another Try/Sweet Sixteen (12")	30

BEN BROWN

67	Polydor 56198	Ask The Lonely/Sidewinder	50

BOOTS BROWN & HIS BLOCKBUSTERS

58	RCA RCA 1078	Cerveza/Juicy (78 rpm = £10)	10
59	RCA RCA 1102	Jim Twangy/Trollin' (78 rpm = £15)	10

(see also Shorty Rogers)

BUNNY BROWN

72	Songbird SB 1073	Fat Boy/Fat Boy — Version	12

(see also Noel Brown, Winston Scotland)

BUSTER BROWN

60	Melodisc 1559	Fannie Mae/Lost In A Dream	60
65	Sue WI 368	Fannie Mae/Lost In A Dream (reissue)	20
67	Island WI 3031	My Blue Heaven/Two Women	20
69	Blue Horizon 57-3147	Sugar Babe/I'm Going, But I'll Be Back	20
60s	XX MIN 713	B. AND BUSTER BROWN (EP, with B. Brown)	20

BUSTY BROWN

68	Doctor Bird DB 1158	Here Comes The Night/Don't Look Back	30
69	Upsetter US 304	What A Price/How Can I Forget?	12
69	Upsetter US 308	To Love Somebody/BLEECHERS: Farmer's In The Den	12
69	Punch PH 10	Broken Heart/Tribute To A King	12
70	Punch PH 38	Greatest Love/I Love You Madly	12
70	Escort ES 822	Fight For Your Right/MEDITATORS: Soul Fight (Busty Top A Pop) (B-side actually Soul Fight by Busty Brown)	25
70	Escort ES 845	Man Short (with Gaytones)/DAVE BARKER: She Want It	12
70	Gas GAS 154	I Love You Madly/Greatest Love	10
70	High Note HS 048	Man Short (with Gaytones)/GAYTONES: Another Version	10
71	Punch PH 72	You Inspire Me/UPSETTERS: Version	6
71	Pama Supreme PS 356	Throw Away Your Gun/TWINKLE BROTHERS: Sad Song	18

(see also Llans Thelwell, John Holt, David Isaacs)

CHARLES BROWN (BAND)

56	Vogue V 9061	I'll Always Be In Love With You/Soothe Me (78 rpm = £120)	500+
57	Vogue V 9065	Confidential/Trouble Blues (78 rpm = £120)	500+
61	Parlophone R 4848	It's Christmas All Year Round/Christmas Question	20

(see also Brown Brothers)

CLARENCE 'GATEMOUTH' BROWN

65	Vocalion VE 170161	CLARENCE 'GATEMOUTH' BROWN (EP)	80
72	Python PLP 26	CLARENCE 'GATEMOUTH' BROWN VOL. 1: 1948-1953 (LP)	25
72	Python PLP 27	CLARENCE 'GATEMOUTH' BROWN VOL. 2: 1956-1965 (LP)	25

CLIFFORD BROWN (& HIS GROUP)

56	Emarcy ERE 1501	SWEET CLIFFORD (EP, as Clifford Brown & His Group)	8
58	Emarcy ERE 1565	STUDY IN BROWN VOL. 1 (EP, as Clifford Brown & His Group)	10
58	Emarcy ERE 1566	STUDY IN BROWN VOL. 2 (EP, as Clifford Brown & His Group)	10
58	Emarcy ERE 1572	CLIFFORD BROWN AND MAX ROACH (EP)	10
55	Vogue EPV 1027	GIGI GRYCE — CLIFFORD BROWN ORCHESTRA (EP)	10
55	Vogue EPV 1041	CONCEPTION (EP)	10
56	Vogue EPV 1119	CLIFFORD BROWN ENSEMBLE (EP)	10
54	Vogue LDE 042	CLIFFORD 'BROWNIE' BROWN QUARTET (10" LP)	25
55	Vogue LDE 121	THE CLIFFORD BROWN SEXTET (10" LP)	25
58	Emarcy EJL 1278	STUDY IN BROWN (LP)	15

(see also Art Farmer, Sonny Rollins, Max Roach)

DENNIS BROWN

70	Bamboo BAM 56	Love Grows/SOUND DIMENSION: Less Problem	30
70	Banana BA 309	No Man Is An Island/SOUL SISTERS: Another Night	28
71	Banana BA 336	Never Fall In Love/Make It With You	28
71	Ocean OC 001	Little Green Apples/SOUND DIMENSION: Version	10
72	Duke DU 139	What About The Half/What About The Half Version	20
72	Explosion EX 2068	Black Magic Woman/PHILL PRATT ALL STARS: Black Magic Woman Pt 2	15
72	Pressure Beat PR 5513	Money In My Pocket/JOE GIBBS ALLSTARS: Money Love	12
72	Randy's RAN 526	Cheater/TOMMY McCOOK & IMPACT ALLSTARS: Harvest In The East	15
72	Randy's RAN 528	Meet Me On The Corner (actually unknown instrumental)/IMPACT ALLSTARS: Version	10
72	Songbird SB 1074	Silhouettes/CRYSTALITES: Version	12
73	Ashanti ASH 402	It's Too Late/Song My Mother Used To Sing	12
73	Jackpot JP 813	He Can't Spell/CRYSTALITES: Acid Version	10
73	Smash SMA 2327	Concentration/Version	12
79	Observer OBS 902	Blessed Are The Men (The Pill)/JUNIOR DELGADO : Cry Cry (12")	20
80	High Times HT 001	Blood City/FREDDIE McGREGOR : Natural Collie (12")	35
73	Trojan TRLS 57	SUPER REGGAE & SOUL HITS (LP)	25
75	Trojan TRLS 107	JUST DENNIS (LP)	15
77	DEB DEBLP 01	WOLF AND LEOPARDS (LP)	25

(see also Big Youth & Dennis Brown, Hugh Roy, Big Youth, Sound Dimension)

DENNIS BROWN & ASWAD

80	Simba SM003	Promised Land/More Dub (12")	20

MINT VALUE £

DUSTY BROWN
61	Starlite ST45 058	Please Don't Go/Well You Know	40

ERROL BROWN & CHOSEN FEW
72	Songbird SB 1082	People Make The World Go Round/People Make The World Go Round (Version)	8

(see also Hot Chocolate)

FAITH BROWN
70	CBS 4728	Lock Me In/The Game Of Love	5
71	Penny Farthing PEN 766	Any Way That You Want Me/City Wine	5
72	Regal Zonophone RZ 3063	Take Me With You/If We Only Have Love	5

(see also Carrolls)

FAY BROWN
55	Columbia SCM 5185	Unchained Melody/I Was Wrong	15

FRIDAY BROWN(E)
66	Parlophone R 5396	Getting Nowhere/And (To Me He Meant Everything) (as Friday Browne)	18
66	Fontana TF 736	32nd Love Affair/Born A Woman	75
67	Fontana TF 851	Ask Any Woman/Outdoor Seminar	5
69	Fontana TF 996	Stand By Your Man/I Want To Rain	6
72	Philips 6006 239	Shake A Hand/Everything's Alright	5
73	Philips 6006 324	Groovy Kind Of Love/Salford	5
71	Philips 6308 074	FRIDAY BROWN (LP)	35

(see also Marianne & Mike, High Society, Manchester Mob, Graham Gouldman)

FUNKY BROWN
72	Sioux SI 018	African (Indian Reservation)/JUMBO STERLING: Elizabethan Reggae	6

GABRIEL BROWN
77	Policy Wheel PW 4592	GABRIEL BROWN AND HIS GUITAR (LP, withdrawn)	15

GEORGIA BROWN
55	Decca F 10489	My Crazy L'il Mixed Up Heart/Before We Know It	8
55	Decca F 10551	I Love To Dance With You/That's All I Need	8
55	Decca F 10616	I Went To The Village/Wrong Again	8
63	Decca SKL 4586	SINGS GERSHWIN (LP)	15

GERRY BROWN'S JAZZMEN
61	Fontana TFL 5165	IT'S TRAD TIME! (LP)	12

GLEN BROWN
68	Blue Cat BS 131	Way Of Life (with Joe White & Trevor)/	
		KARL BRYAN & LYN TAITT: I'm So Proud	48
70	Summit SUM 8502	Collie And Wine/BEVERLEY'S ALLSTARS: Version	10
70	Songbird SB 1021	Love I/CRYSTALITES: Heavy Load	12
72	Songbird SB 1081	Smokey Eyes (with Crystalites)/Smokey Eyes (Version)	20
73	Downtown DT 507	Two Wedding Skank/BARRY SIMPSON: Sugar Down Deh	15
79	Kingley REX 4	Marcus Garvey Words/SLYFORD WALKER: Africa (12")	12

GLENMORE BROWN & HOPETON LEWIS
68	Fab FAB 42	Girl You're Cold/Soul Man	40

(see also Hopeton Lewis & Glenmore Brown)

HENRY BROWN
50	Jazz Collector L 55	It Hurts So Good (with Ike Rodgers)/Screenin' The Blues (78)	10
61	'77' LA 12-5	HENRY BROWN BLUES (LP)	40

HUX BROWN & SCOTTY
71	High Note HS 056	Unbelievable Sounds/GAYTONES: Unbelievable Sounds Version	25

HYLO BROWN (& TIMBERLINERS)
59	Capitol CL 15075	You Can't Relive The Past/Thunder Clouds Of Love	5
60	Capitol CL 15139	I've Waited As Long As I Can/Just Any Old Love	5
63	London HAB/SHB 8094	BLUEGRASS GOES TO COLLEGE (LP)	15

IAN BROWN
98	Polydor 571 986-7	My Star/See The Dawn (7", p/s)	5
97	Polydor MYSTAR1	My Star (CD promo, in sealed PVC black sleeve with printed label, few include a b&w transparency)	8
98	Polydor 567 093-1	Can't See Me (Bacon & Quarmby Remix)/(Bacon & Quarmby Vocal Dub)/(Harvey's Invisible Mix)/(Harvey's Instrumenal Mix), Under The Paving Stones: The Beach (Gabriel's 13th Dream Remix) (12", unique Eyesight Test p/s)	10
98	Polydor CAN'T SEE2	Can't See Me (Bacon and Quarmby remix)/(Harvey's Invisible Remix)/(Bacon and Quarmby Vocal Dub)/Album Version (12" promo no p/s)	8
00	Polydor 561 908-1	Thriller/Billie Jean (12", p/s)	15
98	Polydor 539 916-1	UNFINISHED MONKEY BUSINESS (LP, gatefold, p/s)	18
99	Polydor 543 141-1	GOLDEN GREATS (LP, yellow vinyl, p/s)	15
01	Polydor 589 126-1	MUSIC OF THE SPHERES (LP)	12
02	Polydor 065 927-1	REMIXES OF THE SPHERES (LP)	12
02	Polydor SPHERE2	REMIXES OF THE SPHERES (2 x 12" Promo Sampler)	25
05	Fiction 987 287-3	THE GREATEST (2 x CD Deluxe Book Edition)	20

(see also Stone Roses)

IRVING BROWN
70	Bamboo BAM 36	Today/SOUND DIMENSION: Young Gifted And Black Version	12
70	Bamboo BAM 58	I'm Still Around/Run Come	15
70	Bamboo BAM 61	Let's Make It Up (actually by Larry Marshall)/BURNING SPEAR: Free	25
71	Bamboo Now BN 1003	Now I'm Alone/Funky Night	15

(see also Larry Marshall)

JACKIE BROWN
72	High Note HS 057	One Night/GAYTONES: One Night Version	8
72	High Note HS 060	Last Dance/GAYTONES: Last Dance Version	8

JAMES BROWN (& THE FAMOUS FLAMES)

SINGLES

60	Parlophone R 4667	Think/You've Got The Power (with Famous Flames)	40
60	Fontana H 273	This Old Heart/Wonder When You're Coming Home	30
62	Parlophone R 4922	Night Train/Why Does Everything Happen To Me (with Famous Flames)	50
62	Parlophone R 4952	Shout And Shimmy/Come Over Here (with Famous Flames)	40
63	London HL 9730	Prisoner Of Love/Choo-Choo (Locomotion) (with Famous Flames)	20
63	London HL 9775	These Foolish Things/(Can You) Feel It (Part 1) (with Famous Flames)	20
64	Philips BF 1368	Out Of Sight/Maybe The Last Time (& His Orchestra)	20
64	Sue WI 360	Night Train/Why Does Everything Happen To Me (with Famous Flames)	30
65	London HL 9945	Have Mercy Baby/Just Won't Do Right (with Famous Flames)	18
65	London HL 9990	Papa's Got A Brand New Bag Parts 1 & 2 (with Famous Flames)	20
65	Ember EMB S 216	Tell Me What You're Gonna Do/Lost Someone (some in p/s)	40/20
65	Philips BF 1458	Try Me/Papa's Got A Brand New Bag	15
66	Philips BF 1481	New Breed Parts 1 & 2	15
66	Pye International 7N 25350	I Got You (I Feel Good)/I Can't Help It (I Just Do-Do-Do) (with Famous Flames)	22
66	Pye International 7N 25367	Ain't That A Groove Parts 1 & 2 (with Famous Flames)	15
66	Pye International 7N 25371	It's A Man's Man's Man's World/Is It Yes Or Is It No? (with Famous Flames)	15
66	Pye International 7N 25379	Money Won't Change You Parts 1 & 2 (with Famous Flames)	25
66	Pye International 7N 25394	Don't Be A Drop-Out/Tell Me That You Love Me (with Famous Flames)	20
67	Pye International 7N 25411	Bring It Up/Nobody Knows (with Famous Flames)	20
67	Pye International 7N 25418	Kansas City/Stone Fox (with Famous Flames)	20
67	Pye International 7N 25423	Let Yourself Go/Good Rockin' Tonight (with Famous Flames)	15
67	Pye International 7N 25430	Cold Sweat Parts 1 & 2 (with Famous Flames)	20
67	Pye International 7N 25441	Get It Together Parts 1 & 2 (with Famous Flames)	15
68	Polydor 56740	I Can't Stand Myself/There Was A Time	15
68	Polydor 56743	I Got The Feelin'/If I Ruled The World	8
68	Polydor 56744	Licking Stick, Licking Stick Parts 1 & 2	8
68	Polydor 56752	Say It Loud, I'm Black And I'm Proud Parts 1 & 2	10
68	Polydor 56540	That's Life/Please, Please, Please (with Famous Flames)	15
69	Polydor 56776	Mother Popcorn Parts 1 & 2	8
69	Polydor 56780	The World Parts 1 & 2	8
69	Polydor 56783	Let A Man Come In And Do The Popcorn/Sometimes	10
69	Polydor 56787	There Was A Time/I Can't Stand Myself (When You Touch Me)	10
70	Polydor 56793	Ain't It Funky Now Parts 1 & 2	8
70	Polydor 2001 018	It's A New Day/Georgia On My Mind	8
70	Polydor 2001 071	Get Up, I Feel Like Being A Sex Machine Parts 1 & 2 (paper or plastic label)	8/6
70	Polydor 2001 097	Call Me Super Bad Parts 1, 2 & 3	8
71	Polydor 2001 163	Soul Power Parts 1, 2 & 3	8
71	Polydor 2001 190	I Cried/Get Up, Get Into It, Get Involved	8
71	Polydor 2001 213	Hot Pants (She Got To Use What She Got To Get What She Wants) Parts 1, 2 & 3	8
71	Polydor 2001 223	Make It Funky Parts 1 & 2	8
71	Mojo 2093 006	Hey America/Brother Rapp (Part 1)	8
71	Polydor 2066 153	I'm A Greedy Man Parts 1 & 2	8
72	Polydor 2066 185	King Heroin/Theme From King Heroin	18
72	Polydor 2066 210	There It Is Parts 1 & 2	8
72	Polydor 2066 216	Honky Tonk Parts 1 & 2	10
72	Polydor 2066 231	Get On The Good Foot Parts 1 & 2	8
72	Polydor 2066 283	What My Baby Needs Now Is A Little More Lovin'/This Guy's In Love With You (with Lyn Collins)	15
73	Polydor 2066 285	I've Got A Bag Of My Own/I Know It's True	8
73	Polydor 2141 008	Papa's Got A Brand New Bag/Out Of Sight/It's A Man's Man's Man's World (p/s)	6
73	Polydor 2066 296	I Got Ants In My Pants Parts 1, 15 & 16	6
73	Polydor 2066 329	Think/Something	6
73	Polydor 2066 370	Woman Parts 1 & 2	6
74	Polydor 2066 411	Stone To The Bone/Sexy, Sexy, Sexy	6
74	Polydor 2066 485	My Thang/The Payback	6
74	Polydor 2066 513	It's Hell/Papa Don't Take No Mess	6
75	Polydor 2066 520	Funky President (People It's Bad)/Cold Blooded	6
76	Polydor 2066 642	Hot (I Need To Be Loved, Loved, Loved)/Superbad, Superslick (Part 1)	6
76	Polydor 2066 687	Get Up Offa That Thing/Release The Pressure	6
77	Polydor 2066 763	Bodyheat Parts 1, 15 & 16	6
77	Polydor 2066 834	Honky Tonk/Brother Rapp	6
78	Polydor 2066 915	Eyesight/I Never, Never, Never Will Forget	6
78	Polydor 2066 984	Nature Parts 1 & 2	6
79	Polydor POSP 24	For Goodness Sakes, Look At Those Cakes/Get Up, I Feel Like Being A Sex Machine (red or silver label)	8/5
79	Polydor POSPX 24	Get Up, I Feel Like Being A Sex Machine/For Goodness Sakes, Look At Those Cakes (12")	10
79	Polydor POSPX 68	It's Too Funky In Here/Are We Really Dancing? (12")	10
79	Polydor STEP 2	Star Generation/Let The Boogie Do The Rest	5
79	Polydor STEPX 2	Star Generation/Let The Boogie Do The Rest (12")	8
80	Polydor POSP 121	Regrets/Stone Cold Drag	5
80	RCA RCAT 28	Rapp Payback (Where Iz Moses?) (Parts 1 & 2) (12")	8
81	RCA RCAT 44	Stay With Me/Smokin' And Drinkin' (12")	8
81	RCA RCAT 65	Funky Man (Parts 1 & 2)/Mashed Potatoes (12")	8
88	Urban URBX 13	She's The One/Funky President (People It's Bad)/Funky Drummer (9.13)/Funky Drummer (Bonus Beats Reprise) (12", die-cut title sleeve)	10
88	Urban URBA 13	She's The One (Funky Drummer Remix)/Funky President (People It's Bad)/Funky Drummer (Bonus Beats Reprise) (12")	10
88	Urban URBA17	Payback (Final Mixdown)/Give It Up Or Turn It Loose/Coldsweat (12")	15
88	Urban URBX 17 DJ	Coldcut Meets The Godfather (12" promo, same as The Payback Mix)	10

James BROWN

EPs

64	London RE 1410	JAMES BROWN AND THE FAMOUS FLAMES	60
64	Ember EMB EP 4549	I DO JUST WHAT I WANT	50
66	Pye Intl. NEP 44059	I GOT YOU	40
66	Pye Intl. NEP 44068	I'LL GO CRAZY	40
67	Pye Intl. NEP 44072	PRISONER OF LOVE	40
67	Pye Intl. NEP 44076	HOW LONG DARLING	40
67	Pye Intl. NEP 44088	BRING IT UP	40
70	Polydor 580 701	TURN IT LOOSE	40

LPs

64	London HA 8177	PURE DYNAMITE! (as James Brown & Famous Flames)	75
64	London HA 8184	LIVE AT THE APOLLO (as James Brown & Famous Flames)	60
64	Ember EMB 3357	TELL ME WHAT YOU'RE GONNA DO	45
64	Philips BL 7630	SHOWTIME	40
65	London HA 8203	UNBEATABLE 16 HITS	70
65	London HA 8231	PLEASE, PLEASE, PLEASE (as James Brown & Famous Flames)	80
65	Philips BL 7664	GRITS AND SOUL	50
65	London HA 8240	JAMES BROWN TOURS THE U.S.A. (with Famous Flames)	65
66	London HA 8262	PAPA'S GOT A BRAND NEW BAG (as James Brown & Famous Flames)	50
66	Philips BL 7697	JAMES BROWN PLAYS JAMES BROWN TODAY AND YESTERDAY	40
66	Pye Intl. NPL 28074	I GOT YOU (I FEEL GOOD)	50
66	Philips BL 7718	JAMES BROWN PLAYS NEW BREED	25
66	Pye Intl. NPL 28079	IT'S A MAN'S MAN'S MAN'S WORLD	40
66	Pye Intl. NPL 28097	THE JAMES BROWN CHRISTMAS ALBUM	65
67	Pye Intl. NPL 28093	MIGHTY INSTRUMENTALS	40
67	Philips (S)BL 7761	HANDFUL OF SOUL	25
67	Pye Intl. NPL 28099	PAPA'S GOT A BRAND NEW BAG (reissue)	25
67	Pye Intl. NPL 28100	MR. EXCITEMENT	50
67	Polydor 582 703	THE JAMES BROWN SHOW (live)	22
67	Pye Intl. NPL 28103	SINGS RAW SOUL	20
67	Pye Intl. NPL 28104	LIVE AT THE GARDEN	40
68	Philips (S)BL 7823	JAMES BROWN PLAYS THE REAL THING	30
68	Polydor 623 017	JAMES BROWN'S GREATEST HITS	15
68	Polydor 623 032	MR. DYNAMITE	20
68	Polydor 184 100	MR. SOUL	20
68	Polydor 184 136	I CAN'T STAND MYSELF	25
69	Polydor 184 148	SOUL FIRE	20
69	Polydor 184 159	KING OF SOUL	18
60s	Polydor 2852 002	THE SOUL OF JAMES BROWN (reissue of I Can't Stand Myself)	20
69	Mercury 20133 SMCL	JAMES BROWN SINGS OUT OF SIGHT	30
69	Polydor 583 729/30	LIVE AT THE APOLLO VOLUME TWO (2-LP)	25
69	Polydor 583 741	SAY IT LOUD — I'M BLACK AND I'M PROUD	25
69	Polydor 583 765	THE BEST OF JAMES BROWN	15
69	Polydor 583 768	IT'S A MOTHER	25
69	Polydor 643 317	THIS IS ... JAMES BROWN	20
70	Polydor 583 742	GETTIN' DOWN TO IT	25
70	Polydor 184 319	THE POPCORN	30
70	Polydor 2343 010	AIN'T IT FUNKY	30
70	Polydor 2612 005	LIVE AT THE APOLLO VOLUME TWO (2-LP, reissue)	15
70	Polydor 2334 009	PAPA'S GOT A BRAND NEW BAG	15
71	Polydor 2625 004	SEX MACHINE (2-LP)	25
71	Polydor 2310 022	SOUL ON TOP	25
71	Polydor 2310 029	IT'S A NEW DAY	25
71	Polydor 2310 089	SUPER BAD	20
71	Polydor 2343 036	SOUL BROTHER, NUMBER ONE	15
71	Polydor 2425 086	HOT PANTS	15
72	Polydor 2659 011	REVOLUTION OF THE MIND: RECORDED LIVE AT THE APOLLO VOL. III (2-LP)	25
72	Polydor 2391 033	THERE IT IS	25
73	Polydor 2659 018	GET ON THE GOOD FOOT (2-LP)	30
73	Polydor 2391 057	SOUL CLASSICS (also issued as record club edition [ACB 00222])	15
73	Polydor 2490 117	BLACK CAESAR (soundtrack)	50
73	Polydor 2391 084	SLAUGHTER'S BIG RIP-OFF (soundtrack)	50
74	Polydor 2391 116	SOUL CLASSICS VOLUME TWO	15
74	Polydor 2659 030	THE PAYBACK (2-LP)	30
74	Polydor 2659 036	IT'S HELL (2-LP)	30
75	Polydor 2391 164	REALITY	15
75	Polydor 2391 166	SOUL CLASSICS VOLUME THREE	15
75	Polydor 2391 175	SEX MACHINE TODAY	20
75	Polydor 2391 197	EVERYBODY'S DOIN' THE HUSTLE AND DEAD ON THE DOUBLE BUMP	15
76	Polydor 2391 228	GET UP OFFA THAT THING	15
77	Polydor 2391 258	BODYHEAT	15
77	Polydor 2391 300	MUTHA'S NATURE (by James Brown & the New J.B.'s)	15
85	Polydor 821 231-1	AIN'T THAT A GROOVE — THE J.B. STORY 1966-69	15
85	Polydor 821 232-1	DOING IT TOO DEATH — THE J.B. STORY 1970-73	15
86	Boiling Point 827 439-1	DEAD ON THE HEAVY FUNK — THE J.B. STORY 1974-76	15
86	Polydor 829 417-1	JAMES BROWN'S FUNKY PEOPLE VOL. 1 (with other artists)	15
88	Urban URBLP 14	JAMES BROWN'S FUNKY PEOPLE VOL. 2 (with other artists)	15
88	Urban URBLP 11	IN THE JUNGLE GROOVE (2-LP)	15
91	Polydor 849 108-2	STAR TIME (4-CD, with booklet)	20

(see also Lyn Collins, JBs, Maceo & All King's Men, Nat Kendrick & Swans)

JAMES BROWN (Jamaica)

71	Punch PH 76	Don't Say/TRANS AM ALLSTARS: Don't Say Version	8
72	Ashanti ASH 408	Mama Don't Want To See You/Mama Don't Want To See You Version	7
75	Mango MAN 1001	Stop The War In Babylon/Dub In Peace	15

JERICHO BROWN
60	Warner Bros WB 14	Don'tcha Know (That I Love You)/Look For A Star	10
64	Warner Bros WB 141	I'm Watching You/Wisdom Of A Fool	5

JIM EDWARD BROWN
66	RCA RCX 7179	INTRODUCING JIM EDWARD BROWN (EP)	15

(see also Browns)

JIM EDWARD (BROWN) & MAXINE BROWN
55	London HL 8123	Itsy Witsy Bitsy Me/Why Am I Falling? (78 rpm = £12)	40
55	London HLU 8166	Your Love Is Wild As The West Wind/Draggin' Mainstreet (78 rpm = £15)	40
55	London HLU 8200	You Thought I Thought/Here Today And Gone Tomorrow	
		(B-side with Bonnie) (78 rpm = £12)	40
55	London R-EP 1024	COUNTRY SONGS (EP)	25
55	London R-EU 1044	COUNTRY SONGS VOLUME 3 (EP)	25

JOE BROWN (& BRUVVERS)
59	Decca F 11185	People Gotta Talk/Comes The Day (solo, triangular centre) (78 rpm = £20)	20
60	Decca F 11207	Darktown Strutter's Ball/Swagger (solo)	12
60	Decca F 11246	Jellied Eels/Dinah	12
60	Pye 7N 15322	Shine/The Switch	7
61	Piccadilly 7N 35000	Crazy Mixed Up Kid/Stick Around	6
61	Piccadilly 7N 35005	Good Luck & Goodbye/I'm Henery The Eighth I Am	6
62	Piccadilly 7N 35024	What A Crazy World We're Living In/Popcorn	6
62	Decca F 11496	Comes The Day/People Gotta Talk (reissue)	5
62	Piccadilly 7N 35047	A Picture Of You/A Lay-About's Lament	5
62	Piccadilly 7N 35058	Your Tender Look/The Other Side Of The Town	5
62	Piccadilly 7N 35082	It Only Took A Minute/All Things Bright And Beautiful	5
63	Piccadilly 7N 35106	That's What Love Will Do/Hava Nagila (The Hora)	5
63	Piccadilly 7N 35129	Nature's Time For Love/The Spanish Bit	5
63	Piccadilly 7N 35138	Sally Ann/There's Only One Of You	5
63	Piccadilly 7N 35150	Little Ukelele/Hercules Unchained	5
64	Piccadilly 7N 35163	You Do Things To Me/Everybody Calls Me Joe	5
62	Decca DFE8500	A PICTURE OF JOE BROWN (EP)	20
62	Picadilly NEP 34025	JOE BROWN HIT PARADE (EP)	20
62	Picadilly NEP 34026	ALL THINGS BRIGHT AND BEAUTIFUL (EP)	20
62	Ace of Clubs ACL 1127	A PICTURE OF JOE BROWN (LP)	15
63	Picadilly NPL38006	JOE BROWN – LIVE! (LP)	15

(see also Vicki Brown)

JOE BROWN/MARK WYNTER
63	Piccadilly NEP 24167	JUST FOR FUN (EP, soundtrack, 2 tracks each)	12
64	Golden Guinea WO 1	BIG HITS OF JOE BROWN AND MARK WYNTER (EP)	10
63	Golden Guinea GGL 0179	JOE BROWN/MARK WYNTER (LP, 6 tracks each)	12

(see also Mark Wynter)

JOHNNY BROWN
61	Philips PB 1119	Walkin' Talkin' Kissin' Doll/Sundown	10

KAY BROWN
56	Brunswick 05595	Me 'N' You 'N' The Moon/What Do You Think It Does To Me?	10

KENT BROWN & RAINBOWS
68	Fab FAB 53	When You Going To Show Me How/Come Ya Come Ya	10

(see also Kent & Jeannie, Sir D's Group)

LENNOX BROWN
72	Green Door GD 4023	High School Serenade/WINSTON SCOTLAND: On The Track (1st issue)	7
72	Bullet BU 501	High School Serenade/WINSTON SCOTLAND: On The Track (2nd issue)	7

(see also Jeff Barnes, Peter Tosh)

LEROY BROWN
78	Revue REVD 10	Taxi/Blood A Go Run (12")	30

LES BROWN & HIS BAND OF RENOWN
54	Vogue Coral Q 2034	Ramona/Hot Point	10
54	Vogue Coral Q 2042	St. Louis Blues Mambo/Moon Song	10
55	Vogue Coral Q 72049	The Man That Got Away/Doodle-Doo-Doo	10
55	Capitol CL 14331	Frenesi/Perfidia	6
55	Capitol CL 14350	He Needs Me/Simplicity	6
55	Vogue Coral Q 72107	Lullaby Of Birdland/Bernie's Tune	6
56	Vogue Coral Q 72123	Hong Kong Blues (with Hoagy Carmichael & Band Of Renown)/	
		It's All Right With Me	10
56	Vogue Coral Q 72215	Flamingo/Midnight Sun	5
56	Capitol CL 14512	Sincerely Yours/Take Back Your Mink	5
56	Capitol CL 14611	That Certain Feeling/Hit The Road To Dreamland	5
56	Capitol CL 14631	Talk About A Party/Ancient History	5
57	Capitol CL 14675	Priscilla/The Best Years Of My Life	10
57	Capitol CL 14706	Original Joe/If I Had The Money	5
57	Vogue Coral Q 72242	Forty Cups Of Coffee/I'm Forever Blowing Bubbles	10
54	Vogue Coral LVC 10002	LES DANCE (10" LP)	15
55	Vogue Coral LVC 10017	INVITATION (10" LP)	15
55	Vogue Coral LVC 10033	LES BROWN (10" LP)	15

MAXINE BROWN
61	London HLU 9286	All In My Mind/Harry, Let's Marry	40
62	HMV POP 1102	Am I Falling In Love/Promise Me Anything	150
63	Stateside SS 188	Ask Me/Yesterday's Kisses	30
64	Pye International 7N 25272	Oh No Not My Baby/You Upset My Soul	30
65	Pye International 7N 25299	It's Gonna Be Alright/You Do Something To Me	25
65	Pye International 7N 25317	One Step At A Time/Anything For A Laugh	40

67	Pye International 7N 25410	I've Got A Lot Of Love Left In Me/Hold On (I'm Comin')	
		(B-side with Chuck Jackson)	40
67	Pye International 7N 25434	Since I Found You/Gotta Find A Way	20
70	Major Minor MM 709	Reason To Believe/I Can't Get Along Without You	25
73	Avco 6105 022	Picked Up, Packed Up And Put Away/Bella Mia	15
75	Pye Disco Demand DDS 117	One In A Million/Let Me Give You My Lovin'	15
90s	Kent TOWN 110	It's Torture/I Got Love	12

(see also Chuck Jackson & Maxine Brown)

NAPPY BROWN (& HIS BAND)

55	London HL 8145	Don't Be Angry/It's Really You (78 rpm = £40)	500
55	London HLC 8182	Pitter Patter/There'll Come A Day (78 rpm = £30)	400
57	London HLC 8384	Little By Little/I'm Getting Lonesome (& His Band)	
		(gold or silver lettering on label) (78 rpm = £18)	300/150
58	London HLC 8760	It Don't Hurt No More/My Baby (78 rpm = £18)	75

NOEL BROWN

50s	Parlophone MP 134	Take Me Back To Africa/Virgin Islands (Get Happy In A Hurry) (78, export)	5
68	Island WI 3149	Man's Temptation/Heartbreak Girl	22
69	Songbird SB 1012	By The Time I Get To Phoenix/Heartbreak Girl	5

(see also Bunny Brown)

O'CHI BROWN

85	Magnet MAGT 288	Whenever You Need Somebody (Mixes)/I Play Games (12", p/s)	10
85	Magnet MAGT 288R	Whenever You Need Somebody (Pull It Off Mixes)/I Play Games (12" promo)	18
86	Magnet MAGT 296	100% Pure Pain (Mixes)/I Just Want To Be Loved (12", p/s)	10
86	Magnet MAGT 296R	100% Pure Pain (Mixes)/I Just want To Be Loved (12", p/s)	15
86	Magnet MAGT 297	Two Hearts Beating As One (Mixes)/Another Broken Heart (12", p/s)	10
86	Magnet MAGT 297R	Two Hearts Beating As One (Mixes)/Another Broken Heart (12", p/s)	15
87	Magnet MAGDT 9	Whenever You Need Somebody/Mixes (12", promo)	18

OSCAR BROWN JNR

61	Philips PB 1097	But I Was Cool/Dat Dere	5
61	Philips BBL 7478	SIN AND SOUL (LP)	10
73	Atlantic K 40452	MOVIN' ON (LP)	10

PAMELA BROWN

70	Joe JRS 8	People Are Running/CRITICS: School Days	15

PETE BROWN('S PIBLOKTO)

69	Parlophone R 5767	The Week Looked Good On Paper/Morning Call	
		(as Pete Brown & His Battered Ornaments, promo p/s)	60
69	Parlophone R 5767	The Week Looked Good On Paper/Morning Call	
		(as Pete Brown & His Battered Ornaments)	22
69	Harvest HAR 5008	Living Life Backwards/High Flying Electric Bird (as Pete Brown & Piblokto!)	15
70	Harvest HAR 5023	Can't Get Off The Planet/Broken Magic (with His Battered Ornaments)	15
70	Harvest HAR 5028	Flying Hero Sandwich/My Last Band (as Pete Brown & Piblokto!)	25
69	Harvest SHVL 752	A MEAL YOU CAN SHAKE HANDS WITH IN THE DARK (LP,	
		as Pete Brown & His Battered Ornaments, mono or stereo)	150
70	Harvest SHVL 768	THE ART SCHOOL DANCE GOES ON FOREVER	
		(LP, as Pete Brown & Piblokto!)	140
70	Harvest SHVL 782	THOUSANDS ON A RAFT (LP, as Pete Brown & Piblokto!)	125
73	Deram SML 1103	THE NOT FORGOTTEN ASSOCIATION (LP, with Graham Bond)	90
77	Harvest SHSM 2017	MY LAST BAND (LP, as Pete Brown & Piblokto)	25
82	Discs Intl. INTLP 1	PARTY IN THE RAIN (LP, with Ian Lynn, private pressing)	25

(see also Battered Ornaments, Graham Bond & Pete Brown, Deke Leonard)

PINEY BROWN

54	Esquire 10-330	That's Right Little Girl/EDDIE CHAMBLEE: Blues For Eddie (78)	15

POLLY BROWN

73	Pye NSPL 18396	POLLY BROWN (LP)	18

RANDY BROWN

80	Casablanca CANL 190	I Wanna Make Love To You/We Ought To Be Doin' It (12", p/s)	12

ROY BROWN

57	London HLP 8398	I'm Sticking With You/Party Doll (gold label print, later silver)	600+/300
57	London HLP 8398	I'm Sticking With You/Party Doll (78)	50
57	London HLP 8448	Saturday Night/Everybody (78 rpm = £65)	500

RUTH BROWN (& HER RHYTHMAKERS)

55	London HL 8153	Mambo Baby/Mama (He Treats Your Daughter Mean) (with Rhythmakers)	
		(78 = £30)	350
55	London HLE 8210	As Long As I'm Moving/R.B. Blues (with Her Rhythmakers) (78 rpm = £30)	350
56	London HLE 8310	I Want To Do More/Sweet Baby Of Mine (78 rpm = £30)	200
57	London HLE 8401	Mom Oh Mom/I Want To Be Loved (But Only By You) (78 rpm = £50)	150
57	Columbia DB 3913	Lucky Lips/My Heart Is Breaking Over You (78 rpm = £40)	400
57	London HLE 8483	When I Get You Baby/One More Time (78 rpm = £40)	100
58	London HLE 8552	A New Love/Look Me Up (78 rpm = £30)	100
58	London HLE 8645	Just Too Much/Book Of Lies (78 rpm = £40)	100
58	London HLE 8757	This Little Girl's Gone Rockin'/Why Me (78 rpm = £35)	75
58	London HL 7061	This Little Girl's Gone Rockin'/Why Me (export issue)	75
59	London HLE 8887	Jack O' Diamonds/I Can't Hear A Word You Say (78 rpm = £45)	50
59	London HLE 8946	I Don't Know/Papa Daddy (78 rpm = £45)	50
60	London HLE 9093	Don't Deceive Me/I Burned Your Letter	40
61	London HLK 9304	Sure 'Nuff/Here He Comes	38
64	Brunswick 05904	Yes Sir That's My Baby/What Happened To You	25
76	President PT 457	Sugar Babe/Stop Knocking	6
55	London REE 1038	THE QUEEN OF R&B (EP)	200
63	Philips BE 12537	GOSPEL TIME (EP)	50

60	London Jazz LTZ-K 15187	LAST DATE WITH RUTH BROWN (LP)	50
62	Philips 652 012 BL	ALONG COMES RUTH (LP)	50
63	Philips 652 020 BL	GOSPEL TIME (LP)	40
64	Atlantic ATL 5007	THE BEST OF RUTH BROWN (LP, plum label)	100
76	President PTLS 1067	SUGAR BABE (LP)	20

RUTH BROWN/JOE TURNER
56	London REE 1047	THE KING AND QUEEN OF R&B (EP, 2 tracks each)	225

SAMMI BROWN
68	Fontana TF 947	Daydream/Stop The Music	5

SANDY BROWN('S JAZZ BAND)
51	S&M SN 1002	Irish Black Bottom/Alexander (78)	5
58	Tempo A 124	African Queen/Special Delivery (as Sandy Brown's Jazz Band)	5
53	Esquire EP 28	SANDY BROWN'S JAZZ BAND (EP)	10
55	Tempo EXA 13	SANDY BROWN'S JAZZ BAND (EP)	10
55	Tempo EXA 33	SANDY BROWN'S JAZZ BAND (EP)	10
56	Tempo EXA 49	TRADITIONAL JAZZ SCENE '56 (EP)	10
57	Nixa NJE 1054	BLUE McJAZZ (EP)	10
57	Nixa NJE 1056	AFRO McJAZZ (EP)	10
53	Esquire 20-022	SANDY BROWN (10" LP, with Bobby Mickleburgh)	15
56	Tempo TAP 3	SANDY'S SIDEMEN PLAYING COMPOSITIONS BY AL FAIRWEATHER (LP)	40
57	Nixa Jazz Today NJL 9	McJAZZ (LP)	15
66	Fontana TE1 7473	SANDY BROWN ALL STARS (LP)	15
69	Fontana SFJL 921	HAIR AT ITS HAIRIEST (LP, as Sandy Brown & His Gentlemen Friends)	20
71	77 SEU 12/49	WITH THE BRIAN LEMON TRIO (LP)	15

(see also Wally Fawkes, Sandy & Teachers, Al Fairweather)

SAVOY BROWN
(see under 'S')

SHIRLEY BROWN
75	Stax STXS 2019	Woman To Woman/Yes Sir, Brother	6
75	Stax STXS 2032	I Can't Give You Up/It Ain't No Fun	5
75	Stax STX 1031	WOMAN TO WOMAN (LP)	20

(see also Oliver Sain)

STU BROWN & BLUESOLOGY
67	Polydor 56195	Since I Found You Baby/Just A Little Bit	300

(see also Bluesology, Elton John)

BROWN SUGAR
80	Studio 16 WE 092	Dreaming Of Zion (12")	40
80	Studio 16 WE 106	Confession Hurts (12")	35
80	Studio 16 WE 113	Runaway Love (12")	40

TEDDY BROWN
70	Trojan TR 7793	What Greater Love/Lady Love	6
71	Trojan TR 7827	Walk The World Away/Senorita Rita	6

TINY BROWN
50	Capitol CL 13306	No More Blues/Slow-Motion Baby (78)	15

VEDA BROWN
74	Stax STXS 2008	Short Stopping/I Can See Every Woman's Man But Mine	8

VERNON BROWN
71	Mojo 2093 002	I'm A Lover/Of Your Life	10

VIC BROWN COMBO
63	Rio R 7	Swanee River/Robert E. Lee	15

(se also Alan Martin)

VINCENT BROWN
70	Gas GAS 128	Look What You're Going To Do/Hold On To What You Have Got	8

WATSON T. BROWN (& EXPLOSIVE)
68	President PT 207	Some Lovin'/Home Is Where Your Heart Lies	6
68	President PT 221	Crying All Night/I Close My Eyes	10
70	Bell BLL 1109	Will You Still Love Me Tomorrow/Save The Last Dance For Me (solo)	6

(see also Explosive)

WILLIAM BROWN
71	Ackee ACK 128	I'm Alone/BELTONES: Soul People	10

BROWN BROTHERS
59	Vogue V 9131	Let The Good Times Roll/You're Right, I'm Left (78 rpm = £100)	200

(see also Charles Brown)

DUNCAN BROWNE
68	Immediate IM 070	On The Bombsite/Alfred Bell	25
70	Bell BLL 1119	Resurrection Joe/Final Asylum	6
73	Rak RAK 162	Send Me The Bill/My Only Son	6
78	Logo GO 329	Wild Places/Camino Real	6
68	Immediate IMSP 018	GIVE ME, TAKE YOU (LP, with insert)	250
73	RAK SRKA 6754	DUNCAN BROWNE (LP, gatefold sleeve)	18

GEORGE BROWNE
54	Parlophone CMSP 6	Calypso Mambo/The Peanut Vendor (export issue)	7
54	Parlophone CMSP 17	Somebody Bad Stole De Wedding Bell (Who's Got De Ding Dong?)/Matilda, Matilda! (export issue)	5
57	Columbia DB 3940	Sound Barrier/Te-Le-Le (78 rpm = £6)	7

(see also Humphrey Lyttleton)

MINT VALUE £

JACKSON BROWNE
86	Elektra EKR 35P	For America (Edit)/Till I Go Down (Statue Of Liberty-shaped picture disc)	5
86	Elektra EKR 42P	In The Shape Of A Heart/Voice Of America (heart-shaped picture disc)	5
74	Asylum K2 43007	LATE FOR THE SKY (LP, quadrophonic)	15

SANDRA BROWNE (& BOYFRIENDS)
63	Columbia DB 4998	By Hook Or By Crook/Johnny Boy (as Sandra Browne & Boyfriends)	15
63	Columbia DB 7109	You'd Think He Didn't Know Me/Mama Never Told Me	15
65	Columbia DB 7465	Knock On Any Door/I Want Love	15

TEDDY BROWN(E)
59	Capitol CL 15059	A Corner In Paradise/The Everglades	10
61	Starlite ST45 033	Pretty Little Baby/Genevieve (as Teddy Brown)	20

THOMAS F. BROWNE
71	Vertigo 6325 250	WEDNESDAY'S CHILD (LP, gatefold sleeve, swirl label)	120

(see also Gary Wright)

TOM BROWNE
80	Arista ARIST 12357	Funkin' For Jamaica (N.Y.)/Her Silent Smile (12")	8

DUKE BROWNER
79	Grapevine GRP 145	Crying Over You/Crying Over You (Instrumental)	20

(see also Kaddo Strings)

BROWNHILL'S STAMP DUTY
69	Columbia DB 8625	Maxwell's Silver Hammer/My Woman's Back	8

BROWNS
59	RCA RCA 1140	The Three Bells/Heaven Fell Last Night (78 rpm = £6)	5
59	RCA RCA 1157	Scarlet Ribbons (For Her Hair)/Blue Bells Ring (78 rpm = £6)	5
60	RCA RCA 1176	Teen-Ex/The Old Lamplighter	5
60	RCA RCA 1193	Margo (The Ninth Of May)/Lonely Little Robin	5
60	RCA RCA 1218	Send Me The Pillow You Dream On/You're So Much A Part Of Me	5
60	RCA RCX 587/SRC 7036	IN THE COUNTRY (EP, mono/stereo)	22/25
59	RCA RD 27153/SF 5052	SWEET SOUNDS BY THE BROWNS (LP, mono/stereo)	25/28

(see also Jim Edward & Maxine Brown)

BROWN'S FERRY FOUR
54	Parlophone CMSP 11	I Need The Prayers/Through The Pearly Gates (with Clyde Moody, export issue)	25

(see also Delmore Brothers, Grandpa Jones, Merle Travis)

BROWN SUGAR
70s	Lovers Rock CJ 613	I'm In Love With A Dreadlocks/Version	15

ANNETTE (Reis) & VICTOR BROX
65	Fontana TF 536	I've Got The World In A Jug/Wake Me And Shake Me	15
74	Sonet SNTF 663	ROLLIN' BACK (LP)	15

(see also Aynsley Dunbar Retaliation)

DAVE BRUBECK (QUARTET)
53	Vogue 45-2156	A Foggy Day/Lyons Busy	6
53	Vogue 45-2157	Mam'selle/Me And My Shadow	6
53	Vogue 45-2158	Frenesi/At A Perfume Counter	6
53	Vogue 45-2159	Body And Soul/Let's Fall In Love	6
53	Vogue 45-2160	I'll Remember April/Singin' In The Rain	6
53	Vogue 45-2161	Lullaby In Rhythm/You Stepped Out Of A Dream	6
54	Vogue V 2171	At A Perfume Counter/Me And My Shadow	6
54	Vogue V 2206	Frenesi/Mam'selle	6
60	Philips JAZ 106	I'm In A Dancing Mood/Lover (p/s)	6
61	Fontana H 339	Take Five/Blue Rondo A La Turk	5
61	CBS AAG 102	The Unsquare Dance/Camptown Races	5
62	Fontana H 352	It's A Raggy Waltz/Blue Shadows In The Street	5
54	Vogue LDE 090	DAVE BRUBECK TRIO (10" LP)	15
54	Vogue LDE 095	DAVE BRUBECK QUARTET (10" LP)	15
54	Vogue LDE 104	DAVE BRUBECK QUARTET VOL. 2 (10" LP)	15
55	Vogue LDE 114	DAVE BRUBECK QUARTET VOL. 3 (10" LP)	18
57	Fontana TFL 5017	DAVE DIGS DISNEY (LP)	15
57	Philips BBL 7147	AT NEWPORT (LP, with J.J. Johnson and Kei Winding)	12
59	Vogue LAE 12008	THE FABULOUS DAVE BRUBECK TRIO AND OCTET (LP)	15
59	Fontana TFL 5071	GONE WITH THE WIND (LP, also stereo STFL 501)	15
60	Vogue LAE 12114	DAVE BRUBECK QUARTET FEATURING PAUL DESMOND (LP)	15
66	CBS 62643	MY FAVOURITE THINGS (LP)	15
67	CBS 62921	ANYTHING GOES — THE MUSIC OF COLE PORTER (LP)	15

(see also Jimmy Rushing, Carmen McRae)

JACK BRUCE
65	Polydor BM 56036	I'm Getting Tired (Of Drinking And Gambling)/Rootin' Tootin'	50
71	Polydor 2058 153	The Consul At Sunset/Letter Of Thanks	5
74	RSO 2090 141	Keep It Down/Golden Days	5
69	Polydor 583 058	SONGS FOR A TAILOR (LP, gatefold sleeve)	25
70	Polydor 2343 033	THINGS WE LIKE (LP)	18
71	Polydor 2310 070	THINGS WE LIKE (LP, reissue)	12
71	Polydor 2310 107	HARMONY ROW (LP, gatefold sleeve)	15
74	RSO 2394 143	OUT OF THE STORM (LP, with insert)	12

*(see also Alexis Korner's Blues Incorporated, Cream, Manfred Mann, Graham Bond Organisation,
John Mayall, West Bruce & Laing, Lifetime, Rocket 88, Carla Bley, Duffy Power, Cozy Powell)*

LENNY BRUCE
69	Transatlantic TRA 195	BERKELEY CONCERT (2-LP)	22

TOMMY BRUCE (& BRUISERS)

60	Columbia DB 4453	Ain't Misbehavin'/Got The Water Boilin' (with Bruisers)	5
60	Columbia DB 4498	Broken Doll/I'm On Fire (with Bruisers)	8
60	Columbia DB 4532	On The Sunny Side Of The Street/My Little Girl (with Bruisers)	8
61	Columbia DB 4581	You Make Love So Well/I'm Crazy 'Bout My Baby (with Bruisers)	8
61	Columbia DB 4682	Love, Honour And Oh! Baby/I'm Gonna Sit Right Down And Write	10
62	Columbia DB 4776	Babette/Honey Girl, You're Lonely	10
62	Columbia DB 4850	Horror Movies/It's You	12
62	Columbia DB 4927	Buttons And Bows/London Boys	5
63	Columbia DB 7025	Let's Do It, Let's Fall In Love/Two Feet Left	5
63	Columbia DB 7132	Lavender Blue/Sixteen Years Ago Tonight	5
64	Columbia DB 7241	Let It Be Me/No More	5
64	Columbia DB 7387	Over Suzanne/It's Drivin' Me Wild	5
65	Polydor BM 56006	Boom Boom/Can Your Monkey Do The Dog (with Bruisers)	20
66	RCA RCA 1535	Monster Gonzales/I Hate Getting Up In The Morning	18
68	CBS CBS 3405	I've Been Around Too Long/Where The Colour Of The Soil Is Different	5
68	CBS CBS 3937	Heartbreak Melody/The Reason Why	7
61	Columbia SEG 8077	KNOCKOUT (EP)	100+

BRUCE & ROBIN ROCKERS

66	Marble Arch MAL 626	THE BATMAN THEME (LP)	18

CLAUDIA BRÜCKEN

90	Island 12ISX 471	Absolut[e] (Bastille Mix)/Absolut[e] (Shooting Star Mix) (12", remix, stickered title sleeve, promo only)	8

(see also Propaganda, Act, Glenn Gregory & Claudia Brücken)

HEIDI BRÜHL

60	Philips PB 1095	Ring Of Gold/I'll Belong To You Forever (some in p/s)	10/5
63	Philips 345 579 BF	Marcel/Talk It Over With Someone	5

BRUISERS

63	Parlophone R 5042	Blue Girl/Don't Cry	15
63	Parlophone R 5092	Your Turn To Cry/Give It To Me	15

(see also [Peter] Lee Stirling & Bruisers)

BRUMBEATS

64	Decca F 11834	Cry Little Girl, Cry/I Don't Understand	20

BEAU BRUMMEL ESQUIRE

65	Columbia DB 7447	I Know Know Know/Shoppin' Around	6
65	Columbia DB 7538	The Next Kiss/Come And Get Me	6
65	Columbia DB 7675	A Better Man Than I/Teardrops	6
66	Columbia DB 7878	You Don't Know What You've Got/Take Me Like I Am	6

GEORGE BRUNIS

54	London AL 3536	NEW ORLEANS RHYTHM KINGS (LP)	20

BRUNNING (HALL) SUNFLOWER BLUES BAND

68	Saga FID 2118	BULLEN STREET BLUES (LP, as Brunning Sunflower Blues Band)	20
69	Saga EROS 8132	TRACKSIDE BLUES (LP)	40
70	Saga EROS 8150	I WISH YOU WOULD (LP, as Brunning Sunflower Blues Band)	55
71	Gemini GM 2010	THE BRUNNING/HALL SUNFLOWER BLUES BAND (LP)	65

(see also Five's Company, Fleetwood Mac, Leaf Hound)

BRUNO

66	Parlophone R5450	Wonderboy/Window In My Room	28

TONY BRUNO

68	Capitol CL 15534	What's Yesterday/Small Town, Bring Down	40

BRUTE FORCE

69	Apple APPLE 8	King Of Fuh/Nobody Knows (unissued)	600+

BRUTUS

75	Purple PUR 126	Payroll/New Deal Princess	7

CARL BRYAN

69	Trojan TR 673	Red Ash/SILVERTONES: Bluebirds Flying Over	20
69	Duke DU 13	Soul Pipe/Overproof	15
69	Camel CA 22	Run For Your Life/TWO SPARKS: When We Were Young	12
69	Gas GAS 133	Stagger Back/The Creeper	15
69	Gas GAS 134	Walking The Dead/TREVOR & KEITH: Got What You Want	12

(see also Cannon Ball & Johnny Melody, King Cannon, Vincent Foster, Hugh Malcolm, King Cannonball, Glen Brown, Shenley Duffas, Alton Ellis, Kid Gungo, Jackie Mittoo, Johnny Moore, Joe White, Royals)

DORA BRYAN

55	HMV POP 133	My Only Love With Men/Why Did You Call Me Lily (78)	6
63	Fontana TF 427	All I Want For Christmas Is A Beatle/If I Were A Fairy	5

FITZVAUGHN BRYAN'S ORCHESTRA

60	Melodisc 45-1560	Evening News/Hold Up Your Head And Smile (with Kenrick Patrick)	10

RAD BRYAN

71	Techniques TE 909	Jumping Jack/ANSELL COLLINS: Point Blank	12
71	Bullet BU 463	Shock Attack/Cuban Waltz	12
71	Big Shot BI 559	Just Do The Right Things/Corporal Jones	10
71	Big Shot BI 591	I'll Be Right There (actually by Techniques)/PLAYBOYS: Hot Pants Rock	12
71	Big Shot BI 592	My Best Girl/My Best Girl Version	12
72	Attack ATT 8040	Standing In The Rain (actually by Neville Grant)/Standing In The Rain Version	8
75	Love 1	Rock Children/Version	7

V. BRYAN ORCHESTRA

55	Kay CRS 028	Tan Tan — Calypso/CYRIL DIAS: Brass Crown (Vocal: Lord Superior) (78)	10

WES BRYAN

58	London HLU 8607	Lonesome Love/Tiny Spaceman (78 rpm = £20)	40
59	London HLU 8978	Honey Baby/So Blue Over You (78 rpm = £35)	50

BRYAN & BRUNELLES

65	HMV POP 1394	Jacqueline/Louie Louie	60

ANITA BRYANT

59	London HLL 8983	Six Boys And Seven Girls/The Blessings Of Love (78 rpm = £15)	10
60	London HLL 9075	Little George (Got The Hiccoughs)/Love Look Away	10
60	London HLL 9114	Paper Roses/Mixed Emotions	5
60	London HLL 9171	In My Little Corner Of The World/Just In Time	5
60	London HLL 9219	One Of the Lucky Ones/The Party's Over	6
60	London HLL 9247	Wonderland By Night/Pictures	6
61	London HLL 9281	Till There Was You/A Texan And A Girl From Mexico	6
61	London HLL 9353	Do-Re-Mi/An Angel Cried	6
61	Philips BF 1182	The Wedding/Seven Kinds Of Lonesome	6
66	CBS 202026	Another Year, Another Love/My Mind's Playing Tricks On Me Again	75
62	CBS AAG 20005	KISSES SWEETER THAN WINE (EP)	18
61	London HA-L 2381	IN MY LITTLE CORNER OF THE WORLD (LP)	55

BOOD & FILEECE (Boudleaux & Felice) BRYANT

51	MGM MGM 452	Overweight Blues/I Dreamed Of A Wedding (78)	6

BOUDLEAUX BRYANT

60	Polydor NH 66952	Hot Spot/Touché (with Sparks)	10
	(see also Bood & Fileece Bryant)		

DON BRYANT

70	London HA-U/SH-U 8409	PRECIOUS SOUL (LP)	50

JOHN BRYANT

65	Fontana H 625	Tell Me What You See/Poor Unfortunate Me	15

LAURA K. BRYANT

58	London HLU 8551	Bobby/Angel Tears (78 rpm = £20)	40

MARIE/MARGARET BRYANT

54	Lyragon J 724	The Lost Watch (Tick Tick)/S. BETTANCOURT: Beater Pam (78)	6
54	Lyragon J 725	My Handy Man/RUSSEL HENDERSON: Bacchanal (78)	6
54	Lyragon J 726	Banana Woman/"SHAKE" KEANE: Creole Honey (78)	6
61	Kalypso XX 27	Water Melon/Tomato	6
61	Kalypso XX 28	Don't Touch Me Nylon/Little Boy	6
60s	Melodisc MLP 12 132	DON'T TOUCH ME NYLONS (LP, with or without sleeve)	25/15

MATT BRYANT & LINDA JOYCE

60	Embassy WB 420	Goodness Gracious Me/STEVE STANNARD & HIS GROUP: Man Of Mystery	5
	(see also Maureen Evans)		

RAY BRYANT TRIO/COMBO

60	Pye International 7N 25052	Little Susie Parts 2 & 4	6
60	Philips PB 1003	Little Susie Parts 1 & 3	6
60	Philips PB 1014	The Madison Time Parts 1 & 2	10

RUSTY BRYANT

57	London HB-D 1066	RUSTY BRYANT (10" LP)	70+
72	Prestige PRST 10014	FIRE EATER (LP)	15

SANDRA BRYANT

67	Major Minor MM 523	Girl With Money/Golden Hours	5
68	Major Minor MM 553	Out To Get You/There's No Lock Upon My Door	25

GAVIN BRYARS

75	Obscure 1	THE SINKING OF THE TITANIC (LP)	12
	(see also Brian Eno)		

CALUM BRYCE

68	Condor PS 1001	Lovemaker/I'm Glad	300+

BERYL BRYDEN('S BACK-ROOM SKIFFLE)

56	Decca F 10823	Casey Jones/Kansas City Blues (78 rpm = £15)	40
57	Decca (no cat. no.)	Rock Me/This Train (test pressing, with Alexis Korner & Cyril Davies)	150+
56	Melodisc EPM 7-69	BERYL BRYDEN WITH FATTY GEORGE'S JAZZ BAND (EP)	10
63	Columbia DB 7010	I'm Living With The Blues/Big Daddy	15
	(see also Alexis Korner, Cyril Davies)		

BETSY BRYE

59	Columbia DB 4350	Sleep Walk/Daddy Daddy (Gotta Get A Phone In My Room)	25

B.T.

94	Perfecto SAM 1517	EMBRACING THE SUNSHINE (Original & Sasha Mixes) (12", double pack, promo only)	12
94	Perfecto SAM 1652	LOVING YOU MORE (12", double pack, promo only)	10
95	Perfecto SAM 1688	TRIPPING THE LIGHT FANTASTIC (12", 1-sided LP sampler, promo only)	20
95	Perfecto SAM 1690	DIVINITY (12", 1-sided LP sampler, promo only)	15
95	Perfecto SAM 1691	QUARK (12", 1-sided LP sampler, promo only)	15

B.T.B.

68	Liberty LBF 15067	Do It To 'Em/Sparrows And Daisies	20

B.T. EXPRESS

75	Pye International 7N 25674	Express (Parts 1 & 2)	6
75	Pye International 7N 25682	Once You Get It/This House Is Smokin'	8
75	Pye Intl. NSPL 28207	DO IT (TIL YOU'RE SATISFIED) (LP)	20
75	EMI International INA 1501	NON-STOP (LP)	15

B.T.P. FOLDERS
80	Future Earth FER 005	Radio/All Of A Sudden (p/s)	50

B12
93	Warp WAPLP 9LTD	ELECTRO — SOMA (2-LP, orange vinyl)	40
93	B12 09 CASSETTE	PRELUDE PART 1 (cassette, 400 only)	20
93	B12 09 CD	PRELUDE PT 1 (CD, 500 only)	25
93	B12 CD 1	REDCELL & STASIS (CD, 1500 only)	20
94	B12 15	B12 (12", 4-track promo only, 10 copies pressed)	40

(see also Redcell, Musicology)

BUBA & SHOP ASSISTANTS
85	Villa 21 002	Something To Do/Dreaming Backwards (p/s, with insert in poly bag)	25

(see also Shop Assistants, Pastels)

BUBBLES
63	Duke DK 1001	The Wasp/Bopping In The Barnyard (matrix: DK 1001A-1, plays Rocking Crickets by Hot Toddy's)	25

BUCCA
82	Plant Life PLR 039	THE HOLE IN THE HARPERS HEAD (LP)	20

BUCHANAN BROTHERS
69	Page One POF 139	Medicine Man Part 1/Part 2	6

LINDSAY BUCKINGHAM
81	Mercury MER 85	Trouble/That's How We Do It In L.A. (p/s)	5
82	Mercury MER 96	The Visitor (Bwana)/A Satisfied Mind (p/s)	6
82	Mercury MER 102	Mary Lee Jones/September Song (p/s)	6
83	Mercury MER 150	Holiday Road/Mary Lee Jones (p/s)	8
84	Mercury MER 168	Go Insane/Play In The Rain (p/s)	5
84	Mercury MER 176	Slow Dancing/D.W. Suite (p/s)	8
92	Mercury MER 371	Countdown/This Nearly Was Mine (p/s)	5
92	Mercury MER 380	Soul Drifter/Say You'll Meet Again (p/s)	5

BUCKINGHAM-NICKS
74	Polydor 2066 398	Don't Let Me Down Again/Races Are Run	15
76	Polydor 2066 700	Don't Let Me Down Again/Crystal	10
73	Polydor 2391 013	BUCKINGHAM-NICKS (LP, with insert, some with stickered sleeve)	30/35
81	Polydor 2482 378	BUCKINGHAM-NICKS (LP, reissue with insert)	25

(see also Lindsay Buckingham, Stevie Nicks, Fleetwood Mac)

BUCKINGHAMS (U.K.)
65	Pye 7N 15848	I'll Never Hurt You No More/She Lied	7
65	Pye 7N 15921	To Be Or Not To Be/I Was Your First Guy	10

BUCKINGHAMS (U.S.)
67	Stateside SS 588	Kind Of A Drag/You Make Me Feel So Good	20
68	CBS 2640	Don't You Care/Why Don't You Love Me	30
68	CBS 3559	Back In Love Again/You Misunderstand Me	6

JEFF BUCKLEY
95	Columbia 662042 1	Last Goodbye (Edit)/Lover, You Should've Come Over (Live And Acoustic In Japan)/Tongue (Live) (10", p/s, 5000 only)	12
93	Big Cat ABB 61XCD	LIVE AT SIN-E EP (Mojo Pin/Eternal Life/Je N'en Connais Pas La Fin/The Way Young Lovers Do (CD)	12
95	Columbia 661107 2	THE GRACE EP (Grace (Edit)/Tongue/Kanga-Roo/Grace) (CD)	8
94	Columbia 475928	GRACE (LP)	12
98	Columbia 3C 67228	SKETCHES (FOR MY SWEETHEART, THE DRUNK) (3-LP, gatefold sleeve)	20
00	Columbia 4979721	MYSTERY WHITE BOY LIVE 95-96 (LP)	12

SEAN BUCKLEY & BREADCRUMBS
65	Stateside SS 421	It Hurts Me When I Cry/Everybody Knows	70

TIM BUCKLEY
67	Elektra EKSN 45008	Aren't You The Girl/Strange Street Affair Under Blue	12
67	Elektra EKSN 45018	Morning Glory/Knight-Errant	7
68	Elektra EKSN 45023	Once I Was/Phantasmagoria In Two	7
68	Elektra EKSN 45031	Wings/I Can't See You	7
68	Elektra EKSN 45041	Pleasant Street/Carnival Song	7
70	Straight S 4799	Happy Time/So Lonely	7
66	Elektra EKL/EKS 4004	TIM BUCKLEY (LP, orange label)	60
67	Elektra EKL/EKS 318	GOODBYE AND HELLO (LP, orange label, gatefold sleeve)	40
68	Elektra 74045	HAPPY SAD (LP, orange label)	30
69	Straight STS 1060	BLUE AFTERNOON (LP)	30
70	Elektra 2410 005	LORCA (LP)	30
71	Straight STS 1064	STARSAILOR (LP)	35
72	Warner Bros K 46176	GREETINGS FROM L.A. (LP, gatefold sleeve)	20
74	Discreet K 49201	SEFRONIA (LP)	20
74	Discreet K 59204	LOOK AT THE FOOL (LP)	22
91	Strange Fruit SFPS082	THE PEEL SESSIONS: Morning Glory/Coming Home To You/Sing A Song For You/Hallucinations/Troubadour/Once I Was (12", p/s)	10

VERNON BUCKLEY
73	Grape GR 3057	Mr Softhand/G.G. ALLSTARS: Dub	6
73	Grape GR 3058	Ital Queen/G.G. ALLSTARS: Dub	6

MILT BUCKNER & HIS MUSIC
56	Capitol CL 14662	Night Mist/Good Time Express	5

TEDDY BUCKNER & HIS BAND
56	Vogue V 2369	Oh, Didn't He Ramble/Battle Hymn Of The Republic	7
56	Vogue V 2375	When The Saints Go Marching In/West End Blues	7
57	Vogue V 2414	Sweet Georgia Brown/That's My Home	7

BUCKY & STRINGS
62	Salvo SLO 1807	Lolita's On The Loose/Lonely Island (99 copies only)	30

BUD & HIS BUDDIES
58	Starlite ST45 006	June, July And August/Sing A Little Sweeter	5

BUD & TRAVIS
59	London HLU 8965	Bonsoir Dame/Truly Do (78 rpm = £12)	10
60	London HLG 9211	The Ballad Of The Alamo/The Green Leaves Of Summer	10
61	London HA-G 2328	BUD AND TRAVIS IN CONCERT (LP, also stereo SAH-G 6128)	18/20

ROY BUDD
65	Pye 7N 15807	Birth Of The Budd/M'Ghee M'Ghee	6
66	Parlophone R 5514	Summer Samba/Bahama Sound	5
67	Pye 7N 17279	Mr Rose/Summer Rain	6
68	Pye 7N 17652	Pavanne/Whizz Ball	5
69	Pye 7N 17773	Tijuana Piano/Lead On	5
70	Pye 7N 17987	Borsalino (Theme)/It Only Goes To Show	5
70	Pye 7N 45051	Carter (Theme)/Plaything (some in p/s)	50/60
67	Pye N(S)PL 18177	PICK YOURSELF UP — THIS IS ROY BUDD (LP)	25
67	Pye N(S)PL 18195	THE SOUND OF MUSIC (LP)	15
68	Pye NPL 18212	AT NEWPORT (LP)	25
69	Pye N(S)PL 18305	LEAD ON (LP)	20
71	Pye NSPL 18348	PLAYS SOLDIER BLUE AND OTHER THEMES (LP)	40
71	Pye NSPL 18354	BUDD 'N' BOSSA (LP)	25
71	Pye NSPL 18373	GREAT SONGS AND THEMES FROM GREAT FILMS (LP)	50
72	Pye NSPL 18389	CONCERTO FOR HARRY — SOMETHING TO HIDE (LP, soundtrack)	35
72	Polydor 2383 102	KIDNAPPED (LP, soundtrack, with Mary Hopkin)	25
73	Pye NSPL 18398	FEAR IS THE KEY (LP, soundtrack)	85
76	Bradley's BRADS 8002	DIAMONDS (LP, soundtrack)	20
70s	Pye NSPL 19494	EVERYTHING'S COMING UP (LP)	15

BUDDY & JUNIORS
(see under Buddy Guy)

BUDDY & SKETTO
62	Dice 45/CC 7	Little Schoolgirl/Hush Baby	12

(see also Father Sketto, Ruddy & Sketto, Sketto Rich)

BUDGIE
71	MCA MK 5072	Crash Course In Brain Surgery/Nude Disintegrating Parachutist Woman	15
72	MCA MK 5085	Whisky River/Guts	10
74	MCA MCA 133	Zoom Club (Edited Version)/Wondering What Everyone Knows	8
75	MCA MCA 175	I Ain't No Mountain/Honey	8
78	A&M AMS 7342	Smile Boy Smile/All At Sea	8
80	Active BUDGE	Wildfire/Wildfire (promo only)	12
80	Active BUDGE 1	IF SWALLOWED DO NOT INDUCE VOMITING (12" EP)	12
80	Active BUDGE 2	Crime Against The World/Hellbender (p/s)	8
81	RCA BUDGE 3	Keeping A Rendezvous/Apparatus (p/s)	5
81	RCA BUDGE 3	Keeping A Rendezvous/Apparatus (picture disc)	5
81	RCA BUDGE 4	I Turned To Stone (Part 1)/I Turned To Stone (Part 2) (orange vinyl)	6
82	RCA RCA 271	Bored With Russia/Don't Cry (poster p/s)	6
82	RCA RCAP 271	Bored With Russia/Don't Cry (picture disc)	5
71	MCA MKPS 2018	BUDGIE (LP, pink/red label, initially with poster)	40/25
71	MCA MKPS 2018	BUDGIE (LP, later pressing with blue/black label)	20
73	MCA MCF 2506	BUDGIE (LP, reissue, rainbow label)	12
72	MCA MKPS 2023	SQUAWK (LP, blue/black label)	15
73	MCA MDKS 8010	NEVER TURN YOUR BACK ON A FRIEND (LP, blue/black label, g/fold sleeve)	15
74	MCA MCF 2546	IN FOR THE KILL (LP)	12
75	MCA MCF 2723	BANDOLIER (LP)	12
75	MCA MCF 2766	THE BEST OF BUDGIE (LP)	12
76	A&M AMLH 68377	IF I WAS BRITANNIA I'D WAIVE THE RULES (LP)	12
78	A&M AMLH 64675	IMPECKABLE (LP)	12
80	Active ACTLP 1	POWER SUPPLY (LP, with insert)	12
81	RCA RCALP 3046	POWER SUPPLY (LP, reissue, with different back sleeve)	12
81	RCA RCALP 6003	NIGHT FLIGHT (LP)	12
82	RCA RCALP 6054	DELIVER US FROM EVIL (LP)	12

(see also Tredegar, Phenomena, George Hatcher Band)

DENNIS BUDLIMAR
67	Fontana TL 5307	THE CREEPER (LP)	15

BUENA VISTAS
66	Stateside SS 525	Hot Shot/T.N.T.	30

BUFFALO
81	Heavy Metal HEAVY 3	Battle Torn Heroes/Women Of The Night (p/s)	30
82	Heavy Metal HEAVY 15	Mean Machine/The Rumour (p/s)	25

BUFFALO SPRINGFIELD
67	Atlantic 584 077	For What It's Worth (Stop Hey What's That Sound)/Do I Have To Come Right Out And Say It	10
67	Atlantic 584 145	Rock'n'Roll Woman/A Child's Claim To Fame	10
68	Atlantic 584 165	Expecting To Fly/Everydays	10
68	Atlantic 584 189	Uno-Mundo/Merry-Go-Round	10
69	Atco 226 006	Pretty Girl Why/Questions	10
72	Atlantic K 10237	Bluebird/Mr Soul/Rock'n'Roll Woman/Expecting To Fly (p/s)	5
67	Atlantic 587/588 070	BUFFALO SPRINGFIELD (LP, plum label, mispressing, lists For What It's Worth but plays Baby Don't Scold Me; matrix no. ends '1'; mono/stereo)	60/40
67	Atlantic 587/588 070	BUFFALO SPRINGFIELD (LP, plum label, plays For What It's Worth)	40/30

MINT VALUE £

68	Atlantic 587/588 091	BUFFALO SPRINGFIELD AGAIN (LP, plum label, mono/stereo) 40/30
69	Atco 228 024	LAST TIME AROUND (LP, plum label, gatefold sleeve) 20
69	Atco 228 012	RETROSPECTIVE (LP, plum label) 15
70	Atlantic 2464 012	EXPECTING TO FLY (LP, plum label) 20
72	Atlantic K 40014	BUFFALO SPRINGFIELD AGAIN (LP, reissue, green & orange label) 20
72	Atlantic K 40077	LAST TIME AROUND (LP, reissue, green & orange label, gatefold sleeve) 12
73	Atlantic K 30028	BEGINNINGS (ATLANTIC MASTERS) (LP, green & orange label) 12

(see also Neil Young, Stephen Stills, Poco, Au-Go-Go Singers, Crosby Stills Nash & Young)

BUFFALO TOM
| 89 | Caff CAFF 6 | Enemy/Deep In The Ground (p/s) . . . . 25 |

BUFF MEDWAYS
| 00s | Transcopic TRAN 012 | A Strange Kind Of Happyness/BILLY CHILDISH: Hound Dog (p/s, 500 only) . . . . . . 8 |
| 00s | Transcopic TRAN 015 | Troubled Mind/BILLY CHILDISH: Leave My Kitten Alone (p/s, 500 only) . . . . 8 |

BUFFOONS
| 67 | Columbia DB 8317 | My World Fell Down/Tomorrow Is Another Day . . . . 18 |

THE BUG
| 99 | Fat Cat 12FAT 032 | LOWRIDER EP (12", custom sleeve) . . . . 8 |

BUG CENTRAL
| 00 | BBP/Yellow Fever BBPV 5 | MONEY & RIOTS EP (with inserts) . . . . 8 |
| 99 | Helen Of Troy HOO 48 | THE MEEK WILL INHERIT NOTHING (LP, with inserts) . . . . 15 |

SANDY BULL
| 69 | Vanguard 19040 | E PLURIBUS UNUM (LP) . . . . 20 |

BULLAMAKANKA
| 83 | BBC REL 454 | Dr Who Is Gonna Fix It/Harlequin . . . . 6 |

JOHN BULL BREED
| 66 | Polydor BM 56065 | Can't Chance A Breakup/I'm A Man . . . . 350 |

BULLDOG BREED
| 69 | Deram DM 270 | Portcullis Gate/Halo In My Hair . . . . 55 |
| 70 | Deram Nova (S)DN 5 | MADE IN ENGLAND (LP) . . . . 100 |

(see also Flies)

BULLDOGS
| 64 | Mercury MF 808 | John, Paul, George And Ringo/What Do I See . . . . 10 |

BULLET
| 71 | Purple PUR 101 | Hobo/Sinister Minister . . . . 8 |

(see also Hard Stuff)

BULLET
| 75 | Contour 2870 437 | THE HANGED MAN (LP, TV soundtrack) . . . . 60 |

BULLSEYE
| 80 | Kennet K1 | No. 10,553/Why Don't You Let Me Know . . . . 8 |

BULLY BOYS BAND
| 70 | Stateside SSL 5032 | MOVIE SCENE — HEAVY SOUNDS FROM TODAY'S FILMS (LP) . . . . 15 |

BULLY WEE (BAND)
75	Folksound	BULLYWEE (LP) 20
76	Red Rag RRR 007	THE ENCHANTED LADY (LP) 15
70s	Red Rag RRR 017	SILVERMINES (LP, as Bullywee Band) 12
81	Jigsaw SAW 1	THE MADMAN OF GOTHAM (LP) 20

B. BUMBLE & STINGERS
61	Top Rank JAR 561	Bumble Boogie/School Day Blues 15
62	Top Rank JAR 611	Nut Rocker/Nautilus 10
62	Stateside SS 113	Apple Knocker/The Moon And The Sea 12
62	Stateside SS 131	Dawn Cracker/Scales 12
63	Stateside SS 192	Baby Mash/Night Time Madness 12
67	Mercury MF 977	Silent Movies/Twelfth Street Rag 10
72	Pye International 7N 25597	Down At Mother's Place/Manhattan Spiritual 10
62	Stateside SE 1001	THE PIANO STYLINGS OF B. BUMBLE (EP) 30

(see also Kim Fowley)

BUMBLE BEE SLIM
| 60s | Fontana 688 138ZL | BEE'S BACK IN TOWN (LP) . . . . 30 |

BUMBLES
| 72 | Purple PUR 107 | Beep Beep/Buzz Off (some in promo only p/s) . . . . 25/8 |

BUNCH
67	CBS 202506	We're Not What We Appear To Be/You Never Came Home 70
67	CBS 2740	Don't Come Back To Me/You Can't Do This 15
67	CBS 3060	Looking Glass Alice/Spare A Shilling 150
68	CBS 3692	Birthday/Still 30
68	CBS 3709	Birthday/Still (reissue) 15

(see also Peter & The Wolves, Sounds Around, John Pantry)

BUNCH
| 69 | Beacon BEA 128 | Red Rover, Red Rover/Happy Like This . . . . 5 |

BUNCH
| 72 | Island WIP 6130 | When Will I Be Loved/Willie And The Hand Jive . . . . 8 |
| 72 | Island ILPS 9189 | ROCK ON (LP, some with 1-sided flexi: Let There Be Drums [WI 4002]) . . . . 40/18 |

(see also Fairport Convention, Sandy Denny, Richard & Linda Thompson, Ashley Hutchings, Trevor Lucas)

MINT VALUE £

BUNCH OF FIVES
66	Parlophone R 5494	Go Home Baby/At The Station.	70

(see also Viv Prince, Egg, Hullaballoos, Junior's Eyes, Outsiders [U.K.])

BUNDLE
70	Polydor 2058 029	Dirty La Rue/Progressive Underground	15

ROGER BUNN
70	Major Minor SMLP 70	PIECE OF MIND (LP)	75

BUNNIES
66	Decca F 12350	Thumper/Ja Da	5

BUNNIES (OF LONDON)
68	Decca LK4951	CAUGHT LIVE AT THE PLAYBOY CLUB (LP).	18
69	Decca SKL5026	THE BUNNIES AGAIN SINGIN' AND SWINGIN' AT THE LONDON PLAYBOY CLUB (LP)	18

BINGY BUNNY & BONGO LES
73	Ackee ACK 506	International Scout/International Scout Version	12

(see also Bongo Les, Mediators)

BUNNY & RUDDY
68	Nu Beet NB 007	Rhythm & Soul/MONTY MORRIS: True Romance	25
68	Nu Beat NB 011	On The Town/MONTY MORRIS: Simple Simon	18

BUNNY WAILER
76	Island BUINNY 1	Blackheart Man/Amagideon (12")	20
77	Island IPR 2003	Get up stand up/This train (12")	20
78	Island IPR 2015	Love fire/Love's version (12")	15
78	Island IPR 2025	Roots, Radics, Rockers and Reggae/Fig tree/Armagideon (12")	25
79	Solomonic SM 001	Riding/Version (12")	30
81	Solomonic SM 01	Rise & Shine/Riding	18
81	Solomonic SM07	Rise & Shine/Solomonic Dub (12")	30
83	Solomonic SM 018	Boderation/THE SOLOMONIC PLAYERS - Badder ridim (12")	25

BOB BUNTING
68	Transatlantic TRA 166	YOU'VE GOT TO GO DOWN THIS WAY (LP)	45

VASHTI BUNYAN
70	Philips 6308 019	JUST ANOTHER DIAMOND DAY (LP)	600

(see also Vashti, Fairport Convention, Dave Swarbrick, Robin Williamson)

ERIC BURDON (BAND)
75	Capitol E-ST 11359	SUN SECRETS (LP, as Eric Burdon Band)	12
75	Capitol E-ST 11426	STOP (LP, as Eric Burdon Band)	12
78	Polydor 2302 078	SURVIVOR (LP, with 8-page booklet)	12
80	Polydor 2344 147	DARKNESS — DARKNESS (LP)	12

ERIC BURDON & THE ANIMALS
66	Decca F 12502	Mama Told Me Not To Come/See See Rider (unreleased)	
66	Decca F 12502	Help Me Girl/See See Rider (amended issue with new A-side)	8
67	MGM MGM 1340	When I Was Young/A Girl Named Sandoz	8
67	MGM MGM 1344	Good Times/Ain't That So	8
67	MGM MGM 1359	San Franciscan Nights/Gratefully Dead	15
68	MGM MGM 1373	Sky Pilot (Parts 1 & 2).	6
68	MGM MGM 1412	Monterey/Anything	8
69	MGM MGM 1461	Ring Of Fire/I'm An Animal.	10
69	MGM MGM 1481	River Deep Mountain High/Help Me Girl.	12
67	MGM C(S) 8052	WINDS OF CHANGE (LP)	30
68	MGM C(S) 8074	THE TWAIN SHALL MEET (LP)	30
68	MGM C(S) 8105	LOVE IS (LP)	30
71	MGM 2619 002	LOVE IS (2-LP; individual LP nos.: 2354 006/7)	40

(see also Animals, Stud, Zoot Money's Big Roll Band)

ERIC BURDON & WAR
70	Polydor 2001 072	Spill The Wine/Magic Mountain	5
71	Liberty LBF 15434	They Can't Take Away Our Music/Home Cookin'	5
71	United Artists UP 35217	Paint It Black/Spirit	5
70	Polydor 2310 041	ERIC BURDON DECLARES WAR (LP)	12
70	Liberty LDS 8400	BLACKMAN'S BURDON (2-LP, some with banned track "P.C. 3")	30/20
76	ABC ABCL 5207	LOVE IS ALL AROUND (LP)	12

(see also War)

ERIC BURDON & JIMMY WITHERSPOON
71	United Artists UP 35287	Soledad/Headin' For Home.	6
71	United Artists UAG 29251	GUILTY! (LP, gatefold sleeve)	15

(see also Jimmy Witherspoon)

DAVE BURGESS (TRIO)
55	London HLB 8175	I Love Paris/Five Foot Two, Eyes Of Blue (Has Anybody Seen My Girl)	30
55	London HLB 8175	I Love Paris/Five Foot Two, Eyes Of Blue (Has Anybody Seen My Girl) (78)	10
58	Oriole CB 1413	I'm Available/Who's Gonna Cry? (78 rpm = £15)	100

SONNY BURGESS
60	London HLS 9064	Sadie's Back In Town/A Kiss Goodnight	250

JIM BURGETT
61	Philips PB 1133	Let's Investigate/The Living Dead	48

CHRIS DE BURGH
75	A&M AMS 7148	Hold On/Sin City	5
75	A&M AMS 7185	Flying/Watching The World	5
76	A&M AMS 7196	Lonely Sky/The Song For You	5
76	A&M AMS 7224	Patricia The Stripper/Old Friend	5

76	A&M AMS 7267	A Spaceman Came Travelling/Just A Poor Boy (initially in p/s)	6
77	A&M AMS 7320	Broken Wings/I Will	5
78	A&M AMS 7336	Discovery/Round And Around	5
78	A&M AMS 7347	Spanish Train/Perfect Day (initially in p/s)	5
80	A&M AMS 7546	Shadows And Lights/Walls Of Silence (initially in p/s)	5
80	A&M AMS 7562	The Traveller/Eastern Wind (initially in p/s)	5
81	A&M AMS 8160	Waiting For The Hurricane/Broken Wings (p/s)	5
82	A&M AMS 8268	The Getaway/Living On The Island (p/s)	5

KEVIN BURKE
| 78 | Rockburgh ROC 105 | IF THE CAP FITS (LP) | 25 |

SOLOMON BURKE
61	London HLK 9454	Just Out Of Reach/Be Bop Grandma	40
62	London HLK 9512	Cry To Me/I Almost Lost My Mind	75
62	London HLK 9560	Down In The Valley/I'm Hanging Up My Heart For You	20
63	London HLK 9715	If You Need Me/You Can Make It If You Try	20
63	London HLK 9763	Can't Nobody Love You/Stupidity	30
64	London HLK 9849	He'll Have To Go/Rockin' Soul	20
64	London HLK 9887	Goodbye Baby (Baby Goodbye)/Someone To Love Me	20
64	Atlantic AT 4004	Everybody Needs Somebody To Love/Looking For My Baby	20
64	Atlantic AT 4014	The Price/More Rockin' Soul	15
65	Atlantic AT 4022	Got To Get You Off My Mind/Peepin'	15
65	Atlantic AT 4030	Maggie's Farm/Tonight's The Night	20
65	Atlantic AT 4044	Someone Is Watching/Dance, Dance, Dance	15
65	Atlantic AT 4061	Only Love (Can Save Me Now)/Little Girl That Loves Me	15
66	Atlantic AT 4073	Baby Come On Home/No, No, No, I Can't Stop Lovin' You Now	15
66	Atlantic 584 005	I Feel A Sin Comin' On/Mountain Of Pride	8
66	Atlantic 584 026	Keep Lookin'/Suddenly	8
67	Atlantic 584 100	Keep A Light In The Window Till I Come Home/Time Is A Thief	8
67	Atlantic 584 122	Take Me (Just As I Am)/I Stayed Away Too Long	8
68	Atlantic 584 191	I Wish I Knew (How It Would Feel To Be Free)/It's Just A Matter Of Time	7
68	Atlantic 584 204	Save It/Meet Me In Church	7
68	Bell BLL 1047	Uptight Good Woman/I Can't Stop (No No No)	6
69	Bell BLL 1062	Proud Mary/What Am I Living For	10
74	Anchor ABC 4002	Midnight And You/I Have A Dream	5
63	London REK 1379	TONIGHT MY HEART SHE IS CRYING (EP)	75
65	Atlantic AET 6008	ROCK'N'SOUL (EP)	60
63	London HA-K 8018	SOLOMON BURKE'S GREATEST (LP)	75
64	Atlantic ATL 5009	ROCK'N'SOUL (LP)	50
66	Atlantic 587/588 016	THE BEST OF SOLOMON BURKE (LP)	50
66	Atlantic 590 004	KING OF ROCK'N'SOUL (LP, reissue)	20
68	Atlantic 587 105	KING SOLOMON (LP)	35
68	Atlantic 587/588 117	I WISH I KNEW (LP)	30
69	Bell MBLL/SBLL 118	PROUD MARY (LP)	20
72	MGM 2315 048	THE ELECTRONIC MAGNETISM (LP)	15

(see also Soul Clan)

SONNY BURKE (U.K.)
64	Black Swan WI 457	I Love You Still/It's Always A Pleasure	15
64	Black Swan WI 458	City In The Sky/Everyday I Love You More	15
65	Black Swan WI 469	Glad/Jeanie	15
65	Black Swan WI 470	Dance With Me/My Girl Can't Cook	15
65	Black Swan WI 471	Wicked People/Good Heaven Knows	15
66	Blue Beat BB 363	Blue Island/You Came And Left	12
67	Blue Beat BB 371	Look In Her Eyes/LLOYD CLARKE: Love Is Strange	12
67	Ska Beat JB272	Have Faith/Guinea Pig	18
68	Island ILP 972	THE SOUNDS OF SONNY BURKE (LP, mono only)	125

(see also Bob Andy, Gaylads, Ken Parker, Eddie Thornton Outfit, Glen Adams, Stranger Cole, Gaylads, Sonny & Yvonne)

SONNY BURKE OUTFIT
| 68 | Instant IN 003 | Baby Be My Girl/All You | 20 |

(see also Sonny Burke)

DAVE BURLAND
71	Trailer LER 2029	A DALESMAN'S LITANY (LP, red label)	25
72	Trailer LER 2082	DAVE BURLAND (LP)	20
75	Rubber RUB 012	SONGS AND BUTTERED HAYCOCKS (LP)	18
79	Rubber RUB 036	YOU CAN'T FOOL THE FAT MAN (LP)	15
80	Rubber RUB 012/036	DOUBLE TAKE (2-LP, reissue)	18

SASCHA BURLAND
| 61 | Philips PB 1152 | Gorilla Walk/Hole In My Soul | 5 |

BURMOE BROTHERS
| 85 | Wild Blue Yonder WBY 121 | Skin/Leber Oder Lippenstift/Under The Blanket Of Love (12", p/s) | 15 |

(see also Marc Almond, Nick Cave)

BURN
| 00s | Virgin HUTCDP 146 | Facing The Music (1-sided, numbered gold-embossed p/s, 1000 only) | 20 |

JEAN-JACQUES BURNEL
79	United Artists UP 36500	Freddie Laker (Concorde And Eurobus)/Ozymandias (p/s)	5
80	United Artists BP 361	Girl From The Snow Country/Ode To Joy (live)/	
		Do The European (live) (p/s, unissued)	350+
88	Stranglers Information Service S.I.S. 003	Goebbels, Mosley, God And Ingrams (fan club flexidisc, with issue 27 of *Strangled* fanzine)	8/5
88	Mau Mau P MAU 601	EUROMAN COMETH (LP, picture disc reissue)	12

JEAN-JACQUES BURNEL & DAVE GREENFIELD
84	Epic EPCA 4076	Rain And Dole And Tea/Consequences (p/s)	5

(see also, Blue Maxi, Stranglers)

FRANCES BURNETT
59	Coral Q 72374	Please Remember Me/How I Miss You So (triangular or round centre)	100/75
59	Coral Q 72374	Please Remember Me/How I Miss You So (78)	15

REV. J.C. BURNETT/REV. GATES/REV. MOSELEY
60	Fontana TFE 17265	TREASURES OF NORTH AMERICAN NEGRO MUSIC VOLUME 6: PREACHERS AND CONGREGATIONS (EP)	22

KING BURNETT
75	Dip DL 5056	I Man Free/UPSETTERS: Version	15
75	Dip DL 5073	Key Card/UPSETTERS: Domino Game	15

DORSEY BURNETTE
60	London HLN 9047	Juarez Town/(There Was A) Tall Oak Tree	22
60	London HLN 9160	Hey Little One/Big Rock Candy Mountain	30
61	London HLN 9365	(It's No) Sin/Hard Rock Mine	20
65	Tamla Motown TMG 534	Jimmy Brown/Everybody's Angel (DJ copy = £120)	75
69	Liberty LBF 15190	The Greatest Love/Thin Little, Simple Little, Plain Little Girl	8
63	London RE-D 1402	DORSEY BURNETTE SINGS (EP)	80
63	London HA-D 8050	DORSEY BURNETTE (LP)	100

(see also Johnny & Dorsey Burnette)

JOHNNY BURNETTE (TRIO)
96	Cruisin' The 50s CASB 003	The Train Kept A Rollin'/Sweet Love On My Mind (300 copies only) (78)	40
56	Vogue Coral Q 72177	Tear It Up/You're Undecided (as Johnny Burnette & Rock'N'Roll Trio)	500
56	Vogue Coral Q 72177	Tear It Up/You're Undecided (as Johnny Burnette & Rock'N'Roll Trio) (78)	200
57	Vogue Coral Q 72227	Honey Hush/Lonesome Train (as Johnny Burnette Trio) (78 rpm = £200)	500
57	Vogue Coral Q 72283	Touch Me/Eager Beaver Baby (as Johnny Burnette Trio) (78 rpm = £150)	200
60	London HLG 9172	Dreamin'/Cincinnati Fireball (78 rpm = £400)	15
60	London HLG 9254	You're Sixteen/I Beg Your Pardon	10
61	London HLG 9315	Little Boy Sad/Pledge Of Love	10
61	London HLG 9388	Girls/I've Got A Lot Of Things To Do	10
61	London HLG 9453	God Country And My Baby/Honestly I Do (withdrawn)	15
61	London HLG 9458	Settin' The Woods On Fire/I'm Still Dreaming	15
61	London HLG 9473	Big Big World/The Fool	15
62	Liberty LIB 55416	Clown Shoes/The Way I Am	15
62	Liberty LIB 55489	Damn The Defiant/Lonesome Waters	15
66	Liberty LIB 10235	Dreamin'/Little Boy Sad	6
62	Pye International 7N 25158	I Wanna Thank Your Folks/The Giant	10
63	Pye International 7N 25187	Remember Me/Time Is Not Enough	10
63	Capitol CL 15322	All Week Long/It Isn't There	25
64	Capitol CL 15347	Sweet Suzie/Walking Talking Doll	30

EXPORT SINGLES
60	London HLG 7104	You're Sixteen/Settin' The Woods On Fire	30
61	London HL 7109	Little Boy Sad/I Go Down To The River	30

EPs
60	London RE-G 1263	DREAMING	50
61	London RE-G 1291	LITTLE BOY SAD	60
61	London RE-G 1309	BIG BIG WORLD	50
61	London RE-G 1327	GIRLS	60
63	Liberty LEP 2091	HIT AFTER HIT	50
64	Capitol EAP 20645	FOUR BY BURNETTE	150

LPs
56	Coral LVC 10041	ROCK AND ROLL TRIO (10", as Johnny Burnette Trio)	750
61	London HA-G 2306	DREAMIN'	60
61	London HA-G 2349	YOU'RE SIXTEEN	60
61	London HA-G 2375	JOHNNY BURNETTE SINGS (also stereo SAH-G 6175)	100/120
62	Liberty LBY 1006	BURNETTE'S HITS AND OTHER FAVOURITES	50
64	Liberty LBY 1231	THE JOHNNY BURNETTE STORY	70
66	Ace Of Hearts AH 120	ROCK AND ROLL TRIO (reissue, as Johnny Burnette Trio)	30
68	Sunset SLS 50007E	DREAMIN'	15
68	Coral CP 10	TEAR IT UP (as Johnny Burnette Trio)	40

(see also Johnny & Dorsey Burnette)

JOHNNY & DORSEY BURNETTE
63	Reprise R 20153	Hey Sue/It Doesn't Matter Much	60

(see also Johnny Burnette, Dorsey Burnette)

SMILEY BURNETTE
50	Capitol CL 13388	Rudolph The Red-Nosed Reindeer/Grandaddy Frog (78)	10
54	London HL 8071	Lazy Locomotive/That Long White Line (78 rpm = £15)	75
54	London HL 8085	Chuggin' On Down "66"/Mucho Gusto (78 rpm = £15)	75

BURNING SPEAR
75	Fab FAB 240	Foggy Road/Version	20
78	Island Pre IPR 2027	Civilised Reggae/Social Living (12")	15
75	Island ILPS 9377	MARCUS GARVEY (LP)	12

(see also Irving Brown, King Cry Cry)

BURNING WITCH
98	Trip 005	CRIPPLED LUCIFER (CD, digipack)	20

BURNIN' RED IVANHOE
71	Warner Bros K 44062	BURNIN' RED IVANHOE (LP)	25
72	Dandelion 2310 145	W.W.W. (LP, gatefold sleeve)	30

JAN BURNNETTE
62	Oriole CB 1716	I Could Have Loved You So Well/The Miracle Of Life	15
62	Oriole CB 1742	All At Once/Does My Heartache Show?	10
62	Oriole CB 1761	Teddy/Trust In Me	15
63	Oriole CB 1807	The Boy I Used To Know/Unimportant Things	15
63	Oriole CB 1841	Till I Hear The Truth From You/Fall In Love	10
64	Oriole CB 1905	Let Me Make You Smile Again/No Regrets	15
64	Oriole CB 1920	Too Young/The Four Winds And The Seven Seas	15
64	Oriole CB 1949	Love, Let Me Not Hunger/The One I Love (Belongs To Somebody Else)	10

DENNIS BURNS
(see Mark Perry)

EDDIE 'GUITAR' BURNS
72	Action ACMP 100	BOTTLE UP AND GO (LP)	25
75	Big Bear BEAR 7	DETROIT BLACKBOTTOM (LP)	15

GILLIAN BURNS
69	Fontana TF 1044	Hop Skip And Jump/Merry Go Round	12

JACKIE BURNS & BELLES
63	MGM MGM 1226	He's My Guy/I Do The Best I Can	100

JIMMY BURNS
79	Grapevine GRP 118	I Really Love You/I Love You Girl	15

LISA BURNS
78	MCA MCF 2849	LISA BURNS (LP)	18

RANDY BURNS
68	Fontana STL 5520	EVENING OF THE MAGICIAN (LP)	30

RAY BURNS
53	Columbia SCM 5077	Rags To Riches/Begorrah	12
54	Columbia SCM 5153	I Can't Tell A Waltz From A Tango/Lonely Nightingale	12
56	Columbia DB 3811	Condemned For Life (With A Rock And Roll Life)/The Mare Piccola	40
57	Columbia DB 3966	Wonderful! Wonderful!/Bernadine	6
58	Columbia DB 4107	Are You Sincere/The Best Dream Of All	7
55	Columbia SEG 7594	RAY BURNS (EP)	20

(see also Ruby Murray, Ronnie Harris, Diana Decker, Ray Martin)

WILFRED BURNS
53	MGM SP 1059	There Was An Old Lady/Broken Horseshoe	6

BURNT OFFERING
94	Misanthropy 001	HVIS LYSET TAR OST (LP)	12
94	Misanthropy 002	DET SOMEGAG VAR (LP)	12

HAROLD BURRAGE
65	Sue WI 353	I'll Take One/A Long Ways Together	40
68	President PT 130	You Made Me So Happy/Take Me Now	22

KENNY BURRELL
61	Esquire 32-140	ALL NIGHT LONG (LP, as Kenny Burrell All Stars)	25
64	Verve VLP 9058	BLUE BLASH (LP, with Jimmy Smith)	20
65	Verve VLP 9099	GUITAR FORMS (LP)	15
66	Stateside SL 10163	CRASH! (LP, with Brother Jack McDuff)	15
68	Verve (S)VLP 9217	BLUES, THE COMMON GROUND (LP)	20
69	Verve SVLP 9246	NIGHT SONG (LP)	12
70	Verve SVLP 9250	ASPHALT CANYON SUITE (LP)	12

(see also Brother Jack McDuff, Jimmy Smith)

WILLIAM S. BURROUGHS
80	Industrial IR 0016	NOTHING HERE NOW BUT THE RECORDINGS (LP)	30

BUDDY BURTON
(see under Dixie Four)

HAL BURTON
58	Embassy WB 290	Rave On/Big Man (78)	10
58	Embassy WB 308	Move It/Susie Darling	22

GARY BURTON (QUARTET)
68	RCA Victor SF 7923	LOFTY FAKE ANAGRAM (LP)	30
69	RCA Victor SF 8015	GENUINE TONGUE FUNERAL (LP)	20
71	Atlantic 2400 107	GOOD VIBES (LP)	20
72	Atlantic K 40305	ALONE AT LAST (LP)	15
72	Atlantic K 40378	PARIS ENCOUNTER (LP, with Stefan Grappelli)	15

(see also Michael Gibbs)

JAMES BURTON
71	A&M AMLS 64293	THE GUITAR SOUNDS OF JAMES BURTON (LP)	65

(see also Jim & Joe, Shindogs)

TOMMY BURTON COMBO
64	Blue Beat BB 237	Lavender Blue/I'm Walking	20

TREVOR BURTON
71	Wizard WIZ 103	Fight For My Country/Janie Slow Down	20

(see also B,L&G; Uglys, Move, Balls, Denny Laine, Danny King's Mayfair Set, Magic Christians, Idle Race)

BURUNDI STEPHENSON BLACK
71	Barclay BAR 3	Burundi Black Parts 1 & 2 (some with p/s)	8/4

MINT VALUE £

BURZUM

93	Amazon 001	HVIS LYSET TAR OSS (LP, marbled vinyl)	40
94	Misanthropy 001	HVIS LYSET TAR OSS (LP)	20
94	Misanthropy 002	DET SOM ENGANG VAR (LP)	20
94	Amazon 002	DET SOM ENGANG VAR (LP, with poster)	40
95	Amazon 003	VURZUM/ASKE (LP)	40
96	Amazon 009	FILOSOFEM (3 – sided etched LP)	40
97	Amazon 013	DAUDI BALDRS (LP, with postcards)	25
99	Amazon 021	HILDSKJALF (LP)	20

BURU

83	CSA CSALP 04	BURO (LP)	30

LOU BUSCH & HIS ORCHESTRA

56	Capitol CL 14504	Zambesi/Rainbow's End	5

(see also Joe 'Fingers' Carr)

ERNIE BUSH

75	Contempo CS 2020	Breakaway/(Version 2)	8

KATE BUSH

78	EMI EMI 2719	Wuthering Heights/Kite (p/s)	30
78	EMI EMI 2806	The Man With The Child In His Eyes/Moving (p/s)	15
78	EMI EMI 2887	Hammer Horror/Coffee Homeground (p/s)	7
79	EMI EMI 2911	Wow/Fullhouse (p/s)	7
79	EMI MIEP 2991	KATE BUSH ON STAGE (EP, gatefold sleeve)	10
79	EMI PSR 442/3	KATE BUSH ON STAGE (EP, double pack, gatefold sleeve, promo only)	60
80	Sound For Industry SFI 562	Selected Highlights from Never Forever (flexidisc, black vinyl)	8
80	Sound For Industry SFI 562	Selected Highlights from Never Forever (square flexidisc, black vinyl)	8
81	EMI EMI 5201	Sat In Your Lap/Lord Of The Reedy River (p/s)	5
82	EMI EMI 5350	There Goes A Tenner/Ne T'Enfuis Pas (thick card, p/s)	5
84	EMI KBS 1	THE SINGLE FILE (13 x 7" box set with lyric booklet)	90
85	EMI KB 1	Running Up That Hill/Under The Ivy (gatefold p/s)	5
85	EMI 12 KB 2	Cloudbusting (Organon Mix)/Burning Bridges/My Lagan Love (12", p/s)	8
86	EMI KBP 4	The Big Sky (Single Mix)/Not This Time (picture disc)	8
89	EMI EMPD 119	This Woman's Work/Be Kind To My Mistakes (picture disc, with insert, PVC sleeve)	5
89	EMI 12EMP 119	This Woman's Work/Be Kind To My Mistakes/I'm Still Waiting (12", poster p/s)	8
89	EMI CDEM 119	This Woman's Work/Be Kind To My Mistakes/I'm Still Waiting (CD)	8
91	Rocket TRICD 2	Rocket Man/Candle In The Wind/Rocket Man (Instrumental) (CD, digipak)	8
93	EMI GIRL 1	Rubberband Girl (CD, 1-track "lyrical teaser", promo only)	15
93	EMI EM 280	Eat The Music/Big Stripey Lie (p/s, picture labels, release cancelled, 17 copies only)	1,500
93	EMI 12EMPD 280	Eat The Music/Eat The Music (Madagascan Remix)/Big Stripey Lie (12", picture disc, unissued)	
93	EMI CDEM 280	Eat The Music/(Madagascan Remix)/Big Stripey Lie (CD, unissued)	
93	EMI MUSIC 1	Eat The Music (CD, 1-track promo for unissued single, no inlay, withdrawn)	150
94	EMI EMPD 355	And So Is Love/Rubberband Girl (USA Mix) (picture disc, PVC sleeve, with 60" x 40" poster, unnumbered or 15,000 numbered)	18/6
05	EMI PROMO SAMPLER	KATE BUSH (CD in card sleeve, 9-track promotional back catalogue sampler Sent out prior to release of AERIAL album	20
05	EMI CDEMDJ674	KING OF THE MOUNTAIN (1-track promo single)	8

(The King Of The Mountain 12" remix single 'Kick Inside Remix/Cloudbusting Dub (600 copies) is an unofficial bootleg)

79	EMI EM CP 3223	THE KICK INSIDE (LP, picture disc, stickered sleeve)	50
79	EMI EM CP 3223	THE KICK INSIDE (LP, picture disc, stickered sleeve, second pressing with "manufactured in the U.K. by EMI Records Ltd" wording)	40
79	EMI EM CP 3223	THE KICK INSIDE (LP, picture disc, mispress with same picture both sides)	150
90	EMI KBBX 1	THIS WOMAN'S WORK (9-LP, box set)	150
90	EMI CKBBX 1	THIS WOMAN'S WORK (cassette, box set)	40
90	EMI CDKBBX 1	THIS WOMAN'S WORK (CD, box set)	100

(see also Peter Gabriel & Kate Bush, Lesley Duncan)

RAY BUSH & AVON CITIES' SKIFFLE

56	Tempo A 146	Hey Hey Daddy Blues/Green Corn (78 rpm = £12)	25
56	Tempo A 149	Fisherman's Blues/This Little Light Of Mine (78 rpm = £12)	25
57	Tempo A 156	How Long, How Long, Blues/Julian Johnson (78 rpm = £12)	25
57	Tempo A 157	Lonesome Day Blues/I Don't Know (78 rpm = £12)	25
57	Tempo EXA 40	RAY BUSH & AVON CITIES' SKIFFLE (EP)	30
57	Tempo EXA 50	RAY BUSH & AVON CITIES' SKIFFLE NO. 2 (EP)	30

(see also Avon Cities Jazz Band)

BUSH BOYS

59	Capitol CL 15082	A Broken Vow/Never Before	10

BUSHKILLER

92	Danger001	92 Salute/Bushkiller Draw (12")	30
94	Danger002	Troublemakers (EP)	45

BUSH TETRAS

81	Fetish FET 007	Things That Go Boom In The Night/Das Ah Riot (p/s)	6
82	Fetish FE 15	Can't Be Funky (unissued, stamped white label only, custom plain sleeve)	10
82	Fetish FET 16EP	RITUALS (12" EP)	15

BUSINESS

81	Secret SHH 123	Harry May/National Insurance Blacklist (p/s)	12
82	Secret SHH 132	SMASH THE DISCOS EP: Day-O (The Banana Boat Song)/Disco Girls/Smash The Disco (p/s)	10
83	Secret SHH 150	OUT OF BUSINESS (12" EP, unissued, white label promo, 10 copies only)	100+
85	Wonderful World Of... 121	Get Out Of My House/All Out Tonight/Foreign Girl/Outlaw (12", p/s)	25
85	Diamond DIA 001	Drinking N Driving/H-Bomb (live) (p/s)	15

85	Diamond DIA 001T	Drinking N Driving/H-Bomb (live)/Hurry Up Harry/Drinking 'N' Driving (original version) (12", p/s)	25
80s	Link LINK 1201	DO A RUNNER (12" EP)	12
83	Secret SEC 11	SUBURBAN REBELS (LP)	20
83	Syndicate SYNLP 2	1980-81 OFFICIAL BOOTLEGS (LP)	30
84	Syndicate SYNLP 6	LOUD, PROUD 'N' PUNK, LIVE (LP)	20
85	Harry May SE 13	SATURDAY HEROES (LP)	20
86	Dojo DOJO LP 35	SINGALONGABUSINESS (LP)	15
88	Link LINK LP 035	WELCOME TO THE REAL WORLD (LP)	12
90	Link LRMO 1	IN AND OUT OF BUSINESS (LP, mail-order, 550 only)	20

(see also UK)

BUSKERS
| 73 | Rubber RUB 007 | LIFE OF A MAN (LP) | 18 |
| 75 | Hawk HALPX 142 | THE BUSKERS (LP) | 15 |

GEORGE HENRY BUSSEY/JIM BUNKLEY
| 71 | Revival RVS 1003 | GEORGE HENRY BUSSEY/JIM BUNKLEY (LP) | 15 |

BUSTERS
| 63 | Stateside SS 231 | Bust Out/Astronauts | 22 |

BUSTER('S) ALLSTARS
64	Blue Beat BB 244	Prince Royal/COSMO: One God	25
64	Blue Beat BB 269	The Tickler/COSMO: Rice And Badge	35
65	Blue Beat BB 294	Eye For Eye/South Virginia	35
65	Blue Beat BB 322	Happy Independence 65/STRANGER COLE: When The Party Is Over	25
65	Blue Beat BB 325	Congo Revolution/Little Darlin' – No One	75
65	Blue Beat BB 333	When The Party Is Over/Matilda (with Stranger Cole)	25
66	Blue Beat BB 342	Cincinnatti Kid/Sammy Dead	50
67	Blue Beat BB 372	Sounds And Pressure/My Darling (both actually by Hopeton Lewis)	35
67	Blue Beat BB 384	Take It Easy/Why Must I Cry (both actually by Hopeton Lewis)	30
69	Fab FAB 101	Pum Pum A Go Kill You/Oh Lady Oh	15
70	Fab FAB 124	The Rebel/The Preacher	15

(see also Prince Buster, Teddy King, Little Darling, Khandars, Higgs & Wilson, Owen Gray, Charmers, Fitzroy D Long, Maytals, Derrick Morgan, Eric Morris, Personalities, Roy & Millie, Zoot Simms, Spanish Boys, Spanish Town Skabeats)

BUSTER'S GROUP
| 61 | Starlite ST45 052 | Buster's Shack/ERIC MORRIS: Search The World | 40 |

(see also Prince Buster, Rico, Owen Gray)

BUSTY & COOL
| 62 | Blue Beat BB 144 | Mr Policeman/What A World | 18 |

TONY BUTALA
| 62 | Salvo SLO 1801 | Long Black Stockings/Rumors (99 copies only) | 60 |

BUTCHER
| 82 | Inept INEPT 002 | On The Ground/Grow Up Don't Blow Up (p/s) | 5 |

(see also Intestines)

EDDIE BUTCHER
| 76 | Free Reed FRR 003 | I ONCE WAS A DAYSMAN (LP, with insert) | 12 |

SAM BUTERA (& WITNESSES)
58	HMV POP 476	Good Gracious Baby/It's Better Than Nothing At All (78 rpm = £15)	60
58	Capitol CL 14913	Bim Bam/Twinkle In Your Eye (as Sam Butera & Witnesses)	250
59	Capitol CL 14988	Handle With Care/French Poodle	20
64	Prima PR 1003	Skinnie Minnie/Little Liza Jane	15
56	HMV 7EG 8087	SAX SERENADE (EP)	40
60	London HA-D 2288	THE RAT RACE (LP, as Sam Butera & Witnesses)	30

(see also Louis Prima)

BILLY BUTLER (& ENCHANTERS)
| 69 | Soul City SC 113 | The Right Track/Boston Monkey | 28 |
| 74 | Epic S EPC 2508 | The Right Track/Can't Live Without Her | 10 |

CHAMP BUTLER
| 56 | Vogue Coral Q 72163 | The Joshua Tree/Down In Mexico | 10 |

(see also Johnny Bond's Red River Valley Boys)

JERRY BUTLER
58	London	For Your Precious Love/Sweet Was The Wine (as Jerry Butler & the Impressions) (78 rpm = £100)	200+
60	Top Rank JAR 389	I Found A Love/A Lonely Soldier	40
60	Top Rank JAR 531	He Will Break Your Heart/Thanks To You	50
61	Top Rank JAR 562	Find Another Girl/When Trouble Calls	30
61	Columbia DB 4743	Moon River/Aware Of Love	20
62	Stateside SS 121	Make It Easy On Yourself/It's Too Late	20
63	Stateside SS 158	You Can Run But You Can't Hide/I'm The One	30
63	Stateside SS 170	You Go Right Through Me/The Wishing Star	20
63	Stateside SS 195	Whatever You Want/You Won't Be Sorry	20
64	Stateside SS 252	Need To Belong/Give Me Your Love	20
64	Stateside SS 300	Giving Up On Love/I've Been Trying	20
65	Fontana TF 553	Good Times/I've Grown Accustomed To Her Face	20
65	Fontana TF 588	I Can't Stand To See You Cry/Nobody Needs Your Love	15
65	Mercury MF 932	Love (Oh, How Sweet It Is)/Loneliness	15
66	Sue WI 4003	I Stand Accused/I Don't Want To Hear Anymore	40
66	Sue WI 4009	Just For You/Believe In Me	40
67	Mercury MF 964	I Dig You Baby/Some Kinda Magic	15
67	Mercury MF 1005	Mr. Dream Merchant/'Cause I Love You So	10

Jerry BUTLER

68	Mercury MF 1035	Never Give You Up/Beside You	10
68	Mercury MF 1058	Hey Mr Western Union Man (Send A Telegram)/Just Can't Forget About You	10
69	Mercury MF 1078	Are You Happy/Strange I Still Love You	8
69	Mercury MF 1094	Only The Strong Survive/Just Because I Really Love You	10
69	Mercury MF 1122	Moody Woman/Go Away And Find Yourself (DJ copy = £100)	20
69	Mercury MF 1132	A Brand New Me/What's The Use Of Breaking Up	10
70	President PT 299	Make It Easy On Yourself/Moon River	8
72	Mercury 6052 036	One Night Affair/What's So Good About It (You're My Baby)	8
72	Mercury 6052 119	Moody Woman/A Brand New Me	10
72	Mercury 6052 155	I Only Have Eyes For You/Ain't Understanding Mellow	5
72	Mercury 6052 168	One Night Affair/What's So Good About It (You're My Baby) (reissue)	5
63	Stateside SL 10032	HE WILL BREAK YOUR HEART (LP)	100
63	Stateside SL 10050	FOLK SONGS (LP)	60
68	Fontana (S)TL 5246	LOVE ME (LP)	40
68	Mercury 20118 (S)MCL	MR. DREAM MERCHANT (LP)	30
69	Mercury 20144 (S)MCL	SOUL GOES ON (LP)	30
69	Mercury 20154 (S)MCL	THE ICE MAN COMETH (LP)	30
70	Joy JOYS 171	MAKE IT EASY ON YOURSELF (LP)	15
72	Mercury 6338 102	SPICE OF LIFE (LP)	15
72	Mercury 6430 401	THE VERY BEST OF JERRY BUTLER (LP)	15

(see also Betty Everett & Jerry Butler, Impressions, Gene & Jerry)

LESLIE BUTLER (& FUGITIVES)

67	Island WI 3069	Hornpipe Rock Steady/You Don't Have To Say You Love Me	35
67	Doctor Bird DB 1083	Winchester Rocksteady (with Fugitives)/	
		ASTON CAMPBELL & CONQUERORS: Ramona	35
68	High Note HS 008	Top Cat/WEBBER SISTERS: Stars Above	25
68	High Note HS 009	Revival/GAYLADS: Over The Rainbow's End	12

(see also Ken Boothe, Fugitives, Gaylads)

BUTTERCUPS

68	Pama PM 742	If I Love You/Loving You	15
69	Pama PM 760	Come Put My Life In Order/If I Love You	10

BILLY BUTTERFIELD & HIS ORCHESTRA

55	London HLF 8181	The Magnificent Matador/Sugar Blues Mambo (78 rpm = £6)	30

(PAUL) BUTTERFIELD BLUES BAND

66	London HLZ 10100	Come On In/I Got A Mind To Give Up Living	15
67	Elektra EKSN 45007	All These Blues/Never Say No	8
67	Elektra EKSN 45020	Run Out Of Time/One More Heartache	8
68	Elektra EKSN 45047	Get Yourself Together/Mine To Love	8
69	Elektra EKSN 45069	Where Did My Baby Go/In My Own Dream	8
70	Elektra 2101 012	Love March/Love Disease	6
65	Elektra EKL/EKS 294	PAUL BUTTERFIELD BLUES BAND (LP, orange label)	40
66	Elektra EKL/EKS 315	EAST — WEST (LP, orange label)	45
67	Elek. EKL 4015/EKS 74015	THE RESURRECTION OF PIGBOY CRABSHAW (LP, orange label)	35
68	Elektra EKL 4025	IN MY OWN DREAM (LP, orange label, also stereo EKS 74025)	30
69	Elektra EKS 74053	KEEP ON MOVIN' (LP)	18
71	Elektra EKD 2001	LIVE (2-LP)	20
72	Elektra K 62011	GOLDEN BUTTER (LP, gatefold sleeve)	12

(see also John Mayall's Bluesbreakers, Mike Bloomfield)

BUTTERFLIES

68	President PT 192	Love Me Forever/He's Got Everything	7

BUTTERFLYS

64	Red Bird RB 10009	Goodnight Baby/The Swim	20

BUTTERSCOTCH

70	RCA 1983	Surprise, Surprise/In This World Of Loving You	5

BUTTERSCOTCH CABOOSE

68	Bell BLL 1023	Melinda/Let A Little Sunshine In	6

BUTTHOLE SURFERS

84	Alt. Tentacles VIRUS 22	BUTTHOLE SURFERS (mini-LP, black & white sleeve)	8
89	Blast First BFF P41	WIDOWMAKER! (10" EP, with Reading Festival insert)	8
91	Rough Trade R 2081 2601	PIOUGHD (LP, with bonus 12")	12

BUTTONDOWN BRASS

67	Fontana LPS 16255	HA HA HA (HEE-HEE-HEE) (LP)	15
76	DJM DJS 22046	FUNK IN HELL (LP)	40
76	DJM DJSLM2023	FIREDOG (LP)	15
77	DJM DJS 22076	COPS N'ROBBERS (LP)	15

(see also Ray Davies & Buttondown Brass)·

BUTTS BAND

75	ABC ABC4050	Get Up, Stand Up/Mike's Blues	12

SHEILA BUXTON

55	Columbia SCM 5193	Thank You For The Waltz/Just Between Friends	5
57	Columbia DB 3887	Perfect Love/I Love You Baby (My Baby Loves Me)	5
57	Columbia DB 4051	The In-Between Age/Charm (78 rpm = £6)	5
59	Top Rank JAR 113	Soldier, Won't You Marry Me?/Li Per Li (78 rpm = £6)	6
59	Top Rank JAR 144	The Valley Of Love/The Wonder Of You (78 rpm = £8)	5
59	Top Rank JAR 240	All I Do Is Dream Of You/Shakedown	5
60	Top Rank JAR 356	Sixteen Reasons/Goodnight, God I Love You	10

(see also Craig Douglas)

BUZZ
66	Columbia DB 7887	You're Holding Me Down/I've Gotta Buzz	250

(see also Boston Dexters, Tam White)

BUZZ
79	Redball RR 06	Insanity/Him Not Me/Sick At Heart (p/s)	50
90s	Detour DR004	Tell Her No/Well, I Think It's Already Dead (p/s)	6

BUZZ & BUCKY
65	Stateside SS 428	Tiger A Go Go/Bay City	40

(see also Ronny & The Daytonas)

BUZZCOCKS
77	New Hormones ORG 1	SPIRAL SCRATCH (EP, plastic labels, p/s doesn't credit Howard Devoto)	40
77	United Artists UP 36316	Orgasm Addict/Whatever Happened To...? (p/s)	7
77	United Artists UP 36316B	Whatever Happened To? (1-sided test pressing)	50
78	United Artists UP36348	What Do I Get?/Oh Shit (Mispress, plays Stranglers Peaches)	75
78	United Artists UP 36433	Love You More/Noise Annoys (p/s)	5
78	United Artists UP 36455	Ever Fallen In Love (With Someone You Shouldn't've?)/Just Lust (p/s, mispressed with Gerry Rafferty track on B-side)	20
78	United Artists UP 36471	Promises/Lipstick (p/s)	5
78	New Hormones ORG 1	SPIRAL SCRATCH (EP, reissue, p/s credits Howard Devoto, paper label)	6
78	United Artists UALP 15	Moving Away From The Pulsebeat (12", 1-sided, die-cut co. sl., promo only)	20
79	United Artists UP 36499	Everybody's Happy Nowadays/Why Can't I Touch It? (p/s, available in 3 different colours)	each 5
79	United Artists	Everybody's Happy Nowadays (1-sided Portland Recording Studio Ltd Acetate)	200
79	United Artists UP 36541	Harmony In My Head/Something's Gone Wrong Again (p/s)	5
80	United Artists BP 365	Why She's A Girl From The Chainstore/Are Everything (p/s)	6
80	United Artists BP 365 DJ	Why She's A girl From The Chainstore/Are Everything (DJ promo)	20
89	EMI EM104	Ever Fallen In Love/Promises/Everybody's Happy Nowdays/Harmony In My Head (p/s)	8
91	New Hormones ORG 1	SPIRAL SCRATCH (EP, 2nd reissue, promo only 7")	10
95	One Stop Music ONE 7001	Noise Annoys/Isolation (live) (p/s, 1,500 only)	5
95	United Artists ESP001	What Do I Get?/Mad Mad Judy/Raison D'Etre (Demo)	10
78	United Artists UAG 30159	ANOTHER MUSIC IN A DIFFERENT KITCHEN (LP, black inner sleeve, initially in printed carrier bag)	30/14
78	United Artists UAG 30159	ANOTHER MUSIC IN A DIFFERENT KITCHEN (LP, mispressing without "I Need")	20
78	United Artists UAG 30197	LOVE BITES (LP, with embossed sleeve with insert)	12
79	United Artists UAG 30260	A DIFFERENT KIND OF TENSION (LP, with inner sleeve)	12
89	Absolutely Free FREELP 02	LIVE AT THE ROXY (LP)	15
91	Document DLP 2	TIME'S UP (LP, mock bootleg, with bonus 33rpm interview single [FDLP 2])	20

(see also Pete Shelley, Things, Stevie's Buzz)

JAKI BYARD
68	Transatlantic PR 7463	FREEDOM TOGETHER! (LP)	10

DON BYAS & HIS RHYTHM
56	Vogue V 2390	On The Way To Your Heart/The Portuguese Washerwomen	10

BYE LAWS
68	Pye 7N 17481	Then You Can Tell Me Goodbye/Come On Over To My Place	8
69	Pye 7N 17701	Run Baby Run/To Sir With Love	10

TREVOR BYFIELD
80	Ethnic Fight EF 086	Jah Guide/TREVOR & CLIVE: Sea Of Love (12")	35

MAX BYGRAVES
55	HMV 7EG 8061	PETER BROUGH, ARCHIE ANDREWS AND MAX BYGRAVES (EP)	10
56	HMV 7EG 8203	A GOOD IDEA SON (EP)	8

(see also Joan Regan)

JUNIOR BYLES
71	Bullet BU 499	Beat Down Babylon/UPSETTERS: Version	18
71	Upsetter US 365	Palace Called Africa/UPSETTERS: Earthquake	20
72	Upsetter US 387	Festival Da Da/UPSETTERS: Version	18
72	Pama PM 857	Fever/GROOVERS: Soul Sister (B-side actually by Heptones)	15
72	Dynamic DYN 432	Pharaoh Hiding/Hail To Power	10
72	Randy's RAN 523	King Of Babylon/UPSETTERS: Nebuchadnezzer	18
72	Punch PH 109	Pharaoh Hiding/UPSETTERS: Hail To Power	18
73	Pama PM 878	Education Rock/KEN McKAY: Nobody Knows	7
74	Magnet MAG 27	Curly Locks/Now Generation	8
74	Dip DL 5035	Curly Locks/Now Generation	10
75	Dip DL 5074	Long Way/All The Way	12
75	Ethnic ETH 26	Mumbling And Grumbling/King Size Mumble	7
76	Jessus JI 006	Know Where You Are Going/Going To Zion	12
76	Ethnic Fight EF 042	Bury O Boy/ THE THING MUSIC CO: Version	6
76	Black Wax WAX 17	Pitchy Patchy/THE JA-MAN ALL STARS: 129 Beat Street	6
72	Trojan TRL 52	BEAT DOWN BABYLON (LP, beware of Canadian imports)	40

(see also King Chubby, Lloyd Terrell, Dennis Alcapone, Upsetters, Bob Marley, Lee & Junior)

JUNIOR BYLES & RUPERT REID
76	Black Wax WAX 15	Chant Down Babylon/THE JA-MAN ALL STARS: Version	12

JAMES BYNUM
79	Grapevine GRP 117	Time Passes By/Love You	10

BOBBY BYRD
71	Mojo 2001 118	I Need Help Parts 1 & 2	15
71	Mojo 2027 003	I Know You Got Soul/If You Don't Work You Can't Eat	15
71	Mojo 2093 004	Hot Pants ... I'm Coming, I'm Coming, I'm Coming/Hang It Up	15
72	Mojo 2093 013	Keep On Doin' What You're Doin'/Let Me Know	15

72	Mojo 2093 017	If You Got A Love You'd Better Keep Hold Of It/You've Got To Change Your Mind . .	15
72	Mojo 2093 020	Never Get Enough/My Concerto	10
73	Warner Bros K 16291	Try It Again/I'm On The Move	8
73	Mojo 2093 028	Saying It And Doing It Are Two Different Things/VICKI ANDERSON: Don't Throw Your Love In Garbage/In The Land Of Milk And Honey	15
75	Seville SEV 1003	Back From The Dead/The Way To Get Down	8
75	Seville SEV 1005	Headquarters/Headquarters (Instrumental Version)	8
76	Contempo CS 2096	Here For The Party/Thank You For Your Love	8
87	Urban URB 8	I Know You Got Soul/Hot Pants	7
87	Urban URBX 8	I Know You Got Soul/Hot Pants ... I'm Coming, I'm Coming, I'm Coming/ I Know You Got Soul (Version) (12", die-cut company sleeve)	10
72	Mojo 2918 002	I NEED HELP — LIVE (LP)	50

(see also JB's, James Brown, Anna King & Bobby Byrd, Vicki Anderson)

C. BYRD & SIR D.'s GROUP

60	Blue Beat BB 49	Baa Baa Black Sheep/LLOYD & CECIL: Come Over Here	12

CHARLIE BYRD

63	Riverside 106910	Meditation/Little Boat	8
62	Riverside RLP 436	BOSSA NOVA PELOS PASSAROS (LP)	12
66	CBS 62610	TRAVELLIN' MAN LIVE (LP)	10
66	CBS 62958	BYRDLAND (LP)	10

DONALD BYRD

66	Verve VS 532	Boom Boom/See See Rider	8
80	United Artists UP 622	Dominoes/Wind Parade	5
55	Esquire 32-013	BYRDS EYE VIEW (LP)	35

(see also Blackbyrds, Art Farmer)

GARY BYRD (& THE G.B.E.)

83	Motown TMG 1312	The Crown/(Instrumental Version) (12", p/s)	8

MICHAEL BYRD & COMMERCIALS

80	Another AN 002	SELL OUT BEFORE THE FALL OUT (EP, gatefold p/s, 500 copies only)	6

(see also Cardiac Arrest, Selecter)

RUSSELL BYRD

64	Sue WI 305	Hitch Hike Parts 1 & 2	50

BYRDS

65	CBS 201765	Mr. Tambourine Man/I Knew I'd Want You	8
65	CBS 201796	All I Really Want To Do/Feel A Whole Lot Better	8
65	CBS 202008	Turn! Turn! Turn! (To Everything There Is A Season)/ She Don't Care About Time	8
66	CBS 202037	Set You Free This Time/It Won't Be Wrong	12
66	CBS 202067	Eight Miles High/Why	10
66	CBS 202259	5D (Fifth Dimension)/Captain Soul	8
66	CBS 202295	Mr Spaceman/What's Happening?!?!	10
67	CBS 202559	So You Want To Be A Rock'n'Roll Star/Everybody's Been Burned	10
67	CBS 2648	My Back Pages/Renaissance Fair	10
67	CBS 2924	Lady Friend/Don't Make Waves	18
67	CBS 3093	Goin' Back/Change Is Now	12
68	CBS 3411	You Ain't Goin' Nowhere/Artificial Energy	8
68	CBS 3752	I Am A Pilgrim/Pretty Boy Floyd	8
69	CBS 4055	Bad Night At The Whiskey/Drug Store Truck Drivin' Man	10
69	CBS 4284	Lay Lady Lay/Old Blue	10
69	CBS 4572	Wasn't Born To Follow/Child Of The Universe	8
70	CBS 4753	Jesus Is Just Alright/It's All Over Now Baby Blue	7
71	CBS 5322	Chestnut Mare/Just A Season	7
71	CBS 7253	I Trust/This Is My Destiny	7
72	CBS 7712	America's Great National Pastime/Farther Along (unreleased)	
73	Asylum AYM 516	Things Will Be Better/For Free (promos in p/s)	12/6
73	Asylum AYM 517	Full Circle/Long Live The King	6
66	CBS EP 6069	THE TIMES THEY ARE A' CHANGIN' (EP)	22
66	CBS EP 6077	EIGHT MILES HIGH (EP)	30
90	CBS 656544 5	FOUR DIMENSIONS EP (CD, picture disc)	8
65	CBS (S)BPG 62571	MR TAMBOURINE MAN (LP, mono/stereo)	35/25
66	CBS (S)BPG 62652	TURN! TURN! TURN! (LP, mono/stereo)	40/35
66	CBS (S)BPG 62783	FIFTH DIMENSION (LP, mono/stereo)	40/35
67	CBS (S)BPG 62988	YOUNGER THAN YESTERDAY (LP, mono/stereo)	40/35
68	CBS BPG 63107	THE BYRDS' GREATEST HITS (LP, mono)	12
68	CBS (S)BPG 63169	THE NOTORIOUS BYRD BROTHERS (LP, mono/stereo)	35/30
68	CBS 63353	SWEETHEART OF THE RODEO (LP, mono/stereo)	30/25
69	CBS 63545	DR BYRDS & MR HYDE (LP, mono)	15

(Original copies of the above LPs were issued with rough-textured, plain orange labels & laminated sleeves; later copies are worth two-thirds these values.)

71	Bumble GEXP 8001	PRE-FLYTE (LP)	20
73	Asylum SYLA 8754	THE BYRDS (LP, gatefold sleeve)	12

(see also Beefeaters, Roger McGuinn, David Crosby, Gene Clark, Gram Parsons, Gene Parsons, Skip Battin, Earl Scruggs, Flying Burrito Brothers, Evergreen Blueshoes, Dillard & Clark, Kentucky Colonels)

JERRY BYRNE

76	Specialty SON 5011	Lights Out/Honey Baby	5

PACKIE BYRNE (& BONNIE SHALJEAN)

69	EFDSS LP 1009	PACKIE BYRNE (LP)	22

EDD/EDWARD BYRNES
60	Warner Bros WB 5	Kookie, Kookie (Lend Me Your Comb) (with Connie Stevens)/You're The Top	10
60	Warner Bros WB 27	Lonely Christmas/Yulesville (as Edd Byrnes)	12
60	Warner Bros WEP 6010	KOOKIE (EP, also stereo WSEP 2010)	15/8
63	Warner Bros W(S)EP 6108	KOOKIE VOLUME 2 (EP)	20

(see also Connie Stevens)

MARTIN BYRNES
70	Leader LEA 2004	BYRNES (LP)	15

PAUL BYRON
60	Decca F 11210	Pale Moon/Year Ago Tonight	10

SOL BYRON & IMPACTS
60s	Flamingo PR 5027	Pride And Joy/Thou Shall Not Steal	12

BYSTANDERS
65	Pylot WD 501	That's The End/This Time	150
66	Piccadilly 7N 35330	(You're Gonna) Hurt Yourself/Have I Offended The Girl	20
66	Piccadilly 7N 35351	My Love — Come Home/If You Walk Away	30
67	Piccadilly 7N 35363	98.6/Stubborn Kind Of Fellow	15
67	Piccadilly 7N 35382	Royal Blue Summer Sunshine Day/Make Up Your Mind	30
67	Piccadilly 7N 35399	Pattern People/Green Grass	15
68	Pye 7N 17476	When Jezamine Goes/Cave Of Clear Light	50
68	Pye 7N 17540	This World Is My World/Painting The Time	15

(see also Man)

BYZANTIUM
73	A&M AMS 7064	What A Coincidence/My Seasons Changing With The Sun	7
72	private pressing	LIVE AND STUDIO ('BLACK AND WHITE') (LP, 100 only)	150
72	A&M AMLH 68104	BYZANTIUM (LP, some with poster)	60/45
73	A&M AMLH 68163	SEASONS CHANGING (LP, poster sleeve)	60

(see also Ora)

FANTASTIC JOHNNY C
67	London HL 10169	Boogaloo Down Broadway/Look What Love Can Make You Do	12
68	London HL 10212	Hitch It To The Horse/Cool Broadway	12
69	Action ACT 4543	Is There Anything Better Than Making Love/New Love	2
75	Island USA 8	Don't Depend On Me (Parts 1 & 2)	10
69	Action ACLP 6001	BOOGALOO DOWN BROADWAY (LP)	55

ROY C
66	Island WI 273	Shotgun Wedding/I'm Going To Make It	20
66	Island WI 273	Shotgun Wedding/High School Dropout (different B-side)	20
67	Ember EMB S 230	Twistin' Pneumonia/Tear Avenue	15
66	Ember NR 5055	THE SHOTGUN WEDDING MAN (LP)	30
75	Mercury 9100 017	SEX AND SOUL (LP)	15

CABARET VOLTAIRE
79	Rough Trade RT 018	Nag Nag Nag/Is That Me (p/s)	8
79	Rough Trade RT 035	Silent Command/Chance Versus Causality (p/s)	8
80	Rough Trade RT 060	Seconds Too Late/Control Addict (p/s)	8
81	Rough Trade RT 096	Eddie's Out/Walls Of Jericho (12", p/s, with bonus 7" Jazz The Glass/Burnt To The Ground [pink die-cut sleeve, RT 095] in plastic wallet)	8
82	Masterbag BAG 004	Gut Level (live) (flexidisc free with *Masterbag* magazine)	7/5
76	(no label or cat. no.)	LIMITED EDITION (private cassette)	30

(see also Richard H. Kirk, Hafler Trio, Peter Hope & Richard H. Kirk, Stephen Mallinder, Pressure Co., Eric Random)

CABLES
68	Coxsone CS 7072	What Kind Of World?/My Broken Heart	35
68	Studio One SO 2060	Baby Why?/Be A Man	25
68	Studio One SO 2071	Love Is A Pleasure/Cheer Up	30
69	Studio One SO 2085	Got To Find Someone/ALEXANDER HENRY: Please Be True	25
69	Bamboo BAM 12	So Long/PRESSURE BOYS: More Love	15
70	Bamboo BAM 19	How Can I Trust You?/SOUND DIMENSIONS: How Can I Trust You? (Inst.)	12
70	Trojan TR 7792	Salt Of The Earth/Ring A Bell	10
70	Harry J. HJ 6614	Didn't I/JAY BOYS: Tilly	10
70	Harry J. HJ 6620	Feel Alright/Equal Rights	7
71	Big Shot BI 598	A Sometime Girl/IN CROWD BAND: A Sometime Girl Version	6
72	Jackpot JP 787	Come On/Come On Version	6
73	Attack ATT 8053	Give Me A Chance/JAH FISH: King Of Zion	6

(see also K. Drummond, Dingle Brothers, Alton Ellis)

CABOOSE
70	Stax STAX 151	Black Hands, White Cotton/In My Hour Of Need	6

CACOPHONY
87	Roadrunner RR 349577	SPEED METAL SYMPHONY (LP)	12
88	Roadrunner RR 9577	GO OFF (LP, as Marty Friedman, Jason Becker & Cacophony)	12

(see also Marty Friedman, Megadeth)

MINT VALUE £

CACTUS
70	Atco 2400 020	CACTUS (LP)	22
71	Atco 2400 114	ONE WAY ... OR ANOTHER (LP, reissue of above LP)	20
72	Atlantic K 40307	RESTRICTIONS (LP)	12
72	Atlantic K 50013	'OT AND SWEATY (LP)	12

(see also Vanilla Fudge, Leaf Hound, Beck Bogert Appice)

BILL CADDICK
79	Highway SHY 7006	REASONS BRIEFLY SET DOWN (LP)	15

ALAN CADDY
64	HMV POP 1286	Tornado/Workout	40

(see also Tornados)

CADETS (U.K.)
63	Decca F 11677	Hello Trouble/Our First Quarrel	10
64	Pye 7N 15693	Chapel Of Love/I Gave My Wedding Dress Away	10
65	Pye 7N 15769	Are You Teasing Me?/My Heart Skips A Beat	5
65	Pye 7N 15852	Jealous Heart/Right Or Wrong	10
65	Pye 7N 15947	Baby Roo/Raining In My Heart	10
66	Pye 7N 17024	If I Had My Life To Live Over/Best Of All	5
66	Pye 7N 17167	At The Close Of A Long Long Day/True Love	5
69	Pye 7N 17762	Dying Ranger/Storeen Bawn	5

CADETS (U.S.)
56	London HLU 8313	Stranded In The Jungle/I Want You (gold or silver label lettering)	700/300
56	London HLU 8313	Stranded In The Jungle/I Want You (78)	50

CADILLAC
86	CBS A 7180	Valentino/Valentino (p/s)	8

EARL CADILLAC & HIS ORCHESTRA
59	Vogue V 9133	Zon, Zon, Zon/Il Suffit D'Une Melodie (78 rpm = £12)	18
59	Vogue V 9138	The Fish Seller/Tremendo Cha Cha Cha (Plegaria) (78 rpm = £12)	15

CADILLACS
59	London HLJ 8786	Peek-A-Boo/Oh, Oh, Lolita (78 rpm = £25)	50

SUSAN CADOGAN
74	Dip DL 5030	Hurt So Good/UPSETTERS: Loving Is Good	7
75	Lucky LY 5078	Feeling Right/Congratulations	7

CAEDMON
78	private pressing	CAEDMON (LP, with insert, some with bonus 7": Beyond The Second Mile/Give Me Jesus)	250+/275+

CAERN
70s	Gem DES 1015	A COLLECTION OF SCOTCH FOLK (LP)	18

CAESAR & CLEO
65	Reprise R 20419	Love Is Strange/Let The Good Times Roll (some in p/s)	25/15
65	Reprise R 30056	CAESAR AND CLEO (EP, 2 tracks each by Caesar & Cleo and Sonny & Cher)	15

(see also Sonny & Cher)

CAESARS
65	Decca F 12251	On The Outside Looking In/Can You Blame Me?	15
66	Decca F 12462	Five In The Morning/It's Superman	12

CAESARS
00s	Dolores 5468797	Fun And Games/Crackin' Up/Only You/Since You've Been Gone	8

CAFE SOCIETY
75	Konk KOS 5	Whitby Two-Step/Maybe It's Me	6
75	Konk KONK 102	CAFE SOCIETY (LP, with inner sleeve)	15

(see also Tom Robinson Band, Claire Hamill)

BUTCH CAGE/MABEL LEE WILLIAMS
60s	Storyville SLP 129	COUNTRY BLUES (LP)	20

AUBREY CAGLE
62	Starlite ST45 082	Come Along Little Girl/Blue Lonely World	200

CAGLIOSTRO
86	él GPO 22	Libera Me/Madmen And Lovers (p/s)	8

JAMES CAGNEY
70	United Artists UP 36385	Yankee Doodle Dandy/Over There (B-side with Frances Langford) (p/s)	8

JEREMY CAHILL
70s	Solent	September Blues/Yesterday	15

(see also Shide & Acorn)

PATRICIA CAHILL
70	Deram DM 320	Little Altar Boy/Rain	7
71	Deram DM 324	Colm Ban/Eighteen	7
70	Deram Nova SDN 22	SUMMER'S DAUGHTER (LP)	25
72	Rex RPS 104	IRELAND (LP)	15

CAIN
68	Page One POF 054	Her Emotion/Take Me Back One Time	32

CAIN
80s	private pressing	CAIN (2-LP)	30

TUBAL CAINE
70	Attack ATT 8023	I'm A Drifter Part 1/CIMMARONS: I'm A Drifter Part 2	7

AL CAIOLA (ORCHESTRA)

56	London HLC 8285	Flamenco Love/From The Heart	20
61	London HLT 9294	The Magnificent Seven/The Lonely Rebel	12
61	London HLT 9325	Bonanza/Bounty Hunter	12
61	HMV POP 884	Bonanza/Bounty Hunter (as Al Caiola Orchestra, reissue)	10
61	HMV POP 889	The Magnificent Seven/The Lonely Rebel (as Al Caiola Orchestra)	10
62	Oriole CB 1732	Mambo Jambo/Twistin' At The Woodchoppers Mill	10
66	United Artists UEP 1018	HIT T.V. THEMES (EP)	15
56	London HA-C 2017	DEEP IN A DREAM (LP)	22
57	London HA-C 2022	SERENADE IN BLUE (LP)	22
64	United Artists UAL 8053	CIAO	22
64	United Artists ULP 1090	TUFF GUITAR (LP)	20
66	United Artists (S)ULP 1115	SOUNDS FOR SPIES AND PRIVATE EYES (LP)	35

CAIRN

70s	GES 1015	A COLLECTION OF SCOTCH FOLK (LP)	15

JOHN CAIRNEY

57	HMV POP 424	Two Strangers/A Certain Girl I Know (with Sammy San)	10
68	Waverley SLP 543	Please/Deep Purple	5

FORRIE CAIRNS

62	Fontana 267240 TF	Salty Dog/Cockles And Mussels	7

CAIRO

80	Absurd ASK 15	Movie Stars/Cuthbert's Birthday Treat (p/s)	5

CAJUN MOON

76	Chrysalis CHR 1116	CAJUN MOON (LP)	12

CAKE

68	MCA MUPS 303	THE CAKE (LP)	12
69	MCA MUPS 390	A SLICE OF CAKE (LP)	12

BOBBY CALDWELL

78	TK 7529	What You Want Me To Do/Version	10

J.J. CALE

66	Liberty LIB 55881	Outside Lookin' In/In Our Time	18
72	A&M AMS 7018	Cajun Moon/Starbound	6
72	A&M AMS 7022	After Midnight/Crazy Mama	6
72	A&M AMLS 68105	NATURALLY (LP, tan label)	15
72	A&M AMLS 68157	REALLY (LP, tan label)	15
79	Shelter ISA 5018	FIVE (LP, with bonus single "Katy Cool"/"Juan And Maria Juarez Blues" [JJ-1])	15

(see also Leathercoated Minds)

JOHN CALE

74	Island WIP 6202	The Man Who Couldn't Afford To Orgy/Sylvia Said	10
77	Illegal IL 006	Jack The Ripper In The Moulin Rouge/Memphis (unissued, test pressings only)	25
81	A&M AMS 8130	Dead Or Alive/Honi Soit	5
83	Ze IS 113	Close Watch/I Keep A Close Watch (p/s)	5
84	Ze IS 157	Caribbean Sunset/(same) (unissued, promo only)	8
84	Ze IS 197	Ooh La La/Magazines (p/s)	5
77	Illegal IL 003	ANIMAL JUSTICE (EP)	6
77	Illegal IL 003	ANIMAL JUSTICE (12" EP)	10
71	CBS 64256	VINTAGE VIOLENCE (LP, orange label)	18
71	CBS 64259	CHURCH OF ANTHRAX (LP, with Terry Riley)	18
72	Reprise K 44212	ACADEMY IN PERIL (LP)	15
73	Reprise K 44239	PARIS 1919 (LP, with lyric insert)	15
75	Island ILPS 9350	HELEN OF TROY (LP)	12
77	Island ILPS 9459	GUTS (LP)	12

(see also Velvet Underground, Nico, Terry Riley, Ayers Cale Nico & Eno, Judy Nylon)

CALEB (Quaye)

67	Philips BF 1588	Baby Your Phrasing Is Bad/Woman Of Distinction (300-500 pressed)	750

(see also Mirage, Hookfoot, Bread & Beer Band, Elton John)

CALEDONIANS

69	Fab FAB 103	Funny Way Of Laughing/Don't Please	15

(see also Clarendonians, Prince Buster)

CALENDAR

75	All Platinum 6146 308	Hypertension Parts 1 & 2	6

CALENNIG

80	Greenwich Village GVR 214	SONGS AND TUNES FROM WALES (LP)	15

CALIFORNIA IN-CROWD

66	Fontana TF 779	Questions And Answers/Happiness In My Heart	45

CALIFORNIA MUSIC

74	RCA RCA 2488	Don't Worry Baby/Ten Years Harmony	10
76	RCA RCA 2661	Jamaica Farewell/California Farewell	10
78	RSO 014	I Can Hear Music/Love's Supposed To Be That Way (as California)	7

(see also Bruce Johnston, Beach Boys)

CALIFORNIANS

67	CBS 2263	Golden Apples/Little Ship With A Red Sail	60
67	Decca F 12678	Follow Me/What Love Can Do	20
67	Decca F 12712	Sunday Will Never Be The Same/Can't Get You Out Of My Mind	7
68	Decca F 12758	Congratulations/What Is Happy, Baby?	7
68	Decca F 12802	Out In The Sun/The Sound	7
69	Fontana TF 991	Mandy/The Cooks Of Cake And Kindness	90

| 69 | Fontana TF 1052 | Sad Old Song/Weep No More | 8 |
| 69 | Chapter One CH 112 | You've Got Your Troubles/Early Morning Sun | 7 |

(see also Warren Zevon)

CALLAN & JOHN
| 69 | CBS 4447 | House Of Delight/Long Shadow Day | 22 |

CALL GIRLS
| 88 | 53rd & 3rd AGAR 001 | Primal World/VATICAN SHOTGUN SCARE: Thick Fat Heat Source (p/s) | 8 |

(MISSISSIPPI) JOE CALLICOTT
| 68 | Blue Horizon 7-63227 | PRESENTING THE COUNTRY BLUES (LP) | 125 |
| 71 | Revival RVS 1002 | DEAL GONE DOWN (LP, as Joe Callicott) | 30 |

TERRY CALLIER
79	Elektra K 12372	Sign Of The Times/Occasional Rain	8
90	Acid Jazz JAZID 27T	I Don't Want To See Myself (Without You)/(If I Could Make You) Change Your Mind (12")	25
78	Elektra K 52096	FIRE ON ICE (LP)	30
79	Elektra K 52140	TURN YOU TO LOVE (LP)	25

CALLIES
| 71 | Rubber RUB 002 | ON YOUR SIDE (LP, gatefold sleeve) | 18 |

CALLINAN-FLYNN
| 72 | Mushroom 150 MR 18 | FREEDOM'S LAMENT (LP) | 200 |

JO CALLIS
| 81 | Pop: Aural POP 12 | Woah Yeah/Sinistrale/Dodo Boys (p/s) | 5 |

(see also Rezillos, Shake, Human League)

CAB CALLOWAY
66	Stateside SS 509	History Repeats Itself/After Taxes	5
58	Gala 45XP 1016	CAB CALLOWAY (EP)	8
60	Fontana TFE 17216	CAB CALLOWAY (EP)	10
70s	Vintage Jazz VEP 22	CABULOUS CALLOWAY (EP)	8
70s	Vintage Jazz VEP 35	CABULOUS CALLOWAY VOL. 2 (EP)	8

GEORGE CALSTOCK
| 78 | Hit Run DD2 | The Ungodly (Feat. U Black)/DOCTOR PABLO: Righteous Melody (12") | 60+ |

EDDIE CALVERT
53	Columbia SCM 5003	My Yiddishe Momme/Hora Staccato	6
53	Columbia SCM 5004	Ave Maria/Just A-Wearyin' For You (as Eddie Calvert Orchestra)	6
54	Columbia SCM 5129	My Son, My Son/Sherpa Song	6
55	Columbia SCM 5168	Cherry Pink And Apple Blossom White/Roses Of Picardy	10
56	Columbia SCM 5237	The Man With The Golden Arm/Memories Of You	5
56	Columbia SCM 5277	Moonglow & Theme From Picnic/If I Loved You	5
58	Melodisc EPM 7	MISERLOU (EP)	8
55	Columbia SEG 7591	GOLDEN MELODIES OF THE GOLDEN TRUMPET (EP)	8
56	Columbia SEG 7637	GOLDEN TRUMPET — GOLDEN MELODIES No. 2 (EP)	8

(see also Gerry Brereton)

ROBERT CALVERT
72	United Artists UP 35543	Ejection/Catch A Falling Starfighter (p/s)	15
79	Wake Up WUR 5	Cricket Star (p/s, 33rpm flexidisc, as Robert Calvert & 1st XI)	10
80	Flicknife FLS 204	Lord Of The Hornets/The Greenfly & The Rose (purple print p/s)	10
81	Flicknife FLS 204	Lord Of The Hornets/The Greenfly & The Rose (reissue, black print p/s)	5
74	United Artists UAG 29507	CAPTAIN LOCKHEED AND THE STARFIGHTERS (LP, gatefold sleeve, with booklet and inner sleeve)	22
75	United Artists UAG 29852	LUCKY LIEF AND THE LONGSHIPS (LP, gatefold sleeve)	20
81	A-Side IF 0311	HYPE (SONGS OF TOM MAHLER) (LP)	15
84	Flicknife SHARP 021	FREQ (LP)	12
86	Demi Monde DMLP 1010	TEST TUBE CONCEIVED (LP)	12
86	Harbour (no cat. no.)	THE CELLAR TAPES VOLUME ONE (cassette only)	15
86	Harbour (no cat. no.)	THE CELLAR TAPES VOLUME TWO (cassette only)	15
88	Harbour (no cat. no.)	ROBERT CALVERT READS THE EARTH RITUAL (cassette, limited edition)	15
88	Beat Goes On BGOLP 2	LUCKY LIEF AND THE LONGSHIPS (LP, gatefold sleeve, reissue)	12
88	Beat Goes On BGOLP 5	CAPTAIN LOCKHEED AND THE STARFIGHTERS (LP, gatefold sleeve with booklet, reissue)	12
89	Clear BLACK 1	ROBERT CALVERT AT THE QUEEN ELIZABETH HALL (LP, mail order only, with badge, poster & T-shirt, gatefold sleeve)	40
92	Cyborg (no cat. no.)	REVENGE (cassette only)	12

(see also Hawkwind, Imperial Pompadours, Catapilla, Adrian Wagner, John Stevens Away)

TABBY CALVIN & ROUNDERS
| 56 | Capitol CL 14640 | False Alarm/I Came Back To Say I'm Sorry | 10 |

CAMARATA
59	Top Rank JAR 160	Love Theme Sleeping Beauty/Medley Sleeping Beauty (as Walt Disney Studio Orchestra) (78 rpm = £6)	5
59	Top Rank JAR 162	On The Trail/Trumpeter's Prayer (as Tutti's Trumpets) (78 rpm = £6)	6
65	London SHU 8257	THINK YOUNG! (LP, as Camarata Orchestra)	12
70	Deram SML 1053	THE VELVET GENTLEMAN: THE MUSIC OF ERIK SATIE (LP)	40

CAMBODIANS
| 70 | Duke DU 101 | Coolie Man/J.J. ALLSTARS: Coolie Version | 12 |

CAMEL
73	MCA MUPS 1177	Never Let Go/Curiosity	6
80	Decca FR 13871	Your Love Is Stranger Than Mine/Neon Magic (p/s)	6
84	Decca CAMEL 1	Cloak And Dagger Man/Pressure Point (p/s)	5

| 73 | MCA MUPS 473 | CAMEL (LP, black/blue label) | 18 |
| 74 | Deram SML 1107 | MIRAGE (LP, with insert) | 12 |

(see also Pete Bardens, Gong/Camel, Hatfield & The North)

CAMEL DRIVERS
| 68 | Pye International 7N 25471 | Sunday Morning 6 O'Clock/Give It A Try | 8 |

CAMEO
78	Casablanca CAN 121	It's Serious/Inflation (12")	8
80	Casablanca CAN 199	On The One/Cameosis (12")	8
77	Casablanca CAL 2015	CARDIAC ARREST (LP)	20
78	Casablanca CAL 2026	WE ALL KNOW WHO WE ARE (LP)	15

CAMEOS
| 63 | Columbia DB 7092 | Powercut/High Low And Lonesomely | 45 |
| 64 | Columbia DB 7201 | My Baby's Coming Home/Where E'er You Walk | 45 |

CAMEOS
| 67 | Toast TT 503 | A Pretty Shade Of Blue/You Didn't Have To Be So Nice | 8 |
| 68 | Toast TT 508 | On The Good Ship Lollipop/The Love Of A Boy | 8 |

CAMERA OBSCURA
| 80 | Small Wonder SMALL 28 | Destitution/Race In Athens (p/s) | 6 |

DION CAMERON & THREE TOPS
| 66 | Rio R 111 | Lord Have Mercy/Get Ready | 12 |

(see also Dion & Three Tops)

G.C. CAMERON
| 76 | Tamla Motown TMG 1033 | Me And My Life/Act Like A Shotgun | 8 |

(see also Detroit Spinners)

ISLA CAMERON
| 64 | Transatlantic TRAEP 109 | LOST LOVE (EP) | 25 |

(see also Ewan MacColl)

JOHN CAMERON (QUARTET)
67	Columbia DB 8120	You Owe Me/Walk Small (solo)	8
69	Deram DM 256	Troublemaker/Off Centre	90
67	Columbia SCX 6116	COVER LOVER (LP)	40
69	Deram DML/SML 1044	OFF CENTRE (LP)	65

(see also Frog)

JOHNNY CAMERON
| 60 | Top Rank JAR 396 | I Double Dare You/Fantasy | 10 |

RAY CAMERON
| 67 | Island WIP 6003 | Doin' My Time/Getaway, Getaway Car | 10 |

CAMOUFLAGE
| 90 | Atlantic | STRANGERS THOUGHTS (CD video) | 50 |
| 90 | Atlantic | THE GREAT COMMANDMENT (CD) | 30 |

AL CAMPBELL
78	Deb DEB 018	Love The Way It Should Be/Version (12")	20
80	JB JBD 019	You Jamming/You Jamming (Part 2) (12")	20
79	Burning Sounds BS 1036	DIAMONDS (LP)	20
79	Hawkeye HLD 03	RAINY DAYS (LP)	30
80	JB JBLP 002	LATE NIGHT BLUES (LP)	30

AL CAMPBELL & TRINITY
| 78 | Deb DEB 013 | Reggae Dance/Dragon Dance/AL CAMPBELL: Roots Man Style (12") | 20 |

ALEX CAMPBELL
65	Transatlantic TRASP 4	Been On The Road So Long/The Night Visiting Song (some in p/s)	10/6
68	Saga OPP 2	Victoria Dines Alone/Pack Up Your Sorrows	20
63	Arc ARC 36	OUT WEST WITH ALEX CAMPBELL (EP)	8
63	Society SOC 912	WAY OUT WEST (LP)	15
63	Society SOC 960	FOLK SESSION (LP)	15
64	Fidelity FID 2171	FOLK SESSION (LP, reissue)	12
64	Xtra XTRA 1064	ALEX CAMPBELL (LP, with Martin Carthy)	22
65	Polydor 623 035	IN COPENHAGEN (LP)	18
67	Saga ERO 8021	ALEX CAMPBELL AND HIS FRIENDS (LP, with Sandy Denny)	30
71	Ad-Rhythm/Tepee ARPS 1	THIS IS ALEX CAMPBELL VOL. 1 (LP)	30
71	Ad-Rhythm/Tepee ARPS 2	THIS IS ALEX CAMPBELL VOL. 2 (LP)	30
71	Boulevard 4007	16 BEST LOVED SONGS OF BONNIE SCOTLAND (LP)	15
72	Boulevard 4073	AT HIS BEST (LP)	20
76	Look LKLP 6043	NO REGRETS (LP)	12
79	Burlington BURL 002	ALEX CAMPBELL, ALAN ROBERTS AND DOUGIE MACLEAN (LP)	12
87	Sundown SDLP 2048	WITH THE GREATEST RESPECT (2-LP, reissue of "This Is..." Vols. 1 & 2)	18

(see also Sandy Denny)

AMBROSE ADEKOYA CAMPBELL'S WEST AFRICAN RHYTHM BROTHERS
| 52 | Melodisc SP 1 | Sing The Blues/Omo Lo' Fu Ja (78) | 8 |

BILL & PETE CAMPBELL
| 71 | Duke DU 123 | Come On Home Girl/You Are Mine | 7 |

CAT CAMPBELL & NICKY THOMAS
| 72 | Pressure Beat PB 5511 | Hammering/PETER TOSH: Medicine Man | 20 |

CHOKER CAMPBELL
| 65 | Tamla Motown TMG 517 | Mickey's Monkey/Pride And Joy (as Choker Campbell's Big Band) (DJ copy = £225) | 150 |
| 65 | Tamla Motown TML 11011 | HITS OF THE SIXTIES (LP, as Choker Campbell & His 16-Piece Band) | 150 |

MINT VALUE £

CORNELL CAMPBELL

63	Island WI 039	Rosabelle/Turndown Date (B-side actually "Under The Old Oak Tree")	30
63	Island WI 083	Each Lonely Night/ROLAND ALPHONSO: Steamline	20
64	Port-O-Jam PJ 4008	Jericho Road (with Dimple Hinds)/DON DRUMMOND & GROUP:	
		Roll On Sweet Don	60
64	Rio R 38	Gloria/I'll Be True	25
72	Dynamic DYN 446	My Confession/AGGROVATORS: Version	12
72	Green Door GD 4042	Dearest Darling/Star Dust	15
72	Jackpot JP 801	Queen And The Minstrel/Put Yourself In My Place	12
73	Jackpot JP 809	Pity The Children/You're No Good	15
73	Jackpot JP 814	Harry Hippy/Just One Kiss	6
73	Green Door GD 4057	Give Me Love/Help Them O Lord	12
73	Duke DU 158	Shotgun Wedding/Girl Of My Dreams	10
73	Duke DU 159	The Very Best I Can/Heading For The Mountains	6
73	Ackee ACK 513	Give Me A Love/SHORTY PERRY: Message Of Love	6
76	Daddy Kool DK001	I Heart Is Clean/KING TUBBY AND THE OBSERVERS : Zinc Fence	10
77	Nationwide 1018	Let Me Go Girl/Version	7
78	D-Roy 3	Listen Dread/Version	8
78	Third World 7529	Blessed Are They/New York City (With I ROY)	8
80	Cha Cha CHAD25	Rainbow/PETER BROGGS: Never Forget Jah (12")	30
72	Trojan TBL 199	CORNELL CAMPBELL (LP)	40
76	Angen ANGL 03	GORGON (LP)	32
79	Striker Lee TSL 104	NATTY DREAD IN A GREENWICH FARM (LP)	40
79	Burning Sounds BS 1034	SWEET BABY (LP)	20

(see also Eternals, Don Cornel & Eternals, Clarendonians, Charmers, Stranger & Patsy, GG Allstars)

DAVID CAMPBELL

67	Transatlantic TRA 141	DAVID CAMPBELL (LP)	25
72	Decca SKL 5139	SUN WHEEL (LP)	18

ETHNA CAMPBELL

64	Mercury MF 804	What's Easy For Two Is Hard For One/Again	20
64	Mercury MF 816	Girls Like Boys/Five Minutes More	10
75	Philips 6382138	FOR THE GOOD TIMES (LP)	15

GLEN CAMPBELL

61	Top Rank JAR 596	Turn Around, Look At Me/Brenda	20
62	Capitol CL 15268	Too Late To Worry, Too Blue To Cry/How Do I Tell My Heart Not To Break?	10
62	Capitol CL 15278	Here I Am/Long Black Limousine	10
63	Capitol CL 15295	Prima Donna/Oh My Darling	10
67	Speciality SPE 1002	Satisfied Mind/Can't You See I'm Trying	7
68	Ember EMB S 252	I Wanna Live/Hey Little One	5
68	Ember EMB S 255	Dreams Of The Everyday Housewife/Combine	5
68	Ember EMB S 258	Straight Life/That's Not Home	5
69	Ember EMB S 261	Wichita Lineman/Back In The Race (p/s)	5
69	Ember EMB S 263	Galveston/Everytime I Itch I Wind Up Scratching You	5
69	Capitol CL 15615	True Grit/Hava Nagila	5
66	London HA-F/SH-F 8291	SWINGING 12-STRING (LP)	18

(see also Sagittarius, Jimmy Slade)

CAMPBELL FAMILY

65	Topic 12T 120	THE SINGING CAMPBELLS — TRADITIONS OF AN ABERDEEN FAMILY	
		(LP, blue label)	15

IAN CAMPBELL (FOLK) GROUP

63	Topic STOP 102	The Sun Is Burning/The Crow On The Cradle (some in title p/s)	15/7
64	Decca F 11802	Marilyn Monroe/The Bells Of Rhymney	7
65	Transatlantic TRASP 2	Kelly From Killane/Boys Of Wexford (with Boys From Wexford)	7
65	Transatlantic TRASP 5	The Times They Are A-Changin'/Across The Hills (some in p/s)	20/12
66	Transatlantic TRASP 6	Come Kiss Me/The First Time I Ever Saw Your Face (some in p/s)	12/7
66	Transatlantic TRASP 7	Guantanamera/Mary Anne	6
66	Transatlantic TRASP 10	One Eyed Reilly/Snow Is Falling (solo)	6
67	Big T BIG 103	Lover Let Me In/Private Harold Harris (as Ian Campbell Four)	6
69	Major Minor MM 639	Break My Mind/Govan Cross Special (solo)	6
62	Topic TOP 82	SONGS OF PROTEST (EP)	15
64	Decca DFE 8592	IAN CAMPBELL FOLK GROUP (EP)	15
65	Transatlantic TRAEP 128	SAMPLER (EP)	12
63	Transatlantic TRA 110	THIS IS THE IAN CAMPBELL FOLK GROUP (LP)	30
64	Transatlantic TRA 118	ACROSS THE HILLS (LP)	25
64	Contour 2870 314	PRESENTING THE IAN CAMPBELL FOLK GROUP (LP, reissue of 1st LP)	12
68	Transatlantic TRA 163	THE CIRCLE GAME (LP)	22
68	Xtra XTRA 1074	TAM O'SHANTER (LP, as Ian Campbell & John Dunkerley)	18
69	Transatlantic TRASAM 4	THE IAN CAMPBELL FOLK GROUP SAMPLER (LP)	12
69	Transatlantic TRASAM 12	SAMPLER 2 (LP, as Ian Campbell Folk Four)	12
69	MFP SMFP 1349	IAN CAMPBELL & FOLK GROUP WITH DAVE SWARBRICK (LP)	12
71	Argo ZFB 13	THE SUN IS BURNING (LP)	25
72	Pye PKL 5506	SOMETHING TO SING ABOUT (LP)	15

(see also Dave Swarbrick)

JEAN CAMPBELL

60	Embassy WB 372	The Big Hurt/I Can't Begin To Tell You (78)	5
60	Embassy WB 395	Sweet Nuthin's/PAUL RICH: Standing On The Corner (78)	7
60	Embassy WB 398	Robot Man/BOBBY BRENT: Lucky Five (78)	7
60	Embassy WB 407	I'm Sorry/Everybody's Somebody's Fool (78)	9
60	Embassy WB 408	Paper Roses/Train Of Love (78)	9
60	Embassy WB 417	My Heart Has A Mind Of It's Own/I Want To Be Wanted (78)	9

JIMMY CAMPBELL

69	Fontana TF 1009	On A Monday/Dear Marge (some in p/s)	10/6
70	Fontana TF 1076	Lyanna/Frankie Joe	6

70	Fontana 6007 025	Don't Leave Me Now/So Lonely Without You	6
69	Fontana STL 5508	SON OF ANASTASIA (LP)	25
70	Vertigo 6360 010	HALF BAKED (LP, gatefold sleeve, swirl label)	15
72	Philips 6308 100	JIMMY CAMPBELL'S ALBUM (LP)	18

(see also Kirkbys, 23rd Turnoff, Rockin' Horse)

JO-ANN CAMPBELL
58	London HLU 8536	Wait A Minute/It's True (78 rpm = £20)	65
60	HMV POP 776	Bobby, Bobby, Bobby/A Kookie Little Paradise	20
61	HMV POP 873	Motorcycle Michael/Puka Puka Pants	20
62	HMV POP 1003	You Made Me Love You/I Changed My Mind Jack	20
62	Columbia DB 4889	Sloppy Joe/I'm The Girl From Wolverton Mountain	10
62	Cameo Parkway CP 237	Mr Fix It Man/Let Me Do It My Way	15
63	Cameo Parkway CP 249	Mother Please/Waiting For Love	15

JUNIOR CAMPBELL
74	Deram SML 1106	SECOND TIME AROUND (LP)	15

(see also Marmalade, Clan, Dean Ford & Gaylords)

MICHAEL CAMPBELL
(see Dread At The Controls)

MURRAY CAMPBELL
58	Philips PB 880	Hey Cabby/One Day I'll Buy A Trumpet (78)	8
58	Philips PB 774	Shangri-La/Balmoral Melody (78)	6

ROY CAMPBELL (& JAZZBO JASPERS)
68	Giant GN 41	Another Saturday Night/Wonderful World (with Jazzbo Jaspers)	7
68	Jolly JY 003	Suzette/Engine Engine Number Nine	7

PATRICK CAMPBELL-LYONS
73	Sovereign SOV 115	Everybody Should Fly A Kite/I Think I Want Him Too	15
73	Sovereign SOV 119	Out On The Road/Me And My Friend	15
77	Electric WOT 12	That's What My Guru Said Last Night/The Whistling Fiddler	5
73	Sovereign SVNA 7258	ME AND MY FRIEND (LP, gatefold sleeve)	90
81	Public PUBL 1	THE ELECTRIC PLOUGH (LP)	20

(see also Nirvana [U.K.], Pica, Hat & Tie, Aquila)

CAN
73	United Artists UP 35506	Spoon/I'm So Green	6
73	United Artists UP 35596	Moonshake/Future Days (Edit)	6
74	United Artists UP 35749	Dizzy Dizzy (Edit)/Splash (Edit)	6
76	Virgin VS 153	I Want More/... And More	5
76	Virgin VS 166	Silent Night/Cascade Waltz	5
77	Virgin VS 172	Don't Say No/Return	5
78	Lightning LIG 545	Can-Can/Can Be	5
69	United Artists UAS 29094	MONSTER MOVIE (LP, burgundy label)	40
70	United Artists UAS 29283	SOUNDTRACKS (LP)	35
71	Utd. Artists UAD 60009/10	TAGO MAGO (2-LP, flip-top sleeve)	45
72	United Artists UAS 29414	EGE BAMYASI (LP, with inner sleeve)	35
73	United Artists UAS 29505	FUTURE DAYS (LP)	20
74	United Artists UAG 29673	SOON OVER BABALUMA (LP, original silver sleeve)	18
74	United Artists USP 103	LIMITED EDITION (LP)	20
75	Virgin V 2041	LANDED (LP)	15
76	Caroline CAD 3001	UNLIMITED EDITION (2-LP, gatefold sleeve)	20
76	Sunset SLS 50400	OPENER (LP, reissue of "Monster Movie")	15
77	Virgin V 2079	SAW DELIGHT (LP, with insert)	12
78	United Artists UDM 105/6	CANNIBALISM (2-LP, gatefold sleeve)	20

CANAAN
73	Dovetail DOVE 3	CANAAN (LP)	25
76	Myrrh MYR 1042	OUT OF THE WILDERNESS (LP, with inner sleeve)	20

LOS CANARIOS
67	Major Minor MM 502	Three Two One Ah/What Can I Do For You	15
67	Major Minor MM 532	Get On Your Knees/Keep On The Right Side	40

CANDIDO
57	HMV DLP 1182	THE VOLCANIC (10" LP)	20
79	Salsoul SSLP 1517	DANCIN' AND PRANCIN' (LP)	12

CANDLE FACTORY
70s	CAVS	NIGHTSHIFT (LP, private pressing)	55

CONTE CANDOLI
56	London Jazz LZ-N 14010	SINCERELY, CONTE (10" LP)	15

PETER CANDOLI & HIS ORCHESTRA
56	Capitol CL 14615	St. Louis Blues — Boogie/The Big Top (Entry Of The Gladiators)	10
60	Warner Bros WB 2	Sunset Strip Cha-Cha/DON RALKE: 77 Sunset Strip	5

CANDY
69	Emerald MD 1119	Little Bit Of Soul/Signs Of Love	12
69	Grape GR 3017	Ace Of Hearts/BILLY JACK: Bet Yer Life I Do	10

PENNY CANDY
60	Top Rank JAR 328	Come On Over/They Said	10

CANDY & KISSES
65	Cameo Parkway C 336	The 81/Two Happy People (DJ copy = £175)	100
85	Kent TOWN 104	Mr Creator/CHUCK JACKSON: Hand It Over (withdrawn)	50

CANDY CHOIR
66	Parlophone R 5472	Silence Is Golden/Shake Hands (And Come Out Crying)	18
67	CBS 3061	Children And Flowers/Marianne	8
68	CBS 3305	Alexander's Ragtime Band/No Grey Skies	8
70	Polydor 56369	Why Do You Cry My Love/Lucky Jim	6

(see also Summer Set, Barry Ryan)

CANDY DATES
65	Pye 7N 15944	A Day Just Like That/Well I Do	10

CANDYMEN
67	HMV POP 1612	Georgia Pines/Movies In My Mind	8

CANE
78	Lightning GIL 31	3 BY 3 EP (p/s)	15

BOB CANN
70s	Topic 12TS 275	WEST COUNTRY MELODEON (LP)	18

CANNED HEAT
68	Liberty	Rollin' And Tumblin'/Bullfrog Blues (unreleased)	
68	Liberty LBF 15090	On The Road Again/The World In A Jug	8
69	Liberty LBF 15169	Going Up The Country/One Kind Favour	8
69	Liberty LBF 15200	Time Was/Low Down	8
69	Liberty LBF 15255	Poor Moon/Sic 'Em Pigs	8
69	Liberty LBF 15302	Let's Work Together/I'm Her Man	8
70	Liberty LBF 15350	Sugar Bee/Shake It And Break It	8
70	Pye International 7N 25513	Spoonful/Big Road Blues	8
70	Liberty LBF 15395	Future Blues/Skat	6
70	Liberty LBF 15429	Christmas Blues/Do Not Enter	6
71	Liberty LBF 15439	Wooly Bully/My Time Ain't Long	6
72	United Artists UP 35348	Rockin' With The King (with Little Richard)/I Don't Care What You Tell Me	6
73	United Artists UP 35562	Keep It Clean/You Can Run But You Sure Can't Hide	6
67	Liberty LBL/LBS 83059E	CANNED HEAT (LP)	30
68	Liberty LBL/LBS 83103	BOOGIE WITH CANNED HEAT (LP)	30
69	Liberty LDS 84001E	LIVING THE BLUES (2-LP, gatefold sleeve)	30
69	Liberty LBS 83239	HALLELUJAH (LP, gatefold sleeve)	20
70	Pye Intl. NSPL 28129	VINTAGE HEAT (LP)	22
70	Liberty LBS 83303	CANNED HEAT COOKBOOK (LP)	18
70	Liberty LBS 83333	CANNED HEAT '70 CONCERT (RECORDED LIVE IN EUROPE) (LP, g/fold sleeve)	12
70	Liberty LBS 83364	FUTURE BLUES (LP, gatefold sleeve)	20
71	Liberty LPS 103/4	HOOKER'N'HEAT (2-LP, gatefold sleeve, with John Lee Hooker)	35
72	United Artists UAG 29304	HISTORICAL FIGURES AND ANCIENT HEADS (LP, gatefold sleeve)	12
73	United Artists UAS 29455	THE NEW AGE (LP)	12

(see also Harvey Mandel)

CANNIBAL & HEADHUNTERS
65	Stateside SS 403	Land Of A Thousand Dances/I'll Show You How To Love Me	25
67	CBS 62942	LAND OF A 1000 DANCES (LP)	30

CANNIBALS
78	Big Cock F-UK 1	Good Guys/Nothing Takes The Place Of You (printed paper bag sleeve)	5
85	Hit Records REEBEE 2	Christmas Rock 'n' Roll/New Year's Eve Song (doublepack in stocking)	6

(see also Count Bishops)

ACE CANNON
62	London HLU 9498	Tuff/Sittin'	10
62	London HLU 9546	Blues Stay Away From Me/Blues In My Heart	10
63	London HLU 9745	Cottonfields/Mildew	10
64	London HLU 9866	Searchin'/Love Letters In The Sand	10
67	London HLU 10105	Wonderland By Night/As Time Goes By	5
70	London HA-U/SH-U 8407	ACE OF SAX (LP)	20

CONROY CANNON
69	Pama PM 769	Oh Happy Day/Can't Get Along Without You	8

FREDDY CANNON
59	Top Rank JAR 135	Tallahassee Lassie/You Know (78 rpm = £25)	30
59	Top Rank JAR 207	Okefenokee/Kookie Hat	10
59	Top Rank JAR 247	Way Down Yonder In New Orleans/Fractured	10
60	Top Rank JAR 309	California, Here I Come/Indiana	10
60	Top Rank JAR 334	Chattanooga Shoeshine Boy/Boston (My Home Town)	10
60	Top Rank JAR 369	The Urge/Jump Over	12
60	Top Rank JAR 407	Happy Shades Of Blue/Guernavaca Choo Choo	10
60	Top Rank JAR 518	Humdinger/My Blue Heaven	10
61	Top Rank JAR 548	Muskrat Rumble/Two Thousand 88	10
61	Top Rank JAR 568	Buzz Buzz A Diddle It/Opportunity	25
61	Top Rank JAR 579	Transistor Sister/Walk To The Moon	10
61	Top Rank JAR 592	For Me And My Gal/Blue Plate Special	10
62	Top Rank JAR 609	Teen Queen Of The Week/Wild Guy	10
62	Stateside SS 101	Palisades Park/June July And August	10
62	Stateside SS 118	What's Gonna Happen When Summer's Done/Broadway	10
62	Stateside SS 134	If You Were A Rock & Roll Record/The Truth Ruth	20
63	Stateside SS 155	Come On And Love Me/Four Letter Man	10
63	Stateside SS 183	The Ups And Downs Of Love/It's Been Nice	10
63	Stateside SS 201	Patty Baby/Betty Jean	15
63	Stateside SS 220	Everybody Monkey/Oh Gloria	10
64	Stateside SS 260	That's The Way Girls Are/Do What The Hippies Do	10
64	Warner Bros WB 123	Abigail Beecher/All American Girl	5
64	Stateside SS 298	Sweet Georgia Brown/What A Party	10
65	Warner Bros WB 5645	Action/Beechwood City	10

66	Warner Bros WB 5693	The Dedication Song/Come On Come On	5
69	London HLK 10252	Beautiful Downtown Burbank/If You Give Me A Title	5
60	Top Rank JKP 2058	THE EXPLOSIVE FREDDY (BOOM! BOOM!) CANNON (EP)	40
60	Top Rank JKP 2066	FOUR DIRECT HITS (EP)	35
61	Top Rank JKP 3010	ON TARGET (EP)	40
62	Stateside SE 1002	BLAST OFF WITH FREDDY CANNON (EP)	50
60	Top Rank 25/018	THE EXPLOSIVE FREDDY CANNON (LP)	30
61	Top Rank 35/106	FREDDY CANNON SINGS HAPPY SHADES OF BLUE (LP)	50
61	Top Rank 35/113	FREDDY CANNON FAVOURITES (LP)	50
63	Stateside SL 10013	BANG ON (LP)	50
64	Stateside SL 10062	STEPS OUT (LP)	60
64	Warner Bros WM/WS 8153	FREDDY CANNON (LP)	30

(see also Danny & Juniors)

JUDY CANNON
65	Pye 7N 15900	The Very First Day I Met You/Hello Heartache	50

SEAN CANNON
60s	Cottage COT 411	ROVING JOURNEYMAN (LP)	20

CANNON BALL & JOHNNY MELODY
69	Big Shot BI 518	Parapinto/Cool Hand Luke	15

(see also Carl Bryan, King Cannon, Johnny Moore, Jackie Mittoo, Royals)

CANNONBALLS
61	Coral Q 72428	Cannonball Caboose/New Orleans Beat	10
61	Coral Q 72431	Lullaby Of Birdland/Calliope Boogie	10

CANNON BROTHERS
65	Brit WI 1003	Turn Your Eyes To Me/Don't Stop Now	18

CANNONS
60	Decca F 11269	I Didn't Know The Gun Was Loaded/My Guy's Come Back	15
61	Columbia DB 4724	Bush Fire/Juicy	20

CANNON'S JUG STOMPERS
66	Tax LP 2	CANNON'S JUG STOMPERS/CLIFFORD'S LOUISVILLE JUG BAND (LP, 1 side each)	22

CANNY FETTLE
75	Tradition TSR 023	VARRY CANNY (LP)	30
77	Tradition TSR 027	TRIP TO HARROGATE (LP)	18

EDDIE CANTOR
61	Capitol EAP1 20113	MA HE'S MAKING EYES AT ME (EP)	12

CAPABILITY BROWN
72	Charisma CB 193	Wake Up Little Sister/Windfall	6
73	Charisma CB 207	Midnight Cruiser/Silent Sounds	6
73	Charisma CB 217	Liar/Keep Death Off The Road	6
70s	Charisma BCP 7	War (p/s)	6
72	Charisma CAS 1056	FROM SCRATCH (LP)	18
73	Charisma CAS 1068	VOICE (LP)	18

(see also Unit 4+2, Tony Rivers & Castaways)

JIM CAPALDI
74	Island WIP 6198	It's All Up To You/Whale Meat Again	6
72	Island ILPS 9187	OH HOW WE DANCED (LP, gatefold sleeve)	15
77	Island ILPS 9497	PLAY IT BY EAR (LP)	15

(see also Hellions, Traffic)

CAPE KENNEDY CONSTRUCTION CO.
69	President PT 265	The First Steps On The Moon/Armageddon	40

CAPERCAILLIE
84	Etive/ERC 333	CASCADE (cassette)	15
84	Etive/SRT 4KL 178	CASCADE (LP)	15
87	Grampian TV GPN 1001	THE BLOOD IS STRONG (LP, with insert)	12
87	Green Linnet SIF 1077	CROSSWINDS (LP, with insert)	12

(see also Etives)

CAPES & MASKS
65	Fontana TL 5339	COMIC BOOK HEROES (LP)	60
65	Nevis NEV R005	COMIC BOOK HEROES (LP)	50

CAPES OF GOOD HOPE
66	Stateside SS 577	Winter's Children/If My Monique Could Only Dance	10

CAPITAL LETTERS
77	Greensleeves GRED 2	Smoking My Ganja/Natty Walk (12")	15
79	Greensleeves GRED 16	UK Skanking/Run Run Run (12")	10
79	Greensleeves GREL 7	HEADLINE NEWS (LP)	12

CAPITOLS (U.K.)
66	Pye 7N 17025	Honey And Wine/Boulavogue	12

CAPITOLS (U.S.)
66	Atlantic 584 004	Cool Jerk/Hello Stranger	25

(see also Three Caps)

ANDY CAPP
69	Treasure Isle TI 7052	Pop-A-Top/RICO: The Lion Speaks	12
70	Duke DU 69	The Law Parts 1 & 2	6
70	Duke DU 71	Poppy Show/Pop-A-Top (Part 2)	10

MINT VALUE £

AL CAPPS
73	Stateside SS 2214	Shangri-La/Magician	7

CAPREEZ
79	Grapevine GRP 113	How To Make A Sad Man Glad/It's Good To Be Home Again	10

DANNY CAPRI
55	Capitol CL 14265	Desirable/I Do, I Do	10
55	Capitol CL 14302	Don't Make A Liar Out Of Me/Angelica	15

CAPRICORN
70	MCA MK 5050	Liverpool Hello/How Did You Find Me	6
(see also Marty Wilde)			

CAPRIS
61	Columbia DB 4605	There's A Moon Out Tonight/Indian Girl	150

CAPTAIN BEEFHEART & HIS MAGIC BAND
SINGLES
68	Pye International 7N 25443	Yellow Brick Road/Abba Zabba	40
68	A&M AMS 726	Moonchild/Who Do You Think You're Fooling	45
73	Reprise K 14233	Too Much Time/My Head Is My Only House Unless It Rains	6
74	Virgin VS 110	Upon The My-Oh-My/Magic Be	5
78	Buddah BDS 466	Sure 'Nuff 'N Yes I Do/Electricity	7
78	MCA MCA 366	Hard Workin' Man (Jack Nitzsche featuring Captain Beefheart)/ JACK NITZSCHE: Coke Machine	6

EPs
71	A&M AME 600	DIDDY WAH DIDDY (promo only)	375
79	Virgin SIXPACK 1	SIX-PACK/SIX TRACK (picture disc, die-cut p/s with stand, 5,000 only)	18
82	Virgin VS 534 12	LIGHT REFLECTED OFF THE OCEANS OF THE MOON (12" EP, p/s)	12
84	A&M AMY 226	THE LEGENDARY A&M SESSIONS (12" EP/mini-LP, Diddy Wah Diddy EP plus Where I Am, I Always Am")	15
86	Edsel BLIMP 902	THE LEGENDARY A&M SESSIONS (12" EP, reissue)	15

ORIGINAL LPs
68	Pye Intl. NPL 28110	SAFE AS MILK (mono, flipback sleeve)	50
68	Liberty LBL/LBS 83172	STRICTLY PERSONAL (gatefold sleeve, mono/stereo)	40/35
69	Straight STS 1053	TROUT MASK REPLICA (2-LP, gatefold sleeve)	50
70	Straight STS 1063	LICK MY DECALS OFF, BABY	50
71	Buddah 2365 002	MIRROR MAN (gatefold die-cut sleeve)	30
72	Reprise K 44162	THE SPOTLIGHT KID (tan 'riverboat' label, some with lyric card insert)	25/20
72	Reprise K 54007	CLEAR SPOT (PVC sleeve with card insert)	30
74	Virgin V 2015	UNCONDITIONALLY GUARANTEED ('two virgins' label)	20
74	Virgin V 2023	BLUEJEANS & MOONBEAMS ('two virgins' label)	12
79	Virgin V 2149	SHINY BEAST (BAT CHAIN PULLER)	12
80	Virgin V 2172	DOC AT THE RADAR STATION	12
82	Virgin V 2237	ICE CREAM FOR CROW (with inner sleeve)	12

REISSUE LPs
70	Buddah 2349 002	DROPOUT BOOGIE (stereo reissue of SAFE AS MILK)	20
73	Reprise K 44244	LICK MY DECALS OFF, BABY	25
74	Buddah BDLP 4004	MIRROR MAN	20
75	Reprise K 64026	TROUT MASK REPLICA (2-LP, gatefold sleeve, tan 'riverboat' label, matt sleeve)	25
70s	Reprise K 64026	TROUT MASK REPLICA (2-LP, gatefold sleeve, 2nd re-pressing, tan 'riverboat' label, soft laminated sleeve)	20
76	Reprise K 84006	TWO ORIGINALS OF CAPTAIN BEEFHEART (2-LP, reissue of LICK, MY DECALS OFF, BABY & SPOTLIGHT KID)	20
77	Pye FILD 008	THE FILE SERIES (2-LP, reissue of SAFE AS MILK & MIRROR MAN die-cut sleeve with inners)	18
(see also Mu, Frank Zappa, Jack Nitzsche)			

CAPTAIN BEYOND
72	Capricorn K 47503	CAPTAIN BEYOND (LP)	30
(see also Deep Purple)			

CAPTAIN LOCKHEED & THE STARFIGHTERS
73	United Artists UP 35543	Ejection/Catch A Falling Starfighter (p/s)	25
73	United Artists UP 35543	Ejection/Catch A Falling Starfighter (different mix of A-side, no p/s)	10
(see also Robert Calvert)			

CAPTAIN SCARLET
(see under Century 21)

CAPTAIN SINBAD
83	Oak Sound OSLP 002	AGAIN (LP)	30
84	Greensleeves GREL 34	THE SEVEN VOYAGES OF SINBAD (LP)	35

C.A. QUINTET
83	Psycho PSYCHO 12	TRIP THROUGH HELL (LP, reissue of U.S. 60s LP)	15

CARAVAN
69	Verve VS 1518	A Place Of My Own/Ride	45
70	Decca F 13063	If I Could Do It All Over Again, I'd Do It All Over You/Hello, Hello	15
71	Decca F 23125	Love To Love You (And Tonight Pigs Will Fly)/Golf Girl	15
75	Decca FR 13599	Stuck In A Hole/Lover	5
76	BTM SBT 104	All The Way (With John Wayne's Single-Handed Liberation Of Paris)/ Chiefs And Indians (p/s)	6
77	Arista ARIST 110	Better By Far/Silver Strings	5
80	Kingdom KV 8009	Heartbreaker/It's Never Too Late (p/s)	6
68	Verve (S)VLP 6011	CARAVAN (LP, 'pillar' sleeve, mono/stereo)	160

70	Decca SKL 5052	IF I COULD DO IT ALL OVER AGAIN, I'D DO IT ALL OVER YOU (LP)	25
71	Deram SDL-R 1	IN THE LAND OF GREY AND PINK (LP, gatefold sleeve)	25
72	Deram SDL 8	WATERLOO LILY (LP, gatefold sleeve)	25
72	MGM 2353 058	CARAVAN (LP, reissue)	20
73	Deram SDL-R 12	FOR GIRLS WHO GROW PLUMP IN THE NIGHT (LP, gatefold sleeve)	15
74	Deram SML 1110	CARAVAN AND THE NEW SYMPHONIA (LIVE AT DRURY LANE) (LP)	15
75	Decca SKLR 5210	CUNNING STUNTS (LP)	12

(see also Gringo, Matching Mole, Hatfield & The North, Spiro Gyra)

CARAVELLES
63	Decca F 11697	You Don't Have To Be A Baby To Cry/The Last One To Know	5
63	Decca F 11758	I Really Don't Want To Know/I Was Wrong	5
64	Decca F 11816	Have You Ever Been Lonely?/Gonna Get Along Without Ya Now	5
64	Fontana TF 466	You Are Here/How Can I Be Sure?	5
64	Fontana TF 509	I Don't Care If The Sun Don't Shine/I Like A Man	5
64	Polydor NH 59034	True Love Never Runs Smooth/Georgia Boy	5
66	Polydor 56137	Hey Mama You've Been On My Mind/New York	10
67	Polydor 56156	I Want To Love You Again/I Had To Walk Home Myself	5
68	Pye 7N 17654	The Other Side Of Love/I Hear A New Kind Of Music	5
63	Decca LK 4565	THE CARAVELLES (LP)	30

(see also Lois Lane)

GUY CARAWAN
58	Pye Nixa 7N 15132	Old Man Atom (Talking Atomic Blues)/Michael Row The Boat Ashore (78 rpm = £7)	8
67	Columbia SX 6065	A GUY CALLED CARAWAN (LP)	30

(see also Peggy Seeger & Guy Carawan)

CARCASS
88	Earache MOSH 06	REEK OF PUTREFACTION (LP)	25
89	Earache MOSH 18	SYMPHONIES OF SICKNESS (LP, picture disc)	30

CARDBOARD ORCHESTRA
69	CBS 4176	Zebady Zak/Mary Tell Me Why	8
69	CBS 4633	Nothing But A Sad Sad Show/Yes I Heard A Little Bird	8

(see also Zior, Monument)

CARDBOARD CATS
88	Reflector FLEX 3	Warm In The Sewer/Your Friend,Icky (500 only)	6

CARDIAC ARREST
79	Another Record AN 1	Running In The Street/T.V. Friends (p/s, 500 only)	10
79	Tortch TOR 002	A BUS FOR A BUS ON A BUS (EP)	20

(see also Cardiacs)

CARDIACS
81	private label	TOY WORLD (cassette)	20
81	private label	THE OBVIOUS IDENTITY (cassette)	20
86	Alphabet ALPH 002	SEASIDE TREATS (12" EP, with poster & lyric insert)	8
87	Alphabet ALPH 006	THERE'S TOO MANY IRONS IN THE FIRE (12" EP, with poster)	8
88	Alphabet ALPH 008	Is This The Life/I'm Eating In Bed (p/s)	7
88	Alphabet ALPHT 008	Is This The Life/Loosefish Goosegash/I'm Eating In Bed (12", p/s)	10
88	Alphabet ALPH 009	Susannah's Still Alive/Blind In Safety And Leafy In Love (p/s)	5
91	Alphabet ALPH 015	DAY IS GONE (12" EP, with lyric sheet)	8
80s	Alphabet ALPH 000	ARCHIVE CARDIACS (cassette, fan club issue, compilation of Toy World & The Obvious Identity)	10
83	Alphabet ALPH 01	THE SEASIDE (13-track cassette, colour inlay)	20
86	Alphabet ALPH 003	MR & MRS SMITH & MR DRAKE (cassette, fan club issue)	10
87	Alphabet ALPH 004	BIG SHIP (mini LP, with lyric insert)	12
87	Alphabet ALPH 005	RUDE BOOTLEG — LIVE AT READING '86 (LP, stamped sleeve with insert)	15
87	Alphabet ALPH MC005	RUDE BOOTLEG — LIVE AT READING '86 (cassette)	12
88	Torso CD 060	A LITTLE MAN AND A HOUSE AND THE WHOLE WORLD WINDOW (CD)	18
88	Alphabet ALPH 009T	Susannah's Still Alive/Blind In Safety And Leafy In Love/All His Geese Are Swans (12", p/s)	8
89	Alphabet ALPH 011	Baby Heart Dirt/I Hold My Love In My Arms (p/s)	5
88	Night Tracks SFNT 013	RADIO ONE EVENING SESSION: R.E.S./ Buds And Spawn/In A City Lining/ Is This The Life/Cameras (12" EP)	10
88	Alphabet ALPHLP 010	CARDIACS LIVE (LP)	15
88	Alphabet ALPH 012	ON LAND AND IN THE SEA (LP)	15
91	Alphabet ALPHLP 014	SONGS FOR SHIPS AND IRONS (LP)	12
92	Alphabet ALPHLP 017	HEAVEN BORN AND EVER BRIGHT (LP)	12

CARDIGANS
58	Mercury AMT 1007	Poor Boy/Each Other (78 rpm = £12)	10

CARDIGANS
99	Simply Vinyl SVLP 114	LIFE (LP, reissue)	12
96	Stockholm CARDBOXCD 1	FIRST BAND ON THE MOON (CD, box set with poster & T-shirt)	18
00	Simply Vinyl SVLP 175	GRAN TURISMO (LP, 180gm vinyl)	15

CARDINALS
72	Nelmwood Audio	ON TOP OF THE WORLD (LP)	22

JACK CARDWELL
54	Parlophone CMSP 24	Whiskey, Women And Loaded Dice/Slap-Ka-Dab (export issue)	30
54	Parlophone DP 400	Whiskey, Women And Loaded Dice/Slap-Ka-Dab (78, export issue)	5
54	Parlophone CMSP 27	Blue Love/Diddle Diddle Dumpling (export issue)	30
54	Parlophone DP 406	Blue Love/Diddle Diddle Dumpling (78, export issue)	5
50s	Parlophone DP 424	Ko Ko Mo (I Love You So)/Are You Mine? (with Jackie Hill) (78)	10

CARE
83	Arista KBIRD 2	Flaming Sword/Misericorde (picture disc)	5

(see also Wild Swans, Lotus Eaters, Lightning Seeds)

CAREFREES

63	Oriole CB 1916	We Love You Beatles/Hot Blooded Lover	25
64	Oriole CB 1931	Aren't You Glad You're You/Paddy Wack	12

DAVE CAREY (JAZZ BAND)

53	Columbia SCM 5030	Broken Wings/Oh, Happy Day (as David Carey)	8
56	Tempo A 122	Kater Street Rag/Kansas City Kitty	10
56	Tempo A 133	I've Found A New Baby/Brown Skin Mama	10
56	Tempo A 138	Sunset Cafe Stomp/Sweet Georgia Brown	10
56	Tempo A 150	Ida, Sweet As Apple Cider/Button Up Your Overcoat	8
61	Philips PB 1158	Bingo (I'm In Love)/Paddlin' Madelin' Home (some in p/s)	8
56	Tempo EXA 38	DAVE CAREY JAZZ BAND (EP)	8
56	Tempo EXA 43	DAVE CAREY JAZZ BAND (EP)	8
56	Tempo EXA 51	DAVE CAREY JAZZ BAND (EP)	15
55	Tempo LAP 4	DAVE CAREY JAZZ BAND (LP)	15
57	Tempo TAP 16	JAZZ AT THE RAILWAY ARMS (LP)	15

MARIAH CAREY

90	Columbia 655 932-2	Vision Of Love/Sent From Up Above/Medley (CD)	20
90	Columbia 656 364-2	Love Takes Time/Vanishing/You Need Me (CD)	20
90	Columbia 656 364-5	Love Takes Time/Vanishing/You Need Me/Vision Of Love (CD, picture disc)	20
91	Columbia 656 583-2	Someday (7" Jackswing Mix)/(12" Jackswing Mix)/Love/Love Takes Time (CD)	15
91	Columbia 656 583-5	Someday (7" Jackswing Mix)/Vision Of Love/Love Takes Time/Alone In Love (CD, picture disc)	12
91	Columbia 656 931-2	There's Got To Be A Way (Album Version)/(12" Remix)/(ALT Vocal Club Mix) (CD)	15
91	Columbia 656 931-5	There's Got To Be A Way/(Album Version)/(7" Remix)/Someday (7" Jackswing Mix)/Vision Of Love (CD, picture disc)	15
91	Columbia 657 403-2	Emotions/Vanishing/Vision Of Love (CD)	8
92	Columbia 657 662-2	Can't Let Go (Edit)/To Be Around You/The Wind (CD, slimline jewel case)	12
92	Columbia 657 941-7	Make It Happen/Emotions (Special Motion Edit) (p/s)	5
92	Columbia 657 941-2	Make It Happen (Radio Edit)/(Ext. Version)/(Dub)/(C&C Classic Mix)/(LP Version) (CD)	8
92	Columbia 658 137-9	I'll Be There (live)/Vision Of Love (live)/If It's Over/All In Your Mind (CD, picture disc)	12

TONY CAREY

84	MCA MCA 873	Fine Fine Day/Say It's Over (p/s)	6
84	MCA MCFC 3212	SOME TOUGH CITY (LP, with inner sleeve)	12
	(see also Rainbow)		

CAREY & LLOYD

72	Attack ATT 8032	Do It Again (as Carey/Lloyd)/GARY RANGLIN: Watch It	6
72	Grape GR 3025	Come Down Part 1/DYNAMITES: Come Down Part 2	6
	(see also Carey Johnson, Lloyd Young, Lloyd & Carey)		

HENSON CARGILL

68	Monument MON 1015	Skip A Rope/Very Well-Travelled Man	6

PATRICK CARGILL

71	Hit HIT 16	Father Dear Father/Theme (Instrumental)	6

CARIBBEANS

69	Doctor Bird DB 1181	Let Me Walk By/AMBLINGS: Tell Me Why	18
69	Crab CR 14	Please Please/MATADORS: The Destroyer	15

CARIBBEATS

66	Ska Beat JB 246	The Bells Of St. Mary's/WINSTON RICHARDS: Loki	22
67	Double D DD 101	Highway 300/I Think Of You (actually by Merlene McKenzie)	15
67	Double D DD 103	I'll Try/If I Did Look	15
68	Double D DD 111	One Step/HAZEL WRIGHT: Please Help Me	50
	(see also Bobby Aitken, Itals)		

CARIBS

60	Starlite ST45 012	Taboo/Mathilda Cha Cha Cha!	10

CARIFTA ALLSTARS

72	Green Door GD 4040	The Harder They Come (actually by Charlie Ace)/Time Is Still Here	8

CARL & COMMANDERS

61	Columbia DB 4719	Farmer John/Cleanin' Up	20

BELINDA CARLISLE

88	I.R.S. DIRM 118	Mad About You/I Never Wanted A Rich Man/Mad About You (Extended Mix) (3" CD)	20
87	Virgin VSCD 1036	Heaven Is A Place On Earth/We Can Change/Heaven Is A Place On Earth (Heavenly Version)/Heaven Is A Place On Earth (Acapella Version) (CD)	15
88	Virgin VSCD 1046	I Get Weak (7" Version)/Should I Let You In/I Get Weak (12" Version) (CD, picture disc)	8
88	Virgin VSTY 1074	Circle In The Sand/(Beach Party Mix)/(Seaside Groove Mix) (12", picture disc)	10
88	Virgin VSCD 1074	Circle In The Sand (7" Version)/(Seaside Mood Groove Mix)/(Sandblast Multi-Mix)/(Beach Party Mix) (CD)	8
88	Virgin VSX 1114	World Without You (Remix)/Nobody Owns Me (box set, 2 cards & lyric sheet)	12
88	Virgin VSTP 1114	World Without You (Extended World-wide Mix)/World Without You (7" Remix)/Nobody Owns Me (12", poster p/s)	8
88	Virgin VSCD 1114	World Without You (Extended World-wide Mix)/World Without You (7" Remix)/World Without You (Panavision Mix) (CD)	8
88	Virgin VSCD 1150	Love Never Dies... (Full Length Version)/I Feel Free (live)/Circle In The Sand (live)/Heaven Is A Place On Earth (live) (CD, with prints)	12
89	Virgin VSCD 1210	Leave A Light On (7" Version)/Shades Of Michaelangelo/Leave A Light On (Extended Mix) (3" CD in card sl., also 5" CD in jewel case [662 719/211], £12)	8

89	Virgin VSCD 1230DJ	La Luna/Whatever It Takes (3" CD, picture disc, promo only) 60
89	Virgin VSCDT 1230	La Luna (Single Version)/La Luna (Extended Dance Mix)/
		La Luna (12" Dub Mix) (5" CD, slimline jewel case) 8
90	Virgin VSCD 1244	Runaway Horses/Heaven Is A Place On Earth (live)/Circle In The Sand
		(Beach Party Mix) (3" CD, card sleeve)............................... 8
90	Virgin VSCDT 1244	Runaway Horses/Heaven Is A Place On Earth (Live)/Circle In The Sand
		(Beach Party Mix) (5" CD, slimline jewel case) 8
87	Virgin VSCD 1036	HEAVEN ON EARTH (CD, picture disc, stickered case) 35
	(see also Go-Go's, Smithereens)	

BILL CARLISLE & CARLISLES
| 59 | Mercury AMT 1063 | Down Boy/Union Suit .... 50 |
| 64 | Hickory 45-1254 | Shanghai Rooster/Big John Henry's Girl .... 10 |

CARLISLE BROTHERS
| 59 | Parlophone GEP 8799 | FRESH FROM THE COUNTRY (EP) .... 30 |

DON CARLOS ORCHESTRA
54	HMV 7 MC 4	Delicado/Anything Can Happen (export issue) 6
56	HMV 7 MC 48	The Bandit/Mexicana (export issue) 6
60	Top Rank JAR 376	Mustapha/Josita 6

DON CARLOS
81	Negus Roots NERT 004	Gimme Gimme Your Love/PAP TULLO: Gimme More Love (12") 20
82	Negus Roots NERT 015	Magic Man/Magic Dub (12") 12
80s	Rusty International RI 001	Isabel/BILLY BOYO: One Morning/CAPTAIN SINBAD & ROOTS RADICALS:
		Radication Dehbout (12") 12
82	Negus Roots NERLP 001	SUFFERING (LP) 40
82	Negus Roots NERLP 005	HARVEST TIME (LP) 60
	(see also Black Uhuru)	

DAVE CARLSEN
| 73 | Spark SRLP 110 | A PALE HORSE (LP) .... 35 |

RAY CARLSON
| 67 | MGM MGM 1362 | Speak No Sorrow/It's Getting Me Down Girl .... 7 |

(LITTLE) CARL CARLTON
68	Action ACT 4501	Competition Ain't Nothin'/Three Way Love 45
68	Action ACT 4514	46 Drums 1 Guitar/Why Don't They Leave Us Alone...................... 20
69	Action ACT 4537	Look At Mary Wonder/Bad For Each Other (as Carl Carlton)............. 20
75	ABC ABC 4040	Smokin' Room/Signed, Sealed, Delivered, I'm Yours (as Carl Carlton)....... 6
90s	Kent TOWN 105	Competition Ain't Nothin'/HESITATIONS: I'm Not Built That Way 8

EDDIE CARLTON
| 76 | Cream CRM 5001 | It Will Be Done (Parts 1 & 2) .... 10 |

CARLTON & HIS SHOES
68	Coxsone CS 7065	Love Me Forever/Happy Land 38
68	Studio One SO 2062	This Feeling/You And Me (Love Is A Treasure) 38
70s	Studio One PSOL 003	LOVE ME FOREVER (LP) 60
	(see also Lee 'Scratch' Perry, Roy & Enid)	

CARMEN
74	Regal Zonophone RZ 3086	Flamenco Fever/Lonely House 6
74	Regal Zonophone RZ 3090	Bulerias/Stepping Stone. 6
73	R. Zonophone SRZA 8518	FANDANGOS IN SPACE (LP, gatefold sleeve) 20
75	R. Zonophone SLRZ 1040	DANCING ON A COLD WIND (LP, with inner sleeve)..................... 30

HOAGY CARMICHAEL
55	Vogue Coral Q 72078	Crazy Otto Rag/Happy Hoagy's Medley 10
55	Vogue Coral Q 72095	Lazy River/I'm Just Wild About Mary 8
56	Vogue Coral Q 72123	Hong Kong Blues/LES BROWN: It's All Right With Me. 8
56	Vogue Coral Q 72206	I Walk The Line/Flight To Hong Kong 8
54	HMV 7EG 8037	STARDUST (EP). 12
54	Brunswick OE 9023	THE STARDUST ROAD (EP).. 12
58	Vogue VE 170113	HOAGY CARMICHAEL (EP) 12

IAN CARMICHAEL
| 57 | HMV POP 406 | Lucky Jim (How I Envy Him)/Tomorrow, Tomorrow .... 6 |

CARMITA
| 58 | Fontana H 160 | The Crowd/Waterwagon Blues (78 rpm = £8)........................... 6 |

CARNABY
| 65 | Piccadilly 7N 35272 | Jump And Dance/My Love Will Stay .... 100 |
| 84 | SOS SOS 004 | Jump & Dance/BOBBY PARIS: I Walked Away .... 12 |

CARNABY STREET POP ORCHESTRA & CHOIR
| 69 | Carnaby CNLS 6003 | CARNABY STREET POP (LP) .... 40 |

CARNATIONS
| 65 | Blue Beat BB 285 | Mighty Man/What Are You Selling .... 22 |

JUDY CARNE
61	Decca F 11347	Late Last Evening (with David Kernan)/A Plea For The Throne
		(with Betty Marsden & Pip Hinton) ('On The Brighter Side' cast) 5
69	Reprise RS 20680	Right, Said Fred/Sock It To Me 5

CARNEGY HALL
| 68 | Polydor 56224 | The Bells Of San Francisco/Slightly Cracked .... 12 |

CARNIVAL
67	Columbia DB 8255	The Big Bright Green Pleasure Machine/Silver Dreams And Scarlet Memories	7
70	Liberty LBF 15252	Son Of A Preacher Man/Walk On By	6
70	Liberty LBS 83305	THE CARNIVAL (LP)	18

CAROL & MEMORIES
66	CBS 202086	Tears On My Pillow/Crying My Eyes Out	20

BOBBI CAROL
63	Fontana 267 260TF	Will You Love Me Tomorrow/It Doesn't Matter	9

CAROLE & SHERRY
62	Fontana 270 107 TF	I Ain't Ready Yet/Like I Gotta Get Away	10

CAROLINA SLIM
72	Flyright LP 4702	CAROLINA BLUES AND BOOGIE (LP)	20

CAROLINES
65	Polydor BM 56027	Love Made A Fool Of Me/Believe In Me	15

CAROLLS
65	Polydor BM 56046	Give Me Time/Darling I Want You So Much	20

(see also Carols, Carrolls)

CAROLS
70	Revolution REV 013	Everyday I Have To Cry Some/FIRE SESSION: Sleeping Reggae	5

(see also Carolls, Carrolls)

THELMA CARPENTER
61	Coral Q 72422	Yes, I'm Lonesome Tonight/Gimme A Little Kiss	10
61	Coral Q 72442	Back Street/I Ought To Know	10

CARPENTERS
69	A&M AMS 716	Merry Christmas Darling/Close To You (gatefold p/s)	7
71	A&M AMS 832	Love Is Surrender/For All We Know	5
71	A&M AMS 851	Rainy Days And Mondays/Saturday	5
71	A&M AMS 868	Merry Xmas Darling/Bless The Beasts And The Children	5
72	A&M AMS 885	Hurting Each Other/Maybe It's You	5
70s	MFP MFP 50431	TICKET TO RIDE (LP)	12

CARPENTER'S APPRENTICE
72	SRS 12107	CHANGES (LP, with insert)	100

CARPET BAGGERS
67	Spin SP 2006	Flea Teacher/On Sunday	20

CARPETTES
77	Small Wonder SMALL 3	RADIO WUNDERBAR (EP)	12
78	Small Wonder SMALL 9	Small Wonder?/2 Ne 1 (p/s)	15
79	Beggars Banquet BEG 27	I Don't Mean It/Easy Way Out (p/s)	10
80	Beggars Banquet BEG 32	Johnny Won't Hurt You/Frustration Paradise/Keys To Your Heart/Total Insecurity (double pack)	10
80	Beggars Banquet BEG 47	Nothing Ever Changes/You Never Realise/Frustration Paradise (live p/s)	10
80	Beggars Banquet BEG 49	The Last Lone Ranger/Love So Strong/Fan Club (p/s)	10
79	Beggars Banquet BEGA 14	FRUSTRATION PARADISE (LP)	12
80	Beggars Banquet BEGA 21	FIGHT AMONGST YOURSELVES (LP)	18

CATHY CARR
56	London HLH 8274	Ivory Tower/Please, Please Believe Me	40
56	Vogue Coral Q 72175	Heartbroken/I'll Cry At Your Wedding	10
59	Columbia DB 4270	First Anniversary/With Love (78 rpm = £10)	10
59	Columbia DB 4317	I'm Gonna Change Him/The Little Things You Do	10
60	Columbia DB 4408	Little Sister/Dark River	15
63	Stateside SS 147	Sailor Boy/The Next Time The Band Plays A Waltz	15

IAN CARR
(see under Nucleus)

JAMES CARR
66	Stateside SS 507	You've Got My Mind Messed Up/That's What I Want To Know (DJ Copy = £150)	75
66	Stateside SS 535	Love Attack/Coming Back To Me Baby (DJ copy = £75)	40
66	Stateside SS 545	You're Pouring Water On A Drowning Man/Forgetting You	30
67	Stateside SS 2001	The Dark End Of the Street/Loveable Girl	30
67	Stateside SS 2038	Let It Happen/A Losing Game (DJ copy = £75)	50
67	Stateside SS 2052	I'm A Fool For You/Gonna Send You Back To Georgia	25
68	Bell BLL 1004	A Man Needs A Woman/Stronger Than Love	30
69	B&C CB 101	Freedom Train/That's The Way Love Turned Out For Me	10
72	Mojo 2092 053	Freedom Train/That's What I Want To Know	15
67	Stateside SL 10205	YOU GOT MY MIND MESSED UP (LP)	120
69	Bell MBLL/SBLL 113	A MAN NEEDS A WOMAN (LP)	50

JOE 'FINGERS' CARR
54	Capitol CL 14169	Piccadilly Rag/Fiddle-A-Delphia	6
55	Capitol CL 14359	The Barky-roll Stomp/Deep In The Heart Of Texas (with Carr-Hops)	6
55	Capitol CL 14372	Give Me A Band And My Baby/Zig-A-Zig (with Joy-Riders)	6

(see also Lou Busch, Vicki Young)

JOHNNY CARR (& CADILLACS)
64	Decca F 11854	Remember That Night/Respectable	20
65	Fontana TF 600	Do You Love That Girl?/Give Him A Little Time	15
66	Fontana TF 681	Then So Do I/I'm Just A Little Bit Shy (solo)	10
67	Fontana TF 823	Things Get Better/You Got Me Baby (solo)	30

LEROY CARR
58	Fontana TFE 17051	TREASURES OF NORTH AMERICAN NEGRO MUSIC VOLUME 1 (EP)	25
64	RCA RCX 7168	R.C.A. VICTOR RACE SERIES VOL. 2 (EP)	15
63	CBS BPG 62206	BLUES BEFORE SUNRISE (LP)	50

LINDA CARR
67	Stateside SS 2058	Everytime/Trying To Be Good For You (DJ copy = £50)	30

MIKE CARR
68	Columbia SCX 6248	UNDER PRESSURE (LP)	20
73	Ad-Rhythm ARPS	MIKE CARR (LP)	18

ROMEY CARR
70	Columbia DB 8710	These Things Will Keep Me Loving You/Stand Up And Fight	30

VALERIE CARR
58	Columbia DB 4083	You're The Greatest/Over The Rainbow	5
58	Columbia DB 4131	When The Boys Talk About The Girls/Padre	8
58	Columbia DB 4225	Bad Girl/Look Forward	5
59	Columbia DB 4365	The Way To My Heart/I'm Only Asking	5
59	Columbia SEG 7860	VALERIE CARR (EP)	10
59	Columbia 33S 1137	VALERIE CARR (10" LP)	20
61	Columbia 33SX 1228	EV'RY HOUR, EV'RY DAY OF MY LIFE (LP, also stereo SCX 3307)	15/18

VIKKI CARR
64	Liberty LBY 1208	DISCOVERY (LP)	12
65	Liberty LBY 1284	ANATOMY OF LOVE (lP)	12

WYNONA CARR
61	Reprise R 20033	I Gotta Stand Tall/My Faith	18

DAVID CARRADINE
75	Jet JETLP 10	GRASSHOPPER (LP)	12

JOE 'KING' CARRASCO & THE CROWNS
80	Stiff CROWN 1	Bueno/Tuff Enuff (vinyl 78, p/s)	15

CARRICK FOLK FOUR
65	Thistle TM 90	Radio Scotland/Blue Nose	7

ANDREA CARROLL
63	London HLX 9772	It Hurts To Be Sixteen/Why Am I So Shy	18

BARBARA CARROLL
59	London HLR 8981	North By Northwest/Far Away (78 rpm = £12)	15

BERNADETTE CARROLL
64	Stateside SS 311	Party Girl/I Don't Wanna Know	20

BOB CARROLL
55	MGM SP 1132	I Love You So Much It Hurts/My Dearest, My Darling, My Love	10
56	London HLU 8299	Red Confetti, Pink Balloons And Tambourines/Handwriting On The Wall	25
56	London HLU 8299	Red Confetti, Pink Balloons And Tambourines/Handwriting On The Wall (78)	8
58	London HLT 8724	Hi Yo Silver/Tonto The Brave (78 rpm = £10)	20
59	London HLT 8888	I Can't Get You Out Of My Heart/Since I'm Out Of Your Arms (78 rpm = £10)	15

CATHY CARROLL
62	Warner Bros WB 72	Poor Little Puppet/Love And Learn	12

DIAHANN CARROLL
59	London HLT 8788	The Big Country/Guiding Light (78 rpm = £15)	20

DON CARROLL
57	Capitol CL 14812	At Your Front Door/The Gods Were Angry With Me	10
58	Capitol CL 14823	In My Arms/The Things I Might Have Been	5

GINA CARROLL
65	Decca F 12297	Bye Bye Big Boy/Down The Street	20

JOHNNY CARROLL & HOT ROCKS
56	Brunswick 05580	Corrine Corrina/Wild Wild Women (78 rpm = £120)	750
56	Brunswick 05603	Crazy, Crazy Lovin'/Hot Rock (78 rpm = £120)	750
74	UK USA 1	Black Leather Rebel/Be-Bop-A-Lula (as Johnny Carroll & Blue Caps)	10

PAT CARROLL
72	Pye International 7N 25592	To The Sun/Out Of My Mind	7

RONNIE CARROLL
56	Philips PB 605	Walk Hand In Hand/Sweet Heartaches (78)	7
60	Philips PB 1004	Footsteps/Where My True Love Walks	5
62	Philips PB 1222	Ring-A-Ding Girl/The Girls In Their Summer Dresses	5
62	Philips 326 550 BF	If Only Tomorrow/Think Of Her (p/s)	5
	(see also Millicent Martin)		

TONI CARROLL
58	MGM MGM 987	Dreamsville/I've Never Felt This Way Before	15
58	MGM EP 689	THIS ONE IS TONI (EP)	20

CARROLLS
66	Polydor BM 56081	Surrender Your Love/The Folk I Love	6
68	CBS 3414	So Gently Falls The Rain/Nice To See You Darling	5
68	CBS 3710	Ever Since/Come On	6
68	CBS 3875	A Lemon Balloon And A Blue Sky/Make Me Belong To You	10
69	CBS 4401	We're In This Thing Together/We Know Better	15
	(see also Carols, Carolls, Faith Brown, Brotherly Love)		

BEN CARRUTHERS & DEEP
65	Parlophone R 5295	Jack O' Diamonds/Right Behind You	40

MINT VALUE £

CHAD CARSON
63   HMV POP 1156   They Were Wrong/Stop Picking On Me. 55

DEL CARSON
59   Decca F 11135   Jean/I Told Myself A Lie (78 rpm = £6) 6

JOHNNY CARSON
60   Fontana H 243   Fraulein/I Wish It Were You 8
60   Fontana H 259   The Train Of Love/First Proposal 8
60   Fontana H 277   You Talk Too Much/Now And Always 8
62   Ember EMB S 150   Teenage Bachelor/Are You Anyone's Girl? 10
63   Ember EMB S 161   The Tears Came Rolling Down/One Track Mind 10

KAY CARSON
56   Capitol CL 14565   Those Who Have Loved/The Fellow Over There 8
56   Capitol CL 14634   There's A Shadow Between Us/This Man 8
     (see also Kit Carson)

KEN CARSON
55   London HLF 8213   Hawkeye/I've Been Working On The Railroad (78 rpm = £12) 30
56   London HLF 8237   Let Her Go, Let Her Go/The Song Of Daniel Boone
                                   (The Daddy Of Them All) (78 rpm = £8) 10

KIT CARSON
56   Capitol CL 14524   Band Of Gold/Cast Your Bread Upon The Waters 12
     (see also Kay Carson)

MINDY CARSON
58   Philips PB 822   The Sentimental Touch/I Was Born 5

MINDY CARSON & GUY MITCHELL
53   Columbia SCM 5022   That's A Why/Train Of Love 40
     (see also Guy Mitchell)

VINCE CARSON
55   HMV 7M 313   Sweetie, Sweet, Sweet Sue/My Possession 10

ANITA CARTER
58   London HLA 8693   Blue Doll/Go Away Johnnie 25
60   London HLW 9102   Moon Girl/Mama Don't Cry At My Wedding 17

BENNY CARTER
54   HMV 7M 189   Blue Mountain/Sunday Afternoon 6
62   HMV CLP 1624/CSD1480   FURTHER DEFINITIONS (LP, mono/stereo) 22
66   HMV CLP/CSD 3576   FURTHER DEFINITIONS (LP, mono/stereo) 22
     (see also Helen Humes)

BETTY CARTER
63   London HLK 9748   The Good Life/Nothing More To Look Forward To 10
     (see also Ray Charles)

CAROLINE CARTER
65   Decca F 12239   The Ballad Of Possibilities/We Want Love 10

CAROLYN CARTER
65   London HL 9959   It Hurts/I'm Thru 40

CHRIS CARTER
81   Industrial IRC 32   THE SPACE BETWEEN (cassette) 12
     (see also Throbbing Gristle, Chris & Cosey)

CLARENCE CARTER
68   Atlantic 584 154   Thread The Needle/Don't Make My Baby Cry. 15
68   Atlantic 584 176   Looking For A Fox/I Can't See Myself (Crying About You). 20
68   Atlantic 584 187   Funky Fever/Slip Away 12
68   Atlantic 584 223   Too Weak To Fight/Let Me Comfort You 12
69   Atlantic 584 248   Snatchin' It Back/Making Love (At The Dark End Of The Street). 12
69   Atlantic 584 272   The Feeling Is Right/You Can't Miss When You Can't Measure. 8
70   Atlantic 584 309   Take It Off Him And Put It On Me/The Few Troubles I've Had 8
70   Atlantic 2091 030   Patches/I Can't Leave Your Love Alone 8
71   Atlantic 2091 045   It's All In Your Mind/Willie And Laura Mae Jones 8
71   Atlantic 2091 093   The Court Room/Getting The Bills (But No Merchandise) 8
71   Atlantic 2091 139   Slipped, Tripped And Fell In Love/I Hate To Love And Run 10
68   Atlantic 588 152   THIS IS CLARENCE CARTER (LP) 25
69   Atlantic 588 172   THE DYNAMIC CLARENCE CARTER (LP) 25
69   Atlantic 588 191   TESTIFYIN' (LP) 20
70   Atlantic 2400 027   PATCHES (LP) 20

HAL CARTER FIVE
62   Oriole CB 1709   Come On And Twist Me/Twistin' Time Is Here 10

HERBIE CARTER
68   Duke DU 4   Happy Time (actually by Keble Drummond)/BOYS: Smashville 7

JEAN CARTER & CENTREPIECES
68   Stateside SS 2114   No Good Jim/And None 15

JOHN CARTER & RUSS ALQUIST
68   Spark SRL 1017   The Laughing Man/Midsummer Dreaming 25
     (see also Carter-Lewis & Southerners, Ivy League, Flowerpot Men)

LYNDA CARTER
78   CBS EPC 83052   LYNDA CARTER (aka WONDER WOMAN) 18

MARTIN CARTER
72   Tradition TSR 012   UPS & DOWNS (LP) 40

MEL CARTER
63	Pye International 7N 25212	When A Boy Falls In Love/So Wonderful	10
66	Liberty LIB 66113	Hold Me, Thrill Me, Kiss Me/Sweet Little Girl	30
65	Liberty LIB 66138	(All Of A Sudden) My Heart Sings/When I Hold The Hand Of The One I Love	12
66	Liberty LIB 66148	Love Is All We Need/I Wish I Didn't Love You So	12
66	Liberty LIB 66165	Band Of Gold/Detour	12
66	Liberty LIB 66183	You You You/If You Lose Her	10

MOTHER MAYBELLE CARTER
64	London HA-R 8214	QUEEN OF THE AUTOHARP (LP)	15

NEL CARTER
74	RCA 2503	Send Him Back To Me/Dreams	20

SHEILA CARTER & EPISODE SIX
66	Pye 7N 17194	I Will Warm Your Heart/Incense	40
	(see also Episode, Episode Six)		

SONNY CARTER with EARL BOSTIC & HIS ORCHESTRA
55	Parlophone MSP 6167	There Is No Greater Love/Oh Baby (78 rpm = £10)	30
	(see also Earl Bostic)		

SYDNEY CARTER
66	Elektra EPK 801	LORD OF THE DANCE (EP)	18

CARTER FAMILY
55	Brunswick OE 9168	MOUNTAIN MUSIC VOL. 2 (EP)	15
62	RCA RCX 7100	THE ORIGINAL AND GREAT CARTER FAMILY VOL. 1 (EP)	10
62	RCA RCX 7101	THE ORIGINAL AND GREAT CARTER FAMILY VOL. 2 (EP)	10
62	RCA RCX 7102	THE ORIGINAL AND GREAT CARTER FAMILY VOL. 3 (EP)	10
63	RCA RCX 7109	THE ORIGINAL AND GREAT CARTER FAMILY VOL. 4 (EP)	10
63	RCA RCX 7110	THE ORIGINAL AND GREAT CARTER FAMILY VOL. 5 (EP)	10
63	RCA RCX 7111	THE ORIGINAL AND GREAT CARTER FAMILY VOL. 6 (EP)	10

CARTER-LEWIS & SOUTHERNERS
61	Piccadilly 7N 35004	So Much In Love/Back On The Scene	30
61	Ember EMB S 145	Two Timing Baby/Will It Happen To Me?	50
62	Piccadilly 7N 35085	Here's Hopin'/Poor Joe	30
62	Ember EMB S 165	Tell Me/My Broken Heart	50
63	Oriole CB 1835	Sweet And Tender Romance/Who Told You?	20
63	Oriole CB 1868	Your Momma's Out Of Town/Somebody Told My Girl	25
64	Oriole CB 1919	Skinny Minnie/Easy To Cry	40
	(see also Ivy League, Flowerpot Men, White Plains, John Carter & Russ Alquist, Jimmy Page, Dawn Chorus)		

MARTIN CARTHY
76	Topic STOP 7002	The Bonny Lass Of Anglesey/Palaces Of Gold	6
65	Fontana (S)TL 5269	MARTIN CARTHY (LP)	30
71	Philips 6308 049	LANDFALL (LP)	30
72	Pegasus PEG 12	SHEARWATER (LP, with insert)	22
72	Philips 6282 022	THIS IS MARTIN CARTHY (LP)	15
74	Deram SML 1111	SWEET WIVELSFIELD (LP)	18

MARTIN CARTHY & DAVE SWARBRICK
67	Fontana TE 17490	NO SONGS (EP)	35
66	Fontana STL 5362	SECOND ALBUM (LP)	30
67	Fontana STL 5434	BYKER HILL (LP)	30
68	Fontana STL 5477	BUT TWO CAME BY (LP)	30
70	Fontana STL 5529	PRINCE HEATHEN (LP)	30
71	Pegasus PEG 6	SELECTIONS (LP, gatefold sleeve)	25
	(see also Dave Swarbrick, Three City Four, Steeleye Span, Leon Rosselson, Alex Campbell, Nigel Denver)		

CARTOONE
69	Atlantic 584 240	Knick Knack Man/A Penny For The Sun	10
69	Atlantic 588 174	CARTOONE (LP)	25
	(see also Jimmy Page)		

FLIP CARTRIDGE
66	London HLU 10076	Dear Mrs Applebee/Don't Take The Lovers From The World	12

DAVE CARTWRIGHT
70	Harmony DB 0001	MIDDLE OF THE ROAD (LP, private pressing with insert)	30
72	Transatlantic TRA 255	A LITTLE BIT OF GLORY (LP)	15
73	Transatlantic TRA 267	BACK TO THE GARDEN (LP)	15
75	Transatlantic TRA 284	DON'T LET YOUR FAMILY DOWN (LP)	15
	(see also Bev Pegg, Away From The Sand)		

DICK CARUSO
60	MGM MGM 1077	Two Long Years/Yes Sir, That's My Baby	10
60	MGM MGM 1099	Pretty Little Dancin' Doll/We've Never Met	10

ALAN CARVELL
76	United Artists UP 36124	Georgia On My Mind/Never Give Your Love (To A New York Woman)	5
	(see also Steve Allan, Carvells, Five Sapphires, Telegrams)		

CARVELLS
77	Creole CR 143	The L.A. Run/Your Sweet Love	5
78	Rocket ROKN 540	Skateboard Queen/Skateboard Surfing	6
78	Rocket ROKN 544	Skateboard Riders/Skateboard King	6
78	Rocket ROLL 15	SKATEBOARD RAMPAGE (LP)	18
	(see also Steve Allan, Alan Carvell, Five Sapphires, Telegrams)		

CASABLANCA
74	Rocket PIGL 7	CASABLANCA (LP, die-cut sleeve with inner lyric sleeve)	15
	(see also Trees)		

CASANOVAS
00s Singles Society 7STAS 3320 Nasty/Too Cool (numbered die-cut p/s, 500 only) 10

CASCADES
63	Warner Bros WB 98	Shy Girl/The Last Leaf 10
63	Warner Bros WB 103	I Wanna Be Your Lover/My First Day Alone 7
63	RCA Victor RCA 1358	Cinderella/A Little Like Loving. 7
64	RCA Victor RCA 1378	Jeannie/For Your Sweet Love 5
65	Liberty LIB 55822	I Bet You Won't Stay/She'll Love Again 5
66	Stateside SS 515	Cheryl's Goin' Home/Truly Julie's Blues 10
69	Uni UN 508	Maybe The Rain Will Fall/Naggin' Cries 6
63	Warner Bros WEP/WSE 6106	RHYTHM OF THE RAIN (EP, mono/stereo) 40/45
63	Warner Bros WM 8127	RHYTHM OF THE RAIN (LP) 40/50

AL CASEY & K.C. ETTES
63	Pye International 7N 25215	Surfin' Hootenanny/Easy Picking 18
	(see also Sanford Clark, Duane Eddy)	

HOWIE CASEY & SENIORS
62	Fontana H 364	Double Twist/True Fine Mama 25
62	Fontana H 381	I Ain't Mad At You/Twist At The Top 20
63	Fontana TF 403	The Boll Weevil Song/Bony Moronie 20
62	Fontana TFL 5108	TWIST AT THE TOP (LP). 90
65	Wing WL 1022	LET'S TWIST (LP, reissue of Twist At The Top) 25
	(see also Freddie Starr)	

ALVIN CASH (& REGISTERS)
65	Stateside SS 386	Twine Time/The Bump (as Alvin Cash & Crawlers).............................. 40
66	Stateside SS 543	Philly Freeze/No Deposits, No Returns (as Alvin Cash & Registers) 30
68	President PT 115	Philly Freeze/No Deposits, No Returns (as Alvin Cash & Registers) (reissue) ... 8
68	President PT 119	Alvin's Boo-Ga-Loo/Let's Do Some Good Timing (as Alvin Cash & Registers)... 12
68	President PT 129	Doin' The Ali Shuffle/Feel So Good. 12
68	President PT 147	Charge/Diff'rent Strokes For Diff'rent Folks 15
71	President PT 351	Twine Time/Twine Awhile 10
72	President PT 383	Barracuda/Do It One More Time 10
67	President PTL 1000	THE PHILLY FREEZE (LP) 50

JOHNNY CASH (& TENNESSEE TWO)
78s
57	London HL 8358	I Walk The Line/Get Rhythm 25
57	London HLS 8427	Train Of Love/There You Go. 25
57	London HLS 8461	Next In Line/Don't Make Me Go. 25
57	London HLS 8514	Home Of The Blues/Give My Love To Rose 30
58	London HLS 8586	Big River (with Tennessee Two)/Ballad Of A Teenage Queen 25
58	London HLS 8656	Guess Things Happen That Way/Come In, Stranger. 20
58	London HLS 8709	The Ways Of A Woman In Love/You're The Nearest Thing To Heaven 30
59	Philips PB 874	All Over Again/What Do I Care. 50
59	Philips PB 897	Don't Take Your Guns To Town/I Still Miss Someone 55
59	London HLS 8789	It's Just About Time/I Just Thought You'd Like To Know. 35
59	London HLS 8847	Luther Played The Boogie/Thanks A Lot 40
59	Philips PB 928	Frankie's Man, Johnny/You Dreamer You. 35
59	London HLS 8928	Katy Too/I Forgot To Remember To Forget 45
59	Philips PB 953	I Got Stripes/Five Feet High And Rising. 55
59	London HLS 8979	You Tell Me/Goodbye, Little Darlin', Goodbye 50
59	Philips PB 979	The Little Drummer Boy/I'll Remember You. 60

SINGLES
57	London HL 8358	I Walk The Line/Get Rhythm (gold label lettering, later silver) 150/80
57	London HLS 8427	Train Of Love/There You Go. 45
57	London HLS 8461	Next In Line/Don't Make Me Go. 50
57	London HLS 8514	Home Of The Blues/Give My Love To Rose 45
58	London HLS 8586	Big River (with Tennessee Two)/Ballad Of A Teenage Queen 35
58	London HLS 8656	Guess Things Happen That Way/Come In, Stranger (with Tennessee Two)...... 20
58	London HLS 8709	The Ways Of A Woman In Love/You're The Nearest Thing To Heaven
		(with Tennessee Two) 20
59	Philips PB 874	All Over Again/What Do I Care. 12
59	Philips PB 897	Don't Take Your Guns To Town/I Still Miss Someone 12
59	London HLS 8789	It's Just About Time/I Just Thought You'd Like To Know (with Tennessee Two). . 25
59	London HLS 8847	Luther Played The Boogie/Thanks A Lot 25
59	Philips PB 928	Frankie's Man, Johnny/You Dreamer You. 12
59	London HLS 8928	Katy Too/I Forgot To Remember To Forget 25
59	Philips PB 953	I Got Stripes/Five Feet High And Rising. 12
59	London HLS 8979	You Tell Me/Goodbye, Little Darlin', Goodbye 15
59	Philips PB 979	The Little Drummer Boy/I'll Remember You. 5
60	London HLS 9070	Straight A's In Love/I Love You Because 15
60	Philips PB 1017	Seasons Of My Heart/Smiling Bill McCall. 5
60	London HLS 9182	Down The Street To 301/Story Of A Broken Heart. 18
60	Philips PB 1075	Going To Memphis/Loading Coal 12
61	London HLS 9314	Oh Lonesome Me/Life Goes On. 15
61	Philips PB 1148	The Rebel — Johnny Yuma/Forty Shades Of Green 5
61	Philips PB 1200	Tennessee Flat-Top Box/Tall Man 12
63	CBS AAG 159	Ring Of Fire/I'd Still Be There 5
63	CBS AAG 173	The Matador/Still In Town. 5
63	CBS AAG 200	Understand Your Man/Dark As A Dungeon 5
65	CBS 201741	Orange Blossom Special/All God's Children Ain't Free 5
65	CBS 201760	It Ain't Me Babe/Time And Time Again 5
65	CBS 201809	Ring Of Fire/Streets Of Laredo 5
66	CBS 202046	The One On The Right Is On The Left/Cotton Pickin' Hands 5
66	CBS 202256	Everybody Loves A Nut/Austin Prison 5

MINT VALUE £

67	CBS 202546	You Beat All I Ever Saw/Put The Sugar To Bed	5
67	CBS 3268	Rosanna's Going Wild/Long-Legged Guitar-Pickin' Man (with June Carter)	5
68	CBS 3438	Certain Kind Of Hurtin'/Another Song To Sing	5
68	CBS 3549	Folsom Prison Blues (live)/The Folk Singer	5
68	CBS 3878	Daddy Sang Bass/He Turned The Water Into Wine	5
69	CBS 4460	A Boy Named Sue (live) /San Quentin (live)	5
69	CBS 4638	Blistered/See Ruby Fall	5
76	CBS S 4287	One Piece At A Time/Go On Blues	5

EXPORT SINGLES
57	London HL 7020	Next In Line/Don't Make Me Go	35
57	London HL 7023	Home Of The Blues/Give My Love To Rose	35
58	London HL 7032	Ballad Of A Teenage Queen/Big River	25
58	London HL 7053	The Ways Of A Woman In Love/You're The Nearest Thing To Heaven	25
57	London HL 7131	Folsom Prison Blues/I Walk The Line	30

EPs
58	London RES 1120	JOHNNY CASH (triangular or round centre)	40/20
59	London RES 1193	JOHNNY CASH SINGS HANK WILLIAMS (triangular or round centre)	40/20
59	London RES 1212	COUNTRY BOY (triangular or round centre)	40/20
59	London RES 1230	JOHNNY CASH NO. 2 (triangular or round centre)	40/20
60	Philips BBE 12377	THE TROUBADOR	20
60	Philips BBE 12318	GRANDFATHER'S CLOCK	20
60	Philips BBE 12395	SONGS OF OUR SOIL	20
61	Philips BBE 12494	STRICTLY CASH	20
64	CBS AGG 20050	FORTY SHADES OF GREEN	15
64	CBS EP 5576	FABULOUS JOHNNY CASH	15
64	CBS EP 5735	ORANGE BLOSSOM SPECIAL	15
64	CBS EP 5744	EVERYBODY LOVES A NUT	15
64	CBS EP 5964	RING OF FIRE	15
65	CBS EP 6061	IT AIN'T ME BABE	15
66	CBS EP 6073	MEAN AS HELL! — BALLADS FROM THE TRUE WEST (with Statler Brothers & Carter Family)	15
65	CBS EP 6109	SONGS OF KATIE ELDER	15
65	CBS EP 6147	HAPPINESS IS YOU	15
69	CBS EP 6601	FOLSOM PRISON BLUES	15
72	CBS EP 9155	LITTLE FAUSS AND BIG HALSY	10

LPs
59	London HA-S 2157	SINGS THE SONGS THAT MADE HIM FAMOUS	40
59	London HA-S 2179	WITH HIS HOT AND BLUE GUITAR	45
59	Philips BBL 7298	THE FABULOUS JOHNNY CASH (also stereo SBBL 554)	20/30
59	Philips BBL 7353	SONGS OF OUR SOIL	22
59	Philips BBL 7373	HYMNS BY JOHNNY CASH	30
60	Philips BBL 7358	NOW THERE WAS A SONG! (also stereo SBBL 580)	20/22
60	Philips BBL 7417	RIDE THIS TRAIN	18
61	CBS (S)BPG 62042	THE FABULOUS JOHNNY CASH (mono/stereo)	each 15
62	CBS (S)BPG 62015	HYMNS FROM THE HEART (mono/stereo)	each 15
62	CBS (S)BPG 62073	THE SOUND OF JOHNNY CASH (mono/stereo)	each 15
63	CBS BPG 62119	BLOOD SWEAT AND TEARS	15
63	CBS (S)BPG 62171	RING OF FIRE (mono/stereo)	each 15
63	CBS (S)BPG 62284	THE CHRISTMAS SPIRIT (mono/stereo)	each 15
64	CBS (S)BPG 62371	I WALK THE LINE (mono/stereo)	each 15
64	CBS (S)BPG 62463	BITTER TEARS (mono/stereo)	each 15
65	CBS (S)BPG 62501	ORANGE BLOSSOM SPECIAL (mono/stereo)	each 15
65	Fontana FJS 301	JOHNNY CASH'S COUNTRY ROUND-UP (4 tracks only)	12
65	London HA-S 8220	THE ORIGINAL SUN SOUND OF JOHNNY CASH	35
65	CBS (S)BPG 62538	BALLADS OF THE TRUE WEST VOL. 1	15
65	CBS (S)BPG 62575	RIDE THIS TRAIN	12
65	CBS (S)BPG 62591	BALLADS OF THE TRUE WEST VOL. 2	15
66	London HA-S 8253	LONESOME ME	25
84	Charley SUN BOX-105	THE SUN YEARS (5-LP box set)	30

CASH CREW
89	Vinyl Solution Storm 07	You Can't Stop This (12")	8
89	Vinyl Solution STORM 12	One Decade vs. Amo (12")	8
90	Scream WTST1	Green Grass (EP)	8
91	Scream WTSTLP1	WILL IT MAKE MY BROWN EYES BLUE? (LP)	12

CASH PUSSIES
79	The Label TLR 010	99% Is Shit/Cash Flow (p/s)	6

(see also Sex Pistols)

CASINO
81	Ellie Jay EJSP 9609	More Than Ever/Tonight (p/s)	10

CASINO ROYALES
67	London HLU 10122	When I Tell You That I Love You/Love In The Open Air	5

CASINOS
67	Ember EMB S 241	That's The Way/Too Good To Be True	40
67	President PT 123	Then You Can Tell Me Goodbye/I Still Love You	10
68	President PT 140	To Be Loved/Tailor Made	6
68	President PT 156	When I Stop Dreaming/Please Love Me	6
68	President PTL 1007	THEN YOU CAN TELL ME GOODBYE (LP)	30

TONY CASO
68	London HL 10178	Shadow On The Ground/I Don't Care Who Knows It	6

MAMA CASS
(see under Mama Cass Elliot, Mamas & Papas, Mugwumps, Big Three)

MINT VALUE £

CASSANDRA
79	D Roy DRDD 19	Sitting In The Park/D ROY BAND: Hyde Park Dub	20
80	D Roy DRDD 29	My Angel Baby/Thank You For The Many Things You've Done (12")	30
80	D Roy DRDD 31	I Must Be Dreaming/Trading Dub (12")	30

CASSETTE
79	1 track CAS 001	THE FAST FORWARD EP: What's The Point/Product/All The Rage	10

CASSETTES
81	Zip ZIP 101	Reverberate/Don't Label Me (die-cut sleeve)	7

DAVID CASSIDY
71	Bell BELL 1189	Cherish/All I Wanna Do Is Touch You	7
85	Arista ARISD 589	The Last Kiss/The Letter (shaped picture disc with calendar, 6500 only)	5
	(see also Partridge Family, Samantha Fox)		

STEVE CASSIDY
63	Ember EMB S 177	Ecstasy/I'm A Worrying	5

TED CASSIDY
65	Capitol CL 15423	The Lurch/Wesley	30

CAST
94	(no label) GRA 001	CAST SAMPLER (Sandstorm/Follow Me Down/Tell It Like It Is) (10", white label, white stamped sleeve, promo only, 700 copies)	25
	(see also La's)		

CASTANARC
74	Peninsula PENCIL 10	JOURNEY TO THE EAST (LP, private pressing)	18

CASTAWAYS
65	London HL 10003	Liar Liar/Sam	40

CASTE
68	President PT 211	Don't Cast Aside/One Step Closer	6

JOEY CASTELL
57	Decca F 10966	I'm Left, You're Right, She's Gone/Tryin' To Get To You (78 rpm = £45)	150

LACKSLEY CASTELL
79	Sufferers Heights SUFF 01	What A great Day/PRINCE JAMMY: Slaughter House 5 (12")	40
80	Negus Roots NERT 001	African Queen/Queen In Dub (12")	25
80	Negus Roots NERT 003	I Love Jah/Version	30
80	Black Joy DH 805	Jah Love Is Sweeter/ROCKERS BAND: Sweeter Rockers (12")	25
81	Negus Roots NERT 008	Government Man/P. TULLO: Straight To The Government (12" blue/black vinyl)	25
83	Negus Roots NERT 019	Johnny Brown/Mrs Brown (12")	12
83	Csa SPCSA 12006	Tug A War Game/EARL SIXTEEN: Rise In The Morning (12")	30
82	Negus Roots NERT LP 002	MORNING GLORY (LP)	60
83	Negus Roots NERT LP 008	AFRICAN LADY (LP)	40

CASTELLS
61	London HLN 9392	Sacred/I Get Dreamy	25
62	London HLN 9551	So This Is Love/On The Street Of Tears	25

CASTELLS
67	Masquerade MA 500	Two Lovers/Jerusalem	5

LEE CASTLE & BARONS
64	Parlophone R 5151	A Love She Can Count On/Foolin'	15

ROY CASTLE
58	Pye 7N 15173	In My Heart/Mister Music Man	5
59	Pye 7N 15215	The Chosen Few/Bimbo	5
60	Philips PB 1087	Little White Berry/Crazy Little Thorn	10
65	CBS 201736	Doctor Terror's House Of Horrors/Voodoo Girl (with Tubby Hayes)	150
68	Olga OLE 12	Wonderful World/For All The World	7
61	Philips BBL 7457	CASTLEWISE (LP, also stereo SBBL 626)	each 15

CASTLE SISTERS (Jamaica)
66	Ska Beat JB 257	Stop Your Lying/Don't Be A Fool	30

CASTLE SISTERS (USA)
59	Columbia DB 4335	Drifting And Dreaming/Lucky Girl	7

CAST OF THOUSANDS
66	Stateside SS 546	My Jenny Wears A Mini/Girl Do What You Gonna Do	15

CASTON & MAJORS
75	Tamla Motown TMG 938	Child Of Love/No One Will Know	15
	(see also Radiants)		

JIMMY CASTOR (BUNCH)
66	Philips BF 1543	Hey Leroy, Your Mama's Callin'/Hamhock's Espanol	25
67	Philips BF 1590	Magic Saxophone/Just You Girl	30
71	Mercury 6052 110	Hey Leroy, Your Mama's Callin'/Hamhock's Espanol (reissue)	10
73	RCA Victor APD1 0103	DIMENSION III (LP, quadrophonic)	18
74	Atlantic K 50052	THE EVERYTHING MAN (LP)	15
76	Atlantic K 50295	E-MAN GROOVIN' (LP)	15

FRANKIE CASTRO
56	Mercury MT 114	Goodbye, So Long, I'm Gone/Too Much (78)	18

CASUAL FOUR
60s	Specially Made For Us 102	I Can Tell/Love Potion No. 9	50

CASUALEERS
74	Pye Disco Demand DDS 103	Dance Dance Dance/Something About This Girl	10

CASUALS

65	Fontana TF 635	If You Walk Out/Please Don't Hide	10
68	Decca F 12737	Adios Amor (Goodbye My Love)/Don't Dream Of Yesterday	6
68	Decca F 22784	Jesamine/I've Got Something Too	7
68	Decca F 22852	Toy/Touched (some in p/s)	15/7
69	Decca F 22900	Fools Paradise/7 X 7	6
69	Decca F 22943	Sunflower Eyes/Never My Love	6
69	Decca F 22969	Caroline/Naughty Boy	8
70	Decca F 23027	My Name Is Love/I Can't Say	6
71	Decca F 23112	Someday Rock 'n' Roll Lady/A Letter Every Day	6
72	Parlophone R 5959	Tara Tiger Girl/Nature's Girl	6
74	Dawn DNS 1069	Witch/Good Times	6
69	Decca LK-R/SKL-R 5001	HOUR WORLD (LP)	40

JOHNNY CASWELL

85	Kent TOWN 106	You Don't Love Me No More/STEINWAYS: You've Been Leading Me On	20

CATAPILLA

71	Vertigo 6360 029	CATAPILLA (LP, gatefold sleeve, swirl label)	140
72	Vertigo 6360 074L	CHANGES (LP, gatefold sleeve, swirl label)	375

CATATONIA

94	Crai CRAI C 039L	Hooked/Fall Beside Her/Difrydreulyd (cassette)	8
94	Crai CRAICD 039	Hooked/Fall Beside Her/Difrydreulyd (CD)	12
94	Rough Trade 45rev33	Whale/You Can (p/s, 'Singles Club' release)	20
95	Nursery NYS 12L	Bleed/This Boy Can't Swim (red vinyl, numbered p/s, 1,000 only)	10
95	Nursery NYSCD 12	Bleed/This Boy Can't Swim/Painful (CD)	12
95	Blanco Y Negro SAM 1746	Blow The Millennium Blow/Beautiful Sailor (p/s, white vinyl Xmas 45, freebie)	12
96	Blanco Y Negro NEGAT 8X	Lost Cat/To And Fro (yellow vinyl, p/s)	6
96	Blanco Y Negro NEG 85X	Sweet Catatonia/Tourist (no'd p/s, clear vinyl, 5,000 only)	6
96	Blanco Y Negro NEG 93	You've Got A Lot To Answer For/Do You Believe In Me (red vinyl)	6
96	Blanco Y Negro NEG 97CD1	Bleed/This Boy Can't Swim/Painful (CD, reissue, one of a pair)	8
99	Blanco Y Negro NEG 116CDDJ	Karaoke Queen (CD, card sleeve, withdrawn, promo only)	15
93	Crai C 039L	FOR TINKERBELL EP (cassette)	10
93	Crai CD 039B	FOR TINKERBELL EP (CD)	12
96	Blanco Y Negro 16305-1	WAY BEYOND BLUE (LP, deleted after one week, with free 7")	18
98	Blanco Y Negro 20834-1	INTERNATIONAL VELVET (LP, 1,000 only, with free 12")	20

CATCH (featuring Marilyn Middleton)

76	London HLZ 10543	Mr. Nice Guy/Mephisto's Nightmare	8

CATCH

77	Logo GO 103	Borderline/Black Blood (company sleeve)	30
	(see also Tourists, Eurythmics)		

GEORGE CATES & HIS ORCHESTRA

55	Vogue Coral Q 72106	Autumn Leaves (with Steve Allen)/High And Dry	5
56	Vogue Coral Q 72162	Moonglow/Theme From "Picnic"/Rio Batucada	5
	(see also Steve Allen & Orchestra)		

CATE BROTHERS

76	Asylum 13062	Where Can We Go/Instrumental	10

CATFISH

70	CBS 64006	GET DOWN (LP, orange label)	18
71	Epic 64408	LIVE CATFISH (LP)	12

CATHEDRAL

95	Earache MOSH 130	THE CARNIVAL BIZARRE (2 x 10" LP, gatefold sleeve)	12

CATHERINE WHEEL

91	Wilde Club WILDE 4	SHE'S MY FRIEND (12", p/s, barcode on sleeve)	8
91	Wilde Club WILDE 5	PAINFUL THING EP (12", p/s)	8

RAY CATHODE (BBC RADIOPHONICS)

62	Parlophone R 4901	Time Beat/Waltz In Orbit	15
	(see also BBC Radiophonic Workshop, George Martin)		

CAT IRON

69	Xtra XTRA 1087	CAT IRON (LP)	20

CAT MOTHER & ALL NIGHT NEWSBOYS

69	Polydor 56543	Good Old Rock'N'Roll/Bad News	12
70	Polydor 2066 026	I Must Be Dreaming/Last Go Round	6
69	Polydor 184 300	THE STREET GIVETH AND THE STREET TAKETH AWAY (LP)	20
70	Polydor 2425 021	ALBION DOO-WAH (LP, gatefold sleeve)	15
72	United Artists UAG 29313	CAT MOTHER & ALL NIGHT NEWS BOYS (LP, gatefold sleeve)	15
73	United Artists UAG 29381	LAST CHANCE DANCE (LP)	12

CATS

69	Baf BAF 1	Swan Lake/Swing Low	15
69	Baf BAF 2	My Girl/The Hog	10
69	Baf BAF 3	The Hig/Blues For Justice	10
69	Baf BAF 4	William Tell/Love Walk Right In	10

CATS

67	Parlophone R 5558	What A Crazy Life/Hopeless Try	5
68	Parlophone R 5663	What Is The World Coming To/How Could I Be So Blind?	5
69	Columbia DB 8524	I Gotta Know What's Going On/Lea	5
69	Columbia DB 8571	Why/Mandy, My Dear	5
70	Columbia DB 8655	Marian/Somewhere Up There	5
71	Columbia DB 8748	I Love You, I Do/Where Have I Been Wrong	5
71	Columbia DB 8816	One Way Mind/Country Woman	5

72	Columbia DB 8850	Dance, Dance, Dance/My Friend Joe 5
72	Columbia DB 8909	Let's Dance/I've Been In Love Before.. 5
71	Columbia SCX 6459	TAKE ME WITH YOU (LP) 12

CATS EYES
68	Deram DM 190	Smile Girl For Me/In A Fantasy World.. 10
68	Deram DM 209	I Thank You Marianne/Turn Around. 8
69	Deram DM 251	Where Is She Now?/Tom Drum 25
70	MCA MK 5028	Loser/Circus 5
70	MCA MK 5043	Circus/Come Away Melinda 5
70	MCA MK 5056	The Wizard/Hey (Open Your Eyes) 20

CAT'S PYJAMAS
68	Direction 58-3235	Virginia Waters/Baby I Love You 25
68	Direction 58-3482	Camera Man/House For Sale 25
	(see also Kenny Bernard)	

CLEM CATTINI ORK
65	Decca F 12135	No Time To Think/Impact 40
	(see also Tornados, Aquarian Age, Rumplestiltskin, Spaghetti Head, Sounds Nice)	

NADIA CATTOUSE
61	Parlophone R 4725	The Boy Without A Heart/Long Time, Boy 5
65	Parlophone R 5240	Port Mahon/A Little More Oil 5
66	Reality RE 503	Beautiful Barbados/Turn Around. 10
60s	Church Miss. Soc. LIV/SP/81	The Larder/PAULINE FILBY: I'm Hungry.............................. 10
66	Reality RY 1001	NADIA CATTOUSE (LP) 60
70	RCA Victor SF 8070	EARTH MOTHER (LP) 40

CAUSTIC WINDOW
92	Rephlex CAT 004	JOYREX J4 EP (12", 6-track) 35
92	Rephlex CAT 005	JOYREX J5 EP (12", 4-track, black or white vinyl)............................... 45/35
93	Rephlex CAT 009 i	JOYREX J9 EP (10", picture disc, with bonus track HMNA, 300 only) 70
93	Rephlex CAT 009 ii	JOYREX J9 EP (12" 4-track, initially in card mailer with bag of "space dust") 55/45
	(see slso Aphex Twin)	

CAVALIERS
86	él GPO 11	It's A Beautiful Game/The I.T. Man (p/s) 10
86	él ACME 4	A PERFECT ACTION (LP) 18

EDDIE CAVE & FYX
66	Pye 7N 17161	Fresh Out Of Tears/It's Almost Good 40

NICK CAVE (& BAD SEEDS)
84	Mute 7 MUTE 32	In The Ghetto/The Moon Is In The Gutter (p/s) 8
85	Mute 7 MUTE 30	Tupelo/The Six Strings That Drew Blood (p/s)...................................... 8
86	Lyntone LYN 18038	Scum (green vinyl flexidisc, some with poster, concert freebie) 12/18
88	Mute MUTE 86	Oh Deanna/The Girl At The Bottom Of My Class (no p/s, DJ-only)............... 8
92	Mute LMUTE 140	Straight To You/Jack The Ripper (Acoustic Version) (limited issue, p/s) 8
92	Mute MUTE 148	I Had A Dream, Joe/The Good Son (live) (numbered p/s, 2,000 only) 8
94	Mute MUTE 160	Do You Love Me? (Single Version)/Cassiel's Song/Sail Away (silver vinyl, p/s, 1,000 copies) 10
94	Mute MUTE 169	Loverman (Single Version)/(I'll Love You) Till The End Of The World (picture disc, 2,000 only) 10
94	Mute MUTE 172	Red Right Hand/That's What Jazz Is To Me (red vinyl, p/s, with 2 different stickers & labels, 2,000 only) 10
97	Mute RCD STUMM 138	MURDER BALLADS (CD, 4-track sampler, promo only)..................... 10
86	Mute STUMM 34	YOUR FUNERAL ... MY TRIAL (2 x 12", with lyric inner sleeves) 10
88	Mute LSTUMM 52	TENDER PREY (LP, with bonus spoken word 12" And The Ass Saw The Angel [P STUMM 52]: "Autumn"/ Animal Static/Mah Sanctum/Lamentation, 5,000 only) 15
90	Mute LSTUMM 76	THE GOOD SON (LP, with bonus 7" Acoustic Versions From Tender Prey [P STUMM 76]: The Mercy Seat/City Of Refuge/Deanna) 10
90	Mute CDSTUMM 76	THE GOOD SON (CD, with bonus CD Acoustic Versions From Tender Prey [P STUMM 76]: The Mercy Seat/City Of Refuge/Deanna) 15
92	Mute LSTUMM 92	HENRY'S DREAM (LP, with photographic print) 12
93	LCD STUMM 122	LIVE SEEDS (CD, with book in slip case). 18
94	Mute LSTUMM 123	LET LOVE IN (LP, with set of postcards or poster)........................... 12
96	Mute CAVESPEAK 1CD	MURDER BALLADS: THE INTERVIEW (CD, promo only)................. 18
97	Mute CAVESPEAK 2CD	THE BOATMAN'S CALL: THE INTERVIEW (CD, promo only)............... 18
	(see also Birthday Party, Annie Hogan, Burmoe Brothers)	

CAVEMAN
91	Profile Proft 330 DJ	I'm Ready/Pages & Pages/Back To Cause Mayhem (12").................... 12
90	Profile PROFT286	Fry You Like Fish (12") 10
90	Profile PROFT296	Victory (12")... 8
91	Profile FILER406	Positive Reaction (LP) 12

ANDY CAVELL
62	HMV POP 1024	Hey There Cruel Heart/Lonely Soldier Boy 38
62	HMV POP 1080	Always On Saturday/Hey There, Senorita 38
63	Pye 7N 15539	Andy/There Was A Boy 50
64	Pye 7N 15610	Shut Up/Tell The Truth 40

JIMMY CAVELLO & HIS HOUSE ROCKERS
57	Vogue Coral Q 72226	Rock, Rock, Rock/The Big Beat (78 rpm = £30).......................... 250
57	Vogue Coral Q 72240	Foot Stompin'/Ooh-Wee (78 rpm = £30) 250
	(see also Alan Freed)	

CAVEMAN
91	Profile PROFIT330DJ	I'm Ready/Pages & Pages/Back To Cause Mayhem (EP) 12

CAVE OF THE LIVING STREAMS
74 UHC 1   SIXTEEN SONGS (LP, private pressing) 75

TERRY CAVENDISH ORCHESTRA
73 Pye NSPL 41023   ALL IN AN AFTERNOON'S WORK (LP). 12

MONTE CAZAZZA
79 Industrial IR 0005   To Mom On Mother's Day/Candy Man
     (p/s, with outer polystyrene sleeve & insert, 2,500 only) 12
80 Industrial IR 0010   SOMETHING FOR NOBODY (EP). 8
81 Industrial IRC 28   LIVE AT LEEDS FAN CLUB (cassette) 10
(see also Psychic TV)

C.C.S. (Collective Consciousness Society)
73 Rak RAK 154   The Band Played The Boogie/Hang It On Me. 5
70 Rak SRAK 6751   C.C.S. (LP, gatefold sleeve) 18
72 Rak SRAK 503   C.C.S. (LP) 15
73 Rak SRAK 504   THE BEST BAND IN THE LAND (LP). 12
(see also Alexis Korner)

CEDARS
68 Decca F 22720   For Your Information/Hide If You Want To Hide 50
68 Decca F 22772   I Like The Way/I Don't Know Why 50
(see also Seaders)

CELIA & THE MUTATIONS
77 United Artists UP 36262   Mony Mony/Mean To Me (p/s) 6
77 United Artists UP 36318   You Better Believe Me/Round And Around (p/s) 8
(see also Stranglers, Tonight)

CELLOPHANE
(see under Selofane)

CELTIC F.C.
67 Thistle   Celtic Celtic (p/s) 12
73 Polydor 2058332   Celtic Your Favourites In Green/Saturday 5

CELTIC FROST
84 Noise N 0017   MORBID TALES (mini LP, some with poster) 25/35

CENOTAPH CORNER
76 Cottage COT 501   UPS AND DOWNS (LP) 20
79 Cottage COT 031   EVERY DAY BUT WEDNESDAY (LP) 25

CENTIPEDE
71 RCA Neon NE 9   SEPTOBER ENERGY (2-LP). 60
74 RCA DPS 2054   SEPTOBER ENERGY (2-LP, reissue, different cover) 20
(see also Mark Charig, Ian Carr, Elton Dean, Zoot Money, Alan Skidmore, Keith Tippett, Julie Tippetts, Mike Patto, Robert Wyatt)

CENTURION
82 Centurion 0001   Two Wheels/Bitch (private pressing) 50
82 Centurion 0001   Two Wheels/Bitch (private pressing, mislabelled 'Nikki'). 30

CENTURY 21 (Gerry Anderson TV spin-offs)
65 Century 21 MA 100   JOURNEY TO THE MOON (EP) 15
65 Century 21 MA 101   INTO ACTION WITH TROY TEMPEST (EP) 15
65 Century 21 MA 102   A TRIP TO MARINEVILLE (EP). 15
65 Century 21 MA 103   INTRODUCING THUNDERBIRDS (EP). 15
65 Century 21 MA 104   MARINA SPEAKS (EP) 15
65 Century 21 MA 105   TV CENTURY 21 THEMES (EP) 15
66 Century 21 MA 106   THE DALEKS (EP). 50
66 Century 21 MA 107   F.A.B. (EP) 18
66 Century 21 MA 108   THUNDERBIRD 1 (EP). 18
66 Century 21 MA 109   THUNDERBIRD 2 (EP). 18
66 Century 21 MA 110   THE STATELY HOME ROBBERIES (EP) 25
66 Century 21 MA 111   LADY PENELOPE & OTHER TV THEMES (EP) 25
66 Century 21 MA 112   THUNDERBIRD 3 (EP). 25
66 Century 21 MA 113   THUNDERBIRD 4 (EP). 25
66 Century 21 MA 114   THE PERILS OF PENELOPE (EP) 30
66 Century 21 MA 115   TOPO GIGIO IN LONDON (EP). 45
67 Century 21 MA 116   GREAT THEMES FROM GERRY ANDERSON'S THUNDERBIRDS (EP) 30
67 Century 21 MA 117   SPACE AGE NURSERY RHYMES (EP) 35
67 Century 21 MA 118   LADY PENELOPE AND PARKER (EP). 35
67 Century 21 MA 119   BRAINS AND TIN TIN (EP) 35
67 Century 21 MA 120   INTERNATIONAL RESCUE (EP) 35
67 Century 21 MA 121   THUNDERBIRDS (EP) 35
67 Century 21 MA 122   LADY PENELOPE (EP) 35
67 Century 21 MA 123   BRAINS (EP) 35
67 Century 21 MA 124   BRINK OF DISASTER (EP) 35
67 Century 21 MA 125   ATLANTIC INFERNO (EP). 35
67 Century 21 MA 126   RICOCHET (EP) 35
67 Century 21 MA 127   TINGHA & TUCKER & THE WOMBAVILLE BAND (EP) 35
67 Century 21 MA 128   ONE MOVE & YOU'RE DEAD (EP). 35
67 Century 21 MA 129   30 MINUTES AFTER NOON (EP) 35
67 Century 21 MA 130   TINGHA & TUCKER IN NURSERY RHYME TIME (EP) 35
67 Century 21 MA 131   INTRODUCING CAPTAIN SCARLET (EP) 30
67 Century 21 MA 132   CAPTAIN SCARLET AND THE MYSTERONS (EP). 30
67 Century 21 MA 133   CAPTAIN SCARLET IS INDESTRUCTIBLE (EP). 25
67 Century 21 MA 134   CAPTAIN SCARLET OF SPECTRUM (EP). 25
67 Century 21 MA 135   CAPTAIN SCARLET VS. CAPTAIN BLACK (EP). 25
67 Century 21 MA 136   THEMES FROM GERRY ANDERSON'S CAPTAIN SCARLET (EP) 25

65	Century 21 LA 100	JOURNEY TO THE MOON (LP)	70
66	Century 21 LA 1	THE WORLD OF TOMORROW (LP)	50
66	Century 21 LA 2	LADY PENELOPE PRESENTS (LP)	50
66	Century 21 LA 3	JEFF TRACY INTRODUCES INTERNATIONAL RESCUE (LP)	50
66	Century 21 LA 4	LADY PENELOPE INVESTIGATES (LP)	50
66	Century 21 LA 5	THE TINGHA & TUCKER CLUB SONG BOOK (LP)	50
67	Century 21 LA 6	FAVOURITE TELEVISION THEMES (LP)	50
68	Marble Arch MAL 770	TV FAVOURITES VOL. 1 (LP)	20
68	Marble Arch MAL 771	TV FAVOURITES VOL. 2 (LP)	20

(see also Barry Gray, Dr. Who)

CEOLBEG
| 90 | Ceolbeg Music CB 001 | NOT THE BUNNY HOP (LP) | 20 |

CERTAIN LIONS & TIGERS
| 70 | Polydor 2344 002 | SOUL CONDOR (LP) | 40 |

CHAD (STUART) & JEREMY (CLYDE)
64	Ember EMB S 180	Yesterday's Gone/Lemon Tree (as Chad Stuart & Jeremy Clyde)	6
64	Ember EMB S 186	Early In The Morning/Like I Love You Today (as Chad Stuart & Jeremy Clyde)	6
64	United Artists UP 1062	Summer Song/No Tears For Johnnie (as Chad Stuart & Jeremy Clyde)	5
64	United Artists UP 1070	Willow Weep For Me/If She Was Mine	5
65	Ember EMB S 205	If I Loved You/No Tears For Johnnie	5
65	CBS 201769	Before And After/Evil-Hearted Me	7
65	CBS 201814	I Don't Want To Lose You/Pennies	5
64	Ember EMB EP 4543	YESTERDAY'S GONE (EP)	10
65	United Artists UEP 1008	CHAD STUART AND JEREMY CLYDE (EP)	10
65	Ember NR 5021	SING FOR YOU (LP)	18
66	Ember NR 5031	SECOND ALBUM (LP)	18

(see also John Barry, Jeremy Clyde)

ERNIE CHAFFIN
| 57 | London HLS 8409 | Feelin' Low/Lonesome For My Baby (78 rpm = £50) | 150 |

CHAINSAW
80	Square SQSP 2	Police And Politicians (p/s)	45
80	Pot Belly EJSP 9462	Lonely Without You/On The Highway	35
84	GMC CS 001	Long Legged Woman/Midnight Blue	30
84	Thunderbolt THBE 1006	MASSACRE (12" EP)	8

CHAIRMEN OF THE BOARD
70	Invictus INV 501	Give Me Just A Little More Time/Since The Days Of Pigtails	6
70	Invictus INV 504	You've Got Me Dangling On A String/Patches	6
71	Invictus INV 507	Everything's Tuesday/Bless You	6
71	Invictus INV 511	Pay To The Piper/When Will She Tell Me She Needs Me?	6
71	Invictus INV 516	Chairman Of The Board/Hanging On To A Memory	5
71	Invictus INV 516	Chairman Of The Board/When Will She Tell Me She Needs Me? (different B-side)	5
72	Invictus INV 519	Working On A Building Of Love/Try On My Love For Size	5
72	Invictus INV 524	Elmo James/Bittersweet	5
72	Invictus INV 527	I'm On My Way To A Better Place/So Glad You're Mine	5
73	Invictus INV 530	Finders Keepers/Finders Keepers (Instrumental)	5
70	Invictus SVT 1002	CHAIRMEN OF THE BOARD (LP)	30
71	Invictus SVT 1003	IN SESSION (LP)	30
72	Invictus SVT 1006	BITTERSWEET (LP)	20
73	Invictus SVT 1009	GREATEST HITS (LP)	15
74	Invictus 65868	SKIN I'M IN (LP)	20

(see also Showmen, General Johnson, Norman Johnson)

CHAKACHAS
61	RCA RCA 1264	Twist Twist/Baila La Bamba	6
72	Polydor 2121 093	Jungle Fever/Chaka Cha	8
72	Polydor 2489 050	JUNGLE FEVER (LP)	20
73	Young Blood SYB 3003	CHAKACHAS (LP)	20

GEORGE CHAKIRIS
| 59 | Saga SAG 45-2905 | Cool/I Got Rhythm | 5 |
| 60 | Triumph RGM 1010 | Heart Of A Teenage Girl/I'm Always Chasing Rainbows | 35 |

BRYAN CHALKER('S NEW FRONTIER)
70	Amity OTS 502	Ned Kelly/Four Girls From The Town Of Boston	6
72	Columbia DB 8883	Daddy Sang Bass/Lot 69	6
72	Chapter One SCH 179	Help Me Make It Through The Night/Eskimo Song	6
72	Chapter One SCH 185	Daisy A Day/Life Gets Tee-jus, Don't It	6
71	Avenue AVE 071	THE HANGING OF SAMUEL HALL (LP, as Bryan Chalker's New Frontier)	30
72	Chapter One CMS 1010	BRYAN CHALKER'S NEW FRONTIER (LP)	18
73	Chapter One CMS 1017	BRYAN CHALKER (LP)	18
74	Chapter One CMS 1020	DADDY SING ME A SONG (LP, as Brian Chalker & The Road Band)	15

CHALLENGER
| 81 | CMC CM 0001 | So Sure Of Yourself | 20 |

CHALLENGERS (U.K.)
| 61 | Parlophone R 4773 | Cry Of The Wild Goose/Deadline | 15 |

CHALLENGERS (U.S.)
63	Stateside SS 177	Torquay/Bulldog	20
65	Vocalion V 9253	The Man From U.N.C.L.E./The Streets Of London	20
66	Vocalion V 9270	Walk With Me/How Could I	10
63	Stateside SL 10030	SURFBEAT (LP)	70
67	Vocalion VA-N/SAV-N 8069	WIPE OUT (LP, mono/stereo)	60/70

RICHARD CHAMBERLAIN
62	MGM MGM-EP 776	HITS (EP)	10
62	MGM MGM-EP 778	I'LL BE AROUND (EP)	10
62	MGM MGM-EP 781	DREAM (EP)	10

CHAMBER POP ENSEMBLE
68	Decca F 12789	Walk Away Renee/59th Street Bridge Song (Feeling Groovy)	6
68	Decca LK/SKL 4933	CHAMBER POP ENSEMBLE (LP)	15

JAMES CHAMBERS
71	Summit SUM 8523	Bongo Man/KEN BOOTHE: Now I Know	10

(see also Jimmy Cliff)

CHAMBERS BROTHERS
66	Vocalion VL 9267	Love Me Like The Rain/Pretty Girls Everywhere	20
66	Vocalion VL 9276	Call Me/Seventeen	20
67	CBS 202565	All Strung Out Over You/Falling In Love	10
68	Direction 58-3215	Up Town/Love Me Like The Rain	7
68	Direction 58-3671	Time Has Come Today/Dinah	10
68	Direction 58-3760	Time Has Come Today/Dinah (reissue)	7
68	Direction 58-3865	I Can't Turn You Loose/Do Your Thing	8
69	Direction 58-4098	Are You Ready/You Got The Power To Turn Me On	6
69	Direction 58-4318	People Get Ready/No, No, No, Don't Say Goodbye	6
69	Direction 58-4367	Wake Up/Everybody Needs Someone	8
70	Direction 58-4846	Love Peace And Happiness/If You Want Me To	7
70	Direction 58-5033	Let's Do It/To Love Somebody	7
71	CBS 5389	Funky/Love, Peace And Happiness	12
71	CBS 7689	By The Hair On My Chinny Chin Chin/Heaven	6
66	Vocalion VA-L/SAV-L 8058	PEOPLE GET READY (LP)	55
68	Liberty LBS 83272	SHOUT! (LP, blue label)	25
68	Direction 8-63407	THE TIME HAS COME (LP)	30
69	Direction 8-63451	A NEW TIME — A NEW DAY (LP)	30
70	Direction 8-66228	LOVE PEACE AND HAPPINESS (Live At Bill Graham's Fillmore West) (2-LP)	30
70	Liberty LBS 83276	FEELIN' THE BLUES (LP)	18
71	CBS 64156	A NEW GENERATION (LP)	15

EDDIE CHAMBLEE & HIS RHYTHM & BLUES BAND
53	Esquire 10-329	All Out/TOMMY DEAN R&B BAND: Scamon Boogie (78)	8
53	Esquire 10-330	Blues For Eddie/PINEY BROWN: That's Right, Little Girl (78)	8
54	Esquire 10-340	Cradle Rock/Back Street (78)	8

CHAMELEONS
82	Epic EPCA 2210	In Shreds/Less Than Human (p/s)	15
83	Statik STAT 30	As High As You Can Go/Pleasure And Pain (p/s)	6
83	Statik STAT 3012	As High As You Can Go/Pleasure And Pain/Paper Tigers (12", p/s)	10
83	Statik TAK 6	A Person Isn't Safe Anywhere These Days/Thursday's Child (p/s)	7
83	Statik TAK 6/12	A Person Isn't Safe Anywhere These Days/Thursday's Child/ Prisoners Of The Sun (12", p/s)	10
85	Statik TAK 29	In Shreds/Nostalgia (p/s)	7
85	Statik TAK 29/12	In Shreds/Less Than Human/Nostalgia (12", p/s)	10
85	Statik TAK 35	Singing Rule Britannia (While The Walls Close In)/Singing Rule Britannia (Radio 1 'Saturday Live' Session Version) (p/s)	6
85	Statik TAK 35/12	Singing Rule Britannia (While The Walls Close In)/Singing Rule Britannia (Radio 1 'Saturday Live' Session Version) (12", p/s)	8
86	Geffen GEF 4	Tears/Paradiso (p/s)	5
86	Geffen GEF 4F/SAM 287	Tears/Paradiso//Swamp Thing/Inside Out (double pack, gatefold p/s)	8
86	Geffen GEF 4T	Tears/Paradiso/Inside Out (12", p/s)	8
86	Geffen GEF 10	Swamp Thing/John, I'm Only Dancing (p/s)	5
86	Geffen GEF 10T	Swamp Thing/John, I'm Only Dancing/Tears (Original Arrangement) (12", p/s)	8
90	Glass Pyramid EMC 1	TONY FLETCHER WALKED ON WATER (12" EP)	35
90	Glass Pyramid EMCD 1	TONY FLETCHER WALKED ON WATER (CD EP)	35
85	Statik STATLP 17	SCRIPT OF THE BRIDGE (LP, picture disc)	20
85	Statik STATLP 22	WHAT DOES ANYTHING MEAN? BASICALLY (LP, gatefold sleeve, with insert)	12

(see also Sun & Moon, Reegs)

TEDDY CHAMES
68	Blue Cat BS 141	I Want It Girl/She Is Gone (actually by Teddy Charmes)	30

CHAMPIONS
63	Oriole CB 1854	Circlorama/Pinky	15

CHAMPIONS OF NATURE
00	White FOFF 1	The Fuck Off Song/An Undercurrent/360/Carpe Diem (EP)	30
00	White FOFF 2	Finalisation/Cold Dessert/Breakfast Of Champions (EP)	30
01	White SALSA001	Salsa Smurph/Jazzy Styles (12")	22

CHAMPS (Jamaica)
64	Blue Beat BB 267	Walk Between Your Enemies/Do What I Say	18

CHAMPS (U.S.)
58	London HLU 8580	Tequila/Train To Nowhere (78 rpm = £12)	18
58	London HL 8655	Midnighter/El Rancho Rock (78 rpm = £12)	18
58	London HL 8715	Chariot Rock/Subway (78 rpm = £15)	18
59	London HLH 8811	Beatnik/Gone Train (78 rpm = £15)	15
59	London HLH 8864	Caramba/Moonlight Bay (78 rpm = £18)	15
60	London HLH 9052	Too Much Tequila/Twenty Thousand Leagues	12
61	London HLH 9430	Cantina/Panic Button	12
62	London HLH 9506	Tequila Twist/Limbo Rock	12
62	London HLH 9539	Experiment In Terror/La Cucaracha	12
62	London HLH 9604	Limbo Dance/Latin Limbo	12
59	London RE 1176	FOUR BY THE CHAMPS (EP)	40

59	London RE-H 1209	ANOTHER FOUR BY THE CHAMPS (EP)	40
59	London RE-H 1223	STILL MORE BY THE CHAMPS (EP)	40
61	London RE-H 1250	KNOCKOUTS! (EP)	70
58	London HA-H 2152	GO CHAMPS GO! (LP)	70
59	London HA-H 2184	EVERYBODY'S ROCKIN' WITH THE CHAMPS (LP)	70
62	London HA-H 2451	GREAT DANCE HITS (LP, early issues with flipback cover)	50/35

JACQUI CHAN
| 60 | Pye 7N 15273 | But No One Knows/Gentlemen Please! | 5 |

(see also Simon Dupree & Big Sound)

ROB CHANCE & CHANCES-R
| 67 | CBS 3130 | At The End Of The Day/I've Got The Power | 12 |

(see also Chances-R)

CHANCES ARE
| 67 | Columbia DB 8144 | Fragile Child/What Went Wrong | 40 |

CHANCES-R
| 67 | CBS 202614 | Talking Out The Back Of My Head/I Aimed Too High | 12 |
| 67 | CBS 2940 | Do It Yourself/Turn A New Leaf Over | 12 |

(see also Ron Chance & Chances-R)

DANY CHANDELLE
| 65 | Columbia DB 7540 | Lying Awake/I Love You | 30 |

BARBARA CHANDLER
| 63 | London HLR 9823 | Do You Really Love Me Too?/I Live To Love You | 20 |
| 64 | London HLR 9861 | I'm Going Out With The Girls/Lonely New Year | 25 |

E.J. CHANDLER
| 80 | Destiny DS 1026 | I Can't Stand To Lose You/Believe In Me | 8 |

GENE CHANDLER
62	Columbia DB 4793	Duke Of Earl/Kissing In The Kitchen	22
63	Stateside SS 185	Rainbow/You Threw A Lucky Punch	40
64	Stateside SS 331	Just Be True/A Song Called Soul	20
64	Stateside SS 364	Bless Our Love/London Town	20
65	Stateside SS 388	What Now/If You Can't Be True (Find A Part Time Love)	30
65	Stateside SS 401	You Can't Hurt Me No More/Everybody Let's Dance	20
65	Stateside SS 425	Nothing Can Stop Me/The Big Lie (DJ copy = £150)	60
65	Stateside SS 458	Good Times/No One Can Love You (Like I Do)	30
66	Stateside SS 500	(I'm Just A) Fool For You/Buddy Ain't It A Shame	30
66	Chess CRS 8047	I Fooled You This Time/Such A Pretty Thing (DJ copy = £100)	50
67	Coral Q 72490	The Girl Don't Care/My Love	20
68	Soul City SC 102	Nothing Can Stop Me/The Big Lie (reissue)	15
69	Action ACT 4551	I Can't Save It/I Can Take Care Of Myself	50
69	President PT 234	Duke Of Earl/Stand By Me	6
70	Mercury 6052 033	Groovy Situation/Not The Marrying Kind	6
71	Mercury 6052 098	You're A Lady/Stone Cold Feeling	15
76	Brunswick BR 39	There Was A Time/ARTISTICS: I'm Gonna Miss You	10
65	Fontana TL 5247	DUKE OF EARL (LP)	80
67	Coral LVA 9236	THE GIRL DON'T CARE (LP)	50
69	MCA MUPS 367	THERE WAS A TIME (LP)	30
69	Action ACLP 6010	LIVE ON STAGE (LP)	50
71	Mercury 6338 037	SITUATION (LP)	20
74	Joy JOYS 136	A GENE CHANDLER ALBUM (LP)	15

GENE CHANDLER & BARBARA ACKLIN
| 69 | MCA Soul Bag BAG 1 | Little Green Apples/Will I Find Love | 15 |
| 74 | Brunswick BR 30 | From The Teacher To The Preacher/Little Green Apples | 10 |

(see also Barbara Acklin, Gene & Jerry)

GEORGE CHANDLER
| 77 | RCA 5020 | Make Up Your Mind/Instrumental | 10 |
| 82 | Polydor 436 | Can't Go Back No More/This Could Be The Night | 18 |

JEFF CHANDLER
54	Brunswick 05264	I Should Care/More Than Anyone	10
55	Brunswick 05380	Everything Happens To Me/Always	10
55	Brunswick 05417	My Prayer/When Spring Comes	10
55	Brunswick 05441	Foxfire/Shaner Maidel	10
55	Brunswick 05465	Only The Very Young/A Little Love Can Go A Long, Long Way	10
57	London HLU 8484	Half Of My Heart/Hold Me (78 rpm = £8)	10
58	London HA-U 2100	JEFF CHANDLER SINGS TO YOU (LP)	50

KAREN CHANDLER
55	Vogue Coral Q 72091	The Price You Pay For Love/The Man In The Raincoat	10
56	Brunswick 05570	Love Is The $64,000 Question/(I'm Just A) Beginner	10
56	Brunswick 05596	Tonight You Belong To Me/Crazy Arms (with Jimmy Wakely) (78 rpm = £8)	10
57	Brunswick 05662	Your Wild Heart/It's An International Language (78 rpm = £8)	10
62	Salvo SLO 1803	My Own True Love/You Made Me Love You (99 copies only)	15

(see also Jimmy Wakely)

KENNY CHANDLER
| 63 | Stateside SS 166 | Heart/Wait For Me | 15 |
| 68 | Stateside SS 2110 | Beyond Love/Charity (DJ Copy = £85) | 50 |

LEN CHANDLER
| 67 | CBS 62931 | TO BE A MAN (LP) | 20 |

LORRAINE CHANDLER
| 75 | Black Magic BM 105 | Love You Baby/What Can I Do | 10 |

CHANDONS
68	RCA RCA 1704	Timber/Never Been Loved Before	5

CHANGIN' TIMES
65	Phillips BF 1442	Pied Piper/Thank You Babe	10
68	Bell BLL 1009	When The Good Sun Shines/Show Me The Way To Go Home	6

BRUCE CHANNEL
62	Mercury AMT 1171	Hey! Baby/Dream Girl	10
62	Mercury AMT 1177	Number One Man/If Only I Had Known	10
62	Pye International 7N 25137	Run Romance Run/Don't Leave Me	20
63	London HLU 9776	I Don't Wanna/Blue And Lonesome	20
64	London HLU 9841	Going Back To Louisiana/Forget Me Not	15
67	Stateside SS 2066	Mr. Bus Driver/It's Me	15
68	Bell BLL 1010	Keep On/Barbara Allen	6
68	Bell BLL 1030	Try Me/Water The Family Tree	7
62	Mercury MMC 14104	HEY! BABY! (LP)	80
68	Bell MBLL/SBLL 1110	KEEP ON (LP)	25

CHANNEL 4
79	Ripping RIP 1	Vampire/Channel 4 (numbered p/s with insert)	6

CHANNEL 3
82	No Future OI 11	I've Got A Gun/Manzanar/Mannequin (p/s)	10

CHANTAYS
63	London HLD 9696	Pipeline/Move It	15
64	King KG 1018	Beyond/I'll Be Back Someday	20
66	Dot DS 26757	Pipeline/Move It (reissue)	7
63	London RED 1397	PIPELINE (EP)	60
63	London HA-D/SH-D 8087	PIPELINE (LP, mono/stereo)	60/75

CHANTELLES
65	Parlophone R 5271	I Want That Boy/London My Home Town	25
65	Parlophone R 5303	The Secret Of My Success/Sticks And Stones	15
65	Parlophone R 5350	Gonna Get Burned/Gonna Give Him Some Love	15
66	Parlophone R 5431	I Think Of You/Please Don't Kiss Me	15
66	Polydor 56119	There's Something About You/Just Another Fool	20
67	CBS 2777	Blue Mood/The Man I Love	15

(see also Lana Sisters)

CHANTELS
58	London HLU 8561	Maybe/Come My Little Baby (78 rpm = £60)	500
62	London HLL 9428	Look In My Eyes/Glad To Be Back	50
62	London HLL 9480	Well I Told You/Still	60
62	London HLL 9532	Here It Comes Again/Summertime	40
63	Capitol CL 15297	Swamp Water/Eternally	40
70	Roulette RO 514	Maybe/He's Gone	8

(see also Richard Barrett)

CHANTER
77	Expert ELP 1	SUBURBAN ETHNIA	
		(LP, private pressing)	12

IRENE CHANTER
75	Polydor 2058 608	Make Me Happy/Funky Music	6

(see also Birds Of A Feather, Chanters, Chanter Sisters)

CHANTERS
66	CBS 202454	Every Night (I Sit And Cry)/Where	7
67	CBS 202616	You Can't Fool Me/All Day Long	20
68	CBS 3400	What's Wrong With You/Right By Your Side	6
68	CBS 3668	My Love Is For You/Mississippi Paddleboat	8

(see also Birds Of A Feather, Chanter Sisters, Irene Chanter)

CHANTER SISTERS
76	Polydor 2058 679	Halfway To Paradise/My Love	8

(see also Birds Of A Feather, Chanters, Irene Chanter)

CHANTS (U.K.)
63	Pye 7N 15557	I Don't Care/Come Go With Me	18
64	Pye 7N 15591	I Could Write A Book/A Thousand Stars	18
64	Pye 7N 15643	She's Mine/Then I'll Be Home	18
64	Pye 7N 15691	Sweet Was The Wine/One Star	10
66	Fontana TF 716	Come Back And Get This Loving Baby/Love Light	10
67	Decca F 12650	A Lover's Story/Wearing A Smile	15
67	Page One POF 016	Ain't Nobody Home/For You	10
68	RCA Victor RCA 1754	A Man Without A Face/Baby I Don't Need Your Love	75
69	RCA Victor RCA 1823	I Get The Sweetest Feeling/Candy	20
76	Chipping Norton CHIP 2	I've Been Trying/Lucky Old Me	40

(see also Real Thing)

CHANTS (U.S.)
58	Capitol CL 14876	Close Friends/Lost And Found	35

CHAOS
79	Chaotic Records VD 1	Summer Of Hate/I Want To Be Left Alone (p/s, 500 only)	100

(originals have a rim around the label — counterfeits have no rim)

CHAOS & JULIA SET
93	Recoil RCL 001	VOL. 1 (12", plain sleeve)	10
93	Recoil RCL 002	VOL. 2 — FEAR OF THE FUTURE (12", plain sleeve)	10

(see also Global Communications)

MINT VALUE £

CHAOS U.K.
82	Riot City RIOT 6	BURNING BRITAIN (EP)	8
82	Riot City RIOT 12	LOUD, POLITICAL AND UNCOMPROMISING (EP)	10

CHAOTIC DISCHORD
82	Riot City RIOT 10	FUCK THE WORLD (EP)	10
83	Beat The System	SAD SOCIETY (EP)	8
83	Riot City CITY 004	FUCK RELIGION, FUCK POLITICS, AND FUCK THE LOT OF YOU (LP)	12
84	Syndicate SYNLP 12	FUCK OFF YOU CUNT WHAT A LOAD OF BOLLOCKS (LP)	12
88	Not Very Nice GRR 3RV	VERY FUCKIN' BAD (LP)	12

HARRY CHAPIN
60s	Elektra 7E 1012	VERITIES & BALDERDASH (LP)	15
60s	Elektra K 42155	SHORT STORIES (LP, gatefold sleeve)	15
60s	Elektra K 52089	LIVING ROOM SUITE (LP)	15

PAUL CHAPLAIN & HIS EMERALDS
60	London HLU 9205	Shortnin' Bread/Nicotine	30

MICHAEL CHAPLIN
65	Decca F 12142	I Am What I Am/Restless	6

COLIN CHAPMAN
60s	CCLP 1001	FOLK SONGS VOL 1 (LP)	15

GENE CHAPMAN
63	Starlite ST45 102	Oklahoma Blues/Don't Come Crying	150

GRADY CHAPMAN
60	Mercury AMT 1107	Sweet Thing/I Know What I Want	30

MICHAEL CHAPMAN
69	Harvest HAR 5002	It Didn't Work Out/Mozart Lives Upstairs	7
69	Harvest SHVL 755	RAINMAKER (LP, gatefold sleeve)	35
70	Harvest SHVL 764	FULLY QUALIFIED SURVIVOR (LP, gatefold sleeve)	30
70	Harvest SHVL 786	WINDOW (LP, gatefold sleeve)	40
71	Harvest SHVL 798	WRECKED AGAIN (LP, gatefold sleeve)	35
73	Deram SML 1105	MILLSTONE GRIT (LP)	15
74	Deram SML 1114	DEAL GONE DOWN (LP)	12
76	Decca SKL-R 5242	SAVAGE AMUSEMENT (LP, with lyric sheet)	12
70s	Standard ESL 146	GUITARS (LP, library issue)	50

CHAPS
62	Parlophone R 4979	Poppin' Medley (Parts 1 & 2)	20

(see also Outlaws)

CHAPTER FIVE
66	CBS 202395	Anything You Do Is Alright/You Can't Mean It	600
67	CBS 2696	One In A Million/Hey Hey (unissued, demos only)	250

CHAPTER FOUR (U.K.)
60s	GSP 11009/10	CHAPTER FOUR (EP, no p/s)	90

CHAPTER FOUR (U.K.)
80	Bridge BR 001	HANGING AROUND STERLING (LP)	35

CHAPTER FOUR (U.S.)
66	United Artists UP 1143	In My Life/In Each Other's Arms	200

(see also Jay & Americans)

CHAPTERS
65	Pye 7N 15815	Can't Stop Thinking About Her/Dance Little Lady	50

CHAPTER THREE (U.K.)
67	CBS 2971	Cold And Lonely Hours/Wrecking Crew	7
67	CBS BPG 63007	RAMBLE AWAY (LP)	18

CHAPTER FIVE
90s	Goldmine/Soul Supply GS 009	You Can't Mean It/One In A Million	8

CHAQUITO & HIS ORCHESTRA
72	Philips 6006 225	Hawaii 5-0/Ironside	5

(see also Johnny Gregory)

CHARGE
70	private pressing	Zeugma/Boring Song (art sleeve)	20

CHARGE
73	SRT private pressing	CHARGE (LP, 1 known copy)	500+
92	Kissing Spell KSLP 9205	CHARGE (LP, reissue, revised sleeve, 500 only)	12

CHARGE
80	YCAFO Records	You Get What You Deserve/Rather B Crazy/Angel Deceast (p/s)	25
81	Test Pressing	You Deserve More Than A Maybe (p/s, 500 only)	20
82	Test Pressing TP 3	Kings Cross/Brave New World (p/s)	12

MARK CHARIG
77	Ogun OG 710	PIPEDREAM (LP)	15

(see also Bluesology, B.B. Blunder, Reg King, Centipede, Keith Tippett, Julie Tippett, Brotherhood Of Breath, Elton Dean, Ninensense)

CHARIOT
84	Shades SHADE 2	ALL ALONE AGAIN (EP)	12
84	Shades SHADE 1	THE WARRIOR (LP)	20
86	Shades SHADE 4	BURNING AMBITION (LP)	15

CHARLATANS (U.K.)

89	Dead Dead Good no cat.no	OCTOBER '89 (demo cassette, sold at gigs)	40
90	Dead Dead Good GOOD ONE TWELVE	Indian Rope/You Can Talk To Me/Who Wants To Know (12", 1st issue with barcode on p/s)	10
90	Dead Dead Good SIT 70T	The Only One I Know/Imperial 109 (Edit)/Everything Changed (12", p/s)	8
90	Dead Dead Good SIT 74T	Then/Taurus Moaner/Then (Alternate Take)/Taurus Moaner (Instrumental) (12", p/s)	10
91	D. D. G. GOOD 1CD	Indian Rope/You Can Talk To Me/Who Wants To Know (CD)	8
91	Situation Two SIT 84T	Me In Time/Occupation/Monster (12" p/s)	8
90	Situation Two SIT 74T	Then/Taurus Moaner/Then (Alternate Take)/Taurus Moaner (Instrumental) (12", mispressing with vocal version of Taurus Moaner on both sides)	8
90	Situation Two SIT 74T	Polar Bear/Taurus Moaner (12", white label test pressing, around 10 only)	80
91	Beggars Banquet CHAR 1	Happen To Die (1-sided, green die-cut sleeve, promo only)	10
92	Situation Two SIT 88T	Weirdo/Theme From The Wish/Sproston Green (U.S. Version)/ Weirdo (Alternate Take) (12", with art print)	8
93	Beggars Banquet CHAR 7	Subterranean (CD, free with *109* fan club magazine)	12/8
94	Beggars Banquet BBQ 31CD1	I Never Want An Easy Life If Me And He Were Ever To Get There/ Only A Boho/Subterranean/Can't Get Out Of Bed (Demo Version) (CD, oblong box set with 3 postcards, numbered)	15
96	Beggars Banq. BBQ 301DJ	One To Another (Radio Edit) (CD, promo)	12
01	12 KEY 1	Love Is The Key (orig. version)/Love Is The Key (So Solid Remix)/ The Bell And The Butterfly (12", no p/s, white label promo)	8
90	Situation Two SITU 30L	SOME FRIENDLY (LP, 'some friendly edition' in white PVC sleeve with inner)	12
91	Live Live Good CB 2	ISOLATION 21.2.91 (LP, official live bootleg, sold via fan club, 1,000 only)	20
92	Situation Two SITU 37	BETWEEN 10TH AND 11TH (CD, box set with cassette & video, promo only)	35
94	Beggars Banquet BBCD 147	UP TO OUR HIPS (CD, box set with cassette & video, promo only)	35

(see also Electric Crayons, Makin' Time)

CHARLATANS (U.S.)

69	Philips SBL 7903	THE CHARLATANS (LP)	70

(see also Mike Wilhelm, Tongue & Groove)

BOBBY CHARLES

56	London HLU 8247	See You Later, Alligator/On Bended Knee	2,500
56	London HLU 8247	See You Later, Alligator/On Bended Knee (78)	300+

BOBBY CHARLES

78	Bearsville J 15508	Small Town Talk/Grow Too Old	10
72	Bearsville K 45516	BOBBY CHARLES (LP)	15

DON CHARLES

62	Decca F 11424	Walk With Me My Angel/Crazy Man, Crazy	10
62	Decca F 11464	The Hermit Of Misty Mountain/Moonlight Rendezvous	25
62	Decca F 11528	It's My Way Of Loving You/Guess That's The Way It Goes	20
63	Decca F 11602	Angel Of Love/Lucky Star	20
63	Decca F 11645	Heart's Ice Cold/Daybreak	20
63	HMV POP 1271	Tower Tall/Look Before You Love	6
64	HMV POP 1307	If You Don't Know I Ain't Gonna Tell Ya/Voice On The Phone	6
64	HMV POP 1332	Big Talk From A Little Man/She's Mine	15
65	HMV POP 1382	Forgetting Me, Loving Him/A Long Time Ago	6
65	HMV POP 1420	Dream On Little Dreamer/We Only Live Once	6
65	HMV POP 1478	I Could Conquer The World/Time Will Tell	6
66	HMV POP 1542	Out Of This Cold/From The Beginning	6
67	Parlophone R 5564	So Let It Be/Bring Your Love To Me	6
67	Parlophone R 5596	Have I Told You Lately/Time Waits For Nobody	6
68	Parlophone R 5659	If I Had The Chance/(I've Got Everything) I've Got You	6
68	Parlophone R 5688	The Drifter/Great To Be Livin'	60
68	Parlophone R 5712	Your Name Is On My Heart/How Can I	5
63	Decca DFE 8530	DON CHARLES (EP)	110
67	Parlophone PMC/PCS 7021	HAVE I TOLD YOU LATELY (LP, mono/stereo)	20

JIMMY CHARLES

60	London HLU 9206	A Million To One/Hop Scotch Hop	25
63	Windsor WPS 120	Pitter Patter/How You Gonna Treat Me Now	10

JOHN CHARLES

60	Cetra SP 785	Sixteen Tons/Love In Portofino	5
60	Cetra SP 786	La Fine (The End)/Non Dimenticar	5

RAY CHARLES

78s

58	London HLE 8768	Rockhouse (Parts 1 & 2)	20
59	London HLE 8917	What'd I Say (Parts 1 & 2)	25
59	London HLE 9009	I'm Movin' On/I Believe To My Soul	35
60	HMV POP 792	Georgia On My Mind/Carry Me Back To Old Virginny	100

SINGLES

58	London HLE 8768	Rockhouse (Parts 1 & 2)	40
59	London HLE 8917	What'd I Say (Parts 1 & 2)	25
59	London HLE 9009	I'm Movin' On/I Believe To My Soul	20
60	London HLE 9058	Let The Good Times Roll/Don't Let The Sun Catch You Cryin'	20
60	HMV POP 774	Sticks And Stones/Worried Life Blues	15
60	London HLK 9181	Tell The Truth/You Be My Baby	15
60	HMV POP 792	Georgia On My Mind/Carry Me Back To Old Virginny	7
60	London HLK 9251	Come Rain Or Come Shine/Tell Me You'll Wait For Me	6
61	HMV POP 825	Ruby/Hard Hearted Hannah	6
61	HMV POP 838	Them That Got/I Wonder	25
61	London HLK 9364	Early In The Mornin'/A Bit Of Soul	15
61	HMV POP 862	One Mint Julep/Let's Go	15
61	HMV POP 935	Hit The Road Jack/The Danger Zone	10

Ray CHARLES

61	London HLK 9435	I Wonder Who/Hard Times	12
62	HMV POP 969	Unchain My Heart/But On The Other Hand Baby	10
62	HMV POP 1017	Hide Nor Hair/At The Club	10
63	HMV POP 1133	Don't Set Me Free/The Brightest Smile In Town	10
63	HMV POP 1161	Take These Chains From My Heart/No Letter Today	6
63	HMV POP 1202	No One/Without Love (There Is Nothing)	6
63	HMV POP 1221	Busted/Making Believe	12
64	HMV POP 1251	That Lucky Old Sun/Mississippi Mud	6
64	HMV POP 1272	Baby Don't You Cry/My Heart Cries For You	6
64	HMV POP 1315	My Baby Don't Dig Me/Something's Wrong	6
64	HMV POP 1333	No One To Cry To/A Tear Fell	6
64	HMV POP 1350	Smack Dab In The Middle/I Wake Up Crying	6
65	HMV POP 1383	Makin' Whoopee/Move It On Over	6
65	HMV POP 1392	Cry/Teardrops From My Eye	6
65	HMV POP 1414	Light Out Of Darkness/Please Forgive And Forget	6
65	HMV POP 1437	I Gotta Woman/Without A Song	6
65	HMV POP 1457	Love's Gonna Live Here/I'm A Fool To Care	6
65	HMV POP 1484	The Cincinnati Kid/That's All I Am To You	6
66	HMV POP 1502	Crying Time/When My Dreamboat Comes Home	6
66	HMV POP 1519	Together Again/You're Just About To Lose Your Clown	6
66	HMV POP 1537	Let's Go Get Stoned/The Train	15
66	HMV POP 1551	I Chose To Sing The Blues/Hopelessly	25
66	HMV POP 1566	Please Say You're Fooling/I Don't Need No Doctor	60
67	Atlantic 584 093	What'd I Say/I Got A Woman	5
67	HMV POP 1589	You Win Again/Bye Bye Love	5
67	HMV POP 1595	Somebody Oughta Write A Book About It/Here We Go Again	5
67	HMV POP 1607	In The Heat Of The Night/Something's Got To Change	5
67	Stateside SS 2071	Yesterday/Never Had Enough Of Nothing Yet	5
68	Stateside SS 2120	Eleanor Rigby/Understanding	5
71	Tangerine 6121 001	Booty Butt/Zig Zag	5

EPs

59	London Jazz EZK 19043	THE GREAT RAY CHARLES	15
59	London Jazz EZK 19048	SOUL BROTHERS (with Milt Jackson)	15
61	London REK 1306	WHAT'D I SAY	18
61	London REK 1317	RAY CHARLES AT NEWPORT	15
62	HMV 7EG 8729	HIT THE ROAD JACK	15
62	HMV 7EG 8781	I CAN'T STOP LOVING YOU	15
63	HMV 7EG 8783	THE BALLAD STYLE OF RAY CHARLES	12
63	HMV 7EG 8801	THE SWINGING STYLE OF RAY CHARLES	12
63	HMV 7EG 8807	BABY IT'S COLD OUTSIDE (with Betty Carter)	12
63	HMV 7EG 8812	TAKE THESE CHAINS FROM MY HEART	12
63	London REB 1407	THE ORIGINAL RAY CHARLES VOLUME ONE	15
63	London REB 1408	THE ORIGINAL RAY CHARLES VOLUME TWO	15
63	London REB 1409	THE ORIGINAL RAY CHARLES VOLUME THREE	15
64	HMV 7EG 8841	BUSTED	12
64	HMV 7EG 8861	RAY CHARLES SINGS	12
64	Realm REP 4001	THE YOUNG RAY CHARLES	10
66	HMV 7EG 8932	RAY CHARLES LIVE IN CONCERT	12
66	HMV 7EG 8951	RAY CHARLES SINGS SONGS OF BUCK OWENS	12

LPs

58	London Jazz LTZ-K 15134	THE GREAT RAY CHARLES	50
59	London Jazz LTZ-K 15146	SOUL BROTHERS (with Milt Jackson, also stereo SAH-K 6030)	25/35
59	London Jazz LTZ-K 15149	RAY CHARLES AT NEWPORT (also stereo SAH-K 6008)	25/35
59	London HA-E 2168	YES INDEED	40
59	London HA-E 2226	WHAT'D I SAY	35
60	London Jazz LTZ-K 15190	THE GENIUS OF RAY CHARLES	35
60	HMV CLP 1387/CSD 1320	THE GENIUS HITS THE ROAD (mono/stereo)	18/25
60	London HA-K 2284	RAY CHARLES IN PERSON	25
61	HMV CLP 1449/CSD 1362	DEDICATED TO YOU (mono/stereo)	15/18
61	HMV CLP 1475/CSD 1384	GENIUS + SOUL = JAZZ (mono/stereo)	15/18
62	HMV CLP 1520/CSD 1414	RAY CHARLES AND BETTY CARTER (mono/stereo)	15/18
62	London Jazz LJZ-K 15238	THE GENIUS SINGS THE BLUES	25
62	HMV CLP 1580/CSD 1451	MODERN SOUNDS IN COUNTRY & WESTERN (mono/stereo)	22/25
63	HMV CLP 1613/CSD 1477	MODERN SOUNDS IN COUNTRY & WESTERN VOL. TWO (mono/stereo)	15/18
63	London HA-K 8022	THE ORIGINAL RAY CHARLES	25
63	London HA-K 8023	THE RAY CHARLES STORY VOL. 1	15
63	London HA-K 8024	THE RAY CHARLES STORY VOL. 2	15
63	London HA-K 8035	THE GENIUS AFTER HOURS	20
63	HMV CLP 1626/CSD 1482	GREATEST HITS (mono/stereo)	15/18
63	London HA-K/SH-K 8045	SOUL MEETING (with Milt Jackson)	20
63	HMV CLP 1678	INGREDIENTS IN A RECIPE FOR SOUL	15
63	Realm RM 101	RAY CHARLES IN R&B GREATS	15
64	HMV CLP 1728/CSD 1537	SWEET AND SOUR TEARS (mono/stereo)	15/18
64	HMV CLP 1795/CSD 1566	HAVE A SMILE WITH ME (mono/stereo)	15/18
65	HMV CLP 1872/CSD 1696	LIVE IN CONCERT (mono/stereo)	15/18
65	HMV CLP 1914/CSD 1630	C&W MEETS R&B mono/stereo)	15/18
65	Summit ATL 4144	THE INCOMPARABLE RAY CHARLES (LP, mono, some tracks by Memphis Slim)	12
60s	WRC T 827	C&W MEETS R&B (LP)	12
60s	WRC T 566	DEDICATED TO YOU (LP)	12
66	HMV CLP/CSD 3533	CRYIN' TIME (with Raelets)	15
66	HMV CLP/CSD 3574	RAY'S MOODS	15
67	Atlantic 587/588 056	HALLELUJAH I LOVE HER SO	15
67	HMV CLP/CSD 3630	RAY CHARLES INVITES YOU TO LISTEN	15

(see also Raelets, Milt Jackson)

SONNY CHARLES (& CHECKMATES LTD)
67	Ember EMB S 240	Mastered The Art Of Love/Please Don't Take My World Away	40
69	A&M AMS 752	Black Pearl/Lazy Susan	15

(see also Checkmates Ltd)

CHARLES, PAULETTE & GEE
71	G.G. GG 4515	Shock And Shake (Version 3)/WINSTON WRIGHT: Roll On (Version 2) (as Charlie, Paulette & Gee)	10
71	G.G. GG 4517	Rock And Shake (Version 3) (actually Lover's Affair by Charlie Ace & Maytones)/Roll On (Version 2) (actually My Love And I by Winston Wright)	10

(see also Charlie Ace)

DICK CHARLESWORTH (& HIS CITY GENTS)
61	Top Rank JAR 558	Billy Boy/Night Fall	7
61	Top Rank 35-104	MEET THE GENTS (LP)	18
62	HMV CLP 1495	YES INDEED IT'S THE GENTS (LP)	18

CHARLIE & MELODIANS
(see under Charlie Ace)

CHARLIE BOY
71	Trojan TR 7823	Funky Strip/UPSETTERS: Mellow Mood	25

(see also Lee Perry/Upsetters)

CHARLIE PARKAS
80	Paranoid Plastics PPS 1	The Ballad Of Robin Hood/Space Invaders (p/s)	7

(see also Alberto Y Los Trios Paranoias)

CHARLIE, PAULETTE & GEE
(see under Charles, Paulette & Gee)

CHARLY & THE BOURBON FAMILY
71	Decca F 23164	Acapulco Gold/Boogachi	8

CHARMER
56	Melodisc MEL 1353	Back To Back, Belly To Belly/Is She Is Or Is She Ain't (78)	15

CHARMERS (Jamaica)
61	Blue Beat BB 42	Lonely Boy/I Am Going Back Home	18
62	Blue Beat BB 114	Crying Over You/Now You Want To Cry	18
63	Blue Beat BB 157	Time After Time/Done Me Wrong (with Prince Buster's Band)	18
60s	Blue Beat	How Could I Forget/Why Won't You Come Home? (with Prince Buster's Band) (white label only)	75
63	R&B JB 118	Angel Love/My Heart	20
63	R&B JB 121	Oh Why Baby/ROLAND ALPHONSO: Perhaps	30
64	R&B JB 151	What's The Use/I Am Through	20
64	R&B JB 156	In My Soul/Beware	20
64	Blue Beat BB 204	I'm Back/It's A Dream	20
64	Blue Beat BB 238	Waiting For You/You Are My Sunshine	20
64	Blue Beat BB 251	Dig Them Prince (actually Dip Them Prince)/Girl Of My Dreams (as The Charmer)	25
65	Blue Beat BB 279	Nobody Takes My Baby Away From Me/BUSTER ALLSTARS: Mules Mules Mules	25
66	Blue Beat BB 345	Oh My Baby/STRANGER COLE: When The Party Is Over	20
66	Ska Beat JB 237	Best Friend/MAYTALS: My Darling	25
66	Rio R 78	You Don't Know/CORNELL CAMPBELL & ROY PANTON: Sweetest Girl	20
68	Coxsone CS 7043	Things Going Wrong/KEN BOOTHE: You Keep Me Hanging On	30
68	Treasure Isle TI 7036	Keep On Going (actually by Lloyd Charmers)/SILVERTONES: Don't Say No	22
70	Duke DU 87	Colour Him Father/Version	12
70	Trojan TR 7773	Sweeter She Is (actually by Lloyd Charmers, Dave Barker & Slim Smith)/Fire Fire (actually by Lloyd Charmers)	10
70	Explosion EX 2026	Can I Get Next To You?/Big Five	7
70	Explosion EX 2035	Sweet Back/Music Talk (actually by Lloyd Charmers)	7
71	Explosion EX 2045	Skinhead Train/TONY & CHARMERS: Everstrong (B-side with Tony Binns)	30
71	Explosion EX 2055	Reggae In Wonderland/Wonder — Version (both actually by Byron Lee & Dragonaires)	7
71	Supreme SUP 220	Just My Imagination/Gotta Get A Message To You (actually by Dave Barker)	7
71	Green Door GD 4000	Rasta Never Fails (actually by Lloyd Charmers & Ken Boothe)/CHARMERS ALL STARS: Rasta Version	7
71	Green Door GD 4001	One Big Unhappy Family/CONSCIOUS MINDS: Africa Is Paradise	12
71	Pama Supreme PS 340	Red Head Duck/Jingle Jangle	6

(see also Spanishtown Skabeats, Lloyd & Ken, Lloydie & Lowbites, Lloyd Terrell)

CHARMERS (U.S.)
58	Vogue V 9095	He's Gone/Oh! Yes (78 rpm = £40)	500

LLOYD CHARMERS
67	Coxsone CS 7023	Time Is Getting Hard/TONY GREGORY: I Sit By The Shore	40+
69	Duke DU 15	Cooyah/UNIQUES: Forever	15
69	Duke DU 16	Follow This Sound/Why Pretend	12
69	Duke DU 25	5 To 5/SOUL STIRRERS: Come See About Me	12
69	Duke DU 36	Safari (The Far East)/Last Laugh	12
69	Songbird SB 1001	Ling Ting Tong/LLOYD ROBINSON: Sweet Sweet	10
69	Songbird SB 1007	Duckey Luckey/In The Spirit	20
69	Camel CA 30	Confidential/TOMMY COWAN: House In Session	12
69	Explosion EX 2001	Death A Come/Zylon	20
70	Explosion EX 2032	Vengeance/Look A-Py-Py	10
70	Explosion EX 2034	Ready Talk/There Is Something About You	7
70	Trojan TR 7788	Oh Me Oh My/I Did It	12
70	Bullet BU 435	Dollars And Bonds/Sounds Familiar	12
70	Bullet BU 442	Reggae A Bye Bye/DAVE BARKER: Doctor Jekyll	15
70	Escort ES 820	Soul Of England/Shang I	18
70	Escort ES 836	Hi Shan/Soul At Large	12

Lloyd CHARMERS

70	Smash SMA 2302	Big Red Bum Ball/BUNNIE LEE ALLSTARS: Big Bum Ball Version	7
73	Green Door GD 4064	Save The People (as L. Charmers)/SCOTTY: Salvation Train	10
74	Harry J. HJ 6662	I'm Gonna Love You Just A Little Bit More/Have I Sinned	6
71	Pama Supreme PS 339	Shaft/Harry's Mood	8
71	Pama Supreme PS 346	Show Business/DEBBY & LLOYD: Gloria	6
72	Pama Supreme PS 355	Desiderata/Desiderata Music	6
70	Trojan TTL 25	REGGAE IS TIGHT (LP)	25
70	Trojan TTL 30	REGGAE CHARM (LP)	25
70	Pama SECO 25	HOUSE IN SESSION (LP, with Hippy Boys)	80

(see also Charmers, Lloyd Tyrell/Terrell, Ken Boothe, Hippy Boys, Wayne Howard, Martia Riley, Eric Donaldson)

CHARMETTES
63	London HLR 9820	Please Don't Kiss Me Again/What Is A Tear	40

CHARMS (Jamaica)
64	Island WI 154	Carry, Go, Bring Home (actually by Justin Hinds & Dominoes)/ Hill And Gully (actually by L. Reid's Group)	15
66	Rio R 98	Everybody Say Yeah/This World Is Yours	20

CHARMS (U.S.)
55	Parlophone MSP 6155	Hearts Of Stone/Ko Ko Mo (I Love You So) (78 rpm Parlophone R3988 = £55)	675
55	Parlophone DP 412	Hearts Of Stone/Bazoom, I Need Your Lovin' (78) (export issue)	50
55	Parlophone DP 423	Two Hearts/The First Time We Met (78) (export issue)	60

(see also Otis Williams & Charms, Tiny Topsy, Harmonizing Four)

CHARTBUSTERS
64	London HLU 9906	She's The One/Slippin' Thru Your Fingers	15
64	London HLU 9934	Why/Stop The Music	10

LINCOLN CHASE
57	London HLU 8495	Johnny Klingeringding/You're Driving Me Crazy (What Did I Do) (78 rpm = £10)	25
61	Philips PB 1103	Miss Orangutang/Walking Slowly	25

CHASERS
65	Decca F 12302	Hey Little Girl/That's What They Call Love (some in p/s)	100/50
66	Parlophone R 5451	Inspiration/She's Gone Away	100
67	Philips BF 1546	The Ways Of A Man/Summer Girl	15

CHASERS
01	Changes One ChangesCD-002	ONWARDS & UPWARDS EP (CD EP, 1,060 copies only, many signed)	18/10

(see also Energetic Krusher, Wildhearts)

CHATEAUX
83	Ebony EBON 13	CHAINED AND DESPERATE (LP)	12
84	Ebony EBON 18	FIRE POWER (LP)	12
85	Ebony EBON 31	HIGHLY STRUNG (LP)	12

ROBERT CHAUVIGNY
59	Top Rank JAR 142	The Bottle Theme/French Rockin' Waltz (Eux) (78 rpm = £10)	7

CHEAP BOOTS
70	Fontana 6001 020	Baby I Do Need You/Come And Stay With Me	6

CHEAP TRICK
78	Epic S EPC 6199	So Good To See You/You're All Talk (withdrawn)	20
79	Epic S EPC 7144	Voices/Surrender (withdrawn)	5
79	Epic S EPC 7258	I Want You To Want Me (live)/I Want You To Want Me (studio) (DJ only)	6
79	Epic CT-1	Dream Police/Voice/I'll Be With You Tonight (sampler, promo only)	10
78	Epic EPC 86083	AT THE BUDOKAN (LP, yellow vinyl, with booklet)	12

CHEATIN' HEARTS
66	Columbia DB 8048	Zip-Tease/The Bad Kind	12

CHUBBY CHECKER
59	Top Rank JAR 154	The Class/Schooldays, Oh, Schooldays (78 rpm = £20)	45
60	Columbia DB 4503	The Twist/Toot	20
60	Columbia DB 4541	The Huckelbuck/Whole Lotta Shakin' Goin' On	15
61	Columbia DB 4591	Pony Time/Oh Susannah	12
61	Columbia DB 4652	Good Good Loving/Mess Around	15
61	Columbia DB 4691	Let's Twist Again/Everything's Gonna Be All Right	7
61	Columbia DB 4728	The Fly/That's The Way It Goes	10
62	Columbia DB 4808	Slow Twistin'/The Lose Your Inhibitions Twist	6
62	Columbia DB 4876	Dancin' Party/Gotta Get Myself Together	6
62	Pye International 7N 25160	Dancin' Party/Gotta Get Myself Together (reissue)	6
62	Cameo Parkway P 806	What Do You Say/Something To Shout About	6
62	Cameo Parkway P 824	Let's Twist Again/The Twist	6
62	Cameo Parkway P 849	Limbo Rock/Hitch Hiker	8
63	Cameo Parkway P 862	Let's Limbo Some More/Twenty Miles	6
63	Cameo Parkway P 873	Black Cloud/Birdland	10
63	Cameo Parkway P 879	Twist It Up/Surf Party	10
64	Cameo Parkway P 907	Hey Bobba Needle/Spread Joy	15
64	Cameo Parkway P 920	Lazy Elsie Molly/Rosie	10
64	Cameo Parkway P 922	She Wants T'Swim/You Better Believe It Baby	20
65	Cameo Parkway P 936	Lovely, Lovely/The Weekend's Here	28
65	Cameo Parkway P 949	(At The) Discotheque/Do The Freddie (DJ copy = £150)	50
65	Cameo Parkway P 959	Everything's Wrong/Cu Ma La Be Stay (DJ copy = £120)	40
65	Cameo Parkway P 965	Two Hearts Make One Love/You Just Don't Know (What You Do To Me) (DJ copy = £300)	250
65	Cameo Parkway P 989	Hey You Little Boogaloo/Pussy Cat	25
69	Buddah 201 045	Back In The U.S.S.R./Windy Cream	5
71	London HL 10331	Let's Go Down/Goodbye Victoria	5

73	Pye Int 25620	Gypsy/Reggae My Way	25
76	London HLU 10515	(At The) Discotheque/Slow Twistin'	6
78	London HLU 10557	You Just Don't Know (What You Do To Me)/	
		Two Hearts Make One Love (reissue)	10
62	Columbia SEG 8155	KING OF THE TWIST (EP)	12
63	Cameo Parkway CPE 550	DANCING PARTY (EP)	15
61	Columbia 33SX 1315	TWIST WITH CHUBBY CHECKER (LP)	35
61	Columbia 33SX 1341	FOR TWISTERS ONLY (LP)	30
61	Columbia 33SX 1365	IT'S PONY TIME (LP)	30
62	Columbia 33SX 1445	TWIST ALONG WITH CHUBBY CHECKER (LP)	20
62	Golden Guinea GGL 0236	TWISTIN' ROUND THE WORLD (LP)	22
63	Cameo Parkway P 7014	ALL THE HITS (LP)	22
63	Cameo Parkway P 7020	LIMBO PARTY (LP)	20
63	Cameo Parkway P 7036	CHUBBY CHECKER (LP)	22
71	London SHZ 8419	CHEQUERED (LP)	15

CHUBBY CHECKER & BOBBY RYDELL

62	Columbia DB 4802	Teach Me To Twist/Swingin' Together	12
62	Cameo Parkway C 205	Jingle Bell Rock/What Are You Doing New Year's Eve?	10
64	Cameo Parkway CPE 554	CHUBBY CHECKER AND BOBBY RYDELL IN LONDON (EP)	25
62	Columbia 33SX 1424	CHECKER AND RYDELL (LP)	30
63	Cameo Parkway C 1063	GOLDEN HITS (LP)	20

CHUBBY CHECKER & DEE DEE SHARP

| 62 | Cameo Parkway C 1029 | DOWN TO EARTH (LP) | 50 |

(see also Dream Lovers, Bobby Rydell, Dee Dee Sharp)

CHECKERS

| 54 | Parlophone DP 403 | Over The Rainbow/CECIL YOUNG QUARTET: Oooh-Diga-Gow | |
| | | (78, export issue) | 65 |

CHECKMATES

61	Piccadilly 7N 35010	Rockin' Minstrel/Pompeii	10
63	Decca F 11603	You've Gotta Have A Gimmick Today/Westpoint	20
64	Decca F 11844	Sticks And Stones/Please Listen To Me	30
65	Decca F 12114	Around/I've Got To Know Now	15
65	Parlophone R 5337	Stop That Music/I've Been In Love Before	15
66	Parlophone R 5402	(You Got) The Gamma Goochie/It Ain't Right	20
66	Parlophone R 5495	Every Day Is Just The Same/I'll Be Keeping The Score	20
61	Pye NPL 18061	THE CHECKMATES (LP)	45

(see also Original Checkmates)

CHECKMATES LTD

67	Ember EMB S 235	Do The Walk (The Temptation Walk)/Glad For You	15
69	A&M AMS 747	Love Is All I Have To Give/I Never Should Have Lied	10
69	A&M AMS 769	Proud Mary/Spanish Harlem	5
69	A&M AMLS 943	LOVE IS ALL I HAVE TO GIVE (LP)	15
70	Ember NR 5048	LIVE AT CAESAR'S PALACE (LP)	15

(see also Sonny Charles & Checkmates Ltd)

CHEEKY

| 80 | Woodbine St. WSR 005 | Don't Mess Around/Get Outa My 'Ouse (no p/s) | 100 |

CHEERS

54	Capitol CL 14189	Bazoom (I Need Your Lovin')/Arrivederci (78 rpm = £10)	40
55	Capitol CL 14248	Bernie's Tune/Whadaya Want? (78 rpm = £10)	25
55	Capitol CL 14280	Blueberries/Can't We Be More Than Friends (78 rpm = £10)	30
55	Capitol CL 14337	I Must Be Dreaming/Fancy Meeting You Here (78 rpm = £10)	25
55	Capitol CL 14377	Black Denim Trousers And Motorcycle Boots/Some Night In Alaska	40
55	Capitol CL 14377	Black Denim Trousers And Motorcycle Boots/Some Night In Alaska (78)	12
56	Capitol CL 14561	Chicken/Don't Do Anything (78 rpm = £15)	25
56	Capitol CL 14601	Que Pasa Muchacha/BERT CONVY: Heaven On Earth (78 rpm = £12)	20
56	Capitol EAP1 584	THE CHEERS (EP)	80

(see also Bert Convy [& Thunderbirds])

CHEETAHS

64	Philips BF 1362	Mecca/Goodnight Kiss	18
65	Philips BF 1383	Soldier Boy/Johnny	18
65	Philips BF 1412	Goodbye Baby (Baby Goodbye)/That's How It Goes	15
65	Philips BF 1453	Whole Lotta Love/Party	15
66	Philips BF 1499	The Russian Boat Song/Gamble	15

(see also Carl Wayne & Cheetahs)

CHELSEA

77	Step Forward SF 2	Right To Work/The Loner (p/s, originals in card p/s)	15/8
77	Step Forward SF 5	High Rise Living/No Admission (p/s)	10
78	Step Forward SF 8	Urban Kids/No Flowers (p/s)	8
80	Step Forward SF 14	No One's Coming Outside/What Would You Do (p/s)	6
80	Step Forward SF 15	Look At the Outside/Don't Get Me Wrong (p/s)	6
80	Step Forward SF 16	No Escape/Decide (p/s)	6
82	Step Forward SF 22	Stand Out/Last Drink (p/s)	5
84	Chelsea CH 001	Give Me More/Sympathy For The Devil (p/s)	5
79	Step Forward SFLP 2	CHELSEA (LP, with inner sleeve)	20
81	Step Forward SFLP 5	ALTERNATIVE HITS (LP)	15
82	Step Forward SFLP 7	EVACUATE (LP)	15
84	Picasso PIK 003	LIVE AND WELL (LP)	12

CHELSEA LADS

| 66 | CBS 202047 | English Tea/Hump A Dink | 5 |

CHELSEA SQUAD
72	Penny Farthing PEN 782	Blue Is The Colour/All Sing Together	7
84	W&A YZ 23	Back On The Ball/(Club Mix) (blue vinyl, p/s)	5

CHEMICAL ALICE
81	Acidic GNOME 1	The Judge/Goodnight Vienna/Lands Of Home/Henry The King (12", p/s)	50
	(see also Marillion)		

CHEMICAL BROTHERS
91	Eastern Bloc	Sea Of Beats/Sea Of Beats (Justin Robertson Mix) (12", p/s, as Ariel)	80
91	Deconstruction PT 44888	Rollercoaster/Mustn't Grumble/Mustn't Grumble (God's Grumble Mix) (12", as Ariel)	30
93	Dust Brothers DB's 333	Song To The Siren (12", as Dust Brothers, no p/s, 500 only)	70
93	Junior Boys Own JBO 10	Song To The Siren/Song To The Siren (Sabres Of Paradise Mixes) (12", p/s)	30
94	Boys Own COLLECT 004	14TH CENTURY SKY EP (12", no p/s, as Dust Brothers)	20
94	Junior Boys Own JBO 20	MY MERCURY MOUTH EP (12", JBO sleeve, as Dust Brothers)	25
95	Junior Boys Own CHEMS TI	Leave Home/Leave Home (Sabres Of Paradise)/Let Me In Mate (12", p/s)	20
95	Junior Boys Own CHEMS TXI	Leave Home (Underworld Mix One)/Leave Home (Underworld Mix Two) (12", p/s)	20

CHEQUERED PAST
85	Heavy Metal America HMUSA53	CHEQUERED PAST (LP, picture disc, 1,000 only)	30
	(see also Steve Jones)		

CLIFTON CHENIER
69	Action ACT 4550	Black Gal/Frogs Legs	15
70	Specialty SNTF 5012	BAYOU BLUES (LP)	15
70	Harvest MHSP 4002	CLIFTON CHENIER'S VERY BEST (LP)	30
79	Flyright FLY 539	ZYDECO BLUES (LP, with other artists)	15

CHER
65	Liberty LIB 66114	All I Really Want To Do/I'm Gonna Love You	10
66	Liberty LIB 66136	Where Do You Go/See See Rider	10
66	Liberty LIB 66160	Bang Bang (My Baby Shot Me Down)/Our Day Will Come	10
66	Liberty LIB 12034	I Feel Something In The Air/Come To Your Window	10
66	Liberty LIB 12038	Sunny/She's No Better Than Me	10
67	Liberty LIB 12046	Mama (When My Dollies Have Babies)/Behind The Door	10
67	Liberty LBF 15038	You Better Sit Down Kids/Elusive Butterfly	10
69	Atlantic 584 278	Walk On Gilded Splinters/Tonight I'll Be Staying Here With You	15
69	Atco 226 003	For What It's Worth/Hangin' On	5
71	MCA MU 1137	Classified 1A/Don't Put It On Me	5
72	MCA MU 1148	The Way Of Love/Fire And Rain	5
72	MCA MU 1158	Living In A House Divided/One Honest Man	5
72	MCA MU 1168	Don't Hide Your Love/First Time	5
75	Phil Spector Intl. 2010 006	A Love Like Yours (with Nilsson)/Hangin' On	15
76	Phil Spector Intl. 2010 013	A Woman's Story/Baby I Love You	12
66	Liberty LEP 4047	THE HITS OF CHER (EP)	20
65	Liberty (S)LBY 3058	ALL I REALLY WANT TO DO (LP, mono/stereo)	15/18
66	Liberty (S)LBY 3072	THE SONNY SIDE OF CHER (LP, mono/stereo)	15/18
66	Liberty (S)LBY 3081	CHER (LP, mono/stereo)	15/18
68	Liberty LBL/LBS 83051	WITH LOVE, CHER (LP)	20
68	Liberty LBL/LBS 83105E	GOLDEN GREATS (LP)	15
68	Liberty LBL 83156E	BACKSTAGE (LP)	15
69	Atco 226 026/228 026	3614 JACKSON HIGHWAY (LP, gatefold sleeve, mono/stereo)	15
	(see also Sonny & Cher, Caesar & Cleo, Nilsson)		

VIVIENNE CHERING
66	Decca F 12360	I'll Do My Crying Tomorrow/Make My Dreams Come True	10
	(see also Flip & Dateliners)		

CHEROKEES (U.S.)
61	Pye International 7N 25066	Cherokee/Harlem Nocturne	15

CHEROKEES (U.K.)
64	Decca F 11915	You've Done It Again Little Girl/Girl Girl Girl	12
64	Columbia DB 7341	Seven Daffodils/Are You Back In My World Now	15
65	Columbia DB 7473	Wondrous Place/Send Me All Your Love	12
65	Columbia DB 7704	I Will Never Turn My Back On You/Dig A Little Deeper	12
66	Columbia DB 7822	Land Of A 1000 Dances/Everybody's Needs	20
	(see also Lee Diamond)		

CHERRY
80s	Crashed Records CAR 91	He's A Bum/He Rides With Me	7

DON CHERRY
56	Brunswick 05538	Wanted Someone To Love/The Thrill Is Gone	10
57	Philips PB 755	I Keep Running Away From You/A Ferryboat Called Minerva (78)	6
57	Philips JK 1013	The Last Dance/Don't You Worry (jukebox edition)	15
58	Philips PB 816	Another Time, Another Place/The Golden Age	5
59	Philips PB 911	Hasty Heart/I Look For A Love (78 rpm = £8)	5
66	London HLU 10045	I Love You Drops/Don't Change	5
56	Philips BBL 7128	SWINGIN' FOR TWO (LP)	15
	(see also John Coltrane, Jazz Composers Orchestra)		

CHERRY PEOPLE
68	MGM MGM 1438	And Suddenly/Imagination (DJ copy = £60)	40
69	MGM MGM 1472	Gotta Get Back/I'm The One Who Loves You	15
69	MGM MGM 1489	Light Of Love/On To Something New	8
75	Black Magic BM 112	And Suddenly/Imagination (reissue)	8

CHERRY PIES
64	Black Swan WI 448	Do You Keep Dreaming/Sweeter Than Cherry Pie	20

CHERRY SMASH
67	Track 604 017	Sing Songs Of Love/Movie Star	12
68	Decca F 12838	Goodtime Sunshine/Little Old Country Home Town	18
69	Decca F 12884	Fade Away Maureen/Green Plant	35

FRANKIE CHERVAL
62	MGM MGM 1183	How Come/Tag Along	10

PETE CHESTER
60	Pye 7N 15305	Ten Swinging Bottles/Whole Lotta Shakin' On The Range (with Consulates)	30
61	Pye International 7N 25074	Three Old Maids/Forest Fire (as Pete Chester & Group)	30
	(see also Five Chesternuts)		

VIC CHESTER
57	Decca F 10882	Rock-A-Billy/First Date, First Kiss, First Love (78 rpm = £8)	25

CHESTERFIELDS
87	Subway Org. SUBORG 003	KETTLE (LP)	12
87	Subway Org. SUBORG 005	WESTWARD HO (LP)	12

MORRIS CHESTNUT
79	Grapevine GRP 128	Too Darn Soulful/You Don't Love Me Anymore	20

CHEVIOT RANTERS
73	Topic 12TS 222	THE CHEVIOT HILLS (LP)	18
74	Topic 12TS 245	CHEVIOT BARN DANCE (LP)	18

CHEVLONS
66	Pye 7N 17145	Too Long Alone/It's My Problem	6

CHEVRONS
60	Top Rank JAR 308	Lullaby/Day After Forever	10

CHEVY
80	Avatar AAA 104	Too Much Loving/See The Light (company sleeve)	20
80	Avatar AAA 107	The Taker/Life On The Run (p/s)	20
81	Avatar AAA 114	Just Another Day/Rock On	12
80	Avatar AALP 5001	THE TAKER (LP, with inner sleeve)	20

CHEYNES
63	Columbia DB 7153	Respectable/It's Gonna Happen To You	80
64	Columbia DB 7368	Going To The River/Cheyne-Re-La	75
65	Columbia DB 7464	Down And Out/Stop Running Around	80
	(see also Peter Bardens, Peter B's, Fleetwood Mac, Mark Leeman Five, Bo Street Runners)		

CHEYNES
71	Bell BLL 1144	April Fool/Gotta Get Back	6

CHIC
84	Atlantic AT 9604	Chic Cheers/Savoir Faire/Dance Dance Dance (12")	8
86	Atlantic K 11209	Le Freak/Savoir Faire/Chic (12")	8
87	Atlantic AT 9198	Jack The Freak/Savoir Faire (12")	8
88	Atlantic AT 9107	Good Times/Warm Summer Nights (12", p/s)	8

CHICAGO
69	CBS 4381	Questions 67 And 68/Listen	6
69	CBS 4503	I'm A Man (Parts 1 & 2) (withdrawn)	20
69	CBS 66221	CHICAGO TRANSIT AUTHORITY (2-LP, orange label)	18
71	CBS 66405	IV (AT CARNEGIE HALL) (4-LP, orange label)	25

CHICAGO BILL
	(see under Big Bill Broonzy)

CHICAGO LINE
66	Philips BF 1488	Shimmy Shimmy Ko Ko Bop/Jump Back	110
	(see also Mike Patto, Bo Street Runners, Viv Prince)		

CHICAGO LOOP
66	Stateside SS 564	(When She Needs Good Lovin') She Comes To Me/This Must Be The Place	7

CHICK with TED CAMERON & D.J.'s
60	Pye 7N 15292	Early In The Morning/Cool Water	40

CHICKEN SHACK
67	Blue Horizon 57-3135	It's OK With Me Baby/When My Left Eye Jumps	15
68	Blue Horizon 57-3143	Worried About My Woman/Six Nights In Seven	15
68	Blue Horizon 57-3146	When The Train Comes Back/Hey Baby	15
69	Blue Horizon 57-3153	I'd Rather Go Blind/Night Life	15
69	Blue Horizon 57-3160	Tears In The Wind/The Things You Put Me Through	15
70	Blue Horizon 57-3168	Maudie/Andalucian Blues	15
70	Blue Horizon 57-3176	Sad Clown/Tired Eyes	15
73	Deram DM 381	Time Goes Passing By/Poor Boy	8
73	Deram DM 396	You Know You Could Be Right/The Loser	8
74	CBS 1832	I'd Rather Go Blind/Sad Clown	6
68	Blue Horizon 7-63203	FORTY BLUE FINGERS FRESHLY PACKED AND READY TO SERVE (LP)	60
69	Blue Horizon 7-63209	O.K. KEN? (LP, gatefold sleeve)	40
69	Blue Horizon 7-63218	100 TON CHICKEN (LP)	45
70	Blue Horizon 7-63861	ACCEPT CHICKEN SHACK (LP, gatefold sleeve)	35
72	Deram SDL 5	IMAGINATION LADY (LP, gatefold sleeve)	30
73	Deram SML 1100	UNLUCKY BOY (LP)	25
	(see also Errol Dixon, Fleetwood Mac, Christine Perfect, Carmen Macrae)		

MINT VALUE £

CHICKEN SHED
77	Colby AJ 370	ALICE (LP)	70

CHICKS
63	Oriole CB 1828	What Are Boys Made Of?/Over The Mountain	20

CHIEFS
58	London HLU 8624	Apache/Dee's Dream (78 rpm = £18)	30
58	London HLU 8720	Enchiladas!/Moments To Remember (78 rpm = £15)	20

CHIFFONS
63	Stateside SS 172	He's So Fine/Oh! My Lover	10
63	Stateside SS 202	One Fine Day/Why Am I So Shy	10
63	Stateside SS 230	A Love So Fine/Only My Friend	10
64	Stateside SS 254	I Have A Boyfriend/I'm Gonna Dry Your Eyes	18
64	Stateside SS 332	Sailor Boy/When Summer's Through	20
65	Stateside SS 437	Nobody Knows What's Going On (In My Mind But Me)/The Real Thing	25
66	Stateside SS 512	Sweet Talkin' Guy/Did You Ever Go Steady	10
66	Stateside SS 533	Out Of This World/Just A Boy	15
66	Stateside SS 559	Stop, Look And Listen/March	18
67	Stateside SS 578	My Boyfriend's Back/I Got Plenty Of Nuttin'	22
64	Stateside SE 1012	THEY'RE SO FINE (EP)	90
63	Stateside SL 10040	THE CHIFFONS (LP)	100
66	Stateside S(S)L 10190	SWEET TALKIN' GUY (LP)	90

(see also Four Pennies)

ANTHONY CHILD/ANDREW READ
99	Fat Cat 12FAT 031	Speedranch/Jansky Noise (12" EP, 'bullet hole' sleeve)	12

LORRAINE CHILD
64	Decca F 11969	You/Not This Time	15

SONNY CHILDE (& T.N.T.)
65	Decca F 12218	Giving Up On Love/Mighty Nice	150
66	Polydor 56108	Two Lovers/Ain't That Good News	15
66	Polydor 56141	Heartbreak/I Still Love You (as Sonny Childe & T.N.T.)	20
66	Polydor 582 003	TO BE CONTINUED (LP)	40

CHILD HAROLDS
68	Trident TRA 201	Diary Of My Mind/Loophole	30

BILLY CHILDISH
87	Hangman HANG 9-UP	THE 1982 CASSETTES (LP, pink & black sleeve)	15

(see also Milkshakes, Thee Mighty Caesars)

DR. A.A. CHILDS & CONGREGATION
50s	Esquire 10-414	The Healing Prayer (Parts 1 & 2) (78)	8
60	Starlite ST45 009	The Healing Prayer (Parts 1 & 2)	8

CHI-LITES
69	Beacon BEA 119	Pretty Girl/Love Bandit	40
71	MCA MU 1138	(For God's Sake) Give More Power To The People/Trouble's A' Comin'	6
71	MCA 1143DJ	What Do I Wish For (1-sided DJ copy)	12
73	Brunswick BR 7	Stoned Out Of My Mind/Someone Else's Arms	8
70	MCA MUPS 397	GIVE IT AWAY (LP)	15
71	MCA MUPS 437	(FOR GOD'S SAKE) GIVE MORE POWER TO THE PEOPLE (LP)	15
72	MCA MUPS 457	A LONELY MAN (LP)	15

(see also Jackie Wilson)

CHILLIWACK
71	London HLU 10327	Everyday/Sundown	5
71	London SHU 8418	CHILLIWACK (LP)	12

(see also Collectors, Electric Prunes)

CHILLI WILLI & RED HOT PEPPERS
75	Mooncrest MOON 40	Breathe A Little/Friday Song	6
72	Revelation REV 002	KINGS OF THE ROBOT RHYTHM (LP)	25
74	Mooncrest CREST 21	BONGOS OVER BALHAM (LP)	15

(see also Brinsley Schwarz, Jo-Ann Kelly)

CHILLUM
71	Mushroom 100 MR 11	CHILLUM (LP, with photo insert)	75

(see also Secondhand)

ALEX CHILTON
80	Aura AUS 117	Hey! Little Child/No More The Moon Shines Lorena (p/s)	8

(see also Box Tops, Big Star)

CHIMES (U.S.)
61	London HLU 9283	Once In A While/Summer Night	40

CHIMES featuring DENISE (U.K.)
63	Decca F 11783	Say It Again/Can This Be Love?	7
64	Decca F 11885	I'll Be Waiting, I'll Be Here/Hello Heartache	7

(see also Little Frankie)

CHIMNEYS
80	Tagmemics 45-003	Do The Big Baby/Take Your Brain Out For A Walk (p/s, 500 only)	15

CHINA DOLL
80	Wessex WEX 273	Oysters And Wine/Past Tense (p/s)	200

CHINA DOLLS
82	Speed FIRED 1	One Hit Wonder/Ain't Love Ain't Bad (p/s)	35

(see also Slade, Dummies)

CHINA STREET
78	Criminal CRM 1	You're A Ruin/(I Wanna Be) Your M.P. (foldout lyric p/s in poly bag & badge)	10

CHINATOWN
81	Airship AP 138	Short And Sweet/How Many Times (p/s)	60
81	Airship AP 343	PLAY IT TO DEATH (LP)	85

CHINAWITE
83	Future Earth FER 014	Blood On The Streets/Ready To Satisfy (p/s)	30

KES CHINS
62	Starlite ST45 089	Annie/Moody	8

CHIPMUNKS
(see under David Seville)

GEORGE CHISHOLM & BLUENOTES
56	Beltona BL 2671	Honky Tonk/D.R. Rock (with Bert Weedon) (78 rpm = £8)	12
56	Decca LK 4147	CHIS (LP)	18
60s	Philips SBBL 612	TRAD TREAT (LP)	15
64	Wing WL 1043	TRAD SPECIAL (LP)	15
60s	77 SEU 12/43	ALONG THE CHISHOLM TRAIL (LP)	15
65	Philips BL 7694	MUSIC FOR ROMANTICS (LP)	12
67	Columbia SCX 6195	THE MAGNIFICENT SEVEN (LP)	15

(see also Bert Weedon)

CHITINIOUS ENSEMBLE
72	Deram SML 1093	CHITINIOUS ENSEMBLE (LP)	100+

CHOCOLATE BOYS
74	Decca F 13556	El Bimbo/Voltaire Pier	6

CHOCOLATE FROG
68	Atlantic 584 207	Butchers And Bakers/I Forgive You	25

(see also Fleur De Lys)

CHOCOLATE MILK
75	RCA RCA 2592	Action Speaks Louder Than Words/Ain't Nothing But A Thing	10
75	RCA RCAT 2592	Action Speaks Louder Than Words/Ain't Nothing But A Thing (12")	20
77	RCA PL 11830	COMIN' (LP)	20

CHOCOLATE WATCH BAND
67	Decca F 12649	The Sound Of The Summer/The Only One In Sight	30
67	Decca F 12704	Requiem/What's It To You	30

CHOIR
68	Major Minor MM 537	It's Cold Outside/I'm Going Home	50
68	Major Minor MM 557	When You Were With Me/Changin' My Mind	40

CHOPYN
75	Jet LPO 8	GRAND SLAM (LP)	12

(see also Ann Odell, Ray Russell)

CHORALERNA
60s	Myrrh MYRRH 1047	LET THERE BE LIGHT (LP)	20
60s	Key KL 018	POWER (LP)	20

CHORDETTES
54	Columbia SCM 5158	Mr. Sandman/I Don't Wanna See You Cryin' (78 rpm Columbia DB 3553 = £20)	225
55	London HLA 8169	Humming Bird/Lonely Lips (78 rpm = £12)	65
56	London HLA 8217	Dudelsack Polka/I Told A Lie (78 rpm = £12)	50
56	London HLA 8264	Eddie My Love/Our Melody (triangular or round centre) (78 rpm = £12)	75/40
56	London HLA 8302	Born To Be With You/Love Never Changes (78 rpm = £7)	50
56	London HA 7011	Born To Be With You/Love Never Changes (export issue)	35
56	London HLA 8323	Lay Down Your Arms/Teenage Goodnight (78 rpm = £8)	40
57	London HLA 8473	Echo Of Love/Just Between You And Me (78 rpm = £12)	40
57	London HLA 8497	Like A Baby/Soft Sands (78 rpm = £12)	40
58	London HLA 8566	Baby Of Mine/Photographs (78 rpm = £12)	30
58	London HLA 8584	Lollipop/Baby, Come-A-Back-A (78 rpm = £12)	20
58	London HLA 8654	Love Is A Two-Way Street/I Don't Know, I Don't Care (78 rpm = £14)	15
59	London HLA 8809	We Should Be Together/No Other Arms, No Other Lips (78 rpm = £14)	15
59	London HLA 8926	A Girl's Work Is Never Done/No Wheels (B-side with Jeff Crom & Jackie Ertel) (78 rpm = £15)	20
61	London HLA 9400	Never On Sunday/Faraway Star	10
62	London HLA 9519	The White Rose Of Athens/Adios (Goodbye My Love)	5
60	London RE-A 1228	THE CHORDETTES (EP)	70
58	London HA-A 2088	THE CHORDETTES (LP)	125
62	London HA-A 2441	THE CHORDETTES SING (LP)	60

CHORDS (U.K.)
79	Polydor 2059 141	Now It's Gone/Don't Go Back (p/s)	6
80	Polydor POSP 101	Maybe Tomorrow/I Don't Wanna Know/Hey Girl (p/s)	6
80	Polydor POSP 146	Something's Missing/This Is What They Want (p/s)	6
80	Polydor 2059 258	The British Way Of Life/The Way It's Got To Be (p/s)	6
80	Polydor POSP 185	In My Street/I'll Keep On Holding On (p/s)	6
81	Polydor POSP 270	One More Minute/Who's Killing Who (p/s)	6
81	Polydor POSP 288	Turn Away Again/Turn Away Again (Again) (p/s)	8
80	Polydor Super POLS 1019	SO FAR AWAY (LP, some with stickered sleeve & 7" Now It's Gone/Things We Said [KRODS 1])	30/15
90s	Detour DRLP028	AT THE BBC (LP)	12

(see also Rage)

MINT VALUE £

CHORDS (U.S.)
54	Columbia SCM 5133	Sh-Boom (Life Could Be A Dream)/Little Maiden	2,000
54	Columbia DB 3512	Sh-Boom (Life Could Be A Dream)/Little Maiden (78)	100

CHORDS FIVE
67	Island WI 3044	I'm Only Dreaming/Universal Vagrant	100
68	Polydor 56261	Same Old Fat Man/Hold On To Everythin' You've Got	50
69	Jay Boy BOY 6	Some People/Battersea Fair	30

(see also Smoke)

CHOSEN FEW (U.K.)
65	Pye 7N 15905	It Won't Be Around You Anymore/Big City	20
65	Pye 7N 15942	So Much To Look Forward To/Today, Tonight & Tomorrow	20

(see also Alan Hull, Lindisfarne, Skip Bifferty)

CHOSEN FEW (Jamaica)
70	Songbird SB 1031	Time Is Hard/CRYSTALITES: Time Is Hard Part Two	12
70	Songbird SB 1032	Going Back Home/CRYSTALITES: Going Back Home Part Two	10
70	Songbird SB 1046	Why Can't I Touch You/INNER CIRCLE BAND: Touch You Version	12
71	Songbird SB 1061	Shaft/Shaft (Version)	12
71	Songbird SB 1067	Everybody Just A Stall/Everybody (Version)	10
72	Songbird SB 1070	Do Your Thing/Your Thing (Version)	18
72	Trojan TR 7864	Ebony Eyes/Ebony Eyes (Version)	6
72	Trojan TR 7882	Everybody Plays The Fool/You're A Big Girl Now	12
73	Trojan TR 7894	Am I Black Enough For You/Message From A Blackman	8
73	Duke DU 162	Children Of The Night/LLOYD CHARMERS: For The Good Times	7
73	Duke DU 163	Stoned In Love/MIKE CHUNG & NOW GENERATION: Stoned In Love (Version)	7
73	Duke DU 164	It's Too Late/MIKE CHUNG & NOW GENERATION: It's Too Late (Version)	7
73	Trojan TRLS 56	HIT AFTER HIT (LP)	30

CHOSEN FEW (U.K.)
74	Action ACT 4623	Funky Butter/Wondering	20
76	Polydor 2058 721	I Can Make Your Dreams Come True/Pretty Face	20
76	Miami MIA401	Night And Day/Funky Buttercup	70
78	Polydor 2058 975	You Mean Everything To Me/It Won't Be Long	30

CHOU PAHROT
79	Klub KEP 101	Buzgo Tram Chorus/Gwizgweela Gwamhnoo/Lemons (p/s)	10
79	Klub KLP 19	LIVE (LP, private pressing)	12

CHRIS & COSEY/CREATIVE TECHNOLOGY INSTITUTE
81	Rough Trade RT 078	October (Love Song)/Little Houses (p/s)	5
81	Rough Trade RTT 078	October (Love Song)/Little Houses (12", p/s)	7
80s	Electronic Sound Maker	Sweet Surprise (magazine with free cassette)	20
84	Intl. One CTI 002	Conspiracy International/The Gift Of Tongues/The Need (p/s)	7
84	C.T.I. CTI 1	HAMMER HOUSE EP (12")	10
84	C.T.I. CTI 2	GIFT OF TONGUES (12")	10
85	Rough Trade RTT 148	Sweet Surprise 1 (1984)/2 (1985) (12", p/s, with Annie Lennox & Dave Stewart)	8
91	World Serpent WS7 004	Passion (p/s, 1-sided, other side etched)	5
80s	Sinn And Form	City Of Spirit (cassette magazine)	10
81	Rough Trade ROUGH 34	HEARTBEAT (LP, with insert)	12
81	Rough Trade COPY 008	HEARTBEAT (cassette, with 2 extra tracks "Pressure Drop" & "Tight Fit")	12
82	Rough Trade ROUGH 44	TRANCE (LP)	12

(see also Throbbing Gristle, Chris Carter, Eurythmics, Cosey Fanni Tutti)

CHRIS & STUDENTS
61	Parlophone R 4806	Lass Of Richmond Hill/Ducks Away From My Fishin'	20

PETER CHRIS & OUTCASTS
66	Columbia DB 7923	Over The Hill/The Right Girl For Me	40

FUD CHRISTIAN ALL STARS
71	Big Shot BI 571	Never Fall In Love (actually by Winston Heywood)/Never Fall In Love Version	8

HANS CHRISTIAN
68	Parlophone R 5676	All Of The Time/Never My Love	50
68	Parlophone R 5698	(The Autobiography Of) Mississippi Hobo/Sonata Of Love	90

(see also Jon Anderson, Yes)

LIZ CHRISTIAN
67	CBS 202520	Suddenly You Find Love/Make It Work Out (DJ copy = £100)	75
69	Spark SRL 1004	Call My Name/Think Of You Baby	8

(see also James Royal)

MARIA CHRISTIAN
85	MCA MCA 974	Wait Until The Weekend Comes/(Instrumental) (p/s)	15

NEIL CHRISTIAN (& CRUSADERS)
60/61	Private Pressing	Restless/Red Sails In The Sunset/Your Cheating Heart/Danny (one-sided 4 track 12" demo acetate, only 6 made, 2 known to survive. Jimmy Page's first studio recording)	2,500+
62	Columbia DB 4938	The Road To Love/The Big Beat Drum	40
63	Columbia DB 7075	A Little Bit Of Someone Else/Get A Load Of This (with Crusaders)	15
66	Strike JH 301	That's Nice/She's Got The Action	10
66	Strike JH 313	Oops/She Said Yeah	10
66	Strike JH 319	Two At A Time/Wanna Lover	10
67	Pye 7N 17372	You're All Things Bright And Beautiful/I'm Gonna Love You Baby	15
73	Youngblood YB 1044	That's Nice/She's Got The Action	6
66	Columbia SEG 8492	A LITTLE BIT OF SOMETHING ELSE (EP)	85

(see also Christian's Crusaders, Guy Hamilton, Jimmy Page, Ritchie Blackmore, Nicky Hopkins, Miki Dallon, Screaming Lord Sutch)

CHRISTIAN DEATH
83	No Future FL 2	ONLY THEATRE OF PAIN (LP, with insert)	25
86	Jungle NOS 006	OFFICIAL ANTHOLOGY OF LIVE BOOTLEGS (LP, black & yellow sleeve)	25
86	Jungle NOS 006	OFFICIAL ANTHOLOGY OF LIVE BOOTLEGS (LP, pink vinyl)	12

JOHN CHRISTIAN DEE
68	Pye 7N 17566	Take Me Along/The World Can Pack Its Bags And Go Away	6
69	Decca F 12901	The World Can Pack Its Bags And Go Away/Stick To Your Guns	6
70	London HLH 10317	Come Forward The Man/Mr. & Mrs. Jones	6

CHRISTIAN'S CRUSADERS
64	Columbia DB 7289	Honey Hush/One For The Money	40
	(see also Neil Christian & Crusaders)		

CHRISTIE
71	CBS 9130	Everything's Gonna Be Alright/Freewheelin' Man/Magic Highway (p/s)	6
70	CBS 64108	CHRISTIE (LP)	15
71	CBS 64397	FOR ALL MANKIND (LP)	18
	(see also Acid Gallery, Epics, Outer Limits)		

JOHN CHRISTIE
74	Polydor 2058 496	4th Of July (written by Paul McCartney)/Old Enough To Know Better (some in p/s)	30/15
74	Polydor 2058 528	Everybody Knows/How Does It Feel (p/s)	6

LOU CHRISTIE
63	Columbia DB 4983	The Gypsy Cried/Red Sails In The Sunset	20
63	Columbia DB 7031	Two Faces Have I/All That Glitters Isn't Gold	15
63	Columbia DB 7096	How Many Teardrops/You And I (Have A Right To Cry)	15
66	MGM MGM 1297	Lightnin' Strikes/Cryin' In The Streets	15
66	MGM MGM 1308	Rhapsody In The Rain/Trapeze	10
66	MGM MGM 1317	Painter/Du Ronda	10
66	MGM MGM 1325	If My Car Could Only Talk/Song Of Lita	15
66	Colpix PX 735	Merry Go Round/Guitars And Bongos	10
67	King KG 1036	Outside The Gates Of Heaven/All That Glitters Isn't Gold	9
67	CBS 2718	Shake Hands And Walk Away Cryin'/Escape	12
67	CBS 2922	Gina/Back To The Days Of The Romans	10
69	Buddah 201 057	I'm Gonna Make You Mine/I'm Gonna Get Married	5
69	Buddah 201 073	She Sold Me Magic/Are You Gettin' Any Sunshine?	5
66	MGM MGM-C(S) 8008	LIGHTNIN' STRIKES (LP)	25
66	Colpix PXL 551	STRIKES AGAIN (LP)	30
69	Buddah 203 029	I'M GONNA MAKE YOU MINE (LP)	12
71	Buddah 2318 035	PAINT AMERICA LOVE (LP)	12
74	CTI CTL 24	LOU CHRISTIE (LP)	12

CHRISTIE BROTHERS STOMPERS
59	Parlophone GEP 8719	TOGETHER AGAIN (EP)	10
60	Esquire EP233	RUM & COCA COLA (EP)	25
60	Esquire EP243	STOMPIN' (EP)	25

KEITH CHRISTIE
54	Esquire 20-047	HOMAGE TO THE DUKE (LP)	20

TONY CHRISTIE (& TRACKERS)
66	CBS 202097	Life's Too Good To Waste/Just The Two Of Us	10
67	MGM MGM 1365	Turn Around/When Will I Ever Love Again?	10
68	MGM MGM 1386	I Don't Want To Hurt You Anymore/Say No More	10
68	MGM MGM 1440	My Prayer/I Need You	10
73	MCA MKS 5101	Avenues And Alleyways/I Never Was A Child	7

DEREK CHRISTIEN
70	Major Minor MM 676	When A Woman Has A Baby/Please Don't Go Away	25
70	Major Minor MM 713	Suddenly There's A Valley/I'll Be Coming Home	100
	(see also Christien Brothers)		

CHRISTIEN BROTHERS
69	Major Minor MM 628	I Reached For You/Answer Me	7

KEITH CHRISTMAS
69	RCA Victor SF 8059	STIMULUS (LP, with Mighty Baby)	120
70	B&C CAS 1015	FABLE OF THE WINGS (LP)	22
71	B&C CAS 1041	PIGMY (LP, gatefold sleeve)	22
74	Manticore K 53503	BRIGHTER DAY (LP. with inner sleeve)	15
76	Manticore K 53509	STORIES FROM THE HUMAN ZOO (LP, with insert)	12
	(see also Mighty Baby, Magic Muscle)		

JUNE CHRISTY
55	Capitol CL 14355	Pete Kelly's Blues/Kicks	8
55	Capitol EAP 516	SOMETHING COOL (EP)	8
54	Capitol LC 6682	SOMETHING COOL (10" LP)	18
56	Capitol T 725	JUNE CHRISTY (LP)	18
57	Capitol T 833	JUNE — FAIR AND WARMER (LP)	15
58	Capitol T 902	GONE FOR THE DAY (LP)	15
58	Capitol T 1006	JUNE CHRISTY (LP)	15
59	Capitol (S)T 1076	JUNE'S GOT RHYTHM (LP)	15
59	Capitol (S)T 1114	THE SONG IS JUNE (LP)	15
59	Capitol T 1202	JUNE CHRISTY RECALLS THOSE KENTON DAYS (LP)	15
60	Capitol (S)T 1308	BALLADS FOR NIGHT PEOPLE (LP)	15
61	Capitol (S)T 1398	COOL SCHOOL (LP, with Joe Castro Quartet)	15
	(see also Stan Kenton)		

CHROME

80	Red RS 12007	READ ONLY MEMORY (12" EP, some with poster)	12/10
80	Beggars Banquet BEG 36	New Age/Information (p/s)	6
81	D. F. O. T. Mountain Y3	INWORLDS - In A Dream/Danger Zone (12")	12
82	D. F. O. T. Mountain Z17	Firebomb/Shadows Of A Thousand Years (p/s)	8
80	Beggars Banquet BEGA 15	RED EXPOSURE (LP, with inner sleeve)	12
80	Beggars Banquet BEGA 18	HALF MACHINE LIP MOVES (LP, some with poster insert)	15/12
81	D. F. O. T. Mountain X6	BLOOD ON THE MOON (LP, with inner sleeve)	12
82	D. F. O. T. Mountain X18	3RD FROM THE SUN (LP, with insert)	12

CHRON GEN

81	Gargoyle GRGL 780	PUPPETS OF WAR (EP)	10
81	Gargoyle/Fresh GRGL 780	PUPPETS OF WAR (EP, reissue, silver & black label)	7
81	Step Forward SF 19	Reality/Subway Sadist (p/s)	5
82	Secret SEC 3	LIVING NEXT DOOR TO ALICE (EP, some with *Chronic Generation Oi* magazine No. 1)	8/5
82	Secret SHH 129	Jet Boy Jet Girl/Abortions/Subway Sadist (p/s)	5
82	Secret SHH 139	Outlaw/Behind Closed Doors/Disco (p/s)	6
83	Secret SEC 3	CHRONIC GENERATION (LP, some with free 7")	15/12

CHROMING ROSE

90	EMI 5667 93774	LOUIS XIV (LP, some as picture disc)	12

CHUBBY & HONEYSUCKERS

66	Rio R 75	Emergency Ward/LEN & HONEYSUCKERS: One More River	12

CHUBUKOS

73	Mainstream MSS 303	Witch Doctor Bump/House Of The Rising Funk	10

CHUCK & BETTY

59	Brunswick 05815	Sissy Britches/Come Back Little Girl (78 rpm = £15)	40

CHUCK (Josephs) & DOBBY (Dobson)

60	Blue Beat BB 19	Til The End Of Time/DUKE REID & HIS GROUP: What Makes Honey	20
60	Blue Beat BB 23	Cool School/DUKE REID & HIS GROUP: Joker	20
61	Starlite ST45 043	Sad Over You/Sweeter Than Honey	20
61	Starlite ST45 044	Lovey Dovey/Sitting Square	20
61	Blue Beat BB 39	Du Du Wap/I Love My Teacher (with Aubrey Adams & Du Droppers)	18
61	Blue Beat BB 59	Oh Fanny/Running Around	18
64	Blue Beat BB 246	Tell Me/I'm Going Home	15

CHUCK & GARY

58	HMV POP 466	Teenie Weenie Jeanie/Can't Make Up My Mind (78 rpm = £22)	70

CHUCK & GIDEON

63	Parlophone R 5011	Cherry Berry Lips/The Tender Touch	10

CHUCK & JOE WHITE

(see under Joe White)

CHUCKLES

72	Duke DU 144	Reggae Limbo/ZAP POW: Broken Contract	12

CHUCKS

63	Decca F 11569	Loo Be Loo/Anytime Is The Right Time	10
63	Decca F 11617	Mulberry Bush/That's All I Need	10
63	Decca F 11777	The Hitch Hiker/Humpity Dumpity	10
64	Decca DFE 8562	THE CHUCKS (EP)	45

CHUMBAWAMBA

88	Agit Prop PROP 3	ENGLISH REBEL SONGS 1381-1914 (10" LP, with die-cut sleeve)	15

MIKIE CHUNG & NOW GENERATION

72	Green Door GD 4032	Breezing/NOW GENERATION: Breezing — Version	8
73	Duke DU 163	Stoned In Love/CHOSEN FEW: Stoned In Love	7
73	Duke DU 164	It's Too Late/CHOSEN FEW: It's Too Late	7

CHURCH

82	Carrere CAR 212	Unguarded Moment/Busdriver (p/s)	5
82	Carrere CAR 247	Almost With You/Life Speeds Up (p/s)	5
82	Carrere CAR EP 257	Unguarded Moment/Interlude/Golden Dawn/Sisters (10", p/s)	8
83	Carrere CHURCH R5A	Different Man/I Am A Rock (no p/s)	7
86	Bucketfull Of Brains BOB 9	Warm Spell (hard vinyl test pressing, 20 copies only)	20
86	Bucketfull Of Brains BOB 9	Warm Spell (flexi with *Bucketfull Of Brains* magazine 15)	5
88	Arista 659 778CD	Under The Milky Way/Musk/The Warm Spell (CD, picture disc)	8
83	Carrere CHURCH 5	SING SONGS (12" EP)	10
88	Arista 208895	STARFISH (LP, with bonus 5-track numbered 12")	15

EUGENE CHURCH

59	London HL 8940	Miami/I Ain't Goin' For That (triangular or round centre) (78 rpm = £30)	75/40

CHICK CHURCHILL

73	Chrysalis CHR 1051	YOU AND ME (LP)	12

(see also Ten Years After, Cozy Powell, Jethro Tull, Bernie Marsden)

SAVANNAH CHURCHILL

53	Brunswick 05218	Shake A Hand/Shed A Tear (78)	25

CICCONE YOUTH

86	Blast First BFFP 8	INTO THE GROOVE(Y) EP: Tuff Titty Rap/Into The Groove/Burning Up (12")	10
88	Blast First BFUS 28P	WHITEY ALBUM PROMO (EP, promo only)	10

(see also Sonic Youth)

CIGARETTES
78	Dead Good KEVIN 1	THE CIGARETTES (EP, unreleased)	
79	Company CIGCO 008	They're Back Again, Here They Come/I've Forgot My Number/ All We Want Is Your Money (gatefold p/s, red or later black labels)	70/60
80	Dead Good DEAD 10	Can't Sleep At Night/It's The Only Way To Live (Die) (p/s)	40

CIM(M)AR(R)ONS
70	Hot Rod HR 105	Grandfather Clock/Kick Me Or I Kick You (as Cimarrons)	12
70	Reggae REG 3003	Bad Day At Black Rock (with Cimmaron Kid)/Fragile	20
71	Big Shot BI 562	Funky Fight/You Turned Me Down	10
71	Spinning Wheel SW 107	Soul For Sale/Bogus-ism	7
71	Downtown DT 486	Oh Mammy Blue/Oh Mammy Blue — Version	6
71	Downtown DT 487	Holy Christmas/Silent Night/White Christmas	6
74	Trojan TR7919	Over The Rainbow/We Are Not The Same	15
78	Cimarak CR002	Paul Bogle/Greedy Man (12")	40
82	IMP IMPS 50	With A Little Luck/Peggy Sue	
82	Safari/MPL SAFE 49	Big Girls Don't Cry/How Can I Prove Myself To You?	10
82	Safari/MPL SAFEL 49	Big Girls Don't Cry/How Can I Prove Myself To You? (12")	15
82	Safari/MPL SAFELX 49	Big Girls Don't Cry/How Can I Prove Myself To You? (12", picture disc)	20
83	MPL/Cimarons CIM 001	Love And Affection	18
83	MPL/Cimarons 12CIM 001	Love And Affection (12", less than 1000 pressed)	60
74	Trojan TRLS 77	IN TIME (LP)	15
82	MPL/Pickwick SHM 3106	REGGAEBILITY (LP)	18
	(see also Reaction, Winston Groovy)		

CINDERELLAS
59	Brunswick 05794	Mister Dee-Jay/Yum Yum Yum (78 rpm = £20)	45
60	Philips PB 1012	The Trouble With Boys/Puppy Dog	25

CINDERELLAS
64	Colpix PX 11026	Baby, Baby (I Still Love You)/Please Don't Wake Me	80
	(see also Cookies)		

CINDERS
63	Warner Bros WB 86	The Cinnamon Cinder/C'mon Wobble	18
	(see also Darlene Love)		

CINDY & LINDY
57	HMV POP 409	The Language Of Love/Tell Me Something Sweet (78 rpm = £8)	10
59	Coral Q 72368	Saturday Night In Tijuana/The Wonder That Is You (78 rpm = £12)	10

CINEMATICS
80s	Pulsebeat CINE 001	FAREWELL TO THE PLAYGROUND (EP, foldover p/s)	25
	(see also Razorcuts)		

CINNAMON
69	Beacon BEA 111	You Won't See Me Leaving/Leaves Of Love	6

CINNAMON QUILL
69	Morgan MRS 17	Girl On A Swing/Take It Or Leave It	20
69	Morgan MRS 21	Candy/Hello, It's Me	30

CIRCLE
60s	Circle GR 1	IN AID OF THE MILLFIELD BUILDING FUND (EP, private pressing)	150

CIRCLES
66	Island WI 279	Take Your Time/Don't You Love Me No More	65
	(see also Plastic Penny, Savages, Tony Dangerfield & Thrills, Screaming Lord Sutch)		

CIRCLES
72	Sioux SIOUX 017	Mammy Blue/POOCH JACKSON & HARRY J. ALLSTARS: King Of The Road	7
	(see also Bob Andy)		

CIRCLES
79	Graduate GRAD 4	Opening Up/Billy (p/s)	20
80	Vertigo ANGRY 1	Angry Voices/Summer Nights (p/s)	8
80	Chrysalis CHS 2418	Opening Up/Billy (p/s, reissue)	8
85	Graduate GRAD 17	Circles/Summer Nights (p/s)	18

CIRCUS
67	Parlophone R 5633	Gone Are The Songs Of Yesterday/Sink Or Swim	18
68	Parlophone R 5672	Do You Dream/House Of Wood	40
69	Transatlantic TRA 207	CIRCUS (LP, gatefold sleeve)	60
	(see also Philip Goodhand-Tait)		

CIRCUS MAXIMUS
67	Vanguard VSD 79260	CIRCUS MAXIMUS (LP)	30
68	Vanguard VSD 79274	NEVERLAND REVISITED (LP)	30

CIRKUS
80	Guardian GRCA 4	Melissa/Amsterdam/Pick Up A Phone (EP)	20
73	RCB 1	CIRKUS ONE (LP, private pressing with gatefold sleeve)	100
77	Shock SHOCK 1	FUTURE SHOCK (LP)	50

CIRRUS
81	Jet JET 123	Rollin' On/Keep On Rolling (p/s, 'Yorkie™'-shaped brown vinyl)	5

CITATIONS
63	Columbia DB 7068	Moon Race/Slippin' And Slidin'	35

CITY LIMITS CREW
85	Survival 12-034	Fresher Than Ever (12")	8

CITY OF WESTMINSTER STRING BAND
68	Pye 7N 17620	A Touch Of Velvet And A Sting Of Brass/Tommy Tucker	8

CITY RAMBLERS SKIFFLE GROUP

57	Tempo A 158	Ella Speed/2.19 Blues (78 rpm = £13)	20
57	Tempo A 161	Mama Don't Allow/Tom Dooley (78 rpm = £13)	18
57	Tempo A 165	Delia's Gone/Boodle-Am Shake (78 rpm = £13)	20
58	Topic TRC 101	Round And Round The Picket Lines/Nine Hundred Miles (78, with Hylda Sims)	12
57	Storyville SEP 327	I WANT A GIRL (EP)	40
57	Storyville SEP 345	I SHALL NOT BE MOVED (EP)	40
57	Tempo EXA 59	I WANT A GIRL (EP)	40
57	Tempo EXA 71	GOOD MORNING BLUES (EP)	40
57	Tempo EXA 77	DELIA'S GONE (EP)	40

(see also Henrik Johansen)

CITY SMOKE

66	Mercury MF 971	Sunday Morning/A Little Bit Of Love	6

CITY WAITES

74	EMI EMI 2149	The Fox/One Of My Aunts	5
74	EMI EMC 3027	A GORGEOUS GALLERY OF GALLANT INVENTIONS (LP)	25
76	Decca SKL 5264	THE CITY WAITES (LP)	25
81	Hyperion A 66008	HOW THE WORLD WAGS (LP, gatefold sleeve, some with Hyperion insert)	40

C-JAM BLUES

66	Columbia DB 8064	Candy/Stay At Home Girl	40

CLAGUE

69	Dandelion S 4493	Mandy Lee/Bottle Up And Go (with Kevin Coyne)	12

(see also Coyne-Clague, Kevin Coyne, Siren)

CLAN

72	Deram DM 356	Pretty Belinda/Ode To Karen	7

(see also Junior Campbell)

CLANCY'S ALLSTARS

68	Pama PM 722	C.N. Express Parts 1 & 2 (B-side actually "You Were Meant For Me" by Lee Perry)	25

(see also Owen Gray)

CLANNAD & BONO

89	RCA PA42995A	In A Lifetime (7" picture disc)	15

see also U2, Bono & Gavin Friday, The Passengers)

JIMMY CLANTON

58	London HLS 8699	Just A Dream/You Aim To Please (as Jimmy Clanton & His Rockets) (78 rpm = £18)	30
58	London HL 7066	A Letter To An Angel/A Part Of Me (as Jimmy Clanton & Aces) (export issue)	30
59	London HLS 8779	A Letter To An Angel/A Part Of Me (as Jimmy Clanton & Aces) (78 rpm = £18)	30
59	Top Rank JAR 189	My Own True Love/Little Boy In Love (78 rpm = £20)	25
60	Top Rank JAR 269	Go, Jimmy, Go/I Trusted You	25
60	Top Rank JAR 382	Another Sleepless Night/I'm Gonna Try	20
60	Top Rank JAR 509	Come Back (To Me)/Wait	20
61	Top Rank JAR 544	What Am I Gonna Do/If I	15
62	Stateside SS 120	Venus In Blue Jeans/Highway Bound	15
63	Stateside SS 159	Darkest Street In Town/Dreams Of A Fool	15
65	Stateside SS 410	Hurting Each Other/Don't Keep Your Friends Away	75
69	London HLP 10289	Curly/I'll Never Forget Your Love	5
59	London RES 1224	JUST A DREAM (EP)	100

CLAP

79	SRTS SRTS/79/CUS	Hey Little Girl/20 Watts Of Power (p/s)	10

CLAPHAM SOUTH ESCALATORS

81	Upright UP YOUR 1	Get Me To The World On Time/Leave Me Alone/Cardboard Cut Outs (p/s)	8

(see also Meteors)

ERIC CLAPTON

66	Purdah 45-3502	Lonely Years/Bernard Jenkins (with John Mayall, 500 copies only)	300
70	Polydor 2001 096	I Am Yours (unissued)	
70	Polydor 2001 096	After Midnight/Easy Now	10
74	RSO 2090 139	Willie And The Hand Jive/I Can't Hold Out Much Longer (p/s)	5
76	RSO 2090 208	Hello Old Friend/All Our Pastimes (p/s)	8
80	RSO JON 1	Wonderful Tonight (live)/Further On Up The Road (live) (promo only)	10
80	RSO JONX 1	Wonderful Tonight (live)/Further On Up The Road (live) (12", numbered p/s)	10
81	RSO RSO 75	Another Ticket/Rita Mae (p/s)	5
83	Duck W 9701P	The Shape You're In/Crosscut Saw (picture disc)	6
87	Duck W 8461F	Behind The Mask/Grand Illusion//Crossroads (live)/White Room (live) (double pack, gatefold p/s)	8
87	Duck W 8397F	It's In The Way That You Use It/Bad Influence//Behind The Mask/Grand Illusion (double pack, shrinkwrapped with sticker)	6
88	Polydor PZCD 8	After Midnight (Extended Version)/I Can't Stand It/Whatcha Gonna Do/Sunshine Of Your Love (CD, card sleeve)	20
89	BBC CD RSL 178	Edge Of Darkness/Shoot Out/Obituary/Escape From Northmoor/Oxford Circus/Northmoor (with Michael Kamen, 3" CD with adaptor, 5" case)	20
89	Duck W 2644B	Bad Love/I Shot The Sheriff (live) (box set with family tree & 2 colour prints)	6
90	Duck W 2644CD	Bad Love/Badge (live)/Let It Rain (live) (CD)	12
90	Duck W 9981CD	No Alibis/Running On Faith/Behind The Mask (live)/Cocaine (CD)	8
90	Duck W 9970CD	Pretending/Hard Times/Knock On Wood/Behind The Sun (CD)	8
70	Polydor 2383 021	ERIC CLAPTON (LP)	12
73	RSO 2479 702	CLAPTON (LP, withdrawn)	55
74	RSO QD 4801	461 OCEAN BOULEVARD (LP, quadrophonic)	18
82	RSO RSDX 3	TIME PIECES (2-LP, unissued)	

83	WEA W 37734	MONEY AND CIGARETTES (cassette, with interview)	12
84	Aston PD 20118	TOO MUCH MONKEY BUSINESS (LP, picture disc, with Yardbirds)	15
99	Reprise SAM 00189	A SELECTION FROM THE BEST OF (CD, 9-track sampler, promo only)	20

(see also Yardbirds, John Mayall, Cream, Blind Faith, Delaney & Bonnie, Derek & The Dominos, Viv Stanshall, King Curtis, Randy Crawford)

THE CLAQUE
69	Dandelion 4494	The Stride/I Wonder Where	10
69	Dandelion 4493	Mandy Lee/Battle Up & Go	10

ALAN CLARE GROUP
62	Parlophone R 4938	Screwball/Love For Sale	5
65	Pye 7N 15764	Dog's Body/Mulligatawny	5
56	Decca DFE 6368	THE IMPROVISATIONS OF... (EP)	40
56	Decca DFE 6391	ALAN CLARE TRIO WITH BOB BURNS (EP)	35
58	Decca LK 4260	JAZZ AROUND THE CLOCK (LP)	40
68	Decca SKL 4965	YOUNG GIRL (LP)	15

KENNY CLARE
67	Columbia DB 8216	If I Were A Buddy Rich Man/Hum-Drum	5

KENNY CLARE & RONNIE STEPHENSON
67	Columbia SCX 6168	DRUM SPECTACULAR (LP, with Tubby Hayes, also mono Columbia SX 6168).	30

CLARENDONIANS
65	Ska Beat JB 219	Muy Bien (My Friend)/You Are A Fool	22
66	Ska Beat JB 261	Doing The Jerk/You Won't See Me	22
66	Island WI 284	Try Me One More Time/Can't Keep A Good Man Down	22
66	Island WI 3005	I'll Never Change/Rules Of Life	22
67	Island WI 3032	Shoo-Be-Doo-Be (I Love You)/Sweet Heart Of Beauty	22
67	Island WI 3041	You Can't Be Happy/Goodbye Forever	22
67	Studio One SO 2004	The Table's Going To Turn/I Can't Go On	35
67	Studio One SO 2007	He Who Laughs Last/GAYLADS: Just A Kiss From You	30
67	Studio One SO 2017	Love Me With All Your Heart/Love Don't Mean Much To Me	30
67	Rio R 112	Rudie Bam Bam/Be Bop Boy	18
67	Rio R 115	Musical Train/Lowdown Girl	18
68	Caltone TONE 114	Baby Baby/Bye Bye Bye	30
69	Duke DU 97	Come Along/Try To Be Happy	10
69	Gas GAS 131	When I Am Gone/She Brings Me Joy	12
70	Trojan TR 7714	Lick It Back/BEVERLEY'S ALLSTARS: Busy Bee	8
70	Trojan TR 7719	Baby Don't Do It/BEVERLEY'S ALLSTARS: Touch Down	8
71	Green Door GD 4009	Seven In One (Medley) (both sides)	6
72	Attack ATT 8039	Bound In Chains/STUD ALLSTARS: Version	6
72	Pama PM 847	This Is My Story/VAL BENNETT: Caledonia	6
73	Pama PM 856	Good Hearted Woman/CORNELL CAMPBELL: What Happens	8
73	Techniques TE 925	Just One Look/Sinner Man	6
73	Dragon DRA 1006	Walking Up A One Way Street/DYNAMITES: Instrumental	20

(see also Lee & Clarendonians, Desmond Baker & Clarendonians, Four Aces, Prince Buster, Dennis Walks)

ALICE CLARK
69	Action ACT 4520	You Got A Deal/Say You'll Never	25

CHRIS CLARK
67	Tamla Motown TMG 591	Love's Gone Bad/Put Yourself In My Place	50
67	Tamla Motown TMG 624	From Head To Toe/The Beginning Of The End	30
68	Tamla Motown TMG 638	I Want To Go Back There Again/I Love You	25
68	T. Motown (S)TML 11069	SOUL SOUNDS (LP)	100

CLAUDINE CLARK
62	Pye International 7N 25157	Party Lights/Disappointed	20
63	Pye International 7N 25186	Walk Me Home From The Party/Who Will You Hurt?	20
67	Sue WI 4039	The Strength To Be Strong/Moon Madness	40

DAVE CLARK FIVE
62	Ember EMB S 156	Chaquita/In Your Heart (grey/pink or red/yellow labels)	55/45
62	Piccadilly 7N 35088	First Love/I Walk The Line	45
62	Piccadilly 7N 35088	That's What I Said/I Knew It All The Time	45
63	Columbia DB 7011	The Mulberry Bush/Chaquita	30
63	Columbia DB 7112	Do You Love Me/Doo-Dah	12
63	Columbia DB 7154	Glad All Over/I Know You	6
64	Columbia DB 7210	Bits And Pieces/All Of The Time	6
64	Columbia DB 7291	Can't You See That She's Mine/Because	6
64	Columbia DB 7335	Thinking Of You Baby/Whenever You're Around	6
64	Columbia DB 7377	Any Way You Want It/Crying Over You	7
65	Columbia DB 7453	Everybody Knows/Say You Want Me	7
65	Columbia DB 7503	Reelin' And Rockin'/Little Bitty Pretty One	7
65	Columbia DB 7580	Come Home/Mighty Good Loving (in p/s)	18
65	Columbia DB 7625	Catch Us If You Can/Move On	6
65	Columbia DB 7744	Over And Over/I'll Be Yours	6
66	Columbia DB 7863	Try Too Hard/All Night Long	10
66	Columbia DB 7909	Look Before You Leap/Please Tell Me Why	10
66	Columbia DB 8028	Nineteen Days/I Need Love	7
67	Columbia DB 8152	You Got What It Takes/Sitting Here Baby	7
67	Columbia DB 8194	Tabatha Twitchit/Man In A Pin-Striped Suit (some in export p/s)	20/5
67	Columbia DB 8286	Everybody Knows/Concentration Baby	5
68	Columbia DB 8342	No One Can Break A Like You/You Don't Want My Lovin'	5
68	Columbia DB 8465	The Red Balloon/Maze Of Love	5
68	Columbia DB 8505	Live In The Sky/Children	5
69	Columbia DB 8545	The Mulberry Tree/Small Talk	5
69	Columbia DB 8591	Get It On Now/Maze Of Life (unreleased, acetates exist)	

MINT VALUE £

69	Columbia DB 8624	Put A Little Love In Your Heart/34-06 5
69	Columbia DB 8638	Good Old Rock'N'Roll Medley (Parts 1 & 2) (in p/s) 6
70	Columbia DB 8660	Everybody Get Together/Darling I Love You 5
70	Columbia DB 8681	Julia/Five By Five 7
70	Columbia DB 8689	Here Comes Summer/Break Down And Cry. 7
70	Columbia DB 8724	Play More Good Old Rock'N'Roll Medley (Parts 1 & 2) (in p/s) 7
71	Columbia DB 8749	Southern Man/If You Wanna See Me Cry 6
71	Columbia DB 8791	Won't You Be My Lady/Into Your Life 6
72	Columbia DB 8963	All Time Greats Medley (Glad All Over/Do You Love Me/Bits & Pieces/ Glad All Over)/Wild Weekend (p/s) 8
64	Columbia SEG 8289	THE DAVE CLARK FIVE (EP) 20
65	Columbia SEG 8381	THE HITS OF THE DAVE CLARK FIVE (EP) 25
65	Columbia SEG 8447	WILD WEEKEND (EP) 30
64	Columbia 33SX 1598	SESSION WITH THE DAVE CLARK FIVE (LP, blue/black label) 30
64	Ember FA 2003	DAVE CLARK FIVE AND THE WASHINGTON D.C.'s (LP) 40
65	EMI Regal REG 2017	IN SESSION (LP, export issue). 45
65	Columbia SX 1756	CATCH US IF YOU CAN (LP, soundtrack, blue/black label) . . . . 50+
67	Columbia SX 6105	THE DAVE CLARK FIVE'S GREATEST HITS (LP, blue/black label) . . . 25
68	Columbia SX 6207	EVERYBODY KNOWS (LP, blue/black label) 35
69	Columbia SX 6309	5 BY 5 1964-69: 14 TITLES BY THE DAVE CLARK FIVE (LP, blue/black label). 35
70	Columbia SCX 6437	IF SOMEBODY LOVES YOU (LP). 30

(see also Dave Clark & Friends, Smith D'Abo, Mike Smith, Washington D.C.s)

DAVE CLARK & FRIENDS

71	Columbia DB 8834	Draggin' The Line/One Eyed, Blues Suited, Gun Totin' Man 5
72	Columbia DB 8862	Think Of Me/Right Or Wrong 5
72	Columbia DB 8907	Rub It In/I'm Sorry Baby 5
73	EMI EMI 2013	Sweet City Woman/Love Comes But Once 5
73	EMI EMI 2082	Sha-Na-Na/I Don't Know 5
72	Columbia SCX 6494	DAVE CLARK AND FRIENDS (LP) 15

(see also Dave Clark Five)

DEE CLARK

59	London HL 8802	Nobody But You/When I Call On You (78 rpm = £25) 30
59	London HL 8915	Just Keep It Up (And See What Happens)/ Whispering Grass(Don't Tell The Trees) (78 rpm = £30) 35
59	Top Rank JAR 196	Hey, Little Girl/If It Wasn't For Love (78 rpm = £40). 30
60	Top Rank JAR 284	How About That/Blues Get Off My Shoulder 15
60	Top Rank JAR 373	At My Front Door/Cling-A-Ling 22
60	Top Rank JAR 501	Gloria/You're Looking Good 15
61	Top Rank JAR 551	Your Friends/Because I Love You 15
61	Top Rank JAR 570	Raindrops/I Want To Love You 15
62	Columbia DB 4768	Don't Walk Away From Me/You're Telling Our Secrets 40
63	Stateside SS 180	I'm A Soldier Boy/Shook Up Over You 20
64	Stateside SS 355	Heartbreak/Warm Summer Breeze 15
65	Stateside SS 400	T.C.B./It's Impossible 15
70	Liberty LBF 15334	Where Did All The Good Times Go?/24 Hours Of Loneliness 10
60	Top Rank BUY 044	HOW ABOUT THAT! (LP) 40
70	Joy JOYS 130	YOU'RE LOOKING GOOD (LP) 15

DOTTY CLARK

61	London HLX 9418	It's Been A Long, Long Time/That's A Step In The Right Direction 10

GENE CLARK

67	CBS 202523	Echoes/I Found You 20
74	Asylum AYM 536	No Other/The True One. 6
74	Asylum AYM 540	Life's Greatest Fool/From A Silver Phial. 6
88	Bucketfull of Brains BOB 18	Gypsy Rider/SEERS: Flyaway (flexidisc with Bucketfull Of Brains magazine, issue 24) 7/5
92	Demon GENE 1	GENE CLARK AND CARLA OLSON SING 3 SONGS BY THE BYRDS (CD, picture disc, no inlay, promo only). 12
67	CBS 62934	GENE CLARK WITH THE GOSDIN BROTHERS (LP) 38
72	A&M AMLS 64297	WHITE LIGHT (LP). 25
74	Asylum SYL 9020	NO OTHER (LP). 20
77	RSO 2394 175	TWO SIDES TO EVERY STORY (LP) 12
84	Making Waves SPIN 122	FIREBYRD (LP) 12

(see also Byrds, Dillard & Clark)

GUY CLARK

75	RCA Victor APL1-130	OLD NO. 1 (LP) 15
76	RCA Victor RS 1097	TEXAS COOKIN' (LP) 15

JAMES CLARK(E) + SOUNDS

68	Fontana TF 918	"A Man Of Our Times" T.V. Series Theme/Spring Bossa 6
68	Fontana SFJL 966	A MAN OF OUR TIMES (LP). 30

JIMMY 'SOUL' CLARK

76	Black Magic BM 115	Sweet Darlin'/Sweet Darlin' (Instrumental) 10

MICHAEL CLARK

66	Liberty LIB 5893	None Of These Girls/Work Out 20

NOBBY CLARK

76	Epic S EPC 4381	Steady Love/Give Me The Heart 10

PAUL CLARK & FRIENDS

77	Myrrh MYR 1054	GOOD TO BE HOME (LP, with inner sleeve) 20
78	Myrrh MYR 1059	HAND TO THE PLOUGH (LP). 20

PETULA CLARK
SINGLES

57	Pye Nixa 7N 15096	With All My Heart/Gonna Find Me A Bluebird	22
57	Pye Nixa 7N 15112	Alone/Long Before I Knew You	8
58	Pye Nixa 7N 15126	Baby Lover/The Little Blue Man	10
58	Pye Nixa 7N 15135	Love Me Again/In A Little Moment	10
58	Pye Nixa 7N 15152	St. Tropez (Sur La Plage)/Devotion	12
58	Pye Nixa 7N 15168	I Wish I Knew/Fibbin'	110
59	Pye Nixa 7N 15182	Ever Been In Love/Lucky Day	10
59	Pye Nixa 7N 15191	Watch Your Heart/Suddenly	10
59	Pye Nixa 7N 15208	Where Do I Go From Here?/Mama's Talking Soft (78 rpm = £6)	12
59	Pye Nixa 7N 15220	Adonis/If I Had My Way (78 rpm £10)	12
59	Pye Nixa 7N 15230	Dear Daddy/Through The Livelong Day (78 rpm = £6)	15
59	Pye 7N 15244	I Love A Violin/Guitare Et Tambourin (78 rpm = £7)	15
60	Pye 7N 15281	Cinderella Jones/All Over Now	5
61	Pye 7N 15324	Sailor/My Heart	5
61	Pye 7N 15337	Something Missing/Isn't This A Lovely Day?	8
61	Pye 7N 15355	Welcome Home/Les Gens Diront	8
61	Pye 7N 15361	Romeo/You're Getting To Be A Habit With Me	5
61	Pye 7N 15389	My Friend The Sea/With All My Love	5
62	Pye 7N 15407	I'm Counting On You/Some Other World	7
62	Pye 7N 15437	Whistlin' For The Moon/Tender Love	5
62	Pye 7N 15448	Ya Ya Twist/Si C'est Oui, C'est Oui	5
62	Pye 7N 15456	Jumble Sale/Too Late	5
62	Pye 7N 15478	The Road/No Love, No Nothin'	5
63	Pye 7N 15495	I Will Follow Him/Darling Cheri	5
63	Pye 7N 15517	Valentino/Imagination	5
63	Pye 7N 15522	Chariot/Casanova	5
63	Pye 7N 15551	Let Me Tell You/Be Good To Me	5
63	Pye 7N 15573	Baby It's Me/This Is Goodbye	5
64	Pye 7N 15606	Thank You/Crying Through A Sleepless Night	8
64	Pye 7N 15639	In Love/Forgetting You (J'ai Tout Oublié)	5
64	Pye 7N 15668	True Love Never Runs Smooth/Saturday Sunshine	5
65	Pye 7N 15991	You're The One/Gotta Tell The World (some in export p/s)	15/5
66	Pye 7N 17071	A Sign Of The Times/Time For Love	15
66	Pye 7N 17187	Who Am I/Love Is A Long Journey	6
67	Pye 7N 17377	The Cat In The Window/Fancy Dancin' Man	6
68	Pye 7N 17466	Kiss Me Goodbye/I've Got Love Going For Me	8
71	Pye 7N 45026	The Song Of My Life/For Love	7
71	Pye 7N 45091	The World Song/I Know What Love Is About	5
71	Pye 7N 45112	I Don't Know How To Love Him/Song Went Wrong	7
72	Polydor 2058 295	Wedding Song (There Is Love)/Song Without End	6
73	Polydor 2058 413	Lead Me On/Taking It On (both with Sacha Distel)	8
74	Polydor 2058 519	Let's Sing A Love Song/I'm The Woman You Need	7
75	Polydor 2058 560	I Am Your Song/Super Loving Lady	8
75	Pye 7N 45473	Wind Of Change (edit)/Memories Are Made Of This	5
75	Pye 7N 45506	What I Did For Love/I Believe In Love	5
76	Pye 7N 45650	Downtown (Disco Version)/Two Rivers	5

EPs

56	Pye Nixa NEP 24006	CHILDREN'S CHOICE	20
56	Pye Nixa NEP 24016	PETULA CLARK HIT PARADE	20
57	Pye Nixa NEP 24056	PETULA CLARK HIT PARADE NO. 2	15
57	Pye Nixa NEP 24060	YOU ARE MY LUCKY STAR PART 1	20
57	Pye Nixa NEP 24061	YOU ARE MY LUCKY STAR PART 2	20
57	Pye Nixa NEP 24062	YOU ARE MY LUCKY STAR PART 3	20
58	Pye Nixa NEP 24080	PETULA CLARK HIT PARADE NO. 3	18
58	Pye Nixa NEP 24089	PETULA CLARK SINGS IN FRENCH	15
58	Pye Nixa NEP 24094	A CHRISTMAS CAROL (also stereo NSEP 85001)	18/25
59	Pye NEP 24121	ENCORE	15
61	Pye NEP 24137	PETULA CLARK HIT PARADE 4	15
61	Pye NEP 24150	PETULA CLARK HIT PARADE 5	15
62	Pye NEP 24157	PET-OOH-LA-LA	15
63	Pye NEP 24182	EN FRANÇAIS	12
64	Pye NEP 24189	ENCORE EN FRANÇAIS	12
65	Pye-Vogue VRE 5004	LES DISQUES D'OR DE LA CHANSON	18
65	Pye-Vogue VRE 5007	PETULA CLARK CHANTE EN ITALIEN	20
66	Pye NEP 24237	CALL ME	15
66	Pye NEP 24246	MY LOVE	12
66	Pye NEP 24259	JUST SAY GOODBYE	12
66	Pye NEP 24266	I COULDN'T LIVE WITHOUT YOUR LOVE	12
67	Pye NEP 24279	THIS IS MY SONG	12
66	Pye-Vogue VRE 5019	L'AGENT SECRET	15
66	Pye-Vogue VRE 5023	HELLO MISTER BROWN	15
67	Pye-Vogue VRE 5025	C'EST MA CHANSON	15
67	Pye NEP 24280	THE MANY FACES OF PETULA CLARK	12
67	Pye NEP 24286	HERE, THERE AND EVERYWHERE	12
68	Pye-Vogue VRE 5026	L'AMOUR VIENDRA	12
68	Pye-Vogue VRE 5028	DIS-MOI AU REVOIR	12
68	Pye NEP 24301	DON'T GIVE UP	12

LPs

56	Pye Nixa NPT 19002	PETULA CLARK SINGS (10")	80
56	Pye Nixa NPT 19014	A DATE WITH PET (10")	60
57	Pye Nixa NPL 18007	YOU ARE MY LUCKY STAR	50
59	Pye Nixa NPL 18039	PETULA CLARK IN HOLLYWOOD	45
62	Pye NPL 18070	IN OTHER WORDS — PETULA CLARK	35

63	Pye NPL 18098	PETULA 20
64	Pye-Vogue VRL 3001	LES JAMES DEAN. 32
65	Pye-Vogue VRL 3010	PETULA '65 (in French) 30
66	Pye-Vogue VRL 3016	HELLO PARIS VOL. 1 25
66	Pye-Vogue VRL 3019	HELLO PARIS VOL. 2 25
66	Pye-Vogue VRL 3022	PETULA '66 20
68	Warner Bros WF(S) 2550	FINIAN'S RAINBOW (soundtrack) 25
68	Pye-Vogue VRLS 3035	PETULA CLARK A PARIS 20

ROY CLARK

59	HMV POP 581	Please Mr. Mayor/Puddin' (78 rpm = £40) 130
63	Capitol CL 15288	In The Mood/Texas Twist 22
63	Capitol CL 15317	Tips Of My Fingers/Spooky Movies 20
69	Dot DOT 126	Yesterday When I Was Wrong/Just Another Man 5
69	Dot DOT 131	September Song/For All The Life Of Me 5
62	Capitol (S)T 1780	THE LIGHTNING FINGERS OF ROY CLARK (LP) 50

SANFORD CLARK

56	London HLD 8320	The Fool/Lonesome For A Letter (with Al Casey)
		(gold label print, later silver) (78 rpm = £20) 220/125
56	London HL 7014	The Fool/Lonesome For A Letter (with Al Casey) (export issue) 50
59	London HLW 8959	Run, Boy Run/New Kind Of Fool (triangular or round centre) 30/20
59	London HLW 8959	Run, Boy Run/New Kind Of Fool (78) 50
60	London HLW 9026	Son-Of-A-Gun/I Can't Help It (If I'm Still In Love With You) 22
60	London HLW 9095	Go On Home/Pledging My Love 22
68	Ember EMB S 250	Shades/Once Upon A Time 10
57	London RED 1105	PRESENTING SANFORD CLARK (EP) 90
60	London REW 1256	LOWDOWN BLUES (EP). 90
72	Ember CW 131	THEY CALL ME COUNTRY (LP) 15
	(see also Al Casey)	

TERRY CLARK

| 60s | Myrrh MYR 1071 | WELCOME (LP) . . . . 20 |

ALLAN CLARKE

72	RCA RCA 2244	You're Losing Me/A Coward By Name 8
78	Polydor 2058 979	I Don't Know When I'm Beat/The passenger 6
72	RCA SF 8283	MY REAL NAME IS 'AROLD (LP) 12
73	EMI EMA 752	HEADROOM (LP). 12
74	EMI EMC 3041	ALLAN CLARKE (LP) 12
76	EMI EMC 3130	I'VE GOT TIME (LP). 12
	(see also Hollies)	

ANNETTE CLARKE

| 73 | Techniques TE 925 | Just One Look/Sinner Man. . . . . 10 |

DAVE CLARKE

| 94 | Bush 1012 | Red 1 (of 3) (Protective Custody)/Zeno Xero (12", p/s, red vinyl) . . . . 15 |
| 94 | Bush 1015 | Red 2 (of 3) (Wisdom To The Wise)/Gonk (12", p/s, red vinyl). . . . . 12 |

ERIC CLARKE

| 78 | Baal BAL 89004 | LOVE THAT GROWS AND GROWS BAAL (LP) . . . . 60 |

JOHN COOPER CLARKE

79	Epic S EPC 12 7009	¡Gimmix!/I Married A Monster From Outer Space (Third Version)
		(p/s, triangular disc, orange vinyl) 5
79	Epic S EPC 7982	Splat/Twat/Sleepwalk (double-grooved A-side, p/s, with Epic inner sleeve) 5
78	Rabid TOSH 103	INNOCENTS (EP, orange p/s, green labels) 5
78	Rabid TOSH 103	INNOCENTS (EP, 2nd pressing, blue foldout p/s, blue labels) 5
78	CBS 83132	DISGUISE IN LOVE (LP) 25
80	Epic EPC 84083	SNAP, CRACKLE [&] BOP (LP, with 48-page book in sleeve pocket) 15

JOHNNY CLARKE

74	Explosion EX 2089	None Shall Escape The Judgement/Every Rasta Is A Star. 12
74	Pyramid PYR 7013	My Desire/Lemon Tree 6
74	Lord Koos KOOS42	Enter Int This Gate With Praise 8
74	Atra ATRA019	Everyday Wondering. 7
74	Cactus CTEP32	Jump Back Baby. 15
74	Harry J HJ6706	Move Out A Babylon. 10
74	Explosion EX2089	None Shall Escape The Judgement 12
75	Horse HOSS86	Move out Of Babylon 7
75	Horse HOSS100	Too Much War 7
75	Vulcan VUL 1001	I'm Gonna Put It On/KING TUBBY AND THE AGGROVATORS – Version 6
76	Virgin VS159	Crazy Baldhead. 8
77	Virgin VS173	Roots, Natty Roots, Natty Congo 8
78	Star PTP1009	Every Knee Shall Bow (With U Roy) (12") 25
79	Greensleeves GRED20	Jah Love Is With I/Bad Days Are Going (12") 50
80	Cha Cha CHAD17	Babylon/One Man Live (as J. Clark) (12"). 30
81	Chrysalis 122849	Babylon/Than You For The Many Things You've Done – Cassandra (12") 20
82	Black Joy DH822	Too Much War 12
83	Top Notch TOP005	Young Rebel (10") 15
89	Jah Shaka SHAKA 876	Rosie/Rosie Dub (12") 12
75	Attack ATLP 1015	ENTER INTO HIS GATES WITH PRAISE (LP) 25
75	Vulcan VULP 001	PUT IT ON (LP) 25
76	Virgin V2076	AUTHORISED VERSION (LP) 12
77	Justice JUSLP 001	GIRL I LOVE YOU (LP) 40
77	Paradise PDLP 001	DON'T STAY OUT LATE (LP) 25
78	Third World TWS 932	KING IN THE ARENA (LP). 40
82	Art and Craft ACDLP001	CAN'T GET ENOUGH 25
83	Ariwa ARI 007 LP	YARD STYLE (LP) 30

MINT VALUE £

KENNY CLARKE (with Francy Boland Big Band)
57	Columbia SEG 7830	KENNY CLARKE QT. (EP)..	20
63	London HA-K 8085	JAZZ IS UNIVERSAL (LP, with Francy Boland Big Band)...................	12

(see also Francey Boland)

LINDA CLARKE
67	Decca F 12709	Your Hurtin' Kinda Love/Send Me The Pillow You Dream On	10
68	Decca F 12787	Society's Child/Rain In My Heart.................................	20

LLOYD CLARKE
62	Blue Beat BB 99	Good Morning/Now I Know A Reason (with Smithie's Sextet)..............	12
62	Blue Beat BB 104	Fool's Day/You're A Cheat (with Reco's All Stars).....................	12
62	Island WI 007	Love You The Most/LLOYD ROBINSON: You Said You Loved Me.............	15
62	Island WI 045	Japanese Girl/He's Coming	15
63	Rio R 16	Love Me/Half As Much	15
64	Rio R 23	Stop Your Talking/A Penny..	15
64	Rio R 24	Fellow Jamaican/PATRICK & GEORGE: My Love	15
68	Island WI 3116	Summertime/VAL BENNETT: Soul Survivor...........................	25
68	Blue Cat BS 136	Young Love/UNTOUCHABLES: Wall Flower...........................	25
70	Escort ERT 849	Chicken Thief/STRANGER COLE: Tomorrow...........................	7
71	Black Swan BW 1405	Love You The Most/LOW BITES:Version	12

(see also Derrick & Lloyd, Theo Beckford, Soulettes, Delroy Wilson, Laurel Aitken, Sonny Burke, Uniques)

MICKEY CLARKE
66	HMV 1483	Help Me/For Me	20

TONY CLARKE
64	Pye International 7N 25251	Ain't Love Good, Ain't Love Proud/Coming Back Strong..................	20
65	Chess CRS 8011	The Entertainer/This Heart Of Mine.................................	30
69	Chess CRS 8091	The Entertainer/Ain't Love Good, Ain't Love Proud	15
74	Chess 6145 030	Landslide/The Entertainer	10

CLARK-HUTCHINSON
70	Decca Nova (S)DN-R 2	A = MH²(LP)	42
70	Deram SML 1076	RETRIBUTION (LP)	40
71	Deram SML 1090	GESTALT (LP)	40

(see also Sam Gopal, Vamp, Upp)

CLARK SISTERS
59	London HLD 8791	Chicago/Opus 1 (78 rpm = £8)......................................	10
58	London RE-D 1198	SING, SING, SING (EP)	10
58	London HA-D 2128	SING, SING, SING (LP)..	20
59	London HA-D 2177	THE CLARK SISTERS SWING AGAIN (LP, also stereo SAH-D 6025)	20/25

CLARO INTELECTO
02	Ai AI 003	PEACE OF MIND (12", first pressings in blue p/s)	15

CLASH
77	CBS S CBS 5058	White Riot/1977 (p/s, 'The Clash' or 'The CLASH' on label)...............	12
77	CBS CL 1	CAPITAL RADIO (EP, NME freebie, p/s)	80
77	CBS S CBS 5293	Remote Control/London's Burning (live) (p/s).........................	7
77	CBS Promo S CBS 5293	Remote Control/London's Burning (Studio Version) ('A' Label Promo)	50
77	CBS S CBS 5664	Complete Control/The City Of The Dead (p/s)	8
78	CBS S CBS 6383	(White Man) In Hammersmith Palais/The Prisoner (initially green, then pink, blue or yellow die-cut sleeve)...........................	7
79	CBS S CBS 7324	THE COST OF LIVING (EP, gatefold p/s & inner sleeve)..................	8
79	CBS S CBS 8087	London Calling/Armageddon Time (p/s, green or red shaded sleeve, white or yellow/orange label).....................................	6

(All the early Clash singles were re-pressed in 1979 with picture sleeves.)
81	CBS A12 1133	The Magnificent Seven/The Magnificent Dance (12", p/s)...............	10
81	CBS S 2309	Know Your Rights/First Night Back In London (p/s, with free sticker)	10
82	CBS A 2479	Rock The Casbah/Long Time Jerk (p/s, with free stickers)	10
82	CBS A 11 2479	Rock The Casbah/Long Time Jerk (picture disc)	10
82	CBS A 2646	Should I Stay Or Should I Go/Straight To Hell (p/s)....................	10
82	CBS A 11 2646	Should I Stay Or Should I Go/Straight To Hell (picture disc)...............	10
82	CBS A 12 2646	Should I Stay Or Should I Go/Straight To Hell (12")	12
88	CBS CLASHB 2	London Calling/Brand New Cadillac/Rudie Don't Fail (box set)	12
91	Columbia 656 667-5	Should I Stay Or Should I Go/London Calling/ Train In Vain/I Fought The Law (CD in tin)	10
91	Columbia 656 814-5	Rock The Casbah/Tommy Gun/(White Man) In Hammersmith Palais/ Straight To Hell (CD in tin)..	10
91	Columbia 656 946-5	London Calling/Clampdown/The Call Up/London's Burning (CD in tin)...........	8
78	CBS 82431	GIVE 'EM ENOUGH ROPE (LP, promo-only package with poster in folder).....	200

(see also 101'ers, Big Audio Dynamite, Janie Jones & Lash, Tymon Dogg, Ellen Foley, Futura 2000)

CLASSICS (Jamaica)
69	Doctor Bird DB 1190	Worried Over Me/LAUREL AITKEN: Rice And Peas	18
70	New Beat NB 061	Same Old Feeling/So Much Love	7
70	New Beat NB 071	History Of Africa/Honeybee	7
70	Pama PM 830	Sex Education/POWER: Soul Flash	10
71	Punch PH 79	Cheerio Baby/Civilization..	7

CLASSICS (U.S.)
61	Mercury AMT 1152	Life Is But A Dream/That's The Way	110
63	Stateside SS 215	Till Then/Enie Minie Mo	35
66	Capitol CL 15470	Pollyanna/Cry Baby	30

CLASSICS IV
68	Liberty LBF 15051	Spooky/Poor People..	12
69	Liberty LBF 15177	Stormy/Twenty Four Hours Of Loneliness............................	15

69	Liberty LBF 15196	Traces/Mary, Mary Row Your Boat	6
69	Liberty LBF 15231	Everyday With You Girl/Sentimental Lady	6
(see also Dennis Yost & Classics IV)			

CLASSMATES
63	Decca F 11736	Let's Get Together Tonight/It's No Game	5
63	Decca F 11779	Go Tell It On The Mountain/Give Me A Girl	5
64	Decca F 11806	In Morocco/I Feel	5
64	Decca F 12047	Go Away/Pay Day	10

CLAUDETTE (& CORPORATION)
69	Jackpot JP 712	Let's Fall In Love/PROPHETS: Purple Moon	30+
70	Grape GR 3020	Skinheads A Bash Them (with Corporation)/	
		CORPORATION: Walkin' Thru Jerusalem	75
(see also Corporation)			

CASSIUS CLAY
64	CBS AAG 190	Stand By Me/I Am The Greatest	40
66	CBS 202190	Stand By Me/I Am The Greatest (reissue)	20
63	CBS BPG 62274	I AM THE GREATEST! (LP)	50

JUDY CLAY
67	Stax 601 022	You Can't Run Away From Your Heart/It Takes A Lotta Good Love	15
(see also Billy Vera & Judy Clay, Booker T. & M.G.'s)			

JUDY CLAY & WILLIAM BELL
68	Stax STAX 101	Private Number/Love Eye 'Tis	12
69	Stax STAX 115	My Baby Specialises/Left Over Love	10
(see also William Bell, Billy Vera & Judy Clay)			

OTIS CLAY
67	President PT 121	It's Easier Said Than Done/Flame In Your Heart	10
68	President PT 132	I'm Satisfied/I Testify	10
68	President PT 148	That's How It Is/Show Place	20
68	President PT 176	A Lasting Love/Got To Find A Way	10
69	Atlantic 584 282	Baby Jane/You Hurt Me For The Last Time	75
72	London HLU 10397	Trying To Live My Life Without You/Let Me Be The One	10
74	London HLU 10467	You Did Something To Me/It Was Jealousy	10
73	London SH-U 8446	TRYING TO LIVE MY LIFE WITHOUT YOU (LP)	30

TOM CLAY
72	Tamla Motown TMG 801	What The World Needs Now/The Victors	10

CLAY FAV
79	own label	CONSIGNMENT STOCK (EP, 1,000, 200 with stamped "consignment Stock' sleeve, no p/s)	150/50

ALASDAIR CLAYRE
67	Elektra EUK 255	ALASDAIR CLAYRE (LP)	55
76	Acorn CF 252	ADAM AND THE BEASTS (LP)	25

ADAM CLAYTON & LARRY MULLEN
96	Mother MUM 75	Theme From Mission: Impossible/Theme From Mission: Impossible (Junior's Hard Mix Edit) (jukebox issue, no p/s, promo only)	10
96	Mother 12MUMDJ 75-1	THEME FROM MISSION: IMPOSSIBLE — REMIXES BY JUNIOR VASQUEZ (12", brown die-cut sleeve with title sticker, promo only)	18
96	Mother 12MUMDJ 75-2	THEME FROM MISSION: IMPOSSIBLE — REMIXES BY GOLDIE & ROB PLAYFORD (12", grey die-cut sleeve with title sticker, promo only)	18
96	Mother MUMCD 75DJ	Theme From Mission: Impossible/(Junior's Hard Mix Edit)/ (Junior's Hard Mix)/Mission Accomplished — Cut The Red Not The Blue/ (Dave Clarke's Remix)/(Guru Mix) (CD, digipak, promo only)	25
(see also U2)			

BUCK CLAYTON
57	Pye/Vanguard PPT 12006	BUCK MEETS RUBY (10" LP, with Ruby Braff)	15
(see also Humphrey Lyttelton, Jimmy Rushing)			

DOCTOR CLAYTON
65	RCA Victor RCX 7177	RCA RACE SERIES VOLUME 6 (EP)	20
70	RCA Intl. INTS 1176	PEARL HARBOUR BLUES (LP)	20

MERRY CLAYTON
70	A&M AMS 802	Gimme Shelter/Good Girls	15
73	Ode ODS 66301	Acid Queen/Underture (p/s)	15
70	A&M AMLS 995	GIMME SHELTER (LP)	15
72	A&M AMLS 67012	MERRY CLAYTON (LP)	15
(see also Raelets)			

PAUL CLAYTON
61	London HLU 9285	Wings Of A Dove/So Long (It's Been Good To Know You)	15
61	London REU 1276	PAUL CLAYTON (EP)	130

STEVE CLAYTON
56	Vogue Coral Q 72200	Two Different Worlds/It Happened Again	7
57	Vogue Coral Q 72253	The Boy With The Golden Kazoo/I Wanna Put My Arms Around You	7
60	London HLU 9033	Let's Tell Them Now/They Say In Time	7

VIKKI CLAYTON
88	Dambuster DAM 021	LOST LADY FOUND (LP)	20
(see also Fairport Convention)			

CLAYTON SQUARES
65	Decca F 12250	Come And Get It/And Tears Fell	40+
66	Decca F 12456	There She Is/Imagination	150+
(see also Liverpool Scene, Andy Roberts, Mike Hart)			

DAVID CLAYTON-THOMAS
72	CBS 64755	DAVID CLAYTON-THOMAS (LP, plain orange label)	15
72	CBS 65237	TEQUILA SUNRISE (LP, plain orange label)	15
73	RCA SF 8381	DAVID CLAYTON-THOMAS (LP, gatefold sleeve)	15

(see also Blood Sweat & Tears)

CLEAR BLUE SKY
70	Vertigo 6360 013	CLEAR BLUE SKY (LP, gatefold sleeve, swirl label)	125
90	Saturn SRLP 101	DESTINY (LP)	15

CLEAR LIGHT
67	Elektra EKSN 45019	Black Roses/She's Ready To Be Free	12
68	Elektra EKSN 45027	Night Sounds Loud/How Many Days Have Passed	20
67	Elektra EKL 4011	CLEAR LIGHT (LP, orange label, also stereo EKS 74011)	45

CLEARLIGHT
75	Virgin V 2029	SYMPHONY (LP, stickered sleeve)	18
75	Virgin V 2039	FOREVER BLOWING BUBBLES (LP)	18

(see also Gong, Steve Hillage)

CLEAR SPOT
98	Duophonic Super 45s	Psycho's Blues/Moonman Bop (33rpm, 300 copies on blue vinyl, 1700 on black, p/s)	8/6

(see also Stereolab)

CLEARWAYS
64	Columbia DB 7333	I'll Be Here/I've Just Got A Letter	10

JOHN CLEESE (& 1948 CHOIR)
67	Pye 7N 17336	The Ferret Song — From 'At Last The 1948 Show'/The Rhubarb Tart Song	10
67	Parlophone PMC 7024	I'M SORRY I'LL READ THAT AGAIN (LP)	20

(see also Monty Python)

CLEFS
62	Salvo SLO 1810	Don't Cry/The Dream Train Special (99 copies only)	22

CLEFTONES
56	Columbia DB 3801	You Baby, You/Little Girl Of Mine (78 rpm = £60)	550
61	Columbia DB 4678	Heart And Soul/How Do You Feel	175
61	Columbia DB 4720	(I Love You) For Sentimental Reasons/Deed I Do	120
63	Columbia DB 4988	Lover Come Back To Me/There She Goes	60

PAT CLEMENCE
64	HMV POP 1360	While I Live/Since I Don't Have You	5

JACK CLEMENT
58	London HLS 8691	Ten Years/Your Lover Boy (78 rpm = £50)	100

SOUL JOE CLEMENTS
69	Plexium PXM 10	Smoke And Ashes/Ever, Ever	200

CLEO
64	Decca F 11817	To Know Him Is To Love Him/ANDREW OLDHAM ORCHESTRA: There Are But Five Rolling Stones	40

(see also Andrew Oldham Orchestra, This 'N' That)

CLERKS
80	Rok ROK VIII/VII	No Good For Me/HAZARD: Gotta Change My Life (company sleeve)	6
84	Puddisc SRT8 KS 1538	Dancing With My Girl/On The Telephone/All I Want Is You (p/s)	5

CLEVELANDS
64	Philips BF 1315	Big Town/Lonely, Weary And Blue	7
64	Philips BF 1342	Little Girl In Calico/Everything Is Fine	7

CLIENTELLE
79	Quest BRS 003	Can't Forget (p/s)	125
81	Banana BANANA 505	DESTINATION UNKNOWN (LP)	120

JIMMY CLIFF
62	Blue Beat BB 78	I'm Sorry (with Cavaliers Combo)/BLUE BEATS: Roarin' (with Red Price)	30
62	Island WI 012	Hurricane Hatty/Dearest Beverley	18
62	Island WI 016	Miss Jamaica/Gold Digger	25
62	Island WI 025	Since Lately/I'm Free	25
63	Island WI 062	My Lucky Day/One-Eyed Jacks	25
63	Island WI 070	King Of Kings/SIR PERCY: Oh Yeah	25
63	Island WI 112	Miss Universe/The Prodigal	18
63	Black Swan WI 403	The Man/You Are Never Too Old	20
64	Stateside SS 342	One Eyed Jacks/King Of Kings	18
66	Fontana TF 641	Call On Me/Pride And Passion	12
67	Island WIP 6004	Aim And Ambition/Give And Take	10
67	Island WIP 6011	I Got A Feeling/Hard Road To Travel	10
67	Island WIP 6024	That's The Way Life Goes/Thank You	10
68	Island WIP 6039	Waterfall/Reward	30
69	Trojan TR 690	Wonderful World, Beautiful People/Hard Road To Travel (some in p/s)	7/5
70	Trojan TR 7722	Vietnam/She Does It Right	5
70	Trojan TR 7745	Suffering/Come Into My Life	5
70	Trojan TR 7745	Those Good Good Old Days/Pack Up Hang Ups	5
70	Trojan TR 7767	You Can Get It If You Really Want/Be Aware	5
70	Island WIP 6087	Wild World/Be Aware	5
70	Island WIP 6097	Synthetic World/I Go To Pieces	5

71	Island WIP 6103	Goodbye Yesterday/Breakdown	5
71	Island WIP 6100	Sitting In Limbo/The Bigger They Come	5
72	Island WIP 6132	Trapped/Struggling Man	5
68	Island ILP 962	HARD ROAD TO TRAVEL (LP)	50
69	Trojan TRLS 16	JIMMY CLIFF (LP)	20
71	Island ILPS 9159	ANOTHER CYCLE (LP)	12

(see also Jackie Edwards & Jimmy Cliff, James Chambers)

CLIFF & HANK
(see under Cliff Richard)

BUZZ CLIFFORD
61	Fontana H 297	Baby Sittin' Boogie/Driftwood	12
61	Fontana H 312	Three Little Fishes/Simply Because	10
62	Columbia DB 4903	More Dead Than Alive/Nobody Loves Me Like You	10
61	Fontana TFL 5147	BABY SITTIN' WITH BUZZ CLIFFORD (LP, also stereo [STFL 567])	55/65

JOHN & JULIA CLIFFORD
| 77 | Topic 12TS 311 | THE HUMOURS OF LISHEEN (LP) | 22 |

LINDA CLIFFORD
74	Paramount PARA 3051	After Loving You/Check Out Your Heart	8
78	Curtom K 17163	If My Friends Could See Me Now/Runaway Love	10
78	Curtom K 17163T	If My Friends Could See Me Now/Runaway Love (12")	12
79	RSO RSO 37	Don't Give It Up/Don't Let Me Have Another Bad Dream (12")	8

CLIFFTERS
| 62 | Philips PB 1242 | Django/Amapola (Pretty Little Poppy) | 10 |

BILL CLIFTON
60	Melodisc 1554	You Don't Think About Me/Mail Carrier's Warning	6
63	Decca F 11793	Beatle Crazy/Little Girl Dressed In Blue	6
58	Mercury MEP 9546	BILL CLIFTON AND THE DIXIE MOUNTAIN BOYS (EP)	12
62	London HA-B 8004	CARTER FAMILY MEMORIAL ALBUM (LP)	15
62	London HA-B 8020	THE BLUEGRASS SOUND OF BILL CLIFTON (LP)	15

BILL CLIFTON & JIM EANES
| 60s | Melodisc EPM 7102 | BLUE RIVER HOEDOWN (EP) | 10 |

CLIMAX (CHICAGO) BLUES BAND
69	Parlophone R 5809	Like Uncle Charlie/Loving Machine	20
70	Harvest HAR 5029	Reap What I've Sowed/Spoonful	6
71	Harvest HAR 5041	Towards The Sun/Everyday (as Climax Chicago)	6
69	Parlophone PMC/PCS 7069	CLIMAX CHICAGO BLUES BAND (LP, yellow/black label)	50
70	Parlophone PCS 7084	PLAYS ON (LP)	40
70	Harvest SHSP 4009	A LOT OF BOTTLE (LP)	25
71	Harvest SHSP 4015	TIGHTLY KNIT (LP)	25
72	Harvest SHSP 4024	RICH MAN (LP)	12

PATSY CLINE
57	Brunswick 05660	A Poor Man's Roses (Or A Rich Man's Gold)/Walkin' After Midnight (78 rpm = £25)	90
61	Brunswick 05855	I Fall To Pieces/Lovin' In Vain	15
61	Brunswick 05861	Crazy/Who Can I Count On	25
62	Brunswick 05866	She's Got You/Strange	10
62	Brunswick 05869	When I Get Through With You/Imagine That	10
62	Brunswick 05874	So Wrong/You're Stronger Than Me	10
62	Brunswick 05878	Heartaches/Why Can't He Be You	8
63	Brunswick 05883	Leavin' On Your Mind/Tra Le La Le La Triangle	10
63	Brunswick 05888	Sweet Dreams/Back In My Baby's Arms	15
63	Decca 31262	Blue Moon Of Kentucky/Faded Love (export)	40
62	Brunswick OE 9490	SWEET DREAMS (EP)	32
62	Brunswick LAT 8394	SHOWCASE (LP)	30
62	Brunswick LAT/STA 8510	SENTIMENTALLY YOURS (LP, mono/stereo)	28/30
63	Brunswick LAT 8549	A TRIBUTE TO PATSY CLINE (LP)	30
64	Brunswick LAT/STA 8589	A PORTRAIT OF PATSY CLINE (LP, mono/stereo)	28/30
65	Ember CW 16	IN MEMORIAM (LP)	15
65	Fontana FJL 302	TODAY TOMORROW AND FOREVER (LP)	20
66	Fontana FJL 309	I CAN'T FORGET YOU (LP)	20
68	Ember CW 134	WALKING AFTER MIDNIGHT (LP)	12
68	MCA MUP 316	THE SOUND OF PATSY CLINE (LP)	12
68	MCA MUP(S) 326	HEARTACHES (LP)	12

CLINIC
97	Aladdin's Cave Of Golf GOLF001	IPC Subeditors Dictate Our Youth/Porno/D.I.Y. (p/s, 500 copies only)	18
98	Aladdin's C.O.G. GOLF002	Monkey On Your Back/D.T. (p/s, 500 copies only)	6
98	Aladdin's C.O.G. GOLF003	Cement Mixer/Kimberley (p/s, 1,000 copies only)	5

BUDDY CLINTON
| 60 | Top Rank JAR 287 | Across The Street From Your House/How My Prayers Have Changed | 20 |

GEORGE CLINTON
| 79 | ABC ABC 4053 | Please Don't Run From Me/Life And Breath | 10 |

(do not see also Parliament, Funkadelic)

LARRY CLINTON
| 79 | Grapevine GRP 120 | She's Wanted In Three States/If I Knew | 20 |

CLINTONES
| 73 | Ackee ACK 515 | Equal Rights/Version | 6 |

CLIQUE (U.K.)
65	Pye 7N 15786	She Ain't No Good/Time Time Time	90
65	Pye 7N 15853	We Didn't Kiss, Didn't Love, But Now We Do/You've Been Unfair	150
60s	private pressing	THE CLIQUE (EP, no p/s)	550+

(see also Hammersmith Gorillas)

CLIQUE
93	Detour DR 006	THE EARLY DAYS EP (EP, purple, orange or blue p/s, 130 on green vinyl; rest on black, white or yellow vinyl	6/5
94	Detour DR 014	Reggie/She Doesn't Need You Anymore (p/s, red vinyl)	5
94	Detour DR 014	Reggie/She Doesn't Need You Anymore (pic disc, 200 only)	5

CLIQUE (U.S.)
| 69 | London HLU 10286 | Sugar On Sunday/Superman | 30 |

JIMMY CLITHEROE
| 65 | Parlophone R 5387 | They All Blame Jim/Jim Plays Hookies | 7 |

CLIVE & GLORIA
63	R&B JB 113	Change Of Plan/Little Gloria	18
64	R&B JB 173	Money Money Money/Have I Told You Lately	18
64	King KG 1004	Do The Ska/You Made Me Cry	20

CLIVE & NAOMI
| 65 | Ska Beat JB 181 | You Are Mine/Open The Door | 20 |

(see also Desmond Dekker)

CLOCK DVA
81	Fetish FET 008	Four Hours (Re-mixed)/Sensorium (p/s)	8
85	Fetish FET 008	FOUR HOURS EP (12", p/s)	8
80	private cassette	DEEP FLOOR (cassette)	12
80	private cassette	FRAGMENT DVATION (cassette)	12
81	Fetish FR 2002	THIRST (LP, with insert)	12
81	Industrial IRC 31	WHITE SOULS IN BLACK SUITS (cassette, with booklet)	15

CLOCKHOUSE
| 83 | Picturesque PIC 1 | Vanishing Point/Everyman (p/s) | 7 |

CLOCKWORK CRIMINALS
| 82 | Ace ACE 38 | YOUNG AND BOLD (EP) | 10 |

CLOCKWORK ORANGES
| 66 | Ember EMB S 227 | Ready Steady/After Tonight | 22 |

CLOCKWORK SOLDIERS
| 84 | Rot ASS 5 | Wet Dreams/Suicide/In The Name Of Science (p/s) | 5 |

BETTY CLOONEY
| 55 | HMV 7M 311 | I Love You A Mountain/Can't Do Without You | 15 |

(see also Rosemary Clooney)

ROSEMARY CLOONEY
50	Columbia DB 2708	Me And My Teddy Bear/I Found My Mama (78)	6
51	Columbia DB 2861	Shot Gun Boogie/Beautiful Brown Eyes (78)	6
51	Columbia DB 2892	Alice In Wonderland Medley (Parts 1 & 2) (78)	8
53	Columbia SCM 5019	Half As Much/Botch-A-Me (Ba-Ba-Baciami Piccina)	20
53	Columbia SCM 5027	If I Had A Penny/You're After My Own Heart	12
53	Columbia SCM 5028	On The First Warm Day/If Teardrops Were Pennies (78 rpm = £6)	15
53	Columbia SCM 5040	(Remember Me) I'm The One Who Loves You/Lover's Gold	15
53	Columbia SCM 5049	Blues In The Night/Who Kissed Me Last Night?	12
54	Columbia SCM 5093	I Still Feel The Same About You (with Betty Clooney)/Why Fight The Feeling	12
56	Philips JB 100	The Teddy Bear's Picnic/Kitty Kat's Party (78, picture label)	10
57	Philips PB 744	You Can't Lose The Blues With Colours/That's How It Is (78)	8
57	Philips JK 1010	Mangos/All The Pretty Little Horses (jukebox issue) (78 rpm = £7)	14
58	Philips PB 792	I Can't Stop Crying/Love And Affection (78)	8
58	Philips PB 800	I Could Have Danced All Night/I've Grown Accustomed To Your Face (78 = £8)	6
58	MGM MGM 990	The Loudenboomer Bird/It's A Boy (78 rpm = £8)	8
59	Philips PB 900	Tonight/Come Rain Or Come Shine (78 rpm = £12)	8
59	Coral Q 72357	Diga Me (Deega May-Tell Me)/A Touch Of The Blues (78 rpm = £12)	8
59	MGM MGM 1010	Love Eyes/Flattery (B-side with Jose Ferrer)	6
60	Coral Q 72388	Love, Love Away/I Wish I Were In Love Again	5
60	MGM MGM 1062	For You/I Wonder	5
60	RCA RCA 1203	Many A Wonderful Moment/Vaya, Vaya	5
54	Columbia SEG 7552	ROSEMARY CLOONEY AND HARRY JAMES (EP)	10
55	Philips BBE 12004	ROSEMARY CLOONEY (EP)	12
56	Philips BBE 12051	ROSEMARY CLOONEY (EP)	12
60	Coral FEP 2045	SWING AROUND ROSIE VOL. 1 (EP)	10
60	Coral FEP 2046	SWING AROUND ROSIE VOL. 2 (EP)	10
54	Philips BBR 8022	WHITE CHRISTMAS (10" LP)	25
55	Philips BBR 8047	ROSEMARY CLOONEY (10" LP)	25
56	Philips BBR 8073	AT THE LONDON PALLADIUM (10" LP)	25
56	Philips BBL 7090	HEY BABY (LP, with Duke Ellington)	18
57	Philips BBL 7156	RING AROUND ROSIE (LP, with Hi-Lo's)	18
57	Philips BBL 7191	CHILDREN'S FAVOURITES (LP)	18
59	Philips BBL 7301	SHOWCASE OF HITS (LP)	18
59	Coral LVA 9112	SWING AROUND ROSIE (LP)	18
61	RCA RD 27189	CLAP HANDS, HERE COMES ROSIE! (LP, also stereo SF 5075)	12
61	MGM C 838	SWINGS SOFTLY (LP)	12
63	Reprise R 6008	LOVE (LP)	12

(see also Bing Crosby)

MINT VALUE £

ROSEMARY CLOONEY & MARLENE DIETRICH
53	Columbia SCM 5010	Too Old To Cut The Mustard/Good For Nothin'	15

(see also Marlene Dietrich, Betty Clooney, Bob Hope & Rosemary Clooney, Guy Mitchell)

CLOSE LOBSTERS
89	Caff CAFF 4	Just Too Bloody Stupid/All The Little Boys And Girls (p/s)	8

CLOUD
75	Kingsway DOVE 16	FREE TO FLY (LP)	20
77	Kingsway DOVE 44	WATERED GARDEN (LP, gatefold sleeve)	30
70s	private pressing	THE RESTING PLACE (LP)	25
85	Songs Of Fellow. SFR103	THE PROMISE (LP)	15

CLAUDE CLOUD
55	MGM MGM 820	Cloudburst/One Bone (78, as Claude Cloud & Thunderclaps)	22
57	MGM MGM 946	The Beat/Around The Horn (as Claude Cloud & His Orchestra)	15
55	MGM MGM-EP 517	LET'S GO CATSTATIC NO. 1 (EP, as Claude Cloud & Thunderclaps)	45
56	MGM MGM-D 142	ROCK 'N' ROLL (10" LP)	120

(see also Sonny Thompson, Sam 'The Man' Taylor)

CLOUD NINE
90s	Acid Jazz JAZID 87P	I Feel It (12", p/s, promo-only, withdrawn)	20
90s	Acid Jazz JAZID 78	MILLENNIUM (LP, withdrawn)	35

CLOUDS
69	Island WIP 6055	Heritage/Make No Bones About It	15
69	Island WIP 6067	Scrapbook/Carpenter	15
69	Island ILPS 9100	THE CLOUDS SCRAPBOOK (LP, pink label or 'pink rim palm tree')	40
71	Chrysalis ILPS 9151	WATERCOLOUR DAYS (LP, gatefold sleeve, 'pink rim palm tree' label)	18

CLOUDS
86	Sha La La Ba Ba Ba 001	Throwaway/CLOUDS: Jenny Nowhere (p/s, flexi free with various fanzines)	8/6
88	Subway Org. SUBWAY 12	Tranquil/Get Out Of My Dream (p/s)	5
88	Subway Org. SUBWAY 12T	Tranquil/Get Out Of My Dream/Village Green (12", p/s)	8

(see also Boy Hairdressers, Teenage Fanclub)

CLOUT
90	Mooncrest JWL 1000	We'll Bring The House Down/Jim Jam (p/s)	7

(see also Slade)

CLOVEN HOOF
82	Elemental EM 001	OPENING RITUAL (12" EP)	80
84	Neat NEAT 1013	CLOVEN HOOF (LP)	15
86	Trojan CH 002	FIGHTING BACK (LP, some with poster)	15

CLOVER
70	Liberty LBF 15341	Wade In The Water/Stealin'	10
77	Vertigo LYN 4277	There Is No Substitute For Real Magic (flexidisc, promo only)	7
69	Liberty LBS 83340	CLOVER (LP)	25
71	Liberty LBS 83487	FORTY-NINER (LP)	25

(see also Huey Lewis & News)

CLOVERLEAFS
56	MGM MGM 933	Step Right Up And Say Howdy/With Plenty Of Money And You (Gold Digger's Lullaby)	8

(see also Art Mooney)

CLOVERS
56	London HLE 8229	Nip Sip/If I Could Be Loved By You (gold or silver label lettering)	900/400
56	London HLE 8229	Nip Sip/If I Could Be Loved By You (78)	45
56	London HLE 8314	Love, Love, Love/Hey, Doll Baby (78 rpm = £55)	600
56	London HLE 8334	From The Bottom Of My Heart/Your Tender Lips (78 rpm = £65)	650
58	London HL 7048	Wishing For Your Love/All About You (export issue) (78 rpm = £55)	250
58	HMV POP 542	In The Good Old Summertime/Idaho (78 rpm = £30)	40
59	London HLT 8949	Love Potion No. 9/Stay Awhile (triangular or round centre)	75/40
59	London HLT 8949	Love Potion No. 9/Stay Awhile (78)	50
60	London HLT 9122	Lovey/One Mint Julep	40
60	London HLT 9154	Easy Lovin'/I'm Confessin' (That I Love You)	45
61	HMV POP 883	Honey Dripper/Have Gun	25
68	Atlantic 584 160	Your Cash Ain't Nothin' But Trash/I've Got My Eyes On You	15
69	Atlantic 587 162	LOVE BUG (LP)	60

CLUES
81	Clues CLU 001	NO VACANCIES (EP)	10

CLUTHA (FOLK GROUP)
71	Argo ZFB 18	SCOTIA! (LP, as Clutha Folk Group)	15
74	Topic 12TS 242	SCOTS BALLADS, SONGS AND DANCE TUNES (LP, as Clutha)	12

JEREMY CLYDE
65	CBS 201823	I Love My Love/Anytime	5

(see also Chad & Jeremy)

CLYDE VALLEY STOMPERS
56	Beltona BL 2648	Uist Tramping Song/Keep Right On To The End Of The Road (78)	6
56	Beltona BL 2649	I Love A Lassie/Old Rustic Bridge By The Mill (78)	6
56	Beltona BL 2650	Old Time Religion/Pearly Gates (78)	6
57	Decca FJ 10897	Bill Bailey Won't You Please Come Home (with Mary McGowan)/Milenberg Joys (78 rpm = £6)	7
60	Pye NJL 23	HAVE TARTAN — WILL TRAD (LP)	20

(see also Ian Menzies)

C.M.J.
68	Impression IMP 102	I Can't Do It All By Myself/Nothing At All	45
71	Mother MOT 3	La La La/Step Around It	12
65	Impression EPIM 501	THE C.M.J. TRIO (EP)	80
69	Impression IMPL 1001	C.M.J. LIVE AT THE BANKHOUSE (LP, private pressing)	110

C.M.U. (Contemporary Music Unit)
72	Transatlantic BIG 508	Heart Of The Sun/Doctor Am I Normal?	10
71	Transatlantic TRA 237	OPEN SPACES (LP, gatefold sleeve)	55
72	Transatlantic TRA 259	SPACE CABARET (LP)	40

COACHMEN
59	Vogue V 9154	Those Brown Eyes/Bald Mountain (78 rpm = £10)	5
61	Vogue VAE 170149	HERE COME THE COACHMEN (EP)	8

COACHMEN
66	Columbia DB 8057	Gabrielle/Seasons In The Sun	8

COASTERS
57	London HLE 8450	Searchin'/Young Blood (78 rpm = £12)	80
57	London HL 7021	Searchin'/Young Blood (export issue)	35
58	London HLE 8665	Yakety Yak/Zing! Went The Strings Of My Heart (78 rpm = £18)	20
58	London HLE 8729	The Shadow Knows/Sorry But I'm Gonna Have To Pass (78 rpm = £30)	65
59	London HLE 8819	Charlie Brown/Three Cool Cats (78 rpm = £18)	15
59	London HL 7073	Charlie Brown/Three Cool Cats (export issue)	15
59	London HLE 8882	Along Came Jones/That Is Rock And Roll (silver top label) (78 rpm = £30)	20
59	London HLE 8938	Poison Ivy/I'm A Hog For You (78 rpm = £35+)	20

(The above 45s were originally issued with triangular centres, later round centre copies are worth half to two-thirds these values.)

60	London HLE 9020	What About Us/Run Red Run (78 rpm = £70)	20
60	London HLK 9111	Besame Mucho (Parts 1 & 2) (78 rpm = £80)	25
60	London HLK 9151	Wake Me, Shake Me/Stewball	20
60	London HLK 9208	Shoppin' For Clothes/The Snake And The Bookworm	30
61	London HLK 9293	Wait A Minute/Thumbin' A Ride	18
61	London HLK 9349	Little Egypt/Keep On Rolling	18
61	London HLK 9413	Girls! Girls! Girls! (Parts 1 & 2)	18
62	London HLK 9493	(Ain't That) Just Like Me/Bad Blood	18
64	London HLK 9863	T'Ain't Nothin' To Me/Speedo's Back In Town	18
66	Atlantic 584 033	She's A Yum Yum/Saturday Night Fish Fry	10
67	Atlantic 584 087	Searchin'/Yakety Yak	10
67	CBS 2749	Soul Pad/Down Home Girl	15
68	Direction 58-3701	She Can/Everybody's Woman	18
71	Parlophone R 5931	Love Potion No. 9/D.W. Washburn	20
72	Stateside SS 2201	Cool Jerk/Talkin' 'Bout A Woman	25
59	London REE 1203	THE COASTERS (EP)	60
60	London HA-E 2237	GREATEST HITS (LP)	100
63	London HA-K 8033	COASTIN' ALONG WITH THE COASTERS (LP)	100
66	Atlantic 588 134	COASTIN' ALONG WITH THE COASTERS (LP, reissue)	25
67	Atlantic 590 015	ALL TIME GREATEST HITS (LP)	20
71	Joy JOYS 189	HUNGRY (LP)	20
74	London SHZ 8460	ON BROADWAY (LP)	15

COAST ROAD DRIVE
74	Deram SML 1113	DELICIOUS AND REFRESHING (LP)	35

COAST TO COAST
82	Polydor POSP 451	The Bell/How Can I Be Sure	8

(see also Status Quo)

C.O.B. (Clive's Original Band)
72	Polydor 2058 260	Blue Morning/Bones	30
71	CBS 69010	SPIRIT OF LOVE (LP, gatefold sleeve)	70
72	Polydor Folk Mill 2383 161	MOYSHE McSTIFF & THE TARTAN LANCERS OF THE SACRED HEART (LP, gatefold sleeve)	250

(see also Famous Jug Band, Incredible String Band)

COBBLERS LAST
79	Banshee BAN 1012	BOOT IN THE DOOR (LP, with insert)	110

COBBS
69	Amalgamated AMG 845	Hot Buttered Corn/COUNT MACHUKI: It Is I	20
69	Amalgamated AMG 849	Space Doctor/LLOYD & DEVON: Baby Reggae	20

JUNIE COBB'S HOMETOWN BAND
59	Collector JDL 38	Chicago Buzz/East Coast Trot	10

BILLY COBHAM
73	Atlantic K 40406	SPECTRUM (LP, gatefold sleeve)	12
74	Atlantic K 50098	TOTAL ECLIPSE (LP)	12
74	Atlantic K 50037	CROSSWINDS (LP)	12
75	Atlantic K 50147	SHABAZZ (LP)	12
75	Atlantic K 50185	A FUNKY SIDE OF THINGS (LP)	12

COBRA
78	Rip Off RIP 3	Graveyard Boogie/Looking For A Lady (p/s)	30

(see also Speed)

COCHISE
70	United Artists UP 35134	Watch This Space/59th St. Bridge Song	6
70	Liberty LBS 15425	Love's Made A Fool Of You/Words Of A Dying Man	6
71	Liberty LBF 15460	Why I Sing The Blues/Jed Colider	6

70	United Artists UAS 29117	COCHISE (LP, gatefold sleeve)	20
70	Liberty LBS 83428	SWALLOW TALES (LP)	15
72	United Artists UAS 29286	SO FAR (LP)	15

(see also B.J. Cole, Mick Grabham)

DIB COCHRAN & EARWIGS
70	Bell BLL 1121	Oh Baby/Universal Love	700

(see also Marc Bolan, Tyrannosaurus Rex, Tony Visconti, Rick Wakeman)

EDDIE COCHRAN
78s
57	London HLU 8386	20 Flight Rock/Dark Lonely Street	80
57	London HLU 8433	Sittin' In The Balcony/Completely Sweet	110
58	London HLU 8702	Summertime Blues/Love Again	100
59	London HLU 8792	C'mon Everybody/Don't Ever Let Me Go	150
59	London HLU 8880	Teenage Heaven/I Remember	325
59	London HLU 8944	Somethin' Else/Boll Weevil Song	325
60	London HLW 9022	Hallelujah, I Love Her So/Little Angel	400
60	London HLG 9115	Three Steps To Heaven/Cut Across Shorty	550
95	Cruisin' The 50s CASS 001	Three Steps To Heaven/Cut Across Shorty (reissue, 300 only)	40
96	Cruisin' The 50s CASB 004	Week-End/Cherished Memories (reissue, 400 only)	30

SINGLES
57	London HLU 8386	20 Flight Rock/Dark Lonely Street (triangular centre; also silver-top label with triangular centre; later round centre)	200/50
57	London HLU 8433	Sittin' In The Balcony/Completely Sweet	400
58	London HLU 8702	Summertime Blues/Love Again	35
59	London HLU 8792	C'mon Everybody/Don't Ever Let Me Go	35
59	London HLU 8880	Teenage Heaven/I Remember	40
59	London HL 7082	Teenage Heaven/Boll Weevil Song (export issue)	80
59	London HLU 8944	Somethin' Else/Boll Weevil Song	55
60	London HLW 9022	Hallelujah, I Love Her So/Little Angel (triangular centre) (Later round centre = £25)	60

(The above singles were originally issued with triangular centres, later round centre copies are worth half these values unless stated.)

60	London HLG 9115	Three Steps To Heaven/Cut Across Shorty	20
60	London HLG 9196	Sweetie Pie/Lonely	40
61	London HLG 9362	Weekend/Cherished Memories	25
61	London HLG 9460	Jeannie, Jeannie, Jeannie/Pocketful Of Hearts	40
61	London HLG 9464	Pretty Girl/Teresa	45
61	London HLG 9467	Undying Love/Stockin's 'n' Shoes	50
62	Liberty LIB 10049	Never/Think Of Me	20
63	Liberty LIB 10088	My Way/Rock And Roll Blues	18
63	Liberty LIB 10108	Drive-In Show/I Almost Lost My Mind	18
64	Liberty LIB 10151	Skinny Jim/Nervous Breakdown	60
66	Liberty LIB 10233	C'mon Everybody/Summertime Blues	20
66	Liberty LIB 10249	Three Stars/Somethin' Else	60
67	Liberty LIB 10276	Three Steps To Heaven/Eddie's Blues	50
68	Liberty LBF 15071	Summertime Blues/Let's Get Together	20
68	Liberty LBF 15109	Somethin' Else/Milk Cow Blues	20
70	Liberty LBF 15366	C'mon Everybody/Mean When I'm Mad	20

EPs
59	London REU 1214	C'MON EVERYBODY (orange sleeve, triangular or round centre)	125/75
59	London REU 1214	C'MON EVERYBODY (yellow sleeve, silver-top label, round centre)	125
60	London REU 1239	SOMETHIN' ELSE (triangular or round centre)	125/90
60	London REG 1262	EDDIE'S HITS	90
61	London REG 1301	CHERISHED MEMORIES OF EDDIE COCHRAN	90
62	Liberty LEP 2052	NEVER TO BE FORGOTTEN	50
63	Liberty LEP 2090	CHERISHED MEMORIES (VOL.1)	50
63	Liberty LEP 2111	C'MON EVERYBODY (reissue)	30
63	Liberty LEP 2122	SOMETHIN' ELSE (reissue)	30
63	Liberty LEP 2123	CHERISHED MEMORIES OF EDDIE COCHRAN (reissue)	40
63	Liberty LEP 2124	EDDIE'S HITS (reissue)	40
64	Liberty LEP 2165	C'MON AGAIN	50
64	Liberty LEP 2180	STOCKIN'S 'N' SHOES	50

LPs
58	London HA-U 2093	SINGIN' TO MY BABY (initially with laminated rear sleeve)	250/200
60	London HA-G 2267	THE EDDIE COCHRAN MEMORIAL ALBUM	100
62	Liberty LBY 1109	CHERISHED MEMORIES	55
63	Liberty LBY 1127	THE EDDIE COCHRAN MEMORIAL ALBUM (reissue)	40
63	Liberty LBY 1158	SINGIN' TO MY BABY (reissue)	50
64	Liberty LBY 1205	MY WAY	70
68	Liberty LBL/LBS 83009	THE EDDIE COCHRAN MEMORIAL ALBUM (2nd reissue)	15
68	Liberty LBL/LBS 83072E	CHERISHED MEMORIES (reissue)	15
68	Liberty LBL 83104	MY WAY (reissue in different sleeve)	15
68	Liberty LBL/LBS 83152	SINGIN' TO MY BABY (2nd reissue in different sleeve)	15
70	Liberty LBS 83337	THE VERY BEST OF EDDIE COCHRAN	15
80	United Artists UP ECSP 20	20TH ANNIVERSARY ALBUM (4-LP, box set)	30
88	Liberty ECB 1	THE EDDIE COCHRAN BOX SET (6-LP box set with booklet)	25

HANK COCHRAN
68	Monument LMO 5020	HEART OF HANK (LP)	15

JACKIE LEE COCHRAN
57	Brunswick 05669	Ruby Pearl (with Jimmy Pruett)/Mama Don't You Think I Know	2,500
57	Brunswick 05669	Ruby Pearl (with Jimmy Pruett)/Mama Don't You Think I Know (78)	200

COCK & WOODPECKERS
71	Newbeat 93	Every Day And Every Night/I Fall In Love Everyday	15

BRUCE COCKBURN
71	True North WTN 003	HIGH WINDS WHITE SKY (LP)	15
71	True North TNX 7	SUNWHEEL DANCE (LP)	15

COCKERAL CHORUS
72	Young Blood YB 1017	Nice One Cyril/Cyril Marches On	5
73	Young Blood YB 107	NICE ONE CYRIL (LP)	20

JOE COCKER
64	Decca F 11974	I'll Cry Instead/Precious Words	75
68	Regal Zonophone RZ 3006	Marjorine/New Age Of The Lily	10
68	Regal Zonophone RZ 3013	With A Little Help From My Friends/Something's Coming On	6
69	Regal Zonophone RZ 3024	Delta Lady/She's So Good To Me	6
70	Regal Zonophone RZ 3027	The Letter/Space Captain	6
70	Fly BUG 3	Cry Me A River/Give Peace A Chance (p/s)	6
71	Fly BUG 9	High Time We Went/Black-Eyed Blues	6
72	Magni Fly ECHO 103	With A Little Help From My Friends/Delta Lady/The Letter (p/s)	6
72	Cube BUG 25	Woman To Woman/Midnight Rider (with Chris Stanton Band)	5
83	Island WIP 6818	Ruby Lee/Talking Back To The Night (export issue)	7
60s	Oak	JOE COCKER (EP, existence unconfirmed)	500+
67	Action ACT 002 EP	RAG GOES MAD AT THE MOJO (33rpm EP, 2 tracks by Joe Cocker's Blues Band, in conjunction with Sheffield University rag magazine *Twikker*)	70
69	Regal Zono. SLRZ 1006	WITH A LITTLE HELP FROM MY FRIENDS (LP)	30
69	Regal Zono. SLRZ 1011	JOE COCKER! (LP)	25
71	Fly HIFLY 3	COCKER HAPPY (LP)	12
74	Fly HIFLY 18	I CAN STAND A LITTLE RAIN (LP)	12

(see also Grease Band, Made In Sheffield)

COCKNEY REBEL
(see under Steve Harley/Cockney Rebel)

COCKNEY REJECTS
79	Small Wonder SW 19	Flares'N'Slippers/Police Star/I Wanna Be A Star (p/s)	8
79	EMI EMI 5008	I'm Not A Fool/East End (p/s)	6
80	EMI EMI 5035	Bad Man!/The New Song (p/s)	6
80	Zonophone Z 2	The Greatest Cockney Rip-Off/Hate Of The City (p/s, yellow vinyl)	7
80	Zonophone Z 4	I'm Forever Blowing Bubbles/West Side Boys (p/s)	8
80	Zonophone Z 6	We Can Do Anything/15 Nights (p/s)	6
80	Zonophone Z 10	We Are The Firm/War On The Terraces (p/s)	8
81	Zonophone Z 20	Easy Life/Motorhead/Hang 'Em High (p/s)	5
80	Zonophone ZONO 101	GREATEST HITS VOLUME 1 (LP)	18
80	Zonophone ZONO 102	GREATEST HITS VOLUME 2 (LP, with inner sleeve & poster)	15
81	Zonophone ZEM 101	GREATEST HITS VOLUME 3 (LIVE AND LOUD) (LP)	15

COCKNEYS
64	Philips BF 1303	After Tomorrow/I'll Cry Each Night	15
64	Philips BF 1338	After Tomorrow/I'll Cry Each Night (reissue)	15
64	Philips BF 1360	I Know You're Gonna Be Mine/Oh No You Won't	15

COCK SPARRER
77	Decca FR 13710	Runnin' Riot/Sister Suzie (no p/s; demos in p/s £100)	20
77	Decca FR 13732	We Love You/Chip On My Shoulder (no p/s)	20
77	Decca LFR 13732	We Love You/Chip On My Shoulder (12" p/s, with photo insert, 7,500 only)	25
82	Carrere CAR 255	England Belongs To Me/Argy Bargy (p/s)	25
83	Razor RAZ 9	SHOCK TROOPS (LP)	20
84	Syndicate SYNLP 7	RUNNIN' RIOT IN 84	15
86	Razor RAZ 26	TRUE GRIT (LP)	12

(see also Little Roosters, Guttersnipes)

COCKTAIL CABINET
67	Page One POF 046	Puppet On A String/Breathalyser	15

COCTEAU TWINS
83	4AD AD 303	Peppermint Pig/Laugh Lines (p/s)	12
84	4AD AD 314	Sugar Hiccup (1-sided, promo only)	15
88	4AD CAD 807	BLUE BELL KNOLL (LP, tri-foldout sleeve)	12

(see also This Mortal Coil, Felt)

C.O.D.s
66	Stateside SS 489	Michael (The Lover)/Cry No More (DJ copy = £60)	30

JAMIE COE
59	Parlophone R 4600	Summertime Symphony/There's Gonna Be A Day	150
60	Parlophone R 4621	School Day Blues/I'll Go On Loving You	100
61	HMV POP 991	How Low Is Low/Little Dear Little Darling	20
63	London HLX 9713	The Fool/I've Got That Feeling Again	20

PETER & CHRIS COE
72	Trailer LER 2077	OPEN THE DOOR AND LET US IN (LP)	25
76	Trailer LER 2098	OUT OF SEASON, OUT OF RHYME (LP)	20
79	Highway SHY 7007	GAME OF ALL FOURS (LP)	15

(see also Bandoggs)

TONY COE (QUINTET)
61	Philips B 10784L	SWINGIN' TILL THE GIRLS COME HOME (LP)	50
67	Columbia SCX 6170	TONY'S BASEMENT (LP)	70

TONY COE & BRIAN LEMON TRIO
68	'77' SEU 12/41	TONY COE AND BRIAN LEMON TRIO (LP)	30

(see also Robert Farnon & Tony Coe)

Jack & Charlie COEN

MINT VALUE £

JACK & CHARLIE COEN
77	Topic 12TS 337	THE BRANCH LINE (LP)	22

COFFEE BAR SKIFFLERS
58	Embassy WEP 1008	SKIFFLE SESSION (EP)	10

(see also Chas McDevitt Skiffle Group)

DENNIS COFFEY
72	A&M AMS 7010	Getting It On/Ride Sally Ride	8
70	A&M AMLS 68035	EVOLUTION (LP)	18
71	A&M AMLS 68072	GOIN' FOR MYSELF (LP)	18
74	Sussex LPSX 9	INSTANT COFFEY (LP)	15

ALMA COGAN
53	HMV 7M 166	Over And Over Again/Isn't Life Wonderful (with Les Howerd)	35
53	HMV 7M 106	I Went To Your Wedding/You Belong To Me	40
53	HMV 7M 107	To Be Loved By You/The Homing Waltz (B-side with Larry Day)	40
54	HMV 7M 173	Ricochet (Rick-O-Shay)/The Moon Is Blue	40
54	HMV 7M 188	Bell Bottom Blues/Love Me Again	60
54	HMV 7M 196	Make Love To Me/Said The Little Moment	35
54	HMV 7M 219	The Little Shoemaker/Chiqui-Chaqui (Chick-ee Chock-ee)	40
54	HMV 7M 228	Little Things Mean A Lot/Canoodlin' Rag	45
54	HMV 7M 239	Skinnie Minnie (Fishtail)/What Am I Going To Do, Ma (The Doo-Ma Song)	75
54	HMV 7M 269	This Ole House/Skokiaan	45
54	HMV 7M 271	I Can't Tell A Waltz From A Tango/Christmas Cards	35
55	HMV 7M 286	Paper Kisses/Softly, Softly	35
55	HMV 7M 293	Chee-Chee-Oo-Chee (Sang The Little Bird)/Tika Tika Tok	35
55	HMV 7M 301	Tweedlee-Dee/More Than Ever Now	35
55	HMV 7M 316	Got'n Idea/Give A Fool A Chance	35
55	HMV 7M 337	Never Do A Tango With An Eskimo/Twenty Tiny Fingers	40
56	HMV 7M 367	Love And Marriage/Sycamore Tree	35
56	HMV 7M 415	Why Do Fools Fall In Love?/(The Same Thing Happen With) The Birds And The Bees?	50
56	HMV POP 239	Mama Teach Me To Dance/I'm In Love Again	30
56	HMV POP 261	In The Middle Of The House/Two Innocent Hearts	30
57	HMV POP 284	You, Me And Us/Three Brothers	30
57	HMV POP 317	Whatever Lola Wants (Lola Gets)/Lucky Lips	40
57	HMV POP 336	Chantez, Chantez/Funny, Funny, Funny	25
57	HMV POP 367	Fabulous/Summer Love	30
57	HMV POP 392	That's Happiness/What You've Done To Me	20
57	HMV POP 415	Party Time/Please Mister Brown (Mister Jones, Mister Smith)	20
58	HMV POP 433	The Story Of My Life/Love Is	15
58	HMV POP 450	Sugartime/Gettin' Ready For Freddy	15
58	HMV POP 482	Stairway Of Love/Comes Love	15
58	HMV POP 500	Sorry, Sorry, Sorry/Fly Away Lovers	15
58	HMV POP 531	There's Never Been A Night/If This Isn't Love (78 rpm = £6)	15
59	HMV POP 573	Last Night On The Back Porch/Mama Says (78 rpm = £8)	15
59	HMV POP 608	Pink Shoelaces/The Universe	15
59	HMV POP 670	We Got Love/I Don't Mind Being All Alone (78 rpm = £18)	10
60	HMV POP 728	O Dio Mio/Dream Talk	10
60	HMV POP 760	The Train Of Love/The 'I Love You' Bit	15
60	HMV POP 815	Must Be Santa/Just Couldn't Resist Her With Her Pocket Transistor	10
61	Columbia DB 4607	Cowboy Jimmy Joe/Don't Read This Letter	7
61	Columbia DB 4679	With You In Mind/Ja-Da	7
61	Columbia DB 4749	All Alone/Keep Me In Your Heart	7
62	Columbia DB 4794	She's Got You/In The Shade Of The Old Apple Tree	7
62	Columbia DB 4912	Goodbye Joe/I Can't Give You Anything But Love	7
63	Columbia DB 4965	Tell Him/Fly Me To The Moon (Bossa Nova)	7
63	Columbia DB 7059	Hold Out Your Hand You Naughty Boy/Just Once More	7
64	Columbia DB 7233	The Tennessee Waltz/I Love You Too Much	7
64	Columbia DB 7390	It's You/I Knew Right Away	7
65	Columbia DB 7652	Snakes And Snails (And Puppy Dog Tails)/How Many Days, How Many Nights	15
65	Columbia DB 7786	Eight Days A Week/Help!	7
66	Columbia DB 8088	Now That I've Found You/More	7
55	HMV 7EG 8122	THE GIRL WITH A LAUGH IN HER VOICE (EP)	25
55	HMV 7EG 8151	THE GIRL WITH A LAUGH IN HER VOICE NO. 2 (EP)	25
56	HMV 7EG 8169	THE GIRL WITH A LAUGH IN HER VOICE NO. 3 (EP)	25
57	HMV 7EG 8437	SHE LOVES TO SING (EP)	35
58	HMV CLP 1152	I LOVE TO SING (LP)	60
61	HMV CLP 1459	OLIVER! (LP, with others, also stereo CSD 1370)	40/50
61	Columbia 33SX 1345	ALMA SINGS WITH YOU IN MIND (LP, also stereo SCX 3391)	60/70
62	Columbia 33SX 1469	HOW ABOUT LOVE! (LP, also stereo SCX 3459)	60/70
67	Columbia SX 6130	ALMA (LP)	40

(see also Ronnie Hilton, Angela & Fans)

ALMA COGAN & RONNIE HILTON
57	HMV 7EG 8352	THE HITS FROM 'MY FAIR LADY' (EP, 1 side each)	10

(see also Ronnie Hilton)

ALMA COGAN & FRANKIE VAUGHAN
54	HMV 7M 226	Do, Do, Do, Do, Do, Do, Do It Again/Jilted (78 rpm, HMV B 10712 = £7)	22

(see also Frankie Vaughan)

DON COGAN
58	MGM MGM 984	The Fountain Of Love/I'm Takin' Over (78 rpm = £6)	25

SHAYE COGAN
58	Columbia DB 4055	Billy Be Sure/Doodle Doodle Doo	15
60	MGM MGM 1063	Mean To Me/They Said It Couldn't Be Done	75

(see also Buddy Morrow)

ALAN COHEN BAND
72	Argo ZDA 159	BLACK, BROWN AND BEIGE (LP)	65

LEONARD COHEN
68	CBS 3337	Suzanne/So Long, Marianne	7
69	CBS 4245	Bird On The Wire/Seems So Long Ago, Nancy	8
71	CBS 7292	Joan Of Arc/Diamonds In The Mine	7
74	CBS 2494	Bird On The Wire (live)/Tonight Will Be Fine (live)	7
74	CBS 2699	Lover Lover Lover/Who By Fire	6
76	CBS 4306	Suzanne/Take This Longing	6
77	CBS 5882	Memories/Don't Go Home With Your Hard-On	6
78	CBS 6095	True Love Leaves No Traces/I Left A Woman Waiting	6
72	CBS EP 9162	McCABE AND MRS MILLER (EP, p/s)	10
68	CBS (S)BPG 63241	SONGS OF LEONARD COHEN (LP, orange label, some with stickered sleeve; mono/stereo)	20/15
68	CBS 63241	SONGS OF LEONARD COHEN (LP, orange label, re-pressing w/out prefix)	15/12

COIL
79	North'ton Wood H. HAV 1	Motor Industry/Alcoholic Stork (p/s)	15

COIL
85	F & F/K.422 FFK 512	Panic/Tainted Love/Aqua Regis (12", red or black vinyl, 'hair'-textured p/s)	18/12
86	Force & Form/K.422 ROTA 121	The Anal Staircase/Blood From The Air/Ravenous (12", p/s, some on clear vinyl)	18/12
87	Solar Lodge 001	HELLRAISER (10" EP, coloured vinyl [clear or pink, 500 each], or black)	20/7
90	Shock SX 002	Wrong Eye/Scope (pink p/s, signed & lettered A-Z, 26 only)	25
90	Shock SX 002	Wrong Eye/Scope (974 w/ no'd white p/s; or 1,000 w/ unno'd yellow p/s)	12/10
90	Shock SX 002	Wrong Eye/Scope (green p/s, 300 only, some with gold/black sticker)	20
92	Clawfist 22	Airborne Bells/Is Suicide A Solution (p/s, 1,250 only)	20
94	Loci S1	Themes From Blue (p/s, 23 on yellow vinyl, 1,000 on blue vinyl)	50/20
94	Eskaton 001	Nasa Arab/First Dark Ride (12", stickered plain black sleeve, 2,500 only)	15
95	Eskaton 003	PHILM (10" EP, with poster, 2,000 only, 50 on clear vinyl in handmade p/s)	45/12
86	Threshold ROTA 1	HORSE ROTORVATOR (LP, with A5 card insert & stickers)	15
87	Threshold House LOCI 1	GOLD IS THE METAL (LP, red vinyl; with bonus 7": The Wheel/The Wheal, unfinished proof sleeve without writing, 25 only)	150
87	Threshold House LOCI 1	GOLD IS THE METAL (LP, red [150 only] or clear vinyl [500 only], with inner sleeve; with bonus 7": The Wheel/The Wheal)	40/25
87	Threshold House LOCI 1	GOLD IS THE METAL (LP, box set with 7", The Wheel/The Wheal, poster & booklet in black linen folder, embossed sleeve, autographed, 55 only)	300
87	Threshold House LOCI CD1	GOLD IS THE METAL (CD, 1,000 only)	15
90	Normal NORMAL 77	GOLD IS THE METAL (LP, black vinyl re-pressing with 7": The Wheel/Keel Hauler)	18
93	Loci CD 4b	STOLEN AND CONTAMINATED SONGS (CD, 1st edit with different artwork)	20
90s	Loci CD 6	ANGELIC CONVERSATION (CD, gold disc, 1,000 only)	18
95	Eskaton 007	WORSHIP THE GLITCH (2 x 10" LP, as Coil Vs. Elph, with insert, 2,000 only, 50 with white optical plastic cover)	45/20
95	Eskaton 006	WORSHIP THE GLITCH (CD, as Coil Vs. Elph, 500 only in black optical plastic)	20
99	Acme/Prescription DRUG8	ASTRAL DISASTER (LP, 99 copies signed and numbered by Balance and Christopherson, with insert, artwork in plastic bag)	50
99	Chalice GRAAL LP002	MUSICK TO PLAY IN THE DARK VOL 1 (LP, 500 only, white vinyl)	20
00	Threshold House LOC114	ASTRAL DISASTER (LP re-issue, 100 copies, grey vinyl signed lyricsheet and artwork)	30
00	Chalice GRAAL LP004	MUSICK TO PLAY IN THE DARK VOL 2 (2 x LP, white vinyl, one side etched)	25
00	Chalice GRAAL LP004	MUSICK TO PLAY IN THE DARK VOL 2 (2 x LP, 100 copies with blue/green vinyl)	30
00	Chalice GRAAL LP004	MUSICK VOL 2 (26 copy 'trauma edition' lettered A-Z white sleeves smeared with Balance's blood)	50
02	Eskaton 28	TIME MACHINES (Coil as Time Machines) (2 x LP, 1,000 only/55 copies, clear vinyl, signed)	18/25

(see also Psychic TV, Throbbing Gristle, Current 93, Thighpaulsandra)

COINS
69	Toast TT 513	Love Power/You Can't Get Away From It	6
69	Toast TT 515	Don't You Know It's Just A Game, Love? (actually by Miss White & Mr. Green)/Crying Over You	6

ALVADEAN COKER
55	London HLU 8191	Do Dee Oodle De Do I'm In Love/We're Gonna Bop (78 rpm = £50)	400

SANDY COKER & HIS BAND
54	London HL 8109	Meadowlark Melody/Toss Over (78 rpm = £8)	80

RIC COLBECK QUARTET
70	Fontana 6383 001	THE SUN IS COMING UP (LP)	30

COLD BLOOD
70	Atlantic 584 319	You Got Me Hummin'/If You Will	8
70	Atlantic 588 218	COLD BLOOD (LP, plum/red label)	18
71	Atlantic 2400 102	SISYPHUS (LP, gatefold sleeve, plum/red label)	18
74	Warner Bros K 56047	LYDIA (LP)	15

COLDCUT
	Ahead Of Our Time AHED1201	Beats & Pieces (12")	60
	Ahead Of Our Time AHED1201	Beats & Pieces (Mo Bass Remix) (12")	30
88	Urban URBX17DJ	Coldcut Meets The Godfather (12")	10

COLDCUT Feat. QUEEN LATIFAH
89	Big Life CCUT8T	Find A Way/Ride The Pleasure (12")	8

BEN COLDER
64 MGM MGM-EP 791 MAKE THE WORLD GO BY (EP) 15
(see also Sheb Wooley)

COLDPLAY
98	private pressing HGCD 633	SAFETY EP: Bigger, Stronger/No More Keeping My Feet On The Ground/ Such A Rush (CD, 500 only)	500
99	Fierce Panda NING 68	Brothers And Sisters/Easy To Please (wraparound p/s, 1000 only)	40
99	Fierce Panda NING 68CD	Brothers And Sisters/Easy To Please/Only Superstition	10
99	EMI EMI CDR 6528	THE BLUE ROOM EP (Bigger, Stronger/Don't Panic/See You Soon/High Speed/ Such A Rush) (CD, digipak)	20
99	EMI EMI 12R 6528	THE BLUE ROOM EP (Bigger, Stronger/Don't Panic/See You Soon/High Speed/ Such A Rush) (12")	20
00	Parlophone R 6536	Shiver/For You/Careful Where You Stand (p/s)	10
00	Parlophone R 6536	Shiver/For You/Careful Where You Stand (CD, digipak)	10
00	Parlophone R 6538	Yellow/Help Is Around The Corner (7" ltd edn. Numbered single p/s)	10
00	Parlophone TCR 6538	Yellow/Help Is Around The Corner (Cassette single p/s)	8
00	Parlophone R 6549	Trouble/Brothers And Sisters (p/s, numbered, stickered poly outer)	10
00	Parlophone TCR 6549	Trouble/Brothers And Sisters (Cassette single)	8
01	COLDXMAS01	Have Yourself A Merry Little Christmas/Yellow (Alpha Mix) (CD EP, 1000 only, given away with *Coldplayground* fanzine)	75
02	Parlophone R 6588	The Scientist/1:36/I Ran Away (p/s)	6
03	Parlophone R 6594	Clocks/Crest Of Waves (p/s)	5
03	Parlophone 12 R 6594	Clocks (Royksopp Trembling Heart Mix)/Roykdopp Trembling Heart InstrumentalMix/God Put A Smile Upon Your Face (Def Inc. Remix feat. Mr. Thing) (12", die-cut sleeve, 1000 only in UK)	25
00	Parlophone 5277831	PARACHUTES (LP)	15
02	Parlophone 540 5041	A RUSH OF BLOOD TO THE HEAD (LP, gatefold sleeve, with inner)	15
05	Parlophone 474 7861	X&Y (LP, gatefold sleeve with slip case and poster)	15
05	Parlophone 474 7862	X&Y (CD, with carrier bag, T shirt, key ring and wrist band)	20

PROMOS
98	None	Ode To Deodorant/Brothers And Sisters (2-track cassette sent to concert promoters and radio DJ's. White label, attributed to The Coldplay with "contact Phil" and 0777 mobile no)	400
99	Parlophone CDRDJ 6528	THE BLUE ROOM EP (Bigger, Stronger/Don't Panic/See You Soon/ High Speed/Such A Rush) (CD digipak)	30
99	Parlophone 12RDJ 6528	THE BLUE ROOM EP (Bigger, Stronger/Don't Panic/See You Soon/ High Speed/Such A Rush) (12")	25
00	EMI EMISAMP/13	You're Keeping Me Up All Night (EMI CD sampler with alternative version of Spies)	20
00	Parlophone CDRDJ 6538	Yellow/Help Is Round The Corner/No More Keeping My Feet On The Ground (CD)	10
00	Parlophone 12RDJ 6538	Yellow/Help Is Round The Corner/No More Keeping My Feet On The Ground (12")	15
00	Parlophone CDRDJ 6549	Trouble (1-track CD)	8
00	Parlophone 12RDJ 6549	Trouble/Brothers & Sisters/Shiver (12")	10
01	Parlophone PANIC01	Don't Panic (CD)	8
02	Parlophone CDRJX	The Scientist (Edit)/1.36/I Ran Away (CD)	8
00	Parlophone CHUTE001	PARACHUTES (CD, blue card sleeve)	20
02	Parlophone COLDADJ001	A RUSH OF BLOOD TO THE HEAD (CD, numbered and sealed card sleeve)	15
02	Parlophone COLDINT001	A RUSH OF BLOOD TO THE HEAD (CD interview disc)	15
03	Parlophone CPLIVE	LIVE (2xCD)	30
05	Parlophone COLDINT2	X&Y (CD interview disc)	15

B.J. COLE
73 United Artists UAS 29418 NEW HOVERING DOG (LP) 15
(see also Cochise)

BOBBY COLE
68 CBS 3626 Mister Bo Jangles/Bus 22 To Jerusalem 5

CINDY COLE
65 Columbia DB 7519 A Love Like Yours/He's Sure The Boy I Love 20
66 Columbia DB 7973 Just Being Your Baby (Turns Me On)/Lonely City Blue Boy 30
(see also Jeannie & Big Guys)

CLAY COLE
62 London HLP 9499 Twist Around The Clock/Don't Twist 10

COZY COLE
58	London HL 8750	Topsy (Parts 1 & 2) (78 rpm = £6)	10
58	London HL 7065	Topsy (Parts 1 & 2) (export issue)	10
59	Mercury AMT 1015	St. Louis Blues/Father Co-operates (78 rpm = £8)	10
59	London HL 8843	Turvy (Parts 1 & 2) (78 rpm = £9)	10
62	Coral Q 72457	Big Noise From Winnetka (Parts 1 & 2)	10
57	MGM MGM-EP 622	COZY COLE ALL STARS (EP)	15

DON COLE & ALLEYNE
65 Fontana TF 522 Gotta Find My Baby/Something's Gotta Hold Of Me 5

JERRY COLE
65 Capitol CL 15397 Every Window In The City/Come On Over To My Place 20

KEITH COLE
71 Big BG 315 Musical Attack/RUPIE EDWARDS ALLSTARS: Shack Attack 8
71 Big BG 316 Music Alone Version 3/RUPIE EDWARDS ALLSTARS: Behold Another Version . . . 8

KING COLE TRIO/QUINTET
(see under Nat 'King' Cole)

LLOYD COLE & COMMOTIONS

84	Welcome To L. Vegas LC 1	Are You Ready To Be Heartbroken?/Down At The Mission	
		(p/s, withdrawn)	30
85	Polydor COLET 5	Lost Weekend (extended)/Big World/Lost Weekend – (7" version)	
		(10" p/s)	8

NAT COLE

70	Jackpot JP 717	Pack Of Cards/RITA & NAT COLE: Spread Joy	5
70	Jackpot JP 718	Love Making/SONNY BINNS & RITA: My Love	5
70	Jackpot JP 722	Sugar Sugar/SONNY BINNS & RITA: Sign Off	5
70	Explosion EX 2022	In The Summertime/Apollo Moon Walk	8
70	Creole CR 1002	Me And My Life/Instrumental	5

(see also Rita Alston)

(NAT) 'KING' COLE

78s

50	Melodisc 8011	Heads/It Had To Be You (as King Cole Quintet)	10
50	Melodisc 8012	Pro-Sky/I Can't Give You Anything But Love (as King Cole Quintet)	10
54	Vogue V 2214	Nat's Kicks (Parts 1 & 2) (as Nat 'King' Cole Quintet)	8
55	Capitol CL 14215	Long Long Ago/Open Up The Doghouse (with Dean Martin)	12
58	Capitol CL 14820	Angel Smile/Back In My Arms	8
58	Capitol CL 14853	With You On My Mind/The Song Of Raintree County	8
58	Capitol CL 14898	Come Closer To Me/Nothing In The World	8
58	Capitol CL 14937	Non Dimenticar (Don't Forget)/Bend A Little My Way	8
59	Capitol CL 14987	Madrid/Give Me Your Love	8
59	Capitol CL 15017	You Made Me Love You/I Must Be Dreaming	10
59	Capitol CL 15056	Midnight Flyer/Sweet Bird Of Truth	12
59	Capitol CL 15087	Buon Natale/The Happiest Little Christmas Tree	20

SINGLES

54	Capitol CL 14149	Smile (Theme From 'Modern Times')/Make Her Mine	20
54	Capitol CL 14155	Unbelievable/Hajji Baba (Persian Lament)	15
54	Capitol CL 14172	I Am In Love/There Goes My Heart	15
54	Capitol CL 14203	If I Give My Heart To You/Hold My Hand	15
54	Capitol CL 14207	Papa Loves Mambo/Teach Me Tonight	15
55	Capitol CL 14215	Long Long Ago/Open Up The Doghouse (with Dean Martin)	15
55	Capitol CL 14235	A Blossom Fell/Alone Too Long	15
55	Capitol CL 14251	The Sand And The Sea/Darling, Je Vous Aime Beaucoup	15
55	Capitol CL 14295	If I May (with Four Knights)/I Envy	15
55	Capitol CL 14317	Annabelle/I'd Rather Have The Blues ('Kiss Me Deadly' Theme)	15
55	Capitol CL 14351	My One Sin/Don't Hurt The Girl	15
55	Capitol CL 14364	Love Is A Many-Splendored Thing/Autumn Leaves	15
55	Capitol CL 14378	Someone You Love/Forgive My Heart	15

(The above 45s were originally issued with triangular centres.)

EPs

55	Capitol EAP 1-514	TENTH ANNIVERSARY ALBUM PART 1	10
55	Capitol EAP 2-514	TENTH ANNIVERSARY ALBUM PART 2	10
55	Capitol EAP 3-514	TENTH ANNIVERSARY ALBUM PART 3	10
55	Capitol EAP 4-514	TENTH ANNIVERSARY ALBUM PART 4	10
55	Capitol EAP 1-633	MOODS IN SONG	10
56	Capitol EAP 1010	LOVE IS A MANY-SPLENDORED THING	10
56	Capitol EAP 1036	THE CHRISTMAS SONG	10
56	Capitol EAP 1040	STRIP FOR ACTION	10
57	Capitol EAP 1-801	NIGHT LIGHTS	8
57	Capitol EAP 1-813	AROUND THE WORLD (with Nelson Riddle)	8
58	Capitol EAP 1-824	LOVE IS THE THING PART 1	8
58	Capitol EAP 2-824	LOVE IS THE THING PART 2	8
58	Capitol EAP 3-824	LOVE IS THE THING PART 3	8
58	Capitol EAP 1-960	LOOKING BACK	8
58	Capitol EAP 1-993	ST. LOUIS BLUES PART 1	10
58	Capitol EAP 2-993	ST. LOUIS BLUES PART 2	10
58	Capitol EAP 3-993	ST. LOUIS BLUES PART 3	10
58	Capitol EAP 1-782	AFTER MIDNIGHT PART 1	8
58	Capitol EAP 2-782	AFTER MIDNIGHT PART 2	8
58	Capitol EAP 3-782	AFTER MIDNIGHT PART 3	8
58	Capitol EAP 4-782	AFTER MIDNIGHT PART 4	8

LPs

53	Capitol LC 6569	CAPITOL PRESENTS NAT KING COLE (10")	35
53	Capitol LC 6587	CAPITOL PRESENTS NAT KING COLE AND HIS TRIO VOLUME 1 (10")	35
53	Capitol LC 6593	CAPITOL PRESENTS NAT KING COLE AT THE PIANO (10")	35
53	Capitol LC 6594	CAPITOL PRESENTS NAT KING COLE AND HIS TRIO VOLUME 2 (10")	35
53	Capitol LC 6627	NAT KING COLE SINGS FOR TWO IN LOVE (10")	25
54	Capitol LCT 6003	NAT KING COLE TENTH ANNIVERSARY ALBUM	20
56	Capitol LC 6818	BALLADS OF THE DAY (10")	20
56	Capitol LC 6830	THE PIANO STYLE OF NAT KING COLE (10")	20
56	Brunswick LAT 8123	IN THE BEGINNING (as King Cole Trio)	20
57	Capitol (S)LCT 6129	LOVE IS THE THING	12
57	Capitol LCT 6133	AFTER MIDNIGHT (as Nat King Cole & His Trio)	12
57	Capitol LCT 6142	THIS IS NAT KING COLE	12
58	Capitol (S)LCT 6149	JUST ONE OF THOSE THINGS	12
58	Capitol (S)LCT 6156	ST LOUIS BLUES — SONGS OF W.C. HANDY	12
59	Capitol (S)LCT 6173	THE VERY THOUGHT OF YOU (mono/stereo)	each 12
59	Capitol (S)LCT 6176	WELCOME TO THE CLUB (mono/stereo)	each 12
59	Capitol (S)LCT 6182	TO WHOM IT MAY CONCERN (mono/stereo)	each 12
60	Capitol (S)W 1220	A MIS AMIGOS (mono/stereo)	each 12
60	Capitol (S)W 1444	THE MAGIC OF CHRISTMAS (mono/stereo)	each 12
61	Capitol (S)W 1392	WILD IS LOVE (mono/stereo)	each 12

61	Capitol (S)W 1331	TELL ME ALL ABOUT YOURSELF (mono/stereo) .... each 12
61	Capitol (S)W 1574	THE TOUCH OF YOUR LIPS (mono/stereo) .... each 12
65	Capitol (S)W340	CAT BALLOU AND OTHER MOTION PICTURE SONGS................. each 12

(see also Dean Martin, Four Knights)

PATSY COLE
| 66 | Island WI 271 | Disappointed Bride/EARL BOSTIC: Honeymoon Night .... 18 |

ROCKY COLE
| 61 | Oriole CB 1635 | Heaven And Earth/Huey's Song... 5 |

STRANGER COLE
63	R&B JB 133	Out Of Many/Nothing Tried 22
63	Island WI 110	Stranger At The Door/Conqueror 22
63	Island WI 114	Last Love/STRANGER & KEN: Hush Baby............................ 25
63	Island WI 126	We Are Rolling/Millie Maw 22
64	Island WI 137	Goodbye Peggy (actually plays Goodbye Peggy Darling by Roy Panton)/ BABA BROOKS: Portrait Of My Love 22
64	R&B JB 129	Morning Star/Beat Up Your Gum.................................. 18
64	Island WI 133	Til My Dying Days/STRANGER & PATSY: I Need You 22
64	Black Swan WI 413	Uno Dos Tres (act. with Ken Boothe)/Look (B-side actually by unknown artist) 22
64	Black Swan WI 415	Summer Day/Loving You Always (both actually by Dottie & Bonnie)... 22
64	Black Swan WI 435	Little Boy Blue/ERIC MORRIS: Words Of Wisdom 22
65	Ska Beat JB 192	Pussy Cat/MAYTALS: Sweet Sweet Jenny 25
65	Island WI 169	Koo Koo Doo (with Owen & Leon)/GLORIA & DREAMLETTS: Stay Where You Are 22
65	Island WI 177	Run Joe (with Baba Brooks)/Make Believe 22
65	Blue Beat BB 322	When The Party Is Over/BUSTER'S ALLSTARS: Happy Independence '65 20
65	Blue Beat BB 333	Matilda (actually with Prince Buster)/BUSTER'S ALL STARS: When The Party Is Over 35
66	Doctor Bird DB 1025	We Shall Overcome/Do You Really Love Me (as Stranger Cole & Seraphines)... 25
66	Doctor Bird DB 1040	Drop The Ratchet/Oh Yee Mahee (as Stranger Cole & Conquerors)........... 25
67	Doctor Bird DB 1066	You Took My Love (actually by Patsy Todd)/FUGITIVES: Living Soul 25
68	Island WI 3154	Jeboza Macoo/Now I Know (B-side actually with Gladdy Anderson) 45
68	Amalgamated AMG 801	Just Like A River (as Stranger Cole & Gladdy)/LEADERS: Hope Someday 20
69	Amalgamated AMG 838	What Mama Na Want She Get/We Two 18
69	Duke DU 27	Glad You're Living/Help Wanted 10
69	Unity UN 501	Last Flight To Reggae City (w/ Tommy McCook)/JUNIOR SMITH: Watch Dem Go... 8
69	Unity UN 514	When I Get My Freedom/Life Can Be Beautiful 7
69	Escort ES 810	Pretty Cottage/To Me 10
69	Escort ES 819	Leana Leana/Na Na Na 7
69	Escort ES 826	Loneliness/Remember 7
70	Escort ES 830	Little Things/Till The Well Runs Dry 6
70	Escort ES 831	Everything With You/Picture On The Wall 6
70	Escort ES 832	Pussy/Let Me In.. 6
70	Pama PM 790	Come Dance With Me/Dance With Me.............................. 7
71	Camel CA 72	Crying Every Night/DENNIS ALCAPONE & DELROY WILSON: It Must Come ... 10
71	Escort ERT 849	Tomorrow/SONNY BURKE: Chicken Thief 7
72	Tropical AL 0011	Mail Man (with Charlie Ace)/Mail Man (Version).................... 7
72	Jackpot JP 791	My Confession/LASCELS & HORTENSE: The Might Organ............. 6
72	Pama PM 848	The House Where Bombo Lives/Our High School Dance 5

(see also Stranger, Stranger & Gladys, Stranger & Patsy, Stranger & Ken, Rob Walker, Charmers, Lloyd Clarke, Don Drummond, Tommy McCook, Ernest Wilson, Delroy Wilson, Lester Sterling, Baba Brooks, Roland Alphonso)

BOBBY COLEMAN
| 66 | Pye International 7N 25365 | (Baby) You Don't Have To Tell Me/Pleasure Girl .... 70 |

FITZROY COLEMAN
| 61 | Starlite ST45 064 | Lucilla/Caribbean Sunset...................................... 12 |

LONNIE COLEMAN & JESSE ROBERTSON
| 56 | London HLU 8335 | Dolores Diane/Oh Honey, Why Don'tcha (78 rpm = £10) .... 75 |

ORNETTE COLEMAN
60	Contemporary LAC 12228	TOMORROW IS THE QUESTION (LP)............................... 20
61	London Jazz LTZ-K 15199	CHANGE OF THE CENTURY (LP, also stereo SAH-K 5099)........... 20
61	London Jazz LTZ-K 15228	THIS IS OUR MUSIC (LP, also stereo SAH-K 6181)................. 20
62	London Jazz LTZ-K 15241	THE ORNETTE COLEMAN QUARTET (LP, also stereo SAH-K 6235)... 20
67	CBS 66023	CHAPPAQUA SUITE (2-LP).. 20
68	Polydor 623 246/7	AN EVENING WITH ORNETTE COLEMAN (2-LP)..................... 15

ROGER COLEMAN
| 60 | Top Rank JAR 311 | Nobody's Fool/Endlessly .... 10 |

COLETTE & BANDITS
| 65 | Stateside SS 416 | A Ladies Man/Lost Love.. 15 |

COLLAGE
| 73 | Studio Two TWO 410 | MISTY (LP)... 50 |

(see also Brian Bennett)

COLLECTIVE HORIZONTAL
| 79 | Dolmen DO 1 | COLLECTIVE HORIZONTAL EP (gatefold p/s, stickered white labels) .... 5 |

COLLECTORS (Canada)
| 70 | London HLU 10304 | I Must Have Been Blind/The Beginning .... 6 |
| 69 | Warner Bros WS 1774 | GRASS AND WILD STRAWBERRIES (LP) .... 25 |

(see also Chilliwack, Electric Prunes)

COLLECTORS (U.K.)
| 80 | Central Collection COL 1 | Different World/Talking Hands (p/s) .... 6 |

MINT VALUE £

COLLEGE BOYS (Jamaica)
64	Blue Beat BB 202	Love Is A Treasure/Someone Will Be There	25

COLLEGE BOYS (U.K.)
64	Columbia DB 7306	I Just Don't Understand/I'm Gonna Cry	20
67	Pye 7N 17294	Good Times/San Antonio Rose	10

GRAHAM COLLIER SEXTET/SEPTET
67	Deram DML/SML 1005	DEEP DARK BLUE CENTRE (LP)	60
69	Fontana SFJL 922	DOWN ANOTHER ROAD (LP)	70
70	Fontana 6309 006	SONGS FOR MY FATHER (LP, as Graham Collier Music featuring Harry Beckett)	50
71	Philips 6308 051	MOSAICS (LP, live, as Graham Collier Music featuring Harry Beckett)	40
72	Saydisc SDL 244	PORTRAITS (LP)	20
	(see also Harry Beckett)		

MITTY COLLIER
64	Pye International 7N 25275	I Had A Talk With My Man/Free Girl	30

ALBERT COLLINS
69	Liberty LBS 83238	LOVE CAN BE FOUND ANYWHERE (LP)	35
73	Tumbleweed TW 3501	THERE'S GOTTA BE A CHANGE (LP)	25

ANSEL(L) COLLINS
69	Trojan TR 699	Night Of Love/DERRICK MORGAN: Copy Cat	12
69	Trojan TR 7712	Cotton Dandy/CARL DAWKINS: Don't Get Weary	12
70	Trojan TR 7729	Moon Dust/Fat Cat	15
70	Trojan TR 7730	Monkey (Version I)/(Version II) (plays "High Voltage"/"High Voltage Version": B-side actually by Beverley All Stars)	15
70	J-Dan JDN 4401	Cock Robin/KING DENNIS: Seven Zero	12
70	Techniques TE 907	Top Secret/Crazy Rhythm (both actually by Winston Wright)	15
71	Techniques TE 913	Nuclear Weapon/TECHNIQUES ALL STARS: La, La, La	15
	(see also Dave & Ansell Collins, Conquerors, Lloyd Young, Prince Buster, Les Foster, Ethiopians, Eternals, Pam Brooks, Dennis Alcapone, Rad Bryan)		

BOOTSY COLLINS
(see under Bootsy's Rubber Band)

DAVE & ANSELL COLLINS
(see under 'D')

DONIE COLLINS SHOWBAND
68	Pye 7N 17682	Get Down With It/I Can't Help Myself (Sugar Pie Honey Bunch)	10

DOROTHY COLLINS
51	MGM MGM 354	Me And My Imagination/I'm Playing With Fire (78)	7
52	Brunswick 05010	So Madly In Love (with Gordon Jenkins Orchestra)/GORDON JENKINS, ORCHESTRA & CHORUS: Just Say The Word (78)	7
53	Brunswick 05042	Jump Back Honey/I Will Still Love You (with Snooky Lanson) (78)	8
53	Brunswick 05051	If'n'Puppy Love (with Raymond Scott Orchestra) (78)	8
55	Vogue Coral Q 72111	My Boy — Flat Top/In Love (78 rpm = £15)	40
56	Vogue Coral Q 72116	Moments To Remember/Love And Marriage (78 rpm = £8)	10
56	Vogue Coral Q 72137	Seven Days/Manuello (78 rpm = £12)	25
56	Vogue Coral Q 72173	Treasure Of Love/He's Got Me, Hook, Line And Sinker (78 rpm £10)	20
56	Vogue Coral Q 72193	Love Me As Though There Were No Tomorrow/Rock And Roll Train (78 rpm £12)	40
56	Vogue Coral Q 72198	The Italian Theme/Cool It, Baby (78 rpm = £12)	40
56	Vogue Coral Q 72208	The Twelve Gifts Of Christmas/Mr. Santa	15
57	Vogue Coral Q 72232	Baby Can Rock/Would You Ever (78 rpm = £12)	25
57	Vogue Coral Q 72252	Mr. Wonderful/I Miss You Already	10
57	Vogue Coral Q 72262	Four Walls/Big Dreams (78 rpm = £6)	8
57	Vogue Coral Q 72287	Soft Sands/Sing It, Children, Sing It	6
59	Top Rank JAR 259	Baciare, Baciare/Everything I Have Is Yours	6
60	Top Rank JAR 401	Banjo Boy/Tintarella Di Luna	6
60	Top Rank JAR 523	Unlock Those Chains/I'll Be Yours, You'll be Mine	6
55	London REP 1025	DOROTHY COLLINS SINGS (EP)	35
57	Coral LVA 9058	AT HOME WITH DOROTHY AND RAYMOND (LP)	30

EDWYN COLLINS
87	Creation CRE 047T	Don't Shilly Shally/If Ever You're Ready (7" & 12", white label test pressing only)	40/35
87	Elevation ACIDB 6	My Beloved Girl/50 Shades Of Blue (Acoustic Version)/Clouds (Fogging Up My Mind)/What's The Big Idea? (box set with 3 postcards)	6
	(see also Orange Juice, Paul Quinn & Edwyn Collins)		

GLENDA COLLINS
60	Decca F 11280	Take A Chance/Crazy Guy	15
61	Decca F 11321	Oh How I Miss You Tonight/Age For Love	15
61	Decca F 11417	Head Over Heels In Love/Find Another Fool	15
63	HMV POP 1163	I Lost My Heart In The Fairground/I Feel So Good	55
63	HMV POP 1233	If You Gotta Pick A Baby/In The First Place	70
64	HMV POP 1283	Baby It Hurts/Nice Wasn't It	55
64	HMV POP 1323	Lollipop/Everybody's Got To Fall In Love	55
65	HMV POP 1439	Johnny Loves Me/Paradise for Two	55
65	HMV POP 1475	Thou Shall Not Steal/Been Invited To A Party	70
66	Pye 7N 17044	Something I've Got To Tell You/My Heart Didn't Lie	75
66	Pye 7N 17150	It's Hard To Believe It/Don't Let It Rain On Sunday	50
90	Document CSAP LP 108	BEEN INVITED TO A PARTY (LP)	20

JOHNNY COLLINS
75	Tradition TSR 020	JOHNNY'S PRIVATE ARMY (LP)	18

JOHNNY COLLINS & FRIENDS
73	Tradition TSR 014	THE TRAVELLER'S REST (LP)	18

JUDY COLLINS
66	London HLZ 10029	I'll Keep It With Mine/Thirsty Boots	10
67	Elektra EKSN 45011	In My Life/Hard Lovin' Loser	5
69	Elektra EKSN 45053	Some Day Soon/My Father	5
69	Elektra EKSN 45073	Chelsea Morning/Pretty Polly	5
69	Elektra EKSN 45077	Turn, Turn, Turn/Mr. Tambourine Man	5
65	Elektra EKL 209	MAID OF CONSTANT SORROW (LP)	25
65	Elektra EKS 7300	FIFTH ALBUM (LP, orange label)	15
68	Elektra EKL 4012	WILD FLOWERS (LP, orange label, also stereo EKS 74012)	15
69	Elektra EKL 4033	WHO KNOWS WHERE THE TIME GOES (LP, gatefold sleeve, orange label; also stereo EKS 74033)	15

KEANYA COLLINS
78	Grapevine GRP 108	Barnabus Collins — Love Bandit/I Call You Daddy	10

LYN COLLINS
64	Sabre SA 0002	What Am I Gonna Do Without You?/When A Girl Meets A Bad, Bad Boy	20
74	Polydor 2066 490	Rock Me Again And Again And Again/Wide Awake In A Dream	25
74	Mojo 2093 029	Think (About It)/Me And My Baby Got Our Own Thing Going	10
88	Urban URBX 15	Rock Me Again And Again And Again (12")	10
72	Polydor 2918 006	THINK (ABOUT IT) (LP)	50
88	Urban URBLP 7	LYN COLLINS (THE FEMALE PREACHER) (LP)	15
	(see also James Brown)		

PETER COLLINS
70	Decca F 13048	Get In A Boat/Girl By The Sea	7
70	Decca Nova SDN 21	PETER COLLINS (LP)	25

PHIL COLLINS
81	Virgin VSK 102	In The Air Tonight/The Roof Is Leaking (12-page cartoon booklet p/s)	6
82	Virgin VSY 524	Thru' These Walls/Do You Know, Do You Care? (7" picture disc)	6
82	Virgin VSY 531	You Can't Hurry Love/I Cannot Believe It's True (7" picture disc)	6
85	Virgin VSS 735	One More Night/I Like The Way (12" picture disc)	8
85	Virgin VS 777	Take Me Home/We Said Hello Goodbye (7", p/s with luggage tag)	8
	(see also Genesis, Flaming Youth, Brand X, Peter Banks)		

PHIL COLLINS & MARILYN MARTIN
85	Virgin VSSD 818	Separate Lives/Only You Know And I Know (2 interlocking picture discs)	5
	(see also Brand X, Peter Banks, Genesis, Flaming Youth, Marilyn Martin)		

RODGER COLLINS
67	Vocalion VF 9285	She's Looking Good/I'm Serving Time (DJ copy = £60)	20

SHIRLEY COLLINS
60	Collector JEI 1508	SINGS IRISH (EP)	65
60	Collector JEB 3	THE FOGGY DEW (EP)	65
60	Collector JEB 5	ENGLISH SONGS (EP)	65
64	Collector JEB 9	ENGLISH SONGS VOL. 2 (EP, with Robin Hall)	65
63	Topic TOP 95	HEROES IN LOVE (EP)	65
59	Folkways FG 3564	FALSE TRUE LOVERS (LP)	130
60	Argo RG 150	SWEET ENGLAND (LP)	130
64	Decca LK 4652	FOLK ROOTS, NEW ROUTES (LP, with Davy Graham)	150
67	Topic 12T 170	THE SWEET PRIMROSES (LP, originally with blue label)	40/25
68	Polydor 583 025	THE POWER OF THE TRUE LOVE KNOT (LP, with Incredible String Band)	100
71	Pegasus PEG 7	NO ROSES (LP, gatefold sleeve, with Albion Country Band)	30
74	Topic 12T 238	ADIEU TO OLD ENGLAND (LP, originally with blue label)	35/25
75	Deram SML 1117	A FAVOURITE GARLAND (LP)	30
76	Harvest SHSM 2008	AMARANTH (LP)	20
78	Topic 12T 380	FOR AS MANY AS WILL (LP)	18
83	Hannibal HNBL 1327	THE POWER OF THE TRUE LOVE KNOT (LP, reissue)	12

SHIRLEY & DOLLY COLLINS
69	Harvest SHVL 754	ANTHEMS IN EDEN (LP, gatefold sleeve)	90
70	Harvest SHVL 771	LOVE, DEATH AND THE LADY (LP, gatefold sleeve)	100
	(see also Davy Graham, Albion Country Band, Conundrum)		

SIR COLLINS
(see under 'S')

TOMMY COLLINS
58	Capitol CL 14838	Think It Over Boys/All Of The Monkeys Ain't In The Zoo	15
58	Capitol CL 14894	Let Down/It Tickles	10
59	Capitol CL 15076	Little June/A Hundred Years From Now	10
60	Capitol CL 15118	Wreck Of The Old '97/You Belong In My Arms	10
57	Capitol T 776	WORDS AND MUSIC COUNTRY STYLE (LP)	25
59	Capitol T 1196	THIS IS TOMMY COLLINS (LP)	25

COLLINS BAND & BOB STACKIE
68	Collins Downbeat CRC 0017	Bob Stackie In Soho/LORD CHARLES & HIS BAND: Jamaican Bits And Pieces	45
	(see also Sir Collins)		

JOE COLMAN
90	Blast First FU10	INFERNAL MACHINE (LP, picture disc, 1,000 only)	18

COLONEL
75	Ring O' 2017 104	Cokey Cokey/Away In A Manger (company sleeve)	10

COLONEL
80	Virgin VS 380	Too Many Cooks (In The Kitchen)/I Need Protection (p/s)	6
	(see also XTC, Mr. Partridge)		

JERRY COLONNA

			MINT VALUE £
54	Brunswick 05243	Ebb Tide/The Velvet Glove	15
54	Brunswick 05342	It Might As Well Be Spring/Ja-Da	10
55	Parlophone MSP 6165	Let Me Go, Lover/I Want To Love You, Cara Mia	10
55	London HL 8143	Chicago Style/Baffi	25
56	HMV 7M 369	The Shifting, Whispering Sands/Waltz Me Around	20
59	London HA-U 2190	LET'S ALL SING (LP)	20
65	Ace Of Hearts AH 102	JERRY COLONNA AND GROUCHO MARX (LP)	15

COLORADOS

64	Oriole CB 1972	Lips Are Redder On You/Who You Gonna Hurt?	30

COLOR TAPES

79	Wavelength HURT 4	Cold Anger/Leaves Of China (p/s)	6

COLOSSEUM

69	Fontana TF 1029	Walking In The Park/Those About To Die	10
69	Fontana STL 5510	THOSE WHO ARE ABOUT TO DIE SALUTE YOU (LP, gatefold sleeve)	30
69	Vertigo VO 1	VALENTYNE SUITE (LP, gatefold sleeve, swirl label & inner bag)	30
70	Vertigo 6360 017	DAUGHTER OF TIME (LP, gatefold sleeve, some with swirl label & bag)	40/20

(see also Dick Heckstall-Smith, Chris Farlowe, Greenslade, John Mayall, Howard Riley Trio, Tempest, Mogul Thrash)

COLOURBOX

82	4AD AD 215	Breakdown/Tarantula (p/s)	6
82	4AD BAD 215	Breakdown/Tarantula (12", p/s)	8
83	4AD AD 314	Breakdown (Second Version)/Tarantula (Second Version) (different p/s)	5
86	4AD 605	The Official Colourbox World Cup Theme/Philip Glass (p/s)	5
85	4AD CAD 508	COLOURBOX (LP, stickered sleeve, 10,000 only, with bonus LP MAD 509)	18

(see also M/A/R/R/S)

COLOURED RAISINS

70	Trojan TR 7700	One Way Love/No More Heartaches	7

(see also Raisins)

COLOURFIELD

84	Chrysalis COLF D2	Thinking Of You/Wild Flames//Little Things/Thinking Of You (double pack)	5
85	Chrysalis COLF D4	Castles In The Air/Your Love Was Smashing//I Can't Get Enough Of You Baby/Castles In The Air (Instrumental Mix) (double pack, gatefold p/s)	5
87	Chrysalis CCD 1546	DECEPTION (CD)	22
89	Chrysalis CHR 1480	VIRGINS AND PHILISTINES (CD)	50

(see also Specials)

COLOURFUL SEASONS

68	MGM MGM 1433	Out Of The Blue/It's Gonna Break My Heart	6

COLO(U)RS OF LOVE

68	Page One POF 060	I'm A Train/Up On A Cotton Cloud	8
68	Page One POF 086	Just Another Fly/Twenty Ten	8
69	Page One POF 124	Mother Of Convention/Music Mother Made	8

CHRISTOPHER COLT

68	Decca F 12726	Virgin Sunrise/Girl In The Mirror	30

TONY COLTON('S BIG BOSS BAND)

64	Decca F 11879	Lose My Mind/So Used To Loving You (solo)	25
65	Pye 7N 15886	I Stand Accused/Further On Down The Track (with Big Boss Band)	170+
66	Pye 7N 17046	You're Wrong There Baby/Have You Lost Your Mind	25
66	Pye 7N 17117	I've Laid Some Down In My Time/Run Pony Rider	40
68	Columbia DB 8385	In The World Of Marnie Dreaming/Who Is She? (solo)	15

(see also Poet & One Man Band, Head Hands & Feet, Real McCoy, Peter B's)

JOHN COLTRANE

60	Esquire EP 229	SOUL OF 'TRANE (EP)	8
61	Esquire EP 239	BASS BLUES (EP)	8
64	Fontana 469 203TE	WHILE MY LADY SLEEPS (EP)	8
58	Esquire 32-079	THE FIRST TRANE (LP)	20
58	Esquire 32-089	SOUL TRANE (LP)	20
59	Esquire 32-091	TRANEING IN (LP)	20
60	London Jazz LTZ-K 15197	GIANT STEPS (LP)	25
61	Esquire 32-129	LUSH LIFE (LP)	20
61	London Jazz LTZ-K 15219	COLTRANE JAZZ (LP, also stereo SAH-K 6162)	20
62	London Jazz LTZ-K 15232	BAGS AND TRANE (LP, also stereo SAH-K 6192)	20
62	Columbia 33SX 1399	THE BIRDLAND STORY VOL. 1: ECHOES OF AN ERA (LP)	15
62	London Jazz LTZ-K 15239	OLE COLTRANE (LP, also stereo SAH-K 6223)	20
62	HMV CLP 1548	AFRICA/BRASS (LP, also stereo CSD 1431)	20
62	HMV CLP 1590	LIVE AT THE VILLAGE VANGUARD (LP, also stereo CSD 1456)	20
63	United Artists (S)ULP 1018	COLTRANE TIME (LP)	20
63	London HA-K/SH-K 8017	COLTRANE PLAYS THE BLUES (LP, as John Coltrane Group)	25
63	Esquire 32-179	STANDARD COLTRANE (LP)	25
63	HMV CLP 1629	COLTRANE (LP, also stereo CSD 1483)	20
63	HMV CLP 1647	BALLADS (LP, also stereo CSD 1496)	20
63	HMV CLP 1657	DUKE ELLINGTON & JOHN COLTRANE (LP, also stereo CSD 1502)	20
64	HMV CLP 1695	IMPRESSIONS (LP, also stereo CSD 1509)	20
64	HMV CLP 1700	JOHN COLTRANE WITH JOHNNY HARTMAN (LP)	20
64	Realm RM 157	ON WEST 42ND STREET (LP)	20
64	Realm RM 181	TRANE RIDE (LP)	20
64	HMV CLP 1741	LIVE AT BIRDLAND (LP, also stereo CSD 1544)	20
65	HMV CLP 1799	CRESCENT (LP, also stereo CSD 1567)	20
65	Stateside SL 10124	BLACK PEARLS (LP)	20
65	HMV CLP 1869	A LOVE SUPREME (LP, also stereo CSD 1605)	20
65	Atlantic ATL/SAL 5022	MY FAVOURITE THINGS (LP)	20
65	Realm RM 52226	TANGANYIKA STRUT (LP)	15

John COLTRANE

65	HMV CLP 1897	COLTRANE PLAYS (LP, also stereo CSD 1619)	15
66	Stateside SL 10162	BAHIA (LP)	15
66	HMV CLP/CSD 3543	ASCENSION (LP, as John Coltrane Orchestra)	15
66	HMV CLP/CSD 3551	NEW THING AT NEWPORT (LP, with Archie Shepp)	15
66	Atlantic 587/588 004	THE AVANT-GARDE (LP, with Don Cherry)	15
66	HMV CLP/CSD 3575	MEDITATIONS (LP)	15
67	Atlantic 587/588 039	COLTRANE'S SOUND (LP)	15
67	HMV CLP/CSD 3599	COLTRANE LIVE AT THE VILLAGE VANGUARD AGAIN! (LP)	15
67	HMV CLP/CSD 3617	OM (LP, withdrawn)	25
67	HMV CLP/CSD 3617	KULU SE MAMA (LP)	15
68	Transatlantic PR 7280	DAKAR (LP)	15
68	Transatlantic PR 7378	LAST TRANE (LP)	15
68	Impulse MIPL/SIPL 502	EXPRESSION (LP)	15
69	Atlantic 588 139	THREE LITTLE WORDS (LP)	15
69	Impulse MIPL/SIPL 515	COSMIC MUSIC (LP, by Alice & John Coltrane)	15
70	Impulse SIPL 522	SELFLESSNESS (LP)	15
71	Probe SPB 1025	AFRO BLUE (LP)	15
72	Prestige PR 24003	JOHN COLTRANE (2-LP)	15
73	CBS PR 24014	MORE LASTING THAN BRONZE (2-LP)	15
74	Atlantic K 60052	THE ART OF JOHN COLTRANE: THE ATLANTIC YEARS (2-LP)	15
74	CBS PR 24037	BLACK PEARLS (2-LP)	15

(see also Miles Davis, Thelonious Monk, Cannonball Adderley, Don Cherry, Archie Shepp)

COLTS
65	Pye 7N 15955	San Miguel/Where Has Our Love Gone?	5

COLUMBIA BOYS
68	Pye 7N 17513	Baby Come Back/Born To Lose	8
69	Pye 7N 17763	That's My Pa/She Thinks I Still Care	7

COLUMBUS
70	Deram DM 294	Ev'rybody Loves The U.S. Marshall/Tired	10

KEN COLYER('S JAZZMEN)
55	Decca F 10504	Early Hours/Cataract Rag	10
55	Decca F 10519	If I Ever Cease To Love/The Entertainer	10
55	Decca F 10565	It Looks Like A Big Time Tonight/Red Wing	10
56	Tempo A 117	Just A Closer Walk With Thee/Sheik Of Araby	10
56	Tempo A 120	If I Ever Cease To Love You/Isle Of Capri	10
56	Tempo A 126	My Bucket's Got A Hole In It/Wabash Blues	10
56	Tempo A 136	Maryland, My Maryland/The World Is Waiting For The Sunrise	10
56	Decca FJ 10755	All The Girls Go Crazy About The Way I Walk/Dippermouth Blues	10
61	Columbia DB 4676	The Happy Wanderer/Maryland, My Maryland	9
55	Decca DFE 6268	AND BACK TO NEW ORLEANS VOL. 1 (EP)	12
55	Decca DFE 6299	AND BACK TO NEW ORLEANS VOL. 2 (EP)	12
55	Vogue EPV 1202	KEN COLYER IN NEW ORLEANS (EP)	12
55	Tempo EXA 26	KEN COLYER JAZZMEN (EP)	12
56	Melodisc EPM7 59	KEN COLYER JAZZMEN AND THE CRANE RIVER JAZZ BAND (EP)	15
56	Vogue EPV 1102	KEN COLYER IN NEW ORLEANS (EP)	12
56	Tempo EXA 31	KEN COLYER JAZZMEN (EP)	12
57	Tempo EXA 53	KEN COLYER IN NEW ORLEANS (EP)	12
58	Decca DFE 6435	KEN COLYER AND HIS OMEGA BRASS (EP)	10
58	Decca DFE 6466	THEY ALL PLAYED RAGTIME (EP)	12
59	Esquire EP 233	RUM AND COCA COLA (EP, with Christie Brothers Stompers)	12
60	Storyville SEP 301	KEN COLYER JAZZMEN (EP)	15
60	Storyville SEP 305	KEN COLYER'S JAZZMEN (EP)	15
60	Storyville SEP 309	KEN COLYER'S JAZZMEN (EP)	12
60	Decca DFE 6645	WALKING THE BLUES (EP, also stereo STO 143)	each 20
60	Columbia SEG 8038	THIS IS JAZZ (EP)	15
61	Storyville SEP 392	TRAD JAZZ SCENE IN EUROPE VOL. 2 (EP)	15
61	Storyville SEP 412	WILDCAT BLUES (EP)	12
61	Columbia SEG 8104	THIS IS JAZZ VOL. 1 NO. 2 (EP)	18
61	Esquire EP 243	STOMPING (EP)	15
62	Columbia SEG 8145	THIS IS JAZZ VOL. 2 (EP)	12
62	Columbia SEG 8180	TOO BUSY (EP)	15
60s	Melodisc EPM7 105	KEN COLYER (EP)	15
66	K.C. KCS 11EP	GREEN CORN (EP)	12
54	Decca LF 1152	NEW ORLEANS TO LONDON (10" LP)	40
54	Decca LF 1196	BACK TO THE DELTA (10" LP, as Ken Colyer's Jazzmen & Skiffle Group)	35
55	Vogue LDE 161	KEN COLYER IN NEW ORLEANS (10" LP)	20
56	Tempo LAP 11	KEN COLYER'S JAZZMEN (10" LP)	20
57	Decca LK 4178	CLUB SESSION (LP)	18
58	Decca LF 1301	IN GLORY LAND (10" LP, as Ken Colyer & His Omega Brass Band)	15
59	Decca LF 1319	COLYER IN HAMBURG (10" LP)	15
59	Decca LK 4294	PLAYS STANDARDS (LP)	20
60	Columbia 33SX 1220	THIS IS JAZZ (LP)	15
61	Columbia 33SX 1297	THIS IS JAZZ VOL. 2 (LP, also stereo SCX 3360)	15
61	Columbia 33SX 1363	THIS IS THE BLUES VOL. 1 (LP)	25
63	Society SOC 914	COLYER'S PLEASURE (LP)	20
64	77 LEU 12/7	KEN COLYER AND THE ORIGINAL CRANE RIVER BAND (LP)	20
64	77 LEU 12/10	THE REAL KEN COLYER (LP)	20
65	K.C. KCS 1001	WANDERING (LP)	30

KEN COLYER'S SKIFFLE GROUP
55	Decca F 10631	Down By The Riverside/Take This Hammer (78 rpm = £8)	22
56	Decca FJ 10711	Streamline Train/Go Down Old Hannah (78 rpm = £8)	22
56	Decca FJ 10751	Down Bound Train/Mule Skinner (78 rpm = £8)	15
56	Decca FJ 10772	Old Riley/Stack O'Lee Blues	15

MINT VALUE £

57	Decca FJ 10889	The Grey Goose/I Can't Sleep (78 rpm = £8)	15
57	Decca FJ 10926	Sporting Life/House Rent Stomp (78 rpm = £8)	15
57	Decca FJ 10972	Ella Speed/Go Down Sunshine (78 rpm = £10)	15
55	Decca DFE 6286	KEN COLYER'S SKIFFLE GROUP (EP, various coloured sleeves)	22
58	Decca DFE 6444	KEN COLYER'S SKIFFLE GROUP NO. 2 (EP)	20
60	Decca DFE 6563	KEN COLYER'S SKIFFLE GROUP IN HAMBURG (EP)	22

(see also Crane Skiffle Group)

COMBAT 84
82	Victory VIC 1	ORDERS OF THE DAY (EP, wraparound p/s)	20
83	Victory VIC 2	Rapist/The Right To Choose/Barry Prudom (p/s)	20

COMBINATIONS
72	Punch PH 99	1 2 3 A B C/Zee	6

COME
79	Come Org. WDC 88001	Come Sunday/Shaved Slits	15
79	Come Org. WDC 88203	PRESENT RAMPTON (LP)	40
81	Come Org. WDC 881012	I'M JACK (LP, orange vinyl with insert)	30

(see also Whitehouse, New Order)

RORY COMMANDORE
(see under Tindersticks)

COMMANCHES
64	Pye 7N 15609	Tomorrow/Missed Your Loving	10

(see also Bobby Allen)

COMMANDERS
55	Brunswick 05366	The Elephants' Tango/Commanders Overture	5
55	Brunswick 05433	The Cat From Coos Bay/Camptown Boogie	5
55	Brunswick 05467	The Monster/Cornball No. 1	5

(see also Louis Armstrong)

COMMENDABLES
80	Lip CC 1	London E1/Decaying House	10

COMMERCIALS
81	Fast Product COM 1	Sixteen Again And Again/The Heroine Dies/Simon (p/s)	8

COMMITTED
79	Ace ACE 006	Crash Victim/British Crimes/Fast Lane/Advertising (500 only)	100

COMMITTEE
68	Liberty LBF 15154	Hard Way/Hey You	15

COMMITTEE
69	Pye 7N 17826	Sleep Tight Honey/Memories Of Melinda	6

COMMODORES
55	London HLD 8209	Riding On A Train/Uranium (78 rpm = £100)	1000
56	London HLD 8251	Speedo/Whole Lotta Shakin' Goin' On (78 rpm = £100)	1000

COMMODORES
69	Atlantic 584 273	Keep On Dancing/Rise Up	30

(see also Lionel Richie)

COMMON ROUND
70s	Galliard GAL 4015	FOUR PENCE A DAY (LP)	15

PERRY COMO
59	RCA RCA 1156	A Still Small Voice/No Well On Earth (78)	8
60	RCA RCA 1170	Delaware/I Know What God Is (78)	20
53	HMV 7M 102	The Ruby And The Pearl/My Love And Devotion	15
53	HMV 7M 110	Some Enchanted Evening/Bali Ha'i	15
53	HMV 7M 118	Don't Let The Stars Get In Your Eyes/To Know You (Is To Love You) (B-side with Fontane Sisters) (78 rpm, HMV B 10400 = £8)	40
53	HMV 7M 124	Wild Horses/Please Believe Me	15
53	HMV 7M 138	My Lady Loves To Dance/A Bushel And A Peck (B-side with Betty Hutton)	15
53	HMV 7M 149	My One And Only Heart/Say You're Mine Again	15
53	HMV 7M 155	Hello, Young Lovers/We Kiss In A Shadow	15
53	HMV 7M 163	Pa-Paya Mama/Why Did You Leave Me?	15
54	HMV 7M 175	You Alone/Surprising	15
54	HMV 7M 200	Idle Gossip/Look Out The Window	15
54	HMV 7M 215	Wanted/Give Me Your Hand	15
54	HMV 7M 241	Hit And Run Affair/If You Were Only Mine	15
54	HMV 7M 263	There Never Was A Night So Beautiful/Papa Loves Mambo	15
54	HMV 7M 278	Frosty The Snowman/The Twelve Days Of Christmas	15
55	HMV 7M 296	Ko Ko Mo (I Love You So)/You'll Always Be My Lifetime Love	15
55	HMV 7M 305	Door Of Dreams/Nobody	12
55	HMV 7M 326	There's No Place Like Home For The Holidays/Tina Marie	12
56	HMV 7M 366	Fooled/The Rose Tattoo	12
56	HMV 7M 404	Hot Diggity (Dog Ziggity Boom)/My Funny Valentine	15
56	HMV 7MC 39	Hot Diggity (Dog Ziggity Boom)/Juke Box Baby (export issue)	20
56	HMV POP 240	Glendora/More	15
56	HMV 7MC 49	Glendora/More (export issue)	15
56	HMV POP 271	Moonlight Love/Chincherinchee	8
57	HMV POP 304	Somebody Up There Likes Me/Dream Along With Me (I'm On My Way To A Star)	8
57	HMV 7MC 51	Somebody Up There Likes Me/Dream Along With Me (I'm On My Way To A Star) (export issue)	8
57	HMV POP 328	Round And Round/My House Is Your House	8
57	RCA RCA 1001	The Girl With The Golden Braids/My Little Baby	8

MINT VALUE £

57	HMV POP 369	Silk Stockings/Childhood Is A Meadow	8
57	HMV POP 394	As Time Goes By/All At Once You Love Her	8
56	HMV 7EG 8192	COMO SWINGS (EP)	8
57	HMV 7EG 8244	WITH A SONG IN MY HEART (EP)	8
54	HMV DLP 1026	PERRY COMO SINGS (10" LP)	28
57	RCA RD 27035	WE GET LETTERS (LP)	15
57	RCA RD 27070	WE GET LETTERS VOL. 2 (LP)	15
57	RCA RD 27078/SF 5011	DEAR PERRY (LP mono/stereo)	15
57	RCA RD 27082	SINGS MERRY CHRISTMAS MUSIC (LP)	12
58	RCA RD 27100	COMO'S GOLDEN RECORDS (LP)	12
58	RCA RD 27106/SF 5021	WHEN YOU COME TO THE END OF THE DAY (LP, mono/stereo)	each 12
58	RCA RD 27139/SF 5045	SINGS THE SONGS OF CHRISTMAS (LP, mono/stereo)	each 12
59	RCA RD 27154/SF 5053	COMO SWINGS (LP, mono/stereo)	each 12
60	RCA RD 27206/SF 5089	FOR THE YOUNG AT HEART (LP, mono/stereo)	each 12
61	RCA RD 27232	SING TO ME, MR. C (LP)	12
63	RCA Victor RD 7582	THE SONGS I LOVE (LP)	12
66	RCA Victor RD 7802	LIGHTLY LATIN (LP)	12
66	RCA Victor RD 7836	IN ITALY (LP)	12
	(see also Fontane Sisters, Betty Hutton)		

LES COMPAGNONS DE LA CHANSON
53	Columbia SCM 5005	The Three Bells (The Jimmy Brown Song)/Ave Maria	20
53	Columbia SCM 5056	The Galley Slave/Dreams Never Grow Old	15

COMPANY
80	Incus INCUS 36	FABLES (LP)	50
80	Incus INCUS 38	FICTIONS (LP)	50
82	Incus INCUS 46	EPIPHANY (LP)	50
82	Incus INCUS 47	EPIPHANIES (LP)	50
83	Incus INCUS 51	TRIOS (LP)	50

COMPANY
79	United Artists BP 326	We Wish You Well/Right Time For Love	30
	(see also Whitesnake)		

COMPLEX
70	CLPM 001	COMPLEX (LP, private pressing, 99 copies only)	600+
71	Deroy	THE WAY WE FEEL (LP, private pressing, 99 copies only)	400+
	(see also Monsoon, Misfits)		

COMPROMISE
66	CBS 202050	You Will Think Of Me/Love Minus Zero	7

COMSAT ANGELS
79	Junta JUNTA 1	Red Planet/I Get Excited/Specimen No. 2 (p/s, later reissued on red vinyl)	6/8

BOBBY COMSTOCK (& COUNTS)
59	Top Rank JAR 223	The Tennessee Waltz/Sweet Talk	10
60	London HLE 9080	Jambalaya/Let's Talk It Over (as Bobby Comstock & Counts)	20
63	Stateside SS 163	Let's Stomp/I Want To Do It	15
63	Stateside SS 221	Susie Baby/Take A Walk	15
65	United Artists UP 1086	I'm A Man/I'll Make You Glad	20

COMUS
71	Dawn DNX 2506	Diana/In The Lost Queen's Eyes/Winter Is A Coloured Bird (p/s)	25
71	Dawn DNLS 3019	FIRST UTTERANCE (LP, gatefold sleeve with lyric sheet)	150
74	Virgin V 2018	TO KEEP FROM CRYING (LP)	25
	(see also Gong, Henry Cow, Esperanto Rock Orchestra)		

CON-CHORDS
65	Polydor BM 56059	You Can't Take It Away/Let Me Walk With You	25

CONCORDE
70	Attack ATT 8020	Let Me Out/I Belong To You	12

CONCORDS
66	Emblem JDR 303	SOUL PURPOSE (LP)	25

CONCORDS
69	Blue Cat BS 170	Buttoo/I Need Your Loving	25

CONDEMNED 84
86	RFB SIN 2	Oi Ain't Dead!/Under Her Thumb/Follow The Leader/The Nutter (12", p/s, blue vinyl)	25
86	RFB SIN 2	Oi Ain't Dead!/Under Her Thumb/Follow The Leader/The Nutter (7", p/s, blue vinyl)	20
87	RFB SIN 3	IN SEARCH OF THE NEW BREED (12" EP)	25
88	Oi! OIR 003	BATTLE SCARRED (LP)	22

JEFF CONDON
63	MGM MGM 1221	(Walkin' In) Freddy's Footsteps/Never You Mind	7

HOWIE G. CONDOR
65	Fontana TF 613	Big Noise From Winnetka/The Fix	10

CONEY ISLAND KIDS
55	London HLJ 8207	Baby, Baby You/Moonlight Beach (78 rpm = £15)	50

CONFLICT
82	Crass 221984/1	THE HOUSE THAT MAN BUILT (EP, foldout poster p/s)	8
82	Xntrix XN 2001	LIVE AT THE CENTRE IBERICO (EP, with insert)	8
83	Corp. Christi CHRIST IT'S 4	A Nation Of Animal Lovers/Liberate (poster p/s)	6
85	Mortarhate MORT 15	The Battle Continues (both sides) (p/s, different colours, with insert)	5
88	FUND 1	FROM PROTEST TO RESISTANCE (LP, mail order, w/I, stickered plain sleeve)	12

CONGO ASHANTI ROY
82	On-U Sound DP 08	Hands & Feet/African Blood (10")	15

CONGOS
81	Go-Feet BEAT 2	HEART OF THE CONGOS (LP)	20

ARTHUR CONLEY
67	Atlantic 584 083	Sweet Soul Music/Let's Go Steady	10
67	Atlantic 584 121	Shake, Rattle And Roll/You Don't Have To See Me	10
67	Atlantic 584 143	Whole Lotta Woman/Love Comes And Goes	10
68	Atlantic 584 175	Funky Street/Put Our Love Together	10
68	Atlantic 584 197	People Sure Act Funny/Burning Fire	10
68	Atlantic 584 224	Aunt Dora's Love Soul Shack/Is That You Love	10
69	Atco 226 004	Star Revue/Love Sure Is A Powerful Thing	7
70	Atco 226 011	They Call The Wind Maria/Hurt	5
70	Atlantic 2091 025	All Day Singing/God Bless	5
71	Atlantic 2091 106	Sweet Soul Music/Shake, Rattle And Roll	5
71	Atlantic 2091 120	I'm Living Good/I'm So Glad You're Here	5
72	Capricorn K 17506	Rita/More Sweet Soul Music	5
67	Atlantic 587 069	SWEET SOUL MUSIC (LP)	30
68	Atlantic 587 084	SHAKE, RATTLE AND ROLL (LP)	25
68	Atlantic 587/588 128	SOUL DIRECTION (LP)	25
69	Atco 228 019	MORE SWEET SOUL (LP)	20
	(see also Soul Clan)		

CONNARD
68	Spot JW 11	Amadhan/Desdemona	50

BRIAN CONNELL & ROUND SOUND
66	Mercury MF 956	Just My Kind Of Loving/Something You've Got	10
66	Mercury MF 991	The Same Thing's Happened To Me/Mister Porter	10
68	Philips BF 1661	What Good Am I/Just Another Wedding Day	10
68	Philips BF 1718	I Know/Mister Travel Company	10

RAY CONNIFF & ROCKIN' RHYTHM BOYS
55	Vogue Coral QW 5001	Piggy Bank Boogie/Short Stuff (78 rpm = £6)	20
68	CBS (S)BPG 63276	HOW TO SAVE A MARRIAGE AND RUIN YOUR LIFE (LP, soundtrack)	20

BILLY CONNOLLY
72	Transatlantic TRA 258	LIVE! (LP)	12
	(see also Humblebums; George Harrison, Ringo Starr & Eric Clapton appear on "Freedom")		

BRIAN CONNOLLY
82	Carrere CAR 231	Hypnotised/Fade Away (p/s)	18
	(see also Sweet)		

CHRIS CONNOR
59	London HLE 8869	Hallelujah I Love Him So/I Won't Cry Anymore (78 rpm = £18)	15
60	London HLK 9124	I Only Want Some/That's My Desire	10
56	London EZ-N 19010	CHRIS CONNOR SINGS LULLABYS OF BIRDLAND (EP, with Ellis Larkin Trio)	15
57	London RE-N 1093	LONDON'S GIRL FRIENDS — NO. 2 (EP)	15
56	London HA-K 2030	PRESENTING CHRIS CONNOR (LP, also stereo SAH-K 6032)	20
56	London LZ-N 14007	SINGS LULLABYS FOR LOVERS (10" LP)	15
57	London HB-N 1074	CHRIS (10" LP)	20
57	London HA-K 2066	HE LOVES ME, HE LOVES ME NOT (LP)	20
60	London LZ-N 14036	THIS IS CHRIS (10" LP)	20
60	London LTZ-K 15142	A JAZZ DATE WITH (LP)	20
60	London LTZ-K 15151	CHRIS CRAFT (LP)	15
60	London Jazz LTZ-K 15183	THE BALLAD OF THE SAD CAFÉ (LP)	15
60	London Jazz LTZ-K 15185	WITCHCRAFT (LP)	15
60	London Jazz LTZ-K 15195	CHRIS IN PERSON (LP, also stereo SAH-K 6088)	15
61	London SAH-K 6190	DOUPLE EXPOSURE (LP, with Maynard Ferguson)	15

EDRIC CONNOR
57	Oriole CB 1362	Manchester United Calypso/Yorumba Highlife (78)	8

KENNETH CONNOR
59	Top Rank JAR 138	Rail Road Rock/Ramona (78 rpm = £10)	10

CAROL CONNORS
62	London HLN 9619	Big Big Love/Two Rivers	20
	(see also Teddy Bears)		

CONNY
61	Columbia DB 4714	No One Can Tell Me I'm Too Young/Lovable	20
62	Columbia DB 4845	Gino/Midi-Midinette	20

CONQUERORS
67	Doctor Bird DB 1119	Won't You Come Home Now?/Oh That Day	25
67	Treasure Isle TI 7035	Lonely Street/I Fell In Love	20
69	Amalgamated AMG 832	Secret Weapon (actually by Ansell Collins)/Jumpy Jumpy Girl	18
69	High Note HS 016	If You Can't Beat Them/Anywhere You Want To Go	12
69	High Note HS 025	National Dish/Mr D.J.	12
	(see also Stranger Cole & Conquerors, Baba Brooks)		

JESS CONRAD
60	Decca F 11236	Cherry Pie/There's Gonna Be A Day	8
60	Decca F 11259	Unless You Meant It/Out Of Luck	10
61	Decca F 11315	Mystery Girl/The Big White House	8
61	Decca F 11348	This Pullover/Why Am I Living?	10
61	Decca F 11375	Oh You Beautiful Doll/I See You	6
61	Decca F 11394	Walkaway/Every Breath I Take	6
61	Decca F 11412	Twist My Wrist/Hey Little Girl (some in p/s)	12/5

MINT VALUE £

62	Decca F 11511	Pretty Jenny/You Can Do It If You Try	6
63	Decca F 11620	It's About Time/As You Like It	5
63	Columbia DB 4969	Take Your Time/I Know You	5
64	Columbia DB 7223	Pussycat/Tempted	5
65	Columbia DB 7561	Things I'd Like To Say/Don't Turn Around	5
65	Pye 7N 15849	Hurt Me/It Can Happen To You	20
69	President PT 269	Other Side Of Life/See The Tinker Ride	5
70	President PT 292	Crystal Ball Dream/Pussycat	5
71	President PT 357	Here She Comes Again/My Idea	5
60	Decca DFE 6666	JESS CONRAD (EP)	22
62	Decca DFE 6702	TWIST MY WRIST (EP)	22
63	Decca DFE 8524	THE HUMAN JUNGLE (EP)	22
61	Decca LK 4390	JESS FOR YOU (LP)	50

(see also Guvners)

TONI CONRAD & FAUST
| 72 | Caroline C 1501 | OUTSIDE THE DREAM SYNDICATE (LP) | 25 |

(see also Faust)

CONSCIOUS MINDS
71	Big BG 318	Jamaican Boy/Brainwash	10
71	Ackee ACK 141	Paul, Marcus And Norman/Version	7
71	Punch PH 97	Paul, Marcus And Norman/Version (reissue)	6
71	Escort ERT 857	Peace Treaty/Brainwash	7

(see also Ken Boothe, Jamaicans, B.B.Seaton, Charmers)

CONSOLERS
| 67 | President PT165 | Someone Must Answer/No One | 8 |

CONSORTIUM
68	Pye 7N 17635	All The Love In The World/Spending My Life Saying Goodbye	10
69	Pye 7N 17725	When The Day Breaks/Day The Train Never Came	18
69	Pye 7N 17797	Beggar Man/Cynthia Serenity	10
69	Pye 7N 17841	I Don't Want Her Anymore/The House Upon The Hill	7
70	Trend TNT 52	Melanie Cries Alone/Copper Coloured Years	7

CONSTRUCTION
| 89 | White PA4799 | Transmission (12") | 50 |

CONSUMATES
| 68 | Coxsone CS 7054 | What Is It/ROLAND ALPHONSO: Musical Happiness | 25 |

CONTACT
| 79 | Object Music OM 11 | FUTURE/PAST (EP) | 5 |

(see also Passage)

CONTINENTALS
| 62 | Island WI 010 | Going Crazy/Give Me All Your Love | 25 |

CONTINUUM
| 70 | RCA Victor SF 8157 | CONTINUUM (LP) | 12 |
| 71 | RCA Victor SF 8196 | AUTUMN GRASS (LP, gatefold sleeve) | 30 |

CONTOURS
62	Oriole CB 1763	Do You Love Me/Move Mister Man	25
63	Oriole CB 1799	Shake Sherry/You Better Get In Line	50
63	Oriole CB 1831	Don't Let Him Be Your Baby/It Must Be Love	70
64	Stateside SS 299	Can You Do It/I'll Stand By You	45
65	Stateside SS 381	Can You Jerk Like Me/That Day She Needed Me	45
65	Tamla Motown TMG 531	First I Look At The Purse/Searching For A Girl	60
66	Tamla Motown TMG 564	Determination/Just A Little Misunderstanding	50
67	Tamla Motown TMG 605	It's So Hard Being A Loser/Your Love Grows More Precious Every Day	30
70	Tamla Motown TMG 723	Just A Little Misunderstanding/First I Look At The Purse	10
65	Tamla Motown TME 2002	THE CONTOURS (EP)	100
63	Oriole PS 40043	DO YOU LOVE ME (LP)	200

CONTRABAND
| 74 | Transatlantic BIG 518 | Lady For Today/On The Road | 6 |
| 74 | Transatlantic TRA 278 | CONTRABAND (LP, with lyric insert) | 25 |

(see also Mae McKenna)

CONTRAST
| 69 | Orange OAS 202 | Hey That's No Way To Say Goodbye/We Can Make It If We Try | 8 |

CONTRASTS featuring BOB MORRISON
64	Parlophone R 5095	I Can't Get You Out Of My Mind/Click When You're In Love	5
64	Parlophone R 5190	Call Me/Come On Let's Go	5
68	Monument MON 1018	What A Day/Lonely Child	5

(see also Bill Forbes)

CONTROLLED BLEEDING
| 86 | Sterile SR 11 | HEADCRACK (LP) | 20 |

CONUNDRUM & RICHARD HARVEY
| 78 | Streetsong No. 1 | Black Birds Of Brittany/SHIRLEY COLLINS & ANNIE POWER: The Mariners Farewell (poster p/s) | 18 |

(see also Bert Jansch, Shirley Collins)

CONVAIRS
| 66 | HMV POP 1549 | Tomorrow Is A Long Time/Midnight Mary | 10 |

BERT CONVY & THUNDERBIRDS
| 55 | London HLB 8190 | C'mon Back/Hoo Bop De Bow (78 rpm = £40) | 150 |
| 56 | Capitol CL 14601 | Heaven On Earth/CHEERS: Que Pasa Muchacha (78 rpm = £20) | 25 |

(see also Cheers, Thunderbirds)

CONNIE CONWAY
60   London HA-W 2214   CONNIE CONWAY (LP) 20

MIKE CONWAY
68   Plexium PXM 1   Reign Of King Sadness/I'm Gonna Get Me A Woman 5

RUSS CONWAY
60   Columbia DB 4418   Royal Event/Rule Britannia! (78) 8
      (see also John Barry, Ronnie Harris, Olivers)

STEVE CONWAY
55   Columbia SEG 7573   MEMORIES OF STEVE CONWAY (EP, company sleeve) 10
56   Columbia SEG 7649   MORE MEMORIES OF STEVE CONWAY (EP) 10

JIMMY CONWELL
72   Jay Boy BOY 64   Cigarette Ashes/Second Hand Happiness 10

COO-COO RACHAS
59   Capitol CL 15024   Chili Beans/Track Down 15

RY COODER
71   Reprise RS 23497   How Can A Poor Man Stand Such Times And Live/Goin' To Brownsville 7
71   Reprise RSLP 6402   RY COODER (LP). 18
72   Reprise K 44142   INTO THE PURPLE VALLEY (LP, with lyric sheet) 15
      (see also Don Everly)

ENGLAND COOK
72   Explosion EX 2063   Samba Girl/NOW GENERATION: Samba (Version) 5

LITTLE JOE COOK (U.K.)
65   Sue WI 385   Stormy Monday Blues (Parts 1 & 2) 50
      (see also Chris Farlowe, Beazers)

LITTLE JOE COOK (U.S.)
68   Sonet SON 2002   Don't You Have Feelings?/Hold On To Your Money 10
74   Sonet SON 2041   Hold On To Your Money/Don't You Have Feelings? (reissue, sides reversed) 5

PETER COOK
65   Pye 7N 15847   Georgia/There And Bach Again 40
      (see also Peter London)

PETER COOK
65   Decca F 12182   The Ballad Of Spotty Muldoon/Lovely Lady Of The Roses 18
61   Parlophone PMC 1145   BEYOND THE FRINGE (LP, with other artists) 20
63   Parlophone PMC 1190   BRIDGE ON THE RIVER WYE (LP, with other artists; also stereo PCS 3036) . . 20/25
63   Parlophone PMC 1198   PETER COOK PRESENTS THE ESTABLISHMENT (LP, with other artists) 20
65   Decca LK 4722   PETER COOK PRESENTS MISTY MR. WISTY (LP) 25
65   Transatlantic TRA 131   PRIVATE EYE'S BLUE RECORD (LP, with other artists) 25

PETER COOK & DUDLEY MOORE
62   Parlophone R 4969   Excerpts From Beyond The Fringe: Sitting On The Bench/The End Of The
                                           World (with Alan Bennett & Jonathan Miller) 15
65   Decca F 12158   Goodbyeee (& Dudley Moore Trio)/DUDLEY MOORE TRIO: Not Only But Also . . . 10
66   Decca F 12380   Isn't She A Sweetie/Bo Dudley 12
67   Decca F 12551   The L.S. Bumble Bee/The Bee Side 30
67   Decca F 12710   Bedazzled/Love Me 40
65   Parlophone GEP 8940   PETER COOK AND DUDLEY MOORE (EP) 12
65   Decca DFE 8644   BY APPOINTMENT (EP) 12
65   Decca LK 4703   NOT ONLY PETER COOK BUT ALSO DUDLEY MOORE (LP) 22
66   Decca LK 4785   ONCE MOORE WITH COOK (LP) 22
68   Decca LK/SKL 4923   BEDAZZLED (LP, soundtrack) 100
68   Decca LK 4981   GOODBYE AGAIN (LP, excerpts from TV series) 20
71   Decca LK 5080   NOT ONLY BUT ALSO (LP) 20
      (see also Dudley Moore Trio)

PAUL COOKE
71   Ackee ACK 129   That Girl Was Mine/No Harm 5

ROGER (JAMES) COOKE
68   NEMS 56 3719   If I Didn't Have You/I Know It's You. 7
69   Columbia DB 8510   Not That It Matters Anymore/Paper Chase 6
69   Columbia DB 8556   Stop/Someday 6
69   Columbia DB 8596   Smiling Through My Tears/Ain't That A Wonderful Thing (with Eve Graham) 6
71   Columbia DB 8761   If You Would Stay/Mama Packed A Picnic Tea. 6
71   Columbia DB 8806   People I Gotta Dream/Today I Killed A Man I Didn't Know 6
70   Columbia SCX 6388   STUDY (LP) 20
72   Regal Zono. SRZA 8508   MEANWHILE ... BACK AT THE WORLD (LP, gatefold sleeve) 20
73   Regal Zono. SLRZ 1035   MINSTREL IN FLIGHT (LP) 20
      (see also David & Jonathan)

SAM COOKE
57   London HLU 8506   You Send Me/Summertime (78 rpm = £18) 40
58   London HLU 8615   That's All I Need To Know/I Don't Want To Cry (78 rpm = £30) 60
58   HMV POP 568   Love You Most Of All/Win Your Love For Me (78 rpm = £40) 45
59   HMV POP 610   Everybody Likes To Cha Cha Cha/The Little Things You Do (78 rpm = £50) 45
59   HMV POP 642   Only Sixteen/Let's Go Steady Again (78 rpm = £80) 15
59   HMV POP 675   There, I've Said It Again/One Hour Ahead Of The Posse 40
60   London HLU 9046   Happy In Love/I Need You Now 50
60   RCA RCA 1184   Teenage Sonata/If You Were The Only Girl 22
60   HMV POP 754   Wonderful World/Along The Navajo Trail 30
60   RCA RCA 1202   Chain Gang/I Fall In Love Everyday 15
61   RCA RCA 1221   Sad Mood/Love Me 15
61   RCA RCA 1230   That's It, I Quit, I'm Movin' On/What Do You Say 15
61   RCA RCA 1242   Cupid/Farewell, My Darling 15

Sam COOKE

61	RCA RCA 1260	Feel It/It's Alright	15
62	RCA RCA 1277	Twisting The Night Away/One More Time	10
62	RCA RCA 1296	Bring It On Home To Me/Having A Party	10
62	RCA RCA 1310	Nothing Can Change This Love/Somebody Have Mercy	10
63	RCA RCA 1327	Send Me Some Loving/Baby Baby Baby	10
63	RCA RCA 1341	Another Saturday Night/Love Will Find A Way	10
63	RCA RCA 1361	Frankie And Johnny/Cool Train	10
63	RCA RCA 1367	Little Red Rooster/Shake Rattle And Roll	15
64	RCA RCA 1386	Good News/Basin Street Blues	10
64	RCA RCA 1405	Good Times/Tennessee Waltz	12
64	RCA RCA 1420	Cousin Of Mine/That's Where It's At	15
65	RCA RCA 1436	Shake/A Change Is Gonna Come	15
65	RCA RCA 1452	It's Got The Whole World Shakin'/Ease My Troublin' Mind	20
65	RCA RCA 1476	Sugar Dumpling/Bridge Of Tears	50
68	RCA RCA 1701	Another Saturday Night/DUANE EDDY: Dance With The Guitar Man (withdrawn)	15+
69	RCA RCA 1817	Cupid/Farewell, My Darling (reissue)	5
63	RCA RCX 7117	HEART AND SOUL (EP)	35
64	RCA RCX 7128	SWING SWEETLY (EP)	50
58	HMV CLP 1261	SAM COOKE (LP, with Bumps Blackwell Orchestra)	130
59	HMV CLP 1273	ENCORE (LP)	100
61	RCA RD 27190	COOKE'S TOUR (LP, also stereo SF 5076)	45/60
61	RCA RD 27215	HITS OF THE FIFTIES (LP, also stereo SF 5098)	45/60
61	RCA RD 27222	SWING LOW (LP)	50
62	RCA RD 27245	MY KIND OF BLUES (LP, also stereo SF 5120)	50/65
62	RCA RD 27263	TWISTIN' THE NIGHT AWAY (LP, also stereo SF 5133)	50/65
63	RCA RD/SF 7539	MR. SOUL (LP, mono/stereo)	50/60
63	RCA RD/SF 7583	NIGHT BEAT (LP)	50/75
64	RCA RD/SF 7635	AIN'T THAT GOOD NEWS (LP, mono/stereo)	40/55
65	RCA RD/SF 7674	AT THE COPA (LP, mono/stereo)	40/55
65	RCA RD/SF 7730	SHAKE (LP, mono/stereo)	45/60
65	London HA-U 8232	THE SOUL STIRRERS FEATURING SAM COOKE (LP)	100
66	RCA RD/SF 7764	TRY A LITTLE LOVE (LP)	45
66	Immediate IMLP 002	THE WONDERFUL WORLD OF SAM COOKE (LP)	60
74	BBC	SAM COOKE AND OTHERS (LP, for radio use)	100

COOKIE CREW
87	Rhythm King LEFT12T	Females (12")	8

COOKIES
62	London HLU 9634	Chains/Stranger In My Arms	22
63	London HLU 9704	Don't Say Nothin' Bad About My Baby/Softly In The Night	22
63	Colpix PX 11012	Will Power/I Want A Boy For My Birthday	22
64	Colpix PX 11020	Girls Grow Up Faster Than Boys/Only To Other People	25

(see also Earl-Jean, Cinderellas, Dorothy Jones)

COOL
69	DeWolfe DW/LP 3136	POP SOUNDS (LP, music library only)	40

(see also Elastic Band)

JOE COOL & KILLERS
77	Ariola ARO 165	I Just Don't Care/My Way	6

(see also Killers)

OLIVER COOL
60	Columbia DB 4552	Oliver Cool/I Like Girls	10
61	Columbia DB 4616	Give Me The Summertime/I Said Yeah	10

COOL BREEZE
71	Patheway PAT 103	People Ask What Love Is/There'll Be No More Sad Tomorrows	20
72	Decca F 13324	Summertime Sunshine/Sing Out Your Love	6
75	Bus Stop BUS 1023	Do It Some More/Citizen Jones	6

COOL CATS
68	Jolly JY 007	What Kind Of Man/HELMSLEY MORRIS: Little Things	40
69	Jolly JY 009	Hold Your Love/ALVA LEWIS: Hang My Head And Cry	30

COOLERS
73	Bread BR 1112	The Youth Of Today/TYRONE TAYLOR: Close Observation	6

EDDIE COOLEY & DIMPLES
57	Columbia DB 3873	Priscilla/Got A Little Woman (78 rpm = £65)	250

SPADE COOLEY & HIS FIDDLIN' FRIENDS
51	Brunswick 04812	Horse Hair Boogie/Down Yonder (78)	10

RITA COOLIDGE
83	A&M AM 007	All Time High/All Time High (Extended Instrumental) (p/s)	6
83	Scanlite BOND 1	All Time High/All Time High (Extended Instrumental) (p/s)	12

COOL MEN
58	Parlophone GEP 8739	COOL FOR CATS NO. 1 (EP)	25
58	Parlophone GEP 8752	COOL FOR CATS NO. 2 (EP)	25

COOL NOTES
80	Jama JADC 0008	Billy The Kid/Kidnap My Baby (12")	12
80	Jama JADC 0024	My Tune (Re-Mix)/Version (12")	30

COOL SPIN
67	Coxsone CS 7032	Yakety Yak/SOUL VENDORS : Drum Song	10

COOL SPOON (Jeff Dixon & Alton Ellis)
67	Coxsone CS 7031	Yakety Yak/SOUL VENDORS: Drum Song	25

COOL STICKY

68	Amalgamated AMG 825	Train To Soulsville/ERIC MONTY MORRIS: Cinderella (actually by Errol Dunkley)	30

CHRIS COOMBES

65	Holyground HG 110	WHERE IT'S AT (EP, 99 only)	35

ALICE COOPER

71	Straight W 7209	Eighteen/Body	50
71	Warner Bros K 16127	Under My Wheels/Desperado	8
72	Warner Bros K 16188	School's Out/Gutter Cat (p/s)	10
72	Warner Bros K 16214	Elected/Luney Tune (p/s)	10
73	Warner Bros/ Lyntone LYN 2585/6	Slick Black Limousine/Extracts From: Unfinished Sweet/Elected/No More Mr Nice Guy/Billion Dollar Babies/I Love The Dead (33rpm flexi free with *NME*)	10
74	Warner Bros K 16409	School's Out/No More Mr. Nice Guy/Elected/Billion Dollar Babies (maxi-45)	5
74	Chrysalis CHS 2069	I'm Flash/ELKIE BROOKS: Sacrifice (p/s, promo only)	35
75	Anchor ANC 1012	Department Of Youth/Cold Ethyl (p/s)	6
75	Anchor ANC 1018	Only Women Bleed/Devil's Food	5
75	Anchor ANC 1025	Welcome To My Nightmare/Black Widow	5
75	Anchor ANE 7001	Welcome To My Nightmare/Department Of Youth/Black Widow/ Only Women Bleed (EP, p/s)	6
75	Anchor ANE 12001	Welcome To My Nightmare/Department Of Youth/Black Widow/ Only Women Bleed (12" EP, p/s)	8
76	Warner Bros K 16792	I Never Cry/Got To Hell (p/s)	5
77	Warner Bros K 16935	(No More) Love At Your Convenience/It's Hot Tonight (p/s, gothic type on label)	5
80	Warner Bros K 17598	Clones (We're All)/Model Citizen (p/s)	7
86	MCA MCA 1090	He's Back (The Man Behind The Mask)/Billion Dollar Babies (poster p/s)	6
89	Epic ALICE 3	Bed Of Nails/I'm Your Gun (p/s, with poster)	8
89	Epic ALICE 3	Bed Of Nails/I'm Your Gun/Go To Hell (live) (12", picture disc)	8
89	Epic 655 061-2	Poison/Trash/Ballad Of Dwight Fry (live)/I Got A Line On You (CD, 'bottle' pack)	12
89	Epic ALICEP 4	House Of Fire/This Maniac's In Love With You (shaped picture disc)	6
91	Epic 657 438-9	Love's A Loaded Gun/Fire/Eighteen (live) (CD, gun-shaped p/s)	8
69	Straight STS 1051	PRETTIES FOR YOU (LP, purple label, gatefold sleeve)	65
69	Straight STS 1061	EASY ACTION (LP, purple label, gatefold sleeve)	60
71	Straight STS 1065	LOVE IT TO DEATH (LP, purple label, gatefold sleeve)	60
71	Warner Bros K 56005	KILLER (LP, green label, gatefold sleeve with perforated foldout calendar)	25
72	Warner Bros K 56007	SCHOOL'S OUT (LP, green label, 'desktop' gatefold sleeve, with 'paper panties' inner)	75
73	Warner Bros K 56013	BILLION DOLLAR BABIES (LP, green label, gatefold embossed sleeve with attached perforated cards, with $ billion note & inner sleeve)	18
73	Warner Bros K 46177	LOVE IT TO DEATH (LP, reissue, green label, gatefold sleeve)	18
73	Warner Bros K 66021	SCHOOL DAYS (2-LP, gatefold sleeve, reissue of STS 1051 & 1061)	18
74	Warner Bros K 56018	MUSCLE OF LOVE (LP, 'cardboard box' sleeve, with insert & inner sleeve)	15

(see also Billion Dollar Babies)

GARNELL COOPER & KINFOLKS

63	London HL 9757	Green Monkey/Long Distance	20

HENRY COOPER

76	DJM DJS 10734	Knock Me Down With A Feather/Knocked Out For Your Love (p/s)	10/6

LES COOPER & SOUL ROCKERS

62	Stateside SS 142	Wiggle Wobble/Dig Yourself	15

MARTY COOPER CLAN

63	RCA Victor RD 7596	NEW SOUNDS — OLD GOODIES (LP)	15

MIKE COOPER

70	Dawn DNX 2501	Your Lovely Ways (Parts 1 & 2)/Watching You Fall (Parts 1 & 2) (p/s)	7
71	Dawn DNX 2511	Too Late Now/The Ballad Of Fulton Allen/Good Times (p/s)	7
72	Dawn DNS 1022	Time In Hand/Schwabisch Hall	6
60s	Saydisc SD 137	UP THE COUNTRY BLUES (EP)	70
68	Matchbox SDM 159	THE INVERTED WORLD (LP, with Ian A. Anderson)	60
69	Pye NSPL 18281	OH REALLY!? (LP)	30
70	Dawn DNLS 3005	DO I KNOW YOU? (LP)	20
70	Dawn DNLS 3011	TROUT STEEL (LP, with poster insert)	25
71	Dawn DNLS 3026	PLACES I KNOW (LP, with insert)	20
72	Dawn DNLS 3031	THE MACHINE GUN COMPANY (LP)	18
74	Fresh Air 6370 500	LIFE AND DEATH IN PARADISE (LP)	12

(see also Ian A. Anderson, Heron)

TOMMY COOPER

61	Palette PG 9019	Don't Jump Off The Roof Dad/How Come There's No Dog Day?	18
67	Pye 7N 17259	Happy Tommy/Tom Tom The Piper's Son	6

COOPER TEMPLE CLAUSE

00s	private pressing	The Crayon Demos/Who Needs Enemies?/Let's Kill Music/Devil Walks In The Sand Demos (CD-R, in hand-crayoned sleeve)	100
00s	Morning MORNING 27	A.I.M. (1-track promo-only CD, avaiable on mail order from *NME*)	15
01	Morning MORNING 2	THE HARDWARE EP (Way Out West/Sister Soul//The Devil Walks In The Sand/ Solitude) (2 x 7", 1 black and 1 white vinyl, poly sleeves in box, 500 only)	40
01	Morning MORNING 6	THE WARFARE EP (Panzer Attack/ I'll Still Write/I'll Still Write [Acoustic]/Mansell) (2 x 7", 1 black and white 1 vinyl in box, 1000 only)	15
01	Morning MORNING 5	THE WARFARE EP (Panzer Attack/ I'll Still Write/Mansell) (CD, digipak)	12
02	Morning MORNING 20	SEE THIS THROUGH AND LEAVE (6 x 7", limited, numbered box set)	20

COWBOY COPAS

51	Vogue V 9001	The Feudin' Boogie (with Grandpa Jones)/Strange Little Girl (78)	10
53	Parlophone R 3708	It's No Sin To Love You/I've Grown So Used To You (78)	10

MINT VALUE £

53	Parlophone R 3756	Doll Of Clay/If Wishes Were Horses (78)	10
54	Parlophone CMSP 10	I Can't Go On/A Wreath On The Door Of My Heart (export issue) (78 rpm = £10)	30
54	Parlophone MSP 6079	Tennessee Senorita/If You Will Let Me Be Your Love (78 rpm, R3812 = £10)	30
54	Parlophone DP 384	Look What I Got/Will You Forget (78, export issue)	10
54	Parlophone DP 390	The Man Upstairs/He Stands By The Window (78, export issue)	10
54	Parlophone MSP 6109	A Heartbreak Ago/The Blue Waltz (78 rpm, R3880 = £10)	30
55	Parlophone MSP 6164	I'll Waltz With You In My Dreams/Return To Sender (78 rpm, R 4005 = £10)	30
60	Melodisc M 1566	Alabam/I Can	20
55	Parlophone GEP 8527	FAVOURITE COWBOY SONGS (EP)	22
56	Parlophone GEP 8575	WESTERN STYLE (EP)	22
50s	Parlophone CGEP 3	COWBOY COPAS (EP, export issue)	22
62	Top Rank JKP 3014	COUNTRY MUSIC (EP)	22
63	Stateside SE 1003	COUNTRY HITS (EP)	15
64	London R-ED 1418	THE UNFORGETTABLE COWBOY COPAS VOLUME 1 (EP)	15
64	London R-ED 1419	THE UNFORGETTABLE COWBOY COPAS VOLUME 2 (EP)	15
64	London R-ED 1420	THE UNFORGETTABLE COWBOY COPAS VOLUME 3 (EP)	15
61	Melodisc MLP 12-119	COWBOY COPAS (LP)	15
63	Stateside SL 10035	SONGS THAT MADE HIM FAMOUS (LP)	15
63	London HA-B 8088	COUNTRY ENTERTAINER NO. 1 (LP)	25
64	London HA-B 8180	STARS OF THE GRAND OLE OPRY — COWBOY COPAS (LP)	20

(see also Johnny Bond)

JULIAN COPE

84	Mercury MADOX 004	Head Hang Low/Elegant Chaos/Strasbourg/Lunatic And Fire Pistol (excerpts), (tracks by Spirit) (flexidisc sampler, printed plain sleeve)	5
85	Mercury MER 1822	Sunspots/I Went On A Chourney/Mik Mak Mok/Land Of Fear (double pack)	6
86	Island ISBN 290	World Shut Your Mouth/World Shut Your Mouth (Trouble Funk Remix)/Umpteenth Unnatural Blues/Levitation (double pack box set with biography, photos & stickers)	8
87	Antar 4503	Interview/Christmas Mourning/Transmitting (fan club box set, with card, biography, membership card, letter, photos & stickers)	7
91	Island JC 1	Safesurfer/If You Love Me At All (33rpm, sold at gigs, stickered white sleeve)	12
94	K.A.K. (no cat. no.)	Paranormal In The West Country (Original Version)/(String Quartet Version)/ (Acoustic Version)/(Krankenhausmusik Version) (mail-order only via offer with Queen Elizabeth LP)	12
87	Island ILPS 9861	SAINT JULIAN (LP, with free 12" interview LP [JCCLP 1])	12

(see also Teardrop Explodes, Rabbi Joseph Gordan)

KEN COPE & BREAKAWAYS

63	Pye 7N 15524	Hands Off, Stop Muckin' About/Why Am I So Shy	5

(see also Breakaways)

SUZY COPE

61	HMV POP 941	Teenage Fool/Juvenile Delinquent	25
62	HMV POP 1047	Not Never Not Now/Kisses And Tears	25
63	HMV POP 1167	Biggity Big/Doing What You Know Is Wrong	25
65	CBS 201792	You Can't Say I Never Told You/And Now I Don't Want You	25

AL(L)AN COPELAND

57	Vogue Coral Q 72237	Feeling Happy/You Don't Know	15
57	Vogue Coral Q 72277	How Will I Know?/Will You Still Be Mine	5
59	Pye International 7N 25007	Flip Flop/Lots More Love (as Allan Copeland) (78 rpm = £10)	25

KEN COPELAND

57	London HLP 8423	Pledge Of Love/MINTS: Night Air (78 rpm = £75)	300

BOB & RON COPPER

63	EFDSS 1002	BOB & RON COPPER (LP)	35

COPPER FAMILY

71	Leader LED 2067	A SONG FOR EVERY SEASON (LP, sampler, tracks from 4-LP set)	40

COPPERFIELD

69	Instant IN 004	Any Old Time/I'm No Good For Her	12
69	Parlophone R 5818	I'll Hold Out My Hand/Far Away Love	6

(see also Quartz)

COPS 'N ROBBERS

64	Decca F 12019	St. James Infirmary/There's Gotta Be A Reason	50
65	Pye 7N 15870	I Could Have Danced All Night/Just Keep Right On	25
65	Pye 7N 15928	It's All Over Now Baby Blue/I've Found Out	25

(see also Fairies)

COPY CATS

69	Bullet BU 419	Copy Cat (with Derrick Morgan)/BUNNY LEE ALL STARRS: Hot Lead	12

CORAL

01	Deltasonic DLT 1	SHADOWS FALL EP (Shadows Fall/The Ballad Of Simon Diamond/A Sparrow's Song) (CD, 1000 only)	50
01	Deltasonic DLTCD 3	THE OLDEST PATH EP (The Oldest Path/God Knows/Short Balled/Flys (CD, 1000 only, picture disc)	18

CORBAN

78	Acorn AC 002	A BREAK IN THE CLOUDS (LP, with insert)	18

HARRY H. CORBETT

62	Pye 7N 15468	Junk Shop/The Isle Of Clerkenwell	8
63	Pye 7N 15552	Like The Big Guys Do/The Green Eye	8
63	Pye 7N 15584	The Table And The Chair/Things We Never Had	8
67	Decca F 12714	Flower Power Fred/(I'm) Saving All My Love (with Unidentified Flower Objects)	12
71	Columbia DB 8840	Harry You Love Her/It's The End Of A Beautiful Night	8

(see also Wilfred Brambell, Wilfred Brambell & Harry H. Corbett, Faraway Folk)

MIKE CORBETT & JAY HIRSH
71	Atlantic 2400 141	MIKE CORBETT & JAY HIRSH (LP, gatefold sleeve)	20

(see also Mr. Flood's Party)

RONNIE CORBETT
68	Columbia DB 8512	Big Man/Fancy You Fancying Me	5
70	Philips 6006 070	It's All Going Up, Up, Up/Put On A Happy Face	5

CORBY & CHAMPAGNE
66	Pye 7N 17203	Time Marches On/I'll Be Back	5

JASON CORD
69	Chapter One CH 102	I've Got My Eyes On You/I Can't Take No More Of Your Lies	6
69	Chapter One CH 110	Why Shouldn't I/Spring Never Came Twice	6

FRANK CORDELL & HIS ORCHESTRA
56	HMV 7M 397	Port-Au-Prince/Double Cross TV Theme	6
56	HMV 7M 419	Sadie's Shawl/Flamenco Love	12
59	HMV POP 576	Granada/Lovely Is The Evening (78)	6
61	HMV POP 824	The Black Bear/Darling Charlie	8
61	HMV POP 852	Theme From 'The Rebel'/Ou La La	6
63	HMV CSD 1475	HERE THIS! (LP)	15

PHIL CORDELL
69	Warner Bros WB 8001	Pumping The Water/Red Lady	7

(see also Thursday's Children)

CORDES
65	Cavern Sound IMSTL 1	Give Her Time/She's Leaving	60

LOUISE CORDET
62	Decca F 11476	I'm Just A Baby/In A Matter Of Moments	8
62	Decca F 11520	Sweet Enough/Someone Else's Fool	6
63	Decca F 11673	Around And Around/Which Way The Wind Blows	10
64	Decca F 11824	Don't Let The Sun Catch You Crying/Loving Baby	10
64	Decca F 11875	Don't Make Me Over/Two Lovers	15
62	Decca DFE 8515	THE SWEET BEAT OF LOUISE CORDET (EP)	60

CORDUROYS
66	Planet PLF 122	Tick Tock/Too Much Of A Woman	40

CHICK COREA (& RETURN TO FOREVER)
72	ECM ECM 1018/9	PARIS CONCERT FEBRUARY 1971 (2-LP, as Corea & Braxton & Holland)	15
74	Atlantic K 60081	INNER SPACE (2-LP)	15
74	People PLEO 9	SUNDANCE (LP)	15

(see also Return To Forever)

PADDY COREA
72	Explosion EX 2066	Soul And Inspiration/STAGS: You Must Be Trying My Faith	6

CORKSCREW
79	Highway SHY 7005	FOR OPENERS (LP)	25

CORNBREAD & JERRY
61	London HLG 9352	L'il Ole Me/Loco Moto	12

DON CORNEL & ETERNALS
70	Moodisc MU 3506	Christmas Joy/WINSTON & RUPERT: Musically Beat	7

CORNELIUS BROTHERS & SISTER ROSE
71	United Artists UP 35218	Treat Her Like A Lady/Over At My Place	8
72	United Artists UP 35378	Too Late To Turn Back Now/Lift Your Love Higher	20
73	United Artists UP 35502	I'm Never Gonna Be Alone Anymore/Let's Stay Together	8

DON CORNELL
51	HMV JO 212	I Need You So/It Couldn't Happen To A Sweeter Girl (78)	6
54	Vogue Coral Q 2013	Hold My Hand/I'm Blessed	20
54	Vogue Coral Q 2037	S'Posin'/I Was Lucky	18
55	Vogue Coral Q 72058	No Man Is An Island/All At Once	10
55	Vogue Coral Q 72070	Give Me Your Love/When You Are In Love	10
55	Vogue Coral Q 72071	Athena/Size 12	10
55	Vogue Coral Q 72073	Stranger In Paradise/The Devil's In Your Eyes	18
55	Vogue Coral Q 72080	Unchained Melody/Most Of All (78 rpm = £8)	12
55	Vogue Coral Q 72104	Love Is A Many Splendored Thing/The Bible Tells Me So	10
56	Vogue Coral Q 72132	There Once Was A Beautiful/Make A Wish	12
56	Vogue Coral Q 72144	Teenage Meeting (Gonna Rock It Right)/I Still Have A Prayer (78 rpm = £8)	35
56	Vogue Coral Q 72152	Rock Island Line/Na-Ne Na-Na (78 rpm = £8)	22
56	Vogue Coral Q 72164	But Love Me (Love But Me)/Fort Knox	18
56	Vogue Coral Q 72203	All Of You/Heaven Only Knows	15
57	Vogue Coral Q 72218	See-Saw/From The Bottom Of My Heart	20
57	Vogue Coral Q 72234	Let's Be Friends/Afternoon In Madrid	15
57	Vogue Coral Q 72257	Sittin' In The Balcony/Let's Get Lost (78 rpm = £10)	30
57	Vogue Coral Q 72276	Mama Guitar/A Face In The Crowd (78 rpm = £10)	30
57	Vogue Coral Q 72291	There's Only You/Non Dimenticar	12
58	Coral Q 72308	Before It's Time To Say Goodnight/Mailman, Bring Me No More Blues	10
58	Coral Q 72308	Before It's Time To Say Goodnight/Mailman, Bring Me No More Blues (78)	12
58	Coral Q 72313	I've Got Bells On My Heart/Keep God In The Home (78 rpm = £14)	10
59	Pye International 7N 25041	Sempre Amore/Forever Couldn't Be Long Enough (78 rpm = £12)	10
59	London HLD 8937	This Earth Of Mine/The Gang That Sang "Heart Of My Heart" (78 rpm = £15)	10
54	Vogue Coral LVC 10004	DON CORNELL FOR YOU (10" LP)	20
56	Coral LVA 9037	LET'S GET LOST (LP)	20

JERRY CORNELL
55	London HL 8157	Please Don't Talk About Me When I'm Gone/St. Louis Blues	25

MINT VALUE £

LYN CORNELL

60	Decca F 11227	Like Love/Demon Lover	22
60	Decca F 11260	Teaser/What A Feeling	10
60	Decca F 11277	Never On Sunday/Swain Kelly	5
60	Decca F 11301	The Angel And The Stranger/Xmas Stocking	5
61	Decca F 11326	The Sweet Life (La Dolce Vita)/When Is Someday	5
61	Decca F 11374	Surely In Love/Adios My Love	5
62	Decca F 11430	African Waltz/Moanin'	6
62	Decca F 11469	I Sold My Heart To The Junkman/Step Up And Rescue Me	18
63	Decca F 11775	Sally Go Round The Roses/You Can Kiss Me If You Like	10

CORNFLAKES

62	Fontana 267 227TF	Oh, Listen To The Band/Moonstruck	8

ARNOLD CORNS

71	B&C CB 149	Moonage Daydream/Hang Onto Yourself (as 'The Arnold Corns')	75
72	B&C CB 189	Hang Onto Yourself/Man In The Middle	60
74	Mooncrest MOON 25	Hang Onto Yourself/Man In The Middle (reissue)	18
	(see also David Bowie)		

CORONADOS

64	London HL 9895	Love Me With All Your Heart/Querida	10
67	Stateside SS 2043	Johnny B. Goode/Shook Me Down	10

CORONETS

54	Columbia SCM 5117	Do, Do, Do, Do, Do, Do, Do It Again/I Ain't Gonna Do It No More	15
56	Columbia SCM 5235	Lizzie Borden/My Believing Heart	10
56	Columbia SCM 5261	There's No Song Like An Old Song/The Magic Touch	10
56	Columbia DB 3827	Someone To Love/The Rocking Horse Cowboy	10
56	Columbia SEG 7603	RHYTHM AND BLUES (EP, as Coronets with Eric Jupp Orchestra)	18
56	Columbia SEG 7621	THE PERFECT COMBINATION (EP, as Coronets with Eric Jupp Orchestra)	10
56	Columbia SEG 7714	SONG SHOW (EP)	10
	(see also Chris Sandford & Coronets, Tony Brent, Ronnie Harris, Benny Hill, Eric Jupp, Lee Lawrence)		

CORONETS

68	Stresa BEV SP 1104/1105	I Wonder Why/You're Leaving Tomorrow	45

CORPORATION (Jamaica)

70	Grape GR 3022	Sweet Musille/Walking Thru' Jerusalem	12
	(see also Claudette & Corporation, Billy Jack)		

CORPORATION (U.S.)

69	Capitol E-T/E-ST 175	THE CORPORATION (LP)	25

CORRIE FOLK TRIO/CORRIES

63	Waverley SLP 530	Love Is Teasing/O, Waly Waly (p/s)	8
63	Waverley ELP 129	CORRIE FOLK TRIO (EP)	14
63	Waverley ELP 131	YON FOLK SONGS IS FOR THE BURDS (EP)	14
63	Waverley ELP 132	MORE FOLK SONGS FOR THE BURDS (EP)	14
65	Waverley ZLP 2042	CORRIE FOLK TRIO WITH PADDIE BELL (LP, also stereo SZLP 2043)	16
65	Waverley ZLP 2050	THE PROMISE OF THE DAY (LP)	16

CORRS

95	Atlantic A 5727CD	Runaway/Leave Me Alone (CD)	8
96	Atlantic A 5662 CD	Love To Love You (radio edit)/Rainy Day/Carraroe Jig (CD, includes 6 cards)	10
99	Atlantic PC1/C01	Lifting Me (Mixes)/Interactive CD-Rom Interview	10
98	Atlantic 80917 2	TALK ON CORNERS (CD, with 4 prints & cassette)	10

CORSAIRS (Jamaica)

70	Unity UN 558	Goodnight My Love/Lover Girl	8

CORSAIRS (U.K.)

67	CBS 202624	Pay You Back With Interest/I'm Gonna Shut You Down	15

CORSAIRS (U.S.)

62	Pye International 7N 25142	I'll Take You Home/Sitting On Your Doorstep (with Jay 'Bird' Uzzel)	15

BOB CORT (SKIFFLE GROUP)

57	Decca FJ 10831	It Takes A Worried Man To Sing A Worried Blues/	
		Don't You Rock Me Daddy-O (78 rpm = £8)	20
57	Decca F 10892	Six-Five Special/Roll Jen Jenkins (78 rpm = £8)	20
57	Decca F 10899	Maggie May/Jessamine (with Liz Winters)	8
57	Decca F 10905	Schoolday (Ring! Ring! Goes The Bell)/Ain't It A Shame	
		(To Sing Skiffle On Sunday)	20
57	Decca F 10951	'Bob Cort Skiffle Party' Medley (Parts 1 & 2)	5
58	Decca F 10989	The Ark (Noah Found Grace In The Eyes Of God)/Yes! Suh!	8
59	Decca F 11109	Foggy Foggy Dew/On Top Of Old Smokey (solo) (78 rpm = £10)	5
59	Decca F 11145	Waterloo/Battle Of New Orleans (solo) (78 rpm = £8)	7
59	Decca F 11160	Kissin' Time/I'm Gonna Get Married (solo) (78 rpm = £8)	7
	William Timpson Ltd	The Shop In The Cellar (1-sided 78, 200 only)	15
60	Decca F 11197	El Paso/A Handful Of Gold (solo)	5
60	Decca F 11256	Mule Skinner Blues/The Ballad Of Walter Williams (solo) (78 rpm = £10)	12
60	Decca F 11285	The Ballad Of The Alamo/Five Brothers (solo)	5
59	Decca DFE 6630	BARRACK ROOM BALLADS (EP)	10
61	Decca DFE 6686	BOB CORT'S GENTLEFOLK (EP, as Bob Cort's Gentlefolk)	10
57	Decca LK 4222	AIN'T IT A SHAME (LP)	30
59	Decca LK 4301	ESKIMO NELL (LP)	18
	(see also Liz Winters & Bob Cort)		

DAVE 'BABY' CORTEZ

59	London HLU 8852	The Happy Organ/Love Me As I Love You (78 rpm = £6)	12
59	London HLU 8919	The Whistling Organ/I'm Happy (78 rpm = £6)	5
60	Columbia DB 4404	Piano Shuffle/Dave's Special	5

60	London HLU 9126	Deep In The Heart Of Texas/You're Just Right.	15
62	Pye International 7N 25159	Rinky Dink/Getting Right	20
66	Roulette RK 7001	Countdown/Summertime	10
60	London RE-U 1233	DAVE 'BABY' CORTEZ (EP)	40
64	London HA-U 8142	THE GOLDEN HITS OF DAVE 'BABY' CORTEZ (LP)	30

CORTINAS
68	Polydor 56255	Phoebe's Flower Shop/Too Much In Love	20

(see also Octopus)

CORTINAS
77	Step Forward SF 1	Fascist Dictator/Television Families (p/s, first 1,000 in card sleeve)	20/12
78	Step Forward SF 6	Defiant Pose/Independence (p/s).	12
78	Step Forward SF 6	Defiant Pose/Independence (12", pink die-cut sleeve)	12
78	CBS CBS 6759	Heartache/Ask Mr. Waverley (p/s)	8
78	CBS CBS 82831	TRUE ROMANCES (LP, with photo insert)	20

LEE CORVETTE
62	Decca	The Heart You Break (May Be Your Own)/Tender Love.	10

CORVETTES
82	Bitchin BIT 100	Surf, Don't Walk/She'll Be Blonde (p/s)	10
84	Bitchin BIT 101	Girls Cars Girls Sun Girls Surf Girls Fun Girls/The Beach Is Not Enough (p/s)	10

LARRY CORYELL
69	Vanguard SVRL 19051	LADY CORYELL (LP)	15
69	Vanguard SVRL 19059	CORYELL (LP)	15
71	Vanguard 6359 005	SPACES (LP)	30

(see also Jazz Composers Orchestra)

BILL COSBY
67	Warner Bros WB 7072	Little Ole Man (Uptight! Everything's Alright)/Don'cha Know (some in p/s)	40/25
65	Warner Bros W(S) 1567	I STARTED OUT AS A CHILD (LP)	15
66	Warner W(S) 1634	WONDERFULNESS (LP)	15
68	Warner W(S) 1770	IT'S TRUE, IT'S TRUE (LP)	15

COSMIC BABY/VANGELIS
94	East West SAM 1484	A TRIBUTE TO BLADERUNNER (12", double pack, promo only)	20

(see also Vangelis)

COSMIC EYE
72	Regal Zono. SLRZ 1030	DREAM SEQUENCE (LP)	140

COSMO
63	Blue Beat BB 175	Gypsy Woman/Do Unto Others	10
64	Blue Beat BB 244	One God/BUSTER'S ALL STARS: Prince Royal (actually "Reincarnation")	30
64	Blue Beat BB 269	Rice And Badgee/BUSTER'S ALL STARS: The Tickler	40

(see also Cosmo & Dennis, Denzil Dennis)

FRANK COSMO
63	Island WI 058	Revenge/Laughin' At You (B-side actually with Bobby Aitken)	15
63	Island WI 073	Dear Dreams/Go Go Go	15
63	Island WI 100	Merry Christmas/Greetings From Beverley's	20
63	R&B JB 119	I Love You/DON DRUMMOND: Close Of Play	22
64	Island WI 135	Better Get Right/Ameletia	20
64	Black Swan WI 446	Alone/Beautiful Book	20

(see also Two Kings)

COSMO & DENNIS (alias Denzil)
62	Blue Beat BB 145	Bed Of Roses/Tonight And Evermore (as Cosmo & Denzil).	10
65	Blue Beat BB 296	Sweet Rosemarie/Lollipop I'm In Love	12
65	Blue Beat BB 312	Come On Come On/I Don't Want You	12

(see also Cosmo)

COSMOTHEKA
70s	Shy SHY 7001	WINES & SPIRITS (LP)	30

DON COSTA, HIS ORCHESTRA & CHORUS
55	London HLF 8186	Love Is A Many Splendoured Thing/Safe In The Harbour.	40
59	London HLT 8992	I Walk The Line/Cat Walk (78 rpm = £8)	10
60	London HLT 9137	Theme From The Unforgiven/Streets Of Paris	5
60	London HLT 7103	Theme From The Unforgiven/FERRANTE & TEICHER: Theme From The Apartment (export issue)	5

SAM COSTA
61	Palette PG 9026	I'm Changing My Hat To A Bowler/Oh Dear	5

JACK CONSTANZO
61	London HLG 9401	Theme From Route 66/Naked City Theme	5

JACK CONSTANZO & TUBBY HAYES
62	Fontana TFL 5190/ STFL 598	COSTANZO PLUS TUBBS — EQUATION IN RHYTHM (LP, mono/stereo)	60/30

(see also Tubby Hayes)

CELIA COSTELLO
75	Leader LEE 4054	CELIA COSTELLO (LP, with insert)	20

DANNY COSTELLO
57	Oriole CB 1393	Like A Brook Gets Lost In A River/That's Where I Shine	5

DAY COSTELLO
71	Spark SRL 1042	The Long And Winding Road/Free (Unlimited Horizons)	10

(see also Ross McManus)

Elvis COSTELLO

ELVIS COSTELLO (& ATTRACTIONS)

77	Stiff BUY 14	Alison/Welcome To The Working Week (p/s, A-side mispress on white vinyl)	300
77	Stiff BUY 15	Red Shoes/Mystery Dance (p/s, mispress, plays Dream Tobacco by Max Wall)	8

(The above singles were later re-pressed with 'Made In England' on label; these are worth £3 each.)

78	Radar ADA 24	Radio Radio/Tiny Steps (12", promo-only, 500 pressed)	15
78	Radar RG 1	Talking In The Dark/Wednesday Week (p/s, gig freebie)	8
80	F-Beat XX 5P	New Amsterdam/Just A Memory/Dr Luther's Assistant/Ghost Train (picture disc)	6
80	2-Tone CHS TT 7	I Can't Stand Up For Falling Down/Girls Talk (unreleased, later a gig freebie, more common issue has XX1 in run-off groove, 13,000 pressed)	20/12
80	Stiff GRAB 3	STIFF SINGLES FOUR PACK (BUY 11, 14, 15 & 20 in clear plastic wallet)	12
81	F-Beat XX 17	A Good Year For The Roses/Your Angel Steps Out Of Heaven (withdrawn p/s)	10
93	Demon ECPROMO 1	TWO AND A HALF YEARS IN 31 MINUTES (CD, fold-out digipak, promo only)	10
94	Demon ECPROMO 2	HIGHLIGHTS FROM ALMOST BLUE AND IMPERIAL BEDROOM (CD, fold-out digipak, promo only)	10
95	Demon ECPROMO 3	SELECTIONS FROM THE KING OF AMERICA (CD, fold-out digipak, promo only)	10
78	Radar RAD 3	THIS YEAR'S MODEL (LP, with free 7" Stranger In The House/Neat Neat Neat (live) [die-cut company sleeve, SAM 83], 50,000 pressed; 1st 5,000 shrinkwrapped & stickered)	12
79	Radar RAD 15	ARMED FORCES (LP, foldout stickered sleeve with free EP Live At Hollywood High [p/s, SAM 90] & postcards)	12
79	Radar RAD 15	ARMED FORCES (LP, mispress, plays What's So Funny 'Bout Peace, Love & Understanding instead of Two Little Hitlers; sticker on insert)	15
86	IMP FIEND CD 21	ARMED FORCES (CD, with Peace, Love & Understanding)	18
94	Warner Bros PRO-CD 6955	BRUTAL YOUTH WORDS AND MUSIC PROGRAMME (CD, promo only)	18

(see also Nick Lowe, George Jones, Coward Brothers)

JAMES COTTON (BLUES BAND)

78	Buddah BDS 471	Rock'n'Roll Music/Help Me	6
68	Vanguard SVRL 19035	CUT YOU LOOSE! (LP, as James Cotton Blues Band)	25

JIMMY COTTON

62	Columbia SEG 8141	CHRIS BARBER PRESENTS JIMMY COTTON (EP)	25
62	Columbia SEG 8189	CHRIS BARBER PRESENTS JIMMY COTTON NO. 2 (EP)	25

(see also James Cotton Blues Band, Alexis Korner)

MIKE COTTON (SOUND)

62	Columbia DB 4910	The Tinker/Zulu Warrior (as the Mike Cotton Jazz Band)	10
63	Columbia DB 7029	Swing That Hammer/Heartaches (as Mike Cotton Jazzmen)	10
63	Columbia DB 7134	Midnite Flyer/One Mint Julep (as Mike Cotton Band)	10
64	Columbia DB 7267	I Don't Wanna Know/This Little Pig	40
64	Columbia DB 7382	Round And Round/Beau Dudley	50
65	Columbia DB 7623	Make Up Your Mind/I've Got My Eye On You	50
66	Polydor BM 56096	Harlem Shuffle/Like That	50
62	Columbia SEG 8144	COTTON PICKING (EP)	40
63	Columbia SEG 8190	THE WILD AND THE WILLING (EP)	40
64	Columbia 33SX 1647	MIKE COTTON SOUND (LP)	400+

(see also Lucas & Mike Cotton Sound, Satisfaction)

JOHN(NY) COUGAR

78	Riva RIVA 14	I Need A Lover/Born Reckless (as Johnny Cougar, p/s)	7
78	Riva RIVA 16	Factory/Alley Of The Angels (as Johnny Cougar, p/s)	10

(see also John Cougar Mellencamp)

COUGARS

63	Parlophone R 4989	Saturday Night At The Duckpond/See You In Dreamland	15
63	Parlophone R 5038	Red Square/Fly-By-Nite	15
64	Parlophone R 5115	Caviare And Chips/While The City Sleeps	18
63	Parlophone GEP 8886	SATURDAY NIGHT WITH THE COUGARS (EP)	50

ROGER COULAM QUARTET

67	CBS 52399	ORGAN IN ORBIT (LP)	20
70	Fontana 16009	BLOW HOT, BLOW COLD (LP)	20

DENIS COULDRY (& SMILE)

68	Decca F 12734	James In The Basement (solo)/DENIS COULDRY & NEXT COLLECTION: I Am Nearly There	30
68	Decca F 12786	Penny For The Wind/Tea And Toast, Mr. Watson? (as Denis Couldry & Smile)	15

(see also Felius Andromeda)

DENNIS COULSON

73	Elektra K 42148	DENNIS COULSON (LP, gatefold sleeve)	15

COULSON, DEAN, McGUINNESS, FLINT

72	DJM DJLPS 424	LO AND BEHOLD (LP, gatefold sleeve)	18

(see also Manfred Mann, McGuinness Flint, Dennis Coulson, Lyle McGuinness Band)

PHIL COULTER ORCHESTRA

68	Pye 7N 17511	Congratulations/Gold Rush	22

COUNCIL COLLECTIVE

84	Polydor MINEX 1	Soul Deep (Club Mix)/Soul Deep (12", stickered black die-cut sleeve)	8

(see also Style Council, Jimmy Ruffin)

COUNT

74	Purple PUR 122	Gazaroody/The So, So Long	10

(COUNT) BISHOPS

75	Chiswick SW 1	SPEEDBALL (EP, 1st 1,000 in glossy p/s, promos £10)	8
78	Chiswick NS 35	Mr Jones/Human Bean/Route 66/Too Much Too Soon (unissued, test pressings only, as Bishops)	18
77	Chiswick WIK 1	THE COUNT BISHOPS (LP)	12
78	Chiswick CH 7	LIVE AT THE ROUNDHOUSE (10" mini-LP)	12

(see also Cannibals)

COUNT BUSTY & RUDIES
68	Melody MRC 003	You Like It/The Reggay	10

COUNT DOWNE & ZEROS
64	Ember EMB S 189	Hello My Angel/Don't Shed A Tear	40

(see also Peter & Headlines)

COUNTDOWNS
63	United Artists UP 1024	Mouse On The Moon/The Big Safari	10

(see also John Barry)

COUNT FIVE
66	Pye International 7N 25393	Psychotic Reaction/They're Gonna Get You	40

COUNT HOUSE FOLK MUSIC CLUB
65	own label MSCH 2	MORE SINGING AT THE COUNT HOUSE (LP, private pressing)	250

COUNT OSSIE & HIS MYSTIC REVELATION
71	Ashanti ASH 404	Rasta Reggae/Samia	12
71	Moodisc MU 3515	Whispering Drums/SLIM SMITH & UNIQUES: Give Me Some More Loving	15
71	Moodisc HM 105	Whispering Drums/SLIM SMITH & UNIQUES: Give Me Some More Loving	15
74	Ashanti NTI 1301	GROUNATION (3-LP, with Mystic Revelation Of Rastafari)	60

(see also Jackie Estick, Gaylads, Soul Defenders)

COUNT PRINCE
(see under Count Prince Miller)

COUNTRY BOY
64	Blue Beat BB 236	I'm A Lonely Boy (actually by Shenley Duffas)/EDWARD'S ALL STARS: He's Gone Ska	20

COUNTRY CATS
56	Parlophone DP 521	Mountain Mambo/Hot Strings (78, export issue)	6

COUNTRY FOLK
70s	Thule SLP 101	THE COUNTRY FOLK (LP, private pressing)	70

COUNTRY FUNK
70	Polydor 248 2018	COUNTRY FUNK (LP)	22

COUNTRY GAZETTE
72	United Artists UAG 29404	TRAITOR IN OUR MIDST (LP)	15
73	United Artists UAS 29491	DON'T GIVE UP YOUR DAY JOB (LP)	15

(see also Flying Burrito Brothers)

COUNTRY GENTLEMEN
63	Decca F 11766	Greensleeves/Baby Jean	10

(see also High Society, Peter Cowap)

COUNTRY HAMS
74	EMI EMI 2220	Walking In The Park With Eloise/Bridge On The River Suite (p/s, red & brown label)	55
82	EMI EMI 2220	Walking In The Park With Eloise/Bridge On The River Suite (p/s, reissue, beige label)	15

(see also Paul McCartney/Wings, Chet Atkins, Floyd Cramer)

COUNTRY JOE & THE FISH
67	Fontana TF 882	Not So Sweet Martha Lorraine/Love	15
69	Vanguard VA 3	Here I Go Again/It's So Nice To Have Love	7
70	Vanguard 6076 250	I-Feel-Like-I'm-Fixin'-To-Die Rag/Maria	10
67	Fontana TFL 6081	ELECTRIC MUSIC FOR THE MIND AND BODY (LP)	40
68	Fontana TFL 6086	I-FEEL-LIKE-I'M-FIXIN'-TO-DIE (LP)	35
68	Vanguard SVRL 19006	TOGETHER (LP)	20
69	Vanguard SVRL 19026	ELECTRIC MUSIC FOR THE MIND AND BODY (LP, reissue)	15
69	Vanguard SVRL 19029	I-FEEL-LIKE-I'M-FIXIN'-TO-DIE (LP, reissue)	15
69	Vanguard SVRL 19048	HERE WE ARE AGAIN (LP)	20
70	Vanguard SVRL 19058	THE BEST OF COUNTRY JOE AND THE FISH (LP)	15
70	Vanguard 6359 002	C.J. FISH (LP)	18
73	Vanguard VSD 27/28	THE LIFE AND TIMES OF (2-LP, gatefold sleeve, quadrophonic/stereo)	20/15
80	Piccadilly PIC 3009	THE EARLY YEARS (LP, private pressing, withdrawn)	50+

(see also Country Joe McDonald)

COUNTRY JUG
72	Decca F 13270	I'm Sorry/Do You Wanna?/Flying	22

(see also Ray Dorset)

COUNTRYMEN
62	Piccadilly 7N 35029	I Know Where I'm Going/Swamp Legend	8
62	Piccadilly 7N 34012	I KNOW WHERE I'M GOING (EP)	10
62	Piccadilly NPL 38003	A FLYING VISIT BY THE COUNTRYMEN (LP)	10

COUNTRYMEN
69	Jayboy BOY 3	After All/White Rose Of Athens	6

COUNTS
72	Janus 6146 013	(Why Not) Start All Over Again/Thinking Single	10

COUNT VICTORS
62	Coral Q 72456	Peepin' 'N' Hidin'/Don't Laugh At Me ('Cos I'm A Fool)	25
63	Coral Q 72462	Road Runner/Lorie	20

WAYNE/JAYNE COUNTY (& ELECTRIC CHAIRS)
77	Illegal IL 002	Stuck On You/Paranoia Paradise/The Last Time (p/s)	8
77	Sweet F.A. WC 1	Fuck Off/On The Crest (p/s)	12
78	Safari SAFE 1	Eddie And Sheena/Rock And Roll Cleopatra (p/s, some with cartoon insert)	10
78	Safari SAFE 6	I Had Too Much To Dream Last Night/Fuck Off (unissued)	

Wayne/Jayne COUNTY

78	Safari WC 2	BLATANTLY OFFENZIVE (EP, gold vinyl) 8
78	Safari SAFE 9	Trying To Get On The Radio/Evil Minded Momma (p/s) 5
79	Illegal IL 005	Thunder When She Walks/What You Got (p/s) 5
78	Safari SAFELS 13	Berlin (Long Version)/Waiting For The Marines/Midnight Pal (12", p/s, pink vinyl) . . 8
83	Safari WCP 3	Fuck Off/Toilet Love (picture disc) 7
78	Safari GOOD 1	STORM THE GATES OF HEAVEN (LP, multicoloured or grey marbled vinyl)..... 12
	(see also Mystere Five's)	

DIANA COUPLAND
59	HMV POP 690	Love Him/I Am Loved 5

COURIERS
66	Ember EMB S 218	Take Away/Done Me Wrong (some with p/s)........................... 100/30
	(see also William E. Kimber)	

COURIERS
69	Ash ALP 201	PACK UP YOUR SORROWS (LP)... 30

TOM COURTENAY
63	Decca F 11729	Mrs. Brown You've Got A Lovely Daughter/Knocking On The Door 5

COURT MARTIAL
82	Riot City RIOT 5	GOTTA GET OUT (EP)... 5
82	Riot City RIOT 11	NO SOLUTION (EP)... 5

BILL COURTNEY
59	RCA RCA 1142	Judy Is/Without Her Love 5
60	Columbia DB 4512	Petticoats Fly/Blanket On The Beach 5

COURTYARD MUSIC GROUP
74	Deroy	JUST OUR WAY OF SAYING HELLO (LP, private pressing) 200

COUSIN EMMY & HER KINFOLK
56	Brunswick OE 9258	KENTUCKY MOUNTAIN BALLADS VOL. 1 (EP)........................... 18
56	Brunswick OE 9259	KENTUCKY MOUNTAIN BALLADS VOL. 2 (EP)........................... 18

COUSINS (Belgium)
61	Palette PG 9011	Kili Watch/Feugo 10
61	Palette PG 9017	Bouddha/Kana Kapila 10
62	Palette PG 9035	Anda/Danseuse 10

COUSINS (U.K.)
64	Decca F 11924	Yes Sir That's My Baby/Two Lovely Black Eyes 5

DAVE COUSINS
72	A&M AMS 7032	Going Home/Ways And Means 6
72	A&M AMLS 68118	TWO WEEKS LAST SUMMER (LP) 20
79	Old School SLURP 1	OLD SCHOOL SONGS (LP, private pressing with Brian Willoughby) 25
80	Passport PVC 8901	OLD SCHOOL SONGS (LP, reissue with different sleeve) 15
	(see also The Strawbs)	

DON COVAY (& GOODTIMERS)
61	Pye International 7N 25075	Pony Time/Love Boat 25
61	Philips PB 1140	Shake Wid The Shake/Every Which Way 35
62	Cameo Parkway C 239	The Popeye Waddle/One Little Boy Had Money 30
64	Atlantic AT 4006	Mercy, Mercy/Can't Stay Away.. 12
65	Atlantic AT 4016	Take This Hurt Off Me/Please Don't Let Me Know........................ 12
65	Atlantic AT 4056	See Saw/I Never Get Enough Of Your Love............................. 15
66	Atlantic AT 4078	Sookie Sookie/Watching The Late Late Show 15
66	Atlantic 584 025	You Put Something In Me/Iron Out The Rough Spots..................... 10
66	Atlantic 584 059	See Saw/Somebody's Got To Love You 10
67	Atlantic 584 082	Shingaling '67/I Was There... 10
67	Atlantic 584 094	Sookie Sookie/Mercy Mercy.. 10
67	Atlantic 584 114	40 Days — 40 Nights/The Usual Place 10
70	Atlantic 2091 018	Everything I Do Goin' Be Funky/Key To The Highway 10
65	Atlantic ATL 5025	MERCY! (LP, plum label).. 80
67	Atlantic 587 062	SEE-SAW (LP) 25
69	Atlantic K 50225	HOUSE OF BLUE LIGHT (LP).. 25
73	Mercury 6338 211	SUPERDUDE (LP) 15
75	Mercury 9100 010	HOT BLOOD (LP)... 15
	(see also Soul Clan)	

DAVID COVERDALE
77	Purple PUR 133	Hole In The Sky/Blindman 12
78	Purple PUR 136	Breakdown/Only My Soul 12
90	Epic 656 292 7	Last Note Of Freedom/HANS ZIMMER: Car Building (poster p/s) 10
90	Epic 656 292 6	Last Note Of Freedom/HANS ZIMMER: Car Building (12", p/s) 8
77	Purple TPS 3509	DAVID COVERDALE'S WHITESNAKE (LP)............................... 12
77	Purple TPS 3509TC	DAVID COVERDALE'S WHITESNAKE (LP, white label promo, plain sleeve, with insert) 25
78	Purple TPS 3513	NORTHWINDS (LP, with inner sleeve)................................... 12
	(see also Coverdale-Page, Whitesnake, Deep Purple, Wizard's Convention, Roger Glover, Jimmy Page)	

COVERDALE-PAGE
93	EMI EMPD 279	Take A Look At Yourself/Waiting On You (picture disc in numbered p/s)........ 6
93	EMI CDEMS 270	TAKE ME FOR A LITTLE WHILE (CD EP, in box with colour prints) 8

JULIAN COVEY & MACHINE
67	Island WIP 6009	A Little Bit Hurt/Sweet Bacon 45
67	Island WIP 6442	A Little Bit Hurt/Sweet Bacon (reissue) 10

JULIE COVINGTON
70	Columbia DB 8649	The Magic Wasn't There/The Way Things Ought To Be 15
70	Columbia DB 8705	Tonight Your Love Is Over/If I Had My Time Again 15

| 72 | RCA RCA 2181 | Day By Day/With Me It Goes Deeper | 6 |
| 71 | Columbia SCX 6466 | THE BEAUTIFUL CHANGES (LP) | 120 |

(see also Rock Follies)

COWBOY
| 71 | Atlantic 2466 022 | REACH FOR THE SKY (LP) | 15 |
| 72 | Atlantic K 40312 | 5'LL GETCHA TEN (LP, with insert) | 15 |

COWBOY CHURCH SUNDAY SCHOOL
55	Brunswick 05371	Open Up Your Heart/The Lord Is Counting On You	6
55	Brunswick 05455	Go On By/The Little Black Sheep	5
56	Brunswick 05533	These Bad Bad Kids/A Handful Of Shame	5
56	Brunswick 05598	It Is No Secret/Don't Send Those Kids To Sunday School	5

COWBOYS INTERNATIONAL
| 79 | Virgin VS 253 | Aftermath/Pt. 2 (orange vinyl, p/s) | 10 |

(see also Public Image Ltd.)

STANLEY COWELL
| 72 | Freedom FLP40104 | BRILLIANT CIRCLES (LP) | 20 |

COWSILLS
67	MGM MGM 1353	The Rain, The Park And Other Things/River Blue	25
68	MGM MGM 1383	We Can Fly/A Time For Remembrance	10
68	MGM MGM 1400	In Need Of A Friend/Mr. Flynn	10
68	MGM MGM 1424	Indian Lake/Newspaper Blanket	10
68	MGM MGM 1441	Poor Baby/Meet Me At The Wishing Well	8
69	MGM MGM 1469	Hair/What Is Happy	8
69	MGM MGM 1484	The Prophecy Of Daniel And John The Divine/Gotta Get Away From It All	8
69	MGM MGM 1490	Love American Style/Silver Threads And Golden Needles	8
71	London HLU 10329	On My Side/There Is A Child	8
67	MGM C/CS 8059	THE COWSILLS (LP)	25
68	MGM CS 8077	WE CAN FLY (LP)	25
68	MGM CS 8095	CAPTAIN SAD AND HIS SHIP OF FOOLS (LP)	20

BILLY COX
| 71 | Pye Intl. NSPL 25158 | NITRO FUNCTION (LP) | 40 |

(see also Jimi Hendrix)

HARRY COX
| 65 | EFDSS LP 1004 | ENGLISH FOLK SINGER (LP) | 15 |

IDA COX
52	Jazz Collector L 22	Graveyard Dream Blues/Weary Way Blues (78)	6
52	Jazz Collector L76	Mama Do Shee Blues/Worried Mama Blues (78)	6
59	Fontana TFE 17136	IDA COX (EP)	25
54	London AL 3517	SINGS THE BLUES (10" LP)	80
60s	Riverside RLP 374	BLUES FOR RAMPART STREET (LP)	30
75	Gannet GEN 5371-5376	PARAMOUNT RECORDINGS (6-LP box set)	30

(see also Ma Rainey)

IDA COX/ETHEL WATERS
| 50s | Poydras 104 | IDA COX AND ETHEL WATERS (EP) | 25 |

MICHAEL COX
59	Decca F 11166	Boy Meets Girl/Teenage Love (78 rpm = £12)	25
59	Decca F 11182	Too Hot To Handle/Serious (78 rpm = £12)	25
60	Triumph RGM 1011	Angela Jones/Don't Want To Know	20
60	Ember EMB S 103	Angela Jones/Don't Want To Know (export issue)	60
60	HMV POP 789	Along Came Caroline/Lonely Road	25
61	HMV POP 830	Teenage Love/Linda	20
61	HMV POP 905	Sweet Little Sixteen/Cover Girl	25
62	HMV POP 972	Young Only Once/Honey Cause I Love You	20
62	HMV POP 1065	Stand Up/In April	25
63	HMV POP 1137	Don't You Break My Heart/Hark Is That A Cannon I Hear	25
63	HMV POP 1220	Gee What A Party/See That Again	25
64	HMV POP 1293	Rave On/Just Say Hello	30
65	HMV POP 1417	Gypsy/It Ain't Right	20
66	Parlophone R 5436	I Hate Getting Up In The Morning/Love 'Em And Leave 'Em	10
67	Parlophone R 5580	I'll Always Love You/You Never Can Tell (Till You Try)	20

SONNY COX
| 70 | Pama PM 815 | Choking Kind/Chocolate Candy | 10 |

WALLY COX
| 61 | Vogue V 9175 | I Can't Help It/The Heebie Jeebies | 30 |
| 74 | Pye Disco Demand DDS 105 | This Man/I've Had Enough | 10 |

LOL COXHILL
78	Chiltern Sound CS 100	MURDER IN THE AIR (12" EP)	35
71	Dandelion DSD 8008	EAR OF THE BEHOLDER (2-LP, gatefold sleeve, also with cat. no. 69001)	60
72	Mushroom 150 MR 23	TOVERBAL SWEET (LP)	70
73	Caroline C 1503	COXHILL MILLER (LP, with Stephen Miller)	20
74	Caroline C 1507	THE STORY SO FAR … OH REALLY? (LP, with Stephen Miller)	20
75	Caroline C 1514	LOL COXHILL & WELFARE STATE (LP)	15
75	Caroline C 1515	FLEAS IN THE CUSTARD (LP)	20
76	Ogun OG 510	DIVERSE (LP)	15
78	Ogun OG 525	THE JOY OF PARANOIA (LP)	15
78	Ictus 0008	MOOT (LP)	15
80	Pipe PIPE 1	SLOW MUSIC (LP)	20

(see also Stephen Miller & Lol Coxhill, Kevin Ayers, Steve York's Camelo Pardalis)

MINT VALUE £

COXHILL BEDFORD DUO
71	Polydor 2001 253	Pretty Little Girl (Parts 1 & 2)	6
72	Dandelion 2058 214	Mood/WILL DANDY & DANDYLETTES: Sonny Boy/Oh Mein Papa	6

(see also David Bedford, Lol Coxhill)

GRAHAM COXON
02	Transcopic TRAN020	Escape Song/Mountain Of Regret (p/s)	5
04	EMI R 6632	Freakin' Out/Feel Right (numbered p/s)	5
00	Transcopic 10 RDJ 6541	Oochy Woochy/That's When I Reach For My Revolver (10" promo p/s)	40
98	Transcopic TRANLP 005	THE SKY IS TOO HIGH (LP, inner sleeve, 4 postcards)	18
01	Transcopic TRANLP 010	CROW SIT ON BLOOD TREE (2-LP, with inners & print, some signed, 1,000 only)	35/25
02	Transcopic TRANLP 018	THE KISS OF MORNING (2xLP, 10" x 10" picture book)	14
04	EMI 5775191	HAPPINESS IN MAGAZINES (LP)	12

(see also Blur)

JIM COYLE & MAL SHARPE
63	Warner Bros WM 8130	THE ABSURD IMPOSTERS (LP)	10

KEVIN COYNE
72	Dandelion 2001 357	Cheat Me/Flowering Cherry	7
80	Virgin VGD 3504	SANITY STOMP (EP, double pack)	8
72	Dandelion 2310 228	CASE HISTORY (LP)	60
73	Virgin VD 2501	MARJORY RAZORBLADE (2-LP)	20

(see also Clague, Coyne-Clague, Siren, Gordon Smith)

COYNE-CLAGUE
69	Dandelion S 4494	The Stride/I Wonder Where	8

(see Clague, Kevin Coyne)

CRABBY APPLETON
70	Elektra 2101 006	Go Back/Try	6
71	Elektra EK 45716	Grabon/Can't Live My Life	6
70	Elektra EKS 74067	CRABBY APPLETON (LP)	18
71	Elektra EKS 74106	ROTTEN TO THE CORE (LP)	18

CRACK
80	JSO EAT 4	Making The Effort/Easy Street	8

CRACK
82	RCA RCA 214	Don't You Ever Let Me Down/I Can't Take It (die-cut 'Battle of the Bands' sleeve)	25
82	RCA RCA 255	Going Out/The Troops Have Landed (p/s)	15
83	RCA CRACK 1	All Or Nothing/I Caught You Out (p/s)	20

CRACKED MIRROR
83	CMLP 001	CRACKED MIRROR (LP, private pressing, 200 only)	80

CRACKERS
69	Fontana TF 995	Honey Do/It Happens All The Time	12

(see also Merseys)

CRACK THE SKY
76	Lifesong ELS 45016	We Want Mine/Invaders From Mars	8
76	Lifesong LSLP 6005	ANIMAL NOTES (LP, with inner sleeve)	15

SARAH CRACKNELL
87	3 Bears TED 001	Love Is All You Need/Coastal Town (p/s)	20
97	Gut CDGUT 7	Goldie (Radio Edit)/(Original Version)/Empire State High/ Aussie Soap Girl (CD, slimline jewel case, withdrawn)	20

(see also St. Etienne, 50 Year Void, Lovecut D.B.)

CRACKOUS ROCK 'N' ROLL
89	HTB BAR 6	Back Home/Barrelhouse Cam In Vietnam (flexi, with *Hit The Bar* fanzine)	5

(BILLY) 'CRASH' CRADDOCK
59	Philips PB 966	Boom Boom Baby/Don't Destroy Me (as 'Crash' Craddock) (78 rpm = £20)	30
60	Philips PB 1006	Since She Turned Seventeen/I Want That (as 'Crash' Craddock)	30
60	Philips PB 1092	Good Time Billy (Is A Happiness Fool)/Heavenly Love	30
61	Mercury AMT 1146	How Lonely He Must Be/Truly True	15

CRADLE OF FILTH
94	Cacophonous NIHIL1	THE PRINCIPLE OF EVIL MADE FLESH (LP)	15

CRAIG
65	King KG 1022	Ain't That A Shame/International Blues	18

CRAIG
66	Fontana TF 665	A Little Bit Of Soap/Ready Steady Let's Go	55
66	Fontana TF 715	I Must Be Mad/Suspense	350

(see also Galliard)

PAUL CRAIG
66	CBS 202406	Midnight Girl/Autumn	10

DON CRAINE'S NEW DOWNLINERS SECT
67	Pye 7N 17261	I Can't Get Away From You/Roses	210

(see also Downliners Sect)

FLOYD CRAMER
54	London HL 8012	Fancy Pants/Five Foot Two Eyes Of Blue (78 rpm = £10)	50
54	London HL 8062	Jolly Cholly/Oh! Suzanna (78 rpm = £10)	60
55	London HLU 8195	Rag-A-Tag/Aunt Dinah's Quiltin' Party (78 rpm = £12)	35
58	RCA RCA 1050	Flip Flop And Bop/Sophisticated Swing (78 rpm = £15)	30
60	RCA RCA 1211	Last Date/Sweetie Baby	5
65	London REP 1023	PIANO HAYRIDE (EP, with Louisiana Hayride Band)	50

63	RCA RCX 7120	THAT HANDSOME PIANO (EP)	15
61	RCA RD 27221/SF 5103	ON THE REBOUND (LP, mono/stereo)	15
62	RCA RD 27250/SF 5124	AMERICA'S BIGGEST SELLING PIANIST (LP, mono/stereo)	15

(see also Country Hams)

FLOYD CRAMER/HOUSTON ROBERTS
| 65 | Fontana FJL 308 | FLOYD CRAMER/HOUSTON ROBERTS (LP, one side each) | 12 |

CRAMP
| 78 | Rip Off RIP 7 | She Doesn't Love Me/Suzy Lie Down (p/s) | 10 |

CRAMPS
79	Illegal ILS 12013	GRAVEST HITS (12" EP, blue or black vinyl)	30/8
80	Illegal ILS 0017	Fever/Garbage Man (withdrawn 1st 'full band' p/s; re-pressed in different p/s with 4 separate shots)	20/15
80	Illegal ILS 0017	Garbage Man/Mystery Plane (Unreleased test pressing)	150+
80	Illegal ILS 021	Drug Train/Love Me/I Can't Hardly Stand It (p/s)	10
81	IRS PFS 1003	Goo Goo Muck/She Said (p/s, yellow vinyl)	14
81	IRS PFSX 1008	The Crusher/Save It/New Kind Of Kick (12", p/s)	12
85	Big Beat NS 110	Can Your Pussy Do The Dog?/Blue Moon Baby (p/s, orange see-through vinyl)	5
86	Big Beat NS 115	What's Inside A Girl/Give Me A Woman (p/s, purple vinyl)	5
86	Big Beat NS 115	What's Inside A Girl/Get Off The Road/Give Me A Woman (12", p/s, white vinyl)	10
89	Enigma ENVPD 17	Bikini Girls With Machine Guns/Jackyard Backoff (picture disc)	8
89	Enigma ENV 19	All Women Are Bad/King Of The Drapes/Teenage Rage/High School Hellcats (12", pic disc)	10
80	Illegal ILP 005	SONGS THE LORD TAUGHT US (LP, white label with Drug Train in place of TV Set)	175+
80	Illegal ILP 005	SONGS THE LORD TAUGHT US (LP, with TV Set)	15
81	IRS SP 70016	PSYCHEDELIC JUNGLE (LP)	15
83	Illegal ILP 012	OFF THE BONE (LP, white label, with different mix of Drug Train, around 50 copies pressed, unreleased)	100+
83	Illegal ILP 012	OFF THE BONE (LP, with 3-D sleeve & glasses)	15
83	Illegal ILP 012	OFF THE BONE (LP, picture disc with extra track)	15
84	Big Beat NED 6	SMELL OF FEMALE (LP, red see-through vinyl)	15
84	Big Beat BEDP 6	SMELL OF FEMALE (LP, picture disc)	20
86	Big Beat WIKA 46	A DATE WITH ELVIS (LP, with poster)	12
86	Big Beat WIKA 46	A DATE WITH ELVIS (LP, blue vinyl)	20
91	Big Beat WIKPD 101	LOOK MOM NO HEAD (LP, picture disc)	15
91	Windsong WINDSONG 4	LUX (3 x 12" box set, with poster, T-shirt & book, numbered, withdrawn)	50

CRANBERRIES
91	Xeric XER 014	Uncertain/Nothing Left At All (p/s)	15
91	Xeric XER 014T	Uncertain/Nothing Left At All/Pathetic Senses/Them (12", p/s)	20
91	Xeric XER 014CD	Uncertain/Nothing Left At All/Pathetic Senses/Them (CD)	30
92	Mlah FAN 2	Fields Of Athenry/Little Green Apes (1-sided flexi, with 'Spudsound' fanzine)	7

LES CRANE
| 71 | Warner Bros K16119 | Deiderata/A different Drummer | 10 |

TONY CRANE
65	Polydor BM 56008	Ideal Love/Little You	5
66	CBS 202022	Even The Bravest/I Still Remember	5
67	Pye 7N 17337	Anonymous Mr Brown/In This World	10
68	Pye 7N 17517	Scratchin' Ma Head/Patterns In The Sky	12

(see also Bob Miller, Merseys/Merseybeats)

CRANE/FARLOWE
| 73 | Dawn DNS 1034 | Can't Find A Reason/Moods | 7 |

(see also Atomic Rooster, Crazy World Of Arthur Brown, Chris Farlowe, Katmandu)

CRANE RIVER JAZZ BAND
53	Parlophone MSP 6008	Lily Of The Valley/Till We Meet Again	5
57	77 LP/4	ORIGINAL CRANE RIVER JAZZ BAND (LP)	20
57	77 LP/5	ORIGINAL CRANE RIVER JAZZ BAND (LP)	20
57	77 LP/17	ORIGINAL CRANE RIVER JAZZ BAND (LP)	20
57	77 LP/18	ORIGINAL CRANE RIVER JAZZ BAND (LP)	20

(see also Ken Colyer)

CRANES SKIFFLE GROUP
| 57 | Embassy WB 238 | Freight Train/Cumberland Gap (78) | 5 |

(see also Ken Colyer, Chas McDevitt)

CRASH
| 82 | Crash EJSP 9819 | FIGHT FOR YOUR LIFE (EP, no p/s) | 8 |

CRASHERS
| 69 | Amalgamated AMG 834 | Hurry Come Up/Off Track | 18 |

CRASS
78	Small Wonder WEENY 2	THE FEEDING OF THE 5000 (12" EP, with 4-page insert & poster)	15
78	Crass 621984	THE FEEDING OF THE 5000 (12" EP, reissue with "Reality Asylum")	8
79	Crass 521984/1	Reality Asylum/Shaved Women (brown cardboard gatefold p/s; later in white newspaper foldout sleeve)	20/6
80	Crass/Xntrix 421984/1	Bloody Revolutions/POISON GIRLS: Persons Unknown (foldout p/s)	8
80	Crass 421984/5	Nagasaki Nightmare/Big A Little A (foldout p/s, some with patch)	12/6
81	Crass 421984/6	Rival Tribal Rebel Revel/Bully Boys Out Fighting (flexidisc with *Toxic Graffiti* fanzine)	20/8
81	Crass 421984/6	Rival Tribal Rebel Revel/Bully Boys Out Fighting (hard vinyl promo, p/s)	40
81	Crass COLD TURKEY 1	Merry Crassmass/Merry Crassmass — Have Fun (p/s)	6

81	Crass 321984/IF flexi	Our Wedding (free flexi sent to readers of *Loving* - 'for the price of a Stamp'. By Creative Recording And Sound Services – CRASS' with/without mailer envelope	200+/300+
82	Crass 221984/6	How Does It Feel (To Be The Mother Of 1000 Dead?)/The Immortal Death/ Don't Tell Me You Care (foldout p/s)	8
83	Crass 121984/3	Sheep Farming In The Falklands/Gotcha! (live) (foldout p/s with lyric insert)	6
83	(no label)	Gotcha! (clear flexidisc)	10
83	Crass 121984/4	Who Dunnit? (Parts 1 & 2) (p/s, brown vinyl)	6
82	Crass BOLLOX 2U2	CHRIST THE ALBUM (2-LP, box set with booklet)	20

(see also Joy De Vivre, Eve Libertine, Poison Girls)

CRAVATS
78	The Cravats CH 004	Gordon/Situations (p/s)	12
79	Small Wonder SMALL 15	The End/Burning Bridges/I Hate The Universe (p/s)	8
80	Small Wonder SMALL 24	Precinct/Who's In Here With Me? (p/s, some with free flexidisc Fireman/ A FLUX IN 3D: Divide)	8/6
80	Small Wonder SMALL 25	You're Driving Me Mad/I Am The Dregs (p/s)	10
81	Small Wonder SMALL 26	Off The Beach/And The Sun Shone On (p/s)	8
82	Crass 221984/2	RUB ME OUT (EP, 21" x 14" poster p/s)	8
85	Reflex 12 RE 10	THE LAND OF THE GIANTS (12" EP)	10
80	Small Wonder CRAVAT 1	THE CRAVATS IN TOYTOWN (LP, with inner sleeve)	15

(see also Very Things)

CAROLYN CRAWFORD
65	Stateside SS 384	When Someone's Good To You/My Heart	150

HANK CRAWFORD
63	London HAK 8103	SOUL OF THE BALLAD (LP)	30

JAMES 'SUGARBOY' CRAWFORD
73	Chess 6145 024	Jock-o-mo (Iko Iko)/BOBBY CHARLES: See You Later, Alligator	6

JIMMY CRAWFORD
60	Columbia DB 4525	Long Stringy Baby/Unkind	55
61	Columbia DB 4633	Love Or Money/Does My Heartache Show	15
61	Columbia DB 4717	I Love How You Love Me/Our Last Embrace	5
62	Columbia DB 4841	I Shoulda Listened To Mama/A Boy Without A Girl	15
62	Columbia DB 4895	Thank You/There'll Be No Goodbyes	15
63	Columbia DB 4957	Another Of Your Toys/Young And Afraid	5
63	Columbia DB 7175	Don't Worry About Bobby/Take This Rose	15

JOHNNY CRAWFORD
62	Pye International 7N 25145	Cindy's Birthday/Patti Ann	10
62	London HL 9605	Your Nose Is Gonna Grow/Something Special	10
62	London HL 9638	Rumors/No One Really Loves A Clown	10
63	London HL 9669	Proud/Lonesome Town	10
64	London HL 9836	Judy Loves Me/Living In The Past	10
62	London RE 1343	JOHNNY CRAWFORD (EP)	35
64	London RE 1416	WHEN I FALL IN LOVE (EP)	30
63	London HA 8060	RUMORS (LP)	35
64	London HA 8197	JOHNNY CRAWFORD – HIS GREATEST HITS (LP)	35

MICHAEL CRAWFORD
65	United Artists UP 1095	The Knack/Oh That Girl	5

ROSETTA CRAWFORD
51	Vocalion V 1002	Stop It Joe/My Man Jumped Salty On Me (78)	10

CRAWFORD BROTHERS
57	Vogue V 9077	Midnight Mover Groover/Midnight Happenings (78 rpm = £75)	250
59	Vogue V 9140	It Feels Good/I Ain't Guilty (triangular or round centre) (78 rpm = £70)	275

CRAWLING CHAOS
80	Factory FAC 17	Sex Machine/Berlin (p/s)	15

CRAYS
65	Polydor BM 56033	Nancy's Minuet/Don't Pity Me	5

CRAZE
79	Cobra COB 3	Motions/Spartans (p/s)	5
80	Harvest HAR 5200	Motions/Spartans (reissue in different p/s)	5
80	Harvest HAR 5205	Lucy/Stop Living In The Past (p/s)	6

(see also Skunks, Hard Corps)

CRAZY CAVAN AND THE RHYTHM ROCKERS
73	Crazy Rhythm CR 01	Teddy Boy Boogie/Bop Little Baby	8
74	Crazy Rhythm CR 02	Teddy Boy Rock'N'Roll/Rockabilly Star/Wildest Cat In Town/Little Teddy Girl	10

CRAZY ELEPHANT
69	Major Minor MM 609	Gimme Gimme Good Lovin'/Dark Part Of My Mind	8
69	Major Minor MM 623	Sunshine Red Wine/Pam	5
70	Major Minor MM 672	There's A Better Day Coming/Space Buggy	5
69	Major Minor SMLP 62	CRAZY ELEPHANT (LP)	18

CRAZY FEELINGS
67	Polydor NH 56723	Please Lie/Time Is Running Out	6

CRAZY HORSE
72	Reprise RSLP 6438	CRAZY HORSE (LP)	18
72	Reprise K 44171	LOOSE (LP, gatefold sleeve)	15

(see also Neil Young, Nils Lofgren, Jack Nitzsche)

CRAZY ROCKERS
64	King KG 1001	Third Man Theme/Mama Papa	5

PAPA JOHN CREACH
71	Grunt FTR 1003	PAPA JOHN CREACH (LP)	15
73	Grunt FTR 1009	FILTHY (LP)	15

(see also Jefferson Airplane)

CREAM
66	Reaction 591 007	Wrapping Paper/Cat's Squirrel	18
66	Reaction 591 011	I Feel Free/N.S.U.	15
67	Reaction 591 015	Strange Brew/Tales Of Brave Ulysses	15
68	Polydor 56258	Anyone For Tennis (The Savage Seven Theme)/Pressed Rat And Warthog	10
68	Polydor 56286	Sunshine Of Your Love/SWLABR	7
68	Polydor 56300	White Room/Those Were The Days	7
69	Polydor 56315	Strange Brew/Wrapping Paper (unissued)	
69	Polydor 56315	Badge/What A Bringdown	7
71	Polydor 2058 120	I Feel Free/Wrapping Paper	6
72	Polydor 2058 285	Badge/What A Bringdown (reissue)	6
66	Reaction 593/594 001	FRESH CREAM (LP, mono/stereo)	60/50
67	Reaction 593/594 003	DISRAELI GEARS (LP, sleeve laminated on front & back, mono/stereo)	55/45
68	Reaction 593/594 003	DISRAELI GEARS (LP, sleeve laminated on front only, mono/stereo)	50/40
68	Polydor 582/583 031/2	WHEELS OF FIRE (2-LP, gatefold sleeve, mono/stereo; set no. 2612 001)	60/45
68	Polydor 582/583 033	WHEELS OF FIRE — IN THE STUDIO (LP, mono/stereo)	40/25
68	Polydor 582/583 040	WHEELS OF FIRE — LIVE AT THE FILLMORE (LP, mono/stereo)	40/25
69	Polydor 583 053	GOODBYE (LP, gatefold sleeve)	20
69	Polydor 583 060	THE BEST OF CREAM (LP)	12
70	Polydor 2383 016	LIVE CREAM (LP)	15
71	Polydor 2855 002	CREAM ON TOP (LP, mail-order compilation)	65
72	Polydor 2383 119	LIVE CREAM VOL. 2 (LP)	15
75	Polydor 2384 067	CREAM (LP, reissue of Fresh Cream with 2 extra tracks)	12
75	RSO 2394 179	GOODBYE (LP, gatefold sleeve, reissue)	12
80	RSO 2658 142	CREAM (7-LP set including Fresh Cream, Disraeli Gears, Wheels Of Fire, Goodbye, Live Cream & Live Cream Vol. 2)	40
92	UFO CR 1	CREAM IN GEAR (96-page book packaged with Disraeli Gears CD)	20

(see also Eric Clapton, Jack Bruce, Ginger Baker, Blind Faith)

CREAMERS
89	Fierce FRIGHT 045	Sunday Head/Think I'm Gonna Be Sick (p/s)	10

JOAN CREARY
71	Fab FAB 181	Your Best Friend/Version	7

CREATION (U.K.)
66	Planet PLF 116	Making Time/Try And Stop Me	40/35
66	Planet PLF 119	Painter Man/Biff Bang Pow	40/35
67	Polydor 56177	If I Stay Too Long/Nightmares	40
67	Polydor 56207	Life Is Just Beginning/Through My Eyes	80
68	Polydor 56230	How Does It Feel To Feel/Tom Tom	50
68	Polydor 56246	Midway Down/The Girls Are Naked	45
73	Charisma CB 213	Making Time/Painter Man	5
77	Raw RAW 4	Making Time/Painter Man (reissue, p/s)	10
84	Edsel E 5006	Making Time/Uncle Bert (p/s)	10
73	Charisma Perspective CS 8	THE CREATION '66-67 (LP)	40
82	Edsel ED 106	HOW DOES IT FEEL TO FEEL (LP, with foldout insert)	15

(see also Mark Four, Birds, Ashton Gardner & Dyke, Kennedy Express, Eddy Phillips, Smiley, Spectrum)

CREATION (U.S.)
72	Stateside SS 2205	I Got The Fever/Soul Control	15

(see also Prophets)

CREATION REBEL
79	Hit Run HIT DD8	Beware/Natty Conscience Free (12")	40
81	On-U Sound DP3	Independent Man Dub/CREATION REBEL : Dub	30
79	Hit Run APLP 9004	REBEL VIBRATIONS (LP)	70
81	4D Rhythms 4DLP1	STARSHIP AFRICA (LP)	30
81	Static STATLP 04	PSYCHOTIC JONKANOO (LP)	30
82	On-U Sound ON-U LP08	STARSHIP AFRICA (LP)	30
82	Cherry Red BRED 21	THREAT TO CREATION (LP)(With the New Age Steppers)	15

CREATION STEPPERS
79	Tribesman TM 22	What You Are Not Supposed To Do/Children Obey Your Parents (12")	15
80	Nationwide NWD 015	Homeward Bound/version (12")	25

CREATIONS
67	Rio R 133	Meet Me At Eight/Searching	18
68	Amalgamated AMG 818	Holding Out/Get On Up	20
69	Punch PH 2	Mix Up Girl/Qua Kue Shut	10

(see also Little Roys)

CREATOR & NORMA
63	Island WI 105	We Will Be Lovers/Come On Pretty Baby	10

CREATURES
66	CBS 202048	Turn Out The Light/It Must Be Love	6
66	CBS 202350	String Along/Night Is Warm	6
67	CBS 2666	Looking At Tomorrow/Someone Needs You	6

CREATURES
83	Wonderland SHE 1	Miss The Girl/Hot Springs In The Snow (p/s)	5
98	Sioux 1V	Sad Cunt/Sad Cunt (Chix'n'Dix mix) (p/s)	5
98	Sioux 2	ERASER CUT (10" EP, p/s)	8

(see also Siouxsie & Banshees)

CREEDENCE CLEARWATER REVIVAL

69	Liberty LBF 15223	Proud Mary/I Put A Spell On You (withdrawn)	20
69	Liberty LBF 15223	Proud Mary/Born On The Bayou	6
69	Liberty LBF 15230	Bad Moon Rising/Lodi	7
69	Liberty LBF 15250	Green River/Commotion	6
70	Liberty LBF 15283	Down On The Corner/Fortunate Son	6
70	Liberty LBF 15310	Travellin' Band/Who'll Stop The Rain	8
70	Liberty LBF 15354	Up Around The Bend/Run Through The Jungle (initially in p/s)	10/5
70	Liberty LBF 15384	Long As I Can See The Light/Lookin' Out My Back Door (initially in p/s)	10/5
71	Liberty LBF 15440	Have You Ever Seen The Rain/Hey Tonight	5
71	United Artists UP 35210	Hey Tonight/Have You Ever Seen The Rain (reissue)	6
71	United Artists UP 35261	Sweet Hitch-Hiker/Door To Door	6
72	Fantasy F 676	Someday Never Comes/Tearin' Up The Country	5
72	Fantasy FTC 101	Born On The Bayou/I Put A Spell On You	5
73	Fantasy FTC 104	It Came Out Of The Sky/Side O' The Road	5
69	Liberty LBS 83259	CREEDENCE CLEARWATER REVIVAL (LP)	20
69	Liberty LBS 83261	BAYOU COUNTRY (LP)	18
69	Liberty LBS 83273	GREEN RIVER (LP)	18
70	Liberty LBS 83338	WILLY AND THE POORBOYS (LP)	15
70	Liberty LBS 83388	COSMO'S FACTORY (LP)	15
71	Liberty LBG 83400	PENDULUM (LP, gatefold sleeve)	12

(see also Golliwogs, John Fogerty, Tom Fogerty, Blue Ridge Rangers)

CREEPERS

66	Blue Beat BB 366	Beat Of My Soul/LLOYD ADAMS: I Wish Your Picture Was You	20
69	Gas GAS 135	Stagger Back/The Creeper	20

CREME CARAMEL

69	Pye International 7N 25495	My Idea/Excursion	5

CRESCENDOS

58	London HLU 8563	Oh Julie/My Little Girl (78 rpm = £20)	110

CRESCENTS

58	Columbia DB 4093	Wrong/Baby, Baby, Baby	120

CRESCENTS

64	London HLN 9851	Pink Dominos/Breakout	20

CRESSIDA

70	Vertigo VO 7	CRESSIDA (LP, gatefold sleeve, swirl label)	125
71	Vertigo 6360 025	ASYLUM (LP, gatefold sleeve, swirl label)	225

CRESTAS

65	Fontana TF 551	To Be Loved/When I Fall In Love	25

CRESTERS

64	HMV POP 1249	I Just Don't Understand/I Want You	15
64	HMV POP 1296	Put Your Arms Around Me/Do It With Me	10

(see also Mike Sagar & Cresters, Richard Harding)

CRESTS

59	London HL 8794	Sixteen Candles/Beside You (78 rpm = £30)	85
59	Top Rank JAR 150	Flower Of Love/Molly Mae (78 rpm = £22)	25
59	Top Rank JAR 168	Six Nights A Week/I Do (78 rpm = £28)	25
59	London HL 8954	The Angels Listened In/I Thank The Moon (78 rpm = £35+)	55
60	Top Rank JAR 302	A Year Ago Tonight/Paper Crown	30
60	Top Rank JAR 372	Step By Step/Gee (But I'd Give The World)	30
60	HMV POP 768	Always You/Trouble In Paradise	30
60	HMV POP 808	Isn't It Amazing/Molly Mae	30
61	HMV POP 848	Model Girl/We've Got To Tell Them	28
62	HMV POP 976	Little Miracles/Baby I Gotta Know	28
63	London HLU 9671	Guilty/Number One With Me	28

(see also Johnny Maestro)

CREW

69	Plexium PXM 12	Marty/Danger Signs	7
70	Decca F 13000	Cecilia/1970	7

CREW-CUTS

53	Mercury MB 3135	Crazy 'Bout You Baby/Angela Mia (78)	10
54	Mercury MB 3140	Sh-Boom/I Spoke Too Soon (78)	12
54	Mercury MB 3159	Oop-Shoop/Do Me Good, Baby (78)	12
54	Mercury MB 3177	Twinkle Toes/Dance Mr. Snowman Dance (78)	6
54	Mercury MB 3185	Barking Dog/All I Wanna Do (78)	8
55	Mercury MB 3202	Earth Angel/Ko Ko Mo (78)	8
55	Mercury MB 3222	Unchained Melody/Two Hearts, Two Kisses (78)	6
55	Mercury MB 3228	Don't Be Angry/Chop Chop Boom (78)	7
56	Mercury MT 100	Angels In The Sky/Seven Days (78)	7
56	Mercury 7MT 2	Angels In The Sky/Seven Days (export issue)	30
56	Mercury MT 108	A Story Untold/Honey Hair, Sugar Lips, Eyes Of Blue (78)	7
56	Mercury MT 127	Rebel In Town/Bei Mir Bist Du Shoen (78)	7
57	Mercury MT 140	Young Love/Little By Little (78)	8
57	Mercury MT 161	Susie-Q/Such A Shame (78)	20
57	Mercury MT 178	I Sit In My Window/Hey, You Face (78)	18
58	RCA RCA 1075	Hey, Stella!/Forever, My Darling (78 rpm = £18)	30
56	Mercury MEP 9002	PRESENTING THE CREW-CUTS (EP)	60
56	Mercury MPT 7501	THE CREW-CUTS ON PARADE (10" LP)	80

BOB CREWE (GENERATION)

60	London HLI 9077	Water Boy/Voglio Cantare (solo)	6
64	Stateside SS 356	Maggie Maggie May/We Almost Made It	6

67	Stateside SS 582	Music To Watch Girls By/Girls On The Rocks	12
67	Stateside SS 2032	You Only Live Twice/A Lover's Concerto	10
67	Philips BL 7788	PLAY THE FOUR SEASONS HITS (LP, as Bob Crewe Orch.)	18
67	Stateside SL 10210	MUSIC TO WATCH GIRLS BY (LP)	30
68	Stateside S(S)L 10260	BARBARELLA (LP, soundtrack)	100

BERNARD CRIBBINS

60	Parlophone R 4712	Folk Song/My Kind Of Someone (B-side with Joyce Blair)	6
62	Parlophone R 4869	The Hole In The Ground/Winkle Picker Shoes	5
62	Parlophone R 4923	Right Said Fred/Quietly Bonkers	5
62	Parlophone R 4961	Gossip Calypso/One Man Band	5
67	Parlophone R 5603	When I'm Sixty-Four/Oh My Word	7
62	Parlophone GEP 8859	THE HOLE IN THE GROUND (EP)	12
62	Parlophone PMC 1186	A COMBINATION OF CRIBBINS (LP, also stereo [PCS 3035])	each 15

THE CRIBS

03	Squirrel No 3	Jen Schande Split Single (blue vinyl, p/s)	7
03	Wichita WEBB051S	Baby Don't Sweat/Another Number (p/s)	6
04	Wichita WEBB059S	You Were Always The One/Song From Practice 1 (p/s)	7
04	B-Unique KAISER	Plays Kaiser Chiefs (gig only 7" given away free, stickered sleeve)	15
04	Wichita WEBB061S	What About Me/Feelin' It (yellow vinyl, p/s)	7

CRICKETS (featuring Buddy Holly)

78s

57	Vogue Coral Q 72279	That'll Be The Day/I'm Lookin' For Someone To Love	20
57	Coral Q 72298	Oh Boy!/Not Fade Away	15
58	Coral Q 72279	That'll Be The Day/I'm Lookin' For Someone To Love	15
58	Coral Q 72307	Maybe Baby/Tell Me How	20
58	Coral Q 72329	Think It Over/Fool's Paradise	25
58	Coral Q 72343	It's So Easy/Lonesome Tears	35

SINGLES

57	Vogue Coral Q 72279	That'll Be The Day/I'm Lookin' For Someone To Love	25
57	Coral Q 72298	Oh Boy!/Not Fade Away	20
58	Coral Q 72279	That'll Be The Day/I'm Lookin' For Someone To Love (2nd issue)	20
58	Coral Q 72307	Maybe Baby/Tell Me How	20
58	Coral Q 72329	Think It Over/Fool's Paradise	20
58	Coral Q 72343	It's So Easy/Lonesome Tears	20

(All the above 45s were originally issued with triangular centres; later round centre copies are worth around half these values. Although some round centres are more rare!)

| 68 | Decca AD 1012 | Oh, Boy/That'll Be The Day (export issue) | 75 |

EPs

58	Coral FEP 2003	THE SOUND OF THE CRICKETS (triangular or round centre)	each 35
59	Coral FEP 2014	IT'S SO EASY (triangular or round centre)	each 35
60	Coral FEP 2060	FOUR MORE BY THE CRICKETS	45
60	Coral FEP 2062	THAT'LL BE THE DAY	45

LP

| 58 | Vogue Coral LVA 9081 | THE CHIRPING CRICKETS (Vogue-Coral labels & Coral sleeve) | 140 |
| 58 | Coral LVA 9081 | THE CHIRPING CRICKETS (re-pressing with Coral labels & sleeve) | 110 |

(see also Buddy Holly)

CRICKETS

78s

| 59 | Coral Q 72365 | Love's Made A Fool Of You/Someone, Someone | 75 |
| 59 | Coral Q 72382 | When You Ask About Love/Deborah | 100 |

SINGLES

59	Coral Q 72365	Love's Made A Fool Of You/Someone, Someone	15
59	Coral Q 72382	When You Ask About Love/Deborah	15
60	Coral Q 72395	More Than I Can Say/Baby My Heart	15
61	Coral Q 72417	Peggy Sue Got Married/Don'tcha Know	15
61	Coral Q 72440	I Fought The Law/A Sweet Love	15
61	London HLG 9486	He's Old Enough To Know Better/I'm Feeling Better	15
62	Liberty LIB 55441	Don't Ever Change/I Am Not A Bad Guy	8
62	Liberty LIB 55495	Little Hollywood Girl/Parisian Girl	12
63	Liberty LIB 10067	My Little Girl/Teardrops Fall Like Rain	8
63	Liberty LIB 10092	Don't Try To Change Me/Lost And Alone	8
63	Liberty LIB 10113	Right Or Wrong/You Can't Be In Between	5
64	Liberty LIB 10145	Lonely Avenue/Playboy	5
64	Liberty LIB 55696	(They Call Her) La Bamba/All Over You	5
64	Liberty LIB 10174	I Think I've Caught The Blues/We Gotta Get Together	10
66	Liberty LIB 55603	April Avenue/Don't Say You Love Me	5
68	Liberty LBF 15089	My Little Girl/Lonely Avenue	5
72	United Artists UP 35457	Don't Ever Change/Playboy	5
73	Philips 6006 269	My Rockin' Days/Lovesick Blues	8
73	Philips 6006 294	Hayride/Wasn't It Nice In New York City (some in p/s)	20/12
74	Mercury 6008 006	Ooh Las Vegas/Rhyme And Time	5
79	Rollercoaster RRC 2001	Cruise In It/Rock Around With Ollie Vee	
		(1st 2,000 with 'single photo' p/s)	8/5
87	Rollercoaster RRC 2007	Forever In Mind/The Weekend/Your M-M-Memory/Three-Piece	
		(tri-centre in overprinted p/s)	8
88	MPL/CBS TSH 1	T-Shirt/Hollywould (p/s)	8

EPs

60	Coral FEP 2053	THE CRICKETS (initially trangular centre, later round centre)	55/45
61	Coral FEP 2064	THE CRICKETS DON'T EVER CHANGE	40
63	Liberty (S)LEP 2094	STRAIGHT NO STRINGS (mono/stereo)	30
64	Liberty LEP 2173	COME ON	40

MINT VALUE £

LPs
61	Coral LVA 9142	IN STYLE WITH THE CRICKETS	50
62	Liberty (S)LBY 1120	SOMETHING OLD, SOMETHING NEW, SOMETHING BLUE, SOMETHING ELSE! (mono/stereo)	30/40
65	Liberty LBY 1258	THE CRICKETS — A COLLECTION	25
71	CBS 64301	ROCKIN' FIFTIES, ROCK 'N' ROLL	20
73	Philips 6308 149	BUBBLEGUM, POP, BALLADS & BOOGIES	20
74	Mercury 6310 007	A LONG WAY FROM LUBBOCK	15

(see also Buddy Holly, Jerry Allison & Crickets, Ivan, Sonny Curtis, Earl Sinks, Sinx Mitchell, David Box)

CRICKETS & BOBBY VEE
63	Liberty LEP 2084	JUST FOR FUN (EP)	25
63	Liberty (S)LEP 2116	BOBBY VEE MEETS THE CRICKETS (EP, mono/stereo)	25/35
63	Liberty LEP 2149	BOBBY VEE MEETS THE CRICKETS VOL. 2 (EP)	30
62	Liberty (S)LBY 1086	BOBBY VEE MEETS THE CRICKETS (LP, mono/stereo)	25/35

(see also Bobby Vee)

JIMMY CRIKIT
70	MCA MK 5047	Isabella/Love Is A See Saw	10

CRIME
80	Punk Products PP 1	Johnny Come Home/Generation Gap (p/s)	100

CRIMINAL CLASS
82	Inferno HELL 7	Fighting The System/Soldier (p/s)	8

CRIMSON BRIDGE
72	Myrrh Ms 6224	FILL YOUR HEAD WITH...	40

GEOFF CRIPPS & LOUISA RUGG
85	Steam Pie SPR 1003S	ICARUS (LP)	15

CRISIS
79	Peckham Action NOTH 1	No Town Hall (Southwark)/Holocaust/P.C. One Nine Eight Four (p/s)	15
79	Ardkor CRI 002	UK '79/White Youth (p/s)	10
80	Ardkor CRI 003	HYMNS OF FAITH (12" EP)	20
81	Ardkor CRI 004	Alienation/Brückwood/Hospital (p/s, with insert)	10
82	Crisis NOTH 1/CRI 002	HOLOCAUST UK (12" EP)	15

(see also Death In June, Current 93, Theatre Of Hate)

CRISIS
70s	private pressing	ANOTHER FINE MESS (LP)	35

CRISPY AMBULANCE
79	Aural Assault AAR 001	From The Cradle To The Grave/4 Minutes From The Frontline (glossy or matt p/s)	15/8
81	Factory FAC 32	Unsightly And Serene: Not What I Expected/Deaf (10", p/s)	8
83	CBST 7	THE BLUE AND YELLOW OF THE YACHT CLUB (cassette)	8
83	CBST 8	OPEN GATES OF FIRE (cassette)	8
89	Temps Moderne LTMV:X	FIN (LP)	12

(see also Ram Ram Kino)

GARY CRISS
62	Stateside SS 104	Our Favourite Melodies/Welcome Home To My Heart	10
62	Stateside SS 123	My Little Heavenly Angel/The Girl That I Told You About	10
63	Stateside SS 164	Long Lonely Nights/I Still Miss You So	10
63	Stateside SS 265	Sweet, Warm And Soft/Little Joe	10
65	Stateside SS 427	Hands Off Buddy/If This Is Goodbye	10

PETER CRISS
79	Casablanca CAN 139	You Matter To Me/Hooked On Rock And Roll (p/s, green vinyl with mask)	30
79	Casablanca CAN 139	You Matter To Me/Hooked On Rock And Roll (p/s, black vinyl)	15
80	Mercury 6302 065	OUT OF CONTROL (LP)	15

(see also Kiss)

LINDA CRISTAL
59	Coral Q 72350	Strictly For Pleasure (A Perfect Romance)/It's Better In Spanish (78 rpm = £6)	8

BOBBY CRISTO & REBELS
64	Decca F 11913	The Other Side Of The Track/I've Got You Out Of My Mind	40

MARY CRISTY
76	Polydor 2056 513	Thank You For Rushing Into My Life/We Can't Hide This Time	10

CRITICS & NYAH SHUFFLE
70	Joe JRS 1	Behold/SEXY FRANKIE: Tea, Patty, Sex And Ganja	12

CRITICS GROUP
66	Argo ZDA 46	A MERRY PROGRESS TO LONDON (LP, with insert)	18
68	Argo ZDA 82	THE FEMALE FROLIC (LP, with insert)	18
68	Argo DA 86	WATERLOO PETERLOO (LP, with insert)	15

CRITTERS
66	London HLR 10047	Younger Girl/Gone For Awhile	18
66	London HLR 10071	Mr. Dieingly Sad/It Just Won't Be That Way	18
66	London HLR 10101	Bad Misunderstanding/Forever Or No More	20
67	London HLR 10119	Marryin' Kind Of Love/New York Bound	20
67	London HLR 10149	Don't Let The Rain Fall Down On Me/Walk Like A Man Again	14
67	London HA-R 8302	THE CRITTERS (LP)	35

JIM CROCE
72	Vertigo 6073 251	Operator/Rapid Roy	6
72	Vertigo 6360 700	YOU DON'T MESS AROUND WITH JIM (LP, gatefold sleeve, swirl label)	30
72	Vertigo 6360 702	I GOT A NAME (LP)	12
70s	Life Song 35000	TIME IN A BOTTLE (LP)	12

CROCHETED DOUGHNUT RING
67	Polydor 56204	Two Little Ladies (Azalea And Rhododendron)/Nice	30
67	Deram DM 169	Havana Anna/Happy Castle	40
68	Deram DM 180	Maxine's Parlour/Get Out Your Rock And Roll Shoes	25

(see also Force Five, Doughnut Ring, Fingers, Daddy Lindberg)

CROCODILE RIDE
80s	Thunderball Surfacer 002	Ex-Hipster/Satellite/14 ICED BEARS: Falling Backwards/World I Love (Speed Mix) (1,000 only, numbered & stickered mailer)	8

CROFTERS
69	Say Disc SD 113	PILL FERRY (EP)	10
69	Beltona SBE 103	CROFTERS (LP)	15

NICOLE CROISILLE
77	Decca F 13708	The Loving Song/Tell Me What I Want To Hear/Telephone Moi	6

TONY CROMBIE
54	Decca F 10424	Stop It All/All Of Me (& His Orchestra)	8
55	Decca F 10454	Perdido/Love You Madly (& His Orchestra)	8
55	Decca F 10547	Early One Morning/Flying Home (& His Orchestra)	8
55	Decca F 10592	Flying Hickory/String Of Pearls (& His Orchestra)	8
55	Decca F 10637	I Want You To Be My Baby (with Annie Ross)/Three Little Words (78 rpm = £10)	6
56	Columbia DB 3822	Teach You To Rock/Short'nin' Bread Rock (as Tony Crombie & Rockets)	45
56	Columbia DB 3822	Teach You To Rock/Short'nin' Bread Rock (as Tony Crombie & Rockets) (78)	10
56	Columbia DB 3859	Sham Rock/Let's You And I Rock (as Tony Crombie & Rockets) (78 rpm = £10)	40
57	Columbia DB 3880	Rock, Rock, Rock/The Big Beat (as Tony Crombie & Rockets) (78)	15
57	Columbia DB 3881	Lonesome Train (On A Lonesome Track)/We're Gonna Rock Tonight (78, as Tony Crombie & Rockets)	20
57	Columbia DB 3921	London Rock/Brighton Rock (as Tony Crombie & Rockets) (78 rpm = £15)	30
57	Columbia DB 4000	Sweet Beat/Sweet Georgia Brown (as Tony Crombie & His Sweet Beat)	10
57	Columbia DB 4000	Sweet Beat/Sweet Georgia Brown (as Tony Crombie & His Sweet Beat) (78)	10
58	Columbia DB 4076	Dumplin's/Tw'on Special (78 rpm = £12)	10
58	Columbia DB 4145	Unguaua/Piakukaungchung (as Tony Crombie Men) (78 rpm = £8)	7
58	Columbia DB 4189	Rock-Cha-Cha/The Gigglin' Gurgleburp (as Tony Crombie Men) (78 rpm = £12)	6
59	Columbia DB 4253	Champagne Cha Cha/Shepherd's Cha Cha (as Tony Crombie Men) (78 = £10)	5
59	Top Rank JAR 182	"Man From Interpol" Theme/Interpol Cha Cha Cha & Chase (as Tony Crombie Orchestra) (78 rpm = £20)	10
62	Ember JBS 706	Gutbucket/Just Like Old Times	5
56	Decca DFE 6247	PRESENTING TONY CROMBIE NO. 1 (EP)	15
56	Decca DFE 6281	PRESENTING TONY CROMBIE NO. 2 (EP)	15
57	Columbia SEG 7676	ROCK ROCK ROCK (EP)	90
57	Columbia SEG 7686	LET'S YOU AND I ROCK (EP)	90
61	Decca DFE 6670	FOUR FAVOURITE FILM THEMES (EP)	10
59	Columbia SEG 7882	SWINGIN' DANCE BEAT NO. 1 (EP)	10
59	Columbia SEG 7896	SWINGIN' DANCE BEAT NO. 2 (EP)	10
59	Columbia SEG 7918	ATMOSPHERE (EP, as Tony Crombie & His Men)	10
56	Columbia 33S 1117	TONY CROMBIE & HIS SWEETBEAT (10" LP)	40
57	Columbia 33S 1108	ROCKIN' WITH TONY CROMBIE & ROCKETS (10" LP)	100
58	Columbia SCX 3262	ATMOSPHERE (LP)	35
59	Top Rank 35/043	MAN FROM INTERPOL (LP, TV series music, by Tony Crombie & Band)	25
60	Top Rank BUY 027	DRUMS! DRUMS! DRUMS! (LP, as Tony Crombie & His Band)	20
61	Tempo TAP 30	JAZZ INC. (LP)	100
61	Decca SKL 4114	SWEET WIDE AND BLUE (LP)	30
61	Decca LK 4385	TWELVE FAVOURITE FILM THEMES (LP, also stereo SKL 4127)	30
61	Ember EMB 3336	WHOLE LOTTA TONY (LP)	40

(see also Annie Ross, Ray Ellington, London Jazz Quartet)

BILL CROMPTON
58	Fontana H 152	A Hoot An' A Holler/The Popocatepetl Beetle	10
59	Fontana H 178	Out Of Sight, Out Of Mind/My Lover	10

CROMWELL
75	Cromwell WELL 006	First Day	20
75	Cromwell WELL 005	AT THE GALLOP (LP, private pressing)	140

(see also Establishment)

LINK CROMWELL (Lenny Kaye)
66	London HLB 10040	Crazy Like A Fox/Shock Me	20

(see also Patti Smith Group)

ANDREW CRONSHAW
77	Trailer LREP 1	CLOUD VALLEY (EP)	10
74	Xtra XTRA 1139	A IS FOR ANDREW, Z IS FOR ZITHER (LP)	15
77	Trailer LER 2104	EARTHED IN CLOUD VALLEY (LP)	15

CROOKED OAK
76	Folkland FL 0102	FROM LITTLE ACORNS GROW (LP, 500 only)	50
79	Eron ERON 019	THE FOOT O'WOR STAIRS (LP)	25

CROOKS
79	Blue Print BLU 2002	Modern Boys/The Beat Goes On (die-cut p/s)	6
80	Blue Print BLU 2006	All The Time In The World/Bangin' My Head (p/s)	8
80	Blue Print BLUP 5002	JUST RELEASED (LP)	12

DAVID CROOKS
70	Jackpot JP 759	I Won't Hold It Against You (actually by Dave Barker)/ BOBBY JAMES: King Of Hearts	7

(see also Dave Barker)

MINT VALUE £

STEVE CROPPER
70	Stax STAX 147	Funky Broadway/Crop Dustin'.	10
69	Stax SXATS 1008	WITH A LITTLE HELP FROM MY FRIENDS (LP).	25

STEVE CROPPER & ALBERT KING
69	Stax SXATS 1020	JAMMED TOGETHER (LP, with Pops Staples).	18

(see also Booker T. & M.G.'s, Albert King)

BING CROSBY
SINGLES
54	Brunswick 03384	White Christmas/Let's Start The New Year Right	10
54	Brunswick 03929	Silent Night, Holy Night/Adeste Fideles	7
54	Brunswick 05224	What A Little Moonlight Can Do/Down By The Riverside (with Gary Crosby)	8
54	Brunswick 05244	Changing Partners/Y'All Come	15
54	Brunswick 05269	Secret Love/My Love, My Love	12
54	Brunswick 05277	Young At Heart/I Get So Lonely	8
54	Brunswick 05304	If There's Anybody Here (From Out Of Town)/Back In The Old Routine (with Donald O'Connor)	7
54	Brunswick 05315	Cornbelt Symphony/The Call Of The South (with Gary Crosby)	7
54	Brunswick 05339	Count Your Blessings Instead Of Sheep/What Can You Do With A General	12
54	Brunswick 05354	White Christmas/Snow (with Danny Kaye, Peggy Lee & Trudy Stevens)	8
51	Brunswick LA 8513	SINGS COLE PORTER SONGS (10")	15
51	Brunswick LA 8514	STARDUST (10")	15
51	Brunswick LA 8529	EL BINGO — A SELECTION OF LATIN AMERICAN FAVOURITES (10")	15
52	Brunswick LA 8505	SINGS JEROME KERN SONGS (10")	15
54	Columbia 33S 1036	CROSBY CLASSICS (10").	15
53	Brunswick LA 8602	BLUE SKIES (10", with Fred Astaire)	12
54	Brunswick LAT 8051-8055	BING — A MUSICAL AUTOBIOGRAPHY (5-LP box set)	30

(see also Gary Crosby, Louis Armstrong, Bob Hope, Fred Astaire, Peggy Lee)

BOB CROSBY & HIS BOBCATS
59	London HLD 8828	Petite Fleur/Such A Long Night (78 rpm = £6)	8
60	London HLD 9228	The Dark At The Top Of The Stairs/Night Theme.	7

(see also Modernaires)

DAVID CROSBY
93	Atlantic A 7360	Hero/Coverage/Fare Thee Well (CD)	8
71	Atlantic 2401 005	IF I COULD ONLY REMEMBER MY NAME (LP, gatefold sleeve, red/plum label)	18

(see also Byrds, Crosby [Stills] Nash [& Young])

GARY CROSBY
58	HMV POP 550	Judy, Judy/Cheatin' On Me (78 rpm = £10)	50
59	HMV POP 648	The Happy Bachelor/This Little Girl Of Mine	6
57	Vogue VA 160118	GARY CROSBY (LP)	15

(see also Bing Crosby, Louis Armstrong)

CROSBY & NASH
72	Atlantic K 10192	Southbound Train/Whole Cloth	7
72	Atlantic K 50011	GRAHAM NASH & DAVID CROSBY (LP, foldout sleeve).	20

CROSBY, STILLS & NASH
69	Atlantic 584 283	Marrakesh Express/Helplessly Hoping.	10
69	Atlantic 584 304	Suite: Judy Blue Eyes/Long Time Gone.	8
69	Atlantic 588 189	CROSBY, STILLS & NASH (LP, gatefold sleeve, with lyric sheet)	22

CROSBY, STILLS, NASH & YOUNG
70	Atlantic 2091 002	Teach Your Children/Country Girl	7
70	Atlantic 2091 010	Woodstock/Helpless.	8
70	Atlantic 2091 023	Ohio/Find The Cost Of Freedom	7
70	Atlantic 2091 039	Our House/Deja Vu	10
88	Atlantic A 9003TX	American Dream/Compass/Soldiers Of Peace/Ohio (12", p/s)	8
70	Atlantic 2401 001	DÉJA VU (LP, gatefold sleeve, pasted-on photo on front, plum/red label)	25
71	Atlantic 2657 007	FOUR WAY STREET (2-LP, gatefold sleeve with lyric sheet)	25

(see also David Crosby, Stephen Stills [Manassas], Graham Nash, Neil Young)

CROSS
87	Virgin VST 1007	Cowboys And Indians (Full Length Version 5.53)/Love Lies Bleeding (She's A Wicked Wily Waitress) (12", p/s)	12
87	Virgin CDEP 10	Cowboys And Indians (4.20)/Cowboys And Indians (Full Length Version 6.12)/ Love Lies Bleeding (She's A Wicked Wily Waitress) (CD, promo only)	30
88	Virgin VST 1026	Shove It! (Extended Mix)/Shove It! (Metropolix)/Rough Justice (12", p/s)	10
88	Virgin VST 1062	Heaven For Everyone/Love On A Tightrope (Like An Animal)/Contact (12", p/s)	10
88	Virgin VST 1100	Manipulator (Extended)/Stand Up For Love/Manipulator (7" Version) (12", p/s)	10
90	Parlophone 12R 6251	Power To Love (Extended Version)/Passion For Trash/ Power To Love (7" Version) (12", p/s).	10
90	Parlophone PCS 7342	MAD, BAD AND DANGEROUS TO KNOW (LP)	15
90	Parlophone CDPCS 7342	MAD, BAD AND DANGEROUS TO KNOW (CD)	35
90	(no label)	OFFICIAL BOOTLEG (fan club-only cassette, featuring Brian May)	12
91	(no label)	LIVE IN GERMANY (fan club-only cassette).	12

(see also Roger Taylor, Queen)

JIMMIE CROSS
66	Red Bird RB 10042	Super Duper Man/Hey Little Girl	20
78	Wanted Cult 101	I Want My Baby Back/Play The Other Side (p/s)	5

(Keith) CROSS & (Peter) ROSS
71	Decca F 13224	Can You Believe It?/Blind Willie Johnson	7
72	Decca F 13316	Peace In The End/Prophets Guiders	7
72	Decca SKL 5129	BORED CIVILIANS (LP)	60

(see also T2)

CROSSBEATS
67	Pilgrim PSR 7003	Step Aside/Forgive Me (p/s or art sleeve)	8
60s	Pilgrim PSR 7004	Busy Man/Change (p/s)	6
60s	Pilgrim KLP 12	CRAZY MIXED UP GENERATION (LP)	20

ANDRAE CROUCH (& DISCIPLES)
70s	Light LS 7014	JUST ANDRAE (LP)	25
70s	Light LS 7018	DISCIPLES LIVE AT CARNEGIE HALL (LP)	25
70s	Light LS 7019	KEEP ON SWINGIN' (LP)	25
70s	Light LS 7025	TAKE ME BACK (LP)	25
70s	Myrrh MYR 1188	NO TIME TO LOSE (LP)	25

CROW
70	Stateside SS 2159	Evil Woman, Don't Play Your Games With Me/Gonna Leave A Mark	6
70	Stateside SS 2171	Slow Down/Cottage Cheese	6
70	Stateside SS 2180	Don't Try To Lay No Boogie Woogie On The King Of Rock And Roll/Satisfied	6
75	Right On R101	Your Autumn Of Tomorrow/Uncle Funk	30
70	Stateside SSL 10301	CROW MUSIC (LP)	20
70	Stateside SSL 10310	CROW BY CROW (LP)	18

SHERYL CROW
93	A&M 580 380-7	Run, Baby, Run/All By Myself (p/s)	7
93	A&M 580 381-2	Run, Baby, Run/All By Myself/The Na-Na Song/Reach Around Jerk (CD)	15
94	A&M 580 462-7	What Can I Do For You (Radio Edit)/Volvo Cowgirl 99 (p/s)	6
94	A&M 580 462-7	What Can I Do For You (Radio Edit)/What Can I Do For You (LP Version)/Volvo Cowgirl 99/I Shall Believe (CD)	10
94	A&M 580 568-7	Run, Baby, Run/Leaving Las Vegas (Acoustic Version) (p/s)	6
94	A&M 580 569-2	Run, Baby, Run/Leaving Las Vegas (Acoustic Version)/All By Myself/Reach Around Jerk (CD)	10
94	A&M 581 147-2	Run, Baby, Run/Can't Cry Anymore/Reach Around Jerk/I Shall Believe (CD, The Nashville Sessions, box set with poster & no'd 'obi')	15
94	A&M 580 644-7	Leaving Las Vegas/Leaving Las Vegas (Live In Nashville) (p/s, with postcard)	5
94	A&M 580 645-2	Leaving Las Vegas/I Shall Believe/What Can I Do For You (Live At Borderline) (CD, stickered digipak with space for 2nd CD)	10
96	A&M 581 902-7	If It Makes You Happy (Edit)/All I Wanna Do (jukebox issue, no p/s)	7
96	A&M SCJB 2	Strong Enough/All I Wanna Do (Remix) (jukebox issue, no p/s)	7
96	A&M 580 918-7	Strong Enough/No One Said It Would Be Easy (p/s)	5
95	A&M 540 368-2/ 540 126-2-18	TUESDAY NIGHT MUSIC CLUB (CD, 2nd issue, with patchwork/montage cover and bonus 6-track CD Sheryl Crow Live [540 367-2])	25

CROWBAR
84	Skinhead SKIN 1	Hippie Punks/White Riot (p/s)	35

CROWD
79	SRT SRTS/79/CUS 377	Ronnie (Is A Headbanger)/A Little Of What I Fancy/Let's Fly Together (p/s)	6

CROWDED HOUSE
87	Capitol CDCL 416	World Where You Live (Extended Version)/Something So Strong/Don't Dream It's Over/That's What I Call Love (CD, card sleeve)	15
88	Capitol CDCL 498	Better Be Home Soon/Kill Eye/Don't Dream It's Over (live)/Better Be Home Soon (CD)	18
88	Capitol CDCL 509	Sister Madly/Mansion In The Slums/Something So Strong (live) (CD)	18
92	Capitol CDCL 655	Four Seasons In One Day (LP)/Dr. Livingstone/Recurring Dream/Anyone Can Tell (CD, in collector's box)	10
92	Capitol CDCL 5642	Weather With You (2 x CD set)	15
91	Capitol CDP 793 559-2	WOODFACE (CD, foldout pack)	18
92	Capitol CDCL 5661	WOODFACE (8 x CD singles in box)	45
92	Capitol CH 1/2	LIVE AT THE TOWN AND COUNTRY CLUB, LONDON, NOVEMBER 9 1991 (2-CD, in PVC gatefold wallet & inserts, promo only)	35
92	Capitol CH 1/2	LIVE AT THE TOWN AND COUNTRY CLUB, LONDON, NOVEMBER 9 1991 (2-CD, in 5" x 5" black box with sampler cassette, promo only)	40
96	EMI FINNTERVIEW 2	THE FINAL INTERVIEW...? (CD, promo only)	18

(see also Split Enz, Tim Finn)

CROWDY CRAWN
(see under Brenda Wootton)

CROWFOOT
70	Paramount PARA 3008	California Rock 'N' Roll/Maybe I Can Learn To Live	5
70	Paramount SPFL 265	CROWFOOT (LP)	12

DON CROWN & HIS BUSKING BUDGIES
71	President PT 340	Mrs Wilson's Budgie/Flying Machines	15

CROWNS
68	Pama PM 725	I Know, It's Alright/I Surrender	20
68	Pama PM 736	Jerking The Dog/Keep Me Going	25
68	Pama PM 745	She Ain't Gonna Do Right/I Need Your Loving	20
68	Pama PM 759	Since You Been Gone/Call Me	20
68	Pama PMLP 6	MADE OF GOLD (LP)	40

CROWS
54	Columbia SCM 5119	Gee/I Love You So (78 rpm Columbia DB 3478 = £175+)	2,000

TREVOR CROZIER'S BROKEN CONSORT
72	Argo AFB 60	PARCEL OF OLD CRAMS (LP)	30

CRUCIFIXION
80	Miramar MIR 4	The Fox/Death Sentence (no p/s)	80
82	Neat NEAT 19	Take It Or Leave It/On The Run (p/s)	5
84	Neat NEAT 37	Green Eyes/Moon Rising/Jailbait (p/s)	5
84	Neat NEAT 3712	Green Eyes/Jailbait/Moon Rising (12", p/s, some on purple or green vinyl)	18/8

MINT VALUE £

ARTHUR 'BIG BOY' CRUDUP
64	RCA RCA 1401	My Baby Left Me/I Don't Know It	40
64	RCA RCX 7161	RHYTHM AND BLUES VOL. 4 (EP)	25
69	Blue Horizon 7-63855	MEAN OLE FRISCO (LP)	70
70	Delmark DS 614	LOOK ON YONDERS WALL (LP)	25
71	Delmark DS 621	CRUDUP'S MOOD (LP)	25
72	RCA RD 8224	THE FATHER OF ROCK 'N' ROLL (LP)	25
74	United Artists UAS 29092	ROEBUCK MAN (LP)	40

CRUISERS
65	Decca F 12098	It Ain't Me Babe/Baby What You Want Me To Do	25

(see also Dave Berry, Godley & Creme)

SIMON CRUM
58	Capitol CL 14965	Country Music Is Here To Stay/Stand Up, Sit Down, Shut Your Mouth	25
59	Capitol CL 15077	I Fell Out Of Love With Love/Morgan Poisoned The Water Hole	15
61	Capitol CL 15183	Enormity In Motion/Cuzz Yore So Sweet	15

(see also Ferlin Husky)

RAY CRUMLEY
77	Magnet MAG 103	It's Uncanny/All The Way In Love With You	25

CRUSADERS
71	Rare Earth SRE 3001	OLD SOCKS NEW SHOES (LP)	15
72	Blue Thumb ILPS 9218	CRUSADERS (2-LP)	15
73	Mowest MWS 7004	HOLLYWOOD (LP)	20
75	ABC ABCD 607	SOUTHERN COMFORT (2-LP)	15

(see also Jazz Crusaders)

CRUX/CRASH
82	No Future OI 18	KEEP ON RUNNING (12" EP)	15

CRY
87	Crazy Flowerpot CFP 001	Party After Dark (some with p/s)	80/15
87	Crazy Flowerpot CFP 002	Give Her An Ice Cream (no p/s)	20

CRYAN' SHAMES
(see under Shames)

CRYER
80	Happy Face MM 124	The Single/Hesitate (p/s, with 2 inserts)	65

BARRY CRYER
58	Fontana H 139	The Purple People Eater/Hey! Eula (78 rpm = £7)	12
58	Fontana H 151	Nothin' Shakin'/Seven Daughters (78 rpm = £9)	12
59	Fontana H 177	Angelina/Kissin' (78 rpm = £8)	10

CRYIN' SHAMES
66	Decca F 12340	Please Stay/What's News Pussycat	25
66	Decca F 12425	Nobody Waved Goodbye/You	30

(see also Paul & Ritchie & Cryin' Shames, Gary Walker & Rain)

CRYING SHAMES
80	Logo GO 385	That's Rock'n'Roll/Too Late (p/s)	12

CRYSTALITES
69	Big Shot BI 510	Biafra/Drop Pan	15
69	Nu Beat NB 036	Splash Down/Finders Keepers	20
69	Songbird SB 1015	Musical Madness Parts 1 & 2	12
69	Songbird SB 1016	The Bad Parts 1 & 2	12
69	Explosion EX 2002	Doctor Who (Parts 1 & 2)	12
69	Explosion EX 2003	Barefoot Brigade/Slippery	12
69	Explosion EX 2005	Bombshell/Bag-A-Wire (B-side actually by Bobby Ellis & Crystalites)	15
69	Explosion EX 2006	A Fistful Of Dollars/The Emperor (B-side actually by Bobby Ellis & Crystalites)	15
70	Explosion EX 2010	The Bad/The Bad Version	12
70	Bullet BU 424	A Fistful Of Dollars/BOBBY ELLIS: Crystal	12
70	Songbird SB 1017	The Undertaker/Stop That Man (B-side actually "Easy Ride" by Ike Bennett & Crystalites)	15
70	Songbird SB 1020	Lady Madonna/Ghost Rider	8
70	Songbird SB 1024	Isies/Isies (Version 2)	12
70	Songbird SB 1025	Stranger In Town/Stranger In Town (Version 2)	12
70	Songbird SB 1030	Sic Him Rover/Drop Pon	12
70	Songbird SB 1034	Overtaker (Version I)/Overtaker (Version II)	10
70	Songbird SB 1035	Undertaker's Burial/Ghost Rider	12
71	Songbird SB 1057	Earthly Sounds/Version	12
73	Grape GR 3050	Blacula/Version	12

(see also Chosen Few, Scotty, Ramon & Crystalites, Kingstonians, Bongo Herman, Denzil Laing, Derrick Harriot, Ethiopians, Dennis Brown, Glen Brown, Big Youth)

CRYSTALS
62	Parlophone R 4867	There's No Other Like My Baby/Oh Yeah Maybe Baby	150
62	London HLU 9611	He's A Rebel/I Love You Eddie	18
63	London HLU 9661	He's Sure The Boy I Love/Walking Along (La-La-La)	15
63	London HLU 9732	Da Doo Ron Ron/Git It	8
63	London HLU 9773	Then He Kissed Me/Brother Julius	8
64	London HLU 9837	Little Boy/Uptown (withdrawn)	100
64	London HLU 9852	I Wonder/Little Boy	50
64	London HLU 9909	All Grown Up/PHIL SPECTOR GROUP: Irving (Jaggered Sixteenths)	15
65	United Artists UP 1110	My Place/You Can't Tie A Girl Down	50
69	London HLU 10239	Da Doo Ron Ron/He's A Rebel	5

MINT VALUE £

74	Warners/Spector K 19010	Da Doo Ron Ron/Then Kissed Me (blue vinyl)	5
76	Phil Spector Intl. 2010 020	All Grown Up/The Twist	5
63	London RE-U 1381	DA DOO RON RON (EP)	100
63	London HA-U 8120	HE'S A REBEL (LP)	150

(see also Darlene Love, Bob B. Soxx & Blue Jeans, Phil Spector)

CRYTUFF & THE ORIGINALS
| 79 | Hitrun APLP 9006 | DUB TO AFRICA (LP) (Pre-release) | 45 |

C.S.A.
| 96 | Squariel Records SQ003 | Don't/'Till I Waltz Again With You (p/s) | 6 |

JOE CUBA SEXTET
| 66 | Pye International 7N 25401 | Bang! Bang!/Push, Push, Push | 20 |

CUBAN HEELS
| 78 | Housewives' Choice JY 1/2 | Downtown/Do The Smoke Walk (p/s) | 30 |

CUBY & BLIZZARDS
68	Philips BF 1638	Distant Smile/Don't Know Which Way To Go	15
68	Philips BF 1719	Windows Of My Eyes/Checkin' Up On My Baby	10
69	Philips BF 1827	Apple Knocker's Flophouse/Go Down Sunshine	15
69	Philips (S)BL 7874	DESOLATION (LP)	40
69	Philips SBL 7918	APPLE KNOCKERS FLOPHOUSE (LP)	40

'CUDDLY' DUDLEY (Heslop)
59	HMV POP 586	Lots More Love/Later (78 rpm = £10)	20
60	HMV POP 725	Too Pooped To Pop/Miss In-Between	25
61	Ember EMB S 136	Sitting On A Train/One Thing I Like	10
62	Piccadilly 7N 35090	Monkey Party/The Ferryboat Ride (as Cudley Dudley)	10
64	Oriole International ICB 9	Blarney Blues/Peace On Earth	10
64	Oriole International ICB 10	Way Of Life/When Will You Say You'll Be Mine	15

CUDDLY TOYS
81	Parole PURLE 9	Astral Joe/Slowdown (p/s)	12
81	Fresh FRESH 10	Mothman/Jo In The Girls (p/s, with 5 stickers)	12
81	Fresh FRESH 20	Astral Joe/Slowdown (p/s, reissue)	12
81	Fresh FRESH 25	Someone's Crying/Bring On The Ravers (p/s)	8

(see also Raped)

CUES
56	Capitol CL 14501	Burn That Candle/O My Darlin' (78 rpm = £25)	250
56	Capitol CL 14651	Crackerjack/The Girl I Love (featuring Jimmy Breedlove) (78 rpm = £25)	200
57	Capitol CL 14682	Prince Or Pauper/Why (78 rpm = £20)	200

(see also Jimmy Breedlove)

CUFF-LINKS
| 70 | MCA MU 1128 | Robin's World/Lay A Little Love On Me | 6 |
| 70 | MCA MUP(S) 398 | TRACY (LP) | 18 |

XAVIER CUGAT
54	Columbia SCMC 2	Spanish Dance/The Bells Of San Raquel (export issue)	5
54	Columbia SCMC 4	Yo Ta Namora/Anna Boroco Tinde (export issue)	5
54	HMV 7MC 35	MI Espanan/Society Conga (export issue)	5
63	Mercury AMT 1202	Watermelon Man/Swinging Shepherd Blues	10

CULPEPPER'S ORCHARD
| 72 | Polydor 2480 123 | SECOND SIGHT (LP) | 120 |

JAMIE CULLUM TRIO
| 99 | own label | HEARD IT ALL BEFORE (CD, private pressing, 700 only) | 100 |

CULT
80s	Beggars Banquet 235H	Sun King/Edie (Ciao Baby)/She Sells Sanctuary (12", holographic plastic sl.)	12
84	B. Banquet BEGA 57P	DREAMTIME (LP, picture disc)	12
84	B. Banquet BEGA 57	DREAMTIME (white label test pressing, with unique version of Go West)	30
80s	Beggars Banquet	ELECTRIC (LP, gold vinyl)	15
91	Beggars Banquet CBOX 1	SINGLES COLLECTION (10-CD box set, picture discs with booklet)	30

(see also Death Cult, Lonesome No More, Theatre Of Hate, Studio Sweethearts)

CULT FIGURES
| 79 | Rather GEAR 4/RT 020 | Zip Nolan (Highway Patrolman)/P.W.T. (Playing With Toys)/ Zip Dub (gatefold p/s) | 8 |

(see also Swell Maps)

CULT HERO
| 79 | Fiction FICS 006 | I'm A Cult Hero/I Dig You (p/s, 2,000 only) | 50 |
(see also Cure)

CULT MANIAX
| 82 | Elephant Rock | Blitz/Lucy Looe (p/s) | 6 |
| 82 | Next Wave NXT 2/BAK 1 | Frenzie/The Russians Are Coming/Black Horse/Death March (p/s) | 6 |

CULTURE
77	Sky Note DD 003	The Cultures Trod On/THE REVOLUTIONARIES, CULTURE AND RANKING TREVOR: Trod On In Dub (A-side as The Cultures) (12" white pasted sleeve)	25
78	Lightning LIG 515	Jah Pretty Face/Natty Dread Taking Over	5
78	Sky Note SKY LP 016	IN DUB (LP)	50
78	Lightning LIP 1	TWO SEVENS CLASH (LP)	15

CULTURE CLUB
82	Virgin VSY 518	Do You Really Want To Hurt Me/Do You Really Want To Hurt Me (Dub Version) (picture disc)	5
82	Virgin (no cat. no.)	I'll Tumble 4 Ya/BLUE RONDO: Change (blue 1-sided flexi with *Noise* mag)	6
82	Virgin VSY 558	Time (Clock Of The Heart)/White Boys Can't Control It (picture disc)	5

MINT VALUE £

84	Virgin VSY 694	The War Song/La Cancion De Guerra (picture disc, withdrawn)	65
86	Virgin VSX 845	Move Away/Sexuality (5", picture disc, 33rpm, with booklet & gatefold p/s)	5
86	Virgin VSY 861	God Thank You Woman/From Luxury To Heartache (picture disc)	18
82	Virgin VP 2232	KISSING TO BE CLEVER (LP, picture disc, with insert)	12
83	Virgin VP 2285	COLOUR BY NUMBERS (LP, picture disc)	12
84	Virgin VP 2330	WAKING UP WITH THE HOUSE ON FIRE (LP, picture disc, with insert)	12

(see also Boy George, Jesus Loves You, The Edge)

CULVER STREET PLAYGROUND
| 68 | President PT 145 | Alley Pond Park/A Decent Sort Of Guy | 12 |

CUMBERLAND THREE
60	Columbia DB 4460	Johnny Reb/Come Along Julie	5
64	Parlophone R 5113	The Cumberland Crew/Chilly Winds	5
61	Columbia 33SX 1302	FOLK SCENE, U.S.A. (LP, also stereo SCX 3364)	12

(see also John Stewart)

BARBARA CUMMINGS
| 67 | London HLU 10110 | She's The Woman/There's Something Funny Going On | 6 |

DAVID CUNNINGHAM
| 80 | Piano PIANO 001 | GREY SCALE (LP) | 12 |

H. CUNNINGHAM
| 71 | Tropical AL 004 | Ethiopian Son/TROPICAL ALLSTARS: Version 2 | 5 |

RUPERT CUNNINGHAM
| 70 | Duke DU 98 | Funky/Sugar Cane | 5 |

CUPIDS
| 58 | Vogue V 9102 | Now You Tell Me/Lillie Mae (78 rpm = £150) | 900 |

CUPID'S INSPIRATION
68	NEMS 56-3500	Yesterday Has Gone/Dream	8
68	NEMS 56-3702	My Love/Everything Is Meant To Be	8
69	Bell BLL 1069	The Sad Thing/Look At Me	8
70	CBS 4722	Without Your Love/Different Guy	7
70	CBS 4994	Are You Growing Tired Of My Love/Sunshine	7
69	NEMS 6-63553	YESTERDAY HAS GONE (LP, as Cupid's Inspiration Featuring T. Rice-Milton)	30

(see also Gordon Haskell, Paper Blitz Tissue)

CUPOL
| 80 | 4AD BAD 9 | Like This For Ages/Kluba Cupol (12", p/s, 45/33rpm) | 12 |

(see also Wire)

CUPPA T
| 67 | Deram DM 144 | Miss Pinkerton/Brand New World | 12 |
| 68 | Deram DM 185 | Streatham Hippodrome/One Man Band | 12 |

(see also Overlanders)

CUPS
| 68 | Polydor 56777 | Good As Gold/Life And Times | 12 |

(see also Gallagher & Lyle)

MIKE CURB CONGREGATION
| 70 | Polydor 2058 075 | Burning Bridges/Sweet Gingerbread Man | 8 |

CURE
SINGLES
78	Small Wonder SMALL 11	Killing An Arab/10.15 Saturday Night (p/s, 15,000 only, beware of counterfeits)	30
79	Fiction FICS 001	Killing An Arab/10.15 Saturday Night (p/s, reissue)	18
79	Fiction FICS 002	Boys Don't Cry/Plastic Passion ('soldier' p/s)	18
79	Fiction FICS 005	Jumping Someone Else's Train/I'm Cold (p/s)	25
80	Fiction FICS 010	A Forest/Another Journey By Train (p/s or 'radiophonic' die-cut sleeve)	15/10
80	Fiction FICSX 010	A Forest (Extended Version)/Another Journey By Train (12", p/s)	30
81	Fiction FICS 012	Primary/Descent (p/s)	15
81	Fiction FICSX 012	Primary (Extended)/Descent (12", p/s)	25
81	Fiction FICS 014	Charlotte Sometimes/Splintered In Her Head (p/s)	12
81	Fiction FICSX 014	Charlotte Sometimes/Splintered In Her Head/Faith (live) (12", p/s)	18
82	Fiction FICS 015	The Hanging Garden/Killing An Arab (live) (p/s)	12
82	Fiction FICG 015	The Hanging Garden/100 Years//A Forest/Killing An Arab (double pack, gatefold p/s, 5,000 only)	15
82	Lyntone LYN 12011	Lament (1-sided flexidisc, red or green vinyl)	35/12
82	Lyntone LYN 12011	Lament (1-sided flexidisc, red or green vinyl, with *Flexipop* issue 22)	40/15
82	Fiction FICSX 017	Let's Go To Bed (Extended)/Just One Kiss (Extended) (12", p/s)	10
83	Fiction FICS 018	The Walk/The Dream (paper labels, poster p/s)	15
83	Fiction FICS 018	The Walk/The Dream (plastic labels, standard p/s)	7
83	Fiction FICSP 018	The Walk/The Dream (picture disc)	35
83	Fiction FICSX 018	Upstairs Room/The Dream/The Walk/Lament//Let's Go To Bed (Extended)/Just One Kiss (Extended) (12" double pack, shrinkwrapped with sticker)	25
83	Fiction FICSP 019	The Lovecats/Speak My Language (picture disc, PVC sleeve)	30
84	Fiction FIXSP 020	The Caterpillar/Happy The Man (picture disc, printed PVC sleeve)	30
85	Fiction FICSX 22	In Between Days/The Exploding Boy/A Few Hours After This (12", p/s)	10
85	Fiction 080182-2	In Between Days/The Exploding Boy/A Few Hours After This/Six Different Ways (live)/Push (live) (CD Video)	40
85	Fiction FICSG 23	Close To Me (Remix)/A Man Inside My Mouth (poster p/s; some copies with blue & white 'Head On The Door' sticker)	12
85	Fiction FICST 23	HALF AN OCTOPUS: Close To Me (Remix)/A Man Inside My Mouth/New Day/Stop Dead (10" EP, p/s)	15
85	Fiction 080180-2	Close To Me (12" Remix)/A Man Inside My Mouth/Stop Dead/New Day (CD Video)	40
86	Fiction FICSX 24	Boys Don't Cry (New Voice Club Mix)/Pill Box Tales/Do The Hansa (12", p/s)	12

87	Fiction FICSG 25	Why Can't I Be You?/A Japanese Dream//Six Different Ways (live)/ Push (live) (numbered double pack, gatefold p/s)..........................15
87	Fiction FICS 26	Catch/Breathe (p/s, in carrier bag) 8
87	Fiction FICSP 26	Catch/Breathe (clear vinyl, printed PVC sleeve) 15
87	Fiction FICSE 26	Catch/Breath/Kyoto Song (live)/A Night Like This (live) (12")..............12
87	Fiction 080186-2	Catch/Breathe/A Chain Of Flowers/Icing Sugar (Remix) (CD Video)............40
87	Fiction FICS 27	Just Like Heaven/Snow In Summer (p/s, numbered, white vinyl)..............12
87	Fiction FICS 27	Just Like Heaven/Snow In Summer (p/s, mispress, A-side plays both sides)....20
87	Fiction FICSP 27	Just Like Heaven/Snow In Summer (picture disc in custom PVC sleeve)........20
87	Fiction FICSX 27	Just Like Heaven/Snow In Summer/Sugar Girl (12", p/s)......................9
87	Fiction FIXCD 27	Just Like Heaven (Remix)/Snow In Summer/Sugar Girl (CD, card sleeve).......25
88	Fiction FIXCD 28	Hot Hot Hot!!! (Extended Remix)/Hot Hot Hot!!! (Remix)/Hey You!!! (Extended Remix) (CD, card sleeve with insert for *10 Imaginary Years* book)....25
89	Fiction FICSG 29	Lullaby (Remix)/Babble (gatefold p/s, numbered with sticker)..........................8
89	Fiction FICSP 29	Lullaby (Remix)/Babble (clear vinyl, numbered printed 'spider web' PVC sleeve) 15
89	Fiction FICVX 29	Lullaby (Remix)/Babble/Out Of Mind (12", pink vinyl, numbered with stickers) ..20
89	Fiction FICCD 29	Lullaby (Remix)/Babble/Out Of Mind/Lullaby (Extended Remix) (3" CD, gatefold p/s)............................20
89	Fiction FICSG 30	Lovesong/2 Late ('The Love Box' set with linen print)......................15
89	Fiction FICCD 30	Lovesong (7" Mix)/2 Late/Fear Of Ghosts/Lovesong (Extended Mix) (CD).......15
90	Fiction FICPA 34	Pictures Of You (Remix)/Last Dance (live) (p/s, green vinyl, no'd sticker).......8
90	Fiction FICPA 34	Pictures Of You (Remix)/Last Dance (live) (p/s, green vinyl, mispress, plays "Last Dance" both sides)...........................25
90	Fiction FICPB 34	Pictures Of You (Remix)/Prayers For Rain (p/s, purple vinyl, numbered sticker) .12
90	Fiction FIXPA 34	Pictures Of You (Extended Remix)/Last Dance (live)/Fascination Street (live) (12", p/s, green vinyl, numbered sticker)..........................12
90	Fiction FIXPB 34	Pictures Of You (Strange Mix)/Prayers For Rain (live)/Disintegration (live) (12", p/s, purple vinyl, numbered sticker).........................15
90	Fiction FICCDA 34	Pictures Of You (Remix)/Last Dance (live)/Fascination Street (live) (CD).......10
90	Fiction FICCDB 34	Pictures Of You (Strange Mix)/Prayers For Rain (live)/Disintegration (live) (CD)..12
90	Fiction FICSX 35	Never Enough (Big Mix)/Harold & Joe/Let's Go To Bed (Milk Mix) (12", p/s)....10
90	Fiction FICDP 35	Never Enough (Big Mix)/Harold & Joe/Let's Go To Bed (Milk Mix) (CD, with window sticker, numbered slimline jewel case)....................12
90	Fiction 080184-2	Why Can't I Be You? (12" Remix)/A Japanese Dream (5.40 Remix)/Hey You!!! (CD Video)............................40
91	Fiction FICDR 36	Close To Me (Closer Mix)/Just Like Heaven (Dizzy Mix)/Why Can't I Be You (12" remix) (CD, with poster, shrinkwrapped with card insert & numbered sticker)........12
92	Fiction FICCD 39	High/This Twilight Garden/Play/High (Harki-Mix) (CD, box set).............10
92	Fiction FICPA 42	Friday I'm In Love/Halo/Scared Of You/Friday I'm In Love (Strangelove Mix) (12", p/s, numerous different coloured or marbled vinyls)....................10
96	Fiction FICDD 53	Gone! (Radio Mix)/(Critter Mix)/(Ultraliving Mix)/ (Spacer Mix) (CD, 3-CD inlay)..........................12

PROMOS

79	Fiction	Boys Don't Cry 45
79	Fiction CUR 1	Grinding Halt/Meat Hook (12", stickered sleeve)........................60
81	Fiction FICS 12	Primary (1-sided, no p/s)............................25
82	Lyntone LYN 12011	Lament (hard vinyl test pressing, no p/s)........................220+
82	Fiction CURE 1	One Hundred Years/The Hanging Garden (12", p/s, promo/gig freebie)........60
88	Fiction FICSDJ 28	Hot Hot Hot!!! (Remix)/Hey You!!! (Remix) (die-cut title p/s)..............15
84	Fiction KAREN 1	THE TOP (12", 1-sided, 3-track sampler)..........................55
94	Fiction FICCS 50	LOST WISHES (cassette, 4-track, mail order only)......................55
96	Fiction FICSTX 53	Gone! (Ultraliving Mix) (12", same track both sides, with 'DJ' insert)......12
97	Fiction FICSX 54	Wrong Number (Single Mix)/(ISDN Mix)/(Digital Exchange Mix)/ (Dub Analogue Exchange Mix)/(Crossed Line Mix)/(Engaged Mix)/ (P2P Mix) (12", double pack, p/s, promo only)........................25
89	Fiction DISIN 1	DISINTEGRATION (CD, 4-track sampler) 20
89	Fiction CIFCD 3	STRANGER THAN FICTION (CD, 6-track sampler, 1000 only) 120
90	Fiction CUREPROCD 1	MIXED UP (CD, 4-track sampler) 15
90	Fiction CUREPROCD 3	THE CURE — AN INTERVIEW (CD) 22
92	Fiction CURE 1	CLASSIC CURE: Love Cats/Close To Me (Closer Mix)/Lovesong/ Charlotte Sometimes/Lullaby/Why Can't I Be You/A Forest (CD, sampler, inlay) .22
93	Fiction SHOWPRO 1	SHOWPRO: Just Like Heaven/Doing The Unstuck (CD, 2-track sampler) 20
93	Fiction PARISPRO 01	PARISPRO: Catch/Play For Today (CD, 2-track sampler)..................25
97	Fixtion FIXCD.COM 1	FIVE SWING LIVE (CD, 5-track sampler, available via the internet, 5,000 only)....30

LPs

79	Fiction FIX 1	THREE IMAGINARY BOYS (with inner sleeve, postcard & badge) 35
80	Fiction FIXC 6	FAITH/CARNAGE VISORS (original double-play cassette, b&w cover, paper labels) 15
84	Fiction FIXS 9	THE TOP (with badge & poster, green inner sleeve).....................20
84	Fiction FIXS 9	THE TOP (with promo plastic snake & top).........................35
86	Fiction 815 011-2	BOYS DON'T CRY (CD, original non-picture disc, with Object & World War & without So What)..........................30
87	Fiction FIXH 13/FIXHA 13	KISS ME, KISS ME, KISS ME (with bonus orange vinyl 6-track 12" [FIXHA 13], in custom PVC sleeve)........................50
89	Fiction FIXHP 14	DISINTEGRATION (picture disc, printed PVC sleeve) 25
90	Fiction FIXCD 17	ENTREAT (CD, exclusive to HMV, card p/s, yellow photo)................25
92	Fiction 513 600-0	LIMITED EDITION CD BOX (15 x CD hinged box set, 2,500 only) 200
04	Fiction CUREBOX1	JOIN THE DOTS (CD, sampler in card sleeve).......................25

(see also Cult Hero, Siouxsie & Banshees, Glove, Fools Dance, Tim Pope, Lockjaw, Obtainers)

MARTIN CURE & PEEPS

67	Philips BF 1605	It's All Over Now/I Can Make The Rain Fall Up 50

(see also Peeps, Rainbows)

MINT VALUE £

JOHNNY CURIOUS & STRANGERS
78	Illegal IL 009	In Tune/Road To Cheltenham/Pissheadsville/Jennifer (p/s)	10
79	Bugle BLAST 2	Someone Else's Home/Backwards In The Night (p/s)	12

CURIOSITY SHOPPE
68	Deram DM 220	Baby I Need You/So Sad	75

CURLEW
85	Topic 12TS 435	FIDDLE MUSIC FROM SHETLAND AND BEYOND (LP)	12

CURRANT KRAZE
70	Deram DM 292	Lady Pearl/Breaking The Heart Of A Good Man	5

CURRENT 93
83	L.A.Y.L.A.H. L.A.Y. 1	Lashtal/Salt/Caresse (12", white p/s [reissued in 1988 with dark p/s and "1988" on label])	22/18
85	L.A.Y.L.A.H. L.A.Y. 14	NIGHTMARE CULTURE (12" EP, with Sickness Of Snakes [i.e. Coil feat. Boyd Rice]; matt black & red sleeve)	22
87	L.A.Y.L.A.H. L.A.Y. 18	HAPPY BIRTHDAY PIGFACE CHRISTUS (12" EP)	22
87	Maldoror MAL 108	Crowleymass/Christmassacre/Crowleymass (Mix Mix Mix) (12", p/s)	28
88	Yangki 002	FAITH'S FAVOURITES EP (Ballad Of The Pale Girl/NURSE WITH WOUND: Swamp Rat) (12", laminated p/s)	28
88	Maldoror MAL 088	The Red Face Of God/The Breath And The Pain Of God (12", p/s, with insert, 666 only)	40
89	Yangki 003	DEATH OF THE CORN (12" EP, with Sol Invictus; 'art' sleeve)	18
90	Harbinger 001	No Hiding From The Blackbird/NURSE WITH WOUND: Burial Of The Stoned Sardine (p/s, remixed reissue of giveaway 7")	12
90	Shock SX 003	She Is Dead And All Fall Down/God Has Three Faces And Wood Has No Name (folded sleeve in bag, 1,000 only, 26 signed/lettered)	45/22
90	Cerne 004	This Ain't The Summer Of Love (live) (with Sol Invictus, gig freebie, printed labels, 93 copies with ticket)	30/18
92	Durtro DURTRO 004	LOONEY RUNES (12", love EP, 2,000 only, with poster)	22
94	Ptolemaic Terrascope POT6	Broken Birds Fly/RANDY CALIFORNIA: The American Society/The Whale Song (free with *Ptolemaic Terrascope* mag)	10/8
94	Durtro DURTRO 022	THE FIRE OF THE MIND (CD EP, free with book 'Simply Being')	55
95	Durtro DURTRO 025	Tamlin/How The Great Satanic Glory Faded (12", numbered with insert, 2,000 only)	28
95	Durtro DURTRO 025	Tamlin/How The Great Satanic Glory Faded (CD, numbered, 3,000 only)	18
95	Durtro DURTRO 028	Where The Long Shadows Fall (12", 1-sided clear vinyl with insert, 2,000 only)	18
96	Durtro DURTRO 033	The Seven Seals/(various artists) (CD, mail order)	18
84	L.A.Y.L.A.H. LAY 008	DOGS BLOOD RISING (LP; CDs £18)	18
86	Maldoror UDO 22M	IN MENSTRUAL NIGHT (LP, 25 with handmade inserts & cover)	115/22
86	United Dairies UD 022	IN MENSTRUAL NIGHT (LP, picture disc)	28
87	L.A.Y.L.A.H. LAY 20	SWASTIKAS FOR NODDY (LP, with insert)	25
88	Maldoror MAL 666	CHRIST AND THE PALE QUEENS MIGHTY IN SORROW (3-sided LP, with inserts, 93 copies only)	110
88	Maldoror MAL 777	IMPERIUM (LP, black label, with insert, later copies have white label)	28/18
89	Maldoror MAL 093	DAWN (LP)	60
89	Durtro DURTRO 001	LIVE AT BAR MALDOROR (LP, white label, 1,000 only)	55
80s	Maldoror MAL 123	NATURE UNVEILED (LP, some with insert & free 7": No Hiding From The Blackbird/NURSE WITH WOUND: Burial Of The Sardine)	30/20
90	United Dairies UD 029	EARTH COVERS EARTH (mini-LP)	35
90	Cerne 00123	THE CERNE BOX SET (3-LP set, includes Horse; other LPs by Sol Invictus & Nurse With Wound, 2,000 only)	70
90	United Dairies UD 033CD	CROOKED CROSSES FOR THE NODDING DOG (CD)	18
90	NER BADVC 693	1888 (LP, split with Death In June, 500 each on clear & red vinyl; also on black vinyl)	35/25
92	Durtro DURTRO 006	ISLAND (LP, with insert, 2,000 only)	22
92	Durtro DURTRO 011	THUNDER PERFECT MIND (2-LP, with insert)	22
94	Durtro DURTRO 018	OF RUINE, OR SOME BLAZING STARRE (LP, blue vinyl w/insert, 2,000 only)	18
94	Durtrohoho 019	LUCIFER OVER LONDON (LP, red vinyl with insert, 2,000 only)	20
96	Durtro DURTRO 026	ALL THE PRETTY LITTLE HORSES (LP, clear vinyl with insert, 2,000 only)	12
96	United Dairies UDOR 4	WHEN THE MAY RAIN COMES (CD, mail order, free with Ultrasonic Seraphim [2-CD by SAND])	15
01	United Durtro UDOR 8	BRIGHT YELLOW MOON (CD, with Nurse With Wound, first 1,000 with bonus CD)	28

(see also Nurse With Wound, 23 Skidoo, Psychic TV, Crisis, Death In June, Sol Invictus, Steven Stapleton & David Tibet, Tibet & Stapleton)

CLIFFORD CURRY
69	Action ACT 4549	She Shot A Hole In My Soul/We're Gonna Hate Ourselves In The Morning	20
69	Pama PM 793	You Turn Out The Light/Good Humour Man	12
69	Pama PM 797	I Can't Get A Hold Of Myself/Ain't No Danger	25

TIM CURRY
74	UK UK 67	Sweet Transvestite/Time Warp	7

CURTAINS
95	Detour DR 025	In My Street/Family Affair (p/s, blue vinyl, 100 only)	7

DAN CURTIN
94	Peacefrog PF 018X	PARALLEL EP (12", sampler, plain sleeve)	10
94	Peacefrog PF 018	THE SILICON DAWN (2-LP)	18
94	Peacefrog PF 018CD	THE SILICON DAWN CD (CD)	15
95	Peacefrog PF 023	PURVEYORS OF FINE FUNK — HEIGHTS TRAX VOL 1 EP (12", plain sleeve)	15
95	Peacefrog PF 024	DREAMS NOT OF TODAY EP (12", plain sleeve)	10
95	Peacefrog PF 032	PURVEYORS OF FINE FUNK — HEIGHTS TRAX VOL 2 EP (12", plain sleeve)	10
95	Peacefrog PF 038	WEB OF LIFE (2-LP)	18
96	Peacefrog PF 058	PURVEYORS OF FINE FUNK VOL 3 EP (12", plain sleeve)	10
97	Peacefrog PF 064	PURVEYORS OF FINE FUNK VOL 4 EP (12", plain sleeve)	10

ALLEN CURTIS
64	Hickory 45-1226	Fireball Mail/The Hole He Said He'd Dig For Me	9

CHRIS CURTIS
66	Pye 7N 17132	Aggravation/Have I Done Something Wrong	40
(see also Searchers)			

DENNY CURTIS
68	Plexium PXM 2	Crying Over You/You Don't Love Me No More	6
69	Plexium PXM 6	Message/You Gotta Be Mine	6

JOHNNY CURTIS
66	Parlophone R 5529	Our Love's Disintegrating/(I'd Be) A Legend In My Time	70
67	Parlophone R 5582	Jack And The Beanstalk/Go On Back	30
68	Major Minor MM 564	Pickin' Up Pebbles/Gentle On My Mind	7

KING CURTIS
(see under 'K')

LEE CURTIS (& ALL STARS)
63	Decca F 11622	Little Girl/Just One More Dance (solo)	15
63	Decca F 11690	Let's Stomp/Poor Unlucky Me	20
64	Decca F 11830	What About Me/I've Got My Eyes On You	15
64	Philips BF 1385	Ecstasy/A Shot Of Rhythm And Blues	15
(see also Pete Best Four)			

MAC CURTIS
57	Parlophone R 4279	The Low Road/You Ain't Treatin' Me Right (78 rpm = £250)	1,750
74	Polydor 2310 293	ROCKABILLY KINGS (LP, with Charlie Feathers)	25

SONNY CURTIS
60	Coral Q 72400	The Red Headed Stranger/Talk About My Baby	40
64	Colpix PX 11024	A Beatle I Want To Be/So Used To Loving You	15
64	Liberty LIB 55710	Bo Diddley Bach/I Pledged My Love To You	20
85	Songworks S1	I Think I'm In Love/A Whole Lot Less To Me Than Meets The Eye	5
85	Songworks S2	Heart Of Gold/Why Did You Say 'I Do' To Me	5
(see also Crickets)			

DAVE CURTISS & TREMORS
63	Philips BF 1257	You Don't Love Me/Sweet Girl Of Mine	8
63	Philips BF 1285	What Kind Of Girl Are You?/Dreamer's Funfair	8
64	Philips BF 1330	Summertime Blues/I'm A Hog For You Baby	8

ROCKY CURTISS & HARMONY FLAMES
59	Fontana TFE 17172	U.S.A. HIT PARADE (EP)	50

CURTISS MALLDOON
71	Regal Zonophone 3038	You Make Me Happy (And You Make Me Sad)/Amber Man	5
72	Purple PUR 106	One Way Ticket/Next Time	7

BOBBY CURTOLA (& MARTELLS)
61	Columbia DB 4672	Don't You Sweetheart Me/My Heart's Tongue-Tied (solo)	20
62	London HL 9577	Fortune Teller/Johnny Take Your Time (solo)	20
62	London HL 9639	Aladdin/I Don't Want To Go On Without You (solo)	20
63	Decca F 11670	Gypsy Heart/I'm Sorry	20
63	Decca F 11725	Three Rows Over/Indian Giver	20

CURVE
91	Anxious ANXP 27	Blindfold/Ten Little Girls (picture disc)	8
93	Anxious	FALLING FREE — APHEX TWIN REMIX (12", 1-sided promo only, 500 only)	20
93	Anxious ANXCDS 42	BLACKERTHREETRACKERTWO EP (CD, with Future Sound Of London mix)	10

CURVED AIR
71	Warner Bros WB 8023	It Happened Today/What Happens When You Blow Yourself Up	8
72	Warner Bros K 16164	Sarah's Concern/Phantasmagoria	6
84	Pearl Key PK 07350	Renegade/We're Only Human (p/s)	10
70	Warner Bros K 56004	AIR CONDITIONING (LP, picture disc, some with booklet, 10,000 only)	45/20
70	Warner Bros WSX 3012	AIR CONDITIONING (LP, green label)	18
70	Warner Bros K 56004	AIR CONDITIONING (LP, green label)	12
71	Warner Bros K 46090	SECOND ALBUM (LP, die-cut 'leaves' fold-out sleeve, green label)	20
72	Warner Bros K 46158	PHANTASMAGORIA (LP, green label, with inner lyric card)	15
73	Warner Bros K 46224	AIR CUT (LP, green label, gatefold sleeve)	15
(see also Kirby, Sonja Kristina, [Darryl Way's] Wolf, Trace, Legs, Stretch)			

IVOR CUTLER TRIO
67	Parlophone R 5624	I Had A Little Boat/A Great Grey Grasshopper	5
59	Fontana TFE 17144	OF Y'HUP (EP)	20
61	Decca DFE 6677	GET AWAY FROM THE WALL (EP)	20
61	Decca LK 4405	WHO TORE YOUR TROUSERS? (LP)	40
67	Parlophone PCS 7040	LUDO (LP)	70

T. TOMMY CUTRER (& GINNY WRIGHT)
54	London HL 8093	Mexico Gal/Wonderful World (B-side with Ginny Wright) (78 rpm = £10)	65
(see also Ginny Wright)			

CUTTERS
59	Decca F 11110	I've Had It/Rockaroo (78 rpm = £20)	18
(see also Neville Taylor & Cutters)			

CYANIDE
78	Pye 7N 46048	I'm A Boy/Do It (p/s)	35
78	Pye 7N 46094	Mac The Flash/Hate The State (demo copies in p/s)	60/15
79	Pinnacle PIN 23	Fireball/Your Old Man (p/s)	45
78	Pye NSPL 18554	CYANIDE (LP)	40

MINT VALUE £

CYAN THREE
66	Decca F 12371	Since I Lost My Baby/Face Of A Loser	20

CYBERMEN
78	Rockaway AERE 101	THE CYBERMEN (EP, available in 2 different sleeves with/without info sheet)	100/40
79	Rockaway LUV 002	You're To Blame/It's You I Want (with inserts)	10

CYBOTRON FEATURING DILLINJA
96	Prototype PRO004	Threshold/Hot TO (12")	10
98	Prototype PRO 010	Light Years/Revelations (12")	10
00	Valve CYBX 001	NASTY WAYZ (EP)	15
	(see also Dillinja)		

CYCLONES
64	Oriole CB 1898	Nobody/Little Egypt	40

CYCLONES
71	Banana BA 338	My Sweet Lord/DENNIS BROWN: Silky (B-side actually by Monty Alexander & Cyclones)	12

CYLOB
95	Rephlex CAT 015	INDUSTRIAL FOLKSONGS (12", initially in polystyrene sleeve)	12

CYMANDE
73	Alaska ALA 4	The Message/Zion I	10
73	Alaska ALA 10	Bras/Ras Tafarian Folk Song	10
74	Contempo CS 2019	Brothers On The Slide/Pon De Dungle	10
73	Alaska ALKA 100	CYMANDE (LP)	30
74	Contempo CLP 508	PROMISED HEIGHT (LP)	30

JOHNNY CYMBAL
60	MGM MGM 1106	It'll Be Me/Always, Always	28
63	London HLR 9682	Mr Bass Man/Sacred Lovers Vow	15
63	London HLR 9731	Teenage Heaven/Cinderella Baby	20
63	London HLR 9762	Dum Dum Dee Dum/Surfing At Tijuana	20
64	London HLR 9911	Mitsou/Robinson Crusoe On Mars	20
65	United Artists UP 1093	Go V.W. Go/Sorrow And Pain	25
63	London RER 1375	MISTER BASS MAN (EP)	48
64	London RER 1406	CYMBAL SMASHES (EP)	48
	(see also Derek)		

CYMBALINE
65	Pye 7N 15916	Please Little Girl/Coming Home Baby	30
65	Mercury MF 918	Top Girl/Can You Hear Me?	25
66	Mercury MF 961	I Don't Want It/Where Did Love Go Wrong	8
66	Mercury MF 975	Peanuts And Chewy Macs/Found My Girl	8
67	Philips BF 1624	Matrimonial Fears/You Will Never Love Me	55
68	Philips BF 1681	Down By The Seaside/Fire	15
69	Philips BF 1749	Turn Around/Come Back Baby	5

CYMERONS
64	Decca F 11976	I'll Be There/Making Love To Another	15
66	Polydor 56098	Everyday (Will Change)/I Can See You	7

CYNIC
83	Cynic CYN 1	Suicide/No Time At All (no p/s)	130

CYNTHIA & ARCHIE
64	R&B JB 168	Every Beat/DELROY WILSON: Sammy Dead	25

CYRKLE
66	CBS 202064	Red Rubber Ball/How Can I Leave Her	7
66	CBS 202246	Turn Down Day/Big Little Woman	7
67	CBS 202516	Bony Maronie/Please Don't Ever Leave Me	7
67	CBS 202577	I Wish You Could Be There/The Visit (She Was Here)	7
67	CBS 2790	We Had A Good Thing Goin'/Two Rooms	7
67	CBS 2917	Penny Arcade/Words	7

KIM D
65	Pye 7N 15953	The Real Thing/Come On Baby	22
	(see also Kim Davis)		

ROB D
95	Mo' Wax MW 037	Clubbed To Death/(Mixes) (12", p/s)	25

TONY D & SHAKEOUTS
64	Piccadilly 7N 35168	Is It True/Never Let Her Go	25

DA BAND
78	Rip Off RIP 2	I Like It/Pirate's Lullaby (p/s)	20

DA BIZ
80	Small Operations SO 002	On The Beach/This Is No Audition (p/s)	10
80	Sire SIR 4045	On The Beach/This Is No Audition (p/s, reissue)	6

MIKE D'ABO
69	Immediate IM 075	See The Little People — Gulliver's Travels/Anthology Of Gulliver's Travels Part 2 (withdrawn)	20
70	Uni UNS 525	Let It Roar/California Line	7
70	Bell BLL 1134	Miss Me In The Morning/Arabella, Cinderella	6
72	A&M AMS 7016	Belinda/Little Miss Understood	6
74	A&M AMS 7121	Fuel To Burn/Hold On Darlin'	6
70	Uni UNLS 114	D'ABO (LP, gatefold sleeve)	20
72	A&M AMLH 68097	DOWN AT RACHEL'S PLACE (LP, with inner sleeve)	15
74	A&M AMLH 63634	BROKEN RAINBOWS (LP)	15

(see also Manfred Mann, Band Of Angels, Gulliver's Travels, Smith & D'Abo)

RITA DACOSTA
75	Contempo CS 2060	Don't Bring Me Down/No! No! No!	20

DADA
71	Atco 2400 030	DADA (LP)	25

(see also Robert Palmer, Elkie Brooks, Paul Korda, Vinegar Joe)

DADDY LONGLEGS
70	Warner Bros WB 8012	High Again/To The Rescue (Wet Putso)	5
70	Warner Bros WS 3004	DADDY LONGLEGS (LP)	20
71	Vertigo 6360 038	OAKDOWN FARM (LP, gatefold sleeve, swirl label)	30
72	Polydor 2371 261	THREE MUSICIANS (LP)	15
73	Polydor 2371 323	SHIFTING SANDS (LP)	18

(see also Daylight)

DADDY-O'S
58	Oriole CB 1454	Got A Match?/Have A Cigar (78 rpm = £8)	15

DADDY'S ACT
67	Columbia DB 8242	Eight Days A Week/Gonna Get You	18

D.A.F. (Deutsche Amerikanische Freundschaft)
81	Virgin VS 418	Der Mussolini/Der Räuber Und Der Prinz (co. sleeve, possibly promo only)	5
81	Virgin VS 418-12	Der Mussolini/Der Räuber Und Der Prinz (12", p/s, original issue)	8

CALVIN DAFOS
66	Blue Beat BB 347	Brown Sugar/I'm Gone	22
69	Doctor Bird DB 1174	Lash Them/CDs: Medicine Master	20

DAFT PUNK
94	Soma 014	ALIVE/THE NEW WAVE (12" EP, company sleeve)	15
95	Soma 025	DA FUNK (12" EP, company sleeve)	12

DAGABAND
80	Rutland RX 100	Test Flight/Images (p/s)	5
83	MHM A-M 094	Second Time Around/Reds Under The Beds/I Can See For Miles (p/s)	25

DAGGERMEN
86	Empire UPW 258J	INTRODUCING THE DAGGERMEN (EP, die-cut company sleeve)	10
86	Own Up DAG 001	DAGGERS IN MY MIND (LP)	12

(see also James Taylor Quartet)

DAILY FLASH
84	Psycho PSYCHO 32	I FLASH DAILY (LP)	15

TONY DAINES
63	Fontana TF 433	Chapel In The Moonlight/Echo Of Footsteps	10
64	Fontana TF 472	Too Late/I Told You So	5

DAISY CHAINSAW
90s	Deva 82TP7	Pink Flower/Room Eleven (p/s)	8
90s	Deva 82TP12	Pink Flower/All The Kids Agree/Room Eleven (12", p/s)	8
90s	Deva/One Little Indian 92TP12	Hope Your Dreams Come True/Propeller Punch/Queue For Transatlantic Alien (12", p/s)	8
90s	One Little Indian 100TP7	Love Me Forever/Diamond Of The Desert (white vinyl, p/s)	7

DAISY PLANET
60s	Oak (no cat. no.)	DAISY PLANET (EP, no p/s)	60

DAKOTA JIM
66	Blue Beat BB 358	Only Soul Can Tell (actually by Slim Smith)/DAKOTA'S ALLSTARS: Call Me Master (actually by Prince Buster All Stars)	60

(see also Slim Smith)

DAKOTA OAK
01	Twisted Nerve TN 021	How Danny's Friends Became A Force For Good/How Danny's Sorrowing Friends Defied Conventions/Helpless (p/s, wraparound p/s in outer)	5

DAKOTAS
63	Parlophone R 5044	The Cruel Sea/The Millionaire	10
63	Parlophone R 5064	Magic Carpet/Humdinger	12
64	Parlophone R 5203	Oyeh/My Girl Josephine	28
67	Page One POF 018	I'm 'N 'Ardworkin' Barrow Boy/Seven Pounds Of Potatoes	25
68	Philips BF 1645	I Can't Break The News To Myself/The Spider And The Fly	100
63	Parlophone GEP 8888	MEET THE DAKOTAS (EP)	45

(see also Billy J. Kramer & Dakotas)

MICHAEL D'ALBUQUERQUE
74	RCA SF 8383	WE MAY BE CATTLE BUT WE ALL HAVE NAMES (LP, with lyric sheet)	15
76	Warner Bros K 56276	STALKING THE SLEEPER (LP)	12

(see also E.L.O., Michael Albuquerque)

DALE & GRACE
63	London HL 9807	I'm Leaving It Up To You/That's What I Like About You	16
64	London HL 9857	Stop And Think It Over/Bad Luck	16
69	London HL 10249	I'm Leaving It Up To You/Love Is Strange	8
64	London RE 1428	DALE AND GRACE NO. 1 (EP)	40
64	London RE 1429	DALE AND GRACE NO. 2 (EP)	40
64	London RE 1430	DALE AND GRACE NO. 3 (EP)	40

ALAN DALE
55	Vogue Coral Q 72072	Cherry Pink And Apple Blossom White/I'm Sincere	9
55	Vogue Coral Q 72089	Sweet And Gentle/You Still Mean The Same To Me	9
55	Vogue Coral Q 72105	Rockin' The Cha-Cha/Wham! (There I Go In Love Again)	20
56	Vogue Coral Q 72121	Robin Hood/Lisbon Antigua	9
56	Vogue Coral Q 72156	Dance On/Mr. Moon	9
56	Vogue Coral Q 72166	The Birds And The Bees/I Promise	9
56	Vogue Coral Q 72191	Be My Guest/Pardners (with Buddy Hackett)	9
56	Vogue Coral Q 72194	The Test Of Time/I Cry More (78 rpm = £8)	9
57	Vogue Coral Q 72225	Don't Knock The Rock/Your Love Is My Love (78 rpm = £8)	32
57	Vogue Coral Q 72231	The Girl Can't Help It/Lonesome Road (78 rpm = £10)	32
58	MGM MGM 986	Volare/Weeping Willow In The Wind	6

(see also Johnny Desmond)

DICK DALE & HIS DELTONES
63	Capitol CL 15296	Peppermint Man/Surf Beat	20
63	Capitol CL 15320	The Scavenger/Wild Ideas	20
88	Pulch Wave PSC 666	Pick And Play/The Wedge (p/s)	6
63	Capitol T 1886	SURFERS' CHOICE (LP)	70
63	Capitol T/ST 1930	KING OF THE SURF GUITAR (LP, mono/stereo)	70

GLEN DALE
66	Decca F 12475	Good Day Sunshine/Make Me Belong To You	9
68	Page One POF 059	I've Got You On My Mind/Now I See You	5
68	Page One POF 105	I've Got Something Too/Something's Gotten Hold Of My Heart	5

(see also Fortunes)

JIM DALE
57	Parlophone R 4329	Piccadilly Line/I Didn't Mean It (78 rpm = £8)	15
57	Parlophone R 4343	Be My Girl/You Shouldn't Do That	12
57	Parlophone R 4356	All Shook Up/Wandering Eyes (with Vipers & King Brothers) (78 rpm = £10)	18
57	Parlophone R 4376	Just Born (To Be Your Baby)/Crazy Dream	10
58	Parlophone R 4402	Sugartime/Don't Let Go	10
58	Parlophone R 4424	Tread Softly Stranger/Jane Belinda	8
59	Parlophone R 4522	Gotta Find A Girl/The Legend Of Nellie D. (78 rpm = £10)	7
60	Academy AD 001	Somewhere There's A Someone/If You Come Back	6
62	Piccadilly 7N 35039	One Boy, One Girl/My Resistance is Low	5
63	Piccadilly 7N 35100	Start All Over Again/It's For Them	5
69	Pye 7N 17839	Twinky/Plenty More Days	7
73	United Artists UA 35483	Milligan's Blues/It's Gonna Be A Good War	6
57	Parlophone GEP 8656	JIM DALE (EP)	38
58	Parlophone PMD 1055	JIM (10" LP)	75

PAUL DALE BAND
82	KA KA 6/PAUL 1	Alright On The Night/Hold On (p/s, some on clear vinyl)	12/6

(see also Marseille)

SYD DALE ORCHESTRA
65	Decca F 22300	C'mon In/Disc A Go Go	7

DALEKS
(see under Century 21)

DALE SISTERS
60	HMV POP 781	The Kiss/Billy Boy, Billy Boy	13
61	Ember EMB S 140	My Sunday Baby/All My Life	14
62	Ember EMB S 151	Secrets/Road To Love	11

DÄLEX
81	Dodgy DODGY 1	Juvenile/Action Man Touched (p/s)	6

BASIL DALEY
68	Studio One SO 2054	Hold Me Baby/HEPTONES: I Got A Feeling	20

JIMMY DALEY & DING-A-LINGS
57	Brunswick 05648	Rock, Pretty Baby/Can I Steal A Little Love (78 rpm = £35)	110

SALVADOR DALI
62	Decca SET 230	DALI IN VENICE (LP, gatefold sleeve with booklet)	75

DALLAS BOYS
67	Major Minor MM 534	He Won't Love You (Like I Do)/What Do You Know About Losin'	5

(see also Five Dallas Boys)

DALLIONS
62	Oriole CB 1794	Teardrops In The Rain/Loop De Loop	10

MIKI DALLON
65	RCA RCA 1438	Do You Call That Love?/Apple Pie	20
65	RCA RCA 1478	I Care About You/I'll Give You Love	60
66	Strike JH 306	Cheat And Lie/(I'm Gonna Find A) Cave	30
66	Strike JH 318	What Will Your Mama Say Now?/Two At A Time	8

(see also Neil Christian & Crusaders)

DAVID & MARIANNE DALMOUR

60s	Columbia 33SX 1715	INTRODUCING (LP)	12
66	Columbia SCX 6005	STRANGE ENCHANTMENT (LP)	25

DALTONS

67	Fab FAB 30	Never Kiss You Again/RIGHTEOUS FLAMES: When A Girl Loves A Boy	15

(see also Prince Buster)

ROGER DALTREY

73	Track 2094 014	Thinking/There Is Love	6
75	A&M AMS 7206	Orpheus Song/Love's Dream	6
75	Lyntone LYN 3176/7	Wagner's Dream/Love's Theme/RICK WAKEMAN: Count Your Blessings (flexidisc with *19* magazine)	10/6
77	Polydor 2058 896	One Of The Boys/You Better Put Something Inside Me	6
77	Polydor 2058 948	Say It Ain't So Joe/Satin And Lace (withdrawn, existence unconfirmed)	20+
77	Polydor 2121 319	Written On The Wind/Dear John	8
78	Polydor 2058 986	Say It Ain't So Joe/The Prisoner	8
86	10 TEND 81	Under A Raging Moon/Move Better In The Night//Behind Blue Eyes/5:15 (double pack, gatefold p/s)	10
86	10 TENG 8110	Under A Raging Moon (6.43)/Move Better In The Night/Under A Raging Moon/5:15 (10" double pack, gatefold p/s)	12
86	10 TENG 8112	Under A Raging Moon (6.43)/Move Better In The Night/Under A Raging Moon (4.30) (12", gatefold p/s)	10
86	10 TEND 103	The Pride You Hide/Don't Talk To Strangers//Pictures Of Lily (live)/Break Out (double pack)	8
80	Polydor POLD 5034	McVICAR (LP, soundtrack, some on clear vinyl)	25/18

(see also Who, High Numbers, McEnroe & Cash)

GLEN DALY

61	Piccadilly 7N 35017	The Celtic Song/If Only We Had Old Ireland Over Here	10

TONI DALY

66	Columbia DB 8043	Like The Big Man Said/You Can't Get No Water	8

(see also Antoinette)

DALYS

65	Fontana TF 546	Me Japanese Boy/Never Kind Of Love	6
65	Fontana TF 637	She's My Girl/When Love Has Gone	6
66	Strike JH 317	Don't Go Breaking My Heart/Little Stranger	8
67	Fontana TF 809	Sweet Maria/Leaving Time	6
67	Fontana TF 841	A Fistful Of Dollars/Man With No Name	8
68	Fontana TF 907	Let Me Go Lover/A Place In The Sun	6
69	Fontana TF 988	Early Morning Rain/Chanson D'Amour	6

DAMASCUS

80s	private pressing	OPEN YOUR EYES (12" EP, later with different back sleeve, some with insert)	100/75

(see also Thin End Of The Wedge)

DAMBALA

81	Blank IS 1002	Rally Round/Version (12" p/s)	30

DAMITA JO

54	HMV 7MC 2	I'd Do It Again/Do I, Do I, Do I (B-side with Steve Gibson) (export issue)	20
54	HMV 7MC 2	I'd Do It Again/Do I, Do I, Do I (B-side with Steve Gibson) (78)	12
60	Mercury AMT 1085	Widow Walk/Dearest Darling	5
60	Mercury AMT 1116	I'll Save The Last Dance For You/Forgive	10
60	Mercury AMT 1133	Keep Your Hands Off Him/Hush, Somebody's Calling My Name	5
61	Mercury AMT 1141	Do What You Want/Sweet Georgia Brown	5
61	Mercury AMT 1155	I'll Be There/Love Laid Its Hands On Me	5
61	Mercury ZEP 10118	I'LL SAVE THE LAST DANCE FOR YOU (EP)	18
61	Mercury MMC 14089	I'LL SAVE THE LAST DANCE FOR YOU (LP, also stereo [CMS 18059])	18/25
62	Mercury MMC 14105	LIVE AT THE DIPLOMAT (LP)	15

DAMNED

76	Stiff BUY 6	New Rose/Help! (first pressing with push-out centre & 'Delga' credit on p/s)	25
76	Stiff BUY 6	New Rose/Help! (p/s, later issues)	5
77	Stiff BUY 10	Neat Neat Neat/Stab Yor Back/Singalongascabies (glossy p/s, first pressing with push-out centre & gothic lettering; later centres solid)	20/6
77	Stiff DAMNED 1	Stretcher Case Baby/Sick Of Being Sick (p/s, *NME* competition & gig freebie)	80
77	Stiff BUY 18	Problem Child/You Take My Money (p/s, originally with press-out centre)	10/5
77	Stiff BUY 24	Don't Cry Wolf/One Way Love (20,000 on pink vinyl, no p/s; later black vinyl)	10/5
78	Dodgy Demo Co. SGS 105	Love Song/Burglar (mail order issue/gig freebie, plain sleeve, stickered labels)	25
79	Chiswick CHIS 112	Love Song/Noise Noise Noise/Suicide (red vinyl, 4 different sleeves)	each 8
79	Chiswick CHIS 112	Love Song/Noise Noise Noise/Suicide (4 different sleeves)	each 5
79	Chiswick CHIS 116	Smash It Up/Burglar (p/s)	5
79	Chiswick CHIS 120	I Just Can't Be Happy Today/Ballroom Blitz/The Turkey Song (p/s)	5
79	Chiswick CHIS 120 ADJ-1	I Just Can't Be Happy Today/Ballroom Blitz ('A' Label DJ promo copy)	250
80	Chiswick CHIS 130	White Rabbit/Rabid (Over You)/Seagulls (unissued in U.K., Europe-only, 2 x 1-sided white-label test pressings exist, hand-written labels)	400+
80	Chiswick CHIS 135	The History Of The World Part 1/I Believe The Impossible/Sugar And Spite (p/s)	5
80	Chiswick CHIS 12 135	The History Of The World Part 1/I Believe The Impossible/Sugar And Spite (12", p/s)	8
80	Chiswick CHIS 139	There Ain't No Sanity Clause/Hit Or Miss/Looking At You (live) (p/s)	5
81	NEMS TRY 1	FRIDAY THE 13TH (EP, p/s)	5
81	Stiff GRAB 2	FOUR PACK (4 x 7" [BUY 6, 10, 18 & 24], in a plastic wallet)	60
82	Big Beat NS 75	Love Song/Noise Noise Noise/Suicide (3 different sleeves, blue vinyl)	6
82	Big Beat NS 76	Smash It Up/Burglar (p/s, red vinyl)	6
82	Big Beat NS 77	Wait For The Blackout/CAPTAIN SENSIBLE & SOFTIES: Jet Boy, Jet Girl (p/s, red/black 'Damned' labels)	5

MINT VALUE £

82	Big Beat NSP 77	Wait For The Blackout/CAPTAIN SENSIBLE & SOFTIES: Jet Boy, Jet Girl (picture disc) 5
82	Big Beat NS 80	Lively Arts/Teenage Dream (p/s, green vinyl) 10
82	Bronze BRO 149	Lovely Money/Lovely Money (Disco Mix)/I Think I'm Wonderful (p/s) 6
82	Bronze BROP 149	Lovely Money/Lovely Money (Disco Mix)/I Think I'm Wonderful (picture disc) 7
82	Bronze BRO 156	Dozen Girls/Take That/Mine's A Large One, Landlord/Torture Me (p/s) 6
82	Bronze BRO 159	Generals/Disguise/Citadel Zombies (p/s) 10
83	Big Beat NS 85	White Rabbit/Rabid (Over You)/Seagulls (p/s) 5
84	Plus One DAMNED 1P	Thanks For The Night/Nasty (picture disc) 6
84	Plus One DAMNED 1	Thanks For The Night/Nasty (p/s, 1,000 each on red, white & blue vinyl).... each 7
84	Plus One DAMNED 1T	Thanks For The Night/Nasty/Do The Blitz (12", no'd p/s, multicoloured vinyl) 15
84	Plus One DAMNED 1T	Thanks For The Night/Nasty ('woman'-shaped pic disc w/ plinth, 1,000 only) .. 25
85	MCA GRIM 1	Grimly Fiendish/Edward The Bear (autographed gatefold p/s, 1,000 only) 8
85	MCA GRIMP 1	Grimly Fiendish/Edward The Bear (picture disc). 5
85	MCA GRIMT 1	Grimly Fiendish (Spic'n'Span Mix)/Edward The Bear (12", autographed p/s) 10
85	MCA GRIM 2/GRIMY 2	Edition Premier: The Shadow Of Love/Nightshift/Let There Be Rats/ Wiped Out (double pack) 5
85	MCA GRIM 3	Is It A Dream (Wild West End Mix)/Street Of Dreams (live) (p/s, with 5 badges) ... 5
86	MCA GRIMT 4	Eloise/Temptation/Beat Girl (12", p/s, 2,000 on blue vinyl) 8
86	Stiff BUY 6/BUYDJ 6A	New Rose/Help!//I'm So Bored (1-sided) (double pack, stickered PVC sleeve with insert, 1st disc on white vinyl, 2nd disc actually plays "I Fall" [live]) 12
86	Stiff BUY 6	New Rose/Help! (reissue, red vinyl, PVC sleeve, with card insert) 12
91	Deltic DELT 7T	Fun Factory/CAPTAIN SENSIBLE: Freedom/Pasties/A Riot On Eastbourne Pier (12" p/s, blue vinyl, mail-order only, 2000 only)........................ 8
77	Stiff SEEZ 1	DAMNED DAMNED DAMNED (LP)..................................... 16
77	Stiff SEEZ 1	DAMNED DAMNED DAMNED (LP, 2,000 with Eddie & Hot Rods photograph on rear sleeve; some shrinkwrapped with title sticker) 220/80
79	Chiswick CWK 3011	MACHINE GUN ETIQUETTE (LP, with inner sleeve) 15
81	Ace DAM 1	THE BEST OF THE DAMNED (LP, red or blue vinyl) 12
82	Ace DAM 2	MACHINE GUN ETIQUETTE (LP, reissue, blue or white/clear vinyl with inner) 12
82	Ace DAM 3	THE BLACK ALBUM (LP, single reissue, 12,000 with lyrics & poster) 12
82	Big Beat NED 1	LIVE SHEPPERTON 1980 (LP, with 'Collectors Catalogue', 5,000 only) 12
83	Stiff MAIL 2	DAMNED DAMNED DAMNED/MUSIC FOR PLEASURE (2-LP, reissue, gatefold sleeve, mail-order, 5000 only) 20
83	Damned DAMU 2	LIVE IN NEWCASTLE (LP, 5,000 by mail-order only)..................... 15
83	Damned PDAMU 2	LIVE IN NEWCASTLE (LP, picture disc, 5,000 only) 15
85	MCA MCFW 3275	PHANTASMAGORIA (LP, white vinyl, with inner). 12
86	Stiff GET 4	THE CAPTAIN'S BIRTHDAY PARTY — LIVE AT THE ROUNDHOUSE (mini-LP, 45rpm, blue vinyl, stickered plain white sleeve) 12
86	Stiff MAIL 2	DAMNED, DAMNED, DAMNED/MUSIC FOR PLEASURE (2-LP, reissue, yellow vinyl, 4000 by mail-order only) 18
86	Dojo DOJOPD 46	STRAWBERRIES (LP, reissue picture disc) 12
87	Demon PFIEND 91	DAMNED DAMNED DAMNED (LP, reissue picture disc)................... 12
87	Demon FIEND 108	MUSIC FOR PLEASURE (LP, reissue, orange vinyl) 12
89	Essential ESCLP 008	FINAL DAMNATION (LP, green vinyl, with poster) 12
92	Reviewer RRLP 159	LIVE AT THE LYCEUM (LP, clear vinyl) 12

(see also Captain Sensible, Rat Scabies, Rat & Whale, Edge, Magic Michael, Maxim's Thrash, Naz Nomad & Nightmares, Auntiepus, Disco Brothers, Phantom Chords, Tank, Eddie & Hot Rods, U.F.O., Tanz Der Youth)

KENNY DAMON

65	Mercury MF 907	While I Live/Fountain In Capri 10
66	Mercury MF 936	World Of No Return/You Are Everything That's Beautiful 5
68	Mercury MF 1014	Turn Her Away/Till Then My Love 5

(see also Kenny Roberts)

RUSS DAMON

64	Stateside SS 258	Hip Huggers/Heaven Sent 12

STUART DAMON

70	Reflection REF L7	STUART 'CHAMPION' DAMON (LP) 25

DAMON & NAOMI

97	Earworm WORM 3	The Navigator/Awake In A Muddle (p/s) 5

(see also Galaxie 500)

VIC DAMONE

57	MGM MGM 949	And This Is My Beloved (with Howard Keel)/Night Of My Nights 5
57	MGM MGM 950	Stranger In Paradise (with Ann Blyth)/ANN BLYTH:Baubles, Bangles And Pearls 5
54	Mercury EP1 3121	WALKING MY BABY BACK HOME (EP) 8
57	Philips BBE 12099	VIC DAMONE (EP)... 8
58	Philips BBE 12197	DAMONE FAVOURITES (EP) 8
58	Philips BBE 12222	VIC DAMONE (EP)... 8
58	Mercury MEP 9534	THE VOICE OF VIC DAMONE (EP) 8
57	Mercury MPT 7514	ALL-TIME SONG HITS (10" LP) 25
57	Philips BBL 7144	THAT TOWERING FEELING! (LP) 15
58	Philips BBL 7259	CLOSER THAN A KISS (LP).. 15
60	Philips BBL 7347	THIS GAME OF LOVE (LP) 12

(see also Howard Keel, Easy Riders)

VIC DANA

62	Liberty LIB 51	I Will/Proud 15
64	Liberty LIB 92	Warm And Tender/Shangri-La 5
65	Liberty LIB 309	Moonlight And Roses/What'll I Do. 5
65	Liberty LIB 313	Crystal Chandelier/What Now My Love (Et Maintenant) 5
66	Liberty LIB 319	I Love You Drops/Sunny Skies 5
66	Liberty LIB 322	Million And One/My Baby Wouldn't Leave Me 5

DANCE CHAPTER

80	4AD AD 18	Anonymity/New Dance (p/s, some with card insert)	8/6
81	4AD BAD 115	CHAPTER II (12" EP, most with mismatched A&B-side labels)	10
85	Pleasantly Surprised PS 10	WHEN THE SPIRIT MOVES THEM (cassette, in bag with inserts)	15

DANCER, PRANCER & NERVOUS

59	Capitol CL 15097	The Happy Reindeer/Dancer's Waltz (some with p/s)	12/6

(see also Singing Reindeer)

DANCING DID

79	Fruit & Veg F&V 1	Dancing Did/Lorry Pirates (p/s)	8
80	Fruit & Veg F&V 2	The Haunted Tearooms/Squashed Things On The Road (p/s)	5
82	Stiff BUY 136	The Lost Platoon/The Human Chicken (withdrawn 'cavalry' p/s)	8

DANDO SHAFT

70	Youngblood YB 1012	Cold Wind/Cat Song	10
72	RCA RCA 2246	Sun Clog Dance/This Gift	10
70	Youngblood SSYB 6	AN EVENING WITH DANDO SHAFT (LP)	75
71	RCA Neon NE 5	DANDO SHAFT (LP, gatefold sleeve)	80
72	RCA Victor SF 8256	LANTALOON (LP, initially with poster)	80/45
77	Rubber RUB 034	KINGDOM (LP)	40

(see also Hedgehog Pie)

DANDY (& SUPERBOYS)

64	Dice CC 21	Rudie Don't Go/It's Just Got To Be	15
65	Dice CC 24	You Got To Pray/I Got To Have You (as Dandy & Barbara)	15
65	Blue Beat BB 308	To Love You/I'm Looking For Love	18
65	Blue Beat BB 319	Hey Boy Hey Girl/So Long Baby (as Dandy & Del)	18
65	Blue Beat BB 327	My Baby/I'm Gonna Stop Loving You	15
65	Blue Beat BB 336	I Found Love/You've Got Something Nice	15
66	Dice CC 29	The Operation/A Little More Ska	15
66	Ska Beat JB 247	The Fight/Do You Know	22
67	Ska Beat JB 269	One Scotch One Bourbon One Beer/Maximum Pressure	22
67	Ska Beat JB 273	Rudie A Message To You/Til Death Do Us Part	10
67	Ska Beat JB 279	You're No Hustler/No No	18
67	Giant GN 3	My Time Now/East Of Suez (with Superboys)	18
67	Giant GN 5	Puppet On A String/Have Your Fun (with Superboys)	10
67	Giant GN 7	We Are Still Rude/Let's Do Rocksteady (with Superboys)	10
67	Giant GN 10	Somewhere My Love/My Kind Of Love (with Superboys)	10
67	Giant GN 15	There Is A Mountain/This Music Got Soul (with Superboys)	8
68	Giant GN 20	Charlie Brown/Groovin' At The Cue (as Dandy & Charlie Griffiths)	10
68	Giant GN 27	Sweet Ride/Up The Hill (with Superboys)	10
68	Giant GN 30	Tears On My Pillow/Mad Them (with Superboys)	10
68	Giant GN 36	I'm Back With A Bang Bang/Jungle Walk (with Superboys)	10
68	Trojan TR 618	The Toast/Kicks Out	10
68	Trojan TR 629	Sentence (as Dandy & Lee)/LEE PERRY: You Crummy	15
69	Columbia Blue Beat DB 112	Play It Cool/Rude With Me	8
68	Downtown DT 401	Move Your Mule/Reggae Me This	7
69	Downtown DT 402	Come Back Girl/Shake Me Wake Me	10
69	Downtown DT 404	Tell Me Darling/Cool Hand Luke	10
69	Downtown DT 406	Doctor Sure Shot/Put On Your Dancing Shoes	7
69	Downtown DT 410	Reggae In Your Jeggae/DREAMERS: Reggae Shuffle	5
69	Downtown DT 411	You Don't Care/Tryer (both sides with Audrey)	5
69	Downtown DT 415	Rocksteady Gone/Walking Down	7
69	Downtown DT 416	I'm Your Puppet/Water Boy	7
69	Downtown DT 421	Games People Play/AUDREY: One Fine Day	7
69	Downtown DT 429	People Get Ready/RUDIES: Near East	7
69	Downtown DT 434	Be Natural, Be Proud/Who Do You Want To Run To	7
69	Downtown DT 437	Come On Home/Love Is All You Need	7
69	Downtown DT 442	Everybody Loves A Winner/Try Me One More Time	7
69	Downtown DT 445	Let's Come Together (with Israelites)/JAKE WADE: Music Fever	7
69	Downtown DT 453	Won't You Come Home/Baby Make It Soon	7
70	Downtown DT 456	Raining In My Heart/First Note	7
70	Downtown DT 458	Build Your Love (On Solid Foundation)/Let's Talk It Over	7
70	Downtown DT 462	Morning Side Of The Mountain (as Dandy & Audrey)/AUDREY: Show Me Baby	7
70	Downtown DT 468	How Glad I Am/I'm So Glad (as Dandy & Audrey)	7
70	Trojan TR 7800	Take A Letter Maria/You're Coming Back	6
71	Downtown DT 483	Could It Be True/Your Eyes Are Dreaming (as Dandy & Jackie)	6
71	Downtown DT 484	Daddy's Home/Everyman	6
71	Trojan TR 7816	Same Old Fashioned Way/Out Of Many, One People	6
72	Trojan TR 7857	What Do You Want To Make Those Eyes At Me For/Talking About Sally	6
67	Giant GNL 1000	ROCKSTEADY WITH DANDY (LP)	75
68	Trojan TRL 2	DANDY RETURNS (LP)	30
69	Trojan TRL 17	I NEED YOU (LP, with Audrey)	25
70	Trojan TTL 26	YOUR MUSICAL DOCTOR (LP)	22
70	Trojan TBL 118	MORNINGSIDE OF THE MOUNTAIN (LP, with Audrey)	30

(see also Bobby Thompson, Sugar & Dandy, Rub A Dubs, Don Martin, Boy Friday, Audrey, Little Sal with Dandy & Superboys)

CHRIS DANE

55	London HLA 8165	Cynthia's In Love/My Ideal (78 rpm = £12)	48

JERRY DANE

60	Decca F 11234	You're My Only Girl/Nothing But The Truth	7
60	Decca F 11284	Let's/Awhile In Love	8
63	Windsor WPS 127	Everybody Go Wild/Watcha Want (p/s)	15/8

MINT VALUE £

PATRICK DANE
65	Columbia DB 7466	In My Baby's Eyes/The Only One (with Quiet Five)	6
65	Columbia DB 7749	Go Out And Get Somebody/Go On Your Way (with Club '69)	6
68	MGM MGM 1403	When You Lose The One You Love/Home (as Patrick Dane & Mark 7)	6
(see also Quiet Five)			

SHELLEY DANE
60	Pye International 7N 25064	Hannah Lee/This Is The Time In My Life	5

CAL DANGER
62	Fontana 267 225 TF	Restless/Teenage Girlie Blues	100
(see also Tony Dangerfield)			

A.P. DANGERFIELD
68	Fontana TF 935	Conversations (In A Station Light Refreshment Bar)/Further Conversations	30

KEITH DANGERFIELD
68	Plexium P 1237	No Life Child/She's A Witch	200

TONY DANGERFIELD & THRILLS
64	Pye 7N 15695	I've Seen Such Things/She's Too Way Out	75
(see also Savages, Circles, Cal Danger)			

DANI
74	Pye International 7N 25667	La Vie A 25 Ans/Pour Que Ça Dure (p/s)	6
74	Pye International 7N 25667	That Old Familiar Feeling/Pour Que Ça Dure	12

DANIEL IN THE LION'S DEN
70	Trojan TR 7797	Dancing In The Sun/LION'S DEN: Chick A Bow	6

ERROLL DANIEL
69	Paradox PAR 45902	No Excuses/Go Back	15

DANIELLE
66	Philips BF 1532	I'm Gonna Marry The Boy/Magic Carpet Of Love	8
67	Philips BF 1574	Oh Mama/Come A Little Closer	7

BILLY DANIELS
56	Vogue V 2386	I Live For You/Medley: Easy To Love, etc.	7
56	Oriole CB 1087	I Get A Kick Out Of You/Too Marvelous For Words	7
56	Oriole CB 1095	That Old Black Magic/I Concentrate On You	7
60	Vogue V 9172	That Old Black Magic/My Yiddishe Mamma	12
56	Mercury MEP 9001	BILLY DANIELS (EP)	12
60	Mercury ZEP 10066	THAT OLD BLACK MAGIC (EP)	12
53	Oriole/Mercury MG 10003	TORCH HOUR (10" LP, Oriole label with stickered U.S. Mercury sleeve)	25
54	Mercury MG 25103	TORCH HOUR (10" LP, reissue)	18
54	Mercury MG 25163	SONGS AT MIDNIGHT (10" LP)	25
56	Mercury MPT 7505	SONGS AT MIDNIGHT (10" LP, reissue)	15
56	Vogue LAE 12021	AT THE CRESCENDO (LP)	12
58	HMV DLP 1174	YOU GO TO MY HEAD (10" LP)	12

JOE DANIELS' JAZZ GROUP
54	Parlophone MSP 6111	I Wish I Could Shimmy Like My Sister Kate/Susie	7
54	Parlophone MSP 6129	Little Brown Jug/Mountain Wine	7
54	Parlophone MSP 6143	Crazy Rhythm/The Champagne Touch	6
56	Parlophone R 4236	"Dixieland Party (No. 2)" Medley (both sides)	5
57	Parlophone R 4273	When The Saints Go Marching In/Spanish Shawl (solo)	5
57	Parlophone R 4330	Oi! Oi! Oi!/Bottle Beatin' Blues	5
57	Parlophone R 4378	"Juke Box Jazz" Medley (both sides)	5

JULIUS DANIELS
65	RCA RCX 7175	R.C.A. VICTOR RACE SERIES VOL. 4 (EP)	20

MAXINE DANIELS
57	Oriole CB 1366	Coffee-Bar Calypso/Cha-Cha Calypso (78 rpm = £6)	8
57	Oriole CB 1372	Why Should I Care/London Is A Village (78)	6
58	Oriole CB 1402	I Never Realised/Moonlight Serenade (78 rpm = £6)	8
58	Oriole CB 1440	You Brought A New Kind Of Love To Me/Somebody Else Is Taking My Place	8
58	Oriole CB 1440	You Brought A New Kind Of Love To Me/Somebody Else Is Taking My Place (78)	6
58	Oriole CB 1449	When It's Springtime In The Rockies/My Summer Heart (78 rpm = £6)	8
58	Oriole CB 1462	Passionate Summer/Lola's Heart (78 rpm = £6)	8

MIKE DANIELS & HIS BAND
57	Columbia 33SX 1256	MIKE ON MIKE (LP)	45

REV R.A. DANIELS
51	Capitol CL 13530	He's The Lily Of The Valley/I Shall Wear A Crown (78)	35

ROLY "YO YO" DANIELS
60s	Stardisc SD 101	Yo Yo Boy/The Teacher (p/s)	15
61	Parlophone R 4759	Late Last Evening/Bella Bella Marie	7
62	Decca F 11501	Yo Yo Boy/The Teacher (reissue)	8

SAM DANIELS
63	Sway SW 003	Tell Me Baby/ERNIE FAULKENER: Beautiful Girl (both with Planets)	12

JOHNNY DANKWORTH ORCHESTRA
53	Parlophone MSP 6026	Honeysuckle Rose (with Cleo Laine)/Swingin'	12
53	Parlophone MSP 6032	Moon Flowers/Two Ticks	12
53	Parlophone MSP 6037	I Get A Kick Out Of You (with Frank Holder)/Easy Living (with Cleo Laine)	12
54	Parlophone MSP 6067	S' Wonderful/Younger Every Day	12
54	Parlophone MSP 6077	The Slider/It's The Talk Of The Town	12
54	Parlophone MSP 6083	The Jerky Thing/My Buddy	12
54	Parlophone MSP 6092	Runnin' Wild/Oo-Be-Doop	12
54	Parlophone MSP 6113	Perdido/Four Of A Kind	12

MINT VALUE £

54	Parlophone MSP 6139	Bugle Call Rag/You Go To My Head	12
55	Capitol CL 14285	Singin' In The Rain/Non-Stop London	12
56	Parlophone MSP 6255	Experiments With Mice/Applecake	14
57	Parlophone R 4274	All Clare/Melbourne Marathon	6
57	Parlophone R 4294	Duke's Joke/Coquette	6
57	Parlophone R 4321	Big Jazz Story/Firth Of Fourths	6
58	Parlophone R 4456	The Colonel's Tune/Jim And Andy's	6
59	Top Rank JAR 209	We Are The Lambeth Boys/Duet For 16 (78 rpm = £10)	7
61	Columbia DB 4590	African Waltz/Moanin'	5
61	Columbia DB 4695	The Avengers/Chano	15
61	Columbia DB 4751	String Of Camels/Winter Wail	6
62	Columbia DB 4852	Cannonball/S.O. Blues	6
62	Columbia DB 4943	Opato/Abandonado	5
63	Fontana TF 422	The Avengers/Off The Cuff	15
64	Fontana TF 512	Beefeaters/Down A Tone	25
65	Fontana TF 643	Sands Of The Kalahari/Night Thoughts	6
66	Fontana TF 675	Return From The Ashes/Piano Theme	5
66	Fontana TF 700	Modesty Blaise Theme/The Frost Report	7
67	Fontana TF 805	(Ain't That) Just Like A Woman/Accident	6
73	Philips 6006 337	Tomorrows World/Bitter Lemons	6
78	BBC RESL 63	Telford's Change/Serenade For Sylvia (p/s)	8
61	Columbia SEG 8137	AFRICAN WALTZ (EP)	15
58	Parlophone GEP 8653	DANKWORTH WORKSHOP NO. 1 (EP)	20
58	Parlophone GEP 8697	DANKWORTH WORKSHOP NO. 2 — EXPERIMENTS WITH DANKWORTH (EP)	15
60	Columbia SEG 8037	THE CRIMINALS (EP, soundtrack; also stereo ESG 7825) each	15
56	Parlophone PMD 1042	JOURNEY INTO JAZZ (10" LP)	20
58	Parlophone PMC 1076	THE VINTAGE YEARS (LP)	20
59	Parlophone PMC 1043	FIVE STEPS TO DANKWORTH (LP)	20
60	Top Rank 25/019	LONDON TO NEWPORT (LP)	40
61	Columbia 33SX 1280	JAZZ ROUTES (LP, also stereo SCX 3347) each	30
63	Columbia 33SX 1572	CURTAIN UP (LP)	15
64	Fontana TL/STL 5203	WHAT THE DICKENS! (LP)	25
64	Encore ENC 165	FROM 7 ON (LP)	20
65	Fontana TL/STL 5229	THE ZODIAC VARIATIONS (LP, mono/stereo) each	15
67	Stateside S(S)L 10213	FATHOM (LP, soundtrack)	45
68	Fontana TL 5445	THE $1,000,000 COLLECTION (LP)	25
72	Philips 6308 122	FULL CIRCLE (LP)	18
73	Philips 6308 169	LIFELINE (LP)	18
80s	Sepia RRT 1007	FAIR OAK FUSIONS (LP)	15

(see also Cleo Laine, Philip Green, Tony Mansell, Kenny Wheeler & Johnny Dankworth)

DANLEERS
58	Mercury AMT 1003	One Summer Night/Wheelin' And A-Dealin' (78 rpm = £40)	200

DANNY & THE JUNIORS
58	HMV POP 436	At The Hop/Sometimes (When I'm All Alone) (78 rpm = £10)	25
58	HMV POP 467	Rock And Roll Is Here To Stay/School Boy Romance (78 rpm = £18)	40
58	HMV POP 504	Dottie/In The Meantime (78 rpm = £25)	25
60	Top Rank JAR 510	Twistin' U.S.A./Thousand Miles Away	15
61	Top Rank JAR 552	Pony Express/Daydreamer	15
61	Top Rank JAR 587	Back To The Hop/The Charleston Fish	15
62	Top Rank JAR 604	Twistin' All Night Long/Twistin' England (with Freddy Cannon)	18
63	London HL 9666	Oo-La-La-Limbo/Now And Then	12
68	Stateside SS 2117	At The Hop/LLOYD PRICE: (You've Got) Personality	5

C. DANOVAN
73	Randy's RAN 529	Sweet Caroline/IMPACT ALL STARS: Caroline (Version)	5

DANSE SOCIETY
81	Society SOC 3-81	The Clock/Continent (brown, black & white foldout p/s)	15
81	Society SOC 3-81	The Clock/Continent (re-pressing, black & white foldout p/s)	5
81	Pax PAX 2	There Is No Shame In Death/Dolphins/These Frayed Edges (12", p/s, blue or black vinyl)	20/6
82	Pax SOC 5	Woman's Own/We're So Happy (p/s)	8
82	Pax PAX 5	Woman's Own/Continent/We're So Happy/Belief (12", with spined p/s)	10

DANSETTE DAMAGE
78	Shoestring LACE 001	New Musical Express/The Only Sound (p/s)	100
79	Pinnacle PIN 30	2001¾ Approximately/Must Be Love (p/s)	8
94	Shoestring BLOO 2LP	SOLD AS SEEN (LP, gatefold sleeve)	15

DANTALIAN'S CHARIOT
67	Columbia DB 8260	The Madman Running Through The Fields/The Sun Came Bursting Through My Cloud	150
95	Tenth Planet TP 015	CHARIOT RISING (LP, numbered, 1,000 only)	25

(see also Zoot Money's Big Roll Band)

DANTE
61	Brunswick 05857	Bye Bye Baby/That's Why	12

DANTE & EVERGREENS
60	Top Rank JAR 402	Alley-Oop/The Right Time	30

RONNIE DANTE
64	Stateside SS 351	Don't Stand Up In A Canoe/If You Love Me Laurie	6

TROY DANTE (& INFERNOS)
63	Decca F 11639	The Face/Give Me Some More	8
63	Decca F 11746	It's Alright/Tell Me (as Troy Dante & Infernos)	8
64	Fontana TF 445	Tell Me When/It Had To Be (as Troy Dante & Infernos)	8
64	Fontana TF 477	This Little Girl/Loving Eyes (as Troy Dante & Infernos)	18

64	Fontana TF 498	Baby/Tell Me Now	8
65	Fontana TF 541	I Wish I Knew/Sad Tears	8
66	Polydor NH 56110	I'll Never Know/Security	7
68	Columbia DB 8381	My Friend The Scarecrow/Emma May Kingston	7
69	MCA MK 5003	It's About Time/Behold	8

JOE DARENSBOURG & HIS DIXIE FLYERS

58	Vogue V 2409	Yellow Dog Blues/Careless Love	6
58	Vogue LAE 12149	JOE DARENSBOURG & HIS DIXIE FLYERS (LP)	15

DARIEN SPIRIT

73	Charisma CAS 1065	ELEGY TO MARILYN (LP)	15

BOBBY DARIN

78s

56	Brunswick 05561	Rock Island Line/Timber (as Bobby Darin & Jaybirds)	50
58	London HLE 8666	Splish Splash/Judy Don't Be Moody	25
58	London HLE 8679	Early In The Morning/Now We're One	40
58	London HLE 8737	Queen Of The Hop/Lost Love	45
59	London HLE 8793	Mighty Mighty Man/You're Mine (as Bobby Darin with Rinky Dinks)	50
59	London HLE 8815	Plain Jane/While I'm Gone	50
59	London HLE 8867	Dream Lover/Bullmoose	30
59	London HLK 8939	Mack The Knife/Was There A Call For Me	35
60	London HLK 9034	La Mer (Beyond The Sea)/That's The Way Love Is	50
60	London HLK 9086	Clementine/Down With Love	55
60	London HLK 9142	Bill Bailey Won't You Please Come Home/Tall Story	65

SINGLES

56	Brunswick 05561	Rock Island Line/Timber (as Bobby Darin & Jaybirds)	170
58	London HLE 8666	Splish Splash/Judy Don't Be Moody	30
58	London HLE 8679	Early In The Morning/Now We're One (as Rinky-Dinks featuring Bobby Darin)	40
58	London HLE 8737	Queen Of The Hop/Lost Love	25
58	London HL 7060	Queen Of The Hop/Lost Love (export issue)	20
59	London HLE 8793	Mighty Mighty Man/You're Mine (as Bobby Darin with Rinky Dinks)	40
59	London HLE 8815	Plain Jane/While I'm Gone	30
59	London HL 7078	Plain Jane/Dream Lover (export issue)	25
59	London HLE 8867	Dream Lover/Bullmoose	6
59	London HLK 8939	Mack The Knife/Was There A Call For Me	6
60	London HLK 9034	La Mer (Beyond The Sea)/That's The Way Love Is	5

(The above 45s were originally issued with triangular centres, later round centre pressings are worth around two-thirds these values.)

60	London HLK 9086	Clementine/Down With Love	5
60	London HLK 9142	Bill Bailey Won't You Please Come Home/Tall Story	5
60	Brunswick 05831	Hear Them Bells/The Greatest Builder	15
60	London HLK 9197	Beachcomber/Autumn Blues (credited to 'Bobby Darin At The Piano')	12
60	Lonson HLK 9215	Somebody To Love/I'll Be There	5
61	London HLK 9303	Lazy River/Oo-Ee-Train	5
61	London HLK 9375	Nature Boy/Look For My True Love	5
61	London HLK 9407	Theme From "Come September"/Walk Bach To Me (with Orchestra)	8
61	London HLK 9429	You Must Have Been A Beautiful Baby/Sorrow Tomorrow	5
61	London HLK 9474	Multiplication (From "Come September")/Irresistible You	5
62	London HLK 9540	What'd I Say/Ain't That Love	6
62	London HLK 9575	Things/Jailer Bring Me Water	6
62	Capitol CL 15272	If A Man Answers/A True, True Love	8
62	London HLK 9624	Baby Face/You Know How	6
63	London HLK 9663	I've Found A New Baby/Keep A-Walkin'	7
63	Capitol CL 15286	You're The Reason I'm Living/Now You're Gone	6
63	Capitol CL 15306	Eighteen Yellow Roses/Not For Me	8
63	Capitol CL 15328	Be Mad Little Girl/Since You've Been Gone	10
64	Capitol CL 15338	I Wonder Who's Kissing Her Now/As Long As I'm Singing	6
64	Atlantic AT 4002	Milord/Golden Earrings	6
64	Capitol CL 15360	The Things In This House/Wait By The Water	6
65	Capitol CL 15401	When I Get Home/Lonely Road	6
65	Capitol CL 15414	Gyp The Cat/That Funny Feeling	6
65	Atlantic AT 4046	We Didn't Ask To Be Brought Here/Funny What Love Can Do	10
66	Atlantic 584 014	Mame/Walking In The Shadow Of Love	6
66	Atlantic 584 051	If I Were A Carpenter/Rainin'	6
67	Atlantic 584 063	The Girl That Stood Beside Me/Reason To Believe	6
67	Atlantic 584 079	Lovin' You/Amy	6
67	Atlantic 584 105	The Lady Came From Baltimore/I Am	6
67	Atlantic 584 147	At The Crossroads/She Knows	5
68	Bell BLL 1040	Change/Long Line Rider	8
69	Bell BLL 1090	Sugar-Man/Jive	8
70	Major Minor MM 697	Maybe We Can Get It Together/RX-Pyro (Prescription: Fire) (as Bob Darin)	8
74	Mowest MW 3014	Blue Monday/Moritat: Mack The Knife	8

EPs

59	London REE 1173	BOBBY DARIN (tri/round centre)	75/60
59	London REE 1225	BOBBY DARIN NO. 2 (tri/round centre)	70/50
60	London REK 1243	THAT'S ALL	28
61	London REK 1286	FOR TEENAGERS ONLY	40
61	London REK 1290	UP A LAZY RIVER	25
61	London REK 1310	TWO OF A KIND (with Johnny Mercer)	35
61	London REK 1321	THE 25TH DAY OF DECEMBER	40
61	London REK 1334	LOVE SWINGS	30
62	London REK 1338	TWIST WITH BOBBY DARIN	30
62	London REK 1342	THINGS!	22
65	Atlantic AET 6013	MILORD	22

LPs

58	London HA-E 2140	BOBBY DARIN	75
59	London HA-E 2172	THAT'S ALL	30
59	London HA-K 2235	THIS IS DARIN (also stereo SAH-K 6067)	30/40
60	London HA-K 2291	DARIN AT THE COPA (also stereo SAH-K 6103)	25/35
60	London HA-K 2311	FOR TEENAGERS ONLY	45
61	London HA-K 2363	TWO OF A KIND (with Johnny Mercer; also stereo SAH-K 6164)	35/45
61	London HA-K 2372	THE BOBBY DARIN STORY	30
61	London HA-K 2394	LOVE SWINGS (also stereo SAH-K 6194)	30/40
62	London HA-K 2456	DARIN SINGS RAY CHARLES (also stereo SAH-K 6243)	30/40
62	Capitol T 1791	OH! LOOK AT ME NOW	25
62	London HA-K 8030	THINGS AND OTHER THINGS	35
63	London HA-K/SH-K 8102	IT'S YOU OR NO-ONE (mono/stereo)	35/45
63	Capitol T 1826	EARTHY	20
63	Capitol T 1866	YOU'RE THE REASON I'M LIVING	25
63	Capitol (S)T 1942	EIGHTEEN YELLOW ROSES & 11 OTHER HITS (mono/stereo)	30/40
64	Capitol (S)T 2007	GOLDEN FOLK HITS (mono/stereo)	30/40
65	Capitol T 2194	FROM HELLO DOLLY TO GOODBYE CHARLIE	20
65	Atlantic ATL 5014	BOBBY DARIN WINNERS	30
65	Capitol T 2322	I WANNA BE AROUND	30
66	Capitol T 2571	THE BEST OF BOBBY DARIN	20
66	Atlantic 587/588 014	SINGS THE SHADOW OF YOUR SMILE	22
66	Atlantic 587/588 020	IN A BROADWAY BAG (MAME)	18
66	Atlantic 587/588 051	IF I WERE A CARPENTER	18
67	Atlantic 587 065	THE BOBBY DARIN STORY	18
67	Atlantic 587 073	SOMETHING SPECIAL	40
67	Atlantic 587 076	INSIDE OUT	18
	(see also Rinky Dinks)		

DARK

72	SIS 0102	DARK ROUND THE EDGES (LP, private pressing, 12 copies with colour gatefold sleeve & booklet)	1,800
72	SIS 0102	DARK ROUND THE EDGES (LP, private pressing, 8 copies with black & white gatefold sleeve)	1,300
72	SIS 0102	DARK ROUND THE EDGES (LP, private pressing, 40 copies with single black & white sleeve)	1,000
90	Swank	DARK ROUND THE EDGES (LP, reissue, U.K. pressing marketed in U.S.)	30
91	Swank/Darkside 001	DARK ROUND THE EDGES (LP, as above, with different insert, 225 only)	25
92	Kissing Spell KSCD 9204	DARK ROUND THE EDGES (CD, with 8-page booklet, 1,500 only)	20
95	Acme AC 8009LP	ARTEFACTS FROM THE BLACK MUSEUM (LP, 500 only, with insert)	15

DARKER SHADE OF BLACK

71	Jackpot JP 758	War/JEFF BARNES: People's Version	8

DARKNESS

02	Must Destroy DUSTY 001CD	I Believe In A Thing Called Love/Love On The Rocks With No Ice/Love Is Only A Feeling (CD)	100
02	Must Destroy DUSTY CD 001	I Believe In A Thing Called Love (Single Version)/(Album Version) (CD)	20
03	Must Destroy DESTROYER 6	Get Your Hands Off My Woman (Clean Version)/(Dirty Version)/Best Of Me (p/s, 2000 only)	40
03	Must Destroy DESTROYER 10	Growing On Me/How Dare You Call This Love (p/s)	18
03	Must Destroy DUSTY 010 CD/DVD	Growing On Me/How Dare You Call This Love?/Bareback//Growing On Me/Growing On Me (Video)/Out-takes (DVD/CD, double disc pack)	10
03	Must Destroy DARK 01CD/DVD	I Believe In A Thing Called Love/Makin' Out/Physical Sex/I Believe In A Thing Called Love/Out Of My Hands/I Believe In A Thing Called Love (Video)/Video Clips (DVD/CD, double disc pack, with poster)	12
03	Must Destroy DARK 01	I Believe In A Thing Called Love/Makin' Out (picture disc, sticker-sealed PVC sleeve, with inlay)	5
03	Must Destroy DARK 02	Christmas Time (Don't Let The Bells End)/I Love You 5 Times (die-cut picture disc)	7
03	Must Destroy DARK 02	Christmas Time (Don't Let The Bells End)/I Love You 5 Times (custom sleeve, with rub-on tattoo)	
03	Must Destroy DARK 02	Christmas Time (Don't Let The Bells End)/I Love You 5 Times (promo-only box set, in giftwrap, with card)	60
04	Atlantic SAM 00932	Love Is Only A Feeling (1-track CD promo in heart shaped fold out sleeve)	15
03	Must Destroy 50466 74521	PERMISSION TO LAND (LP)	12

DARKSIDE

90	Situation 2 SITU 29P	ALL THAT NOISE (LP, picture disc, die-cut sleeve)	12
91	Acid Ray DARK 2	PSYCHEDELIZE SUBURBIA (LP, mail-order only, with poster)	12
93	Situation 2 SITU 34P	MELOMANIA (LP, picture disc, die-cut sleeve)	12
	(see also Spacemen 3)		

DARK STAR

81	Avatar AAA 105	Lady Of Mars/Rock 'N' Romancin' (company sleeve)	12
81	Steel Strike no cat. no.	Lady Of Mars/Rock 'N' Romancin' (12", 250 pressed)	90
81	Avatar AALP 5003	DARK STAR (LP, some with patch)	22/18
87	FM WKFMLP 97	REAL TO REEL (LP)	15

DARKTHRONE

91	Peaceville VILE 22	SOULSIDE JOURNEY (LP, picture disc)	25
92	Peaceville VILE 28	A BLAZE IN THE NORTHERN SKY (LP)	30
93	Peaceville VILE 35	UNDER A FUNERAL MOON (LP)	30
94	Peaceville VILE 43	TRANSILVANIAN HUNGER (LP)	30

DARLETTES

70	President PT 317	Lost/Sweet Kind Of Loneliness	20

DARLING BUDS

DARLING BUDS
87	Darling Buds DAR 1	If I Said/Just To Be Seen (p/s, some with insert, 2,000 only)	15/8
88	Bonk On 001	Spin/BUBBLEGUM SPLASH track (flexidisc free with *So Naive* fanzine)	8/6
90	Native NTV 54	Shame On You/Valentine//It's All Up To You/Spin//Think Of Me/	
		That's The Reason (triple-pack in envelope sleeve)	8

BILL DARNEL
55	London HLU 8204	My Little Mother/Bring Me A Bluebird (with Frank Weir & His Orchestra) (78 = £6)	45
56	London HLU 8234	The Last Frontier/Rock-A-Boogie Baby (78 rpm = £10)	50
56	London HLU 8267	Guilty Lips/Ain't Misbehavin' (78 rpm = £10)	40
56	London HLU 8292	Tell Me More/Satin Doll (78 rpm = £10)	40
	(see also Frank Weir & His Orchestra)		

GLENN DARRELL
54	London HL 8023	Write And Tell Me Why/Don't Let Me Down (78)	8

GUY DARRELL (& MIDNIGHTERS)
63	Oriole CB 1932	Go Home Girl/You Won't Come Home (as Guy Darrell & Midnighters)	15
64	Oriole CB 1964	Sorry/Sweet Dreams (as Guy Darrell & Midnighters)	15
65	CBS 201806	Stupidity/One Of These Days	10
66	CBS 202033	Somewhere They Can't Find Me/It Takes A Lot To Laugh	10
66	CBS 202082	I've Been Hurt/Blessed	22
66	CBS 202296	Big Louie/My Way Of Thinking	6
67	CBS 202510	Hard Lovin'/I've Never Had A Love Like That	6
67	CBS 202642	Crystal Ball/Didn't I	6
67	Piccadilly 7N 35406	Evil Woman/What You Do About That	20
67	Pye 7N 17435	Cupid/What's Happened To Our Love	6
68	Pye 7N 17586	Skyline Pigeon/Everything	6
69	Page One POF 120	Turn To Me/What's Her Name	5
69	Page One POF 141	Birds Of A Feather/Keep The Rain From My Door	5
69	Page One POF 155	How Are You/Turtle Turquoise And The Hare (as Guy Darrell Syndicate)	5
72	CBS 53364	GUY DARRELL (LP)	22

JAMES DARREN
59	Pye International 7N 25019	Gidget/There's No Such Thing (as Jimmy Darren) (78 rpm = £6)	15
59	Pye International 7N 25034	Angel Face/I Don't Wanna Lose You (as Jimmy Darren) (78 rpm = £6)	12
60	Pye International 7N 25059	Because They're Young/Let There Be Love	8
61	Pye International 7N 25116	Goodbye Cruel World/Valerie	8
62	Pye International 7N 25125	Her Royal Majesty/If I Could Only Tell You	8
62	Pye International 7N 25138	Conscience/Dream Big	8
62	Pye International 7N 25155	Mary's Little Lamb/The Life Of The Party	8
62	Pye International 7N 25168	Too Young To Go Steady/Hail To The Conquering Hero	8
63	Pye International 7N 25170	Pin A Medal On Joey/I'll Be Loving You	8
63	Colpix PX 708	Backstage/Gegetta	8
65	Warner Bros WB 5648	Because You're Mine/Millions Of Roses	5
66	Warner Bros WB 5689	Tom Hawk/I Want To Be Lonely	5
67	Warner Bros WB 5874	All/Misty Morning Eyes	5
59	Pye Intl. NEP 44004	P.S. I LOVE YOU (EP)	20
62	Pye Intl. NEP 44008	JAMES DARREN HIT PARADE (EP)	20
63	Pye Intl. NPL 28021	LOVE AMONG THE YOUNG (LP)	25

JEANNIE DARREN & SECOND CITY SOUND
69	Major Minor MM 611	River Deep, Mountain High/Julie	5

MAXINE DARREN
65	Pye 7N 15796	How Can I Hide It From My Heart/Don't You Know	10

CHRIS DARROW
73	United Artists UAG 29453	CHRIS DARROW (LP)	15
74	United Artists UAG 29634	UNDER MY OWN DISGUISE (LP)	15
	(see also Kaleidoscope)		

DARTELLS
63	London HLD 9719	Dartell Stomp/Hot Pastrami	22

BARRY DARVELL
60	London HL 9191	Geronimo Stomp/How Will It End?	80

DARWIN'S THEORY
67	Major Minor MM 503	Daytime/Hosanna	50

NITAE DASGUPTA
72	Mushroom 100 MR 22	SONGS OF INDIA (LP)	42

DAS SCHNITZ
79	Ellie Jay EJSP 9249	4 AM (EP, custom sleeve)	70

DATE WITH SOUL
67	Stateside SS 2062	Yes Sir, That's My Baby/PRISCILLA: He Noticed Me	75
	(see also Jack Nitzsche, Brian Wilson, Sonny & Cher, Darlene Love/Blossoms, Jackie De Shannon, the Paris Sisters)		

DAUGHTERS OF ALBION
69	Fontana STL 5486	DAUGHTERS OF ALBION (LP)	20

CLAUDE DAUPHIN
59	Top Rank JAR 195	From The French/JOE PARADISE TRIO: From The French	8

DAVE & ANSELL COLLINS
72	Techniques TE 915	Karate/Doing Your Own Thing	8
72	Rhino RNO 106	Keep On Trying/Give Me Some Light	6
73	Rhino RNO 111	Hot Life/Sunshine Rock (label credits 'Dave Collins')	6
73	Trojan TR 7891	Bandwagon/Ton Up Kids	6
71	Trojan TBL 162	DOUBLE BARREL (LP)	18
	(see also Ansel Collins, Les Foster & Ansell Collins, Dave Barker)		

DAVE DAVANI & D MEN
63	Columbia DB 7125	Don't Fool Around/She's The Best For Me	15
64	Decca F 11896	Midnight Special/Sho' Know A Lot About Love	20

DAVE DAVANI (FOUR)
65	Parlophone R 5329	Top Of The Pops/Workin' Out	20
66	Parlophone R 5490	Tossin' And Turnin'/Jupe	40
66	Parlophone R 5525	One Track Mind/On The Cooler Side	30
72	Philips 6006 195	King Kong Blues/Come Back Baby (solo)	8
65	Parlophone PMC 1258	FUSED (LP)	75

DAVE & DIAMONDS
65	Columbia DB 7692	I Walk The Lonely Night/You Do Love (some in p/s)	35/15

(see also Dave Russell)

DAVE & DON
67	Polydor 56212	What A Feeling/That's My Way	6

BOB DAVENPORT (& RAKES)
60	Collector JEB 4	GEORDIE SONGS (EP)	15
62	Topic TOP 83	WOR GEORDIE (EP, with Rakes)	15
66	Columbia SX 1786	BOB DAVENPORT AND THE RAKES (LP, with Rakes)	20

ALAN DAVEY
87	Hawkfan HWFB 3/4	THE ELF EP (double pack, 2 x 7" with insert in wraparound p/s in poly bag)	10

(see also Hawkwind)

(Shaun) DAVEY & (James) MORRIS
73	York FYK 417	DAVEY AND MORRIS (LP, with insert)	110

(see also Strawbs)

DAVID
69	Philips BF 1776	Please Mister Postman/Light Of Your Mind	75
69	President PT286	The Who The Why/President	6
70	Fontana TF 1081	I'm Going Back/Selppin	7

ALAN DAVID
64	Decca F 11956	I Want So Much To Know You/I Can't Go Wrong	7
65	Decca F 12130	Crazy 'Bout My Baby/A Thousand Years Too Late	7
67	Polydor BM 56201	Flower Power/Completely Free	12
65	Decca LK 4674	ALAN DAVID (LP)	40

DAVID & EMBERS
63	Decca F 11717	What Is This/Teddy Bear Special	7

(see also Embers)

DAVID & GIANTS
68	Capitol CL 15915	Ten Miles High/Super Love	8

DAVID & JONATHAN
67	Columbia S(C)X 6031	DAVID AND JONATHAN (LP)	25

(see also Roger Cook, Edison Lighthouse, White Plains)

DAVID & ROZAA
70	Philips 6006 040	Time Of Our Life/We Can Reach An Understanding	20
71	Philips 6006 094	The Spark That Lights The Flame/Two Can Share	20

(see also David Essex)

DIANNE DAVIDSON
72	Janus 6146 019	Sympathy/All I Wanted	10
72	Janus 6146 021	Ain't Gonna Be Treated This Way/All I Wanted (All The Time)	5
72	Janus 6310 209	BACKWOODS WOMAN (LP)	15

FRANKIE DAVIDSON & HI MARKS
61	Starlite ST45 5037	You're Driving Me Crazy/I Care For You (B-side with Unicords)	22
61	London HL 9309	Detour/Just For Today	12
64	HMV POP 1256	Lickin' And A-Stickin'/I Love To Shake	18
68	Decca F 22780	Hector The Trash Collector/Somebody Come And Take My Wife	6

TOMMY DAVIDSON
56	London HLU 8219	Half Past Kissing Time/I Don't Know Yet But I'm Learning (78 rpm = £20)	90

HUTCH DAVIE
58	London HLE 8667	At The Woodchopper's Ball/Honky Tonk Train Blues (& Honky Tonkers) (78 rpm=£5)	10
60	London HLE 9076	Sweet Georgia Brown/Heartaches	5
62	Pye International 7N 25149	But I Do/Time Was (& Orchestra)	5
60	London HA-E 2216	MUCH HUTCH (LP)	20

ALUN DAVIES
65	Parlophone R 5384	Girls Were Made To Love And Kiss/Rose Marie	6
68	Mercury MF 1043	One Day Soon/Pretend You Don't See Her	6
72	CBS 65108	DAYDO (LP)	15

(see also Cat Stevens)

BOB DAVIES
63	London HLU 9767	Rock'N'Roll Show/With You Tonight	30

CYRIL DAVIES (R&B ALLSTARS)
63	Pye International 7N 25194	Country Line Special/Chicago Calling	30
63	Pye International 7N 25221	Preachin' The Blues/Sweet Mary	40
69	Pye 7N 17663	Country Line Special/Sweet Mary	15
64	Pye Intl. NEP 44025	THE SOUND OF CYRIL DAVIES (EP)	75
57	'77' LP 2	THE LEGENDARY CYRIL DAVIES (10" LP, 99 only, with Alexis Korner)	350+
70	Folklore F-LEAT 9	THE LEGENDARY CYRIL DAVIES (LP, reissue)	75

(see also Alexis Korner, Beryl Bryden)

MINT VALUE £

DAVE DAVIES

67	Pye 7N 17356	Death Of A Clown/Love Me Till The Sun Shines	7
67	Pye 7N 17429	Susannah's Still Alive/Funny Face	10
68	Pye 7N 17514	Lincoln County/There's No Life Without Love	20
69	Pye 7N 17678	Hold My Hand/Creeping Jean	20
68	Pye NEP 24289	DAVE DAVIES HITS (EP)	320
69		UNTITLED (Test pressing of untitled solo album – only 1 copy known to exist)	1000+

(see also Kinks)

IRVING DAVIES & METHOD MEN

62	Decca F 11456	The Method/ABC The Method	6

JACKIE DAVIES & HIS QUARTET

57	Pye Nixa N 15115	Land Of Make Believe/Over The Rainbow (78)	80

(see also Chico Arnez)

MARION DAVIES

69	Columbia DB 8589	Walk Out Of My Mind/This Is My Lonely Life	7

(see also Ladybirds)

MIAR DAVIES

64	Decca F 11805	Ten Good Reasons/I Won't Remember You	10
64	Decca F 11894	I Hear You Knocking/Navy Blue	10

NICOLA DAVIES

68	SNB 55-3627	Infatuation/My Boy	6

RAY DAVIES & BUTTONDOWN BRASS

73	Pye NSPL 41021	I BELIEVE IN MUSIC (LP)	15
74	Philips 6382 103	THEMES FROM THE EXORCIST, FRENCH CONNECTION AND OTHER GREAT FILMS (LP)	15
75	Philips 6382 111	FLASHPOINT (LP)	15

(see also Buttondown Brass; the above is not Ray Davies of the Kinks)

RAY DAVIES

86	Virgin VS 865-12	Quiet Life/Voices In The Dark/GIL EVANS: Va Va Voom (12", p/s)	8
86	Virgin VS 865	Quiet Life/Voices In The Dark (p/s)	5

(see also Kinks)

RUPERT DAVIES

63	Parlophone R 5067	October Dreams/Smoking My Pipe (La Pipa)	5

BARRINGTON DAVIS

72	Montague MONS 2	TRACKS OF MIND (LP, with lyric insert)	50

BETTE DAVIS & DEBBIE BURTON

63	London HLU 9711	Whatever Happened To Baby Jane?/I've Written A Letter To Daddy	12
76	EMI EMA 778	MISS BETTE DAVIS (LP)	20

BETTY DAVIS

75	Island USA 2011	Shut Off The Light/He Was A Big Freak	6
75	Island ILPS 9329	NASTY GIRL (LP)	22

BILLIE DAVIS

63	Decca F 11572	Tell Him/I'm Thankful	7
63	Decca F 11658	He's The One/V.I.P.	12
63	Columbia DB 7115	Bedtime Stories/You And I	15
64	Columbia DB 7195	That Boy John/Say Nothin' Don't Tell	15
64	Columbia DB 7246	School Is Over/Give Me Love	15
64	Columbia DB 7346	Whatcha Gonna Do/Everybody Knows (as Billie Davis & Le Roys)	25
65	Piccadilly 7N 35227	Last One To Be Loved/You Don't Know	10
65	Piccadilly 7N 35266	No Other Baby/Hands Off	10
66	Piccadilly 7N 35308	Heart And Soul/Don't Take All Night	10
66	Piccadilly 7N 35350	Just Walk In My Shoes/Ev'ry Day	40
67	Decca F 12620	Wasn't It You?/Until It's Time For You To Go	7
67	Decca F 12696	Angel Of The Morning/Darling Be Home Soon	6
68	Decca F 12823	I Want You To Be My Baby/Suffer	6
69	Decca F 12870	I'll Come Home/Make The Feeling Go Away	8
69	Decca F 12923	I Can Remember/Nobody's Home To Go Home To	20
69	Decca F 12977	Nights In White Satin/It's Over	18
70	Decca F 13049	Venid Con Migo/Love (Spanish export issue)	7
70	Decca F 13085	There Must Be A Reason/Love	6
72	Regal Zonophone RZ 3050	I Tried/Touch My Love	6
78	Magnet MAG 124	Run Joey Run/East Come Easy Go	6
70	Decca LK/SKL 5029	BILLIE DAVIS (LP, mono/stereo)	60/55

(see also Keith & Billie, Le Roys, Mike Sarne)

BLIND GARY DAVIS/REVEREND GARY DAVIS

63	'77' LA 12-14	PURE RELIGION AND BAD COMPANY (LP)	45
60s	Fontana 688 303 ZL	HARLEM STREET SINGER (LP)	40
64	Xtra XTRA 1009	REV. GARY DAVIS/SHORT STUFF MACON (LP, 1 side each)	22
66	Xtra XTRA 5014	SAY NO TO THE DEVIL (LP)	25
67	Xtra XTRA 5042	A LITTLE MORE FAITH (LP)	25
69	Fontana SFJL 914	BRING YOUR MONEY HONEY (LP)	28
71	Transatlantic TRA 244	RAGTIME GUITAR (LP)	15
72	Transatlantic TRA 249	CHILDREN OF ZION (LP)	15
74	Kicking Mule SNKD 1	LO I BE WITH YOU ALWAYS (2-LP)	15

BLIND JOHNNY DAVIS

52	MGM MGM 463	Your Love Belongs To Me/Magic Carpet (78)	10

BOBBY DAVIS (Jamaica)
71	Banana BA 342	Got To Get Away/We'll Cry Together (with Barbera Dunkley)	12
71	Banana BA 344	Return Your Love/RILEY'S ALLSTARS: Version	10
71	Beacon 114	Strange Days/I Wish It would Rain	12

(see also Barbara Dunkley)

BOBBY DAVIS (U.S.)
61	Starlite ST45 056	I Was Wrong/Hype You Into Selling Your Head	50

BONNIE DAVIS
55	Brunswick 05507	Pepper-Hot Baby/For Always, Darling (78 rpm = £12)	55

CLIFFORD DAVIS
69	Reprise RS 27003	Before The Beginning/Man Of The World	10
70	Reprise RS 27008	Come On Down And Follow Me/Homework	7
71	Reprise K 14282	Before The Beginning/Man Of The World (reissue)	7

DANNY DAVIS (U.K.)
60	Parlophone R 4657	Love Me/You're My Only Girl	22
60	Parlophone R 4796	Talking In My Sleep/Lullaby Of Love	15
61	Pye 7N 15391	Tell All The World/Rumours	10
62	Pye 7N 15427	Rome Wasn't Built In A Day/Tell Me	5
62	Pye 7N 15470	Patches/September In The Rain	5

(see also Marauders)

DANNY DAVIS ORCHESTRA (U.S.)
58	London HL 8766	Trumpet Cha-Cha-Cha/Lonesome Trumpet	8
65	MGM MGM 1277	Main Theme From "The Saint"/Little Bandits Of Juarez	10
64	London HAR 8204	THEY'RE PLAYING OUR SONG (LP, with Ruby & Romantics)	40

(see also Ruby & Romantics, Byron Lee)

EDDIE ('LOCKJAW') DAVIS
56	Parlophone GEP 8587	EDDIE 'LOCKJAW' DAVIS TRIO (EP)	10
57	Parlophone GEP 8678	LOCKJAW (EP)	10
58	Parlophone GEP 8685	EDDIE 'LOCKJAW' DAVIS TRIO (EP)	10
59	Esquire EP 217	EDDIE 'LOCKJAW' DAVIS (EP)	10
61	Esquire EP 237	EDDIE 'LOCKJAW' DAVIS QUARTET (EP)	10
60	Esquire 32-104	THE EDDIE 'LOCKJAW' DAVIS COOK BOOK (LP)	22
60	Esquire 32-117	VERY SAXY (LP, with Coleman Hawkins, Arnett Cobb & Bobby Tate)	22
61	Esquire 32-128	JAWS IN ORBIT (LP)	22
64	Stateside SL 10102	THE FIRST SET — LIVE AT MINTONS (LP, with Johnny Griffin)	20

(see also Coleman Hawkins, Johnny Griffin)

EDWARD H. DAVIS
74	Sain SAIN 1016M	HEN FFORDD GYMREIG O FYW (LP)	20
76	Sain SAIN 1053M	SNEB YN BECSO DAM (LP)	15

JESSE (ED) DAVIS
71	Atlantic 2091 076	Every Night Is Saturday Night/Washita Love Child (as Jesse Davis)	6
71	Atco 2400 106	JESSE 'ED' DAVIS (LP)	15
72	Atlantic K 40329	ULULU (LP)	15

KIM DAVIS
66	Decca F 12387	Don't Take Your Lovin' Away/Feelin' Blue	20
67	CBS 202568	Tell It Like It Is/Losing Kind	12
68	CBS 3260	Until It's Time For You To Go/I Hold No Grudge	7
69	CBS 4210	Are You Ready For Love/Taste Of Excitement	7

(see also Kim D, Kim & Kinetics)

LARRY DAVIS/FENTON ROBINSON
72	Python PLP 24	LARRY DAVIS AND FENTON ROBINSON (LP, 99 copies only)	70

MAXWELL DAVIS
66	Ember FA 2040	BATMAN THEME AND OTHER BAT SONGS (LP)	35

MAXWELL STREET JIMMY DAVIS
66	Bounty BY 6009	MAXWELL STREET JIMMY DAVIS (LP)	30

MELVIN DAVIS
69	Action ACT 4531	Save It/This Love Was Meant To Be	30

MILES DAVIS
LPs
55	Esquire 20-041	MILES DAVIS QUINTET (10")	40
53	Esquire 20-017	MILES DAVIS PLAYS (10")	40
53	Esquire 20-021	MILES DAVIS ALL STARS (10")	40
54	Esquire 20-052	MILES DAVIS ALL STARS (A HIFI MODERN JAZZ JAM SESSION) (10")	40
54	Vogue LDE 064	MILES DAVIS AND HIS ORCHESTRA (10")	40
54	Esquire 20-056	MILES DAVIS ALL STARS (A SECOND HIFI MODERN JAZZ JAM SESSION) (10")	40
54	Capitol LC 6683	CLASSICS IN JAZZ (10")	35
55	Esquire 20-062	MILES DAVIS ALL STARS SEXTET (10")	35
55	Esquire 20-072	MILES DAVIS QUINTET (10")	35
56	Philips BBL 7140	'ROUND ABOUT MIDNIGHT	25
57	Fontana TFL 5007	MILES AHEAD	25
58	Fontana TFL 5035	MILESTONES	18
58	Esquire 32-068	RELAXIN' WITH THE MILES DAVIS QUARTET	40
59	Fontana TFL 5056	PORGY AND BESS (also stereo [STFL 507])	20/25
59	Esquire 32-012	THE MUSINGS OF MILES	25
60	Fontana TFL 5081	JAZZ TRACK — "L'ANSCENSEUR POUR L'ECHAFAUD"	20
60	Fontana TFL 5089	THE "MOST" OF MILES	25
60	Fontana STFL 513	KIND OF BLUE (also mono [TFL 5072])	20/15
60	Esquire 32-098	WALKIN'	25
60	Esquire 32-100	MILES DAVIS AND THE MODERN JAZZ GIANTS VOL. 2	25

MINT VALUE £

60	Esquire 32-108	WORKIN' WITH THE MILES DAVIS QUINTET	25
61	Font. TFL 5100/STFL 531	SKETCHES OF SPAIN	25
61	Esquire 32-118	EARLY MILES	20
61	Esquire 32-138	STEAMIN' WITH THE MILES DAVIS QUINTET	25
61	Fontana TFL 5163	FRIDAY NIGHT AT THE BLACKHAWK, SAN FRANCISCO (VOL. 1)	
		(with Cannonball Adderley & John Coltrane; also stereo STFL 580)	each 15
61	Fontana TFL 5164	SATURDAY NIGHT AT THE BLACKHAWK, SAN FRANCISCO (VOL. 2)	
		(with Cannonball Adderley & John Coltrane; also stereo STFL 581)	each 15
62	Fontana TFL 5172	SOMEDAY MY PRINCE WILL COME (also stereo STFL 587)	each 15
70	CBS 66236	BITCHES BREW (2-LP)	15
71	CBS 66257	MILES DAVIS AT FILLMORE (2-LP)	15
72	CBS 64575	LIVE-EVIL (2-LP)	20
72	Prestige PR 24001	MILES DAVIS (2-LP)	15
72	Prestige PR 24012	TALLEST TREES (2-LP)	15
73	CBS CQ 30997/Q 66236	BITCHES BREW (2-LP, quadrophonic)	20
73	CBS GQ 30954/Q 67219	LIVE-EVIL (2-LP, quadrophonic)	20
88	CBS 4632461	CBS YEARS 1955 – 1985 (5xLP box set)	35

MILES DAVIS/ART BLAKEY

66	Fontana FJL 135	L'ASCENSEUR POUR L'ECHAFAUD/LA FEMME DISPARAISSANTE	
		(LP, soundtrack, 1 side each)	50

(see also Art Blakey, Thelonius Monk, Dizzy Gillespie, Milt Jackson, Cannonball Adderley, Charlie Parker)

MILES DAVIS & JOHN COLTRANE
(see under Miles Davis, John Coltrane)

RONNIE DAVIS

77	Third World TWDIS 005	Anywhere Don't Watch Your Woman (with Dillinger)/	
		BARRY BROWN : Mr Money Man (12")	25

SAMMY DAVIS (Jnr.)

54	Brunswick 05326	Because Of You (Parts 1 & 2)	8
55	Brunswick 05383	The Birth Of The Blues/Love (Your Magic Spell Is Everywhere)	8
55	Brunswick 05389	Six Bridges To Cross/Glad To Be Unhappy	8
55	Brunswick 05409	And This Is My Beloved/The Red Grapes	8
55	Brunswick 05428	Love Me Or Leave Me/Something's Gotta Give	8
55	Brunswick 05450	That Old Black Magic/Give A Fool A Chance	8
55	Brunswick 05469	Hey There/My Funny Valentine	8
55	Brunswick 05478	Backtrack/It's Bigger Than You And Me	8
56	Brunswick 05518	In A Persian Market/The Man With The Golden Arm	8
56	Capitol CL 14562	Azure/Dedicated To You	5
56	Brunswick 05583	Adelaide/I'll Know	5
56	Brunswick 05594	Earthbound/Five	5
56	Brunswick 05611	Frankie And Johnny/Circus	5
56	Brunswick 05617	You're Sensational/Don't Let Her Go	5
56	Brunswick 05629	All Of You/Just One Of Those Things	7
57	Brunswick 05637	The Golden Key/All About Love	5
57	Brunswick 05647	Dangerous/The World Is Mine Tonight	5
57	Brunswick 05668	Too Close For Comfort/Jacques D'Iraque	7
57	Brunswick 05694	Goodbye, So Long, I'm Gone/French Fried Potatoes And Ketchup	5
57	Brunswick 05717	Mad Ball/The Nearness Of You	5
57	Brunswick 05724	Long Before I Knew You/Never Like This	5
58	Brunswick 05732	I'm Comin' Home/Hallelujah, I Love Her	5
59	Brunswick 05778	That's Anna/I Never Got Out Of Paris (78)	6
60	Brunswick 05830	Happy To Make Your Acquaintance/Baby, It's Cold Outside (with Carmen McRae)	5
64	Reprise R 20227	The Shelter Of Your Arms/Falling In Love With You	25
64	Reprise R 20289	Not For Me/Bang Bang	10
69	MCA MK 5016	Rhythm Of Life/Pompeii Club/Rich Man's Frug	5
72	MGM 2006 095	The Candy Man/I Want To Be Happy	6
76	20th Century BTC 2292	Baretta's Theme/I Heard A Song	6
50	Brunswick OE 9445	BOY MEETS GIRL (EP, with Carmen McRae)	10
56	Capitol EAP1 555	SAMMY DAVIS JNR. (EP)	10
56	Brunswick LAT 8088	JUST FOR LOVERS (LP)	15
56	Brunswick LAT 8153	STARRING SAMMY DAVIS (LP)	15
70	Tamla Motown STML 11160	SOMETHING FOR EVERYONE (LP)	20

(see also Dean Martin)

SILKIE DAVIS

70	Torpedo TOR 2	Conversations/TWINKLE: Peace & Tranquility	5
70	Torpedo TOR 12	When I Was A Little Girl/I'm So Lonely	5

SKEETER DAVIS

60	RCA Victor RCA 1201	No Never/(I Can't Help You) I'm Falling Too	8
61	RCA Victor RCA 1222	My Last Date With You/Someone I'd Like To Forget	6
63	RCA Victor RCA 1328	The End Of The World/Somebody Loves You	10
63	RCA Victor RCA 1345	I'm Saving My Love/Somebody Else On Your Mind	6
63	RCA Victor RCA 1363	I Can't Stay Mad At You/It Was Only My Heart	10
64	RCA Victor RCA 1384	He Says The Same Things To Me/How Much	6
64	RCA Victor RCA 1398	Now You're Gone/Gonna Get Along Without You Now	6
65	RCA Victor RCA 1474	Sun Glasses/He Loved Me Too Little	6
64	RCA Victor RCX 7153	SILVER THREADS AND GOLDEN NEEDLES (EP)	22
63	RCA Victor RD/SF 7563	THE END OF THE WORLD (LP, mono/stereo)	25/30
63	RCA Victor RD/SF 7604	CLOUDY, WITH OCCASIONAL TEARS (LP, mono/stereo)	20/25
64	RCA Victor RD 7676	LET ME GET CLOSE TO YOU (LP)	20
69	RCA Victor SF 8068	MARY FRANCES (LP)	20

SKEETER DAVIS & BOBBY BARE

65	RCA RD 7711	TUNES FOR TWO (LP)	20

(see also Bobby Bare)

SMILEY DAVIS
53	London L 1189	Big Mamou/Play Girl (78, actually by Smiley Lewis)	130

SPENCER DAVIS (GROUP)
64	Fontana TF 471	Dimples/Sittin' And Thinkin'	30
64	Fontana TF 499	I Can't Stand It/Midnight Train	25
65	Fontana TF 530	Every Little Bit Hurts/It Hurts Me So	15
65	Fontana TF 571	Strong Love/This Hammer	20
65	Fontana TF 632	Keep On Running/High Time Baby	10
66	Fontana TF 679	Somebody Help Me/Stevie's Blues	10
66	Fontana TF 739	When I Come Home/Trampoline	15
66	Fontana TF 762	Gimme Some Loving/Blues In F	10
67	Fontana TF 771	I'm A Man/I Can't Get Enough Of It	12
67	Fontana TF 854	Time Seller/Don't Want You No More	10
67	United Artists UP 1203	Mr. Second Class/Sanity Inspector	6
68	United Artists UP 2213	After Tea/Moonshine	6
68	United Artists UP 2226	Short Change/Picture Of Heaven	8
73	Vertigo 6059 087	Livin' In A Back Street/Sure Need A Helping Hand	6
65	Fontana TE 17444	YOU PUT THE HURT ON ME (EP)	25
65	Fontana TE 17450	EVERY LITTLE BIT HURTS (EP)	30
66	Fontana TE 17463	SITTIN' AND THINKIN' (EP)	35
65	Fontana TL 5242	THEIR FIRST LP (LP)	48
66	Fontana TL 5295	THE SECOND ALBUM (LP)	48
66	Fontana TL 5359	AUTUMN '66 (LP)	48
67	United Artists (S)ULP 1186	HERE WE GO ROUND THE MULBERRY BUSH (LP, soundtrack, with Traffic, mono/stereo)	35/30
68	United Artists (S)ULP 1192	WITH THEIR NEW FACE ON (LP, mono/stereo)	30/25
68	Wing WL 1165	EVERY LITTLE BIT HURTS (LP, reissue of Their First LP)	15
68	Island ILP 970/ILPS 9070	THE BEST OF THE SPENCER DAVIS GROUP FEATURING STEVIE WINWOOD (LP, plain pink label, flipback sleeve; sleeve lists Please Do Something but plays Together Till The End Of Time; mono/stereo)	20/15
69	CBS 63842	LETTERS FROM EDITH (LP, unissued, 50 white label test pressings only)	200+
71	United Artists UAS 29177	IT'S BEEN SO LONG (LP, solo with Peter Jameson, 'envelope' cover)	15
72	United Artists UAS 29361	MOUSETRAP (LP, solo)	15
73	Vertigo 6360 088	GLUGGO (LP, gatefold sleeve)	12
74	Vertigo 6360 105	LIVIN' IN A BACK STREET (LP)	12

(see also Stevie Winwood, Traffic, Anglos, Blind Faith, Ray Fenwick, Pete York, Hardin & York, Murgatroyd Band, Mirage, Portobello Explosion, Shotgun Express)

STEVE DAVIS
68	Fontana TF 922	Takes Time To Know Her/She Said Yeah	55+

TYRONE DAVIS
68	Stateside SS 2092	What If A Man/Bet You Win	30
69	Atlantic 584 253	Can I Change My Mind/A Woman Needs To Be Loved	12
69	Atlantic 584 265	Is It Something You've Got?/Undying Love	12
69	Atlantic 584 288	All The Waiting Is Not In Vain/Need Your Lovin' Everyday	12
70	Atlantic 2091 003	Turn Back The Hands Of Time/I Keep Coming Back	15
71	Atlantic 2091 078	Could I Forget You/Just My Way Of Loving You	10
71	Atlantic 2091 131	One Way Ticket/We Got A Love	10
72	Atlantic K 10207	Can I Change My Mind/Turn Back The Hands Of Time/One Way Ticket	8
73	Brunswick BR 4	Without You In My Life/How Could I Forget You	10
73	Brunswick BR 6	There It Is/You Wouldn't Believe	10
74	Brunswick BR 10	I Wish It Was Me/You Don't Have To Beg To Stay	10
76	Brunswick BR 31	Turning Point/Don't Let It Be Too Late	10
77	Brunswick BR 40	Ever Lovin' Girl/Forever	10
70	Atlantic 588 209	CAN I CHANGE MY MIND (LP)	30
71	Atlantic 2465 021	TURN BACK THE HANDS OF TIME (LP)	30
73	Brunswick BRLS 3002	I HAD IT ALL THE TIME (LP)	30
73	Brunswick BRLS 3005	GREATEST HITS (LP)	18

WALTER DAVIS
64	RCA RCX 7169	R.C.A. VICTOR RACE SERIES VOL. 3 (EP)	22
70	RCA Intl. INTS 1085	THINK YOU NEED A SHOT (LP)	20

WARREN DAVIS MONDAY BAND
67	Columbia DB 8190	Wait For Me/I Don't Wanna Hurt You	18
67	Columbia DB 8270	Love Is A Hurtin' Thing/Without Fear	15

(see also Boardwalkers)

DAVIS SISTERS
53	HMV B 10582	Rock-A-Bye Boogie/I Forgot More Than You'll Ever Know (78)	15

BRIAN DAVISON
70	Charisma CAS 1021	BRIAN DAVISON'S EVERY WHICH WAY (LP, pink label)	15

(see also Habits, Nice, Every Which Way)

WILD BILL DAVISON
55	Melodisc MLP 501	WILD BILL DAVISON (LP)	15

TIM DAWE
69	Straight ST(S) 1058	PENROD (LP)	30

CARL DAWKINS
67	Rio R 136	All Of A Sudden/Running Shoes	18
67	Rio R 137	Baby I Love You/Hard Time	18
68	Blue Cat BS 114	I Love The Way You Are/DERMOTT LYNCH: I Can't Stand It	20
68	Duke DU 3	I'll Make It Up/J.J. ALL STARS: One Dollar Of Music	12
69	Nu Beat NB 030	Rodney's History/DYNAMITES: Tribute To Drumbage	12
70	Duke DU 93	Get Together/FAMILY MAN: Instalment Plan	8
70	Duke DU 95	This Land/J.J. ALL STARS: Land Version	8

Carl DAWKINS

70	Trojan TR 7765	Satisfaction/Things A Get Bad To Worse	7
71	Big Shot BI 570	Perseverence/J.J. ALL STARS: Perseverence (Version)	8
71	Explosion EX 2051	I Feel Good/J.J. ALL STARS: I Feel Good Version Two	6
71	Explosion EX 2059	Make It Great/STONE: What A Day	6
71	New Beat NB 086	Walk A Little Prouder/YOUTH PROFESSIONALS: Walk (Version)	6
72	Duke DU 133	My Whole World/Men A Broken Heart	6

(see also Rass Dawkins, Untouchables, Winston Wright, Ansell Collins, Roland Alphonso, West Indians)

HORRELL DAWKINS
66	Ska Beat JB 240	Cling To Me/Butterfly	25

JIMMY DAWKINS
73	Mojo 2027 011	The Things I Used To Do/Put It On The Hawg	8
71	Delmark DS 623	FAST FINGERS (LP)	20
78	Sonet SNTF 758	TRANSATLANTIC 770 (LP)	15

RASS DAWKINS (& WAILERS)
71	Upsetter US 368	Picture On The Wall/UPSETTERS: Picture Version	25

(see also Bob Marley/Wailers, Carl Dawkins)

JULIE DAWN
53	Columbia SCM 5035	Wild Horses/A Whistling Kettle And A Dancing Cat	15

(see also Tony Brent & Julie Dawn, Cyril Stapleton)

DAWN & DEEJAYS
65	RCA RCA 1470	These Are The Things About You/I Will Think Of You	15

DAWNBREAKERS
65	Decca F 12110	Let's Live/Lovin' For You	15

DAWN CHORUS
69	MCA MK 5004	A Night To Be Remembered/Crying All Night	10

(see also Carter-Lewis)

DAWN CHORUS
85	Dawn DAWN 1	Teenage Kicks/Dream Lover (p/s)	15

DAWN TRADER
80	AFE 1980	NO ONE GONNA BETTER ME (EP, private pressing)	40

DAWNWATCHER
80	Dawnwatcher DWS 001	Spellbound	100
82	Dawnwatcher DWS 002	Backlash (p/s)	20

DAWNWIND
76	Amron ARN 5003	LOOKING BACK ON THE FUTURE (LP, private pressing)	80

DONNA DAWSON
73	Trojan TR 7892	You Can't Buy Me Love/First Cut Is The Deepest	6

LES DAWSON SYNDICATE
(see under Johnny Stevens and Les Dawson Syndicate)

LESLEY DAWSON
66	Mercury MF 924	Pastel Shades Of Love/The Time Has Come	5
67	Mercury MF 946	Just Say Goodbye/Just A Passing Phase	8
67	Mercury MF 965	Run For Shelter/I'll Climb On A Rainbow	30

DANIELLE DAX
83	Initial IRC 009	POP-EYES (LP, with 'Meat Harvest' cover & lyric sheet)	20

(see also Lemon Kittens)

DAY
94	Detour DR 019	Another Country/Gospel (p/s, 100 on green vinyl)	7

BING DAY
59	Mercury AMT 1047	I Can't Help It/Mama's Place	120

BOBBY DAY (& SATELLITES)
57	HMV POP 425	Little Bitty Pretty One/When The Swallows Come Back To Capistrano (as Bobby Day & Satellites) (78 rpm = £25)	175
58	London HL 8726	Rockin' Robin/Over And Over (78 rpm = £20)	28
59	London HL 8800	The Bluebird, The Buzzard And The Oriole/Alone Too Long (78 rpm = £40)	50
59	London HL 8964	Love Is A One Time Affair/Ain't Gonna Cry No More (78 rpm = £30)	30
60	London HLY 9044	My Blue Heaven/I Don't Want To	25
61	Top Rank JAR 538	Over And Over/Gee Whiz	20
65	Sue WI 388	Rockin' Robin/Over And Over (reissue)	30

DORIS DAY
59	Philips PB 949	The Tunnel Of Love/Run Away, Skidaddle, Skidoo (78)	6
59	Philips PB 958	Possess Me/Roly Poly (78)	6
53	Columbia SCM 5038	April In Paris/Your Mother And Mine (with Four Lads)	15
53	Columbia SCM 5039	That's What Makes Paris Paree/I Know A Place	15
53	Columbia SCM 5044	A Bushel And A Peck/If I Were A Bell	15
53	Columbia SCM 5045	The Second Star To The Right (with Four Lads) I'm Gonna Ring The Bell Tonight	15
53	Columbia SCM 5059	The Cherries/Papa, Won't You Dance With Me?	15
53	Columbia SCM 5062	Mister Tap-Toe/Why Should We Both Be Lonely?	15
53	Columbia SCM 5067	We Kiss In A Shadow/Something Wonderful	15
53	Columbia SCM 5075	That's The Way He Does It/Cuddle Up A Little Closer	15
54	Columbia SCM 5087	A Load Of Hay/It Had To Be You	15
55	Columbia SCM 5171	Just One Of Those Things/Sometimes I'm Happy	15
57	Philips JK 1020	Twelve O'Clock Tonight/Today Will Be Yesterday Tomorrow! (jukebox issue)	15
57	Philips JK 1031	The Party's Over/Rickety-Rackety Rendezvous (jukebox issue)	12
64	CBS AAG 219	Oowee Baby/The Rainbow's End	10

EPs

55	Philips BBE 12007	DORIS DAY	8
55	Philips BBE 12011	I'LL NEVER STOP LOVING YOU	8
56	Philips BBE 12089	DORIS DAY NO. 2	8
57	Philips BBE 12151	DAY DREAMS	8
58	Philips BBE 12167	DORIS	8
58	Philips BBE 12187	THE SONG IS YOU	8
58	Philips BBE 12213	DREAM A LITTLE DREAM OF ME	8
59	Philips BBE 12298	LET'S FLY AWAY (also stereo SBBE 9006)	each 8
59	Philips BBE 12339	PILLOW TALK	8
60	Philips BBE 12388	YOU CAN'T HAVE EVERYTHING (also stereo SBBE 9021)	each 8

LPs

54	Columbia 33S 1038	LULLABY OF BROADWAY (10", 2 different sleeve designs)	each 28
54	Philips BBR 8026	THE VOICE OF YOUR CHOICE (10")	20
55	Philips BBR 8040	YOUNG AT HEART (10", with Frank Sinatra)	25
55	Philips BBL 7047	LOVE ME OR LEAVE ME	25
56	Philips BBR 8094	DORIS DAY FAVOURITES (10")	18
56	Philips BBR 8104	CALAMITY JANE (10", with Howard Keel)	18
57	Philips BBL 7120	DAY DREAMS	22
57	Philips BBL 7137	DORIS AND FRANK (6 tracks each by Doris Day & Frank Sinatra)	22
57	Philips BBL 7142	DAY BY DAY	25
58	Philips BBL 7175	DAY IN HOLLYWOOD	20
58	Philips BBL 7197	THE PYJAMA GAME (with other artists, 5 tracks by Doris Day)	15
58	Philips BBL 7211	DAY BY NIGHT	30
58	Philips BBL 7247	HOORAY FOR HOLLYWOOD VOL. 1	25
58	Philips BBL 7248	HOORAY FOR HOLLYWOOD VOL. 2	20
59	Philips BBL 7296	CUTTIN' CAPERS (also stereo SBBL 540)	each 15
59	Philips BBL 7297	SHOWCASE OF HITS	15
59	Philips SBBL 519	HOORAY FOR HOLLYWOOD (stereo reissue)	20
59	Philips SBBL 548	DAY BY NIGHT (stereo reissue)	20
60	Philips BBL 7377	WHAT EVERY GIRL SHOULD KNOW (also stereo SBBL 563)	each 15
60	Philips SBBL 537	IN THE STILL OF THE NIGHT	15
60	Philips BBL 7392	SHOW TIME (also stereo SBBL 577)	each 15
61	Philips BBL 7471	BRIGHT AND SHINY (also stereo SBBL 619)	each 18
61	Philips BBL 7496	I HAVE DREAMED (also stereo SBBL 643)	each 18
63	CBS (S)BPG 62101	YOU'LL NEVER WALK ALONE (mono/stereo)	each 18
63	CBS (S)BPG 62129	ANNIE GET YOUR GUN (with Robert Goulet, mono/stereo)	each 12
64	CBS (S)BPG 62226	LOVE HIM (mono/stereo)	each 18
65	CBS (S)BPG 62461	WITH A SMILE AND A SONG	12

(see also Four Lads, Frank Sinatra, Frankie Laine, Howard Keel)

DORIS DAY & JOHNNIE RAY
53	Columbia SCM 5033	Ma Says, Pa Says/A Full Time Job	30

(see also Johnnie Ray)

JACKIE DAY
67	Sue WI 4040	Before It's Too Late/Without A Love	200

JILL DAY
55	Parlophone MSP 6169	Sincerely/Chee-Chee-Oo Chee (Sang The Little Bird)	12
55	Parlophone MSP 6177	Promises/Whistlin' Willie	12
56	HMV 7M 362	I Hear You Knocking/Far Away From Everybody	12
56	HMV 7M 391	A Tear Fell/Holiday Affair	12
56	HMV POP 254	Happiness Street (Corner Sunshine Square)/Somewhere In The Great Beyond	10
57	HMV POP 288	I Dreamed/Give Her My Love When You See Her	10
57	HMV POP 320	Mangos/Cinco Robles (Five Oaks)	10

KENNY DAY
60	Top Rank JAR 339	Teenage Sonata/My Love Doesn't Love Me At All (some with p/s)	10/6
61	Top Rank JAR 400	Why Don't We Do This More Often/The Sheik Of Morocco (some with p/s)	10/6

MURIEL DAY
69	CBS 4115	The Wages Of Love/Thinking Of You	15
69	Page One POF 151	Optimistic Fool/Nine Times Out Of Ten (DJ copy = £100)	50

TANYA DAY & NU-NOTES
64	Polydor NH 52331	His Lips Get In The Way/I Get So Lonely	6

TERRY DAY
62	CBS AAG 104	That's All I Want/I Waited Too Long	20

(see also Rip-Chords, Rogues)

DAY BROTHERS
60	Oriole CB 1575	Angel/Just One More Kiss	20

JOHNNY DAY
69	Stax STAX 111	Stay Baby Stay/I Love Love	15

JENNIFER DAYE
80	Arawak ARK DD 018	Together/Version (12")	20

DAYLIGHT
71	RCA RCA 2106	Lady Of St. Clare/Wednesday People	10
71	RCA SF 8194	DAYLIGHT (LP)	40

(see also Daddy Longlegs)

DAYLIGHTERS
64	Sue WI 343	Oh Mom! (Teach Me How To Uncle Willie)/Hard-Headed Girl	45

DAY OF THE PHOENIX
70	Greenwich GLSPR 1002	WIDE OPEN N-WAY (LP)	40
72	Chapter One CNSR 812	THE NEIGHBOUR'S SON (LP)	50

MINT VALUE £

DAYTRIPPERS
71	Trojan TR 7839	The Birds And The Bees/My Family	5

DAYTON
83	Capitol 12 CL 318	The Sound Of Music/Eyes On You/Love You Anyway (12", p/s)	8
83	Capitol EST 712 2971	FEEL THE MUSIC (LP)	20

DAZZLE
75	DJM DJS 384	Jim'll Fix It/Leave It Up To Jim	6

DBX
93	Peacefrog PF 015	ALIEN EP (12", plain sleeve)	12
94	Peacefrog PF 022	Losing Control/Beat Phreak/Live Wire/Spock's Brain (12", plain sleeve)	22
95	Peacefrog PR 025	LOSING CONTROL REMIXES (12", plain sleeve)	15

D.C. 10's
80	Certain Euphoria ACE 451	Bermuda/I Can See Through Walls	10

BOBBY DEACON
60	Pye 7N 15270	Fool Was I/Where's My Love	18
60	Pye 7N 15299	I Love You So/Your Kisses Are Fine	15

GEORGE DEACON & MARION ROSS
73	Xtra XTRA 1130	SWEET WILLIAM'S GHOST (LP, with lyric insert)	80

DEACON BLUE
88	CBS CP DEAC 5	When Will You (Make My Telephone Ring)/That Brilliant Feeling No. 2/ Punch And Judy Man/Disney World (CD, picture disc)	8
88	CBS 450 549-0	RAINTOWN (LP, with bonus LP RICHES [XPR 1361] & sticker)	12
88	CBS XPR 1361	RICHES (LP, white embossed sleeve, available separately via fan club)	12

DEAD 60's
04	Deltasonic DLT021B	You're Not The Law/Too Much TV (Dub) (Red vinyl, sticker, p/s)	10
04	Deltasonic DLTCD021	You're Not The Law/Too Much TV (Dub) (CD, p/s)	10
04	Deltasonic DLT025	Riot Radio/No Good Town (Dub) (yellow vinyl, p/s)	7

DEADBEATS
80	Red Rhino RED 3	Choose You/Julie's New Boyfriend (p/s)	8

DEAD BOYS
77	Sire SRE 1004	Sonic Reducer/Down In Flames (no p/s)	25
77	Sire 6078 609	Sonic Reducer/Little Girl/Down In Flames (12", p/s)	15
78	Sire SRE 1029	Tell Me/Not Anymore/Ain't Nothin' To Do (p/s)	25
77	Sire 9103 329	YOUNG, LOUD & SNOTTY (LP)	25
78	Sire SRK 6054	WE HAVE COME FOR YOUR CHILDREN (LP)	15
87	Line LILP 400200	NIGHT OF THE LIVING DEAD BOYS (LP)	15

(see also Stiv Bators, Lords Of The New Church, Wanderers)

DEAD ELVIS
95	Concrete HARD 612	Opium Shuffle (Skank Mix)/(Dead Elvis Mix) (12", p/s)	15

(see also Death In Vegas)

DEAD KENNEDYS
80	Fast Products FAST 12	California Uber Alles/Man With The Dogs (p/s, moulded or paper labels)	6
81	Statik STAT EP 2	IN GOD WE TRUST (12" EP, with insert)	8
81	Cherry Red CHERRY 13	Holiday In Cambodia/Police Truck ('digger' p/s)	5
81	Cherry Red CHERRY 13	Holiday In Cambodia/Police Truck ('burning man' p/s, with lyric sheet)	6
81	Cherry CHERRY 16	Kill The Poor/In-Sight (p/s, with badge)	10
81	Cherry CHERRY 24	Too Drunk To Fuck/The Prey (p/s, with lyric sheet)	5
82	Statik STAT 24	Nazi Punks Fuck Off/Moral Majority (p/s)	5
81	Cherry Red B RED 10	FRESH FRUIT FOR ROTTING VEGETABLES (LP, with insert and 'Heads' pic on rear)	18
87	Alternative Tent. VIRUS 57	GIVE ME CONVENIENCE... (LP, with "Buzzbomb From Pasadena" flexidisc)	15

(see also East Bay Ray, Lard)

DEADLY TOYS
79	Bonhard/Hunt DT 1	Nice Weather/Roll On Doomsday/I'm Logical/Deadly Mess Around (EP, some in hand made gatefold sleeve)	25

DEAD MAN'S SHADOW
80	Hog HOG 1	Neighbours/Poxy Politics/War Ploys/Morons (p/s)	5
81	Subversive ANARCHO 1	HEATHROW TOUCHDOWN (EP, 1 side by Action Pact)	6
82	Rondelet ROUND 16	BOMB SCARE (EP)	6
84	Criminal Damage CRILP 110	TO MOHAMMED ... A MOUNTAIN (LP)	12

DEAD OR ALIVE
80	Inevitable INEV 005	I'm Falling/Flowers (foldout p/s)	12
81	Inevitable INEV 008	Number Eleven/Name Game (live) (p/s)	8
82	Black Eyes BE 1	It's Been Hours Now/Whirlpool/Nowhere To Nowhere/ It's Been Hours Now (Alternative Mix) (12", p/s)	15
82	Black Eyes BE 2	The Stranger/Some Of That (p/s)	8
83	Epic A 3399	Misty Circles/Misty Circles (Instrumental) (p/s)	6
83	Epic TA 3399	Misty Circles (Dance Mix)/Misty Circles (Dub Mix)/Selfish Side (12", p/s)	10
83	Epic A 3676	What I Want/The Stranger (Remix) (white 'floppy hat' p/s, withdrawn)	25
83	Epic A 3676	What I Want/The Stranger (black p/s)	6
83	Epic TA 3676	What I Want (Dance Mix)/The Stranger (12", p/s, some with poster)	15/8
84	Epic A 4069	I'd Do Anything/Anything (Dub) (p/s)	5
84	Epic QA 4069	I'd Do Anything/Anything (Dub)/Give It To Me (10", p/s)	10
84	Epic TA 4069	I'd Do Anything/Misty Circles/What I Want/Give It To Me (12", p/s)	10
84	Epic WA 4271	That's The Way (I Like It)/Keep That Body Strong (That's The Way) (picture disc)	6
84	Epic A 4510	What I Want (Remix)/The Stranger (poster p/s)	10

84	Epic TA 4510	What I Want (Dance Mix)/The Stranger (12", p/s, some with poster)	10/8
84	Epic XPR 1257	MIGHTY MIX: Wish You Were Here/What I Want/Do It/Misty Circles/ Absolutely Nothing/Sit On It/You Make Me Wanna/That's The Way (I Like It) (12", white label, promo only)	12
84	Epic	You Spin Me Round (Big Ben Mix) (1-sided, stickered p/s, promo only)	15
84	Epic TX 4861/TA 4510	You Spin Me Round (Like A Record) (Murder Mix)/Misty Circles (Extended Mix)// What I Want (Dance Mix)/The Stranger (12", p/s, double pack, shrinkwrapped)	15
85	Epic A 6086	Lover Come Back To Me/Far Too Hard (blue p/s, withdrawn)	60
85	Epic WA 6086	Lover Come Back To Me/Far Too Hard (fan-shaped picture disc with plinth)	10
85	Epic QTA 6086	Lover Come Back To Me (Extended Remix)/Far Too Hard (12", poster p/s)	15
87	Epic XPR 1328	CLEAN AND DIRTY: Something In My House (Naughty XXX Mix) (12", white label, plain white sleeve)	50
88	Epic BURNSQ 4	Turn Around And Count 2 Ten (I Had A Disco Dream Mix)/Something In My House (Instru-Mental)/Then There Was You/Come Inside (12", p/s)	18
88	Epic BURNSC 4	Turn Around And Count 2 Ten/Something In My House (Instru-Mental)/ Turn Around And Count 2 Ten (I Love BPM Mix)/ (Instru-Mental) (CD, picture disc)	18

(see also Nightmares In Wax, Sisters Of Mercy, Pauline Murray & Invisible Girls, International Chrysis, Mission)

DEAD SEA FRUIT
67	Camp 602 001	Kensington High Street/Put Another Record On	15
68	Camp 602 004	Love At The Hippiedrome/My Naughty Bluebell	15
67	Camp 603 001	DEAD SEA FRUIT (LP)	100

DEAD WRETCHED
82	Inferno HELL 2	NO HOPE FOR ANYONE (EP)	5
82	Inferno HELL 5	Convicted/Infiltrator (p/s)	5

BILL DEAL & RHONDELLS
69	MGM MGM 1466	May I/Day By Day My Love Grows Stronger	6
69	MGM MGM 1479	I've Been Hurt/I've Got My Needs	15
69	MGM MGM 1488	What Kind Of Fool Do You Think I Am/Are You Ready For This	10

DEALER
83	Windrush WR 1030	Better Things To Do/Suspected Foul Play (p/s)	100
86	Ebony EBON 42	FIRST STRIKE (LP)	12

ALAN DEAN
55	MGM SP 1116	The Song From Desiree/Tonight, My Love	6
55	MGM SP 1139	Remember Me, Wherever You Go/Love Is All That Matters	6
56	MGM SP 1173	Without You/Take A Bow	6
57	Columbia DB 3932	Rock 'n' Roll Tarantella/Life Is But A Dream	20

ALAN DEAN & HIS PROBLEMS
64	Decca F 11947	The Time It Takes/Dizzy Heights	30
65	Pye 7N 15749	Thunder And Rain/As Time Goes By	60

LITTLE BILLY DEAN
67	Strike JH 325	That's Always Like You/Tic Toc	25

BOBBY DEAN
65	Parlophone R 5254	More And More/Saint James' Infirmary	8

DEREK DEAN & FRESHMEN
66	Pye 7N 17037	So This Is Love/King Cole Yenka	8

(see also Derek & Freshmen)

ELTON DEAN
71	CBS 64539	ELTON DEAN (LP)	50
77	Ogun OG 610	THE CHEQUE IS IN THE MAIL (LP, with Joe Gallivan & Kenny Wheeler)	15

(see also Bluesology, Soft Machine, Centipede, Ninesense, Julie Tippetts, Hugh Hopper, Mike Hugg, Reg King, Keith Tippett)

EMIL DEAN
68	Island WIP 6033	This Is Our Anniversary/Lonely Boy	6

(see also Nirvana [UK])

HAZELL DEAN
75	Decca F 13613	Our Day Will Come/Instrumental	6
76	Decca F 13668	Got You Where I Want You/You Were There	6
77	Decca F 13683	Look What I've Found At The End Of A Rainbow/Where Are We Going	6
77	Decca F 13736	No One's Ever Gonna Love You (The Way That I Love You)/ Just One More Time	6
77	Decca F 13751	Who Was That Lady (I Saw You With)/One Bad Mistake	6
81	Carlin Music Corp. CMC1004	THE SOUND OF BACHARACH & DAVID (LP, promo only)	25

JIMMY DEAN
57	Phillips PB 747	Deep Blue Sea/Love Me So I'll Know (78)	9
58	Phillips PB 813	Makin' My Mind Up/Starlight Starbright (78)	8
59	Philips PB 940	Weekend Blues/Sing Along (78 rpm = £10)	8
60	Philips PB 984	There's Still Time, Brother/Thanks For The Dream	6
61	Philips PB 1187	Big Bad John/I Won't Go Hunting With You Jake	5
61	Philips PB 1210	To A Sleeping Beauty/The Cajun Queen	6
62	Philips PB 1223	Smoke Smoke (Smoke) That Cigarette/Dear Ivan	5
62	CBS AAG 107	Steel Men/Little Bitty Big John	5
62	CBS AAG 122	Little Black Book/Please Pass The Biscuits	5
61	Philips BBE 12501	JIMMY DEAN (EP)	15
66	CBS EP 6075	THE BEST OF JIMMY DEAN (EP)	20
63	CBS	PORTRAIT OF JIMMY DEAN (LP)	15
65	Fontana FJL 303	GOLDEN FAVOURITES (LP)	15

NORA DEAN
69	Upsetter US 322	The Same Thing You Gave To Daddy/UPSETTER PILGRIMS: A Testimony	50+
70	Trojan TR 7735	Barbwire/BARONS: Calypso Mama.	7
71	Randy's RAN 508	Want Man/RANDY'S ALL STARS: Man	7
71	High Note HS 050	I Must Get A Man/The Valet	5
71	Bullet BU 472	Peace Begins Within/SLICKERS: Go Back Home	8
71	Gas GAS 165	Greedy Boy/KEITH: Please Stay (B-side actually by Slim Smith)	8
72	Big Shot BI 611	Night Food Reggae/PROPHETS: Jaco	6
73	Bread BR 1117	Mama/Man A Walk And Talk	6

(see also Hugh Roy)

PAUL DEAN (& SOUL SAVAGES)
65	Decca F 12136	You Don't Own Me/Hole In The Head (as Paul Dean & Thoughts).	18
66	Reaction 591 002	She Can Build A Mountain/A Day Gone By (as Paul Dean & Soul Savages)	15

(see also Oscar, Thoughts)

PAULA DEAN & NYAH SHUFFLE
70	Joe's JRS 2	Since I Met You Baby/Jug Head.	10

ROGER DEAN'S LYSIS
77	Mosaic GCM 762	LYSIS LIVE (LP)	15
77	Mosaic GCM 774	CYCLE (LP)	15

TERRI DEAN
59	Top Rank JAR 141	I'm Confessin' (That I Love You)/I Blew Out The Flame (78 rpm = £8)	10
59	Top Rank JAR 179	Adonis/You Treat Me Like A Boy (78 rpm = £8)	10

DEAN & JEAN
64	Stateside SS 249	Tra La La La Suzy/I Love The Summertime	20
64	Stateside SS 283	Hey Jean Hey Dean/Please Don't Tell Me How	20
64	Stateside SS 313	Thread Your Needle/I Wanna Be Loved	20

(see also Brenda Lee Jones)

DEAN & MARK
64	Hickory 45-1227	With Tears In My Eyes/Kissin' Games.	10
64	Hickory 45-1249	When I Stop Dreaming/There Oughta Be A Law	10
65	Hickory 45-1294	Just A Step Away/Fallen Star	10

(see also Newbeats, Larry Henley)

JASON DEANE
66	King KG 1049	Make Believe/Don't Ever Want To See You No More.	30
67	King KG 1060	Down In The Street/Ain't Got No Love	40

(see also Jason Dene)

PETER DE ANGELIS ORCHESTRA & CHORUS
58	London HL 8743	The Happy Mandolin/Holiday In Naples	6

DEANO
65	Columbia DB 7728	Just A Child In This World/Little Miss With-It	12
66	Columbia DB 7898	Starlight, Starbright/I'm So Happy	22
66	Columbia DB 7965	Please Don't Talk To The Lifeguard/When You Wish Upon A Star.	12
67	Columbia DB 8233	What's The Matter With The Matador?/Baby, Let Me Be Your Baby	10
65	Columbia SEG 8470	DEANO (EP)	38

BLOSSOM DEARIE
66	Fontana TF 719	I'm Hip/Wallflower Lonely, Cornflower Blue	6
67	Fontana TF 788	Sweet Georgie Fame/One Note Samba.	8
67	Fontana TF 886	Once I Loved/Sunny	6
67	Fontana TF 934	The Music Played/Discover Who I Am	6
68	Fontana TF 986	Hey John/59th Street Bridge Song	6
67	Fontana TL 5399	SWEET BLOSSOM DEARIE (LP)	40
67	Fontana TL 5352	BLOSSOM TIME AT RONNIE'S (LP)	60
67	Fontana STL 5454	SOON IT'S GONNA RAIN (LP)	40
70	Fontana 6309 015	THAT'S THE WAY I WANT IT TO BE (LP)	100

DEARLY BELOVED
66	CBS 202398	Peep Peep Pop Pop/It Is Better	10

DEAR MR. TIME
70	Square SQ 3	Prayer For Her/Light Up A Light	50
71	Square SQA 101	GRANDFATHER (LP)	90

DEATH ADDICT
83	Stench STN 1	Killing Time/Dead And Buried (p/s)	12

DEATH CULT
83	Situation 2 SIT 29	God's Zoo/God's Zoo (These Times) (p/s)	5
83	Situation 2 SIT 29 T	God's Zoo/God's Zoo (These Times) (12", p/s)	8

(see also Cult)

DEATH FROM ABOVE
05	Sony DFA01	Black History Month (Alan Brake & Fred Falke Remix)/(Sammy Danger NLS Edit)/ (Alan Brake & Fred Falke Instrumental) (12", 300 only die-cut sleeve)	10

DEATH IN JUNE
84	New European SA 29634	Heaven Street/We Drive East/In The Night Time (12", 2,000 with brown/gold embossed/textured sleeve, later 2,000 with blue/white sleeve)	50/40
84	New European SA 30634	State Laughter/Holy Water (p/s)	40
84	New European BADVC 6	She Said Destroy/The Calling (p/s)	25
84	New European 12BADVC 6	The Calling/She Said Destroy/Doubt To Nothing (12", p/s with insert)	40
85	New European BADVC 69	Born Again/The Calling (Mk II)/Carousel (Bolt Mix) (12", p/s)	25
85	New European BADVC 73	...And Murder Love/A.M.L. (Instrumental) (p/s)	25
85	New European 12BADVC73	Come Before Christ And Murder Love/Torture By Roses (12", p/s)	30
87	New European BADVC 10	To Drown A Rose/Zimmerit/Europa/The Gates Of Heaven (10", p/s)	20

88	Cenaz CENAZ 09	Born Again/The Calling (Mk II)/Carousel (Remix) (12" picture disc, 1st pressing with silver print & rim, 970 only; 2nd pressing bronze)	25/20
94	Twilight Command NERO I	SUNDOGS (Rose Clouds Of Holocaust/13 Years Of Carrion) (p/s with sticker)	7
92	New European BADVC 8	CATHEDRAL OF TEARS (12" EP, picture disc with sticker)	20
93	New European BADVC 63	PARADISE RISING (12" EP)	18
96	Twil. Command NERO XIII	Kapo!/Occidental Martyr (p/s)	18
85	New European BADVC 3	THE GUILTY HAVE NO PRIDE (LP)	25
80s	Leprosy UBADVC 4	BURIAL (LP, 'quilted' sleeve, brown, pink, white & other coloured vinyl)	30
90s	Leprosy UBADVC 4	BURIAL (LP, textured sleeve, various coloured vinyls)	30
92	Leprosy UBADVC 4	BURIAL (LP, standard sleeve, green vinyl)	30
85	New European BADVC 13	NADA (LP, blue or brown sleeve; also picture disc)	40/25/15
86	New European BADVC 726	LESSON ONE: MISANTHROPY (LP, embossed sleeve with insert)	20
87	New European BADVC 11	BROWN BOOK (LP, textured sleeve with inner & insert; export copies had extra inserts & postcards)	35/25
88	New European BADVC 9	THE WORLD THAT SUMMER (2-LP, gatefold textured sleeve)	30
88	New European BADVC 88	WALL OF SACRIFICE (LP, red sleeve or green/yellow sleeve)	60/40
89	New European BADVC 93	93 DEAD SUN WHEELS (mini-LP, with Current 93)	20
92	Leprosy LEPER 2	NIGHT AND FOG (LP, red vinyl, 1,000 only)	30
93	New European BADVC 36	BUT WHAT ENDS WHEN THE SYMBOLS SHATTER (LP, with inner & insert, 500 on purple vinyl, 3,000 on black vinyl)	35/20
93	New Euro'n BADVCCD 36	BUT WHAT ENDS WHEN THE SYMBOLS SHATTER (CD, gold disc digipak, 5,000 only)	20
93	New European BADVC 96	SOMETHING IS COMING (2-CD, digipak, 5,000 only)	25
94	New European BADVC 38	ROSE CLOUDS OF HOLOCAUST (LP, with insert & inner)	12
94	New Euro'n BADVCCD 38	ROSE CLOUDS OF HOLOCAUST (CD, digipak, 5,000 only)	20
95	New European BADVC 39	BLACK WHOLE OF LOVE (box set with 12", 10", 7" & CDs with inserts)	30
96	New European BADVC 96	SOMETHING IS COMING (2-LP, textured sleeve with insert)	15

(see also Crisis, Current 93, Boyd Rice & Friends, Sol Invictus)

DEATH IN VEGAS
99	Concrete YAWNING 1	Blood Yawning (12", 1-sided promo-only, etched, p/s)	8
00	Concrete HARD 4510	One More Time (featuring Bobby Gillespie) (1-sided 10", red vinyl, p/s)	5
01	Concrete SCORPIO 1	Scorpio (12", no p/s, 1-sided DJ white label, 1,000 copies only)	12
02	Concrete HARD 5112	Leather Girls (Original Mix)/Natja (LAMF Mix)/Natja (Zoo Station) (12", double pack, p/s)	8

(see also Dead Elvis)

DEATH SENTENCE
82	Beat The System DEATH 1	DEATH & PURE DESTRUCTION (EP)	6

DEBONAIRES (U.K.)
66	Pye 7N 17151	A Love Of Our Own/The Night Meets The Dawn	5
66	Pye 7N 17204	Crying Behind Your Smile/Forever More	5

DEBONAIRES (U.S.)
70	Track 604 035	I'm In Love Again/Headache In My Heart	50

DEBONAIRS
63	Parlophone R 5054	That's Right/When True Love Comes Your Way	5

DEBS
65	Mercury MF 888	Sloopy's Gonna Hang On/Under A Street Light	20

DEB-TONES
59	RCA RCA 1137	Knock, Knock — Who's There?/I'm In Love Again (78 rpm = £20)	25

DEBUTANTES
80	Rok ROK XVII/XVIII	Man In The Street/INNOCENT BYSTANDERS: Where Is Johnny (company sleeve)	6

DECAMERON
73	Vertigo 6360 097	SAY HELLO TO THE BAND (LP)	12

YVONNE DE CARLO
55	Capitol CL 14380	Take It Or Leave It/Three Little Stars	12

PAULO DE CARVALHO
74	Pye International 7N 25647	(And Then) After Love/E Depois Do Adeus (p/s)	10

DE CASTRO SISTERS
54	London HL 8104	Teach Me Tonight/It's Love (78 rpm = £6)	50
55	London HL 8137	Boom Boom Boomerang/Let Your Love Walk In (78 rpm = £10)	50
55	London HL 8158	I'm Bewildered/To Say You're Mine (78 rpm = £10)	50
55	London HLU 8189	If I Ever Fall In Love/Cuckoo In The Clock (78 rpm = £10)	30
55	London HLU 8212	Christmas Is A-Comin'/Snowbound For Christmas	28
56	London HLU 8228	Give Me Time/Too Late Now (78 rpm = £12)	28
56	London HLU 8296	No One To Blame But You/Cowboys Don't Cry (78 rpm = £12)	28
58	HMV POP 527	Who Are They To Say?/When You Look At Me (78 rpm = £15)	12
59	HMV POP 583	Teach Me Tonight Cha Cha/The Things I Tell My Pillow (78 rpm = £20)	12
61	Capitol CL 15199	Red Sails In The Sunset/Bells	7

DECISIONS
68	MCA MU 1027	In The Shade Of Your Love/Constable Jones	5

DIANA DECKER
54	Columbia SCM 5083	Oh, My Papa/Crystal Ball	20
54	Columbia SCM 5096	The Happy Wanderer/Till We Two Are One	20
54	Columbia SCM 5120	Jilted/The Man With The Banjo	20
54	Columbia SCM 5123	Kitty In The Basket/Never Never Land	18
54	Columbia SCM 5130	Mama Mia/Percy The Penguin	20
54	Columbia SCM 5145	Sisters/Abracadabra	20
55	Columbia SCM 5166	Open The Window Of Your Heart/The Violin Song	15

MINT VALUE £

55	Columbia SCM 5173	Apples, Peaches And Cherries/Paper Valentine	40
56	Columbia SCM 5246	Rock-A-Boogie Baby/Willie Can	35
	(see also Ray Burns, Ruby Murray)		

DECORATORS
81	New Hormones ORG 5	Twilight View/Reflections (p/s)	5

DE COURCY'S
65	Egmont EGM 9220	SALUTE TO THE SHADOWS (LP)	15

DE DANAAN
82	Cara CARA 1	Hey Jude/St. Jude's Hornpipe/Trip To Taum Reel/Teetotaller	5
75	Polydor 2904 005	DE DANAAN (LP)	15
77	Decca SKL-R 5287	DE DANAAN — SELECTED JIGS AND REELS (LP)	20
80	Decca SKL 5318	BANKS OF THE NILE (LP)	12

DEDICATED MEN'S JUG BAND
65	Piccadilly 7N 35245	Boodle-Am-Shake/Come On Boys	6
66	Piccadilly 7N 35283	Don't Come Knocking/Out Time Blues	6

DEDRINGER
80	DinDisc DIN 10	Sunday Drivers/We Don't Mind (p/s)	5
80	DinDisc DIN 11	Innocent 'Till Proven Guilty/Maxine//Took A Long Time/ We Don't Mind (double pack)	10
81	DinDisc DIN 12	Direct Line/She's Not Ready (p/s)	5
82	Neat NEAT 18	Hot Lady/Hot Licks And Rock'N'Roll (p/s)	5
81	DinDisc DID 7	DIRECT LINE (LP)	15
83	Neat NEAT 1009	SECOND RISING (LP, with inner sleeve)	12

DAVE DEE
70	Fontana TF 1074	My Woman's Man/Gotta Make You Part Of Me	5
70	Fontana 6007 021	Annabella/Kelly	5
70	Philips 6006 061	Everything About Her/If I Believed In Tomorrow	5
71	Philips 6006 100	Wedding Bells/Sweden	5
71	Philips 6006 154	Hold On/Mary Morning, Mary Evening	5
71	Philips 6006 180	Swingy/Don't You Ever Change Your Mind	5
	(see also Dave Dee, Dozy, Beaky, Mick & Tich)		

DAVE DEE, DOZY, BEAKY, MICK & TICH
65	Fontana TF 531	No Time/Is It Love	28
65	Fontana TF 586	All I Want/It Seems A Pity	25
65	Fontana TF 630	You Make It Move/I Can't Stop	10
67	Fontana TF 798	Touch Me Touch Me/Marina	6
68	Fontana TF 903	The Legend Of Xanadu/Please	6
69	Fontana TF 1020	Snake In The Grass/Bora Bora	6
74	Antic K 11510	She's My Lady/Babeigh	6
67	Fontana TE 17488	LOOS OF ENGLAND (EP)	12
66	Fontana TL 5350	DAVE DEE, DOZY, BEAKY, MICK & TICH (LP)	22
66	Fontana (S)TL 5388	IF MUSIC BE THE FOOD OF LOVE PREPARE FOR INDIGESTION (LP)	25
67	Fontana (S)TL 5441	GOLDEN HITS OF DAVE DEE, DOZY, BEAKY, MICK & TICH (LP)	15
68	Fontana (S)TL 5471	IF NO-ONE SANG (LP)	22
69	Fontana SFL 13002	DDDBM&T (LP)	20
70	Fontana SFL 13173	TOGETHER (LP)	20
	(see also Dozy Beaky Mick & Tich [D,B,M & T], Dave Dee)		

JEANNIE DEE
69	Beacon BEA 115	Come Into My Arms/Sun Shine On Me	7
69	Beacon BEA 142	Don't Go Home My Little Darling/Come See About Me	15

JOEY DEE & STARLI(GH)TERS
61	Columbia DB 4758	Peppermint Twist (Parts 1 & 2)	10
62	Columbia DB 4803	Hey, Let's Twist/Roly Poly	7
62	Columbia DB 4842	Shout (Parts 1 & 2)	10
62	Columbia DB 4862	Ya Ya/Fanny Mae	7
62	Columbia DB 4905	What Kind Of Love Is This?/Wing Ding	7
63	Columbia DB 4955	I Lost My Baby/Keep Your Mind On What You're Doin'	5
63	Columbia DB 7005	Baby You're Driving Me Crazy/Help Me Pick Up The Pieces	5
63	Columbia DB 7055	Hot Pastrami With Mashed Potatoes (Parts 1 & 2)	10
63	Columbia DB 7102	Dance, Dance, Dance/Let's Have A Party (features Ronettes uncredited)	12
63	Columbia DB 7277	Down By The Riverside/Getting Nearer (features Ronettes uncredited)	12
61	Columbia 33SX 1406	DOIN' THE TWIST LIVE AT THE PEPPERMINT LOUNGE (LP)	25
62	Columbia 33SX 1461	BACK AT THE PEPPERMINT LOUNGE (LP)	25
62	Columbia 33SX 1502	ALL THE WORLD IS TWISTIN' (LP)	25
63	Columbia 33SX 1532	JOEY DEE (LP)	25
63	Columbia 33SX 1607	DANCE DANCE DANCE (LP, with Starlighters, also with Ronettes uncredited)	32
	(see also Young Rascals)		

JOHNNIE DEE
65	Columbia DB 7612	Frankie's Angel/Everything's Upside Down	7

JOHNNY DEE
57	Oriole CB 1367	Sittin' In The Balcony/A-Plus Love (78 rpm = £35)	140
	(see also John D. Loudermilk)		

KIKI DEE
63	Fontana TF 394	Early Night/Lucky High Heels	15
63	Fontana TF 414	I Was Only Kidding/Don't Put Your Heart In His Hand	12
64	Fontana TF 443	Miracles/That's Right, Walk On By	18
64	Fontana TF 490	(You Don't Know) How Glad I Am/Baby I Don't Care	12
65	Fontana TF 596	Runnin' Out Of Fools/There He Goes	10
66	Fontana TF 669	Why Don't I Run Away From You?/Small Town	20
67	Fontana TF 792	I'm Going Out (The Same Way I Came In)/We've Got Everything Going For Us	10

67	Fontana TF 833	I/Stop And Think	10
67	Fontana TF 870	Excuse Me/Patterns	10
68	Fontana TF 926	Can't Take My Eyes Off You/Hungry Heart	10
68	Fontana TF 983	Now The Flowers Cry/On A Magic Carpet Ride	150
70	Tamla Motown TMG 739	The Day Will Come Between Sunday And Monday/ My Whole World Ended (The Moment You Left Me)	15
73	Rocket PIG 2	Lonnie And Josie/The Last Good Man In My Life	7
65	Fontana TE 17443	KIKI DEE (EP)	38
66	Fontana TE 17470	KIKI DEE IN CLOVER (EP)	32
68	Fontana (S)TL 5455	I'M KIKI DEE (LP)	40
70	Tamla Motown STML 11158	GREAT EXPECTATIONS (LP)	55
	(see also Elton John)		

LENNY DEE
55	Brunswick 05440	Plantation Boogie/Birth Of The Blues	10

RICKY DEE & EMBERS
62	Stateside SS 136	Workout/JOHN MOBLEY: Tunnel Of Love	15

SANDRA DEE
61	Brunswick 05858	Tammy Tell Me True/Let's Fall In Love	10

SIMON DEE
69	Chapter One CH 105	Julie/Whatever Happened To Us?	6

TAMMI DEE
71	Downtown DT 479	Val/MUSIC DOCTORS: Bank Raid	12

TOMMY DEE
59	Melodisc 1516	Three Stars/TEEN JONES (TONES): I'll Never Change (tri or round centre)	75/50
59	Melodisc 1516	Three Stars/TEEN JONES (TONES): I'll Never Change (78)	25

DEE & DYNAMITES
60	Philips PB 1081	Blaze Away/South Bound Gasser	12

MAURICE DEEBANK
84	Cherry Red MRED 61	INNER THOUGHT ZONE (LP)	12
	(see also Felt)		

DEEJAYS
65	Polydor BM 56034	Dimples/Coming On Strong	50
65	Polydor BM 56501	Blackeyed Woman/I Just Can't Go To Sleep	110

ANTHONY DEELEY
68	Pama PM 728	Anytime Man/Don't Change Your Mind About Me	7

ANGELA DEEN
64	Fontana TF 491	There's So Much About My Baby That I Love/Gotta Hand It To The Boy	12

CAROL DEENE
61	HMV POP 922	Sad Movies/Don't Forget	8
62	HMV POP 973	Norman/On The Outside Looking In	6
62	HMV POP 1027	Johnny Get Angry/Somebody's Smiling	8
62	HMV POP 1058	Some People/Kissin'	8
62	HMV POP 1086	James/It Happened Last Night	8
63	HMV POP 1123	Let Me Do It My Way/Growin' Up	8
63	HMV POP 1200	Oh Oh Oh Willie/I Want To Stay Here	8
64	HMV POP 1275	Who's Been Sleeping In My Bed?/Love Is Wonderful	8
64	HMV POP 1337	Very First Kiss/Hard To Say Goodnight	8
65	HMV POP 1405	Most People Do/I Can't Forget Someone Like You	8
65	Columbia DB 7743	He Just Don't Know/Up In The Penthouse	8
66	Columbia DB 7890	Dancing In Your Eyes/Please Don't Be Unfaithful Again	6
67	Columbia DB 8107	Love Not Have I/Time	6
68	CBS 3206	When He Wants A Woman/I'm Not Crying	6
69	Conquest CXT 102	One More Chance/Invisible Tears	6
70	World Records ST 1031	A LOVE AFFAIR (LP)	20

DEEP END
78	private pressing	BEGGED AND BORROWED (LP, listed as CPLP 016)	15

DEEP FEELING
70	Page One POF 165	Do You Love Me/Move On	5
70	Page One POF 177	Skyline Pigeon/We've Thrown It All Away	6
71	DJM DJLPS 419	DEEP FEELING (LP)	55

DEEP FREEZE
70s	Guardian GRL 43	Keeping You In Furs/Don't Look Back	5

DEEP FREEZE MICE
80s	Cordelia ERICAT 002	THESE FLOORS ARE SMOOTH (EP)	10
80s	Cordelia ERICAT 016	NEURON MUSIC (12" EP)	8
79	Mole Embalming MOLE 1	MY GERANIUMS ARE BULLETPROOF (LP, 1st 200 with paste-on sleeve, 8-page booklet & various A4 inserts)	60/30
81	Mole Embalming MOLE 2	TEENAGE HEAD IN MY REFRIGERATOR (LP)	30
81	Inedible MOLE 3	GATES OF LUNCH (LP)	15
83	Mole Embalming MOLE 4	SAW A RANCH BURNING LAST NIGHT (LP)	15

DEEP PURPLE
68	Parlophone R 5708	Hush/One More Rainy Day (some in promo-only p/s)	350+/35
68	Parlophone R 5745	Kentucky Woman/Wring That Neck (withdrawn)	50+
69	Parlophone R 5763	Emmaretta/Wring That Neck	35
69	Harvest HAR 5006	Hallelujah (I Am The Preacher)/April Part 1 (some in promo-only p/s)	250/20
70	Harvest PSR 325	Concerto, 1st Movement (edit)/Concerto, 2nd Movement (edit) (promo, possibly some commercial)	30

DEEP PURPLE

70	Harvest HAR 5020	Black Night/Speed King	6
71	Harvest HAR 5033	Strange Kind Of Woman/I'm Alone	6
71	Harvest HAR 5045	Fireball/Demon's Eye	6
72	Purple PUR 102	Never Before/When A Blind Man Cries	6
74	Purple PUR 117	Might Just Take Your Life/Coronarias Redig	7
76	Purple PUR 130	You Keep On Moving/Love Child	7
77	Purple PUR 132	Smoke On The Water/Woman From Tokyo/Child In Time (10,000 with p/s)	7
85	Polydor POSPP 719	Perfect Strangers (edit)/Son Of Alerik (edit) (picture disc)	7
87	Polydor POSPP 843	Call Of The Wild/Strange Ways (12", picture disc)	10
88	Polydor POC 4	Hush ('88 Re-recording)/Dead Or Alive (Live) (blue vinyl, p/s)	5
88	Polydor RX 4	Hush ('88 Re-recording)/Dead Or Alive (Live)/Bad Attitude (12", gatefold p/s)	8
88	Polydor PZCD 4	Hush ('88 Re-recording)/Dead Or Alive/Bad Attitude (CD)	12
88	Polydor 080 088-2	Bad Attitude/Black And White/Unwritten Law/Strangeways (CD Video)	25
90	RCA PT 49224	Love Conquers All (Edit)/Truth Hurts (die-cut picture disc, with insert)	7
95	EMI 7243 8 82214 67	Black Night (Remix)/Black Night (Original Mix)/Speed King (12", purple vinyl, numbered limited edition)	8
77	Purple PUR 135	NEW LIVE AND RARE VOL. 1 (EP, 15,000 on purple vinyl)	8
78	Purple PUR 137	NEW LIVE AND RARE VOL. 2 (EP)	8
80	Harvest SHEP 101	NEW LIVE AND RARE VOL. 3 (EP)	8
68	Parlophone PMC/PCS 7055	SHADES OF DEEP PURPLE (LP, yellow/black label, mono/stereo)	100/70
69	Parlophone PCS 7055	SHADES OF DEEP PURPLE (LP, stereo repressing, white/black label)	20
69	Harvest SHVL 751	THE BOOK OF TALIESYN (LP)	30
69	Harvest SHVL 759	DEEP PURPLE (LP, laminated gatefold sleeve)	25
70	Harvest SHVL 767	CONCERTO FOR GROUP AND ORCHESTRA (LP, laminated gatefold sleeve)	18
70	Harvest SHVL 777	IN ROCK (LP, laminated gatefold sleeve)	20
71	Harvest SHVL 793	FIREBALL (LP, textured gatefold sleeve, with insert)	15
72	Purple TPSP 351	MADE IN JAPAN LP, double gatefold)	12
72	Purple TPSA 7504	MACHINE HEAD (LP, laminated gatefold sleeve, with lyric insert)	12
73	Purple TPSA 7508	WHO DO WE THINK WE ARE (LP, laminated gatefold sleeve, with insert)	12
74	Purple Q4TPS 7504	MACHINE HEAD (LP, laminated gatefold sleeve, quadrophonic)	35
74	Purple TPS 3505	BURN (LP)	12
74	Purple TPS 3508	STORMBRINGER (LP)	12
75	Purple TPSA 7515	COME TASTE THE BAND (LP, gatefold sleeve with inner)	12
78	Harvest SHSM 2026	THE SINGLES A's AND B's (LP, purple vinyl)	20
79	Purple TPS 3514	THE MARK 2 PURPLE SINGLES (LP, purple vinyl)	15
80	Harvest SHSM 2016	SHADES OF DEEP PURPLE (LP, 'dismembered doll-limb' sleeve, withdrawn)	75
84	Polydor POLHP 16	PERFECT STRANGERS (LP, picture disc, with extra track & die-cut sleeve)	12
84	Polydor DEEP 1A	DEEP PURPLE INTERVIEW (LP, 1-sided, promo-only, stickered white sleeve)	15
85	EMI EJ 26 0343 0	IN ROCK (LP, picture disc with poster)	15
85	EMI EJ 34 0344 0	FIREBALL (LP, picture disc with poster)	15
85	EMI EG 26 0345 0	MACHINE HEAD (LP, picture disc with poster)	15
85	EMI PUR 1/E 2606131	DEEP PURPLE — ANTHOLOGY (2-LP, blue vinyl)	30
86	Polydor DEEP 2A	HOUSE OF BLUE LIGHT (interview LP, promo-only, plays same both sides, stickered black sleeve)	15
87	Polydor 831 318-2	HOUSE OF BLUE LIGHT (CD)	20
88	Connoisseur VSOP 125	SCANDINAVIAN NIGHTS (2-LP, gatefold sleeve, with booklet)	18
91	EMI 96129	ANTHOLOGY (3-LP)	20
93	BMG 74321 15420-1	THE BATTLE RAGES ON (LP, with inner sleeve)	15
95	EMI 7243 8 34019 18	DEEP PURPLE IN ROCK (2-LP, purple vinyl, gatefold sleeve with inners)	15
97	EMI DEEPP 3	MACHINE HEAD (2-LP, 'EMI 100' remixed anniversary edition, purple vinyl, gatefold sleeve, with insert)	18
97	EMI LPCENT 25	SHADES OF DEEP PURPLE (LP, 'EMI 100', 180gm vinyl edition, yellow/black label)	15
97	EMI DEEPP 2	FIREBALL (2-LP, gatefold sleeve with inners & limited edition print)	15
98	EMI PP 074	VERY BEST OF (2-LP, purple vinyl)	18
98	EMI 7243 8 57864 19	MADE IN JAPAN (2-LP, numbered, purple vinyl, gatefold sleeve with inners)	15
99	Harvest 7243 4 99469 10	BOOK OF TALIESYN (LP, 180gm vinyl, gatefold sleeve in stickered PVC outer)	15

(see also Ritchie Blackmore, Rainbow, Gillan, [David Coverdale's] Whitesnake, Tommy Bolin, [Sheila Carter &] Episode Six, Jon Lord, Roger Glover, Green Bullfrog, Wizard's Convention, Elf, Maze, M.I. Five, Warhorse, Captain Beyond, John Lawton, Hell Preachers Inc., Glen Hughes, Trapeze, Leading Figures, Paice Ashton & Lord, Silverhead, Pete York Percussion Band)

DEEP RIVER BOYS

54	HMV 7M 174	Sweet Mama Tree Top Tall/A Kiss And Cuddle Polka	25
54	HMV 7M 280	Shake, Rattle And Roll/St. Louis Blues	45
56	HMV 7M 361	Rock-A-Beatin' Boogie/Just A Little Bit More!	45
56	HMV POP 263	That's Right/Honey Honey	20
57	HMV POP 395	Whole Lotta Shakin' Goin' On/There's A Goldmine In The Sky	30
57	HMV POP 395	Whole Lotta Shakin' Goin' On/There's A Goldmine In The Sky (78)	10
58	HMV POP 449	Not Too Old To Rock And Roll/Slow Train To Nowhere (78 rpm = £10)	25
58	HMV POP 537	Itchy Twitchy Feeling/I Shall Not Be Moved (78 rpm = £10)	22
59	Top Rank JAR 172	Nola/Kissin' (78 rpm = £10)	8
59	Top Rank JAR 174	I Don't Know Why (I Just Do)/Timbers Gotta Roll (with Harry Douglass)	5
60	Top Rank JAR 352	Go Galloway, Go/Dum Dum De Dum (with Harry Douglass)	5
62	HMV POP 1081	Settle Down/Ashes Of Roses	7
55	Nixa 45EP 113	GO ON BOARD LITTLE CHILDREN (EP)	10
55	Nixa 45EP 114	SWING LOW SWEET CHARIOT (EP)	10
55	Nixa 45EP 130	WALK TOGETHER CHILDREN (EP)	10
55	Nixa 45EP 131	EZEKIEL SAW THE WHEEL (EP)	10
55	HMV 7EG 8133	DEEP RIVER BOYS (EP)	10
57	HMV 7EG 8321	ROMANCE A LA MODE (EP)	10
57	HMV 7EG 8445	NEGRO SPIRITUALS (EP)	10
54	Nixa XLTY 135	SPIRITUALS SUNG BY THE DEEP RIVER BOYS (10" LP)	25
54	Nixa XLTY 138	SPIRITUALS SUNG BY THE DEEP RIVER BOYS (10" LP)	25
60	Top Rank 35/108	THE BLUE DEEPS (LP)	25

(see also Fats Waller, Harry Douglass & Deep River Boys)

DEEP SET
68	Pye 7N 17594	That's The Way Life Goes/Hello Amy	7
69	Major Minor MM 607	I Started A Joke/Spicks And Specks	10

DEEP SIX
66	Liberty LIB 55882	Counting/When Morning Breaks	6

DEEP SWITCH
86	SWITCH 1	NINE INCHES OF GOD (LP, private pressing)	20

DEEP TIMBRE
72	Westwood WR 5006	DEEP TIMBRE (LP)	40

BRIAN DEE
75	Atlantic 2460 255	HAMMOND EXCITEMENT (LP)	12

SAM DEES
69	Major Minor MM 655	If It's All Wrong (It's All Right)/Don't Keep Me Hangin' On	20
75	Atlantic K 10676	Fragile, Handle With Care/Save The Love At Any Cost	100
89	RCA PB 43129	After All/Always Something (p/s)	10
97	Goldmine/Soul Supply GS 0002	Lonely For You Baby/SAM FLETCHER: I'd Think It Over (promos [GS 0002X] £12)	10
75	Atlantic K 50142	THE SHOW MUST GO ON (LP)	75

SAM DEES & BETTYE SWANN
76	Atlantic K 10719	Storybook Children/Just As Sure	12
(see also Bettye Swann)			

DEE SET
68	Blue Cat BS 146	I Know A Place/ROY BENNETT: I Dangerous	20

DEFENDANTS
80s	Edible EAT 001	Headmaster/Such A Spiv (stickered insert cover & stickered labels)	12

DEFENDERS
68	Doctor Bird DB 1104	Set Them Free/Don't Blame The Children (actually by Lee Perry & Sensations)	30
(see also Lee Perry)			

DEF J
92	Kold Sweat KS122	Just Save It (12")	8

DEF LEPPARD
79	Bludgeon Riffola SRT/CUS/232	THE DEF LEPPARD EP: Ride Into The Sun/Getcha Rocks Off/The Overture (red label, p/s with lyric insert, 150 only)	300
79	Bludgeon Riffola SRT/CUS/232	THE DEF LEPPARD EP: Ride Into The Sun/Getcha Rocks Off/The Overture (red label, with/without p/s, 850 only)	250/60
79	Bludgeon Riffola MSB 001	Ride Into The Sun/Getcha Rocks Off/The Overture (reissue, yellow label, 15,000 pressed, no p/s)	18
79	Phonogram 6059 240	Getcha Rocks Off/Ride Into The Sun/The Overture (2nd reissue, no p/s)	10
79	Phonogram 6059 240	Getcha Rocks Off/Ride Into The Sun/The Overture (mispressing, both sides play "The Overture")	40
79	Phonogram 6059 247	Wasted/Hello America (p/s)	12
80	Phonogram LEPP 1	Hello America/Good Morning Freedom (p/s)	12
81	Phonogram LEPP 2	Let It Go/Switch 625 (p/s, 10,000 shrinkwrapped with patch)	15/12
82	Phonogram LEPP 3	Bringin' On The Heartbreak/Me And My Wine (p/s)	35
82	Phonogram LEPP 312	Bringin' On The Heartbreak/Me And My Wine/You Got Me Runnin' (12", p/s)	20
83	Phonogram VER 5	Photograph/Bringin' On The Heartbreak (p/s)	10
83	Phonogram VERP 5	Photograph/Bringin' On The Heartbreak (camera-shaped fold-out/pop-up sleeve, 500 only)	25
83	Phonogram VERX 5	Photograph/Bringin' On The Heartbreak/Mirror, Mirror (12", p/s)	20
83	Phonogram VER 6	Rock Of Ages/Action! Not Words (p/s)	7
83	Phonogram VERP 6	Rock Of Ages/Action! Not Words (guitar-shaped picture disc)	35
83	Phonogram VERQ 6	Rock Of Ages/Action! Not Words (foldout 'rock box' cube sleeve, 500 only)	40
83	Phonogram VERX 6	Rock Of Ages/Action! Not Words (12", p/s)	18
83	Phonogram VERDJ 8	Too Late/Foolin' (p/s, DJ-only promo with rear band photo in football kit)	150
83	Phonogram VER 8	Too Late For Love/Foolin' (p/s)	12
83	Phonogram VERX 8	Too Late For Love/Foolin'/High And Dry (12", p/s)	20
84	Phonogram VER 9	Photograph/Bringin' On The Heartbreak (reissue, 'wallet' p/s)	10
84	Phonogram VERG 9	Photograph/Bringin' On The Heartbreak (g/fold printed 'wallet' p/s, 500 only)	40
84	Phonogram VERX 9	Photograph/Bringin' On The Heartbreak/Mirror, Mirror (12", p/s)	20
87	Phonogram LEPX 1	Animal/Animal (Extended Mix)/Tear It Down (12", p/s, black vinyl)	8
87	Phonogram LEPC 1	Animal/Animal (Extended Mix)/Tear It Down (12", p/s, red vinyl)	20
87	Phonogram LEPCD 1	Animal/Women/Animal (Extended Mix)/Tear It Down (CD, no'd, 1,000 only)	25
87	Phonogram LEPS 2	Pour Some Sugar On Me/I Wanna Be Your Hero (tri-shaped picture disc in silver 12" foldout p/s with tour dates)	15
87	Phonogram LEPMC 2	Pour Some Sugar On Me/I Wanna Be Your Hero (cassette)	7
87	Phonogram LEPX 2	Pour Some Sugar On Me (Extended Version)/Pour Some Sugar On Me/I Wanna Be Your Hero (12", p/s)	8
87	Phonogram LEPPX 2	Pour Some Sugar On Me (Extended Version)/Pour Some Sugar On Me (Extended)/I Wanna Be Your Hero (12", picture disc, unissued)	
87	Phonogram LEPMC 333	Hysteria/Ride Into The Sun (1987 Version) (cassette)	8
87	Phonogram LEPS 3	Hysteria/Ride Into The Sun (1987 Version) (p/s, shrinkwrapped with patch)	10
87	Phonogram LEPX 3	Hysteria/Ride Into The Sun (1987 Version)/Love And Affection (live) (12", p/s)	8
87	Phonogram LEPX 313	Hysteria/Ride Into The Sun (1987 Version)/Love And Affection (live) (12", envelope box sleeve with poster & international discography, 5,000 only)	15
87	Phonogram LEPCD 3	Hysteria/Ride Into The Sun (1987 Version)/Love And Affection (live)/I Wanna Be Your Hero (CD, 5,000 only with titles in red, numbered)	15
88	Phonogram LEPP 4	Armageddon It! (The Atomic Mix)/Ring Of Fire (poster p/s)	7
88	Phonogram LEPX 4	Armageddon It!/Armageddon It! (The Atomic Mix)/Ring Of Fire (12", p/s)	8
88	Phonogram LEPXB 4	Armageddon It!/Armageddon It! (The Atomic Mix)/Ring Of Fire (12", numbered box set with poster, enamel badge & 5 postcards, 5,000 only)	18

MINT VALUE £

88	Phonogram LEPCD 4	Armageddon It! (The Atomic Mix)/Ring Of Fire/Animal/ Pour Some Sugar On Me (CD, picture disc)................. 15
88	Phonogram LEPG 5	Love Bites/Billy's Got A Gun (live)/(no'd gatefold p/s with 8-page lyric book) 8
88	Phonogram LEPX 5	Love Bites/Billy's Got A Gun (live)/Excitable (Orgasmic Mix) (12", p/s) 8
88	Phonogram LEPXB 5	Love Bites/Billy's Got A Gun (live)/Excitable (Orgasmic Mix) (12", box set with 4 cardboard inserts, 5,000 only)................. 18
88	Phonogram LEPCD 5	Love Bites/Rocket (The Lunar Mix)/Billy's Got A Gun (live) (CD, card sleeve) ... 15
89	Phonogram LEPC 6	Rocket/Release Me (foldout 'Brit' pack, envelope sleeve with 3 inserts) 8
89	Phonogram LEPXP 6	Rocket (The Lunar Mix)/(Radio Edit)/Release Me (12", picture disc, some numbered) 15/10
89	Phonogram LEPX 6	Rocket (The Lunar Mix)/Release Me/Rock Of Ages (live) (12", p/s)............. 8
89	Phonogram LEPXC 6	Rocket (The Lunar Mix)/Release Me/Rock Of Ages (live) (12", calendar pack) ... 20
89	Phonogram LEPCD 6	Rocket (The Lunar Mix)/Rock Of Ages (live)/Release Me (CD)................. 15
92	Phonogram DEFXP 7	Let's Get Rocked/Only After Dark/Too Late For Love (live) (12", picture disc, with insert) 10
92	Phonogram DEFCD 7	Let's Get Rocked/Only After Dark/Women (live) (CD, picture disc, in box with space for 4 CDs) 15
88	Bludgeon Riffola 080 458-2	Love Bites/Rocket (Lunar Mix)/Billy's Got A Gun (live)/ Love Bites (Video) (CD Video)................................. 25
89	Bludgeon Riffola 080 034-2	Rock Of Ages/Stagefright/Billy's Got A Gun/Too Late For Love/ Rock Of Ages (Video) (CD Video)............................. 25
89	Bludgeon Riffola 080 626-2	Animal (Extended Version)/Animal/Tear It Down/Animal (Video) (CD Video)..... 25
90	Bludgeon Riffola 080 990-2	Rocket (Radio Edit)/Release Me/Rock Of Ages/Rocket (Video) (CD Video)..... 25
87	Phonogram HYSPD 1	HYSTERIA (LP, picture disc) 15
89	Phonogram 836 606-2	THE FOUR ALBUMS (4-CD box set, with booklet)............... 50
92	Phonogram 510 978-1	ADRENALIZE (LP, picture disc, 5,000 only, numbered, die-cut sleeve) 15
94	Phonogram (no cat. no.)	ADRENALIZE — MAHOGANY BOX SET (CD, picture disc, with interview picture CD, 3 booklets, signed/no'd certificate, signed photo & plectrum, 1,000 only).. 200
95	Mercury DLINT 3	1980-1995 VAULT — AN INTERVIEW WITH JOE ELLIOT & RICK SAVAGE (CD, promo only)... 30

(see also Lucy, Gogmagog)

DEF TEX
01	Monkey Face MF01	Sing Sad Songs (7")..................................... 10
92	Sound Clash SCR003	MASTER BLASTER (EP)................................... 25
94	Sound Clash CLASH003	HERBS & VERBS (EP) 15
95	Sound Clash SCR007	MOON MEDITATION (EP) 10

ZION DE GALLIER
68	Parlophone R 5686	Me/Winter Will Be Cold 30
68	Parlophone R 5710	Dream Dream Dream/Geraldine............................ 18

(see also Mark Wirtz)

GLORIA DE HAVEN
55	Brunswick 05369	So This Is Paris/The Two Of Us........................... 10
55	Brunswick 05457	Red Hot Pepper Pot/Won't You Save Me? 15
59	Oriole CB 1524	Dearly Beloved/Life.................................... 10

DE-HEMS
72	President PT 388	Don't Cross That Line/Lover Let Me Go..................... 8

DEIGHTON TASK FORCE
89	White REACT1	Neighbourhood (12") 30

DE JOHN SISTERS
57	Mercury MT 174	What Am I/Where Would I Be (78 rpm = £7)................. 10
60	London HLT 9127	Yes Indeed/Be Anything (But Be Mine)................... 10

DEK & JERRY
66	Philips BF 1494	What's The Matter With Me?/Don't Waste Your Time 8

DESMOND DEKKER (& ACES)
63	Island WI 054	Honour Your Mother And Father (as Desmond Decker & Beverley's Allstars)/ Madgie ('63) (with Beverley's Allstars) 18
63	Island WI 111	Parents/Labour For Learning (solo) 28
64	Island WI 158	Jeserine/King Of Ska (as Desmond Dekkar & His Cherry Pies) 28
64	Black Swan WI 455	Dracula (as Desmond Dekkar)/DON DRUMMOND: Spitfire 35
65	Island WI 181	Get Up Adine (as Desmond Dekkar, actually with Four Aces)/Be Mine Forever (as Patsy & Desmond; song is act. Down Down Down by Clive & Naomi) 32
65	Island WI 202	This Woman (as Desmond Dekker & Four Aces)/ LEE PERRY & UPSETTERS: Si Senora (B-side actually by Ossie & Upsetters) .. 20
67	Pyramid PYR 6003	Wise Man/ROLAND ALPHONSO: Middle East................... 15
67	Pyramid PYR 6004	007 (Shanty Town)/ROLAND ALPHONSO: El Torro............. 7
67	Pyramid PYR 6006	It's A Shame/ROLAND ALPHONSO: On The Move 15
67	Pyramid PYR 6008	Rudy Got Soul/ROLAND ALPHONSO: The Cat 22
67	Pyramid PYR 6011	Rude Boy Train/ROLAND ALPHONSO: Nothing For Nothing... 25
67	Pyramid PYR 6012	Mother's Young Girl/SOUL BROTHERS: Confucious 45
67	Pyramid PYR 6017	Unity/Sweet Music..................................... 15
67	Pyramid PYR 6020	Sabotage/Pretty Africa 15
67	Pyramid PYR 6020	Sabotage/It Pays 15
67	Pyramid PYR 6026	It Pays/Young Generation............................... 15
68	Pyramid PYR 6031	Beautiful And Dangerous/I've Got The Blues 15
68	Pyramid PYR 6035	Bongo Gal/Shing A Ling 15
68	Pyramid PYR 6037	To Sir, With Love/Fu Manchu............................. 45
68	Pyramid PYR 6044	Mother Pepper/Don't Blame Me........................... 15
68	Pyramid PYR 6047	Hey Grandma/Young Generation.......................... 15
68	Pyramid PYR 6051	Music Like Dirt (Intensified)/Coconut Water................ 15
68	Pyramid PYR 6054	It Mek/Writing On The Wall 8
68	Pyramid PYR 6058	Israelites/BEVERLEY'S ALLSTARS: The Man 7
68	Pyramid PYR 6059	Christmas Day/I've Got The Blues 10

69	Pyramid PYR 6068	It Mek/Problems.	5
69	J.J. PYR 6058	Israelites/BEVERLEY'S ALLSTARS: The Man (reissue, mis-labelled copy)	5
70	Trojan TR 7777	You Can Get It If You Really Want/Perseverance	5
70	Trojan TR 7802	The Song We Used To Sing/Get Up Little Suzie	5
71	Trojan TR 7847	Lightning Stick/Troubles And Miseries.	5
72	Trojan TR 7876	It Gotta Be So/The First Time For A Long Time.	5
73	Rhino RNO 115	Sing A Little Song/I'm A Busted Lad.	5
67	Doctor Bird DLM 5007	007 SHANTY TOWN (LP)	100
69	Doctor Bird DLM 5013	THE ISRAELITES (LP, solo)	90
69	Trojan TTL 4	THIS IS DESMOND DEKKAR (LP, label credits Dekker)	28
70	Trojan TBL 146	YOU CAN GET IT IF YOU REALLY WANT (LP).	18
73	Trojan TRLD 401	DOUBLE DEKKER (2-LP)	15

(all the above LPs have orange labels)
(see also Al Barry, Skatalites, Maytals)

GEORGE DEKKER

71	Trojan TR 7879	Time Hard/SYDNEY, GEORGE & JACKIE: Fall In Love	6

DEL AMITRI

82	Lyntone LYN 1548	What She Calls It (flexi, free with *Stand & Deliver*)	8
83	No Strings NOSP 1	Sense Sickness/The Difference Is (p/s)	30
85	Chrysalis CHS 12 2925	Hammering Heart/Lines Running North/Brown Eyed Girl (12", p/s)	12
89	A&M AM 527	Stone Cold Sober/The Return Of Maggie Brown/Talk It To Death (p/s)	10
89	A&M CDEE 515	Kiss This Thing Goodbye/No Holding On/Slowly, It's Coming Back (3" CD, card sleeve)	10
80s	Fan Club	Charlie's Bar (flexi, 1-track)	10
90	A&M AMX 589	Spit In The Rain/Scared To Love/The Return Of Maggie Brown/Talk It To Death (10", in box with lyric insert)	12

DELACARDOS

61	HMV POP 890	Hold Back The Tears/Mister Dillon	95

DE LAINE SISTERS

62	Piccadilly 7N 35070	It Might As Well Rain Until September/Puppet On A String	10

(see also Ladybirds, Breakaways)

ERIC DELANEY BAND

56	Pye N 15069	Rockin' The Tymphs/Ain't She Sweet (78)	8
60	Parlophone R 4646	Bass Drum Boogie/Let's Get Organised.	6
62	Parlophone R 4925	Manhattan Spiritual/Down Home	7
50s	Pye	HI-FI DELANEY (10" LP)	28

ERIC DELANEY'S BIG BEAT SIX

65	Pye 7N 15782	The Big Beat/Big Noise From Winnetka	6

DELANEY & BONNIE (& FRIENDS)

69	Elektra EKSN 45066	Get Ourselves Together/Soldiers Of The Cross (withdrawn)	20+
69	Apple SAPCOR 7	THE ORIGINAL DELANEY & BONNIE (LP, unreleased, no sleeve)	800
69	Elektra EKS 74039	THE ORIGINAL DELANEY & BONNIE — ACCEPT NO SUBSTITUTE (LP, commercial release of above LP).	18
69	Stax SXATS 1029	HOME (LP)	18
70	Atlantic 2400 013	ON TOUR WITH ERIC CLAPTON (LP)	15
71	Atco 2400 029	TO BONNIE FROM DELANEY (LP)	12
71	London ZGL 113	GENESIS (LP)	12
71	Atlantic 2400 119	MOTEL SHOT (LP).	12
72	CBS 64959	TOGETHER (LP)	12

(see also Eric Clapton, Delaney Bramlett, King Curtis with Delaney & Friends, Shindogs)

THE DELAYS

04	Rough Trade RTRADES 136	Long Time Coming/Hand Me Down (Mustard vinyl, p/s).	5

DEL-CAPRIS

79	Grapevine GRP 112	Hey Little Way Out Girl (actually by Construction)/EULA COOPER: Beggars Can't Be Choosey (p/s).	10

DELFONICS

68	Bell BLL 1005	La La Means I Love You/Can't Get Over Losing You.	10
68	Bell BLL 1016	Together We Can Make Such Sweet Music/Bad Bad Weather	10
69	Bell BLL 1066	You Can't Be Loving Him	12
69	Bell BLL 1073	Funny Feeling/You Got Yours	12
68	Bell SBLL 106	LA-LA MEANS I LOVE YOU (LP)	25
69	Bell SBLL 121	THE SOUND OF SEXY SOUL (LP)	25
71	Bell SBLL 137	THE DELFONICS (LP)	20
74	Bell BELLS 245	ALIVE AND KICKING (LP).	20

TERESA DEL FUEGO

81	Satril HH 155	Don't Hang Up/Wonder Wonder (no p/s)	8

(see also Swing Out Sister)

DELGADOS

95	Chemikal Underground CHEM 001	Monica Webster/Brand New Car (p/s)	6
96	Chemikal Underground CHEM 004	Cinecentre/Thirteen Gliding Prices/Mule Emulator (p/s).	5
96	Boa HISS 4	Liquidation Girl/VAN IMPE: Piranha (hand-painted brown paper bag p/s, 500 only)	15
95	Radar SCAN 07	THE LAZARWALKER EP (p/s)	10

DELICATES

59	London HLT 8953	Ronnie Is My Lover/Black And White Thunderbird (78 rpm = £50)	110
60	London HLT 9176	Too Young To Date/The Kiss	80

DELICATESSAN
67	Vocalion VN 9286	The Red Baron's Revenge/The Dog Fight (Der Hundkampf)	10

DELITES
80	Grapevine GRP 127	Lover/Tell Me Why	10

JOHNNY DE LITTLE
61	Columbia DB 4578	Not Guilty/They	10
62	Columbia DB 4907	Lover/You Made Me Love You	10
63	Columbia DB 7023	Days Of Wine And Roses/Ride On	10
63	Columbia DB 7044	The Wind And The Rain/Unchained Melody	8
65	CBS 201790	The Knack/What To Do With Laurie	8

(see also John Barry)

DELIVERANCE
87	Metalworks VOV 664	DEVIL'S MEAT (LP)	15
89	Metalworks VOV 673	EVIL FRIENDSHIP (LP, lyric inner)	15
90	Metalworks VOV 679	THE BOOK OF LIES (LP)	15

DENNIS D'ELL
67	CBS 202605	It Breaks My Heart In Two/Better Use Your Head (withdrawn: DJ copy = £300	400+
67	Decca F 12647	A Woman Called Sorrow/The Night Has A Thousand Eyes (as Denny D'Ell)	8
76	Polydor 2058 715	Home Is Home/Morning Without You (as Denis D'Ell)	7

(see also Honeycombs)

JIMMY DELL
58	RCA RCA 1066	Teeny Weeny/BARRY DE VORZON: Barbara Jean (78 rpm = £35)	70

DELLINGER
77	Carib Gems GG 004	Melting Pot/Version	7

(see also Dillinger)

PETE DELLO & FRIENDS
71	Nepentha 6437 001	INTO YOUR EARS (LP, gatefold sleeve)	150

(see also Honeybus, Lace, Red Herring, Leah, John Killigrew, Magic Valley, Grant Tracy & Sunsets, Sunsets)

DELLS
63	Pye International 7N 25178	The (Bossa Nova) Bird/Eternally	22
67	Chess CRS 8066	O-O I Love You/There Is	15
68	Chess CRS 8071	Wear It On Our Face/Please Don't Change Me Now	15
68	Chess CRS 8079	Stay In My Corner/Love Is So Simple	12
68	President PT 223	It's Not Unusual/Stay In My Corner	15
68	Chess CRS 8084	Always Together/I Want My Momma	8
69	Chess CRS 8099	I Can Sing A Rainbow/Love Is Blue-Hallelujah Baby	6
69	Chess CRS 8102	Oh What A Night/Believe Me	8
69	President PT 270	Oh What A Night/Moving On	7
69	Chess CRS 8105	On The Dock Of The Bay/When I'm In Your Arms	7
72	Chess 6145 008	It's All Up To You/Oh, My Dear	6
73	Chess 6145 022	Give Your Baby A Standing Ovation/Run For Cover	30
68	Chess CRLS 4554	GREATEST HITS (LP)	8
69	Chess CRLS 4555	LOVE IS BLUE/OH, WHAT A NIGHT (LP)	30
71	Joy JOYS 186	OH WHAT A NIGHT (LP)	15

DELKOM
91	Wau! Mr Modo MWS 034R	Superjack — Orbital Infusion 2000/Neutron 9000 Mix (12", 500 only)	12

ELAINE DELMAR
68	CBS 63511	Sneakin' Up On You	50
70	CBS 5329	Hurt So Bad/The Train	5

DANNY DELMONTE
63	Oriole CB 1894	John Kennedy/Come Summer	6
64	Oriole CB 1958	Worry/'Till I'm Back With You Darlin' Again	6

DELMORE BROTHERS
58	Parlophone GEP 8728	COUNTRY AND WESTERN (EP)	40

(see also Brown's Ferry Four, Grandpa Jones, Merle Travis)

DELMONTES
80s	Rational RATE 3	Don't Cry Your Tears/So It's Not To Be (yellow or blue p/s)	8

AL DE LORY
65	London HLU 9999	Yesterday/Traffic Jam	22
70	Capitol CL 15644	Song From M*A*S*H/Feeling Of Love	8

DELROY & SPORTY
71	Banana BA 322	Lovers Version/DUDLEY SIBLEY: Having A Party	15

DELROY & TENNORS
71	Camel CA 62	Donkey Shank/MURPHY'S ALL STARS: Donkey Track	10

DELTA CATS
69	Bamboo BAM 3	I Can't Re-Live (song actually "I Can't Believe")/I've Been Hurt	18

(see also Thrillers)

DELTA 5
79	Rough Trade RT 31	Mind Your Own Business/Now That You've Gone (p/s)	10
80	Rough Trade RT 41	Anticipation/You (p/s)	7
81	Rough Trade RT 61	Try/Colour (p/s)	7

DELTA KINGS
61	London RE-R 1318	AT SUNDOWN (EP)	10
61	London Jazz LTZ-R 15204	AT SUNDOWN (LP, also stereo SAH-R 6118)	15/18

DELTA RHYTHM BOYS
51	London L 1145	Blow Out The Candle/All The Things You Are (78)	12
54	Brunswick 05353	Mood Indigo/Have A Hope, Have A Wish, Have A Prayer	12
52	Esquire 15-001	DELTA RHYTHM BOYS WITH THE METRONOME ALLSTARS (10" LP)	28

DELTAS
64	Blue Beat BB 265	Georgia/The Party	20
65	Blue Beat BB 275	The Visitor/SKATALITES: Hanging The Beam	40

DELTA SKIFFLE GROUP
57	Esquire 10-504	Skip To My Lou/John Brown's Body (78)	10
57	Esquire 10-507	K.C. Moan/Pick A Bale Of Cotton (78)	10
58	Esquire 10-517	Ain't You Glad?/Open Up Them Pearly Gates (78)	12
58	Esquire EP 162	DELTA SKIFFLE GROUP (EP)	55

DELTONES (Jamaica)
71	Green Door GD 4010	Chopsticks/DES BRYAN: Belmont Street	8
72	Trojan TRM 9001	Chopsticks/I Got It/Put It On	6

DELTONES (U.K.)
70	Columbia DB 8719	Gimme Some Lovin'/Have A Little Talk With Myself	20

DEL-TONES (U.S.)
59	Top Rank JAR 171	Moonlight Party/Rockin' Blues (78 rpm = £30)	85

(see also Beau-Marks)

MILTON DE LUGG ORCHESTRA
65	Columbia DB 7474	The Addams Family Theme/The Alfred Hitchcock Theme	15
66	Columbia DB 7762	The Munsters Theme/The Addams Family Theme	15

(see also Beau-Marks)

DELUSION
80s	Wizzo WIZZO 2	Pessimists Paradise/Desert Island (gatefold p/s)	8

DEL(L)-VIKINGS
57	London HLD 8405	Come Go With Me/How Can I Find A True Love (gold or silver label lettering)	155/68
57	London HLD 8405	Come Go With Me/How Can I Find A True Love (78)	15
57	London HLD 8464	Whispering Bells/Little Billy Boy (78 rpm = £12)	65
57	Mercury MT 169	Cool Shake/Jitterbug Mary (78)	30
58	Mercury 7MT 199	The Voodoo Man/Can't Wait (78 rpm = £35)	65
59	Mercury AMT 1027	Flat Tyre/How Could You (78 rpm = £45)	60
62	HMV POP 1072	Confession Of Love/Kilimanjaro	30
63	HMV POP 1145	An Angel Up In Heaven/The Fishing Chant	30
71	Contour 2870 388	COME GO WITH ME (LP)	12

(see also Chuck Jackson)

LEO DE LYON
54	MGM SP 1087	The Band Played On/Say It Isn't So	7
60	Oriole CB 1561	Rich In Love/The Blue Train	7
60	Oriole MG 20053	LEO DE LYON (LP)	18

RALPH DE MARCO
59	London HLL 9010	Old Shep/More Than Riches (78 rpm = £30)	10

ARIN DEMAIN
90s	Goldmine/Soul Supply GS 028	Silent Treatment/PARIS: Sleepless Nights	8

DEMENSIONS
60	Top Rank JAR 505	Over The Rainbow/Nursery Rhyme Rock	90
61	Coral Q 72437	Count Your Blessings Instead Of Sheep/Again	20+

(ROD) DEMICK & (HERBIE) ARMSTRONG
70	Decca F 13056	We're On The Right Track/Dreaming (as Demick-Armstrong)	6
71	Mam MAM 10	If I Ever Get To You/Girl	5
71	Mam MAM-AS 1001	LITTLE WILLY RAMBLE (LP)	15
72	A&M AMLH 68908	LOOKIN' THROUGH (LP)	15

(see also Wheels, James Brothers, Fox)

DEMOB
81	Round Ear ROUND 1	Anti Police/Teenage Adolescence (foldout p/s, later standard p/s)	12/10
81	Round Ear EAR 3	No Room For You/Think Straight/New Breed (p/s)	10

DEMON
81	Clay CLAY 4	Liar/Wild Woman (p/s, red vinyl)	8
82	Carrere CAR 226	One Helluva Night/Into The Nightmare (picture disc)	6
83	Clay CLAY 25	The Plague/The Only Sane Man (p/s)	6
84	Clay CLAY 41	Wonderland/Blackheath (p/s)	6
84	Clay 12CLAY 41	Wonderland/Blackheath/Nowhere To Run (12", p/s)	8
88	Clay CLAY 48D	Tonight (The Hero Is Back)/Hurricane//Night Of The Demon/ Don't Break The Circle (double pack)	5
83	Clay CLAYLP 6	THE PLAGUE (LP, gatefold sleeve, with insert)	15
83	Clay CLAYLP 6P	THE PLAGUE (LP, picture disc)	20
90	Sonic SONICLP 1	NIGHT OF THE DEMON (LP)	12
90	Flametrader LP 1	ONE HELLUVA NIGHT (2-LP)	18

DEMON BOYZ
88	Music Of Life Note 013	Northside/Rougher Than An Animal (12")	20
88	Music Of Life Note 022	Vibes (12")	12
89	Music Of Life NOTE26	Recognition/Lyrical Culture (12")	15
90	Mango 12 MNS 738	International Karate (12")	10
92	Tribal Bass Tribe4	DETT (12")	10
92	Tribal Bass Tribe9	Glimity Glamity/Junglist (12")	20

DEMON BOYZ

89	Music Of Life DEMON1	RECOGNITION (LP)	18
92	Tribal Bass Tribe11	ORIGINAL GUIDANCE – THE SECOND CHAPTER (LP)	15

DEMON FUZZ
70	Dawn DNX 2504	I Put A Spell On You/Message To Mankind/Fuzz Oriental Blues (some in p/s)	12/10
70	Dawn DNLS 3013	AFREAKA! (LP)	80

DEMON PACT
81	Slime PACT 1	Eaten Alive/Raiders (p/s)	50
81	Slime PACT 2	Escape/Demon Pact (unreleased, labels only)	

DEMON PREACHER
78	Illegal SRTS/CUS/78110	Royal Northern (N7)/Laughing At Me/	
		Steal Your Love/Dead End Kidz (numbered p/s)	80
78	Small Wonder SMALL TEN	Little Miss Perfect/Perfect Dub (p/s)	10

(see also Demons, Alien Sex Fiend, Fenzyx)

DEMONS (Jamaica)
69	Big Shot BI 523	You Belong To My Heart/Bless You	10

DEMONS (U.K.)
80	Crypt Music DEM 1	Action By Example/I Wish I Was A Dog (p/s)	12

(see also Alien Sex Fiend, Demon Preacher)

DEMONSTRATORS
64	Warner Bros WB 132	Sweet Violets/Ultra Violet	15

JASON DENE
66	Parlophone R 5485	Opportunity/It's Me	8

(see also Jason Deane)

TERRY DENE
57	Decca F 10895	A White Sport Coat/The Man In The Phone Booth (78 rpm = £8)	40
57	Decca F 10914	Start Movin'/Green Corn (78 rpm = £7)	25
57	Decca F 10938	Come And Get It/Teenage Dream (78 rpm = £7)	25
57	Decca F 10964	Lucky Lucky Bobby/Baby, She's Gone (78 rpm = £8)	25
58	Decca F 10977	The Golden Age/C'Min And Be Loved (78 rpm = £7)	20
58	Decca F 11016	Stairway Of Love/Lover, Lover! (78 rmp = £7)	12
58	Decca F 11037	Seven Steps To Love/Can I Walk You Home (78 rpm = £8)	18
58	Decca F 11076	Who Baby Who/Pretty Little Pearly (78 rpm = £10)	20
59	Decca F 11100	I've Got A Good Thing Going/Bimbombey (78 rpm = £8)	15
59	Decca F 11136	There's No Fool Like A Young Fool/I've Come Of Age (78 rpm = £10)	15
59	Decca F 11154	Thank You Pretty Baby/A Boy Without A Girl (78 rpm = £12)	20
60	Oriole CB 1562	Geraldine/Love Me Or Leave Me	25
61	Oriole CB 1594	Like A Baby/Next Stop Paradise	22
63	Aral PS 107	The Feminine Look/Fever (all in p/s)	20
57	Decca DFE 6427	THE GOLDEN DISC (EP)	45
58	Decca DFE 6459	TERRY DENE NO. 1 (EP)	60
58	Decca DFE 6507	TERRY DENE NO. 2 (EP)	45
66	Herald ELR 107	TERRY DENE NOW (EP)	20
74	Decca SPA 368	I THOUGHT TERRY DENE WAS DEAD (LP)	12

DENE BOYS
57	HMV POP 374	Bye Bye Love/Love Is The Thing	20
58	HMV POP 455	Skylark/I Walk Down The Street	8

DENE FOUR
59	HMV POP 666	Hush-a-bye/Something New	25

(see also Dene Boys)

DENIGH
80	Ace ACE 16	No Way/Running (no p/s)	80

DENIM
97	DISC009	Summer Smash/Sun's Out (p/s)	7

(see also Felt)

DENIMS
65	CBS 201807	I'm Your Man/Ya Ya	75

CLAUDE DENJEAN
71	Decca PFS 4212	MOOG! (LP)	12

ROGER DENISON
66	Parlophone R 5545	I'm On An Island/I'm Running Out Of Time	12
67	Parlophone R 5566	She Wanders Through My Mind/This Just Doesn't Seem To Be My Day	30+

WADE DENNING & PORT WASHINGTONS
67	MGM MGM 1339	Tarzan's March/Batman	15

D.D DENNIS (Brother Lloyd's All-Stars)
68	Mercury MF 1064	Save The Last Dance For Me/Will You Still Love Me Tomorrow?	8

D.D. (Denzil) DENNIS
70	Crab CRAB 60	Having A Party/Man With Ambition	5
70	Pama Supreme PS 301	My Way/Happy Days	5
71	Punch PH 93	Christmas Message/Cool It Girl	5
71	Pama Supreme PS 330	I'm A Believer/I'll Make The Way Easy	5
74	Pama Supreme PS 391	Women And Money/UPSETTERS: Ten Cent Skank	8

(see also Denzil Dennis)

DENZIL DENNIS
63	Blue Beat BB 181	Seven Nights In Rome/Love Is For Fools	15
68	Trojan TR 614	Donkey Train/Down By The Riverside	12
68	Trojan TR 615	Me Nah Worry/Hush Don't You Cry	12

68	Jolly JY 011	Oh Carol/Where Has My Little Girl Gone	8
70	Pama Supreme PS 304	Painful Situation/Nothing Has Changed	5
71	Pama Supreme PS 350	South Of The Border/GRAHAM: Long Island	10
72	Pama Supreme PS 375	Mama We're All Crazy Now/ROY SHIRLEY: A Lady's A Man's Best Friend	7
72	Duke DU 142	I Forgot To Be Your Lover/I've Got To Settle Down	5
73	Grape GR 3059	People Got To Be Friends/Ups And Downs (actually by Pat Rhoden)	5

(see also D.D. Dennis, Cosmo & Dennis, Denzil & Pat, Denzil & Jennifer, Les & Silkie)

JACKIE DENNIS
58	Decca F 10992	La Dee Dah/You're The Greatest	12
58	Decca F 11011	Miss Valerie/My Dream (78 rpm = £7)	18
58	Decca F 11033	The Purple People Eater/You-Oo (78 rpm = £7)	18
58	Decca F 11060	More Than Ever (Come Prima)/Linton Addie (78 rpm = £8)	12
58	Decca F 11090	Gingerbread/Lucky Ladybug (78 rpm = £8)	12
59	Top Rank JAR 129	Summer Snow/Night Bird (78 rpm = £8)	10
58	Decca DFE 6513	JACKIE DENNIS NO. 1 (EP)	45

DENNIS & LIZZY
| 70 | Camel CA 56 | Everybody Bawlin'/Mr Brown | 10 |
| 73 | Pyramid PYR 7002 | Ba-Ba-Ri-Ba-Shank/TOMMY McCOOK ALL STARS: Buck And The Preacher | 12 |

(see also Dennis Alcapone, Lizzy & Dennis)

DENNISONS
63	Decca F 11691	(Come On) Be My Girl/Little Latin Lupe Lu	20
64	Decca F 11880	Walkin' The Dog/You Don't Know What Love Is	25
64	Decca F 11990	Nobody Like My Babe/Lucy (You Sure Did It This Time)	20

DENNY & WILSON
| 72 | Hillcrest HCT 6 | Hey Hey Girl/CARLTON ALPHONSO: Girl I Love You | 6 |

MARTIN DENNY (& HIS ORCHESTRA)
59	London HLU 8860	Quiet Village/Llama Serenade	7
59	London SLW 4004	Quiet Village/Llama Serenade (stereo export issue)	10
59	London HLU 8976	The Enchanted Sea/Martinique (78 rpm = £6)	6
62	Liberty LIB 55470	A Taste Of Honey/The Brighter Side	6
60	London REU 1241	THE EXOTIC SOUNDS OF MARTIN DENNY (EP)	20
58	London HB-U 1079	EXOTICA (10" LP, mono only)	30
58	London SAH-U 6004	FORBIDDEN ISLAND (LP, stereo only)	30
59	London HA-U 2196	AFRO-DESIA (LP, also stereo SAH-U 6048) each	20
60	London HA-U 2208	QUIET VILLAGE (LP, also stereo SAH-U 6055) each	25
60	London SAH-W 6062	EXOTICA (12" LP, stereo reissue with extra tracks "Busy Port" & "Waipio")	25
60	London HA-G 2253	EXOTICA – VOL. 2 (LP, also stereo SAH-G 6076)	25
60	London HA-W 2239	EXOTICA – VOL. 3 (LP, also stereo SAH-W 6069)	25
60	London HA-G 2281	THE ENCHANTED SEA (LP, also stereo SAH-G 6098) each	25
61	London HA-G 2317	THE SILVER SCREEN (LP, also stereo SAH-G 6122) each	12
61	London HA-G 2387	EXOTIC PERCUSSION (LP, also stereo SAH-G 6187) each	12
62	London HA-G 2417	ROMANTICA (LP, also stereo SAH-G 6215) each	12
64	Liberty LBY 1241	HAWAII TATTOO (LP)	12
65	Liberty (S)LBY 1221	LATIN VILLAGE (LP)	12

SANDY DENNY
72	Island WIP 6141	Here In Silence/Man Of Iron (theme from *Pass Of Arms* film, some in p/s)	25/40
72	Island WIP 6142	Listen Listen/Tomorrow Is A Long Time	6
73	Island WIP 6176	Whispering Grass/Friends (some in p/s)	6/10
74	Island WIP 6195	Like An Old Fashioned Waltz (unissued)	
76	Mooncrest MOON 54	Make Me A Pallet On Your Floor/This Train	6
77	Island WIP 6391	Candle In The Wind/Still Waters Run Deep (unissued, promo only)	30
67	Saga EROS 8041	SANDY AND JOHNNY (LP, with Johnny Silvo)	40
70	Saga EROS 8153	SANDY DENNY (LP)	30
71	Island ILPS 9165	THE NORTH STAR GRASSMAN AND THE RAVENS (LP, gatefold sleeve, 'pink rim palm tree' label)	30
72	Island ILPS 9207	SANDY (LP, gatefold sleeve, originally with 'pink rim palm tree' label)	12/25
73	Island ILPS 9258	LIKE AN OLD FASHIONED WALTZ (LP, gatefold sleeve, 'pink rim palm tree' label)	25
73	Hallmark SHM 813	ALL OUR OWN WORK (LP, with Strawbs)	15
77	Island ILPS 9433	RENDEZVOUS (LP, with insert)	18
78	Mooncrest CREST 28	THE ORIGINAL SANDY DENNY (LP)	20
85	Island SDSP 100	WHO KNOWS WHERE THE TIME GOES? (4-LP box set)	30
97	Strange Fruit SFRSCD 006	THE BBC SESSIONS 1971-73 (CD, limited edition, withdrawn – beware of bootlegs)	30

(see also Fairport Convention, Bunch, Strawbs, Fotheringay, Alex Campbell, Trevor Lucas, Richard Thompson)

SUSAN DENNY
| 65 | Melodisc MEL 1596 | Don't Touch Me/Johnny | 15 |

DENTISTS
85	Spruck SP 003	Strawberries Are Growing In My Garden (And It's Wintertime)/Burning The Thoughts From My Skin/Doreen (p/s)	10
85	Spruck SP 004	YOU AND YOUR BLOODY ORANGES (12" EP, p/s)	10
86	Tambourine SP 006	DOWN AND OUT IN PARIS AND CHATHAM (12" EP, brown/white or group p/s)	8
87	Tambourine URINE 3	Writhing On The Shagpile/Just Like Oliver Reed/A Strange Way To Go About Things/Calm You Down/The Turquoise Castle (12", p/s)	8
85	Spruck SPR 001	SOME PEOPLE ARE ON THE PITCH THEY THINK IT'S ALL OVER IT IS NOW (LP)	15

MICKEY DENTON
| 61 | London HLX 9398 | The Steady Kind/Now You Can't Give Them Away | 12 |

KARL DENVER

61	Decca F 11360	Marcheta/Joe Sweeney	6
61	Decca F 11395	Mexicali Rose/Bonny Scotland	6
62	Decca F 11420	Wimoweh/Gypsy Davy	7
62	Decca F 11431	Never Goodbye/Highland Fling	6
62	Decca F 11470	A Little Love, A Little Kiss/Lonely Sailor	6
62	Decca F 11505	Blue Weekend/My Mother's Eyes	6
62	Decca F 11553	Dry Tears/Pastures Of Plenty	7
63	Decca F 11608	Can You Forgive Me/Love From A Heart Of Gold	7
63	Decca F 11674	Indian Love Call/My Melancholy Baby	7
63	Decca F 11720	Still/My Canary Has Circles Under His Eyes	7
64	Decca F 11828	My World Of Blue/The Green Grass Grows All Round	7
64	Decca F 11905	Love Me With All Your Heart/Am I That Easy To Forget?	7
64	Decca F 12025	Sally/Swanee River	7
65	Mercury MF 878	Cry A Little Sometimes/Today Will Be Yesterday Tomorrow	7
65	Mercury MF 904	Marta/I'll Never Forget To Remember	7
65	Mercury MF 926	The Tips Of My Fingers/I'm Alone Because I Love You	7
68	Page One POF 063	You've Still Got A Place In My Heart/I Still Miss Someone (as Karl Denver Trio)	8
62	Decca DFE 8501	BY A SLEEPY LAGOON (EP)	15
62	Decca DFE 8504	KARL DENVER HITS (EP)	10
61	Ace Of Clubs ACL 1098	WIMOWEH (LP)	22
62	Ace Of Clubs ACL 1131	KARL DENVER (LP)	22
63	Decca LK 4540	LIVE AT THE YEW TREE (LP)	28
64	Decca LK 4596	WITH LOVE (LP)	28

NIGEL DENVER

66	Decca LK 4728	MOVIN' ON (LP, featuring Martin Carthy)	50
67	Major Minor MMLP 1	SCOTTISH REPUBLICAN SONGS (LP)	25
68	Decca SKL 4943	FOLK OLD AND NEW (LP)	25

DENZIL & JENNIFER

70	Escort ES 824	Young, Gifted And Black/OWEN GRAY: I Am Satisfied	7

DENZIL (Dennis) & PAT (Rhoden)

69	Downtown DT 403	Dream/Sincerely	7

WILBUR DE PARIS' NEW ORLEANS BAND

59	London HLE 8816	Petite Fleur/Over And Over Again	7

DEPARTURE

04	Parlophone CDR6642	All Mapped Out/Dirty Words (CD, silver embossed card sleeve)	8
04	Parlophone R6642	All Mapped Out/Dirty Words (Silver embossed sleeve)	8

DEPECHE MODE

81	Lyntone LYN 10209	Sometimes I Wish I Was Dead/FAD GADGET: King Of The Flies (red flexidisc free with *Flexipop* magazine, issue 11)	25/15
81	Lyntone LYN 10209	Sometimes I Wish I Was Dead/FAD GADGET: King Of The Flies (test pressing)	250
81	Mute MUTE 013	Dreaming Of Me/Ice Machine (p/s)	5
83	Mute L12BONG 2	Get The Balance Right/My Secret Garden (live)/See You (live)/Satellite (live) (12", numbered p/s)	10
83	Mute L12BONG 3	Everything Counts/Boys Say Go (live)/New Life (live)/Nothing To Fear (live)/The Meaning Of Love (live) (12", numbered p/s)	10
83	Mute L12BONG 4	Love In Itself (2)/Just Can't Get Enough (live)/Photograph Of You (live)/Shout (live)/Photographic (live) (12", numbered p/s)	10
84	Mute L12BONG 5	People Are People (On-U-Sound Remix)/In Your Memory/People Are People (12", numbered in die-cut p/s)	10
84	Mute L12BONG 6	Master And Servant (On-U-Sound Science Fiction Dancehall Classic)/Are People People?/(Set Me Free) Remotivate Me (12", numbered p/s)	10
85	Mute L12 BONG 8	Edit The Shake/Master And Servant (live)/Flexible (Pre-Deportation Mix)/Something To Do (Metal Mix) (12", p/s)	10
85	Mute 7BONG 9	It's Called A Heart/Fly On The Windscreen (p/s, sealed with poster)	5
85	Mute D12BONG 9	It's Called A Heart (Mixes)/Fly On The Windscreen (Mixes) (12", p/s, dbl-pack)	10
86	Mute CBONG 11	A Question Of Lust (Flood Mix)/If You Want (live)/Shame (live)/Blasphemous Rumours (live) (cassette in 7" pack with book & badge)	8
86	Mute L12BONG 12	A Question Of Time (Mixes)/Black Celebration (Black Tulip Mix)/More Than A Party (Live Remix) (12", p/s)	8
87	Mute L12 BONG 13	Strangelove (Blind Mix)/PIMPF/Strangelove (Pain Mix)/Agent Orange (12", p/s)	8
87	Mute CDBONG 13	Strangelove (Maxi-Mix)/Strangelove (Midi-Mix)/Strangelove (LP Mix)/PIMPF/Agent Orange (CD, card p/s)	8
87	Mute L12BONG 14	Never Let Me Down Again (Tsangarides Mix)/Pleasure Little Treasure (Join Mix)/To Have And To Hold (Spanish Taster) (12", p/s)	8
87	Mute CDBONG 14	Never Let Me Down Again (Split Mix)/Pleasure Little Treasure (Join Mix)/To Have And To Hold (Spanish Taster)/Never Let Me Down Again (Aggro Mix) (CD in pouch)	12
88	Mute L12BONG 15	Behind The Wheel (Beatmasters Remix)/Route 66 (Casuality Mix) (12", p/s)	8
89	Mute 10BONG 16	Everything Counts (Absolute Mix)/(1983 12" Mix)/Nothing (US 7" Mix) (10", envelope p/s, with 2 postcards & window sticker)	12
89	Mute L12BONG 16	Everything Counts (Tim Simenon & M. Saunders Remix)/Nothing (Justin Strauss Remix)/Strangelove (Tim Simenon & M. Saunders Remix) (12", p/s)	8
89	Mute LCDBONG 16	Everything Counts (Tim Simenon & M. Saunders Remix)/Nothing (Justin Strauss Remix)/Strangelove (Tim Simenon & M. Saunders Remix) (3" CD, 'filofax page' in p/s)	15
89	Mute GBONG 17	Personal Jesus/(Acoustic)/Dangerous (Hazchemix) (gatefold p/s with photos)	5
89	Mute L12BONG 17	Personal Jesus (Mixes)/Dangerous (Hazchemix) (12", p/s)	8
89	Mute LCDBONG 17	Personal Jesus (Pump Mix)/Personal Jesus (Telephone Stomp Mix)/Dangerous (Hazchemix) (3" CD)	15
90	Mute XL12BONG 18	Enjoy The Silence (The Quad: Final Mix) (12", 1-side etched, p/s)	10

90	Mute LCDBONG 18	Enjoy The Silence (Bassline): Bassline/Harmonium/Ricki Tick Tick Mix/ Memphisto (CD)	10
90	Mute XLCDBONG 18	Enjoy The Silence (The Quad: Final Mix) (3" CD, 1-track)	25
90	Mute L12BONG 19	Policy Of Truth (Trancentral Mix)/Policy Of Truth (Pavlov's Dub)/ Kaleid (remix) (12", gatefold p/s)	8
90	Mute L12BONG 20	World In My Eyes (Dub In My Eyes)/Happiest Girl (The Pulsating Orbital Mix) (12", p/s with inner, in sealed blue PVC pack)	10
90	Mute LCDBONG 20	World In My Eyes (Dub In My Eyes)/World In My Eyes (Mode To Joy)/ Happiest Girl (The Pulsating Orbital Vocal Mix)/Sea Of Sin (Sensoria)/ World In My Eyes (Mayhem Mode)/Happiest Girl (Jack Mix) (CD)	25
91	Mute DMBX 1	1 (6-CD single box set, with booklet)	25
91	Mute DMBX 2	2 (6-CD single box set, with booklet)	25
91	Mute DMBX 3	3 (6-CD single box set, with booklet)	25
94	Mute XLCDBONG 24	In Your Room (Mixes)/Higher Love (Adrenaline Mix) (CD)	10
02	Mute MUTE 12BONG 33	Goodnight Lovers (ISAN Falling Leaf Mix)/When The Body Speaks (Acoustic Version/The Dead Of Night (Electronicat Remix) (12", red vinyl, p/s)	25
87	Mute STUMM 47	MUSIC FOR THE MASSES (LP, clear vinyl)	20
87	Mute STUMM 47	MUSIC FOR THE MASSES (LP, with bonus 12" "Strangelove (Maximix)"/ "Never Let Me Down Again (Split Mix)" [HMV 1])	30
88	Mute CDSTUMM 5	SPEAK AND SPELL (CD)	18
89	Mute CD TUMM 100	101 (2-CD, tri-fold card sleeve, with booklet in slip case)	20
89	Mute (no cat. no.)	B-SIDES (4-LP set, plain white box, unreleased, test pressings only)	1,000
93	Mute LCDSTUMM 106	SONGS OF FAITH AND DEVOTION LIVE (CD, in slipcase with photo-book)	20
98	Mute MUTEL 5	SINGLES 86-98 (3-LP box set, numbered, with booklet)	25

PROMOS

86	Mute BONG 12	A Question Of Time (Edit)/Black Celebration (Live) (white label)	70
87	Mute BONG 13R	Strangelove (Radio Edit)/Strangelove (p/s)	80
87	Mute DANCE BONG 13	Strangelove (Blind Mix)/(Fresh Ground Mix) (12", promo-only remix)	50
87	Mute BONG 14R	Never Let Me Down Again/Pleasure Little Treasure	70
87	Mute P12BONG 14	Never Let Me Down Again (Split Mix)/Pleasure Little Treasure (Glitter Mix)/ Never Let Me Down Again (Aggro Mix) (12")	10
87	Mute DJBONG 15	Behind The Wheel (DJ Remix)/Behind The Wheel (LP Mix)	90
89	Mute BONG 17	Personal Jesus/Dangerous (censored black rear p/s)	40
89	Mute PP12BONG 16	Strangelove (Hijack Mix)/Nothing (12")	18
89	Mute BONG 16R	Everything Counts (Live – Radio Edit)/Nothing (Live Mix) (stickered p/s)	20
90	Mute BONG 18	Enjoy The Silence/Memphisto ('A' label)	25
90	Mute RCDBONG 18	Enjoy The Silence (7")/Memphisto (7") (CD)	25
90	Mute CDBONG 19R	Policy Of Truth (7" Version)/Kaleid (Remix) (CD)	25
90	Mute PSTUMM 64	VIOLATOR (12" EP, 4-track sampler)	15
90	Mute 12BONG 20	World In My Eyes (Oil Tank Mix)/Happiest Girl (Kiss-A-Mix)/Sea Of Sin (Sensoria) (12", white label, numbered, stickered sleeve)	25
93	Mute PL12BONG 23	Rush (Spiritual Guidance Mix)/Rush (Amylnitrate Mix)/Rush (Wild Planet Vocal Mix) (12")	50
97	Mute BONG 26	It's No Good (Club 69 Future Mix)/It's No Good (Club 69 Future Dub)/ It's No Good (Club 69 Funk Dub) (12")	60
97	Mute PL12BONG 26	It's No Good (Club 69 mixes) (12")	70
97	Mute XLCDBONG 26	It's No Good (Live) (CD)	70
97	Mute P12BONG 28	Useless (CJ Bolland Funky Sub Mix)/Useless (the Kruder & Dorfmeister Session™) (12", die-cut p/s)	18
98	Mute P12BONG 29	Only When I Lose Myself (Dan The Automator Mix)/Only When I Lose Myself (Subsonic Legacy Mix)/Painkiller (Kill The Pain — DJ Shadow Vs Depeche Mode)/Headstar (12", die-cut p/s)	10
01	Mute P12BONG 30	Dream On (Bushwacka Tough Guy mixes) (12", p/s)	18
01	Mute P12BONG 30	Dream On (Dave Clarke Club Mix)/Dream On (Bushwacka Blunt Mixes) (12", p/s)	18
01	Mute P12BONG 30	Dream On (Octagon Man mixes)/(Dave Clarke Acoustic Mix)/Dream On (Kid 606 Mix) (12", p/s)	18
01	Mute PL12BONG 31	I Feel Loved (Danny Tenaglia mixes) (12", p/s)	20
01	Mute PL12BONG 32	Freelove (Deep Dish Freedom Mix)/Freelove (Josh Wink Vocal Interpretation)/Freelove (Deep Dish Freedom Dub)/Freelove (Powder Productions Remix) (12", doublepack, p/s)	25
87	Mute (no cat. no.)	THE B-SIDES (4-LP test pressings in title box)	800+
87	Mute (no cat. no.)	THE B-SIDES (4-cassette set)	250+
90	Mute (no cat. no.)	VIOLATOR (LP, CD & cassette in 12" x 12" picture box with insert)	140
93	Mute VERBONG 1	SONGS OF FAITH & DEVOTION (interview CD)	70
93	Mute (no cat. no.)	SONGS OF FAITH & DEVOTION (4-CD box set)	300
94	Mute DEPRO 1	DEPRO 1 (13-track compilation CD)	90
97	Mute BXSTUMM 148	ULTRA (box set, with CD, T-shirt, stickers & EPK video, soap box pack)	150
98	Mute (no cat. no.)	THE SINGLES 86>98 (15" x 6" box set, with 3 CDs, video tape & cards)	120
01	Mute IPKSTUMM 190	EXCITER (interview CD with bonus multimedia disc)	70
01	Mute BCDSTUMM 190	EXCITER (interview CD with bonus multimedia disc, in long box)	110
04	Mute P12BONG34	REMIXES 81 – 04 SAMPLER : Enjoy The Silence (Richard X Extended Mix)/ (EwanPearson Extended Instrumental)/Timo Maas Extended Remix)/ Ewan Pearson Extended Remix) (2 x 12" singles)	25
04	Mute PXL12BONG34	Halo (Goldfrapp Remix)/(Clean Colder Version)/Little 15 (Ulrich Schauss Remix) (12")	15
05	Mute PCDBONG35	Precious (Sasha's Spooky Mix – Edit)/(Sasha's Gargantuan Vocal Mix Edit)/ Michael Mayer Balearic Mix)/(Full Vocal Mix)/Crunch Mix)/(Motor Remix) (CD)	20

DEPRAVED

86	Children Of Rev. GURT 6	COME ON DOWN (LP, with lyric inner)	12

DEPRESSIONS

77	Barn 2014 112	Living On Dreams/Family Planning (p/s)	20
78	Barn 2014 119	Messing With Your Heart/Street Kid (p/s)	18
78	Barn 2014 122	Get Out Of This Town/Basement Daze (p/s)	10
78	Barn 2314 105	THE DEPRESSIONS (LP)	15

MINT VALUE £

DEPTH CHARGE
89	Vinyl Solution STORM 08	Depth Charge (12")	8
89	Vinyl Solution STORM 13	Bounty Killers (12")	8

DEPUTIES
66	Strike JH 305	Given Half A Chance/Where Do People Go	10

DEPUTY DAWG
96	Peacefrog P F053	GUN SLINGER EP (12", plain sleeve)	10

(see also Luke Slater)

DEREK
68	London HLZ 10230	Cinnamon/This Is My Story	10

(see also Johnny Cymbal)

DEREK & THE DOMINOES
70	Polydor 2058 057	Tell The Truth/Roll It Over (withdrawn)	80+
71	Polydor 2058 130	Layla/Bell Bottom Blues (original, red paper label)	5
74	RSO 2090 104	Why Does Love Got To Be Sad?/Presence Of The Lord	5
82	RSO RSO 87	Layla/ERIC CLAPTON: Wonderful Tonight (p/s)	5
82	RSO RSOX 87	Layla/ERIC CLAPTON: Wonderful Tonight (live) (12", p/s)	8
71	Polydor 2625 005	LAYLA AND OTHER ASSORTED LOVE SONGS (2-LP)	18

(see also Eric Clapton, Bobby Whitlock)

DEREK & FRESHMEN
65	Oriole CB 305	Gone Away/I Stand Alone	15

(see also Derek Dean & Freshmen)

DEREK B
87	Music Of Life NOTE 3	Rock The Beat (12")	8

FRANK DE ROSA & HIS ORCHESTRA
58	London HLD 8576	Big Guitar/Irish Rock	30

DERRICK (Morgan) & JENNIFER
70	Crab CRAB 47	Need To Belong/Let's Have Some Fun	5
70	Crab CRAB 54	Rocking Good Way/Wipe These Tears	5

(see also Derrick Morgan)

DERRICK (Morgan) & LLOYDS (Clarke)
62	Blue Beat BB 135	Love And Leave Me (actually by Lloyd Clarke)/Merry Twist (actually "Whistle Stop Tour" by Roy Richards)	15

(see also Derrick Morgan, Lloyd Clarke)

DERRICK (Morgan) & NAOMI (Campbell)
65	Island WI 193	Two Of A Kind/I Want A Lover (credited to Derrick Morgan)	20
65	Ska Beat JB 185	Heart Of Stone/DERRICK MORGAN: Let Me Go	18
65	Ska Beat JB 188	I Wish I Were An Apple/DERRICK MORGAN: Around The Corner	18

(see also Derrick Morgan, Naomi, Don Drummond)

DERRICK (Morgan) & PATSY (Todd)
61	Blue Beat BB 57	Feel So Fine/ROLAND ALPHONSO & GROUP: Mean To Me	18
61	Blue Beat BB 65	Baby Please Don't Leave Me/Let The Good Times Roll	16
62	Blue Beat BB 97	Love Not To Brag/DRUMBAGO'S ALL STARS: Duck Soup	14
62	Blue Beat BB 100	In My Heart (actually by Derrick Morgan)/BELL'S GROUP: Kingston 13	14
62	Blue Beat BB 106	Oh Shirley/BASIL GABIDON'S GROUP: Sam The Fisherman (B-side actually by Roland Alphonso)	18
62	Blue Beat BB 121	Crying In The Chapel/Come Back My Love	15
62	Blue Beat BB 123	Oh My Love/Let's Go To The Party	15
62	Island WI 018	Housewife's Choice/Gypsy Woman	15
63	Blue Beat BB 152	Little Brown Jug/Mow Sen Wa (with Lloyd Clarke)	15
63	Blue Beat BB 160	Trying To Make You Mine (actually "Baby Please Don't Leave Me" by Derrick Morgan)/Hold Me	15
63	Island WI 055	Sea Wave/Look Before You Leap	18
64	Blue Beat BB 207	Lover Boy/The Moon	15
64	Blue Beat BB 224	Steal Away/Money	15
64	Blue Beat BB 247	Troubles/Right (B-side actually "Baby Face")	15
65	Blue Beat BB 291	You I Love/Let Me Hold Your hand (song actually "Steal Away")	15
65	Blue Beat BB 318	Eternity/Want My Baby	15
65	Island WI 224	The National Dance/DESMOND DEKKER & FOUR ACES: Mount Zion	25
66	Island WI 288	I Found A Queen/It's True My Darling	15
68	Nu Beat NB 008	Hey Boy, Hey Girl/Music Is The Food Of Life	12

(see also Derrick Morgan, Patsy Todd)

DERRICK (Morgan) & PAULETTE
69	Nu Beat NB 027	I'll Do It/Give You My Love	12

(see also Derrick Morgan, Paulette)

DERRICK (Morgan) & PAULINE (Morgan)
68	Pyramid PYR 6027	You Never Miss Your Water/DERRICK MORGAN: Got You On My Mind	12
68	Pyramid/J.J. PYR 6063	Don't Say/DERRICK MORGAN: Johnny Pram Pram	15

(see also Derrick Morgan, Patsy Todd, Basil Gabbidon)

DERRICK & SOUNDS
68	Pye 7N 17601	Power Of Love/I'll Take You Home	5
69	Pye 7N 17709	My Sly Sadie/I Can't Lose That Girl	5
69	Pye 7N 17801	Morning Papers And Margarine/Winter Of Your Love	12

DERRINGERS
61	Capitol CL 15189	(If You Cry) True Love, True Love/Sheree	20

GLEN DERRY ORCHESTRA
61	Oriole CB 1609	Blue Sax/Beatnik	8

HENRI DES
70	United Artists UP 35109	Return/Retour	18

DES (Bryan) ALLSTARS
70	Grape GR 3014	Night Food Reggae/Walk With Des	12
70	Grape GR 3015	If I Had A Hammer/Hammer Reggae	12
70	Grape GR 3016	Henry The Great/Black Scorcher	12

SUGAR PIE DE SANTO
64	Pye International 7N 25249	Soulful Dress/Use What You Got	30
64	Pye International 7N 25267	I Don't Wanna Fuss/I Love You So Much	30
66	Chess CRS 8034	There's Gonna Be Trouble/In The Basement (B-side with Etta James)	28
69	Chess CRS 8093	Soulful Dress/There's Gonna Be Trouble	15

(see also Etta James & Sugar Pie De Santo)

MICHAEL DES BARRES
74	Purple PUR 123	Leon/New Moon Tonight	8

(see also Silverhead, Detective, Phoenix)

DESCENDANTS
67	CBS 202545	Garden Of Eden/Lela	70

DESECTORS
70	GAS GAS 137	King Kong/Please Stay	6

DESERT WOLVES
87	Ugly Man UGLY 6T	Love Shattered Lives/Stopped In My Tracks/Desolation/Sunday Morning (12", p/s)	10
88	Ugly Man UGLY 9	Speak To Me Rochelle/Besotted (p/s)	6
88	Ugly Man UGLY 9T	Speak To Me Rochelle/Mexico/Besotted/La Petite Rochelle (12", p/s)	12

JACKIE DE SHANNON
62	Liberty LIB 55497	You Won't Forget Me/I Don't Think So Much	20
63	Liberty LIB 55563	Needles And Pins/Did He Call Today Mama?	20
64	Liberty LIB 55645	When You Walk In The Room/Till You Say You'll Be Mine	18
64	Liberty LIB 10165	Dancing Silhouettes/Hold Your Head High	12
64	Liberty LIB 10175	Don't Turn Your Back On Me/Be Good Baby	12
65	Liberty LIB 10192	She Don't Understand Him Like I Do/The Prince	12
65	Liberty LIB 10202	What The World Needs Now Is Love/It's Love Baby	7
65	Liberty LIB 12019	A Lifetime Of Loneliness/I Remember The Boy	10
66	Liberty LIB 66171	Come And Get Me/Splendour In The Grass	7
66	Liberty LIB 66202	I Can Make It With You/To Be Myself	7
66	Liberty LIB 66224	Come On Down/Find Me Love	20
68	Liberty LBF 15133	The Weight/Effervescent Blue	7
69	Liberty LBF 15238	Put A Little Love In Your Heart/Always Together	7
70	Liberty LBF 15281	Love Will Find A Way/I Let Go Completely	7
70	Liberty LBF 15324	What The World Needs Now/Keep Me In Mind	5
72	Atlantic K 10184	Vanilla Olay/I Wanna Roo You	5
72	Atlantic K 10241	Only Love Can Break Your Heart/Would You Like To Learn To Dance	5
65	Liberty LEP 2233	JACKIE (EP)	40
64	Liberty LBY 1182	THIS IS JACKIE DE SHANNON (LP)	20
65	Liberty LBY 1245	DON'T TURN YOUR BACK ON ME (LP)	20
65	Liberty LBY 3063	THIS IS JACKIE DE SHANNON (LP)	20
66	Liberty (S)BLY 3085	ARE YOU READY FOR THIS? (LP)	20
68	Liberty LBS 83117E	GREAT PERFORMANCES (LP)	20
69	Liberty LBS 83148E	ME ABOUT YOU (LP)	20
70	Liberty LBS 83304	PUT A LITTLE LOVE IN YOUR HEART (LP)	20
72	Atlantic K 40396	JACKIE (LP)	15

(see also Date With Soul)

DESIGN
70	CBS 5112	Willow Stream/Coloured Mile	7
71	Epic EPC 7119	Jet Song/Minstrel's Theme	10
72	Regal Zonophone RZ 3044	Colour All The World/Lazy Song	7
72	Regal Zonophone RZ 3060	Mayday/Yellow Bird	6
73	Regal Zonophone RZ 3082	One Sunny Day/End Of The Party	6
71	Epic EPC 64322	DESIGN (LP)	15
71	Epic EPC64653	TOMORROW IS SO FAR AWAY (LP, with insert)	30
73	Regal Zono. SLRZ 1037	DAY OF THE FOX (LP)	25

DESI ROOTS
79	Hawkeye HD 018	Hung-Up/Up-Town Rebel (12")	20
80	Hawkeye HD 025	Weed Fields/HAWKEYE ALL STARS: Burning (12")	40
80	Hawkeye HD 033	Go Deh Right/REVOLUTIONARIES: Go Right Deh (12")	25
80	Hawkeye HLP 007	DO IT RIGHT (LP)	45

DESIRELESS
88	CBS 565 902-9	FRANCOIS (CD)	22

JOHNNY DESMOND
53	MGM SP 1042	A Bushel And A Peck/ART LUND: If I Were A Bell	10
54	Vogue Coral Q 2019	The High And The Mighty/Got No Time	10
55	Vogue Coral Q 72055	Don't/There's No Happiness For Me (with Alan Dale & Buddy Greco)	10
55	Vogue Coral Q 72076	Play Me Hearts And Flowers/I'm So Ashamed	10
55	Vogue Coral Q 72090	Togetherness/A Straw Hat And A Cane	10
55	Vogue Coral Q 72099	Yellow Rose Of Texas/You're In Love With Someone	10
55	Vogue Coral Q 72110	Land Of The Pharaohs/This Too Shall Pass	8
56	Vogue Coral Q 72115	Sixteen Tons/Ballo Italiano	8
56	Vogue Coral Q 72153	Without You/I'll Cry Tomorrow	8
56	Vogue Coral Q 72170	A Little Love Can Go A Long Way/Please Don't Forget Me	8
56	Vogue Coral Q 72190	"The Proud Ones" Theme/I Only Know I Love You	8

Johnny DESMOND

56	Vogue Coral Q 72207	A Girl Named Mary/Run For The Sun Theme	8
57	Vogue Coral Q 72235	Where The River Meets The Sea/18th Century Music Box	
		(B-side with Jimmy Saunders)	8
57	Vogue Coral Q 72246	That's Where I Shine/I Just Want You To Want Me	8
57	Vogue Coral Q 72261	A White Sports Coat (And A Pink Carnation)/Just Lookin'.	12
57	Vogue Coral Q 72269	Shenandoah Rose/Consideration	8
58	MGM MGM 994	Hot Cha Cha/I'll Close My Eyes	5
60	Coral Q 72398	The Most Happy Fella/LANCERS: Joey, Joey, Joey	5
60	Philips PB 1044	Hawk/Playing The Field	25
62	Top Rank JAR 612	Twistin' Rose Of Texas/ Hello Honey	10
56	Vogue Coral LVA 9035	SOUVENIR D'ITALIE (LP)	25

LORRAE DESMOND (& REBELS)

54	Decca F 10375	Hold My Hand/On The Waterfront (78 rpm = £7)	12
54	Decca F 10398	Far Away (My Love Is Far Away)/No One But You (78 rpm = £6)	12
54	Decca F 10404	I Can't Tell A Waltz From A Tango/For Better, For Worse	
		(with Johnston Brothers)	12
55	Decca F 10461	A Boy On Saturday Night/Why — Oh Why? (78 rpm = £6)	12
55	Decca F 10510	Don't/Where Will The Baby's Dimple Be? (78 rpm = £6)	12
55	Decca F 10533	Stowaway/Heartbroken (B-side with Johnston Brothers) (78 rpm = £6)	10
55	Decca F 10612	You Should Know/Wake The Town And Tell The People (78 rpm = £6)	10
56	Parlophone R 4239	Written On The Wind/A House With Love In It (78 rpm = £6)	10
57	Parlophone R 4287	You Won't Be Around/Play The Music (as Lorrae Desmond & Rebels)	10
57	Parlophone R 4287	You Won't Be Around/Play The Music (as Lorrae Desmond & Rebels) (78)	6
57	Parlophone R 4320	Kansas City Special/Preacher, Preacher (as Lorrae Desmond & Rebels)	10
57	Parlophone R 4320	Kansas City Special/Preacher, Preacher (as Lorrae Desmond & Rebels) (78)	8
57	Parlophone R 4361	Ding-Dong Rock-a-billy Weddin'/Cabin Boy (as Lorrae Desmond & Rebels)	25
57	Parlophone R 4361	Ding-Dong Rock-a-billy Weddin'/Cabin Boy (as Lorrae Desmond & Rebels) (78)	9
58	Parlophone R 4400	Two Ships/Little David (78 rpm = £7)	8
58	Parlophone R 4430	Down By The River/The Secret Of Happiness (78 rpm = £10)	8
58	Parlophone R 4463	Soda Pop Hop/Blue, Blue Day (78 rpm = £10)	20
59	Parlophone R 4534	Tall Paul/Wait For It (78 rpm = £9)	10
60	Parlophone R 4670	Tell Me Again/Get Your Daddie's Car Tonight	10

MIKE DESMOND

57	Columbia DB 3954	Young And In Love/Two Loves (as Michael Desmond)	6
57	Columbia DB 4018	Chances Are/If You're Not Completely Satisfied (as Michael Desmond)	6
59	Top Rank JAR 225	If I Were The Sky/Tua	5
60	Top Rank JAR 298	The Happy Muleteer/Oh, So Wunderbar	5

PAUL DESMOND

| 60 | RCA 1373 | Take Ten/Embarcadero | 6 |

(see also Gerry Mulligan, Dave Brubeck)

DESOLATION ANGELS

| 84 | AM AM 266 | Valhalla/Boadicea (p/s) | 40 |
| 85 | Thameside TRR 111 | DESOLATION ANGELS (LP) | 50 |

DESPERATE BICYCLES

77	Refill RR 1	Smokescreen/Handlebars (p/s, same tracks both sides)	12
77	Refill RR 2	The Medium Was Tedium/Don't Back The Front (p/s, same tracks both sides)	12
78	Refill RR 4	Occupied Territory/Skill (p/s)	7
78	Refill RR 7	Grief Is Very Private/Obstructive/Conundrum (some copies may be in p/s)	8
80	Refill RR 6	REMORSE CODE (LP)	15

DESSIE & JOHN

| 69 | Downtown DT 440 | Boss Sound/Everything Is Alright | 10 |

DESTROY ALL MONSTERS

79	Cherry Red CHERRY 3	Bored/You're Gonna Die (p/s, red vinyl)	5
79	Cherry Red CHERRY 7	Meet The Creeper/November 22nd 1963 (p/s)	5
79	Cherry Red CHERRY 9	Nobody Knows/What Do I Get? (p/s)	5

(see also MC5)

DESTROYER

| 81 | Clean Kill SJP 829 | Evil Place/Stand And Deliver (no p/s) | 50 |

DESTROYERS

| 70 | Amalgamated AMG 856 | Niney Special/Danger Zone | 15 |
| 70 | Pressure Beat PR 5505 | Pressure Tonic/Machuki's Cooking (B-side actually with Count Machuki) | 20 |

(see also Soul Brothers, Nicky Thomas)

DESTRUCTORS (V)

82	Carnage BOOK 2	Meaningless Names/AK 47/Police State/Dachau/Death Squad (p/s)	5
82	Carnage Benelux KILL 2	Religion/Soldier Boy/Agent Orange/Corpse Gas (p/s)	5
80s		EXORCISE THE DEMONS OF YOUTH (EP, with insert)	8

(see also Blanks)

DETAILS

| 80 | Energy NRG 2 | Keep On Running/Run'ins (p/s) | 5 |
| 80 | Energy NRG 002 | Keep On Running/Run'ins (12", stickered plain sleeve, promo only) | 8 |

DETECTIVE

| 78 | Swansong SS 8504 | IT TAKES ONE TO KNOW ONE (LP, with inner sleeve) | 12 |

(see also Michael Des Barres)

DETERGENTS

| 65 | Columbia DB 7513 | Leader Of The Laundromat/Ulcers | 18 |
| 65 | Columbia DB 7591 | I Don't Know/The Blue Kangaroo | 10 |

DETONATORS

| 78 | Local LR 1 | Need Love Tonight/Great Big Ghetto/Shoob Shooby Do/ | |
| | | Give Me A Helping Hand (p/s) | 6 |

DETOURS
68	CBS 3213	Run To Me Baby/Hangin' On	30+
68	CBS 3401	Whole Lotta Lovin'/Pieces Of You	60

(see also Gene Latter)

DETROIT with MITCH RYDER
72	Paramount PARA 3022	It Ain't Easy/Long Neck Goose	5
72	Paramount SPFL 277	DETROIT (LP)	20

(see also Mitch Ryder)

DETROIT EMERALDS
71	Pye International 7N 25544	Do Me Right/Just Now And Then	10
71	Janus 6146 004	Wear This Ring/I Bet You Get The One	6
72	Janus 6146 007	You Want It, You Got It/Till You Decide To Come Home	6
72	Janus 6146 015	Do Me Right/Baby Let Me Take You In My Arms	6
72	Janus 6146 020	Feel The Need In Me/And I Love Her	8
73	Westbound 6146108	You're Getting A Little Too Smart/Lee	10
71	Janus 6310 204	DO ME RIGHT (LP)	20
72	Janus 6310 207	YOU WANT IT, YOU GOT IT (LP)	20
73	Janus 6309 101	ABE, JAMES AND IVORY (LP)	12

DETROIT ESCALATOR CO.
96	Ferox FERLP 2	SOUNDTRACK (313) (LP)	20

DETROITS
70	Fontana 6438 006	'TIS US OURSELVES (LP)	12

DETROIT SPINNERS
65	Tamla Motown TMG 514	Sweet Thing/How Can I? (demos credited to either 'Spinners' or 'Detroit Spinners' = £300/225)	200
65	Tamla Motown TMG 514	Sweet Thing/How Can I? (stock copies credited to 'Spinners')	200
65	Tamla Motown TMG 523	I'll Always Love You/Tomorrow May Never Come (as 'Spinners' or 'Detroit Spinners') (DJ copy = £175)	100/75
67	Tamla Motown TMG 627	For All We Know/I'll Always Love You	20/18
70	Tamla Motown TMG 755	It's A Shame/Together We Can Make Such Sweet Music (unissued)	
70	Tamla Motown TMG 755	It's A Shame/Sweet Thing (as Motown Spinners)	12
71	Tamla Motown TMG 766	Together We Can Make Such Sweet Music/Truly Yours (as Motown Spinners)	10
74	Tamla Motown TMG 871	Together We Can Make Such Sweet Music/Bad Bad Weather	12
80	Atlantic K 11558	Split Decision/Now That You're Mine Again	10
80	Atlantic K 11558	Split Decision/Now That You're Mine Again (12")	25
68	T. Motown (S)TML 11060	THE DETROIT SPINNERS (LP)	55
71	T. Motown STML 11182	SECOND TIME AROUND (LP, as Motown Spinners)	15

(see also Spinners, G.C. Cameron)

DEUCE COUP
67	Mercury MF 1013	A Clown In One Town/Angela (some in p/s)	12/6

DEUCE OF HEARTS
66	CBS 202345	Closer Together/The Times They Are A Changin'	7

JIMMY DEUCHAR
58	Tempo A 167	Bewitched/My Funny Valentine (as Jimmy Deuchar & His Pals) (78 rpm = £6)	6
55	Tempo EXA 18	JIMMY DEUCHAR ENSEMBLE (EP)	40
56	Esquire EP 93	JIMMY DEUCHAR QUARTET (EP)	40
56	Esquire EP 103	JIMMY DEUCHAR QUARTET (EP)	40
58	Tempo EXA 79	OPUS DE FUNK (EP, as Jimmy Deuchar Sextet)	40
58	Tempo EXA 81	SWINGIN' IN STUDIO TWO (EP)	40
59	Tempo EXA 88	WAIL (EP, with Victor Feldman Quintet)	40
54	Esquire 20-059	DIG DEUCHAR, DON'T DANCE (LP)	80
55	Tempo LAP 2	JIMMY DEUCHAR ENSEMBLE (10" LP)	250
56	Tempo TAP 4	TOP TRUMPETS (LP)	250
56	Vogue LDE	SHOWCASE (LP)	60
58	Tempo TAP 20	PAL JIMMY (LP)	400

(see also Victor Feldman)

BIG PETE DEUCHAR/DEUKER
63	Fontana 267 278 TF	Google Eye/There's A Hand Leading Me (as Big Pete Deuchar)	10
65	Columbia DB 7763	Goin' In Training/I Saw Your Face In The Moon	8

DEVIANTS
68	Stable STA 5601	You Got To Hold On/Let's Loot The Supermarket	30
67	Underground Imp. IMP 1	PTOOFF! (LP, foldout sleeve, private pressing via *IT* magazine)	140
68	Stable SLP 007	DISPOSABLE (LP, gatefold sleeve)	100
69	Transatlantic TRA 204	THE DEVIANTS THREE (LP, some with booklet)	80/60
69	Decca LK-R/SKL-R 4993	PTOOFF! (LP, reissue)	60
84	Psycho PSYCHO 25	HUMAN GARBAGE (LIVE AT DINGWALLS '84) (LP)	12

(see also Mick Farren, Pink Fairies, Larry Wallis)

DEVIL'S HOLE GANG
70s	Slow Burning Fuse SSSS 1	Free The People/Isn't It/Something To Look Forward To (p/s, with insert)	12

JOHNNY DEVLIN (& DETOURS)
64	Pye 7N 15598	Sometimes/If You Want Someone (as Johnny Devlin & Detours)	10
66	CBS 202085	Hung On You/Prove It	8
66	CBS 202339	My Strength; Heart Of Soul/I Can't Get You Off My Mind	8
67	CBS 202452	Tender Lovin' Care/Five O'Clock World	8
67	CBS 2751	Hurtin'/You Gotta Tell Me	7

DEVO
78	Stiff DEV 1	Jocko Homo/Mongoloid (foldout p/s)	6
78	Stiff DEV 2/BOY 1	(I Can't Get No) Satisfaction/Sloppy (I Saw My Baby Getting) (p/s)	6
78	Stiff BOY 1	(I Can't Get No) Satisfaction/Sloppy (I Saw My Baby Getting) (12", stickered p/s)	6

MINT VALUE £

78	Stiff ODD 1	BE STIFF (12" EP, white label)	8
79	Elevator NICE 1	Mechanical Man/Blockhead/Blackout/Auto-Modern (official bootleg, red/yellow stamped sleeves with plastic outer sleeve)	10
78	Virgin V 2106	Q: ARE WE NOT MEN? (LP, various colour vinyls)	12
78	Virgin VP 2106	Q: ARE WE NOT MEN? (LP, picture disc, with 'Flimsy Wrap' 33rpm 1-sided flexidisc [VDJ 27/Lyntone LYN 6260])	12

DEVON (Russell) & TARTANS
| 68 | Nu Beat NB 021 | Let's Have Some Fun/Making Love | 10 |

(see also Tartans)

DEVON (Russell) & SEDRIC (Myton)
| 69 | Blue Cat BS 158 | What A Sin Thing/Short Up Dress | 25 |

DEVONNES
| 75 | UK USA 5 | I'm Gonna Pick Up My Toys/Limits | 8 |

BARRY DE VORZON
| 58 | RCA RCA 1066 | Barbara Jean/JIMMY DELL: Teeny Weeny (78 rpm = £30) | 65 |
| 60 | Philips PB 993 | Betty Betty (Go Steady With Me)/Across The Street | 25 |

(see also Barry & Tamerlanes, Jimmy Dell)

DEVOTED
| 68 | Page One POF 076 | I Love George Best/United (initially in p/s) | 25/15 |

DEVOTIONS
| 64 | Columbia DB 7256 | Rip Van Winkle/I Love You For Sentimental Reasons | 100 |

JANINE DE WAYLENE & HER MARTENOT
| 60 | Top Rank JAR 363 | Faces In The Dark/Martenot Theme/Farewell Christina | 7 |
| 60 | Oriole CB 1576 | Faces In The Dark/Martenot Theme/Farewell Christina | 8 |

DEWDROPS
| 67 | Blue Beat BB 381 | Somebody's Knocking/By And By | 18 |

BRIAN DEWHURST
| 75 | Folk Heritage FHR 075 | THE HUNTER & THE HUNTED (LP) | 20 |

KEITH DEWHURST & ALBION BAND
| 80 | Charisma CDS 4020 | LARK RISE TO CANDLEFORD (A COUNTRY TAPESTRY) (LP, soundtrack) | 12 |

(see also Albion Band)

FAY DEWITT
| 54 | London HL 8021 | Misirlou/Snap Snap Snap Your Fingers (78) | 6 |

DANNY DEXTER
| 63 | London HLU 9690 | Sweet Mama/Go On | 20 |

EDDIE DEXTER & HIS BAND
| 55 | Capitol CL 14371 | Moonlight/The Verse Of Stardust | 8 |

RAY DEXTER & LAYABOUTS
| 62 | Decca F 11538 | The Coalman's Lament/Lonely Weekend | 30 |

DEXYS MIDNIGHT RUNNERS
| 85 | Mercury DEXYS 13 | An Extract From 'This Is What She's Like'/'This Is What She's Like' Finale (p/s) | 5 |
| 85 | Mercury DEXYSD 13 | An Extract From 'This Is What She's Like'/'This Is What She's Like' Finale// Marguerita Time/Reminisce Part One (double pack, gatefold p/s) | 8 |

(see also Killjoys, Kevin Rowland)

TRACEY DEY
| 64 | Stateside SS 287 | Go Away/Gonna Get Along Without You Now | 18 |

BARRY D'FANO
| 62 | Palette PG 9038 | Message Of Love/The Kiss That Broke My Heart | 10 |

DHARMA B featuring ACE OF CLUBS
| 90s | Acid Jazz JAZID 35T | Everything Is Going To The Beat (12", company sleeve) | 20 |

DHARMA BLUES BAND
| 69 | Major Minor SMPC 5017 | DHARMA BLUES (LP) | 45+ |

DIALS (Jamaica)
| 69 | Duke DU 48 | Bye Bye Love/It's Love | 7 |
| 69 | Duke DU 49 | Love Is A Treasure/DIAMONDS: I Want To Be | 7 |

DIALS (U.K.)
| 79 | Wessex WEX 266 | Maxine/Hey Denise (p/s) | 7 |
| 79 | Scene ACT1 | All I Hear/Running (p/s) | 10 |

DHAIMA
| 78 | Lightning LIG 528 | Ina Jah Children/THE MIGHTY TWO: Save The Children (12") | 10 |

BRIAN DIAMOND & THE CUTTERS
63	Decca F 11724	Jealousy Will Get You Nowhere/Brady Brady	18
64	Fontana TF 452	Shake, Shout And Go/Whatcha Gonna Do Now Pretty Baby	18
65	Pye 7N 15779	Big Bad Wolf/See If I Care	15
65	Pye 7N 15952	Bone Idol/Sands Of Time	15

(GREGG DIAMOND'S) BIONIC BOOGIE
79	Polydor PB 50	Chains/Hot Butterfly	5
79	Polydor POSPX 50	Chains/Hot Butterfly (12")	5
88	Urban URBX 16	Hot Butterfly/Mess Up The Boogie/When The Shit Hits The Fan (12", p/s)	8
79	Polydor 2391 322	BIONIC BOOGIE (LP)	12

JERRY DIAMOND
| 57 | London HLE 8496 | Sunburned Lips/Don't Trust Love (78 rpm = £20) | 40 |

LEE DIAMOND (& CHEROKEES)
61	Fontana H 310	I'll Step Down/Josephine (as Lee Diamond & Cherokees)	18
61	Fontana H 345	Stop Your Crying/You'll Want Me	18

(see also Cherokees)

NEIL DIAMOND
66	London HLZ 10049	Solitary Man/Do It	10
66	London HLZ 10072	Cherry, Cherry/I'll Come Running	10
66	London HLZ 10092	I Got The Feelin' (Oh No No)/The Boat That I Row	9
67	London HLZ 10111	You Got To Me/Someday Baby	9
67	London HLZ 10126	Girl, You'll Be A Woman Soon/You'll Forget	9
67	London HLZ 10151	Thank The Lord For The Night Time/The Long Way Home	9
67	London HLZ 10161	Kentucky Woman/The Time Is Now	8
68	London HLZ 10177	New Orleans/Hanky Panky	8
68	London HLZ 10187	Red Red Wine/Red Rubber Ball	8
68	Uni UN 503	Brooklyn Roads/Holiday Inn Blues	5
68	MCA MU 1033	Two-Bit Manchild/Broad Old Woman	5
69	MCA MU 1070	Brother Love's Travelling Salvation Show/A Modern Day Version Of Love	5
69	MCA MU 1087	Sweet Caroline (Good Times Never Seemed So Good)/Dig In	5
71	President PT 335	Kentucky Woman/Cherry, Cherry/I Thank The Lord For The Night Time (p/s)	7
87	CBS 651 201-7	I Dreamed A Dream/Sweet Caroline (box set with calendar)	6
66	London HA-Z 8307	THE FEEL OF NEIL DIAMOND (LP)	40
74	CBS Q 69067	SERENADE (LP, quadrophonic)	15
76	CBS Q 86004	BEAUTIFUL NOISE (LP, quadrophonic)	15
81	World Records ALBUM 91	THE BEST OF NEIL DIAMOND (4-LP box set, mail-order only)	22
96	Sony Publishing XPCD 708	THE NEIL DIAMOND SONG BOOK (CD, promo only)	20

DIAMOND BOYS
62	Parlophone GIB 102	Fool In Love/New Orleans (export issue)	25
63	RCA RCA 1351	Hey Little Girl/What'd I Say	15

(see also Albert Ammons)

DIAMOND HEAD
80	Happy Face MMDH 120	Shoot Out The Lights/Helpless (p/s)	15
80	Media SCREEN 1	Sweet And Innocent/Streets Of Gold (p/s)	15
81	DHM DHM 004	Waited Too Long/Play It Loud (p/s)	7
81	DHM DHM 005	DIAMOND LIGHTS EP (Diamond Lights/ We Won't Be Back/I Don't Got/It's Electric) (12", p/s)	30
82	MCA DHM 101	FOUR CUTS (EP, p/s)	7
82	MCA DHMT 101	FOUR CUTS (12" EP, with insert)	12
82	MCA DHM 102/MSAM 23	In The Heat Of The Night/Play It Loud (live)//Sweet And Innocent (live)/ (Interview With Tommy Vance) (double pack, gatefold p/s)	8
82	MCA DHMT 102	In The Heat Of The Night (Full Length Version)/Play It Loud (live) (12", p/s)	10
83	MCA DHM 103	Makin' Music/(Andy Peebles Interview) (p/s)	8
83	MCA DHMT 103	Makin' Music/(Andy Peebles Interview) (12", p/s)	15
83	MCA DHM 104	Out Of Phase/The Kingmaker (p/s)	5
83	MCA DHMP 104	Out Of Phase/The Kingmaker (picture disc)	6
83	MCA DHMT 104	Out Of Phase/The Kingmaker/Sucking My Love (live) (12", p/s)	30
92	Bronze	Wild In The Streets (12", p/s, 1 side etched)	8
80	DHM MMDHLP 105	LIGHTNING TO THE NATIONS (LP, plain or printed white labels, plain white sleeve, sold at gigs, a few signed in blue ink & available via *Sounds*)	60/50
81	MCA DH 1001	LIVING ON BORROWED TIME (LP, gatefold sleeve with inner sleeve, some with poster & fan club insert)	25/15
83	MCA DH 1002	CANTERBURY (LP)	12
86	Metal Masters METALP 110	BEHOLD THE BEGINNING (LP, remixed reissue of 1st LP)	15
87	FM WKFMLP 92	AM I EVIL (LP, with inner sleeve)	20

DIAMONDS (Jamaica)
72	Songbird SB 1079	Mash Up/DYNAMITES: Mash Up (Version)	6

(see also Dymonds, Sir Collins Band)

DIAMONDS (U.K.)
63	Philips BF 1264	The Lost City/Chasey Chasey	15

DIAMONDS (U.S.)
55	Vogue Coral Q 72109	Black Denim Trousers And Motorcycle Boots/Nip Sip (78 rpm = £25)	50
55	Mercury MT 121	Love, Love, Love/Ev'ry Night About This Time (78)	2
57	Mercury MT 148	Little Darlin'/Faithful And True (78)	8
57	Mercury MT 167	Don't Say Goodbye/Words Of Love (78)	15
57	Mercury MT 179	Oh, How I Wish/Zip Zip (78)	12
58	Mercury 7MT 187	Silhouettes/Honey Bird (78 rpm, Mercury MT 187 = £12)	40
58	Mercury 7MT 195	The Stroll/Land Of Beauty (78 rpm, Mercury MT 195 = £15)	35
58	Mercury 7MT 207	Don't Let Me Down/High Sign (78 rpm, Mercury MT 207 = £18)	35
58	Mercury 7MT 208	Straight Skirts/Patsy (78 rpm, Mercury MT208 = £20)	50
58	Mercury 7MT 233	Where Mary Go?/Kathy-O (78 rpm, Mercury MT 233 = £15)	8
58	Mercury AMT 1004	Eternal Lovers/Walking Along (78 rpm = £15)	12
59	Mercury AMT 1024	She Say (Oom Dooby Doom)/From The Bottom Of My Heart (78 rpm = £30)	12
60	Mercury AMT 1086	Tell The Truth/Real True Love	25
61	Mercury AMT 1156	One Summer Night/It's A Doggone Shame	15
57	Mercury MEP 9515	PRESENTING THE DIAMONDS (EP)	35
57	Mercury MEP 9523	THE DIAMONDS VOL. 1 (EP)	45
58	Mercury MEP 9527	THE DIAMONDS VOL. 2 (EP)	45
58	Mercury MEP 9530	THE DIAMONDS VOL. 3 (EP)	45
59	Mercury ZEP 10003	DIG THE DIAMONDS (EP)	45
59	Mercury ZEP 10020	THE DIAMONDS MEET PETE RUGOLO (EP)	22
59	Mercury ZEP 10026	DIAMONDS ARE TRUMPS (EP)	45
60	Mercury ZEP 10053	STAR STUDDED DIAMONDS (EP)	45

DIAMONDS

61	Mercury ZEP 10097	PETE RUGOLO LEADS THE DIAMONDS (EP, also stereo SEZ 10912)....... 25/35
57	Mercury MPT 7526	THE DIAMONDS (10" LP)... 150
60	Mercury MMC 14039	SONGS FROM THE OLD WEST (LP)...................................... 22
	(see also Pete Rugolo)	

DIAMOND TWINS
| 66 | HMV POP 1508 | Crying The Night Away/Start The World Spinning Again................... 6 |
| | (see also Sonia Kent) | |

DIANE & JAVELINS
| 66 | Columbia DB 7819 | Heart And Soul/Who's The Girl...................................... 55 |

DIANE & THE NEW WORLDS
| 71 | Stereo Gold Award MER 350 | TAMLA HITS (LP)... 12 |

(PAUL) DI'ANNO
84	FM VHF 1	Heart User/Road Rat (p/s)... 8
84	FM WKFM LP1	DI'ANNO (LP, blue vinyl)... 15
84	FM WKFM PD1	DI'ANNO (LP, picture disc)... 18
	(see also Gogmagog, Iron Maiden)	

DIATONES
| 61 | Starlite ST45 057 | Ruby Has Gone/Oh Baby Come Dance With Me....................... 100 |

MANU DIBANGO
73	London HL 10423	Soul Makossa/Lily.. 8
73	London SH 8451	O BOSO (LP).. 20
75	Creole CRLP 503	MAKOSSA MUSIC (LP)... 15
78	Decca SKL-R 5296	AFROVISION (LP)... 12
79	Decca SKL-R 5303	MANU '76 (LP)... 12

BILLY DICE & SHENLEY DUFFUS
| 73 | Pama 874 | Women Smarter/Standing On The Hill................................ 8 |

LLOYD DICE
| 70 | Joe JRS 5 | Trial Of Pama Dice/JOE: Jughead Returns........................... 15 |
| | (see also Trevor Lloyd) | |

DICE THE BOSS
69	Duke/Joe DU 51	Gun The Man Down/JOE MANSANO: The Thief...................... 20
69	Duke/Joe DU 52	But Officer/JOE'S ALL STARS: Reggae On The Shore................. 15
70	Duke/Joe DU 57	Your Boss D.J./TITO SIMON: Read The News....................... 20
70	Joe's JRS 17	The Informer/Cool It... 20
70	Explosion EX 2017	Funky Monkey/JOE'S ALL STARS: Funky Monkey Version............ 15
70	Explosion EX 2020	Funky Duck/Dunkier Than Duck..................................... 15
	(see also Pama Dice, Joe The Boss)	

PAMA DICE
69	Jackpot JP 715	Honky Tonk Popcorn/Bongo Man..................................... 12
69	Jackpot JP 716	Sin, Sun And Sex/Reggae Popcorn.................................. 12
	(see also Dice The Boss, Joe The Boss)	

DICK & DEE DEE
61	London HLG 9408	The Mountain's High/I Want Someone................................ 12
62	London HLG 9483	Goodbye To Love/Swing Low.. 12
62	Liberty LIB 55412	Tell Me/Will You Always Love Me.................................... 6
63	Warner Bros WB 96	Young And In Love/Say To Me....................................... 6
63	Warner Bros WB 111	Where Did The Good Times Go/Guess Our Love Must Show.......... 6
63	Warner Bros WB 119	Turn Around/Don't Leave Me.. 6
64	Warner Bros WB 126	All My Trails/Don't Twice, It's All Right............................. 7
64	Warner Bros WB 138	Remember When/You Were Mine..................................... 7
64	Warner Bros WB 145	Thou Shalt Not Steal/Just 'Round The River Bend.................... 6
65	Warner Bros WB 156	Be My Baby/Room 404... 16
65	Warner Bros WB 5671	Use What You've Got/P.S. 1402..................................... 6
63	Warner Bros WM/WS 8132	YOUNG AND IN LOVE (LP, mono/stereo)........................... 30/40
63	Warner Bros WM/WS 8150	TURN AROUND (LP, mono/stereo).................................. 30/40

DOLES DICKEN'S BAND
| 58 | London HLD 8639 | Piakukaungchung (Pie-ah-coo-ka-ung-chung)/Our Melody................. 10 |

DICKENS
| 80 | Hawkmoon ROCK 101 | STANDING OUT (LP, private pressing)................................ 12 |
| | (see also Ice) | |

CHARLES DICKENS
65	Pye 7N 15887	That's The Way Love Goes/In The City................................ 10
65	Pye 7N 15938	I Stand Alone/Hey Little Girl.. 10
66	Immediate IM 025	So Much In Love/Our Soul Brothers................................. 22
	(see also Habits)	

LITTLE JIMMY DICKENS
| 54 | Columbia DC 670 | Then I Had To Turn Around/Hot Diggity Dog (78, export issue)............. 10 |
| 65 | CBS 201969 | May The Bird Of Paradise Fly Up Your Nose/My Eyes Are Jealous......... 6 |

DICKIES
78	A&M AMS 7368	Paranoid/I'm OK, You're OK (p/s, clear, black or milky vinyl)............ 5/6/7
78	A&M AMS 7373	Eve Of Destruction/Doggie Do (p/s, pink or black vinyl)................ 5
78	A&M AMS 7391	Give It Back/You Drive Me Ape (p/s, white or black vinyl)............... 5
78	A&M AMS 7403	Silent Night/The Sounds Of Silence (p/s, white or black vinyl)........... 6/5
79	A&M AMS 7431	Banana Splits/Hideous/Got It At The Store
		(p/s, opaque or translucent yellow vinyl; also black vinyl)............. 5/7/6
79	A&M AMS 7469	Nights In White Satin/Waterslide (p/s, white vinyl).................... 5
79	A&M AMS 7491	Manny, Moe And Jack/She Loves Me Not (p/s, black vinyl only)............. 10

80	A&M AMS 7504	Fan Mail/Tricia Toyota (I'm Stuck In A Pagoda) (opaque or translucent red vinyl, poster p/s)	8
80	A&M AMS 7544	Gigantor/Bowling With Bedrock Barney (yellow vinyl, p/s with full colour or b&w reverse)	10
90	Overground OVER 12	Just Say Yes/Ayatollah You So (p/s with lyric sheet, mauve, blue or white vinyl, 2,000 of each colour)	6
90	Overground OVER 12	Just Say Yes/Ayatollah You So (black vinyl test pressing, 50 only)	15
90	Overground OVER 017	Roadkill (flexidisc available on 'Just Say Yes' European Tour, no p/s, 5000 only)	5
95	Plastic Head HOLE 008	Make It So/Oh Baby (p/s, black vinyl, 1,000 only)	6
79	A&M AMLE 64742	THE INCREDIBLE SHRINKING DICKIES (LP, black or yellow vinyl) each 14
79	A&M AMLE 64742	THE INCREDIBLE SHRINKING DICKIES (LP, blue or orange vinyl, with black or red-and-black on sleeve)	18/22
79	A&M AMLH 68510	DAWN OF THE DICKIES (LP, blue or black vinyl)	20/14

(see also Chuck Wagon)

BRUCE DICKINSON

90	EMI EM 138	Tattooed Millionaire/Ballad Of Mutt (paper label, glossy p/s)	6
90	EMI EMPD 138	Tattooed Millionaire/Ballad Of Mutt (shaped picture disc)	12
90	EMI EMPD 142	All The Young Dudes/Darkness Be My Friend (shaped picture disc with plinth)	12
90	EMI EMCD 142	All The Young Dudes/Darkness Be My Friend/Sin City (CD picture disc)	12
90	EMI EMPD 151	Dive! Dive! Dive!/Riding With The Angels (live)/Sin City (live)/ Black Night (live) (12", picture disc)	12
94	EMI EM 341	Shoot All The Clowns/Over And Out (p/s, clear vinyl with insert)	5

(see also Iron Maiden, Samson, Xero, Rock Aid Armenia)

BARBARA DICKSON

74	RSO 2090 144	Here Comes The Sun/The Long And Winding Road	5
69	Trailer LER 3002	THE FATE O'CHARLIE (LP)	45
70	Decca SKL 5041	THRO' RECENT YEARS (LP, with Archie Fisher)	35
71	Decca SKL 5058	DO RIGHT WOMAN (LP)	40
72	Decca SKL 5116	FROM THE BEGGAR'S MANTLE FRINGED WITH GOLD (LP)	40
74	RSO 2394 141	JOHN, PAUL, GEORGE, RINGO AND BERT (LP, with London cast)	30

DICTATORS with TONY & HOWARD

63	Oriole CB 1934	So Long Little Girl/Say Little Girl	20

(see also Tony & Howard)

DICTATORS

77	Asylum K 13091	Search And Destroy/Sleepin' With The TV On (no p/s)	8
77	Asylum K 53061	MANIFEST DESTINY (LP)	12

BO DIDDLEY

59	London HLM 8913	The Great Grandfather/Crackin' Up (78 rpm = £40)	78
59	London HLM 8975	Say Man/The Clock Strikes Twelve (78 rpm = £40)	78
60	London HLM 9035	Say Man, Back Again/She's Alright	75
60	London HLM 9112	Road Runner/My Story	55
62	Pye Intl. 7N 25165	You Can't Judge A Book By The Cover/I Can Tell	29
63	Pye Intl. 7N 25193	Who Do You Love?/The Twister	18
63	Pye Intl. 7N 25210	Bo Diddley/Detour	18
63	Pye Intl. 7N 25216	You Can't Judge A Book By The Cover/I Can Tell (reissue)	12
63	Pye Intl. 7N 25217	Pretty Thing/Road Runner	15
63	Pye Intl. 7N 25217	Bo Diddley Is A Lover/Doin' The Jaguar	15
64	Pye Intl. 7N 25235	Memphis/Monkey Diddle	15
64	Pye Intl. 7N 25243	Mona/Gimme Gimme	16
64	Pye Intl. 7N 25258	Mama Keep Your Big Mouth Shut/Jo-Ann	15
65	Chess CRS 8000	Hey Good Lookin'/You Ain't Bad (As You Claim To Be)	15
65	Chess CRS 8014	Somebody Beat Me/Mush Mouth Millie	15
65	Chess CRS 8021	Let The Kids Dance/Let Me Pass	15
66	Chess CRS 8026	500% More Man/Stop My Monkey	15
66	Chess CRS 8036	We're Gonna Get Married/Easy	15
67	Chess CRS 8053	Ooh Baby/Back To School	12
67	Chess CRS 8057	Wrecking My Love Life/Boo-Ga-Loo Before You Go	18
68	Chess CRS 8078	Another Sugar Daddy/I'm High Again	10
69	Chess CRS 8088	Bo Diddley 1969/Soul Train	10
72	Chess 6145 002	I Said Shut Up Woman/I Love You More Than You'll Ever Know	8
56	London RE-U 1054	RHYTHM AND BLUES WITH BO DIDDLEY (EP, gold label lettering)	225
63	Pye Intl. NEP 44014	HEY! BO DIDDLEY (EP)	25
64	Pye Intl. NEP 44019	THE STORY OF BO DIDDLEY (EP)	25
64	Pye Intl. NEP 44031	BO DIDDLEY IS A LUMBERJACK (EP)	28
64	Pye Intl. NEP 44036	DIDDLING (EP)	28
65	Chess CRE 6008	I'M A MAN (EP)	30
66	Chess CRE 6023	ROOSTER STEW (EP)	30
59	London HA-M 2230	GO BO DIDDLEY (LP)	325
62	Pye Jazz NJL 33	BO DIDDLEY IS A GUNSLINGER (LP)	40
63	Pye Intl. NPL 28025	HEY! BO DIDDLEY (LP)	25
63	Pye Intl. NPL 28026	BO DIDDLEY (LP)	25
63	Pye Intl. NPL 28029	BO DIDDLEY RIDES AGAIN (LP)	25
63	Pye Intl. NPL 28032	BO DIDDLEY'S BEACH PARTY (LP)	22
64	Pye Intl. NPL 28034	BO DIDDLEY IN THE SPOTLIGHT (LP)	35
64	Pye Intl. NPL 28049	16 ALL-TIME HITS (LP)	25
64	Chess CRL 4002	HEY GOOD LOOKIN' (LP)	32
65	Chess CRL 4507	LET ME PASS (LP)	32
67	Chess CRL 4525	THE ORIGINATOR (LP)	32
68	Chess CRL 4529	SUPER BLUES (LP, with Muddy Waters & Little Walter)	40
68	Chess CRL 4537	THE SUPER SUPER BLUES BAND (LP, with Muddy Waters & Howlin' Wolf)	50

71	Chess 6310107	ANOTHER DIMENSION (LP)	30
73	Chess 6499 476	THE LONDON SESSIONS (LP)	15

(see also Chuck Berry & Bo Diddley)

DIDDY MEN
65	Columbia DB 7782	The Song Of The Diddy Men/Hello Doddy	8

DIDJITS
95	Touch & Go RCRPA 11	Pigs (1-sided white label)	5

DIE ELECTRIC EELS
78	Rough Trade RT 008	Agitated/Cyclotron (p/s)	15

DIESEL M
94	Choci's Chewns CCB 001	M FOR MULTIPLE (12", blue vinyl, 666 only)	25
95	Choci's Chewns DDL 001	M FOR MANGOES (12", red vinyl, 666 only)	25

(see also µ-Ziq)

MARLENE DIETRICH
52	Columbia SCM 5010	Too Old To Cut The Mustard/Good For Nothing (with Rosemary Clooney)	15
53	Philips PB 164	Dot's Nice — Donna Fights/It's The Same (with Rosemary Clooney) (78)	6
54	Philips PB 314	Besides/Land, Sea And Air (with Rosemary Clooney) (78)	6
57	London HLD 8492	Near You/Another Spring, Another Love	18
63	HMV POP 1196	Lili Marlene/Sag Mir Wo Die Blumen Sind?	6
65	HMV POP 1379	Where Have All The Flowers Gone?/Blowin' In The Wind	6
65	Pye 7N 15770	Go Away From My Window/Shir Hatan	6
57	HMV 7EG 8257	MARLENE DIETRICH IN 'THE BLUE ANGEL' (EP)	25
58	London RED 1146	MARLENE DIETRICH (EP)	20
64	HMV 7EG 8844	RETURNS TO GERMANY (EP)	15
53	Brunswick LA 8591	SOUVENIR ALBUM (10" LP)	25
54	Philips BBR 8006	AT THE CAFÉ DE PARIS (10" LP, introduced by Noel Coward)	25
59	Philips BBL 7322	LILI MARLENE (LP)	15
60	Philips BBL 7386	DIETRICH IN RIO (LP, also stereo SBBL 571)	each 15
63	HMV CLP 1659	RETURNS TO GERMANY (LP)	15
65	Pye NPL 18113	DIETRICH IN LONDON (LP)	15

(see also Rosemary Clooney)

DIF JUZ
81	4AD BAD 109	HU/RE/MI/CS (12" EP)	15
81	4AD BAD 116	VIBRATING AIR: Heset/Diselt/Gunet/Soarn (12" EP)	12
83	Red Flame RFM 24	WHO SAYS SO (LP)	15
85	Pleasantly Surprised PS 9	TIME CLOCK TURNS BACK (cassette, with inserts)	40

RICHARD DIGANCE
70s	Coast COASTAL 4	SONG FROM A BOOK (LP)	12

DIGA RHYTHM BAND
76	United Artists UAG 29975	DIGA RHYTHM BAND (LP)	22

(see also Grateful Dead, Mickey Hart, Jerry Garcia)

STEVE DIGGLE
80	Faulty Products FEP 7000	Fifty Years Of Comparative Wealth/Shut Out The Light/ Here Comes The Fire Brigade (unreleased)	25

(see also Buzzcocks, Flag Of Convenience)

DIGITAL PRINCESS
02	Mosquito MSQ 019	LISTEN TO ME TENDER (12" EP)	8

MOSES & JOSHUA (DILLARD)
67	Stateside SS 2059	My Elusive Dreams/What's Better Than Love (as Moses & Joshua Dillard) (DJ copy = £45)	20
68	Bell BELL 1018	Get Out Of My Heart/They Don't Want Us Together (as Moses & Joshua)	20
72	Mojo 2092 054	My Elusive Dreams/Get Out Of My Heart	8

DILLARD & CLARK
69	A&M AMS 764	Radio Song/Why Not Your Baby	6
69	A&M AMLS 939	THE FANTASTIC EXPEDITION OF DILLARD & CLARK (LP)	20
69	A&M AMLS 966	THROUGH THE MORNING, THROUGHTHENIGHT (LP)	20

(see also Gene Clark, Byrds, Dillards)

DILLARDS
65	Capitol CL 15420	Nobody Knows/Ebo Walker	7
69	Elektra EKSN 45048	Reason To Believe/Nobody Knows	7
69	Elektra EKSN 45062	She Sang Hymns Out Of Tune/Single Saddle	6
69	Elektra EKSN 45081	Rainmaker/West Montana Hanna	6
68	Elektra EKS 74035	WHEATSHEAF SUITE (LP)	15
69	Polydor 236 559	BACK PORCH BLUE GRASS (LP)	15
70	Elektra EKS 74054	COPPERFIELDS (LP)	15

(see also Dillard & Clark)

DILLINGER
73	Duke DU 149	Headquarters (as Dellenger)/CHENLEY DUFFAS: Black Girl In My Bed	10
73	Downtown DT 512	Tighten Up Skank/Middle East Rock	10
76	Black Swan WIP 6355	Bionic Dread/Eastman Skank	10
79	Island ISL 976	Cokane In My Brain/Power	5
77	Black Swan WIP 6380	Natty BSc/Buckingham Palace	10
77	Black Swan BS 7	Cocaine In My Brain/Buckingham Palace/Ragnampiza (12")	15
79	Jamaica Sound JSD 921	Dread Call Fred/Lamb's Bread (let go the dread) (12", with Sugar Minott)	8
76	Black Swan ILPS 9455	BIONIC DREAD (LP)	50
77	Magnum DEAD 1001	TALKIN' BLUES (LP)	50

(see also David Isaacs)

DILLINGER V TRINITY
78	Burning Sounds BSLP 1003	CLASH (LP)	35

DILLINJA
93	Cybotron DILL 01	Steal The Way/Forever Fierce (1-sided 12")	20
93	Cybotron DILL 03	From Beyond/Ride It Hard (1-sided 12")	20
93	Cybotron DILL 04	Sine/Dark Science (1-sided 12")	20
94	Deadly Vinyl D2	Deadly Ceremonies/Soverign Melody (12")	15
94	Deadly Vinyl D3	Deadly Deep Subs/Calculus Beats (12")	15
94	Logic Productions DM 003	You Don't Know (Remix)/Heavenly Bass (12")	20
	(Cybotron featuring Dillinja)		

TODD DILLINGHAM
95	Woronzow WOO 25	SGT. KIPPER (2-LP)	18

PHYLLIS DILLON
66	Doctor Bird DB 1061	Don't Stay Away (as Phillis Dillon)/TOMMY McCOOK & SUPERSONICS: What Now	50
67	Trojan TR 006	This Is A Lovely Way/Thing Of The Past (as Phyllis Dellon)	30
67	Treasure Isle TI 7003	This Is A Lovely Way/Thing Of The Past	25
67	Treasure Isle TI 7015	Perfidia/It's Rocking Time	50
68	Treasure Isle TI 7041	I Wear This Ring/Don't Touch Me Tomato	18
69	Trojan TR 651	Love Is All I Had/Boys And Girls Reggae (as Phillis Dylon)	50
69	Trojan TR 671	The Right Track/TOMMY McCOOK & SUPERSONICS: Moonshot	12
69	Trojan TR 686	Lipstick On Your Collar (as Phillis Dillon)/TOMMY McCOOK & SUPERSONICS: Tribute To Rameses	12
70	Duke Reid DR 2508	This Is Me/Skabuvie (act. If Your Name Is Andy/Ska Vovi by Dorothy Reid)	12
70	Duke DU 76	Walk Through This World/The Rooster	8
71	Treasure Isle TI 7058	One Life To Live, One Love To Give/TOMMY McCOOK: My Best Dress	12
71	Treasure Isle TI 7070	Midnight Confession/TOMMY McCOOK & SOUL SYNDICATE: Version	12
72	Sioux SI 009	In The Ghetto/NYAH EARTH: Knight Of The Long Knives	12
72	Trojan TRL 41	ONE LIFE TO GIVE (LP)	45

DIMENSIONALS
53	London L 1217	Sleepy Time Gal/DON BAKER/DIMENSIONALS: Drinkin' Pop-Sodee Odee (78)	30

DIMENSIONS
65	Parlophone R 5294	Tears On My Pillow/You Don't Have To Whisper	35

DIMPLES
66	Decca F 12537	The Love Of A Lifetime/My Heart Is Tied To You	40
	(see also Gospel Garden, Amazing Blondel)		

DIMPLES & EDDIE with RICO's COMBO
62	Planetone RC 3	Fleet Street/Good Bye World	20

D INFLUENCE
90s	Acid Jazz JAZID 30T	I'm The One (12", p/s)	15

DINGER
85	Face Value FVRA 221	Air Of Mystery/I Love To Love (no p/s)	35
	(see also Erasure)		

DINGLE BROTHERS
71	Dynamic DYN 418	You Don't Know/CABLES: Rich Man, Poor Man	6

BOB DINI
53	London L 1213	Too Long/Remember Me (78)	8
54	London HL 8019	Good-bye My Love/Sometime (78)	10

MARK DINNING
60	MGM MGM 1053	Teen Angel/Bye Now Baby	15
60	MGM MGM 1069	You Win Again/A Star Is Born (A Love Is Dead)	10
60	MGM MGM 1101	The Lovin' Touch/Come Back To Me (My Love)	10
61	MGM MGM 1125	Top Forty, News, Weather And Sport/Suddenly	12
62	MGM MGM 1148	In A Matter Of Moments/What Will My Mary Say	10
62	MGM MGM 1155	All Of This For Sally/The Pickup	10
65	Hickory 45-1293	Dial Al 1-4883/I'm Glad We Fell In Love	8

DINNING SISTERS
55	Polygon P 1161	Goofus/Mama (He Treats Your Daughter Mean) (78)	12
55	London HLF 8179	Drifting And Dreaming/Truly (78 rpm = £20)	55
56	London HLF 8218	Hold Me Tight/Uncle Joe (78 rpm = £20)	55
	(see also 'Tennessee' Ernie Ford)		

KENNY DINO
61	HMV POP 960	Your Ma Said You Cried In Your Sleep Last Night/Dream A Girl	12

DINO, DESI & BILLY
65	Reprise R 20367	I'm A Fool/So Many Ways	12
66	Reprise R 23047	Not The Loving Kind/Chimes Of Freedom	12

DINOSAUR JR
88	Blast First BFFP 30	Freak Scene/Keep The Glove (p/s)	5
88	Blast First BFFP 30	Freak Scene (censored)/Keep The Glove (plain white labels, no p/s, promo only)	5
89	The Catalogue CAT 069/2	Just Like Heaven/LUNACHICKS: Get Off The Road (33rpm square flexidisc free with *The Catalogue* magazine)	10/6
89	Blast First BFFP 47	Just Like Heaven/Throw Down (p/s)	5
89	Blast First BFFP 47T	Just Like Heaven/Throw Down/Chunks (A Last Rites Tune) (12", p/s)	8
89	Blast First BFFP 47CD	Just Like Heaven/Throw Down/Chunks (A Last Rites Tune)/Freak Scene (Uncensored Version)/Keep The Glove (CD, picture disc)	12
97	Trade 2 TRDSC 009	I'm Insane (2000 copies pressed)	8

DIO

75	Purple PUR 128	Sitting In A Dream (as Ronnie Dio featuring Roger Glover & Guests)/	
		JOHN LAWTON: Little Chalk Blue	10
83	Vertigo DIOP 2	Rainbow In The Dark/Stand Up And Shout (live) (picture disc)	7
84	Vertigo DIOP 4	Mystery/Eat Your Heart Out (live) (picture disc)	6
85	Vertigo DIOD 5	Rock'n'Roll Children/Sacred Heart (gatefold p/s)	5
85	Vertigo DIOW 512	Rock'n'Roll Children/We Rock (live)/The Last In Line (live)	
		(12", white vinyl, stickered PVC sleeve)	8
85	Vertigo DIOFP 6	Hungry For Heaven/King Of Rock And Roll (p/s, with poster & sticker)	5
85	Vertigo DIOP 6	Hungry For Heaven/King Of Rock And Roll (dragon-shaped picture disc)	8
85	Vertigo DIOW 612	Hungry For Heaven/The Message (12", white vinyl)	8
86	Vertigo DIOP 710	THE DIO EP (10", shaped picture disc)	8
86	Vertigo DIO 712	THE DIO EP (12", p/s with family tree)	8
87	Vertigo DIOP 912	Hey Angel/Why Are They Watching Me?/Rock'n'Roll Children/Mystery	
		(12", picture disc with insert)	8
86	Vertigo VERB 40	INTERMISSION (mini-LP with postcards & discography,	
		stickered sleeve)	12

(see also Elf, Rainbow, Roger Glover, Black Sabbath, John Lawton)

DION (& BELMONTS)

78s

58	London HL 8646	I Wonder Why/Teen Angel (as Dion & Belmonts)	85
58	London HL 8718	I Can't Go On (Rosalie)/No One Knows (as Dion & Belmonts)	55
59	London HL 8799	Don't Pity Me/Just You (as Dion & Belmonts)	55
59	London HLU 8874	A Teenager In Love/I've Cried Before (as Dion & Belmonts)	50
59	Pye International 7N 25038	A Lover's Prayer/Every Little Thing I Do (as Dion & Belmonts).	90
60	London HLU 9030	Where Or When/That's My Desire (as Dion & Belmonts)	120

SINGLES

58	London HL 8646	I Wonder Why/Teen Angel (as Dion & Belmonts)	70
58	London HL 8718	I Can't Go On (Rosalie)/No One Knows (as Dion & Belmonts)	55
59	London HL 8799	Don't Pity Me/Just You (as Dion & Belmonts)	55
59	London HL 8874	A Teenager In Love/I've Cried Before (mispressing as Dion & Delmonts) ...	45
59	London HLU 8874	A Teenager In Love/I've Cried Before (as Dion & Belmonts)	42

(The above 45s were originally issued with triangular centres, round-centre re-pressings are worth two-thirds these values.)

59	Pye International 7N 25038	A Lover's Prayer/Every Little Thing I Do (as Dion & Belmonts).	50
60	London HLU 9030	Where Or When/That's My Desire (as Dion & Belmonts)	28
60	Top Rank JAR 368	When You Wish Upon A Star/My Private Joy (as Dion & Belmonts)	20
60	Top Rank JAR 503	In The Still Of The Night/Swinging On A Star (as Dion & Belmonts)	20
60	Top Rank JAR 521	Lonely Teenager/Little Miss Blue	20
61	Top Rank JAR 545	Havin' Fun/North-East End Of The Corner	15
61	Top Rank JAR 586	Runaround Sue/Runaway Girl	12
62	HMV POP 971	The Wanderer/The Majestic	12
62	HMV POP 1020	Lovers Who Wander/(I Was) Born To Cry	10
62	Stateside SS 115	Little Diane/Lost For Sure	10
62	Stateside SS 139	Love Came To Me/Little Girl.	8
63	CBS AAG 133	Ruby Baby/He'll Only Hurt You	10
63	Stateside SS 161	Sandy/Faith	20
63	CBS AAG 145	This Little Girl/The Loneliest Man In The World	8
63	Stateside SS 209	Come Go With Me/King Without A Queen	15
63	CBS AAG 161	Be Careful Of Stones That You Throw/I Can't Believe	
		(That You Don't Love Me Anymore)	10
63	CBS AAG 169	Donna, The Prima Donna/You're Mine	8
63	CBS AAG 177	Drip Drop/No One's Waiting For Me	10
64	CBS AAG 188	I'm Your Hoochie Coochie Man/The Road I'm On (Gloria)	12
64	CBS AAG 224	Johnnie B. Goode/Chicago Blues	15
65	CBS 201728	Sweet, Sweet Baby/Unloved, Unwanted Me (as Dion Di Mucci)	12
65	CBS 201780	Spoonful/Kickin' Child	12
66	HMV POP 1565	My Girl The Month Of May/Berimbau (as Dion & Belmonts)	20
67	HMV POP 1586	Movin' Man/For Bobbie (as Dion & Belmonts).	12
68	London HLP 10229	Abraham, Martin And John/Daddy Rollin'	8
69	London HLP 10277	Both Sides Now/You Better Watch Yourself (Sonny Boy)	7
70	Warner Bros WB 7356	If We Only Have Love/Natural Man	7
70	Warner Bros WB 7401	Your Own Back Yard/Sit Down, Old Friend	6
71	Warner Bros WB 6120	Close To It All/Windows	6
71	Warner Bros K 16100	Peaceful Place/Sunniland.	6
72	Warner Bros K 16132	Sanctuary/Brand New Morning	6
75	Phil Spector Intl. 2010 012	Born To Be With You/Good Lovin' Man	5

EPs

62	HMV 7EG 8749	SWINGALONG WITH DION.	100
63	Stateside SE 1006	DION'S HITS.	65

LPs

59	London HA-U 2194	PRESENTING DION AND THE BELMONTS (as Dion & Belmonts)	300+
60	Top Rank 25-027	THE TOPPERMOST — VOL. 1 (as Dion & Belmonts, with others)	75
61	HMV CLP 1539	RUNAROUND SUE	100
63	Stateside SL 10034	LOVERS WHO WANDER.	80
63	CBS (S) BPG 62137	RUBY BABY (mono/stereo). .... each 25
64	CBS (S) BPG 62203	DONNA THE PRIMA DONNA (mono/stereo) 25
67	HMV CLP 3618	TOGETHER AGAIN (as Dion & Belmonts, also stereo CSD 3618) ... each 40
70	London HA-P/SH-P 8390	DION.	15
70	Warner Brothers WS 1826	SIT DOWN OLD FRIEND	15
71	Warner Brothers WS 1872	YOU'RE NOT ALONE	15
72	Warner Brothers K 46122	SANCTUARY	15
72	Warner Brothers K 46199	SUITE FOR LATE SUMMER	15
73	Warner Brothers K 46208	REUNION — LIVE AT MADISON SQUARE GARDEN, 1972 (with Belmonts) ...	15
75	Phil Spector Intl. 2307 002	BORN TO BE WITH YOU	15

(see also Belmonts)

DION (Cameron) & THREE TOPS
67	Doctor Bird DB 1101	Miserable Friday/This World Has A Feeling	28
72	Big BG 331	Three Tops Time/UNDERGROUND PEOPLE: Tops (Version)	10

(see also Three Tops)

CELINE DION
91	Epic 656 326-7	Where Does My Heart Beat Now?/I Feel Too Much (p/s)	6
91	Epic 656 326-6	Where Does My Heart Beat Now?/I'm Loving Every Moment With You/I Feel Too Much (12", p/s)	8
91	Epic 656 326-2/5	Where Does My Heart Beat Now?/I'm Loving Every Moment With You/I Feel Too Much (CD, card sleeve or jewel case)	each 15
91	Epic 657 333-7	The Last To Know/Unison (p/s)	5
91	Epic 657 333-0	The Last To Know/Unison (poster p/s)	10
92	Epic 657 660-7	Beauty And The Beast (duet with Peabo Bryson)/The Beast Lets Belle Go (Instrumental) (p/s)	5
92	Epic 657 660-5	Beauty And The Beast (duet with Peabo Bryson)/The Beast Lets Belle Go (Instrumental) (CD, textured blue digipak)	15
92	Epic 658 192-7	If You Asked Me To/Love You Blind (p/s)	5
92	Epic 658 778-2	Love Can Move Mountains (Remix)/Love Can Move Mountains (Club Mix)/Cry Just A Little/Beauty And The Beast (duet with Peabo Bryson) (CD)	15
91	Epic 467 203-1	UNISON (LP)	15
92	Epic 471 508-1	CELINE DION (LP, some with bonus track Where Does My Heart Beat Now)	15

DIPLOMATS
67	Caltone TONE 108	Meet Me At The Corner/Do It To Me Baby (by Lloyd & Groovers)	25
68	Caltone TONE 109	Going Alone/My Heart My Soul (by Lloyd & Groovers)	30
68	Caltone TONE 112	Strong Man/Listen To The Music (by Lloyd & Groovers)	30

DIPLOMATS
68	Direction 58-3899	I Can Give You Love/I'm So Glad I Found You	10

(see also Sam, Erv & Tom)

DIPLOMATS
82	Exchange EX 1	Memories Of You/I'll Keep Holding On (p/s)	7

(see also Scene)

DIRECT HITS
82	Whaam! WHAAM 007	Modesty Blaise/Sunny Honey Girl (p/s)	15
85	Direct POP 001	Christopher Cooper/She Really Didn't Care (p/s)	7
84	Whaam! BIG 7	BLOW UP (LP)	30

(see also Exits)

DIRECTION
93	Detour DR 003	Yesterday/The Kids Wanna New Direction (p/s, 1,000 only)	6

DIRECTIONS
79	Tortch TOR 004	Three Bands Tonite/On The Train (p/s, some with badge)	80/75

(see also Big Sound Authority)

DIRECTIONS IN JAZZ UNIT
64	Philips BL 7625	DIRECTIONS IN JAZZ (LP)	120

DIRE STRAITS
82	Vertigo DSTR 101	Private Investigations/Badges Posters Stickers T-Shirts (10", p/s)	7
84	Vertigo DSTR 610	Love Over Gold (live)/Solid Rock (live) (10", p/s)	7
85	Vertigo DSTR 910	So Far Away/Walk Of Life (10", p/s)	7
85	Vertigo DSTR 1010	Money For Nothing/Love Over Gold (live) (10", p/s)	7
85	Vertigo DSPIC 10	Money For Nothing/Love Over Gold (live) (shaped picture disc with plinth)	8
85	Vertigo DSPIC 11	Brothers In Arms/Going Home — Theme From Local Hero (Live Version) (oblong picture disc in stickered PVC sleeve)	12
85	Vertigo DSTR 1110	Brothers In Arms/Going Home — Theme From Local Hero (Live Version) (10", p/s)	7
85	Vertigo 884 285-2	Brothers In Arms (short)/Going Home (live)/Brothers In Arms (long)/Why Worry (CD, promo only)	50
88	Vertigo DSCD 15	Sultans Of Swing/Portobello Belle (live)/Romeo And Juliet/Money For Nothing (CD, card sleeve)	10
88	Vertigo 080 130-2	Money For Nothing (Full Length Version)/One World/So Far Away (CD Video)	20
88	Vertigo 080 134-2	Walk Of Life/Why Worry (LP Version)/Ride Across The River (CD Video)	20
89	Vertigo 080 128-2	Sultans Of Swing/Wild West End/Down The Waterline (CD Video)	20
89	Vertigo 080 132-2	Brothers In Arms (Full Length Version)/Your Latest Trick/Ride Across The River (CD Video)	20
89	Vertigo 080 136-2	Twisting By The Pool/Two Young Lovers/If I Had You/Twisting By The Pool (live) (CD Video)	20
82	Vertigo HS 6359 034	MAKING MOVIES (LP, half-speed master recording)	15
82	Vertigo HS 9102 021	DIRE STRAITS (LP, half-speed master recording)	15

(see also Mark Knopfler, David Knopfler)

DIRK & STIG
78	Ring O' 2017 109/DIB 1	Ging Gang Goolie/Mr. Sheene (unissued)	
79	EMI EMI 2852	Ging Gang Goolie/Mr. Sheene (p/s, black or khaki vinyl)	18/10

(see also Rutles, Neil Innes)

DIRTY BLUES BAND
68	Stateside S(S)L 10234	DIRTY BLUES BAND (LP)	32
69	Stateside S(S)L 10268	STONE DIRT (LP)	25

(see also Baconfat)

DIRTY DOG
78	Lightning GIL 511	Let Go Of My Hand/Shouldn't Do It/Gonna Quit/Guitar In My Hand (p/s)	15

DIRTY HARRY
73	Unity UN 573	Big Haire/YOUNG DOUG: Skank In Skank	5

DIRTY STRANGERS

DIRTY STRANGERS
89	Thrill TH 3	Bathing Belles/Oh Yeah/Hands Up (p/s, featuring Keith Richards)	8

(see also Rolling Stones)

DIRTY TRICKS
75	Polydor 2383351	DIRTY TRICKS (LP)	20

DISCHARGE
80	Clay CLAY 1	Realities Of War/They Declare It/But After The Gig/Society's Victim (p/s)	8
80	Clay CLAY 3	Fight Back/War's No Fairy Tale/Always Restrictions/You Take Part In Creating This System/Religion Instigates (p/s)	7
80	Clay CLAY 5	Decontrol/It's No TV Sketch/Tomorrow Belongs To Us (p/s)	7
81	Clay CLAY 6	Never Again/Death Dealers/Two Monstrous Nuclear Stock-Piles (p/s)	7
82	Clay CLAY 14	State Violence, State Control/Doomsday (p/s)	7
83	Clay CLAY 29	Price Of Silence/Born To Die In The Gutter (p/s)	7
81	Clay PLATE 2	WHY (12" EP)	10
82	Clay CLAYLP 3	HEAR NOTHING, SEE NOTHING, SAY NOTHING (LP)	15
84	Clay CLAYLP 12	NEVER AGAIN (LP, red vinyl)	18

DISCO BROTHERS
76	United Artists	THE DISCO BROTHERS/THE TARTAN HORDE (EP, p/s)	6

(see also Nick Lowe, Tartan Horde, Roogalator, Damned, Brinsley Schwartz)

DISCO STUDENTS
79	Yeah Yeah Yeah UHHUH 1	South Africa House/Kafkaesque (no p/s)	15
80	Yeah Yeah Yeah UHHUH 2	A Boy With A Penchant For Open-Necked Shirts/Pink Triangles/Credit (no p/s)	15

DISCO 2000
87	KLF Comms. D 2001	I Gotta CD (7" Edit) (unissued, white labels only)	18
87	KLF Comms. D 2000	I Gotta CD/I Love Disco 2000 (12", p/s)	12

(see also J.A.M.s, KLF, Timelords, Bill Drummond, Space)

DISCO ZOMBIES
79	South Circular SGS 106	Drums Over London/Heartbeats Love (black, white & pink or black, white & green handmade wraparound p/s)	30
79	Uptown/Wizzo WIZZO 1	THE INVISIBLE (EP)	15
81	Dining Out TUX 2	Here Come The Buts/Mary Millington (p/s)	15

(see also Steppes, Fifty Fantastics)

DISCS
65	Columbia DB 7477	Not Meant To Be/Come Back To Me	7

BABA DISE
69	Gas GAS 118	Wanted/SENSATIONS: I'll Always Love You	16

DISORDER
80	Durham B. Centre BOOK 1	Reality Crisis/1984 (oversized p/s)	15

DISORDER
80	Ace ACE 12	Air Raid/Law And Disorder (1st 100 in custom 'war book' p/s)	80/50
81	Disorder ORDER 1	Complete Disorder/Insane Youth/Today's World/Violent Crime (p/s)	6
81	Disorder ORDER 2	Distortion To Deafness/More Than Fights/Daily Life/ You've Got To Be Someone (p/s)	5
82	Disorder 12ORDER 3	PERDITION (12" EP)	8
83	Disorder ORDER 4	MENTAL DISORDER (EP)	6
84	Disorder 12 ORDER 5	THE SINGLES COLLECTION (12" EP)	10

TOM DISSIVELT
65	Philips BL 7681	FANTASY IN ORBIT (LP)	40

DISTANT COUSINS
66	CBS 202352	She Ain't Loving You/Here Today, Gone Tomorrow	18
67	CBS 2800	Mister Sebastian/Empty House	7

DISTINCTIVE DRONE
79	Antrim House 42-7	The Count/The Count (Version)	5

DISTRACTIONS
79	Factory FAC 12	Time Goes By So Slow/Pillow Fight (p/s)	15
79	TJM TJM 2	YOU'RE NOT GOING OUT DRESSED LIKE THAT (12" EP)	12

DISTRIBUTORS
80	Tap TAP 1	TV Me/Wireless (various foldover p/s)	6
81	Red Rhino RED 9	Hold/Get Rid Of These Things/Wages For Lovers (12", p/s)	8

DIVINE
84	Proto ENAT 118	You Think You're A Man/You Think You're A Man (Remix)/Give It Up (12", p/s)	15

DIVINE COMEDY
91	Setanta SET 008	Timewatch/Jerusalem/The Rise And Fall (12", p/s)	30
92	Setanta SET 011	Europop: New Wave/Intifada/Monitor/Timewatch/Jerusalem/ The Rise And Fall (12", p/s)	30
92	Setanta SET 011CD	Europop: New Wave/Intifada/Monitor/Timewatch/Jerusalem/ The Rise And Fall (CD)	40
93	Setanta CAO 008	Lucy/The Pop Singer's Fear Of The Pollen Count/ I Was Born Yesterday (mail order, p/s)	18
93	Setanta CAO 009	Your Daddy's Car (Demo)/THE GLEE CLUB: Free To Believe (33 rpm clear vinyl flexi)	18
93	Setanta DC 001	Indulgence No. 1: Hate My Way/Untitled Melody/Europe By Train (picture disc)	20
94	Setanta DC 002	Indulgence No. 2: A Drinking Song/When The Lights Go Out All Over Europe/ Tonight We Fly (handfinished wraparound p/s, stamped labels)	25
98	TC 12TC BJD 001	I've Been To A Marvellous Party (Mixes) (12", p/s, double pack promo)	22
90	Setanta SETLPM 002	FANFARE FOR THE COMIC MUSE (LP, with inner sleeve)	80
90	Setanta SETCD 002	FANFARE FOR THE COMIC MUSE (CD, beware of counterfeits)	80
93	Setanta SETLP 011	LIBERATION (LP)	15

93	Setanta SETCD 011	LIBERATION (CD)	20
94	Setanta SETCD 013	PROMENADE (CD, with bonus 4-track live CD)	45
97	Setanta SETCDL 036	A SHORT ALBUM ABOUT LOVE (numbered boxed digipak, with 3 postcards)	22
98	Setanta SET CDL 057	FIN DE SIÈCLE (CD, gatefold digipak with lyric booklet)	20
99	Setanta SETCDL 100	A SECRET HISTORY (2-CD, with hardback book)	25

DIXIE BELLES

63	London HLU 9797	Down At Papa Joe's/Rock, Rock, Rock	15
64	London HLU 9842	Southtown, U.S.A./Why Don't You Set Me Free?	10
64	London REU 1434	THE DIXIE BELLES (EP)	25
64	London HA-U/SH-U 8152	DOWN AT PAPA JOE'S (LP, with Cornbread & Jerry)	30

DIXIE CUPS

64	Pye International 7N 25245	Chapel Of Love/Ain't That Nice	10
64	Red Bird RB 10006	People Say/Girls Can Tell (some copies on Pye label)	10
64	Red Bird RB 10012	You Should Have Seen The Way He Looked At Me/No True Love	12
64	Red Bird RB 10017	Little Bell/Another Boy Like Mine	12
65	Red Bird RB 10024	Iko Iko/Gee Baby Gee	10
65	Red Bird RB 10032	Gee The Moon Is Shining Bright/I'm Gonna Get You Yet	20
65	HMV POP 1453	Two Way Poc A Way/That's Where It's At	18
66	HMV POP 1524	What Kind Of Fool/Danny Boy	22
66	HMV POP 1557	Love Ain't So Bad (After All)/Daddy Said No	12
71	Buddah 2011 079	Chapel Of Love/People Say	5
65	Red Bird RB 20100	CHAPEL OF LOVE (LP)	60
66	HMV CLP 1916	RIDING HIGH (LP)	50

DIXIE DRIFTER

| 65 | Columbia DB 7710 | Soul Heaven/Three Chairs Theme | 12 |

DIXIE FOUR

| 60s | Rarities RA 3 | THE DIXIE FOUR (EP) | 25 |

DIXIE HUMMINGBIRDS

| 64 | Vogue V 2422 | Have A Talk With Jesus/In The Morning | 15 |
| 64 | Vogue LAE-P 588 | PRAYER FOR PEACE (LP) | 25 |

DIXIELANDERS

| 63 | Vocalion V 9209 | Cyclone/Mardyke | 38 |

DIXIELAND JUG BLOWERS

54	HMV 7M 223	Memphis Shake/Boodle-Am-Shake	18
54	HMV 7M 233	Hen Party Blues/Carpet Alley Breakdown	18
	(see also Johnny Dodds)		

ERROL DIXON

60	Blue Beat BB 27	Midnight Track/Anytime Anywhere	15
61	Blue Beat BB 46	Mama Shut Your Door/Too Much Whisky	15
62	Blue Beat BB 86	Bad Bad Woman/Early This Morning	15
62	Island WI 017	Morning Train/Lonely Heart	18
63	Island WI 069	I Love You/Tell Me More	18
63	Carnival CV 7001	Oo Wee Baby/Twisting And Shaking	10
63	Carnival CV 7004	Mean And Evil Woman/Tutti Frutti	10
64	Oriole CB 1945	Rocks In My Pillow/Give Me More Time (as Errol Dixon & Bluebeaters)	75
66	Blue Beat BB 337	Gloria/Heavy Shuffle	12
66	Blue Beat BB 344	You're No Good/Midnight Bus	12
66	Rainbow RAI 104	I Need Someone To Love/I Want (as Errol Dixon & Goodtime Band)	20
66	Fab EP 1	I Need Someone To Love/I Want (reissue)	15
67	Ska Beat JB 271	Midnight Party/It Makes No Difference	20
67	Direct DS 5002	I Don't Want/The Hoop	150
67	Decca F 12613	Six Questions/Not Again	15
67	Decca F 12717	True Love Never Runs Smooth/What Ya Gonna Do (B-side with Judy Kay)	8
68	Decca F 12826	Back To The Chicken Shack (as Big City Blues Of Errol Dixon)/ I Done Found Out	8
69	Doctor Bird DB 1197	Why Hurt Yourself/She Started To Scream	18
70	Gas GAS 148	Something On Your Mind/I Need Love	8
65	Decca DFE 8626	SINGS FATS (EP, with Honeydrippers)	60
68	Decca LK/SKL 4962	BLUES IN THE POT (LP, with Chicken Shack)	85
70	Transatlantic TRA 225	THAT'S HOW YOU GOT KILLED BEFORE (LP)	35
	(see also Chicken Shack)		

HUGH DIXON

| 64 | London HA-U 8188 | FRANTIC GUITARS (LP) | 15 |

JEFF DIXON

| 67 | Coxsone CS 7015 | The Rock/HAMBOYS: Harder On The Rock | 25 |
| 68 | Studio One SO 2051 | Tickle Me/ENFORCERS: Forgive Me | 30 |

TEX DIXON

| 70 | Ackee ACK 111 | Funky Trombone/Crying Horn | 10 |
| 70 | Ackee ACK 112 | My Ring/Here I Am | 10 |

WILLIE DIXON & ALLSTARS

| 56 | London HLU 8297 | Walking The Blues/Crazy For My Baby (78 rpm = £125+) | 1,500 |
| 64 | Pye International 7N 25270 | Crazy For My Baby/Walkin' The Blues (reissue) | 30 |

DIXXY SISTERS

| 54 | Columbia SCM 5105 | Spin The Bottle Polka/The Game Of Broken Hearts | 15 |

DJ CRYSTL

92	Lucky Spin LSR 001	Suicidal/Drop XTC (12")	12
93	Dee Jay Recordings DJX 008	Crystlize/Deep Space (12")	10
93	Dee Jay Recordings DJX 010	Meditation/Warpdrive (12")	20

94	Dee Jay Recordings DJX 020	Let It Roll/Paradise (12")	12
94	Lucky Spin STU 01	Untitled (1-sided, white label 12")	15

DJ CRYSTL & SLIPMASTER J
92	Lucky Spin LSR 004	Frantic Situation/Drop XTC (12")	40

DJ CYCLONE
96	Acid Fever MDMA 9612	909 TRAX EP: Trak 101/Trak 3/4/Trak 303/Trak 23 (12")	20
96	Acid Fever MDMA 9613	Innersense (Halfcore remix)/Innersense (original hardcore mix)/ Mushroom Of Fire/Non-sense (12")	20
96	Acid Fever MDMA 9614 303	Joy Ride/Cycloid Spiral Motion/Circular Motion/ Cycloid Spiral Slow Motion (12")	20

DJ EXCEL
91	(No company) EDUC 2	Just when you thought it was safe/Breakbeat 1/Breakbeat 2/Breakbeat 3 /Breakbeat 4 (12")	30

DJ FOOD
	Ninja Tune 1221 ZEN	Peace/Dark Blood/Well Swung (12")	6
	Open 013 OPENT	Peace (Remixes)/Peace (Part 1 & 2)/Peace (Part 3) (12")	8
95	Ninja Tune 1020 ZEN	A DUB PLATE OF FOOD (2 x 10")	10
95	Ninja Tune 1229	Freedom (Fila Brazilia Mix)/Cosmic Consciousness (Ashley Beadle Mix) (12")	8
96	Ninja Tune 212 ZEN	REFRIED FOOD PT 1 & 2 (2 x 12")	8
96	Ninja Tune 1233 ZEN	REFRIED FOOD PT 2 (Journeymen Mix)/(Autechre Mix)	8
	Ninja Tune 1233 ZEN	REFRIED FOOD PART 2 (12")	10
96	Ninja Tune 2113 ZEN	REFRIED FOOD PT 3 & 4 (2 x 12")	8
96	Ninja Tune 2116 ZEN	REFRIED FOOD PT 5 & 6 (2 x 12")	8
96	Ninja Tune 1 ZENKLON	Spiral/THE HERBALISER: Up For The Get Downs (12", 1-sided, some etched)	10
90s	Ninja Tune	FUNGLE JUNK (2 x 10")	8
	Ninja Tune 2 ZEN	JAZZ BRAKES VOLUME 1 (LP)	15
	Ninja Tune 3 ZEN	JAZZ BRAKES VOLUME 2 (LP)	15
	Ninja Tune 4 ZEN	JAZZ BRAKES VOLUME 3 (2-LP)	15
90s	Ninja Tune 106267	REFRIED FOOD LUNCHBOX (3-LP)	25

DJ KRUSH
95	Mo' Wax MW 033	A Whim/89.9 Megamix (12", stickered p/s)	15
95	Mo' Wax MWCD 033	A Whim/89.9 Megamix (CD, in slipcase, with inner)	8
95	Mo' Wax MW 042	Meiso/(mixes) (12", p/s)	8
96	Mo' Wax MW 060	Only The Strong Survive/(mixes) (12", p/s)	10
93	Mo' Wax MWLP 001	JAZZ HIP JAP (LP)	30
94	Mo' Wax MWLP 025	STRICTLY TURNTABLIZED (2-LP)	15
95	Mo' Wax MWLP 039	MEISO (2-LP, die-cut sleeve)	20
	(see also DJ Shadow)		

DJ MINK Feat. THE K.I.D & C
90	Warp WAR4	Hey Hey Can U Relate (12")	12

DJ SHADOW
93	Mo' Wax MW 014	In/ Flux/Hindsight (12", plain sleeve, with obi sticker, with the Groove Robbers)	50
93	Mo' Wax MW 014	In/ Flux/Hindsight (12", reissue, title sleeve, with the Groove Robbers)	15
93	Mo' Wax MW 014	In/ Flux/Hindsight (12" picture disc, plastic sleeve, with the Groove Robbers)	30
93	Mo' Wax MWCD 014	In/ Flux/Hindsight (CD, with the Groove Robbers)	10
94	Mo' Wax MW 024	Lost And Found/DJ KRUSH: Kemuri (12", p/s)	15
94	Mo' Wax MWCD 024	Lost And Found/DJ KRUSH: Kemuri (CD)	10
94	Mo' Wax MW 027	What Does Your Soul Look Like (parts 1, 3 & 4) (p/s)	10
96	Mo' Wax MW 057	Midnight In A Perfect World (remixes)/Mutual Slump (12", p/s)	12
96	Mo' Wax MWCD 057	Midnight In A Perfect World (remixes)/Mutual Slump (CD, card sleeve with inner)	15
96	Mo' Wax MW 058	Stem/Red Bus Needs To Leave (p/s)	10
97	Mo' Wax MW 063s	High Noon/Organ Donor (Extended Overhaul) (p/s)	10
97	Mo' Wax MW 063	High Noon/Devil's Advocate/Organ Donor (Extended Overhaul) (p/s)	8
97	Mo' Wax MWCD 063	High Noon/Devil's Advocate/Organ Donor (Extended Overhaul) (CD)	10
98	Mo' Wax MW 059	ENDTRODUCING (LP)	15
	(see also Q-Bert, U.N.K.L.E.)		

DJ TRACE
91	Orbital 12 ORBIT 11	Inception/Ain't Gonna Wait No More/Love Dove Sound (12")	20
92	(No company, no number)	Rudeboy Hardcore/Untitled/Untitled (white label 12" with 'DJ Trace' and phone number stamped on labels. A-side samples 'Orinoco flow')	20
93	Lucky Spin LSR 003	Lost entity (London side)/Lost entity (New York side) (12")	30
	DJ Trace and Ed Rush		

DJ TRACE & ED RUSH
93	Lucky Spin LSR 008	Don Bad Man/Clean Gun (12")	20

DJ VADIM
99	Ninja Tune ZEN1279	Friction/Raps Don't Grow On Trees (12")	12
94	Jazz Fudge JF001	ABSTRACT HALLUCINATING GASSES EP (12")	15
96	Ninja Tune ZEN1245	AURAL PROSTITUTION (EP)	20

D'JURANN JURANN
74	Dawn DNS 1068	Streakin'/Oh! Janine	10
	(see also Paul King, King Earl Boogie Band, Mungo Jerry)		

JED(RZEZ) DMOCHOWSKI
83	Whaam! WHAAM 009	Sha-La-La-La (Dance With Me)/Ruined City (with or without 'Jed' on p/s)	8/10
82	Whaam! WHAAM 84	STALLIONS OF MY HEART (LP)	12
	(see also V.I.P.'s)		

DNA
90	Raw Bass 12 RBASS 006	LA SERENISSIMA (12" EP)	10

DNV
79	New Pleasures Z2	Mafia/Death In Venice/Goodbye 70s (foldout p/s)	20

(see also Another Pretty Face, Funhouse, Waterboys, TV21)

D.O.A.
93	Alt. Tentacles VIRUS 120	It's Not Unusual/Dead Men Tell No Tales (yellow vinyl)	5
81	Alt. Tentacles VIRUS 7	POSITIVELY D.O.A. (EP)	7
83	Alt. Tentacles VIRUS 31	BLOODIED BUT UNBOWED — THE DAMAGE TO DATE 1978-84 (12" EP)	8
84	Alt. Tentacles VIRUS 24	WAR ON 45 (12" EP)	8
85	Alt. Tentacles VIRUS 42	DON'T TURN YOUR BACK (ON DESPERATE TIMES) (LP)	12
85	Alt. Tentacles VIRUS 44	LET'S WRECK THE PARTY (LP, with insert & small 'spy' logo)	12

CARL DOBKINS JNR.
59	Brunswick 05804	My Heart Is An Open Book/My Pledge To You (78 rpm = £15)	15
59	Brunswick 05811	If You Don't Want My Lovin'/Love Is Everything (78 rpm = £15)	25
60	Brunswick 05817	Lucky Devil/(There's A Little Song A-Singing) In My Heart	12
60	Brunswick 05832	Exclusively Yours/One Little Girl	12
60	Brunswick LAT 8329	CARL DOBKINS JNR. (LP)	75

BOBBY DOBSON
69	Punch PH 4	Strange/Your New Love	10

(see also Dobby Dobson)

BONNIE DOBSON
69	RCA RCA 1901	I'm Your Woman/I Got Stung	6
70	RCA SF 8079	BONNIE DOBSON (LP)	25
72	Argo ZFB 79	BONNIE DOBSON (LP)	40
76	Polydor 2383 400	MORNING DEW (LP)	12

DOBBY DOBSON (& DELTAS)
65	King KG 1008	Cry A Little Cry/Diamonds And Pearls (as Dobby Dobson & Deltas)	15
67	Trojan TR 011	Loving Pauper/TOMMY McCOOK & SUPERSONICS: Sir Don	18
68	Studio One SO 2068	Walking In The Footsteps/SOUL VENDORS: Studio Rock	30
68	Coxsone CS 7058	Seems To Me I'm Losing You/GAYLADS: Red Rose	30
69	Blue Cat BS 171	Strange/Your New Love	25
69	Punch PH 12	The Masquerade Is Over/Love For Ambition	10
70	Success RE 906	Crazy/RUPIE EDWARDS ALL STARS: Your New Love	6
70	Big BG 303	That Wonderful Sound/I Wasn't Born Yesterday	6
70	Big BG 310	Halfway To Paradise/Utopia	5
71	Dynamic DYN 426	Carry That Weight/More Weight	5
69	Pama SECO 33	STRANGE (LP)	50
70	Trojan TBL 145	THAT WONDERFUL SOUND (LP)	35

(see also Bobby Dobson, Chuck & Dobby, Bruce Bennett, Ernest Wilson & Freddy)

LYN DOBSON
74	Fresh Air 6370 501	JAM SANDWICH (LP)	25

(see also Manfred Mann, Soft Machine, Miller Anderson)

ROY DOCKER
68	Domain D3	Mellow Moonlight/MUSIC THROUGH SIX: Riff Raff	15
69	Pama PM 750	When/Go	8
69	Pama PM 756	I'm An Outcast/Everyday Will Be A Holiday	8

DOCTOR & THE MEDICS
82	Whaam! WHAAM 6	The Druids Are Here/The Goats Are Trying To Kill Me (p/s)	8
85		Miracle Of The Age (1-sided acetate)	12

DOCTOR BROWN
95	Magic Gnome	ANOTHER REALM (LP, 500 only)	15

DR. ALIMANTADO
78	Greensleeves GREL 1	BEST DRESSED CHICKEN IN TOWN (LP)	20

DR. CALCULUS
86	10 Records TEN 131	Perfume From Spain/Straight To Stereo	5
86	10 DIX 45	DESIGNER BEATNIK (LP)	12
86	10 DIXCD 45	DESIGNER BEATNIK (CD)	18

(see also Stephen 'Tin Tin' Duffy)

DOCTOR DARK
76	Target TGT 102	Red Hot Passion/Instrumental (no p/s)	7

(see also Snivelling Shits)

DOCTOR FATHER
70	Pye 7N 17977	Umbopo/Roll On	7

(see also 10cc, Godley & Creme, Hotlegs)

DR. FEELGOOD & THE INTERNS (U.S.)
62	Columbia DB 4838	Dr. Feelgood/Mister Moonlight	25
64	Columbia DB 7228	The Doctor's Doogie/Blang Dong	25
66	CBS 202099	Don't Tell Me No Dirty/Where Did You Go	20
68	Capitol CL 15569	Sugar Bee/You're So Used To It	20
64	Columbia SEG 8310	DR. FEELGOOD AND THE INTERNS (EP)	70

(see also Piano Red)

DR. FEELGOOD (U.K.)
74	United Artists UP 35760	Roxette/(Get Your Kicks On) Route 66 (no p/s)	5
75	United Artists UP 35815	She Does It Right/I Don't Mind (no p/s)	5
75	United Artists UP 35857	Back In The Night/I'm A Man	5
77	United Artists UP 36304	She's A Windup/Hi-Rise (p/s)	5
77	United Artists 12UP 36304	She's A Windup/Hi-Rise/Homework (12", die-cut sleeve)	8
77	United Artists UP 36332	Baby Jane/Looking Back	7
77	United Artists 12UP 36332	Baby Jane/Looking Back/You Upset Me Baby (live) (12", p/s)	8
79	United Artists UP 36468	Milk And Alcohol/Every Kind Of Vice (p/s, brown or white vinyl)	5

DR. FEELGOOD

79	United Artists X/Y/ZUP 36506	As Long As The Price Is Right/Down At The (Other) Doctors (p/s, either black, blue, brown or violet vinyl, 3 different p/s designs)	each 5
86	Stiff BUY 253	Don't Wait Up/Something Good (shrink-wrapped with bonus 45: Back In The Night/Milk And Alcohol [FBUY 56]) (p/s)	6
75	United Artists UAS 29727	DOWN BY THE JETTY (LP, mono only)	12
75	United Artists UAS 29880	MALPRACTICE (LP)	12
76	United Artists UAS 29990	STUPIDITY (LP initially with stickered covers & bonus 7": Riot In Cell Block No. 9/Johnny B. Goode [FEEL 1])	12
79	United Artists UAK 30239	AS IT HAPPENS (LP, with inner sleeve & bonus 7" "Encore EP": Riot In Cell Block No. 9"/The Blues Had A Baby And They Named It Rock'N'Roll/ Lights Out/Great Balls Of Fire [p/s, FEEL 2], with inner sleeve)	12

(see also Wilko Johnson, Lew Lewis, Oil City Sheiks)

DR. HOOK

73	CBS 1037	The Cover Of "Radio Times" (1-sided, promo only, by Dr. Hook & Friends)	75
78	Capitol CL 15992	The Radio/Only Sixteen/I'm A Lamb (p/s)	8
78	Capitol PSLP 314	FOR YOU FROM DR. HOOK (EP, promo only)	10
71	CBS 64754	DR. HOOK AND THE MEDICINE SHOW (LP, plain orange label)	15
71	CBS 65132	SLOPPY SECONDS (LP, plain orange label)	15

DR. JOHN (The Night Tripper)

70	Atco 2091 019	Wash Mama Wash/Mama Roux	6
72	Atlantic K 10158	Iko Iko/Huey Smith Medley	6
72	Atlantic K 10214	Wang Dang Doodle/Big Chief	5
73	Atlantic K 10291	Right Place, Wrong Time/I Been Hoodooed	10
73	Atlantic K 10329	Such A Night/Life	8
68	Atlantic 587/588 147	GRIS GRIS (LP, plum label, mono/stereo)	30
69	Atco 228 018	BABYLON (LP, plum label)	18
70	Atco 2400 015	REMEDIES (LP, plum label)	18
71	Atlantic 2400 161	THE SUN, MOON AND HERBS (LP, plum label, gatefold sleeve with insert)	25
72	Atlantic K 40384	GUMBO (LP, green & orange label, gatefold sleeve)	15
72	Atlantic K 40168	GRIS GRIS (LP, reissue, green & orange label)	15
72	Atlantic K 40250	THE SUN, MOON AND HERBS (LP, reissue, green & orange label, gatefold sleeve with insert)	15
73	Atco K 50017	IN THE RIGHT PLACE (LP, U.K. disc in U.S. stickered 3-way gatefold sleeve)	20
73	CBS 65659	TRIUMVIRATE (LP, with John Hammond & Mike Bloomfield)	15
74	Atlantic K 50035	DESITIVELY BONNAROO (LP)	15
75	United Artists UAG 29902	HOLLYWOOD BE THY NAME (LP, with inner sleeve)	15

DR. K'S BLUES BAND

68	Spark SRLP 101	DR. K'S BLUES BAND (LP)	60

DR. MARIGOLD'S PRESCRIPTION

68	Pye 7N 17493	My Old Man's A Groovy Old Man/People Get Ready	6
69	Pye 7N 17832	You've Got To Build Your Love/My Picture Of Love	6
70	Bell BLL 1096	Breaking The Heart Of A Good Man/Night Hurries On By	6
70	Bell BLL 1126	Sing Along, Sing Along, Sing Along/Father Jim	6
71	Bell BLL 1149	Muddy Water/Come With Me	6

DR. OCTAGON

96	Mo' Wax MWLP 046	OCTAGONECOLOGYST (3-LP)	25
96	Mo' Wax MW064LP	INSTRUMENTALYST (OCTAGON BEATS) (LP)	25

DOCTOR ROCKIT

96	Clear CLR 411	READY TO ROCKIT EP (2 x 10", p/s)	8
96	Clear CLR 416	D FOR DOKTOR EP (12", p/s)	12

DR. STRANGELY STRANGE

69	Island ILPS 9106	KIP OF THE SERENES (LP, pink label, later 'palm-tree' with remix)	120/150
70	Vertigo 6360 009	HEAVY PETTING (LP, gatefold sleeve, swirl label; beware of counterfeits)	120

(see also Sweeney's Men, Gary Moore)

DR. TECHNICAL & MACHINES

83	Hawkfan HWFB 1	Zones/Processed (1-sided with insert, mail-order issue, no p/s)	12

(see also Dave Brock, Hawkwind)

DR. WEST'S MEDICINE SHOW & JUNK BAND

67	CBS 202492	The Eggplant That Ate Chicago/You Can't Fight City Hall Blues	8
67	CBS 202658	Gondoliers, Shakespeares, Overseers/Daddy I Know	8
68	Page One POF 061	Bullets La Verne/Jigsaw	35
70	Page One POF 176	Gondoliers, Shakespeares, Overseers/Daddy I Know (reissue)	6
69	Page One POLS 017	THE EGGPLANT THAT ATE CHICAGO (LP)	30

(see also Norman Greenbaum)

DR. WHO

76	Argo ZSW 564	DR. WHO AND THE PESCATONS (LP, spoken word, read by Tom Baker & Elizabeth Sladen)	15
79	BBC REC 364	GENESIS OF THE DALEKS (LP, spoken word)	15
81	RNIB	TALKING BOOK (reel-to-reel tape, read by Gabriel Wolf)	20
82	BBC 2LP-22001	DOCTOR WHO COLLECTOR'S EDITION (2-LP, includes "Genesis Of The Daleks" [BBC 22364], "Sound Effects" [BBC 22316], & bonus 7" "Doctor Who"/"The Astronauts" [RESL 451], with poster)	30

(see also BBC Radiophonic Workshop, Century 21, Jon Pertwee)

DR. Z

70	Fontana 6007 023	Lady Ladybird/People In The Street	60
71	Vertigo 6360 048	THREE PARTS TO MY SOUL (LP, gatefold sleeve, swirl label)	425

PAT DODD

59	Pye International 7N 25030	Stag Party/Odds'n'Dodds (78 rpm, Pye N 25030 = £12)	7

DODD'S ALLSTARS

69	Coxsone CS 7096	Mother Aitken (actually by Lord Power)/What A Love (actually by Denzil Laing)	25

JOHNNY DODDS

53	London AL 3505	JOHNNY DODDS VOLUME 1 (10" LP)	15
54	London AL 3513	JOHNNY DODDS VOLUME 2 (10" LP)	15
55	Vogue Coral LRA 10025	JOHNNY DODDS VOL. 1 (10" LP)	25
55	HMV DLP 1073	JOHNNY DODDS WASHBOARD STOMP (10" LP)	15
56	London AL 3555	JOHNNY DODDS VOLUME 3 (10" LP)	15
57	London AL 3560	JOHNNY DODDS VOLUME 4 (10" LP)	15

(see also Dixieland Jugblowers)

MALCOLM DODDS

59	Brunswick 05774	This Is Real (This Is Love)/I'll Always Be With You	5
59	Brunswick 05796	Tremble/Deep Inside	5

NELLA DODDS

65	Pye 7N 25281	Come See About Me/You Don't Love Me Anymore (DJ copy = £75)	40
65	Pye 7N 25291	Finders Keepers, Losers Weepers/A Girl's Life (DJ copy = £50)	30

DODGERS

60	Downbeat CHA 2	Let's Make A Whole Lot Of Love/You Make Me Happy	28

DODO'S

67	Polydor BM 56153	I Made Up My Mind/Can't Make It Out	30

ERNIE K-DOE

(see under 'K')

DOGFEET

71	Reflection HRS 7	Sad Story/On The Road	35
71	Reflection HRS 12	Since I Went Away/Evil Woman	35
70	Reflection REFL 8	DOGFEET (LP)	400
94	Kissing Spell CA 36001	DOGFEET (LP, reissue)	15

TYMON DOGG

81	Ghost Dance GHO 1	Lose This Skin (featuring the Clash)/Indestructable (p/s)	6

(see also Timon, Clash)

DOGGEREL BANK

73	Charisma CAS 1079	SILVER FACES (LP)	12
75	Charisma CAS 1102	MISTER SKILLCORN DANCES (LP)	15

BILL DOGGETT

55	Parlophone DP 411	Gumbo/Tara's Theme (78, export issue)	18
55	Parlophone DP 432	Christmas Song/Winter Wonderland (78, export issue)	18
56	Parlophone CMSP 39	Honky Tonk (Parts 1 & 2) (gold label lettering, export issue)	20
56	Parlophone R 4231	Honky Tonk (Parts 1 & 2) (gold label lettering, later silver)	25
56	Parlophone R 4231	Honky Tonk (Parts 1 & 2) (78)	6
57	Parlophone R 4265	Slow Walk/Peacock Alley (78 rpm = £8)	15
57	Parlophone R 4306	Ram-Bunk-Shush/Blue Largo (78 rpm = £10)	15
57	Parlophone R 4379	Hot Ginger/Soft (78 rpm = £10)	18
58	Parlophone R 4413	Leaps And Bounds (Parts 1 & 2) (78 rpm = £12)	10
60	Parlophone R 4629	Smokie/Evening Dreams	10
61	Warner Bros WB 32	The Hully Gully Twist/Jackrabbit	10
61	Warner Bros WB 46	You Can't Sit Down (Parts 1 & 2)	15
57	Parlophone GEP 8644	HONKY TONK (EP)	30
57	Parlophone GEP 8674	PLAYS DUKE ELLINGTON (EP)	10
58	Parlophone GEP 8711	BILL DOGGETT (EP)	10
58	Parlophone GEP 8727	RAINBOW RIOT (EP)	10
59	Parlophone GEP 8771	A JOLLY CHRISTMAS (EP)	10
58	Parlophone PMD 1067	DAME DREAMING (10" LP)	30
59	Parlophone PMD 1073	DANCE AWHILE WITH DOGGETT (10" LP)	30
60	Parlophone PMC 1118	DOGGETT'S BIG CITY DANCE PARTY (LP)	20
60	Parlophone PMC 1124	ON TOUR (LP)	18
61	Warner Bros WM 402	3046 PEOPLE DANCED 'TIL 4 A.M. (LP, live, as Bill Doggett & His Combo)	15
62	Parlophone PMC 1165	BACK WITH MORE BILL DOGGETT (LP)	18
62	Warner Bros WM 4056	THE BAND WITH THE BEAT (LP, with His Combo)	15
65	HMV CLP 1884	WOW (LP)	18

(see also Ella Fitzgerald, Earl Bostic)

DOGROSE

73	Satril SAT 6	All For The Love Of City Lights/Each Other	6
72	Satril SATL 4002	ALL FOR THE LOVE OF DOGROSE (LP)	22

DOGS

05	Fallout IS874/986	London Bridge/End Of An Era (Custom printed parcel tape label)	20
05	Fallout IS874/986791-8	London Bridge/End Of An Era (CD, custom printed parcel tape sleeve)	20

DOGS D'AMOUR

88	China WOL 7	THE (UN)AUTHORISED BOOTLEG (LP)	30

THE DOG THAT BIT PEOPLE

71	Parlophone R 5880	Lovely Lady/Merry-Go-Round	25
71	Parlophone PCS 7125	THE DOG THAT BIT PEOPLE (LP)	240

(see also Norman Haines, Locomotive)

DOGS DIE IN HOT CARS

03	Radiate RDTS11	I Love You 'Cause I Have To/Celebrity Sanctum (p/s)	6
05	Island ISX891/IS981	Tuned To A Different Station/It's Not Right/Tuned To A Different Station/Candy Came (2 x 7", p/s)	8

DOGWATCH

79	Bridgehouse BHLP 002	PENFRIEND (LP, with insert)	20

MINT VALUE £

NED DOHENY
| 81 | CBS 9481 | To Prove My Love/On The Swing Shift (p/s) | 8 |
| 81 | CBS 13-9481 | To Prove My Love/On The Swing Shift (12", p/s) | 10 |

DOKKEN
| 82 | Carrere CAR 229 | We're Illegal/Paris Is Burning (p/s) | 5 |
| 82 | Carrere CAL 136 | BREAKIN' THE CHAINS (LP) | 12 |

JOE DOLAN
| 67 | Piccadilly 7N 35368 | House With The Whitewashed Gable/Work Day Blues | 6 |
| 67 | Pye 7N 17354 | Tar And Cement/Time Of My Life | 7 |

RAMBLIN' JIMMY DOLAN
| 51 | Capitol CL 13600 | Wine, Women, And Pink Elephants /GENE O'QUIN: Boogie Woogie Fever (78) | 8 |
| 53 | Capitol CL 13982 | The Wheel That Does The Squeakin'/Playin' Dominoes And Shootin' Dice (78) | 8 |

DOLE
| 78 | Ultimate ULT 402 | New Wave Love/Hungry Men No Longer Steal Sheep But Are There Hanging Judges? (die-cut p/s) | 20 |

MICKY DOLENZ
67	London HLH 10117	Don't Do It/FINDERS KEEPERS: (We Wear) Lavender Blue	15
67	London HLH 10152	Huff Puff/OBVIOUS: Fate	15
73	MGM 2006 265	Daybreak/Love War	10
74	MGM 2006 392	Ooh She's Young/Love War	6
79	Chrysalis CHS 2297	Love Light/Alicia (p/s)	5
83	A&M BUGSY 1	Tomorrow/BUGSY MALONE GANG: Fat Sam's Grand Slam (with poster)	10
	(hey! hey! see also Monkees)		

ANDY DOLL
| 62 | Starlite ST45 068 | Wild Desire/Wyat | 15 |
| 63 | Starlite STLP II | ON STAGE (LP, by Andy Doll Band & Guests) | 15 |

LINDA DOLL & SUNDOWNERS
| 64 | Piccadilly 7N 35166 | Bonie Maronie/He Don't Want Your Love Anymore | 15 |

DOLLIES
| 65 | CBS 201788 | You Touch Me Baby/I Can't Go On | 10 |

DOLPHIN
76	Private Stock PVT 67	Goin' Back/Think Ahead	8
80	Gale 5	Hey Joe/Dubby Dubby	5
77	Private Stock PVLP 1055	GOODBYE (LP)	12
80	Gale GALELP 02	MOLECULES (LP)	12

DOLPHINS
| 65 | Stateside SS 375 | Hey Da Da Dow/I Don't Want To Go On Without You | 15 |

ERIC DOLPHY
61	Esquire 32-123	THE ERIC DOLPHY QUINTET (LP)	35
64	Esquire 21-123	OUTWARD BOUND (LP)	35
64	Esquire 32-153	OUT THERE (LP)	30
61	Esquire 32-173	AT THE 5 SPOT VOL. 1.(LP)	40
64	Fontana TL5284	LAST DATE (LP)	80
65	Fontana 688521XL	MEMORIAL ALBUM (LP)	30
69	Transatlantic PR 7311	OUTWARD BOUND (LP)	12

ERIC DOLPHY & BOOKER LITTLE
| 66 | Stateside SL 10160 | ERIC DOLPHY AND BOOKER LITTLE MEMORIAL ALBUM (LP) | 15 |

BILLY DOLTON
| 61 | Parlophone R 4733 | Winkie Doll/Girls | 15 |

DOME
81	Dome DOME 3	Jasz (1-sided flexidisc)	10
80	4AD CAD 16	3R4 (mini-LP)	15
80	Dome DOME 1	DOME ONE (LP)	15
80	Dome DOME 2	DOME 2 (LP)	15
81	Dome DOME 3	DOME 3 (LP)	15
	(see also Wire, Gilbert & Lewis)		

DOMINANT FORCE
| 91 | Gangster GAGR001 | Criminals/Raptivity (12") | 28 |
| 92 | Ital Juice DOMF 12 002 | We're Ready/When We Flex (12") | 10 |

ANNA DOMINO
| 86 | Factory FAC 158 | Summer (p/s) | 12 |

FATS DOMINO
78s
54	London HL 8007	Rose Mary/You Said You Love Me	60
54	London HL 8063	Little School Girl/You Done Me Wrong	50
54	London HL 8096	Don't Leave Me This Way/Something's Wrong	45
55	London HL 8124	Love Me/Don't You Hear Me Calling You	40
55	London HL 8133	Thinking Of You/I Know	25
55	London HLU 8173	Ain't That A Shame/La La	12
56	London HLU 8256	Bo Weevil/Don't Blame It On Me	18
56	London HLU 8280	I'm In Love Again/My Blue Heaven	10
56	London HLU 8309	When My Dream Boat Comes Home/So Long	12
56	London HLU 8330	Blueberry Hill/I Can't Go On (Rosalie)	10
57	London HLU 8356	Honey Chile/Don't You Know	12
57	London HLP 8377	Blue Monday/What's The Reason I'm Not Pleasing You	12
57	London HLP 8407	I'm Walkin'/I'm In The Mood For Love	12
57	London HLP 8449	The Valley Of Tears/It's You I Love	12
57	London HLP 8471	What Will I Tell My Heart/When I See You	12

57	London HLP 8519	Wait And See/I Still Love You	12
58	London HLP 8575	The Big Beat (from the film)/I Want You To Know	12
58	London HLP 8628	Sick And Tired/No, No	12
58	London HLP 8663	Little Mary/The Prisoner's Song	15
58	London HLP 8727	Young School Girl/It Must Be Love	20
58	London HLP 8759	Whole Lotta Loving/Coquette	20
59	London HLP 8822	When The Saints Go Marching In/Telling Lies	30
59	London HLP 8865	Margie/I'm Ready	35
59	London HLP 8942	I Want To Walk You Home/I'm Gonna Be A Wheel Some Day	45
59	London HLP 9005	Be My Guest/I've Been Around	55
60	London HLP 9073	Country Boy/If You Need Me	65
60	London HLP 9163	Walking To New Orleans/Don't Come Knockin'	100

SINGLES

55	London HL 8124	Love Me/Don't You Hear Me Calling You	175
55	London HL 8133	Thinking Of You/I Know	150
55	London HLU 8173	Ain't That A Shame/La La	70
56	London HLU 8256	Bo Weevil/Don't Blame It On Me	100
56	London HLU 8280	I'm In Love Again/My Blue Heaven	80
56	London HLU 8309	When My Dream Boat Comes Home/So Long	60
56	London HLU 8330	Blueberry Hill/I Can't Go On (Rosalie)	60
57	London HLU 8356	Honey Chile/Don't You Know	60
57	London HLP 8377	Blue Monday/What's The Reason I'm Not Pleasing You	55

(The above 45s were originally issued with triangular centres & gold lettering labels; later silver-label re-pressings are worth around half these values.)

57	London HLP 8407	I'm Walkin'/I'm In The Mood For Love	28
57	London HLP 8449	The Valley Of Tears/It's You I Love	28
57	London HLP 8471	What Will I Tell My Heart/When I See You	28
57	London HLP 8519	Wait And See/I Still Love You	25
58	London HLP 8575	The Big Beat (From The Film)/I Want You To Know	22
58	London HLP 8628	Sick And Tired/No, No	22
58	London HLP 8663	Little Mary/The Prisoner's Song	25
58	London HLP 8727	Young School Girl/It Must Be Love	28
58	London HLP 8759	Whole Lotta Loving/Coquette	25
59	London HLP 8822	When The Saints Go Marching In/Telling Lies	15

(HLP 8407 through to 8822 45s were issued with triangular centres & silver lettering on all-black labels; later copies are worth around half these values.)

59	London HLP 8865	Margie/I'm Ready (triangular centre & silver-top label, later round centre)	15/8
59	London HLP 8942	I Want To Walk You Home/I'm Gonna Be A Wheel Some Day (tri or round)	18/10
59	London HLP 9005	Be My Guest/I've Been Around (triangular or round centre)	40/12

(All subsequent London 45s were issued with round centres & silver-top labels.)

60	London HLP 9073	Country Boy/If You Need Me	12
60	London HLP 9133	Tell Me That You Love Me/Before I Grow Too Old	15
60	London HLP 9163	Walking To New Orleans/Don't Come Knockin'	15
60	London HLP 9198	Three Nights A Week/Put Your Arms Around Me, Honey	15
60	London HLP 9244	My Girl Josephine/Natural Born Lover	10
61	London HLP 9301	What A Price/Ain't That Just Like A Woman	15
61	London HLP 9327	Fell In Love On Monday/Shu-Rah	15
61	London HLP 9374	It Keeps Rainin'/I Just Cry	30
61	London HLP 9415	Let The Four Winds Blow/Good Hearted Man	15
61	London HLP 9456	What A Party/Rockin' Bicycle	15
62	London HLP 9520	Jambalaya/You Win Again	10
62	London HLP 9557	My Real Name/My Heart Is Bleeding	15
62	London HLP 9590	Dance With Mr. Domino/Nothing New (Same Old Thing)	15
62	London HLP 9616	Did You Ever See A Dream Walking/Stop The Clock	15
63	London HLP 9738	You Always Hurt The One You Love/Trouble Blues	12
63	HMV POP 1164	There Goes My Heart Again/Can't Go On Without You	12
63	HMV POP 1197	When I'm Walkin'/I've Got A Right To Cry	10
63	HMV POP 1219	Red Sails In The Sunset/Song For Rosemary	7
63	HMV POP 1265	Just A Lonely Man/Who Cares	10
64	HMV POP 1281	I Don't Want To Set The World On Fire/Lazy Lady	7
64	HMV POP 1303	If You Don't Know What Love Is/Something You Got Baby	40
64	HMV POP 1324	Mary Oh Mary/Packin' Up	10
64	HMV POP 1370	Kansas City/Heartbreak Hill	10
65	Mercury MF 869	(I Left My Heart) In San Francisco/I Done Got Over It	10
65	Mercury MF 873	What's That You Got?/It's Never Too Late	10
65	HMV POP 1421	Why Don't You Do Right?/Wigs	10
67	HMV POP 1582	I'm Livin' Right/I Don't Want To Set The World On Fire	10
67	Liberty LBF 12055	It Keeps Rainin'/Blue Monday	15
68	Liberty LBF 15098	Walking To New Orleans/Blueberry Hill	5
68	Reprise RS 20696	Honest Mamas Love Their Papas Better/One For The Highway (withdrawn)	25
68	Reprise RS 20763	Lady Madonna/One For The Highway	6
69	Reprise RS 20810	Everybody's Got Something To Hide Except Me And My Monkey/So Swell When You're Well	6
69	Liberty LBF 15274	I'm Ready/The Fat Man	6
69	Mercury MF 1104	What's That You Got?/Jambalaya (On The Bayou)	6
78	Sonet SON 2168	Sleeping On The Job/After Hours	5

EXPORT SINGLES

57	London HL 7028	Wait And See/I Still Love You	32
58	London HL 7040	Sick And Tired/No, No	32
58	London HL 7054	The Big Beat (From The Film)/Little Mary	32

EPs

55	London RE-P 1022	BLUES FOR LOVE (1st pressing with gold lettering label, later silver)	70/40
56	London RE-U 1062	BLUES FOR LOVE VOL. 2 (1st pressing with gold label, later silver)	70/40
57	London RE-U 1073	FATS (export issue, plain sleeve)	100
57	London RE-P 1079	HERE COMES FATS VOL. 1	50

Fats DOMINO

58	London RE-P 1080	HERE COMES FATS VOL. 2	50
58	London RE-P 1115	CARRY ON ROCKIN' PART 1	70
58	London RE-P 1116	CARRY ON ROCKIN' PART 2	70
58	London RE-P 1117	BLUES FOR LOVE VOL. 3	45
58	London RE-P 1121	BLUES FOR LOVE VOL. 4	45
58	London RE-P 1138	HERE COMES FATS VOL. 3	40
59	London RE-P 1206	THE ROCKIN' MR. D VOL. 1	40
59	London RE-P 1207	THE ROCKIN' MR. D VOL. 2	40

(The above EPs were originally issued with triangular centres; round-centre re-pressings are worth two-thirds these values.)

60	London RE-P 1261	BE MY GUEST	35
60	London RE-P 1265	THE ROCKIN' MR. D VOL. 3	38
62	London RE-P 1340	WHAT A PARTY	38
64	HMV 7EG 8862	RED SAILS IN THE SUNSET	25
65	Liberty LEP 4026	MY BLUE HEAVEN	25
66	Liberty LEP 4045	ROLLIN'	25

LPs

56	London HA-U 2028	FATS' ROCK AND ROLLIN'	110
56	London HA-P 2041	CARRY ON ROCKIN'	110
57	London HA-P 2052	HERE STANDS FATS DOMINO	110
56	London HA-P 2073	THIS IS FATS DOMINO	70
58	London HA-P 2087	THIS IS FATS	70
58	London HA-P 2135	THE FABULOUS "MR. D"	65
59	London HA-P 2223	LET'S PLAY FATS DOMINO	65
60	London HA-P 2312	A LOT OF DOMINOES!	55
61	London HA-P 2364	I MISS YOU SO	55
61	London HA-P 2420	LET THE FOUR WINDS BLOW	50
61	London HA-P 2426	WHAT A PARTY	50
62	London HA-P 2447	TWISTIN' THE STOMP	50
63	London HA-P 8039	JUST DOMINO	50
63	London HA-P 8084	WALKING TO NEW ORLEANS	50
63	HMV CLP 1690	HERE COMES FATS DOMINO (also stereo CSD 1520)	each 30
63	HMV CLP 1740	FATS ON FIRE (also stereo CSD 1543)	30
65	Liberty LBY 3033	MILLION SELLERS BY FATS VOL. 1	15
65	Liberty LBY 3046	MILLION SELLERS BY FATS VOL. 2	15
65	HMV CLP 1821	GETAWAY WITH FATS DOMINO (also stereo CSD 1580)	each 20
65	Mercury (S)MCL 20070	DOMINO '65 (mono/stereo)	15
68	Stateside (S)SL 10240	FANTASTIC FATS	15

DOMINOES (Jamaica)

68	Melody MRC 002	A Tribute (actually by Ann Reid)/Hooray (actually by Uniques)	10

DOMINOES (U.K.)

60	Reading Rag LYN 545	Bye Bye Johnny/Yakety Yak	15

DOMINOES (U.S.)

51	Vogue V 9012	Sixty Minute Man/I Can't Escape From You (78)	50
52	Vogue V 2135	Have Mercy, Baby/That's What You're Doing To Me (78)	45
67	Vogue V 212	Sixty Minute Man/I Can't Escape From You	28
56	Vogue EPV 1113	RHYTHM AND BLUES (EP, 2 tracks by Swallows)	300+

(see also Billy Ward & Dominoes, Clyde McPhatter, Jackie Wilson)

SAM DONAHUE & HIS ORCHESTRA

55	Capitol CL 14349	Saxaboogie/September In The Rain	15

TROY DONAHUE

63	Warner Bros WB 111	Live Young/Somebody Loves Me	10

MIKE DONALD

71	Folk Heritage FHR 021	YORKSHIRE SONGS OF THE BROAD ACRES (LP)	25

ERIC DONALDSON

71	Dynamic DYN 420	Cherry Oh Baby/LLOYD CHARMERS: Sir Charmers Special	8
71	Dynamic DYN 423	Love Of The Common People/DRAGONAIRES: The Dragon's Net	8
71	Dynamic DYN 425	Just Can't (Happen This Way)/Just Can't (Happen This Way) Version	6
72	Dynamic DYN 431	I'm Indebted/I'm Indebted (Version)	6
72	Dynamic DYN 439	Miserable Woman/The Lion Sleeps	8
72	Dynamic DYN 445	Blue Boot/Blue Boot (Version)	6
72	Dynamic DYN 452	Little Did You Know/Little Did You Know (Version)	5
73	Dragon DRA 1017	What A Festival/I ROY & ERIC: Festival Version	5
73	Dragon DRA 1018	The Way You Do The Things You Do/Version	5
73	Dragon DRA 1020	Watch What You're Doing To Me/You Must Believe Me	5
73	Dragon DRA 1027	A Weh We A Go Go/SOUL DEFENDERS: Version	5
72	Trojan TRL 42	ERIC DONALDSON (LP)	15

(see also Prunes, Satchmo)

DON & DEWEY

64	London HL 9897	Get Your Hat/Annie Lee	30
66	Cameo Parkway CP 750	Soul Motion/Stretchin' Out	30
67	Sue WI 4032	Soul Motion/Stretchin' Out (reissue)	30
71	Specialty SNTF 5006	DON AND DEWEY (LP)	15

(see also Dewey Terry)

DON & GOODTIMES

67	Columbia DB 8199	I Could Be So Good To You/And It's So Good	10
67	Columbia DB 8266	Happy And Me/If You Love Her, Cherish Her And Such	8

DON & JUAN

62	London HLX 9529	What's Your Name?/Chicken Necks	40

DON & PETE

66	Columbia DB 7881	And I'm Crying Again/Time Will Tell	5

DONAYS
| 62 | Oriole CBA 1770 | Devil In His Heart/Bad Boy..150 |

DON, DICK & JIMMY
54	Columbia SCM 5110	Brand Me With Your Kisses/Angela Mia.................................15
55	London HL 8117	You Can't Have Your Cake And Eat It Too/That's What I Like (78 rpm = £8)......35
55	London HL 8144	Make Yourself Comfortable/(Whatever Happened To The) Piano Players (That Played Like This) (78 rpm = £8)..................................20
56	HMV POP 280	That's The Way I Feel/Two Voices In The Night..........................10
55	London RE-U 1043	DON, DICK AND JIMMY (EP) 30

DOROTHY DONEGAN
| 56 | MGM MGM-EP 532 | DOROTHY DONEGAN TRIO (EP)..8 |

LONNIE DONEGAN
78s
56	Oriole CB 1329	The Passing Stranger/TOMMY REILLY: The Intimate Stranger 6
56	Columbia DB 3850	On A Christmas Day/Take My Hand, Precious Lord 6
59	Pye Nixa N 15181	Does Your Chewing Gum Lose Its Flavour/Aunt Rhody....................8
59	Pye Nixa N 15206	Battle Of New Orleans/Darling Corey`.................................8
60	Pye N 15256	My Old Man's A Dustman/The Golden Vanity ....15+
60	Pye N 15267	I Wanna Go Home (The Wreck Of The John B)/Jimmy Brown The Newsboy ...15+

SINGLES
55	Decca F 10647	Rock Island Line/John Henry (as Lonnie Donegan Skiffle Group) (tri-centre) 25
56	Decca FJ 10695	Diggin' My Potatoes/Bury My Body (as Lonnie Donegan Skiffle Group) (tri-centre) (78 rpm = £6)..25
56	Columbia DB 3850	On A Christmas Day/Take My Hand, Precious Lord (as Lonnie Donegan with Chris Barber's Jazz Band) 25
57	Pye Nixa 7N 15116	Jack O' Diamonds/Ham 'N' Eggs......................................10
58	Pye Nixa 7N 15129	The Grand Coolie Dam/Nobody Loves Like An Irishman 10
58	Pye Jazz 7NJ 2006	Midnight Special/When The Sun Goes Down 25
58	Pye Nixa 7N 15148	Sally, Don't You Grieve/Betty, Betty, Betty 10
58	Pye Nixa 7N 15158	Lonesome Traveller/Times Are Getting Hard Boys (78 rpm = £6) 5
58	Pye Nixa 7N 15165	Lonnie's Skiffle Party (Parts 1 & 2) (78 rpm = £6) 5
58	Pye Nixa 7N 15172	Tom Dooley/Rock O' My Soul (78 rpm = £6).............................5
59	Pye Nixa 7N 15198	Fort Worth Jail/Whoa Buck (78 rpm = £6) 5
59	Pye 7N 15223	Sal's Got A Sugar Lip/Chesapeake Bay (78 rpm = £10) 5
59	Pye 7N 15237	San Miguel/Talking Guitar Blues (78 rpm = £12) 5
60	Pye 7N 15275	Lorelei/In All My Wildest Dreams (78 rpm = £30+).....................5
60	Pye 7N 15312	Lively/Black Cat (Cross My Path Today)...............................5
60	Pye 7N 15315	Virgin Mary/Beyond The Sunset 5
61	Pye 7N 15330	(Bury Me) Beneath The Willow/Leave My Woman Alone 5
61	Pye 7N 15371	Michael Row The Boat/Lumbered 5
61	Pye 7N 15410	The Comancheros/Ramblin' Round 5
62	Pye 7N 15455	Pick A Bale Of Cotton/Steal Away (some in p/s) 6
66	Pye 7N 15993	World Cup Willie/Where In This World Are We Going (some in p/s) 40/20

EPs
56	Decca DFE 6345	THE LONNIE DONEGAN SKIFFLE GROUP (tri-centre, later round)............20
56	Jazz Today JTE 107	BACKSTAIRS SESSION 30
56	Pye Nixa Jazz NJE 1014	BACKSTAIRS SESSION (reissue) 10
56	Pye Nixa Jazz NJE 1017	SKIFFLE SESSION 15
57	Pye Nixa NEP 24031	HIT PARADE..10
57	Pye Nixa NEP 24040	HIT PARADE VOL. 2 10
58	Pye Nixa NEP 24067	HIT PARADE VOL. 3 10
58	Pye Nixa NEP 24075	DONEGAN ON STAGE 10
58	Pye Nixa NEP 24081	HIT PARADE VOL. 4 10
59	Pye Nixa NEP 24104	HIT PARADE VOL. 5 10
59	Pye Nixa NEP 24107	RELAX WITH LONNIE 10
59	Pye Nixa NEP 24114	HIT PARADE VOL. 6 10
60	Pye Nixa NEP 24127	YANKEE DOODLE DONEGAN 10
61	Pye Nixa NEP 24134	HIT PARADE VOL. 7 10
61	Pye Nixa NEP 24149	HIT PARADE VOL. 8 10

LPs
56	Pye Nixa NPT 19012	LONNIE DONEGAN SHOWCASE (10")..25
57	Pye Nixa NPT 19027	LONNIE (10", also stereo NSPT 84000)............................each 25
58	Pye NPL 18034	TOPS WITH LONNIE 15
59	Pye NPL 18043	LONNIE RIDES AGAIN 15
61	Pye NPL 18063	MORE TOPS WITH LONNIE 15
62	Pye NPL 18073	SING HALLELUJAH 20
65	Pye NPL 18126	THE LONNIE DONEGAN FOLK ALBUM 20

(see also Monty Sunshine, Chris Barber, Max Miller)

DONKEYS
80	Rhesus GO APE 102	What I Want/Four Letters (yellow or orange label, p/s)................20
80	Rhesus GO APE 3	No Way/You Jane (p/s) 20
80	Rhesus GO APE 105	Don't Go/Living Legends (p/s)..20
80	Back Door DOOR 006	No Way/You Jane (reissue, p/s).......................................7
80	Deram DM-R 431	What I Want/Four Letters (reissue, p/s) 8
81	MCA MCA 721	Let's Float/Watched By Everyone (p/s)................................7
81	MCA MCA 737	Listen To Your Radio/Watched By Everyone (as Donkees) (p/s)..........7

JIMMY DONLEY
| 57 | Brunswick 05715 | South Of The Border/The Trail Of The Lonesome Pine ....20 |
| 59 | Brunswick 05807 | The Shape You Left Me In/What Must I Do (78 rpm = £20) ....120 |

DONNA & FREEDOM SINGERS
| 70 | Bamboo BAM 53 | Oh Me Oh My (actually by Jerry Jones)/JACKIE MITTOO: Gold Mine ....18 |

RAL DONNER

61	Parlophone R 4820	You Don't Know What You've Got/So Close To Heaven	15
61	Parlophone R 4859	Please Don't Go/I Didn't Figure On Him	20
62	Parlophone R 4889	I Don't Need You/She's Everything (I Wanted You To Be)	20
62	Stateside SS 109	Bells Of Love/Loveless Life	20
63	Reprise R 20141	I Got Burned/A Tear In My Eye	35

DONNIE & DREAMERS

61	Top Rank JAR 571	Count Every Star/Dorothy	45

DONOVAN

65	Pye 7N 15801	Catch The Wind/Why Do You Treat Me Like You Do	7
65	Pye 7N 15866	Colours/To Sing For You	7
65	Pye 7N 15984	Turquoise/Hey Gyp (Dig The Slowness)	8
66	Pye 7N 17067	Josie/Little Tin Soldier	7
66	Pye 7N 17088	Remember The Alamo/The Ballad Of A Crystal Man	15
66	Pye 7N 17241	Sunshine Superman/The Trip	7
67	Pye 7N 17267	Mellow Yellow/Preachin' Love	6
67	Pye 7N 17403	There Is A Mountain/Sand And Foam	6
68	Pye 7N 17457	Jennifer Juniper/Poor Cow	6
68	Pye 7N 17537	Hurdy Gurdy Man/Teen Angel	6
68	Pye 7N 17660	To Susan On The West Coast Waiting/Atlantis (unreleased)	
68	Pye 7N 17660	Atlantis/I Love My Shirt	6
69	Pye 7N 17778	Goo Goo Barabajagal (Love Is Hot)/Bed With Me (with Jeff Beck Group)	12
69	Pye 7N 17778	Barabajagal/Trudi (shortened A-side title & retitled B-side)	8
70	Dawn DNS 1006	Ricki Tavi/Roots Of Oak (as Donovan with Open Road)	6
70	Dawn DNS 1006	Riki Tiki Tavi (shortened spelling of A-side)/Roots Of Oak (with Open Road)	5
70	Dawn DNS 1007	Celia Of The Seals (with Danny Thompson)/Mr. Wind	6
72	private pressing	The Music Makers (one-sided, paper sleeve, 50 only)	50
73	Epic EPC 1471	I Like You/Earth Sign Man	5
73	Epic EPC 1644	Maria Magenta/Intergalactic Laxative (p/s)	8
73	Epic EPC 1960	Sailing Homeward/Lazy Daze (p/s)	6
74	Epic EPC 1960	Sailing Homeward/Yellow Star (p/s, reissue with different B-side; some copies list both Donovan & Andrew Oldham as producers)	each 6
75	Epic EPC 2661	Rock'n'Roll With Me/Divine Daze Of Deathless Delight (some in p/s)	30/6
75	Epic EPC 3037	Rock And Roll Souijer/Love Of My Life	5
77	Rak RAK 265	The Light/The International Man (some in p/s)	8/5
92	Silhouette MDCDKR 3	Newest Bath Guide/Moira MacCavendish/Brother Sun, Sister Moon (CD)	18
65	Pye NEP 24219	THE UNIVERSAL SOLDIER (EP, some incorrectly list 'Summer 1955' instead of 'Summer 1965' as date on rear sleeve)	each 12
65	Pye NEP 24229	COLOURS (EP)	22
66	Pye NEP 24239	DONOVAN VOL. 1 (EP)	22
68	Pye NEP 24287	CATCH THE WIND (EP)	22
68	Pye NEP 24299	HURDY GURDY DONOVAN (EP)	22
65	Pye NPL 18117	WHAT'S BIN DID AND WHAT'S BIN HID (LP, some with misprinted Side 2 label)	30
65	Pye NPL 18128	FAIRYTALE (LP, some copies with blank rear sleeve)	25
66	World Records ST 951	DONOVAN (LP)	15
67	Pye NPL 18181	SUNSHINE SUPERMAN (LP)	30
68	Pye N(S)PL 20000	A GIFT FROM A FLOWER TO A GARDEN (2-LP, black or navy blue box set, separate halves or with taped hinge; with 12 inserts in folder, mono/stereo)	55/45
68	Pye N(S)PL 18237	DONOVAN IN CONCERT (LP, mono/stereo)	20/18
69	Pye N(S)PL 18283	DONOVAN'S GREATEST HITS (LP, gatefold sleeve with booklet, mono/stereo)	15/12
70	Dawn DNLS 3009	OPEN ROAD (LP, gatefold sleeve)	20
71	Dawn DNLD 4001	H.M.S. DONOVAN (2-LP, gatefold sleeve, some with foldout poster)	55/22
73	Pye 11PP 102	FOUR SHADES ("H.M.S. Donovan"/"Greatest Hits"/"Open Road") (4-LP box set)	50
73	Epic EPC 65490	COSMIC WHEELS (LP, gatefold sleeve with inner sleeve & poster)	12
90	Permanent PERMLP 2	DONOVAN RISING (LP, 500 only)	20
	(see also Jeff Beck, Open Road)		

DONTELLS

65	Fontana TF 566	In Your Heart/Nothing But Nothing	75
74	President PT 373	In Your Heart/Nothing But Nothing (reissue)	20

DICKY DOO & DON'TS

58	London HLU 8589	Click Click/Did You Cry (78 rpm = £20)	30
58	London HLU 8754	Leave Me Alone/Wild, Wild Party (with Orchestra) (78 rpm = £30)	40
60	Top Rank JAR 318	Wabash Cannonball/WEST TEXAS MARCHING BAND: The Drums Of Richard A Doo	25

DOOF

80	Doof	EXIST (10" mini-LP, with booklet)	8
	(see also Exhibit A)		

DOOLEY SISTERS

55	London HL 8128	Ko Ko Mo (I Love You So)/Heart Throb	45+

JOHN DOONAN

72	Leader LEA 2043	FLUTE FOR THE FEIS (LP)	15

DOONICANS

87	Probe Plus PP 23T	THE FISHERMAN'S WAY (12" EP)	10

DOOR & THE WINDOW

79	NB Records NB 3	He Feels Like A Doris/I Like Sound/Innocent/Dig/Production Line (white label with stickers & insert p/s in poly bag)	5
80	NB Records NB 5	DETAILED TWANG (LP, blank labels)	12
80	NB Records NB 9	MUSIC AND MOVEMENT (live cassette)	12
	(see also Alternative TV)		

DOORS

SINGLES

67	Elektra EKSN 45009	Break On Through (To The Other Side)/End Of The Night	42
67	Elektra EKSN 45012	Alabama Song (Whisky Bar)/Take It As It Comes	22
67	Elektra EKSN 45014	Light My Fire/The Crystal Ship	20
67	Elektra EKSN 45017	People Are Strange/Unhappy Girl	20
67	Elektra EKSN 45022	Love Me Two Times/Moonlight Drive	12
68	Elektra EKSN 45030	We Could Be So Good Together/The Unknown Soldier	12
68	Elektra EKSN 45037	Hello, I Love You/Love Street.	10
69	Elektra EKSN 45050	Touch Me/Wild Child	10
69	Elektra EKSN 45059	Wishful Sinful/Who Scared You?	10
69	Elektra EKSN 45065	Tell All The People/Easy Ride	10
70	Elektra 2101 004	You Make Me Real/The Spy	7
70	Elektra 2101 008	Roadhouse Blues/Blue Sunday	7
71	Elektra EK 45726	Love Her Madly/(You Need Meat) Don't Go No Further	6
71	Elektra K 12021	Riders On The Storm/The Changeling	6
72	Elektra K 12036	Tightrope Ride/Variety Is The Spice Of Life	5
72	Elektra K 12048	Ship W/ Sails/In The Eye Of The Sun	5
72	Elektra K 12059	Get Up And Dance/Tree Trunks	5
79	Elektra K 12215/SAM 94	Love Me Two Times/Hello, I Love You//	
		Ghost Song/Roadhouse Blues (double pack)	8
83	Elektra E 9974T	Gloria/Love Me Two Times (12", p/s with poster)	10
89	Elektra 969 344-2	Riders On The Storm/The End (3" CD, card sleeve)	8
91	Elektra EKR 125TW	Light My Fire/People Are Strange/Soul Kitchen (12", p/s, with poster).	8
92	Final Vinyl FV 1/2	INTERVIEW TAPES (2 x 7" box set, with 7 inserts, numbered, 500 only).	10

ORIGINAL LPs

67	Elektra EKL 4007	THE DOORS (orange label, also stereo EKS 74007)	65/35
68	Elektra EKL 4014	STRANGE DAYS (textured orange label, inner sleeve,	
		also stereo EKS 74014)	65/35
68	Elektra EKL 4024	WAITING FOR THE SUN (orange label, gatefold sleeve with insert,	
		also stereo EKS 74024)	65/35
69	Elektra EKS 75005	THE SOFT PARADE (orange label, gatefold sleeve, with lyric sheet)	25
70	Elektra EKS 75007	MORRISON HOTEL (orange label, gatefold sleeve)	20
70	Elektra 2665 002	ABSOLUTELY LIVE (2-LP, orange label, gatefold sleeve)	20
71	Elektra EKS 74079	13 ('butterfly' label, compilation)	15
71	Elektra K 42090	L.A. WOMAN ('butterfly' label, round-cornered, die-cut PVC 'window'	
		sleeve & yellow inner sleeve)	15
71	Elektra K 42104	OTHER VOICES ('butterfly' label, gatefold sleeve)	15
72	Elektra K 62009	WEIRD SCENES INSIDE THE GOLDMINE	
		(2-LP, 'butterfly' label, gatefold sleeve)	20
72	Elektra K 62116	FULL CIRCLE ('butterfly label', gatefold sleeve)	15
78	Elektra K 52111	AN AMERICAN PRAYER ('butterfly' label, gatefold sleeve,	
		with 8-page booklet)	25
88	HMV C 8816	L.A. WOMAN (CD, HMV box set, 2,500 only, numbered with booklet)	18
91	Elektra 7559 61082-2	IN CONCERT (2-CD)	20
98	Elektra 7559 62295-2	THE DOORS BOX SET VOL. I (2-CD, with booklet)	22
98	Elektra 7559 62296-2	THE DOORS BOX SET VOL. II (2-CD, with booklet)	22

(see also Ray Manzarek)

DOORS OF PERCEPTION

91	Lizard Nation LN 002	ACID DREAMS (12" EP, includes Jim Morrison sample, withdrawn)	8
91	Lizard Nation LN 001	SO JOIN MR. DREAMS (LP, with inner sleeve, some with booklet,	
		850 only)	15/12

MIKE DORANE & CIMARONS

71	Ackee ACK 144	Penguin Funk/Ad-Lib	8

DOREEN (Campbell) & ALL STARS

67	Rainbow RAI 114	Rude Girls/Please Stay	15

DOREEN (Shaffer) & JACKIE (Opel)

65	Ska Beat JB 208	Welcome Home/You And I	25

(see also Jackie & Doreen)

KENNY DORHAM & SONNY ROLLINS

58	London LTZU 15133	JAZZ CONTRASTS (LP)	15

DORIAN

70	Ember EMB S 285	Psychedelic Lipstick/Help For My Waiting	6

DORIS

81	ABCD ABCD 1	Sitting Here Waiting (no p/s)	5
82	ABCD ABCD 3	GYPSY LADY (LP, actually credited to A Band Called Doris)	250

DORIS

98	EMI/Mr. Bongo MRBLP 010	DID YOU GIVE THE WORLD SOME LOVE TODAY, BABY?	
		(LP, reissue of Swedish 60s LP)	12

HAROLD DORMAN

60	Top Rank JAR 357	Mountain Of Love/To Be With You	25
61	London HLS 9386	There They Go/I'll Stick By You	30

STACY DORNING

74	Scratchy CHR 1070	STACY DORNING (LP, with Duncan Browne)	12

DOROTHY

80	Industrial IR 0014	I Confess/Softness (p/s)	8

RALPH DORPER

83	Operation Twilight OPT 18	THE ERASERHEAD EP (12")	12

(see also Propaganda)

Chris DORS

CHRIS DORS
61	Fontana H 329	That's When Your Heartaches Begin/They Called It Love 12

DIANA DORS
53	HMV B 10613	I Feel So Mmm…/A Kiss And A Cuddle (78). 18
60	Pye 7N 15242	April Heart/Point Of No Return (78 rpm, Pye N 15242 = £25). 8
64	Fontana TF 506	So Little Time/It's Too Late. 12
66	Polydor BM 56111	Security/Gary. 10
77	EMI EMI 2705	Passing By/It's A Small World 8
82	Nomis NOM 1	Where Did They Go/It's You Again (with Gary Dors). 8
60	Pye NPL 18044	SWINGIN' DORS (LP, foldout sleeve, red vinyl). 100

RAY DORSET (WITH MUNGO JERRY)
72	Dawn DNS 1018	Cold Blue Excursion/I Need It (solo). 10
77	Polydor 2230 103	MUNGO BOX (EP, as Ray Dorset & Mungo Jerry, p/s). 8
79	Polydor 2059 127	Dancin' In The Street/Rockin' On The Road
		(as Ray Dorset & Mungo Jerry, p/s). 8
79	Satellite RAY 001	Forgotten Land/New Way Of Life (solo, unreleased; 100 promos only). 10
81	Stagecoach TRI 101	Knocking On Heaven's Door/Hazel Eyes (as Ray Dorset with Mungo Jerry). 8
72	Dawn DNLS 3033	COLD BLUE EXCURSION (LP, solo; gatefold sleeve with lyric inner). 20
(see also Mungo Jerry, Good Earth, County Jug, Macon Jug, Katmandu, Insiders, Panache, Made In England)		

DORSETS
65	Sue WI 391	Pork Chops/Cool It 40

GERRY DORSEY
59	Decca F 11108	Mister Music Man/Crazy Bells (78 rpm = £10) 15
59	Parlophone R 4595	I'll Never Fall In Love Again/Every Day Is A Wonderful Day. 10
61	Parlophone R 4739	Big Wheel/The Sentimental Joker. 10
64	Pye 7N 15622	Baby I Do/Take Your Time 10
65	Hickory 45-1337	Baby Turn Around/Things I Wanna Do 12

JACK DORSEY ORCHESTRA
65	Polydor 56020	Dance Of The Daleks/Likely Lads 18
68	Pye 7N 17501	Soul Coaxing/Elizabeth's Waltz. 8

JIMMY DORSEY ORCHESTRA
57	HMV POP 324	So Rare/Sophisticated Swing 5
57	HMV POP 383	Jay-Dee's Boogie Woogie/June Night. 8

LEE DORSEY
62	Top Rank JAR 606	Do-Re-Mi/People Gonna Talk 25
65	Sue WI 367	Do-Re-Mi/Ya Ya 30
65	Stateside SS 441	Ride Your Pony/The Kitty Cat Song 10
65	Stateside SS 465	Work Work Work/Can You Hear Me. 10
66	Sue WI 399	Messed Around/When I Meet My Baby 40
66	Stateside SS 485	Get Out Of My Life, Woman/So Long 10
66	Stateside SS 506	Confusion/Neighbour's Daughter 8
66	Stateside SS 528	Working In A Coalmine/Mexico (with yellow vinyl = £20+) 10
66	Stateside SS 552	Holy Cow/Operation Heartache 10
67	Stateside SS 593	Rain Rain Go Away/Gotta Find A Job 6
67	Stateside SS 2017	My Old Car/Why Wait Until Tomorrow 6
67	Stateside SS 2055	Go-Go Girl/I Can Hear You Callin' 6
68	President PT 226	Ya Ya/Give Me You 6
68	Bell BLL 1006	Can You Hear Me/Cynthia. 6
69	Bell BLL 1051	I'm Gonna Sit Right Down And Write Myself A Letter/Little Baby 6
69	Bell BLL 1060	Ride Your Pony/Get Out Of My Life, Woman 6
69	Bell BLL 1074	Everything I Do Gonh Be Funky/There Should Be A Book. 12
71	Mojo 2066 063	Occapella/Yes We Can Part 1. 5
72	Mojo 2093 009	Freedom For The Stallion/If She Won't (Find Someone Who Will) 5
66	Stateside SE 1038	RIDE YOUR PONY (EP). 25
66	Stateside SE 1043	YOU'RE BREAKING ME UP (EP). 30
65	Sue ILP 924	THE BEST OF LEE DORSEY (LP). 65
66	Stateside S(S)L 10177	LEE DORSEY — RIDE YOUR PONY (LP). 25
66	Stateside S(S)L 10192	THE NEW LEE DORSEY (LP). 25
71	Polydor 2489 006	YES WE CAN (LP). 22

LEE DORSEY & BETTY HARRIS
69	Buffalo BFS 1002	Love Lots Of Lovin'/Take Care Of Your Love. 15
(see also Betty Harris)		

TOMMY DORSEY ORCHESTRA
58	RCA RD 27069	FRANKIE AND TOMMY (LP, with Frank Sinatra) 12
(see also Frank Sinatra, Jo Stafford)		

D.O.S.E.
95	Colosseum TOGA 001TJX	Plug Myself In (with Mark E. Smith) (p/s, numbered, 1-sided, 500 only). 5
(see also Fall)		

JOHNNY DOT & DASHERS
62	Salvo SLO 1805	I Love An Angel/Just For You (99 copies only) 50

DOTTY & BONNIE
64	Rio R 43	I'm So Glad/DOUGLAS BROTHERS: Got You On My Mind 12
64	Island WI 143	Your Kisses/Why Worry 15
64	Island WI 148	Dearest/Tears Are Falling 12
65	Ska Beat JB 183	Foul Play/ROLAND ALPHONSO & GROUP: Yard Broom 35
67	Ska Beat JB 274	I'll Know/Love Is Great 15
(see also Bonnie Frankson, Eric Morris, Don Drummond, Skatalites, Baba Brooks)		

DOUBLE FEATURE
67	Deram DM 115	Baby Get Your Head Screwed On/Come On Baby . . . . 50+
67	Deram DM 165	Handbags And Gladrags/Just Another Lonely Night 18

DOUBLES with GAY BLADES
59	HMV POP 613	Hey Girl!/Little Joe	120

SUZANNE DOUCET
68	Liberty LBF 15150	Swan Song/Cry My Heart	12

DOUGHNUT RING
68	Deram DM 215	Dance Around Julie/The Bandit	38

(see also Crocheted Doughnut Ring)

JOHNNY DOUGHTY
77	Topic 12TS 324	ROUND RYE BAY FOR MORE (LP, with insert)	15

CARL DOUGLAS (& BIG STAMPEDE)
66	Go AJ 11401	Crazy Feeling/PETER PERRY SOUL BAND: Keep It To Myself	30
67	Go AJ 11408	Let The Birds Sing/Something For Nothing	30
67	United Artists UP 1206	Nobody Cries/Serving A Sentence Of Life (solo)	150
68	United Artists UP 2227	Sell My Soul To The Devil/Good Hard Worker	30
71	CBS 7101	Do You Need My Love/Lean On Me	50
72	Blue Mountain BM 1007	Somebody Stop This Madness/Ain't No Use (as Karl Douglas)	10

CHIC DOUGLAS
58	Fontana H 121	I'm Not Afraid Anymore/Jo-Ann	10

CRAIG DOUGLAS
58	Decca F 11055	Nothin' Shakin'/Sitting In A Tree House (78 rpm = £10)	25
58	Decca F 11075	Go Chase A Moonbeam/Are You Really Mine (78 rpm = £8)	18
59	Top Rank JAR 110	Come Softly To Me/Golden Girl (78 rpm = £10)	7
59	Top Rank JAR 133	Teenager In Love/The 39 Steps (78 rpm = £12)	7
59	Top Rank JAR 159	Only Sixteen/My First Love Affair (78 rpm = £12)	6
59	Top Rank JAR 204	The Riddle Of Love/Wish It Were Me	6
59	Top Rank TR 5004	Battle Of New Orleans/Dream Lover/SHEILA BUXTON: Personality/ Where Were You On Our Wedding Day/BERT WEEDON: I Need Your Love Tonight ('King-Size' 7", special sleeve)	15
60	Top Rank JAR 268	Pretty Blue Eyes/Sandy	6
60	Top Rank JAR 340	Heart Of A Teenage Girl/New Boy	6
60	Top Rank JAR 406	Oh, What A Day/Why, Why, Why	6
60	Top Rank JAR 515	Where's The Girl (I Never Met)/My Hour Of Love	6
61	Top Rank JAR 543	The Girl Next Door/Hey Mister Conscience	6
61	Top Rank JAR 555	A Hundred Pounds Of Clay/Hello Spring	12
61	Top Rank JAR 556	A Hundred Pounds Of Clay (censored version)/Hello Spring (some in p/s)	20/7
61	Top Rank JAR 569	Time/After All	6
61	Top Rank JAR 589	No Greater Love/We'll Have A Lot To Tell	6
62	Top Rank JAR 603	A Change Of Heart/Another You	7
62	Top Rank JAR 610	When My Little Girl Is Smiling/Ring A Ding	7
62	Columbia DB 4854	Our Favourite Melodies/Rainbows	7
62	Decca F 11523	Oh Lonesome Me/Please Don't Take My Heart	5
62	Decca F 11575	Town Crier/I'd Be Smiling Now	5
63	Decca F 11665	Danke Shoen/Teenage Mona Lisa	5
63	Decca F 11722	I'm So Glad I Found Her/Love Her While She's Young	5
63	Decca F 11763	Counting Up The Kisses/From Russia With Love	6
64	Fontana TF 458	Silly Boy/Love Leave Me Alone	10
64	Fontana TF 475	Come Closer/She's Smiling At Me (as Craig Douglas & Tridents)	15
65	Fontana TF 525	Across The Street/Party Girl	10
65	Fontana TF 580	Around The Corner/Find The Girl	10
66	Fontana TF 690	I'm On The Outside Looking In/Knock On Any Door	8
69	Pye 7N 17746	How Do You Feel About That/Then	7
69	Pye 7N 17863	Raindrops Keep Falling On My Head/Don't Mind If I Cry	8
59	Top Rank JKR 8033	CRAIG SINGS FOR 'ROXY' (EP)	25
60	Decca DFE 6633	CRAIG (EP)	30
62	Decca DFE 8509	CUDDLE UP WITH CRAIG (EP)	22
63	Columbia SEG 8219	CRAIG MOVIE SONGS (EP)	35
60	Top Rank BUY 049	CRAIG DOUGLAS (LP)	60
61	Top Rank 35-103	BANDWAGON BALL (LP)	42
62	Columbia 33SX 1468	OUR FAVOURITE MELODIES (LP)	80

(see also Bert Weedon)

DONNA DOUGLAS
58	Fontana H 158	The Shepherd/I'm Dancing With Tears In My Eyes	8
59	Fontana H 223	Six Boys And Seven Girls/Into Each Life Some Rain Must Fall (78 rpm = £8)	8
61	Piccadilly 7N 35014	Tammy Tell Me True/Memory Lane	8
62	Piccadilly 7N 35031	The Message In A Bottle/If This Is Love	9
62	Piccadilly 7N 35042	Matelot/All The Other Girls	8
63	Piccadilly 7N 35111	It's A Pity To Say Goodnight/Do I Know	8
63	Piccadilly 7N 35135	He's So Near/Turn Around	8
64	Pye 7N 15654	Blue Star/Java Jones	8

JOHNNY DOUGLAS (& HIS ORCHESTRA/COMBO)
54	Decca F 10276	Ballet Of The Bells/Solfeggio (as Johnny Douglas & His Orchestra)	6
63	Speyside SK 1501	Ski Jump/Clementine (as Johnny Douglas Combo)	6
65	RCA 1444	Crack In The World/Time	12

KIRK DOUGLAS & MELLOMEN
55	Brunswick 05408	A Whale Of A Tale/And The Moon Grew Brighter And Brighter	15

LEW DOUGLAS & HIS ORCHESTRA
54	MGM SP 1093	Caesar's Boogie/Turn Around Boy	15

MARK DOUGLAS
62	Ember EMB S 166	It Matters Not/Upside Down	75

MINT VALUE £

NORMA DOUGLAS
57   London HLZ 8475   Be It Resolved/Joe He Gone 25

ROB & DEAN DOUGLAS
67   Deram DM 132   I Can Make It With You/Phone Me 40

DOUGLAS BROTHERS
66   Rio R 57   Valley Of Tears/CHARMERS: Where Do I Turn. 15
66   Rio R 63   Down And Out/RONALD WILSON: Lonely Man . . . . 80+
     (see also Dotty & Bonnie)

HARRY DOUGLASS & DEEP RIVER BOYS
60   Top Rank JAR 352   Dum Dum De Dum/Go Galloway, Go. 7
     (see also Deep River Boys)

RONNIE DOVE
64   Stateside SS 314   Sweeter Than Sugar/I Believed In You 7
64   Stateside SS 346   Say You/Let Me Stay Today 7
64   Stateside SS 366   Right Or Wrong/Baby, Put Your Arms Around Me 7
65   Stateside SS 392   Hello Pretty Girl/Keep It A Secret 7
65   Stateside SS 412   One Kiss For Old Times' Sake/Bluebird 8
65   Stateside SS 436   A Little Bit Of Heaven/If I Live To Be A Hundred 8
65   Stateside SS 462   I'll Make All Your Dreams Come True/I Had To Lose You 7
65   Stateside SS 480   Kiss Away/Where In The World 7
66   Stateside SS 492   When Liking Turns To Loving/I'm Learning How To Smile Again 7
66   Stateside SS 510   Let's Start All Over Again/That Empty Feeling 7
66   Stateside SS 524   Happy Summer Days/Long After 7
66   Stateside SS 542   I Really Don't Want To Know/Years Of Tears 7
66   Stateside SS 571   Cry/Autumn Rhapsody 7
70   Stateside SS 2003   One More Mountain To Climb/All. 7
70   Stateside SS 2018   My Babe/Put My Mind At Ease. 7
70   Stateside SS 2047   I Want To Love You For What You Are/I Thank You For Your Love 7
70   Stateside SS 2086   Dancin' Out Of My Heart/Back From Baltimore 7
68   Stateside SS 2119   Mountain Of Love/Never Gonna Cry (The Way I'll Cry Tonight). 8
65   Stateside SL 10149   RONNIE DOVE (LP) 40

DOVELLS
61   Columbia DB 4718   The Bristol Stomp/Out In The Cold Again 20
62   Columbia DB 4810   Do The New Continental/Mopitty Mope Stomp 20
62   Columbia DB 4877   Bristol Twistin' Annie/The Actor 20
62   Cameo Parkway P 845   Hully Gully Baby/Your Last Chance 10
63   Cameo Parkway P 861   You Can't Run Away From Yourself/Save Me Baby 10
63   Cameo Parkway P 867   You Can't Sit Down/Stompin' Everywhere 15
63   Cameo Parkway P 882   Betty In Bermudas/Dance The Froog 12
63   Cameo Parkway P 901   Be My Girl/Dragster On The Prowl 22
79   London HAU 8515   CAMEO PARKWAY SESSIONS (LP). 15
     (see also Len Barry)

DOVES
98   Manchester MANC 9   Seven Day Smile (with Jane Weaver)/ANDY VOTEL & JANE WEAVER: Gutter
                              Girl (p/s) 10
98   Manchester MANCCD 9   Seven Day Smile (with Jane Weaver)/ANDY VOTEL & JANE WEAVER: Gutter . . . .
                              Girl/JANE WEAVER: You're Not The Only Person That I Used To Know (CD) 12
99   Casino CHIP 003   Here It Comes/Meet Me At The Pier/(Acoustic Version) (10", p/s) 20
02   Heavenly HVN 111-10   There Goes The Fear/Hit The Ground Running (10", p/s). 8
98   Casino CHIP 001   CEDAR EP: Cedar Room/Rise/Zither (10", wraparound p/s) 70
99   Casino CHIP 002   SEA EP (10", p/s). 20
99   Casino CHIP 002CD   SEA EP (CD, gatefold card sleeve) 40
     (see also Badly Drawn Boy, Sub Sub, Jane Weaver v Doves)

NICK DOW
79   Dingles DIN 306   BURD MARGARET (LP) 15

BRENT DOWE
71   Summit SUM 8521   Knock Three Times/GAYLADS: This Time I Won't Hurt You 6
71   Summit SUM 8525   Put Your Hand In The Hand/Miracle (B-side actually
                              "It Took A Miracle Version" by Beverley's All Stars). 6
71   Summit SUM 8530   Freedom Train/BEVERLEY'S ALL STARS: Freedom Train (Version) 6
73   Green Door GD 4061   Reggae Makossa/No Nola (B-side actually by Melodians) 8
     (see also Melodians)

JOE DOWELL
61   Mercury AMT 1161   The Bridge Of Love/Just My Love 7
62   Mercury AMT 1180   Little Red Rented Rowboat/The One I Left For You. 7
60s Wing   WOODEN HEART (LP) 20

DOWLANDS
62   Oriole CB 1748   Little Sue/Julie (as Dowlands & Soundtracks). 45
62   Oriole CB 1781   Big Big Fella/Don't Ever Change 100
63   Oriole CB 1815   Break Ups/A Love Like Ours 45
63   Oriole CB 1892   Lonely Johnny (song actually titled "Lucky Johnny")/
                              Do You Have To Have Me Blue? . . . . 850+
64   Oriole CB 1897   All My Loving/Hey Sally (as Dowlands & Soundtracks) 15
64   Oriole CB 1926   I Walk The Line/Happy Endings. 40
64   Oriole CB 1947   Wishing And Hoping/You Will Regret It 80
65   Columbia DB 7547   Don't Make Me Over/Someone Must Be Feeling Sad 40

DOWNBEATS
61   Starlite ST45 051   Thinkin' Of You/Midnight Love . . . . 25+

BRUCE DOWNER
71	Summit SUM 8524	Free The People (actually by Bruce Ruffin)/BEVERLEY'S ALL STARS: Free The People (Version)	6

BOB DOWNES
70	Vertigo 6059 011	No Time Like The Present/Keep Off The Grass	7
70	Philips SBL 7922	BOB DOWNES' OPEN MUSIC (LP)	100
70	Vertigo 6360 005	ELECTRIC CITY (LP, gatefold sleeve, swirl label)	35
73	Ophenian BDOM 001	DIVERSIONS (LP)	20
74	Ophenian BDOM 002	EPISODES AT 4AM (LP, with insert)	20
75	Ophenian BDOM 003	HELLS ANGELS (LP)	25

DEIRDRE DOWNES & BROADSIDERS
69	Pye 7N 17781	Lady Mary/Did He Mention My Name	7

DOWN HOME
70s	Lismor Folk LIFL 7011	FIDDLE MUSIC VOLUME ONE (LP)	15

BIG AL DOWNING
64	Sue WI 341	Yes I'm Loving You/Please Come Home	40

DOWNLINERS SECT
64	Columbia DB 7300	Baby What's Wrong/Be A Sect Maniac	28
64	Columbia DB 7347	Little Egypt/Sect Appeal	28
64	Columbia DB 7415	Find Out What's Happening/Insecticide	28
65	Columbia DB 7509	Wreck Of The Old '97/Leader Of The Sect	28
65	Columbia DB 7597	I Got Mine/Waiting In Heaven Somewhere	28
65	Columbia DB 7712	Bad Storm Coming/Lonely And Blue	28
66	Columbia DB 7817	All Night Worker/He Was A Square	28
66	Columbia DB 7939	Glendora/I'll Find Out	65
66	Columbia DB 8008	The Cost Of Living/Everything I've Got To Give	30
64	Contrast Sound RBCSP 1	NITE IN GREAT NEWPORT STREET (EP)	300
65	Columbia SEG 8438	THE SECT SING SICK SONGS (EP)	125
64	Columbia 33SX 1658	THE SECT (LP)	150
65	Columbia 33SX 1745	THE COUNTRY SECT (LP)	125
66	Columbia S(C)X 6028	THE ROCK SECT'S IN (LP, mono/stereo)	100/120

(see also Don Crane's Downliners Sect)

DOWN TO EARTH
71	Downtown DT 485	Under The Boardwalk/Under The Boardwalk (Version) (B-side actually "Double Barrel Version")	7

DOWNTOWN ALL STARS
69	Downtown DT 426	Everybody Feel Good/RUDIES: Downtown Jump	8

DOYAL & GROVES (MELODY BOYS)
60	Top Rank JKP 2057	COUNTRY AND WESTERN EXPRESS VOL. 3 (EP)	8

GENE DOZIER & UNITED FRONT
74	Mercury 6167 007	Give The Women What They Want/The Best Girl I Ever Had	25

LAMONT DOZIER
74	Probe PRO 618	Trying To Hold On To My Woman/We Don't Want Nobody To Come	10
74	Anchor ABC 4003	Fish Ain't Bitin'/Breaking Out All Over	5
75	Anchor ABC 4056	All Cried Out/Rose	5
77	Warner Bros K 16942	Going Back To My Roots/Going Back To My Roots (Version)	8
81	CBS A 1235	To Cool Me Out/Starting Over	10
74	ABC ABCL 5042	OUT HERE ON MY OWN (LP)	18
75	ABC ABCL 5096	BLACK BACH (LP)	18
77	Warner Bros K 56396	PEDDLIN' MUSIC ON THE SIDE (LP)	15

(see also Holland & Dozier)

DOZY, BEAKY, MICK & TICH (D.B.M.&T.)
69	Fontana TF 1061	Tonight Today/Bad News	6
70	Fontana TF 1075	Mr. President/Frisco Annie (as D.B.M.&T)	5
70	Philips 6006 066	Festival/Leader Of A Rock'N'Roll Band	5
70	Philips 6308 029	FRESH EAR (LP, gatefold sleeve, credited to D.B.M.&T)	15

(see also Dave Dee Dozy Beaky Mick & Tich)

DRAGON
76	Acorn CF 268	DRAGON (LP, gatefold sleeve)	30

DRAGONFLY
74	Retreat RTS 257	Gondola/Almost Abandoned (demo)	15
75	Retreat RTS 261	Driving Around The World/Since I Left My Home	8
74	Retreat RTL 6002	ALMOST ABANDONED (LP)	15

DRAGONFLY
80s	Dragonfly DF 001	SILENT NIGHTS EP (p/s, private pressing)	200

DRAGONSFIRE
82	Belltree BTR 001	RISING PHOENIX (LP, with insert)	25

(see also Spinning Wheel)

DRAG SET
66	Go AJ 11405	Get Out Of My Way/Day And Night	250

(see also Open Mind)

DRAGSTER
81	Heavy Metal HEAVY 4	Ambition/Won't Bring You Back (p/s)	30

CHARLIE DRAKE
58	Parlophone R 4461	Splish Splash/Hello, My Darlings (78 rpm = £8)	10
58	Parlophone R 4478	Volare/Itchy Twitchy Feeling (78 rpm = £9)	10
58	Parlophone R 4496	Tom Thumb's Tune/Goggle Eye Ghee (78 rpm = £10)	7

59	Parlophone R 4552	Sea Cruise/Starkle, Starkle Little Twink (78 rpm = £10)	12
60	Parlophone R 4675	Naughty/Old Mr. Shadow	7
60	Parlophone R 4701	Mr. Custer/Glow Worm	7
61	Parlophone R 4824	My Boomerang Won't Come Back/She's My Girl.	5
62	Parlophone R 4875	Tanglefoot/Drake's Progress	5
62	Parlophone R 4918	I Bent My Assigai/Sweet Freddy Green	5
63	Parlophone R 5057	I've Lost The End Of My Yodel/I Can Can't I	5
64	Parlophone R 5143	I'm Too Heavy For The Light Brigade/The Reluctant Tight-Rope Walker	5
64	Parlophone R 5209	Charles Drake 007/Bumpanology (Bump Head Blues)	5
71	Columbia DB 8829	Puckwudgie/Toffee And Tears	5
75	Charisma CB 270	You Never Know/I'm Big Enough For Me (produced by Peter Gabriel)	9
76	Sol Doon SDRO 24S	Super Punk/Someone	9
58	Parlophone GEP 8720	HELLO MY DARLINGS (EP)	20
60	Parlophone GEP 8812	NAUGHTY CHARLIE DRAKE (EP)	18
64	Parlophone GEP 8903	HITS FROM THE MAN IN THE MOON (EP)	15

NICK DRAKE

79	Island RSS 7	Introduction/Hazy Jane II/Time Has Told Me/Fruit Tree/Rider On The Wheel ("Fruit Tree" sampler, 1-sided promo only)	250
69	Island ILPS 9105	FIVE LEAVES LEFT (LP, 1st pressing, pink label, black 'circle' logo, g/fold sleeve)	300+
69	Island ILPS 9105	FIVE LEAVES LEFT (LP, gatefold sleeve, 2nd pressing, 'pink rim label, 'palm tree' logo)	50+
70	Island ILPS 9134	BRYTER LAYTER (LP, 'pink rim label, 'palm tree' logo)	150+
72	Island ILPS 9184	PINK MOON (LP, 'pink rim label, 'palm tree' logo, gatefold sleeve)	100+
79	Island NDSP 100	FRUIT TREE (3-LP, box set with booklet)	70
85	Island ILPS 9826	HEAVEN IN A WILD FLOWER (THE BEST OF NICK DRAKE) (LP)	22
86	Hannibal HNBX 5302	FRUIT TREE (4-LP, expanded reissue with booklet)	75
87	Hannibal HNBL 1318	TIME OF NO REPLY (LP)	18
89	Island ILPS 9105	FIVE LEAVES LEFT (LP, reissue, 'blue with white palm tree' label)	18
89	Island ILPS 9134	BRYTER LAYTER (LP, reissue, 'blue with white palm tree' label)	18
89	Island ILPS 9184	PINK MOON (LP, reissue, 'blue with white palm tree' label).	18
91	Hannibal HNCD 5402	FRUIT TREE (4-CD, with booklet in 12" x 12" box)	70

PETE DRAKE

63	Philips BF 1332	Forever/Sleep Walk	10

DRAMATICS

72	Stax 2025 053	Whatcha See Is Whatcha Get/Thankful For Your Love	8
72	Stax 2025 101	In The Rain/Get Up And Get Down	6
73	Stax 2025 117	Toast To A Fool/Your Love Was Strange	12
73	Stax 2025 181	Hey You, Get Off My Mountain/Devil Is Dope.	6
76	ABC ABC 4101	You're Fooling You/I'll Make It So Good	6
72	Stax 2362 025	WHATCHA SEE IS WHATCHA GET (LP)	20
74	Stax STX 1021	A DRAMATIC EXPERIENCE (LP)	20
75	ABC ABCL 5121	DRAMATIC JACKPOT (LP, gatefold sleeve)	12
75	ABC ABCL 5150	DRAMA V (LP, gatefold sleeve)	12

DRAMATIS

82	Rocket XPRES 79-12	The Shame (Dance Party Mix 1)/Only Find Rewind (12", p/s, with poster)	8

(see also Gary Numan, Paul Gardiner)

BARRY DRANSFIELD

72	Polydor Folk Mill 2383 160	BARRY DRANSFIELD (LP)	240

(see also Robin & Barry Dransfield, Dransfields)

ROBIN DRANSFIELD

80	Topic 12TS 414	TIDEWAVE (LP)	18

(see also Robin & Barry Dransfield, Dransfields)

ROBIN & BARRY DRANSFIELD

70	Trailer LER 2011	THE ROUT OF THE BLUES (LP yellow label)	40
71	Trailer LER 2026	LORD OF ALL I BEHOLD (LP)	35

(see also Robin Dransfield, Barry Dransfield, Dransfields)

DRANSFIELDS

76	Transatlantic TRA 322	THE FIDDLER'S DREAM (LP)	22
77	Free Reed 018	POPULAR TO CONTRARY BELIEF (LP)	15
78	Transatlantic TRA 386	BOWIN' AND SCRAPIN' (LP)	15

(see also Robin & Barry Dransfield, Robin Dransfield, Barry Dransfield)

RUSTY DRAPER

56	Mercury MT 101	Are You Satisfied?/Wabash Cannonball (78)	10
56	Mercury MT 113	Rock And Roll Ruby/House Of Cards (78)	12
56	Mercury MT 128	In The Middle Of The House/Pink Cadillac (78)	15
57	Mercury MT 137	Giant (from the film)/Tiger Lilly (with Jack Halloran Singers) (78).	8
57	Mercury MT 147	Let's Go Calypso/Should I Never Love Again (78).	8
58	Mercury MT 194	Buzz Buzz Buzz/I Get The Blues When It Rains (78).	12
58	Mercury 7MT 211	Gamblin' Gal/That's My Doll (78 rpm, Mercury MT211 = £10).	15
58	Mercury 7MT 229	Chicken-Pickin' Hawk/June, July And August (78 rpm, Mercury MT229 = £10).	15
59	Mercury AMT 1019	Shoppin' Around/With This Ring (78 rpm = £12)	30
59	Mercury AMT 1034	The Sun Will Always Shine/Hey Li Lee Li Lee Li	12
60	Mercury AMT 1101	Mule Skinner Blues/Please Help Me, I'm Falling	8
60	Mercury AMT 1110	Luck Of The Irish/It's A Little More Like Heaven	7
61	Mercury AMT 1127	Jealous Heart/Ten Thousand Years Ago.	12
63	London HLU 9786	Night Life/That's Why I Love You Like I Do	12
65	London HLU 9989	Folsom Prison Blues/You Can't Be True, Dear	12
56	Mercury MEP 9506	PRESENTING RUSTY DRAPER (EP).	40
59	Mercury ZEP 10016	RUSTY DRAPER (EP)	22
60	Mercury ZEP 10059	RUSTY IN GAMBLING MOOD (EP)	22

60	Mercury ZEP 10095	MULE SKINNER BLUES (EP)	25
64	London RE-U 1431	RUSTY DRAPER NO. 1 (EP)	20
64	London RE-U 1432	RUSTY DRAPER NO. 2 (EP)	20
60	Mercury MMC 14040	HITS THAT SOLD A MILLION (LP)	25

MIKEY DREAD (AKA MICKEY CAMPBELL (AKA DREAD AT THE CONTROLS)

81	Dread At The Controls DATC 003	Warrior Stylee/Israel Stylee (12")	15
82	Dread... DATCD 008	Roots & Culture/Jungle Dread (12")	15
77	Hawkeye HALP 001	DUB (LP)	15
79	Dread... DTCLP 002	AFRICAN ANTHEM – THE MIKEY DREAD SHOW DUBWISE (LP)	20
80	Dread... DTCLP 006	WORLD WAR III (LP)	15
80	Dread... DTLP 001	MASTER SHOWCASE (LP)	35
83	Dread... DTLP 009	DUB MERCHANT (LP)	25

DREAMERS
68	Columbia DB 8340	The Maybe Song/The Long Road	10

(see also Freddie & Dreamers)

DREAMERS
69	Downtown DT 407	Sweet Chariot/Let's Go Downtown	7
69	Downtown DT 408	I Second That Emotion/Dear Love	7

DREAMLETS
65	Ska Beat JB 182	Really Now/SKATALITES: Street Corner	40

DREAMLOVERS
61	Columbia DB 4711	When We Get Married/Just Because	200

(see also Chubby Checker)

DREAM MERCHANTS
67	Decca F 12617	Rattler/I'll Be With You In Apple Blossom Time	8

DREAM POLICE
70	Decca F 12998	I'll Be Home (In A Day Or So)/Living Is Easy	10
70	Decca F 13078	Our Song/Much Too Much	6
70	Decca F 13105	I've Got No Choice/What's The Cure For Happiness?	6

DREAMS
68	United Artists UP 2249	I Will See You There/A Boy Needs A Girl	35
69	CBS 4247	Baby I'm Your Man/Softly, Softly	7
69	Dolphin 4432	Casatschok/Don't You Ask Me	7
70	CBS 64203	DREAMS (LP)	20
72	CBS 64597	IMAGINE MY SURPRISE (LP)	20

DREAM SYNDICATE
88	Bucketfull Of Brains BOB 21	Blind Willie McTell/THE BEVIS FROND: High In A Flat (free with *Bucketfull Of Brains* issue 27, 33rpm, yellow die-cut sleeve)	10/6

DREAM THEATER
93	East West	Another Day/Status Seeker (live) (cassette)	12
94	East West A 5835	Lie/Space-Dye Vest/To Live Forever/Another Day (live) (p/s)	8
94	East West A 5835 T	Lie/Take The Time (Demo)/Space-Dye Vest (12", p/s)	20
89	MCA MCF 3445	WHEN DREAM AND DAY UNITE (LP)	12
92	Atco 7567 92148 1	IMAGES AND WORDS (LP)	15

DREAMTIMERS
61	London HLU 9368	The Dancin' Lady/An Invitation	25

DREAM WEAVERS
56	Brunswick 05515	It's Almost Tomorrow/You've Got Me Wondering (gold label lettering, later silver)	40/25
56	Brunswick 05568	A Little Love Can Go A Long, Long Way/Into The Night (featuring Wade Buff)	22
56	Brunswick 05607	You're Mine/Is There Somebody Else? (featuring Wade Buff)	15

DREGS
79	Disturbing DRO 1	THE DREGS EP (p/s, numbered, stamped sleeve, 500 only)	50

LEN DRESSLAR
56	Mercury 7MT 3	Chain Gang/These Hands (export issue)	15

JOHN DREVAR('S EXPRESSION)
67	MGM MGM 1367	The Closer She Gets/When I Come Home	70
68	Polydor BM 56290	What Greater Love/I've Decided (solo)	8

ALAN DREW
63	Columbia DB 7090	Here Comes The Rain/Always The Lonely One	6

PATTI DREW
68	Capitol CL 15557	Workin' On A Groovy Thing/Without A Doubt	15
68	Capitol CL 15575	Hard To Handle/Just Can't Forget About You	15

DREXCIYA
93	Rephlex CAT 017	3 — MOLECULAR ENHANCEMENT (12", 4-track)	10
95	Warp WAP 57	THE JOURNEY HOME (12", company sleeve)	10

DRIFTERS (U.K.)
59	Columbia DB 4263	Feelin' Fine/Don't Be A Fool (With Love) (78 rpm = £65)	50
59	Columbia DB 4325	Driftin'/Jet Black	45

(see also Shadows, Cliff Richard, Jet Harris, Tony Meehan)

MINT VALUE £

DRIFTERS (U.S.)
78s
56	London HLE 8344	Soldier Of Fortune/I Gotta Get Myself A Woman	100
58	London HLE 8686	Moonlight Bay/Drip-Drop	60
59	London HLE 8892	There Goes My Baby/Oh, My Love	100
59	London HLE 8988	Dance With Me/True Love, True Love	110
60	London HLE 9081	This Magic Moment/Baltimore	130

SINGLES
56	London HLE 8344	Soldier Of Fortune/I Gotta Get Myself A Woman	1,500
58	London HLE 8686	Moonlight Bay/Drip-Drop	150
59	London HLE 8892	There Goes My Baby/Oh, My Love	35
59	London HLE 8988	Dance With Me/True Love, True Love	20
60	London HLE 9081	This Magic Moment/Baltimore	18
60	London HLK 9145	Lonely Winds/Hey Senorita	18
60	London HLK 9201	Save The Last Dance For Me/Nobody But Me	12
61	London HLK 7114	Save The Last Dance For Me/This Magic Moment (export issue)	15
61	London HLK 7115	I Count The Tears/Dance With Me (export issue)	20
61	London HLK 9287	I Count The Tears/Sadie My Lady	20
61	London HLK 9326	Some Kind Of Wonderful/Honey Bee	15
61	London HLK 9382	Please Stay/No Sweet Lovin'	15
61	London HLK 9427	Sweets For My Sweet/Loneliness Or Happiness	12
62	London HLK 9500	Room Full Of Tears/Somebody New Dancin' With You	12
62	London HLK 9522	When My Little Girl Is Smiling/Mexican Divorce	10
62	London HLK 9554	Stranger On The Shore/What To Do	10
62	London HLK 9626	Up On The Roof/Another Night With The Boys	8
63	London HLK 9699	On Broadway/Let The Music Play	20
63	London HLK 9750	Rat Race/If You Don't Come Back	20
63	London HLK 9785	I'll Take You Home/I Feel Good All Over	10
64	London HLK 9848	Vaya Con Dios/In The Land Of Make Believe	10
64	London HLK 9886	One Way Love/Didn't It	10
64	Atlantic AT 4001	Under The Boardwalk/I Don't Want To Go On Without You	15
64	Atlantic AT 4008	I've Got Sand In My Shoes/He's Just A Playboy	15
64	Atlantic AT 4012	Saturday Night At The Movies/Spanish Lace	15
65	Atlantic AT 4019	At The Club/Answer The Phone	15
65	Atlantic AT 4023	Come On Over To My Place/Chains Of Love	20
65	Atlantic AT 4034	Follow Me/The Outside World	20
65	Atlantic AT 4040	I'll Take You Where The Music's Playing/Far From The Maddening Crowd	15
66	Atlantic AT 4062	We Gotta Sing/Nylon Stockings	22
66	Atlantic AT 4084	Memories Are Made Of This/My Island In The Sun	15
66	Atlantic 584 020	Up In The Streets Of Harlem/You Can't Love 'Em All	25
67	Atlantic 584 065	Baby What I Mean/Aretha	10
68	Atlantic 584 152	I'll Take You Where The Music's Playing/On Broadway	8
68	Atlantic 584 195	Still Burning In My Heart/I Need You Now	8
69	Atlantic 584 246	Saturday Night At The Movies/Under The Boardwalk	6
71	Atlantic 2091 064	A Rose By Any Other Name/Be My Lady	6
76	Atlantic K 10700	You Gotta Pay Your Dues/Black Silk	15
79	Epic EPC 7806	Pour Your Little Heart Out Parts 1 & 2	40

EPs
61	London RE-K 1282	THE DRIFTERS' GREATEST HITS	42
63	London RE-K 1355	THE DRIFTERS	45
63	London RE-K 1385	DRIFTIN'	45
64	Atlantic AET 6003	DRIFTIN' VOL. 2	40
65	Atlantic AET 6012	TONIGHT	38

LPs
60	London HA-K 2318	THE DRIFTERS' GREATEST HITS	60
62	London HA-K 2450	SAVE THE LAST DANCE FOR ME	70
65	Atlantic ATL 5015	OUR BIGGEST HITS	40
65	Atlantic ATL/STL 5023	THE GOOD LIFE WITH THE DRIFTERS (mono/stereo)	40
66	Atlantic ATL/STL 5039	I'LL TAKE YOU WHERE THE MUSIC'S PLAYING (mono/stereo)	40
67	Atlantic 587 038	BIGGEST HITS	20
67	Atlantic 587 061	I'LL TAKE YOU WHERE THE MUSIC'S PLAYING (reissue)	18
67	Atlantic 590 010	SOUVENIRS	25
67	Atlantic 587 063	SAVE THE LAST DANCE FOR ME (reissue)	20
68	Atlantic 587/588 103	THE DRIFTERS' GOLDEN HITS	15
68	Atlantic 587 123	ROCKIN' AND DRIFTIN'	32
68	Atlantic 587 144	GOOD GRAVY (as Clyde McPhatter & Drifters)	45
69	Atlantic 587/588 160	UP ON THE ROOF	20

(see also Clyde McPhatter, Ben E. King, Bobby Hendricks)

DRIFTING SLIM
66	Blue Horizon 45-1005	Good Morning Baby/My Sweet Woman (99 copies only)	100

DRIFTWOOD
70	Decca F 13084	Shylock Bay/The Wind Cries Above You	6
71	Decca F 13139	Say The Right Things/Still I'll Stay With You	6
70	Decca SKL 5069	DRIFTWOOD (LP)	48

(see also Neil Harrison)

JIMMY DRIFTWOOD
60	RCA RCX 191	COUNTRY GUITAR VOL. 13 (EP)	8
60	RCA RCX 193	TALL TALES IN SONG VOL. 1 (EP)	8
60	RCA RCX 195	TALL TALES IN SONG VOL. 2 (EP)	8
60	RCA RCX 198	TALL TALES IN SONG VOL. 3 (EP)	8

JULIE DRISCOLL
63	Columbia DB 7118	Take Me By The Hand/Stay Away From Me	40
65	Parlophone R 5296	Don't Do It No More/I Know You	35

66	Parlophone R 5444	I Didn't Want To Have To Do It/Don't Do It No More	20
67	Parlophone R 5588	I Know You Love Me Not/If You Should Ever Leave Me	20
67	Marmalade 598 005	Save Me	20
71	Polydor 2480 074	JULIE DRISCOLL — 1969 (LP)	45

JULIE DRISCOLL, BRIAN AUGER & TRINITY

68	Marmalade 598 006	This Wheel's On Fire/A Kind Of Love In	10
68	Marmalade 598 011	Road To Cairo/Shadows Of You	10
69	Marmalade 598 018	Take Me To The Water/Indian Rope Man	30
67	Marmalade 607/608 002	OPEN (LP, mono/stereo)	90/70
68	M. For Pleasure MFP 1265	JOOLS/BRIAN (LP, tracks shared by Julie Driscoll & Brian Auger)	30
69	Marmalade 608 005/6	STREET NOISE (2-LP)	150
69	Marmalade 608 014	STREET NOISE PART 1 (LP)	40
69	Marmalade 608 015	STREET NOISE PART 2 (LP)	40

(see also Brian Auger & Trinity, Working Week, Julie Tippetts, B.B. Blunder)

DRISCOLLS
| 80s | Woosh | Father's Name Is Dad/STRAWBERRY STORY: Tell Me Now (p/s) | 7 |

DRIVE
| 78 | NRG NE 467 | Jerkin'/Push'N'Shove (no p/s) | 50 |

DRIVE
| 93 | Ninja Tune DRIVE 1 | Curfew (Beatmasters 12" Mix)/(Rebel Funk Mix)/(Beatmasters Instrumental) (12", p/s) | 8 |
| 93 | Ninja Tune DRIVE CD 1 | Curfew (Rebel Radio Mix)/(Beatmasters 12" Mix)/(Rebel Funk Mix) (Beatmasters Instrumental) (CD) | 10 |

(see also All Saints)

DRIVER
| 80 | Rods Hot 1 | YOU BETTER TAKE IT (LP, 300 only) | 110 |

DRIVERS
83	Greyhound GRK 701	Talk All Night/Sister (p/s)	6
84	Nouveau NMS 5	Things/Stolen Treasure (p/s)	6
83	Greyhound GRK 3301	SHORT CUTS (LP)	12

(see also Nick Van Eede)

DRIZABONE
| 91 | 4th & Broadway BRW 223 | Real Love/Instrumental Version | 50 |
| 94 | 4th & Broadway 12 BRW 264 | Pressure (Roger's Soul Sensation Mix)/Pressure (Album Version)/Pressure (Bonus Beats Mix)/Pressure (Bone Idol Remix)/Pressure (Nu Solution Mix)/ Pressure (Underground Network Mix) (12", p/s) | 15 |

D-ROK
| 91 | Warhammer DROK 08722 | Get Out Of My Way (D-Mix)/Renegade/Get Out Of My Way (Airnix) (12", p/s) | 10 |
| 91 | Warhammer DROK 08710 | OBLIVION (LP) | 12 |

(see also Brian May)

FRANK D'RONE
60	Mercury AMT 1123	Strawberry Blonde (The Band Rocked On)/Time Hurries By	10
59	Mercury ZEP 10033	FRANK D'RONE SINGS (EP)	15
59	Mercury ZEP 10083	BLUE SERENADE (EP)	10
59	Mercury ZEP 10116	THE BAND ROCKED ON (EP)	30
60	Mercury MMC 14053	AFTER THE BALL (LP)	30

DRONES
77	Valer VRS 1	Bone Idle/I Just Wanna Be Myself (gatefold p/s, made in France or England)	12/6
77	Fifth Avenue CAS 107	Bone Idle/I Just Wanna Be Myself (cassette, flip-open 'cigarette box' sleeve)	30
77	Valer VRSP 1	Be My Baby/Lift Off The Bans (12", white label, unreleased)	50
77	Valer	Be My Baby (Take Two)/The Clique (white label, unrel., many autographed)	20
77	Ohms GOOD MIX 1	TEMPTATIONS OF A WHITE COLLAR WORKER (EP, different coloured sleeves, some with writing on inner sleeve)	15
80	Fabulous JC 4	Can't See/Fooled Today (p/s)	7
77	Valer VRLP 1	FURTHER TEMPTATIONS (LP)	30

DROWNING CRAZE
81	Situation 2 SIT 3	Storage Case (p/s)	8
81	Situation 2 SIT 13	Trance/I Love The Fjords (p/s)	8
82	Situation 2 SIT 16	Heat (p/s)	8

DRUG ADDIX
| 78 | Chiswick SW 39 | MAKE A RECORD (EP) | 10 |

(see also Kirsty MacColl)

DRUID
| 75 | EMI EMC 3081 | TOWARDS THE SUN (LP, with inner sleeve) | 12 |
| 76 | EMI EMC 3128 | FLUID DRUID (LP, with inner sleeve) | 12 |

DRUID CHASE
| 67 | CBS 3053 | Take Me In Your Garden/I Wanna Get My Hands On You | 30 |

DRUIDS
| 63 | Parlophone R 5097 | Long Tall Texan/Love So Blue | 20 |
| 64 | Parlophone R 5134 | It's Just A Little Bit Too Late/See What You've Done | 20 |

DRUIDS
| 71 | Argo ZFB 22 | BURNT OFFERING (LP) | 80 |
| 73 | Argo ZFB 39 | PASTIME WITH GOOD COMPANY (LP) | 60 |

(see also Giles Farnaby's Dream Band)

MINT VALUE £

DRUMBAGO

63	Island WI 085	I Am Drunk (actually by Raymond Harper & Drumbago's Group)/Sea Breeze (actually by Sammy & Drumbago's Group)	20
68	Blue Cat BS 145	Reggae Jeggae (with Blenders)/TYRONE TAYLOR: Delilah	30
69	Trojan TR 638	Dulcemania (with Dynamites)/CLANCY ECCLES: China Man	10

(see also Derrick Patsy, Dennis Walks)

BILL DRUMMOND

87	Creation CRE 039T	King Of Joy/The Manager (12", p/s)	25

(see also Big In Japan, Lori & Chameleons, J.A.M.s, KLF, Disco 2000, Timelords)

DON DRUMMOND

62	Island WI 021	Schooling The Duke/Bitter Rose (as Don Drummond Orchestra; B-side is actually by Shenley Duffus)	30
63	Black Swan WI 406	Scrap Iron/DRAGONAIRE: Prevention	25
63	Blue Beat BB 179	Reload/Far East	20
63	Island WI 094	Scandal/My Ideal (B-side actually by W. Sparks)	25
63	R&B JB 103	Royal Flush/MAYTALS: Matthew Mark	30
63	R&B JB 105	The Shock/TONETTES: Tell Me You're Mine	22
64	Ska Beat JB 178	Silver Dollar/TOMMY McCOOK: My Business	30
64	Island WI 149	Eastern Standard Time/DOTTY & BONNIE: Sun Rises	22
64	Island WI 153	Musical Storeroom/STRANGER COLE: He Who Feels	22
64	Island WI 162	Garden Of Love/STRANGER COLE: Cherry May	35
65	Island WI 192	Stampede (with Drumbago)/JUSTIN HINDS & DOMINOES: Come Bail Me	22
65	Island WI 204	Coolie Baby/LORD ANTICS: You May Stray	22
65	Island WI 208	Man In The Street/RITA & BENNY: You Are My Only Love	35
65	Island WI 242	University Goes Ska/DERRICK & NAOMI: Pain In My Heart	35
69	Studio One SO 2078	Heavenless/GLEN BROWN & DAVE BARKER: Lady Lovelight	40
69	Trojan TR 678	Memory Of Don/JOHN HOLT: Darling I Love You	15
69	Studio One SO 9008	THE BEST OF DON DRUMMOND (LP)	100
69	Trojan TTL 23	MEMORIAL ALBUM (LP)	25

(see also Joe White, Rhythm Aces, Roy & Millie, Movers, Desmond Dekker, Shenley Duffas, Hi-Tones, Duke Reid, Soul Brothers, Baba Brooks, Bonnie & Skitto, Eric Morris, Pioneers, Stranger & Patsy, Techniques, Winston Wright)

DON DRUMMOND JUNIOR

67	Caltone TONE 104	Sir Pratt Special/HEMSLEY MORRIS: Love Is Strange	40
68	Caltone TONE 124	Dirty Dozen/PHIL PRATT: Reach Out	50
70	Jackpot JP 710	Memory Of Don Drummond/TOBIES: Resting	12

(see also Vincent Gordon)

K. DRUMMOND

73	Jackpot JP 810	Your Pretty Face/Your Pretty Face (Version)	5

(see also Cables)

PETE DRUMMOND & THE VHF BAND

72	Warner Bros K 16232	Rocking At The BBC/Goodbye (vinyl 78)	20

ROY DRUSKY

59	Brunswick 05785	Wait 'N' See/Just About That Time (78 rpm = £8)	10

DRY ICE

69	B&C CB 115	Running To The Convent/Nowhere To Go	25

(see also Pluto)

DRY RIB

79	Clockwork COR 001	THE DRY SEASON (EP, 33rpm, photocopied foldover p/s, screen-printed labels)	30

(see also Television Personalities, Times, L'Orange Mechanik)

AMANCIO D'SILVA

69	Columbia S(C)X 6322	INTEGRATION (LP)	200
71	Columbia SCX 6465	REFLECTIONS (LP)	20

(see also Cosmic Eye)

D TO THE K

88	BPM BP12004	Hard But Live/Ease Up Your Mind (12")	28

D-TRAIN

82	Prelude EPCA 12-2016	You're The One For Me/You're The One For Me (Version) (12", p/s)	8

DUALS

61	London HL 9450	Stick Shift/Cruising	40

DUBBING IN THE U.K.

81	Star Light SDLP 902	DUBBING IN THE U.K.(LP)	35

DUBLINERS

60s	Transatlantic TRAEP 136	MAINLY BLARNEY (EP)	8
66	Transatlantic TRA 139	FINNEGAN WAKES (LP)	20
69	Columbia SCX 6380	AT HOME WITH THE DUBLINERS (LP)	15

DUBS

57	London HLU 8526	Could This Be Magic/Such Lovin' (78 rpm = £30)	250
58	London HL 8684	Gonna Make A Change/Beside My Love 78 rpm = £30)	300

DIANE DUCANE

79	Contact WN 2	Better Late Than Never/One Day	15

JOHN DU CANN

77	Arista ARIST 128	Throw Him In Jail/Street Stutter	5
77	Arista ARIST 145	Where's The Show/Hang Around	5
79	Vertigo 6059 241	Don't Be A Dummy/If I'm Makin' (p/s)	5

(see also Attack, Andromeda, Five Day Week Straw People, Atomic Rooster, Hard Stuff, Status Quo)

MINT VALUE £

DUCKS DELUXE
73	RCA RCA 2438	Coast To Coast/Bring Back That Packard Car	6
75	RCA RCA 2531	I Fought The Law/Cherry Pie	6
74	RCA LPL1 5008	DUCKS DELUXE (LP)	15
74	RCA SF 8402	TAXI TO THE TERMINAL ZONE (LP)	15
82	Blue Moon BMLP 001	LAST NIGHT OF A PUB ROCK BAND (2-LP)	18

(see also Motors, Tyla Gang, Brinsley Schwarz)

DUDLEY
60	Vogue V 9171	Lone Prairie Rock/El Pizza	20

DAVE DUDLEY
63	United Artists UP 1029	Six Days On The Road/I Feel A Cry Coming On	12
67	Mercury MF 1003	Trucker's Prayer/Don't Come Cryin' To Me	8
68	Mercury MF 1037	There Ain't No Easy Run/Why Can't I Be With You? (It's A Shame)	6

ROBERTA DUDLEY
50	Tempo R 22	Krooked Blues/When You're Alone (78)	15
51	Poydras 3	Krooked Blues/When You're Alone (shellac 45)	8

(see also Kid Ory)

DU-ETTES
72	President PT 382	Every Beat Of My Heart/Sugar Daddy	15
72	President PT 398	Please Forgive Me/Lonely Days	15

SHENLEY DUFFAS
62	Island WI 036	Give To Get/What You Gonna Do (as S. Duffas; B-side actually with Millie Small)	15
63	Island WI 063	Fret Man Fret/Doreen	15
63	Island WI 093	What A Disaster/I Am Rich	15
63	Island WI 115	Know The Lord/TOMMY McCOOK: Ska Ba	35
63	Island WI 125	Easy Squeal/Things Ain't Going Right	15
63	R&B JB 134	No More Wedding Bells/Let Them Fret	15
64	R&B JB 146	Big Mouth/FRANKIE ANDERSON: Peanut Vendor	18
64	R&B JB 152	Christopher Columbus/CARL BRYAN ORCHESTRA: Barber Chair	18
64	R&B JB 154	Mother-In-Law/DON DRUMMOND & GROUP: Festival	18
64	Black Swan WI 440	Digging A Ditch/He's Coming Down	18
64	Black Swan WI 443	Gather Them In/Crucifixion	20
64	Rio R 41	I Will Be Glad/Heariso (as Shandly Duffus)	18
65	Island WI 182	La La La/UPCOMING WILLOWS: Jonestown Special	30
65	Island WI 184	You Are Mine/UPCOMING WILLOWS: Red China	30
65	Island WI 186	Rukumbine/One Morning	15
72	Upsetter US 380	Bet You Don't Know/UPSETTERS: Ring Of Fire	18
72	Dynamic DYN 451	Peace (with Soul Avengers)/UPSETTER: Peace — Version	7
72	Grape GR 3031	Sincerely/Sincerely — Version (with Upsetters)	8

(see also Chenley Duffus, Billy Dyce)

CHENLEY DUFFUS
72	Pama PM 859	At The End/Good Night My Love	8

(see also Shenley Duffas)

DUFFY
73	Chapter One SCHR 184	The Joker/Running Away	18
70	Chapter One CHSR 814	SCRUFFY DUFFY (LP)	100

STEPHEN 'TIN TIN' DUFFY
82	WEA TIN 1T	Kiss Me (Dub Version)/Love's Duet (Dub Version) (12", p/s)	8
85	10	She Loves Me/She Loves It (p/s, withdrawn)	60
85	10	Baby Impossible (p/s, withdrawn)	60
86	10 TENP 91	I Love You (Aversion)/I Love You/Love Is Driving Me Insane (gatefold p/s with poster, withdrawn)	6
86	10 TIN 91-12	I Love You/Love Is Driving Me Insane/I Love You (The Inversion)/Wednesday Jones/Icing On The Kake/Kiss Me (12", p/s)	8
86	10 TIND 5-10	I Love You (Inversion)/Wednesday Jones (Dixie)//Icing On The Cake/Kiss Me (10", double pack, gatefold p/s)	7
97	Indolent DOLE064	MEMORY & DESIRE (CD)	40

(see also Hawks, Tin Tin, Dr. Calculus, Lilac Time)

DUFFY'S NUCLEUS
67	Decca F 22547	Hound Dog/Mary Open The Door	50

(see also Duffy Power, Pentangle, John McLaughlin)

DON DUGGAN
68	Pye 7N 17633	Let Her Dance/Westmeath Bachelor (with Savoys)	8

BILLY DUKE
62	Ember EMB S 153	Walking Cane/Amen	7
62	Ember EMB S 160	Ain't She Pretty/Timbuctu	7
64	London HLU 9907	While The Bloom Is On The Rose/I'm The Lonesomest Guy In Town	10
65	London HLU 9960	Sugar'N'Spice/Prisoner Of Love	10

DENVER DUKE & JEFFREY NULL BLUEGRASS BOYS
63	Starlite STEP 33	DENVER DUKE & JEFFREY NULL BLUEGRASS BOYS (EP)	15

DON DUKE
60	Embassy WB 402	Please Don't Tease/Made You (78)	8
60	Embassy WB 405	When Will I Be Loved/Look For A Star (78)	8
60	Embassy WB 414	Only The Lonely/Chain Gang (78)	10
60	Embassy WB 416	So Sad (To See Good Love Go Bad)/Please Help Me I'm Falling (78)	12
60	Embassy WB 418	Dreamin'/Let's Think About Living (78)	12

(see also Dick Jordan, Bud Ashton)

MINT VALUE £

DORIS DUKE
71	Mojo 2092 005	To The Other Woman/I Don't Care Anymore	8
71	Mojo 2092 017	If She's Your Wife Who Am I?/It Sure Was Fun	8
73	Mainstream MSS 302	Business Deal/Nobody But You	8
74	Contempo 7703	Grasshopper/Please Come Back	8
76	Contempo CX15	Woman Of The Ghetto/TAMIKO JONES: Let It Flow	12
71	Mojo 2916 001	I'M A LOSER (LP)	40
71	Mojo 2916 006	A LEGEND IN HER OWN TIME (LP)	40
75	Contempo CRM 111	A LEGEND IN HER OWN TIME (LP, reissue)	15
75	Contempo CLP 519	WOMAN (LP)	30

PATTY DUKE
65	United Artists UP 1103	Don't Just Stand There/Everything But Love	12
65	United Artists UP 1116	Say Something Funny/Funny Little Butterflies	8
65	United Artists (S)ULP 1123	DON'T JUST STAND THERE (LP, mono/stereo)	40

DUKE ALL STARS
68	Blue Cat BS 111	Letter To Mummy And Daddy (Parts 1 & 2)	20

DUKE & DUCHESS
55	London HLU 8206	Borrowed Sunshine/Get Ready For Love (with Sir Hubert Pimm)	40
	(see also Sir Hubert Pimm)		

AGGIE DUKES
57	Vogue V 9090	John John/Well Of Loneliness (78 rpm = £70)	400+

DUKES OF STRATOSPHEAR
85	Virgin VS 763	The Mole From The Ministry/My Love Explodes (no p/s)	5
87	Virgin VSY 982	You're A Good Man Albert Brown/Vanishing Girl (p/s, 5,000 on multi-coloured vinyl)	5
85	Virgin WOW 1	25 O'CLOCK (LP)	12
87	Virgin VP 2440	PSONIC PSUNSPOT (LP, gatefold sleeve, 5,000 on multi-coloured vinyl)	30
	(see also XTC, Mr. Partridge)		

DULCIMER
71	Nepentha 6437 003	AND I TURNED AS I HAD TURNED AS A BOY (LP, gatefold sleeve)	60
80	Happy Face MMLP 1021	A LAND FIT FOR HEROES (LP, private pressing)	18

LIZA DULITTLE
68	Pye 7N 17590	I've Got To Get A Grip Of Myself/Did You Hear A Heart Break Last Night?	8
	(see also Margo & Marvettes)		

DUM
74	RAK RAK 179	In The Mood/Watching The Clock	6
	(see also Mud)		

DUMB ANGELS
88	Fierce FRIGHT 033	Love And Mercy/Love And Mercy (p/s, numbered)	45
	(see also Pooh Sticks)		

DUMBELLES
80	Polydor POSP 209/EGO 3	Giddy Up/A Christmas Dream (no p/s)	10
	(see also Roxy Music)		

JOHN DUMMER (BLUES BAND)
68	Mercury MF 1040	Travelling Man/40 Days (as John Dummer Blues Band)	20
69	Mercury MF 1119	Try Me One More Time/Riding At Midnight (as John Dummer Blues Band)	15
70	Fontana 6007 027	Happy/Nightingale (unissued in U.K.; France-only)	
70	Philips 6006 111	Nine By Nine/Going In The Out (credited to either Famous Music Band or John Dummer Band)	12
71	Philips 6006 176	Medicine Weasel/The Endgame (with Nick Pickett)	7
73	Vertigo 6059 074	Ooblee-Dooblee Jubilee/The Monkey Speaks His Mind (as John Dummer Oobleedooblee Band)	6
69	Mercury SMCL 20136	CABAL (LP)	100
69	Mercury SMCL 20167	JOHN DUMMER BAND (LP)	135
70	Philips 6309 008	FAMOUS MUSIC BAND (LP)	55
72	Philips 6382 039	THIS IS THE JOHN DUMMER BLUES BAND (LP)	25
73	Philips 6382 040	VOLUME II — TRY ME ONE MORE TIME (LP)	25
72	Vertigo 6360 056	BLUE (LP, gatefold sleeve, swirl label)	200
73	Vertigo 6360 083	OOBLEEDOOBLEE JUBILEE (LP, as John Dummer Oobleedooblee Band, swirl label)	40
	(see also Nick Pickett, Dave Kelly, Famous Music Band, Tony McPhee)		

DUMMIES
79	Cheapskate FWL 001	When The Lights Are Out/She's The Only Woman (no p/s)	8
80	Pye 7P 163	When The Lights Are Out/She's The Only Woman (no p/s, reissue)	8
80	Cheapskate CHEAP 003	Didn't You Used To Use To Be You?/Miles Out To Sea (p/s)	10
81	Cheapskate CHEAP 014	Maybe Tonite/When I'm Dancin' I Ain't Fightin' (p/s)	12
	(see also China Dolls, Slade)		

DUMPY'S RUSTY NUTS
81	Cool King CNK 006	Just For Kicks/Ride With Me (p/s, reissued as Dumpy's Rusty Bolts)	8/5
82	Cool King CK 008	Boxhill Or Bust/It's Got To Be Blues (p/s, initially with free patch)	6/5
90	A Side DRN 21	Run Run Run/Rock City (withdrawn, promos more common)	5
84	Landslide LDLP 101	SOMEWHERE IN ENGLAND (LP)	12

DUNAMIS
79	Daybreak DB 2602	I CAN FLY (LP, some signed)	20/15

AYNSLEY DUNBAR (RETALIATION)
67	Blue Horizon 3109	Warning/Cobwebs (some in p/s)	60/25
68	Liberty LBF 15132	Watch 'N' Chain/Roamin' And Ramblin'	15
68	Liberty LBL/LBS 83154	AYNSLEY DUNBAR RETALIATION (LP, mono/stereo)	50
68	Liberty LBL/LBS 83177	DR. DUNBAR'S PRESCRIPTION (LP, mono/stereo)	50

69	Liberty LBS 83223	RETALIATION (LP)	50
70	Liberty LBS 83316	REMAINS TO BE HEARD (LP)	40
71	Warner Bros WS 3010	BLUE WHALE (LP)	22

(see also John Mayall & Bluesbreakers, Heavy Jelly, Annette & Victor Brox, Excheckers)

SCOTT DUNBAR

71	Ahura Mazda AMS SDS 1	FROM LAKE MARY (LP)	30

JOHNNY DUNCAN (& BLUE GRASS BOYS)

57	Columbia DB 3925	Kaw-Liga/Ella Speed (gold label lettering, later silver) (78 rpm = £12)	25/15
57	Columbia DB 3959	Last Train To San Fernando/Rock-A-Billy Baby (gold label lettering, later silver)	25/12
57	Columbia DB 3996	Blue, Blue Heartache/Jig Along Home	10
57	Columbia DB 4029	Footprints In The Snow/Get Along Home, Cindy	10
58	Columbia DB 4074	Goodnight Irene/If You Love Me Baby (78 rpm = £8)	15
58	Columbia DB 4118	Itching For My Baby/I Heard The Bluebirds Sing (78 rpm = £10)	10
58	Columbia DB 4167	All Of The Monkeys Ain't In The Zoo/More And More (78 rpm = £10)	10
58	Columbia DB 4179	My Lucky Love/Geisha Girl (78 rpm = £10)	10
59	Columbia DB 4282	Rosalie/This Train (78 rpm = £12)	10
59	Columbia DB 4311	Kansas City/That's All Right Darlin' (78 rpm = £15)	12
60	Columbia DB 4415	Any Time/Yellow, Yellow Moon (solo)	7
61	Pye 7N 15358	Tobacco Road/Sleepy-Eyed John (solo)	6
61	Pye 7N 15380	The Legend Of Gunga Din/Hannah (solo)	6
62	Pye 7N 15420	A Long Time Gone/Waitin' For The Sandman (solo)	6
63	Columbia DB 7164	The Ballad Of Jed Clampett/Will You Be Mine? (as Johnny Duncan & Kingpins)	6
64	Columbia DB 7334	Dang Me/Which Way Did He Go? (solo)	6
66	Columbia DB 7833	My Little Baby/I Thank My Lucky Stars (solo)	5
57	Columbia SEG 7708	JOHNNY DUNCAN AND HIS BLUE GRASS BOYS (EP)	25
57	Columbia SEG 7773	JOHNNY DUNCAN AND HIS BLUE GRASS BOYS NO. 2 (EP)	25
58	Columbia SEG 7753	FOOTPRINTS IN THE SNOW (EP)	25
58	Columbia SEG 7850	TENNESSEE SING SONG (EP)	25
57	Columbia 33S 1122	TENNESSEE SONG BAG (10" LP)	50
58	Columbia 33S 1129	JOHNNY DUNCAN SALUTES HANK WILLIAMS (10" LP)	40
61	Columbia 33SX 1328	BEYOND THE SUNSET (LP)	3

(see also Chris Barber's Skiffle Group)

LESLEY DUNCAN (& JOKERS)

63	Parlophone R 5034	I Want A Steady Guy/Movin' Away (as Lesley Duncan & Jokers)	10
64	Parlophone R 5106	Tell Me/You Kissed Me Boy	10
64	Mercury MF 830	When My Baby Cries/Did It Hurt?	10
65	Mercury MF 847	Just For The Boy/See That Guy	10
65	Mercury MF 876	Run To Love/Only The Lonely And Me	15
65	Mercury MF 939	Hey Boy/I Go To Sleep	10
79	CBS 8061	Sing Children Sing/Rainbow Games (p/s, with Kate Bush)	10
71	CBS 64202	SING CHILDREN SING (LP)	15
72	CBS 64807	EARTH MOTHER (LP)	15
74	GM GML 1007	EVERYTHING CHANGES (LP)	15

(see also Mitchell/Coe Mysteries)

TOMMY DUNCAN

66	Sue WI 4002	Dance, Dance, Dance/Let's Try It Over Again	40

TOMMY DUNCAN & HIS WESTERN ALL STARS

50	Capitol CL 13261	Gamblin' Polka Dot Blues/Chattanooga Shoe Shine Boy (78)	12

DIANE DUNCANE

79	Contact 2	Better Late Than Never/One Day	20

BARBARA DUNKLEY

71	Banana BA 342	We'll Cry Together/BOBBY DAVIS: Got To Get Away	7

DELROY DUNKLEY

70	Hot Rod HR 109	I Wish You Well/TONY & DELROY: Impossible Love	10

ERROL(L) DUNKLEY

67	Rio R 109	Love Me Forever/VIETNAM ALLSTARS: The Toughest	55
67	Rio R 131	You're Gonna Need Me/Seek And You'll Find	35
68	Island WI 3150	Once More/I'm Not Your Man	20
68	Amalgamated AMG 800	Please Stop Your Lying/Feel So Fine (B-side actually by Tommy McCook & Band)	35
68	Amalgamated AMG 805	I'm Going Home/I'm Not Your Man	30
68	Amalgamated AMG 807	The Scorcher/Do It Right Tonight	35
68	Amalgamated AMG 820	Love Brother/I Spy	35
69	Fab FAB 117	I'll Take You In My Arms/KING CANNON: Daphney Reggae	10
70	Unity UN 554	My Special Prayer/Never Hurt The One You Love	7
70	Banana BA 302	Satisfaction/CECIL LOCKE: Sing Out Loud	15
71	Big BG 324	Deep Meditation/RUPIE EDWARDS ALL STARS: Meditation Version	20
71	Big BG 327	Three In One/RUPIE EDWARDS ALL STARS: One In Three	6
71	Nu Beat NB 091	Three In One/RUPIE EDWARDS ALL STARS: One In Three	6
71	Explosion EX 2053	O Lord/KEITH with IMPACT ALL STARS: Raindrops (B-side actually My Baby by Lloyd Charmers)	6
72	Camel CA 87	Black Cinderella/PHIL PRATT ALLSTARS: Our Anniversary (B-side actually Tropic Shadows)	12
73	Grape GR 3039	Why Did You Do It/One Love	8
73	Count Shelley CS 3039	Girl You Cried/Where Must I Go	6
73	Ackee 507	Keep The Pressure Down/Version	35
70s	Attack AT 1003	YOU NEVER KNOW (LP)	30
73	Attack ATLP 1003	DARLING OOH (LP)	20
79	Black Joy DH 802	DISCO SHOWCASE (LP)	45

(see also Errol & His Group, Gaynor & Erroll], Mister Versatile, Don Lee, Ken Parker, Bongo Herman)

MINT VALUE £

BLIND WILLIE DUNN'S GIN BOTTLE FOUR with KING OLIVER

54	Columbia SCM 5100	Jet Black Blues/Blue Blood Blues (78 rpm, Columbia DB 3440 = £20)	25

(see also Eddie Lang & Lonnie Johnson)

GEORGE DUNN

73	Leader LEE 4042	GEORGE DUNN (LP, with insert)	18

TONY DUNNING (& TREMELOS)

60	Palette PG 9006	Seventeen Tomorrow/Be My Girl	10
61	Palette PG 9018	Pretend/Don't Bother To Call	10
61	Palette PG 9027	Under Moscow Skies/Sixteen Candles	10

DUPARS

76	Contempo 2104	Love Cookin'/Instrumental	20

CHAMPION JACK DUPREE

51	Jazz Parade B 16	Fisherman's Blues/County Jail Special (78)	30
62	Storyville A 45051	Whiskey Head Woman/Shirley May	20
67	Decca F 12611	Barrelhouse Woman/Under Your Hood	20
67	Blue Horizon 45-1007	Get Your Head Happy/Easy Is The Way (with T.S. McPhee)	115
68	Blue Horizon 57-3140	I Haven't Done No-One No Harm/How Am I Doing It (with Stan Webb)	20
69	Blue Horizon 57-3152	Ba'la Fouche/Kansas City	20
69	Blue Horizon 57-3158	I Want To Be A Hippy/Goin' Back To Louisiana	20
61	Storyville SEP 381	BLUES ANTHOLOGY VOL. 1 (EP)	30
64	RCA RCX 7137	RHYTHM AND BLUES VOL. 1 (EP)	30
64	Decca DFE 8586	LONDON SPECIAL (EP, with Keith Smith Climax Band)	60
65	Ember EMB 4564	JACK DUPREE (EP)	25
60s	XX MIN 716	CHAMPION JACK DUPREE (EP)	20
59	London Jazz LTZ-K 15171	BLUES FROM THE GUTTER (LP)	85
61	London Jazz LTZ-K 15217	CHAMPION JACK'S NATURAL AND SOULFUL BLUES LP, stereo = SAH-K 6151)	75/100
65	Storyville SLP 145	TROUBLE TROUBLE (LP)	35
65	Xtra XTRA 1028	CABBAGE GREENS (LP)	25
65	Storyville SLP 161	PORTRAITS IN BLUES (LP)	35
66	Decca LK/SKL 4747	FROM NEW ORLEANS TO CHICAGO (LP)	100
67	Storyville 670 194	CHAMPION JACK DUPREE (LP)	40
67	Decca SKL 4871	CHAMPION JACK DUPREE AND HIS BIG BLUES BAND (LP)	100
68	Blue Horizon 7-63206	WHEN YOU FEEL THE FEELING YOU WAS FEELING (LP)	90
69	Blue Horizon 7-63214	SCOOBYDOOBYDOO (LP)	90
70	Sonet SNTF 614	THE INCREDIBLE CHAMPION JACK DUPREE (LP)	15
72	Sonet SNTF 626	LEGACY OF THE BLUES (LP)	15

(see also T.S. McPhee)

CHAMPION JACK DUPREE/JIMMY RUSHING

64	Ember CJS 800	TWO SHADES OF BLUE (LP)	30

(see also Jimmy Rushing)

CHAMPION JACK DUPREE & KING CURTIS

73	Atlantic K 40434	BLUES FROM MONTREUX (LP)	12

(see also King Curtis)

SIMON DUPREE & BIG SOUND

66	Parlophone R 5542	I See The Light/It Is Finished	10
67	Parlophone R 5574	Reservations/You Need A Man	10
67	Parlophone R 5594	Day Time, Night Time/I've Seen It All Before	10
67	Parlophone R 5646	Kites/Like The Sun Like The Fire (with Jacqui Chan)	20+
68	Parlophone R 5670	For Whom The Bell Tolls/Sleep	6
68	Parlophone R 5697	Part Of My Past/This Story Never Ends	8
68	Parlophone R 5727	Thinking About My Life/Velvet And Lace	8
69	Parlophone R 5757	Broken Hearted Pirates/She Gave Me The Sun	10
69	Parlophone R 5816	The Eagle Flies Tonight/Give It All Back	10
67	Parlophone PMC/PCS 7029	WITHOUT RESERVATIONS (LP, yellow & black label)	55

(see also Moles, Gentle Giant, Jacqui Chan)

DUPREES

62	HMV POP 1073	You Belong To Me/Take Me As I Am	40
62	Stateside SS 143	My Own True Love/Ginny	18
63	London HLU 9678	I'd Rather Be Here In Your Arms/I Wish I Could Believe You	22
63	London HLU 9709	Gone With The Wind/Let's Make Love Again	20
63	London HLU 9774	Why Don't You Believe Me?/My Dearest One	20
63	London HLU 9813	Have You Heard?/Love Eyes	20
64	London HLU 9843	It's No Sin/The Sand And The Sea	20
65	CBS 201803	Around The Corner/They Said It Couldn't Be Done	20
66	CBS 202028	She Waits For Him/Norma Jean	15
68	MGM MGM 460	My Special Angel/Ring Of Love	10
70	Polydor 2058 077	Check Yourself/The Sky's The Limit	20

DURAN DURAN

81	EMI EMI 5137	Planet Earth/Late Bar (glossy p/s)	6
81	EMI 12EMI 5137	Planet Earth (Night Version)/Planet Earth/Late Bar (12", p/s)	6
81	EMI EMI 5168	Careless Memories/Khanada (p/s)	6
81	EMI 12EMI 5168	Careless Memories/Fame/Khanada (12", p/s)	8
81	EMI 12EMI 5206	Girls On Film (Night Version)/Girls On Film/Faster Than Light (12", p/s)	8
81	EMI EMI 5254	My Own Way/Like An Angel (p/s)	5
81	EMI 12EMI 5254	My Own Way (Night Version)/Like An Angel/My Own Way (Short Version)(12", p/s)	8
82	EMI 12EMI 5327	Save A Prayer/Hold Back The Rain (12" remix) (12", p/s)	8
82	EMI 12EMI 5346	Rio (Part 1)/Rio (Part 2)/My Own Way (12", p/s)	8
83	Flexi (no cat. no.)	The Smash Hits Interview (flexidisc free with Smash Hits)	8/5
84	EMI DURANP 2	The Reflex/Make Me Smile (poster p/s)	6

84	EMI 12 DURANP 2	The Reflex (Dance Mix)/Make Me Smile/The Reflex (12", picture disc)	10
84	EMI DURAN (A-E) 3	The Wild Boys/Cracks In The Pavement (Live) (5 different p/s)	5
85	Parlophone DURANG 007	A View To A Kill/A View To A Kill (That Fatal Kiss) (white vinyl, gatefold p/s)	6
86	Parlophone 12 DDNX 45	Notorious (Latin Rascals Mix)/Winter Marches On/Notorious (12", p/s)	10
87	Parlophone TRADEX 1	Skin Trade/We Need You (poster p/s)	8
87	Parlophone TC TRADE 1	Skin Trade (Stretch Mix)/We Need You/Skin Trade (cassette in 'video' case)	10
87	Parlophone TOUR 1	Meet El Presidente/Vertigo (Do The Demolition) (non-gatefold p/s)	8
88	Parlophone 12 YOUR 1	I Don't Want Your Love (Big Mix)/(7" Mix)/(Album Version) (12", p/s)	8
88	Parlophone 12 YOUR S1	I Don't Want Your Love (Big Mix)/I Don't Want Your Love (Album Version) (12", p/s, 1 side etched)	8
88	Parlophone CD YOUR 1	I Don't Want Your Love (7" Mix)/I Don't Want Your Love (Album Version)/I Don't Want Your Love (Big Mix) (CD, stickered case)	10
88	Parlophone 12DDX 11	All She Wants Is (US Master Mix)/All She Wants Is (45 Mix)/I Believe — All I Need To Know (Medley) (12", p/s)	8
88	Parlophone CDDD 11	All She Wants Is (45 Mix)/Skin Trade (Parisian Mix)/I Believe — All I Need To Know (Medley) (3" CD)	15
89	Parlophone DDA/B/C 12	Do You Believe In Shame?/The Krush Brothers LSD Edit/Do You Believe In Shame?/God (London)/This Is How A Road Gets Made/Palomino//Do You Believe In Shame?/Drug — It's Just A State Of Mind (triple-pack, foldout p/s & 3 cards)	18
89	Parlophone 10DD 12	Do You Believe In Shame?/The Krush Brothers LSD Edit/Notorious (live) (10", numbered or unnumbered p/s)	10/8
89	Parlophone CDDD 12	Do You Believe In Shame?/The Krush Brothers LSD Edit/Notorious (live)/God (London)/This Is How A Road Gets Made (3" CD)	20
89	Parlophone CDDD 13	Burning The Ground/Decadance/Decadance (Extended Mix) (CD, 2,000 only)	35
93	Parlophone CDDDS 16	Ordinary World (Single Version)/Save A Prayer/Skin Trade/My Antarctica (CD, fold-out pack, withdrawn)	25
94	Parlophone CDDDB 35	DURAN DURAN (2-CD, fold-out digipak with 2 booklets)	25

PROMOS

81	EMI 12EMI 5137	Planet Earth (1-sided 12")	20
87	Parlophone CLUBTOUR 1	THE PRESIDENTIAL SUITE EP (12")	12
88	Parlophone 12YOURDJ 1	I Don't Want Your Love (Big Mix)/ (Dub Mix) (12")	12
88	Parlophone 12DDDJ 11	All She Wants Is (Euro Dub Mix)/(Mixes) (12")	12
93	Parlophone 12DDDJ 17	Come Undone (FGI Phumpin' 12" Mix)/(Mixes) (12")	25
93	Parlophone CDDDDJ 17	Come Undone (Edit)/(Mixes)/Ordinary World (Acoustic Versions) (CD)	20
95	Parlophone CDINTPR 01	Perfect Day (CD export promo, pink title sleeve)	15
95	Parlophone 12DD DJ 007	White Lines (70's Club Mix)/(Oakland Funk Mix)/(Album Version) (12", pearl vinyl, promo only)	15
97	Parlophone BARBDJ 97	Electric Barbarella (Radio Edit)/(Album Version) (CD, card sleeve)	20
97	Virgin VSTDJ 1639	Out Of My Mind/(Mixes) (12", stickered title sleeve)	15
98	Parlophone 12GOF 1	Girls On Film (Tall Paul Mix)/(Instrumental) (12")	18
98	EMI GREATEST 001	GREATEST (CD, card sleeve)	20

(see also Arcadia, Power Station)

JIMMY DURANTE

55	Brunswick 05395	Pupalina (My Little Doll)/Little People	8
55	Brunswick 05445	It's Bigger Than Both Of Us (with Patty Andrews)/When The Circus Leaves Town	8
55	Brunswick 05495	Swingin' With Rhythm And Blues (with Peter Lawford)/I Love You, I Do (with Eddie Jackson)	8
60	Brunswick 05829	Shine On Harvest Moon/The Best Things In Life Are Free	7
63	Warner Bros WB 112	September Song/Young At Heart	7
64	Warner Bros WB 149	Old Man Time/I Came Here To Swim	6
54	MGM EPC 2	JIMMY DURANTE (EP, export issue)	15
57	MGM MGM-EP 508	JIMMY DURANTE (EP)	12
57	MGM MGM-EP 597	SCHNOZZLES (EP)	15
52	MGM MGM-D 102	IN PERSON (10" LP)	30
53	Brunswick LA 8582	JIMMY DURANTE SINGS (10" LP)	30
57	Brunswick LAT 8216	CLUB DURANTE (LP)	20

(see also Ethel Merman, Groucho Marx)

ALLISON DURBIN

69	Decca LK-R/SKL-R 4996	I HAVE LOVED ME A MAN (LP)	40

JUDITH DURHAM

67	Columbia DB 8207	The Olive Tree/The Non Performing Lion Quickstep	6
67	Columbia DB 8290	Again And Again/Memories	20
70	A&M AMS 777	The Light Is Dark Enough/Wanderlove	6
69	Columbia S(C)X 6374	FOR CHRISTMAS WITH LOVE (LP)	15
70	A&M AMLS 967	GIFT OF SONG (LP)	15

(see also Seekers, Keith Potger)

KENNY DURHAM

58	London LTZU 15133	JAZZ CONTRASTS (LP, with Sonny Rollins)	15

TERRY DURHAM

69	Deram DML/SML 1042	CRYSTAL TELEPHONE (LP, with insert)	22

(see also Storyteller)

DURUTTI COLUMN

82	Factory FAC 64	I Get Along Without You Very Well/Prayer (p/s)	7
80	Factory FACT 14	THE RETURN OF THE DURUTTI COLUMN (LP, with sandpaper sleeve, some with Martin Hannett's "Testcard" flexidisc [FAC 14C])	50/35
83	Factory FACT 74	ANOTHER SETTING (LP, with perfumed cut-out insert)	12
83	VU VINI 1	LIVE AT THE VENUE LONDON (LP)	18
88	Factory FACT 244	VINI REILLY (LP, with free p/s 7" I Know Very Well How I Got My Note Wrong [FAC 244++] by Vincent Gerard & Steven Patrick)	20
88	Factory FACD 244	VINI REILLY (CD, with 3" CD, I Know Very Well How I Got My Note Wrong [FAC CD 244++] by Vincent Gerard & Steven Patrick)	30

(see also Nosebleeds, Gammer & His Familiars, Morrissey)

IAN DURY (& THE BLOCKHEADS)
78	Stiff BUY 2712	What A Waste/Wake Up (12", plain white sleeve)	20
78	Stiff BUY 38	Hit Me With Your Rhythm Stick/There Ain't Half Been Some Clever Bastards (red vinyl, p/s, one copy known)	400
78	Stiff FREEBIE 1	Sex And Drugs And Rock And Roll/England's Glory/Two Steep Hills (p/s, free at *NME* party/competition)	8
77	Stiff SEEZ 4	NEW BOOTS AND PANTIES!! (LP, with bonus track 'Sex And Drugs And Rock And Roll')	20
77	Stiff SEEZ 4	NEW BOOTS AND PANTIES!! (LP, limited edition gold vinyl)	25

(see also Kilburn & The High Roads, Greatest Show On Earth, Loving Awareness)

ANDREW DURYER
75	Real RR 2003	BALLADS OF A WANDERER (LP)	25

JEAN DUSHON
65	Chess CRL 4000	MAKE WAY FOR JEAN DUSHON (LP)	40

DUSK
71	Bell BLL 1167	I Hear Those Church Bells Ringing/I Cannot See To See You	10

PAT DUSKY AND MARINES
67	Stardust STP 1	I Fall To Pieces/This Can Be The Night.	6

LA DÜSSELDORF
78	Radar ADA 5	La Düsseldorf/Silver Cloud (unissued, white label promo only)	25
81	Albion ION 1025	Tintarella Di (some might have p/s)	10

DUST BROTHERS
93	Dust Brothers DB's 333	Song To The Siren (12", no p/s, 500 only)	75
93	Junior Boys Own JBO 10	Song To The Siren/Song To The Siren (Sabres Of Paradise Mixes) (12", p/s)	25
94	Boys Own COLLECT 004	14TH CENTURY SKY EP (12", no p/s)	20
94	Junior Boys Own JBO 20	MY MERCURY MOUTH EP (12", JBO sleeve)	15

(see also Chemical Brothers)

SLIM DUSTY
58	Columbia DB 4212	A Pub With No Beer/Once When I Was Mustering (with His Country Rockers)	8
59	Columbia DB 4294	The Answer To A Pub With No Beer/Winter Winds (with His Bushlanders)	6
60	Columbia SEG 8009	SLIM DUSTY AND HIS COUNTRY ROCKERS (EP)	25
63	Decca LK 4551	SLIM DUSTY SINGSONG (LP)	20

DUTCH SWING COLLEGE BAND
51	Saturn EGX 106	Alexander's Ragtime Band/Birthday Blues (78 picture disc)	75

DUTCHESS
81	B'kreig Waxworks EJSP 9580	Your Love/Dead And Gone	120

JACQUES DUTRONC
66	Vogue VRS 7015	Et Moi, Et Moi, Et Moi/Mini-Mini-Mini	12
66	Vogue VRS 7021	Les Cactus/L'Espace D'Une Felle	7
66	Vogue VRS 7024	J'Aime Les Filles/L'Idole.	6
67	Vogue VRS 7027	Le Plus Difficile/Les Rois De La Reforme.	6
67	Vogue VRL 3029	JACQUES DUTRONC (LP)	25

JOSE DUVAL
57	London HLR 8458	Message Of Love/That's What You Mean To Me	25

MARK DWAYNE
62	Oriole CB 1712	Remember Me Huh/Poorest Boy In Town	12
62	Oriole CB 1744	Today's Teardrops/Little Bitty Heart	12

BILLY DYCE
72	G.G. GG 4532	Be My Guest/HUGH ROY: Way Down South	10
72	G.G. GG 4534	Take Warning/TYPHOON ALL STARS: Warning (Version)	8
72	G.G. GG 4537	Time Is Still Here/G.G. ALL STARS: Time — Version	7
72	Pama PM 835	Be My Guest/HUGH ROY: Way Down South	10
73	Pama PM 874	Woman Smarter/SHENLEY DUFFAS: Standing On The Hill	6
73	Bread BR 1115	You Need Love (with Millions)/G.G. ALL STARS: Love — Dub	6

DYKE & BLAZERS
67	Pye International 7N 25413	Funky Broadway (Parts 1 & 2)	25

BOB DYLAN
65	CBS 201751	The Times They Are A-Changin'/Honey, Just Allow Me One More Chance (white promo label)	40
65	CBS 201751	The Times They Are A-Changin'/Honey, Just Allow Me One More Chance (orange label, special sleeve)	250
65	CBS 201751	The Times They Are A-Changin'/Honey, Just Allow Me One More Chance ('BOB DYLAN' below titles, orange label)	8
65	CBS 201751	The Times They Are A-Changin'/Honey, Just Allow Me One More Chance ('BOB DYLAN' vertically on left, orange label).	12
65	CBS 201751	The Times They Are A-Changin'/Honey, Just Allow Me One More Chance (yellow/red label, labelled mono, plays stereo. Matrix no's 201751 A5054/5 2/2B-1)	5
65	CBS 201751	The Times They Are A-Changin'/Honey, Just Allow Me One More Chance (yellow/red label, labelled stereo, plays stereo. Matrix no's S 1751 A3/CBS S 1751 B3)	5
65	CBS 201751	The Times They Are A-Changin'/Honey, Just Allow Me One More Chance (yellow/red label labelled stereo, plays mono. Matrix no's 20.1751/CBS 20.1751)	20
65	CBS 201753	Subterranean Homesick Blues/She Belongs To Me (white promo label)	40
65	CBS 201753	Subterranean Homesick Blues/She Belongs To Me (orange label, push out center/ solid centre)	7/9
65	CBS 201771	Maggie's Farm/On The Road Again (white promo label)	40
65	CBS 201771	Maggie's Farm/On The Road Again (orange label, push-out centre both sides have LP reference)	7

65	CBS 201771	Maggie's Farm/On The Road Again (orange label, push out centre, no LP ref)	7
65	CBS 201771	Maggie's Farm/On The Road Again (orange label with LP reference on B-side only)	15
65	CBS 201811	Like A Rolling Stone (Part 1)/Like A Rolling Stone (Part 2) (white promo label)	125
65	CBS 201811	Like A Rolling Stone/Gates Of Eden (Test Pressing. Side 1 white label with CBS logo, handwritten title + A5175. Side 2 black)	200
65	CBS 201811	Like A Rolling Stone/Gates Of Eden (white promo label)	40
65	CBS 201811	Like A Rolling Stone/Gates Of Eden (orange label with LP reference on B-side only. 'Side A/B' between cat. no and matrix no)	7
65	CBS 201811	Like A Rolling Stone/Gates Of Eden (orange label with LP reference on B-side only. 'Side A/B' not stated)	7
65	CBS 201811	Like A Rolling Stone/Gates Of Eden (orange label, no LP reference)	15
74	CBS 1811	Like A Rolling Stone/Gates Of Eden (Test Pressing. Both sides red with black printing 'Advance Copy Test Pressing...' Handwritten: 5175.3 A/5176.2)	180
74	CBS 201811	Like A Rolling Stone/Gates Of Eden (yellow/red label. With cat. no. 201811)	15
74	CBS 1811	Like A Rolling Stone/Gates Of Eden (yellow red label with cat. no. 1811 'BOB DYLAN' on left 16mm, solid centre)	5
74	CBS 1811	Like A Rolling Stone/Gates Of Eden (yellow red label with cat. no. 1811 'BOB DYLAN' on left 24mm, solid centre)	5
74	CBS 1811	Like A Rolling Stone/Gates Of Eden (yellow red label with cat. no. 1811 'BOB DYLAN' on left 28mm, solid centre)	5
74	CBS 1811	Like A Rolling Stone/Gates Of Eden (yellow red label with cat. no. 1811 'BOB DYLAN' on left 26mm, open centre)	5
65	CBS 201824	Positively 4th Street/From A Buick 6 (white promo label)	40
65	CBS 201824	Positively 4th Street/From A Buick 6 (orange label 'Side A/B' between cat. no. and matrix no. "BLOSSOM MUSIC" on right)	10
65	CBS 201824	Positively 4th Street/From A Buick 6 (orange label 'Side A/B' not stated, 'BLOSSOM MUSIC LTD' on right)	12
66	CBS 201900	Can You Please Crawl Out Of Your Window?/Highway 61 revisited (white promo)	40
66	CBS 201900	Can You Please Crawl Out Of Your Window?/Highway 61 revisited (orange label)	12
66	CBS	Queen Jane Approximately/Positively 4th Street/Can You Please Crawl Over Your Window? (7" unreleased EP acetate. White blank labels Matrix EP7011)	400
66	CBS 202053	One Of Us Must Know (Sooner Or Later)/Queen Jane Approximately (white promo label)	40
66	CBS 202053	One Of Us Must Know (Sooner Or Later)/Queen Jane Approximately (orange label)	20
66	CBS 02307	Rainy Day Women Nos. 12 & 35 (edit 2.26)/Pledging My Time (edit 2.06) (Test Pressing. Side 1 white label CBS logo, handwritten title +A 5368/9 B-side black)	200
66	CBS 02307	Rainy Day Women Nos. 12 & 35 (edit 2.26)/Pledging My Time (white promo label)	40
66	CBS 02307	Rainy Day Women Nos. 12 & 35 (edit 2.26)/Pledging My Time (orange label, 'B Feldman' below catalogue numbers)	10
66	CBS 02307	Rainy Day Women Nos. 12 & 35 (edit 2.26)/Pledging My Time (orange label, 'Dwarf Music LTD' below catalogue numbers)	12
66	CBS 202258	I Want You/Just Like Tom Thumb's Blues (live) (white promo label)	40
66	CBS 202258	I Want You/Just Like Tom Thumb's Blues (live) (orange label, push out/solid centre)	12/12
66	CBS	Absolutely Sweet Marie (1-sided 10" acetate, 45RPM white label, typed title)	300
67	CBS 2700	Leopard-Skin Pill-Box Hat/Most Likely You Go Your Way And I'll Go Mine (White promo label)	40
67	CBS 2700	Leopard-Skin Pill-Box Hat/Most Likely You Go Your Way And I'll Go Mine (orange label, p/s)	45
67	CBS 2700	Leopard-Skin Pill-Box Hat/Most Likely You Go Your Way And I'll Go Mine (orange label)	10
69	CBS 4219	I Threw It All Away/Drifter's Escape (white promo label)	30
69	CBS 4219	I Threw It All Away/Drifter's Escape (orange label push out/solid centre)	6/5
69	CBS 4434	Lay, Lady, Lay/Peggy Day (White promo label)	30
69	CBS 4434	Lay, Lady, Lay/Peggy Day (orange label, song titles smaller letters than 'BOB DYLAN' on left, solid centre. 'U.S.A Production' below 'produced by Bob Johnston')	5
69	CBS 4434	Lay, Lady, Lay/Peggy Day (orange label, songtitles equally large letters Solid centre, no 'U.S.A Production')	6
69	CBS 4434	Lay, Lady, Lay/Peggy Day (orange label, songtitles equally large letters Push-out cente, no 'U.S.A Production')	6
75	CBS 4434	Lay, Lady, Lay/Peggy Day (yellow/red label, overall length of 'BOB DYLAN' 24mm in bolt print, push-out centre)	5
75	CBS 4434	Lay, Lady, Lay/Peggy Day (yellow/red label, overall length of 'BOB DYLAN' 16mm in bolt print, solid centre)	5
75	CBS 4434	Lay, Lady, Lay/Peggy Day (yellow/red label, overall length of 'BOB DYLAN' 24mm in bolt print, solid centre)	5
69	CBS 4611	Tonight I'll Be Staying Here With You/Country Pie (white promo label)	35
69	CBS 4611	Tonight I'll Be Staying Here With You/Country Pie (orange label)	6
70	CBS 5122	Wigwam/Copper Kettle (The Pale Moonlight) (white promo label, misprint: label side-2 on both sides)	40
70	CBS 5122	Wigwam/Copper Kettle (The Pale Moonlight) (white promo label, correct labelling, CBS Newsletter added)	40
70	CBS 5122	Wigwam, Copper Kettle (The Pale Moonlight) (Orange label)	5
71	CBS 7092	If Not For You/New Morning (white promo label)	35
71	CBS 7092	If Not For You/New Morning (orange label, solid/push-out centre)	8/8
71	CBS 7329	Watching The River Flow/Spanish Is The Loving Tongue (white promo label)	35

Bob DYLAN

71	CBS 7329	Watching The river Flow/Spanish Is The Loving Tongue (orange label, solid/push-out centre). 6/6
71	CBS	George Jackson (Acoustic)/George Jackson (Big Band Version) (10" acetate) . 300
71	CBS 7688	George Jackson (Acoustic)/George Jackson (Big Band Version) (white promo label). 35
71	CBS 7688	George Jackson (Acoustic)/George Jackson (Big Band Version) (orange label, solid/push-out centre). 8/8
80	CBS 7688	George Jackson (Acoustic)/George Jackson (big band version) (yellow/red label. "(Acoustic)"/'(BIG BAND VERSION)' next to song titles). 6
80	CBS 7688	George Jackson (Acoustic)/George Jackson (Big Band Version) (yellow/red label. '(ACOUSTIC)'/'(BIG BAND VERSION)' below song titles). 6
73	CBS 1158	Just Like A Woman (full album version)/I Want You (extended version) (Hall Of Fame series, orange label push out centre, stereo, p/s) 8
73	CBS 1158	Just Like A Woman (full album version)/I Want You (extended version) (Hall Of Fame series, orange label solid centre, stereo, p/s). 8
75	CBS 1158	Just Like A Woman (full album version)/I Want You (extended version) (testpressing. Both sides red with black printing 'ADVANCE COPY TEST PRESSING…' Handwritten 'A' is added on A side) 180
75	CBS 1158	Just Like A Woman (full album version)/I Want You (extended version) (Hall Of Fame series. Yellow/red label, standard sleeve 'BOB DYLAN' 25mm. 5
75	CBS 1158	Just Like A Woman (full album version)/I Want You (extended version) (Hall Of Fame series. Yellow/red label, standard sleeve 'BOB DYLAN' 16mm. 5
79	CBS 1158	Just Like A Woman (full album version)/I Want You (extended version) (Hall Of Fame series. Yellow/red label, standard sleeve 'BOB DYLAN' 28mm. 5
73	CBS 1158	Knockin' On Heaven's Door/Turkey Chase (white promo label) 35
73	CBS 1158	Knockin' On Heaven's Door/Turkey Chase (orange label push-out/solid centre). 6/6
75	CBS 1158	Knockin' On Heaven's Door/Turkey (yellow/red label 'U.S.A. Production' below song titles and credits, open/solid centre) 6/6
76	CBS 1158	Knockin' On Heaven's Door/Turkey Chase (yellow/red label, 'Exclusive licencees' below credits, open/solid centre) 6/6
73	CBS 1158	Knockin' On Heaven's Door/Turkey (yellow/red 'U.S.A. Production' below Song titles/credits, 'BOB DYLAN' on 2 lines on left, 'LC' above cat. Solid centre . 6
74	CBS 2006	A Fool Such As I/Lily Of The West (White promo label) 35
74	CBS 2006	A Fool Such As I/Lily Of The West (orange label, push out/solid centre). 8
74	Island WIP618	On A Night Like This/Forever Young (promo label). 35
74	Island WIP618	On A Night Like This/Forever Young. 8
74	Island	Most Likely You Go Your Way And I'll Go Mine (live) (7" acetate, no UK release) 350
75	CBS 3160	Tangled Up In Blue/If You See Her, Say Hello (white promo label) 35
75	CBS 3160	Tangled Up In Blue/If You See Her, Say Hello (yellow/red label, push-out/solid centre) 8
75	CBS 3160	Tangled Up In Blue/If You See Her, Say Hello (yellow/red label, open centre, 'Engineer: Paul Martinson' below LP reference). 8
75	CBS 3665	Million Dollar Bash/Tears Of Rage (white promo label) 35
75	CBS 3665	Million Dollar Bash/Tears Of Rage (yellow/red label) 7
76	CBS 3878JB	Hurricane (Part 1)/Hurricane (Part 2) (mis-labelled, B-side plays full-length Version. Side 3 plays at 45rpm, swear word bleeped) 10
76	CBS 3878JB	Hurricane (Part 1)/Hurricane (Part 2) (mis-labelled, B-side plays full-length Version. Side 3 plays at 33⅓ rpm, swear word bleeped) 10
76	CBS 3878	Hurricane (Part 1)/Hurricane (full lenth version) (white promo label, swear-word Bleeped. Full-length version plays at 33⅓ rpm. Regular p/s) 35
76	CBS 3878JB	Hurricane (Part 1)/Hurricane (full lenth version at 33⅓ rpm) (with "Taken from the LP 'DESIRE' S 86003) 8
76	CBS 3878JB	Hurricane (Part 1)/Hurricane (full lenth version at 33⅓ rpm) (without LP reference 45/33⅓ in large figures 'full length version' below 'stereo') 8
76	CBS 3878JB	Hurricane (Part 1)/Hurricane (full lenth version at 33⅓ rpm) (without LP reference '45/33⅓' in small figures 'full length version' not below 'stereo'. Length of 'BOB DYLAN' is 20mm) 8
76	CBS 3878JB	Hurricane (part 1)/Hurricane (full lenth version at 33⅓ rpm) (without LP reference '45/33⅓' in small figures, "full-length version" not below STEREO, overall length Of BOB DYLAN 28mm. Mislabelled, B-side plays 45rpm) 10
76	CBS 3878JB	Hurricane (part 1)/Hurricane (full lenth version at 33⅓ rpm) (A-side with LP reference B-side without. '45/33⅓' in large figures) 8
76	CBS	Hurricane (for John Hammond live) (12" unreleased UK acetate, white sticker with typed song title, broadcast Dec 13th 1975) 350

(All Hurricane singles come with the same p/s although it is not uncommon to find late runs in standard p/s)

76	CBS 3945	Lay, Lady, Lay/I Threw It All Away (Hall Of Fame series 'Produced by Bob Johnston' above LP reference, p/s or standard sleeve) 8/5
76	CBS 3945	Lay, Lady, Lay/I Threw It All Away (Hall Of Fame series 'Produced by Bob Johnston' below LP reference, p/s or standard sleeve) 8/5
76	CBS 4113	Mozambique/Oh, Sister (white promo label) 15
76	CBS 4113	Mozambique/Oh, Sister (open/solid centre) 6/6
77	CBS 4859	Rita May/Stuck Inside Of Mobile With The Memphis Blues Again (Live) (white promo label, commercial p/s). 15
77	CBS 4859	Rita May/Stuck Inside Of Mobile With The Memphis Blues Again (Live) 'exclusive licensees' below title. Credits end with abbreviation 'UK'. Rita May as A-Side p/s version which unlike labels, lists Rita May as B-side). 7
77	CBS 4859	Rita May/Stuck Inside Of Mobile With The Memphis Blues Again (Live) "exclusive licensees" ends with United Kingdom. Rita May as A-side p/s version which unlike labels, lists Rita May as B-side) 7
78	CBS 6499	Baby Stop Crying/New Pony (test pressing, both sides red with black printing 'ADVANCE COPY….' Handwritten A is added on A-side) 150
78	CBS 6499	Baby, Stop Crying/New Pony (white promo label). 15

78	CBS 6499	Baby, Stop Crying/New Pony (yellow/red label, 'Produced By Don DeVito' above LP reference, open/solid centre)	5/5
78	CBS 6499	Baby, Stop Crying/New Pony (yellow/red label, 'Produced By Don DeVito' below LP reference, open/solid centre. 'stereo'on both sides, solid centre)	5
78	CBS 6499	Baby, Stop Crying/New Pony (yellow/red label, "Produced By Don DeVito below LP reference, open/solid centre. 'stereo' on Side 1 only, misprint, solid centre)	20
78	CBS 6499	Baby, Stop Crying/New Pony (plastic dark red embossed)	8
78	CBS 12-6499	Baby, Stop Crying/New Pony (12" p/s)	10
78	CBS 6718	Is Your Love In Vain?/We Better Talk This Over (white promo label)	20
78	CBS 6718	Is Your Love In Vain?/We Better Talk This Over (open/solid centre)	6/6
78	CBS 12-6718	Is Your Love In Vain?/We Better Talk This Over (test pressing, black on white labels with 'not for resale or distribution' in red)	150
78	CBS 12-6718	Is Your Love In Vain?/We Better Talk This Over (12" p/s)	10
78	CBS 6935	Changing Of The Guards (edit 3.39)/Changing Of The Guards (5.36) (white promo)	17
78	CBS 6935	Changing Of The Guards/Senor (Tales Of Yankee Power)	5
79	CBS 7071	Lay Lady Lay/I Threw It All Away (Golden Decade Series. Yellow/red label without 'LC' capsule, archline starts with 'Made In England')	5
79	CBS 7071	Lay, Lady, Lay/I Threw It All Away (Golden Decade Series. Yellow/red label with 'LC' capsule, archline starts with 'Made In England')	5
79	CBS 7071	Lay, Lady, Lay/I Threw It All Away (Golden Decade Series. Yellow/red label with 'LC' capsule, archline ends with 'Made In England')	10
79	CBS 7071	Lay, Lady, Lay/I Threw It All Away (Golden Decade Series. red label with 'LC' capsule, archline ends with 'Made In England')	10
79	CBS 7473	Forever Young (short version live)/Forever Young (long version live) (white label)	17
79	CBS 7473	Forever Young (live)/All Along The Watchtower (live)/I Want you (live)	10
79	CBS 7828	Precious Angel/Trouble In Mind (white label promo)	15
79	CBS 7828	Precious Angel/Trouble In Mind (open/solid centre)	5/5
79	CBS 7970	Man Gave Names To All The Animals/When He Returns (white label promo)	15
79	CBS 7970	Man Gave Names To All The Animals/When He Returns	5
80	CBS 8134	Gotta Serve Somebody/Gonna Change My Way Of Thinking (white label promo)	15
80	CBS 8134	Gotta Serve Somebody/Gonna Change My Way Of Thinking	5
80	CBS 8743	Saved/Are You Ready? (white label promo)	15
80	CBS 8743	Saved/Are You Ready?	5
81	CBS	Heart Of Mine (3.30) (1-sided 7" acetate 'PYRAL' sleeve, shorter than single version)	250
81	CBS A1406	Heart Of Mine/Let It Be Me (white promo label)	15
81	CBS A1406	Heart Of Mine/Let It Be Me (white promo label with blue release date stamp)	15
81	CBS A1406	Heart Of Mine/Let It Be Me (yellow/orange label)	5
81	CBS A1406	Heart Of Mine/Let It Be Me (plastic ochre embossed label)	5
81	CBS A1406	Lenny Bruce/Dead Man, Dead Man (white label promo commercial p/s)	15
81	CBS A1406	Lenny Bruce/Dead Man, Dead Man (white label promo, blue release date stamp p/s)	15
81	CBS A1406	Lenny Bruce/Dead Man, Dead Man (sleeve misprint with 'Lennie Bruce')	200
81	CBS A1406	Lenny Bruce/Dead Man, Dead Man	8
83	CBS	Union Sundown/License To Kill (7" acetate blue on white CBS labels with 'MASTERING STUDIOS', 'PYRAL' standard sleeve)	250
83	CBS	Angel Flying Too Close To The Ground (7" 1-sided acetate)	250
83	CBS A3916	Union Sundown/Angel Flying Too Close To The Ground (white promo label, commerical p/s 'Angels' mistakenly credited to Bob Dylan)	15
83	CBS A3916	Union Sundown/Angel Flying Too Close To The Ground (yellow/red label p/s 'Angels' mistakenly credited to Bob Dylan)	7
83	CBS A3916	Union Sundown/Angel Flying Too Close To The Ground (plastic ochre embossed label p/s 'Angels' mistakenly credited to Bob Dylan)	7
83	CBS A3916	Union Sundown/Angel Flying Too Close To The Ground (yellow/red label 'Angels' correctly credited to Willy Nelson)	10
83	CBS A4055	Jokerman (full length version)/Jokerman (faded version for radio play) (white label promo, standard sleeve 'exclusive licensees' below song titles)	15
83	CBS A4055	Jokerman (full length version)/Jokerman (faded version for radio play) (white label promo, 'exclusive licensees' vertically on left)	15
83	CBS A4055	Jokerman/Licence To Kill (yellow/red label, 'exclusive licencees' below song titles, p/s)	6
83	CBS A4055	Jokerman/Licence To Kill (yellow/red label, 'exclusive licencees' vertically on left, p/s)	6
83	CBS A4055	Jokerman/Licence To Kill (plastic ochre embossed label, p/s)	6
84	CBS A4595	Lay Lady Lay/I Threw It All Away ("BACKTRACK" series)	25
85	CBS A5020	Highway 61 Revisited (live)/It Ain't Me Babe (live) (yellow/red label promo with 'A' on one side, commerical p/s)	15
85	CBS A5020	Highway 61 Revisited (live)/It Ain't Me Babe (live) (yellow/red/plastic ochre label p/s)	8/8
85	CBS A5020	Highway 61 Revisited (live)/It Ain't Me Babe (live) ("Souvenir" edn. Fold out p/s)	10
85	CBS A6303	Tight Connection To My Heart(short version)/Tight Connection To My Heart (long version) (yellow/red label Promo with 'A' on one side. Commercial p/s)	15
85	CBS A6303	Tight Connection To My Heart(short version)/Tight Connection To My Heart (long version) (p/s)	7
85	CBS A6469	When The Night Comes Falling From The Sky (edit)/Dark Eyes (yellow/red promo label with 'A' on one side)	15
85	CBS A6469	When The Night Comes Falling From The Sky (edit)/Dark Eyes (different A-side mix, p/s)	25
85	CBS A6469	When The Night Comes Falling From The Sky (edit)/Dark Eyes (Disco Mix, p/s)	8
85	CBS A6469	When The Night Comes Falling From The Sky (edit)/Dark Eyes (12" p/s)	10
86	MCA 1076	Band Of The Hand/M RUBINI: Theme From Joe's Death (promo)	20

Bob DYLAN

86	MCA 1076	Band Of The Hand/M RUBINI: Theme From Joe's Death (plastic blue/silver embossed p/s)	8/8
86	MCA 1076	Band Of The Hand/M RUBINI: Theme From Joe's Death (12" p/s)	10
87	CBS 6511486	The Usual/Got My Mind Made Up/They Killed Him (12" mis-pressing, plays 'Drifting Too Far From Shore' instead of 'They Killed Him' p/s)	10
87	CBS 6511487	The Usual/Got My Mind Made Up (regular label with red promo release date sticker on commercial p/s)	10
87	CBS 6511487	The Usual/Got My Mind Made Up (p/s)	8
88	CBS	Silvio/When Did You Leave Heaven?/Drifting Too Far From Shore (12" acetate 'CBS MASTER STUDIOS', white labels, blue lettering, handwritten titles)	300
88	CBS 6514066	Silvio/When Did You Leave Heaven?/Drifting Too Far From Shore (12" p/s)	10
88	CBS 6514067	Silvio/When Did You Leave Heaven? (regular label, red promo sticker on p/s)	10
88	CBS 6514067	Silvio/When Did You Leave Heaven? (p/s)	8
89	CBS	Everything Is Broken/Dead Man, Dead Man/I Want You (live) (12" acetate STUDIO WEST, white label, blue lettering, blue logo, hand written song titles)	300
89	CBS 6553586	Everything Is Broken/Dead Man, Dead Man/I Want You (live) (12" p/s with CBS promo sticker)	12
89	CBS 6553586	Everything Is Broken/Dead Man, Dead Man/I Want You (live) (12" p/s)	10
89	CBS 6553588	Everything Is Broken/Dead Man, Dead Man/I Want You (live) (12" p/s with limited edition numbered album sleeve print)	20
89	CBS	Everything Is Broken/Death Is Not The End (10" acetate, STUDIO WEST, white label, blue lettering, blue logo hand-written song titles)	300
89	CBS 6553587	Everything Is Broken/Death Is Not The End (regular label with red promo release date sticker on commercial p/s)	10
89	CBS 6553587	Everything Is Broken/Death Is Not The End (p/s)	8
90	CBS 6556436	Political World/Ring Them Bells/Silvio/All Along The Watchtower (live) (12" p/s)	8
90	CBS 6556437	Political World/Ring Them Bells (test pressing, blank labels p/s)	100
90	CBS 6556437	Political World/Ring Them Bells (regular label with red promo release date sticker on commerical p/s and CBS promo letter)	10
90	CBS 6556437	Political World/Ring Them Bells (p/s)	8
90	CBS 6563047	Unbelievable/10,000 Men (test pressing, yellow labels commercial p/s)	100
90	CBS 6563047	Unbelievable/10,000 Men (regular label with red promo release date sticker on commercial p/s and CBS promo letter)	10
90	CBS 6563047	Unbelievable/10,000 Men (p/s grey shaded not laminated/brown shaded laminated)	8/8
00	Columbia 6693797	Things Have Changed/Blind Willy McTell (numbered p/s)	8

EPs

64	CBS 6051	DYLAN (Bob Dylan below song titles, solid/push-out centre, designer credits in bottom right corner, p/s)	40/40
64	CBS 6051	DYLAN (Bob Dylan vertically on left: 'EXTENDED PLAY' on 1 line above 'EP 6051', push out centre – no designer credits, p/s)	45
65	CBS 6051	DYLAN (Bob Dylan vertically on left: 'EXTENDED PLAY' on 2 lines above 'EP 6051', solid centre, no designer credits, p/s)	45
66	CBS 6070	ONE TOO MANY MORNINGS (Only EP in Europe with five songs, p/s)	50
66	CBS 6070	MR. TAMBOURINE MAN (length of EP on both sides: 27mm 'EXTENDED PLAY' on 1 line, 'Blossom Music LTD' on both sides. Solid/push-out centre, p/s)	50/50
66	CBS 6078	MR. TAMBOURINE MAN (length of EP on side 1, 'EXTENDED PLAY' divided over 2 lines, 'Blossom Music' (side 1) 'Blossom Music Ltd' (Side 2), push out centre, p/s)	50

(Contrary to popular belief the following EPs were never officially released. On the verge of release with some copies sent to record stores Phonogram cancelled the project as permission from CBS was refused. Planned release date was May 1965 and all tracks were taken live from the Newport Folk Festival in July 1963)

65	Fontana TFE 18009	WITH GOD ON OUR SIDE (Joan Baez and Bob Dylan title track)/ PETE SEEGER: The Bells of Rhymney/JOAN BAEZ: Waggoner's Lad, p/s)	75
65	Fontana TFE 18010	BLOWING IN THE WIND (BOB DYLAN: Blowing In The Wind/ JOAN BAEZ: Oh Freedom/PETE SEEGER: Careless Love, p/s)	75
65	Fontana TFE 18011	YE PLAYBOYS AND PLAYGIRLS (Bob Dylan and Pete Seeger title track/ JOAN BAEZ: Te Ador, Te Manha/PETE SEEGER: This Land Is Mine, p/s)	75

LPS

62	CBS BPG 62022	BOB DYLAN (mono, 33⅓ on orange labels, condensed logo, 3 rear flaps)	30
62	CBS SBPG 62022	BOB DYLAN (stereo 33⅓ on orange labels, condensed logo, 3 rear flaps)	30

(STEREO cover editions come in 4 versions: 1 mono cover with no stereo indications. 2 gold 'STEREO' sticker on rear cover. 3 rubber-stamped 'STEREO' indication on rear cover. 4 printed 'STEREO' indication on front -and rear cover.)

69	CBS SBPG 62022	BOB DYLAN (stereo 33⅓ on orange labels, regular logo, 3 rear flaps)	25
75	CBS BPG 62022	BOB DYLAN (stereo 33⅓ on orange/yellow labels, mono prefix, stereo LP)	17
99	Columbia 62022/SVLP 0085	BOB DYLAN (180gm Simply Vinyl pressing)	18
63	CBS BPG 62193	THE FREEWHEELIN' BOB DYLAN (mono 33⅓ on orange labels, condensed logo, 3 rear flaps)	30
63	CBS SBPG 62193	THE FREEWHEELIN' BOB DYLAN (stereo, 33⅓ on orange label, condensed logo, 3 rear flaps)	30
64	CBS SBPG 62193	THE FREEWHEELIN' BOB DYLAN (stereo, 33⅓ on orange label, condensed logo, 3 rear flaps)	30

(STEREO cover editions come in 4 versions: 1 mono cover with no stereo indications. 2 gold 'STEREO' sticker on rear cover. 3 rubber-stamped 'STEREO' indication on rear cover. 4 printed 'STEREO' indication on front -and rear cover.)

75	CBS BPG 62193	THE FREEWHEELIN' BOB DYLAN (orange/yellow labels)	15
99	Columbia 63193/SVLP 0003	THE FREEWHEELIN' BOB DYLAN (180gm Simply Vinyl pressing)	18
01	Columbia 8786/8125017	THE FREEWHEELIN' BOB DYLAN (125gm Simply Vinyl pressing, silver sticker)	15
03	Columbia 8786/8125017	THE FREEWHEELIN' BOB DYLAN (125gm Simply Vinyl pressing, silver sticker)	15

64	CBS BPG 62251	THE TIMES THEY ARE A-CHANGIN' (mono, 33⅓ on orange labels, condensed logo, 3 rear flaps)	30
64	CBS SBPG 62251	THE TIMES THEY ARE A-CHANGIN' (white label test pressing)	80
64	CBS SBPG 62251	THE TIMES THEY ARE A-CHANGIN' (stereo, 33⅓ on orange labels, condensed Logo 3 rear flaps)	30

(STEREO cover editions come in 4 versions: 1 mono cover with no stereo indications. 2 gold 'STEREO' sticker on rear cover. 3 rubber-stamped 'STEREO' indication on rear cover. 4 printed 'STEREO' indication on front -and rear cover.)

65	CBS SBPG 62251	THE TIMES THEY ARE A-CHANGIN' (stereo, 33⅓ on light orange labels)	27
75	CBS SBPG 62251	THE TIMES THEY ARE A-CHANGIN' (orange/yellow labels)	15
79	CBS BPG 62251	THE TIMES THEY ARE A-CHANGIN' (orange/yellow labels, mono prefix, stereo LP)	15
99	Columbia 62251/SVLP 0031	THE TIMES THEY ARE A-CHANGIN' (180gm Simply Vinyl pressing)	18

64	CBS BPG 62429	ANOTHER SIDE OF BOB DYLAN (mono, orange labels, condensed logo, 3 rear flaps)	30
64	CBS SBPG 62429	ANOTHER SIDE OF BOB DYLAN (stereo, orange labels, condensed logo, 3 rear flaps)	30
65	CBS BPG 62429	ANOTHER SIDE OF BOB DYLAN (stereo 33⅓ on orange labels)	27
64	CBS BPG 62429	ANOTHER SIDE OF BOB DYLAN (stereo 33⅓ on orange labels, STEREO story on rear)	27

(STEREO cover editions come in 4 versions: 1 mono cover with no stereo indications. 2 gold 'STEREO' sticker on rear cover. 3 rubber-stamped 'STEREO' indication on rear cover. 4 printed 'STEREO' indication on front -and rear cover.)

| 75 | CBS SBPG 62429 | ANOTHER SIDE OF BOB DYLAN (orange/yellow labels) | 15 |
| 99 | Columbia 62429/SVLP 0078 | ANOTHER SIDE OF BOB DYLAN (180g Simply Vinyl pressing) | 18 |

65	CBS BPG 62515	BRINGING IT ALL BACK HOME (mono on orange labels, condensed logo, 3 rear flaps)	30
65	CBS SBPG 62515	BRINGING IT ALL BACK HOME (stereo on orange labels, condensed logo, 3 rear flaps)	30
66	CBS SBPG 62515	BRINGING IT ALL BACK HOME (stereo, 33⅓ on orange labels STEREO story on rear)	27

(STEREO cover editions come in 4 versions: 1 mono cover with no stereo indications. 2 gold 'STEREO' sticker on rear cover. 3 rubber-stamped 'STEREO' indication on rear cover. 4 printed 'STEREO' indication on front -and rear cover.)

| 75 | CBS SBPG 62515 | BRINGING IT ALL BACK HOME (orange/yellow labels) | 15 |
| 99 | Columbia 62515/SVLP 0036 | BRINGING IT ALL BACK HOME (180gm Simply Vinyl pressing) | 18 |

65	CBS BPG 62572	HIGHWAY 61 REVISITED (mono on orange labels, condensed logo, 3 rear flaps)	30
65	CBS SBPG 62572	HIGHWAY 61 REVISITED (stereo on orange labels, condensed logo, 3 rear flaps)	30
66	CBS SBPG 62572	HIGHWAY 61 REVISITED (stereo 33⅓ on orange labels STEREO story on rear)	27

(STEREO cover editions come in 4 versions: 1 mono cover with no stereo indications. 2 gold 'STEREO' sticker on rear cover. 3 rubber-stamped 'STEREO' indication on rear cover. 4 printed 'STEREO' indication on front -and rear cover.)

75	CBS SBPG 62572	HIGHWAY 61 REVISITED (orange/yellow labels)	15
98	Columbia 62572	HIGHWAY 61 REVISITED (180gm 'Absolute Analogue' re-release)	20
00	Columbia 62572	HIGHWAY 61 REVISITED (180gm Simply Vinyl pressing)	18

66	CBS DDP 66012	BLONDE ON BLONDE (mono, 33⅓ on orange labels, gatefold, 4 rear flaps)	60
66	CBS DDP 66012	BLONDE ON BLONDE (mono 33⅓ on orange labels, condensed logo, 4 rear flaps)	60
66	CBS SDDP 66012	BLONDE ON BLONDE (stereo, 33⅓ on orange labels, condensed logo gatefold, 4 rear flaps)	45
67	CBS SDDP 66012	BLONDE ON BLONDE (stereo, 33⅓ on orange labels condensed logo, gatefold)	35

(STEREO cover editions come in 4 versions: 1 mono cover with no stereo indications. 2 gold 'STEREO' sticker on rear cover. 3 rubber-stamped 'STEREO' indication on rear cover. 4 printed 'STEREO' indication on front -and rear cover.)

75	CBS SDDP 66012	BLONDE ON BLONDE (orange/yellow labels, gatefold, 7 photos inside)	18
79	CBS C2S 841	BLONDE ON BLONDE (USA import, stickers over Columbia info, gatefold, 7 photos)	15
85	CBS 22130	BLONDE ON BLONDE (red labels, cover not gatefold)	12
99	Columbia 66012/SVLP063	BLONDE ON BLONDE (180gm Simply Vinyl pressing, silver sticker front/rear)	25
03	Columbia 66012/SVLP063	BLONDE ON BLONDE (180gm Simply Vinyl pressing, gold sticker front/rear)	25

67	CBS SBPG 62847	GREATEST HITS (stereo on orange labels, 3 rear flaps)	18
67	CBS BPG 62847	GREATEST HITS (mono 33⅓ on orange labels)	15
68	CBS SBPG 62847	GREATEST HITS (stereo 33⅓ on orange labels, STEREO story on rear)	12

(STEREO cover editions come in 4 versions: 1 mono cover with no stereo indications. 2 gold 'STEREO' sticker on rear cover. 3 rubber-stamped 'STEREO' indication on rear cover. 4 printed 'STEREO' indication on front -and rear cover.)

| 68 | CBS BPG 63252 | JOHN WESLEY HARDING (mono, 33⅓ on orange labels. Spain and UK only) | 30 |
| 68 | CBS CBPG 63252 | JOHN WESLEY HARDING (stereo, 33⅓ on orange labels) | 15 |

(STEREO cover editions come in 4 versions: 1] mono cover with no stereo indications. 2] gold "STEREO" sticker on rear cover. 3] rubber-stamped "STEREO" indication on rear cover. 4] printed "STEREO" indication on front -and rear cover.)

| 75 | CBS CBPG 63252 | JOHN WESLEY HARDING (orange/yellow labels) | 12 |
| 99 | Columbia 63252/SVLP 0056 | JOHN WESLEY HARDING (180gm Simply Vinyl pressing) | 18 |

| 69 | CBS M 63601 | NASHVILLE SKYLINE (mono, 33⅓ on orange labels. Spain and UK only) | 30 |
| 69 | CBS S 63601 | NASHVILLE SKYLINE (stereo, 33⅓ on orange labels) | 15 |

(STEREO cover editions come in 4 versions: 1 mono cover with no stereo indications. 2 gold "STEREO" sticker on rear cover. 3 rubber-stamped "STEREO" indication on rear cover. 4 printed "STEREO" indication on front -and rear cover.)

Bob DYLAN

75	CBS S 63601	NASHVILLE SKYLINE (orange/yellow labels)	12
99	Columbia 63601/SVLP071	NASHVILLE SKYLINE (180gm Simply Vinyl pressing)	18
03	Columbia 63601/S125036	NASHVILLE SKYLINE (125gm Simply Vinyl pressing)	15
70	CBS S 64085/6	SELF PORTRAIT (stereo, 33⅓ on orange labels, gatefold)	15
75	CBS S 64085/6	SELF PORTRAIT (orange/yellow labels)	12
70	CBS S 69001	NEW MORNING (Test pressing, b/w logos with TEST PRESSING)	80
70	CBS S 69001	NEW MORNING (stereo 33⅓ on orange labels	15
75	CBS 32267	NEW MORNING (orange/yellow labels)	12
01	Columbia 69001/SVLP341	NEW MORNING (180gm Simply Vinyl pressing)	18
71	CBS S 67239	MORE BOB DYLAN GREATEST HITS (orange labels, gatefold, opening inside)	15
75	CBS S 67239	MORE BOB DYLAN GREATEST HITS (orange/yellow labels, opening outside)	12
73	CBS S 69049	DYLAN (LP, orange labels)	15
75	CBS 32286	DYLAN (LP, orange/yellow labels)	12
74	Island ILPS.9261	PLANET WAVES (gold on white back cover insert)	15
01	Columbia 321541/SVLP331	PLANET WAVES (Simply Vinyl pressing)	18
74	Island IDBD-1	BEFORE THE FLOOD (LP)	16
75	CBS S 69097	BLOOD ON THE TRACKS (test pressing, plain white labels)	80
75	CBS S 69097	BLOOD ON THE TRACKS (orange labels)	15
76	CBS S 69097	BLOOD ON THE TRACKS (orange/yellow labels)	12
98	Columbia 69097	BLOOD ON THE TRACKS (180gm "Absolute Analogue" re-release)	20
01	Columbia 690971/SVLP 192	BLOOD ON THE TRACKS (180gm simply Vinyl, silver sticker front/rear)	18
03	Columbia 690971/SVLP 192	BLOOD ON THE TRACKS (180gm simply Vinyl, golden sticker front/rear)	18
75	CBS S 88147	THE BASEMENT TAPES (test pressing, plain white labels)	100
75	CBS S 88147	THE BASEMENT TAPES (with info sticker)	17

(From Basement Tapes onwards all standard LP's come with orange/yellow labels)

76	CBS S 86003	DESIRE (with info sticker)	15
85	CBS 32388	DESIRE (red label, mispressing, Emmylou Harris says "He fucked it up" at the end of 'Oh Sister')	100
01	Columbia 86003 1/SVLP 350	DESIRE (180gm Simply Vinyl pressing)	18

(Quadrophonic issues of Nashville Skyline and Desire LP's were imports and not pressed in the UK)

76	CBS CBS 86016	HARD RAIN	12
78	CBS CBS 86067	STREET LEGAL	12
00	Columbia 86067/SVLP 197	STREET LEGAL (180gm Simply Vinyl pressing)	18
79	CBS CBS 96004	AT BUDOKAN (test pressing, plain white labels)	100
79	CBS CBS 96004	AT BUDOKAN (white on black info sticker)	17
01	Col'bia 4658001000/SVLP319	OH MERCY (180gm Simply Vinyl pressing)	18
00	Col'bia 4783741/SVLP100	MTV UNPLUGGED (180gm Simply Vinyl pressing)	25
80	CBS 7950	JOES GARAGE (When You Gonna Make Up appears instead of Catholic Girls, This track was only officially released in USA and Canada in 1979)	100

(Pat Garrett & Billy The Kid, Slow Train Coming, Saved, Shot Of Love, Infidels, Real Live, Dylan & The Dead and Under The Red Sky are all worth between £8-10)

PROMOS
| 88 | CBS SAMPCD 1224 | FOREVER YOUNG (CD, 18 tracks) | 40 |
| 90 | CBS XPCD 116 | FOREVER YOUNG (CD, 13 tracks) | 40 |

MISPRESSING: FRANK ZAPPA
| 80 | CBS 7950 | JOES GARAGE ('When You Gonna Make Up' appears instead of 'Catholic Girls', This track was only officially released in USA and Canada in 1979) | 100 |

Dylan appears as a sideman on the following releases

DOUG SAHM
| 73 | Atlantic K 10293 | Is Anybody Goin' To San Anton/Don't Turn Around (Dylan on A-side) | 8 |

BETTE MIDLER
| 76 | Atlantic K 11260 | Buckets of Rain/La Vie En Rose (Dylan on A-side) | 7 |

LEONARD COHEN
| 77 | CBS 5882 | Memories/Don't Go Home With Your Hard-On (Dylan on B-side) | 7 |

LONE JUSTICE
| 85 | Geffen TX 6426 | Sweet, Sweet Baby (remix)/Go Away Little Boy (Dylan)/Pass It On (12" p/s) | 20 |

USA FOR AFRICA
| 85 | CBS A 6112 | We Are The World (7" p/s or 12" p/s with promo stamp) | 5/8 |

(see also Dick Farina, Band, George Harrison, Traveling Wilburys, Doug Sahm, Earl Scruggs)

DYMONDS
| 71 | Big BG 326 | Girl You Are Too Young/RUPIE EDWARDS ALL STARS: Version | 6 |

DYNAMIC CORVETTES
| 75 | Contempo CS 2059 | Funky Music Is The Thing (Parts 1 & 2) | 7 |

DYNAMIC GANG (Bob Andy & Marcia Griffiths)
| 71 | Moodisc MU 3511 | I'll Never Believe In You/LLOYD WILLIS: Black Attack | 8 |

DYNAMIC MCS
| 87 | Tuff GrooveTUFF002 | I Feel Dynamic (12") | 20 |

DYNAMICS (Jamaica)
| 68 | Blue Cat BS 104 | My Friends/NEVILLE IRONS: Soul Glide | 50 |
| 69 | Punch PH 1 | The Burner/Jackie Juckie (B-side actually by Tommy McCook & Carl Bryan) | 12 |

DYNAMICS (U.S.)
63	London HLX 9809	Misery/I'm The Man	40
64	King KG 1007	So In Love With Me/Say You Will	20
69	Atlantic 584 270	Ice Cream Song/The Love That I Need	10

DYNAMITES
69	Duke DU 30	John Public/CLANCY ECCLES: Fire Corner (B-side actually by King Stitt)	10
69	Duke DU 31	I Don't Care (actually by Dingle Brothers)/CLANCY ECCLES: Shoo-Be-Do	8
69	Clandisc CLA 200	Mr. Midnight (Skokiaan)/KING STITT: Who Yeah	10
70	Clandisc CLA 212	Black Beret/BARRY & AFFECTIONS: Love Me Tender	10
70	Clandisc CLA 219	Sha La La La/Pop It Up	10
71	Clandisc CLA 237	Hello Mother/FABULOUS FLAMES: Hi-De-Ho	7
69	Trojan/Clandisc TTL 21	FIRE CORNER (LP, with King Stitt)	20

(see also Clancy Eccles & Dynamites, Baba Brooks, Dennis Alcapone, Diamonds, Joe Higgs, Silvertones, Carl Dawkins, Chris Leon, Hopeton Lewis, Melodians, Cynthia Richards, Soul Twins, Stranger & Gladys, Carey & Lloyd)

DYNATONES
59	Top Rank JAR 149	Steel Guitar Rag/The Girl I'm Searching For (78 rpm = £20)	25

DYNATONES
66	Pye International 7N 25389	The Fife Piper/And I Always Will	50

RONNIE DYSON
71	CBS 7449	When You Get Right Down To It/Sleeping Sun	6
74	CBS 2430	We Can Make It Last Forever/Just A Little Love From Me	15

VINCE EAGER (& THE VAGABONDS)
58	Decca F 11023	Tread Softly Stranger & Yea Yea (as Vince Eager & The Vagabonds; unissued, 2 x 1-sided demos only)	each 28
58	Parlophone R 4482	Five Days, Five Days/No More (78 rpm = £15)	35
59	Parlophone R 4531	When's Your Birthday, Baby?/The Railroad Song (78 rpm = £25+)	20
59	Parlophone R 4550	This Should Go On Forever/No Other Arms, No Other Lips	20
59	Top Rank JAR 191	Makin' Love/Primrose Lane (78 rpm = £30+)	7
60	Top Rank JAR 275	Why/El Paso	6
60	Top Rank JAR 307	No Love Have I/Lonely Blue Boy	8
61	Top Rank JAR 539	(I Wanna) Love My Life Away/I Know What I Want	7
61	Top Rank JAR 593	The World's Loneliest Man/Created In A Dream	7
63	Piccadilly 7N 35110	Any Time Is The Right Time/Heavenly	7
63	Piccadilly 7N 35157	I Shall Not Be Moved/It's Only Make Believe	6
58	Decca DFE 6504	VINCE EAGER AND THE VAGABONDS NO. 1 (EP)	125
71	Avenue AVE 093	VINCE EAGER PAYS TRIBUTE TO ELVIS PRESLEY (LP)	16
78	Nevis NEV LP 143	TWENTY YEARDS ON (LP)	15

EAGLE
70	Pye International 7N 25530	Kickin' It Back To You/Come In, It's All For Free	15
69	Pye Intl. NSPL 28138	COME UNDER NANCY'S TENT (LP)	30

EAGLES (Jamaica)
69	Songbird SB 1006	Rudam Bam/Prodigal Boy (B-side actually "Any Little Bit" by Crystals)	8
72	Duke Reid DR 2522	Your Enemies Can't Hurt You/Version	7
73	Techniques TE 927	Rub It Down/TOMMY McCOOK ALL STARS: Rub It Down — Version	6

(see also Jamaican Eagles, Roy Richards)

EAGLES (U.K.)
62	Pye 7N 15451	Bristol Express/Johnny's Tune	10
62	Pye 7N 15473	Exodus: The Main Theme/March Of The Eagles	10
62	Pye 7N 15503	The Desperados/Special Agent	10
63	Pye 7N 15550	Come On Baby (To The Floral Dance)/Theme From Station Six Sahara	10
63	Pye 7N 15571	Eagles Nest/Poinciana (unreleased)	
64	Pye 7N 15613	Andorra/Moonstruck	10
64	Pye 7N 15650	Write Me A Letter/Wishin' And Hopin'	12
62	Pye NEP 24166	NEW SOUND T.V. THEMES (EP)	15
63	Pye NPL 18084	SMASH HITS (LP)	50

(see also Valerie Mountain)

EAGLES (U.S.)
72	Asylum AYM 505	Take It Easy/Get You In The Mood (promo only p/s)	8
75	Asylum K 53003	DESPERADO (LP, audiophile pressing, mail-order via *Hi-Fi Today* mag)	25

SNOOKS EAGLIN
60s	Storyville A 45056	Country Boy/Alberta (some with p/s)	15
60s	Storyville SEP 386	BLUES ANTHOLOGY VOL. 6 (EP)	15
61	Heritage HLP 1002	SNOOKS EAGLIN (LP, 99 only)	90+
63	Storyville SLP 119	NEW ORLEANS STREET SINGER (LP)	20
64	Storyville SLP 140	VOL. 2 — BLUES FROM NEW ORLEANS (LP)	20
70s	Storyville 670 146	PORTRAITS IN BLUES VOLUME 1 (LP)	20

JIM EANES
59	Melodisc 1530	Christmas Doll/It Won't Seem Like Christmas	18

EARCANDY
93	Poor Person Prod. PPPR 1	SPACE IS JUST A PLACE (LP, handmade sleeve, 500 only)	15
94	Poor Person Prod. PPPR 2	TIME IS JUST A STATE OF MIND (LP, handmade sleeve)	15
95	Poor Person Prod. PPPR 5	SOUND IS JUST THE WAY YOU EAR IT (LP, handmade sleeve, insert, 600 only)	15

95	Poor Person Prod. PPPR 8	TASTING 1,2,3, TASTING (LP, handmade sleeve & insert, numbered, 500 only)	15

ROBERT EARL
58	Philips PB 805	I May Never Pass This Way Again/Someone	6
58	Philips PB 867	More Than Ever (Come Prima)/No One But You (In My Heart)	6
59	Philips PB 891	The Wonderful Secret Of Love/The Boulevard Of Broken Dreams	6
59	Philips PB 960	The Test Of Time/The Key (78 rpm = £6)	6
62	Philips PB 1029	Shalom/When You're In Love	6
62	Philips 326556 BF	Lonely/Time Will Tell	6
58	Philips BBE 12032	ROBERT EARL (EP)	14
59	Philips BBE 12240	THE WONDERFUL SECRET OF LOVE (EP)	14
67	Philips BE 12598	SHALOM (EP)	10
60	Philips BBL 7394	SHOWCASE (LP)	20

EARL & DEAN
66	Strike JH 323	Slowly Goin' Out Of My Head/Little Buddy	7

KENNETH EARLE
60	Decca F 11205	The New Frankie And Johnny/40-30-40	12
60	Decca F 11224	Standing On The Corner/Put Your Arms Around Me, Honey	5

EARL-JEAN
64	Colpix PX 729	I'm Into Somethin' Good/We Love And Learn	25
64	Colpix PX 748	Randy/They're Jealous Of Me	28

(see also Cookies)

EARLS
63	Stateside SS 153	Remember Then/Let's Waddle	45
63	London HL 9702	Never/I Keep-A Tellin' You	55
71	Atlantic 2091 129	Remember Then/I Believe	10

EARTH
69	CBS 4671	Resurrection City/Comical Man	40
69	Decca F 22908	Stranger Of Fortune/Everybody Sing The Song	15

EARTH & FIRE
70	Penny Farthing PEN 741	Mechanical Lover/Ruby Is The One	8
70	Polydor 56790	Seasons/Paradise	20
71	Nepentha 6129 001	Invitation/Wild And Exciting	20
72	Polydor 2001 356	Memories/From The End To The Beginning	10
73	Polydor 2001 435	Maybe Tomorrow/Theme From Atlantis	6
74	Polydor 2121 235	Love Of Life/Tuffy The Cat	6
71	Nepentha 6437 004	EARTH AND FIRE (LP, gatefold sleeve)	200
73	Polydor 2310 262	ATLANTIS (LP)	18
75	Polydor 2925 033	TO THE WORLD A FUTURE (LP)	15

EARTH & STONE
79	Cha Cha CHAD 09	Sweet Africa/Dance With Me (12")	15
79	Cha Cha CHAD 015	Slave Driver/Magic Woman (12")	20
79	Cha Cha CHADLP 007	KOOL ROOTS (LP)	45

EARTH BAND
(see under Manfred Mann's Earth Band)

EARTH BOYS
59	Capitol CL 14979	Barbara Ann/Space Girl	20

EARTHLINGS
65	Parlophone R 5242	Landing Of The Daleks/March Of The Robots	40

EARTH OPERA
68	Elektra EKSN 45035	Close Your Eyes And Shut The Door/Dreamless	8
69	Elektra EKSN 45049	American Eagle Tragedy/When You Were Full Of Wonder	7
69	Elektra EKSN 45061	Alfie Finney/Home To You	7
68	Elektra EKS 74016	EARTH OPERA (LP, gatefold sleeve)	40
69	Elektra EKS 74038	GREAT AMERICAN EAGLE TRAGEDY (LP)	22

(see also Rowan Brothers)

EARTHQUAKE
74	Cloud One HIT 4	Friday On My Mind/Madness	5
75	United Artists UP 35787	Tall Order For A Short Guy/Mr Security	5
75	United Artists UAS 29853	LIVE (LP)	12

EARTHQUAKERS
67	Stateside SS 2050	Whistling In The Sunshine/Dreaming In The Moonlight	8

EARTHQUAKES
69	Duke DU 54	Pair Of Wings/I Can't Stop Loving You	12
69	Duke DU 56	Earthquake/Simmering	12

(see also Sir Collins & Earthquakes)

EARTH, WIND & FIRE
71	Warner Bros WB 6125	Help Somebody/Love Is Life	6
73	CBS 1792	Evil/Clover	6
74	CBS 2033	Keep Your Head To The Sky/Build Your Nest	6
74	CBS 2284	Mighty Mighty/Drum Song	6
74	CBS 2782	Kalimba Story/The Nine Chee Bit	6
71	Warner Bros WS 1905	EARTH, WIND & FIRE (LP, with insert)	35
73	CBS 65208	LAST DAYS AND TIME (LP)	15
73	CBS Q 65604	HEAD TO THE SKY (LP, quadrophonic)	15
73	CBS 65604	HEAD TO THE SKY (LP)	15
74	CBS 65844	OPEN OUR EYES (LP, with inner sleeve)	12

TIM EASLEY
68	Bell BLL 1036	Susie Q (Parts 1 & 2)	8

EAST BAY RAY
84	Alt. Tentacles VIRUS 34	Trouble In Town/Poisonheart (p/s)	5

(see also Dead Kennedys)

EAST MAIN ST. EXPLOSION
69	Fontana TF 1039	Hop, Skip And Jump/Little Jackie Horner	6

EAST OF EDEN
68	Atlantic 584 198	King Of Siam/Ballad Of Harvey Kaye	30
69	Deram DM 242	Northern Hemisphere/Communion	20
70	Deram DM 297	Jig-A-Jig/Marcus Junior	6
71	Deram DM 338	Ramadhan/In The Snow For A Blow/Better Git It In Your Soul/ Have To Whack It Up A Bit	15
72	Harvest HAR 5055	Boogie Woogie 'Flu/Last Dance Of The Clown (p/s)	12
73	United Artists UP 35567	Sin City Girls/All Our Yesterdays	8
69	Deram DML/DML 1038	MERCATOR PROJECTED (LP, mono/stereo)	40/35
70	Deram SML 1050	SNAFU (LP)	30
71	Decca SPA 157	WORLD OF EAST OF EDEN (LP)	15
71	Harvest SHVL 792	EAST OF EDEN (LP)	30
71	Harvest SHVL 796	NEW LEAF (LP)	30

BUGSY EASTWOOD
68	President PT 209	Blackbird Charlie/My Sun	6

(see also Exception)

CLINT EASTWOOD
62	Cameo Parkway C 240	Rowdy/Cowboy Wedding Song (some in p/s)	20/10

CLINT EASTWOOD
77	Jamaica Sounds JSLP 0010	JAH LIGHTS SHINING (LP)	15
78	Cha Cha CHALP003	DEATH IN THE ARENA (LP)	45
78	Third World TWS933	AFRICAN YOUTH (LP)	35

EASYBEATS
66	United Artists UP 1144	Come And See Her/Make You Feel Alright (Women)	22
66	United Artists UP 1157	Friday On My Mind/Made My Bed, Gonna Lie In It	10
66	United Artists UP 1175	Who'll Be The One?/Saturday Night	13
67	United Artists UP 1183	Heaven And Hell/Pretty Girl	13
67	United Artists UP 1201	The Music Goes Round My Head/Come In, You'll Get Pneumonia	13
68	United Artists UP 2209	Hello, How Are You?/Falling Off The Edge Of The World	10
68	United Artists UP 2219	The Land Of Make-Believe/We All Live Happily	10
68	United Artists UP 2243	Good Times/Lay Me Down And Die	10
69	Polydor 56335	St. Louis/Can't Find Love	10
70	Polydor 2001 028	(Who Are My) Friends?/Rock'n'Roll Boogie	12
67	United Artists (S)ULP 1167	GOOD FRIDAY (LP)	100
68	United Artists (S)ULP 1193	VIGIL (LP)	60
70	Polydor Special 2482 010	FRIENDS (LP)	60

(see also Paintbox, Haffy's Whisky Sour, Harry Vanda, Grapefruit)

EASY RIDERS
58	Philips PB 823	Salute To Windjammer/Kari Waits For Me	5
60	London HLR 9204	Young In Love/Saturday's Child	6
60	London HA-R 2323	REMEMBER THE ALAMO (LP, also stereo SAH-R 6126)	12/14

(see also Terry Gilkyson & Easy Riders, Vic Damone, Frankie Laine)

EASY STREET
76	Polydor 2058807	Feels Like Heaven/Shadows On The Wall (no p/s)	10
70s	Muscle Music AP 591	Person To Person/Easy Come Easy Go	30
77	Polydor 2383 444	UNDER THE GLASS (LP)	15

EASYWORLD
90s	Fierce Panda NING 103	Hundredweight/U Make Me Want To Drink Bleach (orange vinyl, 500 only)	15
90s	Zomba 9253377	Try Not To Think/Everyone Knows (die-cut, numbered p/s, 500 only)	8

EATER
77	The Label TLR 001	Outside View/You (p/s)	10
77	The Label TLR 003	Thinkin' Of The USA/Space Dreamin'/Michael's Monetary System (p/s)	10
77	The Label TLR 004	Lock It Up/Jeepster (p/s)	10
77	The Label TLR 004/12	Lock It Up/Jeepster (12", p/s)	8
78	The Label TLR 007	GET YOUR YO-YO'S OUT (EP, white vinyl; blue, green or red p/s)	8
78	The Label TLR 007	GET YOUR YO-YO'S OUT (12" EP, white vinyl; (blue, green or red p/s)	10
78	The Label TLR 009	What She Wants She Needs/Reaching For The Sky (p/s)	6
78	The Label TLRLP 001	THE ALBUM (LP, with inner sleeve)	30
85	De Lorean EAT 1	THE HISTORY OF EATER (LP, 1,000 each on red, white & blue vinyl, with bonus 7" [EAT FREEBIE 1])	12
85	De Lorean EAT 1	THE HISTORY OF EATER (LP, green vinyl)	12

(see also Andy Blade)

EATHOPIANS
69	Nu Beat NB 038	Buss Your Mouth (actually Contention by Ethiopians)/REGGAE BOYS: Rough Way Ahead (B-side actually by Keith Blake & Hi-Tals)	12

(see also Ethiopians)

EAZIE RYDER
78	Graduate GRAD 1	Motorbikin'/City Lights (p/s)	15

EBONIES
68	Philips BF 1648	Never Gonna Break Your Heart Again/Shoeshine Boy	10

EBONYS
71	CBS 7384	You're The Reason Why/Sexy Ways	8

EBONY SISTERS

69	Bullet BU 401	Let Me Tell You Boy/RHYTHM RULERS: Mannix	
		(B-side actually by Rhythm Rulers)	12
70	Bullet BU 420	Each Time/BUNNY LEE ALLSTARS: Boss Waik	10

(see also Sister)

KATJA EBSTEIN

70	Liberty LBF 15317	No More Love For Me/Without Love	15

ECCENTRICS

65	Pye 7N 15850	What You Got/Fe Fi Fo Fum	45

CLANCY ECCLES (& DYNAMITES)

61	Blue Beat BB 34	River Jordan/I Live And I Love (with Hersan & His City Slickers)	20
61	Blue Beat BB 67	Freedom/More Proof	22
63	Island WI 044	Judgement/Baby Please (B-side actually with Paulette)	22
63	Island WI 098	Glory Hallelujah/Hot Rod (B-side actually by Roland Alphonso)	24
65	Ska Beat JB 194	Sammy No Dead/Roam Jerusalem	18
65	Ska Beat JB 198	Miss Ida/KING ROCKY: What Is Katty	20
67	Doctor Bird DB 1156	Feel The Rhythm/Easy Snapping (B-side actually by Theo Beckford)	20
67	Pama PM 701	What Will Your Mama Say/Darling Don't Do That	20
67	Pama PMB 703	Western Organ/Mother's Advice (actually by The Clancy Set)	15
68	Pama PM 712	The Fight/Great	15
68	Nu Beat NB 006	Festival '68/I Really Love You	24
69	Trojan TR 639	Sweet Africa/Let Us Be Lovers	12
69	Trojan TR 647	Bangarang Crash/DYNAMITES: Rahthid	14
69	Trojan TR 648	Constantinople/Deacon Sun	14
69	Trojan TR 649	Demonstration/VAL BENNETT: My Girl	14
69	Trojan TR 658	Fattie Fattie/SILVERSTARS: Last Call	14
69	Duke DU 9	Auntie Lulu/SLICKERS: Bag A Boo	10
69	Duke DU 31	Shoo-Be-Do/DYNAMITES: I Don't Care (B-side actually by Dingle Brothers)	10
69	Clandisc CLA 201	The World Needs Loving/DYNAMITES: Dollar Train	
		(B-side actually by Clancy Eccles)	20
69	Clandisc CLA 206	Dance Beat/KING STITT: The Ugly One	10
70	Clandisc CLA 209	Open Up/HIGGS & WILSON: Agane (B-side actually "Again")	10
70	Clandisc CLA 211	Promises/Real Sweet (both sides with Dynamites)	8
70	Clandisc CLA 212	Black Beret (with Dynamites)/BARRY & AFFECTIONS: Love Me Tender	10
70	Clandisc CLA 213	Phantom/Skank Me (both sides with Dynamites)	
		(B-side actually by Barry & Affections)	12
70	Clandisc CLA 214	Africa/Africa Part Two (both sides with Dynamites)	6
70	Clandisc CLA 221	Unite Tonight/Uncle Joe	6
70	Clandisc CLA 227	Credit Squeeze/DYNAMITES: Credit Squeeze	6
71	Clandisc CLA 231	Sweet Jamaica/DYNAMITES: Going Up West	6
71	Clandisc CLA 232	Rod Of Correction/Rod Of Correction Version	6
71	Clandisc CLA 235	John Crow Skank/KING STITT: Merry Rhythm	10
71	Clandisc CLA 236	Power For The People/DYNAMITES: Power For The People — Version	6
71	Pama Supreme PS 332	What Will Your Mama Say/TIGER: United We Stand	9
72	Clandisc CLA 239	Hallelujah, Free At Last/DYNAMITES: Sha-La-La	9
69	Trojan TTL 22	FREEDOM (LP)	35
70	Clandisc TBL 124	HERBSMAN REGGAE (LP)	35

(see also Dynamites, Drumbago, Marlene Webber, Westmorelites)

JIMMY ECHO

65	Columbia DB 7629	After Tonight/Practise What You Preach	6

ECHO & BUNNYMEN

79	Zoo CAGE 004	The Pictures On My Wall/Read It In Books (p/s, original issue with yellow or grey labels, with The Revenge Of Voodoo Billy scratched in B-side run-off)	6
80	Korova KOW 1	Rescue/Simple Stuff (2 different p/s designs)	each 6
80	Korova KOW 1T	Rescue/Simple Stuff/Pride (12", p/s)	8
80	Korova KOW 15	The Puppet/Do It Clean (p/s, limited issue)	7
81	Korova KOW 15T	A Promise/Broke My Neck (Long Version) (12", p/s)	8
83	Korova KOW 26	The Cutter/Way Out And Up We Go/Zimbo (12", with bonus Peel Session cassette [KOW 26C])	10
83	Korova KOW 26T	The Cutter/Way Out And Up We Go/Zimbo (live) (12", with poster)	8
84	Korova KOW 35F/ SAM 202	Seven Seas/All You Need Is Love//The Killing Moon/Stars Are Stars/ Villiers Terrace (numbered double pack, gatefold p/s)	6
88	Korova KOW 43P	Bring On The Dancing Horses/Over Your Shoulder ('cow'-shaped picture disc in stickered PVC sleeve)	8
88	Korova KOW 43F/SAM 269	Bring On The Dancing Horses/Over Your Shoulder/Villiers Terrace/Monkeys (double pack)	6
87	WEA YZ 134	The Game/Lost And Found (unreleased alternate p/s without title, promo only)	7
87	WEA YZ 144B	Lips Like Sugar/Rollercoaster (box set with 3 postcards)	6
91	Imaginary FREE 001	Foggy Notion/MOCK TURTLES: Pale Blue Eyes (no p/s, promo only)	5
81	Korova KODE 1	CROCODILES (LP, with bonus 7", Do It Clean/Read It In Books [SAM 128] & inner sleeve)	12
83	Korova KODE 6	PORCUPINE (LP, with bonus Peel Session cassette [KOW 26C])	15
85	Korova KODE 13	SONGS TO LEARN AND SING (LP, with lyric booklet & 7": The Pictures On My Wall/Read It In Books [p/s, yellow/blue labels, CAGE 004], no Voodoo Billy run-off groove message; some signed)	25/15
85	Korova KODE 13P	SONGS TO LEARN AND SING (LP, picture disc)	12

(see also Ian McCulloch, Will Sergeant)

ECHO BASE

84	DEP International DEP 14	Out Of My Reach/Splash Down (p/s)	15
85	DEP International DEP 19	Puppet At The Go Go/Genius + Soul = Jazz (p/s)	15
85	DEP International LPDEP 9	BUY ME (LP)	18

(see also Ocean Colour Scene)

ECHOES (U.K.)

62	Fontana 267254 TF	Cloak And Dagger/Sounds Like Winter	10
62	Fontana TF 392	The Happy Whistler/Sticks And Stones	9
63	Fontana TF 415	The Jog/Marching Thru'	10
64	Fontana TF 439	My Little Girl/More	10
64	Philips BF 1370	Don't You Believe Them/I'll Get Over You	10
66	Philips BF 1480	Got To Run/Thanks A Lot	10
68	Philips BF 1687	Searchin' For You Baby/Listen To Me Baby	17

ECHOES (U.S.)

60	Top Rank JAR 399	Born To Be With You/My Guiding Light	20
61	Top Rank JAR 553	Baby Blue/Boomerang	22

ECHOES & CELESTIALS (Jamaica)

61	Hornet H 1004	Are You Mine/I'll Love You Forever	18
62	Blue Beat BB 89	Are You Mine/I'll Love You Forever (reissue)	10

BILLY ECKSTINE

53	MGM SP 1011	Kiss Of Fire/I Apologise	15
53	MGM SP 1020	Come To The Mardi Gras/Be Fair	7
53	MGM SP 1040	Coquette/A Fool In Love	7
53	MGM SP 1055	I've Never Been In Love Before/I'll Know	7
53	MGM SP 1060	St. Louis Blues (Parts 1 & 2) (as Billy Eckstine & Metronome All Stars)	7
54	MGM SP 1082	Tenderly/Fortune Telling Cards	8
54	MGM SP 1084	Rendezvous/Don't Get Around Much Anymore	7
54	MGM SP 1095	Seabreeze/Sophisticated Lady	7
54	MGM SP 1101	No One But You/I Let A Song Go Out Of My Heart	16
54	MGM SP 1107	Beloved/Olay Olay (The Bullfighter's Song)	7
55	MGM SP 1117	Mood Indigo/Do Nothin' Till You Hear From Me	7
55	MGM SP 1124	What More Is There To Say?/Prelude To A Kiss	7
55	MGM SP 1136	Love Me Or Leave Me/The Life Of The Party	8
55	MGM SP 1140	More Than You Know/La De Do De Do (Honey Bug Song)	7
56	MGM SP 1153	Farewell To Romance/Lost In Loveliness	7
56	MGM SP 1167	Good-bye/You've Got Me Crying Again	7
56	MGM SP 1170	The Show Must Go On/You'll Get Yours	7
56	MGM MGM 925	Solitude/I Got It Bad (And That Ain't Good)	8
57	MGM MGM 948	A Man Doesn't Know/My Fickle Heart	7
57	HMV POP 341	Pretty, Pretty/Blue Illusion	6
57	MGM MGM 970	Bring Back The Thrill/Over The Rainbow	6
58	Mercury 7MT 191	Boulevard Of Broken Dreams/If I Can Help Somebody	6
58	Mercury 7MT 224	Vertigo/In The Rain (78 rpm, Mercury MT 224 = £8)	6
58	Mercury AMT 1008	Prisoner Of Love/Funny (78 rpm = £10)	5
59	Mercury AMT 1018	Gigi/Trust In Me (78 rpm = £10)	6
59	Columbia DB 4334	I Want A Little Girl/Lonesome Lover Blues (with Count Basie Orchestra)	5
59	Columbia DB 4334	I Want A Little Girl/Lonesome Lover Blues (with Count Basie Orchestra) (78)	10
60	Columbia DB 4407	Anything You Wanna Do (I Wanna Do With You)/Like Wow	5
62	Ember JBS 703	Good Jelly Blues/If That's The Way You Feel	5
65	Tamla Motown TMG 533	Had You Been Around/Down To Earth (DJ copy = £150)	100
54	MGM EPC 6	BILLY ECKSTINE (EP, export issue)	12
55	MGM MGM-EP 511	BILLY ECKSTINE (EP)	12
55	MGM MGM-EP 523	THE CASHMERE VOICE (EP)	12
57	MGM MGM-EP 598	FOUR GREAT STANDARDS (EP)	12
57	Parlophone GEP 8672	A DATE WITH RHYTHM (EP, with His All Star Band)	12
57	Mercury ZEP 10005	THE BEST OF MISTER B. NO. 1 (EP)	12
57	Mercury ZEP 10110	BOULEVARD OF BROKEN DREAMS (EP)	12
60	Emarcy JAZZYEP 9509	THE BEST OF MISTER B. NO. 2 (EP)	12
61	Columbia SEG 8042	BASIE-ECKSTINE INCORPORATED (EP; also stereo ESG 7827)	12/15
54	MGM MGM-D 126	TENDERLY (10" LP)	20
56	MGM MGM-D 138	THAT OLD FEELING (10" LP)	20
58	MGM MGM-D 151	A WEAVER OF DREAMS (10" LP)	20
59	Mercury MMB 12002	BILLY ECKSTINE'S IMAGINATION (LP)	12
60	Mercury MMC 14043	BILLY'S BEST (LP)	12
60	Columbia 33SX 1249	ONCE MORE WITH FEELING (LP, also stereo SCX 3322) each	12
61	Columbia 33SX 1327	NO COVER, NO MINIMUM (LP, also stereo SCX 3381) each	12
62	Ember EMB 3338	MR. B (LP)	12
62	Mercury MMC 14100	AT BASIN STREET EAST (LP, also stereo CMS 18066)	12/15
64	Mercury 20102 MCL	NOW SINGING 12 GREAT MOVIES (LP)	15
66	T. Motown (S)TML 11025	THE PRIME OF MY LIFE (LP, mono/stereo)	55/65
67	T. Motown (S)TML 11046	MY WAY (LP, mono/stereo)	45/55
69	T. Motown (S)TML 11101	GENTLE ON MY MIND (LP)	40
71	Stax 2362 013	STORMY (LP)	12
72	Stax 2325 084	SENIOR SOUL (LP)	12

(see also Sarah Vaughan & Billy Eckstine)

ECLECTION

68	Elektra EKSN 45033	Nevertheless/Mark Time	12
68	Elektra EKSN 45040	Another Time, Another Place/Betty Brown	12
68	Elektra EKSN 45042	Please/Saint George And The Dragon	12
68	Elektra EKSN 45046	Please (Mark II)/In The Early Days	10
76	Elektra K 12196	Nevertheless/Please	5
68	Elektra EKL 4023	ECLECTION (LP, gatefold sleeve, also stereo EKS 74023)	45

(see also Fotheringay, Dorris Henderson, Trevor Lucas, Mogul Thrash)

ECSTASY CLUB

88	Hardware HWR 001	JESUS LOVES THE ACID (EP)	8

ECSTASY, PASSION & PAIN

74	Pye International 7N 25641	Don't Burn Your Bridges Behind You/I Wouldn't Give You Up	10
74	Pye International 7N 25660	Good Things Don't Last Forever/Born To Lose You	8
74	Pye International 7N 25669	Ask Me/I'll Take The Blame	10
74	Pye Intl. NSPL 28204	ECSTASY, PASSION & PAIN (LP)	20

ECTOMORPH

90s	Woronzow WOO 15	THE FURIOUS SLEEPER (LP, with poster & inserts, 500 only)	20

JASON EDDIE & THE CENTREMEN

65	Parlophone R 5388	Whatcha Gonna Do Baby/Come On Baby (as Jason Eddie & the Centremen)	150
66	Parlophone R 5473	Singing The Blues/True To You (as Jason Eddie & the Centremen)	175
69	Tangerine DP 0010	Heart And Soul/Playing The Clown (solo)	50

EDDIE & THE CRAZY JETS

64	King KG 1000	Come On Let's Slop/Down By The Riverside	6

EDDIE & THE HOT RODS

76	Island WIP 6270DJ	Writing On The Wall/Cruisin' (In The Lincoln) (promos in generic title p/s)	15
76	Island WIP 6270	Writing On The Wall/Cruisin' (In The Lincoln) (some in black & white p/s)	15/5
76	Island WIP 6306	Wooly Bully/Horseplay (Weary Of The Schmaltz) (p/s)	8
76	Island IEP 2	LIVE AT THE MARQUEE (EP, p/s)	6
76	Island WIP 6354	Teenage Depression/Shake	6
77	Island WIP 6388	I Might Be Lying/Ignore Them	6
77	Island WIP 6401	Do Anything You Wanna Do/Schoolgirl Love (p/s)	6
77	Island 12WIP 6401	Do Anything You Wanna Do/Schoolgirl Love (12", white stickered sleeve)	8
77	Island IEP 5	AT THE SPEED OF SOUND (EP, p/s)	8
77	Island IEP 5	AT THE SPEED OF SOUND (12", plain sleeve)	8
77	Island WIP 6411	Quit This Town/Distortion May Be Expected (p/s)	5
77	Island WIP 6438	Life On The Line/Do Anything You Wanna Do (live) (p/s)	5
77	Island 12WIP 6438	Life On The Line/Do Anything You Wanna Do (live)/(I Don't Know) What's Really Going On (live)/Why Can't It Be (live) (12", p/s)	8
76	Island ILPS 9457	TEENAGE DEPRESSION (LP, with poster)	15
94	Windsong WINCD 062	BBC RADIO ONE LIVE IN CONCERT (CD, withdrawn)	20

(see also Rods, Rob Tyner & Hot Rods, Lew Lewis)

EDDIE & JERRY

72	Hillcrest HCT 4	Hail Rasta Man Hail/UPSETTERS: Scorcher	8

EDDIE'S CROWD

66	CBS 202078	Baby Don't Look Down/Take It Easy Baby	70

DUANE EDDY (& THE REBELS)

78s

58	London HL 8669	Rebel-Rouser/Stalkin'	20
58	London HL 8723	Ramrod/The Walker (as Duane Eddy & Rebels, actually by Al Casey)	25
58	London HL 8764	Cannonball/Mason-Dixon Lion (as Duane Eddy & Rebels)	25
59	London HLW 8821	The Lonely One/Detour	30
59	London HLW 8879	Peter Gunn/Yep!	40
59	London HLW 8929	Forty Miles Of Bad Road/The Quiet Three	30
59	London HLW 9007	Some Kind-A Earthquake/First Love, First Tears	65
60	London HLW 9050	Bonnie Came Back/Movin 'N' Groovin'	80
60	London HLW 9104	Shazam!/The Secret Seven	120
60	London HLW 9162	Because They're Young/Rebel Walk	110

SINGLES

58	London HL 8669	Rebel-Rouser/Stalkin' (initially with triangular centre, later round centre)	15/10
58	London HL 8723	Ramrod/The Walker (as Duane Eddy & Rebels, actually by Al Casey tri-centre or round centre)	15/10
58	London HL 8764	Cannonball/Mason-Dixon Lion (as Duane Eddy & Rebels, tri or round centre)	15/10
59	London HLW 8821	The Lonely One/Detour (triangular centre or round centre)	15/10
59	London HLW 8879	Peter Gunn/Yep! (triangular or round centre)	12
59	London HLW 8929	Forty Miles Of Bad Road/The Quiet Three (triangular or round centre)	10/15
59	London HLW 9007	Some Kind-A Earthquake/First Love, First Tears	8
60	London HLW 9050	Bonnie Came Back/Movin 'N' Groovin'	5
60	London HLW 9104	Shazam!/The Secret Seven	8
60	London HLW 9162	Because They're Young/Rebel Walk	5
60	London HLW 9225	Kommotion/Theme For Moon Children	8
61	London HLW 9257	Pepe/Lost Friend	5
61	London HLW 9324	Theme From Dixie/The Battle	10
61	London HLW 9370	Ring Of Fire/Gidget Goes Hawaiian	5
61	London HLW 9406	Drivin' Home/My Blue Heaven	10
61	London HLW 9477	The Avenger/Londonderry Air	10
61	Parlophone R 4826	Caravan (Parts 1 & 2) (actually by Al Casey)	10
62	RCA RCA 1288	Deep In The Heart Of Texas/Saints And Sinners	5
62	RCA RCA 1300	The Ballad Of Paladin/Wild Westerner	5
62	RCA RCA 1316	(Dance With The) Guitar Man/Stretchin' Out (with Rebelettes)	8
63	RCA RCA 1329	Boss Guitar/Desert Rat (with Rebelettes)	8
63	RCA RCA 1344	Lonely Boy, Lonely Guitar/Joshin'	8
63	RCA RCA 1357	You're Baby's Gone Surfin'/Shuckin'	10
63	RCA RCA 1369	My Baby Plays The Same Old Song On His Guitar All Night Long/ Guitar'd And Feather'd	10
64	RCA RCA 1389	The Son Of Rebel Rouser/The Story Of Three Loves	10
64	RCA RCA 1425	Guitar Star/The Iguana	10
65	Colpix PX 779	Trash/South Phoenix	10
65	Colpix PX 788	The House Of The Rising Sun/Don't Think Twice, It's All Right	15
66	Reprise RS 20504	Daydream/This Guitar Was Made For Twangin'	15
67	Reprise RS 20557	Monsoon/Roarin'	15
68	Reprise RS 20690	Niki Hoeky/Velvet Nights (Theme From "Elvira Madigan")	15

MINT VALUE £

68	RCA RCA 1701	Dance With The Guitar Man/SAM COOKE: Another Saturday Night (withdrawn) .	15
68	London HLW 10191	Peter Gunn/Rebel-Rouser	8
69	CBS 3962	Break My Mind/Loving Bird	8
75	Target 101	Love Confusion/Love Is A Warm Emotion	10

EXPORT SINGLES

58	London HL 7057	Ramrod/The Walker (as Duane Eddy & Rebels)	20
59	London HL 7072	The Lonely One/Detour	20
59	London HL 7076	Yep!/Three-30-Blues	30
59	London SLW 4001	Peter Gunn/Yep! (stereo)	90
59	London HL 7080	Forty Miles Of Bad Road/The Quiet Three	15
60	London HL 7090	Bonnie Come Back/Lost Island	15
60	London HL 7096	Because They're Young/Rebel Walk	15

EPs

58	London RE 1175	REBEL ROUSER (as Douane Eddy)	20
59	London RE-W 1216	THE LONELY ONE	25
59	London RE-W 1217	YEP!	20
60	London RE-W 1252	BECAUSE THEY'RE YOUNG	15
60	London RE-W 1257	TWANGY	15
61	London RE-W 1287	PEPE	15
61	London RE-W 1303	DUANE EDDY PLAYS MOVIE THEMES	15
61	London RE-W 1341	TWANGY NO. 2	20
63	RCA RCX 7115	A COUNTRY TWANG	25
63	RCA RCX 7129	MR. TWANG	35
64	RCA RCX 7146	TWANGIN' UP A SMALL STORM	40
65	Colpix PXE 304	COTTONMOUTH	50

LPs

58	London HA-W 2160	HAVE 'TWANGY' GUITAR, WILL TRAVEL	40
59	London HA-W 2191	ESPECIALLY FOR YOU (also stereo SAH-W 6045 with different version of "Tuxedo Junction")	20/30
60	London HA-W 2236	THE "TWANG'S" THE "THANG!" (also stereo SAH-W 6068)	20/30
60	London HA-W 2285	SONGS OF OUR HERITAGE (gatefold sleeve, also stereo SAH-W 6119)	25/30
61	London HA-W 2325	A MILLION DOLLARS' WORTH OF TWANG	25
61	London HA-W 2373	GIRLS, GIRLS, GIRLS (also stereo SAH-W 6173)	25/30
62	London HA-W 2435	A MILLION DOLLARS' WORTH OF TWANG VOL. 2	30
62	RCA RD 27264/SF 5134	TWISTIN' AND TWANGIN' (mono/stereo)	25
62	RCA RD/SF 7510	TWANGY GUITAR — SILKY STRINGS (mono/stereo)	15/20
63	RCA RD/SF 7545	DANCE WITH THE GUITAR MAN (mono/stereo)	20/25
63	RCA RD/SF 7560	TWANG A COUNTRY SONG (mono/stereo)	20/25
63	RCA RD/SF 7568	TWANGIN' UP A STORM (mono/stereo)	20/25
64	RCA RD/SF 7621	LONELY GUITAR (mono/stereo)	20/25
64	RCA RD/SF 7656	WATER SKIING (mono/stereo)	25/30
65	RCA RD/SF 7689	TWANGIN' THE GOLDEN HITS (mono/stereo)	18/20
65	RCA RD/SF 7754	TWANGSVILLE (mono/stereo)	25/30
65	Colpix PXL 490	DUANE A-GO-GO-GO	20
66	Colpix PXL 494	DUANE EDDY DOES BOB DYLAN	20
67	Reprise R(S)LP 6218	THE BIGGEST TWANG OF THEM ALL (mono/stereo)	15/20
67	Reprise RLP 6240	THE ROARIN' TWANGIES (mono only)	30
67	G. Guinea GG(S)L 10337	DUANE DOES BOB DYLAN (reissue, mono/stereo)	15/20
70	Valiant VS 108	THE BIGGEST TWANG OF THEM ALL	14
84	Magnum Force MFM 023	REBEL ROUSIN' (Duane Eddy Convention anniversary issue, with overprinted labels, 200 only)	12

(see also Lee Hazlewood)

PEARL EDDY

| 54 | HMV 7M 262 | Devil Lips/That's What A Heart Is For | 16 |

EDDY & TEDDY

| 61 | London HLU 9367 | Bye Bye Butterfly/Star Crossed Lovers | 16 |

EDDYSONS

| 68 | Olga OLE 010 | Ups And Downs/Sweet Memories | 7 |

DAVID EDE BAND

60	Pye 7N 15280	Easy Go/The Blue Bird (as David Ede & Rabin Rock)	12
61	Pye 7N 15329	Obsession/Bootnik	12
61	Pye 7N 15370	Last Night/Ding Dong John (as David Ede & Go Man Go Men)	30
61	Pye 7N 15394	Twelfth Street Rag/No Hats On Ilkley	12
62	Pye 7N 15417	Twistin' Those Meeces To Pieces/Twistin' The Trad	12

(see also Oscar Rabin)

TONI EDEN

60	Columbia DB 4409	Teen Street/No One Understands (My Johnny)	25
60	Columbia DB 4458	Grown Up Dreams/Whad'ya Gonna Do	18
60	Columbia DB 4527	Will I Ever/The Waitin' Game	15
61	Decca F 11342	Send Me/Interesting Facts	10

EDEN'S CHILDREN

| 68 | Stateside (S)SL 10235 | EDEN'S CHILDREN (LP) | 50 |

EDEN STREET SKIFFLE GROUP

| 57 | Headquarter & General Stores (no cat. no.) | SKIFFLE ALBUM NO. 1 (10 x 7" 78rpm clear flexidiscs in p/s) | 90 |

EDGE

78	Albion ION 4	Macho Man/I'm Cold (p/s)	5
79	Hurricane FIRE 3	Downhill/American Excess (p/s, white vinyl)	6
79	Chiltern Sound CSLP	UNEASY PEACE (LP)	15
80	Hurricane FLAK 102	SQUARE 1 (LP)	15

(see also Damned, Culture Club)

THE EDGE with SINÉAD O'CONNOR
86	Virgin VS 897	Heroine (Theme From "Captive")/Heroine (Mix II) (p/s)	5
86	Virgin VS 897-12	Heroine (Theme From "Captive")/Heroine (Mix II) (12", p/s)	8
86	Virgin V 2401	CAPTIVE (LP, soundtrack)	12

(see also U2, Jah Wobble)

EDISON LIGHTHOUSE
| 71 | Bell BLL 1153 | What's Happening/Take A Little Time | 6 |
| 72 | Bell BLL 1206 | Find Mr. Zebedee?/Reconsider, My Belinda | 6 |

(see also Flowerpot Men, White Plains, David & Jonathan, First Class)

HARRY 'SWEETS' EDISON SEXTET
| 60 | HMV POP 720 | Hollering At The Watkins/K.M. Blues | 6 |
| 56 | Vogue LDE 118 | HARRY EDISON QUARTET (LP) | 15 |

EDITORS
04	Kitchenware SKCD77	Bullets/You Are Fading/Dust In The Sunlight (CD, 500 only)	20
04	Kitchenware SKX77	You Are Fading/Dust In The Sunlight (500 only)	20
05	Kitchenware SKX78	Munich/Disappear (Numbered, p/s)	7

LADA EDMUND JR
| 75 | MCA MU 172 | The Larue/Soul Au Go-Go | 10 |

DAVE EDMUNDS (& ROCKPILE)
71	Regal Zonophone RZ 3032	I'm-A Comin' Home/Country Roll	15
71	Regal Zonophone RZ 3037	Blue Monday/I'll Get Along	15
72	Regal Zonophone RZ 3059	Down, Down, Down/It Ain't Easy	15
73	Rockfield ROC 1	Baby I Love You/Maybe	6
73	Rockfield ROC 2	Born To Be With You/Pick Axe Rag (with Mickie Gee)	7
74	Rockfield ROC 4	Need A Shot Of Rhythm And Blues/Let It Be Me	7
75	Rockfield ROC 6	I Ain't Never/Some Other Guy	7
90	Capitol 10CL 568	King Of Love/Stay With Me Tonight (45rpm)/King Of Love (78 rpm) (10", p/s)	20
90	Capitol 12CL 568	King Of Love/Stay With Me Tonight/Every Time I See Her (12", p/s)	10
71	Regal Zono. SRZA 8503	ROCKPILE COLLECTION (LP, unreleased)	
72	Regal Zono. SLRZ 1026	ROCKPILE (LP)	30
75	Rockfield RRL 101	SUBTLE AS A FLYING MALLET (LP)	15
82	Arista SPART 1184	DE 7TH (LP, with bonus EP "Live At The Venue" [JUKE 1])	12

(see also Image, Human Beans, Love Sculpture, Rockpile, Andy Fairweather-Low)

EDOUARD
| 66 | CBS 202200 | My Name Is Edouard/N'aie Pas Peur Antoinette (p/s) | 6 |

EDSELS
| 61 | Pye International 7N 25086 | Rama Lama Ding Dong/Bells | 125 |

IAN EDWARD & ZODIACS
(see under Ian & Zodiacs)

(KING) EDWARDS GROUP
63	Island WI 040	Dear Hearts/Oh Mary (B-side actually by Ransford Barnett)	22
63	Island WI 047	Russian Roulette (actually by King Edwards All Stars)/You're Mine (actually by Douglas Brothers)	28
63	Island WI 082	He Gave You To Me/Kings Priests And Prophets (both actually by The Schoolboys)	20
63	Island WI 087	Hey Girl/Skies Are Grey (both actually by Ransford Barnett)	18

ADINA EDWARDS
| 72 | Dynamic DYN 454 | Talk About Love/Don't Forget To Remember | 6 |
| 60s | Tabernacle TLP 1005 | JESUS IS MINE (LP) | 20 |

(see also Coxsone Dodd)

BOBBY EDWARDS
| 61 | Top Rank JAR 584 | You're The Reason/I'm A Fool Loving You | 15 |

BRENT EDWARDS
| 63 | Pye International 7N 25197 | Pride/Over The Weekend | 10 |

C EDWARDS & SYMBOLIC
| 80 | Symbolic BS 02 | Loving Jah/Loving One & All (12") | 80 |

CHUCK EDWARDS
| 68 | Soul City SC 104 | Downtown Soulville/I Need You | 15 |

GARY EDWARDS (COMBO)
62	Oriole CB 1700	Twist Or Bust/The Franz Liszt Twist (as Gary Edwards Combo)	12
62	Oriole CB 1717	The Method/Twistful Thinkin'	10
62	Oriole CB 1733	Africa/One Fifteen A.M.	12
62	Oriole CB 1759	Hopscotch/Theme For A Broken Dream	15

(WILFRED) JACKIE EDWARDS
60	Starlite ST45 016	We're Gonna Love/Your Eyes Are Dreaming (as Wilfred Edwards & Caribs)	18
60	Starlite ST45 026	I Know/Tell Me Darling (as Wilfred Edwards)	18
61	Starlite ST45 046	Whenever There's Moonlight/Heaven Just Knows (as Wilfred Edwards)	18
61	Starlite ST45 062	More Than Words Can Say/I Love You No More (as Wilfred Edwards)	18
62	Starlite ST45 076	Little Bitty Girl/Never Go Away (as Wilfred Edwards)	18
62	Island WI 008	All My Days/Hear Me Cry (as Wilfred Jackie Edwards)	15
62	Island WI 019	One More Week/Tears Like Rain (as Wilfred Edwards)	15
62	Decca F 11547	Lonely Game/Suddenly	15
63	Black Swan WI 404	Why Make Believe/Do You Want Me (as Wilfred Jackie Edwards & Velvetts)	15
64	Black Swan WI 416	The Things You Do/Little Smile (as Wilfred Jackie Edwards)	15
64	Fontana TF 465	Sea Cruise/Little Princess	15
64	Sue WI 329	Stagger Lee/Pretty Girl	22
65	Aladdin WI 601	He'll Have To Go/Gotta Learn To Love Again	12

MINT VALUE £

65	Aladdin WI 605	Hush/I Am In Love With You No More	12
65	Aladdin WI 611	The Same One/I Don't Know	12
65	Island WI 255	White Christmas/My Love And I	12
66	Island WI 270	Sometimes/Come On Home	15
66	Island WI 274	L-O-V-E/What's Your Name	12
66	Island WI 287	Think Twice/Oh Mary	12
66	Island WI 3006	I Feel So Bad/I Don't Want To Be Made A Fool Of	200+
66	Island WI 3018	Royal Telephone/It's No Secret	8
67	Island WI 3030	Only A Fool Breaks His Own Heart/The End	8
67	Island WIP 6008	Come Back Girl/Tell Him You Lied	6
68	Island WIP 6026	Julie On My Mind/If This Is Heaven	6
68	Island WI 3157	You're My Girl/Heaven Only Knows	10
69	Direction 58-4096	Why Must I Be Alone/I'm Gonna Make You Cry	6
69	Direction 58-4402	Too Experienced/Someone To Love	6
69	Direction 58-4630	Oh Manio/Here We Go Again	6
70	CBS 5147	Tell Me Why Say Goodbye/Walter Walter	6
71	Horse HOSS 1	I Must Go Back/Baby I Want To Be Near You (some in p/s)	10/6
66	St. Mary's IEP 701	SACRED HYMNS VOL. 1 (EP, some in p/s)	38/12
66	St. Mary's IEP 702	SACRED HYMNS VOL. 2 (EP, with St. Mary's label, some in p/s)	38/12
66	St. Mary's IEP 702	SACRED HYMNS VOL. 2 (EP, with red-and-white Island label; some in p/s)	38/12
66	Island IEP 708	HUSH! (EP)	40
64	Island ILP 906	THE MOST OF WILFRED JACKIE EDWARDS (LP)	50
64	Island ILP 912	STAND UP FOR JESUS (LP)	50
66	Island ILP 931	COME ON HOME (LP)	50
66	Island ILP 936	THE BEST OF JACKIE EDWARDS (LP)	50
66	Island ILP 940	BY DEMAND (LP)	50
67	Island ILP(S) 960	PREMATURE GOLDEN SANDS (LP)	50
69	Island IWP 4	PUT YOUR TEARS AWAY (LP)	50
69	Direction 8-63977	LET IT BE ME (LP)	20
70	Trojan TTL 40	THE MOST OF WILFRED JACKIE EDWARDS (LP, as Wilfred Jackie Edwards)	18
70	Trojan TTL 45	COME ON HOME (LP)	18
70	Trojan TTL 46	BY DEMAND (LP)	18
70	Trojan TTL 57	PREMATURE GOLDEN SANDS (LP, reissue)	18

(see also Wilfred & Millicent, Wilfred & Millie, Jackie & Millie, Jackie's Boys)

JACKIE EDWARDS & JIMMY CLIFF

| 68 | Island WIP 6036 | Set Me Free/Here I Come | 7 |
| 68 | Island WIP 6042 | You're My Girl/Heaven Only Knows | 7 |

(see also Jackie & Millie, Millie, Jimmy Cliff, Wilfred & Millie, Jackie's Boys)

JIMMY EDWARDS (U.K.)

60	Fontana H 260	I've Never Seen A Straight Banana/Rhymes	12
60	Fontana TFE 17296	JIMMY EDWARDS SINGS "PA GLUM" (EP)	25
60	Fontana TFL 5103	TAKE IT FROM HERE (LP, with Dick Bentley & June Whitfield)	35

(see also Joy Nichols)

JIMMY EDWARDS (U.S.)

| 58 | Mercury 7MT 193 | Love Bug Crawl/Honey Lovin' (78 rpm, Mercury MT 193 = £70+) | 550 |

JIMMY EDWARDS (& PROFILE)

79	Warner Bros K 17415	Nora's Diary/Call Me A Fraud (features Sham 69) (p/s)	20
79	Warner Bros K 17464	Twentieth Century Time/Seven Hail Marys (features Pretenders) (p/s)	6
80	Polydor 2059 240	Toys/Hard Heart (p/s)	5
80	Polydor 2059 256	Cabaret/Drag It Back (p/s, solo)	5
81	Polydor POSP 240	In The City/Five Minute Girl (p/s, solo)	5

(see also Time U.K., Pretenders, Sham 69)

JONATHAN & DARLENE EDWARDS

| 60 | Philips BBL 7412 | JONATHAN & DARLENE EDWARDS IN PARIS (LP, also stereo SBBL 590) | 12 |

(see also Gordon MacRae, Jo Stafford)

MILL EDWARDS

| 73 | Action ACT 4617 | I Found Myself/Don't Forget About Me | 15 |

PAUL EDWARDS

| 76 | Cottage COT 301 | LONGSTONE FARM (LP) | 15 |

R. EDWARDS & SOCIAL EAGLES

| 73 | Dip DL 5014 | One Sunday Morning/Version Sunday Morning (with Allstars) | 6 |
| 73 | Dip DL 5014 | One Sunday Morning/AFRICAN BROTHERS: Mysterious Nature (2nd issue, different B-side) | 10 |

RUPIE EDWARDS (ALL STARS)

62	Blue Beat BB 90	Guilty Convict/Just Because (as Rupert Edwards & Smithie's Sextet)	25
68	Doctor Bird DB 1163	I Can't Forget/I'm Writing Again	25
69	Crab CRAB 35	Long Lost Love/Uncertain Love	12
70	Crab CRAB 41	Sharp Pan Ya Machete/Redemption	12
70	Explosion EX 2030	Full Moon/Moon	20
70	Explosion EX 2031	Love At First Sight/I Need Your Care	8
71	Bullet BU 494	I'm Gonna Live Some Life/RUPIE EDWARDS ALLSTARS: Rock 'In'	6
71	Nu Beat NB 082	Black Man/Tell The People	8
71	Nu Beat NB 091	One In Three/ERROLL DUNKLEY: Three In One	8
71	Big BG 320	Soulful Stew/Soulful Stew — Version Two (as Rupie Edwards Allstars)	8
71	Big BG 324	Deep Meditation (version)/ERROLL DUNKLEY: Deep Meditation	18
71	Big BG 327	One In Three/ERROLL DUNKLEY: Three In One	6
72	Big BG 333	Press Along/Press Along — Version (as Rupie Edwards Allstars)	6
72	Big BG 335	Jimmy As Job Card (actually titled "Jimmy Has A Job Card")/Riot (as Rupie Edwards Allstars)	15
72	Big BG 337	Christmas Parade (actually by Rupie Edwards Allstars)/UNDERGROUND PEOPLE: Santa	5

MINT VALUE £

78	Success SLD 016	Oh Black People/NOEL TEMPO : It's Time To Be Free (12")	30
75	Cactus CTLP 107	DUB BASKET (LP)	60
76	Cactus CTLP 120	JAMAICA SERENADE (LP)	35
77	Success SUCLP	101 DUB CLASSICS (LP)	80

(see also R. Edwards & Social Eagles, Gaylads, Heptones, Ethiopians, Dymonds, Dobby Dobson, Keith Cole, Country Boy, Keith Cole, Laurel Aitken, Dennis Alcapone, Gregory Isaacs, Itals, Hugh Roy, Kingstonians, Little George, Mediators, Max Romeo, I Roy, B.B. Seaton, Soul Kings, Joe White)

SAMUEL EDWARDS
69	Blue Cat BS 159	Want It Want It/SPARKERS: Israel	28

TOM EDWARDS
57	Vogue Coral Q 72236	What Is A Teen Age Girl?/What Is A Teen Age Boy?	8

TOMMY EDWARDS
52	MGM MGM 466	It's All In The Game/My Concerto (78)	6
52	MGM MGM 540	Easy To Say/Greatest Sinner Of Them All (78)	6
52	MGM MGM 567	Piano Bass And Drums/Sinner Or Saint (78)	6
53	MGM MGM 598	(Now And Then, There's) A Fool Such As I/Take These Chains From My Heart (78)	10
53	MGM SP 1030	(Now And Then, There's) A Fool Such As I/Take These Chains From My Heart	10
56	MGM SP 1168	Baby, Let Me Take You Dreaming/MARION SISTERS: Life Could Not Be Better	10
56	MGM MGM 894	Baby, Let Me Take You Dreaming/MARION SISTERS: Life Could Not Be Better (78)	8
58	MGM MGM 989	It's All In The Game/Please Love Me Forever	5
58	MGM MGM 995	Mr. Music Man/Love Is All We Need (78 rpm = £10)	5
59	MGM MGM 1006	Please, Mr. Sun/The Morning Side Of The Mountain (78 rpm = £15)	5
59	MGM MGM 1020	My Melancholy Baby/It's Only The Good Times (78 rpm = £20)	5
59	MGM MGM 1032	I've Been There/I Looked At Heaven	5
59	MGM MGM 1045	(New In) The Ways Of Love/Honestly And Truly	5
60	MGM MGM 1065	Don't Fence Me In/I'm Building Castles Again	5
60	MGM MGM 1080	I Really Don't Want To Know/Unloved	5
60	MGM MGM 1097	Blue Heartaches/It's Not The End Of Everything	5
60	MGM MGM 1113	As You Desire Me/Suzie Wong	5
61	MGM MGM 1130	The Golden Chain/That's The Way With Love	5
62	MGM MGM 1156	The Tables Are Turning/I'll Cry You Out Of My Heart	5
59	MGM MGM-EP 707	I'VE BEEN THERE (EP)	20
60	MGM MGM-EP 712	THE WAYS OF LOVE (EP)	20
59	MGM MGM-C 774	IT'S ALL IN THE GAME (LP)	25
59	MGM MGM-C 791	FOR YOUNG LOVERS (LP)	25
60	MGM MGM-C 824	YOU STARTED ME DREAMING (LP)	25

TYRONE EDWARDS
74	Invictus S INV 2542	Can't Get Enough Of You/You Took Me From A World Outside	15

VINCE EDWARDS (U.K.)
67	United Artists UP 1179	I Can't Turn Back Time/The Lively One	20
68	United Artists UP 2230	County Durham Dream/It's The Same Old Song	6
68	United Artists UP 2236	Aquarius/Hair	5

VINCE EDWARDS (U.S.)
58	Capitol CL 14825	Widget/Lollipop	7
64	Colpix PX 771	No Not Much/See That Girl (p/s)	10
62	Brunswick OE 9498	VINCE EDWARDS SINGS (EP)	10
60s	United Artists	BEN CASEY (LP)	14

WILFRED EDWARDS
(see under Jackie Edwards)

EDWARDS HAND
71	RCA SF 8154	STRANDED (LP)	25
73	Regal Zono. SRZA 8513	RAINSHINE (LP, unissued, demos only)	100+

(see also Picadilly Line)

EDWICK RUMBOLD
66	CBS 202393	Specially When/Come Back	60+
67	Parlophone R 5622	Shades Of Grey/Boggle Woggle	90+

EEK A MOUSE
81	Love Linch LL019	No Wicked/Trying To Be Free (12")	75

E.F. BAND
80	Rok ROK XI/XII	Another Day Gone/SYNCHROMESH: October Friday (die-cut co. sleeve)	30
80	Aerco/EF Band EF 1	Night Angel/Another Day Gone (some with p/s)	30/15
80	Redball RR 026	Self Made Suicide/Sister Syne (some with wraparound p/s)	30/7
80	Redball RR 036	The Devil's Eye/Comprende (some with wraparound p/s)	25/7
83	Bullet CULP 2	DEEP CUT (LP)	15

WILLIE EGANS
70s	Flyright LP 6000	ROCKS, BOOGIES AND ROLLS (LP)	15

JULIE EGE
71	CBS 5431	Love/In One Of Your Weaker Moments	10

JOSEPH EGER
70	Charisma CAS 1008	CLASSICAL HEADS (LP)	15

EGG
69	Deram DM 269	Seven Is A Jolly Good Time/You Are All Princes	20
70	Deram Nova (S)DN 14	EGG (LP)	35
71	Deram SML 1074	THE POLITE FORCE (LP)	40
74	Caroline C 1510	THE CIVIL SURFACE (LP)	28

(see also Hatfield & The North, Arzachel, Bunch Of Fives, Khan)

EGGY
69	Spark SRL 1024	Hookey/You're Still Mine	20

EGYPT
88	HTD 7HTD 1	Crazy Horses /Got No Fear (p/s)	10
88	HTD HTD LP 1	EGYPT (LP, with inner)	15

EIFFEL TOWER
69	Chappell LPC 1032	THE EIFFEL TOWER (LP, library edition)	50

8-EYED SPY
82	Fetish FE 19	Diddy Wah Diddy/Dead You Me B Side (p/s)	12
81	Fetish FR 2003	8-EYED SPY (LP)	20
(see also Lydia Lunch)			

EIGHTH DAY
71	Invictus INV 514	She's Not Just Another Woman/I Can't Fool Myself	8
72	Invictus INV 521	Eeny Meeny Miny Mo/Rocks In My Head	8

801
76	Island ILPS 9444	801 LIVE (LP)	12
(see also Phil Manzanera, Roxy Music, Brian Eno)			

EIGHTH WONDER
85	CBS QTX 6594	Stay With Me/Loser In Love/Open Your Mind (12", poster p/s)	8
88	CBS SCARE Y1	I'm Not Scared/I'm Not Scared (Disco Mix)/J'ai Pas Peur (10", p/s, with PSB)	18
88	CBS SCAREC 1	I'm Not Scared (Disco Mix)/I'm Not Scared/J'ai Pas Peur (CD, with PSB)	25
(see also Pet Shop Boys, Rock Aid Armenia)			

EIGHTIES LADIES
86	Music Of Life MOLIF 6	Turned On To You/Turned On To You (Alternative Mix) (12", p/s)	15
(see also Roy Ayers)			

808 STATE
88	Creed STATE 003	Let Yourself Go (303 Mix)/Let Yourself Go (D50 Mix)/Deepville (12", plain stickered sleeve)	8
89	ZTT ZANG 1TX	Pacific — 909 (Mellow Birds Mega Edit)/Bonus Bird Beats/Cobra Bora (12", plain stickered sleeve)	8
89	ZTT ZANG 1CD	Pacific 202/Pacific State Origin/Pacific 303/Cobra Bora Shortcut (3" CD)	12
93	ZTT SAM 933	10 X 10 (Vox Mix)/10 X 10 (Beats Version) (12", promo only)	10
89	ZTT ZANG 2CD	THE EXTENDED PLEASURES OF DANCE EP (CD, withdrawn)	30
91	ZTT ZANG 14CD	IN YER FACE EP (CD)	10
91	ZTT ZANG 19CD	Ooops!/Ski Family/808091 (live) (CD, featuring Björk)	10
88	Creed STATE 002	NEWBUILD (LP)	15
(see also Hit Squad)			

EINSTÜRZENDE NEUBAUTEN
85	Some Bizzare BART 12	Yü-Gung/Seelebrennt/Sand (12", p/s)	10
85	Some Bizzare BART 451	Das Schaben/Das Schaben (LP freebie, no p/s)	8

EIRE APPARENT
67	Track 604 019	Follow Me/Here I Go Again	20
69	Buddah 201 039	Rock'N'Roll Band/Yes I Need Someone	20
72	Buddah 2011 117	Rock'N'Roll Band/Yes I Need Someone (reissue)	10
69	Buddah 203 021	SUN RISE (LP, featuring Jimi Hendrix)	60
(see also Ernie Graham, Henry McCulloch)			

EJECTED
82	Riot City RIOT 14	HAVE YOU GOT 10p? (EP)	10
82	Riot City RIOT 19	NOISE FOR THE BOYS (EP)	10
83	Riot City RIOT 28	PRESS THE BUTTON (EP)	8
82	Riot City CITY 003	A TOUCH OF CLASS (LP)	25
83	Riot City CITY 007	THE SPIRIT OF REBELLION (LP)	25

BRITT EKLAND
79	Jet JET 161	Do It To Me (Once More With Feeling)/Private Party (gatefold p/s)	5
79	Jet JETP 161	Do It To Me (Once More With Feeling)/Private Party (picture disc)	10
(see also Britt)			

EKSEN TRICK BRICK BAND
78	Aerco AERL 17	SKY STORY (LP, with insert)	30

EKSEPTION
70	Philips 318 992 BF	Air/Dharma For One	5
72	Philips 6012 219	Ava Maria/Dharma For One	5
69	Philips 6314 001	BEGGAR JULIAN'S TIME TRIP (LP)	15
70	Philips 6314 005	EKSEPTION (LP)	18
71	Philips 6423 005	EKSEPTION III (LP)	15
72	Philips 6423 019	00.04 (LP)	15
72	Philips 6423 042	V (LP)	15
74	Philips 6423 079	CLASSICS IN POP (LP)	12

MARGARET ELAINA
73	Bullet BU 522	Ben/RICHIE & NOW GENERATION: Laughing Stock Version	5

ELAINE
63	Columbia DB 7091	I Never Wonder Where My Baby Goes/Look But Don't Touch	10

ELASTICA
93	Deceptive BLUFF 003	Stutter/Pussycat (numbered die-cut sleeve, 1,500 only)	20
93	Deceptive BLUFF 003	Stutter/Pussycat (White label test pressing)	35
94	Deceptive BLUFF 004	Line Up/Vaseline (numbered die-cut sleeve, 1,500 only)	8
94	Deceptive BLUFF 010	Connection/See That Animal (numbered die-cut sleeve, 3,000 only)	7

95	Deceptive BLUFF 011	Waking Up/Gloria (numbered die-cut sleeve, 5,000 only)	7
95	Deceptive BLUFF 011	Waking Up/Gloria (12", p/s)	8
95	Deceptive BLUFF 014LP	ELASTICA (LP, with flexidisc & booklet, no'd & stickered sleeve, 5,000 only)	15

(see also Suede)

ELASTIC BAND
68	Decca F 12763	Think Of You Baby/It's Been A Long Time Baby	28
68	Decca F 12815	Do Unto Others (From Mr. Rose T.V. Series)/8½ Hours Of Paradise	25
69	Decca Nova (S)DN 6	EXPANSIONS ON LIFE (LP, mono/stereo)	55/42

(see also Mayfield's Mule, Sweet, Andy Scott, Love Affair, Northwind)

ELASTICK BAND
67	Stateside SS 2056	Spazz/Papier Mache (unissued, demos only)	300+
68	Decca F 12815	Do Unto Others/8 Half Hours Of Paradise	35

ELASTIC OZ BAND
(see under Bill Elliott)

DONNIE ELBERT
58	Parlophone R 4403	Let's Do The Stroll/Wild Child (78 rpm = £40+)	115
65	Sue WI 377	A Little Piece Of Leather/Do Wat'cha Wanna	25
65	Sue WI 396	You Can Push It (Or Pull It)/Lily Lou	30
67	CBS 2807	Get Ready/Along Came Pride	10
68	Polydor BM 56234	In Between The Heartaches/Too Far Gone	20
68	Polydor BM 56265	This Old Heart Of Mine (Is Weak For You)/Run Little Girl	10
68	New Wave NW 001	Baby Please Come Home/Without You	8
69	Deram DM 235	Without You/Baby Please Come Home (reissue)	8
69	R&B UP 2000	Without You/(different B-side) (white label test pressing only)	8
72	Epic EPC 7943	Get Ready/Alone Came Pride	8
72	Mojo 2092 040	This Old Heart Of Mine (Is Weak For You)/Good To Me	8
72	Jay Boy BOY 70	Half As Old/Baby Let Me Love You Tonite	8
97	Joe Boy JBV 1	So Soon/Can't Get Over Losing You (p/s with numbered certificate, 300 only)	20
69	Polydor 236 560	TRIBUTE TO A KING (LP)	20
73	Ember EMB 3421	THE ROOTS OF DONNIE ELBERT (LP)	20

ELBOW
98	Soft Records Softrec001	NOISEBOX EP: Powder Blue/Red/George Lassoes The Moon (Original version)/Theme From Munroe Kelly/Can't Stop (CD, 200 copies – 50 numbered)	150/175
05	V2 VVR 5032547	Forgot Myself/McGregor (mis-press A side plays Madness' 'Shame and Scandal')	10

ELCORT
66	Parlophone R 5447	Tammy/Searchin'	18

ERIC ELDER
70	Philips 6006 081	San Tokay/Sunflower	5

ELDORADOS (Jamaica)
70	Bullet BU 428	Savage Colt/The Clea Hog	25

ELDORADOS (Rhodesia)
63	Decca DFE 8543	THE ELDORADOS (EP)	115

ELDORADOS (U.S.)
72	Mojo 2092 050	Loose Booty (Parts 1 & 2)	8

ROY ELDRIDGE & CLAUDE BOLLING
56	Vogue V 2373	Wild Man Blues/Fireworks	15

ROY ELDRIDGE QUINTET
58	Columbia/Clef SEB 10085	DIXIELAND BLUES (EP)	10
60	HMV 7EG 8682	SWINGING ON THE TOWN (EP)	10
55	Columbia/Clef 33C 9005	ROY ELDRIDGE QUINTET (LP)	15

ELECAMPANE
75	Dame Jane ODJ 1	WHEN GOD'S ON THE WATER (LP, private pressing with insert)	50
78	Dame Jane ODJ 2	FURTHER ADVENTURES OF MR PUNCH (LP, private pressing with booklet)	20

ELECTRIC BANANA
67	De Wolfe DW/LP 3040	ELECTRIC BANANA (LP, 10", original issue, tricolour label)	80
67	De Wolfe DWLP 3040	ELECTRIC BANANA (LP, second issue, with other artists)	30
68	De Wolfe DWLP 3069	MORE ELECTRIC BANANA (LP)	65
69	De Wolfe DWLP 3123	EVEN MORE ELECTRIC BANANA (LP)	45
73	De Wolfe DWLP 3284	HOT LICKS (LP)	40
76	De Wolfe DWLP 3381	THE RETURN OF THE ELECTRIC BANANA (LP)	25
79	Butt NOTT 001	THE SEVENTIES (LP)	18
80	Butt NOTT 003	THE SIXTIES (LP)	18
97	Tenth Planet TP 031	THE ELECTRIC BANANA BLOWS YOUR MIND (LP, numbered, 1,000 only)	15

(see also Pretty Things, Zac Zolar & Electric Banana)

ELECTRIC CHAIRS
(see under Wayne/Jayne County)

ELECTRIC CRAYONS
89	Emergency MIV 3	Hip Shake Junkie/Happy To Be Hated (p/s)	20

(see also Charlatans)

ELECTRIC EELS (U.S.)
(see under Die Electric Eels)

ELECTRIC FLAG
68	CBS 3584	Groovin' Is Easy/Over-Lovin' You	7
69	CBS 4066	Sunny/Soul Searchin'	7
68	CBS 62394	A LONG TIME COMIN' (LP)	20

69	CBS 63462	THE ELECTRIC FLAG — AN AMERICAN MUSIC BAND (LP)	22
71	CBS 64337	THE BEST OF ELECTRIC FLAG (LP)	14

(see also Mike Bloomfield, Buddy Miles, Barry Goldberg)

ELECTRICIANS
67	Columbia DB 8228	Champion House Theme/DON HARPER & ELECTRICIANS: Shin Bone	7

(see also Don Harper)

ELECTRIC INDIAN
69	United Artists UP 35039	Keem-O-Sabe/Broad Street	7

(see also Len Barry)

ELECTRIC JOHNNY
61	London HLU 9384	Black-Eyes Rock/Johnny On His Strings	40

ELECTRIC LIGHT ORCHESTRA (E.L.O.)
SINGLES
72	Harvest HAR 5053	10538 Overture/1st Movement (Jumping Biz)	6
72	Harvest HAR 5063	Roll Over Beethoven/Manhattan Rumble (49th Street Massacre) (with withdrawn B-side)	12
72	Harvest HAR 5063	Roll Over Beethoven/Queen Of The Hours	6
73	Harvest HAR 5077	Showdown/In Old England Town (Boogie 2) (Instrumental)	8
74	Warner Brothers K 16349	Ma-Ma-Ma Belle/Oh No Not Susan	5
75	Warner Bros K 16510	Can't Get It Out Of My Head/Illusions In G Major	5
75	Jet JET 764	Evil Woman/10538 Overture (live)	5
76	Jet JET 769	Night Rider/Daybreaker (live)	5
76	Jet JET 779	Strange Magic/Showdown (live)	5
76	Jet UP 36184	Livin' Thing/Fire On High (blue vinyl)	7
77	Jet UP 36209	Rockaria!/Poker (p/s)	5
77	Jet UP 36254	Telephone Line/Poor Boy (The Greenwood)/King Of The Universe	5
77	Harvest HAR 5121	Showdown/Roll Over Beethoven (p/s)	5
77	Harvest HAR 12-5121	Showdown/Roll Over Beethoven (12", p/s)	8
77	Harvest PSLP 213	Showdown/Roll Over Beethoven (12", promo-only art sleeve)	12
77	Jet UP 36342	Mr. Blue Sky/One Summer Dream (p/s, some on blue vinyl)	6/7
78	Jet SJET 12-109	Wild West Hero/Eldorado (12", yellow vinyl, die-cut company sleeve, 'Jet' or picture labels)	10/8
78	Jet SJET 121	Sweet Talkin' Woman/Bluebird Is Dead (mauve or black vinyl, p/s)	5/5
78	Jet SJET 12-121	Sweet Talkin' Woman/Bluebird Is Dead (12", mauve vinyl, p/s)	10
79	Jet SJET 144	Shine A Little Love/Jungle (white or black vinyl, p/s)	6/5
79	Jet SJET 12-144	Shine A Little Love/Jungle (12", black vinyl, company sleeve)	12
79	Jet SJET 150	The Diary Of Horace Wimp/Down Home Town (p/s)	5
79	Jet JET 166	Confusion/Last Train To London (p/s, wth sticker)	5
80	Jet JET 185	Xanadu/Fool Country (gatefold p/s, red or Jet label, with Olivia Newton-John)	7
80	Jet JET 10-185	Xanadu/Fool Country (10", pink vinyl, die-cut p/s, with Olivia Newton-John)	10
80	Jet JET 10-195	All Over The World/Midnight Blue (10", blue vinyl, die-cut p/s)	10
80	Jet JET 7004	Don't Walk Away/Across The Border (p/s)	5
81	Jet ELO 2	Mr Blue Sky/Across The Border/Telephone Line/Don't Bring Me Down (withdrawn, some in p/s)	15/20

LPs
71	Harvest SHVL 797	ELECTRIC LIGHT ORCHESTRA (gatefold sleeve, with inner sleeve & lyric insert)	18
73	Harvest Q4SHVL 797	ELECTRIC LIGHT ORCHESTRA (quadrophonic, promo only)	75
73	Harvest SHVL 806	ELECTRIC LIGHT ORCHESTRA II (gatefold sleeve)	12
73	Warner Bros K 56021	ON THE THIRD DAY (cut-out gatefold sleeve)	15
76	Jet JETLP 19	OLE ELO (withdrawn)	15
77	Jet UAG 30091	ON THE THIRD DAY (new mix, new sleeve & inner sleeve)	15
78	Jet JETBX 1	THREE LIGHT YEARS (3-LP, boxed set of "On The Third Day", "Eldorado" & "Face The Music", with booklet & inserts)	18
78	Jet JETLP 200	A NEW WORLD RECORD (red vinyl, with inner sleeve)	15
78	Jet JETLP 201	FACE THE MUSIC (green vinyl, with inner sleeve)	15
78	Jet JETLP 202	ON THE THIRD DAY (clear vinyl, with inner sleeve)	15
78	Jet JETLP 203	ELDORADO (yellow vinyl, with inner sleeve)	15
78	Jet JETDP 400	OUT OF THE BLUE (2-LP, clear or dark blue vinyl, with inner sleeves, with cut-out spaceship, poster & insert)	15
82	Jet JETBX 2	FOUR LIGHT YEARS (4-LP, box set of "A New World Record", "Out Of The Blue" [2-LP] & "Discovery", with booklet & insert)	20

(see also Idle Race, Jeff Lynne, Move, Roy Wood, Michael D'Albuquerque, Wilson Gale & Co., Tandy-Morgan)

ELECTRIC PRUNES
66	Reprise RS 20532	I Had Too Much To Dream (Last Night)/Luvin'	30
67	Reprise RS 20564	Get Me To The World On Time/Are You Lovin' Me More (But Enjoying It Less)	30
67	Reprise RS 20607	The Great Banana Hoax/Wind-Up Toys	20
67	Reprise RS 23212	A Long Day's Flight/The King Is In His Counting House	19
68	Reprise RS 20652	Everybody Knows You're Not In Love/You Never Had It Better	30
73	Elektra K 12102	I Had Too Much To Dream (Last Night)/KNICKERBOCKERS: Lies	7
79	Radar ADA 16	I Had Too Much To Dream (Last Night)/Luvin' (p/s)	8
67	Reprise R(S)LP 6248	THE ELECTRIC PRUNES (LP, mono/stereo)	68
68	Reprise R(S)LP 6275	MASS IN F MINOR (LP, mono/stereo)	48
68	Reprise RSLP 6316	RELEASE OF AN OATH (LP)	48
73	Reprise K 34003	MASS IN F MINOR (LP, reissue)	12
97	Heartbeat HB 67	STOCKHOLM '67 (LP, gatefold sleeve with booklet)	20

ELECTRIC SOFT PARADE
03	BMG 8287658787	Things I've Done Before (white vinyl, numbered, stickered sleeve)	5

ELECTRIC TOILET
83	Psycho PSYCHO 8	IN THE HANDS OF KARMA (LP, reissue of U.S. LP)	15

MINT VALUE £

ELECTRIX
| 79 | ELX 001 | HOLLAND (EP) | 6 |

ELECTRONIC
89	Factory FAC 257	Getting Away With It (white label test pressing)	15
89	Factory FAC 257	Getting Away With It (Full Length Version)/Getting Away With It (Inst.) (12", p/s).	10
93	Parlophone 10RD 6311	Disappointed (7" Mix)/Disappointed (12" Remix) (10", promo only)	10
99	Parlophone 12R651	Late At Night/Make It Happen (Original Version)/Make It Happen (Darren Price Mix) (12" withdrawn)	20

(see also New Order, Smiths, Pet Shop Boys)

ELECTROSCOPE
| 97 | Wurlitzer Jukebox WJ 19 | THE VANISHING PLANET PULSAR EP (p/s) | 8 |
| 97 | Wurlitzer Jukebox WJ 23 | SOMMERSON EP (p/s) | 8 |

ELECTROTUNES
| 80 | Cobra COS 5 | If This Ain't Love/Bodywork (p/s) | 5 |

ELEGANTS
| 58 | HMV POP 520 | Little Star/Getting Dizzy (78 rpm = £25) | 30 |
| 58 | HMV POP 551 | Please Believe Me/Goodnight (78 rpm = £30) | 60 |

ELEKTRIC MUSIC
93	East West YZ 755	TV/Television (p/s).	8
93	East West YZ 755T	TV/Television (12", p/s).	10
93	East West YZ 755CD	TV/Television (CD).	8
93	East West SAM 1252	Lifestyle (Edit-Style Mix)/(Club-Style Mix)/(Phoneme-Style Mix) (10", promo)	50

(see also Kraftwerk)

ELENA
| 65 | Columbia DB 7598 | Evening Time/Road Of Love | 18 |

ELEPHANT BAND
| 72 | Mojo 2092 036 | Stone Penguin/Groovin' At The Apollo | 25 |

ELEPHANT'S MEMORY
69	Buddah 201055	Crossroads Of The Stepping Stones/Yoghurt Song	6
69	Buddah 201067	Old Man Willow/Jungle Gym At The Zoo	15
70	CBS 5207	Mongoose/I Couldn't Dream	6
72	Apple APPLE 45	Power Boogie/Liberation Special (double-A-side)	15
69	Buddah 203 022	ELEPHANT'S MEMORY (LP)	20
72	Apple SAPCOR 22	ELEPHANT'S MEMORY (LP, gatefold sleeve with inner sleeve)	28

(see also John Lennon, Yoko Ono)

ELERI, JANET & DIANE
| 70s | Fanfare FR 2196 | THE ANSWER (LP) | 100 |

11.59
| 74 | Dovetail DOVE 4 | THIS IS OUR SACRIFICE OF PRAISE (LP, with insert) | 80 |

ELEVENTH HOUR
| 75 | 20th Century BTC 2215 | Hollywood Hot/Hollywood Hotter | 5 |

ELF
| 74 | Purple PUR 118 | L.A. 59/Ain't It All Amusing | 10 |
| 74 | Purple TPS 3506 | CAROLINA COUNTRY BALL (LP) | 22 |

(see also Roger Glover, Dio, Rainbow, Deep Purple, Black Sabbath)

ELFLAND ENSEMBLE
| 77 | Chrysalis CHS 2151 | Too Much Magic (feat. Derek Brimstone)/Lizarel (featuring Mary Hopkin) (p/s). | 6 |
| 77 | Chrysalis CHS 2193 | Beyond The Fields We Know/Alveric's Journey | 6 |

(see also Mary Hopkin)

ELGINS
66	Tamla Motown TMG 551	Put Yourself In My Place/Darling Baby	100
66	Tamla Motown TMG 583	Heaven Must Have Sent You/Stay In My Lonely Arms	70
67	Tamla Motown TMG 615	It's Been A Long Long Time/I Understand My Man	30
68	Tamla Motown TMG 642	Put Yourself In My Place/Darling Baby (reissue)	18
71	Tamla Motown TMG 771	Heaven Must Have Sent You/Stay In My Lonely Arms (reissue)	8
71	Tamla Motown TMG 787	Put Yourself In My Place/It's Gonna Be Hard Times	8
68	T. Motown (S)TML 11081	DARLING BABY (LP)	90

ELIAS & HIS ZIG-ZAG JIVE FLUTES
| 58 | Columbia DB 4109 | Tom Hark/Ry-Ry. | 12 |
| 58 | Columbia DB 4146 | Zeph Boogie/Vucka' Magcwabeni (Back From The Dead) (78 rpm = £6) | 12 |

ELIAS HULK
| 70 | Youngblood SSYB 8 | UNCHAINED (LP). | 200 |

ELIGIBLES
59	Capitol CL 15067	Faker, Faker/24 Hours (Till My Date With You)	12
59	Capitol CL 15098	The Little Engine/My First Christmas With You	12
60	Capitol CL 15203	Young Is My Lover/East Of West Berlin	8
60	Capitol (S)T 1310	ALONG THE TRAIL (LP)	20
61	Capitol (S)T 1411	LOVE IS A GAMBLE (LP)	20

ELIJAH
| 71 | Ackee ACK 121 | Selassie High/Mount Zion | 6 |

ELIMINATORS
| 66 | Pye NPL 18160 | GUITARS AND PERCUSSION (LP). | 30 |

ELIXIR
85	Elixir ELIXIR 1	Treachery (Ride Like The Wind)/Winds Of Time (folded p/s with insert)	80
86	Elixir ELIXIR 2	THE SON OF ODIN (LP, private pressing with insert)	60
90	Sonic SONICLP 9	LETHAL POTION (LP, features Clive Burr)	15

(see also Iron Maiden)

ELIZABETH
73	Paramount PARA 3032	Stop Killing Me With Kindness/Oh Bird	6
68	Vanguard SVRL 19010	ELIZABETH (LP)	35

ELKI & OWEN & RIM RAM BAND
69	Revolution REV 004	Groovie Kinda Love	8

(see also Elkie Brooks, Owen Gray)

JIMMY ELLEDGE
62	RCA RCA 1274	Swanee River Rocket/Funny How Time Slips Away	15
65	Hickory 45-1363	Pink Dally Rue/Legend In My Time	10
64	RCA RCX 7132	FUNNY HOW TIME SLIPS AWAY (EP)	45

ELLI
67	Parlophone R 5575	Never Mind/I'll Be Looking Out For You	20

YVONNE ELLIMAN
71	MCA MK 5063	I Don't Know How To Love Him/Jesus Christ Superstar Overture	7
73	Purple PUR 114	I Can't Explain/Hawaii	20
73	Purple TPS 3504	FOOD OF LOVE (LP)	30

DUKE ELLINGTON & HIS (FAMOUS) ORCHESTRA

78s
51	Columbia DC 573	Fancy Dan/The Hawk Talks (export issue)	7
52	Vogue V 2080	Caravan/Indian Summer	8
52	Vogue V 2087	She/The Happening	8
59	Philips PB 946	Anatomy Of A Murder/Flirtibird	8

SINGLES
53	HMV 7M 156	Otto Make That Riff Staccato/Time's A-Wastin'	10
54	HMV 7MC 1	Flamingo/Jump For Joy (export issue)	10
54	HMV 7MC 9	In A Sentimental Mood/I Let A Song Go Out Of My Heart (export issue)	10
54	HMV 7M 170	The Flaming Sword/BARNEY BIGARD ORCHESTRA: A Lull At Dawn	10
54	Capitol CL 14186	Smile/If I Give My Heart To You	10
55	Capitol CL 14229	Twelfth Street Rag (Mambo)/Chile Bowl	9
55	Capitol CL 14260	Tyrolean Tango/All Day Long	9
55	Columbia SCM 5182	Brown Betty/Ting-A-Ling	9
59	Philips PB 946	Anatomy Of A Murder/Flirtibird	8
59	Philips PB 243	Skin Deep (Parts 1 & 2) (with Louis Bellson)	9
60	Philips JAZ 101	Malletoba Skank/All Of Me (p/s)	5
60	Philips JAZ 117	Duke's Place/Jones (p/s)	5

EPs
54	Columbia SEG 7538	DUKE ELLINGTON	8
54	Columbia SEG 7579	DUKE ELLINGTON	8
54	Columbia SEG 7563	DUKE ELLINGTON	8
54	Capitol EAP1 477	THE DUKE PLAYS ELLINGTON	8
54	Capitol EAP2 477	THE DUKE PLAYS ELLINGTON PT. 2	8
54	HMV 7EG 8033	DUKE ELLINGTON AND HIS ORCHESTRA	8
55	HMV 7EG 8158	DUKE ELLINGTON AND AL HIBBLER	8
55	Capitol EAP1 521	ELLINGTON '55	8
55	Capitol EAP2 521	ELLINGTON '55	8
55	Capitol EAP3 521	ELLINGTON '55	8
55	Vogue EPV 1051	DUKE ELLINGTON — BILLY STRAYHORN	8
55	Vogue EPV 1060	DUKE ELLINGTON AND THE CORONETS	8

LPs
53	HMV DLP 1007	ELLINGTON'S GREATEST (10")	15
53	Columbia 33SX 1022	MASTERPIECES	14
53	Vogue LDE 035	DUKE ELLINGTON AND THE CORONETS (10")	15
53	Capitol LC 6616	PREMIERED BY ELLINGTON (10")	15
54	Capitol LC 6670	THE DUKE PLAYS ELLINGTON (10")	15
54	HMV DLP 1025	GREAT ELLINGTON SOLOISTS (10")	15
54	HMV DLP 1034	ELLINGTON HIGHLIGHTS, 1940 (10")	15
54	Columbia 33S 1044	JAZZ COCKTAIL (10")	15
54	Capitol LCT 6008	ELLINGTON '55	15
54	Philips BBL 7003	ELLINGTON UPTOWN	15
55	HMV DLP 1070	PERFUME SUITE/BLACK BROWN AND BEIGE (10")	15
55	HMV DLP 1094	SATURDAY NIGHT FUNCTION (10")	15
55	Vogue Coral LRA 10027	DUKE ELLINGTON AND HIS ORCHESTRA VOL. 1 (10")	15
55	Vogue Coral LRA 10028	DUKE ELLINGTON AND HIS ORCHESTRA VOL. 2 (10")	15
55	Philips BBR 8044	MOOD ELLINGTON (10")	15
56	London AL 3551	THE DUKE — 1926 (10")	15
56	London Jazz LTZ-N 15029	HISTORICALLY SPEAKING — THE DUKE	15
56	Capitol T 679	ELLINGTON SHOWCASE	12
57	Philips BBL 7133	AT NEWPORT	12
57	Philips BBL 7152	AT NEWPORT WITH BUCK CLAYTON	12
57	London LTZ N 15078	PRESENTS	12
58	HMV DLP 1172	A BLUES SERENADE (10")	12
59	RCA RD 27134	IN A MELLOW TONE	12
59	HMV CLP 1316	BACK TO BACK (with Johnny Hodges)	12
60	Philips SBBL 514	ANATOMY OF A MURDER (soundtrack)	15

MARC ELLINGTON
68	Philips BF 1665	I Shall Be Released/Mrs. Whittle	7
69	Philips BF 1742	Did You Give The World Some Love Today Baby/Bless The Executioner	6
69	Philips BF 1779	Four In The Morning/Peggy Day	6
71	Charisma CB 161	Alligator Man/Song For A Friend	6
69	Philips (S)BL 7883	MARC ELLINGTON (LP)	20
71	Charisma CAS 1033	RAINS, REINS OF CHANGES (LP, with lyric insert)	22
72	Philips 6308 120	A QUESTION OF ROADS (LP)	18

Marc ELLINGTON

72	Xtra XTRA 1154	MARC TIME (LP, with Fairport Convention)	25
73	Philips 6308 143	RESTORATION (LP)	15

(see also Fairport Convention, Matthews Southern Comfort)

RAY ELLINGTON QUARTET

53	Columbia SCM 5050	The Little Red Monkey/Kaw-Liga	18
54	Columbia SCM 5088	All's Going Well (My Lady Montmorency) (with Marion Ryan)/Ol' Man River	20
54	Columbia SCM 5104	Rub-A-Dub-Dub/The Owl Song	16
54	Columbia SCM 5147	A.B.C. Boogie/Christmas Cards	30
55	Columbia SCM 5177	Ko Ko Mo (I Love You So)/Woodpecker	30
55	Columbia SCM 5187	Play It Boy, Play/The Irish Were Egyptians Long Ago	18
55	Columbia SCM 5199	Cloudburst/Pet	12
56	Columbia SCM 5250	Hold Him Tight/Who's Got The Money?	12
56	Columbia SCM 5274	Keep The Coffee Hot/Lucky 13	12
56	Columbia DB 3821	Stranded In The Jungle/Left Hand Boogie (78 rpm = £8)	30
56	Columbia DB 3838	Giddy-Up-A Ding Dong/The Green Door (78 rpm = £8)	30
57	Columbia DB 3905	Marianne/That Rock 'N' Rollin' Man (78 rpm = £8)	30
57	Columbia DB 4013	Don't Burn Me Up/Swaller-Tail Coat (78 rpm = £9)	10
58	Columbia DB 4057	Living Doll/Long Black Nylons (78 rpm = £12)	20
58	Pye Nixa 7N 15159	The Sultan Of Bezaaz/You Gotta Love Somebody (78 rpm = £12)	8
59	Pye Nixa 7N 15189	Chip Off The Old Block/Charlie Brown (78 rpm = £15)	15
59	Oriole CB 1512	Carina/I Was A Little Too Lonely (78 rpm = £12)	15
60	Ember EMB S 102	The Madison/Jump Over (with Tony Crombie Orchestra) (p/s with insert)	15
60	Ember EMB S 114	Très Jolie/Dracula's Three Daughters	8
63	Ember EMB S 172	Too Old To Cut The Mustard/She Lied	8
64	Ember EMB S 188	Rhythm Of The World/If You Can't Say Something Nice	8

(see also Tony Crombie, Marion Ryan)

ELLINGTONS

79	Grapevine GRP 114	(I'm Not) Destined To Become A Loser/MILLIONAIRES: You've Got To Love Your Baby	10

DEREK & DOROTHY ELLIOT

72	Trailer LER 2023	DEREK & DOROTHY ELLIOT (LP)	15
76	Tradition TSR 025	YORKSHIRE RELISH (LP)	12

MAMA CASS (ELLIOT)

68	RCA Victor RCA 1726	Dream A Little Dream Of Me/Midnight Voyage (as Mama Cass)	8
68	Stateside SS 8002	California Earthquake/Talkin' To Your Toothbrush	7
69	Stateside SS 8014	I Can Dream Can't I?/Move A Little Closer Baby	7
69	Stateside SS 8021	It's Getting Better/Who's To Blame? (as Mama Cass)	7
69	Stateside SS 8031	Make Your Own Kind Of Music/Lady Love	7
70	Stateside SS 8039	New World Coming/Blow Me A Kiss	7
70	Stateside SS 8057	A Song That Never Comes/I Can Dream, Can't I?	7
71	Probe PRO 512	Good Times Are Comin'/Welcome To The World	6
71	Probe PRO 519	Easy Come, Easy Go/Ain't Nobody Else Like You	6
68	Stateside S(S)L 5004	DREAM A LITTLE DREAM (LP)	22
69	Stateside S(S)L 5014	BUBBLEGUM, LEMONADE AND SOMETHING FOR MAMA (LP)	18

(see also Mamas & Papas, Big Three, Dave Mason & Cass Elliot, Mugwumps)

BERN ELLIOTT (& FENMEN)

63	Decca F 11770	Money/Nobody But Me	10
64	Decca F 11852	New Orleans/Everybody Needs A Little Love	10
64	Decca F 11970	Good Times/What Do You Want With My Baby (as Bern Elliott & Klan)	10
65	Decca F 12051	Guess Who/Make It Easy On Yourself (solo)	12
65	Decca F 12171	Lipstick Traces/Voodoo Woman (solo)	10
64	Decca DFE 8561	BERN ELLIOTT AND THE FENMEN (EP)	32

(see also Fenmen)

BILL ELLIOTT & ELASTIC OZ BAND

71	Apple APPLE 36	God Save Us/Do The Oz (initially with p/s)	45/20

(see also Splinter, John Lennon/Yoko Ono)

JACK ELLIOTT

69	Leader LEA 4001	JACK ELLIOTT OF BIRTLEY (LP, with booklet)	20

(see also Elliotts Of Birtley)

MARI ELLIOTT

76	GTO GT 58	Silly Billy/Half Past One	15

(see also Poly Styrene, X Ray Spex)

MIKE ELLIOTT

72	Ackee ACK 151	Milk And Honey/Burst A Shirt	7

PETER ELLIOTT

57	Parlophone R 4355	To The Aisle/All At Once (You Love Her)	10
58	Parlophone R 4457	Devotion/No Fool Like An Old Fool	7
59	Parlophone R 4529	The Young Have No Time/Over And Over (78 rpm = £6)	5
61	Top Rank JAR 390	Waiting For Robert E. Lee/Toot Toot Tootsie	6
60s	Honey Hit TB 123	The Devil's Workshop/Three Little Peggies (p/s)	7

(RAMBLIN') JACK ELLIOTT

54	Topic TRC 98	Talking Miner Blues/Pretty Boy Floyd (78)	25
65	Fontana TF 575	More Pretty Girls/Roll On Buddy (as Ramblin' Jack Elliott)	6
65	Columbia DB 7593	Rusty Jigs And Sandy Sam/Rocky Mountain Belle (as Ramblin' Jack Elliott)	6
60	Columbia SEG 8046	KID STUFF (EP)	30
63	Collector JEA 5	RAMBLING JACK ELLIOTT (EP)	25
64	Collector JEA 6	BLUES AND COUNTRY (EP)	25
55	Topic T 5	WOODY GUTHRIE'S BLUES (8" mini-LP)	45
57	Topic 10T 15	JACK TAKES THE FLOOR (10" LP)	45
59	Columbia 33SX 1166	RAMBLIN' JACK ELLIOT IN LONDON (LP)	45

59	Encore ENC 194	IN LONDON (LP)	25
60	Columbia 33SX 1291	RAMBLIN' JACK ELLIOTT SINGS WOODY GUTHRIE & JIMMIE RODGERS (LP)..	45
65	Fontana TFL 6044	JACK ELLIOTT (LP)	25
65	Stateside SL 10143	JACK ELLIOTT COUNTRY STYLE (LP)	25
66	Stateside SL 10167	SINGS THE SONGS OF WOODY GUTHRIE (LP)	22
70	Reprise RSLP 6387	BILL DURHAM SACKS AND RAILROAD SACKS (LP)	15

SHAWN ELLIOTT

62	Stateside SS 124	Goodbye My Lover/Ain't That A Shame	9
63	Stateside SS 174	Sincerely And Tenderly/Why Don't You Love Me Anymore	8
64	Rio R 51	Shame And Scandal In The Family/My Girl	9
64	Columbia DB 7418	My Girl/Shame And Scandal In The Family (reissue)	8

ELLIOTTS OF BIRTLEY

| 69 | Xtra XTRA 1091 | A MUSICAL PORTRAIT OF A DURHAM MINING FAMILY (LP) | 15 |

(see also Jack Elliott)

ELLIOTT'S SUNSHINE

| 68 | Philips BF 1649 | Is It Too Late/'Cause I'm Lonely | 7 |

ELLIS

(see under Steve Ellis)

ALTON ELLIS (& FLAMES)

65	Island WI 239	Dance Crasher (with Flames)/BABA BROOKS: Vitamin A	38
65	Island WI 241	You Are Not To Blame/BABA BROOKS: Teenage Ska	32
66	Doctor Bird DB 1044	Blessings Of Love/Nothing Sweeter (as Alton & Flames)	60
66	Doctor Bird DB 1049	The Preacher (as Alton & Flames)/LYNN TAITT & COMETS: Tender Loving Care.	28
66	Doctor Bird DB 1055	Shake It (with Flames)/SILVERTONES: Whoo Baby	30
66	Doctor Bird DB 1059	Girl I've Got A Date (with Flames)/LYN TAITT & TOMMY McCOOK: The Yellow Basket.	28
67	Island WI 3046	Cry Tough (with Flames)/TOMMY McCOOK & SUPERSONICS: Mr Solo.	38
67	Treasure Isle TI 7004	Rocksteady (with Flames)/TOMMY McCOOK & SUPERSONICS: Wall Street Shuffle	30
67	Treasure Isle TI 7010	Duke Of Earl/All My Tears (with Flames)	32
67	Treasure Isle TI 7016	Ain't That Loving You/TOMMY McCOOK/SUPERSONICS: Tommy's Rocksteady	22
67	Treasure Isle TI 7030	Oowee Baby/How Can I (with Flames)	21
67	Treasure Isle TI 7044	Willow Tree/I Can't Stop Now.	22
67	Trojan TR 004	Ain't That Loving You (with Flames)/TOMMY McCOOK & SUPERSONICS: Comet Rocksteady	25
67	Trojan TR 009	Wise Birds Follow Spring/TOMMY McCOOK & SUPERSONICS: Soul Rock..	25
67	Studio One SO 2028	I Am Just A Guy/SOUL VENDORS: Just A Little Bit Of Soul	28
67	Studio One SO 2033	Only Sixteen/Baby (both actually by Heptones)	30
68	Studio One SO 2037	Live And Learn/HEPTONES: Cry Baby Cry	30
68	Trojan TR 630	I Can't Stand It/Trying To Reach My Goal.	18
68	Trojan TR 642	Breaking Up/Party Time	16
68	Nu Beat NB 010	I Can't Stand It/Tonight.	25
68	Nu Beat NB 013	Bye Bye Love/MONTY MORRIS: My Lonely Days	12
68	Nu Beat NB 014	La La Means I Love You/Give Me Your Love	15
68	Pama PM 707	The Message/Some Talk	10
68	Pama PM 717	My Time Is The Right Time/JOHNNY MOORE: Tribute To Sir Alex	10
68	Coxsone CS 7071	A Fool/SOUL VENDORS: West Of The Sun	38
69	Studio One SO 2084	Change Of Plans/CABLES: He'll Break Your Heart (B-side act. by Mad Lads)	22
69	Gas GAS 105	Diana/Some Talk	9
69	Bamboo BAM 2	Better Example/DUKE MORGAN: Lick It Back.	60+
69	Duke DU 14	Diana/Personality	25
70	Duke DU 72	Remember That Sunday/TOMMY McCOOK & SUPERSONICS: Last Lick.	12
70	Gas GAS 151	Suzie/Life Is Down In Denver (some copies credit Alton Ellis & Flames).	10
70	Gas GAS 161	Deliver Us/NEVILLE HINDS: Originator.	10
70	Duke Reid DR 2501	What Does It Take To Win Your Love/TOMMY McCOOK: Reggae Meringue	12
70	Duke Reid DR 2512	You Made Me So Very Happy/TOMMY McCOOK & SUPERSONICS: Continental..	12
70	Bamboo BAM 29	Tumbling Tears/SOUND DIMENSION: Today Version	12
70	Techniques TE 903	It's Your Thing/TECHNIQUES ALL STARS: Get Left	8
70	Techniques TE 905	I'll Be Waiting/TECHNIQUES ALL STARS: I'll Be Waiting Version	8
71	Banana BA 318	Sunday Coming/CARL BRYAN: Sunday Version.	12
71	Banana BA 330	Bam Bye/Keep On Yearning.	12
71	Banana BA 347	Hey World/Harder And Harder	12
71	Gas GAS 164	Back To Africa/NEVILLE HINDS: Originator.	10
71	Fab FAB 165	Good Good Loving/Since I Fell For You.	25
71	Bullet BU 466	Black Man's Pride/LEROY PALMER: Groove With It.	15
71	Bullet BU 485	Don't Care/True Born African.	12
71	Smash SMA 2319	A Little Loving/DELROY WILSON & ALTON ELLIS: Loving Version	7
71	Smash SMA 2320	I'll Be There/ITALS: Rude Boy Train	7
71	Big Shot BI 589	Be True/Be True — Version	5
72	Big Shot BI 602	I'm Trying/Luna's Mood	15
72	Spur SP 3	All That We Need Is Love/KEITH HUDSON: Better Love	30
72	Grape GR 3029	Big Bad Boy/HUDSON'S ALLSTARS: Big Bad Version.	7
72	Ackee ACK 145	Oppression/Oppression Version (both with Zoot Simms)	22
72	Ackee ACK 148	Let's Stay Together/Version	15
72	Ackee ACK 502	Too Late To Turn Back Now/IMPACT ALLSTARS: Version	10
72	Jackpot JP 796	Play It Cool/AGGROVATORS: King Of The Zozas	10
72	Camel CA 94	Wonderful World/FAB DIMENSION: Wonderful Version	6
72	Pama PM 840	Girl I've Got A Date/Eat Bread	5
72	Pama Supreme PS 347	Moon River/I Can't Find Out.	5
72	Pama Supreme PS 361	Working On A Groovy Thing/HARLESDEN SKANKERS: Version	6
73	Ackee ACK 511	Alton's Official Daughter/Aquarius Dub (both with Herman)	15
73	Spur SP 3	All We Need Is Love/KEITH HUDSON: Better Love.	35
73	Harry J. HJ 6653	Deliver Us To Africa/Nyah Medley.	5

Alton ELLIS (& FLAMES)

83	Fashion FAD 013	Too Late To Turn Back Now/Party Mix (12")..........................	12
73	Pyramid PYR 7003	Truly/LLOYD COXSONE SIX: Cruising	5
67	Coxsone CSL 8008	SINGS ROCK AND SOUL (LP)	100
71	Bamboo BDLPS 214	SUNDAY COMING (LP)	70
73	Count Shelly SSLO 02	ALTON ELLIS'S GREATEST HITS (LP)	38

(see also Alton & Eddy, Hortense Ellis, Hortense & Alton, Flames [Jamaica], Righteous Flames, Tony Gordon)

ALTON ELLIS & THE HEPTONES
80	Cha Cha CHAD 21	Mr. Ska Beana/ALTON ELLIS: Ain't No Music (12")..................	25

BOBBY ELLIS
68	Island WI 3136	Dollar A Head (with Crystalites)/RUDY MILLS: I'm Trapped..........	25
74	Dragon DRA 1033	Up Park Camp/Verse 4	6

(see also Jerry Lewis, Derrick Harriot, Rudy Mills, Crystalites, Keith & Tex, Eric Morris, Roy Richards, Soul Vendors)

DON ELLIS (ORCHESTRA)
69	CBS 4518	Eli's Comin'/House In The Country	5
67	Fontana (S)TL 5426	'LIVE' AT MONTEREY (LP)	12
68	Liberty LBL/LBS 83060	THE DON ELLIS ORCHESTRA LIVE (LP)	12
68	CBS 63230	ELECTRIC BATH (LP)	25
68	CBS 63356	SHOCK TREATMENT (LP)	12
69	CBS 63503	AUTUMN (LP)..	12
69	CBS 63680	THE NEW DON ELLIS BAND GOES UNDERGROUND (LP)	12
71	CBS 66261	DON ELLIS AT FILLMORE (2-LP)	15
72	CBS GQ 30927	TEARS OF JOY (LP, quadrophonic)	12

HERB ELLIS-JIMMY GIUFFRE ALL STARS
60	HMV POP 721	Goose Grease/My Old Flame	5

HORTENSE ELLIS
63	R&B JB 101	I'll Come Softly/I'm In Love (with Alton Ellis)...................	20
65	Blue Beat BB 295	I've Been A Fool/Hold Me Tenderly	25
67	Fab FAB 20	Somebody Help Me (with Buster's All Stars)/	
		PRINCE BUSTER & ALL STARS: Rock & Shake	60
70	Bullet BU 427	Last Date/PAT SATCHMO: Cherry Pink..........................	12
70	Gas GAS 160	To The Other Man/MUSIC BLENDERS: Raindrops	7
70	Techniques TE 908	To The Other Man/TECHNIQUES ALL STARS: To The Other Man Version	7
72	Green Door GD 4035	Bringing In The Sheaves (with Stranger Cole)/Version..............	6

(see also Hortense & Alton, Hortense & Delroy, Hortense & Jackie, Alton Ellis, Duke Reid, Three Tops, Jackie Opal)

JO-JO ELLIS
72	Fury FY 302	The Fly/Perdona Mia	30

LARRY ELLIS
58	Felsted AF 110	Buzz Goes The Bee/Nothing You Can Do (78 rpm = £10)............	18

MATTHEW ELLIS
71	Regal Zonophone RZ 3033	Avalon/You Are	6
71	Regal Zonophone RZ 3039	Birthday Song/Salvation.......................................	6
72	Regal Zonophone RZ 3045	Palace Of Plenty/Two By Two	6
71	Regal Zono. SRZA 8501	MATTHEW ELLIS (LP)...	18
72	Regal Zono. SRZA 8505	AM I...? (LP)...	30

(see also Procol Harum, Chris Spedding)

SHIRLEY ELLIS
63	London HLR 9824	The Nitty Gritty/Give Me A List	15
65	London HLR 9946	The Name Game/Whisper To Me Wind	10
65	London HLR 9961	The Clapping Song/This Is Beautiful	7
65	London HLR 9973	The Puzzle Song/I See It, I Like It, I Want It	8
66	London HLR 10021	Ever See A Diver Kiss His Wife While The Bubbles Bounce About Above	
		The Water?/Stardust	8
67	CBS 202606	Soul Time/Waitin' (DJ copy = £75).............................	30
67	CBS 2817	Sugar Let's Shing-A-Ling/How Lonely Is Lonely	15
71	CBS 7463	Soul Time/Waitin' (reissue)...................................	15
77	CBS 4901	Soul Time/Waitin' (2nd reissue, blue coloured vinyl)	10
67	CBS (S)BPG 63044	SOUL TIME WITH SHIRLEY ELLIS (LP)	60

(STEVE) ELLIS
70	CBS 4992	Loot/More More More	5
70	CBS 5199	Evie/Fat Crow	5
71	CBS 7037	Take Your Love/Jingle Jangle Jasmine..........................	5
71	CBS 7411	Hold On/Goody Goody Dancing Shoes	5
72	Epic EPC 64878	RIDING ON THE CREST OF A SLUMP (LP, as Ellis)	18
73	Epic EPC 65650	WHY NOT? (LP, as Ellis)......................................	15

(see also Love Affair, Widowmaker, Zoot Money, Peter Bardens)

ANDY ELLISON
68	Track 604 018	It's Been A Long Time/JOHN'S CHILDREN: Arthur Green	70
68	CBS 3357	Fool From Upper Eden/Another Lucky Lie.......................	50
68	S.N.B. 55-3308	You Can't Do That/Casbah	75
68	S.N.B. 55-3308	You Can't Do That/Cornflake Zoo (second issue, different B-side).....	85

(see also John's Children, Jet, Radio Stars)

LORRAINE ELLISON
66	Warner Bros WB 5850	Stay With Me/I Got My Baby Back (re-pressed in 1969)	10
68	Warner Bros WB 2094	Try (Just A Little Bit Harder)/In My Tomorrow	8
70	Warner Bros WB 7394	You've Really Got A Hold On Me/You Don't Know Anything About Love....	8
71	Mercury 6052 073	Call Me Anytime You Need Some Lovin'/Please Don't Teach Me To Love You ...	25
70	Warner Bros WS 1821	STAY WITH ME (LP)...	30

ELMER HOCKETT'S HURDY GURDY
68	Parlophone R 5716	Fantastic Fair/MOOD MOSAIC: The Yellow Spotted Capricorn	10

(see also Mood Mosaic, Mark Wirtz)

IAN ELMS
82	Squid Marks SMT 013	GOOD NIGHT (LP, with insert)	180

ELOY
83	Heavy Metal HMINT 1	Fools/Heartbeat (p/s)	5
83	Heavy Metal HMPD 1	Fools/Heartbeat (picture disc)	8
83	Heavy Metal HMPD 1	Fools/Heartbeat (clear vinyl)	8
82	Heavy Metal HMILP 1	PLANETS (LP, clear vinyl with inner sleeve)	15
82	Heavy Metal HMIPD 1	PLANETS (LP, picture disc)	18
82	Heavy Metal HMILP 3	TIME TO TURN (LP, clear vinyl with inner sleeve)	12
82	Heavy Metal HMIPD 3	TIME TO TURN (LP, picture disc)	18
83	Heavy Metal HMIPD 12	PERFORMANCE (LP, picture disc)	15
84	Heavy Metal HMIPD 21	METROMANIA (LP, picture disc)	18
84	Heavy Metal HMICD 21	METROMANIA (CD, existence unconfirmed)	20
85	IMS MILCH 014	CODENAME WILDGEESE (LP, soundtrack)	15
89	FM Revolver REV PD120	RA (LP, picture disc)	15

EL PAS(S)O
71	Big Shot BI 572	Out De Light, Baby/Mosquito I (both actually by Dennis Alcapone)	15
71	Punch PH 61	Mosquito One/Out De Light (reissue)	12
	(see also Dennis Alcapone)		

JEFF ELROY & BOYS BLUE
66	Philips BF 1533	Honey Machine/Three Woman	20
	(see also Boys Blue)		

ELTI-FITS
70s	Worthing Street WSEF 1	GOING STRAIGHT (EP, various foldover picture sleeves)	6

ELVES
70	MCA MU 1114	Amber Velvet/West Virginia	7

CAROL ELVIN
63	Columbia DB 7095	'Cos I Know/C'mon Over	11
65	Parlophone R 5228	Don't Leave Me/'Cos I Love You	11

LEE & JAY ELVIN
59	Fontana H 191	So The Story Goes/When You See Her (78 rpm = £15)	20
	(see also Jerry Lordan)		

EMANON
77	Clubland SJP 777	Raging Pain/Rip A Bough (stamped sleeve)	30

BOBBIE EMBER
65	Polydor BM 56062	Why Can't You Bring Me Home/When Love Isn't There	7

EMBERS
63	Decca F 11625	Chelsea Boots/Samantha	20
	(see also David & Embers, Three's A Crowd)		

EMBRACE
96	Fierce Panda NING 29	All You Good Good People/My Weakness Is None Of Your Business (p/s, 1,300 only, some numbered)	25/30
97	Hut CDHUT 46	THE GOOD WILL OUT (CD, digipak with blue cloth cover)	12
98	BBC BOX SET	EMBRACE EPS (6 x 12"s in black box, numbered, 100 only)	200

EMBRYO
80	Rampant RAM 001	I'm Different/You Know He Did (p/s)	8
	(see also Jump Squad)		

EMCEE 5
62	Columbia SEG 8153	LET'S TAKE FIVE (EP)	45

EMERALDS (U.K.)
65	Decca F 12096	Don't Listen To Your Friends/Say You're Mine	7
65	Decca F 12304	King Lonely The Blue/Someone Else's Fool	60

EMERALDS (U.S.)
64	London HL 9839	Donkey Kick Back/Sittin' Bull	10

EMERGENCY
83	Riot City RIOT 21	POINTS OF VIEW (EP)	5

KEITH EMERSON
76	Manticore K 13513	Honky Tonk Train Blues/Barrel House Shake Down (p/s)	6
80	Atlantic K 11612	Taxi Ride (Rome)/Mater Tenebrarum (p/s)	6
81	MCA MCA 697	I'm A Man/Nighthawks Main Title Theme (p/s)	7
	(see also Emerson Lake & Palmer, Nice, V.I.P.'s, Rock Aid Armenia)		

EMERSON, LAKE & PALMER
73	Lyntone/Manticore LYN 2762	Brain Salad Surgery/(excerpts from Brain Salad Surgery LP) (flexidisc in gatefold p/s free with *NME*)	15/7
74	Manticore K 13503	Jerusalem/When The Apple Blossoms Bloom In The Windmills Of Your Mind, I'll Be Your Valentine (some with p/s)	10/6
77	Atlantic K 10946	Fanfare For The Common Man/Brain Salad Surgery (p/s)	6
77	Atlantic K 10946T	Fanfare For The Common Man (Album Version)/Brain Salad Surgery (12", p/s)	15
70	Island ILPS 9123	EMERSON, LAKE AND PALMER (LP, pink label, later 'pink rim palm tree')	30/15
71	Island ILSP 9155	TARKUS (LP, gatefold sleeve)	15
71	Island HELP 1	PICTURES AT AN EXHIBITION (LP, gatefold sleeve)	15
73	Manticore K 53501	BRAIN SALAD SURGERY (LP, fold-out sleeve with poster)	18
	(see also Emerson Lake & Powell, Nice, Keith Emerson, Greg Lake, Shame, Asia, King Crimson, Stray Dog, Atomic Rooster)		

MINT VALUE £

EMERSON, LAKE & POWELL
86	Polydor POSP 804	Touch And Go/Learning To Fly (p/s)	5
86	Polydor POSPX 804	Touch And Go/Learning To Fly/The Locomotion (12", p/s)	10

(see also Emerson Lake & Palmer, Cozy Powell)

KATHLEEN EMERY
97	Jazzman JM001	Sometimes I Feel Like A Motherless Child/Evil Ways	25

DICK EMERY
62	Philips 326559 BF	A Cockney Christmas/(All I Want For Christmas Is) My Two Front Teeth	7
63	Philips BF 1272	I (Who Have Nothing)/Walk With Me, My Angel	5
69	Pye 7N 17644	If You Love Her/Day After Day	5
70	Pye 7N 17888	With Ageing/Wonderful World Of Love	5
72	Pye 7N 45202	You Are Awful/Dance Dance	5
73	Pye 7N 45288	You're Just As Lovely Today/Our Young Idea	5

EMILY
87	Sha La La 007	The Old Stone Bridge/REMEMBER FUN: Hey Hey Hate (flexidisc, p/s)	7
87	Big Fun BIG FUN 001	The Old Stone Bridge/What The Fool Said (flexidisc)	7

EMJAYS
59	Top Rank JAR 145	All My Love All My Life/Cross My Heart (78 rpm = £30)	65

EMMET SPICELAND
68	Page One POF 089	Lowlands Low/Bunclody	7
69	Page One POF 143	So Long Marianne/In Search Of Franklin	7
68	Page One POLS 011	THE FIRST (LP)	75
77	Hawk HALP 166	THE EMMET SPICELAND ALBUM (LP, reissue of above LP)	35

EMMETT
65	Columbia DB 7582	Baby Ain't No Lie/Hard Travelling	7
65	Columbia DB 7695	Nancy/Kilkenny Mountains	6

EMOTIONS
69	Downtown DT 446	Give Me Love/HORACE FAITH: Daddy's Home	10

EMOTIONS (Jamaica)
66	Ska Beat JB 263	Rude Boy Confession/Heartbreaking Gypsy	35
67	Caltone TONE 100	A Rainbow/TONY & DOREEN: Just You And I	40+
68	Caltone TONE 118	Soulful Music/No Use To Cry	20
68	Caltone TONE 129	Careless Hands/TOMMY McCOOK & SUPERSONICS: Caltone Special	35
69	High Note HS 018	The Storm/Easy Squeeze	10
69	High Note HS 026	Rum Bay/PATSY: Find Someone	8
70	Supreme SUP 209	Halleluiah/MATADOR ALLSTARS: Boat Of Joy	6

(see also Romeo & Emotions, Horace Faith)

EMOTIONS (U.K.)
65	Polydor BM 56025	Lonely Man/Line Shooter	6

EMOTIONS (U.S.)
62	London HLR 9640	Echo/Come Dance Baby	45
63	London HLR 9701	L-O-V-E/A Million Reasons	55
63	Stateside SS 237	A Story Untold/One Life One Love One You	35

EMOTIONS (U.S.)
69	Stax STAX 123	So I Can Love You/Got To Be The Man	7
69	Stax STAX 134	I Like It/Best Part Of A Love Affair	15
69	Deep Soul DS 9104	Somebody New/Brushfire	35
75	Stax STXS 2020	Baby I'm Through/I Wanna Come Back	6
70	Stax SXATS 1030	SO I CAN LOVE YOU (LP)	30

EMPEROR
77	Private Stock	EMPEROR (LP)	12

EMPEROR (Norway)
93	Candlelight 002	EMPEROR (LP)	15
95	Candlelight 008	IN THE NIGHTSIDE ECLIPSE (LP)	15
98	Candlelight 023	ANTHEMS TO THE WELKIN AT DUSK (LP, gatefold sleeve)	15
99	Candlelight 035	EQUILIBRIUM IX (LP, gatefold sleeve)	12
01	Candlelight 052	EMPERIAL VINYL PRESENTATION (Numbered box set with 5 picture disc LPs and booklet. 3000 only)	50

EMPERORS
66	Stateside SS 565	Karate/I've Got To Have Her	15

EMPEROR'S NEW CLOTHES
90s	Acid Jazz JAZID 128T	Dark Light (12", company sleeve)	20

EMPIRE
81	Dinosaur DE 004	Hot Seat/All These Things (p/s)	12
80	White Line DE 001	EXPENSIVE SOUND (LP)	12

(see also Generation X)

ENCHANTED FOREST
68	Stateside SS 2080	You're Never Gonna Get My Lovin'/Suzanne	18

ENCHANTERS
67	Warner Bros WB 2054	We Got Love/I've Lost All Communications	10

ENCONA COURSE
91	Edutainment EDUT001	Rhyme Grenade/Tasye Of The Future/Hit Men (EP)	18

THE END
65	Philips BF 1444	I Can't Get Any Joy/Hey Little Girl	20
68	Decca F 22750	Shades Of Orange/Loving, Sacred Loving	45+
69	Decca LK-R/SKL-R 5015	INTROSPECTION (LP)	115

| 96 | Tenth Planet TP 025 | IN THE BEGINNING ... THE END (LP, gatefold sleeve, numbered, 1,000 only) | 15 |
| 97 | Tenth Planet TP 033 | RETROSPECTION (LP, numbered, 1,000 only) | 15 |

(see also Tucky Buzzard, Bill Wyman, Innocents, Bobby Angelo, Tuxedo)

ENDEVERS
68	Decca F 12817	Remember When We Were Young/Taking Care Of Myself	30
68	Decca F 12859	She's My Girl/She's That Kind Of Girl	30
69	Decca F 12939	Sunny And Me/I Really Hope You Do	10

SERGIO ENDRIGO
| 68 | Pye International 7N 25502 | Marianne/Il Dolce Paese | 10 |

MELVIN ENDSLEY
| 57 | RCA RCA 1004 | I Like Your Kind Of Love/Is It True? (78 rpm = £15) | 45 |
| 58 | RCA RCA 1051 | I Got A Feelin'/There's Bound To Be (78 rpm = £20) | 45 |

ENEMY
81	Tin Tin NM 1	50,000 Dead/Society's Fool/Neutral Ground (p/s)	8
82	Fallout FALL 001	Fallen Hero/Tomorrow's Warning/Prisoner Of War (p/s, with inner)	7
82	Fallout FALL 004	Punks Alive/Piccadilly Sidetracks/Twist And Turn (p/s, orange vinyl)	7
83	Fallout FALL 014	Last Rites/Why Not (p/s)	5
84	Rot ASS 9	Last But Not Least/Images (live) (p/s)	6

ENERGETIC KRUSHER
| 89 | Vinyl Solution SOL 17 | PATH TO OBLIVION (LP, with insert, features Danny McCormack) | 20 |

(see also Chasers, Wildhearts)

ENERGY
83	Aros AROS 11233	Nowhere To Hide/Fight For Your Freedom (no p/s)	75
81	GRN 1	CONQUER THE WORLD: Conquer The World/Make It/Law Breaker (EP, no p/s)	100
80s	BIPS BECK 927	ENERGISED (EP)	80

ENERGY IQ
| 80 | Optimistic OPT 008 | THROUGH THE PLUGHOLE (EP) | 6 |

SCOTT ENGEL
58	Vogue V 9125	Blue Bell/Paper Doll (78 rpm = £100+)	450
59	Vogue V 9145	The Livin' End/Good For Nothin' (with Count Dracula & Boys)	550
59	Vogue V 9145	The Livin' End/Good For Nothin' (with Count Dracula & Boys) (78)	150+
59	Vogue V 9150	Charlie Bop/All I Do Is Dream Of You (78 rpm = £75)	400
66	Liberty LEP 2261	SCOTT ENGEL (EP)	50

(see also Scott Walker, Walker Brothers)

SCOTT ENGEL & JOHN STEWART
| 66 | Capitol CL 15440 | I Only Came To Dance With You/Greens | 40 |

(see also Scott Walker, Walker Brothers)

ENGINE
| 87 | Beak BEAK 1 | Getting Away From It All (p/s) | 5 |
| 88 | BH SIXFIFTY 1 | WELL OILED (LP) | 12 |

ENGLAND
| 76 | Deroy DER 1356 | ENGLAND (LP, private pressing) | 200 |

ENGLAND
| 77 | Arista ARIST 88 | Pariffinalea/Nanagram | 6 |
| 77 | Arista ARTY 153 | GARDEN SHED (LP, allegedly some with booklet) | 100+/40 |

ENGLAND'S GLORY
| 73 | Venus VEN 105 | ENGLAND'S GLORY (LP, private pressing, pink label, 25 copies only; beware of white label counterfeits) | 250 |
| 87 | Five Hours Back TOCK 4 | ENGLAND'S GLORY (LP, stickered sleeve) | 12 |

(see also Only Ones)

ENGLAND FOOTBALL SQUAD
70	Pye 7N 17920	Back Home/Cinnamon Stick (some with 'football centre; some in p/s)	7/15/25
70	Pye 7N 17920	Back Home/Cinnamon Stick (in promo 'BOAC' sleeve)	200
88	MCA GOAL 1	All The Way (p/s, as 1988 England Squad with Stock, Aitken & Waterman)	5
82	England ER 1	This Time (We'll Get It Right)/England, We'll Fly The Flag (p/s)	5
82	Ariola ER 1	This Time (We'll Get It Right)/England, We'll Fly The Flag (Instrumental) (p/s)	5
82	Original Sound ERP 1P	This Time (picture disc)	20
86	EMI DB 9128	We've Got The Whole World At Our Feet/When We Are Far From Home (p/s)	5
86	EMI 12DBP 9128	We've Got The Whole World At Our Feet/When We Are Far From Home (12" pic disc)	8
70	Pye NSPL 18337	THE WORLD BEATERS SING THE WORLD BEATERS (LP, round fold-out sleeve)	35
82	K-Tel NE 1169	THIS TIME (LP, gatefold, with booklet)	20
82	Event EV 002	ENGLAND IN THE WORLD CUP 1982 (LP, gatefold sleeve)	20

ENGLAND/NEW ORDER
| 90 | Factory FAC 293-7 | World In Motion/The B-Side (p/s) | 5 |

(see also New Order)

ENGLAND SISTERS
| 60 | HMV POP 710 | Heartbeat/Little Child | 55 |

ENGLISH
| 81 | Albion ION 1008 | Hooray For The English/When You Fly (p/s) | 10 |

BARBARA JEAN ENGLISH
| 74 | Contempo CS 2031 | Breaking Up A Happy Home/Guess Who | 8 |
| 75 | Contempo CS 2062 | I'm Living In A Lie/Key In The Mailbox | 20 |

ERROL(L) ENGLISH
70	Big Shot BI 547	I Don't Want To Love You/Love Is Pure	7
70	Big Shot BI 548	Once In My Life/Rabbit In A Cottage	7
70	Torpedo TOR 8	Open The Door To Your Heart/That Will Do	7
70	Torpedo TOR 9	Where You Lead Me/Hitchin' A Ride	7
70	Torpedo TOR 16	Sad Girl/Welcome Me Back Home	7
70	Torpedo TOR 22	Sha La La La Lee/BOVVER BOYS: A.G.G.R.O.	15
71	Duke DU 99	Sometimes (with Champions)/Sugar Cane	7

(see also Junior English, Errol & Champions)

JUNIOR ENGLISH
69	Camel CA 35	Nobody Knows (with Tony Sexton)/Somewhere	7
71	Pama PM 828	Jesamine/SYDNEY ALL STARS: The Flash	7
72	Pama PM 841	Miss Playgirl/Once In My Life	6
72	Pama PM 866	I Don't Want To Die/Land Of Sea And Sand	6
72	Pama PM 869	Daniel/Perfidia	6
72	Banana BA 368	Anniversary/Girls Like You	7
73	Pama Supreme PS 381	Garden Party/Version	7

(see also Errol English)

ENGLISH COUNTRY BLUES BAND
83	Rogue FMSL 2004	HOME AND DERANGED (LP)	15

ENGLISH ROSE
70	Polydor 2058 040	Yesterday's Hero/To Jackie	6

(see also Neat Change, Love Affair)

ENGLISH SUBTITLES
79	Small Wonder SMALL 22	Time Tunnel/Sweat/Reconstruction (p/s)	5
82	Glass 007/10 SEC 21	Tannoy/Cars On Fire (folded p/s in bag with insert)	6
82	Glass GLASS LP 013	ORIGINAL DIALOGUE (LP, with inner sleeve)	12

ENID
SINGLES
76	Buk BUK 3002	The Lovers/In The Region Of The Summer Stars	12
77	EMI International INT 534	Jubilee/Omega (p/s)	5
77	EMI International INT 540	Golden Earrings/Omega (p/s)	12
79	Pye 7P 106	Dambusters March — Land Of Hope And Glory/The Skye Boat Song (p/s, blue vinyl)	10
80	Pye 7P 187	Fool/Tito (p/s)	10
80	EMI EMI 5109	Golden Earrings/665 The Great Bean (p/s)	10
81	Bronze BRO 127	When You Wish Upon A Star/Jessica (p/s)	10
81	Bronze BRO 134	Heigh Ho/Twinkle Twinkle Little Star (p/s)	8
82	Rak RAK 349	And Then There Were None/Letter From America (p/s)	6
84	EMI 12EMI 5505	And Then There Were None/Letter From America/Raindown (12", p/s)	10
86	Sedition EDITL 3314	Itchycoo Park/Sheets Of Blue (12", p/s)	10
90	Enid ENID 6999	Salome/Salomee (12", p/s)	8

LPs
76	Buk BULP 2014	IN THE REGION OF THE SUMMER STARS (1st issue, white label, with insert, without mention of Enid on front cover; distributed by Decca)	20
77	Buk BULP 2014	IN THE REGION OF THE SUMMER STARS (2nd issue, black label, with Enid on front cover)	15
77	Honeybee INS 3012	AERIE FAIRIE NONSENSE	12
79	Pye NSPH 18593	TOUCH ME (with insert)	12
79	Pye NH 116	SIX PIECES (with insert, 2,000 only)	12
84	The Enid ENID 1	LIVE AT HAMMERSMITH VOL. I (5,500 only)	12
84	The Enid ENID 2	LIVE AT HAMMERSMITH VOL. II (2,000 only)	12
84	The Enid ENID 3	SOMETHING WICKED THIS WAY COMES	12
84	The Enid ENID 4	SIX PIECES ('enhanced' version, 3,500 only)	12
84	The Enid ENID 5	TOUCH ME ('enhanced' version, 4,000 only)	15
84	The Enid ENID 6	AERIE FAERIE NONSENSE (remixed/re-recorded version)	12
84	The Enid ENID 7	IN THE REGION OF THE SUMMER STARS (remastered & re-recorded version)	12
84	The Enid ENID 8	THE SPELL (2-LP, 45rpm, gatefold sleeve)	12
84	The Stand LE 1	"THE LIVERPOOL ALBUM" (untitled mini-album, sold at gigs, 800 only)	30
84	The Stand THE STAND 1	THE STAND (fan club issue, 5,000 only, some autographed)	30+/20
85	The Stand THE STAND 2	THE STAND 1985-1986 (fan club issue, 2,000 only, some autographed)	20+/18
85	The Enid ENID 9	FAND (with re-recorded version of Fand track, 3,000 only)	12
87	Dojo DOJOLP 24	LOVERS AND FOOLS (2-LP)	12
94	The Enid AHOE 1	AN ALTERNATIVE HISTORY VOL 1 (LP, green vinyl, numbered, with insert, 1000 only)	15
94	The Enid AHOE 2	AN ALTERNATIVE HISTORY VOL 2 (LP, pink vinyl, numbered, with insert, 1000 only)	15

(Cassette copies of the above Enid-label albums with Lodge Recording Studios inlays are worth £15 each; copies with typewritten & colour-cover inlays are worth £10 each.)
(see also Robert John Godfrey, Godfrey & Stewart, William Arkle, Glen Baker, Kim Wilde)

ETHEL ENNIS
64	RCA SF 7654	ONCE AGAIN (LP)	15

RAY ENNIS & BLUE JEANS
68	Columbia DB 8431	What Have They Done To Hazel?/Now That You've Got Me (You Don't Seem To Want Me)	25

(see also Swinging Blue Jeans, Blue Jeans)

SEAMUS ENNIS
68	Ember FA 2054	THE BONNY BUNCH OF ROSES (LP, reissue)	12
70	Leader LEA 2003	SEAMUS ENNIS (LP)	12
74	Topic 12TS 250	THE WANDERING MINSTREL (LP)	12
76	Free Reed FROO 1/2	FORTY YEARS OF IRISH PIPING (2-LP with insert)	12

BRIAN ENO

74	Island WIP 6178	Seven Deadly Finns/Later On	8
75	Island WIP 6233	The Lion Sleeps Tonight (Wimoweh)/I'll Come Running	8
78	Polydor 2001 762	The King's Lead Hat/R.A.F. (B-side with Snatch)	5
89	Virgin CDT 41	Another Green World/Dover Beach/Deep Blue Day (3" CD, g/fold card sleeve)	8
74	Island ILPS 9268	HERE COME THE WARM JETS (LP)	15
74	Island ILPS 9309	TAKING TIGER MOUNTAIN (BY STRATEGY) (LP)	15
75	Island ILPS 9351	ANOTHER GREEN WORLD (LP)	15
75	Island HELP 22	EVENING STAR (LP, as Fripp & Eno)	15
75	Obscure OBS 3	DISCREET MUSIC (LP)	12
76	Editions EG EGM 1	MUSIC FOR FILMS (LP, private pressing)	100
77	Polydor 2302 071	BEFORE AND AFTER SCIENCE (LP, with 4 Peter Schmidt prints)	15
83	EG EGBS 002	WORKING BACKWARDS 1983-1973 (9-LP box set with Music For Films, Vol. 2 LP & Rarities" 12)	40

(see also Ayers Cale Nico & Eno, Roxy Music, Passengers, Robert Fripp, Lady June, David Toop, Gavin Bryars, Toto)

BRIAN ENO & DAVID BYRNE

81	EG EGO 1	The Jezebel Spirit/Regiment (p/s)	10

(see also David Byrne, Talking Heads)

ENORMOUS ROOM

86	Sharp CAL 5	100 Different Words/Sylvia's Children/Melanie And Martin/You Wrote A Book (12", p/s)	8
86	Medium Cool MC 001	I Don't Need You/Melanie And Martin (flexidisc, p/s)	6

ENOS & SHEILA

68	Blue Cat BS 138	Tonight You're Mine/UNTOUCHABLES: Your Love	30

(see also Enos McLeod)

ENOUGH'S ENOUGH

68	Tattoo TT 101	Please Remember/Look Around You Baby	300+

ENSLAVED

90s	Candlelight 001MLP	HORDANES LAND (EP)	60

ENTICERS

72	Atlantic 2091 136	Calling For Your Love/Storyteller	50

ENTOMBED

89	Earache MOSH 21P	LEFT HAND PATH (LP, picture disc)	15

JOHN ENTWISTLE('S OX)

71	Track 2094 008	I Believe In Everything/My Size	10
75	Decca FR 13567	Mad Dog/Cell No.7 (as John Entwistle's Ox)	8
81	WEA K 79249P	Too Late The Hero/I'm Coming Back (picture disc, some autographed)	10/6
71	Track 2406 005	SMASH YOUR HEAD AGAINST THE WALL (LP)	28
72	Track 2406 104	WHISTLE RYMES (LP)	28
75	Decca TXS 114	MAD DOG (LP, as John Entwistle's Ox)	22

(see also Who, Rigor Mortis)

ENYA

87	BBC RESL 201	I Want Tomorrow/The Celts Theme (p/s)	7
87	BBC CDRSL 201	I Want Tomorrow/The Celts Theme/To Go Beyond I/To Go Beyond II (CD)	25
88	WEA YZ 312 CD	Orinoco Flow/Smaotin.../Out Of The Blue (3" CD)	18
88	WEA YZ 356 CD	Evening Falls/Oiche Chiun (Silent Night)/Morning Glory (3" CD)	15
89	WEA YZ 368 CD	Storms In Africa (Part II)/Storms In Africa (Part I) (3" CD, card sleeve)	15
89	WEA YZ 368 CDX	Storms In Africa (Part II)/The Celts/Aldebaran/Storms In Africa (Part I) (5" CD, picture disc)	20
91	WEA YZ 580 CD	Exile/On Your Shore/Watermark/River (CD, slimline jewel case)	10
91	WEA YZ 604 CDX	Caribbean Blue/Orinoco Flow/As Baile/Oriel Window (CD, digipak)	8
91	WEA YZ 635 T	How Can I Keep From Singing/O'che Chi'n (Silent Night) (12", metallic p/s)	8
92	WEA YZ 640 CDX	Book Of Days/Watermark/On Your Shore/Exile (CD, box set with 4 prints)	12
92	WEA YZ 705 CDX	The Celts/O'che Chi'n (Silent Night)/Storms In Africa (Pt. II)/Eclipse (CD, with 4 prints)	8
95	WEA WEA023 CDX	ANYWHERE IS (CD EP, limited edition)	10
87	BBC REB 605	ENYA (LP)	15
87	BBC BBCCD 605	ENYA (CD)	35
93	WEA WX 274	WATERMARK (LP)	15
93	WEA 2292-43875-8	WATERMARK (mini-disc)	18
90s	WEA WX 431903175572	SHEPHERDS' MOONS (LP)	15

EPHEBE

96	Ferox FER 019	ONE (12" EP)	8
96	Ferox FER 022	TWO (12" EP)	8

EPICS (U.K.)

65	Pye 7N 15829	There's Just No Pleasing You/My Little Girl	7
66	Pye 7N 17053	Just How Wrong Can You Be/Blue Turns To Grey	8
68	CBS 3564	Travelling Circus/Henry Long	15

(see also Acid Gallery, Christie, T. Rex)

EPICS (Jamaica)

70	Bamboo BAM 37	Your Love/Driving Me Crazy	10

EPILEPTICS

80	Stortbeat/Mirror BEAT 8	1970'S EP (black & white p/s, stencilled white labels)	12
81	Spiderleg SDL 1	1970'S EP (re-recorded, printed labels, folded different printed b&w p/s)	8
81	Spiderleg SDL 2	LAST BUS TO DEBDEN (EP, hand-written labels & photocopied p/s)	10

(see also Licks, Flux Of Pink Indians)

EPISODE

68	MGM MGM 1409	Little One/Wide Smiles	30

(see also Episode Six)

EPISODE SIX

66	Pye 7N 17018	Put Yourself In My Place/That's All I Want	20
66	Pye 7N 17110	I Hear Trumpets Blow/True Love Is Funny That Way	20
66	Pye 7N 17147	Here, There And Everywhere/Mighty Morris Ten	22
67	Pye 7N 17244	Love, Hate, Revenge/Baby Baby Baby	40
67	Pye 7N 17330	Morning Dew/Sunshine Girl	18
67	Pye 7N 17376	I Can See Through You/When I Fall In Love	40
68	Chapter One CH 103	Lucky Sunday/Mr. Universe	20
69	Chapter One CH 104	Mozart Versus The Rest/Jak D'Or	18
87	PRT PYL 6026	PUT YOURSELF IN MY PLACE (LP)	12

(see also Episode, Sheila Carter & Episode Six, Neo Maya, Roger Glover, Jon Lord, Gillan, Deep Purple, Quatermass)

MINNIE EPPERSON

68	Action ACT 4503	Grab Your Clothes (And Get On Out)/No Love At All	40

PRESTON EPPS

59	Top Rank JAR 140	Bongo Rock/Bongo Party (78 rpm = £7)	20
59	Top Rank JAR 180	Bongos In Pastel/Doin' The Cha Cha Cha (78 rpm = £8)	7
60	Top Rank JAR 345	Bongo Boogie/Flamenco Boogie	15
60	Top Rank JAR 413	Bongo Bongo Bongo/Hully Gully Bongo	12
60	Top Rank JAR 522	Bongola/Blue Bongo	8
70	President PT 294	Bongo Rock/SANDY NELSON: Teen Beat	6
60	Top Rank JKP 2060	RUSHING FOR PERCUSSION (EP, with Sandy Nelson)	22

(see also Sandy Nelson)

EQUALS

67	President PT 117	I Won't Be There/Fire	8
67	President PT 135	Baby, Come Back/Hold Me Closer	6
67	President PT 158	Give Love A Try/Another Sad And Lonely Night	7
68	President PT 180	I Get So Excited/Skies Above	6
68	President PT 200	Laurel And Hardy/The Guy Who Made Her A Star	6
68	President PT 222	Softly Softly/Lonely Rita	6
69	President PT 240	Michael And The Slipper Tree/Honey Gum	6
69	President PT 260	Viva Bobby Joe/I Can't Let You Go	6
69	President PT 275	Rub A Dub Dub/After The Lights Go Down Low	6
70	President PT 303	I Can See But You Don't Know/Gigolo Sam	70
70	President PT 325	Black Skin Blue Eyed Boys/Happy Birthday Girl	6
70	President PT 345	Help Me Simone/Love Potion	6
73	President PT 414	Diversion/Here Today Gone Tomorrow	6
75	President PT 436	Georgetown Girl/We've Got It All Worked Out	6
76	Mercury 6007 104	Kaiwana Sunshine Girl/Soul Mother	15
76	Mercury 6007 106	Funky Like A Train/If You Didn't Miss Me	6
76	Mercury 6007 107	Funky Like A Train/If You Didn't Miss Me (12")	20
77	Mercury 6007 139	Irma La Douce/Ar'e Harry	6
77	President PT 464	Beautiful Clown/Daily Love	6
78	Ice GUY 5	Red Dog/Something Beautiful	6
88	Club JAB 58	Funky Like A Train/Born Ya!/Funky Like A Train (extended) (reissue)	7
88	Club JABX 58	Funky Like A Train/Born Ya!/Funky Like A Train (extended) (12", reissue)	12
68	President PTE 1	BABY COME BACK (EP)	20
68	President PTE 2	THE EQUALS (EP)	20
67	President PTL 1006	UNEQUALLED EQUALS (LP)	22
68	President PTL 1015	EQUALS EXPLOSION (LP)	20
68	President PTL(S) 1020	SENSATIONAL EQUALS (LP)	20
68	President PTL(S) 1025	SUPREME (LP)	18
69	President PTLS 1030	THE EQUALS STRIKE AGAIN (LP)	18
69	President PTLS 1050	BEST OF THE EQUALS (LP)	18
70	President PTLS 1038	AT THE TOP (LP)	18
76	Mercury 9109 601	BORN YA! (LP)	25
78	Ice ICEL 1002	MYSTIC SISTER (LP)	25

(see also Little Grants & Eddie, Pyramids, Hickory, Little Brother Grant, Zappata Schmitt, Seven Letters/Syramip, Thirty-Second Turn-Off)

EQUATIONS

69	Fontana TF 1035	Waiting On The Shores Of Nowhere/You Stood Beside Me	6

EQUINOX

73	Boulevard BLVD 4118	HARD ROCK (LP)	18

EQUIPE 84

67	Major Minor MM 517	Auschwitz/Twenty Ninth Of September	20

ERASURE

SINGLES

85	Mute L12MUTE 40	Who Needs Love (Like That) (Mexican Mix)/Push Me Shove Me (Tacos Mix) (12", p/s)	30
85	Mute L12MUTE 42	Heavenly Action (Yellow Brick Mix)/Don't Say No (Ruby Red Mix) (12", p/s, L12 cat. no. must be listed on sleeve & label)	60
85	Mute DMUTE 42	Heavenly Action/Don't Say No (Ruby Red Mix)//Who Needs Love (Like That) (Mexican Mix)/Push Me Shove Me (Tacos Mix) (12", shrinkwrapped double pack)	30
86	Mute 12MUTE 45	Oh L'Amour/March On Down The Line/Gimme! Gimme! Gimme! (12", 'Thomas The Tank Engine' p/s, withdrawn)	15
86	Mute L12MUTE 45	Oh L'Amour (Funky Sisters Mix)/March On Down The Line/Gimme! Gimme! Gimme! (Remix) (12", p/s)	12
86	Mute DMUTE 51	Sometimes/Sexuality//Who Needs Love (Like That)/Push Me Shove Me (double pack, with insert, shrinkwrapped with sticker)	8
86	Mute DMUTE 51	Sometimes/Sexuality//Oh L'Amour/March On Down The Line (double pack, with insert, shrinkwrapped with sticker)	8

Rare Record Price Guide 2008

87	Mute CDMUTE 56	It Doesn't Have To Be/Sometimes/Oh L'Amour/Heavenly Action/Who Needs Love (Like That)/Gimme! Gimme! Gimme!/In The Hall Of The Mountain King (CD, 7"-sized 'tray' p/s)	10
88	Mute LCDMUTE 93	Crackers International II: Stop! (Mark Saunders Remix)/Knocking On Your Door (Mark Saunders Remix)/God Rest Ye Merry Gentlemen (3" CD, Xmas pack with card & gift label, 6" x 3" sleeve)	20
90	Mute XL12MUTE 99	Supernature (Mark Saunders Remix)/You Surround Me (Gareth Jones Remix)/ Supernature (Daniel Miller & Phil Legg Remix) (12", envelope p/s)	10
90	Mute XL12MUTE 109	Blue Savannah (Der Deutsche Mix II)/Blue Savannah (Der Deutsche Mix I) (12", 1-sided, numbered envelope p/s)	10
94	Mute MUTE 166	I Love Saturday/Dodo/Because You're So Sweet (unreleased, p/s only)	50

LPs

99	Mute EBX 1	ERASURE 1 (5-CD box set)	30
99	Mute EBX 2	ERASURE 2 (5-CD box set)	30

PROMOS

86	Mute P12MUTE 45	Oh L'Amour/March On Down The Line/Gimme! Gimme! Gimme! (12", plain white sleeve, dark blue vinyl)	20
89	Mute (no cat. no.)	WILD (CD, promo-only box set, with LP, 12", cassette, stickers, postcard, photo & info sheet)	220
90	Mute ERAS 1	Push Me Shove Me (Moonbeam Mix)/(Catatonic Mix)/Senseless (Avalon Mix) (12", p/s)	20
90	Mute ERAS 2	ERAS 2: Who Needs Love Like That (Winnie Cooper Mix)/ Ship Of Fools (Orbital South Seas Isles Of Holy Beats Mix) (12", die-cut title sleeve)	18
90	Mute ERAS 3	Sometimes (Danny Rampling Mix) (12", die-cut title sleeve)	20
91	Mute P12MUTE 125	Chorus (Youth's Agreessive Dance Mix)/(Pure Dance Mix)/Snappy (Martyn Phillips Mix)/Snappy (Justin Robertson Mix) (12", green label, no p/s)	12
90s	Mute P12MUTE 195	Don't Say Your Love Is Killing Me (Tall Paul Mix)/(John Pleased Wimmin Flashback Vox) Oh L'Amour (Tin Tin Out Remix)/(Matt Darey Mix) (12", white label test pressing with press release & release sheet, 10 copies only)	70
91	Mute CDSTUMM 95	CHORUS (promo CD, with cassette and booklet)	100
92	Mute ERAS 4	ABBA-ESQUE EP: Voulez Vous (Brain Stem Death Mix)/Lay All Your Love On Me (No Panties Mix)/Take A Chance On Me (Take A Trance On Me)/ SOS (Perimeter Mix) (12")	25
92	Mute (no cat. no.)	POP! THE FIRST 20 HITS (CD, promo-only box set, with T-shirt, info sheets, 2-LP, video tape, & cassette)	220
94	Mute PL12 MUTE 166	Ghost (12", 1-sided)	15
97	Mute P12 MUTE 208	Rain (Blue Amazon Twisted Circles Mix)/In My Arms (Dekkard Dub)/ Sometimes (John 00 Flemings Full Vocal Club Mix)/Sometimes (John 00 Flemings Give It Some Welly Dub Mix) (12", p/s)	10
97	Mute PL12 MUTE 208	Rain (John Of The Pleased Wimmin Vocal Mix)/(John Of The Pleased Wimmin Dub)/Sometimes (John "00" Flemings Full Vocal Club Mix)/ In My Arms (BBE Mix) (12", p/s)	10
92	Mute ERAS 5	POP (CD, 19-track compilation, without Take A Chance On Me & Who Needs Love Like That [Hamburg Mix], numbered, promo only)	40
92	Mute ERAS INT 1	POP (CD, interview disc)	40
96	Mute ERAS SAY 1	I SAY I SAY I SAY I SAY (CD, interview disc)	40
96	Mute ERAS SAY 2	ERASURE (CD, interview disc)	40
96	Mute ERAS SAY 3	COWBOY (CD, interview disc)	40
	(see also Depeche Mode, Dinger)		

ERAZERHEAD

81	Test Pressing TP 4	Ape Man/Wipeout/Rock And Roll Zombie (p/s)	5
82	Flicknife FLS 208	Shell Shock/She Can Dance (p/s)	5
82	Flicknife FLS 210	Teenager In Love/All For Me (p/s)	5

EREHWON

81	Harvest HAR 5213	Tiny Goddess/The Hero (p/s)	5
	(see also Patrick Campbell-Lyons)		

ERIC (Sykes) & HATTIE (Jacques)

63	Decca LK 4507	ERIC, HATTIE AND THINGS (LP)	15
	(see also Eric Sykes & Hattie Jacques)		

ERIC HYSTERIC & ESOTERICS

80	Wasted Vinyl WASTE 1	Tropical Vision/Dance And Sing (p/s)	5

ROKY ERICKSON (& THE ALIENS)

77	Virgin VS 180	Bermuda/The Interpreter (p/s)	10
80	CBS 8888	Creature With The Atom Brain/The Wind And More (with The Aliens)	8
80	CBS 9055	Mine Mine Mind/Bloody Hammer (Acoustic Version) (p/s, with The Aliens)	8
87	B'full Of Brains BOB 13	Don't Shake Me Lucifer (live) (flexidisc free with *Bucketfull Of Brains* mag)	6/5
87	Five Hours Back TOCK 7P	CASTING THE RUNES (LP, picture disc)	25
	(see also 13th Floor Elevators)		

ERIK

93	PWL PWCD 252	Looks Like I'm In Love Again (mixes) (CD)	8
93	PWL PWLT 270	The Devil & The Deep Blue Sea (mixes) (12", p/s, withdrawn)	10
93	PWL PWCD 270	The Devil & The Deep Blue Sea (mixes) (CD, withdrawn)	15

ERROL (English) & CHAMPIONS

70	Jackpot JP 732	Lonely Boy/Da Boo	7
70	Jackpot JP 738	Lonely Boy/TONY & CHAMPIONS: All Of My Life	7
	(see also Errol English)		

ERROL (Dunkley) & HIS GROUP

65	Blue Beat BB 284	Gypsy/Miss May (actually by Errol Dunkley & Roy Shirley)	25
	(see also Errol Dunkley)		

ERROL (Dunkley) & U ROY
72	Punch PH 105	Darling Ooh Wee/GOD SONS: Merry Up Version	12

ERSATZ
81	Raw RAW 35	Motorbody Love/One Good Reason/Gimme A Chance (poster p/s)	6
80s	Leisure Sounds SRS 32	Smile In Shadow/House Of Cards (p/s)	6

BOOKER ERVIN
61	Parlophone 1170	THE BOOK (LP)	35

BLUEGRASS ERWIN
59	Top Rank JAR 252	I Won't Cry Alone/I Can't Love You	7

ESCALATORS
83	Big Beat NS 86	Something's Missing/The Edge (p/s)	8
83	Big Beat NS 87	The Munsters Theme/Monday (p/s)	6

ESCORTS (Jamaica)
70	Big Shot BI 535	I'm So Afraid/Mother Nature	7
74	Fab FAB 245	Sixpense/Loving Feeling	7
(see also Sensations)			

ESCORTS (U.K.)
64	Fontana TF 453	Dizzy Miss Lizzy/All I Want Is You	25
64	Fontana TF 474	The One To Cry/Tell Me Baby	25
64	Fontana TF 516	I Don't Want To Go On Without You/Don't Forget To Write	20
65	Fontana TF 570	C'Mon Home Baby/You'll Get No Lovin' That Way	20
66	Fontana TF 651	Let It Be Me/Mad Mad World	25
66	Columbia DB 8061	From Head To Toe/Night Time	40
(see also Big Three, Paddy Klaus & Gibson, Swinging Blue Jeans, Terry Sylvester)			

ESCORTS (U.S.)
63	Coral Q 72458	Submarine Race Watching/Somewhere	20

ESCORTS (U.S.)
75	Contempo CLP 521	ALL WE NEED IS ANOTHER CHANCE (LP)	15

ESCORTS & KAY JUSTICE
54	Columbia SCM 5132	If You Took Your Love From Me/Yes, Indeed	15

ESCOURTS
76	Alaska ALA 1014	Disrespect Can Wreck/Bam A Lam A Boogie	8

ESG
81	Factory FAC 34	You're No Good/UFO (p/s)	35

ESPERANTO ROCK ORCHESTRA
73	A&M AMLH 68175	ESPERANTO ROCK ORCHESTRA (LP)	12
(see also Keith Christmas, Comus)			

ESPRIT DE CORPS
73	Jam JAM 24	If (Would It Turn Out Wrong)/Picture On The Wall	20
73	Jam JAM 32	Lonely/Do You Remember Me	10
(see also David Ballantyne, Just Plain Smith, Just Plain Jones)			

ESPRIT DE CORPS
80s	Come 0001	Anxiety/The Tea Cup Song (hand-made silk-screened sleeve)	10

ESQUERITA
58	Capitol CL 14938	Rockin' The Joint/Esquerita And The Voola	100
72	Specialty SPE 6603	WILDCAT SHAKEOUT (LP)	40

ESQUIRES
67	Stateside SS 2048	Get On Up/Listen To Me	20
68	Stateside SS 2077	And Get Away/Everybody's Laughing	20
73	Action ACT 4618	My Sweet Baby/Henry Ralph	40
68	London HA-Q/SH-Q 8356	GET ON UP AND GET AWAY (LP)	25

ESQUIVEL
63	Reprise R 6046	MORE OF OTHER WORLDS, OTHER SOUNDS (LP)	15

ESSENTIAL LOGIC
78	Cells SELL ONE	Aerosol Burns/World Friction (p/s)	8
79	Rough Trade RT29	Popcorn Boy/Flora Force (p/s)	12
80	Rough Trade RT50	Eugene (p/s)	10
81	Rough Trade RT74	Fanfare In The Garden/The Captain (p/s)	7
(see also X-Ray Spex)			

ESSEX
63	Columbia DB 7077	Easier Said Than Done/Are You Going My Way	20
63	Columbia DB 7122	A Walkin' Miracle/What I Don't Know Won't Hurt Me (with Anita Humes)	15
63	Columbia DB 7178	She's Got Everything/Out Of Sight, Out Of Mind	15
63	Columbia 33SX 1593	EASIER SAID THAN DONE (LP)	60
64	Columbia 33SX 1613	A WALKIN' MIRACLE (LP)	60

DAVID ESSEX
65	Fontana TF 559	And The Tears Came Tumbling Down/You Can't Stop Me Loving You	48
65	Fontana TF 620	Can't Nobody Love You/Baby I Don't Mind	45
66	Fontana TF 680	This Little Girl Of Mine/Brokenhearted	40
66	Fontana TF 733	Thigh High/De Boom Lay Boom	40
68	Uni UN 502	Love Story/Higher Than High	22
68	Pye 7N 17621	Just For Tonight/Goodbye	22
69	Decca F 12935	That Takes Me Back/Lost Without Linda	40
69	Decca F 12967	The Day The Earth Stood Still/Is It So Strange?	40
73	CBS 1693	Rock On/On And On (p/s)	5
73	CBS 1902	Lamplight/We All Insane (p/s)	5

74	CBS 2176	America/Dance Little Girl (p/s)	5
74	CBS 2492	Gonna Make You A Star/Window (p/s)	5
74	CBS 2828	Stardust/Miss Sweetness (p/s)	5
75	CBS 3425	Rollin' Stone/Coconut Ice (p/s)	5
75	CBS 3572	Hold Me Close/Good Old Rock & Roll (p/s)	5
75	CBS 3676	If I Could/Funfair (p/s)	5
75	Sound For Industry SFI 200	Hello It's Me (fan club flexidisc)	15
76	CBS 4050	City Lights/St. Amie (p/s)	5
76	CBS 4486	Coming Home/Good Lovin' (p/s, some copies b/w "Won't Get Burned Again")	5
79	Vertigo 6059 233	M.O.D./M.O.D. (2) (as M.O.D., songwriting credited to D. Cook, p/s, some allegedly mispressed on 2-Tone label)	75+/7
80	United Artists UP 605	World/I Who Am I (p/s)	5
80	Mercury BIKE 1	Silver Dream Machine (Part 1)/(Part 2) (p/s)	5
80	Mercury HOT 1	Hot Love/Rock And Roll Me (p/s)	5
80	Mercury BIKE 2	The Race/Suzuki Warlord (p/s)	5
80	Mercury MER 47	On My Bike/Swim Against The Flow (p/s)	5
	(see also David & Rozaa, Us)		

ESSJAY
71	DJM DJS 254	Twins Of Evil/Fastback	20+

ASTON ESSON
80	Studio 16 STD 01	Woman Of My Dreams/Version (12")	30

NEVILLE ESSON
61	Blue Beat BB 37	Lover's Jive/Wicked And Dreadful (with Clue J. & His Blues Busters)	18

ESTABLISHMENT
81	Foetain	BAD CATHOLICS (LP)	30
	(see also Cromwell)		

'SLEEPY' JOHN ESTES
66	Delmark DJB 3	SLEEPY JOHN'S GOT THE BLUES (EP)	35
63	Esquire 32-195	THE LEGEND OF SLEEPY JOHN ESTES (LP)	55
63	'77' LA 12-27	TENNESSEE JUG BUSTERS — BROKE AND HUNGRY (LP)	40
65	Storyville SLP 172	PORTRAITS IN BLUES VOLUME 10 (LP)	32
72	Delmark DS 619	ELECTRIC SLEEP (LP)	20

JOHN ESTES/FURRY LEWIS/WILL SHADE
71	Revival RVS 1008	OLD ORIGINAL TENNESSEE BLUES (LP)	20

JACKIE ESTICK
61	Blue Beat BB 64	Boss Girl/COUNT OSSIE & GROUP: Cassavubu	28
63	Island WI 042	Since You've Been Gone/Daisy I Love You	12
66	Ska Beat JB 256	The Ska/Daisy I Love You	15

DEON ESTUS
89	Mika MIKCD 2	Heaven Help Me/It's A Party/Love Can't Wait/Me Or The Rumours (Instrumental) (CD, card p/s)	12
	(see also George Michael)		

ETCETERAS
64	Oriole CB 1950	Where Is My Love/Bengawan Solo	15
64	Oriole CB 1973	Little Lady/Now I Know	20

ETERNAL
90	Sarah SARAH 031	Sleep/Breathe/Take Me Down (p/s)	8

ETERNALS (Jamaica)
69	Coxsone CS 7091	Queen Of The Minstrels/Stars	32
70	Moodisc MU 3506	Christmas Joy/WINSTON & RUPERT: Musically Beat	7
71	Moodisc MU 3507	Push Me In The Corner/MUDIE'S ALL STARS: Mudie's Madness (B-side actually by Ansell Collins)	12
71	Moodisc MU 3508	Keep On Dancing/HAZEL WRIGHT: My Jealous Eyes	10
	(see also Don Cornel & Eternals)		

ETERNALS (U.S.)
59	London HL 8995	Rockin' In The Jungle/Rock 'N' Roll Cha-Cha (triangular or round centre)	150/100
59	London HL 8995	Rockin' In The Jungle/Rock 'N' Roll Cha-Cha (78)	45

ETERNAL TRIANGLE
69	Decca F 12954	Turn To Me/Windows	6
69	Decca F 12979	I Guess The Lord Must Be In New York City/Perfumed Candle	6

ETERNITY'S CHILDREN
68	Capitol CL 15558	Mrs Bluebird/Little Boy	25

ETHEL THE FROG
80	Best SRTSFMR 014	Eleanor Rigby/Fight Back	60
80	EMI EMI 5041	Eleanor Rigby/Fight Back (reissue)	10
80	EMI EMC 3329	ETHEL THE FROG (LP, with Terry Hopkinson & Doug Sheppard)	15

ETHIOPIAN IRATION BLOOD RELATIVE & IDREN
79	Greensleeves GRED 21	This Foundation/Elders and Deacons/How Can A Man/Jah Children Come (12")	40

ETHIOPIANS
66	Ska Beat JB 260	Live Good (credited to the Etheopians)/SOUL BROTHERS: Soho	38
66	Island WI 3015	I Am Free/SOUL BROTHERS: Shanty Town	28
67	Rio R 110	Owe Me No Pay Me/SHARKS: I Wouldn't Baby	20
67	Rio R 114	I'm Gonna Take Over Now/JACKIE MITTOO: Home Made	35
67	Rio R 123	What To Do/JACKIE MITTOO: Got My Bugaloo	45
67	Rio R 126	Dun Dead A'Ready/BOB ANDY: Stay In My Lonely Arms	25
67	Rio R 130	Train To Skaville/You Are The Girl (B-side actually by Gladiators)	18
67	Doctor Bird DB 1092	I Need You/Do It Sweet	35

67	Doctor Bird DB 1096	The Whip/Cool It, Amigo	15
67	Doctor Bird DB 1103	Stay Loose, Mama/The World Goes Ska	40
68	Doctor Bird DB 1141	Come On Now/Sh'Boom	25
68	Doctor Bird DB 1147	Engine 54/Give Me Your Love	150+
68	Doctor Bird DB 1148	Train To Glory/You Got The Dough	35
68	Doctor Bird DB 1169	Everything Crash/I'm Not Losing You	25
68	Crab CRAB 2	Fire A Muss Tail/Blacker Black (B-side actually by Count Ossie)	40+
68	Crab CRAB 5	Reggie Hit The Town/Ding Dong Bell	15
69	Crab CRAB 7	I Am A King/What A Big Surprise	12
69	Doctor Bird DB 1172	Not Me/Cut Down	18
69	Doctor Bird DB 1185	Hong Kong Flu/Clap Your Hands	15
69	Doctor Bird DB 1186	What A Fire/You	20
69	Doctor Bird DB 1199	Everyday Talking/Sharing You	20
69	Trojan TR 666	Woman Capture Man/One	10
69	Trojan TR 697	Well Red/J.J. ALLSTARS: R.F.K.	7
69	Nu Beat NB 031	My Testimony/J.J. ALL STARS: One Dollar Of Soul	10
69	Duke DU 35	My Girl/ANSELL COLLINS: Bigger Boss	12
70	Duke DU 61	Mek You Go On So/WINSTON WRIGHT & J.J. ALL STARS: Neck Tie	10
70	Duke Reid DR 2507	Mother's Tender Care/TOMMY McCOOK: Soldier Man	5
70	Bamboo BAM 26	Walkie Talkie/SOUND DIMENSION: Moan And Groan	12
70	Bamboo BAM 38	You'll Want To Come Back/JACKIE MITTOO: Baby Why (Instrumental) (B-side actually by Sound Dimension)	12
70	J.J. JJ 3302	Wreck It Up/Don't Go	8
70	J.J. JJ 3303	Hong Kong Flu/Everything Crash	6
70	Gas GAS 142	Satan Girl/MATADORS: The Pum	6
70	High Note HS 042	Praise For I (actually "Praise Fari")/GAYTONES: Charrie Part II	8
70	Songbird SB 1040	No Baptism/CRYSTALITES: No Baptism (Version Two)	7
70	Songbird SB 1047	Good Ambition/CRYSTALITES: Ambition Version	6
71	Randy's RAN 509	Mi Want Girl/RANDY'S ALL STARS: Girl — Version	7
71	Randy's RAN 510	True Man, Free Man/RANDY'S ALL STARS: Truthful — Version	7
71	Randy's RAN 512	Mr. Tom/Sad News	7
71	Fab FAB 180	Monkey Money/Version	8
71	Treasure Isle TI 7067	Pirate/TOMMY McCOOK & SOUL SYNDICATE: Depth Charge	6
71	Songbird SB 1059	What A Pain/CRYSTALITES: Pain Version	6
71	Songbird SB 1062	Lot's Wife/DERRICK HARRIOTT: Slave	6
71	Songbird SB 1064	Best Of Five (Parts 1 & 2)	6
71	Big Shot BI 569	He's Not A Rebel/J.J. ALL STARS: He's Not A Rebel — Version	15
71	Big Shot BI 574	The Selah/Don't Let Me Go	6
71	Duke DU 102	Drop Him/J.J. ALL STARS: Drop Him Version	6
71	Duke DU 108	Rim Bim Bam/RANDY'S ALL STARS: Rim Bim Bam Version	7
71	Explosion EX 2050	Starvation/TROJAN ALL STARS: Starvation Version	6
71	G.G. GG 4519	Love Bug/Sound Of Our Forefathers	7
71	Supreme SUP 221	Love Bug/Sound Of Our Forefathers	6
71	Supreme SUP 226	Starvation/MAXIE & GLEN: Jordan River	6
71	Big BG 330	Solid As A Rock/RUPIE EDWARDS ALL STARS: Solid As A Rock Version	6
71	Punch PH 96	Solid As A Rock/RUPIE EDWARDS ALL STARS: Solid As A Rock Version	6
72	G.G. GG 4533	Israel Want To be Free/TYPHOON ALL STARS: Israel (Version)	6
72	Prince Buster PB 38	You Are For Me/Playboy	8
72	Techniques TE 919	Promises/TIVOLIS: Promises — Version	6
73	Harry J. HJ 6646	The Word Is Love/The Word Is Love — Version	5
74	Harry J. HJ 6663	Buy You A Ring/Pray Muma	5
75	Dragon DRA 1032	Knowledge Is Power/Power Version	5
68	Doctor Bird DLM 5011	THE ETHIOPIANS GO ROCK STEADY/ENGINE 54 (LP)	220
69	Trojan TTL 10	REGGAE POWER (LP)	35
70	Trojan TBL 112	WOMAN CAPTURE MAN (LP)	40

(see Eathopians, Soul Brothers, Soul Vendors, Hamliins)

ETHNIC FIGHT BAND
| 77 | Ethnic Fight EF 4444 | MUSIC EXPLOSION DUB (LP) | 80 |

ETIVES
81	Ayrespin AYRC 106	A BREATH OF FRESH AIR (cassette)	20
84	Ayrespin AYRC 015	AN GAOL A THUG MI OG (MY LOVE OF EARLY DAYS) (LP)	20
84	Ayrespin AYRC 015	AN GAOL A THUG MI OG (MY LOVE OF EARLY DAYS) (cassette)	12

(see also Capercaillie)

ETTA (James) & HARVEY (Fuqua)
| 60 | London HLM 9180 | If I Can't Have You/My Heart Cries | 55 |

(see also Etta James, Moonglows, Harvey & Moonglows)

JACK EUBANK'S ORCHESTRA
| 61 | London HLU 9312 | What'd I Say/Chiricahua | 12 |
| 62 | London HLU 9501 | Searchin'/Take A Message To Mary | 12 |

EUGENE & BURST
| 71 | Supreme SUP 225 | Let It Fall/DENZIL & BURST: Can't Change | 6 |

EUGENIUS
| 93 | Creation CAUG 005 | Caesar's Vein (p/s) | 7 |
| 93 | Creation CAUG 008CD | EASTER BUNNY EP (CD) | 8 |

(see also Teenage Fanclub)

EUROPEANS
| 79 | Heartbeat PULSE 2 | Europeans/Voices (p/s) | 5 |

EUROPEANS
83	A&M AMLX 68558	VOCABULARY (LP)	12
84	A&M SCOT 1	LIVE (LP)	12
84	A&M AMA 5034	RECURRING DREAMS (LP)	12

(see also Marillion)

EURYTHMICS

81	RCA RCA 68	Never Gonna Cry Again/Le Sinistre (p/s) 8
81	RCA RCAT 68	Never Gonna Cry Again (Extended)/Le Sinistre (Extended) (12", p/s) 25
81	RCA RCA 115	Belinda/Heartbeat, Heartbeat (p/s) 15
82	RCA RCA 199	This Is The House/Home Is Where The Heart Is (p/s) 15
82	RCA RCAT 199	This Is The House/Your Time Will Come (live)/Never Gonna Cry Again/ 4/4 In Leather (live)/Take Me To Your Heart (live) (12", p/s) 35
82	RCA RCA 230	The Walk/Step On The Beast/The Walk (Part 2) (p/s) 12
82	RCA RCAT 230	The Walk/Invisible Hands/Dr Trash/The Walk (Part 2) (12", printed die-cut sl.) ... 35
82	RCA DA 1	Love Is A Stranger/Monkey, Monkey (with reverse print on rear of p/s) 5
82	RCA DAP 1	Love Is A Stranger/Monkey, Monkey (picture disc) 5
82	RCA DAT 1	Love Is A Stranger/Let's Just Close Our Eyes/Monkey, Monkey (12", blue p/s) 8
83	RCA DAP 2	Sweet Dreams (Are Made Of This)/I Could Give You (A Mirror) (picture disc) 6
83	RCA DAT 2	Sweet Dreams (Are Made Of This)/I Could Give You (A Mirror)/ Baby's Gone Blue (12", p/s) 8
83	RCA DAP 3	Who's That Girl?/You Take Some Lentils ... And You Take Some Rice (picture disc) 7
83	RCA DAT 3	Who's That Girl?/You Take Some Lentils ... And You Take Some Rice/ ABC (Freeform) (12", p/s) 8
83	RCA DA 4/EUC 001	Right By Your Side/Right By Your Side (Party Mix) (stickered p/s) 5
83	RCA EUC 001	INTRO SPEECH: Intro Speech/Step On The Beast/ Invisible Hands/Angel (Dub)/Satellite Of Love) 20
83	RCA DAP 4	Right By Your Side/Right By Your Side (Party Mix) (picture disc) 6
83	RCA DAT 4	Right By Your Side/Right By Your Side (Special Mix)/ Pluse Something Else (12", p/s) 8
84	RCA DAP 5	Here Comes The Rain Again/Paint A Rumour (picture disc) 5
84	RCA DAT 5	Here Comes The Rain Again/This City Never Sleeps (live)/ Paint A Rumour (Long Version) (12", p/s) 8
84	Virgin VSY 728-12	Sexcrime (1984) (Extended Mix)/Sexcrime (1984) (Single Version)/ I Did It Just The Same (12" picture disc) 10
85	Virgin VSY 734	Julia/Ministry Of Love (picture disc in pop-up p/s) 8
85	Virgin VSY 734-12	Julia (Extended Version)/Ministry Of Love (12", picture disc, unissued)
85	RCA PB 40375	It's Alright (Baby's Coming Back)/Conditioned Soul ('video still' p/s) 5
85	RCA PB 40375/PB 40101	It's Alright (Baby's Coming Back)/Conditioned Soul//Would I Lie To You?/ Here Comes That Sinking Feeling (double pack, with free coloured vinyl 7") 12
85	RCA PB 40376/PB 40102	It's Alright (Baby's Coming Back)/Conditioned Soul/Tous Les Garçons Et Les Filles//Would I Lie To You? (E.T. Mix)/Would I Lie To You? (Extended Remix)/ Here Comes That Sinking Feeling (12", double pack, gatefold PVC sleeve; 2nd on coloured vinyl) 10
85	RCA BYTI 100	I Love You Like A Ball And Chain (mono)/I Love You Like A Ball And Chain (stereo) (promo only) 8
86	RCA DA 8	Thorn In My Side/In This Town (p/s, with shrinkwrapped enamel badge) 6
86	RCA DA 9P	The Miracle Of Love/When Tomorrow Comes (live) (shaped picture disc) 8
87	RCA DAT 14P	Shame (Dance Mix)/I've Got A Lover (Back In Japan)/Shame (12", p/s & print).... 8
88	RCA DA 15X	I Need A Man/I Need You/There Must Be An Angel (Playing With My Heart) (live)/ Missionary Man (live) (10", p/s) 8
88	RCA DA 15CD	I Need A Man/Missionary Man (Live Version)/I Need You/I Need A Man (Macho Mix) (CD, picture disc in numbered metal tin) 8
83	Lyntone LYN 13916	A CHRISTMAS MESSAGE (fan club flexidisc, no p/s) 8
84	Lyntone LYN 15292	A YULETIDE MESSAGE TO ALL OUR PALS (fan club flexidisc, no p/s) 8
87	Lyntone (no cat. no.)	DAVE AND ANNIE'S CHRISTMAS MESSAGE '87 (fan club flexidisc, no p/s) 5
89	Flexi FLX 880	DAVE AND ANNIE'S CHRISTMAS MESSAGE '89 (fan club flexidisc, foldout p/s) 5
90	Flexi FLX 1000	DAVE AND ANNIE'S CHRISTMAS MESSAGE '90 (fan club flexidisc, foldout p/s) 5
00	BMG BMGSM 2	PEACE IS JUST A WORD (CD EP, with *The Sunday Times Magazine*) 10
83	RCA RCALP 6063	SWEET DREAMS (LP, picture disc) 12
83	RCA PL 70109	TOUCH (LP, picture disc) 12
		(see also David A. Stewart, ACatch, Tourists, Chris & Cosey, Stewart & Harrison)

JOHN EVAN BAND

90	A New Day NRS/CD 1	THE JOHN EVAN BAND LIVE '66 (CD, 500 only) 50
		(see also Jethro Tull)

BARBARA EVANS

59	RCA RCA 1122	Souvenirs/Pray For Me, Mother (triangular centre) (78 rpm = £18) 28
61	Mercury AMT 1151	Charlie Wasn't There/Nothing You Can Do 5

CHRISTINE EVANS

65	Philips BF 1406	Growing Pains/Someone In Love 5
66	Philips BF 1496	Somewhere There's Love/Right Or Wrong 8
67	Melodisc MEL 1620	I'm Gonna Tell Tony/Someone In Love 12

DAVE EVANS

71	Village Thing VTS 6	THE WORDS IN BETWEEN (LP) 12
72	Village Thing VTS 14	ELEPHANTASIA (LP) 12
74	Kicking Mule SNKF 107	SAD PIG DANCE (LP, with booklet) 12

GIL EVANS ORCHESTRA

60	Vogue EPV 1266	GREAT JAZZ STANDARDS (EP) 8
60	Vogue LAE 12234	GREAT JAZZ STANDARDS (LP) 15

JOHN EVANS

62	Palette PG 9040	Melodie Pour Madame/Cry Me A River 10

LARRY EVANS

56	London HLU 8269	Crazy 'Bout My Baby/Henpecked (78 rpm = £70+) .... 700+

MAUREEN EVANS
SINGLES

58	Embassy WB 300	Carolina Moon/Stupid Cupid	9
58	Embassy WB 303	Fever/Born Too Late	9
58	Embassy WB 309	The Hula Hoop Song/Hoopa Hoola	7
58	Embassy WB 313	I'll Get By/Someday (You'll Want Me To Want You)	7
58	Embassy WB 316	You Always Hurt The One You Love/The Day The Rains Came	7
58	Embassy WB 319	To Know Him Is To Love Him/Kiss Me, Honey Honey, Kiss Me	8
59	Embassy WB 344	Goodbye Jimmy, Goodbye/May You Always	7
59	Embassy WB 348	Lipstick On Your Collar/What A Diff'rence A Day Made (78 rpm = £13)	8
59	Embassy WB 356	Broken-Hearted Melody/Plenty Good Lovin' (78 rpm = £10)	8
59	Embassy WB 371	Among My Souvenirs/Happy Anniversary (78 rpm = £12)	8
59	Oriole CB 1517	Don't Want The Moonlight/The Years Between (78 rpm = £10)	9
60	Oriole CB 1533	The Big Hurt/I Can't Begin To Tell You (78 rpm = £15)	10
60	Oriole CB 1540	Love, Kisses And Heartaches/We Just Couldn't Say Goodbye (78 rpm = £15)	7
60	Oriole CB 1550	Paper Roses/Please Understand (78 rpm = £22)	10
61	Oriole CB 1563	Mama Wouldn't Like It/My Little Corner Of The World	7
61	Oriole CB 1578	As Long As He Needs Me/Where Is Love?	8
61	Oriole CB 1581	Till/Why Don't You Believe Me	8
61	Oriole CB 1613	My Foolish Heart/Oh Gypsy Oh Gypsy	8
62	Oriole CB 1743	Never In A Million Years/We Had Words	7
62	Oriole CB 1760	Like I Do/Starlight Starbright	7
63	Oriole CB 1804	Pick The Petals/Melancholy Me	8
63	Oriole CB 1806	Tomorrow Is Another Day/Acapulco Mexico	8
63	Oriole CB 1851	What A Difference A Day Made/Oh What A Guy	6
63	Oriole CB 1875	Like You Used To Do/As You Love Her	6
64	Oriole CB 1906	I Love How You Love Me/John John	8
64	Oriole CB 1939	He Knows I Love Him Too Much/Don't Believe Him	8
64	Oriole CB 1969	Get Away/I've Often Wondered	9
65	CBS 201733	All The Angels Sing/Speak Sugar Speak	9
65	CBS 201752	Never Let Him Go/Poco Sole	9
67	CBS 202621	Somewhere There's Love/It Takes A Little Time	9
68	CBS 3222	I Almost Called Your Name/Searching For Home	9
63	Oriole EP 7076	MELANCHOLY ME (EP)	40
63	Oriole PS 40046	LIKE I DO (LP)	35

(see also Matt Bryant & Linda Joyce)

PAUL EVANS (& CURLS)

59	London HLL 8968	Seven Little Girls Sitting In The Back Seat/Worshipping An Idol (with Curls)	15
59	London HLL 8968	Seven Little Girls Sitting In The Back Seat/Worshipping An Idol (78)	25
60	London HLL 9045	Midnite Special/Since I Met You, Baby	30
60	London HLL 9129	Happy-Go-Lucky Me/Fish In The Ocean	10
60	London HLL 9183	Brigade Of Broken Hearts/Twins	10
60	London HLL 9239	Hushabye Little Guitar/Blind Boy	18
62	London HLR 9636	The Bell That Couldn't Jingle/Gilding The Lily	8
63	London HLR 9770	Even Tan/Ten Thousand Years	13
63	London RE-R 1349	PAUL EVANS (EP)	100
60	London HA-L 2248	PAUL EVANS SINGS THE FABULOUS TEENS (LP)	125

RUSSELL EVANS & NITEHAWKS

66	Atlantic 584 010	Send Me Some Cornbread/The Bold	10

TOMMY EVANS

02	Y n R YNR007	The Four Horsemen/Not Nice (12")	8
00	Y n R YNR003	THE TIME CAPSULE (EP)	12
01	Y n R YNR005	THE FOUR ELEMENTS (EP)	10

EVEN DOZEN JUG BAND

66	Bounty BY 6023	THE EVEN DOZEN JUG BAND (LP)	25

(see also Lovin' Spoonful, John Sebastian)

BETTY EVERETT

64	Stateside SS 259	You're No Good/Chained To Your Love	22
64	Stateside SS 280	It's In His Kiss (The Shoop Shoop Song)/Hands Off	18
64	Stateside SS 321	I Can't Hear You/Can I Get To Know You	20
64	Fontana TF 520	Getting Mighty Crowded/Chained To A Memory	20
64	King KG 1002	Happy I Long To Be/Your Loving Arms	15
65	Sue WI 352	I've Got A Claim On You/Your Love Is Important To Me	50
68	President PT 215	It's In His Kiss (The Shoop Shoop Song)/Getting Mighty Crowded	8
69	President PT 251	You're No Good/Hands Off	8
69	MCA Soul Bag BAG 3	I Can't Say No To You/Better Tomorrow Than Today	8
69	MCA MU 1055	There'll Come A Time/Take Me	8
70	Uni UN 517	Sugar/Hold On	8
71	Liberty LBF 15428	I Got To Tell Somebody/Why Are You Leaving Me	15
72	President PT 372	Trouble Over The Weekend/The Shoe Doesn't Fit	10
65	Fontana TL 5236	IT'S IN HIS KISS (LP)	60
68	Joy JOYS 106	IT'S IN HIS KISS (LP, reissue)	15
69	Uni UNLS 109	THERE'LL COME A TIME (LP)	45

BETTY EVERETT & JERRY BUTLER

64	Stateside SS 339	Let It Be Me/Ain't That Lovin' You Baby	15
65	Fontana TF 528	Smile/Love Is Strange	12
68	President PT 214	Let It Be Me/Smile	6
69	President PT 252	Our Day Will Come/Just Be True	6
65	Fontana TL 5237	DELICIOUS TOGETHER (LP)	55
68	Joy JOYS 123	DELICIOUS TOGETHER (LP, reissue)	15

(see also Jerry Butler)

VINCE EVERETT

65	Fontana TF 606	Bless You/'Til I Lost You	10
67	Fontana TF 818	Endlessly/Who's That Girl?	10
68	Fontana TF 915	Every Now And Then/Barbarella	10

EVERGREEN BLUES

67	Mercury MF 1012	Midnight Confessions/(Yes) That's My Baby	10
68	Mercury MF 1025	Laura (Keep Hangin' On)/Yesterday's Coming	6
68	Mercury 20122 SMCL	7 DO ELEVEN (LP)	18

EVERGREEN BLUESHOES

69	London HA-U/SH-U 8399	THE BALLAD OF THE EVERGREEN BLUESHOES (LP)	22

(see also Skip Battin, Byrds)

EVERLY BROTHERS

78s

57	London HLA 8440	Bye Bye, Love/I Wonder If I Care As Much	10
57	London HLA 8498	Wake Up Little Susie/Maybe Tomorrow	10
58	London HLA 8554	Should We Tell Him/This Little Girl Of Mine	18
58	London HLA 8618	All I Have To Do Is Dream/Claudette	12
58	London HLA 8685	Bird Dog/Devoted To You	15
58	London HLA 8781	Problems/Love Of My Life	30
59	London HLA 8863	Poor Jenny/Take A Message To Mary	40
59	London HLA 8934	('Til) I Kissed You/Oh, What A Feeling	70
60	London HLA 9039	Let It Be Me/Since You Broke My Heart	160
60	Warner Bros WB 1	Cathy's Clown/Always It's You	230
60	London HLA 9157	When Will I Be Loved/Be-Bop-A-Lula	150
60	Warner Bros WB 19	Lucille/So Sad (To Watch Good Love Go Bad)	300

SINGLES

57	London HLA 8440	Bye Bye, Love/I Wonder If I Care As Much	28/10
57	London HLA 8498	Wake Up Little Susie/Maybe Tomorrow	18/10
58	London HLA 8554	Should We Tell Him/This Little Girl Of Mine	30/10
58	London HLA 8618	All I Have To Do Is Dream/Claudette	10/6
58	London HLA 8685	Bird Dog/Devoted To You	10/6
58	London HLA 8781	Problems/Love Of My Life	10/6
59	London HLA 8863	Poor Jenny/Take A Message To Mary	12/6
59	London HLA 8934	('Til) I Kissed You/Oh, What A Feeling	12/6
60	London HLA 9039	Let It Be Me/Since You Broke My Heart	20/8

(Where two prices are listed above, the first refers to original triangular centres, the second to later round centres.)

60	Warner Bros WB 1	Cathy's Clown/Always It's You	8
60	London HLA 9157	When Will I Be Loved/Be-Bop-A-Lula	10
60	Warner Bros WB 19	Lucille/So Sad (To Watch Good Love Go Bad)	8
60	London HLA 9250	Like Strangers/Leave My Woman Alone	10
61	Warner Bros WB 33	Walk Right Back/Ebony Eyes	7
61	Warner Bros WB 42	Temptation/Stick With Me Baby	7
61	Warner Bros WB 50	Muskrat/Don't Blame Me	7
62	Warner Bros WB 56	Crying In The Rain/I'm Not Angry	6
62	Warner Bros WB 67	How Can I Meet Her?/That's Old Fashioned	6
62	Warner Bros WB 79	No One Can Make My Sunshine Smile/Don't Ask Me To Be Friends	6
63	Warner Bros WB 94	So It Will Always Be/Nancy's Minuet	6
63	Warner Bros WB 99	It's Been Nice/I'm Afraid	6
63	Warner Bros WB 109	The Girl Sang The Blues/Love Her	6
64	Warner Bros WB 129	Ain't That Lovin' You Baby/Hello Amy	6
64	Warner Bros WB 135	The Ferris Wheel/Don't Forget To Cry	6
64	Warner Bros WB 143	You're The One I Love/Ring Around My Rosie (withdrawn)	22
64	Warner Bros WB 146	Gone, Gone, Gone/Torture	10
65	Warner Bros WB 154	You're My Girl/Don't Let The Whole World Know	9
65	Warner Bros WB 158	That'll Be The Day/Give Me A Sweetheart	8
65	Warner Bros WB 161	The Price Of Love/It Only Costs A Dime	8
65	Warner Bros WB 5628	The Price Of Love/It Only Costs A Dime (reissue)	5
65	Warner Bros WB 5639	I'll Never Get Over You/Follow Me	8
65	Warner Bros WB 5649	Love Is Strange/Man With Money	8
66	Warner Bros WB 5682	It's All Over/I Used To Love You (unissued)	
66	Warner Bros WB 5743	(You Got) The Power Of Love/Leave My Girl Alone	10
66	Warner Bros WB 5754	I've Been Wrong Before/Hard Hard Year	15
67	Warner Bros WB 7520	Bowling Green/I Don't Want To Love You	15
67	Warner Bros WB 7062	Mary Jane/Talking To The Flowers	15
67	Warner Bros WB 7088	Love Of The Common People/A Voice Within	15
68	Warner Bros WB 7192	It's My Time/Empty Boxes	15
68	Warner Bros WB 7226	Milk Train/Lord Of The Manor	15
69	Warner Bros WB 6056	Cathy's Clown/Walk Right Back	5
70	Warner Bros WB 6074	Good Golly, Miss Molly/Oh, Boy!	12
70	Warner Bros WB 7425	Yves/Human Race	12
72	RCA Victor RCA 2232	Ridin' High/Stories We Could Tell	15
73	RCA Victor RCA 2286	Not Fade Away/Lay It Down	8
77	Warner Bros K 17004	Silent Treatment/Dancing On My Feet	5
80	Old Gold SET 1	THE EVERLY BROTHERS SINGLES SET (15 x p/s 7", box set with book)	30

EPs

58	London RE-A 1113	THE EVERLY BROTHERS	30
58	London RE-A 1148	THE EVERLY BROTHERS — NO. 2	30
58	London RE-A 1149	THE EVERLY BROTHERS — NO. 3	35
59	London RE-A 1174	THE EVERLY BROTHERS — NO. 4	35
59	London RE-A 1195	SONGS OUR DADDY TAUGHT US PART 1	40
59	London RE-A 1196	SONGS OUR DADDY TAUGHT US PART 2	40
59	London RE-A 1197	SONGS OUR DADDY TAUGHT US PART 3	40
60	London RE-A 1229	THE EVERLY BROTHERS — NO. 5	40

(Prices for the above EPs refer to original triangular centre labels, round-centre editions are worth two-thirds these values.)

61	Warners W(S)EP 6034	ESPECIALLY FOR YOU (mono/stereo)	30/40
61	London RE-A 1311	THE EVERLY BROTHERS — NO. 6	40
62	Warners W(S)EP 6049	FOREVERLY YOURS (mono/stereo)	30/40
62	Warners W(S)EP 6056	IT'S EVERLY TIME (mono/stereo)	30/40
63	Warners W(S)EP 6107	A DATE WITH THE EVERLY BROTHERS VOL. 1 (mono/stereo)	30/45
63	Warners W(S)EP 6109	A DATE WITH THE EVERLY BROTHERS VOL. 2 (mono/stereo)	30/45
63	Warners W(S)EP 6111	INSTANT PARTY VOL. 1 (mono/stereo)	30/45
63	Warners W(S)EP 6113	INSTANT PARTY VOL. 2 (mono/stereo)	30/45
63	Warners W(S)EP 6115	BOTH SIDES OF AN EVENING — FOR DANCING VOL. 1 (mono/stereo)	30/45
64	Warners W(S)EP 6117	BOTH SIDES OF AN EVENING — FOR DREAMING VOL. 2 (mono/stereo)	30/45
64	Warners WEP 6128	THE EVERLY BROTHERS SING GREAT COUNTRY HITS VOL. 1	30
64	Warners WEP 6131	THE EVERLY BROTHERS SING GREAT COUNTRY HITS VOL. 2	30
64	Warners WEP 6132	THE EVERLY BROTHERS SING GREAT COUNTRY HITS VOL. 3	30
65	Warner Bros WEP 6138	BOTH SIDES OF AN EVENING — FOR FUN VOL. 3	30
65	Warner Bros WEP 604	THE PRICE OF LOVE	30
65	Warner Bros WEP 608	ROCK'N'SOUL VOL. 1	30
65	Warner Bros WEP 609	ROCK'N'SOUL VOL. 2	30
66	Warner Bros WEP 610	LOVE IS STRANGE	30
66	Warner Bros WEP 612	PEOPLE GET READY	30
66	Warner Bros WEP 618	WHAT AM I LIVING FOR?	30
67	Warner Bros WEP 622	LEAVE MY GIRL ALONE	30
67	Warner Bros WEP 623	SOMEBODY HELP ME	30
72	Warner Bros K 16209	CRYING IN THE RAIN	10
74	Warner Bros K 16407	WAKE UP LITTLE SUSIE	10

LPs

58	London HA-A 2081	THE EVERLY BROTHERS	75
58	London HA-A 2150	SONGS OUR DADDY TAUGHT US	75
60	Warner Bros WM 4012	IT'S EVERLY TIME (also stereo WS 8012)	32/48
60	London HA-A 2266	THE FABULOUS STYLE OF THE EVERLY BROTHERS	40
60	Warner Bros WM 4028	A DATE WITH THE EVERLY BROTHERS (also stereo WS 8028)	35/45
61	Warner Bros WM 4052	BOTH SIDES OF AN EVENING (also stereo WS 8052)	35/45
62	Warner Bros WM 4061	INSTANT PARTY (also stereo WS 8061)	35/45
62	Warner Bros WM/WS 8108	THE GOLDEN HITS OF THE EVERLY BROTHERS (mono/stereo)	18/20
62	Warner Bros WM/WS 8116	CHRISTMAS WITH THE EVERLY BROTHERS AND THE BOYS TOWN CHOIR (mono/stereo)	40/50
63	Warner Bros WM/WS 8138	SING GREAT COUNTRY HITS (mono/stereo)	35/45
64	Warner Bros WM/WS 8163	THE VERY BEST OF THE EVERLY BROTHERS (mono/stereo)	12/15
65	Warner Bros WM/WS 8169	GONE GONE GONE (mono/stereo)	30/40
65	Warner Bros WM/WS 8171	ROCK 'N' SOUL (mono/stereo)	30/40
65	Warner Bros W(S) 1578	ROCK 'N' SOUL (reissue)	20/25
65	Warner Bros W(S) 1605	BEAT 'N' SOUL	30
65	Warner Bros W(S) 1620	IN OUR IMAGE (mono/stereo)	30/40
67	Warner Bros W(S) 1646	TWO YANKS IN ENGLAND (mono/stereo)	30/40
67	Warner Bros W(S) 1676	THE HIT SOUND OF THE EVERLY BROTHERS (mono/stereo)	30/40
67	Warner Bros W(S) 1708	THE EVERLY BROTHERS SING (mono/stereo)	30/40
68	Warner Bros W(S) 1752	ROOTS	22
70	Warner Bros WS 1858	THE EVERLY BROTHERS SHOW (2-LP)	20
72	RCA Victor SF 8270	STORIES WE COULD TELL	12
73	RCA Victor SF 8332	PASS THE CHICKEN AND LISTEN	12
77	Warner Bros K 56415	THE NEW ALBUM	12
80	Marks & Spencer IMP 111	THE VERY BEST OF THE EVERLY BROTHERS	40
90	Knight EVYLP 47004	PERFECT HARMONY (multi-LP box set)	20

(see also Don Everly, Phil Everly)

DON EVERLY

74	Ode ODS 66046	Warmin' Up The Band/Evelyn Swing	5
76	DJM DJS 10692	Yesterday Just Passed Away Again/Never Like This	5
77	DJM DJS 10760	So Sad/Love At Last Sight (p/s)	5
77	DJM DJS 10842	Brother Juke Box/Oh What A Feeling	5
71	A&M AMLS 2007	DON EVERLY (LP, with Ry Cooder)	18
74	Ode ODE 77023	SUNSET TOWERS (LP, with Heads, Hands & Feet)	18

PHIL EVERLY

73	RCA RCA 2409	The Air That I Breathe/God Bless Older Ladies	5
74	Pye 7N 45398	Invisible Man/It's True	5
74	Pye 7N 45415	Sweet Music/Goodbye Line	5
75	Pye 7N 45544	Better Than Now/You And I Are A Song	5
80	Epic EPC 9575	Dare To Dream Again/Lonely Days, Lonely Nights	5
83	Capitol CL 2276	She Means Nothing To Me (with Cliff Richard)/A Man And A Woman (p/s)	5
73	RCA SF 8370	STAR SPANGLED SPRINGER (LP)	18
74	Pye NSPL 18448	THERE'S NOTHING TOO GOOD FOR MY BABY (LP)	18
75	Pye NSPL 18473	MYSTIC LINE (LP)	15

(see also Cliff Richard)

EVERREADY'S

80	Taaga TAG 3	Don't Do It Again/Martian Girl (gatefold p/s)	15

LENNY EVERSONG

57	Vogue Coral Q 72255	Jezebel/Jealousy	10

EVERYBODY'S CHILDREN

70	Fontana TF 1070	Time Is Now/Abide With Me	5

EVERY MOTHER'S SON

67	MGM MGM 1341	Come And Take A Ride In My Boat/I Believe In You	22
67	MGM MGM 1350	Put Your Mind At Ease/Proper Four Leaf Clover	20

MINT VALUE £

67	MGM MGM 1372	Pony With The Golden Mane/Dolls In The Clock	8
67	MGM C(S) 8044	EVERY MOTHER'S SON (LP)	35
68	MGM C(S) 8061	EVERY MOTHER'S SON'S BACK (LP)	30

EVERYONE
| 71 | Charisma CB 146 | Trouble At The Mill/Radio Lady | 5 |
| 71 | Charisma CAS 1028 | EVERYONE (LP) | 12 |

(see also Andy Roberts)

EVERYONE ELSE
| 79 | Woodbine St WSR 001 | Schooldays/Brainwashed/Out Of My Mind/Don't Call Us (p/s) | 100 |

EVERYONE INVOLVED
| 72 | Arcturus ARC 3 | The Circus Keeps On Turning/Motor Car Madness | 30 |
| 72 | Arcturus ARC 4 | EITHER OR (LP, private pressing, embossed plain white sleeve with inserts) | 150 |

EVERYTHING BUT THE GIRL
82	Cherry Red CHERRY 37	Night And Day/Feeling Dizzy/On My Mind (yellow p/s)	5
83	Cherry Red 12CHERRY 37	Night And Day/Feeling Dizzy/On My Mind (12", p/s)	8
84	Blanco Y Negro NEG 1	Each And Every One/Laugh You Out The House/Never Could Have Been Worse (12", p/s)	8
84	Blanco Y Negro NEG 6T	Native Land/Riverbed Dry/Easy As Sin/Gun Cupboard Love/Don't You Go (12", stickered p/s)	8
86	Blanco Y Negro NEG 23F	Don't Leave Me Behind/Alfie//Come On Home (Acoustic)/Always On My Mind (live) (double pack, gatefold p/s)	5
96	Blanco Y Negro SAM 1936	Driving (Masters At Work Extended 12") (Masters At Work Dub)/(Acapella) (T's Master Mix)(T's Frozen Sun Mix)/(Underdog Vocal Mix)/(Underdog Instrumental Mix) (12", double pack, stickered title p/s)	8
97	Virgin VSTXDJ 1589	Wrong (Mood II Swing Dub)/(Deep Dish Remix) (12", stickered sleeve)	8
97	Virgin VSTDJ 1589	Wrong (Todd Terry Remix)/(Everything But The Drums)/(Deep Dish Remix)/(Tee's Beats)/(EBTG Original Mix)/(Deep Dish Dub) (12", double pack, stickered sleeve)	8

(see also Ben Watt, Marine Girls, Tracey Thorn)

EVERYTHING IS EVERYTHING
| 69 | Vanguard VA 1 | Witchi Tai To/Oooh Baby | 12 |
| 68 | Vanguard SVRL 19036 | EVERYTHING IS EVERYTHING (LP) | 18 |

EVERY WHICH WAY
| 70 | Charisma BD 1 | Go Placidly | 6 |

(see also Brian Davison, Griffin, Heavy Jelly, Skip Bifferty, Graham Bell, Bell & Arc)

EVIL ED
| 01 | Y n R YNR4 | THE TOURNAMENT ROUND 1 (EP) | 10 |
| 02 | Hidden Identity HID1 | THE TOURNAMENT ROUND 2 (EP) | 10 |

EWAN (McDermott) & DENVER
| 67 | Giant GN 17 | I Want You So Bad/ERIC McDERMOTT: I'm Gonna Love You | 10 |

EWAN (McDermott) & JERRY (McCarthy)
67	Blue Beat BB 385	Oh Babe/Dance With Me (with Carib Beats)	18
67	Giant GN 5	The Right Track/We Got To Be One	10
67	Giant GN 10	Rock Steady Train/My Baby Is Gone	10
67	Giant GN 14	Tennessee Waltz/You've Got Something	10

DON EWELL
| 57 | Tempo TAP 7 | PIANO SOLOS OF KING OLIVER CREOLE JAZZ BAND TUNES (LP) | 15 |

(see also Mama Yancey/Don Ewell)

EX
| 86 | Ron Johnson ZRON 11 | '1936' THE SPANISH REVOLUTION (double pack with book) | 7 |

EX/ALERTA
| 84 | CNT CNT 017 | THE RED DANCE PACKAGE (12", split EP) | 8 |

EXCALIBUR
88	Clay PLATE 1	HOT FOR LOVE (Hot For Love/Early In The Morning/Come On And Rock/Death's Door (12" EP)	8
90	Active 12ATV 101	Carole Ann (12", p/s)	8
85	Conquest QUEST 5	THE BITTER END (mini-LP)	18

EXCEL
| 79 | ARSS XL1 | If It Rains/Rolling Home/She's One Of The Boys/Rock Show (EP, p/s) | 100 |
| 80 | Polydor POSP 110 | What Went Wrong?/Junita (p/s) | 8 |

EXCELS
| 67 | Atlantic 584 133 | California On My Mind/The Arrival Of Mary | 20 |

EXCELSIOR SPRING
| 69 | Instant IN 002 | Happy Miranda/It | 20 |

EXCEPTION(S)
67	CBS 202632	The Eagle Flies On Friday/Girl Trouble	40
67	CBS 2830	Gaberdine Saturday Night Street Walker/Sunday Night At The Prince Rupert	20
68	President PT 181	Rub It Down/It's Snowing In The Desert	6
68	President PT 205	Helicopter/Back Room	6
68	President PT 218	Tailor Made Babe/Turn Over The Soil	6
69	President PT 236	Jack Rabbit/Keep The Motor Running	6
69	President PT 271	Pendulum/Don't Torture Your Mind	12
69	President PTLS 1026	THE EXCEPTIONAL EXCEPTION (LP)	25

(see also Bugsy Eastwood, Fotheringay, Fairport Convention)

EXCEPTIONS
| 65 | Decca F 12100 | What More Do You Want?/Soldier Boy | 20 |

(see also Orchids)

EXCHECKERS
| 64 | Decca F 11871 | All The World Is Mine/It's All Over | 20 |

(see also Aynsley Dunbar Retaliation)

EXCITERS
63	United Artists UP 1011	Tell Him/Hard Way To Go	20
63	United Artists UP 1017	He's Got The Power/Drama Of Love	20
63	United Artists UP 1026	Get Him/It's So Exciting	18
64	United Artists UP 1041	Do-Wah-Diddy/If Love Came Your Way	20
65	Columbia DB 7479	I Want You To Be My Boy/Tonight, Tonight	20
65	Columbia DB 7544	Just Not Ready/Are You Satisfied	18
65	Columbia DB 7606	Run Mascara/My Father	20
66	London HLZ 10018	A Little Bit Of Soap/I'm Gonna Get Him Someday	15
66	London HLZ 10038	You Better Come Home/Weddings Make Me Cry	30
69	United Artists UP 2274	Do Wah Diddy Diddy/Hard Way To Go	12
71	Jay Boy BOY 38	Soul Motion/You Know It Ain't Right	12
65	United Artists UEP 1005	DO WAH DIDDY DIDDY (EP)	70
64	United Artists ULP 1032	THE EXCITERS (LP)	100

EXCURSION
| 69 | Gemini GMX 5029 | NIGHT TRAIN (LP) | 18 |

EXECUTIVE(S)
64	Columbia DB 7323	March Of The Mods/Why, Why, Why	8
64	Columbia DB 7393	Strictly For The Beat/No Room For Squares	8
65	Columbia DB 7573	It's Been So Long/You're For Me (as Executives)	8
65	Columbia DB 7770	Return Of The Mods/How Sad	10
66	Columbia DB 7919	Lock Your Door/In My Arms (as Executives)	8

EXECUTIVE(S)
67	CBS 202652	Smokey Atmosphere/Sensation	20
67	CBS 3067	Ginza Strip/I'll Always Love You	10
68	CBS 3431	Tracy Took A Trip/Gardena Dreamer (as Executive, some with promo only p/s)	40/25
69	CBS 4013	I Ain't Got Nobody/To Kingdom Come (as Executive)	10

EXECUTIVES
| 80 | Attrix RB 05 | Shy Little Girl/Never Go Home/JOHNNIE & LUBES: I Got Rabies/Terror In The Parking Lot (p/s) | 7 |

EXECUTIVE SUITE
| 75 | Cloud One HIT 1 | When The Fuel Runs Out/(instrumental) | 8 |

EXHIBIT A
| 80 | Irrelevant Wombat DAMP 1 | NO ELEPHANTS THIS SIDE OF THE WATFORD GAP (EP, with insert) | 15 |
| 80 | Irrelevant Wombat DAMP 2 | DISTANCE (EP) | 15 |

(see also Doof)

EXILE
| 77 | Boring BO 1 | DON'T TAX ME (EP, 1,000 only p/s) | 50 |
| 78 | Charly CYS 1033 | The Real People/Tomorrow Today/Disaster Movie (p/s) | 10 |

EXILES
| 66 | Topic 12T 143 | FREEDOM, COME ALL YE (LP) | 15 |
| 67 | Topic 12T 164 | THE HALE AND THE HANGED (LP) | 15 |

EXITS
| 78 | Way Out WOO 1 | YODELLING (EP, numbered, gatefold p/s, hand-stamped labels) | 60 |

EXITS
| 78 | Red Lightning GIL 519 | The Fashion Plague/Cheam (p/s, labels on wrong sides) | 80 |

(see also Direct Hits)

EXODUS (Jamaica)
71	Duke DU 103	Pharaoh's Walk/Little Caesar	8
72	Sioux SI 001	Pharaoh's Walk No. 9/SAMMY JONES: Worried Over You	6
72	Sioux SI 010	Julia Sees Me/LLOYD THE MATADOR: The Train (Engine 54)	8

EXORDIUM
| 70s | Face To Face FTF 1001 | TROUBLE WITH ADAM (LP, private pressing) | 20 |

EXOTICS
| 64 | Decca F 11850 | Cross My Heart/Ooh La La | 10 |

EXOTICS
| 68 | Columbia DB 8418 | Don't Lead Me On/You Can Try | 10 |

EXPELAIRES
| 79 | Zoo CAGE 007 | To See You/Frequency (p/s) | 5 |

(see also Mission)

EXPELLED
82	Riot City RIOT 8	Dreaming/No Life, No Future/What Justice (p/s)	6
82	Riot City RIOT 17	Government Policy/Make It Alone (p/s)	6
84	Riot City 12RIOT 33	THE SINGLES (12" EP)	8

EXPERIMENTS WITH ICE
| 81 | United Dairies EX 001 | EXPERIMENTS WITH ICE (LP) | 20 |

EX PISTOLS
| 84 | Cherry Red/Virgina Pistol 76p | Land Of Hope And Glory/The Flowers of Romansk (Picture disc) | 10 |

EXPLICIT CORPSE
| 81 | Gistol | That Day Before.../I Gotta Gistol (stickered white labels, plastic gatefold p/s) | 5 |

EXPLOITED
81	Exploited EXP 001	Army Life/Fuck The Mods/Crashed Out (p/s)	8
81	Exploited EXP 002	Exploited Barmy Army/I Believe In Anarchy/What You Gonna Do? (p/s)	8
81	Secret SHH 110	Dogs Of War/Blown To Bits (live) (p/s)	5
81	Secret SHH 112	Army Life/Fuck The Mods/Crashed Out (p/s, reissue)	5
81	Secret SHH 120	Dead Cities/Hitler's In The Charts Again/Class War (p/s)	5
83	Blurg/Pax PAX 15	Rival Leaders/Army Style/Singalongabushell (p/s)	6
81	Exploited EXP 003	EXTRACTS FROM EDINBURGH NITE CLUB (EP)	6
81	Exploited EXP 1001	PUNK'S NOT DEAD (LP)	12
81	Exploited EXP 1002	ON STAGE (LP)	12

EXPLORER
84	Rock Shop RSR 006	EXPLODING (LP)	40

EXPLOSIVE
68	President PT 221	Crying All Night/I Close My Eyes	6
69	President PT 244	Cities Make The Country Colder/Step Out Of Line	20
69	President PT 262	Who Planted Thorns In Miss Alice's Garden?/I Get My Kicks From Living	15
70	President PT 286	I'm Gonna Use What I Got To Get What I Need/Am I A Fool? (with Del Taylor)	6
70	President PT 302	This Ain't The Road To Freedom/Today Is Today	6
71	Plexium PXM 20	Hey Presto, Magic Man/Get It Together	60
71	Plexium PXM 24	Love Doesn't Come Easy/See You In The Morning	6

(see also Watson T. Browne & Explosive)

EXPORT
79	Atlantic K 11344	Julie Bitch/Nice To Know You	15
80	His Master's Vice VICE 2	You've Got To Rock/Wheeler Dealer (title sleeve)	18
80	His Master's Vice VICE 1	EXPORT (LP)	18

EXPOSURE
80	Ahgular Music ACUTE 1	Style & Fashion/Video Eyes (p/s)	10

EXPOZER
80	Hit Hard HARD 1	Rock Japan/Exposed At Last (p/s)	12
80	Hit Hard	EXPOSED AT LAST (LP)	12

EXTERNAL MENACE
82	Beat The System MENACE 1	YOUTH OF TODAY (EP)	7
83	Beat The System MENACE 2	NO VIEWS (EP)	7

EXTREEM
66	Strike JH 326	On The Beach/Don't You Ignore Me	15

EXTREME NOISE TERROR/CHAOS U.K.
86	Manic Ears ACHE 01	EAR SLAUGHTER — RADIOACTIVE (LP)	15

EXUMA
71	Mercury 6052 080	Damn Fool/You Don't Know What's Going On	6
72	Mercury 6052 112	We Got To Go/Zandoo	6
72	Kama Sutra 2013 053	Honkberry Moon Delight/Obeah Man Come Back	6
70	Mercury 6338 018	EXUMA (LP)	15

EYE FULL TOWER
67	Polydor BM 56734	How About Me?/Carol Cartoon	7

EYELESS IN GAZA
80	Ambivalent Scale ASR 2	Kodak Ghosts Run Amok/China Blue Vision/The Feeling's Mutual (wraparound p/s)	15
81	Cherry Red CHERRY 20	Invisibility/Three Kittens/Plague Of Years (p/s, with insert)	5
81	Cherry Red CHERRY 31	Others/Jane Dancing/Ever Present/Avenue With Trees (p/s)	5
82	Cherry Red CHERRY 47	Veil Like Calm/Taking Steps (p/s)	8
81	Cherry Red BRED 18	CAUGHT IN THE FLUX (LP, with bonus 12" EP [12 BRED 18], with inner)	12
82	Cherry Red BRED 36	DRUMMING THE BEATING HEART (LP)	12

(see also Martyn Bates)

EYES
65	Mercury MF 881	When The Night Falls/I'm Rowed Out	210
66	Mercury MF 897	The Immediate Pleasure/My Degeneration	150
66	Mercury MF 910	Man With Money/You're Too Much	175
65	Mercury MF 934	Good Day Sunshine/Please Don't Cry	100
78	Raw 16	I Like It/Once Ain't Enough	6
66	Mercury 10035 MCE	THE ARRIVAL OF THE EYES (EP)	400+
84	Bam Caruso KIRI 028	BLINK (LP, 2 different sleeves)	each 18
87	Bam Caruso MARI 038	SCENE BUT NOT HEARD (mini-LP)	15

(see also Pupils)

EYES OF BLUE
66	Deram DM 106	Heart Trouble/Up And Down	75
67	Deram DM 114	Supermarket Full Of Cans/Don't Ask Me To Mend Your Broken Heart	40
68	Mercury MF 1049	Largo/Yesterday	12
69	Mercury SMCL 20134	THE CROSSROADS OF TIME (LP)	45
69	Mercury SMCL 20164	IN FIELDS OF ARDATH (LP)	45

(see also Ancient Grease, Big Sleep, Man, Ritchie Francis, Gary Pickford-Hopkins)

EYNESBURY GIANT
78	Ultimate URL 602	FROM THE CASK (LP, with insert)	20

WILL EZELL
50s	Signature 910	Heifer Dust/Barrelhouse Woman (78)	8
50s	Signature 911	Old Mill Blues/Mixed Up Rag (78)	8
50	Tempo R 31	Old Mill Blues/Mixed Up Rag (78)	8

54	London AL 3539	GIN MILL JAZZ (10" LP)	25

(see also Paramount Allstars)

EZY MEAT
84	Electric Storm ES 0001	NOT FOR WIMPS (LP, with insert, Irish only)	50
86	Electric Storm ES 0002	ROCK YOUR BRAINS OUT (LP, with insert, Irish only)	40

EZY RIDER
82	English Steel	POWER (LP)	150

SHELLEY FABARES
62	Pye International 7N 25132	Johnny Angel/Where's It Gonna Get Me? (blue label, later yellow label)	15
62	Pye International 7N 25133	She Can't Find Her Keys/Very Unlikely (with Paul Peterson)	15
62	Pye International 7N 25151	Johnny Loves Me/I'm Growing Up	15
62	Pye International 7N 25166	The Things We Did Last Summer/Breaking Up Is Hard To Do	15
63	Pye International 7N 25184	Telephone (Won't You Ring)/Big Star	15
65	Fontana TF 592	My Prayer/Pretty Please	15

(see also Paul Peterson & Shelley Fabares)

FABIAN
59	HMV POP 587	I'm A Man/Hypnotized (78 rpm = £35)	38
59	HMV POP 612	Turn Me Loose/Stop Thief!	38
59	HMV POP 643	Tiger/Mighty Cold (To A Warm, Warm Heart)	25
59	HMV POP 659	Got The Feeling/Come On And Get Me	18
60	HMV POP 695	Hound Dog Man/This Friendly World	18
60	HMV POP 724	String Along/About This Thing Called Love	10
60	HMV POP 778	I'm Gonna Sit Right Down And Write Myself A Letter/Strollin' In The Springtime	12
60	HMV POP 800	Tomorrow/King Of Love	12
60	HMV POP 810	Kissin' And Twistin'/Long Before	12
61	HMV POP 829	You Know You Belong To Somebody Else/Hold On	10
61	HMV POP 869	Grapevine/David And Goliath	12
61	HMV POP 934	You're Only Young Once/The Love That I'm Giving To You	12
59	HMV CLP 1301	HOLD THAT TIGER (LP)	78
60	HMV CLP 1345	THE FABULOUS FABIAN (LP)	62
61	HMV CLP 1433	YOUNG AND WONDERFUL (LP, also stereo CSD 1352)	45/65

FABIAN (Jamaica)
78	Tribesman TM 08	Prophecy/JIMMY LINSAY : Easy (12")	55

FABIONS
69	Bullet BU 410	V. Rocket/Smile (B-side actually "My Baby" by Tennors)	15

FABLE
70	Penny Farthing PEN 725	Minstrel Song/She Said Yes	5
71	Penny Farthing PEN 751	With A Boy Like You/She Said Yes	5
74	Magnet MAG 5002	FABLE (LP)	15

(see also Trapeze)

FABULOUS COUNTS
71	Mojo 2092 021	Get Down People/Lunar Funk	15

FABULOUS DIALS
63	Pye International 7N 25200	Bossa Nova Stomp/Forget Me Not	30

FABULOUS FLAMES
70	Clandisc CLA 224	Holly Holy/LORD CREATOR: Kingston Town	12
71	Trojan TR 7822	Growing Up/Lovitis	6

(see also Dynamites)

FABULOUS IMPACT
90	Kent 6T 6	Baby Baby, I Want You/HAMPTONS: No No No No No No Not My Girl (100 Club 6Ts allnighter anniversary disc)	30

FABULOUS SHADES
71	Tropical AL 005	Lonely Man/Version 2	6

FABULOUS SWINGTONES
58	HMV POP 471	Geraldine/You Know Baby (78 rpm = £60)	400

FABULOUS TALBOT BROTHERS
50s	Melodisc M 1507	Bloodshot Eyes/She's Got Freckles (78 rpm = £12)	18

FACES
70	Warner Bros WB 8005	Flying/Three-Button Hand-Me-Down	10
70	Warner Bros WB 8014	Wicked Messenger/Nobody Knows (unissued)	
70	Warner Bros WB 8018	Had Me A Real Good Time/Rear Wheel Skid	10
73	Warner Bros K 16247	Cindy Incidentally/Skewiff (Mend The Fuse) (with lyric insert, no p/s)	10
73	Warner Bros K 16281	Borstal Boys (withdrawn, any pressed?)	20+
73	NME SF1 139	Dishevelment Blues/Ooh La La Preview (flexidisc free with NME)	15/8
74	Warner Bros K 16494	You Can Make Me Dance, Sing Or Anything/As Long As You Tell Him (credited to Rod Stewart and the Faces, p/s)	8

77	Riva RIVA 8	THE FACES (EP, p/s)	8
70	Warner Bros WS 3000	FIRST STEP (LP, orange label, gatefold sleeve)	28
71	Warner Bros WS 3011	LONG PLAYER (LP, blue & silver label, stitched die-cut '78rpm' style sleeve)	25
71	Warner Bros K 46053	FIRST STEP (LP, reissue, green label, gatefold sleeve)	20
71	Warner Bros K 56006	A NOD IS AS GOOD AS A WINK … TO A BLIND HORSE (LP, green label, with poster)	25/12
72	Warner Bros K 46064	LONG PLAYER (LP, reissue, blue & silver label, stitched die-cut '78rpm'-style sleeve)	20
73	Warner Bros K 56011	OOH-LA-LA (LP, green label, 'Faces' sleeve with lyric poster)	20
73	Warner Bros K 56172	SNAKES AND LADDERS: BEST OF (LP)	15
74	Warner Bros K 46053	FIRST STEP (LP, 2nd reissue, 'Burbank' label, gatefold sleeve)	15
74	Warner Bros K 56006	A NOD IS AS GOOD AS A WINK … TO A BLIND HORSE (LP, reissue, 'Burbank' label)	15
74	Warner Bros K 56011	OOH-LA-LA (LP, 'Burbank' label, 'Faces' sleeve, some with lyric poster)	18/12
75	Warner Bros K 66027	TWO ORIGINALS OF … (2-LP, reissue of First Steps & Long Player, gatefold sleeve)	20

(see also Small Faces, Rod Stewart, Ronnie Lane & Slim Chance, Ron Wood, Jeff Beck Group, Kenney Jones)

FACTION feat. PETE WYLIE
| 80s | Inevitable INEV 006 | FACTION (LP, some in plastic bag) | 15/12 |

FACTORY
68	MGM MGM 1444	Path Through The Forest/Gone	650
69	CBS 4540	Try A Little Sunshine/Red Chalk Hill	400
70	OAK RGJ718	Time Machine/Castle On The Hill (99 copies only)	300+

(see also Peter & Wolves, Norman Conquest, John Pantry, Velvet Hush)

FACTORY
| 82 | Future Earth FER 011 | You Are The Music/History Of The World (silver die-cut sleeve) | 20 |

FACTOTUMS
65	Immediate IM 009	In My Lonely Room/Run In The Green And Tangerine Flaked Forest	35
65	Immediate IM 022	You're So Good To Me/Can't Go Home Anymore My Love	30
66	Piccadilly 7N 35333	Here Today/In My Room	22
66	Piccadilly 7N 35355	I Can't Give You Anything But Love/Absolutely Sweet Marie	18
67	Pye 7N 17402	Cloudy/Easy Said, Easy Done	15
69	CBS 4140	Mr And Mrs Regards/Driftwood	12

FADELA
| 88 | Factory FAC 197 | N'sel Fik/Ateni Bniti (12") | 10 |

FADERS
| 79 | Rip Off RIP 8 | Cheatin'/Library Book (in bag p/s) | 50 |

FAD GADGET
| 81 | Lyntone LYN 10209 | King Of The Flies/DEPECHE MODE: Sometimes I Wish I Was Dead (red vinyl flexidisc free with *Flexipop* magazine, issue 11) | 25/10 |

FADING COLOURS
| 66 | Ember EMB S 229 | (Just Like) Romeo And Juliet/Billy Christian | 20 |
| 67 | Ember EMB S 237 | Be With Me/You're No Use | 7 |

(see also Orange Seaweed)

BRIAN FAHEY (& HIS ORCHESTRA)
59	Parlophone R 4655	Street Of A Thousand Bongos/Waltz For Beatniks	8
60	Parlophone R 4686	At The Sign Of The Swingin' Cymbal/The Clanger	18
62	Parlophone R 4909	At The Sign Of The Swingin' Cymbal/The Clanger (reissue, as Brian Faye & His Orchestra)	12
65	Parlophone R 5262	Gidian's Way/Love Theme From "In Harm's Way"	12
65	United Artists UP 1115	Twang You Can't Catch Me	15
67	Parlophone R 5615	The Plank/Stay On the Island	10
68	Columbia DB 8447	Late Night Extra/Oh The Pity Of It All	8
69	Major Minor MM 656	Open House/Countdown	15
67	Studio Two TWO 175	TIME FOR TV (LP)	25

JOHN FAHEY
67	Transatlantic TRA 173	THE TRANSFIGURATION OF BLIND JOE DEATH (LP, some with booklet)	25/15
68	Vanguard SVRL 19033	YELLOW PRINCESS (LP)	22
68	Vanguard SVRL 19055	REQUIA (LP)	22
69	Takoma SNTF 607	BLIND JOE DEATH (LP)	18
69	Takoma SNTF 608	DEATH CHANTS, WALTZES & MILITARY BREAKDOWNS) (LP)	18
72	Reprise K 44213	OF RIVERS AND RELIGION (LP)	15
73	Reprise K 44246	AFTER THE BALL (LP)	15
74	Takoma SNTF 675	JOHN FAHEY, PETER LANG AND LEO KOTTKE (LP)	15

(see also Leo Kottke)

JAD FAIR
| 80 | Armageddon AEP 003 | THE ZOMBIES OF MORA-TAU (EP, die-cut p/s with insert) | 15 |

(see also Half Japanese)

JAD FAIR & PASTELS
| 91 | Paperhouse PAPER 013T | THIS COULD BE THE NIGHT EP (12", p/s) | 12 |
| 92 | Paperhouse PAPER 018CD | HE CHOSE HIS COLOURS WELL (CD, EP) | 10 |

(see also Pastels)

WERLY FAIRBURN & DELTA BOYS
| 56 | London HLC 8349 | I'm A Fool About Your Love/All The Time (78 rpm = £150) | 1,000 |

JOHNNY FAIRE
| 58 | London HLU 8569 | Bertha Lou/Till The Law Says Stop (78 rpm = £100) | 600 |

FAIRFIELD PARLOUR
| 70 | Vertigo 6059 003 | Bordeaux Rosé/Chalk On The Wall | 22 |
| 70 | Vertigo 6059 008 | Just Another Day/Caraminda/I Am All The Animals/Song For You | 22 |

MINT VALUE £

| 76 | Prism PRI 1 | Bordeaux Rosé/Baby Stay For Tonight | 10 |
| 70 | Vertigo 6360 001 | FROM HOME TO HOME (LP, gatefold sleeve, swirl label) | 120 |

(see also Kaleidoscope [U.K.], I Luv Wight)

FAIRIES

64	Decca F 11943	Don't Think Twice, It's Alright/Anytime At All	110
65	HMV POP 1404	Get Yourself Home/I'll Dance	260
65	HMV POP 1445	Don't Mind/Baby Don't	120

(see also Twink, Cops 'N Robbers)

FAIRPORT CONVENTION
SINGLES

67	Track 604 020	If I Had A Ribbon Bow/If (Stomp)	60
68	Island WIP 6047	Meet On The Ledge/Throwaway Street Puzzle (pink label)	18
69	Island WIP 6064	Si Tu Dois Partir/Genesis Hall	6
70	Island WIP 6089	Now Be Thankful/Sir B. McKenzie's Daughter's Lament	10
70	Polydor 2058 014	If (Stomp)/Chelsea Morning	10
71	Island WIP 6128	John Lee/The Time Is Near (some in p/s)	12/6
73	Island WIP 6155	Rosie/Knights Of The Road	6
75	Island WIP 6241	White Dress/Tears (some in p/s)	12/6
78	Hawk HASP 423	Jam's O'Donnell's Jig/The Last Waltz (Irish-only)	15
79	Simons PMW 1	Rubber Band/The Bonny Black Hare	12
86	Sunrise Bong 1	Quazi B Goode/MIKE SILVER: Where Would You Rather Be Tonight	10
87	Island 12IF 324	Meet On The Ledge (Re-recorded)/John Barleycorn (live)/ Sigh Bheg Sigh Mhor (live) (12", p/s, some with poster)	10/8

POLYDOR LP

| 68 | Polydor 582/583 035 | FAIRPORT CONVENTION (mono/stereo) | 100/80 |

ISLAND LPs

69	Island ILPS 9092	WHAT WE DID ON OUR HOLIDAYS (1st pressing, pink label with black 'circle' logo; 2nd pressing, pink label with black 'block' logo)	70/50
69	Island ILPS 9092	WHAT WE DID ON OUR HOLIDAYS (3rd pressing, pink label with 'i' logo)	25
69	Island ILPS 9092	WHAT WE DID ON OUR HOLIDAYS (4th pressing, pink rim label with 'palm tree' logo)	12
69	Island ILPS 9102	UNHALFBRICKING (1st pressing, pink label with black 'circle' logo)	60
69	Island ILPS 9102	UNHALFBRICKING (2nd pressing, pink label with black 'block' logo)	35
69	Island ILPS 9102	UNHALFBRICKING (3rd pressing, pink label with 'i' logo)	25
70	Island ILPS 9102	UNHALFBRICKING (4th pressing, pink rim label with 'palm tree' logo)	12
69	Island ILPS 9115	LIEGE AND LIEF (gatefold sleeve, 1st pressing, pink label with 'i' logo)	25
70	Island ILPS 9115	LIEGE AND LIEF (gatefold sleeve, 2nd pressing, pink rim label with 'palm tree' logo)	15
70	Island ILPS 9130	FULL HOUSE (white label test pressing, with "Poor Will & The Jolly Hangman")	225+
70	Island ILPS 9130	FULL HOUSE (1st pressing, gatefold sleeve lists "Poor Will & The Jolly Hangman")	20
70	Island ILPS 9130	FULL HOUSE (2nd pressing, gatefold sleeve without reference to "Poor Will & The Jolly Hangman")	18
70	Island ILPS 9130	FULL HOUSE (gatefold sleeve, 3rd pressing, pink rim label with 'palm tree' logo)	15
71	Island ILPS 9162	ANGEL DELIGHT (gatefold sleeve with 'stuck-on' photos, pink rim label)	12
71	Island ILPS 9176	BABBACOMBE LEE (gatefold sleeve, with innersleeve and booklet, some with sticker)	35/18
72	Island ICD 4	THE HISTORY OF FAIRPORT CONVENTION (2-LP, with 12-page booklet & blue ribbons; later with book & green, red or light blue ribbons)	20/18
73	Island ILPS 9208	ROSIE	12
73	Island ILPS 9246	FAIRPORT NINE (gatefold sleeve)	12
74	Island ILPS 9285	LIVE CONVENTION (with insert)	12
75	Island ILPS 9313	RISING FOR THE MOON (with insert, 'palm tree' label)	12
75	Island ISS 2	FAIRPORT TOUR SAMPLER (free in *NME* competition, 500 only)	120
76	Island ILPS 9389	GOTTLE O' GEER	15
76	Island HELP 28	LIVE AT THE L.A. TROUBADOR 1974	15

OTHER LPs

77	Vertigo 9102 015	BONNY BUNCH OF ROSES (gatefold sleeve)	18
78	Vertigo 9102 022	TIPPLER'S TALES (with lyric insert)	15
79	Woodworm BEAR 22	FAREWELL FAREWELL (gatefold sleeve)	30
79	Simons GAMA 1	FAREWELL FAREWELL (reissue, gatefold sleeve)	20
82	Woodworm WR 001	MOAT ON THE LEDGE — LIVE 1981	12
83	Woodworm WRC 1	AT 2 (AIRING CUPBOARD TAPES 2) (cassette)	20
84	Woodworm (no cat. no.)	THE BOOT (2-cassette in video box, 1,000 only)	25
87	Woodworm (no cat. no.)	THE OTHER BOOT (2-cassette in video box, 1,000 only)	25
88	Woodworm (no cat. no.)	THE THIRD LEG (2-cassette in video box, 1,000 only)	25
89	BGO BGOCD 72	TIPPLER'S TALES (CD)	20
92	Vertigo 512882	BONNY BUNCH OF ROSES / TIPPLERS TALES (CD)	30

(see also Richard Thompson, Ian Matthews, Dave Swarbrick, Sandy Denny, Ashley Hutchings, Trevor Lucas,
Albion Band, Bunch, Fotheringay, Vashti Bunyan, Trader Horne, Thieves, Pyramid, Allan Taylor, Krysia,
Marc Ellington, Brian Maxine, Steeleye Span, Vikki Clayton)

FAIR WARNING

| 87 | Areba ERA 2 | ROCKING AT THE SPEED OF LIGHT EP (12", p/s) | 30 |

FAIRWAYS (featuring Gary Street)

| 69 | Mercury MF 1116 | Yoko Ono/I Don't Care | 12 |

FAIR WEATHER

70	RCA RCA 1977	Natural Sinner/Haven't I Tried?	6
70	RCA RCA 2040	Road To Freedom/Tutti Frutti	6
71	RCA Neon NE 1000	Lay It On Me/Looking For The Red Label Pt 2	12
71	RCA Neon NE 1	BEGINNING FROM AN END (LP)	25

(see also Andy Fairweather-Low, Amen Corner, Wynder K. Frog)

AL FAIRWEATHER
57	Columbia SEG 7653	AL FAIRWEATHER'S JAZZ BAND (EP)	8
58	Tempo EXA 63	AL FAIRWEATHER'S JAZZMEN (EP, with Henrick Johansen)	10
58	Nixa NJT 511	FAIRWEATHER FRIENDS (LP)	18
60	Columbia 33SX 1159	AL AND SANDY (LP)	18
60	Columbia 33SX 1221	AL'S PALS (LP)	18
61	Columbia 33SX 1306	DOCTOR McJAZZ (LP, also stereo SCX 3367, with Sandy Brown)	25
63	Columbia 33SX 1509	THE INCREDIBLE McJAZZ (LP, with Sandy Brown's All Stars)	20

(see also Sandy Brown, Henrik Johansen, Albert Nicholas)

ANDY FAIRWEATHER-LOW
76	A&M AMLH 64602	BE BOP'N'HOLLA (LP, blue vinyl)	12

(see also Amen Corner, Fair Weather, Gary Pickford-Hopkins & Friends, Dave Edmunds & Rockpile)

FAIRY'S MOKE
75	Deroy 1175	FAIRY'S MOKE (LP, private pressing, actually various artists LP)	75

(see also Baby Sunshine)

FAIRYTALE
67	Decca F 12644	Guess I Was Dreaming/Run And Hide	110
67	Decca F 12665	Lovely People/Listen To Mary Cry	90

ADAM FAITH (& ROULETTES)
SINGLES
58	HMV POP 438	(Got A) Heartsick Feeling/Brother Heartache And Sister Tears (78 rpm = £50)	130
58	HMV POP 557	High School Confidential/Country Music Holiday (78 rpm = £50)	130
59	Top Rank JAR 126	Ah, Poor Little Baby!/Runk Bunk (blue label) (78 rpm £50)	40
59	Parlophone R 4591	What Do You Want?/From Now Until Forever (78 rpm = £30)	6
60	Parlophone R 4665	Made You/When Johnny Comes Marching Home (78 rpm = £40)	6
62	Parlophone R 4864	Lonesome/Watch Your Step	5
62	Parlophone R 4964	Baby Take A Bow/Knocking On Wood	5
63	Parlophone R 4990	What Now/What Have I Got	5
63	Parlophone R 5039	Walkin' Tall/Just Mention My Name	5
63	Parlophone R 5091	We Are In Love/Made For Me (with Roulettes)	5
64	Parlophone R 5109	If He Tells You/Talk To Me	5
64	Parlophone R 5138	I Love Being In Love With You/It's Alright (with Roulettes)	5
64	Parlophone R 5174	I Just Don't Know/Only One Such As You	5
64	Parlophone R 5201	A Message To Martha (Kentucky Bluebird)/It Sounds Good To Me	5
65	Parlophone R 5235	Stop Feeling Sorry For Yourself/I've Gotta See My Baby	5
65	Parlophone R 5260	Hand Me Down Things/Talk About Love	5
65	Parlophone R 5289	Someone's Taken Maria Away/I Can't Think Of Anyone Else (with Roulettes)	7
65	Parlophone R 5349	I Don't Need That Kind Of Lovin'/I'm Used To Losing You	7
66	Parlophone R 5398	Idle Gossip/If You Ever Need Me	5
66	Parlophone R 5412	To Make A Big Man Cry/Here's Another Day	5
66	Parlophone R 5516	Cheryl's Goin' Home/Funny Kind Of Love	7
67	Parlophone R 5556	What More Can Anyone Do/You've Got A Way With Me	7
67	Parlophone R 5635	Cowman Milk Your Cow/Daddy, What'll Happen To Me	7
67	Parlophone R 5649	To Hell With Love/Close The Door	7
68	Parlophone R 5673	You Make My Life Worth While/Hey Little Lovin' Girl	7

EPs
60	Parlophone GEP 8811	ADAM'S HIT PARADE	10
60	Parlophone GEP 8824	ADAM NO. 1 (also stereo SGE 2014)	10/18
60	Parlophone GEP 8826	ADAM NO. 2 (also stereo SGE 2015)	10/18
60	Parlophone GEP 8831	ADAM NO. 3 (also stereo SGE 2018)	10/18
61	Parlophone GEP 8841	ADAM'S HIT PARADE VOL. 2	12
62	Parlophone GEP 8851	ADAM FAITH NO. 1	16
62	Parlophone GEP 8852	ADAM FAITH NO. 2	16
62	Parlophone GEP 8854	ADAM FAITH NO. 3 (with John Barry)	16
62	Columbia SEG 8138	BEAT GIRL (2 Faith tracks, with John Barry Orchestra)	38
62	Parlophone GEP 8862	ADAM'S HIT PARADE VOL. 3	16
63	Parlophone GEP 8877	ADAM'S LATEST HITS	16
64	Parlophone GEP 8893	TOP OF THE POPS (with Roulettes)	20
64	Parlophone GEP 8904	FOR YOU — ADAM	14
65	Parlophone GEP 8929	A MESSAGE TO MARTHA — FROM ADAM	15
65	Parlophone GEP 8939	SONGS AND THINGS	15

LPs
60	Columbia 33SX 1225	BEAT GIRL (soundtrack, with John Barry Orchestra)	60
60	Parlophone PMC 1128	ADAM (also stereo PCS 3010)	18/25
61	Parlophone PMC 1162	ADAM FAITH (also stereo PCS 3025)	18/25
62	Parlophone PMC 1192	FROM ADAM WITH LOVE (also stereo PCS 3038)	15/20
63	Parlophone PMC 1213	FOR YOU — ADAM (also stereo)	18/25
64	Parlophone PMC 1228	ON THE MOVE (with Roulettes)	38
65	Parlophone PMC 1249	FAITH ALIVE! (with Roulettes)	50
60	EMI Regal (S)REG 1033	ADAM (mono/stereo export issue in different sleeve)	15

(see also Roulettes, John Barry)

AUSTIN FAITH
71	Dynamic DYN 407	634 5789/DYNAMIC BOYS: Warm And Tender Love	7

(see also Austin Faithful)

GEORGE FAITH
77	Island IPR 2034	Diana/To Be A Lover (12")	15
79	Warrior WAR 134	Don't Be Afraid/BUNNY SCOTT : What's The Use/Never Had It So Good (act. Jimmy Riley) (12")	10
77	Black Swan ILPS 9504	TO BE A LOVER (LP)	30

HORACE FAITH
69	B&C CB 104	Spinning Wheel/Like I Used To Do	9
69	Downtown DT 446	Daddy's Home/EMOTIONS: Give Me A Love	8

MINT VALUE £

70	Trojan TR 7766	Susie Is Sorrow/DERRICK PEPPER: Don't Go	8
70	Trojan TR 7790	Black Pearl/Help Me Help Myself	6
70	A&M AMS 817	Shame And Scandal In The Family/REGGAE STRINGS: Reggae Strings	6

PERCY FAITH ORCHESTRA
60	Philips PB 989	Theme From 'A Summer Place'/Go-Go-Po-Go	5
64	CBS AAG 226	The Virginian/Judy	5
59	Philips BBE 12397	FAMOUS FILM THEMES (EP)	5
66	CBS 62663	THEMES FOR THE IN CROWD (LP)	15
66	CBS SS 62779	BIG BAM BOOM!!! (LP)	14

AUSTIN FAITHFUL
68	Blue Cat BS 140	Uncle Joe/Can't Understand	20
68	Pyramid PYR 6016	I'm In A Rocking Mood/ROLAND ALPHONSO: Stream Of Life	18
69	Pyramid PYR 6028	Eternal Love/ROLAND ALPHONSO: Goodnight My Love	18
69	Pyramid PYR 6042	Ain't That Peculiar?/Miss Anti-Social	15

(see also Austin Faith)

MARIANNE FAITHFULL
64	Decca F 11923	As Tears Go By/Greensleeves	7
64	Decca F 12007	Blowin' In The Wind/The House Of The Rising Sun	8
65	Decca F 12075	Come And Stay With Me/What Have I Done Wrong?	8
65	Decca F 12162	This Little Bird/Morning Sun	6
65	Decca F 12193	Summer Nights/The Sha La La Song	7
65	Decca F 12268	Yesterday/Oh Look Around You	7
66	Decca F 12408	Tomorrow's Calling/That's Right Baby	7
66	Decca F 12443	Counting/I'd Like To Dial Your Number	12
66	Decca F 22524	Is This What I Get For Loving You?/Tomorrow's Calling	12
69	Decca F 12889	Something Better/Sister Morphine (withdrawn)	55+
75	NEMS NES 004	Dreamin' My Dreams/Lady Madalene	6
76	NEMS NES 013	All I Wanna Do In Life/Wrong Road Again	6
77	NEMS NES 014	Wrong Road Again/The Way You Want Me To Be	6
78	NEMS NES 117	The Way You Want Me To Be/That Was The Day (Nashville)	6
79	Island WIP 6491	The Ballad Of Lucy Jordan/Brain Drain	6
80	Island 12WIP 6542	Broken English/Why D'Ya Do It? (12", p/s)	10
80	Decca F 13890	As Tears Go By/Come And Stay With Me/This Little Bird/Summer Nights (p/s)	6
65	Decca DFE 8624	GO AWAY FROM MY WORLD (EP)	40
65	Decca LK 4688	COME MY WAY (LP)	55
65	Decca LK 4689	MARIANNE FAITHFULL (LP)	58
66	Decca LK 4778	NORTH COUNTRY MAID (LP)	60
67	Decca LK/SKL 4854	LOVEINAMIST (LP)	80
69	Decca (S)PA 17	THE WORLD OF MARIANNE FAITHFULL (LP)	15
76	NEMS NEL 6007	DREAMIN' MY DREAMS (LP)	15

FAITH, HOPE & CHARITY
| 70 | Crewe CRW 3 | So Much Love/Life Won't Be The Same Without You | 8 |
| 70 | Crewe CRW 3 | So Much Love/Let's Try It Over | 8 |

FAITH NO MORE
88	Slash LASH 17	We Care A Lot/Spirit (p/s)	6
88	Slash LASHX 17	We Care A Lot/Spirit/Chinese Arithmetic (Radio Mix) (12", p/s)	8
88	Slash LASH 18	Annie's Song (Remix)/Greed (p/s)	10
88	Slash LASHP 18	Annie's Song (Remix)/Greed (picture disc)	10
88	Slash LASHX 18	Anne's Song (Remix)/Greed (12", p/s)	12
89	Kerrang! FIEND 3	Sweet Emotion/(Balaam & The Angel track) (flexidisc with *Kerrang!*)	10/6
90	Slash LASPD 21	Epic/War Pigs (live) (shaped picture disc)	8
90	Slash LASCD 21	Epic/War Pigs (live)/Surprise You're Dead (live)/Chinese Arithmetic (live) (CD, card sleeve)	10
90	Slash LASCD 24	From Out Of Nowhere/Woodpecker From Mars (live)/The Real Thing (live)/Epic (live) (CD, card sleeve)	8
90	Slash LASPD 26	Epic/Falling To Pieces (live) (shaped picture disc, 12" insert in PVC sleeve)	6
90	Slash LASPD 26	Epic/Falling To Pieces (live)/Epic (live)/As The Worm Turns (live) (CD)	8
90	London/Slash 850 228	KING FOR A DAY, FOOL FOR A LIFETIME (7 x 7" box set)	30
89	Slash 828 217-1	THE REAL THING (LP, picture disc)	18

FAKES
| 79 | Deep Cuts DEEP TWO | Production/Look-Out (p/s) | 5 |

TAV FALCO'S PANTHER BURNS
(see under Panther Burns)

EDDIE FALCON
| 60 | Columbia DB 4420 | The Young Have No Time To Lose/My Thanks To You | 8 |
| 61 | Columbia DB 4646 | Linda Rose/If Ever I Should Fall In Love | 8 |

FALCONS (U.K.)
| 64 | Philips BF 1297 | Stampede/Kazutzka | 18 |

FALCONS (U.S.)
| 59 | London HLT 8876 | You're So Fine/Goddess Of Angels (78 rpm = £70) | 140 |
| 62 | London HLK 9565 | I Found A Love/Swim (some labels credit B-side as "Swin") | 60 |

(see also Wilson Pickett, Eddie Floyd)

THE FALL
78	Step Forward SF 7	BINGO-MASTERS' BREAKOUT! (EP)	10
78	Step Forward SF 9	It's The New Thing/Various Times (p/s)	8
79	Step Forward SF 11	Rowche Rumble/In My Area (p/s)	6
80	Step Forward SF 13	Fiery Jack/Second Dark Age/Psykick Dancehall 2 (black-and-white or yellow p/s)	10/8
80	Rough Trade RT 048	How I Wrote Elastic Man/City Hobgoblins (p/s)	6
80	Rough Trade RT 056	Totally Wired/Putta Block (p/s)	8

81	Rough Trade RT 071	SLATES (10" EP, 33rpm)	10
81	Kamera ERA 001	Lie Dream Of A Casino Soul/Fantastic Life (p/s)	5
82	Kamera ERA 004	Look, Know/I'm Into C.B. (p/s)	6
82	Rough Trade RT 133	The Man Whose Head Expanded/Ludd Gang (p/s)	6
82	Kamera ERA 014	Marquis Cha Cha/Papal Visit (p/s, B-side plays "Room To Live", withdrawn)	30
83	Rough Trade RT 143	Kicker Conspiracy/Wings//Container Drivers/New Puritan (g/fold double pack)	10
84	Beggars Banquet BEG 116	C.R.E.E.P/Pat-Trip Dispenser (p/s)	10
84	Beggars Banquet BEG 116T	C.R.E.E.P/(Extended Version)/Pat-Trip Dispenser (12", p/s, green vinyl)	10
84	B. Banquet BEG 116TP	C.R.E.E.P/(Extended Version)/Pat-Trip Dispenser (12", p/s, with art print)	8
84	Beggars Banquet BEG 120E	CALL FOR ESCAPE ROUTE (7"/12" double pack EP)	8
85	Beggars Banquet BEG 150	Cruiser's Creek (p/s)	6
85	Beggars Banquet BEG 150T	Cruiser's Creek (12", p/s)	8
87	Beggars Banquet BEG 187H	There's A Ghost In My House/Haf Found Bormann (hologram p/s)	5
87	Beggars Banquet BEG 200P	Hit The North (Parts 1 & 2) (picture disc, printed PVC sleeve)	5
87	Beggars Banquet BEG 200T	Hit The North (Parts 1 & 2) (12", gatefold sleeve)	8
87	Beggars Banquet BEG 206B	Victoria/Tuff Life Boogie (box set with inserts & badge)	5
88	Beggars Banquet FALL 2B	Jerusalem (Remix)/Acid Priest 2088 (Remix)//Big New Prinz (Remix)/ Wrong Place Right Time No. 2 (Remix) (double pack box set, with postcard)	5
88	Beggars Banquet FALL 2CD	Jerusalem (Remix)/Acid Priest 2088 (Remix)//Big New Prinz (Remix)/ Wrong Place, Right Time No. 2 (Remix) (3" CD, double pack, gatefold wallet, 4,000 only)	10
90	Cog Sinister SINR 5	Popcorn Double Feature/Zandra (p/s)	6
94	Permanent 10SPERM 14	15 Ways (10", p/s)	10
79	Step Forward SFLP 1	LIVE AT THE WITCH TRIALS (LP)	12
79	Step Forward SFLP 4	DRAGNET (LP, with insert)	15
80	Rough Trade ROUGH 10	TOTALE'S TURNS (IT'S NOW OR NEVER) (LP)	15
80	Rough Trade ROUGH 18	GROTESQUE (AFTER THE GRAMME) (LP)	14
81	Step Forward SFLP 6	THE EARLY YEARS 1977-79 (LP)	15
82	Kamera KAM 005	HEX ENDUCTION HOUR (LP)	12
83	Rough Trade 062	PERVERTED BY LANGUAGE (LP)	15

(see also D.O.S.E.)

FALLEN ANGELS (U.K.)

| 84 | Fallout FALL 12 027 | INNER PLANET LOVE (mini-LP) | 10 |

(see also Knox, Hanoi Rocks, Troops Of Tomorrow)

FALLEN ANGELS (U.S.)

| 67 | London HL 10166 | I Don't Want To Fall/Most Children Do | 7 |
| 68 | London HA-Z/SH-Z 8359 | THE FALLEN ANGELS (LP) | 28 |

JOHNNY FALLIN

| 59 | Capitol CL 15043 | Party Kiss/The Creation Of Love | 45 |
| 59 | Capitol CL 15091 | Wild Streak/If I Could Write A Love Song | 50 |

FALLING LEAVES

| 65 | Parlophone R 5233 | She Loves To Be Loved/Not Guilty | 65+ |
| 66 | Decca F 12420 | Beggar's Parade/Tomorrow Night | 40+ |

FALLOUT

| 83 | Mouth Too Small To F. F2 | SALAMI TACTICS (EP) | 5 |
| 84 | I FLP 2 | BUTCHERY (10" EP, with lyric inner) | 8 |

FALLOUT CLUB

| 79 | Secret SHH104 | The Falling Years/The Beat Boys (p/s) | 14 |
| 81 | Happy Birthday UR3 | Dream Soldiers/Pedestrial Walk Way (p/s) | 14 |

FALSE IDOLS

| 78 | Old Knew Wave BOG 005 | Broken Judy/Marbled Hands/H-Brain (tri-fold p/s) | 5 |
| 78 | Old Knew Wave BOG 007 | Ego Wino/Good Night (p/s, pink vinyl) | 5 |

AGNETHA FALTSKOG

82	Epic EPC A 2824	Never Again/Just For The Fun (p/s, with Tomas Ledin)	12
83	Epic EPC A 3436	The Heat Is On/Man (p/s)	8
83	Epic EPC WA 3436	The Heat Is On/Man (picture disc)	30
83	Epic EPC A 3622	Wrap Your Arms Around Me/Take Good Care Of The Children (p/s)	8
83	Epic EPC TA 3622	Wrap Your Arms Around Me/The Heat Is On/ Take Good Care Of The Children (Extended) (12", p/s)	15
83	Epic EPC A 3812	Can't Shake Loose/To Love (p/s)	8
83	Epic EPC A 3812	Can't Shake Loose/To Love (poster p/s)	15
83	Epic EPC WA 3812	Can't Shake Loose/To Love (picture disc)	25
85	Epic EPC A 6133	I Won't Let You Go/You're There (p/s)	8
85	Epic EPC TA 6133	I Won't Let You Go (Extended)/You're There (12", p/s)	15
86	Sonet SON 2317	The Way You Are/Fly Like The Eagle (p/s, with Ola Hanansson)	10
88	WEA YZ 170	The Last Time/Are You Gonna Throw It All Away (p/s)	8
88	WEA YZ 170T	The Last Time (Extended Remix)/The Last Time/ Are You Gonna Throw It All Away (12", p/s)	15
88	WEA YZ 177	I Wasn't The One (Who Said Goodbye)/If You Need Somebody Tonight (p/s, with Peter Cetera)	8
88	WEA YZ 177T	I Wasn't The One (Who Said Goodbye) (Extended Version)/(Yo No Fui [Quien Dijo Adios])/If You Need Somebody Tonight (12", p/s, with Peter Cetera)	15
88	WEA YZ 300	Let It Shine/Maybe It Was Magic (p/s)	8
88	WEA YZ 300T	Let It Shine (Extended)/('Bright' Mix)/Maybe It Was Magic (12", p/s)	15
98	Polydor POLPROCD 2	The Queen Of Hearts (Nar Du Tar Mej I Din Fam) (CD, promo only)	20
74	Embassy EMB 31094	AGNETHA (LP)	80

(see also Abba)

MINT VALUE £

GEORGIE FAME (& THE BLUE FLAMES)

SINGLES

64	Columbia DB 7193	Do The Dog/Shop Around	22
64	Columbia DB 7255	Green Onions/Do-Re-Mi	15
64	Columbia DB 7328	Bend A Little/I'm In Love With You (solo)	22
64	Columbia DB 7428	Yeh Yeh/Preach And Teach (some copies list "Yeah, Yeah" on label)	10
64	Columbia DB 7428	Yeh Yeh/Preach And Teach (99 promo copies only with p/s)	65+
65	Columbia DB 7494	In The Meantime/Telegram	12
65	Columbia DB 7633	Like We Used To Be/It Ain't Right	12
65	Columbia DB 7727	Something/Outrage	10
66	Columbia DB 7946	Getaway/El Bandido	10

(All the above singles credited to Georgie Fame & Blue Flames unless stated; the singles listed below were solo.)

66	Columbia DB 8015	Sunny/Don't Make Promises	7
66	Columbia DB 8096	Sitting In The Park/Many Happy Returns	7
67	CBS 202587	Because I Love You/Bidin' My Time (p/s)	7
67	CBS 2945	Try My World/No Thanks (p/s)	7
67	CBS 3124	The Ballad Of Bonnie And Clyde/Beware Of The Dog (p/s)	7
69	CBS 4295	Peaceful/Hideaway (with John Barry)	6
69	CBS 4659	Seventh Son/Fully Booked	6
70	CBS 5035	Entertaining Mr. Sloane/Somebody Stole My Thunder	75
70	CBS 5131	Fire And Rain/Someday Man	5

EPs

64	Columbia SEG 8334	RHYTHM AND BLUEBEAT	50
64	Columbia SEG 8382	RHYTHM AND BLUES AT THE FLAMINGO	35
64	Columbia SEG 8393	FAME AT LAST	28
65	Columbia SEG 8406	FATS FOR FAME	32
65	Columbia SEG 8454	MOVE IT ON OVER	32
66	Columbia SEG 8518	GETAWAY	28
67	CBS EP 6363	KNOCK ON WOOD	28

LPs

64	Columbia 33SX 1599	RHYTHM AND BLUES AT THE FLAMINGO	100
64	Columbia 33SX 1638	FAME AT LAST	30
66	Columbia SX 6043	SWEET THINGS	30
66	Columbia SX 6076	SOUND VENTURE	30
67	Columbia SX 6120	HALL OF FAME	20
67	CBS (S)BPG 63018	TWO FACES OF FAME	30
68	CBS (S) 63293	THE THIRD FACE OF FAME (mono/stereo)	15
69	CBS (S) 63650	GEORGIE DOES HIS OWN THING WITH STRINGS (mono/stereo)	15
69	CBS S 63786	SEVENTH SON	15
71	CBS S 64350	GOING HOME	15
72	Reprise K 44183	ALL ME OWN WORK.	20
74	Island ILPS 9293	GEORGIE FAME	25

(see also Blue Flames, Jimmy Nicol, Perry Ford & Sapphires)

FAMILY

67	Liberty LBF 15031	Scene Thru The Eye Of A Lens/Gypsy Woman (mispress, B-side plays Let Me Be Good To You by Otis Redding)	80
67	Liberty LBF 15031	Scene Thru The Eye Of A Lens/Gypsy Woman	200
68	Reprise RS 23270	Me My Friend/Hey Mr. Policeman	15
68	Reprise RS 23315	Second Generation Woman/Home Town	15
69	Reprise RS 27001	No Mule's Fool/Good Friend Of Mine (initially in p/s)	15/5
70	Reprise RS 27005	Today/Song For Lots (initially in p/s)	15/5
70	Reprise RS 27009	The Weaver's Answer/Strange Band/Hung Up Down (in p/s)	5
71	Reprise K 14090	In My Own Time/Seasons (in p/s)	5
71	Reprise SAM 1	Larf And Sing/Children (promo only)	15
73	Raft RA 18501	Boom Bang/Stop This Car	7
73	Raft RA 18503	Sweet Desiree/Drink To You.	7
68	Reprise R(S)LP 6312	MUSIC IN A DOLL'S HOUSE (LP, with insert, mono/stereo)	80/40
69	Reprise RLP 6340	FAMILY ENTERTAINMENT (LP, mono, with poster)	45
69	Reprise RSLP 6340	FAMILY ENTERTAINMENT (LP, stereo, with poster)	50
70	Reprise RSLP 9001	A SONG FOR ME (LP, with lyric sheet, later copies without boat label £15)	25

(The above LPs were originally issued with 'steamboat' label designs, later pressings with same cat. no. are worth £2 less.)

70	Reprise RSX 9005	ANYWAY (LP, custom polythene sleeve)	18
71	Reprise RMP 9007	OLD SONGS NEW SONGS (LP)	15
71	Reprise K 54003	FEARLESS (LP)	15
72	Reprise K 54006	BANDSTAND (LP, 'window' sleeve)	15

(see also Farinas, Stud, Mogul Thrash, Hellions, Ashton Gardner & Dyke, Revolution, Streetwalkers)·

FAMILY CAT

89	Bad Girl BGRIFC 01	Tom Verlaine (Demo Version) (gig freebie flexidisc, hand-sprayed p/s & insert)	5
91	Bad Girl BGRLT 009T	Color Me Grey/I Must Have Been Blind/Great Ugly Place (12", p/s)	8

(see also P.J. Harvey)

FAMILY CIRCLE

69	Attack AT 8001	Phoenix Reggae/BIG L: Music Box	8

FAMILY DOGG

67	MGM MGM 1360	Family Dogg/The Storm	10
68	Fontana TF 921	I Wear A Silly Grin/Couldn't Help It	12
68	Fontana TF 968	Brown-Eyed Girl/Let It Rain	7
69	Bell SBLL 122	A WAY OF LIFE (LP, with members of Led Zeppelin)	25

(see also Steve Rowland, Christine Holmes)

FAMILY FODDER

79	Parole/Fresh PURL 4	Playing Golf/My Baby Takes Valium (p/s)	5

FAMILY MAN (Aston Barrett)
70	Escort ERT 834	Midnight Sunshine/GREGORY & STICKY: You Are My Sunshine	8
72	Downtown DT 491	Herb Tree/STUDIO SOUND: Holy Poly (reissue)	8

(see also Hippy Boys, Upsetters, Bob Marley & Wailers, Carl Dawkins)

FAMILY PLANN
75	President PT 441	Sexy Summer/Can You Get Into The Music	5

FAMILY QUEST
84	Jungle Rhythm SWE-T2	Outerspace 84 Rap	20
86	Streetwave MKHAN74	Sleepwalking (12")	8

FAMOUS ECCLES & MISS FREDA THING
56	Parlophone R 4251	My September Love/JIM MORIARTY: You Gotta Go Oww!	20

(see also Spike Milligan, Goons)

FAMOUS JUG BAND
69	Liberty LBF 15224	The Only Friend I Own/A Leaf Must Fall	10
69	Liberty LBS 83263	SUNSHINE POSSIBILITIES (LP)	38
70	Liberty LBS 83355	CHAMELEON (LP)	35

(see also Incredible String Band, C.O.B.)

FAMOUS MUSIC BAND
69	Philips 6006 111	Nine By Nine/Going In The Out (with John Dummer)	8

(see also John Dummer)

FANATICS
89	Chapter 22 12 CHAP 38	SUBURBAN LOVE SONGS (12" EP)	20

(see also Ocean Colour Scene)

FAN-CLUB
78	M&S SJP 791B	Avenue/Night Caller (p/s, photocopied insert)	15

(see also Transvision Vamp)

FANCY
73	Atlantic K 10383	Wild Thing/Fancy (with p/s)	5
76	Arista ARIST 32	Music Maker/Bluebird	8

(see also Ray Fenwick, Judas Priest)

FANDANGO
(see Nic Simper's Fandango, under 'S')

FANNY
70	Reprise RSLP 6416	FANNY (LP)	15
72	Reprise K 44144	CHARITY BALL (LP)	15

FANS
79	Fried Egg EGG 3	Giving Me That Look in Your Eyes/Stay The Night/He'll Have To Go (p/s)	45
79	Albion ION 0004	True (dayglo inner, inc bonus 7" & lyric sheet)	20
80	Albion FAN 01	Cars And Explosions/Dangerous Goodbyes (p/s)	20
81	Fried Egg EGG 10	You Don't Live Here Anymore/Following You (p/s)	30

FANTASIA
67	Stateside SS 2031	Gotta Get Away/She Needs My Love	7

FANTASTIC BAGGYS
76	United Artists UP 36142	Summer Means Fun/JAN & DEAN: Surf City/Sidewalk Surfin'	12

(see also Jan & Dean, Bruce Johnston)

FANTASTIC FOUR
68	Tamla Motown TMG 678	I Love You Madly/I Love You Madly (Instrumental)	25
69	T. Motown (S)TML 11105	THE FANTASTIC FOUR (LP)	60

FANTASTIC JOHNNY C
(see under 'C')

FANTASTICS
68	MGM MGM 1434	Baby Make Your Own Sweet Music/Who Could Be Lovin' You	20
68	MGM MGM 1434DJ	Baby Make Your Own Sweet Music/ Who Could Be Lovin' You (DJ promo)	30
69	Deram DM 264	Face To Face With Heartache/This Must Be My Rainy Day	6
70	Deram DM 283	Waiting Round For Heartaches/Ask The Lonely	6
71	Deram DM 334	For Old Times Sake/Exodus Main Theme	6
71	Mojo 2027 004	Baby Make Your Own Sweet Music/Who Could Be Lovin' You? (reissue)	6

(see also Velours)

FANTASY
73	Polydor 2058 405	Politely Insane/I Was Once Aware	35
73	Polydor 2383 246	PAINT A PICTURE (LP, gatefold sleeve)	250

BARRY FANTONI
66	Fontana TF 707	Little Man In A Little Box/Fat Man	25
67	Columbia DB 8238	Nothing Today/The Spanish Lady Tango	7

FAPARDOKLY
83	Psycho PSYCHO 5	FAPARDOKLY (LP, 300 only)	15

(see also Mu)

FARAWAY FOLK
70s	Tabitha TAB 3	Shadow Of A Pie/Folsom Prison Blues/Rent A Man/Soulful Shade Of Blue	12
70s	RA EP 7001	INTRODUCING THE FARAWAY FOLK (EP)	30
70s	RA LP 6006ST	LIVE AT THE BOLTON (LP)	35
72	RA LP 6012ST	TIME AND TIDE (LP)	40
73	RA LP 6019	ON THE RADIO (LP)	30
74	RA LP 6022	ONLY AUTHORISED EMPLOYEES TO BREAK BOTTLES (LP, with Harry H. Corbett)	30

75	RA LP 6029	SEASONAL MAN (LP, gatefold sleeve with insert)	110
80s	RA	BATTLE OF THE DRAGONS (cassette)	15

(see also Harry H. Corbett)

FAR CRY
69	Vanguard SVRL 19041	THE FAR CRY (LP)	25

DON FARDON
67	Pye International 7N 25437	(The Lament Of The Cherokee) Indian Reservation/Dreamin' Room	10
68	Pye International 7N 25475	(The Lament Of The Cherokee) Indian Reservation/Dreamin' Room (reissue)	6
69	Pye International 7N 25483	We Can Make It Together/Coming On Strong	6
69	Pye International 7N 25486	Good Lovin'/Ruby's Pictures On My Wall	6
69	Youngblood YB 1003	I'm Alive/Keep On Loving Me	40
69	Young Blood YB 1007	It's Been Nice Loving You/Let The Love Live	7
70	Young Blood YB 1010	Belfast Boy/Echoes Of The Cheers	30
71	Young Blood YB 1013	Delta Queen/Hometown Baby	5
71	Young Blood YB 1021	Girl/Sandiago	5
71	Young Blood YB 1027	Follow Your Drum/Get Away John	5
70	Young Blood SYB 4	I'VE PAID MY DUES! (LP)	20
70	Young Blood SSYB 13	RELEASED (LP)	18

(see also Sorrows)

FAR EAST FAMILY BAND
75	Vertigo 6370 850	NIPPONJIN (LP)	20

DICK FARINA & ERIC VON SCHMIDT
63	Folklore F-LEUT/7	DICK FARINA & ERIC VON SCHMIDT (LP, featuring 'Blind Boy Grunt')	80

(see also Bob Dylan, Richard & Mimi Farina)

RICHARD & MIMI FARINA
65	Fontana STFL 6060	CELEBRATIONS FOR A GREY DAY (LP)	15
65	Fontana STFL 6075	REFLECTIONS IN A CRYSTAL WIND (LP)	15
73	Vanguard VSD 21/22	THE BEST OF RICHARD & MIMI FARINA (2-LP)	15

(see also Dick Farina & Eric Von Schmidt)

FARINAS
64	Victor Buckland Sound Studio	Bye Bye Johnny/All You Gotta Do/Twist And Shout (as James King & Farinas)	500+
64	Fontana TF 493	You'd Better Stop/I Like It Like That	75+

(see also Family)

CHRIS FARLOWE (& THUNDERBIRDS)
62	Decca F 11536	Air Travel/Why Did You Break My Heart?	60
63	Columbia DB 7120	I Remember/Push Push (as Chris Farlowe & Thunderbirds)	30
64	Columbia DB 7237	Girl Trouble/Itty Bitty Pieces (as Chris Farlowe & Thunderbirds)	30
64	Columbia DB 7311	Just A Dream/What You Gonna Do? (as Chris Farlow & Thunderbirds)	28
64	Columbia DB 7379	Hey, Hey, Hey/Hound Dog (as Chris Farlow & Thunderbirds)	20
65	Columbia DB 7614	Buzz With The Fuzz/You're The One (withdrawn, as Chris Farlow & Thunderbirds, demos more common £105)	200
65	Immediate IM 016	The Fool/Treat Her Good	15
66	Immediate IM 023	Don't Just Look At Me/Think	22
66	Immediate IM 035	Out Of Time/Baby Make It Soon	10
66	Columbia DB 7983	Just A Dream/Hey, Hey, Hey	15
66	Immediate IM 038	Ride On Baby/Headlines	15
67	Immediate IM 041	My Way Of Giving/You're So Good To Me	15
67	Immediate IM 049	Yesterday's Papers/Life Is But Nothing	8
67	Immediate IM 056	Moanin'/What Have I Been Doin'?	8
67	Immediate IM 065	Handbags And Gladrags/Everyone Makes A Mistake	10
68	Immediate IM 066	The Last Goodbye/Paperman Fly In The Sky (B-side with Thunderbirds)	12
68	Immediate IM 071	Paint It Black/I Just Need Your Lovin'	12
69	Immediate IM 074	Dawn/April Was The Month	12
70	Polydor 2066 017	Black Sheep/Fifty Years	6
70	Polydor 2066 046	Put Out The Light/Questions (as Chris Farlowe & Hill)	5
75	Polydor 2066 650	We Can Work It Out/Only Women Bleed	5
78	Beeb BEEB 022	Gangsters (as Chris Farlowe & Dave Greenslade)/DAVE GREENSLADE'S GANGSTERS: Sarah Gant Theme	6
65	Decca DFE 8665	CHRIS FARLOWE (EP)	100
65	Immediate IMEP 001	FARLOWE IN THE MIDNIGHT HOUR (EP)	50
66	Immediate IMEP 004	CHRIS FARLOWE HITS (EP)	40
66	Island IEP 709	STORMY MONDAY (EP)	140
66	Columbia SX 6034	CHRIS FARLOWE AND THE THUNDERBIRDS (LP)	150
66	Immediate IMLP 005	14 THINGS TO THINK ABOUT (LP)	60
66	Immediate IMLP 006	THE ART OF CHRIS FARLOWE (LP)	60
67	EMI Regal REG 2025	CHRIS FARLOWE (LP, export issue)	35
68	Immediate IMLP/IMCP 010	THE BEST OF CHRIS FARLOWE VOLUME ONE (LP)	25
69	Immediate IMLP 021	THE LAST GOODBYE (LP)	70
70	Polydor 2425 029	FROM HERE TO MAMA ROSA (LP, as Chris Farlowe & Hill)	20
75	Polydor 2469 259	THE CHRIS FARLOWE BAND LIVE (LP)	15

(see also Thunderbirds, Beazers, Little Joe Cook, Crane/Farlowe, Atomic Rooster, Colosseum, Dave Greenslade, Spectrum)

ART FARMER
56	Vogue EPV 1045	ART FARMER (EP, as Art Farmer New Jazz All Stars)	8
54	Esquire 20-033	ART FARMER SEXTET — WORK OF ART (10" LP)	18
55	Esquire 32-037	MUSIC FOR THAT WILD PARTY (LP)	15
56	Esquire 32-072	TWO TRUMPETS (LP, with Donald Byrd)	15
59	London SAH-T 6028	MODERN ART (LP)	15

60	London Jazz LTZ-T 15184	BRASS SHOUT (LP)	15
60	London Jazz LTZ-T 15198	THE AZTEC SUITE (LP)	15
61	Esquire 32-120	EARTHY (LP)	15
64	London HA-K/SH-K 8135	INTERACTION (LP, as Art Farmer Quartet featuring Jim Hall)	15

(see also Clifford Brown, Benny Golson, Donald Byrd)

JULES FARMER
59	London HLP 8967	Love Me Now/Part Of Me (Is Still With You) (78 rpm = £10)	15

MYLENE FARMER
89	Polydor 080 360-2	Ainsi Soit Je. . . (Maxi Remix)/Ainsi Soit Je. . . (Lamentations)/	
		Ainsi Soit Je. . . (Classic Bonus Beats) (CD Video, export only)	45

FARMLIFE
82	Dining Out TUX 19	Susie's Party/Simple Men	6
83	Whaam! WHAAM 13	Big Country 1 & 2 (unreleased; Echantillan test pressings only)	40

GILES FARNABY'S DREAM BAND
73	Argo AFW 112	Newcastle Brown/29th Of May	12
73	Argo ZDA 158	GILES FARNABY'S DREAM BAND (LP)	55

(see also Druids)

ROBERT FARNON ORCHESTRA
63	Philips BF 1299	Charade/Gina, Gina, Don't You Cry	6
72	MCA MCA 117	Colditz March/That Italian Summer	5
58	Decca DFE 6470	JOURNEY INTO MELODY (EP)	8
55	Decca LK 4119	CANADIAN IMPRESSIONS (LP)	20
56	Vogue Coral LVA 9003	GENTLEMEN MARRY BRUNETTES (LP, soundtrack)	35
60	Delyse ECB 3157/DS 6057	CAPTAIN HORATIO HORNBLOWER (LP, soundtrack, mono/stereo)	60/75
68	Philips SBL 7867	SHALAKO (LP, soundtrack)	15

(see also Jack Saunders)

ROBERT FARNON & TONY COE
70	Chapter One CHS 804	POP MAKES PROGRESS (LP)	25

(see also Tony Coe)

FARON'S FLAMINGOS
63	Oriole CB 1834	Do You Love Me?/See If She Cares	25
63	Oriole CB 1867	Shake Sherry/Give Me Time	28

(see also Big Three, Mojos)

WAYNE FARO'S SCHMALTZ BAND
69	Deram DM 222	There's Still Time/Give It Time	50

GARY FARR (& THE T-BONES)
65	Columbia DB 7608	Give All She's Got/Don't Stop And Stare (as Gary Farr & T-Bones)	50+
68	Marmalade 598 007	Everyday/Green (with Kevin Westlake)	12
69	Marmalade 598 017	Hey Daddy/The Vicar And The Pope	18
71	CBS 5430	Revolution Of The Seasons/Old Man Boulder	8
65	Columbia SEG 8414	DEM BONES, DEM BONES, DEM T-BONES (EP)	150
69	Marmalade 608 013	TAKE SOMETHING WITH YOU (LP)	80
71	CBS 64138	STRANGE FRUIT (LP, with Richard Thompson & Mighty Baby)	40

(see also T-Bones, Richard Thompson, Mighty Baby, Meic Stevens, Kevin Westlake & Gary Farr)

MARY ANN FARRAR & SATIN SOUL
76	Brunswick BR 38	Stoned Out Of My Mind/Living In The Footsteps Of Another Girl	20

BILLY FARRELL
53	MGM MGM 607	Kaw-Liga/You Can't Stop Me From Dreaming (78)	6
55	Mercury MB 3206	It May Sound Silly/Rock Love (78)	8
58	Philips PB 828	Yeah Yeah/Someday (You'll Want Me To Want You) (78 rpm = £8)	22

DO & DENA FARRELL
57	HMV POP 427	Young Magic/New Love Tonight (78 rpm = £10)	15

MICK FARREN
78	Logo GO 321	Half Price Drinks/I Don't Want To Go This Way	6
78	Stiff LAST 4	ALL SCREWED UP (EP, as Mick Farren & Deviants)	8
70	Transatlantic TRA 212	MONA (THE CARNIVOROUS CIRCUS) (LP)	60
78	Logo LOGO 2010	VAMPIRES STOLE MY LUNCH MONEY (LP, with lyric insert)	25
84	Psycho PSYCHO 20	MONA (THE CARNIVOROUS CIRCUS) (LP, reissue)	20

(see also Deviants, Twink)

MIA FARROW
68	Dot DOT 116	Lullaby From Rosemary's Baby (Parts 1 & 2)	8

FASCINATIONS
67	Stateside SS 594	Girls Are Out To Get You/You'll Be Sorry (DJ copy = £150)	75
68	Sue WI 4049	Girls Are Out To Get You/You'll Be Sorry (reissue)	40
71	Mojo 2092 004	Girls Are Out To Get You/You'll Be Sorry (2nd reissue)	15
71	Mojo 2092 018	I'm So Lucky He Loves Me/Say It Isn't So	10

FASCINATORS
58	Capitol CL 14942	Chapel Bells/I Wonder Who	350
59	Capitol CL 15062	Oh, Rose Marie/Fried Chicken And Macaroni	200

FASHIONS
68	Stateside SS 2115	I.O.U. (A Lifetime Of Love)/When Love Slips Away	20
69	Evolution E 2444	I.O.U. (A Lifetime Of Love)/He Gives Me Love	10

FAST BREEDERS & RADIO ACTORS
78	Nuke NUKE 235	Nuclear Waste/Digital Love (some in p/s, with insert)	15/10

(see also Radio Actors)

FAST CARS
79   Streets Ahead SA 3   The Kids Just Wanna Dance/You're So Funny (1,000 only, p/s) 250

FAST EDDIE
82   Well Suspect BLAM 001   My Babe/Help Me/Sweet Sensations (p/s) 8

FAST SET
80   Axis AXIS 1   Junction One/Children Of The Revolution (p/s) 15

FAT
71   RCA LSA 3009   FAT (LP) 20

FATAL CHARM
79   Company CR 005   Paris/Glitterbit/Out Of My Head 8

FATAL MICROBES
79   Small Wonder SMALL 20   Violence Grows/Beautiful Pictures/Cry Baby (p/s) 5
     (see also Pete Fender)

FATAL MICROBES/POISON GIRLS
79   Small Wonder WEENY 3   FATAL MICROBES MEET THE POISON GIRLS (12" EP, with insert) 8
     (see also Poison Girls)

FATBACK BAND
75   Polydor 2066 494   Keep On Steppin'/Breakin' Up Is Hard To Do 5
75   Polydor 2066 524   Wicky Wacky/Can't Fight The Flame 6
75   Polydor 2066 590   Yum, Yum (Gimme Some)/Trompin' 5
75   Polydor 2066 637   (Are You Ready) Do The Bus Stop/Got To Learn How To Dance 5
76   Polydor 2066 682   Par-r-rty Time/Put Your Love In My Tender Care 5
79   Spring POSP78   King Tim III (Personality Jock)/You're My Candy Sweey 6
75   Polydor 2391 143   KEEP ON STEPPIN' (LP) 15
75   Polydor 2391 184   YUM, YUM (LP) 15

FAT CITY
69   Probe SPB 1008   REINCARNATION (LP) 18

FATHEAD
83   Greensleeves GRED 118   Champion/Stop All The Fight (12") 20

FATHER'S ANGELS
68   MGM MGM 1459   Don't Knock It/Bok To Bach (DJ copy = £300) 200
75   Black Magic BM 103   Bok To Bach/Disco Trucking 6

FAT MATTRESS
69   Polydor 56352   Naturally/Iridescent Butterfly 10
69   Polydor 56367   Magic Forest/Bright New Way 15
70   Polydor 2058 053   Highway/Black Sheep Of The Family 15
69   Polydor 582/583 056   FAT MATTRESS (LP, open-out sleeve) 28
70   Polydor 2383 025   FAT MATTRESS II (LP) 20
     (see also Noel Redding Band, Jimi Hendrix Experience, Flowerpot Men)

FATMAN VERSUS JAH SHAKA
80   Live & Love LAP12   DUB CONFRONTATION (LP) 15

FATS & CHESSMEN
62   Pye International 7N 25122 Big Ben Twist/Old Macdonald Had A Twist 8

ERIC FATTER
69   Camel CA 20   Since You've Been Gone (actually Eric Fratter)/WINSTON HINES: Cool Down
                                (B-side actually by Winston Hinds) 12
     (see also Eric Fratter, Afrotones)

FAT TULIPS
88   Sweet William BILLY 001   You Opened My Eyes/ROSEHIPS: Ask Johnny Dee
                                (33rpm flexi, p/s w/insert) 10

ERNIE FAULKNER
63   Sway SW 003   Beautiful Girl/SAM DANIELS: Tell Me Baby (both with The Planets) 10

FAUST
72   Faust/Polydor 2001-299   It's A Bit Of A Pain / So Far 8
79   Recommended RR 2.5   It's A Bit Of A Pain / So Far (p/s, reissue) 5
96   Die Stadt 011   Right Between Yr Eyes (p/s, Uberschall Festival single,with Stereolab and
                                Foetus) 20
90   Chemical Imbalance CI 08   Live In Hamburg (issued free with Chemical Imbalance magazine) 25
97   CRDC 11   Mikrowaves, Magic Brew And R Be Yr Ey (10", p/s) 8
79   Recommended RR 1.5   EXTRACTS FROM FAUST PARTY 3: Extract 1 / Extract 4 (EP) 8
80   Recommended RR 6.5   EXTRACTS FROM FAUST PARTY 3: Extract 2 / Extract 6 (EP) 8
71   Polydor 2310 142   FAUST (LP, initially on clear vinyl, with clear sleeve & clear insert) 45/15
72   Polydor 2310 196   SO FAR (LP, with 9 prints in wallet) 40
73   Virgin VC 501   THE FAUST TAPES (LP) 18
73   Virgin V 2004   FAUST IV (LP) 20
79   Recommended R.R. 2   SO FAR (LP, reissue, with 10 insert prints, numbered, 600 only) 20
80   Recommended RR 6   THE FAUST TAPES (LP, plastic bag cover) 15
90   Table Of The Elements 26   CONCERTS 1: LIVE IN HAMBURG (CD) 30
94   Table Of The Elements 27   CONCERTS 2: LIVE IN LONDON (CD) 30
     (see also Toni Conrad & Faust)

FAVOURITES
80   4 Play FOUR 002   S.O.S./Favourite Shoes (p/s) 10
80   4 Play FOUR 003   Angelica/Cold (p/s) 8

FAVOURITE SONS
65   Mercury MF 911   That Driving Beat/Walkin' Walkin' Walkin' 160

WALLY FAWKES (& HIS TROGLODYTES)

57	Decca FJ 10855	Petite Fleur/Baby Brown (with Sandy Brown Quintet)	15
57	Decca FJ 10936	Sent For You Yesterday And Here You Came Today/Why Can't You Behave	10
58	Decca F 11002	The Pilot Fish And The Whale/Pale Blues	10
56	Decca DFE 6192	TAKIN' IT EASY -- VOL 1 (EP, with Bruce Turner)	8
56	Decca DFE 6193	TAKIN' IT EASY -- VOL 2 (EP, with Bruce Turner)	8
57	Decca DEF 6407	AND HIS TROGLODYTES (EP)	10
60	Decca DFE 6600	FLOOK DIGS JAZZ (EP)	10
61	Decca STO 136	A NIGHT AT THE SIX BELLS (EP)	15
56	Decca LF 1214	TAKIN' IT EASY (LP, with Bruce Turner)	18
58	Decca LF 312	FAWKES ON HOLIDAY (LP)	18

(see also Sandy Brown)

CHARLIE FAWN

80	Warner Bros K 17566	Always Something There To Remind Me/Poet For A Generation	8

BILL FAY

67	Deram DM 143	Some Good Advice/Screams In The Ears	45
70	Deram Nova SDN 12	BILL FAY (LP)	70
71	Deram SML 1079	TIME OF THE LAST PERSECUTION (LP)	200

BRIAN FAYE & ORCHESTRA

(see under Brian Fahey)

FRANCIS FAYE

61	Vogue V 9186	I Wish I Could Shimmy Like My Sister Kate/Night And Day	20
61	HMV POP 898	Frenesi/Miserlou	7
65	Stateside SL 10129	YOU GOTTA GO! GO! GO! (LP)	18

LITTLE RITA FAYE

53	MGM MGM 671	Rock City Boogie/Wait A Little Longer (78)	12
53	MGM MGM 697	I Fell Out Of The Christmas Tree/I'm A Problem Child (78)	10

F.B.I. (FOLK BLUES INC.)

66	Eyemark EMS 1006	Don't Hide/When The Ship Comes In	25
73	A&M AMS 7050	I Wonder What She's Doing Tonight/Boogaloo Boo-Boo	10
76	Good Earth GD 6	F.B.I./The Time Is Right To Leave The City	20
77	Good Earth GDS 802	F.B.I. (LP)	50

FEARN'S BRASS FOUNDRY

68	Decca F 12721	Don't Change It/John White	45
68	Decca F 12835	Now I Taste The Tears/Love, Sink And Drown	10

FEAR OF FALLING

83	Excellent XL 7	Like A Lion/You My Prodigal Son (p/s)	20

CHARLIE FEATHERS/MAC CURTIS

74	Polydor 2310 293	ROCKABILLY KINGS (LP, withdrawn)	25

(see also Mac Curtis)

FEATURES

70s	Progress PR 01	Drab City/Job Satisfaction	60

FEATURES

80	ASM HIT 06	She Makes Me Blue/Don't Let Them Know	20
81	AFM PET 01	Monday-Friday/Cue The Next Army	20

FEDERALMEN

70	London HLU 10303	Soul Serenade/Scorcher	8

FEDERALS (U.K.)

63	Parlophone R 4988	Brazil/In A Persian Market	15
63	Parlophone R 5013	Boot Hill/Keep On Dancing With Me	15
64	Parlophone R 5100	The Climb/Dance With A Dolly	18
64	Parlophone R 5139	Marlena/Please Believe Me	18
64	Parlophone R 5193	Twilight Time/Lost And Alone	18
65	Parlophone R 5320	Bucket Full Of Love/Leah	20

(see also Winston's Fumbs, Yes)

FEDERALS (Jamaica)

67	Island WI 3126	Penny For Your Song/I've Passed This Way Before	30
68	Island WI 3152	Shocking Love/By The River	22
69	High Note HS 024	Wailing Festival/Me And My Baby (B-side actually "By The River")	15
70	Camel CA 40	In This World/You Better Call On Me (B-side actually "Shocking Love")	10

FEEDER

96	Echo ECS 13	TWO COLOURS: Pictures Of Rain/Chicken On A Bone (p/s, clear vinyl)	50
96	Echo ECSCD 13	TWO COLOURS: Pictures Of Rain/Chicken On A Bone (CD, 1,000 only)	50
96	Echo ECS 27	Stereo World/My Perfect Day (p/s)	45
97	Echo ECS 32	Tangerine/Rhubarb (die-cut p/s)	15
97	Echo ECS 36	Cement/Pictures Of Pain (red vinyl, p/s)	8
97	Echo ECS 42	Crash/Here In The Bubble (clear vinyl, numbered p/s)	8
97	Echo ECS 44	High/Wishing For The Sun (sky blue vinyl, p/s)	7
98	Echo ECS 052	Suffocate/Eclipse (purple vinyl, p/s)	7
99	Echo ECS 75	Day In Day Out/Dance To Disco/Honeyfuzz (white vinyl, p/s)	7
01	Echo ECS 106	Buck Rogers/Sex Type Drug (orange vinyl, p/s)	6
01	Echo ECS 107	Seven Days In The Sun/Just A Day (p/s)	5
01	Echo ECS 116	Turn/Come Back Around (purple vinyl, p/s)	7
01	Echo ECS 121	Just A Day/Early (orange vinyl, p/s)	7
01	Echo	Turn/Bad Hair Day (6-12 white label promo competition prizes, 7" die-cut sleeve)	20
03	Echo ECS 145	Find The Colour/Remember The Silence (white vinyl p/s)	5
04	Echo ECS157A/B -1	Tumble and Fall/Victoria (12" white label promos auctioned for Warchild charity)	20

96	Echo ECHLP 9	SWIM (LP)	15
97	Echo ECHLP15	POLYPHENE (LP, re-issue with free High 7")	20
04	Echo ECHLP52	PICTURE OF PERFECT YOUTH (3xLP)	25
04	Echo ECHCD52	PICTURE OF PERFECT YOUTH (CD, internet only release - deleted)	30

FEELIES

79	Stiff (no cat. no.)	Facé La/The Boy With Perpetual Nervousness/ Everybody's Got Something To Hide (Except Me And My Monkey) (flexidisc, promo only, free with Be Stiff fanzine issue 6, 5,000 only)	6
79	Rough Trade RT 24	Facé La/Raised Eyebrows (p/s)	7
80	Stiff BUY 65	Everybody's Got Something To Hide/Original Love (p/s)	7

FELDER'S ORIOLES

65	Piccadilly 7N 35247	Down Home Girl/Misty	30+
65	Piccadilly 7N 35269	Sweet Tasting Wine/Turn On Your Lovelight	18
66	Piccadilly 7N 35311	I Know You Don't Love Me No More/Only Three Can Pay	18
66	Piccadilly 7N 35332	Back Street/Something You Got	25

(see also V.I.P.s, Mike Patto)

MARTY FELDMAN

68	Pye NPL 18258	MARTY (LP)	15
69	Decca LK/SKL 4983	I FEEL A SONG GOING OFF (LP)	15

VICTOR FELDMAN BIG BAND/QUARTET

55	Tempo A 127	Elegy/Maenya (78)	7
56	Tempo A 142	Big Top/Cabaletto	8
57	Tempo A 154	Jackpot/You Are My Heart's Desire	8
55	Tempo EXA 29	BIG BAND (EP)	50
57	Tempo EXA 57	VICTOR FELDMAN IN LONDON -- THE QUARTET VOLUME 1 (EP)	60
57	Tempo EXA 67	VICTOR FELDMAN IN LONDON VOLUME 2 (EP)	60
58	Tempo EXA 85	MUTUAL ADMIRATION (EP, with Dizzy Reece)	50
50s	Esquire EP 43	MODERN JAZZ QUARTET (EP)	40
50s	Esquire EP 54	MODERN JAZZ QUARTET (EP)	20
50s	Esquire EP 64	MODERN JAZZ QUINTET/SEXTET (EP)	25
50s	Esquire EP 84	MODERN JAZZ QUARTET/SEXTET (EP)	20
50s	Esquire EP 104	MODERN JAZZ QUARTET (EP)	40
50s	Esquire EP 114	VIC FELDMAN ENCORE (EP)	15
50s	Esquire 20 - 046	MULTIPLE TALENTS (LP)	30
50s	Esquire 20 - 064	EXPERIMENT IN TIME (LP)	40
55	Tempo LAP 5	VICTOR FELDMAN'S SEXTET (10" LP)	180
56	Tempo LAP 6	VICTOR FELDMAN MODERN JAZZ QUARTET (10" LP)	160
57	Tempo TAP 8	VICTOR FELDMAN IN LONDON VOL. 1 (LP)	130
57	Tempo TAP 12	VICTOR FELDMAN IN LONDON VOL. 2 (LP)	120
58	Tempo TAP 19	TRANSATLANTIC ALLIANCE (LP)	240
59	Contemporary LAC 12172	THE ARRIVAL OF VICTOR FELDMAN (LP)	15
62	Fontana 267233	A Taste Of Honey/Valerie	10
80s	Jasmine JASM 2002	TRANSATLANTIC ALLIANCE (LP, reissue)	12
80s	Jasmine JASM 2023	IN LONDON VOL. 1 (LP, reissue)	12
80s	Jasmine JASM	IN LONDON VOL. 2 (LP, reissue)	12

(see also Dizzy Reece, Tubby Hayes)

VICTOR FELDMAN, TERRY GIBBS & LARRY BUNKER

60	Top Rank 30/007	VIBES TO THE POWER OF THREE (LP)	20

JOSE FELICIANO

68	RCA RCA 1715	Light My Fire/California Dreamin'	8
68	RCA RCA 1769	Hi Heel Sneakers/Hitchcock Railway	5
69	RCA RCA 1871	And The Sun Will Shine/Rain	5
70	RCA RCA 1998	Destiny/Susie-Q	5
74	RCA RCA PB10094	Golden Lady/Virgo	12
60s	RCA LP 4370	FIREWORKS (LP, embossed sleeve)	12

FELIUS ANDROMEDA

67	Decca F 12694	Meditations/Cheadle Heath Delusions	45+

(see also Denis Couldry)

JULIE FELIX

65	Decca DFE 8613	SINGS BOB DYLAN & WOODY GUTHRIE (EP)	18
64	Decca LK 4626	JULIE FELIX (LP)	20
65	Decca LK 4683	SINGS DYLAN AND GUTHRIE (LP)	20
65	Decca LK 4724	SECOND ALBUM (LP)	15
66	Decca LK 4820	THIRD ALBUM (LP)	15
66	Fontana TL 5386	CHANGES (LP)	15
60s	Fontana SFL 13117	GOING TO THE ZOO (LP)	15

MIKE FELIX

66	Pye 7N 17058	You Belong To Me/Booga Dee	22
67	Decca F 12701	Blueberry Hill/I Don't Think You Want Me Anymore	8

FELIX & HIS GUITAR

59	London HLU 8875	Chili Beans/Puerto Rican Riot (78 rpm = £12)	12

FELT

79	Shanghai S79/CUS 321	Index/Break It (p/s, early copies have notes on rear sleeve)	60/50
81	Cherry Red CHERRY 26	Something Sends Me To Sleep/Red Indians/Something Sends Me To Sleep (Version)/Red Indians (p/s)	15
82	Cherry Red CHERRY 45	My Face Is On Fire/Trails Of Colour Dissolve (p/s)	12
83	Cherry Red CHERRY 59	Penelope Tree/A Preacher In New England (p/s)	10
83	Cherry Red 12CHERRY 59	Penelope Tree/A Preacher In New England/ Now Summer's Spread Its Wings Again (12", p/s)	12
84	Cherry Red CHERRY 78	Mexican Bandits/The World Is As Soft As Lace (p/s)	8

84	Cherry Red CHERRY 81	Sunlight Bathed The Golden Glow/Fortune (p/s)....................	15
84	Cherry Red 12CHERRY 81	Sunlight Bathed The Golden Glow/Fortune/Sunlight Strings (12", p/s).......	15
85	Cherry Red 12CHERRY 89	Primitive Painters/Cathedral (12", p/s, with Liz Frazer)..............	10
86	Creation CRE 027	Ballad Of The Band/I Didn't Mean To Hurt You (p/s)..............	8
86	Creation CRE 032	Rain Of Crystal Spires/I Will Die With My Head In Flames (p/s).......	8
88	Cherry Red CDCHERRY 89	Primitive Painters/Cathedral (reissue, picture CD)................	10
88	Creation CRE 060	Space Blues/Tuesday's Secret (ltd. ed. die-cut company sleeve).......	6
89	él GPO F44	Get Out Of My Mirror (flexidisc)........................	7
89	él GPO 44	Get Out Of My Mirror (hard vinyl test pressing, 200 only)..........	20

(see also Denim, Versatile Newts, Maurice Deebank, Cocteau Twins)

FEMININE TOUCH featuring DUKE DURRELL
76	Paladin PAL 11	You Make Me Come Alive/You Make Me Come Alive (Instrumental)...........	5

JAYMES FENDA & VULCANS
64	Parlophone R 5210	Mistletoe Love/The Only Girl.........................	16

JAN FENDER
71	Prince Buster PB 5	Sea Of Love/PRINCE BUSTER: Heaven Help Us All................	15
71	Fab FAB 164	Sweet P/CLIFF & ORGANIZERS: Mr Brown...................	12
71	Fab FAB 166	Holly Holy Version/Old Kentrone Version (as Jal Fender)...........	12

PETE FENDER
81	Xntrix 2002	FOUR FORMULAS (EP, some in 8" silk-screened book p/s)............	30/8

(see also Fatal Microbes, Omega Tribe)

FENDER BENDERS
79	Sticky SL 001	Big Green Thing/Hillman Hunter Paranoia (textured p/s, various colours).......	6

FENDERMEN
60	Top Rank JAR 395	Mule Skinner Blues/Torture..........................	12
60	Top Rank JAR 513	Don't You Just Know It/Beach Party.....................	12

FENMEN
64	Decca F 11955	Rag Doll/Be My Girl..............................	20
65	Decca F 12269	I've Got Everthing You Need Babe/Every Little Day Now............	12
66	CBS 202075	California Dreamin'/Is This Your Way?...................	12
66	CBS 202236	Rejected/Girl Don't Bring Me Down......................	28

(see also Bern Elliott & Fenmen, Pretty Things, Zac Zolar & Electric Banana)

PETER FENTON
66	Fontana TF 748	Marble Breaks, Iron Bends/Small Town....................	15

SHANE FENTON (& FENTONES)
61	Parlophone R 4827	I'm A Moody Guy/Five Foot Two, Eyes Of Blue................	8
62	Parlophone R 4866	Walk Away/Fallen Leaves On The Ground..................	8
62	Parlophone R 4883	It's All Over Now/Why Little Girl......................	8
62	Parlophone R 4921	Cindy's Birthday/It's Gonna Take Magic...................	8
62	Parlophone R 4951	Too Young For Sad Memories/You're Telling Me..............	8
63	Parlophone R 4982	I Ain't Got Nobody/Hey Miss Ruby.....................	8
63	Parlophone R 5020	A Fool's Paradise/You Need Love (solo)..................	8
63	Parlophone R 5047	Don't Do That/I'll Know (solo).......................	8
64	Parlophone R 5131	Hey, Lulu/I Do, Do You?...........................	12
72	Fury FY 305	Eastern Seaboard/Blind Fool........................	25
74	Contour 2870 409	GOOD ROCKIN' TONIGHT (LP).......................	18

(see also Fentones)

FENTONES
62	Parlophone R 4899	The Mexican/Lover's Guitar.........................	15
62	Parlophone R 4937	The Breeze And I/Just For Jerry......................	15

(see also Shane Fenton)

FENWAYS
65	Liberty LIB 66082	Walk/Whip And Jerk.............................	15

RAY FENWICK
78	Mercury 6007 176	Queen Of The Night/I Wanna Boogie....................	6
71	Decca SKL 5090	KEEP AMERICA BEAUTIFUL, GET A HAIRCUT (LP)............	35

(see also Spencer Davis Group, After Tea, Fancy, Ian Gillan Band, Wizard's Convention, Murgatroyd Band, Marlon, Forcefield, Syndicats, South Coast Ska Kings, Rupert's People)

FERDIA
78	Polydor 2904 012	A SIGH FOR OLD TIMES (LP)........................	15

FERDINAND & DILL
70	Pama PM 805	Take Back Your Nicklet/Blueberry Hill...................	6

DOTTIE FERGUSON
57	Mercury MT 182	Happy Happy Birthday Baby/Darling, It's Wonderful (78)...........	10

H-BOMB FERGUSON
54	Esquire 10-372	Feel Like I Do/My Love (78).........................	30

HELENA FERGUSON
67	London HLZ 10164	Where Is The Party?/My Terms.......................	30

JESSIE LEE FERGUSON & OUTER LIMITS
69	Pye International 7N 25492	New Shoes/Puttin' It On, Puttin' It Off...................	15

JOHNNY FERGUSON
60	MGM MGM 1059	Angela Jones/Blue Serge And White Lace..................	12
61	MGM MGM 1119	No One Can Love You/The Valley Of Love.................	8

MINT VALUE £

MAYNARD FERGUSON ORCHESTRA

58	Emarcy EJL 1270	JAM SESSION (LP)	15
58	Emarcy EJL 1275	AROUND THE HORN (LP)	15
58	Emarcy EJL 1287	DIMENSIONS (LP)	15
59	Columbia 33SX 1146	MESSAGE FROM NEWPORT (LP)	15
60	Mercury MMC 14050	THE BOY WITH LOTS OF BRASS (LP, also stereo CMS 18034)	15
60	Columbia 33SX 1210	MESSAGE FROM BIRDLAND (LP, also stereo SCX 3245)	15
60	Columbia 33SX 1270	JAZZ FOR DANCING (LP, also stereo SCX 3338)	15
61	Columbia 33SX 1301	NEWPORT SUITE (LP, also stereo SCX 3368)	15
62	Columbia 33SX 1439	MAYNARD 62 (LP)	15
66	Fontana TL 5274	BLUES REAR (LP)	18
66	Fontana TL 5293	COLOR HIM WILD (LP)	18
67	Fontana TL 5310	SEXTET (LP)	20
68	Atlantic 2464008	FREAKY (LP)	20
69	CBS 63514	BALLAD STLYE OF MAYNARD FERGUSON (LP)	120
70	CBS 64101	WORLD OF (M.F. HORN) (LP)	20
71	CBS 64432	ALIVE AND WELL IN LONDON (LP)	20
72	CBS 65027	M.F. HORN 2 (LP)	20
73	CBS 65589	M.F. HORN 3 (LP)	20
73	CBS 65952	M.F. HORN 4 (LIVE AT JIMMYS) (LP)	20

FERKO STRING BAND

55	London HL 8140	Alabama Jubilee/Sing A Little Melody (78 rpm = £5)	25
55	London HLF 8183	Ma (She's Making Eyes At Me)/You Are My Sunshine (78 rpm = £5)	25
55	London HLF 8215	Happy Days Are Here Again/Deep In The Heart Of Texas (78 rpm = £8)	25
58	London HL 7052	Happy Days Are Here Again/Alabama Jubilee (export issue)	18
56	London RE-F 1041	PHILADELPHIA MUMMERS PARADE VOL. 1 (EP)	10
56	London RE-F 1052	PHILADELPHIA MUMMERS PARADE VOL. 2 (EP)	10
57	London HB-C 1064	THE FERKO STRING BAND VOL. 1 (10" LP)	15

FERMENA

71	Pama PM 839	Come What May/Version (B-side with Ranny)	6
73	Pama PM 879	Wonderful Dreams/Version	6

PHIL FERNANDO

58	Pye Nixa 7N 15142	Blonde Bombshell/Make Ready for Love (78 rpm = £8)	10
62	Palette PG 9029	Do The High Life/High Life Girl	6

ANDY FERNBACH

69	Liberty LBL/LBS 83233	IF YOU MISS YOUR CONNEXION (LP)	110

(see also Groundhogs)

MAJA FERNICK

72	Philips 6006 196	Give Me Your Love Again/Flowers In The City	22

FERRANTE & TEICHER

61	HMV/Utd. Artists 7EG 8700	EXODUS (EP)	10

DIANE FERRAZ & NICKY SCOTT

66	Columbia DB 7824	Me And You/Don't Pretend	8
66	Columbia DB 7897	You've Got To Learn/Like You As You Are	5
66	Columbia DB 7963	Sh-Boom, Sh-Boom/Allah Mobish	5

(see also Nicky Scott, Ferris Wheel)

JOE FERRER & HIS DEVILS BOYS

61	Oriole CB 1629	Rockin' Crickets/Blue Guitar	20

EUGENE FERRIS

66	Planet PLF 112	There Was A Smile In Your Eyes/Soft Moonlight	40

GEORGE FERRIS

71	Ackee ACK 117	With Every Dream/Diana	6

FERRIS WHEEL

67	Pye 7N 17387	I Can't Break The Habit/Number One Guy	10
68	Pye 7N 17538	Let It Be Me/You Look At Me	8
68	Pye 7N 17631	The Na Na Song/Three Cool Cats	8
69	Polydor 56366	Can't Stop Now/I Know You Well	6
67	Pye NPL 18203	CAN'T BREAK THE HABIT (LP)	25
70	Polydor 583 066	FERRIS WHEEL (LP)	15

(see also Linda Lewis, West Five)

BRYAN FERRY

73	Island WIP 6170	A Hard Rain's Gonna Fall/2 HB	5
74	Island WIP 6196	The 'In' Crowd/Chance Meeting (initially in p/s)	8/5
74	Island WIP 6205	Smoke Gets In Your Eyes/Another Place	5
75	Island WIP 6234	You Go To My Head/Re-Make, Re-Model (no p/s)	5
75	Island WIP 6234	You Go To My Head/Re-Make, Re-Model (DJ copies in generic promo p/s)	20
76	Island IEP 1	EXTENDED PLAY (EP, p/s)	6
78	Polydor PPSP 10	Hold On I'm Coming/Take Me To The River (12", unissued, promo only, numbered stamped p/s)	20
85	E.G. FERPX 2	Don't Stop The Dance (Special 12" Remix)/Slave To Love (Special 12" Remix)/Nocturne (12", picture disc, printed PVC sleeve)	10
88	Virgin CDT 10/EGOCD 41	Let's Stick Together/Shame Shame Shame/Chance Meeting/Sea Breezes (3" CD, card sleeve)	8
88	Virgin CDEP 8	The Right Stuff (4.25)/(6.40)/(Dub Mix) (CD, gatefold sleeve)	8
88	Virgin CDEP 19	Kiss And Tell/Kiss And Tell (Dub Mix)/Zamba/Kiss And Tell (Dance Mix) (CD)	8
88	Virgin VSCD 1066	Limbo (Latin Mix)/Bête Noire (Instrumental)/Limbo (Brooklyn Dub Mix) (CD in 6" x 5" cardboard box)	8
88	E.G. EGOCD 44	Let's Stick Together (Westside '88 Mix)/Trash/Sign Of The Times/Casanova (CD)	8
89	E.G. EGOCD 46	The Price Of Love (The R&B '89 Remix)/Don't Stop The Dance (Special 12" Remix)/Slave To Love (12" Remix)/Loner (3" CD, card sleeve)	8

89	E.G. EGOCD 48	He'll Have To Go/Take Me To The River/Broken Wings/Carrickfergus
		(3" CD, card sleeve) 10
73	Island (no cat. no.)	THESE FOOLISH THINGS (2 x 7", white label test pressings)........... 250
73	Island ILPS 9239	THESE FOOLISH THINGS (LP, unissued gatefold sleeve) 500
76	Island ILPS 9367	LET'S STICK TOGETHER (LP, original issue) 15
78	Polydor POLD 5003	THE BRIDE STRIPPED BARE (LP, original with A//3 P matrix,
		includes 'Broken Wings', white label test pressings only,
		some in different proof gatefold sleeve) 200/400

(see also Roxy Music)

CATHERINE FERRY
| 76 | Barclay BAR 42 | One, Two, Three/1, 2, 3. .... 12 |

FESTIVAL
| 78 | Nevis NEV 107 | Something In Your Smile/Let's Make Love. .... 45 |

FEVER TREE
68	MCA MU 1043	San Francisco Girls/Come With Me 10
68	Uni UNLS 102	FEVER TREE (LP) 35
68	MCA MUPS 347	ANOTHER TIME, ANOTHER PLACE (LP) 40

FICKLE FINGER
| 69 | Page One POF 150 | Fickle Lizzie-Anne/Cellophane Mary Jane .... 12 |

(see also Matchmakers, Mark Wirtz)

FICKLE PICKLE
| 70 | Fontana TF 1069 | Millionaire/Sam And Sadie. .... 15 |
| 70 | Philips 6006 038 | Maybe I'm Amazed/Sitting On A Goldmine. .... 6 |

FI-DELS
| 72 | Jay Boy BOY 69 | Try A Little Harder/You Never Do Right .... 15 |
| 70s | DJM DJS 689 | Try A Little Harder/KEYMAN STRINGS: Instrumental Version (DJ copy p/s £20) . 10 |

KEITH FIELD
| 68 | Polydor 56278 | The Day That War Broke Out/Stop Thief. .... 15 |

FIELD MICE
80s	Waaaaah BULL 40	Burning Word (1-sided flexi) 6
90	Sarah SARAH 024	Autumn Store Pt. 1/If You Need Someone/World In Me (p/s) 10
90	Sarah SARAH 025	Autumn Store Pt. 2/Anyone Else Isn't You/Bleak (p/s) 10

JERRY FIELDING & HIS ORCHESTRA
54	London HL 8017	When I Grow Too Old To Dream/Button Up Your Overcoat 50
55	London HL 7001	Faintly Reminiscent/Blues Serenade (export issue) 20
55	London HL 7002	Pea-nut Vendor/Can't Help Lovin' Dat Man (export issue) 20
55	London HL 7003	Tea For Two/Here In My Arms (export issue)........................ 20
55	London HL 7004	I'm In Love/Blue Prelude (export issue) 20
55	Brunswick 05399	The Gypsy In My Soul/The Glory Of Love 10
55	London RE-P 1026	DANCE DATE VOL. 1 (EP) 18
54	London H-APB 1022	FAINTLY REMINISCENT (10" LP) 20
54	London H-APB 1027	PLAYS A DANCE CONCERT (10" LP) 20

FIELD MICE
88	Sarah SARAH 012	Emma's House/When You Sleep/Fabulous Friend/The Last Letter (p/s)........ 10
89	Caff CAFF 2	I Can See Myself Alone Forever/Everything About You
		(foldaround p/s in poly bag with insert) 25
88	Sarah SARAH 18	Sensitive/When Morning Comes To Town/Penguins (foldout p/s, with poster) ... 12
91	Sarah SARAH 44	September's Not So Far Away/Hello And Goodbye (p/s, with insert) 10

FIELDS
| 69 | Uni UNLS 104 | FIELDS (LP) .... 40 |

FIELDS
| 71 | CBS 7555 | Friends Of Mine/Three Minstrels .... 6 |
| 71 | CBS 69009 | FIELDS (LP, with/without poster) .... 40/25 |

(see also Rare Bird)

BILLY FIELDS
| 55 | MGM SP 1126 | Sincerely/Thrilled .... 6 |
| 59 | Mercury AMT 1067 | The Greatest Love In The World/No Other Love .... 10 |

ERNIE FIELDS & HIS ORCHESTRA
59	London HL 8985	In The Mood/Christopher Columbus (some with tri-centre) (78 rpm = £20) 15
60	London HL 9100	Chattanooga Choo Choo/Workin' Out. 12
60	London HL 9227	Raunchy/My Prayer. 10
60	London RE 1260	SAXY (EP) 50
60	London HA 2263	IN THE MOOD (LP) 50

GRACIE FIELDS
| 52 | Decca LF 1080 | NOW IS THE HOUR (10" LP, original pressing) .... 12 |
| 53 | Decca LF 1140 | GRACIE FIELDS (10" LP) .... 12 |

IRVING FIELDS TRIO & ORCHESTRA
| 54 | Parlophone CMSP 9 | Mr. Piano Player/Cuban Carnival (export issue) .... 10 |
| 58 | Oriole CB 1436 | Ragtime Rock/Syncopated Sadie (78 rpm = £6) .... 6 |

KANSAS FIELDS & MILTON SEALEY
| 56 | Ducretet DEP 95017 | KANSAS FIELDS & MILTON SEALEY (EP). .... 10 |

FIELDS OF THE NEPHILIM
84	Tower N1	BURNING THE FIELDS (12" EP, red/black p/s) .... 45+
85	Tower N1/Jung. JUNG 28T	BURNING THE FIELDS (12" EP, green p/s with insert & band photo label) ... 10
85	Tower N1/Jung. JUNG 28T	BURNING THE FIELDS (12" EP, green & other coloured vinyl export issue)..... 10
86	Situation 2 SIT 42	Power/Secrets (7", white label promos only, stickered plain sleeve) 15
87	Situation 2 SIT 46	Preacher Man/Laura II (p/s, some with Beggars Banquet sticker) 38/28

FIELDS OF THE NEPHILIM

87	Situation 2 SIT 48	Blue Water/In Every Dream Home A Heartache (p/s) 10
87	Situation 2 SIT 48T	Blue Water (Electrostatic)/In Every Dream Home A Heartache (live)/
		Blue Water (Hot Wire) (12", p/s, some with poster) 18/8
87	House Of Dolls HOD 15	Dawnrazor (on free EP with *House Of Dolls* magazine, issue 15) 8/6
89	Situation 2 SIT 57	Psychonaut/Celebrate (Second Seal) (blue/green p/s) 6
90	Beggars Banquet BEG 250	Sumerland/Phobia (live) (no p/s) 5
88	Situation 2 SITU 22	THE NEPHILIM (LP, gatefold sleeve, with inner) 15
88	Situation 2 SITU 22L	THE NEPHILIM (LP, 2 x 45rpm 12", gatefold sleeve, numbered) 20

FIESTAS
59	London HL 8870	So Fine/Last Night I Dreamed (78 rpm = £40) 45
71	Atlantic 2091 121	So Fine/Broken Heart 8

FIFE REIVERS
69	Columbia SCX 6371	FIFE REIVERS (LP) 30

FIFTEENTH
86	Tanz TANZ 3	ANDELAIN (12" EP) 10

FIFTH AVENUE
65	Immediate IM 002	The Bells Of Rhymney/Just Like Anyone Would Do 30
	(see also Denny Gerrard, Warm Sounds)	

FIFTH AVENUE BAND
69	Reprise RSPL 6369	FIFTH AVENUE BAND (LP) 25

FIFTH COLUMN
66	Columbia DB 8068	Benjamin Day/There's Nobody There 28
	(see also Gerry Rafferty)	

5TH DIMENSION
67	Liberty LIB 12051	Go Where You Wanna Go/Too Poor To Die 22
67	Liberty LIB 12056	Another Day, Another Heartache/Rosecrans Blvd. 12
67	Liberty LBF 15014	Up Up And Away/Pattern People 10
68	Liberty LBF 15052	Carpet Man/Magic Garden 15
68	Liberty LBF 15072	Stoned Soul Picnic/Sailboat Song 7
68	Liberty LBF 15081	Ticket To Ride/Orange Air 6
68	Liberty LBF 15130	California Soul/It'll Never Be The Same 12
68	Liberty LBF 15143	Sweet Blindness/Good News... 6
69	Liberty LBF 15180	California Soul/I'll Never Be The Same Again 6
69	Liberty LBF 15193	Aquarius — Let The Sun Shine In/Don'tcha Hear Me Callin' To Ya 6
69	Liberty LBF 15288	Wedding Bell Blues/Let It Be Me 6
69	Liberty LBF 15308	Blowing Away/Skinny Man... 6
70	Liberty LBF 15356	I'll Be Lovin' You Forever/Train Keep On Movin' 15
67	Liberty LBL/LBS 83038	UP UP AND AWAY (LP) 18
68	Liberty LBL/LBS 83098E	MAGIC GARDEN (LP) 18
68	Liberty LBL/LBS 83155E	STONED SOUL PICNIC (LP) 20
68	Liberty SBL 135	PORTRAITS (LP) 12
69	Liberty LBS 83205	AGE OF AQUARIUS (LP) 18
70	Liberty LBS 83228	THE FANTASTIC 5TH DIMENSION (LP)..................................... 15

FIFTH ESTATE
67	Stateside SS 2034	Ding Dong The Witch Is Dead/Rub A Dub 10
67	Stateside SS 2068	Heigh Ho/It's Waiting There For You 8
68	Stateside SS 2105	Do Drop In/That's Love.. 7
69	Stateside SS 2125	Coney Island Sally/Tomorrow Is My Turn................................... 7

FIFTY FANTASTICS
79	South Circular SGS 108	God's Got Religion/STEPPES: The Beat Drill (white label) 10
80	Dining Out TUX 5	God's Got Religion/The Beat Drill (reissue, foldout p/s,
		handdone labels).. 8
	(see also Steppes, Disco Zombies)	

FIFTY FOOT HOSE
69	Mercury SLML 4030	CAULDRON (LP) .... 85+

50 YEAR VOID
92	BLADE 1	Blade's Love Machine (1-sided 12", white label promo, 100 only) .... 30+
	(see also St. Etienne, Sarah Cracknell)	

FIGGY DUFF
80	Dingles DIN 326	FIGGY DUFF (LP) 50
85	Celtic CM 023	AFTER THE TEMPEST (LP, with insert) 30

PAULINE FILBY
60s	Church Miss. Soc. LIV/SP/81	I'm Hungry/NADIA CATTOUSE: The Larder 20
68	Herald ELR 1081	MY WORLD BY PAULINE FILBY (EP) 30
69	Herald LLR 567	SHOW ME A RAINBOW (LP) 60
	(see also Narnia, Accolade, Gordon Giltrap)	

FILE UNDER POP
79	Rough Trade RT 011	Heathrow/Corrugate/Heathrow SLB (p/s) 6
	(see also AK Process)	

FILTHY PHIL & FAST EDDIE
89	Receiver RRLP 124	NAUGHTY OLD SANTA'S CHRISTMAS CLASSICS (LP) 15
	(see also Motörhead)	

FILTHY RICH
87	JM TR 102	She's 17 (p/s) 25
	(see also Trident)	

FINAL CONFLICT
89	Futuresound VFS 001	My England/Across The Room (stickered white sleeve) 20
86	Futuresound FS 001	CHANNEL 8 (cassette) 8

86	Futuresound FS 001	EP (EP)	10
86	Futuresound FS 002	THE TIME HAS ARRIVED (EP, with 22-page booklet)	10

FINAL PROGRAM
81	Program FINAL 001	PROTECT AND SURVIVE (EP)	6

FINAL TOUCH
70s	Myrrh MYR 1188	LOVE SONG (LP)	15

FINCH
78	Rockburgh ROC 103	GALLEONS OF PASSION (LP)	15

FINDERS KEEPERS (U.K.)
66	CBS 202249	Light/Power Of Love (withdrawn, promos may exist)	60+
66	CBS 202249	Light/Come On Now	15
67	Fontana TF 892	On The Beach/Friday Kind Of Monday	30
68	Fontana TF 938	Sadie (The Cleaning Lady)/Without Her	18

(see also Trapeze, Glenn Hughes, News)

FINDERS KEEPERS (U.S.)
67	London HLH 10117	Lavender Blue/MICKEY DOLENZ: Don't Do It	16

JEM FINER
00s	no cat. no.	LONGPLAYER (LP, with book)	15

FINGERS
66	Columbia DB 8026	I'll Take You Where The Music's Playing/My Way Of Thinking	10
67	Columbia DB 8112	All Kinds Of People/Circus With A Female Clown	35

(see also Crocheted Doughnut Ring, Legend)

FINI TRIBE (101)
84	Finiflex LT 1001	CURLING & STRETCHING EP (12", p/s, original issue)	10
88	Finiflex FT 002	DESTIMONY EP (12", p/s)	10
91	Finiflex/One Little Indian 54 TP 7	101: Sonic Shuffle (Edit)/101: 303 (3D Bass Edit) (promo only, plain stickered sleeve)	5

LEE FINN & RHYTHM MEN
63	Starlite ST45 103	High Class Feelin'/Pour Me A Glass Of Wine	200

MICKEY FINN & BLUE MEN
(see under 'M')

SIMON FINN
70	Mushroom 100 MR 2	PASS THE DISTANCE (LP, with lyric insert)	200

TIM FINN
83	Epic A 3932	Fraction Too Much Friction/Below The Belt (p/s)	5
86	Virgin VS 849-12	No Thunder No Fire No Rain (Extended Version)/ No Thunder No Fire No Rain/Searching The Streets (12", p/s)	8
86	Virgin VS 866-12	Carve You In Marble/Hole In My Heart (12", p/s)	8
89	Capitol CDCL 542	How'm I Gonna Sleep?/Cruel Black Crow (live)/ Six Months In A Leaky Boat (live) (CD)	8
94	Capitol	LIVE AT THE BORDERLINE (CD, promo only)	25

(see also Split Enz, Crowded House)

LARRY FINNEGAN
62	HMV POP 1022	Dear One/Candy Lips	18
62	London HLU 9613	Pretty Suzy Sunshine/It's Walkin' Talkin' Time	20
65	Ember EMB S 207	The Other Ringo (A Tribute To Ringo Starr)/When My Love Passes By (p/s)	20/10

MIKE FINNIGAN
78	CBS 6656	Just One Minute More/Blood Is Thicker Than Water	20

FINN MACCUILL
77	private pressing	SINK YE SWIM YE (LP)	80

FIRE
68	Decca F 12753	Father's Name Is Dad/Treacle Toffee World	200
68	Decca F 12856	Round The Gum Tree/Toothie Ruthie	30
70	Pye NSPL 18343	THE MAGIC SHOEMAKER (LP)	300
97	Tenth Planet TP 029	UNDERGROUND AND OVERHEAD: THE ALTERNATE FIRE (LP, gatefold sleeve, numbered, 1,000 only)	18

(see also Strawbs, Paul Brett's Sage)

FIREBALLS
59	Top Rank JAR 218	Torquay/Cry Baby	20
60	Top Rank JAR 276	Bulldog/Nearly Sunrise	17
60	Top Rank JAR 354	Foot-Patter/Kissin'	15
60	Top Rank JAR 507	Vaquero (Cowboy)/Chief Whoopin'-Koff	15
61	Pye International 7N 25092	Quite A Party/Gunshot	15
62	Stateside SS 106	Rik-A-Tik/Yacky Doo	10
63	Stateside SS 151	Carioca/Find Me A Golden Street	10
65	Stateside SS 417	Baby What's Wrong/Yummie Yama Papa	10
67	Stateside SS 2095	Bottle Of Wine/Ain't That Rain	6
68	Stateside SS 2106	Goin' Away/Groovy Motions	6
69	Stateside SS 2134	Come On, React!/Woman Help Me	6
69	London HLZ 10260	Long Green/Light In The Window	6
61	Top Rank 35/105	VAQUERO (LP)	70
68	Stateside S(S)L 10237	BOTTLE OF WINE (LP)	30
69	London HA/SH 8396	COME ON, REACT! (LP)	20

(see also Jimmy Gilmer, Buddy Holly)

FIREBALL XL5
(see under Century 21)

MINT VALUE £

FIREBRAND
85	What WR 71	Never Felt This Way Before/I'm Leaving (p/s)	75

FIRECLOWN
83	Fireclown FC 1001	INVASION EP (Magic/Poor Man/Invasion) (10", no p/s)	12

FIRE ENGINES
80	Codex Comms. CDX 01	Get Up And Use Me/Everything's Roses (p/s)	12
81	Pop:Aural POP 010	Candy Skin/Meat Whiplash (foldout p/s in poly bag)	8
81	Pop:Aural POP 013	Big Gold Dream/Sympathetic Anaesthetic (p/s)	6
81	Pop:Aural POP 01312	Big Gold Dream/Sympathetic Anaesthetic/New Thing In Cartons (12", non-gatefold p/s; gatefold p/s £5)	7
81	Accessory ACC 001	LUBRICATE YOUR LIVING ROOM (LP, in plastic bag)	12

FIRE EXIT
79	Time Bomb Explosion 1	Timewall/Talkin' About Myself (p/s, stamped labels)	10

FIREFLIES
59	Top Rank JAR 198	You Were Mine/Stella Got A Fella (78 rpm = £25)	20
60	London HLU 9057	I Can't Say Goodbye/What Did I Do Wrong	50

FIRE ISLAND
92	Boys Own BOIX 11	In Your Bones/Fire Island (12", 4-track)	15
94	Junior Boys Own JBO 18	There But For The Grace Of God (12")	15
95	Junior Boys Own JBO 26	If You Should Need A Friend (12")	15
97	Junior Boys Own JBO 51	White Powder Dreams/mixes (12")	15
	Junior Boys Own JNR 500 1576	Shout To The Top (12", featuring Loleatta Holloway)	15

FIREMAN
99	Hydra HYPRO 12 008	Fluid (12", p/s, promo only)	50
99	Hydra HYPRO CD 008	Fluid (CD, promo only)	25
93	Parlophone FIRE 1	STRAWBERRIES OCEANS SHIPS FOREST (2-LP, clear vinyl, numbered white sleeve, with inners, promo only)	50
93	Parlophone PCSD 145	STRAWBERRIES OCEANS SHIPS FOREST (2-LP, clear vinyl, red sleeve, with inners)	30
93	Parlophone PCSD 145	STRAWBERRIES OCEANS SHIPS FOREST (CD)	20
98	HYPRO CD007	RUSHES (CD 3-track album promo)	20
98	Hydra 4970551	RUSHES (LP)	25
	(see also Paul McCartney, Youth)		

FIRE SESSION
70	Revolution REV 10	Souvenir/Bad Girl	6
70	Revolution REV 13	Sleeping Reggae/CAROLS: Everyday I Have To Cry Some	6
70	Revolution REV 14	Death Of The Ugly One/Big Feet	6

FIRESIGN THEATRE
68	CBS 65129	WAITING FOR THE ELECTRICIAN OR SOMEONE LIKE HIM (LP)	12
68	CBS 65130	HOW TO BE IN TWO PLACES AT ONCE WHEN YOU'RE NOT ANYWHERE AT ALL? (LP)	12
72	CBS CQ 30737	FIRESIGN THEATRE (LP, quadrophonic)	12

FIRESTONES
62	Decca F 11436	Party Twist (Medley) (Parts 1 & 2)	6

FIRING SQUAD
64	Parlophone R 5152	A Little Bit More/Bull Moose	30

FIRKIN THE FOX
84	Woodworm WR 005	BEHIND BARS (LP)	25

FIRM
85	Atlantic A 9586P	Radioactive/Together (shaped picture disc)	10
85	Atlantic AT 9586	Radioactive/Together/City Sirens/Live In Peace (12", p/s)	10
86	Atlantic A 9458	All The King's Horses/Fortune Hunter (p/s)	5
85	Atlantic 781 239-2	THE FIRM (CD)	18
86	Atlantic 781 628-2	THE FIRM MEAN BUSINESS (CD)	18
	(see also Jimmy Page, Rock Aid Armenia)		

FIRST AID
77	Decca TXS 117	NOSTRADAMUS (LP)	22

FIRST CHOICE
73	Pye International 7N 25613	This Is The House Where Love Died/One Step Away (unissued, demos may exist)	acetate 350
74	Bell BLL 1376	The Player (Parts 1 & 2)	8
73	Bell BELLS 229	ARMED AND EXTREMELY DANGEROUS (LP)	20

FIRST CLASS
74	UK UKAL 1008	THE FIRST CLASS (LP)	15
76	UK UKAL 1022	S.S.T. (LP)	15
	(see also White Plains, Edison Lighthouse, Brotherhood Of Man, Carter-Lewis & Southerners, Ivy League)		

FIRST DOWN
90	Cobden Capers FD1	Jaw Warfare/From Now On/Dedication	50
93	Ill Gotten Gains FD002	LET THE BATTLE BEGIN (EP)	25
94	Blitz Vinyl EFA61008	MAD DOGS AND ENGLISHMAN (EP)	25
94	Blitz Vinyl EFA61009	WORLD SERVICE (LP)	30

FIRST EDITION
68	Reprise RS 20655	Just Dropped In (To See What Condition My Condition Was In)/Shadow In The Corner Of Your Mind	12
68	Reprise RS 20693	Charlie The Fer'de Lance/Look Around I'll Be There	5

69	Reprise RS 20799	But You Know I Love You/Homemade Lies	5
68	Reprise RSLP 6276	THE FIRST EDITION (LP)	15
(see also Kenny Rogers)			

FIRST GEAR
| 64 | Pye 7N 15703 | A Certain Girl/Leave My Kitten Alone | 190 |
| 65 | Pye 7N 15763 | The 'In' Crowd/Gotta Make Their Future Bright | 40 |

FIRST IMPRESSION
| 67 | Saga SOC 1045 | BEAT CLUB (LP) | 15 |

FIRST IMPRESSION/GOOD EARTH
| 68 | Saga FID 2117 | SWINGING LONDON (LP) | 15 |
| *(see also Good Earth, Mungo Jerry)* | | | |

FIRST IMPRESSIONS
| 65 | Pye 7N 15797 | I'm Coming Home/Looking For Her | 15 |
| *(see also Legends)* | | | |

FIRST OFFENCE
| 88 | Metal Other OTH 11 | FIRST OFFENCE (LP, some with insert) | 30/25 |

FIRST STEPS
| 80 | English Rose ER I | The Beat Is Back/She Ain't In Love/Let's Go Cuboids (p/s, with insert) | 20 |
| 81 | English Rose ER III | Anywhere Else But Here/Airplay/I Got The News (p/s) | 20 |

CLARE FISCHER
| 62 | Fontana 688124 ZL | FIRST TIME OUT (LP) | 20 |

WILD MAN FISCHER
| 69 | Reprise RSLP 6332 | AN EVENING WITH WILD MAN FISCHER (gatefold sleeve) | 40 |
| *(see also Frank Zappa)* | | | |

FISCHERMAN'S FRIEND
| 91 | EG OP 51 | MONEY (12", with "Orb Clubmix", 500 only) | 12 |

FISH
89	EMI 12EMPD 109	State Of Mind/The Voyeur (I Like To Watch)/State Of Mind (Presidential Mix) (12", picture disc)	8
90	EMI EMPD 135	A Gentleman's Excuse Me/Whiplash (shaped picture disc)	5
90	EMI 12EMPD 135	A Gentleman's Excuse Me/Whiplash/A Gentleman's Excuse Me (Demo Version) (12", picture disc)	8
91	Polydor FISHS 1	Internal Exile/Carnival Man (12" picture disc, numbered die cut sleeve)	8
91	Polydor FISHS 2	Credo/Credo (7" Mix)/Poet's Moon (12", box set with poster & numbered seal)	8
91	Polydor FISHCD 2	Credo/Credo (7" Mix)/Poet's Moon (CD, picture disc, signed numbered digipak)	12
90	EMI EMDPD 1015	VIGIL IN A WILDERNESS OF MIRRORS (LP, picture disc)	12
(see also Marillion)			

ARCHIE FISHER
68	Xtra XTRA 1070	ARCHIE FISHER (LP)	25
70	Decca SKL 5057	ORFEO (LP)	30
82	Celtic Music CM 007	ARCHIE FISHER (LP, reissue)	15
(see also Barbara Dickson)			

ARCHIE FISHER, BARBARA DICKSON & JOHN MacKINNON
| 69 | Trailer LER 3002 | SONGS OF THE JACOBITE REBELLIONS (LP) | 25 |

CHIP FISHER
| 59 | Parlophone R 4604 | Poor Me/No One | 16 |
| 59 | RCA RCX 143 | AT THE SUGAR BOWL (EP) | 75 |

CILLA FISHER & ARTIE TREZISE
| 79 | Kettle KAC 1 | FOR FOUL DAY AND FAIR (LP) | 15 |

EDDIE FISHER
53	HMV 7M 101	I'm Yours/That's The Chance You Take	20
53	HMV 7M 115	Everything I Have Is Yours/You'll Never Know	22
53	HMV 7M 116	Trust In Me/Forgive Me	15
53	HMV 7M 117	Outside Of Heaven/Lady Of Spain	30
53	HMV 7M 125	Even Now/If It Were Up To Me	15
53	HMV 7M 126	Downhearted/Am I Wasting My Time On You	20
53	HMV 7M 133	I'm Walking Behind You (with Sally Sweetland)/Hold Me	20
53	HMV 7M 146	Just Another Polka/When I Was Young (Yes, Very Young)	15
53	HMV 7M 159	Wish You Were Here/A Fool Was I	25
53	HMV 7M 168	Many Times/With These Hands	12
54	HMV 7M 172	Oh My Papa/(I Never Missed You) Until You Said "Goodbye"	18
54	HMV 7M 185	How Deep Is The Ocean?/That Old Feeling	15
54	HMV 7M 201	April Showers/Just To Be With You	15
54	HMV 7M 212	I'm In The Mood For Love/A Girl, A Girl	15
54	HMV 7M 235	May I Sing To You?/My Friend	15
54	HMV 7M 242	How Do You Speak To An Angel?/My Heart, My Love	15
54	HMV 7M 251	I Need You Now/Heaven Was Never Like This	15
54	HMV 7M 257	They Say It's Wonderful/Green Years	15
54	HMV 7M 266	Count Your Blessings Instead Of Sheep/White Christmas	15
55	HMV 7M 294	(I'm Always Hearing) Wedding Bells/A Man Chases A Girl	15
56	HMV 7M 353	Magic Fingers/My One And Only Love	12
56	HMV 7M 374	Dungaree Doll/If It Hadn't Been For You	20
56	HMV 7M 402	Without You/No Other One	12
56	HMV 7M 421	Sweet Heartaches/What Is This Thing Called Love?	12
56	HMV POP 273	Cindy, Oh Cindy/Fanny	20
54	HMV 7EG 8026	NIGHT AND DAY (EP)	10
54	HMV 7EG 8046	APRIL SHOWERS (EP)	10
55	HMV 7EG 8146	HOW DEEP IS THE OCEAN (EP)	10

Eddie FISHER

MINT VALUE £

55	HMV 7EG 8156	EDDIE FISHER SINGS NO. 3 — TAKE MY LOVE (EP)	10
56	HMV 7EG 8207	BUNDLE OF JOY (EP, with Debbie Reynolds)	12
54	HMV DLP 1040	TIME FOR ROMANCE (10" LP)	25
55	HMV DLP 1074	MY SERENADE IS YOU (10" LP)	25
56	HMV CLP 1095	SINGS ACADEMY AWARD WINNING SONGS (LP)	15

FAYE FISHER
65	Columbia DB 7575	Our Love/I Just Don't Know What To Say	7
65	Columbia DB 7732	Oh Heartache You're Bothering Me/It's You	7

MATTHEW FISHER
73	RCA APL1 0195	JOURNEY'S END (LP)	12

(see also Procol Harum, Green Bullfrog)

RAY FISHER
72	Trailer LER 2038	THE BONNY BIRDY (LP, red label, later yellow)	20/15

SONNY FISHER
77	Ace NST 59	Rockin' Daddy/I Can't Lose (78)	30

TONI FISHER
60	Top Rank JAR 261	The Big Hurt/Memphis Belle	8
60	Top Rank JAR 341	How Deep Is The Ocean/Blue, Blue, Blue	10
62	London HLX 9564	West Of The Wall/What Did I Do	10

FISHER BROTHERS
64	London HLN 9928	Big Round Wheel/By The Time You Read This Letter	12

FISHER FAMILY
60s	Topic TOP 67	FAR OVER THE FORTH (EP)	8
66	Topic 12T 137	THE FISHER FAMILY (LP)	15

FISHERFOLK
70s	Celebration CR 1007	WORSHIP WITH THE FISHERFOLK (LP)	18
70s	Celebration CR 1025	THE SUN'S GONNA SHINE (LP)	15
70s	Celebration CR 1028	JOY IN THE MORNING (LP)	18
70s	Celebration CR 1030	WILLING TO ROW (LP)	18

FIST
80	Neat NEAT 04	Name Rank And Serial Number/You'll Never Get Me In One Of Those (p/s, some with poster insert)	10/8
80	MCA MCA 615	Name Rank And Serial Number/You'll Never Get Me (In One Of Those) (p/s, reissue, some with poster insert)	30/20
80	MCA MCA 640	Forever Amber/Brain Damage (p/s)	12
81	MCA MCA 663	Collision Course/Law Of The Jungle (some in p/s)	100/30
82	Neat NEAT 021	The Wanderer/Too Hot (p/s)	10
80	MCA MCF 3082	TURN THE HELL ON (LP)	15
85	Neat NEAT 1003	BACK WITH A VENGEANCE (LP, some on yellow vinyl)	30/15

JOHN FITCH & ASSOCIATES
71	Beacon BEA 117	Romantic Altitude/Stoned Out Of It	15

FITS
82	Rondelet ROUND 13	Think For Yourself: Burial/Straps (p/s)	5
83	Corpus Christi ITS 9	Tears Of A Nation/Bravado/Breaking Point (p/s)	6
84	Trapper FIT 1	Action/Achilles Heel (p/s)	7
85	Trapper FIT 2	Fact Or Fiction/Give Away (p/s)	5
81	Beat The System FIT 1	YOU SAID WE'D NEVER MAKE IT (EP, wraparound p/s)	7
82	Rondelet ABOUT 6	NOTHING AND NOWHERE (LP)	12

FITS OF GLOOM
92	Gem GEMX 002	Differences/mixes (12")	12
94	MCA MCSTD 1981	Heaven/mixes (12")	12
94	MCA MCST 2016	Power Of Love/mixes (12")	12

FITZ & COOLERS
68	Nu Beat NB 003	Cover Me/Darling	12

ELLA FITZGERALD
SINGLES
54	Brunswick 05324	Who's Afraid (Not I, Not I, Not I)/I Wished On The Moon (with Gordon Jenkins)	8
55	Brunswick 05392	Lullaby Of Birdland/Later	8
55	Brunswick 05427	Moanin' Low/Take A Chance On Love	8
55	Brunswick 05468	Lover, Come Back To Me/Old Devil Moon	8
55	Brunswick 05473	Pete Kelly's Blues/Hard Hearted Hannah	8
55	Brunswick 05477	Soldier Boy/Air Mail Special (with Bill Doggett)	8
56	Brunswick 05514	My One And Only Love/(Love Is) The Tender Trap	8
56	Brunswick 05539	Ella's Contribution To The Blues/Early Autumn	8
56	Brunswick 05584	You'll Never Know/But Not Like Mine	8
56	HMV POP 266	The Silent Treatment/The Sun Forgot To Shine This Morning	8
57	HMV POP 290	A Beautiful Friendship/Too Young For The Blues	7
57	HMV POP 316	Hotta Chocolatta/Stay There	7
57	HMV POP 348	Johnny One Note/To Keep My Love Alive	7
57	HMV POP 373	Ev'ry Time We Say Goodbye/Manhattan	7
57	HMV POP 380	Goody Goody/A Tisket, A Tasket	5
58	HMV POP 486	The Swingin' Shepherd Blues/Midnight Sun	7
58	HMV POP 499	Beale Street Blues/St. Louis Blues	5
58	HMV POP 518	Your Red Wagon/Trav'lin Light	5
59	Brunswick 05783	My Happiness/A Satisfied Mind	5
59	HMV POP 657	But Not For Me/You Make Me Feel So Young	5
59	HMV POP 686	The Christmas Song/You Make Me Feel So Young	7
60	HMV POP 701	Like Young/Beat Me Daddy Eight To The Bar	5

MINT VALUE £

60	HMV POP 719	It's All Right With Me/Don'cha Go Way Mad (with Oscar Peterson)	5
60	HMV POP 736	Mack The Knife/Lorelei	7
60	HMV POP 782	How High The Moon (Parts 1 & 2)	7
60	HMV POP 809	Good Morning Blues/Jingle Blues	5
60	HMV POP 817	We Three Kings Of Orient Are/White Christmas	5
61	HMV POP 849	The Lady Is A Tramp/Misty	5
64	Verve VS 502	Desafinado/Stardust	5
65	Verve VS 519	Can't Buy Me Love/Sweetest Sound	10
65	Verve VS 524	Why Was I Born/All The Things You Are	5
66	Stateside SS 569	These Boots Were Made for Walkin'/Stardust	5
69	Reprise RS 20850	Get Ready/Open Your Window	15
69	Polydor 56767	Hey Jude/Sunshine Of Your Love	10
71	Reprise RS 23507	I Heard It Through The Grapevine/Days Of Wine & Roses	5

LPs

53	Brunswick LA 8581	SOUVENIR ALBUM (10")	20
54	Brunswick LA 8648	ELLA SINGS GERSHWIN (10")	20
55	Brunswick LAT 8056	ELLA – SONGS IN A MELLOW MOOD	15
56	Brunswick LAT 8091	SWEET AND HOT	15
56	Brunswick LAT 8115	LULLABIES OF BIRDLAND	15
56	HMV CLP 1083	THE COLE PORTER SONGBOOK VOLUME 1	15
56	HMV CLP 1084	THE COLE PORTER SONGBOOK VOLUME 2	15
57	Brunswick LAT 8223	ELLA AND HER FELLAS	15
57	HMV CLP 1116	THE RODGERS AND HART SONGBOOK VOLUME 1	15
57	HMV CLP 1117	THE RODGERS AND HART SONGBOOK VOLUME 2	15
58	HMV CLP 1166	LIKE SOMEONE IN LOVE	15
58	HMV CLP 1183	THE IRVING BERLIN SONGBOOK VOLUME ONE	12
58	HMV CLP 1184	THE IRVING BERLIN SONGBOOK VOLUME TWO	12
58	HMV CLP 1213/1214	THE DUKE ELLINGTON SONGBOOK NUMBER ONE (2-LP)	15
58	HMV CLP 1227/1228	THE DUKE ELLINGTON SONGBOOK NUMBER TWO (2-LP)	15
59	HMV CLP 1267	ELLA SWINGS LIGHTLY	12
59	HMV CLP 1338	SINGS GERSHWIN VOL. 1 (also stereo CSD 1292)	each 12
59	HMV CLP 1339	SINGS GERSHWIN VOL. 2	12
60	HMV CLP 1347	SINGS GERSHWIN VOL. 3 (also stereo CSD 1299)	each 12
60	HMV CLP 1348	SINGS GERSHWIN VOL. 4 (also stereo CSD 1300)	each 12
60	HMV CLP 1353	SINGS GERSHWIN VOL. 5 (also stereo CSD 1304)	each 12
60	HMV CSD 1287	SWEET SONGS FOR SWINGERS	12
60	HMV CLP 1391	ELLA IN BERLIN – MACK THE KNIFE	12
60	HMV CLP 1396	SONGS FROM THE FILM "LET NO MAN WRITE MY EPITAPH"	12
60	HMV CLP 1397	ELLA WISHES YOU A SWINGING CHRISTMAS	12
61	HMV CLP 1383	HELLO LOVE! (also stereo CSD 1315)	each 12
63	Verve VLP 9020	RHYTHM IS MY BUSINESS	12
65	Verve VLP 9083	ELLA AT JUAN-LES-PINS	12

(see also Oscar Peterson, Count Basie, Ink Spots)

ELLA FITZGERALD & LOUIS ARMSTRONG

56	HMV CLP 1098	ELLA AND LOUIS (LP)	12
57	HMV CLP 1146	ELLA AND LOUIS AGAIN NO. 1 (LP)	12
57	HMV CLP 1147	ELLA AND LOUIS AGAIN NO. 2 (LP)	12
59	HMV CLP 1245	PORGY AND BESS (LP)	12
59	HMV CLP 1246	PORGY AND BESS (LP)	12

(see also Louis Armstrong)

ELLA FITZGERALD/BILLIE HOLIDAY

58	Columbia Clef 33CX 10100	AT NEWPORT (LP)	15

G. F. FITZGERALD

70	Uni UNLS 115	MOUSEPROOF (LP, with insert)	70

(see also Sam Gopal)

PATRICK FITZGERALD

77	Small Wonder SMALL 4	SAFETY PIN STUCK IN MY HEART (EP, with lyrics)	7
78	Small Wonder SMALL 6	Buy Me, Sell Me/The Little Dippers/Trendy/The Backstreet Boys (p/s)	8
78	Small Wonder WEENY ONE	THE PARANOID WARD/THE BEDROOM TAPES (EP, mono/stereo, 33rpm)	7
78	Small Wonder WEENY ONE	THE PARANOID WARD/THE BEDROOM TAPES (12" EP)	10
79	Polydor 2383 533	GRUBBY STORIES (LP)	12
80s	Final Solution FSEP 001	TONIGHT EP	8

MAGGIE FITZGIBBON

59	Pye International N 25047	Kookaburra/The Right Kind Of Man (78)	10

FITZROY (Sterling) & HARRY

70	Bullet BU 439	Freedom Street/Freedom Street Version	7
70	Escort ERT 827	Pop A Top Train/Doing The Moonwalk	10

FIVE AMERICANS

66	Pye International 7N 25354	I See The Light/The Outcasts	20
66	Pye International 7N 25373	Evol – Not Love/Don't Blame Me	35
67	Stateside SS 2012	Western Union/Now That It's All Over	10
67	Stateside SS 2036	Sound Of Love/Sympathy	8
68	Stateside SS 2097	7.30 Guided Tour/See-Saw Man	8

5 A.M. EVENT

66	Pye 7N 17154	Hungry/I Wash My Hands (In Muddy Water)	250+

FIVE & A PENNY

68	Polydor 56282	You Don't Know Where Your Interest Lies/Mary Go Round	40

FIVE BLIND BOYS

64	Vocalion EPVP 1276	NEGRO SPIRITUALS (EP, 2 tracks by Spirits Of Memphis)	25
64	Vocalion EPVP 1282	FIVE BLIND BOYS (EP)	25

FIVE BLOBS
58	Philips PB 881	The Blob/Saturday Night In Tijuana	20
58	Philips PB 881	The Blob/Saturday Night In Tijuana (78)	15

FIVE BY FIVE
68	Pye International 7N 25477	Fire/Hang Up	38

FIVE CARD STUD
67	Philips BF 1567	Beg Me/Once	15

FIVE CHESTERNUTS
58	Columbia DB 4165	Jean Dorothy/Teenage Love (78 rpm = £100)	200

(see also Shadows, Pete Chester)

FIVE COUNTS
62	Oriole CB 1769	Watermelon Walk/Spanish Nights	24

FIVE CRESTAS
66	Excel ES SP 288/289	How Sweet It Is (To Be Loved By You)/You Used To Love Me (private pressing)	65

FIVE DALLAS BOYS
57	Columbia DB 4005	Shangri-La/By The Fireside	10
57	Columbia DB 4041	I Never Had The Blues/All The Way	10
58	Columbia DB 4102	26 Miles (Santa Catalina)/Sail Along, Silv'ry Moon	10
58	Columbia DB 4154	Big Man/Lonesome Traveller	8
58	Columbia DB 4231	Fatty Patty/Do You Wanna Jump Children? (78 rpm = £10)	10
59	Columbia DB 4313	Morning Papers/I'm Aware	5
60	Columbia SEG 8035	THE FIVE DALLAS BOYS (EP)	16

(see also Dallas Boys)

FIVE DAY RAIN
70	private pressing	FIVE DAY RAIN (LP, no sleeve, 20-30 copies only)	500+
93	private pressing	FIVE DAY RAIN (LP, re-pressing in signed, numbered sleeve, signed note in run-out groove & letter of authenticity, 25 only)	80

(see also Scots Of St. James, Hopscotch, One Way Ticket, Glencoe)

FIVE DAY WEEK STRAW PEOPLE
68	Saga FID 2123	FIVE DAY WEEK STRAW PEOPLE (LP)	120

(see also Attack, Andromeda, John Du Cann)

FIVE DE MARCO SISTERS
53	MGM SP 1043	Bouillabasse/I'm Never Satisfied	17
54	Brunswick 05349	Love Me/Just A Girl That Men Forget	17
55	Brunswick 05425	Dreamboat/Two Hearts, Two Kisses (Make One Love)	17
55	Brunswick 05474	The Hot Barcarolle/Sailor Boys Have Talk To Me In English	15
56	Brunswick 05526	Romance Me/This Love Of Mine	15

FIVE DU-TONES
63	Stateside SS 206	Shake A Tail Feather/Divorce Court	25
68	President PT 134	Shake A Tail Feather/Divorce Court (reissue)	10

FIVE EMPREES
65	Stateside SS 470	Little Miss Sad/Hey Lover	18

FIVE FLEETS
58	Felsted AF 103	Oh What A Feeling/I Been Cryin' (78 rpm = £90)	300

FIVE GO DOWN TO THE SEA
83	Kabuki KAFIVE 5	KNOT A FISH (EP)	6
84	Abstract 12 ABS 027	THE GLEE CLUB (12" EP)	8
85	Creation CRE 021T	Singing In Braille/Aunt Nelly/Silk Brain Worm/Women (12", p/s)	8

FIVE HAND REEL
76	Rubber RUB 019	FIVE HAND REEL (LP, with lyric insert)	12
78	RCA PL 25150	EARL O'MORAY (LP)	15

FIVE KEYS
54	Capitol CL 14184	Ling, Ting, Tong/I'm Alone (78)	50
55	Capitol CL 14313	The Verdict/Make Me Um Pow Pow (triangular centre) (78 rpm = £50)	500
55	Capitol CL 14325	(Close Your Eyes) Take A Deep Breath/Doggone It, You Did It (tri centre)	450
55	Capitol CL 14325	(Close Your Eyes) Take A Deep Breath/Doggone It, You Did It (78)	40
56	Capitol CL 14545	Gee Whittakers!/'Cause You're My Lover (78 rpm = £30)	300
56	Capitol CL 14582	She's The Most/I Dreamt I Dwelt In Heaven (78 rpm = £30)	250
56	Capitol CL 14639	That's Right/Out Of Sight, Out Of Mind (78 rpm = £20)	150
57	Capitol CL 14686	The Wisdom Of A Fool/Now Don't That Prove I Love You? (78 rpm = £25)	150
57	Capitol CL 14736	Four Walls/Let There Be You (78 rpm = £30)	100
57	Capitol CL 14756	The Blues Don't Care/This I Promise You (78 rpm = £40)	150
58	Capitol CL 14829	From Me To You/Whippety Whirl (78 rpm = £45)	150
58	Capitol CL 14967	One Great Love/Really-O Truly-O	150
57	Capitol T 828	THE FIVE KEYS ON STAGE! (LP)	180+

FIVE MILES OUT
73	Action ACT 4614	Super Sweet Girl Of Mine/Set Your Mind Free	15

FIVE OF DIAMONDS
65	Oak RGJ 150 FD	FIVE OF DIAMONDS (EP)	375

FIVE OR SIX
81	Cherry Red CHERRY 19	Another Reason/The Trial (p/s)	5
81	Cherry Red 12CHERRY 23	POLAR EXPOSURE (12" EP)	8
82	Cherry Red 12CHERRY 43	FOUR FROM FIVE OR SIX (12" EP)	8
82	Cherry Red FRIZBEE 2	A THRIVING AND HAPPY LAND (LP)	12

FIVE ROYALES
60	Ember EMB S 124	Dedicated To The One I Love/Miracle Of Love	100+

FIVE SAPPHIRES
78	Rocket ROKN 539	Love Music/Where Did All The Good Times Go	5

(see also Steve Allan, Alan Carvell, Carvells, Telegrams)

FIVE SATINS
57	London HL 8501	To The Aisle/Wish I Had My Baby (78 rpm = £160)	1000
59	Top Rank JAR 199	Wonderful Girl/Weeping Willow	45
59	Top Rank JAR 239	Shadows/Toni My Love	45
60	MGM MGM 1087	Your Memory/I Didn't Know	68

FIVE'S COMPANY
66	Pye 7N 17118	Sunday For Seven Days/The Big Kill	10
66	Pye 7N 17162	Some Girls/Big Deal	6
66	Pye 7N 17199	Session Man/Dejection	18
69	Saga FID 2151	THE BALLAD OF FRED THE PIXIE (LP)	20

(see also Brunning Hall Sunflower Blues Band)

FIVE SMITH BROTHERS
54	Decca F 10403	A.B.C. Boogie/Veni-Vidi-Vici (with Dennis Wilson Quartet)	20
55	Decca F 10507	Paper Valentine/You're As Sweet Today (As Yesterday)	15
55	Decca F 10527	Don't Worry/I'm In Favour Of Friendship	15
56	Decca F 10698	You Took My Heart (My Only Heart)/The Grass Is Green	8

FIVE STAIRSTEPS (& CUBIE)
68	Pye International 7N 25448	A Million To One/Something's Missing (with Cubie)	15
69	Buddah 201 026	Stay Close To Me/I Made A Mistake (with Cubie)	20
69	Buddah 201 070	We Must Be In Love/Little Young Lovers (with Cubie)	20
70	Buddah 201 083	Dear Prudence/O-o-h Child	15
70	Buddah 2011 036	O-o-h Child/Who Do You Belong To?	10
70	Buddah 2011 053	Because I Love You/America — Standing	9

(see also Stairsteps)

FIVE STEPS BEYOND
67	CBS 202490	Not So Young Today/Meanwhile Back In My Heart	15
95	Tenth Planet TP 019	FAINT HEARTS AND FAIR MAIDS (LP, 600 only)	15
96	Tenth Planet TP 021	SMILE (LP, with A4 booklet, 600 only)	15

FIVE TOWNS
67	Direction 58-3115	It Isn't What You've Got/Advice	8

FIXER
78	Rainbow RSL 116	Bright And Rosy (no p/s)	40

FIZZARUM
99	City Centre Offices BLOCK 2	Phut Of Plex (clear vinyl, plain black sleeve, with inserts; 650 copies only)	20

FIZZBOMBS
87	Narodnik NRK 003	Sign On The Line/The Lines That (p/s)	8
87	Wild Rumpus SHEP 001	You Worry Me/JESSE GARON & DESPERADOS: Hank Williams Is Dead (p/s, flexidisc)	6
88	Calculus KIT 002	THE SURFIN' WINTER EP (p/s)	5
88	Calculus KIT 002T	THE SURFIN' WINTER EP (12", p/s)	8

ROBERTA FLACK
69	Atlantic 588 204	FIRST TAKE (LP)	15
71	Atlantic K 40097	CHAPTER TWO (LP)	15
72	Atlantic K 40297	QUIET FIRE (LP)	15
73	Atlantic K 50021	KILLING ME SOFTLY (LP)	15
75	Atlantic K 50049	FEEL LIKE MAKIN' LOVE (LP)	15

(see also Donny Hathaway)

FLACK OFF
80	Sofa	FLACK OFF EP: COCKTAILS AT SIX	20

FLAG OF CONVENIENCE
82	Sire SIR 4057	Life On The Telephone/The Other Man's Sin (no p/s)	5

(see also Steve Diggle, Buzzcocks)

FLAIRS
57	Oriole CB 1392	Swing Pretty Mama/I'd Climb The Hills And Mountains	575
57	Oriole CB 1392	Swing Pretty Mama/I'd Climb The Hills And Mountains (78)	110

LES FLAMBEAUX
65	HMV POP 1456	Cachita/Greensleeves	5
71	Mushroom 100 MR 13	LES FLAMBEAUX (LP, 2 different sleeve designs)	15

FLAME
70	Stateside SS 2183	See The Light/Get Your Mind Made Up	15
71	Stateside SSL 10312	THE FLAME (LP)	35

(see also Flames [South Africa], Beach Boys)

FLAME
77	RCA PC 12160	QUEEN OF THE NEIGHBOURHOOD (LP)	12

(see also Aerosmith)

FLAME 'N' KING & BOLD ONES
79	Grapevine GRP 123	Ho Happy Day/Ain't Nobody Jivin'	10

FLAMES
64	Island WI 130	He's The Greatest/Someone Going To Bawl (both actually by the Maytals)	35
64	Island WI 136	Little Flea/Good Idea (both actually by the Maytals)	35
64	Island WI 138	When I Get Home/Neither Silver Nor Gold (both actually by the Maytals)	35
64	Island WI 139	Broadway Jungle/Beat Lied (both actually by the Maytals)	40

(see also Maytals, Vikings)

FLAMES
64	Blue Beat BB 205	Helena Darling/My Darling (both actually by Plamers)	16

FLAMES
68	Nu Beat NB 020	Mini Really Fit Dem/Soul Train (both actually by Alton Ellis & Flames)	10
73	Ackee ACK 528	Feeling Good/Zig Zag	6

(see also Alton Ellis & Flames, Righteous Flames, Larry Marshall)

FLAMES (South Africa)
68	Flame FAN 101/1	Streamliner/Follow The Sun (p/s)	20
68	Page One FOR(S) 009	BURNING SOUL (LP)	40

(see also Flame, Beach Boys)

FLAMING EMERALDS
78	Grapevine GRP 104	Have Some Everybody/Have Some Everybody (Instrumental)	15

JOHNNY FLAMINGO
57	Vogue V 9089	My Teen-Age Girl/When I Lost You (78 rpm = £40)	120
58	Vogue V 9100	So Long/Make Me A Present Of You (78 rpm =- £50)	75

FLAMINGOS
57	London HLN 8373	Would I Be Crying?/Just For A Kick (78 rpm = £100+)	600+
57	Brunswick 05696	The Ladder Of Love/Let's Make Up (78 rpm = £80+)	550
59	Top Rank JAR 213	Love Walked In/Yours	50
60	Top Rank JAR 263	I Only Have Eyes For You/I Was Such A Fool	100
60	Top Rank JAR 367	Nobody Loves Me Like You/You, Me And The Sea	40
60	Top Rank JAR 519	Mio Amore/At Night	35
66	Philips BF 1483	Boogaloo Party/Nearness Of You	22
69	Philips BF 1786	Boogaloo Party/Nearness Of You (reissue, some in p/s)	20/18
69	Philips SBL 7906	HITS NOW AND THEN (LP)	45

FLAMIN' GROOVIES
71	Kama Sutra 2013 031	Teenage Head/Evil-Hearted Ada	12
72	Kama Sutra 2013 042	Gonna Rock Tonite/Keep A-Knockin'/SHA NA NA: Rock'n'Roll Is Here To Stay/At The Hop/Duke Of Earl	8
72	United Artists UP 35392	Slow Death/Talahassie Lassie (some in promo only p/s)	25/7
72	United Artists UP 35464	Married Woman/Get A Shot Of Rhythm And Blues	10
76	Sire 6198 086	Don't You Lie To Me/She Said Yeah/Shake Some Action (p/s)	7
76	Sire 6078 602	Shake Some Action/Teenage Confidential (p/s, 2 different versions of A-side)	6
76	Kama Sutra KSS 707	Teenage Head/Headin' For The Texas Border	5
78	Sire 6078 619	Feel A Whole Lot Better/Paint It Black/Shake Some Action (p/s)	5
78	Sire 6078 619	Feel A Whole Lot Better/Paint It Black/Shake Some Action (12", p/s)	9
76	United Artists REM 406	SLOW DEATH (EP)	10
71	Kama Sutra 2683 003	FLAMIN' GROOVIES (2-LP)	20
77	Sire 9103 251	SHAKE SOME ACTION (LP)	15
78	Sire 9103 333	THE FLAMIN' GROOVIES NOW! (LP)	15

(see also Mike Wilhelm)

FLAMING LIPS
89	Glitterhouse EFA 40153	Drug Machine In Heaven/Strychnine/What's So Funny (About Peace, Love And Understanding) (p/s)	15
91	City Slang 04063-05	Unconsciously Screamin'/Ma, I Didn't Notice/Let Me Be It/Lucifer Rising (clear vinyl, hologram sleeve)	8
92	Warners PRO CD 5401	Everyone Wants To Live Forever (CD promo, title sleeve)	20
92	Warners PRO S 5452	Ballrooms Of Mars/MR BUNGLE: Sudden Death (promo, grey vinyl, no p/s)	15
92	Warners PRO CD 5628	Collector Scum Tantalizor (promo CD)	20
94	Warners W 0246CDX	She Don't Use Jelly/The Process/Moth In The Incubator (CD)	8
94	Warners SAM 1431	She Don't Use Jelly/Translucent Egg/Turn It On (Bluegrass Version)/The Process (12" promo)	15
95	Warners W 0322CD	Bad Days (Edit)/She Don't Use Jelly (Primitive Demo)/Girl With Hair Like An Explosion/Giraffe (Demo Version) (CD)	12
95	Warners W 0322CDX	Bad Days (Edit)/Ice Drummer (Suicide Tribute Album Contribution)/When You Smiled (I Lost My Only Idea)/Put The Waterbug In The Policeman's Ear (Ghetto Blaster Recording At The Art School, Sept. '93) (CD, 'squidgy pack')	15
95	Warners PRO S 7918	What's The New Mary Jane?/Under Pressure (promo, no p/s)	15
96	Warners 9362-43672	This Here Giraffe/The Sun (Live Peel Session Version)/Hit Me Like You Did First Time (Live Peel Session Version) (star-shaped CD)	10
96	Warners WO 370CD	Brainville/Evil Will Prevail (Recorded On 'Brave New World', KCRW, Santa Monica)/Waterbug (Recorded On 'Brave New World', KCRW, Santa Monica)	8
96	Warners WO 370 CDX	Brainville/Brainville (Recorded On 'Brave New World', KCRW, Santa Monica)/Raindrops (Written By Burt Bacharach) (Recorded On 'Brave New World', KCRW, Santa Monica) (CD, holographic sleeve)	10
98	Warners PRO CD 9295	The Big Ol' Bug Is The New Baby Now (Stereo Mix) (enhanced CD-Rom, stickered cardboard sleeve)	15
02	Warners (no cat. no.)	Ego Tripping/It's Summertime (promo CD-R)	20
00s	Rykodisc/Restless PRCD RPRO 270	THE SHAMBOLIC BIRTH AND EARLY LIFE OF THE FLAMING LIPS CATALOG SAMPLER 1983-1991 (promo CD)	18

FLAMING YOUTH
69	Fontana TF 1057	Guide Me Orion/From Now On (Immortal Invisible)	22
70	Fontana 6001 002	Every Man, Woman And Child/Drifting	18
70	Fontana 6001 003	From Now On/Space Child	18
69	Fontana STL 5533	ARK II (LP, with plastic window sleeve)	50

(see also Genesis, Phil Collins, Jackson Heights)

FLAMMA-SHERMAN
68	SNB 55-3488	No Need To Explain/Bassa Love	10
68	SNB 55-3769	Love Is In The Air/Super Day	10
69	SNB 55-4142	Move Me/Where Is He (DJ copy = £75)	

TOMMY FLANAGAN
59	Esquire 32-156	THE CATS (LP)	40

FLANAGAN & ALLEN
53	Columbia SEG 7709	TOGETHER AGAIN (EP)	8
53	Columbia 33S 1010	FLANAGAN AND ALLEN (10" LP)	12
53	Decca LF 1125	FAVOURITES (10" LP)	12

FLANAGAN BROTHERS
58	Vogue Coral Q 72342	Salton City/Early One Evening (78 rpm = £12)	20

TOMMY FLANDERS
69	Verve SVLP 6020	MOONSTONE (LP)	18

(see also Blues Project)

FLARES
61	London HLU 9441	Foot Stompin'/Hotcha Cha-Cha Brown	25
63	London HA-U 8034	FOOT STOMPIN' HITS (LP)	75

FLASH
72	Sovereign SOV 105	Small Beginnings/Morning Haze	7
73	Sovereign SOV 116	Watch Your Step/Lifetime	7
72	Sovereign SVNA 7251	FLASH (LP)	15
72	Sovereign SVNA 7255	FLASH IN THE CAN (LP, some in unissued 'band in studio' proof sleeve)	25/15
73	Sovereign SVNA 7260	OUT OF OUR HANDS (LP)	18

(see also Peter Banks, Yes)

FLASH & BOARD OF DIRECTORS
68	Bell BLL 1007	Busy Signal/Love Ain't Easy	10

FLASHPOINT
87	private pressing FP 01	NO POINT OF REFERENCE (LP)	40

FLAT EARTH SOCIETY
83	Psycho PSYCHO 17	WALEECO (LP)	15

FLATMATES
86	Subway Organisation SUBWAY 6	I Could Be In Heaven/Tell Me Why/So In Love With You (foldaround p/s with insert in poly bag)	6
88	Subway Org. SUBWAY 17T	Shimmer/On My Mind/If Not For You/Bad (12", p/s, with 'flat sharing guide')	8

(Lester) FLATT & (Earl) SCRUGGS
65	CBS 201793	Ballad Of Jed Clampett/Gonna Give Myself A Ball	6
67	CBS 3038	Foggy Mountain Breakdown/California Uptight Band	5
67	Mercury MF 1007	Foggy Mountain Breakdown/My Cabin In Caroline	5
61	Mercury ZEP 10106	C & W TRAIL BLAZERS NO. 4 (EP)	15
64	Mercury 10010 MCE	COUNTRY AND WESTERN ACES (EP)	15
62	Philips BBL 7516	SONGS OF THE FAMOUS CARTER FAMILY (LP)	12
63	CBS BPG 62095	FOLK SONGS OF OUR LAND (LP)	12
63	CBS BPG 62259	AT CARNEGIE HALL (LP)	12

LINDA FLAVELL
66	Decca F 12312	And The Trouble With Me Is You/Over And Over	10

FLAVOUR
68	Direction 58-3597	Sally Had A Party/Shop Around	10

LOS FLECHAZOS
94	Detour Records DRO 13	Try It/You Drove Me Crazy (p/s, 100 red vinyl)	7

GREGORY FLECKNER QUINTET
96	Clear CLR 418	Oi, That's My Bird (12", with Plaid & Dr Rockit mixes, p/s)	8

(FABULOUS) FLEE-REKKERS/FLEE-RAKKERS
60	Triumph RGM 1008	Green Jeans/You Are My Sunshine (as Fabulous Flee-Rakkers)	40
60	Top Rank JAR 431	Green Jeans/You Are My Sunshine (reissue, as Fabulous Flea-Rakkers)	70
60	Pye 7N 15288	Sunday Date/Shiftless Sam	15
60	Pye 7N 15326	Blue Tango/Bitter Rice	15
61	Piccadilly 7N 35006	Lone Rider/Miller Like Wow	15
62	Piccadilly 7N 35048	Stage To Cimarron/Twistin' The Chestnuts	15
62	Piccadilly 7N 35081	Sunburst/Black Buffalo	20
63	Piccadilly 7N 35109	Fireball/Fandango	20
61	Pye NEP 24141	THE FABULOUS FLEE-REKKERS (EP)	75

(see also Ricky Wayne & Fabulous Flee-Rakkers)

(PETER GREEN'S) FLEETWOOD MAC
SINGLES
67	Blue Horizon 57-3051	I Believe My Time Ain't Long/Rambling Pony (as Peter Green's Fleetwood Mac, initially with p/s)	100/20
68	Blue Horizon 57-3138	Black Magic Woman/The Sun Is Shining	10
68	Blue Horizon 57-3139	Need Your Love So Bad/Stop Messin' Around	10
68	Blue Horizon 57-3145	Albatross/Jigsaw Puzzle Blues	6
69	Immediate IM 080	Man Of The World/EARL VINCE & VALIANTS: Somebody's Gonna Get Their Head Kicked In Tonight	10
69	Blue Horizon 57-3157	Need Your Love So Bad/Black Magic Woman (unissued)	
69	Blue Horizon 57-3157	Black Magic Woman/No Place To Go (unissued)	
69	Blue Horizon 57-3157	Need Your Love So Bad/No Place To Go	6
69	CBS 3051	I Believe My Time Ain't Long/Rambling Pony (reissue)	6
69	Reprise RS 27000	Oh Well (Parts 1 & 2)	6
70	Reprise RS 27007	The Green Manalishi (With The Two-Prong Crown)/World In Harmony (initially with p/s)	30/8
71	Reprise RS 27010	Dragonfly/The Purple Dancer	5
71	CBS/Blue Horizon 3145	Albatross/Jigsaw Puzzle Blues (reissue)	5
72	Reprise K 14194	Spare Me A Little Of Your Love/Sunny Side Of Heaven	5

73	Reprise K 14280	Did You Ever Love Me?/The Derelict.	5
73	CBS 1722	Black Magic Woman/Stop Messin' Around.	5
73	CBS 8306	Albatross/Need Your Love So Bad (p/s, 'Hall Of Fame Hits' reissue)	5
74	Reprise K 14315	For Your Love/Hypnotised	5
75	Reprise K 14388	Heroes Are Hard To Find/Born Enchanter	5
75	DJM DJS 10620	Man Of The World/DANNY KIRWAN: Second Chapter	5
75	Reprise K 14403	Warm Ways/Blue Letter (with p/s)	8
76	Reprise K 14413	Over My Head (Edit)/I'm So Afraid.	5
76	Reprise K 14430	Rhiannon/Sugar Daddy (with p/s)	8
76	Reprise K 14447	Say You Love Me/Monday Morning.	5
77	Warner Bros K 16872	Go Your Own Way/Silver Springs (p/s)	8
77	Warner Bros K 16930	Don't Stop/Gold Dust Women	5
77	Warner Bros K 16969	Dreams/Songbird	5
77	Warner Bros K 17013	You Make Loving Fun/Never Going Back Again	5
79	Warner Bros K 17468	Tusk/Never Make Me Cry ('dog' or 'plain' p/s)	each 5
79	Warner Bros K 17533	Sara/That's Enough For Me (p/s).	6
80	Warner Bros K 17577	Not That Funny/Save Me A Place (p/s)	5
80	Warner Bros K 17614	Think About Me/Honey Hi (p/s)	5
81	Warner Bros K 17746	The Farmer's Daughter/Dreams (live) (p/s)	7
82	Warner Bros K 17965	Hold Me/Eyes Of The World (p/s)	5
82	Warner Bros K 17997	Gypsy (Edit)/Cool Water (p/s)	5
82	Warner Bros FLEET 1P	Oh Diane/Rhiannon/The Chain (picture disc).	8
83	Warner Bros W 9848	Can't Go Back/That's Alright (p/s).	5
83	Warner Bros W 9848T	Can't Go Back/Rhiannon/Tusk/Over And Over (12", p/s)	10
87	Warner Bros W 8398	Big Love/You And I Part 1//The Chain/Go Your Own Way (gatefold double pack)	6
87	Warner Bros W 8398TP	Big Love (Extended)/You And I Part 1 (12", picture disc)	10
87	Warner Bros W 8317TP	Seven Wonders (Extended Remix)/Book Of Miracles (Instrumental)/ Seven Wonders (Dub) (12", picture disc)	10
87	Warner Bros W 8291	Little Lies/Ricky (picture disc).	5
87	Warner Bros W 8291TP	Little Lies (Extended)/Little Lies (Dub)/Ricky (12", picture disc)	10

LPs

68	Blue Horizon 7-63200	PETER GREEN'S FLEETWOOD MAC (mono/stereo)	50/40
68	Blue Horizon 7-63205	MR. WONDERFUL (gatefold sleeve)	45
69	Blue Horizon 7-63215	THE PIOUS BIRD OF GOOD OMEN.	20
69	Reprise RSLP 9000	THEN PLAY ON (gatefold sleeve)	15
70	Reprise RSLP 9004	KILN HOUSE (gatefold sleeve, some with insert).	15/12
71	CBS Blue Horizon 63875	THE ORIGINAL FLEETWOOD MAC.	20
72	Reprise K 44181	BARE TREES.	18
77	Reprise K 54043	FLEETWOOD MAC (white vinyl with lyric sheet).	18
77	Warner Bros K 56344	RUMOURS (white vinyl with lyric sheet)	18
90	Warner Bros 7599-26206-2	BEHIND THE MASK (picture disc, box set, with print & graphics software)	20

(see also Mick Fleetwood's Zoo, Peter Green, Stevie Nicks, Buckingham-Nicks, Jeremy Spencer, Christine Perfect, Danny Kirwan, John Mayall, Otis Spann, Eddie Boyd, Duster Bennett, Chicken Shack, Shotgun Express, Bo Street Runners, Cheynes, Tramp, Brunning Hall Sunflower Blues Band)

FLEETWOODS

59	London HLU 8841	Come Softly To Me/I Care So Much (78 rpm = £20).	20
59	London HLU 4003	Come Softly To Me/I Care So Much (stereo export issue)	25
59	London HLU 8895	Graduation's Here/Oh Lord Let It Be Me (78 rpm = £35)	20
59	Top Rank JAR 202	Mr. Blue/You Mean Everything To Me (78 rpm = £40+)	15
60	Top Rank JAR 294	Outside My Window/Magic Star (some in p/s)	20/10
60	Top Rank JAR 383	Runaround/Truly Do	10
61	London HLG 9341	Tragedy/Little Miss Sad One	15
61	London HLG 9426	He's The Great Imposter/Poor Little Girl	12
62	Liberty LIB 62	They Tell Me It's Summer/Lovers By Night Strangers By Day	15
63	Liberty LIB 75	Goodnight My Love Pleasant Dreams/Jimmy Beware	12
64	Liberty LIB 93	Ruby Red Baby Blue/Lonesome Town	12
65	Liberty LIB 10191	Almost There/Before And After (Losing You).	15
60	Top Rank BUY 028	MR BLUE (LP, with 3 tracks by other artists).	30
61	London HA-G 2388	SOFTLY (LP, also stereo SAH-G 6188).	65/85
61	London HA-G 2419	DEEP IN A DREAM (LP)	75

MICK FLEETWOOD'S ZOO

81	RCA RCA 118	You Weren't In Love/O-Niamali (p/s)	5
83	RCA RCA 360	I Want You Back/Put Me Right (p/s)	8

(see also Fleetwood Mac)

HELEN FLEMING

66	Blue Beat BB 341	Eve's Ten Commandments/Don't Take Your Love Away.	15

JOY FLEMING

75	Antic K 11518	A Bridge Of Love/Divorcee.	10
76	Private Stock PVT 54	Are You Ready For Love/Alabama Standby	20

RAY FLEMING

63	MGM MGM 1196	I'm Glad I Have You/Humpty Dumpty	10

WADE FLEMONS

59	Top Rank JAR 206	Slow Motion/Walkin' By The River	15
60	Top Rank JAR 327	What's Happening?/Goodnight, It's Time To Go	15
60	Top Rank JAR 371	Easy Lovin'/Whoops Now	15

FLESHEATERS

81	Initial IRC 007	A MINUTE TO PRAY, A SECOND TO DIE (LP)	18

FLESH VOLCANO

87	Some Bizzare SLUT 1	Slut/The Universal Cesspool/Bruisin' Chain (12", p/s)	10

(see also Marc Almond, Foetus)

DARROW FLETCHER
66	London HLU 10024	The Pain Gets A Little Deeper/My Judgement Day (DJ copy = £150)	85

DON FLETCHER
66	Vocalion VP 9271	Two Wrongs Don't Make A Right/I'm So Glad	25

GUY FLETCHER
69	Pye 7N 17765	Magic Woman/All Fall Down	6

SAM FLETCHER
59	MGM MGM 1024	Time Has A Way/No Such Luck	7
60	RCA RCA 1255	Tall Hope/You're So Far Away From Home	7

FLEUR-DE-LYS
65	Immediate IM 020	Moondreams/Wait For Me	220
66	Immediate IM 032	Circles/So Come On	500
66	Polydor 56124	Mud In Your Eye/I've Been Trying	500
67	Polydor 56200	I Can See A Light/Prodigal Son	60
68	Polydor 56251	The Gong With The Luminous Nose/Hammer Head	130
68	Atlantic 584 193	Stop Crossing The Bridge/Brick By Brick (Stone By Stone)	40
69	Atlantic 584 243	Liar/One Girl City.	75

(see also John Bromley, Terry Durham, Tony & Tandy, Sharon Tandy, Rupert's People, Shyster, Quotations, Bryn Haworth, Chocolate Frog, Gordon Haskell, Waygood Ellis)

VIC FLICK SOUND
70	Chapter One CH 136	Hang On/Wonderful World	8
71	Chapter One CH 155	Quest For Love/Clarice.	6

FLIES
66	Decca F 12533	I'm Not Your Stepping Stone/Talk To Me	175
67	Decca F 12594	House Of Love/It Had To Be You	70
68	RCA RCA 1757	The Magic Train/Gently As You Feel	40

(see also Bulldog Breed, T2)

SHELBY FLINT
61	Warner Bros WB 30	Angel On My Shoulder/Somebody	12
66	London HLT 10068	Cast Your Fate To The Wind/The Lilly	20

FLINTLOCKS
66	Decca F 12412	What Goes On?/I Walked Right Into A Heaven	7

FLINTSTONES
64	HMV POP 1266	Safari/Work Out	20

BUNNY FLIP
72	Pressure Beat PB 5510	Shanky Dog (actually "Skanky Dog" by Winston Scotland)/ JOE GIBBS & NOW GENERATION: Boney Dog	10

(see also Winston Scotland)

FLIP & DATELINERS
64	HMV POP 1359	My Johnny Doesn't Come Around Anymore/Please Listen To Me	70

(see also Vivienne Chering)

FLIPPER
81	Alt. Tentacles VIRUS 8	Ha Ha Ha/Love Canal (p/s, with insert)	8

FLIPS
62	London HLU 9490	Rockin' Twist/Oh, You Beautiful Doll — Twist	20

FLIRTATIONS
68	Deram DM 195	Someone Out There/How Can You Tell Me?.	10
68	Deram DM 216	Nothing But A Heartache/Christmas Time Is Here Again	28
69	Deram DM 252	What's Good About Goodbye My Love?/Once I Had A Love	6
70	Deram DM 281	Keep On Searchin'/Moma I'm Coming Home.	6
70	Deram DM 295	Can't Stop Loving You/Everybody Needs Somebody	6
71	Deram DM 329	Give Me Love/This Must Be The End Of The Line.	6
72	Deram DM 351	Need Your Lovin'/I Wanna Be There	7
71	Polydor 2058 167	Little Darlin'/Take Me In Your Arms And Love Me	18
72	Polydor 2058 249	Love A Little Longer/Hold On To Me Babe.	6
74	Polydor 2058 295	Dirty Work/No Such Thing As A Miracle.	6
73	Mojo 2092 058	Why Didn't I Think Of That?/Oh Mia Bamba	6
98	London Traffic TRAF 1	Nothing But A Heartache (1-sided, reissue promo, 500 only)	8
69	Deram DML/SML 1046	SOUNDS LIKE THE FLIRTATIONS (LP)	40

(see also Pearly Gates, Gypsies)

FLO & EDDIE
73	Reprise K 14261	Afterglow/Carlos And De Bull	6
72	Reprise K 44201	THE PHLORESCENT LEECH AND EDDIE (LP).	15
73	Reprise K 44234	FLO AND EDDIE (LP)	15

(see also Turtles, Frank Zappa/Mothers Of Invention)

FLOATING BRIDGE
69	Liberty LBS 83271	FLOATING BRIDGE (LP).	40

FLOCK
70	CBS 4932	Tired Of Waiting For You/Store Bought — Store Thought	8
69	CBS 63733	THE FLOCK (LP, orange label).	12
70	CBS 64055	DINOSAUR SWAMPS (LP, orange label, gatefold sleeve).	15

(see also Mahavishnu Orchestra)

FLOCK OF SEAGULLS
(see under A Flock Of Seagulls)

DICK FLOOD
59	Felsted AF 125	The Three Bells/Far Away (78 rpm = £15)	10

MINT VALUE £

FLORIBUNDA ROSE
67	Piccadilly 7N 35408	One Way Street/Linda Loves Linda	35

(see also Scrugg, John T. Kongos)

FLOWCHART
90s	Enraptured RAPT 4505	Rainbow Hello/ALPHASTONE: Astro (p/s)	8
90s	Enraptured RAPT 4527	NO. 7 IN THE STRESS FREE SERIES: Gip Part One/Gip Part 2 (in box)	10

FLOWERPOT MEN
67	Deram DM 142	Let's Go To San Francisco (Parts 1 & 2)	5
68	Page One POF 065	Mighty Quinn/Voices From The Sky	10
67	Deram DM 160	A Walk In The Sky/Am I Losing You?	8
68	Deram DM 183	A Man Without A Woman/You Can Never Be Wrong	8
69	Deram DM 248	In A Moment Of Madness/Young Birds Fly	10

(see also Ivy League, Friends, Carter-Lewis & Southerners, Edison Lighthouse, Fat Mattress, Gordon Haskell, Kestrels, One & One)

LLOYD FLOWERS & RECO'S RHYTHM GROUP
62	Blue Beat BB 88	I'm Going Home/Lover's Town	12

PHIL FLOWER(S)
69	A&M AMS 766	Like A Rolling Stone/Keep On Sockin' It Children	10
70	A&M AMS 784	Every Day I Have To Cry/If It Feels Good Do It (miscredited as Phil Flower)	20

(Lloyd) FLOWERS & ALVIN (Ranglin)
72	Explosion EX 2067	Howdy And Tenky/SHORTY PERRY: Sprinkle Some Water	6
72	Grape GR 3028	In De Pum Pum/MAYTONES: If Loving You Was Wrong	6
72	Bullet BU 512	Howdy And Tenky/SHORTY PERRY: Sprinkle Some Water	6
73	Duke DU 150	Rastaman Going Back Home/LITTLE YOUTH: Barble Dove Skank	6

FLOWERS & FROLICS
77	Free Reed FRR 016	BEES ON HORSEBACK (LP, featuring June Tabor & Bob Davenport)	35

FLOWER SERMON
92	Rough Trade 45REV 13	Sugar Lullaby (p/s with insert)	8

FLOWER SHOPPE
72	Polydor 2066 096	You've Come A Long Way/Kill The Monster	8

FLOWER TRAVELLING BAND
71	Atlantic 2091 128	Satori (Enlightment) (Parts 1 & 2)	20

BOBBY FLOYD
72	Pama PM 860	Sound Doctor/YOUNG DILLINGER: Doctor Skank	20

EDDIE FLOYD
66	Atlantic 584 041	Knock On Wood/Got To Make A Comeback	8
67	Stax 601 001	Raise Your Hand/I've Just Been Feeling Bad (dark or light blue label)	10/8
67	London HL 10129	Set My Soul On Fire/Will I Be The One?	10
67	Speciality SPE 1001	Never Get Enough Of Your Love/Bye Bye Baby	10
67	Stax 601 016	Things Get Better/Good Love, Bad Love	15
67	Stax 601 024	On A Saturday Night/Under My Nose	15
68	Stax 601 035	Big Bird/Holding On With Both Hands	15
68	Stax STAX 104	I've Never Found A Girl (To Love Me Like You Do)/I'm Just The Kind Of Fool	15
69	Stax STAX 108	Bring It On Home To Me/Sweet Things You Do	8
69	Stax STAX 116	I've Got To Have Your Love/Girl I Love You	5
69	Stax STAX 125	Don't Tell Your Mama/Consider Me	5
70	Stax STAX 153	My Girl/Laurie	5
72	Polydor 2025 098	Yum Yum Yum/I Want Some/Tears Of Joy	5
74	Stax STXS 2005	Soul Street/The Highway Man	5
81	I-Spy SEE 9	The Beat Song/London ('I-Spy' sleeve)	5
67	Stax 589 006	KNOCK ON WOOD (LP)	35
68	Stax (S)XATS 1003	I'VE NEVER FOUND A GIRL (LP)	30
69	Atco 228 014	KNOCK ON WOOD (LP, reissue)	18
69	Stax SXATS 1023	YOU'VE GOT TO HAVE EDDIE (LP)	20
71	Stax 2363 010	YOU'VE GOT TO HAVE EDDIE (LP, reissue)	15
74	Stax STX 1002	SOUL STREET (LP)	12

(see also Falcons, Primettes/Eddie Floyd)

FLUFF
72	Decca F 13305	The Sun Ain't Gonna Shine (Anymore)/Let's Get Back Together	7

FLUKE
89	Fluke FLUKE 001T	Thumper!/Cool Hand Flute (12", stamped white label with stickered sleeve)	10
90	Creation CRE 090T	PHILLY (12")	10

FLUX (OF PINK INDIANS)
81	Crass 321984/2	NEU SMELL (EP, foldout poster sleeve)	8
85	Spiderleg SDL 16	TAKING A LIBERTY (EP, as Flux, with booklet sleeve)	6
83	Spiderleg SDL 8	STRIVE TO SURVIVE CAUSING THE LEAST SUFFERING POSSIBLE (LP, with booklet)	15
84	Spiderleg SDL 13	THE FUCKING CUNTS TREAT US LIKE PRICKS (2-LP)	18

(see also Epileptics, Licks)

FLYING BURRITO BROTHERS
69	A&M AMS 756	The Train Song/Hot Burrito No. 1	8
70	A&M AMS 794	Older Guys/Down In The Churchyard	5
70	A&M AMS 816	Tried So Hard/Lazy Days	5
72	A&M AMS 871	White Line Fever/Colorado	5
69	A&M AML(S) 931	THE GILDED PALACE OF SIN (LP)	15
70	A&M AMLS 983	BURRITO DELUXE (LP)	15

71	A&M AMLS 64295	THE FLYING BURRITO BROTHERS (LP)	12
72	A&M AMLS 64343	LAST OF THE RED-HOT BURRITOS (LP)	12
73	Bumble GEXD 301	LIVE IN AMSTERDAM (2-LP)	15

(see also Byrds, Gram Parsons, Gene Parsons, Stephen Stills & Manassas, Rick Roberts, Country Gazette, Skip Battin)

FLYING CIRCUS
71	Harvest SHSP 4010	PREPARED IN PEACE (LP)	20

FLYING MACHINE
69	Pye 7N 17722	Smile A Little Smile For Me/Maybe We've Been Loving Too Long	7
69	Pye 7N 17722	Baby Make It Soon/Smile A Little Smile For Me	6
69	Pye 7N 17811	Send My Baby Home Again/Look At Me, Look At Me	6
70	Pye 7N 17914	Hanging On The Edge Of Sadness/Flying Machine	7
70	Pye 7N 45001	The Devil Has Possession Of Your Mind/Hey Little Girl	15
70	Pye 7N 45093	Yes I Understand/Pages Of Your Life	6
70	Pye NSPL 18328	DOWN TO EARTH WITH THE FLYING MACHINE (LP)	22

(see also Pinkertons, Pinkerton's Assorted Colours, Tony Newman)

FLYING SAUCER ATTACK
92	Heartbeat FSA 6	Soaring High/Standing Stone (p/s, 500 only, 1st few with autographed postcards; later with various different designs)	25/20
93	Heartbeat FSA 61	Wish/Oceans (p/s, 700 only)	15
94	Domino RUG 23	Land Beyond The Sun/Everywhere Was Everything (p/s, hand-painted rear sleeve, 500 only)	8
95	Planet PUNK 008	Beach Red Lullaby/Second Hour (p/s, 1,300 only)	6
96	Enraptured RAPT 4505	At Night/JESSAMINE: From Hereto And Now Otherwise (500 on clear vinyl, 2500 black)	12/8
98	Earworm WORMSC 1	Land Beyond The Sun (2-Track Version)/Instrumental For Silence (green vinyl, 500 only)	6
94	Heartbeat FSA 62	FLYING SAUCER ATTACK (LP, 1,000 only)	20

FLYING SAUCERS
76	Nevis NEV LP 114	PLANET OF THE DRAPES (LP)	12

FLYING SQUAD
78	Epic S EPC 6375	Drive On/Baltimore Baby	5
78	Epic S EPC 6542	Backroom Boys (Night After Night)/Tell Me What To Do	5
78	Epic EPC 82875	FLYING SQUAD (LP)	12

(see also Status Quo)

ERROL FLYNN
55	Philips PB 380	Lily Of Laguna/We'll Gather Lilacs (B-side with Patrice Wymore) (78)	10

STEVE FLYNN
67	Parlophone R 5625	Mr Rainbow/Let's Live For Tomorrow	25
68	Parlophone R 5689	Your Life And My Life/Come Tomorrow	8

(see also Mark Wirtz)

FLY ON THE WALL
79	Next Wave NEXT 1	DEVON DUMB (EP, numbered)	20

FLYS
78	EMI EMI 2747	Love And A Molotov Cocktail/Can I Crash Here?/Civilisation (p/s)	10
78	EMI EMI 2795	Fun City/E.C. 4 (p/s)	10
78	EMI EMIY 2867	Waikiki Beach Refugees/We Don't Mind The Rave (p/s, yellow vinyl)	10
78	EMI EMI 2907	Beverley/Don't Moonlight On Me (p/s)	6
79	EMI EMI 2936	Name Dropping/Fly V Fly (p/s, some on green vinyl)	15
79	EMI EMI 2979	Living In The Sticks/We Are The Lucky Ones (p/s)	8
79	Parlophone R 6030	16 Down/Night Creatures/Lois Lane/Today Belongs To Me (p/s)	5
77	Zama ZA 10 EP	BUNCH OF FIVE (33rpm EP, die-cut p/s)	125
80	Parlophone R 6063	FOUR FROM THE SQUARE (EP, p/s, demos £20)	7

FLYTE REACTION
91	Woronzow W0014	SONGS IN A CIRCLE (LP)	15
92	Splendid SPLEN 001	STRAWBERRY LIP SALVATION (LP)	12
93	Splendid SPLEN 002	SPECTRAL FOOTWEAR (LP)	12
95	Splendid SPLEN 003	CREATE A SMILE (LP)	12

FOCAL POINT
68	Deram DM 186	Love You Forever/Sycamore Sid	40

FOCUS
71	Polydor 2001 134	House Of The King/Black Beauty	5
71	Blue Horizon 2094 006	Hocus Pocus/Janis	15
72	Blue Horizon 2096 008	Tommy/Focus II	15
71	Polydor 2344 003	IN AND OUT OF FOCUS (LP, gatefold sleeve)	12
72	Blue Horizon 2096 002	MOVING WAVES (LP, with poster)	20
72	Polydor 2659 016	FOCUS III (2-LP, gatefold sleeve)	12

(see also Jan Akkerman, Thijs Van Leer, Brainbox, Robin Lent)

FOCUS THREE
67	Columbia DB 8279	10,000 Years Behind My Mind/The Sunkeeper	65

FOETUS & CHROME CRANKS
94	PCP 011-2	Vice Squad Dick/Little Johnny Jewel (p/s)	20

FOETUS ART TERRORISM
84	Self Imm. WOMB FAT 11.12	Calamity Crush/Catastrophe Crunch (12")	20

FOETUS CORRUPTUS
91	Rifle RIFLE 1	RIFE (2-LP, stickered black sleeve)	20

MINT VALUE £

FOETUS INC.
90	Big Cat ABB 16T	Butterfly Potion/Free James Brown (12")	20
90	Self Imm. WOMB 6	SINK (LP)	25

FOETUS INTERRUPTUS
88	Self Imm. WOMB FIP 5	THAW (LP)	20

FOETUS ÜBER FRISCO
82	Self Immolation WOMB 125/SUSC 12	Custom Built For Capitalism/1.0.4.5./Birthday (12", p/s)	20
85	Self Imm. WOMB UNC 7.12	Finely Honed Machine/Sick Minutes (12")	20

FOETUS UNDER GLASS
85	Self Imm. WOMB S201	Spite Your Face/OKFM (p/s)	20

(see also You've Got Foetus On Your Breath, Philip & His Foetus Vibrations, Scraping Foetus Off The Wheel, Flesh Volcano)

FOGCUTTERS
64	Liberty LIB 55793	Cry Cry Cry/You Say	15

JOHN FOGERTY
74	Fantasy FTC 111	Comin' Down The Road/Ricochet	6
75	Fantasy FTC 119	Rockin' All Over The World/The Wall	6
75	Fantasy FTC 120	Almost Saturday Night/Sea Cruise	6
76	Fantasy FTC 133	You Got The Magic/Evil Thing	6
75	Fantasy FT 526	JOHN FOGERTY (LP)	15

(see also Creedence Clearwater Revival, Blue Ridge Rangers)

TOM FOGERTY
71	United Artists UP 35264	Goodbye Media Man (Parts 1 & 2)	5
72	Fantasy F 680	Cast The First Stone/Lady Of Fatima	5
73	Fantasy FTC 109	Joyful Resurrection/Heartbeat	5
72	Fantasy FAN 9407	TOM FOGERTY (LP)	15

(see also Creedence Clearwater Revival, Ruby)

FOGGY
72	York SYK 534	How Come The Sun/Take Your Time	7
73	York SYK 542	Kitty Starr/She's Far Away (p/s)	7
72	York FYK 411	SIMPLE GIFTS (LP, with insert, featuring Strawbs)	45
75	Canon CNN 5759	PATCHWORK (LP)	35

(see also Strawbs, Foggy Dew-O)

FOGGY DEW-O
68	Decca F 12776	Reflections/Grandfather's Clock	8
71	York SYK 503	Me And Bobby McGee/Feelin' Groovy	6
68	Decca LK/SKL 4940	THE FOGGY DEW-O (LP)	20
70	Decca LK/SKL 5035	BORN TO TAKE THE HIGHWAY (LP)	15

(see also Strawbs, Foggy)

FOGHAT
72	Bearsville K 45503	FOGHAT (LP)	15
73	Bearsville K 45514	FOGHAT — ROCK'N'ROLL (LP)	12

(see also Black Cat Bones, Savoy Brown, Warren Philips & The Rockets)

FOIL
97	13th Hour HOUR 011	Don't Come Around/Brand New Brain/Molina (p/s, blue vinyl, 1000 only)	7
97	13th Hour HOUR 013	Reviver Gene/Sedate Me (green vinyl, 500 only)	7
97	Mute 13THLP 05	SPREAD IT ALL AROUND (LP, clear vinyl, with inner sleeve)	12

ELLEN FOLEY (& CLASH)
81	Epic EPC A 9522	The Shuttered Palace/Beautiful Waste Of Time (p/s)	6
81	Epic EPC A 1160	Torchlight/Game Of A Man (p/s)	6
81	Epic SEPC 84809	SPIRIT OF ST. LOUIS (LP, with inner sleeve)	14

(see also Clash)

RED FOLEY
53	Brunswick 05076	Hot Toddy/ROBERTA LEE & HARDROCK GUNTER: Sixty Minute Man (78)	10
54	Brunswick 05307	Pin Ball Boogie/Jilted (78)	15
54	Brunswick 05321	Skinnie Minnie (Fishtail)/Thank You For Calling (78 rpm = £12)	18
55	Brunswick 05508	Croce Di Oro (Cross Of Gold) (with Betty Foley)/The Night Watch	18
55	Brunswick 05363	Hearts Of Stone/RED FOLEY & BETTY FOLEY: Never	22
60	Brunswick LAT 8343	SING ALONG WITH RED FOLEY (LP, also stereo STA 3034)	20/25

(see also Roberta Lee)

RED FOLEY & ERNEST TUBB
55	Brunswick OE 9148	COUNTRY DOUBLE DATE (EP, with Minnie Pearl)	20
57	Brunswick LAT 8206	RED AND ERNIE (LP)	25

(see also Ernest Tubb)

SIMON FOLEY
77	Look LKLP 6324	TO STRIVE WITH PRINCES (LP, with booklet)	20

FOLKAL POINT
72	Midas MR 003	FOLKAL POINT (LP)	425

FOLK DEVILS
84	Ganges RAY 1	Hank Turns Blue/Chewin' The Fat (some with p/s)	15/8

CALVIN FOLKES
63	Rio R 5	Someone/Kentucky Home	10
63	Rio R 8	You'll Never Know/Is It Time?	10
64	Port-O-Jam PJ 4117	My Bonnie/What A Day	12
64	Port-O-Jam PJ 4118	Hello Everybody/IRVING SIX: King's Boogie	12

FOLK(S) BROTHERS
61	Blue Beat BB 30	Carolina/I Met A Man (original, blue label, as Folks Brothers)	12
60s	Fab BB 30	Carolina (as Folks Brothers)/ERIC 'HUMPTY DUMPTY' MORRIS:	
		Humpty Dumpty	6
70s	Blue Beat BB 30	Carolina/I Met A Man (reissue, white label, as Folk Brothers)	6

FOLKLANDERS
60s	Urban PB 001	TWO LITTLE FISHES (EP)	10

FOLK SONG CLUB
65	white label (no cat. no.)	IMPERIAL COLLEGE (LP, private pressing)	100

FOLKWAYS
72	Folk Heritage	NO OTHER NAME (LP)	12

FONN
99	Fat Cat 12FAT 018	Untitled (2 x 12", embossed sleeve)	10

EDDIE FONTAINE
55	HMV 7M 304	Rock Love/All My Love Belongs To You (with Neal Hefti & Excels)	350+
55	HMV B 10852	Rock Love/All My Love Belongs To You (with Neal Hefti & Excels) (78).	75
56	Brunswick 05624	Cool It, Baby/Into Each Life Some Rain Must Fall (78 rpm = £50)	200
58	London HLM 8711	Nothin' Shakin' (But The Leaves On The Trees)/Don't Ya Know (78 rpm = £45)	45

ARLENE FONTANA
59	Pye International 7N 25010	I'm In Love/Easy	12
59	Pye International N 25010	I'm In Love/Easy (78)	8

WAYNE FONTANA & THE MINDBENDERS
63	Fontana TF 404	Hello! Josephine/Road Runner	25
63	Fontana TF 418	For You, For You/Love Potion No.9.	15
64	Fontana TF 436	Little Darlin'/Come Dance With Me	15
64	Fontana TF 451	Stop Look And Listen/Duke Of Earl	10
64	Fontana TF 497	Um, Um, Um, Um, Um, Um/First Taste Of Love	6
65	Fontana TF 535	The Game Of Love/Since You've Been Gone.	6
65	Fontana TF 579	It's Just A Little Bit Too Late/Long Time Comin'	10
65	Fontana TF 611	She Needs Love/Like I Did	8
69	Fontana H 1022	Um, Um, Um, Um, Um, Um/The Game Of Love (p/s)	8
64	Fontana TE 17421	ROAD RUNNER (EP).	55
64	Fontana TE 17435	UM, UM, UM, UM, UM, UM (EP)	20
65	Fontana TE 17449	THE GAME OF LOVE (EP)	20
65	Fontana TE 17453	WALKING ON AIR (EP)	50
64	Fontana TL 5230	WAYNE FONTANA AND THE MINDBENDERS (LP)	60
65	Fontana TL 5257	ERIC, RICK, WAYNE, BOB — IT'S WAYNE FONTANA AND THE MINDBENDERS (LP)	60
67	Wing WL 1166	WAYNE FONTANA AND THE MINDBENDERS (LP, reissue)	15

(see also Wayne Fontana, Mindbenders)

WAYNE FONTANA
65	Fontana TF 642	It Was Easier To Hurt Her/You Made Me What I Am Today	10
66	Fontana TF 684	Come On Home/My Eyes Break Out In Tears.	7
66	Fontana TF 737	Goodbye Bluebird/The Sun's So Hot Today.	7
66	Fontana TF 770	Pamela Pamela/Something Keeps Calling Me Back	10
67	Fontana TF 827	24 Sycamore/From A Boy To A Man	7
67	Fontana TF 866	The Impossible Years/In My World	12
67	Fontana TF 889	Gina/We All Love The Human Race	7
68	Fontana TF 911	Storybook Children/I Need To Love You.	7
68	Fontana TF 933	The Words Of Bartholomew/Mind Excursion	7
68	Fontana TF 976	Never An Everyday Thing/Waiting For A Break In The Clouds	8
69	Fontana TF 1008	Dayton Ohio 1903/Say Goodbye To Yesterday	8
69	Fontana TF 1054	Charlie Cass/Linda (withdrawn issue)	20+
69	Fontana TF 1054	We're Building A Love/Charlie Cass	10
69	Fontana H 1027	Come On Home/Pamela Pamela (p/s)	10
70	Philips 6006 035	Give Me Just A Little More Time/I'm In Love (withdrawn) (DJ copy = £100).	150
73	Warner Bros K 16269	Together/One Man Woman.	6
66	Fontana (S)TL 5351	WAYNE ONE (LP)	25
69	Fontana SFL 13144	WAYNE ONE (LP, reissue)	12

(see also Mindbenders)

FONTANE SISTERS
51	HMV B 10021	Tennessee Waltz/As We Are Today (78)	10
54	HMV B 10765	Please Play Our Song/Mexican Joe (78).	10
54	London HL 8099	Happy Days And Lonely Nights/If I Didn't Have You (78 rpm = £15).	100
55	London HL 8113	Hearts Of Stone/Bless Your Heart (78 rpm = £15)	100
55	London HL 8126	Rock Love/You're Mine (78 rpm = £15).	100
55	London HLD 8177	Seventeen/If I Could Be With You (78 rpm = £10)	100
55	London HLD 8211	Rolling Stone/Daddy-O (78 rpm = £12).	85
56	London HLD 8225	Adorable/Playmates (78 rpm = £12)	50
56	London HLD 8265	Eddie My Love/Yum Yum (78 rpm = £12)	50
56	London HL 7009	Eddie My Love/Yum Yum (export issue)	40
56	London HLD 8289	I'm In Love Again/You Always Hurt The One You Love (gold lettering label, later silver) (78 rpm = £15)	45/25
56	London HLD 8318	Voices (with narration by Pat Boone)/Willow Weep For Me (gold lettering label, later silver) (78 rpm = £10)	40/20
56	London HLD 8343	Silver Bells/Nuttin' For Christmas (78 rpm = £15)	25
57	London HLD 8378	The Banana Boat Song/Lonesome Lover Blues (gold or silver lettering) (78 rpm = £8).	30/20
57	London HLD 8415	Please Don't Leave Me/Still (78 rpm = £15)	25
57	London HLD 8488	Fool Around/Which Way To Your Heart? (78 rpm = £12)	25
58	London HLD 8621	Chanson D'Amour (Song Of Love)/Cocoanut Grove (78 rpm = £10).	15
59	London HLD 8861	Billy Boy/Encore D'Amour (78 rpm = £18)	15

FONTANE SISTERS

60	London HLD 9037	Listen To Your Heart/Please Be Kind	10
60	London HLD 9078	Theme From "A Summer Place"/Darling, It's Wonderful	10
55	London RE-D 1029	FONTANE SISTERS NO. 1 (EP)	75
55	London RE-D 1037	FONTANE SISTERS NO. 2 (EP)	65
57	London HA-D 2053	THE FONTANES SING (LP)	135
	(see also Pat Boone, Perry Como)		

SAM FONTEYN
66	Parlophone R 5519	Lost In Space/BERNARD SHARPE: Jorrocks	10

BILLY FONTEYNE
63	Oriole CB 1917	Little Child/Look Before You Leap	13

FOO FIGHTERS
95	Roswell CL 753	This Is A Call/Winnebago	10
95	Roswell 12CL 753	This Is A Call/Winnebago/Podunk (12", luminous vinyl)	18
95	Roswell CDCL 753	This Is A Call/Winnebago/Podunk (CD)	8
95	Roswell CL 757	I'll Stick Around/How I Miss You (red vinyl)	8
95	Roswell 12CL 757	I'll Stick Around/How I Miss You (12" p/s)	8
95	Roswell CL 762	For All The Cows/Watershed (blue vinyl)	8
95	Roswell CDCL 762	For All The Cows/(live version)/Watershed (live) (CD)	8
95	Roswell CL 768	Big Me/Floaty/Gas Chamber (white vinyl)	6
97	Roswell CL 788	Monkey Wrench/Up In Arms (red vinyl)	5
97	Roswell CL 792	Everlong/Drive Me Wild (blue vinyl)	10
97	Roswell CL 796	My Hero/Dear Lover (red vinyl, stickered poly sleeve, with insert)	10
00	RCA 74321 79012-7	Breakout/Stacked Actors (live) (p/s)	5
00	RCA 74321 80926-7	Next Year/Big Me (live)	5
02	RCA 74321 97315-7	All My Life/Sister Europe (numbered p/s)	5
03	RCA 74321 98955-7	Times Like These/Lack Of Illision (numbered p/s)	5
03	RCA 82876 56370-7	Have It All/Darling Nikki (p/s)	5
03	BMG 82876-52256-7	Low/Never Talking To You Again (Live Version) (numbered p/s, 3,000 only)	5
99	BMG 749582	GENERATOR (CD EP)	8
95	Roswell EST 2266	FOO FIGHTERS (LP)	25
05	BMG 82876680381	IN YOUR HONOUR (4 x LP)	18

FOOL
69	Mercury MF 1111	We Are One/Shining Light	10
69	Mercury SMCL 20138	THE FOOL (LP)	30

FOOLS DANCE
87	L. T. T. Slaughter LTS 22	They'll Never Know/Empty Hours (p/s)	10
87	L. T. T. Slaughter LTS 22T	They'll Never Know/The Collector/Empty Hours/The Ring (12", p/s)	15
85	Top Hole Turn TURN 19	FOOLS DANCE (mini-LP)	20
86	Top Hat TH 22	FOOLS DANCE (mini-LP, reissue)	15
	(see also Cure, Stranglers)		

CHUCK FOOTE
62	London HLU 9495	You're Running Out Of Kisses/Come On Back	16

FOOT IN COLD WATER
73	Island WIP 6162	(Isn't Love Unkind) In My Life/Deep Freeze	7
74	Elektra K 52011	OR ALL AROUND US (LP)	20

FORBES
77	Power Exchange PX 253	The Beatles/Sweet Kiss Of Fire	7

BILL FORBES
58	Columbia DB 4232	My Cherie/God's Little Acre (78 rpm = £6)	10
59	Columbia DB 4269	Once More/Believe In Me	12
59	Columbia DB 4386	Too Young/It's Not The End Of The World	15
61	Columbia DB 4566	You're Sixteen, You're Beautiful/Backward Child	15
61	Columbia DB 4619	That's It, I Quit, I'm Moving On/Big City Boy	15
61	Columbia DB 4747	Goodbye Cruel World/Next Time	12
62	Columbia DB 4855	Laughter Or Tears/Like A Good Girl Should	7
62	Columbia DB 4945	Poker Face/Marianne	7
	(see also Contrasts)		

FORCEFIELD
87	President PT 551	Smoke On The Water/Shine It On Me (p/s)	5
88	President PT 578	Heartache/I Lose Again (Instrumental Version) (p/s)	5
	(see also Cozy Powell, Graham Bonnet, Ray Fenwick, Whitesnake)		

FORCE FIVE
64	United Artists UP 1051	Don't Make My Baby Blue/Shaking Postman	20
65	United Artists UP 1089	Yeah, I'm Waiting/I Don't Want To See You Again	33
65	United Artists UP 1102	Baby Don't Care/Come Down To Earth	33
65	United Artists UP 1118	I Want You Babe/Gee Too Tiger	45
66	United Artists UP 1141	Don't Know Which Way To Turn/Baby Let Your Hair Down	45
	(see also Crocheted Doughnut Ring)		

FORCE WEST
65	Decca F 12223	I Can't Give What I Haven't Got/Why Won't She Stay	12
66	Columbia DB 7908	Gotta Find Another Baby/Talkin' About Our Love	15
66	Columbia DB 7963	When The Sun Comes Out (Weatherman)/Gotta Tell Somebody	12
67	Columbia DB 8174	All The Children Sleep/Desolation	15
68	CBS 3632	I'll Walk In The Rain/What's It To Be?	8
68	CBS 3798	I'll Be Moving On/Like The Tide, Like The Ocean	8
69	CBS 4385	Sherry/Mister Blue	8

CLINTON FORD
58	Oriole CB 1425	Sweet Sixteen/Eleven More Months And Ten More Days (78 rpm = £8)	6
59	Oriole CB 1483	I Cried A Tear/(You Were Only) Teasin' (78 rpm = £8)	6

59	Oriole CB 1500	Old Shep/Nellie Dean Rock (78 rpm = £15)	6
59	Oriole CB 1516	Lovesick Blues/Give A Little, Take A Little (78 rpm = £15)	5
59	Oriole CB 1518	Silver Threads Among The Gold/Red Indian Christmas Carol (78 rpm = £12)	5
61	Oriole CB 1551	Mustapha/Two Brothers	5
61	Oriole CB 1612	Oh By Jingo/Get Out And Get Under	5
61	Oriole CB 1623	Too Many Beautiful Girls/Everybody's Doing It	5
62	Oriole CB 1706	Fanlight Fanny/Dreamy City Lullaby	6
67	Piccadilly NEP 34057	DANDY (EP)	10
62	Oriole PS 40021	CLINTON FORD (LP) (with George Chisholm Allstars)	15
63	Columbia 33SX 1560	THE MELODY MAN (LP) (also stereo SCX 3496)	12/15
64	Realm RM 147	BY JINGO (LP)	15
65	Columbia 33SX 1689	LISTEN WITH US (LP) (also stereo SCX 3529)	15/20
67	Pye NPL 18210	CLINTON THE CLOWN (LP)	15
67	Piccadilly N(S)PL 38028	DANDY (LP)	15
67	Piccadilly N(S)PL 38034	BIG WILLY BROKE JAIL TONIGHT LP)	15

(see also Hallelujah Skiffle Group)

DEAN FORD (& GAYLORDS)

64	Columbia DB 7264	Twenty Miles/What's The Matter With Me?	25
64	Columbia DB 7402	Mr Heartbreak's Here Instead/I Won't	25
65	Columbia DB 7610	The Name Game/That Lonely Feeling	25
75	EMI EMC 3079	DEAN FORD (LP)	15

(see also Gaylords, Marmalade, Junior Campbell)

DEE DEE FORD

| 60 | London HLU 9245 | Good-Morning Blues/I Just Can't Believe | 65 |

(see also Don Gardner & Dee Dee Ford)

EDDIE/EDDY FORD

| 72 | Pressure Beat PB 5512 | You Wrong Fe Trouble Joshua/KENNETH POWER: Joshua Row Us Home | 7 |
| 73 | Duke Reid DR 2523 | Guess I This Riddle/Riddle Version (as Eddie Ford) | 5 |

EMILE FORD (& THE CHECKMATES)

59	Pye 7N 15225	What Do You Want To Make Those Eyes At Me For?/Don't Tell Me Your Troubles	6
59	Pye N 15225	What Do You Want To Make Those Eyes At Me For?/	
		Don't Tell Me Your Troubles (78)	15
60	Pye 7N 15245	On A Slow Boat To China/That Lucky Old Sun (78 rpm, Pye N 15245 = £15)	5
60	Pye 7N 15268	You'll Never Know What You're Missin' 'Til You Try/Still	5
60	Pye 7N 15279	Red Sails In The Sunset/Afraid	7
60	Pye 7N 15282	Them There Eyes (solo)/Question	6
60	Pye 7N 15314	Counting Teardrops/White Christmas	6
61	Pye 7N 15331	What Am I Gonna Do/A Kiss To Build A Dream On	7
61	Piccadilly 7N 35003	Half Of My Heart/Gypsy Love (solo)	8
61	Piccadilly 7N 35007	After You've Gone/Hush, Somebody's Calling My Name	8
61	Piccadilly 7N 35019	The Alphabet Song/Keep A-Lovin' Me (solo)	8
62	Piccadilly 7N 35033	I Wonder Who's Kissing Her Now/Doin' The Twist (solo)	8
62	Piccadilly 7N 35078	Your Nose Is Gonna Grow/Rains Come	10
63	Piccadilly 7N 35116	Hold Me Thrill Me Kiss Me/Doin' What You Do To Me	10
69	Decca F 12959	Set Me Free/Don't Remind Me (export issue)	12
59	Pye NEP 24119	EMILE (EP)	18
60	Pye NEP 24124	EMILE FORD HIT PARADE (EP)	15
60	Pye NEP 24133	EMILE FORD HIT PARADE VOL. 2 (EP)	20
60	Pye NPL 18049	NEW TRACKS WITH EMILE (LP)	30
61	Piccadilly NPL 38001	EMILE (LP)	38

FRANKIE FORD

59	London HL 8850	Sea Cruise/Roberta (with Huey 'Piano' Smith & Clowns)	
		(black triangular centre, later silver-top triangular centre)	60/40
59	London HL 8850	Sea Cruise/Roberta (with Huey 'Piano' Smith & Clowns) (78)	40+
59	Top Rank JAR 186	Alimony/Can't Tell My Heart (What To Do)	
		(with Huey 'Piano' Smith & Clowns)	12
59	Top Rank JAR 186	Alimony/Can't Tell My Heart (What To Do) (78)	70
60	Top Rank JAR 282	Cheatin' Woman/HUEY 'PIANO' SMITH & CLOWNS:	
		Don't You Just Know Kokomo	22
60	Top Rank JAR 299	Time After Time/I Want To Be Your Man	10
60	London HLP 9222	You Talk Too Much/If You've Got Troubles	22
65	Sue WI 366	Sea Cruise/Roberta (with Huey 'Piano' Smith & Clowns) (reissue)	22
65	Sue WI 369	What's Going On?/Watchdog	35

(see also Huey 'Piano' Smith)

JASON FORD & THE BULLDOGS

| 62 | Piccadilly 7N 35193 | Nobody Knows/Am I The One | 12 |

JON FORD

68	Philips BF 1690	Two's Company, Three's A Crowd/Place In Your Heart	7
69	Philips BF 1791	I Know It's Love/Look Before You Leap	6
69	Philips BF 1817	Ice Cream Man/This Was The Time	6
70	Philips BF 1833	Yesterday When I Was Young/Running Around	6
70	Philips 6006 030	You've Got Me Where You Want Me/You're All Alone Tonight	
		(DJ copy = £150)	100

LITA FORD & OZZY OSBOURNE

89	Dreamland A 49396	Close My Eyes Forever (Remix)/Under The Gun (p/s)	5
89	Dreamland PA 49396	Close My Eyes Forever (Remix)/Under The Gun/Blueberry	
		(12", picture disc)	8
89	Dreamland PA 49396	Close My Eyes Forever (Remix)/Under The Gun/Blueberry (3" CD, g/fold p/s)	10

(see also Ozzy Osbourne, Runaways)

MIKE FORD & THE CONSULS

| 63 | Piccadilly 7N 35127 | Jump Jeremiah/The Greenman | 15 |

MINT VALUE £

PERRY FORD (& SAPPHIRES)
59	Parlophone R 4573	Bye, Bye Baby, Goodbye/She Came As A Stranger	10
60	Parlophone R 4633	Crazy Over You/Garden Of Happiness	10
60	Parlophone R 4683	Don't Weep (Little Lady)/Little Grown-Up	10
62	Decca F 11497	Baby, Baby (Don't You Worry)/Prince Of Fools (with Sapphires & Blue Flames)	12

(see also Ivy League, Georgie Fame)

RICKY FORD (& TENNESSEANS)
63	Parlophone R 5018	Sweet And Tender Romance/Cheat Cheat	10
64	Parlophone R 5230	You Are My Love/Long Way From Home (with Tennesseans)	7

'TENNESSEE' ERNIE FORD
SINGLES
54	Capitol CL 14005	Give Me Your Word/River Of No Return	18
54	Capitol CL 14006	Catfish Boogie/Kiss Me Big	25
55	Capitol CL 14261	His Hands/I Am A Pilgrim	10
55	Capitol CL 14273	Losing You/There Is Beauty In Everything	10
56	Capitol CL 14500	Sixteen Tons/You Don't Have To Be A Baby To Cry	18
56	Capitol CL 14506	The Ballad Of Davy Crockett/Farewell	15
56	Capitol CL 14557	That's All/Bright Lights And Blonde-Haired Women	9
56	Capitol CL 14616	Who Will Shoe Your Pretty Little Foot?/Gaily The Troubadour	5
56	Capitol CL 14657	First Born/Have You Seen Her?	5
57	Capitol CL 14691	The Watermelon Song/One Suit	5
57	Capitol CL 14734	The Lonely Man/False Hearted Girl	5
57	Capitol CL 14759	In The Middle Of An Island/Ivy League	5
58	Capitol CL 14846	Down Deep/Bless Your Pea Pickin' Heart	5
58	Capitol CL 14896	Love Makes The World Go 'Round/Sunday Barbecue	5
59	Capitol CL 14972	Glad Rags/Sleepin' At The Foot Of The Bed	5
59	Capitol CL 15010	Blackeyed Susie/Code Of The Mountains	5
61	Capitol CL 15210	Little Red Rockin' Hood/I Gotta Have My Baby Back	8
56	Capitol EAP 1014	SIXTEEN TONS (EP)	18
57	Capitol EAP 1-639	'TENNESSEE' ERNIE FORD (EP)	12
60	Capitol EAP1 1227	GATHER ROUND (EP)	12
61	Capitol EAP1 20067	ANTICIPATION BLUES (EP)	20
52	Capitol LC 6573	CAPITOL PRESENTS (10" LP)	32
56	Capitol LC 6825	THIS LUSTY LAND (10" LP)	18
58	Capitol T 888	OL' ROCKIN' ERN (LP)	32
60	Capitol T 1380	SIXTEEN TONS (LP)	28

(see also Dinning Sisters)

'TENNESSEE' ERNIE FORD & BETTY HUTTON
54	Capitol CL 14133	This Must Be The Place/The Honeymoon's Over (green label)	18

FORD THEATRE
69	Stateside SSL 10288	TIME CHANGES (LP)	15

EDDIE 'BUSTER' FOREHAND
69	Action ACT 4519	Young Boy Blues/You Were Meant For Me	22

FOREIGNER
77	Atlantic K 10986	Cold As Ice/I Need You (ice-coloured clear vinyl, printed PVC sleeve)	5
78	Atlantic K 11167	Hot Blooded/Tramontaine (red vinyl, printed PVC sleeve)	5
79	Atlantic K 11236	Blue Morning, Blue Day/I Have Waited So Long (picture disc)	5
85	Atlantic A 9596	I Want To Know What Love Is/Street Thunder ('F'-shaped picture disc)	6

(see also J&B, State Of Mickey & Tommy, Spooky Tooth)

FORERUNNERS
64	Solar SRP 100	Bony Maronie/Pride	60

FORERUNNERS
60s	Key KL 008	THE FORERUNNERS (LP)	20
60s	Key KL 004	RUNNING BACK (LP)	20

JOHN FOREMAN
70s	Reality RY 1004	THE 'OUSES IN BETWEEN (LP)	15

FOREST
69	Harvest HAR 5007	Searching For Shadows/Mirror Of Life	22
69	Harvest SHVL 760	FOREST (LP)	120
70	Harvest SHVL 784	FULL CIRCLE (LP)	175
88	Zap! ZAP 3	FULL CIRCLE (LP, reissue)	12

FOR(R)ESTERS
65	Polydor 56038	Broken Hearted Clown/Lonely Boy	10
65	Polydor 56057	How Can I Tell Her/So Shy	10
66	Polydor 56104	Early Morning Hours/World Is Mine	8
66	Columbia DB 8040	Sometimes When You're Lonely/Today Or Tomorrow (as Forresters)	7
66	Columbia DB 8086	Mr. Smith/Ship On The Sea (as Foresters)	6
67	Columbia DB 8176	Comin' Home In The Evening/Sunshine's On Its Way (as Foresters)	6

FOREVER AMBER
69	Advance (no cat. no.)	THE LOVE CYCLE (LP, private pressing, 99 copies only)	1,250+

FOREVER MORE
70	RCA RCA 2024	Put Your Money On A Pony/Yours	6
70	RCA SF 8016	YOURS FOREVER MORE (LP)	18
71	RCA LSA 3015	WORDS ON BLACK PLASTIC (LP)	15

(see also Scots Of St. James, Hopscotch)

FORGEMASTERS
89	WARP WAP 1	TRACK WITH NO NAME (12", p/s)	10

FORK IN THE ROAD
70 Ember EMB S 311   I Can't Turn Around/Skeleton In My Closet 160

FORMAT
69 CBS 4600   Maxwell's Silver Hammer/Music Man 10
(see also Fourmost)

FORMATIONS
68 MGM MGM 1399   At The Top Of The Stairs/Magic Melody (DJ Copy = £250) 120
71 Mojo 2027 001   At The Top Of The Stairs/Magic Melody (reissue) 7

GEORGE FORMBY
55 Decca DFE 6144   GEORGE FORMBY AND HIS UKULELE GUITAR (EP) 10
56 Decca DFE 6328   GEORGE FORMBY AND HIS UKULELE GUITAR, NO. 2 (EP) 10
56 Decca DFE 6355   GEORGE FORMBY AND HIS UKULELE GUITAR, NO. 3 (EP) 10
61 Ace Of Clubs ACL 1062 GEORGE FORMBY SOUVENIR (LP) 12
63 Ace Of Clubs ACL 1145 TURNED OUT NICE AGAIN (LP) 15

FORMERLY FAT HARRY
71 Harvest SHSP 4016   FORMERLY FAT HARRY (LP) 35
(see also Country Joe and the Fish)

FORMINX
65 Vocalion V 9235   Jenka Beat/Geronimo Jenka 40
(see also Aphrodite's Child, Vangelis)

FORMULA
65 HMV POP 1438   Close To Me/If Ever 8

FORMULA 1
65 Warner Bros WB 155   I Just Can't Go To Sleep/Sure Know A Lot About Love 25

FORMULA TWO
72 CBS SCBS 8285   Easy Times/Girl Who Lives Next Door 6

ANDY FORRAY
68 Parlophone R 5715   Sarah Jane/Don't Care Anymore 8
68 Parlophone R 5729   The Proud One/Messin' Round With Me 8
68 Decca F 12733   Epitaph To You/Dream With Me 60
69 Fontana TF 999   Let The Sunshine In/Baby Is Coming 6

HELEN FORREST
56 Capitol CL 14594   Taking A Chance On Love/I Love You Much Too Much 10

JANE FORREST
56 Columbia SCM 5213   Sincerely Yours/A Girl Can't Say 10

JIMMY FORREST
54 Vogue V 2282   Flight 3D/Sophisticated Lady (78) 12

SHARON FORRESTER
73 Ashanti ASH 403   Silly Wasn't I?/NOW-GEN: Silly Wasn't I? — Version 6

THOMAS FORSTNER
89 Ariola 112 298   Song Of Love/Nur Ein Lied (p/s, withdrawn) 5
89 Ariola 662 298   Song Of Love (12" Version)/Nur Ein Lied/Song Of Love (7") (CD, withdrawn) 8

BRUCE FORSYTH
62 Piccadilly 7N 35086   The Oh-Be-Joyfuls/I Like People 5
64 Piccadilly 7N 35189   The Mysterious People/You've Just Found Out 5
65 Pye 7N 15879   Hush Hush Sweet Charlotte/Don't Say Goodbye 5
68 Mercury MF 1047   Star/Do, Do, Do 5
68 Pye 7N 17460   I'm Backing Britain/There's Not Enough Love In The World (p/s) 6
69 Decca F 12940   When You Gotta Go/By The Fireside 5
60 Parlophone PMC 1132   MR ENTERTAINMENT (LP, also stereo PCS 3031) 12

FORTES MENTUM
68 Parlophone R 5684   Saga Of A Wrinkled Man/Mr. Partridge Passed Away Today 55
68 Parlophone R 5726   I Can't Go On Loving You/Humdiggle We Love You 12
69 Parlophone R 5768   Gotta Go/Marrakesh 12
(see also Angel Pavement, Pussy)

LANCE FORTUNE
60 Pye 7N 15240   Be Mine/Action (with Johnny Prendy, alias John Barry) (78 rpm = £15) 8
60 Pye 7N 15260   All On My Own/This Love I Have For You 12
60 Pye 7N 15297   I Wonder/Will You Still Be My Girl? 12
61 Pye 7N 15347   Who's Gonna Tell Me?/Love Is The Sweetest Thing 12

RITA FORTUNE
74 CBS 2603   Sisters And Brothers/(Part 2) 8

FORTUNES
63 Decca F 11718   Summertime Summertime/I Love Her Still (as Fortunes & Cliftones)
                           (some in p/s) 40/18
64 Decca F 11809   Caroline/If You Don't Want Me Now 25
64 Decca F 11912   Come On Girl/I Like The Look Of You 15
64 Decca F 11985   Look Homeward Angel/I'll Have My Tears To Remind Me 15
65 Decca F 12173   You've Got Your Troubles/I've Got To Go 6
65 Decca F 12243   Here It Comes Again/Things I Should Have Known 6
66 Decca F 12321   This Golden Ring/Someone To Care 7
66 Decca F 12429   You Gave Me Somebody To Love/Silent Street 7
66 Decca F 12485   Is It Really Worth Your While?/Am I Losing My Touch 7
67 Decca F 12612   Our Love Has Gone/Truly Yours 7
67 United Artists UP 1188 The Idol/His Smile Was A Lie 6
68 United Artists UP 2218 Loving Cup/Hour At The Movies 6
68 United Artists UP 2239 Seasons In The Sun/Louise 6

69	United Artists UP 35054	Lifetime Of Love/Sad Sad Sad (withdrawn, existence unconfirmed)	
69	United Artists UP 35054	Books And Films/Sad Sad Sad	7
71	Capitol CL 15671	Here Comes That Rainy Day Feeling Again/Bad Side Of Town	7
65	Decca LK/SKL 4736	THE FORTUNES (LP, mono/stereo)	35/60
72	Capitol ST 21891	THE FORTUNES (LP)	15

(see also Glen Dale)

45's
79	Chopper CHEAP 5	Couldn't Believe A Word/Lonesome Lane (no p/s)	7
79	Stiff BUY 52	Couldn't Believe A Word/Lonesome Lane (no p/s, reissue)	5

48 CHAIRS
79	Absurd ABSURD 3	Snap It Around/Psycle Sluts (p/s)	5

49 AMERICANS
80	No Bad NB 4	THE HIT ALBUM (14-track EP)	6
80	Choo Choo Train CHUG 2	TOO YOUNG TO BE IDEAL (12" EP)	10
80	Choo Choo Train CHUG 1	EL PLURIBUS UNUM (LP)	12

FORUM
67	London HLM 10120	The River Is Wide/I Fall In Love (All Over Again)	12
70	B&C CB 119	The River Is Wide/I Fall In Love (All Over Again) (reissue)	5

FORWARD RUSSIA
05	Dance To The Radio DTTR001	Nine/He Shoots Presidents, Ltd 500 Only red vinyl 7", p/s	10
05	White Heat OPE002	Thirteen/Fourteen (blue vinyl, 1000 only)	7

SHIRLEY FORWOOD
57	London HLD 8402	Two Hearts (With An Arrow Between)/Juke Box Lovers (78 rpm = £7)	30

BOBBY FOSTER
70	Bread BR 1101	Tell Me Why You Say Goodbye/YOUTH: I'll Make Him Believe In You	6

JACKIE FOSTER
63	Planetone RC 13	Oh Leona/I Fell In Love	15

JOHN FOSTER
66	Island ILP 939	JOHN FOSTER SINGS (LP)	40

LARRY FOSTER & SOUL EXPLOSION
70	Fab FAB 130	Boom Biddy Boom/Next To Me (actually by Sugar Simone)	7

(see also Sugar Simone)

LES FOSTER
70	Torpedo TOR 7	Run Like A Thief/Nobody's Fool	8

LES FOSTER & ANSELL COLLINS
73	Camel CA 102	The Man In Your Life/Version	5

(see also Dave & Ansell Collins, Sugar Simone, Lance Hannibal)

LESLIE FOSTER
69	Jolly JY 022	Muriel/Nowhere To Hide	6

VINCENT FOSTER
69	Escort ES 803	Shine Eye Gal/Who Nest (B-side actually "Who Next" by Carl Bryan)	6

FOTHERINGAY
70	Island WIP 6085	Peace In The End/Winter Winds	15
70	Island ILPS 9125	FOTHERINGAY (LP, pink label/'i' logo, gatefold sleeve)	40
70	Island ILPS 9125	FOTHERINGAY (LP, later issue, pink rim label/'palm tree' logo, gatefold sleeve)	22

(see also Sandy Denny, Trevor Lucas, Eclection, Exception[s], Fairport Convention, Mick Greenwood)

FOUL PLAY
92	Oblivion OR 001	VOLUME 1 EP: The Alchemist/Ragatere/Ricochet/Feel The Vibe (12")	25
92	Oblivion OR 002	VOLUME 2 EP: Survival/Dubbing You/Ricochet (no stopping the remix)/Feel the vibe (again) (12")	25
93	Section 5 SECTION 04	Finest illusion/Screwface (12")	40
93	Moving Shadow SHADOW 29	VOLUME III EP: Open Your Mind/Murder Most Foul/Survival (remix)/Dub in U (remix) (12", p/s)	8
93	Moving Shadow SHAD 29R	VOLUME III REMIXES: Open Your Mind (Tango remix)/Open Your Mind (Foul Play remix) (10", p/s)	8
93	Moving Shadow SHAD 29R2	VOLUME III REMIXES PART 2: Open Your Mind (Nookie remix)/Finest Illusion (legal mix)(10", p/s)	10

MR FOUNDATION
(see under 'M')

FOUNDATIONS
67	Pye 7N 17366	Baby, Now That I've Found You/Come On Back To Me	7
68	Pye 7N 17417	Back On My Feet Again/I Can Take Or Leave Your Loving	6
68	Pye 7N 17503	Any Old Time (You're Lonely And Sad)/We Are Happy People	6
68	Pye 7N 17636	Build Me Up Buttercup/New Direction	6
69	Pye 7N 17702	In The Bad Bad Old Days/Give Me Love	6
69	Pye 7N 17809	Born To Live, Born To Die/Why Did You Cry	6
69	Pye 7N 17849	Baby I Couldn't See/Penny, Sir	6
70	Pye 7N 17904	Take A Girl Like You/I'm Gonna Be A Rich Man	6
70	Pye 7N 17956	I'm Gonna Be A Rich Man/Who Am I?	6
71	MCA MCA 5075	Stoney Ground/I'll Give You Love	20
70s	Summit SU 100	Where Were You When I Needed Your Love/Love Me Nice 'n Easy	6
78	Psycho P 2603	Closer To Loving You/Change My Life	300
68	Pye NEP 24297	IT'S ALL RIGHT (EP)	25
67	Pye NPL 18206	FROM THE FOUNDATIONS (LP)	22
68	Pye NPL 18227	ROCKING THE FOUNDATIONS (LP)	22
69	Pye N(S)PL 18290	DIGGING THE FOUNDATIONS (LP)	22

(see also Pluto)

JAMES FOUNTAIN
76	Cream CRM 5002	Seven Day Lover/Malnutrition	15

PETE FOUNTAIN
60	Coral Q 72389	Do You Know What It Means To Miss New Orleans?/A Closer Walk............	5
60	Coral Q 72404	Columbus Stockade Blues/Sentimental Journey (78 rpm = £15).............	5
71	Xtra XTRA 1120	NEW ORLEANS ALL STARS (LP)	12

(see also Brenda Lee)

THE 4
64	Decca F 11999	It's Alright/There's Nothing Like It....................................	18

FOUR ACES (Jamaica)
65	Island WI 178	Hoochy-Koochy-Kai-Po/River Bank Coberly Again..........................	25
65	Island WI 178	Hoochy-Koochy-Kai-Po/SKATALITES: Sucu Sucu (different B-side)	25
65	Island WI 179	Sweet Chariot/Peace And Love	15
65	Island WI 180	Little Girl/CLARENDONIANS: Day Will Come	18

(see also Desmond Dekker)

FOUR ACES (U.K.)
60s	Anton/E.R.S. EAG 178/179	Why Do You/Fortune Teller (private pressing)...........................	250+

FOUR ACES (U.S.)
54	Brunswick 05256	The Gang That Sang "Heart Of My Heart"/Heaven Can Wait	10
54	Brunswick 05308	Three Coins In The Fountain/Wedding Bells	
		(Are Breaking Up This Gang Of Mine)	20
54	Brunswick 05322	It Shall Come To Pass/Dream	10
54	Brunswick 05348	It's A Woman's World/The Cuckoo Bird In The Pickle Tree	12
54	Brunswick 05355	Mister Sandman/(I'll Be With You) In Apple Blossom Time	25
55	Brunswick 05379	Melody Of Love/There Is A Tavern In The Town	12
55	Brunswick 05401	There Goes My Heart/Take Me In Your Arms	6
55	Brunswick 05418	Stranger In Paradise/You'll Always Be The One	20
55	Brunswick 05429	Sluefoot/I'm In The Mood For Love....................................	6
55	Brunswick 05480	Love Is A Many Splendored Thing/Shine On Harvest Moon	22
55	Brunswick 05504	Jingle Bells/The Christmas Song (Merry Christmas To You)	7
55	Brunswick 05562	To Love Again/Charlie Was A Boxer	6
56	Brunswick 05566	The Gal With The Yaller Shoes/Of This I'm Sure	6
56	Brunswick 05573	If You Can Dream/It's The Talk Of The Town	6
56	Brunswick 05589	A Woman In Love/I Only Know I Love You..............................	8
56	Brunswick 05601	Dreamer/Let's Fall In Love	5
56	Brunswick 05613	You Can't Run Away From It/Written On The Wind......................	5
56	Brunswick 05623	Friendly Persuasion (Thee I Love)/Someone To Love	7
57	Brunswick 05651	Heart/What A Difference A Day Made	6
57	Brunswick 05663	Bahama Mama/You're Mine	6
57	Brunswick 05695	Three Sheets To The Wind/Yes, Sir, That's My Baby.....................	5
57	Brunswick 05712	Half Of My Heart/When My Sugar Walks Down The Street................	5
58	Brunswick 05743	Rock And Roll Rhapsody/I Wish I May, I Wish I Might (78 rpm = £6)	6
58	Brunswick 05758	Hangin' Up A Horseshoe/Two Arms, Two Lips, One Heart! (78 rpm = £8)	6
58	Brunswick 05767	The World Outside/The Christmas Tree (78 rpm = £12)	6
59	Brunswick 05773	The World Outside/The Inn Of The Sixth Happiness (78 rpm = £12)........	6
59	Brunswick 05812	Waltzin' Matilda/Roses Of Rio (78 rpm = £10)	6
50s	Decca A 73010	I'm Yours/I Understand (export issue)	10
54	Brunswick OE 9090	PRESENTING THE FOUR ACES (EP)	15
55	Brunswick OE 9157	MOOD FOR LOVE VOL. 1 (EP)...	15
55	Brunswick OE 9192	MOOD FOR LOVE VOL. 2 (EP)...	15
57	Brunswick OE 9324	ACES SING FILM TITLES (EP)	10
59	Brunswick OE 9458	THE FOUR ACES (EP)..	10
53	Brunswick LA 8614	JUST SQUEEZE ME (10" LP)	30
57	Brunswick LAT 8221	SHUFFLIN' ALONG (LP)	22
58	Brunswick LAT 8249	HITS FROM HOLLYWOOD (LP)	20
59	Brunswick STA 3014	THE SWINGIN' ACES (LP, stereo)	22

(see also Al Alberts)

4 DEGREES
65	Oak RGJ 187	4 DEGREES (LP, 1-sided, no sleeve)...................................	425

FOUR DOLLS
57	Capitol CL 14778	Three On A Date/Proud Of You (78 rpm = £6)	15
58	Capitol CL 14845	Whoop-A-Lala/I'm Following You	12

FOUR ESCORTS
54	HMV 7M 277	Loop De Loop Mambo/Love Me (78 rpm, HMV B10795 = £8)	15

FOUR ESQUIRES
55	London HL 8152	The Sphinx Won't Tell/Three Things (A Man Must Do) (78 rpm = £10)	50
56	London HLA 8224	Adorable/Thunderbolt (78 rpm = £10)	40
57	London HL 8376	Look Homeward Angel/Santo Domingo (78) (unreleased on both 78 and 45)	
58	London HLO 8533	Love Me Forever/I Ain't Been Right Since You Left	16
58	London HLO 8579	Always And Forever/I Walk Down The Street (78 rpm = £10).............	15
58	London HL 8746	Hideaway/Repeat After Me (78 rpm = £15)	12
59	Pye Intl. 7N 25012	Non E Cosi/Land Of You And Me (78 rpm = £8)..........................	5
59	Pye Intl. 7N 25027	Act Your Age/So Ends The Night (78 rpm = £12)	5
60	Pye Intl. 7N 25049	Wouldn't It Be Wonderful/Wonderful One	5

FOUR EVERS
66	CBS 202549	A Lovely Way To Say Goodnight/The Girl I Wanna Bring Home	35

FOUR FRESHMEN
54	Capitol CL 14196	Love Turns Winter To Spring/Mood Indigo..............................	8
55	Capitol CL 14338	Day By Day/How Can I Tell Her	8
56	Capitol CL 14580	Love Is Just Around The Corner/Angel Eyes (Four Freshmen/5 Trombones).....	5

56	Capitol CL 14610	Graduation Day/Lonely Night In Paris	6
56	Capitol CL 14633	You're So Far Above Me/He Who Loves And Runs Away	5
54	Capitol LC 6685	VOICES IN MODERN (10" LP)	18
58	Capitol T1008	IN PERSON (LP)	12
59	Capitol ST 1255	FOUR FRESHMEN AND FIVE GUITARS (LP)	12

CURTIS FULLER/TOMMY FLANAGAN
58	Pye PYE28009	IT'S MAGIC (LP)	40

FOUR FULLER BROTHERS
69	MCA MU 1068	Bitter Honey/Groupie	8

FOUR GEES
67	President PT 160	Ethiopia/Rough Rider	7

FOUR GIBSON GIRLS
58	Oriole CB 1447	No School Tomorrow/June, July And August (78 rpm = £6)	20
58	Oriole CB 1453	Safety Sue/VARIOUS ARTISTS: Safety Sue (78 rpm = £10)	15

FOUR GUYS
55	Vogue Coral Q 72054	Half Hearted Kisses/Mine	16
	(see also Modernaires)		

FOUR INSTANTS
66	Society	DISCOTHEQUE (LP)	16

FOUR JACKS
58	Decca F 10984	Hey! Baby/The Prayer Of Love (78 rpm = £8)	20
58	Decca DFE 6460	HEY! BABY (EP)	45

FOUR JACKS & A JILL
68	RCA Victor RCA 1669	Master Jack/I Looked Back	7

FOUR JONES BOYS
55	Decca F 10568	A Real Romance/When I Let You Go	7
55	Decca F 10671	Moments To Remember/Sing-ing-ing-ing	6
56	Decca F 10717	Tutti Frutti/Are You Satisfied? (78 rpm = £8)	20
56	Decca F 10789	Happiness Street (Corner Of Sunshine Square)/Someone To Love	7
56	Decca F 10829	Priscilla/It Isn't Right	11
	(see also Jones Boys, Annette Klooger)		

FOUR JUST MEN
64	Parlophone R 5186	That's My Baby/Things Will Never Be The Same	80
	(see also Just Four Men, Wimple Winch)		

FOUR KENTS
68	RCA RCA 1705	The Moving Finger Writes/Searchin'	20

FOUR KESTRELS
61	Decca F 11333	Sound Off/Can't Say I Do	6

FOUR KINSMEN
67	Decca F 22671	It Looks Like The Daybreak/Forget About Him	8
	(see also Kinsmen)		

FOUR KNIGHTS
54	Capitol CL 14076	I Get So Lonely/Till Then	25
54	Capitol CL 14154	Easy Street/In The Chapel In The Moonlight	20
54	Capitol CL 14204	I Don't Wanna See You Cryin'/Saw Your Eyes	20
55	Capitol CL 14244	Honey Bunch/Write Me, Baby	38
55	Capitol CL 14290	Inside Out/Foolishly Yours	15
56	Capitol CL 14516	Guilty/You	15
59	Coral Q 72355	Foolish Tears/O' Falling Star (78 rpm = £12)	15
55	Capitol EAP1 506	THE FOUR KNIGHTS (EP)	60
53	Capitol LC 6604	SPOTLIGHT SONGS (10" LP)	50
	(see also Nat 'King' Cole)		

FOUR LADS
57	Philips JK 1021	Golly/I Just Don't Know (jukebox issue) (78 rpm = £10)	12
57	Philips PB 769	The Eyes Of God/His Invisible Hand (78)	6
58	Philips PB 839	Enchanted Island/Guess What The Neighbours'll Say (78 rpm = £8)	5
59	Philips PB 894	The Girl On Page 44/The Mocking Bird	5
60	Philips PB 1000	Standing On The Corner/Sunday	5
60	Philips PB 1020	You're Nobody 'Til Somebody Loves You/Goona Goona	5
55	Philips BBE 12044	MOMENTS TO REMEMBER (EP)	10
61	London RE-R 1289	FOUR LADS FOUR HITS (EP)	12
62	London HA-R 2413	DIXIELAND DOIN'S (LP)	15
	(see also Johnnie Ray, Frankie Laine, Doris Day)		

FOUR LEAVED CLOVER
65	Oak RGJ 207	Alright Girl/Why	400

FOUR MACS
64	Parlophone R 5204	Come Back Silly Girl/Darlin'	6
	(see also Sands Of Time)		

FOUR MATADORS
66	Columbia DB 7806	A Man's Gotta Stand Tall/Fast Cars And Money	70

FOURMOST
63	Parlophone R 5056	Hello Little Girl/Just In Case	6
63	Parlophone R 5078	I'm In Love/Respectable	7
64	Parlophone R 5128	A Little Loving/Waiting For You	7
64	Parlophone R 5157	How Can I Tell Her/You Got That Way	9
64	Parlophone R 5194	Baby I Need Your Loving/That's Only What They Say	9

65	Parlophone R 5304	Everything In The Garden/He Could Never	7
65	Parlophone R 5379	Girls Girls Girls/Why Do Fools Fall In Love?	8
66	Parlophone R 5491	Here, There And Everywhere/You've Changed	12
66	Parlophone R 5528	Auntie Maggie's Remedy/Turn The Lights Down	15
68	CBS 3814	Apples, Peaches, Pumpkin Pie/He Could Never	15
69	CBS 4041	Rosetta/Just Like Before (DJ copy = £60)	40
69	CBS 4461	Easy Squeezy/Do I Love You?	20
72	Phoenix SNIX 126	Goodnight Sweet Dreams/Memphis	6
64	Parlophone GEP 8892	THE SOUND OF THE FOURMOST (EP)	65
64	Parlophone GEP 8917	THE FOURMOST (EP)	80
65	Parlophone PMC 1259	FIRST AND FOURMOST (LP)	100

(see also Format)

FOURMYULA
| 69 | Columbia DB 8549 | Honey Chile/Come With Me | 20 |

FOUR PALMS
| 58 | Vogue V 9116 | Jeanie, Joanie, Shirley, Toni/Consideration (78 rpm = £150) | 600 |

FOUR PENNIES (U.K.)
63	Philips BF 1296	Do You Want Me To/Miss Bad Daddy	9
64	Philips BF 1322	Tell Me Girl/Juliet	6
64	Philips BF 1322	Juliet/Tell Me Girl (A- & B-sides supposedly flipped after original release)	10
64	Philips BF 1349	I Found Out The Hard Way/Don't Tell Me You Love Me	5
64	Philips BF 1366	Black Girl/You Went Away	5
65	Philips BF 1398	The Way Of Love/A Place Where No-One Goes	5
65	Philips BF 1435	Until It's Time For You To Go/Till Another Day	5
66	Philips BF 1469	Trouble Is My Middle Name/Way Out Love	5
66	Philips BF 1491	Keep The Freeway Open/Square Peg	5
66	Philips BF 1519	No Sad Songs For Me/Cats	10
64	Philips BBE 12561	THE FOUR PENNIES (EP)	20
64	Philips BBE 12562	SPIN WITH THE PENNIES (EP)	20
64	Philips BBE 12570	THE SWINGING SIDE OF THE FOUR PENNIES (EP)	20
64	Philips BBE 12571	THE SMOOTH SIDE OF THE FOUR PENNIES (EP)	15
64	Philips BL 7642	TWO SIDES OF THE FOUR PENNIES (LP)	50
66	Philips BL 7734	MIXED BAG (LP)	90
67	Wing WL 1146	JULIET (LP)	20

(see also Lionel Morton, Fritz Mike & Mo)

FOUR PENNIES (U.S.)
63	Stateside SS 198	My Block/Dry Your Eyes	30
63	Stateside SS 244	When The Boy's Happy (The Girl's Happy Too)/Hockaday Part 1	28
79	Ensign ENY 23	When The Boy's Happy/CARLO: Little Orphan Girl	5

(see also Chiffons)

FOUR + ONE
| 65 | Parlophone R 5221 | Time Is On My Side/Don't Lie To Me | 100 |

(see also In Crowd, Tomorrow, Keith West)

FOUR PREPS
57	Capitol CL 14727	Falling Star/Where Wuz You	5
57	Capitol CL 14747	I Cried A Million Tears/Moonstruck In Madrid	5
57	Capitol CL 14768	Again 'n' Again 'n' Again/Promise Me Baby	5
57	Capitol CL 14783	Band Of Angels/How About That?	5
58	Capitol CL 14815	26 Miles (Santa Catalina)/Fools Will Be Fools	5
58	Capitol CL 14873	Big Man/Stop, Baby	5
58	Capitol CL 14914	Lazy Summer Night/Summertime Lies	5
59	Capitol CL 14992	The Riddle Of Love/She Was Five And He Was Ten	5
59	Capitol CL 15032	Cinderella/Gidget	5
59	Capitol CL 15044	The Big Surprise/Try My Arms	5
59	Capitol CL 15065	I Ain't Never/Memories, Memories	5
60	Capitol CL 15110	Listen Honey (I'll Be Home)/Down By The Station	5
60	Capitol CL 15128	Got A Girl/(Wait Till You) Hear It From Me	5
61	Capitol CL 15182	Calcutta/Gone Are The Days	5
61	Capitol CL 15217	More Money For You And Me (Medley)/Swing Down Chariot	5
57	Capitol EAP1 862	DREAMY EYES (EP)	15
58	Capitol EAP1 1015	TWENTY SIX MILES (EP)	15
59	Capitol EAP1 1064	BIG MAN (EP)	15
59	Capitol EAP1 1139	LAZY SUMMER NIGHT (EP)	15
61	Capitol EAP4 1647	CAMPUS ENCORES (EP)	12
59	Capitol T 1216	DANCING AND DREAMING (LP)	15
61	Capitol T 1291	DOWN BY THE STATION (LP)	15
61	Capitol T 1566	ON THE CAMPUS (LP)	20
61	Capitol (S)T 1647	CAMPUS ENCORE (LP)	15
62	Capitol (S)T 1814	CAMPUS CONFIDENTIAL (LP)	15
63	Capitol (S)T 1976	SONGS FOR A CAMPUS PARTY (LP)	15
64	Capitol (S)T 2169	HOW TO SUCCEED IN LOVE (LP)	15

4 SAXOPHONES IN 12 TONES
| 56 | Vogue V 2355 | Fantastic/Frankly Speaking | 7 |

FOUR SEASONS
SINGLES
62	Stateside SS 122	Sherry/I've Cried Before	9
63	Stateside SS 145	Big Girls Don't Cry/Connie-O	9
63	Stateside SS 169	Walk Like A Man/Lucky Ladybug	9
63	Stateside SS 194	Ain't That A Shame/Soon (I'll Be Home Again)	9
63	Stateside SS 216	Candy Girl/Marlena	9
63	Stateside SS 241	Santa Claus Is Coming To Town/Christmas Tears	15
64	Stateside SS 262	Peanuts/Silhouettes	9

64	Philips BF 1317	Dawn (Go Away)/No Surfin' Today	6
64	Philips BF 1334	Ronnie/Born To Wander	6
64	Stateside SS 315	Alone/Long Lonely Nights	6
64	Philips BF 1347	Rag Doll/Silence Is Golden	6
64	Stateside SS 343	Since I Don't Have You/Sincerely	10
65	Philips BF 1364	Save It For Me/Funny Face	6
65	Philips BF 1372	Big Man In Town/Little Angel	6
65	Philips BF 1395	Bye Bye Baby (Baby Goodbye)/Searching Wind	6
65	Philips BF 1411	Toy Soldier/Betrayed	6
65	Philips BF 1420	Girl Come Running/Cry Myself To Sleep	6
65	Philips BF 1439	Let's Hang On!/On Broadway Tonight	6
66	Philips BF 1474	Working My Way Back To You/Too Many Memories	6
66	Philips BF 1493	Opus 17 (Don't Worry 'Bout Me)/Beggar's Parade	15
66	Philips BF 1511	I've Got You Under My Skin/Huggin' My Pillow	8
67	Philips BF 1538	Tell It To The Rain/Show Girl	8
67	Philips BF 1556	Beggin'/Dody	7
67	Philips BF 1584	C'mon Marianne/Let's Ride Again	7
67	Philips BF 1600	Around And Around/WONDER WHO: Lonesome Road	8
67	Philips BF 1621	Watch The Flowers Grow/Raven	8
68	Philips BF 1651	Will You Love Me Tomorrow?/Silhouettes	9
68	Philips BF 1685	Saturday's Father/Goodbye Girl	10
69	Philips BF 1743	Electric Stories/Pity	10
69	Philips BF 1763	Rag Doll/Working My Way Back To You (p/s)	7
71	Philips 6051 018	Rag Doll/Let's Hang On/I've Got You Under My Skin (maxi-single)	5
71	Warner Bros K 16107	Whatever You Say/Sleeping Man (withdrawn, 300 only) As Frankie Valli and the Four Seasons)	35

EPs

| 64 | Stateside SE 1011 | THE FOUR SEASONS SING | 50 |
| 68 | Philips MCP 1000 | HITS OF THE FOUR SEASONS (cassette, in plastic tray, card p/s) | 10 |

LPs

63	Stateside SL 10033	SHERRY AND 11 OTHERS	40
63	Stateside SL 10042	AIN'T THAT A SHAME	50
63	Stateside SL 10051	THE FOUR SEASONS' GREETINGS	35
64	Philips BL 7611	BORN TO WANDER	20
64	Philips BL 7621	DAWN (GO AWAY) AND 11 OTHER GREAT SONGS	20
64	Philips BL 7643	RAG DOLL	18
65	Philips BL 7663	ENTERTAIN YOU	20
65	Philips (S)BL 7687	SING BIG HITS BY BURT BACHARACH ... HAL DAVID ... BOB DYLAN	18
65	Philips (S)BL 7699	WORKING MY WAY BACK TO YOU	18
66	Philips (S)BL 7719	GOLD VAULT OF HITS	15
67	Philips (S)BL 7751	SECOND VAULT OF GOLDEN HITS	15
67	Philips (S)BL 7752	LOOKIN' BACK	15
67	Philips (S)BL 7753	CHRISTMAS ALBUM	25
69	Philips (S)BL 7880	THE GENUINE IMITATION LIFE GAZETTE	22

(see also Beverly Hills Blues Band, Frankie Valli, Wonder Who)

FOUR SENSATIONS
| 52 | London L 1137 | Heaven Knows Why/Believing In You (78) | 25 |
| 52 | Melodisc P 216 | Raindrops/When Honeymoon Lane Becomes Memory Lane (78) | 10 |

FOUR SIGHTS
| 64 | Columbia DB 7227 | But I Can Tell/And I Cry | 12 |

4-SKINS
81	Clockwork Fun CF 101	One Law For Them/Brave New World (p/s)	15
81	Secret SHH 125	Yesterday's Heroes/Justice/Get Out Of My Life (p/s)	10
82	Secret SHH 141	Lowlife/Bread Or Blood (p/s)	10
82	Secret SEC 4	THE GOOD, THE BAD AND THE 4-SKINS (LP, with photo inner)	15
83	Syndicate SYN 1	A FISTFUL OF ... 4-SKINS (LP)	15
84	Syndicate SYN LP 5	FROM CHAOS TO 1984 (LP)	20

(see also Plastic Gangsters)

FOUR SPICES
| 57 | MGM MGM 944 | Armen's Theme (Yesterday And You)/Fire Engine Boogie (78 rpm = £25) | 125 |

FOUR SQUARES
| 64 | Hollick & Taylor HT 1009 | FOUR SQUARES (EP) | 70 |

(see also Pink People)

FOURTEEN (14)
68	Olga OLE 002	Through My Door/Meet Mr. Edgar	12
68	Olga OLE 006	Umbrella/Drizzle (Rain) (Demo £20)	12
68	Olga S 051	Easy To Fool/Frosty Stars On A Window Pane	10

FOUR TET
99	Output OPR21	DIALOGUE (LP)	18
01	Domino WIGLP94	PAUSE (LP)	12
02	Domino wIGLP126	ROUNDS (2xLP)	12
05	Domino WIGLP154x	EVERYTHING ECSTATIC (2xLP)	12

14 ICED BEARS
86	Frank COPPOLA 101	Inside/Blue Suit/Cut (hand-printed paper bag sleeve)	25
87	Frank CAPRA 202	Like A Dolphin/Balloon Song/Train Song/Lie To Choose (12", p/s)	10
87	Penetration	Balloon Song (flexidisc)	8
87	Penetration 001	Lie To Choose/SPLENDOUR IN THE GRASS: Twist Me (flexidisc)	6
88	Sarah SARAH 005	Come Get Me/Unhappy Days/Sure To See (poster p/s)	15
89	Thunderball 7TBL 2	Mother Sleep (7", unreleased, Mayking test pressings only)	25
90s	Thunderball Surfacer 002	Falling Backwards/World I Love/CROCODILE RIDE: Ex-Hipster/Satellite (Speed Mix) (numbered & stickered mailer, 1,000 only)	8

FOUR TONES

58	Decca F 11074	Voom Ba Voom/Rickshaw Boy (78 rpm = £9)	15

FOUR TOPHATTERS

55	London HLA 8163	Leave-a My Gal Alone/Go Baby Go (78 rpm = £35)	300
55	London HLA 8198	Forty Five Men In A Telephone Booth/Wild Rosie (78 rpm = £35)	300

FOUR TOPS
SINGLES

64	Stateside SS 336	Baby I Need Your Lovin'/Call On Me (DJ copy = £175)	50
65	Stateside SS 371	Without The One You Love (Life's Not Worthwhile)/Love Has Gone (DJ = £150)	50
65	Tamla Motown TMG 507	Ask The Lonely/Where Did You Go? (DJ copy = £150)	60
65	Tamla Motown TMG 515	I Can't Help Myself/Sad Souvenirs (DJ copy = £150)	20
65	Tamla Motown TMG 528	It's The Same Old Song/Your Love Is Amazing (DJ copy = £125)	25
65	Tamla Motown TMG 542	Something About You/Darling I Hum Our Song (DJ copy = £125)	25
66	Tamla Motown TMG 553	Shake Me, Wake Me (When It's Over)/Just As Long As You Need Me (DJ = £125)	30
66	Tamla Motown TMG 568	Loving You Is Sweeter Than Ever/I Like Everything About You (DJ = £100)	20
66	Tamla Motown TMG 579	Reach Out, I'll Be There/Until You Love Someone (small print, later large) (DJ copy = £85)	12/7
67	Tamla Motown TMG 589	Standing In The Shadows Of Love/Since You've Been Gone (small print, later large) (DJ copy = £85)	15/8
67	Tamla Motown TMG 601	Bernadette/I Got A Feeling (DJ copy = £85)	15
67	Tamla Motown TMG 612	Seven Rooms Of Gloom/I'll Turn To Stone (DJ copy = £85)	15
67	Tamla Motown TMG 623	You Keep Running Away/If You Don't Want My Love (DJ copy = £85)	15
67	Tamla Motown TMG 634	Walk Away Renee/Mame (DJ copy = £75)	10
68	Tamla Motown TMG 647	If I Were A Carpenter/Your Love Is Wonderful (DJ copy = £75)	20
68	Tamla Motown TMG 665	Yesterday's Dreams/For Once In My Life (DJ copy = £75)	10
68	Tamla Motown TMG 675	I'm In A Different World/Remember When (DJ copy = £60)	10
69	Tamla Motown TMG 698	What Is A Man?/Don't Bring Back Memories (DJ copy = £75)	20
69	Tamla Motown TMG 710	Do What You Gotta Do/Can't Seem To Get You Out Of My Mind (DJ copy = £75)	25
70	Tamla Motown TMG 736	It's All In The Game/Love (Is The Answer) (DJ copy = £45)	8
70	Tamla Motown TMG 752	Still Water (Love)/Still Water (Peace) (DJ copy = £45)	8
71	Tamla Motown TMG 770	Just Seven Numbers (Can Straighten Out My Life)/I Wish I Were Your Mirror (DJ copy = £35)	8
71	Tamla Motown TMG 785	Simple Game/You Stole My Love (DJ copy = £35)	8
72	Tamla Motown TMG 803	Bernadette/I Got A Feeling/It's The Same Old Song (DJ copy = £30)	6
72	Tamla Motown TMG 829	I'll Turn To Stone/Love Feels Like Fire (DJ copy = £30)	6
72	Probe PRO 575	Keeper Of The Castle/Jubilee With Soul	5
73	Probe PRO 596	Are You Man Enough/Peace Of Mind	6
74	Probe PRO 612	I Just Can't Get You Out Of My Mind/Am I My Brother's Keeper	15
75	ABC ABC 4057	Seven Lonely Nights/I Can't Hold On Much Longer	5

EPs

66	Tamla Motown TME 2012	THE FOUR TOPS (flipback design covers)	28
67	Tamla Motown TME 2018	FOUR TOP HITS	22

LPs

65	Tamla Motown TML 11010	THE FOUR TOPS	75
66	T. Motown (S)TML 11021	SECOND ALBUM (mono/stereo)	40/50
66	T. Motown (S)TML 11037	FOUR TOPS ON TOP (mono/stereo)	30/40
67	T. Motown (S)TML 11041	FOUR TOPS LIVE! (mono/stereo)	30/40
67	T. Motown (S)TML 11056	REACH OUT	25
68	T. Motown (S)TML 11061	FOUR TOPS GREATEST HITS	18
69	T. Motown (S)TML 11087	YESTERDAY'S DREAMS	22
69	T. Motown (S)TML 11113	FOUR TOPS NOW	22
70	T. Motown (S)TML 11138	SOUL SPIN (mono/stereo)	22/18
70	Tamla Motown STML 11149	STILL WATERS RUN DEEP	15
71	Tamla Motown STML 11173	CHANGING TIMES	15
71	Tamla Motown STML 11195	GREATEST HITS VOL. 2	15
72	Tamla Motown STML 11206	NATURE PLANNED IT	12
73	Probe SPB 1064	KEEPER OF THE CASTLE	15
73	Probe SPB 1077	SHAFT IN AFRICA (soundtrack, with Johnny Pate)	12
73	Probe SPBA 6277	MAIN STREET PEOPLE	12
74	Probe SPBA 6283	MEETING OF THE MINDS	12
74	ABC ABCL 5035	SHAFT IN AFRICA (soundtrack, reissue)	35
74	ABC ABCL 5062	LIVE AND IN CONCERT	12
75	ABC ABCL 5132	NIGHT LIGHTS HARMONY	12

(see also Supremes & Four Tops)

FOUR TUNES

54	London L 1231	I Gambled With Love/Marie (78)	50
54	London HL 8050	Do, Do, Do, Do, Do Do It Again/My Wild Irish Rose (78)	20
55	London HL 8151	I Sold My Heart To A Junkman/The Greatest Feeling In The World (78 rpm = £35)	130
55	London HLJ 8164	Tired Of Waitin'/L'Amour, Toujours L'Amour (Love Everlasting) (78 rpm = £30)	65

FOUR VOICES

56	Philips PB 591	Geronimo/Lovely One (78)	10
58	Philips PB 864	Tell Me You're Mine/Tight Spot (78 rpm = £12)	6

FOUR WINDS

58	London HLU 8556	Short Shorts/Five Minutes More (78 rpm = £20)	45

KIM FOWLEY

66	Parlophone R 5521	Lights/Something New And Different	22
66	CBS 202243	They're Coming To Take Me Away Ha-Haaa!!/You Get More For Your Money On The Flip Side Of This Record Talking Blues	10
66	CBS 202338	Lights (The Blind Can See)/Something New And Different (reissue)	12
68	Island WI 278	The Trip/Beautiful People	12
72	Action ACT 4606	Born To Make You Cry/Thunder Road	7

Kim FOWLEY

73	Capitol CL 15743	International Heroes/E.S.P. Reader	5
78	Mercury 6005 009	Control/Rubber Rainbow	5
79	Illegal ILS 012	Rubber Rainbow/In My Garage (p/s)	5
80	Island WIP 6555	1989: Waiting For The Next Ten Years/1987: Lost Like A Lizard In Snow	5
73	Capitol E-ST 11159	INTERNATIONAL HEROES (LP)	12
80	Island WIP 278	The Trip/Beautiful People (p/s, reissue)	10

(see also Freaks Of Nature, Hollywood Argyles, Napoleon XIV, B. Bumble & Stingers)

HARRY FOWLER & MARIO FABRIZI

61	HMV POP 891	Buddies/HARRY FOWLER: Follow Flogger	8

FOX

68	CBS 3381	Mister Carpenter/Seek And You Find	100+

(see also Top Topham, Dave Mason)

FOX

70	Fontana 6007 016	Second Hand Love/Butterfly	25
70	Fontana 6309 007	FOR FOX SAKE (LP)	80

FOX

76	GTO GT51	S-S-S-Single Bed/Silk Milk	6
75	GTO GTLP 006	TAILS OF ILLUSION (LP)	12
77	GTO GTLP 020	BLUE HOTEL (LP)	12

(see also Wooden Horse, Demick & Armstrong)

FOX

81	BBC RESL 115	Electro People/If You Don't Want My Peaches	8

BOB FOX & STU LUCKLEY

78	Rubber RUB 028	NOWT SO GOOD'LL PASS (LP)	15

DON FOX

57	Decca F 10927	Be My Girl/You'll Never Go To Heaven	12
57	Decca F 10955	The Majesty Of Love/Party Time	12
58	Decca F 10983	Pretend You Don't See Her/Wasteland	12
58	Decca F 11057	She Was Only Seventeen/When You're A Long, Long Way Away	10
60	Triumph RGM 1022	T'ain't What You Do/Out There	40
61	Oriole CB 1643	Don't Fool With Love/If You Go	8
60s	Honey Hit TB 125	Three Swinging Clicks/I Found The Girl I Love In My Home Town (some in p/s)	15/7
69	B & C CB110	Once In A While/You Belong To My Heart	6

SAMANTHA FOX

84	Lamborghini LMG 10	Aim To Win/17 And Holding (12", p/s)	8
84	Lamborghini LMG 10	Aim To Win/17 And Holding (12", picture disc)	8
87	Jive FOXYS 5	Nothing's Gonna Stop Me Now (Extended Mix)/Dream City/Want You To Want Me (12" picture disc)	8
87	Jive FOXTB 5	Nothing's Gonna Stop Me Now (Extended Mix)/Dream City/Want You To Want Me (12", box set)	8
89	Jive FOXY CD 11	I Only Wanna Be With You/Nothing's Gonna Stop Me Now/ I Only Wanna Be With You (Extended Version)/Confession (CD, in circular tin)	8
88	Jive HIPR 39	TOUCH ME (LP, picture disc)	15

(see also David Cassidy)

ROY FOXLEY & HIS LEVEE RAMBLERS

50	Tailgate 4 & 5	South/Weary Blues (78)	7

BRUCE FOXTON

86	Harvest HAR 5239	Play This Game To Win/Welcome To The Hero (p/s)	5

(see also Jam)

FOXX

71	MCA MUPS 419	REVOLT OF EMILY YOUNG (LP)	15

INEZ FOXX

63	Sue WI 301	Mockingbird/He's The One You Love (actually by Inez & Charlie Foxx)	25
64	Sue WI 304	Jaybirds/Broken-Hearted Fool (actually by Inez & Charlie Foxx)	25
64	Sue WI 314	Ask Me/Hi Diddle Diddle (actually by Inez & Charlie Foxx)	25
64	Sue WI 323	Hurt By Love/Confusion (actually by Inez & Charlie Foxx)	25
71	Pye International 7N 25546	You Shouldn't Have Set My Soul On Fire/Live For Today	10
73	Stax 2025 151	You Hurt Me For The Last Time/Watch The Dog (That Brings The Bone)	8

INEZ & CHARLIE FOXX

64	Sue WI 307	Competition/Here We Go Round The Mulberry Bush (as Charlie & Inez Foxx)	30
64	Sue WI 356	La De Da I Love You/Yankee Doodle Dandy	30
65	London HLC 9971	My Momma Told Me/I Feel Alright	10
65	London HLC 10009	Hummingbird/If I Need Anyone (Let It Be You)	10
66	Stateside SS 556	Come By Here/No Stranger To Love	28
67	Stateside SS 586	Tightrope/My Special Prayer (DJ copy = £75)	35
67	Direction 58-2712	I Ain't Goin' For That/Undecided	10
67	Direction 58-3192	(1, 2, 3, 4, 5, 6, 7) Count The Days/A Stranger I Don't Know	10
68	Direction 58-3816	Come On In/Baby Drop Your Dime	10
69	Direction 58-4042	Baby Give It To Me/You Fixed My Heartache	10
69	London HLC 10250	Mockingbird/Hummingbird (unissued)	
69	United Artists UP 2269	Mockingbird/Hurt By Love	8
69	United Artists UP 35013	La De Da I Love You/Don't Do It No More	8
71	Pye International 7N 25561	Tightrope/Baby Take It All	6
83	Sue ENS 2	Mockingbird EP	15
64	Sue ILP 911	MOCKINGBIRD (LP)	100
65	London HA-C 8241	INEZ AND CHARLIE FOXX (LP, plum label, later black)	70/40
68	Direction 8-63085	COME BY HERE (LP)	30
68	Direction 8-63281	GREATEST HITS (LP)	22

69	United Artists UA(S) 29025	MOCKINGBIRD (LP)	15
71	Pye PKL 4406	GREATEST HITS (LP)	12

JOHN FOXX

80	Island Music/Smash Hits	My Face (yellow vinyl 1-sided flexidisc free with *Smash Hits* magazine)	10/5
80	Virgin VS 338	No-One Driving/Glimmer//This City/Mr. No (double pack, gatefold p/s)	6
80	Virgin VS 338	No-One Driving (2.53 DJ Version)/Glimmer//This City/Mr. No (double pack, stickered gatefold p/s, matrix no. VS 338 A5DJ)	15
80	Virgin VS 360	Burning Car/20th Century (picture disc)	5
82	Virgin VS 543	Endlessly/Ghosts On Water//Dance With Me/A Kind Of Wave (double pack)	5
84	Virgin VS 615	Your Dress/Woman On A Stairway//Lifting Sky/Annexe (double pack)	5
84	Virgin VSP 645	Like A Miracle/Wings And A Wind (shaped picture disc)	7
85	Virgin VS 771	The Stars On Fire/What Kind Of Girl (p/s, with bonus single)	5
	(see also Ultravox)		

FRABJOY & RUNCIBLE SPOON

69	Marmalade 598 019	I'm Beside Myself/Animal Song	30
	(see also Godley & Creme, Doctor Father, Hotlegs, Mockingbirds, 10cc)		

FRAME

66	RCA RCA 1556	My Feet Don't Fit In His Shoes/She	18
67	RCA RCA 1571	Doctor Doctor/I Can't Go On	65
70	Pye 7N 45213	Rockin' Machine/One More Time	8

FRAMES

79	Brain Booster BBC 2	False Accusations/69 (no p/s)	6

PETER FRAMPTON

72	A&M AMS 7025	It's A Plain Shame/Oh For Another Day	5
75	A&M AMS 7174	Show Me The Way/Crying Clown	5
81	A&M AMS 8154	Breaking All The Rules/Night Town (p/s)	7
85	Virgin VSS 827	Lying/You Know So Well (shaped disc)	7
72	A&M AMLS 68099	WIND OF CHANGE (LP)	15
74	A&M AMLH 6369	SOMETHING'S HAPPENING (LP)	14
	(see also Preachers, Herd, Humble Pie, Frampton's Camel, Moon's Train)		

FRAMPTON'S CAMEL

73	A&M AMS 7069	All Night Long/Don't Fade Away	5
73	A&M AMLH 68150	FRAMPTON'S CAMEL (LP, with poster)	15
	(see also Peter Frampton, Parrish & Gurvitz)		

FRAN & ALAN

68	MGM MGM 1428	Such A Pity/Mrs Robinson	8

PETER FRANC

73	Dawn DNS 1033	I'll Move Along/Song For Every Season	6
73	Dawn DNS 1039	Ballad Of the Superstar/Strange Kind Of Woman	6
74	Dawn DNS 1088	Flag Of Convenience/At Home With You	6
73	Dawn DNLS 3043	PROFILE (LP)	15
73	Dawn DNLS 3051	EN ROUTE (LP)	12

FRANCIS

67	Blue Beat BB 379	Warn The People (actually by Willie Francis)/SWINGERS: Simpleton (actually by Peter Tosh & Crackers)	60
72	Fab FAB 182	Rocking Machine/SOUL CLANS: Flying Rhythm	12
73	Fab FAB 251	Locks/Version	12

B. FRANCIS

65	Ska Beat JB 193	Judy Crowned/Who Crunch	12

BOBBY FRANCIS

67	Doctor Bird DB 1153	Chain Gang/Venus	20
	(see also Winston Francis)		

CLAIRE FRANCIS

66	Polydor 56079	I've Got My Own Thing Going/Here I Go Again	7
67	Polydor 56142	But I Don't Care/If You Don't Know	7

CONNIE FRANCIS

78s

56	MGM MGM 902	My First Real Love (with Jaybirds)/Believe In Me (Crede Mi)	65
56	MGM MGM 932	My Sailor Boy/Everyone Needs Someone	18
57	MGM MGM 945	Little Blue Wren/I Never Had A Sweetheart	35
57	MGM MGM 962	Eighteen/Faded Orchid	45
58	MGM MGM 998	You Always Hurt The One You Love/In The Valley Of Love	12
59	MGM MGM 1001	My Happiness/Happy Days And Lonely Nights	18
59	MGM MGM 1012	If I Didn't Care/Toward The End Of The Day	35
59	MGM MGM 1018	Lipstick On Your Collar/Frankie	35
59	MGM MGM 1036	Plenty Good Lovin'/You're Gonna Miss Me	35
59	MGM MGM 1046	Among My Souvenirs/Do You Love Me Like You Kiss Me?	40

SINGLES

56	MGM SP 1169	My First Real Love (with Jaybirds)/Believe In Me (Crede Mi)	200
56	MGM MGM 932	My Sailor Boy/Everyone Needs Someone	80
57	MGM MGM 945	Little Blue Wren/I Never Had A Sweetheart	60
57	MGM MGM 962	Eighteen/Faded Orchid	60
58	MGM MGM 975	Who's Sorry Now?/You Were Only Fooling (While I Was Falling In Love)	8
58	MGM MGM 982	I'm Sorry I Made You Cry/Lock Up Your Heart	8
58	MGM MGM 985	Carolina Moon/Stupid Cupid	12
58	MGM MGM 993	I'll Get By/Fallin'	8
58	MGM MGM 998	You Always Hurt The One You Love/In The Valley Of Love	7
59	MGM MGM 1001	My Happiness/Happy Days And Lonely Nights	7
59	MGM MGM 1012	If I Didn't Care/Toward The End Of The Day	10

Connie FRANCIS

59	MGM MGM 1018	Lipstick On Your Collar/Frankie	
59	MGM MGM 1036	Plenty Good Lovin'/You're Gonna Miss Me	
59	MGM MGM 1046	Among My Souvenirs/Do You Love Me Like You Kiss Me?	
60	MGM MGM 1060	Valentino/It Would Be Worth It	
60	MGM MGM 1070	Mama/Teddy (withdrawn; demos more common, £40)	6
60	MGM MGM 1076	Mama/Robot Man	
60	MGM MGM 1086	Everybody's Somebody's Fool/Jealous Of You	
60	MGM MGM 1100	My Heart Has A Mind Of Its Own/Malaguena	
60	MGM MGM 1111	Many Tears Ago/Senza Mama (With No-One)	
61	MGM MGM 1121	Where The Boys Are/Baby Roo	
61	MGM MGM 1136	Breakin' In A Brand New Broken Heart/Someone Else's Boy	
61	MGM MGM 1138	Together/Too Many Rules	
61	MGM MGM 1145	Baby's First Christmas/I'm Falling In Love With You Tonight	
62	MGM MGM 1151	Don't Cry On My Shoulder/Mr. Twister	
62	MGM MGM 1157	Don't Break The Heart That Loves You/Ain't That Better Baby?	
62	MGM MGM 1165	Vacation/It's Gonna Take Me Some Time	2
62	MGM MGM 1171	Playin' Games/I Was Such A Fool	1(
62	MGM MGM 1185	I'm Gonna Be Warm This Winter/Pretty Little Baby	
62	MGM MGM 1193	Follow The Boys/Tonight's My Night	
63	MGM MGM 1202	If My Pillow Could Talk/Lollipop Lips	
63	MGM MGM 1207	Drownin' My Sorrows/Look At Him	8
63	MGM MGM 1212	Your Other Love/Whatever Happened To Rosemary	8
63	MGM MGM 1220	The Summer Of His Years/My Buddy	
63	MGM MGM 1224	Blue Winter/Souvenirs	
63	MGM MGM 1236	Be Anything (But Be Mine)/Tommy	
64	MGM MGM 1253	Don't Ever Leave Me/Waiting For You	1(
65	MGM MGM 1265	Forget Domani/I Don't Want To Be No Better Off	1(
65	MGM MGM 1271	My Child/No One Ever Sends Me Roses	
65	MGM MGM 1282	Roundabout/Love Is Me, Love Is You	1(
66	MGM MGM 1293	Jealous Heart/Can I Rely On You?	9
66	MGM MGM 1295	The Phoenix Love Theme — Senza Fine/Bossa Nova Hand Dance	9
66	MGM MGM 1305	Love Is Me, Love Is You/I'd Let You Break My Heart All Over Again	9
66	MGM MGM 1320	Somewhere My Love (Lara's Theme)/Letter From A Soldier (Dear Mama)	9
66	MGM MGM 1327	Spanish Nights And You/Games That Lovers Play	9
67	MGM MGM 1334	Another Page/Souvenir D'Italie	8
67	MGM MGM 1336	Time Alone Will Tell/Born Free	8
67	MGM MGM 1347	My Heart Cries For You/If My Friends Could See Me Now (Medley)	8
68	MGM MGM 1381	My World Is Slipping Away/Till We're Together	8
68	MGM MGM 1407	Why Say Goodbye?/Addio Mi Amore	8
68	MGM MGM 1446	Somebody Else Is Taking My Place/Brother Can You Spare A Dime?	8
69	MGM MGM 1471	The Wedding Cake/Overhill Underground	1(
69	MGM MGM 1483	Who's Sorry Now?/Vacation	8
69	MGM MGM 1493	Mr. Love/Zingara	1(

EPs

56	MGM MGM-EP 658	A GIRL IN LOVE	30
58	MGM MGM-EP 677	HEARTACHES	25
58	MGM MGM-EP 686	CONNIE FRANCIS	25
59	MGM MGM-EP 697	IF I DIDN'T CARE	25
60	MGM MGM-EP 711	YOU'RE MY EVERYTHING	30
60	MGM MGM-EP 717	ROCK AND ROLL MILLION SELLERS NO. 1	30
60	MGM MGM-EP 720	ROCK AND ROLL MILLION SELLERS NO. 2	30
60	MGM MGM-EP 731	ROCK AND ROLL MILLION SELLERS NO. 3	25
60	MGM MGM-EP 742	FIRST LADY OF RECORD (laminated or matt rear sleeve)	18
61	MGM MGM-EP 756	WHERE THE BOYS ARE	25
61	MGM MGM-EP 759	CONNIE FRANCIS FAVOURITES	30
61	MGM MGM-EP 760	SINGS ITALIAN FAVOURITES	30
63	MGM MGM-EP 769	CONNIE'S AMERICAN HITS	30
63	MGM MGM-EP 773	HEY RING-A-DING	40
63	MGM MGM-EP 775	WHAT KIND OF FOOL AM I?	25
63	MGM MGM-EP 780	MALA FEMMENA	25
63	MGM MGM-EP 783	FROM ITALY ... WITH LOVE	25
65	MGM MGM-EP 789	SINGS FOR MAMA	25
66	MGM MGM-EP 792	JEALOUS HEART	25

LPs

58	MGM MGM-D 153	WHO'S SORRY NOW? (10")	75
59	MGM MGM-C 782	MY THANKS TO YOU	30
59	MGM MGM-C 786	THE EXCITING CONNIE FRANCIS	25
59	MGM MGM-C 797	CHRISTMAS WITH CONNIE	40
60	MGM MGM-C 804	ROCK AND ROLL MILLION SELLERS NO. 1	50
60	MGM MGM-C 812	COUNTRY AND WESTERN GOLDEN HITS	30
60	MGM MGM-C 819	FUN SONGS FOR CHILDREN	30
60	MGM MGM-C 821	SINGS ITALIAN FAVOURITES (also stereo CS 6002)	20/22
60	MGM MGM-C 831	CONNIE'S GREATEST HITS	15
60	MGM MGM-C 836	SPANISH AND LATIN AMERICAN FAVOURITES (also stereo CS 6012)	18/20
61	MGM MGM-C 845	SINGS JEWISH FAVOURITES (also stereo CS 6021)	18/20
61	MGM MGM-C 854	MORE ITALIAN FAVOURITES (also stereo CS 6029)	18/20
61	MGM MGM-C 861	AT THE COPA (also stereo CS 6035)	18/20
61	MGM MGM-C 870	SONGS TO A SWINGIN' BAND (also stereo CS 6044)	18/20
61	MGM MGM-C 875	SINGS 'NEVER ON SUNDAY' AND OTHER TITLE SONGS	
		FROM MOTION PICTURES (also stereo CS 6047)	18/20
61	MGM MGM-C 879	DO THE TWIST	50
62	MGM MGM-C 883	SINGS FOLK SONG FAVOURITES (also stereo CS 6054)	18/20
62	MGM MGM-C 898	SINGS IRISH FAVOURITES (also stereo CS 6056)	25/30
62	MGM MGM-C 916	COUNTRY MUSIC CONNIE STYLE (also stereo CS 6062)	20/25

63	MGM MGM-C 930	SINGS MODERN ITALIAN HITS (also stereo CS 6067)	18/20
63	MGM MGM-C 931	FOLLOW THE BOYS (also stereo CS 6068)	18/20
63	MGM MGM-C 940	SINGS AWARD-WINNING MOTION PICTURE HITS (also stereo CS 6070)	18/20
64	MGM MGM-C 958	GREATEST AMERICAN WALTZES (also stereo CS 6075)	18/20
64	MGM MGM-C 970	16 OF CONNIE'S BIGGEST HITS	15
65	MGM MGM-C 983	LOOKING FOR LOVE (also stereo CS 6079)	20
65	MGM MGM-C 998	A NEW KIND OF CONNIE... (also stereo CS 6080)	18/20
65	MGM MGM-C 1003	SINGS GREAT COUNTRY FAVOURITES (with Hank Williams Jnr, also stereo CS 6081)	20/22
65	MGM MGM-C 1006	SINGS 'FOR MAMA' (also stereo CS 6082)	20/22
65	MGM MGM-C 1012	SINGS THE ALL-TIME INTERNATIONAL HITS (also stereo CS 6083)	18/20
66	MGM MGM-C(S) 8006	WHEN THE BOYS MEET THE GIRLS (soundtrack, mono/stereo)	15/18
66	MGM MGM-C(S) 8009	JEALOUS HEART	20
66	MGM MGM-C(S) 8027	MOVIE GREATS OF THE SIXTIES	20
66	MGM MGM-C(S) 8036	LIVE AT THE SAHARA IN LAS VEGAS	20
67	MGM MGM-C 8041	THE BEST OF CONNIE FRANCIS	15
68	MGM MGM-C(S) 8050	LOVE ITALIAN STYLE (mono/stereo)	18/20
68	MGM MGM-C(S) 8054	MY HEART CRIES FOR YOU (mono/stereo)	18/20
68	MGM MGM-C(S) 8086	CONNIE AND CLYDE	20
69	MGM MGM-C(S) 8110	HAWAII CONNIE	40
70	MGM MGM-CS 8117	SINGS THE SONGS OF LES REED	20
78	United Artists ULP 30182	WHO'S HAPPY NOW? (withdrawn sleeve with different lettering)	100
78	United Artists ULP 30182	WHO'S HAPPY NOW?.	15
81	R/Digest GBCF-A-106	THE BEST OF CONNIE FRANCIS (4-LP)	15

CONNIE FRANCIS & MARVIN RAINWATER

58	MGM MGM 969	The Majesty Of Love/You My Darling You (78 rpm = £30)	50

(see also Marvin Rainwater)

(KING) JOE FRANCIS

65	Blue Beat BB 323	Wicked Woman/King Joe's Ska (as King Joe Francis)	15
66	Ska Beat JB 262	Scarborough Ska/I Got A Scar (as Joe Francis & Ricky Logan & Snowballs)	20
66	Rio R 90	Have My Body (song actually "Have Mercy Baby")/Everybody's Got To Know (as King Joe Francis & Hijackers)	14
66	Rio R 94	Days Are Lonely/My Baby	25
67	Rainbow RAI 114	My Granny/Pull It Out (as J. Francis & Rico's Boys)	15

JOHNNIE FRANCIS

55	Decca F 10440	Funny Thing/Give Me The Right	7

LEE FRANCIS

65	Decca F 12148	Ciao/If He Wants Me	7

(see also Vernons Girls)

NAT FRANCIS

66	Blue Beat BB 346	Mama Kiss Him Goodnight/Tra La La (with Prince Buster Junior & Sunsets)	18
66	Blue Beat BB 361	Just To Keep You (credited to B. Junior)/You Only Want My Money	15
67	Blue Beat BB 376	Seven Nights Of Love/Feeling Blue	20

RITCHIE FRANCIS

72	Pegasus PEG 11	SONGBIRD (LP)	20

(see also Eyes Of Blue, Big Sleep)

STEVE FRANCIS

64	King KG 1012	Watch Your Step/Lovey Dovey	6

WILBERT FRANCIS & VIBRATORS

66	Ska Beat JB 267	Memories Of You/CHUCK JACQUES: Now That You're Gone	18

(see also Little Willie, Vibrators [Jamaica])

WILLIE FRANCIS

69	Bullet BU 415	Motherless Children/I Am Not Afraid	8
71	Escort ERT 848	Burn Them/Poor Boy	7
71	Pama PM 829	Oh What A Mini/Version	6

(see also Martin Riley)

WINSTON FRANCIS

69	Coxsone CS 7089	Reggae And Cry/FREEDOM SINGERS: Easy Come Easy Go (B-side actually by Righteous Flames)	28
69	Studio One SO 2086	The Games People Play/ALBERT GRIFFITHS: The Kicks	30
69	Punch PH 5	Too Experienced/JACKIE MINTO: Mule Jerk (B-side actually by Jackie Mittoo)	15
69	Bamboo BAM 10	The Same Old Song/SOUND DIMENSION: Rattle On	20
70	Bamboo BAM 46	Turn Back The Hands Of Time/Soul Bowl	20
70	Bamboo BAM 48	California Dreaming/JACKIE MITTOO & SOUND DIMENSION: Soul Stew	30
72	Camel CA 99	Ten Times Sweeter Than You/Fat Boy	8
73	Fab FAB 271	Mr Fix It/Version	8
74	Ashanti ASH 415	California Dreaming/SOUND DIMENSION: Soul Food (reissue)	8
70	Bamboo BDLP 207	MR FIX IT (LP)	55
71	Bamboo BDLPS 216	CALIFORNIA DREAMING (LP)	55

(see also Bobby Francis, Jerry & Freedom Singers, Zimm & Dee Dee)

JACQUELINE FRANCOIS

59	Philips BBL 7273	THE SWEET LANGUAGE OF LOVE (LP)	15

JACKSON C. FRANK

65	Columbia DB 7795	Blues Run The Game/Can't Get Away From My Love	50
65	Columbia 33SX 1788	JACKSON C. FRANK (LP)	175
78	B&C BCLP 4	AGAIN (LP, reissue of above LP)	40

FRANK & BARBARIANS

62	Oriole CB 1758	The Bouncer/Concerto In The Stars	10

(see also Frank Barber)

MINT VALUE £

FRANKIE & CLASSICALS
67	Philips BF 1586	I Only Have Eyes For You/What Shall I Do?.........................	200
74	Pye Intl. DDS 101	What Shall I Do?/Goodbye Love, Hello Sadness......................	10

FRANKIE & JOHNNY
66	Decca F 22376	Never Gonna Leave You/I'll Hold You.................................	220
66	Parlophone R 5518	Climb Ev'ry Mountain/I Wanna Make You Understand	15
78	Inferno HEAT 8	I'll Hold You/Never Gonna Leave You (reissue).......................	20

(see also Maggie Bell)

FRANKIE & LARRY
60	Capitol CL 15153	Not Yet/A Fool For You..	16

FRANKIE & TIMEBREAKERS
68	Philips BF 1696	I'll Be Home/Is There Anybody	7

FRANKIE GOES TO HOLLYWOOD
SINGLES
83	ZTT P ZTAS 1	Relax (Move)/One September Monday (picture disc)	6
83	ZTT 12 ZTAS 1	Relax (Original Mix)/Ferry Across The Mersey/Relax Bonus (Again) (12", ZTT sleeve or standard p/s)	18
83	ZTT 12 ZTAS 1	Relax (Original Mix)/Ferry Across The Mersey/Relax Bonus (Again) (12", ZTT sleeve or standard p/s, some copies play at 33rpm but list 45rpm)....	15
83	ZTT 12 ZTAS 1 (matrix no.: 1A 2U)	Relax (Sex Mix [alias 8.20 New York Mix])/Ferry Across The Mersey Relax Bonus (Again) (12", p/s, 45rpm)	12
83	ZTT 12 ZTAS 1 (matrix no.: 1A 5U)	Relax (Sex Mix)/Ferry Across The Mersey/Relax Bonus (Again) (12", p/s, 45rpm, different 'U.S. chequered' p/s)	8
83	ZTT 12P ZTAS 1	Relax (Sex Mix)/Ferry Across The Mersey/Relax Bonus (Again) (12", picture disc)...	8
83	ZTT CTIS 102	Relax: The Party Trick (Acting Dumb)/The Special Act (Adapted From The Sex Mix)/The U.S. Mix (Come Dancing)/The Single (The Act)/Later On (From One September Monday)/Gerry Marsden's Ferry Across The Mersey (And Here I'll Stay) (cassette)	8
84	ZTT P ZTAS 3	Two Tribes (We Don't Want To Die)/One February Friday (picture disc)........	6
84	ZTT CTIS 103	TWO TRIBES (KEEP THE PEACE) (cassette)...........................	5
84	ZTT P ZTAS 5	The Power Of Love/The World Is My Oyster (picture disc)	5
84	ZTT 12X ZTAS 5	The Power Of Love/The World Is My Oyster/Welcome To The Pleasuredome (Pleasurefix)/The Only Star In Heaven (Starfix) (12", g/fold p/s with 5 photos)....	8
84	ZTT CTIS 105	The Power Of Love (Extended Version)/Trapped And Scrapped/Holier Than Thou (cassette, picture 'envelope' box)	8
85	ZTT ZTAS 7	Welcome To The Pleasure Dome (Altered Reel) (actually plays Video Mix 5.05)/Happy Hi Get It On (p/s, blue label)	10
85	ZTT P ZTAS 7	Welcome To The Pleasure Dome (Alternative Reel [Fruitiness Mix])/ Happy Hi/Get It On (apple-shaped picture disc)	7
85	ZTT CTIS 107	Welcome To The Pleasure Dome (Soundtrack From Bernard Rose Video)/ Happy Hi (All In The Mind)/Get It On/How To Remake The World (cassette)	5
86	ZTT ZTAX 22	Rage Hard (Stamped)/(Don't Lose What's Left) Of Your Little Mind (p/s)......	5
86	ZTT ZTD 22	Rage Hard/(Don't Lose What's Left) Of Your Little Mind ('pop-up fists' p/s)	5
86	ZTT 12 ZTAQ 22	Rage Hard/Suffragette City/(Don't Lose What's Left) Of Your Little Mind (extended) (12", stickered p/s with poster)	8
86	ZTT 12 ZTAX B 22	Rage Hard (++ Mix)/Roadhouse Blues/(Don't Lose What's Left) Of Your Little Mind (extended) (12", in 'action series 22' box)..........	8
86	ZTT ZCID 22	Rage Hard +/Rage Hard ++/Rage Hard°/(Don't Lose What's Left) Of Your Little Mind/Suffragette City/Roadhouse Blues (CD, card sleeve)	10
86	ZTT ZCID 25	WARRIORS OF THE WASTELAND (Compacted) (CD EP, card sleeve)...........	8
87	ZTT ZTE 26	Watching The Wildlife (Die Letzen Tag Der Menscheit Mix)/ Watching The Wildlife/The Waves (12", p/s).........................	8
87	ZTT CTIS 26	Watching The Wildlife (Cassetted) (EP, cassette, includes Condom Mix & Orchestral Wildlife)................................	5
00	ZTT ZTT 154TX3	Two Tribes (Almighty Remix) (12", 1-sided, white label)	10

PROMOS
83	ZTT ZTAS 1DJ	Relax — The Last Seven Inches/One September Monday (white label, stamped label, no p/s)	8
84	ZTT XZTAS 3DJ	Two Tribes (Carnage)/Relax (U.S. Mix) (12", ZTT sleeve)	12
84	ZTT XZIP 1	Two Tribes (Hibakusha)/War (Hide Yourself)/Two Tribes/ One February Friday (12", ZTT sleeve)............................	18
84	ZTT ZTAS 5 DJ-A	The Power Of Love (5.28)/The World Is My Oyster (12")	18
86	ZTT 12 ZTAK 25	Warriors (The Attack Mix) (12", white label, featuring Gary Moore)	18
93	ZTT SAM 1231	Relax (Ollie J. Remix) (6.38)/(Trip-Ship Edit) (6.12)/(Ollie J.'s Seven Inches)/ (Jam & Spoon Hi-N-R-G Mix) (7.55)/(C Jam & Spoon Trip-O-Matic Fairy Tale Space Mix) (7.52)/(MCMXCIII) (3.45) (12", double pack, gatefold sleeve)	15
93	ZTT SAM 1275	Welcome To The Pleasuredome (Brothers In Rhythm Rollercoaster Mix) (15.15)/ (Pleasurefix — Original 12" Mix) (9.55)/(Elevatorman's Top Floor Club Mix) (6.02)/(Elevatorman's Deep Down Bass-Ment Dub) (6.00) (12", double pack, gatefold sleeve, promo sleeve)	15
94	ZTT SAM 1331	Two Tribes (The Intermission Mixes): (Legend Mix)/(Legend Instrumental)/ (Workout Mix)/(Workout Instrumental) (12", stickered title sleeve)............	10
94	ZTT (no cat. no)	Two Tribes (808 State Remix) (10", 1-sided red vinyl)...............	15
00	ZTT ZTT 166TP	Welcome To The Pleasuredome (mixes) (12", double pack, p/s)............	20

(see also Holly, Holly Johnson, Spitfire Boys)

ARETHA FRANKLIN
SINGLES
61	Fontana H 271	Love Is The Only Thing/Today I Sing The Blues (with Ray Bryant Combo)......	15
61	Fontana H 343	Rock-A-Bye Your Baby With A Dixie Melody/Operation Heartbreak	10
65	CBS 201732	Can't You Just See Me/You Little Miss Raggedy Anne...................	20
67	CBS 202468	Cry Like A Baby/Swanee	7
67	CBS 3059	Take A Look/Lee Cross..	7
67	Atlantic 584 084	I Never Loved A Man (The Way I Love You)/Do Right Woman – Do Right Man ..	667

	Atlantic 584 115	Respect/Save Me	6
67	Atlantic 584 127	Baby I Love You/Going Down Slow	10
67	Atlantic 584 141	(You Make Me Feel Like A) Natural Woman/Never Let Me Go	6
67	Atlantic 584 157	(I Can't Get No) Satisfaction/Night Life (withdrawn B-side)	10
67	Atlantic 584 157	Chain Of Fools/(I Can't Get No) Satisfaction	10
68	Atlantic 584 172	Since You've Been Gone/Ain't No Way	10
68	Atlantic 584 186	Think/You Send Me	8
68	Atlantic 584 206	I Say A Little Prayer/See-Saw	25
69	Atlantic 584 239	Don't Let Me Lose This Dream/The House That Jack Built	6
69	Atlantic 584 252	The Weight/The Tracks Of My Tears	5
69	Atlantic 584 285	Share Your Love With Me/Pledging My Love/The Clock	5
69	Atlantic 584 306	Eleanor Rigby/It Ain't Fair	5
70	Atlantic 584 322	Call Me/Son Of A Preacher Man	8
70	Atlantic 2091 027	Don't Play That Song/The Thrill Is Gone	5
70	Atlantic 2091 042	Border Song (Holy Moses)/You And Me (unissued)	
70	Atlantic 2091 044	Oh No, Not My Baby/You And Me	6
71	Atlantic 2091 063	You're All I Need To Get By/The Border Song	5
71	Atlantic 2091 111	I Say A Little Prayer/(I Can't Get No) Satisfaction	5
71	Atlantic 2091 127	A Brand New Me/Spirit In The Dark	10
71	Atlantic 2091 168	Rock Steady/Oh Me, Oh My	12
72	Atlantic K 10154	Daydreaming / I've Been Loving You Too Long	8
72	Atlantic K 10224	Rock Steady/All The King's Horses	7
86	Arista ARIST 22624	Freeway Of Love (Pink Cadillac Mix)/Until You Say You Love Me (p/s, pink vinyl)	8
86	Arista ARIST 22657	Another Night / Kind Of Man // Another Night (Nightlife Mix) (double pack)	6
86	Arista ARIST 22678	Jumpin' Jack Flash/Who's Zoomin' Who//Sweet Bitter Love/Integrity (double pack)	20+
89	Arista 612 185	Through The Storm (with Elton John)/Come To Me/Oh Happy Day (live) (with Mavis Staples) (12", p/s)	8
89	Arista 162 185	Through The Storm (with Elton John)/Come To Me/Oh Happy Day (live) (with Mavis Staples) (3" CD, card sleeve)	8
89	Arista 612 545	It Isn't, It Wasn't, It Ain't Never Gonna Be (Extended) (with Whitney Houston)/ (Hip-Hop Remix)/Think 89 (12", p/s)	8
89	Arista 612 683	It Isn't, It Wasn't, It Ain't Never Gonna Be (with Whitney Houston)/ (After Hours Club Mix)/(New Jack Swing Dub Mix (12", no p/s)	8
89	Arista 662 545	It Isn't, It Wasn't, It Ain't Never Gonna Be (Single Remix) (with Whitney Houston)/ (Extended Remix)/(Hip-Hop Remix)/Think 89 (12", p/s)	8

EP
62	Fontana TE 467217	TODAY I SING THE BLUES	35

LPs
61	Fontana TFL 5173	ARETHA	50
65	CBS (S)BPG 62566	YEAH!!! — IN PERSON	40
67	CBS (S)BPG 62744	SOUL SISTER	40
67	Atlantic 587/588 066	I NEVER LOVED A MAN	25
67	CBS (S)BPG 62969	TAKE IT LIKE YOU GIVE IT	25
67	CBS 63160	LEE CROSS	25
67	Atlantic 587/588 085	ARETHA ARRIVES	20
67	CBS 64536	GREATEST HITS	20
68	Atlantic 587/588 099	LADY SOUL	20
68	CBS 63269	TAKE A LOOK AT ARETHA FRANKLIN	30
68	Atlantic 587/588 114	ARETHA NOW	20
68	CBS 63064	GREATEST HITS VOL. 2	20
68	Atlantic 587/588 149	ARETHA IN PARIS — LIVE AT THE OLYMPIA	22
69	Atlantic 588 169	SOUL '69	18
69	Atlantic 588 182	ARETHA'S GOLD	15
69	Chess (S)CRL 54550	SONGS OF FAITH	18
70	Atlantic 2400 004	THIS GIRL'S IN LOVE WITH YOU	18
70	Atlantic 2464 007	I SAY A LITTLE PRAYER	20
70	Atlantic 2400 021	DON'T PLAY THAT SONG	20
71	Atlantic 2400 136	LIVE AT THE FILLMORE WEST (gatefold sleeve)	18
72	Atlantic K 40095	SPIRIT IN THE DARK	15
72	Atlantic K 40323	YOUNG, GIFTED AND BLACK	12
72	Atlantic K 60023	AMAZING GRACE (2-LP)	18
73	Atlantic K 40504	HEY NOW HEY (THE OTHER SIDE OF THE SKY)	12
74	Atlantic K 50031	LET ME IN YOUR LIFE	12
76	Atlantic K 56248	SPARKLE (soundtrack, with Curtis Mayfield)	12

ARETHA FRANKLIN & WHITNEY HOUSTON
89	Arista 612 545	It Isn't, It Wasn't, It Ain't Never Gonna Be (Extended) (with Whitney Houston)/(Hip-Hop Remix)/Think 89 (12")	8
89	Arista 612 683	It Isn't, It Wasn't, It Ain't Never Gonna Be (with Whitney Houston)/(After Hours Club Mix)/(New Jack Swing Dub Mix) (12")	8
89	Arista 662 545	It Isn't, It Wasn't, It Ain't Never Gonna Be (Single Remix) (with Whitney Houston)/(Extended Remix)/(Hip-Hop Remix)/Think 89 (CD)	8

(see also Whitney Houston)

CAROLYN FRANKLIN
69	RCA Victor RCA 1851	Boxer/I Don't Want To Lose You	8
70	RCA Victor RCA 2009	All I Want To Be Is Your Woman/You Really Didn't Mean It	6
69	RCA RD/SF 8035	BABY DYNAMITE! (LP)	22
70s	Joy JOYS 180	THE FIRST TIME I CRIED (LP)	12

ERMA FRANKLIN
67	London HLZ 10170	Piece Of My Heart/Big Boss Man	20
68	London HLZ 10201	Open Up Your Soul/I Just Ain't Ready For Love	10
68	London HLZ 10220	The Right To Cry/Don't Catch The Dog's Bone	10
69	Soul City SC 118	Don't Wait Too Long/Time After Time	25

69	MCA MU 1073	Gotta Find Me A Lover (24 Hours A Day)/Change My Thoughts From You	15
71	Jay Boy BOY 36	I Just Ain't Ready For Love/The Right To Cry	8
71	Jay Boy BOY 41	Piece Of My Heart/Big Boss Man (reissue)	8
70	MCA MUP MUPS 394	SOUL SISTER (LP)	40

MARIE FRANKLIN
68	MGM MGM 1455	You Ain't Changed/Don'tcha Bet No Money	10

GORDON FRANKS
60	Oriole CB 1541	Inn For Trouble/Twinkle Toes	6
62	Parlophone R 4910	Rag Trade Rag/Sid's Tune	7
62	Parlophone R 4929	Outbreak Of Murder/Johnny's Tune	8
63	Decca F 11587	Sam Benedict Theme/Sweet And Sour	7

JOHNNY FRANKS
55	Melodisc P 230	Tweedle Dee/Shake, Rattle And Roll (78)	25
56	Melodisc 1355	Rock Candy Baby/Sing-ing-ing (78)	12
58	Melodisc 1459	Good Old Country Music/Cheatin' On Me (78 rpm = £25)	7

BONNIE (BLUE) FRANKSON
68	Jolly JY 014	Loving You/Shoo Be Do (both with Joe Nolan Band)	12
69	Jolly JY 021	London City/Dearest (both with Joe Nolan & Dynamic Heatwave)	12
69	Columbia Blue Beat DB 114	Dearest/London City	15
73	Ackee ACK 512	Getting Things Together/Version	6

(see also Dotty & Bonnie)

FRANTIC ELEVATORS
79	TJM TJM 5	Voice In The Dark/Passion/Every Day I Die (p/s)	40
80	TJM TJM 6	Hunchback Of Notre Dame/See Nothing And Everything/Don't Judge Me (unreleased; demos only)	150+
80	Eric's ERIC'S 6	You Know What You Told Me/Production Prevention (p/s)	50
81	Crackin' Up CRAK 1	Searching For The Only One/Hunchback Of Notre Dame (p/s)	20
82	No Waiting WAIT 1	Holding Back The Years/Pistols In My Brain (p/s)	20
87	TJM TJM 101	THE EARLY YEARS (mini-LP)	20
88	Receiver KNOB 2	THE EARLY YEARS (mini-LP, reissue with new sleeve & interview disc, as Mick Hucknall & Frantic Elevators)	18

(see also Simply Red)

FRANZ FERDINAND
03	Domino RUG164CDP	Darts Of Pleasure/Van Tango/Shopping For Blood (CD 3-track promo p/s)	25
03	Domino RUG164CD	Darts Of Pleasure/Van Tango/Shopping For Blood (CD, p/s)	20
03	Domino RUG164	Darts Of Pleasure/Shopping For Blood (p/s)	5
03	Domino RUG164T	Darts Of Pleasure/Van Tango/Shopping For Blood (12", p/s 500 only)	12
04	Domino RUG172	Take Me Out/Truck Stop (3,000 only, p/s)	6
04	Domino PRINCIPP01	Take Me Out (Naum Gabo Remix) (7" white label promo)	12
04	Domino RUG172T	Take Me Out/Taken Me Out (Morgan Geist re-version) (12" 2500 only, p/s)	8
04	Domino RUG172TDAFT	Take Me Out (Daft Punk Remix)/Album Version/Naum Gabo Remix (12" white label)	12
03	Chateau CHAT001	LIVE 2003 (LP, 10-track official bootleg/promo 500 copies)	20
05	Domino RUG211TP	Do You Want To (Erol Alkan's Glam Racket Mix/Original Version (12" white label)	14
05	New! NEW001	Get Up and Use Me (Franz Ferdinand)/Jacqueline (The Fire Engines) (7" single)	15
04	Domino WIGCD136P	FRANZ FERDINAND (CD, 11 track promo album p/s)	18
04	Domino WIGCD136X	FRANZ FERDINAND (Ltd edn. 2 CD set with live album p/s)	20

(see also The Karelia, The Ampheta Meanies)

ANDY FRASER BAND
75	CBS 80731	THE ANDY FRASER BAND (LP)	12
75	CBS 81027	IN YOUR EYES (LP)	12

(see also Free, Sharks)

JOHN FRASER
58	Pye N 15098	Bye Bye Love/Why Don't They Understand? (78)	8
58	Pye 7N 15118	Trolley Stop/Don't Take Your Love From Me (78 rpm, Pye N 15118 = £8)	5
59	Pye 7N 15212	Bye Bye, Baby, Goodbye/Golden Cage (78 rpm, Pye N 15212 = £15)	20
58	Pye NEP 24068	PRESENTING JOHN FRASER (EP)	20

NORTON FRASER
57	Columbia DC 709	Rock Around The Clock/Bongalulu (78) (export issue)	10

FRATERNITY BROTHERS
59	HMV POP 582	Passion Flower/A Nobody Like Me (B-side with Gil Fields)	9

FRATERNITY OF MAN
70	Stateside SS 2166	Don't Bogart Me/Wispy Paisley Skies	12

ERIC FRATTER
69	Trojan TR 655	Since You've Been Gone/AFROTONES: Things I Love	9

(see also Eric Fatter)

FRAYS
65	Decca F 12153	Keep Me Covered/Walk On	140
65	Decca F 12229	My Girl Sloopy/For Your Precious Love	50

(see also Mike Patto)

NORMA FRAZER
65	Ska Beat JB 223	Heartaches/Everybody Loves A Lover	60+
67	Coxsone CS 7017	The First Cut Is The Deepest/BUMPS OAKLEY: Rag Doll	25
67	Studio One SO 2024	Come By Here/WAILERS: I Stand Predominate	75
68	Coxsone CS 7060	Respect/Time	30

(see also Sound Dimension, Righteous Homes, Viceroys, Tommy McCook)

MINT VALUE £

DALLAS FRAZIER
66	Capitol CL 15445	Elvira/That Ain't No Stuff	10
66	Capitol CL 15457	Just A Little Bit Of You/Walkin' Wonder	8
59	Capitol EAP 1035	DALLAS FRAZIER (EP)	20

FRAZIER CHORUS
87	Virgin VSCD 1192	Sloppy Heart/Anarchy In The UK/String/Typical (3" CD in heart-shaped box)	12
91	Virgin CDV 2654	RAY (CD, with bonus remix CD)	20

FREAKS OF NATURE
66	Island WI 3017	People! Let's Freak Out/The Shadow Chasers	60

(see also Kim Fowley, Belfast Gypsies, Jackie McAuley)

STAN FREBERG
54	Capitol CL 14187	Sh-Boom (Life Could Be A Dream) (with The Toads)/C'est Ci Bon	30
55	Capitol CL 14316	The Lone Psychiatrist/The Honey-Earthers (with Daws Butler)	25
56	Capitol CL 14509	The Yellow Rose Of Texas/Rock Around Stephen Foster	20
56	Capitol CL 14571	The Great Pretender/The Quest For Bridey Hammerschlaugen (B-side with June Foray)	20
56	Capitol CL 14608	Heartbreak Hotel/Rock Island Line	30
57	Capitol CL 14712	Banana Boat (Day-O)/Tele-vee-shun	20
58	Capitol CL 14966	Green Chritma (with Daws Butler)/The Meaning Of Christmas (with Jud Conlon Chorale)	15
60	Capitol CL 15122	The Old Payola Roll Blues (with Jesse White)/ Sh-Boom (Life Could Be A Dream)	20
55	Capitol EAP1 496	ANY REQUESTS (EP)	15
56	Capitol EAP1 628	THE REAL SAINT GEORGE (EP)	15
61	Capitol EAP1 1101	OMAHA (EP)	15
61	Capitol EAP1 20050	THE GREAT PRETENDER (EP)	15
61	Capitol EAP1 20115	FREBERG AGAIN (EP, with Daws Butler)	15
57	Capitol T 777	A CHILD'S GARDEN OF FREBERG (LP)	30
58	Capitol LCT 6170	THE BEST OF THE STAN FREBERG SHOWS (LP)	15
58	Capitol LCT 6171	THE BEST OF THE STAN FREBERG SHOWS VOL. 2 (LP)	20
61	Capitol W 1573	PRESENTS THE UNITED STATES OF AMERICA (LP)	20
64	Capitol T 2020	THE BEST OF STAN FREBERG (LP)	15

JOHN FRED & HIS PLAYBOY BAND
67	Pye International 7N 25442	Judy In Disguise (With Glasses)/When The Lights Go Out	5
68	Pye International 7N 25453	Hey Hey Bunny/No Letter Today	8
68	Pye International 7N 25462	We Played Games/Lonely Are The Lonely	6
68	Pye International 7N 25470	Little Dum Dum/Tissue Paper	6
68	CBS 3475	Shirley/High Heel Sneakers	10
69	MCA MU 1088	Silly Sarah Carter/Back In The USSR	5
67	Pye Intl. NPL 28111	AGNES ENGLISH (LP)	25

FRED BANANA COMBO
78	Warm AWMR 2004	No Destination Blues/Jerk Off All Nite Long (p/s)	5

FREDDIE & THE DREAMERS
63	Columbia DB 7032	If You Gotta Make A Fool Of Somebody/Feel So Blue	8
64	Columbia DB 7214	Over You/Come Back When You're Ready	6
64	Columbia DB 7286	I Love You Baby/Don't Make Me Cry	6
64	Columbia DB 7322	Just For You/Don't Do That To Me	6
65	Columbia DB 7526	A Little You/Things I'd Like To Say	5
65	Columbia DB 7720	Thou Shalt Not Steal/I Don't Know	6
65	Columbia DC 763	A Windmill In Old Amsterdam/A Love Like You (export issue)	15
66	Columbia DB 7857	If You've Gotta Minute Baby/When I'm Home With You	6
66	Columbia DB 7929	Playboy/Some Day	6
66	Columbia DB 8033	Turn Around/Funny Over You	6
67	Columbia DB 8137	Hello, Hello/All I Ever Want Is You	6
67	EMI Regal	See You Later Alligator (export issue)	35
67	Columbia DB 8200	Brown And Porter's (Meat Exporters) Lorry/Little Brown Eyes	10
68	Columbia DB 8496	Little Big Time/FREDDIE GARRITY: You Belong To Me	10
68	Columbia DB 8517	It's Great/Gaberdine Mac	10
69	Columbia DB 8606	Get Around Downtown Girl/What To Do	10
71	Philips 6006 098	Susan's Tuba/You Hurt Me Girl	9
78	Polydor 2059 041	Here We Go/I Saw Ya	9
63	Columbia SEG 8275	IF YOU GOTTA MAKE A FOOL OF SOMEBODY (EP)	15
63	Columbia SEG 8287	SONGS FROM THE FILM *WHAT A CRAZY WORLD* (EP)	20
64	Columbia SEG 8302	YOU WERE MADE FOR ME (EP)	15
64	Columbia SEG 8323	OVER YOU (EP)	15
64	Columbia SEG 8349	FREDDIE SINGS JUST FOR YOU (EP)	15
65	Columbia SEG 8403	READY, FREDDIE, GO! (EP)	15
65	Columbia SEG 8457	FREDDIE AND THE DREAMERS (EP)	15
63	Columbia 33SX 1577	FREDDIE AND THE DREAMERS (LP)	25
64	Columbia 33SX 1663	YOU WERE MAD FOR ME (LP)	25
65	Columbia SX 1785	SING ALONG PARTY (LP)	20
66	Columbia S(C)X 6069	IN DISNEYLAND (LP, mono/stereo)	20/22
67	Columbia SX 6177	KING FREDDIE AND THE DREAMING KNIGHTS (LP)	25

(see also Freddie Garrity, Dreamers)

FREDDIE & THE DREAMERS/PETER & GORDON
64	Columbia SEG 8337	JUST FOR YOU (EP, 2 tracks each)	22

(see also Peter & Gordon)

DOTTY FREDERICK
59	Top Rank JAR 106	Ricky/Just Wait (78 rpm = £12)	50

TOMMY FREDERICK & HI-NOTES
58	London HLU 8555	Prince Of Players/I'm Not Pretending (78 rpm = £20)	60

Bill FREDERICKS

BILL FREDERICKS
78	Polydor 2059 035	Almost/Wind Of Change	15

DOLORES FREDERICKS
56	Brunswick 05540	Cha Cha Joe/Whole Lotta Shakin' Goin' On	30

MARC FREDERICKS
56	London HLD 8281	Mystic Midnight/Symphony To Anne	35

FRED LOCKS
78	Tribesman TM 20	Love & Only Love/Stricker Ishion	15
78	Revelations FRW 375	Love & Harmony/Joy & Harmony (featuring Brigadier Jerry) (p/s)	12
78	Lloyd Coxsone LC 001	Voice Of The Poor/LEVI ROOTS: Poor Man's Story	12

FREE (Holland)
69	Philips BF 1738	Soul Party/Down To The Bone	10
69	Philips BF 1754	Keep In Touch/Taking It Away	40

FREE (U.K.)
69	Island WIP 6054	Broad Daylight/The Worm	60
69	Island WIP 6062	I'll Be Creepin'/Sugar For Mr Morrison	60
70	Island WIP 6082	All Right Now/Mouthful Of Grass (pink label)	10
70	Island WIP 6093	The Stealer/Lying In The Sunshine	8
71	Island WIP 6100	My Brother Jake/Only My Soul	6
72	Island WIP 6129	Little Bit Of Love/Sail On	6
72	Island WIP 6146	Wishing Well/Let Me Show You	6
73	Island WIP 6160	Travellin' In Style/Easy On My Soul	6
76	Island WIP 6351	The Hunter/Worry	6
85	Island 12 IS 221	Wishing Well/Woman (live)/Walk In My Shadow (live) (12", p/s)	10
78	Island IEP 6	THE FREE EP (p/s)	6
82	Island PIEP 6	THE FREE EP (12", picture disc)	10
69	Island ILPS 9089	TONS OF SOBS (LP, gatefold sleeve, 1st pressing, pink label/black & orange 'circle' logo)	90
69	Island ILPS 9089	TONS OF SOBS (LP, gatefold sleeve, 2nd pressing, pink label/black'block' logo)	30
70	Island ILPS 9089	TONS OF SOBS (LP, gatefold sleeve, 3rd pressing, pink label/'i' logo)	20
71	Island ILPS 9089	TONS OF SOBS (LP, gatefold sleeve, 4th pressing, pink rim label/'palm tree' logo)	15
69	Island ILPS 9104	FREE (LP, gatefold sleeve, 1st pressing, pink label/'i' logo)	70
70	Island ILPS 9104	FREE (LP, gatefold sleeve, 2nd pressing, pink rim label/'palm tree' logo)	15
70	Island ILPS 9120	FIRE AND WATER (LP, 1st pressing, pink label/'i' logo)	30
70	Island ILPS 9120	FIRE AND WATER (LP, 2nd pressing, pink rim label/'palm tree' logo)	15
70	Island ILPS 9138	HIGHWAY (LP)	15
71	Island ILPS 9160	LIVE (LP, in envelope sleeve with inner)	15
72	Island ILPS 9192	FREE AT LAST (LP)	14
74	Island ISLD 4	THE FREE STORY (2-LP, with 4-page booklet, numbered)	18

(see also Paul Kossoff, Rabbit, Kossoff Kirke Tetsu & Rabbit, Sharks, Andy Fraser Band, Black Cat Bones, Rock Aid Armenia)

FREE AGENTS
80	Groovy STP 1	FREE AGENTS (LP, 1000 only, hand-made sleeve)	20

(see also Pete Shelley, Eric Random)

ALAN FREED & HIS ROCK'N'ROLL BAND
57	Vogue Coral Q 72219	Teen Rock/Right Now, Right Now (with Alan Freed's Rock'n'Rollers)	100
57	Vogue Coral Q 72219	Teen Rock/Right Now, Right Now (with Alan Freed's Rock'n'Rollers) (78).	35
57	Vogue Coral Q 72230	Rock'n'Roll Boogie/Teener's Canteen (with Alan Freed's Rock'n'Rollers)	100
57	Vogue Coral Q 72230	Rock'n'Roll Boogie/Teener's Canteen (with Alan Freed's Rock'n'Rollers)	35
56	Vogue Coral LVA 9033	ROCK'N'ROLL DANCE PARTY VOL. 1 (LP, featuring Modernaires)	70
57	Vogue Coral LVA 9066	ROCK'N'ROLL DANCE PARTY VOL. 2 (LP, with Jimmy Cavello)	105

(see also Jimmy Cavello)

BOB FREEDMAN ORCHESTRA
63	Island ILP 101	MUSIC TO STRIP BY (LP, some with free G string)	12/80

FREED UNIT
99	Out-There OTT 06	MASONIC YOUTH (9" EP, triangular clear vinyl, 100 only)	50
01	Out-There OTT 09	SIX SIDED (9" EP, clear vinyl, 100 only)	25
98	Out-There OTTLP 04	FIELD REPORTS FROM OUT-THERE (LP, clear vinyl)	18
98	Enraptured RAPTLP 19	THINGS ARE LOOKING UP... (LP, orange vinyl)	15

FREE DESIGN
69	Project 3	HEAVEN/EARTH (LP)	30

FREEDOM
68	Mercury MF 1033	Where Will You Be Tonight/Trying To Get A Glimpse Of You (some in p/s)	25/12
69	Plexium PXM 3	Escape While You Can/Kandy Kay	15
70	Probe PRO 504	Frustrated Woman/Man Made Laws	30
71	Vertigo 6059 051	Thanks/Miss Little Louise	10
70	Probe SPBA 6252	FREEDOM (LP)	30
71	Vertigo 6360 050	THROUGH THE YEARS (LP, gatefold sleeve, swirl label)	75
72	Vertigo 6360 072	FREEDOM IS MORE THAN A WORD (LP, gatefold sleeve, swirl label)	120

(see also Procol Harum, Snafu)

FREEDOM GROUP
72	Randy's RAN 525	Sing A Song Of Freedom (actually by Max Romeo)/IMPACT ALLSTARS: Song Of Freedom (Version)	7

FREEDOM SINGERS (Jamaica)
67	Studio One SO 2010	Have Faith/Work Crazy	25
70	Bamboo BAM 21	Give Peace A Chance/SOUND DIMENSION: In Cold Blood	18

(see also Winston Francis)

FREEDOM SINGERS (U.K.)
70	New Beat NB 059	Election (with Live Stocks)/FLECE & LIVE SHOCKS: Tomorrow's World	9
71	New Beat NB 074	Your Testimony/Train Coming	6

FREE FERRY
69	CBS 4456	Mary, What Have You Become?/Friend	8
70	CBS 4647	Haverjack Drive/Flying	8

FREEFORM
95	Skam SKA 3	Fane/Recut/Rail/Siamese Telebox/The Brink/Many/Freeform Dub (12")	25

ALAN FREEMAN AND THE TALMY STONE BAND
62	Decca F 11543	Madison Time/Madison Time	6

ART FREEMAN
66	Atlantic 584 053	Slippin' Around/Can't Get You Out Of My Mind	140

BOBBY FREEMAN
58	London HLJ 8644	Do You Want To Dance?/Big Fat Woman (78 rpm = £20)	40
58	London HLJ 8721	Betty Lou Got A New Pair Of Shoes/Starlight (78 rpm = £30)	50
59	London HLJ 8782	Shame On You Miss Johnson/Need Your Love (78 rpm = £30)	50
59	London HLJ 8898	Mary Ann Thomas/Love Me (78 rpm = £35)	45
60	London HLJ 9031	Sinbad/Ebb Tide (The Sea)	15
60	Parlophone R 4684	(I Do The) Shimmy Shimmy/You Don't Understand Me	20
64	Pye International 7N 25260	C'mon And Swim (Parts 1 & 2)	22
64	Pye International 7N 25280	S-W-I-M/That Little Old Heartbreaker Me	28
66	Pye International 7N 25347	The Duck/Cross My Heart	30
66	Pye International 7N 25347	The Duck/The Devil (2nd issue with different B-side)	18

BUD FREEMAN
54	Columbia 33S 1016	COMES JAZZ (10" LP)	12
55	Capitol LC 6706	CLASSICS IN JAZZ (10" LP)	12
66	Fontana TL 5370	BUD FREEMAN ESQ. (LP)	20
68	Fontana TL 5414	FREEMAN & CO (LP)	20
73	Philips 6308 254	SONG OF THE TENOR (LP)	20

CAROL FREEMAN
67	CBS 202579	The Rolling Sea/Leaving You Now	12

ERNIE FREEMAN
57	London HLP 8523	Raunchy/Puddin' (78 rpm = £10)	20
57	London HL 7029	Dumplin's/Beautiful Weekend (export issue)	20
58	London HLP 8558	Dumplin's/Beautiful Weekend (78 rpm = £12)	15
58	London HLP 8660	Indian Love Call/Summer Serenade (78 rpm = £12)	12
60	London HLP 9041	Big River/Night Sounds	10
65	London HLP 9944	Raunchy '65/Jivin' Around	10
56	London RE-U 1059	ERNIE FREEMAN AND HIS RHYTHM GUITAR (EP)	55
59	London RE-P 1210	ERNIE FREEMAN VOL. 2 (EP)	40

EVELYN FREEMAN EXCITING VOICES
69	London HLU 10287	I Heard The Voice/I Dreamed Last Night	5

GEORGE FREEMAN
71	Jay Boy BOY 54	I'm Like A Fish/Why Are You Doing This To Me	28

MARGARET FREEMAN
61	Starlite ST45 040	Forbidden Fruit/Mister Ting A Ling	12

PAUL FREEMAN
71	Punch PH 82	Don't Give Up/UPSETTERS: Give Up (Version)	12

RUSS FREEMAN & CHET BAKER QUARTET
60	Vogue EPV 1255	RUSS FREEMAN & CHET BAKER QUARTET (EP)	12
	(see also Chet Baker)		

FREE MOVEMENT
72	CBS 7768	The Harder I Try/Comin' Home	30

FREE 'N EASY
68	Oak RGJ 628	FREE 'N EASY (LP, private pressing [Warren Coley W.C.P. 001])	110

FREE SOULS
64	Blue Beat BB 264	I Want To Be Free/Angel	20

FREESTYLE ORCHESTRA
89	SBK 12SBKDJ 7011	Keep On Pumping It Up (12", promo only)	15

FREEWAY
79	Decca F 13824	I Love The Music/Sarah Girl (p/s)	6
79	Decca F 13843	That Was The Greatest Song/Lost In A Dream (p/s)	6
79	Decca TXs 131	FREEWAY (LP)	12
	(see also Terry Melcher)		

FREEWHEELERS
65	HMV POP 1406	Why Do You Treat Me Like A Fool?/Ad Lib Blues	8

FREEZE
79	A1.A.1.1.A.1	IN COLOUR (EP, p/s)	10
80	A1 A.1.1.S.1	Celebration/Cross-Over	8

ACE FREHLEY
78	Casablanca CAN 135	New York Groove/Snow Blind (p/s, blue vinyl with mask)	35
78	Casablanca CAN 135	New York Groove/Snow Blind (no p/s, black vinyl)	15
87	Atlantic A 9255T	Into The Night/Fractured Too/Breakout (12", p/s)	10
	(see also Kiss)		

MINT VALUE £

DON FRENCH
59	London HLW 8884	Lonely Saturday Night/Goldilocks (78 rpm = £50)	150
59	London HLW 8989	Little Blonde Girl/I Look Into My Heart (78 rpm = £65)	175

RAY FRENCH
66	Pye 7N 17215	Since I Lost My Baby/Gun Me Down	15

FRENCH IMPRESSIONISTS
82	Operation Twilight OPT 20	Santa Baby/Jingle Bell Rock (p/s)	15
82	Operation T'light 12OPT 20	Santa Baby/Jingle Bell Rock (12", p/s)	10

(see also Aztec Camera)

FRENCH REVOLUTION
69	Decca F 22898	Nine Till Five/Why?	90

FRENZ
70	Sugar SU 101	Mee Lei Moi/I Hear Music	12

FRENZY
81	Frenzy FRENZY 1	This Is The Last Time/Gypsy Dancer (no p/s)	100
81	Frenzy FRENZY 3	Without You/Thanks For Nothing (no p/s)	150
84	Nervous NEP 002	Robot Riot/All Alone (p/s)	6
84	Nervous 12 NEP 002	Robot Riot/All Alone/Cry Or Die/Torment (12", p/s, 1st 500 on blue vinyl)	10/8
86	ABC EYE T7	I See Red/Who's Life/Don't Give Up (12", p/s)	8
85	Nervous NERD 016	HALL OF MIRRORS (LP, orange vinyl)	12
86	ABC EYE T7	I See Red/Whose Life (p/s)	8
86	I.D. NOSE 8	CLOCKWORK TOY (LP)	15
87	I.D. NOSE 19	SALLY'S PINK BEDROOM (LP)	15

FRESH
70	RCA RCA 2003	Stoned In Saigon/Just A Note	7
70	RCA SF 8122	FRESH OUT OF BORSTAL (LP)	18
71	RCA LSA 3027	FRESH TODAY (LP)	15

(see also Paul Korda, Brother Bung, Fruit Machine)

FRESH
92	Magnet MAG 1008CD	Did I Say "Ti Amo" (mixes) (CD)	12

FRESH AIR
69	Pye 7N 17736	Running Wild/Stop, Look, Listen	150+
72	Philips 6006 187	It Takes Too Long/Here Comes Summer	6
72	Columbia DB 8872	Bye Bye Jane/It's All Over	6

FRESHIES
78	Razz RAZZXEP 1	BAISER (EP, with Chris Sievey solo tracks, 33rpm, no'd, handwritten labels)	20
79	Razz RAZZXEP 2	STRAIGHT IN AT NO. 2 (EP, handwritten labels with inserts, 1,000 only, numbered, green or orange p/s)	15
79	Razz RAZZ 3	THE MEN FROM BANANA ISLAND WHOSE STUPID IDEAS NEVER CAUGHT ON IN THE WESTERN WORLD AS WE KNOW IT (EP, black & white photocopied p/s or numbered blue p/s)	each 10
79	Razz RAZZ 5	We're Like You/CHRIS SIEVEY: Hey (p/s)	8
80	Absurd A9	Octopus/Sheet Music	8
80	Razz RAZZ 6	Yellow Spot/If It's News (p/s)	8
80	Razz RAZZ 7	No Money/Oh Girl (p/s)	8
80	Razz RAZZ 8	RED INDIAN MUSIC (EP, with Chris Sievey)	8
80	Razz RAZZ 11	I'm In Love With The Girl On The Virgin Manchester Megastore Checkout Desk/Singalong Version (p/s, some with free lyric book)	12/8
80	Razz RAZZ 12	I'm In Love With The Girl On The Manchester Checkout Desk (Radio Version)/Singalong Version ('bleeped') (white label radio issue, 200 only)	10
80	Razz RAZZ 13	One To One/House Beautiful (unreleased)	
81	MCA MCA 693	Wrap Up The Rockets And It's Gonna Get Better/Tell Her I'm Ill (12")	8
81	CV CVS 1	If You Really Love … Buy Me A Shirt/I Am A Walrus (p/s)	8
81	HANNA 1	Virgin Megastore/Wrap Up The Rockets/Buy Me A Shirt/Tell Her I'm Ill/Frank Talks To Chris (Conversation) (12", white label, stickered sleeve)	8
80	Razz CS-4	ROUGH AND READY (12-track cassette, 1,000 only)	12
81	Razz CS-5	LONDON PLAYS (cassette, live & radio sessions, 1,000 only)	12
85	ETS 1	JOHNNY RADAR STORY (20-track cassette, some with bonus Frank Sidebottom 8-track: "Firm Favourites")	15/12
85	ETS 1	JOHNNY RADAR STORY (LP, vinyl test pressing of cassette)	40

(see also Chris Sievey, Going Red?)

FRESHKI & MO ROCK
87	Tuff GrooveTUFF003	Talking Pays/Pick Up On This (12")	60
91	Conscious CON003	THE LONG AWAITED PAROXYSM (EP)	35

FRESH MAGGOTS
71	RCA RCA 2150	Car Song/What Would You Do	22
71	RCA SF 8205	FRESH MAGGOTS (LP)	220

FRESH MEAT
73	Deram DMR 384	Never Mind The Money/Candy Eyes	7

FRESHMEN
67	Pye 7N 17432	Papa Oom Mow Mow/Let's Dance	10
68	Pye 7N 17592	Go Granny Go/Look At The Sunshine	15
69	Pye 7N 17689	Just To See You Smile/Indian Lake	8
69	Pye 7N 17757	She Sang Hymns Out Of Tune/Mr. Beverly's Heavy Days	8
70	CBS 4842	Halfway To Where/Time Hasn't Changed Her	6
70	CBS 5168	Banquet For The World/Time Hasn't Changed Her	6
71	CBS 7241	One Bad Thing/Everywhere There Is Love	6
72	CBS 7694	Swanee River/Take The Time It Takes	8
68	Pye N(S)PL 18263	MOVIN' ON (LP)	60
70	CBS 64099	PEACE ON EARTH (LP)	30

FRESH WINDOWS
67	Fontana TF 839	Fashion Conscious/Summer Sun Shines	90+

FRIDA
82	Epic EPC A 2603	I Know There's Something Going On/Threnody (p/s)	8
82	Epic EPC A 2863	To Turn To Stone/I Got Something (p/s)	12
83	Epic EPC A 3435	Here We'll Stay/Strangers (p/s)	8
83	Epic EPC A 3983	Time/I Am A Seeker (p/s, with B.A. Robertson)	8
84	Epic EPC A 4717	Shine/That's Tough (p/s)	8
84	Epic EPC TA 4717	Shine (6.27 Version)/That's Tough (12", p/s)	15
84	Epic EPC A 4886	Heart Of The Country/Slowly (p/s)	12
84	Epic EPC TA 4886	Heart Of The Country/Slowly/I Know There's Something Going On (Extended) (12", p/s)	20

(see also Abba)

BOY FRIDAY (& GROOVERS)
70	Downtown DT 470	Version Girl/Grumble Man	15
71	Downtown DT 471	Music So Good/Right Track (both with Groovers)	8
71	Downtown DT 472	Sounds I Remember/JOAN LONG: Reconsider Our Love	6
71	Downtown DT 473	Take A Message Ruby/Second Note	10
71	Downtown DT 476	There'll Always Be Sunshine/Sunshine Track	7
71	Downtown DT 477	Hot Pants Girl/Raunchy	6
71	Downtown DT 481	El Raunchy/Conversation (as Boy Friday & Collins)	6
71	J-Dan JDN 4416	I Don't Want No War/Third Note Swing	7
71	J-Dan JDN 4418	Situation Version/OUR BAND: Keep Tracking	7

(see also Dandy & Superboys)

CAROL FRIDAY
65	Parlophone R 5297	Gone Tomorrow/Show Me The Way	8
65	Parlophone R 5369	Everybody I Know/Wasted Days	30
67	Parlophone R 5567	Big Sister/I Look Around Me	10

FRIDAY KNIGHTS
60	Oriole CB 1579	Poor Man's Roses/Don't Open That Door	8

FRIDGE
98	Earworm WORM 37	Deadly Cube/PORTAL: Hydro-Electric (tracing paper p/s)	5

FRIDGES
80	Ink-Ink II 01	Lynn Freeze/Shower Of B's/That's Why I Took Up The Harmonica/No Room! (p/s, with insert)	5

KINKY FRIEDMAN
74	Vanguard VSD 79333	SOLD AMERICAN (LP)	12
75	ABC ABCL 5134	KINKY FRIEDMAN (LP)	12
76	Epic EPC 81640	LASSO FROM EL PASO (LP)	12

MARTY FRIEDMAN
86	Shrapnel RR 95291	DRAGON'S KISS (LP)	12

(see also Megadeth, Cacophony)

BRIAN JOSEPH FRIEL
74	Dawn DNLS 3054	BRIAN JOSEPH FRIEL (LP)	15
75	Dawn DNLS 3064	ARRIVERDERCI ARDROSSAN (LP)	15

TERRY FRIEND & FRIENDS
77	Tramp (no cat. no.)	COME THE DAY (LP, private pressing, 100 only)	40

(see also Stonefield Tramp)

FRIEND & LOVER
68	Verve VS 1515	Reach Out Of The Darkness/Time Is On Your Side	10

FRIENDLY HOPEFULS
81	Abstract ABS 004	Tribute To The Punks Of '76/Tribute To The Punks Of '76 (Disco Dub Mix) (p/s, coloured vinyl)	5

FRIENDLY PERSUASION
74	Rare Earth RES 120	Remember (Sha La La)/I'll Always Do The Best I Can	5

FRIENDS
68	Deram DM 198	Piccolo Man/Mythological Sunday (B-side is the collectable one!)	30

(see also Flowerpot Men, Ivy League)

FRIENDS
70	United Artists UP 35146	Futz/Costa Del Sol	5

FRIENDS
74	Merlin HF 4	FRIENDS (LP, white label test pressing, 1 copy only!)	1,500+

(see also Ithaca, Alice Through The Looking Glass, Agincourt, Tomorrow Come Someday, BBC Radiophonic Workshop)

FRIENDS
83	Rock Shop RSR 002	Night Walker/Wasted Time (no p/s)	25

FRIENDS AGAIN
83	Moonboot MOON 1	Honey At The Core/Lucky Star (p/s)	6
84	Mercury FAEP 1	THE FRIENDS AGAIN EP: Lullaby No. 2 Love On Board/Wand You Wave/Thank You For Being An Angel/Sunkissed (New Version)/State Of Art (Remix) (double pack, stickered gatefold p/s)	6

FRIENDSHIP
70	B&C CB 133	The World Is Going To Be A Better Place/Million Hearts	5

FRIENDS OF DISTINCTION
69	RCA 1838	Grazing In The Grass/I Really Hope You Do	7
70	RCA 1952	Love Or Let Me Be Lonely/This Generation	8
71	RCA LSP 4408	WHATEVER (LP)	18

FRIENDS O' MINE
72	Westwood WRS 021	FRIENDS O' MINE (LP, 250 copies only)	80

(see also Mark Kjeldsen)

FRIJID PINK
70	Deram DM-R 288	The House Of The Rising Sun/Drivin' Blues	8
70	Deram DM 309	Sing A Song Of Freedom/End Of The Line	8
70	Deram DM 321	Heartbreak Hotel/Bye Bye Blues	10
71	Deram DM 332	Music For The People/Sloony	10
71	Deram DM 336	We're Gonna Be There (When Johnny Comes Marching Home)/Shortly Kline	8
71	Deram DM 347	Lost Son/I Love Her	8
70	Deram SML 1062	FRIJID PINK (LP)	38
70	Deram SML 1077	DEFROSTED (LP)	38

(Robert) FRIPP & (Brian) ENO
73	Island HELP 16	NO PUSSYFOOTIN' (LP)	12
75	Island HELP 22	EVENING STAR (LP)	12

(see also Giles Giles & Fripp, King Crimson, Brian Eno, Roxy Music)

JACKIE FRISCO
63	Decca F 11566	You Can't Catch Me/Sugar Baby	12
63	Decca F 11692	When You Ask About Love/He's So Near	8

VONNIE FRITCHIE
55	London HLU 8178	Sugar Booger Avenue/There I Stood (To Throw Old Shoes And Rice)	65

FRED FRITH
74	Caroline C 1508	GUITAR SOLOS (LP)	12
76	Caroline C 1518	GUITAR SOLOS 2 (LP)	12

(see also Henry Cow)

FRITZ, MIKE & MO
65	Philips BF 1427	Somebody Stole The Sun/Let Me Hear Your Voice	10
65	Philips BF 1441	What Colour Is A Man?/So Now You're Gone	8

(see also Four Pennies)

LEFTY FRIZZELL
51	Columbia MC 3412	Shine Shave Shower/Look What Thoughts Will Do (78, export issue)	18
51	Columbia MC 3422	Travellin' Blues/I Want To Be With You Always (78, export issue)	15
52	Columbia FB 3632	Always Late (With Your Kisses)/Mom & Dad's Waltz (78)	15
63	CBS BPG 62188	THE ONE AND ONLY LEFTY FRIZZELL (LP)	15
66	CBS BPG 62595	THE SAD SIDE OF LOVE (LP)	15

CORNELIA FROBOESS
62	HMV HMV 1671	GERMAN TEENAGERS (LP)	40

FRANK FROEBA
52	Brunswick LA 8547	BACK ROOM PIANO (10" LP)	12
53	Brunswick LA 8611	MOONLIGHT PLAYING TIME (10" LP)	12
53	Brunswick LA 8555	PARLOR PIANO (10" LP)	12

EDGAR FROESE
74	Virgin V 2016	AQUA (LP)	12

(see also Tangerine Dream)

FROG
73	Jam JAM 39	Witch Hunt (Theme From Psychomania)/Living Dead (die-cut company sleeve)	100

(see also John Cameron)

WYNDER K. FROG
(see under 'W')

RAYMOND FROGGATT
68	Polydor 56249	Callow-La-Vita/Lost Autumn	5
68	Polydor 56274	Just A Little Bit Of Love/ABC Gold Fish	5
68	Polydor 56284	The Red Balloon/Lost Autumn	5
68	Polydor 56294	Rosalind/Roly	5
69	Polydor 56314	Ring Ting A Ling/Anything You Want To	5
69	Polydor 56334	Movin' Down South/It's Only Me	5
69	Polydor 56358	Lazy Jack/Hasn't The Lord Blessed Us?	5
72	Bell BLL 1261	Running Water/Rock'n'Roll Song	5
74	Reprise K 14328	Roadshow/Salt	5
75	Jet JET 749	Try To Get You Into My Life/This Could Last All Night	5
69	Polydor 583 044	THE VOICE AND WRITING OF RAYMOND FROGGATT (LP)	20
72	Bell BELLS 207	BLEACH (LP)	20
74	Reprise K 44257	ROGUES AND THIEVES (LP)	15

(see also Monopoly)

FROGMEN
61	Oriole CB 1617	Underwater/Mad Rush (withdrawn)	100+

FROGMORTON
76	Philips 6308 261	AT LAST (LP)	15

JANE FROMAN
55	Capitol CL 14208	The Song From *Desiree* (We Meet Again)/Mine	6
55	Capitol CL 14209	The Finger Of Suspicion Points At You/My Shining Hour	8
55	Capitol CL 14254	I Wonder/I'll Never Be The Same	8
56	Capitol CL 14658	You'll Never Walk Alone/One Little Candle	6
56	Capitol EAP1 600	JANE FROMAN (EP)	8
56	Capitol EAP1 889	SONGS AT SUNSET (EP)	8

56	Capitol EAP2 889	SONGS AT SUNSET (EP)	8
56	Capitol EAP3 889	SONGS AT SUNSET (EP)	8
52	Capitol LC 6554	WITH A SONG IN MY HEART (10" LP)	20
53	Capitol LC 6605	YOURS ALONE (10" LP)	20

FRONT
77	The Label TLR 005	System/Queen's Mafia (p/s)	8

DOM FRONTIERE & HIS ORCHESTRA
57	London HLU 8385	Jet Rink Ballad/Uno Mas (78 rpm = £12)	25

FRONT LINE
65	Atlantic AT 4057	I Don't Care/Got Love	35

FROST
69	Vanguard SVRL 19056	ROCK AND ROLL MUSIC (LP)	20
69	Vanguard SVRL 19052	FROST MUSIC (LP)	20

BERNIE FROST
74	Vertigo 6059 108	The House/What Do You Want To Hear Today	50

(see also Status Quo, Rossi & Frost, Boz Frost)

BOZ FROST
73	Vertigo 6059 083	Foreign Lady/Big White Seagull	25

(see also Status Quo, Rossi & Frost, Bernie Frost)

DAVID FROST (& others)
66	Parlophone R 5441	Zookeeper/Deck Of Cards	5
66	Parlophone PMC 7005	THE FROST REPORT ON BRITAIN (LP)	15
67	Pye NPL 18199	THE FROST REPORT ON EVERYTHING (LP)	15

MAX FROST & TROOPERS
68	Capitol CL 15565	Shape Of Things To Come/Free Lovin'	25

FROST LANE
71	Cutty Wren MM 1	FROST LANE (LP, actually various artists LP)	45

FRUGAL SOUND
66	Pye 7N 17062	Norwegian Wood/Cruel To Be Kind	12
66	Pye 7N 17129	Just Outside The Door/I'm On Your Side	6
67	RCA Victor RCA 1556	Backstreet Girl/Reason To Believe	6
67	RCA Victor RCA 1595	Abilene/Love Is A New Face	5
68	RCA Victor RCA 1659	All Strung Out/Miss Mary	5

FRUIT EATING BEARS
78	DJM DJS 857	Door In My Face/Going Through The Motions (company sleeve)	45
78	Raw RAW 9	Chevy Heavy (p/s)	25

FRUIT GUMS
70	Fab FAB 138	Sweet Pork/Crying All Night	6

FRUIT MACHINE
69	Spark SRL 1003	Follow Me/Cuddly Toy	70
69	Spark SRL 1027	I'm Alone Today/Sunshine Of Your Love (some in title p/s)	130+/80

(see also Rare Bird)

FRUMPY
71	Philips 6003 133	Life Without Pain/Morning	12
71	Philips 6305 067	ALL WILL BE CHANGED (LP)	20
72	Philips 6305 098	FRUMP 2 (LP, black & blue vinyl)	25

(see also Atlantis)

FRUUPP
74	Dawn DNS 1087	Prince Of Heaven/Jaunting Car	10
73	Dawn DNLS 3053	FUTURE LEGENDS (LP)	30
74	Dawn DNLS 3058	SEVEN SECRETS (LP, with lyric insert)	30
74	Dawn DNLH 2	THE PRINCE OF HEAVEN'S EYES (LP, some with book)	45/30
75	Dawn DNLS 3070	MODERN MASQUERADES (LP, with lyric insert)	30

FUCHSIA
71	Pegasus PEG 8	FUCHSIA (LP)	150

FUD (Christian) & DEL
73	Duke DU 165	Beef Sticker/PRINCE HERON: Ten Commandments	6
73	Songbird SB 1086	Dr. Fud/FUD CHRISTIAN ALLSTARS: La-Fud-Del Skank	6

FUD CHRISTIAN ALLSTARS
71	Big Shot BI 571	Never Fall In Love (actually by Winston Heywood)/Never Fall In Love Version	8

(see also Linkers, Ansel Linkers)

FUGI
71	Blue Horizon 2096 005	Red Moon (Parts 1 & 2)	25

FUGITIVE
81	private pressing FMR 050	Need My Freedom	20

FUGITIVES (Jamaica)
67	Doctor Bird DB 1082	Musical Pressure/LESLIE BUTLER & FUGITIVES: Winchester Rocksteady	22

(see also Jo Jo Bennett & Fugitives, Two Kings, Jo Jo Bennett, Stranger Cole)

FUGITIVES (U.S.)
61	Vogue V 9176	Freeway/Fugitive	40

FUGS
68	Big T BIG 115	Crystal Liaison/When The Mode Of The Music Changes	12
68	Transatlantic TRA 180	TENDERNESS JUNCTION (LP, some with poster)	35/20
68	Transatlantic TRA 181	IT CRAWLED INTO MY HAND, HONEST (LP)	25

69	Fontana (S)TL 5501	VIRGIN FUGS (LP)	25
69	Fontana (S)TL 5513	THE FUGS ... FIRST ALBUM (LP)	25
69	Fontana (S)TL 5524	FUGS II (LP)	22
69	Reprise RSLP 6359	THE BELLE OF AVENUE A (LP)	15

FULHAM FURIES
78	GM GMS 9050	These Boots Are Made For Walking/Under Pressure (no p/s)	35

(see also Lurkers)

BLIND BOY FULLER
57	Philips BBL 7512	BLIND BOY FULLER 1935-40 (LP)	45
68	Matchbox SDR 143	BLIND BOY FULLER ON DOWN VOLUME 1 (LP)	22
69	Matchbox SDR 168	BLIND BOY FULLER ON DOWN VOLUME 2 (LP)	22
60s	Flyright LP 105	CAROLINA BLUES (LP)	15

GIL FULLER & DIZZY GILLESPIE
66	Fontana 688 147 ZL	MAN FROM MONTEREY (LP)	15

(see also Dizzy Gillespie)

BOBBY FULLER FOUR
66	London HLU 10030	I Fought The Law/Little Annie Lou	25
66	London HLU 10041	Love's Made A Fool Of You/Don't You Ever Let Me Know	20
73	President PT 394	Another Sad And Lonely Night/Only When I Dream	10
67	President PTL 1003	MEMORIAL ALBUM (LP)	40

(see also Randy Fuller)

JERRY FULLER
59	London HLH 8982	The Tennessee Waltz/Charlene (78 rpm = £25)	15
61	London HLN 9439	Guilty Of Loving You/First Love Never Dies	13
62	Salvo SLO 1802	Lipstick And Rouge/Mother Goose At The Bandstand (99 copies only)	150

JESSE FULLER
65	Good Time Jazz GV 2426	San Francisco Bay Blues/New Midnight Special	10
67	Good Time Jazz GV 2427	Runnin' Wild/The Monkey And The Engineer	10
67	Fontana TF 821	Going Back To My Old Used To Be/Bye And Bye	15
58	Good Time Jazz LAG 12159	JESSE FULLER (LP)	25
60	Good Time Jazz LAG 12279	LONE CAT (LP)	25
60	Topic 10T 59	WORKING ON THE RAILROAD (10" LP)	30
63	Good Time Jazz LAG 574	SAN FRANCISCO BAY BLUES (LP)	15
65	Stateside SL 10154	JESSE FULLER'S FAVOURITES (LP)	15
66	Fontana TL 5313	SESSION WITH JESSE FULLER (LP)	18
66	Topic 12T 134	MOVE ON DOWN THE LINE (LP)	25
66	Stateside SL 10166	SAN FRANCISCAN BAY BLUES (LP, reissue)	15
60s	Vocalion VRLP 574	SAN FRANCISCO BAY BLUES (LP)	20
60s	Evolution Z 1004	LIVE IN LONDON (LP)	15

JOHNNY FULLER
73	Speciality SON 5017	Haunted House/Swinging At The Creek	6

RANDY FULLER
67	President PT 111	It's Love, Come What May/The Things You Do	12

(see also Bobby Fuller Four)

WALTER 'GIL' FULLER
51	Vogue V 2037	The Scene Changes/Mean To Me (78)	8

FULL TIME MEN
86	Shigaku SHIG 1T	I Got Wheels/One More Time/Way Down South (12", p/s)	8

(see also R.E.M.)

LOWELL FULSON/FULSOM
53	London L 1199	I Love My Baby/The Blues Came Rollin' In (78)	60
65	Sue WI 375	Too Many Drivers/Key To Your Heart	28
66	Sue WI 4023	Talking Woman/Blues Around Midnight	40
66	Outasite 45-502	Stop And Think/Baby (with Leon Blue)	70
66	Polydor 56515	Black Nights/Little Angel	20
67	Fontana TF 795	Tramp/Pico	28
76	Jet JET 770	Do You Love Me?/Monday Morning	5
69	Fontana SFJL 920	SAN FRANCISCO BLUES (LP)	45
69	Polydor 2384 038	IN A HEAVY BAG (LP, as Lowell Fulsom)	25

FUMBLE
72	Sovereign SOV 110	Hullo Mary Lou/Hanging On	5
73	Sovereign SOV 118	Million Seller/Get Up	5
72	Sovereign SVNA 7254	FUMBLE (LP, gatefold sleeve)	15

FUNBOY FIVE
80s	Cool Cat Daddy-O PHUN 1	Life After Death/Compulsive Eater (foldover p/s)	6

FUNERAL FOR A FRIEND
02	Mighty Atom MTY 338	Between Order And Model/Juno/Red Is The New Black (CD)	20
03	Infectious EW 269	Juneau/Getaway Plan (white vinyl, p/s)	10
03	Infectious EW 269CD 1	Juneau/Getaway Plan (CD, card sleeve)	8
03	Warner EW 274	She Drove Me To Daytime TV/Bullet Theory (blue vinyl, p/s)	6
03	Infectious INFEC 126S	Four Ways — This Year's Most Open Heartbreak/She Drove Me To Daytime Television/Kiss And Make Up (All Bets Are Off)/Escape Artists Never Die (2 x 7, red vinyl, gatefold p/s)	20
03	Infectious INFEC 12CDS	Four Ways — This Year's Most Open Heartbreak/She Drove Me To Daytime Television/Kiss And Make Up (All Bets Are Off)/Escape Artists Never Die (CD, 2000 only)	15
03	Infectious EW269	Juneau/Getaway Plan (white vinyl, p/s)	7

FUN FOUR
80	NMC NMC 010	Singing In The Showers/By Products/Elevator Crush (p/s)	25

(see also Orange Juice)

FUNGUS
73	Fungus FUN 1	Premonitions Parts 1 & 2 (LP, private pressing)	100+

(see also Secondhand, Seventh Wave)

FUNHOUSE
82	Ensign ENY 222	Out Of Control/This Could Be Hell (p/s)	6
82	Ensign ENYT 222	Out Of Control (Full Version)/This Could Be Hell (12", p/s)	10

(see also Another Pretty Face, DNV, Waterboys)

FARLEY 'JACKMASTER' FUNK
86	London LONX 105	Love Can't Turn Around (12", featuring Darryl Pandy)	8

FUNKADELIC
70	Pye International 7N 25519	I Got A Thing, You Got A Thing, Everybody's Got A Thing/Fish, Chips & Sweat	10
71	Pye International 7N 25548	You & Your Folks, Me & Mine/Funky Dollar Bill	10
71	Janus 6146 001	Can You Get To That/Back In Our Minds	10
78	Warner Bros K 17246	One Nation Under A Groove (Parts 1 & 2)	5
78	Warner Bros K 17246T	One Nation Under A Groove (Parts 1 & 2) (12")	10
79	Warner Bros K 17321	Cholly (Funk Getting Ready To Roll)/Into You	5
79	Warner Bros K 17494	(Not Just) Knee Deep (Parts 1 & 2)	8
81	Warner Bros K 17786	The Electric Spanking Of War Babies/(Instrumental Mix) (p/s)	5
81	Warner Bros K 17786T	The Electric Spanking Of War Babies/(Instrumental Mix) (12")	8
70	Pye Intl. NSPL 28137	FUNKADELIC (LP)	40
71	Pye Intl. NSPL 28144	FREE YOUR MIND AND YOUR ASS WILL FOLLOW (LP)	40
71	Janus 6310 201	MAGGOT BRAIN (LP)	40
75	20th Century W 215	LET'S TAKE IT TO THE STAGE (LP)	12
78	Warner Bros K 56299	HARDCORE JOLLIES (LP)	15
78	Warner Bros K 56539	ONE NATION UNDER A GROOVE (LP, some with free 12" One Nation Under A Groove)	15/12
79	Warner Bros K 56712	UNCLE JAM WANTS YOU (LP, gatefold sleeve)	15

(see also Parliament, Parlet, Brides Of Funkenstein, Bootsy's Rubber Band, Dolby's Cube, P-Funk Allstars)

FUNKEES
76	Black Magic BM 114	Abraka/Ole	7
75	Contempo CS 2058	Tu Lay/Cool It Down	7

FUNKMASTERS
84	Master Funk MF4	It's Over/(Versions) (12")	8

FUNKY BOTTOM CONGREGATION
69	Beacon BEA 122	Hare-Krishna/Things About Yourself	6

FUNKY JUNCTION
73	Stereo Gold Award MER 373	PLAY TRIBUTE TO DEEP PURPLE (LP)	18

(see also Thin Lizzy)

FINBAR & EDDIE FUREY
68	Transatlantic TRA 168	FINBAR AND EDDIE FUREY (LP)	20
69	Xtra XTRA 1077	TRADITIONAL IRISH PIPE MUSIC (LP)	20
69	Transatlantic TRA 191	THE LONESOME BOATMAN (LP)	18
72	Dawn DNLS 3037	THE DAWNING OF THE DAY (LP, with lyric insert)	20

FINBAR FUREY & BOB STEWART
76	Crescent ARS 110	TOMORROW WE PART (LP)	12

FUR FUR
80s	Daark Inc. D.I. 7	FUR FUR (cassette)	12

(see also Karl Blake, Danielle Dax, Lemon Kittens, Gland Shrouds)

FURRY DICE
80	White Line WHLS 001	Rudi Don't Take Your Love To Town/K.G.B. (p/s)	6

TOMMY FURTADO
57	London HLA 8418	Sun Tan Sam/Isabella (78 rpm = £10)	30

BILLY FURY
78s
59	Decca F 11102	Maybe Tomorrow/Gonna Type A Letter	140
59	Decca F 11128	Margo/Don't Knock Upon My Door	200
59	Decca F 11158	Angel Face/Time Has Come	250
59	Decca F 11189	My Christmas Prayer/Last Kiss	350

SINGLES
59	Decca F 11102	Maybe Tomorrow/Gonna Type A Letter (triangular centre, later round)	25
59	Decca F 11128	Margo/Don't Knock Upon My Door (triangular centre, later round)	25/30
59	Decca F 11158	Angel Face/Time Has Come (triangular centre, later round)	30/20
59	Decca F 11189	My Christmas Prayer/Last Kiss (triangular centre, later round)	70/40
60	Decca F 11200	Colette/Baby How I Cried (triangular centre, later round)	40/15
60	Decca F 11237	That's Love/You Don't Know (as Billy Fury & Four Jays)	25
60	Decca F 11267	Wondrous Place/Alright, Goodbye	25
60	Decca F 11311	A Thousand Stars/Push Push	15
61	Decca F 11334	Don't Worry/Talkin' In My Sleep (with Four Kestrels)	15
61	Decca F 11349	Halfway To Paradise/Cross My Heart	10
61	Decca F 11384	Jealousy/Open Your Arms	10
61	Decca F 11409	I'd Never Find Another You/Sleepless Nights	10
62	Decca F 11437	Letter Full Of Tears/Magic Eyes	10
62	Decca F 11458	Last Night Was Made For Love/King For Tonight	10
62	Decca F 11485	Once Upon A Dream/If I Lose You	10
62	Decca F 11508	Because Of Love/Running Around	10
63	Decca F 11582	Like I've Never Been Gone/What Do You Think You're Doing Of?	10

Billy FURY

63	Decca F 11655	When Will You Say I Love You?/All I Wanna Do Is Cry	10
63	Decca F 11701	In Summer/I'll Never Fall In Love Again	10
63	Decca F 11744	Somebody Else's Girl/Go Ahead And Ask Her	10
63	Decca F 11792	Do You Really Love Me Too?/What Am I Gonna Do?	10
64	Decca F 11888	I Will/Nothin' Shakin' (But The Leaves On The Trees) (some B-sides list "Nothin' Shakin' ")	each 18
64	Decca F 11939	It's Only Make Believe/Baby What Do You Want Me To Do?	15
64	Decca F 40719	Hippy Hippy Shake/Glad All Over (export-only, some with p/s)	80/50
65	Decca F 12048	I'm Lost Without You/You Better Believe It, Baby	10
65	Decca F 12178	In Thoughts Of You/Away From You	10
65	Decca F 12230	Run To My Lovin' Arms/Where Do You Run?	10
66	Decca F 12325	I'll Never Quite Get Over You/I Belong To The Wind	10
66	Decca F 12409	Don't Let A Little Pride Stand In Your Way/Didn't See The Real Thing Come Along	12
66	Decca F 12459	Give Me Your Word/She's So Far Out She's In	15
67	Parlophone R 5560	Hurtin' Is Loving/Things Are Changing	20
67	Parlophone R 5605	Loving You/I'll Go Along With It Now	15
67	Parlophone R 5634	Suzanne In The Mirror/It Just Don't Matter Now	18
67	Parlophone R 5658	Beyond The Shadow Of A Doubt/Baby Do You Love Me?	18
68	Parlophone R 5681	Silly Boy Blue/One Minute Woman	35
68	Parlophone R 5723	Phone Box/Any Morning Now	22
68	Parlophone R 5747	Lady/Certain Things	20
69	Parlophone R 5788	I Call For My Rose/Bye Bye	20
69	Parlophone R 5819	All The Way To The U.S.A./Do My Best For You	20
70	Parlophone R 5845	Why Are You Leaving?/Old Sweet Roll (Hi-De-Ho)	35
70	Parlophone R 5874	Paradise Alley/Well ... All Right	40
72	Fury FY 301	Will The Real Man Please Stand Up/At This Stage	25
74	Warner Bros WB 16402	I'll Be Your Sweetheart/Fascinating Candle Flame	30
76	NEMS NES 018	Halfway To Paradise/Turn My Back On You	12
81	Polydor POSP 355	Be Mine Tonight/No Trespassers (p/s)	10
82	Polydor POSP 488	Love Or Money/Love Sweet Love (p/s)	9
82	Polydor POSP 528	Devil Or Angel/Don't Tell Me Lies ('guitar' or 'microphone' p/s)	10/15
83	Polydor POSP 558	Forget Him/Your Words (p/s)	10
83	Polydor POSP 558	Let Me Go Lover/Your Words (same p/s as above but diff. A-side, 500 only)	35
83	Lyntone LYN 13078/BF 1	Devil Or Angel/Lost Without You (flexi free within memorial concert booklet)	20/6
83	private pressing	BILLY FURY IN INTERVIEW WITH STUART COLEMAN (10", 500 white label copies only, 1st 200 numbered)	40/35

EPs

59	Decca DFE 6597	MAYBE TOMORROW (triangular centre, orange/red p/s)	100
59	Decca DFE 6597	MAYBE TOMORROW (round centre, orange/red or yellow p/s)	100/80
61	Decca DFE 6694	BILLY FURY	70
62	Decca DFE 6699	BILLY FURY NO. 2	70
62	Decca DFE 6708	PLAY IT COOL	30
62	Decca DFE 6708	PLAY IT COOL (export issue, blue/green 'crouching' cover)	100+
62	Decca DFE 8505	BILLY FURY HITS	30
63	Decca DFE 8525	BILLY FURY AND THE TORNADOS	40
63	Decca DFE 8558	AM I BLUE	50
65	Decca DFE 8641	BILLY FURY AND THE GAMBLERS	125
73	Ronco MR EP 001	LONG LIVE ROCK (with others, no p/s)	30
83	Decca DFE 8686	MY CHRISTMAS PRAYER	15

LPs

60	Decca LF 1329	THE SOUND OF FURY (10")	200
60	Ace Of Clubs ACL 1047	BILLY FURY	40
61	Ace Of Clubs ACL 1083	HALFWAY TO PARADISE	40
63	Decca LK 4533	BILLY	40
63	Decca LK 4548/SKL 4548	WE WANT BILLY! (with Tornados, mono/stereo)	40/55
65	Decca LK 4677	I'VE GOTTA HORSE (soundtrack)	70
67	Ace Of Clubs ACL 1229	THE BEST OF BILLY FURY	25
71	Decca SPA 188	THE WORLD OF BILLY FURY (mono/stereo)	each 15
72	Decca SPA 575	THE WORLD OF BILLY FURY VOLUME 2	20
76	Decca DPA 3033/4	THE BILLY FURY STORY (2-LP)	15
81	Decca LFT 1329	THE SOUND OF FURY (10", reissue)	20
83	Red Bus BUSLP 1003	THE MISSING YEARS	18

(see also Tornados, Gamblers, Dave Berry, Malcolm Roberts)

FURYS

63	Stateside SS 182	Never More/Zing! Went The Strings Of My Heart	15
72	Jay Boy BOY 61	What Is Soul?/I Lost My Baby	8
72	Jay Boy BOY 68	I'm Satisfied With You/Just A Little Mixed Up	15

FURY'S TORNADOES

74	Warner Bros K 16442	Telstar '74/I Would Give You Anything	12

(see also Billy Fury)

F.U.S.E.

93	Warp WAP38	TRAIN TRACS (12", some white vinyl, p/s)	10/7
93	Warp LP12LTD	DIMENSION INTRUSION (2-LP, white vinyl)	15

FUSION

79	Plastic Fantastic PFUL 1104	COLD OUTSIDE EP (12")	8
80	Telephone TEL 101	TILL I HEAR FROM YOU (LP, blue vinyl)	20

FUSION

95	Ferox FER 015	FREESTYLE EP (12")	8
96	Ferox FER 021	GALAXY OF FUTURE VISIONS (12" EP)	10

FUSION ORCHESTRA
73	EMI EMI 2056	When My Mama's Not At Home/Nuthouse Rock	6
73	EMI EMA 758	A SKELETON IN ARMOUR (LP, gatefold sleeve)	40

FUT
70	Beacon BEA 160	Have You Heard The Word/Futting Around	30

(see also Graham Bonnet, Bee Gees, Marbles, Maurice Gibb, Steve & Stevie; this record has NO Beatles involvement)

FUTURE BEAT ALLIANCE
99	Ferox FER 035	ABACO (12" EP)	10

FUTUREHEADS
01	Private Pressing	The first Demo (4-track CD, handwritten sticker)	50
02	Private Pressing	1-2-3 Nul Demo (5-track CD)	50
02	Project C'naut PCOS 001	Nul Book Standard — Park Inn/Robot/My Rules/Stupid And Shallow (p/s)	25
03	Fantastic Plastic FP7035	1-2-3-NUL! EP: Carnival Kids/Ticket/Cabaret/A Picture Of Dorian Gray (p/s, with sticker and badge)	20
03	Fantastic Plastic FPS035	1-2-3-NUL! EP: Carnival Kids/Ticket/Cabaret/A Picture Of Dorian Gray (CD, p/s)	20
03	Fantastic Plastic FP 7036	First Day/Balsch/Piece Of Crap (red or clear vinyl, p/s, 500 only)	7
03		Hounds Of Love (1-track white label: gig/fanclub 7")	12
04	(No Cat. No.)	Meantime/Decent Days & Nights Remixes (1000, white label gig/fanclub 7")	7

FUTURE PAST
91	B12 03	Our Paths Meet/Harmony Park/Your Hand In My Mind/Dance Intellect/TV People (12", black vinyl)	15

FUTURES
75	Buddah BDS 430	You Better Be Certain/No One Could Compare	15
75	Buddah BDLP 4031	CASTLES IN THE SKY (LP)	25

FUTURE SOUND OF LONDON
SINGLES
91	Jumpin' & Pumpin' TOT 17	Papua New Guinea/Papua New Guinea (Andrew Weatherall Mix) (p/s)	6
94	Virgin PROMO 500	Slider/Snake Hips/You're Creeping Me Out/Herd Killing/Live In New York (double pack, promo only, 500 copies)	25

12" SINGLES
91	Jumpin' & Pumpin' 12TOT 11	PULSE: Bring On The Pulse/In The Mind Of A Child/Hardhead/Pulse State	15
91	Jumpin' & Pumpin' 12TOT 16	PULSE 3: Tingler/Owl/Bite The Bullet/Calcium	12
91	Jumpin' & Pumpin' 12TOT 17	Papua New Guinea (Dali Mix)/(Dumb Child Of Q Mix)/(Qube Mix) (p/s)	12
92	Jumpin' & Pumpin' 12TOT 17R	Papua New Guinea (Andrew Weatherall Mix)/(Dub Mix)/(Journey To Pyramid)/(Monsoon Mix)/(Graham Massey Mix)/(Dumb Child Of Q Mix) (p/s)	8
94	Virgin VST 1540P	Far Out Son Of Lung And The Ramblings Of A Madman/Snake Hips/Smokin' Japanese Babe/Amoeba (white vinyl, promo only)	25
95	Virgin SEMTEX DJ 1	Semtex (Part 1)/Semtex (Part 2)/We Have Explosive/Semtex (stamped sleeve, promo only, 500 copies)	20
97	Virgin VSTDJ 1616	We Have Explosive Mantronix Plastik Formula (Mix 1)/(Mix 2) (stickered sleeve, promo only)	10
97	Virgin VSTXDJ 1616	We Have Explosive (Original Mix)/(Leon Mar Mix)/(Oil Funk Mix)/(Part 4)/(Part 5) (stickered black sleeve, promo only)	8

12" EPs
91	Jumpin' & Pumpin' 12TOT 15	PRINCIPALS OF MOTION EP	8
91	Jumpin' & Pumpin' 12TOT 18	SMART SYSTEMS EP	10
92	Jumpin' & Pumpin' 12TOT 25	PULSE 4 (I'm Not Gonna Let You Do It/The Creator/Shrink/18 Space Virus)	12
92	Union City UCRT 11	METROPOLIS EP	12
93	Virgin VST 1478	CASCADE EP	8

CD SINGLES
92	Jumpin' & Pumpin' CDSTOT 17	Papua New Guinea/(Andrew Weatherall Mix)/(Dub Mix)/(Journey To Pyramid)/(Graham Mix)/(Dumb Child Of Of Q)/(Hamish McDonald Mix)	10
93	Virgin VSCDT 1478	Cascade (Part 1)/(Part 2)/(Part 3)/(Part 4)/(Part 5)/Short Form	8
96	Virgin VCD 1605	MY KINGDOM (5 mixes & radio edits, card slipcase, promo only)	12
96	Virgin VSCDDJ 1805	My Kingdom (Media Mix)/(Part 4) (card sleeve, promo only)	10

ALBUMS
92	Jumpin'/Pumpin' LPTOT 2	ACCELERATOR (2-LP)	15
94	Virgin V 2755	ISDN (LP, embossed, fold-out black sleeve with insert)	25
94	Virgin CDV 2755	ISDN (CD, embossed black wallet)	20
97	Virgin ISDNSHOW 1	ISDN SHOW (CD, promo only, no inlay)	25

(see also Amorphous Androgynous, Art Science Technology, Humanoid, Humanoid featuring Sharon Benson, Intelligent Communications, Mental Cube, Metropolis, Pulse Systems, Semi Real, Smart Systems, Yage, Stakker)

FUZZ
71	Mojo 2092 003	I Love You For All Seasons (Parts 1 & 2)	7
71	Mojo 2092 008	Like An Open Door/Leave It All Behind	7
71	Mojo 2916 010	FUZZ (LP)	30

FUZZ FACE
68	Page One POF 065	Mighty Quinn/Voices From The Sky	6

FUZZTONES
85	ABC S 006	She's Wicked/Epitaph For A Head (p/s)	6

FUZZY DUCK

71	MAM MAM 37	Double Time Woman/Just Look Around You	15
71	MAM MAM 51	Big Brass Band/One More Hour	15
71	MAM AS 1005	FUZZY DUCK (LP, with poster)	140+
90	Reflection MM 05	FUZZY DUCK (LP, reissue with booklet & single "Double Time Woman"/	
		"One More Hour" [MMS 01])	15

(see also Andromeda, Greatest Show On Earth, Alvin Lee)

FX

79	own label	THE SOUTH'S GONNA RISE AGAIN (EP)	100

FYNN McCOOL

70	RCA RCA 1956	U.S. Thumbstyle/Diamond Lil	8
70	RCA SF 8112	FYNN McCOOL (LP, gatefold sleeve)	50

(see also Shakespears, Grapefruit, Sleepy)

TOMMY G & CHARMS

67	London HLB 10107	I Know What I Want/I Want You So Bad	42

WINSTON G (& WICKED)

65	Parlophone R 5266	Please Don't Say/Like A Baby	35
66	Parlophone R 5330	Until You Were Gone/That Way Too (as Winston G. & Wicked)	18
66	Decca F 12444	Cloud Nine/I'll Make You Cry Tomorrow	18
67	Decca F 12559	Mother Ferguson's Love Dust/Judge And Jury	22
67	Decca F 12623	Riding With The Milkman/Bye Bye Baby	22

B(ASIL) GABBIDON

61	Blue Beat BB 069-A	Warpaint Baby (miscredited to B. Cabbidon & Buster's Group)/	
		I Was Wrong (miscredited to Chuck & Dobbie with Buster's Group)	16
62	Blue Beat BB 111-A	Ivoree/Lover Man	18
62	Blue Beat BB 124	Independence Blues/For My Love (as B. Gabbidon)	18
62	Blue Beat BB 129-A	Our Melody/Going Back To Ja (with Randy's All Stars)	18
62	Island WI 033	I Found My Baby (actually by Roy Braham)/No Fault Of Mine	20
63	Island WI 076	I Bet You Don't Know/3 x 7	20
63	Island WI 089	St. Louis Woman/Get On The Ball	20
63	Blue Beat BB 155-A	Eana Mena/Since You Are Gone (with Prince Buster All Stars)	18
63	Blue Beat BB 161	I'll Find Love (with Prince Buster All Stars)/	
		MELLOW LARKS: What You Gonna Do?	18
65	Blue Beat BB 288	Tick Tock (actually by Theo Beckford)/The Streets Of Glory	
		(actually by Theo Beckford & Yvonne Harrison)	18

(see also Derrick Patsy & Basil, Mellow Larks, Derrick Morgan)

PETER GABRIEL

77	Charisma CB 301	Solsbury Hill/Moribund The Burgermeister (p/s)	15
77	Charisma CB 302	Modern Love/Slowburn (no p/s, 'nude' picture label, withdrawn)	40
78	Charisma CB 311	D.I.Y./Perspective (p/s, purple label, Irish-only sleeve)	10
78	Charisma CB 311	D.I.Y./Perspective (p/s, silver label, possibly Irish-only sleeve)	10
78	Charisma CB 319	D.I.Y. (Remix)/Mother Of Violence/Teddy Bear (no p/s, withdrawn)	30
78	Sound For Industry SFI 381	Solsbury Hill (live) (1-sided flexidisc, concert freebie)	8
80	Charisma CB 354	Games Without Frontiers/The Start/I Don't Remember (p/s)	5
80	Charisma CB 370	Biko/Shosholoza/Jetzt Kommt Die Flut (p/s, 33rpm)	5
80	Charisma CB 360	No Self Control/Lead A Normal Life (p/s)	6
82	Charisma SHOCK 1	Shock The Monkey/Soft Dog (Instrumental) (p/s)	6
82	Charisma SHOCK 1	Shock The Monkey/Shock The Monkey (Instrumental) (same p/s as above)	20
82	Charisma SHOCK 122	Shock The Monkey/Soft Dog (Instrumental) (picture disc)	10
82	Charisma SHOCK 350	Shock The Monkey/Shock The Monkey (Instrumental)	
		(12", same p/s as above [SHOCK 12])	20
82	Charisma CB 405	I Have The Touch/Across The River (p/s)	15
83	Charisma GAB 12	I Don't Remember (live)/Solsbury Hill (live)/Kiss Of Life (live)	
		(12", shrinkwrapped stickered double pack, with 12" white label [GAB 122],	
		"Games Without Frontiers"/"Schnappschuss (Ein Familienfoto)", no p/s)	20
88	Charisma/Virgin CDT 33	Solsbury Hill/Moribund The Burgermeister/Solsbury Hill (live) (3" CD, card p/s)	12
92	Virgin PGS 7	Digging In The Dirt/Bashi-Bazouk (black label, jukebox issue)	7
92	Virgin PGSDG 712	Digging In The Dirt/Digging In The Dirt (Instrumental)/Quiet Steam/	
		Bashi-Bazouk (12", p/s, withdrawn)	10
92	Virgin PGSDG 7	Digging In The Dirt/Digging In The Dirt (Instrumental)/Quiet Steam/	
		Bashi-Bazouk (CD, picture disc in box with lyric sheet)	10
92	Virgin PGSDX 8	Steam/Games Without Frontiers (Massive DB Mix)/Steam	
		(Oh, Oh, Let Off Steam Mix)/Games Without Frontiers (live)	
		(CD in fold-out house-shaped box)	15
92	Virgin PGS 9	Blood Of Eden/Mercy Street (p/s)	5
00	Realworld PGDJ2000	Father & Son/Downside Up/The Tower Ate People (Promo CD, card p/s)	10
00	Virgin RWSCDJ14	Father & Son (Radio Edit)/When Your Falling(Long Radio Edit)	
		(Promo CD, card p/s)	10
02	Virgin PGSCDJ14	More Than This/More Than This (Radio Edit) (Promo CD, card p/s)	10
80	Reformation RSR 113	CHROMEDOME (LP)	25

86	Virgin PGCDP 5	SO (CD, picture disc)	18
92	Real World/Virgin PGCDJ7	US (CD promo, in-store play copy in A4 folder with press release)	30
02	Virgin PGCDJ11	UP (CD promo, pre-release in A4 folder with press release)	30

(see also Genesis, Youssou 'Ndour & Peter Gabriel, Colin Scot, Charlie Drake)

PETER GABRIEL & KATE BUSH

86	Charisma/Virgin PGSP 2	Don't Give Up/In Your Eyes (Special Mix) (poster p/s in stickered PVC sleeve)	15
86	Charisma/Virgin PGS 212	Don't Give Up/In Your Eyes (Special Mix)/This Is The Picture (Excellent Birds) (12", p/s)	8

(see also Kate Bush)

RUSS GABRIEL

93	Ferox FER 002	PEACE EP (12", plain sleeve)	20
94	Ferox FER 006	DARWINIAN EP (12", plain sleeve)	20
95	Input Neuron INMD(X)1	FUTURE FUNK VOL. 1 (12", double pack, p/s)	10

(see also Fusion, Too Funk)

RUSS GABRIEL & AFFIE YUSUF

94	Ferox FER 005	Sian's Tune/Deep Space (12")	20

GABRIEL & ANGELS

63	Stateside SS 150	That's Life That's Tough/Don't Wanna Twist No More	15

GABRIELLI BRASS

65	Polydor 56031	Angel Cake/Cat Walk	6
65	Polydor 56047	Ride Your Pony/Anyone Who Had A Heart	10
68	Polydor 56252	'Canterbury Tales' Theme/Working My Way Back To You	15

GABY & CABLES

72	Duke DU 129	Only Love Can Make You Smile/Only Love Version	7

(see also Gaby & Wilton)

GABY & WILTON

72	Camel CA 92	Only Love/CHARLEY ACE: The Ten Commandments Of Joshua	9

(see also Gaby & Cables)

GADGETS

79	Final Solution FSLP 001	GADGETREE (LP, with insert, blue or beige picture on sleeve)	20
80	Final Solution FSLP 002	LOVE, CURIOSITY, FRECKLES & DOUBT (LP)	20
83	Glass GLALP 006	THE BLUE ALBUM (LP, with inner sleeve)	12

(see also The The, Matt Johnson, Colin Lloyd Tucker, Plain Characters)

MEL GADSON

60	London HLX 9105	Comin' Down With Love/I'm Gettin' Sentimental Over You	22

GAGALACTYCA

90	Holyground HG 1135/	GAGALACTYCA (LP, with booklet, actually by Lightyears Away	
	Magic Mixture MM 3	& Thundermother, 425 only)	25

(see also Bill Nelson, David John & Mood)

MAJOR YURI GAGARIN

61	Britone MK 100	CONQUEST OF SPACE (EP)	30

GAGS

79	Look LKLP 6312	DEATH IN BUZZARD'S GULCH (LP)	30

BASIL GAIL

70	Bullet BU 454	I Wish/Black Is Black	7

SLIM GAILLARD (QUARTET/TRIO)

50	Parlophone R 3291	Jam Man/JOHNNY OTIS: Harlem Nocturne (78)	40
51	Vogue V 2029	Voot Boogie/Queen's Boogie (78)	10
51	Vogue V 2044	Central Avenue Breakdown/Sighing Boogie (78)	10
56	Parlophone GEP 8595	SLIM GAILLARD NO. 1 (EP)	20
56	Columbia Clef SEB 10046	MUSICAL AGGREGATIONS (EP)	20
60	London RED 1251	SLIM GAILLARD RIDES AGAIN (EP)	25

(see also Meade 'Lux' Lewis & Slim Gaillard)

DONNA GAINES

71	MCA MK 5060	Sally Go Round The Roses/So Said The Man	7

(see also Donna Summer)

GAINORS

58	London HLU 8734	The Secret/Gonna Rock Tonite (78 rpm = £35)	120

GALACTIC FEDERATION

66	Polydor BM 56093	The March Of The Sky People/Moon Shot	38

GALACTIC SYMPOSIUM

80	Vague VOG 2	Money/In The Navy (gatefold p/s)	6

GALAHAD

87	private pressing G 1001	Dreaming From The Inside/The Opiate (p/s, 500 only)	12

DIAMANDA GALAS

82	Y Y 18	LITANIES DU SATAN (LP)	12
86	Mute STUMM 33	SAINT OF THE PIT (12" EP, p/s with inner)	8

GALAXIE 500

89	Chemical Imbalance C 1005	Oblivious/tracks by other artists (free with issue 8 of *Chemical Imbalance* magazine)	8
89	Catalogue CAT 075	Victory Garden/STRAIGHTJACKET FITS: Hail (1-sided flexi free with *The Catalogue* magazine)	5
90	Caff CAFF 9	Rain/Don't Let Your Youth Go To Waste (p/s, with insert in bag)	25
89	Schemer 8905 CD	TODAY (CD, with 2 extra tracks)	15
89	Rough Trade ROUGH 146	ON FIRE (LP)	12

MINT VALUE £

90	Rough Trade ROUGH 156	THIS IS OUR MUSIC (LP, with sticker and 3 postcards)	12
90	Rough Trade ROUGHCD 156	THIS IS OUR MUSIC (CD, trifold case)	15
91	Rough Trade ROUGH 146L	ON FIRE (LP, reissue with shrinkwrapped CD single)	15
96	Rykodisc RCD 10355	GALAXIE 500 (4-CD box set with booklet)	25

(see also Damon & Naomi)

GALAXIES
60	Capitol CL 15158	The Big Triangle/Until The Next Time	18

DAVID GALBRAITH
57	Columbia DB 3947	Heartbreak Is New To Me/Miracle In Milan	5
58	Columbia DB 4226	Do I Love You/Tonight (78 rpm = £10)	5

EDDIE GALE
69	Blue Note BST 84294	GHETTO MUSIC (LP)	15

SANDRA GALE
63	Ember EMB S 162	Hello Heartbreak/If She's Right For You	8

SUNNY GALE
53	HMV 7M 147	Teardrops On My Pillow/Send My Baby Back To Me	10
54	HMV 7M 243	Goodnight, Well It's Time To Go/Close To Me	10
55	HMV 7M 344	C'est La Vie/Looking Glass	10
57	Brunswick 05659	Two Hearts (With An Arrow Between)/Maybe You'll Be There	10
57	Brunswick 05661	Come Go With Me/Please Go	10
58	Brunswick 05753	A Certain Smile/Just Friends	10
61	London HLU 9322	Please Love Me Forever/Sunny	10

GALE BROTHERS
66	Parlophone R 5535	Every Day Of My Life/All Strung Out	5

GALENS
63	London HLH 9804	Baby I Do Love You/Love Bells	30

FRANCE GALL
65	Philips BF 1408	Poupée De Cire, Poupeé De Son/Le Coeur Qui Jazze	5
88	WEA YZ 316 CD	Ella Elle L'a (CD, slimline jewel case)	15

RORY GALLAGHER
71	Polydor 2383 044	RORY GALLAGHER (LP)	28
71	Polydor 2383 076	DEUCE (LP)	22
72	Polydor 2383 112	LIVE! IN EUROPE (LP, gatefold sleeve)	15
73	Polydor 2383 189	BLUEPRINT (LP)	15
73	Polydor 2383 230	TATTOO (LP)	12
74	Polydor 2659 031	IRISH TOUR '74 (2-LP)	12
87	Capo/Demon XFIEND 98	DEFENDER (LP, with bonus 7", Seems To Me/No Peace For The Wicked)	12

(see also Taste, Killing Floor, Joe O'Donnell)

GALLAGHER-LYLE
67	Polydor BM 56170	Trees/In The Crowd	10
72	Capitol ST 21906	GALLAGHER AND LYLE (LP)	18

(see also James Galt, McGuinness Flint, Cups)

GALLAHADS
55	Capitol CL 14282	Ooh-Ah/Careless (78 rpm = £10)	15

GALLANTS
64	Capitol CL 15366	Happy Beat/Rhino	5
65	Capitol CL 15408	Man From U.N.C.L.E. Theme/Vagabond	15

GALLERY
69	Midas	THE WIND THAT SHAKES THE BARLEY (LP)	250

GALLIANO
88	Acid Jazz JAZID 1	Frederick Lies Still/I Love You Baby (1st pressing, with large centre hole)	20

GALLIARD
70	Deram DM 306	I Wrapped Her In Ribbons/The Hermit And The Knight	10
70	Deram Nova (S)DN 4	STRANGE PLEASURE (LP)	80
70	Deram SML 1075	NEW DAWN (LP)	35

(see also Craig)

GALLIARDS
60	Topic STOP 101	Black And White/Bahnuah	7

BOB GALLION
59	MGM MGM 1028	Out Of A Honky Tonk/You Take The Table And I'll Take The Chairs	12
60	MGM MGM 1057	Froggy Went A Courtin'/Hey! Joe	12
65	Hickory 45-1300	I Don't Have The Right (To Disagree)/Thank The Devil For Hideaways	7

GALLON DRUNK
93	Clawfist XPIG 21	Known, Not Wanted/TINDERSTICKS: We Have All The Time In The World ('singles club' release, p/s, 1,400 only)	15

GALLOW GLASS CEILI BAND
60s	Top Rank RX 30314	COME TO THE CEILI (LP)	20

FRANK GALLUP
58	HMV POP 509	Got A Match?/I Beg Your Pardon	8

JAMES GALT
65	Pye 7N 15936	Comes The Dawn/My Own Way	12
65	Pye 7N 17021	With My Baby/A Most Unusual Feeling	75

(see also Gallagher-Lyle)

GAMBLERS

63	Decca F 11780	You've Really Got A Hold On Me/Can I See You Tonight? 12
64	Decca F 11872	Nobody But Me/It's So Nice 15
65	Decca F 12060	Now I'm All Alone/Find Out What's Happening 20
66	Decca F 12399	Doctor Goldfoot (And His Bikini Machine)/It Seems So Long 17
67	Parlophone R 5557	Cry Me A River/Who Will Buy 20

(see also Billy Fury)

GAME

65	Pye 7N 15889	But I Do/Gotta Keep On Moving Baby 75
66	Decca F 12469	Gonna Get Me Someone/Gotta Wait 160
67	Parlophone R 5553	The Addicted Man/Help Me Mummy's Gone (withdrawn) (demo's = £750) 1000
67	Parlophone R 5569	It's Shocking What They Call Me/Help Me Mummy's Gone 400

GAMMER & HIS FAMILIARS

84	Gammer GAMMER 5	Will The New Baby/All Above (12", p/s) 8

(see also Durutti Column)

GANDALF THE GREY

80s	Heyoka	THE GREY WIZARD AM I (LP, reissue of U.S. LP) 25

RON WARREN GANDERTON

(see under Sound Ceremony)

LITTLE JIMMY GANDY

69	Roulette RO 510	Cool Thirteen/I'm Not Like The Others 20

GANGBUSTERS

63	Fontana TF 419	The Memory Of Your Face/When We Met 5

GANG OF ANGELS

94	Shotgun CDBOR 012	Hello Goodbye/Jim Jam (CD) 8

(see also Slade)

GANG OF FOUR

80	Fast Product FAST 5	DAMAGED GOODS (EP, original with b&w labels, some with sticker) 8/5

GANGSTERS

79	Stortbeat A45/B45	Harlow Town/Record Company (p/s) 10
79	Stortbeat BEAT 3	Best Friend/Best Friend Dub (p/s) 8
79	Stortbeat BEAT 2	GANGSTERS (LP) 20

GANGSTERS

80	Big Bear BB 25	Rudi The Red Nose Reindeer/White Christmas 5
80	Big Bear BB 28	Wooly Bully/We Are The Gangsters 5

GANIM'S ASIA MINORS

58	London HLE 8637	Daddy Lolo/Halvah 15

CECIL GANT

74	Flyright LP 4710	ROCK LITTLE BABY (LP) 15
75	Flyright LP 4714	CECIL'S BOOGIE (LP) 15
79	Magpie 1816	KILLER DILLER BOOGIE (LP) 15

CLENTT GANT

60	Starlite ST45 023	I'm Just A Lucky So-And-So/I Need You So 10

DON GANT

65	Hickory 45-1297	Early In The Morning/Don't Ya Even Cry 10

ELMER GANTRY'S (VELVET) OPERA

67	Direction 58-3083	Flames/Salisbury Plain 20
68	Direction 58-3481	Mary Jane/Dreamy 15
69	Direction 58-3924	Volcano/A Quick 'B' 10
68	Direction 8-63300	ELMER GANTRY'S VELVET OPERA (LP) 70

(see also Velvet Opera, Stretch, Strawbs, Hudson-Ford, Paul Brett's Sage)

GANTS

65	Liberty LIB 55829	Road Runner/My Baby Don't Care 35
67	Liberty LIB 55940	I Wonder/Greener Days 15

GARBAGE

SINGLES

95	Discordant CORD 001	Vow/Torn Apart (embossed metal 'G' logo sleeve, with insert, 3,000 pressed [934 issued], stickered, some sealed) 30/35
95	Discordant CORD 001	Vow/Torn Apart (plain black embossed 'G' logo sleeve, with insert in poly bag, 500 only, some sealed) 12/15
95	Mushroom SX 1138	Subhuman/1 Crush (embossed rubber 'G' logo sleeve, with SX 1138 insert, some in white 'G' logo carrier bag, 3,000 only; some with incorrect insert [S 1138]) 15/20
95	Mushroom S 1138	Subhuman/1 Crush (embossed card 'G' logo sleeve, with insert, 2,000 pressed [1,000 issued]) 12
95	Mushroom D 1138	Subhuman/1 Crush/Vow (CD, embossed inlay, stickered case, 3,000 only) 12
95	Mushroom SX 1199	Only Happy When It Rains/Girl Can't Come/Sleep (double-grooved B-side, stickered 'hologram prismaboard' 'G' logo sleeve, with inner sleeve & insert; some in blue 'G' logo carrier bag, 5,000 only) 6
95	Mushroom SX 1199	Only Happy When It Rains/Girl Can't Come/Sleep (as above, shrinkwrapped) 8
95	Mushroom SX 1237	Queer/Queer (Adrian Sherwood Remix) (p/s, in stickered 'crystal' outer 'G' logo sleeve, 5,000 only, some with 12" pink 'Garbage' carrier bag) 8
96	Mushroom SX 1271	Stupid Girl/Dog New Tricks (The Pal Mix) (jukebox issue, white label, no p/s) 7
96	Mushroom SX 1271/1237	Stupid Girl/Queer (jukebox issue, white label, stamped 'Garbage' logo, no p/s) . . 10
96	Mushroom SX 1271	Stupid Girl/Dog New Tricks (The Pal Mix) (stickered red 'Tak-Tile' cloth 'G' logo sleeve, some with stickered shrinkwrap, 10,000 only) 5/8

96	Mushroom SX 1271	Stupid Girl/Dog New Tricks (The Pal Mix) (stickered blue 'Tak-Tile' cloth 'G' logo sleeve, some with stickered shrinkwrap, 10,000 only)	6/10
96	Mushroom SX 1494	Milk (The Wicked Mix)/(The Tricky Remix) (embossed/hologram 'G' logo sleeve, with inner sleeve & poster, sealed)	5
96	Mushroom DJMILK 1	RABBIT IN THE MOON MILK (Udder Edit)/(Got It Mix)/(Butchered Vegas Mix)/ (12", die-cut white embossed 'G' logo sleeve, day-glo yellow inner sleeve, 500 only)	12
96	Mushroom DJMILK 2	GOLDIE MILK ('Completely Trashed' Mix)/('VIP Refuge Trash Your Shit') (12", die-cut white embossed 'G' logo sleeve, day-glo orange inner sleeve, 500 only)	12
96	Mushroom DJMILK 3	MASSIVE ATTACK MILK ('D' Mix)/('Trance' Mix) (12", die-cut white embossed 'G' logo sleeve, day-glo pink inner sleeve, 500 only)	12

LPs

95	Mushroom L 31450	GARBAGE (as 2 x 45rpm 12", with inner sleeves)	15
95	Mushroom LX 31450	GARBAGE (as 6 x 7" singles in box set with 3 inserts [now import only], most sealed)	15/18

PROMOS

95	Mushroom (no cat. no.)	Subhuman/1 Crush/Vow (cassette, black embossed inlay)	35
95	Mushroom (no cat. no.)	Vow/Queer/Only Happy When It Rains/Fix Me Now/As Heaven Is Fine (cassette, black embossed inlay)	35
95	Mushroom TRASH 02	Vow/Subhuman/1 Crush (CD, embossed rubber sleeve with insert, promo only)	45
96	Mushroom TRASH 09/010	Stupid Girl (Red Snapper Mix)/(Dreadzone Mix) (12", hand-stamped label, plain black die-cut sleeve, 1,000 only)	18
96	Mushroom TRASH 011	Stupid Girl Remixes (Todd Terry)/(Danny Saber) (CD, no inlay, 500 only; 125 distributed)	25
96	Mushroom MILK CDP	Milk (Wicked Mix)/(The Siren Mix)/(Album Version) (CD, hologram inlay)	20
96	Mushroom CDP (no cat no.)	Milk (Garbage Wicked Mix)/(Goldie Completely Trashed Mix)/ (Massive Attack Massive Mix)/(The Tricky Mix)/ (Rabbit In The Moon Utter Mix) (CD, hologram inlay)	20
98	Mushroom TRASH 16	THIS IS A PROMOTIONAL ITEM: Stupid Girl/Only Happy When It Rains/ Queer/Milk (CD, card sleeve in resealable foil bag)	18
98	Mushroom TRASH 19	VERSION 2.0 (CD/CD-ROM, stickered, embossed shaped card sleeve with insert, promo only)	18
01	Mushroom TRASH 33	PREVIOUS GARBAGE (CD sampler, card title sleeve)	20
	(see also Goodbye Mr. MacKenzine)		

GARBO
82	Rarn RARN 201	Dancing Strange/Why Don't You Call Me?/Everyday Hallucinations (p/s)	150

GARBO'S CELLULOID HEROES
78	Big Bear BB 13	Only Death Is Fatal/Won't You Come to my Funeral (p/s)	10

VIN GARBUTT
72	Trailer LER 2078	THE VALLEY OF TREES (LP, red label)	15

DIGNO GARCIA Y SUS CARIOS
61	Palette PG 9024	Brigitte Bardot/Morena	5
66	Pye 7N 17172	Guantanamera/The Bird	5

JERRY GARCIA
71	Douglas DGL 69013	HOOTEROLL? (LP, with Howard Wales)	18
72	Warner Bros K 46139	GARCIA (LP)	15
74	Round RX 59301	GARCIA (LP)	12
76	United Artists UAG 29921	REFLECTIONS (LP)	12
	(see also Grateful Dead, Diga Rhythm Band, Old & In The Way)		

RUSS GARCIA ORCHESTRA
58	London	FANTASTICA! (12" LP)	20+

GARDEN ODYSSEY (ENTERPRISE)
69	Deram DM 267	Sad And Lonely/Sky Pilot (8/M/1) (as Garden Odyssey Enterprise)	22
72	RCA RCA 2159	Joker/Have You Ever Been To Georgia (as Garden Odyssey)	6
	(see also Graham Gouldman)		

PAUL GARDINER
81	Beggars Banquet BEG 61	Stormtrooper In Drag/Night Talk (p/s)	5
84	Numa NU 1	Venus In Furs/No Sense (p/s)	5
84	Numa NUM 1	Venus In Furs (Extended Mix)/No Sense/Venus In Furs (7" Mix) (12", p/s)	10
	(see also Dramatis, Tubeway Army, Gary Numan)		

AVA GARDNER
53	MGM SP 1005	Can't Help Lovin' Dat Man/Bill	15

BORIS GARD(I)NER (& LOVE PEOPLE)
69	High Note HS 010	Lucky Is The Boy/Bobby Sox To Stockings	28
69	Doctor Bird DB 1205	Elizabethan Reggae/Hooked On A Feeling	20
69	Duke DU 21	Never My Love/The Bold One	15
70	Treasure Isle TI 7056	Hooked On A Feeling/MESSAGE: Turn Around Twice	10
70	Big Shot BI 537	Sweet Soul Special/Memories Of Love (with Love People)	10
70	Big Shot BI 538	Darkness/Watch This Music (B-side actually "Keep Out") (with Love People)	8
70	Big Shot BI 539	Hot Shot/Watch This Music (with Love People)	8
70	Dynamic DYN 404	Commanding Wife/Band Of Gold (as Boris Gardner & Happening)	6
70	Trojan TR 7753	Dynamic Pressure/Reggae Me Dis, Reggae Me Dat	6
70	Trojan TBL 121	REGGAE HAPPENING (LP)	32

DAVE GARDNER
58	Brunswick 05740	Hop Along Rock/All By Myself (B-side with Anita Kerr Singers)	30
58	Brunswick 05740	Hop Along Rock/All By Myself (B-side with Anita Kerr Singers) (78)	10

MINT VALUE £

DON GARDNER & DEE DEE FORD
62	Stateside SS 114	I Need Your Loving/Tell Me	20
62	Stateside SS 130	Don't You Worry/I'm Coming Home To Stay	20
68	Soul City SC 101	Don't You Worry/I'm Coming Home To Stay (reissue)	15

(see also Baby Washington & Don Gardner, Dee Dee Ford)

JOANNE GARDNER
70s	Polydor	JOANNE GARDNER (LP)	15

JOHNNY GARFIELD
65	Pye 7N 15758	Stranger In Paradise/Anyone Can Lose A Heart	45

(Art) GARFUNKEL
74	CBS CQ 31474/Q 69021	ANGEL CLARE (LP, quadrophonic)	12

(see also Simon & Garfunkel, Tom & Jerry)

FRANK GARI
60	London HLU 9277	I Ain't Got A Girl/Utopia	10

JUDY GARLAND
53	MGM SP 1001	A Couple Of Swells/Medley: I Love A Piano/Snooky Ookums/When The Midnight Choo Choo Leaves (with Fred Astaire)	12
56	MGM SP 1157	Look For The Silver Lining/Who?	12
57	Capitol CL 14789	Rock-a-bye Your Baby With A Dixie Melody/After You've Gone	6
57	Capitol CL 14790	I Feel A Song Coming On/Just Imagine	6
57	Capitol CL 14791	By Myself/It's Lovely To Be Back In London	6
55	Philips BBE 12012	BORN IN A TRUNK — SELECTIONS FROM A STAR IS BORN (EP)	10
56	MGM MGM-EP 568	IF YOU FEEL LIKE SINGING (EP)	10
56	MGM MGM-EP 641	EASTER PARADE — EXCERPTS (EP, with Fred Astaire & Peter Lawford)	10
56	MGM MGM-EP 672	WORDS AND MUSIC — SOUNDTRACK EXCERPTS (EP, 1 track with June Allyson & Mickey Rooney)	10
59	Capitol EAP1 1036	JUDY IN LOVE (EP)	8
59	Capitol EAP2 1036	JUDY IN LOVE (EP)	8
59	Capitol EAP3 1036	JUDY IN LOVE (EP)	8
59	Capitol EAP7 1569	JUDY AT CARNEGIE HALL (EP)	5
59	Capitol EAP8 1569	JUDY AT CARNEGIE HALL (EP)	5
60	Capitol EAP1 20051	A GARLAND FOR JUDY (EP)	5
55	Brunswick LA 8725	JUDY AT THE PALACE (10" LP)	20
55	MGM MGM-D 134	BORN TO SING (10" LP)	20
55	Philips BBL 7007	A STAR IS BORN (LP, soundtrack)	15
56	Capitol LCT 6103	MISS SHOW BUSINESS (LP)	15
57	Capitol LCT 6121	JUDY (LP)	15
57	Capitol LCT 6136	ALONE (LP)	15
59	Capitol (S)T 1036	JUDY IN LOVE (LP)	15
59	Capitol (S)T 1118	AT THE GROVE (LP)	15
59	Capitol (S)T 1188	THE LETTER (LP)	15
61	Capitol (S)T 1467	JUDY! THAT'S ENTERTAINMENT (LP, mono/stereo) each	15

(see also Fred Astaire)

RED GARLAND
59	Esquire 32-116	RED IN BLUES VILLE (LP)	30
59	Esquire 32-126	AT THE PRELUDE (LP)	25

BILLY GARNER/JACQUELINE JONES
75	Vulcan VUL1005	Tradition/Wicky Wacky	15

ERROL GARNER
60	Philips JAZ 103	Cheek To Cheek/The Way You Look Tonight (p/s)	6
60	Philips JAZ 105	Lullaby Of Birdland/Easy To Love (p/s)	6
53	Vogue LDE 034	ERROL GARNER TRIO VOLUME ONE (10" LP)	12
54	Felsted EDL 87002	MARGIE (10" LP)	12
54	Philips BBR 8002	PLAYS FOR DANCING (10" LP)	12
55	Philips BBR 8045	SOLO FLIGHT (10" LP)	12
55	Columbia 33S 1050	PIANO MOODS (10" LP)	12
55	Columbia 33S 1059	PIANO GEMS (10" LP)	12
55	Oriole MG 26042	GONE WITH GARNER (10" LP)	12
55	Felsted EDL 87015	PASSPORT TO FAME (10" LP)	12

KAY GARNER
60s	Oriole CB 1951	I Still Get Jealous/Squeeze Me	20

REGGIE GARNER
76	Capitol CL 15874	Hot Line/Blessed Be The Name Of My Baby	10

BLIND LEROY GARNET
52	Jazz Collector L 74	Chain 'Em Down/Louisiana Glide (78)	15

COL GARNET
66	Page One POF 002	With A Girl Like You/Monday Monday	13

ALF GARNETT (& FAMILY)
67	CBS 202607	All/Among My Souvenirs	6
68	Pye NPL 18192	SEX AND OTHER THOUGHTS (LP)	18

GALE GARNETT
64	RCA RCA 1418	We'll Sing In The Sunshine/Prism Song	10
65	RCA RCA 1451	I'll Cry Alone/Where Do You Go To Go Away?	60
65	RCA RD 7726	MY KIND OF FOLK SONGS (LP)	30
66	RCA RD 7750	LOVIN' PLACE	20

LAURENT GARNIER
93	Warp WAP 36	A BOUT DE SOUFFLE (12", company sleeve)	8

JESSE GARON & DESPERADOS
(see under 'J')

LIEF GARRETT
79	Scotti Brothers K 11449	Same Goes For You/Give In (p/s)	8

VERNON GARRETT
67	Stateside SS 2006	If I Could Turn Back The Hands Of Time/You And Me Together (DJ copy = £85)	40
67	Stateside SS 2026	Shine It On/Things Are Lookin' Better (DJ copy = £75)	40
68	Action ACT 4508	Shine It On/Things Are Lookin' Better (reissue)	25

DAVID GARRICK
65	Piccadilly 7N 35231	Go/When The World Was Our Own	6
65	Piccadilly 7N 35263	One Little Smile/We Must Be In Love	6
66	Piccadilly 7N 35317	Lady Jane/Let's Go Somewhere	10
66	Piccadilly 7N 35335	Dear Mrs Applebee/You're What I'm Living For	6
67	Piccadilly 7N 35371	I've Found A Love/(You Can't Hide) A Broken Heart	6
67	Piccadilly 7N 35377	A Certain Misunderstanding/I'm Looking Straight At You	6
67	Piccadilly 7N 35402	Don't Go Out In The Rain (You're Gonna Melt, Sugar)/Theme For A Wishing Heart	6
67	Pye 7N 17409	Ave Maria/Please Stay	6
67	Pye 7N 17409	Ave Maria/You Don't Know (different B-side)	6
68	Pye 7N 17509	Rainbow/I'll Be Home	7
68	Pye 7N 17610	A Little Bit Of This (And A Little Bit Of That)/Flutterby Butterfly	6
69	Pye 7N 17685	Maypole Mews/Like To Get To Know You Better	6
69	Pye 7N 17820	Poor Little Me/Molly With The Hair Like Silver	6
69	Columbia DB 8680	Bake Me A Woman/House In The Heather	8
71	Columbia DB 8784	Mary In The Morning/Beautiful People	8
67	Piccadilly NEP 34056	DAVID (EP)	30
66	Piccadilly N(S)PL 38024	A BOY CALLED DAVID (LP, mono/stereo)	20/25
67	Piccadilly N(S)PL 38035	DON'T GO OUT INTO THE RAIN, SUGAR (LP)	20

MICHAEL GARRICK
65	Argo EAF/ZFA 92	ANTHEM — MICHAEL GARRICK QUINTET (EP, mono/stereo)	50
66	Argo EAF 115	BEFORE NIGHT/DAY (EP)	50
63	Airborne	CASE OF JAZZ (LP)	65
64	Airborne	MOONSCAPE (LP)	400+
64	Argo ZDA 26/27	POETRY AND JAZZ IN CONCERT (2-LP, with Norma Winstone)	60
65	Argo (Z)DA 33	OCTOBER WOMAN (LP, as Michael Garrick Quintet, with Joe Harriott)	75
65	Argo (Z)DA 36	PROMISES (LP, as Michael Garrick Sextet, with Ian Carr)	100
68	Argo (Z)DA 88	BLACK MARIGOLDS (LP, as Michael Garrick Septet)	100
68	Airborne NBP 0021	JAZZ PRAISES AT ST. PAULS (LP)	45
69	Argo ZPR 264/5	POETRY AND JAZZ IN CONCERT 250 (2-LP, as Michael Garrick Quintet)	55
70	Argo ZDA 135	HEART IS A LOTUS (LP, as Michael Garrick Sextet with Norma Winstone)	75
72	Argo ZDA 153	COLD MOUNTAIN (LP, as Michael Garrick Trio)	120+
72	Argo ZDA 154	HOME STRETCH BLUES (LP, as Michael Garrick Band with Norma Winstone)	120+
73	Impulse AS 49	ILLUMINATION (LP, as Michael Garrick Sextet)	25
74	Argo ZDA 163	TROPPO (LP)	60
81	Hep Records HEP2011	YOU'VE CHANGED (LP)	20

(see also Ian Carr, Norma Winstone, Joe Harriott, Garrick's Fairground)

GARRICK'S FAIRGROUND
71	Argo AFW 105	Epiphany/Blessed Are The Peacemakers	10
72	Argo ZAGF 1	MR. SMITH'S APOCALYPSE (LP)	70

(see also Michael Garrick)

FREDDIE GARRITY
68	Columbia DB 8348	Little Red Donkey/So Many Different Ways	8
74	Bus Stop BUS 1017	Hello Kids/It's Good For You	8
74	Bus Stop BUS 1022	The Chicken Song/Pooh Pooh Pooh	8
70	Starline SRS 5019	OLIVER IN THE OVERWORLD (LP, soundtrack)	20

(see also Freddie & Dreamers)

ROBIN GARSIDE & PAUL GOUGH
77	Northern Sound NSR 01	SEA SONGS (LP)	15

ROBIN GARTON & HIS BAND
58	Martello MC 100	Topsy/Jump For Me	5

REX GARVIN & MIGHTY CRAVERS
66	Atlantic 584 028	Sock It To 'Em J.B. (Parts 1 & 2)	20
67	Atlantic 584 097	I Gotta Go Now (Up On The Floor)/Believe It Or Not	22

JOHN GARY
59	Top Rank JAR 177	Let Them Talk/Tell My Love (78 rpm = £12)	10
60	Top Rank JAR 392	Little Things Mean A Lot/Ever Since I Met Lucy	7

GARY & ARIELS
64	Fontana TF 476	Say You Love Me/Town Girl	12

(see also Garry Mills)

GARY & STU
72	Carnaby 6151 003	Sweet White Dove/Good Lady Fair	12
72	Carnaby 6302 012	HARLAN FARE (LP)	38

(see also Koobas, March Hare)

GAS
80	Polydor POSP 192	It Shows In Your Face/Tomorrow (p/s)	35
81	Polydor POSP 264	Ignore Me/Do It, Don't Tell Me (p/s)	20
81	Polydor POSP 296	Treatment/That's It (12", p/s)	30
81	Polydor POSP 344	The Finger/Knock It Down (p/s)	25
81	Polydor POLE 1052	EMOTIONAL WARFARE (LP)	20

GASKIN
81	Rondelet ROUND 7	I'm No Fool/Sweet Dream Maker (p/s)	25
82	Rondelet ROUND 21	Mony Mony/Queen Of Hams (p/s)	18
81	Rondelet ABOUT 4	END OF THE WORLD (LP, gatefold sleeve)	25
82	Rondelet ABOUT 8	NO WAY OUT (LP, with inner)	20

GASLIGHT
70	SDE 32732	GASLIGHT (2-LP, private pressing, gatefold sleeve with inserts, 2nd disc by Gaslight Choir)	75

GASS
65	Parlophone R 5344	One Of These Days/I Don't Know Why	15
66	Parlophone R 5456	The New Breed/In The City	35
67	CBS 202647	Dream Baby (How Long Must I Dream?)/Jitterbug Sid	20
71	Polydor 2058 147	Something's Got To Change Your Ways/Mr Banana	6
70	Polydor 2383 022	JUJU (LP, featuring Peter Green)	50
71	Polydor 2383 035	CATCH MY SOUL — THE ROCK-OTHELLO (LP, cast recording featuring Gass)	20

(see also Hummingbird, Humble Pie)

GASS COMPANY
68	President PT 170	Everybody Needs Love/Nightmare	40

(see also Wake)

GAS WORKS
73	Regal Zonophone RZ 3075	Standing Stiff/Keep On Rolling	6
73	Regal Zonophone RZ 3080	God's Great Spaceship/Cider With Rosie	6
73	Regal Zono. SRLZ 1036	GAS WORKS (LP)	18

DAVID GATES
60	Top Rank JAR 504	The Happiest Man Alive/The Road That Leads To Love	40
73	Elektra K 42150	DAVID GATES — FIRST (LP)	15

(see also Bread)

PEARLY GATES
74	Polydor 2058 443	Johnny And The Juke-Box/They Were Good Times	6
78	Bronze BRO 61	Burnin' Love (Parts 1 & 2)	5

(see also Flirtations, Gypsies)

RAY GATES
66	Decca F 12502	It's Such A Shame/Have You Ever Had The Blues	40

REV. J.M. GATES
50s	Square M3	Need Of Prayer/Death's Black Train Is Coming (78)	10

GATES OF EDEN
66	Pye 7N 17195	Too Much On My Mind/I'm Warning You	18
67	Pye 7N 17252	In Your Love/Snoopy Versus The Red Baron	12
67	Pye 7N 17278	1 To 7/Hey Now	24

GATEWAY SINGERS
57	Brunswick LAT 8176	PUTTIN' ON THE STYLE (LP)	18

GATHERERS
73	Duke DU 153	Words Of My Mouth/UPSETTERS: Version	40

LUCHO GATICA
54	Parlophone CMSP 16	Besame Mucho/Las Muchachas De La Plaza De Espana (export issue)	9

GATOR CREEK
71	Mercury 6052 058	Danny's Song/Take A Look	6
71	Mercury 6338 035	GATOR CREEK (LP)	15

DICK GAUGHAN
72	Trailer LER 2072	NO MORE FOREVER (LP, red label)	15

GEORGES GAVARENTZ
69	Philips SBL 7898	THEY CAME TO ROB LAS VEGAS (LP, soundtrack)	80

JIMMY GAVIN
57	London HLU 8478	I Sit In My Window/Lonely Chair	85
57	London HLU 8478	I Sit In My Window/Lonely Chair (78)	22

JOHNNY GAVOTTE
60	Parlophone R 4631	It's Not Too Late/Can't Forget	10

ELAINE GAY
54	Parlophone MSP 6140	Love/Instantly	12
55	Parlophone R 3997	Rock Love/Ebony Eyes (78)	10

MAC GAYDEN
73	EMI EMA 760	McGAVOCK GAYDEN (LP)	20

(see also Area Code 615)

BILLY GAYE & GAYTONES
73	Waverley SLP 501	Oh Honey Love Me/I'll Never Say Never Again	5

MARVIN GAYE
63	Oriole CBA 1803	Stubborn Kind Of Fellow/It Hurt Me Too	125
63	Oriole CBA 1846	Pride And Joy/One Of These Days	125
63	Stateside SS 243	Can I Get A Witness?/I'm Crazy 'Bout My Baby	50
64	Stateside SS 284	You're A Wonderful One/When I'm Alone I Cry	45
64	Stateside SS 326	Try It Baby/If My Heart Could Sing	40
64	Stateside SS 360	How Sweet It Is (To Be Loved By You)/Forever	40
65	Tamla Motown TMG 510	I'll Be Doggone/You've Been A Long Time Coming	45
65	Tamla Motown TMG 524	Pretty Little Baby/Now That You've Won Me	40
65	Tamla Motown TMG 539	Ain't That Peculiar?/She's Got To Be Real	25
66	Tamla Motown TMG 552	One More Heartache/When I Had Your Love	30

Marvin GAYE

66	Tamla Motown TMG 563	Take This Heart Of Mine/Need Your Lovin' (Want You Back)	30
66	Tamla Motown TMG 574	Little Darlin' (I Need You)/Hey Diddle Diddle	30
67	Tamla Motown TMG 618	Your Unchanging Love/I'll Take Care Of You	25
68	Tamla Motown TMG 640	You/Change What You Can	20
68	Tamla Motown TMG 676	Chained/At Last (I Found A Love)	20
69	Tamla Motown TMG 686	I Heard It Through The Grapevine/Need Somebody	8
69	Tamla Motown TMG 705	Too Busy Thinking 'Bout My Baby/Wherever I Lay My Hat	7
69	Tamla Motown TMG 718	That's The Way Love Is/Gonna Keep On Tryin' Till I Win Your Love	7
70	Tamla Motown TMG 734	Abraham, Martin And John/How Can I Forget?	8
71	Tamla Motown TMG 775	What's Going On?/God Is Love	6
71	Tamla Motown TMG 796	Save The Children/Little Darling (I Need You)	8
72	Tamla Motown TMG 802	Mercy Mercy Me/Bad Tomorrows	6
72	Tamla Motown TMG 817	Inner City Blues/Wholly Holy	10
73	Tamla Motown TMG 846	Trouble Man/Don't Mess With Mister 'T'	12
74	Tamla Motown TMG 882	Come Get To This/Distant Lover	15
66	Tamla Motown TME 2016	MARVIN GAYE (EP)	75
67	Tamla Motown TME 2019	ORIGINALS FROM MARVIN GAYE (EP)	55
64	Stateside SL 10100	MARVIN GAYE (LP)	250
65	Tamla Motown TML 11004	HOW SWEET IT IS TO BE LOVED BY YOU (LP)	100
65	Tamla Motown TML 11015	HELLO BROADWAY (LP)	100
66	T. Motown (S)TML 11022	A TRIBUTE TO THE GREAT NAT KING COLE (LP, mono/stereo)	75/100
66	T. Motown (S)TML 11033	MOODS OF MARVIN GAYE (LP, mono/stereo)	75/100
68	T. Motown (S)TML 11065	MARVIN GAYE'S GREATEST HITS (LP, mono/stereo)	30/20
69	T. Motown (S)TML 11091	IN THE GROOVE (LP)	40
69	T. Motown (S)TML 11119	M.P.G. (LP)	30
69	T. Motown (S)TML 11123	MARVIN GAYE AND HIS GIRLS (LP, with T. Terrell, M. Wells & K. Weston)	30
70	T. Motown (S)TML 11136	THAT'S THE WAY LOVE IS (LP)	25
71	Tamla Motown STML 11190	WHAT'S GOING ON? (LP, initially with lyric sheet)	18/12
72	Tamla Motown STML 11201	THE HITS OF MARVIN GAYE (LP)	12
73	Tamla Motown STML 11225	TROUBLE MAN (LP, soundtrack)	20
78	Tamla Motown TMSP 6008	HERE, MY DEAR (2-LP)	20
76	Tamla Motown STML 12025	I WANT YOU (LP)	12

MARVIN GAYE & TAMMI TERRELL

67	Tamla Motown TMG 611	Ain't No Mountain High Enough/Give A Little Love	18
67	Tamla Motown TMG 625	Your Precious Love/Hold Me Oh My Darling	15
67	Tamla Motown TMG 635	If I Could Build My Whole World Around You/If This World Were Mine	12
68	Tamla Motown TMG 655	Ain't Nothin' Like The Real Thing/Little Ole Boy, Little Ole Girl	8
68	Tamla Motown TMG 668	You're All I Need To Get By/Two Can Have A Party	7
69	Tamla Motown TMG 681	You Ain't Livin' Till You're Lovin'/Oh How I'd Miss You	8
69	Tamla Motown TMG 697	Good Lovin' Ain't Easy To Come By/Satisfied Feelin'	7
69	Tamla Motown TMG 715	The Onion Song/I Can't Believe You Love Me (demos in p/s £40)	5
68	T. Motown (S)TML 11062	UNITED (LP)	45
68	T. Motown (S)TML 11084	YOU'RE ALL I NEED (LP)	38
70	T. Motown (S)TML 11132	EASY (LP)	25
70	T. Motown (S)TML 11153	GREATEST HITS (LP)	15

MARVIN GAYE & MARY WELLS

64	Stateside SS 316	Once Upon A Time/What's The Matter With You, Baby?	25
64	Stateside SL 10097	TOGETHER (LP)	125

MARVIN GAYE & KIM WESTON

64	Stateside SS 363	What Good Am I Without You?/I Want You Around	25
67	Tamla Motown TMG 590	It Takes Two/It's Got To Be A Miracle (This Thing Called Love)	15
67	T. Motown (S)TML 11049	TAKE TWO (LP, mono/stereo)	50/60

(see also Diana Ross, Tammi Terrell, Mary Wells, Kim Weston)

GAYLADS

64	R&B JB 159	There'll Come A Day/BILLY COOKE: Iron Bar	28
64	R&B JB 165	What Is Wrong With Me?/Whap Whap	25
66	Island WI 281	Goodbye Daddy/Your Eyes	28
66	Island WI 291	You Never Leave Him/Message To My Girl	25
66	Island WI 3002	Stop Making Love/They Call Her Dawn	20
66	Doctor Bird DB 1014	Lady With The Red Dress/Dinner For Two	15
66	Doctor Bird DB 1031	You Should Never Do That/WINSTON STEWART: I Don't Know Why I Love You	25
66	Rymska RA 104	You Should Never Do That/TECHNIQUES: So Many Times	25
67	Island WI 3022	Don't Say No/SONNY BURKE: You Rule My Heart	22
67	Island WI 3025	You No Good Girl/Yes Girl	22
67	Studio One SO 2002	Tears From My Eyes/Never Let Your Country Down	30
67	Studio One SO 2013	I Am Going To Cool It (actually by Little Roy)/MELODIANS: Let's Join Together	45
67	Studio One SO 2017	Love Me With All Your Heart/I Don't Care	30
67	Rio R 125	Put On Your Style/SOUL BROTHERS: Soul Serenade	22
68	Blue Cat BS 110	Go Away/SOUL VENDORS: Julie On My Mind	30
68	Doctor Bird DB 1124	It's Hard To Confess/I Need Your Loving	25
68	Doctor Bird DB 1145	She Want It/Joy In The Morning	23
68	Fab FAB 62	Looking For A Girl/Aren't You The Guy	30
68	Hi Note HS 001	A B C Rocksteady/LESLIE BUTLER & COUNT OSSIE: Soul Drums	22
69	Trojan TR 688	You Had Your Chance/Wha' She Do Now	12
69	Upsetter US 323	The Same Things/I Wear My Slanders	15
70	Trojan TR 7703	There's A Fire/Last Time	7
70	Trojan TR 7738	That's What Love Will Do/This Time I Won't Hurt You	9
70	Trojan TR 7743	Young, Gifted And Black/BEVERLEY'S ALLSTARS: Moon Glow	9
70	Trojan TR 7763	Tell The Children The Truth/Something Is Wrong Somewhere	7
70	Trojan TR 7771	Soul Sister/BEVERLEY'S ALLSTARS: Soul Version	7
70	Trojan TR 7782	It's All In The Game/BEVERLEY'S ALLSTARS: Version II	7

70	Trojan TR 7799	Fire And Rain/Cold And Lonely Night 6
71	Ackee AC 141	Accept My Apologies (actually by B.B. Seaton & Ken Boothe)/
		My Version (actually by Conscious Minds) 6
71	Big BG 319	Can't Hide The Feeling/RUPIE EDWARDS ALLSTARS: Version 6
71	Camel CA 79	Seven In One Medley (Parts 1 & 2) 6
71	Summit SUM 8514	My Jamaican Girl/BEVERLEY'S ALLSTARS: Version 6
71	Bullet BU 462	My Love/Stranger Love 7
74	Dip DL 5009	You Made A Mistake/Shower Of Blessings 6
67	Coxsone CSL 8005	ROCKSTEADY (LP) 110
67	Coxsone CSL 8006	SUNSHINE IS GOLDEN (LP) 75

(see also Gaylords, Rockstones, Delano Stewart, Ken Boothe, B.B. Seaton, Brent Dowe, Dobby Dobson, Jackie Mittoo, Heptones, Clarendonians, Soul Vendors)

VINLEY GAYLE
| 64 | Black Swan WI 453 | Go-Go/BABA BROOKS: Take Five . . . . 22 |

GAYLET(T)S
68	Island WI 3129	Silent River Runs Deep/You're My Kind Of Man 22
68	Island WI 3141	I Like Your World/Lonely Feeling 22
68	Big Shot BI 502	If You Can't Be Good/Something About My Man 12
69	Big Shot BI 516	Son-Of-A-Preacher-Man/That's How Strong My Love Is 12
70	London HLJ 10302	Son-Of-A-Preacher-Man/I Like Your World 7

(see also Bob Andy)

GAYLORDS (U.S.)
| 55 | Mercury MB 3226 | Mambo Rock/Plantation Boogie (78) . . . . 8 |
| 60 | Mercury MMC 14032 | THAT'S AMORE (LP) . . . . 12 |

GAYLORDS (Jamaica)
| 66 | Island WI 269 | Chipmunk Ska/What Is Wrong? (both actually by Gaylads) . . . . 25 |

(see also Gaylads)

GAYLORDS (U.K.)
| 66 | Columbia DB 7805 | He's A Good Face But He's Down And Out/You Know It Too . . . . 20 |

(see also Dean Ford & Gaylords, Marmalade)

WILTON 'BOGEY' GAYNAIR QUARTET
| 61 | Tempo EXA 103 | BLUE BOGEY VOLUME ONE (EP) . . . . 60 |
| 59 | Tempo TAP 25 | BLUE BOGEY (LP) . . . . 250+ |

GAYNOR (Junior English) & ERROL (Dunkley)
| 65 | Blue Beat BB 286 | My Queen/ROLAND ALPHONSO: Roland Plays Prince |
| | | (B-side actually "Hanging The Beam" by Skatalites) . . . . 50 |

(see also Errol Dunkley)

GLORIA GAYNOR
| 78 | Polydor 2066922 | For The First Time In My Life/This Love Affair . . . . 40 |

MEL GAYNOR
55	Decca F 10497	Just A Man/How Important Can It Be? 7
55	Decca F 10542	With You Beside Me/Oh, My Love 7
55	Decca F 10618	Bella Notte/Sweet Kentucky Rose 7

(see also Oscar Rabin)

MITZI GAYNOR
59	Top Rank JAR 258	Happy Anniversary/Play For Keeps 5
60	Top Rank JAR 289	I Don't Regret A Thing/The Touch Of Time 5
58	HMV 7EG 8460	MITZI (EP) 10

ROSEMARY GAYNOR
| 55 | Columbia SCM 5196 | Ain't That A Shame/A Happy Song . . . . 12 |

PAUL GAYTEN
| 57 | London HL 8503 | Yo, Yo, Walk/TUNE WEAVERS: Happy Happy Birthday Baby (78 rpm = £45) . . . . 200 |
| 59 | London HLM 8998 | The Hunch/Hot Cross Buns (78 rpm = £40) . . . . 150 |

GAYTONES (Jamaica)
70	High Note HS 037	Target (actually "Musical Fight" by Crashers)/PATSY: Find Someone
		(song actually "True Love") 18
70	High Note HS 048	Ten To One/Another Version 9
71	High Note HS 055	Heart Of The Knights/One Toke Over The Line (B-side actually by
		Stranger & Gladdy) 15
71	Green Door GD 4016	Jamaican Hilite (Parts 1 & 2) 8
73	Smash SMA 2330	Blackman Kingdom Come/Swing And Dine (B-side actually by Melodians) 8

(see also Righteous Flames, Max Romeo, Ethiopians, Jackie Brown, Jean & Gaytones, Huxbrown & Scotty, Charlie Ace, Delano Stewart, Teddy & Conquerors)

GAYTONES (U.S.)
| 73 | Action ACT 4610 | Soul Makossa/Soul Makossa (Version) . . . . 16 |

GBH
82	Clay CLAY 8	No Survivors/Self Destruct/Big Women (p/s) 6
82	Clay CLAY 11	Sick Boy/Slit Your Own Throat/Am I Dead Yet? (p/s) 6
82	Clay CLAY 16	Give Me Fire/Mantrap (p/s) 8
82	Clay CLAY 16P	Give Me Fire/Mantrap (picture disc) 10
83	Clay CLAY 22	Catch 23/Hellhole (p/s) 8
84	Clay CLAY 36	Do What You Do/Four Men (p/s) 8
82	Clay CLAYLP 4	CITY BABY ATTACKED BY RATS (LP) 20

G-CLEFS
56	Columbia DB 3851	Ka-Ding Dong/Darla, My Darlin' (78 rpm = £40) 750
61	London HLU 9433	I Understand/Little Girl I Love You 5
62	London HLU 9530	A Girl Has To Know/(There Never Was A Dog Like) Dad 15
62	London HLU 9563	Make Up Your Mind/Call Me Away 15

GEDDES AXE
80	ACS ACS 1	Return Of The Gods/Wildfire/Aftermath (p/s, with insert)	20
81	Steel City AXE 1	Sharpen Your Wits/Rock 'N' Roll (p/s)	50
82	Bullet BOLT 4	Escape From New York/Day The Wells Ran Dry/Six Six Six (12", p/s)	8

MARSHA GEE
80s	Joker JK 001	The Peanut Duck/ENCHANTMENTS: I'm In Love With Your Daughter/ H.B. BARNUM: It Hurts Too Much Too Cry	10

ROY GEE
70	J-Dan JDN 4412	Consider Me/You Walked Away	8
70	J-Dan JDN 4413	Try To Understand/I'd Rather Go Blind	7

RON GEESIN
65	RRG 319/320	RON GEESIN (EP, handmade p/s, 100 only)	80
67	Transatlantic (S)TRA 161	A RAISE OF EYEBROWS (LP)	50
72	KPM KPM 1102	ELECTROSOUND (LP, library issue, 1,000 only)	50
73	Ron Geesin RON 28	AS HE STANDS (LP)	15
75	KPM KPM 1154	ELECTROSOUND VOL. 2 (LP, library issue, 1,000 only)	50
75	Ron Geesin RON 31	PATRUNS (LP)	15
77	Ron Geesin RON 323	RIGHT THROUGH (LP)	15
77	KPM KPM 1201	ATMOSPHERES (LP, library issue, 1,000 only)	50

(see also Bridget St. John, Pink Floyd, Original Downtown Syncopators, Amory Kane)

RON GEESIN & ROGER WATERS
70	Harvest SHSP 4008	MUSIC FROM THE BODY (LP, soundtrack; initially green labels with Waters/Geesin photos)	22

(see also Roger Waters, Pink Floyd)

HERB GELLER QUARTET
56	London RE-U 1067	SENSATIONAL SAX OF HERB GELLER (EP)	12

GEMAGE
80	private pressing BGA 1	Story So Far/Bring Me Death (no p/s)	50

GEMINI (Portugal)
78	Philips 6031 070	Dal-Li-Dou (Falling In Love)/Dal-Li-Dou	12

GEMINI (U.K.)
65	Columbia DB 7638	Space Walk/Goodbye Joe (demos may credit the 'Original Tornados')	45

(see also Tornados)

GEMINI (U.K.)
69	President PT 257	Never Say Die/Something Special	6

GEMINI (U.K.)
81	Airship AP 345	COUNTER BALANCE (LP)	60

GENE
94	Costermonger COST 1	For The Dead/Child's Body (p/s, 1,994 numbered copies only)	25
94	Costermonger COST 2	Be My Light, Be My Guide/This Is Not My Crime (numbered p/s)	12

GENE & DEBBE
67	London HLE 10165	Go With Me/Torch I Carry	8
68	London HLE 10179	Playboy/I'll Come Running	12
68	London HLE 10203	Lovin' Season/Love Will Give Us Wings	8

GENE & EUNICE
56	Vogue V 9062	I Gotta Go Home/Have You Changed Your Mind? (78 rpm = £55)	180
57	Vogue V 9066	Move It Over, Baby/This Is My Story (78 rpm = £60)	155
57	Vogue V 9071	Let's Get Together/I'm So In Love With You (78 rpm = £60)	155
57	Vogue V 9083	Doodle Doodle Doo/Don't Treat Me This Way (78 rpm = £65)	155
58	Vogue V 9106	I Mean Love/The Angels Gave You To Me (78 rpm = £65)	155
58	Vogue V 9126	Strange World/The Vow (78 rpm = £70)	50

(The above 45s were originally issued with triangular centres; later issues with round centres are worth about half the values listed.)

59	Vogue V 9136	Bom Bom Lulu/Hi Diddle Diddle (78 rpm = £95)	100
59	London HL 8956	Poco-Loco/Go-On Kokomo (78 rpm = £120)	48

GENE & GENTS
68	Pye 7N 17532	C'mon Everybody/Hound Dog	7

GENE & JERRY
71	Mercury 6052 050	You Just Can't Win/Sho' Is Groovin'	8
71	Mercury 6052 087	Everybody Is Waiting/Ten And Two	8
71	Mercury 6338 051	ONE AND ONE (LP)	18

(see also Gene Chandler, Jerry Butler)

GENE LOVES JEZEBEL
82	Situation 2 SIT 18T	Shavin' My Neck/Sun & Insanity/Machismo/Glad To Be Alive (12", p/s)	12
82	Situation 2 SIT 20	Screaming (For Emaline) (p/s)	12
82	Situation 2 SIT 24	Bruises/Punch Drunk (p/s)	8

GENERAL JOHNSON
(see under 'J')

GENERAL STRIKE
79	Canal CANAL 01	Part 1: My Body/Part 2: (Parts Of) My Body (p/s)	5

GENERAL WOLF
86	SRT SRT 6KS 1085	I Believe In Love/Take A Dream (p/s)	8

GENERATION GAP
69	Pye 7N 17845	She's Coming Home/Reach The Top	6
70	Pye 7N 17979	Any Old Time You're Lonely And Sad/Rainbows 'N' Sorrows	6

GENERATION X

77	Generation X GX 101	Your Generation/Listen! (white label test pressing, official bootleg sold at gigs, no p/s)	50
77	Chrysalis CHS 2165	Your Generation/Day By Day (p/s, original copies with 'A' on label have band credits on front)	6/5
77	Chrysalis CHS 2165	Your Generation/Day By Day (sleeve only, unissued, featuring 'pre-peroxide' Billy Idol; 1 copy known to exist)	500
77	Chrysalis CHS 2189	Wild Youth/Wild Dub (Version) (p/s)	8
77	Chrysalis CHS 2189	Wild Youth/Wild Dub (Version) (p/s, mispressing, plays "No No No", B-side matrix: CHS 2189 B/1)	30
78	Chrysalis CHS 2207	Ready Steady Go/No No No (p/s)	5
79	Chrysalis CHS(A) 2261	King Rocker/Gimme Some Truth (pink vinyl, Tony James p/s)	8
79	Chrysalis CHS(B) 2261	King Rocker/Gimme Some Truth (red vinyl, Billy Idol p/s)	6
79	Chrysalis CHS(C) 2261	King Rocker/Gimme Some Truth (yellow vinyl, Mark Laff p/s)	10
79	Chrysalis CHS(D) 2261	King Rocker/Gimme Some Truth (orange vinyl, Bob Andrews p/s)	8
79	Chrysalis CHS 2261	King Rocker/Gimme Some Truth (black vinyl, Bob Andrews p/s)	6
79	Chrysalis CHS 2310	Valley Of The Dolls/Shakin' All Over (p/s, marbled brown vinyl)	8
79	Chrysalis CHS 2330	Friday's Angels/Trying For Kicks/This Heat (p/s, red or black vinyl)	8/25
81	Chrysalis CHS 2488	Dancing With Myself/Untouchables/King Rocker/Rock On (as Gen X, p/s, some on clear vinyl)	18/8
78	Chrysalis CHR 1169	GENERATION X (LP, with 'T-shirt offer' wraparound)	35

(see also Billy Idol, Sigue Sigue Sputnik, Empire, Westworld)

GENERATOR (featuring Gary Numan)

94	JVO JVOT 001	Are 'Friends' Electric? (Eccentric Mix)/Bring Back The Love/Going Home (12", p/s)	8
94	JVO JVO 001	Are 'Friends' Electric? (Radio Mix)/Are 'Friends' Electric? (Eccentric Mix)/Bring Back The Love/Going Home (CD)	8

(see also Gary Numan)

GENESIS
SINGLES

68	Decca F 12735	The Silent Sun/That's Me (promos £325)	350
68	Decca F 12775	A Winter's Tale/One Eyed Hound (promos £350)	375
69	Decca F 12949	Where The Sour Turns To Sweet/In Hiding (promos £375)	400
70	Charisma GS 1/2	Looking For Someone/Visions Of Angels (promo only)	600
71	Charisma CB 152	The Knife (Parts 1 & 2) (some in p/s)	450/100
72	Charisma CB 181	Happy The Man/Seven Stones (some belated copies in p/s; beware counterfeits) (promos £150)	450/100
73	Charisma (no cat. no.)	Twilight Alehouse (1-sided flexidisc free with *Zig Zag* & later via fan club, [black vinyl, white label test pressings exist — £70] with/without magazine)	35/20
74	Charisma CB 224	I Know What I Like (In Your Wardrobe)/Twilight Alehouse (promos with press release £95)	8
74	Charisma CB 238	Counting Out Time/Riding The Scree	8
74	Charisma CB 238	Counting Out Time/Counting Out Time (promo)	60
75	Charisma CB 251	The Carpet Crawlers/Evil Jam ("The Waiting Room" live) (promos £65)	25
76	Charisma CB 277	A Trick Of The Tail/Ripples (purple label)	8
77	Charisma CB 300	Your Own Special Way/It's Yourself	6
78	Charisma CB 309	Follow You, Follow Me/Ballad Of Big (p/s)	5
78	Charisma CB 315	Many Too Many/The Day The Light Went Out/Vancouver (p/s)	8
80	Charisma CB 369	Misunderstanding/Evidence Of Autumn (p/s)	8
81	Charisma CB 39	Keep It Dark/Naminanu (p/s)	5
81	Charisma CB 391-12	Keep It Dark/Naminanu/Abacab (Long Version) (12", p/s)	8
82	Charisma CB 393	Man On The Corner/Submarine (blue label, some with p/s)	100/5
82	Charisma GEN 1	3 X 3 (Paperlate/You Might Recall/Me And Virgil) (EP, picture disc)	7
82	Lyntone LYN 11806	The Lady Lies (live) (green flexidisc free with *Flexipop* mag, issue 21)	12/7
83	Lyntone LYN 13143	Firth Of Fifth (live edit) (flexidisc, some with numbered gatefold p/s)	20/5
83	Charisma/Virgin TATA Y-1	That's All/Taking It All Too Hard (shaped picture disc)	20
84	Charisma/Virgin ALS 1	Illegal Alien/Turn It On Again (live) (shaped picture disc)	20
84	Charisma/Virgin CB 300	Your Own Special Way/It's Yourself (blue label reissue, no p/s)	6
84	Charisma/Virgin CB 356	Turn It On Again/Behind The Lines Part 2 (blue label reissue, no p/s)	6
84	Charisma/Virgin CB 369	Misunderstanding/Evidence Of Autumn (blue label reissue, no p/s)	6
86	Charisma/Virgin GENSY 1	Invisible Touch/The Last Domino (clear vinyl, foldout p/s)	6
86	Charisma/Virgin GENSY 2-12	In Too Deep (Unedited)/Do The Neurotic (Unedited) (12" picture disc in stickered sleeve)	10
86	Virgin SNEG 3-12	Land Of Confusion/Land Of Confusion (Extended)/Feeding The Fire/Do The Neurotic (CD, gatefold p/s)	10
87	Virgin GENSG 412	Tonight, Tonight, Tonight (Edit)/In The Glow Of The Night/Paperlate/Tonight, Tonight, Tonight (12" Remix) (12", gatefold p/s)	8
87	Virgin CDEP 1	Tonight, Tonight, Tonight (Edit)/In The Glow Of The Night/Invisible Touch (12" Remix)/Tonight, Tonight, Tonight (CD, gatefold p/s)	65
87	Virgin GENS 512	Throwing It All Away (live)/I'd Rather Be You/Invisible Touch (live) (12", p/s)	8
88	Virgin CDT 5	Mama (Long Version)/It's Gonna Get Better (Long Version) (3" CD, card p/s)	8
88	Charisma/Virgin CDT 40	SPOT THE PIGEON EP (Match Of The Day/Pigeons/Inside And Out) (3" CD, card sleeve)	15
88	Charisma/Virgin CDF 40	SPOT THE PIGEON EP (Match Of The Day/Pigeons/Inside And Out) (5" export CD, card sleeve)	20
89	Virgin VVD 359	Domino: (Part 1) In The Glow Of The Night/(Part 2) The Last Domino (3" CD free with "Invisible Touch Tour" video)	20
92	Virgin GENDG 8	Hold On My Heart/Way Of The World/Your Own Special Way (live) (CD, digipak with 4 postcards)	8
92	Virgin GENDX 9	Jesus He Knows Me (Single Mix)/Hearts On Fire/Land Of Confusion (Rehearsal Version) (CD, 'Invisible Series' box set w/ space for other CDs)	10
92	Virgin GENS 10	Invisible Touch (live)/Abacab (live) (no'd gatefold p/s)	8

MINT VALUE £

92	Virgin GENDX 10	Invisible Touch (live)/Abacab (live)/The Brazilian (live) (CD, numbered box with booklet)	10
98	Virgin GENCDJ 6	CALLING ALL STATIONS (CD, 7-track sampler, promo only)	8
98	Virgin SOLO2	Live Rehearsal: Mama (live)/Calling All Stations (live)/Invisible Touch (live)/ Follow You, Follow Me (live)/Turn It On Again (live) (CD 5-track promo)	80+
99	Virgin SAMPGEN 8	TURN IT ON AGAIN (CD, 3-track sampler, promo only)	10

LPs

69	Decca LK 4990	FROM GENESIS TO REVELATION (mono, with lyric sheet, unboxed logo)	750
69	Decca SKL 4990	FROM GENESIS TO REVELATION (stereo, with lyric sheet, unboxed logo)	270
70	Decca SKL 4990	FROM GENESIS TO REVELATION (stereo, with lyric sheet, boxed logo)	75
70	Decca KSKC 4990	FROM GENESIS TO REVELATION (cassette tape, boxed logo)	35
70	Charisma CAS 1020	TRESPASS (original pink scroll label & gatefold sleeve with lyric sheet)	85
71	Charisma CAS 1052	NURSERY CRYME (original pink scroll label, gatefold sleeve)	75
72	Charisma CAS 1052	NURSERY CRYME (2nd pressing, 'tour' label, gatefold sleeve, only 3 copies known to exist)	550
74	Decca SKL 4990	IN THE BEGINNING (reissue of 1st LP, 'snake' sleeve with lyric insert)	25
75	Charisma CGS 102	GENESIS COLLECTION VOLUME ONE (2-LP, boxed set of "Trespass" & "Nursery Cryme" in original sleeves, with poster)	110
75	Charisma CGS 103	GENESIS COLLECTION VOLUME TWO (2-LP, boxed set of "Foxtrot" & "Selling England By The Pound", with poster)	110
91	Virgin DJG CD 3	We Can't Dance (CD, pre-release promo)	20
91	Virgin Edits 1	We Can't Dance (CD, 6 track promo – tour edition marketed by Volkswagon)	80
91	Virgin GEN CD	We Can't Dance (CD & cassette tape, housed in custom promo box With three hand numbered watercolours)	110
93	Virgin GENBOX1	Live: The Way We Walk (2xCD in wooden box with certificate & badge (1000 only)	160
97	Virgin GENLP6	Calling All Stations (2xLP fourth sided no tracks but etched with band picture)	18
97	Virgin GENCDJ6	Calling All Stations (CD, 7-track promo album sampler)	12
97	Virgin GENCDP6	Calling All Stations (CD, in store play copy, card p/s)	15
98	Virgin CDBOX6	Genesis Archive 1967 - 975 (4 CD Box Set)	35
98	Virgin CDBOX98	Genesis Archive 1967 - 1975 (CD 12-track promo digipack)	35
98	Virgin VCDJBOX98	Genesis Archive 1967 - 1975 The Interviews (2xCD promo, p/s)	100
99	Virgin VGP 000270	Turn It On again – The Hits (CD, in store promo p/s – each song played for 1 min)	65
00	Virgin CDBOX7	Genesis Archive 2: 1976 – 1992 (3xCD Box Set)	30
00	Virgin CDBCXDJ7	Genesis Archive 2: 1976 – 1992 (CD, 12-track promo)	15

(see also Flaming Youth, Phil Collins, Mike Rutherford, Peter Gabriel, Steve Hackett, Anthony Phillips, Brand X, Quiet World)

GENEVA
80	Valiant ROUND1	2.30/Geneva Street (p/s)	10

GENEVEVE
66	CBS 202061	Once/Just A Whisper (some in p/s)	20
66	CBS 202096	Nothing In The World/Summer Days	9
67	CBS 202524	That Can't Be Bad/I Love Him, I Need Him	9

GENGHIS KHAN (Germany)
79	CBS 12-7317	Genghis Khan/Desert Land (12", clear vinyl with p/s insert)	8

GENGHIS KHAN (U.K.)
83	Genghis Khan GK 1	DOUBLE DEALIN' (If Heaven Is Hell/Highway Passion//Midnight Rendezvous Mean Streak) (EP, double pack)	80
83	Wabbit WAB 61/63	Love You/Lady Lady//Mongol Nation/Gone For A Drive (double pack)	40

GENOCIDE
79	Safari SAP 2	IMAGES OF DELUSION (EP)	8

GENTILES (U.K.)
68	Pye 7N 17530	Goodbye Baby/Marlena	8

GENTILES (Jamaica)
70	High Note HS 046	Your Destiny/Lock Love Away (actually by Melodians)	12

(see also Melodians)

JOHNNY GENTLE
59	Philips PB 908	Wendy/Boys And Girls (Were Meant For Each Other) (78 rpm = £10)	15
59	Philips PB 945	Milk From The Coconut/I Like The Way (78 rpm = £15)	10
60	Philips PB 988	Darlin' Won't You Wait/This Friendly World	9
60	Philips PB 1069	After My Laughter Came Tears/Sonja	8
61	Philips PB 1142	Pick A Star/Darlin'	8
59	Philips BBE 12345	THE GENTLE TOUCH (EP)	65

(see also Darren Young)

TIM GENTLE & HIS GENTLEMEN
65	Oriole CB 1988	Without You/Someone's In The Kitchen With Dinah	15

GENTLE GIANT
73	WWA WWP 1001	In A Glass House/An Inmate's Lullaby	12
74	WWA WWS 017	The Power And The Glory/Playing The Game	12
77	Chrysalis CHS 2160	I'm Turning Around/Just The Same (live)	6
70	Vertigo 6360 020	GENTLE GIANT (LP, gatefold sleeve, swirl label)	35
71	Vertigo 6360 041	ACQUIRING THE TASTE (LP, gatefold sleeve)	40
72	Vertigo 6360 070	THREE FRIENDS (LP, gatefold sleeve, swirl label)	30
72	Vertigo 6360 080	OCTOPUS (LP, gatefold sleeve, swirl label)	20
73	WWA WWA 002	IN A GLASS HOUSE (LP, silk-screen cover, with photo insert & lyric inner)	25
74	WWA WWA 010	THE POWER AND THE GLORY (LP, with insert)	20
75	Vertigo 6641 334	GIANT STEPS -- THE FIRST FIVE YEARS (2-LP)	15
76	Chrysalis CHR 1115	INTERVIEW (LP, green label, with lyric inner sleeve)	12

77	Chrysalis CTY 1133	LIVE (PLAYING THE FOOL) (2-LP, with 12-page booklet)	18
77	Chrysalis CHR 1152	THE MISSING PIECE (LP, with inner sleeve)	20
78	Chrysalis CHR 1186	GIANT FOR A DAY (LP, with mask insert & lyric inner sleeve)	12
80	Chrysalis CHR 1285	CIVILIAN (LP, with lyric inner sleeve)	15

(see also Simon Dupree & Big Sound, Moles)

GENTLE INFLUENCE
| 69 | Pye 7N 17666 | Never Trust In Tomorrow/Easy To Love | 15 |
| 69 | Pye 7N 17743 | Always Be A Part Of My Living/Captain Reale | 18 |

GENTLE PEOPLE
| 67 | Columbia DB 8276 | It's Too Late/Sea Of Heartbreak | 15 |

GENTLE PEOPLE
| 95 | Rephlex CAT 040R | JOURNEY (12", Aphex Twin Remix) | 8 |

GENTLE POWER OF SONG
| 67 | Polydor 2310 285 | CIRCUS (LP) | 30 |

GENTLE RAIN
| 73 | Polydor 2310 285 | MOODY (LP) | 200 |

GENTLE RESPITE
| 90 | Sarah SARAH 026 | DARKEST BLUE EP: Summer In Me/Darkest Blue/If I Touch (wraparound p/s, with insert) | 10 |

GENTLE TOUCH
| 65 | London HLR 10175 | Among The First To Know/Merry Go Round | 5 |

BILL GENTLES
69	Gas GAS 104	Long Life/SCHOOLBOYS: O Tell Me	10
70	Pama PM 801	What A Woman/Sleepy Cat	8
70	Punch PH 54	Fight The Good Fight/Fight Beat	8
71	Escort ERT 853	Bachelor Boy/SCORPIONS: Colour Rites	8
72	Bullet BU 506	Pure In Heart/Clean Hands	6

(see also Bill Jentles, Bill Jenties)

ART GENTRY
| 72 | Mojo 2092 048 | Breakthrough/Wonderful Dream | 10 |

BOBBIE GENTRY
67	Capitol CL 15511	Ode To Billie Joe/Mississippi Delta	8
67	Capitol (S)T 2830	ODE TO BILLIE JOE (LP)	18
68	Capitol (S)T 2842	THE DELTA SWEETE (LP)	15
69	Capitol E-(S)T 155	TOUCH 'EM WITH LOVE (LP)	14

BO GENTRY & RITCHIE CORDELL
| 69 | CBS 4299 | Stone Go-Getter/Hung Up | 5 |

GENTRYS
65	MGM MGM 1284	Keep On Dancing/Make Up Your Mind	15
66	MGM MGM 1296	Brown Paper Sack/Spread It On Thick	28
66	MGM MGM 1312	Everyday I Have To Cry/Don't Let It Be	15
68	Bell BLL 1012	I Can't Go Back To Denver/You Better Come Home	7

GENTS
81	Posh POSH 001	The Faker/The Pink Panther	20
82	Kosmic KOS 6886	Schooldays/True Stories (p/s)	8
83	Posh POSH 007	Revenge/Girl (p/s)	5
85	Posh no cat. no.	Lambs To The Slaughter/Friday On My Mind	5
80s	Posh MEGA 1	Revenge/Over Me/The Gent (p/s)	5
77	GG no cat. no.	HOW IT ALL BEGAN (LP)	12

GEOFFREY
| 78 | Music Bank BECK 694 | ABH (Who Wants To Listen To Punk Rock?)/Colt 45 Rock (p/s) | 15 |

GEORDIE
72	Regal Zonophone RZ 3067	Don't Do That/Francis Was A Rocker	12
73	EMI EMI 2008	All Because Of You/Ain't It Just Like A Woman	6
82	EMI EMI 2031	Nutbush City Limits/No Sweat (p/s)	20
73	EMI EMC 3001	HOPE YOU LIKE IT (LP)	15
74	EMI EMA 764	DON'T BE FOOLED BY THE NAME (LP)	15
76	EMI EMC 3134	SAVE THE WORLD (LP)	18
83	Neat NEAT 1008	NO SWEAT (LP)	15

(see also Influence, AC/DC)

BARBARA GEORGE
| 62 | London HL 9513 | I Know/Love | 22 |
| 64 | Sue WI 316 | Send For Me/Bless You | 50 |

EARL GEORGE
| 73 | Count Shelly CS 025 | Gonna Give Her All The Love/PRINCE JAZZBO: Wise Shepherd | 6 |

LLOYD GEORGE
| 62 | London HLP 9562 | Lucy Lee/Sing Real Loud | 75 |

GEORGETTES
| 58 | London HL 8548 | Love Like A Fool/Oh Tonight (78 rpm = £30) | 55 |
| 60 | Pye International 7N 25058 | Down By The River/A Pair Of Eyes | 15 |

GEORGE GOLDEN
| 64 | R&B JB145 | Fire In My Feet/ One More Chance | 20 |
| 64 | R&B JB157 | Don't You Know/ Nancy Tell Me | 20 |

GEORGIA SLIM/WALTER ROLAND
| 59 | Jazz Collector JEL 2 | THE MALE BLUES VOL. 1 (EP) | 20 |

MINT VALUE £

GEORGIA TOM
60s   Riverside RLP 8803   GEORGIA TOM AND FRIENDS (LP)................................. 20
(see also Paramount Allstars)

GEORGIE'S VARSITY 5
61   Vogue Pop V 9189   When My Sugar Walks Down The Street/Five Foot Two, Eyes Of Blue 10

GERBILS
98   Earworm WORM 14   Lucky Girl/Big White Limo (p/s, 1,000 only)................................. 5

WESLEY GERMS
72   Upsetter US 390   Whiplash/UPSETTERS: Whiplash Version..................................... 12

GERONIMO BLACK
72   Uni UNLS 126   GERONIMO BLACK (LP)....................................... 25
(see also Frank Zappa/Mothers Of Invention)

DENNY GERRARD
70   Deram Nova SDN 10   SINISTER MORNING (LP, with High Tide)........................... 55
(see also Warm Sounds, High Tide, Open Road, Fifth Avenue, High Tide)

GERRY & THE HOLOGRAMS
79   Absurd ABSURD 4   Gerry And The Holograms/Increased Resistance (p/s)...................... 5
79   Absurd ABSURD 5   The Emperor's New Music (unplayable record, glued into p/s)............... 8

GERRY & THE PACEMAKERS
63   Columbia DB 4987   How Do You Do It?/Away From You 6
63   Columbia DB 7041   I Like It/It's Happened To Me 6
63   Columbia DB 7126   You'll Never Walk Alone/It's All Right 7
64   Columbia DB 7189   I'm The One/You've Got What I Like 6
64   Columbia DB 7268   Don't Let The Sun Catch You Crying/Show Me That You Care 5
64   Columbia DB 7353   It's Gonna Be Alright/It's Just Because 7
64   Columbia DB 7437   Ferry Cross The Mersey/You You You 7
65   Columbia DB 7504   I'll Be There/Baby, You're So Good To Me 6
65   Columbia DB 7738   Walk Hand In Hand/Dreams 6
66   Columbia DB 7835   La La La/Without You 6
66   Columbia DB 8044   Girl On A Swing/A Fool To Myself 10
74   DJM DJS 298   Remember (The Days Of Rock And Roll)/There's Still Time 7
63   Columbia SEG 8257   HOW DO YOU DO IT? (EP).. 22
64   Columbia SEG 8295   YOU'LL NEVER WALK ALONE (EP, initially in misprinted sleeve
                                  listing It's All Right instead of Jambalaya on front)............... 25/20
64   Columbia SEG 8311   I'M THE ONE (EP) 20
64   Columbia SEG 8346   DON'T LET THE SUN CATCH YOU CRYING (EP)............................... 25
64   Columbia SEG 8367   IT'S GONNA BE ALRIGHT (EP) 25
65   Columbia SEG 8388   GERRY IN CALIFORNIA (EP) 40
65   Columbia SEG 8397   HITS FROM 'FERRY CROSS THE MERSEY' (EP)............................... 35
65   Columbia SEG 8426   RIP IT UP (EP) 45
63   Columbia 33SX 1546   HOW DO YOU LIKE IT? (LP, also stereo SCX 3492)...................... 30/40
65   Columbia 33SX 1693   FERRY CROSS THE MERSEY (LP, soundtrack,
                                  with Cilla Black & Fourmost, also stereo SCX 3544) 40/45
65   EMI Regal REG 2018   YOU'LL NEVER WALK ALONE (LP, export issue) 35
(see also Gerry Marsden)

GESCOM
94   Skam SKA 2   Dan One/Five/Cicada/Sciew Spo (12", card folder p/s)...................... 50
95   Skam SKA 3   Snackwitch/Mag (12", printed card folder p/s)........................... 50
95   Clear CLR 408   THE SOUNDS OF MACHINES OUR PARENTS USED (12", p/s).................... 60
96   Skam SKA 7   KEY NELL 1/2/3/4 (12", bubblewrap sleeve)............................... 20
(see also Autechre)

GESTURES
65   Stateside SS 379   Run Run Run/It Seems To Me 20

STAN GETZ (QUARTET/QUINTET)
50   Melodisc MEL 1109   Five Brothers/Four & One More (78, as Stan Getz Tenor Sax Stars)...... 7
55   Columbia LB 10002   The Way You Look Tonight/Stars Fell On Alabama (78) 7
50s   Esquire EP 16   STAN GETZ QUARTET (EP).. 8
50s   Esquire EP 48   STAN GETZ QUARTET (EP).. 8
50s   Esquire EP 133   STAN GETZ IN RETROSPECT (EP, as Stan Getz Quartet) 8
50s   Esquire EP 134   THE BROTHERS (EP, as Stan Getz & His Four Brothers)................... 8
50s   Esquire EP 173   STAN GETZ QUARTET (EP).. 8
50s   Esquire EP 194   DON'T GET SCARED (EP)... 8
54   Vogue EPV 1016   STAN GETZ QUARTET (EP).. 10
55   Columbia SEB 10001   THE ARTISTRY OF STAN GETZ NO. 1 8
55   Columbia SEB 10021   THE ARTISTRY OF STAN GETZ NO. 2 8
56   Vogue EPV 1084   THE BROTHERS — STAN GETZ VOL. 1 8
56   Columbia SEB 10034   'TIS AUTUMN (as Stan Getz Quintet) 8
57   Columbia SEB 10063   THE ARTISTRY OF STAN GETZ NO. 3 8
57   Columbia SEB 10076   MINOR BLUES 8
57   Columbia SEB 10089   COOL SOUNDS 8
58   Columbia SEB 10117   MORE COOL SOUNDS (as Stan Getz Group) 8
53   Esquire 20-007   STAN GETZ PLAYS (LP, 10") 28
54   Vogue LDE 089   AT STORYVILLE (LP, 10") 28
55   Vogue LDE 147   STAN GETZ QUARTET (LP, 10") 28
55   Columbia Clef 33CX 10000   AT THE SHRINE NO. 1 (LP, as Stan Getz Quintet) 18
55   Columbia Clef 33CX 10001   AT THE SHRINE NO. 2 (LP, as Stan Getz Quintet) 18
62   HMV CLP 1577   FOCUS (LP, also stereo CSD 1448) 12/15
63   Verve (S)VLP 9013   JAZZ SAMBA (LP, with Charlie Byrd, mono/stereo)................... 12/15
63   Verve VLP 9024   BIG BAND BOSSA NOVA (LP)... 12
63   Verve (S)VLP 9038   JAZZ SAMBA ENCORE! (LP, with Luiz Bonfa, mono/stereo).......... 12/15
64   Verve VLP 9065   GETZ—GILBERTO (LP).. 12

64	Verve VLP 9069	REFLECTIONS (LP)	12
65	MGM MGM-C(S) 8001	MICKEY ONE (LP, soundtrack, mono/stereo, with booklet)	20/25
66	Stateside SL 10161	GREATEST HITS (LP)	12

(see also Dizzy Gillespie, Gil Fuller & Dizzy Gillespie, Astrud Gilberto, Joao Gilberto, Johnny Smith)

G-FORCE

80	Jet JET 183	Hot Gossip/Because Of Your Love (p/s)	20
80	Jet JET 194	You/Trust You Lovin' (no p/s)	12
80	Jet JET 7005	White Knuckles/Rockin' And Rollin'/I Look At You (p/s)	15
80	Jet JETLP 229	G-FORCE (LP, with inner sleeve and patch)	20
80	Jet JETPD 229	G-FORCE (LP, picture disc)	18

(see also Gary Moore)

G.G. ALLSTARS

70	Explosion EX 2012	Champion/MAYTONES: Funny Man	10
70	Explosion EX 2014	Barabus/This Kind Of Life	10
70	Explosion EX 2023	Man From Carolina/Gold On Your Dress (B-side actually by Slickers)	10
70	Explosion EX 2024	African Melody/Serious Love (B-side actually by Maytones)	7
70	Explosion EX 2025	Ganja Plane/Deep River	8
70	Gas GAS 153	So Alive/Mercy Mr D.J.	8
70	Escort ERT 835	African Melody/Man From Carolina	7
70	G.G. GG 4501	Music Keep On Playing (actually by Cornell Campbell)/Music Keep On Playing Version	7
71	G.G. GG 4508	Cleanliness Version 2/MAYTONES: Cleanliness	7
71	G.G. GG 4510	Rocking On The G.G. Beat (actually by Maytones)/WINSTON WRIGHT: Rocking On The G.G. Beat Version II	8
71	G.G. GG 4511	Lonely Nights (actually by Eric Donaldson & West Indians)/MAYTONES: Let The Version Play	6
71	G.G. GG 4513	All One Nation (actually by Maytones)/VAL BENNETT: Judgement Warrant	8
71	G.G. GG 4526	Rod Of Righteousness (actually Stretch Forth His Hand by Jah Huntly)/DENNIS ALCAPONE: King Of Kings (B-side actually King Of Glory)	6
72	G.G. GG 4530	Donkey Face Version/MAYTONES: Donkey Face	6
72	Pama PM 846	I'm Feeling Lonely Version/MAYTONES: I'm Feeling Lonely	6
73	Bullet BU 528	People Get Funny Version/MAYTONES: People Get Funny	6
70	Trojan TBL 129	MAN FROM CAROLINA (LP)	35+

(see also Paulette & Gee, Billy Dyce, Maytones, Charlie Ace, Monty Morris, Starlights, Lloyd & Carey, Gladdy & Stranger, Heptones, Shorty Perry, Barbara Jones)

G.G.F.H.

94	Peaceville CC8	Welcome To The Process (green vinyl)	15

G.G. RHYTHM SECTION

69	Blue Cat BS 165	T.N.T./MAYTONES: Botheration	20

GHETTO CHILDREN

73	CBS 1450	I Just Gotta Find Somebody To Love Me/Rat-a-tat-tat	20

WESS & DORI GHEZZI

75	Bradleys BRAD 7515	Fallin'/Era	8

GHOST

69	Gemini GMS 007	When You're Dead/Indian Maid	25
70	Gemini GMS 014	I've Got To Get To Know You/For One Second	22
88	Bam Caruso OPRA 088	Time Is My Enemy/POETS: I Love Her Still (company sleeve, promo only)	6
70	Gemini GME 1004	WHEN YOU'RE DEAD — ONE SECOND (LP, some with extra track, I've Got To Get To Know Her)	170/130
87	Bam Caruso KIRI 077	FOR ONE SECOND (LP, reissue of When You're Dead with extra track)	12

(see also Velvett Fogg, Shirley Kent, Virginia Tree)

GHOST DANCE

86	Karbon KAR 604	The Grip Of Love/Where Spirits Fly (p/s)	8

(see also Skeletal Family, All About Eve, Sisters Of Mercy)

BILL GIANT

61	MGM MGM 1135	Better Let Her Go/When I Grow Too Old To Dream	12

GIANT CRAB

68	Uni UN 509	Hot Line Conversation/E.S.P.	18

GIANTS

60s	Polydor LPHM 46426	IN GERMANY (LP, also stereo SLPHM 237626)	25/30

GIANT SAND

87	B'full Of Brains BOB 14	Wishing Well/PAUL ROLAND: Madhouse (Demo) (hard vinyl test pressing)	6

GIANT SUNFLOWER

67	CBS 2805	February Sunshine/Big Apple	18
67	CBS 3033	Mark Twain/What's So Good About Goodbye?	10

BARRY GIBB

70	Polydor 2058 030	I'll Kiss Your Memory/This Time	8

(see also Bee Gees)

MAURICE GIBB

70	Polydor 2058 013	Railroad/I've Come Back	8

(see also Bee Gees, Fut)

ROBIN GIBB

69	Polydor 56337	Saved By The Bell/Alexandria Good Time (withdrawn)	20
69	Polydor 56337	Saved By The Bell/Mother And Jack	6
69	Polydor 56368	One Million Years/Weekend	8
70	Polydor 56371	August October/Give Me A Smile	7
69	Polydor 583 085	ROBIN'S REIGN (LP)	30

(see also Bee Gees)

MINT VALUE £

STEVE GIBBONS (BAND)
71	Wizard WIZ 102	Alright Now/Lay Some Lovin' Down	10
82	RCA RCA 174	Loving Me, Loving You/That Makes It Tough/No Money Down (picture disc)	5
71	Wizard SWZA 5501	SHORT STORIES (LP)	50

(see also Uglys, Magic Christians, B,L&G)

CALY GIBBS
71	Amalgamated AMG 870	Seeing Is Believing/JOE GIBBS ALLSTARS: Ghost Capturer	20

(see also Carlton Gibbs)

CARLTON GIBBS
70	Amalgamated AMG 872	Ghost Walk/Joy Stick	20

GEORGIA GIBBS
55	Mercury MB 3196	Tweedle Dee/You're Wrong, All Wrong (78)	8
55	Mercury MB 3223	Dance With Me Henry/Ballin' The Jack (78)	6
55	Vogue Coral Q 72088	Ballin' The Jack/I Still Feel The Same About You (78 rpm = £6)	12
56	Mercury MT 110	Kiss Me Another/Rock Right (78)	8
56	Vogue Coral Q 72182	If I Were A Bell/I'll Know	10
57	RCA RCA 1011	Sugar Candy/I'm Walking The Floor Over You (78 rpm = £8)	10
58	RCA RCA 1029	Great Balls Of Fire/I Miss You (78 rpm = £8)	35
58	Mercury 7MT 210	Arriverderci Roma/24 Hours A Day (78 rpm = £6)	18
58	Columbia DB 4201	The Hula Hoop Song/Keep In Touch (78 rpm = £6)	10
59	Columbia DB 4259	The Huckebuck/Better Loved You'll Never Be (78 rpm = £6)	10
60	London HLP 9098	The Stroll That Stole My Heart/Seven Lonely Days	10
65	Stateside SS 423	Let Me Cry On Your Shoulder/Venice Blues	10
55	Mercury EP-1-3265	THE MAN THAT GOT AWAY (EP)	15
56	Mercury MEP 9505	SWEET GEORGIA GIBBS (EP)	15
57	Mercury MEP 9516	SWEET GEORGIA GIBBS VOL. 2 (EP)	15
56	Mercury MPT 7500	SINGS THE OLDIES (10" LP)	28
57	Mercury MPT 7511	HER NIBS MISS GIBBS (10" LP)	28
57	Mercury MPL 6508	SWINGING WITH HER NIBS (LP)	20

JOE GIBBS (& DESTROYERS)
68	Amslgamated AMG 822	People Grudgeful (as Sir Joe)/Pan-Ya Machete (actually the Pioneers)	60
70	Amalgamated AMG 855	Nevada Joe (act. by Johnny Lover)/Straight To The Head (act. by Destroyers)	22
70	Amalgamated AMG 858	Franco Nero (actually by Count Machuki & Destroyers)/Version Two (actually by Destroyers)	23
70	Amalgamated AMG 859	Rock The Clock/Version Two	50
70	Amalgamated AMG 860	Let It Be/Turn Back The Hands Of Time (both actually by Nicky Thomas)	18
70	Amalgamated AMG 865	Hijacked/Life Is Down In Denver	35
70	Amalgamated AMG 867	Movements/Caesar	18
70	Amalgamated AMG 868	Gift Of God (actually by Lizzy)/The Rapper	12
70	Pressure Beat PR 5504	News Flash/Version Two	12
73	Jackpot JP 811	Ration/Version (as Joe Gibbs All Stars)	8

(see also Lizzy, Reggae Boys, Bunny Flip, Destroyers, Dennis Brown, Caly Gibbs, Nicky Thomas)

MICHAEL GIBBS
70	Deram DML/SML 1063	MICHAEL GIBBS (LP)	60
71	Deram SML 1087	TANGLEWOOD '63 (LP)	40
72	Polydor 2683 011	JUST AHEAD (2-LP)	35
74	Polydor 2383 252	IN THE PUBLIC INTEREST (LP, with Gary Burton)	30
70s	Bronze ILPS 9353	ONLY CHROME ... WATERFALL (LP)	15

(see also Neil Ardley, Gary Burton)

TERRY GIBBS SEXTET
56	Vogue Coral LVA 9013	TERRY (LP)	20
56	Vogue Coral LVA 9009	JAZZTIME USA (LP, as Terry Gibbs Quartet & Sextet)	20

(see also Terry Gibbs Big Band)

TERRY GIBBS BIG BAND
59	Mercury CMS 18016	LAUNCHING A NEW BAND (LP)	15
61	HMV/Verve CLP 1560	THE EXCITING TERRY GIBBS BIG BAND (LP, also stereo CSD 1439)	12/15

DON GIBSON
56	MGM SP 1177	Sweet Dreams/The Road Of Life Alone (78 rpm, MGM 909 = £20)	150
58	RCA RCA 1056	Oh Lonesome Me/I Can't Stop Lovin' You (78 rpm = £10)	20
58	RCA RCA 1073	Blue Blue Day/Too Soon (78 rpm = £10)	15
58	RCA RCA 1098	Give Myself A Party/Look Who's Blue (78 rpm = £10)	20
59	RCA RCA 1110	A Stranger To Me/Who Cares? (78 rpm = £18)	18
59	RCA RCA 1150	Don't Tell Me Your Troubles/Heartbreak Avenue (78 rpm = £22)	18
59	RCA RCA 1158	Big Hearted Me/I'm Movin' On (78 rpm = £25)	15

(The above RCA 45s were originally issued with triangular centres; later round-centre copies are worth half these values.)

60	RCA RCA 1183	Just One Time/I May Never Get To Heaven	12
60	RCA RCA 1200	Far Far Away/A Legend In My Time	12
60	RCA RCA 1217	Sweet Dreams/The Same Street	8
61	RCA RCA 1243	Sea Of Heartbreak/I Think It's Best (To Forget Me)	10
62	RCA RCA 1272	Lonesome Number One/The Same Old Trouble	5
62	RCA RCA 1297	I Can Mend Your Broken Heart/I Let Her Get Lonely	5
63	RCA RCA 1335	Head Over Heels In Love With You/It Was Worth It	6
65	RCA RCA 1456	Again/You're Going Away	6
66	RCA RCA 1524	(Yes) I'm Hurting/My Whole World Is Hurt	6
67	RCA RCA 1626	All My Love/No Doubt About It (as Don Gibson & Jordanaires)	6
68	RCA RCA 1680	Ashes Of Love/Good Morning Dear	6
60	RCA RCX 1050	BLUE AND LONESOME (EP)	18
62	RCA RCX 213	LOOK WHO'S BLUE (EP)	18
62	RCA RCX 214	THAT GIBSON BOY (EP)	18
63	RCA RCX 7122	MAY YOU NEVER BE ALONE (EP)	18

60	RCA RD 27158	THE GIBSON BOY (LP)	65
62	RCA Victor RD/SF 7506	SOME FAVOURITES OF MINE (LP)	22
63	RCA Victor RD/SF 7576	I WROTE A SONG (LP)	22
64	RCA Victor RD 7641	GOD WALKS THESE HILLS (LP)	22

GINNY GIBSON
55	MGM SP 1121	Like Ma-a-d/Once There Was A Little Girl	15
58	MGM MGM 953	Whatever Lola Wants (Lola Gets)/If Anything Should Happen	18

JODY GIBSON & MULESKINNERS
59	Parlophone R 4579	Kissin' Time/Man On My Trail	15
60	Parlophone R 4645	If You Don't Know/So You Think You've Got Troubles	18

LORNE GIBSON TRIO
62	Decca F 11519	Little Black Book/What Kind Of Love Is This?	5
63	Decca F 11684	Some Do, Some Don't (Some Will, Some Won't)/Heaven's Above	5
64	Decca F 11814	Hang Up The Phone/I Think It's Best To Forget Me	5
64	Decca F 12005	The Girl I Loved/Don't Go Near The Indians	5

STEVE GIBSON & RED CAPS
57	HMV POP 417	Silhouettes/Flamingo (78 rpm = £30)	200

WAYNE GIBSON (& DYNAMIC SOUNDS)
63	Decca F 11713	Linda Lu/Beachcomber	20
64	Decca F 11800	Come On Let's Go/Pop The Whip	20
64	Pye 7N 15680	Kelly/See You Later Alligator	18
65	Pye 7N 15798	Portland Town/Please Baby Please	12
65	Parlophone R 5357	Ding Dong The Witch Is Dead/In The Night	12
65	Columbia DB 7683	One Little Smile/Baby, Baby, Baby Pity Me	30
66	Columbia DB 7911	Under My Thumb/It Always Happens (Icey) (solo) (DJ copy = £120)	45
66	Columbia DB 7998	For No One/He's Got The Whole World In his Hands (solo)	10

GIBSONS
65	CBS 202015	Any Time That You're Lonely/Born To Be Free	7
66	CBS 202063	Come Summertime/Summer Affair	7
66	Deram DM 103	Two Kinds Of Lovers/Hey Girl	6
67	Deram DM 119	The Magic Book/You Know I Need Your Lovin'	7
67	Major Minor MM 524	Night And Day/City Life	20
67	Major Minor MM 538	Lazy Summer Day/She's Not Like Any Girl	10
67	Major Minor MM 547	Only When You're Lonely/Ode To A Dolls House	7

GIDIAN (& UNIVERSALS)
66	Columbia DB 7826	Try Me Out/There Isn't Anything	20
66	Columbia DB 7916	Fight For Your Love/See If She Cares	8
66	Columbia DB 8041	Feeling/Don't Be Sentimental (as Gidian & Universals)	10
70	UPC UPC 107	That's Love/We Are The Happiest	6

(see also Universals, Chris Lamb & Universals)

GIFT
81	Venus ORBIT 1	Crashing Down/It'll End In Tears (p/s)	20

GIFTED CHILDREN
81	Whaam! WHAAM 001	Painting By Numbers/Lichtenstein Girl (p/s)	30

(see also Television Personalities)

GIGGETTY
78	Pye 7N 46136	Black Country Christmas/Motorway Mess	12
75	GE 100	DAWN TO DUSK IN THE BLACK COUNTRY (LP, with insert)	40
77	Bridge GE 101	TAMBOURINE (LP)	30
80	Bridge GE 103	BLACK COUNTRY TIME (LP, also listed as Revolver REV LP1)	30

GILBERTO GIL
71	Famous SFM 1001	GILBERTO GIL (LP)	20

GILBERT
67	CBS 3089	Disappear/You	18
68	CBS 3399	What Can I Do?/You	18
69	Major Minor MM 613	Mister Moody's Garden/I Wish I Could Cry	20

(see also Gilbert O'Sullivan)

HERSCHEL BURKE GILBERT
63	London HLD 9655	Dick Powell Theme/Nervous Teaser Theme	7

GEORGE GILBERT
74	Mime LPMS 7041	MEDWAY FLOWS SOFTLY (LP, with insert)	15

GILBERT & LEWIS
81	4AD AD 106	Ends With The Sea/Hung Up To Dry Whilst Building An Arch (p/s)	6
82	Cherry Red BRED 27	MZUI (LP, PVC cover, insert sleeve)	12

(see also Wire, Dome, Cupol)

ASTRUD GILBERTO
64	Verve VS 520	Girl From Ipanema (with Stan Getz)/STAN GETZ & JOAO GILBERTO: Blowin' In The Wind	5
66	Verve VEP 5019	AND ROSES AND ROSES (EP, with Antonio Carlos Jobim)	10
66	Verve (S)VLP 9163	A CERTAIN SMILE AND A CERTAIN KIND OF SADNESS (LP)	15
69	Verve (S)VLP 9242	I HAVEN'T GOT ANYTHING BETTER TO DO (LP)	15
72	C.T.I. CTL 1	GILBERTO WITH TURRENTINE (LP, with Stanley Turrentine)	15

(see also Stan Getz, Stanley Turrentine)

JOAO GILBERTO
61	Parlophone PMC 1248	BOSSA-FINADO (LP)	15

(see also Stan Getz)

MINT VALUE £

GILDED CAGE
69	Tepee TPR 1003	Long Long Road (For The Broken Heart)/Baby Grumpling	40

(see also She Trinity)

COSMO GILE
60	Top Rank JAR 410	Bambina D'Amsterdam/Tintarella Di Luna	8

GILES, GILES & FRIPP
68	Deram DM 188	One In A Million/Newly-Weds	60
68	Deram DM 210	Thursday Morning/Elephant Song	50
68	Deram DML/SML 1022	THE CHEERFUL INSANITY OF GILES, GILES AND FRIPP (LP, mono/stereo)	50/60
70	Deram SPA 423	THE CHEERFUL INSANITY OF GILES, GILES AND FRIPP (LP, stereo reissue)	22

(see also Brain, Trendsetters Ltd, League Of Gentlemen, King Crimson, Fripp & Eno, McDonald & Giles)

TOM GILFELLON
72	Trailer LER 2079	LOVING MAD TOM (LP, red label)	15
76	Topic 12TS 282	IN THE MIDDLE OF THE TUNE (LP, blue label)	15

GILGAMESH
75	Caroline CA 2007	GILGAMESH (LP)	18

(see also Hugh Hopper, Colosseum, Whitesnake)

TERRY GILKYSON & EASY RIDERS
58	Philips JK 1007	Marianne/Goodbye Chaquita (jukebox issue)	18
60	Fontana TFE 17326	STROLLING BLUES (EP)	18
60	Fontana TFE 17327	LONESOME RIDER (EP)	15
61	London RER 1333	ROLLIN' (EP)	18
53	Brunswick LA 8618	GOLDEN MINUTES OF FOLK MUSIC (10" LP)	25
61	London HA-R 2301	ROLLIN' (LP, also stereo SAH-R 6111)	15/18
61	London HA-R 2323	REMEMBER THE ALAMO (LP, as Easyriders Including Terry Gilkyson)	15

(see also Easy Riders)

(IAN) GILLAN (BAND)
78	Island R 553-B	Twin Exhausted (live)/Smoke On The Water (live)/ILLUSION: Madonna Blue/Revolutionary (12", promo only, as Ian Gillan Band)	15
78	Island WIP 6423	Mad Elaine/Mercury High (as Ian Gillan Band, company sleeve)	7
79	Acrobat BAT 2	Vengeance/Smoke On The Water (p/s)	6
79	Acrobat BAT 1212	She Tears Me Down/Puget Sound/Vengeance/Mr. Universe (12", stickered card sleeve, promo only)	20
80	Virgin VS 355	Sleeping On The Job/Higher And Higher (p/s, with free patch)	5
80	Virgin VS 362	No Easy Way/Handles On Her Hips/Might As Well Go Home (p/s)	5
80	Virgin VS 377	Trouble/Your Sister's On My List (poster p/s)	5
80	Virgin VS 377	Trouble/Your Sister's On My List/Mr Universe (live)/Vengeance (live)/Smoke On The Water (live) (double pack, gatefold p/s)	7
81	Virgin VSK 103	Mutually Assured Destruction/The Maelstrom (gatefold p/s, with booklet)	6
81	Sounds FREEBIE No. 2	I'll Rip Out Your Spine (extract)/PROFESSIONALS: Little Boys In Blue (extract) (33rpm 1-sided flexi, printed die-cut sleeve, free with *Sounds*)	with mag 7
81	Lyntone LYN 10599	Higher And Higher/Spanish Guitar (1-sided blue flexi with *Flexipop* magazine 13)	with mag 7
81	Lyntone LYN 10599	Higher And Higher/Spanish Guitar (same tracks both sides, hard vinyl test pressing, handwritten white labels)	25
82	Virgin VSY 465	Restless/On The Rocks (live) (picture disc)	5
82	Virgin VSY 519	Living For The City/Purple Sky (picture disc, mispressed, B-side plays "Breaking Chains", some with explanatory sticker)	5
82	Virgin VSY 519	Living For The City/Purple Sky (picture disc)	8
82	Virgin VS 537	Long Gone/Figi (foldout p/s)	5
82	Kerrang!	Purple Sky/GARY MOORE: Wishing Well/TELEPHONE: Squeeze (flexidisc free with *Kerrang!*)	with mag 8
88	Virgin TVS 1088	South Africa (extended mix)/South Africa/John (12", p/s, as Ian Gillan)	8
90	Teldec SAM 678	Talking To You/Moonshine (12", clear vinyl promo, in PVC wallet with insert & postcard)	12
91	East West SAM 906	Toolbox/Hang Me Out To Dry/Dirty Dog/Pictures Of Hell (12" promo, black sl.)	12
76	Polydor/Oyster 2490 136	CHILD IN TIME (LP, gatefold sleeve, as Ian Gillan Band)	15
77	Island ILPS 9511DJ	IAN GILLAN BAND SAMPLER (LP, 1-sided promo for Scarabus, company sleeve)	18
78	Island ILPS 9545	LIVE AT THE BUDO-KAN (LP, unissued)	
80	Virgin V 2171	GLORY ROAD (LP, with bonus LP For Gillan Fans Only [VDJ 32], stickered, embossed sleeve & inner sleeves)	15

(see also Episode Six, Deep Purple, Ray Fenwick, Split Knee Loons, John McCoy, Johnny Gustafson, Bernie Tormé, Thunderstick, Jerusalem, Quatermass, Colin Towns, White Spirit, Zzebra, Rock Aid Armenia)

DANA GILLESPIE
65	Pye 7N 15872	Donna Donna/It's No Use Saying If	12
65	Pye 7N 15962	Thank You Boy/You're A Heartbreak Man	9
67	Pye 7N 17280	Pay You Back With Interest/Adam Can You Beat That	9
68	Decca F 12847	You Just Gotta Know My Mind/He Loves Me, He Loves Me Not	10
74	RCA RCA 0211	Weren't Born A Man/All Gone	8
74	RCA RCA 2466	Andy Warhol/Dizzy Heights	10
75	RCA RCA 2489	Really Love That Man/Hold Me Gently	6
69	Decca SKL 5012	BOX OF SURPRISES (LP)	55
73	RCA APL1 0354	WEREN'T BORN A MAN (LP)	18
74	RCA APL1 0682	AIN'T GONNA PLAY NO SECOND FIDDLE (LP)	15

DIZZY GILLESPIE (QUINTET)
56	Vogue V 2116	The Champ (Parts 1 & 2)	6
59	HMV 7EG 8574	Constantinople/Willow Weep For Me	6
60	HMV POP 705	Doddlin'/Dizzy's Blues	6
55	Vogue EPV 1022	DIZZY GILLESPIE (EP)	10
55	Vogue EPV 1049	DIZZY GILLESPIE WITH STRINGS (EP)	10
56	Vogue EPV 1078	DIZZY GILLESPIE (EP)	10

56	Vogue EPV 1094	THE CHAMP — DIZZY GILLESPIE (EP)	10
56	Vogue EPV 1157	DIZZY GILLESPIE AND HIS ORCHESTRA (EP)	10
56	Vogue EPV 1158	DIZZY GILLESPIE AND HIS ORCHESTRA (EP)	10
52	Esquire 20-003	OPERATIC STRINGS (10" LP)	18
53	Vogue LDE 017	DIZZY GILLESPIE PLAYS (10" LP)	18
53	Vogue LDE 033	DIZZY GILLESPIE PLAYS — JOHNNY RICHARDS CONDUCTS (10" LP)	18
54	Vogue LDE 039	PARIS CONCERT (10" LP)	18
54	Vogue LDE 076	DIZZY GILLESPIE AND ORCHESTRA (10" LP)	18
54	HMV DLP 1047	DIZZY GILLESPIE AND HIS ORCHESTRA (10" LP)	18
54	Felsted EDL 87006	DIZZY GILLESPIE'S OPERATIC STRINGS — JEALOUSY (10" LP)	18
55	Vogue LDE 135	DIZZY GILLESPIE AND HIS ORCHESTRA (10" LP)	18
55	Columbia Clef 33CX 10002	DIZZY GILLESPIE AND HIS ORCHESTRA (LP)	15
58	Columbia Clef 33CX 10144	DIZZY IN GREECE (LP)	15
59	HMV CLP 1318	HAVE TRUMPET, WILL EXCITE! (LP)	12
60	HMV CLP 1381	THE GREATEST TRUMPET OF THEM ALL (LP)	12
61	HMV CLP 1431	PORTRAIT OF DUKE ELLINGTON (LP)	12
62	HMV CLP 1484	GILLESPIANA (LP, also stereo CSD 1392)	15
62	Verve VLP/SVLP 9016	CARNEGIE HALL CONCERT (LP)	12
71	Pye PKL 4403	SOULED OUT (LP)	12

(see also Miles Davis, Lalo Schifrin)

DIZZY GILLESPIE & STAN GETZ

60	HMV 7EG 8596	DIZZY GILLESPIE/STAN GETZ SEXTET (EP)	8
55	Columbia Clef 33C 9009	DIZZY GILLESPIE — STAN GETZ SEXTET (LP)	15
55	Columbia 33C 9027	MORE OF (10" LP)	15

(see also Stan Getz)

DIZZY GILLESPIE & CHARLIE PARKER

| 57 | Columbia Clef SEB 10087 | ONE MORE TIME: WITH BIRD AND DIZ (EP) | 8 |
| 61 | Vogue LAE 12252 | DIZ 'N BIRD IN CONCERT (LP) | 15 |

(see also Charlie Parker)

DIZZY GILLESPIE & HIS ORCHESTRA

| 54 | Felsted 82001 | Blue & Sentimental/Moon Nocturne (78) | 8 |

DIZZY GILLESPIE & ORCHESTRA/DON BYAS QUARTET

| 57 | MGM MGM-EP 579 | DIZZ AND DON (EP, 2 tracks each) | 8 |

DIZZY GILLESPIE/KAI WINDING'S BIRDLANDERS

| 58 | MGM MGM-EP 681 | TWO BY TWO (EP, 2 tracks each) | 8 |

HUGH GILLESPIE

| 78 | Topic 12TS 364 | CLASSIC RECORDINGS OF IRISH TRADITIONAL FIDDLE MUSIC (LP) | 12 |

JAZZ GILLUM

66	RCA Victor RD 7816	JAZZ GILLUM 1938-1947 (LP)	22
70	RCA Intl. INTS 1177	YOU GOT TO REAP WHAT YOU SOW (LP)	15
71	Xtra XTRA 1111	BLUES BY JAZZ GILLUM, WITH ARBEE STIDHAM AND MEMPHIS SLIM (LP)	15

JIMMY GILMER & FIREBALLS

62	London HLD 9632	I'm Gonna Go Walkin'/Born To Be With You (as Chimmy Gilmer)	16
63	London HLD 9789	Sugar Shack/My Heart Is Free	10
64	London HLD 9827	Daisy Petal Pickin'/When My Tears Have Dried	10
64	London HLD 9872	Ain't Gonna Tell Nobody/Young Am I	12
64	London HLD 9898	Look At Me/I'll Send For You	12
65	Stateside SS 418	Thunder 'N' Lightnin'/What Do You Do	15
65	Stateside SS 472	She Belongs To Me/Rambler's Blues	10
68	London HL 10232	Three Squares/Baby	6
64	London HA-D/SH-D 8150	SUGAR SHACK (LP)	40
65	Dot DLP 3577	BUDDY'S BUDDY — BUDDY HOLLY SONGS BY JIMMY GILMER (LP)	55

(see also Fireballs, Jim & Monica)

DAVE GILMOUR

78	Harvest HAR 5167	There's No Way Out Of Here/Deafinitely (no p/s)	7
84	Harvest HAR 5226	Blue Light (LP Version)/Cruise (blue or red titles on p/s)	each 5
84	Harvest 12HAR 5226	Blue Light (LP Version)/Cruise (12", p/s)	10
84	Harvest HAR 5229	Love On The Air/Let's Get Metaphysical (p/s)	5
84	Harvest HARP 5229	Love On The Air/Let's Get Metaphysical (shaped picture disc)	12
84	Harvest 12HAR 5229	Love On The Air/Let's Get Metaphysical (12", p/s)	8

(see also Pink Floyd, Joker's Wild, Rock Aid Armenia, Unicorn)

PETER GILMORE

| 60 | HMV POP 740 | Follow That Girl/Come Away | 8 |

JAMES GILREATH

| 63 | Pye International 7N 25190 | Little Band Of Gold/I'll Walk With You | 12 |
| 63 | Pye International 7N 25213 | Lollipops, Lace And Lipstick/Mean Ole River | 12 |

GORDON GILTRAP (BAND)

73	Philips 6006 344	No Way Of Knowing/I See A Road	15
79	Cube BUG 89	The Waltons Theme/Birds Of A Feather (p/s)	5
79	Electric LWOP 29	Fear Of The Dark/Catwalk Blues/Inner Dream (12", picture disc)	8
68	Transatlantic TRA 175	GORDON GILTRAP (LP)	40
69	Transatlantic TRA 202	PORTRAIT (LP)	40
71	MCA MKPS 2020	A TESTAMENT OF TIME (LP)	25
73	Philips 6308 175	GILTRAP (LP, with lyric insert)	18
81	Themes International	THEMES (LP, by Gordon Giltrap Band, library issue)	18
82	KPM KPM 1292	SOUNDWAVES (LP, by Gordon Giltrap Band, library issue)	15
82	KPM KPM 1330	IN AT THE DEEP END (LP, by Gordon Giltrap Band, library issue)	15

(see also Accolade, Pauline Filby, Catherine Andrews)

MINT VALUE £

GINGER
01	Infernal/Round GINGERCD1	I'm A Lover Not A Fighter/Don't Let Me Die Lonely/ Thailand Uber Alles (CD)	15
01	Infernal/Round GINGERCD2	Cars And Vaginas/You, Me And BT/Not Bitter, Just A Little Disappointed (CD)	12
02	Infernal/Round GINGERCD3	And This Time I'm Serious/Re-Inventing The Wheel/ Blinded By Absinthe (CD)	12
02	Infernal/Round GINGERCD4	The Saga Of Me & You/Naked Innocence/Better Man (CD)	8

(see also SilverGinger 5, Super$hit666, Wildhearts)

GINGER ALE
70	Famous FAM 102	In The Sand/Get Off My Life Woman	5

GINGER JUG BAND
70s	GJB 001	GINGER JUG BAND (LP, private pressing)	22

GINGER SNAPS
65	RCA RCA 1483	The Sh Down Down Song/I've Got Faith In Him	20

GINGRINI
73	Harry J. HJ 6647	Zion 'Iah/Zion 'Iah (Version)	6

GINHOUSE
71	Charisma CAS 1031	GINHOUSE (LP)	60

(see also Kestrel. Mouse)

GINKS
65	Summit ATL 4176	A TRIBUTE TO THE BEATLES (LP)	15

GINO & GINA
58	Mercury 7MT 230	Pretty Baby/Love's A Carousel (78 rpm, Mercury MT 230 = £20)	40

ALLEN GINSBERG
60s	Cape Goliard	Wales: A Visitation (single issued with book of same title)	15
65	Better Books (no cat. no.)	ALLEN GINSBERG READING AT BETTER BOOKS (LP)	20
65	Love Books Ltd. LB 0001	ALLEN GINSBERG, LAURENCE FERLINGHETTI, GREGORY CORSO & ANDREI VOZNESENSKY READING AT THE ARCHITECTURAL ASSOCIATION (LP)	20
68	Transatlantic TRA 192	GINSBERG'S THING (LP)	15

(see also Ginsbergs)

GINSBERGS
67	Saga Psyche PSY 3002	THE GINSBERGS AT THE ICA (LP)	15

(see also Allen Ginsberg)

MARCELLO GIOMBINI
70	United Artists UP 35110	Sabata — Main Title/Banjo Arrives	10

GIORGIO
66	Page One POF 003	Full Stop/Believe Me	6
67	Page One POF 028	How Much Longer Must I Wait/Bla Bla Diddly	12
69	MCA MCA 1094	Happy Birthday/Looky Looky	6

(see also Giorgio Moroder, Giorgio & Marco's Men)

GIORGIO & MARCO'S MEN
66	Polydor 56101	Girl Without A Heart/Run Run	7
68	Electratone EP 1003	Baby I Need You/Maureen	70

GIPSY LOVE
72	BASF BAP 5026	GIPSY LOVE (LP)	22

CHUCK GIRARD
60s	Myrrh MYR 1025	CHUCK GIRARD (LP)	20
60s	Myrrh MYR 1065	WRITTEN ON THE WIND (LP)	20
60s	myrrh MYR 1089	THE STAND (LP)	20

MARTINE GIRAULD
92	Opaz OP 001SRH	REVIVAL (12" EP, p/s)	8

GIRGIO
69	MCA 5023	Stop/Believe Me	20

GIRL
79	Jet JET 159	My Number/My Number (Version) (clear vinyl, PVC sleeve, with 2 stickers)	5
79	Jet JET 159	My Number/My Number (Version) (black vinyl, promo only)	5
80	Jet JET 169	Do You Love Me?/Strawberries (p/s)	6
80	Jet JET 176	Hollywood Tease (Remix)/You Really Got Me/My Number (some in poster p/s)	7/5
80	Jet JET 191	Love Is A Game/Little Miss Ann (white vinyl, patch & sticker in PVC sleeve)	5
80	Jet JET 10 191	Love Is A Game/Little Miss Ann (10", white vinyl with sticker in PVC sleeve)	6
80	Jet JETLP 224	SHEER GREED (LP, stickered sleeve with inner)	12
82	Jet JETLP 238	WASTED YOUTH (LP, with inner sleeve)	12

(see also Def Leppard, Bernie Tormé)

GIRLFRIENDS
63	Colpix PX 712	Jimmy Boy/For My Sake	50

GIRLIE
69	Treasure Isle TI 7053	Boss Cocky/LOVE SHOCKS: Musical True	18
69	Bullet BU 400	Madame Straggae/LAUREL AITKEN: Stupid Married Man	12
69	Duke DU 42	African Meeting (as Girlie & Junior)/JOSH: Higher And Higher	10
70	Joe JRS 7	Small Change/Mind Your Business (as Girlie & Joe [Mansano])	12
70	Ackee ACK 124	Decimilization/Decimilization Version (as Girlie & Paul)	6

(see also Laurel Aitken & Girlie)

GIRLS AT OUR BEST
80	Records RR 001	Getting Nowhere Fast/Warm Girls (p/s)	10
81	Rough Trade RT 055	Politics/It's Fashion (p/s)	5
81	Happy Birthday UR 4	Go For Gold/I'm Beautiful Now (p/s)	8
81	Happy Birthday UR 6	Fast Boyfriends/This Train (p/s)	8
81	Happy Birthday RULP 1	PLEASURE (LP, with lyric insert, 1st 10,000 with free 'pleasure bag' with 2 postcards, sticker & stencil)	12/10

GIRLSCHOOL
79	City NIK 6	Take It All Away/It Could Be Better (p/s, red vinyl, pink p/s, b&w front photo)	7
79	City NIK 6	Take It All Away/It Could Be Better (p/s, black vinyl, orange p/s)	5
79	Mulligan LUNS 723	Take It All Away/It Could Be Better (Irish version, no p/s, red vinyl)	8
81	Bronze BROX 118	Hit And Run/Tonight/Tush (10" EP)	8
81	Bronze BROX 126	C'mon Let's Go/Tonight/Demolition Boys (10" EP)	8
82	Bronze BRO 144	THE WILDLIFE EP: Don't Call It Love/Wildlife/Don't Stop (red vinyl, p/s)	5
81	Bronze BRON 534	HIT AND RUN (LP, red vinyl)	15
(see also Motörhead, Killjoys)			

GIRL TALK
| 84 | Innervision IVST 4 | Can The Rhythm (mixes) (12", p/s) | 12 |

GIST
81	Rough Trade RT 58	This Is Love/Yanks (p/s)	8
81	Rough Trade RT 85	Love At First Sight/Light Aircraft (p/s)	7
83	Rough Trade RT 125	Fool For A Valentine/Fool For A Version (p/s)	7

GITTE
| 64 | Columbia DB 7440 | The Heart That You Break (May Be Your Own)/Seems Just Like Old Times | 12 |

JIMMY GIUFFRE
55	Capitol LC 6699	JIMMY GIUFFRE (10" LP)	20
57	London Jazz LTZK 15059	THE JIMMY GIUFFRE CLARINET (LP)	15
58	London Jazz LTZK 15130	JIMMY GIUFFRE (LP)	15
58	London Jazz LTZK 15137	TRAV'LIN' LIGHT (LP)	15
58	London LTZ-K 15130	JIMMY GIUFFRE 3 (LP)	15
(see also Shelly Manne)			

GLADDY (Anderson) & FOLLOWERS
| 69 | Blue Cat BS 172 | Judas/The World Come To An End | 22 |
| *(see also Stranger & Glady)·* | | | |

GLADDY (Anderson) & STRANGER (Cole)
| 73 | Pama PM 872 | Dedicated To Illiteracy/G.G. ALLSTARS: Dub | 8 |
| *(see also Gladstone Anderson, Stranger Cole, Stranger & Glady)* | | | |

GLADIATORS
| 63 | HMV POP 1134 | Tovaritch/Bleak House | 20 |
| *(see also Nero & Gladiators)* | | | |

GLADIATORS
68	Direction 58-3854	Girl Don't Make Me Wait/Can't Get Away From Heartbreak	10
69	Direction 58-4308	Waiting On The Shores Of Nowhere/I'll Always Love You	10
69	Direction 58-4507	As Long As I Live/Everything	8
69	Direction 58-4660	Twelfth Of Never/Lovin' My Baby Back Home	8
69	Studio One 2086	Kicks/Games People Play	30

GLADIATORS (Jamaica)
69	Doctor Bird DB 1114	The Train Is Coming/So Fine	28
69	Studio One SO 2072	Hello Carol/RICHARD ACE: More Reggae	35
69	Bamboo BAM 7	Anywhere/SOUND DIMENSION: Baby Face	20
70	Duke DU 58	My Girl (actually by Glen Adams)/You Were To Be	12
72	Ackee ACK 149	Sonia/SOUND DIMENSION: Solas	15
70s	Rock Steady Rev. REVR 12	Unusual Reggae/Andue	6

GLADIOLAS
| 57 | London HLO 8435 | Little Darlin'/Sweetheart, Please Don't Go (78 rpm = £65) | 275 |
| *(see also Maurice Williams & Zodiacs)* | | | |

GLASER BROTHERS
| 69 | MGM MGM-CS 8115 | NOW COUNTRY (LP) | 12 |

GLASGOW
| 84 | Neat NEAT 40 | Stranded/Heat Of The Night (p/s) | 15 |
| 84 | Clydebank CLY 001 | GLASGOW'S MILES BETTER (12" EP) | 12 |

GLASGOW RANGERS AFC BOYS CLUB
| 71 | Hallmark SHM 759 | GLORY, GLORY GLASGOW RANGERS (LP) | 20 |

LUD GLASKIN
| 62 | UPC 3428 | To My Good Friend Jack Cotton, the 'Allo Twist (1-sided private pressing) | 25 |

GLASS
| 82 | Glass GLASS1 | New Colours/Sweet Entropy (p/s) | 22 |

PHILIP GLASS
70s	Chatham Square LP 1001/2	MUSIC WITH CHANGING PARTS (2-LP)	25
70s	Chatham Square LP 1003	MUSIC IN FIFTHS/MUSIC IN A SIMILAR MOTION (LP)	15
70s	Folkways FTS 33902	TWO PAGES (LP)	12
76	Cardine LA 2010	MUSIC IN 12 (PARTS 1 & 2) (LP)	12
78	Shandar SHAN 83515	SOLO MUSIC (LP)	12
(see also Ray Manzarek)			

GLASS HARP
| 72 | MCA MUPS 431 | GLASS HARP (LP) | 20 |
| 72 | MCA MUPS 449 | SYNERGY (LP) | 15 |

MINT VALUE £

GLASS HOUSE
70	Invictus INV 506	Stealing Moments From Another Woman's Life/If It Ain't Love, It Don't Matter.	8
71	Invictus INV 510	I Can't Be You/He's In My Life	8

GLASS MENAGERIE
68	Pye 7N 17518	She's A Rainbow/But That's When I Start To Love Her	12
68	Pye 7N 17568	You Didn't Have To Be So Nice/Let's All Run To The Sun	8
68	Pye 7N 17615	Frederick Jordan/I Said Goodbye To Me	200
69	Polydor 56318	Have You Forgotten Who You Are/Do You Ever Think?	6
69	Polydor 56341	Do My Thing Myself/Watching The World Pass By	6

(see also Paladin, Toe-Fat)

GLASS OPENING
68	Plexium P 1236	Silver Bells And Cockle Shells/Does It Really Matter	500

GLAXO BABIES
79	Heartbeat PULSE5	Christine Keeler/Nova Bossanova (p/s)	10

TOM GLAZER & DO-RE-MI CHILDREN'S CHORUS
63	London HLR 9742	On Top Of Spaghetti/Battle Hymn Of The Children	7
63	London HLR 9817	It's A Mad, Mad, Mad, Mad World/Dance With The Dolly	7

JACKIE GLEASON (& ORCHESTRA)
55	Capitol CL 14289	Rain/I'll Never Be The Same (with Orchestra)	6
55	Capitol CL 14363	Autumn Leaves/Oo! What You Do To Me (with Orchestra)	6
60	Brunswick 04775	What Is A Boy?/What Is A Girl?	6
56	Capitol EAP 1-871	TO A SLEEPING BEAUTY (EP)	10

CAPTAIN GLEASON'S GARDEN BAND
55	Capitol CL 14323	In The Good Old Summertime/The Band Played On	6

(see also Jackie Gleason)

GLEN (Brown) & LLOYD (Robinson)
66	Ska Beat JB 250	Live And Let Others Die/Too Late	35
67	Doctor Bird DB 1099	Feel Good Now/What You've Got (credited as Lloyd Glen)	35

GLENCOE
72	Epic EPC 8383	Look Me In The Eye/Telephonia	6
72	Epic EPC 65207	GLENCOE (LP)	18
73	Epic EPC 65717	SPIRIT OF GLENCOE (LP)	15

(see also Hopscotch, Five Day Rain, Greatest Show On Earth, Loving Awareness)

DARRELL GLENN
54	HMV 7MC 23	In The Chapel In The Moonlight/Once And Only Once (export issue)	20

GLIDE
95	Ochre OCH 003	EXCERPTS FROM A SPACE AGE FREAK OUT (Part 1) (orange vinyl, p/s)	5

(see also Echo & Bunnymen)

GLITTERHOUSE
68	Stateside SS 2129	Barbarella/BOB CREWE: An Angel Is Love	15
68	Stateside SS 2129	Barbarella/Love Drags Me Down (different B-side)	18

GLOBAL COMMUNICATIONS
93	Evolution EVO 04	KEONGAKU EP (12", 4-track, plain sleeve)	25
94	Dedicated DEDLP 014L	76: 14 (2-LP, gatefold sleeve with bonus 12")	20
94	Dedicated DEDLP 014	76: 14 (2-LP, gatefold sleeve)	18
94	Dedicated DEDCD 014L	76: 14 (CD, gatefold, wraparound sleeve)	20
94	Dedicated DEDCD 014	76: 14 (CD)	18
96	Dedicated DED 21LP	REMOTION — THE GLOBAL COMMUNICATIONS REMIX ALBUM (LP)	18

(see also Mystic Institue, Link, Reload, Reload & E621, Chaos & Julia Set, Jedi Knights)

GLOBAL VILLAGE TRUCKING COMPANY
76	Caroline C 1516	GLOBAL VILLAGE TRUCKING COMPANY (LP, with insert)	15

GLOBE SHOW
69	Page One POF 128	Yes Or No/Gettin' On Back	7

(see also Chris Shakespeare Globe Show)

GLOBE TROTTERS
54	Parlophone CMSP 18	At Sundown/My Gal Sal (export issue)	15
54	Parlophone GEP 8528	SATURDAY NIGHT HOP (EP)	18

GLOBETROTTERS
70	RCA RCA 2017	Gravy/Cheer Me Up	8
71	RCA SF 8158	THE GLOBETROTTERS (LP)	16

GLOOMYS
68	Columbia DB 8391	Daybreak/Queen And King	12
71	DJM DJS 240	I'm A Bum/Let Me Dream	6

GLORIA MUNDI
78	RCA PB 5068	Fight Back/Do It (p/s)	5
78	RCA PL2 5157	I INDIVIDUAL (LP, with inner sleeve)	12
79	RCA PL2 5244	THE WORD IS OUT (LP, with lyric inner)	12

GLORIES
67	CBS 2786	I Stand Accused (Of Loving You)/Wish They Could Write A Song	28
67	Direction 58-3084	Give Me My Freedom/Security	15
68	Direction 58-3300	Sing Me A Love Song/Oh Baby That's Love	15
68	Direction 58-3646	My Sweet Sweet Baby/Stand By (I'm Comin' Home)	10

GLORY LANDERS
69	IBA SECC 1203	VOLUME 1 (LP)	15

GLOVE

83	Wonderland SHE 3	Like An Animal/Mouth To Mouth (p/s, some sleeves with centre holes)	7
83	Wonderland SHEX 3	Like An Animal (Club, What Club? Mix)/Like Animal/Mouth To Mouth (12", p/s, some sleeves with centre hole)	10
83	Wonderland SHE 5	Punish Me With Kisses/The Tightrope (p/s)	12
83	Wonderland SHELP 2	BLUE SUNSHINE (LP, mispressing with double-printed sleeve)	20

(see also Cure, Siouxsie & Banshees, Creatures)

ROGER GLOVER (& GUESTS)

74	Purple PUR 125	Love Is All/Old Blind Mole/Magician Moth	10
84	Safari SAF EP 1	Love Is All/Old Blind Mole/Magician Moth (p/s, reissue)	5
84	Polydor POSP 678	The Mask/So Remote (p/s, solo)	6
74	Purple TPSA 7514	THE BUTTERFLY BALL (AND THE GRASSHOPPER'S FEAST) (LP, g/fold sleeve)	18
78	Polydor 2391 306	ELEMENTS (LP, solo)	12
84	Polydor POLD 5139	THE MASK (LP, solo, with insert)	12

(see also [Sheila Carter &] Episode [Six], Deep Purple, Elf, Eddie Hardin, Whitesnake, Rainbow, Glenn Hughes, John Lawton, Wizard's Convention, Marlon, Green Bullfrog, David Coverdale, Dio)

JEREMY GLUCK

86	Flicknife SHARP 037	I KNEW BUFFALO BILL (LP)	15

(see also Barracudas)

GMT

91	Mausoleum BONE 12-83102	One By One (12", p/s)	10

GNAC

98	Earworm WORM 29	The Moustache/Armchair Thriller (p/s, black vinyl)	6

GNANK

99	Gnank GNANK 01	Gnank Gnank/Oi, Gnank (p/s)	8

GNASHER

74	Purple PUR 119	Medina Road/Easy Meat	8

GNIDROLOG

72	RCA SF 8261	IN SPITE OF HARRY'S TOE-NAIL (LP)	55
72	RCA SF 8322	LADY LAKE (LP, some with insert)	120/60

GNOMES OF ZURICH

66	Planet PLF 121	Please Mr Sun/I'm Coming Down With The Blues (with custom 'Planet' sleeve)	40/35
67	CBS 202556	Hang On Baby/Blues For My Baby	30
67	CBS 2694	High Hopes/Pretender	30
67	RCA Victor RCA 1606	Second Fiddle/Publicity Girl	35

G-NOTES

58	Oriole CB 1456	Ronnie/I Would (78 rpm = £12)	20

GOAT

82	Real Kavoom ARK 1	REAL KAVOOM (12" EP)	8

GOBBLEDEGOOKS

64	Decca F 12023	Now And Again/Where Have You Been	15

GOBBLINZ

79	Pinnacle P 8454	London/Women In Love (p/s)	80
80s	Bacon SLICE 01	Love Me Too/All Of This And More (no p/s)	80

GO-BETWEENS

80	Postcard 80-4	I Need Two Heads/Stop Before You Say It (brown label & brown co. sleeve)	20
80	Postcard 80-4	I Need Two Heads/Stop Before You Say It (yellow label & cream co. sleeve)	18
80	Postcard 81-9	Your Turn My Turn (company sleeve)	8
82	Rough Trade RT 108	Hammer The Hammer/By Chance (p/s)	6
83	Rough Trade RT 124	Cattle And Cane/Heaven Says (p/s)	6
83	Rough Trade RT 114	Man O'Sand To Girl O'See/This Girl Black Girl (p/s)	6
87	Beggars Banquet BEG 183D	Right Here/When People Are Dead/A Little Romance//Don't Call Me Gone/ A Little Romance (live) (double pack)	6
88	B. Banquet BEG 218B	Streets Of Your Town/Wait Until June (box set)	8

GOBLIN

79	EMI EMC 3222	SUSPIRIA (LP, soundtrack)	45

VIC GODARD (& SUBWAY SECT)

80	Oddball/MCA 585	Split Up The Money/Out Of Touch (p/s, with Subway Sect)	5
81	Rough Trade RT 068	Stop That Girl/Instrumentally Scared/Vertical Integration (p/s, w/Subway Sect)	5
81	Club Left CLUB 1	Stamp Of A Vamp/Hey Now (I'm In Love) (p/s, with Subway Sect)	5
85	El Benelux EL 4	Holiday Hymn/Nice On The Ice (p/s)	5
85	El Benelux EL 4T	Holiday Hymn/Nice On The Ice/Stop That Girl/Ice On The Volcano/ T.R.O.U.B.L.E. (12", p/s)	10
93	Postcard DUBH 937	Won't Turn Back/Won't Turn Back (Version) (p/s, 1,000 only)	5
80	Oddball/MCA MCF 3070	WHAT'S THE MATTER BOY? (LP, with Subway Sect)	12
82	London SH 8549	SONGS FOR SALE (LP, with Subway Sect)	12
85	Rough Trade ROUGH 56	A RETROSPECTIVE (LP, with Subway Sect)	12
85	MCA/EI 01	HOLIDAY HYMN (LP, 10 test pressings only; abandoned issue of T.R.O.U.B.L.E.)	30+
86	Rough Trade ROUGH 86	T.R.O.U.B.L.E. (LP)	12
93	Postcard DUBH 936	END OF THE SURREY PEOPLE (LP)	12

(see also Subway Sect)

KEITH & DONNA GODCHAUX

75	Round RX 104	KEITH & DONNA GODCHAUX (LP)	18

(see also Grateful Dead)

MINT VALUE £

GEOFF GODDARD

61	HMV POP 938	Girl Bride/For Eternity	55
62	HMV POP 1068	My Little Girl's Come Home/Try Once More	65
63	HMV POP 1160	Saturday Dance/Come Back To Me	45
63	HMV POP 1213	Sky Men/Walk With Me My Angel	145

HUGH GODFREY

67	Coxsone CS 7001	A Dey Pon Dem/SOUL BROTHERS: Take Ten	25
67	Studio One SO 2008	My Time/MARCIA GRIFFITHS: Hound Dog	35
67	Studio One SO 2015	Go Tell Him/MARCIA GRIFFITHS: After Laughter	30

(see also Soul Brothers)

RAY GODFREY

78	Grapevine GRP 111	Come And Get These Memories/I'm The Other Half Of You	8

ROBERT JOHN GODFREY

74	Charisma CAS 1084	FALL OF HYPERION (LP)	35

(see also Enid, Godfrey & Stewart, Don Bradshaw)

GODFREY & STEWART

86	The Enid ENID 11	THE SEED AND THE SOWER (LP)	15
80s	The Stand HEARTLP	JOINED BY THE HEART (LP, fan club issue, 2,000 only)	20
80s	The Stand HEARTC	JOINED BY THE HEART (cassette, fan club issue)	12

(see also Robert John Godfrey, Enid)

GODIEGO

78	Satril SATL 4009	THE WATER MARGIN (LP, TV soundtrack)	12

GODLEY & CREME

68	Blinkers 1215	Goodnight Blinkers/Hello Blinkers (die-cut sleeve)	32
79	Mercury SAMP 017	5 O'Clock/The Flood//Lost Weekend/Honolulu (double pack sampler, promo)	10
81	Polydor POSP 322	Under Your Thumb (Short Version)/Power Behind The Throne (2,000 only with p/s)	5
85	Polydor POSP 372	Cry/Love Bombs (picture disc)	5
85	Polydor 080 101 2	Cry/Love Bombs/Cry (CD Video)	12
81	Polydor POLD 543	ISMISM (LP, white sleeve with die-cut holes)	12

(see also Mockingbirds, Hotlegs, 10cc, Dave Berry, Frabjoy & Runcible Spoon, Cruisers, Whirlwinds, Doctor Father)

GODS

67	Polydor 56168	Come On Down To My Boat Baby/Garage Man	140
68	Columbia DB 8486	Baby's Rich/Somewhere In The Street	35
69	Columbia DB 8544	Hey! Bulldog/Real Love Guaranteed	35
69	Columbia DB 8572	Maria/Long Time, Sad Time, Bad Time	35
68	Columbia S(C)X 6286	GENESIS (LP)	150
70	Columbia SCX 6372	TO SAMUEL A SON (LP)	140
76	Harvest SHSM 2011	GODS (LP)	28

(see also Uriah Heep, Shame, Toe-Fat, Birds Birds)

GOD'S GIFT

79	Newmarket no cat. no.	THESE DAYS (EP)	10
81	New Hormones ORG 14	Soldiers/Anthony Perkins/No God/The Hunger Of Millions (12", p/s)	8
83	Pleasantly Surprised PS 7	FOLIE A QUATRE (cassette, in bag with inserts)	12

GOD SONS

72	Green Door GD 4024	Merry Up/Merry Up — Version	10

(see also Errol & U Roy, Carl Masters)

GOD SPEED! YOU BLACK EMPEROR

99	Constellation CST 006	SLOW RIOT FOR NEW ZERO KANADA (12" EP)	15
99	Kranky KRANK 034	SLOW RIOT FOR NEW ZERO KANADA (CD EP)	8

GODZ

67	Fontana STL 5500	CONTACT WITH THE GODZ (LP)	25
69	Fontana STL 5512	GODZ II (LP)	25

GOGMAGOG

85	F. For Thought YUMT 109	I Will Be There/Living In A Timewarp/It's Illegal, It's Immoral, It's Unhealthy But It's Fun (12", p/s & insert)	35

(see also Iron Maiden, Di'Anno, Def Leppard, Whitesnake, Gillan, White Spirit)

GO-GO's (U.K.)

64	Oriole CB 1982	I'm Gonna Spend My Christmas With A Dalek/Big Boss Man (some in p/s)	40/20

GO-GO's (U.S.)

80	Stiff BUY 78	We Got The Beat/How Much More (p/s)	5
81	I.R.S. PFP 1007	Our Lips Are Sealed/Surfing And Spying (p/s, pink vinyl)	10
81	I.R.S. GONP 101	Automatic/Tonite (picture disc)	7
90	A&M AMP 712	Cool Jerk/We Got The Beat (picture disc)	5
90	A&M AMCD 712	Cool Jerk/We Got The Beat (CD)	8

(see also Belinda Carlisle, Jane Wiedlin)

GOING RED?

81	Razz CLEAN 1	Some Boys/Tune Kevin's Strings (p/s)	8
81	MCA MCA 673	Some Boys/Tune Kevin's Strings (reissue, p/s)	5

(see also Freshies, Chris Sievey, Jilted John)

HERBIE GOINS & NIGHT-TIMERS

66	Parlophone R 5478	No. 1 In Your Heart/Cruisin'	125
66	Parlophone R 5533	The Incredible Miss Brown/Comin' Home To You	70
67	Parlophone PMC 7026	NUMBER ONE IN YOUR HEART (LP)	150

(see also Night-Timers, Alexis Korner's Blues Incorporated)

DAVID GOLD

97	Fat Cat 10FAT 001	Respect City Police (10")	40

HARRY GOLD with NORRIE PARAMOR ORCHESTRA
54	Columbia SCM 5144	Be Good To Me/Frou Frou	10

(see also Norrie Paramor)

MARTY GOLD
70	Avco Embassy 6466 001	MOOG PLAYS THE BEATLES (LP)	12

BARRY GOLDBERG (REUNION)
68	Pye International 7N 25465	Another Day/Capricorn Blues (as Barry Goldberg Reunion)	7
68	Pye Intl. NSPL 28116	BARRY GOLDBERG REUNION (LP)	20
69	Buddah 203 020	TWO JEWS BLUES (LP, with Mike Bloomfield)	15
71	Buddah 2318 038	BLASTS FROM MY PAST (LP)	12

(see also Electric Flag, Mike Bloomfield)

GOLDEBRIARS
64	Columbia DB 7384	Sea Of Tears/I've Got To Love Somebody	12

GOLDEN APPLES OF THE SUN
65	Decca F 12194	Monkey Time/Chocolate Rolls, Tea And Monopoly (unissued, test pressings only)	80+
65	Immediate IM 010	Monkey Time/Chocolate Rolls, Tea And Monopoly	40

GOLDEN CRUSADERS
64	Columbia DB 7232	I'm In Love With You/Always On My Mind	15
64	Columbia DB 7357	Hey Good Lookin'/Come On, Come On	15
65	Columbia DB 7485	I Don't Care/That Broken Heart Is Mine	15

GOLDEN DAWN
88	Sarah SARAH 009	My Secret World/Spring-Heeled Jack/The Railway Track (p/s, with poster)	12
89	Sarah SARAH 017	George Hamilton's Dead (p/s, with poster)	12

GOLDEN EARRING(S)
68	Capitol CL 15552	I've Just Lost Somebody/The Truth About Arthur (as Golden Earrings)	20
68	Capitol CL 15567	Dong Dong Di Ki Di Gi Dong/Wake Up — Breakfast (as Golden Earrings)	10
69	Major Minor MM 601	Just A Little Peace In My Heart/Remember My Friend (as Golden Earrings)	15
69	Major Minor MM 633	It's Alright But It Could Be Better/Where Will I Be (as Golden Earrings)	8
70	Major Minor MM 679	Another Forty-Five Miles/I Can't Get Hold Of Her	8
70	Polydor BM 56514	That Day/Words I Need	20
70	Polydor 2001 073	Back Home/This Is The Time Of Year	8
72	Polydor 2001 346	Buddy Joe/Avalanche	5
73	Track 2094 116	Radar Love/Just Like Vince Taylor	5
74	Track 2094 121	Instant Poetry/From Heaven, From Hell	5
74	Track 2094 126	Candy's Going Bad/She Flies On Strange Wings	5
75	Track 2094 130	Ce Soir/Lucky Number	5
76	Polydor 2001 626	Sleepwalking/Babylon (no p/s)	5
77	Polydor 2121 312	Bombay/Faded Jeans (no p/s)	5
69	Major Minor SMLP 65	EIGHT MILES HIGH (LP)	50
71	Polydor 2310 135	SEVEN TEARS (LP)	25
72	Polydor 2310 210	TOGETHER (LP)	20
73	Track 2406 109	HEARING EARRING (LP, braille sleeve)	15
73	Track 2406 112	MOONTAN (LP, gatefold sleeve with insert)	15

GOLDEN FLEECE
67	Decca F 12669	Athens 6 a.m./Girl From Syracuse	6

GOLDEN GATE QUARTET
53	Columbia SCM 5054	Moses Smote The Waters/Bones, Bones, Bones	5
56	Columbia SEG 7700	SINGS GREAT SPIRITUALS (EP)	8
58	Fontana TFR 6009	THAT GOLDEN CHARIOT (10" LP)	15
59	Columbia 33SX 1172	SHOUT FOR JOY! (LP)	15
50s	Columbia 33CSX 9	NEGRO SPIRITUALS (LP)	15
61	Columbia 33SX 1370	GET ON BOARD (LP)	15

GOLDEN GATE STRINGS
65	Columbia DB 7634	Mr. Tambourine Man/With God On Our Side	12

GOLDEN HORDE
80s	Hot Wire HWS 855	Young And Happy/Little UFO/Fiona (p/s)	5
85	Hot Wire WAY OUT 1	DIG THAT CRAZY GRAVE (EP)	5
85	Hot Wire/I.D. NOSE 7	THE CHOCOLATE BISCUIT CONSPIRACY (LP)	12

GOLDFRAPP
00	Mute 12MUTE 247	Lovely Head/(Stare Mesto Mix)/(Miss World Mix) (12", p/s)	15
00	Mute 12MUTE 253	Utopia/(New Ears Mix)/(Sunroof Mix) (12", p/s)	10
01	Mute 12MUTE 259	Human/(Calexico Instrumental)/(Massey's Neanderthal Mix) (12", p/s)	10
00	Mute STUMM 188	FELT MOUNTAIN (LP, with inner)	12
03	Mute STUMM 196	BLACK CHERRY (LP)	12
03	Mute IPKSTUMM196	BLACK CHERRY (CD, card sleeve - enhanced Press Kit)	18
05	Mute STUMM 250	SUPERNATURE (LP)	12

GOLDIE (& GINGERBREADS)
65	Decca F 12070	Can't You Hear My Heartbeat/Little Boy	15
65	Decca F 12126	That's Why I Love You/Skip	15
65	Decca F 12199	Sailor Boy/Please Please	15
66	Immediate IM 026	Goin' Back/Headlines (solo)	20
66	Fontana TF 693	I Do/Think About The Good Times (solo)	15
69	Decca F 12931	Can't You Hear My Heartbeat/That's Why I Love You	7

(see also Ten Wheel Drive)

GOLDIE LOOKIN' CHAIN
	Must Destroy DESTROY12 001	Half Man Half Machine/Self Suicide/Half Man Half Machine (Clean) (12", p/s, 1,000 only)	10
04	Gold Dust	THE MANIFESTO (CD, sold at gigs)	40

JOHN GOLDING
74	Cottage 101S	DISCARDED VERSE (LP, 2,000 only)	12

VIVIEN GOLDMAN
81	Window WIN 1	Launderette/Private Armies (gatefold p/s, with PiL)	8
81	Window 12WIN 1	Launderette/Private Armies (12", p/s, with PiL)	10

(see also Public Image Ltd)

BOBBY GOLDSBORO
63	Stateside SS 193	The Runaround/The Letter	18
63	United Artists UP 1046	See The Funny Little Clown/Hello Loser	10
64	United Artists UP 1054	Whenever He Holds You/If She Was Mine	10
65	United Artists UP 1079	Little Things/I Just Can't Go On Pretending	15
65	United Artists UP 1091	Voodoo Woman/It Breaks My Heart	7
65	United Artists UP 1104	If You Wait For Love/If You've Got A Heart	7
66	United Artists UP 1120	Broomstick Cowboy/Ain't Got Time For Happy	7
66	United Artists UP 1128	It's Too Late/I'm Goin' Home (DJ copy = £45)	15
66	United Artists UP 1135	I Know You Better Than That/When Your Love Has Gone	7
66	United Artists UP 1146	Take Your Love/Longer Than Forever	25
67	United Artists UP 1156	It Hurts Me/Pity The Fool	10
67	United Artists UP 1166	No Fun At The Fair/Hold On	10
67	United Artists UP 1177	Too Many People/Goodbye To All You Women (DJ copy = £85)	50
68	United Artists UP 2223	Autumn Of My Life/She Chased Me	10
69	United Artists UP 2264	Love Arrester/Dissatisfied Man	8
69	United Artists UP 35034	Muddy Mississippi Line/Richer Man Than I	8
69	United Artists UP 35053	Letter To Emily/Tomorrow Is Forgotten	6
65	United Artists UEP 1006	LITTLE THINGS (EP)	48
66	United Artists UEP 1016	THE TALENTED BOBBY GOLDSBORO (EP)	48
65	United Artists ULP 1118	I CAN'T STOP LOVING YOU (LP)	35
66	United Artists (S)ULP 1135	IT'S TOO LATE (LP)	35
67	United Artists (S)ULP 1163	SOLID GOLDSBORO — GREATEST HITS (LP)	22
68	United Artists (S)ULP 1195	HONEY (LP, black label)	25
68	United Artists (S)ULP 1206	WORD PICTURES (LP)	20
69	United Artists UAS 29008	TODAY (LP)	18

GOL GAPPAS
86	él GPO 21	West 14/Roman (p/s)	12

GOLDSMITH
83	Bedlam BLM 001	Life Is Killing Me/Music Man (p/s)	50

JERRY GOLDSMITH
(see under Soundtrack LPs)

GOLGOTHA
84	Golgotha GOTH 002	DANGEROUS GAMES (Dangerous Games/Old England's Green/Air/ The Great Divide (EP, no p/s)	70
90	Communique CMGLP 003	UNMAKER OF WORLDS (EP, p/s)	15

GOLIARD
76	Broadside BRO 127	FORTUNE MY FOE (LP, with booklet)	15

GOLIATH
70	CBS 5312	Port And Lemon Lady/I Heard About A Friend	7
70	CBS 64229	GOLIATH (LP)	55

GOLLIWOGS
66	Vocalion VF 9266	Brown-Eyed Girl/You Better Be Careful	42
67	Vocalion VF 9283	Fragile Child/Fight Fire	42
72	Fantasy FAN 5996	GOLLIWOGS (LP, pressed in U.S. for U.K. distribution)	15

(see also Creedence Clearwater Revival)

BENNY GOLSON
81	CBS A 1223	The New Killer Joe/Walkin' And Stalkin'	8
81	CBS 12A 1223	The New Killer Joe/Walkin' And Stalkin' (12")	7
59	Esquire 32-125	GONE WITH GOLSON (LP)	20
60	Esquire 32-105	GROOVIN' WITH GOLSON (LP)	20

BENNY GOLSON & ART FARMER
62	Pye International 7N 25120	Blues March/Serenata	5
65	Stateside SL 10150	STOCKHOLM SOJOURN (LP)	12

(see also Art Farmer)

GONADS
82	Secret SHH 131	PURE PUNK FOR NOW PEOPLE (EP)	8
82	Secret SHH 134	PEACE ARTISTS (EP)	6
83	Razor RZS 103	DELILAH (THE PUNK EPIC) (EP)	5

GONDOLIERS
58	Starlite ST45 001	Fly, Seagull, Fly/God's Green Acres	12

NAT GONELLA & HIS GEORGIA JAZZ BAND
60	Columbia DB 4465	Show Me The Way To Go Home/My Gal Sal	5
58	Columbia 33S 1146	SALUTE TO SATCHMO (10" LP)	20
61	Columbia 33SX 1380	THE NAT GONELLA STORY (LP)	25

RON GONELLA
60s	Lismor LILP 5017	FIDDLER'S FANCY (LP)	12

GONG
71	Philips 6332 033	CONTINENTAL CIRCUS (LP, soundtrack)	40
73	Virgin V 2002	RADIO GNOME INVISIBLE PART 1 — THE FLYING TEAPOT (LP, originally with black & white label design)	15/12

73	Virgin V 2007	RADIO GNOME INVISIBLE PART 2 — ANGEL'S EGG	
		(LP, gatefold sleeve, initially with b&w label; some with book)	25/12
74	Virgin VC 502	CAMEMBERT ELECTRIQUE (LP)	12
74	Virgin V 2019	YOU (LP, with lyric insert)	12
76	Virgin V 2046	SHAMAL (LP)	12
77	Virgin VGD 3501	LIVE ETC. (2-LP, with cut-out cover & inner sleeves)	12

(see also Mother Gong, Gilli Smyth & Mother Gong, Daevid Allen, Steve Hillage, Clearlight, Radio Actors, Sphynx, Tim Blake, Comus)

GONG/CAMEL/HENRY COW/GLOBAL TRUCKING COMPANY

73	Greasy Truckers GT 4997	GREASY TRUCKERS (2-LP, 1 side each; with insert)	20

(see also Camel, Henry Cow, Global Trucking Company)

GONKS

64	Decca F 11984	The Gonk Song/That's All Right, Mamma	30

(see also Twinkle)

RON GONNELLA

70s	LISMOR LILP 5017	FIDDLERS FANCY (LP)	12

PAUL GONSALVES

64	Vocalion LAE 587	BOOM JACKIE BOOM CHICK (LP)	250
70	Deram SML 1064	HUMMINGBIRD (LP)	60

(see also Tubby Hayes & Paul Gonsalves)

BELLE GONZALEZ

65	Jupiter JEPOC 37	POETS SET IN JAZZ (EP, as Belle Gonzalez & Sextet)	18
66	Jupiter JEPOC 39	CONTEMPORARY POETS SET IN JAZZ (EP)	18
72	Columbia SCX 6484	BELLE (LP)	50

(see also Mark Wirtz)

DOUGLAS GOOD & GINNY PLENTY

68	Stateside SS 2104	Sunny And Me/Living In A World Of Make Believe	6

JACK GOOD'S FAT NOISE

60	Decca F 11233	The Fat Washerwoman/The Fat Noise	12

GOODBYE MR MACKENZIE

84	Scruples YTS 1	Death Of A Salesman/LINDY BERGMAN: Locked Inside Your Prison	
		(no p/s, 500 only)	25
86	Precious Org. JEWEL 2	The Rattler/Candlestick Park (p/s)	6
86	Precious Org. JEWEL 2T	The Rattler/Candlestick Park/The End (12", p/s)	10
86	Clandestine MACK 1	Face To Face/Secrets/Good Deeds (12", p/s, 1,000 only)	10
90	Parlophone PCS 7345	HAMMER AND TONGS (LP, unreleased, white label test pressings only)	40

(see also Garbage)

GOOD EARTH

68	Saga FID 2112	IT'S HARD ROCK AND ALL THAT (LP)	22
70	Saga FID 8157	IN THE SUMMERTIME (LP, with tracks by Macon Jug)	15

(see also First Impression/Good Earth, Mungo Jerry, Ray Dorset)

GOODEES

69	Stax STAX 113	Condition Red/Didn't Know Love Was So Good	15

GOOD GUYS

70	Duke DU 82	Death Rides/Destruction	10
70	Duke DU 83	Wreck It Up/Dynamic Groove	10
70	Duke DU 84	Happiness/Latissimo	8

(see also Byron Lee & Dragonaires)

PHILIP GOODHAND-TAIT (& STORMSVILLE SHAKERS)

66	Parlophone R 5448	I'm Gonna Put Some Hurt On You/It's A Lie (with Stormsville Shakers)	15
66	Parlophone R 5498	No Problem/What More Do You Want (with Stormsville Shakers)	20
66	Parlophone R 5547	You Can't Take Love/J.C. Greaseburger (solo)	15

(see also Circus, Larry Williams, Love Affair)

CUBA GOODING

83	London LONX 41	Happiness Is Just Around The Bend/(Version) (12")	8

JOHNNY GOODISON

70	Deram DM 319	A Little Understanding/One Mistake	20

(see also Quotations, Johnny B. Great)

GOODLETTSVILLE FIVE

64	London HLW 9854	Eef/Baly's Gone Eefing	8

JOHN GOODLUCK

74	Tradition TSR 015	SUFFOLK MIRACLE (LP, with insert)	30
75	Sweet Folk & Country SFA 047	SPEED THE PLOUGH: TRADITIONAL SONGS OF SUFFOLK (LP)	25
88	Big Ben FE 065	THE MAN WHO PUT THE ENGINE IN THE CHIP SHOP: MORE RAILWAY SONGS OF DAVE GOULDER (LP)	15

BENNY GOODMAN

58	Philips BBE 12172	PEGGY WITH BENNY (EP, with Peggy Lee)	10
52	Capitol LC 6526	SESSION FOR SIX (10" LP, as The Benny Goodman Sextet)	15
52	Capitol LC 6557	EASY DOES IT (10" LP)	15
52	Capitol LC 6565	AFTER HOURS (10" LP)	15
53	Capitol LC 6601	THE BENNY GOODMAN BAND (10" LP)	15
53	Capitol LC 6620	THE GOODMAN TOUCH (10" LP)	15
54	Columbia 33S 1048	SESSION FOR SEXTET (10" LP)	15
54	Capitol LC 6680	CLASSICS IN JAZZ (10" LP)	15
55	Philips BBR 8064	LET'S HEAR THE MELODY (10" LP)	15
58	Fontana TFR 6006	BENNY GOODMAN SEXTET (10" LP)	18

Dave GOODMAN

MINT VALUE £

DAVE GOODMAN & FRIENDS
78	The Label TLR 008	Justifiable Homicide/Take Down Your Fences (p/s, 1st 15,000 on red vinyl)	8

(N.B. rumoured copies with 'Steve Jones & Paul Cook' credit on the sleeve DO NOT exist)
(see also Sex Pistols)

GOOD MISSIONARIES
80	Kif KIF'S 1	Good Missionary (Parts 1 & 2) (p/s)	5
80	Unnormality NORM 001	VIBING UP THE SENILE WORLD (The Good Missionary Part 1 [live]/ The Good Missionary Part/Kif Kif's Free Freak Out [live]) (EP, 1,000 only)	5
81	Unnormality NORM 002	DERANGED IN HASTINGS (Keep Going Backwards/Attitudes) (EP, with printed insert, PVC sleeve)	5
79	Deptford Fun City DLP 04	FIRE FROM HEAVEN (LP)	12
80	Conventional (no cat. no.)	SPONTANEOUS EMISSIONS (studio/live cassette)	12

(see also Mark Perry, Alternative TV)

GOOD RATS
69	London HLR 10237	The Hobo/The Truth Is Gone	6

GOOD SHIP LOLLIPOP
69	Ember EMB S 276	Maxwell's Silver Hammer/How Does It Feel (some in p/s)	12/6

GOOD TIME LOSERS
67	Fontana TF 791	Trafalgar Square/Where Did My Heart Go	6

GOODTIMERS
62	Fontana H 360	It's Twistin' Time/Twisting Train	10

GOOD VIBRATIONS
70	Ember EMB S 270	Call Me Lightning/Nantucket Ferry	6

ROD GOODWAY
90	Woronzow WOO 12	ETHEREAL COUNTERBALANCE (LP)	18

RON GOODWIN CONCERT ORCHESTRA
53	Parlophone MSP 6035	Limelight/The Song From Moulin Rouge	12
53	Parlophone MSP 6055	Tropical Mirage/The Man Between	12
54	Parlophone MSP 6103	The Sons Of The High Seas/Guadalcanal March	12
54	Parlophone MSP 6115	Cara Mia/Three Coins In The Fountain	12
54	Parlophone MSP 6136	Midnight Blue/On The Waterfront	12
56	Parlophone 45 R-4235	War And Peace/The Christmas Tree	10
57	Parlophone R 4297	Skiffling Strings (Swinging Sweetheart)/I'll Find You	10
58	Parlophone R 4608	Lolita/All Strung Up	10
55	Parlophone GEP 8555	RON GOODWIN AND HIS CONCERT ORCHESTRA (EP)	10
58	Parlophone GEP 8662	RON GOODWIN SPECIALS (EP)	8
58	Parlophone GEP 8699	RON GOODWIN SPECIALS NO. 2 (EP)	8
60	Parlophone SGE 2010	THE SMOOTH SOUND (EP, stereo)	8
54	Parlophone PMD 1014	FILM FAVOURITES (10" LP)	15
56	Parlophone PMD 1038	MUSIC TO SET YOU DREAMING (10" LP)	15
58	Parlophone PCS 3002	MUSIC FOR AN ARABIAN NIGHT (LP)	15
58	Parlophone PCS 3006	OUT OF THIS WORLD! (LP)	25
64	United Artists ULP 1071	633 SQUADRON (LP, soundtrack)	25
65	Stateside SL 10136	THOSE MAGNIFICENT MEN IN THEIR FLYING MACHINES (LP, soundtrack)	30
66	Polydor 582 004	THE TRAP (LP, soundtrack)	35
68	Stateside (S)SL 10259	DECLINE AND FALL ... OF A BIRDWATCHER (LP, soundtrack)	100
69	Paramount SPFL 255	MONTE CARLO OR BUST! (LP, soundtrack)	45
69	MGM MGM-C(S) 8102	WHERE EAGLES DARE (LP, soundtrack)	12
69	United Artists UAS 29019	BATTLE OF BRITAIN (LP, soundtrack)	12
76	EMI EMC 3148	ESCAPE FROM THE DARK (LP, soundtrack)	15

(see also 20th Century Fox Orchestra, Parlophone Pops Orchestra)

GOOFERS
55	Vogue Coral Q 72051	Hearts Of Stone/You're The One (78 rpm = £20)	60
55	Vogue Coral Q 72074	Flip, Flop And Fly/My Babe (78 rpm = £20)	60
55	Vogue Coral Q 72094	Goofy Drybones/Nare (78 rpm = £15)	35
56	Vogue Coral Q 72124	Sick! Sick! Sick!/Twenty One (78 rpm = £25)	30
56	Vogue Coral Q 72171	Tear Drop Motel/Tennessee Rock And Roll (78 rpm = £25)	40
57	Vogue Coral Q 72267	Wow!/Push, Push, Push Cart (78 rpm = £25)	30
57	Vogue Coral Q 72289	The Dipsy Doodle/Take This Heart (78 rpm = £15)	30

GOONS
56	Decca F 10756	I'm Walking Backwards For Christmas/Bluebottle Blues (78 rpm = £8)	18
56	Decca F 10780	The Ying Tong Song/Bloodnok's Rock 'N' Roll Call (78 rpm = £8)	18
57	Decca F 10885	Eeh! Ah! Oh! Ooh!/I Love You (78 rpm = £8)	15
57	Decca F 10945	A Russian Love Song/Whistle Your Cares Away (78 rpm = £6)	10
56	Decca DFE 6396	THE GOONS (EP)	20
64	Decca LF 1332	UNCHAINED MELODIES (10" LP)	25
59	Parlophone PMC 1108	BEST OF THE GOON SHOWS (LP)	15
60	Parlophone PMC 1129	BEST OF THE GOON SHOWS (NO. 2) (LP)	15

(see also Peter Sellers, Spike Milligan, Michael Bentine, Famous Eccles, Eric Sykes)

SAM GOPAL
69	Stable STA 5602	Horse/Back Door Man (unissued, existence unconfirmed)	
69	Stable SLE 8001	Escalator/Angry Faces/Cold Embrace/The Sky is Burning (LP sampler)	50
69	Stable SLE 8001	ESCALATOR (LP, gatefold sleeve)	130

(see also Hawkwind, Motörhead, Vamp, Isaac Guillory, Clark-Hutchinson, G. F. Fitzgerald)

RABBI JOSEPH GORDAN
(see under 'R')

PETE(R) GORDENO
61	Fontana H 319	Be My Girl/Haven't Got Time (as Pete Gordeno)	12
62	Parlophone R 4862	I Got Eyes/You're Following Me	12
70	Decca PA 78	THE WORLD OF PETER GORDENO (LP)	15

GORDON
(see under Gordon Waller)

ANITA GORDON
55	Brunswick 05456	Lonesome Like Nobody Knows/His Hands	10

BARRY GORDON
56	MGM MGM 928	I Can't Whistle/The Milkman's Polka	12
56	MGM MGM 935	Rock Around Mother Goose/Nuttin' For Christmas	22

CURTIS GORDON
57	Mercury MT 163	Sixteen/Cry, Cry (78)	18

DEXTER GORDON
65	Realm RM 191	DEXTER RIDES AGAIN (LP)	12
60s	Fontana Jazz FJL 907	MASTER SWINGERS (LP, with Wardell Gray)	15

(see also Wardell Gray)

JOE GORDON (FOLK FOUR)
59	HMV POP 600	Gotta Travel On/Ho Ro My Nutbrown Maid (78 rpm = £6)	5
59	HMV POP 634	Dream Lover/Dance To Your Daddy (78 rpm = £10)	15
60	HMV POP 737	Football Crazy/By The Bright Shining Light Of The Moon	6
59	HMV 7EG 8454	JOE GORDON FOLK HOUR (EP)	15

PHIL GORDON
55	Brunswick 05481	Get A Load Of That Crazy Walk/Strip Polka	10
56	Brunswick 05545	Down The Road Apiece/I'm Gonna Move To The Outskirts Of Town	40

ROBERT GORDON WITH LINK WRAY
77	Private Stock PVTS 127	Endless Sleep & The Fool/The Fool (B-side plays at 78rpm)	15

(see also Link Wray)

RONNIE GORDON
63	R&B JB 127	Shake Some Time/Comin' Home	25

ROSCO(E) GORDON
60	Top Rank JAR 332	Just A Little Bit/Goin' Home (as Rosco Gordon)	30
63	Stateside SS 204	Just A Little Bit/What I Wouldn't Do	28
65	Vocalion V-P 9245	Keep On Doggin'/Bad Dream	30
65	Island WI 256	Surely I Love You/What You Do To Me	25
66	Island WI 272	No More Doggin'/Goin' Home	32

TONY GORDON
73	Grape GR 3056	Be True (actually by Alton Ellis)/Navajo Trail	6

(see also Alton Ellis)

VINCENT GORDON
69	Coxsone CS 7085	Soul Trombone/LARRY & ALVIN: Your Cheating Heart	28
69	Duke DU 37	Everybody Bawlin'/SILVERTONES: Come Look Here	15
69	Crab CRAB 16	Walking By/VICEROYS: Promises Promises	12
74	Big Shot BI 630	Come Go With Me/SKIN, FLESH & BONES: Dub Ali Dub	7
75	DIP DLP 5001	MUSICAL BONES (LP, plain sleeve, white label)	40
70s	Trojan TRO 9058	Liquid Horns/JUNIOR: Liquidator	5

(see also Don Drummond Junior)

CHARLIE GORE
54	Parlophone CMSP 19	I'll Find Somebody/Heaven Sent You To Me (export issue)	25
54	Parlophone DP 379	I'll Find Somebody/Heaven Sent You To Me (78)	10
54	Parlophone CMSP 26	Two Of A Kind/It's A Long Walk Back To Town (export issue)	20
54	Parlophone DP 397	Two Of A Kind/It's A Long Walk Back To Town (78)	10
54	Parlophone CMSP 30	I Didn't Know/Oh! Mis'rable Love (export issue)	20

(see also Hawkshaw Hawkins, Ruby Wright)

LESLEY GORE
63	Mercury AMT 1205	It's My Party/Danny	5
63	Mercury AMT 1210	Judy's Turn To Cry/Just Let Me Cry	5
63	Mercury AMT 1213	She's A Fool/The Old Crowd	5
64	Mercury MF 803	You Don't Own Me/Run Bobby Run	10
64	Mercury MF 810	That's The Way Boys Are/That's The Way The Ball Bounces	10
64	Mercury MF 821	I Don't Wanna Be A Loser/It's Gotta Be You	10
64	Mercury MF 829	Maybe I Know/Wonder Boy	5
64	Mercury MF 837	Sometimes I Wish I Were A Boy/Hey Now	10
65	Mercury MF 846	The Look Of Love/Little Girl Go Home	12
65	Mercury MF 862	Sunshine Lollipops And Rainbows/You've Come Back	12
65	Mercury MF 872	My Town, My Guy And Me/Girl In Love	15
65	Mercury MF 889	I Won't Love You Anymore (Sorry)/No Matter What You Do	15
66	Mercury MF 902	Young Love/I Just Don't Know If I Can	12
66	Mercury MF 963	California Nights/I'm Going Out (The Same Way I Came In)	10
66	Mercury MF 984	I'm Fallin' Down/Summer And Sandy	15
68	Mercury MF 1017	Magic Colours/It's A Happening World	12
75	A&M AMS 7184	Immortality/Give It To Me, Sweet Thing	6
64	Mercury 10017 MCE	LESLEY GORE (EP)	40
63	Mercury MMC 14127	I'LL CRY IF I WANT TO (LP)	40
63	Mercury 20001 MCL	SINGS OF MIXED-UP HEARTS (LP)	32
64	Mercury 20020 MCL	BOYS BOYS BOYS (LP)	32
64	Mercury 20033 MCL	GIRL TALK (LP)	32
65	Mercury 20071 MCL	MY TOWN, MY GUY & ME (LP)	25
65	Mercury 20076 MCL	ALL ABOUT LOVE (LP)	30
67	Wing WL 1183	GIRL TALK (LP, reissue)	15

GORGONI, MARTIN & TAYLOR
72	Buddah 2011-137	Toly Toly Guyluesha/I Can Make You Cry	7
72	Buddah 2318 067	GORGONI, MARTIN AND TAYLOR (LP)	15

MINT VALUE £

GORILLAZ
02	EMI SMVG 004	L'IL DUB CHEFIN (10" 4-track sampler)	18

(see also Blur, Damon Albarn)

GORKY'S ZYGOTIC MYNCI
93	Ankst ANKST/GZM 040	PATIO (10" EP)	20
94	Ankst ANKST 048	Merched Yn Neud Gwallt Eu Gilydd/Bocs Angelica/	
		When You Laugh At Your Own Garden In A Blazer (p/s)	6
95	Ankst ANKST 053	Pentref Wrth Y Môr/The Game Of Eyes/Cwpwrdd Sadwrn (p/s)	6
95	Ankst ANKST 058	Gewn Ni Gorffen/12 Impressionistic Soundscapes	
		(clear vinyl, die-cut p/s, mail order only, 1,000 copies)	10
96	Ankst ANKST 068	AMBER GAMBLER EP (10", p/s)	8
97	Fontana 534 769	BARAFUNDLE (LP)	15
98	Mercury ANKST GZM 5	Let's Get Together (In Our Minds)/Billy And The Sugarloaf Mountain/	
		Hwiangerdd Mar (numbered p/s)	7

JOHN GORMAN
73	Island WIP 6151	WPC Hodges/I Remember	5
77	DJM DJF 20491	GO MAN GORMAN (LP)	15

(see also Scaffold, Grimms)

EYDIE GORMÉ
54	Vogue Coral Q 2014	Frenesi/Climb Up The Wall	15
54	Vogue Coral Q 2027	Tea For Two/Sure	15
55	Vogue Coral Q 72092	Give A Fool A Chance/A Girl Can't Say	15
55	Vogue Coral Q 72103	Soldier Boy/What Is The Secret Of Your Success?	15
56	London HL 8227	Sincerely Yours/Come Home (78 rpm = £8)	25
57	HMV POP 400	Kiss In Your Eyes/Your Kisses Kill Me	7
58	HMV POP 432	Love Me Forever/Until They Sail	8
58	HMV POP 493	You Need Hands/The Gentleman Is A Dope	5
58	HMV POP 513	Gotta Have Rain/To You, From Me (78 rpm = £8)	5
58	HMV POP 529	Dormi, Dormi, Dormi/Be Careful, It's My Heart (78 rpm = £8)	5
59	HMV POP 577	Separate Tables/The Voice Of My Heart (78 rpm = £10)	5
59	HMV POP 616	I'm Yours/Don't Take Your Love From Me	5
60	HMV POP 767	The Dance Is Over/Too Young To Know	20
62	CBS AAG 105	Yes, My Darling Daughter/Sonny Boy	5
63	CBS AAG 131	Blame It On The Bossa Nova/Guess I Should Have Loved Him More	5
63	CBS AAG 149	Don't Try To Fight It Baby/Theme From Light Fantastic	8
63	CBS AAG 170	Everybody Go Home/The Message	15
67	CBS 202470	Everybody Go Home/The Message (reissue)	5
59	HMV 7EG 8547	LOVE IS A SEASON (EP, also stereo [GES 5789])	each 10
59	HMV 7EG 8562	I'LL REMEMBER APRIL (EP, also stereo [GES 5795])	each 10
59	HMV 7EG 8409	EXCITING EYDIE (EP)	10
59	HMV 7EG 8474	FINE AND DANDY (EP)	10
59	HMV 7EG 8515	WHEN YOUR LOVER HAS GONE (EP)	10
64	HMV AGG 20047	THE SWEETEST SOUNDS (EP)	5
58	Coral LVA 9086	EYDIE GORME'S DELIGHT (LP)	15
58	HMV CLP 1156	EYDIE GORME (LP)	15
58	HMV CLP 1170	EYDIE SWINGS THE BLUES (LP)	15
58	HMV CLP 1201	VAMPS THE ROARING 20's (LP)	15
59	HMV CLP 1250	EYDIE IN LOVE (LP)	15
59	HMV CLP 1257	GORME SINGS SHOWSTOPPERS (LP)	12
59	HMV CLP 1290	LOVE IS A SEASON (LP)	15
60	HMV CLP 1323	ON STAGE (LP)	12
60	HMV CLP 1392/CSD 1322	EYDIE IN DIXIE-LAND (LP, mono/stereo)	12/15

(see also Steve Lawrence)

FRANK GORSHIN
66	Pye International 7N 25402	The Riddler/Never Let Her Go (some in p/s)	75/35

GOSPEL CLASSICS
68	Chess CRS 8080	More Love, That's What We Need/You Need Faith (DJ copy = £150)	100

GOSPELFOLK
69	Emblem 7DR 324	PRODIGAL (LP)	200

GOSPEL GARDEN
68	Camp 602 006	Finders Keepers/Just A Tear	12

(see also Dimples, Amazing Blondel)

GOSPEL OAK
70	Uni UNS 527	Recollections Of Jessica/Brown Haired Girl	6
70	Uni UNLS 113	GOSPEL OAK (LP)	40

GOSPEL PEARLS
63	Liberty LBY 1191	THE GOSPEL PEARLS (LP)	25

GOTHIC HORIZON
70	Argo AFW 102	The Jason Lodge Poetry Book/Wilhelmina Before Sunrise	20
71	Argo AFW 104	Marjorie/Song	18
72	Argo AFW 107	If You Can Smile/Thoughts	12
72	Argo AFW 108	Girl With Guitar/Can't Bear To Think About You	12
71	Argo ZFB 26	THE JASON LODGE POETRY BOOK (LP)	75
72	Argo ZDA 150	TOMORROW IS ANOTHER DAY (LP)	90

KEVIN GOULD
70s	Myrrh MYR 1028	TRUE STORIES BY (LP)	20

SANDRA GOULD
63	Philips BF 1290	Hello Melvin (This Is Mama)/My Son The Surfer	7

TERRY GOULD
69	Sing SING 1001	SEVERAL KINDS OF LOVING (LP)	12

DAVE GOULDER
73	Big Ben BB 0004	REQUIEM FOR STEAM: THE RAILWAY SONGS OF DAVE GOULDER (LP)	15

DALE GOULDER & LIZ DYER
70	Argo ZFB 10	JANUARY MAN (LP)	30
71	Argo ZFB 30	RAVEN & CROW (LP)	30

GRAHAM GOULDMAN
66	Decca F 12334	Stop! Stop! Stop! (Or Honey I'll Be Gone...)/Better To Have Loved And Lost	85
68	RCA Victor RCA 1667	Upstairs, Downstairs/Chestnut	22
69	Spark SRL 1026	Windmills Of Your Mind/Harvey's Theme (as Graham Gouldman Orchestra)	15
72	CBS 7739	Nowhere To Go/Growing Older	7

(see also 10cc, Whirlwinds, Mockingbirds, High Society, Frabjoy & Runcible Spoon, Manchester Mob, Garden Odyssey Enterprise, Friday Browne, Doctor Father)

GOVE
69	London HLE 10295	Sunday Morning Early/Death Letter Blues	12

JOHN GRAAS SEPTET
54	London RE-P 1003	FRENCH HORN VOL. 1 (EP)	10

GRAB GRAB THE HADDOCK
84	Cherry Red 12CHERRY 83	THREE SONGS BY GRAB GRAB THE HADDOCK (12" EP)	8

(see also Marine Girls, Tracey Thorne)

MICK GRABHAM
72	United Artists UP 35391	On Fire For You Baby/Sweet Blossom Woman	5
72	United Artists UAS 29341	MICK THE LAD (LP)	12

(see also Plastic Penny, Cochise, Procol Harum)

GRACE
80	MCA MCA 628	Fire Of London/Beatnik (p/s)	5
81	MCA MCA 667	Billy Boy/Ad Mad (p/s)	15

CHARLIE GRACIE
57	Parlophone R 4290	Butterfly/Ninety-Nine Ways (initially gold lettering on label, later silver)	85/45
57	Parlophone R 4290	Butterfly/Ninety-Nine Ways (78)	8
57	Parlophone R 4313	Fabulous/Just Lookin' (initially gold lettering on label, later silver)	85/45
57	Parlophone R 4313	Fabulous/Just Lookin' (78)	6
57	London HL 8467	Wandering Eyes/I Love You So Much It Hurts (tri-centre) (78 rpm = £8)	25
57	London HLU 8521	Cool Baby/You Got A Heart Like A Rock (tri-centre) (78 rpm = £10)	32
58	London HLU 8596	Crazy Girl/Dressin' Up (tri-centre) (78 rpm = £12)	38
59	Coral Q 72362	Doodlebug/Hurry Up, Buttercup (tri-centre) (78 rpm = £30)	30
59	Coral Q 72373	Angel Of Love/I'm A Fool, That's Why (tri-centre, later round centre)	22/15
59	Coral Q 72373	Angel Of Love/I'm A Fool, That's Why (78)	30
59	Coral Q 72381	Oh-Well-A/Because I Love You So (78 rpm = £45)	28
60	Columbia DB 4477	The Race/I Looked For You	22
62	London HLU 9603	Pretty Baby/Night And Day, U.S.A.	22
65	Stateside SS 402	He'll Never Love You Like I Do/Keep My Love Next To Your Heart (DJ copy = £150)	60
57	Parlophone GEP 8630	THE FABULOUS CHARLIE GRACIE (EP)	65
78	London HA-U 8513	CAMEO PARKWAY SESSIONS (LP)	18

GRACIOUS!
68	Polydor 56333	Beautiful/What A Lovely Rain	25
70	Vertigo 6059 009	Once On A Windy Day/Fugue In D Minor	12
70	Vertigo 6360 002	GRACIOUS! (LP, gatefold sleeve, swirl label)	120
72	Philips Intl. 6382 004	THIS IS ... GRACIOUS!! (LP, gatefold sleeve)	70

GRADUATE
80	Precision PAR 100	Elvis Should Play Ska/Julie Julie (p/s)	12
80	Precision PAR 104	Ever Met A Day/Shut Up (p/s)	6
80	Precision PAR 111	Ambition/Bad Dreams (p/s)	5
81	Precision PAR 117	Shut Up/Ever Met A Day (reissue, no p/s)	5
80s	Blue Hat 5 BHR	Mad One/Somebody Put Out The Fire	12
80	Precision PART 001	ACTING MY AGE (LP)	12

(see also Tears For Fears)

GRADUATES
79	Graduate GRAD 1	If You Want It/Hey Young Girl (p/s)	6

BILLY GRAHAM & ESCALATORS
67	Atlantic 584 073	Ooh Poo Pah Doo/East 24th Avenue	15

BOBBY/BOBBIE GRAHAM
65	Fontana TF 521	Skin Deep/Zoom Widge And Wag (as Bobbie Graham)	20
66	Fontana TF 667	Teensville/Grotty Drums (as Bobby Graham)	15

(see also Outlaws, Jimmy Page)

CHICK GRAHAM & COASTERS
64	Decca F 11859	Education/I Know	12
64	Decca F 11932	A Little You/Dance Baby Dance	12

DAV(E)Y GRAHAM
68	Decca F 12841	Both Sides Now/Tristano	5
62	Golden Guinea GGL 0224	THE GUITAR PLAYER (LP)	35
64	Decca LK 4649	FOLK, BLUES AND BEYOND (LP)	75
64	Decca LK 4652	FOLK ROOTS, NEW ROUTES (LP, with Shirley Collins)	110
66	Decca LK 4780	MIDNIGHT MAN (LP)	80
68	Decca LK/SKL 4969	LARGE AS LIFE AND TWICE AS NATURAL (LP)	85
69	Decca LK/SKL 5011	HAT (LP)	75
70	Decca SKL 5056	HOLLY KALEIDOSCOPE (LP, as Davy Graham & Holly)	65
70	President PTLS 1039	GODINGTON BOUNDARY (LP, with Holly)	42

76	Eron ERON 007	ALL THAT MOODY (LP, private pressing)..................................... 125
81	Righteous GDC 001	FOLK ROOTS, NEW ROUTES (LP, with Shirley Collins, reissue) 15
97	Rollercoaster ROLL 2022	AFTER HOURS (10" LP)... 12
99	Rollercoaster ROLL 2023	ALL THAT MOODY (10" LP, reissue)...................................... 12

DAVY GRAHAM & ALEXIS KORNER
| 62 | Topic TOP 70 | 3/4 A.D. (EP, first pressing in mauve sleeve with cream label; later pressings with lilac or bronze sleeve and blue label) ..... 225/125/100 |

(see also Alexis Korner)

DAVY GRAHAM/THAMESIDERS
| 63 | Decca DFE 8538 | FROM A LONDON HOOTENANNY (EP, 2 tracks each) .... 18 |

ERNIE GRAHAM
| 78 | Stiff OFF 2 | Romeo And The Lonely Girl/Only Time Will Tell (p/s)...................... 5 |
| 71 | Liberty LBS 83485 | ERNIE GRAHAM (LP) .... 40 |

(see also Clancy, Eire Apparent, Brinsley Schwarz, Help Yourself, Nick Lowe)

KENNY GRAHAM'S AFRO-CUBISTS
60	Starlite ST45 013	Bongo Chant/Beguine 6
57	Pye Jazz NJE 1053	PRESENTING KENNY GRAHAM PART 1 (EP) 20
57	Esquire EP 34	CARIBBEAN SUITE (EP).. 20
57	Esquire EP 68	KENNY GRAHAM'S AFRO CUBISTS (EP)................................ 20
57	Esquire EP 83	KENNY GRAHAM'S AFRO CUBISTS (EP)................................ 25
56	MGM MGM-C 764	MOONDOG AND SUNCAT SUITES (LP, as Kenny Graham & His Satellites) 60
57	Nixa NJL 12	PRESENTING KENNY GRAHAM (LP) 60
57	Esquire 20-012	KENNY GRAHAM AFRO CUBISTS (LP) .... 30+
57	Esquire 20-023	CARIBBEAN SUITE (LP)... 30+

(see also Yolanda)

LEN GRAHAM
| 77 | Topic 12TS 334 | WIND AND WATER (LP) .... 12 |

LEO GRAHAM
| 73 | Upsetter US 399 | News Flash/UPSETTERS: Flashing Echo.................................. 15 |
| 73 | Summit SUM 8539 | Three Blind Mice/UPSETTERS: Mice Skank.............................. 12 |

LOU GRAHAM
| 58 | Coral Q 72322 | Wee Willie Brown/You Were Mean Baby (78 rpm = £130)................... 500 |

LYNDA GRAHAM
62	Philips 326 552BF	As Long As The River Flows/When I'm Sixteen 8
63	Philips BF 1249	Without Your Love/Wait And See...................................... 10
64	Philips BF 1308	You'd Better Believe It/That's The Last Thing I'd Do..................... 12

GRAHAM CENTRAL STATION
| 74 | Warner Bros K 46206 | GRAHAM CENTRAL STATION (LP)..................................... 15 |

(see also Sly & Family Stone)

GRAIN
97	Fat Cat 12FAT 002	Untitled 1 (12", plain sleeve) 8
99	Fat Cat 12FAT 015	Untitled 2 (12", die-cut sleeve)....................................... 8
99	Fat Cat 12FAT 016	Untitled 3 (12", die-cut sleeve)....................................... 8
02	Fat Cat 12FAT 041	Untitled 4 (12", die-cut sleeve)....................................... 8

COLIN GRAINGER & THE FRANK CORDELL ORCHESTRA
| 58 | HMV POP 484 | This I Know/Are You?... 10 |
| 59 | HMV POP 639 | Love Only Me/Plain And Simple Girl.................................. 10 |

RON GRAINER ORCHESTRA
64	HMV POP 1366	Not So Much A Programme, More A Way Of Life/Ascot Gavotte 7
67	Pye 7N 17383	A Man In A Suitcase/Andorra (pink label, later blue)................... 8
67	RCA Victor RCA 1635	The Prisoner/Happening Sunday...................................... 75
68	RCA Victor RCA 1698	Love Theme/Detective 6
69	RCA Victor RCA 1898	The Paul Temple Theme/The Jazz Age 18
72	Pye 7N 45141	Steptoe & Son/Counting The Coaster.................................. 5
79	RK 1021	Tales Of The Unexpected/Malice Aforethought (p/s)................... 10
60	Warner Bros WEP 6012	THEME MUSIC FROM INSPECTOR MAIGRET (EP)...................... 10
79	Six Of One 6 OF 1	THE PRISONER ARRIVAL (EP, fan club issue) 30
69	RCA Intl. INTS 1020	THEMES LIKE... (LP) 15
78	RK LB 003	TALES OF THE UNEXPECTED (LP)..................................... 15

GLENDA GRAINGER
| 60s | Audio Fidelity AFSP 007 | Mr. Kiss Kiss Bang Bang/Who... 12 |

BILLY GRAMMER
58	London HLU 8752	Gotta Travel On/Chasing A Dream (78 rpm = £12)........................ 15
59	Felsted AF 121	Bonaparte's Retreat/The Kissing Tree (78 rpm = £15).................. 12
59	Felsted AF 128	Willy, Quit Your Playing/It Takes You (78 rpm = £15) 10
61	Brunswick 05851	Rainbow Round My Shoulder/Columbus Stockade Blues 8
59	Felsted GEP 1005	BILLY GRAMMER HITS (EP)... 75

GERRY GRANAHAN
| 58 | London HL 8668 | No Chemise, Please/Girl Of My Dreams (78 rpm = £18)................. 30 |
| 60 | Top Rank JAR 262 | It Hurts/RICHIE ROBIN: Strange Dream .... 15 |

ROCCO GRANATA
| 59 | Oriole CB 1525 | Marina/Manuela (78 rpm = £15).. 5 |
| 61 | Oriole CB 1564 | Julia/Rocco Cha Cha .... 5 |

GRAND FUNK RAILROAD
70	Capitol CL 15632	Heartbreaker/Please Don't Worry 6
70	Capitol CL 15661	Closer To Home/Aimless Lady.. 5
71	Capitol CL 15668	Inside Looking Out/Paranoid (33rpm).................................. 5

71	Capitol CL 15689	I Can Feel Him In The Morning/Are You Ready/Mean Mistreater
		(33rpm maxi-single) 5
71	Capitol CL 15705	People, Let's Stop The War/Save The Land 5
72	Capitol CL 15738	Rock And Roll Soul/Flight Of Phoenix 5
69	Capitol E-ST 307	ON TIME (LP) 35
70	Capitol E-ST 406	GRAND FUNK (LP) 30
70	Capitol E-ST 471	CLOSER THAN HOME (LP) 30
71	Capitol E-SW 764	SURVIVAL (LP) 15
72	Capitol E-AS 853	E PLURIBUS FUNK (LP, circular 'silver coin' sleeve) 15
73	Capitol E-AST 11099	PHOENIX (LP, gatefold sleeve) 15

GRANDISONS
| 63 | RCA RCA 1339 | All Right/True Romance . . . . 12 |

GRANDMASTER RICHIE RICH
| 85 | Spin Offs 12off1 | Check It Out/Scratch It Out (12") . . . . 20 |
| 85 | Spin Offs 12off2 | Don't Be Flash/Flash Scratch (12") . . . . 20 |

GRAND PRIX
80	RCA RCA 7	Thinking Of You/Feels Good (p/s) 15
83	Chrysalis PRIX 2	Shout/Keep On Believing (p/s, with patch) 8
83	Chrysalis PRIXP 2	Shout/Keep On Believing (picture disc) 6
83	Chrysalis PRIXX 2	Shout (12", p/s) 12
(see also McAuley Schenker Group, Praying Mantis, Stratus, Uriah Heep)		

GERRI GRANGER
| 63 | London HLX 9759 | Just Tell Him Jane Said Hello/What's Wrong With Me . . . . 15 |

ROY GRANGER ORCHESTRA
| 60 | Top Rank JAR 320 | Manhattan Lullaby/Lazy Baby . . . . 7 |

GRANNIE
| 71 | SRT SRT 71138 | GRANNIE (LP, private pressing of 99 copies only, homemade sleeve) . . . . 500+ |

GRANNY'S INTENTIONS
67	Deram DM 158	The Story Of David/Sandy's On The Phone Again 25
68	Deram DM 184	Julie Don't Love Me Anymore/One Time Lovers 18
68	Deram DM 214	Never An Everyday Thing/Hilda The Bilda 20
70	Deram DM 293	Take Me Back/Maybe 20
70	Deram SML 1060	HONEST INJUN (LP) 60
(see also Gary Moore)		

AMY GRANT
| 70s | Myrrh MYR 1124 | AGE TO AGE (LP) . . . . 20 |

CLINTON GRANT
| 75 | Circle 5 | I've Been Trying/Second Attempt . . . . 10 |

EARL GRANT
58	Brunswick 05762	The End/Hunky Dunky Doo (78 rpm = £7) 7
59	Brunswick 05779	Evening Rain/Kathy-O (78 rpm = £8) 5
59	Brunswick 05792	Last Night (I Went Out Of My Mind)/Imitation Of Life (78 rpm = £6) . . 5
60	Brunswick 05824	House Of Bamboo/Two Loves Have I (78 rpm = £8) 5
60	Brunswick 05841	Not One Minute More/Building Castles 5
62	Brunswick 05865	Tender Is The Night/Honey 5
62	Brunswick 05870	Swingin' Gently/Evening Rain 5
62	Brunswick 05877	Sweet Sixteen Bars/Learnin' The Blues 5
65	Brunswick 05945	Stand By Me/After Hours 5
60	Brunswick OE 9460	EARL GRANT (EP) 10
63	Brunswick OE 9493	SWINGING GENTLY (EP) 10
59	Brunswick LAT 8297	THE END (LP) 12
60	Brunswick LAT 8332	NOTHIN' BUT THE BLUES (LP) 12
60	Brunswick LAT 8351	THE MAGIC OF EARL GRANT (LP) 12
61	Brunswick LAT 8389	EBB TIDE (LP) 15
62	Brunswick LAT 8502	EARL AFTER DARK (LP) 12

ERKEY GRANT & EARWIGS
| 63 | Pye 7N 15521 | I'm A Hog For You/I Can't Get Enough Of You . . . . 38 |

GOGI GRANT
55	London HLB 8192	Suddenly There's A Valley/Love Is 38
56	London HLB 8257	Who Are We/We Believe In Love 38
56	London HLB 8282	Wayward Wind/No More Than Forever 30
57	London HLB 8364	You're In Love/When The Tide Is High 25
58	London HLB 8550	The Golden Ladder/All Of Me 22
58	RCA RCA 1038	It's A Wonderful Thing To Be Loved/What A Beautiful Combination 5
58	RCA RCA 1047	Bonjour Tristesse/Johnny's Dream 5
59	RCA RCA 1101	Say A Prayer For Me Tonight/TONY MARTIN: She Is Not Thinking Of Me 5
59	RCA RCA 1105	Kiss Me Honey Honey Kiss Me/Two Dreams (78 rpm = £8) 6
60	London HLG 9185	Goin' Home/I'm Going To Live The Life 6
56	London REB 1057	GOGI GRANT (EP, export issue) 20
57	London HA-B 2032	SUDDENLY THERE'S GOGI GRANT (LP) 45
58	RCA RD 27054	BOTH ENDS OF THE CANDLE (LP, soundtrack) 15
59	RCA RD 27097	GIGI (LP, with Tony Martin) 15
60	London HA-G 2242	IF YOU WANT TO GET TO HEAVEN — SHOUT!
		(LP, also stereo SAH-G 6072) 25/30
(see also Tony Martin)		

JANIE GRANT
| 61 | Pye International 7N 25093 | Triangle/She's Going Steady With You . . . . 18 |
| 62 | Pye International 7N 25148 | That Greasy Kid Stuff/Trying To Forget You . . . . 18 |

MINT VALUE £

JULIE GRANT

62	Pye 7N 15430	Somebody Tell Him/Ev'ry Letter You Write	10
62	Pye 7N 15447	So Many Ways/Unimportant Things	10
62	Pye 7N 15461	When You're Smiling/Lonely Sixteen	10
62	Pye 7N 15483	Up On The Roof/When You Ask About Love	10
63	Pye 7N 15508	Count On Me/Then, Only Then	15
63	Pye 7N 15526	That's How Heartaches Are Made/Cruel World	15
63	Pye 7N 15545	Don't Ever Let Me Down/Somebody Cares	10
63	Pye 7N 15590	Hello Love/It's Alright	8
64	Pye 7N 15684	Come To Me/Can't Get You Out Of My Mind	8
64	Pye 7N 15615	Every Day I Have To Cry/Watch What You Do With My Baby	12
64	Pye 7N 15652	You Are Nobody 'Til Somebody Loves You/I Only Care About You	10
65	Pye 7N 15756	Baby Baby (I Still Love You)/My World Is Empty Without You	12
65	Pye 7N 15812	Giving Up/Cause I Believe In You	10
65	Pye 7N 15884	Lonely Without You/As Long As I Know He's Mine	10
65	Pye 7N 15937	Stop/When The Lovin' Ends	10
62	Pye NEP 24171	THIS IS JULIE GRANT (EP)	45

LEE GRANT (& CAPITOLS)

66	Parlophone R 5531	Breaking Point/Don't Cry Baby (with Capitols)	20
70	Decca F 13029	A Little Love And Understanding/I Got To Get You Out Of My Mind (solo)	7

LITTLE BROTHER (GRANT)

70	Torpedo TOR 27	Baby Don't Let Me Down/Brother Strong Man (as Little Brother)	7
70	Torpedo TOR 28	Let's Do It Together/Hey Man, Why (as Little Brother Grant & Zapatta Schmidt)	7
	(see also Equals)		

NEVILLE GRANT

73	Downtown DT 509	Sick And Tired/PRINCE DJANGO: Hot Tip	20

NORMAN GRANT ORCHESTRA

61	Starlite ST45 060	Jive Medley/Speak Low	7

TOP GRANT

62	Island WI 034	Searching/David & Goliath	15
62	Island WI 052	Suzie/Jenny	15
63	Island WI 072	Riverbank Coberley (as Top-Grant)/Nancy	15
63	Island WI 074	Money Money Money/Have Mercy On Me	18
63	Island WI 077	War In Africa/The Birds	15
	(see also Rhythm Aces)		

GRANTCHESTER MEADOW

71	Amber ABR 004	Candlelight/Winter Blues	15

GRAPE

92	Pencil Toast PENT 001	Baby In A Plastic Bag/Listen To Your Heart (p/s)	25
	(see also P.J. Harvey)		

GRAPEFRUIT

68	RCA Victor RCA 1656	Dear Delilah/The Dead Boot	10
68	RCA Victor RCA 1677	Elevator/Yes	10
68	RCA Victor RCA 1716	C'mon Marianne/Ain't It Good	6
68	Stateside-Dunhill SS 8005	Someday Soon/Theme For Twiggy	7
69	Stateside-Dunhill SS 8011	Round Going Round/This Little Man	7
69	RCA Victor RCA 1855	Deep Water/Come Down To The Station	7
70	RCA Victor RCA 1907	Lady Godiva/Thunder And Lightning	6
71	Deram DM 343	Universal Party/Sha Sha	6
69	Stateside-Dunhill S(S)L 5008	AROUND GRAPEFRUIT (LP)	40
69	RCA Victor SF 8030	DEEP WATER (LP)	25
	(see also Tony Rivers & Castaways, Easybeats, Fynn McCool, Sleepy)		

GRAPEVINE

68	Liberty LBF 15063	Things Ain't What They Used To Be Anymore/Ace In The Hole	6

GRASSROOTS

66	RCA Victor RCA 1532	Where Were You When I Needed You/These Are Bad Times	8
67	Pye International 7N 25422	Let's Live For Today/Depressed Feeling	10
67	Pye International 7N 25431	Things I Should Have Said/Tip Of My Tongue	6
68	RCA Victor RCA 1682	Melody For You/Hey Friend	5
68	RCA Victor RCA 1737	Midnight Confessions/Who Will You Be Tomorrow	10
69	Stateside-Dunhill SS 8006	Bella Linda/Hot Bright Lights	5
69	Stateside-Dunhill SS 8012	All Good Things Come To An End/Melody For You	5
69	Stateside-Dunhill SS 8018	The River Is Wide/(You Gotta) Live For Love	5
69	Stateside-Dunhill SS 8023	Who Will You Be Tomorrow/Midnight Confessions	5
69	Stateside-Dunhill SS 8029	I'd Wait A Million Years/Fly Me To Havana	10
71	Probe PRO 515	Temptation Eyes/Keepin' Me Down	8
69	Stateside S(S)L 5005	GOLDEN GRASS (LP)	20
70	Stateside SSL 5012	LEAVING IT ALL BEHIND (LP)	20
	(see also P.F. Sloan)		

GRASS-SHOW

96	Food FOOD 94	Freak Show/Sympathetic Television (picture disc, poster sleeve)	5

GRATEFUL DEAD

67	Warner Bros WB 7186	Born Cross-Eyed/Dark Star	50
70	Warner Bros WB 7410	Uncle John's Band/New Speedway Boogie	12
71	Warner Bros.	Truckin'/Johnny B. Goode (unissued)	
72	Warner Bros K 16167	One More Saturday Night (as Grateful Dead with Bobby Ace)/Bertha	7
73	Atlantic K 19301	Let Me Sing Your Blues Away/Here Comes Sunshine	7
74	United Artists UP 36030	U.S. Blues/Loose Lucy	6
77	Warner Bros SAM 79	Dark Star/Born Cross-Eyed (mail-order issue with *Dark Star* magazine)	15

79	Arista ARIST 236	Good Lovin'/Stagger Lee	6
87	Arista RIS 35	Touch Of Grey/My Brother Esau (grey vinyl, p/s)	6
67	Warner Bros W(S) 1689	THE GRATEFUL DEAD (LP, mono/stereo)	90/45
68	Warner Bros WS 1749	ANTHEM OF THE SUN (LP)	45
69	Warner Bros WS 1790	AOXOMOXOA (LP)	40
70	Warner Bros WS 1830	LIVE/DEAD (2-LP)	35
70	Warner Bros WS 1869	WORKINGMAN'S DEAD (LP, matt sleeve)	15
71	Warner Bros WS 1893	AMERICAN BEAUTY (LP)	15
71	Warner Bros K 66009	GRATEFUL DEAD LIVE (SKULL AND ROSES) (2-LP)	20
72	Polydor 2310 171	HISTORIC DEAD (LP)	22
72	Polydor 2310 172	VINTAGE DEAD (LP)	22
72	Warner Bros K 66019	EUROPE '72 (3-LP, triple fold-out sleeve)	22
73	Warner Bros K 46246	HISTORY OF GRATEFUL DEAD (BEAR'S CHOICE) (LP)	15
73	Warner Bros K 49301	WAKE OF THE FLOOD (LP)	15
74	Warner Bros K 56024	SKELETONS FROM THE CLOSET: THE BEST OF GRATEFUL DEAD (LP)	15
74	Warner Bros K 59302	FROM THE MARS HOTEL (LP)	15
76	United Artists UAD 60131/2	STEAL YOUR FACE (2-LP, gatefold sleeve, with sampler LP For Dead Heads Only [FREE 2] in inner sleeve)	30

(see also Jerry Garcia, Mickey Hart, Kingfish, Robert Hunter, Bob Weir, Keith & Donna Godchaux, Silver [U.S.], Diga Rhythm Band)

GRAVE
03	Century Media	MORBID WAYS TO DIE (Numbered box set with 6 picture disc LPs and booklet, 2000 only)	75

GRAVEDIGGAZ
94	Gee Street GEEA 14	NIGGAMORTIS (LP, with inner sleeve)	20

NICK GRAVENITES
69	CBS 63818	MY LABORS (LP)	22

(see also Big Brother & Holding Company)

BILLY GRAVES
59	Felsted AF 119	The Shag (Is Totally Cool)/Uncertain (export issue) (78 rpm = £15)	20

CARL GRAVES
75	A&M AM 7151	Baby Hang Up The Phone/Walk Softly	8
75	A&M AM 7180	The Next Best Thing/Something Teling Me	6

GRAVY TRAIN
73	Dawn DNS 1036	Strength Of A Dream/Tolpuddle Episode	6
74	Dawn DNS 1058	Starbright Starlight/Good Time Thing	6
75	Dawn DNS 1115	Climb Aboard The Gravy Train/Sanctuary	6
70	Vertigo 6360 022	GRAVY TRAIN (LP, gatefold sleeve, swirl label)	90
71	Vertigo 6360 051	BALLAD OF A PEACEFUL MAN (LP, gatefold sleeve, swirl label)	325
73	Dawn DNLS 3046	SECOND BIRTH (LP)	45
74	Dawn DNLH 1	STAIRCASE TO THE DAY (LP)	45

BARRY GRAY (ORCHESTRA)
62	Lyntone LYN 249/250	Sabotage/Supercar Song/Supercar Twist (flexi, p/s may exist)	35+/18
64	Melodisc MEL 1591	Fireball/Zero G (by Barry Gray & His Spacemakers; some in p/s)	55/18
65	Pye 7N 17016	Thunderbirds/Parker — Well Done (some in p/s)	38/18
67	Pye 7N 17391	Captain Scarlet/The Mysterons Theme (some in p/s)	38/18
68	Pye 7N 17625	Joe 90 — Title Theme/Joe 90 — Hijacked (some in p/s)	55/28
62	Golden Guinea GGL 0106	SUPERCAR — FLIGHT OF FANCY (LP, with Edwin Astley)	50
67	United Artists (S)ULP 1159	THUNDERBIRDS ARE GO! (LP, soundtrack, mono/stereo)	115/135

(see also Century 21, Mary Jane with Barry Gray, Richard Harvey)

CLAUDE GRAY
64	Mercury 10012 MCE	COUNTRY AND WESTERN ACES (EP)	20

DAVID GRAY
92	Hut HUT 23	Birds Without Wings/L's Song/The Light (12", p/s)	12
92	Hut HUTCD 23	Birds Without Wings/L's Song/The Light (CD)	8
93	Hut HUT 27	Shine/Brick Walls/The Rice (12", p/s)	12
93	Hut HUT 32	Wisdom/Lovers/4AM (12", p/s)	12

DOBIE GRAY
65	London HL 9953	The In Crowd/Be A Man	15
65	Pye International 7N 25307	See You At The Go Go/Walk With Love	20
69	London HL 10268	The In Crowd/Be A Man (reissue)	7
73	MCA MU 1184	Drift Away/City Stars	8
73	MCA MU 1221	Now That I'm Without You/Loving Arms	6
75	Black Magic BM 107	Out On The Floor/Be A Man	10

DOLORES GRAY
53	Brunswick 05111	Big Mamou/Say You're Mine (78)	10
55	Brunswick 05382	Heat Wave/After You Get What You Want, You Don't Want It	15
55	Brunswick 05407	Rock Love/One (78 rpm = £10)	30
57	Capitol CL 14732	There'll Be Some Changes Made/Fool's Errand	10
57	Capitol CL 14770	I'm Innocent/My Mama Likes You	8
63	Philips 326 582BF	Mornin' Train/Our Day Will Come	7

DORIAN GRAY
67	Parlophone R 5612	Behind The Tear/Walking Down A Back Street	6
68	Parlophone R 5667	I've Got You On My Mind/Move On	6
68	Parlophone R 5705	Love Is All That It Should Be/Let Me Go Home	6
68	Parlophone R 5732	Jingle Down A Hill/Get Goin' Baby	6

HERBIE GRAY
68	Giant GN 38	We're Staying Here/Life Ska	15

(see also Gene Rondo, Owen & Dandy)

JERRY GRAY & HIS ORCHESTRA
54	Brunswick 05351	The Ooh And Ah Mambo/Kettle Drum Hop.	6

JOHNNIE 'THE GASH' GRAY
58	Fontana H 123	Big Guitar/Tequila (78 rpm = £8)	22
58	Fontana H 134	Apache/Zach's Tune (78 rpm = £12)	20
60	Melodisc 45-1500	Any Old Iron Cha Cha/Cocktails For Two Cha Cha (with His Chunks Of Mettle)	5

LORRAINE GRAY
64	Fontana TF 435	Are You Getting Tired Of Your Little Toy?/	
		The Boy That I Want Doesn't Want Me	10
64	Fontana TF 484	The Little Girl That Cries/Talk To Him	7

OWEN GRAY
60	Starlite ST45 015	Far Love/Please Let Me Go	35
60	Starlite ST45 019	Jenny Lee/The Plea.	35
60	Blue Beat BB 8	Cutest Little Woman/Running Around (with Ken Richards Band).	12
61	Blue Beat BB 43	Sinners Weep/Get Drunk (with Hersan & His City Slickers).	12
61	Starlite ST45 032	Mash It (Parts 1 & 2)	20
62	Starlite ST45 078	I Feel Good/Someone To Help Me	18
62	Starlite ST45 088	Let Me Go Free/In My Dreams	18
62	Blue Beat BB 75	Rockin' In My Feet/Nobody Else (with Jets).	12
62	Blue Beat BB 91	Millie Girl (with Buster's Group)/DERRICK MORGAN: Headache	12
62	Blue Beat BB 103	Lonely Days/No Good Woman (with Sonny Bradshaw Quartet)	10
62	Blue Beat BB 108	Keep It In Mind/Do You Want To Jump (with Les Dawson Combo).	10
62	Blue Beat BB 113	Best Twist/Grandma-Grandpa (B-side with Hersan & His City Slickers)	10
62	Blue Beat BB 127	Pretty Girl/Twist So Fine.	10
62	Blue Beat BB 136	They Got To Move/I Love Her.	10
62	Blue Beat BB 139	Tree In The Meadow/Lizebella (with Buster's Group)	10
62	Island WI 002	Patricia/Twist Baby	12
62	Island WI 020	Audrey/Dolly Baby (with Ernest Rauglin [sic] Orchestra)	12
62	Island WI 030	Midnight Trail/Time Will Tell	12
62	Island WI 048	I'm Still Waiting/Last Night.	12
62	Chek TD 101	Come On Baby/My One Desire	12
62	Dice CC 3	On The Beach/Young Lover.	12
63	Blue Beat BB 147	Big Mabel/Don't Come Knocking (with Edwards' Groupe).	10
63	Blue Beat BB 188	Call Me My Pet/Give Me Your Love	10
63	Blue Beat BB 201	Snow Falling/Oowee Baby (as Owen Gray & His Big Brother)	10
64	Blue Beat BB 217	Draw Me Nearer/Daddy's Girl.	10
65	Blue Beat BB 290	Daddy's Gone/BUSTER'S ALLSTARS: Johnny Dark.	20
65	Aladdin WI 603	Gonna Work Out Fine/Dolly Baby	12
65	Aladdin WI 607	Can I Get A Witness/Linda Lu	12
65	Island WI 252	Shook Shimmy And Shake/I'm Going Back	12
65	Island WI 258	You Don't Know Like I Do/Take Me Serious (with Sound System)	12
66	Island WI 267	Paradise/Bye Bye Love.	8
66	Blue Beat BB 365	I'm Gonna Say So Long/The Days I'm Living	12
67	Island WIP 6000	Help Me/Incense	12
67	Collins Downbeat CR 003	Collins Greetings/Rock It Down (with Sir Collins & Band).	40
67	Collins Downbeat CR 004	I'm So Lonely (with Sir Collins & Band)/EL RECO, SIR COLLINS & J. SATCH:	
		Shock Steady.	40
68	Collins Downbeat CR 007	Am Satisfy (with Sir Collins & Band)/BOB STACKIE & SIR COLLINS & BAND:	
		Sweet Music.	100
68	Collins Downbeat CR 009	Grab It, Hold It, Feel It (with Bob Stackie)/DAN SIMMONS: Way Out Sound	50
68	Collins Downbeat CR 010	I'm Gonna Take You Back (with Bob Stackie)/GLEN ADAMS: King Sized	40
68	Coxsone CS 7047	Give Me A Little Sign/Ain't Nobody Home	20
68	Coxsone CS 7053	Give It To Me/Isn't It So.	20
68	Blue Cat BS 123	These Foolish Things/This I Promise	12
69	Blue Cat BS 156	I Can't Stop Loving You/Tell Me Darling.	12
68	Trojan TR 632	Lovey Dovey/Grooving.	6
69	Fab FAB 90	Three Coins In The Fountain/Tennessee Waltz	5
69	Fab FAB 96	Ay Ay Ay/Let It Be Me (with Rudies)	8
69	Fab FAB 120	Understand My Love/Apollo 12	10
69	Fab FAB 126	Swing Low/Release Me.	8
69	Trojan TR 650	I Can't Stop Loving You/Tell Me Darling.	5
69	Trojan TR 670	Too Experienced/I Really Loved You Baby	8
69	Duke DU 12	Reggae Dance/I Know.	8
69	Duke DU 33	Seven Lonely Days/He Don't Love You Like I Do	6
69	Downtown DT 423	Groovin'/HERBIE GRAY & RUDIES: These Memories.	7
69	Downtown DT 428	Lovey Dovey (with Dandy)/HERBIE GRAY & RUDIES: Kitty Wait	5
69	Camel CA 25	Girl What You Doing To Me/Woman A Grumble.	8
69	Camel CA 34	Don't Take Your Love Away/Two Lovers.	5
69	Camel CA 37	Every Beat Of My Heart/Don't Cry.	5
70	Camel CA 50	Don't Sign The Paper/Packing Up Loneliness.	5
70	Camel CA 51	Bring Back Your Love/Got To Come Back	5
70	Upfront UPF 3	Dream Lover/Mudda-Granma-Reggae (with Maximum Breed).	7
70	Bamboo BAM 47	I Can Feel It/I Don't Want (To Lose Your Love)	10
70	Crab CRAB 52	Just A Little Loving/DERRICK MORGAN: Take A Letter Maria.	5
70	Pama PM 810	Sugar Dumpling/I Don't Know Why.	5
70	Pama Supreme PS 299	I Am In Love Again/RANDY WILLIAMS: Version	5
70	Pama Supreme PS 302	Candida/When Will I Find My Way.	5
70	Pama Supreme PS 310	You Gonna Miss Me/I Hear You Knocking	5
70	Supreme SUP 206	Surfin'/All The Love	5
70	Ackee ACK 102	No More/Don't Leave Me (both as Owen Gray & Omen).	5
71	Ackee ACK 123	Whispering Bells/CLANCY'S ALLSTARS: Whiplash	
		(B-side actually Jacket by Dave Barker).	10
71	Camel CA 60	Groove Me/No Other One	7
71	Camel CA 73	Nothing Can Separate Us/Girl I Want You To Understand	6

71	Punch PH 87	Sincerely/Hold On I'm Coming	6
71	Pama Supreme PS 325	Summer Sand/Something To Remind Me	5
71	Pama Supreme PS 332	Greatest Hits (Parts 1 & 2)	5
72	Pama Supreme PS 351	Time/GRAHAM: Harlesden High Street	8
72	Pama Supreme PS 358	Hail The Man/I'll Follow You	5
72	Pama Supreme PS 360	Amazing Grace (with Graham Hawk)/SKETTO RICH: Don't Stay Out Late	5
70s	Rock Steady Rev. REV 004	Groovy Kind Of Love (with Elki & Rim Ram Band)/ RIM RAM BAND: The Whistler	5
61	Starlite STLP 5	OWEN GRAY SINGS (LP)	120
63	Melodisc MLP 12-153	CUPID (LP)	40
69	Trojan TTL 24	REGGAE WITH SOUL (LP)	20
77	Trojan TRLS 139	FIRE AND BULLETS (LP)	20
78	Trojan TRLS 150	DREAMS OF OWEN GRAY (LP)	12

(see also Laurel & Owen, Gray Brothers, Elki & Owen, Owen & Milie, Owen & Dandy, Dennis Lowe, Survivors, Denzil & Jennifer, Brother Dan, Glen Adam)

SHANE GRAY
| 68 | Page One POF 102 | Sing Out Loud/Come Back To My Heart Again | 6 |

WARDELL GRAY
54	Brunswick LA 8646	THE CHASE (LP, with Dexter Gordon)	15
65	Stateside SL 10144	WARDELL GRAY MEMORIAL ALBUM (VOL. 1) (LP)	15
65	Stateside SL 10145	WARDELL GRAY MEMORIAL ALBUM (VOL. 2) (LP)	15

GRAY BROTHERS
| 68 | Blue Cat BS 124 | Always/Big Man | 22 |

(see also Owen Gray)

KATHRYN GRAYSON
53	MGM SP 1002	(All Of A Sudden) My Heart Sings/Jealousy	10
53	MGM SP 1014	Smoke Gets In Your Eyes/The Touch Of Your Hand (B-side with Howard Keel)	10
54	MGM SP 1078	I Hate Men/ANN MILLER & TOMMY RALL: Always True To You In My Way	10
56	MGM EP 636	WANTING YOU (EP)	10

KATHRYN GRAYSON & HOWARD KEEL
53	MGM SP 1003	Why Do I Love You/Make Believe	10
54	MGM SP 1076	So In Love/ANN MILLER: Too Darn Hot	10
54	MGM SP 1077	We Open In Venice (with Ann Miller & Tommy Rall)/Wunderbar/ HOWARD KEEL: Were Thine That Special Face	10
54	MGM SP 1079	So Kiss Me Kate/KEENAN WYNN & JAMES WHITMORE: Brush Up Your Shakespeare/ANN MILLER, TOMMY RALL, BOBBY VAN & BOB FOSSE: From This Moment On	10

(see also Howard Keel, Ann Miller)

LARRY GRAYSON
| 72 | York SYK 529 | Shut That Door/Slack Alice | 6 |
| 72 | York MYK 602 | WHAT A GAY DAY (LP) | 18 |

MILTON GRAYSON
| 60 | London HLU 9068 | Forget You/The Puppet | 8 |

RUDY GRAYZELL
| 54 | London HL 8094 | Looking At The Moon And Wishing On A Star/The Heart That Once Was Mine | 300 |
| 54 | London HL 8094 | Looking At The Moon And Wishing On A Star/The Heart That Once Was Mine (78) | 80 |

GRAZINA
62	HMV POP 1094	Lover Please Believe Me/So What	15
63	HMV POP 1149	Don't Be Shy/Another Like You	15
63	HMV POP 1212	Be My Baby/I Ain't Gonna Knock On Your Door	18
64	Giv-A-Disc LYN 568	Stay Awhile/Let Me Go Lover	12

(see also Lady Murray, Mr & Mrs Murray, Le Roys, Cliff Richard)

GREASE BAND
72	Harvest HAR 5052	Laughed At The Judge/All I Want To Do/Jesse James	6
75	Goodear EAR 602	New Morning/Pontardawe Hop	5
71	Harvest SHVL 790	THE GREASE BAND (LP)	25
75	Goodear EAR 2902	AMAZING GREASE (LP)	15

(see also Joe Cocker, Wynder K. Frog, Made In Sheffield, Henry McCullough)

JOHNNY B. GREAT (& GOODMEN)
| 63 | Decca F 11740 | School Is In/She's A Much Better Lover Than You (with Goodmen) | 9 |
| 64 | Decca F 11804 | Acapulco 1922/You'll Never Leave Him (solo) | 9 |

(see also Quotations, Johnny Goodison)

GREAT ACES
72	Fab FAB 191	Gold And Silver/Liberty Rock	7
72	Fab FAB 200	Liberty Rock/Rock My Soul	7
72	Fab FAB 201	I Didn't Mean It/Boots And Shoes	6
72	Fab FAB 202	Baby Girl/Version	6
73	Fab FAB 203	Banana/My Sweet Lord	6

GREAT BRITISH HEROES (AKA GBH)
| 78 | Lightning Records GIL 534 | Eric Miller/Don't Give A Damn (1 copy only) | 1,000 |

GREAT AWAKENING
| 69 | London HLU 10284 | Amazing Grace/Silver Waterfall | 6 |

GREATEST LITTLE SOUL BAND IN THE LAND
| 69 | MCA Soul Bag BAG 4 | Tenement Halls/Flat, Black And Together | 6 |
| 69 | MCA Soul Bag BAG 6 | Something For My People/Win Lose Or Draw | 8 |

(see also J.J. Jackson)

GREATEST SHOW ON EARTH
70	Harvest HAR 5012	Real Cool World/Again And Again	20
70	Harvest HAR 5026	Tell The Story/Mountain Song	6
77	Harvest HAR 5129	Magic Touch Woman/Again And Again	8
70	Harvest SHVL 769	HORIZONS (LP)	65
70	Harvest SHVL 783	THE GOING'S EASY (LP)	45
75	Harvest SHSM 2004	THE GREATEST SHOW ON EARTH (LP)	15

(see also Living Daylights, Ian Dury & Blockheads, Fuzzy Duck, Glencoe, Naturals)

GREAT METROPOLITAN STEAM BAND
69	MCA MNP/S 403	THE GREAT METROPLITAN STEAM BAND (LP)	30

GREAT SATURDAY NIGHT SWINDLE
77	CBS 82044	GREAT SATURDAY NIGHT SWINDLE (LP, Irish-only issue)	12

(see also Rosemary Taylor)

GREAT SOCIETY
68	CBS 63476	CONSPICUOUS ONLY IN ITS ABSENCE (LP)	30

(see also Jefferson Airplane)

GREAT UNCLE FRED
67	Strike JH 324	I'm In Love With An Ex-Beauty Queen/Singalong Version	6

R.B. GREAVES
69	Atco 226 007	Take A Letter Maria/Big Bad City	7
70	Atco 2091 013	Fire And Rain/Ballad Of Leroy	7
71	Atlantic 2091 170	Paperback Writer/Over You Now	6
75	20th Century BTC 2191	Come On And Get Yourself Some/BMF (Beautiful)	6
70	Atco 228 034	R.B. GREAVES (LP)	20

JOE GRECH
71	Electro ES 152	Marija L-Maltija/In-Nassab (export issue)	6

BUDDY GRECO
57	London HLR 8452	With All My Heart/Game Of Love (with B-G Skiffle Band) (78 rpm = £10)	15
58	London HLR 8613	I've Grown Accustomed To Her Face/On The Street Where You Live (as Buddy Greco & His Quartet)	6
60	Fontana H 255	The Lady Is A Tramp/Like Young	7
62	Columbia DB 4924	Mr. Lonely/Sentimental Fool	5
65	Columbia DB 7790	Mr. Kiss Kiss Bang Bang/Passing Pastels	5
60	Fontana TFE 17322	BUDDY GRECO PLAYS AND SINGS THE LADY IS A TRAMP (EP)	8
56	Vogue Coral LVA 9021	AT MISTER KELLY'S (LP)	18
60	Fontana TFL 5098	MY BUDDY (LP)	15

(see also Johnny Desmond)

JULIETTE GRECO
54	Philips BBR 8023	JULIETTE GRECO SINGS (10" LP)	22

GREEDIES
80	Vertigo GREED 1	A Merry Jingle/A Merry Jangle (p/s)	10

(see also Professionals, Thin Lizzy, Sex Pistols)

AL GREEN(E)
68	Stateside SS 2079	Back Up Train/Don't Leave Me (as Al Greene & Soul Mates) (DJ copy = £60)	30
69	Action ACT 4540	Don't Hurt Me No More/Get Yourself Together (by Al Greene)	20
70	London HLU 10300	You Say It/Gotta Find A New World	6
71	London HLU 10324	I Can't Get Next To You/Ride Sally Ride	6
71	Bell BLL 1188	Back Up Train/Don't Leave Me (as Al Green & Soul Mates, reissue)	12
71	London HLU 10337	Tired Of Being Alone / Right Now, Right Now	5
71	London HLU 10348	Let's Stay Together/Tomorrow's Dream	5
72	London HLU 10369	Look What You've Done For Me/I've Never Found A Girl	5
72	London HLU 10382	I'm Still In Love With You/Old Time Relovin'	5
72	London HLU 10393	You Ought To Be With Me/What Is This Feeling	5
73	London HLU 10406	Call Me/What A Wonderful Thing Love Is	5
73	London HLU 10419	Love And Happiness/So You're Leaving	5
73	London HLU 10426	Here I Am/I'm Glad You're Mine	5
74	London HLU 10443	Living For You/It Ain't No Fun To Me	5
74	London HLU 10452	Let's Get Married/So Good To Be Here	5
74	London HLU 10470	Sha La La (Make Me Happy)/School Days	5
75	London HLU 10482	L.O.V.E./I Wish You Were Here With Me	5
75	London HLU 10493	Oh Me Oh My/Strong As Death	5
75	London HLU 10511	Full Of Fire/Could I Be The One	5
76	London HLU 10527	Let It Shine/There's No Way	5
76	London HLU 10542	Keep Me Crying/There Is Love	5
69	Action ACLP 6008	BACK UP TRAIN (LP)	50
71	London SHU 8424	AL GREEN GETS NEXT TO YOU (LP)	15
72	London SHU 8430	LET'S STAY TOGETHER (LP)	15
72	London SHU 8443	I'M STILL IN LOVE WITH YOU (LP)	15
73	London SHU 8457	CALL ME (LP)	15
74	London SHU 8464	LIVIN' FOR YOU (LP)	15
74	London SHU 8479	EXPLORES YOUR MIND (LP)	15

BARRY GREEN
63	Ember JBS 713	Together/Collective Marriage	6

BRIAN GREEN
68	Fontana SFJL 912	BRIAN GREEN DISPLAY (LP)	35

GARLAND GREEN
69	MCA Soul Bag BAG 9	Jealous Kinda Fella/I Can't Believe You Quit Me	15
75	Polydor 2066 557	Bumpin' And Stompin'/Nothing Can Take You From Me	6

GREEN GINGER THREE
65	Decca DFE 8623	FROM THE LAND OF GREEN GINGER (EP)	20

GRIZ GREEN
58	Mercury AMT 1012	Be Happy/Morocco (78)	6

HUGHIE GREEN
61	Decca F11317	The Valley Of Peppermint Springs/The Puppet Song	10
66	Columbia DB 8085	Cuddle Up Baby/Clap Your Hands (B-side with Monica Rose)	8
77	Philips GB 1	Stand Up And Be Counted/Land Of Hope And Glory	5

IAN GREEN (REVELATION)
67	Polydor 56194	Last Pink Rose/Green Blues (solo)	12
69	CBS 3997	When You Love A Man/Santa Maria	6
69	CBS 4623	Revelation/Groover's Grave	6
70	CBS 63840	REVELATION (LP)	25
	(see also Madeline Bell, Rosetta Hightower)		

JESSE GREEN
77	EMI EMI 2615	Come With Me/Pt 2	10

JIMMY GREEN
73	Duke DU 155	Suspicion/LLOYD'S ALL STARS: Suspicion — Version	7
73	Green Door GD 4062	I'll Be Standing By/LLOYD'S ALL STARS: I'll Be Standing By "Version"	6
	(see also Jimmy London)		

KATHE GREEN
69	Deram DM 279	If I Thought You'd Ever Change Your Mind/Primrose Hill	7
69	Deram SML 1039	RUN THE LENGTH OF YOUR WILDNESS (LP)	30

PETER GREEN
71	Reprise RS 27012	Heavy Heart/No Way Out	14
72	Reprise K 14141	Beast Of Burden/Uganda Woman (with Nigel Watson)	14
78	PVK PV 16	Apostle/Tribal Dance (supposedly withdrawn)	8
79	PVK PV 24	In The Skies/Proud Pinto (p/s)	5
80	PVK PV 36	Walking In The Road/Woman Don't	5
80	PVK PV 41	Loser Two Times/Momma Doncha Cry	5
81	PVK PV 103	Give Me Back My Freedom/Lost My Love	5
81	PVK PV 112	Promised Land/Bizzy Lizzy	5
70	Reprise RSLP 9006	THE END OF THE GAME (LP, with Nigel Watson)	30
72	Reprise K 44106	THE END OF THE GAME (LP, with Nigel Watson, reissue)	12
79	PVK PVLS 101	IN THE SKIES (LP, green vinyl)	12
	(see also Fleetwood Mac, Peter B's, Shotgun Express, John Mayall & Bluesbreakers, Gass, Peter Bardens, Katmandu)		

SALLY GREEN
62	Philips PB 1243	It Hurts Too Much To Laugh/When's He Gonna Kiss Me	20

TOM GREEN
74	Action ACT 4621	Rock Springs Railroad Station/Endless Confusion	50

PHILIP GREEN & PINEWOOD STUDIO ORCHESTRA
60	Top Rank JAR 355	"League Of Gentlemen" March/"Golden Fleece" Theme	6

GREEN ANGELS
65	Parlophone R 5390	Rockin' Red Wing/Let It Happen	15
66	Parlophone R 5512	An Exile's Dream/Hannigan's Hooley	5

NORMAN GREENBAUM
70	Reprise RS 20846	Jubilee/Skyline	6
70	Reprise RS 20919	Canned Ham/Junior Cadillac	6
71	Reprise RS 21008	California Earthquake/Rhode Island Red	6
70	Reprise RSLP 6365	SPIRIT IN THE SKY (LP)	20
70	Page One POLS 017	WITH DR. WEST'S MEDICINE SHOW & JUNK BAND (LP)	15
	(see also Dr. West's Medicine Show & Junk Band)		

GREEN BEAN
69	Regal Zonophone RZ 3017	The Garden's Lovely/Sittin' In The Sunshine	9

GREENBEATS
64	Pye 7N 15718	If This World Were Mine/You Must Be The One	8
65	Pye 7N 15843	So Sad/I'm On Fire	7
67	Spin SP 2007	Pretty Woman/Thing	8

GREEN BULLFROG
72	MCA MKPS 2021	GREEN BULLFROG (LP)	55
	(see also Deep Purple, Ritchie Blackmore, Roger Glover, Tony Ashton, Matthew Fisher)		

GREEN DAY
94	Reprise W 0257	Basket Case/Tired Of Waiting For You (p/s)	12
94	Reprise W 0257 CD	Basket Case/Longview (live)/Burnout (live)/ 2000 Light Years Away (live) (CD)	8
94	Reprise W 0257 CD2	Basket Case/On The Wagon/Tired Of Waiting For You/ 409 In Your Coffee Maker (CD)	8
95	Reprise W 0287X	Longview/Welcome To Paradise (live) (with sticker sheet, p/s)	35
95	Reprise W 0294X	When I Come Around/She (live) (Ltd edn picture disc with insert)	15
95	Reprise W 0320 LC/X	Geek Stink Breath/I Want To Be On TV (p/s, red vinyl)	20
98	Reprise W 0438	Redundant/The Grouch (live) (p/s)	10

GREEN MAN
75	private pressing	WHAT AILS THEE? (LP)	100+

CLAUDE 'FATS' GREENE & ORCHESTRA
66	Island WI 290	Fats Shake 'Em Up Parts 1 & 2 (actually with Al Thomas)	15

JACK GREENE
68	Decca AD 1005	What Locks The Door/My Elusive Dreams (export issue)	8

MINT VALUE £

JEANIE GREENE
69	Atlantic 584 226	Sure As Sin/I've Been A Long Time Loving You	8

KELLIE GREENE
64	Stateside SS 303	Madrigal/Foggy Day	7

LAURA GREENE
79	Grapevine GRP 135	Can't Help Loving Dat Man/It's A Good Day For A Parade	10

(see also Diane Renay)

LORNE GREENE
64	RCA RCA 1428	Ringo/Bonanza	8
63	RCA RD 7566	YOUNG... AT HEART (LP)	22
65	RCA RD 7709	THE MAN (LP)	22

LEE GREENLEE
59	Top Rank JAR 226	Cherry, I'm In Love With You/Starlight	7

GREEN RIVER
90	Tupelo TUP CD17	DRY AS A BONE EP (CD)	30

GREEN RIVER BOYS
63	Capitol ST 1810	BIG BLUEGRASS SPECIAL (LP)	20

(DAVE) GREENSLADE
73	Warner Bros K 16264	Temple Song/An English Western	5
73	Warner Bros K 46207	GREENSLADE (LP)	18
73	Warner Bros K 46259	BEDSIDE MANNERS ARE EXTRA (LP)	15
73	Warner Bros K 56055	SPYGLASS GUEST (LP, gatefold sleeve)	15
75	Warner Bros K 56126	TIME AND TIDE (LP, gatefold sleeve)	12
76	Warner Bros K 56306	CACTUS CHOIR (LP, as Dave Greenslade)	12
80	EMI EMSP 332	THE PENTATEUCH OF THE COSMOGONY (2-LP, with 47-page book, as Dave Greenslade)	20

(see also Wes Minster Five, Alan Price Set, Geno Washington & Ram Jam Band, Chris Farlowe, Colosseum, Samurai, Web)

ARTHUR GREENSLADE (& GEE MEN)
61	Decca F 11363	Rockin' Susannah/Eclipse (with Gee Men)	7
66	Columbia DB 7865	Watermelon Man/Serenade To A Broken Jaw	6
55	Brunswick OE 9171	CASK OF THE AMONTILLADO (EP)	12

ARTHUR GREENSLADE
72	Deram DM 349	Flirt (Pour Un Flirt)/Rainy Day Love	5

GREEN TELESCOPE
86	Imaginary MIRAGE 001	Two By Two/Make Me Stay/Thinkin' About Toady (p/s, various designs)	6
86	Wump BIF 4811	Face In The Crowd/Thoughts Of A Madman (p/s)	5

ELLIE GREENWICH
67	United Artists UP 1180	I Want You To Be My Baby/Goodnight, Goodnight	18
68	United Artists UP 2214	Sunshine After The Rain/A Long Time Comin'	10
70	Bell BLL 1105	I Don't Wanna Be Left Outside/Ain't That Peculiar	10
73	MGM 2315 243	LET IT BE WRITTEN, LET IT BE SUNG (LP)	25

(see also Popsicles, Raindrops [U.S.])

MICHAEL GREENWOOD
64	Oriole CB 1943	Buy Your Kid A Guitar/The Bellringer's Nightmare	5

MICK GREENWOOD
71	MCA MDKS 8003	THE LIVING GAME (LP, gatefold sleeve)	15
72	MCA MKPS 2026	TO FRIENDS (LP)	15

(see also Fotheringay)

NICHOLAS GREENWOOD
72	Kingdom KVLP 9002	COLD CUTS (LP)	450+

(see also Crazy World Of Arthur Brown, Khan, Bryn Howarth)

STOCKER GREENWOOD & FRIENDS
79	Changes	BILLY + NINE (LP)	25

BIG JOHN GREER
51	HMV JO 360	Woman Is A Five Letter Word/Got You On My Mind (78, export issue)	30

GINNY GREER
57	Brunswick 05673	Five Oranges, Four Apples/Kiss Me Hello (But Never Goodbye)	6

GREG
(see under Greg Bright)

BOBBY GREGG & FRIENDS
62	Columbia DB 4825	The Jam (Parts 1 & 2)	15

GREGER
66	Polydor 249 1103	IN THE NIGHT (LP)	25

MAX GREGER
70	Polydor 241 8022	SUNSHINE STARSHINE (LP)	20

BRIAN GREGORY
65	HMV POP 1412	Give Me Your Word/The Ballad Of Dick Turpin	5

GLENN GREGORY & CLAUDIA BRÜCKEN
85	ZTT P ZTAS 15	When Your Heart Runs Out Of Time/(Drumless) (book-shaped picture disc)	5

(see also Heaven 17, Propaganda, Act)

IA(I)N GREGORY
60	Pye 7N 15295	Time Will Tell/The Night You Told A Lie (as Ian Gregory)	30
61	Pye 7N 15397	Can't You Hear The Beat Of A Broken Heart/Because	25

62	Pye 7N 15435	Mr. Lovebug/Pocketful Of Dreams	35
63	Columbia DB 7085	How Many Times/Yellow Teddy Bear·	12

JOHNNY GREGORY & HIS ORCHESTRA

61	Fontana H 341	Route 66/M Squad	5
61	Fontana TFE 17325	MAVERICK! (EP)	10
61	Fontana TFE 17331	BONANZA (EP)	10
62	Fontana TFE 17389	THE T.V. THRILLERS (EP)	10
61	Fontana TFL 5110	T.V. WESTERN THEMES (LP, also stereo STFL 538)	12
62	Fontana TFL 5170/STFL 585	CHANNEL THRILL: THE T.V. THRILLER THEMES (LP)	15
72	Philips 6308 111	SPIES AND DOLLS (LP)	22
74	United Artists UAG 29546	A MAN FOR ALL SEASONS (LP)	40
	(see also Chaquito)		

TONY GREGORY

66	Doctor Bird DB 1007	Baby Come On Home/Marie Elena	18
66	Doctor Bird DB 1016	Give Me One More Chance/I've Lost My Love	18
67	Island WI 3029	Get Out Of My Life/SOUL BROTHERS: Sugar Cane	18
67	Coxsone CS 7013	Only A Fool (Breaks His Own Heart)/Pure Soul	18
71	Horse HOSS 3	Bouncing All Over The World/Tell Me	6
67	Coxsone CSL 8011	TONY GREGORY SINGS (LP)	60
	(see also Lloyd Charmers)		

GREHAN SISTERS

66	Rex EPR 5005	THE GREHAN SISTERS (EP)	10
67	Transatlantic TRA 160	ON GALTYMORE MOUNTAINS (LP)	15

STAN GREIG'S JAZZ BAND

59	Tempo EXA 90	STAN GREIG'S JAZZ BAND (EP)	25
72	Redeffusion ZS 116	BOOGIE WOOGIE (LP)	15
80s	Calligraph CLGLP 004	BLUES EVERY TIME (LP)	20

GREMLINS

66	Mercury MF 981	The Coming Generation/That's What I Want	22
67	Mercury MF 1004	You Gotta Believe It/I Can't Say	22

JOYCE GRENFELL

61	Columbia SCS 2160	Narcissis (Laughing Song)/I Don't 'Arf Love You (with Norman Wisdom) p/s	10
58	HMV 7EG 8787	AT HOME (EP)	8
59	HMV 7EG 8936	OLD TYME DANCING (EP)	8
54	Philips BBL 7004	REQUESTS THE PLEASURE (LP)	18
62	HMV CLP 1155	JOYCE GRENFELL IN A MISCELLANY (LP)	15
64	HMV CLP 1810	ENCORES (LP)	12

JOYCE GRENFELL & STANLEY HOLLOWAY

59	Caedmon TC 1104	BAB BALLADS & CAUTIONARY TALES (LP)	20
	(see also Stanley Holloway)		

JOEL GREY

54	MGM SPC 1	Last Night In The Back Porch/Two-Faced (export issue)	18
57	Capitol CL 14779	Everytime I Ask My Heart/Moonlight Swim	7
58	Capitol CL 14832	Be My Next/Shoppin' Around	18

RONNIE GREY & JETS

55	Capitol CL 14329	Run, Manny, Run/Sweet Baby	32

GREYHOUND

71	Trojan TR 7834	Follow The Leader/Funky Jamaica	5
71	Trojan TR 7848	Moon River/I've Been Trying/Pressure Is Coming On	5
72	Trojan TRLS 27	BLACK AND WHITE (LP)	15
	(see also Tillermen)		

GRID

93	Virgin VSTX 1442	CRYSTAL CLEAR (Orb Mixes) (12", 4-track, clear vinyl)	8
	(see also Timothy Leary Meets The Grid)		

GRIDS

80	Kings Head	NEW ANTHEMS (EP)	20

ROOSEVELT GRIER

68	Action ACT 4515	People Make The World/Hard To Forget	22
69	Pama PM 774	Who's Got The Ball	15
69	Pama PM 784	C'mon Cupid/High Society Woman	20

GRIFFIN

69	Bell BLL 1075	I Am The Noise In Your Head/Don't You Know	40
72	MGM 2006 088	What Happens In The Darkness/Calling You	10
	(see also Heavy Jelly, Skip Bifferty, Every Which Way, Bell & Arc, Happy Magazine, Ginger Baker's Airforce)		

SYLVIA GRIFFIN

88	Rocket BLAST 7	Love's A State Of Mind/Forgive The Girl (p/s, features George Harrison)	8
88	Rocket BLAST 712	Love's A State Of Mind/Forgive The Girl/Lonely Heart (12", p/s, features George Harrison)	12

JOHNNY GRIFFIN

69	Polydor 583734	THE MAN I LOVE (LP)	45

JOHNNY GRIFFIN BIG SOUL BAND

61	Riverside REP 3203	THE BIG SOUL BAND (EP, with Clark Terry & Bobby Timmons)	10
61	Riverside RLP 12-3331	THE BIG SOUL BAND (LP, also stereo [RLP 9331])	20
	(see also Eddie 'Lockjaw' Davis)		

MERV GRIFFIN

61	London HLL 9339	The Charanga/Along Came Joe	10

MINT VALUE £

VINCENT GRIFFIN
77   Topic 12TS 338   TRADITIONAL FIDDLE MUSIC FROM COUNTY CLARE (LP) 12

VIRGIL GRIFFIN
71   Jay Boy BOY 43   La Da Da Da Da/Climbing 10

GRIFFIN BROTHERS' ORCHESTRA
52   Vogue V 2139   Weepin' And Cryin' (with Tommy Brown)/The Teaser Boogie (78) 15

ANDY GRIFFITH
55   Capitol CL 14263   Ko Ko Mo (I Love You So)/Make Yourself Comfortable 25
56   Capitol CL 14619   No Time For Sergeants/Make Yourself Comfortable 10
57   Capitol CL 14766   Mama Guitar/A Face In The Crowd (78 rpm = £15) 25
58   Capitol CL 14936   Midnight Special/She's Bad, Bad Business (with Dixie Seven) 15
59   Capitol CL 15003   Hamlet (Parts 1 & 2) 5
56   Capitol EAP1 630   ANDY GRIFFITH (EP) 15
60   Capitol ST 1105   SHOUTS THE BLUES AND OLD TIMEY SONGS (LP, mono/stereo) 12/15

JOE GRIFFITHS
69   Philips SBL 7902   OUT OF THE HEAD OF... 30

JOHNNY GRIFFITH INC
73   RCA RCA 2386   Grand Central Shuffle/My Love 8

MARCIA GRIFFITHS
66   Island WI 285   Funny/KING SPARROW: Beggars Have No Choice (B-side actually by
                        Leonard Dillon & Wailers; some copies credit Marcia Griffiths on both sides) . . . 45
67   Studio One SO 2008   Hound Dog (actually by Norma Fraser)/HUGH GODFREY: My Time 38
67   Studio One SO 2015   After Laughter/HUGH GODFREY: Go Tell Him 35
68   Coxsone CS 7035   Mojo Girl (actually by Nora Dean)/HAMLINS: Tell Me That You Love Me 35
68   Coxsone CS 7055   Feel Like Jumping/HORACE TAYLOR: Thundering Vibrations 40
68   Coxsone CS 7062   Hold Me Tight/BASIES: Home Sweet Home (B-side actually by Basses) 40
68   Studio One SO 2047   Words (as Marcia Griffiths & Jeff Dixon)/SHARKS: How Could I Live 25
68   Studio One SO 2059   Truly/SIMMS & ROBINSON: Drought 30
69   Gas GAS 111   Tell Me Now/STAN HOPE: The Weight 15
69   High Note HS 029   Talk (Parts 1 & 2) (correct title is actually "Toil") 15
69   Escort ES 808   Don't Let Me Down/REGGAEITES: Romper Room
                        (B-side actually by Peter Tosh) 12
69   Trojan TR 693   Put A Little Love In Your Heart/J BOYS: Jay Fever 8
70   Harry J. HJ 6613   Put A Little Love In Your Heart/JAY BOYS: Bah Oop Ah 7
70   Harry J. HJ 6623   Band Of Gold/JAY BOYS: Cowboy (Version II) 7
70   Bamboo BAM 59   Shimmering Star/SOUND DIMENSION: Mun-Dun-Gu
                        (B-side actually Im & David) 20
(see also Bob & Marcia, Peter Touch/Tosh, Roy Richards, Soul Vendor, Bob Andy, Della Humphrey, Mr. Foundation,
Bob Marley)

VICTOR GRIFFITHS
70   Punch PH 29   I Am Proud Of You/KING VICTOR ALL STARS: Version 7

FERRE GRIGNARD
68   Atlantic 584 158   Yellow You Yellow Me/La Si Do 6
70   Major Minor SMLP 72   CAPTAIN DISASTER (LP) 15

CAROL GRIMES (& DELIVERY)
70   B&C CB 129   Harry Lucky/Homemade Ruin (with Delivery) 7
74   Virgin VS 109   You're The Only One/Southern Boogie 7
70   Charisma CAS 1023   FOOLS MEETING (LP, with Delivery) 75
74   Caroline CA 2001   WARM BLOOD (LP) 15
    (see also Uncle Dog, Babylon)

TINY GRIMES & HIS R&B QUINTET
54   Esquire 10-349   Annie Laurie/Hot In Harlem (78) 6

GRIMMS
75   DJM DJS 393   Backbreaker/The Masked Poet 5
76   DJM DJS 679   The Womble Bashers Of Walthamstow/
                        The Worst Is Yet To Come/Wiggle Waggle 5
73   Island HELP 11   GRIMMS (LP) 15
73   Island ILPS 9248   ROCKIN' DUCK (LP, gatefold sleeve) 18
    (see also Neil Innes, Liverpool Scene, Scaffold, Mike McGear, McGough & McGear, John Gorman, Zoot Money, Patto,
Viv Stanshall, Andy Roberts, Bashers)

GRIM REAPER
83   Ebony EBON 16   SEE YOU IN HELL (LP) 20
85   Ebony EBON 32   FEAR NO EVIL (LP) 20

GRIN
71   CBS 5239   We All Sung Together/See What A Love Can Do 5
71   CBS 7405   Everybody's Missin' The Sun/18 Faced Lover 5
71   Epic EPC 64272   GRIN (LP) 18
72   Epic EPC 64652   1 + 1 (LP) 18
73   Epic EPC 65166   ALL OUT (LP) 18
    (see also Nils Lofgren)

GRINDERSWITCH
76   Capricorn 2089 030   Picking The Blues/The Best I Can 5

JANNY GRINE
70s   Sparrow BIRD 104   FREE INDEED (LP) 20

GRINGO
71   MCA MKS 5067   I'm Another Man/Soft Mud 6
71   MCA MKPS 2107   GRINGO (LP) 30
    (see also Caravan)

JOE GRINNE
69	Coxsone CS 7098	Mr Editor/How I Feel (both sides actually by Melodians)	25

GRISBY DYKE
69	Deram DM 232	The Adventures Of Miss Rosemary La Page/Mary Anne She	6

GRIZZARDS
98	Baban GRIZ 5	Grizzling/The Green Griz (p/s)	8

DEWEY GROOM
62	Starlite ST45 085	Butane Blues/That's All I Want Out Of Life	32
63	Starlite ST45 095	You're Tearing My Heart Out Of Me/Walking Papers	22
63	Starlite ST45 105	Heartaches For Sale/Sometimes If I'm Lucky	18

GROOP
68	CBS 3204	Woman You're Breaking Me/Mad Over You	30
68	CBS 3351	Lovin' Tree/Night Life	12
69	Bell BLL 1070	A Famous Myth/Tears And Joys	10
69	Bell BLL 1080	The Jet Song (When The Weekend's Over)/Nobody At All	12

GROOVE
69	Parlophone R 5783	The Wind/Play The Song	22

GROOVE
80	Trendy WHIP 1	Heart Complaint/I Wanna Be Your Pygmy	15

GROOVE FARM
87	Raving Pop Blast RPBGF 1	SORE HEADS AND HAPPY HEARTS (EP, with insert & handwritten labels)	10
87	Raving Pop Blast RPBGF 2	ONLY THE MOST IGNORANT GUTLESS SHEEP-BRAINED POLTROON CAN DENY THEM NOW (EP)	8
87	Raving Pop Blast RAVE 20	BAGISM (EP, hand-painted gatefold no'd p/s with insert, home-made labels)	5
87	Subway Org. SUBWAY 15T	GOING BANANAS WITH THE GROOVE FARM (12" EP)	8
88	Subway Organisation SUBWAY 19T	The Big Plastic Explosion! (It's Alright, It's Alright) (Dance Mix)/Nancy Sinatra/Baby Blue Marine/Riot On Sunset Strip/Red Dress (p/s)	7
88	Subway Organisation SUBWAY 22N	Driving In Your New Car (Mini Mix)/Expanding Reindeer/I Can't Dance With You/Epistle To Duppy (10", p/s)	6
88	Subway Organisation SUBWAY 22N	Driving In Your New Car (Mini Mix)/Expanding Reindeer/I Can't Dance With You/Epistle To Duppy (12", white label promos only, with press release)	15
88	Kvatch 001/LYN 18632	Baby Blue Marine/SEA URCHINS: Clingfilm (flexi, 1,000 only, 500 with p/s)	15/8
90	Woosh WOOSH 6	Heaven Is Blue/ESMERELDA'S KITE: Vampire Girl (1-sided red flexidisc free with *Woosh* fanzine)	6/5

GROOVERS
71	Camel CA 83	Put Me Down Easy/I Want To Go Back Home	6
71	Escort ERT 863	Bend Down Low/The Burning Feeling	6

(see also Lloyd & Groovers, Alva Lewis, Junior Byles, Dennis Walks)

GROOVE TUNNEL
95	Detour DR 023	Rainy Day/How Do You Feel (p/s, white vinyl)	7

WINSTON GROOV(E)Y
69	Grape GR 3005	Leaving Me Standing/Little Girl	12
69	Grape GR 3008	Merry X-mas/I Am Lonely	8
69	Nu Beat NB 041	Island In The Sun/Work It Up	10
69	Nu Beat NB 042	Josephine/Champagne And Wine	8
70	New Beat NB 053	Standing At The Corner/You Send Me	6
70	New Beat NB 055	Yellow Bird/For Your Love	6
70	New Beat NB 058	Here Is My Heart/Birds And Flowers	6
70	New Beat NB 066	Groovin'/Sugar Mama	6
70	New Beat NB 073	Tennessee Waltz/Old Man Trouble	6
70	Attack ATT 8019	You Can't Turn Your Back On Me/PAMA DICE: The Worm	10
70	Jackpot JP 708	Funky Chicken/CIMARRONS: Part 2 (B-side actually unknown instrumental)	10
70	Jackpot JP 709	Funny/CIMARRONS: Funny Version Two	9
70	Torpedo TOR 11	Please Don't Make Me Cry/Motion On The Ocean	8
70	Crab CRAB 63	I Like The Way/Tell Me Why	8
71	Crab CRAB 64	I've Got The Find A Way To Win Mary Back/Wanna Be There	8
71	Bullet BU 471	I Wanna Be Loved/Get Back Together	8
71	Pama PM 827	Don't Break My Heart/How Long Will This Go On	8
71	Pama Supreme PS 323	Free The People/Not Now	8
72	Pama Supreme PS 349	What You Gonna Do/Why Did You Leave	8
72	Pama Supreme PS 364	Sylvia's Mother/Here Is My Heart	8
73	Explosion EX 2086	Nose For Trouble/RHYTHM RULERS: Version	8
74	Explosion EX 2088	Please Don't Make Me Cry/So Easy	8
69	Pama PMP 2011	FREE THE PEOPLE (LP)	40

(see also King Horror, Upsetters)

WALTER GROSS
54	MGM SP 1070	Blue Moon/Tenderly	7
54	MGM SP 1071	You Won't Forget Me (with India Adams)/Follow Me	7

G.G. GROSSETT
69	Crab CRAB 10	Run Girl Run/DENNIS WALKS: The Drifter	20
69	Crab CRAB 33	Greater Sounds/Live The Life I Love	12

STEFAN GROSSMAN
70	Big T BIG 133	Pretty Little Tune/Little Sally Walker	6
71	Big T BIG 140	'Joe Hill' — Themes	6
68	Fontana (S)TL 5463	AUNT MOLLY'S MURRAY FARM (LP)	22
69	Fontana STL 5485	THE GRAMERCY PARK SHEIK (LP)	22
70	Transatlantic TRA 217	YAZOO BASIN BOOGIE (LP)	15
71	Transatlantic TRA 246	THOSE PLEASANT DAYS (LP, with lyric insert)	12

MINT VALUE £

| 72 | Transatlantic TRA 257 | HOT DOGS (LP) | 12 |
| 73 | Transatlantic TRA 274 | GUITAR INSTRUMENTALS (LP) | 12 |

(see also John Renbourn)

LUTHER GROSVENOR
71	Island WIP 6109	Here Comes The Queen/Heavy Day	6
72	Island WIP 6124	All The People/Waiting	6
71	Island ILPS 9168	UNDER OPEN SKIES (LP)	20

(see also Hellions, Revolution, Art, Spooky Tooth, Mott The Hoople, Widowmaker)

CARL GROSZMANN
70	Decca F 13065	Thunderbird/Missouri Woman	6
75	Ring O' 2017 103	I've Had It/C'mon And Roll	15
77	Ring O' 2017 107	Face Of A Permanent Stranger/Your Own Affair (promo p/s or company sleeve)	15/10
75	Ring O' 2320 102	CARL GROSZMANN (LP, unreleased)	

GROUND ATTACK
| 81 | Ground Attack GAR 001 | THE RED LION EP (Red Lion/Every Mother's Son) (gatefold p/s, later no p/s) | 80/5 |

GROUNDHOGS
68	Liberty LBF 15174	You Don't Love Me/Still A Fool	28
69	Liberty LBF 15263	B.D.D./TONY McPHEE: Gasoline	18
70	Liberty LBF 15346	Eccentric Man/Status People	16
73	W. Wide Artists WWS 006	Sad Go Round/Over Blue	6
74	W. Wide Artists WWS 012	Plea Sing, Plea Sing/TONY McPHEE: Dog Me Bitch	6
76	United Artists UP 36095	Live A Little Lady/Boogie Withus	6
76	United Artists UP 36177	Pastoral Future/Live Right (as Tony McPhee & Groundhogs)	6
68	Liberty LBL/LBS 83199E	SCRATCHING THE SURFACE (LP, mono/stereo)	75/50
69	Liberty LBS 83253	BLUES OBITUARY (LP)	45
70	Liberty LBS 83295	THANK CHRIST FOR THE BOMB (LP, gatefold sleeve)	25
71	Liberty LBS 83401	SPLIT (LP, gatefold sleeve)	20
72	United Artists UAG 29347	WHO WILL SAVE THE WORLD... (LP, gatefold sleeve)	20
72	United Artists UAG 29419	HOGWASH (LP, gatefold sleeve)	18
74	United Artists UDF 31	GROUNDHOGS' BEST 1969-1972 (2-LP)	18
74	W. Wide Artists WWA 004	SOLID (LP, with lyric insert)	15
76	United Artists UAG 29917	CROSSCUT SAW (LP)	12
76	United Artists UAG 29994	BLACK DIAMOND (LP)	12
84	Psycho PSYCHO 24	HOGGIN' THE STAGE (2-LP, with EP, stickered sleeve)	20

(see also John Lee's Groundhogs, Tony McPhee, Herbal Mixture, Home, Andy Fernbach, John Lee Hooker)

GROUP
| 72 | Charisma CB 197 | Bovver Boys/Piraeus Football Club/An Open Letter To George Best | 6 |

(see also Neil Innes)

GROUP B
| 67 | Vocalion VF 9284 | I Know Your Name Girl/I Never Really Know | 22 |

(see also Blue Cheer)

GROUP 1850
| 69 | Philips SBL 7884 | AGEMO'S TRIP TO MOTHER EARTH (LP) | 150 |

GROUP IMAGE
| 69 | Stable SLE 8005 | A MOUTH IN THE CLOUDS (LP) | 45 |

GROUP ONE
| 58 | HMV POP 463 | She's Neat/Made For Each Other (78 rpm = £10) | 28 |
| 58 | HMV POP 492 | Chanson D'Amour/Londonderry Air (78 rpm = £8) | 10 |

GROUP SIX
| 59 | Oriole CB 1488 | Rock-A-Boogie/Rockin' The Blues (78 rpm = £20) | 25 |

GROUP THERAPY
69	Philips BF 1744	River Deep Mountain High/Remember What You Said	6
69	Philips BF 1792	Can't Stop Lovin' You Baby/I Must Go	6
69	Philips SBL 7883	YOU'RE IN NEED OF GROUP THERAPY (LP)	15

GROUP TWO
| 68 | Columbia DB 8374 | It's Raining Outside/Western Man, Eastern Lady | 5 |

GROUP X
| 63 | Fontana 267 274 TF | There Are 8 Million Cossack Melodies — And This Is One Of Them/Teneriffe (some in p/s) | 25/15 |
| 63 | Fontana TF 417 | Roti Calliope/Cross Beat | 20 |

GROUT
| 78 | Urinating Vicar SIDEWAYS GRA | DO IT YOURSELF (EP) (100 only, sound quality very poor) | 400+ |

GRUMBLE
| 73 | RCA Victor RCA 2384 | Da Doo Ron Ron/Pig Bin An' Gone | 5 |

(see also 10cc)

GRUNT FUTTOCK
| 72 | Regal Zonophone RZ 3042 | Rock 'N' Roll Christian/Free Sole | 30 |

(see also Move, Roy Wood)

GRUVY BEATS
| 70 | Nu Beat NB 048 | Share Your Popcorn/LAUREL AITKEN: Mr. Popcorn | 12 |
| 70 | Nu Beat NB 049 | Blue Mink/LAUREL AITKEN: I've Got Your Love | 10 |

GIGI GRYCE
| 60 | Esquire 32-151 | SAYIN' SOMETHIN' (LP) | 20 |

MINT VALUE £

GRYPHON
77	Harvest HAR 5125	Spring Song/Fall Of The Leaf.	6
73	Transatlantic TRA 262	GRYPHON (LP, gatefold sleeve)	18
74	Transatlantic TRA 282	MIDNIGHT MUSHRUMPS (LP)	12
74	Transatlantic TRA 287	RED QUEEN TO GRYPHON THREE (LP)	12
75	Transatlantic TRA 302	RAINDANCE (LP).	12
77	Harvest SHSP 4063	TREASON (LP, with insert).	12

(see also Richard Harvey)

G.T.O.'s
67	Polydor 56721	She Rides With Me/Rudy Vadoo	50

(see also Joey & Continentals)

G.T.O.'s (Girls Together Outrageously)
70	Straight STS 1059	PERMANENT DAMAGE (LP)	100

(see also Jeff Beck, Frank Zappa)

G.T.R.
86	Arista GTR 1	When The Heart Rules The Mind/Reach Out (poster sleeve)	6
86	Arista GTRSD 1	When The Heart Rules The Mind/Reach Out (picture disc)	8

(see also Steve Hackett)

GUANA BATZ
84	Big Beat SW 89	You're So Fine/Rockin' In My Coffin/Jungle Rumble/Guana Rock (p/s)	6
84	Big Beat NS 96	The Cave/Werewolf Blues (p/s)	5
85	I.D. NOSE 4	HELD DOWN ... AT LAST (LP)	12

GUARDIANS OF THE RAINBOW
68	President PT 186	What Do You Do When You've Lost Your Love/Cry Alone	6

JOSE GUARDIOLA & ROSE MARY
63	HMV POP 1147	Algo Prodigioso/Di Papa	20

GUESS WHO
65	Pye International 7N 25305	Shakin' All Over/Till We Kissed	22
66	King KG 1044	His Girl/It's My Pride	32
67	Fontana TF 831	This Time Long Ago/There's No Getting Away From You	16
67	Fontana TF 861	Miss Felicity Grey/Flying On The Ground Is Wrong	12
70	RCA SF 8037	WHEATFIELD SOUL (LP)	12
70	RCA SF 8107	AMERICAN WOMAN (LP)	12
71	RCA SF 8153	SHARE THE LAND (LP)	12

EARL GUEST
62	Columbia DB 4707	Honky Tonk Train Blues/Winkle Picker Stomp.	10
62	Columbia DB 4926	The Girl From The Fair Isle/Twistin' John.	7
64	Columbia DB 7212	Begin The Beguine/Foxy	20

LENNIS GUESS
75	Route RT 11	Just Ask Me/Workin' For My Baby	10

REG GUEST SYNDICATE
65	Mercury MF 927	Underworld/Guys, Guns, Dolls And Danger.	80
66	Mercury 20089MCL	UNDERWORLD (LP)	55

GUGGENHEIM
72	Indigo GOLP 7001	GUGGENHEIM (LP, private pressing)	50

GUILLEMOTS
05	Fantastic Plastic FPS050	I SAW SUCH THINGS IN MY SLEEP EP (CD, p/s)	50
05	Fantastic Plastic FPS050	I SAW SUCH THINGS IN MY SLEEP EP (10", 300 only p/s)	60
05	Fantastic Plastic FPTEN055	Trains To Brazil/My Chosen One/Go Away (10", 1,000 only, p/s)	10
05	Fantastic Plastic FPS055	Trains To Brazi/My Chosen One/Go Away (CD, 3,500 p/s)	7

ISAAC GUILLORY
74	Atlantic K 40521	ISAAC GUILLORY (LP)	12

(see also Shames, Sam Gopal)

GUILLOTEENS
65	Pye International 7N 25324	I Don't Believe/Hey You	55

BONNIE GUITAR
58	London HLD 8591	A Very Precious Love/Johnny Vagabond (78 rpm = £8)	28
59	Top Rank JAR 260	Candy Red Apple/Come To Me, I Love You	8
58	London HA-D 2122	MOONLIGHT AND SHADOWS (LP)	38

GUITAR CRUSHER with JIMMY SPURRILL
69	Blue Horizon 57-3149	Since My Baby Hit The Numbers/Hambone Blues	40

(see also Wild Jimmy Spurrill)

GUITAR RED
63	Pye International 7N 25219	Just You And I/Old Fashioned Love	30

GUITAR SHORTY
72	Flyright LP 500	CAROLINA SLIDE GUITAR (LP)	15

GULLIVER
70	Elektra 2101 011	Every Day's A Lovely Day/Angelina	6
70	Elektra 2101 017	Angelina/Christine.	5
70	Elektra 2410 006	GULLIVER (LP)	20

(see also Daryl Hall & John Oates)

GULLIVER'S PEOPLE
66	Parlophone R 5435	Splendour In The Grass/Took This Land	7
66	Parlophone R 5464	Fi Fo Fum/Over The Hills	6
68	Parlophone R 5709	On A Day Like This/My Life	6
69	Columbia DB 8588	Somehow, Somewhere/I Found Love	6

MINT VALUE £

GULLIVER'S TRAVELS
69	Instant INLP 003	GULLIVER'S TRAVELS (LP, withdrawn)	60

(see also Mike D'Abo, Andrew Oldham)

GUN
68	CBS 3764	Race With The Devil/Sunshine	10
68	CBS 3764	Race With The Devil/3-4 In The Middle (different B-side)	10
69	CBS 4052	Drives You Mad/Rupert's Travels.	6
69	CBS 4443	Hobo/Don't Look Back	6
69	CBS 4443	Hobo/Long Hair Wild Man (different B-side)	8
70	CBS 4952	Runnin' Wild/Drown Yourself In The River	6
69	CBS 63552	GUN (LP)	28
69	CBS 63683	GUNSIGHT (LP)	32

(see also Rupert's People, Three Man Army, Knack)

GUN CLUB
82	Beggars Banquet BEG 80	Ghost On The Highway/Sex Beat (p/s)	6
82	Animal/Chry. CHCAT 2635	The Fire Of Love/Walking With The Beast (p/s)	6
83	Animal/Chrysalis GUN 1	Death Party/House On Highland Avenue/The Lie (p/s)	8
83	Animal/Chrysalis GUN 12	Death Party/House On Highland Avenue/The Lie/Light Of The World/Come Back Jim (12", p/s)	10
88	Red Rhino RED 89	The Breaking Hands/Crabdance (p/s)	8
88	Red Rhino RED 89 12	The Breaking Hands/Crabdance/Nobody's City (12", p/s)	10
90	Fire BLAZE 47T	The Great Divide/Crabdance/St. John's Divine Part 2 (p/s)	10

(see also Jeffrey Lee Pierce, Kid Congo Powers)

JON GUNN
67	Deram DM 133	I Just Made Up My Mind/Now It's My Turn	15
67	Deram DM 166	If You Wish It/I Don't Want To Get Hung Up On You Babe	15

JO JO GUNNE
(see under 'J')

JIM GUNNER
60	Decca F 11276	Hoolee Jump/Footloose (as Jim Gunner & Echoes)	15
61	Fontana H 313	Desperado/Baghdad (as Jim Gunner & His Sidekicks)	15

TONY GUNNER
62	London HLU 9492	Rough Road/You Gotta Get Home	20

GUNS FOR HIRE
80	Korova KOW 6	My Girlfriend's Boyfriend/I'm Famous Now (p/s)	10

(see also Main T. Possee)

GUNSHOT
90	Vinyl Solution STORM18	Battle Creek Brawl (12")	20
91	Vinyl Solution STORM24	Crime Story/No Sell Out (12")	18
91	Vinyl Solution STORM40	Clear From Present Danger (12")	15
92	Vinyl Solution STORM49	Killing Season/Nobody Move (12")	15

GUNS N' ROSES
87	Geffen GEF 22	It's So Easy/Mr Brownstone (p/s)	12
87	Geffen GEF 22T	It's So Easy/Mr Brownstone/Shadow Of Your Love/Move To The City (12", p/s)	15
87	Geffen GEF 22TP	It's So Easy/Mr Brownstone/Shadow Of Your Love/Move To The City (12", picture disc with stickered PVC sleeve)	50
87	Geffen GEF 30	Welcome To The Jungle/Whole Lotta Rosie (live) (red p/s)	10
87	Geffen GEF 30T	Welcome To The Jungle/Whole Lotta Rosie (live)/It's So Easy (live)/Knockin' On Heaven's Door (live) (12", red p/s)	25
87	Geffen GEF 30TW	Welcome To The Jungle/Whole Lotta Rosie (live)/It's So Easy (live)/Knockin' On Heaven's Door (live) (12", poster p/s)	12
87	Geffen GEF 30P	Welcome To The Jungle/Whole Lotta Rosie (live)/It's So Easy (live)/Knockin' On Heaven's Door (live) (12", picture disc)	40
88	Geffen GEF 43	Sweet Child O' Mine/Out Ta Get Me (p/s, with wraparound sticker)	5
88	Geffen GEF 43TE	Sweet Child O' Mine/Out Ta Get Me/Rocket Queen (10", revolving p/s)	20
88	Geffen GEF 43TV	Sweet Child O' Mine/Out Ta Get Me/Rocket Queen (12", metallic p/s)	12
88	Geffen GEF 47	Welcome To The Jungle/Nightrain (p/s)	5
88	Geffen GEF 47TW	Welcome To The Jungle/Nightrain/You're Crazy (Acoustic Version) (12", poster p/s)	8
88	Geffen GEF 47TV	Welcome To The Jungle/Nightrain/You're Crazy (Acoustic Version) (12", p/s, with patch)	12
88	Geffen GEF 47TP	Welcome To The Jungle/Nightrain/You're Crazy (Acoustic Version) (12", picture disc)	12
88	Geffen GEF 47CD	Welcome To The Jungle/Nightrain/You're Crazy (Acoustic Version) (3" CD with adaptor, 5" case)	15
89	Geffen GEF 50P	Paradise City/I Used To Love Her (gun-shaped clear or white picture disc)	12/15
89	Geffen GEF 50X	Paradise City/I Used To Love Her (p/s, slotted in holster p/s)	8
89	Geffen GEF 50T	Paradise City/I Used To Love Her/Anything Goes (12", p/s)	8
89	Geffen GEF 50CD	Paradise City/I Used To Love Her/Anything Goes/Sweet Child O' Mine (3" CD)	8
89	Geffen GEF 55W	Sweet Child O' Mine (Remix)/Out Ta Get Me (stickered p/s, sealed w/ tattoo)	7
89	Geffen GEF 55P	Sweet Child O' Mine/Out Ta Get Me/Rocket Queen (shaped pic disc & sticker)	15
89	Geffen GEF 55P	Sweet Child O' Mine/Out Ta Get Me/Rocket Queen (12" uncut shaped pic disc)	100
89	Geffen GEF 55T	Sweet Child O' Mine (Remix)/Move To The City/Whole Lotta Rosie (live)/It's So Easy (live) (12", p/s)	12
89	Geffen GEF 55CD	Sweet Child O' Mine (Remix)/Move To The City/Whole Lotta Rosie (live)/It's So Easy (live) (3" CD)	12
89	Geffen GEF 56T	Patience/Rocket Queen/W. Axl Rose Interview (12", p/s)	10
89	Geffen GEF 56CD	Patience/Rocket Queen/W. Axl Rose Interview (3" CD, gatefold card sleeve)	12
89	Geffen GEF 60X	Nightrain/Reckless Life (live) (with patch)	12
89	Geffen GEF 60P	Nightrain/Reckless Life (live) (case-shaped picture disc, stickered PVC sleeve)	15

89	Geffen GEF 60CD	Nightrain/Knockin' On Heaven's Door (live)/Reckless Life (live) (3" CD, gatefold card sleeve)	12
91	Geffen GFSTP 6	You Could Be Mine/Civil War (12", clear vinyl with insert in PVC sleeve)	10
91	Geffen GFSTD 6	You Could Be Mine/Civil War (CD, card p/s)	8
91	Geffen GFST 9	Don't Cry/Don't Cry (Alternate Lyrics)/Don't Cry (Demo) (12", hologram p/s)	8
91	Geffen GFSTD 9	Don't Cry/Don't Cry (Alternate Lyrics)/(Demo) (CD, card gatefold p/s w/ sticker)	8
91	Geffen GFSX 17	Live And Let Die (LP Version)/Live And Let Die (live) (12", yellow/orange vinyl, die-cut p/s)	8
91	Geffen GFSTD 17	Live And Let Die (LP Version)/Live And Let Die (live)/ Shadow Of Your Love (live) (CD, stencil p/s)	10
92	Geffen GFST 18	November Rain/Sweet Child O' Mine (live)/Patience (live) (12", p/s, 1 side etched)	10
92	Geffen GFSTD 18	November Rain/Sweet Child O' Mine (live)/Patience (live) (CD)	8
87	Geffen 9240 148	APPETITE FOR DESTRUCTION (LP, withdrawn 'robot' sleeve)	15
91	Geffen GEF 24415	USE YOUR ILLUSION I (2 x LP)	18
91	Geffen GEF 24420	USE YOUR ILLUSION II (2 x LP)	18

ARTHUR GUNTER
| 72 | Blue Horizon 2431 012 | BLUES AFTER HOURS (LP) | 125 |
| 70s | Contempo COLP 119 | BLACK AND BLUES (LP) | 20 |

HARDROCK GUNTER
| 55 | Brunswick OE 9167 | MOUNTAIN MUSIC (EP) | 32 |

(see also Red Foley, Roberta Lee)

GURU GURU
| 73 | Atlantic K 50022 | DON'T CALL US WE'LL CALL YOU (LP) | 12 |
| 74 | Atlantic K 50044 | DANCE OF THE FLAMES (LP) | 12 |

GURU GURU/ULI TREPTE
| 80s | United Dairies UDT 07 | LIVE 72 & 73 (cassette, 1 side each) | 18 |

GURUS
| 66 | United Artists UP 1160 | Blue Snow Night/Come Girl | 25 |

JOHNNY GUSTAFSON
| 65 | Polydor 56022 | Just To Be With You/Sweet Day | 15 |
| 65 | Polydor 56043 | Take Me For A Little While/Make Me Your Number One | 18 |

(see also Big Three, Merseybeats, Quotations, Hard Stuff, Johnny & John, Ian Gillan Band, G-Force)

CARL GUSTAV & 84's
| 81 | Convulsive CN 001 | I Want To Kill Russians/Through Birds, Through Fire, But Not Through Glass (p/s) | 10 |

ARLO GUTHRIE
67	Reprise RS 20644	Motorcycle Song/Now And Then	8
70	Reprise RS 20877	Alice's Rock'N'Roll Restaurant/Coming In To Los Angeles	5
70	Reprise RS 20951	Valley To Pray/Gabriel's Mother's Hiway Ballad No. 16 Blues (demo-only)	7
67	Reprise RLP 6267	ALICE'S RESTAURANT (LP)	20
68	Reprise RSLP 6269	ARLO (LP)	18
69	Reprise RSLP 6346	RUNNING DOWN THE ROAD (LP)	15
70	Reprise RSLP 6411	WASHINGTON COUNTY (LP)	15

GWEN GUTHRIE
| 86 | 4th + Broadway BRW 1252 | Seventh Heaven/It Should Have Been You/Getting Hot (12", p/s) | 12 |

SHEILA GUTHRIE
| 63 | Fontana TF 399 | Mirror Mirror/It Doesn't Mean A Thing | 8 |

WOODY GUTHRIE
51	Melodisc 1141	Ramblin' Blues/Talkin' Columbia Blues (78)	15
55	Melodisc EPM7 84	HARD AIN'T IT HARD (EP)	22
55	Melodisc EPM7 85	WORRIED MAN BLUES (EP)	22
55	Melodisc EPM7 91	HEY LOLLY LOLLY (EP)	22
55	Melodisc MLP 12-106	MORE SONGS BY GUTHRIE (LP)	55
58	Topic 12T 31	BOUND FOR GLORY (LP)	48
64	RCA RD 7642	DUST BOWL BALLADS (LP)	38
65	Xtra XTRA 1012	WOODY GUTHRIE (LP)	22
66	Xtra XTRA 1064	WOODY GUTHRIE (LP)	22
66	Xtra XTRA 1065	POOR BOY (LP)	22
66	Xtra XTRA 1067	SONGS TO GROW ON VOL. 1 (LP)	22
68	Ember CW 129	WOODY GUTHRIE (LP)	22
69	Ember CW 135	CISCO HOUSTON AND WOODY GUTHRIE (LP)	22
69	Ember CW 136	BLIND SONNY TERRY & WOODY GUTHRIE (LP)	22

GUTTERSNIPES
| 88 | Razor GUTT 1 | Addicted To Love/Love's Young Dream (p/s) | 8 |
| 88 | Razor RAZ 42 | THE POOR DRESS UP (LP) | 12 |

(see also Cocksparrer)

GUTTERSNYPES
94	Liberty Grooves LIB 004	TRIALS OF LIFE (Radio Edits) (12" EP)	18
94	Liberty Grooves LIB 005	TRIALS OF LIFE (12" EP)	20
94	Liberty Grooves LIB 006	TRIALS OF LIFE EP (Instrumentals)	18
94	Liberty Grooves LIB004	The Trials Of Life (Green vinyl radio edit) (12")	15
94	Liberty Grooves LIB005	The Trials Of Life (Blue, Red) (12")	10
94	Liberty Grooves LIB005	The Trials Of Life (Black) (12")	8
94	Liberty Grooves LIB005	The Trials Of Life (White) (12")	20
94	Liberty Grooves LIB006	The Trials Of Life (Clear vinyl instrumentals) (12")	40

GUV'NERS
| 63 | Piccadilly 7N 35117 | Let's Make A Habit Of This/The Kissing Had To Stop | 12 |

(see also Jess Conrad, Dickie Pride, Nelson Keene)

BARRY GUY
76	Incus INCUS 22	STATEMENTS V-XI FOR DOUBLE BASS AND VIOLONE (LP)	50

(see also Derek Bailey Barry Guy & Paul Rutherford)

BUDDY GUY
65	Chess CRS 8004	Let Me Love You Baby/Ten Years Ago	22
68	Fontana TF 951	Mary Had A Little Lamb/Sweet Little Angel	18
72	Atlantic K 10195	Honey Dripper/Man Of Many Words	6
91	Silvertone ORE 30	Mustang Sally/Trouble Don't Last (with Jeff Beck, p/s)	5
65	Chess CRE 6004	CRAZY MUSIC (EP)	40
68	Vanguard SVRL 19001	COMING AT YOU (LP)	40
68	Vanguard SVRL 19002	MAN AND HIS BLUES (LP)	40
68	Vanguard SVRL 19004	BLUES TODAY (LP)	30
69	Vanguard SVRL 19008	THIS IS BUDDY GUY! (LP)	30
69	Vanguard SVRL 79290	HOT AND COOL (LP)	22
69	Chess CRL(S) 4546	I LEFT MY BLUES IN SAN FRANCISCO (LP)	40
69	Python KM 2	FIRST TIME I MET THE BLUES (LP)	45
70	Harvest SHSP 4006	BUDDY AND THE JUNIORS (LP, with Junior Mance & Junior Wells)	45
70	Red Lightnin' RL 001	IN THE BEGINNING (LP)	15
72	Atlantic K 40240	PLAY THE BLUES (LP, with Junior Wells)	20
73	Vanguard VSD 79323	HOLD THAT PLANE (LP)	18

(see also Junior Wells, Eddie Boyd/Buddy Guy)

BUDDY GUY with JEFF BECK
91	Silvertone ORE 30	Mustang Sally/Trouble Don't Last (p/s)	5

(see also Jeff Beck)

DERYCK GUYLER
71	Columbia DB 8764	(You Can't Kill An Old) Desert Rat/Ruby	10

GUYS
69	Tepee TPR SP 1001	You Go Your Way/Little Girl	10

(see also Beat Six)

GYGAFO
89	Holyground HG 1155	LEGEND OF THE KINGFISHER (LP, 160 copies only, posthumously designed semi-gatefold sleeve with insert)	45

GYNAECOLOGISTS
81	Teesbeat TB 2	The Red Pullover/The Offence (p/s)	5

GYPSIES
67	CBS 201785	Jerk It/Diamonds, Rubies, Gold And Fame	35

(see also Flirtations, Pearly Gates)

GYPSY
71	United Artists UAG 29155	GYPSY (LP)	18
72	United Artists UAS 29420	BRENDA AND THE RATTLESNAKE (LP)	12

(see also Legay)

JENNY HAAN
78	EMI EMI 2949	We Drove Them All Mad/Forgotten Dreams (p/s)	5

(see also Babe Ruth)

HABIBIYYA
72	Island HELP 7	IF MAN BUT KNEW (LP, with inner sleeve)	30

(see also Mighty Baby)

HABITS
66	Decca F 12348	Elbow Baby/Need You	30

(see also Charles Dickens, Nice, Brian Davison)

HACKENSACK
72	Island WIP 6149	Moving On/River Boat	12
71	Polydor 2383 263	UP THE HARD WAY (LP, with inner sleeve)	75
74	Zel UZ 003	HERE COMES THE JUDGE (LP, private pressing, as Hack & Sack)	100+

(see also Megaton, Tiger [U.K.], Nicky Moore Band)

BOBBY HACKETT & BILLY BUTTERFIELD
68	Verve (S)VLP 9212	BOBBY, BILLY AND BRAZIL (LP)	12

STEVE HACKETT
78	Charisma CB 312	How Can I?/Kim (with Ritchie Havens)	10
78	Charisma CB 318	Narnia (Remix)/Please Don't Touch	8
79	Charisma CB 334	Every Day/Lost Time In Cordoba	5
79	Charisma CB 341	Clocks — The Angel Of Mons/Acoustic Set	5
79	Charisma CB 341-12	Clocks — The Angel Of Mons /Acoustic Set/Tigermoth (12", p/s)	10
80	Charisma CB 357	The Show/Hercules Unchained (p/s)	5
80	Charisma CB 368	Sentimental Institution/The Toast (p/s)	5
83	Charisma CELL 12	Cell 151/Air Conditioned Nightmare/Time Lapse At Milton Keynes (12", p/s; with bonus white label 12" Clocks — The Angel Of Mons/Acoustic Set/Tigermoth [CELL 13], 2,000 only)	10
75	Charisma CAS 111	VOYAGE OF THE ACOLYTE (LP)	12

Rare Record Price Guide 2008

MINT VALUE £

| 01 | Camino CAMCD 23 | LIVE ARCHIVE (4-CD box set) | 30 |
| 01 | Camino CAMCD 23 | LIVE ARCHIVE (5-CD box set, limited edition with extra CD) | 30 |

(see also Peter Banks, Genesis, GTR, Quiet World)

VERNON HADDOCK'S JUBILEE LOVELIES
| 65 | Columbia SX 6011 | VERNON HADDOCK'S JUBILEE LOVELIES (LP) | 250 |

MANOS HADJIDAKIS
| 62 | Columbia SX 6253 | LILACS OUT OF THE DEAD LAND (LP) | 15 |

HAFFY'S WHISKY SOUR
| 71 | Deram DM 345 | Shot In The Head/Bye Bye Bluebird | 7 |

(see also Easybeats, Paintbox)

HAFLER TRIO
84	Doublevision DVR 4	BANG! — AN OPEN LETTER (LP, with insert)	12
86	Charrm 3	THREE WAYS OF SAYING TWO — THE NETHERLANDS LECTURES (LP, stickered sleeve with booklet)	15
86	Touch T 05	THE SEA ORG (10", 'audio/visual' package with booklet)	12

(see also Cabaret Voltaire)

SAMMY HAGAR
| 77 | Capitol E-ST 11599 | SAMMY HAGAR (LP, red vinyl) | 12 |
| 79 | Capitol E-ST 11983 | STREET MACHINE (LP, with free single) | 12 |

(see also Van Halen, Madonna, Montrose)

EARLE HAGEN
| 64 | Colpix PX 740 | Nancy's Theme/New Interns Watusi | 6 |

JOAN HAGER
| 57 | Brunswick 05650 | Happy Is A Girl Named Me/Run Darlin', Don't Walk (78 rpm = £8) | 10 |

MERLE HAGGARD & STRANGERS
68	Capitol CL 15540	The Legend Of Bonnie And Clyde/I Started Loving You Again	5
66	Capitol T/ST 2453	JUST BETWEEN THE TWO OF US (LP, with Bonnie Owens)	15
67	Capitol T/ST 2702	I'M A LONESOME FUGITIVE (LP)	15
68	Capitol T/ST 2912	THE LEGEND OF BONNIE & CLYDE (LP)	15
69	Capitol T/ST 2972	MAMA TRIED (LP)	15
69	Capitol ST 21377	SAME TRAIN, A DIFFERENT TIME (LP)	15
70	Capitol ST 21531	A PORTRAIT OF MERLE HAGGARD (LP)	15
70	Capitol E-ST 451	THE FIGHTIN' SIDE OF ME (LP)	15
71	Capitol E-ST 735	HAG (LP)	12
72	Capitol E-ST 835	SOMEDAY WE'LL LOOK BACK (LP)	12
72	Capitol E-ST 882	LET ME TELL YOU ABOUT A SONG (LP)	12
73	Capitol E-ST 11200	I LOVE DIXIE BLUES (LP)	12
76	Capitol E-ST 11544	MY LOVE AFFAIR WITH TRAINS (LP)	12
77	MCA MCF 2818	MY FAREWELL TO ELVIS (LP)	12
87	Premier PMP 1003	TO ALL THE GIRLS I'VE LOVED BEFORE (LP, withdrawn)	20

MEL HAGUE
| 60s | LK/LP 6558 | MERRY-GO-ROUND (LP, some signed) | 18/12 |

JOYCE HAHN
| 57 | London HLA 8453 | Gonna Find Me A Bluebird/I Saw You, I Saw You (78 rpm = £10) | 25 |

PAUL HAIG
81	Rational no cat. no.	DRAMA (cassette)	15
82	Operation Twilight OPT 03	Running Away/Time (p/s)	5
84	Island ISX 198	The Only Truth (U.S. Remix)/Instrumental/Ghost Rider (12", p/s)	8
80s	Masterbag no cat. no.	Blue (square flexidisc free with *Masterbag* magazine)	6/5
84	Island ILPS 9742	RHYTHM OF LIFE (LP)	12
85	Operation Afterglow OPA 3	THE WARP OF PURE FUN (LP, inner sleeve)	12

(see also Josef K, Rhythm Of Life, Juggernauts)

NORMAN HAINES (BAND)
70	Parlophone R 5871	Daffodil/Autumn Mobile (as Norman Haynes Band)	25
71	Parlophone SPSR 338	Den Of Iniquity/Everything You See (Mr. Armageddon) (promo only)	42
72	Parlophone R 5960	Give It To You Girl/Elaine (as Norman Haines)	25
71	Parlophone PCS 7130	DEN OF INIQUITY (LP)	350+

(see also Avalanche, Brumbeats, The Dog That Bit People, Locomotive)

HAIR
| 69 | Pye NSPL 18314 | RAVE UP (LIVE FROM THE SHAFTESBURY THEATRE) (LP) | 65 |

(see also Alex Harvey, Hairband)

HAIR
| 71 | Columbia SCX 6452 | HAIRPIECE (LP) | 120 |

HAIRBAND
| 69 | Bell BLL 1076 | Big Louis/Travelling Song | 18 |
| 69 | Bell SBLL 69 | BAND ON THE WAGON (LP) | 55 |

(see also Alex Harvey, Hair)

HAIRCUT 100
83	Arista CLIP 5	Whistle Down The Wind (withdrawn)	10+
83	Polydor HCP2	So Tired (silver vinyl, no p/s)	8
82	Arista HCC 101	BLUE HAT FOR A BLUE DAY (LP, withdrawn, test pressings only)	40+

HAIRPOWER
| 70 | CBS 4961 | Royal International Love-in/Be There, Be Hair | 5 |

HAL
| 05 | Heavenly HVN 147 | Keep Love As Your Golden Rule/THE MAGIC NUMBERS: Animla Sola (Double A side tour single – 500 only p/s) | 8 |

DENNIS HALE

55	Parlophone MSP 6153	The Butterscotch Mop/S'posin'	10

(see also Jack Parnell)

BILL HALEY (& HIS COMETS)

78s

53	London L 1190	Crazy Man, Crazy/Whatcha Gonna Do (as Bill Haley with Haley's Comets) (gold label lettering)	30
53	London L 1216	Pat-A-Cake/Fractured (as Bill Haley with Haley's Comets, gold label)	35
54	London HL 1190	Crazy Man, Crazy/Whatcha Gonna Do (as Bill Haley with Haley's Comets) (reissue, silver label lettering)	25
54	London HL 1216	Pat-A-Cake/Fractured (reissue, silver label lettering, as Bill Haley with Haley's Comets)	30
54	Brunswick 05338	Shake, Rattle And Roll/A.B.C. Boogie (gold or silver lettering)	8/4
55	London HL 8142	Green Tree Boogie/Sundown Boogie	18
55	London HLF 8161	Farewell, So Long, Goodbye/I'll Be True	18
55	London HLF 8194	Ten Little Indians/Rocking Chair On The Moon	18
56	Melodisc 1376	I'm Gonna Dry Ev'ry Tear With A Kiss/Why Do I Cry Over You	65
57	London HLF 8371	Rock The Joint/Yes Indeed!	15
57	Brunswick 05658	Forty Cups Of Coffee/Choo Choo Ch'Boogie	12
57	Brunswick 05688	(You Hit The Wrong Note) Billy Goat/Rockin' Rollin' Rover	14
57	Brunswick 05719	Miss You/The Dipsy Doodle	20
58	Brunswick 05735	Mary, Mary Lou/It's A Sin	20
58	Brunswick 05742	Skinny Minnie/How Many	20
58	Brunswick 05752	Lean Jean/Don't Nobody Move	22
58	Brunswick 05766	Whoa Mabel!/Chiquita Linda	30
59	Brunswick 05788	I Got A Woman/Charmaine	35
59	Brunswick 05805	Shaky/Caldonia	40
59	Brunswick 05810	Joey's Song/Ooh! Look-A There, Ain't She Pretty	40

SINGLES

54	Brunswick 05317	(We're Gonna) Rock Around The Clock/Thirteen Women	60/25
54	Brunswick 05338	Shake, Rattle And Roll/A.B.C. Boogie	45/22
55	Brunswick 05373	Happy Baby/Dim, Dim The Lights (I Want Some Atmosphere)	45/22
55	Brunswick 05405	Birth Of The Boogie/Mambo Rock	45/22
55	London HL 8142	Green Tree Boogie/Sundown Boogie	160/60
55	Brunswick 05453	Two Hound Dogs/Razzle Dazzle	45/22
55	London HLF 8161	Farewell, So Long, Goodbye/I'll Be True	125/65
55	London HLF 8194	Ten Little Indians/Rocking Chair On The Moon	140/70
55	Brunswick 05509	Rock-A-Beatin' Boogie/Burn That Candle	45/22
56	Brunswick 05530	See You Later, Alligator/The Paper Boy (On Main Street, USA)	40/20

(When two prices are given for the above 45s, the first refers to original gold-lettering labels & the second to later copies with silver-lettering on label.)

56	Brunswick 05565	The Saints Rock 'N' Roll/R-O-C-K	20
56	Brunswick 05582	Rockin' Through The Rye/Hot Dog Buddy Buddy	20
56	Brunswick 05615	Rip It Up/Teenager's Mother	20
56	Brunswick 05616	Rudy's Rock/Blue Comet Blues	20
57	Brunswick 05640	Don't Knock The Rock/Calling All Comets	20
57	Brunswick 05641	Hook, Line And Sinker/Goofin' Around	20
57	London HLF 8371	Rock The Joint/Yes Indeed! (gold or silver label)	140/70
57	Brunswick 05658	Forty Cups Of Coffee/Choo Choo Ch'Boogie	20
57	Brunswick 05688	(You Hit The Wrong Note) Billy Goat/Rockin' Rollin' Rover	22
57	Brunswick 05719	Miss You/The Dipsy Doodle	20
58	Brunswick 05735	Mary, Mary Lou/It's A Sin	18
58	Brunswick 05742	Skinny Minnie/How Many	18
58	Brunswick 05752	Lean Jean/Don't Nobody Move	18
58	Brunswick 05766	Whoa Mabel!/Chiquita Linda	20
59	Brunswick 05788	I Got A Woman/Charmaine	18
59	Brunswick 05805	Shaky/Caldonia	20
59	Brunswick 05810	Joey's Song/Ooh! Look-A There, Ain't She Pretty	20

(The above 45s were originally issued with triangular centres; later round centres are worth half the value for earlier 45s to two-thirds for later 45s.)

60	Brunswick 05818	Puerto Rican Peddler/Skokiaan	12
60	Warner Bros WB 6	Candy Kisses/Tamiami	10
61	London HLU 9471	Spanish Twist/My Kind Of Woman	15
63	Stateside SS 196	Tenor Man/Up Goes My Love	8
64	Warner Bros WB 133	Rock Around The Clock/Love Letters In The Sand	12
64	Brunswick 05910	Happy Baby/Birth Of The Boogie	15
64	Brunswick 05917	The Green Door/Yeah! She's Evil	15
68	MCA MU 1013	(We're Gonna) Rock Around The Clock/Shake, Rattle And Roll	6
68	Pye International 7N 25455	Crazy Man, Crazy/Dance With A Dolly (With A Hole In Her Stocking)	18
73	Sonet SON 2016	Me And Bobby McGee/I Wouldn't Have Missed It For The World	6
74	Sonet SON 2043	Crazy Man, Crazy/Lawdy Miss Clawdy	6
74	MCA MCA 128	Rock Around The Clock/Rip It Up/Shake, Rattle And Roll	5
74	MCA MCA 142	See You Later Alligator/Rudy's Rock	5

EXPORT SINGLES

54	Decca BM 05317	(We're Gonna) Rock Around The Clock/Thirteen Women	80
55	Decca BM 05405	Birth Of The Boogie/Mambo Rock	65
55	Decca BM 05509	Rock-A-Beatin' Boogie/Burn That Candle	65
56	Decca BM 05530	See You Later Alligator/The Paper Boy (On Main Street, USA)	65
56	Decca BM 31163	The Saints Rock 'N' Roll/R-O-C-K	50
56	Decca BM 31164	Rockin' Through The Rye/Hot Dog Buddy Buddy	50
56	Decca BM 31171	Rip It Up/Teenager's Mother	50
57	Decca BM 31174	Don't Knock The Rock/Choo Choo Ch'Boogie	50
68	Decca AD 1010	(We're Gonna) Rock Around The Clock/Shake, Rattle And Roll	25

EPs

55	Brunswick OE 9129	DIM, DIM THE LIGHTS (gold lettering label, 'stage' p/s, various colours)	40
55	Brunswick OE 9129	DIM, DIM THE LIGHTS (silver lettering label, 'stage' or 'cameo' p/s)	each 35
55	London REF 1031	ROCK AND ROLL	60
56	London REF 1049	LIVE IT UP PART 1	50
56	London REF 1050	LIVE IT UP PART 2	50
56	Brunswick OE 9214	ROCK AND ROLL WITH BILL HALEY	25
56	Brunswick OE 9250	ROCK AROUND THE CLOCK	20
56	Brunswick OE 9250	ROCK AROUND THE CLOCK (round centre, different sleeve, same design as "Bill Haley" [OE 9459])	40
56	London REF 1058	LIVE IT UP PART 3	50
56	Brunswick OE 9278	ROCK'N'ROLL STAGE SHOW PART 1	35
56	Brunswick OE 9279	ROCK'N'ROLL STAGE SHOW PART 2	35
56	Brunswick OE 9280	ROCK'N'ROLL STAGE SHOW PART 3	35
58	Brunswick OE 9349	ROCKIN' THE OLDIES PART 1	50
58	Brunswick OE 9350	ROCKIN' THE OLDIES PART 2	50
58	Brunswick OE 9351	ROCKIN' THE OLDIES PART 3	50
59	Brunswick OE 9446	ROCKIN' AROUND THE WORLD	60
59	Brunswick OE 9459	BILL HALEY	50

(The above EPs were originally issued with triangular centres, later round-centre copies are worth two-thirds these values.)

60	Warners WEP 6001	BILL HALEY AND HIS COMETS	40
61	Warners WEP 6025	BILL HALEY'S JUKE BOX (also stereo WSEP 2025)	40/60
64	Warners WEP 6133	BILL HALEY VOLUME 1	40
64	Warners WEP 6136	BILL HALEY VOLUME 2	40

LPs

55	London H-APB 1042	LIVE IT UP (10", gold or silver lettering on label)	110/65
56	Brunswick LAT 8117	ROCK AROUND THE CLOCK	35
56	Brunswick LAT 8139	ROCK AND ROLL STAGE SHOW	35
57	London HA-F 2037	ROCK THE JOINT	90
57	Brunswick LAT 8219	ROCKIN' THE OLDIES	65
57	Brunswick LAT 8268	ROCKIN' THE JOINT	65
59	Brunswick LAT 8295	BILL HALEY'S CHICKS (also stereo STA 3011)	65/85
60	Brunswick LAT 8326	STRICTLY INSTRUMENTAL	60
61	Ace Of Hearts AH 13	ROCK AROUND THE CLOCK (2 slightly different sleeves)	18/15
62	Columbia 33SX 1460	TWISTIN' KNIGHTS AT THE ROUNDTABLE (LIVE!)	35
62	Ace Of Hearts AH 35	ROCKIN' THE OLDIES	15
64	Ace Of Hearts AH 66	BILL HALEY'S CHICKS	15
64	Golden Guinea GGL 0282	ROCK THE JOINT	15
65	Xtra XTRA 1027	BILL HALEY & THE COMETS	30
65	Warner Bros W 1391	BILL HALEY'S JUKE BOX	50
67	Marble Arch MAL 817	ROCK THE JOINT	12
67	Ember EMB 3386	REAL LIVE ROCK'N'ROLL	15
68	MCA MUP 318	RIP IT UP!	15
68	Ember EMB 3396	KING OF ROCK (reissued 1973)	15/12
69	Ember EMB 3401	MISTER ROCK 'N' ROLL	12
70	Valiant VS 103	BILL HALEY & THE COMETS	15
71	Coral CP 55	ROCK AROUND THE CLOCK	12
71	Sonet SNTF 623	ROCK AROUND THE COUNTRY	12

(see also Kingsmen, Jodimars, Nick Nantos & His Fireballs)

HALF JAPANESE

81	Armageddon AS 009	Spy/I Know How It Feels ... Bad/My Knowledge Was Wrong (p/s)	5
81	Armageddon ABOX 1	1/2 GENTLEMEN NOT BEASTS (3-LP box set with poster, booklet & lyric insert)	25
81	Armageddon ARM 7	LOUD (LP)	12
		(see also Jad Fair)	

HAL HOPPERS

54	London HL 8107	More Love/Do Nothin' Blues (78 rpm = £10)	50
55	London HL 8129	Mother Of Pearl/Baby I've Had It (78 rpm = £10)	40

ADELAIDE HALL

60	Oriole CB 1556	Common Sense/Blue Bird On My Shoulder	10

BOB HALL & ALEXIS KORNER

78	Logo GO 331	Pinetop's Boogie Woogie/All I Got Is You	12
		(see also Brunning Hall Sunflower Blues Band, Alexis Korner)	

CAROLINE HALL

70	Major Minor MM 689	Dream Boy/Julie	6
71	Decca F 13146	Hold My Hand/Put A Light In The Window	6

(DARYL) HALL & (JOHN) OATES

85	RCA PB 49967	Out Of Touch/Dance On Your Knees (square picture disc)	5
88	Arista 661 730	Downtown Life/Downtown Remix/Dubtown Life/ Keep On Pushin' Love (CD, withdrawn)	8
89	RCA PD 49465	Maneater/Delayed Reaction/I Can't Go For That (No Can Do)/ Unguarded Minute (3" CD, gatefold card sleeve)	8

(see also Gulliver)

DARYL HALL & SOUNDS OF BLACKNESS

94	Mercury MERMC 404	Gloryland/(mixes) (picture disc, in poster sleeve)	10

DEREK HALL & MIKE COOPER

60s	Kennet KRS 766	OUT OF THE SHADES (EP)	35

DICKSON HALL (& COUNTRY ALL-STARS)

57	MGM MGM-EP 626	OUTLAWS OF THE OLD WEST (EP)	20
58	London RE-R 1158	FABULOUS COUNTRY HITS NO. 1 (EP)	20
58	London RE-R 1159	FABULOUS COUNTRY HITS NO. 2 (EP)	20
58	London RE-R 1160	FABULOUS COUNTRY HITS NO. 3 (EP)	20
60	Fontana Z 4011	ALL-TIME COUNTRY AND WESTERN HITS (LP)	15

MINT VALUE £

DOLORES HALL
72 Jay Boy BOY 77   Good Lovin' Man/W-O-M-E-N 15
(see also Jackie Lee & Dolores Hall)

DORA HALL
64 King KG 1003   Hello Faithless/You've Got Me Cryin' Again 5

JIMMY GRAY HALL
74 Epic EPC 2312   Be That Way/Possessed By The Moon 15

JUANITA HALL
62 Storyville SEP 382   STORYVILLE BLUES ANTHOLOGY VOL. 2 (EP) 15
64 Society SOC 971   JUANITA HALL SINGS THE BLUES (LP) 15

LANI HALL
83 A&M AM 159   Never Say Never Again/Un Chanson D'Amour (p/s) 8
74 A&M AMLS 64359   SUNDOWN LADY (LP) 15

LARRY HALL
60 Parlophone R 4625   Sandy/Lovin' Tree 12
62 Salvo SLO 1811   Ladder Of Love/The One You Left Behind (99 copies only) 25

RENE HALL'S ORCHESTRA
58 London HLU 8581   Twitchy/Flippin' (78 rpm = £10) 60

ROBIN HALL (& JIMMY MacGREGOR)
60 Collector JDS 3   Football Crazy/Rosin The Beau (some with p/s) 15/10
60 Decca F 11266   Football Crazy/Rosin The Beau (reissue, p/s) 10
61 Ace Of Clubs ACL 1065   SCOTTISH CHOICE (LP, with Jimmie MacGregor) 15
(see also Galliards)

RONNIE HALL
61 Piccadilly 7N 35001   The Code Of Love/Who Cares 6
62 Piccadilly 7N 35040   My Very First Love/The Day After Forever 6
65 Fontana TF 569   I'll Stand Aside/I'm Getting Nowhere 15

ROY HALL
56 Brunswick 05531   See You Later, Alligator/Don't Stop Now (gold label lettering) 500
56 Brunswick 05531   See You Later, Alligator/Don't Stop Now (78) 120
56 Brunswick 05555   Blue Suede Shoes/Luscious (78 rpm = £130) 500
56 Brunswick 05627   Diggin' The Boogie/Three Alley Cats (78 rpm = £110) 500

TONY HALL
77 Free Reed FRR 012   FIELDVOLE MUSIC (LP, with insert) 20

CHANCE HALLADAY
62 Vogue V 9203   John Henry/Thirteen Women 25

HALLELUJAH SKIFFLE GROUP
58 Oriole CB 1429   I Saw The Light/A Closer Walk With Thee (with Clinton Ford)
                            (78 rpm = £12) 20
(see also Clinton Ford)

HALLIARD
67 Saga SOC 1058   IT'S THE IRISH IN ME (LP) 25
68 Broadside BRO 106   THE HALLIARD AND JON RAVEN (LP) 50
(see also Jon Raven, Nic Jones)

GERI HALLIWELL
99 EMI 12 EMDJX 542   Look At Me (Terminalhead Remix)/(Terminalhead dub) (12", die cut sleeve,
                            promo only) 10
99 EMI CDEMDJX 542   Look At Me (CD, sealed card p/s, promo only) 10
99 EMI CD IN 122   Interview (CD, tri-fold digipak, promo only) 15
99 EMI DJ 521 0092   SCHIZOPHRENIC
                            (CD, album sampler in sealed foil wallet, numbered sticker, promo only) 20
(see also Spice Girls)

DICK HALLMAN
56 Brunswick 05608   Two Different Worlds/Love Me As Though There Were No Tomorrow 8
60 Vogue V 9162   Born To Be Loved/Just Squeeze Me But Don't Teeze Me 10

JOHNNY HALLYDAY
62 Philips BF 1238   Shake The Hand Of A Fool/Hold Back The Sun 10
63 Philips 373 012BF   Hey Little Girl/Caravan Of Lonely Men 10
65 Philips BF 1449   Pour Moi Tu Es La Seule/They Call Him A Man 12
62 Philips 432 813BE   ROCKING (EP) 150
66 Vogue VRE 5013   JOHNNY HALLYDAY (EP) 120
61 Philips BBL 7556   SINGS AMERICA'S ROCKIN' HITS (LP) 100

HALOS
61 London HLU 9424   Nag/Copycat 50

CHRIS HAMALTON
53 London L 1177   Farmer's Boy Boogie/Celebration Rag (78) 8
53 London L 1200   Dizzy Fingers/Saturday Rag (78) 10

STUART HAMBLEN
54 HMV 7MC 20   This Ole House/When My Lord Picks Up The 'Phone (export issue) 25
54 HMV 7MC 20   This Ole House/When My Lord Picks Up The 'Phone (export issue) (78) 8
55 HMV JO 434   Ole Pappy Time/The Toy Violin (78, export issue) 10
55 HMV 7MC 30   Go On By/Just A Man (export issue) 20
56 HMV 7M 394   Hell Train/A Few Things To Remember 18

BILLY HAMBRIC
79 Grapevine GRP 139   She Said Goodbye/I Found True Love 15

CLAIRE HAMILL
72	Island WIP 6122	When I Was A Child/Alice In The Streets Of Darlington	6
72	Island WIP 6133	Baseball Blues/Smile Your Blues Away	6
81	WEA K 18440	First Night In New York/Ultraviolet Light (B-side with Gary Numan) (p/s)	7
72	Island ILPS 9182	ONE HOUSE LEFT STANDING (LP)	18
73	Island ILPS 9225	OCTOBER (LP)	15
74	Konk KONK 101	STAGE DOOR JOHNNIES (LP)	12
75	Konk KONK 104	ABRACADABRA (LP, featuring Cafe Society, with insert)	12

(see also Cafe Society, Gary Numan)

BILLY HAMILTON & STRANDSMEN
67	Philips BF 1622	Try To Remember/Don't You Believe It	7

CHICO HAMILTON QUINTET
57	Vogue V 2407	The Sage/The Morning After	6
65	HMV POP 1451	Carol's Walk/Chic Chic Chico	8
58	Vogue LAE 12045	CHICO HAMILTON QUINTET IN HIFI (LP)	15
68	Solid State USS 7010	THE GAMUT (LP)	12

DAVID HAMILTON
70s	Spectre SP 501	A Special Goodnight To You/Just For The Weekend	8

EDWARD HAMILTON & ARABIANS
80	Grapevine GRP 134	Baby Don't You Weep/I'm Gonna Love You	15

GARY HAMILTON
67	Decca F 12697	Let The Music Play/Don't Ask	12
69	CBS 4674	Easy Rider/Hare Krishna	6

(see also Hamilton & [Hamilton] Movement)

GAVIN HAMILTON
67	King KG 1067	It Won't Be The Same/Turn The Key Softly	140

GEORGE HAMILTON IV
57	London HL 8361	A Rose And A Candy Bar/If You Don't Know (gold or silver label print)	150/80
57	London HL 8361	A Rose And A Candy Bar/If You Don't Know (78)	25
57	HMV POP 429	Why Don't They Understand/Even Tho' (78 rpm = £8)	14
58	HMV POP 474	Now And For Always/One Heart (78 rpm = £10)	10
58	HMV POP 505	I Know Where I'm Goin'/Who's Taking You To The Prom? (78 rpm = £8)	10
58	HMV POP 534	Your Cheatin' Heart/When Will I Know? (78 rpm = £10)	10
60	HMV POP 813	Before This Day Ends/Loneliness Is All Around Us	5
63	RCA RCA 1353	Abilene/Oh So Many Years	5
72	Uni UNS 480	Evel Knievel/Boy From The Country	5
58	HMV CLP 1202	ON CAMPUS (LP)	20
59	HMV CLP 1263	SING ME A SAD SONG — A TRIBUTE TO HANK WILLIAMS (LP)	20

GUY HAMILTON
65	HMV POP 1418	A Lifetime Of Loneliness/Give The Game Away	12

(see also Neil Christian)

M. HAMILTON
67	Ska Beat JB 265	Something Gotta Ring/DENNIS LYNWARD & HIS GROUP: Jazz Session	20

MILTON HAMILTON
73	Explosion EX 2069	Long Long Road/Version	5

ROY HAMILTON
58	Fontana H 113	Don't Let Go/The Right To Love (78 rpm = £10)	25
58	Fontana H 143	Crazy Feelin'/In A Dream (78 rpm = £10)	15
59	Fontana H 180	Pledging My Love/My One And Only Love (78 rpm = £10)	15
59	Fontana H 193	I Need Your Loving/Somewhere Along The Way (78 rpm = £15)	15
61	Fontana H 298	You Can Have Her/Abide With Me	15
61	Fontana H 320	You're Gonna Need Magic/To The One I Love	15
63	MGM MGM 1210	Theme From "The VIPs"/The Sinner	12
64	MGM MGM 1251	There She Is/The Panic Is On (DJ copy = £350)	250
65	MGM MGM 1268	A Thousand Tears Ago/Sweet Violet	15
66	RCA RCA 1500	And I Love Her/Tore Up Over You	15
69	Deep Soul DS 9106	Dark End Of The Street/100 Years Ago	30
59	Fontana TFE 17160	WHY FIGHT THE FEELING (EP)	20
60	Fontana TFE 17163	THE MOOD MOVES (EP)	20
61	Fontana TFE 17170	COME OUT SWINGING (EP)	20
63	Columbia 33SX 1473	GREATEST HITS (LP)	40
64	MGM MGM-C 960	WARM SOUL (LP)	45

RUSS HAMILTON
57	Oriole CB 1359	We Will Make Love/Rainbow	7
57	Oriole CB 1388	Wedding Ring/I Still Belong To You	7
57	Oriole CB 1406	I Don't Know Why/My Mother's Eyes	6
58	Oriole CB 1404	Little One/I Had A Dream	5
58	Oriole CB 1451	Drifting And Dreaming/Tip-toe Through The Tulips	5
58	Oriole CB 1459	I Wonder Who's Kissing Her Now/September In The Rain	5
58	Oriole CB 1465	Things I Didn't Say/Strange Are The Ways Of Love	5
59	Oriole CB 1492	The Reprieve Of Tom Dooley/Dreaming Of You (78 rpm = £8)	5
59	Oriole CB 1506	My Unbreakable Heart/I Found You (78 rpm = £15)	5
59	Oriole CB 1508	Smile, Smile, Smile (And Sing, Sing, Sing)/Shadow (78 rpm = £15)	5
60	Oriole CB 1527	Things No Money Can Buy/Mama (78 rpm = £15)	5
60	Oriole CB 1531	It's A Sin To Tell A Lie/Folks Get Married In The Spring (78 rpm = £12)	5
60	MGM MGM 1096	Gonna Find Me A Bluebird/Choir Girl	5
64	Ember EMBS 184	Valley Of Love/Loneliest Boy In Town	5
64	Ember EMBS 193	We Will Make Love/No One Can Love Like You	5
58	Oriole EP 7005	RUSS HAMILTON (EP)	25
58	Oriole MG 20031	WE WILL MAKE LOVE (LP)	40

MINT VALUE £

SCOTT HAMILTON
66	Parlophone R 5492	Good Day Sunshine/For No One	6

HAMILTON & MOVEMENT
65	Polydor BM 56026	Really Saying Something/I Won't See You Tonight	70
67	CBS 202573	I'm Not The Marrying Kind/My Love Belongs To You	38

(see also Gary Hamilton, Paul Stewart Movement)

HAMLINS
67	Coxsone CS 7021	Trying To Keep A Good Man Down/	
		BOB MARLEY/MARCIA GRIFFITHS: Oh My Darling	80
67	Coxsone CS 7022	Soul And Inspiration/ETHIOPIANS: Let's Get Together	25
68	Coxsone CS 7048	Sentimental Reasons/SOUL VENDORS: Last Waltz	25
68	Blue Cat BS 115	Sugar And Spice/SOUL VENDORS: Mercy Mercy Mercy	30

(see also Minstrels)

JACK HAMMER
61	Oriole CB 1634	Young Only Once/Juliette	15
62	Oriole CB 1645	Kissin' Twist/Melancholy Boy	10
62	Oriole CB 1728	Crazy Twist/Twist Talk	12
62	Oriole CB 1753	Don't Let Baby Know/Number 2539	15
66	Polydor 56091	Thanks/Love Ladder	20
69	United Artists UP 35029	What Greater Love/The Mason Dixon Line	50
60s	Youngblood B 1023	Swim	50
63	Oriole PS 40020	HAMMER + BEAT = TWIST (LP)	75
66	Polydor	BRAVE NEW WORLD (LP)	35

HAMMERHEAD
81	Linden Sounds LS 009	Time Will Tell/Lonely Man (p/s)	60

HAMMERS
69	President PT 247	Baby And Me/Little Butterfly	6
69	President PT 276	Sugar Baby/Power Of Love	6

HAMMERS (Jamaica)
70	Gas GAS 162	Hotter Than Scorcher/Someday Could See You	10

(see also Joan Ross)

HAMMERSMITH GORILLAS
74	Penny Farthing PEN 849	You Really Got Me/Leavin' 'Ome	18
77	Raw RAW 2	You Really Got Me/Leavin' 'Ome (reissue, company sleeve)	8

(see also Clique)

PETER HAMMILL
75	Charisma CB 245	Birthday Special/Shingle Song	8
78	Charisma CB 339	The Polaroid (credited to Ricky Nadir)/The Old School Tie	10
78	Charisma PH 001	Crying Wolf/This Side Of The Looking Glass (promo only)	30
81	Virgin VS 424	My Experience/Glue (p/s)	5
82	Naive NAV 3	Paradox Drive/Now More Than Ever (p/s)	6
83	Naive NAV 8	Film Noir/Seven Wonders	6
84	Charisma CB 414	Just Good Friends/Just Good Friends (Instrumental) (p/s)	5
86	Foundry FOUND 3	Painting By Numbers/You Hit Me Where I Live (p/s)	5
86	Foundry FOUND 312	Painting By Numbers (Extended)/You Hit Me Where I Live/Shell (12", p/s)	8
71	Charisma CAS 1037	FOOL'S MATE (LP, gatefold sleeve)	30
73	Charisma CAS 1067	CHAMELEON IN THE SHADOW OF THE NIGHT (LP, gatefold sleeve)	18
74	Charisma CAS 1083	THE SILENT CORNER AND THE EMPTY STAGE (LP, gatefold sl., with inner)	15
74	Charisma CAS 1089	IN CAMERA (LP, with inner sleeve)	15
75	Charisma CAS 1099	NADIR'S BIG CHANCE (LP, with inner sleeve)	15
77	Charisma CAS 1125	OVER (LP, with inner lyric sleeve)	15

(see also Van Der Graaf Generator, Le Orme, Rikki Nadir, Colin Scot)

CLAY HAMMOND
72	Jay Boy BOY 78	Dance Little Girl/Twin Brother	8

JOHN HAMMOND
65	Fontana TF 560	Baby Won't You Tell Me/I Live The Life I Love	15
68	Atlantic 584 190	Brown Eyed Handsome Man/Crosscut Saw	10
64	Fontana TFL 6046	BIG CITY BLUES (LP)	45
65	Fontana TFL 6059	SO MANY ROADS (LP)	38
71	CBS 64365	SOURCE POINT (LP)	25
72	CBS 65051	I'M SATISFIED (LP)	25
72	Vanguard VSD 11/12	THE BEST OF JOHN HAMMOND — SOUTHERN FRIED (2-LP)	20

CURLEY HAMNER & COOPER BROTHERS
59	Felsted SD 80061	Twistin' And Turnin'/King And Queen	10

SUSAN HAMPSHIRE
65	Decca F 12185	When Love Is True/When The World Was Our Own	10

LIONEL HAMPTON (& HIS HAMP-TONES)
52	MGM MGM 468	Samson's Boogie/Helpless (78, & His Hamp-Tones, B-side with Sonny Parker)	8
57	Vogue V 2405	Flying Home/Perdido (with Just Jazz All Stars)	10
57	Vogue V 2406	Hamp's Boogie Woogie/The Blues (with Just Jazz All Stars)	10
56	MGM MGM-EP 552	LIONEL HAMPTON & HIS ORCHESTRA (EP)	10
54	Vogue EPV 1015	LIONEL HAMPTON TRIO (EP)	8
54	Brunswick OE 9007	JUST JAZZ (EP)	8
55	Brunswick OE 9108	JUST JAZZ CONCERT (EP)	8
55	Philips BBE 12017	LIONEL HAMPTON & HIS ORCHESTRA (EP)	8
57	Vogue EPV 1161	GENE NORMAN PRESENTS JUST JAZZ — LIONEL HAMPTON AT THE PASADENA AUDITORIUM (EP)	8
58	Columbia Clef SEB 10108	HAMPS BOOGIE WOOGIE (EP)	8
62	Oriole EP 7046	LIONEL HAMPTON ORCHESTRA (EP)	8

51	Brunswick LA 8527	HAMP'S BOOGIE WOOGIE (10" LP)	15
52	Brunswick LA 8551	MOONGLOW (10" LP)	15
53	Vogue LDE 043	LIONEL HAMPTON'S JAZZ TIME PARIS VOLUME 1 (10" LP)	15
54	Vogue LDE 051	NEW SOUNDS FROM EUROPE VOLUME 2 — FRANCE (10" LP)	15
54	Vogue LDE 063	LIONEL HAMPTON VOLUME 3 (10" LP)	15
54	Felsted EDL 87007	THE HAMP IN PARIS IN PARIS VOLUME 1 (10" LP)	15
54	Felsted EDL 87008	THE HAMP IN PARIS IN PARIS VOLUME 2 (10" LP)	15
55	Felsted PDL 85002	LIONEL HAMPTON AND HIS NEW FRENCH SOUND VOLUME 1 (10" LP)	15
55	HMV CLP 1023	HOT MALLETS (LP)	12
55	Columbia Clef 33C 9011	LIONEL HAMPTON QUARTET (10" LP)	12
55	Philips BBL 7015	APOLLO HALL CONCERT 1954 (LP)	12

(see also Sonny Parker)

PAUL HAMPTON
| 58 | Philips PB 787 | Play It Cool/Classy Babe (78) | 20 |

SLIDE HAMPTON & HIS BAND
| 62 | London HA-K/SH-K 8008 | JAZZ WITH A TWIST (LP) | 18 |
| 62 | London LZT-K 15225 | LONDON JAZZ (LP, as Slide Hampton Octet) | 18 |

HAMPTONS
(see under Fabulous Impact)

HERBIE HANCOCK
63	Blue Note 45-1887	Blind Man, Blind Man (Parts 1 & 2)	20
70	Warner Bros WB 7358	Fat Mama/Wiggle-Waggle	10
74	CBS 2329	Chameleon/Vein Melter	6
75	CBS 3059	Palm Grease/Butterfly	6
71	Warner Bros WS 1834	FAT ALBERT ROTUNDA (LP)	25
71	Warner Bros K 46077	MWANDISHI (LP)	15
72	Warner Bros K 46164	CROSSINGS (LP)	15
74	Warner Bros K 46039	FAT ALBERT ROTUNDA (LP, reissue)	15
74	CBS 80193	THRUST (LP)	15
74	CBS 80546	DEATH WISH (LP, soundtrack)	20
74	CBS 65582	SEXTANT (LP)	12
74	CBS 65928	HEADHUNTERS (LP)	12
75	CBS 69185	MAN CHILD (LP)	12

(see also Headhunters)

SHEILA HANCOCK
| 63 | Decca F 11618 | My Last Cigarette/Landlord And Tenant | 5 |
| 62 | Transatlantic TRA 106 | PUTTING OUT THE DUSTBIN (LP) | 15 |

SHEILA HANCOCK & MALCOLM TAYLOR
| 66 | Eyemark EMS 1007 | I'm Reformed/I Got You (die cut sleeve) | 7 |

TONY HANCOCK
63	Pye 7N 15575	Wing Commander Hancock — Test Pilot/The Threatening Letters (with Kenneth Williams)	15
61	Pye NEP 24146	LITTLE PIECES OF HANCOCK (EP)	10
62	Pye NEP 24161	LITTLE PIECES OF HANCOCK VOL. 2 (EP)	10
62	Pye NEP 24170	HANCOCK'S HALF HOUR (EP)	10
63	Pye NEP 24175	THE BLOOD DONOR (EP)	10
60	Pye NPL 18045	THIS IS HANCOCK (LP)	15
60	Pye NPL 18054	PIECES OF HANCOCK (LP)	15
61	Pye NPL 18068	THE BLOOD DONOR AND THE RADIO HAM (LP)	15
63	Piccadilly FTF 38500	FACE TO FACE (LP, interview disc)	75
65	Decca LK 4740	IT'S HANCOCK (LP)	15

(see also Sidney James, Kenneth Williams)

OWEN HAND
| 61 | Transatlantic TRA 127 | SOMETHING NEW (LP) | 100 |
| 66 | Transatlantic TRA | I LOVED A LASS (LP) | 55 |

JOHNNY HANDLE
| 61 | Topic TOP 78 | STOTTIN' DOON THE WAAL (EP) | 10 |

(see also Louise Killen & Johnny Handle)

HANDSOME BEASTS
81	Heavy Metal HEAVY 1	All Riot Now/Mark Of The Beast (p/s)	25
81	Heavy Metal HEAVY 2	Breaker/One In A Crowd/Crazy (wraparound p/s)	8
82	Heavy Metal HEAVY 11	Sweeties/You're One Your Own (p/s, with card sheet)	8
82	Heavy Metal HMRLP 2	BEASTIALITY (LP)	20

WAYNE HANDY
| 58 | London HL 8547 | Say Yeah/Could It Be (B-side with King Sisters) (78 rpm = £100) | 500 |

PAUL HANFORD
60	Parlophone R 4680	Itsy Bitsy Teenie Weenie Little Polka Dot Bikini/Why Have You Changed Your Mind	10
60	Parlophone R 4694	If You Ain't Got Love/Ev'ry Little Girl	10
61	Parlophone R 4745	Everything/Cigarettes And Coffee Blues	10
61	Parlophone R 4813	Memphis Address/Flutter Flutter	10
62	Oriole CB 1779	Don't Be/Habit Of Loving You	10
63	Oriole CB 1830	Just When I Need You Most/Judy	10
63	Oriole CB 1866	The Minute You're Gone/High School Dance	10

HANGMAN'S BEAUTIFUL DAUGHTERS
| 87 | Dreamworld DREAM 11 | Love Is Blue/Popular Trend (p/s) | 7 |
| 87 | Yo Jo Jo 1 | Darkside/Pushing Me Too Far (flexidisc, p/s) | 8 |

MINT VALUE £

HANK & MELLOWMEN
60s	Lyntone LYN 153/154	Santa Anno/Mosology/(other artists) (Bangor University Rag flexidisc)	7
60s	Lyntone LYN 201	So In Love With You/Michael (Bangor University Rag flexidisc)	7
	(see also Roger Whittaker)		

BOBBY HANNA
67	Decca F 12604	Thanks To You/Here I Stand	6
67	Decca F 12695	Blame It On Me/Goin' Where The Lovin' Is	8
68	Decca F 12738	Too Much Love/What Do I Want For Tomorrow	6
68	Decca F 12783	Written On The Wind/Everybody Needs Love	15
68	Decca F 12833	To Wait For Love (Is To Waste Your Life Away)/Is It Wrong	6
69	Decca F 22917	Winter Love (E' L'Amore)/Time	6
70	Decca PA 109	THE WORLD OF BOBBY HANNA (LP)	12

GEORGE HANNA & SARAH ANNE O'NEILL
78	Topic 12TS 372	ON THE SHORES OF LOUGH NEAGH (LP)	12

JOSH HANNA
65	Parlophone R 5385	When I Love You/Love Me, Love Me	6
66	Decca F 12532	Shut Your Mouth/Sweet To My Soul	15

HANNA BARBERA (cartoon soundtrack EPs)
66	Hanna Barbera HBE 1	FLINTSTONES — HANSEL AND GRETEL (EP)	18
66	Hanna Barbera HBE 2	UNCLE REMUS — BRER RABBIT AND THE TAR BABY (EP)	18
66	Hanna Barbera HBE 3	FLINTSTONES — GOLDILOCKS, BEAROSAURUS (EP)	18
66	Hanna Barbera HBE 4	SNAGGLEPUSS TALES — WIZARD OF OZ (EP)	18
66	Hanna Barbera HBE 5	YOGI BEAR AND BOO BOO TELL JACK AND THE BEANSTALK (EP)	18
66	Hanna Barbera HBE 6	FRED FLINTSTONE & BARNEY RUBBLE — SONG FROM MARY POPPINS (EP)	18
67	Hanna Barbera HBE 7	TOP CAT — ROBIN HOOD (EP)	18
67	Hanna Barbera HBE 8	YOGI BEAR AND BOO BOO — LITTLE RED RIDING HOOD (EP)	18
67	Hanna Barbera HBE 9	FLINTSTONES — THREE LITTLE PIGS (EP)	18
67	Hanna Barbera HBE 10	AUGIE DOGGY AND DOGGY DADDY — SONGS FROM PINOCCHIO (EP)	18
67	Hanna Barbera HBE 11	PEBBLES AND BAMM BAMM — WE WISH YOU A MERRY CHRISTMAS (EP)	18
68	Hanna Barbera HBE 12	MERRY CHRISTMAS — ORGAN AND CHIMES (EP)	18
68	Hanna Barbera HBE 13	MAGILLA GORILLA AND OGEE — ALICE IN WONDERLAND (EP)	18
68	Hanna Barbera HBE 14	PEBBLES AND BAMM BAMM — SONGS FROM THE GOOD SHIP LOLLIPOP (EP)	18

PAUL HANNAH
94	Ferox FER 007	CONTROL EP (12", plain sleeve)	12
95	Ferox FER 010	ADVENTURES IN TECHNO SOUL (12" EP)	8

ROSS HANNAMAN
74	Bellwood BW1	A NIGHT AT FACTOTUM (LP, 100 only, as John and Rosalind)	20

HANNIBAL
74	B&C HB 1	Winds Of Change/Winter	6
70	B&C CAS 1022	HANNIBAL (LP)	45

LANCE HANNIBAL
69	Blue Cat BS 148	Read The News/RECO & RHYTHM ACES: Return Of The Bullet	18
	(see also Sugar Simone, Les Foster)		

HANOI ROCKS
83	Lick LIX 1	Malibu Beach/Rebel On The Run (p/s)	5
83	Lick LIXPD 1	Malibu Beach/Rebel On The Run (picture disc)	8
84	CBS A 4513	Up Around The Bend/Until I Get You (p/s, with free transfer)	8
84	CBS DA 4513	Up Around The Bend/Until I Get You/Under My Wheels/I Feel Alright/ Train Kept A Rollin' (double pack)	8
84	CBS TA 4513	Up Around The Bend/Back To The Mystery City/Until I Get You/ Mental 84 Beat (12", p/s, with free transfer)	8
84	CBS WA 4732	Underwater World/Shakes/Magic Carpet Ride (12", picture disc)	8
84	CBS WA 4685	Don't You Ever Leave Me/Oil And Gasoline/Malibu Beach (Calypso) (12", 3-D picture disc)	8
82	Lick LICLPPD4	SELF DISTRUCTION BLUES (LP, picture disc)	12
83	Lick LICLP 1	BACK TO THE MYSTERY CITY (LP, white vinyl)	12
	(see also Fallen Angels, Dark, Idle Flowers, Urban Dogs, Suicide Twins)		

HANSON & KARLSSON
67	Polydor 184 196	SWEDISH UNDERGROUND (LP)	15
69	Polydor 462 60	MONUMENT (LP)	15
69	Polydor 583 564	MAN AT THE MOON (LP)	18
	(see also Bo Hansson)		

BO HANSSON
72	Charisma CAS 1059	LORD OF THE RINGS (LP, 1978 reissue with different sleeve has same cat no)	15/15

HAPPENINGS
66	Fontana TF 735	See You In September/He Thinks He's A Hero	10
66	Fontana TF 766	Go Away Little Girl/Tea Time	10
67	Pye International 7N 25501	My Mammy/I Believe In Nothing	7
67	Stateside SS 587	Goodnight My Love/Lillies By Monet	10
67	Stateside SS 2013	I Got Rhythm/You're In A Bad Way	10
67	BT Puppy BTS 45532	Why Do Fools Fall In Love/When The Summer Is Through	7
67	BT Puppy BTS 45530	My Mammy/I Believe In Nothing	5
68	BT Puppy BTS 45538	Music Music Music/When I Lock My Door	6
68	BT Puppy BTS 45540	Randy/Love Song Of Mummy And Dad	7
68	BT Puppy BTS 45543	Breaking Up Is Hard To Do/Anyway	6
68	BT Puppy BTS 45545	Crazy Rhythm/Love Song Of Mummy And Dad	5
69	BT Puppy BTS 45546	Where Do I Go, Go-Be-In (Hare Krishna)/New Day Comin'	5
67	Fontana TL 5383	BYE BYE, SO LONG, FAREWELL ... SEE YOU IN SEPTEMBER (LP)	35
67	BT Puppy BTLP 1003	PSYCLE (LP)	30
68	BT Puppy BTLPS 1004	GOLDEN HITS (LP)	20

HAPPY CONFUSION
69   Penny Farthing PEN 706   Yes Sir/Hereditary Impediment 20

HAPPY FAMILY
82   4AD AD 204   Puritans/Innermost Thoughts/The Mistake (p/s) 12
(see also Josef K, Momus)

HAPPY MAGAZINE
68   Polydor 56233   Satisfied Street/Do Right Woman Do Right Man 8
69   Polydor 56307   Who Belongs To You (Ooby Dooby Doo)/Beautiful Land 10
(see also Griffin)

HAPPY MONDAYS
86   Factory FAC 142   Freaky Dancing (Live)/The Egg (p/s). 12
87   Factory FAC 176   Tart Tart/Little Matchstick Owen's Rap (12", p/s). 10
87   Factory FACT 170   SQUIRREL & G-MAN TWENTY FOUR HOUR PARTY PEOPLE PLASTIC FACE
                CARNT SMILE (WHITE OUT) (LP, with Desmond, 5,000 in plastic sleeve) 25/15

HAPSHASH & THE COLOURED COAT
69   Liberty LBF 15188   Colinda/The Wall 22
67   Minit MLS 40001E   FEATURING THE HUMAN HOST AND THE HEAVY METAL KIDS
                (LP, with Art, initially red vinyl with insert; later copies on black vinyl) 70/40
69   Liberty LBL/LBS 83212R   THE WESTERN FLYER (LP, with Mike Batt) 28
(see also Tony McPhee, Warm Sounds, Marc Bolan/T. Rex, Art, Mike Batt)

HARBOUR LITES
65   HMV POP 1426   Come Back Silly Girl/Revenge. 10
65   HMV POP 1465   I Would Give All/They Call The Wind Maria 10
66   Fontana TF 682   Run For Your Life/Lonely Journey 10

HARDBACK
86   Streetwave 7 BOSS 3   The Champ/Bust The Champ. 6

HARD CORPS
84   Hard Corps HC 01   Dirty/To Breathe (12", hand-written white labels, numbered). 25
84   Survival SUR 026   Dirty/Respirer (To Breathe) (white or printed labels,
                stickered plain black sleeve) 10
84   Survival SUR 12 026   Dirty/Respirer (To Breathe) (12", with sticker in plain black sleeve) 12
85   Immaculate 12 IMMAC 2   Je Suis Passée (Extended French Version)/(Extended Club Dub Mix) (12", p/s). . 12
85   Polydor HARDX 1   Je Suis Passée (Extended)/(Instrumental Mix)/(Dub Mix) (12", p/s) 8
85   Polydor HARDA 1   Je Suis Passée (Hard Mix)/(French Mix)/(Dub Mix)
                (12", gatefold PVC sleeve, various colours, with poster) 25
85   Polydor HARD 2   To Breathe/Metal And Flesh (unreleased) 30
85   Polydor HARDX 2   To Breathe/Metal And Flesh/To Breathe (Instrumental) (12", unreleased) 40
87   Rhythm King TYPE 3T   Lucky Charm/Porte-Bonheur/Lucky Charm (The Music) (12", p/s) 8
90   Concrete P. CPPRODLP 011   METAL AND FLESH (LP, clear vinyl) 15
90   Concrete P. CPPRODCD 011   METAL AND FLESH (CD) 25
(see also Craze, Skunks, T.U.F.F.)

HARD-FI
05   Necessary HARDFI01   Cash Machine/Dub Machine/Sick Of It All (3-track CD, 1,500 only, p/s) 10
05   Necessary HARDFI01   Cash Machine/Dub Machine (1,500 only, p/s). 8
05   Necessary HARDFI02   Tied Up Too Tight/Seven Nation Army (yellow vinyl, p/s). 7
05   Necessary HARDFI02TE   Tied Up Too Tight/Middle Eastern Holiday (Chicken Lips Dub) (10" p/s) 8
05   Necessary   STARS OF CCTV (Original CD album, 1,000 only, black and white p/s) 15
05   Necessary 5046786911   STARS OF CCTV (2 x LP, HMV special with bonus Middle Eastern Holiday 7") . . 12

HARDFLOOR
92   Harthouse HARTUK 1   HARDTRANCE ACPERIENCE EP (12", 4-track) 10

EDDIE HARDIN
72   Decca F 13307   Why Does Everybody Put Me Down/Spend Your Money Honey 5
72   Decca TXS 106   HOME IS WHERE YOU FIND IT (LP) 12
(see also Hardin-York, Spencer Davis Group, Roger Glover, Wizards Convention)

TIM HARDIN
66   Verve VS 1504   Hang On To A Dream/A Reason To Believe 12
67   Verve VS 1511   The Lady Came From Baltimore/Black Sheep Boy 8
68   Verve VS 1516   Don't Make Promises/Smugglin' Man 8
69   CBS 4441   A Simple Song Of Freedom/Question Of Birth 6
71   Verve 2009 006   If I Were A Carpenter/Hang On To A Dream 6
66   Verve (S)VLP 5018   TIM HARDIN 1 (LP) 35
67   Verve (S)VLP 6002   TIM HARDIN 2 (LP) 35
67   Atlantic 587/588 082   THIS IS TIM HARDIN (LP, plum label) 32
68   Verve (S)VLP 6010   LIVE IN CONCERT (LP). 25
69   Verve (S)VLP 6016   TIM HARDIN 4 (LP) 25
69   Verve (S)VLP 6019   THE BEST OF (LP) 22
69   CBS (S/M) 63571   SUITE FOR SUSAN MOORE AND DAMIAN (LP, gatefold sleeve, mono/stereo) . . 18
70   CBS 64335   BIRD ON A WIRE (LP). 18
72   CBS 65209   PAINTED HEAD (LP) 18
74   GM GML 1004   NINE (LP) 12
74   Verve 2683 048   TIM HARDIN 1/2 (2-LP, gatefold reissue) 20

(Eddie) HARDIN & (Pete) YORK
69   Bell BLL 1064   Tomorrow Today/Candlelight (as Hardin-York) 40
69   Bell SBLL 125   TOMORROW TODAY (LP). 25
70   Bell SBLL 136   HARDIN & YORK (THE WORLD'S SMALLEST BIG BAND) (LP). 25
71   Bell SBLL 141   FOR THE WORLD (LP) 25
71   Decca SKL 5095   FOR THE WORLD (LP, reissue) 12
(see also Eddie Hardin, Pete York, Spencer Davis Group)

MIKE HARDING
86   Moonraker M 003   BOMBERS MOON (LP) 20

RICHARD HARDIN
61	HMV POP 887	Jezebel/Temptation	20

(see also Cresters, Mike Sagar & Cresters)

ROSEMARY HARDMAN (& BOB AXFORD)
69	Folk Heritage no cat. no.	QUEEN OF HEARTS (LP)	125
71	Trailer LER 2075	FIREBIRD (LP)	28
71	Trailer LER 3018	SECOND SEASON CAME (LP, by Rosemary Hardman & Bob Axford)	28
75	Alida Star Cottage	JERSEY BURGER (LP)	120
78	Plant Life PLR 014	EAGLE OVER BLUE MOUNTAIN (LP, with insert)	12
80	Plant Life PLR 023	ROSIE HARDMAN (LP)	12
83	Plant Life PLR 053	THE WEAKNESS OF EVE (LP, with lyric insert)	12

HARD MEAT
69	Island WIP 6066	Rain/Burning Up Years	15
70	Warner Bros WB 8010	Ballad Of Marmalade Emma And Teddy Grimes/Yesterday, Today, Tomorrow	6
70	Warner Bros WS 1852	HARD MEAT (LP, with photo insert)	25
70	Warner Bros WS 1879	THROUGH A WINDOW (LP)	25

HARDNOISE
89	White HNX001	Untitled (Original recording) (12")	100
90	Music Of Life NOTE40	Untitled (12")	20
91	Music Of Life NOTE48	Serve Tea, The Murder/Mice In The Presence Of Lions (12")	20

HARD ROAD
79	Goodstuff LP 1002	NO PROBLEM (LP, private pressing)	20

HARD ROCK SOUL MOVEMENT
86	Elite DAZZ56	The Beat Is Mine/Double Def Fresh (12")	10
87	Serious OUS2	Elaweaser Just A Skeezer (12")	12

HARDSHIP POST
95	Sub Pop SP 295	Watching You/Your Sunshine (red vinyl)	5

HARD STUFF
72	Purple PUR 103	Jay Time/The Orchestrator	7
73	Purple PUR 116	Inside Your Life/(It's) How Do You Do It!	7
72	Purple TPSA 7505	BULLETPROOF (LP, gatefold sleeve)	30
73	Purple TPSA 7507	BOLEX DEMENTIA (LP)	30

(see also Andromeda, Atomic Rooster, John Du Cann, Five Day Week Straw People, Johnny Gustafson, Bullet, Quatermass)

HARD TRAVELLIN'
71	Flams Ltd PR 1065	HARD TRAVELLIN' (LP, private pressing)	100+

HARDWARE
79	Narc NARC 001	Speed Unit/Wall To Wall/Walking/Fire (folded p/s)	5
79	Narc NARC 002	Rubberface/Face The Flag/The Seven Minutes (p/s)	5

HARDWARE
85	Reset 7REST 7	Dance/Hey (p/s)	10
85	Reset 12REST 7	Dance/Hey (12", p/s)	20

HARDY
71	Ackee ACK 131	Glorious Morning/Hearing's Not Seeing	5

DAVE HARDY
76	Red Rag RRR 008	LEAVING THE DALES (LP)	12

FRANCOISE HARDY
64	Pye 7N 15612	Catch A Falling Star/Only Friends	10
64	Pye 7N 15653	Tous Les Garcons Et Les Filles/L'Amour S'en Va	8
64	Pye 7N 15696	Pourtant Tu M'Aimes/Jaloux	8
64	Pye 7N 15740	Et Meme/Le Temps De L'Amour	8
65	Pye 7N 15802	All Over The World/Another Place	8
66	Vogue VRS 7001	Just Call And I'll Be There/You Just Have To Say The Word	8
66	Vogue VRS 7004	So Many Friends/However Much	10
66	Vogue VRS 7010	This Little Heart/The Rose	8
66	Vogue VRS 7011	La Maison Ou J'ai Grandi/Je Ne Suis La Pour Personne	8
66	Vogue VRS 7014	Autumn Rendezvous/It's My Heart	8
66	Vogue VRS 7020	Si C'est Ca/Je Serai La Pour Toi	8
66	Vogue VRS 7025	Voila/Qui Peut Dire	8
67	Vogue VRS 7026	On Se Quitte Toujours/Les Petits Garcons	10
68	United Artists UP 1208	Now You Want To Be Loved/Tell Him You're Mine	10
68	United Artists UP 2253	Will You Love Me Tomorrow/Loving You	10
69	United Artists UP 35011	Comment Te Dire Adieu/La Mer, Les Etoiles Et Le Vent	10
70	United Artists UP 35070	All Because Of You/Time Passing By	10
70	United Artists UP 35105	Soon Is Slipping Away/The Bells Of Avignon	10
64	Pye NEP 24188	C'EST FAB (EP)	18
64	Pye NEP 24192	FRANCOISE SINGS IN ENGLISH (EP)	18
64	Pye NEP 24193	C'EST FRANCOISE (EP)	18
60s	Vogue VRE 5000	FRANCOISE (EP)	18
60s	Vogue VRE 5001	FRANCOISE HARDY (EP)	18
60s	Vogue VRE 5003	DIS LUI NON (EP)	18
60s	Vogue VRE 5008	LE TEMPS DES SOUVENIRS (EP)	18
60s	Vogue VRE 5012	CHANTE EN ALLEMAND (EP)	18
60s	Vogue VRE 5015	L'AMITIE (EP)	18
60s	Vogue VRE 5017	MON AMIE LA ROSE (EP)	18
60s	Vogue VRE 5018	AUTUMN RENDEZVOUS (EP)	18
64	Pye NPL 18094	FRANCOISE HARDY (LP)	18
64	Pye NPL 18099	IN VOGUE (LP)	18
65	Vogue VRL 3000	FRANCOISE HARDY (LP)	20
66	Vogue VRL 3021	FRANCOISE HARDY (LP)	20
66	Vogue VRL 3023	LE MEILLEUR DE FRANCOISE HARDY (LP)	18

66	Vogue VRL 3025	SINGS IN ENGLISH (LP)	18
67	Vogue VRL 3028	FRANCOISE (LP)	18
67	Vogue VRL 3031	VOILA! FRANCOISE HARDY (LP)	20
68	United Artists SULP 1191	IL N'Y A PAS D'AMOUR HEUREUX (LP)	25
68	United Artists ULP 1207	EN ANGLAIS (LP)	35
70	United Artists UAS 29046	ONE-NINE-SEVEN-ZERO (LP)	30

LAVELL HARDY
| 68 | Direction 58-3261 | Don't Lose Your Groove/Women Of The World | 12 |

COLIN HARE
70	Penny Farthing PEN 736	Grannie, Grannie/For Where Have You Been	8
71	Penny Farthing PEN 750	Underground Girl/Fighting For Peace	7
72	Warner Bros K 16203	Didn't I Tell You/Seek Not In The Wide World	7
71	Penny Farthing PELS 516	MARCH HARE (LP)	150+

(see also Honeybus)

WINSTON HAREWOOD
| 71 | Camel CA 64 | I Will Never Fall In Love Again (actually by Winston Heywood)/ LA-FUD-DIL ALL-STARS: La-Fud-Dil (actually La-Fud-Del) | 8 |

(see also Winston Heywood)

RON HARGRAVE
| 58 | MGM MGM 956 | Latch On/Only A Daydream (78 rpm = £400) | 3,000 |

HARLAN COUNTY
| 70 | Nashville 6076 002 | Dr. Handy's Dandy Candy/Big Heat | 5 |
| 70 | Nashville 6336 002 | HARLAN COUNTY (LP) | 12 |

HARLEM HAMFATS
| 51 | Vocalion V 1005 | Weed Smoker's Dream (Why Don't You Do Now)/ ROSETTA HOWARD: Let Your Linen Hang Low (78) | 15 |
| 63 | Ace Of Hearts AH 27 | HARLEM HAMFATS (LP) | 18 |

HARLEM JONNS RESHUFFLE
(see under 'J')

HARLESDEN MONKS
| 72 | Pama Supreme PS 352 | Time/Harlesden High Street | 7 |

STEVE HARLEY (& COCKNEY REBEL)
73	EMI EMI 2051	Sebastian/Rock And Roll Parade	5
74	EMI EMI 2191	Psychomodo/Such A Dream (unreleased)	
74	EMI EMI 2191	Mr Soft/Such A Dream (with 'Orchestrated by Alan Powell' credit)	5
(The above singles are credited to Cockney Rebel.)
74	EMI EMI 2233	Big Big Deal/Bed In The Corner	12
76	EMI EMI 2539	(I Believe) Love's A Prima Donna/Sidetrack One	5
77	EMI EMI 2673	The Best Years Of Our Lives (live)/Tumbling Down (live) (p/s)	6
(The above singles are credited to Steve Harley & Cockney Rebel; all subsequent singles are solo.)
| 77 | EMI EMI 2922 | Someone's Coming/Riding The Waves (For Virginia Woolf) | 5 |
(see also Anderson Harley & Batt)

LEE HARMER'S POPCORN
| 68 | Page One POF 053 | Love Is Coming/Hello Sunshine | 20 |

HARMONIANS
| 70 | Ackee ACK 107 | Music Street/Group Of Girls | 10 |
(see also Tony & Hippy Boys, Winston Shan)

HARMONICA FATS
| 63 | Stateside SS 184 | Tore Up/I Get So Tired | 40 |
| 68 | Action ACT 4507 | Tore Up/I Get So Tired (reissue) | 20 |

HARMONISERS
| 69 | Duke DU 32 | Mother Hen/WINSTON SINCLAIR: Chastise Them | 8 |

HARMONIZING FOUR
| 66 | Rymska RA 102 | Who Knows/Heart Of Stone (actually by Charms) | 18 |
(see also Charms)

HARMONY BEACH
| 83 | Surf King SK 1 | HARMONY BEACH (EP, private pressing) | 12 |

HARMONY GRASS
68	RCA RCA 1772	Move In A Little Bit Closer Baby/Happiness Is Toy Shaped	8
69	RCA RCA 1828	First Time Loving/What A Groovy Day	7
69	RCA RCA 1885	I Remember/Summer Dreaming	6
70	RCA RCA 1932	Mrs. Richie/Teach Me How (withdrawn)	10+
70	RCA RCA 1932	Cecilia/Mrs. Richie	6
70	RCA RCA 2011	Stand On Your Own Two Feet/Sing In The Sunshine	6
70	RCA SF 8034	THIS IS US (LP)	28
(see also Tony Rivers & Castaways)

HARMONY TRIO
| 69 | Emblem 7DR 323 | LET'S FACE IT (LP) | 12 |

JOE HARNELL
| 62 | London HLR 9637 | Harlem Nocturne/Fly Me To The Moon — Bossa Nova | 5 |
| 78 | MCA MCA 397 | The Incredible Hulk Theme/Love Theme | 5 |

BILLY HARNER
71	Kama Sutra 2013 029	What About The Music/Please Spare Me This Time	20/15
71	Kama Sutra 2013 029	What About The Music/Please Spare MeThis Time/What About The Music (Instrumental)	800+
72	Blue Horizon 2431 013	TRIGGER FINGER (LP)	20

MINT VALUE £

BUD HARPER
65	Vocalion VP 9252	Mr. Soul/Let Me Love You (DJ copy = £100)	70

CHARLIE HARPER
80	Gem GEMS 35	Barmy London Army/Talk Is Cheap (p/s, green or yellow vinyl)	each 5
81	Ramkup CAC 005	Freaked/Jo (p/s)	5

(see also U.K. Subs, Long Tall Shorty, Urban Dogs)

DON HARPER ORCHESTRA
68	Columbia DB 8519	"World Of Sport" March/England 88	6
73	Columbia DB 9023	World Of Sport/"Dr. Who" Theme (as Don Harper's Homo Electronicus)	25

(see also Electricians)

JANICE HARPER
57	HMV POP 376	Bon Voyage/Tell Me That You Love Me Tonight	10
58	Capitol CL 14899	Devotion/In Time	10
59	Capitol CL 14977	I Was Hoping You'd Ask Me/I'm Making Love To You	6
59	Capitol CL 15026	Let Me Call You Sweetheart/Just Whistle (78 rpm = £8)	6
60	Capitol CL 15159	Only Once/Love Me Now, Love Me Never	6
59	Capitol T 1195	WITH FEELING (LP)	25

JESSIE HARPER
92	Kissing Spell KSLP 9203	GUITAR ABSOLUTION IN THE SHADE OF A MIDNIGHT SUN (LP, reissue of acetate-only album)	20

(see also Human Instinct)

JOE 'HARMONICA' HARPER
58	MGM MGM 983	Lazy Train/Her Lips Were Like Velvet (78 rpm = £6)	8

MIKE HARPER
70	Concord CON 026	You've Got Too Much Going For You/This Time	15

ROY HARPER
SINGLES
66	Strike JH 304	Take Me Into Your Eyes/Pretty Baby (some in wraparound p/s)	48/28
67	CBS 203001	Midspring Dithering/Zengem	20
68	CBS 3371	Life Goes By/Nobody's Got Any Money In The Summer	22
72	Harvest HAR 5059	Bank Of The Dead (Valerie's Song)/Little Lady (some in p/s)	10/6
74	Harvest HAR 5080	(Don't You Think We're) Forever/Male Chauvinist Pig Blues	5
74	Harvest HAR 5089	Home (live)/Home (studio)	5
75	Harvest HAR 5096	When An Old Cricketer Leaves The Crease/Hallucinating Light (Acoustic Version) (p/s)	5
75	Harvest HAR 5102	Grown-Ups Are Just Silly Children/Referendum (Legend)	5
75	EMI PSR 407	Referendum/Another Day (live)/Tom Tiddler's Ground (live) (promo only)	8
77	Harvest HAR 5120	One Of Those Days In England/Watford Gap (p/s)	5
77	Harvest HAR 5140	Sail Away/Cherishing The Lonesome (as Roy Harper's Black Sheep)	7
78	Harvest HAR 5160	When An Old Cricketer Leaves The Crease/Home (studio) (p/s)	5
80	Harvest HAR 5203	Playing Games/First Thing In The Morning (p/s)	6
80	Harvest HAR 5207	Short And Sweet/Water Sports (live)/Unknown Soldier (live) (p/s)	6
82	Public PUBS 1001	No One Gets Out Here Alive/Casualty (live) (p/s)	5
83	Public PUBS 1002	I Still Care/Goodbye Ladybird (p/s)	6
85	B. Banquet BEG 131	Elizabeth (Short Version)/Advertisement (Short Version) (p/s)	6
85	B. Banquet BEG 131T	Elizabeth/Advertisement/I Hate The White Man (live) (12", p/s)	8
88	Regal Zonophone HR 1	Laughing Inside/Laughing Inside (p/s, promo only; as Harry Rope)	7
88	EMI EM 46	Laughing Inside/Laughing Inside (Acoustic Version) (p/s)	5

ORIGINAL LPs
66	Strike JHL 105	SOPHISTICATED BEGGAR	300
67	CBS (S)BPG 63184	COME OUT FIGHTING GHENGIS SMITH (mono/stereo)	40/30
69	Liberty LBL/LBS 83231	FOLKJOKEOPUS (mono/stereo)	45/40
69	Harvest SHVL 766	FLAT, BAROQUE AND BERSERK (gatefold sleeve; some with H. Ash label credit)	30
71	Harvest SHVL 789	STORMCOCK (gatefold sleeve with lyric inner)	25
73	Harvest SHVL 808	LIFEMASK (foldout 'door' sleeve, with insert)	20
74	Harvest SHSP 4027	VALENTINE (initially with lyric booklet)	25/15
74	Harvest SHDW 405	FLASHES FROM THE ARCHIVES OF OBLIVION (2-LP, gatefold sleeve)	30
75	Harvest SHSP 4046	HQ (with lyric inner sleeve)	12
77	Harvest SHSP 4060	BULLINAMINGVASE (with inner sleeve and Watford Gap; some with 7", Referendu/Another Day (live)/Tom Tiddler's Ground [PSR 407])	15
77	Harvest SHSP 4060	BULLINAMINGVASE (2nd pressing with Breakfast With You)	18
77	Harvest SHSP 4077	COMMERCIAL BREAK (unreleased; test pressing with proof sleeve)	200+
78	Harvest SHSM 2025	HARPER 1970-1975	12
78	Harvest	HARPER 1970-1975 (6-LP box set)	125
80	Harvest SHVL 820	THE UNKNOWN SOLDIER (with inner sleeve)	12
82	Public TC PUBLP 5001	WORK OF HEART (cassette on 'real time' high quality tape, different sleeve, 250 only)	12
84	Hard Up PUB 5002	BORN IN CAPTIVITY (880 only)	35
92	Hard Up HU 2	BORN IN CAPTIVITY II (LIVE) (cassette)	15

REISSUE ALBUMS
70	Young Blood SSYB 7	RETURN OF THE SOPHISTICATED BEGGAR (LP, with Hup Hup Spiral closed run-out groove, different sleeve)	20
73	Birth RAB 3	RETURN OF THE SOPHISTICATED BEGGAR (LP, 2nd reissue, with Hup Hup Spiral closed run-out groove, different sleeve)	15
75	Sunset SLS 50373	FOLKJOKEOPUS (LP)	12
77	Big Ben BBX 502	THE SOPHISTICATED BEGGAR (LP, different rear sleeve)	12
77	Embassy EMB 31544	THE EARLY YEARS (LP, reissue of Come Out Fighting Ghengis Smith, different sleeve)	12

86	Awareness AWL 1002	WORK OF HEART (LP, different sleeve with inner; 1st 1,000 with 2 x 7": No One Gets Out Here Alive/Casualty (live) [PUBS 1001] & Still Care/ Goodbye Ladybird [PUBS 1002]; later copies with just PUBS 1001)	15/12
86	Awareness AWL 1002	WORK OF HEART (cassette, different sleeve, 250 only on 'real time' quality tape)	12
93	Hard Up HUCD 003	FLAT, BAROQUE & BERSERK (CD, in box with 40-page booklet & poster, signed)	20

(see also Rory Phare, Per Yarroh, Pink Floyd)

TIM HARPER
| 95 | Peacefrog PF 047 | I Feel A Groove (12", plain sleeve) | 8 |

HARPER'S BIZARRE
67	Warner Bros WB 5890	59th Street Bridge Song (Feelin' Groovy)/Lost My Love Today	5
67	Warner Bros WB 7528	Come To The Sunshine/The Debutante's Ball	5
67	Warner Bros WB 7063	Anything Goes/Malibu U.	5
67	Warner Bros WB 7090	Chattanooga Choo Choo/Hey You In The Crowd.	5
68	Warner Bros WB 7172	Cotton Candy Sandman (Sandman's Coming)/Virginia City	5
68	Warner Bros WB 7223	Battle Of New Orleans/Green Apple Tree	5
69	Warner Bros WB 7238	I Love You, Alice B. Toklas!/Look To The Rainbow	5
70	Warner Bros WB 7388	Anything Goes/Virginia City.	5
67	Warner Bros W 1693	FEELIN' GROOVY (LP)	22
67	Warner Bros W 1716	ANYTHING GOES (LP)	18
68	Warner Bros W(S) 1739	THE SECRET LIFE OF HARPER'S BIZARRE (LP)	18

SLIM HARPO
61	Pye International 7N 25098	Rainin' In My Heart/Don't Start Cryin' Now.	25
63	Pye International 7N 25220	Don't Start Cryin' Now/Rainin' In My Heart.	25
66	Stateside SS 491	Baby Scratch My Back/I'm Gonna Miss You (Like The Devil)	30
66	Stateside SS 527	Shake Your Hips/Midnight Blues	30
66	Stateside SS 557	I'm A King Bee/I Got Love If You Want It	30
67	Stateside SS 581	I'm Your Breadmaker Baby/Loving You (The Way I Do)	30
67	President PT 164	I'm Gonna Keep What I've Got/I've Got To Be With You Tonight.	10
68	Liberty LBF 15176	Something Inside Me/PAPPA LIGHTFOOT: Wine Whisky And Women	20
68	President PT 187	Tip On In (Parts 1 & 2)	15
70	Blue Horizon 57-3175	Folsom Prison Blues/Mutual Friend	30
65	Stateside SL 10135	A LONG DRINK OF THE BLUES (LP, with Lightnin' Slim)	65
68	President PTL 1017	TIP ON IN (LP)	30
70	Blue Horizon 7-63854	HE KNEW THE BLUES (LP)	80
72	Blue Horizon 2431 013	TRIGGER FINGER (LP)	120
76	Flyright LP 520	BLUES HANGOVER (LP)	18
78	Sonet SNTF 769	HE KNEW THE BLUES (LP)	15
80	Flyright FLY 558	GOT LOVE IF YOU WANT IT (LP)	15

(see also Lightnin' Slim)

GEORGE HARRASSMENT & HOMOSEXUALS
| 80s | Black Noise 12 NO 6 | MASAI SLEEP WALKING (LP) | 12 |

(see also Homosexuals)

HARRIER
| 84 | Black Horse HARR 1T | OUT ON THE STREET EP (Out On The Street/Nickels And Dimes/Shine On) (12", p/s). | 12 |

DERRICK HARRIOT(T) (& CRYSTALITES)
62	Blue Beat BB 131	I Care/Have Faith In Me (as Derrick Harriott & Vagabonds)	15
63	Blue Beat BB 178	Be True/I Won't Cry.	15
64	Island WI 157	What Can I Do (The Wedding)/Leona	15
65	Island WI 170	I Am Only Human (as Derak Harriott)/ROY PANTON: Good Man.	20
65	Island WI 237	My Three Loves/The Jerk	20
65	Island WI 245	Together/Mama Didn't Lie	25
65	Ska Beat JB 199	Monkey Ska/Derrick!.	22
66	Doctor Bird DB 1002	Jon Tom/AUDREY WILLIAMS: Solas Market	20
67	Island WI 3063	The Loser/Bless You.	35
67	Island WI 3064	Happy Times/You My Everything.	25
67	Island WI 3077	Walk The Streets/BOBBY ELLIS: Step Softly (B-side with Desmond Miles Seven).	45
67	Island WI 3089	Solomon/BOBBY ELLIS: The Emperor (B-side with Desmond Miles Seven).	35
68	Island WI 3135	Do I Worry?/BOBBY ELLIS & CRYSTALITES: Shuntin'.	40
68	Island WI 3147	Born To Love You/IKE & CRYSTALITES: Alfred Hitchcock	30
68	Island WI 3153	Tang Tang Festival Song/CRYSTALITES: James Ray.	25
69	Big Shot BI 505	Standing In/Bumble Bee.	15
69	Big Shot BI 511	Another Lonely Night/Been So Long	15
70	Songbird SB 1013	Riding For A Fall/I'm Not Begging.	10
70	Songbird SB 1014	Sitting On Top/You Were Meant For Me	10
70	Songbird SB 1022	Go Bye Bye/Laugh It Off.	12
70	Songbird SB 1028	Message From A Black Man/(Version II).	10
70	Songbird SB 1029	Psychedelic Train (w/ Chosen Few)/Psychedelic Train (Pt. 2) (with Crystalites).	12
70	Songbird SB 1033	No Man Is An Island/CRYSTALITES: No Man Is An Island Part 2	10
70	Songbird SB 1042	Groovy Situation/CRYSTALITES: The Crystal Groove	10
70	Songbird SB 1043	Psychedelic Train Chapter Three/CRYSTALITES: Groovy Situation Version II	7
71	Songbird SB 1052	Candy/CRYSTALITES: Candy Version	7
71	Songbird SB 1055	Lollipop Girl/CRYSTALITES: Lollipop Version.	15
71	Songbird SB 1063	Medley In 5 (Parts 1 & 2)	7
72	Songbird SB 1065	Have You Seen Her/CRYSTALITES: Have You Seen Her — Version	7
72	Songbird SB 1068	Over The River/River (Version)	7
72	Songbird SB 1071	Since I Lost My Baby/Baby (Version)	7
72	Songbird SB 1078	Being In Love/Love (Version).	6

72	Songbird SB 1084	Don't Rock The Boat/Rock (Version)	7
73	Explosion EX 2071	Let Me Down Easy/Let Me Down Easy — Version	7
74	Harry J. HJ 6675	Some Guys Have All The Luck/Some Guys Have All The Luck — Version	6
65	Island ILP 928	THE BEST OF DERRICK HARRIOTT (LP)	120
67	Island ILP 955	DERRICK HARRIOTT'S ROCKSTEADY PARTY (LP, actually v/a LP)	200
68	Island ILP 983	THE BEST OF VOLUME TWO (LP, as Derrick Harriott & Crystalites)	150
69	Pama SECO 13	SINGS JAMAICA REGGAE (LP)	90
70	Trojan TTL 43	THE BEST OF DERRICK HARRIOTT (LP)	40
70	Trojan TTL 54	ROCKSTEADY PARTY (LP)	50
70	Trojan TBL 114	THE UNDERTAKER (LP, as Derrick Harriott & Crystalites)	20
70	Trojan TBL 141	PSYCHEDELIC TRAIN (LP, as Derrick Harriott & Crystalites)	35

JOE HARRIOTT

56	Jazz Today JTE 106	WITH STRINGS (EP)	20
56	Pye Jazz NJE 1003	NO STRINGS (EP)	50
50s	Melodisc EPM7 117	COOL JAZZ WITH JOE (EP)	20
57	Columbia SEG 7665	JOE HARRIOTT QUARTET (EP)	75
59	Columbia SEG 7939	BLUE HARRIOTT (EP)	35
61	Columbia SEG 8070	A GUY CALLED JOE (EP)	28
60	Jazzland JLP 49	FREE FORM (LP)	55
62	Columbia 33SX 1477	ABSTRACT (LP)	120
63	Columbia 33SX 1627	MOVEMENT (LP)	200
64	Columbia 33SX 1692	HIGH SPIRITS (LP)	120
66	Columbia S(C)X 6025	DOUBLE QUINTET (LP, with John Mayer)	25
67	Melodisc SLP 12150	SWINGS HIGH (LP)	75
67	Columbia S(C) 6122	INDO-JAZZ FUSIONS (LP, with John Mayer)	30
68	Columbia S(C)X 6215	INDO-JAZZ FUSIONS II (LP, with John Mayer)	40
68	Columbia S(C)X 6249	PERSONAL PORTRAIT (LP)	40
69	Columbia SCX 6354	HUM-DONO (LP)	250
73	One Up OU 2011	MEMORIAL 1973 (LP)	25

(see also Tony Kinsey Trio & Joe Harriott, John Mayer, Michael Garrick)

JOE HARRIOTT/DON RENDELL QUARTET

57	MGM MGM-EP 615	JAZZ BRITANNIA (EP, 2 tracks each)	25

(see also Don Rendell)

ANITA HARRIS

61	Parlophone R 4830	I Haven't Got You/Mr One And Only	5
64	Vocalion V 9223	Lies/Don't Think About Love	5
65	Decca F 12082	Willingly/At Last Love	6
65	Pye 7N 15868	Trains And Boats And Planes/Upside Down	5
65	Pye 7N 15894	I Don't Know Anymore/When I Look At You	5
65	Pye 7N 15971	London Life/I Run To Hide	5
66	Pye 7N 17069	Something Must Be Done/Funny Kind Of Feeling	10
66	CBS 2724	Just Loving You/Butterfly With Coloured Wings	5
67	CBS 2991	The Playground/B.A.D. For Me	12
68	CBS 3765	Le Blon/Dusty Road	5
67	Pye NEP 24288	ANITA HARRIS (EP)	15
67	CBS EP 6359	NURSERY RHYMES FOR OUR TIMES (EP)	10
68	CBS EP 6401	DREAM A LITTLE DREAM OF ME (EP)	10
69	CBS 63927	CUDDLY TOY (LP)	12

(see also Brello Cabal)

ARTIE HARRIS & HIS BOYS

63	Oriole CB 1816	Go Go Gaudeamus/Mexicana	8

BETTY HARRIS

63	London HL 9796	Cry To Me/I'll Be A Liar	20
65	Stateside SS 475	What A Sad Feeling/I'm Evil Tonight	30
67	Stateside SS 2045	Nearer To You/12 Red Roses	25
69	Action ACT 4535	Ride Your Pony/Trouble With My Lover	25
69	Action ACLP 6007	SOUL PERFECTION (LP)	100

(see also Betty Harris & Lee Dorsey)

BRENDA JO HARRIS

69	Roulette RO 503	I Can Remember/Play With Fire	15

EDDIE HARRIS

69	Atlantic 584 218	Listen Here/Theme — In Search Of A Movie	10
69	Atlantic 584 232	It's Crazy/Live Right Now (unissued)	
74	Atlantic K 10513	Is It In?/Funkarama	8
75	Atlantic K 10561	I Need Some Money/Don't Want Nobody	6
76	Atlantic K 10741	Get On Up And Dance/Why Must We Part	5
62	Stateside SL 10009	BREAKFAST AT TIFFANY'S (LP)	15
63	Stateside SL 10018	MIGHTY LIKE A ROSE (LP)	15
63	Stateside SL 10049	GOES TO THE MOVIES (LP)	15
65	Atlantic SAL 5045	THE IN SOUND (LP)	15
69	Atlantic 588 177	SILVER CYCLES (LP)	15
71	Atlantic 2466 013	FREE SPEECH (LP)	12
73	Atlantic K 40123	PLUG ME IN (LP)	12
73	Atlantic K 40482	SINGS THE BLUES (LP)	12
73	Atlantic K 40220	THE ELECTRIFYING EDDIE HARRIS (LP)	12
74	Atlantic K 50084	IS IT IN? (LP)	12

EMMYLOU HARRIS

75	Reprise K54037	PIECES OF SKY (LP)	12

JET HARRIS

62	Decca F 11466	Besame Mucho/Chills And Fever	8

62	Decca F 11488	Main Title Theme (from The Man With The Golden Arm)/Some People 8
64	Decca F 11841	Big Bad Bass/Rifka 10
67	Fontana TF 849	My Lady/You Don't Live Twice 8
75	SRT SRT 75355	Theme For A Fallen Idol/This Sportin' Life (initial pressing) 7
75	SRT SRT 75355	Theme/This Sportin' Life (later pressing with shortened A-side title) 5
78	SRT SRT 77389	Guitar Man/Theme 8
62	Decca DFE 8502	JET HARRIS (EP) 25
78	Ellie Jay EJSP 8622	INSIDE JET HARRIS — THE LAST CONCERT (LP, 2,500 only) 20
70s	Q LPMM 1038	ANNIVERSARY ALBUM (LP) 20

(see also Shadows, Jet Harris & Tony Meehan, Keith Meehan, Peter Rawes)

JET HARRIS & TONY MEEHAN

63	Decca F 11563	Diamonds/Footstomp 6
63	Decca F 11644	Scarlett O'Hara/(Doing The) Hully Gully 6
63	Decca F 11710	Applejack/The Tall Texan 7
80	Decca F 13892	Diamonds/Scarlett O'Hara/Applejack/Man With The Golden Arm (p/s) 5
63	Decca DFE 8528	JET AND TONY (EP) 20

(see also Shadows, Jet Harris, Tony Meehan, Vipers Skiffle Group)

JOHNNY HARRIS

65	Mercury MF 942	Mynahg Hop/Here Comes The Boot 5
69	Warner Bros WB 8000	Footprints On The Moon/Lulu's Theme 7
70	Warner Bros WB 8016	Fragment Of Fear/Stepping Stones 8
70	Warner Bros WS 3002	MOVEMENTS (LP) 25
72	Warner Bros K 46054	MOVEMENTS (LP, reissue) 20
73	Warner Bros K 46187	ALL TO BRING YOU MORNING (LP) 12

JUNE HARRIS

| 65 | CBS 201774 | Over And Over Again/Stand Back . . . . 12 |

KURT HARRIS

| 90s | Goldmine/Soul Supply GS 018 | Emperor Of My Baby's Heart/JIM McFARLAND: Lonely Lover . . . . 8 |

PAT HARRIS & BLACKJACKS

| 63 | Pye 7N 15567 | The Hippy Hippy Shake/You Gotta See Your Mama Ev'ry Night . . . . 18 |

(see also Blackjacks)

PHIL HARRIS

54	HMV 7M 199	I Know An Old Lady/Take Your Girlie To The Movies 10
54	HMV 7M 231	I Guess I'll Have To Change My Plan/The Persian Kitten 10
55	HMV 7M 289	I Wouldn't Touch You With A Ten-Foot Pole/There's A Lot More 10
59	RCA Camden CDN 124	THAT'S WHAT I LIKE ABOUT THE SOUTH (LP) 12

RICHARD HARRIS

68	RCA RCA 1699	MacArthur Park/Paper Chase 5
68	Stateside SS 8001	The Yard Went On Forever/Lucky Me 5
70	Stateside SS 8054	Ballad Of 'A Man Called Horse'/The Morning Of The Mourning Of Another Kennedy 5
68	RCA Victor RD/SF 7947	A TRAMP SHINING (LP) 15
68	Stateside (S)SL 5001	THE YARD WENT ON FOREVER (LP) 15

ROLF HARRIS

60	Columbia DB 4483	Tie Me Kangaroo Down, Sport/Nick Teen And Al K. Hall 5
66	Columbia SEG 8531	ROLF HARRIS FAVOURITES (EP) 8
63	Columbia S(C)X 1507	SUN ARISE (LP, mono/stereo) 12

RONNIE HARRIS (& CORONETS)

54	Columbia SCM 5138	Hold My Hand/No One Can Change Destiny 8
54	Columbia SCM 5139	I Love Paris/I Still Believe 8
55	Columbia SCM 5159	Don't Go To Strangers/Surprisingly (as Ronnie Harris & Coronets) 8
55	Columbia SCM 5176	Stranger In Paradise/I Wonder 8
56	Columbia SCM 5242	I've Changed My Mind A Thousand Times/Come To Me (with Coronets) 8
56	Columbia DB 3836	That's Right/A House With Love In It 12
57	Columbia DB 3877	Armen's Theme (Yesterday And You)/Dancing Chandelier 5
57	Columbia DB 3934	Dear To Me/It's Not For Me To Say (B-side with Russ Conway) 5

(see also Coronets, Ruby Murray, Ray Burns, Russ Conway)

ROY HARRIS

| 72 | Topic 12TS 217 | THE BITTER AND THE SWEET (LP, blue label) . . . . 15 |
| 75 | Topic 12TS 256 | CHAMPIONS OF FOLLY (LP) . . . . 12 |

SHAKEY JAKE HARRIS

| 69 | Liberty LBS 83217 | FURTHER ON UP THE ROAD (LP) . . . . 38 |
| 73 | Polydor 2391 015 | THE DEVIL'S HARMONICA (LP) . . . . 28 |

THURSTON HARRIS (& SHARPS)

57	Vogue V 9092	Little Bitty Pretty One/I Hope You Won't Hold It Against Me (with Sharps) 160
57	Vogue V 9092	Little Bitty Pretty One/I Hope You Won't Hold It Against Me (with Sharps) (78) . . 40
58	Vogue V 9098	Do What You Did/I'm Asking Forgiveness (as Thurston Harris & Sharps) 275
58	Vogue V 9098	Do What You Did/I'm Asking Forgiveness (as Thurston Harris & Sharps) (78) . . . 60
58	Vogue V 9108	Be Baba Leba/I'm Out To Getcha (78 rpm = £55) 300
58	Vogue V 9122	Smokey Joe's/Only One Love Is Blessed (78 rpm = £55) 170
58	Vogue V 9127	Tears From My Heart/Over Somebody Else's Shoulder (78 rpm = £95) 130
59	Vogue V 9139	Purple Stew (as Thurston Harris & Masters)/I Hear A Rhapsody (78 = £90) 140
59	Vogue V 9144	You Don't Know How Much I Love You/In The Bottom Of My Heart (78 = £90) . . 120
59	Vogue V 9146	Hey Little Girl/My Love Will Last (78 rpm = £90) 150
59	Vogue V 9149	Runk Bunk/Bless Your Heart (78 rpm = £90) 200
59	Vogue V 9151	Slip-Slop/Paradise Hill (78 rpm = £100) 200
66	Sue WI 4016	Little Bitty Pretty One/I Hope You Won't Hold It Against Me (reissue) 35

(see also Sharps)

WEE WILLIE HARRIS

57	Decca F 10970	Rockin' At The Two 'I's/Back To School Again (78 rpm = £30)	40
58	Decca F 10980	Love Bug Crawl/Rosie Lee (78 rpm = £30)	40
58	Decca F 11044	Got A Match/No Chemise, Please! (78 rpm = £30)	40
60	Decca F 11217	Wild One/Little Bitty Girl	20
63	HMV POP 1198	You Must Be Joking/Better To Have Loved	10
66	Parlophone R 5504	Someone's In The Kitchen With Diana/Walk With Peter And Paul (some A-sides list 'Dina')	10
66	Polydor 56140	Listen To The River Roll Along/Try Moving Baby (writing in black or white)	10
74	Decca F 13516	Together/Rock'n'Roll Jamboree	5
58	Decca DFE 6465	ROCKING WITH WEE WILLIE (EP)	155

WYNONIE 'MR BLUES' HARRIS

51	Vogue V 2006	All She Wants To Do Is Rock/Drinkin' Wine Spo-Dee-O-Dee (78)	40
52	Vogue V 2111	Luscious Woman/Lovin' Machine (78)	35
52	Vogue V 2127	Bloodshot Eyes/Lollipop Mama (78)	25
52	Vogue V 2128	Just Like Two Drops Of Water/Good Mornin' Judge (78)	30
52	Vogue V 2133	Night Train/Do It Again Please (78)	30
52	Vogue V 2134	Rock, Mr. Blues/Put It Back (78)	35
52	Vogue V 2144	Teardrops From My Eyes/Keep On Churnin' (Till The Butter Comes) (78)	35
52	Vogue V 2166	I Like My Baby's Pudding/Adam Come And Get Your Rib (78)	35
56	Vogue V 2127	Bloodshot Eyes/Lollipop Mama (triangular centre)	125
56	Vogue V 2127	Bloodshot Eyes/Lollipop Mama (round centre)	75
56	Vogue EPV 1103	WYNONIE 'MISTER BLUES' HARRIS (EP)	175
61	Blue Beat BBEP 301	BATTLE OF THE BLUES (EP)	90

WYNONIE HARRIS/EDDIE 'CLEANHEAD' VINSON

72	Polydor 2343 048	JUMP BLUES (LP)	20

(see also Tiny Bradshaw/Wynonie Harris, Eddie 'Cleanhead' Vinson)

HARRIS SISTERS

55	Capitol CL 14232	Kissin' Bug/We've Been Walkin' All Night (78 rpm = £12)	20

DANNY HARRISON

62	Starlite ST45 77	No One To Love Me/All The World is Lonely	7
62	Starlite ST45 91	Broken Love Affair/Have I Wasted My Life	7
63	Starlite ST45 108	Have You Ever Been Lonely/Mary Ann I'm Lonesome	7
65	Coral Q 72479	Speak Of The Devil/I'm A Rollin' Stone	15
62	Starlite STEP 23	INTRODUCING DANNY HARRISON (EP)	22

EARL HARRISON

67	London HL 10121	Humphrey Stomp/Can You Forgive Me	45

GEORGE HARRISON
SINGLES

71	Apple R 5884	My Sweet Lord/What Is Life (colour 'head' p/s)	12
71	Apple R 5912	Bangla-Desh/Deep Blue (some with rare p/s [beware of new-looking counterfeits!])	80/5
74	Apple R 6002	Ding Dong, Ding Dong/I Don't Care Anymore (no p/s)	5
75	Apple R 6001	Dark Horse/I Don't Care Anymore (unissued)	
75	Apple R 6001	Dark Horse/Hari's On Tour (Express)	12
75	Apple R 6007	You/World Of Stone (p/s)	8
76	Apple R 6012	This Guitar (Can't Keep From Crying)/Maya Love (no p/s)	35
76	Apple R 5884	My Sweet Lord/What Is Life (reissue, black & white 'gnome' p/s)	12
76	Dark Horse K 16856	This Song/Learning How To Love You (issued with U.S. p/s)	10
77	Dark Horse K 16896	True Love/Pure Smokey (no p/s)	6
77	Dark Horse K 16967	It's What You Value/Woman Don't You Cry For Me (no p/s)	6
79	Dark Horse K 17327	Blow Away/Soft Touch (p/s)	5
79	Dark Horse K 17284	Love Comes To Everyone/Soft Hearted Hana	8
79	Dark Horse K 17423	Faster/Your Love Is Forever (with charity stickered plain white die-cut sleeve)	15
79	Dark Horse K 17423	Faster/Your Love Is Forever (picture disc, stickered PVC sleeve with insert)	35
81	Dark Horse K 17807M	All Those Years Ago/Writings On The Wall (cassette)	
81	Dark Horse K 17837DJ	Teardrops (Edited Version)/Save The World (DJ promo only, no p/s)	25
81	Dark Horse K 17837	Teardrops/Save The World (p/s)	10
82	Dark Horse 929 864-7	Wake Up My Love/Greece (p/s)	8
86	Ganga Publishing B.V.	Shanghai Surprise (with Vicki Brown) (unreleased, 1-sided promo only; no catalogue number, matrix: SHANGHAI 1)	800
87	Dark Horse W 8178	Got My Mind Set On You/Lay His Head (p/s, green label)	8
87	Dark Horse W 8178B	Got My Mind Set On You/Lay His Head (box set with 2 postcards)	20
87	Dark Horse W 8178T	Got My Mind Set On You (Extended Version)/Got My Mind Set On You (Single Version)/Lay His Head (12", p/s with poster)	20
87	Dark Horse W 8178TP	Got My Mind Set On You (Extended Version)/Got My Mind Set On You (Single Version)/Lay His Head (12", picture disc)	20
88	Dark Horse W 8131B	When We Was Fab/Zig Zag (box set with fold-out poster & cut-out)	10
88	Dark Horse W 8131T	When We Was Fab (Unextended Version)/Zig Zag/That's The Way It Goes/ When We Was Fab (Reverse End) (12")	12
88	Dark Horse W 8131TP	When We Was Fab (Unextended Version)/Zig Zag/That's The Way It Goes (Remix)/When We Was Fab (Reverse End) (12", picture disc)	20
88	Dark Horse W 8131CD	When We Was Fab (Unextended Version)/Zig Zag/That's The Way It Goes (Remix)/When We Was Fab (Reverse End) (3" CD with 5" adaptor, 5" case)	12
88	Dark Horse W 7913	This Is Love/Breath Away From Heaven (p/s)	8
88	Dark Horse W 7913T	This Is Love/Breath Away From Heaven/All Those Years Ago (12", p/s)	15
88	Dark Horse W 7913CD	This Is Love/Breath Away From Heaven/All Those Years Ago/Hong Kong Blues (3" CD with adaptor, 5" case)	12
89	Dark Horse W 2696	Cheer Down/That's What It Takes (p/s)	8
89	Dark Horse W 2696T	Cheer Down/That's What It Takes/Crackerbox Palace (12", p/s)	15
89	Dark Horse W 2696CD	Cheer Down/That's What It Takes/Crackerbox Palace (3" CD, gatefold card sleeve)	20

88	Genesis SGH 777	SONGS BY GEORGE HARRISON (Limited Edition) (EP, 33rpm, issued with limited edition book Songs By George Harrison)	800
88	Genesis SGHCD 777	SONGS BY GEORGE HARRISON (CD EP, issued with limited edition book)	750
92	Genesis SGH 778	SONGS BY GEORGE HARRISON VOL. 2 (EP, with limited edition book *Songs By George Harrison Vol. 2*)	400
92	Genesis SGHCD 778	SONGS BY GEORGE HARRISON VOL. 2 (CD EP, with limited edition book)	375

LPs

68	Apple (S)APCOR 1	WONDERWALL MUSIC (soundtrack; with insert, black inner sleeve, mono/stereo)	250/60
69	Zapple ZAPPLE 02	ELECTRONIC SOUND (with inner sleeve)	90
71	Apple STCH 639	ALL THINGS MUST PASS (3-LP box set with poster & lyric inner sleeves; initial batch in U.K. box, later in U.S. box)	35/25
72	Apple STCX 3385	THE CONCERT FOR BANGLA DESH (3-LP box set, with booklet, featuring Bob Dylan)	25
73	Apple PAS 10006	LIVING IN THE MATERIAL WORLD (gatefold sleeve with inner)	18
91	EPIC EPC 468835 1	THE CONCERT FOR BANGLA DESH (3-LP set in single sleeve)	35
92	Apple SAPCOR 1	WONDERWALL MUSIC (reissue, gatefold sleeve with inner sleeve)	20
92	Dark Horse 7599926964-1	LIVE IN JAPAN (2xLP in single sleeve)	40
96	Zapple ZAPPLE 02	ELECTRONIC SOUND (reissue, with inner sleeve)	20
01	Parlophone 5304741	ALL THINGS MUST PASS (3-LP, reissue)	20
02	Dark Horse 5419691	BRAINWASHED (Gatefold LP with sticker on cover)	20

CDs

87	Dark Horse 9256432	CLOUD NINE	20
87	Parlophone CDS 7466888	ALL THINGS MUST PASS (2-CD, some without Apple logo)	20/15
89	Dark Horse K 9257262	THE BEST OF DARK HORSE 1976-1989	40
92	Dark Horse 7599269642	LIVE IN JAPAN (2-CD)	30
02	Dark Horse 580 3450	BRAINWASHED (CD box set)	30

(see also Beatles, Traveling Wilburys, Billy Connolly & Chris Tummings, Sylvia Griffin)

KATHLEEN HARRISON
66	Columbia DB 7871	Mrs. Thursday/Call Round Any Old Time	7

MIKE HARRISON
71	Island ILPS 9170	MIKE HARRISON (LP)	15
72	Island ILPS 9209	SMOKESTACK LIGHTNING (LP)	15

(see also Spirit)

NEIL HARRISON
74	Deram SML 1115	ALL DRESSED UP AND NOWHERE TO GO (LP)	15

(see also Driftwood)

NOEL HARRISON
65	Decca F 12001	Trees/To Ramona	7
66	Decca F 12314	A Young Girl Of Sixteen/Tomorrow Is My Turn	6
66	Decca F 12345	It's All Over Now Baby Blue/Much As I Love You	6
67	Reprise RS 20615	Suzanne/Life Is A Dream	7
68	Reprise RS 20758	Windmills Of Your Mind/Leitch On The Beach	8
69	Decca F 12918	Love Minus Zero/Just Can't Wait	6
57	HMV 7EG 8383	NOEL HARRISON (EP)	18
65	Decca DFE 8616	NOEL HARRISON (EP)	12
65	Decca DFE 8639	TO RAMONA (EP)	15
60	Philips BBL 7399	AT THE BLUE ANGEL (LP)	22
69	Reprise RSLP 6321	THE GREAT ELECTRIC EXPERIMENT IS OVER (LP)	18

REGGIE HARRISON
63	Cameo Parkway P 863	A Lonely Piano/HIPPIES: Memory Lane	20

WILBERT HARRISON
59	Top Rank JAR 132	Kansas City/Listen My Darling (78 rpm = £30)	25
62	Island WI 031	I'm Broke/Off To School	20
65	Sue WI 363	Let's Stick Together/Kansas City Twist	20
70	London HL 10307	Let's Work Together/Stagger Lee	15
73	Action ACT 4613	Get It While You Can/Amen	8
70	London HA/SH 8415	LET'S WORK TOGETHER (LP)	45

WILBERT HARRISON/BABY WASHINGTON
71	Joy JOYS 191	BATTLE OF THE GIANTS (LP, 1 side each)	18

(see also Baby Washington)

YVONNE HARRISON
67	Caltone TONE 102	The Chase/Take My Hand	50

DEBBIE/DEBORAH HARRY
89	Chrysalis CHSCD 3369	I Want That Man (12 Inch Remix)/(7" Version)/(Instrumental)/Bike Boy (CD)	8
89	Chrysalis CHSCD 3452	Brite Side/In Love With Love/Bugeye (CD)	8
93	Chrysalis TC-CHS 4900	I Can See Clearly/Standing In My Way (B-side with Joey Ramone) (cassette)	7

(see also Wind In The Willows, Blondie, New York Blondes)

HARRY & RADCLIFFE
69	Camel CA 26	History/Just Be Alone	8
69	Punch PH 8	History/Just Be Alone	6

HARRY J. ALL STARS
69	Harry J. TR 675	Liquidator/GLEN & DAVE: La La Always Stay (green or white label)	8/5
70	Harry J. HJ 6601	The Big Three/Lavender (B-side actually Lavender Blue by Lloyd Robinson)	6
70	Harry J. HJ 6608	Reach For The Sky/Interrogator	6
70	Harry J. HJ 6621	Return Of The Liquidator (actually Tons Of Gold by Val Bennett)/All Day	12
72	Harry J. HJ 6641	Down Side Up/Down Side Up — Version	8

MINT VALUE £

73	Explosion EX 2073	Chirpy Chirpy Cheep Cheep/Chirpy Chirpy (Instrumental)	5
73	Blue Mountain BM 1028	U.F.O./Reggae With The Birds	5
70	Trojan TBL 104	THE LIQUIDATOR (LP)	15

(see also Jay Boys, Bob Andy, John Holt, Lizzy)

HARSH REALITY
68	Philips PB 1710	Tobacco Ash Sunday/How Do You Feel	18
69	Philips PB 1769	Heaven And Hell/Praying For Reprieve	18
69	Philips (S)BL 7891	HEAVEN AND HELL (LP, gatefold sleeve)	100

CAJUN HART
69	Warner Bros WB 7258	Got To Find A Way/Lover's Prayer (DJ Copy = £300)	200

DERRY HART & HARTBEATS
59	Decca F 11138	Come On Baby/Nowhere In This World (78 rpm = £18)	20

MICKEY HART
73	Warner Bros. K 46182	ROLLING THUNDER (LP)	18

(see also Grateful Dead, Diga Rhythm Band)

MIKE HART
70	Dandelion S 4781	Yawney Morning Song/Almost Liverpool 8	7
74	Deram DM 409	Son Son/Bad News Man	6
70	Dandelion 63756	MIKE HART BLEEDS (LP)	35
72	Dandelion 2310 211	BASHER, CHALKY, PONGO AND ME (LP, as Mike Hart & Comrades)	35

(see also Clayton Squares, Liverpool Scene)

TIM HART
79	Chrysalis CHR 2335	Overseas/Hillman Avenger (p/s)	7
79	Chrysalis CHR 1218	TIM HART (LP)	12

(see also Steeleye Span)

TIM HART & MADDY PRIOR
68	Tepee TPRM 104	FOLK SONGS OF OLDE ENGLAND VOL. 1 (LP, gatefold sleeve)	65
69	Tepee TPRM 105	FOLK SONGS OF OLDE ENGLAND VOL. 2 (LP, gatefold sleeve)	65
69	Ad-Rhythm ARPS 3	FOLK SONGS OF OLDE ENGLAND VOL. 1 (LP, reissue)	30
69	Ad-Rhythm ARPS 4	FOLK SONGS OF OLDE ENGLAND VOL. 2 (LP, reissue)	30
71	Charisma CAS 1035	SUMMER SOLSTICE (LP, gatefold sleeve)	20

(see also Steeleye Span, Maddy Prior, Silly Sisters)

FRANK HARTE
67	Topic 12T 172	DUBLIN STREET SONGS (LP)	18

KEEF HARTLEY (BAND)
69	Deram DM 250	Leave It 'Till The Morning/Just To Cry	12
69	Deram DM 273	Waiting Around/Not Foolish, Not Wise	12
70	Deram DM 316	Roundabout (Parts 1 & 2)	10
73	Deram DM 380	Dance To The Music/You And Me	8
69	Deram DML/SML 1037	HALFBREED (LP, gatefold sleeve, 1st pressing has 'mono/stereo' holes on rear sleeve)	35
69	Deram DML/SML 1054	THE BATTLE OF N.W.6 (LP, gatefold sleeve, 1st pressing has 'mono/stereo' holes on rear sleeve)	30
70	Deram SML 1071	THE TIME IS NEAR (LP, with booklet)	25
71	Deram SDL 2	OVERDOG (LP, gatefold sleeve)	25
71	Deram SDL 4	LITTLE BIG BAND (LP, gatefold sleeve)	25
72	Deram SDL 9	SEVENTY SECOND BRAVE (LP, gatefold sleeve)	25
73	Deram SDL 13	LANCASHIRE HUSTLER (LP, gatefold sleeve)	20
74	Deram DPA 3011/2	THE BEST OF (2-LP, gatefold sleeve)	20
70s	Deram SDN 30251/2	THE BATTLE OF N.W.6/THE TIME IS NEAR (2-LP, gatefold sleeve)	20

(see also Rory Storm & Hurricanes, Artwoods, John Mayall's Bluesbreakers, Miller Anderson, Dog Soldier, Henry Lowther, Wynder K. Frog)

HARVESTERS
72	Westwood WRS 015	THE HARVESTERS (LP)	25

HARVEY (Fuqua) & MOONGLOWS
58	London HLM 8730	Ten Commandments Of Love/Mean Old Blues (78 rpm = £85)	300

(see also Moonglows, Etta & Harvey)

HARVEY BOYS
57	London HLA 8397	Nothing Is Too Good For You/Marina Girl (78 rpm = £15)	50

(SENSATIONAL) ALEX HARVEY (BAND)
64	Polydor NH 52264	I Just Wanna Make Love To You/Let The Good Times Roll	30
64	Polydor NH 52907	Got My Mojo Working/I Ain't Worried Baby (as Alex Harvey & His Soul Band)	45
65	Fontana TF 610	Agent 00 Soul/Go Away Baby	30
66	Fontana TF 764	Work Song/I Can Do Without Your Love	25
67	Decca F 12640	The Sunday Song/Horizon's	35
67	Decca F 12660	Maybe Some Day/Curtains For My Baby	40
69	Fontana TF 1063	Midnight Moses/Roman Wall Blues	25
72	Vertigo 6059 070	There's No Lights On The Christmas Tree Mother, (They're Burning Big Louie Tonight)/Harp	6
64	Polydor LPHM 46424	ALEX HARVEY AND HIS SOUL BAND (LP)	130
64	Polydor LPHM 46441	THE BLUES (LP)	160
69	Fontana (S)TL 5534	ROMAN WALL BLUES (LP)	170
73	Vertigo 6360 081	FRAMED (LP, as The Sensational Alex Harvey Band, gatefold sleeve, swirl label, later spaceship label)	120/30
73	Vertigo 6360 103	NEXT (LP, as The Sensational Alex Harvey Band, spaceship label)	12
77	K-Tel NE 984	ALEX HARVEY PRESENTS THE LOCH NESS MONSTER (LP, withdrawn, gatefold stickered sleeve, with 16-page 'descriptive diary')	40

78	Mountain TOPS 114	ROCK DRILL (initially with 'No Complaints Department'. Later copies with revised Track listing stickered on sleeve) 35/12
79	RCA PL 25257	THE MAFIA STOLE MY GUITAR (LP, as Alex Harvey - The New Band) 15
83	Power Supply AMP 2	THE SOLDIER ON THE WALL (LP, solo) 30
84	Samurai SAH 117PD	S.A.H.B. LIVE (LP, reissue, picture disc) 12

(see also Tear Gas, Hairband, Rock Workshop, Nazareth, Michael Schenker Group, Tandoori Cassette)

FREDERIC HARVEY
60s	HMV 7EG 8847	SINGS WEST COUNTRY SONGS (EP).................................. 10

JANCIS HARVEY
73	Pilgrim King KLPS 47	DISTANCE OF DOORS (LP) 75
74	Westwood WRS 038	JANCIS HARVEY (LP).. 95
75	Westwood WRS 054	TIME WAS NOW (LP) 95
76	Westwood WRS 107	A PORTRAIT OF JANCIS HARVEY (LP) 70
79	Westwood WRS 144	FROM THE DARKNESS CAME LIGHT (LP) 65

JANE HARVEY
60	Pye International 7N 25046	I'm Gonna Go Fishin'/Hundred Dreams From Now........................ 6

LANCE HARVEY & KINGPINS
64	Pye 7N 15647	He's Telling You Lies/How Do You Fix A Broken Heart 7
64	Lyntone LYN 509	SINCE YOU WALKED OUT ON ME (Keele Rag flexidisc EP, with The Escorts)... 15

PETER HARVEY
62	Columbia DB 4873	Rainin' In My Heart/Please Don't Tell Joe.............................. 7
63	Columbia DB 7030	Wishing You The Best Of Luck My Friend/Lovin' Can Be Lonesome 5
64	Columbia DB 7331	Big Man In A Big House/Date With A Heartache 5

P.J. HARVEY
91	Too Pure PURE 5	Dress/Water (demo)/Dry (demo) (12")................................ 15
92	Too Pure PURECD 5	Dress/Water (demo)/Dry (demo) (CD) 15
92	Too Pure PURES 8	Sheela-Na-Gig/Joe (p/s, 400 only) 35
92	Too Pure PURE 8	Sheela-Na-Gig/Hair (demo)/Joe (demo) (12", p/s) 12
92	Too Pure PURECD 8	Sheela-Na-Gig/Hair (demo)/Joe (demo) (CD) 12
93	Island 12IS 538	50 Ft Queenie/Mansize (demo)/Hook (demo)/Reeling (12", p/s)........... 8
93	Island 12IS 569	Mansize/Wang Dang Doodle/Daddy (12", p/s) 10
93	Island CID 569	Mansize/Wang Dang Doodle/Daddy (CD) 10
95	Island IS 607	Down By the Water/Lying In The Sun/Somebody's Down Somebody's Name (p/s) 7
95	Island CID 607	Down By The Water/Living In The Sun/ Somebody's Down Somebody's Name (CD) 10
95	Island 12IS 614	C'Mon Billy/Darling Be There/Maniac (12", p/s) 10
95	Island IS 610	Send His Love To Me/Long Time Coming (Evening Session) (7" picture disc in 12" poster p/s) 12
92	Too Pure PURE(D) 10	DRY (LP, 1st 5,000 with bonus LP, *Demonstrations*, inner sleeve and numbered sticker) 60
92	Too Pure PUREDCD 10	DRY (CD, 1st 5,000 with additional *Demonstrations* LP tracks)............. 60
95	Island 524-178 2	THE B-SIDES CD (picture disc CD, 2,000 only, digipak).................. 15
95	Island CIDZ 8035	TO BRING YOU MY LOVE & THE B-SIDES CD (2-CD)..................... 25
99	Island DESIRE CD1	IS THIS DESIRE? (CD, interview disc, slimline case, promo only) 15

(see also Automatic Dlamini, Family Cat, Grape, John Parish & Polly Jean Harvey)

RICHARD HARVEY
83	Anderburr HX 1010	Theme From Terrahawks (3.00)/Variations On The Theme (3.17) (p/.s)......... 10
83	Anderburr HX 21010	Theme From Terrahawks (4.50)/Variations On The Theme (7.25) (12", p/s with poster).. 12
75	Transatlantic TRA 292	DIVISIONS ON A GROUND (LP)..................................... 20

(see also Gryphon, Barry Gray)

TINA HARVEY
73	UK UK 24	Nowhere To Run/Tina's Second Song 15

HARVEY'S PEOPLE
69	Galliard GAL 4001	LOVING AND LIVING (LP).. 15

CHRISTINE HARWOOD
70	Birth RAB 1	NICE TO MEET MISS CHRISTINE (LP) 48

GORDON HASKELL
69	CBS 4509	Boat Trip/Time Only Knows 12
70	CBS 4795	Oo-La-Di-Doo-Da-Day/Born To Be Together.......................... 12
69	CBS 63741	SAILIN' MY BOAT (LP) 70
72	Atlantic K 40311	IT IS AND IT ISN'T (LP, with lyric insert)............................. 20
73	RCA	SERVE AT ROOM TEMPERATURE (LP, unissued)...................... 200

(see also Fleur-De-Lys, Cupid's Inspiration, Flowerpot Men, King Crimson)

JACK HASKELL (& HONEY-DREAMERS)
57	London HL 8426	Around The World/Away Out West 25
58	Oriole CB 1442	The Night Of The Senior Prom/Hungry For Love (with Honey-Dreamers) 7

MICHAEL HASLAM
65	Parlophone R 5267	There Goes The Forgotten Man/My Heart Won't Say Goodbye 6

JOE HASSELVANDER
85	Pentagram DEVIL 3	LADY KILLER (LP) 15

HASSLES
67	United Artists UP 1199	You Got Me Hummin'/I'm Thinkin'.................................. 18

(see also Billy Joel)

HASTINGS OF MALAWI
81	Papal 003	VIBRANT STAPLER OBSCURES CHARACTERISTIC GROWTH (LP, red vinyl) ... 12

(see also Nurse With Wound)

HAT & TIE
66	President PT 105	Chance For Romance/California Jazz Club U.S.A.	15
67	President PT 122	Bread To Spend/Finding It Rough (demos credit A-side as "Bread")	130

(see also Patrick Campbell-Lyons, Nirvana [U.K.])

TONY HATCH ORCHESTRA
59	Top Rank JAR 107	Chick/Side Saddle (78 rpm = £8)	5
59	Top Rank JAR 165	Rhoom Ba-Cha/Stetson (78 rpm = £10)	5
61	Pye International 7N 25085	Rocking Waltz/Devil's Herd	5
61	Pye International 7N 25068	Tim Frazer's Theme/Girls Of Copenhagen	5
61	Pye 7N 15408	The Ghost Squad/What's That All About	5
62	Pye 7N 15434	Ben Casey Theme/Perry Mason Theme	5
62	Pye 7N 15460	Out Of This World Theme/Cyril's Tune (some in p/s)	10/5
62	Pye 7N 15494	Theme From The Dick Powell Show/Sharon	5
65	Pye 7N 15754	Crossroads Theme/The Marie Celeste (some in p/s)	10/5
65	Pye 7N15972	Man Alive/Crosstown Commuter	8
66	Pye 7N 17169	Crossroads Theme/Round Every Corner (some in p/s)	10/5
67	Pye 7N 17263	Comedy Tonight/You're Lovely	10
69	Pye 7N 17814	Theme From Who-Dun-It/The Champions	35
69	Pye 7N 17864	The Doctors — Theme/Love Song	6
73	Pye 7N 45210	Memories Of Summer/Best In Football	6
74	Pye 7N 45326	The World At War/Sportsnight	5
78	EMI EMI 2780	Sweeney 2/Regan's Key	20
83	Tube TUBE 003	Airline/The Hifi	6
65	Pye NPL/NSPL 18124	THE TONY HATCH SOUND (LP)	15
67	Pye NSPL 18176	BEAUTIFUL IN THE RAIN (LP)	15
74	Pye NSPL 41029	HIT THE ROAD TO THEMELAND (LP)	15

GEORGE HATCHER BAND
77	United Artists UP 36233	Black Moon Rising/Find A New Lover (p/s)	7
76	United Artists UAG 29997	DRY RUN (LP, gatefold sleeve)	12

(see also Budgie)

HATE
70	Famous SFMA 5752	HATE KILLS (LP)	50

BOBBY HATFIELD
68	Verve VS 570	Hang-Ups/Soul Cafe	10
68	Verve VS 576	Only You/The Wonder Of You	10
72	Warner Bros K 16163	Oo-Wee-Baby, I Love You/Rock'n'Roll Woman	12

(see also Righteous Brothers, Ringo Starr)

HATFIELD & THE NORTH
74	Virgin VS 116	Let's Eat (Real Soon)/Fitter Stoke Has A Bath	8
74	Virgin V 2008	HATFIELD AND THE NORTH (LP, gatefold sleeve)	20
75	Virgin V 2030	THE ROTTER'S CLUB (LP)	15
79	Virgin VR 5	AFTERS (LP, withdrawn)	40

(see also Matching Mole, Egg, Khan, Camel, National Health, Caravan)

DONNY HATHAWAY
70	Atco 226 010	The Ghetto (Parts 1 & 2)	10
72	Atlantic K 10193	The Ghetto (Parts 1 & 2)/Little Ghetto Boy	6
73	Atlantic K 10354	Love Love Love/Someday We'll Be Free	6
71	Atco 2465 019	EVERYTHING IS EVERYTHING (LP)	15
71	Atlantic 2400 143	DONNY HATHAWAY (LP)	15
72	Atlantic K 40369	LIVE (LP)	15
73	Atlantic K 40487	EXTENSION OF A MAN (LP)	15

(see also Roberta Flack)

FAY HAUSER
75	Philips 6006 489	You Bring The Sun In The Morning/(Pt. 2)	5

ALAN HAVEN
64	United Artists UP 1057	Theme From A Jolly Bad Fellow/Jee B'ees (with John Barry)	12
65	Fontana TF 542	Image/Romance On The North Sea	8
65	Fontana TF 590	The Knack/Satin Doll (with John Barry)	12
66	Fontana TF 658	Flamingo/Shangri-La	6
67	Fontana TF 835	Image/Romance Of The North Sea (reissue)	8
71	CBS S 63900	ST. ELMO'S FIRE (LP)	12

RICHIE HAVENS
69	Big T BIG 119	Oxford Town/My Own Way	5
69	Verve VS 1512	Three Day Eternity/No Opportunity Necessary No Experience Needed	5
69	Verve VS 1519	Lady Madonna/Indian Rope Man	15
68	Verve (S)VLP 6005	SOMETHIN' ELSE AGAIN (LP)	15
68	Verve (S)VLP 6008	MIXED BAG (LP)	30
69	Verve (S)VLP 6014	1983 (LP)	15
69	Verve (S)VLP 6021	STONEHENGE (LP)	15
69	Transatlantic TRA 187	ELECTRIC HAVENS (LP)	12
69	Transatlantic TRA 199	THE RICHIE HAVENS RECORD (LP)	12

HAVENSTREET
76	Rissole (no cat. no.)	THE END OF THE LINE (LP, private pressing with booklet)	50

PAT HAWES with DAVE CAREY'S RHYTHM
56	Tempo A 141	Snowy Morning Blues/Sheik Of Araby	5
56	Tempo LAP 9	PAT HAWES (10" LP)	20

GRAHAM HAWK & OWEN GRAY
72	Pama Supreme PS 360	Amazing Grace/SKETTO RICH: Don't Stay Out Late	5

HAWK & CO.
81	Epic EPC A 1735	Nite Life/Nite Life (Version)	5
82	Epic EPC A 2223	Livin' For The Good Times/Sweet Talker	5
	(see also Shadows)		

TOMMY HAWKE
60	Top Rank JAR 348	Good Gravy (I'm In Love Again)/Umpteen Years (And A Million Tears)	20

CHIP HAWKES
77	RCA PL 25044	NASHVILLE ALBUM (LP)	12
	(see Tremeloes)		

HAWKEYES
57	Capitol CL 14764	Someone Someday/Who Is He?	20

BUDDY BOY HAWKINS/WILLIAM MOORE
50s	Heritage RE 102	BUDDY BOY HAWKINS/WILLIAM MOORE (EP)	60
	(see also Blind Lemon Jefferson)		

CAROL HAWKINS
73	Polydor 2058 387	Listen/All For One	8

COLEMAN HAWKINS
55	Brunswick 05459	Lucky Duck/Bye 'N' Bye	8
55	Brunswick OE 9166	THE HAWK TALKS (EP)	8
55	Mercury EP1 6029	COLEMAN HAWKINS GROUP (EP)	8
55	HMV 7EG 8057	COLEMAN HAWKINS AND HIS ORCHESTRA (EP)	8
55	Vogue EPV 1021	COLEMAN HAWKINS (EP)	8
56	Vogue EPV 1147	COLEMAN HAWKINS AND HIS ORCHESTRA (EP)	8
57	HMV 7EG 8230	THE BEAN STALKS AGAIN (EP)	8
58	HMV 7EG 8393	HAWKINS ALLSTARS (EP)	8
58	London Jazz EZ-C 19020	THE HAWK RETURNS PART 1 (EP)	8
58	Columbia Clef SEB 10106	AT THE OPERA HOUSE (EP)	8
59	Esquire EP 192	BEAN AND THE BOYS (EP)	8
50s	London EZC 19020	THE HAWK RETURNS PT 1 (EP)	8
60	HMV 7EG 8625	COLEMAN HAWKINS AND HIS CONFRERES (EP)	8
61	Esquire EP 235	COLEMAN HAWKINS SEXTET (EP)	8
53	Capitol LC 6580	CLASSICS IN JAZZ (10" LP)	15
53	Capitol LC 6650	CAPITOL PRESENTS COLEMAN HAWKINS AND SONNY GREER (10" LP)	15
54	HMV DLP 1055	TEN COLEMAN HAWKINS' SPECIALS (10" LP)	15
59	HMC CLP 1293	GENIUS OF COLEMAN HAWKINS (LP)	15
59	Felsted FJA 7005	THE HIGH AND MIGHTY HAWK (LP, also stereo SJA 2005)	15
61	Esquire 32-095	SOUL (LP)	20
61	Esquire 32-102	HAWK EYES (LP)	20
61	Moodsville MV 7	COLEMAN HAWKINS (LP)	18
62	Swingsville SVLP 2001	COLEMAN HAWKINS WITH THE RED GARLAND TRIO (LP)	15
62	Swingsville SVLP 2005	THE COLEMAN HAWKINS ALL STARS (LP)	15
62	Swingsville SVLP 2013	STASCH (LP)	15
63	HMV CLP 1630	DESAFINADO (LP, also stereo CSD 1484)	15
64	Verve VLP 9044	ALIVE! AT THE VILLAGE GATE (LP)	15
64	HMV CLP 1689	TODAY AND NOW (LP)	15
64	CBS BPG 62157	BACK IN BEAN'S BAG (LP, with Clark Terry)	15
64	Fontana FJL 102	SWING' (LP)	15
65	Fontana TL 5273	MEDITATION (LP)	15
66	Fontana SJL 131	CATTIN' (LP)	15
71	Xtra XTRA 1119	COLEMAN HAWKINS (LP)	12
	(see also Hines & Eldridge, Milt Jackson & Coleman Hawkins, Eddie 'Lockjaw' Davis, Sir Charles Thompson)		

COLEMAN HAWKINS & LESTER YOUNG
65	Stateside SL 10117	CLASSIC TENORS (LP)	12

COLEMAN HAWKINS GROUP
60s	London LTZC 15048	COLEMAN HAWKINS GROUP (LP)	15
	(see also Coleman Hawkins)		

DALE HAWKINS
57	London HL 8482	Susie-Q/Don't Treat Me That Way (78 rpm = £80+)	500
58	London HLM 8728	La-Do-Dada/Cross Ties (78 rpm = £60)	50
59	London HLM 8842	Yea-Yea/Lonely Nights (78 rpm = £60)	50
59	London HLM 9016	Liza Jane/Back To School Blues (78 rpm = £80+)	50
60	London HLM 9060	Hot Dog/Our Turn	50
69	Bell SBLL 127	L.A., MEMPHIS AND TYLER, TEXAS (LP)	15
73	Checker 6467 301	OH! SUSIE Q (LP)	15

ERSKINE HAWKINS QUINTET
60	Brunswick LAT 8374	THE HAWK BLOWS AT MIDNIGHT (LP, also stereo STA 3042)	each 15

HAWKSHAW HAWKINS
51	Vogue V 9003	Doghouse Boogie/Yesterday's Kisses (78)	15
51	Vogue V 9027	Slow Coach/Two Roads (78)	12
54	Parlophone CMSP 1	Betty Lorraine/CHARLIE GORE & LOUIS INNIS: Mexican Joe (export issue)	25
50s	Parlophone DP 336	I Hope You're Crying Too/I'm A Lone Wolf (export 78)	10
63	London HL 9737	Lonesome 7-7203/Everything Has Changed	10
58	Parlophone GEP 8742	COUNTRY AND WESTERN (EP)	45
58	Vogue VE 170117	HAWKSHAW HAWKINS — COUNTRY AND WESTERN (EP)	40+
64	London HA 8181	THE ALL NEW HAWKSHAW HAWKINS (LP)	20
	(see also Charlie Gore, Louis Innis)		

JUNE HAWKINS
55	Brunswick 05370	Beat Out Dat Rhythm On A Drum/MURIEL SMITH & CARMEN JONES CHORUS: Dat's Love	8

MINT VALUE £

RONNIE HAWKINS (& HAWKS)

59	Columbia DB 4319	Forty Days (To Come Back Home)/One Of These Days	50
59	Columbia DB 4345	Mary Lou/Need Your Lovin' (Oh So Bad)	50
60	Columbia DB 4412	Southern Love (Whatcha-Gonna' Do)/Love Me Like You Can	25
60	Columbia DB 4442	Clara/Lonely Hours	35
63	Columbia DB 7036	Bo Diddley/Who Do You Love?	30
70	Roulette RO 512	Who Do You Love?/Bo Diddley	5
70	Atlantic 584 320	Down In The Alley/Matchbox	7
70	Atlantic 2091 007	Bitter Green/Forty Days	5
72	Monument MNT 8292	Cora Mae/Ain't That A Shame	5
60	Columbia SEG 7983	ROCKIN' WITH RONNIE (EP, also stereo ESG 7792)	125/200
60	Columbia SEG 7988	ROCKIN' WITH RONNIE (EP, also stereo ESG 7795)	125/200
60	Columbia 33SX 1238	MR. DYNAMO (LP, also stereo SCX 3315)	140/200
60	Columbia 33SX 1295	THE FOLK BALLADS OF RONNIE HAWKINS (LP, also stereo SCX 3358)	85/100
70	Roulette RCP 1003	ARKANSAS ROCK PILE (LP, with The Band)	20
70	Atlantic 2400 009	RONNIE HAWKINS (LP)	15
72	Monument MNT 65122	ROCK AND ROLL RESURRECTION (LP)	12

(see also Band, Levon & Hawks)

SCREAMIN' JAY HAWKINS

58	Fontana H 107	I Put A Spell On You/Little Demon (78)	90+
65	Columbia DB 7460	The Whammy/Strange	25
65	Sue WI 379	I Hear Voices/Just Don't Care	40
66	Sue WI 4008	I Put A Spell On You/Little Demon (unissued)	
69	Direction 58-4097	I Put A Spell On You/Little Demon	22
80	Polydor POSP 183	I Put A Spell On You/Armpit 6 (with Keith Richards)	10
66	Planet PLL 1001	THE NIGHT AND DAY OF SCREAMIN' JAY HAWKINS (LP)	115
69	Direction (S) 8-63481	I PUT A SPELL ON YOU (LP, mono or stereo)	40
69	Mercury SMCL 20178	WHAT THAT IS (LP)	22

(see also Keith Richards)

HAWKLORDS

78	Charisma HL 1	PSI Power/Death Trap (no p/s, promo only)	12
78	Charisma CB 323	PSI Power/Death Trap (no p/s)	8
79	Charisma CB 332	25 Years/(Only) The Dead Dreams Of A Cold War Kid (no p/s)	6
79	Charisma CB 332 12	25 Years/(Only) The Dead Dreams Of A Cold War Kid/PXR 5 (12", grey vinyl; also mispressed on black vinyl)	10/12
82	Flicknife FLS 209	Who's Gonna Win The War?/Time Of (p/s)	6
78	Charisma CDS 4014	25 YEARS ON (LP, with inner sleeve, some sold with separate tour book)	12/15

(see also Hawkwind)

HAWKS

69	Stateside SS 2147	The Grissle/SHEEP: Hide And Seek	12

HAWKS

81	Five Believers FB 001	Words Of Hope/Sense Of Ending (p/s)	12

(see also Lilac Time, Stephen 'Tin Tin' Duffy)

ALAN HAWKSHAW

70	Tangerine DP 0005	Puppet On A String/Everybody Knows	5
79	BBC RESL 64	Grange Hill/Stoned	20
72	Studio Two TWO 391	27 TOP TV THEMES AND COMMERCIALS (LP)	30
72	KPM 1080	FLUTE FOR MODERNS (with Alan Parker) (LP)	35

(see also Shadows)

HAWKSWORTH-VERRELL JAZZ GROUP

56	Decca FJ 10726	Ring Dem Bells/Always	6

JOHNNY HAWKSWORTH (ORCHESTRA)

65	Pye 7N 15969	Lunar Walk/It's Murder (as Johnny Hawksworth Orchestra)	15
66	Columbia DB 8059	Goal/Goal — World Cup 1966 Theme (as Sounds Of Johnny Hawksworth)	6
67	Columbia DB 8129	Wack Wack/On The Tiles	6

(see also Johnny's Jazz)

HAWKWIND

SINGLES

70	Liberty LBF 15382	Hurry On Sundown/Mirror Of Illusion	150
72	United Artists UP 35381	Silver Machine/Seven By Seven ('machine' art p/s)	12
73	United Artists (WD 3637)	Sonic Attack (1-sided promo in cloth sleeve)	185
73	United Artists UP 35566	Urban Guerilla/Brainbox Pollution	12
73	United Artists USEP 1	HURRY ON HAWKWIND (EP)	35
74	United Artists UP 35715	The Psychedelic Warlords (Disappear In Smoke)/It's So Easy	8
75	United Artists UP 35808	Kings Of Speed/Motorhead (some in p/s)	40/6
76	Charisma CB 289	Kerb Crawler/Honky Dorky	7
77	Charisma CB 299	Back On The Streets/The Dream Of Isis (p/s)	6
77	Charisma CB 305	Quark, Strangeness & Charm/Forge Of Vulcan	7
78	United Artists UP 35381	Silver Machine/Seven By Seven (reissue, black-on-white p/s)	5
78	United Artists 12UP 35381	Silver Machine/Seven By Seven (12", silver p/s)	10
80	Bronze BRO 98	Shot Down In The Night/Urban Guerilla (p/s)	5
80	Bronze BRO 98	Shot Down In The Night/Urban Guerilla (1-sided gold vinyl flexidisc)	30
80	Bronze BRO 109	Who's Gonna Win The War?/Nuclear Toy (p/s, cream or green labels)	12/5
81	RCA RCA 137	Angels Of Death/Trans-Dimensional Man (p/s)	5
82	RCA Active RCA 267	Silver Machine/Silver Machine (Full Version)/Psychedelic Warlords (p/s)	5
82	RCA Active RCAP 267	Silver Machine/(Full Version)/Psychedelic Warlords (picture disc)	10
82	Flicknife FLS 005	Motorhead/Valium Ten (p/s)	5
82	Flicknife FLST 005	Motorhead/Valium Ten (extended) (12", p/s)	8
83	United Artists UP 35381	Silver Machine/Seven By Seven (reissue, white-on-black p/s)	5
83	Liberty UPP 35381	Silver Machine/Seven By Seven (picture disc)	12
83	Liberty UPP 35381	Silver Machine/Seven By Seven (mispressed picture disc, plays Beatles' Ask Me Why)	18

83	Flicknife FLS 214	Hawkwind And Co: Your Last Chance (p/s, sampler with Robert Calvert & Michael Moorcock)	6
83	Flicknife FLS 025	Motorway City/Master Of The Universe (p/s)	5
84	Flicknife FLEP 104	THE EARTH RITUAL PREVIEW (12" EP)	5
85	Flicknife FLS 032	Needle Gun/Arioch (p/s)	5
85	Flicknife FLST 032	Needle Gun (extended)/Arioch (p/s)	8
86	Flicknife FLS 033	Zarozinia/Assault And Battery (live) (p/s)	5
86	Samurai HW 001	Silver Machine/Magnu (motorcycle-shaped picture disc)	15
86	Flicknife FLS 034-A	Motorhead/Hurry On Sundown (p/s with insert)	5
90	Receiver REPLAY 3014	THE EARLY YEARS LIVE (12", p/s, blue vinyl)	12
93	4 Real 4R 1	SPIRIT OF THE AGE (SOLSTICE REMIXES) (12" EP)	15
93	4 Real 4R 2	DECIDE YOUR FUTURE (12" EP)	10
94	Emerg. Broadcast EBS 110	QUARK, STRANGENESS & CHARM (12" EP, clear vinyl, 200 only)	15

ALBUMS

70	Liberty LBS 83348	HAWKWIND (LP, gatefold sleeve; blue or black label)	90/55
71	United Artists UAG 29202	IN SEARCH OF SPACE (LP in foldout sleeve, some with 'log book')	30/12
72	United Artists UAG 29364	DOREMI-FASOL-LATIDO (LP, with inner sleeve, some with poster)	35/12
73	Utd. Artists UAD 60037/8	SPACE RITUAL ALIVE (2-LP, foldout sleeve with inners)	30
74	United Artists UAG 29672	HALL OF THE MOUNTAIN GRILL (LP, with inner sleeve)	12
75	United Artists UAG 29766	WARRIOR ON THE EDGE OF TIME (LP, foldout pop-up sleeve with inner)	20
76	United Artists UAK 29919	ROADHAWKS (LP, gatefold sleeve with poster & sticker)	18/12
76	Mushroom	THE XENON CODEX (LP, with inner, gatefold sleeve)	15
79	Charisma CDS 4016	P.X.R.5 (LP, initially with family tree poster)	25/12
80	Charisma BG 2	REPEAT PERFORMANCE (LP)	12
80	Bronze BRON 530	LEVITATION (LP, blue vinyl)	18
81	RCA Active RCALP 6004	SONIC ATTACK (LP, with insert)	15
82	RCA Active RCALP 9004	CHURCH OF HAWKWIND (LP, with lyric booklet)	20
82	RCA Active RCALP 6055	CHOOSE YOUR MASQUES (LP)	18
84	Flicknife PSHARP 014	ZONES (LP, picture disc reissue)	15
84	Flicknife ZSHARP 019	INDEPENDENT DAYS (10" mini-LP)	8
84	Liberty SLP 1972921	HAWKWIND (LP, reissue, picture disc, die-cut)	15
84	Flicknife SHARP 022	STONEHENGE: THIS IS HAWKWIND DO NOT PANIC (LP, with 12", gatefold sleeve or single sleeve with poster)	each 18
85	Flicknife SHARP 033	CHRONICLE OF THE BLACK SWORD (LP, with inner sleeve)	12
85	Flicknife SHARP 033CD	CHRONICLE OF THE BLACK SWORD (CD, with 3 extra tracks)	18
86	Hawkfan HWFB 2	HAWKFAN 12 (LP, with poster, sticker insert & carrier bag, 600 only)	75
86	RCA NL 71150	ANGELS OF DEATH (LP)	22
86	Samurai SMR 046	APPROVED HISTORY OF HAWKWIND 1967-1982 (3-LP, pic discs & booklet)	40
87	Flicknife HWBOX 01	OFFICIAL PICTURE LOG BOOK (4-LP box set, [3 picture discs & interview disc] with badge & insert)	40
94	Emerg. Broadcast EBS 111	THE BUSINESS TRIP (2-LP, clear vinyl, 1,500 only)	18
95	Emerg. B/cast EBSLP 118	ALIEN 4 (2-LP, gatefold sleeve)	18
95	Dojo DOJO CD 244	ELECTRIC TEPEE (CD, picture disc, unreleased)	20

(see also Hawklords, Robert Calvert, Michael Moorcock, Inner City Unit, Sphynx, Dave Brock, Steve Swindells, Tim Blake, Huw Lloyd Langton Group, Alan Davey, Motörhead, Sonic Assassins, Dr. Technical & Machines, Sam Gopal, Magic Muscle, Opal Butterfly, Nik Turner, Widowmaker, Adrian Shaw)

DEANE HAWLEY

| 61 | Liberty LIB 55359 | Pocketful Of Rainbows/That Dream Could Never Be | 12 |

GOLDIE HAWN

| 72 | Reprise K 14211 | Carey/I'll Be Your Baby Tonight | 6 |

BRYN HAWORTH

| 74 | Island ILPS 9287 | LET THE DAYS GO BY (LP, with inner sleeve) | 12 |

(see also Fleur De Lys, Nicholas Greenwood)

HAYDEN HOUSE

| 69 | NEMS 56-4499 | House Beside The Mine/Lady Wants More | 25 |

HAYDOCK'S ROCKHOUSE

| 66 | Columbia DB 8050 | Cupid/She Thinks | 42 |
| 67 | Columbia DB 8135 | Lovin' You/Mix A Fix | 42 |

(see also Hollies)

BILL HAYES

53	MGM SP 1036	The Donkey Song/My Ever-Lovin'	20
55	London HL 8149	The Berry Tree/Blue Black Hair (78 rpm = £10)	35
56	London HLA 8220	Ballad Of Davy Crockett/Farewell	35
56	London HLA 8239	Kwela Kwela/The White Buffalo (78 rpm = £8)	25
56	London HLA 8300	Das Ist Musik/I Know An Old Lady (78 rpm = £8)	25
56	London HLA 8325	The Legend Of Wyatt Earp/That Do Make It Nice (78 rpm = £12)	25
57	London HL 8430	Wringle Wrangle/Westward Ho The Wagons (78 rpm = £8)	20
59	London HLR 8833	Wimoweh/Goin' Down The Road Feelin' Bad (with Buckle Busters)	8
59	London HLR 8833	Wimoweh/Goin' Down The Road Feelin' Bad (with Buckle Busters) (78)	12
56	London RE-A 1051	GREAT PIONEERS OF THE WEST (EP)	40

GEMMA HAYES

| 00s | Source SOUR 051 | Let A Good Thing Go/Pieces Of Glass (p/s) | 5 |

ISAAC HAYES

69	Stax STAX 133	Walk On By/By The Time I Get To Phoenix	6
70	Stax STAX 154	I Stand Accused/I Just Don't Know What To Do With Myself	6
71	Stax 2025 020	You've Lost That Lovin' Feelin'/Our Day Will Come	5
71	Stax 2025 029	Never Can Say Goodbye/I Can't Help It (If I'm Still In Love With You)	5
72	Stax 2025 069	Theme From Shaft/Cafe Regio's	5
72	Stax 2025 089	Let's Stay Together/Ain't That Loving You (For More Reasons Than One) (with David Porter)	5
72	Stax 2025 146	Theme From The Men/Type Thang	5

Isaac HAYES

74	Stax STXS 2004	Title Theme From *Tough Guys*/Hung Up On My Baby	6
75	ABC ABC 4076	Chocolate Chip/Chocolate Chip (Instrumental)	5
76	ABC ABC 4100	Disco Connection/St. Thomas Square	5
76	ABC ABC 4111	Rock Me Easy Baby (Parts 1 & 2)	5
76	ABC ABC 4136	Juicy Fruit (Disco Freak) (Parts 1 & 2)	5
79	Polydor POSPX 23	Zeke The Freak/If We Ever Needed Peace (12")	8
80	Polydor 2001 965	I Ain't Ever/Love Has Been Good For Us	5
86	CBS 650236-7	Hey Girl/Ike's Rap VIII	5
69	Stax SXATS 1028	HOT BUTTERED SOUL (LP)	20
69	Stax SXATS 1032	THE ISAAC HAYES MOVEMENT (LP)	18
70	Stax 2465 016	BLUE HAYES (LP)	18
71	Stax 2325 026	TO BE CONTINUED (LP)	18
71	Stax 2325 014	THE ISAAC HAYES MOVEMENT (LP, reissue)	12
71	Stax 2325 011	HOT BUTTERED SOUL (LP, reissue)	12
71	Stax 2659 007	SHAFT — ORIGINAL SOUNDTRACK (2-LP, soundtrack, gatefold sleeve)	22
72	MGM 2315 115	SHAFT'S BIG SCORE! (LP, soundtrack)	35
72	Atlantic K 40327	IN THE BEGINNING (LP)	12
72	Stax 2628 004	BLACK MOSES (2-LP)	18
74	Stax 2325 111	JOY (LP)	12
74	Stax STXD 4001/2	TRUCK TURNER (2-LP, soundtrack)	12
74	Stax STXH 5001	TOUGH GUYS (LP, soundtrack)	12
75	Stax STX 1043	USE ME (LP)	15
75	ABC ABCL 5129	CHOCOLATE CHIP (LP, gatefold sleeve)	15
75	ABC ABCL 5155	GROOVE-A-THON (LP, gatefold sleeve)	12

LINDA HAYES

55	Parlophone MSP 6174	Please Have Mercy (with Platters)/Oochi Pachi (with Tony Williams)	330
55	Parlophone R 4038	Please Have Mercy (with Platters)/Oochi Pachi (with Tony Williams) (78)	75

(see also Platters)

PETER LIND HAYES

60	Brunswick 05821	Life Gets Tee-jus Don't It/Sing Me A Happy Song	10

(see also Peter & Mary)

TUBBY HAYES

55	Tempo A 109	May Reh/Orient Line (78)	8
55	Tempo A 113	Sophisticated Lady/Deuces Wild (78)	8
55	Tempo A 119	Fidelius/Tootsie Roll (78)	8
55	Tempo A 123	There's No You/Dance Of The Aerophagytes (78)	8
56	Tempo A 148	Ode To Ernie/No, I Woodyn't (78 rpm = £8)	10
62	Fontana H 397	Sally/I Believe In You (as Tubby Hayes Quintet)	30
55	Tempo EXA 14	THE LITTLE GIANT (EP)	40
55	Tempo EXA 17	TUBBY HAYES AND HIS ORCHESTRA (EP)	25
55	Tempo EXA 27	THE SWINGING GIANT NO. 1 (EP, as Tubby Hayes Quartet)	45
56	Tempo EXA 28	THE SWINGING GIANT NO. 2 (EP, as Tubby Hayes Quartet)	45
56	Tempo EXA 36	MODERN JAZZ SCENE (EP, as Tubby Hayes & His Orchestra)	45
57	Tempo EXA 55	AFTER LIGHTS OUT (EP, as Tubby Hayes Quintet)	60+
57	Tempo EXA 75	TUBBY HAYES AND THE JAZZ COURIERS (EP)	60+
58	Tempo EXA 82	THE EIGHTH WONDER (EP, solo)	60+
57	Tempo TAP 6	AFTER LIGHTS OUT (LP, as Tubby Hayes Quintet)	350+
57	Tempo TAP 15	JAZZ COURIERS (LP)	300+
60	Tempo TAP 29	TUBBY'S GROOVE (LP, as Tubby Hayes Quartet)	400+
61	Fontana TFL 5142	TUBBS (LP, also stereo STFL 562)	100
61	Ember EMB 3337	AN EVENING WITH MR. PERCUSSION (LP, with Tony Kinsey)	70
61	Fontana TFL 5183	TUBBS IN NEW YORK (LP, also stereo STFL 595)	100
63	Fontana 680 998 TL	DOWN IN THE VILLAGE (LP, also stereo 886 163TY)	300/200
64	Fontana (S)TL 5195	RETURN VISIT! (LP)	100
64	Fontana TL 5200	LATE SPOT AT SCOTT'S (LP)	250
66	Fontana (S)TL 5221	TUBBY TOURS (LP, with Orchestra)	30
66	Fontana (S)TL 5410	100% PROOF (LP)	60
67	Wing WL 1162	TUBBS IN NEW YORK (LP, reissue)	15
69	Fontana SFJL 911	MEXICAN GREEN (LP)	125
71	Fontana 6309 002	THE TUBBY HAYES ORCHESTRA (LP)	20
72	Philips 6382 041	THIS IS JAZZ — 100% PROOF (LP)	15

(see also Jack Constanzo & Tubby Hayes, Jazz Couriers, London Jazz Quartet, Dave Lee, Ronnie Scott, Roy Castle)

TUBBY HAYES & CLEO LAINE

61	Fontana TFL 5151	PALLADIUM JAZZ DATE (LP, also stereo STFL 570)	70
65	Wing WL 1088	PALLADIUM JAZZ DATE (LP, reissue)	25

(see also Cleo Laine)

TUBBY HAYES ORCHESTRA

81	Mole MOLE 2	MEXICAN GREEN (LP, reissue)	20
81	Mole MOLE 4	TUBBS' TOURS (LP, reissue)	15

TUBBY HAYES & PAUL GONSALVES ALLSTARS

67	Columbia SX 6003	JUST FRIENDS (LP)	110
60s	World Record Club T 631	CHANGE OF SETTING (LP)	120

(see also Paul Gonsalves)

TUBBY HAYES QUARTET

90	MMO 79	67 LIVE — FOR MEMBERS ONLY (LP)	20

TUBBY HAYES QUINTET

80s	Jasmine JASM 2001	TUBBY'S GROOVE (LP, reissue)	15
80s	Jasmine JASM 2015	AFTER LIGHTS OUT (LP, reissue)	15

LOU HAYLES

77	Myrrh MYR 1055	DON'T HIDE AWAY (LP)	20

DICK HAYMES
51	Brunswick LA 8516	IRVING BERLIN SONGS (10" LP)	15
51	Brunswick LA 8530	SOUVENIR ALBUM (10" LP)	15
56	Capitol LC 6823	RAIN OR SHINE (10" LP)	15

ARTHUR HAYNES
| 61 | HMV POP 987 | Not To Worry/Looking Around | 7 |

GOLDIA HAYNES
| 51 | Capitol CL 13486 | That Great Judgement Day/Travelling (78) | 12 |
| 52 | Capitol CL 13550 | Truth In The Gospel/Oh Lord How Long (78) | 18 |

ROY HAYNES, PHINEAS NEWBORN, PAUL CHAMBERS TRIO
| 61 | Esquire 32-103 | WE THREE (LP) | 12 |

STEVE HAYNES BAND
| 78 | Black Bear BLA 2005 | Back In My Arms Again/Walk On By (p/s) | 20 |
| 78 | Black Bear BLA 2008 | Save Me Save Me/Strong Good Lovin' (p/s) | 15 |

HAYSTACK
| 69 | United Artists UP 35024 | Letter To Josephine/Love You're Making A Fool Of Me | 6 |
| 69 | United Artists UP 35035 | Tahiti Farewell/Pantomime People | 6 |

HAYSTACKS BALBOA
| 70 | Polydor 2489 002 | HAYSTACKS BALBOA (LP) | 100 |

JUSTIN HAYWARD
65	Pye 7N 17041	London Is Behind Me/Day Must Come	125
66	Parlophone R 5496	I Can't Face The World Without You/I'll Be Here Tomorrow	145
80	CBS 11-7731	The Eve Of The War/Horsell (12" picture disc)	8

(see also Wilde Three, Moody Blues)

RICK HAYWARD
| 71 | Blue Horizon 2431 006 | RICK HAYWARD (LP) | 125 |

(see also Accent, Christine Perfect)

SUSAN HAYWARD
| 56 | MGM MGM-EP 555 | I'LL CRY TOMORROW — SOUNDTRACK SELECTION (EP) | 15 |

JOE HAYWOOD
| 65 | Island WI 218 | Warm And Tender Love/I Would If I Could | 20 |

LEON HAYWOOD
66	Vocalion VL 9280	Ain't No Use/Hey, Hey, Hey (DJ copy = £60)	30
67	Vocalion VL 9288	Ever Since You Were Sweet Sixteen/Skate Awhile	25
69	MCA Soul Bag BAG 5	Mellow Moonlight/Tennessee Waltz	10
70	Capitol CL 15634	I Wanna Thank You/I Was Sent To Love You	15
73	Pye International 7N 25611	La La Song/There Ain't Enough Hate Around To Make Me Turn Around	5
75	20th Century BTC 2191	Come On And Get Yourself Some/BMF (Beautiful)	5
75	20th Century BTC 2228	I Wanta Do Something Freaky To You/I Know What Love Is	6
78	Fantasy FTC 151	Baby Reconsider/Would I	15
67	Vocalion VAL 8064	SOUL CARGO (LP)	75
69	MCA MUPS 369	IT'S GOT TO BE MELLOW (LP)	25
73	Pye Intl. NSPL 28177	BACK TO STAY (LP)	25
75	20th Century BT 476	COME AND GET YOURSELF SOME (LP)	15

HAZE
| 85 | Gabadon GABS 003 | THE EMBER (12" EP) | 8 |
| 84 | Gabadon GABL 001 | C'EST LA VIE (LP) | 25 |

HAZEL
| 93 | Sub Pop SP74 241 | Jilted (blue vinyl) | 5 |

HAZEL & JOLLY BOYS
| 67 | Doctor Bird DB 1063 | Stop Them/Deep Down | 20 |

RONNIE HAZELHURST
| 78 | Polydor 2384 107 | SIXTEEN SMALL SCREEN GREATS (LP) | 12 |

LEE HAZLEWOOD
60	London HLW 9223	Words Mean Nothing/The Girl On Death Row (with Duane Eddy)	35
66	MGM MGM 1310	Sand/My Autumn's Done Come	10
67	MGM MGM 1348	My Baby Cried All Night Long/These Boots Are Made For Walkin'	12
67	Reprise RS 20613	Ode To Billie Joe/Charlie Bill Nelson	7
68	Reprise RS 20667	Rainbow Woman/I Am, You Are	8
72	RCA RCA 2185	Big Red Balloon/Down From Dover	6
73	Stateside SS 2225	Poet/Come Spend The Morning	6
66	MGM MGM-CS 8014	THE VERY SPECIAL WORLD OF LEE HAZLEWOOD (LP)	32
68	Reprise RSLP 6297	LOVE AND OTHER CRIMES (LP)	25
69	London HA-N/SH-N 8398	TROUBLE IS A LONESOME TOWN (LP)	32
72	Reprise K 44161	REQUIEM FOR AN ALMOST LADY (LP)	20
74	Stateside SSL 10315	POET, FOOL OR BUM (LP)	25

(see also Nancy Sinatra & Lee Hazlewood, Duane Eddy)

TONY HAZZARD
66	Columbia DB 7927	You'll Never Put Shackles On Me/Calling You Home	6
68	CBS 3452	Sound Of The Candyman's Trumpet/Everything's Gone Wrong	5
69	CBS 63608	DEMONSTRATION (LP)	20
71	Bronze ILPS 9174	LOUDWATER HOUSE (LP)	12
73	Bronze ILPS 9222	WAS THAT ALRIGHT THEN? (LP)	12

HEAD
| 79 | Ellie Jay MB1 | Nothing To Do In A Town Like Leatherhead/University '79 | 60+ |

MURRAY HEAD
65	Columbia DB 7635	Alberta/He Was A Friend Of Mine	8
65	Columbia DB 7771	The Bells Of Rhymney/Don't Sing No Sad Songs For Me	10
67	Columbia DB 8102	Someday Soon/You Bore Me	8
67	Immediate IM 053	She Was Perfection/Secondhand Monday	58
69	MCA MK 5019	Superstar/John 1941 (p/s, with Trinidad Singers)	7
71	MCA MKS 5019	Superstar/John 1941 (p/s, reissue)	6
73	CBS 65503	NIGEL LIVED (LP, gatefold sleeve and booklet)	30
75	Island ILPS 9347	SAY IT AIN'T SO (LP, gatefold sleeve)	15

ROY HEAD (& TRAITS)
65	Pye International 7N 25340	Just A Little Bit/Treat Me Right	15
65	Vocalion VP 9248	Treat Her Right/So Long, My Love	20
66	Vocalion VP 9254	Apple Of My Eye/I Pass The Day	15
66	Vocalion VP 9269	My Babe/Pain	15
66	Vocalion VP 9274	Wigglin' And Gigglin'/Driving Wheel	18
66	London HLZ 10097	To Make A Big Man Cry/Don't Cry No More	15
70	Stateside SS 8050	Mama Mama/I'm Not A Fool Anymore	7
75	London HLD 10487	The Most Wanted Woman In Town/Gingers Breadman	8
66	Pye Intl. NEP 44053	JUST A LITTLE BIT OF ROY HEAD (EP)	40
70	Stateside SSL 5033	SAME PEOPLE (LP)	25

(see also Traits)

HEADACHE
77	Lout 001	Can't Stand Still/No Reason For Your Call (p/s)	25

HEADBANGERS
81	Magnet MAG 206	Status Rock/Headbang Boogie (p/s)	5

(see also Biddu, Leaf Hound, Weapon)

THEE HEADCOATS
90	Sub Pop SP71	Time Will Tell/Davey Crockett (Gabba Hey) (p/s)	6
92	Sub Pop SP151	Ballad Of Hollis Brown/Grizzly Bear (p/s, blue vinyl)	8

(see also Milkshakes)

HEADHUNTERS
76	Arista ARTY 116	SURVIVAL OF THE FITTEST (LP)	30
77	Arista SPART 1046	STRAIGHT FROM THE GATE (LP)	20

(see also Herbie Hancock)

HEADLESS CHICKENS
89	Hometown Atrocities 1	THE HOMETOWN ATROCITIES EP (wraparound p/s, 'kylie' or 'glossy')	200/120

(see also Radiohead)

HEADLINERS
59	Parlophone R 4593	The Bubble Car Song/Andy's Theme	8

HEADLINERS
65	Decca F 12209	That's The Way I Must Go/Four Seasons	8

HEAD MACHINE
70	Major Minor SMLP 79	ORGASM (LP)	190

(see also Uriah Heep)

HEAD OF DAVID
89	Blast First WANT 001	WHITE ELEPHANT (LP, mail-order only)	12

HEADS, HANDS & FEET
71	Island ILPS 9149	HEADS, HANDS AND FEET (LP)	20
72	Island ILPS 9185	TRACKS (LP)	20

(see also Don Everly, Tony Colton, Poet & One Man Band)

HEALEY SISTERS
64	HMV POP 1313	Give Me Back My Heart/After The Party	10

JOE HEANEY
63	Topic 12T 91	IRISH TRADITIONAL SONGS IN GAELIC AND ENGLISH (LP)	12

HEART
77	Arista ARISTA 140	Heartless/Here Song (withdrawn)	8
86	Capitol CLP 406	Nothin' At All (Extended Remix)/The Wolf (heart-shaped picture disc)	6
87	Capitol CLP 457	Who Will You Run To?/Nobody Home (picture disc)	10
87	Capitol CDCL 473	There's The Girl (12" Remix)/Bad Animals/There's The Girl (7" Remix) (CD)	8
88	Capitol CDCL 477	These Dreams (7" Version)/Heart Of Darkness/If Looks Could Kill (live)/There's The Girl (Rock-A-Pella Version) (CD)	8
88	Capitol CDCL 482	Never (Extended Remix)/These Dreams (7" Version)/Heart Of Darkness/If Looks Could Kill (live) (CD)	8
88	Capitol CDCL 487	What About Love? (Extended Version)/Shell Shock/Crazy On You/Dreamboat Annie (CD)	8
88	Capitol CDCL 507	Nothin' At All (Ext. Remix)/I've Got The Music In Me/I Want You So Bad (CD)	8
77	Arista SPART 1024	MAGAZINE (LP, withdrawn)	15
77	Arista SPART 1024	MAGAZINE (LP, picture disc)	15
90	Capitol HGIFT 1	HEART BOX SET (3-LP: *Heart, Bad Animals & Brigade* + 24pp booklet)	18

HEART BEATS
80	Red Shadow REDS 2	Talk To Me/Don't Want Romance (p/s)	8
81	Nothing Shaking SHAD 1	Go/One Of The People (p/s, blue vinyl)	15

HEARTBREAKERS
77	Track 2094 135	Chinese Rocks/Born To Lose (p/s)	8
77	Track 2094 135T	Chinese Rocks/Born To Lose (12", p/s)	12
77	Track 2094 137	One Track Mind/Can't Keep My Eyes On You (live)/Do You Love Me (p/s)	10
77	Track 2094 142	It's Not Enough/Let Go (p/s, withdrawn)	250
79	Beggars Banquet BEG 21	Get Off The Phone (live)/I Wanna Be Loved (live) (p/s)	5

88	Jungle JUNG 38 T	SHE WANTS TO MAMBO (12" EP)	8
77	Track 2409 218	L.A.M.F. (LP)	20
81	Jungle FREUD 1	D.T.K. — LIVE AT THE SPEAKEASY (LP, white or pink vinyl)	18
84	Jungle FREUDP 4	L.A.M.F. REVISITED (LP, picture disc)	18
88	Jungle FREUDP 1	D.T.K. — LIVE AT THE SPEAKEASY (LP, reissue, picture disc)	18

(see also New York Dolls, Johnny Thunders)

HEARTS (U.K.)
64	Parlophone R 5147	Young Woman/Black Eyes	25

HEARTS (U.S.)
64	Stateside SS 268	Dear Abby/Dear Abby (Instrumental)	20

HEARTS & FLOWERS
67	Capitol CL 15492	Rock'N'Roll Gypsies/Road To Nowhere	12
68	Capitol CL 15549	She Sang Hymns Out Of Tune/Tin Angel	8

HEARTS OF SOUL
70	Columbia DB 8670	Waterman/Fat Jack	18

HEATERS
70	Upsetter US 329	Melting Pot/UPSETTERS: Kinky Mood	12

HEAT EXCHANGE
79	EMI EMI 2988	Shake Down/You're Gonna Love This (p/s)	5
79	EMI 12EMI 2988	Shake Down/You're Gonna Love This (12", p/s)	8
79	EMI EMC 3306	ONE STEP AHEAD (LP)	12

(see also Brian Bennett)

JIMMY HEATH
60	Riverside RLP 333	REALLY BIG (LP)	15

TED HEATH ORCHESTRA
	Confectioners'	Candy Queen Waltz (with Dennis Lotis)/The Girl On The Candy Box (with	
	Benevolent Fund	Dickie Valentine) (78, promo)	10
54	Decca F 10246	Skin Deep/Walking Shoes	15
51	Decca LF 1037	TEMPO FOR DANCERS (10")	12
52	Decca LF 1060	LISTEN TO MY MUSIC (10")	12
52	Decca LF 1064	SELECTION (10")	12
58	Decca LK 4275	HITS I MISSED (also stereo SKL 4003)	each 15
58	Decca LK 4280	OLDE ENGLYSHE	12
58	Decca SKL 4023	SWINGS IN HI-STEREO (stereo only)	25
59	Decca SKL 4030	SWING SESSION (stereo only)	20
59	Decca SKL 4046	SHALL WE DANCE	15
59	Decca SKL 4079	BEAULIEU JAZZ FESTIVAL (stereo only)	45
59	Decca LK 4208	ALL TIME TOP TWELVE — THE BILLBOARD (also stereo SKL 4054)	each 15
59	Decca LK 4307	PLAYS THE GREAT FILM HITS (also stereo SKL 4055)	each 15
60	Decca LK 4324	PLAYS THE BLUES (also stereo SKL 4074)	each 15
60	Decca LK 4328	THE BIG BAND DIXIE SOUND (also stereo SKL 4076)	each 15
60	Decca LK 4331	IN CONCERT (also stereo SKL 4079)	each 15
60	Decca LK 4344	MY VERY GOOD FRIENDS THE BAND LEADERS (also stereo SKL 4090)	each 15
61	Decca LK 4374	THE INSTRUMENTS OF THE DANCE ORCHESTRA (also stereo SKL 4117)	each 15
61	Decca LK 4389	GOES LATIN (also stereo SKL 4389)	each 15

(Early copies of the above stereo LPs have a "ffss" circle logo at the top of the label & blue back sleeves.)

62	Decca PFM 24004	BIG BAND PERCUSSION (also stereo PFS 34004)	12/20

(see also Joan Regan, Bobbie Britton, Johnston Brothers, Annette Klooger)

HEATHCLIFFE
68	Tangerine DP 0001	Holly Bush And Mistletoe/My World	8

HEATHER
65	King KG 1027	I'll Come Softly/No One In The Whole Wide World	7

HEAVENLY
89	Sarah SARAH 30	I Fell In Love Last Night/Over And Over (p/s)	8

HEAVEN 17
81	Wool City Rocker LYN 9296	Something's Wrong (flexidisc free with fanzine)	8/5
82	Virgin VS 483	Height Of The Fighting (He-La-Hu)/Honeymoon In New York (unissued, no p/s)	15
83	Virgin VSP 570	Temptation/We Live So Fast (picture disc)	5
83	Virgin VSP 607	Come Live With Me/Let's All Make A Bomb (picture disc)	5
83	Virgin VSP 628	Crushed By The Wheels Of Industry/(Version) (picture disc)	5
84	Virgin/fan club	HOW MEN ARE (cassette, studio demo via fan club)	12
86	Virgin TCV 2383	ENDLESS (cassette, double-play in presentation box with booklet)	12

(see also B.E.F., Human League, Glenn Gregory & Claudia Brucken)

HEAVY COCHRAN
78	Psycho P 2611	I've Got Big Balls/Well, Fairly Big	5
79	Psycho P 2619	I've Got A Little Prick/It's 12 Inches Long, But I Don't Use It As A Rule	6

(see also Lieutenant Pigeon)

HEAVY DUTY BREAKS
85	Illuminated ILL 5512	Heavy Duty Breaks (Radio Version)/Bonus Beats (12", p/s)	8
85	Illuminated JAMS 49	HEAVY DUTY BREAKS (LP, remixes of other artists)	12

(see also Youth, Killing Joke)

HEAVY JELLY
69	Island WIP 6049	I Keep Singing The Same Old Song/Blue	15

(see also Skip Bifferty, Griffin, Graham Bell, Arc)

HEAVY JELLY
69	Head HDS 4001	Time Out Chewn In/The Long Wait	20
70	Island HELP	HEAVY JELLY (LP, promo only)	100
84	Psycho PSYCHO 30	TAKE ME DOWN TO THE WATER (LP, reissue of *Heavy Jelly*)	12

(see also Jackie Lomax, Aynsley Dunbar Retaliation)

HEAVY METAL KIDS
74	Atlantic K 50047	HEAVY METAL KIDS (LP, with poster)	12
77	Rak SRAK 523	KITSCH (LP)	12

(see also Gary Holton, Kids)

HEAVY PETTIN'
82	Neat NEAT 17	Roll The Dice/Love Times Love (p/s)	10
83	Polydor HEPP 3	Love Times Love/Shout It Out (shaped picture disc)	8

HEAVYWEIGHTS
69	Spark SRL 1033	Utterly Funky/Shambala	18

BOBBY HEBB
66	Philips BF 1503	Sunny/Bread	8
66	Philips BF 1522	A Satisfied Mind/Love Love Love	30
67	Philips BF 1541	Love Me/Baby I'm Crazy	10
67	Philips BF 1570	I Love Everything About You/Some Kinda Magic	10
67	Philips BF 1610	Everything Is Coming Up Roses/Bound By Love	8
68	Philips BF 1702	You Want To Change Me/Dreamy	50
72	Philips 6051 023	Love Love Love/Sunny	8
72	Philips 6051 025	Some Kind Of Magic/Good Lovin'	6
66	Philips BL 7740	SUNNY (LP)	40

HEBREW CHILDREN & INNER CIRCLE
73	Ackee ACK 508	Dog And Bone/Version	6

DICK HECKSTALL-SMITH (QUINTET)
57	Pye Jazz NJE 1037	VERY SPECIAL OLD JAZZ (EP, as Dick Heckstall-Smith Quintet)	25
72	Bronze ILPS 9196	DUST IN THE AIR SUSPENDED MARKS THE PLACE ...	
		WHERE A STORY ENDED (LP, gatefold sleeve with lyric inner sleeve)	20

(see also Graham Bond Organisation, John Mayall & Bluesbreakers, Alexis Korner, Colosseum, Rocket 88)

JESSE HECTOR
99	No Hit NO HIT EP 1961	Fast Train To Memphis/My Bucket's Got A Hole In It/All By Myself/	
		Nightmares (p/s)	6

HEDGEHOG PIE
76	Rubber ADUB 8	Well I Know/Go With The Flow	6
72	Rubber RUB 002	HIS ROUND (LP, with Tony Capstick)	15
75	Rubber RUB 009	HEDGEHOG PIE (LP)	25
75	Rubber RUB 014	GREEN LADY (LP)	20
78	Rubber RUB 024	JUST ACT NORMAL (LP, with lyric insert)	20

(see also Dando Shaft)

HEDGEHOPPERS ANONYMOUS
65	Decca F 12241	It's Good News Week/Afraid Of Love	5
65	Decca F 12298	Don't Push Me/Please Don't Hurt Your Heart For Me	6
66	Decca F 12400	Baby (You're My Everything)/Remember	8
66	Decca F 12479	Daytime/That's The Time	10
66	Decca F 12530	Stop Press/Little Memories	8

(see also Alan Avon & Toy Shop, Jonathan King, Mick Tinsley)

HEFNER
97	Inertia INERT 0004	Car Chase/Remix (12", p/s)	10
98	Sticky STICKY 23	A Hymn For The Alcohol/My Art College Days Are Over (p/s, 500 only)	8
98	Too Pure PURE 64	THE HEFNER SOUL: Flowers/A Hymn For The Coffee/Broodmare/	
		The Girl From The Coast/More Christian Girls (10" EP)	10
02	Too Pure PURE 125X	THE HEFNER BRAIN: When The Angels Play Their Drum Machines/	
		Dark Hearted Discos/The Baggage Reclaim Song/Can't Help Losing You/	
		All I'll Ever Need (10", p/s)	8

NEAL HEFTI & ORCHESTRA
66	RCA Victor RCA 1521	The Batman Theme/Batman Chase	28
89	RCA PB 49571PD	The Batman Theme (1966 Version)/Batman Chase (picture disc)	7
54	Vogue/Coral LVC 10005	SWINGIN' ON A CORAL REEF (10" LP)	15
65	Warner Bros W 1599	HARLOW (LP, soundtrack)	30
65	United Artists (S)ULP 1098	HOW TO MURDER YOUR WIFE (LP, soundtrack)	35
66	RCA Victor RD 7795	BOEING BOEING (LP, soundtrack)	30
66	United Artists (S)ULP 1141	DUEL AT DIABLO (LP, soundtrack)	20
67	London HA-D 8337	BAREFOOT IN THE PARK (LP, soundtrack)	30
68	Dot (S)LPD 514	THE ODD COUPLE (LP, soundtrack)	30

LUCILLE HEGAMIN
73	VJM VLP 50	BLUE FLAME (LP)	14

DONALD HEIGHT
66	London HLZ 10062	Talk Of The Grapevine/There'll Be No Tomorrow (DJ copy = £150)	100
67	London HLZ 10116	Three Hundred & Sixty Five Days/I'm Willing To Wait (DJ copy = £100)	70
71	Avco Embassy 6105 005	Dancin' To The Music Of Love/Rags To Riches To Rags	75
71	Jay Boy BOY 32	Talk Of The Grapevine/There'll Be No Tomorrow (reissue)	15
72	Jay Boy BOY 51	Three Hundred & Sixty Five Days/I'm Willing To Wait (reissue)	10
72	Jay Boy BOY 60	We Gotta Make Up/I Can't Get Enough	10

RONNIE HEIGHT
59	Decca F 11126	Come Softly To Me/So Young, So Wise (78 rpm = £20)	20
60	London HLN 9144	The One Finger Symphony/Mem'ries & Habits	7

HEINZ (& WILD BOYS)

63	Decca F 11652	Dreams Do Come True/Been Invited To A Party	20
63	Decca F 11693	Just Like Eddie/Don't You Knock At My Door	8
63	Decca F 11768	Country Boy/Long Tall Jack	8
64	Decca F 11831	You Were There/No Matter What They Say	15
64	Decca F 11920	Please Little Girl/For Loving Me This Way	20
64	Columbia DB 7374	Questions I Can't Answer/The Beating Of My Heart	20
65	Columbia DB 7482	Diggin' My Potatoes/She Ain't Comin' Back (with Wild Boys)	35
65	Columbia DB 7559	Don't Think Twice, It's All Right/Big Fat Spider	25
65	Columbia DB 7656	End Of The World/You Make Me Feel So Good	35
65	Columbia DB 7779	Heart Full Of Sorrow/Don't Worry Baby	35
66	Columbia DB 7942	Movin' In/I'm Not A Bad Guy	40
63	Decca DFE 8545	HEINZ (EP)	60
63	Decca DFE 8559	LIVE IT UP (EP)	40
64	Decca LK 4599	TRIBUTE TO EDDIE (LP)	80
	(see also Tornados, Saints)		

HELDEN

83	Zica ZICA 01	Holding On/Once Upon A Time In The ... (p/s)	10
83	Zica 12 ZICA 01	Holding On/Once Upon A Time In The ... (12", p/s)	25
83	In The City ITC 1	Holding On/HOI POLLOI: When It's History (free with In The City magazine)	6/8
	(see also Ultravox)		

RICHARD HELL (& VOIDOIDS)

76	Stiff BUY 7	(I Could Live With You In) Another World/(I Belong To The) Blank Generation/ You Gotta Lose (some with p/s, numbered, 5,000 only; later re-pressed for The Stiff Box Set & numbered '001')	10/6
77	Sire 6078 608	Blank Generation/Love Comes In Spurts (no p/s)	8
77	Sire 6078 608	Blank Generation/Liars Beware/Who Says? (12", p/s)	10
79	Radar ADA 30	The Kid With The Replaceable Head/I'm Your Man (p/s)	7
94	Overground OVER 36	Another World/Blank Generation/Love Comes In Spurts (p/s, reissue, 2,000 only)	5
96	Codex CODE 3X	GO NOW (10", p/s, 1,000 only, etched yellow vinyl)	8
96	Codex CODE 3	GO NOW (CD, 1,000 only)	8
92	Overground OVER 24	3 NEW SONGS (EP, 134 yellow vinyl copies)	6
77	Sire 9103 327	BLANK GENERATION (LP, some with inner sleeve)	15/12
83	I.D. NOSE 2	DESTINY STREET (LP)	12
	(see also Neon Boys)		

HELLANBACH

84	Neat NEAT 1006	NOW HEAR THIS (LP, with inner sleeve)	12
84	Neat NEAT 1019	THE BIG ... H (LP, with insert)	12

HELLACOPTERS

99	Butcher's Hook HOOK 004	A House Is Not A Motel/POWDER MONKEYS: Destination X (p/s)	5
01	Polar 158 801 2	FLIGHT CASE (enhanced CD EP, box set with patch & insert)	12
	(see also Super$hit666)		

HELLHAMMER

84	Noise N 008	APOCALYPTIC RAIDS (12" EP, 45/33rpm)	25

DAVE HELLING

65	Stateside SS 409	It Ain't Me Babe/If You're Gonna Leave Me	10
66	Planet PLF 101	Christine/The Bells	40

HELLIONS

65	Piccadilly 7N 35213	Daydreaming Of You/Shades Of Blue	22
65	Piccadilly 7N 35232	Tomorrow Never Comes/Dream Child	22
65	Piccadilly 7N 35265	A Little Lovin'/Think It Over	22
	(see also Revolution, Traffic, Roaring Sixties, Jim Capaldi, Dave Mason, Luther Grosvenor, Family, Spooky Tooth)		

HELL IS FOR HEROES

00s	Universal HERO 001CD	Sick/Happy (CD, card sleeve)	20
00s	Chrysalis CHS 5143	I Can Climb Mountains/Get Low (blue vinyl, p/s)	7
00s	EMI 5515397	Night Vision/Can't You Hear It (clear vinyl, p/s)	6

HELLO

72	Bell BELL 1238	You Move Me/Ask Your Mama	15
72	Bell BELL 1265	C'mon/Wench	5
73	Bell BELL 1333	Another School Day/C'mon Get Together (p/s)	6

HELL PREACHERS INC.

69	Marble Arch MALS 1169	SUPREME PSYCHEDELIC UNDERGROUND (LP)	45

BOBBY HELMS

57	Brunswick 05711	Fraulein/(Got A) Heartsick Feeling	15
57	Brunswick 05721	My Special Angel/Standing At The End of My World	15
58	Brunswick 05730	No Other Baby/The Magic Song (78 rpm = £8)	20
58	Brunswick 05741	Love My Lady/Just A Little Lonesome (78 rpm = £6)	20
58	Brunswick 05748	Jacqueline/Living In The Shadow Of The Past	15
58	Brunswick 05754	Schoolboy Crush/Borrowed Dreams (78 rpm = £8)	20
58	Brunswick 05765	Jingle Bell Rock/Captain Santa Claus (78 rpm = £25)	25
59	Brunswick 05786	Miss Memory/New River Train (78 rpm = £15)	15
59	Brunswick 05801	Soon It Can Be Told/I Guess I'll Miss The Prom (78 rpm = £18)	15
59	Brunswick 05813	My Lucky Day/Hurry Baby (78 rpm = £20)	15
61	Brunswick 05852	Sad Eyed Baby/You're The One	8
60	Brunswick OE 9461	BOBBY HELMS (EP)	60
57	Brunswick LAT 8250	SINGS TO MY SPECIAL ANGEL (LP)	85

JIMMY HELMS

63	Pye 7N 45440	Ragtime Girl/Romeo & Juliet	150
69	London HL 10255	If You Let Me/I Don't Care Who Knows It	6
73	Capitol CL 15762	My Little Devil/Magnificent Sanctuary Band	15

HELP
71	MCA MWPS 4039	SECOND COMING (LP)	60

HELPLESS HUW
78	US US 001	Still Love You (In My Heart)	5
80	US US 002	Sid Vicious Was Innocent/Going Through The Motions/ Baby We're Not In Love/When You're Weary (p/s in bag)	7

HELP YOURSELF
71	Liberty LBF 15459	Running Down Deep/Paper Leaves	8
72	United Artists UP 35355	Heaven Row/Brown Lady	8
72	United Artists UP 35466	Mommy Won't Be Home For Christmas/Johnny B. Goode	6
71	Liberty LBS 83484	HELP YOURSELF (LP)	25
72	United Artists UAS 29287	STRANGE AFFAIR (LP, with inner sleeve)	25
72	United Artists UAS 29413	BEWARE OF THE SHADOW (LP)	25
73	United Artists UDG 4001 [UAS 29487/FREE 1]	THE RETURN OF KEN WHALEY/HAPPY DAYS (2-LP, box set with individual sleeves)	35
73	United Artists UAS 29487	THE RETURN OF KEN WHALEY (LP)	15

(see also Man, Deke Leonard, Tyla Gang)

HEMLOCK
73	Deram DM 379	Mr Horizontal/Beggar Man	12
73	Deram SML 1102	HEMLOCK (LP)	60

(see also Miller Anderson, Keef Hartley Band, Dog Soldier)

BERTHA HENDERSON/ROSA HENDERSON
60	Jazz Collector JEL 14	THE FEMALE BLUES VOL. 2 (EP)	15

BILL HENDERSON
60	Top Rank JAR 412	Sweet Pumpkin/Joey, Joey, Joey	10
63	Stateside SL 10019	BILL HENDERSON (LP)	15

DICKIE HENDERSON & JUNE LAVERICK
60	Oriole CB 1536	Simpatica/It's So Nice To Sleep With No-One (78)	10

(see also June Laverick)

DORRIS HENDERSON
65	Columbia DB 7567	The Hangman/Leaves That Are Green	15
67	Fontana TF 811	Message To Pretty/Watch The Stars	10
65	Columbia SX 6001	THERE YOU GO (LP, with John Renbourn)	230
67	Fontana (S)TL 5385	WATCH THE STARS (LP, with John Renbourn)	175

(see also Eclection, John Renbourn)

EDMONIA HENDERSON
51	Tempo R 43	Mama Don't Want A Sweet Man Any More/Hateful Blues (78)	10

FINIS HENDERSON
83	Motown TMGT 1304	Skip To My Lou/I'd Rather Be Gone/Vina Del Mar (12")	10

FLETCHER HENDERSON
50s	Jazz Collector JE 111	FLETCHER HENDERSON JAZZ GROUP (EP)	5
50s	Jazz Collector JE 115	BIG BAND STORY VOL. 1 (EP)	5
55	London AL 3547	BIRTH OF BIG BAND JAZZ (10" LP)	15
55	HMV DLP 1066	AT CONNIE'S INN (10" LP)	15
50s	Audubon AAF-AAK	FLETCHER HENDERSON (6 x 10" LP set)	40

(see also Clara Smith & Fletcher Henderson)

JOE HENDERSON
62	London HLU 9553	Snap Your Fingers/If You See Me Cry	12
63	London REU 1376	JOE HENDERSON (EP)	30

LORNA HENDERSON
60	Oriole CB 1549	Lollipops To Lipstick/Steady Eddie (78 rpm = £20)	28
60	Oriole CB 1590	A Thousand Stars/Murray, What's Your Hurry?	10

RICKIE/RIKKI HENDERSON
60	Embassy WB 399	Three Steps To Heaven/The Urge (78)	8
60	Embassy WB 406	Mais Quis/If She Should Come To You (78)	8
60	Embassy WB 419	It's Now Or Never/Save The Last Dance For Me (78)	8
60	Embassy WB 423	My Love For You/Just As Much As Ever (78)	8

RUSS HENDERSON & HIS CALYPSO BAND
57	HMV POP 333	Waiting For The Coconuts To Fall/Nobody's Business (78)	8

(see also Marie Bryant)

SKITCH HENDERSON
59	Brunswick OE 9434	LONDON AT MIDNIGHT (EP)	10

WILLIE HENDERSON (& SOUL EXPLOSIONS)
70	MCA MU 1127	Funky Chicken/Oo Wee Baby, I Love You (with Soul Explosions)	8
73	Contempo C 18	The Dance Master (Parts 1 & 2)	6
74	Contempo CS 9005	The Dance Master (Parts 1 & 2) (reissue)	5
74	Pye International 7N 25668	Gangster Boogie Bump/Let's Merengue	5

BOBBY HENDRICKS
58	London HL 8714	Itchy Twitchy Feeling/A Thousand Dreams (78 rpm = £30)	60
59	Top Rank JAR 193	Little John Green/Sincerely, Your Lover	20
61	Mercury AMT 1163	I'm Coming Home/Every Other Night	10
64	Sue WI 315	Itchy Twitchy Feeling/Thousand Dreams (reissue, as Bobby Henricks)	22

(see also Drifters)

HUGH HENDRICKS & UPSETTERS
70	Spinning Wheel SW 103	Land Of Kinks/O'NEIL HALL: This Man	15

JON HENDRICKS

56	Brunswick 05521	Four Brothers/Cloudburst (with Dave Lambert Singers)	8
68	Verve VS 572	No More/Rainbow's End	5
71	Philips 6006 088	I Got Soul/Slow Train	5
61	Vogue EPV 1268	A GOOD GIT-TOGETHER (EP)	12
60	Vogue LAE 12231	A GOOD GIT-TOGETHER (LP)	15
70	Valiant VS 140	BOSSA MAN (LP)	12
72	Philips 6438 019	LIVE (LP)	12

(see also Dave Lambert)

JIMI HENDRIX (EXPERIENCE)

SINGLES

66	Polydor 56139	Hey Joe/Stone Free	10
67	Track 604 001	Purple Haze/51st Anniversary (white or black label)	18/8
67	Track 604 004	The Wind Cries Mary/Highway Chile	10
67	Track 604 007	The Burning Of The Midnight Lamp/The Stars That Play With Laughing Sam's Dice	10
67	Decca F 22652	How Would You Feel/You Don't Want Me (with Curtis Knight, test pressing, unreleased)	500
67	Track 604 009	How Would You Feel/You Don't Want Me (with Curtis Knight)	10
67	London HL 10160	Hush Now/Flashing (with Curtis Knight; some in export p/s)	30/8
68	Track 604 025	All Along The Watchtower/Long Hot Summer Night	8
69	Track 604 029	Crosstown Traffic/Gypsy Eyes	10
69	Track 604 033	Let Me Light Your Fire/The Burning Of The Midnight Lamp	10
70	London HLZ 10321	Ballad Of Jimi/Gloomy Monday (with Curtis Knight)	8
70	London HL 7126	Ballad Of Jimi/Gloomy Monday (with Curtis Knight, export issue)	30
70	Track 2095 001	Voodoo Chile/Hey Joe/All Along The Watchtower (p/s; later copies have white border on sleeve; also sold without p/s)	12/8/6
71	RCA RCA 2033	No Such Animal (Parts 1 & 2) (initially in p/s, with Curtis Knight uncredited)	18/6
71	Track 2094 007	Angel/Night Bird Flying	7
71	Track 2094 010	Gypsy Eyes/Remember/Purple Haze/Stone Free (initially in p/s)	20/8
72	Polydor 2001 277	Johnny B. Goode/Little Wing	6
73	Reprise K 14286	Hear My Train A-Comin/Rock Me Baby	6
73	Polydor/Sound For Industry SFI 1572	Red House/Spanish Castle Magic (1-sided flexidisc with *Rolling Stone*)	15
80	Polydor 2608 001	6 SINGLES PACK (6 plain sleeve singles [2141 275-280], open-out card p/s)	20
82	CBS CBS A 2749	Fire/Are You Experienced? (p/s)	5
89	Castle Comms. HENPD 01	Hey Joe/Purple Haze/Radio One Theme (12", picture disc)	8
89	Polydor PO 33	Purple Haze/51st Anniversary (p/s, reissue)	5
89	Polydor PZCD 33	Purple Haze/51st Anniversary/All Along The Watchtower/Hey Joe (CD, card p/s)	8
90	Polydor PO 71	Crosstown Traffic/Voodoo Chile (p/s)	5
90	Polydor PO 100	All Along The Watchtower/Voodoo Chile/Hey Joe (p/s)	5
92	BMG 791 168	JIMI PLAYS BERKELEY (CD EP, available with "Jimi Plays Berkeley" video)	8

TRACK LPs

67	Track 612 001	ARE YOU EXPERIENCED (mono, some in laminated (front and back) sleeve. 2nd value for matt sleeve)	200/150
67	Track 612 003	AXIS: BOLD AS LOVE (laminated gatefold sleeve, some with gatefold insert (first value) , mono)	250/60
67	Track 613 003	AXIS: BOLD AS LOVE (laminated gatefold sleeve, some with gatefold insert, stereo)	100/50
68	Track 612 004/613 004	SMASH HITS (mono/stereo)	40/22
68	Track 612 008/009	ELECTRIC LADYLAND (2-LP, plain white non-gatefold sleeve, labels marked "Test Pressing", mono)	1,000+
68	Track 613 008/009	ELECTRIC LADYLAND (2-LP, laminated gatefold sleeve, stereo)	80
68	Track 613 010	ELECTRIC LADYLAND PART 1 (stereo only)	25
68	Track 613 017	ELECTRIC LADYLAND PART 2 (stereo only)	25
70	Track Super 2406 002	BAND OF GYPSYS (original 'puppet' sleeve)	100
70	Track Super 2406 002	BAND OF GYPSYS (repressing, gatefold 'Isle Of Wight' sleeve)	20
70	Track Super 2406 002	BAND OF GYPSYS (2nd repressing, single sleeve)	15
70	Track 2407 010	BACKTRACK 10: ARE YOU EXPERIENCED? (budget reissue, mono)	15
70	Track 2407 011	BACKTRACK 11: AXIS: BOLD AS LOVE (budget reissue, mono)	15
71	Track 2856 002	ELECTRIC JIMI HENDRIX (mail-order only Record Club release)	650
71	Track 2408 101	THE CRY OF LOVE (gatefold sleeve)	15
71	Track 2408 101	THE CRY OF LOVE (red vinyl, factory custom pressing, 3 copies only)	1,500+
88	Track/HMV C 881-16	ARE YOU EXPERIENCED (LP, box set, ltd. ed. of 2,500, no'd, with certificate)	30

POLYDOR LPs

71	Polydor 2302 016	ISLE OF WIGHT	15
71	Polydor 2302 018	HENDRIX IN THE WEST (gatefold sleeve)	15
72	Polydor 2302 020	WAR HEROES	15
72	Polydor 2302 023	THE CRY OF LOVE (gatefold sleeve, reissue)	12
73	Polydor 2302 268	SMASH HITS (stereo reissue)	12
73	Polydor 2480 005	BAND OF GYPSYS (reissue, different gatefold sleeve)	12
73	Polydor 2657 012	ELECTRIC LADYLAND (2-LP, laminated gatefold sleeve, reissue)	28
73	Polydor 2310 271	ELECTRIC LADYLAND PART 1 (reissue)	12
73	Polydor 2310 272	ELECTRIC LADYLAND PART 2 (reissue)	12
74	Polydor 2310 301	LOOSE ENDS	15
75	Polydor 2310 398	CRASH LANDING	12
75	Polydor 2310 415	MIDNIGHT LIGHTNING	12
78	Polydor 2612 034	THE ESSENTIAL JIMI HENDRIX (2-LP, with bonus 1-sided 33rpm 7" Gloria [JIMI 1] in special bag)	18
78	St. Michael 2102/0102	JIMI HENDRIX (cat. no. also listed as Polydor 2891 139)	60
78	St. Michael/Poly. 2891 139	JIMI HENDRIX (cassette)	25
80	Polydor 2625 040	JIMI HENDRIX (13-LP box set [11 x LP + 1 x 2-LP])	75
80	Polydor POLS 1023	NINE TO THE UNIVERSE	15
84	Polydor SPDLP 3	ELECTRIC LADYLAND (2-LP, non-laminate gatefold sleeve, 2nd reissue)	18
87	Polydor 833 004-1	LIVE AT WINTERLAND (2-LP, with poster)	18

MINT VALUE £

| 88 | Polydor/HMV C88 LP 1-16 | ARE YOU EXPERIENCED? (box set sold via HMV stores, 1,500 only) | 12 |
| 90 | Polydor 847 2311 | CORNERSTONES: JIMI HENDRIX 1967-1970 | 12 |

OTHER LPs

68	London HA/SH 8349	GET THAT FEELING (with Curtis Knight)	30
68	London HA/SH 8369	STRANGE THINGS (with Curtis Knight)	30
71	Ember NR 5057	EXPERIENCE — THE ORIGINAL SOUNDTRACK (gatefold sleeve)	15
71	Reprise K 40430	LIVE AT THE MONTEREY INTERNATIONAL POP FESTIVAL (shared with Otis Redding)	32
71	Reprise K 44159	RAINBOW BRIDGE (matt gatefold sleeve, 'steamboat' label, soundtrack)	15
72	Ember NR 5061	MORE EXPERIENCE (soundtrack)	15
73	Reprise K 64017	SOUNDTRACK RECORDINGS FROM THE FILM *JIMI HENDRIX* (2-LP)	15
73	Ember NR 5068	IN THE BEGINNING (textured gatefold sleeve)	15
74	Ember EMB 3428	LOOKING BACK WITH JIMI HENDRIX	15
75	DJM DJLMD 8011	FOR REAL (2-LP, gatefold sleeve)	18
89	Castle Comms. HBLP 100	LIVE AND UNRELEASED — THE RADIO SHOW (5-LP)	30

CDs

84	Track 821 993 2	BAND OF GYPSYS	18
88	Polydor/HMV C88 LP 1-11	ARE YOU EXPERIENCED? (box set via HMV stores, 1,500 only)	18
89	Castle Comms. HBCD 100	LIVE AND UNRELEASED — THE RADIO SHOW (3-CD, box set)	30
89	Polydor 831 312-2	HENDRIX IN THE WEST	18
89	Polydor 837 574-2	LOOSE ENDS	18

(see also Eire Apparent, Jayne Mansfield, McGough & McGear, Noel Redding Band, Fat Mattress, Curtis Knight, Billy Cox, Buddy Miles, Riot Squad)

MARGIE HENDRIX
| 66 | Mercury MF 976 | I Call You Lover But You Ain't Nothin' But A Tramp/The Question | 18 |
| 67 | Mercury MF 1001 | Restless/On The Right Track | 30 |

LARRY HENLEY
| 64 | Hickory 45-1272 | My Reasons For Living/Stickin' Up For My Baby | 12 |

(see also Newbeats, Dean & Mark)

CHRISTIE HENNESSY
| 73 | Westwood | CHRISTIE HENNESSY (LP) | 40 |

HENNESSYS
| 69 | Cambrian CLP 593 | THE ROADS AND THE MILES (LP) | 80 |
| 60s | Music Factory MF 106 | KARDIFF AFTER DARK (LP) | 80 |

ADRIAN HENRI
| 60s | Charivari | ADRIAN HENRI (LP) | 35 |
| 60s | Argo PLP 1194 | ADRIAN HENRI AND HUGO WILLIAMS (LP) | 30 |

(see also Liverpool Scene, McGough & McGear)

ANN HENRY
| 60 | Top Rank JAR 292 | Like Young/Sugar Blues | 10 |

BOB HENRY
| 65 | Philips BF 1450 | I Need Someone/Built Like A Man | 18 |

(see also Robert Henry)

CLARENCE ('FROGMAN') HENRY
57	London HLN 8389	Ain't Got No Home/Troubles Troubles (as Clarence Henry) (gold or silver lettering) (78 rpm = £60)	275/140
61	Pye International 7N 25078	(I Don't Know Why) But I Do/Just My Baby And Me	7
61	Pye International 7N 25089	You Always Hurt The One You Love/Little Suzy	7
61	Pye International 7N 25108	Lonely Street/Why Can't You	10
61	Pye International 7N 25115	On Bended Knees/Standing In The Need Of Love	10
62	Pye International 7N 25123	A Little Too Much/I Wish I Could Say The Same	10
62	Pye International 7N 25141	Dream Myself A Sweetheart/Lost Without You	10
62	Pye International 7N 25169	The Jealous Kind/Come On And Dance	10
64	London HLU 9936	Little Green Frog/Have You Ever Been Lonely?	10
66	London HLU 10025	Ain't Got No Home/Baby, Ain't That Love?	10
61	Pye Intl. NEP 44007	CLARENCE 'FROGMAN' HENRY HIT PARADE (EP)	55
61	Pye Intl. NPL 28017	YOU ALWAYS HURT THE ONE YOU LOVE (LP)	75

MILTON HENRY
| 76 | Cactus CT85 | Gypsy Woman/Dub | 20 |

RICHARD HENRY
| 68 | Regal Zonophone RZ 3014 | Oh Girl/Lay Your Head Upon My Shoulder | 6 |

ROBERT HENRY
| 66 | Philips BF 1476 | Walk Away Like A Winner/That's All I Want | 70 |

(see also Bob Henry)

HENRY COW
73	Virgin V 2005	THE LEGEND (LP)	22
74	Virgin V 2011	UNREST (LP)	20
75	Virgin V 2027	IN PRAISE OF LEARNING (LP)	20
76	Caroline CAD 3002	CONCERTS (LP)	20
79	Broadcast BC 1	WESTERN CULTURE (LP)	15

(see also Slapp Happy, Art Bears, Fred Frith, Gong/Henry Cow/Global Trucking Company)

HENRY ESSENCE
| 79 | Ellie Jay Records EJSP9392 | Margarita/14 Year Old Lover (500 only, p/s) | 100 |

HENRY & LIZA
| 73 | Dragon DRA 1004 | Hole Under Cratches/TIVOLIS: Hole Under Cratches (Instrumental) (actually "Hole Under Crutches") | 6 |

(see also Max Romeo)

HENRY III
67	Island WI 3078	Thank You Girl/Take Me Back	22
67	Island WI 3081	I'll Reach The End/Won't Go Away (B-side actually	
		"Lee's Special" by Don Tony Lee)	22
67	RCA RCA 1568	So Much Love/Sitting In The Park	20
70	Dynamic DYN 402	Out Of Time/VICEROYS: Love For Everyone (both with Hubcap & Wheels)	8

(see also Uniques)

JUDY HENSKE
66	Reprise RS 20485	Road To Nowhere/Sing A Rainbow	15
65	Reprise RS 6203	DEATH DEFYING (LP)	22

JUDY HENSKE & JERRY YESTER
69	Straight STS 1052	FAREWELL ALDEBARAN (LP)	30

ROBERT HENRY HENSLEY
68	Polydor 56295	You're Gonna See Me Cry/Montage	8

NICKY HENSON
63	Parlophone R 4976	Till I See You Cry/What Does It Mean?	18

DAVID HENTSCHEL
75	Ring O' 2017 101	Oh My My/Devil Woman	8

NAT HEPBURN
60s	Jump Up JU 516	River/Political Girl	6

HEP STARS
66	Decca F 22446	Sunny Girl/No Response	45
67	Olga OLE 001	Wedding/Consolation	25
68	Olga OLE 013	Let It Be Me/Groovy Summertime (withdrawn, supposedly reissued 1969)	45
68	Olga OLE 014	Malaika/It's Nice To Be Back (some in export p/s)	55/25

(see also Abba)

HEPTONES
66	Rio R 104	Gunmen Coming To Town/TOMMY McCOOK & SUPERSONICS:	
		Riverton City	50
67	Ska Beat JB 266	We've Got Love/I Am Lonely	70
67	Caltone TONE 105	Schoolgirls/Ain't That Bad?	35
67	Studio One SO 2005	A Change Is Gonna Come/Nobody Knows	25
67	Studio One SO 2014	Fat Girl/DELROY WILSON: Mother Word	20
67	Studio One SO 2021	If I Knew/Festival Day	40
67	Studio One SO 2026	Why Did You Leave?/GAYLADS: Don't Try To Reach Me	22
67	Studio One SO 2027	Why Must I?/SLIM SMITH: Try Again	22
67	Studio One SO 2031	Take Me (actually by The Soul Vendors)/DELROY WILSON: I'm Not A King	22
67	Studio One SO 2033	Only Sixteen/Baby	20
68	Studio One SO 2040	Tripe Girl/DELROY WILSON: Mr. D.J.	22
68	Studio One SO 2049	Cry, Baby, Cry/Mama	22
68	Studio One SO 2052	Dock Of The Bay/KING ROCKY (ELLIS): The Ruler	80+
68	Studio One SO 2055	Party Time/Oil In Your Lamp	22
68	Coxsone CS 7052	Love Won't Come Easy/Gee Wee	22
68	Coxsone CS 7068	Equal Rights/Ting-A-Ling	22
68	Coxsone CS 7082	Soul Power/Love Me Always	22
69	Coxsone CS 7092	Sweet Talking/Ob-La-Di	22
69	Studio One SO 2083	I Shall Be Released/Love Me Always	22
69	Bamboo BAM 11	I Shall Be Released/Love Me Always (Power) (reissue)	12
70	Bamboo BAM 28	Young, Gifted and Black/SOUND DIMENSION: Joyland	12
70	Bamboo BAM 39	Young Generation/You Turned Away	15
70	Bamboo BAM 43	Message From A Blackman/SOUND DIMENSION: Jamaica Underground	12
70	Upsetter US 339	Hurry Up/Thanks We Get	12
70	Banana BA 311	Be A Man/U ROY: Shock Attack	12
71	Banana BA 325	Suspicious Minds/Haven't You Any Fight Left?	10
71	Banana BA 349	Freedom Line/SOUND DIMENSION: Version	15
72	Green Door GD 4020	Hypocrite/JOHNNY LOVER: Straight To The Head	12
72	Prince Buster PB 37	Our Day Will Come/PRINCE BUSTER: Protection	12
72	Ashanti ASH 411	I'm In The Mood For Love/TOMMY McCOOK & NOW GENERATION:	
		Eight Years After	8
72	Duke DU 143	Save The Last Dance For Me/Be The One	6
72	Pama PM 843	You've Lost That Lovin' Feelin'/RUPIE EDWARDS ALLSTARS: Feeling Version	6
72	Pama Supreme PS 367	Save The Last Dance For Me/Save The Last Dance Version	6
72	Ackee ACK 407	I Miss You (Parts 1 & 2)	5
73	Ackee ACK 414	Let Me Hold Your Hand/Version	5
73	Jaguar JAG 103	Drifting Away/BONGO LES: Zion Drum	10
73	Grape GR 3053	Old Time/G.G. ALLSTARS: Dub	7
73	Smash SMA 2328	Soul Sister/IMPACT ALLSTARS: Soul Sister (Version)	7
74	Pama Supreme PS 390	Thanks We Get/Oppression (both actually by Delroy Butler)	10
75	Faith FA 012	Party Time/Version	5
67	Studio One SOL 9002	THE HEPTONES (LP)	100+
68	Studio One SOL 9010	ON TOP (LP)	100+
72	Trojan TBL 183	THE HEPTONES AND THEIR FRIENDS MEET THE NOW GENERATION (LP)	30
75	Island ILPS 9297	BOOK OF RULES (LP)	18
76	Island ILPS 9456	PARTY TIME (LP)	15

(see also Barry Llewellyn, Soul Vendors, Ronald & Lloyd, Ed Nangle, Love Generation, Alton Ellis, Basil Daley, Ken Boothe, Jackie Mittoo)

HERB & KAY
54	Parlophone MSP 6127	This Ole House/Angels In The Sky	30
54	Parlophone CMSP 23	This Ole House/Angels In The Sky (export issue)	30
55	Parlophone CMSP 31	Coffee Blues/Juke Box Jig (export issue)	30

HERBAL MIXTURE
66	Columbia DB 8021	A Love That's Died/Tailor Made	175
66	Columbia DB 8083	Machines/Please Leave My Mind	200

(see also Tony McPhee, Groundhogs)

HERBIE & ROYALISTS
68	Saga FID 2121	SOUL OF THE MATTER (LP)	25

HERBIE'S PEOPLE
65	CBS 202005	Sweet And Tender Romance/You Thrill Me To Pieces	20
66	CBS 202058	One Little Smile/You Never Know	12
67	CBS 202584	Residential Area/Humming Bird	12

HERD
65	Parlophone R 5284	Goodbye Baby, Goodbye/Here Comes The Fool	40
65	Parlophone R 5353	She Was Really Saying Something/It's Been A Long Time Baby	45
66	Parlophone R 5413	So Much In Love/This Boy's Always Been True	45
67	Fontana TF 819	I Can Fly/Diary Of A Narcissist	12
67	Fontana TF 856	From The Underworld/Sweet William	7
67	Fontana TF 887	Paradise Lost/Come On — Believe Me (some in p/s)	20/7
68	Fontana TF 925	I Don't Want Our Loving To Die/Our Fairy Tale	7
68	Fontana TF 975	Sunshine Cottage/Miss Jones	8
69	Fontana TF 1011	The Game/Beauty Queen	8
71	B&C CB 154	You've Got Me Hangin' From Your Lovin' Tree/I Don't Wanna Go To Sleep Again	6
72	Bumble GEX 1	From The Underworld/Paradise Lost/On My Way Home (maxi-single)	5
73	Bumble GE 120	I Don't Want Our Loving To Die/The Game	5
68	Fontana (S)TL 5458	PARADISE LOST (LP)	40
72	Bumble GEMP 5001	NOSTALGIA (LP)	22

(see also Peter Frampton, Humble Pie, Judas Jump, Andy Bown, Preachers)

HERE & NOW
78	Charly CYS 1055	End Of The Beginning/Choke A Koala (p/s)	5
79	Charly CEP 122	A Dog In Hell/Floating Anarchy Radio (p/s)	5
80	Charly NOW 1	Give And Take	5
78	Deptford Fun City DLP 02	WHAT YOU SEE … IS WHAT YOU ARE (LP, 1 side by Alternative TV)	12

(see also Daevid Allen)

HERESY
86	Earache	Thanks (flexidisc, mail-order, 2,000 only [400 each on different coloured vinyl])	8
89	In Your Face FACE 4	WHOSE GENERATION? EP (gatefold p/s)	8

HERESY/CONCRETE SOX
87	Manic Ears MOSH 2	HERESY/CONCRETE SOX (LP, 1 side each)	12

HERETIC
84	Thunderbolt THBE 1004	BURNT AT THE STAKE EP (Water Of Vice/Keep On Telling Those Lies/ Fever Of Love/Watch Me Grow (12", p/s)	28

HERITAGE
81	Rondelet ROUND 8	Strange Place To Be/Misunderstood (p/s)	20
82	Rondelet ABOUT 12	REMORSE CODE (LP, with lyric insert)	35
82	Plant Life PLR 040	LIVING BY THE AIR (LP)	15

HERMAN (Chin-Loy)
71	Big Shot BI 573	El Fishy/HERMAN'S ALLSTARS: Nightmare (B-side actually In The Spirit by Lloyd Charmers)	12
71	Big Shot BI 577	Tar Baby (actually Crazy Baby by U. Roy Jr.)/TOMMY McCOOK: Archie	7
71	Big Shot BI 578	New Love/AUGUSTUS PABLO: The Mood	20
71	Big Shot BI 579	East Of The River Nile Version/AUGUSTO PABLO: East Of The River Nile	25
71	Duke DU 107	To The Fields/HERMAN'S VERSION MEN: Fields Version	12
71	Ackee ACK 133	Dunce Cap/AQUARIANS: Version Cap	8
71	Ackee ACK 140	Youth Man/AQUARIANS: Version	8
71	Explosion EX 2049	Love Brother/Uganda	6
71	Escort ERT 854	Love Brother/Love Brother Version (B-side actually by Tommy McCook)	7
71	Punch PH 55	Hold The Ghost/AQUARIUS SOUL BAND: Duppy Dance	7
71	Punch PH 58	Listen To The Beat/AQUARIANS: Sounds Only	7

(see also Jimbilin)

PRIEST HERMAN
64	Blue Beat BB 266	We Are Praying/BUSTER'S ALLSTARS: Dallas, Texas	22

WOODY HERMAN
78s
52	London L 1156	Celestial Blues/Early Autumn	6
52	London L 1160	Blues In Advance/Terrista	6
53	London L 1222	Men From Mars/Beau Jazz	6
54	London HL 8013	Wooftie/Moten Stomp (as Woody Herman & New Third Herd)	6
54	London HL 8031	Fancy Woman/Eight Babies To Mind (as Woody Herman's Woodchoppers)	6
55	London HL 8122	Sorry 'bout The Whole Darned Thing/Love's A Dog (with New Third Herd)	6

SINGLES
54	London HL 8013	Wooftie/Moten Stomp (as Woody Herman & New Third Herd)	25
54	London HL 8031	Fancy Woman/Eight Babies To Mind (as Woody Herman's Woodchoppers)	25
54	Capitol CL 14183	Muskrat Ramble/Woodchopper's Mambo (Woody Herman & His Orchestra)	15
55	London HL 8122	Sorry 'Bout The Whole Darned Thing/Love's A Dog (with New Third Herd)	15
55	Capitol CL 14231	Mexican Hat Trick/Sleepy Serenade (as Woody Herman & His Orchestra)	8
55	Capitol CL 14278	My Sin Is You/Have it Your Way (with Allen Sisters)	8
55	Capitol CL 14299	Kiss The Baby/Long, Long Night (as Woody Herman & New Third Herd)	8
55	Capitol CL 14333	The Girl Upstairs/You're Here, My Love (as Woody Herman & His Orchestra)	8
55	Capitol CL 14366	Love Is A Many Splendoured Thing/House Of Bamboo (as Woody Herman & His Orchestra & Singers)	7
56	Capitol CL 14522	Skinned/Skinned Again (as Woody Herman & His Orchestra)	5

56	Capitol CL 14578	To Love Again/For All We Know (as Woody Herman & His Orchestra)........... 5
57	HMV POP 371	Comes Love/Makin' Whoopee 5
60	Top Rank TR 5012	Blowin' Up A Storm/It's Coolin' Time (as Woody Herman Orchestra)......... 6
60	Philips JAZ 113	The Third Herd/Keen And Peachy 5
62	Ember JBS 702	Woodchoppers' Ball/Body And Soul.. 8
66	CBS 202522	Sidewinder/Playgirl... 10
69	Chess CRS 8095	Hush/Light My Fire 15
52	Capitol LC 6560	CLASSICS IN JAZZ (10") 12
52	MGM MGM-D 108	AT CARNEGIE HALL VOLUME 1 (10") 12
53	MGM MGM-D 110	AT CARNEGIE HALL VOLUME 2 (10") 12
53	London H-APB 1014	STOMPING AT THE SAVOY (10", as Woody Herman & New Third Herd) 12
54	London H-APB 1018	MEN FROM MARS (10", as Woody Herman & New Third Herd)..................... 12
56	Philips BBL 7123	THREE HERDS 12
57	HMV CLP 1130	SONGS FOR HIP LOVERS 12

(see also David Rose Orchestra)

HERMAN'S HERMITS

64	Columbia DB 7338	I'm Into Something Good/Your Hand In Mine.................................... 6
64	Columbia DB 7408	Show Me Girl/I Know Why 6
65	Columbia DB 7475	Silhouettes/Can't You Hear My Heartbeat? 6
65	Columbia DB 7546	Wonderful World/Dream On.. 6
65	Columbia DB 7670	Just A Little Bit Better/Take Love, Give Love............................... 6
65	Columbia DB 7791	A Must To Avoid/The Man With The Cigar 6
66	Columbia DB 7861	You Won't Be Leaving/Listen People 6
66	Columbia DB 7947	This Door Swings Both Ways/For Love 7
66	Columbia DB 8012	No Milk Today/My Reservation's Been Confirmed 7
66	Columbia DB 8076	East-West/What Is Wrong, What Is Right? 6
67	Columbia DB 8123	There's A Kind Of Hush (All Over The World)/Gaslite Street 6
67	Columbia DB 8235	Museum/Moonshine Man 6
68	Columbia DB 8327	I Can Take Or Leave Your Loving/Marcel's.................................... 6
68	Columbia DB 8404	Sleepy Joe/Just One Girl 6
68	Columbia DB 8446	Sunshine Girl/Nobody Needs To Know 6
68	Columbia DB 8504	Something's Happening/The Most Beautiful Thing In My Life................... 6
69	Columbia DB 8563	My Sentimental Friend/My Lady 6
68	EMI SLES 15	No Milk Today/There's A Kind Of Hush (promo only, white label) 20
68	EMI SLES 16	London Look (promo only, white label) 20
69	Columbia DB 8626	Here Comes The Star/It's Alright Now 6
70	Columbia DB 8656	Years May Come, Years May Go/Smile Please.................................. 6
71	RCA RCA 2135	She's A Lady/Gold Mandala 6
72	RCA RCA 2265	The Man/Effen Curly 6
74	Buddah BDS 700	Train/Ride On The Water (withdrawn)....................................... 30+
65	Columbia SEG 8380	HERMANIA (EP)... 22
65	Columbia SEG 8440	MRS BROWN YOU'VE GOT A LOVELY DAUGHTER (EP) 20
65	Columbia SEG 8442	HERMAN'S HERMITS HITS (EP) 20
66	Columbia SEG 8477	A MUST TO AVOID (EP) 20
66	Columbia SEG 8503	MUSIC FROM THE SOUNDTRACK "HOLD ON" (EP) 22
67	Columbia SEG 8520	DANDY (EP).. 22
65	Columbia 33SX 1727	HERMAN'S HERMITS (LP) 30
65	Columbia S(C)X 6303	MRS BROWN YOU'VE GOT A LOVELY DAUGHTER (LP, soundtrack, mono or stereo, some with manuscript)................. 25/30
66	Columbia SX 6084	BOTH SIDES OF HERMAN'S HERMITS (LP) 30
67	Columbia S(C)X 6174	THERE'S A KIND OF HUSH ALL OVER THE WORLD (LP) 30
60s	Regal SREG 1117	HERMAN'S HERMITS (LP, export issue)..................................... 40
60s	Columbia SCXC 27	THE BEST OF HERMAN'S HERMITS (LP, export issue) 40
60s	Columbia SCXC 32	THE BEST OF HERMAN'S HERMITS VOL. 2 (LP, export issue) 40
60s	Columbia SCXC 34	THERE'S A KIND OF HUSH ALL OVER THE WORLD (LP, export issue)............ 40
60s	Columbia SCXC 35	BLAZE (LP, export issue) 40

(see also Peter Noone)

CORRINE HERMES

83	Polydor POSPE 597	Words Of Love/Si La Vie Est Cadeau (p/s)................................... 6

HEROES

75	United Artists UP 36016	Grown Up/Losing You... 7

(see also Motors)

TED HEROLD

60	Polydor NH 66817	I Don't Know Why/Moonlight 30

HERON

70	Dawn DNS 1015	Take Me Back Home/Minstrel And A King 10
71	Dawn DNX 2509	Bye And Bye/Through Time/Only A Hobo/I'm Ready To Leave (p/s).............. 10
71	Dawn DNLS 3010	HERON (LP, with insert) .... 100+
72	Dawn DNLS 3025	TWICE AS NICE AT HALF THE PRICE (2-LP, some with postcard) .... 40/100+

(see also Mike Cooper)

MIKE HERON('S REPUTATION)

71	Island WIP 6101	Call Me Diamond/Lady Wonder (p/s).. 5
75	Neighbourhood NBH 3109	Evie/Down On My Knees After Memphis (as Mike Heron's Reputation)........... 5
78	Zoom ZUM 5	Sold On Your Love/Portland Rose (p/s) 5
71	Island ILPS 9146	SMILING MEN WITH BAD REPUTATIONS (LP, gatefold sleeve) 15
75	Neighborhood 80637	MIKE HERON'S REPUTATION (LP) 12

(see also Incredible String Band)

BERNARD HERRMANN

69	Phase 4 Stereo PFS 4173	THE GREAT MOVIE THRILLERS (LP) 15
75	Phase 4 Stereo PFS 4309	THE FANTASY FILM WORLD OF BERNARD HERRMANN (LP) 12
76	Phase 4 Stereo PFS 4337	THE MYSTERIOUS FILM WORLD OF BERNARD HERRMANN (LP)....................... 12

HERRMAN & KLEINE
99	City Centre Offices BLOCK 5	TRANSALPIN EP (12", plain sleeve with inserts, 1050 only)	10

KRISTIN HERSH
93	4AD KH 2	Velvet Days (Demo)/Houdini Blues (demo) (promo only, no p/s)	7
94	4AD CADD 4002CD	HIPS & MAKERS (CD, digipak with postcards)	18

(see also Throwing Muses)

PAT HERVEY & TIARAS & ART SNIDER
67	President PT 110	Can't Get You Out Of My Mind/Givin' In	7

HERZFELD
93	Duophonic DS45 07	Two Mothers/Who The Scroungers Are (p/s, mail order only)	6

HESITATIONS
69	London HLR 10180	Born Free/Push A Little Bit Harder	30
68	London HLR 10198	The Impossible Dream (The Quest)/Nobody Knows You When You're Down And Out	8
68	London HA-R/SH-R 8360	THE NEW BORN FREE (LP)	30

CAROLYN HESTER
65	Dot DS 16750	Ain't That Rain?/Ten Thousand Candles	5
65	Dot DS 16751	Playboys And Playgirls/High Flyin' Bird	5
65	Dot DS 26750	Come On Back/Three Young Men	5
65	Dot DS 26751	What Does It Get You?/Now He's Gone	10
66	CBS 202409	A Reason To Believe/Early Morning Rain	5
65	Dot DLP 3604	THAT'S MY SONG (LP)	15
66	Dot DLP 3638	AT TOWN HALL (LP)	15
66	CBS (S)BPG 62033	CAROLYN HESTER (LP)	50
69	Pye Intl. NSPL 28121	THE CAROLYN HESTER COALITION (LP)	12
71	Ember CW 138	THURSDAY'S CHILD HAS FAR TO GO (LP)	12

HEWETT SISTERS
59	HMV POP 567	Baby-O/Jerri-Lee (I Love Him So) (78 rpm = £10)	25

BEN HEWITT
59	Mercury AMT 1041	You Break Me Up/I Ain't Givin' Up Nothin'	50
59	Mercury AMT 1055	For Quite A While/Patricia June	35
59	Mercury AMT 1084	I Want A New Girl Now/My Search	50
60	Mercury ZEP 10035	BREAK IT UP WITH BEN HEWITT (EP)	210

GARTH HEWITT
70s	Myrrh MYR 1051	LOVE SONGS FOR THE EARTH (LP)	25
70s	Myrrh MYR 1078	I'M GRATEFUL (LP)	25

PETE HEWSON
83	Reset RES 2	Take My Hand/Her (p/s)	40
83	Reset REST 2	Take My Hand/Her (12", p/s)	60

ANNE HEYWOOD
59	Top Rank JAR 130	I'd Rather Have Roses (Than Riches)/Love Is (78 rpm = £8)	6

EDDIE HEYWOOD
58	Mercury 7MT 131	Heywood's Bounce/Soft Summer Breeze	8
64	Stateside SS 264	Theme From The Film *The Prize*/Li'l Darlin'	6

(see also Hugo Winterhalter)

WINSTON HEYWOOD (& HOMBRES)
71	Dynamic DYN 424	Bam-Sa-Bo/Version	8
72	Dynamic DYN 441	Stop The War/Version	6
72	Dynamic DYN 457	Seek And You'll Find/Version	6
73	Attack ATT 8046	Da Doo Ron Ron/Version	6

(see also Winston Harewood, Fud Christian All Stars)

LENNIE HIBBERT & COUNT OSSIE BAND
69	Doctor Bird DB 1113	Pure Sole/PATSY: A Man Is Two Faced	22

(see also Sound Dimension)

AL HIBBLER
55	Brunswick 05420	Unchained Melody/Daybreak (gold or silver label)	30/20
55	Brunswick 05454	They Say You're Laughing At Me/I Can't Put My Arms Around A Memory	12
55	London HL 8184	Now I Lay Me Down To Dream/Danny Boy (78 rpm = £8)	35
55	Brunswick 05492	He/Breeze (Blow My Baby Back To Me)	10
56	Brunswick 05523	The Eleventh Hour Melody/Let's Try Again	10
56	Brunswick 05552	After The Lights Go Down Low/Stella By Starlight	10
55	HMV 7EG 8158	DUKE ELLINGTON AND AL HIBBLER (EP)	10
57	HMV 7EG 8326	AL HIBBLER SINGS LOVE SONGS (EP)	10
57	Brunswick OE 9331	HERE'S HIBBLER PT. 1 (EP)	12
57	Brunswick OE 9332	HERE'S HIBBLER PT. 2 (EP)	12
57	Brunswick OE 9333	HERE'S HIBBLER PT. 3 (EP)	12
56	Brunswick LAT 8140	STARRING AL HIBBLER (LP)	20

EDDIE HICKEY
59	Decca F 11153	Lady May/Cap And Gown	10
60	Decca F 11204	Who Could Be Bluer?/Plain Jane	10
60	Decca F 11241	Another Sleepless Night/Barbara	10

ERSEL HICKEY
59	Fontana H 198	You Threw A Dart/Don't Be Afraid Of Love (78 rpm = £20)	70

DWAYNE HICKMAN
60	Capitol CL 15164	I'm A Lover, Not A Fighter/I Pass Your House	10

HICKORY
69	CBS 3963	Green Light/Key	22

(see also Equals)

COLIN HICKS (& CABIN BOYS)
57   Pye 7N 15114   Wild Eyes And Tender Lips/Empty Arms Blues (with Cabin Boys)
                         (78 rpm = £12) 22
57   Pye 7N 15125   La Dee Dah/Wasteland (78 rpm = £12) 12
58   Pye 7N 15163   Little Boy Blue/Jambalaya (78 rpm = £25) 15

DAN HICKS & HIS HOT LICKS
72   Blue Thumb ILPS 9204   STRIKING IT RICH (LP) 18

JIMMY HICKS
72   London HLU 10396   I'm Mr. Big Stuff/Tell Her That I Love You 15

HIDDEN CAMERAS
04   Rough Trade RTRADST 117   PLAY THE CBC SESSIONS EP (10", 2,000 only) 12

HIDDEN IDENTITY
94   Pure RudenessHIDBBB1   Blunted Bumpkin Buskers (EP) 18

HIDDEN STRENGTH
76   United Artists UAS 29949   HIDDEN STRENGTH (LP) 15

HIDEAWAYS
69   Action ACT 4544   Hide Out/Jolly Joe 18
71   Jay Boy BOY 29   Hide Out/Jolly Joe (reissue) 6

HI-FI
84   Butt MGLS 003   Louie Louie/Summertime 8
     (see also Ian Matthews)

HI-FI FOUR
56   Parlophone MSP 6210   Band Of Gold/Davy, You Upset My Life (78 rpm, Parlophone R 4130 = £18) 160

HI FI'S
63   Piccadilly 7N 35130   Take Me Or Leave Me/I'm Struck 8
64   Pye 7N 15635   Will Yer Won't Yer/She's The One 8
64   Pye 7N 15710   I Keep Forgettin'/Why Can't I Stop Loving You? 35
65   Pye 7N 15788   Baby's In Black/Kiss And Run 15
66   Alp 595 010   It's Gonna Be Morning/I Wanna Hear You Say Yeah 50

HI-FI SEVEN
57   Nestles NR 17   Jazz In Piccadilly (There's A Tavern In The Town) (1-sided card flexi, 78rpm) 7
57   Nestles NR 19   Jazz In Piccadilly (Landlord Fill The Flowing Bowl) (1-sided card flexi, 78rpm) ... 7

ALEX 'HURRICANE' HIGGINS
82   Solid STOP 003   One-Four-Seven/Life's In The Pocket (p/s) 8

LIZZIE HIGGINS
75   Topic 12TS 260   UP AND AWA WI THE LAVEROCK (LP, gatefold sleeve) 12

JOE HIGGS
67   Coxsone CS 7004   Neighbour Neighbour/MELODIANS: I Should Have Made It Up .... 40+
67   Island WI 3026   I Am The Song/Worry No More 35
68   Island WI 3131   You Hurt My Soul/LYNN TAITT: Why Am I Treated So Bad? 30
70   Clandisc CLA 208   Mademoiselle/DYNAMITES: Lion 12
71   Big BG 312   Burning Fire/RUPIE EDWARDS ALL STARS: Version 6
71   New Beat NB 087   Mother Radio/DAWN SHARON: Little Deeds 6
71   Supreme SUP 215   Burning Fire/RUPIE EDWARDS ALL STARS: Push And Pull 6
72   Sioux SI 005   The World Is Spinning Around/THE REACTION: Hallelujah 6
72   Sioux SI 014   The Wave Of War/JUMBO STERLING: Shaft 6
72   Sioux SI 021   Lay A Foundation/JACKIE ROWLAND: Lay A Foundation (Version) ... 5
75   Grounation GROL 508   LIFE OF CONTRADICTION (LP) 20
     (see also Higgs & Wilson, Bob Marley/Wailers, Soul Vendors)

(Joe) HIGGS & (Roy) WILSON
60   Blue Beat (B)B 3   Manny Oh/When You Tell Me Baby (white label/blue writing [B3]
                         or blue label/silver writing [BB 3]) (with Ken Richards & His Comets) ..... each 20
61   Starlite ST45 035   Pretty Baby/I Long For The Day 20
61   Starlite ST45 036   Lover's Song/It Is A Day 20
61   Starlite ST45 042   Come On Home/The Robe 20
61   Starlite ST45 053   Sha Ba Ba/Change Of Mind 20
62   Blue Beat BB 95   How Can I Be Sure/Mighty Man 18
63   R&B JB 109   Let Me Know/Bye And Bye 15
63   Blue Beat BB 190   If You Want Pardon/BABA BROOKS BAND: Musical Communion ... 20
63   Island WI 081   Last Saturday Morning/Praise The Lord 18
64   Rio R 29   Love Is Not For Me/Gone Is Yesterday 15
65   Blue Beat BB 277   Pain In My Heart/BUSTER ALL STARS: Going West 25
70   Clandisc CLA 218   Don't Mind Me/GLEN AND ROY: Angel 8
     (see also Clancy Eccles)

HIGH
69   CBS 4164   Long Live The High/Beggar Man Dan 12

HIGH & MIGHTY
66   HMV POP 1548   Tryin' To Stop Cryin'/Escape From Cuba 30

HIGH BROOM
70   Island WI 6088   Dancing In The Moonlight/Percy's On The Run 15
73   Columbia DB 8969   Dancing In The Moonlight/Percy's On The Run (reissue) 7
     (see also Leviathan, Mike Stuart Span, Jason Crest, Holy Mackerel)

HIGH KEYS
63   London HLK 9768   Que Sera Sera/Daddy, Ooh Long Legs 40

HIGH LLAMAS
98	Alpaca Park/V2 no cat. no.	Blinger Suc/Sparkle Up, Sparkle Down (tour single, clear sleeve)	6

HIGH LEVEL RANTERS
68	Topic 12TS 186	NORTHUMBERLAND FOR EVER (LP, blue label, 2 different sleeves)	15
69	Leader/Trailer LER 2007	THE LADS OF NORTHUMBERLAND (LP)	15
70	Trailer LER 2020	KEEP YOUR FEET STILL GEORDIE HINNIE (LP)	12
71	Trailer LER 2030	HIGH LEVEL (LP)	12
75	Topic 2-12TS 271/2	THE BONNY PIT LADDIE (2-LP, blue label)	18
77	Broadside BRO 128	ENGLISH SPORTING BALLADS (LP, 1-side Martin Wyndham-Read, 2,000 only)	20
79	Topic 12TS 388	FOUR IN A BAR (LP)	12
69	Leader/Trailer LER 2007	THE LADS OF NORTHUMBERLAND (LP)	15

HIGHBURY MARCHERS
72	Columbia DB 8930	The Official Arsenal March/Arsenal Boogie	5

HIGHLY LIKELY
74	BBC RESL 10	Whatever Happened To You?/God Bless Everyone	15

(see also Mike Hugg, Rodney Bewes)

HIGH NUMBERS
64	Fontana TF 480	Zoot Suit/I'm The Face	450+
80	Back Door DOOR 4	I'm The Face/Zoot Suit (reissue, die cut sleeve)	20

(see also Who)

HIGH SOCIETY
66	Fontana TF 771	People Passing By/Star Of Eastern Street	22

(see also Friday Browne, Graham Gouldman, Country Gentlemen, Manchester Mob)

HIGH TIDE
69	Liberty LBS 83264	SEA SHANTIES (LP, gatefold sleeve)	65+
70	Liberty LBS 83294	HIGH TIDE (LP)	60+

(see also Misunderstood, Denny Gerrard, Magic Muscle, Third Ear Band)

HIGH TIDE
81	Sunday Morning (no cat. no.)	Baby Dancing/Letter From A Coward (mail-order only)	8

DEAN HIGHTOWER
60	HMV CLP 1360	TWANGY — WITH A BEAT (LP)	50

DONNA HIGHTOWER
59	Capitol CL 15048	Lover, Come Back To Me/Because Of You	7
59	Capitol CL 15049	Ain't That Love/Forgive Them	7
60	Capitol ST 1273	GEE BABY (LP)	25
68	Ember 2051	TAKE ONE (LP)	12

ROSETTA HIGHTOWER
68	Toast TT 506	Pretty Red Balloons/How Can You Mistreat (The One You Love)?	15
68	Toast TT 509	I Can't Give Back The Love I Feel For You/Big Bird	20
69	CBS 4584	One Heart For Sale/What Do I Do?	10
70	CBS 4758	April Fools/I'll Hold Out My Hand	6
70	CBS 4988	Persuader/Come Together	6
71	CBS 7068	Go Pray For Tomorrow/Give Me Just A Little More Line	6
73	Philips 6006 291	The Walls Fell Down/Captain's Army	6
71	CBS 64201	HIGHTOWER (LP)	30
71	Rediffusion ZS 88	ROSETTA HIGHTOWER (LP)	15

(see also Orlons, Ian Green [Revelation])

HIGH TREASON
80	Burlington BURLS 001	Saturday Night Special (no p/s)	30

HIGHWAY
74	EMI EMC 3019	HIGHWAY (LP)	15
75	EMI EMA 770	SMOKING AT THE EDGE (LP)	15

HIGHWAYMEN
61	HMV POP 948	The Gypsy Rover/Cotton Fields	6
62	United Artists UP 1001	Birdman (with narration from Burt Lancaster)/Cindy Oh Cindy	7

HIGH WINDOWS
68	CBS 3208	Maybe Someday/Your Eyes	6
68	CBS 3437	Anybody Need A Lover/El El Israel	8

HIGSONS
82	Two Tone 21 CHSTT	Tear The Whole Thing Down/Ylang Ylang (p/s, paper labels)	10
82	Two Tone 21 CHSTT	Tear The Whole Thing Down/Ylang Ylang (12", p/s)	12
83	Two Tone 24 CHSTT	Run Me Down/Put The Punk Back Into Funk (p/s, paper labels)	10
83	Two Tone 24 CHSTT	Run Me Down/Put The Punk Back Into Funk (12", p/s)	12
81	Waap 1 WAAP	Lost & The Lonely/It Goes Waap (p/s)	5
81	Waap 1 WAAPLP	ATTACK OF THE CANNIBAL ZOMBIE B MEN (LP)	15

HIJACK
88	Music Of Life NOTE016	Style Wars (12")	20
88	Music Of Life NOTE021	Hold No Hostage/Doomsday Of Rap (12")	20
89	Music Of Life NOTE016R	Style Wars Revenge (12")	15
89	Rhyme Syndicate 7599-26386	The Badman is Robbin'/Hold No Hostage/Doomsday (12" EP)	15
91	Syndicate 0 21751	Daddy Rich/Hijack The Terrorist Group (12")	15
91	Rhyme Syndicate 6555176	HORNS OF JERICHO (LP)	60

HILARY HILARY
80	Modern STP 2	How Come You're So Dumb/Rich Kid Blues (p/s)	60

(see also Roger Taylor, Queen)

RAY HILDEBRAND
70s	Myrrh MST 6508	SPECIAL KIND OF MAN (LP) 25

DIANE HILDEBRANDE
69	Elektra EKSN 45055	Jan's Blues/Early Morning Blues And Greens 10
69	Elektra EKL 4031	EARLY MORNING BLUES AND GREENS (LP) 20

HI LITES
65	London HL 9967	Hey Baby/Groovey 15

HI-LITERS
58	Mercury AMT 1011	Dance Me To Death/Cha Cha Rock (78 rpm = £85) 125

ALEX HILL
53	Vocalion V 1027	Stompin' 'Em Down/Track Head Blues (78) 18
(see also Paramount Allstars)		

BENNY HILL
55	Decca F 10442	I Can't Tell A Waltz From A Tango/Teach Me Tonight (78 rpm = £10) 15
56	Columbia SCM 5238	Memories Are Made Of This/Who Done It? (Benny Hill & Coronets) (78 = £10). . 15
61	Pye 7N 15327	Gather In The Mushrooms/Pepys' Diary 6
61	Pye 7N 15359	Transistor Radio/Gypsy Rock 6
62	Pye 7N 15520	Harvest Of Love/Fame 5
65	Pye 7N 15974	What A World/I'll Never Know 5
66	Pye 7N 17026	My Garden Of Love/The Andalucian Gypsies 5
92	EMI ERNPD 1	Ernie/Ting A Ling A Loo (shaped picture disc) 5
61	Pye NEP 24144	BENNY HILL PARADE VOL. 1 (EP) 12
65	Decca LK4723	BENNY AT THE BBC (LP) 20
66	Pye NPL 18133	SINGS? (LP). 15
(see also Coronets)		

BUNKER HILL & RAYMEN
62	Stateside SS 135	Hide & Go Seek Parts 1 & 2 20

CHIPPIE HILL/HOCIEL THOMAS
72	Collectors Edition 1001	CHIPPIE HILL AND HOCIEL THOMAS (LP). 12

DAVID HILL
57	Vogue V 9076	All Shook Up/Melody For Lovers (with Ray Ellis Orchestra) 200
57	Vogue V 9076	All Shook Up/Melody For Lovers (78, with Ray Ellis Orchestra) 70
58	RCA RCA 1041	That's Love/Keep Me In Mind (with Joe Relsman's Orchestra & Chorus) 175
58	RCA RCA 1041	That's Love/Keep Me In Mind (78, with Joe Relsman's Orchestra & Chorus) 75

JESSIE HILL
60	London HLU 9117	Ooh Poo Pah Doo Parts 1 & 2 25

VINCE HILL
62	Piccadilly 7N 35043	The Rivers Run Dry/Not Any More 6
62	Piccadilly 7N 35068	There You Go/Just As Long As (You Belong To Me). 6
63	Piccadilly 7N 35108	A Day At The Seaside/Tricks Of The Trade. 6
63	Piccadilly 7N 35118	As It Was Written/Is There Anyone At Home 6
63	Piccadilly 7N 35148	Blue Velvet/Like Anything 6
64	Piccadilly 7N 35161	If You Knew/Fools & Lovers. 6
64	Piccadilly 7N 35192	It's Only Make Believe/Let The Wind Blow 6
66	Columbia SEG 8509	FOUR SIDES OF VINCE HILL (EP). 12
66	Columbia S(C)X 6018	HAVE YOU MET? (LP) 12
66	Columbia S(C)X 6046	HEARTACHES (LP) 12
67	Columbia S(C)X 6096	AT THE CLUB (LP) 12
67	Columbia S(C)X 6141	EDELWEISS (LP). 12
68	Columbia S(C)X 6185	ALWAYS YOU AND ME (LP) 12
69	Columbia S(C)X 6304	YOU FORGOT TO REMEMBER (LP) 12
(see also [Jackie &] Raindrops, Elmer Bernstein)		

Z.Z. HILL
65	R&B MRB 5005	Someone To Love Me/Have Mercy Someone. 30
69	Action ACT 4532	Make Me Yours/What Am I Living For?. 75
71	Mojo 2092 019	Faithful And True/I Think I'd Do It 8
75	United Artists UP 35727	I Keep On Loving You/Whoever's Thrilling You. 8
77	CBS 5553	Love Is So Good When You're Stealin' It/Need You By My Side 8
66	Sue IEP 711	GIMME GIMME (EP, 2 tracks each by Z.Z. Hill & Intentions; some in p/s) . . . 300/100
69	Action ACLP 6004	WHOLE LOT OF SOUL (LP) 75
72	Mojo 2916 013	THE BRAND NEW Z.Z. HILL (LP) 30
75	Contempo CLP 515	THE BRAND NEW Z.Z. HILL (LP, reissue). 18
(see also Intentions)		

STEVE HILLAGE
76	Virgin VS 161	It's All Too Much/Shimmer 10
77	Virgin VS 171	Hurdy Gurdy Man/Om Nama Shivaya 5
77	Virgin VS 197	Not Fade Away/Saucer Surfing 5
77	Virgin VDJ 23	Leylines To Glassdome/GLEN PHILLIPS: Lies (p/s, gig freebie) 6
78	Virgin VS 212	Getting Better/Palm Trees (Love Guitar) (some in p/s) 8/5
78	Virgin VDJ 25	Getting Better/Palm Trees (Love Guitar) (12", p/s) 12
79	Virgin VS 313	Don't Dither, Do It/Getting In Tune (p/s) 6
82	Virgin VS 551	Alone (p/s) 6
82	Virgin VS 574	Kamikaze Eyes (p/s) 10
79	Virgin SIXPACK 2	SIX PACK/SIX TRACK (EP, picture disc, 5,000 only, die-cut p/s with stand) . . 8
78	Virgin V 2098	GREEN (LP, green vinyl, with insert). 12
79	Virgin VGD 3502	LIVE HERALD (2-LP). 12
83	Virgin V 2244	FOR TO NEXT (LP, with bonus instrumental LP And Not Or) 12
(see also Gong, Khan, Arzachel, Clearlight, Radio Actors, System 7)		

HILLER BROTHERS
60s	Honey Hit TB 124	Little Darlin'/Changin' My Mind (some with p/s). 10/6

JANE HILLERY
66	Columbia DB 7918	You've Got That Hold On Me/Take Me Away	40

(see also Magistrates)

MABLE HILLERY
69	Xtra XTRA 1063	IT'S SO HARD TO BE A NIGGER (LP)	30

GILLIAN HILLS
65	Vogue VRS 7005	Tomorrow Is Another Day/Look At Them	10

HILLTOPPERS
52	Vogue V 9045	Trying/You Made Up My Mind (featuring Jimmy Sacca) (78)	12
53	London L 1204	P.S. I Love You/I'd Rather Die Young (78)	20
54	London HL 8003	Love Walked In/To Be Alone (78)	25
54	London HL 8026	From The Vine Came The Grape/Time Will Tell (78 rpm = £18)	85
54	London HL 8070	Poor Butterfly/Wrapped Up In A Dream (78 rpm = £18)	85
54	London HL 8081	Will You Remember?/The Old Cabaret (78 rpm = £18)	75
54	London HL 8092	If I Didn't Care/Bettina (78 rpm = £18)	75
55	London HL 8116	Time Waits For No One/You Try Somebody Else (78 rpm = £18)	75
55	London HLD 8168	The Kentuckian Song/I Must Be Dreaming (78 rpm = £10)	55
55	London HLD 8208	Searching/All I Need Is You (78 rpm = £15)	55
56	London HLD 8221	Only You (And You Alone)/(It Will Have To Do) Until The Real Thing Comes Along (gold or silver label lettering)	30
56	London HLD 8255	My Treasure/Last Word In Love (78 rpm = £15)	50
56	London HLD 8278	Do The Bop/When You're Alone (78 rpm = £35)	120
56	London HLD 8298	Tryin'/D-A-R-L-I-N' (78 rpm = £10)	35
56	London HLD 8333	So Tired/Faded Rose (78 rpm = £8)	35
57	London HLD 8381	Marianne/You're Wasting Your Time	25
57	London HLD 8441	I'm Serious/I Love My Girl (78 rpm = £10)	25
57	London HLD 8455	A Fallen Star/Footsteps (78 rpm = £12)	25
57	London HLD 8528	The Joker/Chicken, Chicken (78 rpm = £12)	40
58	London HLD 8603	You Sure Look Good To Me/Starry Eyes (78 rpm = £20)	20
60	London HLD 9038	Alone/The Prisoner's Song	15

EPs
55	London RE-P 1012	PRESENTING THE HILLTOPPERS	40
55	London RE-D 1030	THE HILLTOPPERS VOL. 2	40
57	London RE-D 1099	THE HILLTOPPERS VOL. 3	40

LPs
57	London HA-D 2029	THE TOWERING HILLTOPPERS	50
57	London HA-D 2071	TOPS IN POPS	40

(see also Sacca, Billy Vaughn)

HI-LO'S
62	Reprise RS 20095	A Taste Of Honey/My Baby Just Cares For Me	1
57	London RE-U 1077	UNDER GLASS (EP)	15
58	London RE-R 1110	THE HI-LO'S (EP)	15
57	Philips BBE 12127	HERE ARE THE HI-LO'S (EP)	12
59	Philips BBE 12289	AND ALL THAT JAZZ (EP)	12
60	Philips BBE 12425	HERE ARE THE HI-LO'S (EP, also stereo SBBE 9035)	each 12
57	London HA-U 2026	UNDER GLASS (LP)	15
58	Philips BBL 7154	SUDDENLY IT'S THE HI-LO'S (LP)	15
59	Philips BBL 7288	AND ALL THAT JAZZ (LP)	15
60	Philips BBL 7411	ALL OVER THE PLACE (LP, also stereo SBBL 589)	each 15
60s	Omega XSD 11	IN STEREO (LP)	15

RONNIE HILTON
55	HMV 7M 285	Prize Of Gold/A Blossom Fell	20
55	HMV 7M 303	Just Say You Love Her/My Loving Hands	15
56	HMV 7M 336	Bella Notte/He	15
56	HMV 7M 358	Young And Foolish/Moments To Remember	15
56	HMV 7M 382	The Last Frontier/Here Comes My Love	15
56	HMV 7M 390	No Other Love/It's All Been Done Before (B-side with Alma Cogan)	15
56	HMV 7M 413	Who Are We/Give Me My Ranch	15
56	HMV POP 248	A Woman In Love/I Just Found Out About Love	15
56	HMV POP 274	Two Different Worlds/Constant And True	15
57	HMV POP 291	The Wisdom Of A Fool/Amore	15
57	HMV POP 307	For Your Love/Once	15
57	HMV POP 318	Heart/Penny Serenade	
57	HMV POP 338	Around The World/I'd Give You The World	
57	HMV POP 364	The Miracle Of Love/Wonderful! Wonderful!	
57	HMV POP 393	Marching Along To The Blues/She	
57	HMV POP 422	That's Why I Was Born/The Moonraker's Song	
58	HMV POP 437	I'll Buy You A Star/You Should Belong To Me	
58	HMV POP 446	Magic Moments/One Blade Of Grass (In A Meadow)	
58	HMV POP 468	I May Never Pass This Way Again/Love Walked In	
55	HMV 7EG 8121	THE STAR OF SONG (EP)	1
56	HMV 7EG 8149	HEY THERE (EP)	1
57	HMV 7EG 8198	FOR THOSE IN LOVE (EP)	1
57	HMV 7EG 8202	FOR THOSE IN LOVE NO. 2 (EP)	1
58	HMV 7EG 8352	THE HITS FROM 'MY FAIR LADY' (EP, 1 side by Alma Cogan)	1
55	HMV DLP 1109	BY THE FIRESIDE (10" LP)	2
59	HMV CLP 1295	I'M BEGINNING TO SEE THE LIGHT (LP)	2

(see also Alma Cogan)

HILTONAIRES
67	Coxsone CSL 8004	THE BEST OF THE HILTONAIRES (LP)	80

HIM & THE OTHERS
66	Parlophone R 5510	I Mean It/She's Got Eyes That Tell Lies	75

JUSTIN HINDS/HINES (& DOMINOES)
64	Ska Beat JB 176	King Samuel/River Jordan	25
65	Ska Beat JB 187	Mother Banner/DON DRUMMOND & HIS GROUP: Apanga	40
65	Island WI 171	Botheration/Satan (as Justin Hines & Dominoes)	25
65	Island WI 174	Jump Out Of The Frying Pan/Holy Dove (as Justin Hines & Dominoes)	25
65	Island WI 194	Rub Up, Push Up/The Ark	22
65	Island WI 232	Turn Them Back/TOMMY McCOOK: Rocket Ship	40
65	Island WI 236	Peace And Love/Skalarama (B-side actually by Lyn Taitt & Comets)	30
66	Doctor Bird DB 1048	The Higher The Monkey Climbs/Fight For Your Right	40
67	Island WI 3048	On A Saturday Night/Save A Bread	22
67	Treasure Isle TI 7002	Here I Stand/No Good Rudie	18
67	Treasure Isle TI 7005	Carry Go Bring Come/Fight Too Much	20
67	Treasure Isle TI 7014	On A Saturday Night/Save A Bread	18
67	Treasure Isle TI 7017	Once A Man/TOMMY McCOOK & SUPERSONICS: Persian Cat	18
68	Treasure Isle TI 7063	Botheration/VINCENT HINDS: Mouth Trombone	12
68	Treasure Isle TI 7068	Mighty Redeemer (Parts 1 & 2)	15
69	Trojan TR 652	You Should've Known Better/TOMMY McCOOK & SUPERSONICS: Third Figure	10
70	Duke Reid DR 2511	Say Me Say/I Want It	8
70	Duke DU 67	Drink Milk/Everywhere I Go (as Justin Hines & Dominoes)	8
72	Treasure Isle TI 7068	Mighty Redeemer/DUKE REID'S ALL STARS: Version	10
75	Pama PM 4001	Sinners Where You Going To Hide?/If It's Love You Need	7
76	Island ILPS 9416	JEZEBEL (LP)	30

(see also Lyn Taitt, Skatalites, Don Drummond)

NEVILLE HINDS
70	Duke Reid DR 2503	Sunday Gravy (as Neville Hines)/JOHN HOLT: Write Her A Letter	18
70	Camel CA 44	London Bridge/SCORCHERS: Things And Time (B-side act. by Wailing Souls)	12
70	Gas GAS 126	I Who Have Nothing/You Send Me	8
71	Explosion EX 2043	Delivered/Specially For You (B-side actually by Blake Boy)	6
72	Upsetter US 384	Blackman's Time/UPSETTERS: Version	10
73	Harry J HJ 6657	Musical Splendour/JOHN CROW GENERATION: Musical Drum & Bass	6

(see also Neville Irons & Byron Lee & The Dragonaires, Lloyd Robinson, Marvels, Alton Ellis)

RUPERT HINE
72	Purple PUR 105	Hamburgers/A Varlet Lad T'was Samuel Green (Historical Moments — Part 17)	6
76	Electric WOT 8	Snakes Don't Dance Fast/Hopi Smile	6
71	Purple TPSA 7502	PICK UP A BONE (LP, with David MacIver)	30
73	Purple TPSA 7509	UNFINISHED PICTURE (LP)	30

(see also Jon Pertwee)

EARL 'FATHA' HINES
51	Vogue V 304	Daniel/Get On Board, Little Children (78, as Prof. J. Earl Hines & His Goodwill Singers)	7
57	MGM MGM-EP 573	MIDNIGHT IN NEW ORLEANS (EP, as Earl Hines All Stars)	10
56	Vogue EPV 1144	QUINTET (EP)	10
54	Mercury MG 25018	EARL HINES AND HIS ALL STARS (10" LP)	15
55	Vogue Coral LRA 10031	FATS WALLER SONGS (10" LP)	15
55	Columbia 33S 1063	PIANO MOODS (10" LP)	15
56	HMV DLP 1132	GRAND TERRACE SWING (10" LP)	15
60	MGM MGM-C 833	EARL'S PEARLS (LP, as Earl 'Fatha' Hines Quartet)	15

(see also Louis Armstrong)

FRAZER HINES
68	Major Minor MM 579	Who's Dr. Who?/Punch And Judy Man	125

JUSTIN HINES
(see under Justin Hinds)

SONNY HINES
65	King KG 1009	Anytime, Any Day, Anywhere/Nothing Like Your Love	15

HINES & ELDRIDGE
69	Mercury SMWL 21041	HINES AND ELDRIDGE WITH COLEMAN HAWKINS VOLUME 2 (LP)	12

(see also Coleman Hawkins, Earl Hines, Roy Eldridge)

HINES, HINES & DAD
68	CBS 3667	Something Extra/Hambone	5

HINGE
68	RCA RCA 1721	Village Postman/You'd Better Go Home	10

JOE HINTON
64	Vocalion VP 9224	Funny How Time Slips Away/You Gotta Have Love	15
66	Vocalion VP 9258	Just A Kid Named Joe/Pledging My Love	15
66	Vocalion VA-P 8043	FUNNY HOW TIME SLIPS AWAY (LP)	100

HI-NUMBERS
65	Decca F 12233	Heart Of Stone/Dancing In The Street	50

HIPPIES
63	Cameo Parkway P 863	Memory Lane/REGGIE HARRISON: A Lonely Piano	20

HIPPY BOYS
69	Trojan TR 668	Love/The Whole Family	12
69	Trojan TR 669	Michael Row The Boat Ashore/Who Is Coming To Dinner	10
69	Bullet BU 412	Hog In A Me Minte/Lorna Run	25
69	Bullet BU 413	What's Your Excuse?/Tell Me Tell	10
69	Camel CA 29	Cat Nip/Cooyah (both as Hippie Boys)	15
69	High Note HS 021	Doctor No Go/Sailing (B-side actually Faberge by Baba Brooks & Band)	10
69	High Note HS 030	Chicken Lickin'/BABA BROOKS: Old Man Flint	10
69	High Note HS 035	Reggae Pressure/SOUL RHYTHMS: It Hurts (B-side actually Soul Rhythms)	15
69	Unity UN 528	Dreams To Remember/Peace Maker	12
70	High Note HS 038	Piccadilly Hop/Nigeria	10

70	Duke DU 92	Cloud Burst/LLOYD CHARMERS: Message From A Black Man	10
70	Explosion EX 2032	Vengeance/Look-Ea-Py-Py	30+
71	Big Shot 580	Voodoo/LITTLE ROY: Hard Fighter	10
69	Big Shot BSLP 5005	REGGAE WITH THE HIPPY BOYS (LP, actually on High Note label)	55+

(see also Upsetters, Family Man, Danny Williams, Tony, Hippy Boys, Cynthia Richards, Pioneers)

HIPSTER IMAGE
| 65 | Decca F 12137 | Can't Let Her Go/Make Her Mine | 350 |

HIRSCHE NICHT AUFS SOFA
| 86 | United Dairies UD 018 | MELCHIOR (LP, with Insert) | 30 |

AL HIRT
| 67 | RCA RCA 1590 | Theme From "The Monkees"/Tarzan March | 5 |

(see also Ann-Margret)

HIS NAME IS ALIVE
| 90 | 4AD HNIA 1 | How Ghosts Affect Relationships/If July (promo only, no p/s) | 6 |
| 93 | 4AD HNIA 2 | Extracts From "Mouth To Mouth": In Every Ford/Lip/Drink, Dress And Ink/ Can't Go Wrong Without You/The Dirt Eaters (CD, promo only) | 12 |

HI-SPOTS
| 58 | Melodisc 1457 | Lend Me Your Comb/I Don't Hurt Anymore | 22 |
| 58 | Melodisc 1473 | Secretly/I Got (78 rpm = £12) | 22 |

HISS
| 00s | Polydor 065778-7 | Triumph/Street Research (red vinyl, p/s, 750 only) | 5 |

ALFRED HITCHCOCK
| 58 | London HA-P 2130 | MUSIC TO BE MURDERED BY (LP, music by Jeff Alexander Orchestra, also stereo SH-P 6012) | 40/50 |

(see Jeff Alexander)

ROBYN HITCHCOCK (& THE EGYPTIANS)
81	Armageddon AS 008	The Man Who Invented Himself/Dancing On God's Thumb (p/s, some with flexidisc It's A Mystic Trip/Grooving On An Inner Plane [4 SPURT 1])	6/8
82	Albion ION 103	America/It Was The Night/How Do You Work This Thing? (p/s)	8
82	Albion FREEBIE 1	52 Stations/COSMOPOLITANS: How To Keep Your Husband Happy/ MOTOR BOYS MOTOR: Little Boy And Fat Man/dB's: Amplifier (flexidisc free with *Groovy Decay* LP [ALB 110] or at gigs)	6
82	Midnight Music DING 2	Eaten By Her Own Dinner/Listening To The Higsons/Dr. Sticky (p/s)	7
82	Midnight Music DONG 2	Eaten By Her Own Dinner/Grooving On An Inner Plane/Messages Of The Dark The Abandoned Brain/Happy The Golden Prince (12", p/s)	10
84	Midnight Music DONG 8	The Bells Of Rhymney/Falling Leaves/Winter Love/ The Bones In The Ground (12", p/s)	8
85	Midnight Music DONG 12	Heaven/Dwarfbeat/Some Body (12", p/s)	8
85	Midnight Music DONG 17	Brenda's Iron Sledge (live)/Only The Stones Remain/ The Pit Of Souls (Part I-IV) (12", p/s)	8
83	Albion 12 ION 1036	Nightride To Trinidad (Long Version)/Kingdom Of Love/Midnight Fish (12", p/s)	10
86	Glass Fish OOZE 1	If You Were A Priest/The Crawling (p/s)	5
84	Bucketfull/Brains BOB 8	Happy The Golden Prince (flexidisc free with *Bucketfull Of Brains* mag)	8/6
84	Bucketfull/Brains BOB 8	Happy The Golden Prince (hard vinyl white label test pressing, 20 only)	30
81	Armageddon ARM 4	BLACK SNAKE DIAMOND RôLE (LP)	12

(see also Soft Boys, Knox)

HI-TENSION
77	Island IPR 2007	Hi-Tension/Girl I Bet Cha (12")	8
79	Island WIP 6493	There's A Reason/If It Moves You	5
79	Island 12 WIP 6493	There's A Reason/If It Moves You (12")	10
78	Island ILPS 9564	HI-TENSION (LP, with poster)	15

HI-TONES
62	Island WI 029	Going Steady/Darlin' Elaine	20
63	Island WI 086	Ten Virgins (actually by Angelic Brothers)/Too Young To Love (actually by Larry Marshall)	20
63	R&B JB 123	You Hold The Key/DON DRUMMOND: Rock Away	38

HIT PACK
| 65 | Tamla Motown TMG 513 | Never Say No To Your Baby/Let's Dance (DJ copy = £175) | 125 |

HIT PARADE
84	JSH JSH 1	Forever/Stop (die-cut p/s)	8
84	JSH JSH 2	My Favourite Girl/It Rained On Monday Morning (die-cut p/s)	7
85	JSH JSH 3	The Sun Shines In Gerrards Cross/You Hurt Me Too (die-cut p/s)	6
85	JSH JSH 4	You Don't Love Me Then/Huevo's Mexicana (die-cut p/s with card)	6
86	JSH JSH 5	See You In Havana/Wipe Away The Tears (die-cut p/s)	5
87	JSH JSH 6	I Get So Sentimental/Sue (die-cut p/s)	5

HIT SQUAD
| 88 | Eastern Bloc EASTERN 01 | Wax On The Melt/SPM MC Tunes/Shure.4 (12", white label promo only, plain stickered sleeve) | 30 |

(see also 808 State)

HITTERS
| 73 | United Artists UP 35530 | Hypocrite/The Version | 2 |

(see also Brinsley Schwarz)

HOAX
80	Hologram HOAX 1	ONLY THE BLIND CAN SEE IN THE DARK (EP)	25
81	Hologram HOAX 3	SO WHAT (12" EP, p/s, blue vinyl)	15
82	Hologram HOAX 4	Quiet In The Sixpenny 5 (p/s)	10

HOBBIT
| 71 | Deroy | FIRST AND LAST (LP, private pressing) | 60 |

HOBBITS
68	Decca AD 1004	Daffodil Days (The Affection Song)/Sunny Day Girl (export issue)	20
68	MCA MU 1002	Daffodil Days (The Affection Song)/Sunny Day Girl	8
67	MCA MUP 301	DOWN TO MIDDLE EARTH (LP)	40

HOBBS
78	Big SOLD 4	Bop Around The Shop/(You've Got Me In A) Whirl Girl (gatefold p/s & insert)	6

HOBBY HORSE
72	Bell BELL 1248	Summertime, Summertime/Sweet And Low	10

(see also Mary Hopkin)

HOBBY SHOP
68	Columbia DB 8395	Why Must It Be This Way?/Talk To Me	8

LES HOBEAUX
57	HMV POP 377	Oh, Mary Don't You Weep/Toll The Bell Easy (78 rpm = £12)	25
57	HMV POP 403	Mama Don't Allow/Hey, Hey, Daddy Blues (78 rpm = £12)	20
58	HMV POP 444	Dynamo/Two Ships (78 rpm = £18)	25
57	HMV 7EG 8297	SOHO SKIFFLE (EP)	55

HOBOKEN
73	Oak	HOBOKEN (LP, 6 copies only)	300+

TREVOR HOCKEY
70s	Beau Brummie TET 120ST	Happy 'Cos I'm Blue/THE BLUES PLAYERS: Keep Right On To The End Of The Road (p/s)	40

EDMUND HOCKRIDGE
53	Parlophone MSP 6027	Luck Be A Lady/I'll Know	8
53	Parlophone MSP 6028	I've Never Been In Love Before/My Time Of Day	8

GLENN HODDLE ET AL.
80s	Lyntone LYN 11782	Mastermind Of Soccer (Parts 1 & 2) (coloured flexi, with *Match Weekly* magazine)	10/8
80s	Flexi Ltd	Mastermind Of Soccer (Parts 1-3) (coloured flexi, with Peter Withe & Alan Kennedy, with *Match Weekly* magazine)	10/8

CHRIS HODGE
72	Apple APPLE 43	We're On Our Way/Supersoul (initially in p/s)	30/10
74	RCA LPBO 5007	Beautiful Love/Sweet Lady From The Sky	6
74	DJM DJS 10337	I Love You/Old James Dean	5

MARVA HODGE
70	Polydor 56792	The Ghetto/Sometimes	8

CHARLES HODGES
69	Major Minor MM 654	Try A Little Love/Someone To Love	20

(see also Outlaws, Cliff Bennett's Rebellion)

EDDIE HODGES
61	London HLA 9369	I'm Gonna Knock On Your Door/Ain't Gonna Wash For A Week	12
62	London HLA 9505	Bandit Of My Dreams/Mugmates	15
62	London HLA 9576	(Girls, Girls, Girls) Made To Love/I Make Believe It's You	10
63	MGM MGM 1232	Just A Kid In Love/Avalanche	10
65	Stateside SS 442	New Orleans/Hard Times For Young Lovers	10
65	Stateside SS 469	Love Minus Zero — No Limit/The Water Is Over My Head	12
62	London REA 1353	EDDIE HODGES (EP)	75

(see also Hayley Mills & Eddie Hodges)

JOHNNY HODGES & HIS ORCHESTRA
54	Felsted 82004	Frisky/Far Away Blues (78)	7
52	Vogue LD 011	JOHNNY HODGES (10" LP)	15
56	Columbia/Clef C 9051	IN A TENDER MOOD (10"LP)	12

HOFFNER BROTHERS
72	Bullet BU 513	The King Man Is Back/SHALIMAR ALL STARS: Version	5
72	Green Door GD 4039	The King Man Is Back/SHALIMAR ALL STARS: Version (reissue)	5
73	Ackee ACK 521	Open Up The Gates/Version	5
73	Grape GR 3042	Let Me Dream (Parts 1 & 2)	5

ANNIE HOGAN
85	Doublevision DVR 9	PLAYS KICKABYE (12" EP)	15

(see also Marc Almond, Nick Cave, Soft Cell)

CLAIRE HOGAN
59	Top Rank JAR 161	Sing A Smiling Song/I Wonder (78 rpm = £10)	6

(see also Teresa Brewer)

SILAS HOGAN
71	Blue Horizon 2431 008	TROUBLE AT HOME (LP)	125
70s	Flyright FLY 595	I'M A FREE-HEARTED MAN (LP)	15

HOGARTH
68	Liberty LBF 15156	Suzie's Getting Married/I've Been Dreaming	15

SMOKEY HOGG
64	Realm RM 197	I'M SO LONELY (LP)	30
72	Ember EMB 3405	SINGS THE BLUES (LP)	25
70s	Specialty SNTF 5018	U BETTER WATCH THAT JIVE (LP)	15

(see also John Lee Hooker/Lightnin' Hopkins/Smokey Hogg)

HOGS
69	Jay Boy BOY 5	It's All Coming To Me Now/Motor Cycle Rider	6

SUZI JANE HOKUM
66	MGM MGM 1323	Need All The Help I Can Get/Home	18

HOKUM CLONES
03	Rough Trade FOR US FU 25	Breakin' From A Jailhouse Blues/You Ain't Foolin' Me (p/s, 1000 only) 5

HOKUS POKE
72	Vertigo 6360 064	EARTH HARMONY (LP) 150

RON HOLDEN
60	London HLU 9116	My Babe/Love You So. 70

MARK HOLDER & THE POSITIVES
73	Atlantic K10280	Whatever's Fair/Why Dear Lord. 25

RAM JOHN HOLDER
67	Columbia DB 8157	I Need Somebody/She's Alright. 12
67	Columbia DB 8262	My Friend Jones/It Won't Be Long Before I Love You 22
68	Beacon BEA 108	I Just Came To Get My Baby/Yes I Do 10
69	Upfront UPF 2	Goodwill To All Mankind/BLACK VELVET: Goodwill Sermon. 10
70	United Artists UP 35117	Where Do The Dreams Go?/Miracle Happens Every Day 6
63	Melodisc MLP 12-133	RAM BLUES GOSPEL AND SOUL (LP). 55
69	Beacon BEAS 2	BLACK LONDON BLUES (LP) 70
70	Beacon BEAS 17	BOOTLEG BLUES (LP) 50
	(see also Ram Jam Band, Ram Holder Brothers, Geno Washington)	

RAM HOLDER BROTHERS
66	Parlophone R 5471	Just Across The River/Ram Blues 25
	(see also Ram Jam Band, Ram John Holder)	

HOLE
91	City Slang EFA 04070-45/ SLANG 013	Teenage Whore/Drown Soda (p/s, lilac, clear or green vinyl, 500 of each). . . . . each 12
91	City Slang EFA 04070	Teenage Whore/Drown Soda (12") 8
91	City Slang EFA 04070 CD	Teenage Whore/Drown Soda (CD). 8
93	City Slang EFA 04916-45	Beautiful Son/Old Age/20 Years In The Dakota (purple vinyl) 8
93	City Slang EFA 04916-02	Beautiful Son/Old Age/20 Years In The Dakota (12", green vinyl) 12
94	City Slang EFA 04936-7	Miss World/Rock Star (Alternate Mix) (pink vinyl). 8
96	Mirromax 573 164-7	Gold Dust Woman/N.Y. LOOSE: Spit (gatefold p/s, 2 x 1-sided 7"s, with etched B-sides, 5,000 numbered) 8
91	City Slang SLANG 012	PRETTY ON THE INSIDE (LP, blue vinyl) 20
94	City Slang EFA 04935-1	LIVE THROUGH THIS (LP, 3000 on white vinyl) 25/12

BILLIE HOLIDAY
56	Vogue V 2408	Detour Ahead/Blue, Turning Grey Over You (78 rpm = £8). 22
59	MGM MGM 1033	Don't Worry About Me/Just One More Chance 10
55	Brunswick OE 9172	LADY DAY VOL. 1 (EP) 12
55	Columbia Clef SEB 10009	BILLIE HOLIDAY SINGS (EP) 10
55	Vogue EPV 1128	BILLIE HOLIDAY (EP) 15
56	Brunswick OE 9199	LADY DAY VOL. 2 (EP) 10
56	Brunswick OE 9251	LADY DAY VOL. 3 (EP) 10
56	Columbia Clef SEB 10035	AN EVENING WITH BILLIE HOLIDAY (EP) 10
56	Columbia Clef SEB 10048	BILLIE HOLIDAY SINGS (EP) 10
59	Fontana TFE 17010	LADY DAY (EP) 10
59	HMV 7EG 8627	SAY IT ISN'T SO (EP) 10
60	MGM MGM-EP 715	BILLIE HOLIDAY (EP) 10
50s	Melodisc EPM7 125	EMBRACEABLE YOU (EP) 15
60	Fontana TFE 17026	BLUE (EP) 10
60	Fontana TFE 17214	FABULOUS (EP) 8
60	Philips BBE 12359	JAZZ GALLERY (EP). 8
54	Columbia 33S 1034	BILLIE HOLIDAY (10" LP) 50
54	Brunswick LA 8676	LOVER MAN (10" LP) 50
55	Philips BBR 8032	FAVOURITES (10" LP). 40
56	Columbia Clef 33C 9023	AT JAZZ AT THE PHILHARMONIC (10" LP) 15
56	Columbia Clef 33CX 10019	MUSIC FOR TORCHING (LP) 15
57	Columbia Clef 33CX 10064	VELVET MOOD (LP) 15
57	Columbia Clef 33CX 10076	SOLITUDE (LP) 15
57	Columbia Clef 33CX 10092	LADY SINGS THE BLUES (LP). 15
59	Columbia Clef 33CX 10145	SONGS FOR DISTINGUÉ LOVERS (LP) 15
59	MGM MGM-C 792	BILLIE HOLIDAY (LP) 15
59	Fontana TFL 5032	LADY IN SATIN (LP) 15
60	Fontana TFL 5106	A BILLIE HOLIDAY MEMORIAL (LP) 15
61	HMV CLP 1414	THE UNFORGETTABLE LADY DAY (LP). 15
62	Stateside SL 10007	BILLIE HOLIDAY (LP) 20
65	Fontana TL 5262	ONCE UPON A TIME (LP, with Teddy Wilson) 15
66	Fontana TL 5287	BILLIE HOLIDAY (LP) 15
66	Island ILP 929	LAST LIVE RECORDING (LP). 60

CHICO HOLIDAY
59	RCA RCA 1117	Young Ideas/Cuckoo Girl (78 rpm = £12) 35
61	Coral Q 72443	God, Country And My Baby/Fools (withdrawn) 22
59	RCA RCX 171	CHICO HOLIDAY (EP) 65

JIMMY HOLIDAY
63	Vocalion POP V 9206	How Can I Forget/Janet 30
64	London HLY 9868	I Lied/Alison. 22
66	Liberty LIB 12040	Baby I Love You/You Won't Get Away 20
67	Liberty LIB 12048	Give Me Your Love/The Turning Point 20
67	Liberty LIB 12053	Everybody Needs Help/I'm Gonna Move To The City 20
68	Minit MLF 11008	Give Me Your Love/The Beauty Of A Girl In Love 15
69	Minit MLL/MLS 40010	SPREAD YOUR LOVE (LP). 60

JIMMY HOLIDAY & CLYDIE KING
67	Liberty LIB 12058	Ready, Willing And Able/We Got A Good Thing Goin' (DJ copy = £100)	50
72	United Artists UP 35371	Ready, Willing And Able/JIMMY HOLIDAY: Give Me Your Love	15
	(see also Clydie King)		

JOHNNY HOLIDAY
59	London RE 1226	SENTIMENTAL HOLIDAY (EP)	10
59	London RE 1227	HOLIDAY FOR ROMANCE (EP)	10

HOLIDAYMAKERS
89	Woosh WOOSH 4	Cincinnati/Seventh Valley Girl (p/s)	10
89	Maker 00IT	Gay Cowboy (12", p/s)	8

HOLIDAYS
66	Polydor 56720	I'll Love You Forever/Makin' Up Time	125
	(see also Edwin Starr)		

HOLLAND
84	Ebony EBON 17	EARLY WARNING (LP)	12

BRIAN HOLLAND
74	Invictus INV 2553	I'm So Glad/I'm So Glad (Version)	8

EDDIE HOLLAND
62	Fontana H 387	Jamie/Take A Chance On Me	350
63	Oriole CBA 1808	If It's Love (It's All Right)/It's Not Too Late	500

LYNN HOLLAND
64	Ember EMB S 198	And The Angels Sing/I Can't Read Your Writing (For My Tears) (some in p/s)	12/6
65	Polydor BM 56035	Oh Darling How I Miss You/Before	6
67	Polydor 56166	One Man In My Life/Wand'rin Boy (unissued)	
67	Polydor 56187	Come And Love/May God Help You And Protect You (unissued)	
67	Polydor 236217	OH DARLING HOW I MISS YOU (LP)	25
	(see also Holly)		

TONY HOLLAND
63	HMV POP 1135	Sidewalk/Time Goes By	45

(Brian) HOLLAND & (Lamont) DOZIER
72	Invictus INV 525	Why Can't We Be Lovers/Don't Leave Me	10
73	Invictus INV 528	Don't Leave Me Starvin' For Your Love (Parts 1 & 2)	68
	(see also Lamont Dozier, Brian Holland)		

MICHAEL HOLLIDAY
56	Columbia SCM 5221	Sixteen Tons/The Rose Tattoo	22
56	Columbia SCM 5252	Nothin' To Do/Perfume, Candy And Flowers	20
56	Columbia SCM 5273	Hot Diggity (Dog Ziggity)/The Gal With The Yaller Shoes	20
56	Columbia DB 3813	The Runaway Train/Ten Thousand Miles	20
57	Columbia DB 3871	Yaller Yaller Gold/I Saw Esau	15
57	Columbia DB 3919	Love Is Strange/My House Is Your House	15
57	Columbia DB 3948	Four Walls/Wringle Wrangle	15
57	Columbia DB 3973	All Of You/It's The Good Things We Remember	15
57	Columbia DB 3992	Old Cape Cod/Love You Darlin'	12
58	Columbia DB 4058	The Story Of My Life/Keep Your Heart	7
58	Columbia DB 4087	In Love/Rooney	5
58	Columbia DB 4121	Stairway Of Love/May I?	5
58	Columbia DB 4155	I'll Always Be In Love With You/I'll Be Lovin' You, Too	5
58	Columbia DB 4188	She Was Only Seventeen/The Gay Vagabond	5
58	Columbia DB 4216	My Heart Is An Open Book/Careless Hands	5
59	Columbia DB 4255	Palace Of Love/The Girls Of County Armagh	5
59	Columbia DB 4307	Moments Of Love/Dearest	5
59	Columbia DB 4336	For You, For You/Life Is A Circus (78 rpm = £12)	5

EPs
56	Columbia SEG 7638	MY GUITAR AND ME	10
57	Columbia SEG 7683	MUSIC WITH MIKE	10
58	Columbia SEG 7752	RELAX WITH MIKE	10
58	Columbia SEG 7761	ALL TIME FAVOURITES	10
58	Columbia SEG 7818	MELODY MIKE	10
59	Columbia SEG 7836	SENTIMENTAL JOURNEY (with Edna Savage)	10
59	Columbia SEG 7892	MIKE AND THE OTHER FELLA	10
59	Columbia SEG 7972	MIKE NO. 1 (also stereo ESG 7784)	12
60	Columbia SEG 7986	FOUR FEATHER FALLS (also stereo ESG 7793)	20/30
60	Columbia SEG 7996	MIKE NO. 2 (also stereo ESG 7803)	12
61	Columbia SEG 8074	MIKE NO. 3 (also stereo ESG 7842)	12
61	Columbia SEG 8101	MIKE SINGS RAGTIME (also stereo ESG 7856)	12
61	Columbia SEG 8115	MIKE IN A SENTIMENTAL MOOD (also stereo ESG 7864)	12
62	Columbia SEG 8161	HAPPY HOLLIDAY	12
62	Columbia SEG 8186	MORE HAPPY HOLLIDAY	12
61	Columbia SEG 8242	MIKE SINGS COUNTRY AND WESTERN STYLE	18
64	Columbia SEG 8373	MEMORIES OF MIKE	18

LPs
58	Columbia 33S 1114	HI! (10")	25
59	Columbia 33SX 1170	MIKE	18
60	Columbia 33SX 1262	HOLLIDAY MIXTURE (also stereo SCX 3331)	15
61	Columbia 33SX 1354	HAPPY HOLLIDAY (also stereo SCX 3398)	15
62	Columbia 33SX 1426	TO BING FROM MIKE (also stereo SCX 3441)	15
64	Columbia 33SX 1586	THE BEST OF MICHAEL HOLLIDAY	15
	(see also Edna Savage)		

MINT VALUE £

SU(SAN) HOLLIDAY

64	Columbia DB 7363	Dark Despair/The Other Side (demos list A-side as Street Of] Dark Despair)	15
64	Columbia DB 7403	Any Day Now/Don't Come Knocking At My Door	15
65	Columbia DB 7616	Sometimes/Long Haired Boy	15
65	Columbia DB 7709	Nevertheless (I'm In Love With You)/Moonglow	15
66	Columbia SX 6067	I WANNA SAY HELLO (LP, as Su Holliday)	110

(see also Susan Singer)

TIM HOLLIER

70	Fontana TF 1080	In This Room/Love Song	6
71	Philips 6006 130	Circle Is Small/In A Corner Of My Life/Time Stood Still	6
68	United Artists (S)ULP 1211	MESSAGE TO A HARLEQUIN (LP)	50
70	Fontana 6309 003	TIM HOLLIER (LP)	120
71	Philips 6308 044	SKY SAIL (LP)	30

(see also Amory Kane)

HOLLIES

SINGLES

63	Parlophone R 5030	(Ain't That) Just Like Me/Hey, What's Wrong With Me	22
63	Parlophone R 5052	Searchin'/Whole World Over	15
63	Parlophone R 5077	Stay/Now's The Time	12
64	Parlophone R 5104	Just One Look/Keep Off That Friend Of Mine	7
64	Parlophone R 5137	Here I Go Again/Baby That's All	7
64	Parlophone R 5178	We're Through/Come On Back	6
65	Parlophone R 5232	Yes I Will/Nobody	6
65	Parlophone R 5287	I'm Alive/You Know He Did	6
65	Parlophone R 5322	Look Through Any Window/So Lonely	7
65	Parlophone R 5392	If I Needed Someone/I've Got A Way Of My Own	8
66	Parlophone R 5409	I Can't Let Go/Running Through The Night	6
66	Parlophone R 5469	Bus Stop/Don't Run And Hide	6
66	United Artists UP 1152	After The Fox (with Peter Sellers)/BURT BACHARACH: The Fox-Trot	35
66	Parlophone R 5508	Stop! Stop! Stop!/It's You	6
67	Parlophone R 5562	On A Carousel/All The World Is Love	6
67	Parlophone R 5602	Carrie Anne/Signs That Will Never Change	6
67	Parlophone R 5637	King Midas In Reverse/Everything Is Sunshine	10
68	Parlophone R 5680	Jennifer Eccles/Open Up Your Eyes	6
68	Parlophone R 5733	Listen To Me/Do The Best You Can	7
69	Parlophone R 5765	Sorry Suzanne/Not That Way At All	7
69	Parlophone R 5806	He Ain't Heavy, He's My Brother/'Cos You Like To Love Me	7
70	Parlophone R 5837	I Can't Tell The Bottom From The Top/Mad Professor Blyth	5
70	Parlophone R 5862	Gasoline Alley Bred/Dandelion Wine	6
71	Parlophone R 5905	Hey Willy/Row The Boat Together	7
72	Parlophone R 5939	The Baby/Oh Granny	7
72	Polydor 2058 199	Long Cool Woman (In A Black Dress)/Cable Car	6
72	Polydor 2058 289	Magic Woman Touch/Indian Girl	6
73	Polydor 2058 403	The Day That Curly Billy Shot Down Crazy Sam McGee/Born A Man	6
74	Polydor 2058 435	The Air That I Breathe/No More Riders	5
74	Polydor 2058 476	Son Of A Rotten Gambler/Layin' To The Music	6
74	Polydor 2058 533	I'm Down/Hello Lady Goodbye	6
75	Polydor 2058 595	Sandy (Fourth Of July, Asbury Park)/Second-Hand Hangups	6
75	EMI EMI 2353	Long Cool Woman In A Black Dress/Carrie Anne	6
76	Polydor 2058 694	Boulder To Birmingham/Crocodile Woman (She Bites)	6
76	Polydor 2058 719	Star/Love Is The Thing	6
76	Polydor 2058 779	Daddy Don't Mind/C'mon	6
76	Polydor 2058 799	Wiggle That Wotsit/Corrine	6
76	Polydor 2058 880	Hello To Romance/48 Hour Parole	6
77	Polydor 2058 906	Amnesty/Crossfire	6
78	EMI EMI 2813	Look Through Any Window/I'm Alive/Just One Look (p/s)	6
79	Polydor POSP 35	Something To Live For/Song Of The Sun	6
79	Polydor POSPX 35	Something To Live For/Song Of The Sun/The Air That I Breathe (12", p/s)	12
80	Polydor 2059 246	Soldier's Song/Draggin' My Heels	10
80	Polydor POSP 175	Heartbeat/Take Your Time	8
81	EMI EMI 5229	Holliedaze (A Medley)/Holliepops (Medley)	5
81	Polydor POSP 379	Take My Love And Run/Driver	5
82	Parlophome PMS 1001	He Ain't Heavy, He's My Brother/'Cos You Like To Love Me (p/s)	5
83	WEA U 9888	Stop! In The Name Of Love/Musical Pictures (p/s)	5
84	EMI G45 11	Just One Look/Here I Go Again (p/s)	5
84	Columbia DB 9110	Too Many Hearts Get Broken/You're All Woman (p/s)	5
87	Columbia DB 9146	This Is It/You Gave Me Strength (p/s)	5
87	Columbia 12DB 9146	This Is It/You Gave Me Strength/You're All Woman (12", p/s)	8
87	Columbia DB 9151	Reunion Of The Heart/Too Many Hearts Get Broken (p/s)	5
88	EMI CDEM 74	He Ain't Heavy, He's My Brother/Carrie/The Air That I Breathe/Yes I Will (CD)	8
88	EMI CDEM 80	The Air That I Breathe/We're Through/King Midas In Reverse/He Ain't Heavy, He's My Brother (CD)	8
90	SRT 90LS 2407	Purple Rain/Naomi/Two Shadows (12", p/s, available only at gigs)	8

EPs

64	Parlophone GEP 8909	THE HOLLIES	40
64	Parlophone GEP 8911	JUST ONE LOOK	45
64	Parlophone GEP 8915	HERE I GO AGAIN	45
64	Parlophone GEP 8927	WE'RE THROUGH	45
65	Parlophone GEP 8934	IN THE HOLLIES STYLE	50
65	Parlophone GEP 8942	I'M ALIVE	45
66	Parlophone GEP 8951	I CAN'T LET GO	55

LPs

64	Parlophone PMC 1220	STAY WITH THE HOLLIES (also stereo PCS 3054)	50/60
65	Parlophone PMC 1235	IN THE HOLLIES STYLE	50
65	Parlophone PMC 1261	THE HOLLIES	35
66	Parlophone PMC/PCS 7008	WOULD YOU BELIEVE? (mono/stereo)	30/45
66	Parlophone PMC/PCS 7011	FOR CERTAIN BECAUSE (gatefold sleeve, mono/stereo)	30/45
67	Parlophone PMC/PCS 7022	EVOLUTION (mono/stereo)	45/60
67	Parlophone PMC/PCS 7039	BUTTERFLY (mono/stereo)	40/50
67	Parlophone TA-PMC 7039	BUTTERFLY (reel-to-reel tape, mono)	15
67	EMI Regal SREG 2024	THE HOLLIES (export compilation)	38
67	World Records ST 979	THE VINTAGE HOLLIES (stereo reissue of "In The Hollies Style")	35
68	World Records ST 1035	STAY WITH THE HOLLIES (record club reissue)	30
68	Parlophone PMC/PCS 7057	THE HOLLIES' GREATEST	15
68	Parlophone TA-PMC 7057	THE HOLLIES' GREATEST (reel-to-reel tape, mono)	12
69	Parlophone PMC/PCS 7078	THE HOLLIES SING DYLAN (mono/stereo)	30/22
69	Parlophone PCS 7092	HOLLIES SING HOLLIES (gatefold sleeve)	20

(The above Parlophone LPs were originally issued with yellow/black labels; 1970s pressings with silver & black labels are worth £10 each.)

70	Parlophone PCS 7116	CONFESSIONS OF THE MIND (with colour insert)	20
71	Parlophone PAS 10005	DISTANT LIGHT (gatefold sleeve)	20
71	Regal Starline SRS 5013	STOP! STOP! STOP! (reissue of "For Certain Because")	12
71	MFP MFP 5252	THE HOLLIES (budget reissue of "Evolution")	12
72	Parlophone PCS 7148	THE HOLLIES' GREATEST HITS VOL. 2	12
72	Polydor 2383 144	ROMANY (gatefold sleeve)	20
74	Polydor 2383 262	HOLLIES (with lyric insert)	15
75	Polydor 2442 128	ANOTHER NIGHT (gatefold sleeve)	15
76	Polydor 2442 141	WRITE ON (with lyric inner)	15
76	Polydor 2383 421	RUSSIAN ROULETTE (with lyric inner)	15
78	Polydor 2383 474	A CRAZY STEAL (with lyric inner)	12
78	Parlophone PMC 7174	THE BEST OF THE HOLLIES' EPs	12
78	Parlophone PMC 7176	THE OTHER SIDE OF THE HOLLIES	18
79	Polydor 2442 160	FIVE THREE ONE — DOUBLE SEVEN O FOUR (with lyric insert)	12
79	St. Michael 2102/0101	UP FRONT (sold through Marks & Spencer in conjunction with Polydor)	45
79	St. Michael 2102/0101	UP FRONT (cassette, via Marks & Spencer/Polydor)	20
80	Polydor POLTV 12	BUDDY HOLLY (with lyric insert)	15
83	WEA 2501391	WHAT GOES AROUND	12
94	Fast Forward FFCD 822	LEGENDARY TOP TENS 1963 — 1988 (CD, sold via Avon Cosmetics)	25

(see also Allan Clarke, Graham Nash, Terry Sylvester, Haydock's Rockhouse, Peter Sellers & Sophia Loren)

BRENDA HOLLOWAY

64	Stateside SS 307	Every Little Bit Hurts/Land Of A Thousand Boys	50
65	Tamla Motown TMG 508	When I'm Gone/I've Been Good To You (DJ copy = £200)	100
65	Tamla Motown TMG 519	Operator/I'll Be Available (DJ copy = £150)	75
66	Tamla Motown TMG 556	Together Till The End Of Time/Sad Song (DJ copy = £150)	100
66	Tamla Motown TMG 581	Hurt A Little Everyday/Where Were You (demos credit Brenda Holiday) (DJ = £100)	50
67	Tamla Motown TMG 608	Just Look What You've Done/Starting The Hurt All Over Again (DJ copy = £100)	30
67	Tamla Motown TMG 622	You've Made Me So Very Happy/I've Got To Find It	25
69	Tamla Motown TMG 700	Just Look What You've Done/You've Made Me So Very Happy	15
68	T. Motown (S)TML 11083	THE ARTISTRY OF BRENDA HOLLOWAY (LP)	150

LOLEATTA HOLLOWAY

71	United Artists UP 35273	Bring It On Up/Rainbow '71'	8

PATRICE HOLLOWAY

66	Capitol CL 15484	Love And Desire/Ecstasy (DJ Copy = £250)	150

STANLEY HOLLOWAY

59	Philips BBE 12326	MY WORD YOU DO LOOK QUEER (EP)	8
59	Pye NEP 24097	NO TREES IN THE STREET (EP)	8
60	Columbia SEG 8034	ADVENTURES WITH ALBERT (EP)	8
62	Columbia SEG 8118	BRAHN BOOTS AND OTHER FAVOURITES (EP)	8
56	Columbia 33S 1093	FAMOUS ADVENTURES WITH OLD SAM & THE RAMSBOTTOMS (10" LP)	15
58	Philips BBL 7237	'ERE'S 'OLLOWAY (LP)	12
60	Pye NPL 18056	JOIN IN THE CHORUS (LP)	12

(see also Joyce Grenfell & Stanley Holloway)

HOLLOW GROUND

80	Guardian GR/HG C57	FLYING HIGH EP (Flying High/Warlord/Rock On/Don't Chase The Dragon) (some in p/s)	150/30

HOLLY

65	Fontana TF 980	On With The Game/Paradise Lost	8

(see also Lynn Holland)

HOLLY

79	Eric's ERIC'S 003	Yankee Rose/Treasure Island/Desperate Dan (p/s)	25
79	Eric's ERIC'S 007	Hobo Joe/Stars Of The Bars (p/s)	25

(see also Holly Johnson, Frankie Goes To Hollywood, Big In Japan)

BUDDY HOLLY

78s

56	Brunswick 05581	Blue Days — Black Nights/Love Me	300
57	Vogue Coral Q 72293	Peggy Sue/Everyday	160
58	Coral Q 72293	Peggy Sue/Everyday	12
58	Coral Q 72288	Listen To Me/I'm Gonna Love You Too	25
58	Coral Q 72325	Rave On/Take Your Time	35
58	Coral Q 72333	Early In The Morning/Now We're One	35
58	Coral Q 72346	Heartbeat/Well ... All Right	50

59	Coral Q 72360	It Doesn't Matter Anymore/Raining In My Heart.	40
59	Brunswick 05800	Rock Around With Ollie Vee/Midnight Shift	200
59	Coral Q 72376	Peggy Sue Got Married/Crying, Waiting, Hoping.	180
60	Coral Q 72392	Heartbeat/Everyday.	450

SINGLES

56	Brunswick 05581	Blue Days — Black Nights/Love Me	800
57	Vogue Coral Q 72293	Peggy Sue/Everyday.	70
58	Coral Q 72293	Peggy Sue/Everyday.	20
58	Coral Q 72288	Listen To Me/I'm Gonna Love You Too	25
58	Coral Q 72325	Rave On/Take Your Time	25
58	Coral Q 72333	Early In The Morning/Now We're One	25
58	Coral Q 72346	Heartbeat/Well ... All Right.	25
59	Coral Q 72360	It Doesn't Matter Anymore/Raining In My Heart.	15
59	Brunswick 05800	Rock Around With Ollie Vee/Midnight Shift	45
59	Coral Q 72376	Peggy Sue Got Married/Crying, Waiting, Hoping.	25

(The above 45s were originally issued with triangular centres; reissues with round centres are worth two-thirds these values.)

60	Coral Q 72392	Heartbeat/Everyday.	20
60	Coral Q 72397	True Love Ways/Moondreams	15
60	Coral Q 72411	Learning The Game/That Makes It Tough.	12
61	Coral Q 72419	What To Do/That's What They Say	15
61	Coral Q 72432	Baby I Don't Care/Valley Of Tears	10
61	Coral Q 72445	Look At Me/Mailman, Bring Me No More Blues	15
62	Coral Q 72449	Listen To Me/Words Of Love	15
62	Coral Q 72455	Reminiscing/Wait Till The Sun Shines, Nellie	10
63	Coral Q 72459	Brown-Eyed Handsome Man/Slippin' And Slidin'	10
63	Coral Q 72463	Bo Diddley/It's Not My Fault	10
63	Coral Q 72466	Wishing/Because I Love You	10
63	Coral Q 72469	What To Do/Umm Oh Yeah.	15
64	Coral Q 72472	You've Got Love/An Empty Cup (as Buddy Holly & The Crickets)	22
64	Coral Q 72475	Love's Made A Fool Of You/You're The One	18
66	Coral Q 72483	Maybe Baby/That's My Desire	40
68	Decca AD 1009	Rave On/Peggy Sue (p/s, export reissue).	75
68	MCA MU 1012	Peggy Sue/Rave On (reissue)	6
69	MCA MU 1059	Love Is Strange/You're The One	10
69	MCA MU 1081	It Doesn't Matter Anymore/Maybe Baby (reissue)	7
70	MCA MU 1116	Rave On/Umm Oh Yeah (Dearest)	6
73	MCA MMU 1198	That'll Be The Day/Well All Right/Every Day	6
74	MCA MCA 119	It Doesn't Matter Anymore/True Love Ways/Brown Eyed Handsome Man	6
75	MCA MCA 207	Oh Boy!/Every Day (as Buddy Holly & Crickets)	6
76	MCA MCA 252	True Love Ways/It Doesn't Matter Anymore/Raining In My Heart/ Moondreams (p/s)	6
76	MCA MCA 253	Peggy Sue/Rave On/Rock Around With Ollie Vee/Midnight Shift (p/s)	6
76	MCA MCA 254	Maybe Baby/Think It Over/That'll Be The Day/It's So Easy (p/s, as Buddy Holly & Crickets)	6
78	MCA MCA 344	Wishing/Love's Made A Fool Of You (p/s)	6
83	MCA HR 001	That'll Be The Day/True Love Ways (as Buddy Holly & Crickets) (with/without *The History Of Rock* issue 1; 'Made In France' or 'Made In Gt. Britain' on label)	7/5
84	MCA BHB 1	THAT'LL BE THE DAY (10 x 7" box set, comprising BH1-10 in p/s)	40
89	MCA MCAV 1368	Oh Boy!/Well ... All Right/Mailman Bring Me No More Blues/Everyday (10", p/s)	8

EPs

58	Coral FEP 2002	LISTEN TO ME (brown cover, sleeve shows Holly *without* glasses; disc credits title as "Buddy Holly")	400+
58	Coral FEP 2002	LISTEN TO ME (re-pressing, various shades of green/brown p/s, shows Holly *with* glasses; disc credits title as "Buddy Holly").	40
58	Coral FEP 2005	RAVE ON (various shades of green/brown p/s).	50
59	Coral FEP 2014	IT'S SO EASY.	50
59	Coral FEP 2015	HEARTBEAT	50
59	Coral FEP 2032	BUDDY HOLLY.	50
59	Brunswick OE 9456	BUDDY HOLLY NO. 1	75
59	Brunswick OE 9457	BUDDY HOLLY NO. 2	75

(The above EPs were originally issued with triangular centres; later pressings with round-centres are worth between half and two-thirds these values.)

60	Coral FEP 2044	THE LATE GREAT BUDDY HOLLY (tri centre)	55+
60	Coral FEP 2044	THE LATE GREAT BUDDY HOLLY (round centre)	30
64	Coral FEP 2065	BUDDY — BY REQUEST	55
64	Coral FEP 2066	THAT TEX-MEX SOUND	70
64	Coral FEP 2067	WISHING.	60
64	Coral FEP 2068	SHOWCASE VOLUME 1	70
64	Coral FEP 2069	SHOWCASE VOLUME 2	70
65	Coral FEP 2070	BUDDY HOLLY SINGS	75

LPs

58	Vogue Coral LVA 9085	BUDDY HOLLY (Vogue-Coral labels & Coral sleeve).	125
58	Coral LVA 9085	BUDDY HOLLY.	55
59	Coral LVA 9105	THE BUDDY HOLLY STORY('High Fidelity Coral' logo on sleeve).	30
60s	Coral LVA 9105	THE BUDDY HOLLY STORY (reissue, different 'roll-neck sweater' sleeve with small 'Coral' logo).	50
60	Coral LVA 9127	THE BUDDY HOLLY STORY VOL. II.	25
61	Ace Of Hearts AH 3	THAT'LL BE THE DAY	15
63	Coral LVA 9212	REMINISCING	30
64	Coral LVA 9222	SHOWCASE	30
65	Coral LVA 9227	HOLLY IN THE HILLS (with Bob Montgomery, withdrawn mispressing, sleeve & label list "Wishing", plays "Reminiscing"; matrix no's end w/ 1B both sides)	50

65	Coral LVA 9227	HOLLY IN THE HILLS (corrected edition, with Bob Montgomery, plays Wishing, matrix numbers end with 1B on one side & 2B on other) 70
67	Ace Of Hearts AH 148	BUDDY HOLLY'S GREATEST HITS 12
68	MCA MUP(S) 312	LISTEN TO ME (mono/stereo, reissue of *Buddy Holly* [LVA 9085]) 18
68	MCA MUP(S) 313	RAVE ON (mono/stereo, reissue of *The Buddy Holly Story*) 18
68	MCA MUP(S) 314	BROWN-EYED HANDSOME MAN (mono/stereo, reissue of *Reminiscing*) 18
68	MCA MUP(S) 315	HE'S THE ONE (mono/stereo, reissue of *Showcase*) 18
68	MCA MUP(S) 319	TRUE LOVE WAYS (mono/stereo, reissue of *The Buddy Holly Story, Volume II*) 18
68	MCA MUP 320	WISHING (mono only, reissue of *Holly In The Hills*) 30
69	MCA MUPS 371	GIANT 25

(The above MCA albums were originally issued with yellow labels; later variations exist with various twin-toned designs.)

70	Coral CP/CPS 47	BUDDY HOLLY'S GREATEST HITS VOL. 2 (reissue, mono/stereo) 15
75	World Records SM 301/5	THE BUDDY HOLLY STORY (5-LP box set) 30
79	MCA Coral CDMSP 807	THE COMPLETE BUDDY HOLLY (6-LP box set with sepia-tinted book) 35
80	Marks & Spencer IMP 114	HEARTBEAT 60
83	MCA MCM 1002	FOR THE FIRST TIME ANYWHERE 15
86	Rollercoaster ROLL 2013	SOMETHING SPECIAL FROM BUDDY HOLLY 20

(see also Crickets, Fireballs)

STEVIE HOLLY
66	Planet PLF 107	A Strange World/Little Man 30

HOLLY GOLIGHTLY
94	Vinyl Japan PAD 13	JIGGY JIGGY (EP) 5
95	Vinyl Japan PAD 26	MARY ANN (EP) 5
96	Damaged Goods DAMGOOD 110	Come The Day/In You (picture disc) 6

HOLLY & JOEY
82	Virgin VS 478	I Got You Babe/HOLLY & THE ITALIANS: One More Dance (p/s) 15

(see also Ramones, Deborah Harry)

HOLLY & THE ITALIANS
81	Virgin VS 411	I Wanna Go Home/Fanzine (p/s) 15
81	Virgin VS 429	Just For Tonight/Baby Gets It All (p/s) 7
81	Virgin V 2186	THE RIGHT TO BE ITALIAN (LP, with lyric insert) 15

KENNY HOLLYWOOD
62	Decca F 11546	Magic Star/The Wonderful Story Of Love 30

HOLLYWOOD ARGYLES
60	London HLU 9146	Alley Oop/Sho' Knew A Lot About Love (78 rpm = £40) 10
60	Top Rank JAR 530	Gun Totin' Critter Called Jack/GARY PAXTON: Bug-Eye 20

(see also Kim Fowley, Skip & Flip, Gary Paxton)

HOLLYWOOD FLAMES
57	London HL 7030	Buzz Buzz Buzz/Crazy (export issue) 45
58	London HL 8545	Buzz Buzz Buzz/Crazy (78 rpm = £30) 75
59	London HLW 8955	Much Too Much/In The Dark (78 rpm = £60) 75
60	London HLE 9071	If I Thought You Needed Me/Every Day Every Way 50

HOLLYWOOD FREEWAY
72	Deram DM 359	I've Been Moved/Cool Calamares 6
73	Pye 7N 45273	You're The Song (That I Can't Stop Singing)/This Feeling Called Love 8

(see also Tony Rivers)

HOLLYWOOD HURRICANES
64	Prima PR 1009	Beavershot/Have Love Will Travel 6

HOLLYWOOD STRINGS
64	Capitol T 2116	THE BEATLES SONG BOOK (LP) 15

HOLLYWOOD VINES
61	Capitol CL 15191	When Johnny Comes Slidin' Home/Cruisin' 20

BILL HOLMAN OCTET
54	Capitol KC 65000	Cousin Jack/Plain Folks 8

EDDIE HOLMAN
65	Cameo Parkway P 960	This Can't Be True/A Free Country 70
69	Action ACT 4547	I Love You/I Surrender 70
70	Stateside SS 2160	(Hey There) Lonely Girl/It's All In The Game 15
70	Stateside SS 2170	Since I Don't Have You/Don't Stop Now 12
72	GSF GSZ 1	My Mind Keeps Telling Me/Stranded In A Dream 6
77	Salsoul SZ 2026	This Will Be A Night To Remember/Time Will Tell 6

DAVID HOLMES
97	Go Beat GOB 6	Don't Die Just Yet (Mogwai Mix)/Holiday Girl (Arab Strap Mix) (p/s, 500 only) ... 18

(see also Mogwai)

CHRISTINE HOLMES
64	Mercury MF 813	This Is My Prayer/My Dream 10
64	Mercury MF 819	Play Me A Sad Song (Mr DJ)/Doesn't He Know 10
64	Mercury MF 831	Goodbye Boys Goodbye/Is It Love 10
65	Mercury MF 851	Many Things From Your Window/You'd Better Believe It 7
65	Mercury MF 887	Goin' Where The Lovin' Is/Where There's Smoke 7

(see also Family Dogg)

IVAN HOLMES
67	Columbia DB 8119	The Light, The Love And The Life/Cocaine 7

MINT VALUE £

JAKE HOLMES

69	Polydor 56547	How Are You (Parts 1 & 2)	5
70	Ember EMB S 269	Saturday Night/Diner Song	5
70	Polydor 2066 040	So Close/Django And Friend	5
70	Polydor 583 579	JAKE HOLMES (LP)	30
70	Polydor 2425 036	SO CLOSE SO VERY FAR TO GO (LP)	30
72	CBS 64905	HOW MUCH TIME (LP)	25

JOE HOLMES & LEN GRAHAM

79	Topic 12TS 401	AFTER DAWNING (LP)	12

LEROY HOLMES & ORCHESTRA

68	United Artists UP 2222	The Good, The Bad And The Ugly/Live For Life	5

SALTY HOLMES

50	London L 663	I Found My Mama/Don't Shed Your Tears After I'm Gone (78)	8

RICHARD 'GROOVES' HOLMES

67	Transatlantic PR 7435	SOUL MESSAGE (LP)	12
68	Transatlantic PR 7493	RICHARD 'GROOVES' HOLMES (LP)	18

HOLOCAUST

80	Phoenix PSP 1	Heavy Metal Mania/Only As Young As You Feel (p/s)	20
80	Phoenix 12 PSP 1	Heavy Metal Mania/Love's Power/Only As Young As You Feel (12", p/s)	30
80	Phoenix 12 PSP 2	Smokin' Valves/Friend Or Foe (p/s)	10
80	Phoenix 12 PSP 2	Smokin' Valves/Friend Or Foe/Out My Book (12", p/s)	30
81	Phoenix PSP 3P	HOLOCAUST LIVE (EP)	25
82	Phoenix 12 PSP 4	Comin' Through/Don't Wanna Be A Loser/Good Thing Going (12", p/s)	30
81	Phoenix PSLP 1	THE NIGHTCOMERS (LP)	40
83	Phoenix PSPLP 4	LIVE (HOT CURRY AND WINE) (LP)	25
84	Phoenix PSPLP 5	NO MAN'S LAND (LP)	20

HOLOGRAM

82	Phoenix PSPLP 2	STEAL THE STARS (LP)	12

HOLOSADE

88	Powerstation AMP 16	HELL HOUSE (LP)	12

ERROL HOLT

77	Lior ROAR 111	Come Rock Me/Congo Dread (12")	20
79	Hit Run HIT DD25	Sweet Reggae Music/PRINCE FAR I: Hairdressing Salon	90

JOHN HOLT

63	Island WI 041	I Cried A Tear/I'll Stay	
68	Trojan TR 643	Tonight/Oh How It Hurts (B-side actually by Paragons)	22
69	Trojan TR 661	Ali Baba/I'm Your Man	30
69	Trojan TR 674	What You Gonna Do Now/Have You Ever Been To Heaven	10
69	Trojan TR 694	Have Sympathy/HARRY J ALLSTARS: Spyrone	12
69	Trojan TR 7702	Wooden Heart/All My Life	8
70	Duke Reid DR 2506	Come Out Of My Bed/WINSTON WRIGHT: Hide And Seek	12
70	Duke DU 73	Stealing, Stealing/WINSTON WRIGHT: Stealing, Stealing (Volume 2)	8
70	Duke DU 77	The Working Kind/Open Jaw	8
70	Jackpot JP 735	A Little Tear/JEFF BARNS: Get In The Groove	7
70	Bamboo BAM 44	A Love I Can Feel/JOHNNY LAST: Long Liver Man (B-side act. by Hugh Black)	10
70	Bamboo BAM 55	A Stranger In Love/WAILERS: Jailhouse (Good Rudy)	70
70	Bamboo BAM 62	Holly Holy/Do You Love Me?	10
70	Banana BA 314	Why Can't I Touch You/SOUND DIMENSION: Touching Version	8
70	Smash SMA 2303	My Heart Is Gone/PHIL PRATT ALL STARS: Version	6
70	Smash SMA 2305	I Had A Talk With My Woman/MAXINE: Life Is Not The Same Anymore	6
70	Supreme SUP 212	Share My Rest/AL BROWN: Allways	12
70	Unity UN 548	Sometimes/BUNNY LEE ALL STARS: Lash-La-Rue	15
70	Unity UN 549	Sea Cruise/LEE'S ALL STARS: Niney's Hop	8
70	Unity UN 552	Walking Along/LEE'S ALL STARS: Warefare	15
70	Unity UN 556	Give Her All The Love/BUSTY BROWN: Nobody But You	6
71	Banana BA 340	O.K. Fred/Fancy Make-Up	12
71	Banana BA 345	Build Our Dreams/LEROY SIBBLES: Love In Our Nation	12
71	Treasure Isle TI 7061	Let's Build Our Dreams/TOMMY McCOOK & SUPERSONICS: Testify Version	18
71	Treasure Isle TI 7065	Sister Big Stuff/TOMMY McCOOK & SUPERSONICS: Black River	20
71	Treasure Isle TI 7066	Paragons Medley/TOMMY McCOOK & SUPERSONICS: Medley Version	18
71	Ashanti ASH 401	Again/MUDIES ALL STARS: Ten Steps To Soul Version	7
71	Camel CA 78	Linger A While/Version	7
71	Escort ERT 847	Knock On Your Door/URIEL ALDRIDGE: Set Me Free	6
71	Jackpot JP 772	Stick By Me/It's A Pleasure	6
71	Jackpot JP 774	It's A Jam In The Streets/A Man Needs A Woman	6
71	Jackpot JP 784	Anymore/Lost Love	6
71	Moodisc MU 3513	It May Sound Silly/MUDIE ALL STARS: Instrumental	6
71	Moodisc HM 105	It May Sound Silly/MUDIE ALL STARS: Instrumental (reissue)	10
71	Punch PH 60	Strange Things/WINSTON WRIGHT: Want Money (B-side act. G.G. All Stars)	12
71	Smash SMA 2324	Mother And Father Love/AGGROVATORS: Mother Version	6
72	Blue Beat BB 424	O.K. Fred/BIG YOUTH: Chi Chi Run	20
72	Prince Buster PB 40	Close To Me/Version	7
72	Prince Buster PB 41	Get Ready/Version	7
72	Prince Buster PB 42	Rain From The Skies/Version	7
72	Prince Buster PB 43	The First Time/Version	7
72	Prince Buster PB 49	For Your Love/Version	7
72	G.G. GG 4529	Keep It Up/A Love Like Yours	6
72	Fab FAB 188	A Little Happiness/DELROY WILSON: Diamond Rings	10
72	Jackpot JP 790	Don't You Know/Riding For A Fall	6
72	Jackpot JP 807	Looking Back/I'll Be There	6
72	Pama PM 845	I'll Always Love You/SLIM SMITH: 3 x 7 Rock And Roll	6

72	Pama PM 852	Pledging My Love/I Will Know What To Do	6
73	Fab FAB 224	Let's Go Dancing/Version	7
73	Fab FAB 244	Let's Go Dancing/Version (reissue)	7
73	Attack ATT 8045	Time And The River/Version	5
73	Smash SMA 2329	Don't Break Your Promise/I've Been Admiring You	8
73	Ackee ACK 513	Ecstacy/Version	6
70	Bamboo BDLP 210	A LOVE I CAN FEEL (LP)	55
70s	Melodisc MLP 12170	GREATEST HITS (LP)	40
70s	Melodisc MLP 12180	OK FRED (LP)	45
70s	Melodisc MLP 12191	JOHN HOLT & FRIENDS (LP)	45
71	Trojan TRL(S) 37	STILL IN CHAINS (LP)	12
72	Trojan TRL(S) 43	HOLT (LP)	12
72	Trojan TBL 184	PLEDGING MY LOVE (LP)	12
73	Trojan TRLS 55	THE FURTHER YOU LOOK (LP)	12
74	Attack ATLP 1010	A LOVE I CAN FEEL (LP)	15

(see also Jay & Joya, Little John, Neville Hinds, Jeff Barnes, Danny Simpson, Hugh Roy, U Roy Junior, Don Drummond, Interns)

GARY HOLTON
84	Magnet GARY 2	Catch A Falling Star/Angel (star-shaped picture disc)	8

(see also Heavy Metal Kids, Kids, Slade)

ROOSEVELT HOLTS
68	Blue Horizon 7-63201	PRESENTING THE COUNTRY BLUES (LP)	80

HOLY MACKEREL
72	CBS 8447	Rock-A-Bye/New Black Shoes	6
72	CBS 65297	HOLY MACKEREL (LP)	25
93	Tenth Planet TP 005	CLOSER TO HEAVEN (LP, numbered, 500 only)	15

(see also Jason Crest, High Broom)

HOLY MODAL ROUNDERS
68	Elektra EKL 4026	THE MORAY EELS EAT THE HOLY MODALS (LP, mono)	30
68	Elektra EKS 74026	THE MORAY EELS EAT THE HOLY MODALS (LP, stereo)	30
70	Transatlantic TRA 7451	HOLY MODAL ROUNDERS (LP)	30
70	Transatlantic TRA	HOLY MODAL ROUNDERS 2 (LP)	25

HOMBRES
67	Verve VS 1510	Let It Out (Let It All Hang Out)/Go Girl Go	15

HOM BRU
82	Celtic Music CM 009	OBADEEA: MUSIC FROM SHETLAND AND BEYOND (LP)	12

HOME
69	Bell SBLL 119	JOLLIVER ARKANSAW (LP)	65

HOME
72	CBS 7809	Fancy Lady, Hollywood Child/Shady Lady	6
71	CBS 64365	PAUSE FOR A HOARSE HORSE (LP)	40
72	CBS 64752	HOME (LP)	15
73	CBS 65550	THE ALCHEMIST (LP)	15

(see also Groundhogs, AC/DC, Wishbone Ash, Blue Rondos)

HOMER & JETHRO
54	HMV B 10581	How Much Is That Hound Dog/Rudolph The Flat-Nosed Reindeer (78)	8
54	HMV 7M 211	Swappin' Partners/Crazy Mix-Up Song	12
54	Parlophone CMSP 2	Don't Let Your Sweet Love Die/When It's Long Handle Time In Tennessee (export issue)	8
59	RCA RCA 1148	Waterloo/The Battle Of Kookamonga (78 rpm = £10)	6
59	Parlophone GEP 8791	WANTED FOR MURDER OF THE STANDARDS (EP)	18

HOME SERVICE
84	Coda NAT 001	THE MYSTERIES (LP)	15

HOMESICK JAMES
64	Sue WI 319	Crossroads/My Baby's Sweet	40
65	Sue WI 330	Set A Date/Can't Afford To Do It	40

HOMESICK JAMES/SNOOKY PRYOR
74	Caroline C 1502	HOMESICK JAMES AND SNOOKY PRYOR (LP)	22

HOMOSEXUALS
78	L'Orelei PF 151	Hearts In Exile/South South Africans (p/s, with insert)	8
79	Black Noise F12 No. 2	Divorce Proceedings/Mecho Madness (12", plain sleeve with sticker)	10
81	Black Noise BN 1	BIGGER THAN THE NUMBER YET MISSING THE DOT (EP, clear vinyl, fold-around hand-painted sleeve)	8
84	Recommended RR 18	THE HOMOSEXUALS RECORD (LP, with inserts)	12

(see also George Harrassment & Homosexuals, Ice La Bas, Amos & Sara, Nancy Sesay & Melodaires, L-Voag, Sir Alick & Phraser)

MINAKO HONDA
87	Columbia DB 9153	Golden Days (English Version)/Crazy Nights (English Version) (p/s, features Brian May)	35

HONDELLS
64	Mercury MF 834	Little Honda/Hot Rod High	22
65	Mercury MF 925	Younger Girl/All American Girl	22
66	Mercury MF 967	Cheryl's Goin' Home/Show Me Girl	22

HONEST MEN
69	Tamla Motown TMG 706	Cherie/Baby	25

HONEYBOY
71	Trojan TR 7835	Jamaica/ITALS: Sea Wave	7
72	Banana BA 375	Homeward Bound/Peace In The Land	7

HONEYBUS

67	Deram DM 131	Delighted To See You/The Breaking Up Scene	12
67	Deram DM 152	Do I Figure In Your Life?/Throw My Love Away	12
68	Deram DM 182	I Can't Let Maggie Go/Tender Are The Ashes	7
68	Deram DM 207	Girl Of Independent Means/How Long	12
69	Deram DM 254	She Sold Blackpool Rock/Would You Believe	10
70	Deram DM 289	Story/The Right To Choose	7
72	Bell BLL 1205	She Is The Female To My Soul/For Where Have You Been	6
73	Warner Bros K 16250	For You/Little Lovely One	8
76	Decca F 13631	I Can't Let Maggie Go/Julie In My Heart	5
70	Deram DML/SML 1056	STORY (LP)	90
73	Warner Bros K 46248	RECITAL (LP, withdrawn)	150+
79	See For Miles SEE 264	AT THEIR BEST (LP)	25

(see also Pete Dello, Colin Hare, Lace, Magic Valley, Red Herring)

HONEYCOMBS

64	Pye 7N 15664	Have I The Right/Please Don't Pretend Again	6
64	Pye 7N 15705	Is It Because/I'll Cry Tomorrow	6
64	Pye 7N 15736	Eyes/If You've Got To Pick A Baby	12
65	Pye 7N 15781	Don't Love You No More/I'll See You Tomorrow (withdrawn, promo only)	110
65	Pye 7N 15827	Something Better Beginning/I'll See You Tomorrow	12
65	Pye 7N 15890	That's The Way/Can't Get Through To You	6
65	Pye 7N 15979	This Year, Next Year/Not Sleeping Too Well Lately	10
66	Pye 7N 17089	Who Is Sylvia?/How Will I Know	15
66	Pye 7N 17138	It's So Hard/I Fell In Love	15
66	Pye 7N 17173	That Loving Feeling/Should A Man Cry	18
69	Pye 7N 17741	Have I The Right/Please Don't Pretend Again (stereo reissue)	6
65	Pye NEP 24230	THAT'S THE WAY (EP)	45
64	Pye NPL 18097	THE HONEYCOMBS (LP)	70
65	Pye NPL 18132	ALL SYSTEMS GO! (LP)	80
66	Golden Guinea GGL 0350	THE HONEYCOMBS (LP, reissue in different sleeve)	20

(see also Lemmings, Dennis D'Ell, Martin Murray)

HONEYCONE

70	Hot Wax HWX 103	While You're Out Looking For Sugar/The Feeling's Gone	8
71	Hot Wax HWX 105	Girls It Ain't Easy/Take Me With You	6
71	Hot Wax HWX 107	Want Ads/We Belong Together	10
72	Hot Wax HWX 111	One Monkey Don't Stop No Show/Stick Up	6
72	Hot Wax HWX 112	The Day I Found Myself/When Will It End	6
72	Hot Wax HWX 116	Sittin' On A Time Bomb/It's Better To Have Loved And Lost	6
71	Hot Wax SHW 5002	HONEYCONE (LP)	15
71	Hot Wax SHW 5004	SWEET REPLIES (LP)	15
72	Hot Wax SHW 5005	SOULFUL TAPESTRY (LP)	15
73	Hot Wax SHW 5010	LOVE, PEACE AND SOUL (LP)	18

HONEYCRACK

95	PPP1	King Of Misery/5 Minutes (numbered p/s, 1500 only sold at gigs)	15
95	PPPCD1	King Of Misery/5 Minutes (numbered card p/s, 1500 only sold at gigs)	20
96	Epic XPR 2062	Animals (Martin Steib Industrial Remix)/Sitting At Home (Renegade Soundwave Mix) (12", title-stickered plain black sleeve, promo only)	15
96	EG EGO 52-P	Anyway (CD-R, info-stickered case, promo only)	12
96	Epic 484230 0	PROZAC (LP, with inner sleeve, white vinyl, 2000 only)	15
96	Epic 484230 1	PROZAC (LP, with inner sleeve, black vinyl)	15

(see also Jellys, Wildhearts)

HONEYDEW

70	Argo AFW 101	Part Of This Game/To Make You Mine	5
70	Argo	HONEYDEW (LP)	70

HONEYDRIPPERS

84	Es Paranza SAM 220	Sea Of Love/Rickin' At Midnight (7" radio promo)	10
84	Es Paranza 790 220-1	THE HONEYDRIPPERS VOL. ONE (10" LP)	8

(see also Robert Plant)

HONEYEND

72	Spark SRL 1072	Heartbreaker/Beautiful Downtown	60

HONEYS

63	Capitol CL 15299	Surfin' Down The Swanee River/Shoot The Curl	80

(see also American Spring, Beach Boys)

HONEYTONES

58	London HLX 8671	Don't Look Now, But.../I Know, I Know (78 rpm = £35)	60

HONEYTREE

70s	Myrrh MYR 1039	EVERGREEN (LP)	18

HONG GANG

72	Sioux SI 004	Reggae Mento/MONTEGO MELON: Swan Lake	5
73	Sioux SI 025	Smoking Wild/ROOSEVELT SINGERS: Heavy Reggae	5

(see also Bob Andy)

ROBBIN HOOD

56	MGM SP 1178	The Rock-A-Bye Blues/Beautiful, Beautiful Love	15

HOOD

92	Fluff HONEY 4	Sirens/Fault/Your Sixth Sense (p/s, 500 only)	20
93	Fluff HONEY 6	I Didn't Think You Were Going To Hit Me In The Face/In The Trap Of Doing/Choosing A Grimace (wraparound p/s, 500 only)	18
94	Hedonist Prods. 002 F	57 White Bread: My Last August/Experimental Film-Making (flexidisc, p/s, 1000 only)	6

95	Orgasm ORGASM 08	A Harbour Of Thoughts/Disappointed/Uneven Conversation Should Point To Cause/Forced By The Reasoning Hand/John Clyde-Evans/Silo Crash (p/s) 8
95	555 Recordings 555 01	LEE FAUST'S MILLION PIECE ORCHESTRA: Biochemistry Revision Can Wait/ England's Fine Fields/Rocck? I Can't Even Spell The Word/ Stricken Office Worker (EP, 1000 copies only) 10
96	Earworm WORM 1	SECRETS NOW KNOWN TO OTHERS: Forhead/Crow Blown West/ Beware! Falling Ox/I'm Turning Into A Cart/Further Woodland/20X/Visions Of Old Machinery/Sometimes Doomed/You Should Never Feel Alone In This World/ Crushed By Life (EP, p/s, 1000 only). 10
96	Love Train PUBE 11	I've Forgotten How To Live/The Weather Side Of The Stone Mill Tower/ Dimensions TBA 10
98	Rocket Racer ROCKET 04	The Year Of Occasional Lull/Fog Projections (1000 only, numbered, 980 with black artwork, 20 with red) 5/10
98	Happy Go Lucky HGL 12	Filmed Initiative/As Evening Changed The Day (different photo on each p/s). . . . 15
98	555 Recordings 555 13	(The) Weight/Fallen Farmer/We Are Not Promote/Impossible Calm/ Feel The Rush (Coming In From The Avant Garde)/I Know What To Squander/ . . . . Mast-On-Hill/Collapsing Climate Soul (p/s) 6
94	Fluff ARC 01	CABLED LINEAR TRACTION (LP, 200 only) 25
96	Slumberland SLR 59LP	SILENT '88 (LP, with free 7") 12
97	Happy Go Lucky HAPPY 10LP	STRUCTURED DISASTERS (LP, with free 7") 12
98	Domino WIGLP 42	RUSTIC HOUSES, FORLORN VALLEYS (LP) 12
99	Slumberland SLR 46LP	CABLED LINEAR TRACTION (LP, reissue, 1100 only) 12

HOODOO RHYTHM DEVILS
78	Fantasy FTC 147	Gotta Lot Of Love In My Soul/MDR Of Love. 20

HOOK
68	Uni UN 507	In The Beginning/Show You The Way. 8

EARL HOOKER
69	Blue Horizon 57-3166	Boogie Don't Blot/Funky Blues 30
70	Blue Horizon 7-63850	SWEET BLACK ANGEL (LP) 100
70	Stateside SSL 10298	DON'T HAVE TO WORRY (LP) 50

(see also John Lee Hooker)

JOHN LEE HOOKER
78s
52	Vogue V 2102	Hoogie Boogie/Whistlin' And Moanin' Blues 40
54	London HL 8037	Need Somebody/Too Much Boogie. 40

45s
63	Stateside SS 203	Boom Boom/Frisco Blues 25
64	Stateside SS 297	Dimples/I'm Leaving 20
64	Stateside SS 341	I Love You Honey/Send Me Your Pillow 18
64	Pye International 7N 25255	High Priced Woman/Sugar Mama 18
64	Polydor NH 52930	Shake It Baby/Let's Make It Baby 18
65	Sue WI 361	I'm In The Mood/Boogie Chillun 40
66	Chess CRS 8039	Let's Go Out Tonight/In The Mood 20
66	Planet PLF 114	Mai Lee/Don't Be Messing With My Bread (with Groundhogs) 45
70	President PT 295	Dimples/Boom Boom 8

EPs
60	Riverside REP 3202	WEDNESDAY EVENING 25
60	Riverside REP 3207	DEMOCRAT MAN. 25
64	Stateside SE 1019	THE BLUES OF JOHN HOOKER 30
64	Stateside SE 1023	I'M JOHN LEE HOOKER 30
64	Ember EP 4561	THINKING BLUES 40
65	Pye Intl. NEP 44034	LOVE BLUES 35
65	Chess CRE 6000	DOWN AT THE LANDING 35
65	Atlantic AET 6010	JOHN LEE HOOKER 35
66	Chess CRE 6007	WALKING THE BOOGIE 40
66	Chess CRE 6014	THE JOURNEY. 40
66	Chess CRE 6021	REAL FOLK BLUES VOL. 3 40
73	Impulse 9103	SERVES YOU RIGHT TO SUFFER 15

LPs
60	Advent LP 2801	JOHN LEE HOOKER AND HIS GUITAR. 50
62	Riverside RLP 12-838	THE FOLK BLUES OF JOHN LEE HOOKER. 40
62	Stateside SL 10014	THE FOLK LORE OF JOHN LEE HOOKER 45
63	London HA-K 8097	DON'T TURN ME FROM YOUR DOOR. 65
64	Stateside SL 10053	THE BIG SOUL OF JOHN LEE HOOKER 50
64	Stateside SL 10074	I WANT TO SHOUT THE BLUES 45
64	Pye Intl. NPL 28042	HOUSE OF THE BLUES 50
64	Fontana 688 700 ZL	THE FOLK-BLUES OF HOOKER 40
65	Fontana FJL 119	BLUE! 45
65	Ember EMB 3356	SINGS THE BLUES 30
65	Riverside RLP 008	BURNING HELL 30
65	Chess CRL 4500	JOHN LEE HOOKER PLAYS AND SINGS THE BLUES 45
66	HMV CLP 5032/CSD 3542	IT SERVES YOU RIGHT TO SUFFER (mono/stereo). 45/50
66	Ember (ST)EMB 3371	DRIFTIN' THROUGH THE BLUES 30
67	Chess CRL 4527	THE REAL FOLK BLUES 30
67	HMV CLP/CSD 3612	LIVE AT THE CAFE A GO GO 35
67	Atlantic Special 590 003	DRIFTIN' BLUES 20
68	Joy JOY(S) 101	I'M JOHN LEE HOOKER 15
68	Joy JOY(S) 124	BURNIN'. 15
68	Stateside (S)SL 10246	URBAN BLUES 35
69	Joy JOYS 129	TRAVELIN' 12
69	Joy JOYS 133	THE FOLKLORE OF JOHN LEE HOOKER 15
69	Stateside (S)SL 10280	SIMPLY THE TRUTH 30

John Lee HOOKER

69	Joy JOYS 142	CONCERT AT NEWPORT	15
69	Joy JOYS 147	THE BIG SOUL OF JOHN LEE HOOKER	15
69	Storyville 673 005	YOU'RE LEAVIN' ME BABY	15
69	Joy JOYS 152	IN PERSON	15
70	Storyville 673 020	TUPELO BLUES	15
70	Joy JOYS 156	THE BEST OF JOHN LEE HOOKER	15
70	Stax SXATS 1025	THAT'S WHERE IT'S AT	15
71	Probe SPB 1016	IF YOU MISS 'IM ... I GOT 'IM (with Earl Hooker)	18
71	Probe SPB 1034	ENDLESS BOOGIE	15
71	Stax 2362 017	THAT'S WHERE IT'S AT!	15
71	Xtra XTRA 1114	JOHN LEE HOOKER	15
71	United Artists UAS 29235	COAST TO COAST BLUES BAND	20
72	Specialty SNTF 5005	ALONE	12
72	Probe SPB 1057	NEVER GET OUT OF THESE BLUES ALIVE	15
73	Green Bottle GN 4002	JOHNNY LEE	15
75	ABC ABCL 5059	FREE BEER AND CHICKEN	20
77	DJM DJD 28026	DIMPLES (2-LP)	18

(see also Canned Heat, Carlos Santana & Buddy Miles, John Lee's Groundhogs)

JOHN LEE HOOKER/LIGHTNIN' HOPKINS/SMOKEY HOGG
73	Specialty SNTF 5013	HOOKER HOPKINS HOGG (LP)	18

(see also Lightnin' Hopkins, Smokey Hogg)

STEVE HOOKER & HEAT
77	Takeaway TAKE 1/	If You Don't Do The Business/Rock & Roll Doctor/I'm Hooked/	
	EJR 577	Marionette (stamped white sleeve with insert)	8

HOOKFOOT
69	Page One POF 144	Way Of The Musician/Hookfoot	6
71	DJM DJLPS 413	HOOKFOOT (LP)	15
72	DJM DJLPS 422	GOOD TIMES A' COMIN' (LP)	15
73	DJM DJLPS 428	COMMUNICATIONS (LP)	15

(see also Loot, Caleb, Soul Agents)

MARSHALL HOOKS & CO.
71	Blue Horizon 2096 002	I Want The Same Thing Tomorrow/Hookin' It	20
71	Blue Horizon 2431 003	MARSHALL HOOKS & CO. (LP)	80

HOOTEN(ANNY) SINGERS
64	United Artists UP 1082	Gabrielle/Darling (most copies list artist as Hooten Singers)	35

(see also Abba, Hep Stars, Northern Lights)

BOB HOPE
52	Capitol CL 13787	A 4-Legged Friend/There's A Cloud In My Valley Of Sunshine	
		(78, with Jimmy Wakely)	8
58	London HLU 8593	Paris Holiday/Nothing In Common (with Bing Crosby) (78 rpm = £8)	18
59	RCA RCA 1139	Ain't A-Hankerin'/Protection (with Rosemary Clooney) (78 rpm = £10)	6
63	United Artists UP 1023	Call Me Bwana/The Flipside	6
58	HMV DLP 1088	EDDIE FOY AND THE SEVEN LITTLE FOYS (10" LP, soundtrack, with James Cagney)	30
63	Brunswick LAT 8539	IN RUSSIA AND ONE OTHER PLACE (LP)	18

(see also Bing Crosby, Rosemary Clooney)

LYN(N) HOPE
57	Vogue V 9081	Blue Moon/Blues For Anna Bacca (78 rpm = £18)	45
57	Vogue V 9082	Eleven Till Two/Blues For Mary (78 rpm = £18)	45
58	Vogue V 9115	Temptation/The Scrunch (78 rpm £30)	30
60	Blue Beat BB 21	Shockin'/Blue And Sentimental	20
57	Vogue VE 170103	LYNN HOPE AND HIS TENOR SAX (EP)	90
60	Vogue VE 170146	LYNN HOPE AND HIS TENOR SAX (EP)	100

PETER HOPE & RICHARD H. KIRK
85	Doublevision DVR 15	Leather Hands (Master Mix)/(Radio Mix)/(Crash Mix) (12", p/s)	8

(see also Cabaret Voltaire, Richard H. Kirk)

HOPE OF THE STATES
00s	Seeker SEEK 001	Black Dollar Bills/Everything For Everyone (Demo)/Sts'Ikel (Demo) (CD, numbered & signed, 1000 only)	35
00s	Sony 6742577	Enemies/Friends (numbered p/s)	7

HOPETOWN (Lewis) & GLENMORE (Brown)
68	Fab FAB 43	Skinny Leg Girl/Live Like A King	22

MARY HOPKIN
68	Apple APPLE 2	Those Were The Days/Turn Turn Turn (later copies credit Mary Hopkins)	each 6
68	Apple APPLE 2	Those Were The Days/Turn Turn Turn (blank Apple label on A-side)	12
69	Apple APPLE 7	Lontana Dagli Occhi/Game (Europe-only, unreleased in U.K.)	
69	Apple APPLE 9	Prince En Avignon/The Game (France-only, unreleased in U.K.)	
69	Apple APPLE 10	Goodbye/Sparrow	6
69	Apple APPLE 16	Que Sera Sera/Fields Of St. Etienne (unreleased)	
69	Cambrian CSP 703	Aderyn Llwyd/Y Blodyn Gwyn (p/s)	18
70	Cambrian CSP 712	Pleserau Serch/Tyrd Yn Ôl (p/s)	18
70	Apple APPLE 22	Temma Harbour/Lontano Dagli Occhi (black or green lettering on p/s)	each 6
70	Apple APPLE 26	Knock, Knock Who's There?/I'm Going To Fall In Love Again (p/s)	6
70	Apple APPLE 27	Que Sera Sera/Fields Of St. Etienne (unreleased in U.K., acetates only)	
70	Apple APPLE 30	Think About Your Children/Heritage (p/s)	6
71	Apple APPLE 34	Let My Name Be Sorrow/Kew Gardens (p/s)	18
71	Apple APPLE 39	Water, Paper And Clay/Jefferson (p/s)	22
72	Regal Zonophone RZ 3070	Mary Had A Baby/Cherry Tree Carol	6
76	Good Earth GD 2	If You Love Me (I Won't Care): (some copies list "If You Love Me")/Tell Me Now	6
77	Good Earth GD 11	Wrap Me In Your Arms/Just A Dreamer (p/s)	10

68	Cambrian CEP 414	LLAIS SWYNOL MARY HOPKIN (EP)	15
69	Cambrian CEP 420	MARY AC EDWARD (EP, with Edward Morris Jones)	15
69	Apple (S)APCOR 5	POST CARD (LP, with black inner sleeve, mono/stereo)	20/15
71	Apple SAPCOR 21	EARTH SONG — OCEAN SONG (LP, gatefold sleeve, 'Apple' inner sleeve)	25
72	Apple SAPCOR 23	THOSE WERE THE DAYS (LP, with 'Apple' inner sleeve)	65
77	Decca SPA 546	THE WELSH WORLD OF MARY HOPKIN (LP)	25
91	Apple SAPCOR 5	POST CARD (LP, reissue, gatefold sleeve with bonus 12" [SAPCOR 52])	22
92	Apple SAPCOR 21	EARTH SONG/OCEAN SONG (LP, reissue, gatefold sleeve with inner)	22

(see also Hobby Horse, Sundance, Oasis, Elfland Ensemble, Bob Johnson & Pete Knight, Roy Budd, Elmer Bernstein)

JOEL & LIGHTNIN' HOPKINS
60	Heritage H 1000	BLUES FROM EAST TEXAS (LP, 99 copies only)	120

(see also Lightnin' Hopkins)

LIGHTNIN' HOPKINS
61	Bluesville BVLP 1019	LIGHTNIN' HOPKINS (LP)	70
62	'77' LA 12/1	SAM LIGHTNIN' HOPKINS — THE ROOSTER CROWED IN ENGLAND (LP 99 copies only)	80
63	Stateside SL 10031	LIGHTNIN' STRIKES (LP)	50
63	Realm RM 128	LIGHTNIN' HOPKINS SINGS THE BLUES (LP)	38
63	Realm RM 171	DIRTY HOUSE BLUES (LP)	40
64	Stateside SL 10076	BLUES HOOT (LP, some tracks by Sonny Terry & Brownie McGhee)	45
65	Stateside SL 10110	HOOTIN' THE BLUES (LP)	45
65	Stateside SL 10155	DOWN HOME BLUES (LP)	45
65	Fontana AH 183	THE BLUES (LP)	35
65	Fontana 688 301 ZL	LAST NIGHT BLUES (LP)	40
65	Fontana 688 801 ZL	BURNIN' IN L.A. (LP)	40
66	Fontana 688 803 ZL	BLUE BIRD BLUES (LP)	40
66	Fontana 688 807 ZL	BLUES PARTY (LP)	40
66	Ember EMB 3389	A TIME FOR BLUES (LP)	30
66	Ember EMB 3416	LIVE AT THE BIRD LOUNGE (LP)	30
67	Ember EMB 3423	I'VE BEEN BUKED AND SCORNED (LP)	30
66	Verve (S)VLP 5003	ROOTS OF HOPKINS (LP)	30
66	Verve (S)VLP 5014	LIGHTNIN' STRIKES (LP, reissue)	22
66	Saga ERO 8001	LIGHTNIN' HOPKINS (LP)	18
67	Xtra XTRA 5036	BLUES IN MY BOTTLE (LP)	22
68	Xtra XTRA 5044	GOT TO MOVE YOUR BABY (LP, reissue of Fontana 688 301 ZL)	18
68	Minit MLL/MLS 40006	EARTH BLUES (LP)	30
69	Liberty LBL 83254	KING OF DOWLING STREET (LP)	25
69	Joy JOY(S) 115	LIGHTNIN' STRIKES (LP, 2nd reissue)	15
69	Polydor 545 019	THAT'S MY STORY (LP)	20
70	Ace Of Hearts (Z)AHT 183	THE BLUES (LP)	18
70	Poppy PYS 11000	LIGHTNIN'! VOLUME 1 (LP)	18
70	Poppy PYS 11002	LIGHTNIN'! VOLUME 2 (LP)	18
71	Liberty LBS 83293	THE CALIFORNIA MUDSLIDE (AND EARTHQUAKE) (LP)	22
71	Mayfair AMLB 4000 1/2	LIGHTNIN' STRIKES (2-LP)	18
71	Blue Horizon 2431 005	LET'S WORK AWHILE (LP)	125
71	Xtra XTRA 1127	THE ROOTS OF LIGHTNIN' HOPKINS (LP)	20
71	Boulevard BLVD 4001	LIGHTNIN' HOPKINS (LP)	15
72	Carnival 2941 005	LONESOME LIGHTNIN' (LP)	15
73	Mainstream MSL 1001	DIRTY BLUES (LP)	15
74	Sonet SNTF 672	LEGACY OF THE BLUES VOLUME 12 (LP)	15
75	Mainstream MSL 1031	LOW DOWN DIRTY BLUES (LP)	15

(see also Sonny Terry & Brownie McGhee, Joel & Lightnin' Hopkins, Lightnin' Hopkins & John Lee Hooker, Big Joe Williams)

LIGHTNIN' HOPKINS & JOHN LEE HOOKER
69	Storyville 616 001	THERE'S GOOD ROCKIN' TONIGHT! (LP)	48
72	Storyville SLP 174	LIGHTNIN' HOPKINS AND JOHN LEE HOOKER (LP)	40

(see also John Lee Hooker/Lightnin' Hopkins/Smokey Hogg)

LINDA HOPKINS
61	Coral Q 72423	I Diddle Dum Dum/All In My Mind	20
62	Coral Q 72448	Mama's Doin' The Twist/My Mother's Eyes	20

LINDA HOPKINS & JACKIE WILSON
63	Coral Q 72464	Shake A Hand/Say I Do	15
65	Coral Q 72480	Yes Indeed/When The Saints Go Marching In	15

(see also Jackie Wilson)

NICKY HOPKINS
66	CBS 202055	Mr Big/Jenni	18
67	Polydor 56175	Mister Pleasant/Nothing As Yet	18
68	MGM MGM 1419	Top Pops No. 1 (Medley)/(Part 2)	6
68	Fontana TF 906	High On A Hill/Trumpet Serenade (actually by Nigel Hopkins)	6
73	CBS CBS 1328	Speed On/Sundown In Mexico	5
66	CBS (S)BPG 62679	THE REVOLUTIONARY PIANO OF NICKY HOPKINS (LP)	40
73	CBS 65416	THE TIN MAN WAS A DREAMER (LP)	20

(see also Aquarian Age, Neil Christian & Crusaders, Cyril Davies R&B All-Stars, Poet & One Man Band, Quicksilver Messenger Service, Sweet Thursday)

WASH HOPKINS SINGERS
69	Action ACT 4546	He's Got Blessing/Rock In A Weary Land	20

HOPKIRK AND LEE
98	Gallery Records GAL001CD	Beneath The Apple Tree (CD, EP, 1000 copies)	8
98	Rough Trade/For Us 001	Beneath The Apple Tree (7" 1,000 copies)	6

MINT VALUE £

HUGH HOPPER

73	CBS 65466	1984 (LP)	30
76	Compendium FIDARDO 4	CRUEL BUT FAIR (LP)	15
77	Compendium FIDARDO 7	HOPPERTUNITY BOX (LP)	15
78	Ogun OG 527	ROGUE ELEMENT (LP, as Hopper, Dean, Gowen, Sheen — 'Soft Heap')	12

(see also Caravan, Elton Dean, Gilgamesh, Isotope, Matching Mole, Ninesense, Soft Machine)

HOPSCOTCH

69	United Artists UP 2231	Look At The Lights Go Up/Same Old Fat Man	70+
69	United Artists UP 35022	Long Black Veil/Easy To Find	7

(see also Scots Of St. James, Five Day Rain, Forever More, Glencoe)

HORACE & IMPERIALS

68	Nu Beat NB 012	Young Love/Days Like These	15

HORDEN RAIKES

72	Folk Heritage FHR 026	HORDEN RAIKES (LP)	20
73	Folk Heritage FHR 042	KING COTTON (LP)	15

HORIZON

81	SRT SRTS 81432	Stage Struck/Remember The Bad Boys	10

HORIZON

83	Orbit TRIP 4	Sunshine Reggae/Nightlife	6

(see also Mungo Jerry)

PAUL HORN

68	Liberty LBL 83084E	COSMIC CONSCIOUSNESS (LP)	18

JIMMY BO HORNE

80	T.K. STKR 13 7586	Is It In/Spank (12")	10

LENA HORNE

55	HMV 7M 309	Love Me Or Leave Me/I Love To Love	8
55	HMV 7M 319	It's All Right With Me/It's Love	8
56	HMV 7M 423	If You Can Dream/What's Right For You (Is Right For Me)	8
56	MGM MGM 917	Can't Help Lovin' Dat Man/The Man I Love (78 rpm = £8)	7
59	RCA RCA 1120	A New Fangled Tango/Honeysuckle Rose (78 rpm = £15)	5
65	United Artists UP 1101	The Sand And The Sea/It Had Better Be Tonight	25
71	Buddah 2011 078	Maybe I'm Amazed/Feels So Good	12
57	RCA RD 27021/SF 5007	AT THE WALDORF ASTORIA (LP, mono/stereo)	12/15
58	RCA RD 27063	STORMY WEATHER (LP)	15
59	RCA RD 27098/SF 5019	GIVE THE LADY WHAT SHE WANTS (LP, mono/stereo)	12/15
59	RCA RD 27141	A FRIEND OF YOURS (LP)	12
61	RCA RD 27255	LENA AT THE SANDS (LP, also stereo SF 5217)	12
63	RCA RD/SF 7530	LENA LOVELY AND ALIVE (LP)	12
64	Stateside S(S)L 10081	HERE'S LENA (LP)	12

(see also Harry Belafonte)

HANK HORNSBY

57	MGM MGM 955	Pots And Pans/Cotton	6
58	MGM MGM 972	The Legend Of The Birds And Bees/Girls Girls Girls (78 rpm = £8)	6

HORNSEY AT WAR

70s	War WAR 001	DEAD BEAT REVIVAL (EP, numbered p/s)	8

HORRORCOMIC

77	Lightning/B&C BVZ 0007	I'm All Hung Up On Pierrepoint/The Exorcist/Sex In The Afternoon (p/s)	45
78	Lightning GIL 512	I Don't Mind/England 77 (p/s)	80
79	B&C BCS 18	Jesus Crisis/Cut Your Throat (p/s)	200

HORSE

70	RCA Victor SF 8109	HORSE (LP)	100

(see also Saturnalia, Atomic Rooster)

HORSLIPS

73	Oats OAT 1	High Reel/Furniture	5
73	Oats MOO 3	HAPPY TO MEET ... SORRY TO PART (LP, booklet octagonal sleeve)	20
74	Oats MOO 5	THE TAIN (LP)	15
76	Oats MOO 9	DRIVE THE COLD WINTER AWAY (LP)	12

HORTENSE (Ellis) & ALTON (Ellis)

65	Island WI 230	Don't Gamble With Love/Something You Got (B-side actually by Alton Ellis & Flames)	22

(see also Hortense Ellis, Alton Ellis, Mr. Foundation)

HORTENSE (Ellis) & DELROY (Wilson)

66	Rio R 119	We're Gonna Make It/SOUL BROTHERS: Ska Shuffle	25

(see also Hortense Ellis, Delroy Wilson)

HORTENSE (Ellis) & JACKIE (Opel)

64	R&B JB 138	Stand By Me/JACKIE OPEL: Solid Rock	35

(see also Hortense Ellis, Jackie Opel)

JOHNNY HORTON

59	Philips PB 932	The Battle Of New Orleans/All For The Love Of A Girl (78 rpm = £28)	8
59	Philips PB 951	Sal's Got A Sugar Lip/Johnny Reb (78 rpm = £45)	10
59	Philips PB 976	Take Me Like I Am/I'm Ready If You're Willing (78 rpm = £45)	10
60	Philips PB 995	Sink The Bismarck!/The Same Old Tale The Crow Told Me	10
60	Philips PB 1062	North To Alaska/The Mansion You Stole	10
61	Philips PB 1130	When It's Springtime In Alaska/Mr. Moonlight	10
61	Philips PB 1132	Sleepy Eyed John/They'll Never Take Her Love From Me	10
61	Philips PB 1170	Miss Marcy/Ole Slew Foot	10
62	Philips PB 1226	Words/Honky Tonk Man	10
63	CBS AAG 132	All Grown Up/I'm A One Woman Man	10

60	Mercury ZEP 10074	THE FANTASTIC JOHNNY HORTON (EP) 60
64	Mercury 10008 MCE	COUNTRY AND WESTERN ACES (EP) 40
60	Philips BBL 7464	THE SPECTACULAR JOHNNY HORTON (LP) 35
61	Philips BBL 7536	HONKY TONK MAN (LP) 45
63	London HA-U 8096	DONE ROVIN' (LP) 40
65	Fontana FJL 306	VOICE OF JOHNNY HORTON (LP) 18

ROBERT HORTON
| 60 | Pye 7N 15285 | (Roll Along) Wagon Train/Sail Ho! .... 5 |
| 60 | Pye NEP 24118 | SUNDAY NIGHT AT THE LONDON PALLADIUM (EP) .... 5 |

WALTER 'SHAKEY' HORTON
70	London HAK/SHK 8405	SOUTHERN COMFORT (LP, as Shakey Horton) 100
74	Xtra XTRA 1135	WALTER 'SHAKEY' HORTON WITH HOT COTTAGE (LP) 20
74	Sonet SNTF 677	BIG WALTER HORTON (LP, with Carey Bell) 15

LA/THE HOST
| 84 | Orbitone | THE HOST EP (cassette) .... 5 |
| 85 | Quiet QU 1 | The Big Sleep/Just Breaking Away (p/s) .... 8 |

HOT BUTTER
| 73 | Pye NSPL 28169 | POPCORN (LP) .... 12 |
| 73 | Pye NSPL 28181 | MORE HOT BUTTER (LP) .... 15 |

HOT CITY
| 71 | London HLU 10344 | Leaving/I Believe In Life .... 15 |

HOT CLUB
82	RAK 346	The Dirt That She Walks On Is Sacred Ground To Me/Heat (p/s) 12
82	RAK 346	The Dirt That She Walks On Is Sacred Ground To Me/Heat (12", p/s) 10
	(see also Rich Kids, Spectres)	

HOT CHOCOLATE (BAND)
69	Apple APPLE 18	Give Peace A Chance/Living Without Tomorrow (as Hot Chocolate Band) 48
70	Rak RAK 103	Love Is Life/Pretty Girls (with promo p/s) 8
79	Rak RAK 29	Mindless Boogie/Don't Turn It Off (12" p/s) 15
	(see also Errol Brown & Chosen Few, Tony Wilson)	

HOTLEGS
70	Fontana 6007 019	Neanderthal Man/You Didn't Like It Because You Didn't Think Of It 5
71	Philips 6006 140	Lady Sadie/The Loser 8
71	Philips 6308 047	THINKS: SCHOOL STINKS (LP) 30
71	Philips 6308 080	SONG (LP) 35
	(see also 10cc, Mindbenders, Godley & Creme, Tristar Airbus)	

HOT POTATO
| 73 | PMTB 1 | HOT POTATO (LP, private pressing) .... 25 |

HOT ROD
| 69 | Joe's DU 41 | The Judge/RON: Soul Of Soul Of Joel .... 12 |

HOT ROD ALLSTARS
69	Duke DU 59	Lick A Pop/Treasure 20
70	Duke DU 65	Paint Your Wagon/Organ Man 15
70	Duke DU 66	Return Of The Bad Man/Caysoe Reggae 20
70	Trojan TR 7732	Strong Man/Sentimental 15
70	Trojan TR 7733	Virgin Soldier/Brixton Reggae Festival 18
70	Torpedo TOR 1	Pussy Got Nine Life/BOSS SOUNDS: Lick It Back 60
70	Torpedo TOR 5	Skinheads Don't Fear/Ten Commandments From The Devil 60
70	Torpedo TOR 10	Moonhop In London/Skinhead Moondust 40
70	Torpedo TOR 14	Control Your Doggy/Follow The Stars 15
70	Hot Rod HR 104	Skinhead Speaks His Mind/CARL LEVEY: Carnaby Street 45
70	Hot Rod HR 107	Strictly Invitation/PATSY & PEGGY: Dog Your Woman 10
70	Hot Rod HR 108	Beautiful World/Shocks Of A Drugs Man 15
	(see also Setters, Betty Sinclair)	

HOTRODS
| 65 | Columbia DB 7693 | I Don't Love You No More/Ain't Coming Back No More .... 55 |

HOT SPRINGS
| 66 | Columbia DB 7821 | It's All Right/All I Know About Love .... 18 |

HOT-TODDYS
| 59 | Pye International 7N 25020 | Shakin' And Stompin'/Rockin' Crickets (78 rpm = £30) .... 30 |
| | (see also Rockin' Rebels) | |

HOT TUNA
72	Grunt 65-0502	Keep On Truckin'/Water Song 5
76	Grunt RCG 1002	It's So Easy/I Can't Be Satisfied 5
70	RCA SF 8125	HOT TUNA (LP) 15
71	RCA LSP 4550	ELECTRIC LIVE (FIRST PULL UP, THEN PULL DOWN) (LP) 12
72	Grunt FTR 1004	BURGERS (LP, with purple inner sleeve) 12
	(see also Jefferson Airplane)	

HOT VULTURES
| 77 | Red Rag RRR 015 | THE EAST STREET SHAKES (LP) .... 18 |
| 70s | Plant Life PLR 018 | UP THE LINE (LP) .... 15 |

HOT WATER
| 78 | Duff | Different Morning/Premium Bondage .... 8 |
| 79 | Duff DWR 101 | Get Lost!/Bird's Eye View (p/s) .... 7 |

HOUGHTON WEAVERS
| 78 | Folk Heritage FHR 106 | SIT THI DOWN (LP) .... 15 |
| 81 | EMI HW 1002 | ALIVE & KICKING (LP) .... 15 |

MINT VALUE £

HOUNDHEAD HENRY/FRANKIE JAXON
60	Jazz Collector JEL 10	THE MALE BLUES VOLUME 6 (EP)	18

HOUR GLASS
68	Liberty LBL/LBS 83219E	THE HOUR GLASS (LP)	30
74	United Artists USD 303/4	THE HOUR GLASS (2-LP)	18

(see also Allman Brothers)

SON HOUSE
(see under 'S')

HOUSEHOLD
67	United Artists UP 1190	I Guess I'll Learn How To Fly/Nothing You Can Do But Cry	10
68	United Artists UP 2210	Twenty First Summer/Winter's Coming On	10

HOUSEMARTINS
85	Go! Discs GOD 7	Flag Day/Stand At Ease (p/s)	5
85	Go! Discs GOD 7/GOD 9	Flag Day/Stand At Ease//Sheep/Drop Down Dead (shrinkwrapped double pack)	6
85	Go! Discs GODX 7	Flag Day/Stand At Ease/Coal Train To Hatfield Main (12", p/s)	8
86	Go! Discs GODP 9	Sheep/I'll Be Your Shelter/Drop Down Dead (picture disc)	5
86	Go! Discs GODP 11	Happy Hour/The Mighty Ship (shaped picture disc)	5
86	Go! Discs GODP 13	Think For A Minute/Who Needs The Limelight (shaped picture disc)	5
86	Go! Discs GODP 16	Caravan Of Love/When I First Met Jesus (rectangular picture disc)	5
86	Go! Discs GODB 16	THE HOUSEMARTINS' CHRISTMAS BOX SET (4 singles in foldout sleeve, some signed)	25/12
88	Go! Discs GODCD 22	There Is Always Something There To Remind Me/Get Up Off Our Knees/ Get Up Off Our Knees (live)/Johannesburg (CD)	8
84	private pressing	THEMES FROM THE WELL-DRESSED MAN (cassette)	20
84	private pressing	THE HOUSEMARTINS FROM OUTER SPACE (cassette)	20

(see also Beautiful South)

HOUSEMASTER BALDWIN
88	Koolkat KOOLT 21	DELTA HOUSE (12", p/s)	10
88	Koolkat KOOLT 22	DON'T LEAD ME (12", p/s)	10

HOUSE OF LORDS
69	B&C CB 112	In The Land Of Dreams/Ain't Gonna Wait Forever	20

HOUSE OF LOVE
87	Creation CRE 043T	Shine On/Love/Flow (12", p/s, 4,000 only)	10
87	Creation CRE 044T	Real Animal/Plastic/Nothing To Me (12", p/s, 4,000 only)	25
88	Creation CRE 053	Christine/Loneliness Is A Gun (die-cut '99p' sleeve)	7
88	Creation CRE 057	Destroy The Heart/Blind/Mr Jo (p/s)	8
88	Creation CRE 057T	Destroy The Heart/Blind/Mr Jo (12", p/s)	10
92	Fontana HOL 710	YOU DON'T UNDERSTAND EP (10", limited edition, numbered sleeve)	8

BOBBI HOUSTON
74	Action ACT 4622	I Want To Make It With You (Parts 1 & 2)	12

CISCO HOUSTON
60	Top Rank 30/028	THE CISCO SPECIAL (LP)	50
68	Fontana FJL 412	I AIN'T GOT NO HOME (LP)	15
69	Ember CW 135	CISCO HOUSTON AND WOODY GUTHRIE (LP)	15

CISSY HOUSTON
70	Major Minor MM 700	He/I Believe/I'll Be There	6
70	Major Minor MM 716	The Long And Winding Road/Be My Baby	6
70	Pye International 7N 25537	I Just Don't Know What To Do With Myself/This Empty Place	40
71	Pye International 7N 25545	The Long And Winding Road/Be My Baby (reissue)	5
71	Janus 6146 003	Darling Take Me Back/Hang On To A Dream	6
72	Janus 6146 027	Midnight Train To Georgia/I'm So Glad I Can Love Again	6
70	Major Minor SMLP 80	PRESENTING CISSY HOUSTON (LP)	30
71	Pye Intl. NSPL 28146	THE LONG AND WINDING ROAD (LP)	20
78	Private Stock PVLP 1044	THINK IT OVER (LP)	15

(see also Sweet Inspirations)

DAVID HOUSTON
55	London HL 8147	Blue Prelude/I'm Sorry I Made You Cry (78 rpm = £18)	50
63	Columbia DB 7159	Mountain Of Love/Poor Little Angeline	7
66	Columbia DB 7997	Almost Persuaded/We Got Love	7

DAVID HOUSTON & TAMMY WYNETTE
67	Columbia DB 8246	My Elusive Dreams/Marriage On The Rocks	8

SAM HOUSTON
65	Island WI 172	My Mother's Eyes/Danny Boy	12

THELMA HOUSTON
69	Stateside SS 8026	Jumpin' Jack Flash/Sunshower	10
70	Stateside SS 8036	Save The Country/I Just Can't Stay Away	7
70	Stateside SS 8044	I Just Wanna Be Me/Crying In The Sunshine	7
72	Tamla Motown TMG 799	I Want To Go Back There Again/Pick Of The Week	15
72	Mowest MW 3001	No One's Gonna Be A Fool Forever/What If	5
73	Mowest MW 3004	Black California/I'm Letting Go (withdrawn)	10
69	Stateside (S)SL 5010	SUNSHOWER (LP)	20
73	ABC ABCL 5061	SUNSHOWER (LP, reissue)	12
73	Mowest MWS 7003	THELMA HOUSTON (LP)	30

WHITNEY HOUSTON
85	Arista ARIST 640	All At Once (promo only for 'Wogan' TV show, plain sleeve, printed white label)	8

(see also J.A.M.s, Aretha Franklin & Whitney Houston)

LARRY HOVIS
58	Capitol CL 14843	Do I Love You/We Could Have Lots Of Fun	8
59	Capitol CL 15083	My Heart Belongs To Only You/I Want To Fall In Love	8

BRIAN HOWARD & SILHOUETTES
62	Columbia DB 4914	Somebody Help Me/Young And Evil	22
63	Columbia DB 7067	The Worryin' Kind/Come To Me	22
64	Fontana TF 464	Back In The U.S.A./Hooked	20

JAN HOWARD
60	London HL 7088	The One You Slip Around With/I Wish I Could Fall In Love Again (export issue)	25

JOHNNY HOWARD BAND
60	Decca F 11298	Up The Wall/Orbit	5
62	Decca F 11423	Mind Reader/Spanish Gipsy Dance	5
64	Decca F 11925	Rinky Dink/Java	15
65	Decca F 12065	El Pussy Cat/A Tune Called Harry	5
67	Deram DML/SML 1001	THE VELVET TOUCH OF JOHNNY HOWARD (LP)	12

LES HOWARD
53	HMV 7M 127	Love Evermore/I Lived When I Met You	10
53	HMV 7M 171	Rags To Riches/From Here To Eternity	10
57	Conquest CP 103	Priscilla/Singin' The Blues (78)	7

ROLAND S. HOWARD & LYDIA LUNCH
86	4AD BAD 210	Some Velvet Morning/I Fell In Love With A Ghost (12", p/s, with postcard)	12

(see also Lydia Lunch, Birthday Party)

ROSETTA HOWARD
51	Vocalion V 1005	Let Your Linen Hang Low/HARLEM HAMFATS: Weed Smoker's Dream (78)	20

JACK HOWARTH
71	Fontana 6438 040	'Ow Do (LP)	12

WAYNE HOWARD
70	Explosion EX 2042	All Kinds Of Everything/Cool And Easy (B-side actually by Lloyd Charmers)	7

CATHERINE HOWE
71	Reflection HRS 11	Nothing More Than Strangers/It Comes With The Breezes	18
71	Reflection REFL 11	WHAT A BEAUTIFUL PLACE (LP)	200+
75	RCA Victor SF 8407	HARRY (LP)	15
70s	RCA Victor ARL 5013	DRAGONFLY DAYS (LP)	12

STEVE HOWE
75	Atlantic K 50151	BEGINNINGS (LP, gatefold sleeve, some with embossed 'Yes' logo)	12/15

(see also In Crowd, Syndicats, Tomorrow, Bodast, Yes, Asia)

EDDIE HOWELL
76	Warner Bros K 16701	Man From Manhattan/Waiting In The Wings (features members of Queen)	12
77	Warner Bros K 16866	Sweet On You/Miss Amerika (features Gary Moore)	6

(see also Queen, Gary Moore, Brian May, Freddie Mercury)

PETER HOWELL
(see under Friends, Ithaca, Alice Through The Looking Glass, Agincourt, Tomorrow Come Someday, BBC Radiophonic Workshop)

FRANKIE HOWERD
54	Decca F 10420	(Don't Let The) Kiddy Geddin/Abracadabra (78 rpm = £8)	10
58	Columbia DB 4230	It's All Right With Me/Song And Dance Man (78 rpm = £8)	10
64	Decca F 12028	Last Word On The Election/Last Word On The Election (part 2)	5
70	Pye 7N 45061	Up Je T'Aime/All Through The Night	5
71	Columbia DB 8757	Up Pompeii/Salute!	5
63	Decca LK 4556	AT THE ESTABLISHMENT (LP)	15
60s	Pye NPL	SOMETHING FUNNY HAPPENED ON THE WAY TO THE FORUM (LP)	15
72	Carnival 2928 201	TELLS THE STORY OF PETER AND THE WOLF (LP)	15

CHRIS HOWLAND
58	Columbia DB 4114	Mama (Ma, He's Making Eyes At Me)/Fraulein (78 rpm = £6)	7
59	Columbia DB 4194	Susie Darlin'/The Rain Falls On Ev'rybody (78 rpm = £6)	10

HOWLIN' WOLF
61	Pye International 7N 25101	Little Baby/Down In The Bottom	25
63	Pye International 7N 25192	Just Like I Treat You/I Ain't Superstitious	25
64	Pye International 7N 25244	Smokestack Lightnin'/Going Down Slow ('Slow' or 'South' on B-side label)	25/18
64	Pye International 7N 25269	Little Girl/Tail Dragger	22
64	Pye International 7N 25283	Love Me Darling/My Country Sugar Mama	22
65	Chess CRS 8010	Killing Floor/Louise	15
65	Chess CRS 8016	Ooh Baby/Tell Me What I've Done	15
69	Chess CRS 8097	Evil/Tail Dragger	15
56	London REU 1072	RHYTHM AND BLUES WITH HOWLIN' WOLF (EP)	200+
63	Pye Intl. NEP 44015	SMOKESTACK LIGHTNIN' (EP)	30
64	Pye Intl. NEP 44032	TELL ME (EP)	30
66	Chess CRE 6017	REAL FOLK BLUES (EP)	30
64	Chess CRL 4006	MOANIN' IN THE MOONLIGHT (LP)	80
65	Chess CRL 4508	POOR BOY (LP)	50
66	Ember EMB 3370	BIG CITY BLUES (LP)	35
69	Chess CRLS 4543	THE HOWLIN' WOLF ALBUM (LP)	25
71	Syndicate Chapter SC 003	GOING BACK HOME (LP)	18
71	Chess 6310 108	MESSAGE TO THE YOUNG (LP)	22
71	Rolling Stones COC 49101	THE LONDON SESSIONS (LP)	18
71	Python PLP 13	HOWLIN' WOLF (LP)	55

(see also Hubert Sumlin)

MINT VALUE £

HOWLIN' WOLF, MUDDY WATERS & BO DIDDLEY
68	Chess CRL 4537	THE SUPER SUPER BLUES BAND (LP)	50

(see also Muddy Waters, Bo Diddley)

HOWLIN' WOLF/JUNIOR PARKER/BOBBY BLAND
74	Polydor 2383 257	BLUES FOR MR. CRUMP (LP)	30

LINDA HOYLE
70	Vertigo 6059 018	Eli's Coming/United States Of Mind (as Linda Hoyle & Affinity)	20
71	Vertigo 6360 060	PIECES OF ME (LP, gatefold sleeve, swirl label)	275

(see also Affinity, Nucleus)

H.P. LOVECRAFT
67	Philips BF 1620	Wayfarin' Stranger/The Time Machine	7
68	Philips BF 1639	The White Ship (Parts 1 & 2) (unissued)	
68	Philips BF 1639	The White Ship/I've Been Wrong Before	15
67	Philips (S)BL 7830	H.P. LOVECRAFT (LP)	50
68	Philips SBL 7872	H.P. LOVECRAFT II (LP, most with watermark at start of each side)	35/15
72	Philips 6336 210	THIS IS H.P. LOVECRAFT (LP)	15
72	Philips 6336 213	H.P. LOVECRAFT VOL. 2 (LP)	15

HQ SQUAD
89	Music Of Life NOTE33	Burial Proceedings In The Course Of Three Knights/Onslaught (12")	20

H2O
81	Spock PARA 2	Hollywood Dream/Children (with lyric insert)	6

FREDDIE HUBBARD
72	CTI CTL 5	STRAIGHT LIFE (LP)	12
73	CTI CTL 11	SKY DIVE (LP)	12
75	CTI CTI 6056	POLAR AC (LP)	12
75	Atlantic K 60053	THE ART OF FREDDIE HUBBARD: THE ATLANTIC YEARS (2-LP)	12
75	CBS 80478	HIGH ENERGY (LP)	12

HUBCAP & WHEELS
70	Dynamic DYN 403	One Pound Weight/VICEROYS: Come Dance	6

(see also Byron Lee & Dragonaires)

WENDY HUBER
65	Philips BF 1446	Come Away Melinda/I Belong To The Wind	8

ROY HUDD
66	Polydor 56136	Ramsey's Men/The Day We Won The Cup	10
67	Pye 7N 17434	Artificial Jumping Spider Seller/Sir Rhubarb Tansy	5
77	BBC RESL 47	Standing Outside The Palace/I'm Gonna Let Them Get Me Down	5

JACK HUDSON
72	Folk Heritage FHR 041	SUMMER DAYS AND YOU (LP)	20

JOHNNY HUDSON & TEENBEATS
63	Decca F 11679	Charms/Makin' Up Is So Much Fun	10

KEITH HUDSON (& CHUCKLES)
69	Big Shot BI 528	Tambourine Man/Old Fashioned Way (both actually by Ken Boothe)	18
70	Smash SMA 2311	Don't Get Me Confused/D. SMITH: Ball of Confusion (B-side actually by Dennis Alcapone)	16
71	Smash SMA 2526	Light Of Day/I Thought You Knew	16
72	Spur SP 1	Darkest Night On A Wet Looking Road/Version	40
72	Duke DU 145	Satan Side (with Chuckles)/DON T. JUNIOR: Evil Spirit	35
72	Downtown DT 492	True True To My Heart/BIG YOUTH: Ace 90 Skank	15
73	Summit SUM 8541	Melody Maker/Uncover Me	15
75	Atra AT28	Lost All Sense Of Direction/Jah Jah	6
75	Faith FA 025	Blackbelt Jones/Version	8
77	Tunde TR 1000	I Wanna Be Where You Are/Still Water (12")	25
78	Greensleeves GRED 8	Bloody Eyes/Dub	16
79	Greensleeves GRED 26	Hun Skin Up/Felt We Felt The Strain (12")	25
75	Magnet MGT 007	ENTER THE DRAGON (LP)	200
75	Mamba KH1	FLESH OF MY SKIN, BLOOD OF MY BLOOD (LP)	180
75	Mamba MAM 002	TORCH OF FREEDOM (LP)	35
75	Atra LP1001	TORCH OF FREEDOM (LP, same as Mamba issue)	50
75	ATRA ATLP 1002	PICK A DUB (LP)	45
77	BRD 001	BRAND (LP)	50
88	Atra LP 1004	FLESH OF MY FLESH (LP)	20

(see also Big Youth, Alton Ellis, Hugh Roy, Delroy Wilson)

KEITH HUDSON & I ROY
73	Randy's RAN 534	Silver Platter/Jean You Change Everything	20

(see also I Roy)

ROCK HUDSON
59	Brunswick 05816	Pillow Talk/Roly Poly (78 rpm = £8)	10
70	Warner Bros WB 8006	Gone With The Cowboys/Meantime	5

HUDSON BROTHERS
75	Rocket PIG 18	Rendezvous/Medley: These Things We Do/Home and four others	6

HUDSON-FORD
74	A&M AMS 7096	Burn Baby Burn/Angels (p/s)	5
77	Arnakata ARN 5001	REPERTOIRE (LP, for publishers' use)	20

(see also Strawbs, Monks, Elmer Gantry's Velvet Opera)

HUDSON PEOPLE
78	Hithouse HIT 1	Trip To Your Mind (Parts 1 & 2) (12")	50
79	Ensign ENY 2712	Trip To Your Mind (Parts 1 & 2) (12", reissue)	30

HUES CORPORATION
74	RCA RCA 2444	Freedom Of The Stallion/Get Off My Cloud	5
74	RCA APL1 0323	FREEDOM OF THE STALLION (LP)	12
74	RCA APL1 0775	ROCKIN' SOUL (LP)	12

HUEYS
69	London HLU 10264	Coo-Coo Over You/You Ain't No Hippie	12

HUG
75	Polydor 2383 330	NEON DREAM (LP)	12

MIKE HUGG
72	Polydor 2058 265	Blue Suede Shoes Again/Fool No More	5
73	Polydor 2058 359	Stress And Strain/Tonight	5
72	Polydor/Sound For Industry SFI 122	Bonnie Charlie/SLADE: The Whole World's Going Crazee (33rpm flexidisc free with *Music Scene* magazine)	12/8
72	Polydor 2383 140	SOMEWHERE (LP, gatefold sleeve)	15
73	Polydor 2383 213	STRESS AND STRAIN (LP)	12

(see also Manfred Mann, Hug, Highly Likely, Elton Dean)

HUGGY BEAR
93	PUSS 002	February 14th/Into The Mission (1-sided gig freebie, w/l, plain black sleeve)	5

CAROL HUGHES
58	Columbia DB 4094	Lend Me Your Comb/First Date	15

DANNY HUGHES
69	Pye 7N 17750	Hi Ho Silver Lining/I Washed My Hands In Muddy Water	15

(see also Orange Machine)

DAVID HUGHES
59	Top Rank JAR 205	Teach Me (How To Love Him)/You Would Have Done The Same	5
60	Top Rank JAR 316	Looking High, High, High/Mi Amor	5

FRED HUGHES
65	Fontana TF 583	Oo Wee Baby I Love You/Love Me Baby	20
76	Brunswick BR 37	Baby Boy/JOHNNY JONES & KING CASUALS: Purple Haze	10
76	DJM DJS 10717	Oo Wee Baby I Love You/My Cries Oh	6

'FRIDAY' HUGHES
51	MGM MGM 422	Lazy Morning/The Devil Ain't Lazy (78)	8

GLENN HUGHES
79	Safari SAFE 14	I Found A Woman/L.A. Cut Off (p/s)	5
77	Safari LONG 2	PLAY ME OUT (LP)	12

(see also Deep Purple, News, Finders Keepers, Trapeze, Roger Glover, Hughes-Thrall)

JIMMY HUGHES
63	London HL 9680	I'm Qualified/My Loving Time	30
64	Pye International 7N 25254	Steal Away/Lollipops, Lace And Lipstick	25
66	Sue WI 4006	Goodbye My Love/It Was Nice	40
66	Atlantic 584 017	Neighbour, Neighbour/It's A Good Thing	15
67	Atlantic 584 135	Hi-Heel Sneakers/Time Will Bring You Back	15
69	Stax STAX 117	Sweet Things You Do/Let 'Em Down Baby	8
69	Stax STAX 126	I'm Not Ashamed To Beg Or Plead/Chains Of Love	12
67	Atlantic 587 068	WHY NOT TONIGHT? (LP)	75
69	Stax SXATS 1010	SOMETHING SPECIAL (LP)	30

RHETTA HUGHES
70s	Polydor 184 223	RELIGHT MY FIRE (LP)	100

HUGHES-THRALL
82	Epic EPC 25052	HUGHES-THRALL (LP)	15

(see also Glenn Hughes)

HUGO & LUIGI
57	Columbia DB 3978	Rockabilly Party/Shenandoah Rose	18
58	Columbia DB 4156	Twilight In Tennessee/Cha-Hua-Hua (78 rpm = £6)	8
59	RCA RCA 1127	La Plume De Ma Tante/Honolulu Lu (78 rpm = £10)	6
60	RCA RCA 1169	Just Come Home/Lonesome Stranger (78)	15

ALAN HULL
70	Big T BT 129	We Can Swing Together/Obadiah's Grave	10
73	Charisma CB 208	Numbers (Travelling Band)/Drinking Song/One Off Pat (p/s)	6
73	Charisma CB 211	Justanothersadsong/Waiting	5
73	Charisma CAS 1069	PIPEDREAM (LP, gatefold sleeve with booklet)	15
75	Warner Brothers K 56121	SQUIRE (LP)	12
79	Rocket TRAIN 6	PHANTOMS (LP, with inner sleeve)	12
83	Black Crow CRO 206	ON THE OTHER SIDE (LP)	12

(see also Lindisfarne, Chosen Few, Radiator)

ROD HULL & EMU/BRISTOL ROVERS FOOTBALL TEAM
74	EMI EMI 2734	I'd Do Anything/Bristol Rovers All The Way	5

HULLABALLOOS
64	Columbia DB 7392	I'm Gonna Love You Too/Why Do Fools Fall In Love	12
65	Columbia DB 7558	I'll Show You How To Love/Did You Ever	12
65	Columbia DB 7626	Don't Stop/I Won't Turn Away Now	12

(see also Bunch Of Fives)

GEORGE HULTGREEN
70	Warner Bros WB 8017	Say Hello/Before You Say Goodbye	6

(see Eclection, Sailor)

HUMAN BEANS
67	Columbia DB 8230	Morning Dew (Take Me For A Walk)/It's A Wonder	65

(see also Love Sculpture, Dave Edmunds)

HUMAN BEAST
70	Decca LK/SKL 5053	VOLUME ONE (LP)	200+

(see also Bread Love & Dreams)

HUMAN BEINZ
67	Capitol CL 15529	Nobody But Me/Sueno	45
68	Capitol CL 15542	Turn On Your Lovelight/It's Fun To Be Clean...............................	25

HUMAN INSTINCT
65	Mercury MF 951	Can't Stop Around/I Want To Be Loved By You My Friend..................	40
66	Mercury MF 972	The Rich Man/Illusions	45
67	Mercury MF 990	Go-Go/I Can't Live Without You..	35
68	Deram DM 167	A Day In My Mind's Mind/Death Of The Seaside	50
68	Deram DM 177	Renaissance Fair/Pink Dawn	50

(see also Jessie Harper)

HUMAN LEAGUE
78	Fast Product FAST 4	Being Boiled/Circus Of Death (p/s, original issue with b&w picture labels)	8
79	Fast Product FAST 10	THE DIGNITY OF LABOUR (12" EP, with spoken-word flexidisc [F10x/VF 1])	12
79	Virgin VS 294	Empire State Human/Introducing (p/s)	10
80	Virgin SV 105	HOLIDAY '80 (EP, double pack, purple & blue labels, 10,000 only)............	10
80	Virgin VS 351	Empire State Human/Introducing//Only After Dark/Toyota City	
		(Long Version) (double pack, p/s, shrinkwrapped)	20
80	Virgin VS 351	Only After Dark/Toyota City (Long Version) (p/s)	8
80	Virgin VS 351	Empire State Human/Introducing (p/s, reissue).............................	5
80	Virgin VS 351-12	Empire State Human/Introducing (12", p/s).................................	12
81	Virgin VS 395	Boys And Girls/Tom Baker (gatefold or non-gatefold p/s) .... each	5
81	Virgin SV 105	HOLIDAY '80 (EP, reissue double pack, green/red labels, gatefold p/s)	7
81	Virgin SV 105	HOLIDAY '80 (reissue 3-track EP, green/red or blue/pink labels) .... each	5
81	Virgin SV 105-12	HOLIDAY '80 (12", 5-track EP, withdrawn)	30+
82	Virgin VSY 522	Mirror Man/(You Remind Me Of) Gold (picture disc).......................	6
84	Virgin VSY 723	Louise/The Sign (Remix) (picture disc)	6
88	Virgin CDT 6	Hard Times/Love Action (I Believe In Love)/Hard Times Instrumental/	
		Love Action Instrumental (3" CD, card sleeve)	8
88	Virgin VSCD 1025	Love Is All That Matters (Edit)/I Love You Too Much (Dub Version)/	
		Love Is All That Matters (Extended Version) (CD, gatefold card sleeve)	8
88	Virgin CDT 24	(Keep Feeling) Fascination (Extended 12" version)/(Keep Feeling) Fascination	
		(Improvisation 12" Dub Version)/Total Panic (3" CD, card sleeve)	8
03	Virgin 12HL 001	The Sound Of The Crowd (Trisco's PopClash Mix)/Love Action (Salmon &	
		Jenkins Mix)/Open Your Heart (Laid Remix) (12", stickered title sleeve)	10
03	Virgin 12HL 002	The Sound Of The Crowd (Freaksblamredo)/Love Action (Brooks Red Line	
		Vocal Mix)/(Keep Feeling) Fascination (Groove Collision TMC Mix)	
		(12", stickered title Sleeve)	10
03	Virgin 12HL 003	Don't You Want Me (Majik Johnson Original Booty Mix)/Love Action	
		(Salmon & Jenkins Dub)/The Sound Of The Crowd (Freaksoldskooljam)	
		(12", stickered title Sleeve)	10
03	Virgin 10HL 004	Open Your Heart (The Strand Remix)/The Sound Of The Crowd	
		(Extended Family Vocal Mix) (10", stickered title sleeve)...................	10
81	Virgin VP 2192	DARE! (LP, picture disc, die-cut sleeve with insert, black or	
		white vinyl border)	12
88	Virgin CDHLP 1	GREATEST HITS (CD, picture disc)..	18

(see also Heaven 17, Men, Philip Oakey & Giorgio Moroder, Respect, Jo Callis)

HUMANOID
88	Westside WSR 7	Stakker Humanoid (Part 1)/Stakker Humanoid (Part 2) (p/s)	8
88	Westside WSR 12	Stakker Humanoid/Radio Edit/Omen Mix (12", p/s)........................	12
88	Westside WSRT 12	HUMANOID EP (12", no p/s)...	12
88	Westside WSRCD 12	HUMANOID EP (3" CD)...	8
89	Westside WSR 14	Slam/Bass Invaders/Slam Edit/Slam Hip House Version (12", p/s)	12
89	Westside HUMT 2	The Deep (Into The Abyss Mix)/The Deep (Extended LP Version)/	
		Cry Baby/The Deep (W5 Mix) (12", p/s)..................................	12
92	Jumpin' & Pumpin'	Stakker Humanoid (12" Orginal)/(Smart Systems Remix)/(Cobain Mix '94/	
	12TOT 27	(Snowman Mix)/(The Omen Mix)/(303 Tribe)/(Outer Limits)	
		(12", brown or black vinyl, p/s)..	15/12
92	Jumpin' & Pumpin'	Stakker Humanoid (Original Mix)/(Smart Systems Remix)/(Cobain Mix '94/	
	CDSTOT 27	(The Omen Mix)/(303 Mix)/(Outer Limits)/(12" Original) (CD)	15
88	Westside Human 1989	GLOBAL (LP)..	15
88	Westside HUMANCD 1989	GLOBAL (CD)...	15

(see also Future Sound Of London, Art Science Technology)

HUMANOID featuring SHARON BENSON
89	Westside HUMT 1	TonIGHT (12", 3 mixes, p/s)...	8

(see also Future Sound Of London)

HUMBLEBUMS
69	Big T BIG 122	Saturday Roundabout Sunday/Bed Of Mossy Green	6
69	Big T BIG 127	Coconut Tree/Her Father Didn't Like Me Anyway	6
70	Big T BIG 130	Shoeshine Boy/My Apartment	6
69	Transatlantic TRA 186	THE FIRST COLLECTION OF MERRY MELODIES (LP)	12
69	Transatlantic TRA 201	THE NEW HUMBLEBUMS (LP)	12
70	Transatlantic TRA 218	OPEN UP THE DOOR (LP)	15
74	Transatlantic TRA 288	THE COMPLETE HUMBLEBUMS (3-LP, box set of above albums)	20

(see also Gerry Rafferty, Billy Connolly)

HUMBLE PIE
69	Immediate IM 082	Natural Born Bugie/Wrist Job (later in p/s)...............................	14/8
70	A&M AMS 807	Big Black Dog/Strange Days	8
72	A&M AMS 7003	Hot'n'Nasty/You're So Good For Me	6
73	A&M AMS 7052	Black Coffee/Say No More	6

HUMBLE PIE

73	A&M AMS 7070	Get Down To It/Honky Tonk Woman	6
73	A&M AMS 7090	Oh La De Da/Outcrowd	6
75	A&M AMS 7185	Rock'n'Roll Music/Scored Out	6
80	Jet JET 180	Fool For A Pretty Face/You Soppy Pratt (p/s)	6
69	Immediate IMSP 025	AS SAFE AS YESTERDAY IS (LP)	30
69	Immediate IMSP 027	TOWN AND COUNTRY (LP)	30
70	A&M AMLS 986	HUMBLE PIE (LP)	30
71	A&M AMLS 2013	ROCK ON (LP)	25
72	A&M AMLH 63506	PERFORMANCE — ROCKIN' THE FILLMORE (2-LP)	20
72	A&M AMLS 64342	SMOKIN' (LP)	20
73	A&M AMLD 6004	EAT IT (2-LP)	20
74	A&M AMLH 63611	THUNDERBOX (LP)	15

(see also Steve Marriott, Small Faces, Peter Frampton, Herd, Natural Gas)

HUMBUG
| 70 | CBS 4811 | Groovin' With Mr Bloe/Marianna | 6 |
| 70 | CBS 5208 | I Got A Feeling (Vocal)/I Got A Feeling (Instrumental) | 5 |

HELEN HUMES
53	Brunswick 05078	They Raided The Joint/Loud Talking Woman (78)	10
53	Brunswick 05193	I Cried For You/Mean Way Of Loving (78)	15
56	Vogue V 2048	Million Dollar Secret/If I Could Be With You One Hour Of The Day (78 rpm = £10)	10
59	Contemporary CV 2415	When The Saints Come Marching In/Bill Bailey, Won't You Please Come Home (with Benny Carter's All-Stars)	5
59	Contemporary CV 2415	When The Saints Come Marching In/Bill Bailey, Won't You Please Come Home (78, with Benny Carter's All-Stars)	10
61	Contemporary LAC 12245	HELEN HUMES AND THE BENNY CARTER ALL STARS (LP)	15

(see also Benny Carter, Jimmy Witherspoon/Helen Humes)

DELLA HUMPHREY
| 69 | Action ACT 4525 | Don't Make The Good Girls Go Bad/Your Love Is All I Need | 20 |
| 72 | Fab FAB 183 | Dreamland (actually by Marcia Griffiths)/Version | 35 |

HUMPY BONG
| 70 | Parlophone R 5859 | Don't You Be Too Long/We're Alright 'Till Then | 35 |

(see also Bee Gees, Morgan)

HUNGER
| 84 | Psycho PSYCHO 14 | STRICTLY FROM HUNGER (LP, reissue of U.S. LP) | 15 |

HUNGRY WOLF
| 70 | Philips 6308 009 | HUNGRY WOLF (LP) | 80 |

(see also Czar, Alan Parker, Ugly Custard)

GERALDINE HUNT
| 69 | Roulette RO 515 | Never Never Leave Me/Push Sweep | 20 |
| 75 | EMI EMI 2275 | You/It's All For You | 6 |

MARSHA HUNT
69	Track 604 030	Walk On Gilded Splinters/Hot Rod Poppa	10
69	Track 604 034	Desdemona/Hippy Gumbo	18
70	Track 604 037	Keep The Customer Satisfied/Lonesome Holy Roller	10
73	Vertigo 6059 080	Beast Day/Somebody To Love (as Marsha Hunt's 22)	12
71	Track 2410 101	WOMAN CHILD (LP)	40

PEE WEE HUNT & HIS ORCHESTRA
| 55 | Capitol CL 14225 | It's Never Too Late To Fall In Love/A Room In Bloomsbury | 8 |
| 55 | Capitol CL 14286 | Save Your Love For Me/My Extraordinary Gal | 8 |

TOMMY HUNT
62	Top Rank JAR 605	The Door Is Open/I'm Wondering	20
68	Direction 58-3216	I Need A Woman Of My Own/Searchin' For My Baby Looking Everywhere	15
72	Polydor 2058 236	Mind, Body & Soul/One More Mountain To Climb	6
74	Pye 7N 45325	Sleep Tight Honey/Time Alone Will Tell	6
75	Spark SRL 1132	Crackin' Up/Get Out	8
85	Kent TOWN 103	The Work Song/IVORYS: Please Stay	25

(see also Ivorys)

WILLIE AMOS HUNT
| 67 | Camp 602 003 | Would You Believe/My Baby Wants To Dance | 60 |

HUNT & TURNER
| 72 | Village Thing VTS 11 | MAGIC LANDSCAPE (LP) | 22 |

ALBERTA HUNTER
| 52 | Jazz Collector L 94 | Everybody Loves My Baby/Texas Moaner Blues (78) | 8 |

CAROL HUNTER
| 73 | Purple PUR 115 | Look Out Cleveland/5/4 March | 7 |
| 73 | Purple TPS 3503 | THE NEXT VOICE YOU HEAR (LP) | 12 |

DANE HUNTER
| 65 | Oriole CB 1985 | Evergreen Tree/Too Late | 6 |

DANNY HUNTER (& GIANTS)
60	HMV POP 722	Make It Up/Little Girl (as Danny Hunter & Giants)	20
60	HMV POP 775	Who's Gonna Walk Ya Home?/Lonely And Blue	20
61	Fontana H 300	Lost Weekend/Age For Love	15

DAVE HUNTER
| 68 | RCA RCA 1766 | She's A Heartbreaker/Love Me A Lifetime | 15 |
| 69 | RCA RCA 1841 | Don't Throw Your Love To The Wind/Hitchcock Railway | 6 |

GREG HUNTER
| 66 | Parlophone R 5483 | Five O'Clock World/Away From Happiness | 8 |

MINT VALUE £

IAN HUNTER

75	CBS 3486	Who Do You Love/Boy	5
76	CBS 4268	All American Alien Boy (Version)/Rape	6
76	CBS 4479	You Nearly Did Me In/A Letter From Britannia To The Union Jack	15
77	CBS 5229	Justice Of The Peace/The Ballad Of Little Star (as Ian Hunter's Overnight Angels)	8
77	CBS 5497	England Rocks/Wild 'N' Free (as Ian Hunter's Overnight Angels)	5
79	Chrysalis CHS 2324	When The Daylight Comes/Life After Death (p/s, white vinyl with mask)	5
79	Chrysalis CHS 2346	Ships/Wild East (p/s)	5
79	Chrysalis CHS 2390	Cleveland Rocks/Bastard (p/s)	5
80	Chrysalis CHS 2434	We Gotta Get Out/Medley: Once Bitten Twice Shy/Bastard/Cleveland Rocks/ Sons And Daughters/One Of The Boys (live double pack, gatefold p/s)	5
81	Chrysalis CHS 2542	Lisa Likes Rock 'n' Roll/Noises (p/s, clear vinyl)	5
83	CBS A 3541	All Of The Good Ones Are Taken/Death 'N' Glory Boys (p/s)	5
83	CBS TA 3541	All Of The Good Ones Are Taken/Death 'N' Glory Boys/Traitor (12", p/s)	8
83	CBS A 3855	Somethin's Goin' On/All Of The Good Ones Are Taken (Slow Version) (p/s)	5
83	CBS A 3855	Somethin's Goin' On (Radio Edit)/All Of The Good Ones Are Taken (Slow Version) (promo only, no p/s)	5
90	Mercury HRCD 1	American Music/Women's Intuition/Cool/Big Time (CD, with Mick Ronson, promo only)	8
77	CBS	YOU'RE NEVER ALONE WITH A SCHIZOPHRENIC (LP, unissued; later issued on Chrysalis CHR 1214)	12

(see also Mott The Hoople, At Last The 1958 Rock & Roll Show, Apex Rhythm & Blues All Stars, Mick Ronson, Roger Taylor)

IVORY JOE HUNTER

50	MGM MGM 271	I Almost Lost My Mind/S.P. Blues (78, with Orchestra)	30
56	London HLE 8261	A Tear Fell/I Need You By My Side (78 rpm = £30)	300+
57	Columbia DB 3872	Since I Met You, Baby/You Can't Stop This Rockin' And Rollin' (78 rpm = £25)	250
57	London HLE 8486	Love's A Hurting Game/Empty Arms (78 rpm = £30)	150+
61	Capitol CL 15220	I'm Hooked/Because I Love You	30
61	Capitol CL 15226	You Better Believe It, Baby/May The Man Win	30

ROBERT HUNTER

74	Round RX 101	TALES OF THE GREAT RUM RUNNERS (LP)	12
75	Round RX 105	TIGER ROSE (LP)	12
80	Dark Star DSLP 8001	JACK O'ROSES (LP)	15

(see also Grateful Dead)

SUSAN HUNTER

55	Brunswick 05458	Not Yet/Was That The Right Thing To Do?	8

TAB HUNTER

57	London HLD 8380	Young Love/Red Sails In The Sunset (gold or silver label)	30/18
57	London HLD 8410	Ninety-Nine Ways/I Don't Get Around Much Anymore	20
58	London HLD 8535	Don't Let It Get Around/I'm Alone Because I Love You	20
60	Warner Bros WB 8	(What Can I Give) My Only Love/(I'll Be With You) In Apple Blossom Time	5
60	Warner Bros WB 20	Waitin' For The Fall/Our Love	5
61	London HLD 9381	The Wild Side Of Life/My Devotion	5
62	London HLD 9559	Born To Lose/I Can't Stop Lovin' You	5
58	London RE-D 1134	TAB HUNTER (EP)	40
61	Warner Bros WEP 6023	TAB HUNTER (EP, also stereo WSEP 2023)	25/40
60	Warner Bros WM 4008	TAB HUNTER (LP, also stereo WS 8008)	35/40
61	London HA-D 2401	YOUNG LOVE (LP, also stereo SAH-G 6201)	50/65

HUNTER MUSKETT

73	Bradleys BRAD 303	John Blair/Silver Coin (p/s)	6
70	Decca Nova SDN 20	EVERY TIME YOU MOVE (LP)	160
73	Bradleys BRADL 1003	HUNTER MUSKETT (LP)	25

HUNTERS (U.K.)

60	Fontana H 276	Teen Scene/Santa Monica Flyer	25
61	Fontana H 303	Golden Ear-rings/Tally Ho	15
61	Fontana H 323	The Storm/How's M'Chicks?	15
64	Fontana TF 514	Teen Scene/Someone Else's Baby	15
61	Fontana TFL 5140	TEEN SCENE: THE HUNTERS PLAY THE BIG HITS (LP, stereo STFL 561)	55/65
62	Fontana TFL 5175	HITS FROM THE HUNTERS (LP, also stereo STFL 572)	55/65

(see also Dave Sampson & Hunters, Maisie McDaniel)

HUNTERS (Holland)

66	RCA RCA 1541	Russian Spy And I/Spring	18

(see also Jan Akkerman, Brainbox)

HURDY GURDY

72	CBS 64781	HURDY GURDY (LP)	150

RED VINCENT HURLEY

76	Pye 7N 45583	When/Just A Little Love (p/s)	7

HURRICANES

71	Upsetter US 363	Got To Be Mine/UPSETTERS: Version	12

(see also Dave Barker)

HURRICANE STRINGS

63	Columbia DB 7027	Venus/In The Carrick	8

MIKE HURST (& METHOD)

63	Philips BF 1295	The Banjo Song/Any Chance For Me	5
64	Philips BF 1319	Carol Anne/Anytime That You Want Me	5
64	Philips BF 1353	Half Heaven Half Heartache/Look In Your Eyes	5

(see also Springfields, Remo Four, Ashton Gardner & Dyke, Sundance)

MISSISSIPPI JOHN HURT
65	Vanguard SVRL 19005	THE IMMORTAL MISSISSIPPI JOHN HURT (LP)	25
66	Vanguard SVRL 19032	MISSISSIPPI JOHN HURT (LP)	25
67	Fontana TFL 6079	MISSISSIPPI JOHN HURT (LP)	25
71	Spokane SPL 1001	THE ORIGINAL 1928 RECORDINGS (LP)	50
71	Vanguard VSD 19/20	THE BEST OF MISSISSIPPI JOHN HURT (2-LP)	18
73	Vanguard VSD 79327	LAST SESSIONS (LP)	15

HUSH
68	Fontana TF 944	Elephant Rider/Grey	425

HüSKER Dü
84	SST SST 025	Eight Miles High/Masochism World (live) (p/s)	8
85	SST 051	Makes No Sense At All/Love Is All Around (p/s)	5
86	Warner Bros W 8746	Don't Want To Know If You're Lonely/All Work And No Play (p/s)	5
86	Warner Bros W 8746T	Don't Want To Know If You're Lonely/All Work And No Play/ Helter Skelter (live) (12", p/s)	10
86	Warner Bros W 8612	Sorry Somehow/All This I've Done For You (p/s)	5
86	Warner Bros W 8612	Sorry Somehow/All This I've Done For You//Celebrated Summer (Acoustic)/ Flexible Flyer (double pack, gatefold sleeve)	8
86	Warner Bros W 8612T	Sorry Somehow/All This I've Done For You/Celebrated Summer (Acoustic)/ Flexible Flyer/Fattie (12", p/s)	8
87	Warner Bros W 8456	Could You Be The One/Everytime (p/s)	5
87	Warner Bros W 8456T	Could You Be The One/Everytime/Charity, Chastity, Prudence, Hope (12", p/s)	10
87	Warner Bros W 8276	Ice Cold Ice/Gotta Lotta (p/s)	5
87	Warner Bros W 8276T	Ice Cold Ice/Gotta Lotta/Medley (12", p/s)	10

FERLIN HUSKY (& HIS HUSH PUPPIES)
57	Capitol CL 14702	Gone/Missing Persons (as Ferlin Husky & His Hush Puppies) (78 rpm = £10)	15
57	Capitol CL 14753	A Fallen Star/Prize Possession (78 rpm = £15)	20
57	Capitol CL 14785	This Moment Of Love/Make Me Live Again (78 rpm = £15)	8
58	Capitol CL 14824	Wang Dang Doo/What'cha Doin' After School (78 rpm = £18)	20
58	Capitol CL 14883	Slow Down Brother/The Drunken Driver (& His Hush Puppies)	25
58	Capitol CL 14916	I Feel That Old Heartache Again/I Saw God	8
58	Capitol CL 14922	The Kingdom Of Love/Terrific Together	7
58	Capitol CL 14954	I Will/All Of The Time	5
57	Capitol EAP1 718	SONGS OF THE HOME AND HEART (EP)	12
57	Capitol EAP1 837	FERLIN HUSKY HITS (EP)	15
57	Capitol EAP1 921	COUNTRY MUSIC HOLIDAY (EP)	15
59	Parlophone GEP 8795	COUNTRY ROUND UP (EP)	30
60	Capitol EAP1 1280	FERLIN'S FAVOURITES (EP)	15
60	Capitol EAP2 1280	FERLIN'S FAVOURITES (EP)	15
60	Capitol EAP3 1280	FERLIN'S FAVOURITES (EP)	15
58	Capitol T 880	BOULEVARD OF BROKEN DREAMS (LP)	25
59	Capitol T 976	SITTIN' ON A RAINBOW (LP)	25
65	Fontana FJL 304	OLE OPRY FAVOURITES (LP)	15

(see also Simon Crum)

JACQUES HUSTIN
74	EMI EMI 2143	Fleur De Liberté/Freedom For The Man	15

HUSTLER
74	A&M AMLS 68276	HIGH STREET (LP)	12
75	A&M AMLH 33001	PLAY LOUD (LP)	15

HUSTLERS
63	Philips BF 1275	Gimme What I Want/Not Much	7
64	Mercury MF 807	Be True To You/You Can't Sit Down	7
64	Mercury MF 817	Sick Of Giving/Easy To Find	20

WILLIE HUTCH
73	Tamla Motown TMG 862	Brother's Gonna Work It Out/I Choose You	10
73	Tamla Motown STMA 8003	THE MACK (LP, soundtrack)	15
73	Tamla Motown STML 11247	FULLY EXPOSED (LP)	15
74	Tamla Motown STML 11269	FOXY BROWN (LP, soundtrack)	15
74	Tamla Motown STML 11280	THE MARK OF THE BEAST (LP)	20
75	Tamla Motown STML 12015	ODE TO MY LADY (LP)	20
76	Tamla Motown STML 12023	CONCERT IN BLUES (LP)	15

ASHLEY HUTCHINGS
72	Island HELP 5	MORRIS ON (LP, actually by various folk artists)	12
76	Island HELP 24	RATTLEBONE AND ROUGHJACK (LP)	20
76	Harvest SHSM 2012	SON OF MORRIS ON (LP, actually by various folk artists)	12
77	Harvest SHSP 4073	KICKIN' UP THE SAWDUST (LP)	15

(see also Albion Band, Fairport Convention, Steeleye Span, Bunch)

HUTCH HUTCHINS
77	Goodwood GM 12324	FEELS LIKE RAIN (LP)	35

SAM HUTCHINS
69	Bell BLL 1044	Dang Me/I'm Tired Of Pretending	15

LEROY HUTSON
75	Warner Bros K 16536	All Because Of You Parts 1 & 2	10
74	Buddah BDLP 4013	THE MAN (LP)	20
75	Warner Bros K 56139	HUTSON (LP)	50

J.B. HUTTO & HIS HAWKS
73	Delmark DS 617	HAWK SQUAT (LP)	20

MINT VALUE £

BETTY HUTTON
53	HMV 7M 103	Somebody Loves Me/Jealous (B-side with Pat Morgan)	15
56	Capitol CL 14568	Sleepy Head/Hit The Road To Dreamland	10
54	Capitol LC 6639	CAPITOL PRESENTS BETTY HUTTON (10" LP)	35

(see also Hutton Sisters, Perry Como, 'Tennessee' Ernie Ford)

DANNY HUTTON
66	MGM MGM 1314	Funny How Love Can Be/Dreamin' Isn't Good For You	5
65	Pye International 7N 25325	Roses And Rainbows/Monster Shindig	5

(see also Three Dog Night)

HUTTON SISTERS (Betty & Marion)
55	Capitol CL 14250	Ko Ko Mo (I Love You So)/Heart Throb	25

(see also Betty Hutton)

CHARLIE HYATT
65	Island IEP 707	RASS! (EP, as Bam & Charlie Hyatt)	25
66	Island ILP 932	KISS ME NECK (LP)	45

HYDRA
74	Capricorn 2089 008	Glitter Queen/It's So Hard	5
74	Capricorn 2429 120	HYDRA (LP)	12

HYGRADES
65	Columbia DB 7734	She Cared/We're Through	10

BRIAN HYLAND
60	London HLR 9161	Itsy Bitsy Teeny Weeny Yellow Polka Dot Bikini/Don't Dilly Dally, Sally (78)	220
60	London HLR 9113	Rosemary/Library Love Affair	20
60	London HLR 9161	Itsy Bitsy Teeny Weeny Yellow Polka Dot Bikini/Don't Dilly Dally, Sally	8
60	London HLR 9203	Four Little Heels/That's How Much	8
61	London HLR 9262	Lop Sided, Over Loaded/I Gotta Go ('Cause I Love You)	8
61	HMV POP 915	Let Me Belong To You/Let It Die	8
61	HMV POP 955	The Night I Cried/I'll Never Stop Wanting You	8
62	HMV POP 1013	Ginny Come Lately/I Should Be Gettin' Better	7
62	HMV POP 1051	Sealed With A Kiss/Summer Job	7
62	HMV POP 1079	Warmed Over Kisses/Walk A Lonely Mile	7
63	HMV POP 1113	I May Not Live To See Tomorrow/It Ain't That Way At All	7
63	HMV POP 1143	If Mary's There/Remember Me	7
63	HMV POP 1169	Somewhere In The Night/I Wish Today Was Yesterday	7
63	HMV POP 1188	I'm Afraid To Go Home/Save Your Heart For Me	7
63	HMV POP 1237	Let Us Make Our Own Mistakes/Nothing Matters But You	7
64	Philips BF 1326	Here's To Our Love/Two Kinds Of Girls	7
65	Philips BF 1429	Stay Away From Her/I Can't Keep A Secret	7
65	Philips BF 1486	3,000 Miles/Sometimes They Do	7
66	Philips BF 1508	The Joker Went Wild/I Can Hear The Rain	7
62	HMV 7EG 8780	SEALED WITH A KISS (EP)	50
61	London HA-R 2289	THE BASHFUL BLONDE (LP)	150
62	HMV CLP 1553	LET ME BELONG TO YOU (LP)	100
63	HMV CLP 1759	COUNTRY MEETS FOLK (LP)	65
66	Philips BL 7762	THE JOKER WENT WILD (LP)	30
68	Fontana SFL 13008	HERE'S TO OUR LOVE (LP)	22
72	Uni UNLS 118	BRIAN HYLAND (LP)	15

C. HYMAN
65	Ska Beat JB 200	The Ska Rhythm/The Ska Is Moving On	18

DICK HYMAN TRIO
69	Command SCMD 508	MOOG — THE ELECTRIC ECLECTICS OF DICK HYMAN (LP)	15
70	Command SCMD 946	THE AGE OF ELECTRONICUS (LP)	25

PHYLLIS HYMAN
79	Arista ARIST 323	You Know How To Love Me/Give A Little More (12", p/s)	10

I AM KLOOT
00s	Uglyman AMOUR 4CD	Twist/86 TVs (CD)	10

JANIS IAN
67	Verve Folkways VS 1503	Society's Child (Baby I've Been Thinking)/Letter To Jon	20
67	Verve Folkways VS 1506	Society's Child (Baby I've Been Thinking)/Letter To Jon (reissue)	5
68	Verve Folkways VS 1513	Sunflakes Fall, Snowrays Call/Insanity Comes Quietly To The Structured Mind.	10
67	Verve F'ways (S)VLP 6001	JANIS IAN (LP)	25
67	Verve Forecast (S)VLP 6003	FOR ALL THE SEASONS OF YOUR MIND (LP)	20
68	Verve Forecast (S)VLP 6009	THE SECRET LIFE OF J. EDDY FINK (LP)	15
70	Verve Folkways SVLP 6023	WHO REALLY CARES? (LP)	15
71	Capitol E-ST 683	PRESENT COMPANY (LP)	15

IAN (Meeson) & BELINDA (Gillet)
89	Odeon ODO 112	Who Wants To Live Forever?/Who Wants To Live Forever? (Instrumental) (p/s, feat. Brian May)	7
89	Odeon 12ODO 112	Who Wants To Live Forever?/Who Wants To Live Forever? (Instrumental)/ Who Wants To Live Forever? (Original Demo) (12", p/s, feat. Brian May)	10

(see also Brian May)

IAN & SYLVIA
63	Fontana TF 426	Four Strong Winds/Long Lonesome Road	5
65	Fontana TFL 6053	EARLY MORNING RAIN (LP)	15
68	Vanguard SVRL 19004	THE BEST OF IAN & SYLVIA (LP)	12

IAN (EDWARD) & ZODIACS
63	Oriole CB 1849	Beechwood 4-5789/You Can Think Again	52
65	Fontana TF 548	Just The Little Things/This Won't Happen To Me (as Ian Edward with Zodiacs)	35
66	Fontana TF 708	No Money, No Honey/Where Were You?	30
66	Fontana TF 753	Wade In The Water/Come On Along, Girl	65
65	Wing WL 1074	GEAR AGAIN — 12 HITS (LP)	58

(see also Koppykats, Wellington Wade)

I BENJAHMAN
83	Lion Kingdom LKLP 01	INTRODUCING A FRACTION OF JAH ACTION (LP)	30

ICARUS
69	Spark SRL 1012	The Devil Rides Out/You're In Life	50+
72	Pye NSPL 28161	THE MARVEL WORLD OF ICARUS (LP)	95

ICE
67	Decca F 12680	Anniversary (Of Love)/So Many Times	60
68	Decca F 12749	Ice Man/Whisper Her Name (Maria Laine)	100

(see also Affinity)

ICE
79	Storm SR 3307	SAGA OF THE ICE KING (LP, private pressing with booklet)	110

(see also Dickens)

ICED EARTH
02	Century Media	DARK GENESIS (5-CD box set, initial issues with mispressed labels)	30

ICE LA BAS
80s	Storm SR 12 NO 4	ICE LA BAS (12" EP, with booklet)	10

ICEPICK
97	Backbone BR971AA	Phenomenal Criminal/Brixtonites Pt. 1 (12")	20
98	Backbone ICEEP1 BB002	The ICEPICK (EP)	15

ICICLE WORKS
82	Troll Kitchen WORKS 1	Nirvana/Love Hunt/Scirocco (p/s)	5

(see also Ian McNabb, Melting Bear)

IDEALS
61	Pye International 7N 25103	Knee Socks/Mary's Lamb	40

IDES OF MARCH
66	London HLU 10058	You Wouldn't Listen/I'll Keep Searching (as I'des Of March)	12
68	London HLU 10183	Hole In My Soul/Girls Don't Grow On Trees	12
70	Warner Bros WB 7378	Vehicle/Lead Me Home, Gently	6
70	Warner Bros WB 7403	Superman/Home	6
70	Warner Bros WS 1863	THE IDES OF MARCH (LP)	22

IDIOTS
80s	Blue Angle BLI 2	Operation Julie/(Why Does Politics Turn Men Into) Toads (p/s)	5

(see also Tone Deaf & Idiots)

IDLE FLOWERS
84	Miles Ahead AHEAD 1	All I Want Is You/Fizz Music (p/s)	8

(see also Hanoi Rocks)

IDLE RACE
67	Liberty LBF 15026	The Imposters Of Life's Magazine/Sitting In My Tree	35
68	Liberty LBF 15054	The Skeleton And The Roundabout/Knocking Nails Into My House	20
68	Liberty LBF 15101	The End Of The Road/The Morning Sunshine	15
68	Liberty LBF 15129	I Like My Toys/The Birthday (unissued)	
69	Liberty LBF 15218	Days Of Broken Arrows/Warm Red Carpet (B-side act. "Worn Red Carpet")	20
69	Liberty LBF 15242	Come With Me/Reminds Me Of You	22
71	Regal Zonophone RZ 3036	Dancing Flower/Bitter Green	12
76	United Artists UP 36060	The Skeleton And The Roundabout/Morning Sunshine	5
68	Liberty LBL/LBS 83132	THE BIRTHDAY PARTY (LP, mono/stereo)	85/75
69	Liberty LBS 83221	THE IDLE RACE (LP)	100
71	Regal Zono. SLRZ 1017	TIME IS (LP)	130
73	Sunset SLS 50354	ON WITH THE SHOW (LP)	15
76	Sunset SLS 50381	THE BIRTHDAY PARTY (LP, reissue)	15

(see also Mike Sheridan & Nightriders, Nightriders, Mike Sheridan's Lot, Lemon Tree, Jeff Lynne, Move, E.L.O., Trevor Burton, Steve Gibbons Band, Wizzard)

IDLEWILD
97	Human Condition HC 0017	Queen Of The Troubled Teens/Faster/Self Healer (p/s, 1,000 only)	40
97	Fierce Panda NING 42	Chandelier/I Want To Be A Writer (p/s)	20
97	Deceptive BLUFF 057	Satan Polaroid/House Alone (die-cut p/s, numbered, 1,500 only)	25
98	Deceptive BLUFF 058CD	CAPTAIN EP (Self Healer/Annihilate Now!/Last Night I Missed All The Fireworks/ Satan Polaroid/You Just Have To Be Who You Are) (CD)	8
98	Food FOOD 111	A Film For The Future/Mince Showercap Part 1 (wraparound p/s, stickered poly outer sleeve)	5

98	Food FOOD 113	Everyone Says You're So Fragile/Mince Showercap Part 2 (wraparound p/s, stickered poly outer sleeve)	5
98	Food FOOD 114	I'm A Message/Mince Showercap Part 3 (p/s)	5

BILLY IDOL

82	Chrysalis CHS 2543	Mony Mony/Baby Talk (p/s)	5
82	Chrysalis CHS 12 2543	Mony Mony/Baby Talk/Untouchables/Dancing With Myself (12", p/s)	8
82	Chrysalis CHSP 2625	Hot In The City/Dead On Arrival (picture disc)	5
82	Chrysalis IDOL 1	Dancing With Myself/White Wedding (p/s, clear vinyl)	5
83	Chrysalis IDOL 1	White Wedding/Hot In The City (reissue, p/s, clear vinyl)	5
84	Chrysalis IDOL 2	Rebel Yell/Crank Call//White Wedding/Hot In The City (double pack, gatefold p/s)	5
84	Chrysalis IDOLP 2	Rebel Yell/Crank Call (square picture disc)	8
84	Chrysalis IDOLP 3/ CHS 2656	Eyes Without A Face/The Dead Next Door//Dancing With Myself/ Rebel Yell (12" picture disc)	8
84	Chrysalis IDOL 4	Flesh For Fantasy/Blue Highway (gatefold p/s)	6
84	Chrysalis IDOLX 4	Flesh For Fantasy (Extended)/Blue Highway/Flesh For Fantasy (12", p/s, with poster)	8
84	Chrysalis IDOLP 4	Flesh For Fantasy (Extended)/Blue Highway/Flesh For Fantasy (12" picture disc)	8
85	Chrysalis IDOL 5	White Wedding/Flesh For Fantasy (second reissue, p/s, white vinyl)	5
85	Chrysalis IDOLX 5	White Wedding (Shotgun Mix Parts 1& 2)/Mega-Idol-Mix (12", p/s, white vinyl)	8
85	Chrysalis IDOLP 5	White Wedding (Shotgun Mix Parts 1& 2)/Mega-Idol-Mix (12" picture disc)	8
85	Chrysalis IDOLP 6	Rebel Yell/(Do Not) Stand In The Shadows (Live)/Blue Highway (Live) (12" picture disc)	8

(see also Generation X)

IDOLS

65	Mercury MF 840	Don't Walk Away/You Don't Care	15

(see also Mike Sax & Idols)

IDOLS

79	Ork NYC 2	You/Girl That I Love (p/s)	8

(see also New York Dolls)

IF

70	Island WIP 6083	Raise The Level Of Your Conscious Mind/I'm Reaching Out On All Sides	10
71	United Artists UP 35263	Far Beyond/Forgotten Roads	6
72	United Artists UP 35356	You In Your Small Corner/Waterfall	6
70	Island ILPS 9129	IF (LP, 1st pressing, pink label/'i' logo)	38
71	Island ILPS 9129	IF (LP, 2nd pressing, pink rim label/'palm tree' logo)	20
71	Island ILPS 9137	IF2 (LP, pink label, pink rim label/'palm tree' logo)	20
71	United Artists UAG 29158	IF3 (LP)	35/20/15
72	United Artists UAG 29315	IF IV (LP, gatefold sleeve with inner)	18
74	Gull GULP 1007	TEA BREAK OVER – BACK ON YOUR 'EADS (LP)	12

(see also Ferris Wheel)

KRIS IFE

67	MGM MGM 1369	Hush/The Spectator	15
68	MGM MGM 1390	This Woman's Love/I Gotta Feeling	12
68	Music Factory CUB 3	Give And Take/Sands Of Time	15
68	Parlophone R 5741	Imagination/I'm Coming 'Round	15
69	Parlophone R 5770	Haven't We Had A Good Time?/Will I Ever Fall In Love Again?	7

(see also Quiet Five, Judd)

FRANK IFIELD

62	Columbia SCX 3460	I'LL REMEMBER YOU (LP, stereo)	12
65	Columbia 33SX 1723	PORTRAIT IN SONG (LP, also stereo SCX 3551)	12
65	Columbia 33SX 1751	UP JUMPED A SWAGMAN (LP)	12
66	Columbia S(C)X 6009	BABES IN THE WOOD (LP, cast recording, mono/stereo)	12
73	Spark SRLP 111	SOMEONE TO GIVE MY LOVE TO (LP)	12

'IGGINBOTTOM

69	Deram DML/SML 1051	'IGGINBOTTOM'S WRENCH (LP)	125

(see also Soft Machine)

IGGY & STOOGES

(see under Stooges, Iggy Pop)

JULIO IGLESIAS

70	Decca F 23005	Gwendolyne/Bla, Bla, Bla	8

IGNERANTS

79	Rundown ACE 008	Radio Interference/Wrong Place, Wrong Time (p/s)	30

I.G.s

75	RCA RCA 2560	Show And Tell/I Can't Get You Out Of My Mind	20

IGUANA

72	Polydor 2383 108	IGUANA (LP)	20

IGUANAS

65	RCA RCA 1484	This Is What I Was Made For/Don't Come Runnin' To Me	35

I HAICIDEONS & I JARZIF

78	Greensleeves GRED 7	Rise Ethiopians/Signs Of The Messiah (12")	25

I JAH MAN (LEVI)

76	Lucky LY 6016	Jah Heavy Load/Heavy Dub	70
76	Concrete CJ 756	I Am Levi/Part 2	100
78	Island WIP 6458	Heavy Load/I'm A Levi	20

I-JOG & TRACKSUITS

78	Tyger TYG 1	Red Box/Worrying Man (p/s)	6

IKE (B) & CRYSTALITES
68	Island WI 3134	Illya Kuryakin/Anne Marie (B-side miscredited to Bobby Ellis & Crystalites)	60
68	Island WI 3151	Try A Little Merriness/Patricia (as Ike B & Crystalites)	20

IKETTES
62	London HLU 9508	I'm Blue/Find My Baby	25
65	Stateside SS 407	Peaches'N'Cream/The Biggest Players	25
65	Stateside SS 434	(He's Gonna Be) Fine Fine Fine/How Come	20
65	Sue WI 389	Prisoner In Love/Those Words	40
66	Polydor 56506	I'm So Thankful/Don't Feel Sorry For Me	20
66	Polydor 56516	(Never More) Lonely For You/Sally Go Round The Roses	15
66	London HLU 10081	What'cha Gonna Do?/Down, Down	40
67	Polydor 56533	I'm So Thankful/Don't Feel Sorry For Me (reissue)	8
73	Mojo 2092 063	Peaches'N'Cream/Sally Go Round The Roses.	5
65	Stateside SE 1033	FINE FINE FINE (EP)	50
		(see also Ike & Tina Turner, P.P. Arnold)	

ILANIT
77	Pye International 7N 25739	I'm No One (If You Leave Me)/I Can't Say I Love You (p/s)	10

I LIKE TRAINS
04	Dance To The Radio DTTR005	Before The Curtains Close Part 1/Part 2 (500 only, foldover p/s and 2 inserts)	8
05	Kids	A Rook House For Bobby/The Beeching Report (500 only, picture disc)	8

I LIFE
64	R&B JB 140	Kiss You Gave Me/No More	18

ILLUSION
69	Dot DOT 122	Did You See Her Eyes?/Falling In Love	8
70	Dot DOT 133	Together/Don't Push It	5
70	Dot DOT 137	Let's Make Each Other Happy/Beside You (unissued)	
70	Paramount PARA 3007	Let's Make Each Other Happy/Beside You	5
69	Dot (S)LPD 531	ILLUSION (LP)	22
70	Dot SLPD 537	TOGETHER (AS A WAY OF LIFE) (LP)	20
70	Paramount SPFL 264	IF IT'S SO (LP, originally planned for Dot SLPD 539)	18

ILLUSIVE DREAM
69	RCA Victor RCA 1791	Electric Garden/Back Again	30
		(see also Christine Perfect)	

SOLOMON ILORY
63	Blue Note 45-1899	Yabe E (Farewell) (Parts 1 & 2)	12

I LUV WIGHT
70	Philips 6006 043	Let The World Wash In/Mediaeval Masquerade (some in p/s).	90/35
		(see also Kaleidoscope, Fairfield Parlour)	

I'M NOT A GUN
	City Centre Offices BLOCK 018	Make Sense And Loose/(mixes) (12" EP, custom sleeve)	8

IM (Cedric Brooks) & DAVID
70	Bamboo BAM 57	Candid Eye/SOUND DIMENSION: Federated Backdrop	28

IM & COUNT OSSIE
71	Banana CA 357	So Long Rastafari Calling/Give Me Back My Language & Culture	45

IMAGE
65	Parlophone R 5281	Come To The Party/Never Let Me Go	32
65	Parlophone R 5352	Home Is Anywhere/I Hear Your Voice Again.	32
66	Parlophone R 5442	I Can't Stop Myself/Let's Make The Scene	32
		(see also Dave Edmunds)	

IMAGES
65	Polydor 56011	I Only Have Myself To Blame/Head Over Heels	30

NATALIE IMBRUGLIA
98	RCA 74321 52799-2	Torn/Contradictions/Diving In The Deep End (CD, withdrawn)	12

HAMISH IMLACH
67	Xtra XTRA 1050	LIVE! (LP)	12
67	Xtra XTRA 1059	BEFORE AND AFTER (LP)	12

IMMEDIATE
05	Fierce Panda NING161	Never Seen/Say This (p/s)	7

IMMORTALS
69	Amalgamated AMG 851	Bongo Jah/ANSELL COLLINS: My Last Waltz	40

IMMORTALS
86	MCA MCA 1057	No Turning Back/No Turning Back (The Chocks-Away Mix) (p/s)	30
86	MCA MCAT 1057	No Turning Back (Joy Stick Mix)/No Turning Back/No Turning Back (The Chocks-Away Mix) (12", p/s)	35
		(see also Queen)	

IMPAC
66	CBS 202402	Too Far Out/Rat Tat Ta Tat	80

IMPACT ALL STARS
71	Bullet BU 483	Dandy Shandy Version 4/Go Back Version 3	7
71	Randy's RAN 519	Go Back Version 4/Version 3	7
71	Supreme SUP 223	Go Back/Version	8
		(see also Randy's All Stars, Alton Ellis, Gregory Issacs, Errol Dunkley, C. Danovan, Heptones, Dennis Brown, Horace Andy)	

IMPALAS

IMPALAS
59	MGM MGM 1015	Sorry (I Ran All The Way Home)/Fool, Fool, Fool (78 rpm = £40)	32
59	MGM MGM 1031	Oh, What A Fool/Sandy Went Away	35
60	MGM MGM 1068	Peggy Darling/'Bye Everybody	35
59	MGM MGM-EP 696	SORRY (I RAN ALL THE WAY HOME) (EP)	450+

IMPERIAL POMPADOURS
80	Pompadour POMP 001	ERSATZ (LP, actually Inner City Unit with Robert Calvert & Barney Bubbles)	35

(see also Inner City Unit, Robert Calvert)

IMPERIALS
68	Nu Beat NB 012	Young Love/Days Like These	8

IMPERIALS (Jamaica)
69	Bullet BU 417	Black Is Soul/Always With You	12

IMPERIALS
72	Key KL 012	TIME TO GET IT TOGETHER (LP)	18
74	Key KL 025	FOLLOW THE MAN WITH THE MUSIC (LP)	15

IMPERSONATORS
69	Big Shot BI 524	Make It Easy On Yourself/I've Tried Before	12

(see also Moffat Allstars)

IMPOSSIBLE DREAMERS
80	Merciful Release MR 1	Books Books Books/Not A Love Song/Waiting For The Girl/ What Can You Do When You See Someone As Beautiful As You?	8

IMPOSSIBLE YEARS
85	Dreamworld DREAM 1	SCENES WE'D LIKE TO SEE (12" EP)	12

IMPOSTERS
69	Mercury MF 1080	Apache '69/Q Three	20

IMPRESSIONS
58	London HL 8697	For Your Precious Love/Sweet Was The Wine (as Jerry Butler & Impressions)	175
58	London HL 8697	For Your Precious Love/Sweet Was The Wine (78, as Jerry Butler & Impressions)	70
61	HMV POP 961	Gypsy Woman/As Long As You Love Me	50
63	HMV POP 1129	I'm The One Who Loves You/I Need Your Love	35
63	HMV POP 1226	It's Alright/You'll Want Me Back	20
64	HMV POP 1262	Talkin' About My Baby/Never Too Much Love	22
64	HMV POP 1295	I'm So Proud/I Made A Mistake	18
64	HMV POP 1317	Keep On Pushing/I Love You (Yeah)	18
64	HMV POP 1343	You Must Believe Me/See The Real Me	18
65	HMV POP 1408	People Get Ready/I've Been Trying	18
65	HMV POP 1429	Woman's Got Soul/Get Up And Move	18
65	HMV POP 1446	A Meeting Over Yonder/I Found That I've Lost	18
65	HMV POP 1472	I Need You/Never Could You Be	18
65	HMV POP 1492	Amen/Long Long Winter	15
66	HMV POP 1498	You've Been Cheatin'/Just One Kiss From You	30
66	HMV POP 1516	Since I Lost The One I Love/Falling In Love With You	15
66	HMV POP 1526	Too Slow/No One Else	15
66	HMV POP 1545	Can't Satisfy/This Must End	30
67	HMV POP 1581	You Always Hurt Me/Little Girl	22
68	Stateside SS 2083	We're A Winner/You've Got Me Runnin'	12
68	Buddah 201 021	Fool For You/I'm Loving Nothing	8
69	Stateside SS 2139	Can't Satisfy/You've Been Cheatin'	15
69	Buddah 201 062	Choice Of Colors/Mighty Mighty Spade And Whitey	15
70	Buddah 2011 030	Check Out Your Mind/Can't You See?	6
70	Buddah 2011 045	(Baby) Turn On To Me/Soulful Love	6
71	Buddah 2011 068	Ain't Got Time/I'm So Proud	6
71	Buddah 2011 087	Love Me/Do You Want Me To Win	6
71	Buddah 2011 099	Inner City Blues/Amen/Keep On Pushin'	6
72	Buddah 2011 124	Our Love Goes On And On/This Love's For Real	6
73	Probe PRO 584	People Get Ready/We Be Rolling On	6
65	HMV 7EG 8896	IT'S ALL RIGHT (EP)	60
66	HMV 7EG 8954	SOULFULLY (EP)	60
64	HMV CLP 1743	THE NEVER ENDING IMPRESSIONS (LP)	70
65	HMV CLP 1935	BIG SIXTEEN (LP, also stereo CSD 1642)	38/48
66	HMV CLP/CSD 3548	RIDIN' HIGH (LP)	50
67	HMV CLP/CSD 3631	THE FABULOUS IMPRESSIONS (LP)	50
68	Stateside (S)SL 10239	WE'RE A WINNER (LP)	30
68	Joy JOYS 104	FOR YOUR PRECIOUS LOVE (LP, with Jerry Butler)	15
69	Buddah 203 012	THIS IS MY COUNTRY (LP)	20
69	Stateside (S)SL 10279	BIG SIXTEEN (VOL. 2) (LP)	20
70	Buddah 2359 003	THE YOUNG MOD'S FORGOTTEN STORY (LP)	30
70	Buddah 2359 009	AMEN (LP)	18
71	Buddah 2318 017	CHECK OUT YOUR MIND (LP)	18
72	Buddah 2318 059	TIMES HAVE CHANGED (LP)	18
75	ABC ABCL 5104	BIG SIXTEEN (LP, reissue)	15

(see also Curtis Mayfield, Jerry Butler)

IMPS
58	Parlophone R 4398	Dim Dumb Blonde/Let Me Lie (78 rpm = £15)	22

INADEQUATES
59	Capitol CL 15051	Pretty Face/Audie	28

IN-BE-TWEENS
(see under 'N Betweens)

1959, Billy Fury's Maybe Tomorrow 78 rpm single, £140.

1957, the rarest Rockabilly 45 issued in the UK, £2,500.

1958, Johnny Faire's Rockabilly classic Bertha Lou, £600.

1957, King Kong by Big 'T' Tyler on Vogue label, £200+.

1958, Ronnie Pearson's Flippin' Over You, £750.

1958, rare unissued Rusty York demo £1,000+.

Rare Record Price Guide 2008

1957, classic second HMV EP from the King, £200.

1960, Chuck Berry walks the walk on this EP, £220/£125.

1961, initially a Cliff soundalike, *Dave* EP is worth £160.

1960, worth £125 with trianguar centre, £90 for round.

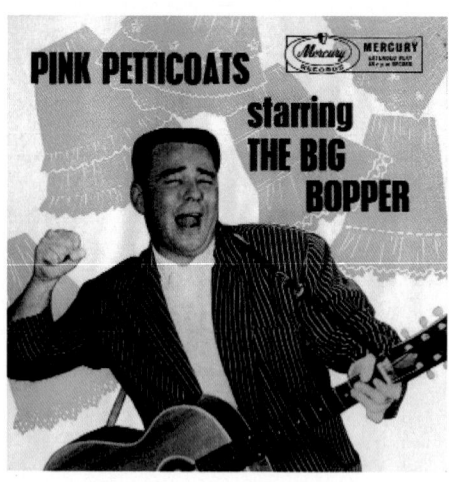

1959, Big Bopper's *Pink Petticoats* EP is worth £300.

1957, Gene Vincent, with gorgeous promo sleeve, £75.

1958, mega-rare 10" LP from original teenager, £500.

1957, this 10" soundrack LP includes The Platters, £175.

1959, only one EP released by Dickie on Columbia, £260.

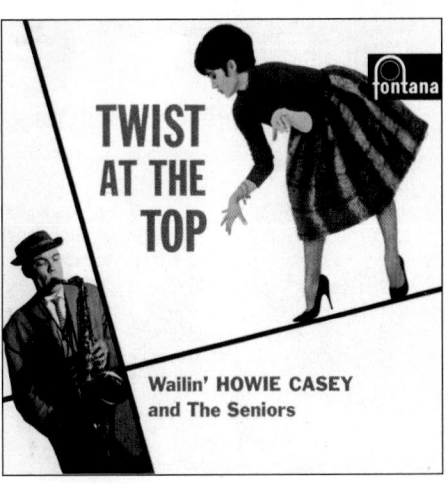

1962, Wailin' Howie Casie and The Seniors LP, £90.

1959, first Bo Diddley album on London label, £325.

1959, not his rarest LP but one of the most sacred, £30.

Rare Record Price Guide 2008

1959, possibly best looking McPhatter EP cover, £175.

1964, Barnum EP popular with Northern Soul fans, £200.

1965, classy Doo Wop/Pop singing act EP, £120.

1966, classic early Motown showcase EP, £250.

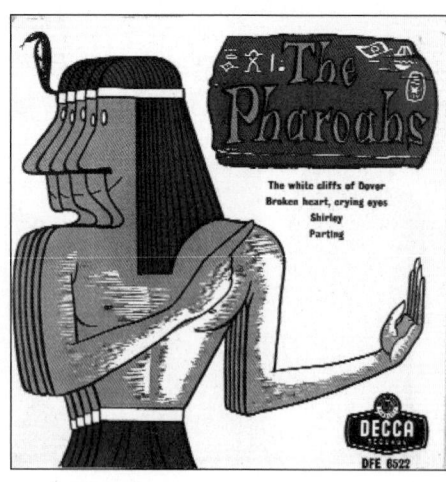

1963, R&B Sonny EP on the Ember label, £65.

1958, very rare Doo Wop EP on Decca, £1,000.

1962, ballad/pop singer Joe Barry, EP £125.

1964, the second of two collectable Fourmost EPs, £80.

1968, final Kinks EP featuring David Watts, £275.

1968, mega-rare Dave Davies EP, £320.

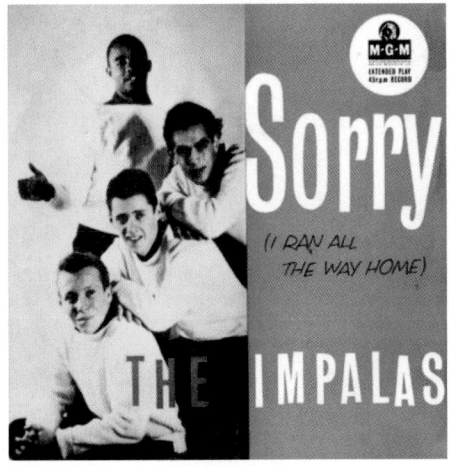

1959, another rare US vocal group on a UK EP, £450+.

1966, British R&B from Zoot Money's band, £275.

1965, Marv "not a plaything" Johnson on Motown, £90.

1965, Candy & Kisses, The 81/Two Happy People, £175.

1965, Invitations, What's Wrong With My Baby? £300.

1966, Patrice Holloway's Love And Desire demo, £250.

1968, Northern Soul classic 45 by Timi Yuro, £500.

1967, Northern Soul on Doctor Bird label, £350.

1969, TMG 720 unissued Blinky & Edwin Starr 7", £250.

1966, Alexander Patton, A Lil Lovin' Sometimes, £350.

1965, demo of The Spinners' I'll Always Love You, £175.

1963, rare Valadiers' I Found A Girl on Oriole, £900.

1963, Topic Folk EP from Anne Briggs, £160.

1962 Davy Graham & Alexis Korner EP, £225.

Rare Record Price Guide 2008

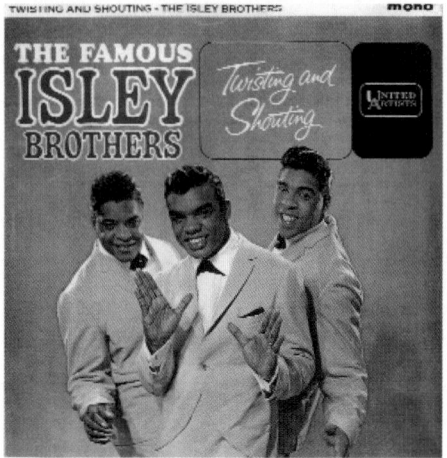

1964, Isley Brothers *Twisting And Shouting* LP, £80.

1967, first Bowie LP, £250 for mono and £280 for stereo.

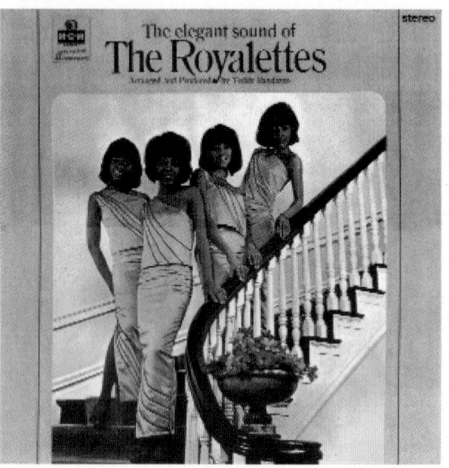

1966, regal looking and sounding US girl group LP, £100.

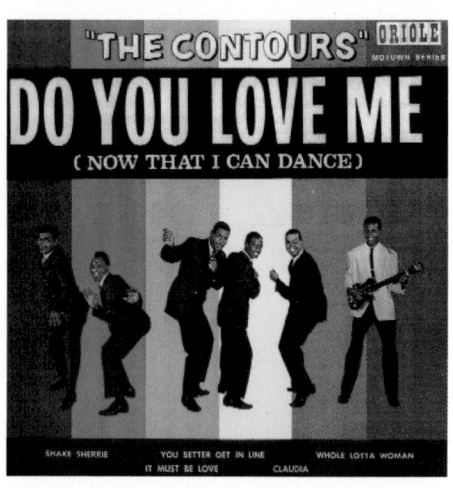

1963, The Contours first LP on UK Oriole label, £200.

1964, Smokey and the gang on Stateside LP, £200.

1957, Lita Roza's *Love Is The Answer* LP, £100.

IN CAMERA
82	4AD BAD 205	FIN (12" EP)	8

INCAS
65	Lyntone LYN 765/6	KEELE RAG RECORD (EP, flexidisc, with 3 other bands)	40
66	Parlophone R 5551	One Night Stand/I'll Keep Holding On	20

INCOGNITO
81	Ensign ENYT 211	Incognito (Remix)/Shine On (live) (12")	10

INCREDIBLE BONGO BAND
73	MGM 2006 161	Bongo Rock/Bongolia	12
72	MGM 2315 255	BONGO ROCK (LP)	30
76	DJM DJS 20452	BONGO ROCK (LP, reissue)	20

INCREDIBLE HOG
73	Dart ART 2026	Lame/Tadpole	12
73	Dart 65372	VOLUME 1 (LP)	100

INCREDIBLE KIDDA BAND
78	Psycho P 2608	Everybody Knows/No Nerve (a few in p/s)	50/30
79	Carrere CAR 119	Fighting My Way Back/Saturday Night Fever	150

INCREDIBLES
67	Stateside SS 2053	There's Nothing Else To Say/Heart And Soul	125
74	Contempo CS 9008	There's Nothing Else To Say/Another Dirty Deal	10
74	Contempo CLP 512	HEART AND SOUL (LP)	15

INCREDIBLE STRING BAND
SINGLES
67	Elektra EKSN 45013	Way Back In The 1960s/Chinese White (white-label promo)	50+
68	Elektra EKSN 45028	Painting Box/No Sleep Blues	12
69	Elektra EKSN 45074	Big Ted/All Writ Down	10
70	Elektra 2101 003	This Moment/Black Jack Davy	6
72	Island WIP 6145	Black Jack David/Moon Hang Low	5
73	Island WIP 6158	At The Lighthouse Dance/Jigs	5

ORIGINAL LPs
66	Elektra EUK 254	THE INCREDIBLE STRING BAND (1st pressing, white label, green logo, black lettering)	100
67	Elektra EUK 257/EUKS 7257	THE 5000 SPIRITS OR THE LAYERS OF THE ONION (mono/stereo, red label)	80/75
68	Elektra EUK 258/EUKS 7258	THE HANGMAN'S BEAUTIFUL DAUGHTER (red label, with lyric insert)	40
68	Elektra EKL 4036/7	WEE TAM/THE BIG HUGE (2-LP, red label, gatefold sleeve, with insert; also stereo EKS 74036/7)	55
69	Elektra EKS 74057	CHANGING HORSES (red label, gatefold sleeve)	25
70	Elektra 2469 002	I LOOKED UP (red label)	25
70	Elektra 2665 001	U (2-LP, red label, gatefold sleeve, some with foldover lyric insert)	30/35
70	Island ILPS 9140	BE GLAD FOR THE SONG HAS NO ENDING (pink rim label/'palm tree' logo)	15
71	Island ILPS 9172	LIQUID ACROBAT AS REGARDS THE AIR (gatefold sleeve, with inner, pink rim label/'palm tree' logo)	18
72	Island ILPS 9211	EARTHSPAN (with lyric inner sleeve, pink rim label/'palm tree' logo)	15
73	Island ILPS 9229	NO RUINOUS FEUD (with inner sleeve, pink rim label/'palm tree' logo)	12
74	Island ILPS 9270	HARD ROPE AND SILKEN TWINE (with inner sleeve, pink rim label/'palm tree' logo)	12
76	Island ISLD 9	SEASONS THEY CHANGE (2-LP, gatefold sleeve)	18

REISSUE LPs
66	Elektra EUK 254	THE INCREDIBLE STRING BAND (2nd pressing, red label)	50
68	Elektra EKL 254	THE INCREDIBLE STRING BAND (3rd pressing, red label)	20
68	Elektra EKS 7257	THE 5000 SPIRITS OR THE LAYERS OF THE ONION (red label)	20
68	Elektra EKL 4036	WEE TAM (red label, also stereo EKS 74036)	15
68	Elektra EKL 4037	THE BIG HUGE (red label, also stereo EKS 74037)	15
72	Elektra K 62002	U (2-LP, 'butterfly' label, gatefold sleeve, with foldover lyric insert)	15

(All other 'butterfly' label re-issues £8-£10 each)
(see also Robin Williamson, Mike Heron, Famous Jug Band, C.O.B., Shirley Collins)

IN CROWD (Jamaica)
71	Spinning Wheel SW 105	Bush Jacket/Soul Face	20
78	Savannah SVN 12-1	Riding High/Version (12")	12

IN CROWD (U.K.)
65	Parlophone R 5276	That's How Strong My Love Is/Things She Says	80
65	Parlophone R 5328	Stop! Wait A Minute/You're On Your Own	65
65	Parlophone R 5364	Why Must They Criticize?/I Don't Mind	55

(see also Tomorrow, Keith West, Steve Howe, Four + One)

INCROWD (U.K.)
69	Deram DM 272	Where In The World/I Can Make Love To You	15

INCUBUS
84	Guardian GRC 2165	TO THE DEVIL A DAUGHTER (LP)	18

INDECENT EXPOSURE
84	Index IS A1	Riots (Single Version)/A Matter Of Time (no p/s)	7

INDEPENDENTS
72	Wand WN 29	Just As Long As You Need Me (Parts 1 & 2)	6
73	Pye 7N 25623	Baby I've Been Missing You/Couldn't Hear Nobody Say	6
74	Pye 7N 252634	It's All Over/Sarah Lee	6

MINT VALUE £

INDIAN SUMMER
71	RCA Neon NE 3	INDIAN SUMMER (LP)	40

(see also Ross)

LOS INDIOS TABAJARAS
63	RCA RCA 1365	Maria Elena/Jungle Dream	5
64	RCA RCX 7135	A LA ORILLA DEL LAGO (EP)	8
64	RCA no cat. no.	LOS INDIOS TABAJARAS (LP)	12

INDO-BRITISH ENSEMBLE
69	MFP 1307	CURRIED JAZZ (LP)	30

INDO JAZZMEN
68	Saga FID 2145	RAGAS AND REFLECTIONS (LP)	15

INERTIA
80s	Inertial ERT 1	The Screen/4 Submarine (p/s)	5

INFANTES JUBILATE
68	Music Factory CUB 5	Exploding Galaxy/Take It Now	58

INFA RIOT
81	Secret SHH 117	Kids Of The 80s/Still Out Of Order (p/s)	6
82	Secret SHH 133	The Winner/School's Out (p/s)	6
82	Secret SEC 7	STILL OUT OF ORDER (LP)	15

(see also Infas)

INFAS
84	Panache PAN 101	Sound And Fury/Triffic Spiff Ya O.K. (p/s)	8
84	Panache PANLP 501	SOUND AND FURY (LP)	12

(see also Infa Riot)

INFINITY PROJECT
89	Fabulous FABU 004	HYPERACTIVE (12" EP, sponged cover)	10
90	Fabulous FABU 005	UPHOLD THE LAW (12" EP)	10
90	Fabulous FABU 016	TRIBADELIC MELTDOWN (12" EP)	8

IN FLAMES
72	Pama PM 842	Rocket Man/I'm All Broke Up	6

INFLUENCE
69	Orange OAS 201	I Want To Live/Driving Me Wild	15

(see also John Miles, Geordie, Smokestack Crumble)

INFORMATION
69	Beacon BEA 121	Orphan/Oh Strange Man	20
70	Evolution E 2461S	Face To The Sun/Lovely To See You	15

NICK INGHAM
75	Studio Two TWOX 1045	TERMINATOR (LP)	22

RED INGLE
50	Capitol CL 13356	Turn Your Head Little Darlin'/You Can't Be As Fit As A Fiddle (78)	6
59	Capitol EAP 20052	CIGAREETS, WHUSKY AND WILD WILD WOMEN (EP)	20

JORGEN INGMANN
61	Fontana H 311	Cherokee/Anna	5
61	Fontana H 333	Milord/Oceans Of Love	5
61	Fontana H 353	Violetta/Pinetop's Boogie Woogie	5
62	Fontana 267 237 TF	Africa/Johnny's Tune	5
63	Columbia DB 7013	I Loved You (Dansevise)/Little Boy (as Grethe & Jorgen Ingmann)	5
64	Columbia SEG 8340	DRINA (EP)	20

LUTHER INGRAM
70	Stax STAX 142	My Honey And Me/Puttin' Game Down	8
70	Stax STAX 148	Home Don't Seem Like A Home/Ain't That Lovin' You?	8

INITIALS
64	London HLR 9860	School Day/Song Is Number One	18

IN-KEEPERS
68	Morgan MR 109P	IN-KEEPERS (LP)	28

INK SPOTS
54	Parlophone DP 368	Ebb Tide/Changing Partners (78, export issue)	15
54	Parlophone MSP 6063	Here In My Lonely Room/Flowers, Mister Florist, Please	20
54	Parlophone MSP 6074	Ebb Tide/If You Should Say Goodbye	20
54	Parlophone MSP 6126	Planting Rice/Yesterdays	20
55	Parlophone MSP 6152	Melody Of Love/Am I Too Late?	20
50s	Parlophone DP 428	Someone's Rocking My Dreamboat/When You Come To The End Of The Day (78, export issue)	5
55	Brunswick OE 9158	SWING HIGH SWING LOW VOL. 1 (EP)	10
56	Brunswick OE 9426	THEY SOLD A MILLION NO. 10 (EP)	10
56	Brunswick OE 9427	THEY SOLD A MILLION NO. 11 (EP)	10
57	HMV 7EG 8410	CHARLIE FUQUA'S INK SPOTS (EP)	10
57	Parlophone GEP 8673	YESTERDAYS (EP)	10
50s	Britone LP 1003	THE INK SPOTS (10" LP)	30
53	Brunswick LA 8590	SOUVENIR ALBUM VOLUME ONE (10" LP)	25
55	Brunswick LA 8710	STREET OF DREAMS (10" LP)	25

(see also Ella Fitzgerald)

AUTREY INMAN
63	Decca DFE 8571	AMERICAN COUNTRY JUBILEE NO. 1 (EP)	15

INMATES
79	Soho SH 7	Dirty Water/Danger Zone (gatefold p/s)	8
79	Radar ADA 47	The Walk/Talkin' Woman (p/s)	5
81	Radar ADA 63	(I Thought I Heard A) Heartbeat/Tallahassie Lassie (p/s)	5

INNER CITY
| 92 | Ten TENX 408 | Praise (F.S.O.L. Conceptual)/(Intergalactic Dub)/(Mayday Mix) (12", p/s) | 12 |
| 93 | Virgin OVD 438 | TESTAMENT 93 (EP, remixes, printed card envelope sleeve) | 10 |

INNER CITY EXPRESS
| 78 | Ebony EYE 5 | Fat On Funk/Sho' Dig Dancin' (12") | 8 |
| 78 | Ebony EYE 15 | Spring Rain/Reggae Strings | 6 |

INNER CITY UNIT
79	Riddle RID 001/ICU 45	Solitary Ashtray/So Try As Id (Dub Version) (plain sleeve with colour insert)	8
79	Riddle RID 003	Paradise Beach/Amyl Nitrate (company die-cut sleeve)	8
81	Avatar AAA 113	Beer, Baccy, Bingo And Benidorm/In The Mood (Nude) (red vinyl, no p/s)	6
82	Avatar AAA 119	Bones Of Elvis/Sid's Song (no p/s)	5
85	Jettisoundz JZ 5	BLOOD AND BONE (12" EP, p/s)	8
79	Riddle RID 002	PASS OUT (THE 360° PSYCHO DELERIA SOUND) (LP)	15
81	Avatar AALP 5004	THE MAXIMUM EFFECT (LP, with insert)	12

(see also Hawkwind, Sphynx, Radio Actors, Imperial Pompadours, Catherine Andrews, Big Amongst Sheep, Nik Turner)

INNER MINDS
70	New Beat NB 067	Witchcraft Man/Night In Cairo	7
70	New Beat NB 069	Pum Pum Girl/Freedom	7
71	Bullet BU 465	Arawak Version/Cuffy Cuffy	7

NEIL INNES
72	United Artists UP 35358	Slush/Rawlinson's End (unissued)	
73	United Artists UP 35495	How Sweet To Be An Idiot/The Age Of Desperation	7
73	United Artists UP 35639	Momma B/Immortal Invisible	7
74	United Artists UP 35676	Re-cycled Vinyl Blues/Fluff On The Needle	7
74	United Artists UP 35745	Lie Down And Be Counted/Bandwagon	7
75	United Artists UP 35772	What Noise Annoys An Oyster/Oo-Chuck-A-Mao-Mao	7
77	Arista ARISTA 106	Lady Mine/Crystal Balls	6
77	Arista ARISTA 123	Silver Jubilee (A Tribute)/Drama On A Saturday Night	6
78	Warner Bros K 17182	Protest Song/The Hard-To-Get	6
82	MMC MMC 100	Them/Rock Of Ages	6
82	MMC MMC 103	Mr. Eurovision/Ungawa	6
73	United Artists UAG 29492	HOW SWEET TO BE AN IDIOT (LP)	25
82	MMC MMC 001	OFF THE RECORD (2-LP)	20

(see also Grimms, Bonzo Dog [Doo Dah] Band, Rutles, World, Dirk & Stig, Group)

INN KEEPERS
| 71 | Banana BA 328 | Duppy Serenade/Sunshine Version (actually by Dennis Alcapone) | 15 |

(see also Winston Matthews)

INNOCENCE
| 66 | Kama Sutra KAS 203 | There's Got To Be A Word!/I Don't Wanna Be Around You | 10 |
| 66 | Kama Sutra KAS 206 | Mairzy Doats And Dozy Doats/Lifetime Of Lovin' You | 10 |

INNOCENT BYSTANDERS
| 80 | Rok ROK XVII/XVIII | Where Is Johnny?/DEBUTANTES: The Man In The Street (company sleeve) | 6 |

INNOCENTS (U.K.)
63	Columbia DB 7098	Stepping Stones/Grazina	15
63	Columbia DB 7173	A Fine, Fine Bird/Spanish Holiday	15
64	Columbia DB 7314	Stick With Me Baby/Not More Than Everything	10

(see also Mike Berry, Innocents & Leroys)

INNOCENTS (U.K.)
| 80 | Kingdom KV 8010 | One Way Love/Every Wednesday Night At Eight (p/s) | 10 |

(see also Woodentops, Advertising, Secret Affair)

INNOCENTS (U.S.)
| 60 | Top Rank JAR 508 | Honest I Do/My Baby Hully Gullys | 30 |
| 61 | Top Rank JAR 541 | Gee Whiz/Please Mr Sun | 40 |

(see also Kathy Young)

INNOCENTS & LEROYS
| 64 | Regal Zonophone RZ 502 | HOT SIX: Don't Throw Your Love Away; My Girl Lollipop; I Love You Because; Not Fade Away (maxi-single, plain sleeve) | 12 |

(see also Innocents [U.K.], Le-Roys)

INQUISITIVE PEOPLE
| 67 | Decca F 12699 | Big White Chief/Rhapsody Of Spring | 10 |

INSANE
82	Insane INSANE 1	Why Die?/War And Violence (p/s)	15
82	Riot City RIOT 3	Politics/Dead And Gone/Last Day (p/s)	10
82	No Future OI 10	El Salvador/Nuclear War/Chinese Rock (p/s)	10

INSECT TRUST
| 69 | Capitol E-(S)T 109 | THE INSECT TRUST (LP) | 75 |

INSIDE OV A BUTCHER'S SHOP
| 98 | Out-There OTT CD 2 | Banking On Death — Carnage (CD, 50 only, numbered hand-made sleeve with fake dollar bill) | 30 |

INSIDE OV A COFFIN
| 98 | Out-There OTT 1 | Banking On Death (7", existence unconfirmed) | |
| 98 | Out-There OTT CD 1 | Banking On Death (CD, 50 only, in hand-made sleeve with fake dollar bill) | 30 |

(see also Freed Unit)

MINT VALUE £

INSIDE OF A ROUGH TRADE SHOP
98	For Us/Out-There FU 005/ OV 003	CARNAGE: LIVE EP (CD, 50 only, numbered, some with full-colour back tray art)	30/20

INSIDERS
80	Satellite SATS 1002	Rollin' & Strollin'/She Had To Go (features Ray Dorset)	10

(see also Ray Dorset)

INSPIRAL CARPETS
80s	own label	SONGS OF SHALLOW INTENSITY (p/s, demo cassette)	25
80s	own label	WAITING FOR OURS (p/s, demo cassette)	25
80s	own label	COW (p/s, demo cassette)	25
87	Debris DEB 06	Garage Full Of Flowers/METRO INFINITY: Stupid Friends (flexidisc, some with *Debris* fanzine)	7/5
88	Playtime AMUSE 2	Keep The Circle Around/Theme From Cow (p/s)	15
88	Playtime AMUSE 2T	PLANE CRASH (12" EP, later 'reissued' as white label without p/s)	15/7
88	Playtime AMUSE 4	Butterfly/You Can't Take The Truth (unreleased, white label promos only)	8
88	Playtime AMUSE 4T	TRAIN SURFING (12" EP, unreleased, white label test pressings only)	15
89	Cow MOO 1	PLANE CRASH (12" EP, unreleased reissue)	8
89	Cow MOO 2	TRAIN SURFING (12" EP, some with rear sticker & scratched-out matrix)	8
89	Cow DUNG 4	Keep The Circle Around/Seeds Of Doubt/Joe/Causeway/Butterfly/26/ Garage Full Of Flowers/96 Tears (demo cassette)	8

INSPIRATIONS (Jamaica)
69	Camel CA 11	Down In The Park/Love Oh Love	10
69	Camel CA 21	Wonder Of Love/Cinderella	8
70	Amalgamated AMG 857	Take Back Your Duck/Nothing For Nothing	12
70	Amalgamated AMG 861	La La/Reggae Fever	15
70	Amalgamated AMG 862	The Train Is Coming/Man Oh Man	10
70	Trojan TTL 27	REGGAE FEVER (LP)	50

(see also Untouchables, Niney)

INSPIRATIONS (U.S.)
67	Polydor 56730	Touch Me, Kiss Me, Hold Me/What Am I Gonna Do With You?	140+

INSTANT AGONY
82	H. Man H. Biscuit DUNK 1	THINK OF ENGLAND (EP)	5
82	H. Man H. Biscuit DUNK 2	FASHION PARADE (EP)	5
83	Flicknife FLS 022	No Sign Of Life/Taste Of Power (p/s)	5
83	Flicknife FLS 028	Nicely Does It/We Don't Need You (p/s)	5

INSTANT SUNSHINE
68	Page One POF 085	Here We Go Again/Methylated	10
68	Page One POL 007	LIVE AT TIDDY DOLS (LP)	28

INSTITUTE OF FORMAL RESEARCH
97	Bubblehead BH 005	VOLUME ONE: FILE UNDER SUBCONSCIOUS (CD, features Zoot Horn Rollo)	20

(see also Mick Taylor, Chris Spedding)

INSYNC VS MYSTERON
95	Peacefrog PF 033	AUDIBLE ILLUSION EP (12", plain sleeve)	10
97	Fat Cat 12FAT 004	TALES FROM THE CRYPT (12", custom sleeve)	15

INTELLIGENT COMMUNICATIONS
91	Jumpin' & Pumpin' 12TOT 15	PRINCIPLES OF MOTION EP (12", p/s)	10

(see also Future Sound Of London)

INTENSIVE CARE
84	Punishment Block CELL 1	COWARDS EP (p/s)	8
87	Back To Back BTB 001	REBBELS, ROCKETS AND RUBBERMEN (12", p/s)	12

INTENTIONS (U.K.)
72	Pye 7N 45123	There's Nobody I'd Sooner Love/Hurry On Home	5

INTENTIONS (U.S.)/Z.Z. HILL
66	Sue IEP 711	GIMME GIMME (EP, 2 tracks each by Intentions & Z.Z. Hill; 2 tracks mistakenly credited to Jackie Day on sleeve; some in p/s)	275/100

INTERNATIONAL CHRYSIS
94	PWL PWLT 303	Rebel Rebel (The Hole Mix)/Rebel Rebel (Extended Mix) (12", promo only)	15

(see also Dead Or Alive)

INTERNATIONAL PENPALS
80s	Radical Wallpaper RADWAL 001	Day They Ate Ronald Reagan (p/s)	12

INTERNS (Jamaica)
64	Jackpot JP 729	See You At Sunrise/LITTLE WONDER: Out Of Reach (B-side actually "Just Out Of Reach" by John Holt)	8

(see also Viceroys, Bob Marley & Wailers)

INTERNS (U.K.)
64	Philips BF 1320	Don't You Dare/Here There Everywhere	15
64	Philips BF 1345	Cry To Me/There's Love For You	15
66	Parlophone R 5479	Is It Really What You Want?/Just Like Me	30
67	Parlophone R 5586	Ray Of Sunshine/Please Say Something Nice	10

(see also Shadows)

INTERPOL
00	CHEM047CD	fukd i.d #3 PDA: Precipitate/Roland/5 (CD, stickered card sleeve, 1,000 only)	60
02	Matador OLE 546-7	PDA/Specialist (p/s)	5
02	Matador OLE 546-2	PDA/NYC/Specialist (CD, digipak, with slipcase)	9
02	Matador OLE 570-7	Obstacle 1/Obstacle 2 (Peel Session Version) (p/s)	5

02	Matador OLE 570 2	Obstacle 1/PDA (Morning Becomes Electric Session)/Hands Away (Peel Session) (CD)	10
00s	Matador OLE 5827	Say Hello To The Angels/NYC (p/s)	8
00s	Matador OLE 582 2	Say Hello To The Angels/NYC/NYC (Demo Version) (CD)	10
00s	Matador OLE 5949	Obstacle 1 (Video)/Specialist (Black Session)/Leif Erikson (Black Session) (DVD)	10
04	Matador (no. cat. no)	ANTICS (5 x 7" box set, only from London Interpol Space Art Gallery)	60

IN THE NURSERY
84	Paragon VIRTUE 5	Witness To A Scream/1984 (p/s)	20
85	New European BADVC 55	Sonority — A Strength (12" EP)	12
83	Paragon VIRTUE 2	WHEN CHERISHED DREAMS COME TRUE (mini-LP, silk-screened g/fold p/s)	30

INTIMATE STRANGERS
| 75 | Alaska ALA 1005 | Love Sounds/The Track | 50 |

INTRA VEIN
| 79 | Bum FP 001 | Speed Of The City/Sick (printed PVC sleeve or stamped plain sleeve) | 40/30 |
| *(see also Veins)* | | | |

INTRIGUES
| 69 | London HL 10293 | In A Moment/Scotchman Rock | 10 |
| 72 | Janus 6146 008 | To Make A World/Mojo Hanna | 6 |

INTRUDERS
| 59 | Top Rank JAR 158 | Frankfurters And Sauerkraut/Creepin' (78 rpm = £10) | 10 |

INTRUDERS
66	London HL 10069	Up And Down The Ladder/United	40
69	Action ACT 4523	Slow Drag/So Glad I'm Yours	15
69	Ember EMB S 254	Cowboys To Girls/Turn Back The Hands Of Time	15
72	Ember EMB S 325	Cowboys To Girls/GOOD VIBRATIONS: Shake A Hand	7

INTURNS
| 79 | Burning Rockers BR 1003 | DETOUR (LP) | 30 |

INVADERS (Jamaica)
67	Columbia Bluebeat DB 105	Limbo Girl/Soul Of The Jungle	10
68	Columbia Bluebeat DB 109	Stop Teasing/Invaders At The Carnival	10
68	Studio One SO 2044	Soulful Music/SOUL VENDORS: Happy Organ	30
71	G.G. GG 4527	Got To Go Home/PAULETTE & GEE: How Long Will You Stay?	7

INVADERS (U.K.)
| 70s | Jovian ZIT 2 | Launderama/Plastic Nose | 5 |

INVICTAS
| 64 | United Artists UP 1013 | Green Bow Tie/Touch Of Orchid | 10 |

INVITATIONS (Jamaica)
| 71 | Crab CRAB 66 | Birmingham Cat/Now You're On Your Own | 8 |

INVITATIONS (U.S.)
65	Stateside SS 453	Hallelujah/Written On The Wall	75
65	Stateside SS 478	What's Wrong With My Baby?/Why Did My Baby Turn Bad? (DJ copy = £300)	150
70	Jay Boy BOY 24	How'd We Ever Get This Way?/Picking Up	10
72	Mojo 2092 055	What's Wrong With My Baby?/Why Did My Baby Turn Bad? (reissue)	10
74	Polydor 2066 366	Let's Love And Find Together/Love Has To Grow	30

INXS
81	RCA RCA 89	Just Keep Walking/Scratch (some in p/s)	40/10
83	Mercury INXS 1	Don't Change/You Never Used To Cry (p/s)	12
83	Mercury INXS 121	Don't Change/You Never Used To Cry/Golden Playpen (12", p/s)	16
83	Mercury INXS 2	The One Thing/The Sax Thing (p/s)	8
83	Mercury INXS 212	The One Thing (6.10)/Black And White (12", p/s)	12
83	Mercury INXS 222	The One Thing/Black And White/Here Comes II (12", p/s)	10
84	Mercury INXS 3	Original Sin/Jan's Song (live)/To Look At You (live) (p/s)	8
84	Mercury INXS 312	Original Sin/Original Sin (Extended Version)/Jan's Song (live)/To Look At You (live) (12", p/s)	12
84	Philips PH 2	I Send A Message/Mechanical (p/s, some in envelope pack with postcard & biography)	20/5
84	Philips PH 212	I Send A Message (Long Distance)/Mechanical/I Send A Message (Local Call) (12", p/s)	15

IONA
| 78 | Silver Scales | CUCKOO (LP) | 35 |
| 70s | Celtic Music CM 001 | IONA (LP) | 35 |

I.O.W. CHEROKEES
| 66 | 69 69EP 001 | I.O.W. CHEROKEES (EP, private pressing) | 10 |

DON IPPOLITO ORCHESTRA
| 55 | Parlophone MSP 6187 | Camptown Racer Mambo/Can't Do It Mambo | 7 |

IPSISSIMUS
| 69 | Parlophone R 5774 | Hold On/Lazy Woman | 40 |

IQ
84	Jim White/IQ PROMO 101	Awake And Nervous/Through The Corridors (12", no p/s, 500 only)	30
84	IQFREEB 1	Hollow Afternoon (1-sided, Marquee gig freebie)	35
86	STAL Other Boxer 1	Nomzamo (Demo) (1-sided fan club single)	18
86	Sahara IQSD 1	It All Stops Here/Intelligence Quotient (shaped picture disc)	18
87	RLOG Another Boxer 1	Fascination/The Bold Grenadier Pt. 1 (fan club single)	18
88	RLOG One More Boxer 1	A Different Magic Roundabout (Honest!)/The Big Balls Of Bert Christ (fan club single)	12

92	MIMP 00000001	BLUBA NEENY NOO: Last Human Gateway (Acoustic Middle Section)/ A Bit Of Love Lost (CD, fan club single, 361 copies only)	18
82	private pressing	SEVEN STORIES INTO EIGHT (cassette, different coloured sleeves, 40 numbered copies only)	10-12
85	STAL BOXER 1	NINE IN A POND IS HERE (2-LP, 1,000 copies only)	22
	(see also Niadem's Ghost)		

IQ PROCEDURE (ROOTS MANUVA)
| 94 | Bluntly Speaking PHAT2 | Run Tings/Can U Get With This/Big Up (12") | 22 |

IQ ZERO
| 79 | Object Music OM 9 | (Everybody Kills) Insects/Electromotion/Quirky Pop Music (p/s) | 20 |
| 79 | Logo GO 374 | She's So Rare/Crazy Dolls (p/s) | 15 |

IRELAND'S FREEMEN
| 75 | Polydor 2908 017 | SEAN SOUTH (LP) | 15 |

IRISH MIST
| 75 | SRT/Custom 012 | ROSIN THE BOW (LP) | 15 |

IRISH ROVERS
67	Brunswick STA 8679	FIRST OF THE IRISH ROVERS (LP)	12
68	MCA MUPS 310	THE UNICORN (LP)	12
69	MCA MUPS 353	LIVERPOOL LOU (LP)	12

IRISH TRADITION
| 79 | Green Linnet SIF 1016 | THE CORNER HOUSE (LP) | 15 |

IRON BUTTERFLY
68	Atlantic 584 188	Possession/Unconscious Power	6
69	Atlantic 584 254	Soul Experience/In The Crowds	6
70	Atlantic 2091 024	In-A-Gadda-Da-Vida/Termination	10
68	Atlantic 587/588 116	IN-A-GADDA-DA-VIDA (LP)	25
69	Atco 2465 015	HEAVY (LP)	18
69	Atco 228 011	BALL (LP, gatefold sleeve)	18
70	Atlantic 2400 014	LIVE (LP)	15
71	Atlantic 2401 003	METAMORPHOSIS (LP)	12
	(see also Ramatam)		

IRON MAIDEN
| 70 | Gemini GMS 006 | Falling/Ned Kelly | 15 |

IRON MAIDEN
80	EMI EMI 5032	Running Free/Burning Ambition (p/s)	25
80	EMI EMI 5032	Running Free (One-sided 7" DJ copy)	50
80	EMI EMI 5065	Sanctuary/Drifter (live)/I've Got The Fire (live) (uncensored p/s)	35
80	EMI EMI 5065	Sanctuary/Drifter (live)/I've Got The Fire (live) (censored p/s)	15
80	EMI EMI 5105	Women In Uniform/Invasion (p/s)	15
80	EMI 12EMI 5105	Women In Uniform/Phantom Of The Opera (live)/Invasion (12", p/s)	15
81	EMI EMI 5145	Twilight Zone/Wrathchild (p/s)	12
81	EMI EMI 5145	Twilight Zone/Wrathchild (p/s, red or clear vinyl)	25/30
81	EMI EMI 5145	Twilight Zone/Wrathchild (p/s, brown vinyl mispressing)	600
81	EMI TCEMI 5145	Twilight Zone/Wrathchild (cassette)	8
81	EMI EMI 5184	Purgatory/Genghis Khan (p/s)	30
82	EMI EMI 5263	Run To The Hills/Total Eclipse (p/s)	6
82	EMI EMIP 5263	Run To The Hills/Total Eclipse (picture disc, mispressed with b-side picture on both sides)	30
82	EMI EMIP 5263	Run To The Hills/Total Eclipse (picture disc)	15
82	EMI EMI 5287	The Number Of The Beast/Remember Tomorrow (live) (p/s)	5
82	EMI EMI 5287	The Number Of The Beast/Remember Tomorrow (live) (p/s, red vinyl)	12
83	EMI EMI 5378	Flight Of Icarus/I've Got The Fire (p/s)	5
83	EMI 12EMIP 5378	Flight Of Icarus/I've Got The Fire (12", picture disc)	20
83	EMI EMI 5397	The Trooper/Cross-Eyed Mary (p/s)	5
83	EMI EMIP 5397	The Trooper/Cross-Eyed Mary (soldier-shaped picture disc)	25
83	EMI EMIP 5397	The Trooper/Cross-Eyed Mary (uncut shaped picture disc)	200+
84	EMI EMI 5489	2 Minutes To Midnight/Rainbow's Gold (p/s)	5
84	EMI 12EMI 5489	2 Minutes To Midnight/Rainbow's Gold/Mission From 'Arry (12", picture disc)	20
84	EMI EMI 5502	Aces High/King Of Twilight (p/s)	5
84	EMI 12EMIP 5502	Aces High/King Of Twilight/The Number Of The Beast (live) (12", picture disc)	18
85	EMI EMI 5532	Running Free (live)/Sanctuary (live) (poster p/s)	7
85	EMI 12EMIP 5532	Running Free (live)/Sanctuary (live)/Murders In The Rue Morgue (live) (12", picture disc)	18
85	EMI EMI 5542	Run To The Hills (live)/Phantom Of The Opera (live) (with Xmas card)	8
85	EMI 12EMIP 5542	Run To The Hills (live)/Phantom Of The Opera (live)/ Losfer Words (The Big 'Orra) (live) (12", picture disc)	15
86	EMI EMIP 5583	Wasted Years/Reach Out (computer-mispressed picture disc)	15
86	EMI EMI 5589	Stranger In A Strange Land/That Girl (foldout poster p/s)	6
86	EMI 12EMIP 5589	Stranger In A Strange Land/That Girl/Juanita (12", picture disc)	18
88	EMI EMS 49	Can I Play With Madness/Black Bart Blues (p/s, with sticker & transfer)	5
88	EMI EMP 49	Can I Play With Madness/Black Bart Blues (shaped picture disc)	15
88	EMI EMP 49	Can I Play With Madness/Black Bart Blues (uncut shaped picture disc)	75+
88	EMI CDEM 49	Can I Play With Madness/Black Bart Blues/Massacre (CD)	10
88	EMI EMP 64	The Evil That Men Do/Prowler '88 (gatefold p/s)	5
88	EMI EMP 64	The Evil That Men Do/Prowler '88 (shaped picture disc)	10
88	EMI EMP 64	The Evil That Men Do/Prowler '88 (uncut shaped picture disc)	75
88	EMI 12EMS 64	The Evil That Men Do/Prowler '88/Charlotte The Harlot '88 (12", poster p/s)	8
88	EMI CDEM 64	The Evil That Men Do/Prowler '88/Charlotte The Harlot '88 (CD, picture disc)	10
88	EMI EMS 79	The Clairvoyant (live)/The Prisoner (live) (clear vinyl, poster p/s)	6
88	EMI EMP 79	The Clairvoyant (live)/The Prisoner (live) (shaped picture disc)	10
88	EMI EMP 79	The Clairvoyant (live)/The Prisoner (live) (uncut shaped picture disc)	50+

88	EMI CDEM 79	The Clairvoyant (live)/The Prisoner (live)/Heaven Can Wait (live) (CD, picture disc)	8
89	EMI EM 117	Infinite Dreams (live)/Killers (live) (with free patch)	5
89	EMI EMPD 117	Infinite Dreams (live)/Killers (live) (shaped picture disc with insert)	7
89	EMI EMPD 117	Infinite Dreams (live)/Killers (live) (uncut shaped picture disc)	50+
89	EMI 12EM 117	Infinite Dreams (live)/Killers (live)/Still Life (live) (12", poster p/s)	8
89	EMI 12EM 117	Infinite Dreams (live)/Killers (live)/Still Life (live) (CD)	8
90	EMI 12EM 158	Holy Smoke (1-sided 7" DJ copy)	50
90	EMI 12EMP 158	Holy Smoke/All In Your Mind/Kill Me Ce Soir (12" picture disc with insert)	8
90	EMI 12EMP 158	Holy Smoke/All In Your Mind/Kill Me Ce Soir (12", gold vinyl test pressing, promo only)	200+
90	EMI EM 171	Bring Your Daughter ... To The Slaughter/I'm A Mover (Clear or white vinyl test pressing for 12" picture disc)	200+
90	EMI EM 171	Bring Your Daughter ... To The Slaughter/I'm A Mover (1-sided etched, p/s)	6
90	EMI EMPD 171	Bring Your Daughter ... To The Slaughter/I'm A Mover (picture disc 'brain' pack)	6
90	EMI 12EMP 171	Bring Your Daughter ... To The Slaughter/I'm A Mover (12", calendar pack)	10
90	EMI 12EMPD 171	Bring Your Daughter ... To The Slaughter/I'm A Mover/ Communication Breakdown (12", picture disc, die-cut sleeve)	12
92	EMI 12EMP 229	Be Quick ...Or Be Dead/Nodding Donkey Blues/Space station No.5 (12" picture disc, with insert)	10
92	EMI EMPD 240	From Here To Eternity/I Can't See My Feeling (shaped picture disc with insert)	8
92	EMI EMPD 240	From Here To Eternity/I Can't See My Feeling (uncut shaped picture disc)	50+
92	EMI EMP 263	Fear Of The Dark (live)/Tailgunner (live) (poster p/s)	5
92	EMI EMPD 263	Fear Of The Dark (live)/Hooks In You (live) (shaped picture disc, with insert)	8
92	EMI EMPD 263	Fear Of The Dark (live)/Hooks In You (live) (uncut shaped picture disc)	50+
92	EMI EMPD 263	Fear Of The Dark (live)/Hooks In You (live) (shaped picture disc, with mispressed B-side "Tailgunner" [live])	12
95	EMI 12EM 398	Man On The Edge/I Live My Way (12", picture disc, with poster)	8
98	EMI EM 507	The Angel And The Gambler/Blood On The World's Hands (Live) (p/s)	5
00	EMI no cat. no.	Tommy Vance Previews: The Wicker Man/Ghost Of The Navigator/ Brave New World/Dream Of Mirrors/The Nomad (CD-R, with Thomas The Vance intros)	100
79	Rock Hard ROK 1	THE SOUNDHOUSE TAPES (EP, p/s; counterfeits have slightly glossier sleeves. Any with different p/s and coloured vinyl are also counterfeit)	100
81	EMI 12EMI 5219	MAIDEN JAPAN EP (12" EP, p/s)	15
93	EMI 12EMP 288	HALLOWED BE THY NAME EP (12", picture disc)	8
03	EMI CDEMDJ633	Rainmaker (CD, 1-track promo in custom card sleeve)	15
03	EMI CDEMDJ627	Wildest Dreams (CD, 1-track promo in custom card sleeve)	15
04	EMI CDEMDJ636	No More Lies (CD, 1-track promo in custom card sleeve)	15
05	EMI CDEMDJ662	The Trooper/The Trooper (live) (CD promo, gatefold card sleeve)	12

ALBUMS

80	EMI EMC 3330	IRON MAIDEN (LP, some with poster)	25/12
82	EMI EMCP 3400	THE NUMBER OF THE BEAST (LP, picture disc, with inner)	40
84	EMI POWERP 1	POWERSLAVE (LP, picture disc, some mispressed and play the title track at 45 RPM)	50/40
88	EMI EMDP 1006	SEVENTH SON OF A SEVENTH SON (LP, picture disc, with banner)	30
90	EMI EMPD 1017	NO PRAYER FOR THE DYING (LP, picture disc, die cut sleeve)	18
90	EMI (no cat. no)	NO PRAYER FOR THE DYING (CD, with interview cassette, photos & bio, promo only)	75
90	EMI (no cat. no)	THE FIRST TEN YEARS — UP THE IRONS (10 x 12" double packs, box set available by mail order with tokens from records)	65
90	EMI (no cat. no)	THE FIRST TEN YEARS — UP THE IRONS (10 x CD, box set available by mail order with tokens from records)	65
93	EMI DON 1	LIVE AT DONINGTON (3-LP)	22
96	EMI IPEMD 1097	BEST OF THE BEAST (4-LP box set, with inners, book and bonus tracks)	65
96	EMI BEST 001	BEST OF THE BEAST (CD, Steve Harris interview disc, commercial CD, video, in 40cm x 30cm, flip-up 3D presentation box with 60-page book, 2 photographs, biography, promo only)	125
98	EMI LPCENT 35	IRON MAIDEN (LP, reissue, 180gm vinyl)	18
98	EMI 4979990	EDDIE'S HEAD (13-CD boxset)	175
99	EMI EDHUNTER 666	ED HUNTER DEMO (CD-ROM, card p/s)	25
00	EMI CDBWDJ001	BRAVE NEW WORLD (5-track sampler CD)	20
00	EMI CDIN 130	BRAVE NEW WORLD (promo interview CD)	25
02	EMI EDDIE 1	EDWARD THE GREAT (5-track promo sampler CD)	20
02	EMI IMRIODJ001	ROCK IN RIO (5-track sampler CD)	20
02	EMI RIOINTCD 001	ROCK IN RIO (promo interview CD)	25
02	EMI 538 6431	ROCK IN RIO (3-LP, picture discs, trifold sleeve)	20
02	EMI 544 2772	EDDIE'S ARCHIVE (6-CD, tin box with insert, shot glass, pewter ring and parchment)	80
02	EMI CDSP255	EDDIE'S ARCHIVE (CD, 8-track sampler in card sleeve)	35
03	EMI DODUKDJoo1	DANCE OF DEATH (5-track sampler CD, card sleeve)	25

(see also Bruce Dickinson, A.S.A.P., Di'Anno, Gogmagog, Samson, Urchin, Xero, Lionheart, Pat Travers, Stratus, Nicko McBrain, Money, White Spirit, McEnroe & Cash)

NEVILLE IRONS

68	Blue Cat BS 104	Soul Glide/DYNAMICS: My Friends	30

(see also Neville Hinds)

IRON VIRGIN

74	Deram DM 416	Rebels Rule/Ain't No Clown	10

I ROY

(see under 'R')

ANDY IRVINE

80	Tara 3002	RAINY SUNDAYS, WINDY DREAMS (LP)	15

MINT VALUE £

ANDY IRVINE & PAUL BRADY
76   Mulligan LUN 008   ANDY IRVINE & PAUL BRADY (LP).. 20

WELDON IRVINE
75   Strata East SES 19749   IN HARMONY (LP).. 12

LONNIE IRVING
60   Melodisc MEL 1546   Pinball Machine/I Got Blues On My Mind........................ 40

(BIG) DEE IRWIN
64   Stateside SS 261   Donkey Walk/Someday You'll Understand Why.................... 15
64   Colpix PX 11040   Heigh-ho/It's My Birthday...................................... 10
64   Colpix PX 11050   Personality/It's Only A Paper Moon............................ 10
65   Stateside SS 450   You Satisfy My Needs/I Wanna Stay Right Here With You (DJ copy = £200) 125
68   Minit MLF 11013   I Can't Stand The Pain/My Hope To Die Girl (as Dee Irwin) 15

BIG DEE IRWIN & LITTLE EVA
63   Colpix PX 11010   Swinging On A Star/Another Night With The Boys (Little Eva uncredited) 6
64   Colpix PX 11021   I Wish You A Merry Christmas/Christmas Song 8
63   Colpix PXE 301   SWINGING ON A STAR (EP).. 22
65   Golden Guinea GSGL 10497 SWINGING ON A STAR (LP)....................................... 20
(see also Little Eva, Suzi & Big Dee Irwin)

DAVID ISAACS
66   Island WI 261   I'd Rather Be Lonely/See That Man........................... 50
68   Trojan TR 616   Place In The Sun/UPSETTER ALL STARS: Handy-Cap............. 18
69   Upsetter US 302   Good Father/SLIM SMITH: What A Situation 12
69   Upsetter US 305   I've Got Memories/I'm Leaving 12
69   Upsetter US 311   He'll Have To Go/Since You're Gone.......................... 12
69   Upsetter US 319   Who To Tell/BUSTY BROWN: I Can't See Myself Cry 12
69   Punch PH 6   I Can't Take It Anymore/LLOYD DOUGLAS: Anyway 10
71   Punch PH 84   You'll Be Sorry/Knock Three Times 8
71   Bullet BU 459   Just Enough/ROY PATIN: Standing (B-side actually by Roy Panton)........... 8
71   Tropical AL 006   Love Has Join Us/MAX ROMEO: Cross Over The Bridge
                        (correct title for A-side is 'Love Has Joined Us') 5
73   Upsetter US 400   Stranger On The Shore/DILLINGER: John Devour 20
73   Bread BR 1118   Just Enough/We Are Neighbours 5
(see also Upsetters)

GREGORY ISAACS
70   Escort ERT 833   While There Is Life/HARRY YOUNG: Come On Over.............. 15
70   Success RE 914   Too Late/KINGSTONIANS: You Can't Wine 12
71   Big Shot BI 584   Lonely Man/RUPIE EDWARDS ALL STARS: Lonely Man Version 12
73   Ackee ACK 522   I'm Coming Home/Version 5
73   Green Door GD 4054   Lonely Soldier/IMPACT ALL STARS: Version..................... 12
74   Pyramid PYR 7012   Innocent People Cry/Version 8
74   Attack ATT 8081   Don't Go/Dubwise... 8
75   Camel CA 2008   Lonely Days/Version.. 8
75   Bullet BU 555   Lonely Days/Version.. 8
77   Observer OBMM-1000   Soul On Fire/CHRISTINE: Saturday Night/TYRONE TAYLOR: Sufferation/
                        In Style (12")... 40
78   Observer P/CHAU   Rock On/DENNIS BROWN & DILLINGER: Jah Is Watching You (12")........... 40
79   Front Line FLS 12112   Soon Forward/Uncle Joe/Come Off Mi Toe (Feat. Prince Far I) (12") 15
80   Solomonic SM 002   Sunday Morning/DENNIS BROWN: Running Around (12")................. 25
88   Greensleeves GRED 221 Rumours/More Rumours (12")..................................... 12
88   Greensleeves GRED 225 Rough Neck/Version (12" with the Mighty Diamonds) 12
89   Greensleeves GRED 256 Report To Me/Report To Me (continued) (12") 12
75   Trojan TRLS 102   IN PERSON (LP)... 15
76   Echo   EXTRA CLASSIC (LP) 12
78   Burning Sounds BS1010 SLUM – GREGORY ISAACS IN DUB (LP) 30
78   DEB DEB LP 04   MR. ISAACS (LP).. 30
79   Virgin Front Line FL1044 SOON FORWARD (LP) 30
83   Burning Sounds BS 1051 SLUM DUB (LP)... 25
(Joel Marvin, I Roy)

IKE ISAACS
74   Decca Eclipse ECS 2163 FOURTEEN GREAT T.V. THEMES (LP) 12

ISCA FAYRE
76   Candle CAN 761   THEN AROUND ME YOUNG AND OLD (LP) 15

JON ISHERWOOD
70   Decca LK/SKL 5051   A LAUGHING CRY (LP).. 15

ISHMAEL & ANDY
73   Myrrh MYR 1005   READY SALTED (LP) 18

ISLAND BOYS
58   London RE-R 1122   GO CALYPSO NO. 1 (EP)....................................... 8
58   London RE-R 1123   GO CALYPSO NO. 2 (EP)....................................... 8
58   London RE-R 1124   GO CALYPSO NO. 3 (EP)....................................... 8

ISLANDERS
59   Top Rank JAR 215   The Enchanted Sea/Pollyanna................................. 5
60   Top Rank JAR 305   Blue Train/Tornado... 5

ISLANDERS
65   Fontana TF 577   It Ain't Me Babe/Four Strong Winds.......................... 10
65   Fontana TF 605   Walkin' Away/Roberta Let Your Hair Hang Down.................. 5

JIMMY ISLE
59   London HLS 8832   Diamond Ring/I've Been Waiting (78 rpm = £25)................ 78
60   Top Rank JAR 274   Billy Boy/Oh Judy.. 18

ISLEY BROTHERS

59	RCA RCA 1149	Shout (Parts 1 & 2)	25
59	RCA RCA 1149	Shout (Parts 1 & 2) (78)	200
60	RCA RCA 1172	Respectable/I'm Gonna Knock On Your Door	20
60	RCA RCA 1190	How Deep Is The Ocean/He's Got The Whole World In His Hands	20
60	RCA RCA 1213	Tell Me Who/Say You Love Me Too	20
62	Stateside SS 112	Twist And Shout/Spanish Twist	15
62	Stateside SS 132	Twistin' With Linda/You Better Come Home	18
63	Stateside SS 218	Nobody But Me/I'm Laughing To Keep From Crying	20
63	United Artists UP 1034	Tango/She's Gone	15
64	United Artists UP 1050	Shake It With Me Baby/Stagger Lee	20
64	Atlantic AT 4010	The Last Girl/Looking For A Love	30
66	Tamla Motown TMG 555	This Old Heart Of Mine (Is Weak For You)/There's No Love Left	
		(1st press has narrow print on label; re-pressed 1968 with wider print)	20/10
66	Tamla Motown TMG 566	Take Some Time Out For Love/Who Could Ever Doubt My Love	30
66	Tamla Motown TMG 572	I Guess I'll Always Love You/I Hear A Symphony	
		(1st pressing has "sold subject to" on centre piece)	30
67	Tamla Motown TMG 606	Got To Have You Back/Just Ain't Enough Love	20
68	Tamla Motown TMG 652	Take Me In Your Arms (Rock Me A Little While)/Why When Love Is Gone	30
69	Tamla Motown TMG 683	I Guess I'll Always Love You/It's Out Of The Question	8
69	Tamla Motown TMG 693	Behind A Painted Smile/One Too Many Heartaches	8
69	Major Minor MM 621	It's Your Thing/Don't Give It Away	8
69	Tamla Motown TMG 708	Put Yourself In My Place/Little Miss Sweetness	10
69	Major Minor MM 631	I Turned You On/I Know Who You Been Socking It To	6
69	Tamla Motown TMG 719	Take Some Time Out For Love/Who Could Ever Doubt My Love (reissue)	8
70	Stateside SS 2162	Was It Good To You?/I Got To Get Myself Together	6
71	Stateside SS 2188	Warpath/I Got To Find Me One	6
71	Stateside SS 2193	Love The One You're With/He's Got Your Love	10
73	Tamla Motown TMG 877	Tell Me It's Just A Rumour, Baby/Save Me From This Misery	5
73	Epic EPC 1980	The Highways Of My Life/Don't Let Me Be Lonely Tonight	5
74	Epic EPC 2803	Need A Little Taste Of Love/If You Were There	5
76	DJM DJS 640	Twist And Shout/Time After Time (reissue)	5
79	RCA PC 9411	Shout/Respectable/Tell Me Who (12", p/s)	8
64	RCA RCX 7149	THE ISLEY BROTHERS (EP)	75
60	RCA RD 27165/SF 7055	SHOUT (LP, mono/stereo)	65/90
64	United Artists ULP 1064	THE FAMOUS ISLEY BROTHERS — TWISTING AND SHOUTING (LP)	80
66	Tamla Motown TML 11034	THIS OLD HEART OF MINE (IS WEAK FOR YOU) (LP, mono/stereo)	40
68	T. Motown (S)TML 11066	SOUL ON THE ROCKS (LP)	45
69	Major Minor SMLP 59	IT'S OUR THING (LP)	25
69	T. Motown (S)TML 11112	BEHIND A PAINTED SMILE (LP, mono/stereo)	30/25
70	Stateside SSL 10300	THE BROTHERS: ISLEY (LP)	22
70	RCA Intl. INTS 1098	SHOUT (LP)	12
73	Epic EPC 65740	3 + 3 (LP, gatefold sleeve)	12
74	Epic EPC 80317	LIVE IT UP (LP)	12
75	Epic EPC 69139	THE HEAT IS ON (LP)	12
76	Epic EPC 81268	HARVEST FOR THE WORLD (LP)	12

ISOLATION

73	Riverside HASLP 2083	ISOLATION (LP, private pressing with insert)	300

ISOTOPE

74	Gull GULP 1002	ISOTOPE (LP)	12
74	Gull GULP 1006	ILLUSION (LP)	12
75	Gull GULP 1017	DEEP END (LP)	12

ISRAELITES

69	Downtown DT 413	Moma Moma/Melody For Two	8
69	Downtown DT 433	Seven Books/Chaka Beat	8
70	J-Dan JDN 4410	Can't Help From Crying/Can't Get Used To Losing You	8
	(see also Music Doctors)		

ISRAEL VIBRATION

78	Harvest HAR 184	The Same Song/Weep And Moan	15
79	Harvest 12 HAR 5189	Crisis/Crisis Dub (feat. Augustus Pablo)	30

ITALS (Jamaica)

67	Giant GN 8	New Loving (with Soul Brothers)/I Told You Little Girl	20
67	Giant GN 12	Don't Throw It Away/Make Up Your Mind (both with Carib-Beats)	35
71	Big BG 325	Ba-Da-Doo-Ba-Dey/RUPIE EDWARDS ALL STARS: Version	10
	(see also Alton Ellis, Honeyboy)		

ITALS (U.K.)

71	Black Swan BW 1404	Dawn Patrol/Whiskey Bonga (DJ and Rhythm)	12
71	Black Swan BW 1407	Judgement Rock (actually by Charlie Ace)/Night West	12

ITHACA

73	Merlin HF 6	A GAME FOR ALL WHO KNOW (LP, with insert)	500+
93	Background	A GAME FOR ALL WHO KNOW (LP, reissue)	15
	(see also Friends, Alice Through The Looking Glass, Agincourt, Tomorrow Come Someday, BBC Radiophonic Workshop)		

IT'S A BEAUTIFUL DAY

69	CBS 4457	White Bird/Wasted Union Blues	8
70	CBS 4933	Soapstone Mountain/Do You Remember The Sun	15
73	CBS 1625	Ain't That Lovin' You Baby/Time	5
69	CBS 63722	IT'S A BEAUTIFUL DAY (LP, gatefold sleeve)	20
70	CBS 64065	MARRYING MAIDEN (LP)	15
72	CBS 64314	CHOICE QUALITY STUFF — ANYTIME (LP)	15

IT'S IMMATERIAL

84	Eternal JF 4	A Gigantic Raft In The Philipines/The Mermaid (p/s)	10

IVAN
58	Coral Q 72341	Real Wild Child/Oh, You Beautiful Doll (78 rpm = £100)	250

(see also Jerry Allison, Crickets)

IVAN D. JUNIORS
63	Oriole CB 1874	Catch You If I Can/On My Mind	20

IVANS MEADS
65	Parlophone R 5342	A Little Sympathy/The Sins Of A Family	70
66	Parlophone R 5503	We'll Talk About It Tomorrow/The Bottle	30

BURL IVES
54	Columbia SCMC 5	I've Got No Use For Women/River Of Smoke (export issue)	10
56	Brunswick 05510	Ballad Of Davy Crockett/Goober Peas	10
56	Brunswick 05551	Dying Stockman/Click Go The Shears	10
56	Brunswick 05604	The Bus Stop Song/That's My Heartstrings	10
56	Decca BM 31183	Marianne/Pretty Girl (with Trinidadies) (export issue)	10
53	Brunswick LA 8552	BALLADS AND FOLK SONGS VOL. 2 (10" LP)	15
53	Brunswick LA 8583	BALLADS AND FOLK SONGS VOL. 1 (10" LP)	15
54	Brunswick LA 8633	FOLK SONGS — DRAMATIC AND HUMOROUS (10" LP)	20
54	Brunswick LA 8641	WOMEN (10" LP)	10
55	Brunswick LAT 8048	CORONATION CONCERT (LP)	15
56	Brunswick LA 8739	AUSTRALIAN FOLK SONGS (10" LP)	18
56	Brunswick LAT 8142	DOWN TO THE SEA IN SHIPS (LP)	15
60	Brunswick LAT 8344	SONGS OF IRELAND (LP)	12
61	Brunswick LAT 8381	THE VERSATILE BURL IVES (LP)	12
62	Brunswick LAT 8395	SONGS OF THE WEST (LP)	12
62	Brunswick LAT 8404	FUNNY WAY OF LAUGHIN' (LP, also stereo STA 3063)	12/12
63	Brunswick LAT 8517	SUNSHINE IN MY SOUL (LP)	15
63	Brunswick LAT/STA 8554	SINGIN' EASY (LP, mono/stereo)	12/12
64	Brunswick LAT 8591	PEARLY SHELLS (LP)	12
66	Brunswick LAT 8665	SOMETHING SPECIAL (LP)	12
60s	American Heritage AH 14	IN THE QUIET OF THE NIGHT (LP)	15
60s	CBS BPG 62588	THE WAYFARING STRANGER (LP)	12
60s	CBS 31717	THE TIMES THEY ARE A-CHANGING (LP)	15
60s	Polydor 3187094	LIVE IN EUROPE (LP)	15
60s	Brunswick LAT 8577	TRUE LOVE (LP)	15
60s	Brunswick LAT 8142	SINGS DOWN TO THE SEA IN SHIPS (LP)	20

IVEYS
68	Apple APPLE 5	Maybe Tomorrow/And Her Daddy's A Millionaire	55
69	Apple APPLE 14	Dear Angie/No Escaping Your Love (unreleased; Europe & Japan only)	
68	Apple SAPCOR 8	MAYBE TOMORROW (LP, unissued; Europe & Japan only)	
92	Apple SAPCOR 8	MAYBE TOMORROW (LP, reissue, gatefold sleeve & bonus 12" [SAPCOR 82])	25
92	Apple SAPCOR 8	MAYBE TOMORROW (CD)	30

(see also Badfinger, Pleasure Garden)

IVOR & SHEILA
81	Eron 027	CHANGING TIMES (LP, with insert)	30

IVORIES
85	Kent TOWN 103	Please Stay/TOMMY HUNT: The Work Song	8

(see also Tommy Hunt)

JACKIE IVORY
66	Atlantic AT 4075	Hi-Heel Sneakers/Do It To Death	20
65	Atlantic ATL 5046	SOUL DISCOVERY (LP, reissued in 1966)	60/18

IVY LEAGUE
64	Piccadilly 7N 35200	What More Do You Want?/Wait A Minute	10
65	Piccadilly 7N 35228	That's Why I'm Crying/A Girl Like You	5
66	Piccadilly 7N 35294	Running Round In Circles/Rain Rain Go Away	5
66	Piccadilly 7N 35326	Willow Tree/One Day	5
66	Piccadilly 7N 35348	My World Fell Down/When You're Young	8
67	Piccadilly 7N 35365	Four And Twenty Hours/Arrivederci Baby	5
67	Piccadilly 7N 35397	Suddenly Things/Tomorrow Is Another Day	5
67	Pye 7N 17386	Thank You For Loving Me/In The Not Too Distant Future	5
65	Piccadilly NEP 34038	FUNNY HOW LOVE CAN BE (EP)	20
65	Piccadilly NEP 34042	TOSSING AND TURNING (EP)	20
65	Piccadilly NEP 34046	THE HOLLY AND THE IVY LEAGUE (EP)	20
66	Piccadilly NEP 34048	OUR LOVE IS SLIPPING AWAY (EP)	30
65	Piccadilly NPL 38015	THIS IS THE IVY LEAGUE (LP)	30

(see also Carter-Lewis, White Plains, Edison Lighthouse, Flowerpot Men, Kestrels, One & One, Johnny Shadow, Perry Ford, First Class, Friends, Warm Sensations)

IVY THREE
60	London HLW 9178	Yogi/Was Judy There	20

IZZY POUND
69	Plexium PXM 9	Pumpkin Miny/Na Na Na Na	60

MINT VALUE £

CLUE J. & HIS BLUES BLASTERS
60	Blue Beat BB 15	Easy Snappin'/Goin' Home (with vocal by Theophilus Beckford)	12
61	Blue Beat BB 37	Lovers' Jive/Wicked And Dreadful (actually with Neville Esson)	12
61	Blue Beat BB 60	Little Willie/Pine Juice	12

DAVID J. (& J. WALKERS)
81	4AD AD 112	Nothing/Armour (as David Jay & René Halkett) (p/s, with lyric sheet)	6
84	GLASS 12032	V For Vendetta: This Viscious Cabaret/V's Theme/Incidental/V's Theme (12" p/s)	8

(see also Bauhaus)

HARRY J. ALL STARS
(see under 'H')

TONY J.
75	Stonehouse 001	Telephone Line/Telephone Version	5

BILLY JACK (& CIMARONS)
70	Grape GR 3018	Let's Work Together/CORPORATION: Jam Monkey	10
70	Big Shot BI 558	Once A Man/Soul Mood (as Billy Jack & Cimarons)	7
70	Big Shot BI 559	Bet Your Life I Do/CANDY & CIMARONS: Ace Of Hearts	7

(see also Candy)

BOBBY JACK
59	Top Rank JAR 190	Tempting Me/Early Mornin'	8

JACK (Bernard) & BEANSTALKS
69	Supreme SUP 203	Work It Up/Chatty Chatty	12

(see also Kingstonians)

JACKAL
86	Crim. Damage CRI 12-134	Underneath The Arches/Thunder Machine (12", p/s)	15

(see also Renegade Soundwave)

JACKIE
78	Fashion FAD 002	It's Too Late Baby/Fashion On Fine Style (12")	20

JACKIE & BRIDIE
68	Major Minor MM 562	Come Me Little Son/We Only Needed Time	6
64	Fontana TL 5212	HOLD BACK THE DAWN (LP)	25
70	Concord CONS 1002	FOLK WORLD OF JACKIE AND BRIDIE (LP)	15
71	Galliard GAL 4009	THE PERFECT ROUND (LP)	15
70s	Nevis NEV LP 102	HELLO FRIEND (LP, as Jacqui & Bridie)	12
77	J & B CNN 5939	COME DAY GO DAY (LP)	12
77	J & B CNN 5949	HOW CAN YOU KEEP FROM SINGING WITH... (LP)	12

(see also Jacqueline & Bridie)

JACKIE & DOREEN
64	Ska Beat JB 168	Every Beat Of My Heart	20
65	Ska Beat JB 209	The New Vow/Adorable You	20

(see also Doreen Shaffer, Jackie Opel)

JACKIE (Edwards) & MILLIE (Small)
65	Island WI 253	This Is My Story/SOUND SYSTEM: Never Again	35
66	Island WI 265	My Desire/MILLIE: That's How Strong My Love Is	25
67	Island WIP 6012	In A Dream/Ooh Ooh	25
67	Island ILP 941	PLEDGING MY LOVE (LP, as Jackie Edwards & Millie Small)	100
68	Island ILP 963	THE BEST OF JACKIE AND MILLIE VOLUME TWO (LP)	90
70	Trojan TTL 52	THE BEST OF JACKIE AND MILLIE VOLUME TWO (LP, reissue)	20
70	Trojan TBL 155	JACKIE & MILLIE (LP)	15

(see also Wilfred & Millicent, Jackie Edwards, Millie)

JACKIE & RAINDROPS
(see under Jackie Lee & Raindrops)

JACKIE & ROY
58	Vogue V 9101	You Smell So Good/Let's Take A Walk Around The Block (78 rpm = £35)	50
59	Vogue VE 1-70131	JACKIE AND ROY (EP)	30
58	Vogue VA 1-60111	JACKIE AND ROY (LP)	40

ALEXANDER JACKSON & TURNKEYS
65	Sue WI 386	The Whip/Tell It Like It Is (actually "Flea Pot"/"Sweetie Lester" by Lala Wilson)	60

BO WEAVIL JACKSON
59	Jazz Collector JDL 127	Some Scream High Yellow/Why Do You Moan? (78 rpm = £8)	6

BULLMOOSE JACKSON & HIS ORCHESTRA
53	Vogue V 2129	Nosey Joe/I Know Who Threw The Whisky In The Well (78)	20

CHRIS JACKSON
69	Soul City SC 112	I'll Never Forget You/Forever I'll Stay With You	35
70	Soul City SC 120	Since There's No Doubt/We Will Be Together (unissued, acetate only)	

MINT VALUE £

CHUCK JACKSON

61	Top Rank JAR 564	I Don't Want To Cry/Just Once	40
62	Top Rank JAR 607	The Breaking Point/My Willow Tree	40
62	Stateside SS 102	Any Day Now/The Prophet	30
62	Stateside SS 127	I Keep Forgettin'/Who's Gonna Pick Up The Pieces	25
63	Stateside SS 171	Tell Him I'm Not Home/Getting Ready For The Heartbreak	25
64	Pye International 7N 25247	Beg Me/For All Time	25
64	Pye International 7N 25276	Any Day Now/The Prophet (reissue)	20
65	Pye International 7N 25287	Since I Don't Have You/Hand It Over	100
65	Pye International 7N 25301	I Need You/Chuck's Soul Brothers Twist	20
65	Pye International 7N 25321	If I Didn't Love You/Just A Little Bit Of Your Soul	22
66	Pye International 7N 25384	Chains Of Love/I Keep Forgettin' (DJ copy = £150)	100
67	Pye International 7N 25439	Shame On Me/Candy	20
68	Tamla Motown TMG 651	Girls, Girls, Girls/(You Can't Let The Boy Overpower) The Man In You	20
70	Tamla Motown TMG 729	Honey Come Back/What Am I Gonna Do Without You	10
73	Probe PRO 595	I Only Get The Feeling/Slowly But Surely	20
74	Probe PRO 617	I Can't Break Away/Just A Little Tear	10
75	All Platinum 6146 310	I've Got The Need/Beautiful Woman	10
75	Disco Demand DDS 116	These Chains Of Love/Any Day Now	10
85	Kent TOWN 104	Hand It Over/CANDY & KISSES: Mr Creator (withdrawn)	30+
80s	Inferno SIN 1	Chains Of Love/Good Things Come To Those Who Wait/Hand It Over/Any Day Now	20
66	Pye Intl. NPL 28082	TRIBUTE TO RHYTHM AND BLUES (LP)	50
68	T. Motown (S)TML 11071	CHUCK JACKSON ARRIVES! (LP)	70
69	T. Motown (S)TML 11117	GOIN' BACK TO CHUCK JACKSON (LP)	50
72	Probe SPB 1084	THROUGH ALL TIMES (LP)	25
74	Anchor ABCL 5040	THROUGH ALL TIMES (LP, reissue)	12

(see also Del[l]-Vikings)

CHUCK JACKSON & MAXINE BROWN

| 65 | Pye International 7N 25308 | Something You Got/Baby Take Me | 25 |
| 65 | Pye Intl. NPL 28091 | SAYING SOMETHING (LP) | 50 |

(see also Maxine Brown, Tammi Terrell)

DEON JACKSON

66	Atlantic AT 4070	Love Makes The World Go Round/You Said You Loved Me	35
66	Atlantic 584 012	Love Takes A Long Time Growing/Hush Little Baby	25
68	Atlantic 584 159	Ooh Baby/All On A Sunny Day	30
76	Contempo CS 9031	Love Makes The World Go Round/I Can't Go On	20

EARL JACKSON

| 76 | ABC ABC 4110 | Soul Self Satisfaction/Looking Thru' The Eyes Of Love | 12 |

GEORGE JACKSON

69	Capitol CL 15605	Find 'Em, Fool 'Em And Forget 'Em/My Desires Are Getting The Best Of Me	25
72	London HLU 10373	Aretha, Sing One For Me/I'm Gonna Wait	12
73	London HLU 10413	Let 'Em Know You Care/Patricia	12

GORDON JACKSON

69	Marmalade 598 010	Me And My Zoo/A Day At The Cottage	10
69	Marmalade 598 021	Song For Freedom/Sing To Me Woman	15
69	Marmalade 608 012	THINKING BACK (LP)	85

(see also Traffic)

HAROLD JACKSON & TORNADOES

| 58 | Vogue V 9105 | Move It On Down The Line Parts 1 & 2 (78 rpm = £60) | 120 |

JACKIE JACKSON

| 74 | T. Motown STML 11249 | JACKIE JACKSON (LP) | 15 |

(see also Jacksons, Jackson 5)

JANET JACKSON

SINGLES

83	A&M AMS 8303	Come Give Your Love To Me/The Magic Is Working (p/s)	8
83	A&M AMSX 8303	Come Give Your Love To Me/The Magic Is Working (12", p/s)	12
83	A&M AM 112	Don't Mess Up This Good Thing/Young Love (p/s)	8
83	A&M AMX 112	Don't Mess Up This Good Thing/Young Love/Forever Yours (12", p/s)	12
86	A&M AMS 337	When I Think Of You/Come Give Your Love To Me/What Have You Done For Me Lately/Young Love (clear vinyl/picture disc double pack in PVC foldout cover)	12
86	A&M AMS 359	Control/Pretty Boy (p/s, with free cassette ["Nasty (Cool Summer Mix)"])	10
87	Breakout USAD 601	Let's Wait A While/Nasty (Cool Summer Mix Pt. 1)/Nasty (Original Mix)/Control/Let's Wait A While (Remix)/Nasty (Cool Summer Mix Part 1 Fade) (picture disc/clear vinyl double pack in PVC foldout sleeve)	10
87	Breakout USAS 613	Funny How Time Flies (When You're Having Fun)/When I Think Of You (poster p/s)	5
89	Breakout USACD 663	Miss You Much (Mamma Mix 3.55)/Miss You Much (Mamma Mix 7.22)/You Need Me (CD)	10
89	Breakout USACD 673	Rhythm Nation (7" Edit)/(12" House Nation Mix)/(12" United Dub) (CD)	10
90	Breakout USAB 681	Come Back To Me (7" I'm Beggin' You Mix)/Alright (7" R&B mix) (box set with metal badge & foldout poster)	6
90	Breakout USACD 681	Come Back To Me (7" I'm Beggin' You Mix)/Alright (7" R + B Mix)/Alright (7" House Mix With Rap) (CD)	10
90	Breakout USAP 684	Escapade (We've Got It Made 7")/Escapade (Housecapade 7") (picture disc with photo & discography)	5

90	Breakout USAS 693	Alright (House Mix)/Vuelve A Mi (Come Back To Me) (shaped picture disc with plinth in printed PVC sleeve)............ 8

JANET JACKSON & CLIFF RICHARD
84	A&M AM 210	Two To The Power Of Love/JANET JACKSON: Rock'n'Roll (p/s) 15
84	A&M AMX 210	Two To The Power Of Love/JANET JACKSON: Rock'n'Roll/Don't Mess Up This Good Thing (12", p/s)........................... 15

(see also Cliff Richard)

JERMAINE JACKSON
84	Epic JMJDJ 1	Tell Me I'm Not Dreamin' (Too Good To Be True) (with Michael Jackson)/ Come To Me/Oh Mother (promo only)....................... 30
85	Arista ARIST 609	Do What You Do/Tell Me I'm Not Dreamin' (Too Good To Be True) (last track with Michael Jackson) (p/s)................. 5
85	Arista ARIST 12609	Do What You Do/Tell Me I'm Not Dreamin' (Too Good To Be True) (last track with Michael Jackson) (12", p/s)............. 8

(see also Jacksons, Jackson 5, Michael Jackson)

JERRY JACKSON
63	London HLR 9689	Gypsy Eyes/Turn Back 40
66	Cameo Parkway P 100	It's Rough Out There/I'm Gonna Paint A Picture (DJ copy = £275)........... 175

JILL JACKSON & CANDLESHINE
90s	PWD 6502	Where Is The Heart/Glider From The Moon 6

JIM JACKSON
66	RCA RCX 7182	R.C.A. VICTOR RACE SERIES VOL. 7 (EP) 18

JIMMY JACKSON('S ROCK 'N' ROLL SKIFFLE)
57	Columbia DB 3898	California Zephyr/I Shall Not Be Moved (78 rpm = £7) 22
57	Columbia DB 3937	Sittin' In The Balcony/Good Morning Blues (78 rpm = £10) 35
57	Columbia DB 3957	River Line/Lonely Road (78 rpm = £7) 18
57	Columbia DB 3988	White Silver Sands/Build Your Love (On A Strong Foundation) (solo) (78 rpm = £7) 10
58	Columbia DB 4085	Love-A Love-A Love A/Photographs (solo) (78 rpm = £8) 10
58	Columbia DB 4153	Swing Down, Sweet Chariot/This Little Light Of Mine (solo) (78 rpm = £8) .. 8
58	Columbia SEG 7750	ROCK 'N' SKIFFLE (EP) 75
58	Columbia SEG 7768	COUNTRY AND BLUES (EP) 80

J.J. JACKSON (& Greatest Little Soul Band In The Land)
67	Polydor 56718	But It's Alright/Do The Boogaloo........................ 20
67	Strike JH 329	Come See Me/Try Me 20
67	Warner Bros WB 2082	Sho Nuff (Got A Good Thing Going)/Here We Go Again........... 15
68	Warner Bros WB 2090	Down, But Not Out/Why Does It Take So Long? 15
68	Warner Bros WB 6029	Courage Ain't Strength/You Do It 'Cause You Wanna 15
69	Warner Bros WB 7276	Ain't Too Proud To Beg/But It's Alright..................... 10
71	Mojo 2092 014	But It's Alright/Do The Boogaloo......................... 10
67	Strike JLH 104	J.J. JACKSON WITH THE GREATEST LITTLE SOUL BAND (LP)....... 50
69	MCA SKA 100	GREATEST LITTLE SOUL BAND (LP) 25
70	RCA Victor SF 8093	J.J. JACKSON'S DILEMMA (LP) 22

(see also Greatest Little Soul Band)

J.J. JACKSON/LINDA JONES
77	Loma/Warners K 56271	THIS IS LOMA — VOL. 7 (LP, 1 side each) 15

LEVI JACKSON
71	Columbia DB 8807	This Beautiful Day/Don't You Be A Sinner 150

(see also Solomon King)

LLOYD JACKSON
71	Pama Supreme PS 308	Cracklin' Rosie/Little Deeds Of Kindness (B-side with Scorpions)............. 5

MAHALIA JACKSON
51	Vogue V 301	Since The Fire Started Burning In My Soul/In My Home Over There (78)........ 10
51	Vogue V 302	The Last Mile Of The Way/I'm Glad Salvation Is Free (78) 8
52	Vogue V 305	I Do, Don't You/Silent Night, Holy Night (78) 10
52	Vogue V 306	I Gave Up/Silent Night, Holy Night (78)..................... 8
55	Philips BB 2005	A Rusty Old Halo/The Treasures Of Love (78, export issue) 12
58	Philips PB 869	For My Good Fortune/Have You Any Rivers (78 rpm = £15)......... 5
59	Philips PB 933	Trouble Of The World/Tell The World About This 5
60	Philips PB 1040	Onward Christian Soldiers/The Lord's Prayer 5
60	Vogue V 2418	The Lord's Prayer/Bless This House 5
60	Top Rank JKP 2038	IN THE UPPER ROOM VOLUME 1 (EP)...................... 8
60	Top Rank JKP 2048	IN THE UPPER ROOM VOLUME 2 (EP)...................... 8
52	Vogue LDE 005	MAHALIA JACKSON (10" LP) 35
59	Philips BBL 7289	NEWPORT 1958 (LP, also stereo SBBL 547)................. 12/15
60	Top Rank 30/006	JUST AS I AM (LP) 15
60	Philips BBL 7362	GREAT GETTIN' UP MORNING (LP) 12
60	Philips BBL 7391	THE POWER AND THE GLORY (LP, also stereo SBBL 576) 12/15
60	Philips BBL 7435	COME ON CHILDREN LET'S SING (LP) 15
61	Philips BBL 7456	I BELIEVE (LP, also stereo SBBL 610)..................... 12/15

MICHAEL JACKSON
SINGLES
72	Tamla Motown TMG 816	Rockin' Robin/Love Is Here And Now You're Gone.............. 5
72	Tamla Motown TMG 834	Ben/You Can Cry On My Shoulder 5
73	Tamla Motown TMG 863	Morning Glow/My Girl................................. 5
74	Tamla Motown TMG 900	Music And Me/Johnny Raven 5
75	Tamla Motown TMG 946	One Day In Your Life/With A Child's Heart 5
75	Tamla Motown TMG 1006	Just A Little Bit Of You/Dear Michael 5
79	Epic S EPC 7135	You Can't Win (Part 1)/You Can't Win (Part 2) (picture disc) 12

Michael JACKSON

79	Epic 12EPC 7135	You Can't Win (Part 1)/You Can't Win (Part 2) (12")	10
79	Epic 12EPC 7763	Don't Stop 'Til You Get Enough/I Can't Help It (12")	8
79	Epic 12EPC 8206	Rock With You/Get On The Floor/You Can't Win (Extended) (12")	8
81	Motown TMG 977	We're Almost There/We've Got A Good Thing Going (p/s)	5
81	Motown TMGT 977	We're Almost There (Album Version)/We've Got A Good Thing Going (12")	8
82	Epic EPCA 11-2729	The Girl Is Mine (with Paul McCartney)/Can't Get Outta The Rain (picture disc)	15
83	Epic EPC 2906	GREATEST ORIGINAL HITS: Don't Stop 'Til You Get Enough/She's Out Of My Life/Off The Wall/Rock With You (EP)	10
83	Epic EPCA 40-2906	GREATEST ORIGINAL HITS: Don't Stop 'Til You Get Enough/She's Out Of My Life/Off The Wall/Rock With You (EP, cassette)	8
83	Motown TMG 986	Happy (Love Theme From 'Lady Sings The Blues')/We're Almost There (poster p/s)	8
83	Motown EPCA 112729	Happy (Love Theme From 'Lady Sings The Blues')/We're Almost There (picture disc)	10
83	Epic EPCA 3643	Thriller/JACKSONS: Things I Do For You (live) (poster p/s)	8
83	Epic TA 3643	Thriller (Album Version)/Thriller (Remix Short Version)/JACKSONS: Things I Do For You (live) (12", 'calendar' p/s)	50
83	Epic MJ 1 (1-9)	MICHAEL JACKSON'S 9 SINGLES PACK (9 x 7", p/s, each on red vinyl, in PVC foldout wallet)	35
84	Arista JMJDJ 1	Tell Me I'm Not Dreamin' (Too Good To Be True)/JERMAINE JACKSON: Come To Me/Oh Mother (promo only)	25
87	Epic 650 202-0	I Just Can't Stop Loving You (with Siedah Garratt)/Baby Be Mine (poster p/s)	10
87	Epic 650 202-6	I Just Can't Stop Loving You (with Siedah Garratt)/Baby Be Mine (12", p/s with poster)	15
87	Epic 651 155-6	Bad (Dance Extended Mix With False Fade)/Bad (7" Single Mix)/Bad (Dance Radio Edit)Bad (Dub)/Bad (A Cappella) (12", p/s, red vinyl)	8
87	Epic 651 275-7	The Way You Make Me Feel/The Way You Make Me Feel (Instrumental) (p/s, with competition leaflet, stickered sleeve)	5
87	Epic 651 275-3	The Way You Make Me Feel (7" Mix)/(A Cappella)/(Dance Radio Edit)/(Dub)/(Get Into The Groove —Put Either Side On The Turntable, Lower The Arm And See Which Your Needle Pix) (12, p/s, double-groove)	12
87	Epic 651 275-9	The Way You Make Me Feel (Dance Extended Mix)/The Way You Make Me Feel (Dub Version)/The Way You Make Me Feel (A Cappella) (CD, card p/s)	12
88	Epic 651 388-9	Man In The Mirror (Single Mix)/Man In The Mirror (Instrumental) (square-shaped picture disc)	15
88	Epic 651 388-2	Man In The Mirror (4.55)/Man In The Mirror (Album Mix)/Man In The Mirror (Instrumental) (CD, card sleeve)	10
88	Epic 651 388-2	Man In The Mirror/Man In The Mirror (Album Mix)/Man In The Mirror (Instrumental) (3" CD with adaptor, card sleeve)	12
88	Epic 651 546-7	Dirty Diana/Dirty Diana (p/s, with 13" cardboard figure)	12
88	Epic 652 864-6	Dirty Diana/Dirty Diana (Instrumental)/Bad (Extended Dance Mix With False Fade) (12", with tour poster p/s)	15
88	Epic 651 546-9	Dirty Diana (4.42)/Dirty Diana (Instrumental)/Bad (Dance Extended Mix Includes "False Fade") (CD, card p/s)	10
88	Epic 651 546-2	Dirty Diana (4.42)/Dirty Diana (Instrumental)/Dirty Diana (Album Version) (3" CD with adaptor, card p/s)	12
88	Epic MJ 5	THE MICHAEL JACKSON BAD SOUVENIR SINGLES PACK (5 x 7" square picture discs in foldout PVC wallet, with lyric book)	40
88	Epic 652 844-9	Another Part Of Me/(Instrumental) (p/s, with Bad tour backstage pass)	12
88	Epic 652 844-0	Another Part Of Me/Another Part Of Me (Instrumental) (poster p/s)	8
88	Epic 652 844-2	Another Part Of Me (Extended Dance Mix)/(Radio Edit)/(Drum Mix)/(A Capella) (CD, card p/s)	10
88	Epic 652 844-3	Another Part Of Me (Extended Dance Mix)/(Radio Edit)/(Dub Mix)/(Instrumental) (3" CD with adaptor, card p/s)	12
88	Epic 653 004-2	Another Part Of Me (Extended Dance Mix)/Another Part Of Me (Radio Edit) Another Part Of Me (Drum Mix)/Another Part Of Me (A Cappella) (CD, pic disc)	12
88	Epic 653 026-0	Smooth Criminal/Smooth Criminal (Instrumental) (pack with 4 postcards)	15
88	Epic 653 170-6	Smooth Criminal (Extended Dance Mix)/Smooth Criminal Extended (Dance Mix Dub Mix)/Smooth Criminal (A Cappella) (12" w/'Moonwalker' advent calendar)	20
88	Epic 653 026-2	Smooth Criminal (Extended Dance Mix)/Smooth Criminal ("Annie" Mix)/Smooth Criminal (A Cappella) (CD, card p/s)	10
89	Epic 654 672-0	Leave Me Alone/Human Nature (pop-up p/s)	25
89	Epic 654 672-2	Leave Me Alone (4.40)/Don't Stop 'Til You Get Enough (3.55)/Human Nature (4.05)/Wanna Be Startin' Something (Extended 6.30) (CD, card sleeve)	10
89	Epic 654 672-3	Leave Me Alone (4.40)/Don't Stop 'Til You Get Enough (6.04)/Human Nature (4.05) (3" CD, gatefold card sleeve)	22
89	Tamla Motown MOTD7 0005	VINTAGE GOLD (3" CD EP, gatefold card sleeve, with Jackson 5)	15
89	Epic 654 947-9	Liberian Girl (Edit)/Girlfriend (star mobile foldout card pack)	15
89	Epic 654 947-2	Liberian Girl (Edit 3.39)/Girlfriend/The Lady In My Life/Get On The Floor (CD, card p/s)	10
89	Epic 654 947-3	Liberian Girl (Edit 3.39)/Get On The Floor/Girlfriend (3" CD, g/fold card p/s)	10
92	Epic MJ 4 (658 281-1/4)	TOUR SOUVENIR PACK (CD, 4-picture disc, box set with booklet)	40
92	Epic 658 360-7	Jam (7" Edit)/Beat It (Moby's Sub Mix) ('picture frame' pack with 2 prints)	5
95	Epic 662 022	Scream (Single Edit)/Childhood (p/s, with 2 page lyric insert)	5
95	Epic 662 127	Scream (Def Radio Mix)/Scream (Single Edit) (limited edition poster sleeve)	5
96	Epic 662 950	They Don't Care About Us (Single Edit 4:43)/They Don't Care About Us (Love To Infinity's Walk In The Park Radio Mix) (jukebox issue, white labels, no p/s)	5
96	Epic 662 950	They Don't Care About Us (LP Mix 4:10)/They Don't Care About Us (Love To Infinity's Walk In The Park Radio Mix) (jukebox issue, white labels, no p/s)	5
97	Epic 663 787	Stranger In Moscow/Stranger In Moscow (Version) (jukebox issue, white labels, no p/s)	5
97	Epic 664 462	Blood On The Dancefloor/Mix (jukebox issue, white labels, no p/s)	5
97	Epic 664 796	History/Ghosts (jukebox issue, white labels, no p/s)	5

Michael JACKSON

97	Epic 665 130 6	Smile/It It Scary (Deep Dish Dark And Scary Remix)/Is It Scary (Eddie's Rub-a-Dub Mix)/Is It Scary (Eddie's Love Mix)/ Off The Wall (Junior Vasquez Remix) (12", p/s withdrawn)	200

PROMOS

92	Epic XPR 1733	Remember The Time: (12" Main Mix)/(New Jack Mix)/(New Jack Main Mix)/ (Silky Soul 12" Mix)/(Silky Soul Dub)/(E-Smoov's Late Nite Mix) (12", company sleeve)	8
92	Epic XPR 1814	Jam: (More Than Enuff Mix)/(Roger's Club Mix)/(E-Smoov Jazzy Jam)/ (Atlanta Techno Mix)/(Roger's Underground Mix)/(Silky 12")/ (More Than Enuff Dub)/(Maurice's Jammin' Dub Mix)/(Roger's Club Dub)/ (Atlanta Techno Dub)/(Roger's Slam Jam Mix)/(Silky Dub)/(A Cappella Mix) (12", double pack, black & orange stickered white sleeve)	25
92	Epic XPR 1797	Who Is It (Patience Mix)/(Patience Beats)/(Most Patient Mix)/(HIS Mix)/ (The P-Man Dub) (12", company sleeve)	10
95	Epic XPR 2265	The Classic Remix Series: Wanna Be Startin' Something (Brothers In Rhythm Mix)/(Tommy D's Main Mix) (12", plain sleeve, sealed with title sticker)	15
95	Epic XPR 2266	DMC Megamix (15.40)/(11.18) (12", custom sleeve)	15
95	Epic XPR 2229	The Classic Remix Series: Rock With You (Frankie's Favorite Club Mix)/ (The Masters At Work Remix) (12", plain sleeve, sealed with title sticker)	12
95	Epic XPCD 7222	The Classic Remix Series: Rock With You (Frankie's Favorite Club Mix Radio Edit)/(Frankie's Favorite Club Mix) (CD)	20
95	Epic XPR 2184	Scream: (Classic Club Mix)/(DM R&B Extended Mix)/(Def Radio Mix)/ (Naughty Main Mix)/(Naughty Main Mix No Rap)/(Dave 'Jam' Hall's Extended Urban Remix)/(Pressurized Dub Part 1)/(Pressurized Dub Part 2)/ (Album Version)/(Single Edit No. 2)/(Naughty Pretty-Pella)/ (Naughty A Cappella) (12", double pack, red title sleeve)	20
96	Epic XPR 2207	Mj Club Megamix (MJ Mega Remix)/(MJ Urban Megamix) (12", blue & purple title sleeve)	15
96	Epic XPR 3020	They Don't Care About Us (The Love To Infinity Mixes): Classic Paradise Mix/ Anthem Of Love/Classic Dub/Anthem Of love Dub/Hacienda Mix (12", p/s)	10
96	Epic XPR 3030	They Don't Care About Us (The R&B Mixes): Track Masters Remix/ Dallas Austin Main Mix/Charles' Full Dirty Mix/LP Edit/Love To Infinity's Walk In The Park/Track Masters' Instrumental (12", p/s)	10
96	Epic XPR 3033	The Classic Remix Series: Don't Stop Til You Get Enough (Roger's Underground Solution Mix)/Beat It (Moby's Sub Mix) (12", plain sleeve sealed with title sticker)	8
96	Epic SAMPCD 3598	This Time Around (DM Radio Mix)/(Dallas Radio Remix)/(Maurice's Club Around Radio Mix)/(Maurice's Hip Hop Around Mix)/ (David Mitson Clean Edit) (CD)	25
97	Epic XPCD 2176	HIStory (Mix 1)/Ghosts/(HIStory (Mix 2) HIStory (Mix 3)/HIStory (Mix 4) (CD)	15
97	Epic XPR 3125	Blood On The Dancefloor (TM's Switchblade Mix)/(TM's O-Postive Dub) (12", blue title p/s)	8
97	Epic XPR 3136	Blood On The Dancefloor (Refugee Camp Mix)/(7" Version) (12", green title p/s)	8
97	Epic XPR 3149	HIStory (Marks! Philly Vocal)/(Marks! Future Dub) (12", yellow title sleeve)	8
97	Epic XPR 3159	HIStory (Tony Moran's HIStory Lesson)/(Tony Moran's HIStorical Dub)	
97	Epic XPR 3168	Is It Scary (Eddie's Love Mix)/(Eddie's Rub-A-Dub Mix)/(Eddie's Love Mix)/ (Radio Edit) (12", white embossed title p/s)	30
97	Epic XPR 3169	HIStory (Ummah Urban Mix)/(Ummah Radio Mix)/(Tony Moran's 7" HIStory Lesson Edit)/(Ummah DJ Mix) (12", green title sleeve)	8
97	Epic XPR 3196	Is It Scary (Deep Dish Dark & Scary Remix)/(Deep Dish Double-O-Jazz Dub)/ (Deep Dish Dark & Scary Remix)/(Radio Edit) (12", black embossed title p/s)	35
97	Epic SAMPCS 4673	Smile (1-track promo CD)	40
97	Epic XPCD 2989	Cheater (1-track promo CD)	15
03	Epic XPR 3744	Twelves (7 x 12" p/s in box with insert)	70

ALBUMS

72	Tamla Motown STML 11205	GOT TO BE THERE (LP)	12
73	Tamla Motown STML 11220	BEN (LP)	12
73	Tamla Motown STML 11235	MUSIC AND ME (LP)	12
75	Tamla Motown STMA 8022	FOREVER, MICHAEL (LP, gatefold sleeve)	12
79	Epic EPC 83458/83468	OFF THE WALL (LP, gatefold sleeve, with 7" picture disc "You Can't Win (Parts 1)/(Part 2)" [S EPC 7135], some with information sheet)	25
79	Epic SXPR 1207	EPIC HITS FROM THE JACKSONS & MICHAEL JACKSON (LP, promo only, stickered sleeve)	12
81	Motown PR 84	JACKSON 5: HISTORY OF MOTOWN (4-LP box set, with 1 Michael Jackson LP)	25
82	Epic EPC 11-85930	THRILLER (LP, picture disc in PVC sleeve)	25
83	MCA MCA 70000	E.T. — THE EXTRA TERRESTRIAL (LP, box set with booklet & poster, narration & "Someone In The Dark", with music by John Williams)	70
82	MCA MCFP 3160	E.T. (THE EXTRA TERRESTRIAL) (LP, picture disc)	15
83	MCA CAC 70000	E.T. — THE EXTRA TERRESTRIAL (cassette, box set with booklet & poster)	20
87	Epic 450 290-0	BAD (LP, picture disc)	12
87	Epic 450 290-8	BAD GIFT PACK (cassette pack, with note pad, highlighter pen & calender)	25
87	Epic 450 290-9	BAD (CD, picture disc, some sealed in long PVC blister pack)	45/25
92	Epic 465 802-9	DANGEROUS (CD, gold disc, 10"x10" pop-up 'Collectors Edition First Printing')	15

(see also Jackson 5, Diana Ross & Michael Jackson, Paul McCartney, Jacksons, Jermaine Jackson)

MILLIE JACKSON

72	Mojo 2093 011	A Child Of God/You're The Joy Of My Life	15
72	Mojo 2093 015	Ask Me What You Want/I Just Can't Stand It	8
72	Mojo 2093 022	My Man, A Sweet Man/I Gotta Get Away (From My Own Self) (paper label)	8
73	Polydor 2066 317	Breakaway/Strange Things	5
75	Polydor 2066 536	If Loving You Is Wrong/The Rap	5
75	Polydor 2006 612	Loving Arms/Left Over	5
76	Spring 2066 713	A House For Sale/There You Are	20
72	Mojo 2918 005	MILLIE JACKSON (LP)	40

(see also Elton John)

MINT VALUE £

MILT JACKSON

57	Esquire EP 74	MILT JACKSON MODERN JAZZ QUARTET (EP)	8
58	London EZ-C 19004	THE MILT JACKSON SEPTET (EP)	8
62	London RE-K 1315	THE BALLAD ARTISTRY OF MILT JACKSON (EP)	8
53	Vogue LDE 044	MILT JACKSON AND HIS NEW GROUP (10" LP)	15
55	Esquire 20-042	MILT JACKSON QUINTET (10" LP)	15
55	London Jazz LZ-C 14006	MILT JACKSON QUARTET (10" LP)	15
57	London Jazz LTZ-K 15064	BALLADS AND BLUES (LP)	12
57	London Jazz LTZ-K 15074	THE JAZZ SKYLINE (LP)	12
57	London Jazz LTZ-K 15091	JACKSONSVILLE (LP)	12
57	Vogue LAE 12046	WIZARD OF THE VIBES (LP)	12
59	London Jazz LTZ-K 15141	PLENTY, PLENTY SOUL (LP)	12
59	London Jazz LTZ-T 15172	BAGS' OPUS (LP, also stereo SAH-T 6049)	12
60	London Jazz LTZ-T 15177	BAGS AND FLUTES (LP)	12
60	London Jazz LTZ-K 15196	BEAN BAGS (LP, also stereo SAH-K 6095; with Coleman Hawkins)	12
61	London Jazz LTZ-K 15220	THE ARTISTRY OF MILT JACKSON (LP, also stereo SAH-K 6163)	each 12
61	London Jazz LTZ-K 15232	BAGS AND TRANE (LP, with John Coltrane; also stereo SAH-K 6192)	each 12
61	Philips BBL 7459	MILT JACKSON (LP)	12
62	Esquire 32-134	MILT JACKSON MODERN JAZZ QUARTET/QUINTET (LP)	12
62	Riverside RLP (9)407	BAGS MEETS WES (LP, with Wes Montgomery)	12
63	Realm RM 119	THE MILT JACKSON QUARTET (LP)	12
63	HMV CLP 1589	STATEMENTS (LP, also stereo CSD 1455)	each 12
63	Realm RM 156	ROLL 'EM BAGS (LP)	12
64	Atlantic ATL/SAL 5012	VIBRATIONS (LP)	12
65	Mercury LML/SML 4008	IN A NEW SETTING (LP)	12
65	Mercury LML/SML 4016	AT THE MUSEUM OF MODERN ART (LP)	12
66	Mercury LML/SML 4028	BORN FREE (LP)	12
73	CTI CTL 8	CHERRY (LP, with Stanley Turrentine)	12

(see also Ray Charles, Modern Jazz Quartet, Stanley Turrentine, Miles Davis/Art Blakey, Coleman Hawkins)

PAPA CHARLIE JACKSON

50	Tempo R 30	Long Gone Lost John/I'm Looking For A Woman Who Knows How To Treat Me Right (78)	15
60	Heritage R 100	PAPA CHARLIE JACKSON (EP) 99 only	80
60	Heritage HLP 1011	PAPA CHARLIE JACKSON (LP) 99 only	110

(see also Paramount Allstars, Blind Blake)

POOCH JACKSON

72	Sioux SI 013	You Just Gotta Get Ready/BROTHER DAN: Django's Valley	5
72	Sioux SI 016	Once Bitten (with Harry J. Allstars)/KING REGGAE: Slave Driver	5

(see also Circles)

PRESTON JACKSON & HIS UPTOWN BAND

50	Tempo R 25	Trombone Man/Yearning For Mandalay (78)	8
50	Tempo R 26	It's Tight, Jim/Harmony Blues (78)	8

PYTHON LEE JACKSON

(see under 'P')

RAY JACKSON

76	EMI EMI 2514	Take Some Time/Working On	5
80	Mercury MER 3	In The Night/Waiting For The Time (p/s)	5
80	Mercury MER 8	Little Town Flirt/Make It Last (p/s)	5
80	Mercury 9109 831	IN THE NIGHT (LP, with inner sleeve)	12

(see also Lindisfarne)

ROOT & JENNY JACKSON

69	Beacon BEA 110	Please Come Home/Lean On Me	15
69	Beacon BEA 136	Let's Go Somewhere/If I Didn't Love You	10

SHAWNE JACKSON

74	Pye 7N 25636	Just As Bad As You/He May Be Your Man	8

SHIRLEY JACKSON

63	Decca F 11612	You Gotta Love And Be Loved/Don't Play Me A Love Song	7
63	Decca F 11788	Broken Home/No Greater Love Than Mine	12

SHOVELVILLE K. JACKSON

60s	Melodisc MEL 1683	Be Careful Of Stones That You Throw/Kentucky Blues	12

SIMONE JACKSON

62	Piccadilly 7N 35087	Pop Pop Popeye/He Ain't Got No Time For Love	12
63	Piccadilly 7N 35124	Ain't Gonna Kiss Ya/Slow Motion	12
63	Piccadilly 7N 35149	Tell Me What To Do/Done What You Know Is Wrong	12

STONEWALL JACKSON

59	Philips PB 941	Waterloo/Smoke Along The Track (78 rpm = £35)	12
60	Philips PB 1073	I'm Gonna Find You/A Little Guy Called Joe	6
65	CBS BPG 62587	GREATEST HITS (LP)	10

TONY JACKSON (& VIBRATIONS)

64	Pye 7N 15685	Bye Bye Baby/Watch Your Step	25
64	Pye 7N 15745	This Little Girl Of Mine/You Beat Me To The Punch	40
65	Pye 7N 15766	Love Potion No. 9/Fortune Teller	55
65	Pye 7N 15876	Stage Door/That's What I Want (as Tony Jackson Group)	35
66	CBS 202039	You're My Number One/Let Me Know (as Tony Jackson Group)	40
66	CBS 202069	Never Leave Your Baby's Side/I'm The One She Really Thinks A Lot Of (solo)	40
66	CBS 202297	Follow Me/Walk That Walk (solo)	65
66	CBS 202408	Anything Else You Want/Come On And Stop (solo)	40
91	Strange Things STZ 5005	JUST LIKE ME (LP)	15

(see also Searchers)

WALTER JACKSON

65	Columbia DB 7620	Welcome Home/Blowin' In The Wind	40
66	Columbia DB 7949	Tear For Tear/It's An Uphill Climb To The Bottom (DJ copy = £125)	75
66	Columbia DB 8054	A Corner In The Sun/Not You	30
67	Columbia DB 8154	Speak Her Name/They Don't Give Medals (To Yesterday's Heroes)	30
70	Atlantic 584 311	Any Way That You Want Me/Life Has Its Ups And Downs	8
73	Brunswick BR 5	Easy Evil/I Never Had It So Good	8

WANDA JACKSON

59	Capitol CL 15033	You're The One For Me/A Date With Jerry	20
59	Capitol CL 15090	Reaching/I'd Rather Have You	20
60	Capitol CL 15147	Let's Have A Party/Cool Love	25
61	Capitol CL 15176	Mean Mean Man/Honey Bop	25
61	Capitol CL 15223	Right Or Wrong/Funnel Of Love	15
62	Capitol CL 15234	In The Middle Of A Heartache/I'd Be Ashamed	12
62	Capitol CL 15249	If I Cried Every Time You Hurt Me/Let My Love Walk In	12
58	Capitol EAP1 1041	WANDA JACKSON (EP)	75
62	Capitol EAP1 20353	A LITTLE BITTY TEAR (EP)	50
58	Capitol T 1041	WANDA JACKSON (LP)	140
60	Capitol T 1384	ROCKIN' WITH WANDA (LP)	100
61	Capitol (S)T 1511	THERE'S A PARTY GOIN' ON (LP, mono/stereo)	75/100
61	Capitol (S)T 1596	RIGHT OR WRONG (LP, mono/stereo)	50/65
62	Capitol T 1776	WONDERFUL WANDA (LP)	35
64	Capitol (S)T 2030	TWO SIDES OF WANDA (LP, mono/stereo)	50/65
64	Capitol (S)T 2306	BLUES IN MY HEART (LP)	15
66	Capitol (S)T 2438	SINGS COUNTRY SONGS (LP, black label)	12
67	Capitol (S)T 2606	SALUTES THE COUNTRY MUSIC HALL OF FAME (LP, black label)	12
67	Capitol (S)T 2812	YOU'LL ALWAYS HAVE MY LOVE (LP)	12
69	Capitol (S)T 2976	CREAM OF THE CROP (LP, with Party Timers)	12
73	Word WST 9514	COUNTRY GOSPEL (LP)	12
70s	Myrrh MUR 1021	NOW I HAVE EVERYTHING (LP)	25

JACKSON & SMITH

65	Polydor 56051	Ain't That Loving You Baby/Every Day I Have The Blues	8
66	Polydor 56086	Party '66/And That's It	6

JACKSON BROTHERS

59	London HLX 8845	Tell Him No/Love Me (78 rpm = £20)	25

JACKSON 5
SINGLES

70	Tamla Motown TMG 724	I Want You Back/Who's Loving You	6
70	Tamla Motown TMG 738	ABC/The Young Folks (some in promo only p/s)	60/6
70	Tamla Motown TMG 746	The Love You Save/I Found That Girl	6
70	Tamla Motown TMG 758	I'll Be There/One More Chance	6
71	Tamla Motown SFI 66	Chartbusters Volume 5: Going Back To Indiana (flexidisc)	8
71	Tamla Motown TMG 769	Mama's Pearl/Darling Dear (some in promo only p/s)	60/6
71	Tamla Motown TMG 778	Never Can Say Goodbye/She's Good	5
72	Tamla Motown TMG 809	Sugar Daddy/I'm So Happy	5
72	Tamla Motown TMG 825	Little Bitty Pretty One/Maybe Tomorrow	5
72	Tamla Motown TMG 833	Lookin' Through The Windows/Love Song (some in promo only p/s)	15/5
72	Tamla Motown TMG 837	THE CHRISTMAS EP: Santa Claus Is Coming To Town/ Someday At Christmas/Christmas Won't Be The Same This Year	12
73	Tamla Motown TMG 842	Doctor My Eyes/My Little Baby	10
73	Tamla Motown TMG 856	Hallelujah Day/To Know	5
73	Tamla Motown TMG 865	Skywriter/Ain't Nothin' Like The Real Thing (some in promo only p/s)	15/5
73	Tamla Motown TMG 878	Get It Together/Touch	5
74	Tamla Motown TMG 895	The Boogie Man/Don't Let Your Baby Catch You	5
74	Tamla Motown TMG 904	Dancing Machine/It's Too Late To Change The Time	5
74	Tamla Motown TMG 927	The Life Of The Party/Whatever You Got I Want	5
74	Lyntone LYN 2639	Talk And Sing Personally To Valentine Readers (33rpm flexidisc free with *Valentine* magazine)	15/10
75	Rice Krispies (no cat. nos.)	Sugar Daddy/Goin' Back To Indiana/Who's Loving You/Mama's Pearl/ ABC/The Love You Save (6 different Rice Krispies cut-out card discs)	each 30
75	Tamla Motown TMG 942	I Am Love (Part 1)/I Am Love (Part 2)	5
75	Tamla Motown TMG 1001	Forever Came Today/I Can't Quit Your Love	5
77	Motown TMG 1081	JUKEBOX GEMS: Skywriter/I Want You Back/The Love You Save (EP)	8
80	Motown SPTMG 2	THE MOTOWN 20TH ANNIVERSARY SINGLES BOX (15 x 7")	30
83	Motown CTME 2034	MOTOWN FLIP HITS — JACKSON 5: I Want You Back/ I'll Be There/Lookin' Through The Windows/ABC (EP, cassette)	10
86	Motown 8000	You Can Cry On My Shoulder/Instrumental (CD)	10
87	Motown ZB 41655	THE CHRISTMAS EP: Santa Claus Is Coming To Town/ Someday At Christmas/Christmas Won't Be The Same This Year (EP, reissue)	5
89	Tamla Motown ZD 41949	VINTAGE GOLD (3" CD, gatefold card sleeve, as Michael Jackson & Jackson 5)	10

LPs

70	T. Motown (S)TML 11142	DIANA ROSS PRESENTS THE JACKSON 5 (flipback sleeve, mono/st.)	25/20
70	T. Motown (S)TML 11156	ABC (flipback sleeve, mono/stereo)	50/40
70	T. Motown STML 11168	THE JACKSON 5 CHRISTMAS ALBUM (flipback sleeve)	20
71	T. Motown STML 11174	THIRD ALBUM (original with flipback sleeve)	18
71	T. Motown STML 11188	MAYBE TOMORROW	15
72	T. Motown STML 11214	LOOKIN' THROUGH THE WINDOWS	20
73	T. Motown STML 11231	SKYWRITER	12
73	T. Motown STML 11243	GET IT TOGETHER (with photo insert)	18
74	T. Motown STML 11275	DANCING MACHINE	18
75	T. Motown STML 11290	MOVING VIOLATIONS	18
76	Motown STML 12046	JOYFUL JUKEBOX MUSIC	12
77	T. Motown TMSP 6004	THE JACKSON 5 ANTHOLOGY (2-LP, original issue)	18

MINT VALUE £

77	Motown STMX 6006	MOTOWN SPECIAL — THE JACKSON 5	15
79	MFP MFP 50418	ZIP-A-DEE-DOO-DAH	15
81	Motown PR 84	JACKSON 5: HISTORY OF MOTOWN (4-LP box set, with 1 Michael Jackson LP)	30
82	Motown/Pickwick TMS 3505	THE JACKSON 5	20

(see also Michael Jackson, Jermaine Jackson, Jacksons)

JACKSON HEIGHTS
70	Charisma JH 1	Doubting Thomas/Insomnia	6
72	Vertigo 6059 068	Maureen/Long Time Dying	6
70	Charisma CAS 1018	KINGS PROGRESS (LP, pink label)	20
72	Vertigo 6360 067	5TH AVENUE BUS (LP, gatefold sleeve, swirl label)	20
72	Vertigo 6360 077	RAGAMUFFIN'S FOOL (LP, swirl label, some with poster)	40/35
73	Vertigo 6360 092	BUMP AND GRIND (LP, 'spaceship label')	25

(see also Nice)

JACKSONS
77	Epic S EPC 5063	Enjoy Yourself (Extended Version 5.48)/Style Of Life (12", p/s)	15
78	Epic S EPC 12-6683	Blame It On The Boogie (LP Version)/Do What You Wanna (12")	10
78	Epic S EPC 12-6983	Destiny (Full Length Album Version)/Blame It On The Boogie (Special 7-Minute Extended Disco Remix)/That's What You Get (For Being Polite) (12", p/s)	10
79	Epic EPC 12-7181	Shake Your Body (Down To The Ground) (Special Disco Remix 8.40)/All Night Dancin' (6.09) (12", p/s)	10
79	Epic EPC 13-7876	Blame It On The Boogie (Album Version)/That's What You Get (For Being Polite)/Blame It On The Boogie (Instrumental) (12")	10
79	Epic E 12-6983	Blame It On The Boogie (Album Version)/That's What You Get (For Being Polite) (7 Minute Remix)/Blame It On The Boogie (12")	10
80	Epic EPC 12-9391	Heartbreak Hotel (Album Version)/Different Kind Of Lady (12")	15
81	Epic EPC A 1294	Walk Right Now/Your Ways (picture disc)	10
79	Epic S XPR 1207	EPIC HITS FROM THE JACKSONS & MICHAEL JACKSON (LP, promo only)	20
84	Epic EPC 86303	VICTORY (LP, picture disc)	35
85	Epic SAI 7561	A TASTE OF VICTORY (LP, picture disc, promo only via Kelloggs offer)	50

(see also Jackson 5, Michael Jackson, Jermaine Jackson)

CHUBBY JACKSON'S BIG BAND
60	Top Rank TR 5015	A Ballad For Jai/Hail, Hail, The Herd's All Here	6

JACKSON SISTERS
73	Mums MUM 18257	I Believe In Miracles/Day In The Blue	75
87	Urban URB 4	I Believe In Miracles/Boy You're Dynamite	18
87	Urban URBX 4	I Believe In Miracles/Boy You're Dynamite (12", p/s)	20

JACKSON SISTERS
00	Fab FAB 004	Rocksteady/STOVELLS: Hang On In There	5

JACK THE LAD
73	Charisma CB 206	One More Dance/Draught Genius (Polka) (p/s)	6
73	Charisma CB 218	Why Can't I Be Satisfied/Make Me Happy	5
75	Charisma CB 242	Home Sweet Home/Big Ocean Liner	5
75	Charisma CB 253	Gentleman Soldier/Oakey Strike Evictions	5
75	Charisma CB 264	My Friend The Drink/Rocking Chair	5
74	Charisma CAS 1085	IT'S JACK THE LAD (LP)	15
74	Charisma CAS 1094	OLD STRAIGHT TRACK (LP, with lyric sheet)	15
75	Charisma CAS 1110	ROUGH DIAMONDS (LP)	15
76	United Artists UAS 29999	JACKPOT (LP)	12

(see also Lindisfarne)

JACKY
68	Philips BF 1647	White Horses/Too Many Chiefs (Not Enough Indians)	8
68	Philips BF 1689	We're Off And Running/Well That's Loving You	6
69	Page One POF 122	Love Is Now/Never Will I Be	7
68	Philips SBL 7851	WHITE HORSES (LP)	25

(see also Jackie & Raindrops, Raindrops, Jackie Lee, Emma Rede, Vince Hill)

DICK JACOBS (& HIS ORCHESTRA)
56	Vogue Coral Q 72147	Saxophone/Never Come Sunday	8
56	Vogue Coral Q 72154	"The Man With The Golden Arm" Theme/Butternut	8
56	Vogue Coral Q 72204	Petticoats Of Portugal/East Of Eden	6
57	Vogue Coral Q 72245	The Big Beat/The Tower Trot (78 rpm = £8)	12
57	Vogue Coral Q 72260	Rock-a-billy Gal/The Golden Strings (78 rpm = £12)	12
57	Vogue Coral Q 72280	Fascination/Summertime In Venice	6
57	Vogue Coral LVA 9076	THE SKIFFLE SOUND (LP, as Dick Jacobs & His Skiffle Group)	45
59	Coral SVL 3008	BROADWAY SONG BOOK (LP)	15
59	Coral LVA 9102	THEMES FROM HORROR MOVIES (LP)	25

HANK JACOBS
64	Sue WI 313	So Far Away/Monkey, Hips And Rice	35
83	Sue ENS 5	SO FAR AWAY EP: So Far Away/Out Of Sight/Hank's Groove/Summertime	10

JIMMY JACOBS & NITESPOTS
60s	Gargoyle ADV 305011	SWINGIN' SOHO — JIMMY SINGS, THE NITESPOTS SWING (LP)	15

JACQUELINE & BRIDIE
64	Fontana TL 5212	HOLD BACK THE DAWN (LP)	20

(see also Jackie & Bridie)

CHUCK JACQUES & LYNN TAITT & COMETS
67	Ska Beat JB 264	Dial 609/VIBRATORS & TOMMY McCOOK & COMETS: Wait For Me	20

(see also Wilbert Francis & Vibrators)

HATTIE JACQUES
71	Avenue NUE 143	THE BUNGLES OF BOJUN (EP)	10

(see also Eric Sykes)

ILLINOIS JACQUET & HIS ORCHESTRA
56	Vogue V 2387	Blow Illinois Blow/Destination Moon	6
53	Vogue LDE 026	ILLINOIS JACQUET (10" LP)	15
56	Columbia Clef 33C 9018	ILLINOIS JACQUET (10" LP)	15
57	Columbia Clef 33CX 10085	GROOVIN' WITH JACQUET (LP)	12
50s	Melodisc MLP 12-301	JAZZ AT THE PHILHARMONIC (LP)	12

JADE
70	DJM DJS 227	Alan's Song/Amongst Anemones	8
70	DJM DJLPS 407	FLY ON STRANGE WINGS (LP)	160

JADE WARRIOR
72	Vertigo 6059 069	The Demon Trucker/Snake	15
78	Island JAD 1	Way Of The Sun/Sun Ra	5
71	Vertigo 6360 033	JADE WARRIOR (LP, gatefold sleeve, swirl label)	65
71	Vertigo 6360 062	RELEASED (LP, gatefold sleeve, swirl label)	100
72	Vertigo 6360 079	LAST AUTUMN'S DREAM (LP, gatefold sleeve, swirl label)	50
74	Island ILPS 9290	FLOATING WORLD (LP)	15
75	Island ILPS 9318	WAVES (LP)	15
76	Island ILPS 9393	KITES (LP)	15
78	Island ILPS 9552	WAY OF THE SUN (LP)	12
79	Butt BUTT 001	REFLECTIONS (LP)	12

(see also July, Joe O'Donnell)

JADIS
84	private pressing	BABOON ENQUIRIES (cassette)	12
87	private pressing DEM 1	G13/Out Of Reach (cassette)	8
88	private pressing DEM 2	Don't Keep Me Waiting/In The Dark (cassette)	8
89	private pressing	Lost For Words/This Changing Face (cassette)	8
90	Back Beat 004-12	THE JADIS ALBUM (LP, numbered)	15

MAX JAFFA (& HIS ORCHESTRA)
56	Columbia SCM 5226	China Boogie/Slap Happy	8

CHRIS JAGGER
73	GM GMS 3	Something New/Joy Of The Ride	6
73	GM GML 1003	CHRIS JAGGER — YOU KNOW THE NAME BUT NOT THE FACE (LP)	15

MICK JAGGER
70	Decca F 13067	Memo From Turner/Natural Magic (some in export p/s)	40/12
84	CBS TA 4431	State Of Shock/Your Ways (picture disc)	8
87	CBS 651028-0	Let's Work/Catch As Catch Can (poster p/s)	8
87	CBS THROW P1	Throwaway/Peace For The Wicked (picture disc)	10
87	CBS THROW C1	Throwaway (Remix)/(Vocal Dub)/Peace For The Wicked (CD, card sleeve)	15
70	United Artists UAS 29108	NED KELLY (LP, soundtrack)	35
70	Warner Bros WS 2554	PERFORMANCE (LP, soundtrack)	35
85	CBS 86310	SHE'S THE BOSS (CD)	15
87	CBS 460 123-2	PRIMITIVE COOL (CD)	15
01	Virgin no cat. no.	GODDESS IN THE DOORWAY (interview CD, promo only)	25

(see also Rolling Stones, Jacksons, Jack Nitzsche)

JAGO
72	Duke DU 134	Rebel Train/Babylon Version	9

JAGS
61	Decca F 11397	The Hunch/Cry Wolf	10

JAGS
79	Island WIP 6501	Back Of My Hand/Double Vision (p/s)	6
79	Island 12SWIP 6501	Back Of My Hand/Double Vision/Single Vision/What Can I Do? (12", p/s)	8
80	Island WIP 6531	Woman's World/Dumb Blonde (p/s)	8
80	Island WIP 6587	Party Games/She's So Considerate (p/s)	10
80	Island WIP 6666	I Never Was A Beach Boy/Tune Into Heaven (p/s)	15
80	Island WIP 6683	The Sound Of G-O-O-D-B-Y-E/The Hurt (no p/s)	10
79	Island ILPS 9603	EVENING STANDARDS (LP)	20
81	Island ILPS 9655	NO TIE LIKE A PRESENT (LP)	20

JAGUAR
81	Heavy Metal HEAVY 10	Back Street Woman/Chasing The Dragon (p/s)	40
82	Neat NEAT 16	Axe Crazy/War Machine (p/s)	22
83	Neat NEAT 1007	POWER GAMES (LP, some on purple vinyl)	30/18
84	Roadrunner RR 9851	THIS TIME (LP)	15

JAGUARS
63	Impression IMP 101	Opus To Spring/The Beat (1,000 only)	35
65	Contest RGJ 152	We'll Live On Happily/Now You Wonder Why	275+

(see also Dave Mason)

JAH BUNNY
80	White Label	DUBBS INTERNATIONAL (LP)	40

JAH FISH
72	Grape GR 3034	Vampire Rock/MOD STARS: El-Sisco Rock	8

JAH LION
76	Island ILPS 9386	COLUMBIA COLLY (LP)	25

(see also Jah Lloyd)

JAH LLOYD
73	Jaguar JAG 102	Channel One (with Douglas Boothe)/SOUL SYNDICATES:Channel Two	6
73	Jaguar JAG 104	Psalm Two/SOUL SYNDICATES: Channel Two	6
74	DIP PL DL 1001	HERBS OF DUB...MORE HERBS (LP)	30
70s	His Majesty MH 1004	REGGAE STICK (LP)	20
70s	His Majesty MH 1003	DREAD LION DUB (LP)	50

(see also Jah Lion)

MINT VALUE £

JAH SCOUSE
85	Better Things BETS 1	Merge/Vegan Mix (foldout p/s)	5

JAH SHAKA
89	Mango MPLM 1001	PRESENTS DUB MASTERS VOL. 1 (LP)	15

JAH SHAKA VS FATMAN
80	Live & Love LP 10	LIVE (LP)	30

JAH STITCH
75	Third World TWS 401	NO DREAD CAN'T DEAD (LP)	40

JAH THOMAS
83	Silver Camel SCLP 03	DANCE HALL CONNECTION (LP)	15

JAH WOBBLE
78	Virgin VOLE 9	Dreadlock Don't Deal In Wedlock/Pthilius Pubis (p/s)	5
78	Virgin 12VOLE 9	Dreadlock Don't Deal In Wedlock/Pthilius Pubis (12", p/s)	8
80	Virgin VS 337	Betrayal/MR. X: Battle Of Britain (p/s)	5
80	Virgin VS 337-12	Betrayal/MR. X: Battle Of Britain (12", p/s)	8
82	Jah Wobble JAH 1	Fading/Nocturnal (p/s, as Jah Wobble With Animal)	5
82	Jah Wobble JAH 2	Long Long Way/Nocturnal (12", p/s)	8
78	Virgin VS 239-12	STEEL LEG MEETS THE ELECTRIC DREAD (12 EP, p/s)	10
92	East West OVAL 103 T	VISIONS OF YOU (12" EP, some with p/s)	8
94	Island CID 587	AMOR (EP, 2-CD in foldout digipak)	12
80	Virgin V 2158	THE LEGEND LIVES ON (mini-LP)	12
	(see also Bartok)		

JAH WOBBLE, THE EDGE & HOLGER CZUKAY
83	Island WOB 1	Snake Charmer/Hold On To Your Dreams (p/s)	5
	(see also Don Letts & Jah Wobble, Dan MacArthur, Joolz, Public Image Ltd, The Edge, Orb, Can)		

JAH WOOSH
75	Lucky DL 5094	Rocking Blues/Version	5
75	Lucky DL 5096	Don't Do That/That Dub	5
78	Freedom Sounds FSD 001	Ales Skank/Different Style (12")	15
76	Cactus CTLP 116	JAH JAG DEY DEY (LP)	25

JAKE & FAMILY JEWELS
70	Polydor 2425 027	JAKE AND THE FAMILY JEWELS (LP)	15

JAKLIN
69	Stable SLE 8003	JAKLIN (LP)	250

JAM
SINGLES
77	Polydor 2058 866	In The City/Takin' My Love (p/s, reissues exist)	10
77	Polydor 2058 903	All Around The World/Carnaby Street (p/s)	8
77	Polydor 2058 945	The Modern World/Sweet Soul Music (live)/Back In My Arms Again (live)/ Bricks And Mortar (Part) [live] (p/s)	8
78	Polydor 2058 995	News Of The World/Aunties And Uncles (Impulsive Youths)/Innocent Man (p/s)	5
78	Polydor 2059 054	David Watts/'A' Bomb In Wardour Street (plastic moulded label, p/s)	5
78	Polydor 2059 054	David Watts/'A' Bomb In Wardour Street (white paper label, no p/s)	5
78	Polydor POSP 8	Down In The Tube Station At Midnight/So Sad About Us/The Night (p/s)	5
79	Polydor POSP 34	Strange Town/The Butterfly Collector (p/s)	5
79	Polydor POSP 69	When You're Young/Smithers-Jones (p/s)	6

(The above singles were reissued twice in their picture sleeves; early originals have curved edges on sleeve openings whereas the reissues are straight. Lettering on the reissue labels tends to be fatter; reissues are worth £3-£4.)

80	Polydor 2059 266	Start!/Liza Radley (p/s)	5
81	Polydor POSP 257	Funeral Pyre/Disguises (p/s)	5
82	Polydor POSP 400	Precious (1-sided promo, company sleeve)	25
82	Polydor POSPJ 540/JAM 1	Beat Surrender/Shopping//Move On Up/Stoned Out Of My Mind/ War (double pack, gatefold p/s)	6
82	Polydor PODJ 540	Beat Surrender (DJ Version)/Shopping (promo, company sleeve)	10
83	Polydor 2059 482	That's Entertainment/Down In The Tube Station At Midnight (live) (U.K. reissue of European import p/s)	5
80	Lyntone LYN 9048/ Flexipop 002	Pop Art Poem/Boy About Town (version) (blue, yellow or green 1-sided flexi with *Flexipop* mag issue 2; add £2 with magazine & £5 with mailer p/s)	7/5/10
80	Lyntone LYN 9048	Pop Art Poem/Boy About Town (version) (same tracks both sides, hard vinyl white label, 300 only, with mail-order mailer p/s)	50/40
81	Lyntone no cat. no.	When You're Young (live) (1-sided fan club flexidisc, 33rpm)	25
82	Fan Club no cat. no.	Tales From The Riverbank (version) (33rpm 1-sided fan club flexidisc)	25
82	Polydor PAOLO 100	Move On Up (live) (flexidisc free with *Melody Maker* paper)	7/5
82	Polydor POSPX400	Town Called Malice (Live at Hammersmith Palais) (12" striped die-cut sleeve)	20
92	Polydor POCS 199	The Dreams Of Children/Away From The Numbers (live) (withdrawn cassette)	15
97	Polydor 2058 266	In The City (1-sided "20th anniversary party invite" promo, die-cut co. sleeve)	25
97	Polydor JAM 1	DIRECTION, REACTION, CREATION (CD, sampler, gatefold card p/s)	12

FRENCH PRESSINGS
79	Polydor POSP 83	The Eton Rifles/See Saw (no p/s)	7
80	Polydor 2059 266	Start!/Liza Radley (p/s)	7
81	Polydor POSP 257	Funeral Pyre/Disguises (no p/s)	7

MISPRESSINGS
78	Polydor 2058 995	News Of The World/Aunties And Uncles/Innocent Man (p/s, plays B-side on both sides)	40
78	Polydor POSP 6	Sandy/Can't Let You Go (by John Travolta, B-side mispressed with "So Sad About Us")	30
78	Polydor 2059 054	David Watts/'A' Bomb In Wardour Street (plastic moulded label; songwriting credit for "David Watts" mis-credited to "Ray Davis", p/s)	20
78	Polydor POSP 8	Down In The Tube Station At Midnight/So Sad About Us/The Night (p/s; with erroneous B-side reference to "All Mod Cons" LP)	15

78	Polydor POSP 8	Down In The Tube Station At Midnight/So Sad About Us/The Night	
		(A-side plays John Travolta's "Sandy")	30
79	Polydor POSP 69	When You're Young/Smithers-Jones (p/s, with B-side on both sides)	40
80	Polydor 2059 266	Start!/Liza Radley (p/s, 1 side plays Village People's "Can't Stop The Music")	15
82	Polydor POSP 400	Town Called Malice/Precious (p/s, silver moulded label, both sides play	
		"Precious")	30

ALBUMS

77	Polydor 2383 477	IN THE CITY (LP, with inner sleeve)	15
79	Polydor 2383 475	THIS IS THE MODERN WORLD (LP, with inner sleeve and picture paper labels)	15
78	Polydor POLD 5008	ALL MOD CONS (LP, with inner sleeve)	12
79	Polydor POLD 5028	SETTING SONS (LP, embossed sleeve with tracklisting sticker on	
		back & inner sleeve)	15
83	Polydor SNAP 1	SNAP! (2-LP, with bonus 4-track EP 'Live At Wembley' [SNAPL 45])	20
84	Polydor 821 712-2	COMPACT SNAP! (CD)	18
91	Receiver	LIVE AT THE ROXY (LP, unissued, 25 test pressings only)	150+
02	Simply Vinyl SVLP	ALL MOD CONS (LP, 180 gm vinyl, limited edition)	20

(see also Style Council, Paul Weller, Bruce Foxton, Time U.K., Sharp)

JAM ON THE MUTHA

90	Wau!/Polydor MAGXR 3	Hotel California (Orb In Cali Mix 1)/(Like Joe Never Left Mix)/	
		(Orbitally Ambient Mix) (12", p/s)	10

JAM TODAY

80s	Stroppy Cow SCJT 1	Stereotyping/Song About Myself (p/s, with insert)	50

JAMAICA FATS

66	Blue Beat BB 368	Jacqueline/Please Come Home (actually by Al T. Joe & Celestials)	22

(see also Al T. Joe)

JAMAICAN ACTIONS

68	Coxsone CS 7070	Catch The Quinella/JACKIE MITTOO: Songbird	35

JAMAICAN CALYPSONIANS

54	Times Record UD 1005	Not Me/Rum & Coconut Water (78)	6
50s	Kalypso RL 102	Hol'im Joe/Bargie (78)	7

JAMAICAN EAGLES

73	Harry J HJ 6661	Country Living/Country Living (Version)	5

(see also Eagles)

JAMAICAN FOUNDATIONS

68	Coxsone CS 7036	Take It Cool/VICEROYS: Try Hard To Leave	25

JAMAICANS

66	Doctor Bird DB 1109	Cool Night/Ma And Pa	40
67	Trojan TR 007	Dedicated To You/The Things I Said To You	25
67	Treasure Isle TI 7007	Things You Say You Love/I've Got A Pain	25
67	Treasure Isle TI 7012	Baba Boom (Festival Song 1967) (actually by Baba Boom)/	
		TOMMY McCOOK & SUPERSONICS: Real Cool	20
67	Treasure Isle TI 7037	Peace And Love/Woman Gone Home	25
69	Escort ES 806	Early In The Morning/Mr. Lonely	12
70	Harry J. HJ 6604	Fire Parts 1 & 2	10
71	Dynamc DYN 410	Love Uprising/My Love For You	7
71	Dynamic DYN 417	Mary/CONSCIOUS MINDS: Soldier Boy	7
71	New Beat NB 084	Mary/CONSCIOUS MINDS: Soldier Boy	7
72	Dynamic DYN 430	I Believe In Music/Music (Version)	5
72	Dynamic DYN 442	Are You Sure/Are You Sure (Version)	5
72	Dynamic DYN 456	Sunshine Love/Sunshine Version	5
74	Dragon DRA 1029	My Heart Just Keeps On Breaking/My Heart Just Keeps On Breaking (Inst'l)	5

(see also Norris Weir & Jamaicans, Tommy Cowan)

JAMAICAN SHADOWS

67	Coxsone CS 7005	Have Mercy/Blending Love	32
69	Upsetter US 320	Dirty Dozen (actually by Upsetters)/Crying Too Long	30

JAMAICA'S OWN VAGABONDS

64	Decca DFE 8588	BEHOLD (EP)	50
64	Decca LK 4617	SKA TIME (LP)	70

(see also Vagabonds, Jimmy James & Vagabonds)

AHMED JAMAL

59	London Jazz LTZ-M 15162	BUT NOT FOR ME (LP)	15
59	London Jazz LTZ-M 15170	AHMED JAMAL (LP)	15
62	Pye Jazz NJL 38	ALHAMBRA (LP)	15
63	Pye Jazz NJL 50	MACANUDO (LP)	15
64	Chess CRL 4001	NAKED CITY THEME (LP)	15
67	Chess CRL 4509	ROAR OF THE GREASE PAINT (LP)	12
68	Chess CRL 4530	STANDARD-EYES (LP)	12
68	Chess CRL 4532	CRY YOUNG (LP)	12

JAMES

86	Sire JIM 3	Chain Mail/Hup Springs (p/s)	10
86	Sire JIM 4	So Many Ways/Withdrawn (p/s)	10
86	Sire JIM 4T	So Many Ways/Just Hipper/Withdrawn (12", p/s)	18
88	Blanco Y Negro NEG 26	Yaho/Mosquito (p/s)	6
88	Blanco Y Negro NEG 26T	Yaho/Mosquito/Left Out Of Her Will/New Nature (12", p/s)	12
88	Blanco Y Negro NEG 31	What For/Island Swing (p/s)	6
88	Blanco Y Negro NEG 31T	What For (Climax Mix)/Island Swing/Not There (12", p/s)	15
88	Blanco Y Negro NEG 31C	What For (Climax Mix)/Island Swing/Not There (cassette, in video-style box)	10
89	Rough Trade RT 225	Sit Down/Sky Is Falling (p/s)	8
89	Rough Trade RTT 225	Sit Down/Goin' Away/Sky Is Falling (12", p/s, 1st 500 with postcard)	12/8

89	Rough Trade RTT 225 CD	Sit Down/Goin' Away/Sky Is Falling (3" CD, card sleeve)	12
89	Rough Trade RT 245	Come Home/Promised Land (p/s)	6
89	Rough Trade RTT 245	Come Home (Long Version)/Come Home (7" Version)/Promised Land/ Slow Right Down (Demo Version) (12", p/s)	10
90	Fontana JIMM 512	How Was It For You?/How Was It For You? (Different Mix)/Lazy/ Undertaker (12", p/s, with stencil)	12
90s	Lyntone	Weather Change (Demo Version) (flexidisc, with tour programme)	12/6
84	Factory FAC 78	JIMONE EP: What's The World/Fire So Close/Folklore (p/s)	12
85	Factory FAC 138	VILLAGE FIRE: What's The World/Fire So Close/Folklore/Hymn From A Village/ If Things Were Perfect (p/s)	12
85	Factory FAC 119	JAMES II: Hymn From A Village/If Things Were Perfect (p/s)	12
86	Sire JIM 3T	SIT DOWN EP: Chain Mail/Uprising/Hup Springs (12", p/s)	15
91	Fontana JIM 812	SIT DOWN (12" EP, recorded live at G-Mex)	10
89	Rough Trade ONEMAN 1LP	ONE MAN CLAPPING (LP, with inner sleeve)	18

B.B. JAMES
| 70 | Upsetter US 328 | Consider Me/Consider Me Version | 12 |

BOB JAMES
| 75 | CTI CTI 6043 | BOB JAMES ONE (LP) | 12 |
| 75 | CTI CTI 6057 | BOB JAMES TWO (LP) | 12 |

BOBBY JAMES & DAVE (Barker)
| 71 | Smash SMA 2314 | You Said It/AGGRO BAND: Hot Sauce | 15 |

BRIAN JAMES
| 68 | Olga OLE 005 | Come Back Silly Girl/It Just Happened That Way | 8 |

CALVIN JAMES
| 65 | Columbia DB 7516 | Some Things You Never Get Used To/Remember | 25 |

(pseudonym for George Underwood; see also Davie Jones & King Bees)

COL JAMES
| 62 | Oriole CB 1736 | Doesn't Anybody Make Short Movies/Oooh Looka There Ain't She Pretty | 12 |

DANNY JAMES
| 72 | Southern Sound BT 100 | Your Gravy Train/Devil Made Me Say That | 5 |

DICK JAMES
53	Parlophone MSP 6039	Mother Nature And Father Time/Don't You Care	5
53	Parlophone MSP 6047	The Joker/Guessing	12
55	Parlophone MSP 6170	Unchained Melody/Come Back (Come Back To Me)	5
55	Parlophone MSP 6190	He/So Must I Love You	5
56	Parlophone MSP 6199	Robin Hood/The Ballad Of Davy Crockett	35
56	Parlophone MSP 6230	"Summer Sing-Song" Medley	5
56	Parlophone R 4220	I Only Know I Love You/Mirabelle	5
56	Parlophone R 4241	"Sing Song Time (No. 3)" Medley	5
57	Parlophone R 4255	The Garden Of Eden/I Accuse	5
57	Parlophone R 4314	Westward Ho The Wagons!/The Gay Cavalier	5
57	Parlophone R 4375	"Skiffling Sing Song" Medley	5
58	Parlophone R 4498	Daddy's Little Girl/When You're Young	5
59	Parlophone R 4606	There But For Your Love Go I/Minus One Heart	5
64	Parlophone R 5212	"Sing A Song Of Beatles With Dick James" Medley (Parts 1 & 2)	8

ELMORE JAMES
64	Sue WI 335	Dust My Blues/Happy Home (as Elmore James & Broom Dusters)	45
65	Sue WI 383	It Hurts Me Too/Bleeding Heart	40
65	Sue WI 392	Knocking At Your Door/Calling The Blues (B-side actually by Junior Wells & Earl Hooker)	120
66	Sue WI 4007	I Need You/Mean Mistreating Mama	30
65	Sue ILP 918	THE BEST OF ELMORE JAMES (LP)	60
65	Sue ILP 927	THE ELMORE JAMES MEMORIAL ALBUM (LP)	60
68	Bell MBLL/SBLL 104	SOMETHING INSIDE OF ME (LP)	45
68	Ember EMB 3397	THE LATE FANTASTICALLY GREAT ELMORE JAMES (LP)	25
70	United Artists UAS 29109	THE LEGEND OF ELMORE JAMES (LP)	22
70	Blue Horizon 7-66230	TO KNOW A MAN (2-LP)	60
70	Blue Horizon 7-63204	TOUGH (LP, with 4 tracks by John Brim)	75
73	Polydor 2383 200	COTTON PATCH HOTFOOTS (LP, shared with Walter Horton)	15
75	DJM DJLMD 8008	ALL THEM BLUES (2-LP)	18
83	Ace CH 68	KING OF THE SLIDE GUITAR (LP, yellow vinyl)	12

ETTA JAMES
60	London HLM 9139	All I Could Do Was Cry/Tough Mary	40
60	London HLM 9234	My Dearest Darling/Girl Of My Dreams	30
61	Pye International 7N 25079	At Last/I Just Want To Make Love To You	25
61	Pye International 7N 25080	Trust In Me/Anything To Say You're Mine	20
61	Pye International 7N 25113	Dream/Fool That I Am	20
62	Pye International 7N 25131	Something's Got A Hold On Me/Waiting For Charlie To Come Home	25
62	Pye International 7N 25162	Stop The Wedding/Street Of Tears	20
63	Pye International 7N 25205	Pushover/I Can't Hold It In Any More	22
65	Sue WI 359	Roll With Me Henry/Good Rockin' Daddy	50
67	Chess CRS 8052	I Prefer You/I'm So Glad (I Found Love In You)	18
67	Chess CRS 8063	Tell Mama/I'd Rather Go Blind	20
67	Chess CRS 8069	Security/I'm Gonna Take What He's Got	15
68	Chess CRS 8076	I Got You Babe/I Worship The Ground You Walk On	15
68	Chess CRS 8082	You Got It/Fire	15
72	Chess 6145 016	Tell Mama/I'd Rather Go Blind/I Found A Love	8
74	Chess 6145 033	Out On The Streets Again/Come A Little Closer	8
78	Warner Brothers K 17173	Piece Of My Heart/Lovesick Blues	8
65	Chess CRL 4502	ETTA JAMES ROCKS THE HOUSE (LP)	75

67	Chess CRL 4524	AT LAST (LP)	70
68	Ember EMB 3390	THE SOUL OF ETTA JAMES (LP)	40
68	Chess CRL 4536	TELL MAMA (LP)	45
72	Chess 6310 126	GOLDEN DECADE (LP)	15
73	Chess 6671 003	PEACHES (2-LP)	25
78	Warner Brothers K 56492	DEEP IN THE NIGHT (LP)	12
81	Ace 10CH 33	GOOD ROCKIN' MAMA (10" LP)	12

(see also Etta & Harvey)

ETTA JAMES & SUGAR PIE DeSANTO
65	Chess CRS 8025	Do I Make Myself Clear/Somewhere Down The Line	25

(see also Sugar Pie DeSanto)

HARRY JAMES & HIS ORCHESTRA
65	Dot DS 16729	Love Theme From In Harm's Way/Green Onions	5

(see also Rosemary Clooney)

JASON JAMES
67	CBS 2705	Miss Pilkington's Maid/Count Me Out	20

JERRY JAMES & BANDITS
64	Solar SRP 101	Sweet Little Sixteen/Three Steps To Heaven	15

JESSE JAMES
54	Vocalion V 1037	Southern Casey Jones/Lonesome Day Blues (78)	15
71	Mojo 2092 016	Don't Nobody Want To Get Married/(Pt. 2)	7

JIMMY JAMES (& THE VAGABONDS)
62	Dice CC 4	Bewildered And Blue/I Don't Want To Cry (solo)	20
63	R&B JB 112	Jump Children/Tell Me (solo)	25
64	Black Swan WI 437	Thinking Of You/Shirley (solo)	30
65	Columbia DB 7653	Shoo Be Doo You're Mine/We'll Never Stop Loving You	20
66	Ska Beat JB 242	Your Love/Someday (solo)	20
66	Piccadilly 7N 35298	I Feel Alright/I Wanna Be Your Everything	30
66	Piccadilly 7N 35320	Hi Diddley Dee Dum Dum (It's A Good Good Feelin')/Come To Me Softly	17
66	Piccadilly 7N 35331	This Heart Of Mine/I Don't Wanna Cry	75
66	Piccadilly 7N 35349	Ain't Love Good, Ain't Love Proud/Don't Know What I'm Gonna Do	15
67	Piccadilly 7N 35360	I Can't Get Back Home To My Baby/Hungry For Love (solo)	12
67	Piccadilly 7N 35374	No Good To Cry/You Showed Me The Way	12
68	Pye 7N 17579	Red Red Wine/Who Could Be Loving You	10
69	Pye 7N 17719	Close The Door/Why (solo)	5
71	Trojan TR 7806	Help Yourself/Why	25
72	Bamboo BAM 67	Riverboat Jenny/If I Wasn't Black	5
72	Stateside SS 2209	A Man Like Me/Survival (DJ copy = £35)	15
75	Pye 7N 45524	Whatever Happened To The Love We Knew/Let's Have Fun	5
75	Pye 7N 45472	Hey Girl/I Am Somebody	45
66	Piccadilly NEP 34053	JIMMY JAMES AND THE VAGABONDS (EP)	50
66	Piccadilly NPL 38027	THE NEW RELIGION (LP)	50
68	Pye N(S)PL 18231	OPEN UP YOUR SOUL (LP)	35
68	Marble Arch MAL 823	THIS IS JIMMY JAMES (LP)	12
70	Marble Arch MAL 1244	THE NEW RELIGION (LP, reissue)	20
75	Pye NSPL 18457	YOU DON'T STAND A CHANCE IF YOU CAN'T DANCE (LP)	18

JIMMY JAMES & THE VAGABONDS/ALAN BOWN SET
67	Pye N(S)PL 18156	LONDON SWINGS — LIVE AT THE MARQUEE CLUB (LP, 1 side each)	50

(see also Vagabonds, Jamaica's Own Vagabonds, Alan Bown Set)

JOHN JAMES
70	Transatlantic TRA 219	MORNING BRINGS THE LIGHT (LP)	15
71	Transatlantic TRA 242	JOHN JAMES (LP)	15
72	Transatlantic TRA 250	SKY IN MY PIE (LP)	15
75	Transatlantic TRA 305	HEAD IN THE CLOUDS (LP)	15
76	Kicking Mule SNKF 128	DESCRIPTIVE GUITAR INSTRUMENTALS (LP)	12
78	Kicking Mule SNKF 136	LIVE IN CONCERT (LP)	12
84	Stoptime STOP 101	ACOUSTICA ECLECTICA (LP, some signed)	20/15

JONI JAMES
53	MGM SP 1013	Why Don't You Believe Me?/Wishing Ring	25
53	MGM SP 1025	Have You Heard/Purple Shades	15
53	MGM SP 1026	Your Cheatin' Heart/I'll Be Waiting For You	15
53	MGM SP 1041	Almost Always/Is It Any Wonder?	15
53	MGM SP 1064	I'll Never Stand In Your Way/Why Can't I	15
54	MGM SP 1081	I Need You Now/You're Nearer	12
54	MGM SP 1089	I'll Be Seeing You/Am I In Love	15
54	MGM SP 1094	You're My Everything/Maybe Next Time	12
54	MGM SP 1100	In A Garden Of Roses/Every Day	12
54	MGM SP 1105	Pa Pa/Mama, Don't Cry At My Wedding	12
55	MGM SP 1125	This Is My Confession/How Important Can It Be?	12
55	MGM SP 1135	When You Wish Upon A Star/Is This The End Of The Line?	12
56	MGM SP 1149	You Are My Love/My Believing Heart	12
57	MGM MGM 918	Give Us This Day/How Lucky You Are	10
57	MGM MGM 954	Only Trust Your Heart/I Need You So	8
58	MGM MGM 973	My Funny Valentine/My Darling, My Darling	7
58	MGM MGM 978	Never 'Till Now/Love Works Miracles	7
58	MGM MGM 991	There Goes My Heart/Funny (78 rpm = £10)	12
59	MGM MGM 1002	There Must Be A Way/I'm Sorry For You, My Friend (78 rpm = £12)	7
59	MGM MGM 1022	Perhaps/I Still Get A Thrill (Thinking Of You)	5
59	MGM MGM 1034	I Still Get Jealous/Prayer Of Love	5
59	MGM MGM 1041	Are You Sorry?/What I Don't Know Won't Hurt Me	5
59	MGM MGM 1050	Little Things Mean A Lot/I Laughed At Love	6

60	MGM MGM 1064	You Belong To Me/I Need You Now	5
60	MGM MGM 1089	We Know/They Really Don't Know You	5
60	MGM MGM 1105	Be My Love/Tall As A Tree	5
54	MGM MGM-EP 504	JONI JAMES (EP)	18
55	MGM MGM-EP 518	SINGS TO YOU (EP)	18
56	MGM MGM-EP 530	LITTLE GIRL BLUE (EP)	18
56	MGM MGM-EP 558	LOVE LETTERS (EP)	15
60	MGM MGM-EP 728	THE SONGS OF HANK WILLIAMS (EP, also stereo MGM-ES 3501)	15/18
54	MGM MGM-D 127	LET THERE BE LOVE (10" LP)	45
59	MGM MGM-C 777	ONE HUNDRED SONGS AND JONI (LP)	30
59	MGM MGM-C 785	JONI SINGS SONGS OF HANK WILLIAMS (LP)	25
60	MGM MGM-C 809	TI VOGLIO BENE (I LOVE YOU SO) (LP)	25
60	MGM MGM-C 823/CS 6005	SINGS IRISH FAVOURITES (LP, mono/stereo)	20/22
60	MGM MGM-C 825	SWINGS SWEET (LP)	22
61	MGM MGM-C 839/CS 6015	100 STRINGS AND JONI IN HOLLYWOOD (LP, mono/stereo)	20/22
63	MGM MGM-C 933	AFTER HOURS (LP)	22

MARK JAMES
67	Liberty LIB 55953	Bimbo Knows/I Can't Let You Go	7

NICKY JAMES (MOVEMENT)
65	Columbia DB 7747	Stagger Lee/I'm Hurtin' Inside (as Nicky James Movement)	30
67	Philips BF 1566	I Need To Be Needed/So Glad We Made It	7
68	Philips BF 1635	Would You Believe/Silver Butterfly	18
68	Philips BF 1694	Lookin' Through Windows/Nobody But Me	7
69	Philips BF 1755	Time/Little Bit Of Paper	8
69	Philips BF 1804	Reaching For The Sun/No Life At All	7
72	Threshold TH 12	Why/Foreign Shore	6
73	Threshold TH 16	Black Dream/She Came To Me	6
73	Threshold TH 17	I Guess I've Always Loved You/My Style	8
71	Philips 6308 069	NICKY JAMES (LP)	25
73	Threshold THS 10	EVERY HOME SHOULD HAVE ONE (LP)	15
76	Threshold THS 19	THUNDERTHROAT (LP)	12

(see also Move)

PHILIP JAMES & BLUES BUSTERS
65	Island WI 219	Wide Awake In A Dream/MAYTALS: Tell Me The Reason	125

(see also Blues Busters)

RICKY JAMES
57	HMV POP 306	Knee Deep in The Blues/Bluer Than Blue (78 rpm = £8)	35
57	HMV POP 334	Party Doll/Ninety-Nine Ways (78 rpm = £8)	40

ROGER JAMES FOUR
65	Columbia DB 7556	Letter From Kathy/Leave Me Alone	7
66	Columbia DB 7813	Better Than Here/You're Gonna Come Home Cryin' (withdrawn)	50
66	Columbia DB 7829	Better Than Here/You're Gonna Come Home Cryin'	30

RUBY JAMES
69	Fontana TF 1051	Gettin' Mighty Crowded/Don't Play That Song	20

SALLY JAMES
74	Philips 6006 418	Isn't It Good/Wake Me When It's Over (p/s)	7

SIDNEY JAMES (& DEAN ROGERS/LIZ FRASER)
61	Decca F 11328	The Ooter Song/Double Bunk (with Liz Fraser)	15
61	HMV POP 886	Kids/One Last Kiss (with Dean Rogers)	10
73	Pye 7N 4528	Our House/She's Gone (solo) (p/s)	15

(see also Tony Hancock)

SKIP JAMES
65	Vanguard VSD 79219	SKIP JAMES TODAY (LP)	25
67	Private PR3	1964-67 (LP, 99 copies only)	45
68	Vanguard VSD 79273	DEVIL GOT MY WOMAN (LP)	25
70	Spokane SPL 1003	THE ORIGINAL 1930/31 RECORDINGS (LP)	45
78	Vanguard VDP 20001	I'M SO GLAD (LP)	20
70s	Storyville 670 185	THE GREATEST OF THE DELTA BLUES SINGERS (LP)	18

SONNY JAMES
56	Capitol CL 14635	The Cat Came Back/Hello Old Broken Heart	25
56	Capitol CL 14664	Twenty Feet Of Muddy Water/For Rent (One Empty Heart)	18
57	Capitol CL 14683	Young Love/You're The Reason I'm In Love	18
57	Capitol CL 14708	First Date, First Kiss, First Love/Speak To Me (78 rpm = £7)	15
57	Capitol CL 14742	Dear Love/Lovesick Blues	10
57	Capitol CL 14788	Love Conquered (Love Came, Love Saw)/A Mighty Lovable Man (78 rpm = £8)	18
57	Capitol CL 14814	Uh-Huh-Mm/Why Can't They Remember? (78 rpm = £15)	30
58	Capitol CL 14848	Kathaleen/Walk To The Dance	15
58	Capitol CL 14879	Are You Mine/Let's Play Love	6
58	Capitol CL 14915	You Got That Touch/I Can See It In Your Eyes	6
58	Capitol CL 14952	I Can't Stay Away From You/Let Me Be The One To Love You	5
59	Capitol CL 14991	Yo-Yo/Dream Big (78 rpm = £22)	12
59	Capitol CL 15022	Talk Of The School/The Table	5
59	Capitol CL 15046	Pure Love/This Love Of Mine	5
59	Capitol CL 15079	Red Mud/Who's Next In Line	5
60	London HL 9132	Jenny Lou/Passin' Through	10
65	Capitol CL 15377	You're The Only World I Know/Tying The Pieces Together	5
57	Capitol EAP1 827	YOUNG LOVE (EP)	35
64	Capitol EAP1 20654	YOU'RE THE ONLY WORLD I KNOW (EP)	22
57	Capitol T 779	SOUTHERN GENTLEMAN (LP)	30
57	Capitol T 867	SONNY (LP)	30
58	Capitol T 988	HONEY (LP)	25
63	London HA-D 8049	YOUNG LOVE (LP)	70

STU(ART) JAMES (& MOJOS)
65	Decca F 12231	Wait A Minute/Wonder If She Knows (as Stu James & Mojos)	12
74	Bradleys BRAD 7406	I Only Wish I Had The Time/Back To Basingstoke (Part 1)	5
76	Bradleys BRAD 7614	I'm In The Mood/Firefly (as Stuart James)	5

(see also Mojos)

SULLIVAN JAMES BAND
66	Parlophone R 5465	Goodbye Mr. Heartache/We're Gonna Make It	7

TOMMY JAMES & SHONDELLS
66	Roulette RK 7000	Hanky Panky/SHONDELLS: Thunderbolt	15
66	Pye International 7N 25398	It's Only Love/Ya! Ya!	10
67	Major Minor MM 511	I Think We're Alone Now/Gone Gone Gone	8
67	Major Minor MM 548	Out Of The Blue/Love's Closing In On Me	6
68	Major Minor MM 558	Wish It Were You/Get Out Now	8
68	Major Minor MM 567	Mony Mony/One, Two, Three And I Fell	7
68	Roulette RO 500	Do Something To Me/Somebody Cares	8
69	Roulette RO 502	Crimson And Clover/Some Kind Of Love	6
69	Roulette RO 506	Sweet Cherry Wine/Breakaway	5
69	Roulette RO 507	Crystal Blue Persuasion/I'm Alive	12
69	Roulette RO 511	Ball Of Fire/Makin' Good Time	5
70	Roulette RO 513	She/Loved One	5
70	Roulette RO 516	Come To Me/Talkin' And Signifyin'	5
70	Roulette RO 518	Ball And Chain/Candy Makers (solo)	5
68	Major Minor MMLP/SMLP 27	SOMETHING SPECIAL (LP)	35
68	Roulette RRLP/SRLP 1	MONY MONY (LP)	30
68	Roulette RRLP/SRLP 2	CRIMSON AND CLOVER (LP)	22
69	Roulette RRLP/SRLP 3	CELLOPHANE SYMPHONY (LP)	22
72	Roulette 2432 002	THE BEST OF TOMMY JAMES & THE SHONDELLS (LP)	15
72	Roulette 2432 005	MY HEAD, MY BED AND MY RED GUITAR (LP, solo)	12

TONY JAMES
68	Jolly JY 002	Treat Me Right/Me Donkey's Dead	12

WINSTON JAMES
70	Hot Rod HR 106	Prison Sentence/JANET FERRON: Darling I Need You	12
70	Torpedo TOR 6	I May Never/Longest Day	25

JAMES BOYS
68	Direction 58-3721	The Mule (Instrumental)/The Horse (Vocal)	10

JAMES BROTHERS
68	Page One POF 077	I Forgot To Give You Love/The Truth About It	8
68	Page One POF 088	Does It Have To Be Me/You Don't Really Love Me	8

(see also Wheels)

JAMES GANG
70	Stateside SS 2158	Funk No. 48/Collage	8
70	Stateside SS 2173	Stop/Take A Look Around (withdrawn)	15
70	Probe PRO 502	Funk 49/Thanks	6
71	Probe PRO 533	Walk Away/Yadig?	5
70	Stateside SSL 10295	YER' ALBUM (LP)	25
70	Probe SPB 6253	RIDES AGAIN (LP)	20
71	Probe SPB 1038	THIRDS (LP)	20
71	Probe SPB 1045	LIVE IN CONCERT (LP)	15
72	Probe SPB 1056	STRAIGHT SHOOTER (LP)	15
73	Probe SPB 1065	PASSIN' THRU (LP)	15

(see also Joe Walsh, Tommy Bolin)

BOBBY JAMESON
64	Decca F 12032	All I Want Is My Baby/Each And Every Day	35
64	London HL 9921	I Wanna Love You/I'm So Lonely	30
65	Brit WI 1001	Rum-Pum/Please Mr. Mailman	20
69	Joy JOYS 193	TOO MANY MORNINGS (LP)	100

STEPHEN JAMESON
70	Pye 7N 45189	Margie Make It March/Happiness Road	5
73	Dawn DNS 1035	Don't Say/Back Together Once Again	5
73	Dawn DNLS 3044	STEPHEN JAMESON (LP)	15

JAMESON RAID
80	Blackbird BRAID 001	The Hypnotist/The Raid/Gettin' Hotter/Straight From The Butchers (p/s)	40
81	GBH GBH 1	Seven Days Of Splendour/It's A Crime/Catcher In The Rye (p/s, with lyric sheet, white sleeve, later black sleeve)	25/20

JAMIES
58	Fontana H 153	Summertime Summertime/Searching For You (78 rpm = £22)	45
62	Columbia DB 4885	Summertime Summertime/Searching For You (reissue)	20

JAMIROQUAI
93	Acid Jazz JAZID 46	When You Gonna Learn/Too Young To Die (p/s)	22
93	Acid Jazz JAZID 46T	When You Gonna Learn/Didgin' Out/Too Young To Die (12", p/s)	15

JAMME
70	Stateside-Dunhill SSL 5024	JAMME (LP)	18

JOE JAMMER
73	Regal Zono. SRZA 8514	BAD NEWS (LP)	28

(see also Mitchell/Coe Mysteries)

J.A.M.s
(see under Justified Ancients Of Mu Mu)

JAN & ARNIE

58	London HL 8653	Jennie Lee/Gotta Getta Date (78 rpm = £35)	50

(see also Jan & Dean)

JAN & DEAN

59	London HLN 8936	Baby Talk/Jeanette, Get Your Hair Done (78 rpm = £100)	32
59	London HLU 8990	There's A Girl/My Heart Sings (78 rpm = £120)	25
60	London HLU 9063	Clementine/You're On My Mind	20
61	London HLH 9395	Heart And Soul/Midsummer Night's Dream	20
62	Liberty LIB 55397	A Sunday Kind Of Love/Poor Little Puppet	15
63	Liberty LIB 55531	Linda/When I Learn How To Cry	15
63	Liberty LIB 55580	Surf City/She's My Summer Girl	10
63	Liberty LIB 55613	Honolulu Lulu/Someday You'll Go Walkin' By	10
64	Liberty LIB 55641	Drag City/Schlock Rod Pt 1	12
64	Liberty LIB 55672	Dead Man's Curve/The New Girl In School	10
64	Liberty LIB 55704	The Little Old Lady From Pasadena/My Mighty GTO	10
64	Liberty LIB 55724	Ride The Wild Surf/The Anaheim, Azusa And Cucamonga Sewing Circle, Book Review And Timing Association	10
65	Liberty LIB 55727	Sidewalk Surfin'/When It's Over	10
65	Liberty LIB 55766	(Here They Come) From All Over The World/Freeway Flyer	10
65	Liberty LIB 55792	You Really Know How To Hurt A Guy/It's As Easy As 1, 2, 3	10
65	Liberty LIB 55833	I Found A Girl/It's A Shame To Say Goodbye	10
66	Liberty LIB 10225	Norwegian Wood/A Beginning From An End	22
66	Liberty LIB 55860	Batman/Bucket 'T'	20
66	Liberty LIB 10244	Popsicle/The Joker Is Wild	20
66	Liberty LIB 55923	The New Girl In School/School Day (Ring Ring Goes The Bell)	8
66	Liberty LIB 10252	Tennessee/Horace The Swinging School Bus Driver	12
67	CBS 202630	Yellow Balloon/A Taste Of Rain	22
65	Liberty LEP 2213	SURF 'N' DRAG HITS (EP)	35
66	Liberty LEP 2258	THE TITANIC TWOSOME (EP)	50
76	United Artists REM 402	REMEMBER JAN & DEAN (EP)	15
63	Liberty LBY 1163	SURF CITY AND OTHER SWINGING CITIES (LP)	40
64	Liberty LBY 1220	DEAD MAN'S CURVE/NEW GIRL IN SCHOOL (LP)	45
64	Liberty LBY 1229	RIDE THE WILD SURF (LP)	40
65	Liberty LBY 1279	GOLDEN HITS (LP)	40
65	Liberty LBY 1304	FOLK 'N' ROLL (LP)	35
66	Liberty LBY 1309	JAN AND DEAN MEET BATMAN (LP)	25
66	Liberty LBY 1339	FILET OF SOUL (A LIVE ONE) (LP)	30

(see also Legendary Masked Surfers, Fantastic Baggys, Jan & Arnie)

JAN & KELLY

62	Philips 326 567 BF	Ooh! 'E Didn't/Prepare To Meet Your Fate Mate	7
62	Philips BF 1253	I Could Have Died/Make Me A Doormat	7
63	Philips BF 1265	Ooh! I Can't/Write Me A Letter	7
64	Philips BF 1323	And Then He Kicked Me/My Country And Western Lover	10
64	Philips BF 1377	There Was A Girl/There Was A Boy/And Then There Was Nothing	7
63	Philips BE 12536	TIME FOR A LAUGH (EP)	25

JAN & KJELD

59	Pye International 7N 25013	Buona Sera/Tiger Rag	6
60	Ember EMB S 101	Banjo Boy/Don't Raise A Storm (some in p/s)	22/10
60	Qualiton PSP 7127	Sweet Sue/Oh! Mein Papa (as Jan & Keld)	6
60	Ember EMB S 109	Down By The Riverside/I Shall Not Be Moved	6
60	Ember EMB 3312	THE KIDS FROM COPENHAGEN (LP, label states "The Boys From Copenhagen")	22

BRUCE JANAWAY

78	Deep Range SRT/CUS/216	PURITANICAL ODES (LP, with insert)	35

JAN DUKES DE GREY

70	Decca Nova (S)DN 8	SORCERERS (LP)	50
71	Transatlantic TRA 234	MICE AND RATS IN THE LOFT (LP)	80

JANE'S ADDICTION

88	WEA W 7520	Mountain Song/Jane Says (p/s)	6
88	WEA W 7520T	Mountain Song/Jane Says/Had A Dad (live) (12", p/s)	8
91	WEA W 0031TP	Classic Girl/No One's Leaving (live)/Ain't No Right (live) (12", picture disc, die-cut sleeve)	8

PETER JANES

67	CBS 203004	Emperors And Armies/Go Home Ulla (some in p/s)	10/6
68	CBS 3299	Do You Believe/For The Sake Of Time	20

JANIE

61	Capitol CL 15180	You Better Not Do That/Only Girls Can Tell	12

(see also Jeanne Black)

JANINE

81	Stiletto JAN 001	Crazy On You/Candy (p/s)	170

JOHNNY JANIS

58	London HLU 8650	The Better To Love You/Can This Be Love (78 rpm = £10)	15
60	Philips PB 1090	Gina/If The Good Lord's Willin'	6
58	HMV 7EG 8365	JOHNNY JANIS (EP)	25
66	London HA-U 8270	ONCE IN A BLUE MOON (LP)	25

BERT JANSCH

67	Big T BIG 102	Life Depends On Love/A Little Sweet Sunshine	12
73	Reprise K 14234	Oh My Father/The First Time Ever I Saw Your Face	7
74	Charisma CB 240	In The Bleak Midwinter/One For Jo	6
75	Charisma CB 267	Dance Lady Dance/Build Another Band	5

79	Kicking Mule SCK 44	Time And Time/Una Linea Di Dolcezza (as Bert Jansch Conundrum)	5
82	Logo GO 409	Heartbreak Hotel/Up To The Stars (p/s)	5
66	Transatlantic EP 145	NEEDLE OF DEATH (EP)	32
65	Transatlantic TRA 125	BERT JANSCH (LP)	28
65	Transatlantic TRA 132	IT DON'T BOTHER ME (LP)	28
66	Transatlantic TRA 143	JACK ORION (LP)	40
67	Transatlantic TRA 157	NICOLA (LP)	28
69	Transatlantic TRA 179	BIRTHDAY BLUES (LP)	25
69	Vanguard VSD 79292	STEPPING STONES (LP)	18
69	Transatlantic TRASAM 10	THE BERT JANSCH SAMPLER (LP)	15
71	Transatlantic TRA 235	ROSEMARY LANE (LP)	22
72	Transatlantic TRASAM 27	BOX OF LOVE — THE BERT JANSCH SAMPLER VOL. 2 (LP)	15
73	Reprise K 44225	MOONSHINE (LP, with lyric insert)	15
74	Charisma CAS 1090	L.A. TURNAROUND (LP, with lyric insert)	12
75	Charisma CAS 1107	SANTA BARBARA HONEYMOON (LP)	12
77	Charisma CAS 1127	A RARE CONUNDRUM (LP)	12
79	Charisma CLASS 6	AVOCET (LP)	12
80	Kicking Mule SNKF 162	THIRTEEN DOWN (LP, as Bert Jansch Conundrum)	12
85	Konexion KOMA 788006	FROM THE OUTSIDE (LP, 500 only)	12

BERT JANSCH & JOHN RENBOURN

| 66 | Transatlantic TRA 144 | BERT AND JOHN (LP) | 25 |

(see also Conundrum, Pentangle, John Renbourn)

JAPAN

78	Ariola Hansa AHA 510	Don't Rain On My Parade/Stateline (solid or press-out centre, no p/s)	15
78	Ariola Hansa AHA 525	The Unconventional/Adolescent Sex (some with p/s)	20/6
78	Ariola Hansa AHA 529	Sometimes I Feel So Low/Love Is Infectious (p/s, initially on blue vinyl)	10/8
79	Ariola Hansa AHA 540	Life In Tokyo (Short Version)/Life In Tokyo Pt 2 (p/s, red vinyl)	8
79	Ariola Hansa AHAD 540	Life In Tokyo (Long Version)/(Short Version) (12", p/s, red vinyl)	12
80	Ariola Hansa AHA 559	I Second That Emotion/Quiet Life (dull red vinyl, card or paper p/s)	8/6
80	Virgin VS 379	Gentlemen Take Polaroids/The Experience of Swimming (fully autographed by band, p/s)	75
80	Virgin VS 379	Gentlemen Take Polaroids/The Experience of Swimming//The Width Of A Room/Burning Bridges (double pack, gatefold p/s)	12
82	Virgin VSY 472	Ghosts/The Art Of Parties (Version) (picture disc, stickered PVC cover)	5
88	Virgin CDT 11	Ghosts/The Art Of Parties (Version)/Visions Of China (3" CD, card sleeve)	8
88	Virgin CDT 32	Gentlemen Take Polaroids/Cantonese Boy (12" Version)/Methods Of Dance (12" Version) (3" CD, gatefold card sleeve)	8
80	Virgin V 2180	GENTLEMEN TAKE POLAROIDS (LP, with misprinted sleeve with sticker, "Some Kind Of Fool" listed instead of "Burning Bridges")	12

(see also David Sylvian)

JOHNNY JAPES & HIS JESTICLES

| 87 | Viz VIZ 1 | Bags Of Fun With Buster/Scrotal Scratch Mix (p/s) | 5 |

(see also XTC, John Otway, Mr. Partridge)

JIMMY JAQUES

58	Fontana H 100	Come Walking/Baby, Don't You Cry (78)	10
58	Fontana H 131	In My Life/Never Let You Go (78 rpm = £10)	12
58	Fontana H 161	Barb'ry Ann/For A Lifetime (78 rpm = £10)	8
60	Parlophone R 4710	Do Me A Favour/Not To Worry	5

JARMELS

| 61 | Top Rank JAR 560 | She Loves To Dance/Little Lonely One | 25 |
| 61 | Top Rank JAR 580 | A Little Bit Of Soap/The Way You Look Tonight | 50 |

COOK E. JARR

| 69 | RCA RCA 1820 | Pledging My Love/If I Were A Carpenter | 6 |

JEAN-MICHEL JARRE
SINGLES

78	Polydor POSP 20	Equinoxe 5/Equinoxe 1 (p/s, with etched autograph on run-off)	8
79	Polydor 2001 896	Equinoxe 4 (Remix)/Equinoxe 3 (p/s)	6
80	Polydor 2001 968	Jarre At The Concorde: Equinoxe 7 (live)/Equinoxe 8 (live) (p/s)	10
81	Polydor POSP 292	Magnetic Fields 2 (Remix)/Magnetic Fields 1 (Excerpt) (p/s)	5
81	Polydor POSP 363	Magnetic Fields 4 (Remix)/Magnetic Fields 1 (Excerpt) (p/s)	10
82	Polydor POSP 430	Orient Express/Fishing Junks At Sunset (p/s)	8
84	Polydor POSPX 718	Zoolook (Remix)/Wooloomooloo/Zoolook (Extended)/Zoolook (Effects) (12", p/s)	15
85	Polydor POSP 740	Zoolookologie (Remix)/Ethnicolor 2 (p/s)	8
85	Polydor POSPG 740	Zoolookologie (Remix)/Ethnicolor 2//Oxygene 4/Oxygene 6 (double pack)	12
85	Polydor POSPX 740	Zoolookologie (Extended Remix)/(Remix)/Ethnicolor 2 (12", p/s)	15
86	Polydor POSPX 788	Rendezvous 4 (Special Remix)/Rendezvous 4/Moon Machine (12", 'face' or 'city skyline' p/s)	each 20
88	Polydor PZ 25	Revolutions (Extended Mix)/Revolutions (LP Mix)/Industrial Revolution 2 (12", p/s)	8
88	Polydor PZCD 25	Revolutions (Extended Mix)/Revolutions/Revolutions (Single Remix) (CD, jewel case)	20
88	Polydor PZCD 32	London Kid (Full Version) (featuring Hank Marvin)/Industrial Revolution 3/Revolutions (Remix) (CD, card sleeve)	20
89	Polydor PZCD 55	Oxygene IV (Single Version)/Industrial Revolution Overture/Oxygene IV (live)/September (CD, card sleeve)	15
90	Polydor PZ 84	Calypso (Extended)/Calypso/Calypso Pt 2 (12", p/s)	10
90	Polydor PZCD 84	Calypso (Extended)/Calypso/Calypso Pt 2 (CD)	8
87	Polydor 833 737-2	THE JEAN-MICHEL JARRE 10TH ANNIVERSARY CD BOX SET (7-CD, 5,000 only)	40
88	Polydor C88 1-3	OXYGENE (LP, HMV-only box set with booklet, 3,300 only)	15
88	Polydor C88-1-3	OXYGENE (CD, HMV-only box set with booklet, 3,500 only)	20

MINT VALUE £

MAURICE JARRE
63	Pye Intl. NPL 28023	LAWRENCE OF ARABIA (LP, soundtrack)	12
65	Fontana (S)TL 5259	THE COLLECTOR (LP, soundtrack)	25
66	MGM MGM-CS 8037	GRAND PRIX (LP, soundtrack)	15
66	CBS (S)BPG 62843	IS PARIS BURNING? (LP, soundtrack)	25
67	RCA RD 7848	NIGHT OF THE GENERALS (LP, soundtrack)	40
67	RCA Victor RD/SF 7876	THE PROFESSIONALS (LP, soundtrack)	50
68	Dot (S)LPD 515	VILLA RIDES (LP, soundtrack)	15
71	MGM 2315 028	RYAN'S DAUGHTER (LP, soundtrack, gatefold sleeve)	12
76	EMI SLCW 1033	THE MESSAGE (LP, soundtrack, gatefold sleeve)	12
77	Pye NSPH 28504	JESUS OF NAZARETH (LP, soundtrack, gatefold sleeve)	15

WAYNE JARRETT
80	Greensleeves GRED 41	Saturday Night Jamboree (12")	20
81	Greensleeves GREL 28	CHIP IN (LP)	12

MARIAN JARVIS
75	Chelsea 2005 038	A Penny For Your Thoughts/A Good Man To Wake Up To	30

JASMIN T
69	Tangerine DP 13	Some Other Guy/Evening (p/s)	150

JASON & THE SCORCHERS
85	EMI EA 200	Shop It Around/Change The Tune (p/s)	5
85	EMI 12EA 200	Shop It Around/Absolutely Sweet Marie/Change The Tune (12", p/s)	8

JASON CREST
68	Philips BF 1633	Turquoise Tandem Cycle/Good Life (some in export p/s)	160/60
68	Philips BF 1650	Juliano The Bull/Two By The Sea	40
68	Philips BF 1687	(Here We Go Round) The Lemon Tree/Patricia's Dream	50
69	Philips BF 1752	Waterloo Road/Education	25
69	Philips BF 1809	A Place In The Sun/Black Mass	140
	(see also Holy Mackerel, High Broom)		

JASON'S GENERATIONS
66	Polydor BM 56042	It's Up To You/Insurance Co.'s Are Very Unfair	40

JASPER
69	Spark SRLP 103	LIBERATION (LP)	220

JAVELLS
77	Pye Disco Demand BD 2003	Goodbye Nothin' To Say/Nothin' To Say	8

JAWBONE
70	Carnaby CNS 4007	How's Ya Pa?/Mister Custer	15
70	Carnaby CNS 4020	Way Way Down/Bulldog Goes West	15
72	B&C CB 190	Gotta Go/Automobile Blues	6
70	Carnaby CNLS 6004	JAWBONE (LP)	90
	(see also Mirage, Portobello Explosion)		

BOB JAXON (& HI-TONES)
55	London HL 8156	Ali Baba/Why Does A Woman Cry (as Bob Jaxon & Hi-Tones) (78 rpm = £20)	45
57	RCA RCA 1019	Beach Party/(Gotta Have Something In The) Bank Frank (78 rpm = £30)	80

FRANKIE JAXON/HOUNDHEAD HENRY
60	Jazz Collector JEL 10	THE MALE BLUES VOLUME 6 (EP)	18

JAY (Black)
64	Coral Q 72471	I Rise, I Fall/How Sweet It Is	30
67	United Artists UP 1174	What Will My Mary Say/Return To Me (as Jay Black)	10
	(see also Jay & The Americans)		

ABNER JAY
63	London HLN 9791	Cleo/Thresher	12

DAVID JAY
	(see under David J.)		

ERIC JAY
59	London HL 9004	The Little Drummer Boy/Blue Champagne Cha Cha (78 rpm = £15)	8

LAURIE JAY COMBO
62	Ember JBS 710	Shades Of Red/Nevada Sunsets	10
63	HMV POP 1234	Teenage Idol/Think Of Me	12
64	HMV POP 1300	Love In My Heart/'Til You're Mine	8
64	HMV POP 1335	Maybe/Be Good To Me	8
65	Decca F 12083	A Song Called Soul/Just A Little Bit	25
	(see also Nero & Gladiators)		

LONNIE JAY & JAYNES
63	Stateside SS 197	Around And Around We Go/Somewhere	10

PETER JAY (& BLUE MEN)
60	Triumph RGM 1000	Just Too Late/Friendship (as Peter Jay & Blue Men)	40
60	Pye 7N 15290	Paradise Garden/Who's The Girl?	40
	(see also Blue Men)		

PETER JAY & JAYWALKERS
62	Decca F 11531	Can Can '62/Redskins	8
63	Decca F 11593	Totem Pole/Jaywalker	7
63	Decca F 11659	Poet And Peasant/Oo La La	10
63	Decca F 11757	Kansas City/The Parade Of Tin Soldiers	10
64	Decca F 11840	You Girl/If You Love Me	1064

	Piccadilly 7N 35199	Where Did Our Love Go/Caroline	12
64	Piccadilly 7N 35212	Tonight You're Gonna Fall In Love/Red Cabbage	10
65	Piccadilly 7N 35220	Parchman Farm/What's Easy For Two Is So Hard For One	20
65	Piccadilly 7N 35259	Before The Beginning/Solitaire	18

(see also Terry Reid, Miller, Big Boy Pete)

JAY & THE AMERICANS

62	HMV POP 1009	She Cried/Dawning	40
63	United Artists UP 1002	This Is It/It's My Turn To Cry	8
63	United Artists UP 1018	What's The Use/Strangers Tomorrow	8
64	United Artists UP 1039	Come Dance With Me/Look Into My Eyes Maria	15
64	United Artists UP 1069	Come A Little Bit Closer/Goodbye Boys Goodbye	8
65	United Artists UP 1075	Let's Lock The Door (And Throw Away The Key)/I'll Remember You	10
65	United Artists UP 1088	Think Of The Good Times/If You Were Mine Girl	8
65	United Artists UP 1094	Cara Mia/When It's All Over	12
65	United Artists UP 1108	Some Enchanted Evening/Girl	8
66	United Artists UP 1119	Sunday And Me/Through This Doorway	12
66	United Artists UP 1129	Why Can't You Bring Me Home/Baby Stop Your Crying	15
66	United Artists UP 1132	Crying/I Don't Need A Friend	8
66	United Artists UP 1142	Livin' Above Your Head/She's The Girl (That's Messing Up My Mind)	45
66	United Artists UP 1162	(He's) Raining In My Sunshine/Reason For Living	7
67	United Artists UP 1178	You Ain't As Hip As All That Baby/Nature Boy	12
67	United Artists UP 1191	(We'll Meet In The) Yellow Forest/Got Hung Up Along The Way	60
68	United Artists UP 2211	French Provincial/Shanghai Noodle Factory	18
69	United Artists UP 2268	This Magic Moment/Since I Don't Have You	7
69	United Artists UP 35008	When You Dance/So Much In Love	8
69	United Artists UP 35026	Hushabye/No I Don't Know Her	6
70	United Artists UP 35074	Walkin' In The Rain/For The Love Of A Lady	10
65	United Artists UEP 1003	COME A LITTLE BIT CLOSER (EP)	50
66	United Artists UEP 1017	LIVING WITH JAY AND THE AMERICANS (EP)	45
66	United Artists (S)ULP 1117	JAY AND THE AMERICANS (LP)	35
66	United Artists (S)ULP 1128	SUNDAY AND ME (LP)	40
67	United Artists (S)ULP 1150	LIVIN' ABOVE YOUR HEAD (LP)	50
67	United Artists (S)ULP 1164	TRY SOME OF THIS (LP)	40

(see also Jay, Chapter Four)

JAY (John Holt) & JOYA (Landis)

68	Trojan TR 633	I'll Be Lonely/SUPERSONICS: Second Fiddle	12

(see also John Holt, Joya Landis)

JAY & TECHNIQUES

67	Philips PB 1597	Apples, Peaches, Pumpkin Pie/Stronger Than Dirt	20
67	Philips PB 1618	Keep The Ball Rollin'/Here We Go Again	15
67	Mercury 6052 302	Apples, Peaches, Pumpkin Pie/Contact	7
68	Philips PB 1644	Strawberry Shortcake/Still (In Love With You)	12
68	Mercury MF 1034	Baby Make Your Own Sweet Music/Help Yourself To All My Lovin'	12
75	Polydor 2066 473	I Feel Love Comin' On/This World Of Mine	20
71	Mercury MCF 127360	Baby Make Your Own Sweet Music/Help Yourself To All My Lovin' (reissue)	6
67	Philips (S)BL 7834	APPLES, PEACHES, PUMPKIN PIE (LP)	40

JAYBIRDS (U.K.)

64	Embassy WB 621	Not Fade Away/Over You	5
64	Embassy WB 624	Tell Me When/You Can't Do That	5
64	Embassy WB 625	Can't Buy Me Love/DEL MARTIN: I Love You Because	5
64	Embassy WB 626	Good Golly Miss Molly/	5
64	Embassy WB 628	Mockin' Bird Hill/Hubble Bubble (Toil And Trouble)	5
64	Embassy WB 632	Baby Let Me Take You Home/BUD ASHTON & HIS GROUP: Rise And Fall Of Fingel Blunt	5
64	Embassy WB 635	Juliet/Here I Go Again	5
64	Embassy WB 651	She's Not There/PAUL RICH: I Wouldn't Trade You For The World	5
64	Embassy WB 663	All Day And All Of The Night/Google Eye	8
64	Embassy WB 672	What Have They Done To The Rain/BUD ASHTON & HIS GROUP: Genie With The Light Brown Lamp	5
65	Embassy WB 673	Go Now/TERRY BRANDON: Ferry 'Cross The Mersey	5

(see also Ray Pilgrim & Beatmen)

JAYBIRDS

66	Sue WI 4013	Somebody Help Me/The Right Kind	45+

JAY BOYS

69	Trojan TR 665	Splendour Splash/TREVOR SHIELD: Please	12
70	Harry J. HJ 6602	The Dog (Parts 1 & 2)	8
70	Harry J. HJ 6607	Jack The Ripper/Don't Let Me Down	8
70	Harry J. HJ 6609	Jay Moon Walk/Elcong	8
70	Harry J. HJ 6610	Je T'Aime/It Ain't Me Babe	8
70	Harry J. HJ 6617	Del Gago/Killer Version	8
70	Harry J. HJ 6618	Can't Get Next To You/(Part 2) (both actually by Charmers)	5
71	Harry J. HJ 6628	The Arcade Walk/The Arcade Walk Vers. II	6
72	Harry J. HJ 6644	African People/HARRY J. ALL STARS: African (Version)	8
72	Ashanti AHS 407	Rough Road/TREVOR SHIELD: Rough Road	5

(see also Roy Panton, Bob & Marcia, Cables)

JERRY JAYE

67	London HLU 10128	My Girl Josephine/Five Miles From Home	35

JAYE SISTERS

59	London HLT 9011	Sure Fire Love/G-3 (78 rpm = £60)	60

JAYHAWKS

56	Parlophone R 4228	Stranded In The Jungle/My Only Darling (78 rpm = £130)	600

JAYLADS
71   Punch PH 95   Royal Chord (actually by Melodians)/Version
                                         (actually "In The Spirit" by Lloyd Charmers) 12

(see also Melodians)

JAYNETTS
63   Stateside SS 227   Sally Go Round The Roses/Sally Go Round The Roses (Instrumental) 18

JAYS
63   Parlophone R 4764   Shock A Boom/Across The Sea. 12

JAYWALKERS
76   Cream CRM 5003   Can't Live Without You/Heartbroken Memories. 10

JAZZATEERS
83   Rough Trade RT 138   Sixteen Reasons/Show Me The Door (p/s) 5
84   Rough Trade ROUGH 46 JAZZATEERS (LP, with insert) 12

JAZZ BUTCHER
83   Glass GLASS 027   Southern Mark Smith/Jazz Butcher Meets Count Dracula (p/s). 20
85   Glass GLASS 12041   Real Men/The Jazz Butcher V The Prime Minister/
                                         Southern Mark Smith (Original) (12", p/s) 20
86   Glass HMMM 001   Christmas With The Pygmies (p/s, promo freebie, given away at gigs) 10

JAZZ COMPOSERS ORCHESTRA
74   JCOA/Virgin JDA 311   JAZZ COMPOSERS ORCHESTRA (2-LP, gatefold sleeve) 15
(see also Carla Bley, Mike Mantler, Don Cherry, Larry Coryell)

JAZZ COURIERS
50s (no cat. no.)   Top Spot Blues/Monk Was Here/Last Minute Blues (square flexi). 100
57   Tempo EXA 75   JAZZ COURIERS (EP). 60
59   Tempo EXA 87   JAZZ COURIERS (EP). 60
58   Tempo TAP 22   IN CONCERT (LP) 400
59   Tempo TAP 26   THE LAST WORD (LP) 350
60   London Jazz LTZ-L 15188 THE COURIERS OF JAZZ! (LP) 200
67   M. For Pleasure MFP 1072 IN CONCERT (LP) 15
80s Jasmine JASM 2004   THE JAZZ COURIERS (LP, reissue). 20
80s Jasmine JASM 2024   THE LAST WORD (LP, reissue) 15
(see also Tubby Hayes, Ronnie Scott)

JAZZ CRUSADERS
66   Fontana 688 149 ZL   THE THING (LP). 20
66   Fontana 688 117 ZL   LOOKING AHEAD (LP) 18
(see also Crusaders)

JAZZ FIVE
61   Tempo TAP 32   THE FIVE OF US (LP) 50
(see also Vic Ash Quartet, Harry Klein Quartet)

JAZZ HIP TRIO
67   Major Minor MMLP 8   JAZZ IN RELIEF (LP). 75

JAZZ MAKERS
66   Ember FA 2023   SWINGIN' SOUNDS (LP) 20

JAZZ MODES
60   London Jazz LTZ-K 15191 THE MOST HAPPY FELLA (LP) 20

JAZZ ROCK EXPERIENCE
70   Deram Nova SDN 19   JAZZ ROCK EXPERIENCE (LP) 40

J & B
66   Polydor 56095   Wow Wow Wow/There She Goes. 50
(see also State Of Micky & Tommy, Foreigner)

J.B.'s
71   Mojo 2001 155   These Are The J.B.'s (Parts 1 & 2). 15
71   Mojo 2027 002   The Grunt (Parts 1 & 2). 15
72   Mojo 2093 007   Gimme Some More/The Rabbit Got The Gun. 15
72   Mojo 2093 016   Hot Pants Road/Pass The Peas. 15
72   Mojo 2093 021   Givin' Up Food For Funk (Parts 1 & 2) 15
72   Mojo 2918 004   PASS THE PEAS (LP) 50
72   Polydor 2391 034   FOOD FOR THOUGHT (LP) 50
74   Polydor 2391 087   DOING IT TO DEATH (LP). 50
75   Polydor 2391 194   HUSTLE WITH SPEED (LP) 50
76   Polydor 2391 204   GIVIN' UP FOOD FOR FUNK — THE BEST OF THE JB's (LP) 40
(see also Fred Wesley & JB's, James Brown, Bobby Byrd)

JC001/DJ D Zire
91   White JCDZ001   Favourite Breaks (12") 12

J.D. (THE ROC)
72   Sioux SI 008   Superbad/MONTEGO MELON: Lucky Dip 8
(see also Jeff Dixon)

BOBBI JEAN
65   Mercury MF 921   Dry Your Tears/Pity The Man 12

CATHY JEAN & ROOMATES
61   Parlophone R 4764   Please Love Me Forever/Canadian Sunset. 60

LANA JEAN
63   Pye International 7N 25214 It Hurts To Be Sixteen/Bad Boy 25

JEAN & GAYTONES
71   Trojan TR 7817   I Shall Sing (actually by Judy Mowatt & Gaytones)/GAYTONES: Target. 12

JEAN & STATESIDES
64	Columbia DB 7287	Putty In Your Hands/One Fine Day	45
64	Columbia DB 7439	You Won't Forget Me/Cold, Cold Winter	30
65	Columbia DB 7651	Mama Didn't Lie/Just Let Me Cry	30

JEAN-ETTES
59	Pye 7N 15185	May You Always/I Saw A Light (78 rpm = £10)	12

JEAN-JACQUES
69	Pye International 7N 25489	Maman/Les Beaux Dimanches	5

JEANNE & JANIE
60	Capitol CL 15146	Journey Of Love/JEANNE BLACK: Lisa	10
60	Capitol CL 15165	Sleep Walkin'/JEANNE BLACK: You'll Find Out	10

(see also Jeanne Black)

JEANNIE (& BIG GUYS)
63	Piccadilly 7N 35147	Don't Lie To Me/Boys (as Jeannie & Big Guys)	12
64	Piccadilly 7N 35164	I Want You/Sticks And Stones (as Jeannie & Big Guys)	12
65	Parlophone R 5343	I Love Him/With Any Other Girl	8

(see also Cindy Cole)

JEANNIE & REDHEADS
64	Decca F 11829	Animal Duds/ANDREW OLDHAM GROUP: Funky And Fleopatra	30

(see also Andrew Oldham Orchestra)

AUDREY JEANS
56	Decca F 10768	Ticky Ticky Tick (I'm Gonna Tell On You)/Will You, Willyum	18
56	Decca F 10788	It's Better In The Dark/The Bus Stop Song (A Paper Of Pins)	7
58	Decca F 11035	Send A Letter To Jeanette — Yet!/Bad Pianna Rag (78 rpm = £10)	7
61	HMV POP 876	How Lovely To Be A Woman/What Did I See In Him	6

JEDDAH
83	Death RIP 2001	Eleanor Rigby (with poster, no p/s)	20

JEDI KNIGHTS
95	Clear CLR 406	MAY THE FUNK BE WITH YOU (12" EP, p/s)	30
95	Clear CLR 406X	MAY THE FUNK BE WITH YOU (12" EP, clear vinyl, embossed sleeve)	50

(see also Global Communications)

JEEPS
66	Strike JH 308	He Saw Eesaw/The Music Goes Round	15
66	Strike JH 315	Ain't It A Great Big Laugh/I Put On My Shoes	15

JEFFERSON
68	Pye 7N 17634	Montage/Did You Hear A Heartbreak Last Night	12
69	Pye 7N 17706	The Colour Of My Love/Look No Further	8
69	Pye 7N 17810	Baby Take Me In Your Arms/I Fell Flat On My Face	8
69	Pye 7N 17855	Love And All The World/I've Got To Tell Her	8
69	Pye NSPL 18316	THE COLOUR OF MY LOVE (LP)	25

(see also Rockin' Berries, Sight & Sound)

BLIND LEMON JEFFERSON
50	Tempo R 38	Weary Dog Blues/Change My Luck Blues (78)	25
50	Tempo R 39	Lock Step Blues/Hangman's Blues (78)	25
51	Tempo R 46	Shuckin' Sugar Blues/Rabbit Foot Blues (78)	25
52	Tempo R 54	Gone Dead On You Blues/One Dime Blues (78)	25
53	Jazz Collector L 91	Shuckin' Sugar Blues/Rabbit Foot Blues (78)	20
53	Jazz Collector L 103	Jack O'Diamonds Blues/Clock House Blues (78)	20
54	Jazz Collector L 126	Gone Dead On You Blues/One Dime Blues (78)	20
50s	Poydras 99	BLIND LEMON JEFFERSON (10" LP)	50
53	London Jazz AL 3508	FOLK BLUES OF BLIND LEMON JEFFERSON (10" LP)	55
55	London Jazz AL 3546	PENITENTIARY BLUES (10" LP)	55
57	London Jazz AL 3564	SINGS THE BLUES (10" LP)	55
69	CBS 63738	THE IMMORTAL (LP)	18
70s	Roots Matchbox RL 301	BLIND LEMON JEFFERSON VOLUME 1 (LP)	20
70s	Roots Matchbox RL 306	BLIND LEMON JEFFERSON VOLUME 2 (LP)	15
70s	Roots Matchbox RL 331	BLIND LEMON JEFFERSON VOLUME 3 (LP)	15

(see also Paramount Allstars)

BLIND LEMON JEFFERSON/ED BELL
60	Jazz Collector JEL 13	THE MALE BLUES VOLUME 7 (EP)	22

BLIND LEMON JEFFERSON/BUDDY BOY HAWKINS
59	Jazz Collector JEL 8	THE MALE BLUES VOLUME 5 (EP)	22

BLIND LEMON JEFFERSON/LEADBELLY
61	Jazz Collector JEL 24	THE MALE BLUES VOLUME 8 (EP)	20

BLIND LEMON JEFFERSON & RAMBLING THOMAS
50s	Heritage HLP 1007	BLIND LEMON JEFFERSON AND RAMBLING THOMAS (LP, 99 only)	100

EDDIE JEFFERSON
67	Stateside SS 591	Some Other Time/When You Look In The Mirror	20

GEORGE PAUL JEFFERSON
68	Fontana TF 923	Looking For My Mind/Out Of Place	12

MARSHALL JEFFERSON
88	ffrr FFRX 18	Open Your Eyes (Celestial Mix)/(Spiritual Mix)/(Marshall's Elevated Dub) (12", p/s)	15

MINT VALUE £

JEFFERSON AIRPLANE

67	RCA Victor RCA 1594	Somebody To Love/She Has Funny Cars	12
67	RCA Victor RCA 1631	White Rabbit/Plastic Fantastic Lover	15
67	RCA Victor RCA 1647	Ballad Of You And Me and Pooneil/Two Heads	10
68	RCA Victor RCA 1711	Greasy Heart/Share A Little Joke (With The World)	15
68	RCA Victor RCA 1736	If You Feel Like China Breaking/Triad	10
70	RCA RCA 1933	Volunteers/We Can Be Together	6
70	RCA RCA 1964	Somebody To Love/White Rabbit	6
70	RCA RCA 1989	Mexico/Have You Seen The Saucers?	6
72	Grunt 65-0500	Pretty As You Feel/Wild Turkey	7
72	Grunt 65-0506	Long John Silver/Milk Train	6
67	RCA Victor RD/SF 7889	SURREALISTIC PILLOW (LP, black label, mono/stereo)	42/30
68	RCA Victor RD/SF 7926	AFTER BATHING AT BAXTERS (LP, black label, mono/stereo)	42/30
68	RCA Victor RD/SF 7976	CROWN OF CREATION (LP, black label, mono/stereo)	25/18
69	RCA RD/SF 8019	BLESS ITS POINTED LITTLE HEAD (LP)	20
69	RCA Victor SF 7889	SURREALISTIC PILLOW (LP, repressing, orange label)	15
69	RCA Victor SF 7926	AFTER BATHING AT BAXTERS (LP, repressing, orange label)	15
69	RCA Victor SF 7976	CROWN OF CREATION (LP, repressing, orange label)	15
70	RCA SF 8076	VOLUNTEERS (LP, gatefold sleeve)	18
71	RCA SF 8164	THE WORST OF JEFFERSON AIRPLANE (LP, matt sleeve)	15
71	Grunt FTR 1001	BARK (LP, bag cover with lyric sheet & brown inner sleeve)	18
71	RCA SF 8195	JEFFERSON AIRPLANE TAKES OFF (LP)	15
72	Grunt FTR 1007	LONG JOHN SILVER (LP, open-out box cover with inner lyric sleeve)	18
73	Grunt FTR 0147	30 SECONDS OVER WINTERLAND (LP, with inner sleeve)	15

(see also Jefferson Starship, Great Society, Paul Kantner, Grace Slick, Papa John Creach, Hot Tuna)

FRAN JEFFRIES

67	Monument MON 1006	My Lonely Corner/Life Goes On	5

JEGA

96	Skam SKA 6	Phlax/Nortom Midgate/Bluette/Ionic/Evil Lee Kirtcele/ Steel Drum/In With The In (12", custom sleeve)	35
97	Skam SKA 9	Card Hore/Oak Hanger/Nausicaa/Stainless Steel Drum/Star Houdini (12", p/s)	15
98	Planet Mu ZIQ 001	TYPE XERO EP (12")	50

JEHST

99	Y n R Productions YNR 001	PREMONITIONS EP: (12", stickered p/s, first pressing has blue text)	25
01	Lowlife LOW 12	THE HIGH PLAINS DRIFTER (EP)	18
01	Lowlife LOW 12 PRO	The Trilogy Remix (12")	55
02	Y n R YNR008	Alcoholic Author/Night Breed (12")	20
02	Lowlife LOW 18	Return Of The Drifter (12")	10

JELLYBEAN

84	EMI 12EAX 210	Sidewalk Talk (featuring Madonna)/Was Dog A Doughnut/Sidewalk Talk (featuring Madonna)/Was Dog A Doughnut (12" remix, p/s)	10

(see also Madonna)

JELLY BEANS

64	Pye International 7N 25252	I Wanna Love Him So Bad/So Long	35
64	Red Bird RB 10011	The Kind Of Boy You Can't Forget/Baby Be Mine	30
75	Right On R 102	You Don't Mean Me No Good/I'm Hip To You	20

JELLYBREAD

69	Blue Horizon 57-3162	Chairman Mao's Boogaloo/No One Else	15
70	Blue Horizon 57-3169	Comment/Funky Wasp	15
70	Blue Horizon 57-3174	Rockin' Pneumonia And The Boogie-Woogie Flu/Readin' The Meters	15
70	Blue Horizon 57-3180	Old Man Hank/Faded Grace	15
71	Blue Horizon 2096 001	Creepin' And Crawlin'/The Loser/The Clergyman's Daughter	12
72	Blue Horizon 2096 006	Down Along The Cove/Sister Lucy	15
60s	Liphook 1	JELLYBREAD (mini-LP)	90
69	Blue Horizon 7-63853	FIRST SLICE (LP)	40
71	Blue Horizon 2431 002	65 PARKWAY (LP)	45
72	Blue Horizon 2931 004	BACK TO THE BEGINNING AGAIN (LP)	120

JELLYFISH

90	Charisma CUSS 2	Baby's Coming Back/All I Want Is Everything (Live) (p/s)	6
90	Charisma CUSCX 2	Baby's Coming Back (CD)	8
91	Charisma CUST 1	The King Is Half Undressed (12", p/s)	8
91	Charisma CUST 3	Now She Knows She's Wrong (12", p/s)	8
91	Charisma CUSCD 3	Now She Knows She's Wrong/Bedspring Kiss, Let 'Em In/That Is Why (Live)/ The King Is Half Undressed (Live) (CD)	8
91	Charisma CUSLP 3	BELLYBUTTON (LP)	12

JELLYS

98	Mission Impossible MIRVL1	WELCOME TO OUR WORLD (LP, with inner sleeve, mail-order only)	12

(see also Honeycrack, Wildhearts)

DIANNE JENKINS

76	Crystal CR 7025	Tow-A-Way-Zone/Anniversary	20

GORDON JENKINS ORCHESTRA

60	London HLR 9089	The Clock Song/Romantica	8

(see also Ella Fitzgerald)

JOHNNY JENKINS

69	Atco 226 009	The Voodoo In You/Backside Blues	10
71	Atco 2400 033	TON-TON MACOUTE (LP)	25

JENNIFER (WARNES)

69	London HLU 10278	Let The Sun Shine In/Easy To Be Hard	7
70	London HLU 10312	Cajun Train/Old Folks (Les Vieux)	8

JENNIFERS
92	Nude NUD 2T	Just Got Back Today/Rocks And Boulders/Danny's Song/	
		Tomorrow's Rain (12")	60
92	Nude NUD 2CD	Just Got Back Today/Rocks And Boulders/Danny's Song/	
		Tomorrow's Rain (CD)	80

(see also Supergrass)

BILL JENNINGS
55	Parlophone MSP 6146	Stuffy/Solitude (as Bill Jennings-Leo Parker Quintet)	6
55	Parlophone MSP 6156	Soft Winds/What's New? (as Bill Jennings Quartet)	6

WAYLON JENNINGS
69	RCA RCA 1866	The Days Of Sand And Shovels/Delia's Gone	6
80	RCA PB 9561	The Dukes Of Hazzard Theme/Storms Never Last (p/s)	5
68	RCA SF 8003	ONLY THE GREATEST (LP)	15
70	A&M Mayfair AMLB 1006	THE COUNTRY SIDE OF WAYLON JENNINGS (LP)	12
70	RCA Victor LSA 3000	BEST OF WAYLON JENNINGS (LP)	12
72	RCA Victor LSA 3053	CEDARTOWN, GEORGIA (LP)	12
74	RCA AFL1-0240	HONKY TONK HEROES (LP)	12
74	RCA AFL1-0539	THIS TIME (LP)	12

JENNORS
67	Coxsone CS 7024	Pressure And Slide (actually by Tennors)/SOUL BROTHERS: One Stop	25

(see also Tennors)

KRIS JENSEN
62	Fontana 267 241 TF	Torture/Let's Sit Down	15
63	Fontana 267 267 TF	Don't Take Her From Me/Claudette	15
64	Hickory 45-1224	Donna Donna/Big As I Can Dream	15
64	Hickory 45-1243	Lookin' For Love/In Time	10
64	Hickory 45-1256	Come Back To Me/You've Only Got Me To Lose	10
65	Hickory 45-1285	The Little Wind-Up Doll/Somebody's Smiling While I'm Crying	10
65	Hickory 45-1311	What Should I Do/That's A Whole Lotta Love	10

KRIS JENSEN/SUE THOMPSON
65	Hickory LPE 1507	INTRODUCING KRIS JENSEN AND SUE THOMPSON (EP, 2 tracks each)	22

(see also Sue Thompson)

PAUL JENSEN & CAR THIEVES
78	Albatross TIT 3	Holiday In Spain/Always Arrive On Time (p/s)	6

JENSENS
68	Philips BF 1686	Deep Thinking/Marguerite	12

(see also Tempus Fugit)

BILL JENTIES
70	Smash SMA 2307	Stop Them (actually by Bill Gentles)/MAXINE: I Don't Care	6

(see also Bill Gentles/Bill Jentles)

BILL JENTLES
70	Pama PM 809	True True Train/JEFF BARNES: Give And Take	12

(see also Bill Jenties)

JERICHO (JONES)
71	A&M AMS 833	Time Is Now/Freedom	5
72	A&M AMS 883	Don't Let Me Down/Mona Mona	10
72	A&M AMS 7017	Hey Man/Champs	10
72	A&M AMS 7037	Mama's Gonna Take You Home/So Come On	10
71	A&M AMLH 68050	JUNKIES, MONKEYS & DONKEYS (LP, as Jericho Jones)	100
72	A&M AMLS 68079	JERICHO (LP, beware of counterfeits with slightly thicker sleeves)	85

JERKS
78	Underground URA 1	Get Your Woofing Dog Off Me/Hold My Hand (p/s)	35
78	Lightning GIL 549	Cool/Jerkin' (p/s)	20
80	Laser LAS 25	Come Back Bogart (I Wish You Would)/Are You Strong Enough?/	
		The Strangest Man Of All (p/s)	15

JERMZ
78	One Way EFP 1	Power Cut/Me And My Baby (p/s)	200

JERRY JEROME
55	MGM SP 1118	Honey/In A Little Spanish Town	5

JERONIMO
70	Major Minor MM695	Hey Ya/Na Na Hey Hey Kiss Him Goodbye	7

JERRY & FREEDOM SINGERS
70	Banana BA 308	It's All In The Game (pseudonym for Winston Francis)/	
		IM: The Way To My Heart (pseudonym for Cedric Brooks)	15

(see also Winston Francis)

JERRY O
67	London HLZ 10162	Karate Boo-ga-loo/The Pearl	10
71	Jay Boy BOY 33	Karate Boo-ga-loo/The Pearl (reissue)	8
72	Jay Boy BOY 62	Dance What 'Cha Wanna/Afro-Twist Time	8

JERUSALEM
72	Deram DM 358	Kamakazi Moth/Frustration	42
72	Deram SDL 6	JERUSALEM (LP, gatefold sleeve)	90

(see also Pussy, Ian Gillan)

JERUSALEM
79	Praise PLP 4	JERUSALEM (LP, with insert)	20
80	Myrrh MYR 1097	VOLUME 2 (LP, with insert)	20
82	Myrrh MYR 1113	WARRIOR (LP)	20

MINT VALUE £

JESS & JAMES
68	MGM MGM 1389	Move/What Was I Born For	20
68	MGM MGM 1420	Something For Nothing/I Let The Day Go By (with J.J. Band)	20
68	MGM MGM 1454	Thank You Show Biz/Motherless Child	10

JESTERS
62	R&L RL 15/16	Little Girl/Casa Pedro (early labels blue and white)	30

JESTERS
73	Jam JAM 35	Fool For A Day/Can't Live Without You	20

JESUS & MARY CHAIN
84	Creation CRE 012	Upside Down/Vegetable Man (black & white wraparound p/s in poly bag with address on rear & name in red)	15
84	Creation CRE 012	Upside Down/Vegetable Man (red & white wraparound p/s with address on rear & name in black)	15
84	Creation CRE 012	Upside Down/Vegetable Man (pink, blue or yellow wraparound p/s in poly bag; some with small T-shirt offer insert)	8
86	Creation CRE 012	Upside Down/Vegetable Man (reissue, different printed p/s)	5
86	Creation CRE 012T	Upside Down/Vegetable Man/Upside Down (demo) (12" white label, no sleeve)	20
85	Blanco Y Negro NEG 008	Never Understand/Suck (p/s)	5
85	Blanco Y Negro NEG 17F	Just Like Honey/Head//Inside Me/Just Like Honey (Demo Oct 84) (double pack, gatefold p/s)	8
87	Blanco Y Negro NEGB 25	Happy When It Rains/Everything Is Alright When You're Down (box set with postcards)	7
89	Blanco Y Negro NEG 41TE	Blues From A Gun/Shimmer/Penetration/Break Me Down (10", gatefold p/s)	8
89	Blanco Y Negro NEG 42/XB/Y/Z	Head On/Terminal Beach//Head On/Deviant Slice//Head On/ I'm Glad I Never//Head On/In The Black (4 x 7" box set; each single sold separately)	12
85	Fierce FRIGHT 004	RIOT (EP, with 'LSD bar' & badge; 2 different sleeves)	25

(see also Acid Angels, Primal Scream, Meat Whiplash)

JESUS IS
70s	Myrrh MYR 1049	JESUS IS (LP)	15

JESUS LIZARD
92	own label	Gladiator (Marquee gig freebie)	8
93	Touch & Go TG 83	Puss/NIRVANA: Oh, The Guilt (p/s, blue vinyl, some with poster)	25/12
93	Touch & Go TG 83	Puss/NIRVANA: Oh, The Guilt (p/s, black vinyl)	18
93	Touch & Go TG 83CD	Puss/NIRVANA: Oh, The Guilt (CD)	20
93	Touch & Go TG 128	Fly On The Wall/White Hole (green vinyl)	5

(see also Nirvana)

JESUS LOVES YOU
89	More Protein PRTOX 12	After The Love (Fon Force Remix)/After The Love (Dub) (12", p/s)	8
89	More Protein PROCD 2	After The Love (10 Glorious Years Edit)/After The Love (10 Glorious Years Mix)/ After The Love (Orbital House Mix) (3" CD, card sleeve)	8
91	More Protein PROT 1312DJ	After The Love (Prophets Of Doom Mix)/(Naughty Norman Normal's Nightie Mix)/Generations Of Love (Absolutely Queer Remix) (12", p/s, promo only)	15
92	Virgin VSCDX 1449	Sweet Toxic Love (Deliverance Mix)/(Hootenanny Mix)/ Am I Losing Control (Disco Mix)/Am I Losing Control (Dizzy Tequila Mix) (CD, plastic clip-shut pack with booklet)	12

(see also Boy George, Culture Club)

JET
75	CBS 80699	JET (LP)	12

(see also Andy Ellison, Nice, Radio Stars, Sparks)

JET (Australia)
03	Warner Bros 7559-62866-1	Are You Gonna Be My Girl (Album Version)/Hey Kids/That's Alright Mama (12", gatefold p/s)	8
03	Warner Bros 7559 628861	DIRTY SWEET EP: Take It Or Leave It/Cold Hard Bitch/Move On/Rollover DJ (12", p/s)	8

JETHRO TULL
SINGLES
68	MGM MGM 1384	Sunshine Day/Aeroplane (miscredited to 'Jethro Toe'; counterfeits credit 'Jethro Tull')	250
68	Island WIP 6043	A Song For Jeffrey/One For John Gee	60
68	Island WIP 6048	Love Story/A Christmas Song (2 different pink label designs)	each 10
68	Island WIP 6048	Love Story/A Christmas Song (mispressing, B-side or both sides credited to Ian Henderson)	each 12
69	Island WIP 6056	Living In The Past/Driving Song (2 different pink labels)	each 15
69	Chrysalis WIP 6070	Sweet Dream/17 (push-out or large centre hole)	7
70	Chrysalis WIP 6077	The Witch's Promise/Teacher (some in p/s)	20/15
70	Chrysalis WIP 6081	Inside/Alive And Well And Living In	10
71	Chrysalis WIP 6098	Lick Your Fingers Clean/Up To Me (unissued)	
71	Chrysalis WIP 6106	Life Is A Long Song/Up The 'Pool/Dr. Bogenbroom/From Later/Nursie (EP, p/s)	8
74	Chrysalis CHS 2054	Bungle In The Jungle/Back Door Angels	6
75	Chrysalis CHS 2075	Minstrel In The Gallery/Summerday Sands	6
76	Chrysalis CHS 2086	Too Old To Rock'n'Roll: Too Young To Die/Rainbow Blues	5
76	Chrysalis CXP 2275	Ring Out Solstice Bells/March The Mad Scientist/A Christmas Song/ Pan Dance (EP)	8
77	Chrysalis CHS 2135	The Whistler/Strip Cartoon (some in p/s)	25/8
78	Chrysalis CHS 2214	Moths/Life Is A Long Song (p/s)	10
78	Chrysalis CHS 2260	A Stitch In Time (3.30 Version)/Sweet Dream (p/s, white or black vinyl)	12/8
78	Chrysalis CHS 2260	A Stitch In Time (4.20 Version)/Sweet Dream (p/s, white or black vinyl)	12/8
79	Chrysalis CHS 2378	North Sea Oil/Elegy (p/s)	10

79	Chrysalis CHS 2394	Home/King Henry's Madrigal (Theme From Mainstream)/Warm Sporran (p/s).... 12
79	Chrysalis CHS 2443	Ring Out Solstice Bells/March The Mad Scientist/A Christmas Song/ Pan Dance (EP, reissue) 7
79	Chrysalis CHS 2468	Working John, Working Joe/Flyingdale Flyer (p/s)......................... 8
80	Chrysalis CHS 2619	Broadsword/Fallen On Hard Times (p/s) 6
80	Chrysalis CHSP 2619	Broadsword/Fallen On Hard Times (picture disc) 12
84	Chrysalis TULLD 1	Lap Of Luxury/Astronomy//Automotive Engineering/Tundra (double pack, gatefold p/s) 10
84	Chrysalis TULL X 1	Lap Of Luxury/Astronomy/Automotive Engineering/Tundra (12", p/s) 10
86	Chrysalis TULL 2	Coronach (with David Palmer)/Jack Frost And The Hooded Crow (p/s)......... 7
86	Chrysalis TULLX 2	Coronach (with David Palmer)/Jack Frost And The Hooded Crow/ Living In The Past/Elegy (12", p/s) 40
87	Chrysalis TULLP 3	Steel Monkey/Down At The End Of Your Road (die-cut picture disc) 20
87	Chrysalis ZTULL 3	Steel Monkey/Down At The End Of Your Road/Too Many Too/I'm Your Gun (cassette, numbered edition of 3,000 with competition pack & badge) 15
87	Chrysalis TULLX 3	Steel Monkey/Down At The End Of Your Road/Too Many Too/I'm Your Gun (12", p/s).. 10
88	Chrysalis TULLX 4	Said She Was A Dancer/Dogs In The Midwinter/The Waking Edge (p/s)......... 8
88	Chrysalis TULLP 4	Said She Was A Dancer/Dogs In The Midwinter (shaped picture disc)......... 10
88	Chrysalis TULL X 4	Said She Was A Dancer/Dogs In The Midwinter (12", p/s) 8
88	Chrysalis TULLCD 4	Said She Was A Dancer/Dogs In The Midwinter/ Down At The End Of The Road/Too Many Too (CD, picture disc, limited issue) 25
88	Chrysalis TULPCD 1	Part Of The Machine (Edit)/Stormy Monday Blues (live)/Lick Your Fingers Clean/ Minstrel In The Gallery (live)/Farm On The Freeway (live) (CD, picture disc) 15
89	Chrysalis TULL 5	Another Christmas Song (p/s)... 10
89	Chrysalis TULLCD 5	Another Christmas Song/Intro — A Christmas Song (live)/Cheap Day Return — Mother Goose (live)/Outro — Locomotive Breath (live) (CD) 10
89	Chrysalis TULLX5	Another Christmas Song/Intro-A Christmas Song/Cheap Day Return-Mother Goose/Outro-Locomotive Breath (12" p/s)................................ 20
91	Chrysalis TULLX 6	This Is Not Love/Night In The Wilderness/Jump Start (12", p/s) 8
92	Chrysalis TULLCD 7	Rocks On The Road/Jack-A-Lynn (Home Demo)/Tall Thin Girl (live)/Fat Man (live)/Rocks On The Road/Bouree (live)/Mother Goose-Jack-A-Lynn (live)/ Aqualung — Locomotive Breath (live) (2-CD, boxed)...................... 8
92	Chrysalis TULLX 7	Rocks On The Road/Jack-A-Lynn (home demo)/ Aqualung-Locomotive Breath (live) (12", picture disc)................... 10
93	Chrysalis 12CHS 3970	Living In The Past (Club Mix)/Living In The Past (7" mix) Living In The Past (Dub Ravey Master)/Living In The Past (Dub N.Y. Mix) (12", p/s) 10
93	Chrysalis 23970/1	Living In The Past (Slightly More Recent) Past (live)/Silver River Turning/Rosa On The Factory Floor/I Don't Want To Be Me/Living In The Past/Truck Stop Runner/Piece Of Cake/Man Of Principle (2-CD set)..................... 8
99	Papillon BTFLYS 0001	Bends Like A Willow (edit)/Dot Com (edit)/It All Trickles Down (CD) 15

PROMOS

76	Chrysalis CHS 3 PDJ	Ring Out/Solstice Bells/March, The Mad Scientist/Christmas Song/ Pan Dance (12", p/s) 25
79	Chrysalis CHS018-PDJ	Dark Ages (Special Edited Version) (12" promo) 15
84	Chrysalis AS 1967	Under Wraps#1 (Electric)/Under Wraps#2 (Acoustic) (12", promo)........... 12
87	Chrysalis VAS 1039	Budapest (Special Radio Edit) (12", promo with illustrated sticker).......... 12
87	Chrysalis VAS 2796	Steel Monkey (12", promo) 12
87	Chrysalis VAS 2866	Farm On The Freeway (Special Rock Radio Edit) (12", promo) 15
88	Chrysalis VAS 1170	Part Of The Machine/Part Of The Machine (Edit) (12" promo with tour dates sticker) 18
89	Chrysalis DPRO 23418	Kissing Willy (CD, 1-track promo)....................................... 8
89	Chrysalis DPRO 04657	A Christmas Song (CD, 1-track promo) 8
95	Chrysalis CD Ian DJ1	Rare And Precious Chain/This Free Will (CD) 8
99	Roadrunner RR Promo 456	Dot.Com (CD, 1-track promo) 8
99	Fuel 2000 FLDPRO 1119	Bends Like A Willow (Radio Edit) (CD, 1-track promo).................... 10
03	RandM RR Promo 743	'Live In Europe 2003' With You There To Help Me (live)/Someday The Sun Won't Shine For You (live) (CD)................................. 12

ORIGINAL LPs

68	Island ILP 985	THIS WAS (1st pressing, pink label/black & orange 'circle' logo, mono) 110
68	Island ILPS 9085	THIS WAS (1st pressing, pink label/black & orange 'circle' logo, stereo, flipback sleeve, some sleeves as mono issues with stereo stickers).......... 45
69	Island ILPS 9103	STAND UP (1st pressing, pop-up sleeve, pink label/black & orange 'circle' logo) 45
70	Chrysalis ILPS 9123	BENEFIT (green Chrysalis or Island pink rim label/'palm tree' logo) 20
71	Island ILPS 9145	AQUALUNG (with gatefold sleeve & inner bag)........................... 20
72	Chrysalis CHR 1003	THICK AS A BRICK (fold-out newspaper sleeve).......................... 20
72	Chrysalis CJT 1	LIVING IN THE PAST (2-LP, with hard sleeve & booklet) 25
73	Chrysalis CHR 1040	A PASSION PLAY (with theatre booklet).................................. 15
74	Chrysalis CHR 1067	WARCHILD (with lyric inner sleeve) 12
75	Chrysalis CHR 1082	MINSTREL IN THE GALLERY (with lyric inner sleeve) 12
76	Chrysalis CHR 1111	TOO OLD TO ROCK 'N' ROLL 12
77	Chrysalis CJT 4	LIVE — BURSTING OUT (2-LP, gatefold sleeve with inners) 15

(First pressings of all above Chrysalis LPs have a white 'I' logo on the label.
Second pressings without this are worth slightly less)

84	Chrysalis CDLP 1461	UNDER WRAPS (picture disc)... 15
84	Chrysalis CHR 1078	MU — THE BEST OF (stickered sleeve, with poster) 15
88	Chrysalis Tbox1	20 YEARS OF JETHRO TULL (5-LP box set with 24-page booklet) 75
88	Chrysalis Tbox CD1	20 YEARS OF JETHRO TULL (3-CD box set with 24-page booklet) 50
89	Chrysalis CHRP 1708	ROCK ISLAND (Picture disc0 18
91	Chrysalis DCHR 1886	CATFISH RISING (Ltd edn. With 3-track 12" and lyric sheet inner sleeve)..... 20
92	Chrysalis CHR 1954	A LITTLE LIGHT MUSIC (2-LP).. 15
93	Chrysalis CDCHR 6004	JETHRO TULL 25th ANNIVERSARY (4-CD cigar box set with 48-page booklet) .. 55
95	Chrysalis CHR 6109	ROOTS TO BRANCHES (2-LP)... 15

MINT VALUE £

LP REPRESSINGS
68	Island ILP 985	THIS WAS (pink label/'i' logo, mono)	45
69	Island ILPS 9085	THIS WAS (pink label/black 'block' logo, 1st mix)	20
70	Island ILPS 9085	THIS WAS (pink label/'i' logo)	20
70	Chrysalis ILPS 9103	STAND UP (pop-up sleeve, pink label/black 'block' logo or pink label/'i' logo)	18/15

(see also Mick Abrahams, Blodwyn Pig, Wild Turkey, The John Even Band)

JETLINERS
66	Blue Beat BB 367	Meditation (actually by Sugar & Dandy)/GIRL SATCHMO: Nature Of Love (actually with Jetliners)	28

JETS
78	Soho SH 3	Rockabilly Baby/James Dean	5

JET SET
62	Delta DW 5001	VC 10/Cruising 600 (some in p/s)	15

JET SET
64	Parlophone R 5199	You Got Me Hooked/True To You	25

(see also Liza & Jet Set, Soulmates)

JETSET
80s	Shadows And Reflections	What Can I Say (Demo)/Christmas Greeting (flexidisc free with fanzine)	6/5
84	Dance Network NET 1	BEST OF THE JETSET (EP)	10
85	Dance Network NET 3	APRIL, MAY, JUNE AND THE JETSET (12" EP)	12
85	Dance Network WORK 1	THERE GOES THE NEIGHBOURHOOD (LP, pink sleeve)	20
86	Dance Network WORK 4	4 GO BANANAS (LP, with lyric insert)	20

(see also Paul Bevoir)

JETSTREAMS
59	Decca F 11149	Bongo Rock/Tiger (78 rpm = £40)	22

JEWELLS (Jamaica)
77	Observer OB 1101	Jah I/LEROY SMART: Jah Is My Light/I-ROY: Wicked Eat Dirt (12")	25

JEWELS
64	Colpix PX 11034	Opportunity/Gotta Find A Way	25
65	Colpix PX 11048	But I Do/Smokey Joe	18

JIGSAW
68	Polydor 56241	I Need Your Love/I've Gotta Get Me Some Money (as Jig-Saw Band)	8
68	Music Factory CUB 4	Mister Job/Great Idea	12
68	Music Factory CUB 6	Let Me Go Home/Tumblin'	80
68	MGM MGM 1410	One Way Street/Then I Found You	100
70	Philips 6006 112	One Way Street/Coffucious Confusion	40
70	Fontana 6007 017	Lollipop And Goody Man/Seven Fishes	40
71	Philips 6006 131	Jesu Joy Of Man's Desiring/No Questions Asked	7
71	Philips 6006 182	Keeping My Head Above Water/It's Nice But It's Wrong	7
71	Philips 6308 033	LETHERSLADE FARM (LP)	65
72	Philips 6308 072	AURORA BOREALIS (LP)	50
73	BASF 29106-5	BROKEN HEARTED (LP, gatefold sleeve)	20
74	BASF BAP 5051	I'VE SEEN THE FILM, I'VE READ THE BOOK (LP)	15

JIH
88	Jungle JUNG 32T/BOV 3	Take Me To The Girl/Come Summer Come Winter/Wake Up (12", unissued, Mayking test pressings only, white proof p/s)	20
88	Jungle JUNG 32T/BOV 3	Take Me To The Girl/Come Summer Come Winter/Wake Up (12", 'small photos' p/s, later blue art p/s)	10/7

(see also Associates)

JILL & BOULEVARDS
62	Columbia DB 4823	And Now I Cry/Eugene	22

JILL & Y'VERNS
60s	Oak RGJ 503	My Soulful Dress/Anything He Wants Me To Do	90

JILTED JOHN
78	Rabid TOSH 105	Jilted John/Going Steady (p/s)	12
78	EMI International INT 567	Jilted John/Going Steady (p/s, reissue)	6
78	EMI International INT 577	True Love/I Was A Pre-Pubescent (p/s)	7
78	EMI International INT 587	The Birthday Kiss/Baz's Party (p/s)	7
78	EMI Intl. INS 3024	TRUE LOVE STORIES (LP, some with board game insert)	18/12

(see also Going Red?)

JIM & JOE
64	London HL 9831	Fireball Mail/Daisy Mae	20

(see also James Burton)

JIM & MONICA
64	Stateside SS 266	Slippin' And Slidin'/Sing Along Without Jim & Monica	20

(see also Jimmy Gilmer & Fireballs)

JIMBILIN
71	Bamboo BAM 68	Human Race/Let Love In (both actually by Herman Chin-Loy & Aquarians)	15
75	Ashanti ASH 421	Balaclava/Tacku	12

JIMMIE & NIGHT HOPPERS
59	London HLP 8830	Cruisin'/Night Hop (78 rpm = £40)	30

JIVA
75	Dark Horse AMLH 22003	JIVA (LP, with inner sleeve)	12

JIV-A-TONES
58	Felsted AF 101	Flirty Gertie/Fire Engine Baby (78 rpm = £160)	275

JIVE FIVE
61	Parlophone R 4822	My True Story/When I Was Single	150
62	Stateside SS 133	What Time Is It?/Begging You Please	90
65	United Artists UP 1106	I'm A Happy Man/Kiss Kiss Kiss	35

JIVERS (U.S.)
56	Vogue V 9060	Little Mama/Cherie (78 rpm = £150)	675
57	Vogue V 9068	Ray Pearl/Dear Little One (78 rpm = £125)	650

JIVERS (Jamaica)
68	Trojan TR 604	Wear My Crown/Down On The Beach	8

(see also Brother Dan Allstars)

JIVING JUNIORS
60	Blue Beat BB 4	Lollipop Girl/Dearest Darling	35
60	Blue Beat BB 5	My Heart's Desire/I Love You	35
60	Starlite ST45 028	Lovers Line/Tu-Woo-Up-Tu-Woo	40
61	Starlite ST45 049	Slop & Mash/My Sweet Angel	40
61	Blue Beat BB 36	Over The River/Hip Rub (with Hersan & His City Slickers)	25
62	Island WI 003	Sugar Dandy/Valerie	20
62	Island WI 027	Andrea/Don't Leave Me	20
63	Island WI 129	Sugar Dandy/Valerie (reissue)	15
73	United Artists UP 35494	Stay/Call Me	5

(see also Duke Reid)

J.J. ALLSTARS
68	Duke DU 3	One Dollar Of Music/CARL DAWKINS: I'll Make It Up	20
69	Trojan TR 691	Memphis Underground (Parts 1 & 2)	18
70	Duke DU 94	Collecting Coins/Cabbage Leaf	12
70	Duke DU 95	This Land (actually by Carl Dawkins)/Land Version	12
70	Escort ES 821	Mango Tree/The Removers (both actually by Winston Wright & J.J. All Stars)	12
71	Big Shot BI 570	Perseverence Version/CARL DAWKINS: Perseverance	12
71	Explosion EX 2051	I Feel Good (Version 2)/CARL DAWKINS: I Feel Good	10

(see also Lloyd Young, Bleechers, Ethiopians)

JJ72
IRISH PRESSING
99	JJ 72 CD 01	Pillows (Oxygen)/Undercover Angel/Surrender (CD demo, some with handwritten note)	90/75

JJ'S POWERHOUSE
83	Sillysybin COX 1657	Running For The Line/Blackrods (no p/s)	250

DAMITA JO
(see under 'D')

MARCY JO & EDDIE RAMBEAU
63	Stateside SS 235	Lover's Medley/When You Wore A Tulip	10

(see also Eddie Rambeau)

ANTONIO CARLOS JOBIM
70	Paramount SPFL 260	THE ADVENTURERS (LP, soundtrack)	12
72	CTI CTL 3	STONE FLOWER (LP)	12

JOBRIATH
73	Elektra K 12129	Take Me I'm Yours/Earthling	5
74	Elektra K 12156	Ooh La La/Gone Tomorrow (demos £20)	5
73	Elektra EKS 75070	JOBRIATH (LP)	12
74	Elektra K 42163	CREATURES OF THE STREET (LP)	12

JO'BURG HAWK
72	Charisma CB 194	Orang Utang/Dark Side Of The Moon	5
73	Charisma CAS 1064	JO'BURG HAWK (LP, gatefold sleeve)	15

JOCK TAMSON'S BAIRNS
80	Temple TP 002	JOCK TAMSON'S BAIRNS (LP, with lyric insert)	12

JODIMARS
56	Capitol CL 14518	Well Now, Dig This/Let's All Rock Together (78 rpm = £20)	75
56	Capitol CL 14627	Rattle My Bones/Lotsa Love (78 rpm = £20)	75
56	Capitol CL 14641	Rattle Shakin' Daddy/Eat Your Heart Out Annie (78 rpm = £20)	75
56	Capitol CL 14642	Dance The Bop/Boom, Boom My Bayou Baby (78 rpm = £20)	75
56	Capitol CL 14663	Midnight/Clarabella (78 rpm = £20)	80
57	Capitol CL 14700	Cloud 99/Later (78 rpm = £25)	80
70s	Bulldog BD 16	Well Now, Dig This/Dance The Bop	5
72	Specialty SPE 6608	WELL NOW DIG THIS (LP)	20

(see also Bill Haley & Comets)

JODY GRIND
69	Transatlantic TRA 210	ONE STEP ON (LP)	60
70	Transatlantic TRA 221	FAR CANAL (LP)	60

AL T. JOE (& CELESTIALS)
62	Dice CC 9	Rise Jamaica/I'm On My Own	15
62	Blue Beat BB 126	You Cheated On Me/This Heart Of Mine (as Al T. Joe & Celestials)	12
63	Blue Beat BB 166	Goodbye Dreamboat/Please Forgive Me	12
63	Blue Beat BB 169	Fatso/Slow Boat	12
70	Duke DU 70	It's A Shame/Desertion	8
72	Duke DU 148	Vision/Young And Unlearned	5
72	Dynamic DYN 429	Oh What A Price/The Prisoners Song	5

(see also Jamaica Fats)

JOE & ANN
65	Black Swan WI 468	Gee Baby/Wherever You May Be	20

CALYPSO JOE

69	Escort ES 801	Adults Only/Calalue	8

BILLY JOE & CHECKMATES
61	London HLU 9502	Percolator/Round & Round & Round & Round	8

JOE COOL (& THE KILLERS)
77	Ariola ARO 105	I Just Don't Care/My Way (p/s)	25

JOE & EDDIE
59	Capitol CL 15038	Green Grass/And I Believed	7
64	Vocalion V 9215	There's A Meetin' Here Tonight/Lonesome Traveller	10
65	Vocalion V 9238	Gabrielle/He's Got The Whole World In His Hands	10
65	Vocalion V 9242	Depend On Yourself/With You In Mind	10
65	Vocalion V-N 9246	Farewell/Hey Nelly Nelly	10
65	Vocalion V-P 9250	Walkin' Down The Line/It Ain't Me Babe	15

BILLY JOEL
72	Philips 6078 001	She's Got A Way/Everybody Loves You Now	6
74	Philips 6078 018	The Ballad Of Billy The Kid/If I Only Had The Words (To Tell You) (some in p/s)	35/25
78	CBS SCBS 6821	My Life/She's Always A Woman	5
79	CBS 7150	Honesty/Root Beer Rag (withdrawn)	20
80	CBS SCBS 8753	It's Still Rock And Roll To Me/Through The Long Night (p/s)	5
83	CBS A 3655	Tell Her About It/Easy Money (p/s)	5
83	CBS A 4280	The Longest Time/Captain Jack (p/s)	5
83	CBS TA 4521	Leave A Tender Moment Alone/Goodnight Saigon/You May Be Right/Movin' Out/Big Shot (12", p/s)	8
83	CBS A 4884	This Night/I'll Cry Instead (p/s; in gatefold p/s [GA 4884])	7
86	CBS DA 7247	Modern Woman/Sleep With The Television On//Up Town/All For Love (double pack)	12
86	CBS 6500 577	A Matter Of Trust/Better Than Nothing (p/s)	5
89	CBS JOEL 1	We Didn't Start The Fire/House Of Blue Light (p/s)	5
72	Philips 6369 150	COLD SPRING HARBOR (LP)	18
73	Philips 6369 160	PIANO MAN (LP, withdrawn)	25
73	Philips 6078 018	BALLAD OF BILLY THE KID (LP)	15
78	CBS H 82311	THE STRANGER (LP, half-speed master version)	15
79	CBS 66352	BILLY JOEL (3-LP box set)	18

(see also Hassles)

JOE 9T & THUNDERBIRDS
80s	Gemme JOE 9T/LYN 6526	Joe 9T Theme/THEY MUST BE RUSSIANS: Psycho Analysis (p/s, stamped white label)	7

(see also They Must Be Russians)

JOE PUBLIC
70s	Wavelength HURT 3	Herman's Back/Travelling With Raymond/Like It (p/s)	8

JOE PUBLIC
85	Capital CLA 55	Anti CND	20

(see also Long Tall Shorty)

JOE'S ALLSTARS
69	Joe/Duke DU 24	Hey Jude/Musical Feet	15
69	Joe/Duke DU 28	Battle Cry Of Biafra/Funky Reggae Part 1	12
69	Joe/Duke DU 50	Brixton Cat/Solitude	15
70	Joe JRS 9	Tony B's Theme/JOE THE BOSS: Skinhead Revolt	100+
72	Sioux SI 012	Tony B's Theme/RAY MARTELL: She Caught The Train	20
70	Trojan TBL 106	BRIXTON CAT (LP)	25

(see also Joe The Boss, Dice The Boss, King Horror, Pattie La Donne)

JOE SOAP
73	Polydor 2383 233	KEEP IT CLEAN (LP)	18

JOE (Mansano) THE BOSS
70	Joe JRS 6	Son Of Al Capone/All My Enemies	22
70	Joe JRS 10	If Life Was A Thing/LLOYD KINGPIN: Daisy Bothering	15

(see also Joe's Allstars, Joe Mansano, Dice The Boss, Pama Dice)

JOEY & CONTINENTALS
70	Polydor 56520	She Rides With Me/Rudy Vadoo	55

(see also G.T.O.'s)

JOEY & GENTLEMEN
64	Fontana TF 444	Like I Love You/I'll Never Let You Go	12
64	Fontana TF 485	Dummy Dum Song/Goodbye Little Girl	6

HENRIK JOHANSEN'S JAZZ BAND
55	Tempo EXA 23	THE TRADITIONAL DANES (EP)	8
57	Tempo EXA 64	HENRIK JOHANSEN'S JAZZ BAND (EP)	8

(see also City Ramblers Skiffle Group, Al Fairweather)

ALEXSANDER JOHN
70s	Myrrh MYR 1010	DAYS GO BY (LP)	18

ANDREW JOHN
71	CBS 7017	Streets Of London/Rick Rack	5
72	CBS 64835	THE MACHINE STOPS (LP)	12

BASIL JOHN
60s	Planetone RC 12	Drink And Drive/MIKE ELLIOTT: J.K. Shuffle	10

CLIVE JOHN
75	United Artists UAS 29733	YOU ALWAYS KNOW WHERE YOU STAND WITH A BUZZARD (LP)	15

(see also Man)

JOHN AND ROSALIND
(see under Ross Hannaman)

DAVID JOHN & MOOD

64	Vocalion V 9220	To Catch That Man/Pretty Thing	225
65	Parlophone R 5255	Bring It To Jerome/I Love To See You Strut	200
65	Parlophone R 5301	Diggin' For Gold/She's Fine	200

(these singles do NOT feature David Bowie; see also Gagalactyca, Astral Navigations, Little Free Rock)

ELTON JOHN
PHILIPS SINGLES

68	Philips BF 1643	I've Been Loving You/Here's To The Next Time	250
69	Philips BF 1739	Lady Samantha/All Across The Havens	75

DJM SINGLES

69	DJM DJS 205	It's Me That You Need/Just Like Strange Rain (some in p/s)	90/50
70	DJM DJS 217	Border Song/Bad Side Of The Moon	25
70	DJM DJS 222	Rock And Roll Madonna/Grey Seal	30
71	DJM DJS 233	Your Song/Into The Old Man's Shoes	7
71	DJM DJS 244	Friends/Honey Roll	12
72	DJM DJX 501	Rocket Man/Holiday Inn/Goodbye (gatefold p/s)	20
72	DJM DJX 501	Rocket Man/Holiday Inn/Goodbye (plain p/s)	7
72	DJM DJS 269	Honky Cat/Lady Samantha/It's Me That You Need	10
72	DJM DJS 271	Crocodile Rock/Elderberry Wine	7
73	DJM DJS 275	Daniel/Skyline Pigeon	7
73	DJM DJX 502	Saturday Night's Alright For Fighting/Jack Rabbit/Whenever You're Ready (We'll Go Steady Again) (p/s)	10
73	DJM DJS 285	Goodbye Yellow Brick Road/Screw You	7
73	DJM DJS 290	Step Into Christmas/Ho! Ho! Ho! (Who'd Be A Turkey At Christmas)	10
73	DJM DJS 10705	Benny And The Jets/Rock 'N' Roll Madonna	7
74	DJM DJS 297	Candle In The Wind/Benny And The Jets	7
74	DJM DJS 302	Don't Let The Sun Go Down On Me/Sick City	7
74	DJM DJS 322	The Bitch Is Back/Cold Highway	7
74	DJM DJS 340	Lucy In The Sky With Diamonds (featuring Dr. Winston O'Boogie [John Lennon] & His Reggae Guitars)/One Day At A Time	9
75	DJM DJS 354	Philadelphia Freedom/I Saw Her Standing There (as Elton John Band; B-side featuring John Lennon with Muscle Shoals Horns) (p/s)	18
75	DJM DJS 385	Someone Saved My Life Tonight/House Of Cards	5
75	DJM DJS 610	Island Girl/Sugar On The Floor (p/s)	9
76	DJM DJS 629	Grow Some Funk Of Your Own/I Feel Like A Bullet (In The Gun Of Robert Ford)	5
76	DJM DJS 652	Pinball Wizard/Harmony	5
77	DJM DJR 18001	FOUR FROM FOUR EYES (EP)	15
78	DJM DJS 10902	Your Song/Border Song (p/s)	15
78	DJM DJS 10903	Honky Cat/Sixty Years On (p/s)	10
78	DJM DJS 10904	Country Comfort/Crocodile Rock (p/s)	10
78	DJM DJS 10905	Rocket Man/Daniel (p/s)	10
78	DJM DJS 10908	Candle In The Wind/I Feel Like A Bullet (In The Gun Of Robert Ford) (p/s, limited edition)	15
78	DJM DJS 10910	Island Girl/Saturday Night's Alright For Fighting (p/s, limited edition)	15
78	DJM DJS 10911	Philadelphia Freedom/Lucy In The Sky With Diamonds (reissue)	15
78	DJM DJS 10912	Pinball Wizard/Benny And The Jets (p/s)	10
78	DJM EJ 12	THE ELTON JOHN SINGLES COLLECTION (12 x 7" box set [DJS 10901-12])	95
78	DJM DJT 15000	FUNERAL FOR A FRIEND (12" EP)	16
80	DJM DJS 10961	Harmony/Mona Lisas And Mad Hatters (glossy p/s)	8
81	DJM DJS 10965	I Saw Her Standing There/Whatever Gets You Thru The Night/Lucy In The Sky With Diamonds (EP, p/s, featuring John Lennon & Muscle Shoals Horns)	14

ROCKET SINGLES

76	Rocket ROKN 512	Don't Go Breaking My Heart/Snow Queen (with Kiki Dee, p/s)	5
76	Rocket ROKN 517	Sorry Seems To Be The Hardest Word/Shoulder Holster (some in p/s)	7/5
77	Rocket ROKN 521	Crazy Water/Chameleon	5
77	Rocket GOALD 1	The Goaldigger Song/Jimmy, Brian, Elton, Eric (mail-order, signed, 500 only)	350
77	Rocket ROKN 526	Bite Your Lip (Get Up And Dance) (Remix)/KIKI DEE: Chicago	5
77	Rocket RU 1	Bite Your Lip (Get Up And Dance) (Remix)/KIKI DEE: Chicago (12", p/s)	10
78	Rocket ROKN 538	Ego/Flintstone Boy (p/s)	7
78	Rocket XPRES 1	Part Time Love/I Cry At Night (p/s)	10
78	Rocket XPRES 5	Song For Guy/Lovesick	5
78	Rocket DJS 10909	The Bitch Is Back/Grow Some Funk Of Your Own (p/s)	15
79	Rocket XPRES 13	Are You Ready For Love Pts 1 & 2	10
79	Rocket XPRES 1312	Are You Ready For Love Pts 1 & 2 (12", p/s)	15
79	Rocket XPRES 20	Mama Can't Buy You Love/Strangers (p/s; withdrawn, misspelt "Mamma")	350
79	Rocket XPRES 21	The Victim Of Love/Strangers (p/s)	10
79	Rocket XPRES 24	Johnny B. Goode/Thunder In The Night (p/s)	5
79	Rocket XPRES 2412	Johnny B. Goode/Thunder In The Night (12", p/s)	14
80	Rocket XPRES 41	Sartorial Eloquence/White Man Danger/Cartier (p/s)	8
80	Rocket XPRES 45	Dear God/Tactics (company sleeve)	45
80	Rocket ELTON 1	Dear God/Tactics//Steal Away Child/Love So Cold (double pack, p/s)	18
81	Rocket XPRES 54	Nobody Wins/Fools In Fashions (p/s)	5
81	Rocket XPRES 59	Just Like Belgium/Can't Get Over Getting Over Losing You (company sleeve)	5
82	Rocket XPRES 77	Empty Garden/Take Me Down To The Ocean (p/s)	5
82	Rocket XPPIC 77	Empty Garden/Take Me Down To The Ocean (picture disc)	15
82	Rocket XPRES 85	Princess/The Retreat (p/s)	5
82	Rocket XPRES 88	All Quiet On The Western Front/Where Have All The Good Times Gone (p/s)	7
82	Rocket XPRPO 88	All Quiet On The Western Front/Where Have All The Good Times Gone (poster p/s)	25
83	Rocket XPRES 91	That's Why They Call It The Blues/Lord Choc Ice Goes Mental ('raised musical note' sleeve with shorter A-side title)	25
83	Rocket XPRES 91	I Guess That's Why They Call It The Blues/Lord Choc Ice Goes Mental ('raised musical note' sleeve)	8

83	Rocket EJPIC 1	I'm Still Standing/Earn While You Learn (piano-shaped picture disc)	25
83	Rocket EJS 112	I'm Still Standing (Extended Mix)/Earn While You Learn (12", p/s)	10
83	Rocket EJS 2/FREEJ 2	Kiss The Bride/Dreamboat//Ego/Song For Guy (double pack, p/s)	25
83	Rocket EJS 212	Kiss The Bride (Full Version)/Dreamboat (12", p/s)	8
83	Rocket EJS 3/2	Cold As Christmas/Crystal//Don't Go Breaking My Heart/Snow Queen (double pack, gatefold p/s, 2nd 45 with Kiki Dee)	25
83	Rocket EJS 312	Cold As Christmas/Crystal/J'Veux De La Tendresse (12", p/s)	8
84	Rocket PHPIC 7	Sad Songs (Say So Much) /Simple Man (hat-shaped picture disc)	10
84	Rocket EJS 512	Passengers/Lonely Boy (12", p/s)	10
85	Rocket EJS 7	Breaking Hearts (Ain't what It Used To Be)/Neon (p/s)	5
85	Rocket EJS 8	Act Of War (Part 1)/(Part 2) (with Millie Jackson, 'concertina pack' of video stills)	15
85	Rocket EJSR 8	Act Of War (Part 5) (1-sided promo, p/s lists 2 tracks & 12" cat. no.)	15
85	Rocket EJSR 812	Act Of War (Part 5)/Act Of War (Part 6) (Instrumental) (12", p/s)	15
85	Rocket EJSD 9	Nikita/The Man Who Never Died//Sorry Seems To Be The Hardest Word (live)/ I'm Still Standing (live) (double pack, gatefold p/s, some pop-up)	10/6
85	Rocket EJS 10/EJS 9	Wrap Her Up/Restless (live)//Nikita/The Man Who Never Died (double pack, stickered gatefold PVC wallet with 2 separate p/s)	20
85	Rocket EJSC 10	Wrap Her Up/Restless (live) (with George Michael, open-out 'cube' p/s)	18
85	Rocket EJPIC 10	Wrap Her Up/Restless (live) (with George Michael, oblong-shaped picture disc)	18
85	Rocket EJSP 10	Wrap Her Up/Restless (live) (with George Michael, oblong-shaped picture disc, with pictures on wrong sides)	55
85	Rocket EJS 1012/ELTON 1	Wrap Her Up (Extended Remix) (with George Michael)/Restless (live)/ Nikita/Cold As Christmas (12", double pack in stickered PVC sleeve)	25
85	Rocket EJS 1112	Cry To Heaven/Candy By The Pound/Your Song (12", p/s)	10
86	Rocket EJSD 11	Cry To Heaven/Candy By The Pound//Rock'n'Roll Medley/Your Song (double pack, gatefold p/s)	8
86	Rocket EJSD 12	Heartache All Over The World/Highlander//Passengers/I'm Still Standing (double pack, gatefold p/s)	7
86	Rocket EJSP 13	Slow Rivers (with Cliff Richard)/Billy & The Kids (picture disc)	18
86	Rocket EJS 13-12	Slow Rivers (with Cliff Richard)/Billy & The Kids/Lord Of The Flies (12", p/s)	12
87	Rocket EJS 14	Your Song (live)/Don't Let The Sun Go Down On Me (live) (p/s)	5
87	Rocket EJS 1412	Your Song/Need You To Turn To/Greatest Discovery/Don't Let The Sun Go Down On Me (all tracks live in Australia) (12", p/s)	12
88	Rocket EJSP 15	Candle In The Wind (live)/Sorry Seems To Be The Hardest Word (live) (picture disc)	15
88	Rocket EJS 1512	Candle In The Wind (live)/Sorry Seems To Be The Hardest Word (live)/ Your Song (live)/Don't Let The Sun Go Down On Me (live) (12", p/s)	12
88	Rocket EJSCD 15	Candle In The Wind (live)/Sorry Seems To Be The Hardest Word (live)/ Your Song (live)/Don't Let The Sun Go Down On Me (live) (CD, card sleeve)	18
88	Rocket EJSIP 16	I Don't Wanna Go On With You Like That/Rope Around A Fool/ (Radio 1 interview) (33rpm, poster sleeve)	18
88	Rocket EJS 1612	I Don't Wanna Go On With You Like That (Remix)//(7" Version)/ Rope Around A Fool (12", blue vinyl factory custom pressing, no p/s)	150
88	Rocket EJSCD 16	I Don't Wanna Go On With You Like That/Rope Around A Fool/ I Don't Wanna Go On With You Like That (Extended Mix) (CD, card p/s)	10
88	Rocket EJSLB 17	Town Of Plenty (with Pete Townshend)/Whipping Boy ('look back' pack in box with 4 photos)	12
88	Rocket EJSCD 17	Town Of Plenty (with Pete Townshend)/Whipping Boy/My Baby's A Saint/ I Guess That's Why They Call It The Blues (CD, card p/s)	12
88	Rocket EJSCD 18	A Word In Spanish/Heavy Traffic/Live Medley (Song For You/Blue Eyes/ I Guess That's Why They Call It The Blues)/Daniel (live) (CD, card p/s)	12
88	Rocket 080 524 2	I Don't Wanna Go On With You Like That (CD Video)	20
88	Rocket 080 272 2	Nikita (CD Video)	20
89	Rocket EJSCD 19	Healing Hands/Sad Songs (Say So Much) (live)/Dancing In The End Zone (CD)	15
89	Rocket EJSCD 20	Sacrifice/Love Is A Cannibal/Durban Deep (CD)	15
90	Rocket EJS 21	Club At The End Of The Street/Give Peace A Chance (p/s, withdrawn)	500
90	Rocket EJSCD 21	Club At The End Of The Street/Give Peace A Chance/ I Don't Wanna Go On With You Like That (Live In Verona) (CD, withdrawn, with "Made In England" credit)	45
90	Rocket EJS 2312	Club At The End Of The Street/Whispers/I Don't Wanna Go On With You Like That (Live in Verona) (12", p/s)	8
90	Rocket EJSG 24	You Gotta Love Someone/Sacrifice (gatefold p/s with discography, dbl A-side)	8
90	Rocket EJSX 25	Step Into Xmas/Cold As Christmas/Easier To Walk Away/ I Swear I Heard The Night Talking ('Xmas EP', 33rpm, gatefold p/s)	12
94	Rocket EJSJB 35	Circle Of Life (Elton's Version)/(Soundtrack Version) (jukebox issue, no p/s)	5
95	Rocket EJSJB 36	Believe/The One (live) (jukebox 7", no p/s)	5
95	Rocket EJSDD 36	Believe/The One/Sorry Seems To Be The Hardest Word//Last Song (live)/ Believe (live) (2-CD, in box)	15
95	Rocket EJSCD 38	Blessed/Made In England (Junior's Sound Factory Mix)/ Made In England (Junior's Joyous Mix) (CD, Part 1 of a 2-CD set, withdrawn)	25
95	Rocket EJSDD 38	Blessed/Honky Cat (live)/Take Me To The Pilot (live)/ The Bitch Is Back (live) (CD, withdrawn)	25
96	Rocket LLHJB 1	Live Like Horses (Studio Version)/(Live Finale Version) (jukebox issue, no p/s)	5
97	Rocket EJSCD 41	Something About The Way You Look Tonight (Edited Version)/ I Know Why I'm In Love/No Valentines/Something About The Way You Look Tonight (Album Version) (CD, card sleeve, unreleased)	40
97	Rocket EJSCX 41	Something About The Way You Look Tonight (Edited Version)/ I Know Why I'm In Love/You Can Make History (Young Again)/ Something About The Way You Look Tonight (Album Version) (CD, digipak, unreleased)	75

OTHER SINGLES

81	Ariola ARO 269	Loving You Is Sweeter Than Ever/Twenty Four Hours (p/s, with Kiki Dee)	7

DJM LPs

69	DJM DJLP 403	EMPTY SKY (gatefold sleeve, mono)	150
69	DJM DJLPS 403	EMPTY SKY (gatefold sleeve, stereo, with 'stereo' sticker on sleeve)	20
70	DJM DJLPS 406	ELTON JOHN (textured gatefold sleeve, later smooth)	15/12
70	DJM DJLPS 410	TUMBLEWEED CONNECTION (gatefold sleeve with stapled booklet)	12
71	DJM DJLPS 414	17.11.70.	12
71	DJM DJLPH 420	MADMAN ACROSS THE WATER (gatefold sleeve)	12
72	DJM DJLPH 427	DON'T SHOOT ME, I'M ONLY THE PIANO PLAYER (gatefold sleeve, with booklet)	12
72	DJM DJLPH 423	HONKY CHATEAU (gatefold sleeve, with foldover flap & pasted photo on cover)	20
74	DJM DJLPH 439	CARIBOU (with inner)	12
75	DJM DJLPH 464	ROCK OF THE WESTIES (with inner & insert)	12
76	DJM DJLPH 473	HERE AND THERE (with inner)	12
76	DJM DJE 29001	GOODBYE YELLOW BRICK ROAD (2-LP, yellow vinyl, triplefold sleeve)	25
77	DJM DJLPH 20473	GREATEST HITS VOLUME TWO (with inner sleeve & lyric booklet)	12
78	DJM DJV 2300	CAPTAIN FANTASTIC AND THE BROWN DIRT COWBOY (picture disc)	75
78	DJM LSP 14512	ELTON JOHN (5-LP, box set)	55
80	DJM DJS 22085	LADY SAMANTHA	12

OTHER LPs

70	Warlock Music WMM 101/2	WARLOCK MUSIC SAMPLER (untitled publishing sampler, 7 tracks by Elton, 4 by Linda Peters)	1,000
71	Paramount SPFL 269	FRIENDS (soundtrack)	25
78	St. Michael 2094 0102	CANDLE IN THE WIND (Marks & Spencer issue)	45
84	Cambra CR 130	SEASONS: THE EARLY LOVE SONGS (2-cassette set, withdrawn, includes unique track, "The Tide Will Turn For Rebecca")	15
87	Rocket EJBXL 1	LIVE IN AUSTRALIA WITH THE MELBOURNE SYMPHONY ORCHESTRA (2-LP box set, numbered banded sleeve, 3,000 only)	30

CDs

87	Rocket EJBXD 1	LIVE IN AUSTRALIA WITH THE MELBOURNE SYMPHONY ORCHESTRA (2-CD box set, 3,000 only)	40
83	DJM CD 4/8100 622	THE SUPERIOR SOUND OF ELTON JOHN 1970-1975	25
91	Rocket 848 236-2	TO BE CONTINUED ... THE VERY BEST OF ELTON JOHN (4-CD, 12" x 8" box set with large colour booklet)	120
93	Happenstance HAPP 001	PLAYS THE SIRAN (private pressing, 50 only)	1000+
93	Happenstance HAPP 002	THE FISHING TRIP (4-CD set, private pressing, 100 only, existence unconfirmed)	700+
97	Rocket ELTON 50	CELEBRATING ELTON JOHN'S 50TH BIRTHDAY (promo only)	50
99	Mercury ADV 1999/1	AIDA (with Sir Tim Rice) (box set with wallet, plinth stand, interview CD, booklet and calender cards, promo only)	75
99	Mercury ADV 1999/1	AIDA PRESS KIT (card box set with wallet, plinth stand, interview CD, booklet, calender cards, scented candle and broadcast CD-R, promo only)	50
99	Rocket STAR 3	ELTON JOHN'S AIDA (export CD, card p/s, promo only)	40

(see also [Stu Brown &] Bluesology, Bread & Beer Band, Neil Sedaka, Kiki Dee, Aretha Franklin, Jennifer Rush, Dionne Warwick Radio Heart)

LITTLE WILLIE JOHN

56	Parlophone DP 510	All Around The World/Don't Leave Me Dear (78, export issue)	50
56	Parlophone R 4209	Fever/Letter From My Darling (78 rpm = £50)	125
58	Parlophone R 4396	Uh, Uh, Baby/Dinner Date (With His Girl Friend) (78 rpm = £45)	50
58	Parlophone R 4432	Talk To Me, Talk To Me/Spasms (78 rpm = £45)	50
58	Parlophone R 4472	Let's Rock While The Rockin's Good/You're A Sweetheart (78 rpm = £55)	70
59	Parlophone R 4571	Leave My Kitten Alone/Let Nobody Love You	50
60	Parlophone R 4674	Heartbreak (It's Hurtin' Me)/Do You Love Me	30
60	Parlophone R 4699	Sleep/There's A Difference	35
61	Parlophone R 4728	Walk Slow/HANK BALLARD: The Hoochie Coochie Coo	40
59	Parlophone PMC 1163	SURE THINGS (LP)	175
64	London HA 8126	COME ON AND JOIN LITTLE WILLIE JOHN (LP)	100

MABLE JOHN

66	Atlantic 584 022	It's Catching/Your Good Thing (Is About To End)	12
67	Stax 601 010	Same Time Same Place/Bigger And Better (dark blue or light blue label)	15/10
68	Stax 601 034	Able Mable/Don't Get Caught	10

ROBERT JOHN

68	CBS 3436	If You Don't Want My Love/Don't.	15
68	CBS 3730	Don't Leave Me/Children	5
68	A&M AMS 835	Raindrops Love And Sunshine/When The Party Is Over	40

SAMMIE JOHN

67	Stateside SS 585	Little John/Boss Bag	20

JOHN & JOHNNY

63	Decca F 11719	I Want You To Be My Girl/It's You	6

JOHN & PAUL

65	London HLU 9997	People Say/I'm Walkin'	15

JOHN LEE'S GROUNDHOGS

66	Planet PLF 104	Over You Baby/I'll Never Fall In Love Again	150

(see also Groundhogs, Tony McPhee)

JOHNNY & JACK

54	HMV 7MC 21	Honey, I Need You/Goodnight, Well It's Time To Go (export issue)	18
55	HMV JO 440	Beware Of "It"/Kiss Crazy Baby (78, export)	15
56	HMV JO 456	Weary Moments/S.O.S. (78, export)	15
59	RCA RCA 1145	Sailor Man/Wild And Wicked World (78 rpm = £22)	6
59	RCA RCX 176	COUNTRY GUITAR VOL. 10 (EP)	12

MINT VALUE £

JOHNNIE & JOE
58	London HLM 8682	Over The Mountain, Across The Sea/My Baby's Gone, On, On (78 rpm = £75)	350

JOHNNY (Osborne) & ATTRACTIONS
67	Doctor Bird DB 1118	Young Wings Can Fly/DUDLEY WILLIAMSON: I'm Moving On	45

JOHNNY (STEVENS) & THE BLUE BEATS
64	Blue Beat BB 229	Shame/Ball And Chain	16

JOHNNY & CHAZ & GUNNERS
61	Decca F 11365	Bobby/Out Of Luck	22

JOHNNY & THE COPYCATS
64	Norco AB 102	I'm A Hog For You Baby/I Can Never See You	60

(see also My Dear Watson)

JOHNNY & THE HURRICANES
59	London HL 8899	Crossfire/Lazy (initially triangular-centre, later round centre)	30/22
59	London HL 8899	Crossfire/Lazy (78)	95
59	London HL 8948	Red River Rock/Buckeye (initially triangular-centre, later round centre)	12/6
59	London HL 8948	Red River Rock/Buckeye (78)	75
59	London HL 9017	Reveille Rock/Time Bomb (initially triangular-centre, later round centre)	15/6
59	London HL 9017	Reveille Rock/Time Bomb(78)	100
60	London HLI 9072	Beatnick Fly/Sand Storm (78 rpm = £110)	7
60	London HLX 9134	Down Yonder/Sheba (78 rpm = £175)	7
60	London HLX 9190	Rocking Goose/Revival (78 rpm = £200)	7
60	London HL 7099	The Hep Canary/Catnip (export issue)	45
61	London HLX 9289	Ja-Da/Mr. Lonely	7
61	London HLX 9378	High Voltage/Old Smokie	7
62	London HLX 9491	Farewell, Farewell/Traffic Jam	7
62	London HLX 7116	You Are My Sunshine/Farewell, Farewell (export issue)	30
62	London HLX 9536	Salvation/Misirlou	18
62	London HLX 9617	Minnesota Fats/Come On Train	6
63	London HLX 9660	Whatever Happened To Baby Jane/Greens And Beans	6
68	London HLX 10199	Rocking Goose/Beatnik Fly (reissue)	5
64	Stateside SS 347	Money Honey/That's All	18
61	London REX 1284	ROCKING GOOSE (EP)	35
62	London REX 1347	JOHNNY AND THE HURRICANES (EP)	35
64	London REX 1414	JOHNNY AND THE HURRICANES VOL. 2 (EP)	40
60	London HA 2227	RED RIVER ROCK (LP, plum label; reissues on black label £18)	55
60	London HA-I 2269	STORMSVILLE (LP)	45
61	London HA-X 2322	THE BIG SOUND OF JOHNNY AND THE HURRICANES (LP)	55

JOHNNY & JAMMERS
79	Big Beat NS 55	School Day Blues/You Know I Love You (p/s)	5

(see also Johnny Winter)

JOHNNY & JOHN
66	Polydor 56087	Bumper To Bumper/Scrape My Boot	15

(see also Johnny Gustafson, Big Three)

JOHNNY & JUDY
59	Vogue Pop V 9128	Bother Me Baby/Who's To Say (78 rpm = £150)	650

(see also John Walker)

JOHNNY & THE SELF ABUSERS
77	Chiswick NS 22	Saints And Sinners/Dead Vandals (p/s)	25

(see also Simple Minds)

JOHNNY & VIBRATONES
63	Warner Bros WB 107	Bird Stompin'/Movin' The Bird	12

JOHNNY F & KLM
92	Liberty Grooves LIB003	TAKIN' LIBERTIES VOL 1 (LP)	20

JOHNNY MOPED
76	Chiswick PROMO 3	BASICALLY, THE ORIGINAL JOHNNY MOPED TAPE (33rpm, no p/s)	15
77	Chiswick S 15	No-One/Incendiary Device (p/s)	7
78	Chiswick NS 27	Darling, Let's Have Another Baby/Something Else/It Really Digs (p/s)	6
78	Chiswick NS 41	Little Queenie/Hard Lovin' Man (p/s)	6
78	Chiswick WIK 8	CYCLEDELIC (LP, some with free single [PROMO 3])	30/12

(see also Slime, Maxim's Trash)

JOHNNY'S BOYS
59	Decca F 11156	Sleep Walk/Ciao Ciao Bambina (78 rpm = £10)	12

JOHNNY'S JAZZ
56	Decca FJ 10663	R.J. Boogie/Get Happy (featuring Johnny Hawksworth)	6

(see also Johnny Hawksworth)

GLYN JOHNS
62	Decca F 11478	January Blues/Sioux Indian	5
63	Decca F 11753	Old Deceiver Time/Dancing With You	5
65	Immediate IM 013	Mary Anne/Like Grains Of Yellow Sand	20
65	Pye 7N 15818	I'll Follow The Sun/I'll Take You Dancing	5
60s	Westcot LYN 827/828	Today You're Gone/Such Stuff Of Dreams (freebie with jeans offer)	5

GLYNIS JOHNS
54	Columbia SCM 5149	I Can't Resist Men/Always You	8

LYNDON JOHNS (& ISRAELITES)
69	Downtown DT 444	Don't Gamble With Love/Song Bird	5
69	Downtown DT 451	Oh Mama Oh Papa/Bring Back The Night (with The Israelites)	5

JOHN'S CHILDREN
66	Columbia DB 8030	The Love I Thought I'd Found/Strange Affair (very few in p/s)	300/175
66	Columbia DB 8030	The Love I Thought I'd Found/Strange Affair (promo)	200+
67	Columbia DB 8124	Just What You Want — Just What You'll Get/But She's Mine	160
67	Track 604 003	Desdemona/Remember Thomas A'Beckett (some in p/s)	125/60
67	Track 604 005	Midsummer Night's Scene/Sara Crazy Child (withdrawn)	4000+
67	Track 604 005	Come And Play With Me In The Garden/Sara Crazy Child (some in p/s)	150/90
67	Track 604 010	Go Go Girl/Jagged Time Lapse	60
87	Bam Caruso KIRI 095	MIDSUMMER NIGHT'S SCENE (LP)	30

(see also Marc Bolan, Andy Ellison, Radio Stars, Jook, Tyrannosaurus Rex)

AL JOHNSON & JEAN CARN
80	CBS 8545	I'm Back For More/You Are My Personal Angel	10

(see also Jean Carn)

ALEC JOHNSON
79	RFP RFP 001	Busman's Holiday (no p/s)	12

(see also Nightwing)

ANTHONY JOHNSON
81	Greensleeves GRED 76	Let Go This One/BILLY BOYO: One Spliff A Day (12")	20

BARRY JOHNSON
58	HMV POP 472	Locked In The Arms Of Love/Are You Sincere (78)	12

BETTY JOHNSON
56	London HLU 8307	I'll Wait/Please Tell Me Why (78 rpm = £15)	55
56	London HLU 8326	Honky Tonk Rock/Say It Isn't So, Joe (78 rpm = £35)	175
57	London HLU 8365	I Dreamed/If It's Wrong To Love You (78 rpm = £15)	50
57	London HLU 8432	1492/Little White Lies (78 rpm = £15)	35
58	London HLE 8557	Little Blue Man/Song You Heard When You Fell In Love (78 rpm = £12)	35
58	London HLE 8678	Dream/How Much (78 rpm = £20)	22
58	London HLE 8701	There's Never Been A Night/Mr. Brown Is Out Of Town (78 rpm = £25)	40
58	London HLE 8725	Hoopa Hoola/One More Time (78 rpm = £25)	35
59	London HLE 8839	Does Your Heart Beat For Me?/You And Only You (78 rpm = £30)	30
59	London RE-E 1221	DREAM (EP)	75
59	London HA-E 2163	THE SONG YOU HEARD WHEN YOU FELL IN LOVE (LP)	80

BLIND WILLIE JOHNSON
50s	Square M1	Dark Was The Night, Cold Was The Ground/Lord I Just Can't Keep From Crying (78)	10
58	Fontana TFE 17052	TREASURES OF NORTH AMERICAN NEGRO MUSIC NO. 2 (EP)	20
70	Xtra XTRA 1098	BLIND WILLIE JOHNSON (LP)	20

BOB JOHNSON & PETE KNIGHT
77	Chrysalis CHR 1137	THE KING OF ELFLAND'S DAUGHTER (LP)	12

(see also Steeleye Span, Mary Hopkin)

BOBBY JOHNSON & ATOMS
67	Ember EMB S 245	Do It Again A Little Bit Slower/Tramp (some in p/s)	20/10

BROWNIE JOHNSON
62	Longhorn BLH 0004	Best Dressed Beggar/Just Pretending	25

BRYAN JOHNSON
60	Decca F 11213	Looking High, High, High/Each Tomorrow (78 rpm = £15)	6
61	Decca DFE 6664	LOOKING HIGH (EP)	18

BUBBER JOHNSON
56	Parlophone R 4161	Keep A Light In The Window For Me/A Wonderful Thing Happens (78)	7
57	Parlophone R 4259	Confidential/Have A Little Faith In Me (78 rpm = £9)	35

BUDDY JOHNSON
55	Mercury MB 3231	Upside Your Head/ELLA JOHNSON: Crazy About A Saxophone (78)	15
59	Mercury ZEP 10009	BUDDY JOHNSON WAILS (EP, with Ella Johnson)	80
57	Mercury MPT 7515	ROCK AND ROLL (10" LP, with Ella Johnson)	165

BUNK JOHNSON (& HIS NEW ORLEANS BAND)
55	HMV 7M 141	When The Saints Go Marching In/Darktown Strutters' Ball	5
50s	Melodisc EPM7 52	ONE YOU LOVE (EP)	10
52	Jazz Man no cat. no.	MANDADISC (LP, with the Original Superior Band)	15
54	Goodtime Jazz LDG 110	BUNK JOHNSON AND THE YERBA BUENA JAZZ BAND (10" LP)	15
54	Columbia 33SX 1015	BUNK JOHNSON AND HIS NEW ORLEANS BAND (LP)	12
59	Melodisc MLP 12-112	BUNK JOHNSON AND HIS NEW ORLEANS JAZZ BAND (LP, w/ George Lewis)	15
50s	Goodtime Jazz	SPIRITUALS AND JAZZ (10" LP)	12
62	Storyville SLP 152	BUNK JOHNSON'S BAND 1944 (LP)	12
70s	Nola LP 3	BUNK JOHNSON AND HIS BAND (LP)	20

CAREY JOHNSON
72	Banana BA 369	Correction Train/SOUL DEFENDERS: Version	18

DANIEL JOHNSON
65	Island WI 250	Come On My People/Brother Nathan	15

DOMINO JOHNSON
72	Green Door GD 4045	Summertime/SWANS: Grazing	5

DOMINO JOHNSON & CHAMPIONS
70	Duke DU 89	You Broke My Heart/TONY & CHAMPIONS: Tell Me The Reason	8

GENERAL JOHNSON
73	Invictus INV 531	Only Time Will Tell/Only Time Will Tell (Instrumental Version)	8
76	Arista ARIST 45	All In The Family/Ready, Willing And Able	6
73	Invictus SVT 1008	GENERALLY SPEAKING (LP)	20

(see also Norman Johnson, Showmen, Chairmen Of The Board)

MINT VALUE £

GINGER JOHNSON AND HIS AFRICAN MESSENGERS
67	Masquerade SM 02001	AFRICAN PARTY (LP)	250

HOLLY JOHNSON
89	MCA DMCA 1306	Love Train (12" Mix)/Love Train (7" Mix)/Murder In Paradise (CD, card sleeve, featuring Brian May)	8
89	MCA DMCAT 1306	Love Train (Ride The 'A' Train Mix)/Love Train (Stoke It Up Mix)/Love Train (7" Mix)/Murder In Paradise (3" CD, featuring Brian May)	8

(see also Holly, Frankie Goes To Hollywood, Big In Japan)

HOWARD JOHNSON
71	Jay Boy BOY 47	The Slide/That Magic Touch Can Send You Flying	15

JAMES P. JOHNSON
54	Columbia SCM 5127	Feeling Blues/Riffs	8
56	HMV 7EG 8164	JAMES P. JOHNSON (EP)	8
57	HMV 7EG 8215	LOUISIANA SUGAR BABIES (EP, with Fats Waller)	8
57	Tempo EXA 65	JAMES P. JOHNSON (EP)	8
54	London AL 3511	EARLY HARLEM PIANO (10" LP)	15
55	London AL 3540	EARLY HARLEM PIANO VOLUME 2 (10" LP)	15

JAMES P. JOHNSON/LUCKEY ROBERTS
56	London HB-U 1057	HARLEM PARTY PIANO (10" LP, 1 side each)	20

JIMMY JOHNSON
65	Sue WI 387	Don't Answer The Door Parts 1 & 2	25

J.J. JOHNSON
55	Vogue LDE 124	J.J. JOHNSON SEXTET (10" LP)	15
55	Vogue LDE 162	J.J. JOHNSON QUINTET (10" LP)	15
60	Fontana TFL 5041	J.J. IN PERSON (LP)	12
61	Fontana TFL 5137	BLUE TROMBONE (LP, also stereo STFL 559)	12/15
63	Verve VLP 9056	J.J.'s BROADWAY (LP)	12
65	RCA RD/SF 7721	J.J.! (LP)	12
73	United Artists UAS 29451	ACROSS 110TH STREET (LP, soundtrack, with Bobby Womack)	20

(see also Sonny Stitt)

(JOHNNY JOHNSON &) THE BANDWAGON
68	Direction 58-3520	Baby Make Your Own Sweet Music/On The Day We Fall In Love (as Bandwagon)	6
68	Direction 58-3670	Breaking Down The Walls Of Heartache/Dancin' Master (as Bandwagon)	6
69	Direction 58-3923	You/You Blew Your Cool And Lost Your Fool	6
69	Direction 58-4180	Let's Hang On/I Ain't Lying (withdrawn)	12
69	Direction 58-4180	Let's Hang On/Don't Let It In	6
72	Stateside SS 2207	Honey Bee/I Don't Know Why	20
69	Direction 8-63500	JOHNNY JOHNSON AND THE BANDWAGON (LP)	30
70	Bell SBLL 138	SOUL SURVIVOR (LP)	25

JUDI JOHNSON (& PERFECTIONS)
64	HMV POP 1371	My Baby's Face/Make The Most Of It (solo)	15
65	HMV POP 1399	How Many Times/A Way Out (as Judi Johnson & Perfections)	15

LARRY JOHNSON
70	Blue Horizon 7-63851	PRESENTING THE COUNTRY BLUES (LP)	125

LAURIE JOHNSON ORCHESTRA
56	HMV 7MC 47	Buttercup/Lullaby Of The Leaves (export issue)	12
57	HMV POP 404	The Moonraker/Call Of The Casbah (78 rpm = £10)	7
60	Pye 7N 15251	No Hiding Place/The Deputy	6
64	Pye 7N 15599	Dr Strangelove Theme/Nevada	6
64	Pye 7N 15715	Call Me Irresponsible/The Beauty Jungle	6
65	Pye 7N 15933	Latin Quarter/M1 (some in p/s)	8/6
65	Pye 7N 17015	The Avengers/Minor Bossa Nova (some in p/s)	50/18
69	MGM MGM 1457	There Is Another Song/Caesar Smith	12
71	Columbia DB 8826	The Jason King Theme/There Comes A Time	50
76	EMI EMI 2562	The New Avengers Theme/A Flavour Of The Avengers (some in p/s)	10/6
80	Unicorn Kachana MCPS 5	The Professionals Main Title/On Target/The New Avengers Main Title (p/s, by Laurie Johnson & London Studio Orchestra)	6
57	Parlophone GEP 8604	THE GOOD COMPANIONS (EP)	15
58	Pye Nixa NPL 18017	SONGS OF THREE SEASONS (LP)	15
62	Golden Guinea GGL 0108	TOP SECRET (LP)	12
63	Pye NPL 18088	THE NEW BIG SOUND OF THE LAURIE JOHNSON ORCHESTRA (LP)	15
65	Pye NPL 18103	THE BIG NEW SOUND STRIKES AGAIN (LP)	18
66	Pye NPL 18136	TWO CITIES SUITE (LP)	15
67	Marble Arch MAL 695	THE AVENGERS AND OTHER FAVOURITES (LP)	25
68	Columbia S(C)X 6206	SOMETHING'S COMING (LP, mono/stereo)	15
69	MGM C(S) 8104	THEMES AND ... (LP)	25
70	Columbia SCX 6412	LAURIE JOHNSON/LONDON JAZZ ORCHESTRA — SYNTHESIS (LP, with Joe Harriott, Tubby Hayes, Stan Tracey & Tony Coe)	55
71	Columbia SCX 6464	CONQUISTADORS (LP)	15
73	Ronco RR 2006	THE BELSTONE FOX (LP, soundtrack, gatefold sleeve)	20
80	Unicorn Kachana KPM 7009	MUSIC FROM THE AVENGERS, THE NEW AVENGERS AND THE PROFESSIONALS (LP, gatefold sleeve, with London Studio Orchestra)	20

(see also Polka Dots)

LONNIE JOHNSON
51	Vogue V 2015	Drunk Again/Jelly Roll Baker (78)	30
51	Vogue V 2079	Happy New Year/Little Rockin' Chair (78)	30
51	Melodisc MEL 1138	Rocks In My Bed/Solid Blues (78)	35
51	Melodisc MEL 1186	Blues For Everybody/In Love Again (78)	35
52	Melodisc MEL 1221	Blues In My Soul/Keep What You Got (78)	35
57	Parlophone GEP 8635	LONESOME ROAD (EP)	50

57	Parlophone GEP 8663	LONNIE'S BLUES (EP)	45
58	Parlophone GEP 8693	LONNIE'S BLUES NO. 2 (EP)	45
64	Storyville SLP 162	PORTRAITS IN BLUES VOL. 6 (LP)	30
64	Storyville 616 010	SEE SEE RIDER (LP, with Otis Spann)	35
60s	Xtra XTRA 1037	LONNIE JOHNSON (LP)	30

(see also Eddie Lang & Lonnie Johnson)

LOU JOHNSON
63	London HLX 9805	Reach Out For Me/Magic Potion (DJ copy = £100)	50
64	London HLX 9917	(There's) Always Something There To Remind Me/ Wouldn't That Be Something	25
64	London HLX 9929	A Message To Martha (Kentucky Bluebird)/The Last One To Be Loved	15
65	London HLX 9965	Please Stop The Wedding/Park Avenue	15
65	London HLX 9994	A Time To Love, A Time To Cry/Unsatisfied (DJ copy = £150)	75
69	London HLX 10269	(There's) Always Something There To Remind Me/Message To Martha	10
64	London REX 1438	THE MAGIC POTION OF LOU JOHNSON (EP)	150

LUTHER 'GEORGIA BOY SNAKE' JOHNSON
| 69 | Transatlantic TRA 188 | THE MUDDY WATERS BLUES BAND (LP, credits Muddy Waters on label) | 30 |

MARGARET JOHNSON
| 52 | Parlophone R 3506 | Cushion Foot Stomp/Take Your Black Bottom Outside (78) | 12 |
| 50s | Jazz Collector L 105 | Death String Blues/Mistreating Man Blues (78) | 8 |

MARV JOHNSON
59	London HLT 8856	Come To Me/Whisper (78 rpm = £75)	110
59	London HLT 9013	You Got What It Takes/Don't Leave Me (78 rpm = £65)	18
60	London HLT 9109	I Love The Way You Love/Let Me Love You	22
60	London HL 7095	I Love The Way You Love/Let Me Love You (export issue)	35
60	London HLT 9165	Ain't Gonna Be That Way/All The Love I've Got	22
60	London HLT 9187	(You've Got To) Move Two Mountains/I Need You	22
61	London HLT 9265	Happy Days/Baby, Baby	22
61	London HLT 9311	Merry-Go-Round/Tell Me That You Love Me	45
65	Tamla Motown TMG 525	Why Do You Want To Let Me Go/I'm Not A Plaything	90
69	United Artists UP 35010	I Love The Way You Love/You Got What It Takes	6
68	Tamla Motown TMG 680	I'll Pick A Rose For My Rose/You Got The Love I Love	10
69	Tamla Motown TMG 713	I Miss You Baby (How I Miss You)/Bad Girl	10
70	Tamla Motown TMG 737	So Glad You Chose Me/I'm Not A Plaything	10
60	London HA-T 2271	MARVELLOUS MARV JOHNSON (LP)	140
69	T. Motown (S)TML 11111	I'LL PICK A ROSE FOR MY ROSE (LP)	40

MATT JOHNSON
| 81 | 4AD CAD 113 | BURNING BLUE SOUL (LP, original 'psychedelic eye' cover) | 25 |

(see also Gadgets, The The)

MIRRIAM JOHNSON
| 61 | London HLW 9337 | Lonesome Road/Young And Innocent | 15 |

NORMAN JOHNSON (& SHOWMEN)
69	Action ACT 4529	You're Everything/Our Love Will Grow	45
69	Action ACT 4545	Take It Baby/In Paradise	45
71	Action ACT 4601	You're Everything/Our Love Will Grow (reissue)	20

(see also General Johnson, Chairmen Of The Board, Showmen)

PETE JOHNSON
51	Vogue V 2007	J.J. Boogie/Yancey Special (78, red or orange label)	15/18
51	Vogue V 2008	Swanee River Boogie/St. Louis Boogie (78, red or orange label)	15/18
51	Vogue V 2019	Hollywood Boogie/Central Avenue Drag (78, orange label)	18
56	Vogue V 2007	J.J. Boogie/Yancey Special	35
56	Vogue V 2008	Swanee River Boogie/St. Louis Boogie	35
55	Vogue EPV 1039	PETE JOHNSON (EP)	35
59	Top Rank JKR 8009	ROLL 'EM BOY (EP)	22
55	London AL 3549	JUMPIN' WITH PETE JOHNSON (10" LP)	55
55	Vogue Coral LRA 10016	BOOGIE WOOGIE MOOD (LP)	35

(see also Joe Turner & Pete Johnson, Albert Ammons & Meade Lux Lewis)

PLAS JOHNSON (ORCHESTRA)
57	Capitol CL 14772	The Big Twist/Come Rain Or Come Shine (78 rpm = £8)	18
57	Capitol CL 14816	Swanee River Rock/You Send Me (78 rpm = £10)	18
58	Capitol CL 14836	Popcorn/Hoppin' Mad (78 rpm = £8)	22
58	Capitol CL 14903	Little Rockin' Deacon/Dinah	22
59	Capitol CL 14973	Robbins Nest Cha Cha/Plaz Jazz	10
57	London HB-U 1078	BOP ME DADDY (10" LP)	60

PROFESSOR JOHNSON & HIS GOSPEL SINGERS
| 51 | Vocalion V 1013 | Give Me That Old Time Religion/Where Shall I Be (78) | 20 |
| 58 | Brunswick OE 9352 | PROFESSOR JOHNSON AND HIS GOSPEL SINGERS (EP) | 22 |

RAY JOHNSON
| 57 | Vogue V 9073 | If You Don't Want Me Baby/Calypso Joe (78 rpm = £20) | 55 |
| 58 | Vogue V 9093 | Calypso Blues/Are You There (78 rpm = £20) | 45 |

ROBERT JOHNSON
62	Philips BBL 7539	ROBERT JOHNSON 1936-1937 (LP)	120
65	CBS BPG 62456	KING OF THE DELTA BLUES SINGERS (LP)	50
67	Kokomo K 1000	ROBERT JOHNSON (LP)	70
60s	Smokestack SS/LP 1	BLUES LEGEND 1936-1937 (LP)	50
70	CBS 64102	KING OF THE DELTA BLUES SINGERS VOL. 2 (LP)	30

ROY LEE JOHNSON
| 69 | Action ACT 4518 | So Anna Just Love Me/Boogaloo No. 3 | 30 |

MINT VALUE £

RUBY JOHNSON
67 Stax 601 020   If I Ever Needed Love (I Sure Do Need It Now)/Keep On Keeping On 20

SPIDER JOHNSON & POPEYE BAND
63 Riverside RIF 106904   Doin' The Popeye/The Gospel Truth 5

SYL JOHNSON
73 London HL 10403   We Did It/Anyway The Wind Blows 10
73 London HL 10438   Back For A Taste Of Your Love/Wind Blow Her Back My Way 6
75 London HL 10476   Let Yourself Go/Please Don't Give Up On Me 6

THEO JOHNSON
65 Aladdin WI 604   Masters Of War/The Water Is Wide 12

TOMMY JOHNSON
60s Saydisc SDM 224   THE LEGACY OF TOMMY JOHNSON (LP) 20

TONY JOHNSON
55 Melodisc 1331   Man Smart Woman Smarter/Give Her Banana (78) 15
50s Parlophone MP 121   Mattie Rag/Linstead Market (78, export issue) 15
50s Parlophone MP 123   Don't Fence Her In/Wheel And Turn Me (78, export issue) 15

WILKO JOHNSON & SOLID SENDERS
78 Virgin V 2105   SOLID SENDERS (LP, with free LP "Live" [VDJ 26]) 12
(see also Dr. Feelgood, Solid Senders, Ian Dury & Blockheads)

BRUCE JOHNSTON COMBO
63 London HL 9780   Original Surfer Stomp/Pajama Party 55
(see also Beach Boys, California Music, Fantastic Baggys, Sagittarius)

DANIEL JOHNSTON
92 Seminal Twang TWANG 13 Laurie/The Monster Inside Of Me/Whiz Kid/The Lennon Song (p/s) 10

JOHNSTON BROTHERS
54 Decca F 10234   The Creep/Crystal Ball 12
54 Decca F 10286   Oh Baby Mine I Get So Lonely/My Love, My Life, My Own 10
54 Decca F 10302   The Bandit/KEYNOTES: A Dime And A Dollar 18
54 Decca F 10364   Sh-Boom (Life Could Be A Dream)/Crazy 'Bout Ya Baby (78 rpm = £8) 15
54 Decca F 10401   Mambo In The Moonlight/Papa Loves Mambo (with Ted Heath Music) 6
54 Decca F 10414   "Join In And Sing" Medley (both sides) 6
55 Decca F 10451   Majorca/Heartbroken 6
55 Decca F 10490   The Right To Be Wrong/Hot Potato Mambo 6
55 Decca F 10513   Chee Chee-Oo Chee (Sang The Little Bird)Hubble Bubble 6
55 Decca F 10526   Dreamboat/Jim, Johnny And Jonas 6
55 Decca F 10608   Hernando's Hideaway/Hey There 20
55 Decca F 10636   "Join In And Sing Again" Medley (both sides) 8
56 Decca F 10721   No Other Love/Flowers Mean Forgiveness 8
56 Decca F 10747   How Little We Know/The Street Musician 6
56 Decca F 10781   In The Middle Of The House (with Keynotes)/Stranded In The Jungle 10
56 Decca F 10814   "Join In And Sing, No. 3" Medley (both sides) 8
56 Decca F 10828   Give Her My Love (When You Meet Her)/A Rose And A Candy Bar 8
57 Decca F 10860   Whatever Lola Wants (Lola Gets)/Heart 7
57 Decca F 10939   I Like Music — You Like Music/Seven Bar Blues 7
57 Decca F 10962   "Join In And Sing, No. 4" Medley (both sides) 5
56 Decca DFE 6249   JOIN THE JOHNSTON BROTHERS (EP) 8
56 Decca DFE 6311   JOIN IN AND SING WITH THE JOHNSTON BROTHERS (EP) 8
57 Decca DFE 6458   JOIN AND SING AGAIN (EP) 8
58 Decca DFE 6503   EASY NO. 1 (EP) 8
58 Decca LK 4266   EASY (LP) 15
(see also Dennis Lotis, Vera Lynn, Joan Regan, Lita Roza, Suzi Miller, Ted Heath, Keynotes)

JOHNSTONS
68 Transatlantic TRA 169   THE JOHNSTONS (LP) 18
68 Transatlantic TRA 184   GIVE A DAMN (LP) 15
68 Transatlantic TRA 185   THE BARLEYCORN (LP) 15
70 Transatlantic TRA 211   BITTER GREEN (LP) 12
71 Transatlantic TRA 231   COLOURS OF THE DAWN (LP) 12
72 Transatlantic TRA 251   IF I SANG MY SONG (LP, gatefold sleeve) 12
(see also Adrienne Johnston)

JOHN THE POSTMAN
78 Bent BIG BENT 2   PUERILE (12" EP, stamped brown paper bag p/s, with inserts) 12
78 Bent BIG BENT 4   PSYCHEDELIC ROCK'N'ROLL FIVE SKINNERS
                                     (12" EP, white label, foldover p/s in bag) 12

JOINER, ARKANSAS, JUNIOR HIGH SCHOOL BAND
60 London HLG 9147   Big Ben/National City 8

JO JO GUNNE (U.K.)
68 Decca F 12807   Every Story Has An End/Should Live Like That 7
69 Decca F 12906   Beggin' You Baby/Bad Penny 7

JO JO GUNNE (U.S.)
72 Asylum AYM 501   Run Run Run/Shake That Fat (withdrawn) 10
72 Asylum AYM 507   Shake That Fat/I Make Love 5
73 Asylum AYM 518   Ready Freddy/Wait A Lifetime 5
74 Asylum AYM 528   I Wanna Love You/Neon City 5
74 Asylum AYM 534   Where Is The Show/Single Man 5
(see also Spirit)

JOKER
84 Lost Moment LM 018   Back On The Road/Pusher (p/s) 6

JOKERS
62	Salvo SLO 1806	Blue Moonbeam/Dog Fight (99 only)	35

JOKER'S WILD
66	Regent Sound RSR 0031	Don't Ask Me/Why Do Fools Fall In Love (handwritten labels, 50 only)	500+
66	Regent Sound RSLP 007	JOKER'S WILD: Don't Ask Me/Why Do Fools Fall In Love/You Don't Know What I Know/That's How Strong My Love Is (12", 1-sided, 50 copies only)	1,000+

(see also Dave Gilmour, Pink Floyd)

JOLLIVER ARKANSAS
69	Bell SBLL 119	HOME (LP)	35

(see also Leslie West, Mountain)

JOLLY BOYS
70	Moodisc MU 3504	On The Water/MUDIES ALL STARS: Cash Register	15

JOLLY BROTHERS
78	Ballistic FORCE 2002	Conscious Man/PRODIGAL CREATOR: Life (actually dub to Lee Perry's Ne Jah Go Run) (12")	15

AL JOLSON
50	Brunswick LA 8502	JOLSON SINGS AGAIN (10" LP)	12
50	Brunswick LA 8509	AL JOLSON SOUVENIR (10" LP)	12
51	Brunswick LA 8512	JOLSON MEMORIES (10" LP)	12
53	Brunswick LA 8554	STEPHEN FOSTER SONGS (10" LP)	12
53	Brunswick LA 8575	AL JOLSON SOUVENIR ALBUM VOLUME 3 (10" LP)	12
53	Brunswick LA 8570	AL JOLSON SOUVENIR ALBUM VOLUME 4 (10" LP)	12
54	Brunswick LA 8655	AL JOLSON SOUVENIR ALBUM VOLUME 6 (10" LP)	12
57	Brunswick LAT 8220	THE JOLSON STORY — AMONG MY SOUVENIRS (LP)	12
58	Brunswick LAT 8267	THE IMMORTAL AL JOLSON (LP)	12

JOLT
77	Polydor 2058 936	You're Cold/All I Can Do (p/s)	12
78	Polydor 2059 008	What'cha Gonna Do About It/Again And Again (die-cut p/s)	12
78	Polydor 2059 039	I Can't Wait/Route 66 (p/s)	12
79	Polydor 2229 215	Maybe Tonight/I'm In Tears/See Saw/Stop Look (p/s)	12
79	Polydor 2229 215DJ	Maybe Tonight/See Saw (promo only, no p/s)	12
78	Polydor 2383 504	THE JOLT (LP)	15

JON
67	Parlophone R 5604	So Much For Mary/Polly Sunday (some in p/s)	32/12
67	Columbia DB 8249	Is It Love/Sing Out	100

(see also Titus Groan, Still Life)

JON & ALUN
63	Decca LK/SKL 4547	RELAX YOUR MIND (LP, mono/stereo)	22/30

JON & DAVE
97	Earworm SS 1	Land Beyond The Sun/Instrumental For Silence (p/s, pale green vinyl, 500 copies only)	8

JON & JEANNIE
68	Beacon 3-105	Lover's Holiday/Something You Got	10
69	Beacon BEA 113	Don't Sign The Papers/We Got Lovin'	10

JON & ROBIN & IN-CROWD
67	Stateside SS 2027	Do It Again A Little Bit Slower/If I Need Someone It's You	12

JON & VANGELIS
81	Polydor POSPX 323	State Of Independence/Beside (12", in blue plastic film canister, promo only)	40+
84	Polydor JV 5/POSP 246	State Of Independence/The Friends Of Mr. Cairo/Chariots Of Fire/Eric's Theme (p/s doublepack, stickered shrinkwrapped p/s)	6
81	Polydor POLD 5039	THE FRIENDS OF MR. CAIRO (LP, promo issue with b&w sleeve, raised figures & logo in left corner)	15

(see also Jon Anderson, Vangelis)

JONATHAN & CHARLES
69	Herald LLR 566	ANOTHER WEEK TO GO (LP)	30+

JONCUNO(O)
(see Juncuno)

AL JONES
58	HMV POP 451	Mad, Mad, World/Lonely Traveller(78 rpm = £80)	275

AL JONES
69	Parlophone PMC/PCS 7081	ALUN ASHWORTH JONES (LP)	70+
72	Village Thing VTS 19	JONESVILLE (LP)	20

(see also Anderson, Jones, Jackson)

ALLAN JONES
53	HMV 7M 111	Why Do I Love You/Make Believe	10
53	HMV 7M 135	I Believe/I Talk To The Trees	10
53	HMV 7M 161	Poppa Piccolino/Why?	10

BARBARA JONES
72	Bullet BU 516	Sad Movies/SIR HARRY: Deejay Version	8
74	Count Shelley CS 045	Baby I'm Yours/Don't Turn Your Back On Me	5
75	Dip DL 5085	Where Do I Turn/G.G. ALL STARS: Version	5

BETTY HALL JONES
50	Capitol CL 13266	This Joint's Too Hip For Me/You've Got To Have What It Takes (78)	25

MINT VALUE £

BEVERLEY JONES (& PRESTONS)
63	HMV POP 1109	The Boy I Saw With You/When It Comes To Love	12
63	HMV POP 1140	Why Do Lovers Break Each Other's Heart/I'm Just An In-Between	15
63	HMV POP 1201	Wait 'Til My Bobby Gets Home/A Boy Like You	12
64	Parlophone R 5189	Heatwave/Hear You Talking (with Prestons)	18

B-LOU JONES & HIS JUPITERS
61	London HLU 9373	Anchors Aweigh (Parts 1 & 2)	10

BRENDA LEE JONES
75	UK USA 8	You're The Love Of My Life/Thread Your Needle (paper label)	10

(see also Dean & Jean)

BRIAN JONES
(see under Pipes Of Pan, Rolling Stones)

CAROL JONES
60	Triumph RGM 1012	The Boy With The Eyes Of Blue/I Gave Him Back His Ring	125

CASEY JONES & THE ENGINEERS
63	Columbia DB 7083	One Way Ticket/I'm Gonna Love	35

CASEY JONES & THE GOVERNERS
64	Golden 12LP 106	DON'T HA HA (LP)	60

(see also Casey Jones & The Engineers)

CURTIS JONES
66	RCA RCX 7184	R.C.A. VICTOR RACE SERIES VOL. 9 (EP)	20
64	Decca LK 4587	CURTIS JONES IN LONDON (LP)	65
68	Blue Horizon 7-63207	NOW RESIDENT IN EUROPE (LP)	45

DAVEY JONES
65	Philips BF 1410	For Your Love/Love Bug	10

DAVIE JONES & THE KING BEES
64	Vocalion Pop V 9221	Liza Jane/Louie, Louie Go Home (beware of counterfeits without centres)	800
78	Decca F 13807	Liza Jane/Louie, Louie Go Home (reissue)	15

(see also David Bowie, Davy Jones, Manish Boys, Calvin James)

DAVY JONES (U.K.)
65	Parlophone R 5315	You've Got A Habit Of Leaving/Baby Loves That Way	650

(see also David Bowie)

DAVY JONES (U.K.) & THE LOWER THIRD/MANISH BOYS
79	EMI EMI 2925	You've Got A Habit Of Leaving/Baby Loves That Way/MANISH BOYS: I Pity The Fool/Take My Tip (p/s)	12
82	Charly CYM 1	You've Got A Habit Of Leaving/Baby Loves That Way/MANISH BOYS: I Pity The Fool/Take My Tip (10", p/s)	20

(see also David Bowie, Davie Jones & King Bees, Manish Boys, Calvin James)

DAVY JONES (U.K.)
65	Colpix PX 784	What Are We Going To Do/This Bouquet	8
67	Pye 7N 17302	It Ain't Me Babe/Baby It's Me (some in p/s)	12/8
67	Pye 7N 17380	Theme For A New Love/Dream Girl (some in p/s)	12/8
67	Pye International 7N 25432	Theme For A New Love/Dream Girl (reissue, withdrawn)	20+
71	Bell BLL 1163	Rainy Jane/Welcome To My Love	8
77	MCA MCA 348	Life Line/It's A Jungle Out There/Gotta Get Up (from 'The Point') (p/s, last track with Micky Dolenz)	8
78	Warner Bros K 17161	(Hey Ra Ra) Happy Birthday Mickey Mouse/You Don't Have To Be A Country Boy To Sing A Country Song (p/s)	8
83	J.J. 2001	I'll Love You Forever/When I Look Back On Christmas	12
67	Pye NPL 18178	DAVY JONES (LP)	25

(see also Davy Jones & Micky Dolenz, Monkees)

DAVY JONES (U.K.) & MICKY DOLENZ
71	Bell BLL 986	Do It In The Name Of Love/Lady Jane	18

(see also Monkees, Davey Jones)

DAVY JONES (U.S.)
60	Pye 7N 15254	Amapola/Mighty Man	10
61	Pye 7N 15318	Shenandoah/Scenery	20
61	Pye International 7N 25072	Model Girl/Scarlet Woman	12
61	Pye International 7N 25095	Bonnie Banks/Baby Baby	10
62	Piccadilly 7N 35038	Jezebel/Don't Come Crying To Me	8

(see also Thelonious Monk)

DILL JONES TRIO
58	Pye Jazz 7NJ 2021	Little Rock Getaway/Carolina Shout	5
56	Jazz Today JTE 104	PIANO MOODS VOL. 2 (EP)	15
56	Pye Jazz NJE 1024	PIANO MOODS VOL. 5 (EP)	20
57	Columbia SEG 7764	TOP OF THE POLL (EP)	10
59	Columbia SEG 7893	DILL JONES PLUS FOUR (EP)	8
60	Columbia 33SX 1336	JONES THE JAZZ (LP)	60

DORIS JONES
76	NEMS NES 9	He's So Irreplaceable/Never Gonna Give Him Up	8
76	NEMS NES 15	Stranded In The Wilderness/(Pt. 2)	8

DOROTHY JONES
61	Philips 322 794 BF	Takin' That Long Walk Home/It's Unbearable	25

(see also Cookies)

FLOYD JONES/EDDIE TAYLOR
60s	XX MIN 712	FLOYD JONES AND EDDIE TAYLOR (EP, 2 tracks each)	15

GEORGE JONES

59	Mercury AMT 1021	The Treasure Of Love/If I Don't Love You (Grits Ain't Groceries) (78 rpm = £25)	22
59	Mercury AMT 1036	White Lightning/Long Time To Forget	50
59	Mercury AMT 1058	Who Shot Sam/Into My Arms Again	30
59	Mercury AMT 1078	Big Harlan Taylor/Money To Burn	15
60	Mercury AMT 1100	Sparkling Brown Eyes/Accidentally On Purpose	15
61	Mercury AMT 1124	Candy Hearts/The Window Up Above	15
62	United Artists POP 1037	She Thinks I Still Care/Geronimo	15
63	United Artists UP 1015	I Saw Me/Not What I Had In Mind (as George Jones with Jones Boys)	12
64	United Artists UP 1044	Your Heart Turned Left (And I Was On The Right)/My Tears Are Overdue	12
65	United Artists UP 1080	The Race Is On/She's So Lonesome Again	15
69	Stateside SS 2145	If My Heart Had Windows/Taggin' Along	8
71	Pye International 7N 25547	It's Been A Good Year For The Roses/Let A Little Come In	6
80	Epic EPC 8560	Stranger In The House (with Elvis Costello)/A Drunk Can't Be A Man (p/s)	6
59	Mercury ZEP 10036	GEORGE JONES (EP)	100
60s	Melodisc EPM7 109	COUNTRY SONG HITS (EP)	42
64	Mercury 10009 MCE	C & W ACES (EP)	22
64	Ember EMB 4548	THE BEST OF AMERICAN COUNTRY MUSIC VOL. 4 (EP)	15
62	United Artists ULP 1007	THE NEW FAVOURITES OF GEORGE JONES (LP)	28
63	United Artists ULP 1014	MY FAVOURITES OF HANK WILLIAMS (LP)	28
63	Ember CW 101	THE CROWN PRINCE OF COUNTRY MUSIC (LP, original pressings have grey & orange label)	18
63	United Artists ULP 1037	HITS OF HIS COUNTRY COUSINS (LP)	25
64	United Artists ULP 1050	I WISH TONIGHT WOULD NEVER END (LP)	25
64	London HA-B 8125	GEORGE JONES SINGS HIS GREATEST HITS (LP)	20
64	United Artists ULP 1070	WHAT'S IN OUR HEARTS (LP, with Melba Montgomery)	18
64	Ember CW 109	THE FABULOUS COUNTRY MUSIC SOUND OF JONES (LP, original pressings have grey & orange label)	15
64	Wing WL 1175	COUNTRY & WESTERN NO. 1 MALE SINGER (LP)	12
64	United Artists ULP 1074	MORE NEW FAVOURITES (LP)	20
65	United Artists ULP 1077	BLUE GRASS HOOTENANNY (LP, with Melba Montgomery)	18
65	United Artists ULP 1091	I GET LONELY IN A HURRY (LP)	20
65	United Artists ULP 1082	JONES SINGS LIKE THE DICKENS (LP)	20
65	United Artists ULP 1101	TROUBLE IN MIND (LP)	20
65	Stateside SL 10147	GEORGE JONES AND GENE PITNEY (LP, with Gene Pitney)	25
65	Stateside SL 10157	MR. COUNTRY AND WESTERN MUSIC (LP)	18
66	London HA-B 8259	GEORGE JONES (LP, with Tommy Hill's Band)	25
66	United Artists (S)ULP 1136	THE GREAT GEORGE JONES (LP)	18
66	United Artists (S)ULP 1137	BLUE MOON OF KENTUCKY (LP, with Melba Montgomery)	18
66	Stateside SL 10173	IT'S COUNTRY TIME AGAIN (LP, with Gene Pitney)	25
66	Stateside S(S)L 10184	LOVE BUG (LP)	20
67	Stateside S(S)L 10195	WE FOUND HEAVEN RIGHT HERE ON EARTH AT '4033' (LP)	20
67	Mercury SMCL 20107	GREATEST HITS (LP)	20
67	London HA-B 8340	THE GEORGE JONES SONG BOOK (LP)	22
67	Stateside S(S)L 10215	VARIETY IS THE SPICE OF ... (LP)	20
68	Stateside S(S)L 10236	SINGS THE SONGS OF DALLAS FRAZIER (LP)	18
68	Mercury SMWL 21003	THE GREAT GEORGE JONES (LP)	20
69	Stateside S(S)L 10256	IF MY HEART HAD WINDOWS (LP)	15
69	Stateside S(S)L 10283	MY COUNTRY (LP)	15
70	Stateside SSL 10308	I'LL SHARE MY WORLD WITH YOU (LP)	15
72	Pye PKL 4412	THE BLUE SIDE OF LONESOME & OTHER COUNTRY FAVOURITES (LP)	12
72	Pye Intl. NSPL 28160	COUNTRY MUSIC '72 (LP)	12
72	CBS EQ 30802	WE GO TOGETHER (LP, with Tammy Wynette, quadrophonic)	12
73	Pye Intl. NSPL 28176	WRAPPED AROUND HER FINGERS (LP)	12

(see also Gene Pitney, Elvis Costello)

GEORGE JONES/JIMMIE SKINNER

59	Mercury ZEP 10012	COUNTRY AND WESTERN (EP, 2 tracks each)	45

GLORIA JONES

66	Capitol CL 15429	Heartbeat (Parts 1 & 2)	35
66	Stateside SS 555	Finders Keepers/Run One Flight Of Stairs	70
74	Tamla Motown TMG 910	Tin Can People/So Tired	10
76	EMI EMI 2437	Get It On/Get It On (Version)	6
76	EMI EMI 2522	I Ain't Going Nowhere/Simplicity Blues	10
77	EMI EMI 2570	Go Now/Drive Me Crazy	6
77	EMI EMI 2720	Bring On The Love/Cry Baby	6
74	Tamla Motown STML 11254	SHARE MY LOVE (LP)	25
76	EMI EMC 3159	VIXEN (LP)	15

(see also Marc Bolan & Gloria Jones)

GRACE JONES

86	Island 12IS 240	Pull Up To The Bumper/La Vie En Rose (12")	8

GRANDPA JONES

57	Brunswick 05676	Eight More Miles To Louisville/Dark As A Dungeon	25
59	Brunswick OE 9455	MOUNTAIN MUSIC VOL. 3 (EP)	30
57	Parlophone GEP 8666	MEET GRANDPA JONES (EP)	30
58	Parlophone GEP 8766	COUNTRY AND WESTERN (EP)	35
59	Parlophone GEP 8781	COUNTRY ROUND UP (EP)	30
64	London RE-U 1417	GRANDPA SINGS JIMMIE RODGERS (EP)	30
62	London HA-U/SH-U 8010	MAKES THE RAFTERS RING (LP)	35
64	London HA-U/SH-U 8119	YODELLING HITS (LP)	35

(see also Brown's Ferry Four)

HUW JONES

69	Sain SAIN 1	Dwr/Fy Ngwlad Fy Hun	20

JACK JONES

65	London HLR 9939	Dear Heart/Where Love Has Gone.	5
65	London HLR 9956	The Race Is On/I Can't Believe I'm Losing You	10
66	London HLR 10088	Impossible Dream/A Day In The Life Of A Fool	5
67	London HLR 10108	Lady/Afraid Of Love	5
63	London RER 1374	JACK JONES (EP)	8
64	London RER 1433	FOUR GREAT SONGS FROM FOUR GREAT SHOWS (EP)	8
64	London HA-R 8167	WIVES AND LOVERS (LP)	12
64	London HA-R/SH-R 8191	SHE LOVES ME (LP)	12
65	London HA-R 8202	BEWITCHED (LP)	12
65	London HA-R/SH-R 8209	WHERE LOVE HAS GONE (LP)	12
65	London HA-R/SH-R 8222	SONGS OF LOVE (LP)	12
65	London HA-R/SH-R 8236	MY KIND OF TOWN (LP)	12
66	London HA-R/SH-R 8254	AND THERE'S LOVE (LP)	12

JANET JONES

74	Midas MR 005	SING TO ME LADY (LP)	80

JANIE JONES (& LASH)

65	HMV POP 1495	Witches Brew/Take-A My Tip	15
66	HMV POP 1514	Gunning For You/Go Go Away From Me	15
67	Columbia DB 8173	Tickle Me Tootsie Wootsies/High And Dry	10
68	Pye 7N 17550	Charlie Smith/Nobody's Perfect	10
68	Major Minor MM 577	The Girl's Song/I've Never Met A Boy Like You	10
70	President PT 309	Back On My Feet Again/Psycho	7
83	Big Beat NS 91	House Of The Ju-Ju Queen/Sex Machine (as Janie Jones & Lash, p/s)	7

(see also The Clash)

JERRY JONES

70	Banana BA 316	Still Waters (Love)/SOUND DIMENSION: Wig Wam	18
71	Bamboo BAM 65	Still Waters (Love)/SOUND DIMENSION: Wig Wam (reissue)	12
71	Bamboo BALPS 213	LIVE AT THE KINGSTON HOTEL, JAMAICA (LP)	50

JIMMY JONES

60	MGM MGM 1051	Handy Man/The Search Is Over (78 rpm = £100)	5
60	MGM MGM 1078	Good Timin'/Too Long Will Be Too Late (78 rpm = £100)	5
60	MGM MGM 1091	I Just Go For You/That's When I Cried	12
60	MGM MGM 1103	Ready For Love/For You	12
61	MGM MGM 1123	I Told You So/You Got It	12
61	MGM MGM 1133	Dear One/I Say Love	12
61	MGM MGM 1146	Mr Music Man/Holler Hey	12
62	MGM MGM 1168	You're Much Too Young/Nights Of Mexico	12
65	Columbia DB 7592	Walkin'/Pardon Me	35
65	Cameo Parkway P 988	Don't You Just Know It	15
67	Stateside SS 2041	39-21-46/Personal Property	15
68	MGM MGM 1405	Good Timin'/Handy Man	8
60	MGM MGM-EP 745	JIMMY HANDYMAN JONES (EP)	60
61	MGM MGMJPJ 1	ORIGINAL HITS (EP)	40
60	MGM MGM-C 832	GOOD TIMIN' (LP)	75

JO JONES TRIO

59	Top Rank 25/039	JO JONES (LP)	12

JOE JONES

60	Columbia DB 4533	You Talk Too Much/I Love You Still	12

JOHN PAUL JONES

64	Pye 7N 15637	Baja/A Foggy Day In Vietnam (B-side actually by Andrew Oldham Orchestra)	80
99	DGM DGMJPJ 1	ZOOMA (CD, advance promo 4-track sampler)	8

(see also Led Zeppelin, Tony Meehan, Andrew Oldham Orchestra)

JOHNNY JONES & KING CASUALS

68	MCA MU 1031	Soul Poppin'/Blues For The Brothers	15
76	Cream CRM 5004	Purple Haze/Horsing Around	15
76	Brunswick BR 37	Purple Haze/FRED HUGHES: Baby Boy	10
80	Sonet SNTF 821	JOHNNY JONES WITH BILLY BOY ARNOLD (LP)	12

JONAH

85	MW MW 7853	Tough/This Is Love (no p/s)	280

JONAH JONES (QUARTET)

59	Mercury AMT 15085	I Dig Chicks/Cherry	5
62	Ember JBS 704	Down By The Riverside/Stars Fell On Alabama	7
65	Brunswick LAT 8633	ON THE SUNNY SIDE OF THE STREET (LP, as Jonah Jones Quartet)	12

JUGGY JONES

76	Contempo CS 2080	Inside America (Parts 1 & 2)	6

JUSTIN JONES

61	London HLU 9463	Dance By Yourself/Love	150

KEN JONES (& HIS ROCK'N'ROLLERS)

60	Parlophone R 4628	Two Way Stretch/Paper Chase	6
61	Parlophone R 4763	Bluesville/On The Rebound	7
61	Parlophone R 4788	Joxville/Just Rollin'.	6
58	Embassy WEP 1004	ROCK'N'ROLL TIME (EP, as Ken Jones & His Rock'n'Rollers)	12

KENNEY JONES

74	GM GMS 027	Ready Or Not/Woman Trouble	8

(see also Small Faces, Faces, Who)

LESLIE JONES

59	Pye NSEP 85004	FOUR FARNON FAVOURITES (EP, stereo)	10
59	Pye NSPL 83008/9	THE MUSIC OF ROBERT FARNON (LP)	15

LINDA JONES
67	Warner Bros WB 2070	Hypnotised/I Can't Stop Lovin' My Baby	50
72	London HLU 10368	For Your Precious Love/Don't Go	15
75	Warner Bros WB 16621	I Just Can't Live My Life/My Heart Will Understand	30

LINDA JONES/J.J. JACKSON
77	Loma/Warners K 56271	THIS IS LOMA — VOL. 7 (LP, 1 side each)	15

LITTLE JOHNNY JONES
73	Pressure Beat PB 5515	More Dub/More Dub — Chapter Two	8
	(see also Johnny Lover)		

LLOYD JONES
70	Bullet BU 429	Rome/RHYTHM RULERS: Version	18

LOUIS JONES ROCK & ROLL BAND
50s	Vogue VE1 70111	ROCK AND ROLL (EP)	90

MAE JONES ENSEMBLE with MARGARET BOND
55	Decca F 10486	I Walked Into The Garden/Tenderly He Watches	7

MAGGIE JONES
70	VJM VLP 23	COLUMBIA RECORDINGS IN CHRONOLOGICAL ORDER VOL. 1 (LP)	15
70	VJM VLP 25	COLUMBIA RECORDINGS IN CHRONOLOGICAL ORDER VOL. 2 (LP)	15

NIC JONES
70	Trailer LER 2014	BALLADS AND SONGS (LP, red label, later with 'highway' label)	20/12
71	Trailer LER 2027	NIC JONES (LP, red label)	15
	(see also Jon Raven, Halliard)		

NIGEL MAZLYN JONES
76	Isle Of Light IOL 666/1	SHIP TO SHORE (LP)	40
78	Avada AVA 105	SENTINEL (LP)	15
82	Isle Of Light IOL 0230	BREAKING COVER (LP)	15

PALMER JONES
68	Direction 58-3603	The Great Magic Of Love/Dancing Master	20

PAUL JONES
66	HMV POP 1554	High Time/I Can't Hold On Much Longer	7
67	HMV POP 1576	I've Been A Bad Bad Boy/Sonny Boy Williamson	7
67	HMV POP 1602	Thinkin' Ain't For Me/Softly (La Vita)	7
67	HMV PSR 5307	Privilege (1-sided demo)	15
67	Columbia DB 8303	Sons And Lovers/Three Sisters	8
68	Columbia DB 8379	And The Sun Will Shine/The Dog Presides	25
68	Columbia DB 8417	When I Was Six Years Old/You Have No Idea	10
68	Columbia DB 8514	Aquarius/Pisces	6
69	Columbia DB 8567	It's Getting Better/Not Before Time	8
71	Vertigo 6059 053	Life After Death/The Mighty Ship	8
73	Philips 6006 282	Perfect Roadie/Mouth Organ	6
78	RSO RSO 003	Sheena Is A Punk Rocker/Pretty Vacant (p/s)	5
67	HMV 7EG 8974	PRIVILEGE (EP)	20
66	HMV CLP/CSD 3586	MY WAY (LP, mono/stereo)	25/30
67	HMV CLP/CSD 3602	LOVE ME, LOVE MY FRIENDS (LP, mono/stereo)	25/30
67	HMV CLP/CSD 3623	PRIVILEGE (LP, soundtrack, with George Bean Group & Mike Leander)	30
69	Columbia SX/SCX 6347	COME INTO MY MUSIC BOX (LP, mono/stereo)	20
71	Vertigo 6360 059	CRUCIFIX IN A HORSESHOE (LP, gatefold sleeve, swirl label)	65
70	President PTLS 1068	DRAKE'S DREAM (LP, soundtrack)	20
	(see also Manfred Mann, Blues Band)		

QUINCY JONES
59	Mercury AMT 1037	Tuxedo Junction/The Syncopated Clock	5
60	Mercury AMT 1111	Love Is Here To Stay/Moonglow	5
62	Mercury AMT 1195	Soul Bossa Nova/On The Street Where You Live	25
65	Mercury MF 844	Seaweed/Golden Boy Theme	5
69	RCA RCA 1850	MacKenna's Gold/Soul Full Of Gold	5
70	A&M AMS 781	Killer Joe/Oh Happy Day	5
72	A&M AMS 888	Ironside/Cast Your Fate To The Wind	5
72	Reprise K 14150	Money Runned	8
72	Atlantic K 10172	Listen To The Melody/Hot Rock Theme	5
60	Mercury ZEP 10047	BIG BAND BASH (EP)	12
61	Mercury ZEP 10109	THE BIRTH OF A BAND (EP, also stereo SEZ 19017)	10/15
61	Columbia SEG 8088	DOUBLE SIX MEET QUINCY JONES (EP)	12
61	Mercury ZEP 10119	THE BIRTH OF A BAND PT. 2 (EP, also stereo SEZ 19021)	10/12
60	Mercury MMC 14038	THE BIRTH OF A BAND (LP, also stereo CMS 18026)	12/15
60	Mercury MMC 14046	THE GREAT WORLD OF QUINCY JONES (LP, also stereo CMS 18031)	12/15
61	Mercury MMC 14080	I DIG DANCERS (LP, also stereo CMS 18055)	each 15
62	HMV CLP 1581	THE QUINTESSENCE (LP, also stereo CSD 1452)	each 15
62	Mercury MMC 14098	AROUND THE WORLD (LP, also stereo CMS 18064)	each 15
63	Mercury MMC 14125	BIG BAND BOSSA NOVA (LP, also stereo CMS 18080)	each 15
63	Mercury MMC 14128	PLAYS HIP HITS (LP)	15
64	Mercury MCL 20016	EXPLORES THE MUSIC OF HENRY MANCINI (LP, also stereo SMCL 20016)	each 15
65	Columbia 33SX 1637	QUINCY'S HOME AGAIN (LP)	15
65	Mercury 20047 MCL	GOLDEN BOY (LP)	15
65	Mercury 20063 SMCL	THE PAWNBROKER (LP, soundtrack)	25
66	Mercury 20072 (S)MCL	"MIRAGE" (LP, soundtrack)	30
66	Mercury 20073 (S)MCL	PLAYS FOR PUSSYCATS (LP)	15
66	Mercury 20078 (S)MCL	QUINCY'S GOT A BRAND NEW BAG (LP)	15
66	Fontana FJL 127	FAB! (LP)	15
67	Mercury SMWL 30003	TRAVELLIN' ON THE QUINCY JONES BANDWAGON (LP)	15
68	RCA Victor RD/SF 7931	IN COLD BLOOD (LP, soundtrack)	45
68	United Artists (S)ULP 1181	IN THE HEAT OF THE NIGHT (LP, soundtrack, with Ray Charles)	25

69	Uni UNLS 103	LOST MAN (LP, soundtrack)	25
69	Paramount SPFL 256	THE ITALIAN JOB (LP, soundtrack, with Matt Monro)	100
69	RCA Victor SF 8017	MACKENNA'S GOLD (LP, soundtrack, with Jose Feliciano)	15
70	United Artists UAS 29128	THEY CALL ME MISTER TIBBS (LP, soundtrack)	60
70	A&M AMLS 961	WALKING IN SPACE (LP; reissued as AMLH 68050)	12
71	A&M AMLS 992	GULA MATIRA (LP)	12
71	A&M AMLS 63037	SMACKWATER JACK (LP)	15
72	WEA K 44168	THE HEIST (LP, soundtrack, with Little Richard)	35
72	Atlantic K 40371	HOW TO STEAL A DIAMOND IN FOUR UNEASY LESSONS (LP, soundtrack)	18
73	A&M AMLS 63041	YOU'VE GOT IT BAD GIRL (LP)	12
74	A&M AMLH 6317	BODY HEAT (LP)	15
75	A&M AMLH 64526	MELLOW MADNESS (LP)	12
75	A&M AMLP 8005	IRONSIDE (LP)	12

(see also Annie Ross, Eddie Barclay & Quincy Jones, Diana Ross & Quincy Jones, John & Joan Shakespeare)

RICK JONES
73	Argo ZDA 156	HIYA MAYA (LP)	12

ROBIN JONES & HIS QUINTET
71	Apollo Sound APPS 5012	DENGA (LP)	40
71	Apollo Sound	EL MAJA (LP)	50

RONNIE JONES
64	Decca F 12012	Let's Pin A Rose On You/I Need Your Loving (B-side with Night Timers)	20
65	Decca F 12066	My Love/It's All Over	20
65	Decca F 12146	Anyone Who Knows What Love Is/Nobody But You	20
65	Parlophone R 5326	You're Lookin' Good/I'm So Clean (with Blue Jays)	40
67	CBS 2699	Little Bitty Pretty One/Put Your Tears Away	18
67	Polydor 56222	In My Love Mind/Mama Come On Home	12
68	CBS 3304	Without Love (There Is Nothing)/Little Bitty Pretty One	12

(see also Night-Timers)

SALENA JONES
66	Columbia DB 7818	A Walk In The Black Forest (Our Walk Of Love)/As Long As I Live	7
66	Columbia DB 7991	I Am Yours/I Only Know I Love You	7
67	Columbia DB 8212	When I Tell You (That I Love You)/Respect	6
73	Indigo GOPOP	Live And Let Die/Some Other World (some in p/s)	15/6
69	CBS 63613	THE MOMENT OF TRUTH (LP)	35
70	CBS 63650	EVERYBODY'S TALKIN' ABOUT SALENA JONES (LP)	35
73	RCA Victor SF 8335	ALONE & TOGETHER (LP)	22
74	RCA LPL 1 5025	THIS'N'THAT (LP)	22
71	CBS 64435	PLATINUM (LP)	25

SALINA JONES
65	Polydor 56012	Longing/Too Late	7

SAMANTHA JONES
65	United Artists UP 1072	It's All Because Of You/I Woke Up Crying	10
65	United Artists UP 1087	Don't Come Any Closer/Just Call And I'll Be There	12
65	United Artists UP 1105	Chained To A Memory/Just For Him	10
66	United Artists UP 1139	That Special Way/Somebody Else's Baby	10
67	United Artists UP 1185	Surrounded By A Ray Of Sunshine/How Do You Say Goodbye (DJ = £150)	80
67	United Artists UP 1200	Why Can't I Remember/Live For Life	8
68	United Artists UP 2248	Lonely Lonely Man/Doll On A Music Box	10
68	United Artists UP 2258	And Suddenly/Go Ahead And Love Me	50
68	Ford	Ford Leads The Way/Go Ahead And Love Me (p/s, Ford cars promo disc)	25
69	Penny Farthing PEN 703	Today (Without You)/The Feelin' That I Get	6
69	Penny Farthing PEN 708	Do I Still Figure In Your Life?/I'm Sorry, But I Think I Love You	6
70	Penny Farthing PEN 734	My Way/Darling Be Home Soon	5
70	Penny Farthing PEN 746	Best Of Both Worlds/Guilty Of Loving You	5
68	United Artists	CALL IT SAMANTHA (LP)	12
70	Contour 2870 003	MY WAY (LP)	12

(see also Vernons Girls, Krimson Kake)

SAMMY JONES
70	Gas GAS 123	You're My Girl/HONEYBOY MARTIN: Unchained Melody	6
72	Sioux SI 002	Mendicino/RUM RUNNERS: Sugar Brown	5
72	Sioux SI 003	Little Caesar/TWINKLE BROTHERS: Happy Song	5
72	Sioux SI 011	You're My Girl/HONEY BOY MARTIN: Unchained Melody	5

SANDIE JONES
72	Polydor 2058 223	Music Of Love/Ceol An Ghra	12

SOLOMON JONES
70	Bullet BU 452	Be Strong/Version	5
70	Pama PM 812	Here Comes The Night/RECO RODRIGUEZ: Jaded Ramble	8

SPIKE JONES
53	HMV 7M 121	Hot Lips/Hotter Than A Pistol (as Spike Jones & His Country Cousins)	12
53	HMV 7M 160	I Saw Mommy Kissing Santa Claus/Winter (as Spike Jones & His City Slickers)	12
54	HMV 7MC 3	Deep Purple/Dragnet (as Spike Jones & His City Slickers, export issue)	10
54	HMV 7MC 17	I Wanna Go Back To West Virginia/Little Bo-Beep Has Lost Her Sheep (as Spike Jones & His City Slickers, export issue)	10
55	HMV 7M 324	Secret Love/I'm In The Mood For Love (as Spike Jones & His City Slickers)	10
61	Warner Bros WB 34	Monster Movie Babe/Teenage Brain Surgeon	10
57	HMV 7EG 8286	FUN IN HI FI (EP)	10
59	RCA RCX 1030	SPIKE JONES NO. 1 (EP)	10
59	RCA RCX 1037	SPIKE JONES NO. 2 (EP)	10
61	Warners W(S) EP 6044	SPIKE JONES IN HI FI (EP, mono/stereo)	10/12
60	Warner Bros WM 4004	THE BAND THAT PLAYS FOR FUN (LP, also stereo WS 8004)	12/15

60	London HA-G 2270	OMNIBUST — T.V. SCHEDULE (LP, also stereo SAH-G 6090)	12/15
61	London HA-G 2298	SIXTY YEARS OF MUSIC AMERICA HATES BEST (LP, stereo SAH-G 6106)	12/15

STAN JONES
58	Pye Disneyland DPL 39000	CREAKIN' LEATHER (LP)	20

STEVE JONES
87	MCA MCA 1184	Mercy/Through The Night (p/s)	7
89	MCA MCAT 1371	Freedom Fighter/Gimme Love/Suffragette City (12", p/s)	8
87	MCA MCF 3384	MERCY (LP)	15
90	MCA CD45 18179	STEVE JONES LIVE (CD sampler, promo only from unissued LP, clear PVC sleeve)	15

(see also Sex Pistols, Professionals)

TAMIKO JONES
75	Arista ARIST 6	Touch Me Baby/Creepin' On My Dreams	6
76	Contempo CS 2079	I'm Spellbound/T.J.'s Magic	8
76	Contempo CX 15	Let It Flow/DORIS DUKE: Woman Of The Ghetto	15

THAD JONES
58	Nixa Jazz NJL 13	LEONARD FEATHER PRESENTS MAD THAD (LP, with others)	15

THELMA JONES
68	Sue WI 4047	Stronger/Never Leave Me	50
69	Soul City SC 110	The House That Jack Built/Give It To Me Straight	30
76	CBS 4711	Salty Tears/You're The Song	15

THUNDERCLAP JONES
56	Oriole CB 1320	Hurricane Boogie/The Laughing Rag (78)	10
56	Oriole CB 1328	Sound Barrier Boogie/Ask For Joe (78)	10

TOM JONES
64	Decca F 11966	Chills And Fever/Breathless	60
65	Decca F 12062	It's Not Unusual/To Wait For Love (Is To Waste Your Life Away)	5
65	Decca F 12121	Once Upon A Time/I Tell The Sea	6
65	Columbia DB 7566	Little Lonely One/That's What We'll All Do	25
65	Decca F 12191	With These Hands/Untrue	6
65	Decca F 12203	What's New Pussycat?/Rose	7
65	Columbia DB 7733	Lonely Joe/I Was A Fool	30
65	Decca F 12292	Thunderball/Key To My Heart	10
66	Decca F 12315	To Make A Big Man Cry/I'll Never Let You Go (export issue)	15
66	Decca F 12349	Stop Breaking My Heart/Never Give Away Love	8
66	Decca F 12390	Once There Was A Time/Not Responsible	12
66	Decca F 12461	This And That/City Girl	7
66	Decca F 12516	Green, Green Grass Of Home/If I Had You (export issue)	15
67	Decca F 22555	Detroit City/If I Had You	6
67	Decca F 22563	Detroit City/Ten Guitars (export issue)	15
68	Decca F 12854	A Minute Of Your Time/Looking Out My Window	10
71	Decca FR 13236	Till//The Sun Died (export issue)	15
71	Decca FR 13237	Till/One Day Soon (export issue)	15
73	Decca F 13434	Today I Started Loving You Again/I Still Love You Enough	6
73	Decca F 13471	Golden Days/Goodbye, God Bless You Baby	6
74	Decca F 13490	La La La (Just Having You Here)/Love Love Love	6
74	Decca F 13564	Pledging My Love/I'm Too Far Gone (To Turn Away)	6
75	Decca F 13575	Ain't No Love/When The Band Goes Home	6
75	Decca F 13590	I Got Your Number/The Pain Of Love	6
75	Decca F 13598	Memories Don't Leave Like People Do/My Helping Hand	6
70s	Decca F 12747/12062	Delilah/It's Not Unusual (double-A-side with different number each side)	6
82	Decca JONES 1	I'll Be Here Where The Heart Is/My Last Goodbye (p/s)	6
87	Epic OLE Q1	A Boy From Nowhere/I'll Dress You In Mourning (poster p/s)	6
65	Decca DFE 8617	ON STAGE (EP)	15
65	Columbia SEG 8464	TOM JONES (EP)	48
65	Decca DFE 8668	WHAT A PARTY (EP)	15
65	Decca LK 4693	ALONG CAME JONES (LP)	15
65	Decca LK/SKL 4743	A-TOM-IC JONES (LP, mono/stereo)	12/15
66	Decca LK 4814	FROM THE HEART (LP)	12
67	Decca SKL 4855	GREEN, GREEN GRASS OF HOME (LP, stereo)	12
67	Decca SKL 4874	LIVE! AT THE TALK OF THE TOWN (LP, stereo)	12
67	Decca SKL 4909	13 SMASH HITS (LP, stereo)	12

(Mono copies of the above three albums are worth around £8 each)

68	Decca LK 4946	DELILAH (LP, mono)	12
68	Decca LK 4982	HELP YOURSELF (LP, mono)	20
69	Decca LK 5007	THIS IS TOM JONES (LP, mono)	15
69	Decca LK 5032	LIVE IN LAS VEGAS — AT THE FLAMINGO (LP, mono)	12

(All the above LPs were issued with unboxed Decca logos on the labels; later boxed label logo copies are worth £8 each)

70	Decca LK 5045	TOM (LP, mono)	12
70	Decca LK 5072	I, WHO HAVE NOTHING (LP, mono)	12

(Stereo copies of the above two albums are worth £10 each)

U.K. JONES
69	Deram DM 231	Let Me Tell Ya/And The Rains Came Down	8
70	Ember EMB S 298	Take Me For What I Am/Love Is Here To Stay	6
	(see also Mike Berry)		

WINSTON JONES
73	Gayfeet GS 208	You Make Me Cry/Version	6

MINT VALUE £

WIZZ JONES

69	United Artists (S)ULP 1029	WIZZ JONES (LP)	120
70	Village Thing VTS 4	LEGENDARY ME (LP)	25
72	CBS 64809	RIGHT NOW (LP)	60
74	Village Thing VTS 24	WHEN I LEAVE BERLIN (LP)	20
77	Plant Life PLR 009	MAGICAL FLIGHT (LP, with insert)	15

(see also Pete Stanley & Wizz Jones, Accolade)

JONES BOYS

57	Columbia DB 4046	Cool Baby/Rock-A-Hula Baby (Ukulele Lady)	15
58	Columbia DB 4170	A Certain Smile/Kathy-O	7
58	Columbia DB 4217	The Day The Rains Came/Hideaway	7
59	Columbia DB 4278	Dream Girl/Straight As An Arrow	6

(see also Four Jones Boys)

JONES GIRLS

82	Philadelphia Intl. PIR 2031	Nights Over Egypt/Love Don't Ever Say Goodbye	8
82	Phil. Intl. PIR 12-2031	Nights Over Egypt/Love Don't Ever Say Goodbye (12")	10
79	Phil. Intl. PIR 83831	THE JONES GIRLS (LP)	15

JONESY

73	Dawn DNS 1030	Ricochet/Every Day's The Same	20
72	Dawn DNLS 3042	NO ALTERNATIVE (LP, gatefold sleeve)	30
73	Dawn DNLS 3048	KEEPING UP (LP)	30
73	Dawn DNLS 3055	GROWING (LP, gatefold sleeve)	30

(see also Alan Bown)

HARLEM JONNS RESHUFFLE

68	Fontana TF 970	You Are The One I Love/Good Lovin'	30
69	Fontana TF 1004	Everything Under The Sun/Let Love Come Between Us	20
69	Fontana (S)TL 5509	HARLEM JONNS RESHUFFLE (LP)	30

JONSTON McPHILBRY

66	Fontana TF 663	She's Gone/Woke Up At Eight	80

JOOK

72	RCA RCA 2279	Alright With Me/Do What You Can	5
73	RCA RCA 2344	Shame/City And Suburban Blues	5
73	RCA RCA 2368	Oo-Oo-Rudi/Jook's On You	5
73	RCA RCA 2431	King Capp/Rumble	5
74	RCA RCA 5024	Bish Bash Bosh/Crazy Kids	5
78	Chiswick SW 30	Watch Your Step/La La Girl/Aggravation Place/Everything I Do (EP)	5

(see also John's Children)

JANIS JOPLIN

69	CBS 3683	Turtle Blues/Piece Of My Heart (withdrawn)	30+
71	CBS 7019	Me And Bobby McGee/Half Moon	6
71	CBS 7217	Cry Baby/Mercedes Benz	6
71	CBS 9136	Move Over/Cry Baby/Try/Piece Of My Heart (maxi-single)	8
72	CBS 8241	Down On Me/Bye Bye Baby	6
76	CBS 3960	Piece Of My Heart/Kozmic Blues (p/s)	7
69	CBS 63546	I GOT DEM OL' KOZMIC BLUES AGAIN, MAMA! (LP)	25
74	CBS CQ 30322/Q 64188	PEARL (LP, quadrophonic)	25

(see also Big Brother & Holding Company)

DANNY JORDAN

61	Mercury AMT 1159	Jeannie/Boom Ditty Boom	10

DICK JORDAN

60	Embassy WB 384	Let It Be Me/Running Bear (78)	8
60	Embassy WB 394	Cathy's Clown/Don't Throw All Those Teardrops (78)	8
60	Oriole CB 1534	Hallelujah, I Love Her So/Sandy (78 rpm = £35)	20
60	Oriole CB 1548	Little Christine/I'll Love You Forever (78 rpm = £35)	18
60	Oriole CB 1566	Garden Of Eden/Alive, Alive Oh!	8
60	Oriole CB 1591	Angel On My Shoulder/The Next Train Home	15
61	Piccadilly 7N 35035	Some Of These Days/I Want Her Back	75
62	Piccadilly 7N 35057	Fortune Teller/My Angel	10
63	Columbia DB 7016	Stop The Music/Dream Chaser	10

(see also Don Duke)

FRED JORDAN

66	Topic 12T 150	SONGS OF A SHROPSHIRE FARM WORKER (LP, blue label)	15

JOHNNY JORDAN

57	HMV POP 349	It's Grand To Be In Love/Home At Last	5

LOUIS JORDAN (& HIS TYMPANY FIVE)

54	Melodisc 1031	Dad Gum Ya Hide Boy/Whiskey Do Your Stuff (78)	15
56	Melodisc 1349	Messy Bessy/I Seen What'cha Done (78)	20
60	Downbeat CHA 3	Ooo-Wee/I'll Die Happy	20
50s	Melodisc EPM7 66	LOUIS JORDAN (EP, as Louis Jordan Tympany Five, 3 different covers)	each 90
57	Mercury MPT 7521	SOMEBODY UP THERE DIGS ME (10" LP, with Tympany Five)	145
58	Mercury MPL 6541	MAN, WE'RE WAILIN' (LP, with Tympany Five)	65
64	HMV CLP 1809	HALLELUJAH, LOUIS JORDAN IS BACK (LP)	48
65	Ace Of Hearts AH 85	LET THE GOOD TIMES ROLL (LP)	18

(see also Louis Armstrong)

LOUIS JORDAN & CHRIS BARBER'S BAND

63	Melodisc 45-1616	Is She Is Or Is She Ain't Your Baby/Fifty Cents	18

(see also Chris Barber)

JORDANAIRES

57	Capitol CL 14687	Sugaree/Baby, Won't You Please Come Home? (78 rpm = £22)	80
57	Capitol CL 14773	Summer Vacation/Each Day (78 rpm = £18)	20
58	Capitol CL 14921	Little Miss Ruby/All I Need Is You	25
63	Capitol CL 15281	Don't Be Cruel/Don't Worry	18
71	Ember EMB S 313	Kentucky/Teach The World To Sing	6
62	Capitol T 1742	SPOTLIGHT ON THE JORDANAIRES (LP)	65

(see also Elvis Presley, Patsy Cline, Don Gibson, Marty Robbins)

JORDAN BROTHERS

59	London HLW 8908	Never, Never/Please Tell Me Now (78 rpm = £35)	30
60	London HLW 9235	Things I Didn't Say/Polly Plays Her Kettle Drum	15
61	London HLW 9308	No Wings On My Angel/Living For The Day	10

JOSEF K

79	Absolute ABS 1	Chance Meeting/Romance (p/s, 1,000 only)	25
80	Postcard 80-3	Radio Drill Time/Crazy To Exist (live) (hand-coloured foldaround p/s, blue labels)	15
80	Postcard 80-3	Radio Drill Time/Crazy To Exist (live) (brown or cream/yellow sleeve & labels)	8/7
80	Postcard 80-5	It's Kinda Funny/Final Request (p/s in poly bag, some with picture insert)	10/6
81	Postcard 81-5	Chance Meeting/Pictures (die-cut sleeve, some with postcard)	8/6
81	Postcard 81-4/TWI 023	Sorry For Laughing/Revelation (p/s)	8
87	Supreme Intl. Edit. 87-7	Heaven Sent/Radio Drill Time/Heads Watch/Fun'n'Frenzy (12", p/s)	8
90	Supreme Intl. Edit.	Young And Stupid (CD)	12
81	Postcard 81-1	SORRY FOR LAUGHING (LP, unreleased, a few with proof sleeve)	
81	Postcard 81-7	THE ONLY FUN IN TOWN (LP, with inner sleeve)	15
87	Supreme Intl. Edit. 87-6	YOUNG AND STUPID (LP)	12

(see also Orange Juice, Paul Haig, Happy Family, Rhythm Of Life)

IRVING JOSEPH

60	London HLT 9027	I Left My Love/Lorena	8

MARGIE JOSEPH (& BLUE MAGIC)

72	Stax 2025 052	Medicine Bend/Same Thing	8
74	Atlantic K 10460	Sweet Surrender/My Love	6
75	Atlantic K 10649	What's Come Over Me/You And Me (as Margie Joseph & Blue Magic)	6
72	Stax 2362 008	MAKES A NEW IMPRESSION (LP)	25
73	Atlantic K 40462	MARGIE JOSEPH (LP)	20

(see also Blue Magic)

JOSH

69	Duke DU 41	Judge/RON: Soul Of Joemel	10
70	Hot Rod HR 111	Leaving Everything/HOT ROD ALL STARS : Psychedelic Bird	20

(see also Girlie)

JOSH & HERBIE

60s	Kalypso AB 107	I'm Nobody's Child/How Can I Believe In You	6

JOSHUA

73	Key KL 014	JOSHUA (LP)	140

MARVA JOSIE

66	Polydor 56711	Crazy Stockings/I'll Get By	16

JOURNEY

82	CBS CBS 11A 1728	Don't Stop Believin'/Natural Thing (12", picture disc)	8
92	Columbia 4728102	TIME3 (3-CD)	25

JOURNEYMEN

67	Ember EMB 3382	INTRODUCING THE JOURNEYMEN (LP)	12

RODDIE JOY

65	Red Bird RB 10021	Come Back Baby/Love Hit Me With A Wallop	50

JOY & DAVID/DAVE

58	Parlophone R 4477	Whoopee!/My Oh My! (as Joy & David)	45
58	Parlophone R 4477	Whoopee!/My Oh My! (78, as Joy & David)	40
59	Decca F 11123	Rocking Away The Blues/If You Pass Me By (as Joy & David)	45
59	Decca F 11123	Rocking Away The Blues/If You Pass Me By (78, as Joy & David)	50
60	Triumph RGM 1002	Let's Go See Gran'ma/Believe Me (as Joy & Dave)	45
60	Decca F 11291	My Very Good Friend The Milkman/Doopey Darling (as Joy & Dave)	35
61	Parlophone R 4855	Joe's Been A-Gittin' There/They Tell Us Not To Love (as Joy & Dave)	30
61	Parlophone R 4855	Joe's Been A-Gittin' There/They Tell Us Not To Love (demo copies with alternate take of B-side)	45

JOHNNY JOYCE

76	Freedom FLP 99003	JOYCE'S CHOICE MIXTURE (LP)	22

(see also Velvet Opera, Levee Breakers)

JOYCE'S ANGELS

67	Major Minor MM 526	Flowers For My Friends/Rodney Reginald Smithfield Harvey Jo	8

(see also Chris White)

JOY DE VIVRE

81	Crass CR & SS ENVY 1	Our Wedding (flexidisc, white vinyl, no p/s, some with mailer)	18/12

(see also Crass)

JOY DIVISION

78	Enigma PSS 139	AN IDEAL FOR LIVING (Warsaw/No Love Lost/Leaders Of Men/Failures) (EP, 1,000 only, foldout p/s; beware of counterfeits)	800
78	Anonymous ANON 1	AN IDEAL FOR LIVING (Warsaw/No Love Lost/Leaders Of Men/Failures) (12" EP reissue, 1,200 only)	400
79	Factory FAC 13	Transmission/Novelty (p/s)	6

80	Factory FAC 28	Komakino/Incubation/(As You Said) (flexidisc, 10,000 only)	5
88	Factory FACD 213	Atmosphere/Love Will Tear Us Apart/Transmission (live) (CD)	8
79	Factory FACT 10	UNKNOWN PLEASURES (LP with inner sleeve, textured sleeve)	18
81	Factory FACT 40	STILL (2-LP, hessian sleeve, card inners & white ribbon)	40

(see also New Order)

COL JOYE & JOYBOYS

59	Brunswick 05806	(Rockin' Rollin') Clementine/Bye Bye Baby Goodbye (78 rpm = £25)	25
60	Top Rank JAR 529	Be My Girl/Yes Sir, That's My Baby	10

JOYFUL SINGERS (with Lynn Tait on organ)

67	Master Time MT 001	Jesus Christ Is Risen/BELIEVERS: Honey In The Rock	6
67	Master Time MT 002	Happy Days/He Watches Over Me	6

(see also Lyn[n] Tait)

JOYFUL SOUND

73	SRT SRT 73278	IT WILL BE WORTH IT ALL (LP)	300

JOY GUESSING

70	Crimson N 034	The Blue Midget/Officer Bud Babe	6

JOY OF COOKING

72	Capitol E-ST 11050	CASTLES (LP)	12

JOYRIDE

69	RCA SF 8027	FRIEND SOUND (LP)	30

JOY UNLIMITED

69	Page One POF 147	Daytime Night Time/Mister Pseudonym	18
69	Page One POF 160	Oh Darlin'/Feeling	10
70	Page One POLS 028	TURBULENCE (LP)	60

J.S.D. BAND

73	Cube BUG 29	Sarah Jane/Paddy Stacks (p/s)	6
71	Regal Zono. SRLZ 1018	COUNTRY OF THE BLIND (LP)	45
72	Cube HIFLY 11	J.S.D. BAND (LP)	12
73	Cube HIFLY 14	TRAVELLING DAYS (LP)	12

JUAN & JUNIOR

67	CBS 2949	The Chase/Nothing	6
68	CBS 3223	To Girls/Andurina	15

JUBILEE STOMPERS

70	Trojan TR 7725	Luciana/I Really Like It	6

JUDAS JUMP

70	Parlophone R 5828	Run For Your Life/Beer Drinking Woman	7
70	Parlophone R 5838	This Feelin' We Feel/Hangman's Playing	8
70	Parlophone R 5873	Beer Drinking Woman/I Have The Right	6
70	Parlophone PAS 10001	SCORCH (LP)	25

(see also Herd, Amen Corner, Andy Bown)

JUDAS PRIEST

74	Gull GULS 6	Rocka-Rolla/Never Satisfied	15
76	Gull GULS 31	The Ripper/Island Of Domination	15
77	CBS S CBS 5222	Diamonds And Rust/Dissident Aggressor	7
78	CBS S CBS 6077	Better By You, Better Than Me/Invader	5
78	CBS S CBS 6719	Evening Star/Starbreaker	5
78	CBS S CBS 6794	Before The Dawn/Rock Forever	5
79	CBS S CBS 6915	Take On The World/Starbreaker	5
79	CBS S CBS 12-6915	Take On The World/Starbreaker/White Heat Red Hot (12", p/s)	8
79	CBS S CBS 7312	Evening Star/Beyond The Realms Of Death	5
79	CBS 12-7312	Evening Star/The Green Manalishi/Beyond The Realms Of Death (12", clear vinyl with picture insert)	8
79	Gull GULS 71	The Ripper/Victims Of Change	8
79	Gull GULS 7112	The Ripper/Never Satisfied/Victim Of Changes (12", p/s)	12
80	CBS TA 4298	United/Grinder (poster p/s)	10
81	CBS A12 1153	Hot Rockin'/Steeler/You Don't Have To Be Old To Be Wise (12", no p/s)	8
82	CBS A 112611	You've Got Another Thing Comin'/Exciter (live) (picture disc)	6
82	CBS A 2822	(Take These) Chains/Judas Priest Audio File (p/s)	5
83	Gull GULS 7612	Tyrant/Rocka-Rolla/Genocide (12", p/s, white vinyl)	12
84	CBS TA 4298	Some Heads Are Gonna Roll/Green Manalishi (Live)/Jawbreaker (12", p/s)	8
86	CBS QTA 7144	Locked In (Extended)/Reckless/Desert Plains (live)/Freewheel Burning (live) (12", poster p/s)	10
88	Atlantic A 9114CD	Johnny B. Goode/Rock You All Around The World (live)/Turbo Lover (live)/Living After Midnight (live) (3" CD, with 5" adaptor in 5" case)	8
90	Columbia 656273 6	Painkiller/United/Better By You, Better Than Me (12" red vinyl, p/s)	8
91	Columbia 656589 0	A Touch Of Evil/Between The Hammer And The Anvil (shaped disc)	10
91	Columbia 656589 6	A Touch Of Evil/Between The Hammer And The Anvil/You've Got Another Thing Coming (Live) (12", p/s, with giant poster)	8
74	Gull GULP 1005	ROCKA ROLLA (LP, original issue, 'bottle top' sleeve)	15
76	Gull PGULP 1015	SAD WINGS OF DESTINY (LP, picture disc)	15
78	Gull PGULP 1026	THE BEST OF JUDAS PRIEST (LP, picture disc)	15
78	CBS 83135	KILLING MACHINE (LP, red vinyl)	15
79	CBS 83852	UNLEASHED IN THE EAST (LP, with free single "Rock Forever"/"Hell Bent For Leather"/"Beyond The Realms Of Death" [SJP 1])	15
79	CBS 66357	BOX SET (3-LP, reissue of "Sin After Sin"/"Stained Class"/"Killing Machine")	20
86	Shanghai PGLP 1026	JUDAS PRIEST (LP, picture disc)	12
93	CBS XPR1896	METAL WORKS (promo single LP, grey vinyl in custom/stickered black sleeve)	20
93	CBS 473050	METAL WORKS (2-LP)	20
98	SPV 0891 8542	98 LIVE MELTDOWN (LP)	12

(see also Trapeze, Fancy)

JUDD
| 70 | Penny Farthing PEN 709 | Snarlin' Mumma Lion/Stronger Than A Man. | 6 |
| 70 | Penny Farthing PEL 504 | JUDD (LP) | 30 |

(see also Kris Ife)

TERRY JUDGE & THE BARRISTERS
63	Oriole CB 1896	Hey Look At Her/Kind Of Girl You Can't Forget.	18
64	Oriole CB 1938	I Don't Care/Try To Forget	18
65	Fontana TF 599	Come With Me And Love Me/Waitin' For The Night To Come	15

JUDGE DREAD
| 72 | Big Shot BI 608 | Big Six/One-Armed Bandit (no p/s) | 5 |
| 74 | Horse HOSS 62 | Hey There Lonely Girl/The Planet Of The Apes (as J.D. Alex, no p/s). | 5 |

JUDGE HAPPINESS
| 85 | Mynah SCS 8501 | Hey Judge/Pig In Pink (very few with p/s) | 25/10 |

(see also Mock Turtles)

JUGGERNAUTS
| 84 | Supreme Int. Editions 84-2 | Come Throw Yourself/My First Million (p/s) | 10 |

(see also Paul Haig)

JUICE ON THE LOOSE
| 81 | Juice JJOS 1 | JUICE ON THE LOOSE (LP) | 12 |

JUICY LUCY
70	Fontana TF 1068	Who Do You Love/Walking Down The Highway (unissued)	
70	Vertigo V1/6059 001	Who Do You Love/Walking Down The Highway.	10
70	Vertigo 6059 015	Pretty Woman/I'm A Thief.	18
72	Polydor 2001 279	It Ain't Easy/Promised Land.	12
69	Vertigo VO 2	JUICY LUCY (LP, swirl label, gatefold sleeve)	40
70	Vertigo 6360 014	LIE BACK AND ENJOY IT (LP, swirl label, gatefold poster sleeve)	40
71	Bronze ILPS 9157	GET A WHIFF OF THIS (LP)	15
72	Polydor 2310 160	PIECES (LP).	15

(see also Misunderstood, Van Der Graaf Generator, Ray Owen, Paul Williams' Big Roll Band)

JULIAN (Judy Mowatt) & CHOSEN FEW
| 71 | High Note HS 054 | Joy To The World/Joyful Version | 8 |

JULIAN (Judy Mowatt) & GAYTONES
| 72 | High Note HS 059 | She Kept On Talking/Version | 15 |

JULIAN (Scott)
| 59 | Pye 7N 15236 | Sue Saturday/Can't Wait (78 rpm, Pye N 15236 = £40) | 35 |

(see also Brian Bennett)

JULIAN KIRSCH
| 69 | Columbia DB 8541 | Clever Little Man/The Adventures Of A Young Cuckoo | 25 |

JULIAN'S TREATMENT
| 70 | Young Blood YB 1009 | Phantom City/Alda, Dark Lady Of The Outer Worlds | 15 |
| 70 | Young Blood SYB 2 | A TIME BEFORE THIS (2-LP) | 130 |

(see also Julian Jay Savarin)

JULY
68	Major Minor MM 568	My Clown/Dandelion Seeds	180+
68	Major Minor MM 580	Hello, Who's There?/The Way	100
68	Major Minor MMLP 29	JULY (LP)	500
87	Bam Caruso KIRI 097	DANDELION SEEDS (LP, reissue of above LP with extra tracks & different sleeve).	22
95	Essex 1011LP	JULY (LP, reissue with bonus 7": "Hello Who's There?"/"The Way" [p/s, 10117]).	20

(see also Jade Warrior, Tom Newman, Tomcats)

JUMBLE LANE
| 71 | Holyground HG 115 | JUMBLE LANE (LP, 99 copies only) | 500 |

JUMP
| 80 | Caveman CLUB 1 | Shake Up/All In Vain (p/s) | 25 |

JUMPIN' JACKS
| 58 | HMV POP 440 | My Girl, My Girl/Tried And Tested (78 rpm = £18) | 25 |

JUMPLEADS
| 82 | Ock OC 001 | THE STAG MUST DIE (LP, with insert) | 20 |

JUMP SQUAD
| 81 | 101 UR 2 | Lord Of The Dance/Debt (p/s) | 20 |

(see also Embryo)

JUNCO PARTNERS
65	Columbia DB 7665	As Long As I Have You/Take This Hammer	60
79	Rigid JUNK 1028	Swinging Sixties Boys/Peepin' And Hidin'.	6
81	Energy NRG 4	Tall Windows/Noizez In My Head (p/s)	5
81	Energy NRGX 4	Tall Windows (Extended)/Noizez In My Head (Extended) (12", stickered white label, plain sleeve, promo only)	10
71	Philips 6308 032	JUNCO PARTNERS (LP).	45

JUNCTION 32
| 75 | Holyground HGS 119 | JUNCTION 32 (LP, 100 copies only) | 500 |

JUNCUNO
| 71 | Banana BA 361 | The End (as Joncuno)/HORACE ANDY: See A Man's Face | 22 |
| 72 | Bamboo BA 69 | Love Is A Stranger/When We Were Children | 8 |

(see also Juncuno Singers)

JUNCUNO SINGERS
| 72 | Banana BA 366 | I'd Like To Teach The World To Sing/Rope Of Sand | 8 |

MINT VALUE £

ROSANNE JUNE
56	London HLU 8352	The Charge Of The Light Brigade/Broken Windows (78 rpm = £12)	30
58	Oriole CB 1430	When A Woman Cries/The Great Chicago Fire (78 rpm = £10)	8

ROSEMARY JUNE
58	Fontana H 141	I'll Always Be In Love With You/Person To Person (78 rpm = £8)	10
59	Pye International 7N 25005	I'll Be With You In Apple Blossom Time/Always A Bridesmaid (78 rpm = £8)	6
59	Pye International 7N 25015	With You Beside Me/I Used To Love You, But It's All Over Now (78 rpm = £8)	6
59	London HLT 9014	The Village Of St. Bernadette/But Not For Me (78 rpm = £15)	10

JUNE BRIDES
84	Pink PINKY 1	In The Rain/Sunday To Saturday (p/s)	10
84	Pink PINKY 2	Every Conversation/Disneyland (die-cut sleeve, some with insert)	8/7
	(see also Phil Wilson)		

JUNG COLLECTIVE
02	Nanny Tango NT 1	Injustice/Street Preacher (Plaid Mix) (clear vinyl, poly sleeve w/sticker insert)	20

HUGH ROY JUNIOR
71	Big BG 329	Papcito/RUPIE EDWARDS: I'm Gonna Live Some Life	8
71	Supreme SUP 211	Double Attack/MURPHY'S ALL STARS: Puzzle	12
72	Ashanti ASH 405	King Of The Road/ROOSEVELT ALL STARS: Version	10
72	Jackpot JP 806	Two Ton Guletto/Version	10
	(see also U Roy Junior)		

U ROY JUNIOR
72	Attack ATT 8030	This Is A Pepper/JOHN HOLT: Justice	8
72	Sioux SI 024	The Wedding/LLOYD'S ALL STARS: Buttercup	8
73	Randy's RAN 532	Froggie/RHYTHM RULERS: Version	10
73	Techniques TE 928	Aunt Kereba/DON RECO: Waterloo Rock (B-side actually by Reco Rodriquez)	12
	(see also Hugh Roy Junior, U Roy)		

JUNIOR (Simpson)
68	Giant GN 18	I'm Gonna Leave You Girl/I Love You I Love You	8
68	Giant GN 25	Come Cure Me/I Want Your Loving	8

JUNIOR BROWN
78	Tempus TEMD 01	Jah Find Babylon Guilty (feat. Ranking Ruben)/Dub (12")	30
80	Jah Shaka 829	Fly Me Away/Travelling Dub	20

JUNIOR ENGLISH
79	Ethnic Fight ETH 1328	Keep On Trying/HORSEMOUTH: Herb Vendor (12")	20
74	Cactus CTLP 102	THE DYNAMIC (LP)	20

JUNIOR DELGADO
78	Deb DEB 019	Trickster/CARLTON & HIS SHOES: Better Days (12")	12
80	Niagra NIADD 108	Fort Augustus/Escape Prisioners (12")	25
86	Incredible IM001	Poverty/Version (12")	50
88	Mango IS 368	Hanging Tree/Hey Good Looking (12")	20

JUNIOR DISPROL
01	SFDB AO27658	Fight Club/Junq Waffle	20

JUNIOR'S EYES
69	Regal Zonophone RZ 3009	Mr. Golden Trumpet Player/Black Snake	20
69	Regal Zonophone RZ 3018	Woman Love/White Light Part 2 (withdrawn B-side)	25
69	Regal Zonophone RZ 3018	Woman Love/Circus Days	20
69	Regal Zonophone RZ 3023	Star Child/Sink Or Swim	20
69	Regal Zono. SLRZ 1008	BATTERSEA POWER STATION (LP)	60
	(see also David Bowie, Tickle, Bunch Of Fives, Outsiders)		

JUNIOR GEE
86	Scorcher 1032	The Truth (12")	18

JUNIOR GEE & THE A TEAM
87	4th & Broadway 63	The Terminator (12")	18

JUNIOR GEE & THE CAPITAL BOYS
84	Tai Wan 1948	Check Us Out/The Break (12")	25

JUNIOR GEE/JUST US
87	Pana 2009	We Want Justice (12")	12

JUNIOR MURVIN
68	Doctor Bird DB 1112	Miss Cushie/LYNN TAITT & JETS: Dr. Paul	30
68	Big Shot BI 503	Chattie Chattie/The Magic Touch	25
69	Big Shot BI 527	The Hustler/The Magic Touch	20
70	Gayfeet GS 205	Jennifer/Slipping	8
77	Island IPR 2001	Tedious/Memories	30
77	Island 12WIP 2010	Upsetter Revue Feat. Junior Murvin: Dread Locks In Moonlight/Closer Together (12")	12
86	Greensleeves GRED 199	Apartheid/Jack Slick (12")	15

JUNIOR REID
81	Negus Roots NERT 09	IF I/Versions (12")	40

JUNIOR ROOTS
81	Black Roots BR 24	Natty Dread Time/BLACK TRAP: Into The Light (12")	12

JUNIORS
64	Columbia DB 7339	There's A Pretty Girl/Pocket Size	55

JUNIPER GREEN
71	Columbia DB 8809	Dreams In The Sky/Cascade Of Ice	25

LENA JUNOFF
68	Olga OLE 8	Yesterday Has Gone/Good Kind Of Hurt	40

Rare Record Price Guide 2008

ERIC JUPP & HIS ORCHESTRA
53	Columbia SCM 5070	Jog Trot/Doina Voda	8
54	Columbia SCM 5081	Ooop De Ooh (Lazy Mambo)/Footsteps In The Fog	8
54	Columbia SCM 5140	They Were Doin' The Mambo/Skokiian (with Coronets)	8
56	Columbia DB 3817	Theme From 'East Of Eden'/When The Lilac Blooms Again	8
57	Columbia DB 4030	Bleep! Bleep!/Three-Two-One-Zero!	10
55	Columbia SEG 7589	ERIC JUPP AND HIS ORCHESTRA (EP)	10
56	Columbia SEG 7603	RHYTHM AND BLUES (EP)	10
56	Columbia SEG 7621	THE PERFECT COMBINATION (EP)	8
56	Columbia 33S 1097	LET'S DANCE (10" LP)	12
58	Columbia 33SX 1072	MUSIC FOR SWEETHEARTS (LP)	12

(see also Coronets, Rockin' Strings)

MICKEY JUPP
83	A&M AM 128	Stormy Sunday Lunchtime/Reading Glasses	5
83	A&M AM 145	Boxes And Tins/Reading Glasses (p/s)	5
83	A&M AMLH 68559	SHAMPOO, HAIRCUT AND SHAVE (LP)	12

(see also Rossi & Frost)

CURT JURGENS
59	Top Rank JAR 151	Ferry To Hong Kong/Live For Love (78 rpm = £15)	8

JUS BADD
87	Tuff GrooveTUFF001	Freestyle/Proud (12")	60

SAMANTHA JUSTE
66	Go AJ 11402	No One Needs My Love Today/If Trees Could Talk	18

JUST FOUR MEN
64	Parlophone R 5186	That's My Baby/Things Will Never Be The Same (withdrawn, as Four Just Men)	80
64	Parlophone R 5208	That's My Baby/Things Will Never Be The Same	60
65	Parlophone R 5241	There's Not One Thing/Don't Come Any Closer	60

(see also Wimple Winch, Four Just Men, Pacific Drift)

JUST FRANK
80	Rok ROK III/IV	You/SPLIT SCREENS: Just Don't Try (die-cut company sleeve)	35

JIMMY JUSTICE
60	Pye 7N 15301	I Understand Just How You Feel/Bloodshot Eyes (as Jimmy Justice & Jury)	20
61	Pye 7N 15351	When Love Has Left You/The Teacher	18
61	Pye 7N 15376	A Little Bit Of Soap/Little Lonely One	15
62	Pye 7N 15421	When My Little Girl Is Smiling/If I Lost Your Love	6
62	Pye 7N 15443	Ain't That Funny/One (some with p/s)	18/7
62	Pye 7N 15457	Spanish Harlem/Write Me A Letter	6
62	Pye 7N 15469	Parade Of Broken Hearts/Dawning	7
63	Pye 7N 15502	The World Of Lonely People/I Wake Up Crying	7
63	Pye 7N 15509	Little Cracked Bell/Lighted Windows	7
63	Pye 7N 15528	The Guitar Player/Don't Let The Stars Get In Your Eyes	7
63	Pye 7N 15558	You're Gonna Need My Lovin'/Since You've Been Gone (with Exchequers)	7
63	Pye 7N 15601	Don't Say That Again/Green Leaves Of Summer	7
69	Decca F 12899	Running Out Of Time/There Goes My World	7
65	Pye 7N 15963	Only Heartbreak For Me/Everything In The Garden	7
68	RCA Victor RCA 1681	I'm Past Forgetting You/Walking Away With My Heart	25
63	Pye NEP 24159	HIT PARADE (EP)	40
62	Pye NPL 18080	TWO SIDES OF JIMMY JUSTICE (LP)	50
62	Pye NPL 18085	SMASH HITS (LP)	50

JUSTIFIED ANCIENTS OF MU MU (J.A.M.s)
87	KLF Comm. JAMS 23	All You Need Is Love (Original) (12", white label, 1-sided, 500 only)	50
87	KLF Comm. JAMS 23(s)	All You Need Is Love (Me Ru Con Mix)/(Ibo Version) (1,000 only, plain sleeve)	10
87	KLF Comm. JAMS 23T	All You Need Is Love/Ivum Naya/Rap, Rhyme And Scratch Yourself (12", 'James Anderton' p/s, 5,000 only)	15
87	KLF Comm. JAMS 24T	Whitney Joins The JAMs (120 bpm) (12", 1-sided, 'Scottish' issue, 500 only)	15
87	KLF Comm. JAMS 25T	1987 — The 45 Edits (12", p/s)	12
87	KLF Comm. JAMS 26T	BURN THE BEAT (12" EP, 5,000 for export only)	10
87	KLF Comm. JAMS 27	Down Town/118 BPM 27 (p/s)	8
87	KLF Comm. JAMS 27	Down Town (A-side Mix) (12", 1-sided, white label, 500 only)	12
87	KLF Comm. JAMS 27	Down Town (B-side Mix) (12", 1-sided, white label, 500 only)	12
87	KLF Comm. JAMS 27	Down Town (A-side Mix)/(B-side Mix) (12", white label)	12
87	KLF Comm. JAMS 27T	Down Town (118 bpm)/Down Town (12", JAMs or mispressed 'album' label, generic sleeve)	10/15
88	KLF Comm. JAMS 28T	It's Grim Up North (Original Vocal Mix) (12", grey vinyl, 1-sided, 350 only)	50
87	KLF Comm. JAMS DS 1	Deep Shit (flexidisc, unreleased)	150
91	KLF Comm. JAMS 028R	It's Grim Up North (Original Vocal Mix) (12", black vinyl, 1-sided promo)	8
88	Fierce FRIGHT 34(T)	20 GREATEST HITS (12" EP; not actually by J.A.M.s!)	12
87	KLF Comm. JAMS LP 1	1987 (WHAT THE FUCK IS GOING ON?) (LP, withdrawn)	50
87	KLF Comm. JAMS LP 1	1987 (WHAT THE FUCK IS GOING ON?) (cassette, withdrawn)	20
88	KLF Comm. JAMS LP 2	WHO KILLED THE JAMS? (LP, stickered sleeve with insert)	25
89	KLF Comm. JAMS DLP 3	SHAG TIMES (2-LP)	20
89	KLF Comm. JAMS CD 3	SHAG TIMES (CD)	20

(see also KLF, Timelords, Disco 2000, Space, Orb, Bill Drummond)

JAY JUSTIN
60	HMV POP 801	Nobody's Darlin' But Mine/Sweet Sensation	7
63	HMV POP 1183	Proud Of You/Love, Love Me, Baby Darling	6
68	Columbia DB 8439	I Sell Summertime/Time (withdrawn)	8

JUSTINS
71	Punch PH 65	Cholera/LLOYD ALL STARS: Black Bird	8

JUSTIN CASE
80	Rok ROK XIX	TV/STRAIGHT UP: One Out All Out (die-cut company sleeve)	40

MINT VALUE £

JUSTINE
69	Dot DOT 121	Leave Me Be/Clown	12
69	Buffalo BFS 1001	Right Now/Place Where Sorrow Hides	20
70	Uni UNS 528	She Brings Back The Morning With Her/Back To Boulder	10
70	Uni UNLS 111	JUSTINE (LP)	100

BILL JUSTIS & HIS ORCHESTRA
57	London HLS 8517	Raunchy/The Midnight Man (78 rpm = £10)	20
58	London HLS 8614	College Man/The Stranger (B-side with Spinners) (78 rpm = £22)	25
63	Mercury AMT 1201	I'm Gonna Learn To Dance/Tamoure	10

JUST BROTHERS
80s	Soul City SC 127	Carlena/IVORIES: Please Stay (die-cut company sleeve)	8

JUST PLAIN JONES
71	CBS CBS 7480	Crazy, Crazy/Should Have Stayed With Mary	5

(see also Just Plain Smith, Micky Manchester, Dave Ballantyne, Esprit De Corps)

JUST PLAIN SMITH
69	Sunshine SUN 7702	February's Child/Don't Open Your Mind (some with p/s)	135/60

(see also Just Plain Jones, Micky Manchester, Esprit De Corps)

JUST US
66	CBS 202068	I Can't Grow Peaches On A Cherry Tree/I Can Save You	8

JUVENILES
66	Pye International 7N 25349	Bo Diddley/Yes I Believe	100

JYNX
64	Columbia DB 7304	How/Do What They Don't Say	60

CAROLINE K
87	Earthly Delights EARTH 1	NOW WAIT FOR LAST YEAR (LP, 1,500 only)	15

KRISSIE K
74	People PEO 110	Stick Up/Who Do You Think You Are	5

JOHNNY K & SINGIN' SWINGIN' 8
63	Fontana H 408	Lemonade/Come Closer Melinda	15

MOSES K & PROPHETS
65	Decca F 12244	I Went Out With My Baby Tonight/So Long	25

(see also Them)

KADDO STRINGS
80	Grapevine GRP 146	Nothing But Love/Crying Over You	20

(see also Duke Browner, Tartans)

KADETTES
82	Blank GET 1	Fireball XL5/Mission Impossible	8

BERT KAEMPFERT
65	Polydor BM 56504	Bye Bye Blues/Remember When	5
66	Brunswick LAT/STA 8651	A MAN COULD GET KILLED (LP, soundtrack)	22

KAINE & ABEL
66	Philips BF 1472	Then You Must Know My Love/Crying In The Rain	8

KAISER CHIEFS
04	Drowned In Sound DIS0003	Oh My God/Born To Be A Dancer/Caroline, Yes (CD, 500 only)	35
04	B-Unique BUN088CD	I Predict A Riot/Wrecking Ball (Original CD release, p/s)	8
04	B-Unique BUN088-7	I Predict A Riot/Take My Temperature (p/s)	8
04	B-Unique BUN088-7	I Predict A Riot/Take My Temperature (150 signed 7" with p/s)	20
05	KAISERCRIBS001	KAISER CHIEFS: Another Number/THE CRIBS: Modern Way (Double 'A' Side sold at gigs during 2005 tour dates. 1000 copies)	15
05	Private Pressing	You Can Have It All (1-sided Xmas 2005 single sent out to first 2000 website subscribers. Christmas card fold-out sleeve. B side with 'I predict Some Quiet' label	15

KAKKO
90	CBS 656023	What Kind Of Fool (mixes)/I Pledge You My Heart (12", p/s)	12
90	CBS 655 710 6	We Should Be Dancing (mixes) (12", p/s)	12
90	CBS 655 710 8	We Should Be Dancing (mixes) (12", p/s)	18
90	CBS 655 710 2	We Should Be Dancing (mixes) (CD)	20

KALA
73	Bradleys BRAD 302	Travelling Home/Still Got Time	5
73	Bradleys BRADL 1002	KALA (LP)	18

(see also Quintessence)

ALAN KALANI
| 59 | Vogue V 9147 | A Touch Of Pink/SURFERS: Mambo Jambo (78 rpm = £20) | 20 |

KALASANDRO!
| 60 | Warner Bros WB 13 | Chi Chi/Forbidden City | 15 |

KALEIDOSCOPE (U.K.)
67	Fontana TF 863	Flight From Ashiya/Holidaymaker (some in p/s)	100/60
68	Fontana TF 895	A Dream For Julie/Please Excuse My Face	40
68	Fontana TF 964	Jenny Artichoke/Just How Much Are You	35
69	Fontana TF 1002	Do It Again For Jeffrey/Poem	50
69	Fontana TF 1048	Balloon/If You So Wish	110
67	Fontana (S)TL 5448	TANGERINE DREAM (LP)	220
69	Fontana STL 5491	FAINTLY BLOWING (LP, gatefold sleeve; most copies with watermark on beginning of each side)	220/150
87	5 Hours Back TOCK 005	TANGERINE DREAM (LP, stereo reissue)	20
87	5 Hours Back TOCK 006	FAINTLY BLOWING (LP, reissue, single sleeve)	20

(see also Fairfield Parlour, I Luv Wight)

KALEIDOSCOPE (U.S.)
| 70 | CBS 64005 | BERNICE (LP, as American Kaleidoscope) | 15 |
| 76 | Island ILPS 9462 | WHEN SCOPES COLLIDE (LP) | 12 |

KALIN TWINS
58	Brunswick 05759	Forget Me Not/Dream Of Me (some B-side labels list "Dream Of You")	10
58	Brunswick 05759	Forget Me Not/Dream Of Me (some B-side labels list "Dream Of You") (78)	10
59	Brunswick 05775	Oh! My Goodness/It's Only The Beginning (78 rpm = £12)	10
59	Brunswick 05797	Cool/When I Look In The Mirror (78 rpm = £14)	10
59	Brunswick 05803	Moody/Sweet Sugar Lips (78 rpm = £14)	8
59	Brunswick 05814	The Meaning Of The Blues/Why Don't You Believe Me?	10
59	Brunswick 05814	The Meaning Of The Blues/Why Don't You Believe Me? (78)	15
60	Brunswick 05826	Chicken Thief/Loneliness	12
60	Brunswick 05844	Zing! Went The Strings Of My Heart/No Money Can Buy	10
61	Brunswick 05848	Momma Poppa/You Mean The World To Me	14
61	Brunswick 05862	One More Time/I'm Forever Blowing Bubbles	12
58	Brunswick OE 9383	WHEN (EP)	50
59	Brunswick OE 9449	THE KALIN TWINS (EP)	50

KITTY KALLEN
54	Brunswick 05261	Are You Looking For A Sweetheart/In The Chapel In The Moonlight	20
54	Brunswick 05287	Little Things Mean A Lot/I Don't Think You Love Me Anymore	20
54	Brunswick 05357	Heartless Heart/The Spirit Of Christmas	20
54	Brunswick 05359	I Want You All To Myself/(Don't Let The) Kiddy Geddin'	15
55	Brunswick 05394	A Little Lie/Take Everything But You	10
55	Brunswick 05402	Polly Pigtails/I'm A Lonely Little Petunia (In A Potato Patch)	10
55	Brunswick 05431	Kitty Who?/By Bayou Bay	10
55	Brunswick 05447	Forgive Me/Lonely	10
55	Brunswick 05475	Let's Make The Most Of Tonight/Just Between Friends	10
55	Brunswick 05494	How Lonely Can I Get?/Sweet Kentucky Rose	10
56	Brunswick 05536	Go On With The Wedding (with Georgie Shaw)/Only Forever	10
56	Brunswick 05612	True Love/Will I Always Be Your Sweetheart?	10
57	Brunswick 05705	Long Lonely Nights/Lasting Love	10
58	Brunswick 05734	Crying Roses/I Never Was The One	5
59	Philips PB 971	If I Give My Heart To You/The Door That Won't Open	5

DICK KALLMAN
56	Brunswick 05608	Two Different Worlds/Love Me As Though There Were No Tomorrow	6
60	Vogue V 9162	Born To Be Loved/Just Squeeze Me But Don't Teeze Me	10
63	HMV POP 1118	Say It Isn't So/From This Day On (A-side with John Barry & His Orchestra)	5
63	HMV CLP 1642	SPEAK SOFTLY (LP)	20

BOBBY KALPHAT
| 68 | Nu Beat NB 007 | Rhythm And Soul/BUNNY & RUDDY: True Romance | 10 |
| 70s | Faith FA 008 | Zion Hill/Dub Hill | 5 |

BOBBY KALPHAT & PHIL PRATT
| 76 | Terminal TERM 001 | ZION HILL DUB (LP) | 200 |

KAMARAS
| 69 | CBS 4199 | Let This Moment Pass Away/I Just Can't Break Away From This Lovin' | 12 |

KIRI TE KANAWA
| 91 | MPL/EMI KIRIS 1 | The World You're Coming Into/Tres Conejos (p/s) | 15 |
| 91 | MPL/EMI KIRIS 2 | Save The Child/The Drinking Song (p/s) | 15 |

AMORY KANE
68	MCA MU 1036	Reflections Of Your Face/Four Ravens	6
70	UNI UNS 518	You Were On My Mind/All The Best Songs And Marches	6
70	CBS 5111	Him Or Me/Forever Waiting	6
68	MCA MUP(S) 348	MEMORIES OF TIME UNWOUND (LP, with insert)	80
70	CBS 63849	JUST TO BE THERE (LP)	60

(see also Ron Geesin)

EDEN KANE
60	Pye 7N 15284	Hot Chocolate Crazy/You Make Love So Well	28
61	Decca F 11353	Well I Ask You/Before I Lose My Mind	5
61	Decca F 11381	Get Lost/I'm Telling You	5
62	Decca F 11418	Forget Me Not/A New Kind Of Lovin'	10
62	Decca F 11460	I Don't Know Why/Music For Strings	5
62	Decca F 11504	House To Let/I Told You	6

MINT VALUE £

63	Decca F 11568	Sounds Funny To Me/Someone Wants To Know	5
63	Fontana TF 398	Tomorrow Night/I Won't Believe You (some in p/s)	5
63	Fontana TF 413	Like I Love You/Come Back (with Earl Preston's TTs)	5
64	Fontana TF 508	Hangin' Around/Gonna Do Something About You	10
65	Fontana TF 582	If You Want This Love/Have I Done Something Wrong	10
66	Decca F 12342	Magic Town/The Whole World Was Crying	20
69	Fontana TF 1023	Boys Cry/Don't Come Cryin' To Me (p/s, reissue)	5
70	Bell BLL 1102	Reason To Believe/I Played It Like A Fool	8
62	Decca DFE 6696	WELL I ASK YOU! (EP)	30
62	Decca DFE 8503	HITS (EP)	25
64	Decca DFE 8567	SIX GREAT NEW SWINGERS (EP)	25
64	Fontana TFE 17424	IT'S EDEN (EP)	25
62	Ace Of Clubs ACL 1133	EDEN KANE (LP)	30
64	Fontana TL 5211	IT'S EDEN (LP)	42
64	Wing WL 1218	SMOKE GETS IN YOUR EYES (LP)	20

(see also Brothers Kane, Sarstedt Brothers)

GARY KANE
67	Pye 7N 17334	Too Good To Miss/Guilty Of Dreaming	5

HELEN KANE
55	MGM EP 549	The Boop-boop-a-doup Girl (EP)	25

LEE KANE
55	Capitol CL 14297	Ev'ry Day/How Would You Have Me?	10
55	Capitol CL 14328	Around And Around/Merci Beaucoup	10

MARIA KANE
65	Decca F 12184	Love Is Slipping Away/Love Is Strange	8

PAUL KANTNER
71	RCA Victor SF 8163	BLOWS AGAINST THE EMPIRE (LP, gatefold sleeve with booklet, as Paul Kantner & Jefferson Starship)	15
71	Grunt FTR 1002	SUNFIGHTER (LP, gatefold sleeve with booklet & inner sleeve; as Paul Kantner, Grace Slick & Jefferson Starship)	12
73	Grunt BFL 1 0148	BARON VON TOLBOOTH (LP, with Grace Slick & David Freiberg)	12

(see also Jefferson Airplane/Starship)

KAPLAN
68	Philips BF 1636	Do You Believe In Magic/I Like	18
68	Philips BF 1699	I Love It/Trousers Down	6

KAPT. KOPTER & FABULOUS TWIRLY BIRDS
73	Epic EPC 65381	KAPT. KOPTER & THE FABULOUS TWIRLY BIRDS (LP)	15

(see also Spirit)

ANTON KARAS
60	Decca F 9235	The "Harry Lime" Theme/The Cafe Mozart Waltz	5
55	Decca DFE 6035	ANTON KARAS ZITHER SOLOS (EP)	10
51	Decca LF 1053	ANTON KARAS (10" LP)	15

THE KARELIA
97	The All Blacks B.V RR88232	DIVORCE AT HIGH NOON (CD, 2005 re-issue has different p/s)	40

(see also Franz Ferdinand, The Amphetameaniest)

KARINA
71	United Artists UP 35205	Tomorrow I'm Coming Your Way/Something	10

BILLY KARLOFF (& EXTREMES)
78	Wanted CULT-45-001	Back Street Billy/Crazy Paving (p/s)	8
81	Warner Bros K 17753	Headbangers/Don't Keep Me Down (p/s)	5

(see also Tom Robinson Band, Stiff Little Fingers)

BORIS KARLOFF
60	Caedmon CAL 102/1	HANS CHRISTIAN ANDERSEN (LP)	15
67	Brunswick LAT 8678	AN EVENING WITH BORIS KARLOFF AND FRIENDS (LP)	50

STEVE KARMEN BIG BAND
75	United Artists UP 35770	Breakaway/Breakaway (Vocal Version) (featuring Jimmy Radcliffe)	10

(see also Jimmy Radcliffe)

KAROO
65	Oak RGJ 193	Mamma's Out Of Town/Lonely Weekend	175

KARRIER
84	Unit TRANS 101	I'm Back/Dreaming (no p/s)	30
85	Unit	WAY BEYOND THE NIGHT (LP)	15

KARYN KARSH
68	RCA Victor RCA 1740	I Wasn't Born To Follow/Musty Dusty	5

KARYOBIN
(see under Spontaneous Music Ensemble)

KASABIAN
03	BMG Paradise 02	Processed Beats (10" 45 rpm screen print sleeve with elastic bands)	25
04	BMG Paradise 04	Reason Is Treason (10" p/s 1,000 only)	18
04	BMG Paradise 06	Club Foot (Jagz Kooner mix) (12" with man-shaped hole sleeve)	7
04	BMG Paradise 09	Club Foot/(Jagz Kooner Vocal Mix)/(Paradise Mix) (with poster p/s)	8
04	BMG Paradise 15	L.S.F (Lost Souls Forever)/Club Foot (Live @ Cabinet War Rooms)/ (Jagz Kooner Mix (Full Version)) (10" poster p/s)	8
04	BMG Paradise 22	Processed Beats/Ovary Stripe(Remix)/Processed Beats (Afrika Bambaata Remix) (10")	8
04	Half Inch Records WHI008	Processed Beats/Waterfall (Mash-up) (12", 1-sided white vinyl)	12
04	BMG Paradise 18	KASABIAN (LP, 2 x 10")	12

KASENETZ-KATZ SINGING ORCHESTRAL CIRCUS

68	Pye International 7N 25472	Down In Tennessee/Mrs. Green	6
69	Pye International 7N 25480	We Can Work It Out/Latin Shake	5
68	Pye Int. NSPL 28119	KASENETZ-KATZ SINGING ORCHESTRAL CIRCUS (LP)	15
69	Buddah 203 018	QUICK JOEY SMALL — I'M IN LOVE WITH YOU (LP, as Kasenetz-Katz Super Circus)	15

AL KASHA

| 60 | Coral Q 72410 | Teardrops Are Falling/No Matter Where You Are | 5 |

KATCH-22

66	Fontana TF 768	Major Catastrophe/Hold Me	50
67	Fontana TF 874	Makin' Up My Mind/While We're Friends	12
68	Fontana TF 930	The World's Gettin' Smaller/Don't Bother	12
68	Fontana TF 984	Pumpkin Mini/100,000 Years	12
69	Fontana TF 1005	Out Of My Life/Baby Love	12
69	CBS 4644	It's The Sunshine/Mrs. Jones	12
68	Saga EROS 8047	IT'S SOFT ROCK & ALLSORTS (LP, with insert)	35

KATCH 22

90	Kold Sweat KS105	Hip Hop Pocrisy/Enter The Dope Zone/2 ? Years (12")	12
91	Kold Sweat KS113	Diary Of A Blackman Living In The Land Of The Lost/Right And Exact (12")	10
92	Kold Sweat KSEP206	RETURN TO THE FUNDAMENTALS (EP)	14
93	Kold Sweat KSEP213	DARK EPOCH (EP)	12
91	Kold Sweat KSLP1	DIARY OF A BLACKMAN LIVING IN THE LAND OF THE LOST (LP)	12
93	Kold Sweat KSLP4	DARK TALE OF TWO CITIES (LP)	12
94	Kold Sweat KSLP10	NON-CONFORMIST RITUALS (LP)	14

KATE

68	CBS 3631	Strange Girl/I Don't Make A Sound	40
68	CBS 3815	Hold Me Now/Empty World	25
69	CBS 4123	Shout It/Sweet Little Thing	50
	(see also Viv Prince, Pretty Things)		

KATHY

| 69 | Morgan MR 14 | Bonjour Monsieur/Long Night | 5 |

KATMANDU

| 86 | Nightflite NTFL 2001 | A CASE FOR THE BLUES (LP) | 12 |
| | *(see also Peter Green, Ray Dorset, Crane/Farlowe)* | | |

KATZ

| 60s | Tetlow TET 118 | LIVE AT THE RUM RUNNER (EP) | 75 |

ARTHUR KAY'S ORIGINALS

80	Red Admiral NYMPH 1	Ska-Wars/Warska (p/s)	8
80	Red Admiral NYMPH 2	Sooty Is A Rudie/Play My Record (p/s)	10
88	Skank MLP 105	RARE 'N' TASTY (mini-LP)	12

BARBARA KAY

65	Columbia DB 8009	The Power And The Glory/I Wanna Walk In Your Sun	5
65	Pye 7N 15774	That's What Angels Are For/What's The Good Of Loving	7
65	Pye 7N 15914	Yes I'm Ready/Someone Has To Cry	20
66	Pye 7N 15997	Chips With Everything/A Lot About Love	5

JOHN KAY

72	Probe SPB 1054	FORGOTTEN SONGS AND UNSUNG HEROES (LP)	12
73	Probe SPBA 6274	MY SPORTIN' LIFE (LP)	12
	(see also Steppenwolf)		

KATHIE KAY(E)

| 55 | HMV 7M 335 | Suddenly There's A Valley/Teddy Bear | 10 |
| 56 | HMV 7M 363 | Jimmy Unknown/Dreams Can Tell A Lie | 10 |

KATHIE KAY & BILLY COTTON

| 62 | Columbia DB 4896 | Til Tomorrow/Someone Nice Like You | 5 |

CAB KAYE

| 61 | Melodisc MEL 1584 | Everything Is Go/Don't You Go Away | 5 |

DANNY KAYE

52	Decca A 73013	Wonderful Copenhagen/Anywhere I Wonder (export issue)	12
58	Capitol CL 14907	The Square On The Hypotenuse/Everything Is Ticketty-Boo	6
59	Capitol CL 15061	Mommy, Gimme A Drinka Water!/Crazy Barbara	6
51	Brunswick LA 8507	DANNY KAYE (10" LP)	15
53	Brunswick LA 8572	HANS CHRISTIAN ANDERSEN (10" LP)	20
54	Brunswick LA 8660	DANNY KAYE AT THE PALACE (10" LP)	15
54	Brunswick LA 8668	KNOCK ON WOOD (10" LP, soundtrack)	25
56	Brunswick LAT 8097	THE COURT JESTER (LP)	18
58	Fontana TFR 6008	PURE DELIGHT (10" LP)	15
58	Capitol T 937	MOMMY, GIMME A DRINKA WATER! (LP)	15
60	Brunswick LAT 8350	FOR CHILDREN (LP)	12
	(see also Bing Crosby, Groucho Marx)		

DANNY KAYE & LOUIS ARMSTRONG

60	London HLU 9346	The Five Pennies Saints/Bill Bailey Won't You Please Come Home	6
60	London HL 7092	The Five Pennies Saints/Bill Bailey Won't You Please Come Home (export issue)	10
	(see also Louis Armstrong)		

DAVE KAYE (& DYKONS)

64	Decca F 11866	A Fool Such As I/It's Nice Isn't It (as Davy Kaye)	38
65	Decca F 12073	In My Way/All The Stars In Heaven (as Dave Kaye)	28
69	Major Minor MM 641	Yesterday When I Was Young/Say You Love Me (as Dave Kaye & Dykons)	12

MINT VALUE £

JANET K(AY)
78   Bushays BFM 108   Silhouette (with Rico)/PRINCE JAZEBO & RICO: Silhouette Gone Clear (12") . . . 20

LINDA KAYE
66   Columbia DB 7915   I Can't Stop Thinking About You/When We Meet Again 25

PETER KAYE
60s   Aral PS 116   Do Me A Favour/You Doll (some in p/s) 10/5

SHIRLEY KAYE
68   Trojan TR 015   Make Me Yours/We Have Happiness 15

STUBBY KAYE
61   Polydor NH 66527   My Wife's A Striptease Dancer/Lydia The Tattooed Lady 5

TONY KAYE & HEARTBEATS
67   Pye International 7N 25412   Hey, Hey Little Orphan Annie/Dream World 8

KAYES
67   Major Minor MM 515   It's No Secret/Remember Me 8
(see also Kaye Sisters)

KAYE SISTERS
58   Philips PB 806   Are You Ready, Freddy?/The Pansy 15
58   Philips PB 832   Stroll Me/Torero 10
58   Philips PB 877   Calla, Calla (The Bride, The Bride)/Oho-Aha (78 rpm = £8) 5
59   Philips PB 892   Jerri-Lee (I Love Him So)/Deeply Devoted (78 rpm = £8) 10
59   Philips PB 925   Goodbye Jimmy, Goodbye/Dancing With My Shadow (78 rpm = £6) 5
59   Philips PB 970   True Love, True Love/Too Young To Marry 6
60   Philips PB 1024   Paper Roses/If Only You'd Be Mine (some in p/s) 6/5
60   Philips PB 1088   Come To Me/A Whole Lot Of Lovin' (some in p/s) 6/5
57   Philips BBE 12166   PRESENTING THE KAYE SISTERS (EP) 18
59   Philips BBE 12256   THE KAYES AT THE COLONY (EP) 15
60   Philips BBE 12392   KAYE SISTERS FAVOURITES (EP) 14
(see also Three Kayes/Three Kaye Sisters, Kayes, Frankie Vaughan)

KAY GEES
76   Polydor 2310 467   HUSTLE WIT' EVERY MUSCLE (LP) 15

KCF & SKELLATON
91   Kold Sweat KS112   Taken To Heart/In Session (12") 14

ERNIE K-DOE
61   London HLU 9330   Mother-In-Law/Wanted, $10,000.00 Reward 20
61   London HLU 9390   Te-Ta-Te-Ta-Ta/Real Man 20
62   London HLU 9487   I Cried My Last Tear/A Certain Girl 25
65   Vocalion VP 9233   My Mother In Law (Is In My Hair Again)/Looking Into The Future 18
68   Action ACT 4502   Dancing Man/Later For Tomorrow. 20
68   Action ACT 4512   Gotta Pack My Bags/How Sweet You Are. 20

PHIL KEAGGY BAND
70s   Myrrh MYR 1046   WHAT A DAY (LP) 15
70s   Myrrh MYR 1066   EMERGING (LP). 15

KEANE
00   Zoomorphic (No cat. no)   Call Me What You Like/Rubbernecking/Closer Now (CD, 500 only) . . . . 100+
01   Zoomorphic ZOO12101   Wolf At The Door/Call Me What You Like/She Has No Time (CD, 50 only p/s) . . 125+
03   Fierce Panda NING 133CD   Everybody's Changing/Bedshaped/The Way You Want It (CD, 1,500 only) 30
03   Fierce Panda NING 147CD   This Is The Last Time/Can't Stop Now/Allemande (CD, 4,000 only) 15
04   Island CID849   Somewhere Only We Know/Snowed Under (numbered, p/s) 8
05   Island KEANE2   The Sun Ain't Gonna Shine Anymore/Your Eyes Open
              (Fan club issue 1000 only p/s). 30

SHAKE KEANE
55   HMV 7MC 38   Akinla/Fire, Fire (export issue) 5
62   Columbia SEG 8140   IN MY CONDITION (EP). 40
65   Decca SKL 4720   SHAKE KEANE WITH THE KEATING SOUND (LP) 22
66   Ace Of Clubs ACL 1219   THAT'S THE NOISE (LP). 25
69   Phase 4 Stereo PFS 4154   DIG IT (LP, with Ivor Raymonde Orchestra) 40
(see also Marie Bryant)

JOHNNY KEATING ORCHESTRA
62   Piccadilly NEP 34011   Z-CARS (EP, with Z-Men) 12
57   Oriole MG 20011   BRITISH JAZZ (LP) 75
58   London LTZ-15122   SWINGIN' SCOTS (LP) 25
64   Decca PFS 4038   SWING REVISITED (LP) 25
64   Decca PFS 4078   STRAIGHT AHEAD (LP) 30
64   Phase 4 Stereo PFS 4060   THE KEATING SOUND (LP, as Johnny Keating & 27 Men). 12
72   Studio Two TWO 393   SPACE EXPERIENCE (LP) 20
72   Studio Two Q4 TWO 393   SPACE EXPERIENCE (LP, quadrophonic) 25
74   Studio Two TWOX 1018   HITS IN HI-FI 1 (LP). 12
75   Studio Two TWOX 1044   SPACE EXPERIENCE 2 (LP). 15

KEEFERS KIDS
67   King KG 1068   Millions Of Hearts/KEEFERS: Lonely Hill. 5

HOWARD KEEL
57   Columbia DB 3969   Love, Wonderful Love/Parisienne 5
(see also Kathryn Grayson & Howard Keel, Vic Damone, Doris Day)

KEELE ROW & KEELE UNIVERSITY STUDENTS
64   Flexi   STANLEY MATTHEWS (EP, flexi) 20

JOHN KEEN
72	Track 2094 103	Old Fashioned Girl/That's The Way It Is	8
73	Track 2094 108	Let Us In/Keep On The Grass	8

(see also Speedy Keen, Thunderclap Newman)

SPEEDY KEEN
71	Track 2406 105	PREVIOUS CONVICTIONS (LP)	12

(see also John Keen, Thunderclap Newman)

MARION KEENE
56	HMV 7M 395	Fortune Teller/A Dangerous Age	7
57	HMV POP 375	In The Middle Of An Island/It's Not For Me To Say	7

NELSON KEENE
60	HMV POP 771	Image Of A Girl/Ocean Of Love	20
60	HMV POP 814	Keep Loving Me/Teenage Troubles	15
61	HMV POP 916	Miracles Are Happening To Me/Poor Little Rich Boy	12

(see also Guv'ners)

REX KEENE
56	Columbia DB 3831	Rebel In Town/Happy Texas Ranger	10

ACE KEFFORD STAND
69	Atlantic 584 260	For Your Love/Gravy Booby Jam (small or large centre hole)	40/35

(see also Move, Cozy Powell, Young Blood, Big Bertha, Bedlam, Carl Wayne)

KEITH
66	Mercury MF 940	Ain't Gonna Lie/It Started All Over Again	8
67	Mercury MF 955	98.6/The Teeny Bopper Song	10
67	Mercury MF 968	Tell Me To My Face/I Can't Go Wrong	8
67	Mercury MF 989	Daylight Savin' Time/Happy Walking Around	15
67	Mercury MF 1002	Sugar Man/Easy As Pie (some in p/s)	12/6
67	Mercury MCL 20103	98.6/AIN'T GONNA LIE (LP)	35

KEITH (Poppin) & IMPACT ALL STARS
71	Randy's RAN 515	Down By The Riverside/IMPACT ALL STARS: Version Two	6

BRIAN KEITH
68	Page One POF 072	The Shelter Of Your Arms/C'est La Vie	7
68	Page One POF 103	When The First Tear Shows/When My Baby Smiles At Me	10
69	Page One POF 152	Till We Meet Again/Lady Butterfly	7

(see also Plastic Penny)

BRYAN KEITH
63	London HLU 9707	Sad Sad Song/Mean Woman	20

RON KEITH
76	A&M AMS 7217	Party Music/Gotta Go By What You Tell Me	100+

KEITH & BILLIE
(see under Keith Powell & Billie Davis; see also Keith Powell, Billie Davis)

KEITH (Stewart) & ENID (Cumberland)
60	Blue Beat BB 6	Worried Over You/Everything Will Be Alright	10
60	Blue Beat BB 11	Send Me/TRENTON SPENCE GROUP: People Will Say We're In Love	10
61	Starlite ST45 047	Never Leave My Throne/Only A Pity (as Keith & Enid with Caribs)	12
61	Starlite ST45 067	You're Gonna Break My Heart/What Have I Done	12
62	Blue Beat BB 125	When It's Spring/True Love (with Sonny Bradshaw Orchestra)	10
63	Dice CC 14	Sacred Vow/My Dreams	8
63	Dice CC 20	Just A Closer Walk/Don't Yield To Temptation	8
64	Black Swan WI 429	Lost My Love/I Cried	10
63	Island ILP 901	KEITH & ENID SING (LP)	60
70	Trojan TTL 37	KEITH & ENID SING (LP, reissue)	15

KEITH (Lyn) & KEN (Lazarus)
65	London HA-R/SH-R 8229	YOU'LL LOVE JAMAICA (LP)	40

KEITH (Rowe) & TEX (Dixon)
67	Island WI 3085	Tonight/LYN TAIT & JETS: You Have Caught Me	65
68	Island WI 3091	Stop That Train/BOBBY ELLIS: Feeling Peckish (with Desmond Miles Seven)	120+
68	Island WI 3137	Hypnotizing Eyes/Lonely Man	25
70	Explosion EX 2008	Tighten Up Your Gird/Look To The Sky	12

JERRY KELLER
59	London HLR 8890	Here Comes Summer/Time Has A Way (triangular or round centre) (78 rpm = £20)	15/10
59	London HLR 8980	If I Had A Girl/Lovable (78 rpm = £20)	8
60	London HLR 9106	Now, Now, Now/Lonesome Lullaby	10
60	London HA-R 2261	HERE COMES JERRY KELLER (LP, also stereo SAH-R 6083)	55/60

PAT KELL(E)Y
68	Giant GN 37	Little Boy Blue/You Are Not Mine (as Pat Kelley & Uniques)	50+
68	Island WI 3121	Somebodies Baby (as Pat Kelly)/BEVERLY SIMMONS: Please Don't Leave Me	45
69	Gas GAS 110	The Workman Song/Never Give Up (as Pat Kelly)	10
69	Gas GAS 115	How Long/Try To Remember (as Pat Kelly)	5
69	Gas GAS 124	Festival Time (Parts 1 & 2) (as Pat Kelley)	8
69	Gas GAS 125	If It Don't Work Out/I Am Coming Home (as Pat Kelley)	5
70	Gas GAS 144	Tammy/I Am Not Your Guy (as Pat Kelley)	7
70	Gas GAS 145	Striving For The Right/When A Boy Fall In Love (as Pat Kelley)	7
70	Gas GAS 157	I Just Don't Know What To Do With Myself/What's He Got That I Ain't Got (B-side actually titled 'Lorna') (as Pat Kelley)	8
70	Jackpot JP 734	I Just Don't Know What To Do With Myself/Lorna (as Pat Kelley)	8
71	Camel CA 65	Talk About Love (as Pat Kelley)/PHIL PRATT ALL STARS: Version	10

71	Gas GAS 171	Love/With All Your Heart (as Pat Kelley)	6
71	Punch PH 88	Soulful Love (as Pat Kelly)/HUGH ROY & PARAGONS: One For All	10
72	Pama Supreme PS 353	I'm Gonna Give Her All The Love I've Got (as Pat Kelley)/	
		MAYTONES: As Long As You Love Me	6
73	Pama Supreme PS 379	Twelfth Of Never (as Pat Kelley)/JERRY LEWIS: 5000 Watts	5
73	Pama Supreme PS 384	I Wish It Could Rain (as Pat Kelly)/PAT KELLY SINGERS: Hallelujah	5
77	Rainbow Stepper RK 231	Carefree Girl/Version	8
69	Pama PMLP 12	PAT KELLEY SINGS (LP)	45
71	Pama PMP 2013	COOL BREEZING (LP)	60

(see also Wonder Boy)

MURRAY KELLUM
| 64 | London HLU 9830 | Long Tall Texan/GLEN SUTTON: I Gotta Leave This Town | 15 |

KELLY
| 66 | RCA RCA 1507 | Be My Man/Here Comes My Baby | 7 |

CHARLIE KELLY
| 68 | Island WI 3155 | So Nice Like Rice/STRANGER & GLADDY: Over Again | 25 |

DAVE KELLY
| 69 | Mercury 20151 SMCL | KEEPS IT IN THE FAMILY (LP) | 100 |
| 71 | Mercury 6310 001 | DAVE KELLY (LP, with Jo-Ann Kelly & Brunning-Hall Sunflower Band) | 150 |

(see also John Dummer Blues Band, Brunning-Hall Sunflower Blues Band)

FRANK KELLY & HUNTERS
62	Fontana 267 242 TF	Send Me The Pillow That You Dream On/'Cept Me	10
63	Fontana 267 261 TF	I Saw Linda Yesterday/Good And True	15
63	Fontana 267 277 TF	What Do You Wanna Do/She Loves Me So	15
64	Fontana TF 454	Some Other Time/Why Baby Why	15

(this is not the same group as [Dave Sampson &] Hunters, also on Fontana)

GENE KELLY
53	MGM SP 1012	Singin' In The Rain/All I Do Is Dream Of You	10
53	MGM SP 1015	'S Wonderful (with Georges Guetary)/I Got Rhythm (with Children's Choir)	5
55	MGM MGM 829	Almost Like Being In Love/I'll Go Home With Bonnie Jean (78)	5
57	MGM MGM 965	The Happy Road (Ca Ca C'est La Vie)/My Baby Just Cares For Me	5
57	MGM MGM 965	The Happy Road (Ca Ca C'est La Vie)/My Baby Just Cares For Me (78)	8
58	RCA RCA 1068	A Very Precious Love/Uncle Samson (78 rpm = £8)	5
57	MGM MGM-EP 671	SINGING IN THE RAIN EXCERPTS (EP, with Donald O'Connor/	
		Debbie Reynolds)	15
53	MGM MGM-D 117	SONG AND DANCE MAN (10" LP)	20
55	MGM MGM-D 133	S'WONDERFUL (10" LP)	20

JO-ANN KELLY
64	GW EP 1	BLUES AND GOSPEL (EP, live at the Bridge House Club)	110
66	Harlequin HAL 1/HW 349	NEW SOUNDS IN FOLK (LP, with other artists)	65
69	CBS 63841	JO-ANN KELLY (LP)	140
76	Red Rag RRR 006	DO IT (LP, with Peter Emery)	30

(see also Chilli Willi & Red Hot Peppers, Dave Kelly, Tramp)

JO-ANN KELLY & TONY McPHEE
| 72 | Sunset SLS 50209 | THE SAME THING ON THEIR MINDS (LP) | 32 |

(see also Tony McPhee, Dave Kelly)

JONATHAN KELLY
69	Parlophone R 5805	Denver/Son John	6
70	Parlophone R 5830	Make A Stranger Your Friend/Daddy Don't Take Me Down Fishing No More	6
70	Parlophone R 5851	Don't You Believe It?/Billy	7
70	Parlophone PCS 7114	JONATHAN KELLY (LP)	45
72	RCA SF 8262	TWICE AROUND THE HOUSES (LP)	12
73	RCA SF 8353	WAIT TILL THEY CHANGE THE BACKDROP (LP)	12

(see also John Ledingham)

KEITH KELLY
60	Parlophone R 4640	(Must You Always) Tease Me/Ooh-La-La	20
60	Parlophone R 4676	Listen Little Girl/Uh-Huh	20
60	Parlophone R 4713	With You/You'll Break My Heart	10
61	Parlophone R 4797	Cold White And Beautiful/When You First Fall In Love	10
65	CBS 201794	Laurie/Save Your Love For Me	8

MARY ANN KELLY
| 53 | London L 1195 | Wilful Lies/If I Ever Fall In Love (78) | 10 |

MONTE KELLY ORCHESTRA
| 59 | London HLL 8777 | Willingly (Melodie Perdue)/The Blue Cha Cha (78 rpm = £6) | 5 |
| 60 | London HLL 9085 | Summer Set/Amalia | 5 |

PAT KELLY
(see under Pat Kelley)

PAUL KELLY
65	Atlantic AT 4053	Chills And Fever/Only Your Love	30
67	Philips BF 1591	Sweet Sweet Lovin'/Cryin' For My Baby	25
72	Atlantic K 10272	Chills And Fever/Only Your Love (reissue)	10

PETE KELLY'S SOULUTION
68	Decca F 12755	Midnight Confessions/If Your Love Don't Swing	25
68	Decca F 22829	Midnight Confessions/BERNIE & BUZZ BAND:	
		The House That Jack Built (export issue)	20

(see also Bernie & Buzz Band, Rhythm & Blues Inc.)

PETER KELLY
| 71 | Polydor 2310 119 | DEALIN' BLUES (LP) | 35 |

SALLY KELLY
59	Decca F 11175	Little Cutie/Come Back To Me	10
60	Decca F 11238	He'll Have To Stay/Honey That's Alright	10
60s	Hit HIT 15	Believe In The Rain/So Much	5

STAN KELLY
60s	Transatlantic TRASP 21	The Ballad Of Armagh Jail/Kelly The Boy From Killang	5
60	Topic TOP 27	LIVERPOOL PACKET (EP)	10
60	Topic TOP 60	SONGS FOR SWINGING LANDLORDS TO (EP)	10

WYNTON KELLY TRIO
65	Verve VLP 9103	UNDILUTED (LP)	15

KELLY BROTHERS
67	Sue WI 4034	Falling In Love Again/Crying Days Are Over	80
68	President PT 143	You Put Your Touch On Me/Hanging In There	25
70	Blue Horizon 57-3177	That's What You Mean To Me/Comin' On In	40
68	President PTL 1019	SWEET SOUL (LP)	100

REV. (Samuel) KELSEY (& CONGREGATION)
52	Vocalion V 1014	The Wedding Ceremony Of Sister Rosetta Tharpe And Russell Morrison (Parts 1 & 2) (78)	20
52	Vocalion V 1020	Little Boy/Low Down The Chariot (78)	20
53	Vocalion V 1028	I'm A Royal Child/Where Is The Lion In The Tribes Of Judea (78)	20
56	Brunswick OE 9256	REV. KELSEY (EP)	25

(see also Sister Rosetta Tharpe)

WAYNE KEMP
66	Atlantic 584 006	Watch That First Step/Little Home Wrecker	10

KEMPION
77	Broadside BRO 123	KEMPION (LP)	15
77	Sweet Folk & C. SFA 044	CAM YE O'ER FRAE FRANCE (LP)	15

KEN & NEW ESTABLISHMENT
73	Fab FAB 264	Soul Mood/Golden Locks	10

KEN & STEPPING TONY
78	Rama RMD 005	Sticks Man Affair/ROCKA & DAVE & GIRL WONDER: Skip-A Dip (12")	50

JOHNNY KENDALL & HERALDS
64	RCA RCA 1416	St. James Infirmary/Little Girl	20

KENDALL SISTERS
58	London HLM 8622	Won't You Be My Baby/Yea, Yea (78 rpm = £25)	50

GRAHAM KENDRICK
73	Key KL 011	FOOTSTEPS ON THE SEA (LP)	15
73	Key KL 016	BRIGHT SIDE UP (LP)	12
74	Key KL 024	PAID ON THE NAIL (LP)	12

LINDA KENDRICK
66	Polydor 56076	It's The Little Things/When Your Love Is Warm	30
66	Polydor 56146	I Fall Apart/Friend Of Mine	10
68	Philips BF 1660	Grey Sunny Day/In Need Of A Friend	7
69	Philips BF 1750	I Will See You There/Inside My Heart	7
69	Philips BF 1818	Hold On/Fah La La	7
70	Philips SBL 7921	LINDA KENDRICK (LP)	22

NAT KENDRICK & SWANS
60	Top Rank JAR 351	(Do The) Mashed Potatoes Parts 1 & 2	20
60	Top Rank JAR 387	Dish Rag Parts 1 & 2	20

(see also James Brown)

EDDIE KENDRICKS
73	Tamla Motown TMG 845	If You Let Me/Just Memories	6
74	Tamla Motown TMG 916	Girl You Need A Change Of Mind Parts 1 & 2	8
75	Tamla Motown TMG 947	Shoe Shine Boy/Hooked On Your Love	6
71	Tamla Motown STML 11186	ALL BY MYSELF (LP)	18
73	Tamla Motown STML 11213	PEOPLE ... HOLD ON (LP)	15
73	Tamla Motown STML 12245	EDDIE KENDRICKS (LP)	15

(see also Temptations)

KENICKIE
95	Slampt U.O. SLAMPT 1	CATSUIT CITY EP	65
96	Fierce Panda NING 16	Come Out 2nite/How I Was Made (p/s)	12
96	Fierce Panda NING 16CD	THE SKILLEX EP (CD)	8
97	EMI CDDISCS 007	PUNKA EP (2-CD, with postcards)	19

CALUM KENNEDY
62	Ember EMB 5167	The Celtic Chorus/Danny Boy	40

CHERYL KENNEDY
67	Columbia DB 8271	Thoroughly Modern Millie/Cradle Song	5
68	Columbia DB 8347	Love Is Blue/I Could Be Happy With You	5

DOUG KENNEDY
65	Columbia DB 7707	Julie/Jailbreak Man	5

GENE KENNEDY
65	Hickory 45-1314	You Better Take Home/Stand In Line	5

JOHN F. KENNEDY
64	Stateside SL 10064	THE PRESIDENTIAL YEARS 1960-1963 (LP)	15

MINT VALUE £

LOU KENNEDY
55	Columbia SCM 5198	Stars Shine In Your Eyes/The Kentuckian Song	10
56	Columbia SCM 5216	Whisper/Sincerely Yours	10

MIKE KENNEDY
69	Major Minor MM 614	I'll Never Forget/I'll Never Get You	6
69	Major Minor MM 629	Johnny Rebel/Golden Memories	6
72	Youngblood YB 1035	Louisiana/Look Up In The Sky	20
(see also Los Bravos)			

CHRIS KENNER
61	London HLU 9410	I Like It Like That Parts 1 & 2	25
65	Sue WI 351	Land Of 1,000 Dances/That's My Girl	30
66	Atlantic 587 008	LAND OF 1000 DANCES (LP)	40+

JAMES KENNEY
58	Pye 7N 15150	The Shrine On The Second Floor/Expresso Party (78 rpm = £6)	10

TONY KENNY & SANDS SHOWBAND
67	Major Minor MM 555	Help Me Rhonda/Some Enchanted Evening	5
68	Major Minor MM 573	Yummy Yummy Yummy/Peanuts	5
71	Hit HIT 1	Knock Three Times/See You In September	5
(see also Sands)			

KENNY (Everett) & (Dave) CASH
65	Decca F 12283	Knees/The B Side	10

KENNY & CORKY
59	London HLX 9002	Nuttin' For Christmas/Suzy Snowflake (78 rpm = £12)	12

KENNY & DENY
65	Decca F 12138	Try To Forget Me/Little Surfer Girl	55
(see also Jimmy Page, Tony Rivers & The Castaways, Harmony Grass, Capability Brown)			

KENNY & WRANGLERS
64	Parlophone R 5224	Somebody Help Me/Who Do You Think I Am?	20
65	Parlophone R 5275	Doobie Doo/Moonshine	20
(see also Kenny Bernard & Wranglers)			

JERRI BO KENO
75	Phil Spector Intl. 2010 001	Here It Comes (And Here I Go)/I Don't Know Why	15

KENT
00s	RCA 560632	If You Were Here/Point Blank/The One To Blame (CD)	12
00s	BMG 645912	747 (Radio Version)/What It Feels Like/Unprofessional (Live Radio Session Version) (CD)	10
00s	Victor 74321812632	Heavenly Junkies (1-track CD)	8
00s	BMG 748507	Music Non Stop/Insects (clear vinyl, withdrawn)	10

AL KENT
67	Track 604 016	You Got To Pay The Price/Where Do I Go From Here	50
71	Mojo 2092 015	You Got To Pay The Price/Where Do I Go From Here (unissued)	

BILL KENT
58	Decca F 10975	The Prettiest Girl In School/Hasty Words	5
58	Decca F 10997	Oh-Oh, I'm Falling In Love/In Love	5

ENOCH KENT
59	Top Rank JAR 238	The Ballad Of Johnny Ramensky/The Bonny Lass Of Fyvie	5
60	Top Rank JAR 386	The Smashing Of The Van/Sean South Of Garryowen	5
62	Topic TOP 81	SINGS THE BUTCHER BOY AND OTHER BALLADS (EP)	10

KLARK KENT
78	Kryptone KK 1	Don't Care/Thrills/Office Girls (p/s, green or rarer black vinyl)	each 5
78	Kryptone KMS 7390	Too Kool To Kalypso/Theme For Kinetic Ritual (p/s, green vinyl)	5
(pseudonym for Stewart Copeland; see also Police, Curved Air)			

PAUL KENT
71	B&C CB 165	Do You/Helpless Harry	6
70	RCA SF 8083	P.C. KENT (LP)	30
71	B&C CAS 1044	PAUL KENT (LP)	25

RICHARD KENT STYLE
66	Columbia DB 7964	No Matter What You Do/Go, Go Children	150
66	Columbia DB 8051	You Can't Put Me Down/All Good Things	80
67	Columbia DB 8182	Marching Off To War/I'm Out	75
68	MCA MU 1032	Love Will Shake The World Awake/Crocodile Tears	40
69	Mercury MF 1090	A Little Bit O' Soul/Don't Tell Lies	40

SHIRLEY KENT
80	Tadpole TAD 001	My Dad/Marianne	6
66	Keele University 103	THE MASTER SINGERS AND SHIRLEY KENT SING FOR CHAREC 67 (EP)	30
89	Magic Spell 0001	FOREVER A WILLOW (LP)	12
(see also Ghost, Virginia Tree)			

SONIA KENT
66	Parlophone R 5401	This Is My Wonderful Day/Somebody Must Care	7
(see also Diamond Twins)			

KENT (Brown) & DIMPLE (Hinds)
63	Island WI 046	Day Is Done/Linger A While	18

KENT (Brown) & JEANNIE with City Slickers
62	Blue Beat BB 98	Daddy/Hello Love	20
(see also Kent Brown & Rainbows)			

RIK KENTON
74	Island WIP 6214	Bungalow Love/Lay It On You (no p/s)	5

(see also Roxy Music)

STAN KENTON & HIS ORCHESTRA
54	Capitol CL 14191	The Lady In Red/Skoot	6
55	Capitol CL 14247	Alone Too Long/Don't Take Your Love From Me	6
55	Capitol CL 14259	A-Ting-A-Ling/Malaguena (with Ann Richards)	10
55	Capitol CL 14269	23 Degrees North, 82 Degrees West/Falling (B-side with Ann Richards)	6
55	Capitol CL 14287	Lover Man/I've Got You Under My Skin	6
55	Capitol CL 14301	Casanova/Dark Eyes (with Ann Richards)	6
55	Capitol CL 14319	Freddy/The Handwriting's On The Wall	6
56	Capitol CL 14537	Winter In Madrid (with Ann Richards)/Baa-Too-Kee	5
56	Capitol CL 14539	Sunset Tower/Opus In Chartreuse	5
56	Capitol CL 14540	My Lady/Frank Speaking	5
56	Capitol CL 14541	Portrait Of A Count/Invention For Guitar And Trumpet	5
56	Capitol CL 14542	Cherokee/Limelight	5
57	Capitol CL 14707	His Feet Too Big For De Bed (with June Christy)/Stardust — Boogie (78 rpm = £6)	5
57	Capitol CL 14806	Lemon Twist/Baby You're Tough	5
58	Capitol CL 14847	Tequila/Cuban Mumble	5
58	Capitol CL 14866	Reverie/More Love Than Your Love	5
59	Capitol CL 15029	Whistle Walk/Tamer-Lane	5
51	Capitol LC 6517	STAN KENTON'S MILESTONES (10" LP)	15
51	Capitol LC 6523	ENCORES (10" LP)	15
52	Capitol LC 6545	ARTISTRY IN RHYTHM (10" LP)	15
52	Capitol LC 6546	A CONCERT IN PROGRESSIVE JAZZ (10" LP)	15
52	Capitol LC 6548	PRESENTS (10" LP)	15
52	Capitol LCT 6006	INNOVATIONS IN MODERN MUSIC (LP)	15
53	Capitol LC 6577	CITY OF GLASS (10" LP)	15
53	Capitol LC 6595	NEW CONCEPTS OF ARTISTRY IN RHYTHM (10" LP)	15
53	Capitol LC 6602	SKETCHES ON STANDARDS (10" LP)	15
54	Capitol LC 6667	THIS MODERN WORLD (10" LP)	15
54	Capitol LC 6676	CLASSICS (10" LP)	15
54	Capitol LCT 6009	KENTON SHOWCASE (LP)	12
55	Capitol LC 6697	PORTRAITS ON STANDARDS (10" LP)	15
56	Capitol LCT 6109	IN HI-FI (LP)	12
56	Capitol LCT 6118	CUBAN FIRE (LP)	12
56	Brunswick LAT 8122	THE FORMATIVE YEARS (LP)	12
57	Capitol LCT 6138	KENTON WITH VOICES (LP)	12
58	Capitol LCT 6157	THE KENTON ERA VOLUME ONE — PROLOGUE (LP)	12
58	Capitol LCT 6158	THE KENTON ERA VOLUME TWO — GROWING PAINS (LP)	12
58	Capitol LCT 6159	THE KENTON ERA VOLUME THREE — PROGRESSIVE JAZZ (LP)	12
58	Capitol LCT 6160	THE KENTON ERA VOLUME FOUR — CONTEMPORARY (LP)	12
58	Capitol (S)T 932	RENDEZVOUS WITH KENTON (LP)	12
58	Capitol T 995	BACK TO BALBOA (LP)	12
59	Capitol (S)T 1068	BALLAD STYLE OF STAN KENTON (LP)	12
59	Capitol T 1130	LUSH INTERLUDE (LP)	12
59	Capitol (S)T 1166	THE STAGE DOOR SWINGS (LP)	12
60	Capitol W 1305	VIVA KENTON (LP)	12

(see also June Christy)

KEN-TONES
56	Parlophone MSP 6229	Get With It/In Port Afrique	12
57	Parlophone R 4257	I Saw Esau/Yaller, Yaller Gold	8

(see also Benny Lee)

KENTUCKY BOYS
55	HMV 7M 312	Don't Fetch It/A Little Fella Like Me	12

KENTUCKY COLONELS
74	United Artists UAS 29514	THE KENTUCKY COLONELS (LP)	18

(see also Byrds)

BILL KENWRIGHT (& RUNAWAYS)
67	Columbia DB 8239	I Want To Go Back There Again/Walk Through Dreams (with Runaways)	10
68	MGM MGM 1430	Giving Up/Love's Black And White (solo)	6
69	MGM MGM 1463	Tiggy/House That Fell On Its Face	6
69	MGM MGM 1478	Baby I Could Be So Good At Loving You/A Boy And A Girl	6
69	Fontana TF 1065	Sugar Man/Epitaph (When Times Were Good)	6

KERBDOG
93	Vertigo VER 80	End Of Green (p/s)	8
94	Vertigo VER 83	Dry Riser/Xena Phobia/Self Inflicted (p/s)	6
94	Vertigo VERR 83	Dry Riser/Xena Phobia/Self Inflicted (p/s, clear vinyl)	8
94	Vertigo VER 86	Dummy Crusher/Too Much Too Young (p/s)	6
94	Vertigo VERX 86	Dummy Crusher/Mr. Clean/Don't Stand In Line (12", picture disc)	10
96	Fontana KER 1	J.J.'s Song/Don't Even Try (clear vinyl)	7

MOIRA KERR
69	Beltona MBE 102	FOLK WARM AND GENTLE (LP, also stereo [SBE 102])	20
71	Beltona SBE 118	SHADOWS OF MY CHILDHOOD (LP)	20

PATRICK KERR
65	Decca F 12069	Magic Potion/It's No Trouble To Love You	30

RICHARD KERR
73	Warner Bros K 46206	FROM NOW UNTIL THEN (LP)	18

KERRIES
67	Major Minor MM 541	Coulters Candy/Gallon Of Whisky And A Barrel Of Beer	5
67	Major Minor MMLP/SMLP 9	THE KERRIES (LP)	15

CHRIS KERRY
65	Mercury MF 957	Seven Deadly Sins/The Place	18
66	Mercury MF 985	Watermelon Man/I've Got My Pride	20

DOUG KERSHAW
69	Warner Bros WB 7304	Feed It To The Fish/You Fight Your Fight (I'll Fight Mine)	6
70	Warner Bros WB 7413	Orange Blossom Special/Swamp Rat	6
71	Warner Bros WS 1906	DOUG KERSHAW (LP)	15
73	Warner Bros K 46196	DEVIL'S ELBOW (LP)	15

(see also Rusty & Doug)

MARY & HARVEY KERSHAW
76	Topic 12TS 302	LANCASHIRE SINGS AGAIN! (LP)	12

KEN KESEY
83	Psycho PSYCHO 4	THE ACID TEST (LP, 300 only)	30

BARNEY KESSEL
69	Polydor 56765	Frank Mills/Quail Bait	5
54	Vogue LDE 085	BARNEY KESSEL (10" LP)	20
55	Contemporary LDC 153	BARNEY KESSEL VOLUME 2 (10" LP)	20
59	Contemporary LAC 12206	SOME LIKE IT HOT (LP)	12
59	Contemorary LAC 12214	BARNEY KESSEL PLAYS CARMEN (LP)	12
77	Phil Spector Intl. 2307 011	SLOW BURN (LP)	15

(see also Rick Nelson)

LARRY KESSLER
96	Lissey's LISS 5S	Radar Eyes/Godz Mix (p/s)	10

KESTREL
75	Cube HIFLY 19	KESTREL (LP)	110

KESTRELS
59	Pye 7N 15234	There Comes A Time/In The Chapel In The Moonlight (78 rpm = £10)	12
60	Pye 7N 15248	I Can't Say Goodbye/We Were Wrong	10
61	Decca F 11391	All These Things/That's It	10
62	Piccadilly 7N 35056	Wolverton Mountain/Little Sacka Sugar	5
62	Piccadilly 7N 35079	Don't Want To Cry/Love Me With All Your Heart	5
63	Piccadilly 7N 35104	Walk Right In/Moving Up The King's Highway	5
63	Piccadilly 7N 35126	There's A Place/Little Star	8
63	Piccadilly 7N 35144	Love Me With All Your Heart/Lazy River	5
60s	Donegal MAU 500	THE KESTRELS (EP)	35
63	Piccadilly NPL 38009	SMASH HITS (LP)	30

(see also Ivy League, Flowerpot Men, White Plains)

KEY CHAINS
66	London HLU 10055	Morgan's Song/Scruggs	5

EBONY KEYES
66	Piccadilly 7N 35358	Sitting In The Ring/If You Knew	100
67	Piccadilly 7N 35375	Cupid's House/If Our Love Should End	10
67	Piccadilly 7N 35390	Country Girl/How Many Times	10
67	Picadilly 7N 35407	Don't/Sweet Mary (Sweeter Than A Rose)	5

KAROL KEYES
64	Fontana TF 517	You Beat Me To The Punch/No-One Can Take Your Place (some in p/s)	30/20
67	Fontana TF 846	Can't You Hear The Music/The Sweetest Touch	12
66	Columbia DB 7899	A Fool In Love/The Good Love, The Bad Love	20
66	Columbia DB 8001	One In A Million/Don't Jump	70

(see also Volunteers)

TROY KEYES
68	Stateside SS 2087	Love Explosions/I'm Crying (Inside)	25
69	Stateside SS 2149	Love Explosions/I'm Crying (Inside) (reissue)	15

KEY LARGO
71	Blue Horizon 57-3178	Voodoo Rhythm/As The Years Go Passing By	20
70	Blue Horizon 7-63859	KEY LARGO (LP)	35

KEY MASSIVE
89	Hat Music HT 001	Oh Girl/Sweet Sensi (12")	25

KEYMEN
59	HMV POP 584	Gazackstahagen/Miss You (78 rpm = £15)	10
62	Columbia DB 4902	Five Weeks In A Balloon/Secretly	6
57	Vogue Coral LVA 9048	THE VOCAL SOUNDS OF THE KEYMEN (LP)	15

KEYNOTES
54	Decca F 10302	A Dime And A Dollar/JOHNSTON BROTHERS: Bandit	15
55	Decca F 10643	Relax-Ay-Voo/Steam Heat	15
56	Decca F 10745	Let's Go Steady/Chincherinchee	8

(see also Bobbie Britton, Johnston Brothers, Dave King, Suzi Miller)

KEYS
64	Oriole CB 1968	Sleep Sleep My Baby/Colour Slide	25
65	CBS 201804	Go Get Her/My Everything	10

K.G.B.
76	MCA MCF 2749	K.G.B. (LP)	12

(see also Barry Goldberg, Mike Bloomfield)

KHAN
72	Deram SDL 11	SPACE SHANTY (LP, later copies in stickered sleeve)	45

(see also Steve Hillage, Egg, Nick Greenwood, Arzachel, Hatfield & The North)

ASHISH KHAN
68	Liberty LBL 83083E	ASHISH KHAN (LP)	15
73	Elektra K 42129	JUGAL BANDI (LP, with John Barham)	12

USTAD ALI AKBAR KHAN
69	HMV ASD 2367	MUSIC FROM INDIA NO. 5 (LP)	12
69	Transatlantic TRA 183	DHUN PALAS KAFI (LP)	12
71	Mushroom 100 MR 14	THE PEACEFUL MUSIC OF USTAD ALI AKBAR KHAN (LP)	25

(see also Ravi Shankar)

USTAD VILAYET KHAN
69	RCA SF 8025	THE GURU (LP, soundtrack)	18
70	Transatlantic TRA 239	RAGA TILAKKAMOD (LP)	15

KHANDARS
65	Blue Beat BB 332	Don't Dig A Hole For Me/BUSTER'S ALL STARS: Skara	40

KHANS
62	London HLU 9555	New Orleans, 2 AM/Blue Mist	15

KHARTOMB
83	Whaam! WHAAM 14	Swahili Lullaby/Teekon Warriors	6

KICK
84	Footwear FWR 01	Let's Get Back Together/A Shot In The Dark/Don't Ever Change (p/s)	6
86	Countdown VAIN 03	I Can't Let Go/Armchair Politician (p/s)	8

KICKS
80	Carrere CAR 138	Get Off The Telephone/Big Boys Don't Cry (p/s)	30
81	Blue Chip BC 102	If Looks Could Kill/Don't She Look Fab	70

KID GUNGO
69	Escort ES 801	Hold The Pussy/KING CANNON: Wha Pen (B-side actually by Carl Bryan)	7

EDDIE KIDD
77	Decca FR 13722	Motorbike Kid/Big Jump At Picket's Lock	8

JOHNNY KIDD (& PIRATES)
59	HMV POP 615	Please Don't Touch/Growl	40
59	HMV POP 674	Feelin'/If You Were The Only Girl In The World (solo)	25
60	HMV POP 698	You Got What It Takes/Longin' Lips	18
60	HMV POP 753	Shakin' All Over/Yes Sir, That's My Baby	12
60	HMV POP 790	Restless/Magic Of Love	18
61	HMV POP 853	Linda Lu/Let's Talk About Us	25
61	HMV POP 919	Please Don't Bring Me Down/So What	25
62	HMV POP 978	Hurry On Back To Love/I Want That (with The Mike Sammes Singers)	25
62	HMV POP 1088	A Shot Of Rhythm And Blues/I Can Tell (blue or black label)	22
63	HMV POP 1173	I'll Never Get Over You/Then I Got Everything	10
63	HMV POP 1228	Hungry For Love/Ecstasy	12
64	HMV POP 1269	Always And Ever/Dr. Feelgood	12
64	HMV POP 1309	Jealous Girl/Shop Around	15
64	HMV POP 1353	Whole Lotta Woman/Your Cheatin' Heart	20
65	HMV POP 1397	The Birds And The Bees/Don't Make The Same Mistake As I Did	20
65	HMV POP 1424	Shakin' All Over '65/Gotta Travel On	25
65	HMV POP 1520	It's Got To Be You/I Hate To Get Up In The Morning (solo)	25
66	HMV POP 1559	Send For That Girl/The Fool	25
60s	HMV JO 674	Feelin'/If You Were The Only Girl In The World (export issue, black label)	40
97	Cruisin' 50 CASB 005	Shakin' All Over/Please Don't Touch (78rpm, 300 only)	50
60	HMV 7EG 8628	SHAKIN' ALL OVER (EP)	60
64	HMV 7EG 8834	JOHNNY KIDD AND THE PIRATES (EP)	70
71	Regal Starline SRS 5100	SHAKIN' ALL OVER (LP)	15

(see also Pirates)

KIDS
75	Atlantic K 50143	ANVIL CHORUS (LP, with inner, stickered sleeve)	12

(see also Heavy Metal Kids, Gary Holton)

KIDS NEXT DOOR
65	London HLR 9993	Inky Dinky Spider/Goodbye Don't Cry	7

KIDZ NEXT DOOR
79	Warner Bros K 17492	What's It All About?/The Kidz Next Door (p/s)	35

KILBURN & HIGH ROADS
74	Dawn DNS 1090	Rough Kids/Billy Bentley	12
75	Dawn DNS 1102	Crippled With Nerves/Huffety Puff	12
78	Warner Bros K 17225	Bentley/Pam's Moods	8
75	Dawn DNLS 3065	HANDSOME (LP)	28

(see also Ian Dury & Blockheads, 999, Nine Days Wonder)

ROY KILDARE
64	Blue Beat BB 226	I Won't Leave/What About It	12

JUDY KILEEN
56	London HLU 8328	Just Walking In The Rain/A Heart Without A Sweetheart (78 rpm = £15)	45

KILFENORA CEILI BAND
74	Transatlantic TRS 108	KILFENORA CEILI BAND (LP)	12

MERLE KILGORE
54	London HL 8103	Seeing Double, Feeling Single/It Can't Rain All The Time (78 rpm = £45)	200
57	London HLP 8392	Ernie/Trying To Find (Someone Like You) (78 rpm = £70)	350
60	Melodisc MEL 1545	Dear Mama/Jimmie Bring Sunshine	15
62	Mercury AMT 1193	42 In Chicago/A Girl Named Liz	18
65	London HA-B 8244	THERE'S GOLD IN THEM THAR HILLS (LP)	25

THEOLA KILGORE
67	Sue WI 4035	I'll Keep Trying/He's Coming Back To Me	40

KILLA INSTINCT
92	Music Of Life NOTE061	The Bambi Murders (12")	14
92	Music Of Life NOTE063	Den Of Thieves/Ununited Kingdom (12")	10
93	European Rhyme ERR02	WHISPERS OF HATRED (EP)	30
94	Move MOVE7013 1	ESCAPISM (EP)	15

LOUIS KILLEN
62	Topic TOP 75	NORTHUMBRIAN GARLAND (EP)	10
66	Topic 12T 126	BALLADS AND BROADSIDES (LP, blue label)	20

LOUIS KILLEN & JOHNNY HANDLE
62	Topic TOP 74	THE COLLIER'S RANT (EP)	10
65	Topic 12T 122	TOMMY ARMSTRONG OF TYNESIDE (LP, with Colin Ross & Tom Gilfellon, blue label with booklet)	15
68	Topic 12T 189	ALONG THE COALY TYNE (LP, with Colin Ross, blue label with booklet)	20

(see also Johnny Handle)

KILLERMETERS
79	Psycho P 2620	Why Should It Happen To Me/Cardiac Arrest (some in p/s)	80/30
80	Gem GEMS 22	Twisted Wheel/SX 225 (p/s, demo copies £50)	90

KILLER
77	Ariola ARL 5003	KILLER (LP)	30

KILLERS
78	Satril SAT 129	Killer (On The Dancefloor) (no p/s)	5

(see also Joe Cool & The Killers)

KILLERS
03	Lizard King LIZARD007	Mr. Brightside/On Top/Smile Like You Mean It/Who Let You Go (CD)	12
03	Lizard King LIZARD007X	Mr. Brightside/Smile Like You Mean It (white vinyl, 500 only p/s)	25
04	Lizard King LIZARD009	Somebody Told Me/The Ballad Of Michael Valentine/Under The Gun (CD, 5000 only)	8
04	Lizard King LIZARD009X	Somebody Told Me/The Ballad Of Michael Valentine (2,000 only, p/s and poster)	8
04	Lizard King LIZARD010X	Mr Brightside/Who Let You Go (red vinyl, p/s and poster)	7
05	Lizard King LIZARD014X	Somebody Told Me/Milo Mix)/The Glimmers (GYPRock Mix) (12" p/s)	8
05	Lizard King (no cat. no)	SINGLES BOX SET (5,000 only,11 x 7" album box set)	35

JOHN KILLIGREW
71	Penny Farthing PELS 513	JOHN KILLIGREW (LP, with Pete Dello)	18

(see also Pete Dello)

KILLING FLOOR
70	Penny Farthing PEN 745	Call For The Politicians/Acid Bean	20
69	Spark (S)RLP 102	KILLING FLOOR (LP)	130
70	Penny Farthing PELS 511	OUT OF URANUS (LP, gatefold sleeve)	120
73	Spark Replay SRLM 2004	ORIGINAL KILLING FLOOR (LP, reissue)	30

(see also Rory Gallagher)

KILLING JOKE
79	Malicious Damage MD 410	Nervous System/Turn To Red/Are You Receiving (10" EP in bag, some with picture & 4 cards)	15/10
80	Island WIP 6550	Turn To Red/Nervous System (p/s)	5
80	Island WIP 6550	Turn To Red/Nervous System ('A' label)	15
80	Island 12 WIP 6550	Almost Red/Nervous System/Are You Receiving/Turn To Red (12", p/s)	10
80	Malicious Damage MD 540	Wardance/Psyche (p/s, some with 'call up label' insert)	10/5
80	Malicious Damage MD 540	Wardance/Psyche (mispressed B-side plays 'unknown artist', p/s)	25
80	E.G. EGMD 1.00	Requiem/Change (p/s)	5
80	E.G. EGMX 1.00	Requiem/Change/Change/Requiem (12", stamped sleeve, later in p/s)	10/8
81	E.G. EGMDX 1.01	Follow The Leaders/Follow The Leaders — Dub/Tension (10", p/s)	7
82	E.G. EGOX 10	Birds Of A Feather/Flock The B-Side (12", p/s)	8
83	E.G. EGOD 14/KILL 1/2	Me Or You/Wilful Days//Feast Of Blaze (double pack, gatefold p/s)	5
83	E.G. EGOXD 14	Me Or You/Feast Of Blaze//Wilful Days//Let's All Go (To The Fire Dances)/The Fall Of Because (live)/Dominator (Version) (12", sealed double pack)	15
84	E.G. EGOX 16	Eighties (Serious Dance Mix)/Eighties/Eighties (Coming Mix) (12", p/s)	8
84	E.G. DJ17	A New Day/Dance Day (DJ promo)	12
85	E.G. EGOY 20	Love Like Blood (Gestalt Mix)/Love Like Blood/Blue Feather (12", p/s)	10
85	E.G. EGOY 21	Kings And Queens (Knave Mix) (12", p/s)	10
85	E.G. EGOX 21	Kings And Queens (The Right Royal Mix)/The Madding Crowd/Kings And Queens (12", different withdrawn p/s)	10
86	E.G. EGOD 27	Adorations/Exile//Ecstasy/Adorations (Instrumental Mix) (double pack)	5
88	E.G. EGOT 43	My Love Of This Land/Follow The Leaders (Dub)/Sun Goes Down (10", p/s, B-side matrix no. EGOT 43B; last track plays "The Gathering")	7
90	ODIC1	Beautiful Dead (1-sided fan club flexi)	10

(see also Youth, Peyr, Heavy Duty Breaks)

KILLJOYS
77	Raw RAW 3	Johnny Won't Get To Heaven/Naive (p/s, 4 different label designs)	25
91	Dam. Goods FNARR LP10	NAIVE (LP, green vinyl)	12

(see also Girlschool)

KILLS
02	Rug RUG 158	Fuck The People (1-sided, stamped card sleeve, 500 only)	25
00s	Domino RUG 144CD	BLACK ROOSTER EP: Cat Claw/Wait/Dropout Boogie/Gum (CD)	8

KILOWATTS
68	Doctor Bird DB 1140	Bring It On Home/What A Wonderful World	35

(see also West Indians)

PAT KILROY
  67   Elektra EKL 311   LIGHT OF DAY (LP) 40

KILTIES
  56   Beltona BL 2666   Teach You To Rock/Giddy-Up-A Ding Dong (78 rpm = £12) 20

KIM & KINETICS
  60s Mortonsound 3032/3033   Without A Song/Stormy Monday 40
  60s Mortonsound 3036/3033   Wee Wee Hours/Stormy Monday 40
  (see also Kim Davis)

WILLIAM KIMBER
  56   EFDSS LP 1001   WILLIAM KIMBER (LP, with booklet) 15
  74   Topic 12T 249   THE ART OF WILLIAM KIMBER (LP, with booklet) 15

WILLIAM E. KIMBER
  68   Parlophone R 5735   Kilburn Towers/Goodbye (withdrawn) 8
  (see also Couriers)

STEVIE KIMBLE
  66   Decca F 12378   Some Things Take A Little Time/All The Time In The World 18

MAX KIMINSKY
  59   Melodisc MLP 12-126   DIXIELAND HORN (LP) 20

KINESIS
  03   Ministry Of Sound   Everything Destroys Itself/Zyklonb/Instinct (CD) 10
      HALL005CD

KINESPHERE
  76   Kinesphere KIN 5001   ALL AROUND YOU (LP) 100

KINETIC EFFECT
  93   Insane 1201   Borderin' Insanity/Beyond The Parameters (12", green vinyl) 30
  93   Insane 1201   Borderin' Insanity/Beyond The Parameters (12") 18

AL KING
  68   Sue WI 4045   Think Twice Before You Speak/The Winner 40

ALLAN KING
  73   Duke DU 151   Africa Wants Us All/JOE GIBBS: Liberation
                           (B-side actually by Joe Gibbs' All Stars) 6

ALBERT KING
  67   Atlantic 584 099   Crosscut Saw/Down Don't Bother Me. 15
  67   Stax 601 015   Born Under A Bad Sign/Personal Manager 10
  68   Stax 601 029   Cold Feet/You Sure Drive A Hard Bargain 10
  68   Stax 601 042   (I Love) Lucy/You're Gonna Need Me 8
  73   Stax 2025 162   Breaking Up Somebody's Home/Little Brother (Make A Way) 5
  67   Polydor 2343 026   TRAVELLIN' TO CALIFORNIA (LP) 35
  68   Stax (S)XATS 1002   LIVE WIRE — BLUES POWER (LP). 35
  69   Atlantic 588 173   KING OF THE BLUES GUITAR (LP). 35
  69   Stax SXATS 1017   KING DOES THE KING'S THINGS (LP) 25
  69   Stax SXATS 1022   YEARS GONE BY (LP) 25
  71   Stax 2363 003   LIVE WIRE — BLUES POWER (LP, reissue). 15
  71   Stax 2325 042   LOVEJOY (LP). 15
  73   Stax 2325 089   I'LL PLAY THE BLUES FOR YOU (LP) 15
  74   Stax STX 1003   I WANNA GET FUNKY (LP). 15
  (se also Steve Cropper & Albert King)

ANNA KING
  65   Philips BF 1402   If Somebody Told You/Baby, Baby, Baby (as Anna King & Bobby Byrd) 15
  65   Philips BBE 12584   BACK TO SOUL (EP). 40
  65   Philips (S)BL 7655   BACK TO SOUL (LP). 90
  (see also Bobby Byrd)

ANTHONY KING
  70s Peer Intl.   ELECTRICAL BAZAAR — SYNTHESIZERS UNLIMITED (LP, library issue) 25

B.B. KING
  62   HMV POP 1101   Tomorrow Night/Mother's Love 20
  64   Ember EMB S 196   Rock Me Baby/I Can't Lose 25
  65   Sue WI 358   The Letter/You Never Know 28
  66   HMV POP 1568   Don't Answer The Door Parts 1 & 2 12
  67   HMV POP 1580   Night Life/Waitin' On You 12
  67   HMV POP 1594   I Don't Want You Cuttin' Your Hair/Think It Over 10
  67   Polydor 56735   Jungle/Long Gone Baby 10
  68   Stateside SS 2112   Paying The Cost To Be The Boss/Having My Say 10
  68   Blue Horizon 57-3144 The Woman I Love/Blues For Me. 20
  69   Stateside SS 2141   Don't Waste My Time/Get Myself Somebody 6
  69   Blue Horizon 57-3161 Everyday I Have The Blues/Five Long Years 22
  70   Stateside SS 2161   The Thrill Is Gone/You're Mean 8
  70   Stateside SS 2169   So Excited/Confessin' The Blues 5
  70   Stateside SS 2176   Hummingbird/Ask Me No Questions. 5
  71   Probe PRO 516   Chains And Things/King's Special 5
  71   Probe PRO 528   Ask Me No Questions/Help The Poor/Humming Bird 5
  71   Probe PRO 546   Ain't Nobody Home/Alexis' Boogie (with Alexis Korner) 10
  72   Probe PRO 573   Summer In The City/Found What I Need 5
  65   HMV CLP 1870   LIVE AT THE REGAL (LP). 45
  66   HMV CLP 3514   CONFESSIN' THE BLUES (LP). 35
  67   HMV CLP 3608   BLUES IS KING (LP). 35
  67   Ember EMB 3379   THE R&B AND SOUL OF B.B. KING (LP) 22
  68   Stateside (S)SL 10238 BLUES ON TOP OF BLUES (LP) 35
  68   Blue Horizon 7-63216 THE B.B. KING STORY CHAPTER 1 (LP) 50

B.B. KING

69	Stateside (S)SL 10272	LUCILLE (LP)	22
69	Stateside SSL 10284	HIS BEST — THE ELECTRIC B.B. KING (LP)	22
69	Blue Horizon 7-63226	THE B.B. KING STORY CHAPTER 2 — BEALE STREET BLUES (LP)	60
70	Stateside SSL 10297	LIVE AND WELL (LP)	22
70	Stateside SSL 10299	COMPLETELY WELL (LP)	22
70	Probe SPBA 6255	INDIANOLA MISSISSIPPI SEEDS (LP)	12
71	Blue Horizon 2431 004	TAKE A SWING WITH ME (LP)	60
71	Probe SPB 1032	LIVE IN COOK COUNTY JAIL (LP)	15
71	Probe SPB 1041	IN LONDON (LP)	15
72	Probe SPB 1051	L.A. MIDNIGHT (LP)	12
72	Probe SPB 1063	GUESS WHO (LP)	12
73	Probe SPB 1069	THE BEST OF B.B. KING (LP)	12
73	Probe SPB 1083	TO KNOW YOU IS TO LOVE YOU (LP)	12

(see also U2)

B.B. KING & BOBBY BLAND

74	ABC ABCD 605	TOGETHER FOR THE FIRST TIME (2-LP)	20

(see also Bobby Bland)

BEN E. KING

61	London HLK 9258	Spanish Harlem/First Taste Of Love	15
61	London HLK 9358	Stand By Me/On The Horizon	20
61	London HLK 9416	Amor, Amor/Souvenir Of Mexico	10
61	London HLK 9457	Here Comes The Night/Young Boy Blues	15
62	London HLK 9517	Ecstasy/Yes	10
62	London HLK 9544	Don't Play That Song (You Lied)/The Hermit Of Misty Mountain	
		(later copies have Atlantic labels instead of *London* Atlantic)	each 10
62	London HLK 9586	Too Bad/My Heart Cries For You	15
63	London HLK 9631	I'm Standing By/Walking In The Footsteps Of A Fool	15
63	London HLK 9691	How Can I Forget/Gloria, Gloria	15
63	London HLK 9778	I (Who Have Nothing)/The Beginning Of Time	10
63	London HLK 9819	I Could Have Danced All Night/Gypsy	15
64	London HLK 9840	Around The Corner/Groovin'	10
64	Atlantic AT 4007	It's All Over/Let The Water Run Down	20
65	Atlantic AT 4018	Seven Letters/River Of Tears	20
65	Atlantic AT 4025	The Record (Baby I Love You)/The Way You Shake It	20
65	Atlantic AT 4043	Cry No More/(There's) No Place To Hide	25
66	Atlantic AT 4065	Goodnight My Love, Pleasant Dreams/Tell Daddy	10
66	Atlantic AT 4065	Goodnight My Love, Pleasant Dreams/I Can't Break The News To Myself	
		(demos with blank label on different B-side)	400+
66	Atlantic 584 008	So Much Love/Don't Drive Me Away	10
66	Atlantic 584 046	I Swear By The Stars Above/Get In A Hurry	10
67	Atlantic 584 069	What Is Soul?/They Don't Give Medals To Yesterday's Heroes	15
67	Atlantic 584 090	Save The Last Dance For Me (as Ben E. King & Drifters)/Stand By Me	10
67	Atlantic 584 106	Tears, Tears, Tears/A Man Without A Dream	15
68	Atlantic 584 149	Seven Letters/Goodnight My Love	10
68	Atlantic 584 184	Don't Take Your Love From Me/Forgive This Fool	22
68	Atlantic 584 205	It's Amazing/Where's The Girl	10
69	Atlantic 584 238	'Till I Can't Take It Any More/It Ain't Fair	10
70	Crewe CRW 2	Goodbye My Old Gal/I Can't Take It Like A Man	5
71	Atlantic 2091 100	It's Amazing/Tears, Tears, Tears	6
71	CBS 7397	White Moon/All Of Your Sorrows	6
72	CBS 7785	Take Me To The Pilot/I Guess It's Goodbye	6
75	Atlantic K 10565	Supernatural Things (Parts 1 & 2)	15
75	Atlantic K 10618	Happiness Is Where You Find It/Drop My Heart Off	5
63	London REK 1361	BEN E. KING (EP)	45
63	London REK 1386	I'M STANDING BY (EP)	45
64	Atlantic AET 6004	WHAT NOW MY LOVE (EP)	40
61	London HA-K 2395	SPANISH HARLEM (LP, also stereo SAH-K 6195)	50/70
62	London HA-K 8012	DON'T PLAY THAT SONG! (LP)	50
63	London HA-K/SH-K 8026	SONGS FOR SOULFUL LOVERS (LP, cover credits	
		"*Sings* For Soulful Lovers"; mono/stereo)	50/50
65	Atlantic ATL 5016	GREATEST HITS (LP, plum label)	45
65	Atlantic ATL 5024	SEVEN LETTERS (LP)	55
66	Atlantic 587/588 055	SONGS FOR SOULFUL LOVERS (LP, cover credits	
		"*Sings* For Soulful Lovers"; reissue)	18
67	Atlantic 590 001	SPANISH HARLEM (LP, reissue)	18
67	Atlantic 587 072	WHAT IS SOUL? (LP)	25
68	Atlantic 588 125	SEVEN LETTERS (LP, reissue)	15
70	Crewe CRWS 203	ROUGH EDGES (LP)	12
71	CBS 64570	THE BEGINNING OF IT ALL (LP)	12
75	Atlantic K 50118	SUPERNATURAL THING (LP)	12

(see also Drifters, Soul Clan)

BRENTON KING

73	Downtown DT 505	Why Do People Have To Cry/Version	6

BOB KING & THE COUNTRY KINGS

59	Oriole CB 1497	My Petite Marie/Hey Honey (78 rpm = £30)	100

BUZZY KING

60	Top Rank JAR 278	Schoolboy Blues/Your Picture	25

CANNON BALL KING

69	Camel CA 14	Danny Boy/Reggae Happiness	10
70s	Junior JR 103	Reggay Got Soul/Land Of Love (actually by Soul Cats)	10

(see also Carl Bryan, King Cannon, Cannon Ball & Johnny Melody)

CARL KING
| 66 | CBS 202407 | Out Of My Depth/Keep It Coming | 20 |
| 67 | CBS 202553 | You And Me/Satin Doll | 8 |

CAROLE KING
62	London HLU 9591	It Might As Well Rain Until September/Nobody's Perfect	10
66	London HLU 10036	Road To Nowhere/Some Of Your Lovin'	40
72	Ode ODS 66031	Been To Canaan/Bitter With The Sweet	5
71	A&M AMLS 996	WRITER — CAROLE KING (LP)	20
72	Ode ODE 77016	RHYMES AND REASONS (LP)	15
80	Capitol EA-ST 12073	PEARLS (LP, picture card inner)	15

CLAUDE KING
61	Philips PB 1173	Big River Big Man/Sweet Loving	10
61	Philips PB 1199	The Comancheros/I Can't Get Over The Way You Got Over Me	10
62	CBS AAG 108	Wolverton Mountain/Little Bitty Heart	12
62	CBS AAG 119	Burning Of Atlanta/Don't That Moon Look Lonesome	10
65	CBS EP 6067	TIGER WOMAN (EP)	20
62	CBS BPG 62114	MEET CLAUDE KING (LP)	25

CLYDIE KING
69	Minit MLF 11014	One Part, Two Part/Love Now Pay Later	15
75	UK USA 11	Punish Me/Punish Me (Instrumental Version)	6
		(see also Jimmy Holiday & Clydie King, Raelets)	

DANNY KING('S MAYFAIR SET)
64	Columbia DB 7276	Tossin' And Turnin'/Young Blood	35
65	Columbia DB 7456	Pretty Things/Outside Of My Room	40
65	Columbia DB 7792	Amen (My Teenage Prayer)/It's Such A Shame (as Danny King's Mayfair Set)	25
		(see also Trevor Burton, Lemon Tree, Roy Wood)	

DAVE KING
56	Decca F 10684	Memories Are Made Of This (& Keynotes)/I've Changed My Mind A 1000 Times	12
56	Decca F 10720	You Can't Be True To Two/A Little Bit Independent	10
56	Decca F 10741	The Birds And The Bees/Hot Chocolatta (with Keynotes)	10
56	Decca F 10791	Christmas And You/You Make Nice	10
57	Decca F 10865	Love Is A Golden Ring/If Your Heart Wants To Dance	5
57	Decca F 10910	With All My Heart/Red Shutters	5
57	Decca F 10947	Shake Me I Rattle/Chances Are	5
58	Decca F 10973	The Story Of My Life/I'll Buy You A Star	6
58	Decca F 11012	I Suddenly/There's Only One Of You	5
58	Decca F 11061	The Story/Home	5
59	Pye International 7N 25032	High Hopes/Night And Day (78 rpm, N25032 = £6)	5
60	Pye 7N 15283	Many A Wonderful Moment/Goody Goody	6
61	Pye International 7N 25076	Young In Love/C'est La Vie, C'est L'amour	5
56	Decca DFE 6385	A DAVE KING SELECTION (EP)	15
58	Decca DFE 6514	DAVE KING NO. 2 (EP)	15
62	Ace Of Hearts ACL 1095	MEMORIES ARE MADE OF THIS (LP)	20

DAVE KING REGGAE BAND
| 70 | Attack ATT 8014 | Hey Little Girl/Why Don't You Try Me | 6 |

DEE KING
| 66 | Piccadilly 7N 35316 | Sally Go Round The Roses/It's So Fine | 12 |

DENNIS KING
| 77 | EMI EMI 2578 | Regan's Theme From The Film 'Sweeney'/F.J.'s Tune | 20 |
| | | *(see also King Brothers)* | |

EARL (CONNELLY) KING
| 56 | Parlophone DP 511 | Gratefully/Don't Take It So Hard (78, export issue) | 20 |

EDDIE KING
| 65 | Columbia DB 7572 | Always At A Distance/If You Wish | 8 |
| 65 | Columbia DB 7654 | I Wanna Love Her So Bad/If All You Need | 10 |

FREDDY/FREDDIE KING
61	Parlophone R 4777	Hideaway/I Love The Woman	40
65	Sue WI 349	Driving Sideways/Hideaway	40
69	Atlantic 584 235	Play It Cool/Funky	10
73	A&M AMS 7076	Woman Across The River/Help Me Through The Day	5
69	Atlantic 588 036	FREDDIE IS A BLUES MASTER (LP)	30
69	Polydor 2343 009	KING OF R&B VOL. 2 (LP)	15
69	Python PLP-KM 5	FREDDY KING VOLUME 1 (LP, 99 copies only)	42
69	Python PLP-KM 7	FREDDY KING VOLUME 2 (LP, 99 copies only)	42
69	Python PLP-KM 11	FREDDY KING VOLUME 3 (LP, 99 copies only)	42
		(Pre-1970 releases are usually credited to Freddy King, post-1970 releases to Freddie King.)	
71	A&M AMLS 65004	GETTING READY (LP)	15
72	Polydor 2343 047	HIS EARLY YEARS VOLUME 1 (LP)	12
72	A&M AMLS 68113	TEXAS CANNONBALL (LP)	12
72	Black Bear 904	LIVE PERFORMANCES VOLUME 1 (LP)	20
72	Black Bear 905	LIVE PERFORMANCES VOLUME 2 (LP)	20
73	A&M AMLS 68919	WOMAN ACROSS THE RIVER (LP)	12
		(see also Lula Reed & Freddy King)	

HAMILTON KING
64	HMV POP 1289	Not Until/I Wanna Live	10
64	HMV POP 1356	Ain't It Time/Money, Money	15
63	HMV POP 1425	Bird Without Wings/Shoppin'	15

| 60s | Toast TT 511 | This Love Of Mine/The Cup Is Fuller | 5 |

HANK KING
| 63 | Starlite STEP 41 | COUNTRY AND WESTERN (EP) | 25 |
| 66 | Starlite GRK 510 | COUNTRY AND WESTERN (EP, reissue) | 10 |

JAY W. KING
| 66 | Stateside SS 505 | I'm So Afraid/I Don't Have To Worry (Not Anymore) | 22 |

JONATHAN KING
67	Decca LK/SKL 4908	OR THEN AGAIN... (LP)	20
72	Decca SKL 5127	TRY SOMETHING DIFFERENT (LP)	12
75	UK UKAL 1010	A ROSE IN A FISTED GLOVE (LP)	12

(see also Weathermen, Hedgehoppers Anonymous, Pleasure Garden)

DR. MARTIN LUTHER KING
68	Pama PM 732	I Have A Dream/Top Of The Mountain	15
68	Tamla Motown TML 11076	THE GREAT MARCH TO FREEDOM (LP)	100
60s	Hallmark CHM 631	IN THE STRUGGLE FOR FREEDOM (LP)	12

P. KING
| 83 | Red Bus RBUS 79 | Hey Rosalyn/Lyin' Again | 6 |

(see also Paul King)

PAUL KING
| 72 | Dawn DNS 1023 | Whoa Buck/Zoe | 7 |
| 72 | Dawn DNLS 3035 | BEEN IN THE PEN TOO LONG (LP, with lyric insert) | 25 |

(see also Mungo Jerry, P. King, P. Rufus King, King Earl Boogie Band, D'Jurann Jurran, Jigilo Jug Band, Russian Roulette)

PEE WEE KING & HIS BAND
52	HMV B 10229	Bull Fiddle Boogie (with Golden West Cowboys)/Silver And Gold (78)	10
52	HMV B 10275	Busybody (with Redd Stewart)/I Don't Mind (with Golden West Trio) (78)	10
53	HMV B 10415	Tennessee Tango/The Crazy Waltz (78)	10
54	HMV 7MC 14	Bimbo/Changing Partners (export issue)	20

(see also Hank Snow)

PETE KING CHORALE & ORCHESTRA
| 61 | London HLR 9437 | Hey! Look Me Over/Tall Hope | 5 |

PETER KING
| 68 | Crab CRAB 3 | Reggae Limbo/DERRICK MORGAN: River To The Bank | 7 |

P. RUFUS KING
| 73 | Dawn DNS 1031 | Look At Me Now/Nobody Knows | 6 |

(see also Paul King, Mungo Jerry)

RAMONA KING
| 64 | Warner Bros WB 125 | It's In His Kiss/It Couldn't Happen To A Nicer Guy | 25 |

RAY KING SOUL BAND
| 67 | Piccadilly 7N 35394 | Behold/Soon You'll Be Gone | 18 |

REG KING
| 71 | United Artists UP 35204 | Little Boy/10,000 Miles (as Reg King & B.B. Blunder) | 7 |
| 71 | United Artists UAG 29157 | REG KING (LP) | 35 |

(see also Action, Andy Leigh, B.B. Blunder, Mark Charig, Elton Dean, Mighty Baby)

SAMMY KING (& VOLTAIRS)
64	HMV POP 1285	What's The Secret/Great Balls Of Fire (as Sammy King & Voltairs)	10
64	HMV POP 1330	Rag Doll/We're Through	7
65	HMV POP 1384	Only You (And You Alone)/A Kiss, A Promise	10
66	HMV POP 1540	If You Can Find Someone To Love You/Past Caring (with Voltairs)	7

SID KING & FIVE STRINGS
| 56 | Philips PB 589 | Booger Red/Oobie-Doobie (78) | 120 |

SOLOMON KING
67	Columbia DB 8306	She Wears My Ring/Try Try (withdrawn B-side)	10
68	Columbia DB 8402	When We Were Young/Those Gentle Hands	5
68	Columbia DB 8454	Somewhere In The Crowd/Hava Nagila	5
68	Columbia DB 8508	Goodbye My Old Gal/Hundred Years Or More	5
69	Columbia DB 8554	Cry Softly/Time Alone Will Tell	5
69	Columbia DB 8586	For Each Question/If I Had Three Wishes	5
70	Columbia DB 8676	Say A Prayer/This Beautiful Day (demos = £150)	100
70	Columbia DB 8739	November Snow/Echoes Of A Million Kisses	5
71	Columbia DB 8771	Answer Me/Don't You Be A Sinner	5
68	Columbia S(C)X 6250	SHE WEARS MY RING (LP)	18
71	Columbia SCX 6458	YOU'LL NEVER WALK ALONE (LP)	15

(see also Levi Jackson)

SONNY KING
| 60 | Pye Intl. NPL 28001 | FOR LOSERS ONLY (LP) | 15 |

TEDDI KING
56	Vogue Coral Q 72142	My Funny Little Lover/I'll Never Be The Same	5
50s	Vogue EPV 1204	STORYVILLE PRESENTS MISS TEDDI KING (EP)	15
55	Vogue LDE 142	MISS TEDDI KING WITH RUBY BRAFF (10" LP)	15
57	Vogue VA 160109	NOW IN VOGUE (LP)	15

(see also George Shearing)

TEDDY KING & BUSTER'S ALLSTARS
| 67 | Fab FAB 27 | Mexican Divorce/SOUL TOPS: Baby I Got News | 18 |

TONY KING (& HIPPY BOYS)
69	Trojan TR 667	Proud Mary/My Devotion (as Tony King & Hippy Boys)	6
70	Gas GAS 156	Daddy, Daddy Don't Cry/I Like It	6

(see also Maytals)

KINGBEES
66	Tempo TPO 103	I'm A Kingbee/My Little Red Book (Irish-only, some in p/s)	350/250

KING ADORA
00s	SQR RQS 007	Bionic/The Law (numbered wraparound sleeve, stickered plastic outer sleeve, 500 only, with promo postcard)	15
00s	SQR RQS 008	Big Isn't Beautiful/Scream And Shout (numbered wraparound sleeve, 1000 only)	5

KING BEE
90	Big One RUFF6X	Back By Dope Demand/Oral Excitement (12")	15
90	1st Bass Ruff6r	Back By Dope Demand (12")	15

KING BISCUIT BOY
70	Paramount SPFL 270	OFFICIAL MUSIC (LP)	20
71	Paramount SPFA 7001	GOODUNS (LP)	20

(see also Bobby Bland)

KING BROTHERS
57	Conquest CP 104	The Cradle Rock/Crazy Little Palace (78)	10
57	Conquest CP 109	Steamboat Railroad/Heart (78)	10
57	Parlophone R 4288	Marianne/Little By Little	10
57	Parlophone R 4310	A White Sport Coat (And A Pink Carnation)/Minne-Minnehaha!	10
57	Parlophone R 4338	In The Middle Of An Island/Rockin' Shoes	7
57	Parlophone R 4367	Wake Up Little Susie/Winter Wonderland	8
57	Parlophone R 4389	Put A Light In The Window/Miss Otis Regrets	7
58	Parlophone R 4410	Hand Me Down My Walking Cane/6-5 Jive (78 rpm = £8)	12
58	Parlophone R 4438	Torero/Moonlight And Roses (78 rpm = £6)	6
58	Parlophone R 4469	Sitting In A Tree House/Father Time (78 rpm = £8)	5
59	Parlophone R 4513	Leaning On A Lamp-Post/Thank Heaven For Little Girls (78 rpm = £8)	5
59	Parlophone R 4554	Hop, Skip And Jump/Civilization (Bongo, Bongo, Bongo) (78 rpm = £10)	10
59	Parlophone R 4577	Makin' Love/Caribbean	6
60	Parlophone R 4639	The Waiter And The Porter And The Upstairs Maid/Standing On The Corner	5
60	Parlophone R 4672	Mais Oui/Gotta Feeling	5
60	Parlophone R 4715	Doll House/Si Si Si	5
61	Parlophone R 4737	Seventy-Six Trombones/I Like Everybody	5
61	Parlophone R 4778	Goodbye Little Darling/Tuxedo Junction	5
61	Parlophone R 4825	The Next Train Out Of Town/Sabre Dance	6
57	Parlophone GEP 8638	HARMONY KINGS (EP)	10
57	Parlophone GEP 8651	SING AL JOLSON (EP)	10
57	Parlophone GEP 8665	LULLABIES OF BROADWAY (EP)	10
58	Parlophone GEP 8726	THAT'S ENTERTAINMENT (EP)	10
58	Parlophone GEP 8760	KINGS OF SONG (EP)	10
61	Parlophone GEP 8838	KING SIZE HITS (EP)	10
61	Encore ENC 106	KINGS OF SONG (EP)	10
58	Parlophone PMC 1060	THREE KINGS AND AN ACE (LP)	20

(see also Jim Dale, Dennis King)

KING CANNON
69	Trojan TR 663	Soul Scorcher/GLEN & DAVE: Lucky Boy	15
69	Trojan TR 644	Soul Special/TREVOR SHIELD: Moon Is Playing Tricks On Me	15
69	Crab CRAB 6	Mellow Trumpet/VAL BENNETT: Reggae City	12
71	Hillcrest HCT 2	Reggay Got Soul/SOUL CATS: Land Of Love	7
71	Moodisc HME 109	Raw Deal (as King Cannon Allout; actually by Carl Bryan)/MUDIE'S ALL STARS: Shirley's Hide Out	6

(see also Cannon Ball & Johnny Melody, Carl Bryan, Max Romeo, Lester Sterling, Kid Gungo, Erroll Dunkley)

KING CANNON (BALL)
68	Trojan TR 636	Thunderstorm/BURT WALTERS: Honey Love	15

KING CHUBBY
70	Pama Supreme PS 297	What's The World Coming To/Live As One	10
70	Supreme PS 297	What's The World Coming To/Live As One (reissue)	10

(see also Junior Byles)

KING COLE TRIO
(see under Nat 'King' Cole)

KING CRIMSON
69	Island WIP 6071	The Court Of The Crimson King (Parts 1 & 2)	15
70	Island WIP 6080	Cat Food/Groon (some in p/s)	20/6
74	Island WIP 6189	The Night Watch/The Great Deceiver	5
76	Island WIP 6274	21st Century Schizoid Man/Epitaph (some in p/s)	25/7
91	Caroline 1467	THE ABBREVIATED KING CRIMSON: HEARTBEAT (CD EP, digipak)	20
69	Island ILPS 9111	IN THE COURT OF THE CRIMSON KING (LP, 1st pressing, pink label/'i' logo)	50
70	Island ILPS 9111	IN THE COURT OF THE CRIMSON KING (LP, 2nd pressing, pink rim label/'palm tree' logo)	15
70	Island ILPS 9127	IN THE WAKE OF POSEIDON (LP, 1st pressing, pink label/'i' logo)	35
70	Island ILPS 9127	IN THE WAKE OF POSEIDON (LP, 2nd pressing, pink rim label/'palm tree' logo)	15
70	Island ILPS 9141	LIZARD (LP, pink rim label/'palm tree' logo)	22
71	Island ILPS 9175	ISLANDS (LP, pink rim label/'palm tree' logo, gatefold sleeve with inner)	15
72	Island HELP 6	EARTHBOUND (LP, black/pink label)	12
73	Island ILPS 9230	LARKS' TONGUES IN ASPIC (LP, pink rim label/'palm tree' logo, with inner)	15
74	Island ILPS 9275	STARLESS AND BIBLE BLACK (LP, pink rim label/'palm tree' logo, with inner)	15

74	Island ILPS 9308	RED (LP, pink rim label/'palm tree' logo, with inner sleeve)	15
75	Island ILPS 9316	U.S.A. (LP, pink rim label/'palm tree' logo, with inner)	15
76	Island ISLP 7	A YOUNG PERSON'S GUIDE (2-LP, with booklet)	18
90s	EG/Virgin CDVKCX 13	THRAK (CD, in metal box, with tour programme)	20

(see also Giles Giles & Fripp, Fripp & Eno, Andy Summers & Robert Fripp, Gordon Haskell, Shame, McDonald & Giles, Emerson Lake & Palmer, Uriah Heep, Boz, Trendsetters Ltd., Pete Sinfield)

KING CRY CRY (Prince Far I)
71	Banana BA 356	I Had A Talk/BURNING SPEAR: Zion Higher	25

KING CURTIS
62	London HLU 9547	Soul Twist/Twistin' Time (as King Curtis & Noble Knights)	20
64	Capitol CL 15346	Soul Serenade/More Soul	20
67	Atlantic 584 109	Good To Me/Hold On I'm Comin'	10
67	Atlantic 584 134	Memphis Soul Stew/Blue Nocturne	15
68	Speciality SPE 1000	Wiggle Wobble/Night Train	8
69	Atlantic 584 287	Little Green Apples/La Jeanne	8
70	Atco 2091 012	Teasin'/Soulin' (as King Curtis & Delaney Bramlett, Eric Clapton & Friends)	15
60	London RE-K 1307	HAVE TENOR SAX, WILL BLOW (EP)	48
60	London HA-K 2247	HAVE TENOR SAX, WILL BLOW (LP)	65
62	RCA RD 27252	ARTHUR MURRAY'S MUSIC FOR DANCING — THE TWIST (LP)	30
62	Esquire 32-161	THE NEW SCENE OF KING CURTIS (LP)	35
67	Atlantic 587 067	PLAYS THE GREAT MEMPHIS HITS (LP)	22
68	Ember SPE/LP 6600	SOUL SERENADE (LP)	18
68	Atlantic 587 093	KINGSIZE SOUL (LP, as King Curtis & Kingpins)	18
68	Atlantic 587/588 115	SWEET SOUL (LP)	18
69	Atco 228 002	BEST OF KING CURTIS (LP)	15
69	Atco 228 027	INSTANT GROOVE (LP)	15
70	Wand WNS 4	ETERNALLY SOUL (LP, as King Curtis & Shirelles)	12
71	Atlantic K 40214	LIVE AT FILLMORE WEST (LP)	15
72	Atlantic K 40360	EVERYBODY'S TALKIN' (LP)	12
72	Speciality SPE 6600	SOUL SERENADE (LP, reissue)	12
72	Speciality SPE 6607	MISTER SOUL (LP, reissue)	12
73	Atlantic K 40434	BLUES AT MONTREUX (LP, with Champion Jack Dupree)	12

(see also Champion Jack Dupree, Eric Clapton)

KING CURTIS, OLIVER NELSON & JIMMY FORREST
63	Esquire 32-189	SOUL BATTLE (LP)	35

KING DIAMOND
89	Road Runner RR 94616	CONSPIRACY (LP, picture disc)	20

BOBBY KINGDOM/BLUE BEATS
61	Bluebeat BB 44	Honey Please/BLUE BEATS: That's My Girl	25
62	Blue Beat 45/BB/77	Spanish Town Twist/Brand New Automobile	12

KINGDOM COME (U.K.)
71	Polydor 2001 234	Eternal Messenger/I D Side To B Side The C Side	5
72	Polydor 2001 416	Spirit Of Joy/Come Alive	5
72	Polydor 2310 130	GALACTIC ZOO DOSSIER (LP, gatefold sleeve, some with poster)	42/20
72	Polydor 2310 178	KINGDOM COME (LP)	15
73	Polydor 2310 254	JOURNEY (LP)	15

(see also Arthur Brown)

KING-EARL BOOGIE BAND
72	Dawn DNS 1024	Plastic Jesus/If The Lord Don't Get You	6
72	Dawn DNS 1028	Starlight/Goin' To Germany	6
72	Dawn DNLS 3040	TROUBLE AT MILL (LP, with poster)	18

(see also Mungo Jerry, Paul King, Skeleton Crew)

KING FIGHTER
60s	Jump Up JU 518	People Will Talk/Same Thing	8

KINGFISH
76	United Artists UAG 29922	KINGFISH (LP)	12
77	United Artists UAG 30080	LIVE AND KICKIN' (LP)	12

(see also Grateful Dead, Bob Weir)

KING GEORGE
67	RCA RCA 1573	Drive On James/I'm Gonna Be Somebody Someday	30

KING HARVEST
73	Pye NSPL 28174	DANCING IN THE MOONLIGHT (LP)	12

KING HORROR
69	Joe/Duke DU 34	Dracula Prince Of Darkness/JOE'S ALL STARS: Honky	30
69	Grape GR 3003	Cutting Blade/Vampire	25
69	Grape GR 3006	The Hole/WINSTON GROOVY: Lover Come Back	25
69	Grape GR 3007	Lochness Monster/VISIONS: Zion I	25
69	Jackpot JP 713	Wood In The Fire/The Naked City	15
69	Jackpot JP 714	Police/PAMA DICE: Honky Tonk Popcorn	18
70	Nu Beat NB 051	Frankenstein/WINSTON GROOVY: I Can't Stand It	25
70	Reggae REG 3005	Slave Driver	20

(see also Laurel Aitken)

KING KONG
86	Greensleeves GRED 206	Paro Them Paro/Paranoia (12")	30

KING OF LUXEMBOURG
86	él GPO 14	Valleri/Sketches Of Luxembourg (p/s)	12

KINGLY BAND
69	Decca F 12926	The Bitter And The Sweet/Standing At The Crossroads	7

KING MIGUEL
73   Bullet BU 524   The Word Is Black/Town Talk.....5

KING OLIVER
53   London AL 3510   PLAYS THE BLUES (10" LP).....20
53   Columbia 33S 1065   KING JOE (10" LP).....15
55   Vogue/Coral LRA 10020   DIXIE SYNCOPATORS (10" LP).....15

KINGPINS (U.S.)
58   London HLU 8658   Ungaua Parts 1 & 2 (78 rpm = £18).....20

KINGPINS (U.K.)
65   Oriole CB 1986   Two Right Feet/That's The Way It Should Be.....20

KING ROCK & WILLOWS
67   Caltone TONE 111   You Are The One/ALVA LEWIS: Return Home.....45

KING ROCKY
68   Studio One SO 2045   The King Is Back/THREE TOPS: Vex Till Yuh Buss.....30
(see also Leroy & Rocky, Clancy Eccles, Heptones)

KINGS IV
59   London HLT 8914   Some Like It Hot/The World Goes On (78 rpm = £18).....18

KING'S HENCHMEN
59   Coral FEP 2025   ALAN FREED PRESENTS VOL. 1 (EP).....150+

KING SCRATCH
70s   Ethnic ETH 16   Spiritual Whip/Version.....12
70s   Ethnic ETH 30   Mash Finger/Version.....8
(see also Lee Perry/Upsetters, Skatalites)

KING SISTERS
57   Capitol CL 14711   While The Lights Are Low/In Hamburg (When The Nights Are Long).....7
57   Capitol CL 14729   Imagination/You're My Thrill.....7
57   Capitol CL 14777   Easy To Love/That Old Feeling.....7
58   Capitol CL 14865   Deep Purple/Unbelievable.....7
58   Capitol CL 14893   What's New?/The Thrill Was New.....6
58   Capitol CL 14934   Autumn In Pleasant Grove/The Guy In The Foreign Sports Car.....6
59   Capitol CL 15012   Keep Smiling (Keep Laughin', Be Happy)/The Maids Of Cadiz.....6
59   Capitol CL 15069   Lovin' Up A Storm/What Would I Do Without You.....6
59   Capitol CL 15096   Over The River (And Through The Woods)/Holiday Of Love (with Their Family).....6
57   Capitol EAP1 919   IMAGINATION (EP).....10
57   Capitol T 808   ALOHA (LP).....15

CHARLES KINGSLEY CREATION
65   Columbia DB 7758   Summer Without Sun/Still In Love With You.....70

EVELYN KINGSLEY & TOWERS
58   Capitol CL 14944   To Know Him Is To Love Him/FRANK PERRY & TOWERS: Let Me Be The One.....25
(see also Towers)

KINGSMEN
58   London HLE 8735   Better Believe It/Week-End (78 rpm = £25).....30
59   London HLE 8812   Conga Rock/The Cat Walk (78 rpm = £35).....35
59   London REE 1211   THE KINGSMEN (EP).....85
(see also Bill Haley & Comets)

KINGSMEN
63   Pye International 7N 25231   Louie Louie/Haunted Castle.....35
64   Pye International 7N 25262   Little Latin Lu/David's Mood.....12
64   Pye International 7N 25273   Death Of An Angel/Searching For Love.....15
65   Pye International 7N 25292   The Jolly Green Giant/Long Green.....10
65   Pye International 7N 25311   The Climb/Waiting.....15
65   Pye International 7N 25322   Annie Fanny/Something's Got A Hold On Me.....10
66   Pye International 7N 25366   Little Latin Lu/Louie Louie.....10
66   Pye International 7N 25370   Killer Joe/Little Green Thing.....15
67   Pye International 7N 25406   Daytime Shadows/Trouble.....12
71   Wand WN 14   Louie Louie/If I Needed Someone.....15
64   Pye Intl. NEP 44023   THE KINGSMEN (EP).....35
65   Pye Intl. NEP 44040   MOJO WORKOUT (EP).....35
66   Pye Intl. NEP 44063   FEVER (EP).....30
63   Pye Intl. NPL 28050   THE KINGSMEN IN PERSON (LP, live).....28
64   Pye Intl. NPL 28054   THE KINGSMEN VOLUME II (LP).....28
65   Pye Intl. NPL 28068   THE KINGSMEN ON CAMPUS (LP).....28
66   Pye Intl. NPL 28085   15 GREAT HITS (LP).....28
68   Marble Arch MAL 829   THE KINGSMEN'S GREATEST HITS (LP).....15
71   Wand WNS 6   UP AND AWAY (LP).....12

KING SOUNDS
78   Grove Music GMDM5   Spend One Night In Babylon (feat. Trinity)/Keep Us Down In Poverty (feat. Jah Woosh) (12").....25
79   Grove Music GMDM 11   They That Hate Us (wrongfully)/Ungrateful Bretheren (12").....15
79   Grove Music GMDM 20   Kill Them Dead/Look Into Youself (12").....15

KING SPARROW
58   Melodisc MEL 1447   Leading Calypsonians/BILLY MOORE: Love Is Everywhere (78 rpm = £8).....7
58   Melodisc MEL 1475   Familysize Cokes/Clara Honey Bunch (78 rpm = £8).....7
59   Melodisc MEL 1491   Goaty/I Confess (78 rpm = £12).....7
66   Island WI 285   Beggars Have No Choice (actually by Leonard Dillon & Wailers)/MARCIA GRIFFITHS: Funny.....35
69   Trojan TRLS 8   SPARROW MEETS THE DRAGON (LP).....12
(see also Mighty Sparrow, Sparrow)

KING SPORTY

70	Banana BA 321	Inspiration/Choice Of Music	12
70	Banana BA 322	Lover's Version (as Sporty & Wilson)/DUDLEY SIBLEY: Having A Party	7
70	Punch PH 44	For Our Desire/WINSTON WRIGHT: Version	15
71	Banana BA 323	D.J. Special/RICHARD & MAD: Creation Version	12
73	Green Door GD 4063	Yearful Of Sundays/Version	6

KING STITT
(see under 'S')

KINGSTON ALLSTARS

66	Dice CC 25	Happy Hunter/LITTLE NORMA: Ten Commandments Of Woman	25

KINGSTONIANS

67	Rio R 140	Winey Winey/I Don't Care	15
68	Coxsone CS 7066	Mother Miserable/I Make A Woman	25
68	Doctor Bird DB 1120	Put Down Your Fire/Girls Like Dirt	25
68	Doctor Bird DB 1123	Mummy And Daddy/False Witness	20
68	Doctor Bird DB 1126	Fun Galore/Crime Don't Pay	20
68	Trojan TR 627	Mix It Up/I'll Be Around	20
69	Big Shot BI 508	Sufferer/Kiss A Little Finger	15
69	Big Shot BI 526	Nice Nice/I'll Be Around	12
69	Crab CRAB 19	Hold Down/BARRY YORK: Who Will She Be	15
69	Bullet BU 409	I Am Just A Minstrel/Yesterday	6
69	Songbird SB 1011	The Clip/BRUCE ANTHONY: Little Miss Muffett	10
70	Songbird SB 1019	Singer Man/CRYSTALITES: Version	8
70	Songbird SB 1041	Rumble Rumble/CRYSTALITES: Version	10
70	Songbird SB 1045	Out There/CRYSTALITES: Out There Version II	12
70	Trojan TR 7708	I'll Need You Tomorrow/I'm Gonna Make It	5
70	Duke DU 88	You Can't Wine/RUPIE EDWARDS ALLSTARS: Bee Sting	8
72	Duke DU 126	Lion's Den/Version	8
70	Trojan TBL 113	SUFFERER (LP)	30

(see also Jack (Bernard) & Beanstalks, Gregory Isaacs)

KINGS OF LEON

03	Handmedown HMD 28	Molly's Chambers/Holy Roller Novocaine (10", limited issue, numbered p/s)	8
03	Handmedown HMD 31	Wasted Time/Molly's Hangover (10", silver vinyl, numbered p/s)	8
03	Handmedown HMD 20	HOLY ROLLER NOVOCAINE EP: Molly's Chambers/California Waiting/ Holy Roller Novocaine (10", clear red vinyl, numbered p/s, 1000 only)	30
03	Handmedown HMD 21	HOLY ROLLER NOVOCAINE EP (CD, digipak, 1000 only)	12
03	Handmedown HMD 22	WHAT I SAW EP: Red Morning Light/Wicker Chair (10", blue vinyl, numbered p/s)	12
03	Handmedown HMD	YOUTH & YOUNG MANHOOD (2 x 10", p/s with picture inners)	12

KINGSTON JOE

64	Blue Beat BB 253	Time Is On My Friend (actually by Lloyd Barnes)/Wear And Tear (B-side actually by Lascelles Perkins)	20

KINGSTON PETE & BUSTER'S ALL STARS

67	Blue Beat BB 403	Little Boy Blue/I'm A Lover Try Me (actually by Larry Marshall)	50

(see also Larry Marshall)

KINGSTON TRIO

58	Capitol CL 14918	Scarlet Ribbons/Three Jolly Coachmen	5
58	Capitol CL 14951	Tom Dooley/Ruby Red	5
59	Capitol CL 14985	Raspberries, Strawberries/Sally (78 rpm = £12)	5
59	Capitol CL 15002	The Tijuana Jail/Oh Cindy	5
59	Capitol CL 15040	M.T.A./All My Sorrows (78 rpm = £15)	5
59	Capitol CL 15073	San Miguel/A Worried Man (78 rpm = £20)	5
60	Capitol CL 15113	Green Grasses/Coo Coo U	5
60	Capitol CL 15199	El Matador/Home From The Hill	5
60	Capitol CL 15138	Bad Man's Blunder/The Escape Of Old John Webb	5
60	Capitol CL 15161	Everglades/This Mornin', This Evenin', So Soon	5
63	Capitol CL 15287	Greenback Dollar/The New Frontier	7

EPs

59	Capitol EAP1 1119	M.T.A.	10
59	Capitol EAP1 1136	TOM DOOLEY	10
59	Capitol EAP1 1182	RASPBERRIES STRAWBERRIES	10
60	Capitol EAP1 1258	HERE WE GO AGAIN (also stereo SEP1 1258)	8/10
60	Capitol EAP2 1258	HERE WE GO AGAIN (also stereo SEP2 1258)	8/10
60	Capitol EAP3 1258	HERE WE GO AGAIN (also stereo SEP3 1258)	8/10
60	Capitol EAP1 1322	A WORRIED MAN	10
62	Capitol EAP4 2011	TIME TO THINK	10
63	Capitol EAP1 20460	GREENBACK DOLLAR	10
64	Capitol EAP1 20655	LEMON TREE	10
65	Brunswick OE 9511	THE KINGSTON TRIO	10

LPs

58	Capitol T 996	THE KINGSTON TRIO	12
59	Capitol T 1107	FROM THE HUNGRY I	12
59	Capitol T 1199	AT LARGE	12
60	Capitol (S)T 1258	HERE WE GO AGAIN	12
60	Capitol (S)T 1352	SOLD OUT	12
60	Capitol (S)T 1407	STRING ALONG	12
60	Capitol ST 1183	STEREO CONCERT	12
60	Capitol (S)T 1446	LAST MONTH OF THE YEAR	12
61	Capitol (S)T 1474	MAKE WAY!	12
61	Capitol (S)T 1564	GOIN' PLACES	12
61	Capitol (S)T 1612	ENCORES	12
61	Capitol (S)T 1642	CLOSE UP	12

62	Capitol (S)T 1658	COLLEGE CONCERT	12
62	Capitol (S)T 1747	SOMETHING SPECIAL	12
63	Capitol (S)T 1809	NEW FRONTIER	12
63	Capitol (S)T 1871	NUMBER SIXTEEN	12
63	Capitol (S)T 1935	SUNNY SIDE	12
64	Capitol (S)T 2011	TIME TO THINK	12
64	Capitol (S)T 2081	BACK IN TOWN	12
64	Capitol (S)T 2180	FOLK ERA	12
69	Polydor 583 751/2	ONCE UPON A TIME (2 x LP)	15

(see also John Stewart)

KING TIMOTH
53	Melodisc 1247	Gerrard Street/Nylon (78)	6

KING TRUMAN
89	Acid Jazz JAZID 9T	Like A Gun (Safe Sax Mix)/(Dub Version)/(Radio Edit) (12", p/s)	120

(see also Style Council, Paul Weller)

KING TUBBY & LEE PERRY
75	Live & Love LALP 02	MEETS THE AGROVATORS AT THE DUB STATION (LP)	75
76	Prophets (no. cat. no)	PROPHECY OF DUB (LP, in plain sleeve)	120
76	Fay FMLP 307	SURROUNDED BY DREAD AT THE NATIONAL ARENA (LP)	55
76	Klik KLIP 9002	SHALOM DUB (LP)	40
77	Fay Music FMLP 304	KING TUBBY MEETS THE UPSETTER AT THE GRASS ROOTS OF DUB (LP)	25
78	Studio 16 WE 102	SURROUNDED BY DREAD AT THE NATIONAL ARENA (LP, reissue)	35
79	Star PTLP 1029	MAJESTIC DUB (LP)	25
81	Live & Love LAP 015	UPSETS THE UPSETTER (LP)	35

KING TUBBY, PRINCE JAMMY & SCIENTIST
81	K&G Imperial KGLP 002	FIRST, SECOND AND THIRD GENERATION OF DUB (LP)	35

KINKS
PYE SINGLES
64	Pye 7N 15611	Long Tall Sally/I Took My Baby Home (Demo £100+)	120
64	Pye 7N 15636	You Still Want Me/You Do Something To Me (Demo £100+)	170
64	Pye 7N 15673	You Really Got Me/It's All Right	12
64	Pye 7N 15714	All Day And All Of The Night/I Gotta Move	10
65	Pye 7N 15759	Tired Of Waiting For You/Come On Now	10
65	Pye 7N 15813	Everybody's Gonna Be Happy/Who'll Be The Next In Line	10
65	Pye 7N 15854	Set Me Free/I Need You	10
65	Pye 7N 15919	See My Friend/Never Met A Girl Like You Before	10
65	Pye 7N 15981	Till The End Of The Day/Where Have All The Good Times Gone	10
66	Pye 7N 17064	Dedicated Follower Of Fashion/Sittin' On My Sofa	10
66	Pye 7N 17125	Sunny Afternoon/I'm Not Like Everybody Else	10
66	Pye 7N 17222	Dead End Street/Big Black Smoke (some labels list "Deadend")	each 10
67	Pye 7N 17321	Waterloo Sunset/Act Nice And Gentle	10
67	Pye 7N 17400	Autumn Almanac/Mr. Pleasant	10
68	Pye 7N 17468	Wonderboy/Polly	15
68	Pye 7N 17573	Days/She's Got Everything	15
69	Pye 7N 17724	Plastic Man/King Kong	15
69	Pye 7N 17776	Drivin'/Mindless Child Of Motherhood	25
69	Pye 7N 17812	Shangri-La/Last Of The Steam-Powered Trains (unissued, acetates only)	
69	Pye 7N 17812	Shangri-La/This Man He Weeps Tonight	25
69	Pye 7N 17865	Victoria/Mr Churchill Says	14
70	Pye 7N 17961	Lola/Berkeley Mews	7
70	Pye 7N 45016	Apeman/Rats	8
71	Pye PMM 100	You Really Got Me/Set Me Free/Wonder Boy/Long Tall Shorty (maxi-single, p/s)	8
71	Pye 7NX 8001	PERCY (33rpm 4-track maxi-single, p/s)	18
74	Pye 7N 45313	Where Have All The Good Times Gone/Lola (p/s)	20
83	PRT KPD 1	You Really Got Me/Misty Water (picture disc)	10
84	PRT KIS 003	All Day And All Of The Night/I Gotta Move (picture disc)	10

EXPORT SINGLES
65	Pye 7N 15981	Till The End Of The Day/Where Have All The Good Times Gone (export p/s)	150
66	Pye 7N 17100	Well Respected Man/Milk Cow Blues	110
67	Pye 7N 17314	Mr. Pleasant/This Is Where I Belong	90
67	Pye 7N 17405	Autumn Almanac/David Watts	90
71	Pye 7N 8001	God's Children/Moments (some in p/s)	60/30

RCA SINGLES
72	RCA RCA 2211	Supersonic Rocket Ship/You Don't Know My Name	8
72	RCA RCA 2299	Celluloid Heroes/Hot Potatoes	8
73	RCA RCA 2387	Sitting In The Midday Sun/One Of The Survivors	8
73	RCA RCA 2418	Sweet Lady Genevieve/Sitting In My Hotel	8
74	RCA RCA 5015	Mirror Of Love/Cricket	12
74	RCA RCA 5042	Mirror Of Love/He's Evil	12
74	RCA RCA 2478	Holiday Romance/Shepherds Of The Nation	10
75	RCA RCA 2546	Ducks On The Wall/Rush Hour Blues	10
75	RCA RCA 2567	You Can't Stop The Music/Have Another Drink	10
76	RCA RCM 1	No More Looking Back/Jack The Idiot Dunce/The Hard Way (p/s)	12

ARISTA SINGLES
77	Arista ARIST 153	Father Christmas/Prince Of The Punks (p/s)	10
78	Arista ARIST 189	A Rock'n'Roll Fantasy/Artificial Light	8
78	Arista ARIST 210	Black Messiah/Misfits (p/s)	8
79	Arista ARIST 300	Moving Pictures/In A Space (p/s)	8
80	Arista ARIST 404	Lola (live)/Celluloid Heroes (live) (export only)	12
81	Arista ARIST 415	Better Things/Massive Reductions (p/s)	10
81	Arista ARIST 415/KINKS 1	Better Things/Massive Reductions//Lola (live)/David Watts (live) (double pack, gatefold p/s)	8

MINT VALUE £

81	Arista ARIPD 426	Predictable/Back To Front (picture disc)	8
83	Arista ARIST 524	Don't Forget To Dance/Bernadette (p/s)	7
83	Arista ARIST 524	Don't Forget To Dance/Bernadette//Predictable/Back To Front (shrink wrapped with free picture disc)	14

OTHER SINGLES

84	Music Week	How Are You (freebie with *Music Week* magazine)	7
86	London LON 119	How Are You/Killing Time (p/s)	12
87	London LONX 132	Lost And Found/Killing Time (p/s, shrink wrapped with bonus 7" "The Official Ray Davies Interview"/"Extracts From The LP 'Think Visual' ")	12
88	London LON 165	The Road (7" Edit)/Art Lover (p/s)	8
89	London LONCD 239	Down All The Days (Til 1992)/You Really Got Me (live)/Entertainment (CD)	14
89	London LON 239	Down All The Days (Til 1992)/You Really Got Me (live) (p/s)	6
90	London LONCD 250	How Do I Get Close/War Is Over (CD, card sleeve)	14
90	London LON 250	How Do I Get Close/War Is Over (p/s)	6
91	Columbia COL 657593-2	Did Ya/Gotta Move (live)/New World/Days/Look Through Any Doorway (1991) (CD)	14
94	Konk Grapevine KNKD 2	Waterloo Sunset 94/You Really Got Me (live)/Elevator Man/On The Outside (CD)	8

EPs

64	Pye NEP 24200	KINKSIZE SESSION	40
64	Pye NEP 24203	KINKSIZE HITS	30
65	Pye NEP 24221	KWYET KINKS	45
66	Pye NEP 24258	DEDICATED KINKS	120
68	Pye NEP 24296	THE KINKS	275
75	Pye AMEP 1001	THE KINKS ('Yesteryear' export issue, red or blue vinyl)	22

PYE LPs

64	Pye NPL 18096	THE KINKS (mono)	90
64	Pye NSPL 83021	THE KINKS (stereo, export only)	225
65	Pye NSPL 18096	THE KINKS (stereo, export only, reissue)	260
65	Pye NPL 18112	KINDA KINKS	90
65	Pye NPL 18131	THE KINK KONTROVERSY	80
65	Pye NSPL 18131	THE KINK KONTROVERSY (reprocessed stereo with stickered catalogue number, export only)	270
66	Pye NPL 18149	FACE TO FACE (mono)	100
66	Pye NSPL 18149	FACE TO FACE (stereo, stickered sleeve "export only")	175
66	Pye ZCP 18149	FACE TO FACE (cassette, original issue)	18
67	Golden Guinea GGL 0357	THE KINKS (reissue, also stereo GSGL 10357)	14/18
67	Pye N(S)PL 18191	LIVE AT KELVIN HALL (mono/stereo)	90/130

(The above Pye LPs were originally issued with laminated flipback sleeves, pink labels & light blue labels)

67	Pye N(S)PL 18193	SOMETHING ELSE BY THE KINKS (mono/stereo)	200/140
68	Pye N(S)PL 18233	THE KINKS ARE THE VILLAGE GREEN PRESERVATION SOCIETY (unissued, 12-track version, 2 test pressings only)	800+
68	Pye N(S)PL 18233	THE KINKS ARE THE VILLAGE GREEN PRESERVATION SOCIETY (15-track version, mono/stereo)	140/90
69	Pye N(S)PL 18317	ARTHUR (mono/stereo)	75/40
70	Pye NPL 18326	THE KINKS (2-LP, gatefold sleeve)	20
70	Pye NSPL 18359	THE KINKS PT 1 — LOLA VS POWERMAN & THE MONEY-GO-ROUND (gatefold sleeve)	25
71	Pye NSPL 18365	SOUNDTRACK FROM THE FILM 'PERCY' (soundtrack)	35
73	Pye 11PP 100	ALL THE GOOD TIMES (4-LP, box set)	50+
83	PRT KINK 1	GREATEST HITS (with bonus 10" EP of unreleased material)	40

OTHER LPs

71	RCA SF 8243	MUSWELL HILLBILLIES (gatefold sleeve)	30
72	RCA DPS 2035	EVERYBODY'S IN SHOWBIZ, EVERYBODY'S A STAR (2-LP, gatefold sleeve)	25
73	RCA SF 8392	PRESERVATION ACT 1	25
74	RCA LPL2 5040	PRESERVATION ACT 2 (2-LP, gatefold sleeve)	30
75	RCA SF 8411	SOAP OPERA	18
75	RCA RS 1028	SCHOOLBOYS IN DISGRACE	20
76	RCA RS 1059	CELLULOID HEROES	18
93	Sony 472489-1	PHOBIA (omits 2 tracks from CD)	70
94	Konk Grapevine KNK LP 1	TO THE BONE	15

(see also Dave Davies, Ray Davies, Maple Oak, Leapy Lee, Phoenix)

TONY KINSEY (QUARTET)

55	Decca F 10548	She's Funny That Way/Fascinatin' Rhythm	20
55	Decca F 10606	Close Your Eyes/Pierrot	15
55	Decca F 10648	Hey! There/Ballet	25
56	Decca F 10708	Stompin' At The Savoy/China Boy (with Dill Jones)	6
56	Decca F 10709	Moonglow/One O'Clock Jump	6
56	Decca FJ 10725	Starboard Bow/Body And Soul	6
56	Decca FJ 10760	Lullaby Of The Leaves/Isolation	12
56	Decca FJ 10773	In A Ditch/A Smooth One	6
57	Decca FJ 10851	Mean To Me/Supper Party	12
57	Decca F 10952	The Midgets/Blue Eyes	6
62	Ember JBS 707	Girl In Blue/Weber The Great	20
56	Decca DFE 6282	PRESENTING THE TONY KINSEY QUARTET NO. 1 (EP)	40
56	Decca DFE 6285	PRESENTING THE TONY KINSEY QUARTET NO. 2 (EP)	40
58	Decca DFE 6461	MY FAIR LADY (EP)	15
59	Parlophone SGE 2004	RED BIRD — JAZZ AND POETRY (EP, mono [GEP 8765]/stereo, with Christopher Logue)	each 25
59	Parlophone SGE 2008	FOURSOME (EP, stereo)	10
57	Decca LK 4186	INTRODUCING THE QUINTET (LP)	100
57	Decca LK 4207	JAZZ AT THE FLAMINGO (LP)	75
58	Decca LK 4274	TIME GENTLEMEN PLEASE (LP)	80
61	Ember EMB 3337	AN EVENING WITH ... (LP)	60
63	Decca LK 4534	HOW TO SUCCEED (LP, with Gordon Beck)	60

TONY KINSEY TRIO & JOE HARRIOTT
54	Esquire 10-382	How Deep Is The Ocean/Last Resort (78)	7
54	Esquire 10-392	Get Happy/Best Behaviour (78)	7
54	Esquire 10-402	Raymond/Can't We Be Friends (78)	7
54	Esquire 10-412	Nice Work If You Can Get It/Jump For Me (78)	7
54	Esquire EP 36	TONY KINSEY TRIO & JOE HARRIOTT (EP)	35
54	Esquire EP 52	TONY KINSEY TRIO & JOE HARRIOTT (EP)	35
54	Esquire EP 82	TONY KINSEY TRIO & JOE HARRIOTT (EP)	35

(see also Joe Harriott)

KINSMEN
| 68 | Decca F 22724 | Glasshouse Green, Splinter Red/It's Started To Rain Again | 30 |
| 68 | Decca F 22777 | It's Good To See You/Always The Loser | 10 |

(see also Four Kinsmen)

KIPPER FAMILY
| 84 | Dambuster DAM 005 | SINCE TIME IMMORAL (LP) | 18 |

KIPPINGTON LODGE
67	Parlophone R 5645	Shy Boy/Lady On A Bicycle	35
68	Parlophone R 5677	Rumours/And She Cried	35
68	Parlophone R 5717	Tell Me A Story/Understand A Woman	40
68	Parlophone R 5750	Tomorrow Today/Turn Out The Light	40
69	Parlophone R 5776	In My Life/I Can See Her Face	40
78	EMI NUT 2894	KIPPINGTON LODGE (EP)	12

(see also Brinsley Schwartz, Nick Lowe)

KIRBY
76	Anchor ANC 1031	Love Letters/Flasher	12
78	Hot Wax WAX 1/ANCHO 1	Bottom Line/That's Some Dream	10
78	Hot Wax HW 2	COMPOSITION (LP)	75

(see also Curved Air, Stretch)

KATHY KIRBY
60	Pye 7N 15313	Love Can Be/Crush Me	25
61	Pye 7N 15342	Danny/Now You're Crying	22
62	Decca F 11506	Big Man/Slowly	20
63	Decca F 11682	Dance On/Playboy	10
63	Decca F 11759	Secret Love/You Have To Want To Touch Him	5
64	Decca F 11832	Let Me Go, Lover!/The Sweetest Sounds	5
64	Decca F 11892	You're The One/Love Me Baby	5
64	Decca F 11992	Don't Walk Away/No Regrets	7
65	Decca F 12087	I Belong/I'll Try Not To Cry	5
65	Decca F 12177	The Way Of Love/Oh Darling, How I Miss You	5
65	Decca F 12280	Where In The World?/That Wonderful Feeling Of Love	6
66	Decca F 12338	Spanish Flea/Till The End Of Time	5
66	Decca F 12432	The Adam Adamant Theme/Will I Never Learn?	35
67	Columbia DB 8139	No One's Gonna Hurt You Anymore/My Yiddishe Momme	8
67	Columbia DB 8192	In All The World/Time	8
67	Columbia DB 8302	Turn Around/Golden Days	6
68	Columbia DB 8400	I Almost Called Your Name/Let The Music Start	10
68	Columbia DB 8521	Come Back Here With My Heart/Antonio	10
69	Columbia DB 8559	I'll Catch The Sun/Please Help Me I'm Falling	10
69	Columbia DB 8634	Is That All There Is?/Knowing When To Leave	10
70	Columbia DB 8682	Wheel Of Fortune/Lucky	10
70	Columbia DB 8721	My Way/Little Green Apples	10
71	Columbia DB 8795	So Here I Go/Yes — I've Got (A-side titled "Here I Go Again" on demos)	10
71	Decca F 13228	Bill/Can't Help Lovin' Dat Man	10
72	Columbia DB 8910	Do You Really Have A Heart/Dream On, Dreamer	10
73	Columbia DB 8965	Little Song For You/Here, There And Everywhere	10
73	Orange OAS 216	Singer With The Band/Hello Morning	65
76	President PT 455	My Prayer/Nobody Loves Me Like You Do	6
63	Decca DFE 8547	KATHY KIRBY (EP)	15
65	Decca DFE 8596	KATHY KIRBY VOL. 2 (EP)	15
65	Decca DFE 8611	A SONG FOR EUROPE (EP)	15
65	Decca LK 4575	16 HITS FROM STARS AND GARTERS (LP)	22
67	Decca LK 4746	MAKE SOMEONE HAPPY (LP)	22
68	Ace Of Clubs ACL 1235	THE BEST OF KATHY KIRBY (LP)	15
68	Columbia S(C)X 6259	MY THANKS TO YOU (LP)	75

LARRY KIRBY & ENCORES
| 59 | Top Rank JAR 143 | My Baby Don't Love Me/My Rose Of Kentucky (78 rpm = £10) | 20 |

PAT KIRBY
56	Brunswick 05560	Happiness Is A Thing Called Joe/Don't Tell Me Not To	7
56	Brunswick 05575	What A Heavenly Night For Love/Greensleeves	7
57	Brunswick 05697	Tammy/Don't Keep Silent	7
58	Brunswick 05731	Sayonara/Please Be Gentle With Me	7

KIRBY STONE FOUR
| 62 | CBS BPG 62040 | GUYS & DOLLS (LP, gatefold sleeve) | 12 |

BASIL KIRCHIN (BAND)
57	Parlophone R 4344	White Silver Sands/Waiting For The Robert E. Lee	5
58	Parlophone R 4511	Cha Cha Bells/Oh Dear What Can The Cha Cha Be (with Rock-A-Cha Cha Band)	5
59	Parlophone R 4527	Rock-A-Conga/Skin Tight (as Basil Kirchin Band)	7
71	Columbia SCX 6463	A WORLD WITHIN WORLDS (LP)	300+
74	Island HELP18	A WORLD WITHIN WORLDS (LP) (reissue)	50

(IVOR & BASIL) KIRCHIN BAND

54	Parlophone MSP 6144	Mambo Macoco/Tangerine (as Kirchin Band)	10
55	Decca F 10434	Minor Mambo/Mother Goose Jumps (as Kirchin Band)	15
56	Parlophone R 4222	The Roller/St. Louis Blues (as Ivor & Basil Kirchin)	7
56	Parlophone R 4237	Rockin' & Rollin' Thru The Darktown Strutters' Ball/Ambush	20
57	Parlophone R 4266	"Rock Around The World Medley" (with Shani Wallis) (78 rpm = £6)	15
57	Parlophone R 4284	Calypso!!/Jungle Fire Dance (as Ivor & Basil Kirchin with Wendy Windows)	5
57	Parlophone R 4335	Teenage World/So Rare (as Kirchin Band & Bandits)	10
55	Parlophone GEP 8531	KIRCHIN BANDBOX (EP)	15
56	Parlophone GEP 8569	THE IVOR AND BASIL KIRCHIN BAND (EP)	22

(see also Basil Kirchin, London Studio Group)

DEE KIRK

62	Salvo SLO 1809	I'll Cry/My Used To Be	25

KEVIN KIRK

62	Columbia DB 4909	Sweet/Don't Waste Your Tears On Him	5
62	Columbia DB 4863	Teenage Heartache/Midnight	5

RICHARD H. KIRK

81	Industrial IRC 34	DISPOSABLE HALF TRUTHS (cassette)	8

(see also Cabaret Voltaire, Peter Hope & Richard H. Kirk)

(RAHSAAN) ROLAND KIRK

64	Mercury 10015 MCE	THE KIRK QUARTET MEETS THE BENNY GOLSON ORCHESTRA (EP)	10
65	Mercury 10016 MCE	ROLAND SPEAKS (EP, with Benny Golson Orchestra)	10
62	Esquire 32-164	KIRK'S WORK (LP, with Jack McDuff)	25
63	Mercury MMC 14126	WE FREE KINGS (LP)	20
64	Mercury MCL 20002	THE KIRK QUARTET MEETS THE BENNY GOLSON ORCHESTRA (LP)	20
64	Mercury MCL 20021	KIRK IN COPENHAGEN (LP)	20
64	Mercury MCL 20037	WE FREE KINGS (LP, reissue)	12
65	Mercury MCL 20045	DOMINO (LP)	20
65	Fontana FJL 114	HIP! (LP)	20
65	Mercury (S)LML 4005	I TALK WITH THE SPIRITS (LP)	15
66	Mercury (S)LML 4015	RIP, RIG AND PANIC (LP)	15
67	Mercury (S)LML 4019	SLIGHTLY LATIN (LP)	18
71	Atlantic 2400 110	RAHSAAN, RAHSAAN (LP, as Rahsaan Roland Kirk)	12
72	Atlantic K 40358	BLACKNUSS (LP)	12
73	Atlantic K 40457	MEETING OF THE TIMES (LP, with Al Hibbler)	12

KIRKBYS

66	RCA RCA 1542	It's A Crime/I've Never Been So Much In Love	130

(see also 23rd Turnoff, Jimmy Campbell, Rockin' Horse, Merseybeats)

KEN KIRKHAM

56	Columbia SCM 5244	It's Almost Tomorrow/No Not Much	10
58	Columbia DB 4116	Now And For Always/Cathy	6

JOHN KIRKPATRICK (& SUE HARRIS)

72	Trailer LER 2033	JUMP AT THE SUN (LP, with Sue Harris)	15
76	Topic 12TS 295	AMONG THE MANY ATTRACTIONS AT THE SHOW WILL BE A REALLY HIGH-CLASS BAND (LP, with Sue Harris)	12
76	Free Reed FRR 010	PLAIN CAPERS (LP, with booklet)	12
77	Topic 12TS 355	SHREDS AND PATCHES (LP, with Sue Harris)	12

(see also Jon Raven)

JULIAN KIRSCH

(see under 'J')

DANNY KIRWAN

75	DJM DJLPS 454	SECOND CHAPTER (LP)	12

(see also Fleetwood Mac, Tramp)

KISS

SINGLES

75	Casablanca CBX 503	Nothin' To Lose/Love Theme From Kiss	25
75	Casablanca CBX 510	Rock And Roll All Nite/Anything For My Baby	20
76	Casablanca CBX 516	Shout It Out Loud/Sweet Pain	15
76	Casablanca CBX 519	Beth/God Of Thunder	15
77	Casablanca CAN 102	Hard Luck Woman/Calling Dr Love/Beth (initially in p/s)	35/10
77	Casablanca CAN 110	Then She Kissed Me/Hooligan/Flaming Youth	15
77	Casablanca CANL 110	Then She Kissed Me/Hooligan/Flaming Youth (12", company sleeve, some stickered)	15/12
78	Casablanca CAN 117	Rocket Ride/Love Gun (live)	8
78	Casablanca CANL 117	Rocket Ride/Detroit Rock City (live)/Love Gun (live) (12", company sleeve)	15
78	Casablanca CAN 126	Rock And Roll All Nite/C'Mon And Love Me (initially in p/s)	25/8
79	Casablanca CAN 152	I Was Made For Lovin' You/Hard Times	8
79	Casablanca CANL 152	I Was Made For Lovin' You (extended)/Charisma (12", p/s)	18
79	Casablanca CAN 163	Sure Know Something/Dirty Livin' (no p/s)	6
80	Casablanca NB 1001	2000 Man/I Was Made For Lovin' You/Sure Know Something (p/s)	15
80	Casablanca NBL 1001	2000 Man/I Was Made For Lovin' You/Sure Know Something (12", co. sleeve)	12
80	Casablanca MER 19	Talk To Me/She's So European (p/s)	10
80	Casablanca KISS 1	What Makes The World Go 'Round/Naked City (p/s)	10
81	Casablanca KISS 2	A World Without Heroes/Mr Blackwell (p/s)	7
81	Casablanca KISSP 002	A World Without Heroes/Mr Blackwell (picture disc)	12
82	Casablanca KISS 3	Killer/I Love It Loud (pull-out tongue p/s)	12
82	Casablanca KISS 312	Killer/I Love It Loud/I Was Made For Lovin' You (12", p/s)	15
82	Casablanca KISS 4	Creatures Of The Night/Rock And Roll All Nite (live) (p/s, pic or silver label)	10/8
82	Casablanca KISS 412	Creatures Of The Night/War Machine/Rock And Roll All Nite (live) (12", p/s)	15
82	Casablanca KISSD 4	Creatures Of The Night/Rock And Roll All Nite (live) (12", double groove, autographs engraved on 1 side)	20

83	Vertigo KISS 5	Lick It Up/Not For The Innocent (p/s) 5
83	Vertigo KISSP 5	Lick It Up/Not For The Innocent (poster p/s) 12
83	Vertigo KPIC 5	Lick It Up/Not For The Innocent (tank-shaped picture disc) 25
83	Vertigo KISS 512	Lick It Up/Not For The Innocent/I Still Love You (12", p/s) 8
84	Vertigo VER 12	Heaven's On Fire/Lonely Is The Hunter (p/s) 5
84	Vertigo VERX 12	Heaven's On Fire/Lonely Is The Hunter/All Hell's Breakin' Loose (12", p/s some with poster) 10/8
85	Vertigo KISS 6	Tears Are Falling/Heaven's On Fire (live) (p/s) 5
87	Vertigo KISSP 7	Crazy Crazy Nights/No No No (poster p/s) 7
87	Vertigo KISSP 712	Crazy Crazy Nights/No No No/Heaven's On Fire/Tears Are Falling (12", picture disc) 8
87	Vertigo KISS 8	Reason To Live/Thief In The Night (p/s, with patch) 7
87	Vertigo KISSP 812	Reason To Live/Thief In The Night/Who Wants To Be Lonely/ Secretly Cruel (12", picture disc) 8
87	Vertigo KISCD 8	Reason To Live/Thief In The Night/Tears Are Falling/Crazy Crazy Nights (CD, card sleeve) 8
87	Vertigo KISSP 9	Turn On The Night/Hell Or High Water (poster p/s) 5
87	Vertigo KISSP 912	Turn On The Night/Hell Or High Water/King Of The Mountain/ Any Way You Slice It (12", picture disc) 8
87	Vertigo KISCD 9	Turn On The Night/Hell Or High Water/Heaven's On Fire/I Love It Loud (CD, card sleeve) 8
88	Vertigo 080 232-2	Crazy Crazy Nights/No, No, No/When Your Walls Come Down/ Thief In The Night (CD Video) 15
88	Mercury 080 100-1	EXPOSED (12" CD Video) 25
89	Mercury 080 044-2	Lick It Up/Dance All Over Your Face/Gimme More/Fits Like A Glove (CD Video) . 15
89	Vertigo 080 059-2	Tears Are Falling/Anyway You Slice It/Who Want To Be Lonely/Secretly Cruel (CD Video) 15
89	Vertigo KISP 1010	Hide Your Heart/Lick It Up/Heaven's On Fire (10", picture disc) 8
90	Vertigo KISXG 11	Forever (Remix)/The Street Giveth And The Street Taketh Away/ Deuce (Demo)/Strutter (Demo) (12", gatefold p/s) 8
92	Mercury KISS 1212	Unholy/Partners In Crime/Deuce (Demo)/Strutter (Demo) (12", picture sleeve, white vinyl) 8
92	Mercury KISCD 12	Unholy/God Gave Rock'N'Roll II You Too/Deuce (Demo)/Strutter (Demo) (CD, digipak, Part 1 of 2-part pack [Part 2 unreleased]) 8
90s	East West SAM 886	God Gave Rock'n'Roll To You (LP Version)/(Edit Version) (12", no p/s, promo only) 12

LPs

75	Casablanca CBC 4003	KISS (blue 'Bogart' label) 20
75	Casablanca CBC 4004	DRESSED TO KILL (blue 'Bogart' label, embossed sleeve) 20
76	Casablanca CBC 4008	DESTROYER (blue 'Bogart' label with inner sleeve) 20
76	Casablanca CBC 4011/2	ALIVE! (2-LP, blue 'Bogart' label, gatefold sleeve with insert, sleeve also lists CBSP 401) 20
77	Casablanca CALH 2001	ROCK AND ROLL OVER ('lovegun' label, red vinyl) 40
77	Casablanca CAL 2006	KISS (reissue, 'lovegun' label, red vinyl) 40
77	Casablanca CAL 2007	HOTTER THAN HELL ('lovegun' label, red vinyl) 40
77	Casablanca CAL 2008	DRESSED TO KILL (reissue, 'lovegun' label, red vinyl) 40
77	Casablanca CAL 2009	DESTROYER (reissue, different sleeve, 'lovegun' label, red vinyl) 40
77	Casablanca CALD 5001	ALIVE! (2-LP, reissue, 'lovegun' label, red vinyl) 50
77	Casablanca CALH 2017	LOVE GUN ('lovegun' label, with picture inner sleeve) 12
77	Casablanca CALH 2017	LOVE GUN ('lovegun' label, red vinyl with picture inner sleeve) 40
77	Casablanca CALD 5004	KISS ALIVE II (2-LP, 'lovegun' label, with colour booklet & transfer sheet) 25
77	Casablanca CALD 5004	KISS ALIVE II (2-LP, 'lovegun' label, red vinyl with colour booklet) 50
78	Casablanca CALD 5005	DOUBLE PLATINUM (2-LP, 'lovegun' label, silver foil embossed sleeve & insert; sleeve & insert pressed in U.S. with U.K. cat. no. sticker) 18
79	Casablanca CALH 2051	DYNASTY ('lovegun' label, black vinyl, colour inner sleeve & poster) 12
80	Mercury 6302 032	UNMASKED (some with poster) 15/12
81	Casablanca 6302 163	(MUSIC FROM) THE ELDER (single sleeve) 12
82	Casa. CANL 4/6302 219	CREATURES OF THE NIGHT ('make-up' sleeve) 12
87	Vertigo 832 903-1	CRAZY NIGHTS (picture disc in stickered PVC wallet) 12

(see also Gene Simmons, Ace Frehley, Peter Criss, Paul Stanley)

KISSING SPELL
93	Essex DELUJO 1001LP	LOS PAJAROS (LP, reissue of Chilean LP, 500 only) 12

KISSING THE PINK
83	Magnet KTP 36/KTP 0	Last Film/Shine//Water In My Eye (Instrumental)/Garden Parties (double pack) . . . 5

KATIE KISSOON
69	Columbia DB 8525	Don't Let It Rain/Will I Never See The Sun 6

(see also Peanut, Marionettes, Rag Dolls [U.K.])

MAC KISSOON
60s	Boulevard (no cat. no.)	Wear It On Your Face/In A Dream 10
69	Youngblood YB 1005	Wear It On Your Face/In A Dream (reissue) 6

(see also Marionettes, Rag Dolls [U.K.])

KITCHENS OF DISTINCTION
87	Gold Rush GRR 3	Escape/The Last Gasp Death Shuffle (p/s) 6

KIT KATS
66	London HLW 10075	Won't Find Better Than Me/That's The Way 15

(see also New Hope)

EARTHA KITT
54	HMV 7M 191	Under The Bridges Of Paris/Lovin' Spree 18
54	HMV 7M 198	Somebody Bad Stole De Wedding Bell/Sandy's Tune 15
54	HMV 7M 234	Santa Baby/Let's Do It (Let's Fall In Love) (78 rpm = £12) 15
54	HMV 7M 246	Easy Does It/Mink Shmink 15
55	HMV 7M 282	Monotonous/African Lullaby 15

MINT VALUE £

55	HMV 7M 288	C'est Si Bon (with Henri René)/Senor	15
56	HMV 7M 422	Honolulu Rock-A-Roll-A/Je Cherche Un Homme (I Want A Man)	25
56	MGM SP 1153	Please Do It/Lady Loves	10
56	MGM SP 1178	Diamonds Are A Girl's Best Friend/Good Little Girls	10
57	HMV POP 309	Just An Old-Fashioned Girl/If I Can't Take It With Me When I Go (gold or silver label)	15/10
57	HMV POP 346	There Is No Cure For L'Amour/Hey Jacque	10
58	RCA RCA 1037	Take My Love/Proceed With Caution	6
58	RCA RCA 1087	Just An Old-Fashioned Girl/If I Can't Take It With Me When I Go (reissue)	7
58	RCA RCA 1093	I Want To Be Evil/Oh John! (78 rpm = £8)	8
59	London HLR 8969	Love Is A Gamble/Sholem (78 rpm = £15)	10
60	RCA RCA 1180	There's No Cure For L'Amour/Let's Do It	10
63	London HL 7119	Shango/In The Evening (When The Sun Goes Down) (export issue)	18
70	Spark SRL 1039	Hurdy Gurdy Man/Catch The Wind	20
71	CBS 7626	A Knight For My Nights/Summer Storm	5
55	HMV 7EG 8079	EARTHA KITT (EP)	10
57	HMV 7EG 8258	EARTHA KITT (EP)	10
58	RCA SRC 7009	SAINT LOUIS BLUES (EP, stereo)	10
58	RCA SRC 7015	THAT BLUE EARTHA (EP, stereo)	10
63	MGM MGM-EP 772	BAD BUT BEAUTIFUL NO. 1 (EP)	10
63	MGM MGM-EP 774	BAD BUT BEAUTIFUL NO. 2 (EP)	10
63	MGM MGM-EP 777	BAD BUT BEAUTIFUL NO. 3 (EP)	10
55	HMV DLP 1067	THAT BAD EARTHA (10" LP)	20
55	HMV DLP 1087	DOWN TO EARTHA (10" LP)	20
58	RCA RD 27076	ST. LOUIS BLUES (LP)	20
60	London HA-R 2207	THE FABULOUS EARTHA KITT (LP, also stereo SAH-R 6058)	15/18
60	London HA-R 2296	EARTHA KITT REVISITED (LP, also stereo SAH-R 6107)	15/18
62	MGM MGM-C 878/CS 6050	BAD BUT BEAUTIFUL (LP, mono/stereo)	15/18

KITTENS
| 64 | Decca F 12036 | Round About Way/Don't Stop Now | 12 |

KLAN
| 67 | Palette PG 9052 | Fifi The Fly/Already Mine | 8 |

KLAXON 5
| 86 | él GPO 20 | Never Underestimate The Ignorance Of The Rich/Great Railway Journeys (p/s) | 8 |

SUSIE KLEE
| 66 | Polydor BM 56082 | Mr Zero/Punch And Judy Girl | 10 |

KLEEER
| 84 | Atlantic 7801451 | INTIMATE CONNECTION (LP) | 12 |

KLEENEX
| 79 | Rough Trade/Sunrise RT 9 | Ain't You/Hedi's Head (poster p/s) | 5 |
| 79 | Rough Trade RT 014 | You/U (p/s) | 5 |

ALAN KLEIN
62	Oriole CB 1719	Striped Purple Shirt/You Gave Me The Blues	32
62	Oriole CB 1737	Three Coins In The Sewer/Danger Ahead	32
65	Parlophone R 5292	It Ain't Worth The Lonely Road Back/I've Cried So Many Tears	5
65	Parlophone R 5370	Age Of Corruption/I'm Counting On You	5
69	Page One POF 119	Honey Pie/You Turned A Nightmare Into A Dream	5
70	Decca F 13033	Dinner's In The Ice Box/Here I Am, There You Are	5
64	Decca LK 4621	WELL, AT LEAST IT'S BRITISH (LP)	18
	(see also New Vaudeville Band)		

HARRY KLEIN QUARTET
56	Jazz Today JTE 105	BRASH BARITONE (EP)	25
56	Nixa NJE 1009	NEW SOUND (EP)	25
56	Nixa NJE 1022	HARRY KLEIN QUARTET (EP)	25
57	Columbia SEG 7647	BARITONE SAX (EP)	15
	(see also Jazz Five)		

KLF
88	KLF Comms. KLF 002	Burn The Beat (II)/The Porpoise Song (p/s)	10
88	KLF Comms. KLF 002T	Burn The Bastards (LP Edit)/Burn The Beat (II) (12", p/s)	15
89	KLF Comms. KLF 004T	What Time Is Love? (Trance Mix)/What Time Is Love? (Mix 2) (12", 'Pure Trance 1', original issue with black/green p/s)	20
89	KLF Comms. KLF 004R	What Time Is Love? ('89 Primal Remix)/What Time Is Love? (Techno Slam)/What Time Is Love? (Trance Mix 1) (12", p/s)	35
89	KLF Comms. KLF 004M	What Time Is Love? (Monster Attack Mix) (12", unissued, 1-sided acetate only, 3 pressed!)	500
90	KLF Comms. KLF 004Y	What Time Is Love? (Moody Boys Vs The KLF)/What Time Is Love? (Echo And The Bunnymen Mix)/What Time Is Love? (Virtual Reality Mix) (12", p/s)	10
90	KLF Comms. KLF 004P	What Time Is Love? (Live At Trancentral)/Wandafull Mix (12", w/l, 1,500 only)	10
90	KLF Comms. KLF 004X	What Time Is Love? (Live At Trancentral)/Techno Gate Mix (12", p/s, mispressing, B-side actually plays "Wandafull Mix", matrix no.: KLF 004X-B)	40
90	KLF Comms. KLF 004CD	What Time Is Love? (Radio)/(Live At Trancentral)/(Trance Mix 1) (CD, mispressing playing part of Knebworth '90 live CD)	15
90	KLF Comms. KLF 005R	3AM Eternal 'Single Edit'/Blue Danube Orbital Mix/Moody Boys Version/3PM Electro (12", original issue with stickered p/s)	20
91	KLF Comms. KLF 005S	3AM Eternal (Live At The S.S.L.) (Radio Freedom Edit) (white label, 500 only)	12
91	KLF Comms. KLF 005X	3AM Eternal (mixes) (12", white label, promo only)	10
91	KLF Comms. KLF 005Y	3AM Eternal (Moody Boys mixes) (12", white label, promo only)	15
92	KLF Comms. KLF 5 TOTP	3AM Eternal (Xmas Top Of The Pops Version) (1-sided, w/Extreme Noise Terror, mail-order only, some with insert & mailing envelope; beware of bootlegs!)	50/10

89	KLF Comms. KLF 008R	Last Train To Trancentral (Remixes 1 & 2) (12", p/s, 'Pure Trance 5', 2,000 pressed, some warped)	50/8
91	KLF Comms. KLF 008X	Last Train To Trancentral (Live From The Lost Continent) (12", white label)	8
91	KLF Comms. KLF 008CD	Last Train To Trancentral (Live From The Lost Continent)/(The Iron Horse)/ (The 1989 Pure Trance Original) (CD)	8
89	KLF PROMO 2	Kylie Said To Jason (Full Length)/Kylie Said Trance (12", promo & press sheet)	15
89	KLF Comms. KLF 010(S)	Kylie Said To Jason (Edit)/Kylie Said Trance (p/s)	10
89	KLF Comms. KLF 010P	Kylie Said To Jason (Full Length)/Kylie Said Trance (12", stickered p/s & pstr)	25
89	KLF Comms. KLF 010R	Kylie Said To Jason (Trance Kylie Express)/Kylie In A Trance/ Kylie Said Harder (12" remix, p/s, export issue)	20
89	KLF Comms. KLF 010RR	Kylie In A Trance/Kylie Said Mu (12", p/s, export edition, 500 only, some shrink wrapped with KLF 010R)	100/50
89	KLF Comms. KLF 010CD	Kylie Said To Jason (Full Length)/Madrugada Eterna/Kylie Said Trance (CD)	50
89	KLF Comms. KLF 006T	Love Trance/What Time Is Love (12", p/s, 3 copies confirmed)	500
90	KLF Comms. KLF 011T	Madrugada Eterna (Club Mix)/Madrugada Eterna (Edit)/Madrugada Eterna (Ambient House Mix) (12", 20 only, beware of counterfeits!)	150
90	KLF Comms. ETERNA 1	Madrugada Eterna (Club Mix) (12", 1-sided, white label, 6 pressed, beware of counterfeits!)	120/10
91	KLF Comms. CHOC ICE 1	Justified And Ancient (All Bound For Mu Mu Land)/Justified And Ancient (Make Mine A '99') (12", white label promo)	15
91	KLF Comms. CHOC ICE 2	Justified And Ancient (Stand By The J.A.M.s)/Justified And Ancient (Let Them Eat Ice Cream) (12", white label promo)	12
91	KLF Comms. CHOC ICE 3	Justified And Ancient (Anti-Acapella Version) (12", 1-sided, w/l, 200 only)	30
91	KLF Comms. LP PROMO 1	Make It Rain/No More Tears (12", promo only, 1,729 pressed)	25
91	KLF Comms. 92PROMO 1	America: What Time Is Love/America No More (12", white label)	8
91	KLF Comms. 92PROMO 2	America: What Time Is January? (12", 1-sided, white label promo, 250 only)	45
91	KLF Comms. 3AM 1	3AM Eternal (feat. Extreme Noise Terror) (p/s, mail order only)	20
92	KLF Comms. 92PROMO 3	What Time Is Love (Acid Mix) (12", 1-sided, w/l promo, perhaps 20 only)	120
92	KLF Comms. USA 4X/ CHOC ICE 2	Justified And Ancient/America: What Time Is Love? (12", 'longboat' picture disc, export edition, 4,000 only)	20
92	KLF Comms. PUB 1	Justified And Ancient/America: What Time Is Love? (jukebox ed., 5,000 only)	8
97	KLF Comms.	Fuck The Millennium (4-track CD, in white carrier bag "Fuck The Millennium" kit, with T-shirt, window sticker, certificate)	50
89	KLF Comms. JAMS LP 4	THE WHAT TIME IS LOVE STORY (LP)	40
89	KLF Comms. JAMS CD 4	THE WHAT TIME IS LOVE STORY (CD)	60
89	KLF Comms. JAMS LP 5	CHILL OUT (LP)	40
89	KLF Comms. JAMS CD 5	CHILL OUT (CD)	25
89	KLF Comms. JAMS LP 6	(TUNES FROM) THE WHITE ROOM (LP, 9-track white label, unreleased, promo only, beware of counterfeits!)	50+
89	KLF Comms. JAMS MC 6	(TUNES FROM) THE WHITE ROOM (cassette, 10-track promo, beware of counterfeits!)	40

(see also J.A.M.s, Timelords, Disco 2000, Bill Drummond, Space, Orb)

TONY KLINGER & MICHAEL LYONS
72	Deram SML 1095	EXTREEMS (LP, soundtrack)	30

PETER KLINT (QUINTET)
66	Mercury MF 997	Walkin' Proud/Shake	20
68	Atlantic 584 208	Hey Diddle Diddle/Just Holding On (solo)	15

ANNETTE KLOOGER
56	Decca F 10701	The Rock And Roll Waltz/Rock Around The Island (with Ted Heath Music)	20
56	Decca F 10726	The Magic Touch/We'll Love Again (with Four Jones Boys)	18
56	Decca F 10738	Why Do Fools Fall In Love?/Lovely One (with Four Jones Boys)	20
56	Decca F 10776	Mama, Teach Me To Dance/Mama, I Long For A Sweetheart (with Edmundo Ros Orchestra)	15
57	Decca F 10844	The Wisdom Of A Fool/Tra La La	15

(see also Four Jones Boys, Ted Heath Orchestra)

KLUBS
68	Cam CAM 681	I Found The Sun/Ever Needed Someone	200

KNACK (U.K.)
65	Decca F 12234	She Ain't No Good/Who'll Be The Next In Line	40+
65	Decca F 12278	It's Love Baby (24 Hours A Day)/Time Time Time	35
66	Piccadilly 7N 35315	Did You Ever Have To Make Up Your Mind?/Red Hearts	12
66	Piccadilly 7N 35322	Stop! (Before You Get Me Going)/Younger Girl	12
66	Piccadilly 7N 35347	Save All My Love For Joey/Take Your Love	12
67	Piccadilly 7N 35367	(Man From The) Marriage Guidance And Advice Bureau/ Dolly Catch Her Man	12

(see also Gun, Sky)

KNACK (U.S.)
79	Capitol E-ST 11948	GET THE KNACK (LP, limited white cover, unissued)	12

BERNIE KNEE QUARTETTE
55	HMV 7M 306	Chocolate Whiskey And Vanilla Gin/Scrape Off De Bark	7

(see also Bernie Nee)

KNEES
74	United Artists UP 35773	Day Tripper/Slow Down	20

(see also Brinsley Schwarz)

KNICKERBOCKERS
66	London HLH 10013	Lies/The Coming Generation	18
66	London HLH 10035	One Track Mind/I Must Be Doing Something Right	18

MINT VALUE £

66	London HLH 10061	High On Love/Stick With Me	18
66	London HLH 10093	Rumours, Gossip, Words Untrue/Love Is A Bird	18
67	London HLH 10102	Can You Help Me/Please Don't Love Him	18
73	Elektra K 12102	Lies/ELECTRIC PRUNES: I Had Too Much To Dream (Last Night)	5
66	London HA-H 8294	THE FABULOUS KNICKERBOCKERS (LP)	50

BAKER KNIGHT
66	Reprise RS 20465	Would You Believe It/Tomorrow's Good Time Girl	12

CURTIS KNIGHT (& ZEUS)
69	RCA RCA 1888	Fancy Meeting You Here/Love In	10
70	RCA RCA 1950	Down In The Village/No Point Of View	12
74	Dawn DNS 1049	Devil Made Me Do It/Oh Rainbow	7
74	Dawn DNS 1065	People Places And Things/Mysterious Lady	7
74	Dawn DNLS 3060	ZEUS, THE SECOND COMING (LP)	35

(see also Jimi Hendrix, Blue Goose)

GLADYS KNIGHT (& PIPS)
SINGLES
64	Stateside SS 318	Giving Up/Maybe Maybe Baby	25
64	Stateside SS 352	Lovers Always Forgive/Another Love	22
65	Sue WI 394	Letter Full Of Tears/You Broke Your Promise	35
66	Tamla Motown TMG 576	Just Walk In My Shoes/Stepping Closer To Your Heart (DJ copy = £150)	60
67	Tamla Motown TMG 604	Take Me In Your Arms And Love Me/Do You Love Me Just A Little Honey	15
67	Tamla Motown TMG 619	Everybody Needs Love/Stepping Closer To Your Heart (demo-only B-side)	90
67	Tamla Motown TMG 619	Everybody Needs Love/Since I've Lost You	15
67	Tamla Motown TMG 629	I Heard It Through The Grapevine/It's Time To Go Now	20
68	Tamla Motown TMG 645	The End Of Our Road/Don't Let Her Take Your Love From Me	12
68	Tamla Motown TMG 660	It Should Have Been Me/You Don't Love Me No More	15
68	Tamla Motown TMG 674	I Wish It Would Rain/It's Summer	12
69	Tamla Motown TMG 714	The Nitty Gritty/Got Myself A Good Man	10
70	Tamla Motown TMG 728	Didn't You Know (You'd Have To Cry Sometime)/Keep An Eye	10
70	Tamla Motown TMG 756	Friendship Train/You Need Love Like I Do (Don't You)	8
71	Tamla Motown TMG 765	If I Were Your Woman/The Tracks Of My Tears	15
72	Tamla Motown TMG 805	Make Me The Woman That You Go Home To/I Don't Want To Do Wrong	15
72	Tamla Motown TMG 813	Just Walk In My Shoes/I'm Losing You	10
73	Ember EMB S 326	Every Beat Of My Heart/Room In Your Heart	6
73	Tamla Motown TMG 844	The Look Of Love/You're My Everything	6
73	Tamla Motown TMG 864	Take Me In Your Arms And Love Me/No One Could Love You More	85
74	Contempo CS 2021	Why Don't You Leave Me/Maybe Baby	6
75	Tamla Motown TMG 945	You've Lost That Loving Feeling/This Child Needs A Father	15
89	MCA MCASP 1339	Licence To Kill/MICHAEL KAMEN: Pain (p/s with postcards & lyric sheet)	6
89	MCA MCAT 1339	Licence To Kill (Extended Version)/MICHAEL KAMEN: Pain (12", picture sleeve)	8

LPs
67	Music F. Pleasure MFP 1187	GLADYS KNIGHT AND THE PIPS	15
67	T. Motown (S)TML 11058	EVERYBODY NEEDS LOVE	35
68	Bell MBLL 103	TASTIEST HITS	30
68	T. Motown (S)TML 11080	FEELIN' BLUESY	35
69	T. Motown (S)TML 11100	SILK'N'SOUL	35
69	T. Motown (S)TML 11135	THE NITTY GRITTY (mono/stereo)	22/20
70	Tamla Motown STML 11148	GREATEST HITS (original with flipback sleeve)	15
71	Tamla Motown STML 11187	IF I WERE YOUR WOMAN	12
75	Buddah BDLP 4038	2ND ANNIVERSARY	12
77	Buddah BDLP 5014	STILL TOGETHER	12
78	Buddah 11PP 602	COLLECTION (4-LP, box set)	30
79	Buddah BDLP 4056	MISS GLADYS KNIGHT (solo)	12

(see also Pips, Dionne Warwick)

JASON KNIGHT
67	Pye 7N 17399	Love Is Getting Stronger/Standing In My Shoes (DJ copy = £130)	70
73	Pye 7N 45287	Love Is Getting Stronger/Standing In My Shoes (reissue)	10

JEAN KNIGHT
71	Stax 2025 049	Mr Big Stuff/Why Do I Keep Living These Memories	10
72	Stax 2025 103	Carry On/Do You Think You're Hot Stuff	8
73	Stax 2025 161	Do Me/Save The Last Kiss For Me	8
72	Stax 2362 022	MR. BIG STUFF (LP)	30

MARIE KNIGHT
61	Fontana H 354	Nothing/Come Tomorrow	22
65	Stateside SS 419	Cry Me A River/Comes The Knight	15
85	Kent TOWN 102	That's No Way To Treat A Girl/JACK MONTGOMERY: Dearly Beloved	20
90s	Soul CITY 125	You Lie So Well/That's No Way To Treat A Girl	12
57	Brunswick OE 9283	GOSPEL SONGS VOL. 1 (EP, with Sam Price Trio)	18
64	Mercury 10001 MCE	THE STORM IS PASSING OVER (EP)	18
64	Mercury 10034 MCE	SONGS OF THE GOSPEL (EP)	15
58	Mercury MPL 6546	SONGS OF THE GOSPEL (LP)	30

(see also Sister Rosetta Tharpe & Sister Marie Knight)

PETER KNIGHT ORCHESTRA/SINGERS
55	Parlophone MSP 6183	Twenty Minutes South (Medley) (both sides, as Peter Knight Singers)	10
62	Pye 7N 15472	Camel Train/Scarlett	6
67	Mercury SML 30023	SGT. PEPPER'S LONELY HEARTS CLUB BAND (LP)	15

PETER KNIGHT & KNIGHT RIDERS
61	Pye 7N 15388	Lucky Stars/Double Trouble	7
64	Pye 7N 15687	Wonderful Day Like Today/It Isn't Enough	8

ROBERT KNIGHT

62	London HLD 9496	Free Me/The Other Half Of Man	20
68	Monument MON 1008	Everlasting Love/Somebody's Baby	10
68	Monument MON 1016	Blessed Are The Lonely/It's Been Worth It All	8
68	Monument MON 1017	The Power Of Love/Love On A Mountain Top	20
68	Bell BLL 1029	Isn't It Lonely Together/We'd Better Stop	8
68	Monument LMO/SMO 5015	EVERLASTING LOVE (LP)	30
71	Monument MNT 65956	LOVE ON A MOUNTAIN TOP (LP)	20

SONNY KNIGHT

57	London HLD 8362	Confidential/Jail Bird (gold or silver label print) (78 rpm = £60)	350/150
57	London HL 7016	Confidential/Jail Bird (export issue)	120
59	Vogue Pop V 9134	But Officer/Dear Wonderful God (78 rpm = £100)	250

TERRY KNIGHT & PACK

66	Cameo Parkway C 102	I (Who Have Nothing)/Numbers	75

TONY KNIGHT

64	Decca F 11989	Did You Ever Hear The Sound?/I Feel So Blue (as Tony Knight & Live Wires)	42
65	Decca F 12109	How Sweet/Surfer Street (as Tony Knight's Chessmen)	38

KNIGHT BROTHERS

65	Chess CRS 8015	Sinking Low/Temptation 'Bout To Get Me	28
66	Chess CRS 8046	That'll Get It/She's A1	30

KNIGHTRIDER

87	Omega KS 1299	Shout Out Loud	25

KNIGHTSBRIDGE STRINGS/BRASS CHORALE

59	Top Rank JAR 170	Cry/The Windows Of Paris (78 rpm = £6)	5
59	Top Rank JAR 216	Wheel Of Fortune/Cow-Cow Boogie (78 rpm = £10)	5
59	Top Rank JAR 220	Eton Boating Song/In A Shanty In Old Shanty Town (78 rpm = £8)	5
60s	Top Rank JKR 8040	ROCKING STRINGS (EP)	8

KNIGHTS OF THE ROUND TABLE

68	Pama PM 734	Lament To Bobby Kennedy/If You Were My Girl	7

K9's

79	Dog Breath WOOF 1	The K9 Hassle/Idi Amin/Sweeney Todd (1st issue in numbered blue p/s, with insert, 1000 only; reissue in white p/s with insert, 500 only)	each 20

KNOCKER JUNGLE

70	Ember EMB S 293	I Don't Know Why/Reality (p/s)	6
71	Ember NR 5052	KNOCKER JUNGLE (LP, gatefold sleeve)	25

KNOCKOUTS

60	Top Rank JAR 279	Riot In Room 3C/Darling Lorraine	30

DAVID KNOPFLER

83	Peach River BBPR 7	Soul Kissing/Come To Me (p/s)	8
83	Peach River BBPR 712	Soul Kissing/Come To Me/The Great Divide (12", p/s)	8
84	Fast Alley FAR 701	Madonna's Daughter/Hey Henry (p/s)	5

(see also Dire Straits)

MARK KNOPFLER

83	Vertigo DSTR 4	Going Home (Theme Of 'Local Hero')/Smooching (p/s)	5
83	Vertigo DSFM 4	Going Home (Theme Of 'Local Hero') (Cinema Version) (promo only)	12
83	Vertigo DSTR 5	Themes From Local Hero: Wild Theme/Going Home (p/s)	5
84	Vertigo DSDJ 7	Joy (from 'Comfort And Joy') (unissued, 1-sided promo only)	20
84	Vertigo DSTR 712	Joy (from 'Comfort And Joy')/Fistful Of Ice Cream (12", p/s)	20
84	Vertigo MARK ONE	Comfort And Joy (12", 1-sided promo)	40
84	Vertigo DSTR 8	The Long Road (Theme From 'Cal')/Irish Boy (p/s)	5
86	Vertigo DSTR 14	Going Home/Wild Theme (reissue, p/s)	5
90	CBS 656377	Poor Boy Blues/There'll Be Some Changes Made (with Chet Atkins) (p/s)	5

(see also Dire Straits, Randy Newman, Chet Atkins)

KNOPOV'S POLITICAL PACKAGE

80	white label	Misadventure/You're In The Army Now	6

(see also Mission)

KNOTT SISTERS

58	London HLX 8713	Undivided Attention/SHADES with KNOTT SISTERS: Sun Glasses	40
58	London HLX 8713	Undivided Attention/SHADES with KNOTT SISTERS: Sun Glasses (78)	18

BUDDY KNOX

57	Columbia DB 3914	Party Doll/My Baby's Gone (gold label print) (78 rpm = £20)	140
57	Columbia DB 3952	Rock Your Little Baby To Sleep/Don't Make Me Cry (as Lieutenant Buddy Knox, gold label print) (78 rpm = £28)	100
57	Columbia DB 4014	Hula Love/Devil Woman (78 rpm = £25)	40
58	Columbia DB 4077	Swingin' Daddy/Whenever I'm Lonely (78 rpm = £25)	40
58	Columbia DB 4180	Somebody Touched Me/C'mon Baby (78 rpm = £25)	25
59	Columbia DB 4302	To Be With You/I Think I'm Gonna Kill Myself	20
61	London HLG 9268	Lovey Dovey/I Got You	15
61	London HLG 9331	Ling Ting Tong/The Kisses (They're All Mine)	15
61	London HLG 9472	Three-Eyed Man/All By Myself	15
62	Liberty LIB 55411	Chi-Hua-Hua/Open Your Loving Arms	15
62	Liberty LIB 55473	She's Gone/Now There's Only Me	10
63	Liberty LIB 55592	Shadaroom/Tomorrow Is Coming	10
64	Liberty LIB 55694	All Time Loser/Good Loving	10
69	United Artists UP 35019	God Knows I Love You/Night Runners	7
70	United Artists UP 35100	Party Doll/God Knows I Love You	5
57	Columbia SEG 7732	ROCK-A-BUDDY KNOX (EP)	125
62	Liberty LBY 1114	GOLDEN HITS (LP)	50
71	Sunset SLS 50206	ROCK REFLECTIONS (LP)	12

KNUCKLEHEAD
93	Saucerman ART 01	Red Eye, Dead Eye/Spirit Matter (p/s, hand-painted label, 150 copies only)	15

KOBALT 60
91	Music Of Life NOTE57	Chaos From Order/Concrete Show (12")	20

KOCK
83	Hard ON 11	One-Eyed Giant/Hickory Dickory Kock (p/s)	6

KODIAKS
69	Decca F 12942	All Because You Wanna See Me Cry/Tell Me Rhonda	18

(SPIDER) JOHN KOERNER
67	Elektra EKSN 45005	Won't You Give Me Some Love/Don't Stop	12
69	Elektra EKSN 45063	Friends And Lovers/Magazine Lady (with Willie Murphy)	10
65	Elektra EKL 290	SPIDER BLUES (LP)	35
68	Elek. EKL 4041/EKS 74041	RUNNING JUMPING STANDING STILL (LP, with Willie Murphy)	25
71	Elektra K 42026	RUNNING JUMPING STANDING STILL (LP, reissue)	12

MOE KOFFMAN
74	CBS S 73245	FOUR SEASONS IN ROCK (LP)	15

KOLETTES
64	Pye International 7N 25278	Who's That Guy?/Just How Much	40
73	Chess 6145 021	Who's That Guy?/Just How Much (reissue)	10

BONNIE KOLOC
72	London HLO 10377	Jazz Man/Got To Get What You Can	6
72	London HLO 10392	Burgundy Wine/We Are Ships	6
72	London SHO 8432	AFTER ALL THIS TIME (LP)	25
72	London SHO 8440	HOLD ON TO ME (LP)	20

JIMMIE KOMACK
54	Vogue Coral Q 2031	Cold Summer Blues/The Nic-Name Song	10
55	Vogue Coral Q 72061	Wabash 4-7473/An Old Beer Bottle	10
55	Vogue Coral Q 72087	Rock-A-Bye Your Baby With A Dixie Melody/This Is The Place	10

CHRISTOPHER KOMEDA
66	Polydor 580001	CUL DE SAC (soundtrack EP)	300
68	Dot (S)LPD 519	ROSEMARY'S BABY (LP, as Kryzstophe Komeda)	35

JOHN (T.) KONGOS
66	Piccadilly 7N 35341	I Love Mary/Goodtime Party Companion (as John T. Kongos)	6
69	Dawn DNS 1002	Flim Flam Pharisee/Blood	6
69	Dawn DNLS 3002	CONFUSIONS ABOUT A GOLDFISH (LP)	20
	(see also Scrugg, Floribunda Rose)		

V. KONGS
63	Halagala HG 18	Tomorrow Will Soon Be Here/Pretty Little Girl	20

KONRADS
65	CBS 201812	Baby It's Too Late Now/I'm Over You	30+

KONSTRUKTIVITS
80s	Third Mind TM 02	PSYKO GENETIKA (LP)	20
86	Sterile SR 10	GLENACAUL (LP)	20
	(see also Whitehouse)		

KOOBAS
65	Pye 7N 17012	Take Me For A Little While/Somewhere In The Night	50
66	Pye 7N 17087	You'd Better Make Up Your Mind/A Place I Know	60
66	Columbia DB 7988	Sweet Music/Face	60
67	Columbia DB 8103	Sally/Champagne And Caviar	40
67	Columbia DB 8187	Gypsy Fred/City Girl	50
68	Columbia DB 8419	The First Cut Is The Deepest/Walking Out	55
69	Columbia S(C)X 6271	THE KOOBAS (LP)	600
88	Bam Caruso KIRI 047	BARRICADES (LP)	20
	(see also Kubas, Van Der Graaf Generator, Gary & Stu, March Hare)		

KOOGA
88	Kooga KO 001	Don't Break My Heart (p/s, private pressing)	8
	(see also Skin)		

KOOKS
05	Private Pressing	Slave To The Game (1-sided, stamped label, tour single, 500 only)	10

KOOL
67	CBS 203003	Look At Me, Look At Me/Room At The Top	10
69	CBS 2865	Step Out Of Your Mind/Funny (What A Fool A Man Can Be)	20
69	MCA MU 1085	Lovin'/Baby's Out Of Reach	12

KOOL KEITH/PHAROE MONCH/AKINYELLE
95	Liberty Grooves	Freestyle Frenzy/Gotta Go Down (7")	45
	LIB 008/DOLO 002		

KOOL & THE GANG
70	London HLZ 10308	Kool And The Gang/Raw Hamburgers	8
71	Mojo 2027 005	Funky Man/Kool And The Gang/Let The Music Take Your Mind	6
71	Mojo 2027 006	Love The Life You Live/The Penguin	6
72	Mojo 2027 009	Music Is The Message (Parts 1 & 2)	6
73	Polydor 2001 474	Funky Stuff/More Funky Stuff	6
74	Polydor 2001 500	Jungle Boogie/North, South, East, West	6
74	Polydor 2001 530	Hollywood Swinging/Dujii	6
74	Polydor 2001 541	Higher Plane/Wild Is Love	6
75	Polydor 2001 558	Rhyme Tyme People/Father, Father	6
75	Polydor 2001 566	Spirit Of The Boogie/Jungle Jazz	6

76	Polydor 2058 645	Love And Understanding/Sunshine And Love	6
77	Contempo CS 1001	Super Band/Open Sesame	5
81	De-Lite GANG 11	Jones Vs Jones/Summer Madness//
		Funky Stuff/Hollywood Swinging (double pack)	5
71	Mojo 2347 001	LIVE AT P.J.'S (LP)	55
71	Mojo 2347 002	THE BEST OF KOOL AND THE GANG (LP)	45
72	Mojo 2347 003	LIVE AT THE SEX MACHINE (LP)	25
73	Mojo 2347 004	MUSIC IS THE MESSAGE (LP)	30
74	Polydor 2310 299	WILD AND PEACEFUL (LP)	15
74	Polydor 2310 357	LIGHT OF WORLDS (LP)	12
75	Polydor 2310 416	SPIRIT OF THE BOOGIE (LP)	12
76	Polydor 2343 083	LIVE AT THE SEX MACHINE (LP, reissue)	12

AL KOOPER
65	Mercury MF 885	Parchman Farm/You're The Lovin' End (as Alan Kooper)	12
69	CBS 4011	You Never Know Who Are Your Friends Are/Soft Landing On The Moon	6
69	CBS 4160	Hey Western Union Man/I Stand Alone	8
71	CBS 5146	Brand New Lady/The Landlord (Love Theme)	5
71	CBS 7376	John The Baptist/Back On My Feet	5
72	CBS 8084	Monkey Time/Bended Knees (Please Don't Let Me Down)	10
69	CBS 63538	I STAND ALONE (LP, orange label)	20
69	CBS 63651	YOU NEVER KNOW WHO YOUR FRIENDS ARE (LP, orange label)	18
70	CBS 63797	KOOPER SESSION — WITH SHUGGIE OTIS (LP, orange label)	18
70	CBS 66252	EASY DOES IT (2-LP, orange label)	20
71	United Artists UAS 29120	THE LANDLORD (LP, soundtrack, with Staple Singers & Lorraine Ellison)	20
71	CBS 64340	NEW YORK CITY (YOU'RE A WOMAN) (LP, gatefold sleeve, orange label)	12
72	CBS 64208	A POSSIBLE PROJECTION OF THE FUTURE/CHILDHOOD'S END
		(LP, orange label)	12
73	CBS 65193	NAKED SONGS (LP)	12

(see also Blues Project, Blood Sweat & Tears, Shuggie Otis)

AL KOOPER, MIKE BLOOMFIELD & STEPHEN STILLS
68	CBS 3770	Season Of The Witch/Albert's Shuffle	12
68	CBS 63396	SUPER SESSION (LP)	20
73	CBS CQ 30991	SUPER SESSION (LP, quadrophonic)	20

(see also Mike Bloomfield & Al Kooper, Stephen Stills)

KOP CHOIR
| 72 | Hallmark SHM 794 | THE KOP CHOIR (LP) | 30 |

KOPPYKATS
| 68 | Fontana SFT 13052/3 | BEATLES' BEST (2-LP) | 40 |

(see also Ian [Edward] & Zodiacs)

TAMARA KORAN WITH PERCEPTION
| 68 | Domain D 7 | Veils Of Mourning Lace/Don't Throw Our Love Away | 100+ |

TOMMY KÖRBERG
| 69 | Sonet SON 2005 | Dear Mrs. Jones/Bird You Must Fly | 8 |

PAUL KORDA
66	Columbia DB 7994	Go On Home/Just Come Closer To Me	25
69	Parlophone R 5778	Seagull (West Coast Oil Tragedy Of '68)/Night Of The Next Day	5
71	MAM MAM 20	Between The Road/English Country Garden	5
71	MAM AS 1003	PASSING STRANGER (LP)	30

(see also Tim Andrews & Paul Korda, Dada, Fresh)

ALEXIS KORNER (BLUES INCORPORATED)
58	Tempo A 166	I Ain't Gonna Worry No More/County Jail (as Alexis Korner Skiffle Group)	100
58	Tempo A 166	I Ain't Gonna Worry No More/County Jail (78)	50
63	Lyntone LYN 299	Blaydon Races/Up-Town (as Blues Incorporated With Alexis Korner,
		free with women's magazine *Trio*)	130
63	Parlophone R 5206	I Need Your Loving/Please Please Please (as Alexis Korner's Blues Inc.)	28
65	Parlophone R 5247	Little Baby/Roberta (as Alexis Korner's Blues Inc.)	25
65	King KG 1017	See See Rider/Blues A La King (as Alexis Korner's All Stars)	45
66	Fontana TF 706	River's Invitation/Everyday (I Have The Blues)	25
67	Fontana TF 817	Rosie/Rock Me	25
75	CBS 3520	Get Off My Cloud/Strange'n'Deranged	10
76	CBS 3877	Ain't That Peculiar/Tree Top Fever	8
58	Tempo EXA 76	BLUES FROM THE ROUNDHOUSE VOL. 1 (EP, as Alexis Korner
		Skiffle Group)	175
59	Tempo EXA 102	BLUES FROM THE ROUNDHOUSE VOL. 2 (EP, as Alexis Korner's
		Blues Inc.)	220
62	Topic TOP 70	3/4 A.D. (EP, with Davy Graham, first pressing in mauve sleeve with
		cream label; later pressings with lilac or bronze sleeve and blue label)	225/125/100
57	'77' LP/2	BLUES FROM THE ROUNDHOUSE (10" LP, 99 only, as Alexis Korner
		Breakdown Group)	1000+
62	Ace of Clubs ACL 1130	R&B FROM THE MARQUEE (LP, claret labels, with Long John Baldry)	120
64	Transatlantic TRA 117	RED HOT FROM ALEX (LP, with Herbie Goins)	150
64	Oriole PS 40058	AT THE CAVERN (LP, live, with Herbie Goins)	350
65	Ace of Clubs ACL 1187	ALEXIS KORNER'S BLUES INCORPORATED (LP)	170
65	Spot JW 551	SKY HIGH (LP, featuring Duffy Power)	350
67	Fontana (S)TL 5381	I WONDER WHO (LP, mono/stereo)	150/160
67	Polydor Special 236 206	BLUES INCORPORATED (LP, reissue of Spot LP with fewer tracks)	50
68	Liberty LBL/LBS 83147	A NEW GENERATION OF BLUES (LP)	85
69	Transatlantic TRASAM 7	ALEXIS KORNER'S ALL STAR BLUES INCORPORATED
		(LP, reissue of "Red Hot From Alex", different cover)	50

71	Rak SRAK 501	ALEXIS (LP)!	40
72	Rak SRAKSP 51	BOOTLEG HIM! (2-LP, with booklet)	60
73	Transatlantic TRA 269	ACCIDENTALLY BORN IN NEW ORLEANS (LP, as Snape)	35
75	CBS 69155	GET OFF MY CLOUD (LP)	30

(see also Cyril Davies, C.C.S., Bob Hall & Alexis Korner, Herbie Goins, Duffy Power, Long John Baldry, Rocket 88, Davy Graham, Beryl Bryden, Jimmy Cotton, Ken Colyer, Jack Bruce, Snape & Little Brother Montgomery)

ARTIE KORNFELD'S TREE
72	Neighbourhood NBH 3	Island Song/Feel	5
70	Probe SPB 1022	A TIME TO REMEMBER (LP)	20

KORPERAYSHUN
89	BPM BP12007	K Factor/Non Stop (12")	35

KOSMIC KOMMANDO
94	Rephlex CAT 007EP	Cat 007 (I)/Cat 007 (II)/Cat 007 (III)/Cat 007 (IV) (12", clear vinyl)	15

(see also Aphex Twin)

PAUL KOSSOFF
73	Island ILPS 9264	BACK STREET CRAWLER (LP)	15
83	St. Tunes SDLP 0012PD	MR. BIG/BLUE SOUL (LP, picture disc)	12

(see also Free, Kossoff Kirke Tetsu & Rabbit, Creepy John Thomas)

KOSSOFF, KIRKE, TETSU & RABBIT
71	Island ILPS 9188	KOSSOFF, KIRKE, TETSU AND RABBIT (LP)	40

(see also Paul Kossoff, Rabbit, Free)

CHIM KOTHARI
66	Deram DM 108	Sitar'N'Spice/Indian Bat	12
66	Deram DML 1002	SOUND OF THE SITAR (LP)	30

LEO KOTTKE
72	Sonet SNTF 629	LEO KOTTKE & HIS 6 & 12-STRING GUITAR (LP)	12

(see also John Fahey)

KOUMBA
82	Greensleeves GRED 105	We Are Leggo/Billy (12")	10

KRACKER
73	Rolling Stones RS 19106	A Song For Polly/Medicated Goo	5
74	Rolling Stones COC 49102	KRACKER BRAND (LP, gatefold sleeve)	12

KRAFTWERK
SINGLES
75	Vertigo 6147 012	Autobahn/Kometenmelodie 1	15
75	Vertigo 6147 015	Comet Melody 2/Kristallo	12
76	Capitol CL 15853	Radio Activity/Antenna (some in p/s)	12/5
77	Capitol CL 104	Showroom Dummies/Europe Endless	6
77	Capitol CLX 104	Showroom Dummies/Europe Endless (12", 'train station' p/s)	15
77	Capitol CL 15917	Trans-Europe Express/Franz Schubert	6
78	Capitol CL 15981	The Robots/Spacelab (foldout p/s)	15
78	Capitol CL 15981	The Robots (alternative mix)/Spacelab (foldout p/s)	30
78	Capitol CL 15998	Neon Lights/Trans-Europe Express/The Model	10
78	Capitol 12CL 15998	Neon Lights/Trans-Europe Express/The Model (12", luminous vinyl, dayglo sleeve)	15
78	Capitol CL 16098	Showroom Dummies/Spacelab/Europe Endless (12", reissue, 'red shirts' p/s)	15
81	EMI EMI 5175	Pocket Calculator/Dentaku (p/s)	5
81	EMI TCEMI 5175	Pocket Calculator/Numbers/Dentaku (cassette, 'cigarette'-pack style box)	35
81	EMI 12EMI 5175	Pocket Calculator/Numbers/Dentaku (12", p/s)	12
81	Vertigo VER 3	Kometenmelodie 2/Vom Himmel Hoch (p/s)	12
81	EMI EMI 5207	Computer Love/The Model (p/s, original issue)	6
81	EMI 12EMI 5207	Computer Love/The Model (12", p/s, original issue)	15
82	EMI EMI 5272	Showroom Dummies/Numbers (p/s, some with mispressed B-side "The Model")	8/5
82	EMI 12EMI 5272	Showroom Dummies/Numbers/Pocket Calculator (12", p/s)	12
83	EMI EMI 5413	Tour De France/Tour De France (Instrumental) (p/s, red or yellow labels)	6
83	EMI TCEMI 5413	Tour De France/Tour De France (Short Version)/Tour De France (2" Etape) (cassette)	35
83	EMI 12EMI 5413	Tour De France (Long Version)/(7" Version)/(2" Etape) (12", p/s, red or yellow labels)	20
84	EMI EMI 5413	Tour De France (Kevorkian Remix)/Tour De France (Original 7" Version) (reissue, 'Breakdance' p/s)	7
84	EMI 12EMI 5413	Tour De France (Kevorkian Remix)/Tour De France (Different Extended Version)/Tour De France (Original 7" Version) (12", reissue, 'Breakdance' p/s)	18
86	EMI EMI 5588	Musique Non-Stop/Musique Non-Stop (Different Version) (p/s)	5
86	EMI 12EMI 5588	Musique Non-Stop (6.15)/Musique Non-Stop (7" Version) (12", p/s)	15
87	EMI EMI 5602	The Telephone Call/Der Telefon Anruf (p/s)	6
87	EMI 12EMI 5602	The Telephone Call (Remix)/House Phone/Der Telefon Anruf (12", p/s)	20
91	EMI EM 192	The Robots (re-recorded version)/Robotronik (p/s, red/black or white/black song title box)	5
91	EMI 12EM 192	Robotronik/The Robots (Single Mix)/The Robots (Album Version) (12", p/s, red/black or white/black song title box)	8
91	EMI CDEM 192	Robotronik/Robotnik/The Robots (Single Edit) (CD, mispressing, plays 'Robotronik [mix]' in place of 'The Robots', red/black song title box)	18
91	EMI CDEM 192	Robotronik/Robotnik/The Robots (Single Edit) (CD, white/black song title box)	18
91	EMI EM 201	Radioactivity (Francois Kevorkian Remix)/(William Orbit Mix) (p/s)	6
91	EMI TCEM 201	Radioactivity (Francois Kevorkian Remix)/(William Orbit Mix) (cassette)	15
91	EMI 12EM 201	Radioactivity (Francois Kevorkian 12" Remix)/(Francois Kevorkian 7" Remix)/(William Orbit 12" Remix) (12", p/s)	891

	EMI CDEM 201	Radioactivity (Francois Kevorkian 7" Remix)/	
		(Francois Kevorkian 12" Remix)/(William Orbit 12" Remix) (CD)	18
97	EMI KLANG DJ 101	Trans Europe Express/Trans Europe Express (Inst.) (12", p/s, promo only)	40
97	EMI KLANG DJ 102	Numbers/Numbers (12", p/s, same track both sides, promo only)	40
97	EMI KLANG DJ 103	Musique Non Stop/Musique Non Stop	
		(12", p/s, same track both sides, promo only)	40
97	EMI KLANG DJ 104	Homecomputer/It's More Fun To Compute (12", p/s, promo only)	40
97	EMI KLANG BOX 101	KRAFTWERK (4 x 12" box set, including "Trans Europe Express", "Numbers",	
		"Musique Non Stop" & "Homecomputer"; *without* T-shirt, promo only)	100+
97	EMI KLANG BOX 101	KRAFTWERK (4 x 12" box set, including "Trans Europe Express",	
		"Numbers", "Musique Non Stop" & "Homecomputer";	
		with separate white or black T-shirt, promo only)	500

LPs

72	Vertigo 6641 077	KRAFTWERK (2-LP, gatefold sleeve, 'swirl' or 'spacecraft' labels)	120/50
74	Vertigo 6360 616	RALF AND FLORIAN (gatefold sleeve, 'spacecraft' label)	110/45
74	Vertigo 6360 620	AUTOBAHN (embossed blue sleeve)	30
75	Vertigo 6360 629	EXCELLER 8 (some with stickered sleeve)	22
75	Vertigo 6360 629	EXCELLER 8 (cassette)	15
76	Capitol EST 11457	RADIOACTIVITY (with insert)	15
81	Vertigo 6449 006	ELEKTROKINETIK	25
81	Vertigo 6449 006	ELEKTROKINETIK (cassette)	15
83	EMI EMC 3407	TECHNOPOP (unissued, sleeves only)	
91	EMI EM 1408	THE MIX (2-LP, with inner sleeves)	20
03	EMI EMI 591 708 1	TOUR DE FRANCE SOUNDTRACKS (2-LP, single stickered sleeve	
		with inners)	15
04	EMI KLANG BOX 001	THE CATALOGUE (8-CD, in card box, 1,000 only)	400+
	(see also Organisation, Elektric Music)		

KRAKEN
81	Knave EJSP 9370	FANTASY REALITY (EP, no p/s)	50

BILLY J. KRAMER
66	Parlophone R 5482	You Make Me Feel Like Someone/Take My Hand	6
67	Parlophone R 5552	Sorry/Going Going Gone	10
67	Reaction 591 014	Town Of Tuxley Toymakers/Chinese Girl	35
68	CBS 56-3396	1941/His Love Is Just A Lie	5
68	NEMS 56-3635	A World Without Love/Going Through It	5
69	MGM MGM 1474	The Colour Of My Love/I'm Running Away	10
73	Decca F 13426	A Fool Like You/I'll Keep You Satisfied	7
73	Decca F 13442	Darlin' Come To Me/Walking	7
74	BASF BA 1006	Stayin' Power/Blue Jean Queen	7
77	EMI EMI 2661	San Diego/Warm Summer Rain	5
78	EMI EMI 2740	Ships That Pass In The Night/Is There Anymore At Home Like You	5
79	Hobo HOS 010	Blue Christmas/Little Love (p/s, blue vinyl)	9
80	JM JM 1005	Silver Dream/Lonely Lady	5
82	Runaway BJK 1	Rock It/Dum Dum	5
83	Rak RAK 359	You Can't Live On Memories/Stood Up (p/s)	5

BILLY J. KRAMER & THE DAKOTAS
63	Parlophone R 5049	Bad To Me/I Call Your Name	6
64	Parlophone R 5156	From A Window/Second To None	6
65	Parlophone R 5285	Trains And Boats And Planes/That's The Way I Feel	9
65	Parlophone R 5362	Neon City/I'll Be Doggone	10
66	Parlophone R 5408	We're Doing Fine/Forgive Me	10
63	Parlophone GEP 8885	THE BILLY J. KRAMER HITS (EP)	25
63	Parlophone GEP 8895	I'LL KEEP YOU SATISFIED (EP)	25
64	Parlophone GEP 8907	LITTLE CHILDREN (EP)	25
64	Parlophone GEP 8921	FROM A WINDOW (EP)	28
65	Parlophone GEP 8928	BILLY J. PLAYS THE STATES (EP)	50
63	Parlophone PMC 1209	LISTEN (LP, also stereo PCS 3047)	30
65	Regal REG 1057	BILLY J (LP, export only)	38
66	MFP MFP 1134	BILLY BOY (LP)	12
	(see also Dakotas)		

WAYNE KRAMER
78	Stiffwick DEA/SUK 1	Ramblin' Rose/Get Some (numbered p/s)	8
79	Radar ADA 41	The Harder They Come/East Side Girl (p/s)	6
	(see also MC5)		

KRAY CHERUBS
88	Fierce FRIGHT 014	No (p/s, 1-sided)	20
89	Snakeskin SS 002	Rot In Hell Mom/SAUCERMAN: Motor Drag (numbered black p/s,	
		300 only; later reissued in purple p/s)	12/8
89	Forced Exposure FE 18	Teen Camel/I Hate My Job (p/s)	15
	(see also Art Attacks, Savage Pencil)		

BILL KRENZ & HIS RAGTIMERS
56	London HLU 8258	There'll Be No New Tunes On This Old Piano/Goofus (78 rpm = £12)	30

KREW KATS
61	HMV POP 840	Trambone/Peak Hour	25
61	HMV POP 894	Samovar/Jack's Good	25
	(see also Shadows, Brian Bennett)		

KRIMSON KAKE
69	Penny Farthing PEN 707	Feelin' Better/Waiter	8
	(see also Samantha Jones, Vernons Girls)		

DAVE KRISS
	80s private pressing	EMIGRATING (2-LP)	15

MINT VALUE £

KRISSI K
74 People PEO110   Stick Up/Who Do You Think You Are? 10

SONJA KRISTINA
68 Polydor 56299   Let The Sunshine In/Frank Mills 15
80 Chopper CHOP 101   St Tropez/Mr Skin (p/s) 10
80 Chopper CHOPE 5   SONJA KRISTINA (LP) 30
(see also Curved Air)

KRIS KRISTOFFERSON
70 Monument SMO 5042   KRISTOFFERSON (LP) 15
71 Monument MNT 64636   THE SILVER TONGUED DEVIL AND ME (LP) 12
72 Monument MNT 64963   BORDER LORD (LP) 12
73 Monument MNT 64631   ME AND BOBBY McGEE (LP, reissue of "Kristofferson") 12
73 Monument MNT 65391   JESUS WAS A CAPRICORN (LP) 12
73 Monument ZQ 31909   JESUS WAS A CAPRICORN (LP, quadrophonic) 15

KRIS KRISTOFFERSON & RITA COOLIDGE
73 A&M AMLH 64403   FULL MOON (LP) 12
75 Monument MNT 80547   BREAKAWAY (LP) 12

KROKODIL
69 Liberty LBS 83306   KROKODIL (LP) 20
70 Liberty LBS 83417   SWAMP (LP) 20

KRONSTADT UPRISING
80s Spider SDL 12   The Unknown Revolution (p/s) 5

HARDY KRUGER
59 Top Rank TR 5005   Blind Date (I'm A Lonely Man)/PINEWOOD ORCHESTRA: Blind Date (p/s) 10

GENE KRUPA (& HIS ORCHESTRA)
59 HMV 7EG 8595   DRUM BOOGIE (EP) 8
58 Columbia/Clef CX 10133   KRUPA ROCKS (LP) 15
61 Verve VLP/SVLP 9005   PERCUSSION KING (LP) 15

GENE KRUPA & BUDDY RICH
64 Verve VS 503   Perdida/Night Train 5
62 Verve SVLP 9014   BURNIN' BEAT (LP) 12

KRYPTON TUNES
78 Black & Red FIRE 1   Behind Your Smile/Coming To See You (p/s) 7
78 Lightning GIL 546   Limited Vision/All In Jail 5

KRYSIA (Kocjan)
74 RCA LPL1 5052   KRYSIA (LP) 15
(see also Natural Acoustic Band, Fairport Convention)

KRYSTAL GENERATION
72 Mercury 6052 120   Wanted Dead Or Alive/Every Man Seems To Be For Himself 7

BOB KUBAN & INMEN
66 Stateside SS 488   The Cheater/Try Me Baby (DJ copy = £100) 50
66 Stateside SS 514   The Teaser/All I Want 20
68 Bell BLL 1027   The Cheater/Try Me Baby (reissue) 12

KUBAS
65 Columbia DB 7451   I Love Her/Magic Potion 40
(see also Koobas)

KUF-LINX
58 London HLU 8583   So Tough/What'cha Gonna Do (78 rpm = £50) 175

LENNY KUHR
69 Philips BF 1777   The Troubadour/Oh No Monsieur 15

KUKL
84 Crass 1984/1   THE EYE (LP, foldout sleeve) 18
85 Crass No. 4   HOLIDAYS IN EUROPE (LP, with inner sleeve) 15
(see also Sugarcubes)

KULT
69 CBS 4276   No Home Today/Mister Number One. 200

PRAMOD KUMAR
72 Philips 6460 854   THIS IS THE MUSIC OF INDIA (LP) 12

CHARLIE KUNZ
54 Decca F 10419   Charlie Kunz Piano Medley, No. 114 15
54 Decca F 10441   Charlie Kunz Piano Medley, No. 115 5
54 Decca F 10481   Charlie Kunz Piano Medley, No. 116 5

KURASS
70 Escort ES 825   Stampede/KING STITT: You Were Meant For Me (B-side actually by
    Lee Perry). 30

FELA RANSOME KUTI (& AFRICA '70)
72 Regal Zonophone RZ 3052   Chop And Quench/Egbe Mi O (with Africa '70 & Ginger Baker) 5
72 Regal Zono. SLRZ 1023   FELI RANSOME-KUTI & THE AFRICA '70 WITH GINGER BAKER LIVE! (LP) 22
75 Creole CRLP 501   SHAKARA (LP, with Africa '70) 15
77 Creole CRLP 511   ZOMBIE (LP, with Africa '70) 12
78 Phase 4 Stereo PFS 4412   YELLOW FEVER (LP) 12
79 Creole CRLP 502   GENTLEMEN (LP) 12
79 Creole CRLP 509   EVERYTHING SCATTER (LP) 12
81 Arista SPART 1167   BLACK PRESIDENT (LP) 12
(see also Ginger Baker)

JIM KWESKIN JUG BAND
65	Fontana TFL 6036	JIM KWESKIN JUG BAND (LP)	15
67	Fontana (S)TFL 6080	SEE REVERSE SIDE FOR TITLE (LP)	15
68	Vanguard SVRL 19046	WHATEVER HAPPENED TO THOSE GOOD OLD DAYS AT CLUB 47 (LP)	15

CHARLES KYNARD
73	Mainstream MSL 1017	YOUR MAMA DON'T DANCE (LP)	25

KYTES
66	Pye 7N 17136	Blessed/Call Me Darling	10
66	Pye 7N 17179	Frosted Panes/I'll Give You Better Love	35
68	Island WI 6027	Running In The Water/The End Of The Day	50

KYTTOCK KYND
70	Dorian 4782	KYTTOCK KYND (LP)	40

L.A.
70	CBS 5017	Speak Of Peace, Sing Of Joy/Brings My Whole World Tumbling Down	7
70	CBS 64109	NEW DAY (LP)	22
	(see also Love Affair)		

PATTI LA BELLE (& BLUE BELLES)
64	Sue WI 324	Down The Aisle/C'est La Vie	30
65	Cameo Parkway P 935	Danny Boy/I Believe	20
65	Atlantic AT 4055	All Or Nothing/You Forgot How To Love (as Patty La Belle & Her Belles)	22
66	Atlantic AT 4064	Over The Rainbow/Groovy Kind Of Love (as Patty La Belle & Her Belles)	12
66	Atlantic 584 007	Patti's Prayer/Family Man (as Patti La Belle & Her Belles)	10
67	Atlantic 584 072	Take Me For A Little While/I Don't Want To Go On Without You (solo)	10
66	Atlantic 587 001	OVER THE RAINBOW (LP)	50
	(see also Blue-Belles)		

LACE
68	Columbia DB 8499	People People/The Nun	25
69	Page One POF 135	I'm A Gambler/Go Away	10
	(see also Universals, Pete Dello, Honeybus, Red Herring, Gary Walker & Rain)		

DAVE LACEY & CORVETTES
65	Philips BF 1419	That's What They All Say/I've Had Enough	10

LACKEY & SWEENEY
73	Village Thing VTS 23	JUNK STORE SONGS FOR SALE (LP)	15

STEVE LACY
72	Emanem 301	SOLO (LP)	25
73	Emanem 304	THE CRUST (LP)	25

STEVE LACY & DEREK BAILEY
76	Incus 26	COMPANY 4 (LP)	25
	(see also Derek Bailey)		

LADDERS
83	Statik TAK 2	Gotta See Jane/Krugerrands (p/s)	6
83	Statik TAK 2-12	Gotta See Jane/Krugerrands (12", p/s)	10

LADD'S BLACK ACES
56	London AL 3556	LADD'S BLACK ACES (10" LP)	15

LA-DE-DA BAND
69	Parlophone R 5810	Come Together/Here Is Love	18

LADIES
80s	Music Of Life MOLIS 6	Turned On To You/I Knew That Love (12")	15

TOMMY LADNIER
54	London AL 3524	BLUES AND STOMPS VOLUME ONE — TOMMY LADNIER (10" LP)	38
55	London AL 3548	PLAYS THE BLUES WITH MA RAINEY & EDMONIA HENDERSON (10" LP)	38
	(see also Ma Rainey)		

PATTIE LA DONNE
69	Joe/Duke DU 23	Friends And Lovers/JOE'S ALLSTARS: Hot Line	12

LA DüSSELDORF
78	Radar ADA 5	La Dusseldorf/Silver Cloud (unissued, white label promos only, no p/s)	25
80	Teldec	Dampfrieman/Individuellos (12", p/s)	10
	(see also Neu!)		

LADYBIRDS
64	Columbia DB 7197	Lady Bird/I Don't Care Any More	12
64	Columbia DB 7250	The White Cliffs Of Dover/It's Not The Same Without A Boy	10
64	Columbia DB 7351	Memories/Try A Little Love	12
65	Columbia DB 7523	I Wanna Fly/O.K. Fred	12
	(see also Sharades, Russ Loader, Marion Davies, De Laine Sisters)		

MINT VALUE £

LADY JANE & VERITY
59	Pye International 7N 25036	The Slow Look/Cry Baby (78 rpm = £10)	8

LADY JUNE
74	Caroline C 1509	LADY JUNE'S LINGUISTIC LEPROSY (LP, with perforated lyric sheet)	20

(see also Kevin Ayers, Eno)

LADY LEE
64	Decca F 11961	I'm Into Something Good/When Love Comes Along	10
65	Decca F 12147	99 Times Out Of 100/I Can Feel It	8
65	Columbia DB 7121	My Whole World (Seems To Be Tumbling Down)/Girl	10

LADY LUCK & LULLABIES
62	Philips PB 1245	Young Stranger/Dance	5

LADYTRON
01	Invicta LIQ 008CD	Play Girl/Commodore Rock/Took Her To A Movie (Bertrand Mix) (CD, digipak)	10
01	Invicta Hi-Fi LIQO 12	The Way That I Found You/Holiday 601 (p/s)	8
00s	Telstar 7STAS 3311	Blue Jeans (Single Version)/Blue Jeans (Interpol Remix) (p/s, 1000 only)	8

LAFAYETTES
62	RCA RCA 1299	Life's Too Short/Nobody But You	10
62	RCA RCA 1308	Caravan Of Lonely Men/I Still Do	15

LA FUNK MOB
95	Mo' Wax MW 023R	Ravers Suck Our Sound (Carl Craig Mix)/Motor Bass Get Phunked Up (Electrofunk Remix)/Ravers Suck Our Sound (Mystic Mix)/Ravers Suck Our Sound (Gangbang Mix)/Ravers Suck Our Sound (New Mix) (2 x 10")	25
96	Mo' Wax MW 017	Tribulations Extra Sensorielles (2 x 12")	10
96	Mo' Wax MW 023	Breaking Boundaries Messing Up Heads/(mixes) (2 x 12")	10

FRANCIS LAI
67	United Artists SULP 1155	A MAN AND A WOMAN (LP, soundtrack)	18
67	United Artists (S)ULP 1185	VIVRE POUR VIVRE (LIVE FOR LIFE) (LP, soundtrack)	18
67	Brunswick LAT/STA 8689	I'LL NEVER FORGET WHAT'S 'ISNAME (LP, soundtrack)	40
69	United Artists SULP 1231	HANNIBAL BROOKS (LP)	15
69	Philips SBL 7876	MAYERLING (Francis Lai)	60
70	United Artists UAS 29137	RIDER IN THE RAIN (LP)	15
71	M. F. Pleasure MFP 50034	THE LEGEND OF FRENCHIE KING (LP)	15
76	Warner Bros K 56231	EMMANUELLE 2 (LP)	15
77	Warner Bros K 56375	BILITIS (LP, gatefold sleeve)	15

LAIBACH
84	L.A.Y.L.A.H. LAY 002	Boji/Sila/Brat Moj (12", p/s)	12
84	East West 12 EWS 3	Panarama/Decree (12", p/s)	10
85	Cherry Red 12CHERRY 91	Die Liebe/Die Liebe Ist Grösste Kraft, Die Alles Schafft (12", p/s)	10
88	Mute PMUTE 80T	SYMPATHY FOR THE DEVIL (12" EP, picture disc)	10
86	Side Effects SER 08	OCCUPIED EUROPE TOUR '85 (LP)	15
92	Mute STUMM 82	KAPITAL (LP)	12
94	NSK NSK 2CDX	OCCUPIED EUROPE NATO TOUR (EPK, in numbered box, with CD, video & booklet)	22
96	Mute STUMM 136	JESUS CHRIST SUPERSTARS (LP)	15
98	Mute STUMM 121	MCMXCIV (LP, with poster and inner)	15

CLEO LAINE
54	Parlophone MSP 6107	I Got Rhythm/I Know You're Mine (with Johnny Dankworth Orchestra)	8
55	Parlophone MSP 6147	Ain't Misbehavin'/I Got It Bad, And That Ain't Good (with Johnny Dankworth Orchestra)	8
57	Pye Jazz 7NJ 2013	I'm Beginning To See The Light/Jeepers Creepers	5
58	Pye 7N 15143	Hand Me Down Love/They Were Right	5
60	Fontana H 269	Let's Slip Away/Thieving Boy	12
61	Columbia DB 4723	It Was A Lover And His Lass/O Mistress Mine	5
61	Fontana H 326	You'll Answer To Me/I Only Have Eyes For You	6
62	Fontana TF 267257	You Gotta Have Love/I Can Dream, Can't I?	5
65	Fontana TF 532	Little Boat/The Exciting Mr. Fitch	5
65	Fontana TF 622	If We Live On The Top Of A Mountain/Don't You Pass Me By	5
66	Fontana TF 759	There Is Nothing Left To Say/Life Is A Wheel	5
70	Philips 6006 016	It Will Soon Be Spring/Feeling Good	5
71	Philips 6006 077	Model City's Programme/Night Owl	10
57	Parlophone GEP 8613	I GOT RHYTHM (EP)	10
57	Pye Nixa Jazz NJE 1010	CLEO LAINE (EP)	10
57	Pye Nixa Jazz NJE 1026	THE APRIL AGE (EP, as Cleo Laine & Dave Lee Quintet)	25
57	Esquire EP 102	CLEO LAINE (EP, as Cleo Laine & Keith Christie Quintet)	25
57	Esquire EP 122	CLEO LAINE (EP, as Cleo Laine & Keith Christie Quintet)	25
59	Columbia SEG 7938	CLEO SINGS ELIZABETHAN (EP)	10
61	Fontana TFE 17381	THE FABULOUS CLEO (EP)	10
64	Fontana TFE 17404	CLEO (EP)	15
55	Esquire 15-007	CLEO LAINE (10" LP)	50
58	Pye Nixa NPT 19024	CLEO'S CHOICE (10" LP)	50
58	MGM MGM-C 765	SHE'S THE TOPS (LP)	25
62	Fontana 680 992 TL	ALL ABOUT ME (LP, also stereo 886 159 TY)	20
64	Fontana (S)TL 5209	SHAKESPEARE & ALL THAT JAZZ (LP)	20
66	Fontana (S)TL 5316	WOMAN TALK (LP)	20
68	Fontana STL 5483	SOLILOQUY (LP)	25

(see also Johnny Dankworth, Tubby Hayes & Cleo Laine)

DENNY LAINE
67	Deram DM 122	Say You Don't Mind/Ask The People	18
68	Deram DM 171	Too Much In Love/Catherine's Wheel	22
69	Deram DM 227	Say You Don't Mind/Ask The People (reissue)	10

| 73 | Wizard WIZ 104 | Find A Way Somehow/Move Me To Another Place | 6 |
| 77 | Palladin PAL 5014 | Caroline/Blues | 6 |

(see also Moody Blues, Paul McCartney/Wings, Balls, Trevor Burton, Magic Christians, Ginger Baker's Airforce, BL&G)

FRANKIE LAINE

53	Columbia SCM 5016	The Ruby And The Pearl/The Mermaid	40
53	Columbia SCM 5017	Jealousy/The Gandy Dancers' Ball	40
53	Columbia SCM 5031	I'm Just A Poor Bachelor/Tonight You Belong To Me	40
53	Columbia SCM 5064	September In The Rain/Chow Willy	30
53	Columbia SCM 5073	The Swan Song/My Ohio Home	28
54	Columbia SCM 5085	Tomorrow Mountain/I'd Give My Life	28
56	Philips JK 1000	Moonlight Gambler/Only If We Love (jukebox issue)	25
56	Philips PB 607	Champion The Wonder Horse/Ticky Ticky Tick (I'm Gonna Tell On You) (78)	8
57	Philips JK 1009	Love Is A Golden Ring (with Easy Riders)/There's Not A Moment To Spare	25
57	Philips JK 1017	Lonely Man/Without Him (jukebox issue) (78 rpm = £8)	25
57	Philips JK 1032	The Greater Sin/East Is East (jukebox issue) (78 rpm = £8)	25
58	Philips PB 797	Shine/Annabel Lee (78 rpm = £8)	10
58	Philips PB 821	The Lonesome Road/My Gal And A Prayer (78 rpm = £8)	10
58	Philips PB 836	Lovin' Up A Storm/A Kiss Can Change The World (78 rpm = £8)	10
58	Philips PB 848	Choombala Bay/I Have To Cry (78 rpm = £10)	10
58	Philips PB 886	When I Speak Your Name/Cottage For Sale (78 rpm = £15)	7
59	Philips PB 905	That's My Desire/In My Wildest Dreams (78 rpm = £30)	7
59	Philips PB 965	Rawhide/Journey's End (78 rpm = £40)	6
60	Philips PB 997	Jelly Coal Man/Rocks And Gravel	7
60	Philips PB 1011	St. James Infirmary/Et Voila!	7
60	Philips PB 1064	And Doesn't She Roll/Seven Women	7

EPs

54	Columbia SEG 7505	JEZEBEL (company die-cut sleeve)	15
54	Philips BBE 12005	FRANKIE LAINE (I BELIEVE)	15
56	Mercury MEP 9000	FRANKIE LAINE SINGS	15
56	Mercury MEP 9500	MORE HITS BY FRANKIE LAINE	15
56	Philips BBE 12087	FRANKIE LAINE NO. 2	15
56	Philips BBE 12103	JUBA JUBA JUBALEE (as Frankie Laine & Four Lads)	12
57	Philips BBE 12130	FRANKIE LAINE NO. 3	15
57	Mercury MEP 9520	FRANKIE LAINE SINGS VOL. 2	15
58	Philips BBE 12216	FRANKIE LAINE (PHILIPS TV SERIES)	15
60	Mercury ZEP 10062	FRANKIE LAINE'S ALL TIME HITS	15
61	Philips BBE 12447	WESTERN FAVOURITES	15
62	CBS AGG 20003	DEUCES WILD NO. 1	15
62	CBS AGG 20007	DEUCES WILD NO. 2	15
62	CBS AGG 20011	DEUCES WILD NO. 3	15
64	CBS AGG 20036	SONG OF THE OPEN ROAD	15

LPs

52	Oriole/Mercury MG 10001	MR RHYTHM SINGS (10", stickered U.S. "Mr Rhythm" sleeve)	50
52	Oriole/Mercury MG 10002	SONGS BY FRANKIE LAINE (10")	50
54	Mercury MG 25097	MR. RHYTHM SINGS (10", reissue)	40
54	Mercury MG 25098	SONGS BY FRANKIE LAINE (10", reissue)	40
54	Columbia 33S 1047	ONE FOR MY BABY (10")	45
54	Philips BBR 8014	THE VOICE OF YOUR CHOICE (10")	40
55	Philips BBR 8068	MR. RHYTHM (10")	35
56	Mercury MPT 7007	CRY OF THE WILD GOOSE (10")	50
56	Philips BBL 7080	JAZZ SPECTACULAR (with Buck Clayton & His Orchestra)	20
56	Philips BBL 7111	JUBA JUBA JUBILEE (with Four Lads)	20
57	Philips BBL 7155	ROCKIN'	30
57	Mercury MPT 7513	THAT'S MY DESIRE (10")	35
58	Philips BBL 7238	FOREIGN AFFAIR	22
58	Philips BBL 7260	TORCHING	22
58	Philips BBL 7263	SHOWCASE OF HITS (flipback or non-flipback sleeve)	25/20
59	Philips BBL 7294	REUNION IN RHYTHM (with Michel Legrand, also stereo SBBL 541)	18/22
60	Philips BBL 7357	FRANKIE LAINE BALLADEER	18
61	Philips BBL 7468	HELL BENT FOR LEATHER (also stereo SBBL 616)	15/20
61	Ember EMB 3334	FRANKIE LAINE SINGS	15
62	Philips BBL 7535	DEUCES WILD (also stereo SBBL 663)	18/22
62	CBS (S)BPG 62082	CALL OF THE WILD (mono/stereo)	18
63	CBS (S)BPG 62126	WANDERLUST	18
60s	World Records SM 531/536	THE FRANKIE LAINE SONGBOOK (6-LP box set)	25

(see also Jo Stafford & Frankie Laine, Four Lads, Doris Day, Easy Riders)

FRANKIE LAINE & JOHNNIE RAY

57	Philips JK 1026	Up Above My Head, I Hear Music In The Air/Good Evening Friends (jukebox issue)	25
57	Philips PB 708	Up Above My Head, I Hear Music In The Air/Good Evening Friends (78)	8
57	Philips BBE 12153	FRANKIE AND JOHNNIE (EP, 1 track each, 2 together)	20

(see also Johnnie Ray)

LINDA LAINE (& SINNERS)

64	Columbia DB 7204	Doncha Know, Doncha Know, Doncha Know/Ain't That Fun	15
64	Columbia DB 7370	Low Grades And High Fever/After Today	15
65	Columbia DB 7549	Don't Do It Baby/All I Want To Do Is Run	15

(see also Sinners)

SCOTT LAINE

| 63 | Windsor WB 114 | Tearaway Johnnie/John Silver | 35 |

DENZIL LAING

| 71 | Songbird SB 1054 | Medicine Stick/CRYSTALITES: Short Cut | 12 |

(see also Soul Vendors, Dennis Alcapone)

ALAN LAKE
70	Ember EMB S 278	Good Times/Got To Have Tenderness (p/s)	15

BONNIE LAKE & HER BEAUX
56	Brunswick 05622	Thirteen Black Cats/The Miracle Of Love (78 rpm = £10)	22
(see also Jack Pleis)			

GREG LAKE
75	Manticore K 13511	I Believe In Father Christmas/Humbug (p/s)	6
77	Atlantic K 10990	C'est La Vie/EMERSON, LAKE & PALMER: Jeremy Bender (p/s)	8
78	Atlantic K 11061	Watching Over You/EMERSON, LAKE & PALMER: Hallowed Be Thy Name (p/s)	5
81	Chrysalis CHS 2553	Love You Too Much/Someone (p/s)	6
82	Chrysalis CHS 2567	It Hurts/Retribution Drive	8
(see also Emerson Lake & Palmer, King Crimson, Asia, Pete Sinfield, Gary Moore)			

LEE LAMAR & HIS ORCHESTRA
57	London HLB 8508	Teenage Pedal Pushers/Sophia (78 rpm = £30)	75

CHRIS LAMB & UNIVERSALS
65	Decca F 12176	Mysterious Land/If You Ask Me	8
(see also Universals, Gidian)			

KEVIN LAMB
70	Concord CON 23	Who Is The Hero?/The Road To Antibes	6
73	Birth RAB 1004	Who Is The Hero?/Who Stole The Ice	5
72	Birth RAB 4	WHO IS THE HERO? (LP)	12

LAMBCHOP
00	City Slang 20174-2	THE QUEEN'S ROYAL TRIMMA (CD EP, sold at gigs)	10

JEANNIE LAMBE
67	CBS 202636	Miss Disc/Montano Blues (with Gordon Beck Orchestra)	20
67	CBS 2731	Day After Day After Day/City At Night	20
67	CBS 3000	This Is My Love/Where Have All The Endings Gone (as Jeanne Lam)	8

DAVE LAMBERT, JON HENDRICKS & ANNIE ROSS
60	Philips BBL 7368	DAVE LAMBERT, JON HENDRICKS & ANNIE ROSS (LP, stereo SBBL 562)	15
(see also Jon Hendricks, Annie Ross)			

DAVE LAMBERT & BUDDY STEWART
51	Vogue V 2039	Bopelbaby/Bopelground (78, with Al Haig)	9

TREVOR LAMBERT
72	Duke DU 132	Bald Head Teacher (act. by Max Romeo)/HEADMASTERS: Bald Head Version	8

LAMB LANCE
95	Long LENGTH 8	THE JOY OF JOUSTING (LP)	12

LAMBRETTAS
79	Rocket XPRES 23	Go Steady/Listen Listen/Cortinas (p/s)	8
80	Rocket XPRES 25	Poison Ivy/Runaround (with '2-Stroke' die-cut sleeve & label)	12
80	Rocket XPRES 25	Poison Ivy/Runaround (with ROCKET die-cut sleeve & label)	12
80	Rocket XPRES 333	Da-a-a-ance/(Can't You) Feel The Beat (picture disc; 2 different shades, red, white & blue or pink, white & blue)	5/8
80	Rocket XPRES 36	Page 3/Steppin' Out (Of Line) (withdrawn; one copy known to exist with p/s)	500/300
80	Rocket XPRES 36	Another Day (Another Girl)/Steppin' Out (Of Line) ('emergency' p/s)	8
81	Rocket XPRES 48	Good Times/Lamba Samba (p/s)	8
81	Rocket XPRES 52	Anything You Want/Ambience (Rocket die-cut sleeve)	6
81	Rocket XPRES 62	Decent Town/Da-a-a-ance (p/s)	6
81	Rocket XPRES 6212	Decent Town/Da-a-a-ance/Total Strangers/Young Girls (12", p/s)	12
82	Rocket XPRES 74	Somebody To Love/Nobody's Watching Me (p/s)	8
82	Rocket XPRES 74	Somebody To Love/Nobody's Watching Me (p/s, mispressing, crediting "Leap Before You Look" on label & sleeve)	8

TONI LAMOND
68	Philips BF 1722	Silent Voices/They Don't Give Medals (To Yesterday's Heroes)	15

DUNCAN LAMONT
67	Studio Two TWO 159	LATIN A LA LAMONT (LP)	12
68	Morgan MRSAM 2	THIS GUY (LP)	15

LAMPLIGHTERS
55	Parlophone DP 416	Salty Dog/Ride Jockey Ride (78, export issue)	120
(see also Thurston Harris)			

LAMP SISTERS
68	Sue WI 4048	A Woman With The Blues/I Thought It Was All Over	40

LANA SISTERS
58	Fontana H 148	Ring-A My Phone/Chimes Of Arcady (78 rpm = £18)	30
59	Fontana H 176	Buzzin'/Cry, Cry, Baby (78 rpm £15)	30
59	Fontana H 190	Mister Dee-Jay/Tell Him No (78 rpm = £18)	30
59	Fontana H 221	(Seven Little Girls) Sitting In The Back Seat (with Al Saxon)/Sitting On The Sidewalk (78 rpm = £28)	20
60	Fontana H 235	My Mother's Eyes/You've Got What It Takes (78 rpm = £28)	20
60	Fontana H 252	Someone Loves You, Joe/Tinatarella Di Luna	15
60	Fontana H 283	Two-some/Down South	15
(see also Al Saxon, Dusty Springfield, Chantelles)			

CYNTHIA LANAGAN
54	Columbia SCMC 8	Body And Soul/I Can't Believe You're In Love With Me (export issue)	15
57	Parlophone R 4316	Jamie Boy/Silent Lips (as Cynthia Lanigan)	10
57	Parlophone R 4383	I'm Available/(Don't Stop, Don't Stop) Tell Me More	10

LANCASHIRE FAYRE
80	Folk Heritage FHR 113	LANCASHIRE FAYRE (LP)	20

STEVE LANCASTER

67	Polydor 56215	San Francisco Street/Miguel Fernando San Sebastian Brown	10

ALAN LANCASTER'S BOMBERS

96	P.J. Rocks PJR002CD	THE MATCHSTICKMEN EP (CD, 4 tracks, card p/s)	15

(see also Status Quo)

LANCASTRIANS

64	Pye 7N 15732	We'll Sing In The Sunshine/Was She Tall	15
65	Pye 7N 15791	Let's Lock The Door (And Throw Away The Key)/If You're Goin' To Leave Me	8
65	Pye 7N 15846	There'll Be No More Goodbyes/Never Gonna Come On Home	8
65	Pye 7N 15927	Lonely Man/I Can't Stand The Pain	8
66	Pye 7N 17043	The World Keeps Going Round/Not The Same Anymore	40
66	Pye 7N 17072	The Ballad Of The Green Berets/My Little Rose	6

MAJOR LANCE

63	Columbia DB 7099	The Monkey Time/Mama Didn't Know (DJ copy = £50)	30
63	Columbia DB 7168	Hey Little Girl/Crying In The Rain	25
64	Columbia DB 7205	Um, Um, Um, Um, Um, Um/Sweet Music	20
64	Columbia DB 7271	The Matador/Gonna Get Married	30
64	Columbia DB 7365	Rhythm/Please Don't Say No More	25
65	Columbia DB 7463	I'm So Lost/Sometimes I Wonder	25
65	Columbia DB 7527	Come See/You Belong To Me, My Love	30
65	Columbia DB 7609	Pride And Joy/I'm The One	30
65	Columbia DB 7688	Too Hot To Hold/Dark And Lonely	30
65	Columbia DB 7787	Everybody Loves A Good Time/I Just Can't Help It	30
66	Columbia DB 7967	Investigate/Little Young Lover (DJ copy = £125)	75
67	Columbia DB 8122	Ain't No Soul (Left In These Ole Shoes)/You'll Want Me Back (DJ copy = £100)	60
69	Atlantic 584 277	Follow The Leader/Since You've Been Gone	15
69	Atlantic 584 302	Sweeter As The Days Go By/Shadows Of A Memory	15
69	Soul City SC 114	The Beat/You'll Want Me Back	25
70	Buddah 2011 046	Gypsy Woman/Stay Away From Me	15
72	Stax 2025 124	I Wanna Make Up/That's The Story Of My Life	15
72	Epic EPC 8404	Um, Um, Um, Um, Um, Um/Sweet Music (reissue)	5
73	Contempo C 1	The Right Track/Um, Um, Um, Um, Um, Um	6
73	Contempo C 9	Ain't No Soul (Left In These Ole Shoes)/Investigate	8
73	Contempo C 26	Dark And Lonely/My Girl	20
73	Warner Bros K 16334	Sweeter/Wild & Free	6
74	Warner Bros K 16385	Without A Doubt/Open The Door To Your Heart	15
74	Contempo CS 2017	Gimme Little Sign/How Can You Say Goodbye	20
74	Contempo CS 9015	The Right Track/Ain't No Soul (Left In These Ole Shoes)	6
75	Contempo CS 2045	Don't You Know I Love You (Parts 1 & 2)	20
75	Pye 7N 45487	You're Everything I Need (Parts 1 & 2)	10
76	Pye International 7N 25705	Nothing Can Stop Me/Follow The Leader	8
64	Columbia SEG 8318	UM UM UM UM UM UM (EP)	90
65	Columbia 33SX 1728	THE RHYTHM OF MAJOR LANCE (LP)	170
73	Contempo COLP 1001	GREATEST HITS LIVE AT THE TORCH (LP, sitting under a tree is first pressing/Second is a 'negative' b/w cover)	30/20
76	Epic EPC 81519	THE BEST OF MAJOR LANCE (LP)	30
78	Tamla Motown STML 12094	NOW ARRIVING (LP)	15

DICK LANCELOT & SEVEN KNIGHTS

66	RCA RCA 1502	Say Girl/Live Like A Lion	15

LANCERS

54	London HL 8002	Sweet Mama Tree Top Tall/Were You Ever Mine To Lose (78)	8
54	London HL 8108	Live And Let Live/I Should Have Never Let You Go (78)	8
54	London HL 8027	Stop Chasin' Me Baby/Peggy O'Neil (78 rpm = £12)	60
54	London HL 8079	So High, So Low, So Wide/It's You, It's You I Love (78 rpm = £12)	60
54	Vogue Coral Q 2038	Mister Sandman/The Little White Light (78 rpm = £10)	25
54	Vogue Coral Q 72062	Timberjack/C-r-a-z-y Music	20
55	Vogue Coral Q 72081	Get Out Of The Car (as Lancers & Georgie Auld)/Close Your Eyes	20
55	Vogue Coral Q 72081	Get Out Of The Car (as Lancers & Georgie Auld)/Close Your Eyes (78)	10
55	Vogue Coral Q 72100	Jo-Ann/The Bonnie Banks Of Loch Lomon'	10
56	Vogue Coral Q 72128	Alphabet Rock/Rock Around The Island (78 rpm = £20)	40
56	Vogue Coral Q 72157	Little Fool/A Man Is As Good As His Word (78 rpm = £12)	10
56	Vogue Coral Q 72183	The First Travelling Saleslady/Free	5
57	Vogue Coral Q 72220	Never Leave Me/I Came Back To Say I'm Sorry (78 rpm = £6)	5
57	Vogue Coral Q 72254	It Happened In Monterey/Ramona/Freckled-Face Sara Jane	5
57	Vogue Coral Q 72282	Charm Bracelet/And It Don't Feel Bad (78 rpm = £10)	10
58	Coral Q 72300	The Stroll/Don't Go Near The Water (78 rpm = £15)	8
60	Coral Q 72398	Joey, Joey, Joey/JOHNNY DESMOND: The Most Happy Fella	5
61	Warner Bros WB 39	Young In Love/Lonesome Town	5
55	London REP 1027	PRESENTING THE LANCERS (EP)	40
54	London H-APB 1029	OH SWEET MAMA (10" LP)	50
61	London HA-P 2307	CONCERT IN CONTRASTS (LP)	15

ELSA LANCHESTER

58	Vogue VA 160126	SONGS FOR A SMOKE-FILLED ROOM (LP, with Charles Laughton)	20
59	Vogue VA 160139	SONGS FOR A SHUTTERED PARLOUR (LP, with Charles Laughton)	20

BILLY LAND

62	Oriole CB 1750	I Go Walking/You're Too Much	12

HAROLD LAND

58	Contemporary LAC 12178	HAROLD IN THE LAND OF JAZZ (LP)	15

BOB LANDER & SPOTNICKS

62	Oriole CB 1784	Midnight Special/My Old Kentucky Home	12

(see also Spotnicks)

MINT VALUE

BILL & BRETT LANDIS
59	Parlophone R 4516	Since You've Gone/Bright Eyes (78 rpm = £12)	1
59	Parlophone R 4551	By You, By You/Forgive Me	1
59	Parlophone R 4570	Baby Talk/Love Me True	1

JERRY LANDIS
62	Oriole CB 1930	Carlos Dominquez/He Was My Brother	3

(see also Paul Simon)

JOYA LANDIS
68	Trojan TR 620	Kansas City/Out The Light	1
69	Trojan TR 641	Moonlight Lover/I Love You True	1

(see also Jay & Joya, Hugh Roy)

HOAGY LANDS
67	Stateside SS 2030	The Next In Line/Please Don't Talk About Me When I'm Gone (DJ copy = £300)	25
68	Stateside SS 2085	I'm Yours/Only You	2
72	Action ACT 4605	Why Didn't You Let Me Know/Do You Know What Life Is All About	2
75	UK USA 13	Friends And Lovers Don't Go Together/True Love At Last	3
75	UK USA 14	The Next In Line/I'm Yours	1

NEIL LANDSTRUMM
95	Mosquito MSQ 02	PASCAL EP (12", custom sleeve)	2

(see also Blue Arsed Fly)

DES(MOND) LANE
56	Decca F 10821	Penny-Whistle Rock/Penny-Whistle Polka	1
57	Decca F 10847	Rock Mister Piper/Plymouth Rock	1
59	Top Rank JAR 203	Moonbird/The Clanger March (as Des Lane Orchestra, with John Barry)	1
59	Top Rank JAR 203	Moonbird/The Clanger March (as Des Lane Orchestra, with John Barry) (78)	1
68	Pye 7N 17546	Sadie/No More Wild Oats (as Des Lane)	1

(see also Cyril Stapleton, John Barry)

GARY LANE & GARRISONS
61	Fontana H 338	Start Walking Boy/How Wrong Can You Be	1
62	Fontana 267221 TF	I'm A Lucky Boy/A Love Like You	1

LOIS LANE
67	RCA RCA 1570	One Little Voice/Sing To Me	1
68	Mercury MF 1042	Punky's Dilemma/Lazy Summer Day	1
69	Mercury MF 1092	Brontasaurus Named Bert/Windmills Of Your Mind	1
69	Mercury MF 1115	Lovin' Time/Winds Of Heaven	1
70	Philips BF 1829	Putting My Baby To Sleep/Far From The Madding Crowd	1
70	DJM DJS 2280	Day By Day/Cloud Of Blue	1
68	Mercury SMCL 20125	LOIS LANE (LP)	2

(see also Caravelles)

MICKEY LEE LANE
64	Stateside SS 354	Shaggy Dog/Oo Oo	1
65	Stateside SS 456	Hey Sah-Lo-Ney/Of Yesterday (DJ copy = £150)	7

PENNY LANE
68	Columbia DB 8377	Loving Or Losing You/Deep Down Inside	1
68	CBS 3718	The Boy Who Never Grew Up/I'm Going Back	1
70	CBS 4749	Bouzouki/Make Up Or Break Up	1
70	CBS 4905	Heartbreak House/He's Got A Hold Of My Heart	1
70	CBS 5311	Rock Me In The Cradle (Of Your Loving Arms)/I'm Free	1

RONNIE LANE & SLIM CHANCE
73	GM GMS 011	How Come/Tell Everyone/Done This One Before (p/s)	1
77	Polydor 2058 944	Street In The City/Annie (with Pete Townshend)	1
77	Polydor 2058 944	Street In The City/Annie (12", with Pete Townshend)	1
79	Gem GEMS 12	Kuschty Rye/You're So Right (p/s)	1
74	GM GMS 1024	ANYMORE FOR ANYMORE (LP)	2
74	GM GMS 024	The Poacher/Bye & Bye (Gonna See The King)	1
74	GM GMS 033	Roll on Babe/Anymore For Anymore	1
74	Island WIP 6216	What Went Down (That Night With You)/Lovely	1
75	Island WIP 6229	Brother Can You Spare A Dime/Ain't No Lady	1
76	Island WIP 6258	Don't Try And Change My Mind/Well, well, Hello (The Party)	1
80	GEM GEMS 19	One Step/Lad's Got Money	1
74	GM GMS 1024	ANYMORE FOR ANYMORE (LP)	2
75	Island ILPS 9321	RONNIE LANE AND SLIM CHANCE (LP)	2
75	Island ILPS 9366	ONE FOR THE ROAD (LP)	1
76	Atlantic K 50308	MAHONEY'S LAST STAND (LP, with Ron Wood, soundtrack)	2
77	Polydor 2442 147	ROUGH MIX (LP, with Pete Townshend)	1
80	Gem GEMLP 107	SEE ME (LP, with insert)	1
88	Thunderbolt THBL 067P	MAHONEY'S LAST STAND (LP, reissue, picture disc)	1

(see also Small Faces, Faces, Pete Townshend & Ronnie Lane)

ROSEMARY LANE
60	Philips PB 1041	Down By The River/My First Love Letter	1
61	Philips BF 1127	Lyin' Kisses/The Nightingale Who Sang Off Key	1
61	Philips BF 1172	Who Does He Think He Is/What Is The Age	1
63	Oriole CB 1871	Like You Should/Baby Please Be Kind	1

TONY LANE & DELTONES
64	Sabre SA-45-5	It's Great/Now She's Mine	1

LANE BROTHERS
60	London HLR 9150	Mimi/Two Dozen And A Half	1

LANE SISTERS
61	Columbia DB 4671	Peek A Boo Moon/Birmingham Rag	1

DON LANG (& HIS "FRANTIC" FIVE)

56	HMV 7M 354	Four Brothers/I Want You To Be My Baby (solo)	30
56	HMV 7M 381	Rock Around The Island/Jumpin' To Conclusions (solo)	30
56	HMV 7M 416	Rock And Roll Blues/Stop The World I Wanna Get Off (solo) (78 rpm = £8)	30
56	HMV POP 260	Sweet Sue — Just You/Lazy Latin (solo) (78 rpm = £10)	20
57	HMV POP 289	Rock Around The Cookhouse/Rock Mister Piper (78 rpm = £12)	35
57	HMV POP 335	Rock-A-Billy/Come Go With Me (B-side with Skifflers) (78 rpm = £12)	30
57	HMV POP 350	School Day (Ring! Ring!) Goes The Bell)/Six-Five Special (78 rpm = £12)	30
57	HMV POP 382	White Silver Sands/Again 'N' Again 'N' Again	15
57	HMV POP 414	Red Planet Rock/Texas Tambourine (78 rpm = £14)	35
58	HMV POP 434	Ramshackle Daddy/6-5 Hand Jive (78 rpm = £12)	25
58	HMV POP 465	Tequila/Junior Hand Jive (78 rpm = £15)	25
58	HMV POP 488	Witch Doctor/Cool Baby Cool	15
58	HMV POP 510	Hey Daddy!/The Bird On My Head (78 rpm = £15)	15
58	HMV POP 547	Queen Of The Hop/La-Do-Da-Da (solo) (78 rpm = £20)	15
59	HMV POP 585	Wiggle Wiggle/(You Were Only) Teasin' (solo) (78 rpm = £25)	15
59	HMV POP 623	Percy Green/Phineas McCoy (solo) (78 rpm = £30)	15
59	HMV POP 649	A Hoot An' A Holler/See You Friday (78 rpm = £35)	12
59	HMV POP 682	Reveille Rock/Frankie And Johnny	15
60	HMV POP 714	Sink The Bismarck!/They Call Him Cliff (solo)	28
60	HMV POP 805	Time Machine/Don't Open That Door	15
62	Decca F 11483	Wicked Women/Play Money (as Don Lang & Boulder Rollers)	12
57	HMV 7EG 8208	ROCK 'N' ROLL (EP)	100
57	HMV DLP 1151	SKIFFLE SPECIAL (LP, 10", by Don Lang & His Skiffle Group)	120
58	HMV DLP 1179	INTRODUCING THE HAND JIVE (LP, 10")	120
62	Ace Of Clubs ACL 1111	TWENTY TOP-TWENTY TWISTS (LP)	20

(see also Gordon Langhorn)

EDDIE LANG & LONNIE JOHNSON

67	Parlophone PMC 7019	BLUE GUITARS (LP)	40
70	Parlophone PMC 7106	BLUE GUITARS VOLUME 2 (LP)	30

(see also Blind Willie Dunn's Gin Bottle Four)

K.D. LANG

87	Sire W 8465	Rose Garden/High Time For A Detour (unissued in U.K.)	
88	Sire W 7841	Sugar Moon/Honky Tonk Medley (p/s)	25
88	Sire W 7841T	Sugar Moon/Honky Tonk Medley/I'm Down To My Last Cigarette (12", p/s)	50
88	Sire W 7697	Our Day Will Come/Three Cigarettes In An Ashtray (live) (p/s)	15
88	Sire W 7697T	Our Day Will Come/Three Cigarettes In An Ashtray (live)/Johnny Get Angry (live) (12", p/s)	50
90	Warner Brothers W 9535	Ridin' The Rails (with Take Six)/DARLENE LOVE: Mr Fix-It (some with p/s)	20/15
92	Sire W 0100	Constant Craving (Edit)/Barefoot (Rhythmic Version) (p/s)	5
92	Sire W 0100T	Constant Craving (Edit)/Barefoot (Rhythmic Version)/Season Of Hollow Soul (12", p/s)	10
92	Sire W 0100CD	Constant Craving (Edit)/Barefoot (Rhythmic Version)/Season Of Hollow Soul (CD)	15

RAY LANG & JAMAICAN ROOM ORCHESTRA

57	Brunswick 05683	Last Train (Biddi-Biddi Bum-Bum)/Keetch (Hey! Bernice) (78 rpm = £10)	10

STEVIE LANGE

81	RCA RCA 152	Remember My Name/I Don't Want To Know (1st issue, p/s)	8
81	RCA LIM 1	Remember My Name/I Don't Want To Know (2nd issue, p/s)	6

LANGFORDS

60s	Torino TSP 341	Send Me An Angel/Candy (label credits to Langford Boys, some with p/s)	10/6

GORDON LANGHORN

55	Decca F 10591	Give A Fool A Chance/Don't Stay Away Too Long	20

(see also Don Lang, Cyril Stapleton)

JERRY LANGLEY

65	Parlophone R 5325	Little Grey Man/Bitter Sweets	5
67	CBS 2935	Joanna Jones/How Long	5

(see also Langleys)

MARY LANGLEY

67	CBS 2862	Stay In My World/Summer Love	5
67	CBS 3032	It Always Rains On Sunday/All My Life Is You	5

(see also Perpetual Langley, Langleys)

PERPETUAL LANGLEY

66	Planet PLF 110	We Wanna Stay Home/So Sad	30
66	Planet PLF 115	Surrender/Two By Two	30

(see also Mary Langley, Langleys)

LANGLEYS

64	Fontana TF 483	Snakes And Ladders/I Wander Everywhere	5
65	Fontana TF 544	Green Island/You Know I Love You	5

(see also Jerry Langley, Mary Langley, Perpetual Langley)

(HUW) LLOYD LANGTON (GROUP)

83	Flicknife FLS 021	Wind Of Change/Outside The Law (as Lloyd Langton Group, p/s)	5
83	Flicknife SHARP 015	OUTSIDE THE LAW (LP, 1,000 only with bonus 7": "Working Time"/"I See You" [FREE 001], as Huw Lloyd Langton)	15/12
86	Gas GAS 4014	LIKE AN ARROW (THROUGH THE HEART) (LP)	12

(see also Hawkwind, Widowmaker)

PHIL LANGTON TRIO

60s	Holyground	PHIL LANGTON TRIO (LP)	18

CYNTHIA LANIGAN

57	Parlophone R 4316	Silent Lips/Jamie Boy (78)	12

LESTER LANIN & HIS ORCHESTRA
| 62 | Columbia 33SX 1442 | TWISTIN' IN HIGH SOCIETY! (LP) | 12 |

SNOOKY LANSON
50	London L 555	The Old Master Painter/Did You Ever See A Dream Walking? (78)	10
50	London L 682	Roses/Where Are You Gonna Be When The Moon Shines (78)	10
56	London HLD 8223	It's Almost Tomorrow/Why Don't You Write (78 rpm = £12)	110
56	London HLD 8236	Stop (Let Me Off The Bus)/Last Minute Love (78 rpm = £20)	200
56	London HLD 8249	Seven Days/Tippity Top (78 rpm = £20)	200
56	London HL 7005	Seven Days/Tippity Top (export issue)	85

(see also Teresa Brewer)

MARIO LANZA
53	HMV 7R 128	The First Noel/Silent Night	5
53	HMV 7R 129	Questa O Quello (Verdi)/Recondita Armonia (Puccini)	5
53	HMV 7R 130	Be My Love/The Bayou Lullaby	5
53	HMV 7R 131	Serenade (Troselli)/Serenade (Drigo)	5
53	HMV 7R 139	Because/For You Alone	5
53	HMV 7R 144	Because You're Mine/The Song Angels Sing	5
53	HMV 7R 145	Lee-Ah-Loo/You Do Something To Me	5
53	HMV 7R 146	Mi Batte Il Cor ... O Paradiso!/Mamma, Quel Vino E Generoso	5
53	HMV 7R 147	O Come, All Ye Faithful/Oh! Little Town Of Bethlehem	5
53	HMV 7R 157	Granada/Lolita	5
53	HMV 7R 168	M'Appari Tutt' Amor (Flotow)/Libiamo, Libiamo Ne' Lieti Calici (B-side with Elaine Malbin)	5
53	HMV 7R 178	Valencia/Besame Mucho	5
60	RCA RCA 1155	O Come All Ye Faithful/Silent Night, Holy Night (78)	8
60	RCA RCA 1166	Because You're Mine/The Donkey Serenade (78 rpm = £8)	5
53	HMV ALP 1071	THE GREAT CARUSO (LP, soundtrack)	12
54	HMV ALP 1202	OPERATIC ARIAS (LP)	12
55	HMV BLP 1071	SONGS OF ROMANCE (10" LP)	12
56	HMV ALP 1365	SERENADE (LP, soundtrack)	12
57	HMV BLP 1091	LANZA ON BROADWAY (10" LP)	12
57	HMV BLP 1094	THE TOUCH OF YOUR HAND (10" LP)	12
57	RCA RB 16002	IN A CAVALCADE OF SHOW TUNES (LP)	12
58	RCA RA 13001	THE SEVEN HILLS OF ROME (10" LP)	12
59	RCA RB 16085	SINGS A KISS AND OTHER LOVE SONGS (LP)	12
59	RCA RB 16113	THE STUDENT PRINCE (LP, soundtrack)	12
59	RCA RB 16158	FOR THE FIRST TIME (LP, soundtrack)	12
59	RCA RB 16167	LANZA ON BROADWAY (LP, soundtrack)	12
59	RCA RB 16171/SB 2054	LANZA SINGS CHRISTMAS CAROLS (LP, stereo)	12

LARKS
| 64 | Pye International 7N 25284 | The Jerk/Forget Me (DJ copy = £70) | 40 |

SAM LARNER
| 61 | Folkways FG 3507 | NOW IS THE TIME FOR FISHING (LP) | 15 |
| 74 | Topic 12T 244 | A GARLAND FOR SAM (LP, blue label) | 15 |

LARO
| 60s | Kalypso XX 21 | Jamaican Referendum Calypso/Wrong Impressions Of A Soldier | 8 |

WINSTON LARO
| 70 | Downtown DT 461 | Goodnight My Love/BOYSIE: I Don't Want To Be Hurt | 5 |

JULIUS LA ROSA
55	London HL 8154	Mobile/Pass It On (78 rpm = £10)	30
55	London HLA 8170	Domani/Mama Rosa	30
55	London HLA 8193	Suddenly There's A Valley/Everytime I Kiss Carrie	30
56	HMV 7M 384	Lipstick And Candy And Rubber-Sole Shoe/Winter In New England (78 rpm = £8)	10
56	London HLA 8272	No Other Love/Rosanne (78 rpm = £8)	20
56	London HLA 8353	Jingle Bells (Campanelle)/Jingle Dingle (78 rpm = £8)	18
58	RCA RCA 1063	Torero/Milano (78 rpm = £6)	8
54	London RE-P 1005	SINGS (EP)	20
57	London HA-A 2031	JULIUS LA ROSA (LP)	35

LARRY'S ALL STARS
| 71 | Ackee ACK 130 | Pre-Fight/The Prayer | 5 |

(see also Larry Lawrence, Delroy Wilson, Hugh Roy, Sensations)

LARRY (Marshall) & ALVIN
68	Studio One SO 2065	Nanny Goat/Smell You Crep.	15
68	Studio One SO 2067	Can't You Understand/Hush Up	40
69	Studio One SO 2080	Lonely Room (No One To Give Me Love)/You Mean To Me	30
69	Coxsone CS 7081	Love Got Me/BOB ANDY: Lady With The Bright Light (both sides actually by Glen [Brown] & Dave [Barker])	25

(see also Larry Marshall, Sound Dimension, Vincent Gordon)

LARRY & JOHNNY
| 65 | Outasite 45 501 | Beatle Time Parts 1 & 2 (99 copies only) | 130 |

(see also Larry Williams & Johnny 'Guitar' Watson)

LARRY & TOMMY
| 68 | Polydor 56741 | You've Gotta Bend A Little/Yo-Yo | 10 |

JACK LARSON
| 61 | Top Rank JAR 573 | I Love The Way She Laughs/The Hammer Bell Song | 8 |

LA'S
87	Go! Discs GOLAS 1	Way Out/Endless (p/s)	18
87	Go! Discs GOLAS 112	Way Out/Knock Me Down/Endless (12", red & silver p/s)	20
87	Go! Discs GOLAR 112	Way Out/Knock Me Down/Endless/Liberty Ship (Demo)/Freedom Song (Demo) (12", blue & silver stickered p/s listing 4 tracks)	20

87	Go! Discs GOLAR 112	Way Out/Knock Me Down/Endless/Liberty Ship (Demo)/Freedom Song (Demo) (12", blue & silver stickered p/s listing 5 tracks)	20
88	Go! Discs GOLAS 2	There She Goes/Come In Come Out (red p/s)	15
88	Go! Discs LASEP 2	There She Goes/Way Out/Who Knows/Come In Come Out (EP, blue p/s, 5,000 only)	22
88	Go! Discs GOLAS 212	There She Goes/Come In Come Out/Who Knows/ Man I'm Only Human (12", red sleeve)	18
88	Go! Discs LASCD 2	There She Goes/Come In Come Out/Who Knows/Man I'm Only Human (CD)	15
89	Go! Discs GOLAS 3	Timeless Melody/Clean Prophet (p/s, unissued; 10 test pressings only)	60+
89	Go! Discs LASEP 3	Timeless Melody (10", unissued)	
89	Go! Discs LASDJ 312	Timeless Melody/Clean Prophet/All By Myself/Rider Yer Camel (12", promo, 500 only)	50+
89	Go! Discs GOLAS 4	Timeless Melody/Clean Prophet (blue p/s)	7
89	Go! Discs GOLAS 412	Timeless Melody/Clean Prophet/Knock Me Down/Over (12", purple p/s)	10
89	Go! Discs LASCD 4	Timeless Melody/Clean Prophet/Knock Me Down/Over (CD, orange card p/s)	15
90	Go! Discs GOLAB 5	There She Goes/Freedom Song (numbered box set with badge & 3 stickers)	10
90	Go! Discs GOLAS 5	There She Goes/Freedom Song (reissue, white sleeve)	7
90	Go! Discs GOLAS 512	There She Goes/Freedom Song/All By Myself (12", reissue, white p/s)	10
90	Go! Discs LASCD 5	There She Goes/Freedom Song/All By Myself (CD)	15
91	Go! Discs GOLAS 6	Feelin'/Doledrum (p/s)	5
91	Go! Discs GOLAB 6	Feelin'/IOU (Alternate Version)/Feelin' (Alternate Version)/Doledrum (numbered box set with badge & 3 stickers)	15
90	Go! Discs LASCD 1	THE LA'S SOUND SAMPLER (CD, promo, 1,000 only)	12
91	Go! Discs 828 202-1	THE LA'S (LP)	30

(see also Cast)

COUNT LASHER
| 60s | Kalypso 100 AB | Calypso Cha Cha Cha/Perseverance | 5 |
| 60s | Kalypso 105 AB | Slide Mongoose/Miss Constance | 5 |

LASSIES & RAY CHARLES SINGERS
| 56 | Brunswick 05571 | Sleepy Head/This I Offer You | 5 |

LASSIES
| 63/4 | Brunswick 89408 | This I Offer You (1-sided demo) | 8 |

LAST BANDITS
| 80s | Solid ROK 722 | The Angels Are Calling/The Dalkey Rake (p/s) | 5 |

(see also Swell Maps, Nikki Sudden)

LAST CHANT
| 81 | Chicken Jazz JAZZ 4 | Run Of The Dove/Strength Alone/Tradition (p/s) | 8 |

(see also Waterboys)

LAST EXIT
| 75 | Wudwink WUD 01 | Whispering Voices/Evensong (no p/s) | 35 |
| 75 | Wudwink WUD.C.101 | FIRST FROM LAST EXIT (cassette only, pink card insert, sold at gigs, only 3 copies known to exist) | 100 |

(see also Newcastle Big Band, Police, Sting)

LAST FLIGHT
| 81 | Heavy Metal HEAVY 5 | Dance To The Music/I'm Ready (p/s) | 8 |

LAST MAN IN EUROPE
| 85 | Cocteau CO 22 | A Certain Bridge/TV Addict (p/s) | 15 |

LAST POETS
| 72 | Douglas DGL 69012 | THIS IS MADNESS (LP) | 20 |

LAST RESORT
| 78 | Red Meat RMRS 01 | Having Fun?/F.U.2 (die-cut printed paper sleeve) | 20 |

LAST RESORT
81	own label	Violence In Our Minds/Help Hostage/Soul Boys (cassette; 4-track issue)	20
81	own label	Violence In Our Minds/Help Hostage (cassette; 3-track issue)	20
82	Last Resort LR 1	SKINHEAD ANTHEMS (LP, red vinyl; also white, blue & black vinyl)	20/20/20/40

LAST RITES
| 83 | Flicknife FLS 219 | We Don't Care/Step Down (p/s) | 5 |
| 84 | Essential 004 | FASCISM MEANS WAR (EP, gatefold p/s) | 5 |

LAST STAND
| 81 | Silly Symbol SJP 825 | Just A Number/Caviare (p/s) | 15 |

LAST STRAW
| 78 | Solent SS 049 | Oh Lady/Fly By Night (p/s) | 50 |

LAST WORD
| 74 | Polydor 2066 429 | Keep On Bumping Before You Run Out Of Gas/Funky And Some | 8 |

LAST WORDS
79	Rough Trade RT 022	Animal World/No Music In The World Today (p/s)	8
79	Remand REMAND 2	Todays Kidz/There's Something Wrong (p/s)	6
81	Armageddon ARM 2	THE LAST WORDS (LP)	12

BILL LASWELL
| 88 | Venture VE12 | HEAR NO EVIL (LP) | 25 |

LATE SHOW
| 78 | Decca F 13777 | Drop Dead/Ain't Gonna Stamp On His Face (p/s) | 15 |
| 79 | Decca F 13822 | BRISTOL STOMP EP (p/s) | 10 |

MINT VALUE £

YUSEF LATEEF
58	Esquire 32-069	THE SOUNDS OF YUSEF (LP)	30
58	Columbia Clef 33CX 10124	BEFORE DAWN (LP)	25
72	Atlantic K 40359	GENTLE GIANT (LP)	12
73	Prestige PR 24007	YUSEF LATEEF (LP)	15
74	Atlantic K 50041	PART OF THE SEARCH (LP)	12
74	Milestone ML 47009	THE MANY FACES OF YUSEF LATEEF (LP)	12

GENE LATTER
66	Decca F 12364	Just A Minute Or Two/Dream Lover	12
66	Decca F 12397	Mother's Little Helper/Please Come Back To Me Again	15
67	CBS 202483	Something Inside Me Died/Don't Go	8
67	CBS 202655	Always/A Woman Called Sorrow	8
67	CBS 2843	A Little Piece Of Leather/Funny Face Girl (DJ copy = £50)	30
67	CBS 2986	With A Child's Heart/Ways	15
68	Direction 58-3245	A Tribute To Otis/Bring Your Love Home	8
68	Spark SRL 1015	My Life Ain't Easy/Angie (as Gene Latter & Detours)	6
69	Spark SRL 1022	Sign On The Dotted Line/I Love You	15
69	Spark SRL 1031	The Old Iron Bell/Holding A Dream	6
69	Parlophone R 5800	Help Me Judy, Help Me/On The Highway	7
69	Parlophone R 5815	Tiger Bay/We Can Make Out	7
70	Parlophone R 5853	Someday You'll Need My Love/Come On Home	6
71	Parlophone R 5896	Catch My Soul/Happiness	10
71	Parlophone R 5913	Sing A Song Of Freedom/Too Busy Thinking About My Baby	10

(see also Detours)

STANLEY LAUDAN
58	Oriole CB 1434	Two Guitars/Blue Shawl (78 rpm = £8)	10

THE LAUGHING APPLE
81	Autonomy AUT 001	HA HA HEE HEE (EP)	8
81	Autonomy AUT 002	Participate!/Wouldn't You? (foldover p/s)	6
82	Essential ESS 001	Precious Feeling/Celebration (p/s)	8
83	Creation Artefact LYN 12903	Wouldn't You?/THE PASTELS: I Wonder Why! (live) (33rpm flexidisc, initially free with The Legend! 7" "'73 In '83" [CRE 001])	8/5

(see also Biff Bang Pow!, Revolving Paint Dream)

LAUGHING GAS
70	RCA RCA 2006	All Shapes And Sizes/Opus No. 1	8

CYNDI LAUPER
84	Portrait WA 4290	Time After Time/I'll Kiss You (picture disc)	5
84	Portrait WA 4620	She Bop/Witness (Cyndi-shaped picture disc)	5

(see also Blue Angel)

LAUREL (Aitken) & OWEN (Gray)
62	Blue Beat BB 149	She's Going To Napoli/Have Mercy Mr Percy	10

(see also Laurel Aitken, Owen Gray)

LAURELS
68	RCA Victor RCA 1741	Sunshine Thursday/Threepence A Tune	6
69	RCA Victor RCA 1836	Making It Groovy/Rainmaker	10

ROD LAUREN
59	RCA RCA 1165	If I Had A Girl/No Wonder (78 rpm = £10)	10

ZACK LAURENCE (ORCHESTRA)
61	Parlophone R 4802	Teenage Concerto/Saratoga	5
63	Parlophone R 5000	Tempo Seven/Sleeve Shaker	5
66	HMV 7EG 8968	BEATLE CONCERTO (EP)	8

JOHN LAURENZ
55	London HL 8138	Goodbye, Stranger, Goodbye/Red Roses (78 rpm = £10)	30
65	Decca F 12147	99 Times Out Of 100/I Can Feel It	5

LAURIE
66	Decca F 12347	He Understands Me/Fools Never Learn	10
66	Decca F 12424	I Love Onions/I Want Him	5

CY LAURIE JAZZ BAND
55	Esquire EP 29	CY LAURIE BAND (EP)	20
55	Esquire EP 39	CY LAURIE BAND (EP)	10
56	Esquire EP 89	CY LAURIE BAND (EP)	10
56	Esquire EP 120	CY LAURIE BAND (EP)	20
56	Tempo EXA 32	JAZZ IN DENMARK (EP)	12
57	Esquire EP 124	CY LAURIE BAND (EP)	15
57	Esquire EP 140	CY PLAYS LIL (EP)	10
57	Melodisc EPM 7-71	CY LAURIE'S JAZZ BAND (EP)	10
58	Esquire EP 200	YOU'RE NEXT (EP)	10
59	Esquire EP 210	CY LAURIE BAND (EP)	15
60	Esquire EP 234	CY LAURIE BAND (EP)	15
58	Parlophone GEP 8710	JUNGLE JAZZ (EP)	10
60s	Storyville SEP 395	CY LAURIE BAND VOL. 5 (EP)	8
55	Esquire 20-037	CY LAURIE JAZZ BAND (10" LP)	20
50s	Esquire 32-008	CY LAURIE JAZZ BAND (LP)	20

LINDA LAURIE
59	London HL 8807	Ambrose/Ooh, What A Lover (78 rpm = £8)	12
60	Top Rank JAR 277	Stay With Me/All Winter Long	10

LAURIE SISTERS
60	MGM MGM 1083	Don't Forget (To Sign Your Name With A Kiss)/I Surrender Dear	7
61	MGM MGM 1128	Live It Up/Lonesome And Sorry	7

MISS LAVELL
65	Vocalion VP 9236	Everybody's Got Somebody/The Best Part Of Me	30

DALIAH LAVI
70	Pye Intl. 7N 25533	Won't You Join Me/Karriere	5
71	Pye Intl. 7N 25582	I'm Leaving/Here's To You	6
70	Pye Intl. NSPL 28141	DALIAH LAVI (LP)	15

JUNE LAVERICK
60	Oriole CB 1537	Stop/JOHNNY WEBB: Concertino (78 rpm = £12)	10

(see also Dickie Henderson & June Laverick, Johnny Webb)

ROGER La VERN & MICRONS
63	Decca F 11791	Christmas Stocking/Reindeer Ride	45
75	SRT SRTS/CUS/042	Sing-A-Long Piano Party Parts 1 & 2 (maxi-single, p/s)	8

(see also Tornados)

BETTY LAVETTE
67	Stateside SS 2015	I Feel Good All Over/Only Your Love Can Save Me (DJ copy = £75)	50
68	Pama PM 748	Only Your Love Can Save Me/I Feel Good All Over (reissue)	30
70	Polydor 56786	He Made A Woman Out Of Me/Nearer To You	10
72	Mojo 2092 030	Let Me Down Easy/I Feel Good All Over/What I Don't Know Won't Hurt Me	10
73	Atlantic K 10299	Your Turn To Cry/Soul Tambourine	10
78	Atlantic K 11198	Doin' The Best I Can Parts 1 & 2	6

AZIE LAWRENCE
59	Mezzotone ME 7001/7002	West Indians In England/Jump Up	7
59	Mezzotone ME 7004	Love In Every Land/No Dice	7
60	Starlite ST45 022	West Indians In England/Jump Up (with Carib Serenaders)	8
61	Starlite ST45 041	No Dice/Love In Every Land	8
61	Melodisc M 1563	Jamaica Blues/Come Rumble & Tumble With Me	7
61	Melodisc M 1572	You Didn't Want To Know	6
61	Blue Beat BB 71	So Far Apart/Palms Of Victory (with Melobeats)	8
64	Blue Beat BB 222	Pempelem/Lovers Understand	8

DIANE LAWRENCE
67	Doctor Bird DB 1075	I Won't Hang Around Like A Hound Dog/Read It Over	28
68	Jolly JY 005	Treat Me Nice/I'll Be Loving You	12

EDDIE LAWRENCE
59	Coral Q 72361	The Salesman's Philosopher/Mother Philosopher (78 rpm = £8)	5

ELLIOTT LAWRENCE BAND
51	Vogue V 9024	Sixty-Minute Man/Quick (78)	10
58	Vogue LAE 12057	PLAYS GERRY MULLIGAN ARRANGEMENTS (LP)	12

GENE LAWRENCE
67	Jump Up JU 505	Longest Day Meringue/Bachelor Boy	6
67	Jump Up JU 510	Meringue Triniana/Devil Woman	6

LARRY LAWRENCE (Jamaica)
63	Island WI 091	Garden Of Eden/DERRICK MORGAN: Sendin' This Message	12

(see also Larry's Allstars, McBean Scott & Champions)

LARRY LAWRENCE (U.S.)
59	Pye International 7N 25042	Goofin' Off/Bongo Boogie (as Larry Lawrence & Band Of Gold) (78 rpm = £10)	10
60	Ember EMB S 106	Squad Car Theme/Jug-A-Roo (with Beatniks, some in art p/s)	15/10

LEE LAWRENCE (& CORONETS)
53	Decca F 10177	Crying In The Chapel/To Live My Life With You (78)	10
54	Decca F 10285	The Little Mustard Seed/My Love For You	15
54	Decca F 10367	The Story Of Tina/For You My Love	15
54	Decca F 10408	The Things I Didn't Do/You Still Mean The Same To Me	12
55	Decca F 10422	My Own True Love (Tara's Theme)/Beware Now!	12
55	Decca F 10438	Lights Of Paris/A Love Like Ours	10
55	Decca F 10485	Wedding Bells And Silver Horse-Shoes/Will You Be Mine Alone?	15
55	Columbia SCM 5175	Beyond The Stars/Give Me Your Word	15
55	Columbia SCM 5181	My World Stood Still/Don't Worry	15
55	Columbia SCM 5190	More Than A Millionaire/Overnight	15
55	Columbia SCM 5201	Suddenly There's A Valley/Mi Muchacha (Little Girl)	15
56	Columbia SCM 5228	Young And Foolish/Don't Tell Me Not To Love You	15
56	Columbia SCM 5254	We Believe In Love/Welcome To My Heart	15
56	Columbia SCM 5283	Come Back, My Love/Valley Valparaiso	15
56	Columbia DB 3830	From The Candy Store On The Corner/High Upon A Mountain	18
57	Columbia DB 3855	Rock 'n' Roll Opera/Don't Nobody Move (78 rpm = £12)	25
57	Columbia DB 3885	Your Love Is My Love/By You, By You, By You	10
57	Columbia DB 3922	Sold To The Man With The Broken Heart/Chapel Of The Roses	10
57	Columbia DB 3981	His Servant/Lonely Ballerina	8
59	Top Rank JAR 175	The Man I Could Be/Be My Love	7
58	Columbia SEG 7780	LEE LAWRENCE (EP)	22
53	Decca LF 1132	PRESENTING LEE LAWRENCE (10" LP)	35

STEVE LAWRENCE
53	Parlophone MSP 6038	Say It Isn't True/This Night (Madalena) (as Steve & Bernie Lawrence)	25
54	Parlophone MSP 6080	Remember Me (You Taught Me To Love)/Too Little Time	25
54	Parlophone MSP 6106	You Can't Hold A Memory In Your Arms/King For A Day	25
55	Vogue Coral Q 72114	Open Up The Gates Of Mercy/My Impression Of Janie	15
56	Vogue Coral Q 72133	Speedo/The Chicken And The Hawk (78 rpm = £15)	22
57	Vogue Coral Q 72228	The Banana Boat Song/If You Would Say You're Mine	20
57	Vogue Coral Q 72243	Party Doll/Pum-Pa-Lum (The Bad Donkey) (78 rpm = £10)	20
57	Vogue Coral Q 72264	Fabulous/Can't Wait For The Summer (with Dick Jacobs Band) (78 rpm = £8)	20
57	Vogue Coral Q 72281	Fraulein/Blue Rememberin' You (78 rpm = £8)	15
57	Vogue Coral Q 72286	Never Mind/Long Before I Knew You	15

MINT VALUE £

58	Coral Q 72304	Geisha Girl/I Don't Know	6
58	Coral Q 72335	Those Nights At The Round Table (with Guinevere)/Stranger In Mexico	6
58	Coral Q 72335	Those Nights At The Round Table (with Guinevere)/Stranger In Mexico (78)	8
59	Coral Q 72353	These Things Are Free/I Only Have Eyes For You (78 rpm = £20)	7
59	HMV POP 604	Only Love Me (Angelina)/Loving Is A Way Of Living	6
60	HMV POP 689	Pretty Blue Eyes/You're Nearer (78 rpm = £50)	10
60	HMV POP 726	Footsteps/You Don't Know (78 rpm = £55)	10
60	Top Rank JAR 416	Say It Isn't True/My Shawl	6
60	HMV POP 763	Why, Why, Why/You're Everything Wonderful	5
60	London HLT 9166	Girls, Girls, Girls/Little Boy Blue	12
60	HMV POP 795	Going Steady/Come Back, Silly Girl	5
61	HMV POP 914	In Time/Oh How You Lied	5
61	HMV POP 950	Somewhere Along The Way/While There's Still Time	5
59	Coral FEP 2010	HERE'S STEVE LAWRENCE NO. 1 (EP)	20
59	Coral FEP 2012	HERE'S STEVE LAWRENCE NO. 2 (EP)	20
60	HMV CLP 1326	SWING SOFTLY WITH ME (LP)	25
60	Top Rank BUY 033	STEVE LAWRENCE (LP)	22
61	HMV CLP 1462	THE STEVE LAWRENCE SOUND (also stereo CSD 1374) (LP)	20/22
62	HMV CLP 1504	PORTRAIT OF MY LOVE (also stereo CSD 1404) (LP)	20/22
63	CBS (S)BPG 62088	COME WALTZ WITH ME (LP)	12
63	United Artists (S)ULP 1022	LAWRENCE GOES LATIN (LP)	12

STEVE LAWRENCE & EYDIE GORMÉ

55	Vogue Coral Q 72044	Make Yourself Comfortable/EYDIE GORME: Chain Reaction	10
55	Vogue Coral Q 72085	Besame Mucho/Take A Deep Breath	10
61	London HLT 9290	The Facts Of Life/I'm A Girl, You're A Boy	8
63	CBS AAG 163	I Want To Stay Here/Ain't Love (some in p/s)	10/5
59	Vogue Coral FEP 2017	STEVE LAWRENCE AND EYDIE GORME (EP)	15
63	CBS AGG 20035	STEVE AND EYDIE (EP)	10
60	HMV CLP 1372/CSD 1310	STEVE AND EYDIE — WE GOT US (LP)	15
61	HMV CLP 1404/CSD 1329	THE GOLDEN HITS (LP)	15
61	HMV CLP 1463	COZY (LP)	15
62	HMV CLP 1517	COME SING WITH ME (LP)	15
	(see also Eydie Gormé)		

BILLY (M.) LAWRIE

69	Polydor 56363	Roll Over Beethoven/Come Back Joanna (as Billy M. Lawrie)	25
73	RCA RCA 2439	Rock And Roller/Shalee Shala	6
73	RCA SF 8395	SHIP IMAGINATION (LP)	25

ELOISE LAWS

69	CBS 4056	I'd Do It All Again/To Know Him Is To Love Him	6
70	CBS 4990	You Make Me Feel Like Someone/The Only Boy In My Life	6
77	Invictus INV 5247	Love Goes Deeper Than That/Camouflage	15

RONNIE LAWS

75	Blue Note BNLA 452	PRESSURE SENSITIVE (LP)	15
76	Blue Note UAG 20007	FEVER (LP)	15
77	Blue Note UAG 30079	FRIENDS AND STRANGERS (LP)	12
78	Blue Note UAG 30204	FLAME (LP)	12

LAWSON-HAGGART ROCKIN' BAND

59	Brunswick OE 9451	BOPPING AT THE HOP (EP)	72
53	Brunswick LA 8576	JELLY ROLL'S JAZZ (10" LP)	15
53	Brunswick LA 8580	BLUES ON THE RIVER (10" LP)	18
53	Brunswick LA 8593	KING OLIVER'S JAZZ (10" LP)	15
54	Brunswick LA 8635	RAGTIME JAMBOREE (10" LP)	15
54	Brunswick LA 8639	WINDY CITY JAZZ (10" LP)	15
55	Brunswick LA 8703	SOUTH OF THE MASON-DIXON LINE (10" LP)	15
59	Brunswick STA 3010	BOPPING AT THE HOP (LP)	95

JULIET LAWSON

72	Sovereign SOV 111	Only A Week Away/Weeds In The Yard	7
72	Sovereign SVNA 7257	BOO (LP)	35
	(see also Trees)		

SHIRLEY LAWSON

| 68 | Soul City SC 108 | The Star/One More Chance | 150 |

JOHN LAWTON (featuring Roger Glover & Guests)

| 75 | Purple PUR 128 | Little Chalk Blue/RONNIE DIO: Sitting In A Dream | 10 |
| | (see also Roger Glover, Ronnie Dio, Deep Purple, Uriah Heep, Lucifer's Friend) | | |

LOU LAWTON

| 67 | Ember EMB S 232 | Doin' The Philly Dog/I Am Searching | 30 |
| 68 | Speciality SPE 1005 | I'm Just A Fool/Wrapped In A Dream | 30 |

LAXTON & OLIVER

| 69 | Blue Cat BS 168 | Wickeder/Stay In My Arms | 20 |

LAY-A-BAHTS

| 60 | Parlophone R 4641 | Fings Ain't Wot They Used T'be/Layin' Abaht/The Ceiling | 5 |

OSSIE LAYNE

| 65 | R&B MRB 5006 | Come Back/Never Answer That 'Phone | 30 |

EDDIE LAYTON

| 58 | Mercury 7MT 221 | Over The Waves/Bright Lights Over Brussels | 5 |
| 59 | Mercury AMT 1064 | Duck Walk/Doodles | 10 |

TEDDY LAYTON JAZZ BAND

| 58 | Parlophone R 4411 | Down By The Riverside/Wooden Joe's Weary Blues | 5 |

KEN LAZ(A)RUS (& CREW)

65	Island WI 220	Funny (as Ken Lazrus & Byron Lee Orchestra)/	
		BYRON LEE ORCHESTRA: Walk Like A Dragon	15
70	London HLJ 10301	Monkey Man/Bongo Nyah	5
71	Explosion EX 2056	Girl/TOMORROW'S CHILDREN: Sister Big Stuff	8
72	Explosion EX 2064	Hail The Man/Where Do I Go	7
72	London HLH 10379	Hail The Man/Where I Go	6
70	London HA-J 8412	REGGAE SCORCHER (LP, unissued)	
70	London LGJ/ZGJ 102	REGGAE SCORCHER (LP)	12
70	London ZGJ 107	REGGAE — GREATEST HITS VOL. 1 (LP)	12
70	London ZGJ 108	REGGAE — GREATEST HITS VOL. 2 (LP)	12

LAZY LATINS

67	Morgan MR 110 P	LAZY LATIN (LP)	12

LAZY SMOKE

80s	Heyoka	CORRIDOR OF FACES (LP, reissue of U.S. LP)	15

LCD SOUNDSYSTEM

02	Output OPRDFA004	Give It Up/Tired (promo, p/s 1000 only)	6
05	DFA DFAEMI2138LP	LCD SOUNDSYSTEM (2xLP)	12

BARBARA LEA

56	London HB-U 1058	A WOMAN IN LOVE (10" LP)	22
56	Esquire 32/043	NOBODY ELSE BUT ME (LP)	15
57	Esquire 32/063	IN LOVE (LP)	15

JIMMY LEA

85	Trojan KANE 001	Citizen Kane/Poland (p/s)	15

(see also Slade)

LEADBELLY (HUDDIE LEDBETTER)

78s

50	Capitol CL 13282	Eagle Rock Rag/Backwater Blues	12
51	Melodisc 1140	How Long/Good Morning Blues	20
51	Melodisc 1151	Goodnight Irene/Ain't You Glad	20
51	Melodisc 1187	On A Monday/John Henry	20
54	Jazz Collector L 108	New Black Snake Moan/Fore Day Worry Blues	20
55	Jazz Collector L 124	Pig Meat Papa/Becky Beem	20
55	HMV MH 190	Alabama Bound/Pick A Bale Of Cotton	30

EPs

56	Melodisc EPM7 63	HOW LONG BLUES	22
58	Melodisc EPM7 77	LEADBELLY	22
58	Melodisc EPM7 82	SEE SEE RIDER	22
59	Melodisc EPM7 87	PARTY PLAYS AND SONGS	20
59	RCA RCX 146	ROCK ISLAND LINE	15
61	Capitol EAP1 1821	HUDDIE LEDBETTER'S BEST NO. 1	15
61	Capitol EAP4 1821	HUDDIE LEDBETTER'S BEST NO. 2	15
61	Capitol EAP1 20111	LEADBELLY	15
61	Storyville SEP 337	LEADBELLY	15
62	Storyville SEP 387	STORYVILLE BLUES ANTHOLOGY VOL. 7	15

LPs

53	Capitol LC 6597	LEADBELLY SINGS CLASSICS IN JAZZ (10")	38
57	Melodisc MLP 511	LEADBELLY VOL. 1 (10", green & silver labels)	28
57	Melodisc MLP 512	LEADBELLY VOL. 2 (10", green & silver labels)	28
58	Melodisc MLP 515	LEADBELLY VOL. 3 (10", green & silver labels)	28
58	Melodisc MLP 517	PLAYS PARTY SONGS (10", green & silver labels)	28
58	Melodisc MLP 12-107	THE SAGA OF LEADBELLY (green & silver or blue & black labels)	25
59	Melodisc MLP 12-113	LEADBELLY'S LAST SESSIONS VOLUME 2 PART 1	25
59	Melodisc MLP 12-114	LEADBELLY'S LAST SESSIONS VOLUME 2 PART 2	25
62	Storyville SLP 124	A DEMON OF A MAN — BLUES ANTHOLOGY	22
63	Storyville SLP 139	LEADBELLY 2 — T.B. BLUES	20
63	Capitol T 1821	HIS GUITAR, HIS VOICE, HIS PIANO: HUDDIE LEDBETTER'S BEST	15
63	RCA Victor RD 7567	GOOD MORNING BLUES	20
65	Verve (S)VLP 5002	TAKE THIS HAMMER	20
65	Society SOC 994	LEADBELLY PLAYS AND SINGS	20
66	Elektra EKL 301/2	THE LIBRARY OF CONGRESS RECORDINGS (3-LP)	25
67	Verve (S)VLP 5011	KEEP YOUR HANDS OFF HER	20
69	Xtra XTRA 1046	LEADBELLY SINGS FOLK SONGS	22
69	Xtra XTRA 1126	SHOUT ON	22
69	Storyville 616 003	IN THE EVENING WHEN THE SUN GOES DOWN	15
69	Storyville 616 004	GOODNIGHT IRENE	15
70	CBS 64103	LEADBELLY	15
72	Ember CW 132	LEADBELLY	12
70s	Xtra XTRAD 1017	THE LEADBELLY BOX SET (2-LP)	18

LEADBELLY & BLIND LEMON JEFFERSON

61	Jazz Collector JEL 124	THE MALE BLUES VOLUME 8 (EP)	18

(see also Blind Lemon Jefferson)

HARRY LEADER BAND

65	Parlophone R 5386	Dragon Fly/Rush Hour	5

LEADERBEATS

60	Top Rank JAR 405	Dance, Dance, Dance/Washington Square	12

LEADERS (Jamaica)

68	Amalgamated AMG 804	Tit For Tat (actually by Lynn Taitt & Jets)/MARVETTS: You Take Too Long	22

(see also Pioneers, Stranger Cole, Versatiles)

MINT VALUE £

LEADERS (U.K.)
65	Fontana TF 602	Night People/Love Will Find A Way	10

LEADING FIGURES
67	Deram DML/SML 1006	OSCILLATION 67! (LP)	22
67	Ace Of Clubs SCL 1225	SOUND AND MOVEMENT (LP)	35

(see also Jon Lord, Deep Purple)

LEAF HOUND
71	Decca SKL-R 5094	GROWERS OF MUSHROOM (LP)	550

(see also Brunning Sunflower Blues Band, Black Cat Bones, Atomic Rooster, Cactus, Headbangers)

LEAGUE OF GENTLEMEN
65	Columbia DB 7666	Each Little Falling Tear/And I Do Now	70
66	Planet PLF 109	How Can You Tell/How Do They Know (with Planet company sleeve)	70
80	EG/Virgin EGEDS 1	Heptaparaparshinokh/Marriagemuzic	6

(see also Giles Giles & Fripp, Brain)

LEAH
73	GM GMS 10	Arise Sir Henry/Uptight Basil	5

(see also Pete Dello, Red Herring)

JOE LEAHY (ORCHESTRA)
55	Parlophone MSP 6149	Desiree/Milano	5
55	Parlophone MSP 6168	Green Fire/Secretly Mine	5
57	London HBZ 1072	LOVELY LADY (10" LP)	12

MIKE LEANDER ORCHESTRA
69	MCA MUPS 383	MIGRATION (LP)	12

VICKY LEANDROS
72	Philips 6000 025	I Am/Love Tell Me Where Is Your Home	8

(see also Vicky)

BOB LEAPER
65	Pye 7N 15700	High Wire (Theme From 'Danger Man')/The Lost World	40
64	Decca LK 4639	BIG BAND, BEATLE SONGS (LP)	20

LEAPERS CREEPERS SLEEPERS
66	Island WI 275	Precious Words/Ba Boo	25

KEVIN 'KING' LEAR
67	Polydor 56203	Count Me Out/Pretty Woman	25
68	Page One POF 087	Power Of Love/Mr. Pearly	25
68	Page One POF 109	Cry Me A River/Shoe Shine Sam	20
69	Page One POF 132	The Snake/Man In The Funnies	30

ERNEST LEARDEE
50	Felstead SDL 86015	CARNIVAL IN MARTINIQUE (10" LP)	15

TIMOTHY LEARY MEETS THE GRID
90	Evolution EVO 1	Origins Of Dance (Electronic Future Mix)/(Hi-Tec Pagan Mix) (12")	10

(see also the Grid)

LEATHERCOATED MINDS
67	Fontana (S)TL 5412	A TRIP DOWN THE SUNSET STRIP (LP)	65

(see also J.J. Cale)

LEATHERHEAD
74	Philips 6006 371	Gimme Your Money Please/Epitaph (die-cut 'Leatherhead' sleeve)	15

LEATHER NUN
79	Industrial IR 0006	Slow Death (EP)	10
84	Subterranean SUB 40	Prime Mover/F.F.A. (p/s)	5
79	Industrial IRC 27	THE LEATHER NUN AT THE SCALA CINEMA (cassette)	12

BILL LEATHERWOOD
60	Top Rank JAR 506	The Long Walk/My Foolish Heart	5

LEA VALLEY SKIFFLE GROUP
57	Esquire 10-508	Streamline Train/Railroad Bill (78)	25
58	Esquire 10-518	I'm Gonna Walk And Talk With Jesus/Oh Mary, Don't You Weep (78)	25
58	Esquire EP 163	LEA VALLEY SKIFFLE GROUP (EP)	65

LEAVES
66	Fontana TF 713	Hey Joe/Funny Little World	45

OTIS LEAVILL(E)
70	Atlantic 2091 015	I Love You/I Need You	15
70	Atlantic 2091 035	Love Uprising/Glad I Met You	10
71	Atlantic 2091 160	There's Nothing Better/I'm So Jealous	10

LE CHEILE
78	Inchecronin INC 7423	AIRIS (LP)	12
78	Inchecronin INC 7424	LORD MAYO (LP)	12

LECUONDA CUBAN BOYS
55	Columbia 33S 1075	BENEATH THE CUBAN MOON (10" LP)	15

JOHN LEDINGHAM
68	Pye 7N 17488	Love Is A Toy/Thank You Mrs. Gilbert	6

(see also Jonathan Kelly)

LED ZEPPELIN
SINGLES
69	Atlantic 584 268	Good Times, Bad Times (unissued, 1-sided acetates only) 400
69	Atlantic 584 269	Communication Breakdown/Good Times, Bad Times (unissued, promo only) . . 500
69	Atlantic 584 309	Whole Lotta Love (Edit)/Livin' Lovin' Maid (She's A Woman) (withdrawn, large centre hole) 500
69	Atlantic 584 309	Whole Lotta Love (Edit)/Livin' Lovin' Maid (She's A Woman) (withdrawn, solid centre with small centre hole, 1 copy known) 1,500
73	Atlantic K 10296	D'Yer Mak'er/Over The Hills And Far Away (unreleased, promo only) 250
75	Swan Song DC 1	Trampled Underfoot/Black Country Woman (freebie, die-cut title sleeve) 20
75	Swan Song DC 1	Trampled Underfoot/Black Country Woman (test pressing, white labels) 350
75	Swan Song SSK 19403	Trampled Underfoot/Black Country Woman (push mispressed cat. no.) 100
79	Swan Song SSK 19421	Wearing And Tearing/Darlene (cancelled Knebworth 45, existence unconfirmed)
90	Atlantic LZ 2	Stairway To Heaven/Immigrant Song/Whole Lotta Love/ Good Times Bad Times (10", p/s, promo only) 25
90	Atlantic LZ 2	Stairway To Heaven/Immigrant Song/Whole Lotta Love/ Good Times Bad Times (10", test pressing, white labels) 350
90	Atlantic CD LZ 1	Stairway To Heaven/Immigrant Song/Whole Lotta Love/ Good Times Bad Times (CD, promo only, in Zeppelin-design long box) 30
90	Atlantic LZ 3	Stairway To Heaven/Whole Lotta Love (with memo, 150 copies only, promo). . . 100
90	Atlantic LZ 3 LC	Stairway To Heaven/Whole Lotta Love (jukebox single, push-out centre) 30
97	Atlantic PRCD 923	BBC SESSIONS SAMPLER: The Girl I Love/Whole Lotta Love/ Communication Breakdown (CD, promo only) 20
97	Atlantic AT 0031CD	Whole Lotta Love (Edit)/Baby Come On Home/Travelling Riverside Blues (CD, numbered digipak) 10
97	Atlantic AT 0031LC	Whole Lotta Love (Edit)/Whole Lotta Love (Edit) (jukebox issue, with pushout centre) 12
03	Warner Vision PR 03945	What Is And What Should Never Be/In My Time Of Dying/Rock And Roll (DVD, promo sampler) 20

ALBUMS
69	Atlantic 588 171	LED ZEPPELIN (LP, 1st pressing, red/maroon label, turquoise sleeve lettering, "Superhype" publishing credit) 500
69	Atlantic 588 171	LED ZEPPELIN (LP, 2nd pressing, red/maroon label, orange sleeve lettering, "Warner Bros" or "Superhype" publishing credit) . . . . 40+/25+
69	Atlantic 588 198	LED ZEPPELIN II (LP, 1st pressing, red/maroon label, with "Living Loving Wreck" miscredit, light brown gatefold sleeve with blue-green edge) . . . . 100+
69	Atlantic 588 198	LED ZEPPELIN II (LP, 1st pressing, red/maroon label, with "The Lemon Song" credit, light brown gatefold sleeve with blue-green edge) . . . . 30+
70	Atlantic 588 198	LED ZEPPELIN II (LP, light brown sleeve, 2nd pressing, credits "Killing Floor" instead of "The Lemon Song" on label) 20
70	Atlantic Deluxe 2401 002	LED ZEPPELIN III (LP, red/maroon label, gatefold rotating-wheel sleeve, "Do What Thou Wilt" in run-off) 35
71	Atlantic Deluxe 2401 012	LED ZEPPELIN IV (FOUR SYMBOLS) (LP, red/maroon label). 25
73	Atlantic K 50014	HOUSES OF THE HOLY (LP; original pressings have an 'obi' around the sleeve) 12
76	Swan Song SSK 59402	PRESENCE (LP, shrinkwrapped gatefold sleeve) 12
78	Atlantic K 50008	LED ZEPPELIN IV (FOUR SYMBOLS) (LP, lilac vinyl reissue) 40
79	Swan Song SSK 59410 A-F	IN THROUGH THE OUT DOOR (LP, 6 different covers with inner sleeves; set labelled 'A' to F, each in individual paper outer; available separately with paper outer £12 each). 250
88	Atlantic K 50008/C 88 1-4	FOUR SYMBOLS (LP, HMV 'Classic Collection' box set, with booklet, no'd) 25
88	Atlantic 250008/C 88 1-4	FOUR SYMBOLS (CD, HMV 'Classic Collection' box set, with booklet, no'd) 25
90	Atlantic ZEP 1	REMASTERS (3-LP, triple gatefold sleeve) 18
90	Atlantic 7567 82144-1	LED ZEPPELIN (5-LP, box set). 50
97	Atlantic 7567 83061-1	BBC SESSIONS (4-LP, box set) 50
99	Atlantic 7567 83268-1	EARLY DAYS – THE BEST OF LED ZEPPELIN VOLUME 1 (LP). 15
00	Atlantic 7567 83278-1	LATTER DAYS – THE BEST OF LED ZEPPELIN VOLUME 2 (LP). 15

(see also Jimmy Page, Robert Plant, John Paul Jones, Listen, Family Dogg, Ian Whitcomb, P.J. Proby, Lord Sutch, Yardbirds)

ALVIN LEE
74	Chrysalis CHS 2020	The World Is Changing/Riffin' (with Myron Le Fevre) 6
73	Chrysalis CHR 1054	ON THE ROAD TO FREEDOM (LP, with Myron Le Fevre) 15
75	Chrysalis CHR 1094	PUMP IRON! (LP) 12
78	Chrysalis CHR 1190	LET IT ROCK (LP) 12

(see also Ten Years After)

ARTHUR LEE
72	A&M AMLS 64356	VINDICATOR (LP) 12

(see also Love)

BENNY LEE (& KEN-TONES)
56	Parlophone MSP 6214	Love Plays The Strings Of My Banjo (with Ken-Tones)/Born To Sing The Blues . . 6
56	Parlophone MSP 6252	Sweet Heartaches/How Long Has This Been Going On? 6
56	Parlophone R 4245	Rock 'N' Rollin' Santa Claus/Life Was Made For Livin' (with Ken-Tones) 25
57	Nestles NR 08	Last Train To San Fernando (as Benny Lee & Jackson Boys) (1-sided card flexi, 78rpm) 6

(see also Ken-Tones)

BRENDA LEE
78s
56	Brunswick 05628	I'm Gonna Lasso Santa Claus/Christy Christmas (as Little Brenda Lee) 85
57	Brunswick 05685	Dynamite/Love You Til I Die 60
57	Brunswick 05720	Ain't That Love/One Teenager To Another 60
58	Brunswick 05755	Ring-A-My-Phone/Little Jonah (Rock On Your Little Steel Guitar) 75
59	Brunswick 05780	Bill Bailey, Won't You Please Come Home/Hummin' The Blues Over You 75
60	Brunswick 05819	Sweet Nuthin's/Weep No More My Baby 160

Brenda LEE

SINGLES

56	Brunswick 05628	I'm Gonna Lasso Santa Claus/Christy Christmas (triangular centre)	200
57	Brunswick 05685	Dynamite/Love You Til I Die (with Anita Kerr Singers, triangular centre)	140
57	Brunswick 05720	Ain't That Love/One Teenager To Another (w/ Anita Kerr Singers, tri-centre)	125
58	Brunswick 05755	Ring-A-My-Phone/Little Jonah (Rock On Your Little Steel Guitar) (tri-centre)	140
58	Decca BM 31186	Fairyland/One Step At A Time (export issue, triangular centre)	75
59	Brunswick 05780	Bill Bailey, Won't You Please Come Home/Hummin' The Blues Over You (triangular or round centre)	20/15
60	Brunswick 05819	Sweet Nuthin's/Weep No More My Baby (round centre)	25
60	Brunswick 05823	Let's Jump The Broomstick/Rock-A-Bye Baby Blues	10
60	Brunswick 05833	I'm Sorry/That's All You Gotta Do	5
60	Brunswick 05839	I Want To Be Wanted/Just A Little	5
61	Brunswick 05847	Emotions/I'm Learning About Love	5
61	Brunswick 05849	You Can Depend On Me/It's Never Too Late	5
61	Brunswick 05854	Dum Dum/Eventually	6
61	Brunswick 05860	Fool No. 1/Anybody But Me	5
62	Brunswick 05864	Break It To Me Gently/So Deep	5
62	Brunswick 05867	Speak To Me Pretty/Lover, Come Back To Me	5
62	Brunswick 05871	Here Comes That Feeling/Everybody Loves Me But You	5
62	Brunswick 05876	It Started All Over Again/Heart In Hand	5
62	Brunswick 05880	Rockin' Around The Christmas Tree/Papa Noel	10
63	Brunswick 05882	All Alone Am I/Save All Your Lovin' For Me	5
63	Brunswick 05886	Losing You/He's So Heavenly	6
63	Brunswick 05891	I Wonder/My Whole World Is Falling Down	6
63	Brunswick 05896	Sweet Impossible You/The Grass Is Greener	6
64	Brunswick 05899	As Usual/Lonely Lonely Lonely Me	5
64	Brunswick 05903	Think/The Waiting Game	5
64	Brunswick 05911	Alone With You/My Dreams	5
64	Brunswick 05915	Is It True/What'd I Say	10
64	Brunswick 05921	Christmas Will Be Just Another Lonely Day/Winter Wonderland	6
65	Brunswick 05927	Thanks A Lot/Just Behind The Rainbow	6
65	Brunswick 05933	Truly, Truly True/I Still Miss Someone	6
65	Brunswick 05936	Too Many Rivers/No One	6
65	Brunswick 05943	Rusty Bells/If You Don't	5
66	Brunswick 05957	Too Little Time/Time And Time Again	30
66	Brunswick 05963	Ain't Gonna Cry No More/It Takes One To Know One	10
66	Brunswick 05967	Coming On Strong/You Keep Coming Back To Me	15
67	Brunswick 05970	Ride, Ride, Ride/Lonely People Do Foolish Things	5
67	Brunswick 05976	Where's The Melody?/Born To Be By Your Side	20
68	Decca AD 1003	That's All Right/Baby, Won't You Please Come Home (export issue)	15
68	MCA MU 1001	That's All Right/Baby, Won't You Please Come Home	5
68	MCA MU 1021	Let's Jump The Broomstick/All Alone Am I	5

EPs

59	Brunswick OE 9462	ROCK THE BOP (green p/s & tri-centre or blue p/s & round centre)	95/65
62	Brunswick OE 9482	PRETEND	40
62	Brunswick OE 9488	SPEAK TO ME PRETTY	40
63	Brunswick OE 9492	ALL ALONE AM I	30
64	Brunswick OE 9499	BRENDA LEE'S TRIBUTE TO AL JOLSON	30
65	Brunswick OE 9510	FOUR FROM '64	30

LPs

59	Brunswick LAT 8319	GRANDMA WHAT GREAT SONGS YOU SANG	50
60	Brunswick LAT 8347	MISS DYNAMITE	40
61	Brunswick LAT 8360	THIS IS BRENDA	40
61	Brunswick LAT 8376	EMOTIONS (also stereo STA 3044)	22
61	Brunswick LAT 8383	ALL THE WAY (also stereo STA 3048)	22
61	Brunswick LAT 8396	SINCERELY (also stereo STA 3056)	22
62	Brunswick LAT/STA 8516	BRENDA, THAT'S ALL (mono/stereo)	22
62	Brunswick LAT/STA 8530	ALL ALONE AM I (mono/stereo)	15
63	Ace of Hearts AH 59	LOVE YOU	25
63	Brunswick LAT/STA 8548	LET ME SING (mono/stereo)	18
64	Brunswick LAT/STA 8576	BY REQUEST (mono/stereo)	18
64	Brunswick LAT/STA 8590	MERRY CHRISTMAS FROM BRENDA (mono/stereo)	25
65	Brunswick LAT/STA 8603	TOP TEEN HITS (mono/stereo)	18
65	Brunswick LAT 8614	THE VERSATILE BRENDA LEE	18
65	Brunswick LAT/STA 8622	TOO MANY RIVERS (mono/stereo)	18
66	Brunswick LAT/STA 8649	BYE BYE BLUES (mono/stereo)	18
67	Brunswick LAT/STA 8672	COMING ON STRONG (mono/stereo)	18
68	MCA MUP(S) 306	REFLECTIONS IN BLUE	15
68	MCA MUP(S) 321	CALL ME	15
68	MCA MUP(S) 322	THE GOOD LIFE	12
68	MCA MUP(S) 330	MERRY CHRISTMAS FROM BRENDA LEE	12
68	MCA MUP(S) 332	BRENDA AND PETE — FOR THE FIRST TIME (with Pete Fountain)	12
70	MCA MUP(S) 396	JOHNNY ONE TIME	12

BUNNY LEE ALLSTARS

70	Pama PM 803	Annie Pama/Mr Magoo	12
71	Smash SMA 2304	Stanley (Parts 1 & 2) (as Bunnie Lee Allstars)	10

(see also Lloyd Charmers, Sonny Binns & Rudies, Copy Cats, John Holt, Lloyd & Doreen, Delroy Wilson)

BYRON LEE & DRAGONAIR(E)S

60	Blue Beat B 2	Dumplin's/Kissin' Gal (vocal: Buddy Davidson) (white label, blue print)	12
60	Blue Beat BB 2	Dumplin's/Kissin' Gal (vocal: Buddy Davidson) (2nd pressing, blue label, silver print)	8
61	Blue Beat BB 28	Mash! Mr. Lee/Help Me Forget (vocal: Keith Lyn)	10
61	Starlite ST45 045	Joy Ride/Over The Rainbow	12
64	Parlophone R 5124	River Bank/Musical Communion	8
64	Parlophone R 5125	Sour Apples/Hanging Up My Heart	8

MINT VALUE £

64	Parlophone R 5140	Sammy Dead/Say Bye Bye (both actually by Eric Morris with Byron Lee)	8
64	Parlophone R 5177	Beautiful Garden/Too Late	8
64	Parlophone R 5182	Come Back/Jamaica Ska	8
64	MGM MGM 1256	Night Train From Jamaica/Ska Dee Wah (with Danny Davis)	10
66	Doctor Bird DB 1003	Sloopy/Gold Finger	10
67	Pyramid PYR 6015	Sloopy/Gold Finger (reissue)	8
68	Trojan TR 624	Soul Limbo/The Whistling Song	5
68	Trojan TR 631	Mr Walker/Sunset Jump Up	5
69	Major Minor MM 615	Every Day Will Be Like A Holiday/Oh What A Feeling	5
70	Trojan TR 7731	Squeeze Up (Parts 1 & 2)	10
70	Trojan TR 7736	Birth Control/Love At First Sight	6
70	Trojan TR 7747	Bond In Bliss/Musical Scorcher	6
70	Trojan TR 7761	Julianne/We Five	5
70	Duke DU 39	Elizabethan Reggae/Soul Serenade	5
70	Duke DU 91	Cashbox/WINSTON WRIGHT: Strolling Thru' The Park	6
71	Dynamic DYN 405	Hitching A Ride/Hitching A Ride Version	6
71	Dynamic DYN 409	My Sweet Lord/Shock Attack	7
71	Dynamic DYN 414	Way Back Home/Version	6
72	Dynamic DYN 435	Make It Reggae/DENNIS ALCAPONE: Go Johnny Go	8
73	Dragon DRA 1008	In The Mood/Black On	6
65	Atlantic AET 6014	SKA TIME (EP, as Byron Lee Ska Kings)	35
64	Island ILP 905	CARIBBEAN JOY RIDE (LP)	40
69	Trojan TTL 5	ROCKSTEADY EXPLOSION (LP)	40
69	Major Minor Sm 53	BYRON LEE & THE DRAGONAIRES (LP)	15
70	Trojan TRLS 18	REGGAE WITH BYRON LEE (LP)	12
70	Trojan TBL 110	REGGAE BLAST OFF (LP)	12
71	Trojan TRL 26	REGGAY SPLASHDOWN (LP)	12

(see also Mighty Avengers, Ken Lazarus, Hopeton Lewis, Danny Davis Orchestra, Good Guys, Neville Hinds, Hubcaps & Wheels, Mighty Sparrow, Blues Busters)

CHRISTOPHER LEE
74	Studio Two TWOA 5001	HAMMER PRESENTS DRACULA (LP, gatefold sleeve)	12
74	Studio Two TWOA Q4 5001	HAMMER PRESENTS DRACULA (LP, gatefold sleeve, quadrophonic)	15

C.P. LEE
80	New Hormones	RADIO SWEAT (cassette, with booklet & stickers in plastic 'radio' bag)	12

(see also Alberto Y Los Trios Paranoias)

CURTIS LEE
60	Top Rank JAR 317	With All My Heart (I Love You)/Pure Love	65
61	London HLX 9313	Pledge Of Love/Then I'll Know	25
61	London HLX 9397	Pretty Little Angel Eyes/Gee How I Wish You Were Here	25
61	London HLX 9445	Under The Moon Of Love/Beverly Jean	25
62	London HLX 9533	A Night At Daddy Gee's/Just Another Fool	22
67	CBS 2717	Get My Bag/Everybody's Going Wild (as Curtis Lee & K.C.P.s)	40
		(DJ copy = £70)	
72	Stateside SS 2208	Under The Moon Of Love/Beverly Jean (reissue)	6

DAVE LEE (& STAGGERLEES)
63	Decca F 11600	Take Four/Five To Four On	8
63	Oriole CB 1864	Dance Dance Dance/Love Me (as Dave Lee & Staggerlees)	8
63	Oriole CB 1907	Sweet & Lovely/Forever And Always (as Dave Lee & Staggerlees)	8
66	Fontana TF 723	Adam Adamant/Georgie's Theme (as Dave Lee & His Orchestra)	13

DAVE LEE
66	Colpix PXL 550	OUR MAN CRICHTON (LP, with Tubby Hayes)	90

(see also Tubby Hayes)

DAVID H. LEE
65	Pye 7N 15809	Heaven With No Angel	8
69	Morgan MR 1	Johnny's Eyes/You're The Only One	7

DEREK LEE
66	Parlophone R 5468	Girl/You've Done Something To My Heart	10

DICK LEE
53	Columbia SCM 5066	All I Want Is A Chance/The Show Is Ended	10
53	Columbia SCM 5078	I Thought You Might Be Lonely/Happy Bells	10
54	Columbia SCM 5094	Book/Stay In My Arms Cinderella	12

DICKIE/DICKEY LEE
59	MGM MGM 1013	A Penny A Kiss — A Penny A Hug/Bermuda (as Dick Lee)	10
62	Mercury AMT 1190	Patches/More Or Less	10
62	Mercury AMT 1196	I Saw Linda Yesterday/The Girl I Can't Forget	10
62	Mercury AMT 1200	Don't Wanna Think About Paula/Just A Friend	10
65	Stateside SS 433	Laurie (Strange Things Happen)/Party Doll (as Dickey Lee)	10
65	Stateside SS 464	The Girl From Peyton Place/A Girl I Used To Know (as Dickey Lee)	5

DINAH LEE
65	Aladdin WI 606	I'll Forgive You Then Forget You/Nitty Gritty	30
65	Aladdin WI 608	I Can't Believe What You Say/Pushin' A Good Thing Too Far	40

DON (TONY) LEE
68	Big Shot BI 504	It's Reggae Time (as Don Tony Lee)/ERROL DUNKLEY: The Clamp Is On	25
68	Doctor Bird DB 1106	Lee's Special (as Don Tony Lee)/LLOYD & GROOVERS: My Heart And Soul	25
68	Island WI 3160	It's Reggae Time (as D. Tony Lee)/ERROL DUNKLEY: The Clamp Is On	22
69	Unity UN 519	Peyton Place/Red Gal In The Ring (as Don Tony Lee)	12

EDNA LEE
68	President PT 175	I Really Think I'm Crying 'Cause I Love You/	
		Don't Let My Friends See What You Do	7

(Freddie) 'FINGERS' LEE (& UPPER HAND)

65	Fontana TF 619	The Friendly Undertaker/Little Bit More (as 'Fingers' Lee)	22
66	Fontana TF 655	I'm Gonna Buy Me A Dog/I Can't Drive (as 'Fingers' Lee)	20
66	Columbia DB 8002	Bossy Boss/Don't Run Away (as Fingers Lee & Upper Hand)	15

(see also At Last The 1958 Rock & Roll Show)

GEORGE LEE (& MUSIC DOCTORS)

69	Downtown DT 443	Talking Boss/Jungle Fever (solo)	8
70	J-Dan JDN 4407	Johnny Dollar/Tough Of Poison (with Music Doctors)	8

(see also Desmond Riley)

HUBERT LEE

73	Ackee ACK 504	I Love Verona/Version	5
73	Downtown DT 498	Something On Your Mind/IMPACT ALL STARS: Mind Version	8
73	Green Door GD 4050	High School Dance/PRINCE TONY'S ALL STARS: Version	5
74	Ackee ACK 524	Tonight Will You Still Love Me/IMPACT ALL STARS: Version	6

JACKIE LEE (U.K.)

55	Decca F 10550	I Was Wrong/For As Long As I Live	10
65	Decca F 12068	I Cry Alone/Cause I Love Him	10
65	Columbia DB 7685	Lonely Clown/Love Is Gone	10
66	Columbia DB 7860	I Know, Know, Know I'll Never Love/So Love Me	7
66	Columbia DB 8052	The Town I Live In/You Too	10
67	Decca F 12663	Born To Lose/Saying Goodbye	8
69	Pye 7N 17829	Love Is a Gamble/Something Borrowed, Something Blue	8
71	Pye PKL 5503	JACKIE'S JUNIOR CHOICE (LP)	15

(see also Jacky, Jackie Lee & Raindrops, Emma Rede)

JACKIE LEE & RAINDROPS (U.K.)

62	Oriole CB 1702	I Was The Last One To Know/There's No One In The Whole World	12
62	Oriole CB 1727	There Goes The Lucky One/I Built My Whole World Around You	15
62	Oriole CB 1757	Party Lights/Midnight	12
63	Oriole CB 1800	The End Of The World/Goodbye Is Such A Lonely Word	12
63	Philips BF 1283	Down Our Street/My Heart Is Your Heart (as Jackie & Raindrops)	15
64	Philips BF 1328	Here I Go Again/Come On Dream Come On (as Jackie & Raindrops)	12

(see also Jacky, Jackie Lee [U.K.], Raindrops [U.K.], Emma Rede)

JACKIE LEE (U.S.)

60	Top Rank JAR 286	Rancho/Like Sunset	10

JACKIE LEE (U.S.)

65	Fontana TF 646	The Duck/Let Your Conscience Be Your Guide	30
66	Jay Boy BOY 28	Would You Believe/You're Everything	10
68	London HLM 10233	The Duck/Dancing In The Street	10
70	Jay Boy BOY 26	Do The Temptation Walk/The Shotgun And The Duck	10
72	Jay Boy BOY 66	Oh! My Darlin'/Don't Be Ashamed (DJ copy = £30)	15
72	Jay Boy BOY 76	African Boo-Ga-Loo/Bring It Home	8
73	Contempo CR 5	The Duck (Parts 1 & 2)	5
85	Kent TOWN 107	Darkest Days/EDDIE BISHOP: Call Me	20
67	London HA-M 8336	THE DUCK (LP)	40
71	Joy JOYS 192	THE DUCK (LP, reissue)	20

(see also Bob & Earl, Earl Nelson, Jackie Lee & Delores Hall)

JACKIE LEE & DELORES HALL

69	B&C CB 105	Whether It's Right Or Wrong/Baby I'm Satisfied	10
72	Jay Boy BOY 52	Whether It's Right Or Wrong/Baby I'm Satisfied (reissue)	6

(see also Jackie Lee [U.S.], Delores Hall)

JAMIE LEE & ATLANTICS

63	Decca F 11571	In The Night/Little Girl In Blue	40

JIMMY LEE

61	Starlite ST45 059	All My Life/Chicago Jump	30

JOHN LEE'S GROUNDHOGS

(see under 'J')

JOHN LEE

72	Explosion EX 2060	Stagger Lee/Musical Version (both sides actually by John Holt)	5

JOHNNIE LEE

59	Pye 7N 15201	Echo/It's-A Me, It's-A Me, It's-A Me My Love (78 rpm = £7)	10
59	Pye 7N 15233	I'm Finally Free/I Fell (with The King's Men)	10
60	Fontana H 257	They're Wrong/Cindy Lou	8
60	Fontana H 280	Poetry In Motion/Let It Come True	10
61	Fontana H 306	Lonely Joe/Nobody	8
67	CBS 202591	Kiss Tomorrow Goodbye/Love No Longer Sounds	5
67	CBS 2802	I Forgot What It Was Like/Lonely Is The Willow	5
67	CBS 3112	Because You're Mine/I'll Not Forget	5

JULIA LEE (& HER BOYFRIENDS)

50	Capitol CL 13321	Nobody Knows You When You're Down And Out/Decent Woman Blues (78)	12
50	Capitol CL 13323	Cold Hearted Daddy/Snatch And Grab It (78)	12
51	Capitol LC 6535	PARTY TIME (10" LP, 2 different sleeves)	90

LAURA LEE (U.K.)

60	Triumph RGM 1030	Tell Tommy I Miss Him/I'm Sending Back Your Roses	50
62	Decca F 11513	Too Young To Be In Love/Brand New Heartbeat	15
68	Columbia DB 8495	Love In Every Room/Master Jack	12
71	Columbia DB 8770	Someone To Love Me/Look Left-Look Right	8

LAURA LEE (U.S.)

67	Chess CRS 8062	Dirty Man/It's Mighty Hard	10
68	Chess CRS 8070	As Long As I Got You/A Man With Some Backbone	10
72	Tamla Motown TMG 831	To Win Your Heart/So Will I (DJ copy = £30)	15
72	Hot Wax HWX 115	Rip Off/Two Lovely Pillows	8
73	Hot Wax HWX 118	Wedlock Is A Padlock/Since I Fell For You	8
73	Hot Wax HWX 119	You've Got The Love To Save Me/Crumbs Off The Table	15
74	Invictus INV 2654	I Need It Just As Bad As You/If I'm Good Enough To Love	8
71	Hot Wax SHW 5006	WOMEN'S LOVE RIGHTS (LP)	20
73	Hot Wax SHW 5009	TWO SIDES OF LAURA LEE (LP)	20

LEAPY LEE

65	Pye 7N 17001	It's All Happening/In The Meantime	5
66	Decca F 12369	King Of The Whole Wide World/Shake Hands (featuring the Kinks)	65
67	CBS 202550	The Man On The Flying Trapeze/My Mixed-Up Mind	5
68	Pye 7N 17619	It's All Happening/It's Great	5
69	MCA MK 5021	Good Morning/Teresa	6

LITTLE MR. LEE & CHEROKEES

66	Vocalion VP 9268	Young Lover/I Don't Want To Go	40

MANDY LEE

50s	Poydras 76	I'm A Harmony Baby/If Your Man Is Like My Man	5

MANDY LEE

69	Dandelion S 4494	Bottle Up And Go (Parts 1 & 2)	6

MICHELLE LEE

68	CBS 3350	L. David Sloan/Everybody Loves My Baby	6

MICKEY LEE

73	Smash SMA 2332	Hello My Little Queen/AUGUSTUS PABLO: African Queen	10

NICKIE LEE

69	Deep Soul DS 9103	And Black Is Beautiful/Faith Within	25

NORMA LEE

67	CBM CBM 002	Hurt/Rollin' On	6

PEGGY LEE

54	Brunswick 05286	Johnny Guitar/I Didn't Know What Time It Was	18
54	Brunswick 05345	Love, You Didn't Do Right By Me/Sisters	15
55	Brunswick 05360	Let Me Go, Lover/Bouquet Of Blues	15
55	Brunswick 05368	Straight Ahead/It Must Be So (with Mills Brothers)	12
55	Brunswick 05421	Baubles, Bangles And Beads/Summer Vacation	12
55	Brunswick 05435	I Belong To You/How Bitter, My Sweet	12
55	Brunswick 05461	Ooh That Kiss/Oh! No! (Please Don't Go)	12
55	Brunswick 05471	Sugar/What Can I Say After I Say I'm Sorry	12
55	Brunswick 05472	He Needs Me/Sing A Rainbow	15
55	Brunswick 05482	He's A Tramp (with Pound Hounds)/The Siamese Cat Song (with Oliver Wallace)	18
55	Brunswick 05483	Bella Notte/La La Lu	12

(The above 45s were originally issued with gold label lettering; silver reissues are worth two-thirds these values.)

56	Brunswick 05549	Three Cheers For Mister Magoo/Mister Magoo Does The Cha Cha Cha (with Jim Backus)	12
56	Brunswick 05554	The Come Back/You've Got To See Mama Every Night	7
56	Brunswick 05593	That's All Right Honey/Love You So	7
56	Brunswick 05625	We Laughed At Love/They Can't Take That Away From Me	7
57	Brunswick 05671	Mr. Wonderful/The Gypsy With Fire In His Shoes	9
57	Brunswick 05714	I Don't Know Enough About You/Where Flamingos Fly	8
57	Capitol CL 14741	Baby, Baby Wait For Me/Every Night (78 rpm = £8)	8
57	Capitol CL 14795	Uninvited Dreams/Listen To The Rockin' Bird (78 rpm = £8)	8
58	Capitol CL 14902	Fever/You Don't Know (78 rpm = £18)	8
58	Capitol CL 14955	Light Of Love/Sweetheart (78 rpm = £15)	8
59	Capitol CL 14984	Alright, Okay, You Win/My Man	5
59	Brunswick 05798	It Ain't Necessarily So/Swing Low, Sweet Chariot (78 rpm = £12)	5
59	Capitol CL 15025	Hallelujah, I Love Him So/I'm Lookin' Out The Window	5
59	Capitol CL 15058	You Came A Long Way From St. Louis/I Lost My Sugar In Salt Lake City (with George Shearing Quintet)	5
59	Capitol CL 15103	You Deserve/Things Are Swingin'	8
61	Capitol CL 15184	Till There Was You/Bucket Of Tears	5
61	Capitol CL 15214	Mañana/The Folks Who Live On The Hill	5
65	Capitol CL 15376	Pass Me By/That's What It Takes	7
65	Capitol CL 15413	I Go To Sleep/Stop Living In The Past	9
69	Capitol CL 15614	Is That All There Is?/I'm A Woman (2nd pressing with different A-side)	18

EPs

55	Brunswick OE 9153	PETE KELLY'S BLUES NO. 1	10
55	Brunswick OE 9154	PETE KELLY'S BLUES NO. 2	10
56	Brunswick OE 9282	PRESENTING PEGGY LEE	10
58	Brunswick OE 9400	SEA SHELLS PT. 1	10
58	Brunswick OE 9401	SEA SHELLS PT. 2	10
58	Philips BBE 12172	PEGGY WITH BENNY (with Benny Goodman)	10
59	Capitol EAP1 1052	FEVER	15
59	Capitol EAP1 1213	ALRIGHT OKAY YOU WIN	10
63	Capitol EAP1 1857	I'M A WOMAN	10

LPs

53	Capitol LC 6584	CAPITOL PRESENTS PEGGY LEE (10")	25
53	Brunswick LA 8629	BLACK COFFEE (10")	20
55	Brunswick LA 8717	SONGS IN AN INTIMATE STYLE (10")	20
55	Brunswick LAT 8078	PETE KELLY'S BLUES (with Ella Fitzgerald)	18
56	Brunswick LA 8731	SONGS FROM 'LADY AND THE TRAMP' (10")	25

56	Capitol LC 6817	MY BEST TO YOU (10")	25
56	Capitol T 864	THE MAN I LOVE	20
57	Brunswick LAT 8171	DREAM STREET	20
58	Capitol (S)T 979	JUMP FOR JOY	15
58	Brunswick LAT 8266	SEA SHELLS	15
59	Capitol T 1049	THINGS ARE SWINGIN'	15
59	Capitol (S)T 1131	I LIKE MEN!	15
59	Brunswick LAT 8287	MISS WONDERFUL	15
60	Capitol (S)T 1219	BEAUTY AND THE BEAT! (with George Shearing Quintet, mono/stereo)	12
60	Capitol (S)T 1401	PRETTY EYES (mono/stereo)	12
61	Capitol T 1366	ALL AGLOW AGAIN!	12
61	Capitol (S)T 1423	CHRISTMAS CAROUSEL	12
62	Capitol (S)T 1520	BASIN STREET EAST PRESENTS PEGGY LEE (mono/stereo)	12
62	Capitol (S)T 1630	IF YOU GO (mono/stereo)	12
62	Ace Of Hearts AH 26	PEGGY LEE	12
62	Capitol (S)T1 1671	BLUES CROSS COUNTRY (mono/stereo)	12
63	Capitol T 1743	BEWITCHING-LEE!	12
63	Capitol (S)T 1857	I'M A WOMAN (mono/stereo)	12
64	Capitol (S)T 1850	MINK JAZZ (mono/stereo)	12
64	Capitol (S)T 1969	IN LOVE AGAIN (mono/stereo)	12
64	Capitol (S)T 2096	IN THE NAME OF LOVE (mono/stereo)	12
65	Capitol (S)T 2320	PASS ME BY	12
66	Capitol (S)T 1475	OLE A LA LEE!	12
66	Ace Of Hearts AH 107	THE FABULOUS PEGGY LEE	12
66	Capitol (S)T 2388	THEN WAS THEN, NOW IS NOW!	12
67	Capitol (S)T 2469	GUITARS A LA LEE	12
67	Capitol (S)T 2475	BIG SPENDER	12
69	Capitol (S)T 21141	IS THAT ALL THERE IS?	12

(see also Bing Crosby, George Shearing)

ROBERTA LEE

52	Brunswick 04876	The Little White Cloud That Cried/Tell Me Why (78, with Grady Martin)	10
53	Brunswick 05076	Sixty Minute Man (with Hardrock Gunter)/RED FOLEY: Hot Toddy (78)	15
53	Brunswick 05116	Say It Isn't So/Dear Joe (78)	7
53	Brunswick 05123	Don't Call My Name/Hey Mister Cottonpicker (78, with Tex Williams)	7
53	Brunswick 05134	Ill Wind (You're Blowing Me No Good)/Fare-Thee-Well (78)	7
53	Brunswick 05205	Caribbean/Let's Go Home (78)	7
54	HMV 7M 261	True Love And Tender Care/When The Organ Played At Twilight	10
55	Brunswick 05388	Ridin' To Tennessee/I'll Be There If Ever You Want Me	10

(see also Red Foley, Hardrock Gunter)

ROBIN LEE

62	Reprise R 20068	Gamblin' Man/An Angel With A Broken Wing	18

ROY LEE

61	Decca F 11406	Two Initials/Honey Lies	6

TONY LEE

68	Doctor Bird DB 1106	Lee's Special/LLOYD & GROOVERS: My Heart My Soul	32

TONY LEE TRIO

71	Contour 2870142	ELECTRIC PIANO (LP)	15
76	Lambert 3416	TONY LEE TRIO (LP)	20
79	Lambert LAM105	STREET OF DREAMS (LP)	20

VINNY LEE & RIDERS

61	HMV POP 856	Mule Train/Gambler's Guitar	15

WARREN LEE

69	Pama PM 762	Underdog Backstreet/Come Put My Life In Order	15

WILMA LEE & STONEY COOPER

64	Hickory 45-1257	Big John's Wife/Pirate King	5

LEE & CLARENDONIANS

72	Green Door GD 4038	Night Owl/Night Owl Version	5

LEE (Perry) & JIMMY (Riley)

75	Dip DL 5075	Rasta Train/Yagga Yagga	18

LEE (Perry) & JUNIOR (Byles)

75	Dip DL 5060	Dreader Locks/Militant Rock	12

LEE & PAUL

59	Philips PB 912	The Chick/Valentina, My Valentina	5

BRAD LEEDS

60	Pye International 7N 25050	A Teenage Love Is Born/I'm Walking Behind You	6

PHIL LEEDS

66	London HLR 10044	Would You Believe It?/FRANK GALLOP: The Ballad Of Irving	8

MARK LEEMAN FIVE

65	Columbia DB 7452	Portland Town/Gotta Get Myself Together	25
65	Columbia DB 7648	Blow My Blues Away/On The Horizon	30
66	Columbia DB 7812	Forbidden Fruit/Goin' To Bluesville	30
66	Columbia DB 7955	Follow Me/Gather Up The Pieces	25

(see also Cheynes)

THOMAS LEER

78	Oblique ER 101	Private Plane/International (folded photocopied p/s, hand-stamped labels)	10
78	Company/Oblique OBCO 1	Private Plane/International (reissue, printed p/s)	6
82	Cherry Red CHERRY 52	All About You/Saving Grace (p/s)	5

MINT VALUE £

82	Cherry Red 12CHERRY 52	All About You/Saving Grace (12", p/s) 8
82	Cherry Red ERED 26	CONTRADICTIONS EP (12", double pack) 8
79	Industrial IR 0007	THE BRIDGE (LP, with Robert Rental) 15
	(see also Act, Robert Rental)	

JOHN LEES
74	Polydor 2058 513	Best Of My Love/You Can't Get It 15
77	Harvest HAR 5132	Child Of The Universe/Kes (A Major Fancy)....................... 5
73	Harvest SHVL 811	A MAJOR FANCY (LP) 15
	(see also Barclay James Harvest)	

JACK LE FORGE
| 65 | Stateside SS 444 | Our Crazy Affair/Bossa Bossa Nova (withdrawn) .... 20 |

LEFT BANKE
66	Philips BF 1517	Walk Away Renee/I Haven't Got The Nerve 12
67	Philips BF 1540	Pretty Ballerina/Lazy Day 12
67	Philips BF 1575	Ivy Ivy/And Suddenly 10
67	Philips BF 1614	Desiree/I've Got Something On My Mind 7
87	Bam Caruso OPRA 023	Walk Away Renee/Ivy Ivy (DJ/jukebox issue)...................... 6
67	Philips (S)BL 7773	WALK AWAY RENEE/PRETTY BALLERINA (LP) 50

LEFTFIELD
90	Outer Rhythm FOOT 9R	More Than I Know (10K Remix)/(More Mix)/(Even More Mix) (12") 15
91	Outer Rhythm FOOT 009	More Than I Know (12" Mix)/Not Forgotten (Hard Hands Mix) (12") 20
92	Hard Hands HAND 001T	Release The Pressure/Release The Pressure (Instrumental)/
		Release The Pressure (with Earl Sixteen) (12") 10
92	Hard Hands HAND 001R	Release The Dubs (Dub 1)/(Dub 2)/(Dub 3)/(Dub 4) (12") 15
92	Hard Hands HAND 002T	Song Of Life/Song Of Life (Dub Of Life)/Song Of Life (Fanfare Of Life) (12") 10
92	Hard Hands HAND 002R	Song Of Life (Underworld Remix)/Release The Pressure
		(Release The Horns Mix)/Release The Pressure (Lemon Interrupt Mix) (12") 15
94	Hard Hands LEFT EP1	LEFTISM (12", 4-track sampler, promo only) 10
95	Hard Hands LEFT EP2	Original/Original (Jam)/Filter Fish/Original (Drift) (12", double pack,
		as Leftfield & Halliday, promo only) 12
95	Hard Hands HAND 29P	RELEASE THE PRESSURE (12", double pack, promo only) 10
95	Hard Hands AFRO EP	AFRO-LEFT EP (12", with Djum Djum, double pack, promo only) 12
	(see also A Man Called Adam, Curve)	

LEFT-HANDED MARRIAGE
67	private pressing	ON THE RIGHT SIDE OF THE LEFT-HANDED MARRIAGE (LP)............ 400
96	Tenth Planet TP 022	ON THE RIGHT SIDE OF THE LEFT-HANDED MARRIAGE (LP,
		reissue, gatefold sleeve) 15

LEFT HAND DRIVE
| 79 | Bancrupt BAN 012 | Who Said Rock & Roll Is Dead/I Know Where I Am (p/s) .... 5 |

LEFT SIDE
| 69 | Columbia DB 8575 | Welcome To My House/This Little Village .... 6 |

LANCE LE GAULT
| 68 | United Artists UP 2255 | Billie/Louisiana Swamp Fox.................................... 5 |

LEGAY
| 69 | Fontana TF 904 | No-One/The Fantastic Story Of The Steam Driven Banana .... 125 |
| | (see also Gypsy) | |

LEGEND
69	Bell BLL 1048	National Gas/Wouldn't You 18
69	Bell BLL 1082	Georgia George Part 1/July 15
70	Vertigo 6059 021	Life/Late Last Night.. 10
71	Vertigo 6059 036	Don't You Know/Someday 10
69	Bell MBLL/SBLL 115	LEGEND (LP) 60
71	Vertigo 6360 019	LEGEND ('RED BOOT') (LP, gatefold sleeve, swirl label) 60
72	Vertigo 6360 063	MOONSHINE (LP, gatefold sleeve, swirl label)..................... 65
	(see also Procol Harum, Fingers)	

LEGEND
| 81 | Legend LEG 1 | Hideaway/Heaven Sent (p/s) .... 70 |

LEGEND
82	Workshop WR 3478	FRONTLINE EP (Frontline/Sabre & Chatila/
		Stormers Of Heaven/Open The Skies (12") 25
81	Workshop WR 2007	LEGEND (LP)... 90
82	Workshop WR 3477	DEATH IN THE NURSERY (LP, with insert)....................... 20

LEGEND!
83	Creation CRE 001/	'73 In '83/You (Chunka Chunka) Were Glamorous (foldaround p/s in poly bag,
	Lyntone LYN 12903	some with 33rpm flexidisc "I Wonder Why! (live)" by The Pastels/"Wouldn't
		You?" by The Laughing Apple)................................15/12
84	Creation CRE 010	The Legend Destroys The Blues/Arrogant Bastards
		(foldaround p/s in poly bag)................................... 6

TOBI LEGEND
| 78 | RK RK 1004 | Time Will Pass You By/DEAN PARRISH: I'm On My Way/ |
| | | JIMMY RADCLIFFE: Long After Tonight Is All Over (some with p/s) .... 20/15 |

LEGENDARY LONNIE
| 81 | Nervous NER 002 | Constipation Shake/Devil's Guitar (p/s) .... 6 |

LEGENDARY MASKED SURFERS
| 73 | United Artists UP 35542 | Gonna Hustle You/Summertime, Summertime........................ 15 |
| | (see also Beach Boys, Jan & Dean) | |

LEGENDARY PINK DOTS
82	In Phaze IPNER 1	THE TOWER (LP)	18
83	In Phaze PHA 2	CURSE (LP)	15
84	In Phaze PHA 3	LEGENDARY PINK DOTS (LP)	15

LEGENDS
65	Pye 7N 15904	I've Found Her/Something's Gonna Happen	18
67	Parlophone R 5581	Tomorrow's Gonna Be Another Day/Nobody Laughs Anymore	40
67	Parlophone R 5613	Under The Sky/Twenty-Four Hours A Day	20

(see also First Impressions)

B. LEGGS
| 71 | Green Door GD 4004 | Drums Of Passion/Love And Emotion (Version) | 6 |

(see also Morgan's All Stars)

LEGO FEET
| 91 | Skam SKAM 1 | Untitled1/Untitled 2 (12", die cut sleeve) | 120 |

MICHEL LEGRAND
73	Tamla Motown TMG 848	Love Theme From "Lady Sings The Blues"/Any Happy Home (with Gil Askey)	5
73	Tamla Motown TMG 848	Love Theme From "Lady Sings The Blues"/Any Happy Home (demo in p/s)	15
58	Philips SBBL 510	LEGRAND JAZZ (LP)	12
64	Philips BL 7605	PLAYS RICHARD ROGERS (LP)	12
64	Mercury SML 30020	VIOLENT VIOLINS (LP)	12
66	Philips (S)BL 7792	THE YOUNG GIRLS OF ROCHEFORT (LP, soundtrack)	25
68	United Artists SULP 1218	THE THOMAS CROWN AFFAIR (LP, soundtrack)	35
68	Sunset SLS 50519	THE THOMAS CROWN AFFAIR (LP, reissue)	20
68	CBS (S)BPG 63276	HOW TO SAVE A MARRIAGE AND RUIN YOUR LIFE (LP, soundtrack)	18
69	MGM MGM-C(S) 8101	ICE STATION ZEBRA (LP, soundtrack)	20
70	United Artists UAS 29084	THE HAPPY ENDING (LP, soundtrack)	20
71	Warner Bros K 46098	SUMMER OF '42 (LP, soundtrack)	12
73	Bell BELLS 235	THE THREE MUSKETEERS (LP, soundtrack)	18

LE GRIFFE
83	Bullet BOL 1	Fast Bikes/Where Are You? (p/s)	8
83	Bullet BOLT 1	Fast Bikes/Where Are You?/The Actor (12", p/s)	15
84	Bullet BOL 7	You're Killing Me (p/s)	8
83	Bullet BOLT 7	You're Killing Me/E.T.A. (12", p/s)	20
84	Bullet BULP 2	BREAKING STRAIN (mini-LP)	20

LEGS
| 74 | Warner Bros K 16317 | So Many Faces/You Bet You Have | 5 |

(see also Curved Air, Stretch)

TOM LEHRER
60	Decca F 11243	Poisoning Pigeons In The Park/The Masochism Tango (some in p/s)	15/7
66	Reprise RS 23049	Pollution/Folk Song Army	5
58	Decca LF 1311	SONGS BY TOM LEHRER (10" LP)	15
59	Decca LF 1323	MORE OF TOM LEHRER (10" LP)	15
59	Decca LK 4332/SKL 4097	AN EVENING WASTED WITH... (LP)	15
60	Decca LK 4375	TOM LEHRER REVISITED (LP)	12
65	Reprise R 6179	THAT WAS THE YEAR THAT WAS (LP)	12

LEIBER-STOLLER ORCHESTRA
| 62 | HMV POP 1050 | Cafe Expresso/Blue Baion | 20 |

LEIBSTANDARTE SS MB
| 81 | Come Organisation | TRIUMPH OF THE WILL (LP, 500 only) | 60 |
| 80s | Come Organisation | WELTANSCHAUUNG (LP) | 40 |

ADELE LEIGH
| 59 | Philips PB 887 | O My Beloved Father/Voi Che Sapete (78) | 10 |

ANDREW LEIGH
| 70 | Polydor 2343 034 | MAGICIAN (LP) | 22 |

(see also Reg King)

BERNIE LEIGHTON
| 63 | Pye International 7N 25177 | Lawrence Of Arabia Theme/The Wonderful World We Live In (some in p/s) | 8/5 |

GARY LeMEL
| 67 | London HLM 7124 | Beautiful People/Take Me With You (export issue) | 20 |

LEMMINGS
| 65 | Pye 7N 15837 | Out Of My Mind/My Little Girl | 20 |
| 65 | Pye 7N 15899 | You Can't Blame Me For Trying/Bring Your Heart With You | 20 |

(see also Honeycombs, Martin Murray)

JACK LEMMON
| 60 | Fontana H 262 | Theme From "The Apartment"/Lemmon-Flavoured Blues | 5 |

LEMMY & UPSETTERS with MICK GREEN
| 90 | Sunnyside STYLE 777 | Blue Suede Shoes/Paradise (p/s) | 6 |

(see also Motörhead, Rockin' Vickers, Sam Gopal)

LEMON DIPS
| 69 | De Wolfe DW/LP 3114 | WHO'S GONNA BUY? (LP, library issue) | 75 |

LEMONHEADS
| 91 | Atlantic A 7709 | Gonna Get Along Without Ya Now/Half The Time (p/s, withdrawn) | 10 |
| 96 | Warner Bros | CAR BUTTON CLOTH (CD, includes track 'Purple Parallelagram', promo-only) | 60 |

LEMON INTERRUPT
| 93 | Jnr. Boys Own JBO 12002 | Eclipse/Bigmouth (12") | 15 |
| 93 | Junior Boys Own JBO 712 | Dirty/Minneapolis/Minneapolis (Airwaves) (12") | 15 |

(see also Underworld)

LEMON JELLY

01	Soft Rock SOFTROCK 001	Soft/Rock (blue vinyl, denim sleeve with condom, 1000 only)	40
02	XL IFXLT 147P	Space Walk/Return To Patagonia (10", leather title sleeve, 3000 only)	20
03	Rolled Oats RO 01	Rolled/Oats (gold vinyl, hessian sleeve, 1200 only)	8
98	Impotent Fury IF 001	THE BATH EP: In The Bath/Nervous Tension/A Tune For Jack (10", 1000 only, stickered cardboard sleeve, 1st 250 in hand-printed p/s)	120/40
99	Impotent Fury IF 002	THE YELLOW EP: His Majesty King Raam/The Staunton Lick/Homage To Patagonia (10", 1000 only, stickered cardboard sleeve, 1st 240 in hand-printed p/s)	100/40
00	Impotent Fury IF 003	THE MIDNIGHT EP: Kneel Before Your God/Page One/Come (10", 1000 only, stickered cardboard sleeve, 1st 350 in hand-printed p/s)	50/20
02	XL IFXLLP 160	LOST HORIZONS (2-LP, gatefold sleeve, with booklet)	20

LEMON KITTENS

79	Step Forward SF 10	SPOONFED AND WRITHING (EP)	25
81	United Dairies UD 07	CAKE BEAST (12" EP, with inner sleeve & insert)	30
80	United Dairies UD 02	WE BUY A HAMMER FOR DADDY (LP, with inner sheet)	40
83	Illuminated JAMS 131	THE BIG DENTIST (LP)	30

(see also Danielle Dax, Shock Headed Peters, Underneath, Gland Shrouds, Karl Blake, Fur Fur)

LEMON LINE

67	Decca F 12688	For Your Precious Love/You Made Me See The Light	6

LEMON MEN

69	Polydor 56365	I've Seen You Cut Lemons/Lemon Strip/Lemon Walk	5

LEMON PIPERS

68	Pye International 7N 25444	Green Tambourine/No Help From Me	7
68	Pye International 7N 25454	Rice Is Nice/Blueberry Blue	6
68	Pye International 7N 25464	Jelly Jungle (Of Orange Marmalade)/Shoeshine Boy	6
68	Pye Intl. NPL 28112	GREEN TAMBOURINE (LP)	25
68	Pye Intl. NSPL 28118	JUNGLE MARMALADE (LP)	18
69	Marble Arch MAL 1120	THE LEMON PIPERS (LP)	12

(see also Ram Jam)

LEMON PIPERS/1910 FRUITGUM CO.

68	Pye Intl. NEP 44091	PRESENTING ... (EP, 1 side each)	15

(see also 1910 Fruitgum Co.)

LEMON TREE

68	Parlophone R 5671	I Can Touch A Rainbow/William Chalker's Time Machine	40
68	Parlophone R 5739	It's So Nice To Come Home/Come On Girl	25

(see also Idle Race, Uglys, Danny King's Mayfair Set, Balls)

LEN & HONEYSUCKERS

66	Rio R 75	One More River/Emergency Ward	10

FREDDIE LENNON

66	Piccadilly 7N 35290	That's My Life (My Love And My Home)/The Next Time You Feel Important	75

(see also Loving Kind)

JIMMY LENNON & ATLANTICS

64	Decca F 11825	Louisiana Mama/I Learned To Yodel	35

JOHN LENNON/PLASTIC ONO BAND

SINGLES

69	Apple APPLE 13/R 5795	Give Peace A Chance/Remember Love (p/s, as Plastic Ono Band; some with Parlophone catalogue number, dark green label)	18/10
69	Apple APPLES 1001	Cold Turkey/Don't Worry Kyoko (Mummy's Only Looking For A Hand In The Snow) (p/s, as Plastic Ono Band)	15
69	Apple APPLES 1002	You Know My Name (Look Up The Number)/What's The New Mary Jane? (as Plastic Ono Band, unreleased; vinyl test pressings only with typed Apple 'Custom Recording' labels & handwritten catalogue number)	3,000+
70	Apple APPLES 1003	Instant Karma!/Who Has Seen The Wind? (p/s, as Lennon/Ono with Plastic Ono Band)	12
71	Apple R 5892	Power To The People/YOKO ONO & PLASTIC ONO BAND: Open Your Box (p/s, full apple label both sides or full/half apple label)	15
72	Apple R 5970	Happy Xmas (War Is Over) (as John & Yoko/Plastic Ono Band with Harlem Community Choir)/YOKO ONO & PLASTIC ONO BAND: Listen, The Snow Is Falling (p/s, green vinyl)	15
72	Apple R 5953	Woman Is The Nigger Of The World/Sisters O Sisters (unreleased, test pressings only)	2,500+
73	Apple R 5994	Mind Games/Meat City (p/s)	6
74	EMI PSR 369	Interview With John Lennon By Bob Mercer And Message To The Salesmen/Whatever Gets You Thru' The Night (promo only)	2,000
75	Apple R 6003	9 Dream (Edited Version)/What You Got (demo only)	80
75	Apple R 6009	Imagine/Working Class Hero (p/s)	12
80	WEA Geffen K 79186	(Just Like) Starting Over/ YOKO ONO : Kiss Kiss Kiss (green vinyl, promo)	500+
81	WEA K 79207	Watching The Wheels/YOKO ONO: I'm Your Angel (pink vinyl "in house" promo)	500+
84	Polydor PODJ 700	Nobody Told Me (1-sided white label promo)	60
84	Polydor PODJ 701	Borrowed Time (Edited Version)/YOKO ONO: Your Hands (promo only)	25
84	Polydor POSP 712	Every Man Has A Woman Who Loves Him/SEAN ONO LENNON: It's Alright (p/s, some with poster)	10/5
88	Parlophone RP 6199	Imagine/Jealous Guy (picture disc)	15
97	Parlophone IMAGINE 001	Imagine (CD, 1-track, card p/s, promo only)	10
97	Parlophone IMAGINE 002	Happy Xmas (War Is Over) (CD, 1-track, card p/s, promo only)	10
98	Parlophone LENNON 002	Happy Xmas (War Is Over) (rough mix)/Be Bop A Lula (CD, card p/s, promo only)	15

MINT VALUE £

LPs

68	Apple APCOR 2	UNFINISHED MUSIC NO. 1: TWO VIRGINS (with Yoko Ono, mono; black inner, no track listing, with "Merrie In England..." blurb on *front* sleeve)	3,000
68	Apple SAPCOR 2/ Track 613 012	UNFINISHED MUSIC NO. 1: TWO VIRGINS (with Yoko Ono, stereo; black inner, with track listing & "Merrie In England..." blurb on *back* sleeve & Track Records logo on label)	500
69	Zapple ZAPPLE 01	UNFINISHED MUSIC NO. 2: LIFE WITH THE LIONS (with Yoko Ono, with inner sleeve)	200
69	Apple SAPCOR 11	WEDDING ALBUM (with Yoko Ono; gatefold sleeve in box set, includes wedding certificate glued to inside box lid, press booklet, poster, white 'Bagism' bag, passport photographs, postcard & picture of wedding cake)	300
69	Apple CORE 2001	LIVE PEACE IN TORONTO 1969 (as Plastic Ono Band, with stapled calendar, some sealed)	125/60
72	Apple PAS 10004	IMAGINE (LP, with inner sleeve, poster & postcard)	50
72	Apple Q4PAS 10004	IMAGINE (LP, quadrophonic, with inner sleeve, poster & postcard)	125
81	Parlophone JLB 8	THE JOHN LENNON BOX (9-LP set, with insert)	100
84	Polydor POLH P5	MILK AND HONEY (picture disc, original pressing, thin vinyl, 2,000 only)	40
84	Polydor POLH P5	MILK AND HONEY (picture disc, 2nd pressing, thicker vinyl, 1,000 only)	50
98	Parlophone 8306142	ANTHOLOGY (4-CDR, jewel cases with Abbey Road studio inlays, incorrect track listing and missing "Grow Old With Me" from CD4, promo only)	80

(see also Beatles, Yoko Ono, Bill Elliott/Elastic Oz Band, Elephant's Memory, Musketeer Gripweed, Elton John)

JOHN LENNON & BLEECHERS (Jamaica)
70	Punch PH 23	Ram You Hard/UPSETTERS: Soul Stew	20

LENNON SISTERS
56	Vogue Coral Q 72176	Graduation Day/Toy Tiger	15
57	Vogue Coral Q 72259	Young And In Love/Teenage Waltz	15
57	Vogue Coral Q 72285	Shake Me I Rattle/Pocohontas	15
61	London HLD 9417	Sad Movies/I Don't Know Why	15
64	London HA-D/SH-D 8154	GREAT FOLK SONGS (LP, as Lennon Sisters & Cousins)	20

ANNIE LENNOX
93	RCA 74321 12883-1	LITTLE BIRD EP (12", remixes by N-Joi et al.)	10

LENNY THE LION (with Terry Hall)
59	Parlophone R 4609	I Wish That I Could Be Father Christmas/I Want A Hippopotamus For Christmas	5

J.B. LENOIR (& AFRICAN HUNCH RHYTHM)
65	Sue WI 339	I Sing Um The Way I Feel/I Feel So Good (with His African Hunch Rhythm)	50
65	Bootleg 503	Man Watch Your Woman/Mama Talk To Your Daughter (99 copies only)	60
66	Blue Horizon 45-1004	Mojo Boogie/I Don't Care What Nobody Say (99 copies only)	115
68	Python PLP 25	J.B. LENOIR (LP, 99 copies only)	75
70	Polydor 2482 014	CRUSADE (LP)	20
75	Rarity LP 2	J.B. LENOIR (LP)	20
70s	CBS 62593	ALABAMA BLUES (LP)	30

ROBIN LENT
71	Nepentha 6347 002	SCARECROW'S JOURNEY (LP, gatefold sleeve, with Focus)	45

(see also Focus, Jan Akkerman)

VAL LENTON
65	Immediate IM 008	Gotta Get Away/You Don't Care	40

CHRIS LEON
72	Dynamic DYN 450	(Last Night) I Didn't Get To Sleep At All/DYNAMITES: Instrumental Version	5

LEON (Silvera) & OWEN (Gray)
62	Blue Beat BB 117	Murder (with Drumbago All Stars)/ROY PANTON: Forty Four	12

(see also Owen & Leon, Owen & Millie)

DEKE LEONARD
73	United Artists UAS 29464	ICEBERG (LP)	12
74	United Artists UAG 29544	KAMIKAZE (LP)	12

(see also Man, Marty Wilde, Help Yourself, Pete Brown's Piblokto, Gary Pickford-Hopkins & Friends)

LEONARD FAMILY
72	Beacon BEA 186	Once You Understand/It Won't Happen Again	6

ANN LEONARDO
57	Capitol CL 14723	Straws In The Wind/Travelling Stranger	15
57	Capitol CL 14755	Lottery/One And Only	10
57	Capitol CL 14797	Three Time Loser/I'll Wait Till Monday	6

TOMMY LEONETTI
54	Capitol CL 14199	That's What You Made Me/I Love My Mama	5
55	Capitol CL 14272	Ever Since You Went Away/Untied	5
56	Capitol CL 14556	Heartless/Sometime	5
56	Capitol CL 14598	It's Wild/Free	5
56	Capitol CL 14654	Too Proud/Wrong	5
58	RCA RCA 1107	Dream Lover/Moonlight Serenade (78 rpm = £12)	5

LEONIE & JOE NOLAN BAND
68	Jolly JY 015	Move And Groove/Don't Let Me Do It	8

LE ORME
(see under 'O')

LEO'S SUNSHIPP
79	Grapevine RED 3	Give Me The Sunshine/I'm Back For More	15
79	Grapevine REDC 3	Give Me The Sunshine/I'm Back For More (12")	20

LEPRECHAUN
81	Excalibur EXC 508	Loc It Up/Party Freaks (12")	8

LE RITZ
77	Breaker BS 2001	Punker/What A Sucker (p/s)	35

LEROY & ROCKY (Ellis)
68	Studio One SO 2042	Love Me Girl/WRIGGLERS: Reel Up	25

(see also King Rocky)

LE ROYS
64	Give A Disc LYN 504/505	Money/Swinging On A Star (flexidisc)	10
64	HMV POP 1274	Gotta Lotta Love (Ciribiribin)/Don't Cry Baby	10
64	HMV POP 1312	Chills/Lost Out On Love	15
64	HMV POP 1368	I Come Smiling On Through/California GL 903	10

(see also Mike Sarne, Simon Scott, John Leyton, Mike Berry, Grazina, Billie Davis, Billy Boyle, Don Spencer)

LEROYS & INNOCENTS
64	Regal Zonophone RZ 502	HOT SIX: Don't Throw Your Love Away; My Girl Lollipop; I Love You Because; Not Fade Away (maxi-single, plain sleeve)	10

(see also Innocents [U.K])

BILL LE SAGE
60s	World Records	PRESENTING THE BILL LESAGE/RONNIE ROSS QUARTET (LP)	20

(see also Ronnie Ross)

BONGO LES (Chen) & BUNNY (Herman)
72	Attack ATT 8041	Feel Nice (Version)/WINSTON SCOTLAND: Quick And Slick	8

(see also Bongo Herman)

LES & SILKIE
70	Torpedo TOR 13	I Don't Want To Tell You/DENZIL DENNIS: Come On In	5

LORNE LESLEY
59	Parlophone R 4518	Some Of These Days/When Love Has Let You Down (78 rpm = £6)	10
59	Parlophone R 4567	Warm/You Ought To Be Mine	6
59	Parlophone R 4581	So High, So Low/I Don't Know	10
60	Polydor NH 66928	Take All My Love/Ritroviamoci (Till We Meet Again)	10
60	Polydor NH 66956	Bloodshot Eyes/We're Gonna Dance	10
65	Philips BF 1403	Someone Like You/Where My Heart Never Wandered	5
65	Philips BF 1434	Rainy Days Were Made For Lonely People/Fire Down Below	5
66	Philips BF 1487	Somebody's Gonna Be Sorry/(I'm Afraid) The Masquerade Is Over	5
66	Parlophone R 5538	Little Snowflakes/Would You	5

MICHAEL LESLEY
65	Pye 7N 15835	Momma Didn't Know/I Don't Wanna Know	6
65	Pye 7N 15908	Penny Arcade/Bye Bye Baby	12
65	Pye 7N 15959	Make Up Or Break Up/She Can't See Me	10
66	Decca F 12531	Right Or Wrong/Office Girl (credited to Michael Leslie)	5

JOHN & CHRIS LESLIE
76	Cottage COT 901	THE SHIP OF TIME (LP)	15

LES RITA MITSOUKO
(see under 'R')

LES SAUTERELLES
(see under 'S')

HEDDY LESTER
77	Sonet SON 2013	The World Keeps Turning/Never Saw Him Laughing (p/s)	6

KETTY LESTER
62	London HLN 9527	Love Letters/I'm A Fool To Want You	10
62	London HLN 9574	But Not For Me/Moscow Nights	7
62	London HLN 9608	You Can't Lie To A Liar/River Of Salt	7
62	London HLN 9635	This Land Is Your Land/Love Belongs To Everyone	7
63	London HLN 9698	A Warm Summer Day/I'll Never Stop Loving You	7
64	RCA Victor RCA 1394	Some Things Are Better Left Unsaid/The House Is Haunted (DJ copy = £125)	80
64	RCA Victor RCA 1403	Roses Grow With Thorns/Please Don't Cry Anymore	40
64	RCA Victor RCA 1421	I Trust You Baby/Theme From "The Luck Of Ginger Coffey"	15
65	RCA Victor RCA 1460	Looking For A Better World/Pretty Eyes	7
65	Capitol CL 15427	West Coast/I'll Be Looking Back	30
66	Capitol CL 15447	When A Man Loves A Woman/We'll Be Together Again	8
62	London RE-N 1348	KETTY LESTER (EP)	45
63	London HA-N 2455	LOVE LETTERS (LP)	60
64	RCA Victor RD 7669	THE SOUL OF ME (LP)	40
65	RCA Victor RD 7712	WHERE IS LOVE (LP)	40
67	Stateside S(S)L 10196	WHEN A MAN LOVES A WOMAN (LP)	100

LAZY LESTER
64	Stateside SS 277	I'm A Lover Not A Fighter/Sugar Coated Love	35
71	Blue Horizon 2431 007	MADE UP MY MIND (LP)	100
77	Flyright FLYLP 526	THEY CALL ME LAZY (LP)	15
79	Flyright FLYLP 544	POOR BOY BLUES (LP)	15

ROBIE LESTER
62	Polydor NH 66963	Ballad Of Cheating John/Miracle Of Love	5

LES YPER SOUND
67	Fontana TF 880	Too Fortiche/Psyche Rock	78

JOE LETHAL
78	Lethal Cl 200526	Don't Come Back (no p/s)	35

LETTERMEN
61	Capitol CL 15222	The Way You Look Tonight/That's My Desire	6
65	Capitol CL 15405	Theme From A Summer Place/Sealed With A Kiss	5

MINT VALUE £

68	Capitol CL 15526	Goin' Out Of My Head/Can't Take My Eyes Off You — I Believe	5
69	Capitol CL 15609	Hurt So Bad/Traces	5
61	Capitol EAP 41669	THE LETTERMEN (EP)	12
62	Capitol (S)T 1669	A SONG FOR YOUNG LOVE (LP)	15
62	Capitol (S)T 1711	ONCE UPON A TIME (LP)	15
62	Capitol (S)T 1761	THE LETTERMEN (LP)	15
63	Capitol (S)T 1829	COLLEGE STANDARDS (LP)	15
63	Capitol (S)T 1936	IN CONCERT (LP)	15
64	Capitol (S)T 2083	LOOK AT LOVE (LP)	15
64	Capitol (S)T 2142	SHE CRIED (LP)	15
65	Capitol T 2270	PORTRAIT OF MY LOVE (LP)	15

LETTERMEN
74	Stag SG 10075	FIRST CLASS (LP, private pressing)	90

LETTERS
79	Heartbeat PULSE 9	Nobody Loves Me/Don't Want You Back (p/s)	100

DON LETTS & JAH WOBBLE
79	Virgin VS 239	Steel Leg: Stratetime & The Wide Man/Electric Dread: Haile Unlikely (p/s)	8
79	Virgin VS 239-12	Steel Leg: Stratetime & The Wide Man/Electric Dread: Haile Unlikely (12", p/s)	10

(see also Jah Wobble, PiL)

LEVEE BREAKERS
65	Parlophone R 5291	Babe I'm Leaving You/Wild About My Loving	25

(see also Beverley, Johnny Joyce)

LEVEE CAMP MOAN
69	County	LEVEE CAMP MOAN (LP, private pressing)	600
69	County	PEACOCK FARM (LP, private pressing)	600

LEVEL 42
79	Elite DAZZ 4	Sandstorm/ATMOSFEAR: Journey To The Powerline (Remix) (12", white label test pressing, no p/s)	25
80	Elite DAZZ 5	Love Meeting Love/Instrumental Love (7", unreleased)	
80	Elite DAZZ 5	Love Meeting Love/Instrumental Love (12", company die-cut stickered sleeve)	8
81	Elite LEVLP 1	STRATEGY (LP, unreleased, 6 white label test pressings only)	100+
91	Polydor 511 635-2	THE COMPLETE LEVEL 42 (9-CD box set)	40

LEVELLERS
89	Hag HAG 005	Carry Me/What's In The Way/The Last Days Of Winter/England My Home (12" EP; first 1,000 copies with Brighton contact address on p/s)	each 10
89	Hag HAG 006	Outside Inside/I Have No Answers (500 promo copies only, no p/s)	6
91	On The Fiddle OTF EP 1	Police On My Back/Where The Hell Are We Going To Love?/Travelogue (4am Mix) (12", fan club issue, p/s)	12
92	On The Fiddle OTF LP 2	LIVE 1992 (LP, fan club issue, 2,000 only)	15

GERRY LEVENE (& AVENGERS)
64	Decca F 11815	It's Driving Me Wild (solo)/Dr. Feelgood	55

(see also Moody Blues)

ANNABEL LEVENTON
69	Morgan MR 20	Easy To Be Hard/My Dear Friend	6

LEVIATHAN
68	Elektra EKSN 45052	Remember The Times/Second Production	60
69	Elektra EKSN 45057	The War Machine/Time	35
69	Elektra EKSN 45052/45057	(WAY IN) THE FOUR FACES OF LEVIATHAN (Remember The Times/Second Production/The War Machine/Time)(2 x 7" press pack, A4 folder sleeve, some overprinted with "Harrods" logo, with biog & photo, promo, some commercial)	150
69	Elektra EKSN 45075	Flames/Just Forget Tomorrow	40
90s	(no cat.no.)	ELEKTRA DAZE (CD EP, private pressing)	25
69	Elektra EKS 74046	LEVIATHAN (2-LP, unissued, acetates only, 1 copy known)	1000+

(see also Mike Stuart Span, High Broom)

HANK LEVINE ORCHESTRA
61	HMV POP 947	Image (Parts 1 & 2)	15
65	HMV POP 1390	Image (Parts 1 & 2) (reissue)	5

LEVITTS
69	ESP Disk/Fontana STL 5518	WE ARE THE LEVITTS (LP)	25

LEVON & HAWKS
65	Atlantic AT 4054	The Stones I Throw/He Don't Love You	50

(see also Band)

BARRINGTON LEVY
79	JB JBD	Call You On The Phone/RANKING TOYAN: London Girl (12")	10
79	Burning Rockers BRD 033	Shine Eye Gal/Dub version (12". Jah Thomas toasts on A-side but is uncredited)	15
79	Burning Sounds BRD 029	Hunting Man (feat. Jah Thomas)/Hunting Dub (12")	25
79	Greensleeves GRED 27	Lose Respect (feat. Trinity)/ROMAN STEWART & TRINITY: Since You're Gone (12")	15
80	Greensleeves GRED 40	Crucifixion/Eventide Fire A Disaster (red vinyl 12")	15
80	Cha Cha CHAD 22	Warm And Sunny Day/GENERAL SAINT - DJ cut (12")	50
80	His Majesty HMD 004	Shaolin Temple/Version (12")	20
80	Strong Like Sampson SLSD8	Wicked Intention/ROD TAYLOR (12")	20
80	Lovelinch LL 03	Skylarking/HORTENSE ELLIS - You Done Me Wrong (12")	40
82	Greensleeves GRED 80	Tomorrow Is Another Day/PAPA TULLO: Delaware (12")	20
82	Oak Sounds OSD 008	Open Book/Open version (12")	15
84	Greensleeves GRED 136	Prison Oval Rock (Master Mix)/Prison Oval Rock (Dub Plate Mix) (12")	10
84	Greensleeves GRED 145	Pon Your Toe/Girl I love you (12")	8

79	Greensleeves GREL 9	ENGLISHMAN (LP)	30
79	Burning Sounds BS 1039	SHINE EYE GAL (LP)	40
80	Jah Guidance JA CC 14	ROBIN HOOD (LP)	40
83	GG's GG 0032	BARRINGTON LEVY'S LIFE STYLE (LP)	40
83	Burning Sounds BS 1050	HUNTER MAN (LP)	20

BEN LEVY
66	Ska Beat JB 245	Doren/Never Knew Love	10
66	Ska Beat JB 255	I'll Make You Glad/Keep Smiling	10

CARL LEV(E)Y & CIMARRONS
70	Hot Rod HR 100	Walk The Hot Street/PEGGY & CIMARRONS: You Say You Don't Love Me	12
70	Hot Rod HR 101	Remember Easter Monday/PEGGY & JIMMY: Pum Pum Lover	10

(see also Hot Rod Allstars, Rita Alston, Peggy)

JONA LEWIE
74	Sonet SON 2048	Piggy Back Sue/Papa Don't Go	6
75	Sonet SON 2056	The Swan/Custer's Last Stand	5
76	Sonet SON 2081	Hallelujah Europe Parts 1 & 2	5
77	Sonet SON 2117	Rocking Yobs/After We Swum	5

(see also Brett Marvin & Thunderbolts)

CARL LEWIN
71	Bullet BU 456	Knock Three Times/SIDNEY ALL STARS: The Whealing Mouse	8
71	Punch PH 98	Nobody Told Me/WING: Don't Play That Song Again (version)	7

ALVA (REGGIE) LEWIS
67	Caltone TONE 111	Return Home/KING ROCK & WILLOWS: You Are The One	42
67	Island WI 3080	I'm Indebted/GROOVERS: You've Got To Cry	35
68	Jolly HY 009	Hang My Head And Cry/COOL CATS: Hold Your Love	50
72	Upsetter US 391	Natty Natty (as Alva Reggie Lewis)/UPSETTERS: Version	12

(see also Reggae Boys, Webber Sisters, Lester Sterling, Cool Cats)

ANDY LEWIS & KEN BURKE
90s	Acid Jazz AJX 147S	(Love Is Alive) In Your Heart (pink vinyl, p/s)	10

BARBARA LEWIS
63	London HLK 9724	Hello Stranger/Think A Little Sugar	30
63	London HLK 9779	Straighten Up Your Heart/If You Love Her	25
64	London HLK 9832	Snap Your Fingers/Puppy Love	25
64	Atlantic AT 4013	Pushin' A Good Thing Too Far/Come Home	40
65	Atlantic AT 4031	Baby I'm Yours/Hello Stranger	15
65	Atlantic AT 4041	Make Me Your Baby/Love To Be Loved	15
66	Atlantic AT 4068	Don't Forget About Me/It's Magic	20
66	Atlantic 584 037	Make Me Belong To You/Girls Need Loving Care	15
67	Atlantic 584 061	Baby What Do You Want Me To Do/I Remember The Feeling	50
68	Atlantic 584 153	Hello Stranger/Baby I'm Yours (reissue)	8
68	Atlantic 584 174	Sho Nuff (It's Got To Be Your Love)/Thankful For What I Got	20
71	Atlantic 2091 143	Someday We're Gonna Love Again/Baby I'm Yours	15
72	Atlantic K 10128	Someday We're Gonne Love Again/Baby I'm Yours (reissue)	10
65	Atlantic AET 6015	SNAP YOUR FINGERS (EP)	80
66	Atlantic ATL 5042	BABY I'M YOURS (LP)	75
66	Atlantic 587 002	IT'S MAGIC (LP)	80
70	Stax SXATS 1035	THE MANY GROOVES OF BARBARA LEWIS (LP)	75

BOB LEWIS
57	Parlophone R 4309	Far Away/The Mayflower Song	5

BOBBY LEWIS
61	Parlophone R 4794	Tossin' And Turnin'/Oh Yes, I Love You	25
61	Parlophone R 4831	One Track Mind/Are You Ready	25
62	Stateside SS 126	I'm Tossin' And Turnin' Again/Nothin' But The Blues	25

CAPPY LEWIS
61	Vogue V 9184	Bullfight/OLYMPICS: Little Pedro	20

(see also Olympics)

DAVE LEWIS
66	Pye Intl. NEP 44057	GIVIN' GAS (EP)	35

DAVID LEWIS
70	AX 1	SONGS OF DAVID LEWIS (LP, private pressing, paste-on sleeve)	300+

(see also Andwella['s Dream], David Baxter)

FURRY LEWIS
69	Blue Horizon 7-63228	PRESENTING THE COUNTRY BLUES (LP)	90
70	Matchbox SDR 190	IN MEMPHIS (LP)	25
71	Xtra XTRA 1116	FURRY LEWIS (LP)	20
71	Spokane SPL 1004	THE EARLY YEARS 1927-1929 (LP)	50

(see also John Estes)

GARY LEWIS & PLAYBOYS
65	Liberty LIB 10187	This Diamond Ring/Tijuana Wedding	15
65	Liberty LIB 55778	Count Me In/Little Miss Go-Go	15
65	Liberty LIB 55809	Save Your Heart For Me/Without A Word Of Warning	7
65	Liberty LIB 55818	Everybody Loves A Clown/Time Stands Still	7
66	Liberty LIB 55846	She's Just My Style/I Won't Make That Mistake Again	15
66	Liberty LIB 55865	Sure Gonna Miss Her/I Don't Wanna Say Goodnight	8
66	Liberty LIB 55880	Green Grass/I Can Read Between The Lines	8
66	Liberty LIB 55898	My Heart's Symphony/Tina	12
66	Liberty LIB 55914	(You Don't Have To) Paint Me A Picture/Looking For The Stars	12
67	Liberty LIB 55933	Where Will The Words Come From/The Best Man	7

Gary LEWIS & PLAYBOYS

67	Liberty LIB 55949	Loser (With A Broken Heart)/Ice Melts In The Sun	7
67	Liberty LIB 55971	Girls In Love/Let's Be More Than Friends	7
67	Liberty LBF 15025	Jill/Needles And Pins	12
68	Liberty LBF 15131	Sealed With A Kiss/Pretty Thing	7
70	Liberty LBF 15335	Orangutan/Something Is Wrong	6
75	United Artists UP 35780	My Heart's Symphony/Tina (reissue)	8
65	Liberty LBY 1259	THIS DIAMOND RING (LP)	48
66	Liberty LBY 1322	JUST OUR STYLE (LP)	35

GEORGE LEWIS & HIS NEW ORLEANS STOMPERS/BAND

56	Vogue V 2051	Climax Rag/Deep Bayou Blues	8
56	Vogue V 2052	Millenberg Joys/Two Jim Blues	8
56	Vogue V 2053	Just A Closer Walk With Thee/Just A Little While To Stay Here	8
56	Vogue V 2054	Fidgety Feet/Dauphine Street Blues	8
56	Vogue V 2055	Don't Go 'Way Nobody/Careless Love Blues	8
60	HMV POP 707	South Rampart Street Parade/Chinatown My Chinatown (with Band)	7
55	Vogue EPV 1066	GEORGE LEWIS AND HIS NEW ORLEANS STOMPERS (EP)	12
55	Vogue EPV 1081	GEORGE LEWIS AND HIS NEW ORLEANS STOMPERS (EP)	12
55	Tempo EXA 15	GEORGE LEWIS AND HIS NEW ORLEANS STOMPERS (EP)	10
57	Tempo EXA 62	GEORGE LEWIS (EP, as George Lewis' Ragtime Band)	10
57	Tempo EXA 66	GEORGE LEWIS (EP, as George Lewis' Ragtime Band)	10
57	Tempo EXA 70	GEORGE LEWIS' RAGTIME BAND (EP)	10
59	Tempo EXA 97	GEORGE LEWIS (EP, as George Lewis & His New Orleans Rhythm Boys)	10
59	Tempo EXA 101	GEORGE LEWIS (EP)	10
59	Vogue EPV 1220	GEORGE LEWIS IN HI-FI (EP)	10
59	Vogue EPV 1252	GEORGE LEWIS IN HI-FI (EP)	10
52	Vogue LDE 012	GEORGE LEWIS AND HIS NEW ORLEANS ALLSTARS (10" LP)	15
54	Vogue LDE 082	GEORGE LEWIS JAM SESSION (10" LP)	15
55	Vogue LAE 12005	GEORGE LEWIS AND HIS NEW ORLEANS STOMPERS (LP)	40
55	London H-APB 1041	VOL. 1 JAZZ BAND (10" LP, with New Orleans Jazz Band & Quartet)	18
56	London HB-U 1045	VOL. 2 ALL STARS (10" LP, with New Orleans All Stars & Quartet)	18
57	Tempo TAP 13	GEORGE LEWIS RAGTIME BAND (LP)	30
57	Melodisc MLP 12-101	NEW ORLEANS PARADE LP)	15
50s	Esquire 20-067	GEORGE LEWIS RAGTIME BAND (10" LP)	15
50s	Esquire 20-073	GEORGE LEWIS RAGTIME BAND (10" LP)	15
50s	'77' LA 12/28	SMILE, DARN YA, SMILE (LP, as George Lewis with Barry Martyn's Band)	20
59	Columbia Clef 33C 9042	RAGGIN' AND STOMPIN' (10" LP)	15
60	HMV CLP 1371/CSD 1309	BLUES FROM THE BAYOU (LP, mono/stereo)	15/18
61	HMV CLP 1413/CSD 1337	DOCTOR JAZZ (LP, mono/stereo)	15/18
64	London HA-K/SH-K 8165	JAZZ AT PRESERVATION HALL VOL. 4 (LP, with Band Of New Orleans)	15

GEORGE LEWIS/FREDDIE KOHLMAN

53	Brunswick LA 8627	NEW ORLEANS JAZZ CONCERT (10" LP)	15

HOPETON LEWIS

67	Island WI 3054	Rock Steady/Cool Collie	90
67	Island WI 3055	Finder's Keepers/ROLAND ALPHONSO: Shanty Town Curfew	30
67	Island WI 3056	Let Me Come On Home/Hardships Of Life (with Merritone All Stars)	25
67	Island WI 3057	Run Down/Pick Yourself Up	25
67	Island WI 3059	Let The Little Girl Dance/This Music Got Soul	35
67	Island WI 3068	Rock A Shacka/I Don't Want Trouble	75
68	Island WI 3076	Everybody Rocking/Stars Shining So Bright	32
68	Fab FAB 43	Skinny Leg Girl/Live Like A King (as Hopetown Lewis & Glenmore Brown)	25
70	Duke Reid DR 2505	Boom Shaka Lacka/TOMMY McCOOK QUINTET: Dynamite	15
70	Duke Reid DR 2516	Testify/TOMMY McCOOK: Super Soul	15
71	Duke DU 112	Grooving Out Of Life (with Byron Lee & Dragonaires) (actually titled "Grooving Out On Life")/BYRON LEE & DRAGONAIRES: Fire Fire	8
71	Treasure Isle TI 7060	To The Other Man/TOMMY McCOOK: Stampede	12
72	Treasure Isle TI 7071	Judgement Day (actually by Hopeton Lewis & Dennis Alcapone)/EARL LINDO: Version Day	10
72	Attack ATT 8035	Starting All Over Again/DYNAMITES: Instrumental Version	5
72	Dynamic DYN 436	Come Together/Going Back To My Hometown	5
72	Dynamic DYN 447	Good Together/Version	5
73	Dragon DRA 1001	City Of New Orleans/The Wind Cries Mary	5
73	Dragon DRA 1011	Groovin' Out On Life/God Bless Whoever Sent You	5
67	Island ILP 957	TAKE IT EASY: ROCKSTEADY WITH HOPETON LEWIS (LP)	160
71	Trojan TRL 36	GROOVING OUT ON LIFE (LP)	30

(see also Glenmore Brown & Hopeton Lewis)

HUGH X. LEWIS

66	London HLR 10032	Looking In The Future/Too Late	8
66	London HA-R 8293	THE HUGH X. LEWIS ALBUM (LP)	15
67	London HA-R 8303	JUST BEFORE DAWN (LP)	15

JENNIFER LEWIS & ANGELA STRANGE

65	Columbia DB 7662	Bring It To Me/You Know	10
66	Columbia DB 7814	I've Heard It All Before/Bad Storm Coming	12

JERRY LEWIS

56	Capitol CL 14626	Buckskin Beauty/Pardners (with Dean Martin)	5
53	Capitol LC 6591	CAPITOL PRESENTS JERRY LEWIS (10" LP)	20

(see also Dean Martin)

JERRY LEWIS (Jamaica)

72	Pama PM 862	The Godfather/ALTON ELLIS: Some Day	15
73	Explosion EX 2077	Rhythm Pleasure/AGGROVATORS: Doctor Seaton	12

(see also I Roy)

JERRY LEE LEWIS

78s

57	London HLS 8457	Whole Lotta Shakin' Goin' On/It'll Be Me	15
57	London HLS 8529	Great Balls Of Fire/Mean Woman Blues	12
58	London HLS 8559	You Win Again/I'm Feelin' Sorry	28
58	London HLS 8592	Breathless/Down The Line	28
58	London HLS 8700	Break-Up/I'll Make It All Up To You	40
59	London HLS 8780	High School Confidential/Fools Like Me	50
59	London HLS 8840	Lovin' Up A Storm/Big Blon' Baby	65
59	London HLS 8941	Let's Talk About Us/The Ballad Of Billy Joe	95
59	London HLS 8993	Little Queenie/I Could Never Be Ashamed Of You	160
96	Cruisin' The 50s CASB 002	Wild One/Old Black Joe (numbered, 300 only)	30

SINGLES

57	London HLS 8457	Whole Lotta Shakin' Goin' On/It'll Be Me	35
57	London HLS 8529	Great Balls Of Fire/Mean Woman Blues	25
58	London HLS 8559	You Win Again/I'm Feelin' Sorry	40
58	London HLS 8592	Breathless/Down The Line	20
58	London HLS 8700	Break-Up/I'll Make It All Up To You	20
59	London HLS 8780	High School Confidential/Fools Like Me	20
59	London HLS 8840	Lovin' Up A Storm/Big Blon' Baby	25
59	London HLS 8941	Let's Talk About Us/The Ballad Of Billy Joe (probably no triangular centre)	20
59	London HLS 8993	Little Queenie/I Could Never Be Ashamed Of You (probably no triangular centre)	20

(The above 45s were originally issued with triangular centres; round-centre pressings are worth two-thirds of these values.)

60	London HLS 9083	I'll Sail My Ship Alone/It Hurt Me So	20
60	London HLS 9131	Baby, Baby, Bye Bye/Old Black Joe	20
60	London HLS 9202	John Henry/Hang Up My Rock And Roll Shoes	20
61	London HLS 9335	What'd I Say?/Livin' Lovin' Wreck	10
61	London HLS 9414	It Won't Happen With Me/Cold Cold Heart	15
61	London HLS 9446	As Long As I Live/When I Get Paid	12
62	London HLS 9526	I've Been Twistin'/Ramblin' Rose	10
62	London HLS 9584	Sweet Little Sixteen/How's My Ex Treating You	10
63	London HLS 9688	Good Golly Miss Molly/I Can't Trust Me (In Your Arms Anymore)	10
63	London HLS 9722	Teenage Letter/Seasons Of My Heart (B-side with Linda Gail Lewis)	12
63	Mercury AMT 1216	Hit The Road Jack/Pen And Paper	8
64	Philips BF 1324	I'm On Fire/Bread And Butter Man	10
64	London HLS 9867	Lewis Boogie/Bonnie B	20
65	Philips BF 1371	Hi-Heel Sneakers/You Went Back On Your Word	7
65	Philips BF 1407	Baby Hold Me Close/I Believe In You	8
65	Philips BF 1425	Rockin' Pneumonia And The Boogie Woogie Flu/This Must Be The Place	8
65	London HLS 9980	Carry Me Back To Old Virginia/I Know What It Means	12
66	Philips BF 1521	Memphis Beat/If I Had It All To Do Over	8
67	Philips BF 1594	It's A Hang-Up Baby/Holdin' On	8
67	Philips BF 1615	Turn On Your Love Light/Shotgun Man	10
68	Mercury MF 1020	Another Place, Another Time/Walking The Floor Over You	6
69	Mercury MF 1088	To Make Love Sweeter For You/Let's Talk About Us	5
69	Mercury MF 1105	Long Tall Sally/Jenny, Jenny (some in p/s)	10/6
69	Mercury MF 1110	Great Balls Of Fire/Whole Lotta Shakin' Goin' On (some in p/s)	10/6
73	Mercury 6052 378	(Taking My) Music To The Man/Jack Daniels (Old No. 7) (some in p/s)	8/6
79	Elektra K 12374	Rocking My Life Away/Rita May (p/s)	8
80	Elektra K 12399	Everyday I Have To Cry/Who Will The Next Fool Be	5
80	Elektra K 12432	Rockin' Jerry Lee/Good Time Charles Got The Blues	5

EXPORT SINGLES

58	London HL 7050	High School Confidential/Fools Like Me	30
62	London HL 7117	Save The Last Dance For Me/Hello Josephine	40
63	London HL 7120	Good Golly Miss Molly/I Can't Trust Me (In Your Arms Anymore)	25
63	London HL 7123	In The Mood/I'm Feelin' Sorry	40

EPs

58	London RE-S 1140	JERRY LEE LEWIS — NO. 1 (initially with triangular centre)	65/40
59	London RE-S 1186	JERRY LEE LEWIS — NO. 2 (initially with triangular centre)	65/40
59	London RE-S 1187	JERRY LEE LEWIS — NO. 3 (initially with triangular centre)	65/40
61	London RE-S 1296	JERRY LEE LEWIS — NO. 4	45
62	London RE-S 1336	JERRY LEE LEWIS — NO. 5	40
63	London RE-S 1351	JERRY LEE LEWIS — NO. 6	40
63	London RE-S 1378	FOUR MORE FROM JERRY LEE LEWIS	45
66	Philips BE 12599	COUNTRY STYLE	30
84	Sun JLL EP 001	THE FABULOUS JERRY LEE LEWIS VOL. 1 (Fan Club issue)	15
84	Sun JLL EP 002	THE FABULOUS JERRY LEE LEWIS VOL. 2 (Fan Club issue)	15

LPs

59	London HA-S 2138	JERRY LEE LEWIS	100
62	London HA-S 2440	JERRY LEE'S GREATEST	65
64	Philips (S)BL 7622	GOLDEN HITS	20
65	Philips (S)BL 7646	LIVE AT THE STAR CLUB, HAMBURG (with Nashville Teens)	25
65	Philips BL 7650	THE GREATEST LIVE SHOW ON EARTH	18
65	Philips BL 7668	THE RETURN OF ROCK	20
65	London HA-S 8251	WHOLE LOTTA SHAKIN' GOIN' ON	68
66	Philips BL 7688	COUNTRY SONGS FOR CITY FOLKS	18
66	Philips (S)BL 7706	MEMPHIS BEAT	18
66	Ember NR 5038	SUNSTROKE (shared with Carl Perkins)	12
67	Philips (S)BL 7746	BY REQUEST — MORE GREATEST LIVE SHOW ON EARTH (mono/stereo)	15/18
67	London HA-S 8323	BREATHLESS	75

(The above London LPs were originally issued with plum labels; later black label reissues are worth £15-£20.)

68	Mercury 20117 (S)MCL	SOUL MY WAY	16
68	Fontana SFJL 964	GOT YOU ON MY MIND	18

Jerry Lee LEWIS

MINT VALUE £

69	Mercury 21011 SMWL	ANOTHER PLACE, ANOTHER TIME	15
69	Mercury 21047 SMCL	SHE STILL COMES AROUND (TO WHAT'S LEFT OF ME) (stereo only)	15
69	Mercury 20156 SMCL	I'M ON FIRE	15
69	Mercury 20157 SMCL	SINGS THE COUNTRY MUSIC HALL OF FAME HITS VOL. 1	12
69	Mercury 20158 SMCL	SINGS THE COUNTRY MUSIC HALL OF FAME HITS VOL. 2	12
70	Mercury 20172 SMCL	TOGETHER (with Linda Gail Lewis)	15
70	Mercury 6338 010	SHE EVEN WOKE ME UP TO SAY GOODBYE	15
71	Mercury 6338 045	THERE MUST BE MORE TO LOVE THAN THIS	15
72	Mercury 6338 071	WOULD YOU TAKE ANOTHER CHANCE ON ME?	15
72	Mercury 6336 300	ROCKIN' WITH JERRY LEE LEWIS	15
72	Mercury 6338 088	THE KILLER ROCKS ON	15
73	Mercury 6672 008	THE SESSION (2-LP)	18
73	Mercury 6338 148	LIVE AT THE INTERNATIONAL HOTEL, LAS VEGAS	15
74	Mercury 6338 452	SOUTHERN ROOTS	15
74	Mercury 6338 496	FAN CLUB CHOICE	15
84	Sun SUN 102	THE SUN YEARS (12-LP, box set with booklet)	70

(see also Nashville Teens)

JIMMY LEWIS
68	Minit MLF 11002	The Girls From Texas/Let Me Know	30

JOE 'CANNONBALL' LEWIS
51	MGM MGM 430	Train Whistle Nightmare/Trust Me Again (78)	10

JOHN LEWIS
60	London Jazz LTZ-K 15186	IMPROVISED MEDITATIONS AND EXCURSIONS (LP)	15
61	London Jazz LTZ-K 15218	THE GOLDEN STRIKER (LP, also stereo SAH-K 6152)	15

(see also Modern Jazz Quartet)

JOHN LEWIS AND SACHA DISTELL
59	UK Oriole mg20036	AFTERNOON IN PARIS (LP)	40

LEW LEWIS (REFORMER)
76	Stiff BUY 5	Caravan Man/Boogie On The Street (p/s, with Dr. Feelgood)	5
77	United Artists UP 36217	Out For A Lark/Watch Yourself	5
78	Lew Lewis LEW 1	Lucky Seven/Night Talk (500 only, plain white sleeve)	8

(see also Oil City Sheiks, Dr. Feelgood, Eddie & the Hot Rods)

LINDA LEWIS
67	Polydor 56173	You Turned My Bitter Into Sweet/Do You Believe In Love	100
71	Reprise K 14096	We Can Win/Hampstead Way	6
72	Reprise K 14209	Old Smokey/It's The Frame	6
75	Arista ARIST 17	It's In His Kiss/Walk About (p/s)	6
73	Raft RA 18502	Rock A Doodle Doo/Reach For The Truth	6
72	Reprise K 44208	LARK (LP)	20
73	Raft RA 48501	FATHOMS DEEP (LP)	12
79	Ariola ARL 5033	HACIENDA VIEW (LP)	12

(see also Ferris Wheel)

MARGARET LEWIS
62	Starlite ST45 081	Sometin's Wrong Baby/John De Lee	40

MEADE 'LUX' LEWIS
50	Melodisc 1006	Boogie Woogie At The Philharmonic — Fast/(Medium) (78)	8
50	Melodisc 1007	Boogie Woogie At The Philharmonic — Slow/Honky Tonk Train (78)	8
50	Melodisc 1130	Boogie Tidal/Yancey's Pride (78)	12
50	Melodisc 1136	Glendale Glide/Denapas Parade (78)	12
51	Melodisc 1153	Randini's Boogie/Lux's Boogie (78)	12
52	Vogue V 2123	Blues Whistle/Chicago Flyer (78)	12
54	Vogue V 2229	Six Wheel Chaser Boogie/Bass On Top Boogie (78)	12
55	Vogue EPV 1065	MEADE 'LUX' LEWIS (EP)	25
56	Melodisc EPM7 107	BOOGIE WOOGIE AND BLUES (EP)	25
56	Columbia Clef SEB 10030	BOOGIE WOOGIE PIANO AND DRUMS NO. 1 (EP)	15
56	Columbia Clef SEB 10052	BOOGIE WOOGIE PIANO AND DRUMS NO. 2 (EP)	15
57	Columbia Clef 33CX 10094	YANCEY'S LAST RIDE (LP)	15
57	HMV DLP 1176	OUT OF THE ROARING TWENTIES (10" LP)	15
60s	Philips 652 014 BL	HOUSE PARTY (LP)	15

(see also Albert Ammons, [Big] Joe Turner)

MEADE 'LUX' LEWIS & SLIM GAILLARD
56	Columbia Clef 33C 9021	JAZZ AT THE PHILHARMONIC (10" LP)	20

(see also Slim Gaillard)

MIA LEWIS
65	Decca F 12117	Wish I Didn't Love Him/This Is The End	12
65	Decca F 12240	It's Goodbye Now/The Luckiest Girl	12
66	Parlophone R 5526	Nothing Lasts Forever/(Baby) I'm Feeling Good	20
67	Parlophone R 5585	No Time For Lovin'/Onion	5
67	Parlophone R 5617	Woman's Love/You Won't Get Away	5

MICHAEL LEWIS
73	United Artists UP 35569	Theatre Of Blood Theme/Edwina's Theme	22

MONICA LEWIS
56	Parlophone R 4224	I Wish You Love/Stay After School	5

NIGEL LEWIS
86	Media Burn MB10	WHAT I FEEL NOW (LP)	20

PATTI LEWIS
56	Columbia DB 3825	Earthbound/Happiness Street (Corner Sunshine Square)	10
57	Columbia DB 3923	Your Wild Heart/A Poor Man's Roses (Or A Rich Man's Gold)	8
57	Columbia DB 3967	Pull Down De Shade/Speak For Yourself John	8

Rare Record Price Guide 2008

PHILLIPPA LEWIS
| 65 | Decca F 12152 | Just Like In The Movies/Get Along Without You | 10 |

RAMSEY LEWIS (TRIO)
65	Chess CRS 8020	The 'In' Crowd/Since I Fell For You (as Ramsey Lewis Trio)	15
65	Chess CRS 8024	Hang On Sloopy/Movin' Easy (as Ramsey Lewis Trio)	8
66	Chess CRS 8029	A Hard Day's Night/'Tout A Doubt (as Ramsey Lewis Trio)	8
66	Chess CRS 8031	Hi-Heel Sneakers (Parts 1 & 2) (as Ramsey Lewis Trio)	10
66	Chess CRS 8041	Wade In The Water/Ain't That Peculiar (Ramsey Lewis Trio) (DJ copy = £150)	40
66	Chess CRS 8044	Uptight (Everything's Alright)/Money In The Pocket	10
67	Chess CRS 8051	Day Tripper/Hurt So Bad	20
67	Chess CRS 8055	1-2-3/Down By The Riverside	8
67	Chess CRS 8058	Function At The Junction/Hey Mrs. Jones	10
67	Chess CRS 8060	Saturday Night After The Movies/China Gate	8
67	Chess CRS 8061	Girl Talk/Dancing In The Street	8
67	Chess CRS 8064	Soul Man/Struttin' Lightly	10
69	Chess CRS 8096	Cry Baby Cry/Wade In The Water (DJ copy = £45)	20
70	Chess CRS 8104	Julia/Do What You Wanna	10
72	Chess 6145 004	Wade In The Water/Ain't That Peculiar (paper label)	15
72	Chess 6145 013	The 'In' Crowd/Soul Man	6
72	CBS 8280	Slipping Into Darkness/Collage	8
66	Chess CRE 6019	A HARD DAY'S NIGHT (EP, as Ramsey Lewis Trio)	28
65	Pye Jazz NJL 55	AT THE BOHEMIAN CAVERNS (LP)	20
65	Chess CRL 4511	THE 'IN' CROWD (LP)	25
65	Chess CRL 4518	CHOICE! THE BEST OF RAMSEY LEWIS (LP)	25
66	Chess CRL 4520	HANG ON RAMSEY! (LP)	20
66	Chess CRL 4522	WADE IN THE WATER (LP)	40
67	Chess CRL 4528	GOIN' LATIN (LP)	25
67	Chess CRL 4531	THE MOVIE ALBUM (LP)	20
68	Chess CRL(S) 4533	DANCIN' IN THE STREET (LP)	25
68	Chess CRLS 4535	UP POPS RAMSEY LEWIS (LP)	25
68	Chess CRLS 4539	MAIDEN VOYAGE (LP)	25
69	Chess CRLS 4545	MOTHER NATURE'S SON (LP)	30
60s	Fontana SFJL 962	DOWN TO EARTH (LP)	20
72	Chess 6310 106	BACK TO THE ROOTS (LP)	15
72	Chess 6310 114	THE BEST OF RAMSEY LEWIS (LP)	15
72	Chess 6310 124	TOBACCO ROAD (LP)	15
72	CBS 64718	UPENDO NI PAMOJA (LP)	12
73	CBS 65307	FUNKY SERENITY (LP)	20
73	CBS CQ 31096	UPENDO NI PAMOJA (LP, quadrophonic)	15
74	CBS S80677	SUN GODDESS (LP)	18

(see also Young-Holt Unlimited)

RICHARD LEWIS & HIS BAND
| 60 | Downbeat CHA 1 | Hey, Little Girl/Hey, Little Boy | 40 |

SMILEY LEWIS
53	London L 1189	Big Mamou/Play Girl (78, some copies miscredited to Smiley Davis)	120
56	London HLU 8312	One Night/Ain't Gonna Do It (78 rpm = £115)	800
56	London HLU 8337	Down Yonder We Go Ballin'/Don't Be That Way (Please Listen To Me)	800
56	London HLU 8337	Down Yonder We Go Ballin'/Don't Be That Way (Please Listen To Me) (78)	110
57	London HLP 8367	Shame, Shame, Shame/No, No (gold or silver label lettering)	500/400
57	London HLP 8367	Shame, Shame, Shame/No, No (78)	100
70	Liberty LBF 15337	I Hear You Knocking/Play Girl	10
70	Liberty LBS 83308	SHAME, SHAME, SHAME (LP)	25
78	United Artists UAS 30167	I HEAR YOU KNOCKING (LP)	15

STEVIE LEWIS
65	Mercury MF 871	Take Me For A Little While/My Whole World Seems To Be Tumbling Down	22
65	Mercury MF 919	Sometimes When You're Lonely/Under The Smile Of Love	5
65	Polydor 56003	Heard It All Before/Wild	5
69	RCA RCA 1840	Take A Little Warning/I Can Try	5

TAMALA LEWIS
| 79 | Destiny DS 1010 | You Won't Say Nothing/If You Can Stand Me (DJ copy = £20) | 10 |

TINY LEWIS
| 60 | Parlophone R 4617 | Too Much Rockin'/I Get Weak | 150 |

VIC LEWIS
55	Philips PB 503	Scramble/Walk, Don't Run (78)	6
55	Philips PB 411	Barwick Green ("The Archers" Theme Tune)/Don't Say Goodbye (78)	6
63	HMV POP 1127	Bossa Nova Scotia/Vic's Tune	5
62	Columbia SEG 8202	SWINGS NELSON RIDDLE (EP)	12
55	Decca LF 1216	PROGRESSIVE JAZZ (10" LP)	20
62	HMV CLP 1641	PLAY BOSSA NOVA HOME AND AWAY (LP)	30
60s	Ember CJS 807	AT THE BEAULIEU FESTIVAL (LP)	30
60s	Ember SE 8018	BIG BAND EXPLOSION (LP)	40
70s	DJM SPECB 103	MY LIFE MY WAY (LP)	20

LEWIS & CLARKE EXPEDITION
| 67 | RCA Victor RCA 1633 | I Feel Good/Blue Revelations | 8 |

LEWIS SISTERS
| 65 | Tamla Motown TMG 536 | You Need Me/Moonlight On The Beach | 100 |

DAVE LEWRY
| 72 | Westwood WRS 019 | ALL I WANT TO DO IS PLAY GUITAR (LP) | 35 |

MONIQUE LEYRAC
| 68 | SNB 55-3309 | Time Time/Love Is Blue | 5 |

John LEYTON

JOHN LEYTON

60	Top Rank JAR 426	Tell Laura I Love Her/Goodbye To Teenage Love	55
60	HMV POP 798	The Girl On The Floor Above/Terry Brown's In Love With Mary Dee	100
61	Top Rank JAR 577	Johnny Remember Me/There Must Be	7
61	Top Rank JAR 585	Wild Wind/You Took My Love For Granted.	7
61	HMV POP 956	Son This Is She/Six White Horses.	6
62	HMV POP 992	Lone Rider/Heart Of Stone.	15
62	HMV POP 1014	Lonely City/It Would Be Easy	10
62	HMV POP 1054	Down The River Nile/I Think I'm Falling In Love	10
62	HMV POP 1076	Lonely Johnny/Keep On Loving You	10
63	HMV POP 1122	Cupboard Love/Land Of Love	10
63	HMV POP 1175	I'll Cut Your Tail Off/The Great Escape	6
63	HMV POP 1204	On Lover's Hill/Lovers Lane	6
63	HMV POP 1230	I Guess You Are Always On My Mind/Beautiful Dreamer	6
64	HMV POP 1264	Make Love To Me/Missing You (as John Leyton & Le Roys)	15
64	HMV POP 1338	Don't Let Her Go Away/I Want A Love I Can See.	10
64	HMV POP 1374	All I Want Is You/Every Day Is A Holiday (with Grazina Frame & Mike Sarne)	10
73	York SYK 551	Dancing In The Graveyard/Riversong.	8
74	York YR 210	Rock 'N' Roll/Highway Song	7
62	Top Rank JKP 3016	JOHN LEYTON (EP)	40
62	HMV 7EG 8747	HIT PARADE (EP)	40
64	HMV 7EG 8843	BEAUTIFUL DREAMER (EP)	40
64	HMV 7EG 8854	TELL LAURA I LOVE HER (EP)	50
61	HMV CLP 1497	THE TWO SIDES OF JOHN LEYTON (LP).	60
62	HMV CLP 1664	ALWAYS YOURS (LP, with Charles Blackwell's Orchestra)	80
73	York FYK 416	JOHN LEYTON (LP).	40
	(see also Le Roys)		

LEYTON BUZZARDS

78	Small Wonder SMALL 7	19 And Mad/Villain/Youthanasia (p/s)	6
79	Chrysalis CHS 2288	Saturday Night Beneath The Plastic Palm Trees/Trough With You (p/s).	5
79	Chrysalis CHS 2328	I'm Hanging Around/I Don't Want To Go/No Dry Ice (p/s, green vinyl)	5
79	Chrysalis CHR 1213	JELLIED EELS TO RECORD DEALS (LP, as Buzzards)	12

L.F.O.

90	Warp WAP 5	L.F.O. (The Leeds Warehouse Mix)/L.F.O. (Track 4)/Probe (The Cuba Edit) (12").	15

LIAISON

82	Catweazle CR 001	Play It With A Passion/Caught In A ... (some in grey or yellow p/s).	35/10
83	Liaison LIC 101	LOOKING AFTER NUMBER ONE (EP).	5
84	Liaison LSN 0020	Only Heaven Knows/Ease The Pain Away (p/s).	5

LIAR

79	Bearsville K 55524	SET THE WORLD ON FIRE (LP, picture disc).	12

LIBERACE

56	Columbia DB 3834	I Don't Care (As Long As You Care For Me)/As Time Goes By	5

LIBERATION SUITE

70s	Myrrh MYR 1027	LIBERATION SUITE (LP).	18

LIBERATORS

65	Stateside SS 424	It Hurts So Much/You Look So Fine	12
	(see also Pinkerton's Assorted Colours)		

EVE LIBERTINE & CRASS

84	Crass 1984/4	ACTS OF LOVE (LP, with book).	12
	(see also Crass)		

LIBERTINES

02	Rough Trade RTRADES 054	What A Waster/I Get Along (p/s, 2000 only)	30
	Rough Trade RTRADESCD 054	What A Waster/I Get Along (CD)	25
02	Rough Trade RTRADES 064	Up The Bracket/Boys In The Band (p/s).	8
03	Rough Trade RTRADES 074	Time For Heroes/The 7 Deadly Sins (demo version) (p/s)	10
03	Rough Trade RTRADS 119	Don't Look Back Into The Sun/Death On The Stairs (blue vinyl, fold-out poster sleeve in PVC slipcase, 3000 only)	15
04	Rough Trade RTRADS 163	Can't Stand Me Now/The Tide That Left Never Came Back/ (I've Got) Sweets (p/s)	5
04	Rough Trade RTRADS 215	What Became Of The Likely Lads?/(Reworked)/Boys In The Band (Live at Brixton Sat 6/3/04) (with free LP poster p/s)	8
02	Rough Trade RTRADELP 065	UP THE BRACKET (LP)	15
04	Rough Trade RTRADELPX166	THE LIBERTINES (2 x LP, gatefold 3000 only)	18
04	Rough Trade RTRADELP166	THE LIBERTINES (white label test pressing, 10 only)	50
	(see also Babyshambles, Wolfman)		

LIBERTY BELLES

71	Jay Boy BOY 40	Shing-A-Ling Time/Just Try Me	10

LICKS

79	Stortbeat BEAT 8	1970S EP	15
	(see also Epileptics, Flux Of Pink Indians)		

JAMIE LIDELL

97	Mosquito MSQ 08	FREAKIN' THE FRAME (12" EP)	20

LIEUTENANT BUDDY KNOX

	(see under 'K')

LIEUTENANT PIGEON

73	Decca SKL 5154	MOULDY OLD MUSIC (LP).	12
	(see also Shel Naylor, Stavely Makepeace, Heavy Cochran)		

LIFE
69	Polydor 56778	Hands Of The Clock/Ain't I Told You Before	22
74	Polydor 2058 500	Woman/Bless My Soul	6
74	Polydor 2383 295	LIFE AFTER DEATH (LP)	40

LIFE
73	Philips 6006 280	Cats Eyes/Death In The Family (paper or moulded label)	20/10

LIFE AFTER LIFE
85	Timetrack SRTSKL 453	LIFE AFTER LIFE (LP, private pressing)	120

KEALOHA LIFE & HIS ROYAL SAMOANS
57	Lambda BB 3003	The Beauty Hula/HARMONY HAWAIIANS: Auwei (78)	10

LIFE 'N' SOUL
67	Decca F 12659	Ode To Billy Joe/Peacefully Asleep	35
68	Decca F 12851	Here Comes Yesterday Again/Dear Paul	15

LIFE SUPPORT
79	Slug SLUG 1	Leader Deceiver/Confusion (p/s, white labels)	6

LIFETIME
70	Polydor 2066 050	One Word/Two Worlds	15
	(see also Tony Williams [Lifetime], Jack Bruce, John McLaughlin)		

JOE LIGES
63	Blue Beat BB 172	Spit In The Sky/Tell Me What (both actually by Delroy Wilson)	25
	(see also Delroy Wilson)		

JOE LIGGINS & HONEYDRIPPERS
50	Parlophone R 3309	I've Got The Right To Cry/Blue Moods (78)	30
76	Specialty SDN 5006	Pink Champagne/Honey Dripper	5

BEN LIGHT
56	HMV 7M 350	Bring Me A Bluebird/You	8

ENOCH LIGHT
59	Top Rank JAR 134	With My Eyes Wide Open/I Cried For You (as Enoch Light & Light Brigade)	5
59	Top Rank JAR 134	With My Eyes Wide Open/I Cried For You (Enoch Light & Light Brigade) (78)	6
59	Top Rank JAR 234	Scarlet Ribbons/Greensleeves (as Enoch Light & His Vibrant Strings)	5
69	Studio Two TWO 312	SPACED OUT (LP)	25
70	Project 3	PERMISSIVE POLYPHONICS (LP)	25

LIGHT FANTASTIC
73	RCA RCA 2331	Jeanie/You Don't Care	20

GORDON LIGHTFOOT
62	Decca F 11527	(Remember Me) I'm The One/Daisy-Doo (as Gord Lightfoot)	20
63	Fontana 267 275TF	Negotiations/It's Too Late, He Wins (as Gordie Lightfoot)	5
63	Fontana TF 405	The Day Before Yesterday/Take Care Of Yourself (as Gordie Lightfoot)	5
65	United Artists UP 1109	Just Like Tom Thumb's Blues/Ribbon Of Darkness	5
66	Warner Bros WB 5621	I'm Not Sayin'/For Lovin' Me	5
68	President PT 138	Adios Adios/Is My Baby Blue Tonight (as Gordie Lightfoot)	5
68	United Artists UP 2216	Black Day In July/Pussy Willow's Cat Tails	5
69	United Artists UP 2272	The Circle Is Small/Does Your Mother Know	5
69	United Artists UP 35020	Bitter Green/May I	5
68	United Artists SULP 1199	DID SHE MENTION MY NAME (LP)	12
69	United Artists SULP 1239	BACK HERE ON EARTH (LP)	12
69	Utd. Artists UAL/UAS 29012	EARLY LIGHTFOOT (LP)	12
71	Reprise RSLP 6392	IF YOU COULD READ MY MIND (LP)	12

PADDY LIGHTFOOT
50s	Melodisc EPM7 100	PADDY LIGHTFOOT (EP)	10

PAPA (GEORGE) LIGHTFOOT
69	Liberty LBF 15176	Wine Whiskey And Woman/SLIM HARPO: Something Inside Me	20
60s	Jan & Dil JR 451	MORE DOWN HOME BLUES (EP)	35
71	Liberty LBS 83353	NATCHEZ TRACE (LP, as Papa George Lightfoot)	30

TERRY LIGHTFOOT'S (NEW ORLEANS) JAZZMEN
61	Columbia DB 4696	True Love/Black Bottom Stomp	5
61	Columbia SCD 2165	King Kong/Riverside Blues (some with p/s)	5
65	Columbia DB 7534	Alley Cat/Petite Fleur	5
58	Columbia SEG 7851	PLAYS TRAD (EP)	20
59	Columbia SEG 7917	MORE TRAD (EP)	10
60	Columbia SEG 7976	TRAD AGAIN (EP)	10
56	Nixa Jazz NJT 503	JAZZ GUMBO VOLUME ONE (10" LP)	15
58	Columbia 33SX 1073	TRADITION IN COLOUR (LP)	15
61	Columbia 33SX 1290	TRAD PARADE (LP, with New Orleans Jazzmen, also stereo SCX 3354) ... each	15
61	Columbia 33SX 1353	WORLD OF TRAD (LP)	20
62	Columbia 33SX 1449	LIGHTFOOT AT LANSDOWNE (LP)	15
63	Columbia 33SX 1551	TERRY (LP)	12
65	Columbia 33SX 1721	ALLEYCAT (LP, as Terry Lightfoot's Jazzmen)	15

LIGHTHOUSE
69	RCA RCA 1884	Eight Miles High/If There Ever Was A Time	7
71	Vertigo 6073 150	Hats Off (To The Strangers)/Sing Sing Sing	7
72	Philips 6073 152	One Fine Morning/Little Kind Words	6
72	Philips 6073 153	Take It Slow/Sweet Lullaby	6
70	RCA SF 8103	SUITE FEELING (LP)	18
70	RCA SF 8121	PEACING IT ALL TOGETHER (LP)	15
71	Vertigo 6342 010	ONE FINE MORNING (LP, gatefold sleeve, swirl label)	40
71	Vertigo 6342 011	THOUGHTS OF MOVIN' ON (LP, gatefold sleeve, swirl label)	40

MINT VALUE £

LIGHTNIN' SLIM
72	Blue Horizon 2096 013	Just A Little Bit/You're Old Enough To Understand/Mind Your Own Business . . .	30
65	Stateside SL 10135	A LONG DRINK OF BLUES (LP, with Slim Harpo)	70
69	Python PLP 8	THE DOWNHOME BLUES PART 1 (LP, 99 copies only)	60
70	Blue Horizon 7-63863	ROOSTER BLUES (LP)	65
72	Blue Horizon 2931 005	LONDON GUMBO (LP)	100
78	Flyright FLYLP 533	TRIP TO CHICAGO (LP)	15
79	Flyright FLYLP 583	THE FEATURE SIDES 1954 (LP)	15
80	Flyright FLYLP 612	WE GOTTA ROCK TONIGHT (LP)	15

(see also Slim Harpo)

LIGHTNING LEON
60s	Jan & Dil JR 450	DOWN HOME BLUES — SIXTIES STYLE (EP)	38

LIGHTNING RAIDERS
80	Arista ARIST 341	Psychedelik Musik ('adult' version)/Views (p/s)	20
80	Arista ARIST 341DJ	Psychedelik Musik ('censored' version)/Views (promo only, no p/s)	35
81	Revenge REVS 200	Criminal World/Citizens (p/s)	25
81	Revenge RSS 39	Sweet Revenge/Rowdies/Addiction/Soul Rescue (12", promo only)	45

(see also Pink Fairies, Professionals)

LIGHTNING SEEDS
89	Ghetto CDGTG 4	Pure/Fools/God Help Them/All I Want (CD, card sleeve)	8
89	Ghetto CDGTG 6	Joy/Frenzy/Control The Flame (CD, card sleeve)	8

(see also Big In Japan, Care)

LIGHT OF THE WORLD
80	Ensign ENY 4312	London Town/Pete's Crusade (12")	12
82	EMI EMI 5319	No. 1 Girl/Don't Run	10
82	EMI 12EMI 5319	No. 1 Girl/Don't Run (12")	15
79	Ensign ENVY 7	LIGHT OF THE WORLD (LP)	12
80	Ensign ENVY 14	ROUND TRIP (LP)	12
82	EMI EMC 3410	CHECK US OUT (LP)	15

LIKE A SONG
73	De Wolfe DW/LP 3273	LIKE A SONG (LP, library issue)	18

LILAC TIME
88	Swordfish LILAC 1	Return To Yesterday/Trumpets From Montparnasse (no p/s)	8
88	Swordfish 12 LILAC 1	Return To Yesterday/Railway Bazaar/Trumpets From Montparnasse/ Reunion Ball (12", p/s)	15
88	Fontana LILCD 2	Return To Yesterday/Rooftrees/Gone For A Burton/ Reunion Ball (CD, card sleeve)	10
88	Fontana LILCD 3	You've Got To Love/Railway Bazaar/Trumpets From Montparnasse (CD, card sleeve)	8
88	Fontana LILAC 4	Black Velvet/Black Dawn (p/s in Xmas card folder)	8
88	Fontana LILCD 4	Black Velvet/Tiger Tea/Street Corner/Black Dawn (CD)	8
89	Fontana LILCD 5	American Eyes/Shepherd's Plaid/The World In Her Arms/Crossing The Line (CD)	8
89	Fontana LILCD 6	The Days Of The Week/The Queen Of Heartless/Spin A Cavalu (CD)	8
89	Fontana LILCD 7	The Girl Who Waves At Trains/If The Stars Shine Tonight (Acoustic Version)/ Ounce Of Nails/American Eyes (Acoustic Version) (CD)	8
90	Caff CAFF 12	Madresfield/Bird On The Wire (p/s, with insert)	20
88	Swordfish SWF LP 6	THE LILAC TIME (LP, original issue)	15
88	Swordfish SWF CD 6	THE LILAC TIME (CD, original issue)	30
88	Fontana 836 744-2	THE LILAC TIME (LP, reissue, with inner sleeve)	12
89	Fontana 838 641-2	PARADISE CIRCUS (CD)	20

(see also Hawks, Stephen Duffy)

LIL & RENEE
63	Reprise R 20206	Tennessee Waltz/Keep A Lite	5

LILYS
96	Ché CHE 51	Returns Every Morning/Touch The Water (white vinyl, p/s, 500 only)	6
96	Ché CHE 65	A Nanny In Manhattan/More Than Is Deserved (coffee-coloured vinyl, p/s, 500 only)	6

LIMELIGHT
75	United Artists UP 35779	I Should Have Known Better/Tell Me Why	12

(see also Brinsley Schwarz)

LIMELIGHT
80	Future Earth FER 006	Metal Man/Hold Me Touch Me (p/s)	12
82	Future Earth FER 010	Ashes To Ashes/Knife In Your Back (p/s, some with insert)	12/10
80	Future Earth FER 008	LIMELIGHT (LP)	30
81	Avatar AALP 5005	LIMITED LIMELIGHT (LP, some with bonus single)	35/20

LIMELITERS
63	RCA RCX 7126	FUN FOLK (EP)	10
64	RCA RCX 7151	FOUR FOLK SONGS (EP)	10
60	Elektra EKL 180	FOLK SONGS FOR MODERNS (LP)	12
61	RCA RD 27254	SLIGHTLY FABULOUS LIMELITERS (LP)	12
63	RCA Victor RD/SF 7581	FOURTEEN 14K FOLK SONGS (LP)	12

ALISON LIMERICK
90	Arista 113509	Where Love Lives/Where Love Lives (Classic Mix) (p/s)	5

LIMEYS
65	Pye 7N 15820	I Can't Find My Way Through/Don't Cry (My Love)	5
65	Pye 7N 15909	Some Tears Fall Dry/Half Glass Of Wine	5
66	Decca F 12382	Cara-Lin/Feel So Blue	30
66	Decca F 12466	The Mountain's High/Lovin' Yourself	5

LIMIT
78	Private Stock PVT 156	Please Please Me/My World At Night (company sleeve)	90

PETER LINCOLN
67	Major Minor MM 520	In The Day Of My Youth/My Monkey Is A Junkie	10

(see also Peter Sarstedt, Sarstedt Brothers, Brothers Kane)

PHILAMORE LINCOLN
68	NEMS 56-3711	Running By The River/Rainy Day	20

LINCOLNS
66	Parlophone R 5418	Mister Loneliness/Only Love Will Break Your Heart	6

LINCOLN X
63	Oriole CB 1823	Heartaches And Happiness/Stand In For Her Past	5

BOB LIND
66	Fontana TF 670	Elusive Butterfly/Cheryl's Goin' Home	6
66	Fontana TF 702	Remember The Rain/Truly Julie's Blues (I'll Be There)	5
66	Fontana TF 750	San Francisco Woman/Oh Babe Take Me Home	5
67	Verve VS 1501	Hey Nellie Nellie/Wandering	5
66	Fontana (S)TL 5340	DON'T BE CONCERNED (LP)	20
66	Verve F'ways (S)VLP 5015	THE ELUSIVE BOB LIND (LP)	20
67	Fontana (S)TL 5395	PHOTOGRAPHS OF FEELINGS (LP)	15

ROSA LINDA
53	London L 1215	Flight 88/Taboo (78)	12

LINDA & FUNKY BOYS
76	Spark SRL 1149	Climbing The Steps Of Love/Baby Are You Satisfied	8

DADDY LINDBERG
67	Columbia DB 8138	Shirl/Wade In The Shade	40

(see also Crocheted Doughnut Ring, Fingers)

ANITA LINDBLOM
62	Fontana 267223 TF	Uptown/Mr Big Wheel	8

DENNIS LINDE
73	Elektra K 42149	DENNIS LINDE (LP)	12
74	Elektra K 52013	TRAPPED IN THE SUBURBS (LP)	12

KATHY LINDEN
58	Felsted AF 102	Billy/If I Could Hold You In My Arms (78 rpm = £12)	15
58	Felsted AF 105	You'd Be Surprised/Why Oh Why (78 rpm = £15)	15
58	Felsted AF 108	Oh! Johnny, Oh!/Georgie (78 rpm = £15)	12
58	Felsted AF 111	Kissin' Conversation/Just A Sandy Haired Boy Called Sandy (78 rpm = £20)	15
59	Felsted AF 122	Goodbye Jimmy, Goodbye/Heartaches At Sweet Sixteen (78 rpm = £15)	9
59	Felsted AF 124	So Close To My Heart/You Don't Know Girls (78 rpm = £20)	10
60	Felsted AF 130	Think Love/Mary Lou Wilson And Johnny Brown	10
59	Felsted GEP 1001	KATHY (EP)	25
59	Felsted GEP 1002	KATHY'S IN LOVE VOLUME ONE (EP)	25
59	Felsted GEP 1004	KATHY'S IN LOVE VOLUME TWO (EP)	25

LINDISFARNE
SINGLES
70	Charisma CB 137	Clear White Light Part II/Knackers Yard Blues	12
71	Charisma CB 153	Lady Eleanor/Nothing But The Marvellous Is Beautiful (some with p/s)	8/5
72	Charisma CB 173	Meet Me On The Corner/Scotch Mist/No Time To Lose (p/s)	6
72	Charisma CB 191	All Fall Down/We Can Swing Together (live) (p/s)	6
72	Charisma CB 199	Court In The Act/Don't Ask Me	5
74	Charisma CB 228	Taking Care Of Business/North Country Boy	6
74	Charisma CB 232	Fog On The Tyne/Mandolin King	6
75	Warner Brothers K 16489	Tonight/No Need To Tell Me	6
75	Charisma CB 266	Lady Eleanor/Fog On The Tyne	5
78	Mercury 6007 177	Run For Home/Stick Together (p/s)	5
78	Mercury 6007 195	Brand New Day/Winter Song	5
79	Mercury 6007 205	Warm Feeling/Clear White Light (live) (p/s)	5
79	Mercury NEWS 1	Easy And Free/When Friday Comes Along (p/s)	5
79	Mercury 6007 241	Call Of The Wild/Dedicated Hound	5
90	Best ZA 44207	Fog On The Tyne (Revisited)/Fog On The Tyne (Revisited) (Instrumental) (picture disc, by Gazza [Paul Gascoigne] & Lindisfarne)	5
70	Charisma CAS 1025	NICELY OUT OF TUNE (LP, pink or 'mad hatter' label)	18/15
71	Charisma CAS 1050	FOG ON THE TYNE (LP, gatefold sleeve)	12
72	Charisma CAS 1057	DINGLY DELL (LP, with inner sleeve & poster)	12
73	Charisma CLASS 2	LINDISFARNE LIVE (LP)	12
73	Charisma CAS 1076	ROLL ON RUBY (LP, gatefold sleeve & poster)	12

(see also Alan Hull, Jack The Lad, Chosen Few, Radiator, Ray Jackson)

MARK LINDSAY
69	CBS 4699	Arizona/Man From Houston	8
70	CBS 5055	Silver Bird/So Hard To Leave You	8
70	CBS 5219	And The Grass Won't Pay No Mind/Funny How Little Men Care	8
71	CBS 5408	Problem Child/Bookends	8
71	CBS 7330	Been Too Long On The Road/All I Really See Is You	8
71	CBS 7551	Are You Old Enough/Don't You Know	8
71	CBS 7690	Something Big/Pretty Pretty	8

(see also Paul Revere & Raiders)

TERRY LINDSEY
69	President PT 232	It's Over/One Day Up, Next Day Down	6

MINT VALUE £

DAVID LINDUP ORCHESTRA
66	Columbia DB 7979	Informer Theme/Blue Mountain	8
66	Polydor 56106	Survival Theme/New Forest	20
70	Aristocrat AR 1021	WHEN THE SAINTS GO (LP)	25

LINDYS
60	Decca F 11253	The Train Of Love/You Know How Things Get Around	15
60	Decca F 11272	Boy With The Eyes Of Blue/Someone Else's Roses	15

LING FAMILY
77	Topic 12TS 292	SINGING TRADITIONS OF A SUFFOLK FAMILY (LP)	15

LINES
78	Linear SJP 782	White Night/Barbican (p/s)	7
79	Illegal ILS 0011	White Night/Barbican (p/s, reissue)	5
80	Red Linear RL 007	Nerve Pylon/Over The Brow (screen-printed p/s)	5
80s	Red Linear RL12 005	COOL SNAP EP (12")	15

LINK
92	Evolution EVO 05	THE FIRST LINK EP (12", plain sleeve)	50
93	Symbiotic SYM 001	THE LINK EP (12", plain sleeve, no credits on label)	50
95	Warp WAP 59	ANTACID EP (12", p/s)	15
95	Warp WAP 59R	ANTACID REMIXES EP (12", p/s)	15
	(see also Reload, Global Communications, Mystic Institute)		

LINKERS
71	Big Shot BI 567	Bongo Man/FUD CHRISTIAN ALLSTARS: Creation Version	6
	(see also Links)		

ANSEL LINKERS & FUD CHRISTIAN ALL STARS
73	Summit SUM 8540	Memories By The Score/FUD CHRISTIAN ALL STARS: Scorer	7
	(see also Links)		

LINKS
72	Tropical AL 0010	Sing A Song Of Freedom/TROPICAL ALL STARS:	
		Love Rhythm (A-side actually by Linkers)	6

ELMO LINN
63	Starlite ST45 101	Another Man's Arms/Sam Houston	15

LINN COUNTY
68	Mercury SMCL 20142	PROUD FLESH SOOTHSEER (LP)	15
69	Mercury SMCL 20165	FEVER SHOT (LP)	15
70	Philips SBL 7923	TILL THE BREAK OF DAWN (LP)	15

LINOLEUM
96	Lino Vinyl LINO 001	Dissent/Twisted (lino sleeve, some sealed, 1,000 only)	10/7
96	Lino Vinyl LINO 002	Smear/Tired (lino sleeve, some sealed, 2,000 only)	7/5

JOE LINTHECOME
50s	Poydras 87	Pretty Mama Blues/Hummingbird Blues	15

LINUS & LITTLE PEOPLE
70	Evolution	Lovin' La La	10

LION (& His Calypso Cubs)
51	Sagomes SG 117	Ugly Woman/The Lost Watch (78)	10
52	Parlophone MP 114	Mary Ann/Little Mary Had No Lamb (export 78)	10
52	Parlophone MP 115	Tick! Tick!/Ugly Woman (export 78)	10
53	Melodisc 1236	Coronation Of Elizabeth 2/Crosby Cavalcade (78, with Caribbean Rhythm)	10
54	Parlophone MP 129	The Royal Tour/The Weather Man (export 78)	10
54	Parlophone MP 132	I Ain't Gonna Do It No More/Trinidad, The Land Of Calypso (export 78)	10
55	Parlophone MP 135	Bananas/The Devil Fly (export 78, with His Calypso Cubs)	12
55	Parlophone MP 140	Go Away Miss Tina/Love Thy Neighbour (export 78, with His Calypso Cubs)	10
56	Parlophone MP 146	Merry Merry Christmas/Christmas Prayer Meeting	
		(export 78, with His Calypso Cubs)	10
56	Parlophone MP 147	Money, Money, Money/Kalenda March (J'ouvert Barriot)	
		(export 78, with His Calypso Cubs)	10

LIONHEART
85	Epic A 5001	Die For Love/Dangerous Games (p/s)	7
84	Epic EPC26214	HOT TONIGHT (LP)	12
	(see also Iron Maiden, Wildfire)		

LIONROCK
92	M.E.R.C. 002	Roots'n'Culture (Part One)/Lionrock (12", original issue)	10
92	De Construc. 74321124381	Lionrock — The Remixes: (Most Excellent Mix)/	
		(Roots 'n' Culture)/(A Trumpet Jamboree In Edinburgh)/	
		(A Dubtastic Jamboree In Edinburgh) (12")	10
93	De Construc. 74321144371	Packet Of Peace (Prankster Sound System Mix)/(Instrumental)/	
		(No More Fucking Trumpets) (12")	8
93	Distort & Cavort	Dub Plate No. 1 (12")	10
94	De Construc. DUB PLATE 1	The Guide/Don't Be Foolish (12")	8
98	Concrete HARD 3112	Rude Boy Rock/Best Foot Forward/Push Button Cocktail (p/s)	8

LIONS
69	Polydor 56757	Twisted Nerve/My Friend The Blackbird	35

LIONS OF JUDAH
69	Fontana TF 1016	Our Love's A Growin' Thing/Katja	15

JOE LIPMAN ORCHESTRA
54	MGM SP 1108	Looking Back To See/Stop	5

LIP MOVES
79	Tichonderoga HP 1	Guest/What Is (p/s with insert, stickered white labels, some signed)	35/30

LIQUID CRYSTAL

91	Bizarre BIZZ 2	Inner Sense/Dischord (12")	25
92	Bizarre BIZZ 3	The Power Within/Let It Go/Inner Sense ('92 Remix) (12")	25
92	Bizarre BIZZ 3R T	The Power Within (Remix)/Radiate/Inner Sense (Original) (12", p/s)	25
92	Ruff On Wax ROWT 1	CHROMATIC EP (12", stickered plain sleeve)	80
92	Ruff On Wax ROWTR 1	CHROMATIC 2 EP (12", stickered plain sleeve)	80

LIQUID SMOKE

75	Pye Int. 7N 25677	Dance Dance Dance/Where Is Our Love	6
70	Avco Embassy 646 6003	LIQUID SMOKE (LP)	45

LISTEN

65	CBS 202456	You'd Better Run/Everybody's Gonna Say	300

(see also Robert Plant, Led Zeppelin)

LITTER

69	Probe CLPS 4504	EMERGE (LP)	45

'BIG' TINY LITTLE

57	Vogue Coral Q 72263	School Day/That's The Only Way To Live (78 rpm = £20)	40
60	Coral FEP 2058	HONKY TONK PIANO VOL. 1 (EP)	15
60	Coral FEP 2059	HONKY TONK PIANO VOL. 2 (EP)	15

KENNY LITTLE & LITTLE PEOPLE

65	United Artists UP 1074	A Shot In The Dark/Never On A Sunday	5

MARIE LITTLE

71	Argo ZFB 19	FACTORY GIRL (LP)	110
73	Trailer LER 2084	MARIE LITTLE (LP)	55
87	private pressing	MY ELDORADO (LP)	12

LITTLE ABNER

57	Oriole CB 1380	Not Here, Not There/You Mean Everything To Me (78)	6

LITTLE ANGELS

87	Little Angels LAN 001	LITTLE ANGELS '87 (12" EP)	30
89	Polydor LTLCD 2	THE BIG BAD EP (CD)	10
87	Powerstation AMP 14	TOO POSH TO MOSH (mini-LP)	18

LITTLE ANN

98	Kent TOWN 111	What Should I Do/O.C. TALBOT: I'm Shooting High (I Reach For The Sky)	15
99	Kent TOWN 112	Who Are You Trying To Fool/I Got To Have You	20

LITTLE ANTHONY & IMPERIALS

58	London HLH 8704	Tears On My Pillow/Two People In The World (78 rpm = £35)	50
59	London HL 8848	So Much/Oh Yeah (78 rpm = £40+)	50
59	Top Rank JAR 256	Shimmy, Shimmy, Ko-Ko Bop/I'm Still In Love With You	30
60	Top Rank JAR 366	My Empty Room/Bayou, Bayou, Baby	25
64	United Artists UP 1065	I'm On The Outside Looking In/Please Go	20
64	United Artists UP 1073	Goin' Out Of My Head/Make It Easy On Yourself	20
65	United Artists UP 1083	Hurt So Bad/Reputation	25
65	United Artists UP 1098	Take Me Back/Our Song	20
65	United Artists UP 1112	I Miss You/Get Out Of My Life	15
66	United Artists UP 1126	Hurt/Never Again	40
66	United Artists UP 1137	Better Use Your Head/The Wonder Of It All (DJ copy = £150)	80
66	United Artists UP 1151	Gonna Fix You Good (Every Time You're Bad)/You Better Take It Easy Baby	75
67	United Artists UP 1189	My Love Is A Rainbow/You Only Live Twice	8
68	United Artists UP 2260	Let The Sunshine In/The Gentle Rain (as Anthony & Imperials)	10
69	United Artists UP 35017	Anthem/Goodbye Goodtimes (as Anthony & Imperials)	8
72	United Artists UP 35345	Gonna Fix You Good (Every Time You're Bad)/You Better Take It Easy Baby (reissue)	10
76	United Artists UP 36118	Better Use Your Head/Gonna Fix You Good (Every Time You're Bad)	10
76	United Artists REM 405	Goin' Out Of My Head/I'm On The Outside Looking In/Hurt So Bad/ Gonna Fix You Good (Every Time You're Bad)	10
65	United Artists UEP 1004	LITTLE ANTHONY AND THE IMPERIALS (EP)	120
64	United Artists ULP 1089	I'M ON THE OUTSIDE LOOKING IN (LP)	150
66	United Artists ULP 1100	GOIN' OUT OF MY HEAD (LP)	100

(see also Anthony & Imperials)

LITTLE ARCHIE

68	Atlantic 584 209	I Need You/I Am A Carpet	25

LITTLE BEAVER

72	President PTLS 1060	JOEY (LP)	22

LITTLE BEVERLEY

68	Pama PM 731	What A Guy/You're Mine	5

(see also Beverley Simmons)

LITTLE BILL & BLUE NOTES

59	Top Rank JAR 176	I Love An Angel/Bye, Bye Baby (78 rpm = £25)	25

(see also Blue Notes)

LITTLE BIRD

84	Magus MGB 1	Zola/Reaching Out For Gold (p/s)	5

LITTLE BO BITCH

79	Cobra COB 1	It's Only Love/I'm Confused (p/s)	5
80	Cobra COB 4	Take It Easy (Lights Out Over London)/Lorraine, Lorraine (p/s)	5
79	Cobra CBR 1002	LITTLE BO BITCH (LP)	12

LITTLE BROTHER

(see under Little Brother Grant)

LITTLE DARLING

LITTLE DARLING
65   Blue Beat BB 325   No One/BUSTER'S ALL STARS: Congo Revolution 30

LITTLE DARLINGS
65   Fontana TF 539   Little Bit O' Soul/Easy To Cry .... 80+

LITTLE DES
70   J-Dan JDN 4400   Somebody's Baby/Spy Man 7

LITTLE DIANA DAY
54   Melodisc P 219   I'm Goin' To Hang Up Mummy's Stocking/Funny Little Snowman (78).......... 5

LITTLE DIPPERS
60   Pye International 7N 25051   Forever/Two By Four 15
61   London HLG 9269   Lonely/I Wonder, I Wonder, I Wonder 25

LITTLE ESTHER
(see under Little Esther Phillips)

LITTLE EVA
62   London HL 9581   The Locomotion/He Is The Boy 10
62   London HLU 9633   Keep Your Hands Off My Baby/Where Do I Go 10
63   London HLU 9687   Let's Turkey Trot/Old Smokey Locomotion 10
63   Colpix PX 11013   The Trouble With Boys/What I Gotta Do (To Make You Jealous).......... 12
63   Colpix PX 11019   Please Hurt Me/Let's Start The Party Again 15
64   Colpix PX 11035   Run To Her/Making With The Magilla 15
65   Stateside SS 477   Stand By Me/That's My Man 22
70s London LOCOX1   The Locomotion (Extended Version)/He Is The Boy/Keep Your Hands Off/
                       Let's Turkey Trot (12" p/s) 10
63   London HA-U 8036   L-L-L-L-LOCO-MOTION (LP, original with plum label & laminated sleeve)....... 60
72   London SH-U 8437   L-L-L-L-LOCO-MOTION (LP, stereo reissue, plum label, boxed label logo) 20
(see also Big Dee Irwin & Little Eva)

LITTLE FOLK
71   Studio Republic CR 1001   LEAVE THEM A FLOWER (LP)... 18

LITTLE FRANKIE (& COUNTRY GENTLEMEN)
65   Columbia DB 7490   The Kind Of Boy You Can't Forget/I'm Not Gonna Do It.................. 15
65   Columbia DB 7578   Make-A-Love/Love Is Just A Game (with Country Gentlemen) 20
65   Columbia DB 7681   It Doesn't Matter Anymore/Happy, That's Me........................... 20
(see also Chimes featuring Denise)

LITTLE FREDDY (McGregor)
70   Unity UN 551   Why Did My Little Girl Cry/PETER AUSTIN: Change Partners 8
(see also Freddie McGregor, Ernest Wilson)

LITTLE FREE ROCK
69   Transatlantic TRA 608   LITTLE FREE ROCK (LP) 80
(see also David John & Mood)

LITTLE GEORGE
64   Rio R 45   Mary Anne/EDWARDS ALLSTARS: Blue Night 18

LITTLE GRANTS & EDDIE (Grant)
67   President PT 159   Rudy's Dead/Everything's Alright 7
67   President PT 172   Rock Steady '67/Bingo 7
(see also Equals, Pyramids)

LITTLE HANK
66   London HLU 10090   Mr. Bang Bang Man/Don't You Know (withdrawn) (DJ copy = £125)........ 150
70   Monument MON 1045   Mr. Bang Bang Man/Don't You Know (reissue) 20

LITTLE JOE (& THRILLERS)
57   Philips PB 759   Peanuts/Lilly Lou (78) 20
60   Fontana H 281   Stay (as Little Joe & Thrillers)/Cherry................................. 25
63   Reprise R 20142   Peanuts/No No I Can't Stop 20

LITTLE JOE (Jamaica)
70   Torpedo TOR 15   Bad Blood/Maxi-Mini War 6
(see also Sexy Girls)

LITTLE JOEY & FLIPS
62   Pye International 7N 25152   Bongo Stomp/Lost Love.. 10

LITTLE JOHN
67   Pama PM 702   Let's Get Married/Around The World 6
70   Unity UN 561   No Love/A Little Tear (both sides actually by John Holt)................. 8
84   Vista VSLP 4061   UNITE (LP) 20
(see also John Holt)

LITTLE JOHN & BILLY BOYO
82   Greensleeves GRED 92   Janet Sinclair/Agony Column Dub (12")............................. 25

LITTLE JOHNNY & THREE TEENAGERS
58   Decca F 10990   Baby Lover/Rickety Rackety Rendezvous (78 rpm = £12) 20

LITTLE LEMMY & BIG JOE
58   Decca F 11054   Little Lemmy Kwela/Kwela No. 5 (78 rpm = £10) 5

LITTLE LUMAN
64   Rio R 44   Hurry Harry/R. ALPHONSE: Hucklebuck (B-side actually by
              Roland Alphonso) 15

LITTLE LUTHER
64   Pye International 7N 25266   Eenie Meenie Minie Moe/Twirl 70

LITTLE MACK & BOSS SOUNDS
66   Atlantic 584 031   In The Midnight Hour/You Can't Love Me (In The Midnight Hour) 20

LITTLE MILTON

65	Pye International 7N 25289	Blind Man/Blues In The Night	20
65	Chess CRS 8013	We're Gonna Make It/Can't Hold Back The Tears	20
65	Chess CRS 8018	Who's Cheating Who?/Ain't No Big Deal On You	22
66	Sue WI 4021	Early In The Morning/Bless Your Heart (actually by Roy Milton)	40
69	Chess CRS 8087	Grits Ain't Groceries/I Can't Quit You Baby	22
69	Chess CRS 8100	Let's Get Together/I'll Always Love You	15
72	Stax 2025 095	That's What Love Will Make You Do/I'm Living Off The Love You Give	8
74	Stax STXS 2003	Behind Closed Doors/Bet You I Win	8
75	Stax STA 100	If That Ain't A Reason/Mr. Mailman	6
69	Chess CRLS 4552	GRITS AIN'T GROCERIES (LP)	75
72	Chess 6310 120	GOLDEN DECADE (LP)	20
74	Stax STX 1013	BLUES 'N' SOUL (LP)	22

LITTLE NELL

76	A&M AMS 7374	Fever/See You Round Like A Record (yellow vinyl)	7

LITTLE NORA

54	Melodisc MEL 1261	Tomato/Nora's Blues (78)	5

LITTLE RICHARD

78s

56	London HLO 8336	Rip It Up/Ready Teddy	18
57	London HLO 8366	Long Tall Sally/Tutti Frutti	18
57	London HLO 8382	The Girl Can't Help It/She's Got It	18
57	London HLO 8446	Lucille/Send Me Some Lovin' (as Little Richard & His Band)	18
57	London HLO 8470	Jenny, Jenny/Miss Ann (as Little Richard & His Band)	18
57	London HLO 8509	Keep A Knockin'/Can't Believe You Wanna Leave	18
58	London HLU 8560	Good Golly Miss Molly/Hey-Hey-Hey-Hey	25
58	London HLO 8647	Ooh! My Soul/True, Fine Mama	30
58	London HLU 8770	Baby Face/I'll Never Let You Go	30
59	London HLU 8831	By The Light Of The Silvery Moon/Early One Morning	55
59	London HLU 8868	Kansas City/She Knows How To Rock	90
60	London HLU 9065	Baby/I Got It	185

SINGLES

56	London HLO 8336	Rip It Up/Ready Teddy (gold label print very rare, later silver)	150/60
50s	London HLO 8336	Rip It Up/Ready Teddy (repressing, silver-top label, round centre)	25
57	London HLO 8366	Long Tall Sally/Tutti Frutti (gold label print very rare, later silver)	150/50
50s	London HLO 8366	Long Tall Sally/Tutti Frutti (repressing, silver-top label, round centre)	20
57	London HLO 8382	The Girl Can't Help It/She's Got It (gold label print very rare, later silver)	175/55
50s	London HLO 8382	The Girl Can't Help It/She's Got It (repressing, silver-top label, round centre)	25
57	London HLO 8446	Lucille/Send Me Some Lovin' (as Little Richard & His Band)	35
57	London HLO 8470	Jenny, Jenny/Miss Ann (as Little Richard & His Band)	35
57	London HLO 8509	Keep A Knockin'/Can't Believe You Wanna Leave	35
58	London HLO 8560	Good Golly Miss Molly/Hey-Hey-Hey-Hey	35
58	London HLO 8647	Ooh! My Soul/True, Fine Mama	15
58	London HLU 8770	Baby Face/I'll Never Let You Go	10
59	London HLU 8831	By The Light Of The Silvery Moon/Early One Morning	10
59	London HLU 8868	Kansas City/She Knows How To Rock	15

(The above 45s were originally issued with triangular centres; later round-centres are worth around half to two-thirds these values.)

60	London HLU 9065	Baby/I Got It	20
61	Mercury AMT 1165	Joy Joy Joy (Down In My Heart)/He's Not Just A Soldier	10
62	Mercury AMT 1189	He Got What He Wanted (But He Lost What He Had)/ Why Don't You Change Your Ways?	12
63	London HLK 9708	Crying In The Chapel/Hole In The Wall	12
63	London HLK 9756	Travelin' Shoes/It Is No Secret	12
64	London HL 9896	Bama Lama Bama Loo/Annie's Back	12
64	Fontana TF 519	Blueberry Hill/Cherry Red	12
64	Stateside SS 340	Whole Lotta Shakin' Goin' On/Goodnight Irene	12
64	Mercury MF 841	Joy, Joy, Joy (Down In My Heart)/Peace In The Valley	8
66	Fontana TF 652	I Don't Know What You've Got But It's Got Me (Parts 1 & 2)	30
66	Stateside SS 508	Holy Mackeral/Baby, Don'tcha Want A Man Like Me?	20
66	Sue WI 4001	Without Love/Dance What You Wanna	40
66	Sue WI 4015	It Ain't Watcha Do (It's The Way How You Do It)/Crossover	40
66	Columbia DB 7974	Poor Dog/Well	28
66	Columbia DB 8058	I Need Love/The Commandments Of Love	22
67	Columbia DB 8116	Get Down With It/Rose Mary	22
67	Columbia DB 8240	A Little Bit Of Something/Money (DJ copy = £75)	50
67	Columbia DB 8263	I Don't Want To Discuss It/Hurry Sundown (DJ copy = £85)	50
68	MCA MU 1006	She's Together/Try Some Of Mine	10
68	London HLU 10194	Good Golly Miss Molly/Lucille	10
68	President PT 201	Whole Lotta Shakin' Goin' On/Lawdy Miss Clawdy	10
69	Action ACT 4528	Baby What Do You Want Me To Do (Parts 1 & 2)	10
70	Reprise RS 20907	Dew Drop In/Freedom Blues	10
71	President PT 329	Without Love/Talkin' 'Bout Soul	5
71	Reprise K 14124	Green Power/Dancing In The Street	8
72	Reprise K 14150	Money Is/Money Runner	5

EXPORT SINGLES

57	London HL 7022	Jenny, Jenny/Miss Ann (as Little Richard & His Band)	35
58	London HL 7049	Ooh! My Soul/True, Fine Mama	30
58	London HL 7056	Baby Face/I'll Never Let You Go	30
59	London HL 7074	She Knows How To Rock/Early One Morning	35
59	London HL 7079	By The Light Of The Silvery Moon/Kansas City	30
59	London HL 7085	Whole Lotta Shakin' Goin' On/All Around The World	70
68	Decca AD 1006	She's Together/Try Some Of Mine	40

LITTLE RICHARD

EPs

57	London RE-O 1071	LITTLE RICHARD AND HIS BAND VOL. 1 (gold tri-centre, later silver)	60/35
57	London RE-O 1074	LITTLE RICHARD AND HIS BAND VOL. 2 (gold tri-centre, later silver)	60/35
57	London RE-O 1103	LITTLE RICHARD AND HIS BAND VOL. 3.	45
57	London RE-O 1106	LITTLE RICHARD AND HIS BAND VOL. 4.	50
59	London RE-U 1208	LITTLE RICHARD AND HIS BAND VOL. 5.	50
60	London RE-U 1234	LITTLE RICHARD AND HIS BAND VOL. 6.	50
60	London RE-U 1235	LITTLE RICHARD AND HIS BAND VOL. 7.	65

(The above EPs were originally issued with triangular centres; later round-centre pressings are worth two-thirds of silver values.)

62	Summit LSE 2049	FOUR DYNAMIC NUMBERS (2 each by Little Richard & Brock Peters)	15
63	London REK 1400	HE'S BACK	40
64	Vocalion VEP 170155	MEMPHIS SLIM AND LITTLE RICHARD	80
66	Stateside SE 1042	DO YOU FEEL IT	35

LPs

57	London HA-O 2055	HERE'S LITTLE RICHARD (flipback, rear sleeve initially in gloss red)	125/70
57	London HA-O 2055	HERE'S LITTLE RICHARD (small flipback or non-flipback sleeve)	75/40
58	London HA-U 2126	LITTLE RICHARD VOL. 2 (flipback or non-flipback sleeve)	75/40
59	RCA Camden CDN 125	LITTLE RICHARD (8 tracks only; others by Buck Ram Orchestra)	22
59	London HA-U 2193	THE FABULOUS LITTLE RICHARD (flipback or non-flipback sleeve)	75/40
60	Top Rank 25/025	PRAY ALONG WITH LITTLE RICHARD VOL. 1: A CLOSER WALK WITH THEE (plain white sleeve, mail-order only)	50
60	Top Rank 25/026	PRAY ALONG WITH LITTLE RICHARD VOL. 2: I'M QUITTING SHOW BUSINESS (plain white sleeve, mail-order only)	100
62	Egmont EGM 9207	SINGS FREEDOM SONGS (reissue of Top Rank 25/025)	15
63	Egmont EGM 9270	PRAY ALONG WITH LITTLE RICHARD (reissue of Top Rank 25/026)	15
64	Stateside SL 10054	SINGS GOSPEL	25
64	Coral LVA 9220	COMING HOME	25
65	Fidelio ATL 4124	SINGS GOSPEL (4 tracks by Brock Peters but credited to Little Richard)	12
65	Summit ATL 4124	SINGS GOSPEL (4 tracks by Brock Peters, overprinted front cover)	12
65	Dial DLP 4124	SINGS GOSPEL (4 tracks by Brock Peters, correctly credited)	12
65	Mercury MCL 20036	IT'S REAL.	15
65	Fontana TL 5235	IS BACK!	25
65	Ember NR 5022	REALLY MOVIN' GOSPEL (3 tracks by Sister Rosetta Tharpe)	12
66	Fontana TL 5314	GREAT HITS.	15
67	Columbia SX/SCX 6136	THE EXPLOSIVE LITTLE RICHARD.	45
67	Polydor 236 202	THE INCREDIBLE LITTLE RICHARD (live)	12
68	Fontana SFL 13010	KING OF THE GOSPEL SINGERS	15
70	Reprise RSLP 6406	THE RILL THING	15
70	Union Pacific UP 003	YOU CAN'T KEEP A GOOD MAN DOWN	20
71	Epic EPC 66285	CAST A LONG SHADOW	15
71	Reprise K 44156	THE KING OF ROCK AND ROLL	12
73	Reprise K 44204	SECOND COMING.	12
75	Rhapsody RHAS 9013	KEEP A KNOCKIN'	12

(see also Canned Heat, Sister Rosetta Tharpe, Buck Ram's Ramrocks)

LITTLE ROOSTERS

79	Pye 7P 152	She Cat Sister Floozie/Roostering With Intent (p/s)	6
80	Ami AIS 101	That's How Strong My Love Is/Suspicious (p/s)	6
80	Ami AIS 107	I Need A Witness/The Age Of Reason (p/s)	6

(see also Cocksparrer, Alison Moyet)

LITTLE ROYS

69	Camel CA 36	Bongonyah/CREATIONS: Dad Name (B-side actually "Bad Name")	10
70	Camel CA 42	Gold Digger (actually by Wailing Soul)/MATADORS: The Mine	10
70	Camel CA 57	Selassie Want Us Back/ROY AND JOY: Make It With You	10

(see also Little Roy, Hippy Boys)

LITTLE SAL with DANDY & SUPERBOYS

68	Giant GN 19	I'm In The Mood/I'm A Lover	8

(see also Dandy & Superboys, Superboys)

LITTLE SISTERS

63	MGM MGM 1192	Goin' To Boston/Where Does It Lead	5

LITTLE SONNY

71	Stax 2363 005	NEW KING OF THE BLUES HARMONICA (LP).	20

LITTLE SUZIE

61	Warner Bros WB 35	Young Love/The Boy I Left Behind	12

LITTLE TONY & HIS BROTHERS

59	Durium DC 16639	Who's That Knockin'/The Beat (78 rpm = £125).	25
59	Durium DC 16657	Four An' Twenty Thousand Kisses/Bella Marie	20
59	Decca F 11164	I Can't Help It/Arrivederci Baby (78 rpm = £105)	10
59	Decca F 11169	The Hippy Hippy Shake/Hey Little Girl (78 rpm = £125)	10
59	Decca F 11190	Too Good/Foxy Little Mama (78 rpm = £105)	8
60	Decca F 21218	I Love You/The Magic Of Love	10
60	Decca F 21223	Princess/I Love You	10
60	Decca F 21247	Teddy Girl/Kiss Me, Kiss Me	10
66	Durium DRS 54008	Let Her Go/What Did I Do	10
67	Durium DRS 54012	Long Is The Lonely Night/People Talk To Me About You (as Little Tony)	10
58	Durium U 20058	PRESENTING LITTLE TONY AND HIS BROTHERS (EP)	65
65	Durium DRL 50006	I SUCCESSI DI LITTLE TONY (LP).	30
66	Durium DRL 50020	LET HER GO (LP).	25

LITTLE WALTER

60	London HLM 9175	My Babe/Blue Midnight.	50
64	Pye International 7N 25263	My Babe/You Better Watch Yourself.	20
56	London RE-U 1061	LITTLE WALTER AND HIS JUKES (EP).	200

64	Pye Intl. NPL 28043	LITTLE WALTER (LP)	60
67	Chess CRL 4529	SUPER BLUES (LP, with Bo Diddley & Muddy Waters)	50
68	Marble Arch MAL 815	LITTLE WALTER (LP, reissue)	15
69	Python PLP-KM 20	LITTLE WALTER AND HIS DUKES (LP, 99 copies only)	40
71	Syndicate Chapter SC 004	THUNDERBIRD (LP)	15

LITTLE WILBUR (& PLEASERS)
57	Vogue V 9091	Plaything/I Don't Care (78 rpm = £150)	650
58	Vogue V 9097	Heart To Heart/Alone In The Night (solo) (78 rpm = £175)	800

(see also Wilbur Whitfield)

LITTLE WILLIE (Francis)
63	Blue Beat BB 151	Settle Down/I'm Ashamed	8

(see also Wilbert Francis & Vibrators)

LIVE HUMAN
98	Fat Cat 12FAT 005	IMPROVISESSIONS (12" EP, custom sleeve)	8
99	Fat Cat 12FAT 019	ORANGEBUSHMONKEYFLOWER (12" EP, custom sleeve)	8

LIVELY ONES
63	London HA 8082	SURF DRUMS (LP)	60
63	London HA/SH 8107	SURF RIDER (LP, mono/stereo)	60/75

LIVELY SET
65	Pye 7N 15880	Don't Call My Name/What Kind Of Love	6
66	Capitol CL 15472	Let The Trumpets Sound/The Green Years	6

LIVERPOOL ECHO
73	Spark	LIVERPOOL ECHO (LP)	12

(see also Mandrake Paddle Steamers)

LIVERPOOL F.C.
78	Logo GO 339	Hail To The Kop/We Are Liverpool (p/s)	5
80	no label	Liverpool's FA Cup Finals (gold flexi)	10
83	Mean MEAN 102	Liverpool We're Never Gonna Stop/Liverpool Anthem (red vinyl)	5
65	Seddon SED 100	EE AYE ADDIO: SEVENTY YEARS WAITING (LP)	50
84	Extra-Terrestrial KOP 1	CONQUERING LIONS OF ANFIELD (LP, picture disc, gatefold sleeve, with booklet, stickers & photographs)	25

LIVERPOOL F.C. & LIVERPOOL SUPPORTERS
72	Penny Farthing PEN 794	Sing A Song For Liverpool/Liverpool, Liverpool	8

LIVERPOOL FISHERMEN
71	Mushroom 150 MR 9	SWALLOW THE ANCHOR (LP)	100

LIVERPOOL SCENE
68	RCA RCA 1762	Son Son/Baby	6
69	RCA RCA 1816	The Woo-Woo/Love Is	6
67	CBS 63045	THE INCREDIBLE NEW LIVERPOOL SCENE (LP)	22
68	RCA SF 7995	THE AMAZING ADVENTURES OF THE LIVERPOOL SCENE (LP)	18
69	RCA SF 8057	BREAD ON THE NIGHT (LP)	18
70	RCA SF 8100	ST. ADRIAN AND CO. BROADWAY & 3RD (LP)	18
70	RCA SF 8134	HEIRLOON (LP)	18
72	Charisma CS 3	RECOLLECTIONS (LP)	12

(see also Clayton Squares, Adrian Henri, Brian Patten, Mike Hart, Andy Roberts, Grimms)

LIVERPOOL SPINNERS
61	Topic TOP 69	SONGS SPUN IN LIVERPOOL (EP)	10

(see also Spinners [U.K.])

RICKY LIVID & TONE DEAFS
64	Parlophone R 5136	Tomorrow/Nuts And Bolts	18

(see also Bill Oddie)

LIVING DAYLIGHTS
67	Philips BF 1561	Let's Live For Today/I'm Real (B-side actually titled "It's Real")	30
67	Philips BF 1613	Always With Him/Baila Maria	30

(see also Greatest Show On Earth, Naturals)

LIVING DAYLIGHTS
79	E.S.R. S/79/CUS 523	HEARTSTOP EP (Personality Changes/Outdoor Girl/Don't Fit/Let Me Know (33¹/₃, die-cut p/s, also listed as ESR 3)	45

LIZA & JET SET
65	Parlophone R 5248	How Can I Know?/Dancing Yet	15

(see also Liza Strike, Jet Set)

LIZZIE & DELROY WILSON
71	Jackpot JP 771	Double Attack/AGGRAVATORS: The Sniper	8

LIZZY
70	Harry J HJ 6625	More Heartaches/HARRY J ALL STARS: Version	8
70	Pressure Beat PB 5508	Ten Feet Tall (actually "Wear You From The Ball"/JOE GIBBS & DESTROYERS: Chapter (actually "Harmony Hall" by Mr Nigel)	10
73	Duke DU 161	Love Is A Treasure/FREDDIE McKAY: Love Is A Treasure	7

LIZZY & DENNIS (Alcapone)
70	Ackee ACK 114	Happy Go Lucky Girl/BOBBY & DAVE: Sammy	12

LIZZY & PARAGONS
71	Ackee ACK 118	On The Beach/DAVE BARKER: Maria	15

LJ IV
69	CBS 63512	AN ELIZABETHAN SONGBOOK (LP)	75

(see also London Jazz Four)

LLAN
66	CBS 202405	Realise/Anytime	35

(see also Vogues)

BARRY LLEWELLYN
73	Downtown DT 515	Meaning Of Life/MORWELL ESQ: Version Of Life	20

(see also Heptones, Sound Dimension)

A.L. LLOYD
60	Topic 12T 51	OUTBACK BALLADS (LP, blue label)	40
64	Topic 12T 103	ENGLISH AND SCOTTISH FOLK BALLADS	
		(LP, with Ewan MacColl, initially with blue label & booklet)	30/20
65	Topic 12T 135	BIRD IN THE BUSH (LP, with Anne Briggs & Frankie Armstrong, blue label)	60
66	Topic 12T 118	FIRST PERSON (LP, blue label)	30
67	Topic 12T 174	LEVIATHAN! (LP, blue label with booklet)	30

(see also Frankie Armstrong, Anne Briggs)

A.L. LLOYD & MARTYN WYNDHAM-READ
71	Topic 12TS 203	THE GREAT AUSTRALIAN LEGEND (LP, blue label with booklet)	65

(see also Ewan MacColl, Peggy Seeger, Martin Wyndham-Read)

CHARLES LLOYD (QUARTET)
67	Atlantic 584 125	Sombrero Sam (Parts 1 & 2)	5
67	Atlantic 587/588 077	LOVE-IN (LP)	15
68	Atlantic 587/588 101	JOURNEY WITHIN (LP)	15
68	Atlantic 588 108	IN EUROPE (LP)	12
71	Atlantic 2400 108	IN THE SOVIET UNION (LP)	12

FRED LLOYD
65	Polydor BM 56055	Girl From Chelsea/You Kissed Him	6

JERRY LLOYD
60	Top Rank JAR 411	Be Faithful, Be True/Sooner Or Later	7

JIMMY LLOYD
58	Philips PB 827	Witch Doctor/For Your Love (78 rpm = £6)	9
58	Philips PB 871	The End/Street In The Rain (78 rpm = £6)	6
59	Philips PB 909	I Kneel At Your Throne/Sapphire (78 rpm = £8)	10
60	Philips PB 1010	Teenage Sonata/Falling	9
60	Philips PB 1055	I Double Dare You/Just For A Thrill	9
61	Philips PB 1120	Pony Time/Three Handed Woman	9
61	Philips PB 1157	Yellow Bird/Without The Sun	5
61	Philips PB 1201	I'm Coming Home/You Are My Sunshine	5
62	Philips 326 527 BF	True Love/Mother Nature And Father Time	5
63	Philips 326 568 BF	Call On Me/Humma Humma Humma Humming Bird	5
59	Philips BBE 12186	FOCUS ON JIMMY LLOYD (EP)	15
62	Philips BBE 12509	YOU ARE MY SUNSHINE (EP)	15

(see also Jimmy Logsdon)

KATHY LLOYD
54	Decca F 10386	It Worries Me/Tomorrow Night	10
54	Decca F 10418	Teach Me Tonight/It's A Woman's World	10
55	Decca F 10464	Our Future Has Only Begun/Unsuspecting Heart	10
55	Decca F 10567	Experience Unnecessary/This Must Be Wrong (with Ted Heath Music)	10

PEGGY LLOYD
55	London RE-P 1017	DIXIELAND HONKY-TONK (EP, with Bill Stegmeyer & His Orchestra)	20

RUE LLOYD
72	Green Door GD 4033	Loving You/Version	7
72	Green Door GD 4036	Cheer Up/Version	7

(see also Joe White)

TREVOR LLOYD
70	Explosion EX 2018	Chinee Brush/DICE & CUMMIE: Real Colley	10
70	Explosion EX 2019	Give Me Back Your Love/Hold Me	5

LLOYD & BARBARA
73	Grape GR 3045	Dear Lonely Hearts/LLOYD BANTAM: I Tried To Love You	5

LLOYD & CAREY WITH G.G. ALL STARS
72	Attack ATT 8029	Scorpion/MAYTONES: Hands And Feet	5

(see also Carey & Lloyd, Pat Satchmo)

LLOYD & CLAUDETTE
70	Big Shot BI 546	Queen Of The World/PROPHETS: Top Of The World	12

LLOYD (Robinson) & DEVON (Russell)
69	Punch PH 14	Love Is The Key/VIRTUES: High Tide	25
69	Blue Cat BS 151	Out Of The Fire/Can't Understand (B-side actually by Austin Faithful)	60

(see also Cobbs, Derrick Morgan)

LLOYD & DOREEN
71	Jackpot JP 762	Midnight/BUNNY LEE'S ALL STARS: Midnight — Version	7

(see also Lloyd Clarke/Doreen Shaeffer)

LLOYD (Robinson) & GLEN (Brown)
67	Coxsone CS 7011	That Girl/You Got Me Wrong	35
67	Doctor Bird DB 1058	Jezebel/TOMMY McCOOK & SUPERSONICS: Jam Session	35
67	Doctor Bird DB 1071	Keep On Pushing/BOBBY AITKEN & CARIBBEATS: You Won't Regret	
		(B-side actually by Lloyd & Glen)	35

LLOYD (Jackson) & GROOVERS

67	Caltone TONE 108	Do It To Me Baby/DIPLOMATS: Meet Me At The Corner	25
68	Caltone TONE 109	My Heart My Soul/DIPLOMATS with TOMMY McCOOK & SUPERSONICS:	
		Going Along	25
68	Caltone TONE 112	Listen To The Music/DIPLOMATS: Strong Man	25

(see also Groovers, Don Lett, Tony Lee)

LLOYD & JOHNNY

68	Island WI 3158	My Argument (actually by Lloyd Terrell)/JOHNNY MELODY: Foey Man	
		(actually by George Dekker)	35

(see also Lloyd Terrell)

LLOYD & JOY

71	Explosion EX 2047	Back To Africa (actually by Alton Ellis)/Born To Lose	15

LLOYD & KEN

72	Punch PH 110	Have I Sinned/Version	7

(see also Lloyd Charmers/Ken Boothe)

LLOYD & LARRY

70s	New Beat NB 080	Monkey Spanner/LLOYD & LARRY'S ALL STARS: Version	6

LLOYD & THE PROPHETS

70	Big Shot BI 553	Bush Beat/PATRICK & PROPHETS: Please Come Come	10
70	Big Shot BI 556	Jaco/Soul Reggae	10

(see also Prophets [Jamaica], Patrick & Lloyd)

LLOYD, DICE & HIS MUM

70	Joe JRS 5	Trial Of Pama Dice/NYAH SHUFFLE: Jughead Returns Version 1	15

LLOYD, DICE & THE BARRISTER

70	Joe JRS 14	Appeal Of Pama Dice/BOSS ALL STARS: Young And Strong Version 2	15

LLOYDIE & LOWBITES

73	Harry J HJ 6660	Pussy Cat/Skanky Pussy	6
71	Lowbite LOW 001	CENSORED! (LP, green/silver label)	20

(see also Lloyd Tyrell/Charmers)

LLOYD'S ALLSTARS

69	Doctor Bird DB 1178	Love Kiss Blue/UNIQUES: Secretly	45

(see also Justins, U Roy Junior, Jimmy Green, Victors)

LLOYD (Campbell) THE MATADOR

72	Sioux SI 010	The Train/Julia Sees Me (Exodus)	8

LLYGOD FFYRNIG

78	Pwdwr PWDWR 1	N.C.B./Sais/Cariad Y Bus Stop (p/s, stamped or printed white labels)	100/130

LOADED FORTY-FOURS

81	X-S TL 44/1	Thunderbirds (Are Go!)/T.V. Child (p/s)	5

DICKIE LOADER

61	Palette PG 9015	Heatwave/Happiness	20

RUSS LOADER

65	Columbia DB 7522	When Your Heart Is Broken/That Girl Of Mine (with Breakaways Orchestra)	10
65	Columbia DB 7643	Just Lies/Mona Lisa	10
65	Columbia DB 7696	Count The Stars/Triyng Too Hard (with Ladybirds)	10
66	Columbia DB 7839	Too Soon/Just A Little Step To Heaven	10
69	Conquest CXT 2	Just Lies/Take Me Tonight	5

(see also Mark Wirtz)

JOSEF LOCKE

53	Columbia SCM 5008	My Heart And I/Goodbye	10
53	Columbia SCM 5009	Hear My Song, Violetta/The Soldier's Dream	10
92	EMI 78EM 231	Hear My Song, Violetta/Charmaine/Count Your Blessings/Goodbye (12" 78)	8

LOCKETS

63	Pye International 7N 25232	Don't Cha Know/Little Boy	40

LOCKJAW

77	Raw RAW 8	Radio Call Sign/The Young Ones (p/s)	20
78	Raw RAW 19	Journalist Jive/I'm A Virgin/A Doonga Doonga (p/s, beware of counterfeits)	80

(see also the Cure)

HANK LOCKLIN

60	RCA RCA 1188	Please Help Me, I'm Falling/My Old Home Town (78 rpm = £22)	6
61	RCA RCA 1252	You're The Reason/Happy Birthday To Me	6
62	RCA RCA 1273	From Here To There To You/This Song Is Just for You	6
62	RCA RCA 1305	We're Gonna Go Fishin'/Welcome Home, Mr. Blues	6
63	RCA RCA 1336	Flyin' South/Behind The Footlights	6
58	RCA RCX 115	COUNTRY GUITAR VOL. 3 (EP)	15
62	RCA RCX 217	SEVEN DAYS (EP)	15
63	Parlophone GEP 8875	ENCORES (EP)	20
63	RCA RCX 7116	WALTZ OF THE WIND (EP)	15
64	RCA RCX 7150	IRISH SONGS COUNTRY STYLE (EP)	15
61	RCA RD 27201	PLEASE HELP ME, I'M FALLING (LP)	20
64	RCA RD 7623	IRISH SONGS COUNTRY STYLE (LP)	15
65	Fontana FJL 305	BORN TO RAMBLE (LP)	12

GERRY LOCKRAN

69	Decca F 12873	Hey Jude/This Train	6
69	Decca F 12919	Standing On Your Own/You're Not There	20
67	Planet PLL 1002	HOLD ON, I'M COMING (LP)	90
68	Waverley ZLP 2091	BLUES VENDETTA (LP)	40
69	Spark SRLP 104	THE ESSENTIAL GERRY LOCKRAN (LP)	25

72	Polydor 2383 122	WUN (LP)	12
76	Decca SKL-R 5257	RAGS TO GLADRAGS (LP)	12

GERRY LOCKRAN, REDD SULLIVAN, DAVE TRAVIS
69	Fidelity FID 2165	BLUES AT SUNRISE (LP)	18

ANNA LOCKWOOD
70	Tangent TGS 104	THE GLASS WORLD OF ANNA LOCKWOOD (LP)	40

MALCOLM LOCKYER ORCHESTRA
54	Decca F 10304	I'm Gonna Rock, Rock, Rock/Changing Partners (78, as Malcolm Lockyer & His Strict Tempo Music For Dancing)	10
61	HMV POP 929	"The Pursuers" T.V. Theme/Stranger Than Fiction	9
65	Columbia DB 7552	The Intelligence Men/Brighton Run	12
65	Columbia DB 7663	The Eccentric Dr. Who/Daleks And Thals	55
75	Contour 2870 439	TOP TV THEMES (LP)	12

LOCOMOTIVE
67	Direction 58-3814	Rudy A Message To You/Broken Heart	15
68	Parlophone R 5718	Rudi's In Love/Never Set Me Free	15
69	Parlophone R 5758	Mr. Armageddon/There's Got To Be A Way (some in promos p/s)	30/15
69	Parlophone R 5801	I'm Never Gonna Let You Go/You Must Be Joking	20
70	Parlophone R 5835	Movin' Down The Line/Roll Over Mary	10
71	Parlophone R 5915	Rudi's In Love/You Must Be Joking	20
69	Parlophone PCS 7093	WE ARE EVERYTHING YOU SEE (LP)	220
		(see also Norman Haines Band, Dog That Bit People, Steam-Shovel)	

NILS LOFGREN
76	CBS 4339	Soft Fun/Slippery Fingers (actually by Grin)	5
79	A&M AMS 7455	Shine Silently/Kool Skool (p/s, coloured or black vinyl)	5
		(see also Grin, Crazy Horse, Bruce Springsteen)	

LOFT
84	Creation CRE 009	Why Does The Rain/Like (foldaround p/s in poly bag)	10
85	Creation CRE 015	Up The Hill And Down The Slope/Lonely Street (foldaround p/s in poly bag)	6
		(see also Weather Prophets, Wishing Stones)	

CRIPPLE CLARENCE LOFTON
59	Vogue EPV 1209	CRIPPLE CLARENCE LOFTON (EP)	60
54	London AL 3531	A LOST RECORDING DATE (10" LP)	50
55	Vogue LDE 122	JAZZ IMMORTALS NO. 1 (10" LP)	50

LOGIC CONTROLS
90	Conscious CONN2	High Pursuit/Gangster Trip (12")	20

JIMMY LOGSDON
54	Brunswick 05226	Pa-Paya Mama/In The Mission Of St. Augustine (78)	15

L.O.K.
79	Fetish FET 001	Fun House/Starlet Love/Tell Me (p/s)	5

LOLITA
60	Polydor NH 66818	Sailor (Your Home Is The Sea)/La Luna (Quanda La Luna)	5

LOLITA STORM
99	Rabid Badger NANG 09	Goodbye America/Get Back (I'm Evil) (p/s)	5

LOLLIPOPS
71	Atlantic 2091 114	Nothing's Gonna Stop Our Love/I Believe In Love	15

LAURIE LOMAN
54	London HL 8101	Whither Thou Goest/I Was The Last One To Know (gold triangular centre)	50
54	London HL 8101	Whither Thou Goest/I Was The Last One To Know (78)	15

ALAN LOMAX (& RAMBLERS)
56	Decca F 10787	Dirty Old Town/Hard Case (as Alan Lomax & Ramblers)	10
56	Decca DFE 6367	OH LULA (EP)	10
58	Pye Jazz NJE 1055	SINGS (EP, with Dave Lee's Bandits)	15
58	Pye Jazz NJE 1062	MURDERER'S HOME PT. 1 (EP)	15
58	Pye Jazz NJE 1063	MURDERER'S HOME PT. 2 (EP)	15
58	Pye Jazz NJE 1064	MURDERER'S HOME PT. 3 (EP)	15
58	Pye Jazz NJE 1065	MURDERER'S HOME PT. 4 (EP)	15
59	Melodisc EPM7 88	SONGS FROM TEXAS (EP)	12
57	Nixa Jazz NJL 8	PRESENTS BLUES IN THE MISSISSIPPI NIGHT (LP, with others)	15
57	Nixa Jazz NJL 11	MURDERER'S HOME (LP)	15
58	Pye Nixa NPL 18013	PRESENTS AMERICAN SONG TRAIN VOLUME ONE (LP)	12
58	HMV CLP 1192	GREAT AMERICAN BALLADS (LP, with Alexis Korner & Guy Carawan)	25

JACKIE LOMAX
68	CBS 2554	Genuine Imitation Life/One Minute Woman	20
68	Apple APPLE 3	Sour Milk Sea/The Eagle Laughs At You	15
69	Apple APPLE 11	New Day/I Fall Inside Your Eyes	15
70	Apple APPLE 23	How The Web Was Woven/Thumbin' A Ride (some in p/s)	30/15
69	Apple (S)APCOR 6	IS THIS WHAT YOU WANT (LP, with inner sleeve, mono/stereo)	90/60
91	Apple SAPCOR 6	IS THIS WHAT YOU WANT (LP, reissue, gatefold sleeve with bonus 12" [SAPCOR 62])	25
91	Apple SAPCOR 6	IS THIS WHAT YOU WANT (CD)	35
		(see also Lomax Alliance, Undertakers, Takers, Heavy Jelly, Badger)	

LOMAX ALLIANCE
67	CBS 2729	Try As You May/See The People	40
		(see also Jackie Lomax)	

GUY LOMBARDO (& ROYAL CANADIANS)

55	Brunswick 05372	No More/Pupalina	5
55	Brunswick 05412	Softly Softly/(I'm Always Hearing) Wedding Bells	5
55	Brunswick 05413	Hey, Mr. Banjo/Blue Mirage	5
55	Brunswick 05443	Cherry Pink And Apple Blossom White/Marty	5
56	Capitol CL 14585	Charleston Parisien/Rinka Tinka Man	5

AL LOMBARDY & HIS ORCHESTRA

54	London HL 8076	The Blues/The Boogie (78 rpm = £10)	60
55	London HL 8127	In A Little Spanish Town/Flying Home (78 rpm = £10)	30

LONDON

77	MCA MCA 305	Everyone's A Winner/Handcuffed	5
77	MCA MCA 336	Animal Games/Us Kids Cold	5
77	MCA MCA 319	SUMMER OF LOVE (EP, p/s)	6
77	MCA 12 MCA 319	SUMMER OF LOVE (12" EP, p/s)	10
78	MCA MCF 2823	ANIMAL GAMES (LP)	15

EDDIE LONDON & CHIMES

57	Decca F 10859	Song Of The Moonlight/I'll Thank You	5

FRANCO LONDON ORCHESTRA

66	Philips BF 1470	Theme From Robinson Crusoe/Adrift	15

JIMMY LONDON

71	Randy's RAN 514	Shake A Hand/CARL MURPHY: Lick I Pipe	6
71	Randy's RAN 517	Bridge Over Troubled Waters/RANDY'S ALLSTARS: War	8
71	Randy's RAN 518	Hip Hip Hooray/IMPACT ALLSTARS: Version	5
71	Randy's RAN 520	A Little Love/IMPACT ALLSTARS: Version	8
72	Randy's RAN 521	It's Now Or Never/IMPACT ALLSTARS: Version	5
72	Randy's RAN 527	Jamaica Festival '72 (with Rocking Horse)/IMPACT ALLSTARS: Version	5
73	Explosion EX 2080	I'll Never Find Another You/IMPACT ALLSTARS: Version	5
73	Dragon DRA 1010	Jennie/I Wonder If I Care As Much (as Jimmi London)	5
74	Dragon DRA 1019	No Letter Today/The Road Is Rough	5
74	Ackee ACK 531	Till I Kiss You/Version	5
72	Trojan TRL 39	BRIDGE OVER TROUBLED WATERS (LP)	20
	(see also Jimmy Green, The Inspirations)		

JOE LONDON

59	London HLW 9008	Lonesome Whistle/It Might Have Been (78 rpm = £10)	12

JULIE LONDON

56	London HLU 8240	Cry Me A River/S'Wonderful (gold label print, later silver) (78 rpm = £15)	80/35
56	London HLU 8279	Baby, Baby All The Time/Shadow Woman (gold label print) (78 rpm = £15)	45
57	London HLU 8394	The Meaning Of The Blues/Now! Baby, Now! (gold label print, later silver)	35/20
57	London HLU 8394	The Meaning Of The Blues/Now! Baby, Now! (78)	10
57	London HLU 8414	The Boy On A Dolphin/Tall Boy (78 rpm = £12)	18
58	London HLU 8602	Saddle The Wind/It Had To Be You (78 rpm = £12)	12
58	London HLU 8657	My Strange Affair/It's Easy (78 rpm = £12)	12
58	London HLU 8769	Man Of The West/Blue Moon (78 rpm = £22)	12
59	London HLU 8891	Come On-A My House/Must Be Catchin' (78 rpm = £35)	25
61	London HLG 9360	Sanctuary/Every Chance I Get	7
63	Liberty LIB 10078	There'll Be Some Changes Made/Love On The Rocks	7
63	Liberty LIB 55605	I'm Coming Back To You/When Snowflakes Fall In The Summer	8
64	Liberty LIB 55666	I Want To Find Out For Myself/Guilty Heart	6
65	Liberty LIB 10189	Send For Me/Bye Bye Blackbird	6
65	Liberty LIB 10205	Charade/Wives And Lovers	6
67	Liberty LIB 10274	Girl Talk/The Mickey Mouse March	6

EPs

57	London RE-U 1076	JULIE SINGS FILM SONGS (gold label print, silver print labels £10)	20
57	London RE-N 1092	LONDON'S GIRL FRIENDS VOL. 1	20
58	London RE-U 1151	MAKE LOVE TO ME — PART ONE	20
58	London RE-U 1152	MAKE LOVE TO ME — PART TWO	20
58	London RE-U 1153	MAKE LOVE TO ME — PART THREE	20
59	London RE-U 1180	JULIE — PART ONE	20
59	London RE-U 1181	JULIE — PART TWO	20
59	London RE-U 1182	JULIE — PART THREE	20
63	Liberty LEP 2103	DESAFINADO	15
66	Liberty LEP 2260	ALL THROUGH THE NIGHT	15

LPs

56	London HA-U 2005	JULIE IS HER NAME	40
57	London HA-U 2038	CALENDAR GIRL	38
58	London HA-U 2083	MAKE LOVE TO ME	40
58	London HA-U 2091	ABOUT THE BLUES	40
58	London HA-U 2112	JULIE	40
59	London HA-U 2171	LONDON BY NIGHT	35
59	London HA-U 2186	JULIE IS HER NAME VOL. 2 (also stereo SAH-U 6042)	30
60	London HA-W 2225	SWING ME AN OLD SONG	30
60	London HA-W 2229	YOUR NUMBER PLEASE	30
60	London HA-G 2280	JULIE AT HOME (also stereo SAH-G 6097)	28/30
61	London HA-G 2299	AROUND MIDNIGHT	30
61	London HA-G 2353	SEND FOR ME (also stereo SAH-G 6154)	28/30
62	London HA-G 2405	WHATEVER JULIE WANTS (aso stereo SAH-G 6205)	28/30
62	Liberty LBY 1023	THE BEST OF JULIE LONDON	15
62	Liberty (S)LBY 1083	LOVE LETTERS	18
63	Liberty (S)LBY 1113	LOVE ON THE ROCKS	18
63	Liberty (S)LBY 1136	SINGS LATIN IN A SATIN MOOD	18
64	Liberty (S)LBY 1185	THE WONDERFUL WORLD OF JULIE LONDON	18
65	Liberty LBY 1222	IN PERSON AT THE AMERICANA	18

MINT VALUE £

65	Liberty (S)LBY 1251	OUR FAIR LADY	18
66	Liberty (S)LBY 1281	FEELING GOOD (with Gerald Wilson Big Band)	15
66	Liberty (S)LBY 1300	ALL THROUGH THE NIGHT	15
67	Liberty (S)LBY 1334	FOR THE NIGHT PEOPLE	15
67	Liberty (S)LBY 1364	NICE GIRLS DON'T STAY FOR BREAKFAST	15
68	Liberty LBL/LBS 83049	GREAT PERFORMANCES	15
69	Liberty LBL/LBS 83183E	YUMMY, YUMMY, YUMMY	15

LAURIE LONDON

57	Parlophone R 4359	He's Got The Whole World In His Hands/The Cradle Rock	10
57	Parlophone R 4388	Handed Down/She Sells Sea Shells	10
58	Parlophone R 4408	The Gospel Train/Boomerang (78 rpm = £6)	10
58	Parlophone R 4426	I Gotta Robe/Casey Jones (78 rpm = £8)	6
58	Parlophone R 4450	Basin Street Blues/Joshua (Fit The Battle Of Jericho) (78 rpm = £10)	10
58	Parlophone R 4474	My Mother/Darktown Strutters' Ball (78 rpm = £10)	10
58	Parlophone R 4499	Up Above My Head/Three O'Clock (78 rpm = £10)	10
59	Parlophone R 4557	Pretty-Eyed Baby (with Gitte)/Boom-Ladda-Boom-Boom (78 rpm = £15)	10
57	Parlophone GEP 8664	LAURIE LONDON (EP)	28
58	Parlophone GEP 8689	LITTLE LAURIE LONDON No. 2 (EP)	28

MARK LONDON

65	Pye 7N 15825	Stranger In The World/Moanin'	10

MICHAEL LONDON

62	HMV POP 1026	Miracles Sometimes Happen/Stranger On The Shore (with Acker Bilk)	7
62	HMV POP 1085	Mutiny On The Bounty Love Song/For The Very Young	7

PETER LONDON

65	Pye 7N 15957	Bless You/Baby I Like The Look Of You	50

(see also Peter Cook)

LONDON POSSE

88	JusticeJT003	Money Mad (12")	30
87	Big LifeBLR2T	London Posse/My Beatbox Reggae Style (12")	20
89	Mango 12 MNG 735	Live Like The Other Half Do/Money Mad(12")	8
90	Mango 12 MNG 752	Tell Me Something/Original London Style (12")	8
91	Mango 12 MNG 774	Jump Around/Gangster Chronicle (12")	8
93	Bullet BULT 2	How's Life In London?/Shut The Fuck Up/How I Make Papes (12")	15
94	Bullet BULT 3	Here Comes The Rugged One/Super Model (12")	10
90	Mango MLPS1066	GANGSTER CHRONICLE (LP)	15

LONDON & BRIDGES

66	CBS 202056	It Just Ain't Right/Leave Her Alone	35

LONDON BALALAIKA ENSEMBLE

68	Deram DML/SML 712	LONDON BALALAIKA ENSEMBLE (LP)	15

LONDON JAZZ CHAMBER GROUP

72	Ember CJS 823	ADAM'S RIB SUITE (LP)	20

(see also Ken Moule's London Jazz Chamber Group, Ken Moule Seven)

LONDON JAZZ FOUR

67	Polydor 56214	It Strikes A Chord/Song For Hilary	20
67	Polydor 582 005	TAKE A NEW LOOK AT THE BEATLES (LP)	70

(see also London Jazz Quartet, LJ IV)

LONDON JAZZ QUARTET

66	Polydor 56092	Norwegian Wood/I Feel Fine	6
60	Tempo TAP 28	LONDON JAZZ QUARTET (LP, with Tubby Hayes & Tony Crombie)	350
60s	Ember EMB 3306	LONDON JAZZ QUARTET (LP)	150

(see also London Jazz Four, Tubby Hayes, Tony Crombie)

LONDON POPS ORCHESTRA

68	Pye 7N 17630	Eleanor Rigby/If I Only Had Time	6
68	Pye NSPL 18241	THE LONDON POPS ORCHESTRA (LP)	12

LONDON PX

80	New Puritan NP 1	Orders/Eviction (p/s)	20
82	Terrapyn SYD 1	Arnold Layne/Indian Summer (1-sided flexidisc)	12

LONDON RHYME SYNDICATE

88	Rhyme & Reason 12LRS001	Hard To The Core (12")	10
88	Rhyme & Reason 12LRS002	London Rhyme Syndicate/Poetry/Armed And Extremely Dangerous (EP)	8

LONDON STUDIO GROUP

66	De Wolfe DW/LP 2974	THE WILD ONE (10" LP, tricolour label)	28

(see also Ivor & Basil Kirchen Band)

LONDON UNDERGROUND

82	On-U Sound ON-U 4	WATCHING WEST INDIANS IN THE COLD (10" EP)	8
83	On-U Sound ON-U 5	STRANGE (10" EP)	8

LONDON WAITS

66	Immediate IM 030	Softly Softly/Serenadio	30

LONDON ZOO

80	Gramophone STB 80	Who's Driving This Car?/You And Your Great Ideas (stamped white labels, no p/s)	6
80	Zoom ZUM 12	Receiving End/London Zoo (p/s)	5

LONDONAIRES

66	Decca F12379	Dearest Emma/Blues A Go-Go	10

LONELY HEARTS
84 Tenacity TROIA   FM Fantasy/Young Girl (p/s) 10

LONE PIGEON
00s Bad Jazz/Fence BEBOP 31   TOUCHED BY TOMOKO EP: Summertime Beeswing/Touched By Tomoko/
                                      Empty Town/The Mean Old Mind Of Man/Waterfall 8
(see also Beta Band)

JOHNNY LONESOME
61 HMV POP 837   Marie Marie/Doctor Heartache 18

LONESOME PINE FIDDLERS
64 London HA-B 8143   MORE BLUEGRASS (LP) 15

LONESOME STONE
73 Reflection RL 306   LONESOME STONE (LP, stage production recording) 22
(see also Sheep)

LONESOME SUNDOWN
71 Blue Horizon 7-63864   LONESOME LONELY BLUES (LP) 80
70s Flyright LP 529   BOUGHT ME A TICKET (LP) 15
70s Flyright LP 587   LONESOME WHISTLER (LP) 15

LONESOME TRAVELLERS
70 Tradition TSR 004   THE LONESOME TRAVELLERS (LP) 25
70s Nebula NEB 100   THE LOST CHILDREN (LP) 15

LONE WOLF
81 Kai KR 02   Fighting For Sommerlund/Vonotar The Traitor (p/s) 15

FITZROY D. LONG & BUSTER ALL STARS
68 Fab FAB 32   Get A New Girl/BUSTER'S ALL STARS: Come And Do It With Me ... 18
(see also Larry Marshall)

SHORTY LONG
65 Tamla Motown TMG 512   Out To Get You/It's A Crying Shame (DJ copy = £175) 100
66 Tamla Motown TMG 573   Function At The Junction/Call On Me (DJ copy = £60) 35
67 Tamla Motown TMG 600   Chantilly Lace/Your Love Is Amazing 25
68 Tamla Motown TMG 644   Night Fo' Last (Vocal)/Night Fo' Last (Instrumental) 20
68 Tamla Motown TMG 663   Here Comes The Judge/Sing What You Wanna 15
68 T. Motown (S)TML 11086   HERE COMES THE JUDGE (LP) 50
70 T. Motown STML 11144   THE PRIME OF SHORTY LONG (LP) 40
(see also Art Mooney)

LONG & SHORT
64 Decca F 11964   The Letter/Love Is A Funny Thing 28
64 Decca F 12043   Choc Ice/Here Comes The Fool 28

LONGBOATMEN
66 Polydor 56115   Take Her Any Time/Only In Her Home Town .... 600+

LONG COLD STARE
90 Rise Above RISE 3   TIRED EYES (LP) 12

CLAUDINE LONGET
67 A&M AMS 708   Good Day Sunshine/The Look Of Love 6
67 A&M AML 903   CLAUDINE (LP) 25

LONG HELLO
73 private pressing   THE LONG HELLO (LP, mail-order only, numbered white sleeve)....... 20
(see also Van Der Graaf Generator)

LONG TALL SHORTY
79 Warner Bros K 17491   By Your Love/1970's Boy (p/s, withdrawn) 100
81 Dr Creation LYN 9904   If I Was You/That's What I Want (flexidisc) 12
81 Ramkup CAC 007   Win Or Lose/Ain't Done Wrong (p/s) 100
85 Diamond DIA 002   On The Streets Again/I Fought The Law/Promises (p/s, some with poster) ... 25/12
86 Diamond DIA 005   What's Going On/Steppin' Stone/Win Or Lose/England (p/s) 12
88 no label or cat. no.   ROCKIN' AT THE SAVOY (LP, official bootleg, some with poster) 18/15
(see also Case, Joe Public, Rage, Charlie Harper)

LOOKING GLASS
72 Epic 65041   LOOKING GLASS (LP) 25

LOOP
86 Head HEAD 5   16 Dreams/Head On/Burning World (12", p/s) 25
87 Head HEAD 7L   Spinning Parts 1 & 2 (large centre, plain black die-cut sleeve) 20
87 Head HEAD 7   Spinning/Deep Hit/I'll Take You There (12", p/s) 25
88 Chapter 22 CAT 065   Torched (flexidisc, with/without *The Catalogue* magazine no. 65) 12/7
89 Situation 2 SIT 64T   ARC LITE EP (12", p/s) 8
89 Situation 2 SIT 64CD   ARC LITE EP (CD) 8
88 Chapter 22 CHAPLLP 34   FADE OUT (LP, 2 x 45rpm 12", gold stickered gatefold sleeve, some signed) . 15/12
91 Reactor REACTORLP 3   WOLF FLOW — JOHN PEEL SESSIONS 1987-90 (2-LP) 15

LOOSE ENDS
66 Decca F 12437   Send The People Away/I Ain't Gonna Eat My Heart Out Anymore 20
66 Decca F 12476   Taxman/That's It 45

LOOT
66 Page One POF 013   Baby Come Closer/Baby 12
67 Page One POF 026   I've Just Gotta Love You/You Need Someone To Love 20
67 CBS 2938   Whenever You're Ready/I Got What You Want 18
68 Page One POF 095   She's A Winner/Radio City (withdrawn B-side) 30
68 Page One POF 095   She's A Winner/Save Me 22
68 CBS 3231   Don't Turn Around/You Are My Sunshine Girl 15
69 Page One POF 115   Try To Keep It A Secret/Radio City 30
(see also Soul Agents, Hookfoot5)

MINT VALUE £

LINDA LOPEZ MAMBO ORCHESTRA
55	Parlophone MSP 6179	Limehouse Blues Mambo/Nursery Mambo	10

TRINI LOPEZ
63	London HL 9808	Jeanie Marie/Love Me Tonight	10
63	Reprise R(9) 6093	LOPEZ AT P.J.'s (LP, mono/stereo)	12
64	London HA 8132	TEENAGE LOVE SONGS (LP)	30
64	London HA 8160	MORE OF TRINI LOPEZ (LP)	25
64	Reprise R 6147	THE FOLK ALBUM (LP)	12

DENISE LOR
54	Parlophone MSP 6120	If I Give My Heart To You/Hallo Darling	10
55	Parlophone MSP 6148	Every Day Of My Life/And One To Grow On	12

KENNY LORAN
59	Capitol CL 15081	Mama's Little Baby/Magic Star	52

L'ORANGE MECHANIK
86	Art Pop POP 44	Symphony/Intermezzo (Sprechstimme)/Scherzo (p/s)	15
	(see also Times)		

BOBBY LORD
64	Hickory 45-1232	Life Can Have Meaning/Pickin' White Gold	6
64	Hickory 45-1259	Take The Bucket To The Well/A Man Needs A Woman	6
65	Hickory 45-1310	That Room In The Corner Of The House/I'm Going Home Next Summer	6

BOBBY LORD/BOB LUMAN
64	Hickory LPE 1501	HICKORY SHOWCASE VOL. 2 (EP, 1 side each)	20
64	Hickory LPE 1504	HICKORY SHOWCASE VOL. 3 (EP, 1 side each)	20
64	Hickory LPM 121	CAN'T TAKE THE COUNTRY FROM THE BOYS (LP, 1 side each)	15
	(see also Bob Luman)		

JON LORD
76	Purple PUR 131	Bourée/Aria	7
82	Harvest HAR 5220	Bach Onto This/Going Home (p/s)	6
71	Purple TPSA 7501	GEMINI SUITE (LP)	15
74	Purple TPSA 7513	WINDOWS (LP)	15
76	Purple TPSA 7516	SARABANDE (LP, die-cut sleeve)	15
82	Harvest SHSP 4123	BEFORE I FORGET (LP)	12

(see also Artwoods, Deep Purple, [Paice] Ashton & Lord, Bernie Marsden, Wizard's Convention, Episode Six, Leading Figures, Whitesnake, Cozy Powell)

TONY LORD
66	Planet PLF 102	World's Champion/It Makes Me Sad	25

JERRY LORDAN
59	Parlophone R 4588	I'll Stay Single/Can We Kiss	10
60	Parlophone R 4627	Who Could Be Bluer?/Do I Worry?	10
60	Parlophone R 4653	Sing Like An Angel/Ev'ry Time	10
60	Parlophone R 4695	Ring, Write Or Call/I've Still Got You	10
61	Parlophone R 4748	You Came A Long Way From St. Louis/Let's Try Again	10
62	Parlophone R 4903	One Good Solid 24 Carat Reason/Second Hand Dress	15
70	CBS 5057	The Old Man And The Sea/Harlequin Melodies	22
61	Parlophone PMC 1133	ALL MY OWN WORK (LP, also stereo PCS 3014)	90/120
	(see also Lee & Jay Elvin)		

LORD BEGINNER
50	Melodisc 1131	Joe Louis Calypso/Trinidad Blues (78)	10
50	Melodisc 1133	Victory Test Match — Calypso/Sergeant Brown (78)	10
50	Melodisc 1134	Straight Hair Girl/Calinda (78)	10
51	Melodisc 1164	Gold Coast Victory/Family Scandal (78)	10
51	Melodisc 1167	Family Scandal/Gold Coast Champion (78)	10
51	Melodisc 1183	Jamaica Hurricane/Pretty Woman (78)	12
51	Melodisc 1193	John Goddard Calypso/Some Girl (78)	10
51	Parlophone MP 112	Federation/Rum, More Rum (78, export)	10
51	Melodisc 1211	Australia V. West Indies/One Morning (78)	10
51	Esquire 5-034	Randolph Turpin's Victory/West Indians And The Steel Band (78, with Kenny Graham's Afro-Cubists)	15
51	Esquire 5-041	Fifty Women To One Man/1951 Festival Of Britain (78, with Kenny Graham's Afro-Cubists)	15
53	Esquire 5-091	England Regains The Ashes/Nobody Wants To Grow Old (78)	15
54	Melodisc 1333	Sir Winston Churchill Calypso/Rhythm Dance (78)	15
54	Melodisc 1334	She Walks Like You/Tambourine (78)	12
50s	Parlophone MP 144	Africa/Syncopation (export 78)	12
60s	Melodisc CAL 1	Victory Test Match — Calypso/Sergeant Brown (reissue)	10
	(see also Lord Kitchener)		

LORD BRISCO(E)
64	Black Swan WI 447	Spiritual Mambo/BABA BROOKS: Fly Right	25
64	Black Swan WI 450	My Love Has Come/BABA BROOKS: Sweet Eileen	25
64	Black Swan WI 454	Trojan/I Am The Least	12
64	Island WI 131	Praise For I/Tell You The Story	12
65	Island WI 187	Jonah (The Master)/Mr. Cleveland	12

LORD BRYNNER & SHEIKS
66	Island WI 266	Congo War/Teach Me To Ska	18
	(see also Roland Alphonso)		

LORD BUCKLEY
62	Fontana 688 010ZL	IN CONCERT (LP)	25
67	Fontana TL 5396	BLOWING HIS MIND (AND YOURS, TOO) (LP)	25
70	Elektra 2410 002	THE BEST OF LORD BUCKLEY (LP)	15

LORD BURGESS & HIS SUN ISLANDERS
67   Pye Intl. NPL 28109   CALYPSO GO-GO (LP) 15

LORD CHARLES & HIS BAND
70s   Sound Of Jamaica JA 1   Jamaican Bits And Pieces/JA Island Soul 8

LORD COMIC
70   Bamboo BAM 66   Rhythm Rebellion/ROY RICHARDS: Reggae Children 20
70   Pressure Beat PR 5507   Jack Of My Trade/CYNTHIA RICHARDS: United We Stand 18
      (see also Sir Lord Comic)

LORD CREATOR
62   Island WI 001   Independant [sic] Jamaica Calypso/Remember (B-side is actually
                                   "Remember Your Mother And Father"). 20
63   Kalypso XX 24   Peeping Tom/Second Hand Piano 8
64   Port-O-Jam PJ 4005   Rhythm Of the Blues/Simple Things. 12
64   Port-O-Jam PJ 4119   Jamaica's Anniversary/Mother's Love 12
64   National Calypso NC 2001   Drive With Care/Sweet Jamaica. 20
65   Blue Beat BB 292   Evening News/Good For Creator. 25
65   Black Swan WI 463   Wicked Lady/MAYTALS: My Little Ruby 25
66   Doctor Bird DB 1029   Obeah Wedding/BERTRAM ENNIS COMBO: Part Two 10
67   Jump Up JU 503   Jamaica Jump Up/Laziest Man 8
67   Jump Up JU 524   Big Bamboo/Marjorie And Harry 8
76   Island WIP 6344   Big Pussy Sally/UPSETTERS: Big Pussy Dub. 6
      (see also Kentrick Patrick, Fabulous Flames)

LORD CRISTO
67   Jump Up JU 515   Dumb Boy And The Parrot/General Hospital 8
67   Jump Up JU 517   Election War Zone/Bad Luck Man 8

LORD DANIEL
60s   Kalypso XX 26   Small Island Gal 6

LORD FLEA & HIS CALYPSONIANS
57   Capitol CL 14704   The Naughty Little Flea/Shake Shake Senora 6

LORD GANDA
57   Melodisc MEL 1417   Everybody Is Rockin' & Rollin'/Landlady Don't Steal My Clothes (78) 15

LORD INVADER & HIS CALYPSO RHYTHM BOYS
59   Pye N 15162   Teddy Boy Calypso/Reincarnation (The Bed Bug) (78). 10
      (see also Fitzroy Alexander Melody)

LORD KITCHENER
50   Parlophone MP 102   Nora/LORD BEGINNER: The Dollar And The Pound (export 78) 12
50   Parlophone MP 103   Underground Train/LORD BEGINNER: I Will Die A Bachelor (export 78) 12
52   Melodisc MEL 1160   Kitch/Food From The West Indies (78) 10
52   Melodisc MEL 1222   Two Timing Josephine/The Tongue Mopsie (78) 10
53   Lyragon J 717   Alec Bedser Calypso/Mistress Jacob (78) 10
55   Melodisc MEL 1325   My Wife's Nightie/Sweet Home (78). 10
56   Melodisc MEL 1400   Rock 'n' Roll Calypso/Life Begins At Forty (78). 10
56   Melodisc MEL 1401   Romeo/Kitch's Calypso Medley (78) 10
59   Melodisc MEL 1498   Black Puddin'/Piccadilly Folk 7
59   Melodisc MEL 1538   If You're Brown/Come Back In The Morning 7
60   Melodisc MEL 1577   Jamaica Turkey/Edna What You Want 7
63   Melodisc CAL 2   Kitch/Rebound Wife 6
63   Melodisc CAL 3   Muriel And The Bug/Nora And The Yankee 6
63   Melodisc CAL 4   Kitch Take It Easy/Redhead 6
63   Melodisc CAL 5   Drink A Rum/Your Wife. 6
63   Melodisc CAL 6   Too Late Kitch/Saxophone Number Two 6
63   Melodisc CAL 7   Wife And Mother/Mango Tree. 6
64   Melodisc CAL 10   Kitch Mambo Calypso/Ghana 6
64   Melodisc CAL 11   Life Begins At Forty/Short Skirts. 6
64   Melodisc CAL 12   Romeo/Kitch Calypso Medley 6
64   Melodisc CAL 14   Federation/Alfonso In Town 6
64   Melodisc CAL 19   Black Puddin'/Piccadilly Folk 6
64   Melodisc CAL 21   Come Back In The Morning/If You're Brown 6
64   Melodisc CAL 22   Jamaica Turkey/Edna What You Want 6
64   Melodisc CAL 23   Carnival/More Rice 6
60s   Jump Up JU 504   Love In The Cemetery/Jamaica Woman 6
60s   Jump Up JU 506   Road/Neighbour 6
64   Jump Up JU 511   Dr. Kitch/Come Back Home Meh Boy 5
65   Jump Up JU 530   Kitch You So Sweet/Ain't That Fun 6
65   Aladdin WI 612   Dr. Kitch/Come Back Home Meh Boy (reissue) 8
71   Duke DU 115   Dr. Kitch/Love In The Cemetary 5
55   Melodisc MLP 500   KITCH — KING OF CALYPSO (10" LP) 22
57   Melodisc MLP 510   KING OF CALYPSO VOL. 2 (10" LP) 22
60s   Melodisc 12-129   CALYPSOS TOO HOT TO HANDLE (LP). 30
60s   Melodisc 12-130   CALYPSOS TOO HOT TO HANDLE VOL. 2 (LP). 20
60s   Melodisc 12-199   CALYPSOS TOO HOT TO HANDLE (LP, reissue with extra tracks) 20
60s   Melodisc 12-200   CALYPSOS TOO HOT TO HANDLE VOL. 2 (LP, reissue with extra tracks). 20
      (see also Lord Beginner)

LORD KITCHENER/FITZROY COLEMAN BAND
56   no label   City And United 1956/The Manchester Football Double (78) 60

LORD LEBBY
58   Kalypso RL 101   Dr Kinsey Report/Ethiopia 15
58   Kalypso XX 05   Sweet Jamaica/Mama Want No Rice No Peas (78 rpm = £12) 12
60   Starlite ST45 018   Caldonia/One Kiss For My Baby 80

MINT VALUE £

LORD MELODY

58	Melodisc MEL 1440	The Devil/No, No (78 rpm = £10)	6
58	Melodisc MEL 1449	Robbery/Men Company (78 rpm = £10)	8
58	Melodisc MEL 1474	Do Able/Happy Holiday (78 rpm = £12)	6
59	Melodisc MEL 1491	I Confess/MIGHTY SPARROW: Goaty (78 rpm = £12)	8
59	Melodisc MEL 1503	Tom Dooley/Jealous Woman	6
59	Melodisc MEL 1504	Romeo/Knock On Any Door	6
60	Kalypso XX 14	Rock 'N' Roll Calypso/Bo Bo Man	5
60s	Melodisc CAL 16	Happy Holiday/Do Able	5

LORD NELSON

63	Stateside SS 189	I Got An Itch/Problems On My Mind	12
64	Stateside SS 281	It's Delinquency/Proud West Indian	12
68	Direction 58-3909	Michael/No Hot Summer	8
64	Stateside SE 1024	PROUD WEST INDIAN (EP)	32

LORD POWER

57	Kalypso XX 02	Chambolina/Penny Reel (78)	12
58	Maracas M 20001	Special Amber Calypso/Mambo La-La (78)	12
69	Coxsone CS 7079	Temptation/AL & VIBRATORS: Change Everything	40

LORD RIGBY

60s	Kalypso XX 29	The Milkman/Old Veterans	6
64	National Calypso NC 1001	Carnival Jamaica/Music Teacher	20

LORD ROCKINGHAM'S XI

58	Decca F 11024	The Squelch/Fried Onions (78 rpm = £8)	15
58	Decca F 11059	Hoots Mon/Blue Train (78 rpm = £6)	8
59	Decca F 11104	Wee Tom/Lady Rockingham, I Presume? (78 rpm = £8)	15
59	Decca F 11139	Ra-Ra Rockingham/Farewell To Rockingham (78 rpm = £15)	10
62	Decca F 11426	Newcastle Twist/Rockingham Twist	12
58	Decca DFE 6555	OH BOY! (EP)	40
68	Columbia S(C)X 6291	THE RETURN OF LORD ROCKINGHAM'S XI (LP, mono/stereo)	40

(see also Robinson Crew, Harry Robinson)

LORD ROSE

60s	Kalypso XX 25	Independent Jamaica/Twistin' Uncle	40

LORDS

67	Columbia DB 8121	Don't Mince Matters/No One Knows	90
68	Columbia DB 8367	Gloryland/Gypsy Boy	18

LORD SITAR

68	Columbia SX/SCX 6256	LORD SITAR (LP)	45

LORDS OF RAP

92	Mad Dog MADDOG001	STIX 'N' STONES (EP)	18

LORD SPOON

70	Escort ERT 839	Woman A Love In The Night Time/World On A Wheel	6

LORD TANAMO

60	Kalypso XX 20	Blues Have Got Me Down/Sweet Dreaming	20
64	Rio R 21	I Had A Dream/OSBOURNE GRAHAM: Be There	12
64	Ska Beat JB 177	Night Food Ska/My Business	20
65	Ska Beat JB 217	Mattie Rag/BABA BROOKS BAND: Mattie Rag	30
65	Ska Beat JB 224	I'm In The Mood For Ska/You Never Know	110
66	Ska Beat JB 243	Mother's Love/Downtown Gal	20
60s	Caribou CRC 3	I Love You Truly/If You Were Only Mine	80
71	Banana BA 319	Keep On Moving/JACKIE MITTOO: Totaly [sic] Together	25

LORELEI

74	CBS 2048	S.T.O.P. (Stop)/I'll Never Let You Down	15

SOPHIA LOREN

58	Philips PB 857	Love Song From "Houseboat"/Bing! Bang! Bong!	6
71	Warner Bros WB 8126	Anyone/There Is A Star	5

(see also Peter Sellers & Sophia Loren)

LORENZO

71	New Beat NB 094	I Will Never Let You Down/This Magic Moment	5

(see also Laurel Aitken)

LORI & CHAMELEONS

78	Zoo CAGE 006	Touch/Love On The Ganges (p/s)	7
79	Sire SIR 4025	Touch/Love On The Ganges (p/s, reissue)	5
80	Korova KOW 5	The Lonely Spy/Peru (p/s)	5
81	Korova KOW 20	Touch/The Lonely Spy (p/s)	5
81	Korova KOW 20T	Touch/The Lonely Spy/Love On The Ganges (12", p/s)	8

(see also Teardrop Explodes, Bill Drummond)

MYRNA LORRIE

55	London HLU 8187	Underway/I'm Your Man, I'm Your Gal (B-side with Buddy DeVal) (78 rpm = £15)	45
56	London HLU 8294	Life's Changing Scene/Listen To My Heartstrings (78 rpm = £15)	45

LORRIES

79	Redball RR 016	The Night/Steal You Anyway/Pushover/Idiot Dances (p/s)	6

DICK LORY

56	London HLD 8348	Cool It Baby/Ball Room Baby (78 rpm = £135)	600
61	London HLG 9284	My Last Date/Broken Hearted	40
62	Liberty LIB 55415	Handsome Guy/The Pain Is Here	10
63	Liberty LIB 55529	Welcome Home Again/I Got Over You	10

LOS BRAVOS
(see under 'B')

JOE LOSS (& HIS ORCHESTRA)
65	HMV POP 1470	Let's Kick/Just For Kicks	8
66	HMV POP 1500	"Thunderbirds" Theme/"The Avengers" Theme	20
66	HMV POP 1517	The England World Cup March/Auld Lang Syne (March)	20
62	HMV 7EG 8749	TWISTING AT THE PALAIS (EP)	10

LOST CHEREES
83	Riot RIOT 3	No Fighting No War (EP)	5
84	Mortarhate MORT 3	A MAN'S DUTY ... A WOMAN'S PLACE (EP)	5
85	Mortarhate MORT 12	UNWANTED CHILDREN (12" EP, with inner)	8
84	Fight Back FIGHT 6	ALL PART OF GROWING UP (LP, with lyric inner)	12

LOST JOCKEY
82	Operation Twilight OPT 11	Professor Slack/Rise And Fall/Animal/Behaviour And Crude Din (p/s)	8

LOTHAR & THE HAND PEOPLE
69	Capitol CL 15610	Sdrawkcab (Backwards)/Today Is Only Yesterday's Tomorrow	20
69	Capitol E-ST 247	SPACE HYMN (LP)	45

DENNIS LOTIS
54	Decca F 10287	Such A Night/Cuddle Me (with Ted Heath Music & Johnston Brothers)	20
54	Decca F 10392	Honey Love/Manhattan Mambo (with Ted Heath Music)	20
55	Decca F 10469	Face Of An Angel, Heart Of A Devil/The Golden Ring	12
55	Decca F 10471	Chain Reaction/Go, Go, Go (with Ted Heath Music)	12
56	Pye 7N 15053	Green Grows The Grass/No Other Love Can Take Your Place	9
57	Columbia DB 3993	Tammy/I Complain	10
57	Columbia DB 4056	Valentina/Good Mornin' Life	10
58	Columbia DB 4090	I May Never Pass This Way Again/Gretna Green	7
58	Columbia DB 4158	The Only Man On The Island/Guessing What The Neighbours'll Say	6
56	Pye NEP 24017	PRESENTING DENNIS LOTIS (EP)	10
57	Pye NEP 24043	LET'S BE HAPPY (EP)	15
57	Pye NEP 24046	HOW ABOUT YOU (EP)	15
57	Pye NEP 24053	HOW ABOUT YOU PT. 2 (EP)	15
57	Pye NEP 24055	HOW ABOUT YOU PT. 3 (EP)	15
59	Columbia SEG 7955	HALLELUJAH IT'S DENNIS LOTIS (EP)	15
57	Nixa NPL 18002	HOW ABOUT YOU (LP)	35
58	Columbia 33SX 1089	BIDIN' MY TIME (LP)	28
(see also Johnstone Brothers)			

PETER LOTIS
60	Ember EMB S 110	Doo-Dah/You're Singing Our Love Song To Somebody Else (some with p/s)	10/6

LOT 39 (STRANGERS)
60s	Eyemark EMS 1004	I'll Get Over You/I Still Love You	6

LOTUS EATERS
84	Sylvan SYL 2	You Don't Need Someone New/Two Virgins Tender (picture disc)	5
84	Sylvan SYL 4	Out Of Your Own/Endless (picture disc)	5
85	Arista FS 5	It Hurts/Evidence//The Soul In Sparks/Church At Llanbadrig (double pack)	5
84	Sylvan 206 263	NO SENSE OF SIN (LP)	12
(see also Wild Swans, Care)			

BONNIE LOU
53	Parlophone MSP 6021	Seven Lonely Days/Dancin' With Someone	50
53	Parlophone MSP 6036	Hand-Me-Down Heart/Scrap Of Paper	50
53	Parlophone MSP 6048	Tennessee Wig Walk/Just Out Of Reach	80
53	Parlophone MSP 6051	Pa-Paya Mama/Since You Said Goodbye	40
54	Parlophone MSP 6072	The Texas Polka/No Heart At All	30
54	Parlophone MSP 6095	Don't Stop Kissing Me Goodnight/The Welcome Mat	30
54	Parlophone MSP 6108	No One/Huckleberry Pie	30
54	Parlophone MSP 6117	Blue Tennessee Rain/Wait For Me, Darling (78 rpm, Parlophone R 3895 = £12)	30
54	Parlophone MSP 6132	Two Step — Side Step/Please Don't Laugh When I Cry (78 rpm, R 3931 = £10)	30
55	Parlophone MSP 6151	Tennessee Mambo/Train Whistle Blues (78 rpm, Parlophone R 3975 = £12)	35
55	Parlophone MSP 6157	Tweedle Dee/The Finger Of Suspicion Points At You (78 rpm, R 3989 = £15)	40
55	Parlophone R 4012	A Rusty Old Halo/Danger! Heartbreak Ahead (78)	15
55	Parlophone MSP 6173	Drop Me A Line/Old Faithful And True Love (78 rpm, Parlophone R 4037 = £12)	25
55	Parlophone MSP 6178	The Barnyard Hop/Tell The World (78 rpm, Parlophone R4054 = £12)	20
55	Parlophone MSP 6188	Dancin' In My Socks/Daddy-O (78 rpm, Parlophone R 4096 = £15)	40
56	Parlophone MSP 6223	Darlin' Why/Miss The Love (That I've Been Dreaming Of) (78 rpm, R4146 = £12)	20
56	Parlophone MSP 6234	Bo Weevil (A Country Song)/Chaperon (78 rpm, Parlophone R4168 = £15)	20
56	Parlophone MSP 6253	Lonesome Lover/Little Miss Bobby Sox (78 rpm, Parlophone R 4194 = £12)	25
56	Parlophone R 4215	No Rock 'N' Roll Tonight/One Track Love (78 rpm = £12)	25
57	Parlophone R 4350	Teenage Wedding/Runnin' Away (78 rpm = £15)	25
58	Parlophone DP 545	I'm Available/Waiting In Vain (export issue)	25

LOU & KEVIN
78	Bushays BFM 103	Reunited/Reunited Stepping Out (12")	20

BONNIE LOU & RUSTY YORK
58	Parlophone R 4409	Let The School Bell Ring Ding-A-Ling/La Dee Dah (78 rpm = £30)	80
(see also Rusty York)			

JOHN D. LOUDERMILK
61	RCA RCA 1269	The Language Of Love/Darling Jane	8
62	RCA RCA 1287	Thou Shalt Not Steal/Mister Jones	8
62	RCA RCA 1323	Angela Jones/Road Hog	10
68	RCA RCA 1761	Sidewalks/The Odd Folks Of Okracoke	5
62	RCA RD 27248/SF 5123	THE LANGUAGE OF LOVE (LP)	40
62	RCA Victor RD/SF 7515	TWELVE SIDES OF JOHN D. LOUDERMILK (LP)	35

John D. LOUDERMILK

67	RCA Victor RD/SF 7890	SINGS A BIZARRE COLLECTION OF SONGS (LP)	22
70	RCA LSA 3159	THE BEST OF JOHN D. LOUDERMILK (LP)	12
	(see also Johnny Dee)		

LOUDNESS
84	Music For Nations MFN 22	DISILLUSION (LP)	12

JOE HILL LOUIS
65	Bootleg 502	Heartache Baby/I Feel Like A Million (99 copies only)	40
60s	Advent LP 2803	MEMPHIS BLUES AND BREAKDOWNS (LP)	60

JOE HILL LOUIS
74	Polydor 2383 214	BLUE IN THE MORNING (LP)	30
	(see also Willie Nix)		

LOUISE
96	EMI EMLH 397	Light Of My Life/Real Love (jukebox only, no p/s)	6
96	EMI CDEM 454	Light Of My Life/Real Love (Tin Tin Out Remix)/Real Love (Stonebridge Remix)/Interview with Louise (CD, with 3 prints)	8
97	EMI LOUPREM 101	SOFT & GENTLE: One Kiss From Louise Pop Megamix/Naked (Tony De Vit Mix)/Real Love (CD, promo/freebie)	8
97	EMI EMLH 490	Arms Around The World (Radio Mix)/Naked (Radio Mix) (jukebox only, no p/s)	5
97	EMI 12EMDJ 490	Arms Around The World (Rated PG Club Mix)/Arms Around The World (Rated PG Dub Mix) (12", p/s, promo only)	8
97	EMI 12DJD 490	Arms Around The World (Farley & Heller's Fire Island Vocal Mix)/Arms Around The World (Farley & Heller's Roach Motel Dub)/ArmsAround The World (T-Empo Club Mix)/Arms Around The World (T-Empo Dub Mix) (12", doublepack, p/s promo only)	8
97	EMI 12EMDJ 500	Let's Go Round Again (Colour Systems Inc. Gold Mix)/Let's Go Round Again (Rated PG Club Mix)/(Rated PG Mr. G Dub) (12", p/s, promo only)	8
97	EMI 12EMDJD 500	Let's Go Round Again (Colour Systems Inc. Amber Vox Mix)/(187 Lockdown Dub Mix)/(Paul Gotel's Peaceful Warrior Mix)/(187 Lockdown Vocal Mix)/(Colour Systems Inc. Amber Dub)/(Paul Gotel's Warrior Dub) (12", double pack, p/s, promo only)	8
98	EMI 12EMDJD 506	All That Matters (DJ Tonka Mix)/All That Matters (Cas Roc Vocal Mix)/All That Matters (Hex Hector Dub Revisited Mix)/All That Matters (Cas Roc Vocal Mix) (12" double pack, p/s, promo only)	8
	(see also Eternal)		

LOUISIANA RED
64	Columbia DB 7270	Keep Your Hands Off My Woman/Don't Cry	40
64	Sue WI 337	I Done Woke Up/I Had A Feeling	45
64	Columbia 33SX 1612	LOWDOWN BACK PORCH BLUES (LP)	60
72	Atlantic K 40436	SINGS THE BLUES (LP)	20
72	Carnival 2941 002	THE SEVENTH SON (LP)	20

LOUISIANA SUGAR BABIES
57	HMV 7EG 8215	LOUISIANA SUGAR BABIES (EP, with Fats Waller & James P. Johnson)	15

LOUVIN BROTHERS
59	Capitol CL 14989	Knoxville Girl/I Wish It Had Been A Dream	25
59	Capitol CL 15078	You're Learning/My Curly Headed Baby	10
56	Capitol EAP1 769	TRAGIC SONGS OF LIFE (EP)	25
58	Capitol EAP1 910	IRA AND CHARLIE (EP)	25
59	Capitol EAP1 1106	COUNTRY LOVE BALLADS (EP)	20

LOVABLES
68	Stateside SS 2108	You're The Cause Of It/Beautiful Idea	22

LOVE
SINGLES
66	London HLZ 10053	My Little Red Book/Hey Joe	35
66	London HLZ 10073	7 And 7 Is/No. Fourteen	40
67	Elektra EKSN 45010	She Comes In Colours/Orange Skies	25
67	Elektra EKSN 45016	Softly To Me/The Castle	22
68	Elektra EKSN 45024	Alone Again Or/Bummer In The Summer	18
68	Elektra EKSN 45026	The Daily Planet/Andmoreagain	20
68	Elektra EKSN 45038	Laughing Stock/Your Mind And We Belong Together	35
70	Elektra EKSN 45086	I'm With You/Robert Montgomery	12
70	Harvest HAR 5014	Stand Out/Doggone	10
70	Harvest HAR 5030	The Everlasting First/Keep On Shining	15
70	Elektra 2101 019	Alone Again Or/Bummer In The Summer (reissue)	6
73	Elektra K 12113	Alone Again Or/Andmoreagain	6
75	RSO 2090 151	Time Is Like A River/You Said You Would	6

ORIGINAL LPs
66	Elek. EKL 4001/EKS 74001	LOVE (LP, gold label, U.K disc in U.S. sleeve)	70
67	Elek. EKL 4005/EKS 74005	DA CAPO (LP, orange label, with U.K. or U.S. sleeve)	60
67	Elek. EKL 4013/EKS 74013	FOREVER CHANGES (LP, orange label)	55
69	Elektra EKL 4049	FOUR SAIL (LP, orange label, mono, existence unconfirmed)	40+
69	Elektra EKS 74049	FOUR SAIL (LP, orange label, stereo)	45
70	Harvest SHDW 3/4	OUT HERE (2-LP, gatefold sleeve)	40
71	Harvest SHVL 787	FALSE START (LP, gatefold sleeve)	35
71	Elektra 2469 009	LOVE REVISITED (LP, gatefold sleeve)	18
73	Elektra K 32002	LOVE MASTERS (LP)	15
74	RSO 2394 145	REEL TO REAL (LP)	15

RE-PRESSINGS
67	Elek. EKL 4001/EKS 74001	LOVE (LP, orange label, with U.K. or U.S. sleeve)	40
72	Elektra K 42068	LOVE (LP, 'butterfly' label)	15
71	Elektra EKS 74005	DA CAPO (LP, 'butterfly' label)	15

72	Elektra K 42011	DA CAPO (LP, 'butterfly' label)	15
72	Elektra K 42015	FOREVER CHANGES (LP, 'butterfly' label)	15
72	Elektra K 42030	FOUR SAIL (LP, 'butterfly' label)	15
	(see also Arthur Lee)		

LOVE
90	Fierce FRIGHT 036	Welsh Girl (1-sided, p/s in bag, hand-finished labels, mail-order only)	20

LOVE & UNITY
80	Studio 16 (no. Cat. No.)	Put It On/(feat Ranking Bogart)/Dub	40
80	Studio 16 WE N1	Just Don't Care/Cut From The Master Tape (12")	30
80	Studio 16 WEA 347	I Adore You/CAPTAIN DESMOND: Lover In Dance (12")	25

CHRISTOPHER LOVE
69	London HLU 10263	The Curse Goes On/You May Be The Next	10

LOVE CONNECTION
77	Strong Like Sampson SLS01	It's My House/Fall In Love (12")	20

DARLENE LOVE
63	London HLU 9725	(Today I Met) The Boy I'm Gonna Marry/Playing For Keeps	40
63	London HLU 9765	Wait 'Til My Bobby Gets Home/Take It From Me	40
63	London HLU 9815	A Fine Fine Boy/Marshmallow World	40
69	London HLU 10244	Wait 'Til My Bobby Gets Home/(Today I Met) The Boy I'm Gonna Marry	15
74	Warner Bros/Spector K 19011	Christmas (Baby Please Come Home)/Wait Till My Bobby Comes Home (blue vinyl)	6
77	Phil Spector Intl. 2010 019	Lord If You're A Woman/Johnny Baby	20
77	Phil Spector Intl. 2010 019	Lord If You're A Woman/Johnny Baby (12", some copies 1-sided)	15
88	CBS 6529357	He's Sure The Man I Love (New Version)/Everybody Needs (p/s)	5
90	Warner Brothers W 9535	Mr Fix-It/k.d. lang with TAKE SIX: Ridin' The Rails (some with p/s)	25/20
64	London RE-U 1411	WAIT TILL MY BOBBY GETS HOME (EP)	200
	(see also Bob B. Soxx & Blue Jeans, Crystals, Phil Spector, Blossoms, Allisons [U.S.], Date With Soul, Cinders)		

GARFIELD LOVE & JIMMY SPRUILL
69	Blue Horizon 57-3150	Next Time You See Me/Part Time Love	35

LOVE AND WAR
80s	SRT SRT9KS 2323	Touch Of Class (p/s)	100

GEOFF LOVE ORCHESTRA
61	Columbia DB 4627	Coronation Street Theme/Sophia	5
62	Columbia DB 4881	Steptoe And Son/Over The Backyard Fence	5
70	Columbia DB 8707	Coronation Street Theme/ALIRIO DIAZ: Aranjuez Mon Amour (Rodgigo)	5
74	EMI EMI 2105	Match Of The Day/Bless This House	5
	(see also Mandingo, Manuel & Music Of The Mountains)		

JILL BABY LOVE
76	Black Magic BM 116	My Way Or Hit The Highway (Parts 1 & 2)	6

MARY LOVE
65	King KG 1024	You Turned My Bitter Into Sweet/I'm In Your Hands	175
67	Stateside SS 2009	Lay This Burden Down/Think It Over Baby (DJ copy = £125)	55
68	Stateside SS 2135	The Hurt Is Just Beginning/If You Change Your Mind	30
82	Kent TOWN 501	You Turned My Bitter Into Sweet/SWEETHEARTS: This Couldn't Be Me	15

MIKE LOVE
83	Creole CR 61	Jingle Bell Rock/Let's Party (p/s)	5
	(see also Beach Boys)		

RONNIE LOVE
61	London HLD 9272	Chills And Fever/Pledging My Love	50
78	Grapevine GRP 108	Let's Make Love/Nothing To It	10

WILLIE LOVE/WILLIE NIX
66	Highway 51 H 700	THE TWO WILLIES FROM MEMPHIS (LP, 99 copies only)	75
	(see also Willie Nix)		

LOVE AFFAIR
67	Decca F 12558	She Smiled Sweetly/Satisfaction Guaranteed	65
67	CBS 3125	Everlasting Love/Gone Are The Songs Of Yesterday	6
68	CBS 3366	Rainbow Valley/Someone Like Us (some in p/s)	20/8
68	CBS 3674	A Day Without Love/I'm Happy	6
69	CBS 3994	One Road/Let Me Know	6
69	CBS 4300	Bringing On Back The Good Times/Another Day	6
69	CBS 4631	Baby I Know/Accept Me For What I Am	10
70	CBS 4780	Lincoln County/Sea Of Tranquility	10
70	Pye 7N 45218	Let Me Dance/Love's Looking Out At You	8
71	Parlophone R 5887	Wake Me I Am Dreaming/That's My Home	12
71	Parlophone R 5918	Help (Get Me Some Help)/Long Way Home	12
73	CBS 1144	Everlasting Love/Bringing On Back The Good Times (p/s, 'Hall Of Fame Hits' series)	5
77	Creole CR 146	Private Lives/Let A Little Love Come In	5
68	CBS 63416	THE EVERLASTING LOVE AFFAIR (LP, mono/stereo)	28
	(see also L.A., Ellis, Steve Ellis, Elastic Band, Widowmaker, Morgan, Phillip Goodhand-Tait, English Rose, Rainbow Ffolly)		

LOVE CHILDREN
69	Deram DM 268	Easy Squeezy/Every Little Step	15
70	Deram DM 303	Paper Chase/My Turkey Snuffed It	10

LOVE COMMITTEE
76	Ariola AA 105	Can't Win For Losing/Love Wins Every Time	10

MINT VALUE £

LOVECUT D.B.
91	Suburbs Of Hell SOH 009EP	Heartspin/Heartspin (Dripping Clock Mix)/(Marisco Disco Mix)/	
		(Porn Cable Mix) (12", p/s)	10
92	Suburbs Of Hell SOH 011EP	JOURNEY TO THE CENTRE OF LOVE EP (12")	10

(see also Sarah Cracknell, St. Etienne)

LOVE GENERATION (Jamaica)
73	Grape GR 3046	Money Raper/HEPTONES: The Magnificent Heptones 3 In One	6
73	Grape GR 3041	Warrika Hill/Battlefield (Third And Fourth Generation)	6

LOVE GENERATION (U.S.)
67	Liberty LBF 15018	She Touched Me/The Love In Me	12
68	Liberty LBL/LBS 83121E	LOVE GENERATION (LP)	25

JOY LOVEJOY
72	Chess 6145 010	In Orbit/Uh! Hum (paper label/moulded label)	12

LOVELITES
78	Grapevine GRP 107	Get It Off My Conscience/Oh, What A Day	15

TONY LOVELLO
59	Top Rank JAR 200	Amore Mio/Dreamy Serenade (78 rpm = £6)	6

LOVE OF LIFE ORCHESTRA
80	Infidelity JMB 227	EXTENDED NICETIES (12" EP)	8

(see also David Byrne)

JOHNNY LOVER
70	Amalgamated AMG 871	Pumpkin Eater/Version	15
70	Amalgamated AMG 873	Two Edged Sword/Version	20

(see also Little Johnny Jones, Heptones)

LOVERS
58	Vogue Pop V 9111	Let's Elope/I Wanna Be Loved (78 rpm = £170)	700

LOVE SCULPTURE
68	Parlophone R 5664	River To Another Day/Brand New Woman	20
68	Parlophone R 5731	Wang-Dang-Doodle/The Stumble	20
68	Parlophone R 5744	Sabre Dance/Think Of Love	6
69	Parlophone R 5807	Seagull/Farandole	15
70	Parlophone R 5831	In The Land Of The Few/People People	20
68	Parlophone PMC/PCS 7059	BLUES HELPING (LP, 1st pressing, yellow/black label, mono/stereo)	50/40
69	Parlophone PCS 7090	FORMS AND FEELINGS (LP, 1st pressing, yellow/black label)	40
70	Parlophone PCS 7059	BLUES HELPING (LP, 2nd pressing, silver/black label)	12
70	Parlophone PCS 7090	FORMS AND FEELINGS (LP, 2nd pressing, silver/black label)	12

(see also Human Beans, Dave Edmunds)

EDDIE LOVETTE
69	Big Shot BI 519	You're My Girl/Let Them Say	8
70	London HLU 10298	Boomerang/Together	5
70	London HLJ 10311	Too Experienced/Little Blue Bird	10
70	London HA-J 8413	TOO EXPERIENCED (LP, unissued)	
70	London LGJ/ZGJ 103	TOO EXPERIENCED (LP)	12

LOVE UNLIMITED
72	Uni UNLS 124	FROM A GIRL'S POINT OF VIEW — LOVE UNLIMITED (LP)	15
73	Pye NSPL 28179	UNDER THE INFLUENCE OF LOVE UNLIMITED (LP)	12
74	20th Century BT 443	IN HEAT (LP)	12

LOVERS DUB
80	Venture	CUT 7 (LP) (actually by Eargasm)	40

(see also Tradition)

LOVEY AUSTIN BLUE SERENADERS/STATE STREET RAMBLERS
60s	Collector JE 123	SMALL JAZZ BANDS VOL. 1 (EP)	8

LENE LOVICH
76	Polydor 2058 812	I Saw Mommy Kissing Santa Claus/The Christmas Song	
		(Merry Christmas To You)/Happy Christmas	10
78	Stiff BUYJ 32	I Think We're Alone Now (Japanese)/Lucky Number (mail-order promo only)	10

LOVIN'
67	Page One POF 035	Keep On Believing/I'm In Command	35
67	Page One POF 041	All I've Got/Do It Again	55

(see also Nerve)

LOVING AWARENESS
76	More Love ML 001	LOVING AWARENESS (LP, gatefold sleeve with 2 posters)	15

(see also Glencoe, Skip Bifferty, Ian Dury)

LOVING KIND
66	Piccadilly 7N 35299	Accidental Love/Nothing Can Change This Love	15
66	Piccadilly 7N 35318	I Love The Things You Do/Treat Me Nice	18
66	Piccadilly 7N 35342	Ain't That Peculiar/With Rhyme And Reason	20

(see also Noel Redding Band, Freddie Lennon)

LOVIN' SPOONFUL
65	Pye International 7N 25327	Do You Believe In Magic?/On The Road Again	15
66	Pye International 7N 25344	You Didn't Have To Be So Nice/My Gal	15
66	Pye International 7N 25361	Daydream/Night Owl Blues	7
66	Kama Sutra KAS 200	Summer In The City/Bald Headed Lena	7
66	Kama Sutra KAS 201	Rain On The Roof/Warm Baby	6
67	Kama Sutra KAS 204	Nashville Cats/Full Measure	8
67	Kama Sutra KAS 207	Darling Be Home Soon/Darlin' Companion	10
67	Kama Sutra KAS 208	Six O'Clock/The Finale	15

67	Kama Sutra KAS 210	She Is Still A Mystery/Only Pretty, What A Pity	8
67	Kama Sutra KAS 211	Money/Close Your Eyes	8
68	Kama Sutra KAS 213	Never Going Back/Forever	10
66	Kama Sutra KEP 300	DID YOU EVER HAVE TO MAKE UP YOUR MIND (EP)	22
66	Kama Sutra KEP 301	JUG BAND MUSIC (EP)	30
66	Kama Sutra KEP 302	SUMMER IN THE CITY (EP)	30
67	Kama Sutra KEP 303	DAY BLUES (EP)	30
67	Kama Sutra KEP 304	NASHVILLE CATS (EP)	35
67	Kama Sutra KEP 305	LOVIN' YOU (EP)	35
67	Kama Sutra KEP 306	SOMETHING IN THE NIGHT (EP)	35
65	Pye Intl. NPL 28069	DO YOU BELIEVE IN MAGIC? (LP)	30
66	Pye Intl. NPL 28078	DAYDREAM (LP)	32
67	Kama Sutra KLP 401	HUMS OF THE LOVIN' SPOONFUL (LP)	32
67	Kama Sutra KLP 402	YOU'RE A BIG BOY NOW (LP, soundtrack)	32
67	Kama Sutra KLP 403	THE BEST OF THE LOVIN' SPOONFUL (LP)	15
68	Kama Sutra KLP 404	EVERYTHING PLAYING (LP)	22
68	Kama Sutra K(S)LP 405	THE BEST OF THE LOVIN' SPOONFUL VOL. 2 (LP)	15
69	Kama Sutra 602 009	REVELATION: REVOLUTION '69 (LP)	18

(see also John Sebastian, Mugwumps, Zalman Yanovsky, Even Dozen Jug Band)

BRUCE LOW
56	HMV JO 464	Just Walking In The Rain/Cindy Oh Cindy (export issue)	20

LOWBITES
70	Black Swan BW 1403	I Got It/I Got It (Version)	6

ARTHUR LOWE
72	Columbia DB 8956	My Little Girl, My Little Boy/How I Won The War	6
69	World Record Club ST 1008	BLESS 'EM ALL! (LP)	12

DENNIS LOWE
70	Downtown DT 465	What's Your Name/MUSIC DOCTORS: Mr Locabe	10
70	Downtown DT 468	Stand Up For The Sound/OWEN & DENNIS: Old Man Trouble	6

JIM LOWE
55	London HLD 8171	Close The Door/Nueva Laredo (gold label print) (78 rpm = £15)	60
56	London HLD 8276	Blue Suede Shoes/Maybellene (silver label print) (78 rpm = £30)	100
56	London HLD 8288	Love Is The $64,000 Dollar Question/Rene La Rue (gold label print)	75
6	London HLD 8288	Love Is The $64,000 Dollar Question/Rene La Rue	15
56	London HLD 8317	The Green Door/The Little Man In Chinatown (as Jim Lowe & High Fives, gold label print, later silver)	55/30
56	London HLD 8317	The Green Door/The Little Man In Chinatown (78)	10
57	London HLD 8368	I Feel The Beat/By You, By You, By You (gold label print, later silver)	45/30
57	London HLD 8368	I Feel The Beat/By You, By You, By You (78)	10
57	London HLD 8431	Four Walls/Talkin' To The Blues (78 rpm = £10)	30
58	London HLD 8538	Roc-A-Chicka/The Bright Light (with Billy Vaughan's Orchestra) (78 rpm = £30)	125
60	London HLD 9043	He'll Have To Go/(This Life Is Just A) Dress Rehearsal	15
65	United Artists UP 1096	Mr Moses/Make Your Back Strong	6
58	London HA-D 2108	SONGS THEY SING BEHIND THE GREEN DOOR (LP)	50
59	London HA-D 2146	WICKED WOMEN (LP)	38

(see also John Barry Seven)

PETER LOWE
57	Parlophone R 4270	The Banana Boat Song/The Wisdom Of A Fool	5

LOWLIFE
88	LOLIF DEMO 1	THE DEMOS (LP, white label test pressings only, hand-written white sleeve)	18

LOW NOISE
81	Happy Birthday UR 5	Jungle Line/Urban Tribal/Jungle Line (Instrumental) (12", p/s)	8

LOW NUMBERS
79	Warner Brothers K 17493	Keep In Touch/Nine All Out (p/s)	40

PHILIP LOWRIE
63	Ember EMB S 179	I Might Have Known (Before)/I Might Have Known (After)	10

ART LOWRY
54	Columbia SCMC 1	The Curse Of An Aching Heart/Heart Of My Heart (export issue)	10

HENRY LOWTHER BAND
70	Deram SML 1070	CHILD SONG (LP)	90

(see also Manfred Mann, John Mayall & Bluesbreakers, Keef Hartley Band, Ricotti & Albuquerque)

MARK LOYD
65	Parlophone R 5277	I Keep Thinking About You/Will It Be The Same	10
65	Parlophone R 5332	Everybody Tries/She Said No	75
66	Parlophone R 5423	When Evening Falls/When I'm Gonna Find Her (DJ copy = £350)	300

L7
92	Slash LACDP42	PRETEND WE'RE DEAD (CD EP gatefold digipak)	8
92	Slash LASCD42	PRETEND WE'RE DEAD (CD EP picture disc, unnumbered sleeve)	8
94	Slash 8576531	Andres/The Bomb/interview (12", poly sleeve, green vinyl, no'd card insert)	8

JEREMY LUBBOCK
58	Parlophone R 4399	Catch A Falling Star/The Man Who Invented Love	5
58	Parlophone R 4421	Lemon Twist/Tonight	5
58	Parlophone R 4473	Odd Man Out/Too Bad You're Not Around	5
58	Parlophone GEP 8745	JUST FOR THE FUN OF IT (EP)	15

LUCAS

LUCAS (& MIKE COTTON SOUND)
66	Polydor 56114	I Saw Pity In The Face Of A Friend/Dance Children Dance (solo)	20
67	Pye 7N 17313	Step Out Of Line/Ain't Love Good, Ain't Love Proud	55
68	MGM MGM 1398	Soul Serenade/We Got A Thing Going Baby	40
68	MGM MGM 1427	Jack And The Beanstalk/Mother-In-Law	20

(see also Mike Cotton Sound, Artwoods)

BUDDY LUCAS BAND
53	London L 1181	Organ Grinder's Swing/Laura (78, as Buddy Lucas & His Orchestra)	25
60	Pye International 7N 25045	I Want To Know/Deacon John (78 rpm = £15)	20

TREVOR LUCAS
66	Reality RE 505	Waltzing Matilda/It's On	30
66	Reality RY 1002	OVERLANDER (LP)	250

(see also Eclection, Fotheringay, Fairport Convention, Bronco, Bunch, Sandy Denny)

LUCID DREAM
91	Euphoric E 9999T	DRIPPY EP (12", p/s)	8

LUCIFER
71	Lucifer L 001	Don't Care/Hypnosis	8
72	Lucifer L 003/004	Fuck You/Bad	8
72	Lucifer L 005/006	Prick/Want It	8
72	Lucifer L 005/006/L 003/004	Prick/Want It//Fuck You/Bad (double pack, black box set)	40
72	Lucifer LLP 1	BIG GUN (LP, private pressing, with poster/inserts, sold via *Oz* mag)	60
72	Lucifer LLP 2	EXIT (LP, private pressing, with poster, sold via *Oz* magazine)	80

LUCIFER'S FRIEND
71	Philips 6003 092	Ride The Sky/Horla	15
71	Philips 6305 068	LUCIFER'S FRIEND (LP)	18

(see also John Lawton, Uriah Heep)

JOHNNY LUCK
58	Fontana H 110	Play Rough/Buzz, Buzz, Buzz (78)	15

LUCY
77	Lightning GIL 516	Never Never/Feel So Good (p/s)	20
78	B&C BCS 8	Really Got Me Goin'/Oy (p/s)	10

(see also Def Leppard)

TOM LUCY
82	Bridgehouse BHS 15	Paris, France/Man Found Dead In Graveyard (no p/s)	6

(see also Wasted Youth)

LUCY SHOW
83	Shout XS 007	Leonardo Da Vinci/Kill The Beast (p/s)	5
85	A&M AMY 261	Ephemeral/White Space (12", p/s)	20

LUDDITES
83	Xcentric Noise SECOND 1	STRENGTH OF YOUR CRY (EP, black or pink foldout p/s)	15/10

LUDLOWS
65	Pye 7N 15946	The Last Thing On My Mind/Kisses Sweeter Than Wine	5
66	Pye 7N 17050	The Sea Around Us/The Butcher Boys	5
66	Pye 7N 17123	The Winds Thro' The Rafters/That's My Song	5
66	Pye 7N 17221	Johnny Lad/Pack Up Your Sorrows	5
67	Pye 7N 17319	Enniskillen Dragoons/Foggy Dew	5
67	Pye 7N 17384	Plaisir D'Amour/Yesterday's Dream	5
66	Pye NPL 18150	THE WIND AND THE SEA (LP)	15

(see also Jim McCann)

LUDUS
80	New Hormones ORG 4	The Visit/Lullaby Cheat/Unveil (12", p/s with insert)	8
81	New Hormones ORG 8	My Cherry Is In Sherry/Anatomy Is Not Destiny (p/s)	5
81	New Hormones CAT 1	PICKPOCKET (C-30 cassette pack with A4 book & button in PVC bag)	12
81	New Hormones ORG 12	Mother's Hour/Patient (p/s, with poster)	5
81	New Hormones ORG 16	THE SEDUCTION (2 x 12" EP, each in p/s; whole package in poly bag)	12
80s	New Hormones	LINDER SINGS BARDOT (cassette)	12
82	New Hormones ORG 20	DANGER CAME SMILING (LP)	12

LUGWORM
97	Guided Missile GUIDE 11	Rococo Negro/BIS: Pop Song (p/s)	5

LUKE & BLAKE
66	CBS 202467	Just You/Wandering Man	8

ROBIN LUKE
58	London HLD 8676	Susie Darlin'/Living's Loving You (78 rpm = £20)	20
58	London HLD 8771	Chicka Chicka Honey/My Girl (78 rpm = £40)	30
59	London RED 1222	ROBIN LUKE (EP)	120

LULU (& LUVVERS)
64	Decca F 11884	Shout/Forget Me Baby (as Lulu & Luvers)	12
64	Decca F 11965	Can't Hear You No More/I Am In Love	15
64	Decca F 12017	Here Comes The Night/That's Really Some Good	10
65	Decca F 12128	Satisfied/Surprise Surprise (as Lulu & Luvers)	18
65	Decca F 12169	Leave A Little Love/He Don't Want Your Love Anymore	10
65	Decca F 12214	Try To Understand/Not In This Whole World	10
65	Decca F 12254	Tell Me Like It Is/Stop Fooling Around	12
66	Decca F 12326	Call Me/After You	12
66	Decca F 12491	What A Wonderful Feeling/Tossin' And Turnin'	12
67	Columbia DB 8169	The Boat That I Row/Dreary Days And Nights	7
67	Columbia DB 8221	Let's Pretend/To Sir With Love	10
67	Columbia DB 8295	Love Loves To Love/You And I	15

68	Columbia DB 8358	Me, The Peaceful Heart/Lookout	10
68	Columbia DB 8425	Boy/Sad Memories	7
68	Columbia DB 8500	I'm A Tiger/Without Him	7
69	Columbia DB 8550	Boom Bang-A-Bang/March!	5
69	Atco 226 008	Oh Me, Oh My (I'm A Fool For You Baby)/Sweep Around Your Own Backyard	5
65	Decca DFE 8597	LULU (EP)	50
65	Decca LK 4719	SOMETHING TO SHOUT ABOUT (LP)	75
67	Ace Of Clubs ACL 1232	LULU! (LP)	25
67	Fontana (S)TL 5446	TO SIR, WITH LOVE (LP, soundtrack, with Ron Grainer & Mindbenders)	60
67	Columbia S(C)X 6201	LOVE LOVES TO LOVE LULU (LP)	35
69	Columbia S(C)X 6365	LULU'S ALBUM (LP)	25
69	Atco 228 031	NEW ROUTES (LP)	25

(see also Luvvers, Scotland World Cup Squad)

LULU BELLE & SCOTTY

50	London L 833	Have I Told You Lately That I Love You/Schrudle Du (78)	10
65	London HA-B 8277	SWEETHEART STILL (LP)	15

BOB LUMAN

60	Warner Bros WB 12	Dreamy Doll/Buttercup	20
60	Warner Bros WB 18	Let's Think About Livin'/You've Got Everything	10
60	Warner Bros WB 28	Why, Why, Bye, Bye/Oh, Lonesome Me	12
61	Warner Bros WB 37	The Great Snow Man/The Pig Latin Song	12
61	Warner Bros WB 49	Private Eye/You Turned Down The Lights	10
62	Warner Bros WB 60	Louisiana Man/Rocks Of Reno (unissued)	
62	Warner Bros WB 75	Hey Joe/The Fool	10
64	Hickory 45-1238	The File/Bigger Men Than I	10
64	Hickory 45-1266	(Empty Walls) A Lonely Room/Run On Home Baby Brother	6
64	Hickory 45-1277	Old George Dickel/Fire Engine Red	6
65	Hickory 45-1289	Bad Bad Day/Tears From Out Of Nowhere	10
65	Hickory 45-1410	Come On And Sing/It's A Sin	6
68	CBS 3602	Ain't Got Time To Be Unhappy/I Can't Remember To Forget	10
61	Warner Bros WEP 6046	LET'S THINK ABOUT LIVIN' (EP, also stereo WSEP 2046)	45/60
62	Warner Bros WEP 6055	LET'S THINK ABOUT LIVIN' NO. 2 (EP, also stereo WSEP 2055)	45/60
62	Warner Bros WEP 6102	LET'S THINK ABOUT LIVIN' NO. 3 (EP, also stereo WSEP 2102)	45/60
60	Warner Bros WM 4025	LET'S THINK ABOUT LIVIN' (LP, also stereo WS 8025)	70/90
64	Hickory LPM 124	LIVIN' LOVIN' SOUNDS (LP)	35
71	London ZGE 115	LIVIN' LOVIN' SOUNDS (LP, reissue)	12

(see also Sue Thompson & Bob Luman)

BOB LUMAN/BOBBY LORD

64	Hickory LPE 1501	HICKORY SHOWCASE VOL. 2 (EP, 1 side each)	20
64	Hickory LPE 1504	HICKORY SHOWCASE VOL. 3 (EP, 1 side each)	20
64	Hickory LPM 121	CAN'T TAKE THE COUNTRY FROM THE BOYS (LP, 1 side each)	15

(see also Bobby Lord)

RUFUS LUMLEY

66	Stateside SS 516	I'm Standing/Let's Hide Away (Me And You) (£400 for demo)	300
78	EMI International INT 556	I'm Standing/Let's Hide Away (Me And You) (reissue)	15

LUNACHICKS

89	Blast First BFFP 44	SUGAR LUV EP (7" double pack)	8

LUNAR TWO

60s	Spot JWS 551	Get It Take It/Don't Ever Leave Me	10

JIMMIE LUNCEFORD

63	Capitol T/ST 1581	THE GREAT JIMMIE LUNCEFORD (LP)	15

LYDIA LUNCH

91	UFO UFOPF 1	Spooky (mono)/Spooky (stereo) (no p/s, promo only)	6
93	Clawfist X-PIG 19	Unearthly Delights/Busted (p/s)	10
82	Situation 2 SITU 6	13.13 (LP, with inner sleeve)	20
84	Doublevision DVR 5	IN LIMBO (LP, red vinyl with inner sleeve)	20
86	Widowspeak SWP 01/07	THE INTIMATE DIARIES OF THE SEXUALLY INSANE (cassette, box set with book, signed)	25
87	Widowspeak WSP 8	HYSTERIE (2-LP, with inners and poster)	20

(see also Eight-Eyed Spy, Roland S. Howard, No Trend)

ART LUND

53	MGM SP 1042	If I Were A Bell/JOHNNY DESMOND: A Bushel And A Peck	5
65	United Artists UP 1100	Branded/Gonna Have A Little Talk	5
57	Vogue Coral LVA 9056	THIS IS ART (LP)	20

TED LUNE

60	Philips PB 1068	Mr Custer/Time Machine	6

(see also Michael Medwin 8 Army Game Cast)

LARRY LUREX

73	EMI EMI 2030	I Can Hear Music/Goin' Back (demo)	300
73	EMI EMI 2030	I Can Hear Music/Goin' Back (press-out centre; beware of solid-centered counterfeits)	200

(see also Queen)

LURKERS

77	Beggars Banquet BEG 1	Free Admission Single: Shadow/Love Story (p/s, black vinyl; reissued on red, blue or white vinyl)	10/12
77	Beggars Banquet BEG 2	Freak Show/Mass Media Believer (p/s)	8
78	Beggars Banquet BEG 6	Ain't Got A Clue/Ooh Ooh I Love You (p/s, 15,000 with gold flexidisc, 'Chaos Brothers Fulham Fallout Fifty Free' [BEG 61/2])	6/4
78	Beggars Banquet BEG 6	Ain't Got A Clue/Ooh Ooh I Love You (reissue, different p/s, with clear vinyl picture flexidisc)	5

79	Beggars Banquet BACK 1	Shadow/Love Story//Freak Show/Mass Media Believer (reissue double pack)	5
79	Beggars Banquet BACK 3	I Don't Need To Tell Her/Pills//Just Thirteen/Countdown (double pack)	5
82	Clay CLAY 17P	Drag You Out/Heroin (It's All Over) (picture disc)	5
78	Beggars Banquet BEGA 2	FULHAM FALLOUT (LP, gatefold sleeve, some with picture disc flexi 'Chaos Brothers Fulham Fallout Forty Free' [BEG 6 1/2] & stickered sleeve)	20/12

(see also Pete Stride & John Plain, Fulham Furies, Rowdies)

DON LUSHER BAND

55	Decca F 10560	Rock 'n' Roll/On With The Don	18
56	Decca F 10740	Fast And Furious/Let's Do It	6

LUSTMØRD

82	Sterile SR 3	LUSTMØRD (LP, with odorous label)	35

NELLIE LUTCHER (& HER RHYTHM)

54	Brunswick 05352	Blues In The Night/Breezin' Along With The Breeze	18
55	Brunswick 05437	It's Been Said/Please Come Back	10
55	Brunswick 05497	Whose Honey Are You?/If I Didn't Love You Like I Do	10
60	Capitol CL 15106	My Mother's Eyes/The Heart Of A Clown	6
60	Capitol EAP 20066	REAL GONE (EP)	50
56	Philips BBE 12045	NELLIE LUTCHER (EP)	35
51	Capitol LC 6500	REAL GONE! (10" LP)	80
57	London HA-U 2036	OUR NEW NELLIE (LP)	60
66	M. For Pleasure MFP 1038	REAL GONE (LP)	15

CLAUDE LUTER ORCHESTRA

59	Vogue V 9132	The Day That The Rains Came/La Grande Coco (78 rpm = £15)	10

LUTHER

76	Cotillion K 10781	It's Good For The Soul (Parts 1 & 2)	18

FRANK LUTHER

53	Brunswick 05124	I'll Ring You Up/Jig A Jig Jig (78)	7
60	Decca F 9050	The Little Red Hen (Song Story) (both sides)	5
60	Decca F 9051	The Three Billy Goats Gruff (Song Story) (both sides)	5

LUTHER & LITTLE EVA

57	Parlophone R 4292	Love Is Strange/Ain't Got No Home (78 rpm = £140)	550
	(do not see also Little Eva)		

LUV BUG

86	Roxy!-Ritz TEASE 2	You Can Count On Me/You Can't Have It (p/s)	7

LUV MACHINE

71	Polydor 2058 080	Witches Wand/In The Early Hours	12
71	Polydor 2460 102	LUV MACHINE (LP)	130

LUVVERS

66	Parlophone R 5459	The House On The Hill/Most Unlovely	35
	(see also Lulu)		

MICK LUVZIT

66	Decca F 12421	Long Time Between Lovers/Though I Still Love You	8

GARY LUX

85	Global LUX 2	Children Of The World/Movies (p/s)	5

L-VOAG

79	Sesame Songs MOVE 1	MOVE (EP, p/s with handmade labels & insert)	15
81	Axis No. 9	THE WAY OUT (LP, with booklet & poster)	30
	(see also Homosexuals)		

LYLE McGUINNESS BAND

83	Cool King CKLP 03	ACTING ON IMPULSE (LP)	12
	(see also McGuinness Flint, Gallagher & Lyle)		

ARTHUR LYMAN GROUP

59	Vogue V 9153	Taboo/Dahil Sayo (78 rpm = £20)	5
59	Vogue VEH 70166	GREATEST HITS VOL. 1 (EP)	12
59	Vogue VEH 70167	GREATEST HITS VOL. 2 (EP)	12
59	Vogue VEH 70168	GREATEST HITS VOL. 3 (EP)	12
59	Vogue VA 160142	TABOO VOL. 1 (LP, also stereo SAV 8002)	15/18
59	Vogue VA 160149	MORE EXOTIC SOUNDS — BWANA A (LP)	12
60	Vogue VA 160166	BAHIA (LP)	12
61	Vogue VA 160171	HAWAIIAN SUNSET (LP)	12
61	Vogue VA 160174	TABOO VOL. 2 (LP, also stereo SAV 8003)	15
63	Vogue SAVH 8030	LOVE FOR SALE (LP)	12

FRANKIE LYMON (& TEENAGERS)

56	Columbia SCM 5265	Why Do Fools Fall In Love?/Please Be Mine (as Teenagers featuring Frankie Lymon) (78 rpm, Columbia DB3772 = £10)	65
56	Columbia SCM 5285	I Want You To Be My Girl/I'm Not A Know It All (78 rpm = £15)	55
56	Columbia DB 3819	Who Can Explain?/I Promise To Remember (78 rpm = £12)	50
56	Columbia DB 3858	Share/The A.B.C.'s Of Love (78 rpm = £15)	50
57	Columbia DB 3878	I'm Not A Juvenile Delinquent/Baby, Baby (78 rpm = £10)	40
57	Columbia DB 3910	Teenage Love/Paper Castles (78 rpm = £12)	40
57	Columbia DB 3942	Miracle In The Rain/Out In The Cold Again (78 rpm = £15)	40
57	Columbia DB 3983	Goody Goody/Creation Of Love (78 rpm = £10)	20
57	Columbia DB 4028	My Girl/So Goes My Love (78 rpm = £20)	30
58	Columbia DB 4073	Thumb Thumb/Footsteps (solo) (78 rpm = £20)	25
58	Columbia DB 4134	Mama Don't Allow It/Portable On My Shoulder (solo) (78 rpm = £25)	20
59	Columbia DB 4245	Melinda/The Only Way To Love (solo) (78 rpm = £40)	20

59	Columbia DB 4295	Up Jumped A Rabbit/No Matter What You've Done (solo)	22
60	Columbia DB 4499	Little Bitty Pretty One/Creation Of Love (solo)	30
66	King KG 1042	Why Do Fools Fall In Love?/I'm Not A Juvenile Delinquent	8
57	Columbia SEG 7662	TEENAGE ROCK (EP)	60
57	Columbia SEG 7694	THE TEENAGERS FEATURING FRANKIE LYMON (EP)	80
57	Columbia SEG 7734	FRANKIE LYMON AND THE TEENAGERS (EP)	80
58	Columbia 33S 1127	FRANKIE LYMON IN LONDON (10" LP, solo)	190
58	Columbia 33S 1134	ROCKIN' WITH FRANKIE LYMON (10" LP, solo)	500

LEWIS LYMON & TEENCHORDS
| 58 | Oriole 45-CB 1419 | Too Young/Your Last Chance (78 rpm, Oriole CB 1419 = £100) | 500 |

DERMOTT LYNCH
68	Blue Cat BS 101	Hot Shot/I've Got Your Number	32
68	Blue Cat BS 122	I Got Everything/Echo	32
68	Doctor Bird DB 1115	Adults Only/Cool It	32

(see also Trevor, Carl Dawkins, Joe White)

JOE LYNCH
| 69 | Spectrum SP 107 | King Child/Johnny Appleseed | 5 |

KENNY LYNCH
60	HMV POP 751	Mountain Of Love/Why Do You Treat Me This Way?	15
60	HMV POP 786	Slowcoach/You Make Love So Well	10
61	HMV POP 841	So/Love Me	10
61	HMV POP 900	The Story Behind My Tears/Steady Kind	10
61	HMV POP 985	There's Never Been A Girl/Doll Face	10
62	HMV POP 1005	It Would Take A Miracle/Strolling Blues	10
62	HMV POP 1057	Puff/Happy That's Me	10
62	HMV POP 1090	Up On The Roof/Jump On Your Broomstick	10
63	HMV POP 1136	Misery/Shut The Door	10
63	HMV POP 1165	You Can Never Stop Me Loving You/Crazy Crazes	6
63	HMV POP 1229	For You (There's Not A Thing I Wouldn't Do)/With Somebody	8
63	HMV POP 1260	Shake And Scream/Harlem Library	10
64	HMV POP 1280	Stand By Me/Baby It's True	8
64	HMV POP 1321	That's What Little Girls Are Made For/What Am I To You?	5
64	HMV POP 1367	My Own Two Feet/So Much To Love You For	25
65	HMV POP 1430	I'll Stay By You/For Loving You Baby	7
65	HMV POP 1476	Nothing But The Real Thing/Don't Ask Me To Stop Loving You	7
65	HMV POP 1496	Get Out Of My Way/One Look At You	10
66	HMV POP 1534	The World I Used To Know/Come On Come On	7
67	HMV POP 1577	I Just Wanna Love You/It's Too Late	8
67	HMV POP 1604	Movin' Away/Could I Count On You	150
68	Columbia DB 8329	Mister Moonlight/The Other Side Of Dreamland	15
68	Columbia DB 8498	Along Comes Love/Sweet Situation	15
69	Columbia DB 8599	The Drifter/Did I Stay Too Long?	40
70	Columbia DB 8703	In Old Kentucky/Loving You Is Sweeter Than Ever	15
63	HMV 7EG 8820	HEY GIRL (EP)	25
64	HMV 7EG 8855	KENNY LYNCH (EP)	25
65	HMV 7EG 8881	WHAT AM I TO YOU (EP)	25
63	HMV CLP 1635	UP ON THE ROOF (LP, also stereo CSD 1489)	60/65
66	Music F. Pleasure MFP 1022	WE LIKE KENNY (LP)	15

LEE LYNCH (& BLUE ANGELS)
66	Decca F 12375	You Won't See Me/You Know There's Me (as Lee Lynch & Blue Angels)	10
69	Ember EMB S 262	Stay Awhile/Bad Time To Stop Loving Me (p/s)	10
70	Ember EMB S 271	Sweet Woman/Can't Take My Eyes Off You (p/s)	10
70	Ember EMB S 282	Joe Poor Loves Daphne Elizabeth Rich/It's Love (p/s)	10

LINDA LYNDELL
| 68 | Stax 601 041 | Bring Your Love Back To Me/Here I Am | 40 |

BARBARA LYNN
64	London HLW 9918	Oh! Baby (We Got A Good Thing Goin')/Unfair	40
65	Immediate IM 011	You Can't Buy My Love/That's What A Friend Will Do	40
66	London HLU 10094	You Left The Water Running/Until I'm Free	40
67	Sue WI 4028	Letter To Mommy And Daddy/Second Fiddle Girl	40
67	Sue WI 4038	You'll Lose A Good Thing/Lonely Heartaches	50
71	Atlantic 2091 133	Take Your Love And Run/(Until Then) I'll Suffer	25
75	Oval OVAL 1006	Letter To Mommy And Daddy/You'll Lose A Good Thing	10
67	Sue ILP 949	THE BARBARA LYNN STORY (LP)	200

BOBBI LYNN
| 68 | Stateside SS 2088 | Earthquake/Opportunity Street (DJ copy = £85) | 45 |
| 71 | Bell BLL 1168 | Earthquake/Opportunity Street (reissue) | 15 |

CHERYL LYNN
| 84 | Streetwave KHAN 23 | Encore/Got To Be Real | 5 |

KARI LYNN
| 61 | Oriole CB 1632 | Yo Yo/Summer Day | 15 |
| 61 | Oriole CB 1644 | You've Got To See Mamma Every Night/Lonesome And Sorry | 15 |

LORETTA LYNN
68	MCA MUP 338	LORETTA LYNN (LP)	15
69	MCA MUP(S) 385	GREATEST HITS (LP)	12
70	MCA MUP(S) 407	HERE'S LORETTA LYNN SINGING WINGS UPON YOUR HORNS (LP)	15
70	MCA MUPS 411	YOUR SQUAW IS ON THE WARPATH (LP)	15
71	MCA MUPS 417	WRITES 'EM AND SINGS 'EM (LP)	12
71	MCA MUPS 427	COAL MINER'S DAUGHTER (LP)	12

(see also Conway Twitty)

MINT VALUE £

PATTI LYNN

62	Fontana H 370	I See It All Now/Someone Else's Valentine	18
62	Fontana H 391	Johnny Angel/Tonight You Belong To Me	18
62	Fontana 267 247 TF	Tell Me Telstar/Big Big Love	20
62	Fontana TFE 17392	PATTI (EP)	55

TAM(M)I LYNN

66	Atlantic AT 4071	I'm Gonna Run Away From You/The Boy Next Door	60
71	Mojo 2092 001	I'm Gonna Run Away From You/The Boy Next Door (reissue)	10
71	Mojo 2092 012	That's Understanding/Never No More	6
75	Contempo CS 9026	I'm Gonna Run Away From You/The Boy Next Door (2nd reissue)	8
71	Mojo 2916 007	LOVE IS HERE AND NOW YOU'RE GONE (LP)	30

VERA LYNN

52	Decca F 9927	Auf Wiederseh'n, Sweetheart/From The Time You Say Goodbye	6
54	Decca F 10253	Two Easter Sunday Sweethearts/Du Bist Mein Liebeshoen	6
54	Decca F 10290	The Homecoming Waltz/Humble People	6
54	Decca F 10372	My Son, My Son/Our Heaven On Earth (with Frank Weir & His Saxophone)	35
56	Decca F 10715	Who Are We?/I'll Be True To You	8
56	Decca F 10799	A House With Love In It/Little Lost Dog	8
57	Decca F 10846	The Faithful Hussar (Don't Cry My Love)/The One Beside You	8
57	Decca F 10903	Travellin' Home/Dear To Me	8
52	Decca LF 1022	SINCERELY YOURS, VERA LYNN (10" LP)	12
53	Decca LF 1102	SINCERELY YOURS, VERA LYNN VOL. 2 (10" LP)	12
53	Decca LF 1183	SINCERELY YOURS, VERA LYNN VOL. 3 (10" LP)	12

(see also Johnstone Brothers, Frank Weir & His Orchestra)

GLORIA LYNNE

64	London HLY 9846	I Wish You Love/Through A Long And Sleeping Night	9
64	London HLY 9888	I Should Care/Indian Love Call	9
59	Top Rank JKP 2024	MEET GLORIA LYNNE (EP, with Wild Bill Davis)	22
60	Top Rank BUY 031	LONELY AND SENTIMENTAL (LP)	22
64	London HA-Y 8112	AT THE LAS VEGAS THUNDERBIRD (LP, with Herman Foster Trio)	20
72	Mojo 2916 016	HAPPY AND IN LOVE (LP)	25

JEFF LYNNE

| 77 | Jet UP 36281 | Doin' That Crazy Thing/Goin' Down To Rio (p/s) | 5 |

(see also Nightriders, Idle Race, Move, E.L.O., Traveling Wilburys)

SUE LYNNE

68	RCA Victor RCA 1724	Reach For The Moon/All Alone	10
69	RCA Victor RCA 1822	You/Don't Pity Me (DJ copy = £200)	150
69	RCA Victor RCA 1874	Baby Baby Baby/You Lose Again	7

PHIL LYNOTT

80	Vertigo LYNT 1	King's Call/Yellow Pearl (12", p/s)	8
80	Vertigo SOLO 2	King's Call/Ode To A Black Man (p/s)	5
81	Vertigo SOLO 3	Yellow Pearl/Girls (p/s, clear vinyl)	5
85	Vertigo SOLO 5	Old Town/Beat Of The Drum (p/s)	6
85	Polydor POSPD 777	19/19 (Dub Version)//THIN LIZZY: Whiskey In The Jar (live) (double pack, 2nd disc 1-sided)	8
80	Vertigo PHIL 1	SOLO IN SOHO (LP, picture disc, die-cut sleeve)	15

(see also Thin Lizzy, Gary Moore & Phil Lynott, John Sykes, Rockers)

JACKIE LYNTON

61	Piccadilly 7N 35012	Over The Rainbow/High In The Sky	10
62	Piccadilly 7N 35055	Don't Take Away Your Love/Wishful Thinking	10
62	Piccadilly 7N 35064	All Of Me/I'd Steal	12
63	Piccadilly 7N 35107	I Believe/The Girl In The Wood	5
63	Piccadilly 7N 35140	Jeannie With The Light Brown Hair/Teddy Bear's Picnic	7
63	Piccadilly 7N 35156	I'm Talkin' About You/Lawdy Miss Clawdy	7
64	Piccadilly 7N 35177	Little Child/Never A Mention	6
64	Piccadilly 7N 35190	Laura/Ebb Tide	6
65	Decca F 12052	Three Blind Mice/Corrina Corrine	6
67	Columbia DB 8097	He'll Have To Go/Only You	6
67	Columbia DB 8180	Decision/Sporting Life	15
67	Columbia DB 8224	Answer Me/I Never Loved A Girl Like You	15
79	Thumb TR003	Dan (The Hedgehog Song)/Farting With The Famous	10
74	WWA WWA 012	THE JACKIE LYNTON ALBUM (LP)	20

(see also Savoy Brown Blues Band)

LYNYRD SKYNYRD

74	MCA MCA 136	Don't Ask Me No Questions/Take Your Time	5
74	MCA MCA 160	Sweet Home Alabama/Take Your Time	5
75	MCA MCA 199	Saturday Night Special/Made In The Shade	5
76	MCA MCA 229	Double Trouble/Roll Gypsy Roll	5
76	MCA MCA 251	Free Bird/Sweet Home Alabama/Double Trouble (p/s)	8
76	MCA MCA 275	Free Bird (Edit)/Gimme Three Steps (p/s)	8
74	MCA MCG 3502	PRONOUNCED LEH-NERD SKIN-NERD (LP, gatefold sleeve)	18
77	MCA MCG 3525	STREET SURVIVORS (LP, gatefold sleeve with tour dates on inner sleeve)	15

BARBARA LYON

55	Columbia SCM 5186	I Love To Dance With You/Yes You Are	15
55	Columbia SCM 5207	Whisper/Where You Are	15
55	Columbia DB 3619	Stowaway	15
56	Columbia SCM 5232	Band Of Gold/Such A Day	12
56	Columbia SCM 5276	Puppy Love/The Birds And The Bees	12
56	Columbia DB 3826	It's Better In The Dark/A Heart Without A Sweetheart	6
56	Columbia DB 3865	Falling In Love/Letter To A Soldier	15
57	Columbia DB 3931	C'est La Vie/Fire Down Below	5
57	Columbia DB 4026	Thanks For The Loan Of A Dream/Third Finger — Left Hand	5

58	Columbia DB 4137	Red Was The Moon/Ring On A Ribbon	5
60	Triumph RGM 1027	My Charlie/Tell Me	40
56	Columbia SEG 7640	MY FOUR FRIENDS (EP)	25

PATTI LYON
62	Fontana H 370	I See It All Now/Someone Else's Valentine	12

RICHARD LYON
59	Fontana H 206	All My Own/Private Eye	22
59	Fontana H 206	All My Own/Private Eye (78)	12

LYONS & MALONE
69	Jay Boy BOY 9	Doctor Gentle/She's Alright	30

LYON ST.
(see under Associates)

LYRICS
67	Coxsone CS 7003	A Get It/KEN PARKER: How Strong	30
68	Coxsone CS 7067	Music Like Dirt/TONETTES: I Give It To You	60
70	Randy's RAN 504	Give Thanks And Praises/TOMMY McCOOK: Get Ready	15
71	Randy's RAN 511	Give Thanks/RANDY'S ALL STARS: Give — Version	15

(see also Randy's All Stars, Viceroys, Jackie Mittoo)

JIMMY LYTELL
59	London HL 8873	Hot Cargo/A Blues Serenade	15

JOHNNY LYTLE
68	Minit MLF 11006	Gonna Get That Boat (Parts 1 & 2)	12

HUMPHREY LYTTELTON (& HIS BAND)
51	Saturn EGX 105	When The Saints Go Marching In/Careless Love (78, picture disc)	85
53	Parlophone MSP 6001	Out Of The Gallion/The Old Grey Mare	8
53	Parlophone MSP 6023	Muskrat Ramble/Mamzelle Josephine	
		(as Lyttelton Paseo Band, B-side with George Brown)	8
53	Parlophone MSP 6033	Maryland, My Maryland/Blue For Waterloo	8
53	Parlophone MSP 6034	Shake It And Break It/Jail Break	8
53	Parlophone MSP 6045	Red For Piccadilly/Kater Street Rag	8
54	Parlophone MSP 6061	Martiniquen Song (Last Year)/Ain't Cha Got Music	7
54	Parlophone MSP 6076	East Coast Trot/Breeze	7
54	Parlophone MSP 6093	Just Once For All Time/Joshua, Fit The Battle Of Jericho	7
54	Parlophone MSP 6097	Mainly Traditional/Oh! Dad (with 'Melody Maker' All Stars)	7
54	Parlophone MSP 6128	Mezzy's Tune/Jelly Bean Blues	7
56	Tempo A 10	When The Saints Go Marching In/Careless Love	7
56	Parlophone R 4212	Love, Love, Love/Echoing The Blues	6
56	Esquire 10-491	The Thin Red Line/Melancholy Blues (78)	8
56	Esquire 10-494	First Of Many/Blues For Two (78)	8
57	Esquire 10-501	Elizabeth/Blue For Waterloo (78)	8
57	Esquire 10-511	Cake Walkin' Babies/If You See Me Comin' (78)	8
57	Parlophone R 4277	Baby Doll/Red Beans And Rice (78)	8
57	Parlophone R 4262	It's Mardi Gras/Sweet And Sour	7
57	Parlophone R 4277	Baby Doll/Red Beans And Rice	7
57	Parlophone R 4333	Early Call (Bermondsey Bounce)/Creole Serenade	5
57	Parlophone R 4368	Dixie Theme/Blues At Dawn	5
58	Parlophone CMSP 41	Bad Penny Blues/Baby Doll (export issue)	30
58	Parlophone R 4392	Buona Sera/Blues In The Afternoon	5
58	Parlophone R 4428	Hand Me Down Love/Here And Gone (Blues In 1890) (78 = £8)	5
58	Decca F 11058	La Paloma/Bodega (78 rpm = £8)	8
59	Parlophone R 4519	Saturday Jump/The Bear Steps Out (78 rpm = £10)	5
61	Summer County LYN 254	Swingin' On The Gate/Jeanie With The Light Brown Hair	
		(flexidisc, some in p/s)	10/5

EPs
55	Parlophone GEP 8503	HUMPHREY LYTTELTON & HIS BAND (EP)	10
55	Parlophone GEP 8514	HUMPHREY LYTTELTON & HIS BAND (EP)	15
55	Parlophone GEP 8546	JAZZ WITH LYTTELTON – 1 (EP)	10
56	Parlophone GEP 8572	JAZZ WITH LYTTELTON – 2 (EP)	12
56	Parlophone GEP 8580	LIGHTLY & POLITELY (EP)	10
56	Parlophone GEP 8584	HUMPH'S BLUES (EP)	12
55	Tempo EXA 1	HUMPHREY LYTTELTON & HIS BAND (EP)	20
56	Esquire EP 111	HUMPHREY LYTTELTON & HIS BAND (EP)	18
57	Esquire EP 141	HUMPHREY LYTTELTON & HIS BAND (EP)	18
57	Esquire EP 153	VINTAGE '49 (EP)	18
57	Parlophone GEP 8599	JAZZ WITH LYTTELTON – 4 (EP)	10
57	Parlophone GEP 8645	HUMPH'S BLUES NO. 2 (EP)	12
58	Parlophone GEP 8700	COLOURFUL HUMPH (EP)	10
58	Parlophone GEP 8734	HUMPH'S JAZZ (EP)	15
58	Esquire EP 171	THAT REVIVAL SOUND (EP)	18
62	Columbia SEG 8163	DO THE BEAULIEU (EP)	15

LPs
53	Parlophone PMD 1006	JAZZ CONCERT (10" LP)	30
54	Parlophone PMC 1012	HUMPH AT THE CONWAY (LP)	30
55	Parlophone PMD 1032	JAZZ AT THE ROYAL FESTIVAL HALL (10" LP)	25
56	Parlophone PMD 1035	JAZZ SESSION WITH HUMPH (10" LP)	20
56	Parlophone PMD 1044	HUMPH SWINGS OUT (10" LP)	30
57	Parlophone PMD 1049	HERE'S HUMPH (10" LP)	20
58	Parlophone PMD 1052	KATH MEETS HUMPH (10" LP, with Kathy Stobart)	30
58	Parlophone PMC 1070	HUMPH IN PERSPECTIVE (LP)	30
58	Decca LK 4276	I PLAY AS I PLEASE (LP)	25
59	Parlophone PMC 1110	TRIPLE EXPOSURE (LP)	40

MINT VALUE £

59	Esquire 32-007	HUMPHREY LYTTELTON AND HIS BAND (LP)	25
60	Columbia 33SX 1239	BLUES IN THE NIGHT (LP)	30
60	Columbia 33SX 1305	HUMPH PLAYS STANDARDS (LP)	30
60	Columbia 33SX 1364	HUMPH MEETS CAB (LP)	50
61	Columbia 33SX 3382	HUMPH RETURNS TO THE CONWAY (LP)	25
61	Columbia SEG 8130	BIG H (EP)	10
62	Columbia 33SX 1484	LATE NIGHT FINAL (LP)	25
65	Society SOC 1003	HUMPHREY LYTTELTON AND HIS BAND (LP)	20
69	Polydor 2460 140	DUKE ELLINGTON CLASSICS (LP)	35
69	Polydor 2661 001	21 YEARS ON (LP)	25

(see also Shirley Abicair, Sidney Bechet, George Brown, Buck Clayton, Helen Shapiro, Radiohead)

M

79	MCA MCAT 413	Pop Musik/M Factor (12", p/s, double groove)	8

(see also Robin Scott)

MABEL

78	Sonet SON 2147	Boom Boom/FBI On The Nail (p/s)	6

MABEL JOY

75	Real RR 2004	MABEL JOY (LP)	25

MOMS MABLEY

69	Mercury MF 1127	Abraham, Martin And John/Sunny	8
71	Mercury 6052 109	That's Pops/I Surrender Dear	6

WILLIE MABON

64	Sue WI 320	Got To Have Some/Why Did It Happen To Me	40
65	Sue WI 331	Just Got Some/That's No Big Thing	40
65	Sue WI 382	I'm The Fixer/Some More	40

MABRAK

78	Different GET A101	DRUM TALK (mixed by King Tubby) (LP)	100

SPENCER MAC

70	Penny Farthing PEN 742	Commuter/Better By You — Better By Me	30

DAN MacARTHUR

79	Virgin VS 275	DAN MacARTHUR (EP)	5
79	Virgin VS 275-12	DAN MacARTHUR (12" EP)	8

(see also Jah Wobble, PiL)

NEIL MacARTHUR

69	Deram DM 225	She's Not There/World Of Glass	20
69	Deram DM 262	Don't Try To Explain/Without Her	12
69	Deram DM 275	It's Not Easy/12.29.	12

(see also Colin Blunstone, Zombies)

GLO MACARI

65	Piccadilly 7N 35218	He Knows I Love Him Too Much/I've Lost You	15

MACARTHUR PARK

70	Columbia DB 8683	Taffeta Rose/Sammy	12
71	Philips 6006 086	Lottie Lottie/Love Is Coming	6

(see also Shadows)

DAVID MACBETH

59	Pye Nixa 7N 15231	Mr. Blue/Here's A Heart (78 rpm = £12)	8
60	Pye 7N 15250	Tell Her From Me/Livin' Dangerously	8
60	Pye 7N 15274	Unhappy/Once Upon A Star	8
60	Pye 7N 15291	Blue Blue Blue/Pigtails In Paris	8
61	Pye 7N 15325	The Puppet Song/Angel On My Shoulder	8
61	Pye 7N 15364	Keep A-Walking/You're Free	8
61	Decca F 11402	Just A Twinkle/While I'm Away	6
62	Piccadilly 7N 35062	Roses Are Red (My Love)/Little Heart	7
62	Piccadilly 7N 35072	Have I Told You Lately That I Love You/A Brother Like You	7
63	Piccadilly 7N 35092	A Very Good Year For Girls/Broken Hearts	6
63	Piccadilly 7N 35114	My Golden Chance/Like A Falling Star	6
69	Pye 7N 17744	Does Anybody Miss Me/The Small Exception Of Me	6

MACATTACK

86	Baad! Records 12HIP1AZ	ART OF DRUMS (12" EP)	15

MACC LADS

89	Renegade RS 1	Jingle Bells/Even Uglier Women (p/s)	5
90	FM Revolver VHF 42	Barrels Round/Jingle Bells (p/s)	5
86	Hectic House HHS 1	EH UP! MACC LADS (EP)	5
85	FM Revolver FMLP 56	BEER AND SEX AND CHIPS'N'GRAVY (LP, white vinyl)	12
88	FM Revolver WKFMLP 115	LIVE AT LEEDS (LP, blue vinyl)	12

EWAN MacCOLL

52	HMV B 10259	Lord Randall/Van Dieman's Land (78)	8
52	HMV B 10260	Sir Patrick Spens/Eppie Morrie (78)	8
58	Topic 10T 26	BARRACK ROOM BALLADS (10" LP)	30
58	Topic 10T 36	BOLD SPORTSMEN ALL (10" LP, with A.L. Lloyd)	32
58	Topic 10T 50	STILL I LOVE HIM (10" LP with booklet, with Isla Cameron)	35
60	Topic 12T 41	STREETS OF SONG (LP, with Dominic Behan, with booklet, originally with blue label)	20/12
61	PRE 13004	THE BEST OF EWAN MacCOLL (LP)	12
62	Topic 12T 79	THE JACOBITE REBELLIONS (LP, originally with blue label)	18/12
64	Topic 12T 103	ENGLISH AND SCOTTISH FOLK BALLADS (LP, with A.L. Lloyd, initially with blue label & booklet)	25/15
67	Topic 12T 130	BUNDOOK BALLADS (LP, originally with blue label)	18
67	Argo ZFB 12	SOLO FLIGHT (LP; reissued 1972)	30
67	Xtra 1052	BLOW BOYS BLOW – SONGS OF THE SEA (LP, with A.L. Lloyd)	15
68	Argo (Z)DA 85	THE WANTON MUSE (LP, with booklet)	30
72	Argo (Z)DA 85	THE WANTON MUSE (LP, reissue)	15
(see also A.L. Lloyd)			

EWAN MacCOLL & PEGGY SEEGER (& CHARLES PARKER)

60s	AUEW AUEW 1	We Are The Engineers/I'm Gonna Be An Engineer (p/s)	6
57	Topic 10T 13	SHUTTLE AND CAGE (10" LP)	38
61	Topic 12T 16	CHORUS FROM THE GALLOWS (LP, originally with blue label)	18/12
64	Topic 12T 104	STEAM WHISTLE BALLADS (LP, blue label, later reissued with booklet)	18/12
65	Argo RG 474	THE BALLAD OF JOHN AXON (LP, by Ewan MacColl & Charles Parker)	25
67	Topic 12T 147	THE MANCHESTER ANGEL (LP, originally with blue label)	18/12
67	Argo DA 140	THE BIG HEWER — A RADIO BALLAD BY EWAN MacCOLL, PEGGY SEEGER, CHARLES PARKER (LP, documentary with music)	28
67	Argo (Z)DA 66	LONG HARVEST 1 (LP)	15
67	Argo (Z)DA 67	LONG HARVEST 2 (LP)	15
67	Argo (Z)DA 68	LONG HARVEST 3 (LP)	15
67	Argo (Z)DA 69	LONG HARVEST 4 (LP)	15
67	Argo RG 502	SINGING THE FISHING (LP, with Charles Parker)	25
67	Argo DA 142	SINGING THE FISHING (LP, reissue, with Charles Parker)	18
68	Argo (Z)DA 70	LONG HARVEST 5 (LP)	15
68	Argo (Z)DA 71	LONG HARVEST 6 (LP)	15
68	Argo (Z)DA 72	LONG HARVEST 7 (LP)	15
68	Argo (Z)DA 73	LONG HARVEST 8 (LP)	15
68	Argo (Z)DA 74	LONG HARVEST 9 (LP)	15
68	Argo (Z)DA 75	LONG HARVEST 10 (LP)	15
68	Argo (Z)DA 84	THE AMOROUS MUSE (LP)	15
68	Argo (Z)DA	THE ANGRY MUSE (LP)	15
69	Argo (Z)DA 98	THE PAPER STAGE 1 (LP, with booklet)	15
69	Argo (Z)DA 99	THE PAPER STAGE 2 (LP)	15
60s	XTRA 1054	SCOTS BALLADS (LP)	30
60s	Folkways FW 8958	SONGS OF ROBERT BURNS (LP)	40
70	Argo SPA-A 102	THE WORLD OF EWAN MacCOLL & PEGGY SEEGER (LP)	20
70	Argo SPA-A 216	THE WORLD OF EWAN MacCOLL & PEGGY SEEGER VOL. 2 — SONGS FROM THE RADIO BALLADS (LP)	15
70	Argo DA 133	THE TRAVELLING PEOPLE (LP, with Charles Parker)	25
71	Argo DA 136	ON THE EDGE (LP)	15
72	Argo ZFB 65	THE ANGRY MUSE (LP, reissue)	12
72	Argo ZFB 66	THE AMOROUS MUSE (LP, reissue)	12
(see also Peggy Seeger, A.L. Lloyd, Isla Cameron)			

KIRSTY MacCOLL

79	Stiff BUY 47	They Don't Know/Motor On (p/s)	8
79	Stiff PBUY 47	They Don't Know/Motor On (picture disc)	6
79	Stiff BUY 57	You Caught Me Out/Boys (with Boomtown Rats, unreleased, demos only)	6
81	Polydor POSP 225	Keep Your Hands Off My Baby/I Don't Need You (p/s)	7
81	Polydor POSP 368	You Still Believe In Me/Queen Of The High Teas (p/s)	10
(see also Drug Addix)			

FINN MacCUILL

79	Radio Edinburgh REL 460	SINK YE — SWIM YE (LP)	200+

AIMI MacDONALD

67	Polydor 56191	Thoroughly Modern Millie/Jimmy	6
70	Philips 6308 011	WHAT'S LOVE ALL ABOUT (LP)	16

BIG MACEO

62	RCA RCX 203	KINGS OF THE BLUES (EP)	22

MACEO & ALL THE KING'S MEN

72	Pye International 7N 25571	Got To Get 'Cha/Thank You For Letting Me Be Myself Again (Part 1)	10
72	Mojo 2916 017	FUNKY MUSIC MACHINE (LP)	60
75	Contempo CRM 114	FUNKY MUSIC MACHINE (LP, reissue)	20

MACEO & THE MACKS

87	Urban URB 1	Cross The Tracks (We Better Go Back)/Soul Power (printed die-cut sleeve)	15
87	Urban URBX 1	Cross The Tracks (We Better Go Back) (Extended Version)/Party Part 1/ Soul Power (12", printed die-cut sleeve)	15
74	Polydor 2391 122	US (LP)	40
88	Urban URBLP 8	US (LP, reissue)	15
(see also Maceo & All The King's Men, James Brown)			

TEO MACERO

57	Esquire 32-113	TEO (LP)	30

MACHINE

67	Granta GR 7STD	Stupidity/Please Stay (private pressing)	20

MACHINE

MACHINE
69	Polydor 56760	Spooky's Day Off/Nobody Wants You	6

(see also Swinging Soul Machine)

MACHINES
78	Wax EAR 1	True Life/Everything's Technical/You Better Hear/Evening Radio (stamped p/s, white labels)	80

MACHITO
50s	Columbia	AFRO CUBAN JAZZ (10" LP)	20

ALURA MACK
50s	Poydras 84	Everybody's Man Is Mine/Monkey Blues	8

JOHNNY MACK
70	Columbia Blue Beat DB 116	Reggae All Night Long/A Million Marvellous Feelings	12

LONNIE MACK
63	Stateside SS 207	Memphis/Down In The Dumps	20
63	Stateside SS 226	Wham!/Susie-Q	20
64	Stateside SS 312	Lonnie On The Move/Say Something Nice To Me	15
65	Stateside SS 393	Sa-Ba-Hoola/Chickin' Pickin'	20
67	President PT 127	Where There's A Will/Baby What's Wrong?	7
67	President PT 142	Save Your Money/Snow On The Mountain	7
68	President PT 198	Soul Express/I Found A Love	10
69	Elektra EKSN 45044	Memphis/Why (Edited Version)	10
69	Elektra EKSN 45060	Save Your Money/In The Band	8
71	Elektra EK 45715	Lay It Down/She Even Woke Me Up To Say Goodbye	6
67	President PTL 1004	THE WHAM OF THAT MEMPHIS MAN (LP)	30
69	Elektra EKL 4040	GLAD I'M IN THE BAND (LP, orange label, also stereo EKS 74040)	30
69	Elektra EKS 74050	WHATEVER'S RIGHT (LP, orange label)	30
70	Elektra 2410 007	FOR COLLECTORS ONLY (LP, reissue of "The Wham Of That Memphis Man")	15
72	Elektra K 42097	THE HILLS OF INDIANA (LP)	15

WARNER MACK
58	Brunswick 05728	Roc-A-Chicka/Since I Lost You (with Anita Kerr Quartet) (78 rpm = £70)	180+
58	Decca	Roc-A-Chicka/Since I Lost You (export issue, with Anita Kerr Quartet)	90
62	London HA-R/SH-R 8002	GOLDEN COUNTRY HITS (LP)	25
63	London HA-R/SH-R 8025	GOLDEN COUNTRY HITS VOL. 2 (LP)	25
66	Brunswick LAT 8658	COUNTRY TOUCH (LP)	18
67	Brunswick LAT 8684	DRIFTING APART (LP)	18

ANDY MACKAY
74	Island WIP 6197	Ride Of The Valkyries/Time Regained	5
75	Island WIP 6243	Wild Weekend/Walking The Whippet (some in promo p/s)	10/5
78	Bronze BRO 64	A Song Of Friendship/Skill And Sweat	5
74	Island ILPS 9278	IN SEARCH OF EDDIE RIFF (LP, 2 different versions)	12

(see also Roxy Music, Rock Follies)

MAHNA MACKAY
69	Parlophone R 5808	Mah Na Mah Na/Daydream	6

RABBIT MacKAY
68	MCA MU 1041	Hard Time Woman/Candy	5
68	MCA MUPS 351	BUG CLOTH (LP)	12

BILLY MacKENZIE
82	WEA MAK 1	Ice Cream Factory/Cream Of Ice Cream Factory (p/s, as MacKenzie Sings Orbidöig)	5
82	WEA MAK 1T	Ice Cream Factory/Cream Of Ice Cream Factory (12", p/s, as MacKenzie Sings Orbidöig)	8
92	Circa YRCD 86	Baby/Sacrifice And Be Sacrificed (CH 8032 Mix)/Grooveature (D 1000 Mix)/Colours Will Come (US 60659 Mix) (CD, solo)	8
92	Circa YRCD 91	Colours Will Come/Opal Krusch/Look What You've Done/Feels Like The Richtergroove (CD)	15
01	Rhythm Of Life ROL 006	Wild Is The Wind/Mother Earth/Baltimore/Give Me Time (Version) (CD, internet-only release)	50
92	Circa CIRCD 22	OUTERNATIONAL (CD)	65

(see also Associates, Orbidöig, Yello, B.E.F., Sweden Through The Ages)

BILLY MacKENZIE with STEVE AUNGLE
01	Rhythm Of Life ROL 005	EUROCENTRIC (CD)	25

BILLY MacKENZIE with PAUL HAIG
00	Rhythm Of Life ROL 003	MEMORY PALACE (CD)	25

GISELE MacKENZIE
53	Capitol CL 13920	Seven Lonely Days/Till I Waltz With You Again (78)	6
55	HMV 7M 318	Hard To Get/Boston Fancy	6
56	Capitol Junior CJ 131	Sings Children's Songs From France Parts 1 & 2 (78, p/s)	6

JUDY MacKENZIE
70	Key KL 005	JUDY (LP)	30
71	Key KL 009	PEACE AND LOVE AND FREEDOM (LP, with poster)	30

MACKENZIE JET COMBO
70	Torpedo TOR 18	Milkman's Theme/Capadulah Recipe	8

MACKERAL
66	Columbia DB 8013	Funny Fish/This Is Mine	5
68	Columbia DB 8388	Trying Again/White Man's Burden	5

KEN MACKINTOSH (& HIS ORCHESTRA)
56	HMV 7M 343	Creeping Tom/Lovers In The Dark	10
56	HMV 7M 359	Start Walking/Curtain Call	10

MINT VALUE £

56	HMV 7M 379	Blues In The Night/Come Next Spring (B-side with Kenny Bardell)	10
56	HMV 7M 403	Sleepwalker/The Berkeley Hunt.	10
56	HMV 7M 417	Dizzy Fingers/The Policeman's Holiday	8
56	HMV POP 270	Soft Summer Breeze/Highway Patrol	8
57	HMV POP 287	The Buccaneers/Regimental Rock	10
57	HMV POP 300	Apple-Jack/Slow Walk	15
57	HMV POP 327	Almost Paradise/Rock Man Rock	15
57	HMV POP 358	Poni Tail/Keep It Movin'	0
57	HMV POP 396	Marching Along To The Blues/Six-Five Blues	8
57	HMV POP 426	Raunchy/Mojo	8
58	HMV POP 441	The Stroll/The Swingin' Shepherd Blues (78 rpm = £6)	6
58	HMV POP 464	Big Guitar/Squatty (78 rpm = £8)	6
58	HMV POP 506	The Swivel/Muchacha (78 rpm = £8)	6
59	HMV POP 592	Rock-A-Conga/Hampden Park (78 rpm = £10)	6
59	HMV POP 656	Sleep Walk/Morgen (One More Sunrise)	6
60	HMV POP 713	No Hiding Place/Tally Ho!.	6
56	HMV 7EG 8170	TEENAGER'S SPECIAL (EP)	20
58	HMV 7EG 8468	DANCING TO THE ROARING TWENTIES (EP)	10
55	HMV DLP 1093	KEN MACKINTOSH (10" LP)	15
58	HMV DLP 1178	ONE NIGHT STAND (10" LP)	20

MACK SISTERS
56	London HLU 8331	Long Range Love/Stop What You're Doing	60

PETE MacLAINE & CLAN
63	Decca F 11699	Yes I Do/U.S. Mail	15

DOUGIE MacLEAN
80	Plant Life PLR 022	SNAIGOW (LP, with lyric insert)	12
88	Dunkeld DUN 008	REAL ESTATE (LP)	20
	(see also Alan Roberts)		

JOHN MacLEOD'S FIRST XI
66	Fontana TF 696	Don't Shoot The Ref/Tomato Crisps	6

JOHN MacLEOD SOUND
60s	Transatlantic TRASP 12	Russian Roulette/West Wind	6

ANGUS MacLISE
87	Fierce FRIGHT 010	Trance (1-sided, with 'Dopechoc' & badge)	10

PATRICK MacNEE & HONOR BLACKMAN
64	Decca F 11843	Kinky Boots/Let's Keep It Friendly	42
	(see also Honor Blackman)		

FLORA MacNEIL
77	Tangent TGS 124	CROABH NAN UBHAL (LP, with insert)	12

MADELINE MacNEIL
60s	Skyline DD 103	PATCHWORK (LP)	25

UNCLE DAVE MACON
63	RCA RCX 7112	UNCLE DAVE MACON NO. 1 (EP)	20
63	RCA RCX 7113	UNCLE DAVE MACON NO. 2 (EP)	20
66	Ace Of Hearts AH 135	UNCLE DAVE MACON (LP)	18

MACON JUG
70	Saga FID 8157	IN THE SUMMERTIME (LP, with tracks by Good Earth)	15
72	Boulevard BLVD 4078	RAY DORSET'S BEST (LP, 4 tracks by Good Earth, 6 tracks by Macon Jug)	12
	(see also Ray Dorset, Mungo Jerry)		

GORDON MacRAE
54	Capitol CL 14168	How Do You Speak To An Angel?/C'est Magnifique	10
54	Capitol CL 14193	Count Your Blessings Instead Of Sheep/Never In A Million Years	10
55	Capitol CL 14222	Here's What I'm Here For/Love Can Change The Stars	7
55	Capitol CL 14276	Stranger In Paradise/High On A Windy Hill	7
55	Capitol CL 14293	You Forget (To Tell Me That You Love Me)/Tik-A-Tee, Tik-A-Tay	7
55	Capitol CL 14334	Jim Bowie/Why Break The Heart That Loves You	7
55	Capitol CL 14361	Bella Notte/Blame It On My Youth	6
56	Capitol CL 14526	Follow Your Heart/Fate	6
56	Capitol CL 14548	Never Before And Never Again/Don't Blame Me	6
56	Capitol CL 14576	Who Are We/There's A Lull In My Life.	6
56	Capitol CL 14606	One Misty Morning/I Asked The Lord	5
56	Capitol CL 14613	People Will Say We're In Love/The Surrey With The Fringe On Top (with Ray Anthony)	5
56	Capitol CL 14622	Woman In Love/I Don't Want To Walk Without You	5
58	Capitol CL 14818	Lonely/Sayonara	5
58	Capitol CL 14864	I've Grown Accustomed To Her Face/Never Till Now	5
58	Capitol CL 14920	The Secret/A Man Once Said (78 rpm = £8)	5
59	Capitol CL 14983	Fly Little Bluebird/Little Do You Know (78 rpm = £8)	5
52	Capitol LC 6564	THE MERRY WIDOW (10" LP, with Lucille Norman)	15
53	Capitol LC 6592	CAPITOL PRESENTS GORDON MACRAE (10" LP)	15
53	Capitol LC 6599	BY THE LIGHT OF THE SILVERY MOON (10" LP, with June Hutton)	15
53	Capitol LC 6606	THE DESERT SONG (10" LP, with Lucille Norman)	15
53	Capitol LC 6613	THE STUDENT PRINCE (10" LP, with Dorothy Warenskjold)	15
54	Capitol LC 6663	NAUGHTY MARIETTA (10" LP, with Lucille Norman)	15
54	Capitol LC 6666	ROBERTA (10" LP, with Lucille Norman)	15
56	Capitol LC 6805	ROMANTIC BALLADS (10" LP)	15
60	Capitol (S)T 1251	SONGS FOR AN EVENING AT HOME (LP)	15
60	Top Rank 25/006	GORDON MACRAE (LP)	15
	(see also Jo Stafford, Ray Anthony, Jonathan & Darlene Edwards)		

JOSH MACRAE
60	Top Rank JAR 290	Talkin' Army Blues/Talkin' Guitar Blues	12
60	Pye 7N 15306	Original Talkin' Blues (Talkin' Southern Blues)/Talkin' Thro' The Mill	7
60	Pye 7N 15307	Let Ramensky Go/Sky High Joe	7
60	Pye 7N 15308	Wild Side Of Life/Dear John	7
61	Pye 7N 15319	Messing About On The River/High Class Feeling	7
61	Pye 7N 15360	Arkansas Rambler/Never Never Man	5
61	Pye 7N 15384	Do It Yourself/Special Place Of Yorn	5
60	Pye NEP 24131	WALKIN', TALKIN', SINGIN' (EP)	15
60	Top Rank JKP 2061	JOSH MACRAE (EP)	15
66	Transatlantic TRA 150	JOSH MACRAE (LP)	18
66	Golden Guinea GGL 0335	MESSING ABOUT ON THE RIVER (LP)	15

JOHNNY MADARA
57	HMV POP 389	Be My Girl/Lovesick	10

MADCAPS
50	London L 786	Nightingale/Sleighride (78)	6
51	Brunswick 04787	Josephine/Casa Loma Stomp	5
53	Brunswick LA 8631	HARMONICATERS (10" LP)	12

MADCAPS & HARMONICATS
54	London H-APB 1016	HARMONICA RHYTHMS (10" LP, 1 side each)	12

MAD DOG
74	Chappell LPC 1053	POP SOUNDS (LP, library edition)	30

MAD DOG
85	Brainy CUTN 1	Sheriff (p/s)	50

JOHNNY MADDOX (& HIS ORCHESTRA)
53	Vogue V 9047	Johnny Maddox Boogie/Little Grass Shack (78)	8
55	London MSD 1503/1504	Nickelodeon Tango/Solitude (unissued, demos only)	50
55	London HL 8056	I Don't Love Nobody/There's A Star-Spangled Banner (78)	10
55	London HL 8134	The Crazy Otto — Medley/Humoresque (78 rpm = £8)	30
55	London HLD 8203	Do, Do, Do/When You Wore A Tulip (And I Wore A Big Red Rose)	20
56	London HLD 8277	Hop Scotch Boogie/Hands Off (78 rpm = £12)	40
56	London HLD 8347	Heart And Soul/Dixieland Band	18
58	London HLD 8540	Yellow Dog Blues/Sugar Train	15
59	London HLD 8826	The Hurdy Gurdy Song/Old Fashioned Love (78 rpm = £12)	10
55	London RE-P 1020	PRESENTING JOHNNY MADDOX AND THE RHYTHMASTERS (EP)	25
55	London RE-P 1040	PRESENTING JOHNNY MADDOX AND THE RHYTHMASTERS NO. 2 (EP)	20
58	London RE-D 1150	HONKY TONK JAZZ (EP)	12
61	London RE-D 1270	OLD FASHIONED LOVE (EP)	12
56	London HB-D 1060	JOHNNY MADDOX PLAYS (10" LP, with His Rhythmasters)	20
58	London HA-D 2101	MY OLD FLAMES (LP)	12

ROSE MADDOX
59	Capitol CL 15023	Gambler's Love/What Makes Me Hang Around	8

MADE IN BRITAIN
91	White MIB001	Break The Crunch/Mellow Infection (12")	24

MADE IN ENGLAND
86	Red Bus RBUS 2208	Prospects/Stay Sharp (A-side with Ray Dorset, p/s)	6
	(see also Ray Dorset)		

MADE IN SHEFFIELD
67	Fontana TF 871	Amelia Jane/Right Satisfied	20
	(see also Joe Cocker, Grease Band, Chris Stainton)		

MADE IN SWEDEN
69	Sonet SLP 71	MADE IN SWEDEN (LP)	20
69	Sonet SLP 2504	SNAKES IN A HOLE (LP)	20
70	Sonet SLP 2506	LIVE AT THE GOLDEN CIRCLE (LP)	20
70	Sonet SLP 2512	MADE IN ENGLAND (LP)	20
71	Sonet SNTF 621	MAD RIVER (LP)	40

BETTY MADIGAN
54	MGM SP 1109	Always You/That Was My Heart You Heard!	6
55	MGM SP 1119	And So I Walked Home/Be A Little Darlin'	6
55	MGM SP 1131	Salute/The Wheels Of Love	6
55	MGM SP 1137	I Had A Heart/Wonderful Words	6
55	MGM SP 1138	Teddy Bear/Strangers	6
69	MGM MGM 1482	I'm Gonna Make You Love Me/Goodnight	6
58	Coral FEP 2009	JEROME KERN SONGBOOK VOL. 1 (EP)	10
59	Coral FEP 2011	JEROME KERN SONGBOOK VOL. 2 (EP)	10

MAD JOCKS & ENGLISHMEN
80	Wild Dog DOGLP 18	TONGUE IN CHEEK (LP)	20
80s	Wild Dog DOGLP 50	THUD & BLUNDER (LP)	20

MAD LADS (U.S.)
65	Atlantic AT 4051	Don't Have To Shop Around/Tear Maker	20
66	Atlantic AT 4083	I Want Someone/Nothing Can Break Through	20
66	Atlantic 584 038	Sugar Sugar/Get Out Of My Life Woman	15

MAD LADS (Jamaica)
69	Coxsone CS 7099	Losing You/WINSTON JARRETT: Peck Up A Pagan	25

MADNESS
SINGLES

79	2-Tone TT 3	The Prince/Madness (paper label, later plastic, company sleeve) 8/5
79	Stiff BUY IT 56	One Step Beyond/Mistakes/Nutty Theme (12", p/s). 10
79	Stiff MAD 1	Don't Quote Me On That/Swan Lake (12", promo only) 20
81	Stiff BUY IT 108	The Return Of The Los Palmas 7/My Girl (Demo)/That's The Way To Do It/
		Swan Lake (live) (12", p/s, with comic). 10
81	Stiff BUY IT 112	Grey Day/Baggy Trousers/Take It Or Leave It/Un Paso Adelante (12", p/s) 20
82	Stiff BUY IT 134	It Must Be Love/Mrs. Hutchinson/Shadow On The House (12", p/s credits
		"Limited Edition Special 12" Dance Mix", record plays standard mix). 8
82	Stiff PBUY 146	House Of Fun/Don't Look Back (picture disc) 5
82	Stiff BUY 153	Driving In My Car/Animal Farm (poster p/s) 5
82	Stiff PBUY 153	Driving In My Car/Animal Farm (picture disc) 5
82	Stiff GRAB 1	THE MADNESS PACK (6 x 7" in clear plastic folder) 20
83	Stiff PBUY 169	Tomorrow's (Just Another Day)/Madness (Is All In The Mind) (picture disc) 5
83	Stiff BUY IT 169	Tomorrow's (Just Another Day) (Warped Mix)/Blue Skinned Beast (warped
		mix)/Tomorrow's (Just Another Day) (Elvis Costello vocal) (12", p/s) 8
83	Stiff BUY 169	Tomorrow's Just Another Day/Madness Is All In The Mind (test pressing,
		pink & blue vinyl, 1 copy known) 350
84	Stiff BUY IT 196	Michael Caine (Extended Version)/Michael Caine/
		If You Think There's Something (12", p/s) 8
85	Zarjazz JAZZ D5	Yesterday's Men/All I Knew (square picture disc)//Yesterday's Men
		(Harmonica Mix)/It Must Be Love (Live) (double pack, gold PVC wallet) 6
85	Zarjazz JAZZY 7	Uncle Sam/Please Don't Go/Insanity Over Christmas (picture disc). 5
86	Zarjazz JAZZ B9-12	(Waiting For) The Ghost-Train/Maybe In Another Life/
		Seven Year Scratch (12", p/s with 8-page booklet) 8
88	Virgin VSX 1054	I Pronounce You/4BF/Patience/11th Hour (as The Madness, box with badge,
		2 cards & sticker) 5
88	Virgin VSCD 1054	I Pronounce You/4BF/Patience/11th Hour (CD, as The Madness) 8

FLEXIDISCS

80	Stiff/Lyntone LYN 8680	Patches Brings You A Few Minutes Of Madness (with *Patches* mag) 10/7
81	Lyntone LYN 10208	Take It or Leave It (free with *Take It Or Leave It* magazine). 12/8
81	Lyn. LYN 10353/EVENT 2	Event — The Madness (free with *Event* magazine) 10/7
82	Lyntone LYN 11546	My Girl (Ballad) (green or white vinyl, with *Flexipop* mag issue 19;
		with/without magazine) 8/6
82	Lyntone LYN 11546	My Girl (Ballad) (hard vinyl test pressing of above) 25
82	Lyntone LYN 10719	Carols On 45 (fan club disc) 8
84	Lyntone LYN 15280/1	Insanity Over Christmas/Visit To Castle Dracstein (fan club disc) 7
85	Lyntone LYN 16676	From Us ... To You (Mad Not Mad tour disc, some with tour programme) 10/6
85	Lyntone LYN 16981	Live From The Mad Not Mad Tour 6
86	Lyntone LYN 18251	Ghost Train (The Demo)/The Final Goodbye (fan club disc) 6

ALBUMS

80	Stiff SEEZ 29	ABSOLUTELY (LP, some in first-issue sleeve) 30/20
84	Stiff PSEEZ 53	KEEP MOVING (LP, picture disc, U.S. running order). 18
82	Madness Info Service	THE M.I.S. RADIO PLAYERS PRESENT 30 MINUTES OF CULTURE
	(no cat. no.)	(fan club cassette) 12
86	Madness Info Service	MADNESS LIVE (fan club cassette) 12

(see also Argonauts, Voice Of The Beehive)

MADONNA
SIRE SINGLES

82	Sire W 9899	Everybody/Everybody (Dub Version) (WEA sleeve, no p/s) 150
82	Sire W 9899T	Everybody/Everybody (Dub Version) (12", WEA sleeve, no p/s) 125
83	Sire W 9522	Lucky Star (Edit)/I Know It ('sunglasses' p/s with no
		Jellybean credit on label) 250
83	Sire W 9522T	Lucky Star (Full Length Version)/I Know It (12", 'sunglasses' p/s;
		some rumoured to come with stickered p/s & poster different to reissue).... 90/65
83	Sire W 9522TV	Lucky Star (U.S Remix)/I Know It (12", stickered plain white die-cut sleeve) 60
83	Sire W 9405	Holiday (Edit)/Think Of Me ('train' p/s) 15
83	Sire W 9405T	Holiday (Full Length Version 6.08)/Think Of Me
		(12", 'train' p/s, some with 'Copyright Control' wording on label) 10/12
84	Sire W 9522	Lucky Star (Edit)/I Know It (reissue, 'bangles & stars' Jellybean credit
		on label, p/s) 7
84	Sire W 9522T	Lucky Star (Full Length Version)/I Know It (12" reissue, stickered 'TV
		screen' p/s) 10
84	Sire W 9522T	Lucky Star (Full Length Version)/I Know It (12" reissue, stickered 'TV
		screen' p/s, with poster). 50
84	Sire W 9260	Borderline (Edit)/Physical Attraction (p/s, large 'A' on paper A-side label) 5
84	Sire W 9260	Borderline (Edit)/Physical Attraction (p/s, large 'A' on paper A-side label
		mispressing with A-Ha's 'Driftwood' on 'B' side) 100
84	Sire W 9260F	Borderline (Edit)/Physical Attraction//Holiday (Edit)/Think Of Me ('map' p/s,
		double pack with European p/s, copies of "Holiday", shrinkwrapped &
		stickered; beware of counterfeits with less-than-Mint picture sleeves!) 250
84	Sire W 9210T	Like A Virgin (U.S. Dance Remix)/Stay (12", p/s, with poster & sticker) 35
85	Sire W 9083	Material Girl/Pretender (p/s) 5
85	Sire W 9083T	Material Girl (Jellybean Dance Mix)/Pretender (12", with poster p/s) 35
85	Sire WA6323	Crazy For You/Sammy Hagar "I'll Fall In Love Again"
		(7" Madonna shaped picture Disc in stickered PVC sleeve. No p/s.) 75
85	Sire WA6323	Crazy For You/Sammy Hagar "I'll Fall In Love Again"
		(Uncut 7" Picture disc on 10" vinyl in PVC sleeve. No p/s.) 1,000
85	Sire W 8934P	Into The Groove/Shoo-Be-Doo (heart-shaped picture disc with 2 stickers)...... 40
85	Sire W 8934P	Into The Groove/Shoo-Be-Doo (12" *uncut* heart-shaped picture disc,
		very few copies) 750
85	Sire W 8934T	Into The Groove/Everybody/Shoo-Be-Doo (12", p/s, initially with poster)...... 30/7
85	Sire W 9405T	Holiday (Full Length Version 6.08)/Think Of Me
		(12", 'cross earring' p/s reissue) 15

85	Sire W 9405P	Holiday (Full Length Version 6.08)/Think Of Me (12", picture disc)	30
85	Sire W 8881P	Angel (Edit)/Burning Up (shaped pic disc, some with cardboard plinth)	45/35
85	SireW8881P	Angel (Edit)/Burning Up (Uncut 7" pic disc on 12" vinyl in	
		PVC sleeve, no p/s)	1000
85	Sire A6585	Gambler/Black 'n' Blue:Nature Of The Beach (7" p/s)	7
85	Sire QA6585	Gambler/Black 'n' Blue:Nature Of The Beach (7" foldout poster p/s)	30
85	Sire TA6585	Gambler (Extended Dance Mix)/(Instrumental Remix) Black 'n' Blue:	
		Nature Of The Beach (12" p/s)	20
85	Sire W 8848T	Dress You Up (12" Formal Mix)/(Casual Instrumental)/I Know It (12", p/s)	8
85	Sire W 8848TF	Dress You Up (12" Formal Mix)/(Casual Instrumental)/I Know It	
		(12", foldout p/s with Virgin Tour Video Advert on back)	35
85	Sire W 8848TF	Dress You Up (12" Formal Mix)/(Casual Instrumental)/I Know It	
		(12", p/s, '4 Track Studio' or 'Live Like A Virgin Tour' rear video advert) . . . . each	7
85	Sire W 8848P	Dress You Up/I Know It ('Xmas tree star'-shaped picture disc)	35
85	Sire W 8848P	Dress You Up (Uncut 7" picture disc on 12" vinyl, no p/s)	750
86	Sire W 9560P	Borderline/Physical Attraction (Madonna-shaped picture disc in	
		pvc sleeve no p/s)	50
86	Sire W 9560P	Borderline/Physical Attraction (Uncut 7" picture disc on 12" vinyl,	
		pvc sleeve no p/s)	750
86	Sire W 8717T(W)	Live To Tell (LP Version)/(Edit)/(Instrumental) (12", p/s, some with poster)	20/5
86	Sire W8636T	Papa Don't Preach(Extended Version)/(LP Vesion) Ain't No Big Deal	
		(12" with poster in stickered p/s)	20
86	Sire W 8636T(W)	Papa Don't Preach (Extended Version)/Papa Don't Preach (LP Version)/	
		Ain't No Big Deal (12", p/s, initially with free poster)	15/8
86	Sire W 8636TP	Papa Don't Preach (Extended Remix)/Ain't No Big Deal (LP Version)/	
		Papa Don't Preach (LP version) (12", picture disc;	
		some copies play last 2 tracks in wrong order) . . . . each	30
86	Sire W 8550TP	True Blue (Extended Dance Version)/Holiday (Full Length Version)	
		(12", picture disc)	25
86	Sire W 8480TP	Open Your Heart (Extended Version)/Open Your Heart (Dub Mix)/	
		Lucky Star (Full Length Version) (12", picture disc)	25
87	Sire W 8378TP	La Isla Bonita (Extended Remix)/(Extended Instrumental) (12", picture disc) . . .	25
87	Sire W 8341TX	Who's That Girl (Extended Version)/Who's That Girl (Dub Mix)/	
		White Heat (12" Remix) (12", p/s)	30
87	Sire W 8341TP	Who's That Girl (Extended Version)/White Heat	
		(12", picture disc; beware of original decaying PVC sleeves)	75
87	Sire W 8224	Causing A Commotion (Silver Screen Single Mix)/Jimmy Jimmy	
		(p/s, with badge shrinkwrapped to p/s)	50
87	Sire W 8224TP	Causing A Commotion (Silver Screen Mix)/Causing A Commotion	
		(Movie House Mix)/Jimmy Jimmy (Fade) (12", picture disc)	20
87	Sire W 8224C	Causing A Commotion (Silver Screen Mix)/Causing A Commotion	
		(Movie House Mix)/Jimmy Jimmy (Fade) (Cassette Single p/s)	30
87	Sire W 8115TW	The Look Of Love/Love Don't Live Here Anymore/I Know It (12",	
		p/s & poster)	20
87	Sire W 8115TP	The Look Of Love/Love Don't Live Here Anymore/I Know It (12", picture disc) . .	20
89	Sire 925 681-2	Papa Don't Preach (7" Version)/(12" Version)/Pretender (Video)	
		(5" CD-Video p/s)	40
89	Sire W 7539T	Like A Prayer/Act Of Contrition (p/s, with free Virgin Megastore poster)	7
89	Sire W 7539TX	Like A Prayer (12" Dance Mix)/(Churchapella Mix)/(7" Remix Edit) (12", p/s)	15
89	Sire W 7539TP	Like A Prayer (12" Extended Remix)/ (12" Club Version)/	
		Act Of Contrition (12", picture disc)	25
89	Sire W 7539C	Like A Prayer (12" Extended Remix)/ (12" Club Version)/	
		Act Of Contrition (Cassette Single p/s)	15
89	Sire W 7539CD	Like A Prayer/(12" Extended Remix)/ (12" Club Version)/Act Of Contrition	
		(3" Gatefold CD)	12
89	Sire W 2948X	Express Yourself (7" Remix)/The Look Of Love (LP) (poster p/s)	25
89	Sire W 2948W	Express Yourself (7" Remix)/The Look Of Love (LP) (cassette single p/s)	15
89	Sire W 2948C	Express Yourself (7" Remix)/The Look Of Love (LP) ('jeans zipper' p/s)	50
89	Sire W 2948CX	Express Yourself (Non-Stop Express Mix)/(Stop + Go Dubs) (cassette)	200
89	Sire W 2948TP	Express Yourself/(Non-Stop Express Mix)/(Stop + Go Dubs)	
		(12", 'nude' picture disc)	25
89	Sire W 2948 CD	Express Yourself/(Non-Stop Express Mix)/(Stop + Go Dubs) (3" CD)	15
89	Sire W 2883C	Cherish/Supernatural (Cassette p/s)	15
89	Sire W 2883TP	Cherish (Extended Version)/(7" Version)/Supernatural (12", mispressed	
		picture disc, plays "Cherish" but pictures feature Fish's "State Of Mind")	50
89	Sire W 2883 CD	Cherish (extended)/Cherish/Supernatural (3" CD)	15
89	Sire W 2668T	Dear Jessie/Till Death Do Us Part (picture disc)	15
89	Sire W 2668C	Dear Jessie/Till Death Do Us Part (Cassette Single, p/s)	10
89	Sire W 2668TW	Dear Jessie/Till Death Do Us Part/Holiday (12" Version) (12", poster p/s)	20
89	Sire W 2268CDX	Dear Jessie/Till Death Do Us Part/Holiday (12" Version) (CD, picture disc)	100
89	Sire 925 681-2	Papa Don't Preach (7" Version)/(12" Version)/Pretender (LP Version)/	
		Papa Don't Preach (CD Video)	65
90	Sire W 9851	Vogue/Keep It Together (Single Remix) (p/s, mispress with B-side twice)	18
90	Sire W 9851P	Vogue/Keep It Together (Single Remix) (picture disc)	15
90	Sire W 9851C	Vogue (Single Version)/Keep It Together (Single Remix) (cassette single, p/s)	7
90	Sire W 9851TW	Vogue (12" Version)/Keep It Together (12" Remix) (12", p/s, with	
		'Face of the 80s' poster)	15
90	Sire W 9851TX	Vogue (12" Version)/Vogue (Strike-A-Pose Dub) (12", p/s, with 'X-rated'	
		30" x 20" poster)	20
90	Sire W 9851TP	Vogue (12" Version)/Keep It Together (12" Remix) (12", picture disc)	20
90	Sire W 9789TP	Hanky Panky/More (cassette single p/s)	7
90	Sire W 9789TP	Hanky Panky (Bare Bottom 12" Mix)/(Bare Bones Single Mix)/More (LP Version)	
		(12", picture disc with gatefold insert & foldout poster)	15
90	Sire W 9000TP	Justify My Love (William Orbit Remix)/Justify My Love/Express Yourself	
		(Shep's 'Spressin' Himself Remix) (12", picture disc with insert)	15

90	Sire W 9000C	Justify My Love/Express Yourself (cassette single, p/s)	10
		(Shep's 'Spressin' Himself Remix) (12", picture disc with insert)	15
90	Sire 7599382253	Justify My Love/Vogue (Live at MTV Awards 1990) (video single, p/s)	8
91	Sire W 0008P	Crazy For You (Remix)/Keep It Together (Single Remix)	
		(shaped picture disc with plinth & insert)	35
91	Sire W 0008C	Crazy For You (Remix)/Keep It Together (Single Remix) (cassette single p/s)	7
91	Sire W 0008CD	Crazy For You (Remix)/Keep It Together (Shep Pettibone Remix)/	
		Into The Groove (Shep Pettibone Remix) (CD, picture disc)	10
91	Sire W0024	Rescue Me/Spotlight (7" p/s)	5
91	Sire W0024C	Rescue Me/Spotlight (cassette single, p/s)	10
91	Sire W0024TW	Rescue (Titanic Mix)/(Houseboat Mix)/(Titanic Mix) (12" with free poster, p/s)	10
91	Sire W0024CD	Rescue (Titanic Mix)/(Houseboat Mix)/(Titanic Mix) (CD, p/s)	25
91	Sire W 0037TP	Holiday/True Blue (12", clear vinyl picture disc with insert in PVC sleeve)	15
91	Sire W0037C	Holiday/True Blue (Edit) (cassette single p/s)	7
91	Sire W 0037CT	THE HOLIDAY COLLECTION (Holiday/True Blue/Who's That Girl/	
		Causing A Commotion) (cassette EP, p/s)	25
91	Sire W 0037CD	THE HOLIDAY COLLECTION (Holiday/True Blue/Who's That Girl/	
		Causing A Commotion) (CD)	10

MAVERICK SINGLES

92	Maverick W 0138TP	Erotica (Album Version 5.12)/Erotica (Instrumental 5.12)/Erotica	
		(Radio Edit 4.31) (12", picture disc with gold insert, withdrawn, 138 only)	2000
92	Maverick W 0138TW	Erotica (Album Version 5.12)/Erotica (Instrumental 5.12)/Erotica	
		(Radio Edit 4.31) (12", Free Poster, p/s)	10
92	Maverick W 0146TP	Deeper And Deeper (Shep's Classic 12")/(Shep's Deep Makeover Mix)/	
		(Shep's Deep Beats)/(David's Klub Mix)/(David's Deep Mix)/	
		(Shep's Deeper Dub) (12", picture disc)	15
93	Maverick W0154TW	Bad Girl (Edit)/Erotica (William Orbit 12")/Erotica (William Orbit Dub)/	
		Erotica (Madonna's In My Jeep Mix) (12", Free Poster, p/s)	10
93	Maverick W 0168P	Fever (Edit)/Fever (Radio Edit Remix) (jukebox 7" white label	
		die-cut sleeve, no p/s)	10
93	Maverick W 0168P	Fever (Edit)/Fever (Radio Edit Remix) (picture disc with numbered insert)	10
93	Maverick W0168T	Fever (Hot Sweat 12")/(Extended 12")/(Shep's Remedy Dub)/(Murk Boys Miami	
		Mix)/(Murk Boys Deep South Mix)/(Oscar G's Dope Dub) (12" stickered, p/s)	10
93	Sire W0190	Rain (Remix Edit)/Open Your Heart (7", stickered p/s)	5
93	Sire W0190	Rain (Remix Edit)/Open Your Heart (jukebox 7" white label	
		die-cut sleeve, no p/s)	7
94	Sire W0240	I'll Remember/Secret Garden (jukebox promo 7" black plastic label, no p/s)	7
94	Sire W0240CD	I'll Remember/(Orbit Remix)/Guerilla Beach Mix)/In This Life (Live)	
		(CD, mispressed, live track plays 'In This Life', p/s)	20
94	Maverick W 0268P	Secret (Edit)/Let Down Your Guard (Rough Mix Edit) (picture disc w/insert)	12
95	Maverick W 0278P	Take A Bow (Edit)/Take A Bow (picture disc with insert)	7
95	Maverick W 0285CDX	Bedtime Story (Junior's Single Mix)/Secret (Allstar Mix)/Secret	
		(Some Bizarre Mix)/Secret (Some Bizarre Single Mix) (CD, booklet sleeve)	10
94	Warner Bros W0268P	Secret (Edit)/Let Down Your Guard (Rough Mix Edit) (picture disc with	
		insert, no p/s)	15
94	Warner Bros W0278	Take A Bow (Edit)/Instrumental (jukebox promo 7" black label, no p/s)	7
94	Warner Bros W0278P	Take A Bow (Edit)/Instrumental (7" picture disc with numbered rear insert,	
		no p/s)	10
95	Warner Bros W0285	Bedtime Story (Album Edit)/(Junior's Single Mix) (Jukebox 7" black label no p/s)	7
95	Warner Bros W0285TX	Bedtime Story (Junior's Sound Factory Mix)/(Junior's Sound Factory Dub)/	
		(Orbital Mix)/Junior's Wet Dream Mix) (12" Glitter Holographic Sleeve)	15
95	Warner Bros W0285CDX	Bedtime Story (Junior's Single Mix)/Secret (Allstar Mix)/Secret	
		(Some Bizarre Mix)/Secret/(Some Bizarre Single Mix) (CD, 'Bedtime	
		Storybook' digipak, p/s)	15
95	Warner Bros W0324LC	You'll See (Edit)/(Instrumental) (jukebox 7" with black plastic label, no p/s)	10
95	Warner Bros W0324LC	You'll See (Edit)/Rain/(Instrumental) (CD, with free 1996 Desk Calendar p/s)	10
95	Warner Bros W0326LC	Oh Father/Live To Tell (Live Edit From Ciao Italia) (Jukebox 7",	
		die-cut sleeve, no p/s)	15
96	Warner Bros W0337LC	One More Chance/You'll See (Spanish Version) (jukebox 7", no p/s)	10
96	Warner Bros W0378LC	You Must Love Me/Rainbow High (jukebox 7" black plastic label, no p/s)	10
96	Warner Bros W0384LC	Don't Cry For Me Argentina/Santa Evita (jukebox 7" no p/s)	10
98	Warner Bros W0433LC	Frozen/Shanti/Ashtangi (jukebox 7", white label no p/s)	10
98	Warner Bros W0444LC	Ray Of Light/Has To Be (jukebox 7" white label, no p/s)	10
98	Warner Bros W0453LC	Drowned World/Substitute For Love/Sky Fits Heaven (Sasha Remix Edit)	
		(jukebox 7", white label, no p/s)	10
98	Warner Bros W459LC	The Power Of Good-Bye/Little Star (jukebox 7", white label, no p/s)	10
99	Warner Bros W495LC	Beautiful Stranger/(Calderone Radio Mix) (jukebox 7", white label, no p/s)	15
00	Warner Bros W519LC	American Pie/(Richard "Humpty" Vission Radio Mix) (Jukebox 7",	
		white label, no p/s)	15
00	Warner Bros W537LC	Music/(Groove Armada's 7" Edit) (jukebox 7", white label, no p/s)	15
00	Warner Bros W547LC	Don't Tell Me (Radio Edit)/Cyba-Raga (jukebox 7", white label, no p/s)	15
02	Warner Bros W595C	Die Another Day (Radio Edit)/(Dirty Vegas Main Mix) (cassette single, p/s)	10
03	Warner Bros W634T	Love Profusion (Passengerz Club Mix)/Nobody Knows Me	
		(Above & Beyond 12" Mix) (12" stickered, p/s)	8
05	Warners W695CD2	Hung Up (Radio Version)/(Tracy Young's Get Up And Dance Groove Edit)	
		/SDP Extended Vocal) (CD, stickered, p/s)	9

OTHER SINGLES

85	Geffen A 6323	Crazy For You/SAMMY HAGAR: I'll Fall In Love Again (p/s)	5
85	Geffen WA 6323	Crazy For You/SAMMY HAGAR: I'll Fall In Love Again	
		(Madonna-shaped picture disc)	65
85	Geffen A 6585	Gambler/BLACK 'N BLUE: Nature Of The Beast (p/s)	5
85	Geffen QA 6585	Gambler/BLACK 'N BLUE: Nature Of The Beast (poster p/s)	25
85	Geffen TA 6585	Gambler (Extended Dance Mix)/Gambler (Instrumental Remix)/	
		BLACK 'N BLUE: Nature Of The Beast (12", p/s)	20

MADONNA

92	Receiver RRSP 1007	Shine A Light/On The Ground (picture disc, withdrawn)	12
92	Receiver RRSPT 1007	Shine A Light/On The Ground/Little Boy (12", p/s, withdrawn)	8
92	Reciever RRSPT 1007	Shine A Light/On The Ground/Little Boy (12", picture disc)	15

PROMOS

83	Sire No cat no	Lucky Star (Edit) (10" acetate, die-cut sleeve)	300
83	Sire W 9522TV	Lucky Star (U.S. Remix)/I Know It (12" in die-cut sleeve "1983" or "1984" on label)	35
83	Sire SAM 193	Lucky Star (Album Version) (12" v/a compilation, die-cut sleeve)	30
83	Sire 238	Holiday (Album Version) (12" white label v/a compilation die-cut sleeve)	30
85	Sire SAM 251	Into The Groove (Edit) Holiday (Edit) (12" white label, die-cut sleeve, stickered)	100
86	Sire W8550	True Blue (Remix)/Holiday (Edit) (test pressing 7" white label, no p/s)	80
87	Sire SAM 412	Spotlight (Dub)/Holiday (Dub)/Over And Over (Dub)/Into The Groove (Dub) 12" white label, die-cut WEA sleeve, no p/s)	50
89	Sire SAM 641	Keep It Together (12" Remix)/(Dub)/(Extended Remix)/(12" Mix)/ (Bonus Beats)/(Instrumental) (12")	30
90	Sire SAM 659	Vogue (12" Version)/Vogue (Strike A Pose Dub) (12")	25
90	Sire SAM 738	Justify My Love (Remix) (1-sided 12" die-cut sleeve, p/s)	20
91	Sire SAM 800	Holiday (Edit) (CD)	150
92	Sire SAM 1103	Erotica (Album Version) (12" white label die-cut no p/s)	35
92	Sire SAM 1118	Deeper And Deeper (Edit)/Shep's Deep Makeover Mix)/Shep's Classic 12" David's Klub Mix)/David's Love Dub)/David's Deeper Dub) (12" white label no p/s)	35
93	Sire SAM 1131	Fever (Hot Sweat 12" Mix)/(Shep's Remedy Dub)/(Dub One)/(Dub Two)/ (Bugged Out Bonzai Mix)/(Peggy's Nightclub Mix)/(Radio Edit)/(Murk Boys Miami Mix)/(Murk Boys Deep South Mix)/(Oscar G's Dope Dub)/ (Back To The Dub One)/(Back To The Dub Two) (2x12" white label, no p/s)	75
94	Warner Bros W 0278 CDDJ	Take A Bow (Edit) (CD with insert, no p/s)	40
94	Warner Bros SAM 1526	Bedtime Story (Junior's Sound Factory Mix)/(Mixes) (12")	15
94	Warner Bros SAM 1653	Human Nature: The Remixes/(Mixes) (12", stickered title sleeve)	15
94	Warner Bros W0300CDDJ	Human Nature (4' 30" Radio Edit) (CD)	20
95	Warner Bros WEA2	Bedtime Story (Album Version) (10" 1-sided acetate with Abbey Road label)	200
95	Warner Bros SAM 1526	Bedtime Story (Junior's Sound Factory Mix)/(Junior's Sound Factory Dub)/ (Orbital Mix)/(Junior's Wet Dream Mix)/(Junior's Wet Dream Dub) (12")	15
95	Warner Bros W 0285 CDDJ2	Bedtime Story (Junior's Singles Mix) (CD in standard p/s)	35
95	Warner Bros W 0326 CDDJ	Oh Father (Edit) (CD)	35
96	Sire SAM 1880	Love Don't Live Here Anymore (Mark!s It's A Girl Dub)/ (Mark!s It's A Boy Dub)/(Mark!s Full On Vocal) (12")	25
96	Warner Bros SAM 1982	Don't Cry For Me Argentina (Miami Mix)/(Mixes) (12", title sleeve)	20
96	Warner Bros W0384CDDJ2	Don't Cry For Me Argentina (Miami Mix edit/Miami Mix) (CD)	20
96	Warner Bros W0388CDDJ	Another Suitcase In Another Hall (CD, title inlay)	15
96	Warner Bros W0337CDDJ	One More Chance (Album Version) (CD, some with p/s)	50/10
97	Warner Bros W 0388 CDDJ	Another Suitcase In Another Hall (CD in stickered unique p/s)	20
98	Warner Bros 3331000037	Drowned World/Substitute For Love (BT & Sasha's Bucklodge Ashram Remix)/ Sky Fits Heaven (Sasha Remix)/Substitute For Love (Victor Calderone Remix Edit) (12")	25
98	Sire SAM 3173	Frozen (Extended Club Mix)/(Stereo MC's Mix)/(Meltdown Mix — Long Version) (12" no p/s, some mispressed on Dive By Boogie)	15/25
98	Sire SAM 3173	Frozen (Extended Club Mix)/(Stereo MC's Mix)/(Meltdown Mix — Long Version) (12", mispress, sleeve & labels credit "Dive Boogie" but play tracks from "Frozen" 12" promo)	15
98	Warner Bros SAM 3247	Ray Of Light (Sasha's Ultra Violet Mix)/(William Orbit's Liquid Mix) (12")	30
98	Warner Bros SAM 3248	Ray Of Light (Calderone Club Mix)/(Album Version) (12" no p/s)	30
98	Warner Bros SAM 3268	Ray Of Light (Sasha's Twilo Mix)/(Victor Calderone Drum Mix) (12")	30
98	Warner Bros SAM 3269	Ray Of Light (Sasha's Strip Down Mix)/(Orbit's Ultra Violet Mix) (12")	30
98	Warner Bros 0444 CDDJ	Ray Of Light (Album Version) (CD, stickered p/s)	15
98	Warner Bros 33331000037	Drowned World/Substitute For Love (BT and Sasha's Bucklodge Ashram Remix)/Sky Fits Heaven (Sasha Remix)/Sky Fits Heaven (Victor Calderone Remix Edit) (12")	10
98	Warner Bros W 459 CDDJ	Little Star (CD, yellow or white stickered)	50
99	Warner Bros SAM 00061	Nothing Really Matters (Club 69 Future Mix)/(Club 69 Future Dub)/(Kruder & Dorfmeister Remix)/Club 69 (Radio) (12" acetate with handwritten labels and Die-cut '777' sleeve, no p/s)	150
99	Warner Bros W 471CDDJ	Nothing Really Matters (Album Version)/Nothing Really Matters (Club 69 Radio Mix) (CD, slimline jewel case)	15
99	Warner Bros (no cat. no.)	Beautiful Stranger (Calderone Club Mix)/(Calderone Radio Mix)/Album Version (12" acetate printed labels, lilac tape to tape p/s, dated 20/05/99)	150
00	Warner Bros PR01802	American Pie (Album Version)/(Richard 'Humpty' Vission Radio Mix) (CD)	15
00	Maverick PRO 261270	American Pie (Pie Mix)/(Orbit Sugar Free Mix) (CD, tin case)	35
00	Warner Bros PRO 6584	Music (mixes) (12" double pack, title-stickered sleeve)	15
00	Warner Bros PR02054	Music (Album Version) (CD)	10
00	Warner Bros (no cat. no)	Music/Impressive Instant (7" test pressing white label, die-cut sleeve)	50
00	Warner Bros (no cat. no)	Music (Calderone Anthem Mix)/(The Young Collective Mix) 12" acetate with handwritten Sonic Arts labels, die-cut sleeve, no p/s)	150
00	Warner Bros (no cat. no)	Madonna EPK December 2000 (radio use interview CD-R, card p/s)	100
00	Warner Bros W 547 LC	Don't Tell Me (Radio Edit)/Cyber-Raga (10" acetate with gold written labels, no p/s)	150
01	Warner Bros PR02296	Don't Tell Me (Thunderpuss Radio Mix)/(mixes) (CD)	15
01	Warner Bros MADZ 01	What It Feels Like For A Girl (Perfecto Mix)/(Above & Beyond Remix) (12" stickered white label, A4 press release, die-cut sleeve no p/s)	100
01	Warner Bros (no cat. no.)	Impressive Instant (Rauhoffers Universal Club Mix)/Impressive Instant (Rauhoffers Drowned World Dub) (CD-R, paper title-sleeve)	35
01	Warner Bros (no cat. no.)	Thunderpuss GHV2 Megamix (Long Edit)/Thunderpuss GHV2 Megamix (Short Edit) (CD-R, paper title-sleeve)	35
01	Warner Bros PROP 05247	GHV2 (CD, slimline jewel case, 'collage' insert)	25

01	Warner Bros SAM 00586	GHV2 (CD, 10" x 10" gatefold p/s).. 80
02	Warner Bros SAM 00721	Die Another Day (Dirty Vegas Main Mix)/(mixes) (12" double pack, stickered title sleeve)... 20
02	Warner Bros (no cat. no.)	Die Another Day (9 mixes) (CD-R, title-sleeve) 45
03	Warner Bros (no cat. no.)	American Life (Missy Elliott American Dream Remix)/(mixes)/Die Another Day (Richard Humpty Vission Electrofried Mix) (CD-R, card sleeve) 25
03	Warner Bros SAM 00824	Hollywood (Oakenfold 12" Full Remix)/Jacques Lu Cont Thin White Duck Mix /Album Version)//(Deepsky Home Sweet Home Vocal Remix) (12")............... 10
03	Warner Bros	Love Profusion (Passengerz Club Mix)/Nobody Knows Me (Above And Beyond 12" Mix) (12" acetate with handwritten labels, die-cut '777' sleeve, no p/s)..... 150
03	Warner Bros W 634 T	Love Profusion (Passengerz Club Mix)/Nobody Knows Me (Above And Beyond 12" Mix) (12" white label test pressing, die-cut sleeve no p/s, press release)... 100

ALBUMS

83	Sire 923 867-1	MADONNA (LP, with inner sleeve)... 10
83	Sire 92-3867-2	MADONNA (CD)... 50
84	Sire 925 157-1	LIKE A VIRGIN (LP, without "Into The Groove", with inner sleeve)........... 15
85	Sire 925 18102	LIKE A VIRGIN (CD, limited number of copies with unique floral rear p/s) 50
85	Sire WX 20P	LIKE A VIRGIN (LP, picture disc in die-cut sleeve)......................... 50
86	Sire WX 54	TRUE BLUE (LP, with tour poster)... 25
87	Sire WX 76	YOU CAN DANCE (LP, with poster & gold 'obi')............................. 20
90	Sire 7599 264932	ROYAL BOX (box set with "Immaculate Collection" CD in satin digipak, video, poster & postcards)... 75
92	Sire WX49	EROTICA (Dirty Version) (2xLP, gatefold, stickered)........................ 15
92	Sire WX49	EROTICA (Clean Version) (2xLP, gatefold, stickered)....................... 15
94	Sire 9362 45767-1	BEDTIME STORIES (2xLP, gatefold).. 20
95	Sire 9362 46100-1	SOMETHING TO REMEMBER (LP).. 40
98	Sire 9362 46847-1	RAY OF LIGHT (2xLP with inner sleeve, stickered)........................ 25
00	Sire 9362 47865-1	MUSIC (2xLP with gold die-cut inners, stickered).......................... 15
00	Sire 9362 47865-2	MUSIC (HMV Oxford Street day of release CD with unique insert autographed in silver, 175 copies only).. 100
00	Sire 9362 47921-2	MUSIC (CD black denim gatefold book and buckle, stickered)............... 100
00	Sire 9362 47921-2	MUSIC (CD tan/grey denim gatefold book and buckle, stickered)............ 75
00	Sire 9362 47921-2	MUSIC (CD pink denim gatefold book and buckle, stickered)............... 30
03	Sire 9362 48454-1	AMERICAN LIFE (2xLP, inner sleeve gatefold) 15
03	Sire 9362 48454-4	AMERICAN LIFE (cassette, stickered)..................................... 25
04	Sire 9362 46847-1	RAY OF LIGHT (Reissue, 2xLP with inner sleeve 180 gm deluxe vinyl, stickered)... 25
06	Sire 9362 494601	CONFESSIONS ON A DANCE FLOOR (2xLP, gatefold)...................... 15

ALBUM PROMOS

84	Sire No cat no	LIKE A VIRGIN (LP, white label, die-cut sleeve, no p/s) 100
89	Sire MER 0120	LIKE A PRAYER (box set in 10" x 7" x 1" box, includes CD, sealed cassette, press release, badge, slides, Rolling Stone re-print, 2 photos)............... 350
92	Sire No cat no	EROTICA (promo cassette with typed promo inlay sleeve, no p/s)............ 20

(see also Jellybean)

MADRIGAL
73	Madrigal MAD 100	BENEATH THE GREENWOOD TREE (LP, private pressing).................. 60+

MAD RIVER
69	Capitol (S)T 2985	MAD RIVER (LP) 32

JOHNNY MAESTRO
61	HMV POP 875	What A Surprise/The Warning Voice...................................... 42
61	HMV POP 909	Mr. Happiness/Test Of Love.. 42
64	United Artists UP 1004	Before I Love Her/Fifty Million Heartbeats 30
71	Buddah 2011 061	Rain Came/Never Knew This Kind Of Hurt Before 8

(see also Crests, Brooklyn Bridge)

MAGAZINE
78	Virgin VS 200	Shot By Both Sides/My Mind Ain't So Open (card or paper p/s) 6/5
78	Virgin VS 207	Touch And Go/Goldfinger (p/s)... 5
78	Virgin VS 237	Give Me Everything/I Love You, You Big Dummy (p/s)..................... 5
79	Virgin VS 251	Rhythm Of Cruelty/T.V. Baby (p/s)....................................... 5
80	Virgin VS 368	Sweetheart Contract/Feed The Enemy//Twenty Years Ago/ Shot By Both Sides (stickered, shrinkwrapped double pack) 8

(see also Buzzcocks)

MAGENTA
78	Cottage COT 821	CANTERBURY MOON (LP, with insert).................................... 60
80	Little Stan LSP 811	RECOLLECTIONS (2-LP, gatefold sleeve with insert)...................... 80
81	Little Stan LSP 831	WOT'S NEXT THEN (LP, with insert)...................................... 60

MAGGIE
68	Columbia DB 8389	L. David Sloane/Too Young To Get Married 6

MAGIC CARPET
72	Mushroom 200 MR 20	MAGIC CARPET (LP).. 125

(see also Clem Alford)

MAGIC CHRISTIANS
69	Major Minor MM 673	If You Want It/Nuts 7
69	Major Minor MM 673	Come And Get It/Nuts (2nd pressing with correct title) 12
70	Major Minor SMLP 71	THE MAGIC CHRISTIANS (LP)... 38

(see also Trevor Burton, Gary Wright, Denny Laine, Steve Gibbons)

MAGICIANS
66	Decca F 12361	Wet Your Whistle/Take The A Train 5
66	Decca F 12374	The Liars/Poggy Goes Pop 6
67	Decca F 12602	The Tarzan March/What A Day For A Metamorphosis...................... 7
68	MCA MU 1046	Painting On Wood/Slow Motion... 22

MAGIC LANTERNS
66	CBS 202250	Rumplestiltskin/I Stumbled	55
67	CBS 202459	Knight In Rusty Armour/Simple Things	10
67	CBS 202637	Auntie Grizelda/Time Will Tell (If I'm A Loser)	10
67	CBS 2750	We'll Meet Again/What Else Can It Be But Love?	10
68	Camp 602 007	Shame Shame/Baby I Gotta Go Now	10
69	Camp 602 009	Melt All Your Troubles Away/Bossa Nova 1940 — Hello You Lovers	10
67	CBS (S) 62935	LIT UP WITH THE MAGIC LANTERNS (LP)	40

MAGIC MICHAEL
80	Atomic MAGIC 1	Millionaire/My Friend And I (p/s)	5

(see also Damned, Captain Sensible)

MAGIC MIXTURE
68	Saga FID 2125	THIS IS MAGIC MIXTURE (LP)	90

MAGIC MUSCLE
88	Five Hours Back TOCK 009	THE PIPE, THE ROAR, THE GRID (LP, with booklet)	15
90	Pilgrim (no cat. no.)	LIVING WEEDS FROM ANCIENT SEEDS (cassette, box set, autographed with booklet, posters & postcard)	15
91	Woronzow WOO 17	GULP! (LP)	20

(see also Keith Christmas, Hawkwind, High Tide, Twink)

MAGIC MUSHROOM BAND
85	Magick Eye MUSH 001	THE MAGIC MUSHROOM BAND (cassette EP)	12
85	Magick Eye MUSH 002	FEED YOUR HEAD (cassette)	12
86	Pagan PM 003	THE POLITICS OF ECSTASY (LP, 100 with A1 poster, 500 with A3 insert)	40/22
87	Aftermath AFT 3	BOMSHAMKAR (LP)	12
90	Fungus FUN 003	PROCESS OF ILLUMINATION (LP, signed with insert & foldaround sleeve & comic in printed PVC sleeve)	12
91	Fungus FUN 005	SPACED OUT (LP, foldout sleeve with A4 booklet)	15

MAGIC NIGHT
75	Pye 7N 25698	If You And I Had Never Met/(Version)	20

MAGIC NOTES
60	Blue Beat BB 9	Album Of Memory/Why Did You Leave Me	8
61	Blue Beat BB 51	Rosabel/I'm Not Worthy2	8

THE MAGIC NUMBERS
04	Heavenly HVN 143	Hymn For Her/Oh Sister (500 only, with 2 stickers of different band members p/s)	30
05	Heavenly HVN 147	Anima Sola/HAL: Keep Love As Your Golden Rule (Tour single – 500 only p/s)	15

MAGIC SAM
69	Python PEN 701	Twenty One Days In Jail/Easy Baby (99 copies only)	50
69	Rooster 707	MEAN MISTREATER (EP)	20
70	Blue Horizon 7-63223	MAGIC SAM: 1937-1969 (LP)	75
70	Delmark DS 615	WEST SIDE SOUL (LP, blue label)	30
71	Delmark DS 620	BLACK MAGIC (LP, blue label)	30

MAGIC SHOP
87	Sha La La Ba Ba 8	It's Time/VISITORS: Goldmining (flexidisc with various fanzines)	7/5

MAGIC SLIM & TEARDROPS
81	Rooster R 707	THREE THUNDERIN' TRACKS (EP)	7

MAGIC VALLEY
69	Penny Farthing PEN 701	Taking The Heart Out Of Love/Uptight Basil	10

(see also Pete Dello, Honeybus)

MAGISTRATES
68	MGM MGM 1425	Here Comes The Judge/Girl	10
68	MGM MGM 1437	After The Fox/Tear Down The Walls (with Jean Hillary)	10

(see also Jane Hillery)

MAGITS
79	Outer H. SRTS/79/CUS/401	Fragmented/Disconnected/Disjointed/Detached (p/s)	7

(see also Rudimentary Peni)

MAGMA
74	A&M AMS 7119	Mekanik Machine/Mekanik Machine (Version)	8
70	Philips 6359 051/2	MAGMA (2-LP)	18
71	Philips 6397 031	1001 CENTIGRADE (LP)	12
74	A&M AMLH 64397	MEKANIK DESTRUCTIW KOMMANDOH (LP)	12
74	A&M AMLH 68260	KOHN TARKOSZ (LP)	12

MAGNA CARTA
69	Fontana TF 1060	Romeo Jack/7 O'Clock Hymn	15
69	Mercury MF 1096	Mid-Winter/Spinning Wheels Of Time	15
70	Vertigo 6059 013	Airport Song/Elizabethan	10
71	Vertigo 6059 043	Time For The Leaving/Wayfarin'	8
72	Vertigo 6059 073	All My Life/Falkland Green	12
73	Vertigo 6059 092	Give Me Luv/Song Of Evening	10
70s	Borough of Camden	When You're Young (charity issue for RoSPA)	5
69	Mercury SMCL 20166	MAGNA CARTA (LP)	40
70	Vertigo 6360 003	SEASONS (LP, gatefold sleeve, swirl label)	20
71	Vertigo 6360 040	SONGS FROM WASTIES ORCHARD (LP, gatefold sleeve, swirl label)	30
72	Vertigo 6360 068	IN CONCERT (LP, gatefold sleeve, swirl label)	18
73	Vertigo 6360 093	LORD OF THE AGES (LP, gatefold sleeve, spaceship label)	20
76	GTO GTLP 012	PUTTING IT BACK TOGETHER (LP)	18
77	GTO GTLP 112	TOOK A LONG TIME (LP)	15

MAGNA JAZZ BAND
57	Parlophone R 4387	Buddy's Habits/Flat Foot	7

(see also Brian White & Magna Jazz Band)

MAGNAPOP
96	Play It Again Sam BIAS 321LP	RUBBING DOESN'T HELP (LP, red vinyl, with inner)	12

MAGNETOPHONE
98	Earworm WORM 26	You Should Write Music/Monitor Rocket Science (p/s, red vinyl)	5

MAGNETS
86	Hurricane FIRE 1	Who's The Fool (Me Or You)/Best	22

MAGNIFICENT MEN
66	Capitol CL 15462	Peace Of Mind/All Your Lovin's Gone To My Head	30
68	Capitol CL 15530	Sweet Soul Medley Parts 1 & 2	10
68	Capitol CL 15570	Save The Country/So Much Love Waiting	6

MAGNIFICENT MERCURY BROTHERS
74	Transatlantic BIG 532	New Girl In School/What About Us	7
74	Transatlantic BIG 536	Why Do Fools Fall In Love/(I'm Not A) Juvenile Delinquent	7

(see also Decameron)

MAGNOG
90s	Enraptured RAPT 4508	Mist Waves Riding The Hills/Moving Ahead Again/Ghost States (p/s)	6

MAGNUM
75	CBS S CBS 2959	Sweets For My Sweet/Movin' On (no p/s)	45
78	Jet SJET 116	Kingdom Of Madness/In The Beginning	6
78	Jet SJET 128	Invasion/Universe	6
79	Jet JET 155	Changes/Lonesome Star (silver p/s, some with sew-on patch)	10/8
79	Jet JET 163	Foolish Heart/Baby Rock Me (p/s)	6
80	Jet JET 175	Magnum Live [All Of My Life (live)/Great Adventure (live)//Invasion (live)/ Kingdom Of Madness (live)] (double pack, stickered p/s)	6
80	Jet JET 188	Changes (live Remix)/Everybody Needs/Changes (live) (black p/s)	7
81	Jet JET 7007	Black Nights (possibly promo only)	12+
82	Jet JET 7020	The Lights Burned Out/Long Days Black Nights (p/s)	6
82	Jet JET 7027	Back To Earth (live)/Hold Back Your Love (live)//Soldier Of The Line (live)/ Sacred Hour (live) (double pack)	8
86	Polydor POSP 798	Lonely Night/Les Morts Dansant (live) (p/s)	5
86	Polydor POSPG 798	Lonely Night/Les Morts Dansant (live)//All England's Eyes (live)/ Hit And Run (live) (double pack)	7
86	Polydor POSPP 833	Midnight (Remix)/Back Street Kid/Kingdom Of Madness (live) (12", picture disc)	10
87	Polydor POSP 850	When The World Comes Down (Edit)/Vigilante (live) (p/s)	5
88	Polydor POSPG 910	Days Of No Trust/Maybe Tonight ('oct-o-pack', gatefold p/s)	8
88	Polydor POSPP 910	Days Of No Trust/Maybe Tonight (p/s, with sew-on patch)	7
88	Polydor POSPG 920	Start Talking Love/C'est La Vie (gatefold pop-up p/s)	5
88	Polydor POSPP 920	Start Talking Love/Days Of No Trust (10", shaped picture disc)	7
88	Polydor POSPG 930	It Must Have Been Love/Crying Time ('prismatic' pack)	5
88	Polydor 080 406-2	Start Talking Love (Extended Remix)/C'est La Vie/Back To Earth (live)/ On A Storyteller's Night (live) (CD Video)	12
78	Jet JETLP 210	KINGDOM OF MADNESS (LP, original 'king' sleeve)	18
83	FM WKFMPD 111	THE ELEVENTH HOUR (LP, picture disc)	15
85	FM WKFM LP 34	ON A STORYTELLER'S NIGHT (LP, with bonus single)	15
85	FM WKFM G/C LP 34	ON A STORYTELLER'S NIGHT (LP, gold or clear vinyl)	15
85	FM WKFM PD 34	ON A STORYTELLER'S NIGHT (LP, picture disc, with poster)	18
86	Polydor POLD 5198	VIGILANTE (LP)	12
88	Polydor POLDP 5221	WINGS OF HEAVEN (LP, picture disc with extra track, die-cut sleeve)	12
88	FM Revolver WKFMPD 110	MAGNUM II (LP, reissue, picture disc)	15
90	FM Revolver WKFMBX 145	FOUNDATION (6-LP box set)	40

TEDDY MAGNUS
71	Green Door GD 4008	Flying Machine/VERSION BOYS: Machine Version	5

MAGOO
95	Noisebox NBX 013	MUDSHARK EP: Tom, Lou And Me/Elsie's Skinny Arms/Hop Your Mouth (orange vinyl, numbered p/s, 500 only)	10
95	Noisebox NBX 016	ROBOT CARNIVAL EP: Robot Carnival/Sampa Calmida (Land Of Joy)/ Candle Buddah/Rocket To Spector City (blue vinyl, p/s)	6
96	Noisebox NBX 020	EYESPY EP: Eye Spy/Motel Mining/Soaterama/Polka Party No.2/ Silver Screen/Word Is Out/Diving Bell (lemon yellow vinyl, p/s, 500 only)	5
98	Fierce Panda NING 47	Black Sabbath/MOGWAI: Sweet Leaf (p/s)	7

MAGPIES
68	Doctor Bird DB 1129	Lulu/Must I Be Lonely	12
68	Doctor Bird DB 1132	Blue Boy/I Guess I'm Crazy	12

ALEX MAGUIRE
87	Incus INCUS 52	LIVE AT OSCARS (LP)	35

JOHN MAGUIRE
73	Leader LEE 4062	COME DAY, GO DAY, GOD SEND SUNDAY (LP, gatefold sleeve with booklet)	12

LEO MAGUIRE
62	Parlophone R 4917	Crying For The Moon/Small World	6

MAGUS
80	Northern Sound NSR 200	BREEZIN' AWAY (LP, private pressing)	50

(see also Blue Epitaph)

TAJ MAHAL
68	Direction 58-3547	Everybody's Got To Change Sometime/Statesboro Blues	8
69	Direction 58-4044	Ee Zee Rider/You Don't Miss Your Water	8
70	Direction 58-4586	Give Your Woman What She Wants/Further On Down The Road	8
71	CBS 7413	Diving Duck Blues/Fishin' Blues	9
67	Direction 8-63279	TAJ MAHAL (LP)	22
69	Direction 8-63397	THE NATCH'L BLUES (LP)	25
69	Direction 8-66226	GIANT STEP/DE OLE FOLKS AT HOME (2-LP)	22
71	CBS 66288	THE REAL THING (2-LP)	20
72	CBS 64447	HAPPY JUST TO BE LIKE I AM (LP)	12
73	CBS 65090	RECYCLING THE BLUES AND OTHER RELATED STUFF (LP)	12
73	CBS 65814	OOOH SO GOOD 'N BLUES (LP)	12
73	CBS 70123	SOUNDER (LP, soundtrack)	15

MAHAVISHNU ORCHESTRA
75	CBS 3007	Can't Stand Your Funk/Eternity's Breath Part 1	6
72	CBS 64717	THE INNER MOUNTING FLAME (LP, with insert)	12
74	CBS CQ 31996	BIRDS OF FIRE (LP, quadrophonic)	15
75	CBS 69108	VISIONS OF THE EMERALD BEYOND (LP, with insert)	12
	(see also John McLaughlin)		

MITCH MAHON & EDITIONS
69	Pye 7N 17844	You've Got What I Need/I've Thrown Our Love Away	5

SKIP MAHONEY & CASUALS
76	Contempo CLP 539	LAND OF LOVE (LP)	20

MAIL
71	Parlophone R 5916	Omnibus/Life Goes On	6

MAINFRAME
84	YYY	INTO TROUBLE WITH THE NOISE OF ART (12", 7-track EP)	10

MAINHORSE
71	Polydor 2383 049	MAINHORSE (LP)	25

MAIN INGREDIENT
74	RCA PB 0305	Happiness Is Just Around The Bend/Why Can't We All Unite	8
71	RCA LSA 3020	TASTEFUL SOUL (LP)	15

MAINLAND
79	Christy ACML 0200	EXPOSURE (LP)	15

MAINLINER
03	Reopse LP 01	MELLOW OUT (LP, red vinyl)	15
	(see also Acid Mothers Temple)		

JULIE MAIRS & CHRIS STOWELL
77	Cottage COT 211	SOFT SEA BLUE (LP)	20

MAISON ROUGE
85	Red Barn RBR 0001	Questions (p/s)	5

DEXTER MAITLAND
69	United Artists UP 35006	Take Ten Terrific Girls (But Only Nine Costumes)/ RUDY VALLEE: The Night They Raided Minsky's	5

MAJAMOOD
66	Doc. Bird/W.I.R.L. DB 1052	Two Hundred Million Red Ants/Faces Amassed	30

MAJESTERIANS
81	Daddy Kool DKR 125	So Many Times/Flute On Fire (12")	20

MAJOR ACCIDENT
82	M. Melodies MAME 1001	Warboots/Terrorist Gang (unissued, test pressings only)	40
83	Step Forward SF 23	Mr. Nobody/That's You (p/s)	12
83	Flicknife FLS 216	Fight To Win/Free Man (p/s)	12
83	Flicknife FLS 023	Leaders Of Tomorrow/Dayo/Breakaway (p/s)	12
84	Flicknife FLS 026	Respectable/Man On The Wall (p/s)	12
83	Step Forward SFLP 9	MASSACRED MELODIES (LP)	20
84	Syndicate SYNLP 9	TORTURED TUNES LIVE (LP)	20
	(see also Accident)		

MAJORETTES
63	Lyntone LYN 982	White Levi's (flexidisc)	12

MAJOR FORCE
94	Mo' Wax	Return Of The Original Artform/(mixes) (12")	8
	(see also Major Force West)		

MAJOR FORCE WEST
94	Mo' Wax MWMFWLP 001	HEADTURNER (LP, with obi)	15
94	Mo' Wax MWMFWCD 001	HEADTURNER (CD)	35
	(see also Major Force)		

MAJORITY
65	Decca F 12186	Pretty Little Girl/I Don't Wanna Be Hurt No More	12
65	Decca F 12271	A Little Bit Of Sunlight/Shut 'Em Down In London Town	18
66	Decca F 12313	We Kiss In A Shadow/Ring The Bells	12
66	Decca F 12453	Simplified/One Third	90
66	Decca F 12504	To Make Me A Man/Tears Won't Help	12
67	Decca F 12573	I Hear A Rhapsody/Wait By The Fire	18
67	Decca F 12638	Running Away With My Baby/Let The Joybells Ring	18
68	Decca F 12727	All Our Christmases/People	12

MAJORS
62	London HLP 9602	A Wonderful Dream/Time Will Tell	22
62	London HLP 9627	She's A Troublemaker/A Little Bit Now	25
63	London HLP 9693	What In The World/Tra La La	22
64	Liberty LBF 66009	Ooh Wee Baby/I'll Be There	22
63	London RE-P 1358	MEET THE MAJORS (EP)	140
63	London HA-P 8068	MEET THE MAJORS (LP)	200

PETER MAKANA & HIS RHYTHM BOYS
| 58 | Oriole CB 1445 | Baboon Shepherd (with Black Duke)/Black John (78 rpm = £8) | 5 |
| 58 | Oriole CB 1446 | Cool Mood/Sweet Baby (78 rpm = £8) | 5 |

MAKIN' TIME
85	Countdown VAIN 1	Here Is My Number/Nothing Else (p/s)	8
86	Countdown TVAIN 1	Here Is My Number/Nothing Else (picture disc)	8
86	Countdown VAIN 5	Pump It Up/Walk A Thin Line (p/s)	8
86	Countdown 12 VAIN 5	PUMP IT UP EP: Once Again/Walk A Thin Line/Eating Up The Cold	8
85	Countdown DOWN 1	RHYTHM 'N' SOUL (LP)	15
86	Ready To Eat READY 1	NO LUMPS OF FAT OR GRISTLE GUARANTEED (LP)	18
87	Re-Elect/President ELECT 1	TIME, TROUBLE AND MONEY (LP)	18

(see also Charlatans)

MAKKA BEES
| 77 | Congo CO 1 | Nation Fiddler/Fire | 20 |

MALAGON SISTERS & CHA CHA RHYTHM BOYS
| 59 | Pye International 7N 25008 | In A Little Spanish Town/Lessons In Cha-Cha-Cha (78 rpm = £8) | 6 |

MAL & PRIMITIVES
| 65 | Pye 7N 15915 | Every Minute Of Every Day/Pretty Little Face | 125 |

(see also Primitives, Mal Ryder & Spirits)

MALARIA!
| 82 | Jungle JUNG 3 | NEW YORK PASSAGE (12" EP) | 8 |

CARL MALCOLM
| 77 | Grove Music GMDM 1 | Repatriation (feat. Ranking Trevor)/Take A Tip From Me (featuring Ranking Trevor) (12") | 20 |

CARLOS MALCOLM & AFRO CARIBS
| 65 | Island WI 173 | Bonanza Ska/Papa Luiga | 25 |

GEORGE MALCOLM
| 53 | Parlophone MSP 6058 | Bach Goes To Town/Bach Before The Mast | 10 |

HUGH MALCOLM
| 68 | Amalgamated AMG 827 | Good Time Rock/LYNN TAITT & JETS: Sleepy Ludy | 35 |
| 68 | Amalgamated AMG 829 | Mortgage/CANNONBALL BRYAN TRIO: Man About Town | 20 |

MALCOLM & ALWYN
| 73 | Pye NSPL 18404 | FOOL'S WISDOM (LP, with poster) | 12 |
| 74 | Key KL 022 | WILDWALL (LP) | 15 |

MALLARD
77	Virgin VS 168	Harvest/Green Coyote	7
76	Virgin V 2045	MALLARD (LP)	12
77	Virgin V 2077	IN A DIFFERENT CLIMATE (LP)	12

(see also Captain Beefheart & His Magic Band)

STEPHEN MALLINDER
| 81 | Fetish FE 12 | Temperature Drop/Cool Down (12", p/s) | 8 |
| 82 | Fetish FM 2010 | POW-WOW (LP) | 12 |

(see also Cabaret Voltaire)

SIW MALMKVIST
59	Oriole CB 1486	Sermonette/The Preacher (78 rpm = £8)	5
61	Parlophone R 4765	Wedding Cake/Red Roses And Little White Lies	5
64	Columbia DB 7411	Sole Sole Sole/Sabato Sera (as Siw Malmkvist & Umberto Marcato)	5
68	Atlantic 584 229	The Man Who Took The Valise Off The Floor/Sadie The Cleaning Lady	5

CINDY MALONE
| 61 | RCA RCA 1254 | Weird Beard/Young Marriage | 8 |

WIL MALONE
| 70 | Fontana STL 5541 | WIL MALONE (LP) | 150+ |

(see also Barnaby Rudge, Motherlight, Wilson Malone Voiceband)

WILSON MALONE VOICEBAND
| 68 | Morgan MR 112P | FUNNY SAD MUSIC (LP) | 25 |

(see also Motherlight, Wil Malone)

RICHARD MALTBY
56	HMV 7M 393	"Man With The Golden Arm" Theme/Heart Of Paris	8
59	Philips PB 955	Theme From The FBI Story/Morgen (78)	10
61	Columbia DB 4606	The Rat Race/Walkie Talkie	20

MAMAS & PAPAS
66	RCA Victor RCA 1503	California Dreamin'/Somebody Groovy	5
66	RCA Victor RCA 1516	Monday, Monday/Got A Feelin'	5
66	RCA Victor RCA 1533	I Saw Her Again/Even If I Could	5
66	RCA Victor RCA 1551	Look Through My Window/Once There Was I Time I Thought	5
67	RCA Victor RCA 1564	Words Of Love/I Can't Wait	5
67	RCA Victor RCA 1576	Dedicated To The One I Love/Free Advice	5
67	RCA Victor RCA 1613	Creeque Alley/No Salt On Her Tail	5
67	RCA Victor RCA 1630	12.30/Straight Shooter	5
67	RCA Victor RCA 1649	Glad To Be Unhappy/Hey Girl	5

MINT VALUE £

68	RCA Victor RCA 1710	Safe In My Garden/Too Late	5
68	RCA Victor RCA 1726	Dream A Little Dream Of Me/Midnight Voyage	5
68	RCA Victor RCA 1744	For The Love Of Ivy/Strange Young Girls	5
66	RCA Victor RD 7803	IF YOU CAN BELIEVE YOUR EYES AND EARS (LP)	20
66	RCA Victor RD/SF 7834	CASS, JOHN, MICHELLE, DENNY (LP)	20
67	RCA Victor RD/SF 7880	DELIVER (LP)	20
68	RCA Victor RD/SF 7960	THE PAPAS AND THE MAMAS (LP)	22
68	Stateside (S)SL 5002	THE MAMAS AND THE PAPAS GOLDEN ERA VOL. 2 (LP)	15
70	Probe SPB 1013/14	A GATHERING OF FLOWERS (2-LP)	20
71	Probe SPB 1048	PEOPLE LIKE US (LP)	15
78	St. Michael MO 101225	CALIFORNIA DREAMIN' (LP, exclusive to Marks & Spencer)	25

(see also Mama Cass [Elliot], John Phillips, Michelle Phillips, Scott McKenzie, Barry McGuire, Mugwumps, Big Three [U.S], Spanky & Our Gang)

MAMA'S BOYS
81	Pussy	Silence Is Out Of Fashion (Irish pressing, p/s)	6
82	Scoff DT 015	Belfast City Blues/Reach For The Top (p/s; Ireland only)	10
83	Spartan 12SP 6	Too Little Of You To Love/Freedom Fighters (12", p/s, with free "Official Bootleg" LP)	10
84	Spartan SP 11	Midnight Promises (p/s)	5
84	Spartan 12SP 11	MIDNIGHT PROMISES (12" EP)	8
85	Jive JIVEP 96	Needle In The Groove/Don't Tell Mama (shaped picture disc)	8
80	Pussy PU 004	OFFICIAL BOOTLEG (LP, Irish pressing)	12
82	Ultra Noise ULTRA 1	PLUG IT IN (LP)	12
85	Jive HIP 24	POWER AND PASSION (LP, with 12" interview picture disc)	12

MAMMATH
84	Neat NEAT 42	Rock Me/Rough 'N' Ready (p/s)	7

MAMMOTH
87	Jive MOTHCD 1	Fatman (Admiral Amour Mix)/Political Animal/Bad Times/Fatman (7" Version) (CD)	8
89	Jive MOTHX 4	All The Days/Fatman/Bet You Wish (12", picture disc, PVC sleeve, withdrawn)	20

(see also John McCoy, Gillan, Samson, Tiger, Nicky Moore Band, Hackensack)

MAN
69	Pye 7N 17684	Sudden Life/Love	18
71	Liberty LBF 15448	Daughter Of The Fireplace/Country Girl	15
74	United Artists UP 35643	Don't Go Away (possibly unissued)	15+
74	United Artists UP 35703	Taking The Easy Way Out Again/California Silks And Satins	6
74	United Artists UP 35739	Day And Night/A Hard Way To Live	5
76	MCA MCA 236	Out Of Your Head/I'm A Love Taker	5
76	United Artists REM 408	BANANAS (EP)	8
69	Pye N(S)PL 18275	REVELATION (LP, mono/stereo, originals have sky blue label with black at top; reissues have black on the *side*)	35/15/12
69	Dawn DNLS 3003	2 OZ'S OF PLASTIC WITH A HOLE IN THE MIDDLE (LP, orange label, g/f sleeve)	30
69	Dawn DNLS 3003	2 OZ'S OF PLASTIC WITH A HOLE IN THE MIDDLE (LP, later pressings with red & blue or purple labels, gatefold sleeve)	15
70	Liberty LBG 83464	MAN (LP, gatefold sleeve)	30
72	United Artists UAS 29236	DO YOU LIKE IT HERE NOW, ARE YOU SETTLING IN? (LP)	22
72	United Artists USP 100	LIVE AT THE PADGET ROOMS, PENARTH (LP)	22
72	United Artists UAG 29417	BE GOOD TO YOURSELF AT LEAST ONCE A DAY (LP, 'map' sleeve with 'family tree' inner)	18
73	United Artists UDX 205/6	CHRISTMAS AT THE PATTI (LP, 2 x 10", with other artists)	20
73	Utd Artists UAD 60053/4	BACK INTO THE FUTURE (2-LP)	15
75	United Artists UAG 29872	MAXIMUM DARKNESS (LP, gatefold sleeve, with poster)	18
77	MCA MCF 2815	ALL'S WELL THAT ENDS WELL (LP, initially with History Of Man booklet)	15/12

(see also Bystanders, Eyes Of Blue, Ancient Grease, Big Sleep, Clive John, Alkatraz, Help Yourself, Deke Leonard, Neutrons, Gary Pickford–Hopkins & Friends, Wild Turkey)

T. MAN & T. BONES
72	Sioux SI 007	True Born African (actually by Winston Jarrett & Righteous Flames)/Tropical Chief	5

(STEPHEN STILLS') MANASSAS
72	Atlantic K 60021	MANASSAS (2-LP, with 2 inner sleeves & lyric poster)	18
73	Atlantic K 40440	DOWN THE ROAD (LP, with inner sleeve)	12

(see also Stephen Stills, Crosby Stills & Nash, Flying Burrito Brothers)

MANASSEH
77	Genesis 12	MANASSEH (LP, with insert)	20

JUNIOR MANCE
60	HMV CLP 1342	JUNIOR (LP)	15
71	Atlantic 2400 028	WITH A LOTTA HELP FROM MY FRIENDS (LP)	25

STEVE MANCHA/J.J. BARNES
69	Stax SXATS 1012	RARE STAMPS (LP)	60

(see also J.J. Barnes)

MICKY MANCHESTER
75	Rainbow RBW 2001	Have You Seen Your Daughter Mrs. Jones/Chamberlain Said	5

(see also Just Plain Smith, Just Plain Jones)·

MANCHESTER CITY SQUAD
72	RCA Victor 2200	The Boys In Blue/Funky City	5

MANCHESTER MEKON
79	Newmarket NEW 102	No Forgetting/Have A Go-Go/Jonathan Livingstone Seafood (hand-painted p/s with insert, 1,000 only)	25

MANCHESTER MOB
67 Parlophone R 5552   Bony Maronie At The Hop/Afro Asian 30
(see also Graham Gouldman, High Society, 10cc, Friday Browne)

MANCHESTERS
66 Ember   TRIBUTE TO THE BEATLES (LP) 25

MANCHESTER'S PLAYBOYS
66 Fontana TF 745   I Feel So Good/I Close My Eyes 150

MANCHESTER UNITED FOOTBALL SQUAD
76 Decca F 13633   Manchester United/MARTIN BUCHAN: Old Trafford Blues 8
79 RCA MAN 1   Onward Sexton's Soldiers/Come On You Reds (red vinyl). 8
94 PolyGram TV MANUP 12   Come On You Reds/(Instrumental) (12" picture disc, with insert) 15
(see also Status Quo)

HENRY MANCINI & HIS ORCHESTRA
59 RCA RCA 1134   Peter Gunn Theme/The Brothers Go To Mother's (78 rpm = £8) 8
61 RCA RCA 1256   Moon River/Breakfast At Tiffanys 5
62 RCA RCA 1285   Experiment In Terror/Tooty Twist 10
62 RCA RCA 1312   Man Of The World Theme/Fluter's Ball. 6
64 RCA RCA 1414   How Soon/The Tiber Twist 5
64 RCA RCA 1431   Dear Heart/A Shot In The Dark. 5
68 RCA RCA 1689   Wait Until Dark/Norma De Guadalajara. 8
70 RCA RCA 1934   Z-Theme/Midnight Cowboy 5
61 RCA RCX 205   BREAKFAST AT TIFFANY'S (EP) 18
62 RCA RCX 7107   HATARI! (EP) 8
64 RCA RCX 7136   THE PINK PANTHER (EP). 12
57 Brunswick LAT 8162   ROCK, PRETTY BABY (LP, soundtrack, with Rod McKuen). 100
59 RCA RD 27123/SF 5033   PETER GUNN (LP, soundtrack) 15
63 RCA SF 7620   CHARADE (LP, soundtrack) 30
64 RCA RD 7667   THE BEST OF MANCINI (LP) 12
65 RCA RD 7759   THE GREAT RACE (LP, soundtrack). 30
66 RCA SF 7818   WHAT DID YOU DO IN THE WAR, DADDY? (LP, soundtrack) 20
66 RCA RD 7817   ARABESQUE (LP, soundtrack) 15
67 RCA RD/SF 7891   TWO FOR THE ROAD (LP, soundtrack) 20
67 RCA RD/SF 7899   GUNN (LP, soundtrack). 20
69 United Artists UAS 29049   CHICAGO, CHICAGO (LP, soundtrack). 12
70 CBS 70061   ME, NATALIE (LP, soundtrack, with Rod McKuen) 12
70 Avco Embassy 6466 002   SUNFLOWER (LP, soundtrack) 18
70 United Artists UAS 29122   MASTER OF THE ISLANDS (LP, soundtrack). 18
70 RCA SF 8138   DARLIN' LILI (LP, soundtrack, gatefold sleeve) 15
72 RCA Victor SF 8127   FILM THEMES A TO Z (LP). 15
73 RCA Victor SF 8366   OKLAHOMA CRUDE (LP, soundtrack) 15
73 RCA Victor SF 8379   VISIONS OF EIGHT (LP, soundtrack) 12
73 Elektra K 46239   THE THIEF WHO CAME TO DINNER (LP, soundtrack) 18
74 RCA Victor APL 1 0270   COUNTRY GENTLEMEN (LP, soundtrack) 12
75 RCA Red Seal RS 1010   THE RETURN OF THE PINK PANTHER (LP, soundtrack) 18
75 MCA MCF 2707   THE GREAT WALDO PEPPER (LP, soundtrack) 15
76 United Artists UAS 30012   THE PINK PANTHER STRIKES AGAIN (LP, soundtrack). 15

MANDALABAND
75 Chrysalis CHR 1095   MANDALABAND (LP) 15
78 Chrysalis CHR 1181   THE EYE OF WENDOR: PROPHECIES (LP, with booklet). 12

HARVEY MANDEL
74 Janus 6146 024   Uno Ino/Shangrenade 6
68 Philips SBL 7873   CRISTO REDENTOR (LP) 25
69 Philips SBL 7904   RIGHTEOUS (LP). 20
70 Philips SBL 7915   GAMES GUITARS PLAY (LP) 15
71 Dawn DNLS 3015   BABY BATTER (LP). 20
71 Philips 6336 009   CRISTO REDENTOR (LP, reissue) 12
72 London SH-O 8426   GET OFF IN CHICAGO (LP) 12
72 Janus 6310 210   THE SNAKE (LP) 15
73 Janus 6499 831   SHANGRENADE (LP) 12
(see also Canned Heat, Dewey Terry)

NELSON MANDELA
64 Ember CEL 905   WHY I'M READY TO DIE (LP, spoken word, narrated by Peter Finch). 25

MANDINGO
73 EMI EMI 2014   Medicine Man/Black Rite 15
73 EMI EMC 3010   MANDINGO 1: SACRIFICE (LP) 15
73 Studio Two TWO 400   MANDINGO 2: PRIMEVAL RHYTHM OF LIFE (LP) 18
73 Studio Two Q4TWO 400   MANDINGO 2: PRIMEVAL RHYTHM OF LIFE (LP, quadrophonic) 15
75 EMI EMC 3038   MANDINGO 3: STORY OF SURVIVAL (LP) 15
77 EMI EMC 3217   MANDINGO 4: SAVAGE RITE (LP) 15
(see also Geoff Love, Manuel & Music Of The Mountains)

MANDRAGORA
86 SAB 01   OVER THE MOON (LP) 30
91 Resonance 33-9133   HEAD FIRST (LP) 12

MANDRAKE
60 Philips PB 1093   Mandrake/The Witch's Twist 10
61 Philips BF 1153   Thank Goodness It's Friday/Queen Of Sheba 7

MANDRAKE MEMORIAL
69 RCA SF 8028   MEDIUM (LP) 35
70 RCA/Poppy PYS 11003   PUZZLE (LP) 40

MINT VALUE £

MANDRAKE PADDLE STEAMERS
69	Parlophone R 5780	Strange Walking Man/Steam	80
88	Bam Caruso NRIC 033	Strange Walking Man/Steam (reissue, gatefold p/s)	12

(see also Liverpool Echo)

MANDRILL
73	Polydor 2066 320	Mandrill/Hang Loose	8
73	Polydor 2066 357	Fencewalk/Polk Street Carnival	8
70	Polydor 2489 028	MANDRILL (LP)	15
72	Polydor 2391 030	MANDRILL IS (LP)	15
73	Polydor 2391 061	COMPOSITE TRUTH (LP)	15
73	Polydor 2391 092	JUST OUTSIDE OF TOWN (LP)	20

MANDY (SMITH)
87	PWL PWLP 1	I Just Can't Wait/Instrumental/You're Never Alone (12" picture disc)	15
88	PWL PWCD 11	Boys & Girls/Mandy's Theme (I Just Can't Wait) (The Cool & Breezy Jazz Mix)/He's My Boy (3" CD)	20
88	PWL PWCD 18	Victim Of Pleasure (Red Rooster Mix)/Say It's Love/Victim Of Pleasure (Instrumental) (3" CD)	20
88	PWL HFCD 2	MANDY (CD)	35

MANEATERS
82	Editions EG EGO 8	Nine To Five/SUZI PINNS: Jerusalem (withdrawn 'Adam & Toyah' p/s)	100
82	Editions EG EGO 8	Nine To Five/SUZI PINNS: Jerusalem (title p/s)	5

(see also Adam & The Ants)

MAN FRIDAY & JIVE JUNIOR
83	Malaco MAL 011	Picking Up Sounds/Picking Up Sounds (Radio Mix) (p/s, features John Deacon)	30
83	Malaco MAL 1211	Picking Up Sounds (Extended)/Picking Up Sounds (Radio Mix) (12", p/s, features John Deacon)	50

(see also Queen)

MAN FROM DELMONTE
87	Ugly Man UGLY 3	Drive Drive Drive/Twenty Two And Still In Love With You/Sun Serious (p/s)	6
87	Ugly Man UGLY 5T	Water In My Eyes/Bred By You (12", p/s)	18
88	Ugly Man UGLY 7T	Will Nobody Save Louise/Good Things In Life/Like A Millionaire (12", p/s)	40
89	Bop Cassettes BIP 502	WAITING FOR ANN (12" EP)	15

MANHATTANS
65	Sue WI 384	I Wanna Be (Your Everything)/Searchin' For My Baby	40
66	Carnival CAR 100	Baby I Need You/Teach Me (The Philly Dog)	20
66	Carnival CAR 101	That New Girl/Can I	20
74	CBS 2117	Soul Train/I'm Not A Run Around	6
73	London SHB 8449	A MILLION TO ONE (LP)	30
76	CBS 81513	THE MANHATTANS (LP)	12
78	CBS 81828	IT FEELS GOOD (LP)	12

MANIACS
77	United Artists UP 36327	Chelsea 1977/Ain't No Legend (p/s)	12

(see also Rings, Physicals)

MANIAX
66	White Label WLR 101/102	Out Of Reach/The Devil's Home	12

MANIC JABS
81	Waldo's MS 009	Autophagus/The Injuns Are Comin'/Thing Wild (p/s)	6

MANIC STREET PREACHERS
SINGLES
88	SBS SBS 002	Suicide Alley/Tennessee (I Get Low) (hand-made p/s with press-cuttings glued to plain card cover)	750
88	SBS SBS 002	Suicide Alley/Tennessee (I Get Low) (blue p/s, 200 only)	600
88	SBS SBS 002	Suicide Alley/Tennessee (I Get Low) (no p/s, 100 only)	300
90	(No Cat. No.)	UK Channel Boredom/LAURENS: I Don't Know What The Trouble Is (p/s flexidisc, some free with *Hopelessly Devoted* or *Goldmining* fanzine; later 're-pressed')	60/45
90	Damaged Goods YUBB 4	NEW ART RIOT EP: New Art Riot/Strip It Down/Last Exit On Yesterday/Teenage 20/20 (12", white label, 100 copies, plain sleeves rubber-stamped with "Made In Wales")	35
90	Damaged Goods YUBB 4	NEW ART RIOT EP: New Art Riot/Strip It Down/Last Exit On Yesterday/Teenage 20/20 (12" EP, p/s, 1st 1,000 black & white label, 2nd 1,000 black-on-yellow; later red, orange & silver & green)	18/15/12
91	Damaged Goods YUBB 004P	NEW ART RIOT EP: New Art Riot/Strip It Down/Last Exit On Yesterday/Teenage 20/20 (12" EP, p/s, reissue on pink vinyl)	25
91	Heavenly HVN 812	Motown Junk/Sorrow 16/We Her Majesty's Prisoners (12", withdrawn p/s)	40
91	Heavenly HVN 8CD	Motown Junk/Sorrow 16/We Her Majesty's Prisoners (CD, withdrawn sleeve)	80
91	Heavenly HVN 10	You Love Us/Spectators Of Suicide (p/s)	20
91	Heavenly HVN 1012	You Love Us/Spectators Of Suicide/Starlover/Strip It Down (live) (12", p/s)	20
91	Heavenly HVN 10CD	You Love Us/Spectators Of Suicide/Starlover/Strip It Down (live) (CD)	25
91	Columbia 657337 6	Stay Beautiful/R.P. McMurphy/Soul Contamination (12", p/s)	10
91	Columbia 657337 8	Stay Beautiful/R.P. McMurphy/Soul Contamination (12", stickered poster p/s)	10
91	Columbia 657582 6	Repeat (U.K.)/Love's Sweet Exile/Democracy Coma (12", p/s)	10
91	Columbia 657582 8	Repeat/Democracy Coma/Love's Sweet Exile/Stay Beautiful (live) (12", gatefold, stickered p/s)	12
91	Caff CAFF 15	FEMININE IS BEAUTIFUL: Repeat After Me/New Art Riot (p/s, 500 only)	125
92	Columbia 657724 6	You Love Us/A Vision Of Dead Desire/It's So Easy (live) (12" gatefold p/s)	10
92	Columbia 657873 7	Slash'N'Burn/Motown Junk (poster p/s)	6
92	Columbia 657873 6	Slash'N'Burn/Motown Junk/Ain't Goin' Down (12", with print, stickered p/s)	12
92	Columbia 657873 2	Slash'N'Burn/Motown Junk/Ain't Goin' Down (gold CD, digipak)	15
92	Columbia 658083 6	Motorcycle Emptiness/Bored Out Of My Mind/Under My Wheels (12", picture disc, stickered PVC sleeve)	15

92	Damaged Goods YUBB 4CD	New Art Riot/Strip It Down/Last Exit On Yesterday/Teenage 20/20 (CD, picture disc, reissue, 3,000 only)	10
92	Columbia 658382 7	Theme From M*A*S*H EP (Suicide Is Painless)/FATIMA MANSIONS: "Everything I Do (I Do It For You)" (poster p/s)	6
92	Columbia 658382 6	Theme From M*A*S*H EP (Suicide Is Painless)/FATIMA MANSIONS: "Everything I Do (I Do It For You)"/Sleeping With The NME (12", p/s)	8
93	Columbia 659727 6	From Despair To Where/Hibernation/Spectators Of Suicide (Heavenly Version) (12", p/s)	8
93	Columbia 659477 6	La Tristesse Durera/Patrick Bateman/Repeat (live)/Tennessee (12", poster p/s)	8
96	Columbia 663070	A Design For Life/Bright Eyes (jukebox issue, no p/s)	5
96	Columbia 663468	Everything Must Go/Raindrops Keep Falling On My Head (Live Acoustic Version) (jukebox issue, no p/s)	5
96	Columbia 664044	Australia/A Design For Life (Live City Hall Sheffield) (jukebox issue, no p/s)	5
97	Columbia MANIC 1-6CD	SIX SINGLES FROM GENERATION TERRORISTS (6-CD box set)	90

PROMOS & MISC. RELEASES

91	Heavenly HVN 10P	You Love Us (Radio Edit) (promo only, some with stickered p/s, 1-sided white label, 500 only)	30
92	Columbia XPCD 171	GENERATION TERRORISTS (CD, 5-track sampler, digipak)	15
92	Columbia XPCD 185	Motorcycle Emptiness/Motorcycle Emptiness (Radio Edit) (CD)	18
93	Columbia XPCD 285	GOLD AGAINST THE SOUL (CD, 4-track sampler, digipak)	20
93	Columbia/Damont XPS 272	Symphony Of Tourette (1-sided, white label, no p/s)	70
94	Columbia	DONE AND DUSTED (12", Chemical Brothers remixes)	20
96	Columbia XPR 3043	A Design For Life (Stealth Sonic Orchestra Remix)/(Instrumental) (12")	20
96	Columbia XPR 3049	Kevin Carter (Stealth Sonic Orchestra Remix) (12", white label, 1-sided, stickered card sleeve, 30 only)	30
96	Columbia XPR 3094	Australia (Lionrock Remix) (12", white label, 1-sided, stickered card sleeve, 20 only)	60
99	Epic XPR 3320	Tsunami (Cornelius Remix)/(Electron Ray Tube Mix by Stereolab) (12", p/s, sealed with sticker, promo only)	10

ALBUMS

92	Columbia 471060 9	GENERATION TERRORISTS (2-LP, picture discs, inner sleeves, 5,000 only)	30
92	Columbia 471060 0	GENERATION TERRORISTS (CD, picture disc, 5,000 only)	40
93	Columbia 4740649 1	GOLD AGAINST THE SOUL (LP, picture disc, inner sleeve, in custom carrier-bag)	15
93	Columbia 4740649 2	GOLD AGAINST THE SOUL (gold CD)	20
94	Epic 477421 9	THE HOLY BIBLE (LP, picture disc)	20
94	Epic 4774212	THE HOLY BIBLE (CD, picture disc)	20
98	Epic 4917031	THIS IS MY TRUTH TELL ME YOURS (LP, picture disc)	18
03	Sony 5123861	LIPSTICK TRACES (3 x LP, 1,000 only, with tactile sleeve)	45

MANICURED NOISE

80	Pre PRE 003	Metronome/Moscow (die-cut p/s with postcard)	5
80	Pre PRE 006	Faith/Free Time (p/s)	5

(see also Weatherman & Friends)

MANIFESTO

80s	Fire BLAZE 66055	Pattern 26 (1-sided white/label in bag with biography)	5

MANISH BOYS

65	Parlophone R 5250	I Pity The Fool/Take My Tip	800+

(see also David Bowie)

MANISH BOYS/DAVY JONES & LOWER THIRD

79	EMI EMI 2925	I Pity The Fool/Take My Tip/DAVY JONES & LOWER THIRD: You've Got A Habit Of Leaving/Baby Loves That Way (p/s)	10
82	Charly CYM 1	I Pity The Fool/Take My Tip/DAVY JONES & LOWER THIRD: You've Got A Habit Of Leaving/Baby Loves That Way (10", p/s, reissue)	7

(see also David Bowie, Davy Jones, Davie Jones & King Bees)

MANITOBA

70	RCA 2016	You'll Never Get Back/Something In You	10

EARLE MANKEY

78	Bronze BRO 53	Mau Mau/Crazy	10

MAN MACHINE

90	Outer Rhythm MMAN 2T	ZEN EP (12")	10
91	Outer Rhythm MMAN 3T	Animal (Primeaval Interface)/Shout (The Communicator)/Shout (Primary Contact) (12")	10

BARRY MANN

61	HMV POP 911	Who Put The Bomp/Love True Love	30
61	HMV POP 949	Little Miss U.S.A./Find Another Fool	20
62	HMV POP 1084	Hey Baby I'm Dancin'/Like I Don't Love You	18
63	HMV POP 1108	Bless You/Teenage Has Been	18
64	Colpix PX 776	Talk To Me Baby/Amy	15
66	Capitol CL 15463	Angelica/Looking At Tomorrow	15
68	Capitol CL 15538	The Young Electric Psychedelic Hippy Flippy Folk And Funky Philosophic Turned On Groovy 12 String Band/Take Your Love	10
63	HMV CLP 1559	WHO PUT THE BOMP IN THE BOMP BOMP BOMP? (LP)	210

CARL MANN

59	London HLS 8935	Mona Lisa/Foolish One (78 rpm = £90)	30
59	London HLS 9006	Pretend/Rockin' Love (78 rpm = £160)	30
60	London HLS 9170	South Of The Border/I'm Comin' Home	25
60	London HA-S 2277	LIKE MANN — CARL MANN SINGS (LP)	325

CHARLES MANN

73	Probe PRO 585	Say You Love Me Too/I Can Feel It	5

GARY MANN ORCHESTRA

73	Penny Farthing PEN 820	The Original 'Big Match' Theme/Newscoop (The Original 'Grandstand' Theme)	10

GEOFF MANN

84	Food For Thought GRUB 4	I MAY SING GRACE (LP)	12
85	Wobbly WOB 1	PSALM ENCHANTED EVENING (LP)	12

GLORIA MANN

56	Brunswick 05569	Why Do Fools Fall In Love/Partners For Life (78 rpm = £10)	20
56	Brunswick 05610	It Happened Again/My Secret Sin	15

HERBIE MANN

66	Atlantic 584 052	Philly Dog/DAVE PIKE: Sunny	8
68	A&M AMS 719	Unchain My Heart/Glory Of Love	10
69	Atlantic 584 297	Memphis Underground/New Orleans	10
72	Atlantic K 10179	Philly Dog/Memphis Underground/It's A Funky Thing	6
75	Atlantic K 10580	Hijack/Orient Express	6
56	London EZN 19006	EAST COAST JAZZ NO. 4 PT. 1 (EP)	10
58	Fontana TFE 17113	HERBIE MANN (EP)	10
59	Columbia Clef SEB 10102	MAGIC FLUTE OF HERBIE MANN (EP)	10
58	Fontana TFL 5013	SALUTE TO THE FLUTE (LP)	15
60	Top Rank 25/015	FLUTE FOR ETERNITY (10" LP, with Buddy Collette)	15
63	London HA-K/SH-K 8043	RIGHT NOW (LP)	15
64	Atlantic ATL 5008	HERBIE MANN AT NEWPORT (LP)	15
65	Atlantic ATL/SAL 5035	THE ROAR OF THE GREASE PAINT (LP)	15
66	CBS (S)BPG 62585	LATIN MANN (LP)	12
66	Atlantic ATL/SAL 5038	STANDING OVATION AT NEWPORT (LP)	15
66	Atlantic 587/588 003	MONDAY NIGHT AT THE VILLAGE GATE (LP)	15
66	Atlantic 587/588 028	NIRVANA (LP, with Bill Evans)	15
67	Atlantic 1471	NEW MANN AT NEWPORT (LP)	12
67	Atlantic 587/588 054	HERBIE MANN AT THE VILLAGE GATE (LP)	12
67	Atlantic Special 590 013	FREE FOR ALL (LP)	12
68	Atlantic 1475	IMPRESSIONS OF THE MIDDLE EAST (LP)	12
68	Atlantic 1490	THE HERBIE MANN STRING ALBUM (LP)	12
69	Solid State USS 7007	ST. THOMAS (LP)	12
69	Atlantic 588 156	INSPIRATION I FEEL (LP)	12
69	A&M AMLS 944	GLORY OF LOVE (LP)	12
69	Atlantic 588 200	MEMPHIS UNDERGROUND (LP)	12
69	SRCP 3002	AFRO-JAZZIAC (LP)	12

LORIE MANN

59	Top Rank JAR 116	A Penny A Kiss, A Penny A Hug/Dream Lover (78 rpm = £10)	7
59	Top Rank JAR 148	Just Keep It Up/You Made Me Care (78 rpm = £10)	10
59	Top Rank JAR 237	So Many Ways/I Wonder	7

MANFRED MANN

63	HMV POP 1189	Why Should We Not/Brother Jack	25
63	HMV POP 1225	Cock-A-Hoop/Now You're Needing Me	22
64	HMV POP 1252	5-4-3-2-1/Without You	8
64	HMV POP 1282	Hubble Bubble (Toil And Trouble)/I'm Your Kingpin	8
64	HMV POP 1320	Do Wah Diddy Diddy/What You Gonna Do?	5
64	HMV POP 1346	Sha La La/John Hardy	5
65	HMV POP 1381	Come Tomorrow/What Did I Do Wrong?	5
65	HMV POP 1413	Oh No Not My Baby/What Am I Doing Wrong	5
65	HMV POP 1466	If You Gotta Go, Go Now/Stay Around	5
66	HMV POP 1523	Pretty Flamingo/You're Standing By	6
66	HMV POP 1541	You Gave Me Somebody To Love/Poison Ivy	12
65	HMV 7TEA 2124	There's No Living Without Your Loving/Tired Of Trying, Bored With Lying, Scared Of Dying (demo-only EP sampler)	30
66	Fontana TF 730	Just Like A Woman/I Wanna Be Rich	5
66	Fontana TF 757	Semi-Detached, Suburban Mr. James/Morning After The Party	5
67	Fontana TF 812	Ha! Ha! Said The Clown/Feeling So Good (in p/s)	8
67	Fontana TF 828	Sweet Pea/One Way	7
67	Fontana TF 862	So Long, Dad/Funniest Gig	7
68	Fontana TF 897	Mighty Quinn/By Request — Edwin Garvey	5
68	Fontana TF 908	Up The Junction/Sleepy Hollow (some in p/s)	15/6
68	Fontana TF 943	My Name Is Jack/There Is A Man	5
68	Fontana TF 985	Fox On The Run/Too Many People	5
69	Fontana TF 1013	Ragamuffin Man/A 'B' Side	5
64	HMV 7EG 8848	MANFRED MANN'S COCK-A-HOOP WITH 54321 (EP)	25
65	HMV 7EG 8876	GROOVIN' WITH MANFRED MANN (EP)	20
65	HMV 7EG 8908	THE ONE IN THE MIDDLE (EP)	20
65	HMV 7EG 8922	NO LIVING WITHOUT LOVING (EP)	20
66	HMV 7EG 8942	MACHINES (EP)	25
66	HMV 7EG 8949	INSTRUMENTAL ASYLUM (EP, with Jack Bruce)	30
66	HMV 7EG 8962	AS WAS (EP)	25
66	Fontana TE 17483	INSTRUMENTAL ASSASSINATION (EP)	10
64	HMV CLP 1731	THE FIVE FACES OF MANFRED MANN (LP)	25
65	HMV CLP 1911/CSD 1628	MANN MADE (LP, mono/stereo)	35/40
66	HMV CLP 3559	MANN MADE HITS (LP)	30
66	HMV TA-CLP 3559	MANN MADE HITS (reel-to-reel tape, mono)	12
66	Fontana (S)TL 5377	AS IS (LP, 'alcove' cover, mono/stereo)	20/30
66	Fontana (S)TL 5377	AS IS (LP, 'locomotive' cover, mono/stereo)	35/45
67	HMV CLP/CSD 3594	SOUL OF MANN (LP, mono/stereo)	40/50
67	HMV TA-CLP 3594	SOUL OF MANN (reel-to-reel tape, mono)	12

68	Fontana (S)TL 5460	UP THE JUNCTION — ORIGINAL SOUNDTRACK RECORDING (LP)	40
68	Fontana SFL 13003	WHAT A MANN (LP)	20
68	Fontana (S)TL 5470	MIGHTY GARVEY! (LP, mono/stereo)	30/15
70	Fontana 6852 005	UP THE JUNCTION — ORIGINAL SOUNDTRACK RECORDING (LP, reissue)	12

(see also Paul Jones, Blues Band, Mike Hugg, Henry Lowther, Mike D'Abo, McGuinness Flint, Jack Bruce, Coulson & Dean, Lyn Dobson, Paddy Klaus & Gibson)

MANFRED MANN & MIKE HUG(G)

71	Ski SKI 1	Ski 'Full-Of-Fitness' Theme/Baby Jane (some in p/s)	15/7
71	Michelin MIC+01	The Michelin Theme (Go Radial, Go Michelin) (1-sided, gatefold p/s)	15

MANFRED MANN'S CHAPTER III

70	Vertigo 6059 012	Happy Being Me/Devil Woman	10
69	Vertigo VO 3	MANFRED MANN CHAPTER III (LP, gatefold sleeve, swirl label)	45
70	Vertigo 6360 012	MANFRED MANN CHAPTER III VOL. 2 (LP, gatefold sleeve, swirl label)	45

MANFRED MANN'S EARTH BAND

70	Lyntone LYN 1981	The Maxwell House Shake (1-sided flexidisc)	8
71	Philips 6006 122	Living Without You/Tribute (as Manfred Mann)	6
71	Philips 6006 159	Mrs Henry/Prayer (as Manfred Mann)	6
72	Philips 6006 251	Meat/Glorified Magnified (as Earth Band)	6
73	Vertigo 6059 078	Get Your Rocks Off/Sadjoy (as Earth Band)	7
79	Bronze BPO 77	Don't Kill It Carol/Blinded By The Light (picture disc)	7
71	Philips 6308 062	STEPPING SIDEWAYS (LP, unissued)	
72	Philips 6308 086	MANFRED MANN'S EARTH BAND (LP)	20
72	Philips 6308 125	GLORIFIED MAGNIFIED (LP)	25
73	Vertigo 6360 087	MESSIN' (LP)	20

(see also Skeleton Crew)

SHADOW MANN

69	Roulette RO 504	Come Live With Me/One By One	12

SHELLY MANNE

68	Atlantic 584 180	Daktari/Out On A Limb	8
54	Vogue LDE 072	SHELLY MANNE AND HIS MEN VOL. 1 (10" LP)	15
55	Contemporary LDC 143	SHELLY MANNE VOL. 2 (10" LP, with Andre Previn & Leroy Vinegar)	15
56	Contemporary LDC 190	SHELLY MANNE, SHORTY ROGERS AND JIMMY GIUFFRE — THE THREE (10" LP)	15
56	Contemporary LDC 192	SHELLY MANNE AND RUSS FREEMAN (10" LP)	15
56	Contemporary LAC 12075	SHELLY MANNE AND HIS FRIENDS (LP, with Andre Previn & Leroy Vinegar)	15
56	Contemporary LAC 12100	MY FAIR LADY (LP)	15
57	Contemporary LAC 12148	SHELLY MANNE AND HIS MEN VOL. 5 (LP)	12
57	Contemporary LAC 12232	SHELLY MANNE AND HIS MEN VOL. 6 (LP)	12
61	Contemporary LAC 12250	AT THE BLACK HAWK VOL. 1 (LP, also stereo SCA 5015)	12
61	Contemporary LAC 12255	AT THE BLACK HAWK VOL. 2 (LP, also stereo SCA 5016)	12
61	Contemporary LAC 12260	AT THE BLACK HAWK VOL. 3 (LP, also stereo SCA 5017)	12
61	Contemporary LAC 12265	AT THE BLACK HAWK VOL. 4 (LP, also stereo SCA 5018)	12
61	Contemporary LAC 12293	THE PROPER TIME (LP, soundtrack)	15
61	Contemporary LAC 12305/6	AT THE MANNE HOLE (2-LP)	18
65	Stateside SL 10125	SHELLY MANNE AND CO. (LP)	12

(see also Gerry Mulligan & Shelly Manne, Shorty Rogers & His Orchestra)

MANNIN FOLK

76	Kelly MAN 2	KING OF THE SEA (LP)	35
70s	Kelly KEP 1	MANNIN FOLK SING (LP)	20

BOB MANNING

54	Capitol CL 14190	I'm A Fool For You/It's All Right With Me	8
55	Capitol CL 14220	The Very Thought Of You/Just For Laughs	8
55	Capitol CL 14256	Majorca (Isle Of Love)/It's My Life	8
55	Capitol CL 14234	My Love Song To You/After My Laughter Came Tears	8
55	Capitol CL 14288	The Mission San Michel/You Are There	8
55	Capitol CL 14318	What A Wonderful Way To Die/Why Didn't You Tell Me?	8

LINDA MANNING

66	King KG 1039	Buy Me Something Pretty, Joey/Downtown Lonely Girl Blues	7

MARTY MANNING & CHEETAHS

67	CBS 2721	Tarzan March/Sunny	12

MICHAEL MANNING

03	Ai Al 007	THE LOST ABERRANT DRAGONFLY EP (12", p/s)	8

EDDIE MANNION

60	HMV POP 804	Just Driftin'/Quiet Girl	50

WINGY MANONE ORCHESTRA

57	Brunswick 05655	Party Doll/Real Gone (78 rpm = £12)	20

MAN ON THE MOON

69	Philips 88457 DE	MAN ON THE MOON (EP, spoken word, 2-part tri-foldout p/s with insert, 'historic souvenir' available via *News Of The World* newspaper)	8

MAN OR ASTROMAN

96	One Louder LOUDER 12	EXPERIMENTAL ZERO (LP, yellow vinyl, with poster)	15

MANOWAR

83	M. F. Nations 12 KUT 102	Defender (featuring Orson Welles)/Gloves Of Metal (12", p/s)	15
84	10 TEN 3012	All Men Play On 10/Mountains (12", p/s, some gatefold)	18/12
87	Atlantic B 9463	Blow Your Speakers/Violence And Bloodshed (p/s)	7
87	Atlantic BT 9463	Blow Your Speakers/Violence And Bloodshed (12", embossed p/s, some with poster)	12/8

(see also Orson Welles)

JOE MANSANO
69	Blue Cat BS 150	Life On Reggae Planet/RECO & RHYTHM ACES: Z.Z. Beat	30
72	Sioux SI 022	The Trial Of Pama Dice/JACKIE ROWLAND: Lonely Man.	20
70	Trojan TBL 106	BRIXTON CAT (LP)	30

(see also Joe The Boss, Joe's Allstars, Dice The Boss)

TONY MANSELL
54	Parlophone MSP 6130	The High And The Mighty/Hold My Hand (with Johnny Dankworth Orchestra). . . .	8
56	Parlophone MSP 6222	Zambesi (Sweet African)/11th Hour Melody (with Johnny Dankworth Orchestra). .	8
58	Parlophone R 4471	Impossible/Who Are They To Say	6

(see also Johnny Dankworth)

KEITH MANSFIELD ORCHESTRA
68	CBS 3895	Beautiful//Soul Thing	15
68	CBS 63426	ALL YOU NEED IS KEITH MANSFIELD (LP).	35
69	CBS 64666	RACE ON THE WIND (LP).	12
70	CBS 70073	LOOT (LP, soundtrack, with Steve Ellis).	60

JAYNE MANSFIELD
67	London HL 10147	As The Clouds Drift By/Suey (with Jimi Hendrix, demos more common, £35) . . .	50

(see also Jimi Hendrix)

CHARLES MANSON
86	Fierce FRIGHT 006	Rise/Sick City (p/s, 1 side etched, handwritten labels).	25
88	Fierce FRIGHT 012	It's Comin' Down Fast (Helter Skelter) (p/s, 1 side etched, hand-made labels) . . .	25
86	Fierce FRIGHT 001	LOVE AND TERROR CULT (LP).	40

EDDY MANSON
55	HMV 7M 325	Oh! No!/The Lovers.	10

JEANE MANSON
79	CBS S CBS 7222	I've Already Seen It In Your Eyes/J'ai Deja Vu Ca Dans Tes Yeux	15

MARILYN MANSON
97	Interscope INVP 95541	The Horrible People/The Not So Beautiful People (10" picture disc)	10
97	Interscope INVP 95552	Tourniquet/(remix) (10" picture disc)	10
97	Interscope INDX 95552	Tourniquet/Lunchbox/Next MF (CD)	8
98	Nothing INVP 95610	The Dope Show/The Dope Show (10" picture disc, same track on both sides). . .	10
99	Interscope SAM 175 CD	I Don't Like Drugs (But The Drugs Like Me) (Radio Edit)/(Album Version) (CD, card sleeve, promo only).	10
00	Nothing/Universe 4974581	Disposable Teens/Five To One/Diamonds & Pollen (12" picture disc, PVC sl.) . .	10
01	Universal 4974911	The Fight Song/(Slipknot Remix)/(Love Song Remix) (12" picture disc, stickered sleeve)	10
03	Universal 9807728	Mobscene/Paranoiac (poster p/s)	5
03	Universal 9810794	This Is The New Shit/(Goldfrapp Version) (10" picture disc)	10
95	Simply Vinyl SVLP 208	SMELLS LIKE CHILDREN (LP, 180 gm vinyl)	18
96	Interscope IND 90086	ANTICHRIST SUPERSTAR (CD, in slipcase)	18
98	Simply Vinyl SVLP 195	MECHANICAL ANIMALS (2-LP, 180 gm vinyl)	20
98	Interscope IND 90273	MECHANICAL ANIMALS (CD, in slipcase)	18
99	Interscope ADV 490 394-2	MECHANICAL ANIMALS (CD, promo, no'd, card sl., with comic, PVC slipcase). .	40
02	Simply Vinyl SVLP 055	ANTICHRIST SUPERSTAR (2-LP, 180 gm vinyl, gatefold sleeve).	20

MANSUN
95	Polygram no cat. no.	Take It Easy Chicken (Demo)/Naked Twister/Drastic Sturgeon (cassette, promo only, with title inlay)	70
95	Sci Fi Hi Fi MANSON 1	Take It Easy Chicken/Take It Easy Chicken (as Manson, same track both sides, die-cut sleeve, 500 only; promos with "Manson Promo" on label £60)	50
95	Regal REG 3	Skin Up Pin Up/Flourella (white vinyl)	18
95	Regal REG 3CD	Skin Up Pin Up/Flourella (CD, PVC sleeve with barcode sticker)	28
96	Parlophone R 6447	Stripper Vicar/No One Knows Us (clear vinyl, p/s)	10
96	Parlophone CDRS 6447	Stripper Vicar/The Edge/Duchess (CD, card p/s with poster)	12
96	Parlophone CDR 6447	Stripper Vicar/An Open Letter/No One Knows Us/Things Keep Falling Off (CD). .	15
96	Parlophone R 6453	Wide Open Space/Rebel Without A Quilt (white vinyl, foldout p/s in PVC sleeve). .	10
96	Parlophone CDR 6453	Wide Open Space/Rebel Without A Quilt/Vision Impaired/ Skin Up, Pin Up (CD, digipak)	20
96	Parlophone CDRS 6453	Wide Open Space/The Gods Of Not Very Much/Moronica (Acoustic Version)/ Lemonade Secret Drinker (Acoustic Version) (CD, fold-out card p/s).	25
97	Parlophone R 6458	She Makes My Nose Bleed/The Holy Blood And The Holy Grail (red vinyl, fold out sleeve)	7
97	Parlophone R 6482	Closed For Business/Egg Shaped Fred (Acoustic Version) (clear vinyl, p/s, with insert)	7
98	EMI R 6497	Legacy/GSOH/Can't Afford To Die (p/s)	7
99	fan club MANSUN 001	Taxloss/Everyone Must Win (live) (fan club-only release)	35
98	Parlophone R 6508	Negative/Mansun's Only Live Song (clear vinyl, PVC sleeve, picture insert).	5
96	Parlophone R 6430	ONE EP (p/s)	18
96	Parlophone CDRS 6430	ONE EP (CD)	22
96	Parlophone CDR 6437	TWO EP (p/s)	15
96	Parlophone CDR 6437	TWO EP (CD)	15
97	Parlophone CDRS 6482	SEVEN EP (CD, digipak with poster).	10
98	Parlophone R 6487	EIGHT EP (p/s, red vinyl)	8
99	Parlophone R 6511	SIX EP (clear vinyl, p/s)	8
97	Parlophone CPCS 7387	ATTACK OF THE GREY LANTERN (2-LP, gatefold sleeve, with inners and poster) .	30

JOHN MANTELL
65	CBS 201783	Remember Child/I'll See You Around	30

MIKE MANTLER
75	Watt WATT 3	13¾ (LP, with Carla Bley; with insert)	15

(see also Carla Bley, Jazz Composers Orchestra)

BOB MANTON
81   Mainstreet MS 101   No Trees In Brixton Prison/Brixton Walkabout (p/s) 8
(see also Purple Hearts)

MANTOVANI (ORCHESTRA)
53   Decca F 10168   Swedish Rhapsody/Jamaican Rumba (gold or silver label lettering) 15/8

MANUEL & MUSIC OF THE MOUNTAINS
78   EMI EMI 2743   Princess Leia's Theme From Star Wars/Mountain Fire 5
(see also Geoff Love, Mandingo)

MANUFACTURED ROMANCE
81   Fresh FRESH 16   The Time Of My Life/Room To Breathe (various colours of p/s) 5

PHIL MANZANERA (& 801)
77   Polydor 2001 733   Flight 19/Car Rhumba 5
(see also Roxy Music, Quiet Sun, 801)

RAY MANZAREK
74   Mercury SRM 1703   THE WHOLE THING STARTED WITH ROCK'N'ROLL (LP) 12
83   A&M AMLX 64945   CARMINA BURANA (LP, with Philip Glass) 12
(see also Doors, Philip Glass)

MAPLEOAK
70   Decca F 13008   Son Of A Gun/Hurt Me So Much 20
71   Decca SKL 5085   MAPLEOAK (LP) 200

LUCILLE MAPP
57   Columbia DB 3916   Mangos/On Treasure Island 10
57   Columbia DB 3949   Jamie Boy/Moonlight In Vermont 8
57   Columbia DB 4040   I'm Available/Lovin' Ya, Lovin' Ya, Lovin' Ya 10
58   Columbia DB 4071   Love Is/The Early Birdie 8
58   Columbia DB 4168   Remember When/I'm A Dreamer, Aren't We All? 7
59   Columbia DB 4261   Chinchilla/Follow Me 15
57   Columbia SEG 7726   STREET OF DREAMS (EP) 15
57   Columbia SEG 7773   LUCILLE MAPP (EP) 15

TOMMY MARA
55   MGM SP 1128   Pledging My Love/Honey Bunch (78 rpm = £8) 10
58   Felsted AF 109   Where The Blues Of The Night/What Makes You So Lonely 10
59   Felsted AF 116   You Don't Know/Marie (78 rpm = £8) 7
59   Felsted AF 123   Until I Hear From You/Now Is The Hour (78 rpm = £10) 7
58   Felsted GEP 1003   PRESENTING TOMMY MARA (EP) 20

MARABAR CAVES
85   Tiki MBAR 1   Sally's Place Crew/Seeds That Never Grew 15

(JOSEPH) MARAIS & MIRANDA
53   Columbia SCM 5025   Old Johnnie Goggabie/The Zulu Warrior 5
59   Fontana H 225   I-Ha-She/The Queen Bee (as Marais & Miranda) (78 rpm = £8) 5

MARATHONS
61   Pye International 7N 25088   Peanut Butter/Down In New Orleans 28
61   Vogue V 9185   Peanut Butter/Talkin' Trash 25

MARAUDERS
63   Decca F 11695   That's What I Want/Hey What'd You Say 18
63   Decca F 11748   Always On My Mind/Heart Full Of Tears 12
64   Decca F 11836   Lucille/Little Egypt 15
65   Fontana TF 609   Baby I Wanna Be Loved/Somebody Told My Girl 12
(see also Danny Davis)

MARBLES
69   Polydor 56310   The Walls Fell Down/Love You 8
70   Polydor 56378   Breaking Up Is Hard To Do/I Can't See Nobody 6
(see also Graham Bonnet, Fut)

MARBLE STAIRCASE
83   Whaam! WHAAM 11   Still Dreaming/Dark Ages (p/s) 12

MARC & MAMBAS
82   Some Bizzare BZS 512   Fun City/Sleaze (Take It, Shake It)/Taking It And Shaking It
    (12", p/s, fan club issue, mail-order only) 20
82   Lyntone LYN 12505   Discipline (*Flexipop* flexidisc, clear or black vinyl, as Marc & Friends) 20/15
82   Some Bizzare BZS 15   Big Louise/Empty Eyes (unreleased, artwork only)
82   Some Bizzare BZS 1512   Big Louise/Empty Eyes/The Dirt Behind The Neon (Sleaze Revisited)
    (12", unreleased, artwork only)
83   Some Bizzare BZS 19   Black Heart/Your Aura (p/s, with postcard insert) 7
83   Some Bizzare BZS 1912   Black Heart/Your Aura/Mamba (12", p/s) 8
83   Some Bizzare BZSDJ 21   Torment/You'll Never See On Sunday (promo) 15
83   Some Bizzare BZS 2112   Torment/First Time/You'll Never See Me On A Sunday/
    Megamillionmania — Multimaniamix (12", p/s) 10
82   Some Bizzare B2A 4   UNTITLED (2-LP, gatefold sleeve) 15
83   Some Bizzare BZA 13   TORMENTS & TOREROS (2-LP) 15
84   Gutterhearts GH 1   BITE BLACK AND BLUES — RAOUL & THE RUINED LIVE
    (LP, fan club issue) 30

(see also Soft Cell, Marc Almond)

LYDIA MARCELLE
66   Sue WI 4025   Another Kind Of Fellow/I've Never Been Hurt Like This Before 45

MUZZY MARCELLINO
56   London HLU 8355   Mary Lou/MR. FORD & MR. GOON-BONES: Ain't She Sweet (78 rpm = £10) 40

MARCELS

61	Pye International 7N 25073	Blue Moon/Goodbye To Love.	8
61	Pye International 7N 25083	Summertime/Teeter Totter Love	12
61	Pye International 7N 25105	You Are My Sunshine/Find Another Fool	20
61	Pye International 7N 25114	Heartaches/My Love For You.	25
62	Pye International 7N 25124	My Melancholy Baby/Really Need Your Love.	40
63	Pye International 7N 25201	I Wanna Be The Leader/Give Me Back Your Love	30
61	Pye Intl. NPL 28016	BLUE MOON (LP)	160

(see also Tommy Regan)

GLORIA MARCH
58	London HLB 8568	Baby Of Mine/Nippon Wishing Well (78 rpm = £15).	25

HAL MARCH
58	London HLD 8534	Hear Me Good/One Dozen Roses (78 rpm = £15)	25

JO MARCH
58	London HLR 8696	Dormi, Dormi, Dormi (Sleep, Sleep, Sleep)/Fare Thee Well, Oh Honey.	12
58	London HLR 8696	Dormi, Dormi, Dormi (Sleep, Sleep, Sleep)/Fare Thee Well, Oh Honey (78).	12
58	London HLR 8763	The Virgin Mary Had One Son/I, Said The Donkey (78 rpm = £12)	10

(LITTLE) PEGGY MARCH
63	RCA RCA 1338	I Will Follow Him/Wind Up Doll (as Little Peggy March)	8
63	RCA RCA 1350	My Teenage Castle/I Wish I Were A Princess (as Little Peggy March)	8
63	RCA RCA 1362	Hello Heartache, Goodbye Love/Boy Crazy (as Little Peggy March)	8
64	RCA RCA 1426	Watch What You Do With My Baby/Can't Stop (as Little Peggy March)	8
65	RCA RCA 1472	Let Her Go/Your Girl	8
68	RCA RCA 1687	If You Loved Me/Thinking Through My Tears (DJ copy = £60).	30
68	RCA RCA 1752	I've Been Here Before/Time And Time Again.	6
69	RCA RCA 1809	What Am I Going To Do Without You/Lilac Skies	6

BOBBY MARCHAN
68	Atlantic 584 155	Get Down With It/Half A Mind.	6
69	Action ACT 4533	Ain't No Reason For Girls To Be Lonely Parts 1 & 2.	10

(see also Huey 'Piano' Smith & Clowns)

VICTOR MARCHESE
53	MGM SP 1018	Fandango/Flamingo	8

MARCH HARE
68	Chapter One CH 101	Cry My Heart/With My Eyes Closed	10
69	Deram DM 258	I Could Make It There With You/Have We Got News For You	7

(see also Gary & Stu, Koobas)

MARCHING GIRLS
81	Pop:Aural POP 011	True Love/First In Line (p/s).	5

MARCH VIOLETS
82	Merciful Release MR 013	Religious As Hell/Fodder/Children On Stun/Bon Bon Babies (p/s)	12
83	Merciful Release MR 017	Grooving In Green/Stream (p/s).	10
84	Rebirth RB 21	Snake Dance/Slow Drip Lizard (snakeskin-embossed stickered p/s with insert)	5

MARCIA & JEFF
68	Studio One SO 2047	Words/SHARKS: How Could I Live	32

MARCUS
76	United Artists UAS 30000	MARCUS (LP)	15

GUY MARDEL
65	Vogue VRS 7000	V'Avoue Jamais (actually "N'Avoue Jamais")/Si Tu N'y Crois Pas	5

JANIE MARDEN
55	Decca F 10600	Soldier Boy/Hard To Get.	12
55	Decca F 10605	I'll Come When You Call/Thank You For The Waltz (with Frank Weir & His Saxophone)	10
55	Decca F 10673	You Are My Love/A Teen Age Prayer	12
56	Decca F 10765	Allegheny Moon/Magic Melody	8
63	Piccadilly 7N 35128	Make The Night A Little Longer/Walk Alone	8
65	Decca F 12101	They Long To Be Close To You/This Empty Place	15
65	Decca F 12155	You Really Didn't Mean It/Only The One You Love	6

MARDEN HILL
86	él GPO 18	Curtain/Let's Make Shane & MacKenzie (p/s)	10
87	él GPO 30	Robe/Hangman (p/s)	10
93	Mo Wax MW 004	Come On/(Mixes) (12", die-cut stickered sleeve).	8

ARIF MARDIN
69	Atlantic 584 295	Glass Onion/How Can I Be Sure	7
73	Atlantic K10309	Theme From Brother Sun, Sister Moon/Yester Year	10

ERNIE MARESCA
62	London HLU 9531	Shout Shout/Crying Like A Baby Over You	18
62	London HLU 9579	Mary Jane/Down On The Beach	25
63	London HLU 9720	Love Express/Lorelei	18
64	London HLU 9834	Rovin' Kind/Please Be Fair.	15
65	London HLU 10008	It's Their World/I Can't Dance	15
66	Stateside SS 560	Rockin' Boulevard Street/Am I Better Off Than Them	20

MARGO & MARVETTES
64	Parlophone R 5154	Say You Will/Cherry Pie	18
64	Parlophone R 5227	Copper Kettle/So Fine.	15
67	Piccadilly 7N 35387	Seven Letters/That's How Love Goes.	12
67	Pye 7N 17423	When Love Slips Away/I'll Be Home (When You Call) (DJ copy = £75).	50

(see also Liza Dulittle)

MARGUERITA
64   Black Swan WI 431   Woman Come/ERIC MORRIS: Number One 40

CHARLES MARGULIS
59   London HLL 8774   Gigi/Malaguena (78 rpm = £10) 10

MARIANNE
68   Columbia DB 8420   As For Marionettes/You Know My Name 20
68   Columbia DB 8456   You Had Better Change Your Evil Ways/Like A See Saw 20

MARIANNE & MIKE
64   Vocalion V 9218   As He Once Was Mine/MARIANNE: Go On 12
64   Vocalion V 9225   You're The Only One/One Good Turn Deserves Another 12
(see also Friday Brown. These records do not feature Mick Jagger or Marianne Faithfull)

CHARLIE MARIANO
56   London LTZN15031   CHARLIE MARIANO QUARTET (LP) 70

MARIAS & MIRANDA
59   Fontana TF 225   I He She/The Queen Bee 6

ANNE MARIE
65   Fontana TF 523   Runaround/There Must Be A Reason 10

MARIE CELESTE
71   private pressing   AND THEN PERHAPS (LP) . . . . 350+

MARIETTA
82   Polydor POSP 305   You're Only Lonely/Making Up My Mind (p/s, with Rick Parfitt & Andy Bown) 8
82   Polydor POSP 483   Do You Wanna Dance/Only In Your Eyes (p/s, with Rick Parfitt & Andy Bown) 8
(see also Status Quo)

MARILLION
82   EMI EMI 5351   Market Square Heroes/Three Boats Down From The Candy (p/s) 5
82   EMI 12 EMI 5351   Market Square Heroes/Three Boats Down From The Candy/Grendel (12", p/s) 8
82   EMI 12 EMIP 5351   Market Square Heroes/Three Boats Down From The Candy/Grendel
                             (12", picture disc, 3,000 only) 25
83   EMI EMI 5362   He Knows, You Know/Charting The Single
                             (p/s, originally with blue plastic label & paper sleeve) 5
83   EMI 12 EMI 5362   He Knows, You Know/Charting The Single/He Knows, You Know
                             (Full Length Version) (12", p/s) 8
83   EMI 12 EMIP 5362   He Knows, You Know/Charting The Single/He Knows, You Know
                             (Full Length Version) (12", picture disc, unreleased)
83   EMI EMI 5393   Garden Party/Margaret (live) (p/s) 5
83   EMI EMIP 5393   Garden Party/Margaret (live) ('jester'-shaped picture disc) 12
83   EMI 12 EMIS 5393   Garden Party (Extended Version)/Charting The Single (live)/
                             Margaret (Extended Live Version) (12", p/s with poster) 10
84   EMI 12 MARILP 1   Punch And Judy/Market Square Heroes (New Version)/
                             Three Boats Down From The Candy (New Version) (12", picture disc) 10
84   EMI MARIL 2   Assassing/Cinderella Search (p/s) 5
84   EMI 12 MARIL 2   Assassing (Full Length Version)/Cinderella Search (Full Length Version)
                             (12", p/s) 15
84   EMI 12 MARILP 2   Assassing (Full Length Version)/Cinderella Search (Full Length Version)
                             (12", picture disc) 10
85   EMI MARILP 3   Kayleigh/Lady Nina (picture disc) 7
85   EMI 12 MARILP 3   Kayleigh (Alternative Mix)/Kayleigh (Extended Version)/
                             Lady Nina (Extended Version) (12", picture disc) 10
85   EMI 12 MARILP 4   Lavender (Remix)/Freaks/Lavender (12", picture disc) 10
85   EMI 12 MARILP 5   Heart Of Lothian (Full Length Version)/Chelsea Monday (live)/
                             Heart Of Lothian (7" Version) (12", picture disc) 12
87   EMI 12MARILP 6   Incommunicado (LP Version)/(Alternative Mix)/Going Under (12", picture disc) . . . 8
87   EMI MARILP 7   Sugar Mice (Radio Edit)/Tux On (picture disc with poster) 8
87   EMI 12MARILP 7   Sugar Mice (Extended Version)/Tux On (12", picture disc) 10
87   EMI CD MARIL 7   Sugar Mice (Radio Edit)/Tux On/Sugar Mice (Radio Edit)/
                             (CD, card p/s, 3,000 only, withdrawn) 15
88   EMI MARILP 9   Freaks (live)/Kayleigh (live) ('jester'-shaped picture disc) 8
99   Raw Power RAWP 2144 MARILLION.COM (CD, 3–track sampler, card p/s, promo only) 12
84   EMI EMCP 3429   SCRIPT FOR A JESTER'S TEAR (LP, picture disc) 20
84   EMI MRLP 1   FUGAZI (LP, picture disc) 18
85   EMI JESTP 1   REAL TO REEL (LP, picture disc) 18
85   EMI MRLP 2   MISPLACED CHILDHOOD (LP, picture disc) 15
(see also Fish, Chemical Alice)

MARINE GIRLS
82   In Phaze COD 2   On My Mind/The Lure Of The Rockpools (p/s, with insert) 12
82   Cherry Red CHERRY 40 On My Mind/The Lure Of The Rockpools (reissue, different p/s) 5
80   private release   A DAY BY THE SEA (cassette, 50 copies only) 12
81   In Phaze Tapes 002 BEACH PARTY (cassette, with photocopied drawings, game & handmade sl.) . . 12
81   Whaam!/In Phaze COD 1 BEACH PARTY (LP, black & white sleeve & labels, with 2 inserts) 12
(see also Tracey Thorn, Everything But The Girl, Jane, Grab Grab The Haddock)

MARINERS
55   London HLA 8201   I Love You Fair Dinkum/(At The) Steamboat River Ball (78 rpm = £8) 25
56   London HA-A 2007   SPIRITUALS (LP) 18

MARION (U.K.)
67   Page One POF 042   I Go To Sleep/Abyssinian Secret 8

MARION (Finland)
73   Columbia DB 8987   Tom Tom Tom/My Son John 15

MARIONETTES
65	Decca F 12056	Whirlpool Of Love/Nobody But You	7
65	Parlophone R 5300	Was It Me?/Under The Boardwalk	10
65	Parlophone R 5356	Raining It's Pouring/Pick Up Your Feet (withdrawn)	12
65	Parlophone R 5374	At The End Of The Day/Pick Up Your Feet	7
66	Parlophone R 5416	Like A Man/Tonight It's Going To Storm	15

(see also Rag Dolls [U.K.], Katie Kissoon, Mac Kissoon)

JON MARK
69	Philips BF 1772	All Neat In Black Stockings/Run To Me	7

(see also Johnny Almond Music Machine, John Mayall, Mark-Almond)

MARK B
95	Jazz Fudge JFR003	ANY MORE QUESTIONS (EP)	15
98	K'Boro KBR 1002	New School Dean/It's Impossible (12")	12

LOUSIA MARKS
78	Bushays BFM 100	Even Though You're Gone/Gone Clear (12")	15
79	Bushays BFM 107	Six Street Six/Instrumental (12")	15
81	Bushays BFM LP 101	BREAKOUT (LP)	25

MARK-ALMOND
71	Harvest SHSP 4011	MARK-ALMOND (LP)	15
73	Harvest SHVL 809	RISING (LP)	12

(see also Johnny Almond Music Machine, Jon Mark)

MARK & JOHN
64	Decca F 12044	Walk Right Back/Karen	6

MARKETTS
62	Liberty LIB 55401	Surfer's Stomp/Start (as Mar-kets)	12
62	Liberty LIB 55443	Balboa Blue/Stompede	12
64	Warner Bros WB 120	Out Of Limits/Bella Delana	35
64	Warner Bros WB 130	Vanishing Point/Borealis	10
66	Warner Bros WB 5696	The Batman Theme/Richie's Theme (some with p/s)	40/20
67	Warner Bros WB 5847	Tarzan's March/Stirrin' Up Some Soul (DJ copy = £75)	50
63	Warner Bros WM 8140	THE MARKETTS TAKE TO WHEELS (LP)	45
64	Warner Bros WM 8147	OUT OF LIMITS (LP)	40
66	Warner Bros W 1642	BATMAN (LP)	55

MAR-KEYS
61	London HLK 9399	Last Night/Night Before	20
61	London HLK 9449	Morning After/Diana	15
62	London HLK 9510	Foxy/One Degree North	20
66	Atlantic AT 4079	Philly Dog/Honey Pot	20
67	Atlantic 584 074	Last Night/Night Before	8
62	London HA-K 8011	DO THE POP-EYE (LP)	70
66	Atlantic 587/588 024	THE GREAT MEMPHIS SOUND (LP)	30
68	Atlantic 587/588 135	MELLOW JELLY (LP)	25
69	Stax SXATS 1021	DAMNIFIKNOW! (LP)	20
69	Stax 2363 008	DAMNIFIKNOW! (LP, reissue)	12

(see also Booker T. & M.G.'s)

MARK FIVE
64	Fontana TF 513	Baby What's Wrong/Tango	50

(see also Nazareth)

MARK FOUR
64	Mercury MF 815	Rock Around The Clock/Slow Down	45
64	Mercury MF 825	Try It Baby/Crazy Country Hop	45
65	Decca F 12204	Hurt Me If You Will/I'm Leaving	75
66	Fontana TF 664	Work All Day (Sleep All Night)/Going Down Fast	90
85	Bam-Caruso OPRA 037	LIVE AT THE BEAT SCENE CLUB (EP, promo, 500 only)	12

(see also Creation)

MARK IV
59	Mercury AMT 1025	Aah-Oo-Gah/I Got A Wife (78 rpm = £18)	12
59	Mercury AMT 1045	Move Over Rover/Dante's Inferno	10
59	Mercury AMT 1060	Ring, Ring, Ring Those Bells/Mairzy Doats	7

MARK II
60	Columbia DB 4549	Night Theme/Confusion	10

PIGMEAT MARKHAM
68	Chess CRS 8077	Here Comes The Judge/The Trial	12
68	Chess CRS 8085	Sock It To 'Em Judge/The Hip Judge	15

ALFRED MARKS
68	RCA RCA 1777	My Young Visitors And Me/When I Wed Miss Ethel Montiche	6

GUY MARKS
68	Stateside SS 2107	Loving You Has Made Me Bananas/Forgive Me My Love	7

MARKSMEN
63	Parlophone R 5075	Smersh/Orbit Three	18

(see also Mark Rogers & Marksmen, Houston Wells & Marksmen)

BOB MARLEY/WAILERS
SINGLES
63	Island WI 088	Judge Not/Do You Still Love Me (as Robert Marley)	270
63	Island WI 128	ERNEST RANGLIN: Exodus/	
		R. MARLEY (as Bobby Martell): One Cup Of Coffee	300
65	Island WI 188	It Hurts To Be Alone/Mr. Talkative	90
65	Island WI 206	Play Boy/Your Love	90

65	Island WI 211	Hoot Nanny Hoot (actually by Peter Tosh & Wailers)/	
		BOB MARLEY: Do You Remember (actually with Wailers)	100
65	Island WI 212	Hooligan/Maga Dog (B-side actually by Peter Tosh & Wailers)	70
65	Island WI 215	Shame And Scandal (as Peter Touch [Tosh] & Wailers)/The Jerk	60
65	Island WI 216	Donna/Don't Ever Leave Me	60
65	Island WI 254	What's New Pussycat/Where Will I Find	60
65	Ska Beat JB 186	Simmer Down/I Don't Need Your Love	75
65	Ska Beat JB 211	Lonesome Feelings/There She Goes	70
65	Ska Beat JB 226	I Made A Mistake/SOUL BROTHERS: Train To Skaville	45
66	Ska Beat JB 228	Love And Affection/Teenager In Love	70
66	Ska Beat JB 230	And I Love Her/Do It Right	70
66	Ska Beat JB 249	Lonesome Tracks/Zimmerman	60

(Most Ska Beat singles have push-out centres with 3 points. Some rarer pressings have 4-point push-out centres. These are generally worth £25 over the usual price)

66	Island WI 260	Jumbie Jamboree/SKATALITES: Independent Anniversary Ska	
		(I Should Have Known Better)	80
66	Island WI 268	Put It On/Love Won't Be Mine	40
66	Island WI 3001	He Who Feels It Knows It/Sunday Morning	90
66	Island WI 3009	Let Him Go (Rude Boy Get Bail)/Sinner Man (B-side matrix: WI-3009B+)	70
66	Island WI 3009	Let Him Go (Rude Boy Get Bail)/The Masher (actually by Beverley's All	
		Stars, or Soul Brothers) (B-side matrix: WI-3009 B+2)	70
66	Rio R 116	Dancing Shoes/Don't Look Back	45
66	Doctor Bird DB 1013	Rude Boy/ROLANDO AL & SOUL BROTHERS: Ringo's Theme (This Boy)	60
66	Doctor Bird DB 1021	Good Good Rudie (Jailhouse)/CITY SLICKERS: Oceans II	60
66	Doctor Bird DB 1039	Rasta Put It On/ROLAND AL & SOUL BROTHERS: Ska With Ringo	65
67	Island WI 3035	Baby I Need You (credited to Ken Boothe)/KEN BOOTHE:	
		I Don't Want To See You Cry	60
67	Island WI 3042	I Am The Toughest (by Peter Touch [Tosh] & Wailers)/	
		MARCIA GRIFFITHS: No Faith	60
67	Island WI 3043	Bend Down Low/Freedom Time	70
67	Coxsone CS 7021	Oh My Darling/HAMLINS: Trying To Keep A Good Man Down	90
67	Doctor Bird DB 1091	Nice Time/Hypocrite	65
67	Studio One SO 2010	Have Faith In The Lord (with Heavenly Sisters; actually by Peter Austin)/	
		JOE HIGGS: Dinah	35
67	Studio One SO 2024	I Stand Predominate/NORMA FRAZER: Come By Here	250
68	Fab FAB 34	Pound Get A Blow/Funeral (white label only)	100
68	Fab FAB 36	Thank You Lord/Mellow Mood (white label only)	100
68	Fab FAB 37	Nice Time/Hypocrites (white label only)	80
68	Fab FAB 41	Burial/Bus Them Shut (existence unconfirmed)	
68	Trojan TR 617	Stir It Up/This Train	60
70	Bamboo BAM 55	Jailhouse (Good Rudy)/JOHN HOLT: A Stranger In Love	50

(All the above singles are credited to Wailers unless stated.)

70	Trojan TR 7759	Soul Shake Down Party/BEVERLY'S ALLSTARS: Version	20
70	Escort ERT 842	Run For Cover/To The Rescue	70
70	Unity UN 562	Duppy Conqueror/UPSETTERS: Duppy Conqueror (Version)	40
70	Jackpot JP 730	Mr Chatterbox (as Wailing Wailers)/DOREEN SHAEFFER:	
		Walk Thru' This World	35
70	Upsetter US 340	My Cup (solo)/LEE PERRY & WAILERS: Son Of Thunder	35
70	Upsetter US 342	Version Of Cup (solo)/UPSETTERS: Dreamland	40
70	Upsetter US 348	Doppy Conqueror (song actually titled "Duppy Conqueror" but plays	
		"Runaway Child" by Dave Barker)/UPSETTERS: Justice	20
70	Upsetter US 349	UPSETTERS: Upsetting Station (actually plays "Dig Your Grave" by	
		Bob Marley & Wailers/UPSETTERS: Justice (Instrumental)	35
71	Upsetter US 354	Mr. Brown/UPSETTERS: Dracula	35
71	Upsetter US 356	Kaya/UPSETTERS: Version	35
71	Upsetter US 357	Small Axe/All In One	20
71	Upsetter US 368	Picture On The Wall (as Rass Dawkins & Wailers)/UPSETTERS: Version	22
71	Upsetter US 369	More Axe (as Bob Marley)/UPSETTERS: Axe Man	22
71	Upsetter US 371	Dreamland (as Wailers)/UPSETTERS: Version	25
71	Upsetter US 372	More Axe (as Bob Marley, different version)/UPSETTERS: Axe Man	22
71	Bullet BU 464	Soultown/Let The Sun Shine On Me	50
71	Bullet BU 493	Lick Samba/Samba	35
71	Punch PH 69	Small Axe/DAVE BARKER: What A Confusion	45
71	Punch PH 77	Down Presser (as Wailers)/JUNIOR BYLES: Got The Tip	40
71	Summit SUM 8526	Stop The Train/Caution (as Wailers)	35
71	Green Door GD 4005	Trench Town Rock/Grooving Kingston 12	12
71	Green Door GD 4022	Lively Yourself Up/TOMMY McCOOK: Lively	12
72	Green Door GD 4025	Guava Jelly/Redder Than Red	20
72	Upsetter US 392	Keep On Moving/African Herbsman	22
72	CBS 8114	Reggae On Broadway/Oh Lord, I Got To Get There (as Wailers)	18
73	Blue Mountain BM 1021	Baby Baby We've Got A Date/Stop That Train	15
73	Punch PH 101	Screw Face/Face Man	22
73	Punch PH 102	Lively Up Yourself/TOMMY McCOOK: Version	20
73	Supreme SUP 216	I Like It Like This (as Bob Marley)/(other artist)	45
73	Island WIP 6164	Concrete Jungle/Reincarnated Soul	8
73	Island WIP 6167	Get Up, Stand Up/Slave Driver (as Wailers)	5
73	Island IDJ 2	I Shot The Sheriff/Pass It On/Duppy Conqueror (promo only)	30
74	Island 12WIP 6244	No Woman No Cry/Jamming (12", p/s)	8
74	Trojan TR 7911	Soul Shake Down Party/Caution	5
74	Trojan TR 7926	Mr Brown/Version	5
75	Island WIP 6212	Natty Dread/So Jah Seh	5
76	Island WIP 6478	Stir It Up/Rat Race (withdrawn, demos only)	15
77	Island WIP 6390	Exodus/Exodus (dub)	5
77	Island WIP 6402	Waiting In Vain/Roots	5

Bob MARLEY

77	Island WIP 6402 1DJ	Promotional Advert For "Exodus" (handwritten label, same track both sides, with Marley commentary)	30
77	Island WIP 6410	Jamming/Punky Reggae Party (p/s)	5
77	Island IPR 2000	Exodus (7:38) / Exodus (3:08, inst. version)(12", pre-release Island sleeve)	8
78	Island WIP 6420	Is This Love?/Crisis (Version) (p/s)	5
78	Island WIP 6440	Satisfy My Soul/Smile Jamaica (p/s)	5
78	Island IPR 2026	War/No More Trouble/Jamming (12", p/s)	8
83	Island ISP 180	Waiting In Vain/Blackman Redemption (picture disc)	8
84	Daddy Kool DK 12101	Rainbow Country (Vocal)/Rainbow Country (Dub)/ PABLO & UPSETTERS: Lama Lava (12", p/s)	15
84	Daddy Kool DK 12102	Natural Mystic/Natural Mystic Rhythm (12", p/s)	15
84	Island 12ISPX 169	One Love/One Love (Dub Version) (p/s)	7
84	Island 12ISP 169	One Love/One Love (Dub Version) (12", white label, p/s)	10
84	Island 12ISPP 169	One Love/One Love (Dub Version) (12", picture disc)	15
80s	Island 12 BMRM 1	Get Up Stand Up/Get Up Stand Up (live) ('Rasta' p/s, promo only)	10
99	Columbia XPR 2533	Turn Your Lights Down Low (with Lauryn Hill)/(Original Version) (die-cut p/s, promo only)	12

(Island singles with the words "DJ Copy" stamped in the middle are worth the same as regular issues. All the above singles are credited to Bob Marley & Wailers unless stated.)

LPs

71	Upsetter TBL 126	SOUL REBEL	75
71	Trojan TBL 126	SOUL REBEL (reissue)	35
71	Trojan TTL 66A/B	SOUL REVOLUTION (LP, white label, test pressing only)	125
72	Island ILPS 9241	CATCH A FIRE (original 'pink rim' label, 'zippo lighter' sleeve)	40
73	Island ILPS 9256	BURNIN' (original label, gatefold sleeve with photos on innner)	15
73	Trojan TRLS 62	AFRICAN HERBSMAN (original issue with "12 Neasden Lane" address and rough orange/white paper labels)	20
73	BBC TS 133425/6	POP SPECTACULAR IN CONCERT (LP, in buff sleeve with printed sheets)	300
74	Trojan TRLS 89	RASTA REVOLUTION (reissue of TBL 126 with 2 extra tracks)	8
75	Island ISS 3	BOB MARLEY & THE WAILERS RADIO SAMPLER (some with photos & press release, promo only)	30/12
77	BBC	ROCK GOES TO COLLEGE IN CONCERT (LP, re-issue of BBC TS 133425/6)	80
83	Island PILPS 97690	CONFRONTATION (picture disc)	50
84	Island PBMW 1	LEGEND — THE BEST OF BOB MARLEY (picture disc)	12
84	Island BMSP 100	THE BOX SET (All 9 Island albums in presentation box – 10,000 only)	125

(see also Peter Tosh, Rita Marley, Ernest Ranglin, Interns, Skatalites, Rass Dawkins & Wailers, Family Man, Norma Frazer)

RITA MARLEY

65	Island WI-226	One More Chance (as Rita & Soulettes)/SKALITES: Dick Tracey	45
67	Rio R 108	Pied Piper/It's Alright	40
67	Island WI 3052	Come To Me/SOUL BOYS: Blood Pressure	38

(see also Soulettes, Soul Brothers)

MICKI MARLO

54	Capitol CL 14086	I'm Gonna Rock-Rock-Rock/Loves Like That (78)	8
55	Capitol CL 14271	Prize Of Gold/Foolish Notion (78 rpm = £8)	15
57	London HL 8481	That's Right/What You've Done To Me (B-side with Paul Anka) (78 rpm = £8)	25

(see also Paul Anka)

MARLON

74	Purple PUR 120	Let's Go To The Disco/Broken Man	7

(see also Roger Glover, Ray Fenwick)

ROBERT MARLOW

83	Reset 7REST 1	Pictures Of Dorian Grey/The Tale Of Dorian Grey (p/s)	5
83	Reset 12REST 1	Pictures Of Dorian Grey/The Tale Of Dorian Grey (12", p/s)	10
83	Reset 7REST 3	I Just Want To Dance/No Heart (p/s)	5
83	Reset 7RESTP 3	I Just Want To Dance/No Heart (picture disc)	6
83	Reset 12REST 3	I Just Want To Dance/No Heart (12", p/s)	10
84	Reset 12REST 4	Claudette/This Happy World (12", p/s)	10
85	Reset 7REST 6	Calling All Destroyers/In Retrospect (p/s)	10
85	Reset 12REST 6	Calling All Destroyers/In Retrosepct (12", p/s, existence unconfirmed)	

(see also Vince Clarke, Erasure)

MARION MARLOWE

56	London HLA 8306	The Hands Of Time/Ring, Phone, Ring (withdrawn) (78 rpm = £70)	100

MARMALADE

66	CBS 202340	It's All Leading Up To Saturday Night/Wait A Minute Baby	10
67	CBS 202643	Can't Stop Now/There Ain't No Use In Hangin' On	10
67	CBS 2948	I See The Rain/Laughing Man	10
67	CBS 3088	Man In A Shop/Cry	7
68	CBS 3412	Lovin' Things/Hey Joe	6
68	CBS 3708	Wait For Me Marianne/Mess Around	6
68	CBS 3892	Ob-La-Di, Ob-La-Da/Chains	6
69	CBS 4287	Baby Make It Soon/Time Is On My Side	6
69	CBS 4615	Butterfly/I Shall Be Released	6
68	CBS 63414	THERE'S A LOT OF IT ABOUT (LP)	20
70	CBS SPR 36	THE BEST OF THE MARMALADE (LP)	18
70	Decca SKL 5047	REFLECTIONS OF THE MARMALADE (LP)	18
71	Decca SKL 5111	SONGS (LP)	18

(see also Dean Ford [& Gaylords], Gaylords, Junior Campbell, Chris McClure Section)

MARQUIS DE SADE

82	Out Of Town HOOT 8	Crystal Grieff/Vampire Affair (p/s)	5

MARQUIS OF KENSINGTON

67	Immediate IM 052	Changing Of The Guard/Reverse Thrust	35

HANK MARR
60	Blue Beat BB 26	Tonk Game/Hob-Nobbin	12

A MARRIAGE OF CONVENIENCE
85	Stranglers Info Service SIS2	My Young Dreams/Two Sides To Every Story (no p/s, fan club issue)	5

(see also Stranglers)

STEVE MARRIOTT
63	Decca F 11619	Give Her My Regards/Imaginary Love	120+
76	A&M AMS 7230	Star In My Life/Midnight Rollin'	6
85	Aura AUS 145	Wha'cha Gonna Do About It/All Shook Up	6
76	A&M AMLH 64572	MARRIOTT (LP)	20
85	Aura AUL 792	PACKET OF THREE (LP)	15

(see also Small Faces, Humble Pie, Spectrum, Pollcats)

M/A/R/R/S
87	4AD BAD 707R	Pump Up The Volume (Remix)/Anitina (The First Time I See She Dance) (Remix) (12", p/s).	8
87	4AD CAD 707R	Pump Up The Volume (Remix)/Anitina/Pump Up The Volume (12" Version)/ Anitina (The First Time I See She Dance) (Remix) (CD, gatefold p/s)	12

(see also A.R. Kane, Colourbox)

BETTY MARS
72	Columbia DB 8879	Come-Comedie/Mon Café Russe	7

JOHNNY MARS
81	Ace NS 73	Born Under A Bad Sign/Horses And Places/Mighty Mars (p/s, withdrawn)	5
72	Polydor 2460 168	BLUES FROM MARS (LP)	15

BERNIE MARSDEN
79	Parlophone PCS 7215	AND ABOUT TIME TOO (LP, with inner sleeve)	12
81	Parlophone PCS 7217	LOOK AT ME NOW (LP, with inner sleeve)	12

(see also Jon Lord, Whitesnake, Cozy Powell, Jack Bruce, Babe Ruth, Bogdon)

BERYL MARSDEN
63	Decca F 11707	I Know/I Only Care About You	20
64	Decca F 11819	When The Lovelight Starts Shining Through His Eyes/ Love Is Going To Happen To Me	20
65	Columbia DB 7718	Who You Gonna Hurt?/Gonna Make Him My Baby	20
65	Columbia DB 7797	Music Talk/Break-A-Way	20
66	Columbia DB 7888	What's She Got/Let's Go Somewhere	20

(see also Shotgun Express, She Trinity)

GERRY MARSDEN
67	CBS 2784	Please Let Them Be/I'm Not Blue	10
67	CBS 2946	Gilbert Green/What Makes Me Love You	10
68	CBS 3575	Liverpool/Charlie Girl (as Gerry Marsden & Derek Nimmo)	10
68	NEMS 56-3831	In The Year Of April/Every Day	5
69	NEMS 56-4229	Every Little Minute/In Days Of Old	5
71	Decca F 13172	I've Got My Ukelele/What A Day	5
72	Phoenix NIX 129	Amo Credo/Come Break Bread	5

(see also Gerry & Pacemakers)

MARSEILLE
84	Ultra Noise ULTRA 3	TOUCH THE NIGHT (LP, with inner sleeve)	12

(see also Paul Dale)

STEVIE MARSH
59	Decca F 11181	If You Were The Only Boy In The World/Leave Me Alone (78 rpm = £18)	8
60	Decca F 11209	You Don't Have To Tell Me (I Know)/Wish	10
60	Decca F 11244	A Girl In Love/Over And Done With	10
62	Ember EMB S 139	I Shouldn't Be Kissing You/Time And Time Again	8

WARNE MARSH
57	London LTZ-P 15080	JAZZ OF TWO CITIES (LP)	20

GARY MARSHALL
61	Parlophone R 4758	One Twitchy Baby/Ev'ry Chance I Get	15

JACK MARSHALL ORCHESTRA & CHORUS
58	Capitol CL 14888	Thunder Road Chase/Finger Poppin'	15

JOY MARSHALL
64	Decca F 11863	Rain On Snow/When You Hold Me Tight	6
65	Decca F 12222	My Love Come Home/When A Girl Really Loves You	6
66	Decca F 12422	The More I See You/Taste Of Honey	10

LARRY MARSHALL
67	Blue Beat BB 374	Move Your Feet/Find A New Baby	20
67	Blue Beat BB 380	Suspicion/Broken Heart	50+
67	Doctor Bird DB 1008	Snake In The Grass/ROLAND ALPHONSO: V.C. 10.	50+
68	Caltone TONE 126	No One To Give Me Love/PHIL PRATT: Safe Travel	40
70	Bamboo BAM 22	Girl Of My Dreams/SOUND DIMENSON: Give It Away	12
70	Bamboo BAM 52	Man From Galilee/Give It Away (as Larry Marshall & Enid Cumberland)	8
70	Banana BA 300	Stay A Little Longer/MAYTALS: He'll Provide	12
71	Banana BA 364	Maga Dog/OSSIE ROBINSON: Economical Heatwave	12
73	Pama PM 873	True Believer/FLAMES: Water Your Garden	6
75	Ocean OC 004	Can't You Understand/KING TUBBY : Locks Of Dub	15

(see also Larry & Alvin, Irving Brown, Fitzroy D. Long, Kingston Pete & Buster's Allstars, Max Romeo, Jackie Mittoo)

LOIS MARSHALL
59	HMV ALP 1671	BRITISH FOLK SONGS (LP)	12

WILLIE MARSHALL
70	Torpedo TOR 20	Loosen Up Strong Man/Strong Man	5

MINT VALUE £

MARSHMALLOW WAY
69	United Artists UP 35031	C'mon Kitty Kitty/Michigan Mints	7

MARSHMELLOW HIGHWAY
68	London HLR 10204	I Don't Wanna Live This Way/Loving You Makes Everything Alright	12

MARSUPILAMI
70	Transatlantic TRA 213	MARSUPILAMI (LP)	60
71	Transatlantic TRA 230	ARENA (LP)	65

PIERA MARTELL
74	CBS S CBS 2293	My Ship Of Love/Mein Ruf Nach Dir	12

RAY MARTELL
70	Joe JRS 3	She Caught The Train/PAMA DICE: Tea House From Emperor Rosko	10
70	Attack ATT 8015	Loving Lover/Cora	6
70	Doctor Bird DB 1503	This Little Light/Lover	6
70	Trojan TR 7787	This Little Light/Lover	6
72	Sioux SI 012	She Caught The Train/JOE'S ALLSTARS: Tony B.'s Theme	6

MARTELLS
66	Decca F 12463	Time To Say Goodnight/The Cherry Song	40+

RALPH MARTERIE & HIS ORCHESTRA
57	Mercury MEP 9517	PRESENTING RALPH MARTERIE (EP)	12
60	Mercury ZEP 10040	SWINGING SOUND OF MARTERIE (EP)	8
60	Mercury ZEP 10068	MUSIC FOR A PRIVATE EYE (EP)	8

MARTHA & THE MUFFINS
80	DinDisc DID 5	TRANCE & DANCE (LP, with bonus 7" [WAS E 20])	12

MARTHA (REEVES) & VANDELLAS
63	Oriole CBA 1814	I'll Have To Let Him Go/My Baby Won't Come Back	400
63	Oriole CBA 1819	Come And Get These Memories/Jealous Lover	200
63	Stateside SS 228	Heatwave/A Love Like Yours (Don't Come Knockin' Every Day) (DJ copy = £150)	85
64	Stateside SS 250	Quicksand/Darling, I Hum Our Song (DJ copy = £100)	45
64	Stateside SS 272	Live Wire/Old Love (Let's Try It Again) (DJ copy = £100)	40
64	Stateside SS 305	In My Lonely Room/A Tear For The Girl (DJ copy = £150)	70
64	Stateside SS 345	Dancing In The Street/There He Is (At My Door) (DJ copy = £100)	22
65	Stateside SS 383	Wild One/Dancing Slow (DJ copy = £100)	45
65	Tamla Motown TMG 502	Nowhere To Run/Motoring (DJ copy = £120)	30
65	Tamla Motown TMG 530	You've Been In Love Too Long/Love (Makes Me Do Foolish Things) (DJ = £100)	30
66	Tamla Motown TMG 549	My Baby Loves Me/Never Leave Your Baby's Side (DJ copy = £120)	40
66	Tamla Motown TMG 567	What Am I Going To Do Without Your Love/Go Ahead And Laugh (DJ = £100)	30
66	Tamla Motown TMG 582	I'm Ready For Love/He Doesn't Love Her Anymore (DJ copy = £50)	15
67	Tamla Motown TMG 599	Jimmy Mack/Third Finger, Left Hand	15
72	Tamla Motown TMG 599	Jimmy Mack/Third Finger, Left Hand (reissue)	6
67	Tamla Motown TMG 621	Love Bug Leave My Heart Alone/One Way Out (DJ copy = £75)	20
68	Tamla Motown TMG 636	Honey Chile/Show Me The Way	15
68	Tamla Motown TMG 657	I Promise To Wait, My Love/Forget Me Not	15
68	Tamla Motown TMG 669	I Can't Dance To That Music You're Playing/I Tried	15
69	Tamla Motown TMG 684	Dancing In The Street/Quicksand	6
69	Tamla Motown TMG 694	Nowhere To Run/Live Wire	6
71	Tamla Motown TMG 762	Forget Me Not/I Gotta Let You Go	6
71	Tamla Motown TMG 794	Bless You/Hope I Don't Get My Heart Broke	6
65	Tamla Motown TME 2009	MARTHA AND THE VANDELLAS (EP)	125
66	Tamla Motown TME 2017	HITTIN' (EP)	125
63	Oriole PS 40052	COME AND GET THESE MEMORIES (LP)	400
65	Tamla Motown TML 11005	HEATWAVE (LP)	80
65	Tamla Motown TML 11013	DANCE PARTY (LP)	100
67	T. Motown (S)TML 11040	GREATEST HITS (LP, original with flipback sleeve, mono/stereo)	25/30
67	T. Motown (S)TML 11040	GREATEST HITS (LP, re-pressing non-flipback sleeve)	15
67	T. Motown (S)TML 11051	WATCH OUT! (LP, mono/stereo)	40/50
68	T. Motown (S)TML 11078	RIDIN' HIGH (LP)	30
69	T. Motown (S)TML 11099	DANCING IN THE STREET (LP)	30
70	T. Motown (S)TML 11134	SUGAR N' SPICE (LP)	25
70	Tamla Motown STML 11166	NATURAL RESOURCES (LP)	25
72	Tamla Motown STML 11204	BLACK MAGIC (LP)	30

MARTIAN SCHOOLGIRLS
79	Red Planet RPR 1	Life In The 1980's/Lonely Nights (p/s)	10

PATRICK D. MARTIN
79	Deram DMR 432	I Like Electric Motors/Time (p/s)	5
80	Deram DM 433	Lucy 'Lectric/I Like Electric Motors/Mutant (p/s)	10
80	IRS/MCA ILS 0023	COMPUTER DATIN' EP	8

MARTIN
68	Coxsone CS 7056	I Second That Emotion (actually by Martin Riley)/ROY TOMLINSON: I Stand For I	35

ALAN MARTIN
63	Rio R 3	The Party/Indeed	8
63	Rio R 6	You Came Late/Dreaming	8
63	Rio R 9	Secretly/Fame And Fortune	8
63	Rio R 10	Mother Brother/Tell Me	8
65	Rio R 66	Must Know I Love You/VIC BROWN'S COMBO: Rio Special	12
65	Rio R 67	Sweet Rosemarie/HONEY DUCKERS: Banjo Man	8
65	Rio R 68	Why Must I Cry/Shirley I Love You	8
65	Rio R 74	Since I Married Dorothy/You Promised Me	8
66	Rio R 94	Days Are Lonely/My Baby	8
66	Rio R 96	Rome Wasn't Built In A Day/I'm Hurt	8

BARRY MARTIN
| 61 | RCA RCA 1234 | Little Lonely One/Are You Sure | 8 |

BENNY MARTIN
| 63 | CBS Realm RM 174 | COUNTRY MUSIC'S SENSATIONAL ENTERTAINER (LP) | 15 |

BILL MARTIN
| 68 | Page One POF 067 | Private Scotty Grant/Singing Vietnam Blues | 5 |

BOBBI MARTIN
| 64 | Coral Q 72477 | Don't Forget I Still Love You/On The Outside (Lookin' In) | 10 |
| 65 | Coral Q 72478 | I Can't Stop Thinking About You/Million Thanks To You | 8 |

CHRIS MARTIN
| 59 | HMV POP 664 | Lonely Street/Swing A Little Lover | 10 |
| 60 | HMV POP 692 | Point Of No Return/I Don't Regret A Thing | 6 |

DAVE MARTIN
| 64 | Port-O-Jam PJ 4112 | Let Them Fight/OSSIE IRVING SIX: Why I Love You | 18 |
| 64 | Port-O-Jam PJ 4115 | All My Dreams/Take Your Belongings | 18 |

DEAN MARTIN
54	Capitol CL 14123	Hey Brother, Pour The Wine/I'd Cry Like A Baby (green or purple labels)	40/25
54	Capitol CL 14138	Sway/Pretty As A Picture	30
54	Capitol CL 14150	How Do You Speak To An Angel?/Ev'ry Street's A Boulevard In Old New York (with Jerry Lewis)	20
54	Capitol CL 14170	The Peddlar Man (Ten I Loved)/Try Again	20
54	Capitol CL 14180	One More Time/If I Could Sing Like Bing	20
55	Capitol CL 14215	Open Up The Doghouse (Two Cats Are Trying To Get In) (with Nat 'King' Cole)/Long, Long Ago	25
55	Capitol CL 14226	Let Me Go, Lover/The Naughty Lady Of Shady Lane	30
55	Capitol CL 14227	Mambo Italiano/That's All I Want From You	30
55	Capitol CL 14253	Belle From Barcelona/Confused	20
55	Capitol CL 14255	What Could Be More Beautiful/Under The Bridges Of Paris	20
55	Capitol CL 14311	Chee Chee-Oo Chee (Sang The Little Bird)/Ridin' Into Love	20
55	Capitol CL 14356	Relax-Ay-Voo/Two Sleepy People (with Line Renaud)	20
55	Capitol CL 14367	Simpatico/Love Is All That Matters	20
55	Capitol CL 14370	In Napoli/I Like Them All	20

(The above 45s were originally issued with triangular centres; round-centre reissues are worth around half these values.)

56	Capitol CL 14505	When You Pretend/The Lucky Song	10
56	Capitol CL 14507	Inamorata/You Look So Familiar	10
56	Capitol CL 14519	Young And Foolish/Just One More Chance	10
56	Capitol CL 14523	Memories Are Made Of This/Change Of Heart	15
56	Capitol CL 14586	Watching The World Go By/The Lady With The Big Umbrella	10
56	Capitol CL 14624	The Test Of Time/I'm Gonna Steal You Away	7
56	Capitol CL 14625	Me 'N' You 'N' The Moon/The Wind, The Wind	7
56	Capitol CL 14626	Pardners (with Jerry Lewis)/Buckskin Beauty	7
56	Capitol CL 14656	Give Me A Sign/Mississippi Dreamboat	7
57	Capitol CL 14690	The Man Who Plays The Mandolino/I Know I Can't Forget	7
57	Capitol CL 14714	Bamboozled/Only Trust Your Heart	6
57	Capitol CL 14737	I Can't Give You Anything But Love/I Never Had A Chance	6
57	Capitol CL 14758	Beau James/Write To Me From Naples	6
57	Capitol CL 14782	The Triche Trache/Promise Her Anything	6
57	Capitol CL 14801	The Look/Just Kiss Me	5
57	Capitol CL 14813	Good Mornin' Life/Makin' Love Ukelele Style	5
58	Capitol CL 14844	Return To Me/Forgetting You	5
58	Capitol CL 14890	Angel Baby/I'll Gladly Make The Same Mistake Again	5
58	Capitol CL 14910	Volare (Nel Blu Dipinto Di Blu)/Outta My Mind	5
58	Capitol CL 14943	Once Upon A Time (It Happened)/The Magician (78 rpm = £8)	5
59	Capitol CL 14990	It Takes So Long (To Say Goodbye)/You Were Made For Love (78 rpm = £12)	5
59	Capitol CL 15015	Rio Bravo/My Rifle, My Pony And Me	15
59	Capitol CL 15039	On An Evening In Roma/You Can't Love 'Em All (78 rpm = £18)	5
59	Capitol CL 15064	Ain't Gonna Lead This Life/Maybe (78 rpm = £25)	6
59	Capitol CL 15102	(Love Is A) Career/For You	6
60	Capitol CL 15127	Who Was That Lady?/Love Me, My Love	7
60	Capitol CL 15145	Napoli/Buttercup A Golden Hair	5
60	Capitol CL 15155	Just In Time/Humdinger	5
60	Capitol CL 15172	Sogni D'Oro (Golden Dreams)/How Sweet It Is	5
61	Capitol CL 15188	Sparklin' Eyes/Tu Sei Bella, Signorina	8
61	Capitol CL 15198	All In A Night's Work/Bella Bella Bambina	8
61	Capitol CL 15209	Giuggiola/The Story Of Life	8
62	Reprise R 20058	Tik A Tee, Tik A Tay/Just Close Your Eyes	8
62	Reprise R 20076	C'est Si Bon!/The Poor People Of Paris	5
62	Reprise R 20082	Dame Su Amor/Baby O	8
63	Reprise R 20116	From The Bottom Of My Heart (Dammi, Dammi, Dammi)/Who's Got The Action?	8
63	Reprise R 20128	Sam's Song (with Sammy Davis Jnr)/SAMMY DAVIS JNR. & FRANK SINATRA: Me And My Shadow	7
63	Capitol CL 15294	Cha Cha Cha D'Amour/I Wish You Love	5
63	Reprise R 20150	Face In A Crowd/Ain't Gonna Try Anymore	5
63	Reprise R 20215	Via Veneto/Mama Roma	10
64	Reprise R 20217	Fugue For Tin Horns/The Oldest Established (Permanent Crap Game In New York) (B-side with Frank Sinatra & Bing Crosby) (some in p/s)	8/6
64	Reprise R 20281	Everybody Loves Somebody Sometime/Little Voice	5
64	Reprise R 20307	The Door Is Still Open/Every Minute, Every Hour	5
64	Capitol CL 15363	Somebody Loves You/Hundred Years From Today	5
67	Pye DMA 1	I'm Not The Marrying Kind (Dean Martin Assoc. issue, 1-sided, promo only)	20
67	Reprise R 20538	Let The Good Times In/I'm Not The Marrying Kind	5
67	Reprise R 20601	In The Chapel In The Moonlight/Welcome To My World	5

67	Reprise R 20608	Little Ole Wine Drinker Me/I Can't Help Remembering You	6
68	Reprise RS 23259	Bumming Around/Home	6
68	Reprise R 20780	Not Enough Indians/Rainbows Are Back in Fashion	5
69	Reprise RS 23343	Gentle On My Mind/That Old Time Feelin'	5
69	Reprise RS 23387	By The Time I Get To Phoenix/Things	5
69	Reprise R 20841	I Take A Lot Of Pride/Drowning In My Tears	5
70	Reprise R 20893	Come On Down/Down Home	10
70	Reprise R 20973	Georgie Sunshine/For The Good Times	5
75	Capitol CL 15821	Memories Are Made Of This/That's Amore (That's Love)	5
81	Reprise K 14512	Gentle On My Mind/King Of The Road (p/s)	5

EPs

55	Capitol EAP 1-9123	DEAN MARTIN	22
55	Capitol EAP 1-481	SUNNY ITALY	22
56	Capitol EAP 1007	SWINGIN' DOWN YONDER NO. 1	15
56	Capitol EAP 1022	SWINGIN' DOWN YONDER NO. 2	15
56	Capitol EAP 1033	DEAN MARTIN AND JERRY LEWIS: "PARDNERS" (with Jerry Lewis)	15
56	Capitol EAP 1037	SWINGIN' DOWN YONDER NO. 3	15
57	Capitol EAP 1-806	HOLLYWOOD OR BUST – FILM SELECTION	15
57	Capitol EAP 1-840	TEN THOUSAND BEDROOMS – FILM SELECTION	20
57	Capitol EAP 1-939	RETURN TO ME	10
58	Capitol EAP 1-1027	VOLARE	8
60	Capitol EAP 1-1285	A WINTER ROMANCE PART 1	12
60	Capitol EAP 2-1285	A WINTER ROMANCE PART 2	12
60	Capitol EAP 3-1285	A WINTER ROMANCE PART 3	12
61	Capitol EAP 1-20072	RELAXIN' WITH DEAN MARTIN	12
61	Capitol EAP 1-20124	DEAN MARTIN IN MOVIELAND	18
61	Capitol EAP 1-20152	I'M YOURS	15
64	Capitol EAP 6-1702	SOMEBODY LOVES YOU	12
65	Capitol EAP 7-1702	CHA CHA DE AMOUR	12
64	Reprise R 30034	EVERYBODY LOVES SOMEBODY	8
65	Reprise R 30036	WE'LL SING IN THE SUNSHINE	10
65	Reprise R 30039	ROBIN AND THE SEVEN HOODS	18
65	Reprise R 30044	I'LL BE SEEING YOU	10
65	Reprise R 30051	SEND ME SOME LOVING	10
66	Reprise R 30059	THE BIRDS AND THE BEES	10
66	Reprise R 30066	RED ROSES FOR A BLUE LADY	10
66	Reprise R 30074	LOVE LOVE LOVE	10
67	Reprise R 30078	SINGS SONGS FROM 'THE SILENCERS': THE GLORY OF LOVE	10
67	Reprise R 30084	MR. HAPPINESS	10
67	Reprise R 30090	WINTER WONDERLAND	10

LPs

53	Capitol LC 6590	CAPITOL PRESENTS DEAN MARTIN (10")	70
56	Britone LP 1002	DEAN MARTIN SINGS, NICOLINI LUCCHESI PLAYS (10")	65
57	Capitol T 849	PRETTY BABY	22
58	Capitol T 1047	THIS IS DEAN MARTIN!	22
59	Capitol (S)T 1150	SLEEP WARM (orchestra conducted by Frank Sinatra, mono/stereo)	20/22
61	Capitol (S)T 1442	THIS TIME I'M SWINGIN'! (mono/stereo)	20/22
62	Encore! ENC 103	DEAN GOES DIXIE	20
62	Reprise R/R9 6021	FRENCH STYLE (mono/stereo)	20/22
62	Capitol (S)T 1659	DINO (mono/stereo)	22/25
63	Reprise R 6054	DINO LATINO	20
63	Capitol (S)T 1702	CHA CHA DE AMOR (mono/stereo)	18/20
63	Reprise R 6061	DEAN (TEX) MARTIN COUNTRY STYLE	20
63	Reprise R 6085	DEAN (TEX) MARTIN RIDES AGAIN	20
64	Regal REG 1010	DEAN MARTIN (export issue)	20
64	Reprise R 6123	DREAM WITH DEAN	20
64	Reprise R 6130	EVERYBODY LOVES SOMEBODY	15
65	Reprise R 6140	THE DOOR IS STILL OPEN TO MY HEART	15
65	Reprise R 6146	MARTIN HITS AGAIN	15
65	Reprise R/R9 6168	HOUSTON (mono/stereo)	12/15
65	Reprise R/R9 6170	(REMEMBER ME) I'M THE ONE WHO LOVES YOU (mono/stereo)	12/15
66	Reprise R 6201	SOMEWHERE THERE'S SOMEONE	12
66	Reprise R 6211	DEAN MARTIN SINGS SONGS FROM "THE SILENCERS"	15
66	Reprise RLP/RSLP 6213	THE HIT SOUND OF DEAN MARTIN	12
66	Reprise RLP 6222	THE DEAN MARTIN CHRISTMAS ALBUM	15
67	Reprise RLP/RSLP 6233	AT EASE WITH DEAN	15
67	Stateside SL/SSL 10201	LOVE IS A CAREER	20
67	Reprise RLP/RSLP 6242	HAPPINESS IS	12
67	Reprise RLP/RSLP 6250	WELCOME TO MY WORLD	12
69	Reprise RLP/RSLP 6330	GENTLE ON MY MIND	12

(see also Jerry Lewis, Line Renaud & Dean Martin, Frank Sinatra)

DEREK MARTIN
64	Sue WI 308	Daddy Rolling Stone/Don't Put Me Down Like This (credited as Derak Martin)	75
65	Columbia DB 7694	You Better Go/You Know	40
68	Stax 601 039	Soul Power/Sly Girl	30

DON MARTIN & DANDY (& SUPERBOYS)
| 67 | Giant GN 6 | Got A Feelin'/CONNECTIONS: At The Junction | 12 |
| 68 | Giant GN 24 | Keep On Fighting/Rock Steady Boogie (with Superboys) | 15 |

(see also Dandy & Superboys)

GEORGE MARTIN & HIS ORCHESTRA
64	Parlophone R 5135	I Saw Her Standing There/All My Loving	12
64	Parlophone R 5166	And I Love Her/Ringo's Theme (This Boy)	12
65	Parlophone R 5222	All Quiet On The Mersey Front/Out Of The Picture	12

65	Parlophone R 5256	I Feel Fine/The Niagara Theme	10
65	Parlophone R 5375	Yesterday/Another Girl	15
66	United Artists UP 1154	By George! — It's The David Frost Theme/Double Scotch	15
66	United Artists UP 1165	Love In The Open Air/Theme From "The Family Way"	20
67	United Artists UP 1194	Theme One/Elephants And Castles	15
72	United Artists UP 35423	Pulp — Theme/Pulp — Love Theme	10
65	Parlophone GEP 8930	MUSIC FROM "A HARD DAY'S NIGHT" (EP)	45
64	Parlophone PMC 1227	OFF THE BEATLE TRACK (LP, also stereo PCS 3057)	30/35
65	Parlophone TA-PMC 1227	OFF THE BEATLE TRACK (reel-to-reel, mono only)	12
65	Columbia SX 1775	PLAYS HELP! (LP, mono)	20
65	Studio Two TWO 102	PLAYS HELP! (LP, stereo)	20
66	United Artists (S)ULP 1157	INSTRUMENTALLY SALUTES THE BEATLES GIRLS (LP)	30
66	Studio Two TWO 141	AND I LOVE HER (LP)	25
67	Decca (S)KL 4847	THE FAMILY WAY (LP, soundtrack)	100
68	United Artists (S)ULP 1196	BRITISH MAID (LP)	30
70	Sunset SLS 50182	BY GEORGE! (LP)	20
73	United Artists UAS 29475	LIVE AND LET DIE (LP, soundtrack, gatefold sleeve)	25
74	Polydor Super 2383 304	BEATLES TO BOND AND BACH (LP)	15
78	St. Michael IMP 105	BEATLES TO BOND AND BACH (LP, exclusive to Marks & Spencer)	30
93	EMI RNB 1	THE BEATLES — GEORGE MARTIN INTERVIEW (CD, card sleeve, promo only)	18

(see also Beatles, Ray Cathode)

GRADY MARTIN & THE SLEWFOOT FIVE
56	Brunswick 05535	Nashville/Don't Take Your Love From Me	15

(see also Jane Turzy)

HONEYBOY MARTIN
67	Caltone TONE 103	Dreader Than Dread (and the Voices)/DANDY: In The Mood	22
70	Gas GAS 123	Unchained Melody/SAMMY JONES: You're My Girl	10
72	Sioux SI 011	Unchained Melody/SAMMY JONES: You're My Girl (reissue)	8
72	Harry J HJ 6643	Have You Ever Seen The Rain/Spanish Harlem	5

(see also Lynn Tait & Jets)

IRVING MARTIN
(see under Martin's Magic Sounds)

JANIS MARTIN
60	Palette PG 9000	Here Today And Gone Tomorrow Love/Hard Times Ahead	40
80	RCA PL 43153	THE COMPLETE RCA JANIS MARTIN (2-LP)	18

JEAN MARTIN
63	Decca F 11751	Ain't Gonna Kiss Ya/Three Times Three Is Love	10
64	Decca F 11897	Save The Last Dance For Me/Will You Still Love Me Tomorrow	10

JERRY MARTIN
63	London HLU 9692	Shake-A Take-A/Exchange Student	15

KERRY MARTIN
58	Parlophone R 4449	Stroll Me/Cold Hands, Warm Heart	15

LUCIA MARTIN
62	Parlophone R 4915	Big Jim/Star From Heaven	12

MARK MARTIN
67	Page One POF 020	Extraordinary Girl/Love Could Be Like Hell	6

MARY MARTIN
64	London HLR 9938	A Spoonful Of Sugar/Feed The Birds	7

MILES MARTIN FOLK GROUP
71	Amber	MILES MARTIN FOLK GROUP (LP, private pressing)	90

MILLICENT MARTIN
64	Parlophone R 5096	In The Summer Of His Years/If I Can Help Somebody	5
64	Parlophone R 5120	Suspicion/Nothing But The Best	6

(see also Ronnie Carroll)

PAUL MARTIN
67	Sue WI 4041	Snake In The Grass/I've Got A New Love	60

RAY MARTIN (& HIS) CONCERT ORCHESTRA
53	Columbia 33S 1011	MUSIC IN THE RAY MARTIN MANNER VOL. 1 (10" LP)	12
54	Columbia 33S 1021	MUSIC IN THE RAY MARTIN MANNER VOL. 2 (10" LP)	12
64	Phase 4 Stereo PFS 4043	THE SOUND OF SIGHT (LP)	18

(see also Ray Burns)

RICKY MARTIN & TYME MACHINE
68	Olga OLE 4	Something Else/Blue Suede Shoes	12

RODGE MARTIN
67	Polydor 56725	When She Touches Me/Lovin' Machine	20

RON MARTIN & JUBILEE STOMPERS
68	Doctor Bird DB 1151	Give Your Love To Me/I Cry My Heart	12

RUPIE MARTIN('S ALLSTARS)
70	Torpedo TOR 24	Last Flight/Super Lotus	18
70	Torpedo TOR 26	Musical Container (Parts 1 & 2)	15
70	Punch PH 43	Death In The Arena (actually by Rupie Martin All Stars)/MAN COMETH: Julia Caesar (actually by Charlie Ace)	12

SETH MARTIN
68	Page One POF 073	Another Day Goes By/Look At Me	20
69	Page One POF 134	What A Lovely Way To Spend Forever/Mystery Lady	5

SHANE MARTIN
68	CBS 2894	You're So Young/I Need You (DJ copy = £350)	275

SKIP MARTIN VIDEO ALL-STARS
60	Golden Guinea GGL 0060	TV JAZZ THEMES (LP, also stereo GGLS 10060)	12/15

STEVE MARTIN
56	Columbia DB 3703	Only You/Lola (78 rpm, Columbia SCM 5212 = £6)	5
58	Philips PB 820	Stairway Of Love/Chanson D'Amour	5
58	Philips PB 853	The Man Inside/Blue-Eyed Sue (78 rpm = £6)	5

TONY MARTIN
53	HMV 7M 105	Tenement Symphony (both sides)	10
53	HMV 7M 136	The Golden Years/April In Portugal	12
54	HMV 7M 203	Here/I Could Write A Book	10
54	HMV 7M 258	I Love Paris/Boulevard Of Nightingales	10
55	HMV 7M 302	Stranger In Paradise/Vera Cruz	15
55	HMV 7M 320	Domani/What's The Time In Nicaragua	10
56	HMV 7M 414	Walk Hand In Hand/Flamenco Love	15
56	HMV 7MC 41	Walk Hand In Hand/Flamenco Love (export issue)	15
57	HMV POP 282	All Of You/Moderation	10
57	RCA RCA 1002	The Man From Idaho/One Is A Lonely Number	5
59	RCA RCA 1101	She Is Not Thinking Of Me/GOGI GRANT: Say A Prayer For Me Tonight (78 = £8)	6
65	Stateside SS 394	Talkin' To Your Picture/Our Rhapsody	100
65	Tamla Motown TMG 537	The Bigger Your Heart Is (The Harder You'll Fall)/The Two Of Us (DJ copy = £125)	85
54	HMV 7EG 8006	TONY MARTIN (EP)	10
55	HMV 7EG 8124	TENEMENT SYMPHONY (EP)	10
57	HMV 7EG 8205	THE DESERT SONG — SOUNDTRACK EXCERPTS (EP)	8
58	RCA RCX 130	SONGS FROM CINDERELLA (EP)	8
55	Brunswick LA 8713	TONY MARTIN SINGS VOL. 1 (10" LP)	18
56	Mercury MPT 7005	TONY MARTIN FAVOURITES (10" LP)	18
57	Mercury MPT 7516	DREAM MUSIC (10" LP)	15
57	HMV DLP 1137	SPEAK TO ME OF LOVE (10" LP)	15
57	RCA RD 27003	A NIGHT AT THE COPACABANA (LP)	15
61	London HA-D 2341	TONY MARTIN'S GREATEST HITS (LP)	15
65	Stateside SL 10113	AT CARNEGIE HALL (LP)	15

(see also Gogi Grant)

TRADE MARTIN
63	London HL 9662	Hula Hula Dancin' Doll/Something In The Wind	15

VINCE MARTIN
59	HMV POP 594	Old Grey Goose (Aunt Rhodie)/Goodnight, Irene (78 rpm = £12)	10

(see also Tarriers)

MARTIN & THE BROWNSHIRTS
78	Lightning GIL 507	Taxi Driver/Boring	35

MARTIN & DERRICK
61	Blue Beat BB 48	Times Are Going/I Love You Baby (with Cavaliers Combo)	10
62	Island WI 024	Come On/MONTY & CYCLONES: Organisation	20

(see also Derrick Morgan)

MARTIN & FINLEY
73	Tamla Motown TMG 867	It's Another Sunday/Best Friends (withdrawn, demo only)	150

WINK MARTINDALE
59	London HLD 8962	Deck Of Cards/Now You Know How It Feels (78 rpm = £20)	5
60	London HLD 9042	Life Gits Tee-Jus Don't It?/I Never See Maggie Alone	5
61	London HLD 9419	Black Land Farmer/Make Him Happy	5
63	London RED 1370	DECK OF CARDS (EP)	15
65	Dot DEP 20000	DECK OF CARDS (EP)	15
60	London HA-D 2240	WINK MARTINDALE (LP)	20
60s	Golden Guinea GGL 0288	DECK OF CARDS (LP)	15

RAY MARTINE
63	Piccadilly NPL 38007	EAST END — WEST END (LP)	12

TONY MARTINEZ QUINTET
54	HMV 7M 264	Cucusa Tune Mambo/Bernie's Tune Mambo	5

MIA MARTINI
77	CBS S CBS 5178	Freedom Is Today/Libera	5

AL MARTINO
54	Capitol CL 14128	Wanted/There'll Be No Teardrops Tonight	30/25
54	Capitol CL 14148	On And On (In Love With You)/Give Me Something To Go With The Wine	30/25
54	Capitol CL 14163	The Story Of Tina/Destiny (No One Can Change)	30/25

(The first prices for the above 45s are for green labels with triangular centres, the second for later pressings with purple labels with triangular centres.)

54	Capitol CL 14192	I Still Believe/When?	20
54	Capitol CL 14202	Not As A Stranger/No One But You	20
55	Capitol CL 14224	Don't Go To Strangers/Say It Again	20
55	Capitol CL 14284	The Snowy, Snowy Mountains/Love Is Eternal	18
55	Capitol CL 14343	The Man From Laramie/To Please My Lady	30
55	Capitol CL 14379	Come Close To Me/Small Talk	20

(All the above 45s were originally issued with triangular centres; round-centre reissues are worth around half these values.)

56	Capitol CL 14550	Journey's End/Sound Advice	10
56	Capitol CL 14614	The Girl I Left In Rome/Some Cloud Above	10
57	Capitol CL 14680	I'm Sorry/A Love To Call My Own	8

59	Top Rank JAR 108	I Can't Get You Out Of My Heart/Two Hearts Are Better Than One	10
59	Top Rank JAR 108	I Can't Get You Out Of My Heart/Two Hearts Are Better Than One (78)	15
59	Top Rank JAR 187	Darling I Love You/The Memory Of You	10
60	Top Rank JAR 312	Summertime/I Sold My Heart	6
60	Top Rank JAR 337	Mama/Dearest (Cara)	6
55	Capitol EAP1 405	AL MARTINO SINGS (EP)	15
61	Capitol EAP1 20153	TO PLEASE MY LADY (EP)	10
63	Ember EMB 4528	DARLING I LOVE YOU (EP)	10
60	Top Rank BUY 030	AL MARTINO (LP)	18
60	Top Rank 25/025	SWING ALONG WITH AL MARTINO LP	18
63	Capitol (S)T 1774	THE EXCITING VOICE OF AL MARTINO (LP, mono/stereo)	each 15
63	Capitol (S)T 1914	I LOVE YOU BECAUSE (LP, mono/stereo)	each 15
64	Capitol (S)T 1975	PAINTED, TAINTED ROSE (LP, mono/stereo)	each 15
64	Capitol (S)T 2040	LIVING A LIE (LP, mono/stereo)	each 15
64	Capitol (S)T 2107	AL MARTINO (LP, mono/stereo)	each 15
65	Capitol (S)T 2200	WE COULD (LP, mono/stereo)	each 15
65	Capitol (S)T 2312	SOMEBODY ELSE IS TAKING MY PLACE (LP, mono/stereo)	each 15
66	Capitol (S)T 2362	MY CHERIE (LP, mono/stereo)	each 15
66	Capitol (S)T 2435	SPANISH EYES (LP, mono/stereo)	each 15

MARTIN'S MAGIC SOUNDS

67	Deram DM 141	Mon Amour, Mon Amour/Midem Melody	6
67	Deram DML/SML 1014	MARTIN'S MAGIC SOUNDS (LP)	12

JOHN MARTYN

71	Island WIP 6116	May You Never/Just Now	7
77	Island WIP 6385	Over The Hill/Head And Heart	6
78	Island WIP 6414	Dancing/Dealer (Version)	6
78	Island WIP	Dancing/Dealer (Version) (promo, 78 rpm)	8
80	Island WIP 6547	Johnny Too Bad/Johnny Too Bad (Version)	6
81	Island IPR 2046	Johnny Too Bad (Extended Dub Version)/Big Muff (Extended Mix) (12", promo)	10
82	WEA K 259987-7	Gun Money (US Remix)/Hiss On the Tape (live)	6
86	Island CID 265	Classic John Martyn: Angeline/Tight Connection To My Heart (Has Anybody Seen My Love)/May You Never/Solid Air/ Glistening Glyndebourne (CD, foldout sleeve)	25
92	Permanent CDPERM 6	Sweet Little Mystery (CD)	12
97	Blueprint BP 276CD	SNOOO... EP (She's A Lover/All In Your Favour/Step It Up/Little Strange) (CD)	8
67	Island ILP 952	LONDON CONVERSATION (LP, 1st pressing, with black & orange 'circle' logo)	90
69	Island ILP 952	LONDON CONVERSATION (LP, 2nd pressing, 'pink rim' label, 'palm tree' logo)	18
68	Island ILP 991/ILPS 9091	THE TUMBLER (LP, 1st pressing, with black 'circle' logo, mono/stereo)	50/35
70	Island ILPS 9091	THE TUMBLER (LP, 2nd pressing, 'pink rim' label, 'palm tree' logo)	18
71	Island ILPS 9167	BLESS THE WEATHER (LP, 'pink rim' label, 'palm tree' logo)	15
73	Island ILPS 9226	SOLID AIR (LP, gatefold sleeve with lyric sheet 'pink rim' label, 'palm tree' logo)	15
73	Island ILPS 9253	INSIDE OUT (LP, gatefold sleeve with inner, 'pink rim' label, 'palm tree' logo)	15
75	Island ILPS 9296	SUNDAY'S CHILD (LP, with lyric inner sleeve, 'palm tree' label)	12
75	Island ILPS 9343	LIVE AT LEEDS (LP, mail-order, 10,000 only, numbered & signed)	40
86	Bodyswerve JMLP 001	PHILENTROPY (LP, red sleeve)	25
91	Permanent PERMLP 4	COOLTIDE (LP, with inner)	25

JOHN & BEVERLEY MARTYN

70	Island WIP 6076	John The Baptist/The Ocean	6
70	Island ILPS 9113	STORMBRINGER (LP, 1st pressing, pink label with 'i' logo)	40
70	Island ILPS 9113	STORMBRINGER (LP, 2nd pressing, 'pink rim' label, 'palm tree' logo)	12
70	Island ILPS 9133	THE ROAD TO RUIN (LP, 'pink rim' label, 'palm tree' logo)	22

(see also Beverley)

KID MARTYN

62	77 77LA 12/20	IN NEW ORLEANS WITH KID SHEIK'S BAND (LP)	15

MARVELETTES

61	Fontana H 355	Please Mr Postman/So Long Baby	50
62	Fontana H 386	Twistin' Postman/I Want A Guy	85
62	Oriole CBA 1764	Beechwood 4-5789/Someday Someway	150
63	Oriole CBA 1817	Locking Up My Heart/Forever	350
64	Stateside SS 251	As Long As I Know He's Mine/Little Girl Blue (DJ copy = £100)	60
64	Stateside SS 273	He's A Good Guy (Yes He Is)/Goddess Of Love (DJ copy = £100)	60
64	Stateside SS 334	You're My Remedy/A Little Bit Of Sympathy, A Little Bit Of Love (DJ copy = £100)	50
65	Stateside SS 369	Too Many Fish In The Sea/Need For Love (DJ copy = £125)	50
65	Tamla Motown TMG 518	I'll Keep Holding On/No Time For Tears (DJ copy = £200)	100
65	Tamla Motown TMG 535	Danger Heartbreak Dead Ahead/Your Cheating Ways (DJ copy = £100)	50
66	Tamla Motown TMG 546	Don't Mess With Bill/Anything You Wanna Do (DJ copy = £85)	40
66	Tamla Motown TMG 562	You're The One/Paper Boy (DJ copy = £75)	40
67	Tamla Motown TMG 594	The Hunter Gets Captured By The Game/I Think I Can Change You (DJ copy = £60)	25
67	Tamla Motown TMG 609	When You're Young And In Love/The Day You Take One, You Have To Take The Other	10
68	Tamla Motown TMG 639	My Baby Must Be A Magician/I Need Someone	20
68	Tamla Motown TMG 659	Here I Am Baby/Keep Off, No Trespassing	20
69	Tamla Motown TMG 701	Reachin' For Something I Can't Have/Destination Anywhere	15
73	Tamla Motown TMG 860	Reachin' For Something I Can't Have/Here I Am Baby (DJ copy plays "My Baby Must Be A Magician" = £100)	10
75	Tamla Motown TMG 1000	Finders Keepers, Losers Weepers/KIM WESTON: Do Like I Do	25
65	Tamla Motown TMG 2003	THE MARVELETTES (EP)	125

65	Tamla Motown TML 11008	THE MARVELLOUS MARVELETTES (LP)	225
67	T. Motown (S)TML 11052	THE MARVELETTES (LP, mono/stereo)	50/60
69	T. Motown (S)TML 11090	SOPHISTICATED SOUL (LP)	40
70	T. Motown STML 11145	IN FULL BLOOM (LP)	25
71	T. Motown STML 11177	THE RETURN OF THE MARVELETTES (LP, unissued)	

MARVELOWS
| 65 | HMV POP 1433 | I Do/My Heart (DJ Copy = £60) | 30 |

MARVELS (Jamaica)
62	Dice CC 8	Come To The Wedding/Angelo	8
63	Blue Beat BB 191	Sonia/The More We Are Together	10
64	Blue Beat BB 221	Millie/Saturday	10
70	Pama PM 813	Love One Another/Falling Rain	5
70	Pama PM 817	Don't Let Him Take Your Love From Me/A Little Smile	5
70	Gas GAS 138	Sail Away/Fight A Broke	12
70	Gas GAS 139	Someday We'll Be Together/MORGAN'S ALL STARS: Instrumental	5
71	Pama PM 819	Oh Lord Why Lord/NEVILLE HINDS: Love Letter	5
71	Pama Supreme PS 338	Rocksteady/ Be My Baby	25
71	New Beat NB 081	Co Co/Hey Girl Don't Bother Me	5
72	Pama PM 832	Do You Know You Have To Cry/Love Power	5
72	Pama Supreme PS 348	What A Hurricane/If You Love Her	5

MARVELS (U.K.)
| 68 | Columbia DB 8341 | Keep On Searching/Heartache | 75 |

MARVELS FIVE
| 65 | HMV POP 1423 | Bye Bye Baby Bunting/In Front Of Her House | 7 |
| 65 | HMV POP 1452 | Don't Play That Song/Forgive | 15 |

MARVETTE
68	Amalgamated AMG 804	Tit For Tat (actually by Lyn Taitt & Jets)/You Take So Long To Know	50
68	Sacred Sound SS 001	We Are Not Divided/He Is So Real To Me	8
68	Sacred Sound SS 002	We Shall Have A Grand Time/Let The Power Fall On Me	8
68	Sacred Sound SS 003	I Was Once Lost In Sin/What A Wonderful Thing	8
68	Tabernacle TS 1001	I Want A Revival/Tell It	15
68	Tabernacle TS 1003	Sweet Jesus/When I Look Back	7
60s	Coxsone TLP 1002	IT'S REVIVAL TIME (LP)	75+

BRETT MARVIN & THUNDERBOLTS
70	Sonet SNTF 616	BRETT MARVIN AND THE THUNDERBOLTS (LP)	12
71	Sonet SNTF 619	12 INCHES OF BRETT MARVIN & THE THUNDERBOLTS (LP)	12
71	Sonet SNTF 620	BEST OF FRIENDS (LP)	12
72	Sonet SNTF 630	ALIAS TERRY DACTYL AND THE DINOSAURS (LP)	12

(see also Jona Lewie)

HANK (B.) MARVIN
68	Columbia DB 8326	London's Not Too Far/SHADOWS: Running Out Of World	15
69	Columbia DB 8552	Goodnight Dick/Wahine	12
69	Columbia DB 8601	Sacha/Sunday For Seven Days	12
69	Columbia DB 8628	Midnight Cowboy/SHADOWS: Slaughter On Tenth Avenue	18
70	Columbia DB 8693	Break Another Dawn/Would You Believe It? (demo-only, unissued B-side)	135
70	Columbia DB 8693	Break Another Dawn/Morning Star	15
78	EMI EMI 2744	Flamingo/Syndicated (as Hank Marvin Guitar Syndicate)	5
69	Columbia SCX 6352	HANK MARVIN (LP, blue/black label, mono/stereo)	35/30
70	Columbia SCX 6352	HANK MARVIN (LP, silver/black label re-pressing)	12

(see also Shadows, Marvin & Farrar, Marvin Welch & Farrar, Bruce Welch, Cliff Richard, Spaghetti Junction, Jean-Michel Jarre)

JOEL MARVIN
| 70 | Explosion EX 2028 | Too Late/Each Day (both actually by Gregory Isaacs) | 15 |

(see also Gregory Isaacs)

MARVIN & FARRAR
73	EMI EMI 2044	Music Makes My Day/Skin Deep (with Olivia Newton-John)	10
75	EMI EMI 2335	Small And Lonely Light/Galadriel (Spirit Of Starlight)	7
73	EMI EMA 755	HANK MARVIN AND JOHN FARRAR (LP, with Olivia Newton-John)	25

(see also Shadows, Hank Marvin, Marvin Welch & Farrar)

MARVIN & JOHNNY
57	Vogue V 9074	Yak Yak/Pretty Eyes (78 rpm = £150)	500
58	Vogue V 9099	Smack, Smack/You're In My Heart (78 rpm = £150)	500
65	Black Swan WI 467	Cherry Pie/Ain't That Right	40

MARVIN, WELCH & FARRAR
71	Regal Zonophone RZ 3030	Faithful/Mr. Sun	8
71	Regal Zonophone RZ 3035	Lady Of The Morning/Tiny Robin	8
72	Regal Zonophone RZ 3048	Marmaduke/Strike A Light	10
71	Regal Zono. SRZA 8502	MARVIN, WELCH AND FARRAR (LP)	15
71	Regal Zono. SRZA 8504	SECOND OPINION (LP)	20
72	Regal Zono. Q4SRZA 8504	SECOND OPINION (LP, quadrophonic)	28

(see also Shadows, Marvin & Farrar, Bruce Welch [& Hank Marvin])

GROUCHO MARX
51	Brunswick 04794	Blackstrap Molasses/How D'ye Do And Shake Hands (78, with Jimmy Durante & Danny Kaye)	8
73	A&M AMS 7057	Show Me A Rose/Lydia The Tattooed Lady	5
72	A&M AMLS 6003	AN EVENING WITH GROUCHO MARX (2-LP)	20

(see also Danny Kaye, Jimmy Durante, Jerry Colonna & Groucho Marx)

GROUCHO & CHICO MARX
| 69 | MCA MCA 758 | Ev'ryone Says I Love You/HARPO MARX: Ev'ryone Says I Love You (p/s) | 6 |

(see also Marx Brothers)

MARX BROTHERS
70   MCA MCF 2533   ORIGINAL VOICE TRACKS FROM THEIR GREATEST MOVIES (LP) 15
(see also Groucho Marx)

MARY JANE with BARRY GRAY & SPACEMAKERS
63   Philips 326 587 BF   Robot Man/Just The Same As I Do (some in p/s) 40/18
(see also Barry Gray)

MARZIPAN
70   Trend 6099 007   My Kind Of Music/Sweet Water Mary 6

MASAI
74   Contempo CS 2007   Across The Track (We Better Go Back) (Parts 1 & 2) 150

MASAI
82   Turbo TURB 01   Stranger To Myself/Lightning (p/s) 8

MASCOTS
63   Pye International 7N 25189   Hey Little Angel/Once Upon A Love 18

HUGH MASEKELA
68   Uni UN 504   Grazing In The Grass/Bajabula Bonke 10
69   Uni UN 510   I Haven't Slept/Where Has All The Grass Gone? 6
68   Uni UNL(S) 101   ALIVE AND WELL AT THE WHISKEY (LP) 20
69   Fontana SFL 13056   HUGH MASEKELA (LP) 18
71   Rare Earth SRE 3002   HUGH MASEKELA AND THE UNION OF SOUTH AFRICA (LP) 25
72   Blue Thumb ICD 3   HOME IS WHERE THE MUSIC IS (LP) 30

SPOKES MASHIYANE
58   Oriole CB 1441   Jika Spokes (with Ben Nkosi)/Boys Of Jo'burg (with France Pilane)
                            (78 rpm = £8) 6

MASKMAN & AGENTS
69   Direction 58-4059   One Eye Open/Y'awll 6

MASON
73   Dawn DNLS 3050   MASON (LP, export issue) 20

BARBARA MASON
65   London HL 9977   Yes, I'm Ready/Keep Him (DJ copy = £75) 40
68   Direction 58-3382   Oh How It Hurts/Ain't Got Nobody 40
69   Action ACT 4542   Slipping Away/Half A Love 20
72   Buddah 2011 133   Bed And Board/Yes It's You 10
73   Buddah 2011 154   Give Me Your Love/You Can Be With The One You Don't Love 7
75   Buddah BDS 425   From His Woman To You/When You Wake Up In Georgia 6
69   Action ACLP 6002   OH HOW IT HURTS (LP) 75
75   Buddah BDLP 4027   TRANSITION (LP) 20
75   Buddah BDLP 4032   LOVE'S THE THING (LP) 20

BARRY MASON
66   Decca F 12401   Misty Morning Eyes/Take Your Time 8
66   Deram DM 104   Over The Hills And Far Away/A Collection Of Recollections 50
69   Decca F 12895   I'm In Love With You, Pom Pom/Mister D.J. Play Me A Sad Song 7
(see also Sounds Of Les & Barry)

CURTISS MASON
71   Columbia DB 8800   Monkberry Moon Delight/Lot Of Lovin' 5

DAVE MASON
68   Island WIP 6032   Just For You/Little Woman 15
70   Harvest HAR 5017   World In Changes/Can't Stop Worrying, Can't Stop Lovin' 6
70   Harvest HAR 5024   Only You Know And I Know/Sad And Deep As You 6
70   Harvest SHTC 251   ALONE TOGETHER (LP) 18
72   Blue Thumb ILPS 9203   HEAD KEEPER (LP) 15
72   Island ICD 2   SCRAPBOOK (2-LP) 15
73   CBS 65258   IT'S LIKE YOU NEVER LEFT (LP, gatefold sleeve) 12
(see also Hellions, Revolution, Traffic, Fox, Jaguars)

DAVE MASON & CASS ELLIOT
71   Probe PRO 513   Something To Make You Happy/Next To You (as Mason & Cass,
                            special sleeve) 6
71   Probe SPBA 6259   DAVE MASON AND CASS ELLIOT (LP) 15
(see also Dave Mason, Mama Cass [Elliot])

GLEN MASON
56   Parlophone MSP 6240   Hot Diggity (Dog Ziggity Boom)/Baby Girl Of Mine 15
56   Parlophone R 4203   Love, Love, Love/Glendora 18
56   Parlophone R 4244   The Green Door/Why Must You Go, Go, Go 18
57   Parlophone R 4271   Don't Forbid Me/Amore 10
57   Parlophone R 4291   Round And Round/Walking And Whistling 6
57   Parlophone R 4334   Crying My Heart Out For You/Why Don't They Understand 6
57   Parlophone R 4357   By My Side/By The Fireside 5
58   Parlophone R 4390   What A Beautiful Combination/I'm Alone Because I Love You 5
58   Parlophone R 4415   I May Never Pass This Way Again/A Moment Ago 7
58   Parlophone R 4451   I Know Where I'm Going/Autumn Souvenir (78 rpm = £6) 6
58   Parlophone R 4485   The End/Fall In Love (78 rpm = £6) 6
59   Parlophone R 4562   The Battle Of New Orleans/I Don't Know (78 rpm = £8) 7
60   Parlophone R 4626   You Got What It Takes/If There's Someone 8
60   Parlophone R 4723   That's What I Want/I Like It When It Rains 6
61   Parlophone R 4834   Don't Move/Shadrack 6
62   Parlophone R 4900   St. Louis Blues/That's Life 6

MARLIN MASON
56   Vogue Coral Q 72168   Don't Throw My Love Away/The Mystery Of Love 10

Nick MASON (& Rick FENN)

NICK MASON (& RICK FENN)
85	Harvest HAR 5238	Lie For A Lie/And The Address (with Rick Fenn, p/s)	5
85	Harvest 12 HAR 5238	Lie For A Lie (Extended 12" Version)/And The Address/	
		Mumbo Jumbo (with Rick Fenn) (12", p/s)	8
85	EMI MAF 1	PROFILES (LP, with Rick Fenn)	12
81	Harvest SHSP 4116	FICTITIOUS SPORTS (LP, solo, with inner sleeve)	12
(see also Pink Floyd, 10cc)			

SANDY MASON
80s	Boot BOS 7234	ONLY LOVE (LP)	12

SPENCER MASON
67	Parlophone R 5555	Flugel In Carnaby Street/Albuferia	8

MASQUERADERS
68	Bell BLL 1023	I Ain't Got To Love Nobody Else/I Got It	15
70	Now! NOW 1001	Love Peace And Understanding/Tell Me You Love Me	10
(see also Lester Tipton)			

MASS
80	4AD AD 14	You And I/Cabbage (some with poster insert in die-cut sleeve)	12/8
81	4AD CAD 107	LABOUR OF LOVE (LP, with inner sleeve)	15
(see also Models, Rema-Rema, Wolfgang Press)			

MASSED ALBERTS
64	Parlophone R 5159	Blaze Away/Goodbye Dolly (Gray)	6

MASSIEL
68	Philips BF 1667	La La La/He Gives Me Love	7

MASSIVE ATTACK
90	Wild Bunch WBRT 1	Daydreaming (mixes) (12", p/s, with cards)	15
91	Wild Bunch WBRT 2	Unfinished Sympathy/Instrumental (12", p/s)	25
91	Wild Bunch WBRR 2	Unfinished Sympathy (Nellee Hooper 12" Mix)/	
		(Nellee Hooper Instrumental Mix)/(Original) (12", p/s)	35
91	Wild Bunch WBRR 3	Safe From Harm (mixes) (12", p/s)	8
98	Circa MASBOX 2	SINGLES 90/98 (11 x 12" singles in numbered heat sensitive box)	60

MASSIVE DREAD
79	His Majesty HM 1001	MASSIVE DREAD (LP)	30

MASTERBOY
91	Spaghetti CIAO 2	Shake It Up And Dance (Mini Live Version)/(Instrumental) (p/s)	5
91	Spaghetti CIAOC 2	Shake It Up And Dance (Mini Live Version)/(Instrumental) (cassette)	6
91	Spaghetti CIAOX	Shake It Up And Dance (Mini Live Version)/(Instrumental) (12", p/s)	8
91	Spaghetti CIAOCD 2	Shake It Up And Dance (Mini Live Version)/(Remix '91)/	
		(Maxi Live Version) (CD)	12

MASTERFLEET
73	Sussex LPSX 5	HIGH ON THE SEA (LP)	25

MASTERMINDS
65	Immediate IM 005	She Belongs To Me/Taken My Love	30
(see also Badfinger)			

MASTERPLAN
78	Satril SAT 136	Love Crazy (Theme From 'Carry On Emmanuel')/	
		Since I've Been Away From My Love (p/s)	10

CARL MASTERS
72	Big Shot BI 604	Va Va Voom/GOD SONS: Rebel	15
(see also Max Romeo, Dennis Alcapone)			

SAMMY MASTERS
60	Warner Bros WB 10	Rockin' Red Wing/Lonely Weekend (78 rpm = £200)	25
65	London HLR 9949	I Fought The Law (And The Law Won)/Big Man Cried	15

VALERIE MASTERS
58	Fontana H 132	Sharing/The Secret Of Happiness	10
58	Fontana H 145	(Well-a, Well-a) Ding-Dong/Merci Beaucoup (78 rpm = £6)	10
59	Fontana H 175	Dreams End At Dawn/Wonder (78 rpm = £6)	10
59	Fontana H 195	Jack O' Diamonds/Say When (78 rpm = £15)	10
59	Fontana H 224	If There Are Stars In My Eyes/Just Squeeze Me (78 rpm = £15)	10
60	Fontana H 238	Oh, Gee/No One Understands	10
60	Fontana H 253	Banjo Boy/Cow Cow Boogie	10
60	Fontana H 268	Sweeter As The Day Goes By/Fools Fall In Love	10
61	Fontana H 293	Too Late For Tears/I Got Rhythm	10
61	Fontana H 322	Birmingham Rag/All The Days Of My Life	7
62	Fontana H 367	African Waltz/All Night Long	7
64	Columbia DB 7426	Christmas Calling/He Didn't Fool Me	75
65	Polydor 56056	It's Up To You/Next Train Out	6
66	Polydor 56135	Don't Ever Go/Say Hello	20
69	Columbia DB 8629	I Don't Wanna Play House/Just Wait A Little While	6

MASTER'S APPRENTICES
71	Regal Zonophone RZ 3031	I'm Your Satisfier/Because I Love Her	35
70	Regal Zono. SLRZ 1016	MASTER'S APPRENTICES (LP)	125
71	Regal Zono. SLRZ 1022	A TOAST TO PANAMA RED (LP)	140

MASTERS AT WORK
96	Talkin' Loud 578795-1	NUYORICAN (6-LP box set)	50

MASTER SINGERS
66	Parlophone R 5523	Weather Forecast/Roadilore	6
66	Parlophone GEP 8962	THE HIGHWAY CODE (EP)	8

MASTERS OF REALITY
88	Def American DEFA 1	The Candy Song/The Blue Garden	10
88	Def American 838 474-1	THE MASTERS OF REALITY (LP)	20
88	Def American 838 474-2	THE MASTERS OF REALITY (CD)	20

MATADOR
71	Big Shot BI 594	Nyah Festival (actually "What Am I Living For" by Derrick Morgan)/ Brixton Serenade	8

MATADORS
69	Crab CRAB 27	Death A Come (actually by Lloyd Robinson)/The Sword (actually "Zylon" by Lloyd Tyrell [Charmers])	12
70	Camel CA 45	Dark Of The Sun (actually by Jackie Mittoo)/Dreader Than Dread	18
71	Green Door GD 4017	I'm Sorry (actually by Tony Brevett)/JOE WHITE: I'm Sorry Version	10

(see also Emotions, Little Roys, Ethiopians)

MATATA (AIR-FIESTA)
72	President PT 380	I Wanna Do My Thing/Wild River	10
73	President PT 406	I Feel Funky/I Want You	12
74	President PT 417	Return To You/Something On My Mind	10
75	President PT 438	Good Good Understanding/Gimme Some Lovin'	10
72	President PTLS 1052	MATATA: AIR FIESTA (LP)	30
75	President PTLS 1057	INDEPENDENCE (LP)	80

MATCHING MOLE
72	CBS 8101	O Caroline/Signed Curtain	15
72	CBS 64850	MATCHING MOLE (LP)	22
72	CBS 65260	MATCHING MOLE'S LITTLE RED RECORD (LP, with inner sleeve)	20

(see also Robert Wyatt, Soft Machine, Caravan, Hatfield & The North)

MATCHMAKERS
71	Chapter One	BUBBLEGUM A GO GO (LP)	20

(see also Mark Wirtz, Philwit & Pegasus, Fickle Finger)

KAREN MATHESON
96	Survival SURCD 020B	THE DREAMING SEA (CD, limited edition in box, with 6 postcards)	20

(see also Capercaillie)

MATHETAI
77	Cavs CAV 017	KNOWING (LP)	50

COUNTRY JOHNNY MATHIS
60	Top Rank JKP 2064	COUNTRY AND WESTERN EXPRESS NO. 5 (EP)	22

JODI MATHIS
75	Capitol CL 15827	Mama/Don't You Care Anymore	10

JOHNNY MATHIS
57	Philips PB 713	Wonderful! Wonderful!/When Sunny Gets Blue (78)	8
57	Philips JK 1029	The Twelfth Of Never/Chances Are (jukebox issue) (78 rpm = £8)	25
57	Fontana H 103	Wild Is The Wind/No Love (But Your Love)	8
58	Fontana H 117	Come To Me/When I Am With You (78 rpm = £8)	6
58	Fontana H 130	Teacher, Teacher/Easy To Love (78 rpm = £8)	7
58	Fontana H 142	A Certain Smile/Let It Rain	7
58	Fontana H 163	Call Me/Stairway To The Sea	6
58	Fontana H 165	Winter Wonderland/Sleigh Ride (78 rpm = £12)	5
59	Fontana H 186	Let's Love/You'd Be So Nice To Come Home To (78 rpm = £12)	5
59	Fontana H 199	Someone/They Say It's Wonderful (78 rpm = £15)	5
59	Fontana H 218	The Best Of Everything/Cherie (78 rpm = £18)	6
59	Fontana H 219	Misty/The Story Of Our Love (78 rpm = £20)	6
59	Fontana H 220	It's Not For Me to Say/Warm And Tender (78 rpm = £20)	5
60	Fontana H 234	You Are Beautiful/Very Much In Love	5
60	Fontana H 248	The Twelfth Of Never/Get Me To The Church On Time	5
60	Fontana H 254	Starbright/All Is Well	5
60	Fontana H 267	My Love For You/Oh That Feeling (some in p/s)	7/5
61	Fontana H 272	Maria/Hey Love	5
61	Fontana H 316	You Set My Heart To Music/Jenny	5
61	Fontana H 328	Laurie, My Love/Should I Wait (Or Should I Run To Her)	5
61	Fontana H 335	Love Look Away/When My Sugar Walks Down The Street	5
62	Fontana H 372	Sweet Thursday/One Look	5
62	CBS AAG 117	Gina/I Love Her, That's Why (with picture insert)	7
63	CBS AAG 135	What Will Mary Say/Quiet Girl	5
63	HMV POP 1217	Your Teenage Dreams/Come Back (some in export p/s)	12/5

EPs
57	Philips BBE 12156	JOHNNY MATHIS	10
58	Fontana TFE 17011	JOHNNY MATHIS	8
58	Fontana TFE 17025	LET ME LOVE YOU	8
58	Fontana TFE 17039	COME TO ME	8
58	Fontana TFE 17047	WHILE WE'RE YOUNG	8
58	Fontana TFE 17056	THE TWELFTH OF NEVER	8
58	Fontana TFE 17064	AVE MARIA	8
58	Fontana TFE 17088	THERE GOES MY HEART	8
58	Fontana TFE 17089	SWING LOW	8
58	Fontana TFE 17091	A HANDFUL OF STARS	8
58	Fontana TFE 17162	CHRISTMAS WITH JOHNNY MATHIS	8
59	Fontana TFE 17177	MEET MISTER MATHIS	8
59	Fontana TFE 17194	IT'S DE LOVELY (also stereo STFE 8001)	8
60	Fontana TFE 17215	SO NICE (also stereo STFE 8000)	8
60	Fontana TFE 17275	FOUR HITS	8
60	Fontana TFE 17281	TENDERLY	8
60	Fontana TFE 17282	ELI ELI	8

MINT VALUE £

60	Fontana TFE 17283	I'LL BE SEEING YOU	8
60	Fontana TFE 17285	LIKE SOMEONE IN LOVE (also stereo STFE 8018)	8

LPs

57	Fontana TFL 5003	WONDERFUL, WONDERFUL	20
58	Fontana TFL 5011	JOHNNY MATHIS	20
58	Fontana TFL 5015	WARM (also stereo STFL 510)	15/18
58	Fontana TFL 5023	HEAVENLY	15
58	Fontana TFL 5031	MERRY CHRISTMAS (also stereo STFL 506)	15/18
59	Fontana TFL 5039	SWING SOFTLY (also stereo STFL 500)	15/18
59	Fontana TFL 5050	OPEN FIRE, TWO GUITARS (also stereo STFL 515)	15/18
59	Fontana TFL 5058	JOHNNY'S GREATEST HITS	15
60	Fontana TFL 5061	RIDE ON A RAINBOW (also stereo STFL 516)	15/18
60	Fontana TFL 5083	MORE OF JOHNNY'S GREATEST HITS (also stereo STFL 517)	15/18
60	Fontana TFL 5084	FAITHFULLY (lso stereo STFL 522)	15/18
60	Fontana SET(S) 101	THE RHYTHMS AND BALLADS OF BROADWAY (2-LP, mono/stereo)	18/22
61	Fontana TFL 5117	JOHNNY'S MOOD (also stereo STFL 545)	15/18
61	Fontana TFL 5134	I'LL BUY YOU A STAR (also stereo STFL 557)	15/18
61	Fontana TFL 5153	PORTRAIT OF JOHNNY (also stereo STFL 571)	15/18
62	Fontana TFL 5177	LIVE IT UP (also stereo STFL 589)	12/15
62	CBS (S)BPG 62077	PORTRAIT OF JOHNNY (reissue, mono/stereo)	12/15
62	CBS (S)BPG 62072	JOHNNY'S MOOD (reissue, mono/stereo)	12/15
63	CBS (S)BPG 62106	RAPTURE	12
63	CBS (S)BPG 62147	JOHNNY'S NEWEST HITS	12
63	CBS (S)BPG 62172	JOHNNY	12
63	HMV CLP 1696/CSD 1521	SOUNDS OF CHRISTMAS (mono/stereo)	12/15
64	CBS (S)BPG 62202	ROMANTICALLY	12
64	HMV CLP 1721	TENDER IS THE NIGHT (also stereo CSD 1535)	12/15
64	CBS (S)BPG 62270	I'LL SEARCH MY SECRET HEART & OTHER GREAT HITS	12
65	HMV CSD 1553	THE WONDERFUL WORLD OF MAKE BELIEVE (stereo only)	25
65	HMV CLP 1818/CSD 1578	OLÉ	30
65	HMV CLP 1859/CSD 1600	THIS IS LOVE (mono/stereo)	30/40
66	HMV CLP 1926/CSD 1638	AWAY FROM HOME	40
66	HMV CLP/CSD 3522	LOVE IS EVERYTHING	15
66	HMV CLP/CSD 3556	THE SHADOW OF YOUR SMILE	15
79	CBS 66355	JOHNNY MATHIS (3-LP box set)	12
81	Readers Digest 034	THE BEST OF JOHNNY MATHIS (4-LP box set, mail-order only)	12

TONY MATOS
62	Salvo SLO 5520-LP	CHA CHA! WITH TONY MATOS (LP, issued with or without sleeve)	18/12

BRIAN MATTHEW
61	Pye 7N 15403	Trad Mad/Sing With Me, Mates	6

BRIAN MATTHEW & PETE MURRAY
60	Decca F 11305	What's It All About Eh?/Gee Ma, I Wanna Go Home	6
see also Matt Bryant)			

IAN MATTHEWS
71	Vertigo 6360 034	IF YOU SAW THRO' MY EYES (LP, gatefold sleeve, swirl label)	30
72	Vertigo 6360 056	TIGERS WILL SURVIVE (LP, gatefold sleeve, swirl label)	30
73	Elektra K 42144	VALLEY HI (LP, gatefold sleeve)	15
74	Elektra K 42160	SOME DAYS YOU EAT THE BEAR, SOME DAYS THE BEAR EATS YOU (LP)	15
76	CBS 81316	GO FOR BROKE (LP)	12
77	CBS 81936	HIT AND RUN (LP)	12
(see also Pyramid, Fairport Convention, Matthews Southern Comfort, Plainsong, Hi-Fi)			

JOE MATTHEWS
68	Sue WI 4046	Sorry Ain't Good Enough/You Better Mend Your Ways	75

MILT MATTHEWS
75	London HLF 10479	All These Changes/When Kids Rule The World	10

RANDY MATTHEWS
70s	Myrrh MXX 1035	NOW DO YOU UNDERSTAND (LP, gatefold sleeve)	35

TOBIN MATTHEWS
63	Warner Brothers WB 117	Can't Stop Talking About You/When You Came Along	6

WINSTON MATTHEWS
71	Banana BA 329	Sun Is Shining/INN KEEPERS: My Friend (B-side actually "The Pressure Is On" by Purpleites)	18

MATTHEWS SOUTHERN COMFORT
70	Uni UNS 513	Colorado Springs Eternal/The Struggle	10
70	Uni UNS 521	Ballad Of Obray Ramsey/Parting	7
70	Uni UNS 526	Woodstock/Scion	5
70	Uni UNLS 108	MATTHEWS SOUTHERN COMFORT (LP)	30
70	Uni UNLS 112	SECOND SPRING (LP, with lyric insert)	15
70	Uni MKPS 2015	LATER THAT SAME YEAR... (LP)	15
(see also Ian Matthews, Marc Ellington, Southern Comfort)			

MATUMBI
73	G.G. GG 4540	Brother Louie Parts 1 & 2	10
77	Matumbi Music Co. MA004	Music In The Air/Guide Us (12")	30

HARVEY MATUSOW'S JEWS HARP BAND
69	Head HDS 4004	Afghan Red/Wet Socks	8
69	Head HDLS 6001	WAR BETWEEN THE FATS & THE THINS (LP)	25

MAUDS
67	Mercury MF 1000	Hold On/C'mon And Move	8
68	Mercury MF 1062	Soul Drippin'/Forever Gone	8

SUSAN MAUGHAN

61	Philips BF 1216	Mama Do The Twist/Blue Night In Yokohama	15
62	Philips BF 1236	Baby Doll Twist/Some Of These Days	15
62	Philips 326 533BF	I've Got To Learn To Forget/I Didn't Mean What I Said	10
62	Philips 326 544BF	Bobby's Girl/Come A Little Closer	6
63	Philips 326 562BF	Hand A Handkerchief To Helen/I'm A Lonely One Too	6
63	Philips 326 586BF	She's New To You/Don't Get Carried Away	8
63	Philips BF 1266	The Verdict Is Guilty/Bachelor Girl	8
64	Philips BF 1301	Hey Lover/Stop Your Foolin'	8
64	Philips BF 1336	Kiss Me Sailor/Call On Me	8
64	Philips BF 1363	Little Things Mean A Lot/That Other Place	30
64	Philips BF 1382	Make Him Mine/South American Joe	8
65	Philips BF 1399	You Can Never Get Away From You/Don't Be Afraid	6
65	Philips BF 1417	When She Walks Away/Come Along Down And See	6
65	Philips BF 1445	Poor Boy/Your Girl	6
66	Philips BF 1495	Come And Get Me/Don't Love Him Too Much	6
66	Philips BF 1518	Where The Bullets Fly/I'll Never Stop Loving You	5
67	Philips BF 1564	Don't Go Home (My Little Darlin')/Somebody To Love	5
68	Philips BF 1713	Cable Car For Two/Off My Mind	5
69	Philips BF 1824	We Really Go Together/I'll Never Forget You	5
62	Philips BBE 12525	HI, I'M SUSAN MAUGHAN AND I SING (EP)	30
63	Philips BBE 12549	FOUR BEAUX AND A BELLE (EP)	30
62	Philips 433 621 BE	EFFERVESCENT MISS MAUGHAN (EP)	30
63	Philips 433 641 BE	MORE OF MAUGHAN (EP)	30
63	Philips 632 300 BL	I WANNA BE BOBBY'S GIRL BUT ... (LP)	55
64	Philips BL 7577	SWINGIN' SUSAN (LP)	35
65	Philips BL 7637	SENTIMENTAL SUSAN (LP)	38
67	Wing WL 1105	BOBBY'S GIRL (LP)	15
69	Fontana SFL 13135	HEY LOOK ME OVER (LP)	12

MAU-MAUS

82	Pax PAX 6	SOCIETY'S REJECTS (EP)	18
82	Pax PAX 8	No Concern/Clampdown/Why Do We Suffer (p/s)	6
83	Pax/Paragon PAX 12	FACTS OF WAR (EP)	15
85	Rebellion REBEL 01	TEAR DOWN THE WALLS (EP)	15
85	Rebellion REBEL 1202	SCARRED FOR LIFE (12" EP)	15
83	Pax PAX 16	LIVE AT THE MARPLES (LP)	20
84	Pax PAX 20	RUNNING WITH THE PACK (LP)	20

MAUREENY WISHFULL

68	Moonshine WO 2388	THE MAUREENY WISHFULL ALBUM (LP, 300 copies, beware of counterfeits)	85

(see also Jimmy Page, Big Jim Sullivan, John Williams)

MAURICE & MAC

68	Chess CRS 8074	You Left The Water Running/You're The One	20
68	Chess CRS 8081	Why Don't You Try Me/Lean On Me	20

(see also Radiants)

MAWAMBA DUB

78	Warrior DRLP 1001	MAWANBA DUB (LP)	60

(see also Dennis Bowell)

MAX & ELAINE

73	Ackee ACK 516	I'm Leaving/(Version)	5

(see also Max Romeo)

MAX & GREGORY

73	Ackee ACK 525	My Jamaican Collie/Push It Down, Rub It Up	5

(see also Max Romeo)

SMILEY MAXEDON & HIS OKAW VALLEY BOYS

54	Columbia SCMC 3	Crazy To Care/In The Window Of My Heart (export issue)	22

JOE S. MAXEY

73	Action ACT 4607	Sign Of The Crab/May The Best Man Win (actually plays Packers' "Hole In The Wall"/"Go Ahead On")	15

MAX HEADROOM & CARPARKS

80	Parlophone R 6034	Don't Panic/Rhythm And Bluebeat (p/s)	6
82	Bandwagon B001	Soldier (no p/s)	30

MAX GROUP

69	Fab FAB 110	Abraham Vision/My Heart Was Breaking	5

MAXI

73	Decca F 13394	Do I Dream/Here Today And Gone Tomorrow	10

MAXIE (Romeo) & GLEN

71	G.G. GG 4520	Jordan River (actually by Max Romeo & Glen Adams)/ GLEN ADAMS: Version Two	10

(see also Max Romeo, Ethiopians)

MAXIMILIAN

61	London HLX 9356	The Snake/The Wanderer	75

(see also Del Shannon)

MAXIMO PARK

03	Billingham Records	Graffiti/Going Missing (red vinyl, 500 only, p/s)	50
05	Warp 7WAP183	The Coast Is Always Changing/The Night I Lost My Head (500 only, p/s)	20

MAXIM'S TRASH

79	Gimp GIMP 1	Disco Girls/Blu Shoes (plastic p/s & inner, hand-stamped white labels, tracks actually recorded in 1975)	40

(see also Sunset Boys, Captain Sensible, Johnny Moped)

MAXIMUM BAND
68	Fab FAB 51	Cupid/Hold Me Tight	5

MAXIMUM BREED
69	Revolution REV 1	Sitting In The Park/You've Got It	5

MAXINE
70	Smash SMA 2301	My Boy Lollipop/Everybody Needs Love	6

BRIAN MAXINE
72	EMI Starline SRS 5140	BRIAN MAXINE SINGS (LP)	35

(see also Fairport Convention)

MAX WEBSTER (BAND)
78	Capitol EST 11776	MEETING UP MY SLEEVE (LP)	12
79	Capitol EST 11937	A MILLION VACATIONS (LP)	12
80	Mercury 6337 144	UNIVERSAL JUVENILES (LP)	12

(see also Rush)

HOLLY MAXWELL
69	Buddah 201 056	Suffer/No-One Else	10

BILLY MAY & HIS ORCHESTRA
55	Capitol CL 14210	Loop-De-Loop Mambo/Rudolph The Red-Nosed Reindeer Mambo	6
55	Capitol CL 14266	How Important Can It Be?/Let It Happen	6
55	Capitol CL 14353	Hernando's Hideaway/Just Between Friends	6
56	Capitol CL 14551	Main Title From "The Man With The Golden Arm"/Suzette	12
56	Capitol CL 14609	Nightmare/The Beat	10
53	Capitol LC 6571	CAPITOL PRESENTS BILLY MAY AND HIS ORCHESTRA (10" LP)	12
53	Capitol LC 6623	BIG BAND BASH (10" LP)	12
54	Capitol LC 6644	BACCHANALIA (10" LP)	12

BRIAN MAY
83	EMI EMI 5436	Starfleet (Single Version)/Son Of Starfleet (p/s)	20
91	Parlophone R 6304	Driven By You (Single Version)/Just One Life (p/s)	5
91	Parlophone RDJ 6304	Driven By You (Edited Version)/(Pollarded Version)/(Special Version)/ (Proper Version) (promo only, no stars on p/s)	150
91	Parlophone 12R 6304	Driven By You (Single Version)/Driven By You (Ford Advert Version)/ Just One Life (Album Version)/Just One Life (Guitar Version) (12", p/s)	8
91	Parlophone CDR 6304	Driven By You (Single Version)/Driven By You (Ford Advert Version)/ Just One Life (Album Version)/Just One Life (Guitar Version) (CD)	10
91	Parlophone CDRDJ 6304	Driven By You (Edited Version)/(Pollarded Version)/(Special Version)/ (Proper Version) (CD, promo only, no stars on p/s)	150
92	Parlophone R 6320	Too Much Love Will Kill You/I'm Scared (Single Version) (p/s)	6
92	Parlophone CDRS 6320	Too Much Love Will Kill You (Album Version)/I'm Scared (Single Version)/ Too Much Love Will Kill You (Guitar Version)/Driven By You (New Version) (CD, red circular gatefold card p/s)	10
92	Parlophone MAYDJ 1	Too Much Love Will Kill You/Resurrection/Last Horizon/Driven By You (CD, promo only "Back To The Light" sampler, blue circular g/fold card p/s)	20
92	Parlophone RDJ 6329	Back To The Light (Radio Version)/Nothin' But Blue (Guitar Version) (promo only, p/s)	80
92	Parlophone CDRX 6329	Back To The Light/Starfleet/Let Me Out (CD)	8
92	Parlophone CDR 6329	Back To The Light/Nothin' But Blue (Guitar Version)/Blues Breaker (CD)	8
92	Parlophone CDRDJ 6329	Back To The Light (Radio Version)/Back To The Light (Album Version)/ Nothin' But Blue (Guitar Version) (CD)	10
93	Parlophone 12RPF 6351	Resurrection/Love Token/Too Much Love Will Kill You (Live Version) (12", with Cozy Powell, picture disc with insert in PVC sleeve)	8
93	Parlophone CDRS 6351	Resurrection/Love Token/Too Much Love Will Kill You (Live Version) (CD)	8
93	Parlophone CDR 6351	Resurrection/Driven By You Two/Back To The Light (live)/ Tie Your Mother Down (live, with Slash) (CD)	8
93	Parlophone R 6371	Last Horizon/39 (live)/Let Your Heart Rule Your Head (p/s)	5
93	Parlophone CDRS 6371	Last Horizon (Radio Version)/(live)/(Album Version)/We Will Rock You (live slow version)/We Will Rock You (live fast version) (CD, pop-up p/s)	8
93	Parlophone HORIZON1	Last Horizon (CD, 1-track, promo only)	30+
83	EMI SFLT 1078061	STARFLEET PROJECT (mini-LP)	15
93	Parlophone 0 7777 80400 19	BACK TO THE LIGHT (LP, textured sleeve)	20
93	Parlophone CDPCSD X123	BACK TO THE LIGHT (Commemorative Issue) (gold CD, 10,000 only, stickered jewel case)	50

(see also Queen, MC Spy-D & 'Friends', Eddie Howell, Holly Johnson, Bad News, D-Rok, Ian & Belinda, Rock Aid Armenia, Cozy Powell, Black Sabbath)

MARY MAY
64	Fontana TF 440	Anyone Who Had A Heart/They Say It's Wonderful	12

JOHN MAYALL (& BLUESBREAKERS)
SINGLES
64	Decca F 11900	Crawling Up A Hill/Mr. James (as John Mayall & Blues Breakers)	50
65	Decca F 12120	Crocodile Walk/Blues City Shakedown	40
65	Immediate IM 012	I'm Your Witchdoctor/Telephone Blues	40
66	Purdah 45-3502	Lonely Years/Bernard Jenkins (as John Mayall & Eric Clapton, 500 copies only)	300
66	Decca F 12490	Parchman Farm (solo)/Key To Love (B-side with Bluesbreakers)	25
66	Decca F 12506	Looking Back/So Many Roads (as John Mayall's Bluesbreakers & Peter Green)	15
67	Decca F 12545	Sitting In The Rain/Out Of Reach (as John Mayall's Bluesbreakers)	15
67	Decca F 12588	Curly/Rubber Duck (as Bluesbreakers)	12
67	Decca F 12621	Double Trouble/It Hurts Me Too (as John Mayall's Bluesbreakers)	15
67	Immediate IM 051	I'm Your Witchdoctor/Telephone Blues (reissue, as John Mayall with Eric Clapton)	15
67	Decca F 12684	Suspicions (Parts 1 & 2) (as John Mayall's Bluesbreakers)	12
68	Decca F 12732	Picture On The Wall/Jenny (as John Mayall)	10

68	Decca F 12792	No Reply/She's Too Young (as John Mayall's Bluesbreakers)...............10
68	Decca F 12846	The Bear/2401 8
69	Polydor 56544	Don't Waste My Time/Don't Pick A Flower 10
70	Polydor 2066 021	Thinking Of My Woman/Plan Your Revolution...............10
67	Decca DFE-R 8673	THE BLUESBREAKERS WITH PAUL BUTTERFIELD (EP) 48

LPs

65	Decca LK 4680	PLAYS JOHN MAYALL — LIVE AT KLOOKS KLEEK! 70
66	Decca LK 4804	BLUES BREAKERS WITH ERIC CLAPTON (original label, mono)...............80
67	Decca LK/SKL 4853	A HARD ROAD (as John Mayall & Bluesbreakers) 40
67	Decca LK/SKL 4890	CRUSADE (as John Mayall & Bluesbreakers) 30
67	Ace of Clubs ACL/SCL 1243	THE BLUES ALONE 22
68	Decca LK/SKL 4918	THE DIARY OF A BAND VOL. 1...............25
68	Decca LK/SKL 4919	THE DIARY OF A BAND VOL. 2...............25
68	Decca LK/SKL 4945	BARE WIRES (gatefold sleeve, as John Mayall & Blues Breakers)...............30
68	Decca LK/SKL 4972	BLUES FROM LAUREL CANYON (gatefold sleeve)...............30

*(The above LPs were originally issued with unboxed Decca label logos.
1970s boxed-logo repressings are worth two-thirds these values.)*

69	Polydor 583 571	THE TURNING POINT 20
69	Decca LK/SKL 5010	LOOKING BACK 22
69	Decca SKL 4804	BLUES BREAKERS WITH ERIC CLAPTON (reissue, original label, stereo).......35
70s	Decca LK/SKL 4804	BLUES BREAKERS WITH ERIC CLAPTON (reissue, boxed logo, mono/stereo) . 18/15
70	Decca (S)PA 47	THE WORLD OF JOHN MAYALL 12
70	Polydor 583 580	EMPTY ROOMS (with lyric insert)...............15
70	Polydor 2425 020	U.S.A. UNION...............15
71	Decca SPA 138	THE WORLD OF JOHN MAYALL VOL. 2...............12
71	Polydor 2657 005	BACK TO THE ROOTS (2-LP)...............25
71	Polydor 2483 016	BEYOND THE TURNING POINT 12
71	Decca SKL 5086	THRU THE YEARS...............15
71	Polydor 2425 085	MEMORIES 12
72	Polydor 2425 103	JAZZ-BLUES FUSION 12
73	Polydor 2391 047	MOVING ON 12
75	ABC ABCL 5115	NEW YEAR, NEW BAND, NEW COMPANY (gatefold sleeve) 12
76	Polydor 2482 272	JOHN MAYALL...............12

(see also Paul Butterfield, Eric Clapton, Jack Bruce, Peter Green, McGuinness Flint, Johnny Almond Music Machine, Alan Skidmore, Mick Taylor, Dick Heckstall-Smith, Keef Hartley, Paul Williams, Ray Warleigh, Colosseum, Henry Lowther, Jon Mark, Aynsley Dunbar, Fleetwood Mac)

MAY BLITZ

70	Vertigo 6360 007	MAY BLITZ (LP, gatefold sleeve, swirl label) 60
71	Vertigo 6360 037	THE 2ND OF MAY (LP, gatefold sleeve, swirl label)...............150

(see also Bakerloo)

MAYDAY

80	Reddingtons R.R. DAN 2	Day After Day/Love In The Spaceage (p/s)...............8

JOHN MAYER (GROUP)

66	Columbia DB 8037	Acka Raga (as John Mayer's I-J-7)/Gana (as John Mayer & Joe Harriott) 8
60s	National Petrol W 1	"Music For People Who Go Your Own Way" Themes 1 & 2 (p/s, with Frank Cordell)...............10
67	Columbia SX 6122	INDO-JAZZ FUSIONS (LP) 30
69	Sonet SNTF 603	ETUDES (LP, as John Mayer Indo-Jazz Fusions) 18

(see also Joe Harriott & John Mayer, Radha Krishna)

NATHANIEL MAYER & FABULOUS TWILIGHTS

62	HMV POP 1041	Village Of Love/I Want A Woman...............80

CURTIS MAYFIELD

70	Buddah 2011 055	(Don't Worry) If There's A Hell Below We're All Going To Go (Edit)/The Makings Of You 8
71	Buddah 2011 080	Move On Up/Give It Up/Beautiful Brother Of Mine (maxi-single)...............15
71	Buddah 2011 101	We Got To Have Peace/People Get Ready 6
72	Buddah 2011 119	Keep On Keepin' On/Stone Junkie 6
72	Buddah 2011 141	Freddie's Dead (Theme From "Superfly")/Underground...............6
72	Buddah 2011 156	Superfly/Give Me Your Love (Love Song)...............6
73	Buddah 2011 187	Back To The World (edit)/The Other Side Of Town 6
74	Buddah BDS 402	Kung Fu/Right On For The Darkness 6
74	Buddah BDS 410	Move On Up/Give It Up 8
75	Buddah BDS 426	Mother's Son/Love Me Right In The Pocket...............6
71	Buddah 2318 015	CURTIS (LP, gatefold sleeve)...............25
71	Buddah 2659 004	CURTIS/LIVE (2-LP)...............22
72	Buddah 2318 045	ROOTS (LP, gatefold sleeve) 20
72	Buddah 2318 065	SUPERFLY (LP, soundtrack, gatefold sleeve) 20
73	Buddah 2318 085	BACK TO THE WORLD (LP, gatefold sleeve) 12
73	Buddah 2318 091	CURTIS IN CHICAGO (LP, TV soundtrack, gatefold sleeve, with Impressions, Jerry Butler, Gene Chandler & Leroy Hutson)...............18
74	Buddah 2318 099	SWEET EXORCIST (LP) 15
74	Buddah BDLP 2001	CURTIS/LIVE (2-LP, reissue) 18
74	Buddah BDLP 4010	CLAUDINE (LP, soundtrack, with Gladys Knight) 15
74	Buddah BDLH 5001	SWEET EXORCIST (LP, reissue) 12
74	Buddah BDLH 5005	CURTIS (LP, reissue)...............12
74	Buddah BDLH 5006	ROOTS (LP, reissue)...............12
74	Buddah BDLP 4015	MOVE ON UP (THE BEST OF CURTIS MAYFIELD) (LP) 12
74	Buddah BDLP 4029	GOT TO FIND A WAY (LP)...............12
75	Buddah BDLP 4033	THERE'S NO PLACE LIKE AMERICA TODAY (LP)...............12
76	Buddah BDLP 4042	GIVE GET TAKE AND HAVE (LP)...............12
76	Atlantic K 56248	SPARKLE (LP, soundtrack, with Aretha Franklin) 12

(see also Impressions, Blow Monkeys)

PERCY MAYFIELD
63	HMV POP 1185	The River's Invitation/Baby Please	10
76	Speciality SPE 5007	Please Send Me Someone To Love/The River's Invitation	6
67	HMV CLP/CSD 3572	MY JUG AND I (LP)	40

MAYFIELD'S MULE
69	Parlophone R 5817	Double Dealing Woman/(Drinking My) Moonshine (some in p/s)	30/15
70	Parlophone R 5843	I See A River/"Queen" Of Rock'n'Roll	20
70	Parlophone R 5858	We Go Rollin'/My Way Of Living	18

(see also Elastic Band, Sweet, Amen Corner, Andy Scott)

MAYHEM
85	Vigilante VIG 1	Bloodrush/Addictive Risk (p/s)	6
85	Vigilante VIG 1T	Bloodrush/Addictive Risk (12", p/s)	10

MAYHEM
97	Amazon 012	WOLF'S LAIR ABYSS (LP)	30

BILL MAYNARD
57	Decca F 10868	Hey Liley, Liley Lo/Who Needs You (78 rpm = £12)	8

JENNY MAYNARD
68	Inter-zel DR 001	He Gives Me Love/Something Here In My Heart	5

(TOOTS &) THE MAYTALS
63	Blue Beat BB 176	Hallelujah/Helping Ages Past	20
64	Blue Beat BB 215	He Is Real/Domino	20
64	Blue Beat BB 220	Pain In My Belly/BUSTER'S ALL STARS: City Riot	25
64	Blue Beat BB 231	Dog War/RECO & CREATORS: I'll Be Home	30
64	Blue Beat BB 245	Little Slea (song actually "Little Flea")/Don't Talk (song actually "Pain In My Belly") (both sides miscredited as V. Maytals)	25
64	Blue Beat BB 254	Sweet Love/PRINCE BUSTER: Wings Of A Dove	25
64	Blue Beat BB 255	Judgement Day/Goodbye Jane	20
64	Blue Beat BB 270	You've Got Me Spinning/Lovely Walking	35
64	R&B JB 130	Hurry Up/Love Divide	18
64	R&B JB 141	Another Chance/FRANKIE ANDERSON: Always On A Sunday	18
64	R&B JB 153	Give Me Your Love/He Will Provide	18
64	R&B JB 164	Hello Honey/ROLAND ALPHONSO: Crime Wave	35
64	R&B JB 174	Christmas Feelings/Let's Kiss	18
65	Blue Beat BB 281	Looking Down The Street/PRINCE BUSTER: Blues Market	20
65	Blue Beat BB 299	Light Of The World/Lovely Walking	25
65	Blue Beat BB 306	Ska War (song actually "Treating Me Bad")/SKATALITES: Perhaps	35
65	Ska Beat JB 202	Let's Jump/Joy And Jean	20
65	Island WI 200	Never You Change/What's On Your Mind	22
65	Island WI 213	My New Name/It's No Use	22
65	Black Swan WI 464	John James/THEO BECKFORD: Sailing On	20
66	Doctor Bird DB 1019	If You Act This Way/SIR LORD COMIC & HIS COWBOYS: Ska-ing West	40
66	Doctor Bird DB 1038	Bam Bam/So Mad In Love	35
68	Pyramid PYR 6030	54-46, That's My Number/ROLAND ALPHONSO: Dreamland	25
68	Pyramid PYR 6043	Struggle/ROLAND ALPHONSO: Stream Of Life	25
68	Pyramid PYR 6048	Just Tell Me/Reborn	18
68	Pyramid PYR 6050	Bim Today, Bam Tomorrow/Hold On	25
68	Pyramid PYR 6052	We Shall Overcome/DESMOND DEKKER & ACES: Fu Manchu	40
68	Pyramid PYR 6055	Schooldays/Big Man	15
68	Pyramid PYR 6057	Do The Reggay/BEVERLEY'S ALLSTARS: Motoring	25
68	Pyramid PYR 6064	Scare Him/In My Heart	15
69	Pyramid PYR 6066	Don't Trouble Trouble/BEVERLEY'S ALLSTARS: Double Action	18
69	Pyramid PYR 6070	Aldina/Hold On	15
69	Pyramid PYR 6073	Pressure Drop/BEVERLEY'S ALLSTARS: Express	15
69	Pyramid PYR 6074	Sweet And Dandy/Oh Yeah	12
69	Trojan TR 7709	Pressure Drop/BEVERLEY'S ALLSTARS: Smoke Screen	10
69	Nu Beat NB 031	My Testimony/JOHNSON BOYS: One Dollar Of Soul (actually by Ethiopians)	10
69	Trojan TR 7711	Monkey Man/Night And Day	8
70	Trojan TR 7726	Sweet And Dandy/54-46, That's My Number	8
70	Trojan TR 7741	Bla Bla Bla/Reborn	6
70	Trojan TR 7757	Water Melon/She's My Scorcher	6
70	Trojan TR 7786	Doctor Lester/Sun, Moon And Star	6
70	Summit SUM 8510	Peeping Tom/BEVERLEY'S ALLSTARS: Version	6
71	Trojan TR 7808	54-46 Was My Number/BEVERLEY'S ALLSTARS: 54-46 Instrumental	6
71	Trojan TR 7849	Johnny Cool Man/BEVERLEY's ALLSTARS: Version	5
71	Summit SUM 8513	Monkey Girl/BEVERLEY'S ALLSTARS: Version	6
71	Summit SUM 8520	One Eye Enos/BEVERLEY'S ALLSTARS: Enos Version	6
71	Summit SUM 8527	It's You/BEVERLEY'S ALLSTARS: Version	6
71	Summit SUM 8529	Walk With Love/BEVERLEY'S ALLSTARS: Version	6
71	Summit SUM 8533	Never You Change/BEVERLEY'S ALLSTARS: Version	6
72	Attack ATT 8042	It Was Written Down/Sweet And Dandy	5
72	Summit SUM 8536	Thy Kingdom Come/BEVERLEY'S ALLSTARS: Version	6
72	Summit SUM 8537	It Must Be True Love/BEVERLEY'S ALLSTARS: Version	6
72	Blue Mountain BM 1020	Christmas Song/I Can't Believe	6
72	Dynamic DYN 438	Redemption Song	6
72	Trojan TR 7865	Louie Louie/Pressure Drop '72	5
73	Dragon DRA 1007	Sit Right Down/Screwface Underground/Pomps & Pride (as Toots & Maytals)	5
73	Dragon DRA 1013	Funky Kingston/Country Road (as Toots & Maytals)	5
73	Dragon DRA 1016	In The Dark/Sailing On (as Toots & Maytals)	5
74	Dragon DRA 1021	Fever/It Was Written Down	5
74	Dragon DRA 1024	Time Tough/Time Tough Version	5
74	Dragon DRA 1026	Sailing On/If You Act This Way (as Toots & Maytals)	5
64	Ska Beat JBL 1113	PRESENTING THE MAYTALS (NEVER GROW OLD) (LP)	180
66	Doctor Bird DLM 5003	THE SENSATIONAL MAYTALS (LP)	180

70	Trojan TBL 107	MONKEY MAN (LP)	25
73	Trojan TRLS 65	FROM THE ROOTS (LP)	20
73	Dragon DRLS 5002	FUNKY KINGSTON (LP)	12
74	Dragon DRLS 5004	IN THE DARK (LP)	12
74	Prince Buster PB 11	ORIGINAL GOLDEN OLDIES VOLUME 3 (LP)	15

(see also Vikings, Flames, Philip James & Blues Busters, Don Drummond, Stranger, Lord Creator, Larry Marshall, Derrick Morgan, Brentwood Road Allstars, Roland Alphonso, Charmers)

MAYTONES

68	Blue Cat BS 149	Billy Goat/Call You Up	15
69	Blue Cat BS 152	Loving Reggae/Musical Beat	18
69	Blue Cat BS 166	Copper Girl/Love	40
69	Blue Cat BS 173	We Nah Tek You Lick/Dig Away De Money	18
69	Camel CA 27	Sentimental Reason/Lover Girl	8
69	Songbird SB 1009	I've Been Loving You/Memphis Reggae	10
69	Songbird SB 1010	Gin Gan Goolie/I'm Thirsty	7
70	Punch PH 35	Serious Love/CHARLIE ACE: Musical Combination	8
70	Explosion EX 2012	Funny Man/G.G. ALLSTARS: Champion	8
70	Explosion EX 2013	Sentimental Reason/Lover Girl	7
70	Explosion EX 2014	Barrabus/G.G. ALLSTARS: Barrabus Part 2 (B-side actually "This Kind Of Life")	8
70	Explosion EX 2027	Cecelia (actually by Keeling Beckford)/Chariot Without Horse (B-side actually "Willie My Darling")	6
70	Explosion EX 2033	Another Festival/Happy Time	6
70	Bullet BU 446	I Don't Like To Interfere/Preaching Love	5
70	Camel CA 47	Black And White/GLORIA'S ALLSTARS: Jumbo Jet	10
70	Camel CA 49	Since You Left/GLORIA'S ALL STARS: Bird Wing	15
71	Duke DU 116	Babylon A Fall/TONY KING: Version Buggy	10
71	Camel CA 61	Judas (actually by Gladstone Anderson & Followers)/Mi Nah Tek	7
71	G.G. GG 4508	Cleanliness/G.G. ALL STARS: Cleanliness Version 2	7
71	G.G. GG 4511	Let The Version Play/Lonely Nights	7
71	G.G. GG 4522	Black And White/TREVOR BROWN: Mr. Brown	6
71	G.G. GG 4525	Bongo Man Rise/ROY & BIM: Remember	6
72	G.G. GG 4530	Donkey Face/G.G. ALL STARS: Donkey Face – Version	8
72	G.G. GG 4531	As Long As You Love Me (Side One)/As Long As You Love Me (Side Two)	6
72	Attack ATT 8029	Hands And Feet/LLOYD & CAREY: Scorpion	6
72	Grape GR 3028	If Loving You Was Wrong/FLOWERS & ALVIN: In De Pum Pum	6
72	Pama PM 846	I'm Feeling Lonely/G.G. ALLSTARS: Version	6
72	Explosion EX 2076	Brown Girl/SHORTY PERRY: Half-Way-Tree Rock	6
73	Pama PM 871	All Over The World People Are Changing/Changing World (Dubwise)	5
73	Bread BR 1114	All Over The World People Are Changing/Changing World (Dubwise)	5
73	Bullet BU 528	People Get Funny/G.G. ALL STARS: Version	5

(see also Vern & Alvin, Vern & Son, Roland Alphonso, G.G. Rhythm Section, Cynthia Richards, Max Romeo, Charlie Ace, Dennis Alcapone)

MAZE (U.K.)

| 66 | Reaction 591 009 | Hello Stranger/Telephone | 80 |
| 67 | MGM MGM 1368 | Catari Catari/Easy Street | 40 |

(see also M.I. Five, Deep Purple)

MAZE (U.S.)

82	Capitol 12CL 211	Joy And Pain/Happy (12")	8
82	Capitol 12CL 244	Before I Let Go/Golden Time Of Day (12")	8
77	Capitol E-ST 11607	MAZE FEATURING FRANKIE BEVERLY (LP)	12

MAZZY STAR

93	R. T. Singles Club 45 rev 19	Five String Serenade/Under My Car (p/s)	12
96	Capitol CL 781	FLOWERS IN DECEMBER (EP, blue vinyl)	12
90	Rough Trade ROUGH 158	SHE HANGS BRIGHTLY (LP)	35
93	Capitol EST2206	SO TONIGHT THAT I MIGHT SEE YOU (LP)	20

JACKIE McAULEY

71	Dawn DNS 1011	Turning Green/It's Alright	7
72	Dawn DNS 1020	Rocking Shoes/One Fine Day	7
71	Dawn DNLS 3023	JACKIE McAULEY (LP)	60

(see also Them, Belfast Gypsies, Trader Horne, Freaks Of Nature)

McAULEY SCHENKER GROUP

90	EMI EMPD 127	Anytime/What We Need/Anytime (Edit) (12", picture disc)	8
90	EMI Electrola CDEM 127	Anytime (LP Version)/What We Need/Anytime (Single Edit) (CD)	8
89	EMI CDP 518941	SAVE YOURSELF SPECIMEN DISC (CD, promo, interviews/album excerpts)	15

(see also Michael Schenker, Michael Schenker Group)

GERRY McAVOY

| 79 | Bridgehouse BHS 004 | Street Talk/Many Rivers To Cross (p/s) | 10 |

JIMMY McBEATH

| 67 | Topic 12T 173 | WILD ROVER NO MORE (LP, blue label with booklet) | 12 |

NICKO McBRAIN

| 91 | EMI NICKO 1 | Rhythm Of The Beast/Beehive Boogie (p/s) | 6 |
| 91 | EMI NICKOPD 1 | Rhythm Of The Beast/McBrain Damage Interview (shaped picture disc with insert & plinth) | 10 |

(see also Iron Maiden, Pat Travers)

FRANKIE McBRIDE

| 67 | Emerald MD 1081 | Five Little Fingers/Do You Mind If You Leave Me Sleeping | 5 |

DAN McCAFFERTY
75	Mountain TOP 5	Watcha Gonna Do About It/Nightingale	5
75	Mountain DAN 1	Stay With Me Baby/Out Of Time/Watcha Gonna Do About It (p/s)	7
75	Mountain TOPS 102	DAN McCAFFERTY (LP, with inner sleeve)	12

(see also Nazareth, Sensational Alex Harvey Band, Mitchell/Coe Mysteries, Roger Glover)

JERRY McCAIN
69	Python 02	Homogenised Love/728 Texas (99 copies only)	45

CASH McCALL
63	Ember EMB S 173	Anytime/From The Very First Rose	12
65	Ember EMB S 204	Many Are The Words (I've Left Unspoken)/Buenos Noches	12

CASH McCALL
67	Chess CRS 8056	It's Wonderful (To Be In Love)/Let's Try It Over	18

DARRELL McCALL
61	Capitol CL 15196	My Kind Of Lovin'/Beyond Imagination	8
63	Philips 304 002 BF	Dear One/I've Been Known	10
63	Philips BF 1259	Hud/No Place To Hide	7

TOUSSAINT McCALL
67	Pye International 7N 25420	Nothing Takes The Place Of You/Shimmy	25
72	Mojo 2092 035	Nothing Takes The Place Of You/Shimmy (reissue)	8

NOEL McCALLA
80	Direction 58-8731	Beggin'/Ain't That Peculiar/One More Heartache/Shake Me, Wake Me	8

(see also Manfred Mann's Earth Band)

DAVID McCALLUM
66	Capitol CL 15439	Communication/My Carousel	7
66	Capitol CL 15474	In The Garden/The House On Breckenridge Lane	5
66	Capitol (S)T 2432	MUSIC ... A PART OF ME (LP)	25
66	Capitol (S)T 2498	MUSIC ... A BIT MORE OF ME (LP)	15

McCALMANS
68	One Up OU 2161	McCALMANS' FOLK (LP)	15

JIM McCANN
72	Polydor 2489 053	McCANNED! (LP)	25

(see also Ludlows)

LES McCANN (LTD)
60	Vogue V 2417	Fish This Week/Vakushna (as Les McCann Ltd)	5
67	Mercury MF 973	All/Bucket O'Grease	15
69	Atlantic 584 284	With These Hands/Burnin' Coal	15
60	Vogue LAE 12238	THE TRUTH (LP)	12
66	Mercury LML 4026	PLAYS THE HITS (LP, mono)	12
69	Atlantic 588 176	MUCH LES (LP)	12
60s	Fontana 688 150ZL	THE WAILERS! (with Gerald Wilson Orchestra)	12

McCARTHY
86	Wall Of Salmon MAC 001	In Purgatory/The Comrade Era/Something Wrong Somewhere (foldover p/s in poly bag, white labels)	20
86	Pink PINKY 12	Red Sleeping Beauty/From The Damned (stickered p/s)	8
86	Pink PINKY 12T	Red Sleeping Beauty/The Comrade Era/From The Damned/ For The Fat Lady (12", p/s with foldover insert)	8
87	Pink PINKY 17	Frans Hals/The Fall (p/s)	5
87	Pink PINKY 17T	Frans Hals/The Fall (Remix)/Kill Kill Kill Kill/Frans Hals (Version) (12", p/s)	8
87	September SEPT 1	The Well Of Loneliness/Antiamericancretin/Unfortunately (p/s)	6
87	September SEPT 1T	The Well Of Loneliness/Bad Dreams/Someone Worse Off/ Antiamericancretin/Unfortunately (12", p/s)	8
88	September SEPTT 4	This Nelson Rockefeller (p/s)	10

(see also Stereolab)

KEITH McCARTHY
67	Coxsone CS 7014	Everybody Rude Now/BASES: Beware	30

LYN & GRAHAM McCARTHY
65	Columbia DB 7584	Seven Doves/Out After Ale	6
66	Columbia DB 7921	I Can't Help But Wonder/There's Got To Be Love	6
66	Columbia DB 8087	The Turkey's Trial/Bitter Withy	6
68	Columbia DB 8422	I Think It's Going To Rain/Once I Was	7
68	RCA RCA 1759	Scarborough Fair — Canticle/Wild Berries	5

MARY McCARTHY
67	CBS 2832	The Folk I Love/You Know He Did	7
67	CBS 2987	Happy Days And Lonely Night/Easy Kind Of Love	6

CECIL McCARTNEY
68	Columbia DB 8474	Hey Aleuthia I Want You/Liquid Blue	15
69	Columbia DB 8595	Orange And Green/Cloudy	7
68	Columbia S(C)X 6283	OM (LP)	22

LINDA McCARTNEY
(see under Suzy & The Red Stripes)

PAUL McCARTNEY/WINGS
SINGLES
71	Apple R 5889	Another Day/Oh Woman, Oh Why	5
71	Apple R 5914	The Back Seat Of My Car/Heart Of The Country (as Paul & Linda McCartney)	5
72	Apple R 5932	Love Is Strange/I Am Your Singer (unreleased)	1500
72	Apple R 5936	Give Ireland Back To The Irish/(Version) (as Wings, yellow 'Wings' die-cut sl.)	10
73	Apple R 5985	My Love/The Mess (as McCartney's Wings, later as Paul McCartney/Wings)	20/5
78	Parlophone R 6020	I've Had Enough/Deliver Your Children (p/s, as Wings)	6

80	Parlophone 12R 6039	Temporary Secretary/Secret Friend (12", p/s)	30
82	Parlophone R 6054	Ebony And Ivory/Rainclouds (unreleased sepia-toned 'studio photo' p/s; beware of clever counterfeits)	50
82	Epic A 11-2729	The Girl Is Mine (with Michael Jackson)/MICHAEL JACKSON: Can't Get Outta The Rain (picture disc)	25
84	Parlophone 12RP 6080	No More Lonely Nights (Extended Version)/Silly Love Songs/No More Lonely Nights (Ballad) (12", picture disc)	20
84	Parlophone 12RDJ 6080T	No More Lonely Nights (Mole Mix) (1-sided promo – only 250 copies)	650
84	Parlophone 12R(DJ) 6080	No More Lonely Nights (Extended Version)/Silly Love Songs/No More Lonely Nights (Ballad) (12", promo, blue 'Give My Regards To Broad Street' label, black die-cut sleeve)	100
84	Parlophone RP 6086	We All Stand Together/We All Stand Together (Humming Version) (with Frog Chorus, shaped picture disc, some in printed PVC sleeve)	25/8
85	Parlophone RP 6118	Spies Like Us/My Carnival (shaped picture disc)	25
85	Parlophone 12RP 6118	Spies Like Us (Party Mix)/Spies Like Us (Alternative Mix)/Spies Like Us (DJ Version)/My Carnival (Party Mix) (12", picture disc)	20
86	Parlophone 10R 6133	Press/It's Not True/Press (Video Edit) (10", circular foldout p/s)	10
86	Parlophone R 6148/ R 6018	Only Love Remains/Tough On A Tightrope/Mull Of Kintyre/Girls' School (p/s, stickered double pack in PVC sleeve, no p/s on R 6018)	10
87	Parlophone CDR 6170	Once Upon A Long Ago/Back On My Feet/Don't Get Around Much Anymore/Kansas City (CD, card sleeve with anti-static inner)	15
87	A&M FREE 21	Long Tall Sally (live)/I Saw Her Standing There (live) (p/s, free with "The Prince's Trust 10th Anniversary Birthday Party" LP [AMA 3906])	6
89	Parlophone RX 6223	This One/The Long And Winding Road (p/s, envelope pack with 6 postcards)	10

PROMO SINGLES

74	EMI R 5997	Band On The Run (Edited Version)/(Full Version) (demo)	150
74	Apple R 5999	Junior's Farm (Edited Version)/Junior's Farm (Full Version) (demo)	100
75	Apple R 5999	Sally G/Junior's Farm (reversed sides, demo)	120
76	Parlophone R 6014	Silly Love Songs (Edited Version)/Silly Love Songs (Full Version) (demo)	50
76	Parlophone R 6015	Let 'Em In (Edited Version)/Let 'Em In (Full Version) (demo)	50
77	Capitol R 6018	Mull Of Kintyre (Edited Version)/Girls' School (Edited Version) (demo)	50
77	MPL Publishing MPL 1	We've Moved! (music publishing sampler with excerpts by Wings, Peggy Lee, Gene Vincent, Frank Sinatra, etc.; some in press pack & insert)	350/250
78	Parlophone R 6019	With A Little Luck (Edited Version)/Backwards Traveller-Cuff Link (demo)	40
80	Parlophone R 6037DJ	Waterfalls (3.22) (edit)/Check My Machine (demo)	40
80	Parlophone R 6039	Temporary Secretary (1-sided demo, no p/s)	75
84	Parlophone 12RDJ 6080T	No More Lonely Nights (Mole Mix) (12", 1-sided, plain white numbered sleeve with plain white inner sleeve & insert, 250 only; beware of counterfeits with scratched [not stamped] matrix)	250
85	Parlophone RDJ 6118	Spies Like Us (DJ Version 3.46)/My Carnival (demo, white printed die-cut sleeve)	35
89	Parl. 12R LOVE 6223	This One (Lovejoy's Remix) (12", 1-sided, plain label, black die-cut sleeve)	35
89	Parlophone GOOD 1	Good Sign (6.51)/Good Sign (Groove Mix) (7.22) (12", black die-cut sleeve)	45
89	Parlophone RDJ 6235	Figure Of Eight (Edited Version 3.59)/Ou Est Le Soleil? (Edited Version 3.57) (demo, standard p/s)	30
89	Parlophone RDJ 6238	Party (Remix By Bruce Forest)/Party (different remix) (12", some copies listed as 'Party Party', some with insert)	50/35
90	Parlophone 12 SOL 1	Où Est Le Soleil? (Tub Dub Mix)/Où Est Le Soleil? (Instrumental Mix) (12", black die-cut stickered sleeve, some with insert)	45/20
93	Parlophone 12 DELIVDJ 1	Deliverance/Deliverance (Dub Mix) (12", green label, plain black die-cut sleeve)	25
93	Parlophone CDRDJ 6338	C'mon People (Radio Edit)/C'mon People (CD)	30
93	Parlophone CDRS 6347	Biker Like An Icon/Things We Said Today/Mean Woman Blues/Midnight Special (CD, unissued)	
93	Parlophone CDRDJ 6347	Biker Like An Icon/Things We Said Today/Mean Woman Blues/Midnight Special (CD, no inlay, jewel case with large sticker; beware of counterfeits with thicker, blurred label print & small sticker on case)	70
93	Parlophone PM LIVE 1	PAUL IS LIVE! (CD, 5-track sampler)	30
99	Parlophone PROMO WC	WORKING CLASSICAL (CD, 4-track sampler, gatefold card sleeve, promo only)	30
99	EMI RDR 004	RUN DEVIL RUN (CD, 2-track sampler, card sleeve, promo only)	18
01	WINDJ 002	Silly Love Songs (Loop Da Loop Mix)/Coming Up (Linus Loves Mix) (12" 50 copies)	500

ALBUM

| 70 | Apple TA/TD-PCS 7102 | McCARTNEY (reel-to-reel tape, jewel case, mono/stereo) | 100/50 |

PROMO ALBUMS

79	Parlophone PCTCP 257	BACK TO THE EGG (LP, as Wings, MPL in-house picture disc; die-cut sleeve, matrix numbers YEX 987-2 & YEX 988-4 or -1; beware counterfeits)	1000+
79	Parlophone PCTC 257	BACK TO THE EGG (LP, box set with badge, booklet, sticker, postcard & 5 cigarette cards; with or without T-shirt; beware of counterfeits with blurred printing)	300/250
79	Capitol (no cat. no.)	MPL PRESENTS (6-LP, box set, hand-numbered, 25 only)	700
88	Parlophone PMBOX 11-19	ALL THE BEST! ('Special Edition') (9 x 7" box set, in black die-cut sleeves, with signed 7" print; some with genuine signatures)	200/75
93	Parlophone CDPMCOLDJ 1	PAUL McCARTNEY COLLECTION (CD, 18-track sampler)	25

(see also Beatles, Country Hams, Percy 'Thrills' Thrillington, Fireman, Mike McGear, Suzy & The Red Stripes, George Martin, Spirit Of Play, Ferry Aid, Michael Jackson)

CAROLINE McCAUSLAND

| 60s | Happy Face MMLP 1022 | SONGS FOR GALA (LP) | 50 |

IAN McLAGAN

79	Mercury MER1	La De Da/Hold On (p/s)	5
80	Mercury 9100 072	TROUBLEMAKER (LP) (with poster)	12
	(see also Faces)		

MINT VALUE £

DAVE McCLAREN
71	Big BG 323	Love Is What I Bring (actually by Dave Barker & Uniques)/
		RUPIE EDWARDS ALL STARS: Love Version (with U Roy Junior) 18

TOMMY McCLENNAN
75	Flyright LP 112	TRAVELIN' HIGHWAY MAN (LP). 15

DELBERT McCLINTON
62	Decca F 11541	Hully Gully/Baby Heartbreak 12

BOBBY McCLURE
(see under Bobby McLure)

CHRIS McCLURE (SECTION)
66	Decca F 12346	The Dying Swan/The Land Of The Golden Tree. 10
68	Polydor 56227	Hazy People/I'm Just A Country Boy 15
68	Polydor 56259	Answer To Everything/Meditation 7
69	RCA RCA 1849	Our Song Of Love/Weather Vane. 7
69	CBS 7646	You're Only Passing Time/Sing Our Song (as Chris McClure Section) 8

(see also Marmalade)

BRIAN McCOLLOM FOLK GROUP
66	Pye 7N 17198	This Dusty Road/Henry Joy McCraken. 5

TOMMY McCOOK & BOBBY ELLIS
75	Grove Music GMLP 002	BLAZING HORNS (LP) 30

TOMMY McCOOK (& SUPERSONICS)
63	Island WI 102	Adam's Apple/MAYTALS: Every Time (B-side actually by Tonettes). 25
63	Island WI 118	Below Zero/LEE PERRY: Never Get Weary. 35
63	Island WI 124	Junior Jive/HORACE SEATON: Power 22
64	R&B JB 139	Sampson/ROY & ANNETTE: My Arms Are Waiting 35
64	R&B JB 163	Bridge View/NAOMI & CO: What Can I Do (B-side actually by Naomi & Clive) . . . 35
64	Port-O-Jam PJ 4001	Exodus (& His Group)/LEE PERRY: Help The Weak 40
64	Port-O-Jam PJ 4003	Jam Rock/LEE PERRY: Band Minded People 40
64	Port-O-Jam PJ 4010	Road Bloack/LEE PERRY: Chatty Chatty Woman . . . . 50+
64	Black Swan WI 422	Two For One/LASCELLES PERKINS: I Don't Know 25
65	Island WI 232	Rocket Ship/JUSTIN HINDS & DOMINOES: Turn Them Back. 40
66	Rio R 100	Jerk Time (with Supersonics)/UNIQUES: The Journey. 22
66	Rio R 101	Out Of Space (with Supersonics)/UNIQUES: Do Me Good. 22
66	Rio R 103	Ska Jam/Smooth Sailing (with Supersonics). 30
66	Rio R 104	Riverton City/HEPTONES: Gunmen Coming To Town 45
66	Doctor Bird DB 1028	More Love/SILVERTONES: True Confession 22
66	Doctor Bird DB 1032	Naked City (with Supersonics)/NORMA FRASER: Heartaches 20
66	Doctor Bird DB 1047	Spanish Eyes (with Lynn Taitt)/STRANGER & HORTENSE: Loving Wine 20
66	Doctor Bird DB 1051	A Little Bit Of Heaven (& His Band)/LLOYD WILLIAMS: Sad World 22
66	Doctor Bird DB 1053	Indian Love Call (with Supersonics)/OWEN & LEON: How Would You Feel 22
66	Doctor Bird DB 1056	Danger Man (with Supersonics)/ERIC MORRIS: If I Didn't Love You 20
66	Doctor Bird DB 1061	What Now/Don't Stay Away 22
67	Doctor Bird DB 1058	Jam Session (with Supersonics)/LLOYD & GLEN: Jezebel 22
67	Island WI 3047	One Two Three Kick/TREASURE ISLE BOYS: What A Fool
		(B-side actually by Silvertones). 40
67	Island WI 3049	Saboo (with Supersonics)/MOVING BROTHERS: Darling I Love You 30
67	Treasure Isle TI 7017	Persian Cat/JUSTIN HINDS: Once A Man. 18
67	Treasure Isle TI 7018	Saboo (with Supersonics)/MOVING BROTHERS: Darling I Love You (reissue). . . 20
67	Treasure Isle TI 7020	Shadow Of Your Smile/SILVERTONES: Cool Down. 20
68	Treasure Isle TI 7027	Soul For Sale/SILVERTONES: In The Midnight Hour. 18
68	Treasure Isle TI 7032	Venus/Music Is My Occupation (with Supersonics) 18
68	Treasure Isle TI 7039	Our Man Flint (with Supersonics)/SILVERTONES: Old Man River. 18
68	Treasure Isle TI 7042	Moving (with Supersonics)/SILVERTONES: Slow And Easy 18
68	Doctor Bird DB 1135	Mad Mad World/Wonderful World (with Lloyd Williams). 22
69	Unity UN 501	Last Flight To Reggie (Reggae) City (with Stranger Cole)/Watch Dem Go 8
69	Trojan TR 642	Breaking Up/Party Time (with Supersonics) (both actually by Alton Ellis) 10
69	Trojan TR 652	Third Figure/You Should've Known Better. 12
69	Trojan TR 657	When The Saints Go Marching In/SOUL OFROUS: Ease Me Up Officer
		(B-side actually by Righteous Flames). 12
69	Trojan TR 671	Moonshot/PHYLLIS DILLON: The Right Shot 15
69	Trojan TR 686	Tribute To Rameses/PHYLLIS DILLION: Lipstick On Your Collar 12
69	Trojan TR 7706	Black Coffee (with Supersonics)/VIC TAYLOR: Heartaches. 12
69	Unity UN 506	The Avengers/LAUREL AITKEN: Donkey Man 12
69	Unity UN 534	Dream Boat/Tommy's Dream 12
69	Unity UN 535	Peanut Vendor/100,000 Tons Of Rock. 15
70	Duke DU 76	The Rooster (with Supersonics) (actually by Jeff Barnes)/
		PHYLLIS DILLON: Walk Through This World. 10
70	Duke DU 77	Open Jaw (with Supersonics)/JOHN HOLT: The Working Kind 10
70	Duke DU 78	Key To The City (with Supersonics)/DOROTHY REID: Give It To Me 10
71	Treasure Isle TI 7058	My Best Dress/PHYLISS DILLON: One Life To Live 15
71	Treasure Isle TI 7061	Testify Version/JOHN HOLT: Let's Build Our Dreams 18
71	Treasure Isle TI 7065	Black River/JOHN HOLT: Sister Big Stuff. 12
71	Treasure Isle TI 7066	Paragon's Medley Version/JOHN HOLT: Paragon's Medley 12
71	Treasure Isle TI 7070	Midnight Confession Version/PHYLLIS DILLON: Midnight Confession 15
71	Big Shot BI 585	Psalm Nine To Keep In Mind (with Observers)/Psalm Nine (Version). 10
71	Spinning Wheel SW 109	Crying Everynight (with Supersonics) (actually by Stranger Cole)/
		HERMAN MARQUIS: Tom's Version 40
71	Spinning Wheel SW 110	Stupid Doctor (with Supersonics)/ROB WALKER: Grooving In Style
		(B-side actually by Ken Parker). 60
73	Technique TE 927	Rub It Down/Rub It Down (Version) (as Tommy McCook Stars) 6
73	G.G. GG 4539	Bad Cow Skank (with Bobby Ellis)/
		GLADSTONE ANDERSON: Drummer Roach 5

70	Trojan TBL 111	GREATER JAMAICA (MOONWALK REGGAE) (LP, actually by various artists) . . .	30
74	Attack ATLP 1007	TOMMY McCOOK (LP)	22
77	Third World TWS 920	HOT LAVA (LP)	20

(see also Denis Alcapone, Dave Barker, Dennis Brown, Chuck & Joe White, Shenley Duffas, Dennis & Lizzy, Dobby Dobson, Dynamics, Alton Ellis, Ethiopians, Eagles, Emotions, Herman, Heptones, Jamaicans, Hopeton Lewis, Lloyd & Glen, Lloyd & Groovers, Bob Marley, Maytals, Melodians, Mellodities, Millions, Paragons, Hugh Roy, Karl Walker & Allstars)

JASON McCORD
| 65 | Pye 7N 15925 | It Was A Very Good Year/Song Of The Pine Tree. . . . . | 20 |

GEORGE McCORMICK
| 55 | MGM SPC 6 | Don't Fix Up The Doghouse/Gold Wedding Band (export issue) . . . . | 18 |

McCORMICK BROTHERS
| 63 | Polydor NH 66986 | Red Hen Boogie/Blue Grass Express. . . . . | 50 |
| 66 | Hickory LPE 1509 | AUTHENTIC BLUEGRASS HITS (EP) . . . . | 22 |

BUDD McCOY
| 58 | RCA RCA 1106 | Hiawatha/The Midnight Ride Of Paul Revere (78 rpm = £20) . . . . | 7 |

CLYDE McCOY
| 57 | Mercury MEP 9513 | DANCING TO THE BLUES (EP) . . . . | 20 |

JOE McCOY
| 59 | Collector JDL 81 | One In A Hundred/One More Greasing . . . . | 30 |

(JOHN) McCOY
83	Legacy LGY 9	Oh Well! (Edit)/Because You Lied (p/s)	5
83	Legacy LLM 109	MINI ALBUM (mini-LP)	10
84	Mausoleum SKULL 8373	THINK HARD (LP, with inner sleeve).	12

(see also Gillan, Samson, Mammoth, Zzebra, Split Knee Loons)

VIOLA McCOY
| 50s | Ristic LP 27 | VIOLA McCOY 1923-1927 (10" LP) . . . . | 60 |

McCOYS
65	Immediate IM 001	Hang On Sloopy/I Can't Explain It.	8
65	Immediate IM 021	Fever/Sorrow	12
66	Immediate IM 028	Don't Worry Mother, Your Son's Heart Is Pure/Ko-Ko.	10
66	Immediate IM 029	Up And Down/If You Tell A Lie	10
66	Immediate IM 034	Runaway/Come On Let's Go	10
66	Immediate IM 037	(You Make Me Feel) So Good/Every Day I Have To Cry	8
67	Immediate IM 046	I Got To Go Back/Dynamite	15
67	London HLZ 10154	Say Those Magic Words/I Wonder If She Remembers Me	25
68	Mercury MF 1067	Jesse Brady/Resurrection	8
69	Immediate IM 076	Hang On Sloopy/This Is Where We Came In	5
66	Immediate IMEP 002	HITS VOL. 1 (EP)	40
66	Immediate IMEP 003	HITS VOL. 2 (EP)	40
65	Immediate IMLP 001	HANG ON SLOOPY (LP)	52
68	Mercury (S)MCL 20128	THE INFINITE McCOYS (LP).	22
71	Joy JOYS 196	HANG ON SLOOPY (LP, reissue)	12

JIMMY McCRACKLIN
58	London HLM 8598	The Walk/I'm To Blame (as Jimmy McCracklin & His Band) (78 rpm = £25).	45
58	London HL 7035	The Walk/I'm To Blame (export issue, as Jimmy McCracklin & His Band)	35
62	Top Rank JAR 617	Just Got To Know/The Drag.	25
65	R&B MRB 5001	I Got Eyes For You/I'm Gonna Tell Your Mother	25
66	Outasite 45 120	Christmas Time (Parts 1 & 2) (99 copies only)	60
65	Liberty LIB 66094	Every Night, Every Day/Can't Raise Me	12
66	Liberty LIB 66129	Think/Steppin' Up In Class.	12
68	Minit MLF 11003	How Do You Like Your Love/Get Together	10
68	Minit MLF 11009	Pretty Little Sweet Thing/A And I.	10
65	Vocalion VEP 170160	JIMMY McCRACKLIN (EP)	120
68	Minit MLL/MLS 40003	A PIECE OF JIMMY McCRACKLIN (LP)	45

GWEN McCRAE
74	President PT 416	It's Worth The Hurt/90% Of Me Is You.	25
82	Atlantic FLAM 1	Keep The Fire Burning/Funky Sensation	15
82	Atlantic FLAM 1T	Keep The Fire Burning/Funky Sensation (12")	15
75	President	GWEN McCRAE (LP).	25

GWEN & GEORGE McCRAE
| 75 | President PTLS 1070 | TOGETHER (LP) . . . . | 20 |

DANNY McCULLOCH
69	Capitol CL 15607	Blackbird/Time Of Man	6
70	Pye Intl./Festival 7N 25514	Colour Of The Sunset/Smokeless Zone	6
69	Capitol E-(S)T 174	WINGS OF A MAN (LP)	15

(see also Animals)

IAN McCULLOCH
| 64 | Decca F11855 | Come On Home/Down By The River. . . . . | 40+ |

IAN McCULLOCH
| 84 | Korowa KOW 40L | September Song/Cockles & Mussels (10", A-side plays at 78rpm) . . . . | 8 |

(see also Echo & The Bunnymen)

HENRY McCULLOUGH
| 75 | Dark Horse AMLH 22005 | MIND YOUR OWN BUSINESS! (LP, some with inner sleeve). . . . . | 20/15 |

(see also Grease Band, Eire Apparent, Paul McCartney & Wings)

ED McCURDY
| 60s | ELK 110 | WHEN DAFFIANCE WAS IN FLOWER (LP, with insert) . . . . | 35 |
| 60s | ELK 140 | WHEN DAFFIANCE WAS IN FLOWER VOL 2 (LP) . . . . | 35 |

MINT VALUE £

GEORGE McCURN
63	London HLH 9705	I'm Just A Country Boy/In My Little Corner Of The World	10

LUKE McDANIEL
55	Parlophone CMSP 29	The Automobile Song/I Can't Steal Another's Bride (export issue)	40
55	Parlophone DP 407	The Automobile Song/I Can't Steal Another's Bride (78)	12

MAISIE McDANIEL
61	Beltona BE 2744	Christmastime In Ireland/The Old Pigsty	6
63	Fontana TF 400	Something Special/This Song Is Just For You	6
63	Fontana TE 17397	MEET MAISIE McDANIEL! (EP, with The Hunters)	15
63	Fontana TE 17398	COUNTRY STYLE (EP, with The Hunters)	15
65	Fontana TL 5215	ARE YOU LONESOME TONIGHT (LP)	15

(see also Hunters)

EUGENE McDANIELS
71	Atlantic 2465 022	OUTLAW (LP)	30

GENE McDANIELS
61	London HLG 9319	A Hundred Pounds Of Clay/Take A Chance On Love	15
61	London HLG 9396	A Tear/She's Come Back	18
61	London HLG 9448	Tower Of Strength/Secret	15
62	Liberty LIB 55405	Chip Chip/Another Tear Falls	10
62	Liberty LIB 55480	Point Of No Return/Warmer Than A Whisper	15
63	Liberty LIB 55510	Spanish Lace/Somebody's Waiting	10
63	Liberty LIB 55541	The Puzzle/Cry Baby Cry	10
63	Liberty LIB 55597	It's A Lonely Town/False Friends	40
63	Liberty LIB 10130	Anyone Else/New Love In Old Mexico	8
64	Liberty LIB 55723	In Times Like These/Make Me A Present Of You	18
65	Liberty LIB 55752	(There Goes The) Forgotten Man	40
65	Liberty LIB 55805	Walk With A Winner/A Miracle(DJ copy = £225)	150
61	London REG 1298	GENE McDANIELS (EP)	65
62	Liberty LEP 2054	A CHANGE OF MOOD (EP)	45
61	London HA-G 2384	A HUNDRED POUNDS OF CLAY (LP, also stereo SAH-G 6184)	80/100
62	Liberty LBY 1003	... SOMETIMES I'M HAPPY (LP)	45
62	Liberty LBY 1021	TOWER OF STRENGTH (LP)	45
63	Liberty (S)LBY 1128	SPANISH LACE (LP)	45
63	Liberty LBY 1179	THE WONDERFUL WORLD OF GENE McDANIELS (LP)	45
68	Sunset SLS 50017E	FACTS OF LIFE (LP)	15

BILL McDAVID
61	Starlite ST45 63	Kiss Me For Christmas/Little Shepherd Boy	8

McDERMOTTS
89	Hag HAGLP 2	THE ENEMY WITHIN (LP)	12

CHAS McDEVITT (SKIFFLE GROUP)
57	Oriole CB 1352	Freight Train (with Nancy Whiskey)/The Cotton Song	22
57	Oriole CB 1357	It Takes A Worried Man/The House Of The Rising Sun (78 rpm = £8)	18
57	Oriole CB 1371	Green Back Dollar (with Nancy Whiskey)/I'm Satisfied (78 rpm = £6)	15
57	Oriole CB 1386	Face In The Rain (with Nancy Whiskey)/Sporting Life (with Tony Kohn)	15
57	Oriole CB 1386	Face In The Rain (with Nancy Whiskey)/Sporting Life (with Tony Kohn) (78)	8
57	Oriole CB 1395	Sing, Sing, Sing/My Old Man (78 rpm = £12)	15
58	Oriole CB 1403	Johnny-O (with Nancy Whiskey)/Bad Man Stack-O-Lee (78 rpm = £10)	15
58	Oriole CB 1405	Across The Bridge (with Shirley Douglas)/Deep Down (78 rpm = £10)	15
58	Oriole CB 1457	Real Love (with Shirley Douglas)/Juke-Box Jumble (78 rpm = £15)	15
59	Oriole CB 1511	Teenage Letter (with Shirley Douglas)/SHIRLEY DOUGLAS: Sad Little Girl	12
59	Oriole CB 1511	Teenage Letter (with Shirley Douglas)/SHIRLEY DOUGLAS: Sad Little Girl (78)	12
60	Top Rank JAR 338	Dream Talk/Forever (with Shirley Douglas)	8
61	HMV POP 845	One Love/Can It Be Love (with Shirley Douglas)	6
61	HMV POP 928	Mommy Out De Light/I've Got A Thing About You (with Shirley Douglas)	6
62	HMV POP 999	Happy Family/Throwing Pebbles In A Pool (with Shirley Douglas)	6
65	Columbia DB 7595	The Most Of What Is Least/Don't Blame Me (with Shirley Douglas)	6
68	Fontana TF 957	City Smoke/One Man Band	6
57	Oriole EP 7002	CHAS AND NANCY (EP, with Nancy Whiskey)	28
57	Oriole MG 10018	THE INTOXICATING MISS WHISKEY (10" LP, with Nancy Whiskey)	55
65	Columbia 33SX 1738	SIXTEEN BIG FOLK HITS (LP, with Shirley Douglas)	12

(see also Nancy Whiskey, Cranes Skiffle Group, Coffee Bar Skifflers)

ALISTAIR McDONALD
69	Major Minor MMLP 51	BATTLE BALLADS (LP)	15

GAVIN McDONALD
72	Regal Zono. SLRZ 1027	LINES (LP)	20

(COUNTRY) JOE McDONALD
71	Vanguard 6076 252	Hold On It's Coming Parts 1 & 2	6
70	Vanguard (S)VRL 19057	THINKING OF WOODY GUTHRIE (LP)	20
71	Vanguard 6359 004	TONIGHT I'M SINGING JUST FOR YOU (LP)	15
71	Sonet SNTF 622	QUIET DAYS IN CLICHY (LP, soundtrack)	15
71	Vanguard VSD 79314	HOLD ON — IT'S COMING (LP)	15
71	Vanguard VSD 79315	WAR WAR WAR (LP)	12
72	Vanguard VSD 79316	INCREDIBLE! LIVE! (LP)	12
73	Vanguard VSD 79328	PARIS SESSIONS (LP)	12

(see also Country Joe & Fish)

LARRY McDONALD & DENZIL LAING
71	Clandisc CLA 228	Name Of The Game/FABULOUS FLAMES: Holly Version	6

RITCHIE McDONALD & GLEN BROWN
72	Duke DU 141	Boat To Progress/Boat To Progress — Version	10

SHELAGH McDONALD
70	B&C CAS 1019	THE SHELAGH McDONALD ALBUM (LP)	40
71	B&C CAS 1043	STAR GAZER (LP, with inner sleeve)	40

SKEETS McDONALD
56	Capitol CL 14566	Fallen Angel/It'll Take Me A Long, Long Time (78 rpm = £18)	30
59	Capitol EAP1 1040	GOING STEADY WITH THE BLUES (EP)	90

TESFA McDONALD
72	Dynamic DYN 455	Life Is The Highest/Recarnate (Re-Incarnate)	
		(actually by Bobby Ellis and Tommy McCook)	18

McDONALD & GILES
70	Island ILPS 9126	McDONALD AND GILES (LP, 1st pressing, pink label, with 'i' logo)	40
70	Island ILPS 9126	McDONALD AND GILES (LP, 2nd pressing, 'pink rim' label, 'palm tree' logo)	12
70	Polydor 2302 070	McDONALD AND GILES (LP)	15

(see also King Crimson; Giles, Giles & Fripp)

ROSE McDOWALL
88	Rio Digital 7RDS 3	Don't Fear The Reaper/Crystal Days (p/s)	5
88	Rio Digital 12RDS 3	Don't Fear The Reaper/Crystal Days (12", p/s)	8

(see also Strawberry Switchblade, Ornamental, Psychic TV, Current 93, Death In June)

(MISSISSIPPI) FRED McDOWELL
66	Bounty BY 6022	MY HOME IS IN THE DELTA (LP)	40
66	Fontana 688 806 ZL	MISSISSIPPI DELTA BLUES (LP)	30
69	CBS 63735	LONG WAY FROM HOME (LP)	30
69	Polydor 236 278	GOING DOWN SOUTH (LP)	25
70	Capitol E-ST 409	I DO NOT PLAY NO ROCK & ROLL (LP)	20
70	Transatlantic TRA 194	LONDON 1 (LP)	18
71	Transatlantic TRA 203	LONDON 2 (LP)	18
71	Revival RVS 1001	EIGHT YEARS RAMBLIN' (LP, with Johnny Woods)	18
74	Xtra XTRA 1136	MISSISSIPPI FRED McDOWELL 1904-1972 (LP)	15

FRED & ANNIE MAE McDOWELL
64	Polydor 236 570	GOING DOWN SOUTH (LP)	18

PAUL McDOWELL
62	Fontana 267228 TF	Frankie/Be A Man	6

(see also Temperance Seven)

(BROTHER) JACK McDUFF
64	Stateside SS 275	Sanctified Samba/Whistle While You Work	10
64	Stateside SS 302	Rock Candy/Real Good 'Un	10
64	Stateside SS 328	Carpetbaggers (Main Theme)/The Pink Panther (Theme)	10
66	Atlantic 584 036	Down In The Valley/A Change Is Gonna Come	8
64	Stateside SL 10060	BROTHER JACK McDUFF LIVE! (LP)	15
64	Stateside SL 10101	THE DYNAMIC JACK McDUFF (LP, as Brother Jack McDuff Quartet)	15
65	Stateside SL 10121	BROTHER JACK McDUFF QUARTET LIVE! AT THE JAZZ WORKSHOP (LP)	15
65	Stateside SL 10142	PRELUDE (LP)	15
66	Stateside SL 10165	THE CONCERT McDUFF (LP)	15
66	Atlantic 587 030	A CHANGE IS GONNA COME (LP)	15
67	Transatlantic PR 7404	SILK AND SOUL (LP)	15
67	Transatlantic PR 7476	WALK ON BY (LP)	15
68	Transatlantic	DYNAMIC JACK McDUFF (LP)	15
72	York FYK 407	IF THE CAP FITS ... WEAR IT (LP, as Jack McDuff Band)	12
72	Prestige PR 24013	ROCK CANDY (LP)	12

(see also Roland Kirk, Kenny Burrell, Jimmy Witherspoon)

MC DUKE
89	Music Of Life NOTE 025DJ	I'm Riffin (English Rasta) (12")	8

McENROE & CASH With The FULL METAL RACKETS
91	M. For Nations KUT 141	Rock'N'Roll (7" Version)/(Instrumental) (p/s)	5
91	M. For Nations 12KUT 141	Rock'N'Roll (Dance Mix)/(7" Version)/(Instrumental) (12", p/s)	10

(see also Iron Maiden, Roger Daltrey)

JOHNNY McEVOY
73	Hawk HALPX 112	JOHNNY McEVOY (LP)	15
74	Hawk HALPX 117	SOUNDS LIKE JOHNNY McEVOY (LP)	20

(see also Rambler)

BOB McFADDEN & DOR
59	Coral Q 72378	The Mummy/The Beat Generation (78 rpm = £12)	20

(see also Rod McKuen)

MC5
69	Elektra EKSN 45056	Kick Out The Jams/Motor City Is Burning	30
69	Elektra EKSN 45067	Ramblin' Rose/Borderline	25
69	Elek. EKL 4042/EKS 74042	KICK OUT THE JAMS (LP, red label, gatefold sleeve, mono/stereo)	80/60
70	Atlantic 2400 016	BACK IN THE U.S.A. (LP)	45
71	Atlantic 2400 135	HIGH TIME (LP)	45

(see also Wayne Kramer, Destroy All Monsters, Rob Tyner & Hot Rods)

MIKE McGEAR
72	Island WIP 6131	Woman/Kill	8
74	Warner Bros K 16446	Leave It/Sweet Baby (p/s)	12/8
75	Warner Bros K 16520	Sea Breezes/Givin' Grease A Ride	8
75	Warner Bros K 16573	Dance The Do/Norton	10
75	Warner Bros K 16658	Simply Love You/What Do We Really Know (some in p/s)	15/8
76	EMI EMI 2485	Doing Nothing All Day/A To Z	6
80	Carrere CAR 144	All The Whales In The Ocean/I Juz Want What You Got — Money!	
		(some in p/s)	30/15

Mike McGEAR

81	Conn SRTS/81/CUS 1112	No Lardidar/God Save The Gracious Queen (some in p/s)	55/35
72	Island ILPS 9191	WOMAN (LP)	25
74	Warner Bros K 56051	*McGEAR (LP, gatefold sleeve with insert)	20
74	Warner Bros KMG 1	McGEAR'S LIMITED EDITION (7-track white label sampler & press kit)	45
80s	Centre Labs	*McGEAR (LP, 6-track reissue, 500 only, numbered & signed)	60

(see also Grimms, Scaffold, McGough & McGear, Paul McCartney)

PAT McGEEGAN
68	Emerald MD 1096	Chance Of A Lifetime/Don't Laugh At Me (If I Cry)	7

BROWNIE McGHEE
51	Melodisc 1127	Secret Mojo Blues/Me And My Dog (78)	25
63	Columbia SEG 8226	BLUES ON PARADE NO. 1 (EP)	35
60s	Xtra 1021	BROWNIE McGHEE (LP)	25
78	Magpie PY 1805	LET'S HAVE A BALL (LP)	12

BROWNIE McGHEE & DAVE LEE
57	Pye Jazz NJE 1060	THE BLUEST (EP)	22

(see also Sonny Terry & Brownie McGhee)

HOWARD McGHEE
61	Fontana FJL906	THE SHARP EDGE (LP)	20

HOWARD McGHEE SEXTET
50	Jazz Parade B1	Dimitar/Al's Tune (78)	7

(Roger) McGOUGH & (Mike) McGEAR
68	Parlophone PMC/PCS 7047	McGOUGH AND McGEAR (LP, with phasing on "So Much"; beware of counterfeits)	160+
89	Parlophone PCS 7332	McGOUGH AND McGEAR (LP, stereo reissue with inner sleeve, without phasing on "So Much")	15
89	Parlophone CDP 7 91877-2	McGOUGH AND McGEAR (CD, without phasing on "So Much")	60

(see also Scaffold, Adrian Henri, Mike McGear, Jimi Hendrix, Grimms)

ROGER McGOUGH & BRIAN PATTEN
75	Argo ZPL 1190	READ THEIR OWN VERSE − BRITISH POETS OF OUR TIME (LP)	15

MAUREEN McGOVERN
73	Pye Intl. 7N 25603	The Morning After/Midnight Storm (p/s)	8

CHRIS McGREGOR('S BROTHERHOOD OF BREATH)
68	Polydor 184 137	VERY URGENT (LP, as Chris McGregor Group)	75
68	Polydor 583 072	UP TO EARTH (LP, unreleased, test pressings only)	150+
70	RCA Neon NE 2	CHRIS McGREGOR'S BROTHERHOOD OF BREATH (LP, gatefold sleeve)	40
72	RCA SF 8260	BROTHERHOOD (LP, gatefold sleeve, as Chris McGregor's Brotherhood Of Breath)	45
74	Ogun OG 100	LIVE, WILLISAU (LP)	15
77	Ogun OG 521	IN HIS OWN TIME (LP)	18
78	Ogun OG 524	PROCESSION (LP)	15

(see also Brotherhood Of Breath, Tunji)

FREDDIE McGREGOR
73	Fab FAB 261	Wise Words/NEW ESTABLISHMENT: Version	20
79	Jackal JALP 7000	FREDDIE McGREGOR (LP)	15
96	Blacker Dread BDTL 05	Mr. Pressure Man/CLIVE HYLTON: Babylon Keep On Knocking (12")	35

(see also Soul Brothers, Young Freddie)

JIMMY McGRIFF
64	Sue WI 303	All About My Girl/M.G. Blues	40
64	Sue WI 310	Last Minute (Parts 1 & 2)	30
64	Sue WI 317	I've Got A Woman (Parts 1 & 2)	35
64	Sue WI 333	'Round Midnight/Lonely Avenue	40
66	United Artists UP 1170	See See Rider/Hallelujah	8
70	United Artists UP 35025	The Worm/What's That	20
64	Sue ILP 907	I'VE GOT A WOMAN (LP)	110
64	Sue ILP 908	GOSPEL TIME (LP)	100
65	London HA-C 8247	BLUES FOR MISTER JIMMY (LP)	60
66	London HA-C 8242	AT THE APOLLO (LP)	75
66	United Artists (S)ULP 1158	A BAG FULL OF SOUL (LP)	30
68	United Artists (S)ULP 1170	THE BIG BAND (LP)	25
69	Solid State USS 7012	I'VE GOT A NEW WOMAN (LP)	12
72	Groove Merchant GM 503	GROOVE GREASE (LP)	15
73	Groove Merchant GM 2205	GOOD THINGS DON'T HAPPEN EVERY DAY (LP, with Junior Parker)	12
74	People PLEO 14	FLY DUDE (LP)	15
74	People PLEO 19	LET'S STAY TOGETHER (LP)	15

BILL McGUFFIE (TRIO)
53	Parlophone MSP 6040	Concerto For Boogie/Begin The Beguine (as Bill McGuffie Trio)	7
59	Philips PB 922	Elmer's Tune/Simple Simon (78)	8
67	Philips BF 1550	Fugue For Thought (from the film 'Dalek Invasion Earth 2150AD')/Fair's Fair	35
55	Philips BBR 8054	JAZZ WITH McGUFFIE (LP)	15
56	Philips BBR 8087	McGUFFIE MAGIC (LP)	28
56	Philips BBL 7072	MORE JAZZ WITH McGUFFIE (LP)	28
58	Philips BBL 7261	CONTINENTAL TOUR (LP)	28
61	Philips BBL 7450	PLAYING FOR PLEASURE (LP)	15
68	Philips LPS 16001	LATIN OVERTONES (LP)	20

ROGER McGUINN
74	CBS 2649	Peace On You/Without You	6
77	CBS 5231	American Girl/Russian Hill	6
73	CBS 65274	ROGER McGUINN (LP)	15

74	CBS 81071	PEACE ON YOU (LP)	12
75	CBS 80877	ROGER McGUINN AND BAND (LP)	12
76	CBS 81369	CARDIFF ROSE (LP)	12

(see also Byrds)

McGUINNESS FLINT
70	Capitol CL 15662	When I'm Dead And Gone/Lazy Afternoon	5
71	Capitol CL 15682	Malt And Barley Blues/Rock On	5
70	Capitol EA-ST 22625	McGUINNESS FLINT (LP, gatefold sleeve)	18
71	Capitol ST 22794	HAPPY BIRTHDAY, RUTHY BABY (LP)	18
73	Bronze ILPS 9244	RAINBOW (LP, gatefold sleeve with inner)	12

(see also Manfred Mann, Blues Band, John Mayall, Coulson Dean McGuinness Flint, Gallagher & Lyle, Paladin)

BARRY McGUIRE
65	Ember EMB S 208	So Long Stay Well/Far Side Of The Hill	8
65	Ember EMB S 224	Greenback Dollar/One By One	8
65	RCA Victor RCA 1469	Eve Of Destruction/What Exactly Is The Matter With Me	6
65	RCA Victor RCA 1493	Child Of Our Times/Upon A Painted Ocean	10
66	RCA Victor RCA 1497	This Precious Time/Don't You Wonder Where It's At	8
66	RCA Victor RCA 1508	Walking My Cat Named Dog/I'd Have To Be Outta My Mind	7
66	RCA Victor RCA 1525	Cloudy Summer Afternoon/You've Got To Hide Your Love Away (B-side with Mamas & Papas)	18
67	RCA Victor RCA 1638	Masters Of War/Why Not Stop And Dig It While You Can	7
65	Envoy VOY 9153	HERE AND NOW (LP, with New Christy Minstrels)	15
65	RCA Victor RD 7751	SINGS EVE OF DESTRUCTION (LP)	40
66	Ember EMB 3362	THE EVE OF DESTRUCTION MAN (LP, with New Christy Minstrels)	25
71	A&M AMLS 2008	BARRY McGUIRE AND THE DOCTOR (LP, with Eric Hord)	15
70s	Sparrow BIRD 105	C'MON ALONG (LP)	30
70s	Sparrow BIRD 111	HAVE YOU HEARD? (LP)	30

(see also Mamas & Papas, New Christy Minstrels)

McGUIRE SISTERS
54	Vogue Coral Q 2028	Lonesome Polecat/Muskrat Ramble	20
55	Vogue Coral Q 72050	Sincerely/No More	25
55	Vogue Coral Q 72052	Melody Of Love/Open Up Your Heart	15
55	Vogue Coral Q 72082	Something's Gotta Give/It May Sound Silly	15
55	Vogue Coral Q 72108	Christmas Alphabet/He	18
56	Vogue Coral Q 72117	Young And Foolish/Doesn't Anybody Love Me?	15
56	Vogue Coral Q 72145	Missing/Be Good To Me (Baby, Baby)	15
56	Vogue Coral Q 72161	Delilah Jones/Picnic	18
56	Vogue Coral Q 72188	Weary Blues/In The Alps	15
56	Vogue Coral Q 72201	My Baby's Got Such Lovin' Ways/Endless	12
56	Vogue Coral Q 72209	Tip Toe Through The Tulips With Me/Do You Remember When?	12
56	Vogue Coral Q 72216	Goodnight My Love, Pleasant Dreams/Mommy	12
57	Vogue Coral Q 72238	Heart/Sometimes I'm Happy	12
57	Vogue Coral Q 72249	Kid Stuff/Without Him	12
57	Vogue Coral Q 72265	Rock Bottom/Beginning To Miss You	18
57	Vogue Coral Q 72272	He's Got Time/Interlude	8
57	Vogue Coral Q 72296	Forgive Me/Kiss Them For Me	8
58	Coral Q 72305	Sugartime/Banana Split	6
58	Coral Q 72327	Ding Dong/Since You Went Away To School (78 rpm = £10)	5
58	Coral Q 72334	Volare/Do You Love Me Like You Kiss Me? (78 rpm = £8)	5
59	Coral Q 72356	May You Always/Achoo-Cha-Cha (78 rpm = £10)	5
59	Coral Q 72379	Red River Valley/Compromise (78 rpm = £10)	5
60	Coral Q 72387	Lovers' Lullaby/Livin' Dangerously	5
60	Coral Q 72399	"The Unforgiven" Theme (The Need For Love)/I Give Thanks	5
60	Coral Q 72406	Nine O'Clock/The Last Dance	5
60	Coral Q 72415	I Don't Know Why/To Be Loved	5
61	Coral Q 72427	Really Neat/Just For Old Time's Sake	5
61	Coral Q 72435	Will There Be Space In The Spaceship/Tears On My Pillow	10
58	Coral FEP 2001	THE McGUIRE SISTERS (EP)	20
58	Coral FEP 2006	VOLARE (EP)	20
59	Coral FEP 2033	MAY YOU ALWAYS (EP)	20
56	Vogue Coral LVA 9024	DO YOU REMEMBER WHEN? (LP)	20
57	Vogue Coral LVA 9072	CHILDREN'S HOLIDAY (LP)	20
58	Coral LVA 9073	TEENAGE PARTY (LP)	20
58	Coral LVA 9082	WHILE THE LIGHTS ARE LOW (LP)	20
59	Coral LVA 9115	MAY YOU ALWAYS (LP)	20
60	Coral LVA 9133	GOLDEN FAVORITES (LP)	20
61	Coral LVA 9140	HIS AND HERS (LP)	20

JOHN McHUGH
| 65 | Columbia SCD 2245 | When The Stars/Strange Harmony | 5 |
| 65 | Columbia SCD 2252 | Goldsmith Of Toledo Serenade/O Vision Entrancing | 5 |

KEN McINTIRE
| 60 | Esquire 32-133 | LOOKING AHEAD (LP, with Eric Dolphy) | 60 |

FREDDIE McKAY
71	Banana BA 348	Picture On The Wall/SOUND DIMENSION: Version	18
71	Banana BA 358	Sweet You, Sour You/High School Dance	15
71	Moodisc HM 110	Old Joe/Too Much Fire	8
72	Banana BA 370	Drunken Sailor/SOUND DIMENSION: Version	18
73	Bullet BU 525	Go On This Way/SANTIC ALL STARS: Santic Dub	10
73	Dragon DRA 1012	Our Rendezvous/Black Beauty	15
73	Grape GR 3060	Our Rendezvous/SOUL DYMAMITES: Version	10
74	Dragon DRA 1022	Dream My Life Over/YOUTH STARS: Version	5

MINT VALUE £

71	Banana BALPS 01	PICTURE ON THE WALL (LP)	45
73	Attack ATLP 1013	PICTURE ON THE WALL (LP, reissue)	15
74	Dragon DRLS 5005	LONELY MAN (LP)	12

(see also Lizzy)

SCOTT McKAY
67	Columbia DB 8147	I Can't Make Your Way/Take A Giant Step	30

SCOTTY McKAY
64	London HLU 9885	Cold Cold Heart/What You Wanna	10

TONY McKAY
66	Polydor BM 56513	Nobody's Perfect/Detroit	8

LONETTE McKEE
75	Sussex SXX 4	Save It/Do It To Me	8

KENNETH McKELLAR
66	Decca F 12341	A Man Without Love/As Long As The Sun Shines	5
66	Decca DFE 8645	SONGS FOR EUROPE (EP)	8

McKENDREE SPRING
69	MCA MUPS 277	McKENDREE SPRING (LP)	12
71	MCA MUPS 433	SECOND THOUGHTS (LP)	12
72	MCA MUPS 454	THREE (LP)	12

MAE McKENNA
75	Transatlantic TRA 297	MAE McKENNA (LP)	12

(see also Contraband)

VAL McKENNA
65	Piccadilly 7N 35237	Baby Do It/I Believe In Love	12
65	Piccadilly 7N 35256	Mixed Up Shook Up Girl/Now That You've Made Up Your Mind	25
66	Piccadilly 7N 35286	I Can't Believe What You Say/Don't Hesitate	12
69	Spark SRL 1005	House For Sale/I'll Be Satisfied	10
69	Spark SRL 1023	It's All In My Imagination/Sweet Sweet Lovin'	7
70	Spark SRL 1038	Love Feeling/It's All In My Imagination	15

McKENNA MENDELSON MAINLINE
69	Liberty LBF 15235	You Better Watch Out/She's Alright	8
69	Liberty LBF 15276	Don't Give Me No Goose For Christmas/Beltmaker	7
69	Liberty LBS 83251	STINK (LP)	40

MARLENE McKENZIE
68	Double D DD 106	Left Me For Another/BOBBY AITKEN & CARIBBEATS: Cell Block Eleven	20

SCOTT McKENZIE
67	CBS 2816	San Francisco (Be Sure To Wear Some Flowers In Your Hair)/What's The Difference	5
67	Capitol CL 15509	Look In Your Eyes/All I Want Is You	20
67	CBS 3009	Like An Old-Time Movie/What's The Difference Chapter II	7
68	CBS 3393	Holy Man/What's The Difference (Chapter 3)	6
73	CBS 1168	San Francisco (Be Sure To Wear Some Flowers In Your Hair)/Reason To Believe ("Hall Of Fame Hits" series, p/s)	5
67	CBS (S)BPG 63157	THE VOICE OF SCOTT McKENZIE (LP)	20

(see also Mamas & Papas)

TOMMY McKENZIE
68	Pama PM 720	Fiddlesticks/Please Stay	12
71	Pama Supreme PS 327	Eastern Promise/Fiddlesticks (as Tommy McKenzie Orchestra)	7

McKENZIE, DOUG & BOB
82	Mercury HOSER 1	Take Off/Elron McKenzie (p/s)	20

(see also Rush)

McKINLEYS
64	Columbia DB 7230	Someone Cares For Me/Million Miles Away	20
64	Columbia DB 7310	When He Comes Along/Then I'll Know It's Love	12
64	Parlophone R 5211	Sweet And Tender Romance/That Lonely Feeling	15
65	Columbia DB 7583	Give Him My Love/Once More	15

ROD McKUEN
57	London HLU 8390	Happy Is A Boy Named Me/Jaydee	45
60	Brunswick 05828	Two Brothers/Time After Time	15
64	Capitol CL 15348	The World I Used To Know/Someplace Green	5
66	Ember EMB 223	Soldiers Who Want To Be Heroes/Wayfarin' Stranger	5
68	RCA Victor RCA 1734	Cat Named Sloopy/Where Are We Now	5
71	Buena Vista DF 482	Pastures Green/Theme From Scandalous John/Train To Quivira (p/s)	5
67	RCA Victor RD 7897	THROUGH EUROPEAN WINDOWS (LP)	12
69	Warner Bros	LONESOME CITIES (LP)	12
69	Stateside (S)SL 10264	JOANNA (LP, soundtrack, with Mike Sarne)	12
69	Stateside (S)SL 10278	THE PRIME OF MISS JEAN BRODIE (LP, soundtrack, with Mike Redway)	15
69	Warner Bros WS 1705	THE EARTH (LP)	12
70	Warner Bros WS 1720	THE SKY (LP)	12
70	Warner Bros WS 1764	HOME TO THE SEA (LP)	12
70	Warner Bros WS 1837	NEW BALLADS (LP)	12
71	Warner Bros WS 3015	THE ROD McKUEN SHOW (LP)	12
71	CBS 70078	THE BOY NAMED CHARLIE BROWN (LP, soundtrack)	12

(see also Bob McFadden & Dor, Mike Redway, Mike Sarne, Henri Mancini)

HAL McKUSICK SEXTET/QUINTET
57	Vogue Coral Q 72258	Kelly And Me (as Sextet)/When I Fall In Love (as Quintet)	6

ALTON McLAIN & DESTINY
78	Polydor 2391 370	IT MUST BE LOVE (LP)	12

TOMMY McLAIN
66	London HL 10065	Sweet Dreams/I Need You So	15
66	London HL 10091	Think It Over/I Can't Take No More	12

JACKIE McLEAN QUINTET
56	Esquire 32-111	JACKIE'S PAL (LP)	30

(MAHAVISHNU) JOHN McLAUGHLIN
69	Marmalade 608 007	EXTRAPOLATION (LP)	45
70	Marmalade 2343 012	EXTRAPOLATION (LP, reissue)	15
71	Douglas DGL 65075	DEVOTION (LP, gatefold sleeve)	18
71	Douglas DGL 69014	MY GOAL'S BEYOND (LP, as Mahavishnu John McLaughlin, gatefold sleeve)	18
73	CBS 69037	LOVE, DEVOTION, SURRENDER (LP, by Mahavishnu John McLaughlin & Carlos Santana)	12
74	CBS Q 69037	LOVE, DEVOTION, SURRENDER (LP, quadrophonic issue)	18

(see also Lifetime, Tony Williams [Lifetime], Mahavishnu Orchestra, John Surman, Santana)

DON McLEAN
71	United Artists UP 35325	American Pie Part 1/American Pie Part 2	5
72	United Artists UP 35359	Vincent/Castles In The Air (p/s)	5

NANA McLEAN
71	Banana BA 355	A Little Love/SOUND DIMENSION: Heavy Beat	22

PHIL McLEAN
61	Top Rank JAR 597	Small Sad Sam/Chicken	5
62	Top Rank JAR 613	Big Mouth Bill/Come With Us	6

GERALD McLEASH
71	G.G. GG 4516	False Reaper/G.G. ALL STARS: Reaping Version	10

LARIS McLENNON
67	CBM 04	Confusion/Turn Me Loose	6

ENOS McLEOD
68	Blue Cat BS 135	You Can Never Get Away/ENOS & SHEILA: La La La Bamba	25

(see also Enos & Sheila)

VINCENT McLEOD
69	Jackpot JP 711	Too Late/SIR COLLINS: Late Night	12

OSCAR McLOLLIE & HIS HONEYJUMPERS
55	London HL 8130	Take Your Shoes Off, Pop/Love Me Tonight (78 rpm = £65)	260

EDDIE McLOYD
75	Brunswick BR 27	Once You Fall In Love/Baby Get Down	20

BOBBY McLURE
66	Chess CRS 8048	Peak Of Love/You Got Me Baby (DJ copy = £75)	40
75	Island USA 006	You Bring Out The Love In Me/SURVIVAL KIT: Daybreak	20

(see also Fontella Bass)

McLYNNS
70	CBS 63836	OLD MARKET ST. (LP)	60

ROSS McMANUS
64	HMV POP 1279	Patsy Girl/I'm The Greatest	8
66	HMV POP 1543	Stop Your Playing Around/Girlie Girlie	6
67	Decca F 12618	Can't Take My Eyes Off Of You/If I Were A Rich Man	6

(see also Day Costello)

MC MELLO
90	Republic LICT033	Open Up Your Mind/Words Spoken (12")	8
90	Republic LICT033R	Open Up Your Mind (Remixes) (12")	12
92	Funki Dreds PA6640	Gone Crazy/Talk Dem Way/Firm Stance (EP)	40
89	Republic LICT007	Bizzie Rhymin'/Comin' Correct/Wize (EP)	20
94	Natural Response 74321208511	THE FIRST CHRONICLES OF DETT (EP)	10
94	Natural Response ASH217	I Teach You Teach Me/Buss A Verse/Sounds Of The DETT(EP)	8
90	Republic 4353ILE	THOUGHTS RELEASED (LP)	15

MARGARET McMILLAN
65	Decca F 12272	You Can't Be True Dear/The Love Of My Man	6

BARBARA McNAIR
66	Tamla Motown TMG 544	You're Gonna Love My Baby/The Touch Of Time (DJ copy = £350)	200
59	Coral FEP 2021	FRONT ROW CENTRE VOL. 1 (EP)	40
64	Warner Bros WEP 6129	I ENJOY BEING A GIRL (EP)	40

(see also Billy Williams & Barbara McNair)

CHARLIE McNAIR'S JAZZ BAND
60	Waverly SLP 504	Big House Blues/Fish Man	6

HAROLD McNAIR
68	RCA Victor RCA 1742	The Hipster/Indecision	75
65	Island ILP 926	AFFECTIONATE FINK (LP, with Ornette Coleman's Sidemen)	350
68	RCA SF 7969	HAROLD McNAIR (LP)	80+
70	RCA Intl. INTS 1096	FLUTE AND NUT (LP)	60
70	B&C CAS 1016	THE FENCE (LP)	45
72	B&C CAS 1045	HAROLD McNAIR (LP)	40

(see also Ginger Baker's Airforce)

John McNALLY

MINT VALUE £

JOHN McNALLY
69	CBS 4517	Mary In The Morning/My Love Forgive Me	5

(this is NOT John McNally of the Searchers)

JOSEPH McNALLY
56	Oriole CB 1325	The March Hare/I'm A Sentimental One	6

TREVOR McNAUGHTON
72	Hillcrest HCT 5	No Sins At All/No Sins At All Version	5

(see also The Melodians)

BIG JAY McNEELY
59	Top Rank JAR 169	There Is Something On Your Mind/...Back...Shac...Track ('vocal: Little Sonny') (78 rpm = £25)	50
65	Sue WI 373	There Is Something On Your Mind/...Back...Shac...Track ('vocal: Little Sonny') (reissue)	40
64	Warner Bros WM 8143	BIG JAY'S PARTY (LP)	40

AARON McNEIL
73	Action ACT 4619	Soul Of A Black Man/Reap What You Sow	12

DAVID McNEIL
68	President PT 212	Don't Let Your Chance Go By/Space Plane	15

PAUL McNEILL
66	Decca LK 4803	TRADITIONALLY AT THE TROUBADOUR (LP)	50

PAUL McNEILL & LINDA PETERS
68	MGM MGM 1408	You Ain't Goin' Nowhere/I'll Show You How To Sing	6

(see also Linda Peters, Richard & Linda Thompson)

McPEAKE FAMILY/FOLK GROUP
60s	Topic TOP 92	WILD MOUNTAIN THYME (EP)	12
60s	Topic	IRISH TRADITIONAL FOLK SONGS AND MUSIC (LP, blue label)	30
60s	Topic 12T 87	THE McPEAKE FAMILY (LP)	20
64	Fontana TL 5214	IRISH FOLK! (LP, as McPeake Family)	30
65	Fontana TL 5358	AT HOME WITH THE McPEAKES (LP)	20
67	Fontana TL 5433	PLEASANT AND DELIGHTFUL (LP, as McPeake Family)	20
69	Evolution Z 1002	WELCOME HOME (LP, as McPeake Folk Group)	40
72	Windmill WMD 151	IRISH TO BE SURE (LP, as McPeake Family)	20

CLYDE McPHATTER
56	London HLE 8250	Seven Days/I'm Not Worthy Of You (78 rpm = £40)	400
56	London HL 7006	Seven Days/I'm Not Worthy Of You (export issue)	125
56	London HLE 8293	Treasure Of Love/When You're Sincere (gold or silver label lettering)	165/80
56	London HLE 8293	Treasure Of Love/When You're Sincere (78)	10
57	London HLE 8462	Just To Hold My Hand/No Matter What (triangular centre) (78 rpm = £25)	150
57	London HLE 8476	Long Lonely Nights/Heartaches (triangular centre) (78 rpm = £30)	115
57	London HLE 8525	Rock And Cry/You'll Be There (triangular centre, later round) (78 rpm = £35)	90/35
58	London HLE 8707	Come What May/Let Me Know (triangular centre) (78 rpm = £35)	65
58	London HLE 8755	A Lover's Question/I Can't Stand Up Alone (triangular centre) (78 rpm = £45)	35
59	MGM MGM 1014	I Told Myself A Lie/(I'm Afraid) The Masquerade Is Over	20
59	London HLE 8878	Lovey Dovey/My Island Of Dreams (triangular centre) (78 rpm = £55)	40
59	London HLE 8906	Since You've Been Gone/Try Try Baby (triangular centre) (78 rpm = £65)	40
59	MGM MGM 1040	Twice As Nice/Where Did I Make My Mistake	18
59	London HLE 9000	You Went Back On Your Word/There You Go (78 rpm = £90)	55
59	MGM MGM 1048	Bless You/Let's Try Again	18
60	London HLE 9079	Just Give Me A Ring/Don't Dog Me	50
60	MGM MGM 1061	Think Me A Kiss/When The Right Time Comes Along	18
60	Mercury AMT 1108	I Ain't Givin' Up Nothin' (If I Can't Get Something)/Ta Ta	15
60	Mercury AMT 1120	You're For Me/I Just Want To Love You	15
61	Mercury AMT 1136	Tomorrow Is A-Comin'/I'll Love You Till The Cows Come Home	40
62	Mercury AMT 1174	Lover Please/Let's Forget About The Past	20
62	Mercury AMT 1181	Little Bitty Pretty One/Next To Me	15
66	Stateside SS 487	Everybody's Somebody's Fool/I Belong To You	18
66	Stateside SS 567	A Shot Of Rhythm And Blues/I'm Not Going To Work Today	20
67	Stateside SS 592	Lavender Lace/Sweet And Innocent	20
68	Deram DM 202	Only A Fool/Thank You Love	15
69	Deram DM 223	Baby I Could Be So Good At Loving You/Baby You've Got It	25
69	Pama PM 775	A Shot Of Rhythm And Blues/I'm Not Going To Work Today (reissue)	10
69	B&C CB 106	Denver/Tell Me	15

EPs
59	London RE-E 1202	CLYDE McPHATTER	340
60	London RE-E 1240	CLYDE MCPHATTER NO. 2 (unissued)	
59	MGM MGM-EP 705	TWICE AS NICE	175
60	MGM MGM-EP 739	THIS IS NOT GOODBYE	175

LPs
63	Mercury MMC 14120	LOVER PLEASE	175
64	Atlantic ATL 5001	THE BEST OF CLYDE McPHATTER	120
71	MCA MUPS 418	WELCOME HOME	20
73	Atlantic K 30033	A TRIBUTE TO CLYDE McPHATTER	20

(see also Drifters, Jackie Wilson, Dominoes, Billy Ward & Dominoes, Jackie Wilson/Clyde McPhatter)

TONY (T.S.) McPHEE
66	Purdah 45-3501	Someone To Love Me/Ain't Gonna Cry No Mo' (as T.S. McPhee)	240
80s	TS 001	Time Of Action/Born To Be With You (sold at gigs)	10
68	Liberty LBL/LBS 83190	ME AND THE DEVIL (LP)	60
71	Sunset SLS 50209	THE SAME THING ON THEIR MINDS (LP, with Jo-Ann Kelly)	35
73	World Wide Artists WWA 1	THE TWO SIDES OF TONY (T.S.) McPHEE (LP, with insert)	25

(see also Groundhogs, Champion Jack Dupree, Jo-Ann Kelly, John Dummer Blues Band, Hapshash & Coloured Coat, Herbal Mixture)

786   Rare Record Price Guide 2008

CHARLES McPHERSON
65	Stateside SL 10151	BEBOP REVISITED (LP)	15
73	Mainstream MSL 1004	SIKU YA BIBI (LP)	12

GILLIAN McPHERSON
71	RCA Victor RCA 2089	It's My Own Way/Is Somebody In Tune With My Song	5
71	RCA Victor SF 8220	POETS AND PAINTERS AND PERFORMERS OF THE BLUES (LP)	60

KEVIN McQUINN
62	Top Rank JAR 598	Every Step Of The Way/Keep Me On Your Mind	8

CARMEN McRAE
55	Brunswick 05502	Love Is Here To Stay/This Will Make You Laugh	8
56	Brunswick 05588	You Don't Know Me/Never Loved Him Anyhow	7
56	Brunswick 05632	Star Eyes/I'm A Dreamer (Aren't We All)	7
57	Brunswick 05652	Whatever Lola Wants (Lola Gets)/Ooh (What 'Cha Doin' To Me) (with Dave Lambert Quartet)	10
57	Brunswick 05723	It's Like Getting A Donkey To Gallop/The Party's Over	7
59	London HLR 8837	Play For Keeps/Which Way Is Love (78 rpm = £18)	15
57	London RE-N 1094	LONDON'S GIRL FRIENDS (EP)	20
56	Brunswick LAT 8104	BY SPECIAL REQUEST (LP)	22
56	Brunswick LAT 8133	TORCHY (LP)	20
56	Brunswick LAT 8147	BLUE MOON (LP)	20
58	Brunswick LAT 8257	AFTER GLOW (LP)	20
59	London HA-R 2185	BOOK OF BALLADS (LP)	20
66	Ember CJS 819	IN LONDON (LP)	15

(see also Sammy Davis Jnr.)

CARMEN McRAE & DAVE BRUBECK FIVE
62	Fontana H 379	Take Five/It's A Raggy Waltz	15

(see also Dave Brubeck)

JAY McSHANN
55	Brunswick LA 8735	KANSAS CITY MEMORIES (10" LP)	25

MC SPY-D & 'FRIENDS'
95	Parlophone 12RPD 6404	The Amazing Spider-Man (Mastermix)/(Sad Bit)/ (The White Trouser Mix) (12", picture disc, with insert)	7
95	Parlophone 12RDJ 6404	The Amazing Spider-Man (Solution Mix)/(Solution Chilled Mix)/ (B&J White Trouser Mix) (12", no p/s, promo only)	30

(see also Brian May)

(BLIND) WILLIE McTELL
66	Transatlantic PR 1040	LAST SESSION (LP)	40
67	Storyville 670 816	BLIND WILLIE McTELL 1940 (LP)	28
60s	Roots RL 324	BLIND WILLIE McTELL 1929-1935 (LP)	25
73	Atlantic K 40400	ATLANTA TWELVE STRING GUITAR (LP)	20

RALPH McTELL
69	Big T BIG 125	Summer Comes Along	5
70	Big T BIG 131	Kew Gardens/Father Forgive Them	5
70	Big T BIG 134	Spiral Staircase/Terminus	5
68	Transatlantic TRA 165	8 FRAMES A SECOND (LP)	20
69	Transatlantic TRA 177	SPIRAL STAIRCASE (LP, with insert)	18
69	Transatlantic TRA 209	MY SIDE OF YOUR WINDOW (LP)	15
70	Transatlantic TRA 227	REVISITED (LP)	15
71	Famous SFMA 5753	YOU, WELL MEANING, BROUGHT ME HERE (LP, gatefold sleeve)	15

McTELLS
87	Frank TRUFFAUT 303	Jesse Man Rae/If Only/Rotten/M.T.B. (p/s in bag)	10

RAY McVAY SOUND
65	Pye 7N 15777	Raunchy/Revenge	35
65	Pye 7N 15816	Kinda Kinky/Kinkdom Come	30
66	Parlophone R 5460	Genesis/House Of Clowns (as Ray MacVay Band)	10
69	Mercury MF 1121	Destination Moon/Mexican Scavenger	7
71	Philips 6006 083	They Call Me Mr. Tibbs (as Ray McVay & Orchestra)	25

CHRISTINE McVIE
84	Warner Bros W 9372T	Got A Hold On Me/Who's Dreaming This Dream (12", p/s)	8
84	Warner Bros W 9372PT	Got A Hold On Me/Who's Dreaming This Dream (12", picture disc)	10

(see also Christine Perfect, Fleetwood Mac, Chicken Shack)

CARL McVOY
58	London HLU 8617	Tootsie/You Are My Sunshine (78 rpm = £80)	250

DAVID McWILLIAMS
66	CBS 202348	God And My Country/Blue Eyes	10
67	Major Minor MM 533	The Days Of Pearly Spencer/Harlem Lady	12
68	Major Minor MM 561	This Side Of Heaven/Mister Satisfied	8
69	Major Minor MM 592	The Stranger/Follow Me	10
69	Major Minor MM 616	Oh Mama Are You My Friend?/I Love Susie In The Summer	8
67	Major Minor MMLP 2	SINGING SONGS BY DAVID McWILLIAMS (LP, also stereo SMLP 2)	25
67	Major Minor MMLP 10	DAVID McWILLIAMS VOL. 2 (LP, also stereo SMLP 10)	25
68	Major Minor MMLP 11	VOLUME III (LP, also stereo SMLP 11)	22
69	Major Minor MCP 5026	THE DAYS OF DAVID McWILLIAMS (LP)	22
72	Dawn DNLS 3039	LORD OFFALY (LP)	18
73	Dawn DNLS 3047	THE BEGGAR AND THE PRIEST (LP)	18
74	Dawn DNLS 3059	LIVING'S JUST A STATE OF MIND (LP)	18

M.D.C.
83	Crass 121984/5	MULTI DEATH CORPORATION (EP)	8

(see also Millions Of Dead Children)

MINT VALUE £

VAUGHN MEADER
63	MGM MGM 1239	No Hiding Place/The Elephant Song	6

ME & THEM
64	Pye 7N 15596	Feels So Good/I Think I'm Gonna Kill Myself	18
64	Pye 7N 15631	Everything I Do Is Wrong/Show You Mean It Too	15
64	Pye 7N 15683	Get Away/Tell Me Why	15

MEANIES
79	Vendetta VD 002	Waiting For You/It's True (p/s)	65

MEAN STREET DEALERS
79	Graduate GRAD 5	Japanese Motorbikes/Tight (p/s)	20
79	Mean St. Dealers MSD 001	BENT NEEDLES (LP)	30
79	Graduate GRADLP 1	BENT NEEDLES (LP, reissue)	18

MEANWHILE BACK IN COMMUNIST RUSSIA...
00	Jitter JTR 1SP	No Cigar/Morning After Pill (p/s, 300 only)	7

MEASLES
65	Columbia DB 7531	Casting My Spell/Bye Birdie Fly	40
65	Columbia DB 7673	Night People/Dog Rough Dan	25
66	Columbia DB 7875	Kicks/No Baby At All	35
66	Columbia DB 8029	Walkin' In/Looking For Love	25

MEAT LOAF
75	Ode ODS 66304	Clap Your Hands, Stamp Your Feet/Stand By Me (withdrawn)	25
78	Epic S EPC 5980	You Took The Words Right Out Of My Mouth/For Crying Out Loud (no p/s)	5
78	Epic S EPC 6281	Two Out Of Three Ain't Bad/For Crying Out Loud (no p/s)	5
78	Epic S EPC 6797	All Revved Up With No Place To Go/Paradise By The Dashboard Light (no p/s)	5
79	Epic S EPC 12-7018	Bat Out Of Hell/Heaven Can Wait (12", p/s, red vinyl)	8
81	Epic EPCA 1580	I'm Gonna Love Her For The Both Of Us/Everything Is Permitted (p/s)	5
81	Epic EPCA 11-1697	Dead Ringer For Love/More Than You Deserve (picture disc)	5
82	Epic EPCA 12-2251	MEAT LOAF IN EUROPE '82 (12" EP)	8
82	Epic EPCA 12-2251	MEAT LOAF IN EUROPE '82 (12" EP, clear vinyl, p/s, Irish issue)	30
83	Epic EPCA WA 3748	Midnight At The Lost And Found (Remix)/Fallen Angel/Bat Out Of Hell (live)/ Dead Ringer For Love (Long Version) (picture disc)	5
83	Epic EPCA A 4080	Razor's Edge (Remix)/Paradise By The Dashboard Light (p/s, with competition insert)	5
84	Arista ARISDP 585	Modern Girl/Take A Number (bike-shaped picture disc, some with poster & plinth)	6/5
84	Arista ARIST 12585D/ ARIPD 12585	Modern Girl (Freeway Mix)/Take A Number (Extended)//Modern Girl (Freeway Mix)/Take A Number (Extended) (12", double pack, 2nd 12" as picture disc)	12
85	Arista ARIPU 600	Nowhere Fast/Clap Your Hands (gatefold pop-up p/s)	5
85	Arista ARISG 600	Nowhere Fast/Clap Your Hands (gatefold p/s with booklet, some signed)	6/5
85	Arista ARISD 600	Nowhere Fast/Clap Your Hands (bike-shaped picture disc)	6
85	Arista ARISD 603	Piece Of The Action/Sailor To A Siren (jaw-shaped picture disc)	6
86	Arista ARIST 10683	Getting Away With Murder/Rock'n'Roll Hero (10", circular p/s)	7
98	Virgin VSCDJX 1718	A Kiss Is A Terrible Thing To Waste (radio edit)/(soft radio edit) (CD, promo only, unreleased versions, card sleeve)	8
82	Epic EPC 11 82419	BAT OUT OF HELL (LP, picture disc)	15
82	Epic EPC 82419	BAT OUT OF HELL (LP, half-speed mastered audiophile pressing with inserts)	12

(see also Stoney & Meat Loaf, Jim Steinman, Rocky Horror Show)

MEAT WHIPLASH
85	Creation CRE 020	Don't Slip Up/Here It Comes (foldaround p/s in poly bag; 1st pressing has photo of band by fence, 2nd pressing has band in field)	15/8

(see also Jesus & Mary Chain)

MECHANICAL HORSETROUGH
70s	Kap KAPS 96	Dogshit On Your Shoes/Jeremy Germoline/Horsetrough Hoedown (p/s)	5
75	Sonet SON 2068	When Santa Lost His Trousers/The Ballad Of Big Bruce	5

MECKENBURG ZINC
70	Orange OAS 205	Hard Working Woman/I'd Like To Help You	5

MEDALLION STRINGS
60	London HLR 9218	Green Leaves Of Summer/Spellbound	5
60	London HLR 9242	Gloria's Theme (From "Butterfield 8")/Suzie Wong	5
61	London HA-R 2331	THE SOUND OF HOLLYWOOD (LP, also stereo SAH-R 6130)	12

Meddy EVILS
65	Pye 7N 15941	Find Somebody To Love/A Place Called Love	125
66	Pye 7M 17091	It's All For You/Ma's Place	125

(see also Stu James and the Mojos, the Quik)

MEDIA
79	Takeaway TA 001	TV Kids/Don't Sit Back/Just For You/Rose And Crown (500 only, p/s)	50

MEDIA
80	Brain Booster Music 4	Back On The Beach Again/South Coast City Rockers (p/s)	5

MEDIATORS
70	Supreme SUP 210	When You Go To A Party (actually by Mediators)/ RUPIE EDWARDS ALLSTARS: Stop The Party	10·

(see also Meditators)

MEDICINE HEAD
69	Dandelion S 4661	His Guiding Hand/This Love Of Old	18
70	Dandelion S 5075	Coast To Coast/All For Tomorrow	12
71	Dandelion DAN 7003	(And The) Pictures In The Sky/Natural Sight (also listed as K 19002) (some in p/s)	10/6

72	Dandelion 2001 276	Kum On/On The Land	6
72	Dandelion 2001 325	Only To Do What Is True/Sittin' In The Sun	6
72	Dandelion 2001 383	How Does It Feel/Morning Light	6
69	Dandelion 63757	NEW BOTTLES, OLD MEDICINE (LP)	45
71	Dandelion DAN 8005	HEAVY ON THE DRUM (LP, gatefold sleeve, also listed as K 49005; some with lyric insert)	35/40
71	Dandelion 2310 166	DARK SIDE OF THE MOON (LP, with insert)	25
73	Polydor 2310 248	ONE & ONE IS ONE (LP, gatefold sleeve)	15
74	Polydor 2383 272	THRU' A FIVE (LP)	12
76	Barn 2314 102	TWO MAN BAND (LP)	12

(see also Ashton Gardner & Dyke, British Lions)

MEDITATIONS
| 68 | Liberty LBF 15045 | Transcendental Meditation/Beautiful Experience | 7 |

MEDITATORS
69	Bullet BU 403	Duba Duba/CECIL NICKY THOMAS: Running Alone	12
70	Big BG 302	When You Go To A Party/Good Morning Mother Cuba	10
71	Big BG 305	Music Alone Shall Live/RUPIE EDWARDS AND ALL STARS: Music Alone — Version	10
73	Pyramid PYR 7010	Great Messiah/Nana Nana	8
73	Smash SMA 2331	Things Not Easy/BONGO HERMAN & BINGY BUNNY: Ration	10

(see also Busty Brown, Pat Satchmo)

MEDIUM
| 68 | CBS 3404 | Edward Never Lies/Colours Of The Rainbow | 28 |

MEDIUM MEDIUM
80	APT SAP-01	Them Or Me/Freeze (p/s)	7
81	Cherry Red CHEER 18	Hungry, So Angry/Nadsat Dream (p/s)	7
81	Cherry Red BRED 19	THE GLITTERHOUSE (LP)	15

BILL MEDLEY
67	Verve VS 564	That Lucky Old Sun/My Darling Clementine	8
68	MGM MGM 1418	I Can't Make It Alone/One Day Girl	6
68	MGM MGM 1432	Brown Eyed Woman/Let The Good Times Roll	6
68	MGM MGM 1456	Peace Brother Peace/Winter Won't Come This Year	8
69	MGM MGM 1475	This Is A Love Song/Something's So Wrong	5
69	MGM MGM 1491	Someone Is Standing Outside/Reaching Back	5
71	A&M AMS 898	You've Lost That Lovin' Feelin'/We've Only Just Begun	5
69	MGM MGM-C(S) 8091	BILL MEDLEY 100% (LP)	22

(see also Righteous Brothers, Garnet Mimms)

JOE MEDLIN
| 59 | Mercury AMT 1032 | I Kneel At Your Throne/Out Of Sight, Out Of Mind (78 rpm = £10) | 25 |

MICHAEL MEDWIN
| 58 | HMV POP 490 | The Army Game/What Do We Do In The Army? (with Bernard Bresslaw, Alfie Bass & Leslie Fyson) | 5 |
| 59 | HMV POP 645 | Blankety-Blankety-Blank/Do It Yourself (with Norman Rossington) | 5 |

KEITH MEEHAN
| 69 | Marmalade 598 016 | Darkness Of My Life/TONY MEEHAN: Hooker Street | 20 |

TONY MEEHAN
| 64 | Decca F 11801 | Song Of Mexico/Kings Go Fifth | 8 |

(see also Shadows, Jet Harris & Tony Meehan, Keith Meehan, John Paul Jones)

JOE MEEK ORCHESTRA
| 63 | Decca F 11796 | The Kennedy March/The Theme Of Freedom | 30 |

(see also Blue Men)

MEGADETH
87	Capitol CL 476	Wake Up Dead/Black Friday (live) (p/s)	8
87	Capitol CLP 476	Wake Up Dead/Black Friday (live) (skull-shaped picture disc with insert)	15
87	Capitol 12CL 476	Wake Up Dead/Black Friday (live)/Devil's Island (live)/Wake Up Dead/Black Friday (live) (12", p/s, some allegedly shrink-wrapped with 7" picture disc)	25/12
87	Capitol 12CL 476	Wake Up Dead/Black Friday (Tommy Vance Show)/Devil's Island (Tommy Vance Show) (12", stickered p/s, with 'Deth' certificate)	15
88	Capitol CL 480	Anarchy In The U.K./Liar (p/s)	5
88	Capitol CLP 480	Anarchy In The U.K./Liar (U.K.-shaped picture disc)	10
88	Capitol CLP 489	Mary Jane/Hook In Mouth (picture disc)	7
90	SBK SBKPD 4	No More Mr. Nice Guy/DEAD ON: "Different Breed" (chair-shaped pic disc)	7
90	SBK 12 SBKP 4	No More Mr. Nice Guy/DEAD ON: "Different Breed"/DANGEROUS TOYS: "Demon Bell [The Ballad Of Horace Pinker]" (12", poster p/s)	8
90	SBK CDSBK 4	No More Mr. Nice Guy/(DEAD ON: "Different Breed")/(DANGEROUS TOYS: "Demon Bell [The Ballad Of Horace Pinker]") (CD)	8
91	Capitol CLS 604	Hangar 18 (MJ 12 Edit)/The Conjuring (live) (p/s, shrink wrapped with patch)	8
91	Capitol CLPD 604	Hangar 18 (MJ 12 Edit)/The Conjuring (live) (Vic-shaped picture disc)	8
91	Capitol CDCL 604	Hangar 18/Conjuring/Hangar 18 (version)/Hangar 18 (Live)/Hook In Mouth (CD)	15
92	Capitol 12CLS 662	Symphony Of Destruction/Breakpoint/Go To Hell (12", p/s, clear vinyl with giant autographed poster)	12
92	Capitol CLP 669	Skin O' My Teeth (LP Version)/Holy Wars... The Punishment Due (The General Schwarzkopf Mix)/High Speed Dirt (live)/The Passes (Mustaine Remarks On Game) (10" bronze Megadeth box with passes & game rules)	15
88	M. For Nations MFN 46P	KILLING IS MY BUSINESS ... AND BUSINESS IS GOOD (LP, picture disc with insert)	20
88	Capitol ESTP 2022	PEACE SELLS ... BUT WHO'S BUYING? (LP, picture disc with insert)	20

88	Capitol ESTP 2053	SO FAR, SO GOOD ... SO WHAT (LP, picture disc with insert) 20
90	Capitol ESTPD 2132	RUST IN PEACE (LP, picture disc, die cut sleeve) 20
94	Capitol ESTPD 2244	YOUTHANASIA (LP, picture disc) 20
94	Capitol ESTPD 2244	YOUTHANASIA (LP, blue vinyl) 18
95	Capitol CDESTS 2244	YOUTHANASIA/HIDDEN TREASURES (2-CD, card sleeve, 2,000 only).......... 30

(see also Marty Friedman, Cacophony)

MEGATON
71	Deram DM-R 331	Out Of Your Own Little World/Niagara 40
71	Deram SML-R 1086	MEGATON (LP) 350

(see also Hackensack)

MEGATON
81	Hot Metal HMM 69	Aluminium Lady/Diehard (p/s).. 40

MEGATONS (Jamaica)
70	Downtown DT 464	Take It Easy/Funk The Beat 10
70	Downtown DT 469	Militant Man/MUSIC DOCTORS: Reggae Jeggae Version.................... 10

(see also Revelation)

MEGATONS (U.S.)
65	Sue WI 325	Shimmy Shimmy Walk (Parts 1 & 2)...................................... 50

(see also Billy Lee Riley)

MEGATRONS
59	Top Rank JAR 146	Velvet Waters/The Merry Piper (78 rpm = 8)................................ 8
59	Top Rank JAR 236	Tootie Flootie/Whispering Winds 8

GEORGE MEGGIE
72	Bullet BU 504	Hard To Believe/MAX ROMEO: Softie...................................... 7
72	Punch PH 112	People Like People/MAX ROMEO: Softie 7

JOHN MEHEGAN TRIO
56	London EZC 19005	THE FIRST MEHEGAN VOLUME ONE (EP) 8
56	London EZC 19015	THE FIRST MEHEGAN VOLUME TWO (EP) 8

MEKONS
78	Fast Products FAST 1	Never Been In A Riot/32 Weeks/Heart And Soul (p/s)....................... 10
78	Fast Products FAST 7	Where Were You?/I'll Have To Dance Then (On My Own) (p/s) 5
80	Virgin SV 101	Teeth/Guardian//Kill/Stay Cool (double pack, gatefold p/s) 5
82	CNT CNT 1	This Sporting Life (6.12)/Frustration (6.21)/(mystery live track) (12", p/s) .. 8
82	CNT CNT 008	This Sporting Life/Fight The Cuts (p/s) 5
82	CNT CNT 014	THE ENGLISH DANCING MASTER (12" EP)................................... 8
80s	Catalogue CAT 075/3	Amnesia (square flexidisc with *The Catalogue* magazine).................. 5

(see also Batfish Boys, Sally Timms & Drifting Cowgirls, Ut)

MEL & DAVE
70	Upsetter US 330	Spinning Wheel/Version 15

MEL & TIM
70	Concord CON 004	Backfield In Motion/Do Right Baby (pink label/multi/Egg desig)........... 10/8/6
73	Stax 2025 125	Starting All Over Again/It Hurts To Want You So Bad 8
73	Stax 2025 171	What's Your Name/Free For All 6
73	Stax 2325 090	STARTING ALL OVER AGAIN (LP) 20

MELANIE
69	Buddah 201 063	Tuning My Guitar/Beautiful People (withdrawn, demos may exist)........... 10+
69	Buddah 203 019	BORN TO BE (LP, gatefold sleeve) 22
69	Buddah 203 028	AFFECTIONATELY MELANIE (LP, with inner lyric sheet) 18
70	Buddah 2318 009	CANDLES IN THE RAIN (LP, gatefold sleeve) 18
70	Buddah 2318 011	LEFTOVER WINE (LP, gatefold sleeve)..................................... 18
71	Buddah 2318 034	ALL THE RIGHT NOISES (LP, soundtrack)................................... 18
71	Buddah 2322 001	THE GOOD BOOK (LP, gatefold sleeve, with booklet) 12
71	Buddah 2322 002	GATHER ME (LP, gatefold sleeve)... 12
72	Buddah 2318 054	GARDEN IN THE CITY (LP, scratch'n'sniff sleeve) 12
72	Buddah 2659 013	THE FOUR SIDES OF MELANIE (2-LP)....................................... 18

TERRY MELCHER
68	Rex R 11039	Indian Lake/Be My Girl 7
74	Reprise K 54016	TERRY MELCHER (LP)... 15

(see also Terry Day, The Rip Chords, Freeway)

GIL MELLE (QUINTET)
55	Vogue LDE 141	GIL MELLE QUINTET (10" LP)... 15

SUSAN MELLEN
75	MAM MAMAS 1014	THE MELLEN BIRD (LP, with insert)....................................... 30

JOHN COUGAR MELLENCAMP
86	Riva JCMDP 5	Small Town/(Version)//Hurts So Good/The Kind Of Fella I Am (p/s, double pack).. 5
89	Mercury 080 212-2	Paper In Fire/Never Too Old/Under The Boardwalk/Cold Sweat/ Paper In Fire (CD Video).. 12
89	Mercury 080 200-2	Pop Singer/J.M.'s Question/Check It Out (live)/Pop Singer (live)/ Pop Singer (CD Video) 12

(see also John Cougar)

MELLODITIES
64	R&B JB 179	Vacation/TOMMY McCOOK: Music Is My Occupation....................... 35

MELLOTONES
57	Beltona BE 2673	Norah/If I Knocked The L Out Of Kelly (78) 8

MELL(O)TONES

68	Amalgamated AMG 812	Fat Girl In Red/VERSATILES: Trust The Book	18
68	Amalgamated AMG 817	Feel Good (actually may be by Bleechers)/Soulful Mood (actually by Tommy McCook & Supersonics)	22
68	Doctor Bird DB 1136	None Such/VAL BENNETT: Popeye On The Shore	20
68	Trojan TR 612	Uncle Charlie/What A Botheration	12
68	Pyramid PYR 6060	Let's Join Together/BEVERLEY'S ALLSTARS: I Don't Know	12
69	Camel CA 18	Facts Of Life/TERMITES: I'll Be Waiting	20
70	Escort ERT 844	Work It/SOUL MAN: Good Lover	10

(see also Sexy Girls)

MELLO & MELLOTONES

72	Summit SUM 8538	Haile Selasie/Old Man River	10

(see also Mellotones)

MELLOW CANDLE

68	SNB 55-3645	Feeling High/Tea With The Sun	60
72	Deram DM 357	Dan The Wing/Silversong	45
72	Deram SDL 7	SWADDLING SONGS (LP)	600

MELLOW CATS (with Count Ossie & Warrickas)

61	Blue Beat BB 68	Rock A Man Soul/MONTO & CYCLONES: Lazy Lou (B-side actually by Monty [Alexander] & Cyclones)	12

(see also Melo Cats)

MELLOW FRUITFULNESS

67	Columbia S(C)X 6242	MEDITATION (LP, mono/stereo)	25

MELLOW LARKS

60	Blue Beat BB 16	Time To Pray (Alleluia)/Love You Baby	8
61	Blue Beat BB 38	No More Wedding/Lite Of My Life	8

(see also Basil Gabbidon)

GEORGE MELLY (& MICK MULLIGAN BAND)

51	Tempo A 96	Rock Island Line/Send Me To The 'Lectric Chair (78, as The George Melly Trio)	15
52	Tempo A 104	Kitchen Man/Jazzbo Brown From Memphis Town (78)	10
55	Decca F 10457	Frankie And Johnny/I'm Down In The Dumps (78 rpm = £10)	8
56	Tempo A 144	Jenny's Ball/Muddy Water (78 rpm = £8)	8
56	Tempo A 147	Death Letter/Cemetery Blues (78 rpm = £8)	8
56	Decca F 10763	Kingdom Coming/I'm A Ding Dong Daddy (78 rpm = £8)	8
56	Decca FJ 10779	Waiting For A Train/Railroadin' Man (78 rpm = £8)	5
56	Decca FJ 10806	My Canary Has Circles Under His Eyes/Heebie Jeebies (78 rpm = £8)	5
57	Decca FJ 10840	Black Bottom/Magnolia (78 rpm = £8)	5
59	Decca F 11115	Abdul Abulbul Amir/Get Away, Old Man, Get Away (78 rpm = £8)	5
60	Pye 7N 15253	Ise A Muggin'/Run Come See Jerusalem	5
75	Warner Bros WB 16532	Ain't Misbehavin'/My Canary Has Circles Under His Eyes (p/s)	5
56	Tempo EXA 41	GEORGE MELLY WITH MICK MULLIGAN'S JAZZ BAND (EP)	8
56	Tempo EXA 47	GEORGE MELLY SINGS DOOM (EP, with Mick Mulligan's Jazz Band)	8
58	Decca DFE 6552	MICHIGAN WATER BLUES (EP)	8
58	Decca DFE 6557	ABDUL ABULBUL AMIR (EP)	8
61	Columbia SEG 8093	THE PSYCHOLOGICAL SIGNIFICANCE OF ANIMAL SYMBOLISM IN AMERICAN NEGRO FOLK MUSIC AND ALL THAT JAZZ (EP)	8

(see also Mick Mulligan Band)

MELO CATS

61	Blue Beat BB 54	Another Moses/ROLAND ALPHONSO & ALLEY CATS: Hully Gully Rock	10

(see also Mellow Cats)

MELODIANS

66	Island WI 3014	Lay It On/Meet Me	30
67	Coxsone CS 7004	I Should Have Made It Up/JOE HIGGS: Neighbour Neighbour	30
67	Treasure Isle TI 7006	You Don't Need Me/I Will Get Along	30
67	Treasure Isle TI 7022	You Have Caught Me/I Know Just How She Feels	30
67	Treasure Isle TI 7023	Last Train To Expo. '67/TOMMY McCOOK & SUPERSONICS: Expo	30
68	Treasure Isle TI 7028	Come On, Little Girl/TOMMY McCOOK & SUPERSONICS: Got Your Soul	30
68	Doctor Bird DB 1125	Little Nut Tree/You Are My Only Love	25
68	Doctor Bird DB 1139	Swing And Dine/I Could Be King	25
68	Fab FAB 61	Sweet Rose/It Comes And Goes	18
69	Gas GAS 108	Ring Of Gold/You've Got It	8
69	Gas GAS 116	Personally Speaking/LLOYD ROBINSON: Trouble Trouble	8
69	Crab CRAB 15	When There Is You/UNIQUES: My Woman's Love	7
69	Trojan TR 660	Everybody Bawlin'/TOMMY McCOOK: Kilowatt	8
69	Trojan TR 695	Sweet Sensation/It's My Delight	5
70	Trojan TR 7720	A Day Seems So Long/BEVERLEY'S ALLSTARS: Project	6
70	Trojan TR 7764	Say Darling Say/Come Rock It To Me	8
70	High Note HS 044	Love Is A Good Thing/No Nola	6
70	Summit SUM 8505	Walking In The Rain/Rivers Of Babylon	7
70	Summit SUM 8508	Rivers Of Babylon/BEVERLEY'S ALL STARS: Babylon Version	6
71	Duke DU 128	The Sensational Melodians (Parts 1 & 2)	5
71	Summit SUM 8512	It Took A Miracle/BEVERLEY'S ALLSTARS: Miraculous Version	5
71	Summit SUM 8522	Come Ethiopians, Come/BEVERLEY'S ALL STARS: Version Two	8
71	Summit SUM 8532	My Love, My Life/My Love, My Life – Version	6
72	Summit SUM 8534	The Time Has Come/BEVERLEY'S ALL STARS: McIntosh (B-side actually "No Sins At All" by Melodians)	6
72	Bullet BU 496	Tropical Land/HUGH ROY & SLIM SMITH: Love I Bring	6
72	Duke DU 130	The Mighty Melodians (Adapted) (Parts 1 & 2)	6
72	Attack ATT 8025	This Beautiful Land/MELODIOUS RHYTHMS: Version	6
72	Attack ATT 8031	Without You (What Would I Do)/DYNAMITES: Instrumental	6
72	Punch PH 111	Round And Round/UPSETTERS: Round Version	6
73	Randy's RAN 530	Passion Love/Love Makes The World Go Round	6

(see also Gentiles, Tony Brevett, Brent Dowe, Jaylads, Trevor McNaughton, Gaylads, Joe Grinne)

MINT VALUE £

BOBBY MELODY
79   Hit Run HIT DD5   Anger & Strife (ft. Jah Lion)/JAH LION: Johnnie Walker (12")................30

JOHNNY MELODY
67   Pyramid PYR 6023   Govern Your Mouth (actually by George Dekker)/
                                ROLAND ALPHONSO: Peace And Love...................................20
    (see also Lloyd & Johnny Melody under 'L', Lloyd Terrell)

MELODY ENCHANTERS
63   Island WI 049   Enchanter's Ball/I'll Be True.................................18
63   R&B JB 117   Gone Gone/Blueberry Hill.....................................18

MELODY FAIR
68   Decca F 12801   Something Happened To Me/Sittin', Watchin', Waitin'..........5

'MELODY MAKER' ALLSTARS
    (see under Humphrey Lyttelton)

MELO'S MARITIME
67   Philips BF 1602   Blow The Man Up/Maneater.....................................5

KANSAS CITY MELROSE/CASINO SIMPSON
72   Chicago Piano 12-001   KANSAS CITY MELROSE/CASINO SIMPSON (LP).....................15

MONIQUE MELSEN
71   Decca F 23170   The Love Beat/Pomme Pomme Pomme..............................12

JOE MELSON
61   Polydor NH 66959   Oh Yeah!/What's The Use I Still Love You.....................30
61   Polydor NH 66961   Hey Mister Cupid/No One Really Cares.........................30
64   Hickory 45-1229   Stay Away From Her/His Girl...................................7

MELTING BEAR
85   Beggars Banquet BEG 144   It Makes No Difference/Nature's Way/Sea Song (unreleased,
                                white label test pressings only)..............................6

    (see also Icicle Works)

MELTON CONSTABLE
70s   SIS private pressing   MELTON CONSTABLE (LP)......................................150

HAROLD MELVIN & BLUE NOTES
72   CBS 8291   I Miss You (Parts 1 & 2).....................................5
72   CBS 8496   If You Don't Know Me By Now/Let Me Into Your World............5
75   Route RT 06   Get Out/You May Not Love Me.................................10
77   ABC 4161   Reaching For The World/Stay Together.........................5
73   CBS 65350   HAROLD MELVIN & THE BLUES NOTES (LP)........................12
73   CBS Q 65859   BLACK AND BLUE (LP, quadrophonic)...........................12

MELVINS
90   Tupelo TUPEP 10   Sweet Young Thing Ain't Sweet No More/STEEL POLE BATH TUB:
                                I Dreamed I Dream (12", p/s, green vinyl, 600 only)..........12

MEMBERS
78   Stiff/One Off OFF 3   Solitary Confinement/Rat Up A Drainpipe (p/s)...............15
79   Virgin VS 242   The Sound Of The Suburbs/Handling The Big Jets (clear vinyl, window p/s).....5
80   Virgin VS 352   Flying Again/Disco Oui Oui/Live In A Lift/Rat Up A Drainpipe
                                (double pack, gatefold p/s)...................................5

MEMOS
59   Parlophone R 4616   The Biddy Leg/My Type Of Girl................................85

MEMPHIS BEND
76   United Artists UP 36132   Ubangi Stomp/Tennessee.......................................8
77   United Artists UAS 30036 GOOD ROCKIN' TONITE (LP)....................................15

MEMPHIS HORNS
71   Atlantic 2091 080   Woolly Bully/I Can't Turn You Loose.........................10
77   RCA PB 0836   Get Up And Dance/Don't Abuse It..............................6
71   Mojo 2466 010   THE MEMPHIS HORNS (LP)......................................22

MEMPHIS JUG BAND
55   HMV 7EG 8073   MEMPHIS JUG BAND (EP, withdrawn)...........................100
69   Saydisc Matchbox RL 33   MEMPHIS JUG BAND (LP).......................................18
71   Saydisc Matchbox RL 337   MEMPHIS JUG BAND VOLUME 2 (LP)..............................18

MEMPHIS MINNIE
64   Heritage H 103   MEMPHIS MINNIE (EP)...75
69   Limited Edition (no cat. no.) MEMPHIS MINNIE 1934-1936 (LP)..........................40
69   Limited Edition (no cat. no.) MEMPHIS MINNIE 1934-1941 (LP)..........................40
69   Sunflower ET 1400   MEMPHIS MINNIE 1941-1949 (LP, 99 copies only)...............50
74   Flyright LP 108   MEMPHIS MINNIE 1934-1941 (LP, reissue)......................12
74   Flyright LP 109   MEMPHIS MINNIE 1941-1949 (LP, reissue)......................12

MEMPHIS SLIM
53   Esquire 10-319   Harlem Bound/ST. LOUIS JIMMY R&B BAND: Holiday For Boogie (78)..32
60   Collector JDN 102   Pinetop's Blues/How Long....................................25
62   Storyville A 45055   Big City Girl/El Capitan....................................15
61   Collector JEN 5   GOING TO KANSAS CITY (EP)...................................25
62   Storyville SEP 385   STORYVILLE BLUES ANTHOLOGY VOL. 5 — BOOGIE WOOGIE AND
                                THE BLUES (EP)..22
63   Vocalion VEP 170155   MEMPHIS SLIM AND LITTLE RICHARD (EP)........................80
63   Summit LSE 2041   WORLD'S FOREMOST BLUES SINGERS (EP).........................12
61   Collector JGN 1004   MEMPHIS SLIM U.S.A. (LP)....................................45
61   Collector JGN 1005   MEMPHIS SLIM U.S.A. (VOL. 2) (LP)...........................45
62   Bluesville BV 1018   JUST BLUES (LP)...25
62   Storyville SLP 118   MEMPHIS SLIM (LP)...25

62	Storyville SLP 138	THIS IS A GOOD TIME TO WRITE A SONG (LP)	25
62	Fontana 688 302 ZL	NO STRAIN (LP)	25
63	United Artists ULP 1042	BROKEN SOUL BLUES (LP)	25
64	Storyville SLP 118	TRAVELLIN' WITH THE BLUES (LP)	22
64	Xtra XTRA 1008	MEMPHIS SLIM (LP)	18
64	Fontana 688 701	ALONE WITH MY FRIENDS (LP)	35
65	Fontana TL 5254	CLAP YOUR HANDS (LP)	25
65	Melodisc MLPS 12-149	FATTENIN' FROGS FOR SNAKES (LP)	35
66	Fontana 688 315 ZL	FRISCO BAY BLUES (LP)	30
67	Polydor 623 211	PINETOP'S BLUES (LP)	22
68	Polydor 623 263	BLUESINGLY YOURS (LP, with Mickey Baker)	22
68	Xtra XTRA 5060	ALL KINDS OF BLUES (LP)	18
69	Xtra XTRA 1085	CHICAGO BLUES (LP)	18
69	Joy JOYS 143	AT THE GATE OF HORN (LP)	12
69	Beacon BEAS 6	LEGEND OF THE BLUES VOL. 2 (LP)	12
72	Barclay 920 214	BLUE MEMPHIS (LP, with Peter Green)	60
72	Barclay 920 332-3	OLD TIMES, NEW TIMES (2-LP)	20
70s	Xtra XTRA 5063	ALL KINDS OF BLUES (LP)	18

(see also Washboard Sam, Ivory Joe Hunter, Otis Spann)

MEMPHIS THREE
| 68 | Page One POF 070 | Wild Thing/She's A Yum Yum | 7 |

MEN
| 79 | Virgin VS 269 | I Don't Depend On You/Cruel (p/s) | 10 |
| 79 | Virgin VS 269-12 | I Don't Depend On You/Cruel (12", p/s) | 15 |

(see also Human League, Philip Oakey & Giorgio Moroder)

MENACE
77	Illegal IL 004	Screwed Up/Insane Society (p/s)	15
77	Illegal IL 004	Screwed Up/Insane Society (12", p/s)	20
77	Small Wonder SMALL 5	G.L.C./I'm Civilized (p/s)	15
78	Illegal IL 008	I Need Nothing/Electrocutioner (p/s)	15
78	Fresh FRESH 14	The Young Ones/Tomorrow's World/Live For Today (p/s)	15
79	Small Wonder SMALL 16	Final Vinyl: Last Year's Youth/Carry No Banners (p/s)	8
86	Razor RAZ 18	GLC — RIP (LP)	25

(see also Aces, Vermilion & Aces)

MENACE
| 01 | Plastica DPFT 004 | Reap What You Sow (12") | 15 |

CARLOS MENDES
| 72 | Pye International 7N 25581 | Shadows/Glow-Worm | 8 |

SERGIO MENDES & BRASIL '66
66	Pye NPL 28089	HERB ALPERT PRESENTS SERGIO MENDES AND BRASIL '66 (LP)	12
67	A&M AML(S) 902	EQUINOX (LP)	12
68	A&M AML 911	LOOK AROUND (LP)	12
69	A&M AMLS 922	FOOL ON THE HILL (LP)	12
70	A&M AMLS 989	LIVE AT EXPO 70 (LP)	15
70	A&M AMLS 2000	STILLNESS (LP)	15

MENDES PREY
83	MP AM 076	On To The Borderline/Runnin' For You (p/s)	20
86	Wag WAG 2	Wonderland/Can You Believe It (p/s)	25
86	Wag 12 WAG 2	Wonderland/Can You Believe It (12", p/s)	25

ENOCH & CHRISTY MENSAH
| 60s | Melodisc M 1569 | Rebecca/Dakuku Dum | 5 |

E.T. MENSAH & HIS TEMPO'S BAND
| 55 | Decca WAL 1001 | DECCA PRESENTS (10" LP) | 22 |

MENSWE@R
| 95 | Laurel LAU 4 | I'll Manage Somehow/Secondhand (p/s, 2,500 only) | 5 |
| 95 | Laurel LAUXDJ 5 | Daydreamer (Radio Mix)/(Student Union Mix) (10", no'd white sl., 5,000 only) | 8 |

MENTAL
| 79 | Kamikaze Pig RAM 1 | God For A Day/18/Kill The Bill/Off The Rails (600 only, p/s) | 60 |

MENTATZ
| 81 | Naff N 001 | Never Trust A Russian/Dead To The World (p/s) | 5 |

MEN WITHOUT HATS
| 85 | Statik CDST 10 | RHYTHM OF YOUTH (CD) | 30+ |

IAN MENZIES
58	Pye Jazz 7NJ 2027	Polly Wolly Doodle/In A Persian Market (with His New Stompers) (78 rpm = £8)	5
58	Pye Jazz 7NJ 2028	Bill Bailey Won't You Please Come Home/Hot Time In The Old Town Tonight (as Ian Menzies & Clyde Valley Stompers)	5
61	Pye Jazz 7NJ 2046	Auf Wiedersehn/Taboo	10
58	Pye Jazz NJE 1049	MELODY MAKER ALL STARS (EP)	10
60	Pye Nixa NJE 1071	SWINGIN' SEAMUS (EP)	12
60	Pye Jazz NJL 26	IAN MENZIES AND THE CLYDE VALLEY STOMPERS (LP)	15

(see also Clyde Valley Stompers)

JOHNNY MERCER
53	Capitol LC 6633	CAPITOL PRESENTS JOHNNY MERCER (10" LP)	12
54	Capitol LC 6640	CAPITOL PRESENTS JOHNNY MERCER VOL. 2 (10" LP)	12
54	Capitol LC 6648	CAPITOL PRESENTS JOHNNY MERCER VOL. 3 (10" LP)	12
54	Capitol LC 6655	CAPITOL PRESENTS JOHNNY MERCER VOL. 4 (10" LP)	12

MINT VALUE £

MARY MAE MERCER
| 65 | Decca DFE 8599 | MARY MAE MERCER (EP) | 60 |

FREDDIE MERCURY
84	CBS A 4735	Love Kills/GEORGIO MORODER: Rotwang's Party (p/s)	5
84	CBS WA 4735	Love Kills/GEORGIO MORODER: Rotwang's Party (picture disc)	40
84	CBS TA 4375	Love Kills (Extended)/GEORGIO MORODER: Rotwang's Party (12", p/s)	10
85	CBS A 6019	I Was Born To Love You/Stop All The Fighting (p/s)	5
85	CBS DA 6019	I Was Born To Love You/Stop All The Fighting//Love Kills (Extended)/ Stop All The Fighting (Extended) (double pack)	20
85	CBS TA 6019	I Was Born To Love You (7.03)/Stop All The Fighting (12", p/s)	12
85	CBS A 6413	Made In Heaven (Remix 3.59)/She Blows Hot And Cold (p/s)	8
85	CBS WA 6413	Made In Heaven (Remix)/She Blows Hot And Cold (shaped picture disc)	35
85	CBS WA 6413	Made In Heaven (Remix)/She Blows Hot And Cold (uncut shaped picture disc)	800
85	CBS TA 6413	Made In Heaven (Extended Remix 4.43)/Made In Heaven (Remix 3.59)/ She Blows Hot And Cold (Extended Version) (12", p/s)	15
85	CBS TA 6555	Living On My Own (Extended 6.38)/My Love Is Dangerous (Extended 6.25) (12", p/s)	12
85	CBS GTA 6555	Living On My Own (Extended 6.38)/My Love Is Dangerous (Extended 6.25) (12", gatefold p/s)	20
85	CBS A 6725	Love Me Like There's No Tomorrow/Let's Turn It On (p/s)	20
85	CBS TA 6725	Love Me Like There's No Tomorrow (Extended Version)/Let's Turn It On (Extended Version) (12", p/s)	40
85	CBS DTA 6725	Love Me Like There's No Tomorrow (Extended Version)//Living On My Own (Extended 6.38)/My Love Is Dangerous (Extended 6.25) (12", double pack, shrinkwrapped with stickers)	80+
85	CBS TA 6725	Love Me Like There's No Tomorrow (Extended Version)/Let's Turn It On (Extended Version) (12", promo, white card sleeve, with sticker)	50+
86	EMI EMI 5559	Time (From The Musical)/Time (Instrumental) (p/s, with inner sleeve)	10
86	EMI 12EMI 5559	Time (From The Musical) (Extended)/Time/Time (Instrumental) (12", p/s)	12
87	Parlophone RP 6151	The Great Pretender/Exercises In Free Love (Mercury Vocal) (shaped picture disc)	50
87	Parlophone RP 6151	The Great Pretender/Exercises In Free Love (Mercury Vocal) (shaped picture disc, with unfolded or folded plinth)	90/70
87	Parlophone RP 6151	The Great Pretender/Exercises In Free Love (Mercury Vocal) (uncut shaped picture disc)	500
87	Parlophone 10R 6151	The Great Pretender (Extended Version)/(7" Version)/Exercises In Free Love (7" Version) (10", 1-sided, printed white label, plain black die-cut sleeve, promo only)	40
87	Parlophone 12R 6151	The Great Pretender (Extended)/(The Great Pretender 7")/ Exercises In Free Love (12", p/s)	8
87	Polydor POSP 887	Barcelona/Exercises In Free Love (Caballé Vocal) (with Montserrat Caballé, with gatefold p/s)	5
87	Polydor POSPX 887	Barcelona (Single Version)/Exercises In Free Love (Caballé Vocal) (12" Version)/Barcelona (Extended) (12", some with gatefold p/s)	18/12
87	Polydor POSPP 887	Barcelona (7" Version)/Exercises In Free Love (Caballé Vocal) (7" Version)/ Barcelona (Extended Version) (12", picture disc)	40
87	Polydor POCD 887	Barcelona (7" Version)/Exercises In Free Love (Caballé Vocal) (7" Version)/ Barcelona (Extended Version) (CD, card p/s)	20
87	Polydor POCD 887	Barcelona/Exercises In Free Love (Version 2) (Caballé Vocal)/ Barcelona (Extended) (CD, autographed card p/s, promo only)	300+
87	Polydor PO 23 DJ	The Golden Boy (with Montserrat Caballé) (radio edit) (1-sided DJ sampler, p/s, with sticker)	200
88	Polydor POSPX 23	The Golden Boy/The Fallen Priest/The Golden Boy (Instrumental) (12", p/s)	20
88	Polydor POCD 23	The Golden Boy/The Fallen Priest/The Golden Boy (Instrumental) (CD)	35
88	Polydor POSP 29	How Can I Go On/Overture Piccante (with Montserrat Caballe) (p/s)	15
88	Polydor POSX 29	How Can I Go On/Overture Piccante (with Montserrat Caballe) (picture disc)	45
89	Polydor PZ 29	How Can I Go On/Guide Me Home/Overture Piccante (12", p/s)	25
89	Polydor PZCD 29	How Can I Go On/Guide Me Home/Overture Piccante (CD, picture disc)	35
88	Polydor CD 3 125 211	The Golden Boy/La Japanese/Barcelona (CD promo, unreleased p/s, jewel case)	100
89	Polydor 0805 548-2	Ensueno/Barcelona (Edit 4.24)/Exercises In Free Love/Barcelona (Extended Version 7.02)/Barcelona (Video) (CD Video)	40
89	Polydor 0805 580-2	The Fallen Priest/The Golden Boy (Album Version)/The Golden Boy (Instrumental Version)/The Golden Boy (Video) (CD Video)	40
92	Polydor PO 234	How Can I Go On/The Golden Boy (yellow p/s)	6
92	Polydor PZCD 234	How Can I Go On/The Golden Boy/The Fallen Priest (CD, yellow p/s)	10
92	Parlophone R 6331	In My Defence/Love Kills (Wolf Euro Mix) (p/s)	6
85	CBS 40-86312	MR. BAD GUY (cassette, with extra remix)	20
85	CBS CD 86312	MR. BAD GUY (CD, with 3 extended mixes; beware of counterfeits)	30
94	Parlophone 7234 8 2814 10	FREDDIE MERCURY REMIXES (LP, unreleased)	150

(see also Queen, Larry Lurex, Eddie Howell, Billy Squier)

MERCURY REV
91	Mint Film MINT 5	Car Wash Hair/Coney Island Cyclone (4 track demo) (200 copies only, p/s)	5
91	Mint Film MINT 5 T	Car Wash Hair/Chasing A Bee (4 track demo)/Coney Island Cyclone (12", p/s)	8
92	Rough Trade 45REV 6	If You Want Me To Stay/Left Handed Raygun of Paul Sharits (Retirement Just Like That) (p/s, with insert)	12
93	Beggars Banquet BBQ 5 T	The Hum Is Coming From Her (as Mercury Theremin Sextet)/So There (as Mercury Rev Orchestra with Robert Creely) (10", p/s)	8
93	Beggars Banquet BBQ 14	Something For Joey/There's Spiders Eggs In Bubbla Yhum (blue vinyl, two different p/s)	5
91	Mint Film MINTLP 4	YERSELF IS STEAM (LP, with bonus LP 'Lego My Ego')	20
93	Beggars Banquet BBQLP 140	BOCES (LP, clear red vinyl)	15
95	B. Banquet BBQLP 176 P	SEE YOU ON THE OTHER SIDE (LP, picture disc)	12
98	V2 VVR 1002772	DESERTER'S SONGS (CD, with cardboard sleeve and stamps)	20

(see also Shady)

MERCY
69	London HLZ 10273	Love (Can Make You Happy)/Fireball	8

BURGESS MEREDITH
63	Colpix PX 690	Home In The Meadow/No Goodbye	8

LOTTIE MERLE
72	Flyright 001	Howling In The Moonlight/Catfish	5

MERLIN
88	Rhythm King LEFTR22T	Born Free (Wizard Mix) (12")	10

ETHEL MERMAN
54	Brunswick 05346	A Husband — A Wife (with Jimmy Durante)/The Lake Song (with Ray Bolger)	8
55	Brunswick 05381	(There's No Business Like) Show Business/Play A Simple Melody (B-side with Dan Dailey)	8
58	RCA RCA 1039	A New-Fangled Tango/Mutual Admiration Society (with Virginia Gibson) (78 = £8)	5
52	Brunswick LAT 8016	SONGS FROM "CALL ME MADAM" (LP)	12
52	Brunswick LA 8539	CALL ME MADAM (LP, with Dick Haymes)	12
54	Brunswick LA 8636	SONGS SHE HAS MADE FAMOUS (10" LP)	12
54	Brunswick LA 8638	DUET FROM FORD 50TH ANNIVERSARY TV SHOW (LP, with Mary Martin)	12
	(see also Jimmy Durante)		

RAY MERRELL
60	Ember EMB S 113	Why Did You Leave Me?/Teenage Love (p/s)	10
60s	Aral PS 115	Battle Of Waterloo/Not Any More (p/s)	10
70	Jay Boy BOY 22	Tears Of Joy/Searchin' (withdrawn) (Beware of bootlegs!) (DJ copy = £250)	200

TONY MERRICK
66	Columbia DB 7913	Lady Jane/Michelle	10
66	Columbia DB 7995	Wake Up/It's For You	6

BOB MERRILL
58	Columbia DB 4086	Nairobi/Jump When I Say Frog	15

BUDDY MERRILL
66	Vocalion VN 9261	Sweet September/Sherk	12

ROBERT MERRILL
59	RCA RCA 1109	À Toujours/Gigi (78 rpm = £8)	5

MERRITTS
70	Hot Rod HR 113	I Don't Want To (Part 1)/HOT ROD ALL STARS: Version	12

MERRYMEN
66	Doctor Bird DB 1004	Big Bamboo/Island Woman	8
69	Trojan TR 7707	Little Drummer Boy/Mary's Boy Child	5
71	Duke DU 113	Big Bamboo/King Ja-Ja (both sides actually with Emille Straker)	5
68	Island ILP 984	CARIBBEAN TREASURE CHEST (LP)	30
	(see also Soul Brothers)		

JASON MERRYWEATHER
69	Crystal CR 001	My Summer Love/Abigail	7
	(see also Ricky Valance)		

MERSEYBEATS
63	Fontana TF 412	It's Love That Really Counts/The Fortune Teller	12
64	Fontana TF 431	I Think Of You/Mister Moonlight	6
64	Fontana TF 459	Don't Turn Around/Really Mystified	6
64	Fontana TF 482	Wishin' And Hopin'/Milkman	6
64	Fontana TF 504	Last Night/See Me Back	8
65	Fontana TF 568	Don't Let It Happen To Us/It Would Take A Long Long Time	10
65	Fontana TF 607	I Love You, Yes I Do/Good Good Lovin'	7
65	Fontana TF 645	I Stand Accused/All My Life	8
69	Fontana TF 1025	I Think Of You/Wishin' And Hopin' (p/s)	10
81	Tudor CR 23	This Is Merseybeat (both sides) (p/s)	6
64	Fontana TE 17422	ON STAGE (EP)	40
64	Fontana TE 17423	I THINK OF YOU (EP)	32
64	Fontana TE 17432	THE MERSEYBEATS (EP)	32
64	Fontana TL 5210	THE MERSEYBEATS (LP)	80
65	Wing WL 1163	THE MERSEYBEATS (LP, reissue)	18
77	Look LKLP 6160	GREATEST HITS (LP)	12
	(see also Merseys, Rockin' Horse, Tony Crane, Kirkbys, Quotations, Johnny Gustavson)		

MERSEYBOYS
64	Ace Of Clubs ACL 1169	15 GREAT SONGS BY JOHN, PAUL AND GEORGE (LP)	20

MERSEYS
66	Fontana TF 694	Sorrow/Some Other Day	6
66	Fontana TF 732	So Sad About Us/Love Will Continue	7
66	Fontana TF 776	Rhythm Of Love/Is It Love?	7
67	Fontana TF 845	The Cat/Change Of Heart	18
68	Fontana TF 916	Penny In My Pocket/I Hope You're Happy	10
68	Fontana TF 955	Lovely Loretta/Dreaming	10
73	Philips 6006 258	Sorrow/MERSEYBEATS: I Think Of You	6
	(see also Merseybeats, Crackers)		

MERSEYSIPPI JAZZ BAND
55	Decca DFE 6251	AT THE ROYAL FESTIVAL HALL (EP)	8
55	Esquire EP 30	THE MERSEYSIPPI JAZZ BAND (EP)	8
55	Esquire EP 60	THE MERSEYSIPPI JAZZ BAND (EP)	8
56	Esquire EP 90	THE MERSEYSIPPI JAZZ BAND (EP)	8
56	Esquire EP 118	THE MERSEYSIPPI JAZZ BAND (EP)	8
57	Esquire EP 130	THE MERSEYSIPPI JAZZ BAND (EP)	8

MINT VALUE £

54	Esquire 20-063	WEST COAST SHOUT (LP)	15
55	Esquire 20-083	ALL THE GIRLS (LP)	15
55	Esquire 20-088	MERSEY TUNNEL JAZZ (LP)	15
56	Esquire 20-093	ANY OLD RAGS (LP)	15

TEDDY MERTENS
63	Oriole CB 1904	Autumn Love/Try To Love Me Again	5
63	Oriole CB 1925	This Is My Prayer/My River Of Memories (as Teddy Mertens' Trumpet)	5

MERTON PARKAS
79	Beggars Banquet BEG 22	You Need Wheels/I Don't Want To Know You (coloured p/s with patch)	10/5
79	Beggars Banquet BEG 25	Plastic Smile/The Man With The Disguise (p/s)	5
79	Beggars Banquet BEG 30	Give It To Me Now/Gi's It (p/s)	5
80	Beggars Banquet BEG 43	Put Me In The Picture/In The Midnight Hour (p/s)	5
83	Well Suspect BLAM 002	Flat 19/Band Of Gold (p/s)	8
80s	Beggars Banquet BEG 22	You Need Wheels/I Don't Want To Know You (reissue, with silver Moulded label, black & white p/s)	7
83	Beggars Banquet BEG 93E	The Singles (6-track mini-LP)	8
79	Beggars Banquet BEGA 11	FACE IN THE CROWD (LP)	20

(see also Style Council)

JUNIOR MERVIN
69	Big Shot BI 527	Hustler/Magic Touch	15

MESCALINE UNITED
92	R&S RS 92019	We Have Arrived (Aphex Twin QQT Reconstruction Mix)/We Have Arrived (Aphex Twin TTQ Reconstruction Mix) (limited issue 12", also known as "PCP Remixed", plain paper sleeve)	80

MESS
80s	Reasonable MEP 1	Tried And Trusted/I'm Falling (p/s)	5

MESSAGE
70	Songbird SB 1503	Rum-Bum-A-Loo/Drummer Boy	8

(see also Boris Gardner)

MESSENGERS
64	Columbia DB 7344	I'm Stealin' Back/This Little Light Of Mine	10
65	Columbia DB 7495	When Did You Leave Heaven/More Pretty Girls Than One	8

MESSENGERS (Jamaica)
73	Attack ATT 8057	Crowded City/Thula Thula	5
73	Bread BR 1116	Cherry Baby/B.B. SEATON: Summertime	5

METABOLISTS
79	Drömm DRO 1	Drömm/Slaves/Eulam's Beat (p/s, rough screen-printed & folded p/s)	12
79	Drömm DRO 1	Drömm/Slaves/Eulam's Beat (p/s, smooth printed & stapled p/s)	10
79	Drömm DRO 3	Identity/Tiz Hoz Nam (p/s)	8
70s	Metabolists	GOATMANAUT (cassette)	12
70s	Drömm D 1	GOATMANAUT (LP)	15
70s	Drömm DRO 2	HANSTEN KLORD (LP)	12

METAL BOYS
79	Rough Trade RT 016	Sweet Marilyn/Fugue For A Darkening Island (p/s)	5

(see also Metal Urbain)

METALLICA
SINGLES
84	Music For Nations 12 KUT 105	Jump In The Fire/Seek And Destroy (live)/Phantom Lord (live) (12", p/s, initially with beige labels [later red/yellow])	20/18
84	Music For Nations CV12 KUT 105	Jump In The Fire/Seek And Destroy (live)/Phantom Lord (live) (12", red vinyl, p/s)	30
84	Music For Nations 12 KUT 105XP	Jump In The Fire/Seek And Destroy (live)/Phantom Lord (live) (12", stickered sleeve with sew-on patch)	25
84	Music For Nations T 12 KUT 105	Jump In The Fire/Seek And Destroy (live)/Phantom Lord (live) (cassette)	8
84	M. F. N. T 12 KUT 112	Creeping Death/Am I Evil?/Blitzkrieg (cassette)	8
84	Music For Nations 12 KUT 112	Creeping Death/Am I Evil?/Blitzkrieg (12", p/s, initially with beige label, later red/yellow)	15/12
84	M. F. N. CV12 KUT 112	Creeping Death/Am I Evil?/Blitzkrieg (12", p/s, blue vinyl, red/yellow or 'Special Anniversary Edition' labels)	30
84	Music For Nations GV12 KUT 112	Creeping Death/Am I Evil?/Blitzkrieg (12", no p/s, 'Anniversary Gold Edition', gold vinyl, 3000 only; some mispressed with 1 side gold, 1 side black vinyl)	60/50
84	Music For Nations P12 KUT 112	Creeping Death/Am I Evil?/Blitzkrieg (12", picture disc, initially without barcode)	30
84	Music For Nations CD12 KUT 112	Creeping Death/Am I Evil?/Blitzkrieg Jump In The Fire/ Seek And Destroy (live)/Phantom Lord (live) (CD)	60
86	Music For Nations PKUT 105	Jump In The Fire/Phantom Lord (live) (shaped picture disc, initially without barcode)	20/18
87	Vertigo METAL 112	$5.98 EP — GARAGE DAYS RE-REVISITED: Helpless/Crash Course In Brain Surgery/The Small Hours/Last Caress - Green Hell (medley) (12", p/s, later copies allegedly add "The Wait")	30
88	Vertigo METAL 212	Harvester Of Sorrow/Breadfan/The Prince (12", p/s, some with 'skull' label)	15
88	Vertigo METAL CD 2	Harvester Of Sorrow/Breadfan/The Prince (CD, card sleeve)	18
89	Vertigo METAL 312	Jump In The Fire/Seek And Destroy (live)/Phantom Lord (live) (12", p/s, reissue)	8
89	Vertigo METAL 412	Creeping Death/Am I Evil?/Blitzkrieg (12", p/s, reissue)	8
89	Vertigo 842-219-2	Creeping Death/Am I Evil?/Blitzkrieg/Jump In The Fire/ Seek And Destroy (live)/Phantom Lord (live) (CD)	50

89	Vertigo METAL 5	One/Seek And Destroy (live) (silver/black labels, paper p/s)	6
89	Vertigo METAP 5	One/Seek And Destroy (live) (card p/s, some stickered, with rolled poster)	12
89	Vertigo METDJ 5	One/One (Edit) (unique blue cover, plus insert)	50
89	Vertigo METPD 510	One/Seek And Destroy (live) (10", picture disc with card)	20
89	Vertigo METAL 512	One (Demo Version)/For Whom The Bell Tolls (live)/Welcome Home (Sanitarium) (live) (12", p/s initially with white labels, later yellow)	12/8
89	Vertigo METAL 512	One (Demo Version)/For Whom The Bell Tolls (live)/Welcome Home (Sanitarium) (live) (12", p/s mis-labelled as "Seek and Destroy" [live])	10
89	Vertigo METG 512	One (Demo Version)/For Whom The Bell Tolls (live)/Welcome Home (Sanitarium) (live) (12", gatefold p/s, with booklet, some mispressed with B-side label both sides)	18
89	Vertigo METCD 5	One/For Whom The Bell Tolls (live)/Welcome Home (Sanitarium) (live) (CD)	18
90	Vertigo 875 487 1	THE GOOD, THE BAD AND THE LIVE — THE 6½ YEARS ANNIVERSARY COLLECTION (6 x 12", with live 4-track EP [METAL 612])	60
91	Vertigo METAL 7	Enter Sandman/Stone Cold Crazy (p/s)	5
91	Vertigo METAL 7	Enter Sandman/Stone Cold Crazy (picture disc in p/s, stickered)	12
91	Vertigo METAL 712	Enter Sandman/Stone Cold Crazy/Holier Than Thou (Demo)/Enter Sandman (Demo) (12", p/s, with stickered sleeve)	8
91	Vertigo METBX 712	Enter Sandman/Stone Cold Crazy/Enter Sandman (Demo) (12", box with 4 photo prints)	20
91	Vertigo METCD 7	Enter Sandman/Stone Cold Crazy/Enter Sandman (Demo) (CD, picture disc in box with room for 3 more CDs)	30
91	Vertigo METAP 812	The Unforgiven/Killing Time /The Unforgiven (Demo) (picture disc, card insert)	8
91	Vertigo METAL 812	The Unforgiven/Killing Time/So What/The Unforgiven (Demo) (12", p/s, some stickered)	8
91	Vertigo METCD 8	The Unforgiven/Killing Time/The Unforgiven (Demo) (CD)	8
92	Vertigo METCB 9	Wherever I May Roam/Last Caress–Am I Evil?–Battery (Live Medley) (digipak CD)	8
92	Vertigo METAL 10	Nothing Else Matters/Enter Sandman (live) (p/s, black & white label)	8
92	Vertigo METCD 10	Nothing Else Matters/Enter Sandman (live)/Harvester Of Sorrow (live)/Nothing Else Matters (Demo) (picture CD)	8
92	Vertigo METCL 10	Nothing Else Matters — Live At Wembley 20/4/92: Enter Sandman/Sad But True/Nothing Else Matters (CD)	25
93	Vertigo METAL 11	Sad But True/Nothing Else Matters (p/s, stickered, no labels)	5
93	Vertigo METAL 1112	Sad But True/Nothing Else Matters (Elevator Version)/Creeping Death (live)/Sad But True (Demo) (12" picture disc with insert)	20
93	Vertigo METCH 11	Sad But True/Nothing Else Matters (live)/Sad But True (Demo) (CD, picture disc)	8
96	Vertigo METJB 12	Until It Sleeps/Until It Sleeps (jukebox issue, no p/s)	10
96	Vertigo METAL 12	Until It Sleeps/2x4 (live)/Until It Sleeps (Moby Remix) (10" red vinyl, stickered)	10
96	Vertigo METCX 12	Until It Sleeps/Kill-Ride (Medley)/Until It Sleeps (Moby Remix) (digipak CD)	10
97	Vertigo METJB 13	Hero Of The Day/Hero Of The Day (jukebox issue, no p/s)	10
96	Vertigo METCY 13	Hero Of The Day/Overkill/Damage Case/Stone Dead Forever/Too Late Too Late (CD, with poster in card cover)	10
96	Vertigo METAL 14	Mama Said/Ain't My Bitch (live) (picture disc with insert)	8

ALBUMS

83	M. For Nations MFN 7	KILL 'EM ALL (LP, 1st issue with beige labels [later red/yellow])	30/20
84	M. For Nations MFN 27	RIDE THE LIGHTNING (LP, with inner sleeve, initially with beige labels & without barcode)	20
86	M. For Nations MFN 27P	RIDE THE LIGHTNING (LP, picture disc, initially lacking barcode)	25/20
86	M. For Nations MFN 7P	KILL 'EM ALL (LP, picture disc, some lacking picture on 1 side, initially lacking barcode)	22/20
86	M. For Nations MFN 60	MASTER OF PUPPETS (LP, with inner sleeve & insert)	15
86	M. For Nations MFN 60	MASTER OF PUPPETS (LP, mispressing, Side 1 label on both sides)	20
86	M. For Nations MFN 60P	MASTER OF PUPPETS (LP, picture disc, initially lacking barcode)	22/18
87	M. For Nations MFN 7DM	KILL 'EM ALL (2-LP, 'direct metal mastered' reissue, gatefold sleeve)	35
87	M. For Nations MFN 60DM	MASTER OF PUPPETS (2-LP, 'direct metal mastered' reissue, gatefold sleeve with poster)	25
87	M. For Nations MFN 27DM	RIDE THE LIGHTNING (2-LP, 'direct metal mastered' reissue, gatefold sleeve with insert)	25
89	Vertigo 838-140-1	RIDE THE LIGHTNING (LP, reissue, mispressing, Side 1 lists "Master Of Puppets" tracks)	15
90	Vertigo 888 788-1	GARAGE DAYS RE-REVISITED (mini-LP)	20
84	M. For Nations MFNCD 7	KILL 'EM ALL (CD)	25
84	M. For Nations MFN 27P	RIDE THE LIGHTNING (CD)	25
86	M. For Nations MFNCD 60	MASTER OF PUPPETS (CD)	25
91	Vertigo MECAN 1/510-022-0	THE METALLICAN (CD, gold disc in metal 'paint can' with video & T-shirt; 35,000 only)	80
93	Vertigo 518-725-0	LIVE SHIT, BINGE & PURGE (3-CD box set with 3 videos & 72-page book)	60

PROMOS

88	Vertigo MET CD 100	THE WHIPLASH SAMPLER (CD)	50
88	Vertigo METDJ 2	Harvester Of Sorrow/Harvester Of Sorrow (unique p/s)	50
89	Vertigo METDJ 512	One (Demo Version)/For Whom The Bell Tolls (live)/Welcome Home (Sanitarium) (live) (12", unissued, promo-only p/s)	60
91	Vertigo METDJ 7	Enter Sandman (Radio Edit)/Stone Cold Crazy (B-side actually silent)	10
96	Vertigo MET INT 1	LOAD — THE INTERVIEW (CD, with cue booklet)	60
96	Mercury MM CJ-1	MANDATORY METALLICA (CD, 7-track sampler)	30
97	Vertigo MMCJ-2	MANDATORY METALLICA 2 (2-CD, 17-track sampler)	40

METAL MIRROR

80	M&M MM 001	Rock 'N Roll Ain't Never Gonna Leave Us/English Booze (some in p/s)	150/50

METAL URBAIN

78	Radar ADA 20	Hysterie Connective/Pas Poubelle	7
79	Rough Trade RT 001	Paris Maquis/Cle De Contact (p/s)	6

MINT VALUE £

METAPHORCE
95	Ill Gotten Gains FDN004	Recipes For Disaster/Behind Enemy Lines (12").	15

METEORS
64	Polydor NH 52263	Get A Load Of This/Ruby Ann	5

METEORS
79	EMI EMI 5000	My Balls Ache/Action (p/s).	5

METEORS
81	Ace SW 65	METEOR MADNESS (EP, some on blue vinyl)	15/10
81	Ace SWT 65	METEOR MADNESS (10" EP, white label test pressings only, custom p/s)	80
81	Chiswick CHIS 147	Radioactive Kid/Graveyard Stomp (p/s)	10
81	Lost Soul LOST 101	The Crazed/Attack Of The Zorch Men (p/s)	10
81	Ace NS 74	Radioactive Kid/Graveyard Stomp (p/s, reissue, some clear or blue vinyl; most on black vinyl)	10/5
82	WXYZ ABCD 5	Mutant Rock/The Hills Have Eyes (p/s)	8
82	I.D. EYE 1	Johnny Remember Me/Fear Of The Dark/Wreckin' Crew (p/s)	5
82	I.D. EYE 1P	Johnny Remember Me/Fear Of The Dark/Wreckin' Crew (picture disc)	7
82	Lyntone LYN 12647	METEORS: Mutant Rock (Instrumental/ANTI NOWHERE LEAGUE: World War Three/DEFECTS: Dance (red flexidisc with *Flexipop* magazine, issue 26)	7/5
84	Mad Pig PORK 1	I'm Just A Dog/Electro Rock (p/s)	6
85	Mad Pig PORK 1T	I'm Just A Dog (Wild Hog Mix Down)/Hoover Rock/Electro (12", p/s)	8
85	Mad Pig PORK 2	Fire, Fire/Little Red Riding Hood (p/s)	5
85	Mad Pig PORK 2T	Fire, Fire/Little Red Riding Hood/Stampede (King Ray Bat Scalator In The Dark Mix) (12", p/s)	8
85	Mad Pig PORK 3	Bad Moon Rising/Rhythm Of The Bell (p/s)	5
85	Mad Pig PORK 3T	Hogs And Cuties /Bad Moon Rising/Rhythm Of The Bell (What? Another Cover Mix) (12", p/s)	8
86	I.D. EYE 10	MUTANT ROCK (EP, green vinyl).	8
86	I.D. EYET 10	MUTANT ROCK (12" EP, green or blue vinyl).	12
86	Anagram ANA 31	Surf City/The Edge (p/s)	10
86	Anagram 12ANA 31	Surf City (Has Beens From Outer Space Mix)/The Edge/Johnny's Here (12", p/s)	10
87	Anagram ANA 35	Go Buddy Go/Wildkat Ways (p/s)	5
87	Anagram 12ANA 35	Go Buddy Go (The Wonkey Donkey Mix)/Wildkat Ways/You Crack Me Up (p/s)	7
81	Ace MAD 1	THE METEORS MEET SCREAMIN' LORD SUTCH (mini-LP, 1 side each, 1,000 only, stickered cartoon print on plain card sleeve).	125
81	Lost Soul LOSTLP 3001	IN HEAVEN (LP).	20
86	Big Beat WIKA 47	TEENAGERS FROM OUTER SPACE (LP).	20
86	Big Beat WIKA 47CD	TEENAGERS FROM OUTER SPACE (CD).	18
87	Dojo LP56P	NIGHT OF THE WEREWOLF (LP, picture disc)	12

(see also Tall Boys, Clapham South Escalators, [Screamin'] Lord Sutch, Deadbeats)

METERS
69	Stateside SS 2140	Sophisticated Cissy/Sehorn's Farm	15
70	Direction 58-4751	Look-Ka-Py-Py/This Is My Last Affair	15
74	Reprise K 14367	People Say/Africa	6
75	Reprise K 14405	Fire On The Bayou/They All Ask'd For You	6
72	Reprise K 44242	CABBAGE ALLEY (LP)	30
74	Reprise K 54027	REJUVENATION (LP)	30
74	Island ILPS 9250	CISSY STRUT (LP)	30
75	Reprise K 54044	FIRE ON THE BAYOU (LP)	22
76	Reprise K 54076	BEST OF THE METERS (LP)	15
76	Reprise K 54078	TRICK BAG (LP)	22
77	Reprise K 56378	NEW DIRECTIONS (LP).	12
79	Pye PKL 5578	GOOD OLD FUNKY MUSIC (LP)	12

METHOD ACTORS
80	Armageddon AS 6	The Method/Can't Act (p/s).	7
81	Armageddon AS 11	Round World/Eye (p/s)	7

METRONOME ALL STARS
51	Capitol CL 13545	Local 802 Blues/Early Spring (78, with Stan Getz & Miles Davis)	12

METROPAK
80	Metropak PAK 001	You're A Rebel/OK Let's Go/Run Run Run (numbered p/s)	6
80	Metropak PAK 002	Here's Looking At You/Walking (foldout card p/s).	5

METROPHASE
79	Neo London MS 01	In Black/Neo Beauty/Cold Rebellion (photocopied p/s with lyric insert)	8
79	Neo London MS 02	New Age/Frames Of Life (foldout p/s, stamped white labels)	8
81	Fresh FRESH 6	In Black/Neo Beauty/Cold Rebellion (reissue, better quality p/s with insert)	6

(see also Swell Maps)

METROPOLITAN POLICE BAND
66	Columbia DB 8095	Thunderbirds March/P.C. ALEXANDER MORGAN: Sussex By The Sea	10

METROTONE
97	Wurlitzer Jukebox WJ 40	Kiss Me Awake/Byddant Fel Y Ser/Four Continuous Tones (p/s, 1,000 only).	5
98	Earworm WORM 21	THE LESS YOU HAVE THE MORE YOU ARE (LP, 4 copies only on black vinyl)	25

PAUL METSERS
81	Highway SHY 7014	CAUTION TO THE WIND (LP).	12

M.E.V.
69	Polydor 583 769	MUSICA ELETTRONICA VIVA (LP).	15

MEW
02	Epic 6728542	Am I Wry?No/Like Paper Cuts/Snowflake (CD)	8
02	Epic 6728547	Am I Wry? No/Snowflake (p/s).	7
02	Epic 6734072	She Came Home For Christmas (1-track original CD)	8

MEXICANS
68	Pye 17613	Alexander Higginbottom/Julie	12
68	Pye 17657	Without Your Love	12

AUGIE MEYERS
70s	Sonet SNTF 883	STILL GROWIN' (LP, with Doug Sahm)	12

(see also Sir Douglas Quintet, Doug Sahm)

ANTHONY MEYNELL
82	Hi-Lo LO 01	HITS FROM 3000 YEARS AGO (LP, purple sleeve)	15

(see also Squire)

LEE MEZA
67	Stateside SS 589	If It Happens/One Good Thing Leads To Another	30

MEZZ MEZZROW
62	Storyville SEP 394	KING JAZZ STORY (EP)	10
55	Vogue LAE 12007	PLEYEL CONCERT (LP)	12

(see also Mezzrow–Bechet Quartet)

MEZZROW–BECHET QUINTET
50	King Jazz KJ 2	Bowin' The Blues/Old School (78)	6
50	King Jazz KJ 3	Where Am I/Funky Butt (12" 78)	6
50	King Jazz KJ 5	Chicago Function Parts 1 & 2 (10" or 12" 78)	7/6
50	King Jazz KJ 7	Tommy's Blues/I'm Going Away From Here (12" 78)	6
50	King Jazz KJ 8	I Want Some/I'm Speaking My Mind (12" 78)	6
51	King Jazz KJ 9	Really The Blues Parts 1 & 2 (78)	6
51	King Jazz KJ 11	Kaiser's Last Break/Delta Mood (12" 78)	6
56	Vogue LAE 12017	THE MEZZROW-BECHET QUINTET (LP)	12

(see also Sidney Bechet)

M.F.Q.
(see under Modern Folk Quartet)

M.F.S.B.
81	Phil. Intl. PIR 12-9501	Mysteries Of The World/Manhattan Skyline (12", no p/s)	8
81	Phil. Intl. PIR 84251	MYSTERIES OF THE WORLD (LP)	12

M-G-M STUDIO ORCHESTRA
55	MGM SP 1144	Rock Around The Clock/"Blackboard Jungle" Love Theme	20

MIAMI
74	Jay Boy BOY 81	Party Freaks/(Part 2)	6
75	Jay Boy BOY 86	Hey Y'all We're Miami/Chicken Yellow	6
75	Jay Boy BOY 96	Funk It Up/Freak On Down My Way	6
76	Jay Boy BOY 111	Kill That Roach/Mr Notorious	7

MIAOW
85	Venus VENUS 1	Belle Vue/Fate (p/s)	6
86	Venus VENUST 1	Belle Vue/Fate/Grocer's Devil Daughter (12", p/s)	10
87	Factory FAC 189	Break The Code/Stolen Ears (p/s)	10

MICHA
65	Pye 7N 15982	Protest Singer/Serpent	8

GEORGE MICHAEL
84	Epic A 4603	Careless Whisper/Careless Whisper (Instrumental) (poster p/s)	30
84	Epic QTA 4603	Careless Whisper (Extended Mix)/Careless Whisper (Special Version Wexler)/Careless Whisper (Instrumental) (12", title p/s)	30
84	Epic WA 4603	Careless Whisper (Extended Mix)/Careless Whisper (Instrumental) (12", picture disc, clear or black rim)	each 20
87	Epic CDLUST 1	I Want Your Sex (Monogamy Mix: Rhythm 1 Lust, Rhythm 2 Brass In Love, Rhythm 3 A Last Request) (CD, gatefold gard p/s)	8
87	Epic EMU C3	Faith/Faith (Instrumental)/Hand To Mouth (cassette)	6
87	Epic EMUP 3	Faith/Faith (Instrumental)/Hand To Mouth (12", picture disc)	20
87	Epic EMU 4	Father Figure/Love's In Need Of Love Today (with calendar & stickered p/s)	8
87	Epic EMUT 4	Father Figure/Love's In Need Of Love Today/Father Figure (Instrumental) (12", stickered p/s with poster)	8
88	Epic EMUP 4	Father Figure/Love's In Need Of Love Today (oblong picture disc in wallet)	10
88	Epic CD EMU 4	Father Figure/Love's In Need Of Love Today/Father Figure (Instrumental) (CD)	8
88	Epic CD EMU 3	Faith/Hand To Mouth/Hard Day (Remix) (CD)	8
88	Epic EMU B5	One More Try/Look At Your Hands (p/s, shrinkwrapped with badge)	8
88	Epic EPC 651 5322	One More Try/Look At Your Hands (3" CD, 5" case with adaptor)	8
88	Epic EMU G6	Monkey/Monkey (A Capella) (gatefold p/s, with photo insert)	5
88	Epic CD EMU 6	Monkey (Extended Version)/(A'Capella)/(Extra Bits)/(7" Edit) (CD)	12
88	Epic CD EMU 7	Kissing A Fool/(Instr.)/A Last Request (I Want Your Sex Part 3) (CD, card p/s)	8
89	Epic Solid Gold 654 601-3	I Want Your Man (Parts 1 & 2)/A Different Corner/Careless Whisper (3" CD)	8
96	Virgin VSLH 1571	Jesus To A Child/One More Try (Live Gospel Version) (jukebox issue, no p/s)	5
96	Virgin VSLH 1579	Fastlove/I'm Your Man (jukebox issue, no p/s)	5
96	Virgin VSLH 1595	Spinning The Wheel (Radio Edit)/You Know That I Want To (jukebox issue, no p/s)	5
97	Virgin VSLH 1626	Older (Radio Edit)/I Can't Make You Love Me (jukebox issue, no p/s)	5
97	Virgin VSLH 1641	Star People '97/Everything She Wants (jukebox issue, no p/s)	5
97	Virgin VSLH 1663	You Have Been Loved/The Strangest Thing '97 (Radio Edit) (jukebox issue, no p/s)	5
87	Epic 460000 9	FAITH (CD, extra tracks, picture disc, PVC box, some sealed)	50/40
90	Epic 467295 2	LISTEN WITHOUT PREJUDICE VOLUME 1 (CD, picture disc, stickered case)	40

PROMOS
99	Virgin GM 99	Roxanne (CD, 1 track, card p/s, promo only)	8
99	Virgin GMX 99	Miss Sarajevo (CD, 1 track, card p/s, promo only)	8
99	Epic GMCD 1	LADIES AND GENTLEMEN — THE BEST OF (CD, sampler, card case, promo only)	20

(see also Wham!, Deon Estus, High, Elton John, Queen)

RAS MICHAEL & THE SONS OF NEGUS

75	Vulcan VUL 005	RASTAFARI (LP)	20
75	Grounation GROL 505	RASTAFARI (LP)	25

CODY MICHAELS

79	Grapevine GRP 121	7 Days — 52 Weeks/VIRTUE ORCHESTRA: Don't Look Back (Instrumental)	10

MARILYN MICHAELS

60	RCA RCA 1208	Tell Tommy I Miss Him/Everyone Was There But You...................	12

MICHAEL SCHENKER GROUP

80	Chrysalis CHS 2455	Armed And Ready/Bijou Pleasurette (p/s, clear vinyl)	6
80	Chrysalis CHS 2471	Cry For The Nations/Into The Arena (live) (p/s, clear vinyl)	5
81	Chrysalis CHS 2541	Ready To Rock/Attack Of The Mad Axeman (p/s, clear vinyl)	5
81	Sounds FREEBIE No. 1	Let Sleeping Dogs Lie/PAT BENATAR: Promises In The Dark (Edit)	
		(flexidisc in red printed sleeve, free with *Sounds*)......................	6/5
82	Chrysalis CHS 2636	Dancer/Girl From Uptown (picture disc)..............................	5
82	Chrysalis CHS 2636	Dancer/Girl From Uptown (p/s, clear vinyl)	5
82	Chysalis PCHR 1393	ASSAULT ATTACK (LP, picture disc)	12
83	Chysalis CHRP 1441	BUILT TO DESTROY (LP, picture disc, U.S. remix)	12

(see also McAuley Schenker Group, Michael Schenker, Scorpions, UFO, Cozy Powell, Graham Bonnet, Alex Harvey Band)

MICHELLE

66	Polydor BM 56070	Sally Fool/I Don't Know Your Name	7

MICHIGAN RAG

72	Blue Horizon 2096 009	Don't Run Away/She's Looking Good................................	18

MICHIGANS

63	Vogue V 9207	Intermission Riff/Tea For Two	15

MICKEY (Baker) & KITTY (Noble)

60	London HLE 9054	Buttercup/My Reverie	35

MICKEY (Baker) & SYLVIA

57	HMV POP 331	Love Is Strange/I'm Going Home (78 rpm = £100)......................	300
58	RCA RCA 1064	Rock And Stroll Room/Bewildered (78 rpm = £65)	40
60	RCA RCA 1206	Sweeter As The Day Goes By/Mommy Out De Light	15
65	RCA Victor RCA 1487	Love Is Strange/Dearest..	25
65	RCA Camden CDN 5133	LOVE IS STRANGE (LP)..	180

(see also Sylvia [Robbins])

MICKEY FINN

64	Blue Beat BB 203	Tom Hark/Please Love Me (as 'Mickey Finn & The Blue Men')	18
64	Oriole CB 1927	Pills/Hush Your Mouth (as 'Mickey Finn & The Blue Men')	50
64	Oriole CB 1940	Reelin' & A'Rockin'/I Still Want You (as 'Mickey Finn').................	50
65	Columbia DB 7510	The Sporting Life/Night Comes Down (as 'The Mickey Finn')	65
66	Polydor 56719	I Do Love You/If I Had You Baby (as 'The Mickey Finn').................	40
67	Direction 58-3086	Garden Of My Mind/Time To Start Loving You (as 'The Mickey Finn')	60
95	Noiseburger 3	Ain't Necessarily So/God Bless The Child (foldaround p/s in poly bag,	
		1,000 only, 1st 500 signed)	10/5

BOBBY "BOBCATS" MICKLEBURGH

53	Esquire 10-327	Tin Roof Blues/Jazz Me Blues (78)	8
54	Esquire 10-337	Mahogany Hall Stomp/Basin Street Blues (78).......................	8
55	Esquire EP 40	MICKLEBURGH'S BOBCATS (EP).................................	15
56	Esquire EP 73	MICKLEBURGH'S BOBCATS (EP).................................	15

MICROBE

69	CBS 4158	Groovy Baby/MICROBOP ENSEMBLE: Your Turn Now	7

MICRODISNEY

82	Kabuki KAMD 2	Hello Rascals/The Helicopter Of The Holy Ghost (p/s)..................	6
83	Kabuki KAMD 4	Pink Skinned Man/Fiction Land (p/s)	5
80s	Virgin V2505	39 MINUTES (LP)	18
80s	Rough Trade ROUGH 75	EVERYBODY IS FANTASTIC (LP)	15
80s	Rough Trade ROUGH 85	THE CLOCK COMES DOWN THE STAIRS (LP)	12
88	Rough Trade RTM 155	WE HATE YOU SOUTH AFRICAN BASTARDS (LP)................	20

MICRON

87	White SG045	Eastenders Rap (12")	30

TONY MIDDLETON

65	London HLR 9983	My Little Red Book (as Burt Bacharach Orchestra with Tony Middleton)/	
		BURT BACHARACH ORCHESTRA: What's New Pussycat..............	30
66	Polydor BM 56704	To The Ends Of The Earth/Don't Ever Leave Me (DJ copy = £700)	450
78	Grapevine GRP 115	Paris Blues/Out Of This World......................................	15
80s	Joker JK 0002	Spanish Maiden/JIMMY MACK: My World Is On Fire/METROS: Since I Found	
		My Baby	8

(see also Willows, Burt Bacharach)

MIDNIGHT CRUISER

77	It IT 2	Rich Bitch/Striker (p/s)..	10

MIDNIGHTERS

55	Parlophone DP 399	Work With Me Annie/Sexy Ways (78, export issue).....................	70
55	Parlophone DP 422	Annie Had A Baby/THUNDERBIRDS: Pledging My Love (78, export issue)	70

(see also Hank Ballard)

MIDNIGHT MOVERS

72	Mojo 2092 038	Why Can't We Do It In The Road Parts 1 & 2...........................	8
73	Contempo C 7	Follow The Wind Parts 1 & 2	8

MIDNIGHT RAGS
80	Ace ACE 005	Public Enemy/Alcatraz/Mamma Said (p/s)	8
80	Velvet Moon VM 1	The Cars That Ate New York/Oscar Automobile (p/s, withdrawn)	8

(see also Paul Roland, Weird Strings)

MIDNIGHTS
66	Ember EMB S 220	(Won'tcha) Show Me Around/Only Two Can Play	15
63	MEP 101/MN 1/EAG-EP-134	MIDNIGHTS (EP, private pressing)	130

MIDNIGHT SHIFT
66	Decca F 12487	Saturday Jump/Living Fast	20

MIDNIGHT SUN
72	MCA MKPS 2019	MIDNIGHT SUN (LP)	25
72	MCA MKPS 2024	WALKING CIRCLES (LP)	25
73	MCA MCF 2687	MIDNIGHT SUN (LP, reissue)	15
73	MCA MCF 2691	WALKING CIRCLES (LP, reissue)	15

M.I. FIVE
66	Parlophone R 5486	You'll Never Stop Me Loving You/Only Time Will Tell	70

(see also Maze, Deep Purple)

MIGHT OF COINCIDENCE
72	Entropia BM 0001	WHY COULDN'T PEOPLE WAIT (LP)	100

MIGHTY AVENGERS (U.K.)
64	Decca F 11891	Hide Your Pride/Hey Senorita	20
64	Decca F 11962	So Much In Love/Sometime They Say	22
65	Decca F 12085	Blue Turns To Grey/I'm Lost Without You	22
65	Decca F 12198	(Walkin' Thru The) Sleepy City/Sir Edward And Lady Jane	35

(see also Andrew Oldham)

MIGHTY AVENGERS (Jamaica)
66	Rymska RA 101	Scatter Shot (actually by Byron Lee & Dragonaires)/BYRON LEE: Like You Do (B-side actually "No One" by Techniques)	20

MIGHTY BABY
71	Blue Horizon 2096 003	Devil's Whisper/Virgin Spring	25
69	Head HDLS 6002	MIGHTY BABY (LP, gatefold sleeve)	160
71	Blue Horizon 2931 001	A JUG OF LOVE (LP, with lyric insert)	300/250
84	Psycho PSYCHO 31	EGYPTIAN TOMB (LP, reissue of "Mighty Baby" in different sleeve)	15

(see also Action, Robin Scott, Habibiyya, Keith Christmas, Gary Farr, Stone's Masonry)

THEE MIGHTY CAESARS
86	Empire LWC 604	Ten Bears Of The Comanches/Baby What's Wrong (p/s)	6
86	Media Burn MB 5	Little By Little/The Swag/What You've Got/Cyclonic (12", p/s)	7
88	Swag SWG 001	She's Just Fifteen Years Old/The Swag (flexi with *Pandora's Box* fanzine)	10/7

(see also Milkshakes, Prisoners, Billy Childish, Thee Headcoats)

MIGHTY DIAMONDS
75	Black Wax WAX13	I Need A Roof/Joe Joe Dub	8
79	Virgin Frontline FLS 122 12	Bodyguard/One Brother Short (12")	10
79	Virgin Frontline FLD 6001	DEEPER ROOTS (LP, with bonus dub LP)	12
80	Mobiliser SRE 31	LEADER OF THE BLACK COUNTRY (LP)	20

MIGHTY DOUGLAS
60s	Jump Up JU 501	Laziest Man/Dance Me Lover	8
60s	Jump Up JU 508	Teacher Teacher/Split Me In Two	8
60s	Jump Up JU 509	Ugliness/My Wicked Boy Child	8

MIGHTY ETHNICZ
90	Laylow LAY101	Harmony Hall/Murder/From Da Mind (12")	10
93	Lowdown LOWT01	Can I Get A Deal?/Bedrock (12")	16

MIGHTY FLEA & MICKEY BAKER
72	Polydor 2058 328	Bloodshot Eyes/Charley Stone	6
73	Polydor 2460 185	LET THE GOOD TIMES ROLL (LP)	22

MIGHTY FLYERS
74	Myrrh MYR 1016	LOW FLYING ANGELS (LP, with insert)	20

(see also Mick Abrahams)

MIGHTY MAYTONES
76	Burning Sounds BS 1002	MADNESS (LP)	15
78	Burning Sounds BS 1022	BOAT TO ZION (LP)	15

(see also Maytones)

MIGHTY MEN
62	Salvo SLO 1804	No Way Out/You Too Much (99 copies only)	35

MIGHTY MO
72	Columbia DB 8851	Ape Call/Heavy Bear	10

MIGHTY POWER
67	Jump Up JU 513	You're Wasting Your Time/Smart Barbarian	8

MIGHTY SAM
66	Stateside SS 534	Sweet Dreams/Good Humor Man	20
66	Stateside SS 544	Fannie Mae/Badmouthin'	20
68	Stateside SS 2076	When She Touches Me/Just Like Old Times	20
70	Soul City SC 115	Papa True Love/I Need A Lot Of Lovin'	25
70	Soul City SCM 004	MIGHTY SOUL (LP)	85

MIGHTY SPARROW

MIGHTY SPARROW

59	Melodisc 1491	Goaty/LORD MELODY: I Confess (78)	12
60	Kalypso XX 22	Mr. Herbert/Simpson	6
68	NEMS 56-3558	Mr. Walker/Carnival In '68	6
60s	Jump Up JU 523	Village Ram/Pull Pistle Gang	6
69	Fab FAB 116	Mr. Walker/Jane	6
70	Fab FAB 147	I Don't Wanna Lose You/The Truth	6
60	Kalypso XXEP 1	THIS IS SPARROW (EP)	10
60	Kalypso XXEP 2	MAN, DIG THIS SPARROW (EP)	10
60	Kalypso XXEP 3	A PARTY WITH SPARROW (EP)	10
61	Kalypso XXEP 4	THIS IS THE SPARROW AGAIN (EP)	10
61	Kalypso XXEP 5	GREETINGS FROM SPARROW (EP)	10
62	Kalypso XXEP 6	SPARROW THE CONQUEROR (EP)	10
63	Island ILP 902	THE SLAVE (LP)	30
66	RCA RD 7516	SPARROW COME BACK (LP)	15
68	Melodisc MLPWI 12-146	CALYPSO CARNIVAL (LP)	25
68	Melodisc MLPWI 12-148	MR WALKER (LP)	30
72	Trojan TRL 49	HOTTER THAN EVER (LP)	12

(see also Sparrow, King Sparrow, Lord Melody)

MIGHTY SPARROW/BYRON LEE & DRAGONAIRES

69	Trojan TRL 8	THE SPARROW MEETS THE DRAGON (LP, gatefold sleeve)	12

(see also Byron Lee & Dragonaires)

MIGHTY TERROR & HIS CALYPSONIANS

50	Melodisc 1033	The Queen Is In/Chinese Children (78)	10
59	Pye N 15177	Women Police In England/Patricia Gone With Millicent (78)	10
59	Pye N 15178	Brown Skin Gal/Kitch Cavalcade (78)	10

MIGHTY VIKINGS

67	Island WI 3060	Do Re Mi/The Sound Of Music	15
67	Island WI 3074	Rockitty Fockitty/Give Me Back My Gal (both actually with Sammy Ismay)	15

MIGIL FIVE

64	Pye 7N 15597	Mockingbird Hill/Long Ago And Far Away	6
64	Pye 7N 15645	Near You/Don't Wanna Go On Shaking	6
64	Pye 7N 15677	Boys And Girls/I Saw Your Picture	7
65	Pye 7N 15757	Just Behind The Rainbow/Seven Lonely Days	7
65	Pye 7N 15874	One Hundred Years/I'm In Love Again	7
66	Pye 7N 17023	Pencil And Paper/Nevertheless (I'm In Love With You)	7
67	Columbia DB 8196	Together/Superstition	22
68	Jay Boy BOY 4	If I Had My Way/Somebody's Stolen The Moon	6
64	Pye NEP 24191	MEET THE MIGIL FIVE (EP)	22
64	Pye NPL 18093	MOCKING BIRD HILL (LP)	45

(see also Migil Four)

MIGIL FOUR

63	Pye 7N 15572	Maybe/Can't I?	10

(see also Migil Five)

MIKE & MECHANICS

85	WEA U 8908P	Silent Running/I Get The Feeling (engine-shaped picture disc)	8
85	WEA U 8765TP	All I Need Is A Miracle/You Are The One/A Call To Arms (12", picture disc)	10
88	WEA U 7789CD	Nobody's Perfect/Nobody's Perfect (Extended)/Nobody Knows (3" CD)	8
89	WEA U 7717CD	The Living Years/Too Many Friends/I Get The Feeling (live) (3" CD)	8
89	WEA U 7602CD	Nobody Knows (Remix)/Why Me/Nobody Knows (Album Version) (3" CD, 5" jewel case or 3" card sleeve)	8
91	Virgin VSCDX 1351	A Time And Place/Yesterday Tomorrow/Word Of Mouth (East West Mix) (CD, in photo wallet with 5 prints)	8
91	Virgin VS 1359	Get Up/I Think I Got The Message (p/s, withdrawn)	6
91	Virgin VSCDG 1359	Get Up/I Think I Got The Message/Before The Next Heartache Falls (CD, withdrawn)	10
92	Virgin VSCDX 1396	Everybody Gets A Second Chance/The Way You Look At Me/At The End Of The Day (CD, with sheet music & lyrics)	8
95	Virgin VSCDX 1535	Beggar On A Beach Of Gold/Boys At The Front/Little Boy/A Beggar On A Beach Of Gold (acoustic) (CD, p/s)	10

(see also Mike Rutherford, Genesis, Paul Carrack)

MIKE & MODIFIERS

62	Oriole CB 1775	I Found Myself A Brand New Baby/It's Too Bad	1000

MIKE STUART SPAN

66	Columbia DB 8066	Come On Over To Our Place/Still Nights	38
67	Columbia DB 8206	Dear/Invitation	45
68	Jewel JL 01	Children Of Tomorrow/Concerto Of Thoughts	400+
68	Fontana TF 959	You Can Understand Me/Baubles And Bangles	25
93	117 CPAT 1171	EXSPANSIONS: Second Production/Rescue Me/Remember The Times/World In My Head (EP)	15
95	Tenth Planet TP 014	TIMESPAN (LP, gatefold sleeve, numbered, 1,000 copies only)	25

(see also Leviathan, High Defenders, Tony's Defenders, High Broom)

MIKI & GRIFF

59	Pye-Nixa 7N 15213	Hold Back Tomorrow/Deedle Dum Doo Die Day (78 rpm = £8)	5
60	Pye 7N 15266	Long Time To Forget/Someday You'll Call My Name	5
64	Pye 7N 15614	Here Today Gone Tomorrow/Changing Partners (p/s)	5

BOBBY MILANO

55	Capitol CL 14252	A King Or A Slave/If You Cared	10
55	Capitol CL 14309	If Tears Could Bring You Back/Make Me A Present Of You	10

MILBURN
03	Private Pressing	Along Comes Mary (no p/s)	35
05	Free Construction FCONS1	Lipstick Lickin'/Send In The Boys (die-cut p/s)	10

AMOS MILBURN
57	Vogue V 9064	Every Day Of The Week/Girl Of My Dreams (triangular or round centre)	150/75
57	Vogue V 9064	Every Day Of The Week/Girl Of My Dreams (78)	40
57	Vogue V 9069	Rum And Coca Cola/Soft Pillow (triangular centre) (78 rpm = £85)	250
57	Vogue V 9080	Thinking Of You Baby/If I Could Be With You (One Hour Tonight) (triangular centre) (78 rpm = £90)	225
60	Vogue V 9163	One Scotch, One Bourbon, One Beer/Bad, Bad Whiskey	150
57	Vogue VE 1-70102	ROCK AND ROLL (EP)	275
78	United Artists UAS 30203	CHICKEN SHACK BOOGIE (LP)	12

AMOS MILBURN JNR
63	London HLU 9795	Gloria/Look At Me Fool	20

PERCY MILEM
66	Stateside SS 566	Crying Baby, Baby, Baby/Call On Me (DJ copy = £150)	100

BARRY MILES
60	Egmont AJS 14	MILES OF GENIUS (LP)	15

BUDDY MILES (EXPRESS)
68	Mercury MF 1065	Train (Parts 1 & 2)	10
69	Mercury MF 1098	Miss Lady/'69 Freedom Special	5
71	Mercury 6052 036	Them Changes/Your Feeling Is Mine (solo)	6
69	Mercury 20137 SMCL	EXPRESSWAY TO YOUR SKULL (LP)	12
69	Mercury 20163 SMCL	ELECTRIC CHURCH (LP)	12
70	Mercury 6338 016	THEM CHANGES (LP)	12
71	Mercury 6338 028	WE GOT TO LIVE TOGETHER (LP)	12
71	Mercury 6338 048	A MESSAGE TO THE PEOPLE (LP)	12
72	Mercury 6641 033	LIVE (2-LP)	15
73	CBS 65406	CHAPTER VII (LP)	12
74	CBS 80349	ALL THE FACES (LP)	12

(see also Electric Flag, Jimi Hendrix, Carlos Santana & Buddy Miles)

DICK & SUE MILES
	Sweet Folk & Country SFA 106	THE DUNMOW FLITCH (LP)	15

GARRY MILES
60	London HLG 9155	Look For A Star/Afraid Of Love	15
60	London REG 1264	LOOK FOR A STAR (EP)	50

JOHN MILES
70	Orange OAS 508	Why Don't You Love Me?/If I Could See Through	5
71	Decca F 13196	Jose/You Make It So Hard	5
72	Orange OAS 207	Come Away Melinda/Walking With My Head Held High	5
72	Orange OAS 208	Yesterday (Was Just The Beginning)/Road To Freedom	10
73	Orange OAS 209	Hard Road/You're Telling Me Lies	5
73	Orange OAS 211	Jacqueline/Keep On Tryin'	5
73	Orange OAS 213	One Minute Every Hour/Hollywood Queen	10
74	Orange OAS 220	Fright Of My Life/Good Time Woman	5
74	Orange OAS 223	What's On Your Mind/Rock'n'Roll Band	5
74	Orange OAS 224	What's On Your Mind/To Be Grateful	5

(see also Influence)

LENNY MILES
61	Top Rank JAR 546	Don't Believe Him Donna/Invisible	18

LIZZIE MILES
56	HMV 7EG 8178	THE BLUES THEY SANG (EP, 1 side by Billy Young, both with Jelly Roll Morton)	25
59	Columbia Clef SEB 10088	SCINTILLATING LIZZIE (EP, with Bob Scobey's Band)	10
50s	Melodisc EPM7 55	NEW ORLEANS BOYS (EP, with New Orleans Boys)	20
57	Capitol T 792	A NIGHT IN NEW ORLEANS (LP)	25

SARAH MILES
65	Fontana TF 552	Where Am I/Here Of All Places	7

MILESTONES & BUTCH BAKER
75	Black Magic BM 111	The Joker Parts 1 & 2	8

MILKSHAKES
82	Bilko BILK-O	Please Don't Tell My Baby/It's You (p/s)	8
83	Upright UP 6	Soldiers Of Love/Shimmy Shimmy (p/s)	6
84	Big Beat NS 94	Brand New Cadillac/Commanche/Jezebel/Jaguar And Thunderbird (p/s)	5
84	Big Beat SW 105	The Ambassadors Of Love/No More/Gringles And Groyles Again/Remarkable (p/s)	5
86	Empire UXF 228	Let Me Love You/She Tells Me She Loves Me (p/s)	5
83	Big Beat NED 4	14 RHYTHM AND BEAT GREATS (LP)	18
83	Upright UPLP 1	AFTER SCHOOL SESSIONS (LP)	18
84	Milkshake HARP-O	NOTHING CAN STOP THESE MEN (LP)	18
85	Big Beat WIK 30	THEY CAME, THEY SAW, THEY CONQUERED (LP)	15
86	Milkshake MILK-O	TALKING 'BOUT MILKSHAKES (LP)	15

(see also Thee Mighty Caesars, Prisoners/Milkshakes, Pop Rivits, Len Bright Combo, Billy Childish, Thee Headcoats)

MILLER
65	Oak RGJ 190	Baby I've Got News For You/The Girl With The Castle	275+
65	Columbia DB 7735	Baby I Got News For You/The Girl With The Castle	300+

(see also Big Boy Pete, Peter Jay & Jaywalkers, Pete Miller, News)

ANN MILLER
54	MGM SP 1076	Too Darn Hot/KATHRYN GRAYSON & HOWARD KEEL: So In Love	10

ANN MILLER & KATHRYN GRAYSON
54	MGM SP 1078	Always True To You In My Fashion/I Hate Men	10

(see also Kathryn Grayson & Howard Keel)

BETTY MILLER
59	Top Rank JAR 115	Pearly Gates/Old Time Religion (78 rpm = £6)	8
59	Top Rank JAR 127	Jack O' Diamonds/(It Took) One Kiss (78 rpm = £7)	10

BOB MILLER & MILLERMEN
57	Columbia DB 4017	The Scamp/The Sack Line (as Bob Miller Music)	7
58	Columbia DB 4140	Square Bash/Muchacha (as Bob Miller Music)	7
59	Fontana H 181	Dig This!/The Poacher (78 rpm = £6)	8
59	Fontana H 192	Little Dipper/The Keel Row (78 rpm = £8)	8
59	Fontana H 228	In The Mood/Joey's Song (78 rpm = £10)	8
60	Fontana H 236	The Busker's Tune/My Guy's Come Back	6
60	Fontana H 245	77 Sunset Strip/Manhunt	6
65	Mercury MF 947	Uptown And Downtown/Carnaby Street Parade	8
65	Polydor 56005	6-5 Special/Dick Van Dyke Theme	10
66	Columbia DB 7877	Get Smart/Bony's Blues (as Bob Miller & His Millermen)	8

BOBBIE MILLER
65	Decca F 12064	What A Guy/You Went Away	40
65	Decca F 12252	Every Beat Of My Heart/Tomorrow	15
66	Decca F 12354	Everywhere I Go/IAN STEWART & RAILROADERS: Stu-Ball	80

(see also Mongrels, Rolling Stones)

CHUCK MILLER
56	Capitol CL 14543	Rogue River Valley/No Baby Like You	15
57	Mercury 7MT 153	The Auctioneer/Me Head's In De Barrel (78 rpm, Mercury MT 153 = £12)	25
57	Mercury MT 157	Bye, Bye Love/Rang Tang Ding Dong (78)	10
57	Mercury MT 181	Plaything/After Yesterday (78)	10
58	Mercury 7MT 215	Down The Road A-Piece/Mad About Her Blues (78 rpm, MT 215 = £12)	90
59	Mercury AMT 1026	The Auctioneer/Baby Doll (78 rpm = £18)	12
60	Mercury ZEP 10058	GOING GOING GONE (EP)	60

COUNT PRINCE (MILLER)
70	Downtown DT 460	I'm Gonna Keep On Trying/Girl I Need You (as Count Prince)	5
70	MCA MK 5042	Mule Train/Lucille (p/s)	5

(see also Jimmy James & The Vagabonds)

FRANKIE MILLER
59	Melodisc MEL 1519	True Blue/Black Land Farmer (78 rpm = £30)	18
59	Melodisc MEL 1529	Poppin' Johnnie/Family Man (78 rpm = £30)	18
60	Melodisc MEL 1552	Rain, Rain/Baby Rocked Her Dolly	18
62	Top Rank JKP 3013	COUNTRY MUSIC (EP)	35
64	Ember CW 107	THE TRUE COUNTRY STYLE OF FRANKIE MILLER (LP)	28

GARY MILLER
58	Pye 7N 15120	The Story Of My Life/Put A Light In The Window	5
58	Pye 7N 15136	Lollipop/Dancing With My Shadow	5
58	Pye 7N 15140	On The Street Where You Live/That's For Me (with Kenny Ball & His Jazz Band)	5
58	Pye 7N 15151	A Couple Of Crazy Kids (with Marion Ryan)/Ivanhoe Of England	5
58	Pye 7N 15164	The First Christmas Day/Nearest And Dearest	5
59	Pye 7N 15188	Jezebel/The Railroad Song	5
59	Pye 7N 15207	Sing Along/Someone To Come Home To	5
59	Pye 7N 15239	Marina/Hold Me, Thrill Me, Kiss Me	5
61	Pye 7N 15404	There Goes That Song Again/The Night Is Young	5
64	Pye 7N 15698	Aqua Marina/Stingray	18
56	Pye NEP 24013	YELLOW ROSE OF TEXAS (EP, 2 different sleeves)	each 20
57	Pye NEP 24047	HIT PARADE VOL. 1 (EP)	20
57	Pye NEP 24057	MEET MISTER MILLER PT. 1 — ON STAGE (EP)	18
57	Pye NEP 24058	MEET MISTER MILLER PT. 2 — FOR THE YOUNG IN LOVE (EP)	18
57	Pye NEP 24059	MEET MISTER MILLER PT. 3 — FOR THE YOUNG IN LOVE (EP)	18
57	Nixa NPL 18008	MEET MISTER MILLER (LP)	30
61	Pye NPL 18059	GARY ON THE BALL (LP)	20

(see also Kenny Ball)

GLEN MILLER
67	Doctor Bird DB 1089	Where Is The Love/Funky Broadway	350
68	Doctor Bird DB 1128	Rocksteady Party/Book Of Memories	25

GLENN MILLER & HIS ORCHESTRA
54	Columbia SCM 5086	I Got Rhythm/Sleepy Time Gal	10
54	HMV 7M 195	Little Brown Jug/Don't Sit Under The Apple Tree	15
53	HMV DLP 1012	GLENN MILLER CONCERT VOL. 1 (10" LP)	12
53	HMV DLP 1013	GLENN MILLER CONCERT VOL. 2 (10" LP)	12
53	HMV DLP 1021	GLENN MILLER CONCERT VOL. 3 (10" LP)	12
54	HMV DLP 1024	THE GLENN MILLER STORY (10" LP)	12
54	HMV DLP 1049	TIME FOR MELODY (10" LP)	12
54	HMV DLP 1059	ORCHESTRA WIVES (10" LP)	12
54	HMV RLS 599	GLENN MILLER LIMITED EDITION (5-LP, presentation set, 'snakeskin' cover)	15
55	HMV DLP 1062	SUNRISE SERENADE (10" LP)	15
55	HMV DLP 1081	GLENN MILLER CONCERT VOL. 4 (10" LP)	15
55	HMV DLP 1104	SUN VALLEY SERENADE (10" LP)	15
55	Philips BBR 8072	GLENN MILLER (10" LP)	15
56	HMV CLPC 6-10/RLS 598	GLENN MILLER LIMITED EDITION VOL. 2 (5-LP, in presentation album)	25
56	HMV RLS 637	GLENN MILLER & THE ARMY AIRFORCE BAND (5-LP, presentation box, [CLP 1077-CLP 1081])	25
56	HMV DLP 1122	MILLER MAGIC (10" LP)	12

56	Philips BBR 8092	GLENN MILLER (10" LP)	12
57	HMV DLP 1145	POLKA DOTS AND MOONBEAMS (10" LP)	12
59	Top Rank 35/023	GLENN MILLER AND HIS ORCHESTRA VOL. 2 (LP)	12
60	RCA RD 27146/RD 27147	FOR THE VERY FIRST TIME (2-LP)	12

JAMES MILLER
| 70 | Trojan TR 7804 | You Got To Me/2001 | 5 |

JIMMY MILLER & (NEW) BARBECUES
57	Columbia DB 4006	Sizzlin' Hot/Free Wheelin' Baby (as Jimmy Miller & Barbecues) (78 rpm = £18)	80
58	Columbia DB 4081	Jelly Baby/Cry, Baby, Cry (as Jimmy Miller & New Barbecues) (78 rpm = £32)	70
	(see also Station Skiffle Group)		

JODY MILLER
64	Capitol CL 15335	He Walks Like A Man/Looking At The World Through A Tear	7
64	Capitol CL 15356	The Fever/In My Room	15
65	Capitol CL 15393	Queen Of The House/The Greatest Actor	7
65	Capitol CL 15404	Silver Threads And Golden Needles/Melody For Robin	6
65	Capitol CL 15415	Home Of The Brave/This Is The Life	10
66	Capitol CL 15482	If You Were A Carpenter/Let Me Walk With You	6
65	Capitol (S) T 2416	HOME OF THE BRAVE (LP)	20/25
66	Capitol (S) T 2446	JODY MILLER SINGS THE GREAT HITS OF BUCK OWENS (LP)	20/25

KENNY MILLER
| 65 | Stateside SS 405 | Restless/Take My Tip | 40 |

MANDY MILLER
| 56 | Parlophone R 4219 | Nellie The Elephant/It's Time To Dream | 8 |
| 58 | Parlophone GEP 8776 | CHILDREN'S CHOICE (EP) | 8 |

MAX MILLER
58	Pye 7N 15141	With A Little Bit Of Luck/Be Sincere	5
59	HMV 7EG 8558	THE CHEEKY CHAPPIE (EP)	8
61	Pye NEP 25154	MAX AT THE MET (EP)	8
62	Pye NEP 25162	MAX AT THE MET VOL. 2 (EP)	8
58	Pye NPT 19026	MAX AT THE MET (10" LP)	20
	(see also Lonnie Donegan)		

MITCH MILLER ORCHESTRA
53	Columbia SCM 5058	Just Dreaming/Without My Lover	5
62	CBS AAG 118	The Longest Day/The Longest Day (Version) (p/s)	5
	(see also Guy Mitchell)		

MRS MILLER
66	Capitol CL 15444	Downtown/A Lover's Concerto	7
66	Capitol T 2494	MRS. MILLER'S GREATEST HITS (LP)	20
66	Capitol T 2579	WILL SUCCESS SPOIL MRS. MILLER (LP)	20

MRS MILLER
| 69 | Jackpot JP 707 | Feel It/LYN BECKFORD: Kiss Me Quick (actually by Keeling Beckford) | 7 |
| | *(see also Lloyd Terrell)* | | |

NED MILLER
63	Capitol CL 15301	Go On Back You Fool/Dark Moon	12
63	London HL 9658	From A Jack To A King/Parade Of Broken Hearts	5
63	London HL 9728	Just Before Dawn/Mona Lisa	6
63	London HL 9766	Another Fool Like Me/Magic Moon	6
64	London HL 9838	Big Love/Sunday Morning Tears	5
64	London HL 9873	Invisible Tears/Old Restless Ocean	5
64	London HL 9937	Do What You Do Do Well/Dusty Guitar	8
63	Capitol EAP1 20492	NED MILLER (EP)	25
63	London RE 1382	NED MILLER (EP)	30
63	London HA 8072	FROM A JACK TO A KING (LP)	30
66	Capitol T 2414	THE BEST OF NED MILLER (LP)	30
69	Capitol ST 2914	IIN THE NAME OF LOVE (LP)	25

PETE MILLER
| 97 | Tenth Planet TP 030 | SUMMERLAND (LP, numbered, 1000 only) | 15 |
| | *(see also Miller, Big Boy Pete)* | | |

ROGER MILLER
64	Philips BF 1354	Dang Me/Got 2 Again	6
64	Philips BF 1365	Chug-A-Lug/Reincarnation	5
65	Philips BF 1390	Do-Wacka-Do/Love Is Not For Me	5
65	Philips BF 1397	King Of The Road/Atta Boy Girl	5
65	Philips BF 1416	Engine Engine No. 9/The Last Word In Lonesome Is Me	6
65	Philips BF 1437	Kansas City Star/One Dyin' And Buryin'	5
65	Philips BF 1456	England Swings/The Good Old Days	5
66	Philips BF 1475	Husbands And Wives/I've Been A Long Time Leavin'	5
66	Philips BF 1498	You Can't Roller Skate In A Buffalo Herd/Train Of Life	5
66	Philips BF 1516	My Uncle Used To Love Me But She Died/You're My Kingdom	5
67	Philips BF 1560	Walkin' In The Sunshine/Home	5
68	Mercury MF 1021	Little Green Apples/Our Little Love	5
69	Mercury MF 1108	England Swings/King Of The Road (p/s)	5
65	Philips BE 12578	ROGER MILLER (EP)	12
65	Camden CDN 5121	SONGS I HAVE WRITTEN (LP)	15
65	Philips BL 7667	ROGER AND OUT! (LP)	15
66	Philips BL 7669	THE RETURN OF ROGER MILLER (LP)	15
66	Philips BL 7676	THE 3RD TIME AROUND (LP)	15
66	Philips BL 7748	WORDS AND MUSIC (LP)	15
67	Philips (S)BL 7822	WALKING IN THE SUNSHINE (LP)	15
67	Philips (S)BL 7833	SINGS THE MUSIC & TELLS THE TALE OF WATERHOLE 3 (LP)	15

RUSS MILLER
57	HMV POP 391	I Sit In My Window/Wait For Me, My Love (78 rpm = £15)	55

STEPHEN MILLER & LOL COXHILL
73	Caroline C 1503	COXHILL MILLER (LP)	30
74	Caroline C 1507	THE STORY SO FAR ... OH REALLY? (LP)	30

(see also Lol Coxhill)

STEVE MILLER BAND
68	Capitol CL 15539	Sittin' In Circles/Roll With It	15
68	Capitol CL 15564	Living In The U.S.A./Quicksilver Girl	15
69	Capitol CL 15604	My Dark Hour/Song For Our Ancestors	15
69	Capitol CL 15618	Little Girl/Don't Let Nobody Turn You Around	7
70	Capitol CL 15656	Going To The Country/Never Kill Another Man	6
72	Capitol CL 15712	My Dark Hour/The Gangster Is Back/Song For Our Ancestors (33rpm)	5
73	Capitol CL 15765	The Joker/Something To Believe In	5
74	Capitol CL 15786	Living In The U.S.A./Kow Kow Calqulator	5
68	Capitol (S)T 2920	CHILDREN OF THE FUTURE (LP, 'rainbow rim' label)	30
69	Capitol (S)T 2984	SAILOR (LP, 'rainbow rim' label)	25
70	Capitol E-(S)T 184	BRAVE NEW WORLD (LP)	15
70	Capitol E-ST 331	YOUR SAVING GRACE (LP)	12
70	Capitol EA-ST 436	NUMBER 5 (LP)	10
82	Mercury HS 9919 916	GREATEST HITS 1974-1978 (LP, half-speed audiophile pressing)	12

(see also Boz Scaggs)

SUZI MILLER
54	Decca F 10389	Happy Days And Lonely Nights/Tell Me, Tell Me (with Johnston Brothers)	25
54	Decca F 10423	Two Step, Side Step (with Johnston Brothers)/	
		Hang My Heart On A Christmas Tree (with Keynotes)	15
55	Decca F 10475	Tweedlee-Dee (with Johnston Brothers)/That's All I Want From You	20
55	Decca F 10512	Dance With Me Henry (Wallflower) (with Johnston Brothers)/	
		Butterfingers (with Marilyn Sisters)	15
55	Decca F 10593	The Banjo's Back In Town/Go On By	10
56	Decca F 10677	Ay-Ay-Senores/Reckless	10
56	Decca F 10722	Get Up! Get Up! (You Sleepy Head)/The Key To My Heart	10
57	Decca F 10848	I Love My Baby/The Money Tree	7

(see also Johnston Brothers)

MILLIE (SMALL)
63	Fontana TF 425	Don't You Know/Until You're Mine	10
64	Fontana TF 449	My Boy Lollipop/Something's Gotta Be Done	5
64	Fontana TF 479	Sweet William/Oh Henry	5
64	Fontana TF 502	I Love The Way You Love/Bring It On Home To Me	8
64	Cadbury's BNVT 01F	The Bournvita Song/Three Nights A Week (p/s)	20
65	Fontana TF 515	I've Fallen In Love With A Snowman/What Am I Living For	7
65	Fontana TF 529	See You Later Alligator/Chilly Kisses	7
65	Fontana TF 591	My Street/It's Too Late	7
65	Fontana TF 617	Bloodshot Eyes/Tongue Tied	10
65	Brit WI 1002	My Street/A Mixed Up, Fickle, Moody, Self-Centred, Spoiled Kind Of Boy	15
66	Fontana TF 740	Killer Joe/Carry Go Bring Come (as Millie Small)	8
67	Fontana TF 796	Chicken Feed/Wings Of A Dove (as Millie Small)	8
67	Island WIP 6021	You Better Forget/I Am In Love	6
68	Fontana TF 948	When I Dance With You/Hey Mr. Love	6
69	Decca F 12948	Readin' Writin' Arithmetic/I Want You Never To Stop	12
70	Pyramid PYR 6080	My Love And I/Tell Me About Yourself	6
70	Trojan TR 7744	Enoch Power/Mayfair	7
70	President PT 306	We're All In A Zoo/Piccaninny Man	5
70	Trojan TR 7801	Honey Hush/Sunday Morning	5
61	Blue Beat BBEP 302	MILLIE (EP, with Little Roy & Owen Gray, most without sleeve)	120/30
64	Fontana TE 17425	MY BOY LOLLIPOP (EP)	45
66	Island IEP 705	MILLIE AND HER BOYFRIENDS (EP)	55
64	Fontana (S)TL 5220	MORE MILLIE (LP, mono/stereo)	45/50
65	Fontana TL 5276	MILLIE SINGS FATS DOMINO (LP)	80
67	Island ILP 953	THE BEST OF MILLIE SMALL (LP)	60
69	Trojan TTL 17	MILLIE AND HER BOYFRIENDS (LP)	12
69	Trojan TTL 49	THE BEST OF MILLIE SMALL (LP, reissue)	15
70	Trojan TBL 108	TIME WILL TELL (LP)	12

(see also Jackie & Millie, Roy & Millie, Owen & Millie)

SPIKE MILLIGAN
58	Parlophone R 4406	Wish I Knew/Will I Find My Love Today? (78 rpm = £15)	10
61	Parlophone R 4839	I'm Walking Out With A Mountain/The Sewers Of The Strand	10
62	Parlophone R 4891	Wormwood Scrubs Tango/Postman's Knock	10
64	Pye 7N 15720	The Olympic Team/Epilogue (with John Bluthal)	8
66	Parlophone R 5513	Purple Aeroplane/Nothing At All	10
66	Parlophone R 5543	Tower Bridge/Silent Night	10
69	Parlophone R 5771	The Q.5 Piano Tune/Ning, Nang, Nong	10
73	Warner Bros. K 16240	Girl On A Pony/Old Man's Protest Song	7
61	Parlophone PMC 1148	MILLIGAN PRESERVED (LP, also in stereo [PCS 18])	20/25
65	Decca LK 4701	MUSES WITH MILLIGAN (LP)	18
68	Pye NPL 18271	THE WORLD OF THE BEACHCOMBER (LP)	18
75	Polydor 2460 235	BADJELLY THE WITCH AND OTHER GOODIES (LP)	12

(see also Goons, Famous Eccles, Peter Sellers)

LUCKY MILLINDER & HIS ORCHESTRA
51	Vogue V 9007	I'm Waiting Just For You/Bongo Boogie (78)	10
51	Vogue V 9021	No One Else Could Be/The Grape Vine (78)	10
52	Vogue V 2138	Ram-Bunk-Shush/Let It Roll Again (78)	10

(see also Wynonie "Mr Blues" Harris)

JEB MILLION
86	WEA YZ 82	Speed Up My Heartbeat/Who Sent You (p/s)	6
86	WEA YZ 82T	Speed Up My Heartbeat (Extended Mix)/Speed Up My Heartbeat/	
		Who Sent You (12", p/s)	12

MILLIONAIRES (Ireland)
66	Decca F 12468	Wishing Well/Chatterbox	75

MILLIONAIRES (U.S.)
67	Mercury 6052301	Never For Me/If I Had You Babe (paper or plastic labels)	25/10

MILLIONS
73	Duke DU 154	Murmuring/TOMMY McCOOK & BOBBY ELLIS: Murmuring (Version)	6
73	Downtown DT 516	Love Of Jah Jah Children/Jah Jah (Version)	7

MILLIONS OF DEAD CHILDREN
85	Radical MDC 3	CHICKENSQUAWK EP (poster p/s)	6
(see also M.D.C.)			

BARBARA MILLS
65	Hickory 45-1323	Queen Of Fools/Make It Last, Take Your Time (DJ copy = £450)	400
65	Hickory 45-1392	Try/Let's Make A Memory	30
75	London HLE 10491	Queen Of Fools/Make It Last, Take Your Time (reissue)	10

GARRY MILLS
59	Top Rank JAR 119	Hey Baby (You're Pretty)/You Alone (78 rpm = £18)	15
59	Top Rank JAR 219	Seven Little Girls Sitting In The Back Seat/The Night You Became 17	10
59	Top Rank JAR 219	Seven Little Girls Sitting In The Back Seat/The Night You Became 17 (78)	17
59	Oriole CB 1529	Living Lord/Big Story Breaking (78 rpm = £8)	7
59	Oriole CB 1530	I Am The Great I Am/Rhythm In Religion (78 rpm = £8)	6
60	Top Rank JAR 301	Running Bear/Teen Angel	10
60	Top Rank JAR 336	Look For A Star/Footsteps	10
60	Top Rank JAR 393	Comin' Down With Love/I'm Gonna Find Out	10
60	Top Rank JAR 500	Top Teen Baby/Don't Cheat Me Again (some in p/s)	18/10
61	Top Rank JAR 542	Who's Gonna Take You Home Tonight?/Christina	10
61	Decca F 11358	I'll Step Down/Your Way Is My Way	12
61	Decca F 11383	Bless You/Footprints In The Sand	10
61	Decca F 11415	Treasure Island/Sad Little Girl	10
62	Decca F 11471	Never Believed In Love/Save A Dream For Me	10
61	Top Rank JKP 3001	LOOK FOR A STAR (EP)	60
(see also Gary & Ariels)			

GORDON MILLS
65	Ace Of Clubs ACL 1191	DO IT YOURSELF (LP)	12
(see also Viscounts)			

HAYLEY MILLS
61	Decca F 21396	Let's Get Together/Cobbler Cobbler	5
62	Decca F 21442	Jeepers Creepers/Johnny Jingo	5
62	Decca LK 4426	LET'S GET TOGETHER (LP)	15

HAYLEY MILLS & EDDIE HODGES
63	HMV POP 1179	Flitterin'/Beautiful Beulah	6
(see also Eddie Hodges)			

JEFF MILLS
61	Ember EMB S 133	Daddy's Home/TIMMY REYNOLDS: Lullaby Of Love	12

MAUDE MILLS
60s	Vintage Jazz VEP 34	MAUDE MILLS (EP)	12

RUDY MILLS
67	Island WI 3092	A Long Story/BOBBY ELLIS: Now We Know	
		(actually with Desmond Miles Seven)	30
68	Island WI 3136	I'm Trapped/BOBBY ELLIS & CRYSTALLITES: Dollar A Head	22
69	Big Shot BI 509	John Jones/A Place Called Happiness	15
69	Explosion EX 2007	Lemi Li/Goody Goody	10
69	Crab CRAB 20	Tears On My Pillow/I'm Trapped	10
69	Crab CRAB 24	A Heavy Load/Wholesale Love	12
69	Pama SECO 12	REGGAE HITS (LP)	75

STEPHANIE MILLS
74	Paramount PARA 3050	I Knew It Was Love/The Passion And The Pain	6
76	Tamla Motown TMG 1020	This Empty Place/I See You For The First Time (unissued, demo only)	70
76	T. Motown STML 12017	FOR THE FIRST TIME (LP)	20

MILLS BROTHERS
54	Brunswick 05325	How Blue?/Why Do I Keep Lovin' You?	10
55	Brunswick 05390	Paper Valentine/The Urge	8
55	Brunswick 05439	Smack Dab In The Middle/Opus One	12
55	Brunswick 05452	You're Nobody Till Somebody Loves You/Yes You Are	8
55	Brunswick 05487	Mi Muchacha (Little Girl)/Gum Drop	18
55	Brunswick 05488	Suddenly There's A Valley/That's All I Ask Of You	8
56	Brunswick 05522	I've Changed My Mind A Thousand Times/All The Way 'Round The World	8
56	Brunswick 05550	Dream Of You/In A Mellow Tone	6
56	Brunswick 05600	Ninety-Eight Cents/King Porter Stomp	5
56	Brunswick 05606	That's Right/Don't Get Caught (Short On Love)	7
57	Brunswick 05680	My Troubled Mind/Queen Of The Senior Prom (78)	7
58	London HLD 8553	Get A Job/I Found A Million Dollar Baby (78 rpm = £12)	30
54	Brunswick OE 9014	PRESENTING THE MILLS BROTHERS (EP)	10
55	Brunswick OE 9060	THE MILLS BROTHERS NO. 2 (EP)	7
56	Brunswick OE 9239	SINGING AND SWINGING PT. 1 (EP)	7
59	London RED 1215	THE MILLS BROTHERS (EP)	12

54	Brunswick LA 8664	MEET THE MILLS BROTHERS (10" LP)	20
55	Brunswick LA 8702	FOUR BOYS AND A GUITAR (10" LP)	18
59	London HA-D 2192	THE MILLS BROTHERS' GREATEST HITS (LP, also stereo SAH-D 6046)	12
60	London HA-D 2250	THE MILLS BROTHERS SING (LP, also stereo SAH-D 6074)	12
61	London HA-D 2319	THE MILLS BROTHERS' GREATEST HITS VOLUME 2 (LP)	12
61	London HA-D 2383	SAN ANTONIO ROSE (LP, also stereo SAH-D 6183)	12
63	London HA-D/SH-D 8058	BEER BARREL POLKA (LP)	12
63	London HA-D/SH-D 8092	THE END OF THE WORLD (LP)	12

(see also Louis Armstrong)

MILLWALL F.C.
| 72 | Decca F1 3350 | Millwall/The Ballad Of Harry Cripps | 8 |

RONNIE MILSAP
66	Pye International 7N 25392	Ain't No Soul (Left In These Old Shoes)/	
		Another Branch From The Same Old Tree (DJ copy = £100)	50
69	Pye International 7N 25490	Denver/Nothing Is As Good As It Used To Be	6
72	Wand WN 26	Ain't No Soul (Left In These Old Shoes)/	
		Another Branch From The Same Old Tree (reissue)	10

RONNIE MILSAP/ROSCOE ROBINSON
| 66 | Pye Intl. NEP 44078 | SOUL SENSATIONS (EP) | 50 |

JOHNNY MILTON & CONDORS
61	Oriole CB 1588	Charleston Cocktail (medley) (as Johnny Milton Band)	5
64	Decca F 11862	A Girl Named Sue/Somethin' Else (as Johnny Milton & Condors)	8
64	Fontana TF 488	Cry Baby/Hurt	6

(see also Symbols)

MILVA
63	Oriole CB 1899	I Can't Believe You're Leaving Me/Loneliness Of Autumn	8
64	Oriole CB 1952	I'll Set My Love To Music/Come Sempre	8
67	Major Minor MM 510	Love Is A Feeling/Seasons Of Love	5

MILWAUKEE COASTERS
68	Pama PM 733	Treat Me Nice/Sick And Tired (Oh Babe)	5
68	Pama PMLP 2	WEST COAST ROCK'N'ROLL 1968 (LP)	15
69	Pama PSP 10	BEST PARTY ALBUM (LP, reissue of PMLP 2)	12

GARNET MIMMS (& ENCHANTERS)
63	United Artists UP 1033	Cry Baby/Don't Change Your Heart (with Enchanters)	25
63	United Artists UP 1038	Baby Don't You Weep/For Your Precious Love (with Enchanters)	20
64	United Artists UP 1048	Tell Me Baby/Anytime You Want Me (with Enchanters)	20
65	United Artists UP 1090	It Was Easier To Hurt Her/So Close	30
66	United Artists UP 1130	I'll Take Good Care Of You/Looking For You (DJ copy = £200)	100
66	United Artists UP 1147	It's Been Such A Long Way Home/Thinkin'	20
66	United Artists UP 1153	My Baby/It Won't Hurt Half As Much	20
66	United Artists UP 1172	All About Love/The Truth Hurts	20
67	United Artists UP 1181	Roll With The Punches/Only Your Love	20
67	United Artists UP 1186	As Long As I Have You/Yesterday	20
68	Verve VS 569	I Can Hear My Baby Crying/Stop And Think It Over	20
68	Verve VS 569	I Can Hear My Baby Crying/BILL MEDLEY: That Lucky Old Sun (mispress)	10
68	Verve VS 574	We Can Find That Love/Can You Top This	25
76	United Artists REM 403	REMEMBER GARNET MIMMS (EP)	10
63	United Artists ULP 1067	CRY BABY AND 11 OTHER HITS (LP, with Enchanters)	120
66	United Artists (S)ULP 1145	WARM AND SOULFUL (LP)	100
67	United Artists (S)ULP 1174	LIVE (LP, as Garnet Mimms & Senate)	80

MINDBENDERS
66	Fontana TF 644	A Groovy Kind Of Love/Love Is Good	6
66	Fontana TF 697	Can't Live With You, Can't Live Without You/One Fine Day	6
66	Fontana TF 731	Ashes To Ashes/You Don't Know About Love	6
66	Fontana TF 780	I Want Her, She Wants Me/The Morning After	18
67	Fontana TF 806	We'll Talk About It Tomorrow/Far Across Town	8
67	Fontana TF 869	The Letter/My New Day And Age	8
67	Fontana TF 877	Schoolgirl/Coming Back	15
68	Fontana TF 910	Blessed Are The Lonely/Yellow Brick Road	9
68	Fontana TF 961	Uncle Joe, The Ice Cream Man/The Man Who Loved Trees	10
69	Fontana H 1026	A Groovy Kind Of Love/Ashes To Ashes (p/s)	10
66	Fontana (S)TL 5324	THE MINDBENDERS (LP, mono/stereo)	45/55
67	Fontana (S)TL 5403	WITH WOMAN IN MIND (LP)	50
68	Fontana SFL 13045	THE MINDBENDERS (LP, reissue)	12

(see also Wayne Fontana & Mindbenders, Hotlegs, Lulu)

SAL MINEO
57	Philips JK 1024	Start Movin' (In My Direction)/Love Affair (jukebox issue)	40
57	Philips PB 733	Lasting Love/You Shouldn't Do That (78)	10
57	Philips PB 764	Party Time/The Words That I Whisper (78)	10
58	Fontana H 118	Little Pigeon/Cuttin' In (78 rpm = £20)	50
58	Fontana H 135	Seven Steps To Love/A Couple Of Crazy Kids (78 rpm = £20)	30
58	Fontana TFL 5004	SAL (LP)	80

CORINA MINETTE
| 60 | HMV POP 752 | He'll Have To Stay/TOMMY THOMAS ORCHESTRA: Young At Cha Cha | 7 |

SEXTON MING
| | Hangman's Daughter
HANG 018UP | 6 MORE MILES TO THE GRAVEYARD (LP) | 12 |

SEXTON MING (& HIS DIAMOND GUSSETS)
| 96 | D. Goods DAMGOOD 71 | I'm In Love With Danny Edwards/Break His Spirit/Son Of Tractor Nits (p/s) | 6 |

CHARLES/CHARLIE MINGUS

60	Philips BBE 12399	CHARLES MINGUS (EP)	8
61	Philips BBE 12451	MINGUS DYNASTY (EP, as Charles Mingus Jazz Groups, also stereo SBBE 9050)	8/10
61	Philips BBE 12453	THINGS AIN'T WHAT THEY USED TO BE (EP, as Charles Mingus Jazz Groups, also stereo SBBE 9052)	8/10
63	Parlophone GEP 8786	SCENES IN THE CITY (EP)	10
65	Mercury 10021 MCE	JAZZ MAKERS (EP, as Charlie Mingus Orchestra)	8
56	Vogue LDE 178	CHARLIE MINGUS PRESENTS JAZZ WORKSHOP VOL. 2 (10" LP)	15
59	Parlophone PMC 1092	EAST COASTING (LP)	15
60	London Jazz LTZ-K 15194	BLUES AND ROOTS (LP, also stereo SAH-K 6087)	15
62	Atlantic SD 8005	CHARLES MINGUS PRESENTS CHARLES MINGUS (LP, U.K. issue of U.S. LP)	15
62	United Artists ULP 1004	JAZZ PORTRAITS (LP)	15
62	London HA-K/SH-K 8007	OH YEAH (LP, by Charlie Mingus & Jazz Group)	15
63	RCA RD/SF 7514	TIJUANA MOODS (LP)	15
63	Vocalion LAE 543	CHAZZ (LP)	15
64	HMV CLP 1694	THE BLACK SAINT AND THE SINNER LADY (LP)	20
65	United Artists ULP 1068	TOWN HALL CONCERT (LP)	15
65	Vocalion LAEF/SEAF 591	CHARLIE MINGUS QUINTET WITH MAX ROACH (LP)	15
65	HMV CLP 1742	MINGUS, MINGUS, MINGUS (LP, also stereo CSD 1545)	15
65	HMV CLP 1796	MINGUS PLAYS PIANO (LP)	15
65	Atlantic ATL/SAL 5019	CHARLIE MINGUS (LP)	15
66	Realm RM 211	JAZZ COMPOSERS WORKSHOP (NO. 1) (LP)	12
66	CBS (S)BPG 62261	MINGUS DYNASTY (LP)	15
68	Polydor 623 215	CHARLIE MINGUS (LP)	12
68	Atlantic 587 131	PITHECANTHROPUS ERECTUS (LP, as Charlie Mingus Jazz Workshop)	12
69	CBS 52346	MINGUS AH-UM! (LP)	12
69	Atlantic 587 166	REINCARNATION OF A LOVEBIRD (LP, as Charlie Mingus Jazz Workshop)	12
69	Mercury SMWL 21056	MINGUS REVISITED (LP)	12
70	Atlantic 545 111	DUKE'S CHOICE (LP, as Charlie Mingus Jazz Workshop)	12
72	CBS 24010	CHARLES MINGUS (2-LP)	15
72	CBS 64715	LET MY CHILDREN HEAR MUSIC (LP)	12
73	Atlantic K 60039	THE ART OF CHARLIE MINGUS: THE ATLANTIC YEARS (2-LP)	15

MINIM

67	Polydor 582 011	WRAPPED IN A UNION JACK (LP)	25

MINISTRY

92	Sire W 0096	Jesus Built My Hotrod/T.V. Song (p/s)	10

MINISTRY OF SOUND

66	Decca F 12449	White Collar Worker/Back Seat Driver	15

LIZA MINNELLI

66	Capitol CL 15483	The Middle Of The Street/I (Who Have Nothing)	8
89	Epic ZEE C1	Losing My Mind (Remix)/(Extended Remix)/Tonight Is Forever (CD, card p/s)	8
89	Epic ZEE 2	Don't Drop Bombs (Extended Remix)/(Dub Mix)/(Acappella) (12", p/s)	10
89	Epic ZEE C2	Don't Drop Bombs (7" Version)/(Extended Remix)/(Acappella) (CD, card p/s)	8
89	Epic ZEE G3	So Sorry, I Said/I Can't Say Goodnight (gatefold p/s)	7
89	Epic ZEE C3	So Sorry, I Said/I Can't Say Goodnight/Losing My Mind (Ultimix)/Losing My Mind (Ultimix Dub) (CD, card sleeve)	8
89	Epic CP ZEE 3	So Sorry, I Said/I Can't Say Goodnight/Losing My Mind (Ultimix Dub) (CD, 'Xmas' pack in pouch with gatefold card & envelope)	12
90	Epic ZEE 4	Love Pains/Love Pains (Steve "Silk" Hurley's Radio Edit) (p/s)	5
90	Epic ZEEQT 4	Love Pains (Deep House Pains)/Love Pains (Steve "Silk" Hurley's Radio Edit)/PET SHOP BOYS: Rent (12", gatefold sleeve)	8
90	Epic CD ZEE 4	Love Pains/Love Pains (Steve "Silk" Hurley's Remix)/PET SHOP BOYS: Rent (CD, card sleeve)	8

(see also Pet Shop Boys)

MINNY POPS

80s	Factory FAC 31	MINNY POPS EP: Goddess/Dolphin Spurt	8

DANNII MINOGUE

91	MCA MCSR 1529	Love And Kisses (7" Mix)/(Instrumental) (poster p/s, some signed)	25/5
97	Warner Bros SAM 3009	All I Wanna Do (Trouser Enthusiasts' Toys Of Desperation Mix)/(Trouser Enthusiasts' Ultra Sensitive Dub)/(Quatara Mix)/(Dizzy's Mix) (12", double pack, blue title sleeve, promo only)	15
97	Warner Bros SAM 3022	All I Wanna Do (12" Extended Mix)/(7" Mix)/(Xenomania Dream House Mix)/(Tiny Tim & The Mekon Dream Dub)/(D-Bop's Innocent Girl Mix)/(Trouser Enthusiasts' Toys Of Desperation Mix) (12", double pack, gold title sleeve, promo only)	20
97	Warner Bros SAM 3106	Everything I Wanted (Jupiter 6 — Soul Surround Mix)/Heaven Can Wait (D'Bop's Melt & Sparkle Mix) (10", promo only)	15
97	Warner Bros SAM 3108	Everything I Wanted (Xenomania 12" Mix)/(Radio Edit)/(Trouser Enthusiasts' Golden Delicious Mix)/(Metro's 7" Edit) (12", metallic green title sleeve, promo only)	12
97	Warner Bros SAM 3105	Everything I Wanted (Xenomania 12" Mix)/(Radio Edit)/(Trouser Enthusiasts' Golden Delicious Mix)/(Hell Fire Club Dub)/(Cloud Nine Mix)/(Liquid Silk Dub) (12" double pack, metallic pink title sleeve, promo only)	15

KYLIE MINOGUE

87	PWL PWLT 8R	I Should Be So Lucky (Bicentennial Mix)/(Instrumental) (12", stickered p/s)	12
88	PWL PWLT 12R	Got To Be Certain (Extra Beat Boys Mix)/Got To Be Certain (7" Mix)/Got To BeCertain (Out For A Duck Bill Platter Plus Dub Mix) (12", stickered p/s)	15
88	PWL PWCD 12	Got To Be Certain (Extended Mix)/Got To Be Certain (Instrumental)/I Should Be So Lucky (Extended Mix 6.03) (CD)	20
88	PWL PWLT 14R	The Loco-Motion (Sankie Mix)/I'll Still Be Loving You (12", stickered p/s)	18

MINT VALUE £

88	PWL PWLP 21	Je Ne Sais Pas Pourquoi/Made In Heaven (poster p/s)	35
88	PWL PWLT 21R	Je Ne Sais Pas Pourquoi (Revolutionary Mix)/Made In Heaven (Maid In England Mix) (12", stickered p/s)	15
88	PWL PWCD 21	Je Ne Sais Pas Pourquoi (Moi Non Plus Mix)/Made In Heaven (Maid In England Mix)/The Loco-Motion (Sankie Mix) (CD)	20
88	PWL PWCD 24	Especially For You (7" Mix)/Especially For You (Extended)/ All I Wanna Do Is Make You Mine (Extended) (with Jason Donovan) (CD)	15
89	PWL PWMC 35	Hand On Your Heart (7" Mix)/Hand On Your Heart (Great Aorta Mix)/ Just Wanna Love You (cassette)	8
89	PWL PWLT 35R	Hand On Your Heart (Heartache Mix)/Hand On Your Heart (Dub mix) Just Wanna Love You (12", with stickered p/s)	35
89	PWL PWCD 35	Hand On Your Heart (Great Aorta Mix)/Just Wanna Love You/ It's No Secret (Extended Mix) (CD)	15
89	PWL PWMC 42	Wouldn't Change A Thing/It's No Secret (Album Version) (cassette)	8
89	PWL PWLT 42R	Wouldn't Change A Thing (Espagna Mix)/Wouldn't Change A Thing (7" Mix)/ It's No Secret (Extended) (12", stickered p/s)	25
89	PWL PWCD 42	Wouldn't Change A Thing (7" Mix)/Wouldn't Change A Thing (Your Thang Mix)/ Je Ne Sais Pas Pourquoi (Revolutionary Mix) (CD)	15
89	PWL PWCD 45	Never Too Late (7" Mix)/(Extended)/(Kylie Smiley Extended Mix) (6.17) (CD)	15
90	PWL PWMC47	Tears On My Pillow (7" Mix)/We Know The Meaning Of Love (7" mix) (cassette)	8
90	PWL PWCD47	Tears On My Pillow (7" Mix)/Tears On My Pillow (Extended Mix)/ We Know The Meaning Of Love (Extended Mix) (CD)	12
90	PWL PWMC 56	Better The Devil You Know (7" Mix)/I'm Over Dreaming Over You (7" Remix)/ (cassette, orange casing)	5
90	PWL PWCD 56	Better The Devil You Know (Mad March Hare Mix)/ I'm Over Dreaming Over You (7" Remix) (CD)	15
90	PWL PWMC 64	Step Back In Time (7" Mix)/Step Back In Time (Instrumental) (cassette, green casing)	5
90	PWL PWCD 64	Step Back In Time (7" Mix)/Step Back In Time (Walkin' Rhythm Mix)/ Step Back In Time (Extended instrumental) (CD)	15
91	PWL PWLP 72	What Do I Have To Do (New Mix)/What Do I Have To Do (Instrumental) (stickered p/s, with postcards)	15
91	PWL PWMC 72	What Do I Have To Do (New Mix)/What Do I Have To Do (Instrumental) (cassette)	5
91	PWL PWLT 72R	What Do I Have To Do (Between The Sheets Mix) (12", withdrawn, no p/s)	80
91	PWL PWCD 72	What Do I Have To Do (New Mix)/What Do I Have To Do (Pumpin Polly Mix)/ What Do I Have To Do (Extended Instrumental) (CD)	15
91	PWL PWL P81	Shocked (DNA 7" Mix)/Shocked (Harding & Curnow 7" Mix) (picture disc)	15
91	PWL PWCD 81	Shocked (DNA 7" Mix)/Shocked (DNA Extended Mix)/Shocked (Harding & Curnow Extended Mix) (CD)	15
91	PWL PWLT204R	Word Is Out (Summer Breeze Remix) (1-sided 12"- Limited Edition with etched Kylie autograph on other side, p/s)	20
91	PWL PWCD 204	Word Is Out (Extended Mix)/Word Is Out (Instrumental)/ Say The Word — I'll Be There (CD)	12
91	PWL PWL 207	Keep On Pumpin' It (Angelic Remix Edit)/(Astral Flight Mix Edit) (with Vision Masters) (p/s)	5
91	PWL PWMC 207	Keep On Pumpin' It (Angelic Remix Edit)/(Astral Flight Mix Edit) (with Vision Masters) (cassette)	5
91	PWL PWLT 207	Keep On Pumpin' It (Angelic Remix)/(Astral Flight Mix) (with Vision Masters) (12", p/s)	10
91	PWL PWCD 207	Keep On Pumpin' It (Angelic Remix Edit)/(Angelic Remix)/ (Astral Flight Mix) (with Vision Masters) (CD)	20
91	PWL PWCD 508	If You Were With Me Now (with Keith Washington) (7" Mix)/(Extended)/ I Guess I Like It Like That (Full Length Version) (CD)	8
92	PWL PWCD 212	Give Me Just A Little More Time (7" Mix)/(Extended)/ Do You Dare (NRG Mix)/(New Rave Mix) (CD)	8
94	Polygram PSPMC 344	Hand On Your Heart/Give Me Just A Little More Time (Woolworths giveaway cassette)	10
94	DeConstruction 278482-0	Confide In Me (Master Mix)/Nothing Can Stop Us/ If You Don't Love Me (CD)	12
95	MUTE MUTE185	Where The Wild Roses Grow (with Nick Cave)/The Ballad of Robert Moore & Betty Coltrane (non-Kylie track) (limited 7", p/s)	8
97	DeCon. 7432 1517257	Some Kind Of Bliss/Love Takes Over Me (numbered limited edition 7", die-cut p/s)	15
98	Arthrob ART021 CD1	GBI/(The Sharp Boys Deee-Liteful Dub)/Boldline (with Towa Tei) (CD)	8
98	Arthrob ART021 CD2	GBI/(Rekut)/(Ebony Boogie Down Mix) (with Towa Tei) (CD)	8
00	Parlophone 12R 6542 A/B	Spinning Around (Sharp Vocal Mix)/(Sharp Double Dub)/ (7th Spinnin' Dizzy Dub)/(7th District Club Mix) (12" double-pack)	10
03	Parlophone 12R6625	Slow (Extended Mix)/Slow (Radio Slave Remix)/Slow (Medicine 8 Remix) (12" picture disc, PVC title sleeve, sealed with sticker)	15
03	BMG BMGSM94	Breathe/Where Is The Feeling? (Little Chef 'Music Collection' giveaway 2-track CD, Includes enhanced CD-Rom section, unique Kylie card p/s)	12
01	Parlophone 12RDJZ6562	Can't Get You Out Of My Head (Extended)/(Extended Instrumental) (limited edition 12", custom Parlophone die-cut sleeve)	20
04	Parlophone 12R6633	Red Blooded Woman (Whitey Mix)/Slow (Chemical Brothers Remix)/ Red Blooded Woman (Narcotic Thrust Mix) (12" picture disc, PVC title sleeve, sealed with sticker)	15
04	Parlophone 12R6639	Chocolate (Tom Middleton Cosmos Mix)/(Radio Edit)/(Emo Mix) (12" picture disc, PVC title sleeve, sealed with sticker)	15
04	Parlophone 12R6656	I Believe In You/(Mylo Dub)/(Skylark Dub) (12" picture disc, PVC, stickered sleeve)	15
05	Parlophone 12R6661	Giving You Up (Riton Re-Rub Dub)/(Single Version)/(Alter Ego Remix) (12" picture disc, PVC title sleeve, sealed with sticker)	15
88	PWL HFD 4	KYLIE (DAT)	100
90	PWL HF 18	Rhythm Of Love (LP, with free poster)	12

90	PWL HFL 18	Rhythm Of Love (LP, gold leaf sleeve, 100 only)	250
91	PWL HFCL 18	Rhythm Of Love (cassette, with 3 bonus tracks, gold case)	15
91	PWL HFCDL 18	Rhythm Of Love (CD, with 3 bonus tracks, gold case)	20
98	DeCon. 74321 58715 1	MIXES (3xLP, inner sleeves, pink silhouette Kylie outer p/s)	30
98	DeCon. 74321 58715 2	MIXES (2xCD, pink silhouette Kylie p/s)	20

PROMOS & TEST PRESSINGS

88	PWL (no cat. no.)	Made In Heaven (3:26) (PWL 1-track in-house promo cassette, custom PWL logo inlay, typed/stickered cassette, 1 only)	50+
90	PWL PWLT 56R	Better The Devil You Know (KC Cohen 'US' Remix) (1-sided 12" promo, withdrawn, die-cut sleeve, 50 only)	150
91	PWL PWLT 72R	What Do I Have To Do (Between The Sheets Mix) (1-sided 12" promo, withdrawn)	65
91	PWL ZR-A1	Keep On Pumpin' It (12" white label issued under pseudonym of 'Angel K', includes 'Angelic Remix' & 'Astral Flight Mix', handwritten/stamped labels, Some with 'I Guess I Like It' titles, die-cut sleeve)	30
91	PWL (no cat. no.)	I Guess I Like It Like That (12" 1-sided white label issued under pseudonym of 'Angel K', includes 'Extended/Album Version', 200 only)	50
		'NRG Mix' & 'New Rave Mix', handwritten labels, die-cut sleeve, 100 only)	60
91	PWL ANGEL-2	Do You Dare (12" white label issued under pseudonym of 'Angel K', includes 'NRG Mix' & 'New Rave Mix', handwritten labels, die-cut sleeve, 100 only)	60
92	PWL PWLT 227	Finer Feelings (Brothers In Rhythm 12" Mix)/Closer (Pleasure Mix) ('Black Diamond' limited promo 12", black diamond label, die cut sleeve)	15
92	PWL PWLT 257	Celebration (Have A Party Mix)/Let's Get To It (Album Version) ('Black Diamond' limited promo 12", Christmas "leaving PWL" promo p/s, black Diamond label)	30
93	Deconstruction K1	Nothing Can Stop Us (1-track CD, considered for early first Deconstruction single. Black card sleeve with white titles, withdrawn, most destroyed)	150+
94	DeCon. 21 227477 JB	Confide In Me (Radio Mix)/(Truth Mix) (7" jukebox issue, no p/s)	10
94	DeCon. 21 246577 JB	Put Yourself In My Place (Radio Mix)/(All Star Mix) (7" jukebox issue, no p/s)	20
94	DeCon. 21 293617 JB	Where Is The Feeling? (BIR Bish Bosh Mix Edit)/(BIR Dolphin Mix) (7" jukebox issue, no p/s)	10
95	DeConstruction FEEL2	Where Is The Feeling? (BIR Dolphin Mix)/(Morales Club Mix) (12", die-cut sleeve, limited quantities)	50
95	DeConstruction FEEL3	Where Is The Feeling? (Da Klubb Feelin' Mix)/(Aphroheadz Powerlite Mix)/ (Three Rad Vid Clash Mix) (12", promo, no p/s, 200 only)	80
95	DeConstruction FEELING1	Where Is The Feeling? (UK 7" Edit) (UK export to Japan promo 1-track CD, unique Custom p/s)	100
95	Deconstruction TIME1	Time Will Pass You By (Paul Masterson's 'Wand Silver Screen Remix') (1-sided 12" White Label, handwritten labels, unreleased mix, withdrawn, 20 only)	150+
97	DeConstruction DID2	Did It Again (Trouser Enthusiasts' Goddess of Contortion Mix)/ (Razor N Go Mix) (12" promo, custom Deconstruction die-cut sleeve, limited to 500 only)	40
97	DeCon. 21 535707 JB	Did It Again (Radio Edit)/Tears (7" jukebox issue, no p/s)	25
98	DeCon. 21 570137 JB	Breathe (Radio Edit)/(Tee's Radio Edit) (7" jukebox issue, no p/s)	25
98	DeConstruction BREATHE02	Breathe (3-track 'edits' promo CD, custom Deconstruction sleeve)	15
98	DeConstruction TOOFAR 1	Too Far (Brothers In Rhythm Mix)/(Junior Vasquez Remix) (12", promo, no p/s)	20
98	Arthrob ART021TJ	GBI (Sharp Boys Deee-Liteful Dub)/(Album Version)/(Kylie-Pella) (with Towa Tei) (UK promo 12" part 1, custom Arthrob sleeve)	15
98	Arthrob ART021TJX	GBI (Rekut/DJ Krust Mix)/(Ebony Boogie Down Mix)/Bold Line (not Kylie) (with Towa Tei) (UK promo 12" part 2, custom Arthrob sleeve)	15
98	Arthrob ART021CDJ	GBI (Radio Edit)/(Album Mix)/(Sharp Boys Deee-Liteful Dub) (with Towa Tei) (UK promo CD, custom Arthrob card slip case)	20
00	Parlophone BUTTERFLO1A	Butterfly (Sandstorm Dub) (12" 1-sided DJ white label, butterfly logo stamped die cut paper sleeve)	80
00	Parlophone 12MINWL 002	Butterfly (Trisco Mix)/Butterfly (Sandstorm Dub) (12" test pressing, white label)	50
00	Parlophone 12MIND 1	Spinning Around (Messy Boyz Remix) (12" 1-sided promo featuring unreleased mix, die cut sleeve, Handwritten label, withdrawn, 10 only)	200+
00	Parlophone SHARP DJ 1	Spinning Around (Sharp Vocal Mix)/Spinning Around (Sharp Double Dub) (12" Pink Promo DJ Vinyl, die-cut sleeve, 100 only)	100
00	Parlophone 12MIND JY 001	Spinning Around (7th District Dub Like This Mix)/Spinning Around (7th District Club-Mental Mix) (12" promo, p/s)	15
00	Parlophone 12MIND JX 001	Spinning Around (Sharp Vocal Mix)/Spinning Around (Sharp Double Dub Mix) (12" promo, p/s)	15
00	Parlophone CDMIND J 001	Spinning Around (CD promo, card insert)	10
00	Parlophone RLH6542	Spinning Around/Paper Dolls (7" jukebox issue, no p/s)	10
00	Parlophone RLH6546	On A Night Like This/Ocean Blue (7" jukebox issue, no p/s)	20
00	Parlophone NLT 001	On A Night Like This (Rob Searle Mix) (12" 1-sided test pressing, white label)	30
00	Parlophone 12MINWLS 002	On A Night Like This (Bini & Martini Club Mix)/On A Night Like This (Bini & Martini Dub Mix) (12" test pressing, white label)	30
00	Parlophone 12MINDJ 002	On A Night Like This (Motiv8 Nocturnal Vocal Mix)/On A Night Like This (Bini & Martini Vocal Mix)/On A Night Like This (Rob Searle Mix)/ Your Disco Needs You (Almighty Mix) (12" promo doublepack, p/s)	25
00	Parlophone CMINDJ 002	On A Night Like This (CD promo, card & paper inners)	10
00	Chrysalis CHSLH5119	Kids (with Robbie Williams)/United (not including Kylie) (7" jukebox issue, no p/s)	10
00	Parlophone RLH6551	Please Stay/Santa Baby (7" jukebox issue, no p/s)	10
00	Parlophone 12RDJ 6551	Please Stay (Metro Mix)/Please Stay (7th District Club Flava Mix)/ Please Stay (7th District Club Dub) (12" promo, p/s, with inner sleeve)	20
00	Parlophone 12MINWL 004	Please Stay (7th District Club Dub)/Please Stay (Hatiras Dreamy Dub)/ Please Stay (7th District Club Flava Mix) (12" promo, title-stickered sleeve)	15
00	Parlophone 12MINWL005	Please Stay (Hatiras Dreamy Dub Mix) (1-sided 12" promo, die-cut sleeve)	20
00	Parlophone CDRDJX6551	Santa Baby/Please Stay (Christmas 2000 promo CD, custom violet metallic slip case with large pink Kylie logo)	20

01	Parlophone LIGHT01A	Light Years (D-Bop Voyager Remix) (1-sided 12" promo, white label, unreleased mix, die cut sleeve, handwritten label, withdrawn)	100+
01	Parlophone (no cat. no)	Light Years (D-Bop Voyager Remix) (Townhouse 1-track CD-R promo, unreleased mix Custom title sleeve, withdrawn)	150+
01	Parlophone RLH6562	Can't Get You Out Of My Head/Boy (7" jukebox issue, no p/s)	20
		NOTE: Clear 7" jukebox pressings carrying this 'RLH6562' catalogue number with 'Can't Get Blue Monday Out Of My Head' as the B-side are unofficial and bootlegs)	
01	Parlophone (no cat. no.)	Can't Get You Out Of My Head (Radio Slave Remix Dub Re-Edit) (1-sided 33rpm 12" 'The Exchange' studio acetate feat. Unreleased mix sampling Roxy Music's 'Angel Eyes', custom studio label, 5 only)	300+
01	Parlophone (no cat. no.)	Can't Get You Out Of My Head (Radio Slave Vocal Re-Edit)/Can't Get You Out Of My Head (Radio Slave Remix Dub Re-Edit) (33rpm 12" 'The Exchange' studio acetate feat. Unreleased mixes sampling Roxy Music's 'Angel Eyes', custom studio label, 10 only)	250+
01	Parlophone 12RDJ 6562	Can't Get Into My Head (Plastika Mix)/Can't Get Into My Head (Time Deluxe Inst.)/Can't Get Into My Head (Time Deluxe Dub) (12" promo, no p/s)	20
01	Parlophone 12RDJY 6562	Can't Get Out Of My Head (Superchumbo Todo Mamado Mix)/Can't Get Out Of My Head (Superchumbo Leadhead Dub)/Can't Get Out Of My Head (Superchumbo Voltapella Mix) (12" promo)	20
01	Parlophone 12RDJX 6562	Can't Get You Out Of My Head (K&M Mindprint Mix)/Can't Get You Out Of My Head (Nick Faber Mix) (12" promo, p/s, frosted PVC outer title sleeve)	25
01	Parlophone 12RDJ6562	"Get Into My Head" – Can't Get You Out Of My Head (Plastika Mix)/(Deluxe's Dirty Dub Instrumental)/(Deluxe's Dirty Dub) (12" promo issued under pseudonym of 'Special K', die-cut sleeve)	20
01	Parlophone 12RDJ6562	"Get Into My Head" – Can't Get You Out Of My Head (Plastika Mix)/(Deluxe's Dirty Dub Instrumental)/(Deluxe's Dirty Dub) (12" 'Limited Tastemaker' white label issued under pseudonym of 'Special K', limited to 100 copies only, die-cut sleeve)	60
01	Parlophone 12RDJY6562	"Get Out Of My Head" – Can't Get You Out Of My Head (Superchumbo Todo Mamado Mix)/(Superchumbo Leadhead Dub)/(Superchumbo Voltapella Mix) (12" promo issued under pseudonym of 'Special K', Die-cut sleeve)	20
01	Parlophone KYLIE-6TRACKS	Can't Get You Out Of My Head 'Remixes' (UK export 6-track remix promo CD housed in custom card p/s)	40
01	Parlophone KBLUE1	Can't Get Blue Monday Out Of My Head (1-sided 12" promo, pink die-cut sl.)	40
02	Parlophone 12RDJ 6569	In Your Eyes (Powder's Spaced Dub)/In Your Eyes (Powder's 12" Dub)/In Your Eyes (Saeed & Palash Mix)/In Your Eyes (Saeed & Palash Nightmare Dub) (12" test pressing, white label, title-stickered sleeve)	25
02	Parlophone 12RDJX 6569	In Your Eyes (The S Man's Release Mix/In Your Eyes (Roger Sanchez Release The Dub Mix)/In Your Eyes (Jean Jacques Smoothie Dub) (12" promo, white sl. with title sticker)	18
02	Tripoli Trax 12RDJY 6569	In Your Eyes (Knuckleheadz Mix)/In Your Eyes (Mr. Bishi Mix) (12" promo, stickered title sleeve)	35
02	Parlophone RLH6569	In Your Eyes/Tightrope (7" jukebox issue, no p/s)	30
02	Parlophone (no cat. no.)	No Better Love (4:18) (1-track internal CD-R promo of unreleased 'Fever' out take, custom inlay, withdrawn)	100+
02	Parlophone RLH6577	Love At First Sight – Can't Get Blue Monday Out Of My Head (7" jukebox issue, no p/s)	20
02	Parlophone 12RDJ 6577	Love At First Sight (The Scumfrog's Beauty & The Beast Vocal)/Love At First Sight (The Scumfrog's Beauty & The Beast Dub)/Love At First Sight (The Scum Frog's Beauty & The Beast Acapella) (12" promo, p/s).	18
02	Parlophone 12RDJX 6577	Love At First Sight (Twin Master Plan Mix)/(Ruff & Jam Vocal 7")/(Ruff & Jam Club Mix) (12" promo, white sl.)	18
02	Parlophone 12RDJY 6577	Love At First Sight (Kid Crème Vocal Dub)/(Kid Crème Vocal-less Dub) (promo 12", custom label, die-cut sleeve, limited to 300 copies only)	20
02	Parlophone 12RDJY 6577	Love At First Sight (Kid Crème Vocal Dub)/(Kid Crème Vocal-less Dub) (promo white label 12", stamped label, die-cut sleeve, 50 only)	80
02	Parlophone RLH6590	Come Into My World (Single Version)/(Fischerspooner Mix) (7" jukebox issue, no p/s)	20
02	Parlophone RDJ 6590	Come Into My World (Fischerspooner Mix)/Come Into My World (Ashtrax Mix) (promo 7", die-cut title sleeve)	40
02	Parlophone 12RDJ 6590	Come Into My World (Robbie Rivera's Hard & Sexy Mix)/(Robbie Rivera's NYC Dub) (12" promo, title sleeve, 400 only)	20
02	Parlophone (no cat. no.)	Whenenever You Feel Like It (4:07) (1-track Parlophone CD-R promo, custom printed inlay, withdrawn)	30+
02	Parlophone (no cat. no.)	Princess Of Pulse 'Electro Eyes' Medley (6:35) (Parlophone 1-track promo DAT used For 'Royal Variety' performance in 2002. Pre-recorded 'live-effect' vocals, unreleased Medley, custom title inlay with cues, 1 only)	100+
03	Parlophone 12MINDJ 006	Slow (Radio Slave Mix)/(Medicine 8 Remix)/(Synth City Mix) (12" promo part 1)	15
03	Parlophone 12MINDJ 006	Slow (Radio Slave Mix)/(Medicine 8 Remix)/(Synth City Mix) (12" white label + press sheet, 50 only)	80+
03	Parlophone 12MINDJX 006	Slow (Extended Mix)/Slow (Extended Instrumental)/Slow (Acapella) (12" promo part 2)	15
03	Parlophone 12MINDJY 006	Slow (Chemical Brothers Remix) (1-sided 12", yellow vinyl promo, 200 only)	60+
03	Parlophone (no cat. no.)	Slow (CD promo, in black card fold-out sleeve)	45
03	Parlophone RLH6625	Slow/Sweet Music (7" jukebox issue, no p/s)	30
04	Parlophone RLH6633	Red Blooded Woman/Almost A Lover (7" jukebox issue, no p/s)	30
04	Parlophone RDJ6633	Red Blooded Woman (Promo 1-sided clear 7" vinyl featuring otherwise unreleased 'Play Paul Radio Edit', 50 only)	150
04	Parlophone 12RDJ6633	Red Blooded Woman (Narcotic Thrust Mix) (1-sided white label 12", stamped title, die cut sleeve)	20
04	Parlophone 12RDJZ6633	Red Blooded Woman (Whitey Mix) (1-sided white label 'DJ friendly' 180gm heavyweight vinyl, stamped title)	20
04	Parlophone 12RDJY6633	Red Blooded Woman (Promo 1-sided 12" featuring otherwise unreleased 'Play Paul Extended Dub', die-cut sleeve, 100 only)	50

04	Parlophone (no cat. no.)	Red Blooded Woman (Celestial Bhangra Club Remix) (6:20) (1-track Parlophone Promo CD-R of unreleased remix, custom inlay, withdrawn) .... 100+
04	Parlophone CDRDJ6639	Chocolate (Radio Edit) (promo CD, fold-out white envelope card sleeve with logo, brown CD) 10
04	Parlophone 12RDJ6639	Chocolate (Tom Middleton Cosmos Mix)/(Emo Mix)/(Emo Dub) (white label 12" promo, stamped label, die-cut sleeve) 15
04	Parlophone (no cat. no)	Chocolate (Violanti's Remix) (1-sided 12" white label, unreleased remix, withdrawn, hand-written label) .... 150+
04	Parlophone CDRDJ6656	I Believe In You (1-track promo CD, custom stripes card slipcase) 10
04	Parlophone 12RDJ6656	I Believe In You (Skylark Mix)/(Mylo Vocal)/(Mylo Dub) (12" promo pressed on 180gm heavy-weight vinyl, promo sleeve with stripes sticker in corner)........ 15
05	Parlophone CDRDJ6661	Giving You Up (1-track promo CD, custom blue stripes card slipcase) 10
05	Parlophone 12RDJ6661	Giving You Up (Riton Re-Rub Vox)/(Riton Re-Rub Dub)/(Alter Ego Remix) (12" promo pressed on 180gm heavy-weight vinyl, promo sleeve with blue stripes sticker in corner) 15
05	Parlophone SHOWGIRL001	Over The Rainbow/Santa Baby (promo 2-track CD-R housed in glossy unique card p/s Of Kylie sitting on a moon from the 'Showgirl Tour', promo only single) .... 100+
93	Deconstruction (no cat. no.)	SESSIONS (8-track demo CD of unreleased sessions recorded with The Rapino Brothers in 1993 as Kylie's demos recorded for Deconstruction, printed inlay, 10 only) .... 800+
94	Deconstruction KYLP1	KYLIE MINOGUE (10 track promo cassette, black p/s with titles)............ 20
94	DeConstruction KM 100	KYLIE MINOGUE (CD, promo, gatefold sl. in lilac slipcase with silver lettering) .... 100+
97	DeConstruction KM001	KYLIE MINOGUE ('Impossible Princess' 6-track 'Interact' sampler cassette issued to fans on the Kylie mailing list with a 'feedback' form to be completed. Snippets of the album tracks with a female introducing each one, custom title inlay) 15
97	DeConstruction KYLIE 1	IMPOSSIBLE PRINCESS (CD, promo, with insert, withdrawn, some with press release from 'Hall Or Nothing' explaining about the withdrawal of the CD & its title due to Princess Diana's death)................................. 120+
97	DeConstruction KM 002	AN INTERVIEW WITH KYLIE MINOGUE (promo interview CD for 'Impossible Princess' album, unique p/s) .... 100+
00	Parlophone LIGHT 001	LIGHT YEARS (CD promo, foldout 22" x 8" pack, does not include 'Kids')...... 70
00	Parlophone LIGHT 002	LIGHT YEARS (CD promo, foldout 22" x 8" pack, includes 'Kids') 60
00	Parlophone LIGHTX 001	LIGHT YEARS (LP promo, unique blue outer 'Kylie' logo sleeve, inner picture sleeve, does not include 'Kids' or 'Password', 100 only)............. 200+
00	Parlophone LIGHTX 002	LIGHT YEARS (LP promo, unique blue outer 'Kylie' logo sleeve, inner picture sleeve, includes 'Kids' but not 'Password', 100 only) .... 150+
00	BMG HITS1	HITS + (CD promo, original withdrawn artwork, card-slip case, withdrawn at Kylie's request when she disliked the picture used, most copies incinerated, few escaped, less than 5 copies)........................... 250+
01	Parlophone FEVER 01	FEVER (CD-ROM promo, DVD-style promo case) 60
01	Parlophone FEVER 02	FEVER (CD promo, card sleeve, frosted PVC outer title sleeve)............. 40
02	PWL 9224680P	GREATEST HITS – THE REMIXES (12" Promo) Hand On Your Heart (WIP 2002 Mix)/What Do I Have To Do? (Movers & Shakers 12" Mix)/ Better The Devil You Know (Movers & Shakers Alternative 12" Mix)/ Step Back In Time (Harding/Curnow Remix) (issued to Promote 2002 revised 'Greatest Hits 87-92' album, custom labels, die-cut sleeve).................. 20
03	Parlophone BODYLANG01	BODY LANGUAGE (promo CD housed in picture card slip case with inner slip-case, copy-control CD) 15
03	Parlophone MININT 02	BODY LANGUAGE INTERVIEW (CD interview promo) 30
04	Parlophone ULTIMATE01	ULTIMATE KYLIE (2xCD promo housed in glossy card slipcase with 2 inner slipcases copy-control CD) 20
04	Parlophone MININT003	ULTIMATE KYLIE – INTERVIEW DISC (promo 40-track interview CD with custom cover, cues and questions, jewel case) 20

MINORBOPS
| 58 | Vogue V 9110 | Need You Tonight/Want You For My Own (78 rpm = £250) .... 800 |

MINOR THREAT
| 85 | Discord DISCORD 15 | Salad Days/Stumped/Good Guys (p/s) .... 6 |

MINSTRELS
| 67 | Studio One SO 2036 | People Get Ready/HAMLINS: Everyone's Got To Be There .... 30 |
| 68 | Studio One SO 2050 | Miss Highty Tighty/WESTMORELITES: Let Me Be Yours Until Tomorrow .... 25 |

MINT
| 69 | Tangerine 014 | Luv/Simone .... 15 |

MINTS
| 57 | London HLP 8423 | Night Air/KEN COPELAND: Pledge Of Love (78 rpm = £80)................. 250 |

MINTY
| 94 | Candy CAN 1V | Useless Man (Version)/(King Rocker Mix)/(The Grid Extended Mix)/ (Dis-Cuss Mix) (12", p/s).. 12 |
| 95 | Sugar SUGA 6V | Plastic Bag/(Foil-Wrapped Mix)/(Partycrashers Mix)/(French Movie Mix) (12", p/s).. 8 |

MINUTE MEN
| 61 | Capitol CL 15206 | Yankee Diddle/Blue Pearl .... 6 |

MINUTEMEN
83	SST SST 002	PARANOID TIME (8-track EP)... 18
84	SST SST 016	BUZZ OR HOWL UNDER THE INFLUENCE OF THE HEAT (12" EP) 20
85	Homestead REFLEX-L	TOUR SPIEL (EP, live 4-track) 10

MINT VALUE £

(SMOKEY ROBINSON &) MIRACLES

61	London HL 9276	Shop Around/Who's Lovin' You	75
61	London HL 9366	Ain't It Baby/The Only One I Love	150
62	Fontana H 384	What's So Good About Goodbye/I've Been So Good To You	200
63	Oriole CBA 1795	You've Really Got A Hold On Me/Happy Landing	130
63	Oriole CBA 1863	Mickey's Monkey/Whatever Makes You Happy	100
64	Stateside SS 263	I Gotta Dance To Keep From Crying/Such Is Love, Such Is Life	50
64	Stateside SS 282	The Man In You/Heartbreak Road	40
64	Stateside SS 324	I Like It Like That/You're So Fine And Sweet	40
64	Stateside SS 353	That's What Love Is Made Of/Would I Love You	30
65	Stateside SS 377	Come On Do The Jerk/Baby Don't You Go	40
65	Tamla Motown TMG 503	Ooo Baby Baby/All That's Good	30
65	Tamla Motown TMG 522	The Tracks Of My Tears/A Fork In The Road	40
65	Tamla Motown TMG 540	My Girl Has Gone/Since You Won My Heart	35
66	Tamla Motown TMG 547	Going To A Go-Go/Choosey Beggar	20
66	Tamla Motown TMG 569	Whole Lotta Shakin' In My Heart/Oh Be My Love	30
66	Tamla Motown TMG 584	(Come 'Round Here) I'm The One You Need/Save Me	15

(The above singles are credited to The Miracles.)

67	Tamla Motown TMG 598	The Love I Saw In You Was Just A Mirage/Swept For You Baby	20
67	Tamla Motown TMG 614	More Love/Swept For You Baby (withdrawn B-side)	120
67	Tamla Motown TMG 614	More Love/Come Spy With Me	25
67	Tamla Motown TMG 631	I Second That Emotion/You Must Be Love	8
68	Tamla Motown TMG 648	If You Can Want/When The Words From Your Heart Get Caught Up In Your Throat	20
68	Tamla Motown TMG 661	Yester-Love/Much Better Off	10
68	Tamla Motown TMG 673	Special Occasion/Give Her Up	10
69	Tamla Motown TMG 687	Baby, Baby Don't Cry/Your Mother's Only Daughter	10
69	Tamla Motown TMG 696	The Tracks Of My Tears/Come On Do The Jerk	8
70	Tamla Motown TMG 745	The Tears Of A Clown/You Must Be Love (with withdrawn B-side)	50
70	Tamla Motown TMG 745	The Tears Of A Clown/Who's Gonna Take The Blame	8
71	Tamla Motown TMG 761	(Come Round Here) I'm The One You Need/We Can Make It, We Can	6
71	Tamla Motown TMG 774	I Don't Blame You At All/That Girl	6
72	Tamla Motown TMG 811	My Girl Has Gone/Crazy 'Bout The La-La-La	6
73	Tamla Motown TMG 853	Going To A Go-Go/Whole Lotta Shakin' In My Heart/Yester-Love	6

(The above singles are credited to Smokey Robinson & The Miracles.)

76	Tamla Motown TMG 1023	Nightlife/The Miracle Workers: Overture (as The Miracles)	6
87	Motown ZB 41147 D	Just To See Her/Te Quiero Como Si No Hubiera Um Manana//Being With You/What's In Your Life For Me? (solo, double pack)	6
61	London RE 1295	SHOP AROUND (EP, as The Miracles)	200
83	Tamla Motown CTME 2028	TEARS OF A CLOWN (cassette EP, as Smokey Robinson & The Miracles)	7
63	Oriole PS 40044	HI! WE'RE THE MIRACLES (LP)	300
64	Stateside SL 10099	THE FABULOUS MIRACLES (LP)	200
65	Tamla Motown TML 11003	I LIKE IT LIKE THAT (LP)	100
66	Tamla Motown TML 11024	GOIN' TO A GO-GO (LP, as Smokey Robinson & The Miracles, mono/stereo)	70/60
66	T. Motown (S)TML 11031	THE MIRACLES FROM THE BEGINNING (LP, mono/stereo)	60/55
67	T. Motown (S)TML 11044	AWAY WE A-GO-GO (LP, mono/stereo)	60/50

(The above albums are credited to The Miracles unless otherwise stated.)

68	T. Motown (S)TML 11067	MAKE IT HAPPEN (LP)	50
68	T. Motown (S)TML 11072	GREATEST HITS (LP)	20
69	T. Motown (S)TML 11089	SPECIAL OCCASION (LP)	30
69	T. Motown (S)TML 11107	SMOKEY ROBINSON & THE MIRACLES LIVE! (LP)	22
70	T. Motown (S)TML 11129	TIME OUT FOR SMOKEY ROBINSON & THE MIRACLES (LP)	20
70	T. Motown STML 11151	FOUR IN BLUE (LP)	30
70	T. Motown STML 11163	WHAT LOVE HAS JOINED TOGETHER (LP, unissued)	
71	T. Motown STML 11172	POCKETFUL OF MIRACLES (LP)	15
73	T. Motown STMA 8008	1957-1972 (LP, gatefold sleeve)	12
73	Motown STMA 8012	SMOKEY (LP, solo)	12

MIRAGE

65	CBS 201772	It's In Her Kiss/What Ye Gonna Do 'Bout It	20
65	CBS 202007	Go Away/Just A Face	20
66	Philips BF 1534	Tomorrow Never Knows/You Can't Be Serious	35
67	Philips BF 1554	Hold On/Can You Hear Me	15
67	Philips BF 1571	The Wedding Of Ramona Blair/Lazy Man	90
68	Page One POF 078	Mystery Lady/Chicago Cottage	12
68	Page One POF 111	Carolyn/World Goes On Around You	12

(see also Yellow Payges, Caleb, Jawbone, Spencer Davis Group, Portobello Explosion)

MIRETTES

68	Uni UN 501	In The Midnight Hour/To Love Somebody	8
68	Uni UN 505	The Real Thing/Take Me For A Little While	8
69	MCA Soul Bag BAG 8	Whirlpool/Ain't You Trying To Cross Over	10
72	Jay Boy BOY 65	Now That I've Found You Baby/He's Alright With Me	10
69	MCA MUP(S) 344	IN THE MIDNIGHT HOUR (LP)	30

(see also Ikettes)

MIRK

79	Mother Earth MUM 1205	MODDANS BOWER (LP)	175
82	Spring Thyme SPR 1009	TAK A DRAM AFOR YE GO (LP)	25

MIRKWOOD

71	Flams Ltd PR 1067	MIRKWOOD (LP)	500+
93	Tenth Planet TP 003	MIRKWOOD (LP, reissue, numbered with insert, 500 only)	20

STEVE MIRO & EYES

78	Object Music OM 03	Up And About/Smiling In Reverse (p/s)	6
79	Object Music OM 10	Dreams Of Desire/Queens Of The Sea (p/s)	5
80	Object Music OBF 008	RUDE INTRUSIONS (LP)	15
81	Object Music OBJ 015	SECOND SENTENCE (LP)	15

(see also Eyes, Noyes Bros)

MIRROR
68	Philips BF 1666	Gingerbread Man/Faster Than Light	65

MIRRORS
78	Lightning GIL 503	Cure For Cancer/Nice Vice (p/s)	15
79	Lightning GIL 540	Dark Glasses/999 (p/s)	15

MISFITS (U.K.)
66	A.S.C.C. PRI 101	You Won't See Me/Hanging Around (Aberdeen Students Charities Campaign)	10

(see also Complex)

MISFITS (U.S.)
81	Plan 9/Cherry Red PLP 9	BEWARE (12" EP)	120

MISSING PRESUMED DEAD
79	Sequel PART 2	Say It With Flowers/Double Life/Driving Home/Family Tree (p/s)	5
80s	Sequel PART 4	MISSING PRESUMED DEAD (LP)	12
80s	Sequel PART 5	REVENGE (LP)	12

MISSING SCIENTISTS
80	Rough Trade RT 057	Big City, Bright Lights/Discotheque X (p/s)	10

(see also Television Personalities, Slaughter)

MISSION
86	Chapter 22 CHAP 6/7	Serpent's Kiss/Wake (p/s)	5
86	Chapter 22 CHAP 7	Garden Of Delight/Like A Hurricane (p/s)	5
86	Chapter 22 L12 CHAP 7	Like A Hurricane/Garden Of Delight/Dancing Barefoot/The Crystal Ocean (12", autographed p/s)	8
86	Mercury MYSG 1	Stay With Me/Blood Brother (autographed, gatefold p/s)	5
88	Mercury MYTH 6	Beyond The Pale (p/s)	5
88	Mercury MYTHCD 6	Beyond The Pale/Tower Of Strength/Tadeusz (CD, card sleeve, numbered)	12
80s	Mercury MYCDB 8	Butterfly On A Wheel (CD, in box)	15
80s	Mercury MYCDB 8	Butterfly On A Wheel (2-CD, in limited box)	20
80s	Flexi FLEX 1	Crazy (1-track flexidisc)	12
90	Mercury MYTH 11	Hands Across The Ocean/Amelia/Love (p/s)	5
90	Phonogram MYTH 910	Deliverance/METAL GURUS: Virginia Plain (10", p/s)	7
90	Phonogram MYTHB 912	Deliverance/(Sorceror's Mix)/METAL GURUS: Virginia Plain (12", in box with poster)	8
90	Mercury MTHCD 9	Deliverance (CD)	8
92	Vertigo MYTH 1310	Like A Child Again/All Tangled Up In You (1-sided 10", etched, numbered p/s)	7
00	Phonogram MYTHB 2	IV: Wasteland/Shelter From The Storm (Live)//Serpent's Kiss (Live)/1969 (Live) (doublepack, in box, with insert and photos)	12
01	Playground PGND 001	Evangeline/Anyone But You//Melt/Swoon (Reprise) (double pack, pink & blue vinyl, gatefold p/s)	8

(see also Sisters Of Mercy, Dead Or Alive, Pauline Murray, Artery, Red Lorry Yellow Lorry, Expelaires, Knopov's Political Package, TV Product)

MISSION BELLES
65	Decca F 12154	Sincerely/When A Girl Really Loves You	15

MISSISSIPPI
70	Fox FOX 1	Mr. Union Railway Man/Main Street	10

MISS JANE
68	Pama PM 704	Bad Mind People/My Heart Is Aching (B-side act. "Witch Doctor" by Coolers)	12

MISS X (Joyce Blair)
63	Ember EMB S 175	Christine/S-E-X	10

MISTER MOST
69	Downtown DT 409	Reggae Train/Pushwood	8

MISTER VERSATILE
69	Jackpot JP 701	Apple Blossom/LITTLE BOY BLUE: Dark End Of The Street (act. by Pat Kelly)	10
69	Jackpot JP 702	Devil's Disciples/ERROL DUNKLEY: Having A Party	8

(see also Lester Sterling)

MISTURA feat. LLOYD MICHAELS
76	Route RT 30	The Flasher/Life Is A Song Worth Singing	6

MISTY
77	Cottage COT 511	MISTY (LP)	20

MISTY IN ROOTS
79	People Unite PU 001	See Them A Come/How Long Jah (12")	10
83	People Unite PU 102	Follow Fashion/Earth/Own Them Control Them/New Day (12")	8
79	People Unite PU 003	LIVE AT THE COUNTER EUROVISION '79 (LP)	20
82	People Unite PU 101 ALB	WISE AND FOOLISH (LP)	20

MISUNDERSTOOD
66	Fontana TF 777	I Can Take You To The Sun/Who Do You Love	55
69	Fontana TF 998	Children Of The Sun/I Unseen (small or large centre hole)	50/40
69	Fontana TF 1028	You're Tuff Enough/Little Red Rooster (as Misunderstood featuring Glenn "Fernando" Campbell, some in p/s)	60/35
69	Fontana TF 1041	Never Had A Girl (Like You Before)/Golden Glass (as Misunderstood featuring Glenn "Fernando" Campbell)	45
81	Cherry Red CHERRY 22	Children Of The Sun/Who Do You Love/I'll Take You To The Sun (p/s)	7
80s	Bucketfull Of Brains BOB 2	You're My Girl (flexidisc with *Bucketfull Of Brains* magazine)	8/5

(see also Juicy Lucy, High Tide, Van Der Graaf Generator, Answers)

MITCH
52	Stardom LA 1005	Cry Of The Wild Goose/Waltzing Matilda (78)	7

BLUE MITCHELL
69	Blue Note BST 84300	COLLISION IN BLACK (LP)	15
73	Mainstream MSL 1002	BLUE'S BLUES (LP)	12

MINT VALUE £

CHAD MITCHELL
62	London HLR 9509	Lizzie Borden/Super Skier	7

DENNY MITCHELL SOUNDSATIONS
64	Decca F 11848	I've Been Crying/For Your Love	8

(see also Preachers, Moon's Train)

GROVER MITCHELL
68	London HLU 10221	Turned On/Blue Over You	15
76	Vanguard VS 5003	What Hurts/Super Hero	60

GUY MITCHELL
53	Columbia SCM 5018	Feet Up (Pat Him On The Po-Po)/Jenny Kissed Me	45
53	Columbia SCM 5022	'Cause I Love Ya, That's A-Why/Train Of Love (both with Mindy Carson)	40
53	Columbia SCM 5032	She Wears Red Feathers/Why Should I Go Home?	45
53	Columbia SCM 5037	Pretty Little Black-Eyed Susie/MITCH MILLER HORNS: Horn Belt Boogie	40
56	Philips JK 1001	Singing The Blues/Crazy With Love (jukebox issue)	65
57	Philips JK 1005	Knee Deep In The Blues/Take Me Back Baby (jukebox issue)	30
57	Philips JK 1015	Rock-A-Billy/Got A Feeling (jukebox issue)	30
57	Philips JK 1023	Sweet Stuff/In The Middle Of A Dark, Dark Night (jukebox issue)	30
57	Philips JK 1027	Call Rosie On The Phone/Cure For The Blues (jukebox issue)	30
58	Philips PB 766	C'mon Let's Go/The Unbeliever (78 rpm = £6)	15
58	Philips PB 798	Wond'rin' And Worryin'/If Ya Don't Like It, Don't Knock It (78 rpm = £7)	10
58	Philips PB 830	Hangin' Around/Honey Brown Eyes (78 rpm = £8)	12
58	Philips PB 858	Let It Shine, Let It Shine/Butterfly Doll (78 rpm = £12)	12
58	Philips PB 885	My Heart Cries For You (2nd Version)/Till We're Engaged (78 rpm = £10)	8
59	Philips PB 915	Alias Jesse James/Pride O' Dixie (78 rpm = £18)	8
59	Philips PB 964	Heartaches By The Number/Two (some with triangular centre) (78 rpm = £20+)	12/6
60	Philips PB 998	The Same Old Me/Build My Gallows High (2nd version)	8
60	Philips PB 1026	Cry Hurtin' Heart/Symphony Of Spring	8
60	Philips PB 1050	Silver Moon Upon The Golden Sands/My Shoes Keep Walking Back To You	8
60	Philips PB 1084	Sunshine Guitar/One Way Street	8
61	Philips PB 1131	Your Goodnight Kiss/Follow Me	8
61	Philips PB 1183	Divorce/I'll Just Pretend	8
62	Philips PB 1202	Soft Rain/Big Big Change	8
63	Pye International 7N 25179	Go, Tiger, Go/If You Ever Go Away (unreleased)	
63	Pye International 7N 25185	Have I Told You Lately That I Love You/Blue Violet	8
66	CBS 202238	Singing The Blues/Rock-A-Billy	15
67	London HLB 10173	Traveling Shoes/Every Night Is A Lifetime	7
68	London HLB 10190	Alabam/Goodbye Road, Hello Home	7
68	London HLB 10218	Before You Take Your Love From Me/Singing The Blues	7
68	London HLB 10234	Just Wish You'd Maybe Change Your Mind/If You Could Cry Me My Tears	7

EPs
54	Columbia SEG 7513	PRETTY LITTLE BLACK EYED SUSIE plain sleeve)	15
55	Columbia SEG 7581	MY TRULY TRULY FAIR (plain sleeve)	15
55	Columbia SEG 7598	JENNY KISSED ME (plain sleeve)	15
55	Philips BBE 12008	GUY MITCHELL	20
56	Philips BBE 12093	GUY MITCHELL NO. 2	22
57	Philips BBE 12112	SINGING THE BLUES WITH GUY MITCHELL	20
58	Philips BBE 12215	GUY MITCHELL PHILIPS TV SERIES	25

LPs
54	Columbia 33S 1028	GUY MITCHELL SINGS (10")	60
55	Philips BBR 8031	THE VOICE OF YOUR CHOICE (10")	40
58	Philips BBL 7246	A GUY IN LOVE	40
58	Philips BBL 7265	SHOWCASE OF HITS	30
61	Philips BBL 7465	SUNSHINE GUITAR	40
66	CBS Realm RM 52336	THE BEST OF GUY MITCHELL	18
68	London HA-B 8364	TRAVELING SHOES (also stereo SH-B 8364)	22/25
77	CBS Embassy 31459	AMERICAN LEGEND	12
79	CBS Warwick PR 5066	20 GOLDEN GREATS	12
81	CBS 22109	THE HIT SINGLES 1950-1960 (2-LP)	18

(see also Mindy Carson)

JONI MITCHELL
68	Reprise RS 20694	Night In The City/I Had A King	10
69	Reprise RS 23402	Chelsea Morning/Both Sides Now	7
70	Reprise RS 20906	Big Yellow Taxi/Woodstock	5
72	Asylum AYM 511	You Turn Me On, I'm A Radio/Urge For Going	5
83	Geffen DA 3122	Chinese Cafe/Ladies Man (double pack, with bonus interview 7")	5
88	Geffen GEF 37CD	My Secret Place (with Peter Gabriel)/Number One/Chinese Cafe-Unchained Melody/Good Friends (3" CD, 5" case)	8
68	Reprise RSLP 6293	JONI MITCHELL (LP, gatefold sleeve, 'steamboat' label)	20
69	Reprise RSLP 6341	CLOUDS (LP, textured single sleeve, 'steamboat' label)	20
69	Reprise RSLP 6341	CLOUDS (LP, 2nd pressing, stickered U.S. gatefold sleeve, 'steamboat' label)	20
70	Reprise RSLP 6376	LADIES OF THE CANYON (LP, gatefold sleeve, 'steamboat' label)	20
71	Reprise K 44128	BLUE (LP, gatefold sleeve, some with blue inner sleeve)	15/12
73	Asylum SYLA 8753	FOR THE ROSES (LP, gatefold sleeve)	15
74	Asylum SYLA 8756	COURT AND SPARK (LP, gatefold sleeve)	15
75	Asylum SYSP 902	MILES OF AISLES (2-LP, gatefold sleeve with inner flap)	20
79	Asylum K 53091	MINGUS (LP, gatefold sleeve)	12
70s	Asylum AS 53002	COURT AND SPARK (LP, reissue)	12
70s	Asylum AS 53007	FOR THE ROSES (LP, reissue)	12
70s	Asylum K 53053	HEJIRA (LP, gatefold sleeve)	15
70s	Reprise REP 44085	LADIES OF THE CANYON (LP, reissue)	12
80	Asylum K 62030	SHADOWS AND LIGHT (2-LP, gatefold sleeve with inners)	20
82	Asylum/Nimbus K 53018	THE HISSING OF SUMMER LAWNS (LP, audiophile pressing, mail order issue)	12
80s	Geffen GEF 26455	DOG EAT DOG (LP)	12

KEITH MITCHELL
	70s	Spark SRLP 109	WORDS WORDS WORDS (LP) 12

McKINLEY 'SOUL' MITCHELL
68	President PT 125	The Town I Live In/No Love Like Your Love 7
68	President PTL 1005	McKINLEY 'SOUL' MITCHELL (LP) 15

PHILIP MITCHELL
71	Jay Boy BOY 37	I'm Gonna Build California From All Over The World/
		The World Needs More People Like You (DJ copy = £50) 40
72	Jay Boy BOY 57	Free For All/Flower Child (DJ copy = £25) 15

RED MITCHELL
| 62 | London LZ-N1 4017 | HAPPY MINORS (10" LP) .... 15 |
| 63 | London SH-K 8027 | HEAR YE!! HEAR YE!! (LP) .... 12 |

RONNIE MITCHELL
| 60 | London HLU 9220 | How Many Times/The Only Love .... 8 |

SINX MITCHELL
| 64 | Hickory 45-1248 | Weird Sensation/Love Is All I'm Asking For .... 20 |
| | *(see also Crickets, Earl Sinks)* | |

VALERIE MITCHELL
65	Oak RGJ 160	There Goes My Heart Again/If I Didn't Love You (p/s) 60
65	HMV POP 1422	Bitter Tears/Forbidden 7
65	HMV POP 1462	There Goes My Heart Again/If I Didn't Love You 7
65	HMV POP 1490	Go My Way/Green Eyes 7
66	HMV POP 1509	Play With Me/Never Let It Be Said 7
66	HMV POP 1529	You Can Go/The Windmill Girls 7
67	Columbia DB 8186	Love Can Be The Sweetest Thing/I'm Sorry. 6
67	Columbia DB 8265	Sunshine/You Belong To Me 6

WILLIE MITCHELL
64	London HLU 9926	20-75/Secret Home 20
65	London HLU 10004	Everything Is Gonna Be Alright/That Driving Beat (Boxed logo = £15) ... 25
66	London HLU 10039	Bad Eye/Sugar T. 10
66	London HLU 10085	Mercy/Sticks And Stones 10
68	London HLU 10186	Soul Serenade/Buster Browne. 20
68	London HLU 10215	Prayer Meetin'/Rum Daddy. 8
68	London HLU 10224	Up Hard/Beale Street Mood 10
70	London HLU 10313	Robbin's Nest/Six To Go 8
73	London HLU 10407	Last Tango In Paris/Six To Go 6
74	London HLU 10545	The Champion (2 parts) 10
67	London HA-U 8319	THE HIT SOUND OF WILLIE MITCHELL (LP) 30
68	London HA-U/SH-U 8365	SOUL SERENADE (LP) 25
68	London HA-U/SH-U 8368	LIVE (LP) 20
69	London HA-U/SH-U 8372	SOLID SOUL (LP) 25
70	London HA-U/SH-U 8388	ON TOP (LP) 25
70	London HA-U/SH-U 8408	SOUL BAG (LP) 25

MITCHELL/COE MYSTERIES
80	RCA PL 25297	EXILED (LP, with inner sleeve, initially with gatefold sleeve) 15/12
	(see also Colin Blunstone, Lesley Duncan, Dan McCafferty, Francis Rossi & Berni Frost, Ray Russell,	
	Joe Jammer, Complex, Monsoon)	

ROBERT MITCHUM
57	Capitol CL 14701	What Is This Generation Coming To?/Mama Looka Boo Boo (78 rpm = £8) 12
62	Capitol CL 15251	The Ballad Of Thunder Road/My Honey's Lovin' Arms. 10
67	Monument MON 1007	Little Ole Wine Drinker Me/Walker's Woods. 7
55	Brunswick OE 9197	RACHEL AND THE STRANGER (EP) 15
67	Monument LMO 5011	THAT MAN (LP) 20

MITHRANDIR
| 82 | New Leaf SVC 01 | MAGICK EP (p/s) .... 75 |
| 82 | New Leaf SVC 570 | Dreamers Of Fortune (p/s) .... 50 |

JACKIE MITTO(O)
66	Island WI 293	Killer Diller (as Jackie Mitto & Soul Brothers)/PATRICK HYTTON: Oh Lady .... 50+
67	Rio R 114	Home Made/ETHIOPIANS: I'm Gonna Take Over Now 25
67	Rio R 123	Got My Buglaoo/ETHIOPIANS: What To Do .... 50+
67	Coxsone CS 7002	Somebody Help Me/GAYLADS & SOUL VENDORS: The Sound Of Silence ... 25
67	Coxsone CS 7009	Ba Ba Boom/SLIM SMITH & FREEDOM SINGERS: Mercy Mercy. 22
67	Coxsone CS 7019	Ram Jam/SUMMERTAIRES: You're Gonna Leave 20
67	Coxsone CS 7026	Something Stupid/LYRICS: Money Lover 25
68	Coxsone CS 7040	Norwegian Wood/GAYLADS: Most Peculiar Man. 25
68	Coxsone CS 7042	Sure Shot/OCTAVES: The Bottle 35
68	Coxsone CS 7046	Man Pon Shot/BOP & BELTONES: Not For A Moment 25
68	Coxsone CS 7050	Napoleon Solo/CANNON BALL BRYAN: You're My Everything. .... 40+
68	Coxsone CS 7075	Mission Impossible/HEPTONES: Giddy Up (B-side actually by Actions) 25
68	Studio One SO 2043	Put It One/SOUL VENDORS: Chinese Chicken 25
68	Studio One SO 2056	Race Track/BASES: I Don't Mind. 30
69	Studio One SO 2082	Hi-Jack/TREVOR CLARKE: Sufferer 30
69	Doctor Bird DB 1177	Dark Of The Sun/MATADOR ALL STARS: Bridge View 35
69	Bamboo BAM 6	Our Thing (with Sound Dimension)/C. MARSHALL: Tra La La Sweet '69 . 18
69	Bamboo BAM 15	Clean Up/Spring Time (as Jackie Mittoo & Sound Dimension) 18
70	Bamboo BAM 17	Dark Of The Moon/Moon Walk (as Jackie Mittoo & Sound Dimension) 30
70	Bamboo BAM 20	Gold Dust/SUPERTONES: Real Gone Loser 18
70	Bamboo BAM 31	Can I Change My Mind/BRENTFORD ALLSTARS: Early Duckling. 18
70	Bamboo BAM 38	Baby Why/ETHIOPIANS: You'll Want To Come Back 18
70	Bamboo BAM 51	Dancing Groove/BLACK & GEORGE: Peanut Butter 22

70	Banana BA 315	Holly Holy/LARRY MARSHALL: I've Got To Make It	15
71	Banana BA 320	Peenie Wallie/ROY RICHARDS: Can't Go On	12
72	London HLU 10357	Wishbone/Soul Bird (as Jackie Mittoo — The Reggae Beat)	7
80	Rite Sound RTA 06	Mystic World/Version (12")	
81	Black Roots BR20	These Eyes/Wall Street/Thriller The Killer (12")	25
67	Coxsone CSL 8009	IN LONDON (LP)	95
68	Coxsone CSL 8014	EVENING TIME (LP, with Soul Vendors)	95
69	Coxsone CSL 8020	KEEP ON DANCING (LP)	110
70	Bamboo BDLP 209	NOW (LP)	55
72	London SHU 8436	WISHBONE (LP)	25

(see also Lord Tanamo, Jamaican Actions, Matadors, Jackie Opel, Soul Vendors, Winston Francis, Donna & Freedom Singers, Skatalites)

MIX BLOOD
| 80 | Creole CR 201 | Last Train To Skaville/Move And Move (p/s) | 10 |

MIXED BAG
| 69 | Decca F 12880 | Potiphar (with Ramases III Orchestra)/Million Dollar Bash | 5 |
| 69 | Decca F 12907 | Round And Round/Have You Ever Been In Love | 5 |

MIXMAN
| 90 | Citizen Kane 12KANE 2 | Bright Child (Manmix)/Bright Child (Dancemix) (12", p/s) | 10 |

MIXTURE
| 65 | Fontana TF 640 | One By One/Monkey Jazz | 8 |
| 69 | Parlophone R 5755 | Sad Old Song/Never Trust In Tomorrow | 7 |

JOHN MIZAROLLI
| 82 | Carrere CAL 142 | MESSAGE FROM THE 5TH STONE (LP) | 12 |

VIC MIZZY, HIS ORCHESTRA & CHORUS
| 65 | RCA RCA 1440 | Addams Family Main Theme/Kentucky James Main Theme | 20 |

M.J.6
| 60 | Decca F 11212 | Tracy's Theme/Private Eye | 6 |

M.J.Q.
(see under Modern Jazz Quartet)

MO & STEVE
| 66 | Pye 7N 17175 | Oh What A Day It's Going To Be/Reach Out For Your Lovin' Touch | 5 |

MOB
68	Mercury MF 1026	Disappear/I Wish You Would Leave Me Alone	6
71	Polydor 2001 127	I Dig Everything About You/Love's Got A Hold On Me	6
71	Polydor 2001 169	Give It To Me/I'd Like To See More Of You	5
71	Polydor 2001 200	Money/Once A Man Twice A Child	5
73	MGM 2006 278	Tear The House Down/One Way Ticket To Nowhere	5
74	UK USA 4	Give It To Me/I'd Like To See More Of You	8
75	Private Stock PVT 32	I Can't Stop This Love Song/Hot Music	12
71	Polydor 2344 001	MOB (LP)	12

MOB
| 80 | Kalida AKB 1/2 | Send Me To Coventry/Mobbed (p/s) | 8 |

MOB
80	All The Madmen MAD 1	Youth/Crying Again (p/s)	7
80	All The Madmen MAD 002	Witch Hunt/Shuffling Souls/What's Going On (EP, handwritten white labels with sticker & foldout, stapled, gatefold p/s)	6
82	Crass 321984/7	No Doves Fly Here/I Hear You Laughing (foldout p/s)	5
83	All The Madmen MAD 6	The Mirror Breaks/Stay (screen-printed p/s, with lyric insert)	5
80s	All/Madmen MADPACK 1	MAD PACK 1 (3 x 7" in 12" pack)	12

JOHN MOBLEY
| 62 | Stateside SS 136 | Tunnel Of Love/Work Out | 10 |

MOBSTER
| 80 | Ensign ENY 41 | The Mobster Shuffle/Simmer Down (p/s) | 6 |
| 81 | Ensign ENY 209 | Perfect Man/Trinidad (p/s) | 5 |

MOBY DICK
| 82 | Ebony EBON 5 | Nothing To Fear/Can't Have My Body Tonight | 6 |

MOBY GRAPE
67	CBS 2953	Omaha/Hey Grandma	25
68	CBS 3555	Can't Be So Bad/Murder In My Heart For The Judge	7
69	CBS 3945	Trucking Man/Ooh Mama Ooh	8
67	CBS (S)BPG 63090	MOBY GRAPE (LP)	30
68	CBS 63271	WOW (LP, mono & stereo)	25
69	CBS 63430	'69 (LP, mono & stereo)	25
69	CBS 63698	TRULY FINE CITIZEN (LP, mono & stereo)	25
72	Reprise K 44152	20 GRANITE CREEK (LP)	18
74	CBS 64743	GREAT GRAPE (LP)	18

MOCEDADES
| 73 | Bell BELL 1303 | Touch The Wind/Eres Tu | 6 |

MOCKINGBIRDS
65	Columbia DB 7480	That's How It's Gonna Stay/I Never Should Have Kissed You	55
65	Columbia DB 7565	I Can Feel We're Parting/The Flight Of The Mockingbird	55
65	Immediate IM 015	You Stole My Love/Skit Skat	110
66	Decca F 12434	One By One/Lovingly Yours	50
66	Decca F 12510	How To Find A Lover/My Story	48

(see also 10cc, Graham Gouldman, Whirlwinds, Doctor Father, Hotlegs, Godley & Greme)

MOCK TURTLES
87 Imaginary MIRAGE 003   POMONA (12" EP, with press sheets & photos) 15
(see also Judge Happiness)

M.O.D.
79 Vertigo 6059 233   M.O.D./M.O.D. (2) (p/s, some allegedly mispressed on 2-Tone label) .... 75+/7
(see also David Essex)

MODE
66 private pressing   THE MODE (EP, white labels, no p/s) 260

MODEL MANIA
79 Boob MM1 A/MM 1AA   No Pride Slow Suicide/Epic Cowboy (250 with handmade stamped label,
750 with black labels) 100/75

MODELS
77 Step Forward SF 3   Freeze/Man Of The Year (p/s)... 20
(see also Adam & The Ants, Mass, Rema Rema, Wolfgang Press)

MODERATES
80 Open Eye OEEP 1001   FETISHES (12" EP) 8

MODERNAIRES (U.K.)
80 Illuminated ILL 2   Life In Our Times/Barbed Up (p/s)....................................... 5
81 Illuminated ILL 4   We Did It Again/And Again (p/s, red vinyl) 5

MODERNAIRES (U.S.)
54 Vogue Coral Q 2024   Teach Me Tonight/Mood Indigo (with Georgie Auld) 8
54 Vogue Coral Q 2035   New Juke Box Saturday Night/Bugle Call Rag 8
55 Vogue Coral Q 72069   Birds And Puppies And Tropical Fish/Mine! Mine! Mine! 8
55 Vogue Coral Q 72084   Wine, Women And Gold/Sluefoot (with Bob Crosby Bob Cats)............. 8
55 Vogue Coral Q 72112   At My Front Door/Alright, Okay, You Win 8
55 Vogue Coral LVC 10012   STOP, LOOK AND LISTEN (10" LP) 22
58 Coral LVA 9080   HERE COME THE MODERNAIRES (LP) 15
(see also Four Guys, Bing Crosby)

MODERN ART
84 Color Disc COLORS 1   Dreams To Live/Beautiful Truth (p/s) 25
86 Color Disc COLORS 5   Penny Valentine/One Way Ticket (1-sided, clear vinyl flexidisc, 1,000 only) .. 12
87 Color Disc COLOR 3   STEREOLAND (LP, hand-stencilled with insert, 300 only) 60
94 Acme 8007 LP   ALL ABOARD THE MIND TRAIN (LP, 500 only, numbered).................. 10
(see also Sun Dial)

MODERN ENGLISH
79 Limp LMP 2   Drowning Man/Silent World (p/s)....................................... 15
80 4AD AD 6   Swans On Glass/Incident (p/s) 7
80 4AD AD 15   Gathering Dust/Tranquility Of A Summer Moment (p/s)................... 6
81 4AD AD 110   Smiles And Laughter/Mesh And Lace (p/s) 5
82 4AD BAD 208   Life In The Gladhouse/The Choicest View (12", p/s)..................... 8
82 4AD AD 212   I Melt With You/The Prize (p/s).. 5
83 4AD AD 309   Someone's Calling/Life In The Gladhouse (p/s)......................... 5
84 4AD AD 401   Chapter 12/Ringing In The Change (p/s) 5
(see also This Mortal Coil)

MODERN EON
80 Modern Eon EON 001   PIECES (EP)... 20
80 Inevitable INEV 3   Euthenics/Waiting For The Cavalry (p/s) 8
81 Dinsales 2   Euthenics/Choreography/Waiting For The Cavalry/The Real Hymn
(12", white label LP sampler)... 30
81 DinDisc DIN 30   Euthenics (New Version)/Cardinal Signs (tri-gatefold folder p/s) 5
81 DinDisc DID 11   FICTION TALES (LP)... 12

MODERN FOLK QUARTET (M.F.Q.)
64 Warner Bros WB 147   The Love Of A Clown/If You All Think.................................. 20
66 RCA RCA 1514   Night Time Girl/Lifetime (as M.F.Q.) 25
63 Warner Bros WM/WS 8135   THE MODERN FOLK QUARTET (LP)................................... 18
85 Off Beat WIK 55   MOONLIGHT SERENADE (LP) 12

MODERN JAZZ QUARTET (M.J.Q.)
50s Esquire EP 106   MODERN JAZZ QUARTET (EP) 8
50s Esquire EP 109   MODERN JAZZ QUARTET (EP) 8
50s Esquire EP 116   GERSHWIN BALLAD MEDLEY (EP) 8
50s Esquire EP 166   FIVE WAYS OF PLAYING LA RONDE (EP) 8
50s Fontana 469 204TE   ALL OF YOU (EP) 8
57 London Jazz EZ-C 19019   THE QUARTET (EP, as The Quartet) 8
59 London Jazz EZ-K 19046   ONE NEVER KNOWS (EP) 8
59 London Jazz EZ-K 19047   THE MODERN JAZZ QUARTET (EP) 8
61 London Jazz RE-K 1314   MODERN JAZZ QUARTET (EP) 8
61 London Jazz RE-K 1320   MODERN JAZZ QUARTET AT MUSIC INN (EP) 10
62 London Jazz RE-K 1319   MODERN JAZZ QUARTET — EUROPEAN CONCERT (EP) 10
55 Esquire 20-069   MODERN JAZZ QUARTET (10" LP) 15
55 Esquire 20-038   MODERN JAZZ QUARTET VOL. 2 (10" LP) 15
55 Esquire 20-090   THE CLASSICAL PERFORMANCES OF... (10" LP).......................... 15
57 London Jazz LTZK 15022   FONTESSA (LP, also stereo SAH-K 6031)...................... each 15
58 London Jazz LTZK 15085   AT THE MUSIC INN (LP) 12
58 London Jazz LTZ 15136   MODERN JAZZ QUARTET (LP) 12
59 London Jazz LTZ-K 15140   PLAYS ONE NEVER KNOWS (LP, also stereo SAH-K 6029) .... each 15
59 London Jazz LTZK 15181   ODDS AGAINST TOMORROW (LP) 15
59 Columbia Clef 33CX 11028   MODERN JAZZ QUARTET & OSCAR PETERSON AT THE OPERA HOUSE (LP) .. 12
60 London Jazz LTZ-K 15193   PYRAMID (LP, also stereo SAH-K 6086).................................. 15
61 London Jazz LTZ-K 15207   THIRD STREAM MUSIC (LP, with Beaux Arts String Quartet
& Jimmy Giuffre Three) 15

MINT VALUE £

61	London Jazz LTZK 15222	EUROPEAN CONCERT (LP)	12
61	Esquire 32-124	LOOKING BACK AT THE MODERN JAZZ QUARTET (LP)	12
63	London HA-K/SH-K 8016	LONELY WOMAN (LP)	15
63	London HA-K/SH-K 8046	THE COMEDY SUITE (LP)	15
64	London HA-K/SH-K 8161	THE SHERIFF (LP)	15
65	Stateside SL 10141	THE BEST OF THE MODERN JAZZ QUARTET (LP)	15
66	Atlantic 587 044	A QUARTET IS A QUARTET IS A QUARTET (LP)	12
68	Atlantic 590 012	STOCKHOLM CONCERT (LP)	12
68	Apple (S)APCOR 4	UNDER THE JASMINE TREE (LP, mono/stereo)	50/30
69	Apple SAPCOR 10	SPACE (LP, gatefold sleeve, dark green label, black inner)	50
70s	Apple SAPCOR 10	SPACE (LP, later pressing, light green label, single sl., white 'Apple' inner)	75
93	Apple SAPCOR 4	UNDER THE JASMINE TREE (LP, reissue, gatefold sleeve with inner)	20
93	Apple SAPCOR 10	SPACE (LP, reissue)	15

(see also John Lewis, Milt Jackson, Sonny Rollins)

MODERN JAZZ SEXTET
56	Columbia Clef 33CX 10048	MODERN JAZZ SEXTET (LP)	15

MODERN JAZZ SOCIETY
56	Columbia Clef 33CX 10038	A CONCERT OF CONTEMPORARY MUSIC (LP)	12

MODERN LOVERS
76	Berkeley BSERK 1	MODERN LOVERS (LP)	12

MODERN TALKING
86	RCA PD 71133	READY FOR ROMANCE (CD)	50

MO-DETTES
79	Mode/Rough Trade MODE 1	White Mice/Masochistic Opposite (pink [card or paper] or white p/s)	4/6
80	S.F.I. SFI 550/MODE 1½	Twist And Shout (gig freebie flexidisc, different label design to later issue)	5
80	Deram DET-R-1/MODE 1½	Paint It Black/Bitta Truth (with free flexidisc "Twist And Shout" & insert, black & white or blue & white p/s)	each 6
81	Deram DET 3	Tonight/Waltz In Blue Minor (p/s)	5
81	Human HUM 10	White Mice/Kray Twins (live) (p/s)	5
80	Deram SML 1120	THE STORY SO FAR (LP, with insert & free colour sticker)	15

MODIFIES
70	Punch PH 45	Bye Bye Happyness/Sufferation We Must Bear	6

MODS
64	RCA RCA 1399	Something On My Mind/You're Making Me Blue	12

MODS
80	Bootlegged Records 007	LOST TOUCH (LP; sold only in Portobello Market, London)	25

MOD '79
79	Casino Classics CC 13	Green Onions/High On Your Love	6

MODULATIONS
74	Buddah BDS 406	I Can't Fight Your Love/Your Love Has Locked Me Up	15
70s	Buddah	THE MODULATIONS (LP)	40

MOE
88	Times Five T5 01	There Were Four Other Guys/One Man Went To Moe (12", p/s)	8

PETER MOESSER'S MUSIC
70	Stateside SS 2182	Hello/Bye Bye (withdrawn)	5

MOFFAT ALL STARS
70	Jackpot JP 719	Riot/IMPERSONATORS: Girls And Boys	12

MOGUL THRASH
70	RCA RCA 2030	Sleeping In The Kitchen/St. Peter	22
71	RCA SF 8156	MOGUL THRASH (LP)	40

(see also Colosseum, Eclection, Family, King Crimson)

MOGWAI
96	Rock Action RAR 01	Tuner/Lower (p/s, 500 only)	50
96	Ché CHE 059	4 TRACK 3 BAND TOUR EP (with Urusei Yatsura & Backwater, p/s, 50 only)	25
96	Ché CHE 61	Angels Vs Aliens/DWEEB: Buzzsong (p/s, 1st 500 on green vinyl)	12/6
96	Love Train PUBE 014	Summer/Ithica 27*9 (p/s, 1,500 only)	20
97	Wurlitzer Jukebox WJ 22	New Paths To Helicon (Parts 1 & 2) (foldover p/s in polythene bag, 1,000 only)	30
97	Flotsam/Jetsam SHAG13.04	Stereo Dee/PH FAMILY: Club Beatroot Part 4 (p/s, 400 only)	45
	Chemikal Underground CHEM 015	4 SATIN EP	8
97	Chemikal Underground CHEM 818LP	YOUNG TEAM (2 x LP)	25
98	Eye EYEUK 032	FEAR SATAN REMIXES: My Bloody Valentine Remix/M-ziq Remix/Surgeon Remix (12", p/s)	12
01	Chrysalis 9460013221	FIVE TRACK TOUR SINGLE: Close Encounters/Drum Machine/D To E/You Don't Know Jesus/Helicon (tour CD, card sleeve)	45
98	Eye Q EYEUKLP 019	KICKING A DEAD PIG (2-LP)	18

(see also Magoo)

ESSRA MOHAWK
75	Mooncrest CREST 24	ESSRA MOHAWK (LP, with insert)	15
77	Private Stock PVLP 1016	ESSRA (LP)	15

MOHAWKS
68	Pama PM 719	The Champ/Sound Of The Witchdoctors (blue label/purple label)	30/20
68	Pama PM 739	Baby Hold On (Parts 1 & 2)	15
68	Pama PM 751	Sweet Soul Music/Hip Jigger	15
68	Pama PM 757	Mony Mony/Pepsi	45
69	Pama PM 758	Ride Your Pony/Western Promise	20

69	Pama PM 798	Skinhead Shuffle/RICO: Red Cow	40
70	Pama PM 796	Landscape/Number 1	20
70	Supreme SUP 204	Let It Be/Looking Back	10
70	Supreme SUP 207	Give Me Some/(Instrumental)	150
86	Pama PM (T) 1	The Champ/Landscape (12", p/s)	8
68	Pama PMLP 5	THE CHAMP (LP)	125+

MOIST

86	Debris DEB 9/LYN 19589	The Cut Up 1/KING OF THE SLUMS: Haemophiliacs On Tacks (33rpm flexidisc free with *Debris* magazine)	8/6
95	Chrysalis 12CHSS 5019	SILVER (12" EP, clear vinyl)	10

MOJO HANNAH

73	Kingdom KV 8008	Six Days On The Road/Moon Dog's Gonna Howl Tonight	5
73	Kingdom KVL 9001	SIX DAYS ON THE ROAD (LP)	15

MOJO MEN

65	Pye International 7N 25336	Dance With Me/The Loneliest Boy In Town	28
66	Reprise RS 20486	Hanky Panky/She's My Baby	38
67	Reprise RS 20539	Sit Down I Think I Love You/Don't Leave Me Crying Like Before	12
67	Reprise RS 20580	Me About You/When You're In Love	12

MOJOS

63	Decca F 11732	They Say/Forever	15
64	Decca F 11853	Everything's Alright/Give Your Lovin' To Me	12
64	Decca F 11918	Why Not Tonight/Don/t Do It Any More	8
64	Decca F 11959	Seven Daffodils/Nothin' At All	8
65	Decca F 12127	Comin' On To Cry/That's The Way It Goes	15
67	Decca F 12557	Goodbye Dolly Gray/I Just Can't Let Her Go	18
68	Liberty LBF 15097	Until My Baby Comes Home/Seven Park Avenue	50
64	Decca DFE 8591	THE MOJOS (EP)	70

(see also Stu James & Mojos, Faron's Flamingos)

MOLES

68	Parlophone R 5743	We Are The Moles (Parts 1 & 2)	35

(see also Simon Dupree & Big Sound)

MOLESTERS

79	Small Wonder SMALL 14	Disco Love/Commuter Man (p/s)	5
79	Small Wonder SMALL 18	End Of Civilisation/Girl Behind The Curtain (p/s)	5

MOMENT

85	Diamond DIA 004	In This Town/Just Once	6
85	Diamond DIA 008	One, Two, They Fly/Karl's New Haircut	5
80s	Tenth Floor	Poor Mr. Diamond (Parts 1 & 2)	10
89	Big Stuff	Ready To Fall (promo only)	8
86	Rave RAVE UP 1	THE WORK GETS DONE (LP, coloured vinyl)	12

MOMENT OF TRUTH

75	Pye Int. 7N 25679	Helplessly/(Part 2)	8
77	Salsoul SZ 2025	You've Got Me Hummin'/At Long Last	5

MOMENTS

63	London HLN 9656	Walk Right In/Walk Right In (Instrumental)	12

MOMENTS

72	London HLU 10378	Love On A Two Way Street/I Won't Do Anything	8
74	London HL 10449	Sexy Mama/Where Can I Find Her	8
74	All Platinum 6146 322	Next Time I See You/It Don't Rain In My Backyard	8
75	All Platinum 6146 309	Look At Me/French Version	6
76	All Platinum 6146313	Nine Times	8
75	All Platinum 9109 302	SHARP (LP)	20

(see also Fabulous Impact)

MOMUS

86	Él GPO 9T	Nicky/Don't Leave/See A Friend In Tears (12")	20
87	Creation CRE 037 T	Murderers, The Hope Of Women (12", p/s)	12
90	Creation CRELP 052	DON'T STOP THE NIGHT (LP)	15
91	Creation CRELP 059	MONSTERS OF LOVE (LP)	12
91	Creation CRELP 097	HIPPOPOTAMOMUS (LP, with "Michelin Man" track & Michelin Man style inlay, withdrawn)	15
91	Creation CRECD 097	HIPPOPOTAMOMUS (CD, with "Michelin Man" track & Michelin Man style inlay, withdrawn)	22
92	Creation	SPACEWALK EP (CD)	20
93	Creation CRECD 151	TIMELORD (CD)	18
94	Creation CRECD 052	DON'T STOP THE NIGHT (CD)	18
94	Creation CRECD 059	MONSTERS OF LOVE (CD)	18
88	Creation CRECD 036	TENDER PERVERT (CD)	18
03	Analogue Baroque	FORBIDDEN SOFTWARE TIME MACHINE: THE BEST OF THE CREATION YEARS 1987-1993 (CD)	18

(see also Happy Family)

MONARCHS

64	London HLU 9862	Look Homeward Angel/What's Made You Change Your Mind	45

JULIE MONDAY

66	London HLU 10080	Come Share The Good Times With Me/Time Is Running Out For Me	8

MONDO KANE

86	Lisson DOLEQ 2	New York Afternoon (mixes)/Manhattan Morning (12", p/s)	10

(see also Georgie Fame)

MONEY
79	Gull GULL 64	Aren't We All Searching/Where Have All The Dancers Gone	8
80	Hobo HOS 011	FAST WORLD (EP, p/s)	80
79	Gull GULP 1031	FIRST INVESTMENT (LP)	25

(see also Iron Maiden)

ZOOT MONEY('S BIG ROLL BAND)
64	Decca F 11954	The Uncle Willie/Zoot's Suit (solo)	50
65	Columbia DB 7518	Good/Bring It Home To Me	28
65	Columbia DB 7600	Please Stay/You Know You'll Cry	32
65	Columbia DB 7697	Something Is Worrying Me/Stubborn Kind Of Fellow	30
65	Columbia DB 7768	The Many Faces Of Love/Jump Back (as Paul Williams & Zoot Money Band)	32
66	Columbia DB 7876	Let's Run For Cover/Self-Discipline	30
66	Columbia DB 7975	Big Time Operator/Zoot's Sermon	20
66	Columbia DB 8090	The Star Of The Show (The La La Song)/The Mound Moves	22
67	Columbia DB 8172	Nick Knack/I Really Learnt How To Cry	22
70	Polydor 2058 020	No One But You/Prisoner	8
80	Magic Moon/MPL MACH 3	Your Feet's Too Big/Ain't Nothin' Shakin' But The Bacon (solo)	12
80	Magic Moon/MPL MACH 6	The Two Of Us/Ain't Nothin' Shakin' But The Bacon (solo)	30
66	Columbia SEG 8519	BIG TIME OPERATOR (EP)	275
66	Columbia S(C)X 6075	ZOOT! — LIVE AT KLOOK'S KLEEK (LP, mono/stereo)	70/80
65	Columbia 33SX 1734	IT SHOULD'VE BEEN ME (LP)	70
68	Direction 8-63231	TRANSITION (LP)	55
70	Polydor 2482 019	ZOOT MONEY (LP)	22
80	Magic Moon/MPL LUNE 1	MR. MONEY (LP, solo)	18

(see also Paul Williams & Big Roll Band, Dantalian's Chariot, Eric Burdon & Animals, Grimms, Centipede, Ellis, Johnny Almond Music Machine)

MONEY MARK
94	Mo' Wax MW 032	Cry/Insects Are All Around Us (p/s)	6
95	Mo' Wax MW 036CD	Cry/(mixes)/Never Stop/Invitation (CD, card sleeve)	10
95	Mo' Wax MW 044	LEGITIMATE POP SONGS?: Untitled Instrumental/Sometimes You Gotta Make It Alone/Untitled Instrumental (EP, die-cut sleeve)	6
98	Mo' Wax MW 089	Maybe I'm Dead/(mixes) (12", die-cut picture disc)	8

(see also Beastie Boys)

MONGREL
73	Polydor 2058 318	Lonely Street/Sing A Little Song	5
73	Polydor 2058 347	Last Night/Twist Her Hand	5
73	Polydor 2383 182	GET YOUR TEETH INTO THIS (LP)	25

MONGRELS
64	Decca F 12003	I Long To Hear/Everywhere	30
65	Decca F 12086	My Love For You/Stewball	30

(see also Bobbie Miller)

MONITORS
69	T. Motown (S)TML 11108	GREETINGS WE'RE THE MONITORS (LP)	100

THELONIOUS MONK
63	CBS AAG 172	Hackensack/Bye Ya	5
56	Vogue EPV 1115	THELONIOUS MONK (EP)	10
50s	Esquire EP 75	THELONIOUS MONK TRIO (EP)	8
50s	Esquire EP 148	SONNY ROLLINS AND THELONIOUS MONK (EP)	8
61	Esquire EP 236	NUTTY MONK (EP)	8
62	Esquire EP 246	BLUE MONK (EP)	8
60s	Riverside REP 3214	NUTTY (EP, as Thelonious Monk & John Coltrane)	8
60s	Riverside REP 3217	RUBY MY DEAR (EP, as Thelonious Monk & John Coltrane)	8
55	Esquire 20-039	THELONIOUS MONK QUINTET (10" LP)	18
55	Esquire 20-049	THELONIOUS MONK (10" LP)	18
56	Esquire 20-075	THELONIOUS MONK PLAYS (10" LP)	18
60	Esquire 32-109	THELONIOUS MONK QUINTETS (LP)	15
61	Esquire 32-115	WORK! (LP, with Art Blakey & Sonny Rollins)	15
61	Esquire 32-119	MONK'S MOODS (LP)	15
61	Riverside RLP 12-201	MONK PLAYS ELLINGTON (LP)	15
61	Philips BBL 1510	THELONIOUS MONK VOL. 1 (LP)	15
61	Riverside RLP 12-226	BRILLIANT CORNERS (LP)	15
61	Riverside RLP 12-262	MONK IN ACTION (LP)	15
62	Riverside RLP 12-300	AT THE TOWN HALL (LP, also stereo RLP 1138)	each 15
62	Riverside RLP 12-323	AT THE BLACK HAWK (LP, also stereo RLP 1171)	each 15
62	Philips BBL 1511	THELONIOUS MONK VOL. 2 (LP)	15
62	Riverside RLP 12-242	MONK'S MUSIC (LP)	15
63	CBS (S)BPG 62135	MONK'S DREAM (LP)	15
63	Riverside RLP 12-235	THELONIOUS HIMSELF (LP)	15
63	Riverside JLP (9)46	THELONIOUS MONK AND JOHN COLTRANE (LP)	15
64	Riverside RLP 002	IN EUROPE (VOL. 1)	15
64	CBS (S)BPG 62173	CRISS-CROSS (LP)	15
64	Blue Note (B)BLP 1510	THE GENIUS OF MODERN MUSIC (VOL. 1) (LP)	15
64	Blue Note (B)BLP 1511	THE GENIUS OF MODERN MUSIC (VOL. 2) (LP)	15
64	Riverside RLP 279	MISTERIOSO (LP)	15
64	CBS (S)BPG 62248	BIG BAND AND QUARTET IN CONCERT (LP)	15
65	CBS (S)BPG 62391	IT'S MONK'S TIME (LP)	15
65	Riverside RLP 305	FIVE BY MONK BY FIVE (LP)	15
65	Riverside RLP 003	IN EUROPE (VOL. 2) (LP)	15
65	CBS (S)BPG 62497	MONK (LP)	15
65	Riverside RLP 312	ALONE IN SAN FRANCISCO (LP)	15
65	Fontana FJL 113	WAY OUT! (LP)	15
65	Realm RM 52223	NICA'S TEMPO (LP, with Gigi Gryce)	12
65	CBS (S)BPG 62549	SOLO (LP)	15

Rare Record Price Guide 2008

MINT VALUE £

65	Stateside SL 10152	THE GOLDEN MONK (LP)	15
66	Riverside RLP 004	IN EUROPE (VOL. 3)	12
66	CBS (S)BPG 62620	MISTERIOSO (LP, reissue)	12
67	CBS (S)BPG 63009	STRAIGHT, NO CHASER (LP)	12
67	Transatlantic PR 7169	WORK (LP)	12
69	CBS 63609	MONK'S BLUES (LP)	12
69	Storyville 673 014	THELONIOUS MONK PLAYS DUKE (LP)	12
69	Storyville 673 022	IN CONCERT (LP)	12
70	Storyville 673 024	*THE* THELONIOUS MONK (LP)	12

(see also John Coltrane, Sonny Rollins, Art Blakey, Miles Davis)

MONKEES
SINGLES

66	RCA Victor RCA 1547	Last Train To Clarksville/Take A Giant Step	8
66	RCA Victor RCA 1560	I'm A Believer/(I'm Not Your) Stepping Stone	5
67	RCA Victor RCA 1580	A Little Bit Me, A Little Bit You/The Girl I Knew Somewhere	7
67	RCA Victor RCA 1604	Alternate Title/Forget That Girl	7
67	RCA Victor RCA 1620	Pleasant Valley Sunday/Words	7
67	RCA Victor RCA 1645	Daydream Believer/Goin' Down	7
68	RCA Victor RCA 1673	Valleri/Tapioca Tundra	8
68	RCA Victor RCA 1706	D.W. Washburn/It's Nice To Be With You	8
69	RCA RCA 1802	Teardrop City/Man Without A Dream	8
69	RCA RCA 1824	Someday Man/Listen To The Band	8
69	RCA RCA 1862	Daddy's Song/The Porpoise Song	10
69	RCA RCA 1887	Mommy And Daddy/Good Clean Fun	10
70	RCA RCA 1958	Oh My My/Love You Better	12
74	Bell BLL 1354	Monkees Theme/I'm A Believer	6
80	Arista ARIST 326	THE MONKEES (EP, p/s)	8
81	Arista ARIST 402	THE MONKEES VOL. 2 (EP, p/s)	8
82	Arista ARIST 487	I'M A BELIEVER (EP, p/s)	8
84	Scoop 7SR 5035	6 TRACK HITS (EP, p/s)	15
84	Scoop 7SC 5035	6 TRACK HITS (EP, cassette)	12
86	Arista ARIST 673	That Was Then, This Is Now/(Theme From) The Monkees (p/s)	6
86	Arista ARIST 1673	That Was Then, This Is Now/(Theme From) The Monkees ('Dolenz' picture disc)	7
86	Arista ARIST 2673	That Was Then, This Is Now/(Theme From) The Monkees ('Tork' picture disc)	7
86	Arista ARIST 3673	That Was Then, This Is Now/(Theme From) The Monkees ('Jones' picture disc)	7
86	Arista ARIST 4673	That Was Then, This Is Now/(Theme From) The Monkees ('group' picture disc)	10
86	Arista ARIST 12673	That Was Then, This Is Now/Pleasant Valley Sunday/(Theme From) The Monkees/Last Train To Clarksville (12", p/s)	12
89	Arista 112 157	THE MONKEES (EP, p/s)	8
89	Arista 112 157	THE MONKEES (EP, box set, with booklet & sew-on patch)	15
89	Arista 112 157	THE MONKEES (10" EP, promo only, no p/s)	20
89	Arista 112 158	THE MONKEES VOL. 2 (EP, p/s)	8
89	Arista 112 158	THE MONKEES VOL. 2 (10" EP, promo only, no p/s)	20
89	Arista 662 158	THE MONKEES VOL. 2 (CD EP, card sleeve with anti-static inner)	15
89	Arista 162 053	Last Train To Clarksville/Take A Giant Step/I'm A Believer/(I'm Not Your) Stepping Stone (3" CD, gatefold card sleeve in blister pack)	10

LPs

67	RCA Victor RD/SF 7844	THE MONKEES (LP, mono/stereo)	18/20
67	RCA Victor RD/SF 7868	MORE OF THE MONKEES (LP, mono/stereo)	18/20
67	RCA Victor RD/SF 7886	HEADQUARTERS (LP, mono/stereo)	20/22
67	RCA Victor RD/SF 7886	HEADQUARTERS (LP, with different 'beard' photo on back, mono/stereo)	25/30
67	RCA Victor RD/SF 7912	PISCES, AQUARIUS, CAPRICORN AND JONES LTD. (LP)	25
68	RCA Victor RD/SF 7948	THE BIRDS, THE BEES & THE MONKEES (LP)	25

(The above albums were originally issued with black labels; later orange label copies are worth the same value.)

69	RCA RD/SF 8016	INSTANT REPLAY (LP, mono/stereo)	35/30
69	RCA RD/SF 8051	HEAD (LP, soundtrack, mono/stereo)	80/55
73	M.F. Pleasure SPR 90032	THE MONKEES (LP, 'Sounds Superb' series, black 'circus' sleeve)	12
79	Arista MONK-1 1/2	MONKEEMANIA (LP)	25
81	Arista DARTY 12	THE MONKEES (2-LP)	18
83	Arista RS 10063	HERE COME THE MONKEES (LP, part of *Reader's Digest* v/a box set)	15
89	Circus BOY 1	IDOLISED, PLASTICISED, PSYCHOANLYSED, STERILISED (LP, spoken-word convention issue, white vinyl)	18
89	Circus BOY 1	IDOLISED, PLASTICISED, PSYCHOANLYSED, STERILISED (LP, spoken-word convention issue, picture disc)	20
93	Arista EMD 018	THE BEST OF THE MONKEES (CD, exclusive via Avon Cosmetics)	22

(see also Micky Dolenz, Davy Jones, Michael Nesmith, Tommy Boyce & Bobby Hart)

BOB MONKHOUSE

69	CBS 3958	I Remember Natalie/In My Dream World	5
69	CBS 4607	Another Time, Another Place, Another World/When I Found You	5

(see also Derek Roy)

MONKS

79	EMI EMI 2999	Johnny B. Rotten/Drugs In My Pocket (p/s)	5

(see also Hudson-Ford)

MONOCHROME SET

79	Rough Trade RT 005	Alphaville/He's Frank (p/s)	8
79	Rough Trade RT 019	Eine Symphonie Des Grauens/Lester Leaps In (1st 1,000 with labels on wrong sides with explanatory insert, p/s)	7/5
79	Rough Trade RT 028	The Monochrome Set/Mr Bizarro (p/s)	6
79	Disquo Bleu BL 1	He's Frank (Slight Return)/Silicon Carne/Fallout (all cuts live) (no p/s)	6
80	DinDisc DID 8	LOVE ZOMBIES (LP, with lithograph)	12

(see also Art Attacks)

MINT VALUE £

MONOGRAMS

59	Parlophone R 4515	Juke Box Cha Cha/The Greatest Mistake Of My Life (78 rpm = £8)	8
59	Parlophone R 4545	Crystal/Teach Me	5

MONOPOLY

67	Polydor 56164	House Of Lords/Magic Carpet	30
67	Polydor 56188	We're All Going To The Seaside/It Isn't Easy	6
70	Pye 7N 17940	We Belong Together/Gone Tomorrow	6
	(see also Raymond Froggatt)		

MONOTONES (U.K.)

64	Pye 7N 15608	What Would I Do/Is It Right	10
64	Pye 7N 15640	It's Great/Anymore	10
65	Pye 7N 15761	No Waiting/Like A Lover Should	10
65	Pye 7N 15814	Something's Hurting Me/A Girl Like That	10

MONOTONES (U.S.)

58	London HLM 8625	Book Of Love/You Never Loved Me (78 rpm = £30)	75

MATT MONRO

56	Decca F 10816	Ev'rybody Falls In Love With Someone/Out Of Sight, Out Of Mind	20
57	Decca F 10845	The Garden Of Eden/Love Me Do (78 rpm = £6)	20
57	Decca F 10870	My House Is Your House/The Bean Song	20
58	Fontana H 122	The Story Of Ireland/Another Time Another Place	15
58	Fontana H 167	Prisoner Of Love/Have Guitar, Will Travel (78 rpm = £10)	15
60	Parlophone R 4638	Love Walked In/I'll Know Her (as Matt Munro)	5
60	Parlophone R 4714	Portrait Of My Love/You're The Top Of My Hit Parade	5
61	Ember EMB S 120	The Ghost Of Your Past/Quite Suddenly	5
63	Parlophone GEP 8889	SINGS THE THEME FROM THE FILM 'FROM RUSSIA FROM LOVE' (EP)	15
64	Parlophone GEP 8898	A SONG FOR EUROPE (EP)	10
57	Decca LF 1276	BLUE AND SENTIMENTAL (10" LP)	65
61	Ace Of Clubs ACL 1069	PORTRAIT (LP)	12
61	Parlophone PMC 1151	LOVE IS THE SAME ANYWHERE (LP, gold/black label, also stereo)	12/18
62	Parl. PMC 1185/PCS 3034	MATT MONRO SINGS HOAGY CARMICHAEL (LP, gold/black label)	18
65	Parlophone PMC 1250	I HAVE DREAMED (LP, yellow/black label, also stereo PCS 3067)	12/15
66	Parlophone PMC 1265	HITS OF YESTERDAY (LP, yellow/black label)	12
66	Capitol (S)T 2540	THIS IS THE LIFE! (LP)	12
67	Capitol (S)T 2608	HERE'S TO MY LADY (LP)	12
67	Capitol (S)T 2683	INVITATION TO BROADWAY (LP)	12
67	Capitol (S)T 2730	INVITATION TO THE MOVIES (LP)	12
68	Capitol (S)T 2801	THESE YEARS (LP)	12
68	Capitol (S)T 2919	THE LATE, LATE SHOW (LP)	12
69	Fontana SFL 13161	TONY BLACKBURN MEETS MATT MONRO (LP)	12
69	RCA Victor SF 8024	THE SOUTHERN STAR (LP, soundtrack, with Georges Garvarentz)	20
70	Capitol ST 22546	WE'RE GONNA CHANGE THE WORLD (LP)	12
71	World Record Club ST 1024	SOFTLY AS I LEAVE YOU (LP)	12
73	Columbia SCX 6525	FOR THE PRESENT (LP)	12
75	Columbia SCX 6578	THE OTHER SIDE OF THE STARS (LP)	12
	(see also John Barry)		

BARRY MONROE

66	Polydor 56088	World Of Broken Hearts/Never Again	6

BILL MONROE (& HIS BLUE GRASS BOYS)

56	Brunswick 05567	New John Henry Blues/Put My Little Shoes Away (78 rpm = £10)	15
57	Brunswick 05681	Four Walls/A Fallen Star (78 rpm = £10)	12
59	Brunswick 05776	Gotta Travel On/No One But My Darlin' (78 rpm = £20)	10
66	Brunswick 05960	Blue Ridge Mountain Blues/John Hardy (solo)	6
55	Brunswick OE 9160	COUNTRY DATE (EP)	20
55	Brunswick OE 9195	COUNTRY WALTZ (EP)	20
63	RCA RCX 7105	COUNTRY GUITAR VOL. 16 (EP, 2 tracks by Monroe Brothers)	12
61	Brunswick LAT 8338	I SAW THE LIGHT (LP)	20
63	Brunswick LAT/STA 8511	BLUEGRASS RAMBLE (LP, mono/stereo)	18/22
65	Brunswick LAT/STA 8579	BLUEGRASS SPECIAL (LP)	15
	(see also Monroe Brothers)		

GERRY MONROE

73	Chapter 1 SCH 187	Goodbye Bobby Boy/I've Got This Feeling	10

MARILYN MONROE

53	MGM MGM 663	Diamonds Are A Girl's Best Friend/Bye Bye Baby (78)	25
54	HMV 7M 232	The River Of No Return/I'm Gonna File My Claim	60
54	HMV B 10723	The River Of No Return/I'm Gonna File My Claim (78)	30
55	HMV B 10847	After You Get What You Want/Heat Wave (78)	40
59	London HLT 8862	I Wanna Be Loved By You/I'm Thru' With Love (78 rpm = £75)	40
78	United Artists UP 36484	I Wanna Be Loved By You/Running Wild/I'm Thru With Love (gatefold p/s)	6
87	Zuma ZOOMP 6	When I Fall In Love/Heat Wave (picture disc)	5
55	HMV 7EG 8090	THERE'S NO BUSINESS LIKE SHOW BUSINESS — SOUNDTRACK EXCERPTS (EP, company sleeve)	40
59	London RET 1231	SOME LIKE IT HOT (EP, soundtrack; triangular centre, later round)	80/50
60	Philips BBE 12414	LET'S MAKE LOVE (EP, with Yves Montand & Frankie Vaughan; also stereo SBBE 9031)	40/55
53	MGM MGM-D 116	GENTLEMEN PREFER BLONDES (10" LP, soundtrack with other artists)	100
59	London HA-T 2176	SOME LIKE IT HOT (LP, s/track with other artists, stereo SAH-T 6040)	90/100
60	Philips BBL 7414/SBBL 592	LET'S MAKE LOVE (LP, soundtrack, with Yves Montand & Frankie Vaughan; mono/stereo)	60/75
63	Stateside S(S)L 10048	MARILYN (LP, soundtrack, mono/stereo)	40/50
83	Liberty UASP 30226	SOME LIKE IT HOT (LP, picture disc)	15
	(see also Frankie Vaughan)		

VAUGHN MONROE (& HIS ORCHESTRA)
53	HMV 7M 144	Less Than Tomorrow (But More Than Yesterday)/Ruby	10
54	HMV 7M 247	They Were Doin' The Mambo/Mister Sandman	10
56	HMV 7M 332	Black Denim Trousers And Motorcycle Boots/All By Myself (78 rpm = £6)	22
57	HMV POP 354	Wringle Wrangle/Westward Ho The Wagons! (78 rpm = £6)	7
59	RCA RCA 1124	The Battle Of New Orleans/Hercules (78 rpm = £20)	8
60	London HLT 9123	Ballerina/Love Me Forever	5
59	RCA RCX 1043	VAUGHAN MONROE'S GREATEST HITS (EP)	12
57	RCA RD 27049	FAMILY SING-SONG (LP)	15

MONROE BROTHERS
63	RCA RCX 7103	COUNTRY GUITAR VOL. 14 (EP)	15
63	RCA RCX 7104	COUNTRY GUITAR VOL. 15 (EP)	15
63	RCA RCX 7105	COUNTRY GUITAR VOL. 16 (EP, 2 tracks by Bill Monroe & Bluegrass Boys)	12

(see also Bill Monroe)

MONSOON
| 71 | Trojan TR 7831 | Hot Honolulu Night/Come Back Jane | 6 |

MONSOON
| 81 | Indipop IND 1 | Ever So Lonely/Sunset Over The Ganges/The Mirror Of Your Mind/ Shout! (Till You're Heard) (in plastic sleeve with insert) | 8 |
| 83 | Mobile Suit Dist. MOBIL 1 | THIRD EYE (LP) | 12 |

(see also Complex)

MONSTER MAGNET
| 98 | A&M 582822-7 | Powertrip (1-sided picture disc) | 5 |
| 98 | A&M 563 274-7 | Space Lord/The Game (picture disc) | 5 |

MONTAG
| 03 | Ai AI 006 | OBJETS PERDUS EP (12", p/s) | 8 |

MONTANAS
65	Piccadilly 7N 35262	All That Is Mine Can Be Yours/How Can I Tell	12
66	Pye 7N 17183	That's When Happiness Began/Goodbye Little Girl	48
67	Pye 7N 17282	Ciao Baby/Anyone There	7
67	Pye 7N 17338	Take My Hand/Top Hat	10
67	Pye 7N 17394	You've Got To Be Loved/Difference Of Opinion	10
68	Pye 7N 17499	A Step In The Right Direction/Someday (You'll Be Breaking My Heart Again)	12
68	Pye 7N 17597	You're Making A Big Mistake/Run To Me	10
69	Pye 7N 17697	Roundabout/Mystery	15
69	Pye 7N 17729	Ciao Baby/Someday (You'll Be Breaking My Heart Again)	6

(see also Trapeze)

MONTANA SEXTET
| 83 | Virgin VS 600 | Who Needs Enemies With A Friend Like You/Friendly Vibes (12") | 15 |
| 87 | 10 TENT 204 | Heavy Vibes pts. 1 & 2 (12") | 8 |

MONTCLAIRS
74	Contempo CS 2008	Make Up For Lost Time/How Can One Man Live	10
75	Contempo CS 2036	Hung Up On Your Love/I Need You More Than Ever	30
74	Contempo CLP 503	DREAMING OF A SEASON (LP)	25

LOU MONTE
54	HMV 7M 176	A Baby Cried/One Moment More	10
54	HMV 7M 190	Darktown Strutters' Ball/I Know How You Feel	12
54	HMV 7M 249	Chain Reaction/Vera's Veranda	10
58	RCA RCA 1048	Lazy Mary (Luna Mezzo Mare)/Angelique-o (78 rpm = £6)	7
59	RCA RCA 1161	Santa Nicola/All Because It's Christmas (78 rpm = £10)	5
60	Columbia DB 4500	Oh! Oh! Rosie/(The New) Darktown Strutters' Ball	5

VINNIE MONTE
| 59 | London HL 8947 | Summer Spree/I'll Walk You Home (78 rpm = £22) | 10 |
| 63 | Stateside SS 156 | Joanie Don't Be Angry/Take Good Care Of Her | 10 |

MONTEGO JOE
| 72 | London HLP 10374 | Stand Up And Be Counted/Glooey (with Seeds Of Life) | 5 |
| 66 | Stateside SL 10159 | JARRIBA! CON MONTEGO JOE (LP) | 12 |

MONTEGO MELON
| 72 | Sioux SI 004 | Swan Lake/HONG GANG: Reggae Mento | 5 |

HUGO MONTENEGRO ORCHESTRA
62	Oriole CB 1765	Palm Canyon Drive/Dark Eyes	7
63	Oriole CB 1792	Get Off The Moon/Sherry	40
68	RCA Victor RCA 1727	The Good, The Bad And The Ugly/Fistful Of Dollars	5
68	RCA Victor RCA 1771	Hang 'Em High/Tomorrow's Love	5
69	RCA RCA 1807	Tony's Theme/Good Vibrations	8
65	RCA Victor RD 7758	THE MAN FROM U.N.C.L.E. (LP, soundtrack)	40
66	RCA Victor RD 7832	MORE MUSIC FROM THE MAN FROM U.N.C.L.E. (LP, soundtrack)	40
67	RCA Victor RD/SF 7877	HURRY SUNDOWN (LP, soundtrack)	28
68	RCA Victor RD 7994	A FISTFUL OF DOLLARS/FOR A FEW DOLLARS MORE/ THE GOOD, THE BAD AND THE UGLY (LP, soundtrack)	15
69	RCA SF 8053	MOOG POWER (LP)	25
69	Stateside S(S)L 10267	LADY IN CEMENT (LP, soundtrack)	40
70	Pye Intl. NSPL 28136	DAWN OF DYLAN (LP)	12
74	RCA APL1 0413	HUGO IN WONDERLAND (LP)	12

BOBBY MONTEZ
| 60 | Vogue V 9165 | Holiday In Havana/Jungle Stars | 8 |

Chris MONTEZ

MINT VALUE £

CHRIS MONTEZ
63	London HLU 9764	My Baby Loves To Dance/In An English Towne.	10
66	Pye International 7N 25348	Call Me/Go 'Head On.	8
66	Pye International 7N 25369	The More I See You/You, I Love You	10
66	Pye International 7N 25381	There Will Never Be Another You/You Can Hurt The One You Love	7
66	Pye International 7N 23599	Time After Time/Keep Talkin'.	7
67	Pye International 7N 25415	Because Of You/Elena	6
68	London HLU 10205	Let's Dance/Some Kinda Fun.	5
73	CBS S CBS 1291	Come On, Let's Go/Somebody Loves You	6
73	CBS S CBS 8343	Dolores, Dolores (I Told You I'd Be Back)/When Your Heart Is Full Of Love (Your Eyes Begin To Overflow)	6
79	Old Gold OG 9011	Let's Dance/LONNIE MACK: Memphis (picture disc)	6
63	London REU 1392	LET'S DANCE (EP)	50
66	Pye Intl. NEP 44071	THE MORE I SEE YOU (EP)	25
66	Pye Intl. NEP 44080	CHRIS MONTEZ (EP).	25
63	London HA-U 8079	LET'S DANCE AND HAVE SOME KINDA FUN!!! (LP)	65
66	Pye Intl. NPL 28080	THE MORE I SEE YOU (LP)	25
67	Pye Intl. N(S)PL 28087	TIME AFTER TIME (LP)	20
68	A&M AML 906	FOOLIN' AROUND (LP)	15
68	A&M AML(S) 925	WATCH WHAT HAPPENS (LP)	12
72	CBS 65408	LET'S DANCE (LP)	15

JACK MONTGOMERY
85	Kent TOWN 102	Dearly Beloved/MARIE KNIGHT: That's No Way To Treat A Girl	20
80s	Soul City 124	My Dear Beloved/Do You Believe It.	10

LITTLE BROTHER MONTGOMERY
50	Jazz Collector L 44	No Special Rider Blues/Vicksburg Blues (78)	15
61	Columbia DB 4595	Pinetop's Boogie Woogie/Cow Cow Blues.	22
61	Columbia 33SX 1289	LITTLE BROTHER MONTGOMERY (LP, with Alexis Korner)	70
62	'77' 77LA 12/21	LITTLE BROTHER MONTGOMERY/SUNNYLAND SLIM (LP)	30
65	Decca LK 4664	LITTLE BROTHER MONTGOMERY (LP)	30
66	Xtra XTRA 1018	LITTLE BROTHER MONTGOMERY (LP)	18
71	Xtra XTRA 1115	FARRO ST. JIVE (LP)	18
71	Saydisc SDR 213	LITTLE BROTHER MONTGOMERY 1930-1969 (LP)	20
72	Saydisc SDM 223	HOME AGAIN (LP).	20

MARIAN MONTGOMERY
65	Capitol CL 15375	When Sunny Gets Blue/Teach Me Tonight	6
67	Reaction 591 018	Love Makes Two People Sing/Monday Thru Saturday	15
68	Pye 7N 17533	Why Say Goodbye/Love Today — Cry Tomorrow	6

ROY MONTGOMERY
97	Enraptured RAPT 4510	Trajectory One/Trajectory Two (p/s, 27 in handmade p/s, 280 clear vinyl)	15/8

STUART MONTGOMERY
69	private pressing	CERTAIN SEA WORDS (LP, with insert)	15

WES MONTGOMERY
60	Fontana FJL 109	GO! (LP)	15
60	Riverside RLP 12-320	THE INCREDIBLE JAZZ GUITAR OF WES MONTGOMERY (LP, mono/stereo)	15/20

MONTROSE
74	Warner Brothers K 16382	Bad Motor Scooter/One Thing On My Mind	5
74	Warner Brothers K 16428	Rock The Nation/One Thing On My Mind	5
74	Warner Brothers/Sound For Industry SFI 175	Rock The Nation/Space Station No. 5/Good Rockin' Tonight (flexidisc).	7

(see also Sammy Hagar)

MONTY, DERRICK & PATSY
65	Blue Beat BB 280	Stir The Pot/Mercy.	20

(see also Monty Morris, Derrick Morgan)

MONTY (Morris) & ROY
61	Blue Beat BB 61	In And Out The Window/Tra La La Boogie (with Dumbago's Orchestra)	8
61	Blue Beat BB 63	Sweetie Pie/ROLAND ALPHONSO'S GROUP: Green Door.	18

(see also Monty Morris)

MONTY PYTHON('S FLYING CIRCUS)
72	Charisma CB 192	Spam Song/The Concert (as Monty Python's Flying Circus, p/s)	6
72	Charisma CB 200	Eric The Half A Bee/The Yangtse Song (Extended) (as Monty Python with Niel [sic] Innes)	5
72	Python Productions	Teach Yourself Heath (flexidisc free with *Zig Zag* magazine).	12
74	Charisma CB 268	Lumberjack Song/Spam Song (p/s)	5
74	NME/Charisma SFI 1259	Monty Python's Tiny Black Round Thing (D.P. Gumby Presents "Election '74"/ The Lumberjack Song) (live flexidisc free with *NME*)	10/6
75	Charisma MP PROMO 1	In Store Commercial (promo only, jukebox single)	5
79	Warner Bros K 17495	Always Look On The Bright Side Of Life/Brian (p/s).	15
80	Charisma CB 374	I Like Chinese/I Bet You They Won't Play This Song On The Radio/ Finland (p/s).	15
83	CBS WA 3495	Galaxy Song/Every Sperm Is Sacred (goldfish bowl-shaped picture disc)	8
88	Warner Bros W 7653	Always Look On The Bright Side Of Life/Brian (p/s, reissue)	10
91	Virgin PYTH 2	Galaxy Song/Every Sperm Is Sacred (p/s, reissue).	5
76	Charisma MP 001	PYTHON ON SONG (EP, double pack [CBS 268/PY 2])	25
70	BBC REB 73M	MONTY PYTHON'S FLYING CIRCUS (LP, mono, pink label).	15
73	Charisma CAS 1063	MONTY PYTHON'S PREVIOUS RECORD (LP, with free flexidisc in p/s, "Teach Yourself Heath" & inner sleeve)	12
73	Charisma CAS 1080	MATCHING TIE AND HANDKERCHIEF (LP, parallel grooves on side 2, die-cut sleeve, 2 inserts).	15
74	Charisma CLASS 4	LIVE AT THE THEATRE ROYAL DRURY LANE (LP).	12

77	Charisma CAS 1134	THE MONTY PYTHON INSTANT RECORD COLLECTION (LP, foldout sleeve)	12
79	Warner Bros K 56751	LIFE OF BRIAN (LP, soundtrack, with inner sleeve)	12
70s	Charisma	INSTANT RECORD COLLECTION (LP, fold out sleeve, with inner)	12

(see also John Cleese, Rutles, Barry Booth)

MONUMENT
71	Beacon BEAS 15	THE FIRST MONUMENT (LP)	60

(see also Zior)

MOOCHE
69	Pye 7N 17735	Hot Smoke And Sasafrass/Seen Through A Light	25

AMEIL MOODIE
69	Blue Cat BS 143	Mello Reggae/Lifeline	20
69	Blue Cat BS 164	Ratchet Knife/Bend The Tree	20

MOOD MOSAIC
66	Columbia DB 7801	A Touch Of Velvet, A Sting Of Brass/Bond Street P.M.	28
67	Columbia DB 8149	Chinese Chequers/The Real Mr. Smith	18
68	Parlophone R 5716	The Yellow Spotted Capricorn/ELMER HOCKETT'S HURDY GURDY: Fantastic Fair	8
69	Columbia DB 8618	A Touch Of Velvet, A Sting Of Brass/Bond Street P.M. (reissue)	15
67	Columbia SX 6153	MOOD MOSAIC (LP, mono)	35
67	Studio Two TWO 160	MOOD MOSAIC (LP, stereo)	25

(see also Mark Wirtz Orchestra & Chorus, Keith West)

MOOD OF HAMILTON
67	Columbia DB 8304	Why Can't There Be More Love?/King's Message	15

MOOD REACTION
70	Pama PSP 1007	LIVE AT THE CUMBERLAND (LP)	20

MOODS
63	Starlite ST45 098	Duckwalk/Easy Going	22

MOOD SIX
82	EMI EMI 5300	Hanging Around/Mood Music (p/s)	5
82	EMI EMI 5336	She's Too Far/Venus (unreleased; white label copies exist with p/s)	30
85	Psycho PSYCHO 2001	Plastic Flowers/It's Your Life (p/s)	5
85	Psycho PSYCHO 4001	PLASTIC FLOWERS (12" EP)	10
85	Psycho PSYCHO 33	THE DIFFERENCE IS... (LP)	12

(see also V.I.P.s)

JAMES MOODY
55	Esquire 20-071	MOODY HI FI (10" LP)	25

RON MOODY
61	Decca F 11371	You've Gotta Pick A Pocket Or Two/Reviewing The Situation	10
64	Parlophone R 5205	Rinkety Tink/Bringing Home My Darling	7

MOODY BLUES
SINGLES
64	Decca F 11971	Steal Your Heart Away/Lose Your Money (But Don't Lose Your Mind) (as Moodyblues)	40
64	Decca F 12022	Go Now!/It's Easy Child	7
65	Decca F 12095	I Don't Want To Go On Without You/Time Is On My Side	7
65	Decca F 12166	From The Bottom Of My Heart (I Love You)/And My Baby's Gone	7
65	Decca F 12266	Everyday/You Don't (All The Time)	8
66	Decca F 12498	Boulevard De La Madelaine/This Is My House (But Nobody Calls)	12
67	Decca F 12543	Life's Not Life/He Can't Win (withdrawn)	50
67	Decca F 12607	Fly Me High/Really Haven't Got The Time	20
67	Decca F 12670	Love And Beauty/Leave This Man Alone	18
67	Deram DM 161	Nights In White Satin/Cities (1st issue, darker labels than later copies)	5
68	Deram DM 196	Voices In The Sky/Doctor Livingstone, I Presume	7
68	Deram DM 213	Ride My See-Saw/A Simple Game	8
69	Deram DM 247	Never Comes The Day/So Deep Within You	7
69	Threshold TH 1	Watching And Waiting/Out And In	8
81	Threshold THPD 29	Talking Out Of Turn/Veteran Cosmic Rocker (picture disc)	7
83	Threshold TH 30	Blue World/Going Nowhere (p/s, with free T-shirt)	6
88	Polydor 080 409-2	Miracle/Vintage Wine/Deep/I Know You're Out There Somewhere/ I Know You're Out There Somewhere (Video) (CD Video)	12
88	Polydor 080 022-2	Your Wildest Dreams/Talkin' Talkin'/It May Be Fire/Rock'n'Roll Over You/ Your Wildest Dreams (Video) (CD Video)	12

EP
65	Decca DFE 8622	THE MOODY BLUES (EP, original label or reissue with boxed Decca logo)	30/10

LPs
65	Decca LK 4711	THE MAGNIFICENT MOODIES (LP, unboxed or boxed Decca label logo)	40/15
67	Deram DML/SML 707	DAYS OF FUTURE PASSED (LP, originally with white band on sleeve & 'DSS' labels, mono/stereo)	25/12
68	Deram DML/SML 711	IN SEARCH OF THE LOST CHORD (LP, gatefold sleeve, mono/stereo)	25/12
69	Deram DML/SML 1035	ON THE THRESHOLD OF A DREAM (LP, gatefold sleeve with stapled booklet, mono/stereo)	25/12
69	Threshold THM/THS 1	TO OUR CHILDREN'S CHILDREN'S CHILDREN (LP, with insert, mono)	15
70	Threshold THS 3	A QUESTION OF BALANCE ('flap' gatefold sleeve with lyric sheet)	12
78	Decca TXS 129	OCTAVE (LP, blue vinyl)	12

(see also Justin Hayward, Denny Laine, Gerry Levene & Avengers, Ray Thomas)

MOOG MACHINE
69	CBS 63807	SWITCHED ON ROCK (LP)	15

MINT VALUE £

MOON
68	Liberty LBF 15076	Someday Girl/Mothers And Fathers	15
70	Liberty LBF 15333	Pirate/Not To Know	10
68	Liberty LBL/LBS 83146	WITHOUT EARTH (LP)	35

(see also Beach Boys)

KEITH MOON
75	Polydor 2058 584	Don't Worry Baby/Together	22
75	Polydor 2442 134	TWO SIDES OF THE MOON (LP)	35

(see also Who)

LARRY MOON
63	Ember EMB 171	Tia Juana Ball/Bouquet Of Roses	20

PERRY MOON
63	Sway SW 002	Nine Five Baby/PLANTES: Water Front	10

TERRY MOON
63	Planetone RC 11	Moon Man/MIKE ELLIOT: This Love Of Mine	10

MOON BOYS
69	Amalgamated AMG 846	Apollo 11/PIONEERS: Love Love Everyday	15

(see also Hippy Boys)

MOONCHILD
75	Look LKSP 5010	War Orphan/Hour Glass	5

MOONDANCE
70	A&M AMS 792	Lazy River/Anna St Claire	5

MOONDOG
54	London REP 1010	ON THE STREETS OF NEW YORK (EP)	40
59	Esquire 32-055	MOONDOG (LP)	80
69	CBS 63906	MOONDOG (LP, gatefold sleeve)	60

MOONDOGS
78	Lyntone LT 002	Heads I Win/Two's A Crowd (p/s)	5

MOONDOGS
79	Good Vibrations GOT 10	She's Nineteen/Ya Don't Do Ya (foldout p/s)	10
80	Real ARE 13	Who's Gonna Tell Mary/Overcaring Parents (p/s)	10
81	Real ARE 14	Talking In The Canteen/Make Her Love Me (p/s, some with neckerchief)	35/10
81	Real ARE 16	Imposter/Baby Snatcher (p/s)	15

ART MOONEY (& HIS ORCHESTRA)
53	MGM SP 1037	I Played The Fool/I Just Couldn't Take It, Baby (with Cathy Ryan)	8
53	MGM SP 1045	Baby Don't Do It/Believe In Me (with Cathy Ryan)	8
54	MGM SP 1088	Oh Boy What Joy We Had/Silhouette D'Amour	6
55	MGM SP 1134	No Regrets/Honey Babe	6
56	MGM SP 1166	Memories Of You/I'm Looking Over	7
56	MGM MGM 899	Tutti Frutti/OCIE SMITH & CLOVERLEAFS: Our Melody (78)	15
57	MGM MGM 923	"Rebel Without A Cause" Theme/"East Of Eden" Theme (78 rpm = £6)	15
57	MGM MGM 943	Giant/There's Never Been Anyone Else But You (78 rpm = £8)	15
57	MGM MGM 951	Rock And Roll Tumbleweed/Is There A Teenager In The House (with Ocie Smith) (78 rpm = £15)	22

(see also Ocie Smith, Shorty Long, Cloverleafs, Cathy Ryan)

HAL MOONEY ORCHESTRA
62	Oriole CB 1782	Small World/Let Us Entertain You	5

MOONGLOWS
57	London HLN 8374	I Knew From The Start/Over And Over Again (78 rpm = £65)	700

(see also Harvey & Moonglows, Etta & Harvey)

MOONKYTE
71	Mother SMOT 1	COUNT ME OUT (LP, with insert, cover has a die-cut spire)	200

MOONLIGHTERS
63	Island WI 043	Going Out/Hold My Hands	20

MOONLIGHTERS
65	Columbia DB 7602	Come On Home/It's Too Late	10
66	Columbia DB 7910	We'll See It Through/Too Late To Come Home	10

MICKY MOONSHINE
74	Decca F 13555	Baby Blue/Name It You Got It (DJ copy = £40)	20
75	Decca F 13555	Baby Blue/Name It You Got It (reissue)	5

MOONSHINERS
65	Stateside SL 10137	THE MOONSHINERS BREAKOUT! (LP)	18
67	Page One POLS 004	HOLD UP (LP)	22

MOONSTONES
65	Parlophone R 5331	Heaven Fell Last Night/Little Roses	6
66	Parlophone R 5497	Violets Of Dawn/Power Of Decision	6
67	Mercury MF 1011	How Many Times/Louisville	6

MOON'S TRAIN
67	MGM MGM 1333	Deed I Do/It's In My Mind	20

(see also Peter Frampton, Denny Mitchell, Preachers)

MOONTREKKERS
61	Parlophone R 4814	Night Of The Vampire/Melodie D'Amour	20
62	Parlophone R 4888	There's Something At The Bottom Of The Well/Hatashiai	25
63	Decca F 11714	Moondust/The Bogey Man	20

MICHAEL MOORCOCK('S DEEP FIX)

80	Flicknife FLS 200	Dodgem Dude/Star Cruiser (p/s)	8
82	Flicknife EJS P9831	Brothel In Rosenstrasse/Time Centre (numbered, 500 only, with autographed lyric sheet)	30
92	Cyborg (no cat. no.)	The Brothel In Rosenstrasse (cassette only)	20
75	United Artists UAG 29732	NEW WORLD'S FAIR (LP, with inner sleeve)	30

(see also Hawkwind)

ALEXANDER MOORE

60	77 77LA 12-7	WHISTLING ALEX MOORE (LP)	18

ALICE MOORE

50s	Poydras MC 66	Prison Blues/My Man Blues	15

ANTHONY MOORE

76	Virgin VS 144	Catch A Falling Star/Back To The Top	5
71	Polydor 2310 062	PIECES FROM THE CLOUDLAND BALLROOM (LP)	35
72	Polydor 2310 079	SECRETS OF THE BLUE BAG (LP)	35
79	Quango HMS 98	FLYING DOESN'T HELP (LP)	12
81	Do It RIDE 7	WORLD SERVICE (LP, with inner)	12

(see also Slapp Happy)

BOB MOORE & ORCHESTRA

61	London HLU 9409	Mexico/Hot Spot	8
62	London HLU 9538	Ooh La La/Aufwiedersehn Marlene	6
63	London HLU 9736	Kentucky/Flowers Of Florence	6
62	London HAU 2439	MEXICO (LP, also stereo [SAHU 6230])	12/15

BOBBY MOORE (& RHYTHM ACES)

66	Chess CRS 8033	Searching For My Love/Hey Mr D.J.	25
75	Pye International 7N 25691	Call Me Your Anything Man/Call Me Your Anything Man (Disco Version) (solo)	6
66	Chess CRL 4521	SEARCHIN' FOR MY LOVE (LP)	75

BUTCH MOORE

65	Pye 7N 15832	Walking The Streets In The Rain/I Stand Still	8

CHRISTY MOORE

69	Mercury 20170 SMCL	PADDY ON THE ROAD (LP)	250
75	Polydor 2383 344	WHATEVER TICKLES YOUR FANCY (LP)	25
76	Polydor 2383 426	CHRISTY MOORE (LP)	25
70s	WEA WX 286	VOYAGE (LP)	15

DUDLEY MOORE (TRIO)

61	Parlophone R 4772	Strictly For The Birds (solo)/Duddly Dell (B-side as Dudley Moore Trio)	15
68	Decca F 12850	30 Is A Dangerous Age, Cynthia/The Real Stuff (solo)	15
69	Decca F 12882	Keep It Up/Gently (as Dudley Moore Trio)	15
65	Decca LK 4732	THE OTHER SIDE OF DUDLEY MOORE (LP)	20
66	Decca LK 4788	GENUINE DUD (LP, as Dudley Moore Trio)	20
68	Decca LK/SKL 4923	BEDAZZLED (LP, soundtrack)	100
69	Decca LK/SKL 4976	THE DUDLEY MOORE TRIO (LP)	40
69	Decca SKL 4980	THE MUSIC OF DUDLEY MOORE (LP)	15
70	Decca SPA 106	THE WORLD OF DUDLEY MOORE (LP)	15
70	Atlantic 2465 017	FROM BEYOND THE FRINGE (LP)	15
72	Atlantic K 40397	TODAY (LP)	22
73	Decca SPA 286	THE WORLD OF DUDLEY MOORE VOL. 2 (LP)	15
74	Black Lion BLP 12151	AT THE WAVENDON FESTIVAL (LP)	15

(see also Peter Cook & Dudley Moore)

GARY MOORE

78	MCA MCA 386	Back On The Streets/Track Nine (some in p/s)	30/5
79	MCA MCA 419	Parisienne Walkways/Fanatical Fascists (p/s)	8
79	MCA MCA 534	Spanish Guitar/Spanish Guitar (instrumental) (p/s)	10
81	Jet JET 12016	Nuclear Attack/Don't Let Me Be Misunderstood/Run To Your Mama (12", company sleeve, as Gary Moore & Friends)	10
82	Kerrang!	Wishing Well/GILLAN: Purple Sky/TELEPHONE: Squeeze (flexidisc with *Kerrang!* magazine)	8/6
82	Virgin VS 528	Always Gonna Love You/Cold Hearted (p/s)	7
82	Virgin VSY 528	Always Gonna Love You/Cold Hearted (picture disc)	8
83	Virgin VSY 564	Falling In Love With You/Falling In Love With You (Instrumental) (picture disc)	12
83	Virgin VS 564	Falling In Love With You/(Instrumental) (p/s, with comic)	10
83	Virgin VS 56412	Falling In Love With You/(Instrumental) (12", p/s)	15
84	10 TEN 13	Hold On To Love/Devil In Her Heart (poster p/s)	7
84	10 TENS 13	Hold On To Love/Devil In Her Heart (plectrum-shaped picture disc)	18
84	10 TEN 1312	Hold On To Love/Devil In Her Heart/Law Of The Jungle (12", p/s)	10
84	10 TEN 19	Shapes Of Things/Blinder (p/s, with patch)	12
84	10 TENS 19	Shapes Of Things/Blinder (explosion-shaped picture disc)	15
84	10 TEN 1912	Shapes Of Things/(Interview) (12", p/s)	8
84	10 TEN 25	Empty Rooms/Nuclear Attack (live) (in poster p/s)	8
84	10 TEN 25-12	Empty Rooms (Ext. Mix)/Empty Rooms//Nuclear Attack (live)/ Empty Rooms (live)/Rockin' Every Night (live) (12", double pack, gatefold p/s with poster)	8
85	10 TEN 58	Empty Rooms (Summer 85 Version)/Out Of My System (p/s)	5
86	10 TENS 134	Over The Hills And Far Away/Crying In The Shadows (guitar-shaped pic disc)	15
86	10 TENG 134	Over The Hills And Far Away (Extended Mix)/Over The Hills And Far Away	
87	10 TENT 178	The Loner/Johnny Boy/The Loner (Extended Version)/The Loner (Live At Hammersmith Odeon (12", p/s)	10
88	Virgin GMSY 1	After The War/This Thing Called Love (picture disc, stickered PVC sleeve)	5
73	CBS 65527	GRINDING STONE (LP, as Gary Moore Band)	12
78	MCA MCF 2853	BACK ON THE STREETS (LP, with inner sleeve)	12
81	Jet JETLP 245	LIVE AT THE MARQUEE (LP, withdrawn test pressing, white sleeve with Jet Info sticker)	50+

82	Virgin V 2245	CORRIDORS OF POWER (LP, with free live EP [VDJ 34])	12
84	EMI OVED 206	VICTIMS OF THE FUTURE (LP, with inner & poster)	20
84	Jet JETLP 241	DIRTY FINGERS (LP)	12
86	10 DIXP 16	RUN FOR COVER (LP, picture disc, die-cut sleeve)	30
87	10 DIXG 56	WILD FRONTIER (2-LP, gatefold sleeve)	18

(see also Granny's Intentions, Dr. Strangely Strange, Skid Row, Thin Lizzy, Gary Moore & Phil Lynott, Greg Lake, Eddie Howell, G-Force, Cozy Powell)

GARY MOORE & PHIL LYNOTT

85	10 TENS 49	Out In The Fields/Military Man (2 1-sided interlocking shaped picture-disc set, stickered gatefold PVC sleeve)	25
85	10 TEND 49	Out In The Fields/Military Man//Still In Love With You/ Stop Messin' Around (live) (double pack)	7
85	10 TEN 49-12	Out In The Fields/Military Man/Still In Love With You (12", gatefold p/s, with poster)	10
85	10 TENC 49-12	Military Man (12", 1-sided, B-side etched with signatures, promo only)	12

(see also Gary Moore, Phil Lynott, Thin Lizzy)

JACKIE MOORE

71	Jay Boy BOY 35	Dear John/Here Am I	8
71	Atlantic 2091 054	Precious Precious/Will Power	8
71	Atlantic 2091 095	Sometimes It's Got To Rain (In Your Love Life)/Wonderful, Marvellous (with Dixie Flyers)	6
74	Atlantic K 10481	Both Ends Against The Middle/Willpower	15

JOHNNY MOORE

| 67 | Caltone TONE 101 | Sound And Soul/ROY SHIRLEY: Get On The Ball | 22 |
| 69 | Doctor Bird DB 1180 | Big Big Boss/CARL CANNONBALL BRYON: Reggae This Reggae | 25 |

(see also Cannonball & Johnny Melody, Alton Ellis)

MATTHEW MOORE

| 66 | Capitol CL 15467 | A Face In The Crowd/St. James Infirmary | 7 |

MERRILL E. MOORE

54	Capitol CL 14057	Bell Bottom Boogie/The House Of Blue Lights (78)	15
54	Capitol CL 14130	Nola/Fly Right Boogie (78)	15
55	Capitol CL 14369	Five Foot Two, Eyes Of Blue/Hard Top Race (as Merrill Moore) (78 rpm = £20)	220
56	Capitol F 3397	King Porter Stomp/Rock Island Line (export only)	160
68	Ember EMB S 253	Down The Road A-Piece/Buttermilk Baby	15
69	B&C CB 100	Sweet Mama Tree Top Tall/Little Green Apples	8
70	Bulldog BD 20	House Of Blue Lights/Red Light	8
67	Ember EMB 3392	BELLYFUL OF BLUE-THUNDER (LP)	40
68	Ember EMB 3394	ROUGH-HOUSE 88 (LP; repressed 1973)	25
69	B&C CAS 1001	TREE TOP TALL (LP)	18

NICKY MOORE BAND

| 81 | Street Tunes STS 006 | Year Of The Lie | 10 |
| 81 | Street Tunes | 7 YEARS OF THE LIE (LP) | 12 |

(see also Tiger, Samson, Hackensack)

PETE MOORE ORCHESTRA

| 70 | Fontana 6438 004 | EXCITING SOUNDS OF TOMORROW (LP) | 15 |

PETE MOORE'S SOLID ROCKIN' BRASS

| 74 | Gold Star 1500 009 | PETE MOORE'S SOLID ROCKIN' BRASS (LP) | 15 |

OSCAR MOORE TRIO

| 55 | London H-APB 1035 | KENYA (10" LP) | 15 |

ROGER MOORE

| 65 | CBS 202014 | Where Does Love Go/Tomorrow After Tomorrow (some in p/s) | 25/10 |

SCOTTY MOORE

| 64 | Columbia 33SX 1680 | THE GUITAR THAT CHANGED THE WORLD! (LP) | 80 |

(see also Elvis Presley)

SHELLEY MOORE (& MOORE SESSIONEERS)

55	Columbia SCM 5197	In The Wee Small Hours Of The Morning/ When You Lose The One You Love (solo)	5
58	Starlite ST45 002	You've Tied Me Up/Gone On The Guy	7
58	Starlite ST45 003	Where Is The Bluebird?/Everything Is Gonna Be All Right	7
57	Starlite ST EP 1	PORTRAIT OF SHELLEY (EP)	8
58	Starlite ST EP 7	KOOOL KANARY (EP)	8

THURSTON MOORE & DON FLEMING

| 97 | Via Satellite V.SAT 6 | Telstar/E.A.R.: Sputnik | 20 |

WHISTLING ALEXANDER MOORE

| 63 | '77' LA 12-6 | WHISTLING ALEXANDER MOORE (LP) | 25 |

ALAN MOORHOUSE ORCHESTRA

66	Pye 7N 17073	(The Ballad Of) The Green Berets/London Bridge	6
68	Page One POF 104	Stop Press/Chloe	7
70	Columbia DB 8674	Haunting Me/Soul Bossa	6

MOOSE

| 70 | Escort ERT 840 | Engine No. 9/KURASS: Do It | 7 |

BIG MOOSE (Walker)

| 68 | Python PKM 1 | Puppy Howl Blues/Rambling Woman | 35 |

MOPEDS

| 68 | Col. Blue Beat DB 108 | Whiskey And Soda/Do It | 5 |

(see also Cindy Starr & Mopeds)

MOQUETTES
64 Columbia DB 7315 Right String, But The Wrong Yo-Yo/You Came Along 75

SANTOS MORADOS
68 Island WIP 6034 Tonopah/Anytime 6

NONO MORALES & HIS ORCHESTRA
54 HMV 7MC 5 Istanbul (Not Constantinople)/Am I Blue (export single) 5

MIKE MORAN
70s Alba TAR 053 PENNY WHISTLES OF ROBERT LOUIS STEVENSON (LP) 20

MORBID ANGEL
94 Earache MOSH 112 LAIBACH REMIXES EP (God Of Emptiness/Sworn To The Black/Sworn To The . . . Black[Laibach Remix]/God Of Emptiness [Laibach Remix]) (12", p/s) 10
89 Earache MOSH11 ALTARS OF MADNESS (LP, picture disc) 30

MORE
80 Atlantic K 11561 We Are The Band/Atomic Rock (with p/s) 6
80 Atlantic K 11561T We Are The Band/Atomic Rock (12", p/s, with patch) 8
82 Atlantic K 11744 Trickster/Hey Joe (p/s) 15
81 Atlantic K 50775 WARHEAD (LP) 12
81 Atlantic K 50875 BLOOD & THUNDER (LP) 12

A. MORE
80 Quango HMGS 10 Judy/Lucia (p/s) 5
(see also Anthony Moore)

MORECAMBE & WISE
61 HMV POP 957 We're The Guys/Me And My Shadow 5
63 HMV POP 1240 Boom Oo Yatta Ta Ta/Why Did I Let You Go 5
64 HMV POP 1373 A-Wassailing/The Happiest Christmas Of All 5
66 HMV POP 1518 Now That You're Here/That Riviera Touch 5
67 Pye 7N 17436 Twelve Days Of Christmas/Bingle Jells 5
69 Columbia DB 8646 Bring Me Sunshine/Just Around The Corner 5
70 Philips 6006 069 Following You Around/Eric & Ernie's Theme 5
71 Columbia DB 8753 Bring Me Sunshine/Just Around The Corner (reissue) 5
74 Lyntone Happy Birthday Record (flexidisc, promotion for Maltesers/Treets, etc, p/s) 8
76 EMI EMI 2475 (We Get Along So Easily) Don't You Agree/Positive Thinking 5
78 (no cat. no.) Morecambe & Wise & Cockram Talk Trio (p/s, promo) 5
64 HMV CLP 1682 MR. MORECAMBE MEETS MR. WISE (LP, also stereo CSD 1522) 12
66 Philips BL 7750 AN EVENING WITH MORECAMBE & WISE (LP) 12
71 BBC RED 128 IT'S MORECAMBE AND WISE (LP) 12

JOE MORELLO
62 RCA LSP 2486 IT'S ABOUT TIME (LP, also stereo [SF 7502]) 12

MORGAN
73 RCA SF 8321 NOVA SOLIS (LP, with insert) 30
78 Cherry Red ARED 1 THE SLEEPER WAKES (LP) 12
(see also Mott The Hoople, Love Affair, Humpy Bong)

MORGAN & MARK SEVEN
66 Polydor BM 56083 I'm Gonna Turn My Life Around/Undercover Man 7

AL MORGAN
58 London HLU 8741 Jealous Heart/Foolish Tears 10
50s London BEP 6043 AL MORGAN (EP, export issue) 12
51 London H-APB 1001 JEALOUS HEART (10" LP) 20
51 London H-APB 1003 LITTLE RED BOOK (10" LP) 20

P.C. ALEXANDER MORGAN
66 Columbia DB 8095 Sussex By The Sea/METROPOLITAN POLICE BAND: Thunderbirds March 10

DAVID/DAVY MORGAN
65 Columbia DB 7624 Tomorrow I'll Be Gone/Ain't Got Much More To See (as Davy Morgan) 45
68 Parlophone R 5692 True To Life/Dawning (as David Morgan) 12
(see also Wishful Thinking)

DERRICK MORGAN
60 Blue Beat BB 7 Fat Man/I'm Gonna Leave You 25
60 Blue Beat BB 12 Don't Cry/I Pray For You (as Derrick Morgan & Ebonies) 10
60 Blue Beat BB 18 Lover Boy/Oh My! 10
61 Blue Beat BB 31 Now We Know/Nights Are Lonely (with Trenton Spence Orchestra) 10
61 Blue Beat BB 35 Leave Earth/Wigger Wee Shuffle (with Clue J. & His Blues Busters) 10
61 Blue Beat BB 62 Shake A Leg/Golden Rule (as Derrick & Drumbago All Stars) 10
62 Blue Beat BB 76 Sunday, Monday/Be Still 10
62 Blue Beat BB 82 Don't You Know Little Girl (actually by Derrick & Basil)/ B. GABBIDON: Hully Gully Miss Molly 10
62 Blue Beat BB 85 Come On Over/Come Back My Darling (with Buster's Group) 10
62 Blue Beat BB 91 Headache/OWEN GRAY: Millie Girl 10
62 Blue Beat BB 94 Meekly Wait/Day In And Day Out (both sides with Yvonne [Sterling]) 10
62 Blue Beat BB 100 In My Heart/BELL'S GROUP: Kingston 13 12
62 Blue Beat BB 110 Are You Going To Marry Me?/Troubles (as Derrick Morgan & Patsy) 8
62 Blue Beat BB 130 Should Be Ashamed/Marjorie (with Buster's Group) 8
62 Blue Beat BB 141 Joybells (with Duke Reid Group)/Going Down To Canaan (with Denzil Dennis) . . . 8
62 Island WI 004 Travel On/Teach Me Baby 12
62 Island WI 006 The Hop/Tell It To Me 12
62 Island WI 011 Forward March/Please Don't Talk About Me (B-side actually with Eric Morris) . . . 12
62 Island WI 013 Cherry Home/See And Blind 12
62 Blue Beat BB 148 Jezebell/Burnette 10
63 Blue Beat BB 177 Patricia My Dear/The Girl I Left Behind 10

Derrick MORGAN

63	Blue Beat BB 187	Tears On My Pillow/You Should Have Known	10
63	Blue Beat BB 196	Telephone/Life Is Tough (B-side actually "Tough Man Tough")	10
63	Island WI 037	Dorothy/Leave Her Alone	12
63	Island WI 051	Blazing Fire/DERRICK & PATSY: I'm In A Jam	8
63	Island WI 053	No Raise, No Praise/Loving Baby	12
63	Island WI 080	Angel With Blue Eyes/Corner Stone	12
63	Rio R 1	Blazing Fire/Edmarine	10
64	Black Swan WI 402	Street Girl/Edmarine	10
64	Black Swan WI 425	Cherry Pie (actually by Frederick Hibbert)/BOB WALLS: Beware	15
64	Blue Beat BB 233	Let Them Talk/Sleeping	10
64	Blue Beat BB 239	Miss Lulu/DERRICK & PALOY: She's So Young (B-side act. by Derrick & Patsy)	10
64	Blue Beat BB 261	The Soldier Man/BUSTER'S ALL STARS: Jet 707	30
64	Blue Beat BB 268	Katy Katy/Call On Me	12
65	Blue Beat BB 276	Weep No More/I Want A Girl	12
65	Blue Beat BB 283	Johnny Grave/BUSTER'S ALL STARS: Yeah Yeah	20
65	Blue Beat BB 311	Throw Them Away/Baby Face	15
65	Blue Beat BB 329	Sweeter Than Honey/You Never Know (with Prince Buster)	15
65	Ska Beat JB 185	Heart Of Stone/Let Me Go (with Baba Brooks Group)	18
65	Ska Beat JB 218	Don't Call Me Daddy/BABA BROOK'S BAND: Girl's Town Ska	30
65	Island WI 193	Two Of A Kind/I Want A Lover (both actually with Naomi)	8
65	Island WI 225	Starvation/I Am A Blackhead Again	20
66	Island WI 277	It's Alright/I Need Someone (both sides actually with Blenders)	22
66	Island WI 289	Ameletia (actually by Frank Cosmo)/Don't You Worry (B-side with Patsy Todd)	12
66	Island WI 3010	Gather Together Now (Jamaican Independence Song)/Soft Hand (actually "So Hard") (both sides actually with Blenders)	25
66	Rio R 122	Cool Off Rudies/Take It Easy	20
67	Island WI 3079	Someone (actually Derrick & Pauline Morgan)/Do You Love Me (with Pauline)	18
67	Pyramid PYR 6010	Tougher Than Tough/ROLAND ALPHONSO: Song For My Father	20
67	Pyramid PYR 6013	Greedy Gal/SOUL BROTHERS: Marcus Junior	20
67	Pyramid PYR 6014	Court Dismiss/FREDERICK McCLEAN: Fine Fine Fine	20
67	Pyramid PYR 6019	Judge Dread In Court/Last Chance	25
67	Pyramid PYR 6021	Kill Me Dead/Don't Be A Fool	15
67	Pyramid PYR 6024	No Dice/I Mean It	15
67	Pyramid PYR 6025	Do The Bang Bang/Revenge	15
68	Island WI 3094	Conquering Ruler/LLOYD & DEVON: Red Rum Ball	25
68	Island WI 3101	Gimme Back/VICEROYS: Send Requests	25
68	Island WI 3159	Hold You Jack/One Morning In May	35
68	Pyramid PYR 6029	I Am The Ruler/I Mean It	15
68	Pyramid PYR 6039	Woman A Grumble/Don't Be A Fool	15
68	Pyramid PYR 6040	Want More/ROLAND ALPHONSO: Goodnight My Love	15
68	Pyramid PYR 6045	Try Me/I'm Leaving (B-side with Pauline)	15
68	Pyramid PYR 6046	King For Tonight (with Pauline)/Last Chance	15
68	Pyramid PYR 6053	Me Naw Give Up/BEVERLEY'S ALLSTARS: Dreadnaught	20
68	Pyramid PYR 6056	Ben Johnson Day/MAYTALS: Ain't Got No Tip	15
68	Pyramid PYR 6061	What's Your Grouse/BEVERLEY'S ALLSTARS: I Don't Know	15
68	Pyramid PYR 6063	Johnny Pram Pram/Don't Say (B-side with Pauline Morgan)	15
68	Amalgamated AMG 824	I Want To Go Home/JACKIE ROBINSON: Let The Little Girl Dance	15
68	Crab CRAB 3	River To The Bank/PETER KING: Reggae Limbo	8
68	Trojan TR 626	Fat Man/VAL BENNETT: South Parkway Rock	18
68	Nu Beat NB 016	I Love You/JUNIOR SMITH: Searching	12
68	Big Shot BI 506	Shower Of Rain/VAL BENNETT: It Might As Well Be Spring	12
69	Crab CRAB 8	Seven Letters/TARTANS: Lonely Heartaches (B-side act. by Clarendonians)	8
69	Crab CRAB 11	My First Taste Of Love/TARTANS: Dance All Night	12
69	Crab CRAB 18	Don't Play That Song/How Can I Forget You?	8
69	Crab CRAB 23	Send Me Some Loving/Come What May	5
69	Crab CRAB 22	Mek It Tan Deah/Gimme Back	8
69	Crab CRAB 28	Hard Time/ROY RICHARDS: Death Rides A Horse	12
69	Crab CRAB 30	Man Pon Spot/What A Thing	5
69	Crab CRAB 32	Moon Hop/Harris Wheel	5
69	Jackpot JP 700	Seven Letters/Too Bad	5
69	Unity UN 507	Belly Woman/PAULETT & LOVERS: Please Stay	5
69	Unity UN 540	Derrick – Top The Pop/GLEN ADAMS: Capone's Revenge	10
70	Unity UN 546	Return Of Jack Slade/Fat Man	10
70	Unity UN 569	The Conquering Ruler/Bedweight	10
70	Crab CRAB 44	A Night At The Hop/Telephone	30
70	Crab CRAB 51	I Wish I Was An Apple/The Story	8
70	Crab CRAB 52	Take A Letter Maria/OWEN GRAY: Just A Little Loving	5
70	Crab CRAB 57	My Dickie/Brixton Hop	5
70	Crab CRAB 58	I Can't Stand It No Longer/Beyond The Wall	5
70	Crab CRAB 59	Endlessly/Who's Making Love	5
70	Crab CRAB 62	Hurt/Julia	5
70	Pama PM 822	Love Bug/My Dickie	5
71	Bullet BU 467	Nobody's Business/Standing By	5
71	Camel CA 84	I Am Just A Sufferer/We Want To Know	5
71	Crab CRAB 67	Searching So Long/MORGAN'S ALL STARS: Drums Of Passion	5
72	Grape GR 3032	Send A Little Rain/DERRICK MORGAN ALL STARS: A Little Rain (Version)	5
72	Jackpot JP 793	Let Them Talk/Bringing In The Guns	5
72	Jackpot JP 794	Won't Be This Way/Ain't No Love	5
72	Jackpot JP 797	Me Naw Run/All Night Long	5
72	Jackpot JP 802	Festival 10/Festival 10 – Version	5
72	Punch PH 107	Forward March/Plenty Of One	5
72	Buster PB 60	Tears On My Pillow/KEITH REID: Worried Over You (actually by Keith & Enid)	5
73	Attack ATT 8048	Derrick's Big Eleven/My Ding A Ling	5
73	Big Shot BI 617	Housewives Choice/Don't You Worry (both sides with Hortense Ellis)	5
73	Bread BR 1119	I Who Have Nothing/I'm Not Home	5

1965, special sleeve for Times They Are A-Changin'...

Rear of sleeve, blank space to write song titles, £250.

1965, unreleased/withdrawn EP featuring Dylan, £75.

1966, *Mr. Tambourine Man* EP, £50.

1965, promo copy of Dylan's first UK single, £40.

1965, test pressing of Like A Rolling Stone, £200.

Rare Record Price Guide 2008

1967, ultra rare Psych 7" by Australian Playboys, £1,000.

1967, One In A Million's Fredereek Hernando, £750.

1968, Mike Stuart Span's Psych classic, £400+.

1968, The Factory find the right forest path, £650.

1968, July's My Clown/Dandelion Seeds, £180+.

1969, Arcadium single in rare Middle Earth sleeve, £150.

1967, Paper Blitz Tissue's Boy Meets Girl/Grey Man, £250.

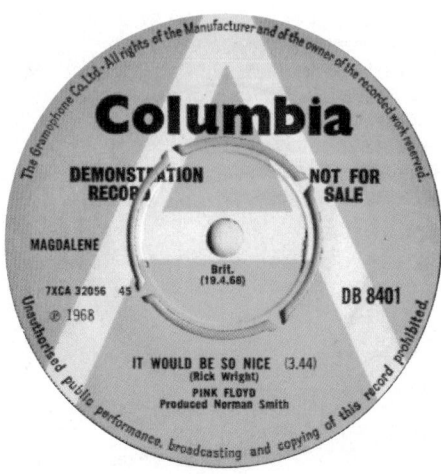

1968, Floyd 1-sided demo of It Would Be So Nice, £650.

1967, famed Pink Floyd debut promo 7", £1,500.

1966, classic EP by the all seeing Eyes, £400+

1968, the Captain's UK debut 45 is worth £40.

1964, before you know who were The Who, £450+.

Rare Record Price Guide 2008

1968, a Swedish export copy of My Generation, £145.

1967, P. P. Arnold's rare withdrawn Immediate LP, £500+.

1960/61, Jimmy Page' s first studio recording, £2,500.

1965, this export EP (Decca SDE 7503) is worth £110.

1965, export copy of Stones' Little Red Rooster, £100.

1964, unreleased Rolling Stones single acetate, £800+.

Rare Record Price Guide 2008

1971, gorgeous looking and sounding UK jazz, £300.

1969, more rare UK jazz from Ronnie Ross, £200.

1966, Cream connection on this rare UK jazz LP, £300+.

1966, even more collectable than Carr's Nucleus, £325.

1969, Joe Harriott's very scarce *Hum Dono* LP, £250.

1968, trumpeter Wheeler and Dankworth Orchestra, £150.

1972, early Genesis single in rare picture sleeve, £450.

1970, withdrawn Tell The Truth, 7" single, £80+.

1969, first pressing of Nick Drake's debut LP, £300+.

1968, B-side of famed Jethro 'Toe' debut single, £250.

1978, sleeve of rarest Queen single, £3,500.

Label detail of this blue vinyl 'Rhapsody'.

Rare Record Price Guide 2008

1966, stock copy of rare Bolan Hippy Gumbo 7", £700.

1968, T-Rex, Deborah demo, £120. £450 with scarce p/s.

1970, Bolan undercover as Dib Cochran, £700.

1971, rare funk from the Phantom Band, £60.

1973, funky B-side to Thank You Baby, £60.

1970, super-rare funk instrumental, £150.

Rare Record Price Guide 2008

1966, mega-rare (99 copies) Blue Horizon LP, £1250.

1971, Mighty Baby *A Jug Of Love* LP, £160.

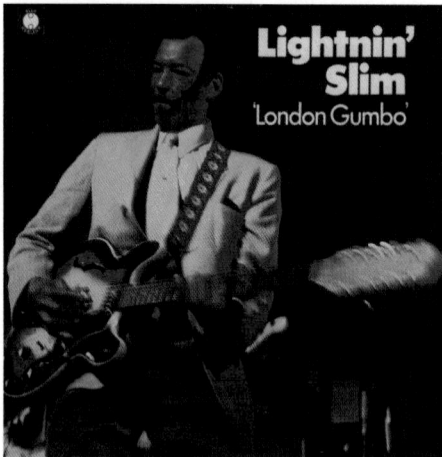

1972, Lightnin' Slim Blue Horizon LP, £100.

1972, rare copies with 'Vertigo Swirl' label, worth £200.

1979, Kevin Ayers debut LP, £60.

1970, rare Tea And Symphony Harvest album, £250.

Rare Record Price Guide 2008

73	Downtown DT 520	Hey Little Girl/Don't Blame The Man	5
73	Pama Supreme PS 387	I'll Never Give Up/I Who Have Nothing	5
75	Klik KL 603	Wet Dreams Part 1/Wet Dreams Part 2	5
63	Island ILP 903	FORWARD MARCH (LP)	150
69	Doctor Bird DLMB 5014	BEST OF DERRICK MORGAN (LP)	95
69	Island ILP 990	DERRICK MORGAN AND HIS FRIENDS (LP)	85
69	Pama ECO 10	DERRICK MORGAN IN LONDON (LP)	60
69	Pama PSP 1006	MOON HOP (LP)	65
69	Trojan TTL 5	SEVEN LETTERS (LP)	25
70	Trojan TTL 38	FORWARD MARCH (LP, reissue)	22
70s	Magnet MGT 004	IN THE MOOD (LP)	12

(see also Roland Alphonso; Frank Cosmo; Copy Cats, Derrick & Lloyd; Derrick, Morris & Patsy; Derrick & Patsy; Derrick & Naomi; Derrick & Paulette; Derrick & Pauline; Morgan's All Stars; Martin & Derrick; Larry Lawrence; Matador, Jackie Robinson)

FREDDY MORGAN
59	London HL 7077	Side Saddle/64 Rue Blondell (export issue)	18

GEORGE MORGAN
68	London HLB 10197	Barbara/Sad Bird	5
57	Philips BBE 12149	COUNTRY AND WESTERN SPECTACULAR (EP)	20
68	London HAB 8353	COUNTRY HITS BY CANDLELIGHT (LP)	22

JANE MORGAN (& TROUBADORS)
55	London HL 8148	Why — Oh Why/The Heart You Break (May Be Your Own) (78 rpm = £10)	48
57	London HLR 8395	From The First Hello To The Last Goodbye/Come Home, Come Home, Come Home	42
57	London HLR 8436	Around The World/It's Not For Me To Say (78 rpm = £10)	25
57	London HLR 8468	Fascination (with Troubadors)/Why Don't They Leave Us Alone	25
58	London HLR 8539	I'm New At The Game Of Romance/It's Been A Long Long Time (with Troubadors) (78 rpm = £6)	20
58	London HLR 8611	I've Got Bells On My Heart/Only One Love (78 rpm = £6)	15
58	London HLR 8649	Enchanted Island/Once More, My Love, Once More (78 rpm = £6)	12
58	London HLR 8751	The Day The Rains Came/Le Jour Ou La Pluie Viendra (78 rpm = £6)	10
58	London HL 7064	The Day The Rains Came/I May Never Pass This Way Again (export issue)	10
59	London HLR 8810	If I Could Only Live My Life Again/To Love And Be Loved (78 rpm = £10)	10
59	London HLR 8925	With Open Arms/I Can't Begin To Tell You (78 rpm = £22)	10
59	London HLR 8999	Happy Anniversary/C'est La Vie, C'est L'Amour (78 rpm = £32)	10
60	London HLR 9087	My Love Doesn't Love Me At All/The Bells Of St. Mary's	10
60	London HLR 9120	Romantica/I Am A Heart	10
60	London HLR 9210	Lord And Master/Where's The Boy (I Never Met)	10
60	London HLR 9249	Somebody/The Angry Sea	6
61	London HLR 9421	It Takes Love/Homesick For Old England	6
62	London HLR 9528	What Now My Love/Forever My Love	6
63	London HLR 9683	Theme From Carnival (Love Makes The World Go 'Round)/The Second Time Around	6
63	Colpix PX 700	Red Sails In The Sunset/My Special Dream	6
64	Colpix PX 713	Bless 'Em All/Does Goodnight Mean Goodbye	6
67	Columbia DB 7645	Maybe/Walking The Streets In The Rain	10
67	Columbia DB 8177	The Three Bells (Jimmy Brown Song)/I Want To Be With You	6
67	HMV POP 1608	This Is My World Without You/Somebody, Someplace	10
68	Stateside SS 2082	Masquerade/Smile	6
58	London RE-R 1161	ALL THE WAY PART 1 (EP, with Troubadours)	20
58	London RE-R 1162	ALL THE WAY PART 2 (EP, with Troubadours)	20
59	London RE-R 1204	THE DAY THAT THE RAINS CAME (EP, triangular or round centre)	22/15
61	London RE-R 1331	JANE MORGAN (EP)	22
57	London HA-R 2086	FASCINATION (LP)	35
58	London HA-R 2110	ALL THE WAY (LP, with Troubadors)	20
58	London HA-R 2133	SOMETHING OLD, SOMETHING NEW, SOMETHING BORROWED, SOMETHING BLUE (LP)	20
59	London HA-R 2136	GREAT SONGS FROM THE GREAT SHOWS OF THE CENTURY VOL. 1 (LP)	20
59	London HA-R 2137	GREAT SONGS FROM THE GREAT SHOWS OF THE CENTURY VOL. 2 (LP)	20
59	London HA-R 2158	THE DAY THE RAINS CAME (LP)	20
60	London HA-R 2244	JANE IN SPAIN (LP)	20
60	London HA-R 2316	THE BALLADS OF LADY JANE (LP)	20
61	London HA-R 2371	JANE MORGAN TIME (LP)	20
61	London HA-R 2377	THE SECOND TIME AROUND (LP, also stereo SAH-R 6177)	20/25
62	London HA-R 2430	AT THE COCONUT GROVE (LP, also stereo SAH-R 6226)	20/25
62	London HA-R/SH-R 8042	WHAT NOW MY LOVE (LP, mono/stereo)	20/25
63	London HA-R/SH-R 8069	LOVE MAKES THE WORLD GO ROUND (LP, mono/stereo)	18/20
63	Colpix PXL 460	JANE MORGAN SERENADES THE VICTORS (LP)	18
65	Columbia SX 6010	IN MY STYLE... (LP)	18

(see also Troubadors, Roger Williams)

JAYE P. MORGAN
54	London HL 8009	Life Is Just A Bowl Of Cherries/Operator 299 (78)	8
55	HMV 7M 327	The Longest Walk/Swanee	15
56	HMV 7M 348	If You Don't Want My Love/Pepper Hot Baby (78 rpm, HMV POP 144 = £8)	25
56	HMV 7M 365	Not One Goodbye/My Bewildered Heart	10
56	Brunswick 05519	Have You Ever Been Lonely?/Baby Don't Do It (78 rpm = £6)	10
57	RCA RCA 1014	You, You Romeo/Graduation Ring (78 rpm = £10)	8
59	MGM MGM 1005	Are You Lonesome Tonight?/Miss You (78 rpm = £15)	10
59	MGM MGM 1021	(It Took) One Kiss/My Reputation	5
59	MGM MGM 1039	Somebody Loses, Somebody Wins/Somebody Else Is Taking My Place	5
60	MGM MGM 1093	I Walk The Line/Wondering Where You Are	6
62	MGM MGM 1182	Heartache Named Johnny/He Thinks I Still Ache	6
62	MGM MGM 1190	Brotherhood Of Man/Nobody's Sweetheart	6

Jaye P. MORGAN

54	London RE-P 1013	JAYE P. SINGS (EP)...22
59	MGM MGM-C 793	SLOW AND EASY (LP) 25
50s	RCA	JUST YOU, JUST ME (LP) 22

JOHN MORGAN
| 72 | Carnaby 6302 010 | KALEIDOSCOPE (LP)..55 |
| 70s | SWP 1007 | LIVE AT DURRANT HOUSE (LP, private pressing) ....90 |

(see also Spirit Of John Morgan)

LEE MORGAN
| 61 | Columbia 33SX 1399 | THE BIRDLAND STORY VOL. 1 (LP)...15 |
| 62 | Stateside SL 10016 | EXPOOBIDENT (LP) ....15 |

MACE MORGAN THUNDERBIRDS
| 63 | Starlite STEP 36 | SHAKE AND SWING (EP)...60 |

MARY MORGAN
56	Parlophone MSP 6204	Jimmy Unknown/You Are My Love 12
56	Parlophone R 4227	From The Candy Store On The Corner/No-One Was There But You............10
57	Parlophone R 4348	A Call To Arms/One For Sorrow, Two For Joy..................................6

RUSS MORGAN ORCHESTRA
55	Brunswick 05464	Alabamy Bound/SCRANTON 7: The Popcorn Song 5
55	Brunswick 05493	Dog Face Soldier/Don't Cry Sweetheart...5
56	Brunswick 05537	The Poor People Of Paris (Poor John)/Silver Moon 5
56	Brunswick 05602	Lay Down Your Arms/My Best You You 5

SAMMY MORGAN
| 70 | Bullet BU 455 | Get Out Of This Land/SYDNEY ALL STARS: Landmark ....5 |
| 70 | Punch PH 57 | Get Out Of This Land/SYDNEY ALL STARS: Landmark ....5 |

MORGAN BROTHERS
| 59 | MGM MGM 1007 | Nola/Guiding Star (78 rpm = £8) ....8 |
| 59 | MGM MGM 1026 | Kissin' On The Red Light/Milk From The Coconut ....6 |

MORGAN'S ALL STARS
| 71 | Camel CA 76 | I Love You The Most (actually by Lloyd Clarke)/I Love You The Most (Version) ... 5 |

(see also B. Leggs, Derrick Morgan, Marvels)

MORGAN TWINS
| 58 | RCA RCA 1083 | T.V. Hop/Let's Get Going (78 rpm = £60)..................................110 |

(Ron Paul) MORIN & (Luke P.) WILSON
| 72 | Sovereign SVNA 7252 | PEACEFUL COMPANY (LP) ....20 |

JOHNNY MORISETTE
| 62 | Stateside SS 107 | Meet Me At The Twistin' Place/Any Time Any Day Any Where...............15 |

MORNING
| 70 | Liberty LBS 83463 | MORNING (LP)..20 |
| 72 | United Artists UAS 29337 | STRUCK LIKE SILVER (LP) ....20 |

MORNING AFTER
| 71 | Sky SKYLP 71014 | BLUE BLOOD (LP) ....80 |

MORNING GLORY
| 73 | Island ILPS 9237 | MORNING GLORY (LP)...20 |

(see also John Surman)

MORNING RUNNER
| 04 | Faith & Hope FH0527 | The Great Escape/Oceans (500 only, p/s).................................40 |
| 05 | EMI 10R6666 | DRAWING SHAPES EP (numbered 10").......................................8 |

GIORGIO MORODER
66	Page One POF 003	Full Stop/Believe Me..5
67	Page One POF 028	How Much Longer Must I Wait/Bla Bla Diddley...............................5
90s	Cause-N-Effect	I Wanna Rock You (Thee Maddcat Mix)/(Thee DrumDrum Mix) (12", no p/s) ...15
90s	Cause-N-Effect	FROM HERE TO ETERNITY (LP) 20
00s	Logic	THE CHASE (2-LP) 20

(see also Phil Oakey & Giorgio Moroder, Freddie Mercury, Giorgio)

ENNIO MORRICONE ORCHESTRA
67	RCA Victor RCA 1596	A Fistful Of Dollars/The Man With No Name 5
67	RCA Victor RCA 1634	For A Few Dollars More/La Resi Dei Conti..................................5
69	RCA RCA 1892	Once Upon A Time In The West (Jill's Theme)/Finale.......................6
67	RCA Victor RD/SF 7875	A FISTFUL OF DOLLARS (LP, soundtrack) 20
68	RCA Victor RD 7994	A FISTFUL OF DOLLARS/FOR A FEW DOLLARS MORE/
		THE GOOD, THE BAD AND THE UGLY (LP, soundtrack) 12
68	United Artists (S)ULP 1197	THE GOOD, THE BAD AND THE UGLY (LP, soundtrack) 20
69	United Artists (S)ULP 1228	THE BIG GUNDOWN (LP, soundtrack).....................................20
69	United Artists UAS 29005	A PROFESSIONAL GUN (LP, soundtrack) 40
70	Stateside SSL 10307	THE SICILIAN CLAN (LP, soundtrack) 20
70	CBS 70067	LOVE CIRCLE (LP, soundtrack)..60
70	MCA MKPS 2013	TWO MULES FOR SISTER SARA (LP, soundtrack)........................30
72	United Artists UAS 29345	A FISTFUL OF DYNAMITE (LP, soundtrack)..............................40
72	Bell BELLS 209	THE BURGLARS (LP, soundtrack)..30
72	Paramount SPFL 275	THE RED TENT (LP, soundtrack)..20

CHRIS MORRIS
| 91 | Flexi FLOP 1 | THE SELECT FLOPPY DISC (EP, 33rpm, poly sleeve, some with magazine) .. 18/15 |

ERIC MORRIS
61	Starlite ST45 052	Search The World/Buster's Shack..30
61	Blue Beat BB 53	Humpty Dumpty/Corn Bread And Butter (as Eric 'Humpty Dumpty' Morris &
		Drumbago All Stars; [B-side actually by Drumbago All Stars])...............10

62	Blue Beat BB 74	My Forty-Five/I've Tried Everybody (as Eric 'Humpty Dumpty' Morris & Drumbago All Stars)	10
62	Blue Beat BB 81	Sinners Repent And Pray/Now And Forever More (B-side act. by Alton Ellis)	10
62	Blue Beat BB 83	Money Can't Buy Life (with Buster's Group)/A. ELLIS: True Love	10
62	Blue Beat BB 105	Pack Up Your Troubles/Oh What A Smile Can Do (with D. Cosmo & Drumbago's All Stars)	10
62	Blue Beat BB 115	G.I. Lady/Going To The River	10
62	Blue Beat BB 128	Over The Hills/Lazy Woman (with Buster's Group)	10
62	Blue Beat BB 137	Miss Peggy's Grandmother/BUSTER'S GROUP: Megaton	10
62	Blue Beat BB 140	Seven Long Years/For Your Love	10
63	Blue Beat BB 153	Lonely Blue Boy/PRINCE BUSTER: Oh We	18
63	Blue Beat BB 184	Sweet Love/BUSTER, DEREK, ERIC: Country Girl	15
64	Blue Beat BB 218	Love Can Break A Man/Worried People	10
64	Blue Beat BB 273	Stitch In Time/For Ever	10
64	Black Swan WI 412	Sampson/BABA BROOKS: Jelly Beans	25
64	Black Swan WI 414	Solomon Grundie/BABA BROOKS: Key To The City	25
64	Black Swan WI 433	Supper In The Gutter/Words Of My Mouth	20
64	Black Swan WI 439	River Come Down/Seek And You'll Find	20
64	Black Swan WI 445	Home Sweet Home/LESTER STERLING: '64 Special	25
64	Island WI 142	Penny-Reel/DUKE REID'S GROUP: Darling When (B-side act. Dotty & Bonnie)	30
64	Island WI 147	Mama No Fret/FRANKIE ANDERSON: Santa Lucia (B-side w/Roland Alphonso)	18
64	Island WI 150	Drop Your Sword/Catch A Fire (B-side actually by Roland Alphonso)	22
64	Island WI 151	What A Man Doeth/DUKE REID'S GROUP: Rude Boy (B-side actually by Baba Brooks)	22
64	Port-O-Jam PJ 4006	Oh My Dear/Lena Belle	12
64	Rio R 39	Little District/True And Just	12
64	Rio R 48	Live As A Man/Man Will Rule	12
65	Rio R 72	By The Sea/I Wasn't Around	12
65	Island WI 183	Love Can Make A Mansion (actually "Love Can Break A Man")/Ungodly People	12
65	Island WI 185	Suddenly/Many Long Years	12
65	Island WI 199	Fast Mouth/The Harder They Come	15
65	Island WI 234	Children Of Today/BABA BROOKS: Greenfield Ska	22
65	Blue Beat BB 298	Those Teardrops/DON DRUMMOND: Ska Town	35
66	Blue Beat BB 349	I'm The Greatest/BUSTER'S ALL STARS: Picket Line	25
60s	Fab BB 30	Humpty Dumpty (as Eric 'Humpty Dumpty' Morris & Buster All Stars)/FOLKS BROTHERS: Carolina	7

(see also Monty Morris, Byron Lee & Dragonaires, Cool Sticky, Tommy McCook, Zoot Simms, Marguerita, Cool Cats)

HELMSLEY MORRIS
67	Caltone TONE 104	Love Is Strange/DON D. JUNIOR: Sir Pratt Special	40
68	Pama PM 720	Stay Loose Mama/You Think I'm A Fool (as Hainsley Morris)	7

JOE MORRIS & ORCHESTRA
54	London HL 8088	I Had A Notion/Just Your Way Baby (78)	60
54	London HL 8098	Travelin' Man/No, It Can't Be Done (78)	35

LIBBY MORRIS
56	Parlophone R 4225	When Liberace Winked At Me/None Of That Now	10
65	RCA RCA 1499	One Of Those Songs/The Phoenix Love Theme (Senza Fine)	5

MILTON MORRIS
69	Upsetter US 318	No Bread And Butter/UPSETTERS: Soulful I	12

MONTY MORRIS
67	Doctor Bird DB 1067	Play It Cool/BABA BROOKS' BAND: Open The Door	22
67	Doctor Bird DB 1081	Put On Your Red Dress/BABA BROOKS' BAND: Faberge	35
68	Doctor Bird DB 1162	Last Laugh/You Really Got A Hold On Me	30
68	Pama PM 721	Say What You're Saying/Tears In Your Eyes	15
68	Nu Beat NB 007	True Romance/BUNNY & RUDDY: Rhythm And Soul	15
68	Nu Beat NB 011	Simple Simon/BUNNY & RUDDY: On The Town	15
69	Doctor Bird DB 1176	Same Face/A Little Bit Of This	18
69	Big Shot BI 513	Deportation/Say I'm Back	12
69	Camel CA 12	Can't Get No Peace/UPSETTERS: For A Few Dollars More	12
69	Camel CA 28	No More Teardrops/Love Me Or Leave Me (as Monty Morris & Maples)	7
70	Unity UN 557	Do It My Way/Where In The World (Are You Going)	6
70	Explosion EX 2016	Higher Than The Highest Mountain/G.G. ALL STARS: Musical Shot	12
73	Ackee ACK 527	I'm Ready To Go/TOMMY McCOOK: Flower Pot	7

(see also Eric Morris, Monty, Derrick & Patsy, Monty & Roy, Alton Ellis)

NAGGO MORRIS
79	Hit Run DD 111	Jah Will Explain/DOCTOR PABLO: Wicked Feel It (12")	25

ROGER MORRIS
72	Regal Zono. SRZA 8509	FIRST ALBUM (LP)	40+

RUSSELL MORRIS
69	Decca F 22964	The Real Thing (Parts I & II)/It's Only A Matter Of Time	70
70	Decca F 23066	Rachel/Slow Joey	5

VICTOR MORRIS
68	Amalgamated AMG 813	Now I'm Alone/Rise And Fall	10

MORRIS & MINORS
80	Round MOR 1	STATE THE OBVIOUS (EP, p/s in poly bag)	10

MORRIS & MITCH
57	Decca F 10900	Cumberland Gap/I'm Not A Juvenile Delinquent (78 rpm = £8)	10
57	Decca F 10929	What Is A Skiffler?/The Tommy Rot Story (78 rpm = £6)	10
58	Decca F 11086	Highway Patrol/Bird Dog (78 rpm = £8)	10
68	Trend TRE 1010	The Magical Musherishi Tourists/Mister D.J. Man	5
58	Decca DFE 6486	SIX FIVE NOTHING SPECIAL (EP)	20

MINT VALUE £

MORRIS FAMILY & GOSPEL JUBILEERS
60	Top Rank JAR 322	Wake Up Jonah/He Never Complained	7

CURLEY JIM MORRISON
61	Starlite ST45 065	Air Force Blues/Didn't I Tell You	150

DOROTHY MORRISON
69	Elektra EKSN 45070	All God's Children Got Soul/Put A Little Love In Your Heart	8

HAROLD MORRISON
65	Brunswick LAT 8639	HOSS HE'S THE BOSS (LP)	12

JAMES MORRISON & TOM ENNIS
80	Topic 12T 390	JAMES MORRISON & TOM ENNIS (LP)	12

PROFESSOR MORRISON'S LOLLIPOP
68	London HLU 10228	You Got The Love/Gypsy Lady	6
69	London HLU 10254	Oo-Poo-Pah Susie/You Take It	6

TOM MORRISON
60	MGM MGM-EP 709	THE ADVENTURES OF MIGHTY MOUSE AND HIS PALS (EP)	8

VAN MORRISON
67	London HLZ 10150	Brown-Eyed Girl/Goodbye Baby (Baby Goodbye)	45
70	Warner Brothers WB 7383	Come Running/Crazy Love	6
70	Warner Brothers WB 7434	Domino/Sweet Jannie	15
70	President PT 328	Brown-Eyed Girl/Goodbye Baby (Baby Goodbye) (reissue)	15
72	Warner Brothers K 16210	Jackie Wilson Said/You've Got The Power	7
74	London HLM 10453	Brown-Eyed Girl/Goodbye Baby (Baby Goodbye) (2nd reissue)	10
74	Warner Brothers K 16392	Caldonia/What's Up, Crazy Pup	10
77	Warner Brothers K 16939	The Eternal Kansas City/Joyous Sound	5
77	Warner Brothers K 16986	Joyous Sound/Mechanical Bliss	6
79	Mercury 6001 121	Bright Side Of The Road/Rolling Hills (p/s)	5
89	Polydor VANX 2	Whenever God Shines His Light (Album Version) (with Cliff Richard)/ Cry For Home/I'd Love To Write Another Song (12", p/s)	8
89	Polydor VANCD 2	Whenever God Shines His Light (7" Version) (with Cliff Richard)/ I'd Love To Write Another Song/Cry For Home/Whenever God Shines His Light (Album Version) (CD)	8
68	London HA-Z 8346	BLOWIN' YOUR MIND (LP)	60
69	Warner Brothers WS 1768	ASTRAL WEEKS (LP, orange or green label)	25/15
70	Warner Brothers WS 1835	MOONDANCE (LP, orange or green label)	25/15
71	Warner Brothers WS 1884	HIS BAND AND STREET CHOIR (LP, green label)	15
71	President PTLS 1045	THE BEST OF VAN MORRISON (LP)	15
71	Warner Brothers K 46114	TUPELO HONEY (LP, gatefold sleeve, green label)	12
72	Warner Brothers K 46172	SAINT DOMINIC'S PREVIEW (LP, with insert, 'Burbank' label)	12
73	Warner Brothers K 46024	ASTRAL WEEKS (LP, reissue, 'Burbank' label)	12
73	Warner Brothers K 46040	MOONDANCE (LP, reissue, 'Burbank' label)	12
73	Warner Brothers K 46066	HIS BAND AND STREET CHOIR (LP, reissue, 'Burbank' label)	12
73	Warner Brothers K 46242	HARD NOSE THE HIGHWAY (LP, gatefold sleeve, 'Burbank' label)	12
74	London HSM 5008	T.B. SHEETS (LP)	12
74	Warner Brothers K 86007	IT'S TOO LATE TO STOP NOW (2-LP, gatefold sleeve, 'Burbank' label)	15
74	Warner Brothers K 56068	VEEDON FLEECE (LP, 'Burbank' label)	12
77	Bang 6467 625	THIS IS WHERE I CAME IN (LP)	12
77	Warner Brothers K 56322	A PERIOD OF TRANSITION (LP)	12
84	Mercury MERH 54	A SENSE OF WONDER (LP, white label test pressings with "Crazy Jane On God")	25
84	Mercury MERH 54	A SENSE OF WONDER (LP, credits but doesn't play "Crazy Jane On God")	12

(see also Them)

MORRISSEY
SINGLES
88	HMV POP 1618	Suedehead/I Know Very Well How I Got My Name (p/s)	6
88	HMV TCPOP 1618	Suedehead/I Know Very Well How I Got My Name/ Hairdresser On Fire/Oh Well, I'll Never Learn (cassette)	22
88	HMV TCPOP 1618	Suedehead/I Know Very Well How I Got My Name/Oh Well, I'll Never Learn (mispressed cassette, plays "Ordinary Boys" instead of "I Know Very Well..."), withdrawn)	15
88	HMV 12 POP 1618	Suedehead/I Know Very Well How I Got My Name/Hairdresser On Fire (12", 1st pressings in brown p/s)	15
88	HMV CDPOP 1618	Suedehead/I Know Very Well How I Got My Name/Hairdresser On Fire/ Oh Well, I'll Never Learn (CD)	20
88	HMV POP 1619	Everyday Is Like Sunday/Disappointed (p/s)	7
88	HMV TCPOP 1619	Everyday Is Like Sunday/Sister I'm A Poet/Disappointed (cassette)	9
88	HMV 12 POP 1619	Everyday Is Like Sunday/Sister I'm A Poet/Disappointed/ Will Never Marry (12", p/s)	12
88	HMV CDPOP 1619	Everyday Is Like Sunday/Sister I'm A Poet/Disappointed/ Will Never Marry (CD)	20
89	HMV TCPOP 1620	The Last Of The Famous International Playboys/Lucky Lisp/ Michaels Bones (cassette)	12
89	HMV CDPOP 1620	The Last Of The Famous International Playboys/Lucky Lisp/ Michaels Bones (CD)	18
89	HMV POP 1621	Interesting Drug/Such A Little Thing Makes Such A Big Difference (p/s)	9
89	HMV TCPOP 1621	Interesting Drug/Such A Little Thing Makes Such A Big Difference (cassette)	12
89	HMV 12 POP 1621	Interesting Drug/Such A Little Thing Makes Such A Big Difference/ Sweet And Tender Hooligan (live) (12", p/s)	10
89	HMV 12 POPS 1621	Interesting Drug/Such A Little Thing Makes Such A Big Difference (12", p/s, 1 side etched)	12
89	HMV CDPOP 1621	Interesting Drug/Such A Little Thing Makes Such A Big Difference/ Sweet And Tender Hooligan (live) (CD)	12

90	HMV POP 1622	Ouija Board, Ouija Board/Yes, I Am Blind (p/s)	6
90	HMV CDPOP 1622	Ouija Board, Ouija Board/Yes, I Am Blind/East West (CD)	10
90	HMV POP 1623	November Spawned A Monster/He Knows I'd Love To See Him (p/s)	6
90	HMV TCPOP 1623	November Spawned A Monster/He Knows I'd Love To See Him (cassette, card slip case)	10
90	HMV 12 POP 1623	November Spawned A Monster/Girl Least Likely To/ He Knows I'd Love To See Him (12", p/s)	10
90	HMV CDPOP 1623	November Spawned A Monster/He Knows I'd Love To See Him/ Girl Least Likely To (CD)	8
90	HMV POP 1624	Piccadilly Palare/Get Off The Stage (p/s)	5
90	HMV TCPOP 1624	Piccadilly Palare/Get Off The Stage (cassette)	10
90	HMV 12 POP 1624	Piccadilly Palare/At Amber/Get Off The Stage (12", p/s)	16
90	HMV CDPOP 1624	Piccadilly Palare/At Amber/Get Off The Stage (CD)	12
91	HMV POP 1625	Our Frank/Journalists Who Lie (p/s)	6
91	HMV TCPOP 1625	Our Frank/Journalists Who Lie (cassette)	10
91	HMV 12 POP 1625	Our Frank/Journalists Who Lie/Tony The Pony (12", p/s)	10
91	HMV CDPOP 1625	Our Frank/Journalists Who Lie/Tony The Pony (CD)	12
91	HMV POP 1626	Sing Your Life/That's Entertainment (p/s)	6
91	HMV TCPOP 1626	Sing Your Life/That's Entertainment (cassette)	10
91	HMV CDPOP 1626	Sing Your Life/That's Entertainment/The Loop (CD)	10
91	HMV POP 1627	Pregnant For The Last Time/Skin Storm (p/s)	6
91	HMV TCPOP 1627	Pregnant For The Last Time/Skin Storm (cassette)	10
91	HMV 12 POP 1627	Pregnant For The Last Time/Skin Storm/Cosmic Dancer (live)/ Disappointed (live) (12", p/s)	10
91	HMV CDPOP 1627	Pregnant For The Last Time/Skin Storm/Cosmic Dancer (live)/ Disappointed (live) (CD)	12
91	HMV CDPOP 1628	My Love Life/I've Changed My Plea To Guilty/There's A Place In Hell For Me And My Friends (live) (CD)	10
92	HMV 12POP 1629	We Hate It When Our Friends Become Successful/Suedehead/I've Changed My Plea To Guilty/Pregnant For The Last Time (12", p/s)	12
92	HMV CDPOP 1629	We Hate It When Our Friends Become Successful/Suedehead/I've Changed My Plea To Guilty/Alsatian Cousin (12", p/s)	12
92	HMV CDPOP 1629	Certain People I Know/You've Had Her/Jack The Ripper (CD)	16
94	Parlophone R 6372	The More You Ignore Me, The Closer I Get/Used To Be A Sweet Boy/ I'd Love To (numbered p/s)	5
94	Parlophone CDR 6383	Hold On To Your Friends/Moon River (CD)	8
95	RCA 74321332947	Boy Racer/London (Live Version) (p/s)	7
95	RCA 74321332952	Boy Racer/Spring Heeled Jim/Why Don't You Find Out For Yourself (CD)	15
95	RCA Victor LC 0316	Dagenham Dave/Nobody Loves Us (p/s)	5
97	Island IS 667	Alma Matters/Heir Apparent (p/s)	5
97	Island IS 671	Roy's Keen/Lost (p/s)	5
97	Island IS 686	Satan Rejected My Soul/Now I Am A Was (p/s)	5
00	EMI EMI 8872932	SINGLES 88-91 (10 x CDs, card sleeves, in box)	28
01	EMI EMI 8797452	SINGLES 91-95 (9 X CDs, card sleeves, in box)	28

PROMOS

92	HMV POP DJ 1629	We Hate It When Our Friends Become Successful/We Hate It When Our Friends Become Sucessful (10", A-side plays at 45rpm, B-side at 78rpm, die-cut sleeve)	32
92	HMV POP DJ 1630	You're The One For Me, Fatty/You're The One For Me, Fatty (10", A-side plays at 45rpm, B-side at 78rpm, die-cut sleeve)	32
93	HMV POPDJ 1631	Certain People I Know/Jack The Ripper (die-cut 'Moz' p/s)	15
93	HMV POPDJ 1632	Jack The Ripper/Sister I'm A Poet (p/s)	12
95	Parlophone CDRDJ 6243	Sunny/Black-Eyed Susan/A Swallow On My Neck (CD)	18
94	Parlophone RDJ 6372	The More You Ignore, Me The Closer I Get/Used To Be A Sweet Boy (yellow p/s)	12
94	Parlophone CDRDJ 6372	The More You Ignore, Me The Closer I Get/Used To Be A Sweet Boy/ I'd Love To (CD, yellow card p/s)	12
94	Parlophone CDRDJ 6372	The More You Ignore, Me The Closer I Get (CD, with "45rpm" logo on disc, withdrawn)	22
94	Parlophone CDRDJ 6383	Hold On To Your Friends/Moonriver (CD, card p/s)	10
95	Parlophone RDJ 6400	Have-A-Go Merchant/Whatever Happens, I Love You (p/s)	25
95	Parlophone CDRDJ 6400	Have-A-Go Merchant/Whatever Happens, I Love You (CD, 'skinhead' card p/s)	20
95	Parlophone CDRDJX 6400	Boxers/Have-A-Go Merchant/Whatever Happens I Love You (CD)	10

(see also Smiths, Durutti Column)

DICK MORRISSEY

61	'77' LEU 12/8	HAVE YOU HEARD? (LP)	250
61	Fontana TFL 5149	IT'S MORRISSEY MAN! (LP)	250
67	Mercury 20093	HERE AND NOW AND SOUNDING GOOD (LP)	200
67	Mercury 20077MCL	STORM WARNING (LP)	200

(see also If, Morrissey-Mullen)

MORRISSEY-MULLEN

| 79 | Harvest SHSP 4098 | CAPE WRATH (LP) | 20 |

(see also Dick Morrissey)

BUDDY MORROW & HIS ORCHESTRA

53	HMV 7M 145	Heap Big Beat/I Can't Get Started	6
53	HMV 7M 151	I Can't Get Started/Heap Big Beat (reissue)	6
53	HMV 7M 162	Dragnet/Your Mouth's Got A Hole In It	8
54	HMV 7M 216	Knock On Wood (with Shaye Cogan)/All Night Long	10
60	RCA RCA 1167	Staccato's Theme/Scraunchy (78 rpm = £10)	6
56	Mercury MPT 7003	SHALL WE DANCE (10" LP)	15

Ella Mae MORSE

ELLA MAE MORSE
52	Capitol CL 13666	Tennessee Saturday Night/A Little Further Down The Road (78) 10
52	Capitol CL 13727	Blacksmith Blues/Love Me Or Leave Me (78)............................ 10
52	Capitol CL 13754	Oakie Boogie/Love Ya' Like Mad (78) 10
52	Capitol CL 13798	Male Call/Sleepin' At The Foot Of The Bed (78)....................... 10
53	Capitol CL 13853	Jump Back Honey/Greyhound (78)..................................... 10
53	Capitol CL 13930	Big Mamou/Is It Any Wonder (78) 10
53	Capitol CL 13960	Forty Cups Of Coffee/Oh! You Crazy Moon (78) 12
54	Capitol CL 14037	T'Ain't What You Do, It's The Way That You Do It/
		It Ain't Necessarily So (78)... 10
54	Capitol CL 14044	The Guy Who Invented Kissin'/Good (78) 10
54	Capitol CL 14116	Goodnight, Well It's Time To Go/Sensational (78)...................... 10
54	Capitol CL 14176	(We've Reached) The Point Of No Return/Give A Little Time (78)......... 10
55	Capitol CL 14223	Bring Back My Baby To Me/Lovey Dovey (78 rpm = £10)................. 60
55	Capitol CL 14303	Smack Dab In The Middle/Yes, Yes I Do (78 rpm = £10)................. 50
55	Capitol CL 14332	Livin', Livin', Livin'/Heart Full Of Hope (78 rpm = £10)................. 50
55	Capitol CL 14341	Razzle-Dazzle/Ain't That A Shame (with Big Dave & His Music) (78 rpm = £20) . 100
55	Capitol CL 14362	Seventeen/Piddily Patter Song (with Big Dave & His Music) (78 rpm = £18) 100
55	Capitol CL 14376	Birmin'ham/An Occasional Man (78 rpm = £10) 50

(The above 45s were originally issued with triangular centres; later round-centres are worth around two-thirds these values.)

56	Capitol CL 14508	When Boy Kiss Girl (It's Love)/Sing-Ing-Ing-Ing (78 rpm = £10) 30
56	Capitol CL 14572	Rock And Roll Wedding/Down In Mexico (78 rpm = £10).................... 40
57	Capitol CL 14726	What Good'll It Do Me/Mister Money Maker (78 rpm = £12)................. 20
57	Capitol CL 14760	I'm Gone/Sway Me (78 rpm = £15)...................................... 20
55	Capitol EAP1 513	BARRELHOUSE BOOGIE AND THE BLUES (EP) 55
54	Capitol LC 6687	BARRELHOUSE BOOGIE AND THE BLUES (10" LP) 100

(see also 'Tennessee' Ernie Ford)

ELLA MAE MORSE & FREDDIE SLACK
67	Ember SPE 6605	ROCKIN' BREW (LP)... 25

AZIE MORTIMER
60	London HLX 9237	Lips/Wrapped Up In A Dream... 100

JELLY ROLL MORTON('S RED HOT PEPPERS)
53	HMV 7M 132	The Chant/Tank Town Bump 7
54	HMV 7M 178	Fat Frances/Pep (solo) 7
54	HMV 7M 187	Wild Man Blues/Smoke-House Blues 7
54	HMV 7M 207	Harmony Blues/Jungle Blues 7
54	HMV 7M 256	Fussy Mabel/Burnin' The Iceberg 7
57	Vogue EPV 1126	JELLY ROLL MORTON (EP).. 8
55	HMV 7EG 8178	THE BLUES THEY SANG (EP).. 8
59	RCA RCX 168	JELLY ROLL MORTON (EP).. 7
50s	Collector JE 120	JAZZ ORIGINATORS VOL. 3 (EP) 7
60	RCA RCX 207	JELLY ROLL MORTON NO. 2 (EP).. 8
60	Fontana TFE 17263	TREASURES OF NORTH AMERICAN NEGRO MUSIC VOL. 4 (EP) 8
61	Storyville SEP 379	JELLY ROLL MORTON (EP).. 8
53	HMV DLP 1016	JELLY ROLL MORTON AND HIS RED HOT PEPPERS (10" LP) 12
54	HMV DLP 1044	MORTON'S RED HOT PEPPERS VOLUME 2(10" LP) 12
54	Vogue LDE 080	NEW ORLEANS MEMORIES (10" LP) 12
54	London AL 3519	JELLY ROLL MORTON SOLOS (10" LP) 12
54	London AL 3520	JELLY ROLL MORTON'S KINGS OF JAZZ (10" LP)......................... 12
54	London AL 3534	CLASSIC JAZZ PIANO VOL. 1 (10" LP) 12
55	HMV DLP 1071	MORTON'S RED HOT PEPPERS NO. 3 (10" LP) 15
56	London AL 3559	CLASSIC JAZZ PIANO VOL. 2 (10" LP) 12

LIONEL MORTON
67	Philips BF 1578	What To Do With Laurie/I'll Just 7
67	Philips BF 1607	First Love Never Dies/Try Not To Cry 7
69	RCA RCA 1875	Waterloo Road/Floral Street... 7

(see also Four Pennies)

MANDY MORTON (BAND)
79	Banshee BANS 791	Song For Me (Music Prince)/Little Inbetween (with Spriguns)................. 15
80	Polydor 2382 101	Ghost Of Christmas Past/Black Nights (p/s) 6
78	Banshee BAN 1011	MAGIC LADY (LP, with lyric insert, 1,000 only) 175
78	Banshee BAN 1011	MAGIC LADY (LP, with lyric insert, blue vinyl, 20 only) 350
80	Polydor 2382 101	SEA OF STORMS (LP, solo, with insert).................................. 40
83	Banshee	VALLEY OF LIGHT (LP, private pressing).................................. 60

(see also Spriguns [Of Tolgus])

MORWELLS
79	Attack TACK 5	Kingston Twelve Tuffie/PRINCE JAMMY: Jammin' For Survival (12")............ 12
77	Burning Sounds BS 1006	CRAB RACE (LP).. 35
79	Bushays BFMLP 100	COOL RUNNING (LP) 35
80	Trojan TRLS 193	A1 DUB (LP)... 35

MOSAICS
66	Columbia DB 7990	Let's Go Drag Racing/Now That You're Here 25

PABLO MOSES
76	Lizzard 001	We Should Be In Angola/Dubbing In Angola 25
80	Island 12WIP	Dubbing Is A Must/Revolutionary Step (12")............................. 25
77	Klik KLP 9026	REVOLUTIONARY DREAM (LP).. 12
78	Different GETL 104	REVOLUTIONARY DREAM (LP).. 12

MOSES & JOSHUA
(see under Moses & Joshua Dillard)

MOSKOW
| 78 | Moskow SRS 2103 | Man From U.N.C.L.E./White Black (p/s) .... 8 |
| 81 | T.W. HIT 103 | Man From U.N.C.L.E./White Black (reissue in different p/s) .... 5 |

BILL MOSS
| 69 | Pama PM 765 | Sock It To 'Em Soul Brother (Parts 1 & 2) .... 15 |
| 70 | Pama PM 796 | Number One.. 8 |

BUDDY MOSS
| 60s | Kokomo K 1003 | GEORGIA BLUES VOLUME 2 (LP) .... 60 |

JENNY MOSS
| 63 | Columbia DB 7061 | Hobbies/Big Boys .... 50 |

STIRLING MOSS
| 61 | Redemption RLP 5004 | THE STIRLING MOSS STORY (LP) .... 15 |

TEDDY MOSS/JOSH WHITE
| 62 | Jazz Collector JEL 5 | THE MALE BLUES (EP) .... 18 |
| | (see also Josh White) | |

MOST
| 79 | SRT SRTS/CUS/570 | Carefree/In And Out (1,000 only stamped lyric insert) .... 60 |

MOST
| 94 | Detour DR 012 | Days, Days, Days/Take You There/Six Fifteen/Our Time (p/s, white vinyl) .... 6 |

ABE MOST OCTET
| 55 | London RE-P 1028 | PRESENTING THE ABE MOST OCTET (EP)................................ 15 |

MOST DOMINANT
| 93 | Kold Sweat KSEP210 | PUSHED TO DA LIMIT (EP) .... 10 |

MICKIE MOST (& GEAR)
63	Decca F 11664	Mr. Porter/Yes Indeed I Do 25
63	Columbia DB 7117	The Feminine Look/Shame On You Boy.................................. 15
63	Columbia DB 7180	Sea Cruise/It's A Little Bit Hot 15
64	Columbia DB 7245	Money Honey/That's Alright (as Mickey Most & Gear) 20
	(see also Most Brothers)	

MR FOUNDATION
| 67 | Studio One SO 2001 | See Them A Come/ KEN PARKER: Have A Good Time...................... 20 |
| 68 | Studio One SO 2061 | Time Oh/DUDLEY SIBLEY & PETER AUSTIN: Hole In Your Soul.............. 40 |

MR MOST
| 69 | Downtown DT 408 | Push Wood/Reggae Train... 12 |

MOST BROTHERS
57	Decca F 10968	Whistle Bait/I'm Comin' Home (78 rpm = £12) 20
58	Decca F 10998	Whole Lotta Woman/Teen Angel (78 rpm = £12) 20
58	Decca F 11040	Don't Go Home/Dottie (78 rpm = £12)................................... 20
	(see also Mickie Most, Alex Murray)	

BENNY MOTEN('S KANSAS CITY ORCHESTRA)
| 54 | HMV DLP 1057 | BENNIE MOTEN PLAYS KAY-CEE JAZZ (10" LP) .... 15 |

MOTHER EARTH
69	Mercury MF 1081	Goodnight Melda Grebe The Telephone Company Has Cut Us Off/I Did My Part .. 8
71	Reprise K 14089	Temptation Took Control Of Me/I'll Be Long Gone 5
68	Mercury SMCL 20143	LIVING WITH THE ANIMALS (LP) 15
69	Mercury SMCL 20173	MAKE A JOYFUL NOISE (LP) 15
69	Mercury SMCL 20179	TRACY NELSON COUNTRY (LP).. 15
71	Mercury 6338 023	SATISFIED (LP) 15
71	Reprise K 44133	BRING ME HOME (LP) 15

MOTHER EARTH
| 90s | Acid Jazz JAZID 100 | Jesse (Live) (company sleeve) .... 25 |
| 90s | Acid Jazz JAZID LP 48 | STONED WOMAN (LP) .... 18 |

MOTHER GONG
81	Butt BUTT 003	ROBOT WOMEN (LP) 12
82	Shanghai HAI 100	ROBOT WOMEN 2 (LP).. 12
83	Shanghai HAI 109	ROBOT WOMEN 3 (LP).. 12
	(see also Gong)	

MOTHERLIGHT
| 69 | Morgan Bluetown BT 5003 | BOBAK, JONS, MALONE (LP) .... 150 |
| | (see also Will Malone [Voice Band], Orange Bicycle) | |

MOTHERLODE
| 69 | Buddah 201 064 | When I Die/Hard Life .... 6 |
| 69 | Buddah 2318 043 | WHEN I DIE (LP) .... 15 |

MOTHERS OF INVENTION
| | (see under Frank Zappa/Mothers Of Invention) | |

MOTHER'S RUIN
81	Spectra SPC 1	Streetfighters/Leaving You (some in p/s) 55/40
82	Spectra SPC 6	Street Lights/Turn A Corner (p/s).................................... 20
82	Spectra SPC 7	Say It's Not True/It's Illogical (p/s)................................. 35
81	Off Course G33303	WANT MORE (LP) 12
82	Spectra SPA 1	ROAD TO RUIN (LP) 12

MOTHER'S SONS
| 70 | J-Dan JDN 4415 | I Want To Tell The World/Underground Man............................. 6 |

MOTHER YOD
| 97 | Prescription DRUG 1 | MOTHER YOD (LP, 99 copies only)..................................... 25 |

MOTHMEN

79	Absurd ABSURD 6	Does It Matter Irene?/Please Let Go (p/s)	5
81	Do It DUN 12	Show Me Your House And Car/People People (p/s, deleted after 1 day)	8
81	Do It DUNIT 12	Show Me Your House And Car/People People (12", p/s, deleted after 1 day)	10
81	Do It DUN 14	Temptation/People People (p/s)	5
82	Do It DUN 19	Wadada/As They Are (p/s)	5
82	Do It RIDE 9	ONE BLACK DOT (LP)	12
80s	On-U-Sound LP 2	PAY ATTENTION (LP)	12

(see also Alberto Y Lost Trios Paranoias)

MOTHS

69	Deroy	MOTHS (LP, private pressing in plain white sleeve)	400

MOTIFFE

72	Deroy 777	MOTIFFE (LP, private pressing in hand-illustrated white sleeve)	300

MOTION

79	DD Records DDLP04	MOTION (LP)	40

(see also Aswad)

MOTIONS

66	Pye International 7N 25390	Stop Your Crying/Every Step I Take	12

MOTIVATION

68	Direction 58-3248	Come On Down/Little Man	40

MÖTLEY CRÜE

84	Elektra E 9756	Looks That Kill/Piece Of The Action (p/s)	5
84	Elektra E 9756T	Looks That Kill/Piece Of The Action/Live Wire (12", p/s with free tattoo)	18
84	Elektra E 9756TP	Looks That Kill/Piece Of The Action/Live Wire (12", picture disc)	30
84	Elektra E 9732	Too Young To Fall In Love/Take Me To The Top (p/s)	5
84	Elektra E 9732T	Too Young To Fall In Love/Take Me To The Top (12", p/s, some with poster)	8
85	Elektra EKR 33T	Smokin' In The Boys' Room/Use It Or Lose It/Shout At The Devil (12", p/s)	8
86	Elektra EKR 16TP	Smokin' In The Boys' Room/Use It Or Lose It (mask-shaped pic disc & sticker)	15
86	Elektra EKR 33P	Smokin' In The Boys' Room/Home Sweet Home (2 different interlocking mask-shaped picture disc set)	18
86	Elektra EKR 33T	Smokin' In The Boys' Room/Home Sweet Home/Shout At The Devil (12", p/s with poster)	8
87	Elektra EKR 59V	Girls, Girls, Girls/Sumthin' For Nuthin' ('X-rated' stickered p/s, 3,000 only)	8
87	Elektra EKR 59T	Girls, Girls, Girls/Sumthin' For Nuthin'/Smokin' In The Boys' Room (12", p/s with patch)	8
87	Elektra EKR 59B	Girls, Girls, Girls/Sumthin' For Nuthin'/Smokin' In The Boys' Room (12", box set with patch)	8
87	Elektra EKR 59TP	Girls, Girls, Girls/Sumthin' For Nuthin'/Smokin' In The Boys' Room (12", picture disc)	8
88	Elektra EKR 65TP	You're All I Need/Wild Side/Home Sweet Home/Looks That Kill (12", picture disc)	8
88	Elektra EKR 65TB	You're All I Need/Wild Side/Home Sweet Home/Looks That Kill (12", box set with poster, tour pass & patch)	12
89	Elektra EKR 97P	Dr Feelgood/Sticky Sweet (shaped picture disc)	8
89	Elektra EKR 109P	Without You/Live Wire (die-cut picture disc)	8
91	Elektra EKR 136TG	Home Sweet Home (12", gatefold sleeve)	8
91	Elektra EKR 136TP	Home Sweet Home (12" picture disc)	8
83	Elektra 9602 89-1	SHOUT AT THE DEVIL (LP, with bonus 12" picture disc & poster)	15
83	Elektra 9602 89-1	SHOUT AT THE DEVIL (LP, gatefold 'pentagram' black sleeve & inner)	12

MOTÖRHEAD

SINGLES

77	Stiff BUY 9	White Line Fever/Leaving Here (p/s, "Stiff Boxed Set" 45, later mail-order)	22
77	Chiswick S 13	Motörhead/City Kids (p/s)	10
77	Chiswick NS 13	Motörhead/City Kids (12", p/s)	12
78	Bronze BRO 60	Louie Louie/Tear Ya Down (p/s)	6
79	Bronze BRO 67	Overkill/Too Late, Too Late (p/s, initially with 'Overkill' badge)	10/5
79	Bronze 12 BRO 67	Overkill/Too Late, Too Late (12", p/s)	10
79	Bronze BRO 78	No Class/Like A Nightmare (3 different sleeves)	each 5
79	Bronze BRO 85	Bomber/Over The Top (p/s, on blue vinyl)	8
79	Big Beat NS 13	Motörhead/City Kids (p/s, black, pink, blue, orange or white vinyl)	5
80	Big Beat NSP 13	Motörhead/City Kids (p/s, black & white or blue & white picture disc)	8/12
80	Bronze BRO 92 DJ	Leaving Here (live)/Stone Dead Forever (live) (2-track promo for Golden Years EP, no p/s)	40
80	Bronze BROX 106	Ace Of Spades/Dirty Love (12", 'Xmas' sleeve)	10
81	Lyntone LYN 9661	The Train Kept-A Rollin' (live) (blue flexi free with *Flexipop* mag, issue 7)	8
81	Bronze BROP 124	Motörhead (live)/Over The Top (live) (picture disc)	6
82	Bronze BRO 146	Iron Fist/Remember Me I'm Gone (p/s, blue or red vinyl)	12/5
82	Bronze BRO 151	Stand By Your Man/No Class/Masterplan (p/s, as Lemmy & Wendy O. Williams)	8
83	Bronze BRO 165	I Got Mine/Turn You Round Again (p/s)	8
83	Bronze BROX 165	I Got Mine/Turn You Round Again (12", p/s)	8
83	Bronze BRO 167	Shine/Hoochie Coochie Man (live) (p/s)	5
83	Bronze BROX 167	Shine/Hoochie Coochie Man (live)/Don't Need Religion (live) (12", p/s)	8
83	Bronze BROX 167/ BROX 92	Shine/Hoochie Coochie Man (live)/Don't Need Religion (live)/ THE GOLDEN YEARS (12", p/s, stickered, shrinkwrapped double pack)	18
83	Lyntone LYN 4383	In Their Own Words/BRONZ: Taken By Storm (flexi free with *Kerrang!* mag)	10/5
84	Bronze BRO 185	Killed By Death/Under The Knife (p/s)	5
84	Bronze BROP 185	Killed By Death/Under The Knife (logo skull-shaped picture disc)	12
84	Bronze BROX 185	Killed By Death (Full Length Version)/Under The Knife/Under The Knife (12", stickered p/s, with poster)	10
88	GWR GWR 15	Ace Of Spades/Dogs/Traitor (sold at concerts & through fan club, no p/s)	15
90	Epic 656578 0	The One To Sing The Blues/Dead Man's Hand (shaped picture disc)	8

80	Big Beat SWT 61	BEER DRINKERS EP (12", p/s, scarce pink or orange vinyl)	8
80	Big Beat SWT 61	BEER DRINKERS EP (12", p/s, brown vinyl)	15
81	Bronze BROX 116	ST. VALENTINES DAY MASSACRE (10" EP, with Girlschool)	12
82	Bronze BROX 116	ST. VALENTINES DAY MASSACRE (7" EP, with Girlschool)	5

ALBUMS

77	Chiswick WIK 2	MOTÖRHEAD (LP, black & silver sleeve with inner, 600 only)	75
77	Chiswick WIK 2	MOTÖRHEAD (LP, black & white laminated sleeve with inner)	15
77	Chiswick CWK 3008	MOTÖRHEAD (LP, white vinyl)	18
79	Bronze BRON 515	OVERKILL (LP, green vinyl)	20
79	Bronze BRON 523	BOMBER (LP, 3 different shades of blue vinyl)	each 15
80	Bronze BRONG 531	ACE OF SPADES (LP, gold vinyl, stickered sleeve)	15
80	Big Beat WIK 2	MOTÖRHEAD (LP, reissue, red or clear vinyl with inner sleeve)	12
81	Bronze BRONG 535	NO SLEEP 'TIL HAMMERSMITH (LP, gold vinyl, stickered sleeve)	15
84	Bronze/Pro MOTOR 1	NO REMORSE (2-LP, leather sleeve with inners)	15
86	GWR GWRLP 1	ORGASMATRON (LP, picture disc)	12
91	Epic 467481-0	1916 (LP, picture disc, stickered PVC sleeve)	12
91	Epic 467481 9	1916 (CD, 'tour' picture disc shrinkwrapped with booklet, stickered case)	18
93	Castle/Bronze CTVCD 125	ALL THE ACES (CD, numbered promo, in box with metal skull, 10 only)	400

(see also Lemmy & Upsetters, Sam Gopal, Hawkwind, Girlschool, Wild Horses, Filthy Phil & Fast Eddie, Young & Moody, Rocking Vickers, Blue Goose)

MOTORS

77	Virgin VS 186	Dancing The Night Away/Whiskey And Wine (p/s)	5
77	Virgin VS 186-12	Dancing The Night Away (extended)/Whiskey and Wine (12" no p/s)	8
77	Virgin VS 194	Be What You Gotta Be/You Beat The Hell Outa Me (p/s)	5
78	Virgin VS 206	Sensation/The Day I Found A Fiver (p/s, 50 with £5 note offer)	7/5
78	Virgin VS 219	Airport/Cold Love (live)	5
78	Virgin VS 219-12	Airport/Cold Love (12", blue vinyl, company sleeve)	8
78	Virgin VS222	Forget About You/Picturama (red/green labels or blue labels/red lettering)	5
78	Virgin VS 222-12	Forget About You/Picturama/The Middle Bit/Soul Surrender (12", red vinyl, stickered company die-cut sleeve)	8
78	Virgin VS236	Today/Here Comes The Hustler	5
79	Virgin VS 263	Love And Loneliness/Time For Make Up (10", red, green, blue or yellow vinyl, die-cut p/s)	each 8
80	Virgin VS349	That's What John Said/Crazy Alice (p/s)	5
80	Virgin VS363	Metropolis/Love Round The Corner (p/s)	5
81	Virgin VS427	Dancing The Night Away (remix)/Be What You Gotta Be (p/s)	5
78	Virgin V 2089	APPROVED BY THE MOTORS (LP, withdrawn group photo sleeve & inner sleeve)	12

(see also Ducks Deluxe, Heroes, Snakes)

MOTOWN SPINNERS
(see under Detroit Spinners)

MOTT

75	CBS 3528	Monte Carlo/Shout It All Out	6
75	CBS 3741	I Can Show You How It Is/By Tonight	5
75	CBS 4005	It Takes One To Know One/I'll Tell You Something	5

(see also Mott The Hoople)

TONY MOTTOLA

61	London HAZ 2442	STRING BAND STRUM-ALONG (LP, also stereo SAHZ 6231)	10/12

MOTT THE HOOPLE

69	Island WIP 6072	Rock And Roll Queen/Road To Birmingham	28
71	Island WIP 6105	Midnight Lady/The Debt (some in p/s)	18/6
71	Island WIP 6112	Downtown/Home (Is Where I Want To Be)	15
74	CBS 2439	Foxy Foxy/Trudi's Song (cherry vinyl)	6
76	CBS 3963	All The Young Dudes/Roll Away The Stone (p/s)	5
89	CBS 654853 3	All The Young Dudes/Roll Away The Stone/All The Way From Memphis/ The Golden Age Of Rock'n'Roll (3" CD, gatefold card sleeve)	8
69	Island ILPS 9108	MOTT THE HOOPLE (LP, pink label; mispress with 5 alternate mixes & "Road To Birmingham" in place of "Backsliding Fearlessly" or 1 alternate mix with "Road To Birmingham", and "Rock And Roll Queen" correctly credited)	60
69	Island ILPS 9108	MOTT THE HOOPLE (LP, pink label; with "Backsliding Fearlessly" in correct order)	40
70	Island ILPS 9119	MAD SHADOWS (LP, pink label, gatefold sleeve)	20
71	Island ILPS 9144	WILD LIFE (LP, pink rim palm tree label)	22
71	Island ILPS 9178	BRAIN CAPERS (LP, pink rim palm tree label & inner sleeve, some with mask)	60/20
72	CBS 65184	ALL THE YOUNG DUDES (LP, with inner sleeve)	12
72	CBS 9215	ROCK AND ROLL QUEEN (LP, 'pink rim palm tree' label)	12
73	CBS 69038	MOTT (LP, die-cut gatefold sleeve with inner)	12
80	Island IRSP 8	TWO MILES FROM HEAVEN (LP, early copies list "Moving On" on rear sleeve)	25/15

(see also Mott, Ian Hunter, At Last The 1958 Rock & Roll Show, Morgan, Mick Ronson, British Lions, Luther Grosvenor, Charlie Woolfe)

KEN MOULE'S LONDON JAZZ CHAMBER GROUP

70	Ember EMB S 275	Mae West/Zsa Zsa Gabor (some in p/s)	25/18
69	Ember CJS 823	ADAM'S RIB SUITE (LP)	55

(see also London Jazz Chamber Group, Ken Moule Seven)

KEN MOULE SEVEN

55	Esquire 10-417	Hallelujah/Bensonality (78)	6
57	Decca LK 4192	KEN MOULE ARRANGES FOR (LP)	25
58	Decca LK 4261	JAZZ AT TOAD HALL (LP)	30

(see also London Jazz Chamber Group)

MINT VALUE £

MATTIE MOULTRIE
67	CBS 202547	That's How Strong My Love Is/The Saddest Story Ever Told................ 20

MOUND CITY BLUE BLOWERS
55	HMV 7EG 8096	MOUND CITY BLUE BLOWERS (EP)................................... 8
60	Collector JEL 1	BLUES BLOWING JAZZ VOL. 1 (EP)................................ 10

MOUNTAIN
70	Bell BLL 1112	Mississippi Queen/The Laird 15
70	Bell BLL 1125	Sittin' On A Rainbow/To My Friend 20
71	Island WIP 6119	Roll Over Beethoven/Crossroader 8
70	Bell SBLL 133	MOUNTAIN CLIMBING! (LP)................................... 20
71	Island ILPS 9148	NANTUCKET SLEIGHRIDE (LP, 'pink rim palm tree' label)............... 20
71	Island ILPS 9179	FLOWERS OF EVIL (LP, 'pink rim palm tree' label).................. 15
72	Island ILPS 9199	LIVE — THE ROAD GOES ON FOREVER (LP, 'pink rim' label, 'palm tree' logo) .. 12

(see also West Bruce & Laing, Leslie West, Jolliver Arkansas)

VALERIE MOUNTAIN
61	Columbia DB 4660	Go It Alone/Gentle Christ 5
62	Pye 7N 15450	Some People/Yes You Did 5
62	Pye NEP 24158	SOME PEOPLE — SOUNDTRACK (EP, some tracks by Eagles) 8

(see also Eagles)

MOUNTAIN ASH
75	Witches Bane LKLP 6036	THE HERMIT (LP, private pressing with insert) 165

MOUNTAIN LINE
74	Xtra XTRA 1140	MOUNTAIN LINE (LP) 12
75	Xtra XTRA 1147	HORSEPOWER (LP) 12

MOUNT RUSHMORE
68	Dot DOT 115	Stone Free/She's No Good To Me 5

MOURNING AFTER
94	Detour DR 017	Doin' Me In/Out For The Count (p/s, 100 blue vinyl) 6

MOURNING PHASE
71	Eden	MOURNING PHASE (LP, private pressing)......................... 200+
91	Eden EDEN 1	EDEN (LP, reissue of "Mourning Phase")........................ 20

MOUSE
73	Sovereign SOV 122	We Can Make It/It's Happening To Me And You..................... 20
74	Sovereign SOV 127	All The Fallen Teen Angels/Just Came Back 12
73	Sovereign SVNA 7262	LADY KILLER (LP) 125

(see also Ray Russell Quartet, Running Man)

MOUSE & TRAPS
68	President PT 174	L.O.V.E. Love/Beg Borrow And Steal 20
68	President PT 210	Sometimes You Just Can't Win/Crying Inside 12

MOUSEFOLK
88	Tea Time Surf's Up 01	Don't Let It Slip Away/Spinning Round (flexidisc, initially with p/s) 7/5
88	Tea Time Surf's Up 02	HAZY TAMBOURINE DAYS EP (p/s) 7
80s	Tea Time SURFS UP 03	Grannie's Cake Crisis/Mrs Marr's Daughter (foldaround p/s, with badge)....... 5
89	Flowerpot 001	Motorcycle Boy/RISK: This Year's Model (p/s flexi, foldaround p/s)............ 5

MOUSE ON MARS
94	Too Pure PURE 36	VULVALAND (LP, with bonus 4-track 12") 12

ALPHONSE MOUZON
76	United Artists UAG 20005	THE MAN INCOGNITO (LP) 12

ALPHONSE MOUZON & LARRY CORYELL
77	Atlantic K 50382	BACK TOGETHER AGAIN (LP) 12

(see also Larry Coryell)

MOVE
66	Deram DM 109	Night Of Fear/Disturbance 8
67	Deram DM 117	I Can Hear The Grass Grow/Wave The Flag And Stop The Train............ 8
67	Regal Zonophone RZ 3001	Flowers In The Rain/(Here We Go Round) The Lemon Tree.............. 6
67	Regal Zonophone	Cherry Blossom Clinic/Vote For Me (unissued)
68	Regal Zonophone RZ 3005	Fire Brigade/Walk Upon The Water.............................. 6
68	Regal Zonophone RZ 3012	Wild Tiger Woman/Omnibus 12
69	Regal Zonophone RZ 3015	Blackberry Way/Something 8
69	Regal Zonophone RZ 3021	Curly/This Time Tomorrow.................................... 8
70	Regal Zonophone RZ 3026	Brontosaurus/Lightnin' Never Strikes Twice 8
70	Fly BUG 2	When Alice Comes Back To The Farm/What? 5
71	Harvest HAR 5036	Ella James/No Time (unissued)
71	Harvest HAR 5038	Tonight/Don't Mess Me Up................................... 5
71	Harvest HAR 5043	Chinatown/Down On The Bay 5
72	MagniFly ECHO 104	Fire Brigade/I Can Hear The Grass Grow/Night Of Fear (p/s) 6
72	Harvest HAR 5050	California Man/Do Ya/Ella James............................... 5
74	Harvest HAR 5086	Do Ya/No Time... 5
68	Regal Zono. TRZ 2001	SOMETHING ELSE FROM THE MOVE (EP, 33rpm) 50
68	Regal Zono. (S)LRZ 1002	THE MOVE (LP, mono/stereo)............................... 75/50
68	Regal Zono. TA-LRZ 1002	THE MOVE (reel-to-reel, mono only)............................ 12
70	Regal Zono. SLRZ 1012	SHAZAM (LP)... 50
70	Fly HIFLY 1	LOOKING ON (LP)... 30
71	Harvest SHSP 4013	MESSAGE FROM THE COUNTRY (LP) 20
72	Fly TOOFA 5/6	THE MOVE/SHAZAM (2-LP reissue) 18
74	Harvest SHSP 4035	CALIFORNIA MAN (LP)...................................... 12

(see also Roy Wood, Jeff Lynne, ELO, Idle Race, Trevor Burton, Nicky James Movement, Ace Kefford Stand, Grunt Futtock, Rick Price, Uglys, Charlie Wayne)

MOVEMENT
68	Pye 7N 17443	Something You've Got/Tell Her 85
68	Target 7N 17443	Something You've Got/Tell Her (Irish issue) 85
68	Big T BIG 112	Head For The Sun/Mister Mann.. 85+

MOVEMENT
80	Ballistic TRIF 2	No Man Is An Island/JAMDOWN PLAYERS: Levi's Choice (dubwise)/
		Togetherness/Deviate/Consolidate/Progression (12") 40

MOVERS
65	Ska Beat JB 191	Jo-Anne/DON DRUMMOND: Don De Lion 35

MOVIES
75	A&M AMLH 33002	THE MOVIES (LP) 12

(see also Ora, Public Foot The Roman)

MOVIETONE
94	Planet PUNK 003	She Smiled Mandarine Like/Orange Zero (p/s) 6
94	Planet PUNK 009	Mono Valley/Under The 3000 Foot Red Ceiling (p/s, 1,000 only) 5

MOVING BROTHERS
67	Island WI 3049	Darling I Love You/TOMMY McCOOK & SUPERSONICS: Saboo 22
67	Treasure Isle TI 7018	Darling I Love You/TOMMY McCOOK & SUPERSONICS: Saboo (reissue) 15

MOVING FINGER
68	Mercury MF 1051	Jeremy The Lamp/Pain Of My Misfortune 40
69	Mercury MF 1077	Higher And Higher/Shake And Fingerpop 20
73	Decca F 13406	So Many People/We're Just As Happy As We Are........................ 8

(see also Anglians)

MOVING IN THE RIGHT DIRECTION
92	Kold Sweat KSEP203	TALES FROM THE SOUTHSIDE (EP) 10

JUDY MOWATT
73	Gayfeet GS 207	Emergency Call/Emergency Call (Version)................................ 8
80	Grove Muzik IPR 2041	Black Woman (feat. Joy Tulloch)/My My People (12") 25

(see also Jean & Gaytones)

MOWREY JNR. & WATSON
76	Riverdale RRL 1000	BUSKER (LP, with insert) 30

MOXY
77	Power Exchange PXL 011	MOXY II (LP).. 12
77	Power Exchange PXL 022	RIDING HIGH (LP) 12
78	Polydor 2480 400	UNDER THE LIGHTS (LP)... 12

MOZABITES
80	Rock Steady MICK 010	Soul To Save/Ananta Snake Dance.................................... 5

MICKEY MOZART QUINTET
59	Columbia DB 4308	Little Dipper/Mexican Hop 5

MP's
80	Moving Plastic WSP 006	Housewives' Choice/Life On The Dole 5

MR. BLOE
70	DJM DJS 216	Groovin' With Mr. Bloe/Sinful.. 8
70	DJM DJLPS 409	GROOVIN' WITH MR. BLOE (LP) 20

(see also Harry Pitch)

MR. CALYPSON
71	Jump Up JU 40	Mohammed Ali/SAMSON DE LARK: Undemocratic Rhodesia.................. 6

MR. DYNAMITE
67	Sue WI 4027	Sh'mon/DYNAMITE ORCHESTRA: Sh'mon (Part Two) 100

MR. FLOOD'S PARTY
71	Ember EMB S 312	Compared To What/Unbreakable Toy (DJ copy = £50) 25
75	Bulldog BD 6	Compared To What/Unbreakable Toy (reissue) 10

(see also Mike Corbett & Jay Hirsch)

MR. FORD & MR. GOON-BONES
56	London HLU 8355	Ain't She Sweet/MUZZY MARCELLINO: Mary Lou 25

(see also Mr. Goon-Bones & Cavaliers)

MR. FOUNDATION
67	Studio One SO 2001	Have A Good Time/KEN PARKER: See Them A Come 30
67	Studio One SO 2003	All Rudies In Jail (actually by Zoot Simms)/
		HORTENSE & ALTON: Easy Squeeze 30
68	Studio One SO 2061	Time-Oh/DUDLEY SIBLEY & PETER AUSTIN: Hole In Your Soul........... 30
68	Studio One SO 2069	Reggae Rumble/MARCIA GRIFFITHS: You Keep Me On The Move............ 30
69	Supreme SUP 201	Time To Pray (actually by Lloyd Robinson)/Young Budd (by Leonard Dillon).... 12

(see also Sound Dimension)

MR. FOX
70	Big T BIG 135	Little Woman/Join Us In Our Game...................................... 8
70	Transatlantic TRA 226	MR FOX (LP).. 40
71	Transatlantic TRA 236	THE GIPSY (LP, gatefold sleeve)...................................... 45
75	Transatlantic TRA 303	THE COMPLETE MR FOX (2-LP, reissue of "Mr Fox" & "The Gipsy")......... 50

(see also Bob Pegg, Bob & Carol Pegg)

MR. MO'S MESSENGERS
67	Columbia DB 8133	Feelin' Good/The Handyman 10

MR. PINK/MR. BLONDE
96	Resevoir BP1	Payin' The Price/Death Before Dishonour (12")........................... 18
97	Resevoir BP2	Jamaica Crime Wave(12") 16

MINT VALUE £

MR. REJECT
71   private pressing   MR. REJECT (LP) 40

MR. TWISTER & TORNADOS
63   Starlite ST45 099   Big Twist (Parts 1 & 2) 7

MU
74   United Artists UAG 29709   LEMURIAN MUSIC (LP) 30
(see also Captain Beefheart, Fapardokly)

MUCKRAM WAKES
76   Trailer LER 2093   MUCKRAM WAKES (LP) 20

MUD
67   CBS 203002   Flower Power/You're My Mother (some in p/s) 28/22
68   CBS 3355   Up The Airy Mountain/Latter Days 15
69   Philips BF 1775   Shangri-La/House On The Hill 15
70   Philips 6006 022   Jumping Jehosaphat/Won't Let It Go 10
74   Rak RAK 187   Lonely This Christmas/I Can't Stand It (p/s) 7
75   Rak RAK 194   The Secrets That You Keep/Still Watching The Clock (p/s) 7
76   Rak RR 6   Tiger Feet/Oh Boy/Dynamite (p/s) 5
76   Private Stock PVT 65   Shake It Down/Laugh, Live, Love (p/s) 5
79   Carrere CAR 117   Drop Everything And Run/Taking The Easy Way Out (picture disc) .. 5
(see also Dum)

MUDHONEY
89   Blast First BFFP 46   Halloween/SONIC YOUTH: Touch Me I'm Sick (12") 8
92   Reprise WO 137   Suck You Dry/Version/Over The Top/Underide (12") 10
92   Reprise WO 137T   Suck You Dry (LP Version)/Deception Pass (12") 10
95   Reprise 9362 458401   MY BROTHER THE COW (LP, with 6-track EP, [PRO S 7492]) 18
(see also Sonic Youth)

MUD HUTTERS
79   Defensive NATO ONE   INFORMATION (EP, foldout p/s, also listed as SRTS/79/CUS 263) 5
79   Defensive NATO TWO   THE DECLARATION (EP, also listed SRTS/79/CUS 496) 5
81   Defensive NATO 3   FACTORY FARMING (LP) 12

MUDIE'S ALL STARS
70   Moodisc HM 3503   Wha Who Wha (Version)/G.G. RUSSELL: Wha Who Wha 12
(see also I Roy, Eternals, King Cannon, John Holt, Niney, Jolly Boys, Jo Jo Bennett)

MUDLARKS
58   Columbia DB 4064   Mutual Admiration Society/A New Love (78 rpm = £8) 10
58   Columbia DB 4099   Lollipop/Young Dove's Calling 5
58   Columbia DB 4133   Book Of Love/Yea, Yea 5
58   Columbia DB 4190   There's Never Been A Night/Lightnin' Never Strikes Twice 5
58   Columbia DB 4210   Which Witch Doctor/My Grandfather's Clock (78 rpm = £8) 5
59   Columbia DB 4250   Abdul The Bulbul Amer Cha Cha/The Love Game (78 rpm = £10) 5
59   Columbia DB 4291   Time Flies/Tell Him No 5
59   Columbia DB 4331   Waterloo/Mary (78 rpm = £15) 5
59   Columbia DB 4374   Tennessee/True Love, True Love 5
60   Columbia DB 4417   Never Marry A Fishmonger/Candy 5
60   Columbia DB 4513   (You've Got To) Move Two Mountains/You're Free To Go 5
61   Columbia DB 4636   When Mexico Gave Up The Rumba/Toy Balloon 5
61   Columbia DB 4708   The Mountain's High/Don't Gamble With Love 5
62   Columbia DB 4788   Them Twistin' Bones/Coney Island Washboard 5
62   Columbia DB 4861   Mañana Pasado Mañana/March Of The Broken Hearts 5
62   Decca F 11537   I've Been Everywhere/Just The Snap Of Your Fingers 5
63   Decca F 11601   The Little Cracked Bell Of San Raquel/La De Da 5
64   Fontana TF 495   Walk Around/Here's Another Day 5
58   Columbia SEG 7854   THE MUDLARKS! (EP) 40

MUGWUMPS
64   Warner Bros WB 144   I'll Remember Tonight/I Don't Wanna Know 10
67   Warner Bros W 1697   THE MUGWUMPS — AN HISTORICAL RECORDING (LP) 25
70   Valiant VS 134   THE MUGWUMPS — AN HISTORICAL RECORDING (LP, reissue) 15
(see also Mamas & Papas, Mama Cass Elliot, Lovin' Spoonful, Zalman Yanovsky)

BOBBY MUIR & BLUEBEATS
60   Blue Beat BB 20   Baby What You Done Me Wrong/Go Pretty Baby Go (as Blue Beats) .. 8
61   Blue Beat BB 44   Honey Please/That's My Girl (as Bobby Kingdom & Blue Beats) 8
62   Blue Beat BB 77   Brand New Automobile/Spanish Town Twist (as Bobby Kingdom & Blue Beats) .. 8

JAMIE MUIR & DEREK BAILEY
81   Incus INCUS 41   DART DRUG (LP) 50
(see also Derek Bailey)

LINDSAY MUIR'S UNTAMED
66   Planet PLF 113   Daddy Long Legs/Trust Yourself A Little Bit
                               (initially with Planet company sleeve) 125/105
(see also Untamed)

MULCAYS
55   London HLF 8188   Harbour Lights/Dipsy Doodle (78 rpm = £10) 30
54   London REP 1016   MERRY CHRISTMAS (EP) 12
56   London REF 1046   HARMONICS BY THE MULCAYS (EP) 12

MULDOONS
65   Decca F 12164   I'm Lost Without You/Come Back Now Baby 30

MULESKINNERS
65   Fontana TF 527   Back Door Man/Need Your Lovin' .... 140+
65   Keepoint KEE-EP-7104   MULESKINNERS (EP, private pressing, no p/s) 750
(see also Small Faces, Faces)

MOON MULLICAN

51	Vogue V 9013	Cherokee Boogie/Love Is The Light That Leads Me Home (78)	55
56	Parlophone DP 503	Yearning (Just For You)/Put Your Arms Around Me, Honey (export 78)	35
56	Parlophone DP 512	San Antonio Rose/Cedarwood Blues (export 78)	35
56	Parlophone MSP 6254	Seven Nights To Rock/Honolulu Rock-A Roll-A	
		(with Boyd Bennett & His Rockets) (78 rpm, Parlophone R 4195 = £70)	400
59	Parlophone GEP 8794	COUNTRY ROUND UP (EP)	60
50s	Parlophone CGEP 13	MOON MULLICAN (EP, export issue)	45
50s	Parlophone CGEP 15	PIANO BREAKDOWN (EP, export issue, company sleeve)	45

(see also Boyd Bennett & His Rockets)

GERRY MULLIGAN

59	London HLT 8901	I Want To Live — Theme/Black Nightgown (as Gerry Mulligan Combo)	
		(78 = £25)	8
60	HMV POP 734	Line For Lyons/Standstill (with Paul Desmond Quartet)	5
60	HMV POP 769	I'm Gonna Go Fishin' (both sides)	5
60	Philips JAZ 102	News From Blueport/Utter Chaos (p/s)	5
55	Capitol EAP1 439	PRESENTING GERRY MULLIGAN AND HIS TENTETTE (EP)	8
55	Capitol EAP2 439	PRESENTING GERRY MULLIGAN AND HIS TENTETTE (EP)	8
58	Emarcy ERE 1553	PRESENTING THE GERRY MULLIGAN SEXTET (EP)	8
58	Emarcy ERE 1556	PRESENTING THE GERRY MULLIGAN SEXTET VOL. 2 (EP)	8
58	Emarcy ERE 1560	PRESENTING THE GERRY MULLIGAN SEXTET VOL. 3 (EP)	8
58	Emarcy ERE 1574	MAINSTREAM VOL. 1 (EP)	8
58	Emarcy ERE 1575	MAINSTREAM VOL. 2 (EP)	8
60	Mercury ZEP 10071	MULLIGAN MANIA (EP)	8
53	Capitol LC 6621	THE GERRY MULLIGAN TENTETTE — ROCKER (10" LP)	15
53	Vogue LDE 029	THE GERRY MULLIGAN QUARTET VOL. 1 (10" LP)	15
53	Vogue LDE 030	THE GERRY MULLIGAN QUARTET VOL. 2 (10" LP)	15
53	Vogue LDE 031	THE GERRY MULLIGAN QUARTET VOL. 3 (10" LP)	15
54	Vogue LDE 075	THE GERRY MULLIGAN QUARTET (10" LP)	15
54	Vogue LDE 083	THE GERRY MULLIGAN QUARTET VOL. 4 (10" LP)	15
54	Esquire 20-032	GERRY MULLIGAN ALLSTARS — MULLIGAN'S TOO (10" LP)	15
55	Vogue LDE 156	GERRY MULLIGAN QUARTET WITH LEE KONITZ (10" LP)	15
56	Esquire 32-014	GERY MULLIGAN ALLSTARS (LP)	15
56	Vogue LAE 12006	THE GERRY MULLIGAN QUARTET (LP)	15
56	Vogue LAE 12015	THE GERRY MULLIGAN QUARTET (LP)	15
56	Emarcy EJL 101	PRESENTING THE GERRY MULLIGAN SEXTET (LP)	15
57	Emarcy EJL 1259	MAINSTREAM OF JAZZ (LP, by Gerry Mulligan Sextet)	15
58	Columbia Clef 33CX 10113	GERRY MULLIGAN AND PAUL DESMOND QUARTET (LP)	15
58	HMV CLP 1204	PHIL SUNKEL'S "JAZZ CONCERTO GROSSO" (LP, with Bob Brookmeyer)	15
59	Philips SBBL 552	WHAT IS THERE TO SAY? (LP, stereo)	15
59	Vogue SEA 5006	GERRY MULLIGAN SONGBOOK (LP, stereo)	15
59	Vogue SEA 5007	REUNION WITH CHET BAKER (LP, stereo, as Gerry Mulligan Quartet)	15
59	London Jazz LTZT 15161	I WANT TO LIVE (LP, with Shelly Manne)	12
60	HMV CLP 1373	GERRY MULLIGAN MEETS BEN WEBSTER (LP)	12
61	HMV CLP 1432	THE CONCERT JAZZ BAND (LP, also stereo CSD 1351)	12
61	Vocalion LAE 12268	THE GENIUS OF GERRY MULLIGAN (LP)	12
62	HMV CLP 1465	GERRY MULLIGAN MEETS JOHNNY HODGES (LP, also stereo CSD 1372)	12
62	HMV CLP 1488	AT THE VILLAGE VANGUARD (LP, also stereo CSD 1396)	12
62	Riverside RLP 12-247	MULLIGAN MEETS MONK (LP, with Thelonious Monk)	15
62	HMV CLP 1549	A CONCERT IN JAZZ (LP, also stereo CSD 1432)	12
62	HMV CLP 1585	ON TOUR (LP, with Zoot Sims)	12

(see also Gerry Mulligan, Chet Baker, Shelly Manne, Annie Ross)

MICK MULLIGAN'S JAZZ BAND

50	Tempo AA 66	Candy Lips/Savoy Blues (12" 78, as Mick Mulligan's Magnolia Jazz Band)	5
56	Tempo A 139	In A Shanty In Old Shanty Town/Snag It	5
56	Tempo A 143	Oriental Strut/Big House Blues	5
56	Tempo A 152	Beale Street Blues/Raver's Edge	5
57	Tempo A 155	St. James' Infirmary/After A While	5
57	Tempo A 164	Old Stack-O-Lee Blues/Double Dee	5
58	Saga STP 7020	YOUNG AND HEALTHY (EP)	10
55	Tempo EXA 25	MICK MULLIGAN'S JAZZ BAND (EP)	10
56	Tempo EXA 37	MICK MULLIGAN'S JAZZ BAND (EP)	10
56	Tempo EXA 41	GEORGE MELLY WITH MICK MULLIGAN'S JAZZ BAND (EP)	15
56	Tempo EXA 47	DOOM (EP, with George Melly)	15
57	Tempo EXA 54	MICK MULLIGAN'S JAZZ BAND (EP)	15
58	Parlophone GEP 8750	MICK BLOWS (EP)	15
57	Tempo TAP 14	JAZZ AT THE RAILWAY ARMS (LP, with George Melly)	50
59	Pye Jazz NJL 21	MEET MICK MULLIGAN (LP)	20
59	Parlophone PMC 1103	THE SAINTS MEET THE SINNERS (LP, with George Melly &	
		Saints Jazz Band)	15

(see also George Melly)

MUM

02	Fat Cat 7FAT 06	Green Grass Of Tunnel/In Through The Lamp (p/s)	5

MUM & DAD

99	Twisted Nerve TN 006	Donington/13th Chime/Monster Truck (p/s)	15

GENE MUMFORD

58	Philips PB 862	More Than You Know/Please Give Me One More Chance	8

HUGH MUNDELL

78	Greensleeves GRE9	Let's All Unite/Unity Dub	12
79	Warrior WAR 131	Stop Them Jah/Push Dawta Push (12")	15
80	J&F 002	Jah Fire Will Be Burning/King Of Israel (12")	20
81	Greensleeves GRED 54	Can't Pop No Style/JUNIOR REID: Know Myself (12")	40

MINT VALUE £

MUNGO JERRY

70	Dawn DNX 2502	In The Summertime/Mighty Man/Dust Pneumonia Blues (p/s)	5
70	Pye 7N 2502	In The Summertime/Mighty Man/Dust Pneumonia Blues (jukebox issue)	8
71	Dawn DNX 2505	Baby Jump/The Man Behind The Piano/Live From Hollywood: Maggie/ Midnight Special/Mighty Man (p/s)	5
71	Dawn DNX 2510	Lady Rose/Have A Whiff On Me/Milk Cow Blues/Little Louis (p/s, withdrawn)	5
71	Dawn DNX 2510	Lady Rose/She Rowed/Milk Cow Blues/Little Louis (re-pressing with different track, p/s)	5
83	Mach 1 MAGIC 008	There Goes My Heart Again/Thinking Of You (featuring Ray Dorset & Tarts)	5
85	Orbit TRIP 4	Sunshine Reggae/Nightlife (reissue of Horizon 45; as Mungo Jerry & Horizon)	6
87	Illegal MUNG 1	In The Summertime '87/Got A Job (as Mungo Jerry & Brothers Grimm, p/s)	5
96	Fan Club 12/1	Sugar In The Bowl/In The Summertime (fan club only, white label, autographed)	5
70	Dawn DNLS 3008	MUNGO JERRY (LP, gatefold sleeve, with 3-D glasses)	15
71	Dawn DNLS 3020	ELECTRONICALLY TESTED (LP, gatefold sleeve)	12
71	Dawn DNLS 3028	YOU DON'T HAVE TO BE IN THE ARMY (LP, gatefold sleeve, with lyric insert)	12
72	Dawn DNLS 3041	BOOT POWER (LP, with 'Dennis The Menace' or 'gun' gatefold sleeve)	each 12

(see also Ray Dorset, Good Earth, King Earl Boogie Band, Horizon, Made In England, Jigilo Jug Band, P. King, Paul King, P. Rufus King, Russian Roulette, First Impression, Good Earth)

RAY MUNNINGS

79	Tammi TAM 102	It Could Happen To You/Let's Boogie	40
79	Tammi TAM 103	Funky Nassau/Jump In The Water	100

CAROLINE MUNRO

67	Columbia DB 8189	Tar And Cement/The Sporting Life	8

CAROLINE MUNRO

85	Numa NU 5	Pump Me Up/The Picture (p/s)	6
85	Numa NUM 5	Pump Me Up (Ext. 6.09)/The Picture/Pump Me Up (4.00 7" Version) (12", p/s)	10

(see also Gary Numan)

HAL MUNRO

58	Embassy WB 284	Breathless/Wear My Ring Around Your Neck	6
59	Embassy WB 336	C'mon Everybody/It's Late (78 rpm = £8)	6
59	Embassy WB 340	Dream Lover/Where Were You (78 rpm = £8)	5
59	Embassy WB 386	You Got What It Takes/California Here I Come (78 rpm = £10)	5
60	Embassy WB 401	Good Timin'/I Wanna Go Home (78 rpm = £12)	5

(see also Neville Taylor)

JANET MUNRO & SEAN CONNERY

59	Top Rank JAR 163	Pretty Irish Girl/Ballamaquilty's Band (78 rpm = £12)	10

LEE MUNRO

86	Numa NU 20	Stereo Headphones/Give Me Your Love (p/s)	6
86	Numa NUM 20	Stereo Headphones (Extended Version)/Give Me Your Love/ Stereo Headphones (7" Version) (12", p/s)	10

PATRICE MUNSEL

53	HMV 7M 152	Is This The Beginning Of Love/The Melba Waltz	6

ADRIAN MUNSEY

79	Virgin VS 266	C'Est Sheep (Part 1)/C'Est Sheep (Part 2) (p/s)	6
79	Virgin VS 266-12	C'Est Sheep (Part 1)/C'Est Sheep (Part 2) (12", p/s)	8

(see also Sparks)

STEPHAN MUNSON & FRIENDS

82	Rhythmic RMNS 2	And David Cried/And Dem Bahnhoff (fold-out photocopied p/s)	8

JERRY MURAD'S HARMONICATS

59	Mercury ZEP 10001	IT'S CHA CHA TIME (EP)	8
67	CBS 63133	GREATEST HITS (LP)	12

MURDER INC.

80	MIL MIL 1	SOUNDS SO FALSE (EP)	8

(see also Business)

MURDER THE DISTURBED

79	Small Wonder SMALL 17	GENETIC DISRUPTION (EP)	7

BILLY MURE (ORCHESTRA)

59	Felsted AF 120	Tea & Trumpets/A String Of Trumpets (78 rpm = £12)	6
60	Top Rank JAR 344	Jambalaya/Kaw Liga (as Billy Mure Orchestra)	5
59	RCA RCX 158	SUPERSONICS IN FLIGHT (EP, also stereo SRC 7032)	12/15
59	Felsted GEP 1006	THE VERSATILE BILLY MURE (EP)	15
60	MGM MGM-C 800	SUPERSONIC GUITARS (LP)	15
60	MGM MGM-C 835/CS 5011	SUPERSONIC GUITARS VOL. 2 (LP, mono/stereo)	15/18

(see also Supersonics)

MURGATROYD BAND

71	Decca F 13256	Magpie (Theme From The TV Series)/Twice A Week (some with p/s)	25/15

(see also Spencer Davis Group, Ray Fenwick)

MURMAIDS

63	Stateside SS 247	Popsicles And Icicles/Comedy And Tragedy	20

MICHAEL MURPHEY

72	Regal Zonophone RZ 3062	Boy From The Country/Geronimo's Cadillac	5
72	Regal Zono. SRZA 8512	GERONIMO'S CADILLAC (LP)	12
73	EMI EMA 754	COSMIC COWBOY SOUVENIR (LP)	12

ARTHUR MURPHY

59	Parlophone R 4523	Sixteen Candles/Molly Malone (78 rpm = £10)	10

DELIA MURPHY
57	HMV 7EG 8295	DELIGHTFUL DELIA (EP)	8

ELLIOT MURPHY
74	Polydor 2391 100	AQUASHOW (LP)	12

LYLE MURPHY
58	Contemporary LAC 12135	GONE WITH THE WOODWINDS (LP)	12

MARK MURPHY
57	Brunswick 05701	Goodbye Baby Blues/The Right Kind Of Woman	6
58	Capitol CL 14962	Belong To Me/Don't Cry My Love (78 rpm = £6)	5
60	Capitol CL 15117	Send For Me/Come To Me	5
63	Riverside RIF 106905	Like Love/Fly Away My Sadness	5
63	Riverside RIF 106908	Fly Me To The Moon/Why Don't You Do Right	40
65	Fontana TF 572	High On Windy Hill/Broken Heart	5
67	Fontana TF 803	(Ain't That) Just Like A Woman/Do You Wonder If I Love You	5
69	Pye 7N 17661	Come Back To Me/Dear Heart	5
57	Brunswick LAT 8172	MEET MARK MURPHY (LP)	15
60	Capitol (S)T 5011	HIT PARADE (LP)	15
64	Fontana (S)TL 5217	MARK TIME! (LP)	15
66	Immediate IMLP/IMSP 004	WHO CAN I TURN TO (LP)	25

NOEL MURPHY
67	Fontana TL 5450	NYA-A-A-H! (LP)	12
73	Village Thing VTS 25	MURF (LP)	12

ROSE MURPHY
52	Oriole/Mercury MG 10004	SONGS BY ROSE MURPHY (10" LP)	18

ALEX MURRAY
60	Decca F 11203	Teen Angel/Paper Doll	15
60	Decca F 11225	All On My Own/String Along	7
61	Decca F 11345	When You Walked Out/Send For Me	7
	(see also Most Brothers)		

LADY MURRAY
66	Clan 597 002	Mister Abercrombie Taught Me/In My Imagination	7
	(see also Grazina, Mr & Mrs Murray)		

MARTIN MURRAY
66	Pye 7N 17070	I Know What I Want/Goodbye Baby	10
	(see also Honeycombs, Lemmings)		

MICKEY MURRAY
67	Polydor 56738	Shout Bama Lama/Lonely Room	8

MISTER MURRAY
65	Fontana TF 623	Down Came The Rain/Whatever Happened To Music?	6
66	Fontana TF 674	I Drink To Your Memory/I Was A Good Song	6
	(see also Mitch Murray Clan, Mr & Mrs Murray)		

MITCH MURRAY CLAN
66	Clan 597 001	Skyliner/Cherokee	12
	(see also Mister Murray, Mr & Mrs Murray)		

MR & MRS MURRAY
68	CBS 3633	You're Outa Your Mind/A Little Bit Of You	6
	(see also Mitch Murray Clan, Lady Murray, Grazina, Mister Murray)		

PETE MURRAY
(see under Pascal Murray, Brian Matthew & Pete Murray)

RUBY MURRAY
55	Columbia SCM 5162	Softly, Softly/What Could Be More Beautiful	22
55	Columbia SCM 5165	Spring, Spring, Spring/Goin' Co'tin (with Ray Burns, Diana Decker & Ronnie Harris)	12
55	Columbia SCM 5169	If Anyone Finds This, I Love You (with Anne Warren)/Before We Know It	15
55	Columbia SCM 5180	Evermore/Bambino	15
56	Columbia SCM 5222	Two Rivers/Boy Meets Girl (with Norman Wisdom)	15
56	Columbia SCM 5225	For Now, For Ever/Oh, Please Make Him Jealous	15
56	Columbia DB 3810	Teddy O'Neil/It Only Hurts For A Little While	15
57	Columbia DB 3849	Knock On Any Door/True Love	15
57	Columbia DB 3852	In Love/O'Malley's Tango	15
57	Columbia DB 3911	From The First Hello — To The Last Goodbye/Heart	15
57	Columbia DB 3933	Mr. Wonderful/Pretty, Pretty	15
57	Columbia DB 3955	Scarlet Ribbons/Macushla Mine	12
57	Columbia DB 3994	Little White Lies/Passing Strangers	8
57	Columbia DB 4042	Ain't That A Grand And Glorious Feeling/I'll Remember Today	8
58	Columbia DB 4075	Forgive Me My Darling/Keep Smiling At Trouble	8
58	Columbia DB 4108	In My Life/Nora Malone (Call Me By 'Phone)	8
58	Columbia DB 4192	Real Love/Little One	8
59	Columbia DB 4266	Nevertheless (I'm In Love With You)/Who Knows	7
59	Columbia DB 4305	Goodbye Jimmy, Goodbye/The Humour Is On Me Now	8
55	Columbia SEG 7588	RUBY IS A GEM (EP)	20
56	Columbia SEG 7620	EVERYBODY'S SWEETHEART NO. 1 (EP)	18
56	Columbia SEG 7631	EVERYBODY'S SWEETHEART NO. 2 (EP)	18
56	Columbia SEG 7636	EVERYBODY'S SWEETHEART NO. 3 (EP)	18
57	Columbia SEG 7748	MUCUSHLA MINE (EP)	18
59	Columbia SEG 7952	ENDEARING YOUNG CHARMS (EP)	18
60	Columbia SEG 8052	LOVE'S OLD SWEET SONG (EP, also stereo ESG 7830)	18/20

55	Columbia 33S 1079	WHEN IRISH EYES ARE SMILING (10" LP)	22
58	Columbia 33S 1135	ENDEARING YOUNG CHARMS (10" LP)	35
60	Columbia 33SX 1201	RUBY (LP, also stereo SCX 3289)	22/25

(see also Norman Wisdom & Ruby Murray, Ray Burns, Ronnie Harris, Diana Decker)

JOHN MURTAUGH

70	Polydor 2482 015	BLUES CURRENT (LP)	20

JUNIOR MURVIN
(see under Junior Murvin)

MUSE

99	Mushroom MUSH 50S	Uno/Agitated (p/s, clear vinyl)	38
99	Mushroom MUSE 1	Uno/Jimmy Kane/Forced In/Agitated (minimax CD, with slipcase)	12
99	Mushroom MUSH 50CDS	Uno/Jimmy Kane/Forced In (CD)	8
99	Mushroom MUSH 58 CDS	Cave/Twin/Cave (Remix) (CD, part 1 of 2-CD set)	8
99	Mushroom MUSH 58 CDX	Cave/Host/Coma (CD, part 2 of 2-CD set)	8
99	Mushroom MUSH 66S	Muscle Museum/Escape (p/s)	8
99	Mushroom MUSH 66S	Muscle Museum/Minimum (clear vinyl, autographed p/s, 1000 only)	35
99	Mushroom MUSH 68S	Sunburn/(Live Acoustic Version) (stickered p/s, clear vinyl)	5
00	Mushroom MUSH 72S	Unintended/Sober (p/s, clear vinyl)	6
01	Mushroom MUSH 89S	Plug In Baby/Nature 1 (p/s)	8
01	Mushroom MUSH 92S	New Born/Shrinking Universe (p/s, limited issue)	8
01	Mushroom MUSH 92T	New Born/Sunburn (Timo Maas Sunstroke Remix)/(Breakz Again Mix) (12", p/s)	8
01	Taste/Mushroom MUSH 968	Bliss/Hyper Chondriac Music (p/s)	8
01	Mushroom MUSH 96S	Bliss/The Gallery (p/s)	8
01	Mushroom MUSH 97S	Hyper Music/Feeling Good (p/s)	8
01	Mushroom MUSH 104S	Dead Star/In Your World (p/s)	7
02	Mushroom MUSH 104S	In Your World/Dead Star (p/s)	8
03	East West EW 272	Time Is Running Out/The Groove (clear vinyl, p/s)	8
03	East West EW 278	Hysteria/Eternally missed (p/s)	8
98	Dangerous DREX CDEP 103	MUSE EP (CD, 999 copies)	110
98	Dangerous DREX CDEP 104	MUSCLE MUSEUM EP: Sober/Uno/Unintended/Instant Messenger/Muscle Museum # 2/Muscle Museum (CD, 999 copies)	90
00	Mushroom MUSH 59LP	SHOWBIZ (2-LP, clear vinyl, gatefold sleeve, with inners)	50
01	Mushroom MUSH 93LP	ORIGIN OF SYMMETRY (2-LP, gatefold sleeve, with lyric inner sleeves, 1500 only)	50
03	East West 5046 68587-1	ABSOLUTION (2 x LP, gatefold sleeve)	15

MUSHROOM

73	Hawk HASP 320	Devil Among The Tailors/Sun Ni Dhuibir/King Of Ireland's Daughter	25
74	Hawk HASP 340	Kings And Queens/Met A Friend	25
73	Hawk HALPX 116	EARLY ONE MORNING (LP, some with poster inner)	375/300

(see also Joe O'Donnell)

MUSIC

01	Fierce Panda NING 107	Take The Long Road And Walk It/The Walls Get Smaller (p/s, 1,000 only)	20
01	Fierce Panda NINGT 107	Take The Long Road And Walk It/The Walls Get Smaller (12", p/s, 250 only)	50
01	Hut HUTT 145	THE MUSIC EP: You Might As Well Try To Fuck Me/Karma/Treat Me Right On/Too High (12", p/s, with inner)	12
02	Hut HUTT 152	THE PEOPLE EP: Let Love Be The Healer/Life/Jag Tune (12", p/s)	8
02	Hut HUT 158	Take The Long Road And Walk It/Alone (picture disc, stickered poly sleeve)	5
03	Hut HUT 164	The Truth Is No Words/What's It For (picture disc, stickered poly sleeve)	5

MUSICAL THEATRE

70	Pye Intl. NSPL 28128	A REVOLUTIONARY REVELATION (LP)	12

MUSIC BOX

72	Westwood MRS 013	SONGS OF SUNSHINE (LP)	110

MUSIC DOCTORS

69	Downtown DT 447	Music Doctor (Parts 1 & 2)	8
70	J-Dan JDN 4402	Electric Shock/KING DENNIS: Black Robin	8
70	J-Dan JDN 4403	Bush Doctor/Lick Your Stick	12
70	J-Dan JDN 4411	The Wild Bunch/ISRAELITES: Born To Be Strong	12
70	J-Dan JDN 4414	In The Summertime/Foundation	6
70	J-Dan JDN 4417	Discretion Version/Doctor Dan, Boy Friday And Friend	6
71	Downtown DT 479	The Pliers (Parts 1 & 2)	6
70	Trojan TBL 117	REGGAE IN THE SUMMERTIME (LP)	22

(see also Dennis Lowe, Audrey, Desmond Riley, Megatons, Prince Of Darkness, Gene Rondo)

MUSIC EMPORIUM

83	Psycho PSYCHO 11	MUSIC EMPORIUM (LP)	15

MUSIC EXPLOSION

67	Stateside SS 2028	A Little Bit O' Soul/I See The Light	20
67	Stateside SS 2054	Sunshine Games/Can't Stop Now	15
67	Philips BF 1547	Little Black Egg/Stay By My Side	7
69	London HLP 10272	A Little Bit O' Soul/Everybody	6
67	London HA-P/SH-P 8352	A LITTLE BIT O' SOUL (LP)	35

MUSICIANS

66	King KG 1055	Jaunty Joe/The Chelsea Set	7

MUSIC MACHINE

67	Pye International 7N 25407	Talk Talk/Come On In	50
67	Pye International 7N 25414	The People In Me/Masculine Intuition	40

MUSIC SPECIALISTS

70	London HLJ 10309	Dynamic Pressure/Flip	7

MUSIC TAPES
98   Earworm WORM 32   The Television Tells Us/Freeing Song By Reindeer
(p/s, pop-up sleeve with 2 inserts, 1,500 copies only) 5

MUSIC THROUGH SIX
68   Domain D3   Riff Raff/ROY DOCKER: Mellow Moonlight 15
(see also Jason Sims & Music Through Six)

MUSKETEER GRIPWEED & THIRD TROOP
66   United Artists UP 1196   How I Won The War/Aftermath (stock copies or demos; stock are much
rarer) 150/100
(see also John Lennon)

MUSKETEERS
69   Philips BF 1773   Fight/Magnifico 5

CHARLIE MUSSELWHITE BLUES BAND
69   Vanguard SVRL 19012   STONE BLUES (LP).. 22

VIDO MUSSO & HIS ORCHESTRA
54   London HL 8077   Vido's Boogie/Blue Night (78) 10

MUSTANG
67   Parlophone R 5579   Why/Here, There And Everywhere..................................... 25

MUS-TWANGS
61   Mercury AMT 1140   Roch Lomond/Marie 12

MUTANT ROCKERS/CITY LIMITS
84   Survival SUR12 028   Keep It On (12") 15

MUTANTS
77   Rox ROX 002   Boss Man/Back Yard Boys (p/s) 6
78   Rox ROX 005   School Teacher/Hard Time/Lady (p/s, red vinyl) 6

MUTE DRIVERS
80s   Mute Drivers MD 001   MUTE DRIVERS (LP, with insert in handmade painted sleeve, 300 only) 15
(see also Anonymes)

MUTT 'N' JEFF
66   Decca F 12335   Don't Nag Me Ma/Strolling The Blues 12

Mµ-ZIQ
93   Rephlex CAT 018   Bluff Limbo (remixes) (2 x 12", 800 only) 40
(see also Rude Ass Tinker)

MY BLOODY VALENTINE
86   Fever FEV 5X   No Place To Go/Moonlight (p/s)...................................... 100
86   Fever FEV 5   GEEK! (12" EP) 25
86   Kaleid. Sound KS 101   THE NEW RECORD BY MY BLOODY VALENTINE (12" EP) 40
87   Lazy LAZY 04   Sunny Sundae Smile/Paint A Rainbow (p/s)........................... 20
87   Lazy LAZY 04T   Sunny Sundae Smile/Paint A Rainbow/Kiss The Eclipse/
Sylvie's Head (12", p/s)... 40
87   Lazy LAZY 07   Strawberry Wine/Never Say Goodbye/Can I Touch You (12", p/s)........... 50
88   Creation CRE 055   You Made Me Realise/Slow (die-cut company sleeve) 6
88   Creation CRE 055T   You Made Me Realise/Slow/Thorn/Cigarette/Drive It All Over Me (12", p/s) 20
88   Creation CRE 061   Feed Me With Your Kiss/Emptiness Inside (plays "I Believe")
(die-cut company sleeve) 20
88   Creation CRE 061T   Feed Me With Your Kiss/I Believe/Emptiness Inside/I Need No Trust (12", p/s)... 15
89   Creation CRE 085   Tremolo/To Hear Knows When (p/s) 8
89   Creation CRE 085T   Tremolo/To Hear Knows When (12", p/s) 8
89   Creation CRECD 085   Tremolo/To Hear Knows When (CD) 10
89   Lyntone CAT 067   Sugar/PACIFIC: December, With The Day (square flexidisc free with
The Catalogue magazine, issue 67) 10/7
90   Creation CRE 073   Soon/Glider (p/s)... 10
90   Creation CRE 073T   GLIDER EP (12", p/s) 10
90   Creation CRE 073T   GLIDER EP (12", remixed by Andy Weatherall, stickered die-cut sleeve) 15
87   Lazy LAZY 08   ECSTACY (mini-LP, 3,000 only) 60
88   Creation CRELP 040   ISN'T ANYTHING (LP, initial 3,000 copies with bonus 7", "Instrumental"/
"Instrumental" [CRE FRE 4, no p/s] & stickered sleeve) 20
89   Lazy LAZY 12   ECSTACY & WINE (LP, compilation of LAZY 07 & LAZY 08) 20
89   Lazy LAZY 12CD   ECSTACY & WINE (CD).. 40
91   Creation CRELP 060   LOVELESS (LP)... 18

MY CAPTAINS
81   4AD AD 103   Fall/Converse/History/Nothing (EP) 8

MY DEAR WATSON
68   Parlophone R 5687   Elusive Face/The Shame Just Drained................................. 30
68   Parlophone R 5737   Make This Day Last/Stop, Stop, I'll Be There........................... 30
70   DJM DJS 224   Have You Seen Your Saviour/White Line Road 10
(see also Johnny & Copycats)

MY DYING BRIDE
94   Peaceville CC5   Sexuality Of Bereavement/Crown Of Sympathy 25
94   Peaceville VILE 45   THE STORIES EP (box set, 1000 only) 75
95   Peaceville VILE 50   THE ANGEL AND THE DARK RIVER (LP, picture disc)..................... 15

MY FOUNDATION
67   Studio One SO 2003   All Rudies In Jail (actually by Zoot Simms)/ALTON ELLIS & HORTENSE
ELLIS: Easy Squeeze 100
(see Zoot Simms)

BILLY MYLES
57   HMV POP 423   The Joker (That's What They Call Me)/Honey Bee (78 rpm = £12)............. 80

MINT VALUE £

MEG MYLES
56   Capitol CL 14555   Sing On, Baby/Will You Shed A Tear For Me? 7

MY LIFE STORY
86   Think Tank CHAPTER 1   HOME SWEET ZOO EP (gatefold p/s, 500 only). 40

MY LORDE SHERIFFE'S COMPLAINTE
79   Frog FROG 1   MY LORDE SHERIFFE'S COMPLAINTE (LP, private pressing). 15

MYND MUZIC
94   Poor Person Prod.   IMAGINE THIS (LP, handmade sleeve, 500 only) 20

MY RED CELL
03   V2 VVR5024797   She's Leaving/50 Quid (red vinyl, p/s) 7

ROWLAND MYRES
74   Deroy DER 1063   JUST FOR THE RECORD (LP, private pressing,
                              also listed as Music Sound Enterprise MSE 1) 120

MYRTELLES
63   Oriole CB 1805   Don't Wanna Cry Again/Just Let Me Cry 40
(see also Sue & Sunshine, Sue & Sunny, Stockingtops)

MY RUIN
99   Snapper SMAS 106   Tainted Love/Blasphemous Girl (p/s, red vinyl, 1,000 only). 6

MYSTERE FIVE'S
80   Flicknife FLS 001   No Message/Shake Some Action (p/s) 5
81   Flicknife FLS 202   Never Say Thank You/Heart Rules The Head (p/s) 5
(see also Wayne County & Electric Chairs)

MYSTERIES
64   Decca F 11919   Give Me Rhythm And Blues/Teardrops. 25

WILLIAM MYSTERIOUS
82   Mezzanine MEZ 1   Security Of Noise/Alright (p/s, with Fay Fife & Revettes). 6
(see also Rezillos, Revillos)

MYSTERY GIRLS
80   Strange HAM 001   SOUNDS LIKE (EP) 5
81   Strange HAM 002   I'm A Believer/Modern Mystery Pop/Walking Backwards (p/s). 6

MYSTERY GUESTS
80   Boys Own/Heater   Wurlitzer Junction/The Merry Shark You Are
       Volume BO 1   (handmade stickered white labels) 6
81   Boys Own BO 3   The Sparrow That Ate New York/The Nude (p/s) 5

MYSTERY MAKER
77   Caves UHC 3   MYSTERY MAKER (LP, private pressing with booklet) 120

MYSTIC INSTITUTE
92   Evolution EVO 06   CYBERDON EP (12"). 50
(see also Global Communications, Reload, Link)

MYSTIC MOODS
73   Warner Bros K 16265   Cosmic Sea/Awakening 15
74   Warner Bros K 46250   AWAKENING (LP) 20

MYSTIC NUMBER NATIONAL BANK
69   Probe SPB 1001   THE MYSTIC NUMBER NATIONAL BANK (LP). 20

MYSTICS
59   HMV POP 646   Hushabye/Adam And Eve. 50
59   Top Rank JAR 243   Don't Take The Stars/So Tenderly 65

MYSTICS (Jamaica)
75   Grounation GRO 2049 God Bless The Youths/Dub 5

MYSTRO
00   Deal Real DR001   Kiss That Arse Goodnight/The Word's Out (12"). 20
01   Camshot CSR002   Open Mic/Keep Smiling/The Burial 99 (EP) 10

MYTHRA
79   Guardian GRMA 16   DEATH & DESTINY: Death And Destiny/Killer/Overload/UFO (EP, no p/s) 8
80   Streetbeat LAMP 2   Death Or Destiny/Killer/U.F.O. (some with p/s) 90/10
80   Streetbeat 12 LAMP 2 Death Or Destiny/Killer/Overlord/U.F.O. (12", some with p/s) 125/20

NABAY
80   Grapevine GRP 143   Believe It Or Not/Believe It Or Not (Instrumental) 75

RICKY NADIR
79   Charisma CB 339   The Polaroid/PETER HAMMILL: The Old School Tie. 10
(see also Peter Hammill)

NA FILI
74   Dolphin DOL 1008   CHANTER'S TUNE (LP) 12

NA H-ORGANAICH
73	Beltona SBE 145	THE GREAT GAELIC SOUND OF (LP)..	15
74	Beltona SBE 160	GAEL FORCE 3 (LP)...	15

NAKED LUNCH
81	Ramkup CAC 003	Rabies/Slipping Again (p/s)...	7

NAKED TRUTH
70	Deram DM 287	Two Little Rooms/Rag Doll Boy......................................	7

NAME
80	Din Disc DIN 14	Forget Art, Let's Dance/Misfits (p/s).................................	10

NAMES
80	Factory FAC 29	Nightshift/I Wish I Could Speak Your Language (p/s)...................	5

NANETTE
70	Columbia DB 8659	Flying Machine/You're Wasting Your Time.............................	6
70	Columbia DB 8673	Every Night When I Cry Myself To Sleep/Jamie........................	6
70	Columbia DB 8733	Let Me Be The One/To Be Loved.....................................	5
71	Columbia DB 8751	Everybody's Singing Right Now/Could I Forget	5
70	Columbia SCX 6398	NANETTE (LP)...	15

ED NANGLE
68	Blue Cat BS 120	Good Girl/ENFORCERS: Musical Fever	30
68	Coxsone CS 7038	Whipping The Prince (actually by Ed Nangle & Alton Ellis & Soul Vendors)/HEPTONES: If You Knew	30

NICK NANTOS & HIS FIREBALLERS
63	Summit LSE 2042	GUITARS ON FIRE (EP)	12
64	Summit ATL 4114	GUITARS ON FIRE (LP)..	16

(see also Bill Haley & Comets)

NAOMI
70	Gayfeet GS 207	You're Not My Kind/GAYTONES: You're Not My Kind (Version II)	10
70	High Note HS 047	Natural Woman/GAYTONES: Natural Woman – Version......................	10

(see also Derrick Morgan, Tommy McCook)

NAPALM DEATH
89	Earache MOSH 014	MENTALLY MURDERED EP (Rise Above/The Missing Link/Mentally Murdered Walls Of Confinement/Cause And Effect/No Mental Effort) (12", p/s)...........	12
90	Earache MOSH 024	Suffer The Children/Siege Of Power/Harmony Corruption (12", p/s)	10
91	Earache MOSH 046	Mass Appeal Madness (12", p/s).....................................	10
92	Earache MOSH 065CD	The World Keeps Turning/A Means To An End/Insanity Excursion (CD)	10
95	Earache MOSH 146	GREED KILLING EP (Greed Kiling/My Own Worst Enemy/Self Betrayal/Finer Truths White Lies/Antibody/All Links Severed/Plague Rages [Live]) (10", p/s)...	10
90	Earache MOSH 19	HARMONY CORRUPTION (2-LP).......................................	25

NAPOLEON XIV
66	Warner Bros WB 5831	They're Coming To Take Me Away Ha-Haa!/!Aah-Ah Yawa Em Ekat Ot Gnimoc Er'Yeht	10
66	Warner Bros WB 5853	I'm In Love With My Little Red Tricycle/Doin' The Napoleon	10
66	Warner Bros W 1661	THEY'RE COMING TO TAKE ME AWAY HA-HA-A! (LP).....................	70

(see also Jerry Samuels, Kim Fowley)

PETER NARDINI
80s	Kettle KS 701	I Think You're Great/Ma Maw's A Mod (some in p/s)	15/8

NARNIA
74	Myrrh MYR 1007	NARNIA – ASLAN IS NOT A TAME LION (LP)............................	100

(see also After The Fire, Pauline Filby)

BILLY NASH
61	Philips PB 1181	Sunset/Nobody Loves Me Like You (as Billy Nash Combo)................	5
63	Philips 370 406 BF	The Madison Step/Madison Rhythm (as Billy Nash Rock Band)..............	5

GENE NASH
59	Capitol CL 15042	I'm An Eskimo Too/Ja, Ja, Ja (Deutsche Rock 'N Roll)...................	25

GRAHAM NASH
71	Atlantic 2091 096	Chicago/Simple Man..	6
71	Atlantic 2091 135	Military Madness/I Used To Be A King	6
71	Atlantic 2401 011	SONGS FOR BEGINNERS (LP)..	18

(see also Hollies, Crosby Stills Nash & Young)

JOHNNY NASH
57	HMV POP 402	Ladder Of Love/I'll Walk Alone (78 rpm = £12)........................	10
58	HMV POP 435	Won't You Let Me Share My Love With You?/A Very Special Love	10
58	HMV POP 435	Won't You Let Me Share My Love With You?/A Very Special Love (78)	10
58	HMV POP 475	It's Easy To Say/My Pledge To You (78 rpm = £12).....................	10
58	HMV POP 553	Almost In Your Arms/Midnight Moonlight (78 rpm = £15).................	7
59	HMV POP 597	Walk With Faith In Your Heart/Roots Of Heaven (78 rpm = £15)	7
59	HMV POP 620	As Time Goes By/Voice Of Love	7
59	HMV POP 651	And The Angels Sing/Baby, Baby, Baby...............................	7
59	HMV POP 673	Take A Giant Step/Imagination......................................	6
60	HMV POP 746	A Place In The Sun/Goodbye..	6
60	HMV POP 822	Somebody/Kisses	6
62	Warner Bros WB 65	Don't Take Away Your Love/Moment Of Weakness......................	25
62	Warner Bros WB 76	Ol' Man River/My Dear Little Sweetheart	25
63	Warner Bros WB 93	Cigareets, Whuskey And Wild, Wild Women/I'm Moving On	20
64	Pye International 7N 25250	Love Ain't Nothin'/Talk To Me	40
65	Chess CRS 8005	Strange Feelin'/Rainin' In My Heart..................................	25
66	Pye International 7N 25353	Let's Move And Groove (Together)/Understanding......................	10

66	Pye International 7N 25363	One More Time/Tryin' To Find Her	20
68	Regal Zono. RZ 3010	Hold Me Tight/Let's Move And Groove Together	8
68	Major Minor MM 586	You've Got Soul/Don't Cry	8
68	Major Minor MM 603	Cupid/People In Love	8
69	MGM MGM 1480	(I'm So) Glad You're My Baby/Stormy	25
64	RCA Victor RCX 7163	PRESENTING JOHNNY NASH (EP)	125
59	HMV CLP 1251	JOHNNY NASH (LP)	40
59	HMV CLP 1299	QUIET HOUR WITH JOHNNY NASH (LP)	28
60	HMV CLP 1325/CSD 1288	I GOT RHYTHM (LP, mono/stereo)	32/42
62	Encore ENC 2005	LET'S GET LOST (LP)	15
69	Major Minor MMLP/SMLP 47	YOU GOT SOUL (LP)	15
69	Major Minor MMLP/SMLP 56	SOUL FOLK (LP)	15
69	Major Minor MMLP/SMLP 63	PRINCE OF PEACE (LP)	15

JOHNNY NASH & KIM WESTON
69	Major Minor SMLP 54	JOHNNY NASH AND KIM WESTON (LP)	30

(see also Kim Weston)

TONY NASH
70	Hot Rod HR 110	Keep On Trying/WINSTON JAMES: Just Can't Do Without Your Love	12

NASH THE SLASH
81	Smash Hits (no cat. no.)	Swing-Shift (Flexi-Version)/ORCHESTRAL MANOEUVRES IN THE DARK: Pretending To See The Future (live) (blue flexidisc with Smash Hits mag)	5
81	Dindisc DIN 28	Dead Man's Curve/Reactor No. 2 (p/s)	5

NASHVILLE FIVE
62	Decca F 11427	Stand Up And Say That/Like Nashville	7
62	Decca F 11484	Some Other Love/Brainwave	7
62	Decca DFE 6706	LIKE NASHVILLE (EP)	40

NASHVILLE TEENS
64	Decca F 11930	Tobacco Road/I Like It Like That	10
64	Decca F 12000	Google Eye (some misspelled "Goggle Eye" on label)/T.N.T.	10
65	Decca F 12089	Find My Way Back Home/Devil-In-Law	10
65	Decca F 12143	This Little Bird/Whatcha Gonna Do?	6
65	Decca F 12255	I Know How It Feels To Be Loved/Soon Forgotten	8
66	Decca F 12316	The Hard Way/Upside Down	15
66	Decca F 12458	Forbidden Fruit/Revived 45 Time	18
66	Decca F 12542	That's My Woman/Words	18
67	Decca F 12580	I'm Coming Home/Searching	10
67	Decca F 12657	The Biggest Night Of Her Life/Last Minute	10
68	Decca F 12754	All Along The Watchtower/Sun-Dog	10
69	Major Minor MM 599	The Lament Of The Cherokee Reservation Indian/Looking For You	18
69	Decca F 12929	Tobacco Road/All Along The Watchtower	6
71	Parlophone R 5925	Ella James/Tennessee Woman	15
72	Parlophone R 5961	You Shouldn't Have Been So Nice/Tell The People (unissued)	
73	Enterprise ENT S101	Lawdy Miss Clawdy/Rocking On The Railroad	7
77	Sky 1007	Tobacco Road/Chips And Peas	5
82	Shanghai HAI 200	LIVE AT THE RED HOUSE (12" EP)	8
65	Decca DFE 8600	THE NASHVILLE TEENS (EP)	60
75	New World NW 6002	THE NASHVILLE TEENS (LP)	30

(see also Arizona Swamp Company, Jerry Lee Lewis, Carl Perkins)

NASTY FACTS
81	5th Column FC 2	Drive My Car/Gotta Get To You/Crazy 'Bout You (p/s)	10

NASTY MEDIA
78	Lightning GIL 542	Spiked Copy/Winter (p/s)	10

NATCHBAND
78	Far In FARS 01	Cadillac (Made In USA)/Being From The Sky (p/s)	6

NATIONAL-ELLS
67	Parlophone R 5609	Mr. Moon/Dance, Dance	5

NATIONAL HEAD BAND
71	Warner Bros K 46094	ALBERT 1 (LP)	25

(see also Caravan, Gary Moore, Toe-Fat, Uriah Heep)

NATIONAL HEALTH
78	Affinity AFF 6	NATIONAL HEALTH (LP)	12
78	Charly CRL 5010	OF QUEUES AND CURES (LP)	12

(see also Hatfield & The North)

NATIONAL LAMPOON
78	Island HELP 8	RADIO DINNER (LP)	12

NATIONAL PINION POLE
66	Planet PLF 111	Make Your Mark Little Man/I Was The One You Came In With (some in Planet sleeve)	12/10

NATIONWIDE ENGLAND SUPPORTERS CLUB
86	Peak PRIDE 1	Oh Sweet England/England Supporter (picture disc, with rosette & beermat)	8

NATURAL ACOUSTIC BAND
73	RCA RCA 2324	Echoes/Is It True Blue	5
72	RCA SF 8272	LEARNING TO LIVE (LP, gatefold sleeve)	25
72	RCA SF 8314	BRANCHING IN (LP)	20

(see also Krysia)

NATURAL BRIDGE BUNCH
69	Atlantic 584 231	Pig Snoots (Parts 1 & 2)	10

NATURAL FOUR
75 Atlantic K 56142   HEAVEN RIGHT HERE ON EARTH (LP) 30

NATURAL GAS
76 Private Stock PVLP 1007 NATURAL GAS (LP, with inner sleeve) 12
(see also Badfinger, Blue Goose, Humble Pie, Uriah Heep, Quiver)

NATURALLY
79 Bushays BFM 111   I'll Get By/All I Have Is Written In Your Eyes (12"). 15

NATURAL MAGIC
75 Oyster OYR 102   Strawberry Fields Forever/Isolated Lady 10
(see also Roger Glover, Eddie Hardin)

NATURAL VIBES
82 Starlight Records SDLP 907 LIFE HARD IN A YARD (LP) 35

NATURALS (U.K.)
64 Parlophone R 5116   Daisy Chain/That Girl 8
64 Parlophone R 5165   I Should Have Known Better/Didn't I? 12
64 Parlophone R 5202   It Was You/Look At Me Now 15
65 Parlophone R 5257   Blue Roses/Shame On You 15
(see also Living Daylights, Greatest Show On Earth)

NATURALS (U.S.)
55 MGM SP 1123   The Finger Of Suspicion Points At You/You Forgot To Remember 12
57 MGM MGM 939   The Buccaneers/The Ballad Of Sir Lancelot 8
(see also Debbie Reynolds)

FATS NAVARRO
56 London LZ-C 14015   MEMORIAL (LP). 15

JERRY NAYLOR
61 Top Rank JAR 591   Stop Your Crying/You're Thirteen 25
67 Stateside SS 2029   Sweet Violets/Temptation Leads Me 6
70 CBS 4882   But For Love/Angeline 5

SHEL NAYLOR
63 Decca F 11776   How Deep Is The Ocean/La Bamba. 20
64 Decca F 11856   One Fine Day/It's Gonna Happen Soon 100
(see also Lieutenant Pigeon, Stavely Makepeace)

NAZARETH
72 Pegasus PGS 2   Dear John/Friends. 18
72 Pegasus PGS 2   Dear John/Friends (2nd issue, PEG label, B-side lists 'Occasional Failure'). 25
72 Pegasus BCP 3   Dear John/Witchdoctor Woman/Morning Dew
    (unreleased, promo only, stamped white labels and insert). 60
72 Pegasus PGS 4   Morning Dew/Spinning Top (PEG label) 20
72 Pegasus BCP 8   Fool About You/Woke Up This Morning/Morning Dew
    (unreleased, promo only, handwritten white labels) 60
72 Pegasus PGS 5   If You See My Baby/Hard Living (PEG label) 20
73 Mooncrest MOON 9   Bad Bad Boy/Hard Living/Spinning Top (in p/s) 10
76 Mountain PSLP 191   I Don't Want To Go On Without You/Waiting For The Man (12" promo) 12
78 Mountain TOP 37   Place In Your Heart/Kentucky Fried Blues
    (mispressing, B-side plays Bee Gees track, company sleeve) 12
79 Mountain NAZ 4   Whatever You Want Babe/Telegram Parts 1, 2 & 3 (p/s, purple vinyl). 7
71 Pegasus PEG 10   NAZARETH (LP, 1st issue, Pegasus picture label/matt sleeve) 30
72 Pegasus PEG 10   NAZARETH (LP, 2nd issue, PEG label/glossy sleeve). 18
72 Pegasus PEG 14   EXERCISES (LP, gatefold sleeve) 20
74 Mooncrest CREST 10   NAZARETH (LP, reissue) 12
74 Mooncrest CREST 14   EXERCISES (LP, reissue, gatefold sleeve) 12
74 Mooncrest CREST 15   RAMPANT (LP, embossed sleeve with inner & dollar sticker insert). 12
85 Sahara SAH 130   SOUND ELIXIR (LP, Marimba label, withdrawn). 12
(see also Dan McCafferty, Mark Five, Sensational Alex Harvey Band, Tandoori Cassette, Billy Rankin)

NAZIS AGAINST FASCISM
79 Truth TRUTH 1   Sid Did It (Intelligible)/Sid Did It (Radio Version) (p/s, 2 different issues). .... each 6
(see also Vibrators)

NAZZ
68 Screen Gems SGC 219001 Open My Eyes/Hello It's Me 10
69 Screen Gems SGC 219002 Hello It's Me/Crowded. 10
69 Screen Gems SGC 219003 Not Wrong Long/Under The Ice. 10
69 Screen Gems SGC 221001 NAZZ (LP). 30

'N BETWEENS
66 Columbia DB 8080   You Better Run/Evil Witchman (demos credit In-Be-Tweens) 420
(see also Slade, Vendors)

YOUSSOU N'DOUR & PETER GABRIEL
89 Virgin VSCD 1207   The Lion (Gaiende)/Macoy/The Lion (Gaiende) (African Mix) (3" CD, card p/s). 8
(see also Peter Gabriel)

CHRIS NEAL
71 Fly BUG 15   Blame It All On Eve/All The Time In The World (p/s). 6

JOHNNY NEAL & STARLINERS
65 Pye 7N 15388   And I Will Love You/Walk Baby Walk 80
70 Parlophone R 5870   Put Your Hand In The Hand/Now. 7
(see also Storyteller)

TOMMY NEAL
68 Vocalion VL 9290   Goin' To A Happening/Tee Ta (DJ copy = £125) 40

NEAT
80s Neatbeat LYN 6269   Hormones In Action/Take Your Chances (p/s) 50

MINT VALUE £

NEAT CHANGE
68   Decca F 12809   I Lied To Auntie May/Sandman (some copies in foldout p/s) 30/15
(see also Peter Banks, English Rose)

NECROMANDUS
90   Reflection MM 09   QUICKSAND DREAM (LP, 500 only) 15

BERNIE NEE
58   Philips PB 794   Lend Me Your Comb/Medal Of Honour (78 rpm = £18) 22
(see also Bernie Knee)

NEEDLES
80   Ellie Jay EJSP 9340   Gotta Know You/Jayneski (no p/s) 150

LOUIS NEEFS
69   Columbia DB 8561   Jennifer Jennings/I Love You 25

ELGIN NEELY
65   Vogue V 9240   Four Walls/I Could Be. 12

NEGATIVES
78   Look LK/SP 6478   Stakeout (50 copies with p/s) 200/40

NEGATIVES
80   Aardvark STEAL 1   Electric Waltz/Money Talks (p/s) 5
81   Aardvark STEAL 3   Scene Of The Crime (p/s) 8

NEGATIVES IN COLOUR
90s own label NEG 1   Caught In Possession. 15

NEGRIL
75   Klik KLP 9005   NEGRIL (LP). 25

NEGUS ROOTS MEETS THE MAD PROFESSOR
83   Negus Roots NERLP 009 DUB ROCKERS VOLUME 2 (LP) 80
(see also Lackley Castell)

FRED NEIL
69   Elektra EKSN 45036   Candy Man/The Water Is Wide. 10
69   Capitol CL 15616   Everybody's Talkin'/Badi-Da 12
67   Elektra EKS 7293   BLEECKER & MACDOUGAL (LP) 40
70   Capitol E-ST 657   OTHER SIDE OF THIS LIFE (LP) 40

DON NEILSON
60   Philips BF 1058   The House Is Haunted/For All We Know. 6
63   Piccadilly 7N 35103   I Will Live My Life For You/How Do You Keep From Crying. 6

NEKTAR
73   United Artists NEK 1   What Ya Gonna Do?/Day In The Life Of A Preacher Pt. One (Edit) (p/s). 15
74   United Artists UP 35706 Fidgety Queen/Little Boy 10
75   United Artists UP 35853 Astral Man/Nelly The Elephant 10
73   United Artists UAD 60041/2 SOUNDS LIKE THIS (2-LP). 30
74   United Artists UAS 29499 A TAB IN THE OCEAN (LP, gatefold sleeve). 22
74   United Artists UAS 29545 REMEMBER THE FUTURE (LP) 22
74   United Artists UAG 29680 DOWN TO EARTH (LP) 20
76   Decca SKL-R 5250   RECYCLED (LP) 18

BILL NELSON('S RED NOISE)
85   Cocteau JEAN 1   PERMANENT FLAME SINGLES BOX (box set of 5 singles). 10
71   Smile LAF 2182/ HG 116 NORTHERN DREAM (LP, 250 only, numbered,
                              in foldover gatefold sleeve with booklet; second pressings £20;
                              reissues on the Butt label £15) 35
85   Cocteau JEAN 2   TRIAL BY INTIMACY (THE BOOK OF SPLENDOURS) (4-LP, box set,
                              with book & postcards, initial copies misspelt as "The Book Splendours") 20
86   KPM/Themes TIM   CHAMELEON — THE MUSIC OF BILL NELSON (LP, library issue) 12
(see also A — Austr, Astral Navigations, Gagalactyca, Be-Bop Deluxe)

CLARE NELSON
59   MGM MGM 1025   The Valley Of Love/You Are My Sunshine 8

DAVID NELSON
64   Philips BF 1321   Somebody Loves Me/Well I Have 8

EARL NELSON
59   London HLW 8950   No Time To Cry/Come On (78 rpm = £20). 30

OZZIE & HARRIET NELSON
59   London HA-P 2145   OZZIE AND HARRIET NELSON (LP) 50

RICK(Y) NELSON
78s
57   HMV POP 355   I'm Walkin'/A Teenager's Romance. 55
57   HMV POP 390   You're My One And Only Love/BARNEY KESSEL: Honey Rock 65
57   London HLP 8499   Be-Bop Baby/Have I Told You Lately That I Love You. 30
58   London HLP 8542   Stood Up/Waitin' In School 30
58   London HLP 8594   Believe What You Say/My Bucket's Got A Hole In It 30
58   London HLP 8670   Poor Little Fool/Don't Leave Me This Way 15
58   London HLP 8732   Someday/I Got A Feeling 30
58   London HLP 8738   Lonesome Town/My Babe 35
59   London HLP 8817   It's Late/Never Be Anyone Else But You. 30
59   London HLP 8927   Just A Little Too Much/Sweeter Than You 45
60   London HLP 9021   I Wanna Be Loved/Mighty Good 80
60   London HLP 9121   Young Emotions/Right By My Side 100
60   London HLP 9188   Yes, Sir, That's My Baby/I'm Not Afraid 125
(All the above 78s were credited to Ricky Nelson.)

45s

57	HMV POP 355	I'm Walkin'/A Teenager's Romance (gold or silver label lettering)	160/90
57	HMV POP 390	You're My One And Only Love/BARNEY KESSEL: Honey Rock	110
57	London HLP 8499	Be-Bop Baby/Have I Told You Lately That I Love You	32
58	London HLP 8542	Stood Up/Waitin' In School	28
58	London HLP 8594	Believe What You Say/My Bucket's Got A Hole In It	32
58	London HLP 8670	Poor Little Fool/Don't Leave Me This Way	10
58	London HLP 8732	Someday/I Got A Feeling	10
58	London HLP 8738	Lonesome Town/My Babe	10
59	London HLP 8817	It's Late/Never Be Anyone Else But You (all black or silver-top label)	10
59	London HLP 8894	Just A Little Too Much/Sweeter Than You (unreleased)	
59	London HLP 8927	Just A Little Too Much/Sweeter Than You (triangular centre)	12

(The above 45s were originally issued with triangular centres; later round-centre copies are worth half to two-thirds the value.)

59	London HL 7081	Just A Little Too Much/Sweeter Than You (export issue)	10
60	London HLP 9021	I Wanna Be Loved/Mighty Good	15
60	London HLP 9121	Young Emotions/Right By My Side	7
60	London HLP 9188	Yes, Sir, That's My Baby/I'm Not Afraid	7
61	London HLP 9260	You Are The Only One/Milk Cow Blues	20
61	London HLP 9260	You Are The One And Only/Milk Cow Blues (with different label credit)	10
61	London HLP 9347	Hello Mary Lou Goodbye Heart/Travelin' Man (later copies as "Hello Marylou Goodbye Heart")	7
61	London HLP 9440	Everlovin'/A Wonder Like You	7

(The above singles were credited to Ricky Nelson; all subsequent singles were credited to Rick Nelson unless stated.)

62	London HLP 9524	Young World/Summertime	10
62	London HLP 9583	Teen Age Idol/I've Got My Eyes On You (And I Like What I See)	8
63	London HLP 9648	It's Up To You/I Need You	8
63	Brunswick 05885	I Got A Woman/You Don't Love Me Anymore	8
63	Brunswick 05889	String Along/Gypsy Woman	10
63	Brunswick 05895	Fools Rush In/Down Home	8
64	Brunswick 05900	For You/That's All She Wrote	8
64	Liberty LIB 66004	Today's Teardrops/Thank You Darling	10
64	Brunswick 05908	The Very Thought Of You/I Wonder	8
64	Brunswick 05918	Lonely Corner/There's Nothing I Can Say	8
64	Brunswick 05924	A Happy Guy/Don't Breathe A Word	8
65	Brunswick 05939	Come Out Dancin'/Yesterday's Love	15
66	Brunswick 05964	Louisiana Man/You Just Can't Quit (as Ricky Nelson)	18
66	Liberty LIB 12033	I Need You/Wonder Like You	10
69	MCA MU 1106	She Belongs To Me/Promises	6
70	MCA MU 1124	Red Balloon/I Shall Be Released	7
71	MCA MU 1135	Life/California (with Stone Canyon Band)	7
72	MCA MU 1147	Love Minus Zero: No Limit/Gypsy Pilot (with Stone Canyon Band)	6
72	MCA MU 1165	Garden Party/So Long Mama	7
73	MCA MUS 1181	Palace Guard/A Flower Opens Gently By Itself	6
73	MCA MUS 1225	Lifestream/Evil Woman Child	6
74	MCA MCA 126	Windfall/Legacy (with Stone Canyon Band)	6
74	MCA MCA 144	One Night Stand/Lifestream (with Stone Canyon Band)	6
75	MCA MCA 198	Try (Try To Fall In Love)/Louisiana Belle (with Stone Canyon Band)	6
77	Epic S EPC 5821	You Can't Dance/It's Another Day	5

EPs

58	London RE-P 1141	RICKY PART 1	40
58	London RE-P 1142	RICKY PART 2	40
58	London RE-P 1143	RICKY PART 3	40
58	London RE-P 1144	RICKY PART 4	40
59	London RE-P 1168	RICKY NELSON PART 1	35
59	London RE-P 1169	RICKY NELSON PART 2	35
59	London RE-P 1170	RICKY NELSON PART 3	35
59	London RE-P 1200	RICKY SINGS AGAIN PART 1	35
59	London RE-P 1201	RICKY SINGS AGAIN PART 2	35
60	London RE-P 1238	I GOT A FEELING	35
60	London RE-P 1249	RICKY SINGS SPIRITUALS	35
61	London RE-P 1300	RICKY NELSON PART 4	40

(The above EPs were credited to Ricky Nelson; all subsequent EPs were credited to Rick Nelson.)

62	London RE-P 1339	IT'S A YOUNG WORLD	35
63	London RE-P 1362	IT'S UP TO YOU	35
63	Brunswick OE 9502	ONE BOY TOO LATE	45
64	Liberty LEP 4001	SINGS FOR YOU	60
64	Liberty LEP 4019	THAT'S ALL	60
65	Liberty LEP 4028	I'M IN LOVE AGAIN	60
65	Brunswick OE 9512	HAPPY GUY	50

LPs

57	London HA-P 2080	RICKY	60
58	London HA-P 2119	RICKY NELSON	60
59	London HA-P 2159	RICKY SINGS AGAIN	55
59	London HA-P 2206	SONGS BY RICKY	55
60	London HA-P 2290	MORE SONGS BY RICKY (gatefold sleeve, also stereo SAH-P 6102)	40/50
61	London HA-P 2379	RICK IS 21 (also stereo SAH-P 6179)	40/50

(The above LPs were credited to Ricky Nelson; all subsequent LPs were credited to Rick Nelson.)

62	London HA-P 2445	ALBUM SEVEN (also stereo SAH-P 6236)	40/50
63	London HA-P 8066	IT'S UP TO YOU	40
63	Brunswick LAT 8545	FOR YOUR SWEET LOVE (also stereo STA 8545)	35/40
64	Brunswick LAT/STA 8562	RICKY SINGS "FOR YOU" (mono/stereo)	50/60
64	Liberty LBY 3027	MILLION SELLERS	45
64	Brunswick LAT/STA 8581	THE VERY THOUGHT OF YOU	50
64	Brunswick LAT/STA 8596	SPOTLIGHT ON RICK	50
65	Brunswick LAT/STA 8615	BEST ALWAYS	50
65	Brunswick LAT/STA 8630	LOVE AND KISSES	50

66	Brunswick LAT/STA 8657	BRIGHT LIGHTS, COUNTRY MUSIC	50
67	Brunswick LAT/STA 8680	COUNTRY FEVER	50
68	Liberty LBL 83020	MILLION SELLERS (reissue)	15
68	MCA MUP(S) 302	ANOTHER SIDE OF RICK	22
70	MCA MUPS 409	IN CONCERT (with Stone Canyon Band)	20
71	MCA MUPS 422	RICK SINGS NELSON (with Stone Canyon Band)	20
72	MCA MUPS 440	RUDY THE FIFTH (with Stone Canyon Band)	20
73	MCA MDKS 8009	GARDEN PARTY (gatefold sleeve, with Stone Canyon Band)	20
74	MCA MCG 3516	WINDFALL	18
77	Epic EPC 81102	INTAKES	15

SANDY NELSON

59	Top Rank JAR 197	Teen Beat/Big Jump	10
59	London HLP 9015	Drum Party/The Big Noise From Winnetka (78 rpm = £45)	10
60	London HLP 9214	I'm Walkin'/Bouncy (as Sandy Nelson & His Combo)	10
61	London HLP 9377	Get With It/Big Noise From The Jungle	10
61	London HLP 9466	Let There Be Drums/Quite A Beat (as Sandy Nelson On The Drums)	6
62	London HLP 9521	Drums Are My Beat/My Girl Josephine	7
62	London HLP 9558	Drummin' Up A Storm/Drum Stomp	10
62	London HLP 9612	...And Then There Were Drums/Live It Up	8
63	London HLP 9717	Ooh Poo Pah Doo/Feel So Good	8
64	Liberty LIB 66060	Teen Beat '65/Kitty's Theme	7
66	Liberty LIB 12062	Hey Joe/Come On Let's Go	7
70	President PT 294	Teen Beat/PRESTON EPPS: Bongo Rock	7
60	Top Rank JKP 2060	RUSHING FOR PERCUSSION (EP, 2 tracks by Preston Epps)	20
62	London REP 1337	LET THERE BE DRUMS (EP)	20
63	London REP 1371	IN THE MOOD (EP)	20
65	Liberty LEP 4033	SANDY NELSON PLAYS (EP)	20
60	London HA-P 2260	TEEN BEAT (LP, also stereo SAH-P 6082)	30/35
61	London HA-P 2425	LET THERE BE DRUMS (LP, also stereo SAH-P 6221)	30/35
62	London HA-P 2446	DRUMS ARE MY BEAT! (LP, also stereo SAH-P 6237)	30/35
62	London HA-P/SH-P 8009	DRUMMIN' UP A STORM (LP)	30/35
63	London HA-P/SH-P 8029	COMPELLING PERCUSSION (LP)	28
63	London HA-P/SH-P 8051	TEENAGE HOUSE PARTY (LP)	28
65	Liberty LBY 3007	SANDY NELSON PLAYS (LP)	20
65	Liberty LBY 3035	LIVE IN LAS VEGAS (LP)	20
66	Liberty LBY 3061	DRUMS A GO-GO (LP)	20
66	Liberty (S)LBY 3080	SUPERDRUMS (LP)	20
67	Liberty LBL/LBS 83043E	THE BEAT GOES ON (LP)	18
68	Liberty LBL/LBS 83094E	SOUL DRUMS (LP)	22
68	Liberty LBL/LBS 83110E	BOOGALOO BEAT (LP)	22
68	Liberty LBL/LBS 83131E	SUPERDRUMS (LP, reissue, different sleeve)	15
69	Liberty LBL/LBS 83165E	ROCK'N'ROLL REVIVAL (LP)	15
70	Liberty LBS 83302E	GROOVY (LP)	15

(see also Preston Epps)

TERRY NELSON (& FIREBALLS)

65	Dice CC 23	Run Run Baby/Bonita (as Terry Nelson & Fireballs)	12
65	Dice CC 25	Bulldog Push/Pretty Little Girl (as Terry Nelson & Fireballs)	12
65	Dice CC 27	Tomorrow Will Soon Be Here/My Blue Eyed Baby	8
65	Blue Beat BB 326	Help/PRINCE BUSTER: Johnny Dollar	25
66	Halagala HG 11	Take These Chains From My Heart/Let-Kiss	6
67	Halagala HG 19	That True Love Must Be Me/Bulldog Walk	5

WILLIE NELSON

63	Liberty LIB 55532	Half A Man/The Last Letter	12
64	Liberty LIB 55697	River Boy/Opportunity To Cry	12
69	RCA RCA 1867	My Own Peculiar Way/Natural To Be Gone	7
66	RCA Victor RD 7749	COUNTRY WILLIE (LP)	25
66	Liberty (S)LBY 1240	AND THEN I WROTE (LP)	22
69	RCA RD 7997	TEXAS IN MY SOUL (LP)	25

NELSON TRIO (U.K.)

57	Oriole CB 1360	Tear It Up/Roll The Carpet Up (78 rpm = £10)	10

NELSON TRIO (U.S.)

60	London HLL 9019	All In Good Time/The Town Crier (78 rpm = £35)	15

CHIITRA NEOGY

68	Gemini GMX 5030	THE PERFUMED GARDEN (LP)	22

NEO MAYA

67	Pye 7N 17371	I Won't Hurt You/U.F.O.	60

(see also Episode Six)

NEON BOYS

90	Overground OVER 11	TIME (EP, purple vinyl, 2,000 only)	6
90	Overground OVER 11	TIME (12" EP, 20 test pressings only)	20
91	Overground OVER 19	That's All I Know (Right Now)/Love Comes In Spurts/High Heeled Wheels/ Don't Die/Time (last 2 tracks credited to Richard Hell & Voidoids [Part III]) (12", p/s, 2,000 only, clear vinyl)	8

(see also Richard Hell, Television)

NEON HEARTS

77	Neon Hearts NEON 1	Venus Eccentric/Regulations (8" p/s)	30
78	Satril SAT 133	Answers/Armchair Thriller (p/s)	8
79	Satril SAT 139	Popular Music/Pretty As A Picture (p/s)	8
79	Satril SATL 4012	POPULAR MUSIC (LP)	15

NEPTUNE'S EMPIRE
71	Polymax PXX 01	NEPTUNE'S EMPIRE (LP)..	120

PETER NERO
69	CBS M 63589	I'VE GOTTA BE ME (LP)...	12

NERO & GLADIATORS
61	Decca F 11329	Entry Of The Gladiators/Boots	12
61	Decca F 11367	In The Hall Of The Mountain King/The Trek To Rome.................	12
61	Decca F 11413	Czardas/That's A Long Time Ago	20

(see also Laurie Jay, Gladiators, Screaming Lord Sutch & Savages, State Of Mickey & Tommy)

PAUL NERO (SOUNDS)
68	Liberty LBL 83100	NERO'S SOUL PARTY (LP)	15

NERVE
67	Page One POF 019	No. 10 Downing Street/Georgie's March..............................	12
68	Page One POF 055	Magic Spectacles/Come The Day	20
68	Page One POF 081	It Is/Mystery Lady	18
68	Page One POF 097	Piece By Piece/Satisfying Kind	15

(see also Lovin')

NERVES
78	Lightning GIL 520	TV Adverts/Sex Education (p/s)......................................	35

NERVES
81	Good Vibrations BIG 3	NOTRE DEMO (LP, official bootleg, foldover sleeve with booklet)	15

NERVES
94	Inflammable Material BURN 2	Bits/SUBSTANDARD: Rostock (p/s)	7

NERVOUS CHOIR
89	Cathexis CRN 5407	O'David/Tonight We Start On Witches/Alsatians/Introducing (p/s, with inserts) ...	5

NERVOUS NORVUS
56	London HLD 8338	Ape Call/Wild Dog Of Kentucky (gold label print, later silver)	110/50
56	London HLD 8338	Ape Call/Wild Dog Of Kentucky (gold label print, later silver) (78)	9
57	London HLD 8383	Dig/Bullfrog Hop (gold label print, later silver) (78 rpm = £9)	135/60
62	Salvo SLO 1812	Does A Chinese Chicken Have A Pigtail/ROD BARTON: Dear Old San Francisco..	60

JIM NESBIT
65	Vocalion V 9241	Tiger In My Tank/I Can't Stand This Living Alone	25

MICHAEL NESMITH (& FIRST/SECOND NATIONAL BAND)
70	RCA RCA 2001	Joanne/The Crippled Lion (with First National Band).....................	5
71	RCA RCA 2053	Silver Moon/Lady Of The Valley (with First National Band)	5
71	RCA RCA 2086	Nevada Fighter/Here I Am (with First National Band)	5
70	RCA SF 8136	MAGNETIC SOUTH (LP, with First National Band)	30
71	RCA SF 8209	NEVADA FIGHTER (LP, with First National Band)	30
72	RCA SF 8276	TANTAMOUNT TO TREASON VOLUME ONE (LP, with Second National Band)...	25
73	RCA APL1 0164	PRETTY MUCH YOUR STANDARD RANCH STASH (LP, solo)	15
75	Island ILPS 9428	THE PRISON (LP, boxed with book, unreleased in U.K.)	
76	RCA RS 1064	THE BEST OF MICHAEL NESMITH (LP)	15
77	Island ILPS 9439	AND THE HITS JUST KEEP ON COMIN' (LP, gatefold sleeve, solo)	12

(see also Monkees, Wichita Train Whistle)

NEU!
73	United Artists UP 35485	Super/Neuschnee	8
75	United Artists UP 35874	Isi/After Eight..	7
72	United Artists UAS 29396	NEU (LP)..	55
73	United Artists UAS 29500	NEU II (LP, gatefold sleeve)	55
75	United Artists UAS 29782	NEU '75 (LP, gatefold sleeve).......................................	30

(see also La Düsseldorf)

NEUTRONS
74	United Artists UP 35704	Dance Of The Psychedelic Lounge Lizard/Suzy And The Wonder Boy	5
74	United Artists UAG 29652	BLACK HOLE STAR (LP, with inner sleeve)............................	15
75	United Artists UAG 29726	TALES FROM THE BLUE COCOONS (LP)	15

(see also Man)

MIKE NEVARD'S MELODY MAKER ALL STARS
54	Atlantic Golden Bell ATL LP2	ACES ANONYMOUS (10" LP)...	20

NEVILLE (Willoughby)
72	Explosion EX 2057	I Love Jamaica/Marry Me Marie......................................	5

(see also Whistling Willie)

AARON NEVILLE
67	Stateside SS 584	Tell It Like It Is/Why Worry	25
69	B&C CB 107	Tell It Like It Is/Why Worry (reissue).................................	8
67	Liberty LBY 3089	HERE 'TIS (LP)...	50

ART NEVILLE
58	Specialty SON 5008	Cha-Dooky-Doo/Zing Zing	25

DEREK NEW QUINTET
63	Ember JBS 711	Scandinavian Nocturne/Nearly Ready To Begin	5

NEW AGE STEPPERS
80	On-U Sound ONU 1	Fade Away/LONDON UNDERGROUND: Learn A Language (p/s)................	7
80	On-U Sound ONULP 1	NEW AGE STEPPERS (LP)...	10
81	Statik 612	My Love/Love Forever (12")..	20

NEWBEATS

64	Hickory 45-1269	Bread And Butter/Tough Little Buggy (pink or black/blue label) .... each 8
64	Hickory 45-1282	Everything's Alright/Pink Dally Rue 10
65	Hickory 45-1290	Break Away/Hey O Daddy O 10
65	Hickory 45-1305	The Birds Are For The Bees/Better Watch Your Step 5
65	Hickory 45-1320	I Can't Hear You No More/Little Child 10
65	Hickory 45-1332	Run Baby Run/Mean Woolly Willie (DJ copy = £70) 25
66	Hickory 45-1366	Shake Hands (And Come Out Crying)/Too Sweet To Be Forgotten........... 20
66	Hickory 45-1387	Crying My Heart Out/Short Of Love (DJ copy = £70 40
66	Hickory 45-1422	My Yesterday Love/Patent On Love 10
65	Hickory LPE 1503	NEWBEATS (EP) 30
65	Hickory LPE 1506	AIN'T THAT LOVIN' YOU BABY (EP) 30
66	Hickory LPE 1510	OH! GIRLS GIRLS (EP) 25
65	Hickory LPM 120	BREAD AND BUTTER (LP) 25

(see also Dean & Mark, Larry Henley)

PHINEAS NEWBORN

61	Columbia 33SX 1311	I LOVE A PIANO (LP, also stereo SCX 3370) 12

(see also Roy Haines)

NEW BREED

65	Decca F 12295	Friends And Lovers Forever/Unto Us 40

MICKEY NEWBURY

72	Elektra K 12047	An American Trilogy/San Francisco Mabel Joy 6

NEWCASTLE BIG BAND

72	Impulse ISS NBB 106	NEWCASTLE BIG BAND (LP, white labels, 2,000 only)................... 150

(see also Last Exit, Police, Sting, Radio Actors)

NEW CENSATION

75	DJM DJS 10371	First Round Knockout/Everybody's Got A Story 8

NEW CHRISTY MINSTRELS

63	CBS BPG 62268	TELL TALL TALES (LP) 12
63	CBS BPG 62269	RAMBLIN' (LP) 12
65	CBS BPG 62492	SING AND PLAY COWBOYS AND INDIANS (LP) 12
66	CBS 63338	ON TOUR THROUGH MOTORTOWN (LP)................................... 12

(see also Barry McGuire)

NEW COLONY SIX

66	London HLZ 10033	I Confess/Dawn Is Breaking... 60
66	Stateside SS 522	At The River's Edge/I Lie Awake 80
68	Mercury MF 1030	I Will Always Think About You/Hold Me With Your Eyes 12
69	Mercury MF 1086	Things I'd Like To Say/Come And Give Your Love To Me.................. 10

NEWCOMERS

72	Stax 2025 063	Pin The Tail On The Donkey/Mannish Boy 6
75	Stax STXS 2023	Keep An Eye On Your Close Friends/(Instrumental Version)................ 8

NEW DAWN

69	private pressing	MAINLINE (LP)... 80

NEW DEAL STRING BAND

69	Argo ZDA 104	DOWN IN THE WILLOW (LP, with insert) 30

NEW DEPARTURES QUARTET

60s	Transatlantic TRA 134	THE NEW DEPARTURES QUARTET (LP, with Stan Tracey)................... 40

(see also Stan Tracey)

NEW ENGLAND

79	Infinity INF 110	P.U.N.K./Shoot (green vinyl, 'lightning' PVC sleeve)....................... 5

DENNIS NEWEY

61	Philips PB 1134	Checkpoint/Title Unknown 7
61	Philips PB 1198	Border Patrol/Yes Yes.. 6
62	Philips 326 588 BF	The Nightriders/The Pied Piper 6

NEW FACES

65	Pye 7N 15842	So Small/Blue Mist 8
65	Pye 7N 15931	Never Gonna Love Again/You'll Be Too Late............................. 8
66	Pye 7N 17029	Like A Man/Shake Up The Party (Myra) 15
67	Pye 7N 17335	Lace Covered Window/The Life That I Lead............................. 8

NEW FORESTERS

65	Lyntone LYN 932/933	Travel/LIZARDS: My Love Goes On (Sheffield Students Rag record).......... 30

NEW FORMULA

67	Piccadilly 7N 35381	Do It Again A Little Bit Slower/I'm On The Outside Looking In 10
67	Piccadilly 7N 35401	I Want To Go Back There Again/Can't You See That She Loves Me........ 10
68	Pye 7N 17552	My Baby's Coming Home/Burning In The Background Of My Mind 20
69	Pye 7N 17818	Stay Indoors/Hare Krishna 25

NEW GENERATION

69	Spark SRL 1000	Sadie And Her Magic Mister Garland/Digger 12
69	Spark SRL 1007	Smokey Blues Away/She's A Soldier Boy 10
70	Spark SRL 1019	Police Is Here/Mister C. 6

NEW HEARTS

77	CBS 5800	Just Another Teenage Anthem/Blood On The Knife (p/s)................. 12
78	CBS 6381	Plain Jane/My Young Teacher (p/s)...................................... 12

(see also Secret Affair)

NEW HERITAGE

73	Westwood WRS 028	ALL MANNER OF THINGS (LP) 50

NEW HOPE
69	London HL 10296	Won't Find Better Than Me/They Call It Love.	12

(see also Kit Kats)

NEW JAZZ GROUP
56	Tempo EXA 39	MODERN JAZZ SCENE (EP)	20

NEW JAZZ ORCHESTRA
65	Decca LK 4690	WESTERN REUNION (LONDON 1965) (LP)	60
69	Verve SVLP 9236	DEJEUNER SUR L'HERBE (LP)	175

(see also Neil Ardley, Nucleus)

NEW JERSEY CONNECTION
82	Nitelife LIFE 1	Love Don't Come Easy/Love Don't Come Easy (Instrumental) (12")	8

NEW JERSEY KINGS
90s	Acid Jazz JAZIDLP 33	PARTY TO THE BUS STOP (LP)	20
90s	Acid Jazz JAZIDCD 33	PARTY TO THE BUS STOP (CD)	18

(see also James Taylor Quartet)

NEW JUMP BAND
68	Domain D 1	The Only Kind Of Girl/Seven Kinds Of Sweet Lovin'	8

ANTHONY NEWLEY
59	Decca F 11127	I've Waited So Long/Sat'day Night Rock-A-Boogie (78 rpm = £10)	10
59	Decca F 11137	Idle On Parade/Idle Rock-A-Boogie (78 rpm = £12)	10
59	Decca F 11142	Personality/My Blue Angel (78 rpm = £12)	5
59	Decca F 11163	Someone To Love/It's All Over (78 rpm = £12)	5
62	Decca F 11419	D-Darling/I'll Walk Beside You	5
62	Decca F 11486	That Noise/The Little Golden Clown	5
63	Decca F 11636	There's No Such Thing As Love/She's Just Another Girl	5
63	Decca F 11767	The Father Of Girls/I Love Everything About You	5
64	Decca F 11818	Tribute/Lament To A Hero	5
66	RCA RCA 1518	Why Can't You Try To Didgeridoo/Is There A Way Back To Your Arms	5
59	Decca DFE 6566	SINGS FOUR SONGS FROM IDLE ON PARADE (EP)	10
60	Decca DFE 6629	TONY'S HITS (EP)	10
60	Decca DFE 6655	MORE HITS FROM TONY (EP)	10
61	Decca DFE 6687	THIS TIME THE DREAM'S ON ME (EP)	10
60	Decca LK 4343	LOVE IS A NOW AND THEN THING (LP)	18
61	Decca LK 4406	TONY (LP)	18
64	Decca LK 4600	IN MY SOLITUDE (LP)	15
64	Decca LK 4654	NEWLEY DELIVERED (LP)	15
65	RCA Victor RD/SF 7737	WHO CAN I TURN TO (LP, mono/stereo)	15
66	RCA Victor RD/SF 7837	NEWLEY RECORDED (LP)	15

ANDY NEWMAN
72	Track 2406 103	RAINBOW (LP)	20

(see also Thunderclap Newman)

BRAD NEWMAN
62	Fontana H 357	Somebody To Love/This Time It's Love	12
62	Fontana H 369	Get A Move On/Here And Now And Evermore	10
62	Fontana 267 220TF	Stay By Me/Candy Lips	10
62	Fontana 267 243TF	Point Of No Return/Now I've Lost You	10
63	Fontana 267 273TF	I'll Find You Another Baby/No Man Should Ever Be Alone	10
64	Piccadilly 7N 35174	Please Don't Cry/Every Hour Of Living	8

COLIN NEWMAN
80	Beggars Banquet BEG 48	B/Classic Remains/Alone On Piano (p/s)	5
81	Beggars Banquet BEG 52	Inventory/This Picture (p/s)	5
82	4AD AD 209	We Means We Starts/Not To (Remix) (p/s)	6

(see also Wire)

DEL NEWMAN SOUND
67	Columbia SCX 6181	FLOWER GARDEN (LP)	30

JIMMY (C.) NEWMAN
57	London HLD 8460	A Fallen Star/I Can't Go On This Way (78 rpm = £12)	32
59	MGM MGM 1009	What'cha Gonna Do/So Soon (78 rpm = £15)	16
59	MGM MGM 1037	Grin And Bear It/The Ballad Of Baby Doe	10
60	MGM MGM 1085	A Lovely Work Of Art/What About Me	7
61	MGM MGM 1112	Now That You're Gone/Wanting You With Me Tonight	7
59	MGM MGM-EP 706	GRIN AND BEAR IT — COUNTRY AND WESTERN STYLE (EP)	45

JOE NEWMAN (SEXTET)
57	Vogue Coral Q 72244	Cocktails For Two/Later For The Happenings	5
57	Vogue Coral LVA 9052	HAPPY CATS (LP)	12
57	Pye/Vanguard PPT 12001	JOE NEWMAN (LP)	12

LIONEL NEWMAN ORCHESTRA
58	Columbia DB 4150	Hey! Eula/Two Butterflies	8

PAUL NEWMAN
66	Mercury MF 969	Ain't You Got A Heart/Tears On My Pillow	50

RANDY NEWMAN
68	Reprise RS 20692	Love Story/I Think It's Going To Rain Today	5
70	Reprise RS 20945	Gone Dead Train/JACK NITZSCHE: Harry Flowers	5
68	Reprise R(S)LP 6286	RANDY NEWMAN CREATES SOMETHING NEW UNDER THE SUN (LP)	15
70	Reprise RSLP 6373	12 SONGS (LP)	15

(see also Harry Nilsson, Tom Petty & Heartbreakers)

MINT VALUE £

TOM NEWMAN
75	Virgin V 2022	FINE OLD TOM (LP, features Mike Oldfield)	15
75	Virgin V 2042	LIVE AT THE ARGONAUT (LP, unreleased, test pressings only)	80
77	Decca TXS 123	FAERIE SYMPHONY (LP, gatefold sleeve)	25
88	Oceandisc	OZYMANDIAS (LP, unissued, 20 test pressings only in proof sleeve)	30

(see also July, Mike Oldfield)

TONY NEWMAN
68	Decca F 12795	Soul Thing/Let The Good Times Roll	20
70	Decca F 13041	Soul Thing/Let The Good Times Roll (reissue)	10

(see also Sounds Incorporated, Flying Machine, Pinkerton['s Assorted Colours], May Blitz, Three Man Army)

THE NEW MASTERHOUNDS
00	Blow It Hard BIH 017	One Note Brown/Burnt Black	20

NEW MODEL
83	Mr. Clean MERC 001	Chilean Warning/The World Thru Our Eyes/Totalitarian Terror (p/s, some in 7" x 10" folder)	10/6

NEW MODEL ARMY
83	Shout QS 002/QF 001	Bittersweet/Betcha/Tension (p/s, with flexi "Fashion"/"The Cause")	5

NEW MONITORS
72	Buddah 2011 118	Fence Around Your Heart/Have You Seen Her	40

NEW ORDER
81	Factory FAC 33	Ceremony/In A Lonely Place (p/s)	10
81	Factory FAC 3312	Ceremony (Re-recording)/In A Lonely Place (Extended) (12", cream & blue p/s)	10
81	Factory FAC 53	Procession/Everything's Gone Green (grey p/s, white writing; also other colours)	8
81	Factory Benelux FBNL 8	Everything's Gone Green/Mesh/Cries & Whispers (12", yellow sleeve)	10
82	Factory FAC 51B	Rocking Carol/Ode To Joy (flexidisc, given away at Hacienda, 4,000 only)	15
82	Factory FAC 63	Temptation/Hurt	7
83	Factory FAC 7312	Blue Monday/The Beach (12", die-cut sleeve, silver insert)	12
83	Factory FAC 93	Confusion (Edit)/(same) (p/s, DJ promo only)	12
84	Factory FAC 103	Thieves Like Us/Lonesome Tonight (p/s)	8
84	Factory FAC 103	Thieves Like Us (Edit)/Lonesome Tonight (Edit) (p/s, DJ promo only)	12
87	Factory FACD 187	Touched By The Hand Of God (Twelve Inch Mix)/Confusion Dub 1987/Temptation (Original Mix) (CD, gatefold card sleeve)	12
88	Factory FAC 73RD	Blue Monday 1988/Blue Monday (DJ-only mix) (12", p/s, DJ promo only)	10
88	Factory FACD 73R	Blue Monday 1988 (12 Inch)/Beach Buggy (12 Inch)/Blue Monday 1988 (7 Inch) (CD)	10
88	Factory FACDV 73R	Blue Monday 1988 (12 Inch)/Blue Monday 1988 (7 Inch)/Beach Buggy/Blue Monday 1988 (Video) (CD Video)	50
88	Factory FACDV 183	True Faith (Remix 12 Inch)/Evil Dust/True Faith (7 Inch) (CD Video)/True Faith (CD Video)	20
89	Factory FAC 263DJ	Round & Round (Ben Grosse Mix)/(12" Mix)/(Detroit Mix) (12", p/s, DJ only)	10
89	Factory FACD 263R	Round & Round (Seven Inch)/Vanishing Point (Instrumental Making Out Mix)/Round & Round (Twelve Inch)/Best & Marsh (Seven Inch) (3" CD, g/f card p/s)	10
89	Factory FAC 273/7	Run 2 (Edit)/MTO (Edit) (DJ promo only, 500 pressed)	20
85	Factory FACTUS 12C	POWER, CORRUPTION & LIES (cassette with 2 extra tracks)	12
86	Factory FACT 150SP	BROTHERHOOD (LP, limited metallic sleeve)	12
86	Factory FACD 150SP	BROTHERHOOD (CD, with "State Of The Nation" & metallic booklet)	20
87	Factory FACT 200	THE GATEFOLD SUBSTANCE (LP, numbered gatefold sleeve, 1,000 only)	35
87	Factory FACT 200C	SUBSTANCE (cassette, 200 only in box set with insert)	15

(see also Joy Division, Electronic, England/New Order, Revenge)

NEW ORDER
81	Come Org. CARA12	BRADFORD RED LIGHT DISTRICT (LP)	110

(see also Come)

NEW ORLEANS ALL STAR BAND
56	Vogue V 2380	Struttin' With Some Barbecue/Basin Street Blues	12
56	Vogue V 2368	Christopher Columbus/Bugle Call Rag (78 rpm = £8)	7

NEW ORLEANS BOOTBLACKS
54	Columbia SCM 5090	Flat Foot/Mad Dog	15

NEW ORLEANS WILD CATS
62	Storyville A 45048	Roll Along Prairie Moon/Well Well Well	5

NEWPORT JAZZ FESTIVAL ALL STARS
61	London Jazz LTZ-K 15202	NEWPORT JAZZ FESTIVAL ALL STARS (LP, also stereo SAH-K 6116)	10/12

NEW RELIGION
72	Bamboo BAM 70	In The Black Caribbean/Black Is Black	12
73	Ackee ACK 526	Walk Away Renee/What's It All About	5

NEWS
66	Decca F 12356	The Entertainer/I Count The Tears	20
66	Decca F 12477	This Is The Moment (from the TV series "Adam Adamant")/Ya Ya Da Da	15

(see also Patto, Glenn Hughes, Finders Keepers, Miller, Big Boy Pete)

NEWS FROM BABEL
86	Recommended RE 6116	NEWS FROM BABEL (LP, hand-screened sleeve)	12
89	ReR 6116 RE 6116	WORK RESUMED ON THE TOWER (LP)	18

BOBBY NEWSOME
72	Mojo 2093 018	Jody Come And Get Your Shoes/Post Office	10

OLIVIA NEWTON-JOHN

66	Decca F 12396	Till You Say You'll Be Mine/For Ever	150
71	Pye International 7N 25543	If Not For You/The Biggest Clown	12
77	EMI (no cat. no.)	Please Mr. Please/PILOT: Love Is (free flexidisc and *Record Mirror* magazine)	6
80	Jet JET 10-185	Xanadu/Fool Country (10" pink vinyl, die-cut p/s, with ELO)	10
80	Jet JETP 196	Magic/Whenever You're Away From Me (picture disc)	5
88	Mercury MERCD 272	The Rumour/Winter Angel/The Rumour (12" Extended Mix) (CD, picture disc, card sleeve)	15
89	Mercury MERCD 313	When You Wish Upon A Star/Rocking/Rock A Bye Baby/ Twinkle Twinkle Little Star (CD)	15
78	EMI EMAP 789	TOTALLY HOT (LP, picture disc)	15
85	Mercury 826 169-2	SOUL KISS (CD)	20

(see also Toomorrow, Marvin & Farrar)

NEWTOWN NEUROTICS

79	No Wonder A 45	Hypocrite/You Said No (no p/s, some with insert & sticker)	25/30/35
80	No Wonder NOW 4	When The Oil Runs Out/Oh No (p/s)	30
82	CNT 4/No Wonder NOW 56	Kick Out The Tories!/Mindless Violence! (p/s)	20
82	CNT CNT 010	Licensing Hours/No Sanctuary (p/s)	15
83	Razor RZS 107	Blitzkrieg Bop/Hypocrite (New Version)/I Remember You (p/s)	10
84	No Wonder NOW 6T	Suzi/Fools (p/s)	10
83	Razor RAZ 6	BEGGARS CAN BE CHOOSERS (LP)	28

NEWTRAMENT

83	Jive 19094	London Bridge Is Falling Down (12")	15

NEW TRENDS

67	Columbia SX 6245	THE NEW TRENDS (LP)	15

NEW VAUDEVILLE BAND

66	Fontana TF 741	Winchester Cathedral/Wait For Me, Baby	5
67	Fontana TF 784	Peek-A-Boo/Amy	5
67	Fontana TF 824	Finchley Central/Rosie (in p/s)	5
67	Fontana TF 853	Green Street Green/Fourteen Lovely Women	5
68	Fontana TF 909	The Bonnie And Clyde/Uncle Gabriel (p/s)	6
67	Fontana (S)TL 5386	WINCHESTER CATHEDRAL (LP)	12
67	Fontana (S)TL 5430	FINCHLEY CENTRAL (LP)	12

(see also Bonzo Dog Doo Dah Band, Alberts, Alan Klein)

NEW VICTORY BAND

78	Topic 12TS 382	ONE MORE DANCE AND THEN (LP)	15

NEW WANDERERS

79	Grapevine GRP 144	This Man In Love/Adam And Eve	10

NEW YORK DOLLS

73	Mercury 6052 402	Jet Boy/Vietnamese Baby	10
74	Mercury 6052 615	Stranded In The Jungle/Who Are The Mystery Girls	8
77	Mercury 6160 008	Jet Boy/Babylon/Who Are The Mystery Girls	6
85	Antler DOLLS 1	Personality Crisis/Subway Train (picture disc)	8
85	Antler DOLLS 2	Looking For A Kiss/Bad Girl (picture disc)	8
73	Mercury 6338 270	NEW YORK DOLLS (LP)	30
74	Mercury 6338 498	TOO MUCH TOO SOON (LP)	25

(see also Johnny Thunders, Heartbreakers, Sylvain Sylvain, Idols)

NEW YORK PORT AUTHORITY

77	Invictus INV 5312	I Got It/I Got It (Version) (7" and 12")	8/10

NEW YORK PUBLIC LIBRARY

66	Columbia DB 7948	I Ain't Gonna Eat Out My Heart Anymore/Rejected	22
68	MCA MU 1025	Gotta Get Away/Time Wastin'	12
68	MCA MU 1045	Love Me Two Times/Which Way To Go	8

NEW YORK ROCK ENSEMBLE

71	CBS 5292	Running Down The Highway/Law And Order	5
69	Atco 228 932	FAITHFUL FRIENDS (LP)	12
71	CBS 64126	ROLL OVER (LP)	12
72	CBS 64324	FREEDOMBURGER (LP)	12

NIADEM'S GHOST

87	Hibination HIDE 002	THIRST (EP, cassette)	15
86	Hibination HIDE 001	IN SHELTERED WINDS (LP)	25

(see also IQ)

NICE

67	Immediate IM 059	The Thoughts Of Emerlist Davjack/Angel Of Death	10
68	Immediate IM 068	America/The Diamond Hard Blue Apples Of The Moon (pink label, some in p/s)	18/10
68	Immediate IM 072	Brandenburger/Happy Freuds	10
70	Charisma CB 132	Country Pie/One Of Those People	6
70s	Immediate IM 068	America/The Diamond Hard Blue Apples Of The Moon (white label, reissue in p/s)	6
67	Immediate IMLP/IMSP 016	THE THOUGHTS OF EMERLIST DAVJACK (LP)	25
67	Immediate AS 2	ALBUM SAMPLER — THE THOUGHTS OF EMERLIST DAVJACK (1-sided LP, promo only)	30
68	Immediate IMSP 020	ARS LONGA VITA BREVIS (LP)	20
69	Immediate IMSP 026	THE NICE (LP)	20
70	Charisma CAS 1014	FIVE BRIDGES (LP, pink label, gatefold sleeve)	18
71	Charisma CAS 1030	ELEGY (LP, pink label)	18

(see also Keith Emerson, Emerson Lake & Palmer, Jackson Heights, Habits, Brian Davison, Refugee, Attack, Jet, P.P. Arnold)

Nick NICELY

NICK NICELY
80	Voxette VOX 1001	D.C.T. Dreams/Treeline (p/s, reissue copies £5)	8
81	EMI EMI 5256	Hillyfields (1892)/49 Cigars (p/s)	8

ALBERT NICHOLAS
56	Tempo A 129	How Long Blues (with Al Fairweather)/Rose Room (with Lise West)	10

(see also Al Fairweather)

PAUL NICHOLAS
68	Polydor 56285	Where Do I Go/Here Comes The Clown	5
69	Polydor 56322	Who Can I Turn To/Sing A Sad Song For Sammy	5
70	Polydor 56374	Freedom City/Run Shaker Life (some with p/s)	30+/50+
71	Polydor 2058 086	The World Is Beautiful/Lamplighter	30

(see also Oscar, Paul Dean)

BILLY NICHOLLS
68	Immediate IM 063	Would You Believe/Daytime Girl (features Small Faces)	42
73	Track 2094 109	Forever's No Time At All/This Song Is Green (with Pete Townshend)	12
68	Immediate IMCP 009	WOULD YOU BELIEVE (LP, withdrawn)	2,500

JANICE NICHOLLS
63	Decca F 11586	Oi'll Give It Foive/The Wednesbury Madison	5

SUE NICHOLLS
68	Pye 7N 17565	Where Will You Be/Every Day	5

JOY NICHOLS
53	Parlophone R 3684	Little Red Monkey/Me An' Johnny (78, with Dick Bentley And Jimmy Edwards)	10

MIKE NICHOLS & ELAINE MAY
62	Mercury AMT 1192	A Little More Gauze/Merry Christmas Doctor	6
59	Mercury MMC 14005	IMPROVISATIONS TO MUSIC (LP)	25
65	Mercury 20031 MCL	THE BEST OF MIKE NICHOLS & ELAINE MAY (LP)	18

SAM NICHOLS (& MELODY RANGERS)
50	MGM MGM 225	Keep Your Motor Hot/Who Puts The Cat Out When Papa's Out Of Town? (78)	12

LEA NICHOLSON
72	Trailer LER 3010	HORSEMUSIC (LP)	20

STEVIE NICKS
81	WEA K 79231	Stop Draggin' My Heart Around/Kind Of Woman (p/s, with Tom Petty & Heartbreakers)	5
81	WEA K 79265	Leather And Lace (edit)/Outside The Rain (p/s)	5
82	WEA K 79264	Edge Of Seventeen/Outside The Rain (p/s)	5
83	WEA U 9870	Stand Back/Garbo (p/s)	5
83	WEA U 9870T	Stand Back/Garbo/Wild Heart (12", p/s)	8
83	WEA X 9590	If Anyone Falls/Gate & Garden (p/s)	5
84	WEA U 9690	Nightbird/Nothing Ever Changes (p/s)	12
86	Parlophone 12R 6110	I Can't Wait (Extended Mix)/Rock A Little (Long)/I Can't Wait (7" Mix) (12", p/s)	8
86	Parlophone 12R 6124	Talk To Me/One More Big Time Rock'n'Roll Star/Imperial Hotel (12", p/s)	8
89	EMI 12EMG 97	Long Way To Go (7" Version)/(Remix)/Real Tears (12", gatefold p/s)	8
91	EMI 12EMS 214	I Can't Wait (Time Space Mix)/I Can't Wait (Dub Mix)/Sleeping Angel (12", p/s with 2 colour photos)	8
89	EMI EMD 1008	THE OTHER SIDE OF THE MIRROR (LP, with hologram)	12

(see also Fleetwood Mac, Buckingham-Nicks, Tom Petty & Heartbreakers)

NICKY AND THE DOTS
78	Small Wonder SMALL 12	Never Been So Stuck/Linoleum Walk (p/s)	20

NICO
65	Immediate IM 003	I'm Not Sayin'/The Last Mile	50+
81	Flicknife FLS 206	Vegas/Saeta (p/s)	8
82	Immediate IMS 003	I'm Not Saying/The Last Mile (p/s, reissue)	5
82	Half 1/2 1	Procession/All Tomorrow's Parties (p/s)	5
83	Aura AUS 137	Heroes/One More Chance (p/s)	5
85	Beggars Banquet BEG 139	My Funny Valentine/My Heart Is Empty (p/s, as Nico & the Faction)	5
68	Elektra EKL 4029	THE MARBLE INDEX (LP, orange label, also stereo EKS 74029)	45/40
71	Reprise RSLP 6424	DESERTSHORE (LP, with John Cale)	30
71	MGM Select 2353 025	CHELSEA GIRL (LP)	30
74	Island ILPS 9311	THE END (LP)	15
81	Aura AUL 715	DRAMA OF EXILE (LP, colour cover)	12

(see also John Cale, Velvet Underground, Ayers Cale Nico & Eno)

NICODEMUS
81	Cha Cha CHAD 44	Gunman Connection/It Have To Ram (12")	15
82	Cha Cha CHALP 011	GUNMAN CONNECTION (LP)	30
82	Black Joy DHLP 2003	DANCE HALL STYLE (LP)	50

JIMMY NICOL (& SHUBDUBS)
64	Pye 7N 15623	Humpty Dumpty/Night Train	20
64	Pye 7N 15666	Husky/Don't Come Back (solo)	18
64	Pye 7N 15699	Baby Please Don't Go/Shub Dubbery (possibly unissued)	20+

(see also Sound Of Jimmy Nicol, Georgie Fame)

WATT NICOLL
71	Xtra XTRA 1122	NICE TO BE NICE (LP)	12

NICOLLETTE
89	Shut Up & Dance SUAD 14	Waking Up (12")	12

NICRA
77	Ogun OG 010	LISTEN/HEAR (LP)	18

(see also Keith Tippett)

NIE ELECTRIKK
80 Synesthesia SYN 1   Cover Girl/Practically Isolate (p/s)... 8

NIGGY HOI!
80s Deli K1Z   Theme From Niggy Hoi!/Titanium Kedi (p/s) 8

NIGHTBIRDS
59 Oriole CB 1490   Cat On A Hot Tin Roof/The Square (78 rpm = £10) 12

NIGHTBLOOMS
90 Fierce FRIGHT 041   Crystal Eyes/Never Dream At All (p/s) 10

NIGHTCRAWLERS
67 London HLR 10109   The Little Black Egg/You're Running Wild 40

NIGHT-HAWKS
58 Fontana H 120   Cool For Cats/Time Will Tell (78) 10

NIGHTIME FLYER
69 Pye 7N 17739   Talk To Me/Spinning Wheel 6
69 Pye 7N 17798   Don't Push Me Baby/Thru' Loving You............................ 7
71 Pye 7N 45046   Love On Borrowed Time/It's A Hurtin' Thing 6

NIGHTIME FLYER
81 Red Eye EYE 2   Out With A Vengeance/Heavy Metal Rules (p/s) 15

NIGHTMARE
84 Ebony EBON 22   WAITING FOR THE TWILIGHT (LP)............................. 12

NIGHTMARES IN WAX
79 Inevitable INEV 0002   BIRTH OF A NATION (EP, with wraparound p/s) 20
84 KY KY 9   Black Leather/Shangri-La (12", 'horror' p/s)...................... 18
85 KY KY 9 1/2   Black Leather/Shangri-La/Girls Song (12", different p/s, 3,000 only) 20
(see also Dead Or Alive)

NIGHTRIDERS
66 Polydor BM 56066   Love Me Right Now/Your Friend (withdrawn, issue or promo).............. 120/85
66 Polydor BM 56116   It's Only The Dog/Your Friend 55
(see also Mike Sheridan & Nightriders, Mike Sheridan's Lot, Idle Race, Jeff Lynne)

NIGHTRIDERS
79 Stardust STR 1001   I Saw Her With Another Guy/London Town (picture insert) 15

NIGHTSHIFT
65 Piccadilly 7N 35243   Corrine Corrina/Lavender Tree 15
65 Piccadilly 7N 35264   That's My Story/Stormy Monday Blues 18

NIGHT-TIMERS
65 Parlophone R 5355   The Music Played On/Yield Not To Temptation (featuring Herbie Goins) 50
(see also Herbie Goins & Night-Timers, Ronnie Jones)

NIGHTWING
80 Ovation OVS 1209   Barrel Of Pain/Nightwing (p/s)................................... 10
84 Gull GULS 75   Treading Water/Call Your Name (p/s) 6
84 Gull GULS 7512   Treading Water/Call Your Name/Barrel Of Pain (12", red vinyl, p/s) 10
84 Gull GULS 77   Night Of Mystery/Dressed To Kill (p/s) 10
84 Gull GULS 7712   Night Of Mystery/Dressed To Kill (12", p/s) 12
85 Gull GULS 80   Strangers Are Welcome/Games To Play//The Devil Walks Behind You/
Cell 151 (double pack, gatefold p/s) 5
79 Ovation OV 1757   SOMETHING IN THE AIR (LP) 15
83 Gull PGULP 1038   STAND UP AND BE COUNTED (LP, picture disc) 15
(see also Alec Johnson Band, Nutz)

NIGHTWISH
04 Back On Black BOBV 003 DPD   ANGELS FALL FIRST (2-LP picture discs, stickered bag) 20
04 Back On Black BOBV 004 DPD   OCEANBORN (2-LP picture discs, stickered bag).................... 20
04 Back On Black BOBV 007 DPD   OVER THE HILLS AND FAR AWAY (2-LP picture discs, stickered bag) 20
04 Back On Black BOBV 006 DPD   WISHMASTER (2-LP picture discs, stickered bag).................. 20
04 Back On Black BOBV 008 DPD   CENTURY CHILD (2-LP picture discs, stickered bag)............... 20
05 Back On Black BOBV 035 DPD   ONCE (2-LP picture discs, stickered bag) 20

NIHILIST SPASM BAND
85 United Dairies UD 016   1X - X = X (LP)... 15

BILL NILE (& HIS GOODTIME BAND)
67 Decca F 12661   Pashionella Grundy/Bric A Brac Man 5
70 Deram DM 290   I Try Not To Laugh/Nobody Knows The Trouble I've Seen 6

WILLY NILLY
84 Ad Hoc AH 1   On The Spur Of The Moment/Half A Job (p/s, with 'time-table' insert) 45

(HARRY) NILSSON
67 RCA Victor RCA 1632   You Can't Do That/Ten Little Indians.................................. 6
68 RCA Victor RCA 1675   One/Sister Marie 12
68 RCA RCA 1707   Everybody's Talkin'/Don't Leave Me 6
68 RCA RCA 1764   Mourning Glory/Rainmaker 6
69 RCA RCA 1864   Maybe/The Puppy Song 6
69 RCA RCA 1876   Everybody's Talkin'/One.. 6
72 RCA RCA 2266   You're Breaking My Heart/Spaceman (possibly withdrawn,
demo stamped copy) 12
68 RCA Victor RD/SF 7928   PANDEMONIUM SHADOW SHOW (LP, mono/stereo)..................... 18/15
68 RCA RD/SF 7973   AERIAL BALLET (LP, mono/stereo) 18/15
69 RCA SF 8010   SKIDOO (LP, soundtrack) 20
69 RCA SF 8046   HARRY (LP) 15
70 RCA SF 8091   NILSSON SINGS NEWMAN (LP, with Randy Newman)................... 15
71 RCA SF 8166   THE POINT (LP, single sleeve or reissue with gatefold sleeve & book) .... each 15

73	RCA SF 8326	AERIAL PANDEMONIUM BALLET (LP)	15
74	Rapple/RCA APL1-0220	SON OF DRACULA (LP, soundtrack, with Ringo Starr, fold-out sleeve)	15

(see also Randy Newman, Ringo Starr, Cher)

NILSSON TWINS
57	Capitol CL 14698	Rain On My Window/I Dance When I Walk	5

LEONARD NIMOY
68	Dot (S)LPD 511	MR. SPOCK PRESENTS MUSIC FROM OUTER SPACE (LP)	25
72	Rediffusion ZS 156	MUSIC FROM OUTER SPACE (LP)	15

NINA
69	CBS 4681	Do You Know How Christmas Trees Are Grown?/The More Things Change	12

NINA & FREDERIK
59	Pye Intl. 7N 25021	Jamaica Farewell/Come Back Liza (78 rpm = £9)	5
59	Pye Intl. 7N 25043	The Formula For Love (with Louis Armstrong)/LOUIS ARMSTRONG with VALMA MIDDLETON: Struttin' With Some Barbecue (78 rpm = £7)	5
59	Columbia DB 4332	Listen To The Ocean/I Would Amor Her (78 rpm = £7)	5
59	Pye Nixa NPT 19023	NINA & FREDERIK (10" LP)	12

NINE BELOW ZERO
81	A&M AMS 8127	Ain't Comin' Back/Liquor Lover (p/s)	5
81	A&M AMS 8110	Three Times Enough/Doghouse (p/s, yellow vinyl)	5
82	A&M AMSX 8210	Wipe Away Your Kiss/True Life Is A Crime (12")	8

NINE BLACK ALPS
04	Melodic MEL0026	Cosmopolitan/Over The Ocean (1,000 only, p/s)	18
05	Island IS885	Shot Down/The Llana Song (blue vinyl, p/s)	6

NINE DAYS WONDER
71	Harvest SHSP 4014	NINE DAYS WONDER (LP)	75

NINE INCH NAILS
90	Island 12IS 482	Down In It (Skin)/Terrible Lie (Mix)/Down In It (Shred - Demo) (12", p/s)	10
91	Island IS 484	Head Like A Hole/Head Like A Hole (Copper Mix) (p/s)	5
91	Island 10ISP 484	Head Like A Hole (Slate)/Head Like A Hole (Copper) (10", poster p/s)	8
91	Island 12IS 484	Head Like A Hole (Slate)/Head Like A Hole (Copper)/Head Like A Hole (Opal) (12", ps)	10
91	Island ISDJ 484	Head Like A Hole (Radio Edit) (promo, stickered p/s, same track both sides)	20
91	Island ISDJ 508	Sin (Radio Edit)/(same) (promo only, stickered p/s)	12
91	Island 9IS 508	Sin (Long)/Sin (Dub)/Get Down Make Love (9", p/s)	10
92	Island IS 552DJ	Wish (Radio Edit) (1-sided, stickered plain sleeve, promo only)	12
94	Island IS 592	March Of The Pigs/A Violent Fluid (p/s, etched disc)	5
94	Island 9IS 592	March Of The Pigs/A Violent Fluid/All The Pigs, All Lined Up/Underneath The Skin (9", numbered p/s)	10
94	Island 12IS 596	Closer (deviation)/Closer (further away)/Closer (6.26)/Closer (precursor)/Closer (internal) (12", p/s)	10
94	Island 12ISX 596	Closer to God/March of the fuckheads/Heresy (blind)/Memorabilia (12", p/s)	10
90	Island CID 482	DOWN IN IT (mixes) (CD EP, numbered case)	20
90	Island CID 484	HEAD LIKE A HOLE (CD EP)	10
92	Interscope IMCD 8004	BROKEN (CD EP, foldout digipak)	10
91	Island ILPS 9973	PRETTY HATE MACHINE (LP)	12
92	Interscope ILPM 8004	BROKEN (1-sided 6 track mini-LP with free 7" 'Physical [Your're So]' / 'Suck')	30
92	Island ILPM 8005	FIXED (remix mini LP)	18
94	Island ILPSD 8012	THE DOWNWARD SPIRAL (2 x LP, gatefold sleeve)	18
99	Island ILPST 8091	THE FRAGILE (3 x LP, inners, booklet)	30

NINE INCH WORMS
97	Martian BEER 05	A NIGHT ON THE TOWN WITH THE NINE INCH WORMS (9" LP)	12

999
77	Labritain LAB 999	I'm Alive/Quite Disappointing (p/s)	18
77	United Artists UP 36299	Nasty Nasty/No Pity (p/s, green or black vinyl)	15/5
77	United Artists FREE 7	Nasty Nasty/No Pity (78rpm promo, 50 copies only)	200+
78	Labritain 12 FREE 10	Waiting/Action (12", mail-order freebie)	8
78	United Artists UP 36399	Emergency/My Street Stinks (p/s)	5
78	United Artists UP 36376	Me And My Desire/Crazy (p/s)	5
78	United Artists UP 36435	Feelin' Alright With The Crew/Titanic (My Over) Reaction (p/s)	8
78	United Artists UP 36467	Homicide/Soldier (p/s, green vinyl)	5
79	Radar ADA 46	Found Out Too Late/Lie, Lie, Lie	50
81	Albion ION 1011	Obsessed/Change/Lie, Lie, Lie (live) (p/s, with laminated sleeve, shrink wrapped with patch)	6
81	Albion ION 1017	Li'l Red Riding Hood/Waiting For Your Number To Be Called/I Ain't Gonna Tell Ya (live) (p/s, with stencil; shrink wrapped)	6
81	Albion ION 1023	Indian Reservation/So Greedy (Remixed)/Taboo (Remix) (p/s, clear vinyl, with sticker)	5
78	United Artists UAG 30199	999 (LP, with inner sleeve)	12
78	United Artists UAG 30209	SEPARATES (LP, with inner sleeve)	15

(see also Kilburn & High Roads)

NINESENSE
76	Ogun OG 900	OH! FOR THE EDGE (LP)	12
77	Ogun OG 910	HAPPY DAZE (LP)	12

(see also Elton Dean, Julie Tippetts, Keith Tippett, Mark Charig, Harold Beckett, Alan Skidmore)

1910 FRUITGUM CO.
68	Pye International 7N 25447	Simon Says/Reflections From The Looking Glass	5
68	Pye International 7N 25458	May I Take A Giant Step (Into Your Heart)/(Poor Old) Mr. Jensen	5
68	Pye Intl. N(S)PL 28115	SIMON SAYS (LP)	18
69	Buddah 203 014	GOODY GOODY GUMDROPS (LP)	15
70	Buddah 2359 006	HARD RIDE (LP)	12

1910 FRUITGUM CO./LEMON PIPERS
| 68 | Pye Intl. NEP 44091 | PRESENTING... (EP, 1 side each) .... 15 |

1984
| 69 | Big T BIG 117 | This Little Boy/Rosalyn .... 10 |
| 69 | Big T BIG 120 | Got To Have Your Love/Here We Are .... 6 |

9.30 FLY
| 72 | Ember NR 5062 | 9.30 FLY (LP) .... 110 |

NINEY (& DESTROYERS/OBSERVERS)
70	Amalgamated AMG 856	Niney Special/Danger Zone 15
70	Pressure Beat PR 5501	Honey No Money/INSPIRATIONS: This Message To You 8
71	Big BG 317	You Must Believe/You Must Believe (Version) 12
71	Big Shot BI 568	Blood And Fire/Mud And Water 8
71	Big Shot BI 586	Message To The Ungodly/Message To The Ungodly (Version) 8
71	Gas GAS 167	Blood And Fire/ROLAND ALPHONSO: 33 66 20
71	Moodisc HME 111	People Let Love Shine/MUDIES ALL STARS: Too Much. 6
72	Big Shot BI 607	Hiding By The Riverside/The Red Sea 5
72	Big Shot BI 609	Beg In The Gutter/Beg In The Gutter (Version) 5
72	Big Shot BI 610	Everyday Music (by The Observers)/Observing The Avenue. 5
72	Bullet BU 503	Aily And Ailaloo (& Max)/(Version) 5
72	Downtown DT 494	Get Out My Life/Get Out My Life (Version) (with the Observers). 5
72	Downtown DT 495	Hi Diddle/Hi Diddle (Version) 5

(see also Niney's All Stars, Observers)

NINEY'S ALL STARS
| 70 | Unity UN 563 | Skankee/Skankee — Version .... 10 |

(see also Niney, Observers)

NINJAMAN & FLOURGON
| 90 | Sure Delight 23 SDT | ZIG IT UP — MAIN ATTRACTION: Zig It Up (Radio/Freestyle/Funke-Club/Funke-Instrumental Mixes) (12", p/s) .... 10 |

NINO & EBBTIDES
| 61 | Top Rank JAR 572 | Those Oldies But Goodies/Don't Run Away .... 50 |

NIPPLE ERECTORS
| 78 | Soho SH 1/2 | King Of The Bop/Nervous Wreck (50 only with glossy p/s, later matt p/s) .... 30/20 |

(see also Nips, Pogues)

NIPS
78	Soho SH 4	All The Time In The World/Private Eyes (foldover p/s) 30
80	Soho SH 9	Gabrielle/Vengeance 18
80	Soho SH 9	Gabrielle/Vengeance (tour copy with 'licensed to cool' stamp). 30
80	Chiswick CHIS 119	Gabrielle/Vengeance (reissue, p/s) 15
81	Test Pressing TP 5	Happy Song/Nobody To Love (p/s) 25
80	Soho HOHO 1	ONLY AT THE END OF THE BEGINNING (LP, with insert, white labels) .. 35

(see also Nipple Erectors, Pogues)

NIRVANA (U.K.)
67	Island WIP 6016	Tiny Goddess/I Believe In Magic. 25
67	Island WIP 6020	Pentecost Hotel/Feelin' Shattered. 20
68	Island WIP 6029	Rainbow Chaser/Flashbulb 22
68	Island WIP 6038	Girl In The Park/C Side In Ocho Rios 12
68	Island WIP 6045	All Of Us (The Touchables)/Trapeze 12
69	Island WIP 6052	Wings Of Love/Requiem To John Coltrane 25
69	Island WIP 6057	Oh! What A Performance/Darling Darlene 20
70	Pye International 7N 25525	The World Is Cold Without You/Christopher Lucifer. 20
71	Vertigo 6059 035	The Saddest Day Of My Life/(I Wanna Go) Home 15
71	Philips 6006 127	Pentecost Hotel/Lazy Day Drift 12
72	Philips 6006 166	Stadium/Please Believe Me 8
76	Bradleys BRAD 7602	Two Of A Kind/Before Midnight 6
76	Island WIP 6180	Rainbow Chaser/Tiny Goddess (p/s). 7
78	Pepper UP 36461	Love Is/Pascale 5
79	Pepper UP 36538	Restless Wind/Thank You And Goodnight 5
81	Zilch ZILCH 8	The Picture Of Dorian Gray/No It Isn't 5
82	Zilch ZILCH 15	Black And White Or Colour/Tall Trees 5
88	Bam Caruso OPRA 45	Black Flower/WIMPLE WINCH: Save My Soul (jukebox issue, die-cut sleeve) 5
68	Island ILP 959/ILPS 9059	THE STORY OF SIMON SIMOPATH (LP, pink label, mono/stereo) 90
68	Island ILPS 9087	ALL OF US (LP, pink label). 90
70	Pye Intl. NSPL 28132	DEDICATED TO MARKOS III (LP) 125
71	Vertigo 6360 031	LOCAL ANAESTHETIC (LP, gatefold sleeve, swirl label) 65
72	Philips 6308 089	SONGS OF LOVE AND PRAISE (LP) 70
87	Bam-Caruso KIRI 061	BLACK FLOWER (LP). 12

(see also Patrick Campbell-Lyons, Ray Singer, Pica, Hat & Tie)

NIRVANA (U.S.)
89	Tupelo TUP EP8	Blew/Love Buzz/Been A Son/Stain (12", p/s) 40
89	Tupelo TUP CD8	Blew/Love Buzz/Been A Son/Stain (CD) 45
90	Tupelo TUP 25	Sliver/Dive (gatefold p/s, green vinyl only, 2,000 pressed). 25
91	Tupelo TUP EP25	Sliver/Dive/About A Girl (live)/Dive (12", p/s) 35
91	Tupelo TUP EP25	Sliver/Dive/About A Girl (live)/Dive (12", repressing, blue vinyl, p/s) ... 45
91	Tupelo TUP CDEP25	Sliver/Dive/About A Girl (live)/Spank Thru (live) (CD) 25
91	Geffen DGCT 5	Smells Like Teen Spirit (Edit)/Even In His Youth/Aneurysm (12", p/s) ... 15
91	Geffen DGCS 5	Smells Like Teen Spirit/Drain You (p/s) 8
91	Geffen DGCTP 5	Smells Like Teen Spirit (Edit)/Drain You (LP Version)/Aneurysm (12", picture disc, die-cut p/s) 40
91	Geffen DGCCD 5	Smells Like Teen Spirit (Edit)/Drain You/Even In His Youth/Aneurysm (CD, digipak with tour dates) 15
92	Geffen DGCTP 7	Come As You Are/Endless, Nameless/School (live) (12", picture disc, die-cut p/s) . 30

92	Geffen DGCTP 9	Lithium/Been A Son (live)/Curmudgeon (12", picture disc, die-cut p/s)	28
92	Geffen DGCTD 9	Lithium/Been A Son (live)/Curmudgeon (CD, digipak)	12
92	Geffen GFS 34	In Bloom/Sliver (live)/Polly (live) (p/s)	10
92	Geffen DGCTP 34	In Bloom/Sliver (live)/Polly (live) (12", picture disc, die-cut p/s)	15
93	Touch & Go TG 83	Oh, The Guilt/JESUS LIZARD: Puss (p/s, blue vinyl, some with poster)	18/10
93	Touch & Go TG 83	Oh, The Guilt/JESUS LIZARD: Puss (p/s, black vinyl)	28
93	Touch & Go TGCD 83	Oh, The Guilt/JESUS LIZARD: Puss (CD)	12
93	Geffen GFST 54	Heart Shaped Box/Milk It/Marigold (12", p/s)	10
93	Geffen GFST 66	All Apologies/Rape Me (12", p/s with 2 art prints)	15
93	Geffen GFSTD 66	All Apologies/Rape Me (CD)	8
94	Geffen (no cat. no.)	Penny Royal Tea (Scott Litt Mix)/Where Did You Sleep Last Night (live) (unreleased, 10 test pressings only)	800+
94	Geffen NIRPRO (no cat. no.)	Penny Royal Tea (Scott Litt Mix) (CD, 1-track, no inlay, promo only)	800+
89	Tupelo TUP LP 6	BLEACH (LP, 300 on white vinyl, 2,000 on green vinyl)	250/80
89	Tupelo TUP LP 6	BLEACH (LP, black vinyl)	20
89	Tupelo TUP CD 6	BLEACH (CD, original issue with extra tracks "Love Buzz" & "Downer")	20
91	Geffen DGC 24425	NEVERMIND (LP, with inner sleeve)	15
91	Geffen DGCCD 24425	NEVERMIND (CD, without uncredited bonus track "Endless, Nameless")	20
94	Geffen GED 24727	UNPLUGGED IN NEW YORK (LP, white vinyl with inner sleeve)	20
02	Sub Pop 9878700341	BLEACH (LP, white vinyl, with inner)	15

(see also Foo Fighters)

NITE-LITERS
72	RCA 2214	K-Jee/Tanga Boo Gonk	8
72	RCA SF 8282	INSTRUMENTAL DIRECTIONS (LP)	20

NITE PEOPLE
66	Fontana TF 747	Sweet Tasting Wine/Nobody But You	18
67	Fontana TF 808	Trying To Find Another Man/Stay As Sweet As You Are	15
67	Fontana TF 885	Summertime Blues/In The Springtime	40
68	Fontana TF 919	Morning Sun/Where You There	18
69	Page One POF 149	Love, Love, Love/Hot Smoke And Sassafras (some with insert)	18/12
69	Page One POF 159	Is This A Dream/Cream Tea	18
70	Page One POF 174	Season Of The Rain/P.M.	12
69	Page One POLS 025	P.M. (LP)	190

(see also Banana Bunch)

NITE ROCKERS
58	RCA RCA 1079	Nite Rock (Lonely Train)/Oh! Baby (78 rpm = £60)	80

NITESHADES
65	CBS 201763	Be My Guest/I Must Reveal	12
65	CBS 201817	Fell So Fast/I'm Not Gonna Worry	10

NITRO FUNCTION
(see under Billy Cox)

NITTY GRITTY DIRT BAND
67	Liberty LIB 55948	Buy Me For The Rain/Candy Man	10
68	Liberty LBF 15099	Collegiana/End Of Your Line	8
70	Liberty LBF 15358	Rave On/The Cure	6
68	Liberty LBL/LBS 83122	PURE DIRT (LP)	28
69	Liberty LBL/LBS 83286	DEAD AND ALIVE (LP)	25
71	Liberty LBG 83345	UNCLE CHARLIE AND HIS DOG TEDDY (LP, gatefold sleeve)	20
72	United Artists UAS 29284	ALL THE GOOD TIMES (LP)	15
74	United Artists USD 307/8	STARS AND STRIPES FOREVER (2-LP)	18

NITZER EBB
85	Power Of Voice NEP 1	Isn't It Funny How Your Body Works/The Way You Live/Crane/Cold War (12", p/s with insert)	8
85	own label	BASIC PAIN PROCEDURE (EP, cassette, given away at gig)	30
86	Power Of Voice NEB 3	Let Your Body Learn/Let Your Body Learn (Instrumental) (12", p/s)	10

JACK NITZSCHE
63	Reprise R 20202	The Lonely Surfer/Song For A Summer Night	25
63	Reprise R 20237	Night Walker/Green Grass Of Texas	12
78	MCA MCA 366	Hard Workin' Man (featuring Captain Beefheart)/Coke Machine	10
74	Warner Bros K 41211	ST GILES CRIPPLEGATE (LP)	25

(see also Date With Soul, Mick Jagger, Captain Beefheart, Randy Newman, Crazy Horse)

NIVENS
88	Woosh WOOSH 1	Let Loose Of My Knee/HOLIDAYMAKERS: Everyday (flexidisc with Woosh fanzine, foldaround p/s in poly bag)	8
89	Woosh WOOSH 5	Yesterday/I Hope You'll Always Be My Friend (p/s)	5

WILLIE NIX
(see under Willie Love, Joe Hill Louis)

NIX-NOMADS
64	HMV POP 1354	You're Nobody (Till Somebody Loves You)/She'll Be Sweeter Than You (demos miscredited to Nix-Nomands)	110

MEL NIXON
75	Alaska ALA 26	Every Beat Of Your Heart/ASTRA NOVA ORCHESTRA: Soul Sleeper	6

N-JOI
90	Deconstruction PT 44042	Anthem/Manic/Techno Gangsters (12", original issue)	15

NMONIC
00	Y n R YNR02	REQUIEM (EP)	12

RAB NOAKES
78	Ring O' 2017 115	Waiting Here For You/Restless (some in p/s)	18/12
78	Ring O' 2017 117	I Won't Let You Down/Long After Dark (unreleased)	
70	Decca SKL 5061	DO YOU SEE THE LIGHTS (LP)	30
72	A&M AMLS 68119	RAB NOAKES (LP, with Stealers Wheel)	15
78	Ring O' 2339 201	RESTLESS (LP)	15

NOBELMEN
59	Top Rank JAR 155	Thunder Wagon/Dragon Walk (78 rpm = £15)	25

NICK NOBLE
57	Mercury MT 165	Fallen Star/Let Me Hold You In My Arms (78, with Dick Noel Singers)	12
60	Coral Q 72403	The Tip Of My Fingers/Sweet Love	6
60	Coral Q 72413	Island Farewell/Excuse Me (I Think I've Got A Heartache)	6
	(see also Dick Noel)		

PATSY ANN NOBLE
61	HMV POP 980	Good Looking Boy/The Guy Who Can Mend A Broken Heart	22
63	Columbia DB 4956	Don't You Ever Change Your Mind/Sour Grapes	18
63	Columbia DB 7008	Heartbreak Avenue/I'm Nobody's Baby	15
63	Columbia DB 7060	I Was Only Foolin' Myself/Ordinary Love	15
63	Columbia DB 7088	Accidents Will Happen/He Tells Me With His Eyes	15
63	Columbia DB 7148	It's Better To Cry Today/Don't Tell Him I Told You	15
64	Columbia DB 7258	I Did Nothing Wrong/Better Late Than Never	15
64	Columbia DB 7318	Private Property/Crack In The Door	15
64	Columbia DB 7386	Tied Up With Mary/Green Eyed People	15
65	Columbia DB 7472	Then You Can Tell Me Goodbye/If You Wanna Be More Than Friends	15
65	Polydor BM 56054	He Who Rides A Tiger/City Of Night	22
	(see also Trisha Noble)		

TRISHA NOBLE
67	MGM MGM 1371	Live For Life/The New Is Rarely Patchka	15
	(see also Patsy Ann Noble)		

WOODROW NOBLE
79	Baby Mother HIT DD10	Reggae A The Best (Feat. Prince Hammer)/Strike The Hammer Wild (12")	30

CLIFF NOBLES (& CO.)
68	Direction 58-3518	The Horse/Love Is Alright	10
68	Direction 58-3738	Judge Baby, I'm Back/Horse Fever (solo)	10
69	Direction 58-4205	Switch It On/Burning Desire	10
68	Direction 8-63477	THE HORSE (LP)	30

NO CHOICE
83	Riot City RIOT 20	SADIST DREAM (EP)	5

NO COVER
82	Guardian GRC 136	200 Voices/Seen Too Much	5

NOCTURNAL EMISSIONS
81	Sterile ION 2	FRUITING BODY (LP)	50
84	Sterile SR 6	NO SACRIFICE (12", p/s, 2,000 only)	12
84	CFC LP 2	CHAOS — LIVE AT THE RITZY (LP)	25
84	Illuminated JAMS LP 33	VIRAL SHEDDING (LP)	25
84	Sterile EMISS 001	TISSUE OF LIES (LP, 1st batch numbered, later in blue sleeve)	50/25
84	Sterile SR 4	DROWNING IN A SEA OF BLISS (LP)	60
84	Sterile SR 5	BEFEHLSNOTSTAND (LP)	25
85	Sterile SRC 003	DEATHDAY (cassette)	10
85	Sterile SR 7	SONGS OF LOVE AND REVOLUTION (LP)	18
86	Sterile SR 9	SHAKE THOSE CHAINS, RATTLE THOSE CAGES (LP)	15
87	Earthly Delights EARTH 02	THE WORLD IS MY WOMB (LP)	20
88	Earhtly Delights EARTH 04	SPIRITFLESH (LP)	20
89	Earthly Delights EARTH 03	STONEFACE (LP)	12
89	Earthly Delights EARTH 05	BEYOND LOGIC (LP, 250 signed)	25/18
90	Earthly Delights EARTH 06	MOUTH OF THE BABES (LP)	30
93	Earthly Delights EARTH 08	THE QUICKENING (LP, 250 signed)	25/18
	(see also Caroline K)		

NOCTURNES
55	MGM SP 1120	Whodat? (Buck Dance)/Hey Punchinello	10
55	MGM SP 1148	Birmin'ham/Toodle-oo Igaloo	10

NOCTURNES
64	Solar SRP 102	Troika/Rawhide	18

NOCTURNES
67	Columbia DB 8158	Wish You Would Show Me Your Mind/I Do, I Do	8
67	Columbia DB 8219	Why (Am I Treated So Bad?)/Save The Last Dance For Me	8
68	Columbia DB 8332	A New Man/Suddenly Free	8
68	Columbia DB 8453	Carpet Man/Look At Me	7
68	Columbia DB 8493	Montage/Fairground Man	40
68	Columbia S(C)X 6223	THE NOCTURNES (LP)	22
68	Columbia S(C)X 6315	WANTED ALIVE (LP)	25
	(see also Lyn Paul)		

NOCTURNS
64	Decca F 12002	Carryin' On/Three Cool Cats	10

PROFESSOR ERNEST NODE & HIS MUG & JUG BAND
67	Columbia DB 8100	The Egg Plant That Ate Chicago/I'm In The Doghouse	10

MINT VALUE £

DICK NOEL
56	London HLH 8295	(The Same Thing Happens With) The Birds And The Bees/Birth Of The Blues	20
56	London HLH 8295	(The Same Thing Happens With) The Birds And The Bees/Birth Of The Blues (78)	8

(see also Nick Nobel)

NO FAITH
81	No Faith NF 001	Double Trouble/Only The Good Die Young (p/s, private pressing)	120

NOIR
71	Dawn DNLS 3029	WE HAD TO LET YOU HAVE IT (LP, with insert)	30

NO KIDDING
74	Wave	NO KIDDING (LP)	15

JOE NOLAN & HIS BAND
69	Jolly JY 013	Cool It With Reggae/Reggae With Me	7
69	Jolly JY 016	Confidential/Poison Reggae	7

(see also Bonnie Frankson)

TERRY NOLAND
58	Coral Q 72311	Oh Baby! Look At Me/Puppy Love (78 rpm = £80)	150+

NOLAN SISTERS/NOLANS
72	Nevis NEVR 009	THE SINGING NOLANS (LP)	12
77	Hanover Grand HG 19751	THE NOLAN SISTERS (LP, sold only at London Room Club, Drury Lane)	12

PIERRE NOLES
63	Oriole CB 1791	Jacqueline/Marilyn	7

NAZ NOMAD & NIGHTMARES
84	Big Beat NS 93	I Had Too Much To Dream (Last Night)/Cold Turkey (p/s)	5
84	Big Beat WIK 21	GIVE DADDY THE KNIFE CINDY (LP, purple vinyl)	12

(see also Damned)

NOMADS
70	Pye 7N 17906	The Singer Sang His Song/Lovin' Him	6

NON
80	Mute MUTE 7	I Can't Look Straight/SMEGMA: Flash Cards (p/s, with 2 centre holes)	10
81	Mute MUTE 015	NON EP: (Rise/Out Out/Romance Fatal Dentro Deun Auto (12", p/s)	12
00	Mute MUTE 250	Solitude/Receive The Flame (p/s, two centre holes, A-side plays at 45 rpm, B-side has closed grooves and plays at *any* speed, 700 copies only)	8

(see also Boyd Rice)

NO NAMES
65	Polydor NH 59080	All Because Of You/She Is Mine	40

PETER NOONE
71	Rak RAK 121	Right On Mother/Walnut Whirl	5
72	Rak RAK 129	Shoo Be Doo Wah/Because You Were There	5

(see also Herman's Hermits)

NO OTHER NAME
79	Daylight LD 500	DEATH INTO LIFE (LP, with insert)	25

NO QUARTER
83	Reel REEL 1	Survivors/Time And Space/Racing For Home (12", foldout p/s)	40
83	Bonzo Bear	BIRDS OF PREY EP (12")	30

NORA/BUNNY
72	Tropical AL 0015	Butterfly/TROPICAL ALL STARS: Fly (Version)	6

KEN NORDINE
57	London RE-D 1091	KEN NORDINE READS (EP, with Billy Vaughn Orchestra)	10
59	London Jazz EZ-D 19040	WORD JAZZ (EP)	10
67	Philips BL 7785	COLOURS (LP)	30

(see also Billy Vaughn & His Orchestra)

NORFOLK & JOY
79	Dara MPA 031	SCOTSOUNDS (LP)	30

NO RIGHT TURN
83	Chelful CHL 001	NO (LP)	25

NORMA & TONY
69	(No Cat. No.)	YOU ARE ALWAYS WELCOME AT OUR HOUSE (LP, private pressing, 100 only)	80

NORMAL
78	Mute MUTE 001	Warm Leatherette/T.V.O.D (p/s)	6

(see also Robert Rental)

NORMAL
03	Ai AI 005	GREEN FUELS EP (12", p/s)	8

GENE NORMAN (JUST JAZZ)
51	Vogue V 2022	Hot House (Parts 1 & 2) (78 rpm = £8)	8
51	Vogue V 2047	Blue Lou (Parts 1 & 2) (78 rpm = £8)	6
57	Vogue V 2272	Four O'Clock Jump/Three O'Clock Jump	6

LARRY NORMAN
69	Key KL 010/Dove DOVE 64	UPON THIS ROCK (LP)	15
73	MGM 2315 135	I'M ONLY VISITING THIS PLANET (LP, with lyric sheet)	12
76	Solid Rock ROCKY 1	IN ANOTHER LAND (LP, gatefold sleeve)	18

MONTY NORMAN
55	HMV 7M 349	The Shifting, Whispering Sands/Bonnie Blue Gal	12
57	HMV POP 281	The Garden Of Eden/Priscilla	12
63	United Artists UEP 1010	DOCTOR NO SOUNDTRACK (EP)	25
63	United Artists (S)ULP 1097	DOCTOR NO (LP, soundtrack, mono/stereo)	30/35

OLIVER NORMAN
67	Polydor 56176	Down In The Basement/Drowning In My Own Despair	25
68	Polydor 56247	People People/You'll Find It Will Come	6

NORMAN & HOOLIGANS
77	President PT 461	I'm A Punk/Re-Entry	15

NORMAN & INVADERS
64	United Artists UP 1031	Stacey/Our Wedding Day	10
64	United Artists UP 1058	Our Wedding Day/Stacey (reissue)	6
65	United Artists UP 1077	Night Train To Surbiton/Likely Lads	12

NORMAN CONQUEST
67	MGM MGM 1376	Two People/Upside Down	30

(see also Factory, Peter & Wolves, John Pantry)

FREDDIE NORTH
72	Mojo 2092 043	Sweeter Than Sweetness/I Did The Woman Wrong	8
72	Mojo 2916 012	FRIEND (LP)	25

ROY NORTH
63	Oak RGJ 107	Blues In Three/Blues In Five	50

NORTH BANK
72	Polydor 2058225	Arsenal We're On Your Side/Half Time	5

NORTHERN LIGHT
75	CBS 3370	Minnesota/Minnesota (DJ Version)	18

NORTHERN LIGHTS
66	United Artists UP 1123	No Time/Time To Move Along	40
66	United Artists UP 1161	Through Darkness, Light/Baby Those Are The Rules	40

(see also Hooten[anny] Singers, Abba)

NORTHSIDE
91	Factory FACT 310	CHICKEN RHYTHMS (LP, with inner sleeve)	15
91	Factory FACTCD 310	CHICKEN RHYTHMS (CD)	20

NORTH STARS
65	Fontana TF 581	For My True Love/Nothing But The Best	8
66	Fontana TF 726	She's So Far Out She's In/Eeenie Meenie Minee Mo	20

NORTHWIND
71	Regal Zono. SLRZ 1020	SISTER, BROTHER, LOVER (LP)	175+

(see also Elastic Band)

NOSEBLEEDS
77	Rabid TOSH 12	Ain't Bin To No Music School/Fascist Pigs (p/s)	15

(see also Durutti Column, Ed Banger, Blue Orchids)

NOSMO KING
74	Pye 7N 45382	Teenage Love/Goodbye	20

NO SWEAT
79	Rip Off RIP 4	Start All Over Again/You Should Be So Lucky (p/s)	8

NOTATIONS (U.K.)
72	Chapter One SCH 174	Need Your Love/Just Nothing Left To Give	40

NOTATIONS (U.S.)
76	Curtom K 16696	Think Before You Stop/I'm Losing	10
76	Curtom K 56212	NOTATIONS (LP)	40

FREDDIE NOTES & RUDIES
69	Downtown DT 427	I Don't Wanna Lose That Girl/Train From Vietnam	12
69	Grape GR 3010	Guns Of Navarone/Yester-Me, Yester-You	40
69	Grape GR 3011	Babylon Girl/Girl I've Got A Date	8
69	Trojan TR 7713	Shanghai/Rome Wasn't Built In A Day	12
70	Bullet BU 421	The Feeling Is Fine/Girl You're Killing Me	7
70	Trojan TR 7724	Rocco/Don't Tell Your Mama	8
70	Trojan TR 7734	Down On The Farm/Easy Street	30
70	Trojan TR 7791	Montego Bay/RUDIES: Blue Mountain	6
70	Trojan TR 7810	Walk A Mile In My Shoes/JOHNNY ARTHEY ORCHESTRA: Reggae Rouser	6
70	Duke DU 63	The Bull/River Ben Come Up	12
70	Duke DU 68	Chicken Inn/Chicken Scratch	12
70	B&C CB 125	It Came Out The Sky/Well Oh Well (p/s)	6
70	Trojan TBL 109	UNITY (LP)	30
70	Trojan TBL 152	MONTEGO BAY (LP)	25

NOTHINGS
65	CBS 201779	At Times Like This/Love So Sweet	8

NO TREND/LYDIA LUNCH
85	Widowspeak WSP 3	HEART OF DARKNESS (12" EP)	8

(see also Lydia Lunch)

NOTSENSIBLES
79	Redball RR 02	(I'm In Love With) Margaret Thatcher/Little Boxes/Gary Bushell's Band Of The Week (p/s)	15
80	Bent SMALL BENT 5	Death To Disco/Coronation Street Hustle/Lying On The Sofa (p/s)	10
80	Snotty Snail NELCOL 1	(I'm In Love With) Margaret Thatcher/Little Boxes/Gary Bushell's Band Of The Week (p/s, reissue)	10
80	Snotty Snail NELCOL 3	I Thought You Were Dead/I Make A Balls Of Everything I Do/Teenage Revolution (p/s)	10
81	Snotty Snail NELCOL 6	I Am The Bishop/The Telephone Rings Again (p/s)	8
80	Bent	INSTANT CLASSICS (LP)	35
80	Snotty Snail SSLP 1	INSTANT CLASSICS (LP, reissue)	25

NOTTS ALLIANCE
72	Tradition TSR 011	THE CHEERFUL 'ORN (LP, with Roy Harris)	15

NOVAK
97	Enraptured WORM 2	Silver Seas/Schmaltz (p/s in outer hand-sewn cloth sleeve with embroidered "Hand-knitted by Novak" label, 200 only, each different)	15
97	Enraptured WORM 2	Silver Seas/Schmaltz (p/s, 800 only)	8
97	Kitty Kitty CHOOSY 007	Rapunzel/Almost Chinook (hand crayoned p/s, 1,000 only)	8

NOVA LOCAL
69	MCA MUPS 377	NOVA 1 (LP)	35

NOVAS
63	RCA RCA 1360	Push A Little Harder/Oh, Gee Baby!	25

NOVAS
65	London HLU 9940	The Crusher/Take 7	50

NOW
69	NEMS 56-4125	Marcia/Hands On My Clock Stand Still	30

NOW
77	Ultimate ULT 401	Development Corporations/Why (p/s, some on blue vinyl)	35/20
79	Raw RAW 31	Into The 1980s/Nine O'Clock (p/s, 800 only)	40

NO WAY
78	Our Own IS/NW/1035	Breaking Point/TV Pox/30 Seconds (p/s)	30

NOW GENERATION
73	Green Door GD 4055	Alone Again, Naturally/MIND-BODY-SOUL: My Part (Version)	5
73	Pyramid PYR 7007	Baby Don't Do It/You'll Never Know	5
	(see also I Roy, B.B. Seaton, Audley Rollins)		

NOYES BROTHERS
80	Object Music OBJ 009/010	SHEEP FROM GOATS (2-LP)	25
	(see also Steve Miro & Eyes, Spherical Objects)		

NOYS OF US
60s	KPS KPS 502	He's Alright Jill/What Can I Do	30

N.R.B.Q. (New Rhythm & Blues Quintet)
69	CBS 4290	Stomp/I Didn't Know Myself	6
69	CBS 4501	C'mon Everybody/Rocket Number 9	6
69	CBS 63653	N.R.B.Q. (LP)	20
72	Buddah 2319 018	SCRAPS (LP)	12
	(see also Carl Perkins)		

N.S.U.
69	Stable SLE 8002	TURN ON OR TURN ME DOWN (LP)	130

GUITAR NUBBIT
64	Bootleg 501	Georgia Chain Gang/Hard Road (99 copies only)	45
60s	XX MIN 705	GUITAR NUBBIT (EP)	20

NUCHA
90	CBS 655885 7	Together/Ha Sempre Alguem	5

NUCLEAR SOCKETTS
81	Subversive SUB 001	HONOR BEFORE GLORY (EP, folded p/s, 33rpm)	10
81	Subversive SUB 002	Play Loud/Shadow On The Map	10

(IAN CARR'S) NUCLEUS
70	Vertigo 6360 008	ELASTIC ROCK (LP, gatefold sleeve, swirl label, later 'spaceship' label)	40/15
71	Vertigo 6360 027	WE'LL TALK ABOUT IT LATER (LP, g/fold sl., swirl or 'spaceship' label)	40/15
71	Vertigo 6360 039	SOLAR PLEXUS (LP, as Ian Carr's Nucleus, gatefold sleeve, swirl or 'spaceship' label)	45/12
72	Vertigo 6360 076	BELLADONNA (LP, as Ian Carr's Nucleus, gatefold sleeve, swirl or 'spaceship' label)	120/12
73	Vertigo 6360 091	LABYRINTH (LP, 'spaceship' label, any with swirl are Italian pressings!)	30
73	Vertigo 6360 100	ROOTS (LP, 'spaceship' label)	20
74	Vertigo 6360 110	UNDER THE SUN (LP, 'spaceship' label)	20
75	Vertigo 6360 119	SNAKE HIPS ETCETERA (LP, 'spaceship' label)	20
75	Vertigo 6360 124	ALLEY CAT (LP, 'spaceship' label)	20
76	Vertigo 9286 019	DIRECT HITS (LP, 'spaceship' label)	15
80	Mood 24000	AWAKENING (LP)	15
	(see also Don Rendell & Ian Carr Quintet, Neil Ardley, Centipede, Michael Garrick, New Jazz Orchestra, Linda Hoyle)		

TED NUGENT (& AMBOY DUKES)
74	Discreet K 19200	Sweet Revenge/Ain't It The Truth (as Ted Nugent & Amboy Dukes)	8
75	Epic S EPC 3900	Stormtroopin'/Hey Baby (some in p/s, orange label)	5
76	Epic S EPC 4796	Dog Eat Dog/Love You So I Told You A Lie	5
77	Epic S EPC 5482	Cat Scratch Fever/A Thousand Nights	5
78	Epic S EPC 9545	Homebound/Death By Misadventure (p/s)	5
75	Discreet K 59203	CALL OF THE WILD (LP)	12
	(see also [American] Amboy Dukes)		

NUGGETS
55	Capitol CL 14216	Quirl Up In My Arms/So Help Me, I Love You	25
55	Capitol CL 14267	Shtiggy Boom/Anxious Heart	25

GARY NUMAN
SINGLES
79	Beggars Banquet BEG 23	Cars/Asylum (p/s,orange plastic labels)	6
79	Beggars Banquet BEG 23	Cars/Asylum (p/s, 'mispressed' on dark red vinyl)	10
79	Beggars Banquet BEG 29	Complex/Bombers (live) (p/s, 'mispressed' on dark red vinyl)	12

80	Beggars Banquet SPC 7	Cars/We Are Glass (cassette, cigarette-pack style box)	8
80	Beggars Banquet BEG 35	We Are Glass/Trois Gymnopedies (1st Movement) (p/s, 'mispressed' on dark red vinyl)	12
80	Beggars Banquet BEG 46	I Die, You Die/Down In The Park (Piano Version) (p/s, dark red vinyl 'mispress')	8
80	Beggars Banquet BEG 46	I Die, You Die/Down In The Park (Piano Version) (p/s, mispressing, plays "Remember I Was Vapour" & "On Broadway" [SAM 126])	12
81	Beggars Banquet BEG 62	She's Got Claws/I Sing Rain (p/s, mispressing, plays Dollar's "Hand Held In Black And White")	18
83	Beggars Banquet BEG 95P	Warriors/My Car Slides (aeroplane-shaped picture disc)	15
84	Beggars Banquet TUB 1	This Is My Life (unissued promo for "The Plan", 300 white label test pressings only)	60
84	Numa NUP 4	Berserker/Empty Bed, Empty Heart (head shaped picture disc)	5
85	Strange Fruit ST 503	JOHN PEEL SESSION ONE (poster p/s)	6
85	Numa NUM 7	THE LIVE EP (12", p/s, blue, white vinyl or black vinyl)	8
85	Numa NUM 7	THE LIVE EP (12", p/s, mispressing on multicoloured vinyl)	80
86	Numa NUMX 16	This Is Love/Survival/Call Out The Dogs (Extended)/No Shelter/This Ship Comes Apart (12", p/s, stickered double pack, shrinkwrapped)	12
86	Numa NUP 17	I Can't Stop/Faces (aeroplane-shaped picture disc)	8
87	B. Banquet BEG 199P	Cars ('E' Reg Model)/Are 'Friends' Electric? (picture disc)	6
88	Polydor POSPP 894	No More Lies (picture disc)	5
88	I.R.S. ILSP 1003	New Anger/I Don't Believe (poster p/s)	5
88	I.R.S. ILSCD 1003	New Anger/I Don't Believe/Creatures (live)/I Can't Stop (live) (CD)	15
88	I.R.S. ILSPD 1004	America/Respect (live) (mispressed picture disc, 'Gary' picture both sides)	30
88	I.R.S. ILSCD 1004	America (Remix)/Respect (live)/New Anger (live)/Call Out The Dogs (live) (CD)	15
89	B. Banquet BBP 5CD	SELECTION (CD EP, picture disc)	8
91	I.R.S. NUMAN 1	Heart/Icehouse (p/s, black vinyl)	5
91	I.R.S. NUMANCD 1	Heart/Icehouse/Tread Careful (CD)	8
91	Numa NUCD 22	Emotion/In A Glass House/Hanoi/Emotion (CD mix) (CD, 'mispressed' disc)	12
92	Numa NU 24DJ	Machine & Soul/Machine & Soul (fan club issue, white label, mail-order only)	8
93	Beggars Banquet BEG 264T	Cars (Multivalve)/Cars (Endurance Model)/Cars (Top Gear Model) (12", black vinyl, promo only)	12
93	Beggars Banquet BEG 264	Cars ('93 Sprint)/Cars (Top Gear) (poster p/s)	5
93	Beggars Banquet BEG 264L	Cars ('93 Sprint)/Cars (Endurance) (McLaren F1-shaped picture disc)	8
93	Beggars Banquet BEG 264CD	Cars ('93 Sprint)/(Multivalve)/(Classic)/(Endurance)/(Top Gear)/(Motorway Mix)/ ('E' Reg Version) (CD, withdrawn, last track mispressed with 12" mix)	15
94	Salvation SACD 1	THE RADIAL PAIR (CD EP, fan club issue, mail order only)	12
94	Numa NU 26	A Question Of Faith/Whisper Of Truth (fan club issue, white label, mail-order only)	18
96	Polygram TV GNRAD 1	Cars (Premier Mix)/Are 'Friends' Electric? (live version)/We Are Glass (CD, promo only)	8
96	The Record Label SPIND 6	Radio (with N.R.G.)/Radio (extended mix) (CD, withdrawn)	60

ALBUMS

80	Beggars Banquet BEGA 19	TELEKON (LP, dark red vinyl 'mispressing', with stickered sleeve; some with bonus single SAM 126 "Remember I Was Vapour [live]"/ "On Broadway [live]")	20/15
81	Beggars Banquet BEGA 28	DANCE (LP, gatefold sleeve with poster)	12
82	Beggars Banquet BEGA 40	I, ASSASSIN (LP, initial copies at Woolworths with colour poster and merchandise sheet)	20
84	B. Banquet BEGA 55P	THE PLAN (LP, picture disc)	12
86	Numa NUMAP 1003	THE FURY (LP, mispress picture disc, "Your Fascination" 12" photo on A-side)	20
86	Numa GNFCDA 1	IMAGES 1 & 2 (2-LP, fan club issue with photo inserts, mail-order only)	20
86	Numa CDNUMA 1003	THE FURY (CD, with original mixes and artwork)	20
86	Numa CDNUMA 1005	STRANGE CHARM (CD)	30
87	Numa GNFCDA 2	IMAGES 3 & 4 (2-LP, fan club issue with photo inserts, mail-order only)	20
87	Numa GNFCDA 3	IMAGES 5 & 6 (2-LP, fan club issue with photo inserts, mail-order only)	20
87	Numa GNFCDA 4	IMAGES 7 & 8 (2-LP, fan club issue with photo inserts, mail-order only)	20
88	I.R.S. ILPPD 035	METAL RHYTHM (LP, picture disc)	12
88	IRS ILPCD 035	METAL RHYTHM (CD)	30
89	IRS EIRSACD 1021	METAL RHYTHM (CD, reissue)	30
89	IRS EIRSACD 1019	THE SKIN MECHANIC — LIVE (CD)	20
89	Numa GNFCDA 5	IMAGES 9 & 10 (2-LP, fan club issue with photo inserts, mail-order only)	20
91	Numa NUMACD 1001	BERSERKER (CD, fan club issue, mail order only, blue text on CD & inlay)	30
91	Numa GNFCCD 11	IMAGES 11 (CD, fan club issue, mail order only)	20
92	Receiver RRLP 170	THE OTHER SIDE OF GARY NUMAN (LP, withdrawn)	12
93	Numa NUMACDX 1009	MACHINE & SOUL (CD, mispressed with 9 tracks instead of 13)	20
94	Numa NUMA 1010	DREAM CORROSION (3-LP, autographed gatefold sleeve; copies bought at HMV with signed 10" x 8" photo)	20
94	Numa NUMA 1011	SACRIFICE (LP, with lyric sheet, stickered sleeve & bonus single: "The Seed Of A Lie [5.26]"/"The Seed Of A Lie [7.07]")	15

(see also Tubeway Army, Paul Gardiner, Dramatis, Claire Hamill, Radio Heart, Nicky Robson, Paper Toys, Caroline Munro, Generator, Bauhaus, Bill Sharpe)

NUMBER NINE BREAD STREET
| 67 | Holy Ground HG 112/1109 | NUMBER NINE BREAD STREET (LP, 250 copies only) | 300+ |

NUMBERS
| 79 | Blasto SRTS 79/CUS/358 | ROCK STARS (EP, with insert) | 8 |

NUMBERS
| 80s | Homegrown HG 701 | Here Today/Put 'Em All To Shame/Another Day/Tear You Down (photocopied or green & white sleeve; some with poster) | 5/4 |

NUMSKULLZ
96	High Noon NUM003	Enough Of That (12")	12
98	Hombre MEX003	Signs Of The End/The Difference (12")	12
98	Hombre MEX005	THE UNEXPECTED (EP)	10
99	Hombre MEX008	VOLCANICS (EP)	8

MINT VALUE £

NU NOTES
63	HMV POP 1232	Hall Of Mirrors/Fury	20
64	HMV POP 1311	Kathy/Sunset	20

(see also Russ Sainty & Nu Notes)

NUNS
81	Butt FUN 2	Wild/Suicide Child (p/s)	5

NURSE WITH WOUND
83	L.A.Y.L.A.H. LAY 3	GYLLENSKÖLD, GEIJERSTAM AND I AT RYDBERG'S (12" EP)	40
84	L.A.Y.L.A.H. LAY 7	BRAINED BY FALLING MASONRY (12" EP)	12
86	Torso 33016	SPIRAL INSANA (12" EP)	12
87	Crystal/Wisewound WW 01	Crank/TERMITE QUEEN: Wisecrack (numbered plain black sleeve with printed band, 500 only)	20
88	Yangki 002	FAITH'S FAVOURITES EP: Swamp Rat (with Current 93)/Ballad Of The Pale Girl (12", laminated p/s)	30
88	Idle Hole MIRROR 003	Cooloorta Moon/Great Empty Space (12", p/s)	20
90	Harbinger 001	The Burial Of The Stoned Sardine/CURRENT 93: No Hiding From The Blackbird	15
90	United Dairies UD 031	SORESUCKER EP: I Am The Poison/Journey Through Cheese (12", p/s, 2,000 only)	20
90	United Dairies UD 031CD	SORESUCKER EP: I Am The Poison/Journey Through Cheese (CD EP)	8
90	Shock SX 004	Sinister Senile: Human Human Human/Psychedelic Underground (45/33rpm, 1,000 only).	25
92	Clawfist 12	Steel Dream March Of The Metal Men/The Dadda's Intoxication ('singles club' release, 33rpm, foldover p/s in poly bag, 1,400 only)	15
93	Clawfist 20	CRUMB DUCK (10" EP, shared with Stereolab, 37 with handmade p/s (Gain/Sadier only), 1450 regular)	100/20
93	World Serpent WS 7003	Alien (1-sided, company sleeve 1,000 only)	25
95	WN 001	ALICE THE GOON (1-sided 12", p/s, 500 only)	75
79	United Dairies UD 01	CHANCE MEETING ON A DISSECTING TABLE OF A SEWING MACHINE AND AN UMBRELLA (LP, 500 only, originals have hand-painted numbers; beware of bootlegs with *printed* numbers)	115
80	United Dairies UD 03	TO THE QUIET MEN FROM A TINY GIRL (LP, numbered, 500 only, originals have hand-painted numbers; beware of bootlegs with *printed* numbers)	75
80	United Dairies UD 04	MERZBILD SCHWET (LP, numbered, 500 only, originals have hand-painted numbers; beware of bootlegs with *printed* numbers)	75
81	United Dairies UD 08	INSECT AND INDIVIDUAL SILENCED (LP, 1,000 only)	60
83	Mi Mort MI MORT iii	GYLLENSKÖLD, GEIJERSTAM & FRIENDS, LIVE AT BAR MALDOROR (LP, some with insert)	50
83	Third Mind TMR 03	OSTRANENIE 1913 (LP, 2,000 only)	45
85	L.A.Y.L.A.H. LAY 15	THE SYLVIE AND BABS HI-FI COMPANION (LP, gatefold sleeve)	25
85	United Dairies UD 110	DRUNK WITH THE OLD MAN OF THE MOUNTAINS (LP)	25
85	United Dairies UD 012	HOMOTOPY TO MARIE (LP, 5,000 only)	35
86	United Dairies UD 019	AUTOMATING VOL. 1 (LP, 3,000 only)	30
86	United Dairies UD 020	A MISSING SENSE (LP, 1 side only; other side by Organum; 2,000 only)	30
87	United Dairies UD 025	DRUNK WITH THE OLD MAN OF THE MOUNTAINS (LP, reissue, handmade custom sleeve, with insert, signed, 100 only)	125
88	United Dairies UD 027	ALAS THE MADONNA DOES NOT FUNCTION (mini-LP, 45/33rpm, 3,000 only)	25
88	Idle Hole MIRROR ONE	SOLILOQUY FOR LILITH (3-LP box set, 1,000 only)	60
88	Idle Hole MIRROR 1C	SOLILOQUY FOR LILITH PTS 5/6 (LP, with insert)	25
89	Idle Hole MIRROR TWO	PRESENTS THE SISTERS OF PATAPHYSICS (LP, 1,000 only)	25
89	United Dairies UD 030	AUTOMATING VOL. II (LP)	20
89	United Dairies UD 032	A SUCKED ORANGE (LP, some with full colour insert)	25/20
89	Yangki 003	LUMBS SISTER (LP)	30
90	United Dairies UD 134	PSILOTRIPITAKA (3-LP [UD 01, 03 & 04], with bonus LP "Registered Nurse" [UD 00], 1,000 only, some possibly in leather bag)	400/125
90	United Dairies UD 134CD	PSILOTRIPITAKA (3-CD [UD 01, 03 & 04], with bonus CD "Registered Nurse" [UD 00CD], 1,000 only, 30 in 'leather bondage bag')	400/60
90	L.A.Y.L.A.H. LAY 30	BRAINED/GYLLENSKÖLD (LP, withdrawn)	35
91	United Dairies UD 038	CREAKINESS (LP, with Spasm)	20
91	United Dairies UD 09	THE 150 MURDEROUS PASSIONS (LP)	25
91	United Dairies UD 09CD	THE 150 MURDEROUS PASSIONS (CD, sealed in black plastic, 500 only)	30
93	United Dairies UD 059	CRUMB DUCK (LP, shared with Stereolab, reissue of Clawfist EP, 50 copies on pink vinyl, 500 on fluorescent yellow vinyl)	50/25
94	United Dairies UD 043	SECOND PIRATE SESSION – ROCK'N'ROLL STATION – SPECIAL EDITION (LP, red vinyl, 500 only)	20
99	United Dairies UD 056	AN AWKWARD PAUSE (2-LP, translucent grey vinyl, 500 only, 1 side not available on CD)	30
01	United Durtro UDOR 8	BRIGHT YELLOW MOON (CD, with Current 93, first 1,000 with bonus CD)	30
02	United Durtro UD 102	MAN WITH THE WOMAN FACE (LP, ltd. edition clear vinyl, poly sleeve, 2 inserts)	15
00s	United Dairies UDX 092	SOLILOQUY FOR LILITH (3-CD box set)	25

(see also Current 93, Organum/New Blockaders, Diana Rogerson, Sol Invictus, Steven Stapleton & David Tibet, Tibet & Stapleton, Whitehouse)

NU-SOUND EXPRESS LTD.
72	Pye Int'l 7N 25580	One More Time Y'all/A Rose For A Lady	20

NUTHIN' FANCY
80s	Dynamic Cat DC 1001	Looking For A Good Time/Too Much Rock'n'Roll (p/s)	250

(see also Terraplane, Thunder)

NU TORNADOS
58	London HLU 8756	Philadelphia U .S.A./Magic Record (78 rpm = £12)	18

NUTRONS
60s	Melodisc M 1593	The Very Best Things/Stop For The Music	18

NUTSHELL
70s	Myrrh MYR 1056	FLYAWAY (LP)	18

MAY'F NUTTER
66	Vocalion VL 1282	Head Shrinker/Don't Know What To Do	15
73	London HLL 10414	I Don't Care/Hitch Hike Nightmare	6

NUTTY SQUIRRELS
59	Pye International 7N 25044	Uh! Oh! Parts 1 & 2 (78 rpm = £12)	6

NUTZ
74	A&M AMLS 68256	NUTZ (LP)	12
75	A&M AMLS 68306	NUTZ TOO (LP)	12

(see also Rage, Nightwing)

NYAH FEARTIES
86	Nya DOPLP 001	A TASTY HEIDFUL (LP)	25

NYAH SHUFFLE
70	Grape GR 3021	Sting Ray/Paradise	10

JUDY NYLON
82	On-U-Sound LP 16	PAL JUDY (LP)	12

(see also John Cale, Snatch)

NYLONS
82	Attic NYLON 1	A Million Ways/Up On The Roof (p/s)	6

LAURA NYRO
67	Verve Forecast VS 1502	Wedding Bell Blues/Stoney End	12
68	CBS 3604	Eli's Coming/Sweet Blindness	6
68	CBS 4031	Once It Was Alright Now (Farmer Joe)/Woman's Blues	6
69	CBS 4719	Time And Love/The Man Who Sends Me Home	6
68	CBS 63346	ELI AND THE THIRTEENTH CONFESSION (LP, gatefold sleeve, orange label)	25
69	CBS 63510	NEW YORK TENDABERRY (LP, orange label)	25
69	Verve Forecast SVLP 6022	THE FIRST SONG	

OAK
71	Topic 12TS 212	WELCOME TO OUR FAIR (LP)	40

(see also Peta Webb)

OAKENSHIELD
82	Acorn OAK 001	ACROSS THE NARROW SEAS (LP)	18
85	Acorn OAK 002	AGAINST THE GRAIN (LP, with insert)	18

PHILIP OAKEY & GIORGIO MORODER
84	Virgin VSY 713	Together In Electric Dreams/(Instrumental) (picture disc)	6

(see also Human League, Men)

OASIS
SINGLES
94	Creation CRE 176	Supersonic/Take Me Away (p/s)	25
94	Creation CRE 182	Shakermaker/D'Yer Wanna Be A Spaceman? (p/s)	22
94	Creation CRESCD 182	Shakermaker/Alive (Demo Version)/Bring It On Down (Live) (CD)	8
94	Creation CRE 185	Live Forever/Up In The Sky (Acoustic) (numbered foldover p/s in stickered poly bag)	22
94	Creation CRE 190	Cigarettes & Alcohol/I Am The Walrus (Live at Glasgow Cathouse June '94) (numbered foldover p/s in poly bag)	15
94	Creation CRECS 190	Cigarettes & Alcohol/I Am The Walrus (Live at Glasgow Cathouse June '94) (cassette, flip-top 'cigarette' pack)	20
94	Creation CRE 195	Whatever/(It's Good) To Be Free (no'd foldover p/s in stickered poly bag)	14
96	Creation CRE 221	Don't Look Back In Anger/Step Out (p/s, with poly outer)	10
97	Creation CRE 278	Stand By Me/I Got The Fever (p/s)	5
02	Big Brother RKID 23	The Hindu Times/Just Getting Older (p/s, limited edition)	6

ALBUMS
94	Creation CRELP 169	DEFINITELY MAYBE (2-LP, gatefold sleeve)	40
95	Creation CRELP 189	(WHAT'S THE STORY) MORNING GLORY? (2-LP, gatefold sleeve)	40
98	Creation CRELP 241	THE MASTERPLAN (3-LP)	40

PROMO SINGLES
93	Creation CTP 8	Columbia (Demo) (12", 1-sided, white label, 510 pressed)	250
94	Creation CRE 176TP	Supersonic/Take Me Away/I Will Believe (Live) (12", company sleeve)	50
94	Creation CRESCD 176P	Supersonic/Take Me Away/I Will Believe (Live)/ Columbia (White Label Demo) (CD)	35
94	Creation CRE 182TP	Shakermaker/D'Yer Wanna Be A Spaceman?/Alive (8 Track Demo) (12")	100
94	Creation CRESCD 182P	Shakermaker/D'Yer Wanna Be A Spaceman?/Alive (8 Track Demo)/ Bring It On Down (Live) (CD)	30
94	Creation CRE 185TP	Live Forever/Up In The Sky (Acoustic)/Cloudburst (12")	70
94	Creation CRESCD 185P	Live Forever/Up In The Sky (Acoustic)/Cloudburst/ Supersonic (Live April '94) (CD)	20
94	Creation CTP 190TP	I Am The Walrus (Live At Glasgow Cathouse June '94) (12", 250 only, co. sl.)	375
94	Creation CTP 190CL	Cigarettes & Alcohol (12", 1-sided)	90

MINT VALUE £

94	Creation CTP 190CL	Cigarettes & Alcohol/I Am The Walrus (live at Glasgow Cathouse June '94)/ Fade Away (12", 300 only)	80
94	Creation CRESCD 190P	Cigarettes & Alcohol/I Am The Walrus (live at Glasgow Cathouse June '94)/ Listen Up/Fade Away (CD)	25
94	Creation CRE 195TP	Whatever (12", 1-sided, 560 only)	100
94	Creation CRESCD 195P	Whatever/(It's Good) To Be Free/Half The World Away/Slide Away (CD)	10
94	Creation CTP 195	(It's Good) To Be Free (12", 1-sided, 360 only)	60
94	Creation CREDM 001	DEFINITELY MAYBE (4 x 7" box set, in silver cigarette-pack-shaped plastic box, with booklet & interview CD)	35
95	Creation CREMG 001	(WHAT'S THE STORY) MORNING GLORY? (4 x 7" box set, in gold cigarette-pack-shaped plastic box, with booklet & interview CD)	35
95	Creation CCD 169	Slide Away (CD, 1-track Brits Awards issue, 1,000 only; beware of counterfeits)	45
95	Creation CCD 204	Some Might Say (CD, 1-track, 350 only)	125
95	Creation CRESCD 204P	Some Might Say/Talk Tonight/Acquiesce/Headshrinker (CD)	20
95	Creation CTP 204	Acquiesce (12", 1-sided, 570 only)	170
95	Creation CCD 204P	Acquiesce (CD, 1-track, 300 only)	170
95	Creation CTP 212	Roll With It (12", 1-sided)	85
95	Creation CRESCD 212P	Roll With It/Better People/Rockin' Chair/ Live Forever (Live at Glastonbury '95) (CD, 3,078 only)	10
95	Creation CRESCD 215P	Wonderwall/Round Are Way/The Swamp Song/The Masterplan (CD, 2,320 only)	10
95	Creation CTP 215	Round Are Way (12", 1-sided, 843 only)	60
96	Creation CTP 221X	Cum On Feel The Noize/Champagne Supernova (Lynchmob Beats Mix) (12", 1,203 pressed, plain die-cut sleeve; beware of counterfeits)	70
96	Creation CCD 221	Cum On Feel The Noize (CD, pic. disc, 1-track, with football motif, no inlay, 500 only)	175
96	Creation CRESCD 221P	Don't Look Back In Anger/Step Out/Underneath The Sky/ Cum On Feel The Noize (CD)	10
96	Creation P 96/1	OASIS (Fade Away/Half The World Away/Acquiesce/The Masterplan) (CD sampler for singles box set)	30

(N.B.: the 4-track 12" "In-Store Sampler" [OASIS 1-12] is a bootleg.)

97	Creation CTP 256	D'You Know What I Mean?/Heroes (12")	30
97	Creation CRESCD 256P	D'You Know What I Mean/Stay Young/Angel Child/Heroes (CD, digipak)	20
97	Creation CCD 256	D'You Know What I Mean (CD, 1-track, black card p/s)	20
97	Creation CCD 256X	D'You Know What I Mean?/Heroes (CD, 2-track, white card title p/s)	25
97	Creation CCD 219PL	Be Here Now (live)/Be Here Now (live with DJ intro) (CD)	25
97	Creation CTP 278	Stand By Me/I Got The Fever (12")	35
97	Creation CCD 278	Stand By Me (CD, 1-track, black card p/s)	20
97	Creation CCD 278X	Stand By Me (CD, 2-track, white card p/s)	18
97	Creation CRESCD 278P	Stand By Me/(I Got) The Fever/My Sister Lover/Going Nowhere (CD, digipak)	12
97	Creation CTP 282	All Around The World/Street Fighting Man (12", black die-cut sleeve)	25
97	Creation CCD 282	All Around The World (Edit) (CD, 1-track, black card sleeve)	15
97	Creation CCD 282X	All Around The World/Street Fighting Man (CD, blue card sleeve)	20
97	Creation CRESCD 282	All Around The World/The Fame/Flashbax/Street Fighting Man (CD)	15
97	Creation (no cat. no.)	VOX BOX (9-CD, wooden guitar-amp-shaped box set in outer box, with booklets from "Silver" & "Gold" CD box sets; contains commerical issues of "Supersonic" through to "Don't Look Back In Anger"; in-house giveaway only)	800+
98	Creation CRELP 241P	THE MASTERPLAN SAMPLER (Acquiesce/Underneath The Sky/ I Am The Walrus/The Masterplan) (12" sampler)	25
98	Creation CCD 241	Acquiesce/Talk Tonight/Rockin' Chair/The Masterplan (CD sampler)	25
98	Sony SAMPMS 6032	Acquiesce/Underneath The Sky/I Am The Walrus/The Masterplan (CD sampler)	40
00	Creation CTP 327	Go Let It Out (12", 1-track, 1-sided, p/s)	45
00	Creation CCD 327	Go Let It Out (CD, 1-track, card sleeve)	15
00	Big Brother FITB 001	Fuckin' In The Bushes (12", 1-sided, white label)	65
00	Big Brother RKID 03TP	Who Feels Love? (12", 1-sided, laminated p/s)	25
00	Big Brother RKID 004TP	Sunday Morning Call (12", 1-sided, flipback laminated p/s)	30
00	Big Brother RKIDSCD 005P	FAMILIAR TO MILLIONS (Gas Panic/Supersonic/Helter Skelter) (live CD, promo-only)	15
01	own label OASIS 10	10 YEARS OF NOISE & CONFUSION (Columbia/Rock & Roll Star (Live)/ Acquiesce/Fuckin' In The Bushes) (10", promo-only, custom labels, die-cut sleeve, 200 only, some with press release)	85/80
02	Big Brother RKID 25TPX	Hung In A Bad Place (12", 1-track, 1-sided, in die-cut mauve/pink sleeve, some in brown sleeve)	30/40
02	Big Brother RKID 24TP	Stop Crying Your Heart Out (Spike Mix) (12", custom sleeve, 250 only)	22
02	Big Brother RKIDSCD 24PX	Stop Crying Your Heart Out (Spike Mix) (CD, custom sleeve, 250 only)	18
02	Big Brother RKID 23TP	The Hindu Times (Spike Mix) (12", promo-only, custom logo sleeve, 250 only)	22
02	Big Brother RKID26TPX	My Generation (12" 1-sided promo with Union Jack Sleeve. 800 only)	30
05	Big Brother RKIDS29TP	Lyla (12" 1-sided promo, 770 only)	20
05	Big Brother RKID31TP	Turn Up The Sun (12" 1-sided promo in card sleeve and inner sleeve, 1,120 only)	30
05	Big Brother RKID32TP	Mucky Fingers (12" 1-sided promo in double p/s, 950 only)	20
05	(No cat. no.)	Oasis Interview – 20 Questions With Noel (CD-R in card sleeve)	20

PROMO ALBUMS

94	Creation CRECD 169P	DEFINITELY MAYBE (CD)	75
95	Creation C-CRE 189PX	(WHAT'S THE STORY) MORNING GLORY? (cassette, 4-track sampler with "Hello"/"[What's The Story] Morning Glory"/ "Wonderwall"/"Don't Look Back In Anger")	18
95	Creation CRECD 189P	(WHAT'S THE STORY) MORNING GLORY? (CD, with "Step Out", black card p/s, withdrawn, beware of counterfeits)	75
95	Creation CRECD 189P	(WHAT'S THE STORY) MORNING GLORY? (CD, without "Step Out", black card p/s)	20

95	Creation C-CRE 189P	(WHAT'S THE STORY) MORNING GLORY? (cassette, with "Step Out", card p/s, withdrawn)	25
95	Creation C-CRE 189P	(WHAT'S THE STORY) MORNING GLORY? (cassette, without "Step Out", card p/s)	15
97	Creation (no cat. no.)	BE HERE NOW (LP, mail-order 12" box set, with "The Making Of Be Here Now" booklet, 1,000 only)	70
97	Creation (no cat. no.)	BE HERE NOW (CD, mail-order 12" box set, with "The Making Of Be Here Now" booklet, 1,000 only)	70
97	Creation C-CRE 219P	BE HERE NOW (cassette)	12
97	Creation C-CRE 219PX	BE HERE NOW (cassette, 4-track sampler with "D'You Know What I Mean?"/ "All Around The World"/"Stand By Me"/"It's Gettin' Better [Man!!]")	18
97	Creation CCD 219	BE HERE NOW (CD, black card sleeve, some in custom picture sleeve)	30/25
98	Sony SAMPCD 5859	THE MASTERPLAN (CD, slimline case, p/s)	35
98	Sony SAMPCD 6034	THE MASTERPLAN INTERVIEW (CD, slimline case, no p/s)	25
00	Big Brother RKIDCD 001P	STANDING ON THE SHOULDER OF GIANTS (cassette, flip-top card box)	25
00	Big Brother RKIDCD 002P	STANDING ON THE SHOULDER OF GIANTS (CD, g/fold card sl. with sticker)	30
02	Big Brother RKIDCD 25P	HEATHEN CHEMISTRY (CD, in promo-only hardback photobook, features hidden track)	30
05	No Cat No	DON'T BELIEVE THE TRUTH (CD-R promo in plastic sleeve with paper insert)	20

*(see also Oas*s)*

OAS*S
95	Fierce Panda NING 12	WIBBLING RIVALRY (interview disc, stickered p/s, without barcode, 1000 only)	8
95	Fierce Panda CDNING 12	WIBBLING RIVALRY (CD)	12

(see also Oasis)

OBERNKIRCHEN CHOIR
60s	GEP 8529	ANGELS IN PIGTAILS (EP)	12
60s	GEP 8706	CHRISTMAS SONGS (EP)	12

OBERON
71	Acorn (no cat. no.)	A MIDSUMMER NIGHT'S DREAM (LP, private pressing)	400+

HUGH O'BRIAN
58	HMV POP 539	Legend Of Wyatt Earp/Down In The Meadow (78 rpm = £7)	10
58	Oriole CB 1480	I'm Looking For A Girl/Ain't Got A Nickel (78 rpm = £7)	7
58	HMV DLP 1189	TV'S WYATT EARP SINGS (10" LP)	20

IAIN O'BRIEN
96	Ferox FERLP 3	DESERT SCORES (2-LP)	12

JIMMY O'BRYANT
60	Heritage RE-101	Famous Original Washboard Band, Vol. 1 (99 copies only) (EP)	30
60	Heritage RE-106	Famous Original Washboard Band, Vol. 2 (99 copies only) (EP)	30

OBSERVERS
71	Big Shot BI 575	Brimstone And Fire/Lightning And Thunder	6
71	Big Shot BI 588	Keep Pushing/Hot Tip	8
72	Big Shot BI 610	Everyday Music/NINEY: Observing The Av	6
72	Songbird SB 1083	International Pum/Reggaematic	5

(see also Niney)

OBSERVERS ALL STARS & KING TUBBY
75	Attack ATLP 017	DUBBING WITH THE OBSERVER (LP)	35

OBTAINERS
79	Dance Fools Dance (no cat. no.)	Yeh Yeh Yeh/Pussy Wussy/MAG-SPYS: Lifeblood/Bombs (stickered plain sleeve, 100 only)	100

(see also Cure)

DIERDRE O'CALLAGHAN
59	Top Rank JAR 164	The Bridal Path/I'll Walk With My Love (78 rpm = £12)	5

OCCASIONALLY DAVID
79	Oven Ready OD 77901	TWIST AND SHOUT (EP)	10
80	Oven Ready OD 1/98002	I Can't Get Used To Losing You (So I'm Coming Back)/ Will You Miss Me Tonight? (foldout p/s)	10

OCCASIONAL WORD ENSEMBLE
69	Dandelion 63753	THE YEAR OF THE GREAT LEAP SIDEWAYS (LP)	18

OCCULT CHEMISTRY
80	Bikini Girl (no. cat. no.)	Water Earth Fire Air (Rough Version) (5" clear flexidisc in stamped envelope with *Bikini Girl* magazine)	15/12
81	Dining Out TUX 4	Water Earth Fire Air/Fire Air Water Earth (handmade p/s)	8

(see also Twilight Zonerz)

OCEAN COLOUR SCENE
90	!Phffft WAVE 1P	One Of These Days/Talk On (p/s, promo only)	50
90	!Phffft WAVE 1	One Of These Days/Talk On (12", p/s, promo only)	50
90	!Phffft FIT 001	Sway/Talk On (p/s)	18
90	!Phffft FITX 001	Sway (Extended)/Lullaby/Sway (7" Version)/One Of These Days (12", p/s)	20
90	!Phffft FITX 001	Sway (Extended)/Lullaby/Sway (7" Version)/One Of These Days (CD)	20
91	!Phffft FIT 002	Yesterday Today/Another Girl's Name/Fly Me (p/s, promos with sticker £20)	7
91	!Phffft FITX 002	Yesterday Today/Another Girl's Name/Fly Me/No One Says (12", p/s)	18
91	!Phffft FITCD 002	Yesterday Today/Another Girl's Name/Fly Me/No One Says (CD)	20
92	Fontana OCSS 1	Sway/My Brother Sarah (p/s)	7
92	Fontana OCS 112	Sway/My Brother Sarah/Mona Lisa Eyes/Bellechoux (12", p/s)	8
92	Fontana OCSS 2	Giving It All Away/Third Shade Of Green (p/s)	6
92	Fontana OCS 212	Giving It All Away/Flowers/Third Shade Of Green/Don't Play (12", p/s)	8
92	Fontana OCSS 3	Do Yourself A Favour/The Seventh Floor (p/s)	7
92	Fontana OCS 312	Do Yourself A Favour/The Seventh Floor/Patsy In Green/Suspended Motion (12", p/s)	8
95	MCA OCS 1	You've Got It Bad/You've Got It Bad (p/s, promo only)	18

96	MCA OCS 2	You've Got It Bad (Full Length Demo Version)/Mona Lisa Eyes (featuring Jimmy Miller) (p/s, mail-order only)	15
97	MCA MCS 40144	Traveller's Tune/Song For The Front Row (gatefold p/s)	7
97	MCA MCD 60034	B-SIDES, SEASIDES AND FREE RIDES (2-LP, with lyric booklet)	25
97	MCA MCD 60034	B-SIDES, SEASIDES AND FREE RIDES (CD, with booklet, in slipcase)	25
92	Fontana 512 269-1	OCEAN COLOUR SCENE (LP, with inner sleeve)	12
92	Fontana 512 269-2	OCEAN COLOUR SCENE (CD)	18
97	MCA MCA 60048	MARCHIN' ALREADY (2-LP, with booklet)	22

(see also Boys, Fanatics, Echo Base)

PHIL OCHS

66	Elektra EKSN 45002	I Ain't Marching Any More/That Was The President	18
68	A&M AMS 716	Outside Of A Small Circle Of Friends/Miranda	8
65	Elektra EKL 269	ALL THE NEWS THAT'S FIT TO SING (LP)	42
65	Elektra EKL 287	I AIN'T MARCHIN' ANYMORE (LP)	42
66	Elektra EKL 310	PHIL OCHS IN CONCERT (LP, gold label)	38
67	A&M AML(S) 913	PLEASURES OF THE HARBOR (LP)	22
68	A&M AMLS 919	TAPE FROM CALIFORNIA (LP)	20
69	A&M AMLS 934	REHEARSALS FOR RETIREMENT (LP)	20
70	A&M AMLS 973	GREATEST HITS (LP)	20

DES O'CONNOR

57	Columbia DB 4011	Moonlight Swim/Sailing Down The Chesapeake Bay (78 rpm = £6)	5
62	Piccadilly 7N 35023	Thin Chow Min/Twist Drive	5

JOHNNY O'CONNOR

53	London L 1171	Fickle Fingers/GUY NELSON: When The World Was Young (78)	10

JOHNNY OCTOBER

59	Capitol CL 15070	Growin' Prettier/Young And In Love	15
60	Capitol CL 15121	So Mean/There'll Always Be A Feeling	15

OCTOPUS

69	Penny Farthing PEN 705	Laugh At The Poor Man/Girl Friend	18
70	Penny Farthing PEN 716	The River/Thief	18
73	Mooncrest MOON 7	Hey Na Na/Future Feelings	6
70	Penny Farthing PELS 508	RESTLESS NIGHT (LP, gatefold sleeve)	160
96	Essex ESSEX 1013LP	RESTLESS NIGHT (LP, reissue, gatefold sleeve)	12

(see also Cortinas)

RAY O'DANIEL

62	Longhorn BLH 0001	What Goes Up Always Comes Down/You're The Only Love For Me	8

ANITA O'DAY

56	HMV POP 245	You're The Top/Honeysuckle Rose	6
60	HMV POP 821	Tea For Two/Sweet Georgia Brown	6
55	Columbia Clef SEB 10042	ANITA O'DAY (EP)	8
56	HMV CLP 1085	ANITA (LP)	18
56	Columbia Clef 33C 9020	ANITA O'DAY COLLATES (10" LP)	20
57	Columbia Clef 33CX 10068	AN EVENING WITH ANITA O'DAY (LP)	18
58	Columbia Clef 33CX 10125	ANITA SINGS THE MOST (LP)	18
58	HMV DLP 1169	PICK YOURSELF UP (10" LP)	20
59	HMV DLP 1203	ANITA AT MISTER KELLY'S (10" LP)	20
60	HMV CLP 1332	ANITA O'DAY SWINGS COLE PORTER WITH BILLY MAY (LP)	15
63	Verve VLP 9125	THE JAZZ STYLINGS OF (LP)	15

PAT O'DAY

55	MGM SP 1129	Earth Angel (Will You Be Mine?)/A Rusty Old Halo (78 rpm = £6)	18
55	MGM SP 1142	Soldier Boy/Annie Oakley	15
60	Pye International 7N 25048	I'll Build A Stairway To Your Paradise/No One Understands	6

ODD

84	OK OK 007	Last Time I Saw You/Look Into My Eyes (p/s)	15

BILL ODDIE

64	Parlophone R 5153	Nothing Better To Do/Traffic Island	6
65	Parlophone R 5346	Knitting Song/Ain't Got Rhythm	6
66	Parlophone R 5433	I Can't Get Through/Because She Is My Love	6
69	Decca F 12903	We Love Jimmy Young/Irish Get Out (as Bill Oddie & Average Mothers)	6
70	Dandelion S 4786	On Ilkla Moor Baht'at/Harry Krishna	10

(see also Ricky Livid)

ODDS

80	Double R RED 001	Saturday Night/Not Another Love Song (p/s)	6
81	JSO EAT 1	Yesterday Man/So You Think (p/s)	20
81	JSO EAT 7	Dread In My Bed/Spare Rib (with press release)	10

ODDSOCKS

75	Sweet Folk & C. SFA 030	MEN OF THE MOMENT (LP)	20

(see also Bevis Frond)

ANN ODELL

73	DJM DJS 10280	Swing Song/Everything's Fine Sunshine	6
73	DJM DJLPS 434	A LITTLE TASTE (LP)	35

(see also Chopyn, Blue Mink)

DOYE O'DELL

57	London HAP-B 1073	DOYE (10" LP)	12

MAC ODELL

54	Parlophone DP 387	What Then/One Day Religion (78, export issue)	10
54	Parlophone CMSP 25	The Stone Was Rolled Away/Heaven-Bound Gospel Train (export issue)	15
54	Parlophone CMSP 25	The Stone Was Rolled Away/Heaven-Bound Gospel Train (78)	10
56	Parlophone DP 507	A Crown He Wore/Are You Practicing His Love? (78, export issue)	10

RONNIE O'DELL & HIS ORCHESTRA
57	London HLD 8439	Melody Of Napoli/Struttin' Down Jane Street	25

ODIN'S PEOPLE
67	Major Minor MM 501	From A Distance/I Need You	7
67	Major Minor MM 506	Tommy Jones/I Need Your Hand In Mine	7

JOE ODOM
69	Capitol CL 15600	Big Love/It's In Your Power	15

AL O'DONNELL
72	Trailer LER 2073	AL O'DONNELL (LP, red label)	20
78	Transatlantic LTRA 501	AL O'DONNELL 2 (LP)	12

JOE O'DONNELL
77	Polydor 2383 465	GAODHAL'S VISION (LP)	20
(see also Mushroom, Rory Gallagher, Jade Warrior)			

ROCK O'DOODLE
73	Decca F 13450	Queen Of Rock & Roll/Woman	5
(see also Patrick Campbell-Lyons)			

ODYSSEY (U.K.)
66	Strike JH 312	How Long Is Time/Beware	20
(see also Sons Of Fred)			

ODYSSEY (U.S.)
73	Mowest MWS 7002	ODYSSEY (LP)	40

OFFSIDE
70	Pye Intl. 25534	Match Of The Day/Small Deal (p/s)	10

OFFSPRING
94	Epitaph EPUK 001	Come Out And Play/Session/Come Out And Play (12", p/s)	8
95	Epitaph 12HOLE 001	Self Esteem/Burn It Up/Jennifer Lost The War (12", p/s)	8

OFO THE BLACK COMPANY
72	London FL12261	Allah Wakbarr/Beautiful Daddy	45

JAMES O'GWYNN
59	Mercury AMT 1052	How Can I Think Of Tomorrow/Were You Ever A Stranger	10

JOHN O'HARA
77	President PT 465	Starsky And Hutch/Sister Rae	5

MAUREEN O'HARA
66	Realm RM 52320	SINGS HER FAVOURITE IRISH SONGS (LP)	12

O'HARA'S PLAYBOYS
66	Fontana TF 763	Start All Over/I've Been Wondering	6
68	Fontana TF 924	In The Shelter Of My Heart/Goodnight Mr. Nightfall	6
68	Fontana TF 974	I Started A Joke/Show Me	15
68	Fontana (S)TL 5461	GET READY (LP)	40

OHIO EXPRESS
68	Pye Intl. TH25439	Yummy Yummy Yummy/Zigzag	5
69	Pye Intl. NSPL 28117	OHIO EXPRESS (LP)	20
69	Buddah 203 015	CHEWY CHEWY (LP)	15
(see also Joey Vine)			

OHIO KNOX
71	Reprise RSLP 6435	OHIO KNOX (LP)	20
(see also Fifth Avenue Band)			

OHIO PLAYERS
69	Capitol CL 15587	Here Today And Gone Tomorrow/Bad Bargain	10
72	Janus 6146 009	Pain (Parts 1 & 2)	5
72	Janus 6146 017	Got Pleasure/I Wanna Hear From You	5
73	Westbound 6146 100	Funky Worm/Paint Me	6
74	Mercury 6167 012	Skin Tight/Heaven Must Be Like This	6
75	Mercury 6167 058	Fire/Together	6
74	Mercury 6338 497	SKIN TIGHT (LP)	15

OH POLO!
03	PPQ PPQ7IN010	Love Buzz/A Thing In E (p/s)	8

OHR MUSIK
97	Prescription DRUG 2	OHR MUSIK (LP, 99 copies only)	20
(see also Spiral Sky)			

OIL CITY SHEIKS
79	United Artists UP 36514	Don't Take But A Few Minutes/Blues Jam (p/s)	7
(see also Dr. Feelgood, Lew Lewis)			

OI POLLOI
80s	Wonderful World WOW 17	OMNICIDE (EP)	8
87	Oi! OIR 011	UNITE AND WIN (LP, with lyric sheet)	12

OISIN
80	Tara 2012	OVER THE MOOR TO MAGGIE (LP)	12
82	Tara 2013	THE JEANNIE C (LP)	12

O'JAYS
65	Liberty LIB 66102	Lipstick Traces/Think It Over Baby (DJ copy = £100)	50
66	Liberty LIB 66197	Stand In For Love/Friday Night	25
67	Stateside SS 2073	I'll Be Sweeter Tomorrow/I Dig Your Act (DJ copy = £130)	75
68	Bell BLL 1020	Look Over Your Shoulder/I'm So Glad I Found You (DJ copy = £75)	30
68	Bell BLL 1033	The Choice/Going Going Gone	15

MINT VALUE £

70	Now! NOW 1002	Don't You Know A True Love/That's Alright	10
72	United Artists UP 35337	Working On Your Case/Hold On	15
73	CBS 1181	Love Train/Who Am I?	6
73	Mojo 2092 052	I Dig Your Act/I'll Be Sweeter Tomorrow (reissue)	10
73	CBS 1546	Time To Get Down/Shifty Shadey Jealous Kind Of People	5
74	Power Exchange PX 101	Peace/Little Brother	5
74	Philadelphia PIR 2186	For The Love Of Money/People Keep Telling Me	6
75	Philadelphia PIR 3297	Give The People What They Want/What Am I Waiting For	6
77	Philadelphia PIR 4834	Darlin' Darlin Baby/Prayer	6
69	Sunset SLS 50038	FULL OF SOUL (LP)	15
72	CBS 65257	BACKSTABBERS (LP)	15

O'KAYSIONS
68	Stateside SS 2126	Girl Watcher/Deal Me In	40

JOHNNY O'KEEFE (& DEE JAYS)
58	Coral Q 72330	Shake Baby Shake/Real Wild Child (as Johnny O'Keefe & Dee Jays) (78 rpm = £85)	150+
60s	Zodiac ZR 0016	Sing/Tell The Blues So Long	22

(ROGER) EARL OKIN
67	Parlophone R 5644	Yellow Petals/I Can't Face The Animals (as Roger Earl Okin)	6
69	CBS 4495	Stop And You'll Become Aware/You're Not There At All (as Earl Okin)	25

OLA (& JANGLERS)
67	Decca F 12646	I Can Wait/Eeny Meeny Miney Moe	12
68	Big T BIG 108	What A Way To Die/That's Why I Cry (solo)	12
69	Sonet SON 2004	Let's Dance/Bird, Bird	5

BABATUNDE OLATUNJI
73	Paramount PARA 3038	Soul Makossa (Parts 1 & 2)	5
73	Paramount SPFL 289	SOUL MAKOSSA (LP)	12

OLD AND IN THE WAY
75	Round RX 103	OLD AND IN THE WAY (LP)	12

(see also Jerry Garcia, Seatrain, Rowan Brothers)

MIKE OLDFIELD
SINGLES
74	Virgin VS 101	Mike Oldfield's Single ("Tubular Bells" Theme)/ Froggy Went A-Courtin' (in p/s)	8
75	Virgin VS 117	Don Alfonso (with David Bedford)/In Dulci Jubilo (For Maureen)	8
76	Virgin VS 163	Portsmouth/Speak (Tho' You Only Say Farewell) (Roger Dean or blue/red label; reissued in brown wraparound p/s)	each 6
78	Virgin VS 238	Take 4 (EP, p/s)	8
78	Virgin VS 238-12	Take 4 (12", white vinyl, stickered p/s)	12
79	Virgin VS 245	Guilty/Excerpt From Incantations (p/s, red/green or white/blue label)	6
79	Virgin VS 317	Blue Peter/Woodhenge (p/s, sudden or 'refined' ending (A7 matrix))	each 6
82	Virgin VSY 464	Five Miles Out/Live Punkadiddle (picture disc)	10
82	Virgin VSY 489	Family Man/Mount Teidi (picture disc)	12
82	Virgin VSY 541	Mistake/Waldberg (The Peak) (picture disc)	5
83	Virgin VSY 586	Moonlight Shadow/Rite Of Man (picture disc)	6
85	Virgin VSD 836	Pictures In The Dark/Legend//Moonlight Shadow/Rite Of Man (double pack in PVC gatefold stickered p/s)	12
86	Virgin VSS 863	Shine (with Jon Anderson)/The Path (shaped picture disc, some uncut)	60/12
88	Virgin CDT 7	Moonlight Shadow (Extended Version)/Rite Of Man/To France/ Jungle Gardenia (3" CD, card p/s)	12
89	Virgin VSCD 1189	Earth Moving (7" Version)/(Disco Mix)/Bridge To Paradise (3" CD, card p/s)	15
89	Virgin VST 1214	Innocent (7" Version)/(12" Mix)/(Club Version) (12", p/s)	10
89	Virgin VSCD 1214	Innocent (7" Version)/(12" Mix)/(Club Version) (3" CD, card p/s)	12
90	Virgin VS 1328	Etude (The Theme Music For The "Nurofen" TV Commercial)/ ONO GAGAKU KAï SOCIETY ORCHESTRA: Gakkain (p/s)	10
90	Virgin VSC 1328	Etude (The Theme Music For The "Nurofen" TV Commercial)/ ONO GAGAKU KAï SOCIETY ORCHESTRA: Gakkain (cassette)	6
90	Virgin AMACD 1	AMAROK X-TRAX 3 extracts from the Amarok album (3" CD EP, 'discount voucher CD' free with W.H. Smith's Insight magazine)	30/25

ALBUMS
73	Virgin V 2001	TUBULAR BELLS (LP, white label)	12
74	Virgin QV 2001	TUBULAR BELLS (LP, quadrophonic, with model plane noise at the end of side 2, stickered sleeve)	20
75	Virgin QVQS 2043	OMMADAWN (LP, quadrophonic, stickered sleeve)	20
75	Virgin VD 2502	V (2-LP, compilation, includes long version of 'Don Alfonso')	30
76	Virgin 2043	OMMADAWN (LP, blue Virgin label)	15
76	Virgin QV 2043	OMMADAWN (LP, different quadrophonic mix, stickered sleeve)	20
76	Virgin VBOX 1	BOXED (4-LP box set, with booklet)	25
78	Virgin VDT 101	INCANTATIONS (2-LP, some with 7" red vinyl of Julie Covington, & poster)	35/30
78	Virgin VP 2001	TUBULAR BELLS (LP, picture disc, die-cut sleeve, stereo remix of 1976 "Boxed" quadrophonic mix; with or without model plane noise)	each 15
78	Virgin VD 2511	EXPOSED (2-LP live, with '100,000 Limited Edition' sticker, and black inners)	12
79	Virgin V 2141	PLATINUM (LP, with inner sleeve & "Sally"; matrix reads "V 2141 B1" or "B2", 30,000 copies, withdrawn)	100
79	Tellydisc TELLY 4	IMPRESSIONS (LP, mail-order only)	25
79	Tellydisc TELLYC 4	IMPRESSIONS (cassette, mail-order only)	30
83	Virgin V 2262	CRISES (LP, with bonus 7" 'Moonlight Shadow')	15
83	Virgin V 2001	TUBULAR BELLS (LP, reissue at 1973 price, with sticker)	15
84	Virgin V 2328	THE KILLING FIELDS (LP, with 20 page film booklet)	25
85	Virgin MOC 1	THE COMPLETE MIKE OLDFIELD (2-LP with bonus 7" 'Pictures In The Dark')	18
93	Virgin CD BOX 2	ELEMENTS (4-CD, remastered best of in special plastic box with 64pp booklet)	60

94	WEA 4509-98581-1	THE SONGS OF DISTANT EARTH (LP, rumoured 1000 copies only, German pressing)	20
97	Virgin LPCENT 18	TUBULAR BELLS (LP, coloured Dean label, audiophile pressing)	20
01	Simply Vinyl SVLP 322	OMMADAWN (LP, audiophile pressing on 180gm vinyl, with 2 stickers)	18
01	Virgin CD BOXY 2	ELEMENTS (4-CD remastered best of, revised "book" sleeve, 64pp booklet)	40

PROMOS

74	Virgin VS 112	Hergest Ridge (1-sided white label)	75
75	Virgin VDJ 1	Extract from The Orchestral Tubular Bells/Extract from The Orchestral Tubular Bells	25
75	Virgin VS 117	Don Alfonso ('A' label)	25
75	Virgin VDJ 9	An Extract From Ommadawn Part 1/An Extract From Ommadawn Part 2 (On Horseback) (12")	50
75	Virgin VS 131	In Dulci Jubilo/On Horseback ('A' label)	10
76	Virgin VS 163	Portsmouth/Speak (Tho' You Only Say Farewell) (Roger Dean label)	8
77	Virgin VS 167	The William Tell Overture/Argiers (blue Virgin 'A' label)	10
78	Virgin VS 238-12	Take 4 EP (12", red vinyl test pressing)	100
79	Virgin VS 245-12	Guilty (Extended Mix)/Guilty/Excerpt From Incantations (12", black vinyl test pressing)	25
79	Virgin VSDJ 317	Blue Peter (1-sided)	25
82	Virgin VS 464	Five Miles Out/Live Punkadiddle (white label test pressing)	20
82	Virgin VSY 541	Mistake/Waldberg (The Peak) (white label test pressing)	20
85	Virgin SWALLOW 1	Etude/Moonlight Shadow/Portsmouth/In Dulci Jubilo (p/s, promo-only for "The Complete Mike Oldfield")	30
85	Virgin	Pictures In The Dark (1-sided Abbey Road acetate)	50
87	Virgin VST 990	Islands (Extended Version)/When The Night's On Fire/The Wind Chimes (Part One) (white label test pressing)	20
87	Virgin CDEP 6	Islands/When The Night's On Fire/The Wind Chimes(Part One)/Islands (Extended Version) (white gatefold stickered card p/s)	25
94	WEA YZ 880 T	Let There Be Light: BT's Pure Luminescence Remix/Hardfloor Remix/Hardfloor Dub (12" p/s, some with 'promo not for sale' sticker)	12/10
89	Virgin VST 1214	Innocent (12" Mix)/7" Mix/Earth Moving (Club Mix) (white label test pressing)	20
90	Virgin AMACD 1DJ	Mike Oldfield Album Sampler (CD, 5 Extracts From Amarok)	30
92	WEA SAM 1085	Sentinel (Single Restructure) (CD, stickered p/s)	15
92	WEA SAM 1094	OLDFIELD V THE ORB: Sentinel (Total Overhaul/Sentinel Nobel Prize Mix/Sentinel Orbular Bells/Sentinel 7" Mix (12")	15
92	WEA SAM 1150	SENTINEL RESTRUCTURE MIXES: Satoshi Tomii Interpretation/Global Lust Mix/TranceMix/Tubular Beats (12", title stickered red sleeve)	20
92	WEA SAM 1470	A SHOT OF MOONSHINE: Jungle Mix (Featuring Rankin' Sean & Peter Lee)/A Shot Of Moonshine (Jungle Instrumental)/A Shot Of Moonshine (Solution Hoedown Mix) (12", lists artist as MOT2)	15
92	WEA YZ 708CDDJ	Tattoo (stickered p/s)	15
76	Virgin QVQS 2043	OMMADAWN (LP, unreleased different quadrophonic mix, promo stickered slve)	50
76	Virgin V BOX 1	COLLABORATIONS (LP, green/yellow label in stamped white sleeve)	30
79	(no cat. no.)	THE SPACE MOVIE (4 x 1-sided acetates of unreleased LP containing music from soundtrack to the 'Space Movie' video; includes Orchestral Hergest Ridge, Orchestral Tubular Bells, Incantations, Ommadawn and Portsmouth, some extracts otherwise unreleased)	500
80	Virgin V 2181	QE2 (LP, white label test pressing in white sleeve)	30
83	Virgin V 2262	CRISES (LP, 2 x 1-sided acetates)	100
92	WEA 4509-90618-2	TUBULAR BELLS 2 (CD, with unique back sleeve)	25
92	WEA WX 2002	TUBULAR BELLS 2 (LP, stickered sleeve)	20
94	WEA SAM 1477	THE SONGS OF DISTANT EARTH (CD in film can, with 2 inserts)	75
94	WEA 4509-98581-1	THE SONGS OF DISTANT EARTH (LP, 2-sided acetate)	100
94	WEA 4509-98581-1	THE SONGS OF DISTANT EARTH (LP, white label test pressing)	60
98	WEA 3331000043	TUBULAR BELLS III (CD, in special 'Waterside Inn' card sleeve)	30
98	WEA 3331000043	TUBULAR BELLS III (CD, in card sleeve, some with bag, TB III tag, press releases and premiere concert details)	50/20
99	WEA (no cat. no.)	MILLENNIUM BELL (CD-R, some tracks with different samples to released album)	75/60

(see also Sallyangie, David Bedford, Kevin Ayers & Whole World, Pekka, Lea Nicholson, Tom Newman)

ANDREW OLDHAM (ORCHESTRA)

64	Decca F 11878	365 Rolling Stones/Oh I Do Like To See Me On The 'B' Side	28
64	Decca F 11987	We Don't All Wear D'Same Size Boots/Right Of Way	20
64	Ace Of Clubs ACL 1180	16 HIP HITS (LP)	45
64	Decca LK 4636	LIONEL BART'S MAGGIE MAY (LP)	25
66	Decca LK/SKL 4796	THE ROLLING STONES SONGBOOK (LP)	80
82	Decca 820 186-1	THE ROLLING STONES SONGBOOK (LP, reissue)	12

(see also Aranbee Pop Symphony, Rolling Stones, Cleo, Bo & Peep, Jeannie & Her Redheads, Gulliver's Travels, Mighty Avengers, John Paul Jones)

OLDHAM TINKERS

74	Topic 12TS 237	BEST O' T' BUNCH (LP, blue label)	18
75	Topic 12TS 276	FOR OLD TIMES SAKE (LP)	15
77	Topic 12TS 323	SIT THEE DOWN (LP)	15
79	Topic 12TS 399	THAT LANCASHIRE BAND (LP)	15

OLD SWAN BAND

71	Dingles DIN 322	GAMESTERS, PICKPOCKETS AND HARLOTS (LP)	15
80	Free Reed 028	OLD SWAN BAND (LP)	15
81	Free Reed FRR 011	NO REELS (LP)	15

OLD TIMERS SKIFFLE GROUP

58	Fontana H 105	The Woman Who Loved A Swine/The Lynching Of Jeff Buckner (78)	15

JOHNNY OLENN & HIS BAND

57	London HLU 8388	I Ain't Gonna Cry No More/My Idea Of Love (78 rpm = £85)	300+
59	Mercury AMT 1050	Born Reckless/You Lovable You (as Johnny Olenn & Blockbusters)	120

MINT VALUE £

O-LEVEL
78	Psycho PSYCHO 2	East Sheen/Pseudo Punk ('map' or 'schoolboy' p/s)	30/35
78	Kings Road KR 002	THE MALCOLM EP (photocopied wraparound or printed p/s)	25/15

(see also Teenage Filmstars, Times, Television Personalities)

OLIVER
69	CBS 4435	Good Morning Starshine/Can't You See	5
70	Crewe CRW 1	Jean/Good Morning Starshine (Arrangement) (p/s)	5

OLIVER
74	Oliv OL 1	STANDING STONE (LP, private pressing, withdrawn blue sleeve, later in green sleeve)	300/200
92	Tenth Planet TP 001	STANDING STONE (LP, reissue, numbered, 500 only)	20

JANE OLIVER
60s	Columbia 35437	STAY THE NIGHT (LP)	25

(see also Johnny Mathis)

JOHNNY OLIVER
56	MGM SP 1165	Chain Gang/These Hands	25
60	Mercury AMT 1095	What A Kiss Won't Do/That's All I'm Living For	12

SY OLIVER & HIS ORCHESTRA
58	London HL 7067	The Mardi Gras March/One More Time (export issue)	10
59	London HLJ 8776	In A Little Spanish Town Cha-Cha/The Mardi Gras March (78 rpm = £8)	10
53	Brunswick LA 8586	FOR DANCERS ONLY (10" LP)	12

OLIVER & TWISTERS
64	Pye Intl. NPL 28018	LOOK WHO'S TWISTIN' (LP)	25

OLIVERS
57	Columbia DB 3995	Ma Curly Headed Baby/Beautiful Dreamer	6

(see also Russ Conway)

OLLIE & NIGHTINGALES
69	Stax STAX 109	You're Leaving Me/Showered With Love	18

OLYMPICS
58	HMV POP 528	Western Movies/Well! (78 rpm = £12)	20
58	HMV POP 564	(I Wanna) Dance With The Teacher/Everybody Needs Love (78 rpm = £20)	20
59	Columbia DB 4346	Private Eye/(Baby) Hully Gully	25
60	Vogue Pop V 9174	I Wish I Could Shimmy Like My Sister Kate/Workin' Hard	22
61	Vogue Pop V 9181	Dance With A Dolly/Dodge City	30
61	Vogue Pop V 9184	Little Pedro/CAPPY LEWIS: Bullfight	20
62	Vogue Pop V 9196	The Twist/Everybody Likes To Cha Cha Cha	15
62	Vogue Pop V 9198	The Stomp/Mash Them 'Taters	18
62	Vogue Pop V 9204	Baby It's Hot/The Scotch	20
63	HMV POP 1155	Sidewalk Serenade/Nothing	15
64	Sue WI 348	The Bounce/Fireworks	40
65	Warner Bros WB 157	Good Lovin'/Olympic Shuffle	15
66	Fontana TF 678	We Go Together (Pretty Baby)/Secret Agents	30
66	Fontana TF 778	Baby, Do The Philly Dog/Western Movies	30
69	Action ACT 4539	Baby, Do The Philly Dog/Mine Exclusively	20
70	Action ACT 4556	I'll Do A Little Bit More/Same Old Thing	28
71	Jay Boy BOY 27	Hully Gully/Big Boy Pete	8
72	Jay Boy BOY 56	Baby, Do The Philly Dog/Secret Agents	8
72	Jay Boy BOY 74	I'll Do A Little Bit More/Same Old Thing (reissue)	15
61	Vocalion VAH 8059	DANCE BY THE LIGHT OF THE MOON (LP)	80
67	London HA-M 8327	SOMETHING OLD, SOMETHING NEW (LP, unissued)	
67	Fontana TL 5407	SOMETHING OLD, SOMETHING NEW (LP)	75
72	Jay Boy JSX 2008	THE OLYMPICS (LP)	30

(see also Cappy Lewis)

PATRICK O'MAGICK
74	Chrysalis CHS 2041	You're A Winner/The Proposal	5

(see also Patrick Campbell-Lyons)

MICHAEL O'MARTIAN
76	Myrrh MYRA 1048	WHITE HORSE (LP, gatefold sleeve, with Larry Carlton)	12
77	Myrrh MYR 1073	SEASONS OF THE SOUL (LP, with Stormie)	18
78	Sparrow BIRD 141	MAINSTREAM (LP)	18

O.M.D.
(see under Orchestral Manoeuvres In The Dark)

OMEGA
76	Decca SKL-R 5219	HALL OF FLOATERS IN THE SKY (LP)	15
76	Decca SKL-R 5243	TIME ROBBER (LP)	15

OMEGA
85	Rock Machine MACH 1	THE PROPHET (LP)	35

OMEGA RED STAR
69	Decca LK/SKL 4974	OMEGA RED STAR (LP)	50

OMEGA TRIBE
83	Crass 221984/10	ANGRY SONGS (EP)	5

(see also Pete Fender)

OMEN SEARCHER
82	OCS 001	Too Much/Teacher Of Sin (p/s)	75
82	OCS 002	Teacher Of Sin/Too Much (p/s)	75

ONDIOLINE BAND
66	London HL 10022	Last Bicycle To Brussels/Lovers Of Cologne	6

ONE
69   Fontana STL 5539   ONE (LP) 55

ONE & ONE
64   Decca F 11948   I'll Give You Lovin'/It's Me 10
(see also Ivy League, Flowerpot Men)

ONE EYED JACKS
78   Pennine PSS 154   TAKE AWAY (LP, some in "One Eyed Jacks" brown paper carrier bag) 28/25

101'ERS
76   Chiswick (N)S 3   Keys To Your Heart/5 Star Rock & Rock Petrol (some with p/s) 20/8
79   Big Beat NS 3   Keys To Your Heart/5 Star Rock & Rock Petrol (reissue, some with p/s) 10/8
80   Big Beat NS 63   Sweet Revenge/Rabies (From The Dogs Of Love) (p/s) 5
81   Andalucia AND 101   ELGIN AVENUE BREAKDOWN (LP) 30
(see also Clash, Alvaro)

100% PROOF
80   Smile SR 929   NEW WAY OF LIVIN' (EP) 25
81   Myrrh MYR 1107   100% PROOF (LP, with insert) 50

100% PROOF AGED IN SOUL
71   Hot Wax HWX 102   Somebody's Been Sleeping/I've Come To Save You 8
71   Hot Wax HWX 108   Somebody's Been Sleeping/I've Come To Save You (reissue) 6
72   Hot Wax HWX 113   Everything Good Is Bad/I'd Rather Fight Than Switch 6
72   Hot Wax HWX 120   Never My Love/Since You've Been Gone 6
71   Hot Wax SHW 5003   SOMEBODY'S BEEN SLEEPING IN MY BED (LP) 25

100% PURE POISON
77   EMI Intl. INS 3001   COMING RIGHT AT YOU (LP) 250

MATTY O'NEIL
54   London L 1037   Don't Sell Daddy Any More Whiskey/Little Rusty (gold label, tri-centre) .... 40+
54   London L 1037   Don't Sell Daddy Any More Whiskey/Little Rusty (silver label, tri-centre) 25
54   London L 1037   Don't Sell Daddy Any More Whiskey/Little Rusty (silver top, round centre) 10

JOHNNY O'NEILL
59   RCA RCA 1114   Wagon Train/Somebody, Just Like You (78 rpm = £8) 10

ONE IN A MILLION
67   CBS 202513   Use Your Imagination/Hold On 110
67   MGM MGM 1370   Fredereek Hernando/Double Sight 750
(see also Thunderclap Newman)

ONE MILLION FUZZTONE GUITARS
82   Monsters In Orbit TVEYE 3 Heaven/Annuese (foldover p/s, at least 2 different designs) 6
83   Monsters In Orbit TVEYE 10 26 (LP) 12

ONENESS OF JUJU
79   Buddah BDS 497   Everyway But Loose/Make A Change 5
79   Buddah BDS 497   Everyway But Loose/Make A Change (12") 8

1,000 MEXICANS
83   Whaam! WHAAM 12   The Art Of Love/News For You (p/s, 1,500 only) 6

1,000 VIOLINS
85   Dreamworld DREAM 2   Halcyon Days/I Remember When Everybody Used To Ride Bikes ...
                                 Now We All Drive Cars (12", p/s, 1,000 only) 20
86   Dreamworld DREAM 8   Please Don't Sandblast My House/Time I Broke Down (p/s, 2,000 only) 12
86   Dreamworld DREAM 8T   Please Don't Sandblast My House/You Ungrateful Bastard/Though It
                                 Poured The Next Day, I Never Noticed The Rain (12", p/s) 12
87   Dreamworld DREAM 14   Locked Out Of The Love-In (p/s) 15
88   Immaculate   If I Were A Bullet (Then For Sure I'd Find A Way To Your Heart) (p/s) 8
88   Immaculate   HEY MAN, THAT'S BEAUTIFUL (LP) 40
(see also Page Boys)

ONE TWO & THREE
65   Decca F 12093   Black Pearl/Bahama Lullaby 15
65   Decca LK 4682   BLACK PEARLS AND GREEN DIAMONDS (LP) 110

ONE WAY SYSTEM
82   Lightbeat WAY 1   Stab The Judge/Riot Torn City/Me And You (p/s) 8
82   Anagram ANA 1   Give Us A Future/Just Another Hero (p/s) 5
83   Anagram ANA 5   Jerusalem/Jackie Was A Jackie (p/s) 10
83   Anagram ANA 9   Cum On Feel The Noise/Breakin' In (p/s) 6
83   Anagram ANA 14   This Is The Age/Into Fires (p/s) 5
84   Anagram ANA 19   Visions Of Angels/Shine Again (p/s) 5
80s   Anagram   ALL SYSTEMS GO (LP, with lyric inner) 15
83   Anagram GRAM 008   WRITING ON THE WALL (LP, with lyric inner) 12

ONE WAY TICKET
78   President PTLS 1069   TIME IS RIGHT (LP, featuring tracks from "Five Day Rain" LP) 90
(see also Five Day Rain)

ONLOOKERS
82   Demon D 1012   You And I/Understand/Julia (p/s) 15

ONLY ONES
77   Vengeance VEN 001   Lovers Of Today/Peter And The Pets (p/s) 12
77   Vengeance VEN 001   Lovers Of Today/Peter And The Pets (12", with 7" x 7" sticker) 12
78   CBS S CBS 6228   Another Girl, Another Planet/Special View (p/s) 10
78   CBS S CBS 6576   Another Girl, Another Planet/As My Wife Says 6
78   CBS S CBS 12-6576   Another Girl, Another Planet/As My Wife Says (12", p/s) 10
79   CBS S CBS 7086   You've Got To Pay/This Ain't All (It's Made Out To Be) (p/s) 6
79   CBS S CBS 7285   Out There In The Night/Lovers Of Today 5

79	CBS S CBS 12-7285	Out There In The Night/Lovers Of Today/Peter And The Pets (12", p/s, blue vinyl, 2 slight sleeve variations)	10
79	CBS S CBS 7963	Trouble In The World/Your Chosen Life (withdrawn 'group' black & red p/s)	350
79	CBS S CBS 7963	Trouble In The World/Your Chosen Life (standard p/s)	5
80	CBS S CBS 8535	Fools/Castle Built On Sand (p/s, with Pauline Murray)	5
83	Vengeance VEN 002	Baby's Got A Gun/PETER PERRETT: Silent Night	5
78	CBS 82830	THE ONLY ONES (LP, orange label)	12
79	CBS 83451	EVEN SERPENTS SHINE (LP, orange label)	12
80	CBS 84089	BABY'S GOT A GUN (LP, orange label)	12

(see also England's Glory)

YOKO ONO

71	Apple APPLE 38	Mrs. Lennon/Midsummer New York	18
72	Apple APPLE 41	Mind Train/Listen, The Snow Is Falling (p/s)	22
73	Apple APPLE 47	Death Of Samantha/Yang Yang	20
73	Apple APPLE 48	Run Run Run/Men Men Men	25
70	Apple SAPCOR 17	YOKO ONO/PLASTIC ONO BAND (LP, with inner sleeve)	55
71	Apple SAPTU 101/2	FLY (2-LP, with inner sleeves, poster & postcard)	60
73	Apple SAPDO 1001	APPROXIMATELY INFINITE UNIVERSE (2-LP, with inner sleeves)	35
73	Apple SAPCOR 26	FEELING THE SPACE (LP)	45

(see also John Lennon, Bill Elliott & Elastic Oz Band)

ONSLAUGHT

83	Complete Control TROL 1	First Strike/State Control/No More (p/s)	8

ONYX

68	Pye 7N 17477	You've Gotta Be With Me/It's All Put On	20
68	Pye 7N 17622	My Son John/Step By Step	20
69	Pye 7N 17768	Tamaris Khan/So Sad Inside	75
69	CBS 4635	Time Off/Movin' In	22
71	Parlophone R 5888	Air/Our House	12
71	Parlophone R 5906	The Next Stop Is Mine/What's That You Say	12

(see also Salamander)

OOBERMAN

98	Transcopic TRAN 002	Sugarbum/Tears From A Willow (p/s, 1,000 copies only)	10
98	Tugboat TUGS 003	SHORLEY WALL EP (12", clear vinyl, 500 copies only)	15

OPAL BUTTERFLY

68	CBS 3576	Beautiful Beige/Speak Up	35
69	CBS 3921	Mary Anne With The Shakey Hand/My Gration Or?	85
70	Polydor 2058 041	You're A Groupie Girl/Gigging Song	60

(see also Hawkwind, Motorhead, Mott The Hoople)

JACKIE OPEL

63	Jump Up JU 512	TV In Jamaica/Worrell's Captaincy	18
64	Black Swan WI 421	You're No Good/King Liges	25
64	R&B JB 138 25	Stand By Me (as Jackie Opel & Hortense Ellis)/Solid Rock	
64	R&B JB 160	Pity The Fool/The Day Will Come	25
65	King KG 1011	Cry Me A River/Eternal Love	30
65	Island WI 203	Wipe Those Tears/Don't Take Your Love	22
65	Island WI 209	Go Whey/Shelter The Storm	20
65	Island WI 227	Old Rockin' Chair/SKATALITES: Song Of Love (B-side is actually "Ska In Vienna Woods")	175
65	Ska Beat JB 190	Done With A Friend/More Wood In The Fire	25
65	Ska Beat JB 227	The Lord Is With Thee/A Little More	25
66	Island WI 264	A Love To Share/ROLAND ALPHONSO: Devoted To You	25
66	Rio R 117	I Am What I Am/JACKIE MITTOO & SKATALITES: Devil's Bug	35
66	Rio R120	I Don't Want Her/SOUL BOYS: Rudie Get Wise	32

(see also Jackie & Doreen, Doreen & Jackie, Hortense & Jackie)

OPEN

03	Loog 9813076	NEVER ENOUGH EP (1,000 only, p/s)	12
04	Loog 9817238	Close My Eyes/The View (mail order only 12" p/s)	12

OPEN MIND

69	Philips BF 1790	Horses And Chariots/Before My Time	65
69	Philips BF 1805	Magic Potion/Cast A Spell	350+
69	Philips SBL 7893	OPEN MIND (LP)	500
86	Antar ANTAR 2	OPEN MIND (LP, reissue)	15

(see also Drag Set)

OPEN ROAD

72	Greenwich GSS 102	Swamp Fever/Lost And Found	6
71	Greenwich GSLP 1001	WINDY HAZE (LP)	40

(see also Warm Sounds, Denny Gerrard, Donovan)

OPPRESSED

83	Firm NICK 1	NEVER SAY DIE (EP)	12
83	Oppressed OPPO 1	Work Together/Victims (p/s)	12
84	Oppressed OPLP 1	OI! OI! MUSIC (LP)	15
85	Skinhead CREW 1	FATAL BLOW (LP)	15

OPTIC EYE

92	Mystic Stones RUNE LP 3	TRANCE (LP)	12
94	Jump/Pumping LPTOT 17	LIGHT SIDE OF THE SUN (LP, coloured vinyl)	12

OPTIMISTS

81	Armageddon AS 018	Mull Of Kintyre/The Plumbers Song (p/s)	12

OPUS

70	Columbia DB 8675	Baby, Come On/Angela Grey	20

ORA
69	Tangerine OPLOP 0025	ORA (LP)	230

(see also Byzantium, Movies)

ORANGE ALABASTER MUSHROOM
98	Earworm WORM 36	The Slug/Ethel Tripped A Mean Gloss (p/s, with sticker)	8

ORANGE BICYCLE
67	Columbia DB 8259	Hyacinth Threads/Amy Peate	25
67	Columbia DB 8311	Laura's Garden/Lavender Girl	22
68	Columbia DB 8352	Early Pearly Morning/Go With Goldie	22
68	Columbia DB 8413	Jenskadajka/Nicely	22
68	Columbia DB 8483	Sing This All Together/Trip On An Orange Bicycle	30
69	Parlophone R 5789	Tonight I'll Be Staying Here With You/Last Cloud Home	15
69	Parlophone R 5811	Carry That Weight/You Never Give Me Your Money/Want To B Side	15
70	Parlophone R 5827	Take Me To The Pilot/It's Not My World	18
70	Parlophone R 5854	Jelly On The Bread/Make It Rain	12
71	Regal Zonophone RZ 3029	Goodbye Stranger/Country Comforts	15
70	Parlophone PCS 7108	ORANGE BICYCLE (LP)	90
88	M'n Blue Town MBT 5003	LET'S TAKE A TRIP ON ON AN ORANGE BICYCLE (LP)	15

(see also Motherlight)

ORANGE BLOSSOM
74	Westwood WRS 038	KEEP ON PUSHING (LP)	100

ORANGE DISASTER
80s	Neuter OD 1	Something's Got To Give/Out Of The Room/Hiding From Frank	6

(see also Varicose Veins)

ORANGE JUICE
80	Postcard 80-1	Falling And Laughing/Moscow Olympics/Moscow (foldover p/s in poly bag, some with postcard; with or without flexidisc "Felicity (live)" [I Wish I Was A Postcard 1], 963 only)	70
80	I Wish I Was A Postcard 1	Felicity (live) (freebie flexidisc, also given away with fanzines)	15
80	Postcard 80-2	Blue Boy/Lovesick (hand-coloured p/s in poly bag, blue labels)	18
80	Postcard 80-2	Blue Boy/Lovesick (brown labels & co. sleeve or yellow labels/cream co. sl.)	4/8
80	Postcard 80-6	Simply Thrilled Honey/Breakfast Time (p/s, with picture insert in poly bag)	12
81	Postcard 81-2	Poor Old Soul/Poor Old Soul Pt. 2 (die-cut co. sleeve, some with postcard)	8/5
81	Postcard 81-6	Wan Light/You Old Eccentric (unreleased)	
83	Polydor POSP 547	Rip It Up/Snake Charmer (p/s, with free live 21/4/79 cassette)	6
84	Polydor OJ 5/JUICE 1	Bridge/Out For The Count (stickered p/s, with free flexidisc "Poor Old Soul [live]")	6
84	Polydor OJ 6/OJC 6	What Presence?!/A Place In My Heart (Dub) (p/s, with free cassette "The Felicity Flexi Session: The Formative Years")	6
92	Postcard DUBH 922	OSTRICH CHURCHYARD (LP, 1,000 with bonus 10" "Irritation Disc" [922TEN])	12

(see also Edwyn Collins, Paul Quinn & Edwyn Collins, Fun Four, Josef K)

ORANGE MACHINE
68	Pye 7N 17559	Three Jolly Little Dwarfs/Real Life Permanent Dream	90
69	Pye 7N 17680	You Can All Join In/Dr. Crippen's Waiting Room	130

(see also Danny Hughes)

ORANGE PEEL
71	Reflection HRS 5	I Got No Time/Searching For A Place To Hide	20

ORANGE SEAWEED
68	Pye 7N 17515	Stay Awhile/Pictures In The Sky	40

(see also Fadin' Colours)

ORB
SINGLES
89	Wau! Mr Modo MWS 010T	KISS (12" EP, 949 only, die-cut company sleeve)	45
90	Wau! Mr Modo MWS 017T	A Huge Ever Growing Pulsating Brain That Rules From The Centre Of The Ultraworld: Loving You (Orbital Mix)/(Bucket And Spade Mix)/Why Is 6 Scared Of 7? (12" p/s, B-side matrix states 'MWS 016T')	15
90	Big Life BLR 270T	A Huge Ever-Growing Pulsating Brain That Rules From The Centre Of The Ultraworld : Loving You (edited)/(Bucket And Spade Mix)/Why Is 6 Scared Of 7? (12", p/s, 8,000 only, B-side matrix: 'MWS 016T')	18
90	Big Life BLR 270CD	A Huge Ever-Growing Pulsating Brain That Rules From The Centre Of The Ultraworld : Loving You (Original Ambient House Mix) (CD)	12
90	Big Life BLR 27T	A Huge Ever-Growing Pulsating Remix (Orbital Dance Mix)/(9am Radio Mix)/(Aubrey Mix I) (12", p/s, 8,000 only)	15
90	Big Life BLR 27CD	A Huge Ever-Growing Pulsating Remix (Orbital Dance Mix)/(9am Radio Mix)/(Aubrey Mix I) (CD)	12
91	Big Life BLRDLP 5	THE ORB'S ADVENTURES BEYOND THE UNDERWORLD (2-LP, with inner sleeve, 'classical pressing' sticker on sleeve)	20
91	Big Life BLRLP 14	THE ORB AUBREY MIXES: THE ULTRAWORLD EXCURSIONS (LP, with inner sleeve, deleted on day of release)	18
92	Big Life BLV 2	ADVENTURES BEYOND THE ULTRAWORLD: PATTERNS AND TEXTURES VERSION (video with 7-track live CD from Brixton Academy)	20

PROMOS
90	Wau! Mr Modo MWS 017T	A Huge Ever-Growing Pulsating Remix/From One Ear To Another/Why Is 6 Scared Of 7? (12", white label, 100 only)	20
90	Wau! Mr Modo MWS 017R	A Huge Ever-Growing Pulsating Brain That Rules From The Centre Of The Ultraworld (Orbital Dance Mix)/(Orbital Radio Mix)/(Aubrey Mix Mk II) (12", stamped white label, 1,000 only)	12
90	Big Life ORB PROMO 1	A Huge Ever-Growing Pulsating Remix (Orbital Dance Mix)/(9am Radio Mix)/(Aubrey Mix Mk 1) (12")	12
90	Big Life ORB PROMO 2	Little Fluffy Clouds (Dance Mk 1)/Into The Fourth Dimension/Little Fluffy Clouds (Ambient Mk 1) (12")	10

ORB

91	Big Life ORB PROMO 3	Perpetual Dawn: Ultrabass/Perpetual Dawn: Solar Flare (12")	15
91	Big Life ORB PICTURE 3	Perpetual Dawn: Ultrabass II (12", 1-sided picture disc, 400 only)	15
91	Big Life ORB PICTURE 3	Perpetual Dawn: Ultrabass II (12", 1-sided picture disc, mispressing, plays "Towers Of Dub (Ambient)", 400 pressed but 300 allegedly destroyed)	20

(see also System 7, KLF, J.A.M.s, Jah Wobble, Apollo XI, Space)

ORBIDÖIG
81	Situation 2 SIT 15	Nocturnal Operation/Down Periscope (p/s)	25

(see also Billy MacKenzie, Sensational Creed)

ROY ORBISON
SINGLES
60	London HLU 9149	Only The Lonely (Know How I Feel)/Here Comes That Song Again	10
60	London HLU 9149	Only The Lonely (Know How I Feel)/Here Comes That Song Again (78)	650
60	London HLU 9207	Blue Angel/Today's Teardrops	15
61	London HLU 9307	I'm Hurtin'/I Can't Stop Loving You	10
61	London HLU 7108	I'm Hurtin'/I Can't Stop Loving You (export issue)	30
61	London HLU 9342	Runnin' Scared/Love Hurts	10
61	London HLU 9405	Cryin'/Candy Man	10
62	London HLU 9511	Dream Baby/The Actress	10
62	London HLU 9561	The Crowd/Mama	10
62	London HLU 9607	Workin' For The Man/Leah	10
63	London HLU 9676	In Dreams/Shahdaroba	7
63	London HLU 9727	Falling/Distant Drums	7
63	London HLU 9777	Blue Bayou/Mean Woman Blues	7
64	London HLU 9845	Borne On The Wind/What'd I Say	7
64	London HLU 9882	It's Over/Indian Wedding	6
64	Ember EMB S 197	Rock House/You're My Baby	20
64	Ember EMB S 200	This Kind Of Love/I Never Knew (some in p/s)	22/12
64	London HLU 9919	Oh, Pretty Woman/Yo Te Amo Maria	6
64	London HLU 9930	Pretty Paper/Summersong	6
65	London HLU 9951	Goodnight/Only With You	7
65	Ember EMB S 209	Sweet And Easy To Love/You're Gonna Cry (some in p/s)	22/12
65	London HLU 9978	(Say) You're My Girl/Sleepy Hollow	8
65	London HLU 9986	Ride Away/Wondering	8
65	London HLU 10000	Crawling Back/If You Can't Say Something Nice	6
66	London HLU 10015	Breakin' Up Is Breakin' My Heart/Wait	8
66	London HLU 10034	Twinkle Toes/Where Is Tomorrow	8
66	London HLU 10051	Lana/House Without Windows	6

(London 45s from HLU 9676 to HLU 9978, and HLU 10051, were originally issued on the London Monument label, as were later pressings of HLU 9149, 9405, 9511, and 9607)

66	London HLU 10067	Too Soon To Know/You'll Never Be Sixteen Again	5
66	London HLU 10096	There Won't Be Many Coming Home/Going Back To Gloria	6
67	London HLU 10113	So Good/Memories	7
67	London HLU 10143	Cry Softly Lonely One/Pistolero	7
67	London HLU 10159	She/Here Comes The Rain Baby	7
68	London HLU 10176	Born To Be Loved By You/Shy Away	7
68	London HLU 10206	Walk On/Flowers	7
68	London HLU 10222	Heartache/Sugar Man	7
69	London HLU 10261	My Friend/Southbound Jerico Parkway	10
69	London HLU 10285	Penny Arcade/Tennessee Owns My Soul	12
69	London HLU 10294	Break My Mind (by Roy Orbison & Art Movement)/How Do You Start Over	10
70	London HLU 10310	So Young/If I Had A Woman Like You	10
71	London HLU 10339	(Love Me Like You Did It) Last Night/Close Again	10
72	Sun 6094 001	Ooby Dooby/Devil Doll	5
72	London HLU 10358	God Love You/Changes	8
72	London HLU 10388	Memphis Tennessee/I Can Read Between The Lines	8
72	London HLU 10388	Memphis Tennessee/I Can Read Between The Lines (export issue with alternate take of A-side: matrix no. MSC-8474-T2-IL)	12
74	Mercury 6167 014	Sweet Mama Blue/Heartache	7
85	ZTT DZTAS 9	Wild Hearts (...Time)/Wild Hearts (Voiceless)//Ooby Dooby/Crying (double pack, p/s)	15
85	ZTT 12 ZTAS 9	Wild Hearts (And Time Again)/Wild Hearts (Voiceless)/Wild Hearts (...Time)/Ooby Dooby (12", p/s)	7
89	Virgin VSG 1166	You Got It/The Only One (gatefold p/s)	5
89	Virgin VST 1166	You Got It/The Only One/Crying (with k.d. lang) (12", p/s)	12
89	Virgin VS 1173	She's A Mystery To Me/Crying (with k.d. lang) (p/s)	7
89	Virgin VS T1173	She's A Mystery To Me/Crying (with k.d. lang)/Dream Baby (12", p/s)	10
89	Virgin VS 1193	California Blue/Blue Bayou (live, with k.d. lang) (p/s)	7
89	Virgin VST 1193	California Blue/Blue Bayou (live, with k.d. lang)/Leah (12", p/s)	10
92	Virgin America VUS 63	Crying (with k.d. lang)/Falling (p/s)	5
92	Virgin America VUS 68	Heartbreak Radio/Crying (with k.d. lang) (p/s)	5

EPs
57	London RE-S 1089	HILLBILLY ROCK (orange p/s, mauve/silver label, triangular centre)	150
57	London RE-S 1089	HILLBILLY ROCK (orange p/s, mauve/silver label, round centre)	120
60	London RE-U 1274	ONLY THE LONELY	35
63	London RE-S 1089	HILLBILLY ROCK (re-pressing, yellow p/s, silver-top, round centre)	90
63	London RE-U 1354	ROY ORBISON	30

(The London EPs listed below were issued on London Monument, as were the later pressings of RE-U 1274 and RE-U 1354)

63	London RE-U 1373	IN DREAMS	25
64	Ember EP 4546	SWEET AND EASY TO LOVE	70
64	Ember EP 4563	TRYIN' TO GET TO YOU	70
64	London RE-U 1435	IT'S OVER	25
64	London RE-U 1437	OH PRETTY WOMAN	25
65	London RE-U 1439	ROY ORBISON'S STAGE SHOW HITS	35

| 65 | Ember EP 4570 | DEVIL DOLL | 75 |
| 65 | London RE-U 1440 | LOVE HURTS | 40 |

LONDON LPs

61	London HA-U 2342	LONELY AND BLUE	50
62	London HA-U 2437	CRYIN' (also stereo SAH-U 6229)	35/45
63	London HA-U/SH-U 8108	IN DREAMS (mono/stereo)	30/35
64	London HA-U 8207	OH, PRETTY WOMAN	25
65	London HA-U/SH-U 8252	THERE IS ONLY ONE ROY ORBISON (mono/stereo)	35/45
66	London HA-U/SH-U 8279	THE ORBISON WAY (mono/stereo)	35/45
66	London HA-U 8297	THE CLASSIC ROY ORBISON (mono)	30
66	London HA-U/SH-U 8297	THE CLASSIC ROY ORBISON (black label mono/blue label stereo)	35/45
67	London HA-U/SH-U 8318	SINGS DON GIBSON (black label mono/blue label stereo)	35/45

(Unless stated, the above London LPs were originally issued with plum labels [mono] or blue labels [stereo]. Later copies were re-pressed with black labels [mono] or plum labels [stereo] with a boxed London logo. They are worth around two-thirds these values.)

68	London HA-U/SH-U 8357	CRY SOFTLY, LONELY ONE	30
68	London HA-U/SH-U 8358	SONGS FROM "THE FASTEST GUITAR ALIVE" FILM SOUNDTRACK	35
70	London HA-U/SH-U 8406	THE BIG "O" (mono/stereo)	35/30
72	London SH-U 8435	ROY ORBISON SINGS	35
73	London SH-U 8445	MEMPHIS	40

OTHER LPs

64	Ember NR 5013	THE EXCITING SOUNDS OF ROY ORBISON (original copies list 'Great Newport Street' address on cover; reissued 1972)	25/18
65	Allegro ALL 778	ROY ORBISON SINGS (some tracks by Jerry Lee Lewis, Tommy Roe; black or blue label)	12
65	Ember FA 2005	ROY ORBISON AND OTHERS (with 4 tracks by Orbison)	15

(Copies of the above LP are rumoured to exist with all tracks solely by Orbison)

67	Monument LMO/SMO 5007	ROY ORBISON'S GREATEST HITS	18
67	Monument LMO/SMO 5004	ORBISONGS	20
68	Monument LMO/SMO 5013	EARLY ORBISON	20
68	Monument LMO/SMO 5014	MORE OF ROY ORBISON'S GREATEST HITS	15
69	RCA Camden CDN 5118	SPECIAL DELIVERY (with other tracks by Bobby Bare & Joey Powers)	12
70	RCA Camden CDS 1077	LITTLE RICHARD AND ROY ORBISON	12
77	Monument SMNT 81808	REGENERATION	15
79	Asylum K 53092	LAMINAR FLOW	15
70s	Fan Club	ROY ORBISON RETURNS (10")	12
70s	Lone Star	THE CONNOISSEURS' ROY ORBISON VOL. 1 (fan club issue)	18
70s	Lone Star	THE CONNOISSEURS' ROY ORBISON VOL. 2 (fan club issue)	18
70s	Fan Club	BIG 'O' LIVE AT THE SNCO (fan club issue)	18

(see also Traveling Wilburys)

WILLIAM ORBIT
| 93 | Virgin VSCDT 1465 | WATER FROM A VINE LEAF (CD) | 20 |

ORBITAL
SINGLES

89	Oh Zone ZONE 1	Chime/Deeper (12", p/s)	20
90	ffrr FRRFX 135	Chime/Deeper (12", reissue, p/s)	8
90	ffrr FRRFXR 135	Chime (JZJ Remix)/Deeper (Bacardi Mix) (12", p/s)	10
90	ffrr FRRCD 135	Chime/Chime (Edit)/Deeper (Edit) (CD)	20
90	ffrr FRRX 145	Omen/2 Deep/Open Mind (12", p/s)	8
90	ffrr FRRXR 145	The Chariot/Wheel Of Fortune/The Fool (12", p/s)	8
90	ffrr FRRCD 145	Omen (7" Version)/Omen (12" Version)/Open Mind (CD)	15
91	ffrr FRRXR 149	Satan (The Rhyme & Reason Vocal Mix)/LC2 (Outer Limits Mix)/Chime (12", p/s)	8
91	ffrr FRRCD 149	Satan/LC1/Belfast (CD)	15
92	ffrr FRRCD 181	MUTATIONS: Chime Crime/Oolaa (Betram Mix)/Farenheit 3D3/ Speed Freak (Moby Mix) (CD)	10
92	Internal LIARX 1	Halcyon/The Naked And The Dub (12", p/s)	12
92	Internal LIAXR 1	The Naked And The Dead/Sunday (12", p/s)	8
92	Internal LIECD 1	Halcyon/The Naked And The Dead/Sunday (CD)	10
93	Internal LIECD 7	Lush 3 – 1/Lush 3 – 2/Lush 3 – 3/Lush 3 – 4/Lush 3 – 5 (CD)	7
94	Internal LIARX 12	PEEL SESSIONS: Lush (Euro Tunnel Disaster '94)/Walk About/ Semi Detached/Attached (12", p/s)	8
94	Internal LIECD 12	PEEL SESSIONS: Lush (Euro Tunnel Disaster '94)/Walk About/ Semi Detached/Attached (CD)	10
95	Internal LIE 23	Times Fly (Slow)/Sad But New/Times Fly (Fast)/The Tranquiliser (double pack, p/s)	6

PROMOS

90	ffrr FRRXDJ 145	Omen (7")/Omen (12")/2 Deep/Open Mind (12")	15
91	ffrr FRRXDJ 149	Satan (2 mixes)/LC1/Belfast (12")	15
91	ffrr FRRDJ 163	Midnight (Radio Edit)/Choice (Radio Edit)	10
91	ffrr FRRXDJ 163	Midnight/Midnight (Sasha Mix)/Choice/Choice Remix (12")	15
91	ffrr FRRX 163	Midnight/Choice (12", p/s)	15
91	ffrr FRRXR 163	Midnight (Sasha Mix)/Choice (Remix) (12", p/s)	15
91	ffrr FRRCD 163	Midnight (Sasha Mix)/Choice/Analogue Test Feb '90 (CD)	15
97	ffrr FRR GUARD 1	Belfast/Impact USA/Sad But New/The Girl With The Sun In Her Head (CD, free with *The Guardian* inside 'M25 Orbital')	10
97	ffrr FRR F 296	The Saint/The Sinner (Industry Standard) (jukebox issue, no p/s)	7
97	ffrr FRR FXDJ 296	The Saint/The Sinner	7
97	ffrr FRR FXXDJ 296	The Sinner (1-sided, withdrawn)	8
96	Internal ORB CD3	EVIL SANTA (3-CD set, including LIECD 37, LICDP 37 & LICDD 37, silver box)	20
96	Internal PromoBox TRUCD 10/LIECD 30	IN SIDES (2-CD, 245mm x 175mm burgundy box with "The Box" video)	30
97	ffrr FRR PromoBox TRCDR10/FCD 296	IN SIDES (2-CD, in 245mm x 175mm burgundy box with gold Orbital logo & "The Saint" second promo video by Activate, custom sleeve)	25

ALBUMS

| 91 | ffrr FRR 828248 - 2 | ORBITAL (CD, green sleeve, with bonus track) | 18 |

MINT VALUE £

ORBIT FIVE
68	Decca F 12799	I Wanna Go To Heaven/Walking (some in p/s)	25/15

ORBITONES
73	Explosion EX 207	Memories Of Love/SONNY EARLE: In Peace	5

ORCHESTRAL MANOEUVRES IN THE DARK (O.M.D.)
79	Factory FAC 6	Electricity/Almost (black 'braille' p/s)	40
79	Din Disc DIN 2	Electricity (Re-Recorded Version)/Almost (p/s, reissue).	8
80	Din Disc DIN 6	Red Frame-White Light/I Betray My Friends (p/s)	6
80	Din Disc DIN 15-10	Messages (Extended)/Waiting For The Man/Taking Sides Again (10", p/s)	8
80	Din Disc DIN 22-12	Enola Gay (Extended)/Annex (p/s)	8
80	Din Disc DIN 24-10	Souvenir (Extended)/Motion And Heart (Amazon Version)/Sacred Heart (10", p/s).	8
81	Flexi/Smash Hits	Pretending To See The Future (Live Version)/NASH THE SLASH: Swing-Shift	
	(no cat. no.)	(Flexi-Version) (blue 33rpm 1-sided flexidisc free with *Smash Hits* mag)	12/6
82	Din Disc DIN 40-12	Maid Of Orleans (The Waltz Joan Of Arc)/Navigation/Of All The Things We've	
		Made (12", 'coin' cover; incorrectly lists "Experiments In Vertical Take-Off")	12
82	Virgin VSY 527	Genetic Engineering/4-Neu (picture disc)	6
83	Virgin VSY 580	Telegraph/66 And Fading (picture disc)	6
84	Virgin VSS 660	Locomotion/Her Body In My Soul (train-shaped picture disc)	12
84	Virgin VSY 685	Talking Loud And Clear/Julia's Song (picture disc)	6
84	Virgin VSY 727	Never Turn Away/Wrappup (picture disc).	6
85	Virgin VS 766	So In Love/Concrete Hands//Maria Gallante/White Trash (live)	
		(double pack, stickered gatefold p/s)	6
85	Virgin VS 796	Secret/Drift (poster p/s)	8
85	Virgin VSS 811	La Femme Accident/Firegun (shaped picture disc).	8
86	Virgin VSD 911	We Love You/(Dub)//If You Leave/88 Seconds In Greensboro' (double pack)	6
80	Din Disc DID 2	ORCHESTRAL MANOEUVRES IN THE DARK (LP, 12" x 12" grid sleeve,	
		black, blue or grey outer sleeves with orange, pink or red inner)	each 12
80	Din Disc DID 6	ORGANISATION (LP, stickered sleeve, with insert & 7": "Introducing Radios"/	
		"Distance Fades Between Us"/"Progress"/"Once When I Was Six" [DEP 2])	15
84	Virgin V 2310	JUNK CULTURE (LP, stickered sleeve, with free 7": "[Angels Keep Turning]	
		The Wheels Of The Universe" [JUNK 1])	15
91	Virgin V 2648	SUGAR TAX (LP, mispressing with extra track "All She Wants Is Everything"	
		instead of "Neon Lights")	15

ORCHIDS
63	Decca F 11743	Gonna Make Him Mine/Stay At Home	25
63	Decca F 11785	Love Hit Me/Don't Make Me Mad	20
64	Decca F 11861	I've Got That Feeling/Larry.	25
(see also Exceptions)			

ORCHIDS
88	Sarah SARAH 002	I've Got A Habit/Give Me Some Peppermint Freedom/Apologies	
		(foldover p/s with poster, 1,000 only)	20
88	Sarah SARAH 011	UNDERNEATH THE WINDOW, UNDERNEATH THE SINK EP (p/s).	10
89	Sarah SARAH 023	WHAT WILL WE DO NEXT? EP (p/s)	12
88	Sha La La BaBaBaBaBa 5	From This Day/SEA URCHINS: Summertime (flexi, 2,500 only, 1,000 in p/s).	10/8
90	Sarah SARAH 029	Something For The Longing/Farewell Dear Bonnie/On A Sunday (p/s, with	
		inserts)	10
90	Caff CAFF 11	An Ill Wind That Blows/All Those Things (p/s, with insert)	20
91	Sarah SARAH 042	PENETRATION EP (12", p/s with insert)	12
95	Sarah SARAH 401	LYCEUM (10" mini-LP)	12
95	Sarah SARAH 611LP	EPICUREAN: A SOUNDTRACK (2-LP).	18

ORDINARY BOYS
04	B-Unique BUN075	Maybe Someday/Laughing From The Sidelines (p/s)	8

ORE
82	Bandit BR 003	Your Time Will Come/Yellow River (p/s)	250

CHARLES ORGANAIRE
64	Blue Beat BB 241	How Did Moses Cross The Red Sea/You May Not Believe (as Big Charlie)	18
64	R&B JB 149	Little Village/It Happens On A Holiday	25
64	Rio R 28	Little Village/It Happens On A Holiday (reissue)	15

ORGANISATION
70	RCA SF 8111	TONE FLOAT (LP)	200
(see also Kraftwerk)			

ORGANISERS
66	Pye 7N 17022	Lonesome Road/The Organiser.	130

ORGANUM/NEW BLOCKADERS
80s	Aeroplane AR 7	Pulp Parts 1 & 2 (gatefold p/s).	30
85	Laylah/Antirecords LAY 19	IN EXTREMIS (LP)	20
88	Laylah LAY 012	TOWER OF SILENCE (LP)	15
(see also Current 93, Nurse With Wound, Eddie Prevost Band)			

ORIGIN UNKNOWN
92	Ram RAMM 002	Untitled (6.03)/Untitled (5.01)/Untitled (5.22)/Untitled (6.12)	
		(12", stamped white labels, promo only, not released).	20
93	Ram RAMM 004	The Touch/Valley Of The Shadows (12")	10
93	Ram RAMM 004R	The Touch (part 2)/Valley Of The Shadows (long dark remix) (12").	10
95	Ram RAMM 014	Truly One/Mission control (12").	80

ORIGINAL BARNSTORMERS SPASM BAND
59	Tempo A 168	That's All There Is/Stormin' The Barn (78 rpm = £18)	8
59	Tempo EXA 95	ORIGINAL BARNSTORMERS SPASM BAND (EP)	18
(see also Barnstormers Spasm Band)			

ORIGINAL BLIND BOYS OF ALABAMA
65	Fontana 688 520 ZL	OLD TIME RELIGION (LP)	22

ORIGINAL CHECKMATES
62	Pye 7N 15428	Hot Toddy/Tuxedo Junction	18
62	Pye 7N 15442	Checkmate Stomp/Begin The Beguine	22
63	Decca F 11688	Union Pacific/The Spy	35

(see also Checkmates)

ORIGINAL DIXIELAND JAZZ BAND
56	HMV DLP 1065	HISTORIC RECORDS OF THE FIRST RECORDED JAZZ (10" LP)	12
56	Columbia 33S 1087	ORIGINAL DIXIELAND JAZZ BAND IN ENGLAND (1919) (10" LP)	12
56	Columbia 33S 1133	ORIGINAL DIXIELAND JAZZ BAND IN ENGLAND NO. 2 (1919-20) (10" LP)	12

ORIGINAL DOWNTOWN SYNCOPATORS
62	VJM VEP 14	ORIGINAL DOWNTOWN SYNCOPATORS (EP)	10
64	Columbia SEG 8293	IT'S JASS (EP)	10
63	J.R.T. Davies DAVLP 301/2	THE ORIGINAL DOWNTOWN SYNCOPATORS (10" LP, white labels only)	35

(see also Ron Geesin)

ORIGINAL DYAKS
67	Columbia DB 8184	Got To Get A Good Thing Going/Would You Love Me Too	10

ORIGINAL NEW ORLEANS RHYTHM KINGS
54	Columbia SCM 5113	Golden Leaf Strut/She's Crying For Me	10

ORIGINALS
62	Top Rank JAR 600	Gimme A Little Kiss, Will Ya, Huh/At Times Like This	35

ORIGINALS
67	Tamla Motown TMG 592	Goodnight Irene/Need Your Lovin', Want You Back (DJ copy = £125)	75
69	Tamla Motown TMG 702	Green Grow The Lilacs/You're The One	25
70	Tamla Motown TMG 733	Baby I'm For Real/The Moment Of Truth	20
72	Tamla Motown TMG 822	God Bless Whoever Sent You/I Like Your Style/Baby I'm For Real	8
76	T. Motown TMGT 1038	Down To Love Town/Just To Be Closer To You (12")	8
76	Tamla Motown TMG 1066	Six Million Dollar Man/Mother Nature's Best (unreleased)	
69	T. Motown (S)TML 11116	GREEN GROW THE LILACS (LP)	50

ORIGINAL SIN
84	Sin S1N	The Shadow/Salvation (12", p/s, private pressing)	25

ORIGINAL TORNADOS
75	SRT SRTS 75350	Telstar/Red Rocket	10

(see also Tornados)

ORIGINELLS 4
64	Columbia DB 7259	My Girl/Kathy (as Origenells)	20
64	Columbia DB 7388	Nights/I Can Make You Mine	18

ORIOLES
53	London L 1180	Hold Me, Thrill Me, Kiss Me/Teardrops On My Pillow (78)	65
53	London L 1201	Crying In The Chapel/Don't You Think I Ought To Know (78)	60
54	London HL 8001	In The Mission Of St. Augustine/Write And Tell Me Why (78)	65

ORION
84	Lost Moment LM 02	Insane In Another World/Storm (p/s)	8

ORION
87	Gypsy GYP 001	JACK ORION (LP)	30

ORION THE HUNTER
84	Portrait PRT 25906	ORION THE HUNTER (LP)	12

(see also Boston)

ORLANDO
69	NEMS 56-4159	Am I The Same Guy/Poor Little Me	6

ORLANDO
96	Blanco Y Negro 0630-19718-2	PASSIVE SOUL (CD)	30

TONY ORLANDO
61	Fontana H 308	Halfway To Paradise/Lonely Tomorrows	20
61	Fontana H 330	Bless You/Am I The Guy	8
61	Fontana H 350	Happy Times (Are Here To Stay)/Lonely Am I	10
62	Fontana H 366	Talkin' About You/My Baby's A Stranger	8
62	Columbia DB 4871	Chills/At The Edge Of Tears	10
63	Columbia DB 4954	Beautiful Dreamer/The Loneliest	10
63	Columbia DB 4991	Shirley/Joanie	8
64	Columbia DB 7288	Tell Me What Can I Do/She Doesn't Know It	8
63	Columbia SEG 8238	BLESS YOU (EP)	80
63	Fontana TFL 5167	BLESS YOU (LP, also stereo STFL 582)	60/75

ORLONS
62	Columbia DB 4865	The Wah Watusi/Holiday Hill	30
62	Cameo Parkway C 231	Don't Hang Up/The Conservative	20
63	Cameo Parkway C 243	South Street/Them Terrible Boots	15
63	Cameo Parkway C 257	Not Me/My Best Friend	15
63	Cameo Parkway C 273	Crossfire/It's No Big Thing	15
63	Cameo Parkway C 287	Bon Doo Wah/Don't Throw Your Love Away	20
63	Cameo Parkway C 295	Shimmy Shimmy/Everything Nice	15
64	Cameo Parkway C 319	Rules Of Love/Heartbreak Hotel	15
64	Cameo Parkway C 332	Knock Knock (Who's There)/Goin' Places	15
66	Planet PLF 117	Spinnin' Top/Anyone Who Had A Heart	80
72	Mojo 2092 029	Spinnin' Top/Anyone Who Had A Heart (reissue)	15
62	Cameo Parkway C 1033	ALL THE HITS (LP)	60
63	Cameo Parkway C 1061	BIGGEST HITS (LP)	55
78	London HA-U 8504	CAMEO PARKWAY SESSIONS (LP)	25

(see also Rosetta Hightower)

LE ORME
73   Charisma CAS 1072   FELONA AND SORONA (LP) 22
(see also Peter Hammill)

CYRIL ORNADEL (ORCHESTRA)
55   MGM SP 1141   King Of Kings (Theme From)/El Cid (Theme From) 7

ORNAMENTAL
88   One Little Indian 18TP 7   Crystal Nights/Yonilingaphonics (p/s) 5
(see also Sugarcubes, Rose McDowall)

OROONIES
91   Demi Monde DMLP 1027   OF HOOF AND HORN (LP) 12

ORPHAN
85   Swoop RTLS 013   Nervous/Little England (p/s) 15

ORPHEUS
66   Red Bird RB 10-041   My Life/Music Minus Orpheus 30

ORPHEUS
68   MGM MGM 1413   I've Never Seen Love Like This/Lesley's World 6
68   MGM MGM-C(S) 8072   ORPHEUS (LP) 22

ORSON FAMILY
83   Orson Enterprises OE 1   Heartbeat/(Be My) Ball And Chain/You Shake My Soul (gatefold p/s) 5

RIZ ORTOLANI
71   United Artists UP 35278   The Hunting Party/CAROL CARMICHAEL: Where's Poppa? 8

BETH ORTON
96   Heavenly HVN 56A   I Wish I Never Saw The Sunshine (p/s, 1-sided limited edition, 500 only) 35
96   Heavenly HVN 6010   She Cries Your Name/Tangent/Safety/It's Not The Spotlight (10", p/s) 8
96   Heavenly HVN 6410   Touch Me With Your Love/Galaxy Of Emptiness/Pedestal/Touch Me With
           Your Love (Instrumental) (10" EP, p/s with insert) 8
97   Heavenly HVN 6510   Someone's Daughter/I Wish I Never Saw The Sunshine/It's This I Am
           I Find (10" EP, p/s) 10
96   Heavenly HVNLP 17   TRAILER PARK (LP, 100 copies only) 40
99   Heavenly HVNLP 22   CENTRAL RESERVATION (2-LP, gatefold sleeve, 1000 copies only) 20
02   Heavenly HVNLP 37   DAYBREAKER (LP) 15
(see also Spill)

KID ORY & HIS CREOLE JAZZ/DIXIELAND BAND
50   Jazz Collector N1   High Society/Panama Rag (78, as Kid Ory's Creole Jazz Band) 8
51   Jazz Man 22   Get Out Of Here/Blues For Jimmy (78) 8
52   Good Time Jazz 65   Oh! Didn't He Ramble/Maryland, My Maryland (78) 8
52   Tempo A 106   Dippermouth Blues/Savoy Blues (78) 8
52   Tempo A 107   High Society/Ballin' The Jack (78) 8
52   Vocalion V 1012   Muskrat Ramble/High Society (78) 8
53   Columbia DB 3351   Tiger Rag/The World's Jazz Crazy, Lawdy So Am I (78) 8
56   Tempo A 106   Dippermouth Blues/Savoy Blues 5
56   Tempo A 107   High Society/Ballin' The Jack 5
56   Vogue V 2011   Tiger Rag/Eh, La-Bas 5
56   Vogue V 2012   12th Street Rag/Savoy Blues 5
54   Goodtime Jazz LDG 055   KID ORY'S CREOLE JAZZ BAND 1944-1945 (10" LP) 12
54   Goodtime Jazz LDG 093   KID ORY'S CREOLE JAZZ BAND 1944-1945 VOL. 2 (10" LP) 12
56   Goodtime Jazz LDG 184   KID ORY'S CREOLE JAZZ BAND 1944-1945 VOL. 3 (10" LP) 12
58   Columbia Clef 33CX 10116   KID ORY IN EUROPE (LP) 12
59   Columbia Clef 33CX 10134   SONG OF THE WANDERER (LP) 12
59   HMV CLP 1303   A KID FROM NEW ORLEANS — ORY, THAT IS (LP) 12
60   HMV CLP 1329   IN THE MOOD (LP) 12
60   HMV CLP 1364   KID ORY PLAYS W.C. HANDY (LP) 12
60   HMV CLP 1395/CSD 1325   DANCE WITH KID ORY — OR JUST LISTEN (LP) 20
61   HMV CLP 1422   WE'VE GOT RHYTHM (LP, with Red Allen) 15
(see also Roberta Dudley)

EILEEN OSBORNE
75   Seagull SG1   SINGING SHORES (LP) 15

MIKE OSBORNE
71   Turtle TUR 300   OUTBACK (LP) 50
73   Cadillac SGC 1002   ORIGINAL (LP, as Mike Osborne & Stan Tracey) 20
77   Ogun OG 210   TANDEM — LIVE AT BRACKNELL FESTIVAL (LP, with Stan Tracey) 18
70s   Ogun OG 300   BORDER CROSSING (LP) 15
70s   Ogun OG 700   ALL NIGHT LONG (LP) 20
70s   Ogun OG 810   MARCEL'S MUSE (LP) 15
(see also Stan Tracey)

OSBORNE BROTHERS
62   MGM MGM 1184   The Banjo Boys/Poor Old Cora 7
59   MGM MGM-EP 691   COUNTRY PICKING AND HILLSIDE SINGING (EP) 25
62   MGM MGM-C 914   BLUE GRASS MUSIC (LP) 20
63   Brunswick LAT 8620   VOICES IN BLUE GRASS (LP) 15
66   Brunswick LAT 8662   UP THIS HILL AND DOWN (LP) 15

TONY OSBOURNE ORCHESTRA
59   HMV GES 5764   THE LATIN TOUCH (EP, stereo) 10

OZZY OSBOURNE
80   Jet JET 197   Crazy Train/You Looking At Me Looking At You (p/s) 8
80   Jet JET 7003   Mr. Crowley (live)/You Said It All (live) (p/s) 8
80   Jet JET 12003   Mr. Crowley (live)/You Said It All (live)/Suicide Solution (live) (12", p/s)........ 10
80   Jet JETP 12003   Mr. Crowley (live)/You Said It All (live)/Suicide Solution (live) (12", picture disc) . 15

81	Jet JET 7017	Over The Mountain/I Don't Know (p/s)	5
81	Jet JET 12017	Over The Mountain/I Don't Know (12", p/s)	8
82	Jet JET 7030	Symptom Of The Universe/N.I.B. (p/s)	6
82	Jet JETP 7030	Symptom Of The Universe/N.I.B. (picture disc)	10
82	Jet JET 12030	Symptom Of The Universe/N.I.B./Children Of The Grave (12", p/s)	8
83	Epic TA 3915	Bark At The Moon/One Up The B-Side (12", p/s, silver vinyl)	15
83	Epic WA 3915	Bark At The Moon/One Up The B-Side (12", picture disc, unreleased)	
84	Epic DA 4452	So Tired/Bark At The Moon (live)/Waiting For Darkness/ Paranoid (live) (double pack)	8
84	Epic TA 4452	So Tired/Bark At The Moon (live)/Waiting For Darkness/ Suicide Solution/Paranoid (live) (12", p/s with free patch)	8
84	Epic WA 4452	So Tired/Bark At The Moon (live)/Waiting For Darkness/ Suicide Solution/Paranoid (live) (12", p/s, gold vinyl)	12
86	Epic A 6859	Shot In The Dark/Rock'n'Roll Rebel (p/s, with signature card)	6
86	Epic QA 6859	Shot In The Dark/Rock'n'Roll Rebel (poster p/s)	8
86	Epic A 7311	The Ultimate Sin/Lightning Strikes (p/s, with free patch)	5
88	Epic 653 063-9	Miracle Man/Crazy Babies (head-shaped picture disc)	8
88	Spiral Scratch 2/Ozzy 1	An Interview With... (no p/s, free with *Spiral Scratch*, issue 2, 5,000 only)	5
90	Adventure ADV TS 102	The Urpney Song/Whirlypad Launch (p/s, some with poster, with Frank Bruno/Billy Connolly)	6/5
90	Adventure ADV TS 102	The Urpney Song/Whirlypad Launch (picture disc, with Frank Bruno/ Billy Connolly)	10
91	Epic 657 4406	No More Tears (extended version)/S.I.N./Party With The Animals (12" pic. disc)	8
93	Epic 659 3406	Changes/Changes (extended version)/No More Tears (extended version)/ Desire (12" picture disc)	8
96	Epic 662 6391	Perry Mason/Living With The Enemy (picture disc)	6
86	Epic EPC 11-26404	THE ULTIMATE SIN (LP, picture disc)	12
89	Epic 463 0862	DIARY OF A MADMAN (CD, promo-only, with diary)	20
91	Epic 467 8592	NO MORE TEARS (CD in embossed wallet)	18
95	Epic XP CD 2007	THE BALLADS OF OZ (CD, promo-only compilation)	40

(see also Black Sabbath, Lita Ford & Ozzy Osbourne)

JOHNNY OSBOURNE (& SENSATIONS)

70	Big Shot BI 549	See And Blind (solo)/THE TECHNIQUES: Scar Face	12
72	Techniques TE 916	See And Blind/TECHNIQUES ALL STARS: Rema Skank	10
70	Trojan TTL 29	COME BACK DARLING (LP, with Sensations)	50
80	Cha Cha CHAD 27	Kiss Somebody/Version (12")	30
80	Black Joy DH 810	Purify Your Heart/Politician (blue vinyl)	20
81	Greensleeves GRED 50	Back Off (with PAPA TULLO).Dub (12")	35
81	Simba LION 1	13 Dead (Nothing Said)/Black Lion Band Murder (12")	15
82	Oak Sounds OSD 006	Yo Yo/ECHO MINOTT: Man In Love (12")	15
73	Big Shot BILP 103	READY OR NOT (LP)	40
81	Cha Cha CHALP 010	IN NAH DISCO STYLE (LP)	20

BOB OSBURN

64	London HLD 9869	Bound To Happen/Think Of Me	15

OSCAR

66	Reaction 591 003	Club Of Lights/Waking Up	22
66	Reaction 591 006	Join My Gang/Days Gone By	32
67	Reaction 591 012	Over The Wall We Go/Every Day Of My Life	32
67	Reaction 591 016	Holiday/Give Her All She Wants	22
68	Polydor 56257	Open Up The Skies/Wild Ones	20

(see also Paul Dean, Paul Nicholas)

OSCAR

74	Buk BULP 2001	OSCAR (LP)	12

OSCAR BICYCLE

68	CBS 3237	On A Quiet Night/The Room Revolves Around Me	50

PETER OSGOOD

70	Penny Farthing PEN 715	Chelsea/Stamford Bridge	10

OSIBISA

71	MCA MDKS 8001	OSIBISA (LP)	18
72	MCA MDKS 8005	WOYOYA (LP)	15
72	MCA MDKS 8007	HEADS (LP)	15
73	Buddah 2318 087	SUPER FLY T.N.T. (LP, soundtrack)	15

OSMOND BROTHERS

63	MGM MGM 1208	Be My Little Baby Bumble Bee/I Wouldn't Know	25
63	MGM MGM 1245	Travels Of Jamie McPheeters/Aura Lee	18
63	MGM MGM-C 1011	NEW SOUND OF THE BROTHERS (LP)	45

OSSIAN

77	Spring Thyme SPR 1004	OSSIAN (LP)	12
79	Iona IR 001	ST. KILDA WEDDING (LP, with lyric insert)	12
81	Iona IR 002	SEAL SONG (LP, with lyric insert)	12

OSSIE & SWEET BOYS

67	Polydor 56167	Nothing Takes The Place Of You/Brixton Boo-Ga-Loo	6

OSSIE & UPSETTERS

66	Doctor Bird DB 1018	Turn Me On/True Love	20

(see also Upsetters, Desmond Dekkar)

AL OSTER

60s	Dominion LP 1321	ECHO OF THE YUKON (LP)	20

Gilbert O'SULLIVAN

GILBERT O'SULLIVAN
71	Columbia DB 8779	I Wish I Could Cry/Mr Moody's Garden.	8
73	MAM MAMSS 505	I'M A WRITER, NOT A FIGHTER (LP).	12

(see also Gilbert)

PETER O'SULLIVAN
70s	Charisma CAS 1160	PETER O'SULLIVAN TALKS TURF (LP)	15

BASHFUL BROTHER OSWALD
64	London HA-B/SH-B 8104	BASHFUL BROTHER OSWALD (LP, mono/stereo)	12/15

OTHER BROTHERS
69	Pama PM 785	Let's Get Together/Little Girl	7

OTHERS
64	Fontana TF 501	Oh Yeah/I'm Taking Her Home	80

(see also Sands, Sundragon; this single does not feature Brian May)

OTHERS
04	Poptones MC5090S	This Is For The Poor/How I Nearly Lost You (signed 7")	12

OTHER TWO
64	Decca F 11911	I Wanna Be With You/Grumbling Guitar	12
65	RCA RCA 1465	Don't You Wanna Love Me Baby/Hold Back The Light Of Dawn	10
66	RCA RCA 1531	I'll Never Let You Go/Hot At Night.	12

(see also Storyteller, J.J. Jackson)

CLYDE OTIS ORCHESTRA
61	Mercury AMT 1143	Jungle Drums/Peanut Vendor	6

JOHNNY OTIS SHOW
50	Parlophone R 3291	Harlem Nocturne (solo)/SLIM GAILLARD: Jam Man (78)	35
57	Capitol CL 14794	Ma (He's Makin' Eyes At Me)/Romance In The Dark	12
58	Capitol CL 14817	Bye Bye Baby (as Johnny Otis Show with Marie Adams)/Good Golly	25
58	Capitol CL 14817	Bye Bye Baby (as Johnny Otis Show with Marie Adams)/Good Golly (78)	10
58	Capitol CL 14837	The Light Still Shines In My Window/All I Want Is Your Love (with Marie Adams).	25
58	Capitol CL 14837	The Light Still Shines In My Window/All I Want Is Your Love (78, with Marie Adams).	15
58	Capitol CL 14854	Well, Well, Well, Well!/You Just Kissed Me Goodbye (with Mel Williams)	25
58	Capitol CL 14854	Well, Well, Well, Well!/You Just Kissed Me Goodbye (with Mel Williams) (78).	10
58	Capitol CL 14875	Ring-A-Ling/The Johnny Otis Hand Jive (78 rpm = £20)	22
58	Capitol CL 14941	Crazy Country Hop/Willie Did The Cha Cha.	22
59	Capitol CL 15008	You/My Dear (as Johnny Otis Show with Mel Williams)	18
59	Capitol CL 15018	Castin' My Spell/Telephone Baby (as Johnny Otis Show with Marci Lee)	25
59	Capitol CL 15057	Three Girls Named Molly Doin' The Hully Gully/I'll Do The Same Thing For You.	20
60	Capitol CL 15112	Mumblin' Mosie/Hey Baby, Don't You Know?	15
64	Ember EMB S 192	Hand Jive One More Time/Baby I Got News For You	12
69	Sonet SON 608	Country Girl/Signifyin' Monkey	6
72	Epic EPC 7896	The Watts Breakaway/You Can Depend On Me	8
72	Epic EPC 8071	The Watts Breakaway/Willie And The Hand Jive	8
59	Capitol EAP1 1134	THE JOHNNY OTIS SHOW (EP)	90
65	Vocalion VEP 170162	JOHNNY OTIS (EP)	105
58	Capitol T 940	THE JOHNNY OTIS SHOW (LP)	105
69	Sonet SNTF 613	COLD SHOT (LP).	15
72	Ember SPE 6604	FORMIDABLE (LP)	20

(see also Marie Adams)

SHUGGIE OTIS
70	CBS 63996	HERE COMES SHUGGIE OTIS (LP).	20

(see also Al Kooper & Shuggie Otis)

NOIT OTNI & PITS
79	Automotive AERS 107	A Heart Can Only Be Broken Once/Moving Target (some in p/s)	35/25

JOHN OTWAY
72	County COUN 215	Gypsy/Misty Mountain (private pressing, with duplicated lyric sheet)	25
76	Viking YRS CF 01	Louisa On A Horse/Beware Of The Flowers (private pressing)	15
78	Polydor 2059 001	Geneve/It's A Long Time Since I Heard Homestead On The Farm (p/s)	5
78	Polydor 2059 060	Baby's In The Club/Julie Julie Julie (p/s).	5
79	Polydor 2059 105	Frightened And Scared (instrumental)/Are You On My Side? (p/s, only 3 copies pressed!)	80+
80	Stiff BUY 101	Green Green Grass Of Home/Wednesday Club (p/s)	5
82	Empire HAM 3	In Dreams/You Ain't Seen Nothing Yet (as John Otway Sweat, p/s)	5
86	'Warner Bros' OTWEAY 1	The New Jerusalem/The Tyger (private pressing)	20
82	Empire HAMLP 1	JOHN OTWAY (ALL BALLS AND NO WILLY) (LP, with Europeans)	12

JOHN OTWAY & WILD WILLY BARRETT
73	Track 2094 111	Murder Man/If I Did	8
76	Track 2094 133	Louisa On A Horse/Misty Mountain.	5
77	Polydor 2058 916	Racing Cars (Jet Spotter Of The Track)/Running From The Law (p/s)	10
77	Polydor 2058 951	Really Free/Beware Of The Flowers (Cos I'm Sure They're Going To Get You Yeh) (p/s or die-cut 'review' sleeve)	6/5
82	Stiff Indie STIN 1	Headbutts/Live Version Headbutts (p/s).	6
82	Empire HAM 5T	12 STITCH EP (12" EP in polythene bag with jay-card)	15
87	VM VMS 6	The Last Of The Mohicans/Fashion (brown paper bag sleeve)	5
77	Extracted EXLP 1	JOHN OTWAY AND WILD WILLY BARRETT (LP, handmade stickered sleeve)	20
77	white label OBL 1	OTWAY AND BARRETT LIVE AT THE ROUNDHOUSE (private pressing LP, freebie, handwritten labels, plain sleeve, 250 numbered copies only)	35
81	Polydor POLS 1039	GONE WITH THE BIN (THE BEST OF OTWAY-BARRETT) (LP)	12
87	VM VM 7	THE WIMP AND THE WILD (LP, 1,000 only)	12

(see also Wild Willy Barrett)

OUR PLASTIC DREAM
67	Go AJ 11411	A Little Bit Of Shangrila/Encapsulated Marigold	150

OUT
79	Rabid TOSH 113	Who Is Innocent/Linda's Just A Statue (p/s)	7

OUTCASTS
78	It IT 4	Frustration/Don't Want To Be No Adult/You're A Disease (p/s)	30
78	Good Vibrations GOT 3	Just Another Teenage Rebel/Love Is For Sops (poster p/s, various colours; 'band' p/s or 'type' p/s)	12/10
79	Good Vibrations GOT 17	Self Conscious Over You/Love You For Never (p/s)	10
81	GBH GBH 001	Magnum Force/Gangland Warfare (p/s)	6
81	Outcasts Only 0001	Programme Love/Beating And Screaming (Parts 1 & 2)/Mania (p/s)	5
79	Good Vibrations BIG 1	SELF CONSCIOUS OVER YOU (LP)	25

OUTER LIMITS
60s	Teldisc TD 154	Paradise For Two/Don't Ever Change	20

OUTER LIMITS
67	Elephant LUR 100	When The Work Is Thru'/5 MAN CARGO: What A Wonderful Feeling (Leeds Students Charity Rag record)	55
67	Deram DM 125	Just One More Chance/Help Me Please	28
68	Immediate IM 067	Great Train Robbery/Sweet Freedom (demo only)	70
68	Instant IN 001	Great Train Robbery/Sweet Freedom	22
71	Decca F 13176	The Dark Side Of The Moon/Black Boots	10
	(see also Christie, Acid Gallery)		

OUTER LIMITS
70s	Snow/Deroy 1049	(I'm Not) Your Stepping Stone/Great Balls Of Fire	40

OUTLAW BLUES BAND
69	Stateside SSL 10290	BREAKING IN (LP)	25

OUTLAW POSSE
90	Gee street Gee A6	My Afro's On Fire (12")	12

OUTLAWS
61	HMV POP 844	Swingin' Low/Spring Is Near	20
61	HMV POP 877	Ambush/Indian Brave	20
61	HMV POP 927	Valley Of The Sioux/Crazy Drums	20
62	HMV POP 990	Ku-pow!/Last Stage West	20
62	HMV POP 1074	Sioux Serenade/Fort Knox	20
63	HMV POP 1124	The Return Of The Outlaws/Texan Spiritual	20
63	HMV POP 1195	That Set The Wild West Free/Hobo	20
63	HMV POP 1241	Law And Order/Do-Da-Day	20
64	HMV POP 1277	Keep-A-Knockin'/Shake With Me	40
61	HMV CLP 1489	DREAM OF THE WEST (LP, mauve label, later black)	120/60
	(see also Mike Berry, Ritchie Blackmore, Bobbie Graham, Chaps, Rally Rounders, Houston Wells [& Marksmen])		

OUT OF DARKNESS
70	Key KL 006	OUT OF DARKNESS (LP)	200

OUTRAGE
70	Kama Sutra 618 027	The Letter/The Way I See It	5

OUTSIDERS (U.K.)
65	Decca F 12213	Keep On Doing It/Songs We Sang Last Summer	20
	(see also Bunch Of Fives, Junior's Eyes, Tickle)		

OUTSIDERS (U.S.)
66	Capitol CL 15435	Time Won't Let You/Was It Really Real? (DJ copy = £50)	35
66	Capitol CL 15450	Girl In Love/What Makes You So Bad, You Weren't Brought Up That Way	15
66	Capitol CL 15468	Respectable/Lost In My World	20
66	Capitol CL 15480	Help Me Girl/You Gotta Look	10
67	Capitol CL 15495	I'll Give You Time/I'm Not Tryin' To Hurt You	20

OUTSIDERS (U.K.)
77	Raw Edge RER 002	ONE TO INFINITY (EP)	20
78	Xciting Plastic	Vital Hours/Take Up (unissued)	
77	Raw Edge RER 001	CALLING ON YOUTH (LP)	25
78	Raw Edge RER 003	CLOSE UP (LP, with insert)	25
	(see also Second Layer, Sound)		

OUTSKIRTS OF INFINITY
87	Woronzow WOO 7	LORD OF THE DARK SKIES (LP)	15
89	Infinity INF 001	SCENES FROM THE DREAMS OF ANGELS (LP)	12
89	Infinity INF 002	STONED CRAZY (LP)	12
94	Dark Skies DSKLP 2	INCIDENT AT PILATUS (2-LP)	18

OVALTINEES
83	BAA 021	BRITISH JUSTICE EP (p/s)	30

OVARY LODGE
73	RCA SF 8372	OVARY LODGE (LP)	50
76	Ogun OG 600	OVARY LODGE (LP)	30
	(see also Keith Tippett)		

OVERDRIVE
81	Boring Grantham BGR 1	ON THE RUN (EP)	80
90	Boring Grantham BGR 11	DISHONEST WORDS (LP)	12

OVERLANDERS
63	Pye 7N 15544	Summer Skies And Golden Sands/Call Of The Wild	12
63	Pye 7N 15568	Movin'/Rainbow	7
64	Pye 7N 15619	Yesterday's Gone/Gone In The Rainbow	5

64	Pye 7N 15678	Don't It Make You Feel Good/Sing A Song Of Sadness	5
64	Pye 7N 15712	If I Gave You/I Wonder Why	5
64	Pye 7N 15719	The Leaves Are Falling/Delia's Gone	5
65	Pye 7N 15804	Along Came Jones/Walking The Soles Off My Shoes	5
65	Pye 7N 15883	Freight Train/Take The Bucket To The Well	5
65	Pye 7N 15967	Room Enough For You And Me/January	5
66	Pye 7N 17034	Michelle/Cradle Of Love	6
66	Pye 7N 17068	My Life/The Girl From Indiana	5
66	Pye 7N 17159	Go Where You Wanna Go/Don't Let It Happen Again	5
66	Pye NEP 24245	MICHELLE (EP)	35
66	Pye NPL 18138	MICHELLE (LP)	40

(see also Paul Arnold, Cuppa T)

OVERLOAD
80	MCA MCA 618	Into Overload/Follow The Lines (p/s)	7
81	MCA MCA 656	Who Are You/Drift Away	7

OVERLORD
78	Airebeat ABT 3	Lucy (p/s)	25

OVERLORD X
88	Hardcore HAKT12	14 Days In May (12")	10
88	Mango 1215 372	Rough In Hackney/Earth Is Moving (12")	8
89	Mango ILPS 9924	WEAPON IS MY LYRIC (LP)	12

RUNE OVERMAN
63	Decca F 11605	Big Bass Boogie/Madison Piano	10

OVERNIGHT PLAYERS
80	Cha Cha CHALP 008	BABYLON DESTRUCTION (LP)	30

OVERTAKERS
68	Amalgamated AMG 803	That's The Way You Like It/The Big Take-Over	15
68	Amalgamated AMG 809	Girl You Ruff/KEITH BLAKE: Woo Oh Oh	25

OWEN (Da Silvera) & LEON
64	Island WI 146	Nextdoor Neighbour/ROLAND ALPHONSO: Feeling Fine	22
64	Island WI 163	My Love For You/How Many Times	22
64	Island WI 164	The Fits Is On Me/SKATALITES: Good News	25
64	Island WI 165	Running Around/SKATALITES: Around The World	25
65	Ska Beat JB 189	Woman/BABA BROOKS with DON DRUMMOND: Doctor Decker	25

(see also Leon & Owen, Tommy McCook)

OWEN (Gray) & DANDY (Livingstone)
69	Downtown DT 428	Lovey Dovey/HERBIE GRAY & RUDIES: Kitty Wait	8

OWEN (Gray) & MILLIE
62	Blue Beat BB 96	Sit And Cry/Do You Know (with City Slickers Orchestra)	10
62	Island WI 014	Sugar Plum/OWEN GRAY: Jezebel	15

(see also Owen Gray, Millie, Owen & Leon, Leon & Owen)

RAY OWEN('S MOON)
69	Fontana TF 1045	Tonight I'll Be Staying Here With You/Down, Don't Bother Me (solo)	5
71	Polydor 2058 095	Hey Sweety/Free Man (as Ray Owen's Moon)	5
71	Polydor 2325 061	RAY OWEN'S MOON (LP)	20

(see also Juicy Lucy)

REG OWEN & HIS ORCHESTRA
56	Parlophone R 4217	Comin' Thru' The Rye Bread/Harlem Swing	5
57	Parlophone R 4303	Easy Now/Sweeping The Floor	5
59	Pye International 7N 25009	Manhattan Spiritual/Ritual Blues (78 rpm = £6)	5
59	Pye International 7N 25040	Ginchy/Kazoo (78 rpm = £8)	5
60	Palette PG 9004	Obsession/Sunday Morn	5
61	Palette PG 9013	Payroll/Swing A Ling-Ling	5
56	Parlophone PMD 1045	SWING ME HIGH (10" LP)	20
59	Pye Intl. NPL 28000	MANHATTAN SPIRITUAL (LP, also stereo NSPL 93000)	15/25

BUCK OWENS (& BUCKAROOS)
59	Capitol CL 15009	Everlasting Love/Second Fiddle	10
60	Capitol CL 15123	Above And Beyond/Til These Dreams Come True	10
60	Capitol CL 15162	Excuse Me (I Think I've Got A Heartache)/I've Got A Right To Know	10
61	Capitol CL 15187	Foolin' Around/High As The Mountain	7
62	Longhorn BLH 0006	Down On The Corner Of Love/Right After The Dance	7
63	Capitol CL 15321	Love's Gonna Live Here/Getting Used To Losing You	6
64	Capitol CL 15364	Together Again/Ain't It Amazin' Gracie (as Buck Owens & Buckaroos)	6
65	Capitol CL 15379	I've Got A Tiger By The Tail/Cryin' Time	7
67	Capitol CL 15501	Sam's Place/Don't Ever Tell Me Goodbye (as Buck Owens & Buckaroos)	7
63	Capitol EAP1 1550	FOOLIN' AROUND (EP)	18
65	Capitol EAP1 20602	ACT NATURALLY (EP)	18
64	Capitol (S)T 2105	THE BEST OF BUCK OWENS (LP)	15
65	Capitol T 2135	TOGETHER AGAIN/MY HEART SKIPS A BEAT (LP)	15
66	Capitol (S)T 2353	BEFORE YOU GO/NO ONE BUT YOU (LP)	15
66	Capitol (S)T 2443	ROLL OUT THE RED CARPET (LP)	15
66	Fontana FJL 307	BUCK OWENS WITH FERLIN HUSKY & FARON YOUNG (LP)	15
66	Capitol (S)T 2283	I'VE GOT A TIGER BY THE TAIL (LP)	15
66	Capitol (S)T 20861	YOURS, COUNTRY STYLE (LP)	18
67	Capitol (S)T 2556	CARNEGIE HALL CONCERT (LP)	15
68	Capitol (S)T 2760	YOUR TENDER LOVING CARE (LP, with His Buckaroos)	15
68	Capitol (S)T 2841	IT TAKES PEOPLE LIKE YOU TO MAKE PEOPLE LIKE ME (LP)	15
68	Capitol (S)T 2897	THE BEST OF BUCK OWENS VOL. 2 (LP)	12
69	Capitol (S)T 2994	THE GUITAR PLAYER (LP)	12

69	Capitol E-(S)T 131	I'VE GOT YOU ON MY MIND AGAIN (LP)	12
69	Capitol E-(S)T 232	BUCK OWENS IN LONDON (LP)	12
70	Capitol E-ST 212	TALL DARK STRANGER (LP)	12
71	Capitol E-ST 628	I WOULDN'T LIVE IN NEW YORK CITY (LP)	12

DONNIE OWENS
| 58 | London HLU 8747 | Need You/If I'm Wrong (78 rpm = £25) | 25 |
| 59 | London HLW 8897 | Ask Me Anything/Between Midnight And Dawn (unissued) | |

OWL
| 68 | United Artists UP 2240 | Run To The Sun/Shades Of Blue And Green Water Flies | 20 |

O.W.L.
| 70s | Shebazz SHE 002 | Shady Tree/4TH STREET ORCHESTRA: Sun Hot | 8 |

TONY OXLEY (QUARTET)
69	CBS 52664	THE BAPTISED TRAVELLER (LP)	110
70	CBS 64071	4 COMPOSITIONS FOR SEXTET (LP, with Derek Bailey)	110
71	RCA SF 8215	ICHNOS (LP)	70
70s	Incus INCUS 8	TONY OXLEY (LP, with Derek Bailey, et al.)	100
70s	Incus INCUS 18	FEBRUARY PAPERS (LP)	50
80s	Bead BEAD 25	THE GLIDER & THE GRINDER (LP)	40
(see also Derek Bailey, Howard Riley)			

OXYM
| 80 | Cargo CRS 003 | Music Power/Mind Key (p/s) | 35 |

OYSTER BAND
89	Cooking Vinyl FRYX 012	Love Vigilantes/Polish Plain/I Fought The Law (Live)/Between The Wars (Live) (10", pink vinyl, poster sleeve)	10
82	Pukka YOP 01	ENGLISH ROCK 'N' ROLL, 1800-1850 (LP)	50
85	Pukka YOP 04	LIE BACK AND THINK OF ENGLAND (LP)	50
85	Pukka YOP 07	LIBERTY HALL (LP)	40

OYSTER CEILIDH BAND
| 80 | Dingles DIN 309 | JACK'S ALIVE (LP) | 30 |

OZRIC TENTACLES
| 94 | Dovetail DOVEBOX 1 | VITAMIN ENHANCED (6-CD box set) | 30 |
| 98 | Snapper SMALP 410 | CURIOUS CORN (LP) | 12 |

OZZ II
| 83 | Streamline | EXPLOITED (LP, red vinyl) | 12 |
| 84 | Zebra ZEB 2 | THE ASSASSIN (LP) | 12 |

AUGUSTUS PABLO
71	Big Shot BI 578	The Mood/HERMAN CHIN-LOY: New Love	20
71	Big Shot BI 579	East Of The River Nile/HERMAN CHIN-LOY: East Of River Nile Version (B-side actually by Aquarians)	45
71	Creole CR 1004	405 (actually "The Mood" by Tommy McCook)/Duck It Up (actually "Confidential Version" by Charmers)	18
71	Ackee ACK 134	Still Yet/AQUARIANS: Version	12
71	Ackee ACK 138	Snowball And Pudding/AQUARIANS: Version	12
71	Duke DU 122	Reggae In The Fields/TOMMY McCOOK: Love Brother	18
73	Randy's RAN 536	Bedroom Mazurka (as Augustus Pablo & Fay)/Melodica Version	20
74	Tropical AL 025	Too Latte/Dub Organiser	10
74	Tropical AL 035	Tales Of Dub/BOOTHE STARS: Tales Dub	10
75	Island WIP 6226	King Tubby Meets The Rockers Uptown/Baby I Love You So	10
75	Island 12 WIP 6226	King Tubby Meets The Rockers Uptown/JACOB MILLER: Baby I Love You So (12")	20
75	Treble C CCC06	Liberation/Dubbing Pablo	12
75	Treble C CCC014	Don Drummond/Thunderbolt Lady	10
78	Rough Trade RT 002	Pablo Meets Mr. Bassie/Mr. Bassie Special (with Rockers All Stars) (with colour sticker)	10
74	Tropical TROPS 101	THIS IS (LP)	35
75	Trojan TRLS 115	ITAL DUB (LP, original issue with "12 Neasden Lane" address on sleeve and rough orange/white paper labels)	25
79	Rockers APD 5	Power Of The Trinity/West Abyssinia Dub (12")	20
79	Rockers APD 6	Twin Seal/Dub/NORRIS REID: Entrance To Jah World (12")	25
79	Rockers AP 1023	Crucial Burial/ROCKERS ALL STARS: Pope Paul Feel It/Sound Of Redemption – Scientist In Dub (12")	30
79	Rockers AB1	Israel In Harmony/HUGH MUNDELL: Feeling Alright/Dub (12")	35
80	Rockers APD 7	Hot Milk/Dub/Robin Bay Step/Dub (12")	25
75	Nationwide NW 03	THRILLER (LP)	25
(see also Mickey Lee, I Roy)			

PACESETTERS
70	Big Chief BC 101	Cool Coffee/Israelites	12
70	Escort ERT 829	Bits And Pieces/Nimrod Leap	8
74	Saga SAGA 8154	REGGAE MEETS POP (LP)	25

PACIFIC DRIFT
70	Deram DM 304	Water Woman/Yes You Do	15
70	Deram Nova (S)DN 13	FEELIN' FREE (LP)	50
	(see also Wimple Winch, Just Four Men)		

PACIFIC GAS & ELECTRIC (P.G. & E.)
70	CBS 5039	Are You Ready?/Staggolee	6
70	CBS 5204	Father Come On Home/Elvira	5
69	B&C CAS 1003	GET IT ON (LP)	25
69	CBS 63822	PACIFIC GAS & ELECTRIC (LP, orange label)	15
70	CBS 64026	ARE YOU READY (LP, orange label)	15
71	CBS 64295	HARD BURN (LP, orange label)	15

PACK
65	Columbia DB 7702	Do You Believe In Magic?/Things Bring Me Down	45

PACK
79	SS PAK 1	Brave New Soldiers/Heathen (p/s, 2,500 only)	12
79	Rough Trade RT 025	King Of Kings/Number 12 (p/s)	8
80	SS SS 1N2/SS 2N1	KIRK BRANDON AND THE PACK OF LIES (EP, with printed inner sleeve)	12
82	Cyclops CYCLOPS 1	LONG LIVE THE PAST (EP)	8
82	Donut DONUT 2	THE PACK LIVE, 1979 (cassette)	15
	(see also Theatre Of Hate, Spear Of Destiny, Senate)		

PACKABEATS
61	Parlophone R 4729	Gypsy Beat/Big Man	20
62	Pye 7N 15480	Evening In Paris/The Traitors	25
63	Pye 7N 15549	Dream Lover/Packabeat	30

PACKERS
66	Pye International 7N 25343	Hole In The Wall/Go 'Head On	25
69	Soul City SC 111	Hole In The Wall/Go 'Head On (reissue)	15
70	Soul City SCM 003	HOLE IN THE WALL (LP)	45

PAC-KEYS
68	Speciality SPE 1003	Stone Fox/Diggin'	15

PADDY, KLAUS & GIBSON
65	Pye 7N 15906	I Wanna Know/I Tried	22
66	Pye 7N 17060	No Good Without You Baby/Rejected	40
66	Pye 7N 17112	Teresa/Quick Before They Catch Us	25
	(see also Manfred Mann, Big Three, Rory Storm & Hurricanes, Kingsize Taylor)		

PADDINGTONS
04	Poptones MC5093S	21/Some Old Girl (p/s)	7

BILLY PAGE
65	London HLU 10006	It's Pop/American Girl	10

CHRIS PAGE
66	Cameo Parkway CP 751	Wait And See/Mine Mine Mine	12

GENE PAGE
75	Atlantic K50105	HOT CITY (LP)	12

HOT LIPS PAGE & HIS ORCHESTRA
55	Parlophone MSP 6172	Ain't Nothing Wrong With That Boy/The Cadillac Song	30

JIMMY PAGE
65	Fontana TF 533	She Just Satisfies/Keep Moving	600
88	Geffen GEF 41	Wasting My Time/Writes Of Winter (p/s, withdrawn)	8
91	Fontana TFCD 533	She Just Satisfies/Keep Moving (CD, in 'Led Zeppelin, A Celebration' pack)	10
	(see also Led Zeppelin, Page & Plant, Firm, Yardbirds, Paul, Carter-Lewis & Southerners, Neil Christian & Crusaders, Bobby Graham, Robert Plant, Honeydrippers, Brian Auger, Cartoone, Maureeny Wishfull, Jimmy Page with Puff Daddy, Coverdale-Page)		

JIMMY PAGE WITH PUFF DADDY
98	Epic/Sony XPR364	Come With Me (12" DJ promo with T.Montana & D. Angelettie mixes)	8

LARRY PAGE (ORCHESTRA)
57	Columbia DB 3965	Cool Shake/Start Movin' (In My Direction) (78 rpm = £15)	25
58	Columbia DB 4012	That'll Be The Day/Please Don't Blame Me (78 rpm = £15)	25
58	Columbia DB 4080	Under Control/This Is My Life (78 rpm = £15)	22
59	Saga SAG 45-2902	Big Blon' Baby/I Vibrate	22
60	Saga SAG 45-2903	How'm I Doing, Hey Hey/Throw All Your Lovin' My Way	12
60	Saga SAG 45-2904	Little Old Fashioned You/Marylin	8
66	Decca F 12320	Waltzing To Jazz/Jo Jo (as Larry Page Orchestra)	5
66	Decca F 12368	Peyton Place Theme/Leanda's Theme (as Larry Page Orchestra)	5
68	Page One POF 068	Take Five/Michelle	5
68	Page One POF 096	Hey Jude/Those Were The Days (as Larry Page Orchestra)	5
60	Saga STP 1024	SINGS HIS PERSONAL CHOICE (EP)	10
65	Decca LK 4692	KINKY MUSIC (LP, as Larry Page Orchestra)	75
68	Page One POL(S) 002	EXECUTIVE SUITE (LP, as Larry Page Orchestra)	30
68	Page One POLS 004	FROM LARRY, WITH LOVE (LP)	12

MALLY PAGE
66	Pye 7N 17105	The Life And Soul Of The Party/You Can Be Wrong About Boys	6

PATTI PAGE

58	Mercury 7MT 184	I'll Remember Today/My, How The Time Goes	8
58	Mercury 7MT 200	Bring Us Together/Belonging To Someone (78 rpm = £6)	8
58	Mercury 7MT 206	These Worldly Wonders/Another Time, Another Place (78 rpm = £6)	8
58	Mercury 7MT 223	Left Right Out Of Your Heart/Longing To Hold You Again	10
58	Mercury AMT 1000	Fibbin'/You Will Find Your Love (In Paris) (78 rpm = £10)	8
59	Mercury AMT 1022	Trust In Me/Under The Sun Valley Moon (78 rpm = £15)	8
59	Mercury AMT 1038	The Walls Have Ears/My Promise	8
59	Mercury AMT 1054	My Mother's Eyes/With My Eyes Wide Open I'm Dreaming (78 rpm = £25)	8
60	Mercury AMT 1089	Promise Me Thomas/Two Thousand, Two Hundred And Twenty-Three Miles	8
60	Mercury AMT 1102	One Of Us (Will Weep Tonight)/What Will My Future Be	8
60	Mercury AMT 1112	I Wish I'd Never Been Born/I Need You	6
61	Mercury AMT 1160	Broken Heart And A Pillow Full Of Tears/Dark Moon	6
63	CBS AAG 136	Just A Simple Melody/Pretty Lonely Boy	6

EPs

56	Mercury MEP 9502	PATTI PAGE	20
59	Mercury ZEP 10006	PATTI PAGE ONE	20
59	Mercury ZEP 10017	PATTI PAGE TWO	20
59	Mercury ZEP 10032	PATTI PAGE THREE	20
59	Mercury ZEP 10045	PATTI PAGE FOUR	20
60	Mercury ZEP 10073	PATTI PAGE FIVE	20
61	Mercury ZEP 10092	THIS LADY IS NO TRAMP (also stereo [SEZ 19008], with Pete Rugolo All Stars)	15/20
61	Mercury ZEP 10114	MY KINDA LOVE (also stereo [SEZ 19020])	15/20

LPs

54	Mercury MG 25101	FOLK SONG FAVOURITES (10")	38
55	Mercury MG 25197	PATTI'S SONGS (10")	38
56	Mercury MPT 7510	CHRISTMAS WITH PATTI PAGE (10")	38
57	Mercury MPT 7531	I'M GETTING SENTIMENTAL OVER YOU (10")	38
57	Mercury MPT 7535	PATTI'S SONGS (10", reissue)	22
57	Emarcy EJL 1252	PATTI PAGE IN THE LAND OF HI-FI	18
57	Mercury MPL 6506	MANHATTAN TOWER	18
58	Mercury MPL 6521	YOU GO TO MY HEAD	18
58	Mercury MPL 6524	PAGE 1 — A COLLECTION OF HER MOST FAMOUS SONGS	18
59	Mercury MMC 14000	LET'S GET AWAY FROM IT ALL	18
59	Mercury MMC 14007	I'VE HEARD THAT SONG BEFORE	18
59	Mercury MMC 14013	I'LL REMEMBER APRIL	18
59	Mercury MMC 14017	INDISCRETION	18
59	Mercury CMS 18004	PATTI PAGE IN THE LAND OF HI-FI (stereo reissue)	18
60	Mercury MMC 14036	THREE LITTLE WORDS	18
61	Mercury MMC 14064	ROMANCE IN RHYTHM	18

(see also Pete Rugolo)

PATTI PAGE & REX ALLEN

54	Oriole CB 1253	Broken-Down Merry-Go-Round/I Want To Be A Cowboy's Sweetheart (78)	8

PAGE & PLANT

94	Fontana PRCDJ 1	Gallows Pole (CD, in special brown or red sleeve, promo only)	each 10
94	Fontana PPCD 2	Gallows Pole/City Don't Cry/The Rain Song (CD, pic. disc, part 1 of 2-CD set)	8
94	Fontana PPDD 2	Gallows Pole/Four Sticks/What Is And What Should Never Be (CD, picture disc, part 2 of 2-CD set)	10
95	Fontana PPCDJ 3	Kashmir (CD promo, withdrawn)	30
95	Fontana PPCDJ 4	The Battle Of Evermore (CD promo)	15
98	Mercury PPMHR 1	Most High (Radio Edit)/Most High (Album Version) (CD, 2-track radio promo)	8
98	Mercury MERJ 506	Shining In The Light (Radio Edit)/(Album Version) (CD, 2-track radio promo)	10
98	Mercury 558 324 2	Walking Into Clarksdale (CD, limited issue digipak)	15
98	Mercury ADV 1998	Walking Into Clarksdale (CD promo, card sleeve)	50
94	Fontana PP ID 1	NO QUARTER UNLEDDED (CD, radio-promo only, with 'question' booklet)	50
94	Fontana 526 3621	NO QUARTER UNLEDDED (LP)	15
98	Mercury ADV 982	TBA (CD, advance promo for WALKING INTO CLARKSDALE)	40
98	Mercury PPTIC 1	WALKING INTO CLARKSDALE AN INTERVIEW (CD radio promo)	40
98	Mercury 558 025 1	WALKING INTO CLARKSDALE (LP)	15

(see also Jimmy Page, Robert Plant)

PAGE BOYS (U.K.)

83	Whaam! WHAAM 10	You're My Kind Of Girl/In Love With You (p/s, 1,000 only)	20

(see also 1,000 Violins)

PAGEBOYS (U.S.)

65	London HLU 9948	When I Meet A Girl Like You/I Have Love	10

PAGE FIVE

66	Parlophone R 5426	Let Sleeping Dogs Lie/I Know All About Her	32

PAGE ONE & THE OBSERVERS

76	Carib Gems CGLP 004	OBSERVATION OF LIFE DUB (LP)	40

PAGE TEN

65	Decca F 12248	Boutique/Colour Talk	12

(see also Niney)

CARLOS PAIAO

81	EMI EMI 5174	Playback (English)/Playback (Portuguese)	7

PAICE, ASHTON & LORD

77	Polydor/Oyster 2391 269	MALICE IN WONDERLAND (LP, with inner sleeve)	15

(see also Deep Purple, Jon Lord, Ashton & Lord, Ashton Gardner & Dyke, Elf, Bernie Marsden)

HAL PAIGE & WHALERS

60	Melodisc MEL 1553	Going Back To My Home Town/After Hours Blues	52

JOEY PAIGE
65	Fontana TF 554	Cause I'm In Love With You/Yeah Yeah Yeah	20

ROSALIND PAIGE
55	London HL 8120	When The Saints Go Marching In/Nobody's Sweetheart Now (78 rpm = £6)	30
57	MGM MGM 937	Love, Oh Careless Love/That Funny Melody	10

PAINTBOX
70	Young Blood YB 1013	Get Ready For Love/Can I Get To Know You	10
71	Young Blood YB 1029	Get Ready For Love/Can I Get To Know You (reissue)	6

(see also Easybeats, Haffy's Whiskey Sour)

PAINTED SHIP
67	Mercury MF 988	Frustration/I Told Those Little White Lies	75+

PAISLEYS
83	Psycho PSYCHO 7	COSMIC MIND AT PLAY (LP, reissue)	20

PALADIN
71	Bronze ILPS 9150	PALADIN (LP)	22
72	Bronze ILPS 9190	CHARGE (LP, gatefold sleeve)	28

(see also Glass Menagerie, McGuinness Flint)

PALE FOUNTAINS
82	Operation Twilight OPT 09	(There's Always) Something On My Mind/Just A Girl (p/s)	30
82	Virgin VS 557	Thank You/Meadow Of Love (picture disc, stickered PVC sleeve)	8
82	Virgin VS 557-12	Thank You/Meadow Of Love/(There's Always) Something On My Mind (12", p/s)	25
83	Virgin VS 568	Palm Of My Hand/(Instrumental)/Love's A Beautiful Place (p/s)	10
83	Virgin VS 568-12	Palm Of My Hand/(Instrumental)/Love's A Beautiful Place (12", p/s)	25
85	Virgin VS 750	From Across The Kitchen Table/Bicycle Thieves//Thank You/Just A Girl (double pack)	12
84	Virgin V 2274	PACIFIC STREET (LP)	20
85	Virgin V 2333	FROM ACROSS THE KITCHEN TABLE (LP, with inner sleeve)	25

(see also Shack)

PALE SAINTS
88	Panic PANIC FIRST	Children Break/SAVLONS: ...And What's More/KERRY FIDDLES: Shiver Me Timbers (33rpm flexidisc, stickered card sleeve, some with postcard)	8
90	4AD CAD 0002	COMFORTS OF MADNESS (LP, with postcards)	15
92	4AD CAD 2004	IN RIBBONS (LP, with free 7" "A Thousand Stars Burst Open"/"A Revelation" [RIB 1])	12

TOM PALEY
69	Argo ZFB 3	SUE COW (LP)	12

PALEY BROTHERS
78	Sire SRE 4005	Come On Let's Go/Magic Power (p/s)	12
78	Sire 6078 613	Ecstacy/Rendezvous/Hide N' Seek/Come Out And Play (12", p/s)	12

(see also Ramones)

PALI GAP
82	Sinister SYN 001	Under The Sun/The Knives Are Out (p/s, with insert)	20

MORTY PALITZ & ACES
59	London HLJ 8778	The Grocer's Cha Cha Cha/Eso Es El Amor (This Is Love) (78 rpm = £10)	8

PALLAS
78	Sue-i-cide PAL/101	THE PALLAS EP (stamped plain die-cut sleeve)	50
82	Granite Wax GWS 1	Arrive Alive/Stranger (On The Edge Of Time) (two different p/s, some w/insert)	50/40

EARL PALMER & HIS TEN PIECE ROCKIN' BAND
58	Capitol CL 14859	Drum Village (Parts 1 & 2)	10
61	Liberty LBY 1008	DRUMSVILLE (LP)	20

EDDIE PALMER
57	Decca F 10873	The Sky/The Twilight Theme	8

JACK PALMER
50	London L 605	Sweet Jennie Lee/All My Baby's Got To Wear Is Minks (78)	6

RICK PALMER
59	London HLL 8900	You Threw A Heart/My Greatest Wish (unreleased)	

ROBERT PALMER
75	Island WIP 6250	Which Of Us Is The Fool/Get Outside (some in p/s)	7/5
76	Island WIP 6272	Gimme An Inch Girl/Pressure Drop	5
76	Island WIP 6345	Man Smart, Woman Smarter/From a Whisper To A Scream	5
78	Island WIP 6425	Every Kinda People/Keep In Touch	5

(see also Alan Bown [Set], Dada, Vinegar Joe)

ROY PALMER & STATE STREET RAMBLERS
54	London AL 3518	A CHICAGO SKIFFLE SESSION (10" LP)	30

PALMETTO KINGS
60	Starlite ST45 021	Ten Rum Bottles/Home Cookin' Mama	10

PALM SKIN PRODUCTIONS
93	Mo' Wax MW 003	Getting Out Of Hell/Like Brothers/A Little Skin (12", die-cut sleeve)	8
93	Mo' Wax MW 013	In A Silent Way/Sunlight On The Garden (12", p/s)	18
93	Mo' Wax MW 009	TIME AND SPACE EP: I/Just Trying To Live/Moon Base Alpha/Spock With A Beard (12")	25

PAMA DICE
69	Jackpot JP 715	Bongo Man/Bear De Pussy	18
69	Jackpot JP 716	Sin, Sun And Sex/Reggae Pop-Corn	15
70	Reggae REG 3001	Brixton Fight/OPENING: Tea House	25

(see also Winston Groovy, King Horror, Ray Martell)

PAN
93	Big Cat ABB 49	HANGIN' OUT FOR JUNE (LP)	15

PANACHE
83	Mach 1 MAGIC 004	I Wanna Dance/Crazy For Your Love (with Ray Dorset)	7

(see also Ray Dorset)

PANAMA FRANCIS BLUES BAND
64	Stateside SL 10070	TOUGH TALK!! (LP)	28

PANAMA LIMITED (JUG BAND)
69	Harvest HAR 5010	Lady Of Shalott/Future Blues	30
70	Harvest HAR 5022	Round And Round/Rotting Wooden In A White Collar's Grave	30
69	Harvest SHVL 753	PANAMA LIMITED JUG BAND (LP)	80
70	Harvest SHVL 779	INDIAN SUMMER (LP, as Panama Limited)	140

GENE PANCHO
68	Giant GN 21	I Like Sweet Music/Seven Days (with Sandy & Superboys)	8

(see also Gene Rondo)

PANDEMONIUM
67	CBS 202462	Season Of The Witch/Today I'm Happy	45
67	CBS 2664	No Presents For Me/The Sun Shines From His Eyes	300
68	CBS 3451	Chocolate Buster Dam/Fly With Me Forever	50

PANDIT PRANNATH
69	Transatlantic TRA 193	EARTH GROOVE (LP)	20

PANHANDLE
72	Decca SKL 5105	PANHANDLE (LP)	25

(see also Chris Spedding)

PANIK
77	Rainy City SHOT 1	IT WON'T SELL (EP)	15

BILL PANNELL
50	London L 623	A Heart Of Stone/I Miss My Miss From Mississippi (78)	10

GARY PANTER & JAY COTTON
90	Blast First FU 7	ONE HELL SOUNDWICH (LP, picture disc)	20

JAN PANTER
65	Oriole CB 1938	My Two Arms Minus You Equals Tears/Does My Heart Show	25
65	CBS 201810	Let It Be Now/Stand By And Cry	22
66	Pye 7N 17097	Scratch My Back/Put Yourself In My Place	150
69	President PT 241	Si Si Senor/Stella In Lights	10

PANTHER BURNS
81	Rough Trade RT 077	Train Kept A Rollin'/Red Headed Woman (p/s)	10

(see also Tav Falco's Panther Burns, Alex Chilton)

ROY PANTON
63	Blue Beat BB 182	Mighty Ruler/Run Old Man	18
64	Blue Beat BB 219	Good From The Bad/Hell Gate	20
64	Rio R 19	Cherita/Seek And You Shall Find	20
64	Rio R 33	You Don't Know Me/KING EDWARD'S ALLSTARS: Doctor No	22
64	Island WI 137	Goodbye Peggy Darling (actually "Goodbye Peggy" by Stranger Cole)/	
		BABA BROOKS: Portrait Of My Love	25
70	Harry J HJ 6624	The Same Old Life/JAYBOYS: Life (Version)	8

(see also Roy & Annette, Roy & Millie, Roy & Paulette, Roy & Yvonne, Roy & Duke Allstars, Roy & Patsy, Derrick Harriot, Leon & Owen, Charmers)

JOHN PANTRY
72	Philips 6006 250	Net Of Concern/Words	10
72	Philips 6308 129	JOHN PANTRY (LP)	20
73	Philips 6308 138	LONG WHITE TRAIL (LP)	18
80s	Tenth Planet TP 040	THE UPSIDE DOWN WORLD OF JOHN PANTRY	
		(LP, 1,000 only)	40

(see also Factory, Peter & Wolves, Norman Conquest, Sounds Around, Bunch)

PAPA DOO RUN RUN
75	RCA RCA 2620	Be True To Your School/Disney Girls	12

PAPA MICHIGAN & GENERAL SMILEY
81	Tuff Gong IPR 2035	One Love Jame Down/FREDDIE McGREGOR: Joggin' (12")	10

PAPA TULLO
82	Negus Roots NERLP 004	TULLO AT HOME (LP)	40

NIKKI PAPAS
59	Parlophone R 4590	49 State Rock/Try Again	45
60	Parlophone R 4652	By The River/Don't Leave Me Alone	18

PAPER BLITZ TISSUE
67	RCA Victor RCA 1652	Boy Meets Girl/Grey Man	250

(see also Cupid's Inspiration)

PAPER BUBBLE
70	Deram DML/SML 1059	SCENERY (LP)	45

PAPER DOLLS
68	Pye 7N 17456	Something Here In My Heart/All The Time In The World	7
68	Pye 7N 17547	My Life Is In Your Hands/There's Nobody I'd Sooner Love	8
68	Pye 7N 17655	Someday/Any Old Time You're Lonely And Sad	7
70	RCA RCA 1919	My Boyfriend's Back/Mister Good Time Friday	7
70	RCA RCA 2007	Remember December/Same Old Story	7
68	Pye N(S)PL 18226	PAPER DOLLS HOUSE (LP)	40

PAPERHOUSE
91   Mystic Stones RUNE LP 11   SPONGY COMESTIBLES (LP) 20

PAPERTOYS
90   Armada ARMAP 003   Cold Surrender (Winston Club Mix)/Cold Surrender (D-Day 7" Radio Mix)/
Cold Surrender (Outland Mix) (12", numbered p/s, 500 only) 8
(see also Gary Numan)

PARADE
67   A&M AMS 701   Sunshine Girl/This Old Melody 15
67   A&M AMS 720   Radio Song/I Can See Love 12

VANESSA PARADIS
87   Polydor POSPG 902   Joe Le Taxi/Varvara Pavlovna (poster p/s) 6
88   Polydor 080 466-2   Joe Le Taxi/Manolo Manolete/Joe Le Taxi (Version Espagnole)/
Joe Le Taxi (Version Longue)/Joe Le Taxi (Video) (CD Video) 15
88   Polydor 080 468-2   Marilyn And John (Version Français) (4.40)/Soldat/Marilyn And John
(Version Anglais)/Marilyn And John (Version Français) (5.44)/
Marilyn And John (Version Français) (Video) (CD Video) 15
88   Polydor 081 312-2   Coup Coup (Remix)/Maxou/Marilyn And John/Coup Coup (Remix) (Video)
(CD Video) 15

JOE PARADIS
59   Top Rank JAR 195   From The French/CLAUDE DAUPHON: From The French 6

PARADONS
60   Top Rank JAR 514   Diamonds And Pearls/I Want Love 150

PARADOX
68   Polydor 56275   The Wednesday Theme/Ring The Changes 150
(see also David Walker)

PARADOX
90   Ronin RDP10   Revolutionary/Dedicated (12") 8

PARAFFIN JACK FLASH LTD
68   Pye NSPL 18252   MOVERS AND GROOVERS (LP) 15

PARAGONS
66   Doctor Bird DB 1060   Happy-Go-Lucky Girl/Love Brings Pain 35
67   Island WI 3045   On The Beach/CAROL & TOMMY McCOOK: Sweet And Gentle
(B-side actually by Tommy McCook & Supersonics) 30
67   Island WI 3067   Talking Love/If I Were You 30
67   Treasure Isle TI 7009   Only A Smile/The Tide Is High 25
67   Treasure Isle TI 7011   Mercy, Mercy, Mercy/Riding On A High And Windy Day 25
67   Treasure Isle TI 7013   The Same Song/TOMMY McCOOK & SUPERSONICS: Soul Serenade 25
67   Treasure Isle TI 7025   Wear You To The Ball/You Mean The World To Me 30
68   Treasure Isle TI 7034   Silver Bird/My Best Girl 25
68   Island WI 3138   Memories By The Score/The Number One For Me 30
69   Studio One SO 2081   Have You Ever Been In Love/Change Your Style 30
69   Duke DU 7   Left With A Broken Heart/I've Got To Get Away 18
67   Doctor Bird DLM 5010   ON THE BEACH (LP) 160
(see also Rosalyn Sweat & Paragons, John Holt, Lester Sterling)

PARALEX
80   Reddingtons R.R. DAN 4   White Lightning/Travelling Man/Black Widow, (12", p/s, green vinyl) 55

PARAMETER
70   Deroy   GALACTIC RAMBLE (LP) 300

NORRIE PARAMOR & HIS ORCHESTRA
53   Columbia SCM 5023   Cotton Reel/Pink Plank Plonk 7
53   Columbia SCM 5034   Fandango/Penny Whistle 7
53   Columbia SCM 5051   April In Portugal/The Song From Moulin Rouge (Where Is Your Heart) 7
53   Columbia SCM 5068   Man Between/Callaghan's Monkey 7
54   Columbia SCM 5126   Johnny Guitar/Paramambo 7
54   Columbia SCM 5136   High And Mighty/Rip Van Twinkle 7
56   Columbia SCM 5251   Theme From The Threepenny Opera/Poor John 7
60   Columbia DB 4419   Summer Place (Theme)/Half Pint 7
62   Columbia DB 4789   Z Cars (Theme)/Ballad Of A Soldier (Theme) 7
65   Columbia DB 7446   Dance Of The Warriors/Dragon Dance 6
70   Polydor 56375   Randall And Hopkirk (Deceased)/A Summer Palace 65
57   Columbia SEG 7720   A KING IN NEW YORK (EP) 10
55   Columbia 33S 1076   JUST WE TWO (10" LP) 15
66   Columbia SX 6012   SHADOWS IN LATIN (LP, also stereo [Studio Two TWO 107]) 12
67   Studio Two TWO 172   PLAYS THE HITS OF CLIFF RICHARD (LP) 20
(see also Harry Gold)

PARAMOUNT ALL-STARS
50   Tempo R 20   Hometown Skiffle (Parts 1 & 2) (78) 25
(see also Blind Blake, Will Ezell, Georgia Tom, Alex Hill, Papa Charlie Jackson, Blind Lemon Jefferson, Charlie Spand)

PARAMOUNTS
63   Parlophone R 5093   Poison Ivy/I Feel Good All Over 15
64   Parlophone R 5107   Little Bitty Pretty One/A Certain Girl 20
64   Parlophone R 5155   I'm The One Who Loves You/It Won't Be Long 20
64   Parlophone R 5187   Bad Blood/Do I 20
65   Parlophone R 5272   Blue Ribbons/Cuttin' In 20
65   Parlophone R 5351   You Never Had It So Good/Don't Ya Like My Love 30
64   Parlophone GEP 8908   THE PARAMOUNTS (EP) 235
(see also Procol Harum)

PARANOIA
84	Rot ASS 8	Dead Man's Dreams/Man In Black (p/s)	5
84	Rot ASS 11	SHATTERED GLASS (LP)	15

PARANOIDS
79	Hurricane FIRE 8	Stupid Guy/Road To Ruin (p/s)	10
80	Hurricane FIRE 14	The Love Job/Theme From Gravity's Rainbow (p/s)	10

PARCEL OF ROGUES
(see under Villagers)

PARCHMENT
72	Pye 7N 45178	Light Up The Fire/Let There Be Light (p/s)	5
72	Pye NSPL 18388	LIGHT UP THE FIRE (LP, with poster insert)	12
73	Pye NSPL 18409	HOLLYWOOD SUNSET (LP)	12
75	Myrrh MYR 1028	SHAMBLEJAM (LP)	30
77	Pilgrim GRAPEVINE 106	REHEARSAL FOR A REUNION (LP)	12

WALTER PARDON
75	Leader LED 2063	A PROPER SORT (LP)	20

TONY PARENTI
57	London EZ V 19022	RAGTIME (EP)	10
57	London LTZU 15072	RAGTIME (LP)	15

PAULA PARFITT
69	Beacon BEA 135	I'm Gonna Give You Back Your Ring/Love Is Wonderful (Beware of bootlegs! – originals have anti-slip grips around the label)	125

TINY PARHAM
50s	Audubon AAC	TINY PARHAM (10" LP)	25

PARIS
72	Avalanche AV 67312	I've Lost The Way/Long Time	8
76	Thunderbird THE 114	Circles/Liar	5
84	Bluebird BRT 9	I Choose You/Punkin' Funkin' (12", p/s)	8

BOBBY PARIS
68	Polydor 56747	Per So Nal Ly/Tragedy	80
69	Polydor 56762	Let The Sun Shine In/You	22
77	London HLU 10553	Night Owl/YVONNE BAKER: You Didn't Say A Word	15

MICA PARIS
91	4th & Broadway 12BRWDJ207	A STAND FOR LOVE EP (12" promo, p/s. Mispress, plays Prince's vocal version of 'A Stand For Love')	100

PRISCILLA PARIS
74	Rak RAK 184	I Love How You Love Me/Over You	10
	(see also Paris Sisters)		

PARIS SISTERS
61	Top Rank JAR 588	I Love How You Love Me/I'll Be Crying Tomorrow	100
64	MGM MGM 1240	Dream Lover/Lonely Girl	50
	(see also Date With Soul, Priscilla Paris)		

JOHN PARISH & POLLY JEAN HARVEY
96	Island IS 648	That Was My Veil/Losing Ground (p/s)	12
96	Island CIDX 8051	DANCE HALL AT LOUSE POINT (CD, 5,000 in digipak with insert)	20
	(see also P.J. Harvey)		

PARISH HALL
70	Liberty LBS 83374	PARISH HALL (LP)	30

ALAN PARKER
70	Aristocrat AR 1022	GUITAR FANTASY (LP)	18
73	MCA MUPS 471	BAND OF ANGELS (LP)	12
	(see also Hungry Wolf, Ugly Custard)		

BENNY PARKER & DYNAMICS
64	Decca F 11944	Boys And Girls/You'll Be On Your Way	45

BILLY PARKER
63	Decca F 11668	Thanks A Lot/Out Of Your Heart	7

BOBBY PARKER
61	London HLU 9393	Watch Your Step/Steal Your Heart Away	50
64	Sue WI 340	Watch Your Step/Steal Your Heart Away (reissue)	40
69	Blue Horizon 57-3151	It's Hard But It's Fair/I Couldn't Quit My Baby	40

CHARLIE PARKER
78s
50	Savoy 928	Buzzy/Donna Lee (78)	10
50	Savoy 939	Ah-Leu-Cha/Constellation (78, as Charlie Parker's All Stars)	6
50	Esquire 10-079	Relaxing At Camarillo/Crazeology – 3 Ways Of Playing a Chorus (78)	6
51	Esquire 10-108	Quasimodo/Dewey Square (78, with Miles Davis)	6
51	Esquire 10-139	Klactoveedsedstene/Charlie's Wig (78, with Miles Davis)	6
51	Savoy 977	Chasing The Bird (as Charlie Parker's All Stars)/MILES DAVIS ALL STARS: Little Willie Leaps (78)	6
52	Vogue V 2132	How Deep Is The Ocean/Scmourphology (78)	6
55	Columbia LB 10006	K.C. Blues/She Rote (78)	6
56	Columbia LB 10034	Laura/Dancing In The Dark (78)	6
57	Columbia LB 10051	Laird Baird/I Hear Music (78)	6

EPs
55	Vogue EPV 1011	CHARLIE PARKER PLAYS	22
55	Columbia Clef SEB 10002	THE MAGNIFICENT CHARLIE PARKER NO. 1	10

Charlie PARKER

56	Columbia Clef SEB 10026	NOW'S THE TIME	12
56	Columbia Clef SEB 10032	PLAYS SOUTH OF THE BORDER	10
56	Columbia Clef SEB 10038	THE MAGNIFICENT CHARLIE PARKER NO. 2 (as Charlie Parker Group)	10
57	Columbia Clef SEB 10053	THE MAGNIFICENT CHARLIE PARKER NO. 3	8
50s	Esquire EP 57	CHARLIE PARKER QUINTET	20
60	Vogue EPV 1264	ALL STARNTET/SEXTET	18
60	HMV 7EG 8626	CHARLIE PARKER BIG BAND	10
64	Realm REP 4008	PARKER'S MOOD (as Charlie Parker All Stars)	8

LPs

52	Vogue LDE 004	CHARLIE PARKER VOLUME ONE (10")	60
53	Vogue LDE 016	CHARLIE PARKER VOLUME TWO (10")	60
58	Vogue LAE 12002	CHARLIE PARKER MEMORIAL ALBUM (gatefold sleeve w/ 2 inserts)	15
55	Melodisc MLP 12-105	BIRD AT ST. NICK'S	30
55	Columbia Clef 33CX 10004	CHARLIE PARKER BIG BAND	55
56	Columbia Clef 33C 9026	BIRD AND DIZ (10", with Dizzy Gillespie)	55
57	Columbia Clef 33CX 10081	APRIL IN PARIS (as Charlie Parker With Strings)	35
57	Columbia Clef 33CX 10090	CHARLIE PARKER PLAYS COLE PORTER	25
58	Columbia Clef 33CX 10117	CHARLIE PARKER JAZZ PERENNIAL	15
58	London Jazz LTZ-C 15104	THE IMMORTAL CHARLIE PARKER VOL. 1	15
58	London Jazz LTZ-C 15105	THE IMMORTAL CHARLIE PARKER VOL. 2	15
58	London Jazz LTZ-C 15106	THE IMMORTAL CHARLIE PARKER VOL. 3	15
58	London Jazz LTZ-C 15107	THE IMMORTAL CHARLIE PARKER VOL. 4	15
58	Mercury MPL 12-105	BIRD AT NICK'S	15
60	Collector JGN 1002	CHARLIE PARKER IN SWEDEN	50
61	HMV CLP 1538	THE ESSENTIAL CHARLIE PARKER	18
62	Verve VLP 9105	"BIRD" SYMBOLS (with insert for Egmont AJS 3)	18
62	Storyville SLP 27	IN SWEDEN 1950	18
62	Esquire 32-157	'BIRD' IS FREE	22

(see also Dizzy Gillespie & Charlie Parker, Sir Charles Thompson)

DAVID PARKER
71	Polydor 2460 101	DAVID PARKER (LP)	40

(see also Andwella's Dream)

DEAN PARKER & REDCAPS
62	Decca F 11555	Stormy Evening/Blue Eyes And Golden Hair	45

DYON PARKER
69	Marble Arch MAL 787	OUT ON THE HIGHWAY (LP)	20

EDDIE PARKER
55	Columbia SCM 5211	Far Away From Everybody/Bella Notte	10
56	Columbia DB 3804	Love Me As Though There Were No Tomorrow/Rich In Love	10

EDDIE PARKER (U.S.)
79	Grapevine GRP 119	Love You Baby (Parts 1 & 2) (some in p/s) (DJ copy = £20)	15/10

EULA PARKER
58	Oriole CB 1411	Silhouettes/Hedgehopper (78 rpm = £12)	22

(see also Frank Weir)

EVAN PARKER
75	Incus INCUS 19	SAXOPHONE SOLOS (LP)	40
78	Incus INCUS 27	MONOCEROS (LP)	30
80	Incus INCUS 39	SIX OF ONE (LP)	30
86	Incus INCUS 49	THE SNAKE DECIDES (LP)	50
89	Cadillac (no cat no)	COLLECTED SOLOS (4 x LP and cassette hand numbered to 200)	60

EVAN PARKER, DEREK BAILEY, HAN BENNINK
70s	Incus INCUS 1	THE TOPOGRAPHY OF THE LUNGS (LP)	50

EVAN PARKER, BARRY GUY & PAUL LYTTON
83	Incus INCUS 42	TRACKS (LP)	40

EVAN PARKER & GEORGE LEWIS
80	Incus INCUS 35	FROM SAXOPHONE & TROMBONE (LP)	40

EVAN PARKER, GEORGE LEWIS, BARRY GUY & PAUL LYTTON
83	Incus INCUS 45	HOOK, DRIFT & SHUFFLE (LP)	50

EVAN PARKER & PAUL LYTTON
72	Incus INCUS 5	COLLECTIVE CALLS (URBAN) (TWO MICROPHONES) (LP)	40
75	Incus INCUS 14	AT THE UNITY THEATRE (LP)	40

(see also Derek Bailey & Evan Parker, Derek Bailey Evan Parker & Han Bennink)

FESS PARKER
57	Oriole CB 1378	Wringle Wrangle/Ballad Of John Colter	15

JIMMY PARKER
62	Top Rank JAR 608	We Gonna/No Word From Betty	18

(LITTLE) JUNIOR PARKER
61	Vogue V 9179	Stand By Me/I'll Forget About You (as Little Junior Parker)	30
62	Vogue V 9193	Mary Jo/Annie Get Your Yo-Yo (as Little Junior Parker)	30
66	Vocalion VP 9256	These Kind Of Blues (Parts 1 & 2) (DJ copy = £60)	40
66	Vocalion VP 9275	Goodbye Little Girl/Walking The Floor Over You	30
67	Mercury SMCL 20097	LIKE IT IS (LP)	50
72	Groove Merchant GM 502	BLUE SHADOWS FALLING (LP)	15
73	Groove Merchant GM 2205	GOOD THINGS DON'T HAPPEN EVERY DAY (LP, with Jimmy McGriff)	15
73	Vogue LDM 30163	MEMORIAL (LP)	15
73	People PLEO 4	YOU DON'T HAVE TO BE BLACK TO LOVE THE BLUES (LP)	20

(see also Howlin' Wolf, Bobby Bland)

KEN PARKER

67	Island WI 3082	How Could I/SONNY BURKE: Choo Choo Train	32
67	Studio One SO 2001	See Them A-Come/MR FOUNDATION: Have A Good Time	32
68	Island WI 3096	Down Low/Sad Mood	32
68	Island WI 3105	Lonely Man/ERROL DUNKLEY: I Am Going Home	32
68	Giant GN 34	Change Is Gonna Come/VAL BENNETT: Jumping With Val	50
69	Bamboo BAM 1	My Whole World Is Falling Down/The Chokin' Kind	15
69	Amalgamated AMG 847	It's Alright/COBBS: One One	20
69	Amalgamated AMG 853	Only Yesterday/COBBS: Joe Gibbs Mood	20
70	Duke DU 79	I Can't Hide/TOMMY McCOOK: Kansas City	10
70	Unity UN 553	When You Were Mine/CLAREDONIANS: The Angels (song actually "The Angels Listened In")	8
71	Duke Reid DR 2504	Sugar Pantie (as Ken Parker & Tommy McCook; actually by Andy Capp)/ TOMMY McCOOK: All Afire	10
71	Duke Reid DR 2521	Jimmy Brown/Version	6
71	Big BG 332	Ain't Misbehaving/Genuine Love	6
72	Jackpot JP 805	Guilty/AGGROVATORS: Guilty (Version)	6
72	Pama PM 844	Shake It Loose/TOMMY McCOOK: Shake It Loose (Version) (actually titled "Help Me Make It Through The Night")	6
72	Treasure Isle TI 7073	Help Me Make It Through The Night/TOMMY McCOOK & ALLSTARS (Version)	8
73	Dragon DRA 1003	Will The Circle Be Unbroken/DYNAMITES: Instrumental	6
73	Dragon DRA 1015	Say Wonderful Things/It's True	6
74	Attack ATT 8063	Kiss An Angel/TOMMY McCOOK: Inez	8
74	Attack ATT 8073	Count Your Blessings/Count Your Blessings (Version)	6
74	Trojan TRLS 80	JIMMY BROWN (LP)	18

(see also Lyrics, Scotty)

LEWIS PARKER

96	Bite It! BITE11	Rise/Visions Of Splendour/Sea Freestyle (12")	34
97	White LEWIS1	Wonderwall (7")	90
98	Melankolic SADTDJ3	Shadows Of Autumn/101 Pianos (12")	28
95	White JED1	B BOY ANTICS (EP)	50
96	Bite It! BITEDJ10	B BOY ANTICS (EP)	30
00	M'lic LEWISTDJ1LC03098	THE OPTIONS (EP)	28
01	White SADTDJ13	It's All Happening Now/Schemes/What The Ancients Say (remixes) (EP)	70
98	Melankolic SADT4	MASQUERADES AND SILHOUETTES (LP)	30

RAYMOND PARKER

66	Sue WI 4024	Ring Around The Roses/She's Coming Home	30

ROBERT PARKER

66	Island WI 286	Barefootin'/Let's Go Baby	18
66	Island WI 3008	Happy Feet/The Scratch	22
74	Island USA 991	Get Ta Steppin'/Get Right On Down	8
74	Contemporaries CS 9010	Barefootin'/I Caught You In A Lie	20
66	Island ILP 942	BAREFOOTIN' (LP)	100

(see also Huey 'Piano' Smith & Clowns)

SONNY PARKER

56	Vogue V 2392	My Soul's On Fire/Disgusted Blues (78 rpm = £110)	450

(see also Lionel Hampton)

WILLIE PARKER

67	President PT 171	You Got Your Finger In My Eye/I Love The Life I Live	15

WINFIELD PARKER

72	Mojo 2093 019	Stop Her On Sight/I'm On My Way	12

JOHNNY PARKER WASHBOARD BAND

55	Pye Nixa NJE 1000	JOHNNY PARKER WASHBOARD BAND (EP)	8
56	Metronome MEP 1092	BARRELHOUSE (EP)	8
57	Storyville SEP 366	JOHNNY PARKER (EP, solo)	8

PARKING LOT

69	Parlophone R 5779	Carpet Man/World Spinning Sadly	35

JIMMY PARKINSON

56	Columbia SCM 5236	The Great Pretender/Hand In Hand	30
56	Columbia SCM 5267	Walk Hand In Hand/Cry Baby	28
56	Columbia DB 3808	Gina/A Lover's Quarrel	15
56	Columbia DB 3833	In The Middle Of The House/You To Me	20
57	Columbia DB 3876	But You/Together (You And I)	12
57	Columbia DB 3912	Round And Round/Whatever Lola Wants (Lola Gets)	12
57	Columbia 33S 1109	SOLO (10" LP)	55

BERNICE PARKS

55	Coral Q 72056	Lovin' Machine/Only Love Me	15

LLOYD PARKS

70	Harry J. HJ 6603	Feel A Little Better/I'll Be Your Man	8
72	Randy's RAN 524	Stars/Stars (Version)	12
74	Fab FAB 273	Schooldays/(Version)	7

(see also L. Sparks)

SIMON PARK

74	EMI EMC 3059	SOMETHING IN THE AIR (LP)	20
75	EMI SM-11581	VENUS FLY TRAP (LP)	15

SONNY PARKS

63	Warner Bros WB 100	New Boy In Town/Us Kids Have Got To Make Up Our Minds	7

Van Dyke PARKS

MINT VALUE £

VAN DYKE PARKS
66	MGM MGM 1301	Number Nine/Do What You Wanta	12
69	Warner Bros W(S) 1727	SONG CYCLE (LP)	25

PARLET
79	Casablanca CAL 2052	INVASION OF THE BOOTY SNATCHERS (LP)	15

(see also Parliament)

PARLIAMENT
71	Invictus INV 513	The Silent Boatman/Livin' The Life	20
72	Invictus INV 522	Come In Out Of The Rain/Little Ole Country Boy	18
75	Casablanca CBX 505	Up On The Down Stroke/Presence Of A Brain	8
76	Casablanca CBX 518	Tear The Roof Off The Sucker (Give Up The Funk)/P. Funk	8
77	Casablanca CAN 103	Tear The Roof Off The Sucker (Give Up The Funk)/Dr. Funkenstein/P. Funk	8
78	Casablanca CAN 115	Bop Gun/I've Been Watching You	7
78	Casablanca CANL 115	Bop Gun/I've Been Watching You (12")	8
78	Casablanca CAN 136	Aqua Boogie/Water Sign	5
79	Casablanca CAN 154	Deep/Flashlight	5
79	Casablanca CANL 154	Deep/Flashlight (12")	8
80	Casablanca CANL 188	Theme From Black Hole/Big Bang Theory (12")	8
81	Casablanca CANL 223	Agony Of De Feet/The Freeze (12")	7
71	Invictus SVT 1004	OSMIUM (LP)	75
74	Casablanca NBLP 7002	UP ON THE DOWN STROKE (LP)	20
75	Casablanca NBLP 7014	CHOCOLATE CITY (LP)	15
76	Casablanca CBC 4009	MOTHERSHIP CONNECTION (LP)	15
76	Casablanca CAL 2003	THE CLONES OF DR. FUNKENSTEIN (LP)	12
77	Casablanca CALD 5002	PARLIAMENT LIVE — P. FUNK EARTH TOUR (2-LP, with poster & transfer)	15
78	Casablanca CALH 2021	FUNKENTELECHY VS. THE PLACEBO SYNDROME (LP, with poster)	12
79	Casablanca CALN 2044	MOTOR BOOTY AFFAIR (LP, picture disc)	12

(see also Parliaments, Funkadelic, Parlet, Brides Of Funkenstein, Bootsy's Rubber Band, P-Funk Allstars)

PARLIAMENTS
67	Track 604 013	I Wanna Testify/I Can Feel The Ice Melting	30
69	Track 604 032	I Wanna Testify/I Can Feel The Ice Melting (reissue)	20

(see also Parliament, Funkadelic)

PARLOPHONE POPS ORCHESTRA
56	Parlophone R 4250	Giddy Up A Ding Dong/(We're Gonna) Rock Around The Clock	12

(see also Ron Goodwin)

PARLOUR BAND
72	Deram SDL 10	IS A FRIEND? (LP)	150

PARLOUR TALK
97	White (Acid Jazz) JAZZID152	Colouring/Super Air Conditioned (12")	22
99	Acid Jazz AJX111T	Vacation/Old, New And Blue (12")	8

CHRIS PARMENTER ORCHESTRA
66	Polydor 56107	Cul De Sac/Donkey	25

JACK PARNELL (ORCHESTRA)
53	Parlophone MSP 6009	Waltzing The Blues/Catherine Wheel (as Jack Parnell Band)	10
53	Parlophone MSP 6031	Night Train/Hawk Talks (as Jack Parnell & His Music Makers)	10
53	Parlophone MSP 6046	Cotton Tail/April In Paris	10
53	Parlophone MSP 6054	Dragnet/Fuller Bounce (as Jack Parnell & His Music Makers)	12
54	Parlophone MSP 6066	Route 66/The Creep	12
54	Parlophone MSP 6078	Skin Deep/Devil's Eyes (B-side with Dennis Hale)	20
54	Parlophone MSP 6094	Knock Out/Blowin' Wild (B-side with Dennis Hale)	12
54	Parlophone MSP 6102	The Bandit (with Dennis Hale)/Annie's Blues (with Annie Ross)	15
54	Parlophone MSP 6138	Sky Blue Shirt And Rainbow Tie/Trip To Mars	12
59	HMV POP 630	Kansas City/The Golden Stalker	12
55	Parlophone GEP 8532	JACK PARNELL AND HIS ORCHESTRA (EP)	10
55	Parlophone GEP 8564	PARNELL ON PARADE (EP)	10
52	Decca LF 1065	THE JACK PARNELL QUARTET (10" LP)	22
58	Parlophone PMD 1053	TRIP TO MARS (10" LP)	60

(see also Dennis Hale)

CATHERINE PARR
65	Decca F 12210	You Belong To Me/He's My Guy	10

DEAN PARRISH
66	Stateside SS 531	Tell Her/Fall On Me (DJ copy = £100)	60
66	Stateside SS 550	Turn On Your Lovelight/Determination (DJ copy = £150)	100
67	Stateside SS 580	Skate (Parts 1 & 2) (DJ copy = £100)	50
75	UK USA 2	I'm On My Way/Watch Out (DJ copy = £20)	10

PARRISH & GURVITZ
71	Regal Zono. SRZA 8506	PARRISH & GURVITZ (LP)	25

(see also Baker Gurvitz Army, Three Man Army, Frampton's Camel)

GAYLORD PARRY
67	CBS 2685	I'm On The Way Up/I'm Coming Home	15

SAM PARRY
73	Argo ZDA 155	IF SADNESS COULD SING (LP)	140

ALAN PARSONS PROJECT
76	Charisma CB 293	(The System Of) Doctor Tarr And Professor Fether/A Dream Within A Dream	5
76	Charisma CB 298	The One In Paradise/The Cask Of Amontillado	5
84	Arista ARISD 553	Don't Answer Me/You Don't Believe (shaped picture disc)	5

BILL PARSONS & HIS ORCHESTRA
59	London HL 8798	The All American Boy/Rubber Dolly (78 rpm = £40)	20

(see also Bobby Bare)

GENE PARSONS
74	Warner Bros K 46257	KINDLING (LP)	18

(see also Byrds, Flying Burrito Brothers)

GRAM PARSONS
73	Reprise K 14245	The New Soft Shoe/She	6
73	Reprise K 44228	GP (LP, gatefold sleeve)	25
74	Reprise K 54018	GRIEVOUS ANGEL (LP, with Emmylou Harris)	25
76	A&M AMLH 65478	SLEEPLESS NIGHTS (LP, with Flying Burrito Brothers & Emmylou Harris)	20
82	Sundown SDLP 003	GRAM PARSONS AND THE FALLEN ANGELS (LP, featuring Emmylou Harris)	15

(see also Byrds, Flying Burrito Brothers)

PARTICULAR PEOPLE
68	Big T BIG 105	Boys Cry/What's The Matter With Juliet	6

PARTISANS
63	E.R.S. EP 63:33	THE PARTISANS (EP, private pressing)	6

PARTISANS
82	No Future OI 2	Police Story/Killing Machine (p/s, with lyric insert)	12
82	No Future OI 12	17 Years Of Hell/The Power And The Greed/Bastards In Blue (p/s)	10
83	Cloak & Dagger PART 1	Blind Ambition/Come Clean (p/s)	12
83	No Future PUNK 4	PARTISANS (LP)	18
84	Cloak & Dagger PARTLP 1	THE TIME WAS RIGHT (LP)	30

PARTISANS
88	Hotwire HWS 863	Open Your Eyes/Partisan (p/s)	8

(see also Blades)

PARTNERS IN CRIME
84	Epic A 4803	Hold On/She's Got Eyes For You (p/s)	6
84	Epic TX 4803	Hold On (Extended)/She's Got Eyes For You (12", p/s)	8
85	Epic A 5040	Miracles/What You Gonna Do? (p/s)	6
85	Epic TX 5040	Miracles (Extended)/What You Gonna Do? (12", p/s)	8
85	Epic A 6170	Hollywood Dreams/She's Got Eyes For You (p/s)	7
85	Epic TX 6170	Hollywood Dreams (Extended)/She's Got Eyes For You (12", p/s)	10
85	Epic EPC 26356	ORGANISED CRIME (LP)	12

(see also Status Quo)

DON PARTRIDGE
69	Columbia DB 8538	Breakfast On Pluto/Stealin'	5
70	Columbia DB 8723	We're All Happy Together/Following Your Fancy	5
60s	CFP CFP 001/002	SINGING SOHO STYLE (EP)	18
68	Columbia S(C)X 6280	DON PARTRIDGE (LP)	15

(see also Accolades)

MR. PARTRIDGE
80	Virgin V 2145	TAKEAWAY — THE LURE OF THE SALVAGE (LP)	12

(see also XTC, Three Wise Men, Dukes Of Stratosphere, Colonel)

PARTRIDGE FAMILY
71	Bell BELL 1150	Doesn't Somebody Want To Be Wanted/You Are Always On My Mind	5
72	Bell MABEL 1	Breaking Up Is Hard To Do/I Think I Love You/I'll Meet You Halfway (p/s, maxi-single)	5

(see also David Cassidy)

PARTY BOYS
87	Epic 651230 0	He's Gonna Step On You Again/She's A Mystery (shaped picture disc)	12

(see also Status Quo)

PASADENA ROOF ORCHESTRA
78	CBS CBS 12-637	Pennies From Heaven/Back In Your Own Back Yard/Pennies From Heaven (p/s, last track plays at 78 rpm)	15

JEAN CLAUDE PASCAL
61	HMV POP 861	Nous Les Amoureux/Les Oubliettes	7

PASHA
69	Liberty LBF 15199	Someone Shot The Lollipop Man/Pussy Willow Dragon	120

(see also Searchers)

PASSAGE
80	Object Music OBJ 11	PINDROP (LP)	12

(see also Contact)

PASSENGERS
95	Island IS 625	Miss Sarajevo/One (live) (7", with poster in 12" card in PVC p/s)	12
95	Island CID 625	Miss Sarajevo/One (live)/Bottoms (Zoo Station Remix)/Via Davidoff (CD, with shrinkwrapped poster, withdrawn)	45
96	Island OST 3	Your Blue Room (CD, 1-track promo, card sleeve, export issue)	100
95	Island OST 2	ORIGINAL SOUNDCHAT 1 (2-CD, music & interview disc, fold-out digipaks, with cue sheet, promo only)	90
95	Island OST1	ORIGINAL SOUNDTRACKS (CD promo in black card sleeve)	25
95	IslanD ILPS8043	ORIGINAL SOUNDTRACKS (LP)	45

(see also U2, Brian Eno)

PASSIONS
58	Capitol CL 14874	My Aching Heart/Jackie Brown	60

PASSIONS

MINT VALUE £

BOBBY PATRICK BIG SIX
64	Decca F 11898	Shake It Easy Baby/Wildwood Days	32
64	Decca F 12030	Monkey Time/Sweet Talk Me Baby	35
64	Decca DFE 8570	TEENBEAT 3 (FROM STAR CLUB, HAMBURG) (EP)	125

(see also Beat Brothers, Tony Sheridan & Beat Brothers)

DAN PATRICK
67	Stateside SS 2004	Tiger Lee/Call Of The Wild	7

KENTRICK PATRICK
63	Island WI 066	Man To Man/ROLAND ALFONSO: Blockade (B-side actually "Hit And Run")	30
63	Island WI 079	Don't Stay Out Late/Forever And Ever	30
63	Island WI 104	The End Of The World/Little Princess	25
63	Island WI 119	Golden Love/Beyond	30
64	Island WI 132	Take Me To The Party/I'm Sorry	25
64	Island WI 140	I Am Wasting Time/RANDY'S GROUP: Royal Charley	70+

(see also Lord Creator)

PATRICK & LLOYD
70	Big Shot BI 550	Return Of The Pollock/PROPHETS: Concorde	15

(see also Lloyd & Prophets)

PATRIOTS
66	Fontana TF 650	Prophet/I'll Be There	15

PATRON OF THE ARTS
66	Page One POF 012	The True Patron Of The Arts/Eleanor Rigby (USA release credits it as Queen City Show Band)	50

PATSY
68	Doctor Bird DB 1122	Little Flea/The Retreat Song	45

(see also Patsy Todd, Derrick & Patsy, Stranger & Patsy, Emotions)

PATSY & PEGGY
70	Hot Rod HR 107	Dog Your Woman/HOT ROD ALLSTARS: Strictly Invitation	10

BRIAN PATTEN
70	Caedmon TC 1300	BRIAN PATTEN (LP)	15
76	Tangent TGS 116	VANISHING TRICK (LP)	25
77	Argo ZSW 607	SLY CORMORANT (LP)	12

(see also Liverpool Scene, Roger McGough & Brian Patten)

PATTERN PEOPLE
68	MGM MGM 1429	Love Is A Lover/Loving To Be Loved	6

BOBBY PATTERSON (& MUSTANGS)
68	Pama PM 735	Broadway Ain't Funky No More/I Met My Match (with Mustangs)	20
68	Pama PM 743	The Good Ol' Days/Don't Be So Mean	15
68	Pama PM 754	Busy Busy Bee/Sweet Taste Of Love (with Mustangs)	15
69	Pama PM 763	T.C.B. Or T.Y.A./What A Wonderful Night For Love (with Mustangs)	22
69	Pama PM 773	My Thing Is Your Thing/Keep It In The Family	15
72	Action ACT 4604	I'm In Love With You/Married Lady	100
72	Mojo 2092 037	How Do You Spell Love/She Don't Have To See You	15

DON PATTERSON
64	Transatlantic PR 733	THE EXCITING NEW ORGAN SOUND OF (LP)	12
67	Transatlantic PR 7430	SATISFACTION! (LP)	12

MANLEY PATTERSON
72	Pama Supreme PS 337	I Stayed Away Too Long/Country Boy	5

OTTILIE PATTERSON
55	Decca F 10472	I Hate A Man Like You/Reckless Blues (with Chris Barber's Jazz Band) (78 = £8)	10
55	Decca F 10621	Weeping Willow Blues/Nobody Knows You When You're Down And Out (78 = £8)	10
57	Pye 7N 15109	Kay-Cee Rider/I Love You Baby (78 rpm = £6)	7
58	Pye Jazz 7NJ 2015	Jailhouse Blues/Beale Street Blues (78 rpm = £6)	10
58	Pye Jazz 7NJ 2025	Trombone Cholly/Lawdy, Lawdy Blues	6
61	Columbia DB 4760	Blueberry Hill/I'm Crazy 'Bout My Baby	15
62	Columbia DB 4834	I Hate Myself/Come On Baby	10
63	Columbia DB 7140	Jealous Heart/Won't Be Long	6
63	Columbia DB 7208	Baby Please Don't Go/I Feel So Good (with Sonny Boy Williamson)	30
65	Columbia DB 7332	Tell Me Where Is Fancy/Oh Me What Eyes	10
69	Marmalade 598 016	Spring Song/Sound Of The Door As It Closes	5
69	Marmalade 598 020	Bitterness Of Death/Spring Song	5
55	Jazz Today JTE 102	THAT PATTERSON GIRL (EP)	18
56	Decca DFE 6303	BLUES (EP)	18
56	Pye Jazz Today NJE 1012	THAT PATTERSON GIRL (EP, reissue)	8
56	Pye Jazz Today NJE 1023	THAT PATTERSON GIRL VOL. 2 (EP)	15
59	Columbia SEG 7915	OTTILIE (EP)	15
60	Columbia SEG 7998	SWINGS THE IRISH (EP)	10
59	Pye NPL 18028	OTTILIE'S IRISH NIGHT (LP)	20
69	Marmalade 608 011	3000 YEARS WITH OTTILIE (LP)	50
69	Polydor 2384 031	SPRING SONG (LP)	50

(see also Chris Barber)

PATTERSONS
69	CBS 63522	AGAIN (LP)	15
69	CBS 63335	TRAVELLING PEOPLE (LP)	12

ROBERT PATTERSON SINGERS
60s	United Artists UAS 2903	THE SOUL OF GOSPEL (LP)	25
65	Fontana 688 516 ZL	I'M SAVED (LP)	18

PATTERSON'S PEOPLE

PATTERSON'S PEOPLE
66	Mercury MF 913	Shake Hands With The Devil/Deadly Nightshade	22

PATTI & PATETTES
75	Dart ART 2053	Bill/It's My Party	6
76	United Artists UP 36077	Summer Heartbreak/Too Much	10

HUBERT PATTISON
66	Pye 7N 17207	Bare Back Rider/The Baby 1 & 2 Problem	5
67	Fontana TF 859	My Home's In My Pocket/Saturday Morning Bride	5

LITTLE JOHN PATTISON
64	Giv-A-Disc LYN 510	Needles And Pins/All My Loving (flexidisc free with *Giv-A-Disc* booklet)	8/6

(MIKE) PATTO
66	Columbia DB 8091	Can't Stop Talking About My Baby/Love (as Mike Patto)	65
74	Goodear EAR 106	Sitting In The Park/Get Up And Dig It (as Mike Patto)	10
70	Vertigo 6360 016	PATTO (LP, gatefold sleeve, swirl label)	75
71	Vertigo 6360 032	HOLD YOUR FIRE (LP, swirl label, foldout sleeve)	220
72	Island ILPS 9210	ROLL 'EM SMOKE 'EM PUT ANOTHER LINE OUT (LP)	35

(see also Bo Street Runners, Breakaways, Boxer, News, Chicago Line, Timebox, Felder's Orioles, Steve York, Centipede, Grimms, V.I.P.s)

ALEXANDER PATTON
66	Capitol CL 15461	A Lil Lovin' Sometimes/No More Dreams (DJ copy = £350)	250

CHARLIE PATTON
50s	Heritage REU 4	CHARLIE PATTON (EP, 99 only)	65

JOHN PATTON
64	Blue Note 45-1889	I'll Never Be Free/Along Came John	8

PATTY & EMBLEMS
64	Stateside SS 322	Mixed Up Shook Up Girl/Ordinary Guy (DJ copy = £75)	50

PATTY FLABBIE'S COUGHED ENGINE
69	Stateside SS 2136	Billy's Got A Goat/Tin Can Eater	6

PAUL
65	Polydor BM 56045	Will You Follow Me/Head Death	80

(see also Jimmy Page)

ANDY PAUL
84	Proto ENA 117	Anna Mari-Elena (Greek)/Anna Mari-Elena (English)/Bistepsememe (p/s, all copies mispressed with Greek version of A-side included twice)	12

BILLY PAUL
73	Epic EPC 65351	360 DEGREES OF BILLY PAUL (LP)	15
73	Epic EPC 65456	EBONY WOMAN (LP)	15
74	Phil. Intl. PIR 65861	WAR OF THE GODS (LP, gatefold sleeve)	15

BUNNY PAUL
54	London HL 8008	Magic Guitar/Never Let me Go (78)	8
54	Columbia SCM 5102	New Love/You'll Never Leave My Side	10
54	Columbia SCM 5112	Such A Night/I'm Gonna Have Some Fun (78 rpm, Columbia DB 3469 = £6)	20
54	Columbia SCM 5131	Lovey Dovey/Answer The Call (78 rpm = £6)	20
54	Columbia SCM 5151	You Came A Long Way From St. Louis/You Are Always In My Heart	12
55	Capitol CL 14279	Please Have Mercy (On A Fool)/These Are The Things We'll Share	12
55	Capitol CL 14304	Leave My Heart Alone/Two Castanets	12
55	Capitol CL 14368	Song Of The Dreamer/For The Very First Time	12

CLARENCE PAUL
75	London HLU 10492	I'm In Love Again/Blue Tuesday	8

DARLENE PAUL
64	Capitol CL 15344	Act Like Nothing Happened/Little Bit Of Heaven	28

DON PAUL
68	RCA 1666	Wise/Ways Of The World	18

EUGENE PAUL
70	Pama Supreme PS 303	Don't Let The Tears Fall/Another Saturday Night	6
70	Pama Supreme PS 305	I Found A Man In My Bed/So Many Things	6
71	Pama Supreme PS 317	Farewell My Darling/Whole Lot Of Woman	6
71	Pama Supreme PS 329	Somebody's Changing My Sweet Baby's Mind/Hard Minded Neighbour	6
72	Pama PM 838	Beautiful Sunday/Take Care Son	6
72	Pama Supreme PS 357	I'll Take You There/Beautiful Baby	6
73	Pama Supreme PS 382	Power To All Our Friends/RANNY WILLIAMS ALLSTARS: Wicked And Dreadful	7

EUGENE PAUL & PILOTS
70	Torpedo TOR 17	Sugar Dumpling/I May Dwell	5

JASON PAUL
69	Pye 7N 17710	Shine A Little Light Into My Room/Paradise Pudding	20

(see also Svensk)

JOHN E. PAUL
67	Decca F 12685	Prince Of Players/I Wanna Know (DJ copy with/without inverted matrix no £100/150)	15

LES PAUL (& MARY FORD)
53	Capitol CL 13943	Vaya Con Dios/ Johnny (78)	6
54	Capitol CL 14185	Mandolino/Whither Thou Goest	18
55	Capitol CL 14212	Mister Sandman/That's What I Like	18
55	Capitol CL 14233	Someday Sweetheart/Song In Blue	18
55	Capitol CL 14300	No Letter Today/Genuine Love	18
55	Capitol CL 14342	Goodbye My Love/Hummingbird	18

56	Capitol CL 14502	Alabamy Bound/Texas Lady	10
56	Capitol CL 14521	Magic Melody/Amukiriki (The Lord Willing)	10
56	Capitol CL 14534	Theme From "The Threepenny Opera" (Moritat) (as Les Paul)/Nuevo Laredo	10
56	Capitol CL 14577	Send Me Some Money/Say The Words I Love To Hear	7
56	Capitol CL 14593	San Antonio Rose/Cimarron (Roll On)	7
56	Capitol CL 14665	Runnin' Wild/Blow The Smoke Away	7
57	Capitol CL 14710	Cinco Robles (Five Oaks)/Ro-Ro-Robinson	6
57	Capitol CL 14738	Hummin' And Waltzin'/Tuxedos And Flowers	5
57	Capitol CL 14776	Strollin' Blues/I Don't Want You No More	7
57	Capitol CL 14809	(I'm Keeping My Heart Away From) Fire/A Pair Of Fools	7
58	Capitol CL 14839	Bewitched/The Night Of The Fourth (as Les Paul solo)	6
58	Capitol CL 14858	More And More Each Day/Small Island	5
58	Philips PB 873	Put A Ring On My Finger/Fantasy (78 rpm = £6)	8
58	Philips PB 882	Jealous Heart/Big Eyed Girl (78 rpm = £6)	7
59	Philips PB 906	At The Sav-A-Penny Super Store/All I Need Is You	7
55	Capitol EAP1 9121	PRESENTING LES PAUL AND MARY FORD (EP)	15
55	Capitol EAP1 540	SITTING ON TOP OF THE WORLD (EP)	15
60	Capitol EAP1 20048	MR AND MRS MUSIC (EP)	15
61	Capitol EAP1 20145	NOLA (EP)	12
65	Capitol EAP1 20540	JAZZ ME BLUES (EP)	12
51	Capitol LC 6514	THE NEW SOUND (LP, 10")	28
53	Capitol LC 6581	THE NEW SOUND VOL. 2 (LP, 10")	28
54	Capitol T 416	HIT MAKERS (LP)	18
55	Capitol LC 6701	LES AND MARY (LP, 10")	25
55	Capitol LC 6704	LES AND MARY PART 2 (LP, 10")	25
56	Capitol LC 6806	BYE BYE BLUES! (LP, 10")	25
57	Capitol T 802	TIME TO DREAM (LP)	15
59	Capitol T 1276	LOVER (LP)	15
59	Philips BBL 7306	LOVER'S LUAU (LP)	15
61	Capitol T 1476	HITS OF LES AND MARY (LP)	12

LYN PAUL

74	Polydor 2058 472	Sail The Summer Winds/Lay Me Down (with John Barry)	7
75	Polydor 2383 340	GIVE ME LOVE (LP)	15

(see also Nocturnes)

RIM D. PAUL

68	Philips BF 1737	Thousand Hours/Downstairs To Meet Her	5

SHELLEY PAUL

69	Jay Boy BOY 10	Clowns Are Coming In/Take Me To Your Heart	6

PAUL & LINDA

69	Page One POF 140	You're Taking My Bag/When I Hear Your Name	6

(this single is not by Paul & Linda McCartney)

PAUL & PAULA

63	Philips 304 012 BF	Hey Paula/Bobby Is The One	10
63	Philips 304 016 BF	Young Lovers/Ba-hey-be	10
63	Philips BF 1256	First Quarrel/School Is Thru	10
63	Philips BF 1269	Something Old, Something New/Flipped Over You	10
63	Philips BF 1281	First Day Back At School/A Perfect Pair	10
64	Philips BF 1380	No Other Baby/Too Dark To See	10
63	Philips BBE 12639	YOUNG LOVERS (EP)	35
63	Philips 652 026BL	SING FOR YOUNG LOVERS (LP)	40
63	Philips BL 7573	WE GO TOGETHER (LP)	45
63	Philips BL 7587	HOLIDAY FOR TEENS (LP)	35

PAUL AND RITCHIE & CRYING SHAMES

66	Decca F 12483	September In The Rain/Come On Back (demos more common, £130)	180

(see also Cryin' Shames, Gary Walker & Rain)

PAULA & JETLINERS

66	Rainbow RAI 102	The Great Pretender/The Legend Of The Man From U.N.C.L.E.	15
66	Rainbow RAI 105	I Know Someday/Something On My Mind (B-side with Carols)	8

PAULETTE (Williams)

68	Major Minor MM 565	One Love In My Heart/Must We Say Goodbye	6
73	Summit SUM 8543	Every Day Is The Same Kind Of Thing/ SHORTY PERRY: The Sweat Of Your Brow	6

(see also Paulette & Gee)

PAULETTE & DELROY

63	Island WI 120	Little Lover/Lovin' Baby	20

(see also Paulette, Paulette & Gee)

PAULETTE & GEE

70	G.G. GG 4506	Hold On Tight/G.G. ALL STARS: Tight (Version)	8

(see also Paulette, Sister, Winston Wright)

PAULETTE SISTERS

55	Capitol CL 14294	Dream Boat/Leave My Honey Be	20
55	Capitol CL 14310	Ring-A-Dang-A-Doo/Lonely One	20
55	Capitol CL 14347	You Win Again/Mama, El Baion	20

PAULINE (& BROWN SUGAR)

80	Studio WE 706	I Am So Proud/NATTY LOCKS: Studio 16 Workshop (12")	25
80	Isis 1	Lion, Me And My Dread/Revelation Side (12")	40

(see also Brown Sugar)

PAUL'S DISCIPLES

65	Decca F 12081	See That My Grave Is Kept Clean/Sixteen Tons	10

MINT VALUE £

PAUL'S TROUBLES
67	Ember EMB S 233	You'll Find Out/You've Got Something	22

PAUPERS
68	Verve Forecast VS 1514	Think I Care/White Song	15
69	Verve Forecast VS 1520	Southdown Road/Numbers	15
68	Verve Forecast (S)VLP 6017	ELLIS ISLAND (LP, mono/stereo)	25

JACKIE PAYNE
77	Barak 4	I Found Myself/Instrumental	12

PAVEMENT
92	Ablaze 8	My First Mine/FLUFF: "Us" (flexi, free with *Ablaze* magazine)	8
92	Big Cat ABB 35S	Trigger Cut/Sue Me Jack/So Stark (You're A Skyscraper) (p/s)	8
92	Big Cat ABB 38P	WATERY, DOMESTIC (12" EP, picture disc, stickered poly sleeve)	10
94	Big Cat ABB 55S	Cut Your Hair/Camera Stare (p/s)	5
95	Big Cat ABB 86S	Rattled By La Rush/False Skorpion/Easily Fooled (p/s)	5
95	Big Cat ABB 91S	Father To A Sister Of Thought/Kris Kraft/Mussle Rock Is A Horse In Transition (p/s)	5
94	Big Cat ABB 56L	CROOKED RAIN CROOKED RAIN (LP, with inner sleeve, some with free 7": "Haunt You Down"/"Jam Kids")	12

PAVLOV'S DOG
75	CBS S CBS 3671	Julia/Episode	5
	(see also Hi-Fi)		

RITA PAVONE
64	RCA RCA 1415	Remember Me/Just Once More	6
66	RCA RCA 1553	Heart/The Man Who Made Music	10
66	RCA RCA 1561	You Only You/Before You Go	7
73	Decca F 13462	He (Didn't Remember My Name)/(Vado Via) Last Summer	6
64	RCA RD/ SF 7657	RITA PAVONE (mono/stereo)	20/25

PAX EXTERNAL
71	Decca F 13167	A Second Chance Mr. Jones/You See Him As Your Brother	6

GARY PAXTON
62	Liberty LIB 55485	Stop Twistin' Baby/Alley Oop Was A Two Dab Man	15
	(see also Skip & Flip)		

TOM PAXTON
66	Elektra EKSN 45001	The Last Thing On My Mind/Goin' To The Zoo	8
66	Elektra EKSN 45003	One Time And One Time Only/Bottle Of Wine	8
67	Elektra EKSN 45006	Leaving London/All The Way Home	8
69	Elektra EKSN 45021	Jennifer's Rabbit/The Marvellous Toy	8
69	Elektra EKSN 45049	Victoria Dines Alone/Clarissa Jones	5
67	Elektra EPK 802	TOM PAXTON (EP)	20
66	Elektra EKL 277/EKS 7277	RAMBLIN' BOY (LP, U.K. pressing in U.S. sleeve)	15
66	Elektra EKL 298/EKS 7298	AIN'T THAT NEWS (LP, U.K. pressing in U.S. sleeve)	15
66	Elektra EKL 317/EKS 7317	OUTWARD BOUND (LP)	15
68	Elek. EKL 4019/EKS 74019	MORNING AGAIN (LP, red label)	15

DAVEY PAYNE & MEDIUM WAVE
69	Ember EMB S 265	Walk In The Sunshine/Looking Towards The Sky (p/s)	6

FREDA PAYNE
62	HMV POP 1091	He Who Laughs Last/Slightly Out Of Tune	30
70	Invictus INV 505	Deeper And Deeper/Unhooked Generation	6
71	Invictus INV 509	Cherish What Is Dear To You (While It's Near To You)/The World Don't Owe You A Thing	6
71	Invictus INV 512	Rock Me In The Cradle (Of Your Lovin' Arms)/Now Is The Time To Say Goodbye	6
71	Invictus INV 515	Bring Home The Boys/Odds And Ends	6
71	Invictus INV 518	You've Got To Love Somebody/Mama's Gone	8
72	Invictus INV 520	You Brought Me Joy/Suddenly It's Yesterday	6
72	Invictus INV 526	Unhooked Generation/Come Back	5
73	Invictus INV 529	I Shall Not Be Moved/Thru' The Memory Of My Mind	5
73	Invictus INV 533	Band Of Gold/The Easiest Way To Fall (reissue, withdrawn)	30
75	ABC ABC 4087	You/Lost In Love	5
70	Invictus SVT 1001	BAND OF GOLD (LP)	20
71	Invictus SVT 1005	CONTACT (LP)	20
72	Invictus SVT 1007	THE BEST OF FREDA PAYNE (LP)	15
78	Capitol E-ST 11864	SUPERNATURAL HIGH (LP)	12
70s	MGM 2351 004	FREDA PAYNE (LP)	25

LEON PAYNE
64	London HA-B 8136	AMERICANA (LP)	12

LAWRENCE PAYTON
74	ABC 4021	Tell Me You Love Me/Instrumental	20
	(see also the Four Tops)		

PAZ
79	Magnus 2	PAZ AT CHICHESTER (LP)	25
83	Spotlight SPJ 507	KANDEEN LOVE SONG (LP)	12
83	Spotlight SPJ 518	PAZ ARE BACH (LP)	10
83	Paladin PALP 001	LOOK INSIDE (LP)	10

P BROTHERS
01	White (Heavy Bronx) PBHB01	HEAVY BRONX EXPERIENCE VOL. 1 (EP)	25

PD3
91	Payday PD001	SYNCOPATED NOISE MUSIC (EP)	20
94	Payday PD004	SYMPHONY (EP)	15

EDDIE PEABODY
55	London RE-D 1034	THE MAN WITH THE BANJO (EP)	12

DAVE PEACE QUARTET
69	Saga FID 2155	GOOD MORNING MR. BLUES (LP)	25

(see also Birmingham)

PEACEFUL COMPANY
(see under Morin & Wilson)

PEACEMAKERS
65	Herald 1070	NOT NOW BUT TOMORROW (EP)	15

PEACHES & HERB
67	CBS 202509	Let's Fall In Love/We're In This Thing Together (DJ copy = £60)	30
67	CBS 2711	Close Your Eyes/I Will Watch Over You	8
67	CBS 2866	For Your Love/I Need Your Love So Desperately (DJ copy = £50)	25
67	Direction 58-3096	Love Is Strange/Two Little Kids	7
68	Direction 58-3415	Let It Be Me/I Need Your Love So Despeartely	7
68	Direction 58-3548	United/Thank You	6
68	Direction 58-3829	Let's Make A Promise/Me And You	7
69	Direction 58-4085	When He Touches Me/Thank You	7
70	Direction 58-4909	Satisfy My Hunger/It's Just A Game, Love	7
70	Direction 58-5249	Soothe Me With Your Love/We're So Much In Love	8
71	CBS 5249	Soothe Me With Your Love/We're So Much In Love (reissue)	6
77	Epic EPC 4903	Soothe Me With Your Love/Satisy My Hunger (coloured vinyl)	6
67	CBS 62966	LET'S FALL IN LOVE (LP)	30
67	CBS 63119	FOR YOUR LOVE (LP)	30
68	Direction 8-63263	GOLDEN DUETS (LP)	25

ANNETTE PEACOCK
72	RCA SF 8255	I'M THE ONE (LP)	18
70s	Aura	LIVE IN PARIS (LP)	18

ANNETTE PEACOCK & PAUL BLEY
73	Freedom 2383 105	DUAL UNITY (LP)	15

(see also Paul Bley, Bley-Peacock Synthesiser Show, Annette Peacock)

ROGER PEACOCK
65	Columbia DB7764	Everybody's Talking About My Baby/Times Have Changed	15

TREVOR PEACOCK
61	Decca F 11414	I Didn't Figure On Him To Come Back/Can I Walk You Home	20

PEANUT
65	Pye 7N 15901	Thank Goodness For The Rain/I'm Not Sad	10
65	Pye 7N 15963	Home Of The Brave/I Wanna Hear It Again	18
66	Columbia DB 8032	I'm Waiting For The Day/Someone's Gonna Be Sorry	20
67	Columbia DB 8104	I Didn't Love Him Anyway/Come Tomorrow	20

(see also Katie Kissoon, Ragdolls U.K.)

PEANUT BUTTER CONSPIRACY
67	CBS 2981	It's A Happening Thing/Twice Is Life	10
68	CBS 3543	Turn On A Friend/Captain Sandwich	7
69	London HLH 10290	Back In L.A./Have A Little Faith	8
68	CBS 63277	THE GREAT CONSPIRACY (LP)	30
80s	Drop Out DO 2000	TURN ON A FRIEND (LP)	12

BOB PEARCE BLUES BAND
74	Westwood WRS 040	LET'S GET DRUNK AGAIN (LP)	18
79	Forest Tracks FT 3015	COLOUR BLIND (LP)	12

(see also Brother Bung)

PEARL JAM
92	Epic 657 572-7	Alive/Once (white vinyl p/s)	5
92	Epic 657 572-6	Alive/Once/Wash (12", poster p/s)	8
93	Epic 657 867-7	Even Flow/Oceans (p/s)	5
93	Epic 657 857-8	Even Flow/Dirty Frank/Oceans (12", white vinyl, p/s)	15
92	Epic 658 258-7	Jeremy/Alive (live) (white vinyl, p/s)	5
92	Epic 658 258-6	Jeremy/Alive (live)/Footsteps (12", picture disc, with card insert)	15
92	Epic 658 258-2	Jeremy/Yellow Ledbetter/Alive (live) (CD, picture disc)	15
93	Epic 660 020-6	Daughter/Blood (Live)/Yellow Ledbetter (Live) (12", ltd. ed. poster sleeve)	15
93	Epic 659 795-6	Go/Alone/Elderly Woman Behind The Counter In A Small Town (Acoustic) (12", with free cassette [plays 'Animal' (Live)])	8
93	Epic 660 020-7	Daughter/Blood (live) (red vinyl p/s)	5
94	Epic 660 441-7	Dissident/Rearviewmirror (live) (stickered poster p/s)	5
92	Epic 468 884-0	TEN (LP, picture disc)	30

(see also Temple Of The Dog)

PEARLS
62	Embassy EMB 564	He's So Fine/BUD ASHTON: Scarlett O'Hara	5

(see also Bud Ashton)

PEARLS
75	Private Stock PVT39	The Cheater/I'm Gonna Steal Your Heart Away	6

PEARLS BEFORE SWINE
68	Fontana STL 5503	BALAKLAVA (LP)	30
68	Fontana STL 5505	ONE NATION UNDERGROUND (LP)	25
69	Reprise RSLP 6364	THESE THINGS TOO (LP)	20
70	Reprise RSLP 6405	THE USE OF ASHES (LP)	20
71	Reprise RSLP 6442	CITY OF GOLD (LP)	20
71	Reprise RSLP 6467	BEAUTIFUL LIES YOU COULD LIVE (LP)	15

PEARLY GATES
70	MCA MU 1109	Free/Carole's Epic Song	9

BUSTER PEARSON BAND
73	Action ACT 4612	Big Funky/Pretty Woman	25
75	K&B 5516	Take It Easy/Instrumental	6

DUKE PEARSON
60s	Polydor	ANGEL EYES (LP)	100

JOHNNY PEARSON
66	Columbia DB 7851	Rat Catcher's Theme/Weaver's Green Theme	18
73	BBC RESL 6	Spy Trap/Playgirl (with Quator)	10

(see also John Barry Seven)

KEITH PEARSON'S RIGHT HAND BAND
76	Eron ER 014	KEITH PEARSON'S RIGHT HAND BAND (LP)	12

RONNIE PEARSON
58	HMV POP 489	Flippin' Over You/Teen-Age Fancy (78 rpm = £175)	750

PEASANTS
65	Columbia DB 7642	Got Some Lovin' For You Baby/Let's Get Together	125

PEBBLES
68	Major Minor MM 574	40 Miles Inside Your Heart/Get Around	7
69	Decca F 22944	Incredible George/Playing Chess	15
70	Deram DM 305	Stand Up And Be Counted/May In The Morning	7
71	Parlophone R 5900	Goodnight Ma/Sadness Of A Summer's Afternoon	7
71	Parlophone R 5921	First Time Loving/Party	7

PEDDLERS
64	Philips BF 1375	Let The Sunshine In/True Girl	6
65	Philips BF 1404	Whatever Happened To The Good Times/Song For The Blues	6
65	Philips BF 1455	Over The Rainbow/You Must Be Having Me On	6
66	Philips BF 1506	Adam's Apple/Anybody's Fool	6
66	Philips BF 1530	I've Got To Hold On/Gassin'	6
67	Philips BF 1557	What'll I Do/Delicious Lady	6
70	Phillips 6006034	Tell The World We're Not In/Rainy Day In London	20
73	Philips 6006 283	Sing Me An Old Song/It's So Easy	25
66	Philips BE 12954	SWINGING SCENE (EP)	22
67	Philips (S)BL 7768	LIVE AT THE PICKWICK (LP)	20
67	CBS (S)BPG 63183	FREE WHEELERS (LP)	15
68	CBS 63411	THREE IN A CELL (LP)	18
68	Fontana SFL 13016	THE FANTASTIC PEDDLERS (LP)	12
70	CBS 63682	BIRTHDAY (LP)	12
70	Philips 6308 028	THREE FOR ALL (LP)	12
71	Philips 6386 066	GEORGIA ON MY MIND (LP)	12

MIKE PEDICIN QUINTET
62	HMV POP 1001	When Cats Come Twistin' In/Gotta Twist	15

BOBBY PEDRICK
58	London HLX 8740	White Bucks And Saddle Shoes/Stranded (78 rpm = £18)	30

ANN PEEBLES
70	London HLU 10322	Part Time Love/I Still Love You	6
71	London HLU 10328	I Pity The Fool/Heartaches, Heartaches	6
71	London HLU 10346	Slipped, Tripped And Fell In Love/99 lbs	5
72	London HLU 10361	Breaking Up Somebody's Home/Troubles, Heartaches And Sadness	5
72	London HLU 10385	Somebody's On Your Case/I've Been There Before	5
73	London HLU 10405	I'm Gonna Tear Your Playhouse Down/One Way Street	6
75	London HLU 10484	Beware/You Got To Feed The Fire	5
75	London HLU 10508	Come On Mama/I'm Leaving You	5
72	London SHU 8434	STRAIGHT FROM THE HEART (LP)	15
74	London SHU 8468	I CAN'T STAND THE RAIN (LP)	15
76	London SHU 8490	TELLIN' IT (LP)	15

PAUL PEEK
61	Pye International 7N 25102	Brother In Law/Through The Teenage Years	20
66	CBS 202073	Pin The Tail On The Donkey/Rockin' Pneumonia	12

(see also Gene Vincent & Blue Caps)

DAVID PEEL (& LOWER EAST SIDE)
68	Elektra EKL 4032	HAVE A MARIJUANA (LP, red label, also stereo EKS 74032)	30/22
70	Elektra 2401 001	AMERICAN REVOLUTION (LP)	15

PEELERS
72	Polydor Folk Mill 2460 165	BANISHED MISFORTUNE (LP)	125+

PEELS
66	Stateside SS 513	Juanita Banana/Fun	10
66	Audio Fidelity AFSP 527	Scrooey Mooey/Time Marches On	32

PEENUTS
67	Ember EMB S 242	The Theme For "The Monkees"/The World's Been Good To Me Tonight (some in p/s)	20/10

PEEPS
65	Philips BF 1421	Now Is The Time/Got Plenty Of Love	12
65	Philips BF 1443	What Can I Say?/Don't Talk About Love	15
66	Philips BF 1478	Gotta Get A Move On/I Told You Before	10
66	Philips BF 1509	Tra La La/Loser Wins	10

(see also Martin Cure & Peeps, Sabres, Rainbows)

PEEP SHOW
67	Polydor 56196	Your Servant, Stephen/Mazy 110
68	Polydor 52226	Esprit De Corps/Mino In A Mix Up 28

BEV PEGG (& HIS GOIN' NOWHERE BAND)
70s	Beaujangle DB 0007	NOSTALGIA IS A THING OF THE PAST (LP, private pressing, with booklet, 100 only; as Bev Pegg & His Goin' Nowhere Band)............ 100
70s	Beaujangle DB 0008	THE FOUNDRY DITTY AND THE INDUSTRIAL AIR (LP, private pressing, 500 only)... 25

(see also David Cartwright, Away From The Sand, Brindley Brae)

BOB PEGG
74	Transatlantic TRA 280	THE SHIPBUILDER (LP, with Nick Strutt) 15
75	Transatlantic TRA 299	ANCIENT MAPS (LP, with insert).. 15

BOB & CAROL PEGG
71	Trailer LER 3016	HE CAME FROM THE MOUNTAIN (LP, red label)............................ 30
72	Galliard GAL 4017	AND NOW IT IS SO EARLY — THE SONGS OF SYDNEY CARTER (LP) 25

(see also Carol Pegg, Mr. Fox)

BOB PEGG & NICK STRUTT
73	Transatlantic TRA 265	BOB PEGG & NICK STRUTT (LP) 18

CAROL PEGG
73	Transatlantic TRA 266	CAROL PEGG (LP, gatefold sleeve) 50

(see also Bob & Carol Pegg)

PEGGY
70	Trojan TR 7752	All Kinds Of Everything Part 1/CARL LEVEY: Instrumental Version 6
70	Hot Rod HR 103	I Shall Follow The Star/CARL LEVEY: Gifted At The Top 8

PEGGY & JIMMY
70	Hot Rod HR 101	Pum Pum Lover/CARL LEVY: Remember Easter Monday 8

PEGGY'S LEG
73	Bunch BAN 2001	GRINILLA (LP, with insert) 250

(see also Skid Row, Jimi Slevin)

PEG LEG SAM
74	Flyright LP 507/8	THE LAST MEDICINE SHOW (2-LP) 15

BERNARD PEIFFER
54	Felsted ED 82010	Strip Tease/Who Is Me? (78) 8

PEKKA
77	Virgin V 2084	THE MATHEMATICIANS AIR DISPLAY (LP, features Mike Oldfield)............ 18

LANA PELLAY
86	Sublime LIMET 101	Pistol In My Pocket/Dirty Harry (Version) (12", p/s)........................ 12

DAVE PELL OCTET
54	London RE-P 1008	IRVING BERLIN GALLERY VOL. 1 (EP)...................................... 12
55	London RE-P 1018	RODGERS AND HART (EP) 12

TRACY PENDARVIS
60	London HLS 9059	A Thousand Guitars/Is It Too Late 32
60	London HLS 9213	Is It Me/South Bound Line 32

MIKE PENDER
86	Sierra FED 23	It's Over/Brothers And Sisters (p/s) 6
86	Sierra FED 23T	It's Over/Brothers And Sisters (12", p/s) 8

(see also The Searchers)

PENDLEFOLK
70	Folk Heritage FHR 007	PENDLEFOLK (LP) 18

PENDRAGON
87	Awareness AWS 101	Red Shoes/Searching/Contact (p/s) 5
89	Toff PENDS 7S	Saved By You/Lady Luck (p/s) 6
85	Elusive ARRLP 100	FIRE IN HARMONY (LP) 12
85	Elusive ARRLP 101	THE JEWEL (LP) 12

PENETRATION
77	Virgin VS 192	Don't Dictate/Money Talks (p/s)... 8
78	Virgin VS 213	Firing Squad/Never (p/s)... 5
78	Virgin VS 226	Life's A Gamble/V.I.P. (p/s) 5
79	Virgin VS 257	Danger Signs/Stone Heroes (live) (p/s)..................................... 5
79	Virgin VS 268	Come Into The Open/Lifeline (p/s)... 5
78	Virgin V 2109	MOVING TARGETS (LP, 15,000 on luminous vinyl)......................... 15

PENGUINS
55	London HL 8114	Earth Angel/Hey Senorita (gold label print, 1st press thick triangular centre) . 1,800+
55	London HL 8114	Earth Angel/Hey Senorita (large centre hole, export issue).................. 900
55	London HL 8114	Earth Angel/Hey Senorita (78) 175

DAWN PENN
66	Rio R 113	Long Days Short Night/Are You There 35
67	Studio One SO 2030	You Don't Love Me/SOUL VENDORS: Portobello Road 42
68	Island WI 3097	I'll Never Let You Go/MARK BROWN: Brown Low Special................... 32

(see also Max Romeo, Viceroys)

TONY PENN
62	Starlite ST45 083	That's What I Like/I Won't Cry Anymore..................................... 40

LEONARD PENNARIO
54	Capitol CL 14173	Midnight On The Cliffs/Dream Rhapsody (with Les Baxter Orchestra).......... 10

(see also Les Baxter)

Barbara PENNINGTON

BARBARA PENNINGTON
76   United Artists UP 36170   24 Hours A Day/I Can't Erase The Thoughts Of You 6

PENNSYLVANIA SIXPENCE
67   Pye 7N 17326   Love Of The Common People/Midweek Excursion 7

PENNY
61   Piccadilly 7N 35009   Who Does He Think He Is/Sparks 10
62   Piccadilly 7N 35045   Shall I Take My Heart And Go/What'd I Do? 10

GEORGE A. PENNY
68   Trojan TR 625   Win Your Love/VAL BENNETT: All In The Game 12

HANK PENNY
56   Parlophone MSP 6202   Bloodshot Eyes/Wham! Bam! Thank You Ma'am (78 rpm, R 4120 = £18) 105

PENNY PEEPS
68   Liberty LBF 15053   Little Man With A Stick/Model Village 200
68   Liberty LBF 15114   I See The Morning/Curly, The Knight Of The Road 25

CHARLES PENROSE
57   COLUMBIA SEG 7743   ADVENTURES OF THE LAUGHING POLICEMAN (EP) 8

LYDIA PENSE & COLD BLOOD
70s   ABC ABC 4109   I Get Off On You/We Came Down Here/Cold Blood Smoking 6

PENTAD
65   Parlophone R 5288   Silver Dagger/Nothing But Love 18
65   Parlophone R 5368   Don't Throw It All Away/Too Many Ways 12
66   Parlophone R 5424   Something Other People Call Love/It Better Be Me 12

PENTAGONS
61   London HLU 9333   To Be Loved Forever/Down At The Beach 100

PENTAGRAM
85   own label DEVIL 4   PENTAGRAM (LP) 12
92   Peaceville   1972-1979 (LP) 12
93   Peaceville VILE 38   RELENTLESS (LP) 12

PENTANGLE
68   Big T BIG 109   Travellin' Song/Mirage (some in title die-cut sleeve) 10/6
69   Big T BIG 124   Once I Had A Sweetheart/I Saw An Angel. 6
70   Big T BIG 128   Light Flight/Cold Mountain. 6
73   Big T BIG 567   Light Flight/Market Song/The Time Has Come 6
68   Transatlantic TRA 162   THE PENTANGLE (LP) 20
68   Transatlantic TRA 178   SWEET CHILD (2-LP) 20
69   Transatlantic TRA 205   BASKET OF LIGHT (LP, gatefold sleeve) 22
70   Transatlantic TRA 228   CRUEL SISTER (LP, gatefold sleeve) 18
71   Transatlantic TRA 240   REFLECTION (LP, gatefold sleeve with inner sleeve) 18
72   Reprise K 44197   SOLOMON'S SEAL (LP, with lyric insert) 25
72   Transatlantic TRASAM 23   HISTORY BOOK (LP). 15
73   Transatlantic TRASAM 29   PENTANGLING (LP) 15
(see also Bert Jansch, John Renbourn, Duffy's Nucleus)

PEOPLE
69   Capitol CL 15553   I Love You/Somebody Tell Me My Name. 22
69   Capitol CL 15599   Ulla/Turnin' Me In. 22
70   RCA RCA 2028   I Am (The Preacher)/September's Son 10
71   Deram DM 346   In Ancient Times/Glastonbury 18
70   Paramount SPFL 261   THERE ARE PEOPLE AND THERE ARE PEOPLE (LP) 25

PEOPLE BAND
70   Transatlantic TRA 214   THE PEOPLE BAND (LP, with Charlie Watts) 60
(see also Charlie Watts, Battered Ornaments)

PEOPLE'S CHOICE
71   Mojo 2092 024   I Like To Do It/Big Ladies Man 8
73   London HLU 10404   Let Me Do My Thing/On A Cloudy Day 5
77   Philadelphia Int. PIR 5891   Jam Jam Jam (All Night Long)/Cold Blooded & Downright Funky 5

PEPPER
68   Pye 7N 17569   We'll Make It Together/I'm On The Way Down 10

ART PEPPER
54   Vogue LDE 067   ART PEPPER QUARTET (10" LP) 15
56   London HLZ V 14038   ART PEPPER QUARTET (10" LP) 40
60   Contemporary LAC 12229   MODERN JAZZ CLASSICS (LP, as Art Pepper Eleven) 15
(see also Chet Baker)

JIM PEPPER
71   Atlantic 2400 149   PEPPER'S POW WOW (LP) 20

KEN PEPPER
61   Top Rank JAR 535   Just A Little At A Time/I Get The Blues When It Rains 7

DANNY PEPPERMINT (& JUMPING JACKS)
61   London HLL 9478   The Peppermint Twist/Somebody Else Is Taking My Place (with Jumping Jacks) . 8
62   London HLL 9516   One More Time/La Dee Dah 8
62   London HLL 9614   Maybe Tomorrow But Not Today/Passing Parade 8
62   London HA-L 2438   TWIST WITH DANNY PEPPERMINT (LP) 75

PEPPERMINT CIRCUS
67   Olga OLE 007   All The King's Horses/It Didn't Take Long 10
68   Polydor 56288   I Won't Be There/Keeping My Head Above Water 6
69   Polydor 56312   Please Be Patient/Take My Love 6

PEPPERMINT RAINBOW
68	MCA MU 1034	Walking In Different Circles/Pink Lemonade	5
69	MCA MU 1076	Will You Be Staying After Sunday/And I'll Be There	12
69	MCA MU 1091	Don't Wake Up In The Morning, Michael/Rosemary	5

PEPPERMINT TROLLEY COMPANY
68	Dot DOT 110	Baby You Come Rolling 'Cross My Mind/Nine O'Clock Business Man	8

PEPPERS
73	Spark SRL 1100	Pepper Box/Pinch Of Salt	5

PEPPI
62	Decca F 11520	Stories/When I Think Of You	5
63	Decca F 11638	Can You Waddle/I Never Danced Before	8
64	Decca F 11991	Pistol Packin' Mama/Roll On Baby	5
64	Fontana TF 446	So Used To Loving You/Don't Trust My Friend	5
65	Decca F 12055	The Skip/Do The Skip	8

PERCELLS
63	HMV POP 1154	What Are Boys Made Of?/Cheek To Cheek	18

NORMAN PERCIVAL
67	United Artists UP 1197	Theme From "Billion Dollar Brain"/Shades Of Green	10

PERCY PAVILION
84	Dead Good Dolly P. DMS 2	Gower Power/You're An Extra Baby (p/s)	5

(see also Captain Sensible)

PEREGRINE
72	Westwood WRS 016	SONGS OF MINE (LP)	100

RAY PEREIRA
70	Baf BAF 5	Don't Mess With Cupid/CATS: Falling In Love	8
70	Baf BAF 6	On Broadway/Hey Chick	6

PERERIN
80	Gwerin SYWM 215	HAUL AR YR EIRA (LP, with insert)	180

PERE UBU
79	Chrysalis CHS 2372	The Fabulous Sequel (Have Shoes Will Walk)/Humour Me (live)/ The Book Is On The Table (p/s)	8
80	Rough Trade RT 049	Final Solution/My Dark Ages (p/s)	8
81	Rough Trade RT 066	Not Happy/Lonesome Cowboy Dave (p/s)	8
78	Radar RDR 1	DATAPANIK IN THE YEAR ZERO (12" EP)	10
78	Blank BLANK 001	THE MODERN DANCE (LP)	15
78	Rough Trade ROUGHUS 14	DUB HOUSING (LP)	15
79	Rough Trade ROUGHUS 20	NEW PICNIC TIME (LP)	15
80	Rough Trade ROUGH 14	THE ART OF WALKING (LP, original with "Miles" & "Arabia")	15
81	Rough Trade ROUGH 23	390° OF SIMULATED STEREO — UBU LIVE: VOLUME 1 (LP)	15

(see also David Thomas)

CHRISTINE PERFECT
69	Blue Horizon 57-3165	When You Say/No Road Is The Right Road	25
70	Blue Horizon 57-3172	I'm Too Far Gone (To Turn Around)/Close To Me	28
70	Blue Horizon 7-63860	CHRISTINE PERFECT (LP)	90

(see also Christine McVie, Fleetwood Mac, Illusive Dream, Chicken Shack, Rick Hayward)

PERFECT PEOPLE
69	MCA MU 1079	House In The Country/Polyanna	12

PERFORMANCE
73	Polydor 2058 324	Funny Little Things/Rejoice	6

PERFORMERS
69	Action ACT 4552	I Can't Stop You/L.A. Stomp	20

EMILIO PERICOLI
62	Warner Brothers WB 69	Al Di La/Sassi	5

PERISHERS
68	Fontana TF 965	How Does It Feel/Bye Bye Baby	40

(see also Seftones)

NICK PERITO ORCHESTRA
60	London HLT 9221	Green Leaves Of Summer/Jennifer	7
62	HMV POP 1032	Jessica/Gina	5

CARL PERKINS
78s
56	London HLU 8271	Blue Suede Shoes/Honey Don't	35
57	London HLS 8408	Matchbox/Your True Love	55
57	London HLS 8527	Glad All Over/Forever Yours	78
58	London HLS 8608	Lend Me Your Comb/That's Right	85
59	Philips PB 983	I Don't See Me In Your Eyes Anymore/One Ticket To Loneliness	120

45s
56	London HLU 8271	Blue Suede Shoes/Honey Don't	250
57	London HLS 8408	Matchbox/Your True Love	200
57	London HLS 8527	Glad All Over/Forever Yours	125
58	London HLS 8608	Lend Me Your Comb/That's Right	125
59	Philips PB 983	I Don't See Me In Your Eyes Anymore/One Ticket To Loneliness	20
61	Philips PB 1179	Anyway The Wind Blows/The Unhappy Girls	20
64	Brunswick 05905	Help Me Find My Baby/I Wouldn't Have You	15
64	Brunswick 05909	Big Bad Blues/Lonely Heart (with Nashville Teens)	15
64	Brunswick 05923	The Monkey Shine/Let My Baby Be	18
67	Stateside SS 599	A Country Boy's Dream/If I Could Come Back	15

Carl PERKINS

68	London HLP 7125	A Country Boy's Dream/Shine Shine Shine (export issue)............... 20
68	Spark SRL 1009	Lake County, Cotton Country/It's You.. 10
68	London HLS 10192	Blue Suede Shoes/Matchbox... 10
69	CBS 3932	Restless/11.43... 10
70	CBS 4991	All Mama's Children/Step Aside (with N.R.B.Q.)............................ 6
77	Mercury ELV 15	The E.P. Express/Big Bad Blues (p/s)...................................... 6
78	Jet UP 36365	Blue Suede Shoes/That's All Right/Rock On Around The World (p/s).......... 5
78	Jet SJET 117	Mustang Wine/The Whole World Misses You (p/s)............................ 5
80	Jet JET 182	Love Sick Blues/Turn Around/Miss Misunderstood/Blue Suede Shoes (p/s)..... 5

LPs

59	London HA-S 2202	THE DANCE ALBUM OF CARL PERKINS
		(plum label, flipback/non-flipback sleeve)............................ 150/90
66	Ember NR 5038	SUNSTROKE (shared with Jerry Lee Lewis)................................ 20
66	CBS Realm 52305	WHOLE LOTTA CARL PERKINS (boxed square logo on originals)......... 55/30
68	CBS 63309	KING OF ROCK 22
68	London HA-P/SH-P 8366	COUNTRY BOY'S DREAM 32
69	CBS 63676	CARL PERKINS' GREATEST HITS...................................... 15
70	CBS 63826	BOPPIN' THE BLUES (with N.R.B.Q.).................................. 12
82	Sun BOX 101	THE SUN YEARS (3-LP, box set with booklet)....................... 20

(see also N.R.B.Q.)

JOE PERKINS
| 63 | London HLU 9794 | Little Eeefin Annie/Encle Eeef .... 7 |
| 72 | Mojo 2092 047 | Wrapped Up In Your Love/Looking For A Woman.................. 8 |

LASCELLES PERKINS
61	Blue Beat BB 41	Creation/Lonely Robin 12
63	Island WI 038	Tango Lips (with Yvonne)/DENNIS SINDREY: Rub Up
		(B-side actually plays "Jamaica's Song")........................... 22
64	R&B JB 175	I Am So Grateful/When I Survey 20
70	Escort ES 814	Please Stay/MATADORS: Voyage From The Moon 25
71	Banana BA 317	Tell It All Brothers/SOUND DIMENSION: Polkadots 18

(see also Tommy McCook)

POLLY PERKINS
63	Decca F 11583	I Reckon You (as Polly Perkins & Bill)/The Girls Are At It Again........ 10
63	Oriole CB 1869	Sweet As Honey/I've Gotta Tell You 10
63	Oriole CB 1929	Young Lover/You Too Can Be A Beatle........................... 10
63	Oriole CB 1979	Faling In Love Again/I Went By Your House Today.............. 10
73	Chapter One CMS 1018	LIBERATED WOMAN (LP) 15

(see also Academy)

TONY PERKINS
| 57 | RCA RCA 1018 | Moonlight Swim/First Romance (78 rpm = £12)............... 12 |

PERMANENTS
| 63 | London HLU 9803 | Oh Dear, What Can The Matter Be/Let Me Be Baby .... 12 |

JEAN-JACQUES PERREY
72	Vanguard VAN 1005	Gossipo Perpetuo/Moog Indigo............................ 8
73	Vanguard VAN 1008	Minuet Of The Robots/Porcupine Rock 8
71	Vanguard VSD 6525	KALEIDOSCOPIC VIBRATIONS — SPOTLIGHT ON THE MOOG
		(LP, 'kaleidoscope' sleeve, with Gershon Kingsley) 18
72	Vanguard VSD 6549	MOOG INDIGO (LP, title sleeve)......................... 25
73	Vanguard VSD 79222	THE IN SOUND FROM WAY OUT! (LP, green/black 'starburst' sleeve,
		with Gershon Kingsley) 20
73	Vanguard VSD 79286	THE AMAZING NEW ELECTRONIC POP SOUND OF... (LP)........ 15
74	Vanguard DPS 2051	THE BEST OF THE MOOG (2-LP) 18

PAT PERRIN
| 68 | Island WI 3115 | Over You/LLOYD TERRELL: Lost Without You .... 25 |

PERRI'S
| 59 | Oriole CB 1481 | Jerri-Lee/Ballad Of A Happy Heart (78 rpm = £15)........ 15 |

BARBARA PERRY
| 70 | Pama PM 795 | Say You Need Me/Unloved................................ 25 |

JEFF PERRY
| 76 | Arista ARIST 51 | Love Don't Come No Stronger/I've Got To See You Right Away .... 5 |

JOHN PERRY
| 73 | Philips 6006 319 | Nancy Sing Me A Song/Crying Eyes..................... 5 |

(see also Summer Wine)

KING PERRY
(see under Lee Perry)

LEE 'SCRATCH' PERRY (& UPSETTERS)
63	R&B JB 102	Prince In The Black/Don't Copy............................ 45
63	R&B JB 104	Old For New/Prince And Duke............................. 45
63	R&B JB 106	Mad Head/Man And Wife................................... 45
63	R&B JB 135	Royalty/Can't Be Wrong.................................. 45
63	Island WI 118	Never Get Weary/TOMMY McCOOK: Below Zero 35
64	Port-O-Jam PJ 4001	Help The Weak/TOMMY McCOOK: Exodus 40
64	Port-O-Jam PJ 4003	Bad Minded People/TOMMY McCOOK & HIS GROUP: Jam Rock......... 40
64	Port-O-Jam PJ 4010	Chatty Chatty Woman/TOMMY McCOOK & HIS GROUP: Road Block 40
65	Island WI 210	Please Don't Go/Bye, St. Peter (both sides with Soulettes)................... 35
65	Island WI 223	Country Girl/Strange Country (as Upsetters; both act. by Ossie & Upsetters) ... 20
65	Ska Beat JB 201	Roast Duck/Hand To Hand, Man To Man 35
65	Ska Beat JB 203	Trail And Crosses/Jon Tom 40
65	Ska Beat JB 212	Wishes Of The Wicked/Hold Down 40

65	Ska Beat JB 215	Open Up/ROLAND ALPHONSO: Twin Double	40
66	Ska Beat JB 251	The Woodman/Give Me Justice	40
66	Island WI 259	Just Keep It Up/ROLAND ALPHONSO: James Bond	45
66	Island WI 292	Doctor Dick (as King Perry)/SOUL BROTHERS: Magic Star	35
66	Island WI 298	Rub And Squeeze (as King Perry & Soulettes)/SOUL BROTHERS: Here Comes The Minx	35
67	Doctor Bird DB 1073	Run For Cover/Something You've Got (as Lee 'King' Perry & Sensations)	30
67	Doctor Bird DB 1098	Whop Whop Man/Wind-Up Doll (with Dynamites)	40
68	Amalgamated AMG 808	The Upsetter/Prisoner Of Love	40
68	Doctor Bird DB 1146	People Funny Boy/BURT WALTERS: Blowing In The Wind	25
68	Trojan TR 644	Uncle Desmond/Bronco (with Upsetters)	20
69	Upsetter US 303	People Funny Fi True/UPSETTERS: Ten To Twelve	20
69	Upsetter US 324	Yakety Yak/Tackio (with Upsetters)	20
70	Upsetter US 325	Kill Them All/Soul Walk (with Upsetters)	20
71	Bullet BU 461	All Combine Pts 1& 2 (as Lee Perry & Upsetters)	12
72	Upsetter US 385	French Connection (with Upsetters)/UPSETTERS: (Version)	15
72	Upsetter US 389	Back Biter (with Dennis Alcapone)/UPSETTERS: (Version)	15
73	Upsetter US 397	Jungle Lion/Freakout Skank	18
73	Upsetter US 398	Cow Thief Skank (actually by Lee Perry & Charlie Ace)/ Seven And Three Quarters Skank	18
73	Bread BR 1111	Station Underground/CARLTON & SHOES: Better Days	25
73	Downtown DT 513	Bucky Skank/Mid East Rock	25
73	Jackpot JP 812	Justice To The People/UPSETTERS: (Version)	20
74	Dip DL 5037	Dub A Pum Pum (with Silvertones)/(Version)	8
74	Dip DL 5060	Dreader Locks (& Junior Byles)/Militant Rock	8
76	Island WIP 6370	Dreadlocks In Moonlight/Cut Throat	6
79	Black Art BH 001	Reggae Music (actually by Hugo Blackwood)/DOC ALIMANTADO: Rastaman Train (12")	35
73	SRNO 8002	CLOAK & DAGGER (LP, as Scratch The Upsetter)	60+
75	Cactus CTLP 112	REVOLUTION DUB (LP)	40
75	DIP DLPD 6002	KUNG FU MEETS THE DRAGON (LP, as The Mighty Upsetter)	50

(see also Upsetters, Defenders, Roland Alphonso, Bob Marley/Wailers, King Scratch, Punchers, Roy Shirley, Pioneers, Desmond Dekker)

MAL PERRY
58	Fontana H 133	That's When Your Heartaches Begin/Make Me A Miracle (78 rpm = £8)	12
58	Fontana H 149	Too Young To Love/Who Are They To Say (78 rpm = £8)	12
58	Fontana H 157	Things I Didn't Say/The Girl Next Door (78 rpm = £8)	12
59	Fontana H 172	Richer Than I/Willingly (78 rpm = £8)	12

MARK PERRY
80	NB NB 7	You Cry Your Tears/Music Death? (with Dennis Burns, p/s in poly bag)	5
80	Deptford Fun City DFC 12	Whole World's Down On Me/I Live — He Dies (p/s)	5
80	Deptford Fun City DLP 06	SNAPPY TURNS (LP)	12

SHORT(L)Y PERRY
72	Attack ATT 8043	Musical Goat/WINSTON GRENNON & J. JACKSON: Stinging Dub	8
72	Explosion EX 2067	Sprinkle Some Water/FLOWERS & ALVIN: Howdy And Tenky	7
72	Bullet BU 512	Sprinkle Some Water/FLOWERS & ALVIN: Howdy And Tenky	7
73	Bullet BU 529	Yama Skank/U ROY JUNIOR: Doctor Run Come Quick	10
73	Downtown DT 517	Dedicated To Illiteracy/G.G. ALL STARS: Illiteracy Dub	7
73	Grape GR 3052	Abusing And Assaulting (by Flowers & Alvin)/Food Control	7
73	Green Door GD 4043	President Mash Up The Resident/President Mash Up The Resident Part Two	7

(see also Shorty, Cornell Campbell, Maytones, Paulette Williams)

STEVE PERRY
60	HMV POP 745	Step By Step/Because They're Young	18
62	Decca F 11462	Ginny Come Lately/Two Of A Kind	12
62	Decca F 11526	Young And In Love/Let It Come True	7
63	Decca F 11656	Find Me A Girl/My Dad	6
64	Decca F 11895	Crooked Little Man/Day Dreams	6

PERRY SISTERS
59	Brunswick 05802	Fabian/Willie Boy (78 rpm = £18)	25

PERSIAN RISK
81	SRT SRTS/81/CUS/1146	Calling For You/Chasing The Dragon (p/s)	175
83	Neat NEAT 24	Ridin' High/Hurt You (p/s)	18
86	Metal Masters METALLP 2	RISE UP (LP)	12

PERSIANS
69	Pama PM 772	I Only Have Eyes For You/The Sun Gotta Shine In Your Heart	12
72	Capitol CL 15726	Baby Come Back Home/I Want To Go Home	8

PERSIMMON'S PECULIAR SHADES
68	Major Minor MM 554	Watchmaker/Coplington	22

PERSONALITIES
65	Dice CC 30	I Remember/Suffering	15
66	Blue Beat BB 354	Push It Down/BUSTER'S ALL STARS: Blues Market	22

PERSUADERS
93	Detour DR 001	Finished Forever/In The Night (p/s, 300 only)	20
94	Detour DR 011	Waiting For The Nowhere Express/Girl/The Paperchase (p/s, 100 on red vinyl)	8/5

PERSUADERS (U.S.)
72	Atlantic K 40370	THE THIN LINE BETWEEN LOVE AND HATE (LP)	20
73	Atlantic K 40476	THE PERSUADERS (LP)	15

PERSUASIONS
65	Columbia DB 7560	I'll Go Crazy/Try Me	25
65	Columbia DB 7700	Big Brother/Deep Down Love	25
66	Columbia DB 7859	La, La, La, La, La/Opportunity	25

PERSUASIONS (U.S.)
69	Minit MLF 11017	Party In The Woods/It's Better To Have Loved And Lost	15
73	MCA MUS 1222	Good Old Acappella/You Must Believe Me	7
70	Straight STS 1062	A CAPPELLA (LP)	38
72	Island ILPS 9201	STREET CORNER SYMPHONY (LP)	20

MORRIS PERT
75	Chantry ABM 21	LUMINOS/CHROMOSPHERE/4 JAPANESE VERSES (LP)	40
80	Chantry CHT 001	LUMINOS/CHROMOSPHERE/4 JAPANESE VERSES (LP, reissue)	30
82	Chantry CHT 007	BOOK OF LOVE/FRAGMENTI I/ULTIMATE DECAY (LP)	30

JON PERTWEE
72	Purple PUR 111	Who Is The Doctor/Pure Mystery	18
85	Safari DOCTOR 1	Who Is The Doctor/Doctor Blood Donor (p/s)	6
62	Phillips BBL 7558	SONGS FOR VULGAR BOATMEN (LP)	22

(see also Rupert Hine, Derek Roy, BBC Radiophonic Workshop)

PESKY GEE!
| 69 | Pye 7N 17708 | Where Is My Mind/A Place Of Heart Break | 40 |
| 69 | Pye N(S)PL 18293 | EXCLAMATION MARK (LP) | 50+ |

(see also Black Widow, Agony Bag)

PETALS
| 63 | Decca F 11650 | Let's Do The Tamoure/Look At Me | 8 |

PETER & ALEX
| 70 | Carnaby 4018 | Big Beat/On The Loose | 7 |

PETER & GORDON
66	Columbia DB 7834	Woman/Wrong From The Start	5
66	Columbia DB 7951	Don't Pity Me/To Show I Love You	5
66	Columbia DB 8003	Lady Godiva/Morning's Calling	5
66	Columbia DB 8075	Knight In Rusty Armour/The Flower Lady	5
67	Columbia DB 8159	Sunday For Tea/Start Trying Someone Else	5
67	Columbia DB 8198	The Jokers/Red, Cream And Velvet	5
68	Columbia DB 8398	I Feel Like Going Out/The Quest For The Holy Grail	5
68	Columbia DB 8451	You've Had Better Times/Sipping My Wine	5
69	Columbia DB 8585	I Can Remember (Not Too Long Ago)/Hard Time, Rainy Day	5
64	Columbia SEG 8337	JUST FOR YOU (EP)	20
64	Columbia SEG 8348	NOBODY I KNOW (EP)	30
64	Columbia 33SX 1630	PETER AND GORDON (LP, also stereo SCX 3518)	20/25
64	Columbia 33SX 1660	IN TOUCH WITH PETER AND GORDON (LP, also stereo SCX 3532)	20/25
65	Columbia 33SX 1761	HURTIN' 'N' LOVIN' (LP, also stereo SCX 3565)	20/25
66	Columbia S(C)X 6045	PETER AND GORDON (LP, mono/stereo)	25/35
66	Columbia S(C)X 6097	SOMEWHERE... (LP, mono/stereo)	20/25
65	Columbia SCXC 25	I GO TO PIECES (LP, export issue)	60
66	Columbia SCXC 29	WOMAN (LP, export issue)	60
66	Columbia SCXC 33	LADY GODIVA (LP, export issue)	70

(see also Gordon Waller)

PETER & HEADLINES
| 64 | Decca F 11980 | Don't Cry Little Girl/It Was Love | 20 |
| 64 | Decca F 12035 | Tears And Kisses/I've Got My Reasons | 20 |

(see also Count Downe & Zeros)

PETER & MARY
| 54 | Columbia SCMC 6 | Crazy Mix Up Song/What Shall We Do With The Lonesome Lover (export issue) | 6 |

(see also Peter Lind Hayes)

PETER & PAUL
| 66 | Blue Beat BB 364 | Hosana/Schoolgirl | 18 |

PETER & PERSUADERS
| 65 | Oak RGJ 197 | The Wanderer/Wine Glass Rock/Oh My Soul/Cross My Heart (EP) | 50 |

(see Legendary Lonnie)

PETER & TEST TUBE BABIES
81	No Future OI 4	Banned From The Pubs/Moped Lads/Peacehaven Wild Lads (p/s)	8
82	No Future OI 15	Run Like Hell/Up Yer Bum (p/s)	8
83	Trapper EARS 1	Zombie Creeping Flesh/No Invitation/Smash And Grab (p/s)	6
83	Trapper EARS 2	The Jinx/Trapper Ain't Got A Bird (p/s)	5
82	No Future Punk 3	PISSED AND PROUD (LP)	15
83	Trapper THIN 1	MATING SOUNDS OF SOUTH AMERICAN FROGS (LP, with lyric inner)	15

PETER & WOLVES
67	MGM MGM 1352	Little Girl Lost And Found/Is Me	20
68	MGM MGM 1374	Lanternlight/Break Up-Break Down	15
68	MGM MGM 1397	Julie/Birthday	12
68	MGM MGM 1452	Woman On My Mind/Old & The New	30
70	UPC UPC 104	Something In The Way She Moves/The Lady And Me	7

(see also Factory, Norman Conquest, John Pantry, Sounds Around, Bunch)

PETER B's
| 66 | Columbia DB 7862 | If You Wanna Be Happy/Jodrell Blues | 70 |

(see also Tony Colton, Peter Bardens, Peter Green, Cheynes, Shotgun Express)

PETER, PAUL & MARY

63	Warner Bros WB 104	Blowing In The Wind/Flora	5
64	Warner Bros WB 142	The Times They Are A-Changin'/Blue	5
63	Warner Bros WSE 6119	MOVING (EP, stereo)	8
63	Warner Bros WSE 6122	PETER, PAUL AND MARY (EP, stereo)	8
63	Warner Bros WM 4064	PETER, PAUL AND MARY (LP, also stereo WS 9064)	12
63	Warner Bros WM/WS 8124	MOVING (LP)	12
65	Warner Bros WM/WS 8142	IN THE WIND (LP)	12
65	Warner Bros WM/WS 8158	IN CONCERT VOL. 1 (LP)	12
65	Warner Bros WM/WS 8159	IN CONCERT VOL. 2 (LP)	12
65	Warner Bros (W)S 1589	A SONG WILL RISE (LP)	12
66	Warner Bros (W)S 1615	SEE WHAT TOMORROW BRINGS (LP)	12
66	Warner Bros W(S) 1648	PETER, PAUL & MARY ALBUM (LP)	12

PETER'S FACES

64	Piccadilly 7N 35178	Why Did You Bring Him To The Dance/She's In Love	12
64	Piccadilly 7N 35196	Try A Little Love My Friend/I Don't Care	12
64	Piccadilly 7N 35205	Just Like Romeo And Juliet/Wait	25
65	Piccadilly 7N 35225	De-Boom-Lay-Boom/Suzie Q	10

(see also Flowerpot Men, White Plains)

JANICE PETERS & PLAYBOYS

58	Columbia DB 4222	This Little Girl's Gone Rockin'/Kiss Cha Cha (78 rpm = £20)	40
59	Columbia DB 4276	A Girl Likes/You're The One (78 rpm = £25)	35

LENNIE PETERS

63	Oriole CB 1887	And My Heart Cried/For A Lifetime	7
64	Oriole CB 1956	Let The Tears Begin/Love Me, Love Me	7

LINDA PETERS

70	Warlock Music WMM 101/2	WARLOCK MUSIC SAMPLER (LP, sampler, 7 tracks by Elton John)	1,000

(see also Paul McNeill & Linda Peters, Richard & Linda Thompson)

MARK PETERS & SILHOUETTES

63	Oriole CB 1836	Fragile (Handle With Care)/Janie	40
64	Oriole CB 1909	Cindy's Gonna Cry/Show Her	40
64	Piccadilly 7N 35207	Don't Cry For Me/I Told You So	15

(see also Rats)

WENDY PETERS

68	Saga OPP 1	Morning Dew/I Don't Understand	12

PAUL PETERSEN

62	Pye International 7N 25153	Keep Your Love Locked/Be Everything To Anyone You Love	7
62	Pye International 7N 25163	Lollipops And Roses/Please Mr Sun	8
63	Pye International 7N 25173	My Dad/Little Boy Sad	7
63	Pye International 7N 25196	Amy/Goody Goody	7
68	Tamla Motown TMG 670	A Little Bit For Sandy/Your Love's Got Me Burnin' Alive	30

PAUL PETERSEN & SHELLEY FABARES

62	Pye International 7N 25133	She Can't Find Her Keys/Very Unlikely	8

(see also Shelley Fabares)

BOBBY PETERSON (QUINTET)

59	Top Rank JAR 232	The Hunch/Love You Pretty Baby (as Bobby Peterson Quintet)	22
64	Sue WI 342	Rockin' Charlie (Parts 1 & 2) (solo)	30
65	Sue WI 346	Piano Rock/One Day (solo)	30

OSCAR PETERSON

55	Columbia Clef SEB 10005	OSCAR PETERSON (EP)	8
56	Columbia Clef SEB 10022	OSCAR PETERSON NO. 2 (EP)	8
55	Columbia 33C 1037	PLAYS PRETTY (10" LP)	40
55	Columbia 33C 9012	PLAYS PRETTY (10" LP, reissue)	15
55	Columbia 33C 1038	THE OSCAR PETERSON QUARTET (10" LP)	15
55	Columbia 33C 1039	OSCAR PETERSON SINGS (10")	15
55	Columbia Clef 33CX 10012	PLAYS DUKE ELLINGTON (LP)	18
55	Columbia Clef 33CX 10016	PLAYS COLE PORTER (LP)	12
55	Columbia Clef 33CX 10028	PLAYS RICHARD RODGERS (LP)	20
55	Columbia Clef 33CX 10039	PLAYS COUNT BASIE (LP)	12
56	Columbia Clef 33C 9025	O LADY BE GOOD (10" LP)	25
56	HMV CLP 1086	IN ROMANTIC MOOD (LP)	12
57	Columbia Clef 33CX 10062	KEYBOARD (LP)	12
57	Columbia Clef 33CX 10073	PLAYS HAROLD ARLEN (LP)	12
58	Columbia Clef 33CX 10096	STRATFORD (CANADA SHAKESPEAREAN FESTIVAL) (LP)	12
59	Columbia Clef 33CX 10135	A NIGHT ON THE TOWN (LP)	12
59	HMV CLP 1278	THE OSCAR PETERSON TRIO SWINGS "MY FAIR LADY" (LP)	12
59	HMV CLP 1317	OSCAR PETERSON AT THE CONCERTGEBOUW (LP)	12
60	HMV CLP 1355	JAZZ PORTRAIT OF SINATRA (LP)	12

(see also Louis Armstrong, Lester Young, Ella Fitzgerald, Sonny Stitt)

RAY PETERSON

59	RCA RCA 1131	The Wonder Of You/I'm Gone (78 rpm = £30)	18
59	RCA RCA 1154	Shirley Purley/Come And Get It (78 rpm = £45)	18
60	RCA RCA 1175	Answer Me/Goodnight My Love, Pleasant Dreams	15
60	RCA RCA 1195	Tell Laura I Love Her/Wedding Day	12
60	London HLX 9246	Corrine, Corrina/Be My Girl	15
61	London HLX 9332	Sweet Little Kathy/You Didn't Care	12
61	London HLX 9379	Missing You/You Thrill Me	10
62	London HLX 9489	I Could Have Loved You So Well/Why Don't You Write Me	15
62	London HLX 9569	You Didn't Care/You Know Me Much Too Well	10
63	London HLX 9746	Without Love/Give Us Your Blessing	10

64	MGM MGM 1249	Oh No/If You Were Here	5
64	MGM MGM 1258	Across The Street/When I Stop Dreaming	5
65	MGM MGM 1273	House Without Windows/Wish I Could Say No To You	5
65	MGM MGM 1288	I'm Only Human/One Lonesome Rose	5
66	MGM MGM 1303	Everybody/Love Hurts	5
61	London REX 1293	CORRINE CORRINA (EP)	85

PETER, SUE & MARC & PFURI, GORPS & KNIRL
79	EMI EMI 2940	Second Hand Company/Troedler & Co.	6

PETEY, PATTY, PEGGY & BRUCE
59	Top Rank JAR 250	The Happy Penguins/IRVING KRASE ORCHESTRA: The Happy Penguin Waltz	5

PET HATE
83	FM 12VHF 2	Roll Away The Stone/Caught/Playing With My Heart (12", p/s)	12
84	Heavy Metal HMRLP 23W	BAD PUBLICITY (LP, white vinyl)	12

(see also Silverwing)

PETITES
60	Philips PB 1035	Get Your Daddy's Car Tonight/Sun Showers	8

MARY PETTI
61	RCA RCA 1239	Hey! Lawdy Lawdy/Gee, But It Hurts	50

PETS
58	London HL 8652	Cha-Hua-Hua/Cha-Kow-Ski (78 rpm = £20)	25
59	Pye International 7N 25004	(You Wandered) Beyond The Sea/Wow-ee!!! (78 rpm = £10)	10

(see also Seph Acre & Pets)

PET SHOP BOYS
SINGLES
84	Epic A 4292	West End Girls/Pet Shop Boys (p/s)	20
84	Epic TA 4292	West End Girls (Extended)/Pet Shop Boys (12", p/s)	30
85	Parlophone R 6097	Opportunities (Let's Make Lots of Money)/In The Night (matrix: A-3-1-2) (1st mix, white p/s)	12
85	Parlophone 12R 6097	Opportunities (Let's Make Lots of Money) (Dance Mix)/In The Night (Extended) (12", white p/s)	20
85	Parlophone 12RA 6097	Opportunities (Let's Make Lots of Money) (Version Latina)/(Dub For Money Remix)/In The Night (Extended Mix) (12", large picture labels, die-cut p/s)	40
85	Parlophone 12R 6097	Opportunities (Let's Make Lots of Money) (Dance Mix)/In The Night (Extended) (12", p/s, mispressing, B-side plays "Opportunities [Dub For Money Remix]")	30
85	Parlophone 12R 6097	Opportunities (Let's Make Lots of Money) (Dance Mix)/In The Night (Extended) (12", p/s, 2nd mispressing, A-side plays "Opportunities [Version Latina]")	30
85	Parlophone 10R 6115	West End Girls (Untitled Mix)/A Man Could Get Arrested (4.09 Mix)/West End Girls (7" Mix) (10", round foldout p/s; some sealed, some stickered)	40/30/30
85	Parlophone 12R 6115	West End Girls (Dance Mix)/A Man Could Get Arrested (4.09 Mix)/West End Girls (7" Mix) (12", with 6" die-cut holes in p/s, 6" picture labels)	8
86	Parlophone 12RA 6115	West End Girls (Shep Pettibone Mastermix)/West End Dub/A Man Could Get Arrested (4.09 Mix) (12", black/blue/red p/s, standard labels)	10
86	Parlophone 12RA 6115	West End Girls (Shep Pettibone Mastermix)/West End Dub/A Man Could Get Arrested (4.09 Mix) (12", same as above with 6" yellow circle on sleeve)	10
86	Parlophone 12RA 6115	West End Girls (Shep Pettibone Mastermix)/West End Dub/A Man Could Get Arrested (4.09 Mix) (12", stickered black/blue/red p/s with 6" die-cut hole & 6" yellow picture labels)	10
86	Parlophone 10R 6116	Love Comes Quickly (Dance Mix)/That's My Impression (Disco Mix) (10", PVC sleeve with poster)	50
86	Parlophone 12R 6116	Love Comes Quickly (Dance Mix)/That's My Impression (Disco Mix) (12", large picture labels, die-cut white sleeve)	10
86	Parlophone RD 6140	Suburbia/Paninaro//Love Comes Quickly (Shep Pettibone Remix)/Jack The Lad/Suburbia Part Two (double pack, gatefold p/s)	6
87	Parlophone 12RX 6158	It's A Sin (Ian Levine Remix)/You Know Where You Went Wrong (Rough Mix) (12", 'video still' p/s)	8
87	Parlophone 12RX 6171	Always On My Mind (Phil Harding Remix)/Do I Have To?/Always On My Mind (Dub) (12", title sleeve)	8
88	Parlophone 12RX 6190	Domino Dancing (Remix)/Don Juan (Demo)/Domino Dancing (Demo) (12", 'hotel' p/s)	8
89	Parlophone 10R 6220	It's Alright (Alternative Mix)/It's Alright (Extended Dance Mix) (10", black title sleeve with poster)	8
89	Parlophone 12RS 6220	It's Alright (Extended)/One Of The Crowd/Your Funny Uncle (12", p/s, with obi)	8
93	Parlophone R 6348	Can You Forgive Her? (7" Version)/Hey Headmaster (red vinyl, factory custom pressing, p/s)	300+
96	Parlophone 12RX 6431	Before (Underground Mix)/(Bonus Dub)/(Underground Instrumental)/(Bonus Beats)/(Classic Paradise Mix)/(Afrodisiac Mix)/(Hedboys Mix)/(Hedboys Dub)/(Joey Negro Extended Mix) (3 x 12", each in p/s, box set)	8
96	Parlophone 12RD 6443	Se A Vida É (That's The Way Life Is) (Mark's Deep And Dark Vocal)/(Mark's Deep And Dark Instrumental)/(Mark's Shelter Dub)/(Deep Dish Liquid Remix)/(Pink Noise Mix)/(Deep Dish Dub)/(7" Version) (12", double pack, yellow & green vinyl, p/s, 2 inner sleeves)	8
97	Parlophone Fan Club	It Doesn't Often Snow At Christmas (CD, fan club issue, in sealed silver bubble wrap)	150

ALBUMS
87	Parlophone PCSDX 104	ACTUALLY (LP, with U.S. import "Always On My Mind" 12", stickered sleeve)	12
87	Parlophone CDPCSDX 104	ACTUALLY (CD, with U.S. import "Always On My Mind" CD single)	25
88	Parlophone PCSX 7325	INTROSPECTIVE (LP, 3 x clear vinyl 12" factory custom pressing, with wraparound paper strip, 10 copies only)	800

88	Parlophone PCSX 7325	INTROSPECTIVE (LP, 3 x black vinyl 12", with picture labels & wraparound paper obi strip)	15
93	Parlophone CDPSDX 143	VERY (CD, with 6-track bonus CD "Relentless" in foldout 'bubble' wallet)	20
96	Parlophone	BILINGUAL (LP)	15
00	Parlophone 724352185719	NIGHTLIFE (LP)	15
02	Parlophone	RELEASE (LP, white vinyl)	12

PROMOS

85	Parlophone R 12R 6097	Opportunities (Let's Make Lots of Money)/In The Night (12", "photocopy" sleeve)	30
85	Parlophone R 6097 (matrix: A-1U-1-1-1)	Opportunities (Let's Make Lots of Money) (New Mix)/In The Night (2nd mix, stickered plain sleeve)	60
86	Parlophone R 6116	Love Comes Quickly (1-sided, p/s)	40
86	Parlophone 12R 6129	Opportunities (Let's Make Lots of Money) (7.18 Shep Pettibone Mastermix)/Opportunities (4.27 Reprise)/Opportunities (6.44 Original Dance Mix)/Was That What it Was (12", autographed black die-cut sleeve, some with press release)	35/30
86	Parlophone 12R 6140	Suburbia (The Full Horror)/Paninaro/Jack The Lad (12", blank red labels)	8
88	Parlophone 12RDJ 6198	Left To My Own Devices (The Disco Mix)/Left To My Own Devices/The Sound Of The Atom Splitting (12", unique title sleeve)	12
90	Parlophone 12RXDJ 6275	Being Boring (Remix)/We All Feel Better In The Dark (After Hours Climax)/We All Feel Better In The Dark (Ambient) (12", black die-cut sleeve)	8
91	Parlophone 12R 6283A	Lose My Mind (Disco Version) (12", 1-sided)	8
91	Parlophone 12RDJ 6301A	D.J. Culture (12", 1-sided)	8
91	Parlophone MFB 6	Music For Boys (12", 3 untitled mixes, hand-stamped white label)	25
91	Parlophone 12MFBX 1	Music For Boys (12", 2 untitled mixes, white label)	12
92	Parlophone CDRX 6332	Go West (7" Version)/West End Girls (Sacha Mix)/Forever/Go West (Extended Dance Mix) (cassette, title sleeve)	150
93	Parlophone 12RXDJ 6348	Can You Forgive Her? (MK Remix)/(MK Bicycle Dub)/I Want To Wake Up (Johnny Marr 1993 Remix)/(Johnny Marr Groove Mix) (12")	10
93	Abbey Road	COMPILED EP (CD-R, Abbey Road title sleeve; autographed by The Boys, 20 only)	500+
94	Parlophone 12RDJ 6386	Yesterday When I Was Mad (Jam & Spoon Mix)/(Junior Vasquez Factory Dub)/(Junior Vasquez Fabulous Dub)/(Junior Vasquez Body Dub)/(Coconut 12" Mix)/(RAF Zone Mix)/(RAF Zone Dub)/Euroboy/Some Speculation (12", double pack, unique p/s)	15
95	Parlophone RLH 6414	Paninaro '95/In The Night (jukebox issue)	5
96	Parlophone RLH 6431	Before/The Truck Driver & His Mate (jukebox issue)	5
96	Parlophone 12RDJD 6431	Before (Classic Paradise Mix)/(Afrodisiac Mix)/(Hedboys Mix)/(Dub)/(Extended Mix) (2 x 12", blue 'penis' p/s)	25
96	Parlophone 12RJD 6431	Before (Underground Mix)/(Bonus Dub)/(Underground Instrumental)/(Bonus Beats) (12", red 'penis' p/s)	25
96	Parlophone CDIN 103	BILINGUAL THE INTERVIEW (CD)	20
97	Parlophone 12 BARDJ 2	The Truck Driver & His Mate/Before (Love To Infinity Classic Paradise Mix) (12", 'two knobs' p/s, 150 copies)	100
97	Parlophone 12RDJ 6460	A Red Letter Day (Trouser Enthusiasts Autoerotic Decapitation Mix)/(Trouser Enthusiasts Congo Dongo Dubstramental) (12")	10
97	Parlophone 12BOYDJ 101	The Boy Who Couldn't Keep His Clothes On (Main Vocal)/(INT... Club Mix)/(Banji Girlfriend Beats)/(On Stage At Twilo)/(Radio Edit) (12", die-cut sleeve)	40
97	Parlophone 12RDJD 6470	Somewhere (Forthright Club Mix)/(Trouser Enthusiasts Mix)/To Step Aside (Brutal Bill Mix)/Somewhere (Forthright Dub)/To Step Aside (Ralphi's Old School Dub)/To Step Aside (Davidson Ospina Dub) (12" double pack, title p/s)	8
97	PSB 97	PET SHOP BOYS TALK (interview CD, promo-only)	15
99	Parlophone (no cat. no.)	NIGHTLIFE (10" x 10" box in PVC slip case, contains interview CD, music CD, book, EPK & 3 photographs)	70
01	10th Planet/PSBP/RUG	FIVE TITLES FROM CLOSER TO HEAVEN: Positive Role Model/Friendly Fire/Shameless/K-Hole/For All Of Us (CD-R, title sleeve, all sung by Neil Tennant)	40+
03	Parlophone 12RDJ 6620	Miracles (Extended Version) (12", 1-sided white label test pressing)	8
03	Parlophone 12RDJX 6620	Miracles (Lemon Jelly Remix) (12", 1-sided white label test pressing)	8
03	Parlophone CDRDJ 6020	Miracles (CD 1- track in "lavender scented" p/s)	8
03	Parlophone LONDON 001	London/(Remix) (12", white label)	8
88	Parlophone (no cat. no.)	INTROSPECTIVE (cassette, video-style case, with lyric booklet)	60
89	Parlophone CDPCSD 113	BEHAVIOUR (CD, commercial issue, different inlay, in white monogrammed pouch, with full-album cassette & chronology)	50
91	Parlophone CDPSBDJ 1	DISCOGRAPHY (CD, with Mark Goodyear spoken-word introductions)	12
93	Parlophone DF 118	RELENTLESS (3 x 12", on pink/yellow/blue vinyl)	60
96	Parlophone BILING 1	BILINGUAL (A4 yellow box set, including "A Taste Of Bilingual" CD: [Discoteca/Electricity/A Red Letter Day/It Always Comes As A Surprise/Se A Vida É], with 2 photos & insert)	40
96	Parlophone PSBCDDJ 1	BILINGUAL (A4 pale blue launch party promo box set including "A Taste Of Bilingual" CD [Before/Se A Vida É], & album cassette, unique inlay)	30
99	Parlophone CDIN 126	INTERVIEW (CD, slipcase)	12
01	Parlophone PSB 001	SAMPLER (CD, 13-track sampler, includes six unreleased versions, part-laminated card sleeve)	15
01	Really Useful Group	CLOSER TO HEAVEN (CD-R, title sleeve; 19 tracks, all sung by Neil Tennant)	80
02	Parlophone RELEASE 01	RELEASE (CD, white card sleeve sealed with title sticker)	30
		cue sheet)	12
03	Parlophone POPART 02	THE INTERVIEW (interview CD for 'PopArt', with cue sheet)	12

(see also Eighth Wonder, Dusty Springfield, Absolutely Fabulous, Electronic, Liza Minnelli, Ian Wright)

FRANK PETTY TRIO

53	MGM SP 1010	St. Louis Blues (Boogie Woogie)/Somebody Stole My Girl	20
53	MGM SP 1033	Side By Side/Who's Sorry Now	10
53	MGM SP 1038	Sugar/Sioux City Sue	10
53	MGM SP 1053	Sweet Jenny Lee/Yes Sir That's My Baby	6
54	MGM SP 1092	Loch Lomond/Pino Pantaloni	6
54	MGM SP 1112	Mr Pogo/Sunday	6

Norman PETTY TRIO

NORMAN PETTY TRIO
54	HMV 7M 274	Mood Indigo/Petty's Little Polka 15

TOM PETTY (& HEARTBREAKERS)
77	Shelter WIP 6377	American Girl/Wild One Forever (some in p/s) 5
77	Shleter WIP 12-6396	Anything That's Rock'n'Roll/Fooled Again (I Don't Like It) (live) (12") 8
77	Shelter WIP 12-6403	American Girl/Luna (live) (12") 8
76	Shelter 1DJ 24A	OFFICIAL LIVE BOOTLEG (LP, with Heartbreakers, 1-sided 5-track, promo only) . . 20

(see also Stevie Nicks, Randy Newman, Traveling Wilburys, k.d. lang & Roy Orbison)

PEYR
(see under Theyr)

P.F.M.
73	Manticore K 43502	PHOTOS OF GHOSTS (LP, gatefold sleeve) 20
74	Manticore K 53502	THE WORLD BECAME THE WORLD (LP) 20
75	Manticore K 53506	COOK (LP) 20
76	Manticore K 53508	CHOCOLATE KINGS (LP, gatefold sleeve with lyric sheet) 18
77	Manticore K 53511	JET LAG (LP) 15

PHANTOM
78	Cool Ghoul COOL 1	Lazy Fascist/Power Dub 6

(see also Tom Robinson, Blazing Sons)

PHANTOM BAND
71	Polydor 2058-176	Loop-Di-Love/Funkin' About 60

PHANTOM CHORDS
92	Camden Town GNAR 003	Town Without Pity/She's A Bad Motorcycle (p/s, 2,000 only) 5

(see also Damned)

PHANTOMS
61	Palette PG 9014	Phantom Guitar/Cachina 20
60s	Arc ARC	GREAT GUITAR HITS (LP) 30

PHARAOHS
58	Decca DFE 6522	THE PHARAOHS (EP) 1,000
86	Ace SW 116	THE PHARAOHS (EP, reissue) 5

RORY PHARE
88	Parlophone RP 1	Laughing Inside/Laughing Inside (actually by Roy Harper; p/s, promo only) 7

(see also Roy Harper)

PHASE 4
66	Decca F 12327	What Do You Say About That/Think I'll Sit Down And Cry (1st issue) 18
66	Fab FAB 1	What Do You Say About That/I'm Gonna Sit Down And Cry (2nd issue) 12
67	Fab FAB 6	Man Am I Worried?/Listen To The Blues 48

PHASE 5
70	Polydor 2058 063	Star Trek/Enterprise 40

JAMES PHELPS
72	Paramount PARA 3019	Check Yourself/My Lover's Prayer 12

PHENOMENA
85	Bronze BRO 193	Dance With The Devil/Hell On Wings (p/s) 7
85	Bronze BROX 193	Dance With The Devil (Midnight Mix)/Hell On Wings (12", p/s with poster) 10

(see also Trapeze, Whitesnake, Cozy Powell, Black Sabbath, Thin Lizzy, Budgie, A-Ha)

PHILADELPHIA SOCIETY
75	Gull GULS 21	100 South Of Broadway (Parts 1 & 2) 6

PHIL & FLINTSTONES
64	Bedrock PR 5371	Love Potion No. 9/Honey Don't (private pressing) 50

PHILIP & HIS FOETUS VIBRATIONS
82	Self Immol. WOMB KX 07	Tell Me, What Is The Bane Of Your Life/Mother I've Killed The Cat (p/s) 25

(see also You've Got Foetus On Your Breath, Foetus Art Terrorism, Foetus Über Frisco, Foetus Under Glass, Scraping Foetus Off The Wheel)

LOUIS PHILIPPE
86	él GPO 15	Like Nobody Do/Twangy Twangy (p/s) 6
89	él GPUT36	YURI GAGARIN (LP) 15

ANTHONY PHILLIPS
79	Arista SPART 1085/AFLP 1	SIDES (LP, 1st 500 copies sealed with free LP "Private Parts & Pieces") 20

(see also Genesis)

CONFREY PHILLIPS (TRIO)
56	Columbia SCM 5223	Love And Marriage/The Others I Like 6
57	Decca F 10835	Am I Going Out Of My Mind?/Afterglow 6
57	Decca F 10866	Shotgun Rock 'n' Roll/Hokey-Kokey Rock 'n' Roll (as Confrey Phillips Trio) 20
57	Decca F 10866	Shotgun Rock 'n' Roll/Hokey-Kokey Rock 'n' Roll (as Confrey Phillips Trio) (78) . . 10

EDDY/EDWIN PHILLIPS
76	Charisma CB 283	Limbo Jimbo/Change My Ways (as Eddy Phillips) 5
85	T-Mac UEZT 003	Life On Earth/(Radio Mix)/(Instrumental) (12", as Edwin Phillips) 7

(see also Creation, Mark Four, Spectrum)

(LITTLE) ESTHER (PHILLIPS)
62	Stateside SS 140	Release Me/Don't Feel Rained On 20
63	Ember EMB S 174	Am I That Easy To Forget/I Really Don't Want To Know
		(as Little Esther Phillips) 12
65	Sue WI 395	The Chains/Feel Like I Wanna Cry (as Esther Philips) 40
65	Atlantic AT 4028	And I Love Him/Shangri-La 15
65	Atlantic AT 4048	Let Me Know When It's Over/I Saw Me 15
66	Atlantic AT 4077	I Could Have Told You/Just Say Goodbye 100

66	Ember EMBS 221	Release Me/Be Honest With Me (as Little Esther Phillips) 8
66	Atlantic 584 013	When A Woman Loves A Man/Ups And Downs 15
67	Atlantic 584 062	Someone Else Is Taking My Place/When Love Comes To The Human Race 8
67	Atlantic 584 103	And I Love Him/Shangri-La (reissue) 6
67	Atlantic 584 126	I'm Sorry/Cheater Man 15
69	Roulette RO 505	Too Late To Worry, Too Blue To Cry/I'm In The Mood For Love
		(Moody's Mood For Love) 8
69	Roulette RO 508	Tonight I'll Be Staying Here With You/Sweet Dreams 6
72	Atlantic K 10168	Catch Me I'm Falling/Release Me. 15
72	Kudu KUS 4000	Home Is Where The Hatred Is/Til My Back Ain't Got No Bone. 20
73	Kudu KUS 4002	I've Never Found A Man/Cherry Red. 15
63	Ember CW 103	REFLECTIONS OF GREAT COUNTRY AND WESTERN STANDARDS (LP) 75
65	Atlantic ATL 5030	AND I LOVE HIM (LP) 70
67	Atlantic 587/588 010	ESTHER PHILLIPS SINGS (LP) 40
72	Kudu KUL 2	FROM A WHISPER TO A SCREAM (LP) 30
73	Kudu KUL 6	ALONE AGAIN, NATURALLY (LP) 15
75	Kudu KU 18	PERFORMANCE (LP) 15
76	Atlantic K 50521	CONFESSIN' THE BLUES (LP, gatefold sleeve) 15

FLIP PHILLIPS
55	Columbia/Clef 33C 9003	FLIP PHILLIPS QUARTET (10" LP) 15

GLENN PHILLIPS
75	Caroline C 1519	LOST AT SEA (LP) 12

GREGORY PHILLIPS
63	Pye 7N 15546	Angie/Please Believe Me 12
64	Pye 7N 15593	Everybody Knows/Closer To Me (with Remo Four). 8
64	Pye 7N 15633	Don't Bother Me/Make Sure That You're Mine 8
65	Immediate IM 004	Down In The Boondocks/That's The One 8
	(see also Remo Four)	

JOHN PHILLIPS
70	Stateside SS 8046	Mississippi/April Anne 6
70	Stateside-Dunhill SSL 5027	JOHN PHILLIPS: THE WOLFKING OF L.A. (LP). 30
	(see also Mamas & Papas)	

LESLIE PHILLIPS
59	Parlophone R 4610	The Navy Lark/The Disc 7
62	Parlophone R 4912	I Must Resist Temptation/Jolly Old Spring. 5
69	Columbia DB 8562	The Man Most Likely To/Marigold 5

MICHELLE PHILLIPS
76	A&M AMS 7250	No Love Today/Aloha Louie. 7
77	A&M AMS 7340	Victim Of Romance/Lady Of Fantasy 12
77	A&M AMLS 64651	VICTIM OF ROMANCE (LP) 25
	(see also Mamas & Papas)	

NOEL PHILLIPS
80	Jammys JM001	Youth Man/Living In The Ghetto (12"). 25

PHIL PHILLIPS & TWILIGHTS
59	Mercury AMT 1059	Sea Of Love/Juella 35
60	Mercury AMT 1072	Take This Heart/Verdi Mae 32
60	Mercury AMT 1093	Your True Love Once More/What Will I Tell My Heart 28
61	Mercury AMT 1139	I Love To Love You/No One Else But You 28

SHAWN PHILLIPS
65	Columbia DB 7611	Hey Nelly Nelly/Solitude. 12
65	Columbia DB 7699	Doesn't Anybody Know My Name?/Nobody Listens. 12
65	Columbia DB 7789	Little Tin Soldier/London Town 8
66	Columbia DB 7956	Summer Came/Storms 8
67	Parlophone R 5606	Stargazer/Woman Mine. 70
70	A&M AMS 819	Christmas Song/Lovely Lady. 6
65	Columbia 33SX 1748	I'M A LONER (LP) 80
66	Columbia S(C)X 6006	SHAWN (LP) 70
70	A&M AMLS 978	CONTRIBUTION (LP). 15
71	A&M AMLS 2006	SECOND CONTRIBUTION (LP, with insert) 15
72	A&M AMLS 64324	COLLABORATION (LP). 15
73	A&M AMLS 64363	FACES (LP) 15
74	A&M AMLH 68278	FURTHERMORE (LP) 15
77	A&M AMLH 64650	SPACED (LP, with inner sleeve). 15

SID PHILLIPS BAND
56	HMV 7M 372	Bugle Call Rag/Memories Of You 8
56	HMV 7M 396	Rockin' Thru' The Rye/Everybody Step 8
56	HMV 7M 406	Juke Box Baby/My Honey's Lovin' Arms 8
56	HMV 7M 418	Mamma Don't Allow/Glad Rag Doll 8
56	HMV POP 269	Farewell Blues (Rock 'N' Roll Style)/It Goes Like This 7
57	HMV POP 416	The Midgets/Tropical Twilight 7
59	HMV POP 549	Weekend/Enchiladas-Cha-Cha. 6
57	HMV 7EG 8253	DIXIELAND RAMBLINGS (EP) 18
59	HMV 7EG 8425	DIXIE SPECIAL (EP) 12
59	HMV 7EG 8461	DIXIE BEAT (EP) 12
61	HMV 7EG 8645	DIXIELAND EXPRESS (EP). 12
55	HMV DLP 1102	HORS D'OEUVRES (10" LP). 15
57	HMV DLP 1164	DOWN DIXIELAND HIGHWAY (10" LP) 15
58	HMV DLP 1194	CRUISING DOWN TO DIXIE (10" LP) 12
58	HMV DLP 1212	FLYING DOWN TO DIXIE (10" LP) 15

MINT VALUE £

STU PHILLIPS
58	London HL 8673	The Champlain And St. Lawrence Line/The Priest Who Slept 100 Years	15
58	London HL 8673	The Champlain And St. Lawrence Line/The Priest Who Slept 100 Years (78)	15
60	Pye International 7N 25062	Strangers When We Meet/BOB MERSEY ORCHESTRA: Song Of India	6
67	RCA RCA 1601	Angel Of Love/The Great El Tigre	5
59	Pye Intl. NEP 44001	STU PHILLIPS (EP)	12

TEDDY PHILLIPS & HIS ORCHESTRA
54	London HL 8032	Ridin' To Tennessee/Alone Tonight (78)	12
54	Parlophone CMSP 4	Down Boy/Meet "Miss Pippin" (export issue)	15
54	Parlophone CMSP 12	The Old Red Barn/JIMMY BLUE CREW: The Old Shoe Cobbler (export issue)	15
54	Parlophone CMSP 28	Life Is Like A Slice Of Cake/One-Sided Love Affair (export issue)	15

WARREN PHILLIPS & THE ROCKETS
69	Decca (S)PA 43	THE WORLD OF ROCK 'N' ROLL (LP)	20
	(see also Savoy Brown, Foghat)		

WOOLF PHILLIPS & HIS ORCHESTRA
54	Melodisc M 1284	Rock, Rock, Rock/Merci Beaucoup (78)	7
54	Decca F 10416	Count Your Blessings Instead Of Sheep/Your Heart, My Heart (B-side with Dennis Morley — Vocal)	6

VINCE PHILPOTT & DRAGS
64	Decca F 11997	The Cramp/Eenie Meenie Miny Mo	15

PHILWIT & PEGASUS
70	Chapter One CHR 130	And She Came — Final Thought/Pauper's Son	8
70	Chapter One CHR 131	And I Try/Pauper's Son	8
70	Chapter One CHR 137	The Elephant Song/Pseudo Phoney Mixed Up Croney	8
70	Chapter One CHSR 805	PHILWIT AND PEGASUS (LP)	35
	(see also Mark Wirtz)		

PHOENIX
69	President PT 246	Tour De France/Time To Go	6

PHOENIX
76	CBS 81621	PHOENIX (LP)	12
80	Charisma CAS 1150	IN FULL VIEW (LP)	12
	(see also Argent, Kinks, Michael Des Barres)		

PHOENIX
81	Rising PR 433032	PHOENIX RISING EP (Lonely Attack/The Minstrel/Understanding/ Phoenix Rising 'Av An 'Am) (12" EP)	35

PHONES SPORTSMAN BAND
81	Rather GEAR 9	I REALLY LIKE YOU (EP)	8
	(see also Swell Maps)		

PHOTOGRAPHED BY LIGHTNING
86	Fierce FRIGHT 008	Sleep's Terminator/Winter Trees (foldaround p/s, hand-coloured labels)	30

PHUTURE PHANTASY
88	Low Fat Vinyl LFV 1	SLAM (12")	15

PHYSICALS
78	Physical PR 001	ALL SEXED UP (EP)	6
79	Big Beat NS 58	Be Like Me/Pain In Love (p/s)	6
	(see also Maniacs)		

EDITH PIAF
53	Columbia DCF 152	Soeur Anne/Misericorde (78)	15
61	Columbia DB 4596	Non, Je Ne Regrette Rien/Les Amants D'Un Jour	6
63	Columbia SEG 8220	GREAT PIAF (EP)	8
64	Columbia SEG 8308	NON, JE NE REGRETTE RIEN (EP)	8
65	Columbia SEG 8387	QU'IL ETAIT TRISTE (EP)	8
57	Columbia SCX 5	MEA CULPA (LP)	15
60	Columbia 33SX 1276	SINCERELY ... EDITH PIAF (LP)	12
61	Columbia 33SX 1330	PIAF AT THE PARIS OLYMPIA (LP)	12

PIANO MAGIC
97	Wurlitzer Jukebox WJ 26	For Engineers A/For Engineers AA (p/s)	7
98	Lissy's LISS 32	Music For Rolex/Matmos (p/s)	6
98	Darla DRL 074	A Trick Of The Sea/Halloween Boat (CD)	12
98	Debut DEBT 001SP	French Mittens/Icebreaker: Melody For Nato (p/s)	9
98	Bad Jazz BEBOP 9	Music For Annahbird/Music For Wasps/Me At 19 (p/s)	8
99	Acetone Solve 010	Amongst The Books, An Angel/C'est Un Mauvais Presage Lorsque Ton Aureole A Tombe (1st 20 copies with interlocking p/s)	10/6
00	Morr MUSIC 008	Panic Amigo — Piano Magic Remixed (12" EP)	10
97	i/Che IRE 2102	POPULAR MECHANICS (LP)	12

PIANO RED
52	HMV B 10244	Rockin' With Red/Red's Boogie (78)	18
52	HMV B 10246	Just Right Bounce/Hey, Good Lookin' (78)	18
52	HMV B 10316	Count The Days I'm Gone/Bouncin' With Red (78)	18
52	HMV JO 244	Rockin' With Red/Red's Boogie (78, export issue)	18
52	HMV JO 276	Layin' The Boogie/Baby What's Wrong (78, export issue)	18
52	HMV JO 296	My Gal Jo/Let's Have A Good Time (78, export issue)	18
53	HMV JO 334	Voo Doopee Doo/Everybody's Boogie (78, export issue)	18
53	HMV 7M 108	Rockin' With Red/Red's Boogie	200
64	RCA RCX 7138	RHYTHM AND BLUES VOL. 2 (EP)	40
	(see also Dr. Feelgood [U.S.])		

PIBLOKTO
(see under Pete Brown & Piblokto)

PICA
70	Polydor 2058 056	Take The Barriers Down/Insurance Man	6
71	Philips 6006 129	Rainbow Chaser/Ad Lib	7

(see also Nirvana [UK])

PIC & BILL
67	Page One POF 024	All I Want Is You/It's Not You	15
67	Page One POF 037	This Is It/Nobody But My Baby	15
68	Page One POF 052	Sad World Without You/Just A Tear	15

PICADILLY LINE
67	CBS 2785	At The Third Stroke/How Could You Say You're Leaving Me	30
67	CBS 2958	Emily Small (The Huge World Thereof)/Gone Gone Gone	18
68	CBS 3595	Yellow Rainbow/Evenings With Corrina	25
68	CBS 3595	Yellow Rainbow/I Know, She Believes (reissue with different B-side)	12
68	CBS 3743	Evenings With Corrina/My Best Friend	20
67	CBS (S)BPG 63129	THE HUGE WORLD OF EMILY SMALL (LP, some with promo insert)	140+

(see also Edwards Hand)

PICARDY
68	Statside SIDE 8004	Montage/How Sweet It Is	5

PICCADILLY STRINGS
61	Piccadilly 7N 35013	Sir Francis Drake Theme/Our House	5

PIERO PICCIONI
67	Fontana TF 898	Main Theme From 'The Tenth Victim'/Part 2 (mono)	12

BUSTER PICKENS
60s	Heritage HLP 1008	TEXAS PIANO (LP, 99 only)	60+

J.B. PICKERS
71	London HLU 10334	Super Soul Sounds/KIM & DAVE: Nobody Knows	15

BOBBY (BORIS) PICKETT & CRYPT-KICKERS
62	London HLU 9597	Monster Mash/Monsters' Mash Party	12
73	London ZGU 133	MONSTER MASH (LP)	32

DAN PICKETT
60s	XX MIN 710	DAN PICKETT (EP)	15

NICK PICKETT
72	Warner Bros K 14156	America/Lady Luck	6
72	Warner Bros K 44172	SILVERSLEEVES (LP)	15

(see also John Dummer Blues Band)

WILSON PICKETT
63	Liberty LIB 10115	It's Too Late/I'm Gonna Love You	25
65	Atlantic AT 4036	In The Midnight Hour/I'm Not Tired	20
65	MGM MGM 1286	Let Me Be Your Boy/My Heart Belongs To You (DJ copies = £100)	60
65	Atlantic AT 4052	Don't Fight It/It's All Over	15
66	Atlantic AT 4072	634-5789/That's A Man's Way	15
66	Atlantic 584 023	99 And A Half (Won't Do)/Danger Zone	10
66	Atlantic 584 039	Land Of 1000 Dances/You're So Fine	12
66	Atlantic 584 066	Mustang Sally/Three Time Loser	15
67	Atlantic 584 101	Everybody Needs Somebody To Love/Nothing You Can Do	12
67	Atlantic 584 107	New Orleans/Soul Dance III	12
67	London HLU 10146	Billy The Kid/I Don't Want No Part-Time Love (with Falcons)	12
67	Atlantic 584 130	Funky Broadway/I'm Sorry About That	12
67	Atlantic 584 142	Stag-O-Lee/I'm In Love	12
68	Atlantic 584 150	In The Midnight Hour/Danger Zone	8
68	Atlantic 584 173	That Kind Of Love/I've Come A Long Way	8
68	Atlantic 584 183	She's Looking Good/We've Got To Have Love	8
68	Atlantic 584 203	I'm A Midnight Mover/Deborah	7
68	Atlantic 584 221	I Found A True Love/For Better Or Worse	7
69	Atlantic 584 236	Hey Jude/Night Owl	6
69	Atlantic 584 261	Mini-Skirt Minnie/Back In Your Arms	10
69	Atlantic 584 281	Hey Joe/Born To Be Wild	6
70	Atlantic 584 313	You Keep Me Hangin' On/Now You See Me, Now You Don't	6
70	Atlantic 2091 005	Sugar, Sugar/Cole, Cooke And Redding	6
70	Atlantic 2091 032	(Get Me Back On Time) Engine No. 9/International Playboy	7
71	Atlantic 2091 086	Fire And Water/Don't Let The Green Grass Fool You	6
71	Atlantic 2091 124	Don't Know My Love (Parts 1 & 2)	6
72	Atlantic K 10166	Don't Let The Green Grass Fool You/Covering The Same Old Ground	8
72	Atlantic K 10181	Funk Factory/One Step Away	6
72	President PT 319	If You Need Me/I'm Gonna Love You	8
73	President PT 322	I Can't Stop/Down To My Last Heartbreak	8
65	Atlantic ATL 5037	IN THE MIDNIGHT HOUR (LP)	70
66	Atlantic 587/588 029	THE EXCITING WILSON PICKETT (LP)	40
66	Atlantic 587 032	IN THE MIDNIGHT HOUR (LP, reissue)	20
67	Atlantic 587/588 057	THE WICKED PICKETT (LP)	25
67	Atlantic 587/588 080	THE SOUND OF WILSON PICKETT (LP)	25
68	Atlantic 587/588 092	THE BEST OF WILSON PICKETT (LP)	20
68	Atlantic 587/588 107	I'M IN LOVE (LP)	25
68	Atlantic 587/588 111	MIDNIGHT MOVER (LP)	22
69	Atlantic 588 170	HEY JUDE (LP)	20
70	Atlantic 2465 002	RIGHT ON (LP)	20
70	Joy JOYS 181	IF YOU NEED ME (LP)	20
71	Atlantic 2400 026	ENGINE NO. 9 — IN PHILADELPHIA (LP)	20
72	Atlantic K 40319	DON'T KNOCK MY LOVE (LP)	15

(see also Falcons)

Gary PICKFORD-HOPKINS

GARY PICKFORD-HOPKINS & FRIENDS
83	Spartan SP 143	Why? (The Song)/Why? (The Story) (p/s)	8
83	Spartan SP 143T	Why? (The Song)/Why? (The Story) (12", p/s)	10

(see also Deke Leonard, Man, Andy Fairweather-Low, Alan Ross, Big Sleep, Eyes Of Blue, Wild Turkey)

PICKWICKS
64	Decca F 11901	Apple Blossom Time/I Don't Wanna Tell You Again	18
64	Decca F 11957	You're Old Enough/Hello Lady	15
65	Warner Bros WB 151	Little By Little/I Took My Baby Home	60+

PICTURES FROM THE GREAT EXHIBITION
80s	Recommended RE/ARC	The Housewife's Nightmare (silkscreened, 1-sided, gatefold p/s)	6

PIED PIPERS
54	Parlophone CMSP 21	Kissin' Drive Rock/Please Understand (export issue)	18

PIED PIPERS
66	Columbia DB 7883	Ragamuffin/Fat Marie	6

BILLY & DEDE PIERCE/JIM ROBINSON
64	London HA-K/SH-K 8163	JAZZ AT PRESERVATION HALL VOL. 2 (LP)	12

WEBB PIERCE
50s	Decca BM 311368	We'll Find A Way/Any Old Time (export issue)	30
56	Brunswick 05630	Teenage Boogie/Any Old Time (78 rpm = £30)	200
57	Brunswick 05682	Bye, Bye Love/Honky Tonk Song (78 rpm = £20)	40
59	Brunswick 05809	I Ain't Never/Shanghaied (78 rpm = £20)	15
60	Brunswick 05820	No Love Have I/Whirlpool Of Love	10
60	Brunswick 05842	Drifting Texas Sand/All I Need Is You	10
56	Brunswick OE 9253	WEBB PIERCE PT. 1 (EP)	25
56	Brunswick OE 9254	WEBB PIERCE PT. 2 (EP)	25
56	Brunswick OE 9255	WEBB PIERCE PT. 3 (EP)	25
62	Ember EMB 4520	COUNTRY AND WESTERN FAVOURITES VOL. 1 (EP)	20
59	Parlophone GEP 8792	COUNTRY ROUND UP (EP)	40
55	Brunswick LA 8716	THE WONDERING BOY (10" LP)	40
60	Brunswick LAT 8324	WEBB! (LP)	22
65	Brunswick LAT 8540	HIDEAWAY HEART (LP)	20
65	Brunswick LAT 8551	CROSS COUNTRY (LP)	15

(see also Red Sovine & Webb Pierce)

CLIVE PIG & THE HOPEFUL CHINAMEN
79	Pinnacle PIN 21	Happy Birthday Sweet Sixteen/Our Movement (p/s)	10

(see also Trixie's Big Red Motorbike)

PIGEON FLYERS
68	Columbia DB 8449	The Heaven We Shared Together/Keep On Sayin'	5

BILLY PIGG
71	Leader LEA 4006	THE BORDER MINSTREL (LP, gatefold sleeve with booklet)	12

PIGGLESWICK FOLK
77	Acorn CF 256	PIG IN THE MIDDLE (LP)	12

PIGS
77	Bristol Recorder NBR 01	Youthenasia/They Say/Psychopath/National Front (p/s)	8

PIGSTY HILL LIGHT ORCHESTRA
70	Village Thing VTS 1	PHLOP! (LP)	15
72	Village Thing VTS 8	PIGGERY JOKERY (LP)	15

DAVE PIKE
63	Starlite ST45 094	Melvalita/Ginha	5
66	Atlantic 584 052	Sunny/HERBIE MANN: Philly Dog	10
66	Atlantic 588 005	JAZZ FOR THE JET SET (LP)	25

PiL
(see under Public Image Ltd)

RAY PILGRIM (& BEATMEN)
60	Oriole CB 1557	Baby Doll/Gambler's Guitar (solo)	12
61	Oriole CB 1616	Little Miss Makebelieve/Granada (solo)	12
64	Embassy WB 645	Kissin' Cousins (with Beatmen)/	
		JAYBIRDS: Some Day We're Gonna Love Again	7

(see also Bud Ashton, Jaybirds, Typhoons)

PILGRIM FATHERS
69	Tangerine 009	Love And The World Will Love/Come A Day	7

PILTDOWN MEN
60	Capitol CL 15149	McDonald's Cave/Brontosaurus Stomp	8
61	Capitol CL 15175	Piltdown Rides Again/Bubbles In The Tar	8
61	Capitol CL 15186	Goodnight Mrs Flintstone/The Great Imposter	8
61	Capitol CL 15211	Gargantua/Fossil Rock	12
62	Capitol CL 15245	A Pretty Girl Is Like A Melody/Big Lizard	12
61	Capitol EAP1 20155	GOODNIGHT MRS. FLINTSTONE (EP)	40

SIR HUBERT PIMM
55	London HL 8155	Goodnight And Cheerio/Honky Tonk Train Blues	35
55	London RE-U 1032	PIMM'S PARTY (EP, with Ellen Sutton)	20

(see also Duke & Duchess)

COURTNEY PINE
88	Island 10ISB 301	CHILDREN OF THE GHETTO (LP, 2 x 10", with 4 prints)	20

PINEAPPLE CHUNKS
65	Mercury MF 922	Drive My Car/Dream About	12

PINEWOOD TOM/TOM TALL
59	Jazz Collector JEL 5	THE MALE BLUES VOLUME 4 (EP)	18

'PING PING' & AL VERLANE
60	Oriole CB 1589	Sucu Sucu/Maria Della Montagna	10

PINKERTON'S ('ASSORTED' COLOURS)
65	Decca F 12307	Mirror Mirror/She Don't Care (as Pinkerton's 'Assorted' Colours)	8
66	Decca F 12377	Don't Stop Loving Me Baby/Will Ya? (as Pinkerton's 'Assorted' Colours)	10
66	Decca F 12493	Magic Rocking Horse/It Ain't Right (as Pinkerton's Colours)	32
67	Pye 7N 17327	Mum And Dad/On A Street Car (as Pinkerton's Colours)	12
67	Pye 7N 17414	There's Nobody I'd Sooner Love/Look At Me (as Pinkerton's)	12
68	Pye 7N 17574	Kentucky Woman/Behind The Mirror (as Pinkerton's)	12

(see also Flying Machine, Liberators, Tony Newman)

PINK FAIRIES
71	Polydor 2058 089	The Snake/Do It	22
72	Polydor 2059 302	Well Well Well/Hold On	25
76	Stiff BUY 2	Between The Lines/Spoiling For A Fight (p/s)	7
71	Polydor 2383 045	NEVERNEVERLAND (LP, printed PVC outer & gatefold card inner, in yellow bag with photos & notes)	60
71	Polydor 2383 045	NEVERNEVERLAND (LP, printed PVC outer & gatefold card inner, pink vinyl & "pink plastic" in text on rear sleeve, around 100 pressed)	250+
71	Polydor 2383 045	NEVERNEVERLAND (LP, black vinyl, standard sleeve)	22
72	Polydor 2383 132	WHAT A BUNCH OF SWEETIES (LP)	22
73	Polydor 2383 212	KINGS OF OBLIVION (LP, with poster)	30
75	Polydor 2384 071	FLASHBACK (LP)	20

(see also Twink, Larry Wallis, Deviants, Lightning Raiders, Shagrat)

PINK FLOYD
SINGLES
67	Columbia DB 8156	Arnold Layne/Candy And A Currant Bun	100
67	Columbia DB 8214	See Emily Play/Scarecrow	80
67	Columbia DB 8310	Apples And Oranges/Paintbox	150
68	Columbia DB 8401	It Would Be So Nice/Julia Dream	70
68	Columbia DB 8511	Point Me At The Sky/Careful With That Axe, Eugene	70
79	Harvest HAR 5194	Another Brick In The Wall (Part 2)/One Of My Turns (initial pressing, plain B-side label without 'window' picture)	6
81	Harvest HAR 5217	Money (Edit)/Let There Be More Light (unreleased)	
81	Harvest 12HAR 5217	Money (Full Length)/Let There Be More Light (12", unreleased)	
82	Harvest HAR 5222	When The Tigers Broke Free/Bring The Boys Back Home (gatefold p/s)	7
82	Harvest HAR 5222	When The Tigers Broke Free/Bring The Boys Back Home (standard p/s)	8
87	EMI EMDJ 26	Learning To Fly (Edited Version)/One Slip (Edited Version)/Terminal Frost (no p/s, mispressing without "One Slip", 1,000 only on pink vinyl, 50 on black)	12/20
87	EMI EM 26	Learning To Fly (Edited Version)/One Slip (Edited Version)/Terminal Frost (p/s)	5
87	EMI 12EM 26	Learning To Fly (Edited Version)/One Slip (Edited Version)/Terminal Frost (DYOL Version) (12", p/s)	7
87	EMI CDEM 26	Learning To Fly (Edited Version)/One Slip (Edited Version)/Terminal Frost (Album Version)/Terminal Frost (DYOL Version) (CD, card sleeve & inner)	15
87	EMI EM 34	On The Turning Away (Album)/Run Like Hell (Live Version) (p/s)	5
87	EMI EMP 34	On The Turning Away (Album)/Run Like Hell (Live Version) (p/s, pink vinyl, 1000 only)	8
87	EMI 12EMP 34	On The Turning Away (Album)/Run Like Hell (Live Version)/On The Turning Away (Live Version) (12", poster p/s)	12
87	EMI CDEM 34	On The Turning Away/Run Like Hell (Live Version)/On The Turning Away (Live Version) (CD)	15
88	EMI EM 52	One Slip/Terminal Frost (p/s)	5
88	EMI EMG 52	One Slip/Terminal Frost (pink vinyl, gatefold p/s with ticket application)	8
88	EMI 12EMP 52	One Slip/Terminal Frost/The Dogs Of War (live) (12", poster p/s)	8
88	EMI CDEM 52	One Slip/Terminal Frost/The Dogs Of War (live) (CD)	12
94	EMI EM 309	Take It Back (Edit)/Astronomy Domine (live) (jukebox issue, black vinyl)	8
94	EMI EM 309	Take It Back (Edit)/Astronomy Domine (live) (red vinyl, p/s)	7
94	EMI CDEMS 309	Take It Back (Album Version)/Astronomy Domine (live)/Take It Back (Edit) (CD, picture disc, with poster)	8
94	EMI EM 342	High Hopes (Radio Edit)/Keep Talking (Radio Edit) (clear vinyl, poster p/s)	5
94	EMI 12EM 342	High Hopes (Album Version)/Keep Talking (Album Version)/One Of These Days (live) (12", 1-sided, laser-etched blue vinyl, p/s in outer gatefold p/s with 7 postcards)	8
94	EMI CDEM 342	High Hopes (Radio Edit)/Keep Talking (Radio Edit)/One Of These Days (live) (CD, with 7 postcards)	8

ALBUMS
67	Columbia S(C)X 6157	THE PIPER AT THE GATES OF DAWN (LP, blue/black label, mono/stereo)	275/175

(second pressings of the above have "File Under Pop" on the right of the flipback; first pressings do not have this. Second pressings are worth half to a third less.)

68	Columbia S(C)X 6258	A SAUCERFUL OF SECRETS (LP, blue/black label, mono/stereo)	250/120
70	Columbia SCX 6157	THE PIPER AT THE GATES OF DAWN (LP, re-pressing, silver & black label)	20
70	Columbia SCX 6258	A SAUCERFUL OF SECRETS (LP, re-pressing, silver & black label)	25
69	Columbia SCX 6346	SOUNDTRACK FROM THE FILM 'MORE' (LP, laminated flipback sleeve, 'couple facing west' photo on green-tinted rear sleeve)	35
70s	Columbia SCX 6346	SOUNDTRACK FROM THE FILM 'MORE' (LP, laminated non-flipback sleeve, 'couple facing west' photo on black-tinted rear sleeve)	25
70s	Columbia SCX 6346	SOUNDTRACK FROM THE FILM 'MORE' (LP, laminated non-flipback sleeve, 'couple facing east' photo on black-tinted rear sleeve)	35

69	Harvest SHDW 1/2	UMMAGUMMA (2-LP, laminated gatefold sleeve) 22
70	MGM 2315 002	ZABRISKIE POINT (LP, soundtrack, with Jerry Garcia/Kaleidoscope, et al) 20
70	Harvest SHVL 781	ATOM HEART MOTHER (LP, gatefold sleeve) 18

(First pressings of the above Harvest LPs have "The Gramophone..." text on label rim and "Harvest" on the left side of the label; second pressings have "The Gramophone..." text with a boxed EMI logo above "Harvest". Second pressings are worth a little less)

71	Harvest SHVL 795	MEDDLE (LP, gatefold sleeve) 12
71	Starline SRS 5071	RELICS (LP, white textured sleeve) 15
72	Harvest SHSP 4020	OBSCURED BY CLOUDS (LP, rounded sleeve) 20
73	Harvest SHVL 804	THE DARK SIDE OF THE MOON (LP, first pressing, solid light blue triangle label, black inner, 2 posters & 2 stickers, gatefold sleeve, only one side opening) ... 200
73	Harvest SHVL 804	THE DARK SIDE OF THE MOON (LP, blue & black label, gatefold sleeve with black inner, 2 posters & 2 stickers, some with stickered sleeve) 20/15
70s	Harvest SHVL 804	THE DARK SIDE OF THE MOON (LP, repressing, blue & silver label, gatefold sleeve with black inner, 2 posters & 2 stickers) 12
73	Harvest Q4 SHVL 781	ATOM HEART MOTHER (LP, quadrophonic, gatefold sleeve, initially with 'quadrophonic' logo on front sleeve, later inside) 30/25
73	Harvest Q4 SHVL 804	THE DARK SIDE OF THE MOON (LP, quadrophonic, gatefold sleeve, no inserts).. 30
73	Harvest SHDW 403	A NICE PAIR (2-LP, gatefold sleeve, with 2 inner sleeves; early copies with 'Mr Phang' dentist cover) 20/15
75	Harvest SHVL 814	WISH YOU WERE HERE (LP, with inner sleeve, postcard & black cellophane wraparound with sticker) 15
76	Harvest Q4 SHVL 814	WISH YOU WERE HERE (LP, quadrophonic, with inner sleeve) 35
77	Harvest SHVL 815	ANIMALS (LP, picture labels, non-barcode gatefold sleeve with inner) 15
78	Harvest SHDW 411	THE WALL (2-LP, plastic stickered gatefold sleeve, with inners) 15
79	Harvest PF 11	THE FIRST XI (11-LP set, original sleeves, plus exclusive "The Dark Side Of The Moon" & "Wish You Were Here" picture discs, 1,000 only) 200
83	Harvest SHPF 1983	THE FINAL CUT (LP, gatefold sleeve with title sticker) 15
87	EMI EMD 1003	A MOMENTARY LAPSE OF REASON (LP, gatefold sleeve with inner) 15
92	EMI CDS 7805572	SHINE ON (9-CD box set, with book and postcards) 100
93	EMI CDDSOM 20	THE DARK SIDE OF THE MOON (CD, 20th anniversary box set with booklet & 5 art cards) 18
94	EMI EMD 1055	THE DIVISION BELL (LP, gatefold sleeve, with inner) 12
95	EMI EMD 578	PULSE (4-LP box set in slipcase with hardback book) 35
97	EMI 859 857-1	THE PIPER AT THE GATES OF DAWN (LP, reissue, gatefold sleeve with inner, mono) 12
97	EMI CDEMD 1110	THE PIPER AT THE GATES OF DAWN (CD, mono, 30th anniversary box set with prints) 18
97	EMI SIGMA 630	'97 VINYL COLLECTION (7-LP set, die-cut box, includes "The Piper At The Gates Of Dawn" [EMD 1110], "The Wall" [EMD 1111], "Atom Heart Mother" [EMD 1112]", "Relics" [EMD 1113], "The Dark Side Of The Moon" [EMD 1114], "Wish You Were Here" [EMD 1115], each in stickered gatefold sleeve & inner [no inner on EMD 1111], withdrawn) .. 80
97	EMI CDEMD 1118	THE FIRST THREE SINGLES (CD, mono, mini album in card gatefold sleeve) ... 20

PROMOS

67	Columbia DB 8156	Arnold Layne/Candy And A Currant Bun (demo copy in promo-only p/s) 1500
67	Columbia DB 8214	See Emily Play/Scarecrow (demo copy in promo-only p/s) 1500
67	Columbia DB 8310	Apples And Oranges/Paintbox (demo copy in promo-only p/s) 1500
68	Columbia DB 8401	It Would Be So Nice (1-sided demo) 650
68	Columbia DB 8511	Point Me At The Sky/Careful With That Axe, Eugene (demo, with newsletter) 650
68	Columbia DB 8511	Point Me At The Sky/Careful With That Axe, Eugene (demo, with postcard) 750
69	Emidisc no cat. no.	The Narrow Way (acetate, different version, 1 copy only) 200
81	Harvest HAR 5217	Money (Edited Version) (1-sided, pink vinyl, 200 only) 35
81	Harvest HAR 5217	Money (Edited Version) (1-sided, pink vinyl, mispressing with "Let There Be More Light" label on B-side) 50
87	EMI EMDJ 34	On The Turning Away (edit)/On The Turning Away (album) (stickered p/s) 8
88	EMI 12PF 1	Delicate Sound Of Thunder Sampler: Another Brick In The Wall Part 2/ One Of These Days/Run Like Hell (12", black & pink sleeve) 20
88	EMI PSLP 1026	Pink Floyd In Europe '88: Money/Shine On/Another Brick In The Wall Part 2/ One Slip/On The Turning Away/Learning To Fly (12", with "Another Brick . . . Part 1" miscredit on back p/s). 20
88	EMI CDPINK 1	Wish You Were Here/Learning To Fly/Run Like Hell (CD). 20
92	EMI SHINE 1	SELECTED TRACKS FROM "SHINE ON" (CD, card sleeve). 18

(see also Syd Barrett, Roger Waters, Dave Gilmour, Rick Wright, Nick Mason, Joker's Wild, Ron Geesin)

PINK INDUSTRY

82	Zulu ZULU 1	Is This The End?/47/Don't Let Go/Final Cry (12", p/s) 8
85	Zulu ZULU RA 8	What I Wouldn't Give 6
83	Zulu ZULU 2	LOW TECHNOLOGY (LP) 12
83	Zulu ZULU 4	WHO TOLD YOU — YOU WERE NAKED (LP) 12

(see also Pink Military, Big In Japan)

PINK MILITARY

79	Last Trumpet LT 001	BUDDHA WALKING DISNEY SLEEPING (EP, foldout sleeve). 8
79	Eric's ERIC'S 002	BLOOD AND LIPSTICK (12" EP, die-cut p/s) 8
80	Eric's ERIC'S 005	Did You See Her/Everyday (p/s). 5
80	Virgin/Eric's ERIC'S 004	DO ANIMALS BELIEVE IN GOD? (LP). 12

(see also Pink Industry, Big In Japan, Ambrose Reynolds)

PINKOES

79	Popular POP1	INTO THE RED (EP). 12

PINK PEOPLE

64	Philips BF 1355	Psychologically Unsound/Cow Catcher 25
64	Philips BF 1356	Indian Hate Call/I Dreamt I Dwelt In Marble Halls 20

(see also Four Squares)

PINKY (& FELLAS)

65	Polydor BM 56009	All Cried Out/Back Where I Belong...............................	6
68	Decca F 12748	Manchester And Liverpool/Come Back Again (as Pinky & Fellas)	5
69	Polydor BM 56338	Let The Music Start/Oh, A Beautiful Day (as Pinky & Fellas).................	5

PINKY & PERKY

58	Decca F 11095	Tom Dooley/The Velvet Glove (Pinky & Perky Theme) (in p/s)................	5
58	Decca F 11095	Tom Dooley/The Velvet Glove (Pinky & Perky Theme) (78, in 10" p/s)	15
59	Decca F 11116	The Little Mountaineer/Does Your Chewing Gum Lose Its Flavour (some in p/s) (78 rpm = £12)	15
59	Decca F 11174	Pinky And Perky's Sing Song Medley (both sides) (78 rpm = £20)	5

PINNACLE

74	Stag HP 125	ASSASSIN (LP)	90

PIONEERS

66	Rio R 102	Good Nannie/Doreen Girl.......................................	40
66	Rio R 106	Too Late/Give Up..	28
68	Blue Cat BS 100	Shake It Up/Rudies Are The Greatest	28
68	Blue Cat BS 103	Give It To Me/LEADERS: Someday Someway	28
68	Blue Cat BS 105	Whip Them/Having A Bawl......................................	28
68	Blue Cat BS 139	Reggae Beat/Miss Eva	45
68	Caltone TONE 119	I Love No Other Girl/MILTON BOOTHE: I Used To Be A Fool...............	50
68	Amalgamated AMG 811	Give Me A Little Loving/This Is Soul (B-side actually by Lyn Tait & Jets)	18
68	Amalgamated AMG 814	Long Shot/Dip And Fall Back....................................	30
68	Amalgamated AMG 821	Jackpot/CREATORS: Kimble (B-side actually by Lee Perry)	32
68	Amalgamated AMG 823	No Dope Me Pony/LORD SALMONS: Great — Great In '68	35
68	Amalgamated AMG 826	Tickle Me For Days/VERSATILES: The Time Has Come	15
68	Amalgamated AMG 828	Catch The Beat/SIR GIBB'S ALLSTARS: Jana (B-side actually Immortals' "Jane Anne")	15
68	Amalgamated AMG 830	Sweet Dreams/DON DRUMMOND JUNIOR: Caterpillar Rock...............	20
68	Pyramid PYR 6062	Easy Come, Easy Go/BEVERLEY'S ALLSTARS: Only A Smile (B-side actually by Lyn Tait & Jets)................................	15
69	Pyramid PYR 6065	Pee Pee Cluck Cluck/BEVERLEY'S ALLSTARS: Exclusively...............	15
69	Amalgamated AMG 833	Don't You Know/Me Naw Go A Believe..............................	15
69	Amalgamated AMG 835	Mama Look Deh/BLENDERS: Decimal Currency.......................	15
69	Amalgamated AMG 840	Who The Cap Fits/I'm Moving On	15
69	Amalgamated AMG 850	Alli Button/HIPPY BOYS: Death Rides	15
69	Trojan TR 672	Long Shot Kick The Bucket/RICO: Jumping The Gun	5
69	Trojan TR 685	Black Bud/Too Late...	7
69	Trojan TR 698	Poor Rameses/BEVERLEY'S ALLSTARS: In Orbit	5
70	Trojan TR 7781	Money Day/BEVERLEY ALL STARS: Ska Ba Do	8
71	Summit SUM 8511	Starvation/BEVERLEY'S ALLSTARS: (Version)........................	7
72	Summit SUM 8535	Story Book Children/SIDNEY, GEORGE AND JACKIE: Gorgeous, Marvellous	5
76	Mercury 6198061	Feel The Rhythm Of You and I/(Version)	8
77	Mercury 6007147	My Good Friend James/Secrets Of You	200
78	Ice GUY 14	My Good Friend James/Secrets Of You (reissue)	150
68	Amalgam. AMGLP 2003	GREETINGS FROM THE PIONEERS (LP)............................	70+
70	Trojan TBL 103	LONGSHOT (LP)	18
70	Trojan TBL 139	BATTLE OF THE GIANTS (LP)....................................	20
71	Trojan TRL 24	YEAH! (LP)...	15

(see also Sir Gibbs, Rebels [Jamaica], Jackey Robinson, Moonboys, Sidney George & Jackie)

PIPES OF PAN

67	Page One POF 038	Monday Morning Rain/Monday Morning Rain (Instrumental Mix)	20

PIPES OF PAN

71	Rolling Stones COC 49100	BRIAN JONES PLAYS WITH THE PIPES OF PAN AT JOUJOUKA (LP, gatefold sleeve with foldout insert; front cover with misprinted title).......	90
71	Rolling Stones COC 49100	BRIAN JONES PRESENTS THE PIPES OF PAN AT JOUJOUKA (LP, gatefold sleeve with foldout insert; "Presents" sticker on misprinted cover)	70
71	Rolling Stones COC 49100	BRIAN JONES PRESENTS THE PIPES OF PAN AT JOUJOUKA (LP, gatefold sleeve with foldout insert; corrected title on front cover)	65

(see also Rolling Stones)

PIPKINS

(see under Sweet)

PIPS

61	Top Rank JAR 574	Every Beat Of My Heart/Room In Your Heart	55

(see also Gladys Knight & Pips)

PIRATES

64	HMV POP 1250	My Babe/Casting My Spell	35
66	Polydor BM 56712	Shades Of Blue/Can't Understand	25
77	Warner Bros K 17002	Sweet Love On My Mind/You Don't Own Me (p/s)	15
78	Warner Bros K 17113	All In It Together/Dr. Feelgood (p/s)	10
78	Warner Bros K 17231	Shakin' All Over/Saturday Night Shoot Out	5
79	Sound For Industry SFI 431	All By Myself/Cat Clothes (1-sided fan club flexidisc, gold vinyl)............	5
79	Cube Hi Fly 33	HAPPY BIRTHDAY ROCK N' ROLL (LP, with flexidisc [PIR 2])..............	12

(see also Johnny Kidd & Pirates, [Billy J. Kramer &] Dakotas)

PISCES

71	Trailer LER 2025	PISCES (LP)..	30

HARRY PITCH

68	MOR MR 101P	HARMONICA JEWEL BOX (LP)	20

(see also Mr. Bloe)

PITCH PIKES

57	Mercury MT 171	Come Back To Me/How Will I Know (78).............................	8

PITCH SHIFTER
92	Earache MOSH 66	SUBMIT EP (12")	8

PITMAN
02	Son/White	Witness The Pitness (12" EP)	10

GENE PITNEY
SINGLES
61	London HL 9270	(I Wanna) Love My Life Away/I Laughed So Hard I Cried	18
61	HMV POP 933	Every Breath I Take/Mr Moon, Mr Cupid & I	30
61	United Artists POP 952	Town Without Pity/Air Mail Special	12
62	United Artists POP 1018	The Man Who Shot Liberty Valance/Take It Like A Man	12
62	United Artists UP 1005	If I Didn't Have A Dime/Only Love Can Break A Heart	7
63	United Artists UP 1012	Half Heaven, Half Heartache/Tower Tall	7
63	United Artists UP 1021	Mecca/Teardrop By Teardrop	7
63	United Artists UP 1030	True Love Never Runs Smooth/Donna Means Heartbreak	6
63	United Artists UP 1035	24 Hours From Tulsa/Lonely Night Dreams (blue or black label)	5
64	United Artists UP 1045	That Girl Belongs To Yesterday/Who Needs It?	6
64	United Artists UP 1055	I'm Gonna Find Myself A Girl/Lips Are Redder On You	10
64	United Artists UP 1063	It Hurts To Be In Love/Hawaii	10
64	Stateside SS 358	I'm Gonna Be Strong/Aladdin's Lamp	6
64	Stateside SS 365	It Hurts To Be In Love/Hawaii (reissue)	6
65	Stateside SS 390	I Must Be Seeing Things/Save Your Love	6
65	Stateside SS 420	Lookin' Thru The Eyes Of Love/Last Chance To Turn Around	6
65	Stateside SS 471	Princess In Rags/Amore Mio	6
66	Stateside SS 490	Backstage/In Love Again	6
66	Stateside SS 518	Nobody Needs Your Love/Dream World	6
66	Stateside SS 558	Just One Smile/The Boss's Daughter	6
67	Stateside SS 597	(In The) Cold Light Of Day/Flower Girl	6
67	Stateside SS 2060	Something's Gotten Hold Of My Heart/Where Did The Magic Go	5
68	Stateside SS 2103	Somewhere In The Country/Lonely Drifter	5
68	Stateside SS 2118	Love Grows/Conquistador	5
68	Stateside SS 2131	Yours Until Tomorrow/She's A Heartbreaker (DJ copy = £30)	15
69	Stateside SS 2142	Maria Elena/The French Horn	5
70	Stateside SS 2177	Shady Lady/Billy, You're My Friend	5
71	Pye International 7N 25564	Run Run Road Runner/Rain Maker	10
72	Pye International 7N 25579	I Just Can't Help Myself/Beautiful Sounds	5

EPs
63	HMV 7EG 8832	TOWN WITHOUT PITY	50
64	United Artists UEP 1001	TWENTY FOUR HOURS FROM TULSA	15
64	United Artists UEP 1002	THAT GIRL BELONGS TO YESTERDAY	15
65	Stateside SE 1027	TWENTY FOUR HOURS FROM TULSA (reissue)	15
65	Stateside SE 1028	THAT GIRL BELONGS TO YESTERDAY (reissue)	12
65	Stateside SE 1030	I MUST BE SEEING THINGS	15
65	Stateside SE 1032	GENE ITALIANO	18
66	Stateside SE 1036	GENE PITNEY SINGS JUST FOR YOU	12
66	Stateside SE 1040	BACKSTAGE	15
66	Stateside SE 1041	SAN REMO WINNERS AND OTHERS	18
67	Stateside SE 1045	THERE'S NO LIVING WITHOUT YOUR LOVING	15
66	Bravo BR 375	GENE PITNEY	10

LPs
62	HMV CLP 1566	THE MANY SIDES OF GENE PITNEY	50
63	United Artists (S)ULP 1028	ONLY LOVE CAN BREAK A HEART (mono/stereo)	30/40
63	United Artists ULP 1043	GENE PITNEY SINGS JUST FOR YOU	22
64	United Artists ULP 1061	BLUE GENE	22
64	United Artists ULP 1064	GENE PITNEY MEETS THE FAIR YOUNG LADIES OF FOLKLAND	22
64	United Artists ULP 1073	GENE PITNEY'S BIG SIXTEEN	20
65	Stateside SL 10118	GENE PITNEY'S BIG SIXTEEN (reissue)	15
65	Stateside SL 10119	BLUE GENE (reissue)	15
65	Stateside SL 10120	I'M GONNA BE STRONG	18
65	Stateside SL 10132	GENE PITNEY'S MORE BIG SIXTEEN (VOL. 2)	20
65	Stateside SL 10147	GEORGE JONES AND GENE PITNEY (with George Jones)	20
65	Stateside SL 10148	LOOKING THRU THE EYES OF LOVE	18
65	Stateside SL 10156	SINGS THE GREAT SONGS OF OUR TIME	20
66	Stateside SL 10173	IT'S COUNTRY TIME AGAIN (with George Jones)	20
66	Stateside S(S)L 10181	BEING TOGETHER (with Melba Montgomery)	18
66	Stateside S(S)L 10183	NOBODY NEEDS YOUR LOVE	18
67	Stateside S(S)L 10194	YOUNG, WARM AND WONDERFUL	18
67	Stateside S(S)L 10199	GENE PITNEY'S BIG SIXTEEN (VOL. 3)	18
67	Stateside S(S)L 10212	JUST ONE SMILE	18
67	Stateside S(S)L 10216	GOLDEN GREATS	15
68	Stateside S(S)L 10242	PITNEY TODAY	15
69	Stateside S(S)L 10286	THE BEST OF GENE PITNEY	12
71	Pye Intl. NSPL 28148	TEN YEARS LATER	12
72	Pye Intl. NSPL 28165	THE NEW SOUNDS OF GENE PITNEY	12

(see also Marc Almond & Gene Pitney, George Jones)

PETE PITTERSON
52	Esquire 5-058	West Indian Folk Music/Bali Game (78)	8

PIXIES
88	4AD BAD 805	Gigantic/River Euphrates/Vamos (live)/In Heaven (Lady In The Radiator Song) (live) (12", p/s)	8
88	4AD BAD 805CD	Gigantic/River Euphrates/Vamos (live)/In Heaven (Lady In The Radiator Song) (live) (CD)	10
89	4AD AD 904	Monkey Gone To Heaven/Manta Ray (p/s)	5
89	4AD PIX ONE	DOOLITTLE SAMPLER: Debaser/Wave Of Mutilation/I Bleed/Gouge Away (12", 1-sided, title sleeve, promo only)	20

89	4AD PIX 2	Into The White/Wave Of Mutilation (U.K. Surf) (12", 1-sided, promo only)	10
90	4AD PIX 3	EXTRACTS FROM BOSSANOVA: Allison/Rock Music/Down To The Well/ The Happening (12", 1-sided, promo only)	15
90	4AD AD 0014	Dig For Fire (p/s)	6
91	4AD PIX 4	EXTRACTS FROM TROMPE LE MONDE: U-Mass/Letter To Memphis/ Subbacultcha (10", same track both sides, promo only)	15
04	4AD PIX 2004CD	BEST OF PIXIES (CD, 5-track sampler, promo only)	20
87	4AD MAD 709	COME ON PILGRIM (mini-LP)	15
88	4AD CAD 803	SURFER ROSA (LP, with inner)	20
89	4AD CAD 905	DOOLITTLE (LP, with lyric booklet & postcard, some in carrier bag)	30/25
90	4AD CAD 0010	BOSSANOVA (LP, with booklet)	20

(see also Breeders, Frank Black)

PIXIES THREE
| 63 | Mercury AMT 1214 | Birthday Party/Our Love | 25 |

PIZZICATO 5
| 97 | Matador OLE 289-7 | Mon Amour Tokyo/Trailer Music (p/s) | 5 |

P.J. HARVEY
(see under 'H')

PLACEBO
95	Fierce Panda NING 13	Bruise Pristine/SOUP: M.E.L.T.D.O.W.N. (foldover p/s, 1500 only)	30
96	Deceptive BLUFF 024	Come Home/Drowning By Numbers (p/s)	10
96	Deceptive BLUFF 024	Come Home/Drowning By Numbers (CD)	25
96	Elevator FLOOR 001	36 degrees/Dark globe (p/s)	10
96	Hut FLOOR 3	Teenage Angst/Hug Bubble/Been Smoking Too Long (part 1 0f 2, p/s)	5
96	Hut FLOORCD 3	Teenage Angst/Hug Bubble/Been Smoking Too Long (CD, card sleeve)	12
96	Hut FLOOR 4	Nancy Boy (Sex Mix)/Slackerbitch (p/s)	6
97	Hut FLOOR 5	Bruise Pristine/(One Punch Remix) (p/s)	5
98	Hut SILVER 1	THE ORIGINAL DEMOS: Nancy Boy/Teenage Angst/36 Degrees/ Bruise Pristine (CD, fan club issue, card sleeve)	18
99	Hut FLOOR TP 10	Without You I'm Nothing (with David Bowie) (UNKLE Remix)/ (Flexirol Mix)/(Brothers In Rhythm Club Mix) (12" promo, 500 only, stickered die-cut sleeve)	20
99	Hut FLOOR CD 10	Without You I'm Nothing (Single Mix)/(UNKLE Remix)/(Flexirol Mix)/ (Brothers In Rhythm Club Mix) (multimedia CD, gatefold card sleeve)	15
99	Elevator SILVER 2	I Feel You (1-track cassette, fan club issue)	50
96	Hut LPFLOORY 2	PLACEBO (LP)	35
96	Hut CD FLOOR 2	PLACEBO (CD, digipak, 5000 only)	30
98	Elevator FLOORLP 8	WITHOUT YOU I'M NOTHING (LP)	25

PLAGUE
| 68 | Decca F 12730 | Looking For The Sun/Here Today, Gone Tomorrow | 150 |

PLAGUE
| 79 | Psycho P2615 | In Love/Wimpey Bar Song (some in p/s) | 100 |

PLAID
92	GPR GENP(X) 7	Scoobs In Columbia (remixes) (12", custom sleeve)	40
94	Clear CLR 409	ANDROID (12" EP, p/s, clear or black vinyl)	40/30
95	Rumble RUMBLE 01	MIND OVER RHYTHM MEET THE MEN FROM PLAID (3 x 10" in p/s)	25
92	Black Dog Prods. LP 1	MBUKI MVUKI (LP)	125

(see also Black Dog)

PLAIN CHARACTERS
(see under Gadgets)

PLAINSONG
72	Elektra K 12976	Even The Guiding Light/Yoko Man/Call The Tune	5
72	Elektra K 42120	IN SEARCH OF AMELIA EARHART (LP, gatefold sleeve with lyric insert)	22
73	Elektra K 42136	PLAINSONG II (LP, white label, promo only)	100

(see also Andy Roberts, Ian Matthews)

PLANET GONG
77	Affinity AF 5101	Opium For The People/Poet For Sale (p/s)	8
78	Charly CYX 202	Opium For The People/Stoned Innocent Frankenstein (10", p/s)	18
78	Charly	FLOATING ANARCHY — LIVE 1977 (LP)	18

(see also Daevid Allen, Gong)

PLANETS
| 60 | Palette PG 9008 | Like Party/Ippy Yippy Beatnik (some in p/s) | 25/18 |

PLANETS
60	HMV POP 818	Chunky/Screwball	15
61	HMV POP 832	Jam Roll/Delaney's Theme	20
61	HMV POP 895	Jungle Street/The Grasshopper	20

ROBERT PLANT
67	CBS 202656	Our Song/Laughin', Cryin', Laughin'	300
67	CBS 202656	Our Song/Laughin' Cryin' Laughin' ('A' label demo)	250+
67	CBS 202858	Long Time Coming/I've Got A Secret	300
67	CBS 202858	Long Time Coming/I've Got A Secret ('A' label demo)	250+
82	Swan Song SSK 19429T	Burning Down One Side/Far Post (12", p/s)	10
83	Es Paranza B 9848	Big Log/Messin' With The Mekon (p/s)	5
83	Es Paranza SAM 220	In The Mood(short version/In The Mood (Long Version) (7" radio promo)	8
85	Es Paranza SAM 2570	Little By Little (12" mix)/Little By Little (Album Version) (12" promo)	8
85	Es Paranza B 9621 F	Little By Little (Remix)/Doo Doo A Do Do/Easily Lead (live)/ Rockin' At Midnight (live) (double pack)	8
88	Es Paranza A 9373 TB	Heaven Knows (Extended Remix)/Walking Towards Paradise/Heaven Knows (Astral Mix) (12", stickered sealed box set with colour poster & 2 prints)	8

Robert PLANT

MINT VALUE £

88	Es Paranza A 9373 CD	Heaven Knows/Walking Towards Paradise/Big Log (3" CD & adaptor, 5" case) . . . 8	
88	Es Paranza A 9348 CD	Tall Cool One/White, Clean And Neat/Tall Cool One (Extended Version)/	
		Little By Little (3" CD, with adaptor, 5" case). 8	
88	Es Paranza A 9281 CDB	Ship Of Fools/Helen Of Troy (live)/Dimples (live) (3" CD, with adaptor & 5" case,	
		inside 5" box set with card, foldout lyric sheet & 2-page biography). 8	
90	Es Paranza A 8985P	Hurting Kind (I've Got My Eyes On You)/I Cried (shaped picture disc). 5	
93	Es Paranza/Fontana FATEX 1	29 Palms (edit) (CD, radio promo). 8	
93	Es Paranza/Fontana	I Believe/Hey Jane/Great Spirit (Acoustic)/Whole Lotta Love (You Need Love)	
	FATE 212	(12" limited edition picture disc). 10	
93	Es Paranza/Fontana	If I Were A Carpenter/I Believe (live)/Tall Cool One (live)	
	FATEX 4	(limited issue, clear plastic sleeve). 5	
02	Mercury MORNCJ 1	Morning Dew (Radio Edit) (CD, radio promo) 8	
03	Mercury LASTCJ 1	Last Time I Saw Her (Remix) (CD, radio promo) 8	
82	Swan Song SAM154	PICTURES AT ELEVEN (LP, promo interview disc with cue sheet). 30	
82	Es Paranza SAM 169	THE PRINCIPLE OF MOVEMENTS (LP, promo interview disc with cue sheet) . . . 30	
88	Es Paranza PR 2244	NON STOP GO! (LP, two disc set interview promo for NOW AND ZEN album) . . . 30	
90	Es Paranza WX 339X	MANIC NIRVANA (LP, gatefold sleeve) 12	
90	Es Paranza (no. cat. no)	MANIC NIRVANA BOX SET (LP promo in presentation box set) 40	
90	Es paranza SAM 653	MANIC NIRVANA (LP, advance promo black label) 15	
90	Es Paranza SAM 645	EXCERPTS FROM MANIC NIRVANA (CD, four track promo) 10	
93	Es Paranza/Fontana FATE 1	FATE OF NATIONS/INTERVIEW (CD, radio promo interview disc) 25	
93	Es Paranza/F'tana 063-994-1	FATE OF NATIONS (LP) 12	
02	Mercury (no cat. no.)	HEAD FIRST (CD, promo, original title for DREAMLAND album) 25	
02	Mercury 063 4652	DREAMLAND COLLECTORS EDITION (CD, limited issue, with bonus CD) 18	
02	Mercury (no cat. no.)	DREAMLAND (CD, promo). 20	
02	Mercury PLANT CJ 1	DREAMLAND (CD, promo, card sleeve) 18	
02	Mercury DREAMINT 1	DREAMLAND INTERVIEW DISC (CD, radio promo). 18	
02	Mercury 063 094 1	DREAMLAND (LP). 15	
03	Mercury PLANT 1/2	66 TO TIMBUKTU (3-CD, promo, with 2CD full album promo plus 9-track	
		sampler CD, in folder with press release) 30	
03	Mercury PLANT 2	66 TO TIMBUKTU (CD, 9-track promo) 12	

(see also Led Zeppelin, Listen, Jimmy Page, Robert Plant & The Strange Sensation, Page & Plant, Honeydrippers)

ROBERT PLANT AND THE STRANGE SENSATION
05	Es Paranza/Sanctuary		
	SANPX 392	All The Kings Horses (edit) (CD, radio promo) 8	
05	Es Paranza/S'ary SANTW405	The Enchanter (12" U.N.K.L.E Reconstruction Mix) (12"). 12	
05	Es Paranza/S'ary SANPR 356	MIGHTY REARRANGER (CD, advance promo) 18	
05	Es Paranza/S'ary SANLP 356	MIGHTY REARRANGER (LP) 15	

PLANXTY
73	Polydor 2383 186	PLANXTY (LP). 12	
73	Polydor 2383 232	THE WELL BELOW THE VALLEY (LP) 12	
74	Polydor 2383 301	COLD BLOW AND RAINY NIGHT (LP). 12	
76	Polydor 2389 387	THE PLANXTY COLLECTION (LP, gatefold sleeve). 12	
79	Tara 3001	AFTER THE BREAK (LP, with poster & lyric insert) 12	
80	Tara 3005	THE WOMAN I LOVED SO WELL (LP) 12	

PLASTIC GANGSTERS
83	Secret SHH 144	Plastic Gangsters/Sretsgnag Citsalp	
		(7", 12", no p/s on 12" stamped p/s on 7", unissued, DJ copies only) . . . . each 200	

(see also 4 Skins)

PLASTIC ONO BAND
(see under John Lennon, Yoko Ono)

PLASTIC PENNY
67	Page One POF 051	Everything I Am/No Pleasure Without Pain My Love 8	
68	Page One POF 062	Nobody Knows It/Just Happy To Be With You. 8	
68	Page One POF 079	Your Way To Tell Me Go/Baby You're Not To Blame 15	
69	Page One POF 107	Hound Dog/Currency 15	
69	Page One POF 146	She Does/Genevieve. 10	
68	Page One POL(S) 005	TWO SIDES OF THE PENNY (LP) 55	
69	Page One POLS 014	CURRENCY (LP) 55	
70	Page One POLS 611	HEADS YOU WIN, TAILS I LOSE (LP) 50	

(see also Universals, Circles, Brian Keith, Mick Grabham)

PLASTIKMAN
94	NovaMute L NO MU 37	MUSIK (2-LP, with bonus 1-sided etched 12") 15	

PLATFORM SIX
65	Piccadilly 7N 35255	Money Will Not Mean A Thing/Girl Down Town 10	

EDDIE PLATT
58	Columbia DB 4101	Tequila/Pop Corn (78 rpm = £25). 25	

PLATTERS
78s
55	Parlophone DP 433	Voo-Vee-Ah-Bee/STRANGERS: Just Don't Care (export issue). 45	
56	Parlophone DP 506	Beer Barrel Boogie/Roses Of Picardy (export issue) 45	
56	Mercury MT 107	(You've Got) The Magic Touch/Winner Takes All. 18	
57	Mercury MT 143	On My Word Of Honour/One In A Million 6	
58	Mercury MT 197	Helpless/Indiff'rent 15	
58	Mercury MT 205	Don't Let Go/Are You Sincere? 15	
58	Mercury MT 214	Twilight Time/Out Of My Mind 15	
58	Mercury MT 227	You're Making A Mistake (featuring Tony Williams)/My Old Flame 15	
58	Mercury AMT 1001	I Wish/It's Raining Outside. 18	
58	Mercury AMT 1016	Smoke Gets In Your Eyes/No Matter What You Are. 20	
59	Mercury AMT 1039	Enchanted/The Sound And The Fury 30	

59	Mercury AMT 1053	Remember When/Love Of A Lifetime (featuring Tony Williams)	40
60	Mercury AMT 1081	Harbour Lights/(By The) Sleepy Lagoon	50

45s

56	Mercury MT 117	The Great Pretender/Only You (And You Alone) (export issue)	40
58	Mercury 7MT 197	Helpless/Indiff'rent	40
58	Mercury 7MT 205	Don't Let Go/Are You Sincere?	30
58	Mercury 7MT 214	Twilight Time/Out Of My Mind	15
58	Mercury 7MT 227	You're Making A Mistake (featuring Tony Williams)/My Old Flame	20
58	Mercury AMT 1001	I Wish/It's Raining Outside.	18
58	Mercury AMT 1016	Smoke Gets In Your Eyes/No Matter What You Are.	10
59	Mercury AMT 1039	Enchanted/The Sound And The Fury	6
59	Mercury AMT 1053	Remember When/Love Of A Lifetime (featuring Tony Williams)	5
59	Mercury AMT 1066	My Blue Heaven/Wish It Were Me	6
60	Mercury AMT 1076	My Secret/What Does It Matter	5
60	Mercury AMT 1081	Harbour Lights/(By The) Sleepy Lagoon	5
60	Mercury AMT 1098	Ebb Tide/(I'll Be With You In) Apple Blossom Time (featuring Tony Williams).	5
60	Mercury AMT 1106	Red Sails In The Sunset/Sad River (featuring Tony Williams)	5
60	Mercury AMT 1118	To Each His Own/Down The River Of Golden Dreams	5
61	Mercury AMT 1128	If I Didn't Care/True Lover	5
61	Mercury AMT 1154	I'll Never Smile Again/You Don't Say	5
62	Ember JBS 701	Only You/Tell The World.	150+
66	Stateside SS 511	I Love You 1000 Times/Hear No Evil, Speak No Evil, See No Evil	20
66	Stateside SS 568	I'll Be Home/(You've Got) The Magic Touch.	12
67	Stateside SS 2007	With This Ring/If I Had A Love.	15
67	Stateside SS 2042	Washed Ashore (On A Lonely Island In The Sea)/	
		What Name Shall I Give You My Love (DJ copy = £60)	25
67	Stateside SS 2067	Sweet Sweet Lovin'/Sonata (DJ copy = £60)	25
69	Stateside SS 2150	With This Ring/If I Had A Love (reissue).	10
71	Pye Intl. 7N 25559	Sweet Sweet Lovin'/Going Back To Detroit	15
71	Pye Intl. 7N 25569	With This Ring/I Washed Ashore (On A Lonely Island In The Sea)	10

EPs

56	Mercury MEP 9504	THE FABULOUS PLATTERS	15
57	Mercury MEP 9514	THE FABULOUS PLATTERS VOL. II	18
57	Mercury MEP 9524	THE FABULOUS PLATTERS VOL. III.	20
58	Mercury MEP 9526	THE FLYING PLATTERS VOL. I	22
58	Mercury MEP 9528	THE FLYING PLATTERS VOL. II.	22
58	Mercury MEP 9537	THE PLATTERS	25
59	Mercury ZEP 10000	PICK OF THE PLATTERS NO. 1.	20
59	Mercury ZEP 10008	PICK OF THE PLATTERS NO. 2.	20
59	Mercury ZEP 10025	PICK OF THE PLATTERS NO. 3.	20
59	Mercury ZEP 10031	PICK OF THE PLATTERS NO. 4.	22
59	Mercury ZEP 10042	PICK OF THE PLATTERS NO. 5	20
60	Mercury ZEP 10056	PICK OF THE PLATTERS NO. 6.	20
60	Mercury ZEP 10070	PICK OF THE PLATTERS NO. 7.	20
61	Mercury ZEP 10112	HARBOUR LIGHTS	22
62	Mercury ZEP 10126	THE PLATTERS ON A PLATTER	32

LPs

57	Mercury MPL 6504	THE PLATTERS	45
57	Mercury MPL 6511	THE PLATTERS VOL. 2.	40
58	Mercury MPL 6528	THE FLYING PLATTERS	35
58	Parlophone PMD 1058	THE PLATTERS (10")	350
59	Mercury MMC 14009	AROUND THE WORLD WITH THE FLYING PLATTERS	35
59	Mercury MMC 14010	THE PLATTERS ON PARADE.	35
59	Mercury MMC 14014	REMEMBER WHEN?.	30
60	Mercury MMC 14045	REFLECTIONS.	25
61	Mercury MMC 14072	LIFE IS JUST A BOWL OF CHERRIES	25
62	Ember EMB 3339	THE BEST OF THE PLATTERS	12
62	Mercury MMC 14091	GOLDEN HITS	15
64	Mercury MCL 20000	THE PLATTERS SING LATINO.	15
64	Concert Hall CJ 1255	THE PLATTERS.	12
66	Wing WL 1044	REFLECTIONS (reissue).	12
67	Stateside S(S)L 10208	GOING BACK TO DETROIT	12
67	Wing WL 1174	TENTH ANNIVERSARY ALBUM	12
68	Stateside S(S)L 10227	THE NEW GOLDEN HITS OF THE PLATTERS	12
68	Stateside S(S)L 10245	SWEET, SWEET LOVIN'	12

(see also Buck Ram's Ramrocks, Linda Hayes)

PLAYBOY CLUB BUNNIES

68	Decca F 12832	Keep The Ball Rollin'/I Only Want To Be With You	6
69	Decca LK 4951	CAUGHT LIVE AT THE PLAYBOY CLUB (LP).	15

PLAYBOYS

60s	Lyntone LYN 549/550	THE PLAYBOYS FOR CHARITY (EP, flexidisc, no p/s)	15

PLAYBOYS (Jamaica)

71	Tropical AL 007	Change Change/TROPICAL ALL STARS: Version 2	5

PLAYBOYS (U.S.)

58	London HLU 8681	Over The Weekend/Double Talk (78 rpm = £25).	45

PLAYBOYS (U.S.)

69	Capitol CL 15621	Let's Get Back To Rock And Roll/Homemade Cookin'	5
	(see also Rad Bryan)		

PLAY DEAD

81	Fresh FRESH 29	Poison Takes A Hold/Introduction (p/s)	7
81	Fresh FRESH 38	T.V. Eye/Final Epitaph (p/s).	7

PLAYERS
63	Oriole CB 1861	Mockingbird/Bizet As It May	18

PLAYGIRLS (Jamaica)
65	Black Swan WI 456	Looks Are Deceiving/BABA BROOKS: Dreadnaught	32

PLAYGIRLS (U.S.)
59	RCA RCA 1133	Hey Sport/Young Love Swings The World (78 rpm = £22)	22

PLAYGROUND
67	MGM MGM 1351	At The Zoo/Yellow Balloon	15
69	NEMS 56-4019	I Could Be So Good/The Girl Behind The Smile	6
69	NEMS 56-4442	Things I Do For You/Lazy Days	6

PLAYMATES
53	London L 1198	My Love Was Wasted On You/You Never Get Too Old To Fall In Love (78)	10
57	Columbia DB 3941	Pretty Woman/Barefoot Girl	15
57	Columbia DB 4033	Island Girl/Darling, It's Wonderful	15
58	Columbia DB 4084	Jo-Ann/You Can't Stop Me From Dreaming	12
58	Columbia DB 4127	Let's Be Lovers/Give Me Another Chance	10
59	Columbia DB 4288	Star Love/The Thing-A-Ma-Jig	6
59	Columbia SEG 7949	PARTY PLAYMATES NO. 1 (EP)	10
59	Columbia SEG 7966	PARTY PLAYMATES NO. 2 (EP)	10
60	Columbia 33SX 1215	BROADWAY SHOW STOPPERS (LP, also stereo SCX 3300)	15

PLAYMATES (Ireland)
70	Emerald MD 1150	Don't Fight It/Jodi	10

PLAYTHINGS
70	Pye 7N 45212	Stop What You're Doing To Me/Sad Songs (re-pressed 1973)	8
73	Pye 7N 45399	Surrounded By A Ray Of Sunshine/Dance The Night Away	5

BOBBY PLEASE
57	London HLB 8507	Your Driver's Licence, Please (unissued, 1-sided demo only)	300+
57	London HLB 8507	Your Driver's Licence, Please/Heartache Street (78)	40+

PLEASERS
77	Solid Gold SGR 104	You Know What I'm Thinking/Hello Little Girl	8
77	Arista ARIST 21	Girl I Know/Don't Go Breaking My Heart (p/s)	5
77	Arista ARIST 152	You Keep Tellin' Lies/I'm In Love/Who Are You (p/s, silver or blue labels)	5/8
78	Arista ARIST 180	The Kids Are Alright/Stay With Me (p/s)	12

PLEASURE
75	Fantasy FTC 115	Dust Yourself Off/Midnight At The Oasis	5
77	Fantasy FTC 138	I'm Mad/Ghetto Of The Mind	6
78	Fantasy FT 543	GET TO THE FEELIN' (LP)	12

PLEASURE BEACH
90s	Acid Jazz AJX 124S	Rollercoaster/Smells Like Teen Spirit (p/s)	20

PLEASURE FAIR
68	Uni UN 500	Morning Glory Blues/Fade Out Fade In	10
67	Uni UNL(S) 100	PLEASURE FAIR (LP)	25
	(see also Bread)		

PLEASURE GARDEN
68	Sound For Industry SFI 31H/32H	Permissive Paradise/EMPEROR ROSKO & JONATHAN KING: Young London (flexidisc, art sleeve)	40
	(see also Iveys)		

PLEASURES
65	Sue WI 357	Music City/If I Had A Little Money	30

PLEBS
64	Decca F 12006	Bad Blood/Babe I'm Gonna Leave You	80
60s	Oak	THE PLEBS (LP, 1-sided, private pressing)	1000+

JACK PLEIS & HIS ORCHESTRA
56	Brunswick 05534	The Trouble With Harry (with Bonnie Lake & Her Beaux)/Pauline	5
57	Brunswick 05634	Giant (with Ralph Young)/Lonesome Without You	5
	(see also Ralph Young, Bonnie Lake & Her Beaux)		

PLEXUS
78	Look LKLP 6175	PLEXUS (LP)	65
79	Hill & Dale HD004	LIFE UP THE CREEK (LP)	55

PLONE
97	Wurlitzer Jukebox WJ 36	Press A Key/Electronic Beauty Parlour (p/s, red vinyl, 300 only)	6

PLUGS
79	Cathedral CATH 1	Too Late/UFO/Sally (gatefold p/s)	20

JEAN PLUM
76	London HLU 10514	Look At The Boy/Back At You	25

PLUM & YOUTH
80s	Checkmount CHK 1	I Got You Babe/Got To Be Moving On (p/s, withdrawn)	15
	(see also Cozy Powell, Rainbow, Bernie Marsden)		

PLUMMERS
64	Blue Beat BB 260	Johnny/Little Stars (actually by Plamers)	22

PLUS
70	Probe SPB 1009	SEVEN DEADLY SINS (LP)	30

PLUTO
71	Dawn DNS 1017	Rag A Bone Joe/Stealing My Thunder	20
72	Dawn DNS 1026	I Really Want It/Something That You Loved	30
71	Dawn DNLS 3030	PLUTO (LP)	60

(see also Dry Ice, Foundations)

PNEUMONIA
68	Oak RGJ 625	I Can See Your Face	400

PNEUMONIA
79	Plastic PLAS 001	Exhibition/Coming Attack/U.K. DECAY: U.K. Decay/Carcrash (folded p/s)	18

(see also U.K. Decay)

POCKETS
77	CBS 5780	Come Go With Me/Pt. 2	8

POCO
71	Epic EQ 30209	DELIVERIN' (LP, quadrophonic)	12

(see also Buffalo Springfield, Au Go-Go Singers)

POEMS
81	Polka DOT 1	ACHIEVING UNITY (EP, initially with booklet)	10

(see also Strawberry Switchblade)

POET & ONE MAN BAND
69	Verve Forecast SVLP 6012	THE POET AND THE ONE MAN BAND (LP)	50

(see also Tony Colton, Nicky Hopkins, Heads Hands & Feet)

POETS
64	Decca F 11995	Now We're Thru/There Are Some	20
65	Decca F 12074	That's The Way It's Got To Be/I'll Cry With The Moon	90
65	Decca F 12195	I Am So Blue/I Love Her Still	50
65	Immediate IM 006	Call Again/Some Things I Can't Forget	100
66	Immediate IM 024	Baby Don't You Do It/I'll Come Home	100
67	Decca F 12569	Wooden Spoon/In Your Tower	500
71	Strike Cola SC 1	Heyla Hola/Fun Buggy	75
88	Bam Caruso OPRA 088	I Love Her Still/GHOST: Time Is My Enemy (company sleeve, promo only)	12

(see also Pathfinders, [White] Trash, Blue)

POETS (Ireland)
68	Pye 7N 17668	Locked In A Room/Alone Am I	200
68	Target 7N 17668	Locked In A Room/Alone Am I (Irish issue, different label)	200

POETS (U.S.)
(see under American Poets)

POGUE MAHONE
84	Pogue Mahone PM 1	Dark Streets Of London/The Band Played Waltzing Mathilda	10
84	Pogue Mahone PM 1	Dark Streets Of London/The Band Played Waltzing Mathilda (white label tour copy with 'harp' stamp, 237 only)	50

(see also Pogues)

POGUES
84	Stiff BUY 207	Dark Streets Of London/The Band Played Waltzing Mathilda (reissue of Pogue Mahone)	10
84	Stiff BUY 212	Boys From The County Hell/Repealing Of The Licensing Laws (green-tinted p/s)	10
84	Stiff BUY 212	Boys From The County Hell/Repealing Of The Licensing Laws (A-label promos in blue-tinted p/s)	12
84	Stiff BUY 207/BUY 212	Dark Streets Of London/The Band Played Waltzing Mathilda//Boys From The County Hell/Repealing Of The Licensing Laws (shrinkwrapped double pack)	20
85	Stiff DBUY 220	A Pair Of Brown Eyes/Whiskey You're The Devil (picture disc)	15
85	Stiff BUYIT 220	A Pair Of Brown Eyes/Whiskey You're The Devil/Muirshin Durkin (12", p/s)	15
85	Stiff BUY 212/BUY 220	Boys From The County Hell/Repealing Of The Licensing Laws//A Pair Of Brown Eyes/Whiskey You're The Devil (shrinkwrapped double pack)	15
85	Stiff BUY 224	Sally MacLennane/Wild Rover (wraparound poster p/s, some green vinyl)	10/7
85	Stiff BUY 224	Sally MacLennane/Wild Rover (standard p/s)	6
85	Stiff PBUY 229	Dirty Old Town/A Pistol For Paddy Garcia (picture disc)	10
85	Stiff BUYIT 229	Dirty Old Town/A Pistol For Paddy Garcia/The Parting Glass (12", some with poster & stickered p/s)	20/15
85	Stiff MAIL 3	Dirty Old Town (live)/Sally MacLennane (live)/(interview) (12", mail-order)	12
86	Stiff PBUY 243	POGUETRY IN MOTION (EP, picture disc)	5
86	MCA MCAT 1084	Haunted/Junk Theme/Hot Dogs With Everything (12", p/s, with poster)	7
87	Stiff/Hell BLOOD 1	The Good, The Bad & The Ugly/Rake At The Gates Of Hell (unreleased)	
87	Stiff/Hell BLOODY 1	The Good, The Bad & The Ugly/Rake At The Gates Of Hell (12", unreleased)	
88	Pogue Mahone SGG 1-12	ST. PATRICK'S NIGHT EP (12")	7
89	WEA SAM 553	Misty Morning Albert Bridge/(same track) (12" promo, green vinyl)	8

(see also Pogue Mahone, Nips, Nipple Erectors, Radiators From Space)

POGUES featuring KIRSTY MacCOLL
87	Pogue Mahone CDNY 7	A Fairytale Of New York/The Battle March Medley/Shane Bradley (CD)	8

POINDEXTER BROTHERS
66	Verve VS 550	(Git Your) Backfield In Motion/(Grandma) Give That Girl Some Slack	20

POINT BLANK MCS
92	Kold Sweat KS120	Planting Semtex (12")	12

POINTED STICKS
79	Stiff BUY 59	Out Of Luck/What Do You Want Me To Do/Somebody's Mom (7" or 12", p/s)	8/10

POINTS PROVEN
92	Payday PD002	Pass The Mic/Noisy Music Pt2/Funky Rhymes, Funky Style (EP)	22
93	Payday PD003	ONLY FOOLS AND HORSES (EP)	18

BONNIE POINTER
78	Motown 1125	Free Me From My Freedom/Tie Me To A Tree	8
78	Motown 1134	I Wanna Make It In Your World/Heaven Must Have Sent You	15

POISON GIRLS
79	Small Wonder WEENY 4	HEX (12" EP, with lyric insert)	8
80	Crass/Xntrix 421984/1	Persons Unknown/CRASS: Bloody Revolutions (folded 21" x 14" poster p/s)	5
81	Crass 421984/10	Pretty Polly/Bully Boys (live) (square red or clear flexidisc free with *In The City* fanzine, with/without magazine)	6/4
81	Crass 421984/8	All Systems Go/Promenade Immortelle/Dirty Work (p/s with lyrics)	5
83	Illuminated ILL 23	One Good Reason/Cinnamon Gardens (p/s)	5
83	Illuminated ILL 25	Are You Happy Now?/Cream Dream (p/s)	5
80	Crass 421984/2	CHAPPAQUIDICK (LP, with free flexidisc "Statement" [421984/7])	12

(see also Crass, Fatal Microbes/Poison Girls)

POISON IDEA
91	Vinyl Solution VS 29	Plastic Bomb/We Got The Beat/Harder They Come/Lawdy Miss Clawdy (double pack, p/s)	8

POISON IVY
64	Granta GR 7EP 1011	CLINGING MEMORIES (EP)	110

POLECAT9S
81	Nervous NER 001	Rockabilly Guy/Chicken Shack (p/s)	6

ROLO POLEY
69	Jackpot JP 704	Zapatoo The Tiger/Music House (both sides actually by Lester Sterling)	40+

POLICE
77	Illegal IL 001	Fall Out/Nothing Achieving (black & white p/s, red & black label, various designs)	10
78	A&M AMS 7348	Roxanne/Peanuts (2.52) ('telephone' p/s, typed matrix no., 'All Rights ...' on top half of label)	5
78	A&M AMS 7348	Roxanne/Peanuts (12", 'telephone' p/s)	15
78	A&M AMS 7381	Can't Stand Losing You/Dead End Job (glossy p/s, original issue, label credited to 'Police', mid-blue or rarer black vinyl)	10/7
78	A&M AMS 7402	So Lonely/Time This Time (p/s, miscredited flip, label credited to 'Police')	5
79	A&M AMS 7348	Roxanne/Peanuts (3.54) (reissue, 'group' p/s, handwritten matrix number, blue or black vinyl)	6/4
79	A&M AMS 7348	Roxanne/Peanuts (2.52) (reissue, 'group' p/s, typed matrix number, blue or black vinyl)	6/4
79	A&M AMSP 7348	Roxanne/Peanuts (12", reissue, 'group' p/s)	10
79	A&M AMS 7381	Can't Stand Losing You/Dead End Job (reissue, label credited to 'The Police'; dark blue or light blue vinyl)	each 10
79	A&M AMS 7381	Can't Stand Losing You/Dead End Job (p/s, reissue, red, yellow, green or white vinyl)	10-12
79	A&M AMS 7381	Can't Stand Losing You/Dead End Job (p/s, mispressed B-side, plays "No Time This Time")	20+
79	A&M AMS 7474	Message In A Bottle/Landlord (p/s, green vinyl)	5
79	Illegal IL 001	Fall Out/Nothing Achieving (reissue, various label designs, green/black p/s)	5
79	Illegal IL 001	Fall Out/Nothing Achieving (reissue, various label designs, purple/blue p/s)	15
79	Illegal IL 001	Fall Out/Nothing Achieving (reissue, various label designs, black & orange p/s)	30
80	A&M AMPP 6001	POLICE PACK (6 x 7" printed foldout PVC pack [AMS 7348, 7381, 7402, 7474 & 7494] & "The Bed's Too Big Without You"/"Truth Hits Everybody" [AMPP 6001/E]; all on blue vinyl with 6 inserts)	25
80	A&M SAMP 5	SIX-TRACK RADIO SAMPLER (custom p/s, promo radio sampler)	15
80	A&M AMS 7564	Don't Stand So Close To Me/Friends (poster p/s)	7
81	A&M AMS 8174	Every Little Thing She Does Is Magic/Flexible Responses (p/s)	5
81	A&M AMS 8194	Spirits (In The Material World)/Low Life (poster p/s, some with badge)	8/5
83	A&M AM 117	Every Breath You Take/Murder By Numbers (p/s, with free badge)	5
83	A&M AM 117/AM 01	Every Breath You Take/Murder By Numbers//Truth Hits Everybody/Man In A Suitcase (double pack, gatefold p/s)	12
83	A&M AMSP 117	Every Breath You Take/Murder By Numbers (picture disc)	12
83	A&M AMP 127	Wrapped Around Your Finger/Someone To Talk To (Sting picture disc)	10
83	A&M AMP 127	Wrapped Around Your Finger/Someone To Talk To (Andy Summers or Stewart Copeland picture disc, 1,000 each)	each 12
86	A&M AMY 354	Don't Stand So Close To Me/Don't Stand So Close To Me (Dance Mix) Friends (12", p/s)	10
95	A&M 581 036 7 A 581 036 7B	Can't Stand Losing You (Live In Boston)/Roxanne (uncut white vinyl test pressing, one copy only)	1,500+
88	A&M AMCD 905	COMPACT HITS (CD EP)	20
78	A&M AMLN 68502	OUTLANDOS D'AMOUR (LP, blue vinyl)	15

(see also Sting, Radio Actors, Zoot Money's Big Roll Band, Last Exit, Newcastle Big Band, Eberhard Schoener, Andy Summers & Robert Fripp)

POLIPHONY
73	Zella JHLPS 136	POLIPHONY (LP, private pressing)	150

POLITICIANS
72	Hot Wax HWX 114	Love Machine/Free Your Mind	15
72	Hot Wax SHW 5007	THE POLITICIANS (LP)	40

FRANK POLK
65	Capitol CL 15389	Trying To Keep Up With The Joneses/Welcome Home, Baby (DJ copy = £125)	75

POLKA DOTS
59	Columbia SEG 7894	SINGIN' AND SWINGIN' (EP)	15
61	Philips BBE 12487	THE POLKA DOTS (EP, also stereo SBBE 9074)	10/12
62	Philips BBE 12528	STRICTLY FOR KICKS (EP)	8
62	Philips BE 12534	RELAX AWHILE (EP)	8
62	Philips 433 625 BE	VOCAL SPECTACULAR (EP)	8
63	Philips BL 7576	NICE WORK AND YOU CAN BUY IT (LP)	18

(see also Teddy Johnson, Laurie Johnson)

RAY POLLARD

65	United Artists UP 1111	The Drifter/Let Him Go (And Let Me Love You) (demo = £400)	250
66	United Artists UP 1133	It's A Sad Thing/All The Things You Are	200

(see also Wanderers)

POLLCATS

90	Community Charge AXT 1	Poll Tax Blues/Poll Tax Blues (same track both sides, p/s)	10

(see also Steve Marriott)

MICHAEL POLNAREFF

66	Vogue VRS 7012	La Poupée Qui Fait Non/Beatnik	10
66	Vogue VRS 7013	No No No No No No/Beatnik	10
66	Vogue VRS 7019	Love Me Please Love Me/L'Amour Avec Toi	10

POLYGON WINDOW

92	Warp WARP LP 7	SURFING ON SINE WAVES (2-LP)	30
93	Warp WARP 33	QUOTH (12" EP, clear vinyl)	25
92	Warp WARP LP 7LTD	SURFING ON SINE WAVES (LP, clear vinyl)	50

(see also Aphex Twin)

POLYPHEMUS

92	Placebo PILL 001	GREAT VILLAGE TRIP EP (10")	8
95	Acme AC 8010LP	SCRAPBOOK OF MADNESS (LP, reissue with insert, 500 only)	18
95	Acme AC 8016LP	STONEHOUSE (LP, gatefold sleeve, 700 only)	18

POLYPHONIC SPREE

02	679 679LO14	ORCHESTRAL: Light And Day/Soldier Girl (p/s, 500 only)	20
03	679 679LO14X	Soldier Girl/(Go! Team Remix) (gatefold p/s, with poster)	8

HERB POMEROY BIG BAND

57	Columbia SX 1091	LIFE IS A MANY SPLENDOURED GIG (LP)	12

POMPHEY

72	Green Door GD 4029	Jamaica Skank/JOHNNY MOORE: Bing Comes To Town	10

PONI-TAILS

58	HMV POP 516	Born Too Late/Come On Joey, Dance With Me (as Pony-Tails) (78 rpm = £10)	10
58	HMV POP 558	Close Friends/Seven Minutes In Heaven (78 rpm = £12)	15
59	HMV POP 596	Early To Bed/Father Time (78 rpm = £12)	15
59	HMV POP 644	Moody/Oom Pah Polka	15
59	HMV POP 663	I'll Be Seeing You/I'll Keep Tryin'	15
58	HMV 7EG 8427	THE PONI-TAILS (EP)	120+

JEAN-LUC PONTY

69	Liberty LBL/LBS 83262	ELECTRIC CONNECTION (LP)	15
70	Liberty LBL/LBS 83375	KING KONG (LP)	15

POOGY

74	EMI EMI 2136	She Looked Me In The Eye (I Gave Her My Life)/Morris And His Turtle	8

POOH STICKS

88	Fierce FRIGHT 011	On Tape (p/s, 1-sided, some with *un*etched B-side)	40/35
88	Fierce FRIGHT 021	1-2-3 Red Light (p/s, 1-sided)	20
88	Fierce FRIGHT 023	Heartbreak (1-sided, etched B-side, hand-coloured promo p/s, with insert)	40
88	Fierce FRIGHT 021-025	FIERCE BOX SET (5 x 1-sided etched discs, hand-coloured labels, with insert)	50
88	Fierce FRIGHT 026	ALAN McGEE (CD EP, with FRIGHT 021-025 tracks plus "On Tape"/ "Please Hue, Please", some in 7" box with booklet)	20/10
88	Fierce FRIGHT 028	HEROES AND VILLAINS (LP, with inner)	18
89	Fierce FRIGHT 034	Dying For It (p/s, sold at U.L.U. gig, 300 only, some signed)	25/15
89	Fierce FRIGHT 034	Dying For It (1-sided, different p/s to above)	15
89	Cheree CHEREE 3	Go Go Girl/Simon E (flexidisc with foldout *Cheree* fanzine/sleeve)	8
89	Woosh WOOSH 007/ WOOSH 6	Hard On Love (yellow flexi with *Pooh Sticks* fanzine)/ GROOVE FARM: Heaven Is Blue/ESMERALDA'S KITE: Vampire Girl (red flexi) (with *Woosh* fanzine 3)	12
89	Anonymous ANON 2	ENCORES (EP, numbered box set, multi-coloured 1-sided 7" with sweet watch, badge, sticker & booklet)	8
92	Fierce/BMG FRIGHT 42	Million Seller (1-sided)	6
89	53rd & 3rd AGAMC 5	ORGASM (LP, pink vinyl with insert for export)	12
89	Fierce FRIGHT 025	THE POOH STICKS (mini-LP, with inner, black & white sleeve, 1-sided, side 2 etched)	12
89	Fierce FRIGHT 035	TRADE MARK OF QUALITY (LP, mail-order only, plain stickered sleeve with insert, numbered)	20

(see also Dumb Angels)

BRIAN POOLE

66	Decca F 12402	Hey Girl/Please Be Mine	8
66	CBS 202349	Everything I Touch Turns To Tears/I Need Her Tonight	22
67	CBS 202661	That Reminds Me Baby/Tomorrow Never Comes	6
67	CBS 3005	Just How Loud/The Other Side Of The Sky	20
69	President PT 239	Send Her To Me/Pretty In The City (as Brian Poole & Seychelles)	5
69	President PT 264	What Do Women Most Desire/Treat Her Like A Woman (with Seychelles)	5

(see also Brian Poole & Tremeloes)

BRIAN POOLE & TREMELOES

62	Decca F 11455	Twist Little Sister/Lost Love	15
62	Decca F 11515	That Ain't Right/Blue	12
63	Decca F 11567	A Very Good Year For Girls/Meet Me Where We Used Meet	6
63	Decca F 11616	Keep On Dancing/Run Back Home	6
63	Decca F 11771	I Can Dance/Are You Loving Me At All	6
64	Decca F 11951	Twelve Steps To Love/Don't Cry	6
65	Decca F 12124	After A While/You Know	8
65	Decca F 12197	I Want Candy/Love Me Baby	8
65	Decca F 12274	Good Lovin'/Could It Be You	10

Brian POOLE & TREMELOES

64	Decca DFE 8566	BRIAN POOLE AND THE TREMELOES (EP)	35
65	Decca DFE 8610	BRIAN POOLE AND THE TREMELOES (EP)	35
63	Ace of Clubs ACL 1146	BIG BIG HITS OF '62 (LP)	22
63	Decca LK 4550	TWIST AND SHOUT WITH BRIAN POOLE AND THE TREMELOES (LP)	50
65	Decca LK 4685	IT'S ABOUT TIME (LP)	60
77	Decca REM 5	REMEMBERING (LP)	12

(see also Brian Poole, Tremeloes)

LOU & LAURA POOLE
72	Jay Boy BOY 63	Only You And I Know/Look At Me	10

POOR SOULS
65	Decca F 12183	When My Baby Cries/My Baby She's Not There	18
66	Alp ALP 595 004	Love Me/Please Don't Change Your Mind	45

POOR THINGS
66	CBS 202431	We Trust In A Better Way Of Life/Danny Boy	50

GROOVY JOE POOVEY
70	Injun 100	Ten Long Fingers On The 88 Keys/Thrill Of Love	12

IGGY POP
77	RCA PB 9093	China Girl/Baby	5
77	RCA PB 9160	Success/The Passenger	5
77	RCA PB 9160	Some Weird Sin/The Passenger	5
78	RCA PB 9213	Sixteen/I Got A Right	5
78	Radar ADA 4	Kill City (with James Williamson)/I Got Nothin'	5
79	Arista ARISP 274	Five Foot One/Pretty Flamingo (picture disc)	6
80	Arista ARIST 327	Loco Mosquito/Take Care Of Me (p/s)	5
82	Chrysalis/Melody Maker	Extracts From "Zombie Birdhouse"/STIFF LITTLE FINGERS: Excerpts From "Now Then" (flexidisc, free with Melody Maker)	6/4
88	A&M AMCD 909	COMPACT HITS (EP)	8
90	Virgin America VUSCD 18	Livin' On The Edge Of The Night (Edit)/The Passenger/Nightclubbing/China Girl (3" CD, card sleeve)	8
73	CBS 65586	RAW POWER (LP, with inner, orange label, as Iggy & Stooges)	30
78	Radar RAD 2	KILL CITY (LP, as Iggy Pop & James Williamson)	12

(see also Stooges)

POPCORNS
63	Columbia DB 4968	Zero Zero/Chinese Twist	15

DAVE POPE
70s	Myrrh MYR 1003	TIME TO TAKE ACCOUNT (LP)	18

TIM POPE
84	Fiction FICS 21	I Want To Be A Tree/The Double Crossing Of Two Faced Fred (p/s)	15
84	Fiction FICSX 21	I Want To Be A Tree/(Elephant) Song/The Double Crossing Of Two Faced Fred (12", p/s)	25

(see also Cure)

POP GROUP
79	Radar ADA 29	She Is Beyond Good And Evil/3.38 (p/s)	10
79	Radar ADA 1229	She Is Beyond Good And Evil/3.38 (12", p/s)	15
79	Rough Trade RT 023	We Are All Prostitutes/Amnesty International Report On British Army Torture Of Irish Prisoners (p/s)	10
80	Rough Trade RT 039/ Y Y1	Where There's A Will There's A Way/SLITS: In The Beginning There Was Rhythm (p/s)	5
79	Radar RAD 20	Y (LP, with foldout colour poster)	20
80	Rough Trade ROUGH 9	FOR HOW MUCH LONGER DO WE TOLERATE MASS MURDER? (LP, with 4 black-and-white posters)	20
80	Y/Rough Trade ROUGH 12	WE ARE TIME (LP, plain black sleeve)	15

(see also Slits)

FRANK POPP ENSEMBLE
01	Blow Up BU026	Hip Teens Don't Wear Blue Jeans/The Catwalk	15

POPPIES
66	Columbia DB 7879	Lullaby Of Love/I Wonder Why	30

KEITH POPPIN
73	Randy's RAN 531	Kick The Bucket/I'm A Man Of My Word	6
76	Mango 1002	Time Slipping Away/King Tubby's Time	12

POPPY FAMILY
70	Decca (S)KL-R 5022	WHICH WAY YOU GOING BILLY? (LP, mono/stereo)	15/12
72	Decca SKL 5114	POPPY SEEDS (LP)	12

POPPYHEADS
88	Sha La La Ba Ba Ba Ba 4	POSTCARD FOR FLOSSY (EP, 1-sided flexidisc, p/s in poly bag)	8
88	Sarah SARAH 006	Cremation Town/Pictures You Weave/Dreamboat (foldaround p/s with large poster in poly bag)	10

POP RIVETS
79	Hypocrite HEP 001	POP RIVITS (EP, no p/s)	12
79	Hypocrite HEP 002	Pop Rivits/Sulphate	15
79	Hypocrite JIM 1	FUN IN THE U.K. (EP, no p/s, double pack)	30
79	Hypocrite HIP-O	EMPTY SOUNDS FROM ANARCHY RANCH (LP, coloured back, stamped labels)	15
80	Hypocrite HIP 007	THE POP RIVETS GREATEST HITS (LP, screen-printed sleeve)	15

(see also Milkshakes)

POPSICLES
65	Vogue V 9243	I Don't Want To Be Your Baby Anymore/Baby I Miss You	40

(see also Ellie Greenwich, Raindrops)

POPULAR 5
68	Minit MLF 11011	I'm A Lovemaker/Little Bitty Pretty One	15

POP WORKSHOP
68	Page One POF 091	Fairyland/When My Little Girl Is Happy	20
69	Page One POF 129	Punch And Judy Man/Love Is A One Way Highway	7

PORCUPINE TREE
94	Delerium DELEC EP 032	Stars Die/Moonloop (12", p/s)	10
00	Snapper SMAS 7111	4 Chords That Made A Million (p/s, 1,000 only)	8
92	Delerium DELEC EP 007	VOYAGE 34 (Astralasia Remix) (12" EP)	12
92	Delerium DELEC EP 010	VOYAGE 34 (12" EP)	18
92	Delerium DELECD EP 010	VOYAGE 34 (CD EP)	18
89	Delerium DELC 0002	TARQUIN'S SEAWEED FARM (cassette, 1st issue, around 50 only)	35
91	Delerium DELC 0002	TARQUIN'S SEAWEED FARM (cassette, 2nd issue, silver print, with A4 booklet, red/black text, 200 only)	25
91	Delerium DELC 0002	TARQUIN'S SEAWEED FARM (cassette, silver print, with photocopied A5 booklet, label on Side 1, 200 only)	20
91	Delerium DELC 0003	THE NOSTALGIA FACTORY (cassette, silver print, with A4 booklet, red/black text, 200 only)	20
91	Delerium DELC 0003	THE NOSTALGIA FACTORY (cassette, with photocopied A5 booklet, label on Side 1, 200 only)	20
92	Delerium DELEC 008	ON THE SUNDAY OF LIFE (2-LP, gatefold sleeve)	20
92	Delerium DELEC 008	ON THE SUNDAY OF LIFE (2-LP, gatefold sleeve)	20
92	Delerium DELEC CD 008	ON THE SUNDAY OF LIFE (CD)	20
94	Magic Gnome MG 4299325	YELLOW HEADGROW DREAMSCAPE (CD, 2,500 only)	30
95	Delerium DELEC LP 028	THE SKY MOVES SIDEWAYS (LP, 2,000 on blue vinyl w/poster)	15

PORK DUKES
77	Wood WOOD 9	Bend And Flush/Throbbing Gristle (p/s)	25
77	Wood BRANCH 9	Making Bacon/Tight Pussy (12", p/s, yellow vinyl)	25
78	Wood Standard WOOD 56	Telephone Masturbator/Melody Makers (p/s)	25
78	Wood PORK 001	THE PORK DUKES (LP, pink vinyl with warning sticker & postcard)	18
80	Wood PORK 2	PIG OUT OF HELL (LP)	15
82	Butt PORK 1	PIG IN A POKE (LP)	15

DAVID PORTER
70	Stax STAX 150	One Part — Two Parts/Can't I See You When I Want To	8
70	Stax SXATS 1034	GRITTY, GROOVY AND GETTIN' IT (LP)	15
71	Stax 2362 006	INTO A REAL THING (LP)	15

NOLAN PORTER
72	Probe PRO 580	If I Could Only Be Sure/Work It Out In The Morning (DJ copy = £125)	75
72	Probe SPB 1067	NOLAN (LP)	40

ROBBIE PORTER
66	MGM 1313	Either Way I Lose/That's The Way Love Goes	25

PORTER & CALYPSO STAR BAND
59	Kalypso XX 11	Cinemascope/Sally Brown (78)	8

PORTER CUNNINGHAM
72	Folk Heritage FHR 027	OBSERVATIONS (LP)	130

PORTION CONTROL
82	In Phaze POR CON 006	Surface And Be Seen/Spinola (Blotch)/Terror Leads To Better Days/Simple As ABC/Monstrous Bulk/He Is A Barbarian (12", p/s, with plastic outer sleeve)	15
84	Illuminated ILL 2612	Raise The Pulse/Collapse/Bite My Head (12", p/s)	10
84	Illuminated ILL 3212	Rough Justice/The Man Who Did Backwards Somersaults (12", p/s with inner)	8
85	Illuminated ILL 4312	Go-Talk/Upside Down/Drag Down (12", p/s)	8
85	Rhythmic/Havoc 7RMIC 7	The Great Divide/Totall Recall (p/s)	5
85	Rhythmic/Havoc 12RMIC 7	The Great Divide/Divided/Bolt It Down (12", p/s)	8
85	Rhythmic/Havoc 12RMICX 7	The Great Divide (Julian Mendelsohn Remix)/Divided/Bolt It Down (12", p/s)	12
86	Dead Man's Curve DMC 1	PRESENT PURGE (12" EP)	8
87	Big Noise In Archgate BNIA 1	LIVE IN EUROPE (10" mini-LP)	10
83	In Phaze EZ 2	HIT THE PULSE (mini-LP, 45/33rpm)	18
84	Illuminated JAMS 44	STEP FORWARD (LP)	12
85	In Phaze PHA 5	SIMULATE SENSUAL (LP, clear vinyl, PVC sleeve with insert)	20
86	Dead Man's Curve DMC 8	PSYCHO-BOD SAVES THE WORLD (LP, with inner sleeve)	12

PORTISHEAD
94	Go Beat GODX 120	Glory Box/Toy Box/Scorn/Sheared Box (12", p/s)	8
97	Go Beat 571 597-1	All Mine/Cowboys/Cowboys (Instrumental) (12", p/s)	8
94	Go Beat GOLCD 116	SOUR TIMES EP (CD, limited edition, with postcards)	15
94	Go Beat GODCD 116	SOUR TIMES EP (CD, limited edition, blue sleeve, with postcards)	10
94	Go Beat 828 522	DUMMY (LP)	15
97	Go Beat 539189-1	PORTISHEAD (LP, gloss sleeve)	12

PORTOBELLO EXPLOSION
69	Carnaby CNS 4001	We Can Fly/Hot Smoke And Sasafrass (label credits *Portebello Explosion*)	30

(see also Mirage, Jawbone, Spencer Davis Group)

PORTWAY PEDLARS
84	Greenwich Village GVR 229	IN GREENWOOD SHADES (LP)	15

SANDY POSEY
66	MGM MGM 1321	Born A Woman/Caution To The Wind	15
66	MGM MGM 1330	Single Girl/Blue Is My Best Colour	5
67	MGM MGM 1335	What A Woman In Love Won't Do/Shattered	5
67	MGM MGM 1342	I Take It Back/The Boy I Love	5
67	MGM MGM 1364	Are You Never Coming Home/I Can Show You How To Live	5
67	MGM MGM-C(S) 8035	BORN A WOMAN (LP)	18

Sandy POSEY

67	MGM MGM-C(S) 8042	SINGLE GIRL (LP)	18
68	MGM MGM-C(S) 8051	SANDY POSEY (LP)	18
68	MGM MGM-C 8060	THE BEST OF SANDY POSEY (LP, original with blue label)	15
68	MGM MGM-C(S) 8073	LOOKING AT YOU (LP)	15

POSITIVE FORCE
79	Sugarhill SH 102	We Got The Funk/Tell Me What You See (12")	8

HOWIE POST & SWIFTIES
63	Fontana TF 421	Tom Swift/The Elephant	10

ADRIENNE POSTER/POSTA
63	Oriole CB 1890	Only Fifteen/There's Nothing You Can Do About That	22
63	Decca F 11797	Only Fifteen/There's Nothing You Can Do About That (reissue)	18
64	Decca F 11864	Shang A Doo Lang/When A Girl Really Loves You	22
65	Decca F 12079	He Doesn't Love Me/The Way You Do The Things You Do	20
65	Decca F 12181	The Winds That Blow/Back Street Girl	20
66	Decca F 12329	Something Beautiful/So Glad You're Mine	30
66	Decca F 12455	They Long To Be Close To You/How Can I Hurt You (as Adrienne Posta)	10

POTATOES
66	Fontana TF 756	The Bend/Bend Ahead	7

KEITH POTGER
69	Mercury MF 1073	The World Would Never Turn Again/Santa Marie (some in p/s)	8/6

(see also Seekers, Judith Durham)

POTLIQUOR
72	Janus 6146 011	Cheer/Chatanooga	6
70	Dawn DNLS 3016	FIRST TASTE (LP, withdrawn)	90
72	Janus 6310 202	LEVEE BLUES (LP)	15
72	Janus 6310 203	FIRST TASTE (LP, reissue)	12

PHIL POTTER
76	Genesis GEN 10	MY SONG IS LOVE UNKNOWN (LP)	20
79	Dove DOVE 61	THE RESTORER (LP)	18
70s	Kingsway KMR 321	LEAD ME ON (LP)	15

POTTERS
72	Trent JT 100	We'll Be With You/Theme For A Team	20

POUND HOUNDS
55	Brunswick 05484	Home Sweet Home/MELLOMEN: Lady	12

(see also Peggy Lee)

ALLEN POUND'S GET RICH
66	Parlophone R 5532	Searchin' In The Wilderness/Hey You (most copies are demos)	500+

BOBBY POWELL
72	Mojo 2092 034	Peace Begins Within/Question	10
75	Contempo CLP 516	THANK YOU (LP)	20

BUD POWELL (TRIO)
55	Vogue EPV 1030	BUD POWELL TRIO (EP)	70
55	Vogue EPV 1033	BUD POWELL'S MODERNISTS (EP)	70
55	Vogue EPV 1036	BUD POWELL TRIO (EP)	60
55	Columbia Clef SEB 10013	BUD POWELL (EP)	70
57	Columbia Clef SEB 10074	GENIUS OF BUD POWELL (EP)	70
58	Columbia Clef SEB 10094	GENIUS OF BUD POWELL NO. 2 (EP)	60
52	Vogue LDE 010	THE BUD POWELL TRIO (10" LP)	30
54	Vogue LDE 053	JAZZ AT THE MASSEY HALL VOL. 2 (10" LP)	25
56	Columbia Clef 33C 9016	BUD POWELL TRIO (10" LP)	30
57	Columbia Clef 33CX 10069	JAZZ ORIGINAL (LP)	40
58	Columbia Clef 33CX 10123	BLUES FOR BUD (LP)	60
59	HMV CLP 1294	THE LONELY ONE (LP)	50
63	Vogue LAE 558	THE BUD POWELL TRIO (LP)	15
63	Columbia 33SX 1575	THE BUD POWELL TRIO FEATURING MAX ROACH (LP)	50
64	Fontana FJL 903	HOT HOUSE (LP)	60
65	Columbia 33SX 1701	THE RETURN OF POWELL (LP)	12
65	Xtra XTRA 1011	BOUNCING WITH BUD (LP)	12
65	Verve VLP 9075	THE VINTAGE YEARS (LP)	12
68	Fontana SFJL 901	BLUES FOR BOUFFEMONT (LP)	90
69	Fontana SFJL 924	AT THE BLUE NOTE CAFE, PARIS 1961 (LP)	12

COZY POWELL
73	Rak RAK 164	Dance With The Devil/And Then There Was Skin (export copy, European diff p/s)	8
73	Rak 4C 006 94962	Dance With The Devil/And Then There Was Skin	
		(export issue, p/s, RAK 164 in run out groove, some on blue or yellow vinyl)	25/15
74	Rak RAK 4C006-95491	The Man In Black/After Dark (export issue, p/s)	12
79	Ariola AROD 189	Theme One/Over The Top (full version) (12", company sleeve)	8
80	Ariola ARL 5038	OVER THE TOP (LP)	12
81	Polydor POLD 5047	TILT (LP, with inner sleeve)	12

(see also Rainbow, Young Blood, Big Bertha, Ace Kefford Stand, Bedlam, Bernie Marsden, Phenomena, Black Sabbath, Jeff Beck, Whitesnake, Michael Schenker Group, Donovan, Gary Moore, Young & Moody, Brian May, Chick Churchill, Graham Bonnet, Forcefield, Emerson Lake & Powell, Jack Bruce, Plum & Youth)

JANE POWELL
53	MGM SP 1061	Something Wonderful/I Whistle A Happy Tune	6
53	MGM SP 1062	Hello, Young Lovers/We Kiss In A Shadow	6
56	HMV POP 267	True Love/Mind If I Make Love To You	10
59	MGM MGM-EP 701	JANE POWELL SINGS (EP)	15
54	Capitol LC 6665	THREE SAILORS AND A GIRL (10" LP)	20
57	HMV CLP 1131	JANE POWELL (LP)	20

(see also Marilyn Monroe)

JIMMY POWELL (& DIMENSIONS)

62	Decca F 11447	Sugar Babe (Parts 1 & 2) (solo)	12
62	Decca F 11544	Tom Hark/Dance Her By Me (solo)	12
63	Decca F 11570	Remember Them/Everyone But You (solo)	8
64	Pye 7N 15663	That's Alright/I'm Looking For A Woman	45
64	Pye 7N 15735	Sugar Babe/I've Been Watching You (as Jimmy Powell & 5 Dimensions)	20
66	Strike JH 309	I Can Go Down/Love Me Right	12
67	Decca F 12664	Unexpected Mirrors/Time Mends Broken Hearts (with Dimensions)	10
68	Decca F 12751	I Just Can't Get Over You/Real Cool (with Dimensions)	8
68	Decca F 12793	Sugar Babe (Parts 1 & 2)	8

JUDITH POWELL

67	RCA RCA 1569	Greener Days/No Goodbyes	6

KEITH POWELL (& VALETS)

63	Columbia DB 7116	The Answer Is No!/Come On And Join The Party (with Valets)	15
64	Columbia DB 7229	Tore Up/You Better Let Him Go (with Valets)	18
64	Columbia DB 7366	I Should Know Better (But I Don't)/Too Much Monkey Business (with Valets)	35
65	Piccadilly 7N 35235	People Get Ready/Paradise	7
65	Piccadilly 7N 35249	Come Home Baby/Beyond The Hill	7
66	Piccadilly 7N 35275	Goodbye Girl/It Was Easier To Hurt Her	7
66	Piccadilly 7N 35300	Victory/Some People Only	7
66	Piccadilly 7N 35353	It Keeps Rainin'/Song of The Moon	10

(see also Move, Carl Wayne & Vikings)

KEITH (POWELL) & BILLIE (DAVIES)

66	Piccadilly 7N 35288	When You Move, You Lose/Tastes Sour, Don't It? (as Keith & Billie)	10
66	Piccadilly 7N 35321	You Don't Know Like I Know/Two Little People	15
66	Piccadilly 7N 35340	Swingin' Tight/That's Really Some Good	10

(see also Keith Powell, Billie Davis)

MARILYN POWELL

64	Fontana TF 448	All My Loving/After The Party	10
65	Fontana TF 526	Please Go Away/Where Did I Go Wrong	8
65	Fontana TF 557	As Long As You Come Back To Me/Go Away	8
65	Fontana TF 687	Showdown/Came The Day	8
68	CBS 2331	Something To Hold On To/Kiss Me Again	8

RAY POWELL

74	RCA 2490	King Kong/Rock Ness Monster	8

POWER

82	Malaco MAL1	Groovin'/Instrumental	8

DUFFY POWER

59	Fontana H 194	Dream Lover/That's My Little Suzie (78 rpm = £20)	20
59	Fontana H 214	Kissin' Time/Ain't She Sweet (78 rpm = £20)	15
59	Fontana H 230	Starry-Eyed/Prettier Than You (78 rpm = £25)	15
60	Fontana H 279	Whole Lotta Shakin' Goin' On/If I Can Dream	30
61	Fontana H 302	I've Got Nobody/When We're Walking Close	15
61	Fontana H 344	No Other Love/What Now	12
63	Parlophone R 4992	It Ain't Necessarily So/If I Get Lucky Someday	12
63	Parlophone R 5024	I Saw Her Standing There (with Graham Bond Quartet)/Farewell Baby	50
63	Parlophone R 5059	Hey Girl/Woman Made Trouble	15
64	Parlophone R 5111	Parchman Farm/Tired, Broke And Busted (with Paramounts)	30
64	Parlophone R 5169	Where Am I?/I Don't Care	30
67	Parlophone R 5631	Davy O'Brien (Leave That Baby Alone)/July Tree	20
70	CBS 5176	Hell Hound/Hummingbird	12
71	Epic EPC 7139	Hummingbird/Hell Hound (reissue)	6
73	GSF GSZ 6	River/Little Soldiers	5
73	GSF GSZ 8	Liberation/Song About Jesus	5
71	Transatlantic TRA 229	INNOVATIONS (LP)	60
73	GSF GS 502	DUFFY POWER (LP)	20
73	Spark SRLM 2005	DUFFY POWER (LP)	20
76	Buk BULP 2010	POWERHOUSE (LP, revised reissue of GSF GS 502)	15

(see also Alexis Korner, John McLaughlin, Jack Bruce, Graham Bond, Duffy's Nucleus)

JIMMY POWER

76	Topic 12TS 306	IRISH FIDDLE PLAYER (LP)	12

POWERCUT CREW

88	PowerCut PC001	Powercut 1/African Beats (12")	60

POWERHOUSE

66	Decca F 12471	Chain Gang/Can You Hear Me?	10
66	Decca F 12507	Raindrops/La Bamba	5

POWERLORDS

89	Pow DOT 001T	British Mic Control (12")	12
90	Commercial DOT005T	The Posse's Ready (12")	10

POWERPACK

66	CBS 202335	It Hurts Me So/What You Gonna Do	40
67	CBS 202551	I'll Be Anything For You/The Lost Summer	18
69	Polydor 56319	Hannibal Brooks/Juliet Simkins	7
70	Polydor 2001 077	Oh Calcutta/Soul Searchin'	15
69	Polydor 583 057	SOUL CURE (LP)	60

(see also Procol Harum, Emperor Rosko & Power Pack)

MINT VALUE £

POWERPILL
92	ffrreedom TABX 110	PAC MAN EP: Powerpill Mix/Ghost Mix/Choci's Hi Score Mix/Mickey Finn's Yum Yum Mix (12", some on limited edition yellow vinyl)................30/20
92	ffrreedom TABX 110	PAC MAN EP: Powerpill Mix/Ghost Mix/Choci's Hi Score Mix/Mickey Finn's Yum Yum Mix (CD)...........................30

(see also Aphex Twin)

JETT POWERS
70	Liberty LBS 83320	CALIFORNIA LICENCE (LP)................................50+

(see also P.J. Proby)

KID CONGO POWERS
89	Night Shift NISHI 208T	In The Heat Of The Night/Cat Tabu/La Historia Des Un Amour (12", p/s).........8

(see also Gun Club)

JOEY POWERS
63	Stateside SS 236	Midnight Mary/Where Do You Want The World Delivered.....................12

POWERS OF BLUE
67	CBS 62953	FLIP OUT! (LP)....................................15

POWER STATION
85	Parlophone 12 RP 6091	Some Like It Hot (Full Length Version)/The Heat Is On/ Some Like It Hot (12", picture disc)...................8

(see also Duran Duran, Robert Palmer)

P.P. & PRIMES
96	Nice (no cat. no.)	Understanding/STEVIE'S BUZZ (i.e. Buzzcocks): Autumn Stone (promo only)...10

(see also Primal Scream, P.P. Arnold)

PEREZ 'PREZ' PRADO & HIS ORCHESTRA
54	HMV 7M 255	Skokiaan — Mambo/The High And The Mighty.....................8
54	HMV GV 203	April In Portugal/Mexicanita (78, export issue).....................7
55	HMV 7M 295	Cherry Pink And Apple Blossom White/Maria Elena.....................15
55	HMV POP 102	Marilyn Monroe Mambo/C'est Si Bon (78).....................8
55	HMV 7MC 29	Mambo De La Telefonista/En Las Calles De La Habana (export issue).....................8
58	RCA RCA 1067	Patricia/Why Wait (78 rpm = £6).....................6
58	RCA RCA 1082	Guaglione/Paris (78 rpm = £6).....................7
59	RCA RCA 1129	Tic Toc Polly Woc/My Roberta (78 rpm = £6).....................5
55	HMV 7EG 8104	KING OF MAMBO (EP).....................10
58	RCA SRC 7004	PREZ (EP).....................10
59	RCA RCX 140	PRADO PLAYS PATRICIA (EP).....................10
59	RCA RCX 1001	PEREZ PRADO (EP).....................10
60	RCA RD 27046	LATIN SATIN (LP).....................20
64	Parlophone PMC 1226	A CAT IN LATIN (LP).....................22

PRAG VEC
78	Spec SP 001	Wolf/Cigarettes/Existential/Bits! (p/s).....................10
79	Spec SP 002	Expert/The Follower! (p/s).....................10
81	Spec RESPECT 1	NO COWBOYS (LP, with insert).....................15

(see also Foetus etc.)

PRAISE
76	No Seven 001	BLESSED QUIETNESS (LP).....................40

PRAMS
81	Product/Ltd. Edition TAKE 3	Nowhere's Safe/TV PRODUCT: Jumping Off Walls (foldout p/s).....................15
86	Classic Quotes CLASS 1	Black Sheep/Classic Quotes (p/s).....................5
80s	Wabbit	WHAT'S THE TIME, MR WOLF? (LP).....................20

ANDY PRATT
69	Polydor 2489 003	RECORDS ARE LIKE LIFE (LP).....................12

GRAHAM & EILEEN PRATT
85	Plant Life PLR 068	HEIROGLYPHICS (LP).....................15
80s	Dingle's DIN 308	TO FRIEND & FOE (LP).....................18

PHIL PRATT
69	Jolly JY 008	Sweet Song For My Baby/THRILLERS: I'm Restless.....................140+

(see also Charlie Ace, Larry Marshall, Don Drummond)

PHIL PRATT ALL STARS
70	Jackpot JP 748	Cut Throat/KEN BOOTHE: You Left The Water Running.....................12
71	Punch PH 94	Winey Winey (actually "Kingstonians Medley" by Kingstonians)/ There Is A Place (actually by Barrington Spence).....................12

(see also Dennis Alcapone, Horace Andy, Dennis Brown, Ken Boothe, Erroll Dunkley, John Holt, Delroy Wilson)

PRAYING MANTIS
79	Ripper/Harvest HAR 5201	THE SOUNDHOUSE TAPES PART 2: Captured City/Johnny Cool (p/s).....................50
79	Ripper/Harvest 12HAR 5201	THE SOUNDHOUSE TAPES PART 2 (12").....................15
80	Gem GEMS 36	Praying Mantis/High Roller (p/s, some with transfer).....................20/18
81	Arista ARIST 397	All Day And All Of The Night/Beads Of Ebony (p/s).....................12
82	Jet JET 7026	Tell Me The Nightmare's Wrong/A Question Of Time/Turn The Tables (p/s)......30
81	Arista SPART 1153	TIME TELLS NO LIES (LP, with inner sleeve).....................30

(see also Stratus, Grand Prix, Uriah Heep)

PREACHERS
65	Columbia DB 7680	Hole In My Soul/Too Old In The Head.....................80

(see also Herd, Peter Frampton, Denny Mitchel & Soundsations, Moon's Train)

PRECISIONS
67	Track 604 014	If This Is Love/You'll Soon Be Gone.....................40
79	Grapevine GRP 129	Such Misery/A Lovers Plea.....................20

PREDATOR
78	Bust! SOL 2	Punk Man/Paperboy Song (with insert).....................40

PREDATOR
85   CTM C 001   Don't Stop/Shotdown (some in p/s) 80/30

PREDATORS
83   Ears And Eyes EER 012   SOCIAL DECAY (LP) 40

PREDATUR
82   Quicksilver QUICK 5   Take A Walk/Seen You Here (p/s) 125

PREFAB SPROUT
82   Candle CANDLE 1   Lions In My Own Garden (Exit Someone)/Radio Love 20

PREGNANT INSOMNIA
67   Direction 58-3132   Wallpaper/You Intrigue Me 60

PRELUDE
70s Crotchet CME 18A/B   PRELUDE (LP, private pressing) 60

PRELUDE
73   Dawn DNLS 3052   HOW LONG IS FOREVER (LP, gatefold sleeve) 15
74   Dawn DNLS 3061   DUTCH COURAGE (LP) 15
75   Dawn DNLH 3   OWL CREEK INCIDENT (LP) 15

PREMIERS (U.K.)
64   Silver Phoenix 1002   Tears, Tears/Bye Bye Johnny 35

PREMIERS (U.S.)
64   Warner Bros WB 134   Farmer John/Duffy's Blues 12
64   Warner Bros W 1565   FARMER JOHN "LIVE" (LP) 58

YVONNE PRENOSILOVA
65   Pye 7N 15775   When My Baby Cries/Come On Home 50

PRESENCE
76   NC SLCW 1031   PRESENCE (LP) 35

PRESENCE
91   Reality LOL 1   In Wonder/Soft (p/s, withdrawn) 5
91   Reality LOLX 1   In Wonder/Soft/In Wonder (Didgeribdub Mix) (12", p/s, withdrawn) ... 8
91   Reality LOLCD 1   In Wonder/Soft/In Wonder (Didgeribdub Mix)/In Wonder (Millies Mix) (CD) .. 8
(see also Cure)

PRESIDENT REAGAN IS CLEVER
86   Hyena HAHA 001   FROM THIS TO THAT EP (12") 8

PRESIDENTS
64   Decca F 11826   Candy Man/Let The Sunshine In 40

PRESIDENTS
72   A&M AMS 856   5-10-15-20 Years Of Love/Triangle Of Love 10
72   Sussex AMLS 65001   5-10-15-20-25-30 (LP) 25

ELVIS PRESLEY
HMV 78s
56   HMV POP 182   Heartbreak Hotel/I Was The One 40
56   HMV POP 213   Blue Suede Shoes/Tutti Frutti 25
56   HMV POP 235   I Want You, I Need You, I Love You/My Baby Left Me 25
56   HMV POP 249   Hound Dog/Don't Be Cruel 15
56   HMV POP 253   Love Me Tender/Anyway You Want Me (That's How I Will Be) 20
56   HMV POP 272   Blue Moon/I Don't Care If The Sun Don't Shine 40
57   HMV POP 295   Mystery Train/Love Me 45
57   HMV POP 305   Rip It Up/Baby, Let's Play House 40
57   HMV POP 330   Too Much/Playing For Keeps 30
57   HMV POP 359   All Shook Up/That's When Your Heartaches Begin 18
57   HMV POP 378   Paralyzed/When My Blue Moon Turns To Gold Again 30
57   HMV POP 408   Tryin' To Get To You/Lawdy, Miss Clawdy 50
58   HMV POP 428   I'm Left, You're Right, She's Gone/How Do You Think I Feel? 50
HMV 45s: PURPLE LABEL/GOLD PRINT
56   HMV 7M 385   Heartbreak Hotel/I Was The One
                                  ('removable/replaceable' or solid centre) 375/200
56   HMV 7M 405   Blue Suede Shoes/Tutti Frutti 300
56   HMV 7M 424   I Want You, I Need You, I Love You/My Baby Left Me 200
56   HMV POP 249   Hound Dog/Don't Be Cruel 140
56   HMV POP 253   Love Me Tender/Anyway You Want Me (That's How I Will Be) 175
56   HMV POP 272   Blue Moon/I Don't Care If The Sun Don't Shine
                                  ('removable/replaceable' centre or solid centre) 200/150
57   HMV POP 295   Mystery Train/Love Me ('removable/replaceable' centre or solid centre) ... 350/290
57   HMV 7MC 42   Mystery Train/I Forgot To Remember To Forget (U.K. issue
                                  of export single, gold label print only, smooth edge to labels) ... 325
57   HMV POP 305   Rip It Up/Baby, Let's Play House ('removable/replaceable' centre
                                  or solid centre) 250/210
57   HMV POP 330   Too Much/Playing For Keeps 140
57   HMV POP 359   All Shook Up/That's When Your Heartaches Begin
                                  (push-out centre or solid centre) 160/100
57   HMV POP 378   Paralyzed/When My Blue Moon Turns To Gold Again 90
HMV 45s: PURPLE LABEL/SILVER PRINT
56   HMV 7M 385   Heartbreak Hotel/I Was The One 240
56   HMV 7M 405   Blue Suede Shoes/Tutti Frutti 300
56   HMV 7M 424   I Want You, I Need You, I Love You/My Baby Left Me 180
56   HMV POP 249   Hound Dog/Don't Be Cruel 120
56   HMV POP 253   Love Me Tender/Anyway You Want Me (That's How I Will Be) 150
56   HMV POP 272   Blue Moon/I Don't Care If The Sun Don't Shine 150
57   HMV POP 295   Mystery Train/Love Me 300

57	HMV POP 305	Rip It Up/Baby, Let's Play House	220
57	HMV POP 330	Too Much/Playing For Keeps	150
57	HMV POP 359	All Shook Up/That's When Your Heartaches Begin ('removable/replaceable' centre or solid centre)	150/50
57	HMV POP 378	Paralyzed/When My Blue Moon Turns To Gold Again	90
57	HMV POP 408	Tryin' To Get To You/Lawdy, Miss Clawdy	70
58	HMV POP 428	I'm Left, You're Right, She's Gone/How Do You Think I Feel?	70

HMV EXPORT 45s

57	HMV 7MC 42	Mystery Train/I Forgot To Remember To Forget (gold label print, serrated edge to labels)	300
57	HMV 7MC 45	I Want You, I Need You, I Love You/My Baby Left Me (gold label print)	325
57	HMV 7MC 50	Hound Dog/Don't Be Cruel (gold label print)	325
57	HMV JO 465	Love Me Tender/Anyway You Want Me (That's How I'll Be) (gold label print)	325
57	HMV JO 466	Too Much/Playing For Keeps (gold label print)	275
57	HMV JO 473	All Shook Up/That's When Your Heartaches Begin (gold label print)	265

RCA 78s

57	RCA RCA 1013	(Let Me Be Your) Teddy Bear/Loving You	15
57	RCA RCA 1020	Party/Got A Lot O' Livin' To Do	15
57	RCA RCA 1025	Santa Bring My Baby Back (To Me)/Santa Claus Is Back In Town	25
58	RCA RCA 1028	Jailhouse Rock/Treat Me Nice	18
58	RCA RCA 1043	Don't/I Beg Of You	25
58	RCA RCA 1058	Wear My Ring Around Your Neck/Doncha' Think It's Time	30
58	RCA RCA 1070	Hard Headed Woman/Don't Ask Me Why	30
58	RCA RCA 1081	King Creole/Dixieland Rock	40
58	RCA RCA 1088	All Shook Up/Heartbreak Hotel	140
58	RCA RCA 1095	Hound Dog/Blue Suede Shoes	150
59	RCA RCA 1100	One Night/I Got Stung (composing credit: Bartholomew or Bartholemew)	60
59	RCA RCA 1113	(Now And Then There's) A Fool Such As I/I Need Your Love Tonight	85
59	RCA RCA 1136	A Big Hunk O' Love/My Wish Came True	120
60	RCA RCA 1187	Stuck On You/Fame And Fortune	750
60	RCA RCA 1194	A Mess Of Blues/The Girl Of My Best Friend	1,000

ORIGINAL RCA 45s: BLACK LABELS

57	RCA RCA 1013	(Let Me Be Your) Teddy Bear/Loving You	25
57	RCA RCA 1020	Party/Got A Lot O' Livin' To Do	20
57	RCA RCA 1025	Santa Bring My Baby Back (To Me)/Santa Claus Is Back In Town	25
58	RCA RCA 1028	Jailhouse Rock/Treat Me Nice	15
58	RCA RCA 1043	Don't/I Beg Of You	15
58	RCA RCA 1058	Wear My Ring Around Your Neck/Doncha' Think It's Time	15
58	RCA RCA 1070	Hard Headed Woman/Don't Ask Me Why	15
58	RCA RCA 1081	King Creole/Dixieland Rock	18
58	RCA RCA 1088	All Shook Up/Heartbreak Hotel	50
58	RCA RCA 1095	Hound Dog/Blue Suede Shoes	50
59	RCA RCA 1100	One Night/I Got Stung	12
59	RCA RCA 1113	(Now And Then There's) A Fool Such As I/I Need Your Love Tonight	15
59	RCA RCA 1136	A Big Hunk O' Love/My Wish Came True	15

(The above RCA 45s were issued with triangular centres, round-centre re-pressings are worth half to two-thirds these values. However, RCA Victor re-pressings are on par with Triangular centre prices)

60	RCA RCA 1187	Stuck On You/Fame And Fortune	6
60	RCA RCA 1194	A Mess Of Blues/The Girl Of My Best Friend	5
60	RCA RCA 1207	It's Now Or Never (O Sole Mio)/Make Me Know It	5
61	RCA RCA 1216	Are You Lonesome Tonight?/I Gotta Know	5
61	RCA RCA 1226	Wooden Heart/Tonight Is So Right For Love	5
61	RCA RCA 1227	Surrender (Torna A Surriento)/Lonely Man	5
61	RCA RCA 1244	Wild In The Country/I Feel So Bad	5
61	RCA RCA 1258	(Marie's The Name) His Latest Flame/Little Sister	5
62	RCA RCA 1270	Rock-A-Hula Baby/Can't Help Falling In Love	5
62	RCA RCA 1280	Good Luck Charm/Anything That's Part Of You	5
62	RCA RCA 1303	She's Not You/Just Tell Her Jim Said Hello	5
62	RCA RCA 1320	Return To Sender/Where Do You Come From	5

ORIGINAL RCA VICTOR 45s: BLACK LABELS

62	RCA Victor RCA 1280	Good Luck Charm/Anything That's Part Of You	6
62	RCA Victor RCA 1303	She's Not You/Just Tell Her Jim Said Hello	6
62	RCA Victor RCA 1320	Return To Sender/Where Do You Come From	6
63	RCA Victor RCA 1337	One Broken Heart For Sale/They Remind Me Too Much Of You	8
63	RCA Victor RCA 1355	(You're The) Devil In Disguise/Please Don't Drag That String Around	5
63	RCA Victor RCA 1374	Bossa Nova Baby/Witchcraft	5
63	RCA Victor RCA 1375	Kiss Me Quick/Something Blue	5
64	RCA Victor RCA 1390	Viva Las Vegas/What'd I Say	6
64	RCA Victor RCA 1404	Kissin' Cousins/It Hurts Me	6
64	RCA Victor RCA 1411	Such A Night/Never Ending	6
64	RCA Victor RCA 1422	Ain't That Loving You Baby/Ask Me	6
64	RCA Victor RCA 1430	Blue Christmas/White Christmas	6
65	RCA Victor RCA 1443	Do The Clam/You'll Be Gone	7
65	RCA Victor RCA 1489	Tell Me Why/Puppet On A String	5
66	RCA Victor RCA 1504	Blue River/Do Not Disturb	6
66	RCA Victor RCA 1509	Frankie And Johnny/Please Don't Stop Loving Me	15
66	RCA Victor RCA 1526	Love Letters/Come What May	7
66	RCA Victor RCA 1545	All That I Am/Spinout	10
66	RCA Victor RCA 1557	If Every Day Was Like Christmas/How Would You Like To Be?	8
67	RCA Victor RCA 1565	Indescribably Blue/Fools Fall In Love	20
67	RCA Victor RCA 1593	The Love Machine/You Gotta Stop	25
67	RCA Victor RCA 1616	Long-Legged Girl (With The Short Dress On)/That's Someone You Never Forget	25
67	RCA Victor RCA 1628	Judy/There's Always Me	55

67	RCA Victor RCA 1642	Big Boss Man/You Don't Know Me	15
68	RCA Victor RCA 1663	Guitar Man/Hi-Heel Sneakers	10
68	RCA Victor RCA 1688	U.S. Male/Stay Away	15
68	RCA Victor RCA 1714	Your Time Hasn't Come Yet Baby/Let Yourself Go	20
68	RCA Victor RCA 1747	You'll Never Walk Alone/We Call On Him	30
68	RCA Victor RCA 1768	A Little Less Conversation/Almost In Love	30

RCA VICTOR 45s: BLACK LABEL REISSUES

64	RCA Victor RCA 1020	Party/Got A Lot O' Livin' To Do	25
64	RCA Victor RCA 1025	Santa Bring My Baby Back (To Me)/Santa Claus Is Back In Town	35
64	RCA Victor RCA 1028	Jailhouse Rock/Treat Me Nice	30
64	RCA Victor RCA 1043	Don't/I Beg Of You	30
64	RCA Victor RCA 1058	Wear My Ring Around Your Neck/Doncha' Think It's Time	25
64	RCA Victor RCA 1070	Hard Headed Woman/Don't Ask Me Why	35
64	RCA Victor RCA 1081	King Creole/Dixieland Rock	35
64	RCA Victor RCA 1088	All Shook Up/Heartbreak Hotel	35
64	RCA Victor RCA 1095	Hound Dog/Blue Suede Shoes	35
64	RCA Victor RCA 1100	One Night/I Got Stung	25
64	RCA Victor RCA 1113	(Now And Then There's) A Fool Such As I/I Need Your Love Tonight	25
64	RCA Victor RCA 1136	A Big Hunk O' Love/My Wish Came True	25
64	RCA Victor RCA 1187	Stuck On You/Fame And Fortune	20
64	RCA Victor RCA 1194	A Mess Of Blues/The Girl Of My Best Friend	15
64	RCA Victor RCA 1207	It's Now Or Never (O Sole Mio)/Make Me Know It	30
64	RCA Victor RCA 1216	Are You Lonesome Tonight?/I Gotta Know	30
64	RCA Victor RCA 1226	Wooden Heart/Tonight Is So Right For Love	10
64	RCA Victor RCA 1227	Surrender (Torna A Surriento)/Lonely Man	10
64	RCA Victor RCA 1244	Wild In The Country/I Feel So Bad	10
64	RCA Victor RCA 1258	(Marie's The Name) His Latest Flame/Little Sister	6
64	RCA Victor RCA 1270	Rock-A-Hula Baby/Can't Help Falling In Love	7

RCA VICTOR 45s: ORANGE LABEL REISSUES

69	RCA Victor RCA 1088	All Shook Up/Heartbreak Hotel	35
69	RCA Victor RCA 1095	Hound Dog/Blue Suede Shoes	35
69	RCA Victor RCA 1207	It's Now Or Never (O Sole Mio)/Make Me Know It	35
69	RCA Victor RCA 1216	Are You Lonesome Tonight?/I Gotta Know	35
69	RCA Victor RCA 1226	Wooden Heart/Tonight Is So Right For Love	50
69	RCA Victor RCA 1688	U.S. Male/Stay Away	110
71	RCA MAXI 2104	Heartbreak Hotel/Hound Dog/Don't Be Cruel ('Maximillion' sleeve)	10
71	RCA MAXI 2153	Jailhouse Rock/Are You Lonesome Tonight?/(Let Me Be Your) Teddy Bear/ Steadfast, Loyal And True ('Maximillion' sleeve)	10
75	RCA MAXI 2601	Blue Moon/You're A Heartbreaker/I'm Left, You're Right, She's Gone ('Maximillion' sleeve)	20

ORIGINAL RCA VICTOR ORANGE LABEL 45s

69	RCA Victor RCA 1795	If I Can Dream/Memories	10
69	RCA Victor RCA 1831	In The Ghetto/Any Day Now	6
69	RCA Victor RCA 1869	Clean Up Your Own Backyard/The Fair's Moving On	6
69	RCA Victor RCA 1900	Suspicious Minds/You'll Think Of Me (p/s)	10
70	RCA Victor RCA 1916	Don't Cry Daddy/Rubberneckin' (p/s)	15
70	RCA Victor RCA 1949	Kentucky Rain/My Little Friend (p/s)	10
70	RCA Victor RCA 1999	I've Lost You/The Next Step Is Love	6
71	RCA Victor RCA 2060	There Goes My Everything/I Really Don't Want To Know (p/s)	10
71	RCA Victor RCA 2084	Rags To Riches/Where Did They Go, Lord (p/s)	10
71	RCA Victor RCA 2125	I'm Leavin'/Heart Of Rome	6
71	RCA Victor RCA 2158	I Just Can't Help Believin'/How The Web Was Woven	6
72	RCA Victor RCA 2188	Until It's Time For You To Go/We Can Make The Morning (p/s)	10
72	RCA Victor RCA 2229	American Trilogy/The First Time Ever I Saw Your Face	12
72	RCA Victor RCA 2267	Burning Love/It's A Matter Of Time	8
72	RCA Victor RCA 2304	Always On My Mind/Separate Ways	7
73	RCA Victor RCA 2359	Polk Salad Annie/See See Rider	7
73	RCA Victor RCA 2393	Fool/Steamroller Blues	7
73	RCA Victor RCA 2435	Raised On Rock/For Ol' Times Sake	7
74	RCA Victor APBO 0196	Take Good Care Of Her/I've Got A Thing About You Baby (solid centre, no p/s; most copies as U.S. imports with large centre hole in U.S. p/s)	250/15
74	RCA Victor APBO 0280	If You Talk In Your Sleep/Help Me	10
74	RCA Victor RCA 2458	My Boy/Loving Arms	5
74	RCA Victor PB 10074	Promised Land/It's Midnight (1st pressing)	5
74	RCA Victor PB 10074	Promised Land/It's Midnight And I Miss You (2nd pressing with correct B-side title)	15
75	RCA Victor RCA 2562	T-R-O-U-B-L-E/Mr. Songman	5
75	RCA Victor RCA 2635	Green Green Grass Of Home/Thinking About You	5
76	RCA Victor RCA 2674	Hurt/For The Heart	10

RETROSPECTIVE RCA BLUE LABEL 45s

78	RCA PB 9265	Don't Be Cruel/Hound Dog (p/s)	5
78	RCA PB 9334	Old Shep/Paralysed (p/s)	5
80	RCA RCA 4	It's Only Love/Beyond The Reef (p/s)	5
80	RCA RCA 16	Santa Claus Is Back In Town/I Believe (p/s)	5
81	RCA RCA 43	Guitar Man/Faded Love (with matt U.K. p/s [cat. no. RCA 43])	50
81	RCA RCA 43	Guitar Man/Faded Love (with glossy U.S. p/s [cat. no. PB 12158])	5
82	RCA RCA 196	Are You Lonesome Tonight? (Laughing Version)/From A Jack To A King (p/s)	6

OTHER RCA 45s

82	RCA RCAP 232	The Sound Of Your Cry/I'll Never Know (picture disc)	5
83	RCA RCAP 1028	Jailhouse Rock/The Elvis Medley (without "Hound Dog" credit on B-side) (reissue, picture disc)	5
83	RCA RCAP 1028	Jailhouse Rock/The Elvis Medley (with "Hound Dog" credit on B-side) (reissue, picture disc)	25

MINT VALUE £

83	RCA RCAP 332	Baby, I Don't Care/One-Sided Love Affair/Tutti Frutti (picture disc)	5
83	RCA RCA 369	I Can Help/The Lady Loves Me (p/s)	5
83	RCA RCAP 369	I Can Help/If Every Day Was Like Christmas/The Lady Loves Me (10", picture disc in clear plastic sleeve)	25
84	RCA RCA 405	Green Green Grass Of Home/Release Me (And Let Me Love Again)/Solitaire (p/s, some with poster)	25/5
84	RCA RCA 459	The Last Farewell/It's Easy for You (p/s)	5
84	RCA RCAT 459	The Last Farewell/It's Easy for You (10", p/s)	15
85	RCA RCA 476	The Elvis Medley/Blue Suede Shoes (p/s)	5
85	RCA PB 49943	Always On My Mind (Alternate Version)/Tomorrow Night (p/s)	5
87	RCA ARON 1	Bossa Nova Baby/Ain't That Loving You Baby (p/s)	5
87	RCA ARONT 1	Bossa Nova Baby/Ain't That Loving You Baby (12", p/s)	15
87	RCA ARON 2	Love Me Tender/If I Can Dream (p/s)	5
87	RCA ARONT 2	Love Me Tender/If I Can Dream (p/s) (12", p/s)	15
88	RCA PB 49177	Are You Lonesome Tonight/Reconsider Baby (p/s)	5
88	RCA PB 49177	Are You Lonesome Tonight/Reconsider Baby (12", p/s)	8
88	RCA PB 49473	Mean Woman Blues/I Beg Of Of You (p/s)	10
88	RCA PT 49474	Mean Woman Blues/I Beg Of Of You (12", p/s)	25
88	RCA PB 49545	Stuck On You/Any Way You Want Me (p/s)	5
88	RCA PT 49546	Stuck On You/Any Way You Want Me (12", p/s)	15
88	RCA PB 49943	Always On My Mind/Tomorrow Night (p/s)	8
88	RCA PT 49944	Always On My Mind/Tomorrow Night (12", p/s)	25
89	RCA PD 49467	Heartbreak Hotel/I Was The One/Don't Be Cruel (To A Heart That's True)/Hound Dog (3" CD, gatefold card sleeve)	8
04	BMG 82876 619211	That's All Right/Blue Moon Of Kentucky (10", brown die-cut sleeve, with 'Sun' labels)	40

SINGLES BOX SET
77	RCA (no cat. no.)	PRESLEY GOLD — 16 NUMBER ONES (16 x 7", each in p/s, black box set)	40

OTHER SINGLES & FLEXIDISCS
57	Weekend Mail (no cat. no.)	THE TRUTH ABOUT ME (1-sided 6" 78 rpm, mail-order only, some in mailer)	70/50
75	Reader's Digest/RCA RD ELV 785/65	Brian Matthew Introduces Excerpts From Elvis Presley's Greatest Hits (6" flexidisc, some with newsletter & advertising leaflet)	7/5
77	RCA Victor 2694-2709	"GOLD 16" SERIES (16 x p/s 7" in foldout cardboard carrier)	35
79	RCA LB 1	The Wonder Of You/Noel Edmonds Introduces Record Year (Lever Brothers premium)	20
81	Chiswick NS 71	Press Conference 1957/DEKE RIVERS: Elvis Presley Medley (picture disc)	6
83	Buttons BUT 3	A.F.N. RADIO INTERVIEW (p/s, fan club interview flexidisc)	5
83	Buttons BUT 4	NEW YORK PRESS CONFERENCE (orange vinyl fan club flexidisc, free with *Elvis Monthly Collector's Special*, issue 2)	5
83	Buttons BUT 5	INTERVIEW BETWEEN ELVIS, PETER NOONE AND TOM MOFFETT (fan club flexidisc free with *Elvis Monthly Collector's Special*, issue 4)	5
84	Buttons BUT 6	GERMAN RADIO INTERVIEW (fan club flexidisc free with *Elvis Monthly Collector's Special*, issue 6)	5
84	Buttons BUT 7	ELVIS' 1964 GREETING TO HIS BRITISH FANS/THE TRUTH ABOUT ME (fan club flexi with *Elvis Monthly Collector's Special*, issue 8)	5
85	Buttons BUT 8	1956 NEW ORLEANS INTERVIEW (fan club flexidisc free with *Elvis Monthly Collector's Special*, issue 10)	5
85	Buttons BUT 9	JACKSON, FLORIDA 1955 INTERVIEW/MEMPHIS 1957 INTERVIEW (fan club flexidisc free with *Elvis Monthly Collector's Special*, issue 10)	5

HMV EPs
57	HMV 7EG 8199	LOVE ME TENDER (soundtrack, round or removeable/replaceable centre)	150/175
57	HMV 7EG 8256	GOOD ROCKIN' TONIGHT (round centre only)	200

RCA EPs: TRIANGULAR CENTRES
57	RCA RCX 101	PEACE IN THE VALLEY	50
57	RCA RCX 104	ELVIS PRESLEY	35
58	RCA RCX 106	JAILHOUSE ROCK (soundtrack)	35
58	RCA RCX 117	KING CREOLE VOL. 1 (soundtrack, black label, cream or white rear p/s)	40
58	RCA RCX 118	KING CREOLE VOL. 2 (soundtrack, cream or white rear sleeve)	40
58	RCA RCX 121	ELVIS SINGS CHRISTMAS SONGS (1st issue, single sleeve)	90
58	RCA RCX 131	ELVIS SAILS (interview record, sleeve laminated front & back)	55
59	RCA RCX 135	ELVIS IN TENDER MOOD (with red print on rear sleeve)	75

*(The above RCA EPs were originally issued with **laminated front and back** sleeves; later copies with front-only laminate are worth three quarters of these values.)*

59	RCA RCX 1045	A TOUCH OF GOLD (laminated front sleeve only)	70
59	RCA RCX 175	STRICTLY ELVIS	55
60	RCA RCX 1048	A TOUCH OF GOLD VOL. 2	150

RCA EPs: ROUND CENTRE RE-PRESSINGS
60s	RCA RCX 101	PEACE IN THE VALLEY	20
60s	RCA RCX 104	ELVIS PRESLEY	15
60s	RCA RCX 106	JAILHOUSE ROCK (soundtrack)	15
60s	RCA RCX 117	KING CREOLE VOL. 1 (soundtrack)	15
60s	RCA RCX 118	KING CREOLE VOL. 2 (soundtrack)	15
60s	RCA RCX 121	ELVIS SINGS CHRISTMAS SONGS (gatefold p/s)	125
60s	RCA RCX 131	ELVIS SAILS (interview record)	25
60s	RCA RCX 135	ELVIS IN TENDER MOOD	20
60s	RCA RCX 1045	A TOUCH OF GOLD	25
60s	RCA RCX 175	STRICTLY ELVIS	10
60s	RCA RCX 1048	A TOUCH OF GOLD VOL. 2	50

ORIGINAL RCA EPs: ROUND CENTRES
60	RCA RCX 190	SUCH A NIGHT	25
62	RCA RCX 211	FOLLOW THAT DREAM (soundtrack)	10
62	RCA RCX 211	FOLLOW THAT DREAM (mispressing, 2nd side features Jim Reeves)	100
62	RCA RCX 7109	KID GALAHAD (soundtrack)	10
64	RCA Victor RCX 7141	LOVE IN LAS VEGAS (soundtrack)	20

64	RCA Victor RCX 7142	ELVIS FOR YOU VOL. 1 75
64	RCA Victor RCX 7143	ELVIS FOR YOU VOL. 2 75
65	RCA Victor RCX 7173	TICKLE ME (soundtrack) 45
65	RCA Victor RCX 7174	TICKLE ME VOL. 2 (soundtrack) 45
67	RCA Victor RCX 7187	EASY COME, EASY GO (soundtrack) 50

RCA VICTOR EPs: BLACK LABEL RE-PRESSINGS

64	RCA Victor RCX 101	PEACE IN THE VALLEY 20
64	RCA Victor RCX 104	ELVIS PRESLEY 15
64	RCA Victor RCX 106	JAILHOUSE ROCK (soundtrack)....................................... 25
64	RCA Victor RCX 117	KING CREOLE VOL. 1 (soundtrack) 15
64	RCA Victor RCX 118	KING CREOLE VOL. 2 (soundtrack) 15
64	RCA Victor RCX 121	ELVIS SINGS CHRISTMAS SONGS (single p/s) 45
64	RCA Victor RCX 131	ELVIS SAILS (interview record) 40
64	RCA Victor RCX 135	ELVIS IN TENDER MOOD 30
64	RCA Victor RCX 1045	A TOUCH OF GOLD 25
64	RCA Victor RCX 175	STRICTLY ELVIS 15
64	RCA Victor RCX 1048	A TOUCH OF GOLD VOL. 2 40
64	RCA Victor RCX 190	SUCH A NIGHT 10
64	RCA Victor RCX 211	FOLLOW THAT DREAM (soundtrack) 10
64	RCA Victor RCX 7109	KID GALAHAD (soundtrack) 10

RCA VICTOR EPs: ORANGE LABEL RE-PRESSINGS

69	RCA Victor RCX 101	PEACE IN THE VALLEY (push-out or solid centre) 15/30
69	RCA Victor RCX 104	ELVIS PRESLEY (push-out or solid centre) 18/12
69	RCA Victor RCX 106	JAILHOUSE ROCK (soundtrack, push-out or solid centre)............ 8/12
69	RCA Victor RCX 117	KING CREOLE VOL. 1 (soundtrack, push-out or solid centre) 18/12
69	RCA Victor RCX 118	KING CREOLE VOL. 2 (soundtrack, push-out or solid centre) 18/12
69	RCA Victor RCX 131	ELVIS SAILS (interview record, push-out or solid centre) ...... each 18
69	RCA Victor RCX 135	ELVIS IN TENDER MOOD (push-out or solid centre, with different take of "Lover Doll") .... each 18
69	RCA Victor RCX 1045	A TOUCH OF GOLD (push-out or solid centre) 22/18
69	RCA Victor RCX 175	STRICTLY ELVIS (push-out or solid centre) .... each 18
69	RCA Victor RCX 1048	A TOUCH OF GOLD VOL. 2 (push-out or solid centre) 22/18
69	RCA Victor RCX 190	SUCH A NIGHT (push-out or solid centre) 18/12

EP BOX SETS

82	RCA EP 1	THE EP COLLECTION (11-EP box set, reissues, with booklet) .. 60
83	RCA EP 2	THE EP COLLECTION VOL. 2 (11-EP box set, reissues, with booklet) 80

LPs: HMV ISSUES

56	HMV CLP 1093	ROCK 'N' ROLL 550
57	HMV CLP 1105	ROCK 'N' ROLL NO. 2 700
57	HMV DLP 1159	THE BEST OF ELVIS (10") 375

LPs: ORIGINAL BLACK/SILVER SPOT RCA ISSUES

57	RCA RC 24001	LOVING YOU (10", soundtrack) 110
57	RCA RD 27052	ELVIS' CHRISTMAS ALBUM (laminated front & back covers with 4 pictures on back cover) 100
58	RCA RD 27088	KING CREOLE (soundtrack) 50
59	RCA RD 27120	ELVIS 75
59	RCA RD 27128	A DATE WITH ELVIS 45
60	RCA RD 27159	ELVIS' GOLDEN RECORDS VOL. 2 30
60	RCA RD 27171/SF 5060	ELVIS IS BACK! (gatefold sleeve, mono/stereo).............. 40/60
60	RCA RD 27192/SF 5078	G.I. BLUES (soundtrack, mono/stereo) 18/45
61	RCA RD 27211/SF 5094	HIS HAND IN MINE (mono/stereo) 25/45
61	RCA RD 27224/SF 5106	SOMETHING FOR EVERYBODY (mono/stereo) 22/45
61	RCA RD 27238/SF 5115	BLUE HAWAII (soundtrack, mono/stereo) 25/40
62	RCA RD 27265/SF 5135	POT LUCK (mono/stereo) 20/40

LPs: SILVER SPOT/'RED SEAL' RCA ISSUES

58	RCA RB 16069	ELVIS' GOLDEN RECORDS (maroon 'silver spot' label, gatefold sleeve with stapled-in 4-page photo booklet) 100
60	RCA RB 16069	ELVIS' GOLDEN RECORDS ('Red Seal'/'silver spot' label, gatefold sleeve with stapled-in 2-page photo booklet)....... 35
63	RCA RB 16069	ELVIS' GOLDEN RECORDS ('Red Seal'/'black spot' label, no booklet, gatefold sleeve).................................... 25
67	RCA RB 16069	ELVIS' GOLDEN RECORDS ('Red Seal'/'black spot' label, no booklet, single sleeve) 18

LPs: ORIGINAL BLACK/SILVER SPOT RCA VICTOR ISSUES

63	RCA Victor RD/SF 7534	GIRLS! GIRLS! GIRLS! (soundtrack, mono/stereo) 20/45
63	RCA Victor RD/SF 7565	IT HAPPENED AT THE WORLD'S FAIR (soundtrack, mono/stereo) .. 20/45
63	RCA Victor RD/SF 7609	FUN IN ACAPULCO (soundtrack, mono/stereo) 20/45

LPs: ORIGINAL BLACK/RED SPOT RCA VICTOR ISSUES

64	RCA Victor RD/SF 7630	ELVIS' GOLDEN RECORDS VOL. 3 (mono/stereo) 18/35
64	RCA Victor RD/SF 7645	KISSIN' COUSINS (soundtrack, mono/stereo) 18/40
64	RCA Victor RD/SF 7678	ROUSTABOUT (soundtrack, mono/stereo) 16/40
65	RCA Victor RD/SF 7714	GIRL HAPPY (soundtrack, mono/stereo)...................... 18/40
65	RCA Victor RD 7723	FLAMING STAR AND SUMMER KISSES (soundtrack, mono only, black label) .. 100
65	RCA Victor RD/SF 7752	ELVIS FOR EVERYONE (mono/stereo, 'orange shirt' sleeve) .. 35/55
65	RCA Victor RD/SF 7767	HAREM HOLIDAY (soundtrack, mono/stereo)................ 20/30
66	RCA Victor RD/SF 7793	FRANKIE AND JOHNNY (soundtrack, mono/stereo) 40/60
66	RCA Victor RD/SF 7810	PARADISE, HAWAIIAN STYLE (soundtrack, mono/stereo) .. 25/40
66	RCA Victor RD/SF 7820	CALIFORNIA HOLIDAY (soundtrack, mono/stereo) 25/40
67	RCA Victor RD/SF 7867	HOW GREAT THOU ART (mono/stereo) 25/40
67	RCA Victor RD/SF 7892	DOUBLE TROUBLE (soundtrack, mono/stereo) 20/30
68	RCA Victor RD/SF 7917	CLAMBAKE (soundtrack, black/red dot labels, mono/stereo) .. 20/30
68	RCA Victor RD/SF 7924	ELVIS' GOLD RECORDS VOLUME 4 (with "Never Ending" listed on sleeve instead of "Love Letters"; mono/stereo) .. 40/60
68	RCA Victor RD/SF 7924	ELVIS' GOLD RECORDS VOLUME 4 (corrected sleeve, mono/stereo)....... 25/30
68	RCA Victor RD/SF 7957	SPEEDWAY (soundtrack, with Nancy Sinatra, mono/stereo) .. 60/40

Elvis PRESLEY

LPs: ORIGINAL ORANGE RCA VICTOR ISSUES

69	RCA Victor RD 8011	ELVIS ("TV Special" Soundtrack)	15
69	RCA Victor RD/SF 8029	FROM ELVIS IN MEMPHIS (mono/stereo)	15/12
70	RCA Victor SF 8080/1	FROM MEMPHIS TO VEGAS — FROM VEGAS TO MEMPHIS (2-LP, with 2 x 10" x 8" photos, glossy or matt cover)	30/25
70	RCA SF 8128	ON STAGE, FEBRUARY 1970 (with 30" x 20" colour poster; glossy or matt cover)	15/12
70	RCA LPM 6401	WORLDWIDE 50 GOLD AWARD HITS VOL. 1 — A TOUCH OF GOLD (4-LP, box set with 20-page photo book)	40
71	RCA LPM 6402	THE OTHER SIDES — WORLDWIDE 50 GOLD AWARD HITS VOL. 2 (4-LP, box with material patch & colour portrait)	40
71	RCA Victor SF 8162	THAT'S THE WAY IT IS (glossy or matt cover)	15/12
71	RCA Victor SF 8172	I'M 10,000 YEARS OLD — ELVIS COUNTRY (with colour print, glossy or matt cover)	15/10
71	RCA Victor SF 8202	LOVE LETTERS FROM ELVIS	18
71	RCA Victor SF 8221	ELVIS SINGS THE WONDERFUL WORLD OF CHRISTMAS	25
72	RCA Victor SF 8266	ELVIS NOW	22
72	RCA Victor SF 8275	HE TOUCHED ME	22
72	RCA Victor SF 8296	ELVIS AS RECORDED AT MADISON SQUARE GARDEN	15
73	RCA Victor SF 8378	ELVIS (with "Fool" sticker, must be UK disc and UK cover!)	50
73	RCA DPS 2040	ALOHA FROM HAWAII VIA SATELLITE (2-LP)	20
73	RCA APL1 0388	RAISED ON ROCK/FOR OL' TIMES SAKE (U.K. disc in U.K. sleeve)	220
74	RCA CPL1 0341	ELVIS — A LEGENDARY PERFORMER VOL. 1	15
74	RCA APL1 0475	GOOD TIMES (back cover credits "Loving Arms" or "Lovin' Arms")	18
74	RCA APL1 0606	ELVIS AS RECORDED ON STAGE IN MEMPHIS	15
74	RCA LPL1 7527	HITS OF THE 70s	15
75	RCA APL1 0873	PROMISED LAND	15
75	RCA APM1 0818	HAVING FUN WITH ELVIS ON STAGE	40
75	RCA RS 1011	TODAY	18
76	RCA CPL1 1349	ELVIS — A LEGENDARY PERFORMER VOL. 2	25
76	RCA RS 1060	FROM ELVIS PRESLEY BOULEVARD, MEMPHIS, TENNESSEE	15
77	RCA LP 3021	MOODY BLUE	12
77	RCA PL 02587	ELVIS IN CONCERT	18
77	RCA PL 12274	WELCOME TO MY WORLD	15
77	RCA PL 12772	HE WALKS BESIDE ME	15
77	RCA PL 42003	ELVIS IN DEMAND	15
80	RCA CPL8 3699	ELVIS ARON PRESLEY (8-LP, box set)	60
83	RCA RCALPP 9020	JAILHOUSE ROCK/LOVE IN LAS VEGAS (picture disc)	12
84	RCA PLP 89287	I CAN HELP (picture disc)	12
84	RCA PL 85172	A GOLDEN CELEBRATION (6-LP box set with inserts)	40

LPs: BLACK/SILVER SPOT RCA VICTOR RE-PRESSINGS

64	RCA Victor RC 24001	LOVING YOU (10" LP, mono only)	125
64	RCA Victor RD 27052	ELVIS' CHRISTMAS ALBUM (laminated front & back covers, no pictures on back cover, mono only)	60
64	RCA Victor RD/SF 7528	ROCK 'N' ROLL NO. 2 (reissue of HMV LP, mono/stereo)	18/25
64	RCA Victor RD 27088	KING CREOLE (soundtrack, mono only)	35
64	RCA Victor RD 27120	ELVIS (mono only)	35
64	RCA Victor RD 27128	A DATE WITH ELVIS (mono only)	20
64	RCA Victor RD 27159	ELVIS' GOLDEN RECORDS VOL. 2 (mono only)	15
64	RCA Victor RD 27171	ELVIS IS BACK! (gatefold sleeve, mono)	30
64	RCA Victor SF 5060	ELVIS IS BACK! (gatefold sleeve, stereo)	40
64	RCA Victor RD 27192	G.I. BLUES (soundtrack, mono)	15
64	RCA Victor SF 5078	G.I. BLUES (soundtrack, stereo)	30
64	RCA Victor RD 27211	HIS HAND IN MINE (mono)	25
64	RCA Victor SF 5094	HIS HAND IN MINE (stereo)	30
64	RCA Victor RD 27224	SOMETHING FOR EVERYBODY (mono)	18
64	RCA Victor SF 5106	SOMETHING FOR EVERYBODY (stereo)	30
64	RCA Victor RD 27238	BLUE HAWAII (soundtrack, mono)	18
64	RCA Victor SF 5115	BLUE HAWAII (soundtrack, stereo)	25
64	RCA Victor RD 27265	POT LUCK (mono)	15
64	RCA Victor SF 5135	POT LUCK (stereo)	30

LPs: BLACK/RED SPOT RCA VICTOR RE-PRESSING

64	RCA Victor RD/SF 7528	ROCK 'N' ROLL NO. 2 (reissue of HMV LP, mono/stereo)	18/25

LPs: 'SMALL' ORANGE RCA VICTOR MONO RE-PRESSINGS

69	RCA Victor RD 27052	ELVIS' CHRISTMAS ALBUM	40
69	RCA Victor RD 27088	KING CREOLE (soundtrack)	30
69	RCA Victor RD 27120	ELVIS	30
69	RCA Victor RD 27128	A DATE WITH ELVIS	30
69	RCA Victor RD 27159	ELVIS' GOLDEN RECORDS VOL. 2	30
69	RCA Victor RD 27171	ELVIS IS BACK! (gatefold sleeve)	30
69	RCA Victor RD 27192	G.I. BLUES (soundtrack)	30
69	RCA Victor RD 27211	HIS HAND IN MINE	30
69	RCA Victor RD 27224	SOMETHING FOR EVERYBODY	30
69	RCA Victor RD 27238	BLUE HAWAII (soundtrack)	30
69	RCA Victor RD 7528	ROCK 'N' ROLL NO. 2	30
69	RCA Victor RD 7630	ELVIS' GOLDEN RECORDS VOL. 3	30
69	RCA Victor RD 7723	FLAMING STAR AND SUMMER KISSES (soundtrack)	500+
69	RCA Victor RD 7810	PARADISE, HAWAIIAN STYLE (soundtrack)	30
69	RCA Victor RD 7867	HOW GREAT THOU ART	30
69	RCA Victor RD 7917	CLAMBAKE (soundtrack)	40
69	RCA Victor RD 7924	ELVIS' GOLD RECORDS VOLUME 4	30
69	RCA Victor RD 7957	SPEEDWAY (soundtrack, with Nancy Sinatra)	30

LPs: 'LARGE' ORANGE RCA VICTOR STEREO RE-PRESSINGS

72	RCA Victor SF 8232	ELVIS FOR EVERYONE ('blue shirt'/'TV Special' sleeve) 40

LPs: GREEN RCA INTERNATIONAL ISSUES

69	RCA Intl. INTS 1012	ELVIS SINGS FLAMING STAR 12
70	RCA Intl. INTS 1103	LET'S BE FRIENDS... 20
70	RCA Intl. INTS 1206	ALMOST IN LOVE 15
72	RCA Intl. INTS 1414	BURNING LOVE AND HITS FROM HIS MOVIES (U.K. disc in U.K. sleeve)...... 40

OTHER LPs

78	St. Michael IMP 113	ELVIS (exclusive to Marks & Spencer) 60
78	St. Michael IMPD 204	THE WONDERFUL WORLD OF ELVIS PRESLEY (2-LP, via Marks & Spencer) . . . 80
79	Hammer HMR 6002	THE KING SPEAKS (green sleeve) 30
84	Imperial Records DR 1124	AMERICAN TRILOGY (3-LP, box set) 25
86	RCA AREP 1	ACUFF-ROSE PRESENTS ELVIS (promo-only, 300 copies) 180

CDs

84	RCA PD 89061/2/3	THE LEGEND (3-CD, gold box set, with booklet, numbered, 5,000 only) 300
84	RCA PD 89061/2/3	THE LEGEND (3-CD, silver box set, 5,000 only, with booklet, numbered) 350

(see also Jordanaires, Scotty Moore, Bill Black's Combo)

REG PRESLEY

69	Page One POF 131	Lucinda Lee/Wichita Lineman 12
73	CBS 1478	'S Down To You Marianne/Hey Little Girl 10

(see also Troggs, Suzi Quatro)

PRESSGANG

89	Vox Pop VOX 022	ROGUES (LP)... 15

RAY PRESSLEY

62	Longhorn BLH 0002	Living, Learning, Trying To Forget/Half A Love 8

PRESSURE CO.

82	Paradox SOLID 1	LIVE IN SHEFFIELD 19 JAN '82 (LP)...................................... 12

(see also Eric Random, Cabaret Voltaire)

BILLY PRESTON

66	Sue WI 4012	Billy's Bag/Don't Let The Sun Catch You Cryin' 30
66	Capitol CL 15458	In The Midnight Hour/Advice (DJ copy = £50) 25
66	Capitol CL 15471	Sunny/Let The Music Play 15
69	President PT 263	Billy's Bag/Don't Let The Sun Catch You Crying (reissue)................... 10
69	President PT 263	Billy's Bag/Goldfinger (different B-side)................................... 15
69	Apple APPLE 12	That's The Way God Planned It/What About You (p/s) 14
69	Apple APPLE 19	Everything's Alright/I Want To Thank You 15
70	Apple APPLE 21	All That I've Got/As I Get Older (some in p/s)........................... 25/8
70	President PT 298	If I Had A Hammer/Ferry 'Cross The Mersey 5
70	Soul City SC 107	Greazee (Parts 1 & 2) 20
67	Capitol (S)T 2532	THE WILDEST ORGAN IN TOWN (LP)..................................... 40
67	Sue ILP 935	THE MOST EXCITING ORGAN EVER (LP) 65
69	President PTLS 1034	APPLE OF MY EYE (LP) 15
69	Apple SAPCOR 9	THAT'S THE WAY GOD PLANNED IT (LP) 35
70	Apple SAPCOR 14	ENCOURAGING WORDS (LP) 40
70	Soul City SCM 002	GREAZEE SOUL (LP) 40
91	Apple SAPCOR 9	THAT'S THE WAY GOD PLANNED IT (LP, gatefold sleeve, with bonus 12" [SAPCOR 92]) 15
93	Apple SAPCOR 14	ENCOURAGING WORDS (LP, gatefold sleeve with bonus 12" [SAPCOR 142]) ... 15

(see also Beatles)

EARL PRESTON

63	Fontana TF 406	I Know Something/Watch Your Step (as Earl Preston & T.T.'s) 22
64	Fontana TF 481	Raindrops/That's For Sure (as Earl Preston & Realms) 22

(see also Realm)

JOHNNY PRESTON

60	Mercury AMT 1079	Running Bear/My Heart Knows (78 rpm = £100) 10
60	Mercury AMT 1092	Cradle Of Love/City Of Tears (some in p/s)........................... 28/10
60	Mercury AMT 1104	Feel So Fine/I'm Starting To Go Steady 15
60	Mercury AMT 1114	Charming Billy/Up In The Air 15
61	Mercury AMT 1129	Leave My Kitten Alone/Do What You Did 15
61	Mercury AMT 1145	Big Chief Heartbreak/Madre De Dios (Mother Of God) 15
61	Mercury AMT 1164	New Baby For Christmas/Rock And Roll Guitar 15
61	Mercury AMT 1167	Free Me/Kissing Tree 15
60	Mercury ZEP 10078	RUNNING BEAR (EP) 90
60	Mercury ZEP 10098	RING TAIL TOOTER (EP) 120
61	Mercury ZEP 10116	TOKEN OF LOVE (EP).. 150
60	Mercury MMC 14051	JOHNNY PRESTON — RUNNING BEAR (LP)............................... 150

MIKE PRESTON

58	Decca F 11053	A House, A Car And A Wedding Ring/My Lucky Love (78 rpm = £10)........... 10
58	Decca F 11087	Why, Why, Why/Whispering Grass (78 rpm = £10) 10
59	Decca F 11120	Dirty Old Town/In Surabaya (78 rpm = £8) 10
59	Decca F 11167	Mr. Blue/Just Ask Your Heart (78 rpm = £10)............................... 7
60	Decca F 11222	A Girl Like You/Too Old (78 rpm = £12). 7
60	Decca F 11255	I'd Do Anything/Where Is Love? (78 rpm = £15) 6
60	Decca F 11287	Togetherness/Farewell My Love 6
60	Decca DFE 6635	FOUR SONGS BY RAY NOBLE (EP) 20
61	Decca DFE 6679	MARRY ME (EP)... 20

PRETENDERS

81	Lyntone LYN 9650	Whatcha Gonna Do About It/Stop Your Sobbin' (orange flexi, with *Flexipop* 6).. 6/4

(see also Jimmy Edwards)

MINT VALUE £

PRETTY BOY FLOYD & GEMS

79	Rip Off RIP OFF 1	Spread The Word Around/Hold Tight (p/s)	15
79	Rip Off RIP 10	Sharon/The Instigator (p/s)	20

PRETTY THINGS

64	Fontana TF 469	Rosalyn/Big Boss Man	22
64	Fontana TF 503	Don't Bring Me Down/We'll Be Together	12
65	Fontana TF 537	Honey I Need/I Can Never Say	12
65	Fontana TF 585	Cry To Me/Get A Buzz	20
65	Fontana TF 647	Midnight To Six Man/Can't Stand The Pain	20
66	Fontana TF 688	Come See Me/£.s.d.	15
66	Fontana TF 722	A House In The Country/Me Needing You	20
66	Fontana TF 773	Progress/Buzz The Jerk	20
67	Fontana TF 829	Children/My Time	18
67	Columbia DB 8300	Defecting Grey/Mr. Evasion	55
68	Columbia DB 8353	Talkin' About The Good Times/Walking Through My Dreams	50
68	Columbia DB 8494	Private Sorrow/Balloon Burning	40
69	Fontana TF 1024	Rosalyn/Don't Bring Me Down (p/s)	12
70	Harvest HAR 5016	The Good Mr. Square/Blue Serge Blues	8
70	Harvest HAR 5031	October 26/Cold Stone	8
71	Harvest HAR 5037	Stone-Hearted Mama/Summertime/Circus Mind	8
72	Warner Bros K 16225	Over The Moon/Havana Bound	5
64	Fontana TE 17434	THE PRETTY THINGS (EP)	60
65	Fontana TE 17442	RAININ' IN MY HEART (EP)	55
66	Fontana TE 17472	ON FILM (EP)	150
65	Fontana TL 5239	THE PRETTY THINGS (LP)	80
65	Fontana TL 5280	GET THE PICTURE (LP)	120
67	Wing WL 1164	BEST OF THE PRETTY THINGS (LP)	25
67	Fontana (S)TL 5425	EMOTIONS (LP, mono/stereo)	60
67	Wing WL 1167	THE PRETTY THINGS (LP, stereo reissue)	18
68	Columbia S(C)X 6306	S.F. SORROW (LP, gatefold sleeve, blue/black label, mono/stereo)	200/120
70	Columbia SCX 6306	S.F. SORROW (LP, gatefold sleeve; silver/black label re-pressing, stereo)	35
70	Harvest SHVL 774	PARACHUTE (LP, gatefold sleeve)	45
72	Fontana Special SFL 13140	EMOTIONS (LP, reissue)	15
72	Warner Bros K 46190	FREEWAY MADNESS (LP, gatefold sleeve)	15
74	Swan Song SSK 59400	SILK TORPEDO (LP, gatefold sleeve with insert)	15
75	Harvest SHDW 406	S.F. SORROW/PARACHUTE (2-LP)	18
75	Swan Song SSL 59401	SAVAGE EYE (LP, gatefold sleeve with inner)	15

(see also Electric Banana, Twink, Viv Prince, Sunshine, Fenmen, Kate, Zac Zolar & Electric Banana)

DORY PREVIN

70	United Artists UAG 29176	ON MY WAY TO WHERE (LP)	12
71	United Artists UAG 29186	MYTHICAL KINGS & IGUNAS (LP, gatefold sleeve)	12
71	United Artists UAG 29346	REFLECTIONS IN A MUD PUDDLE (LP, stickered sleeve with poster)	12
72	United Artists UAG 29435	MARY C. BROWN & THE HOLLYWOOD SIGN (LP, gatefold sleeve)	12
73	United Artists UAD 60045/6	LIVE AT CARNEGIE HALL (2-LP, gatefold sleeve)	15

EDDIE PREVOST BAND

78	Matchless MR 1	LIVE VOLUME 1 (LP, private pressing)	15

(see also Amm, Organum)

JOEL PREVOST

78	CBS SCBS 6300	Somewhere Sometime/Il Y Aura Toujours Des Violins	10

ALAN PRICE (SET)

65	Decca F 12217	Any Day Now (My Wild Beautiful Baby)/Never Be Sick On Sunday	7
66	Decca F 12367	I Put A Spell On You/Iechyd-Da	7
66	Decca F 12518	Willow Weep For Me/Yours Until Tomorrow	6
67	Decca F 12691	Shame/Don't Do That Again	6
68	Decca F 12774	When I Was A Cowboy/Tappy Turquoise (export issue)	20
68	Decca F 12808	Love Story/My Old Kentucky Home	6
69	Deram DM 263	Trimdon Grange Explosion/Falling In Love Again	6
70	Decca F 13017	Sunshine And Rain (The Name Of The Game)/Is There Anybody Out There? (solo)	6
67	Decca DFE 8677	THE AMAZING ALAN PRICE (EP)	30
66	Decca LK 4839	THE PRICE TO PLAY (LP)	30
67	Decca LK/SKL 4907	A PRICE ON HIS HEAD (LP)	20
73	Warner Bros K 46227	O LUCKY MAN! (LP, soundtrack)	20

(see also Animals, Paul Williams Set, Johnny Almond Music Machine, Dave Greenslade)

BILL PRICE

72	Folk Heritage FHR 038	THE FINE OLD YORKSHIRE GENTLEMAN (LP)	22

KENNY PRICE

66	Stateside SS 554	Walking On New Grass/Wasting My Time	8

LLOYD PRICE

57	London HL 8438	Just Because/Why (triangular or round centre) (78 rpm = £30)	150/80
59	HMV POP 580	Stagger Lee/You Need Love (78 rpm = £50)	22
59	HMV POP 598	Where Were You (On Our Wedding Day)?/Is It Really Love? (78 rpm = £55)	10
59	HMV POP 626	Personality/Have You Ever Had The Blues? (78 rpm = £60)	10
59	HMV POP 650	I'm Gonna Get Married/Three Little Pigs (78 rpm = £75)	10
60	HMV POP 712	Lady Luck/Never Let Me Go (78 rpm = £100)	10
60	HMV POP 741	For Love/No If's — No And's	10
60	HMV POP 772	Question/If I Look A Little Blue (as Lloyd Price Orchestra) (78 rpm = £120)	10
60	HMV POP 799	Just Call Me (And I'll Understand)/Who Coulda' Told You (They Lied)	10
61	HMV POP 826	Know What You're Doin'/That's Why Tears Come And Go (as Lloyd Price Orchestra)	10
61	HMV POP 926	Boo Hoo/I Made You Cry	10
62	HMV POP 983	Be A Leader/'Nother Fairy Tale	10

62	HMV POP 1100	Under Your Spell, Again/Happy Birthday Mama	10
63	Liberty LIB 10127	Misty/Cry On	12
73	GSF GSZ 5	Love Music/Just For Baby	10
73	GSF GSZ 11	Trying To Slip Away/They Get Down	10
59	HMV 7EG 8538/GES 5784	THE EXCITING LLOYD PRICE (EP, mono/stereo)	70/90
59	HMV CLP 1285	THE EXCITING LLOYD PRICE (LP)	75
59	HMV CLP 1314	MR. PERSONALITY (LP)	65
60	London HA-U 2213	LLOYD PRICE (LP)	80
60	HMV CLP 1361	MR. PERSONALITY SINGS THE BLUES (LP)	55
60	HMV CLP 1393	THE FANTASTIC LLOYD PRICE (LP, also stereo CSD 1323)	55/75
62	HMV CLP 1519	COOKIN' (LP, also stereo CSD 1413)	55/75
63	Encore ENC 2004	PRICE SINGS THE MILLION DOLLAR SELLERS (LP)	25
69	Major Minor SMLP 57	LLOYD PRICE NOW (LP)	22
70	Regal Starline SRS 5025	THE BEST OF LLOYD PRICE (LP)	12
71	Joy JOYS 202	STAGGER LEE (LP)	12

MALCOLM PRICE (TRIO)

61	Oak RGJ 106	PICKIN' ON THE COUNTRY STRINGS! (EP)	18
64	Decca LK 4627	COUNTRY SESSION (LP, as Malcolm Price Trio)	15
65	Decca LK 4665	WAY DOWN TOWN (LP)	15
69	Saga FID 2156	HIS SONGS, HIS GUITARS (LP)	12
75	Sweet Folk & C. SFA 017	THEN WE ALL GOT UP AND WALKED AWAY (LP)	12

RAY PRICE

52	Columbia MC 342	Weary Blues (From Waiting)/I Made A Mistake And I'm Sorry (export 78)	12
57	Philips BBE 12137	RAY PRICE (EP)	35

(ROCKIN') RED PRICE

56	Decca F 10822	Rocky Mountain Gal/Rock O' The North (as Red Price & His Rockin' Rhythm)	15
56	Decca F 10822	Rocky Mountain Gal/Rock O' The North (78)	12
57	Woodbine	Woodbine Rock (78, some in p/s, promo only)	25/15
58	Pye 7N 15169	Weekend/The Sneeze (78 rpm = £25)	12
60	Pye 7N 15262	Wow!/My Baby's Door	12
61	Parlophone R 4789	Theme From "Danger Man"/Blackjack (as Red Price Combo)	30
	(see also Cherry Wainer)		

RED PRICE & BLUE BEATS

64	Blue Beat BB 209	Blue Beats Over (The White Cliffs Of Dover)/Kiss The Baby (When You Grow Too Old To Dream)	8

RICK PRICE

70	Gemini GMS 012	Davey Has No Dad/Bitter Sweet	8
71	Gemini GMS 017	Top Ten Record/Beautiful Sally	7
70	Gemini GME 1002	THIS IS TO CERTIFY THAT (LP, as Rick Price & Gemini)	25
71	Gemini GME 1017	TALKING TO THE FLOWERS (LP)	22
	(see also Move, Sheridan-Price, Sight & Sound)		

RIKKI PRICE

58	Fontana H 162	Tom Dooley/(It Looks Like Rain In) Cherry Blossom Lane (78 rpm = £8)	6
59	Fontana H 171	Honey, Honey/The Very Thought Of You (78 rpm = £8)	8
59	Fontana H 217	Mr. Blue/Man On My Trail (78 rpm = £10)	6
62	Fontana H 371	You're For Real/When You Pass By	5
58	Fontana TFE 17100	RIKKI PRICE (EP)	20
	(see also Sheridan-Price)		

SAMMY PRICE

63	Storyville A 45 068	Boogieing With Big Sid/133 Street Boogie (some with p/s)	32/22
57	Columbia SEG 7679	ORIGINAL SAMMY BLUES (EP)	20
58	Vogue EPV 1146	SAMMY PRICE (EP)	65
58	Vogue EPV 1151	SAMMY PRICE'S BLUESICIANS (EP)	65
58	Vogue LAE 12027	SWINGIN' PARIS STYLE (LP)	45
62	London Jazz LTZ-R 15240	THE BLUES AIN'T NOTHIN' (LP, also stereo SAH-R 6234)	35/45
	(see also Sister Rosetta Tharpe)		

VINCENT PRICE

77	EMI EMI 2659	The Monster Mash/The Bard's Own Recipe	15
59	Columbia 33SX 1141	VINCENT PRICE (LP)	45

DICKIE PRIDE

59	Columbia DB 4283	Slippin' 'N' Slidin'/Don't Make Me Love You	40
59	Columbia DB 4296	Fabulous Cure/Midnight Oil	35
59	Columbia DB 4340	Frantic/Primrose Lane	35
60	Columbia DB 4403	Betty, Betty (Go Steady With Me)/No John	28
60	Columbia DB 4451	You're Singin' Our Love Song To Somebody Else/Bye Bye Blackbird	8
59	Columbia SEG 7937	SHEIK OF SHAKE (EP)	260
61	Columbia 33SX 1307	PRIDE WITHOUT PREJUDICE (LP, also stereo SCX 3369)	110/130
	(see also Guvners)		

LOUIS PRIMA (& HIS ORCHESTRA)

52	Columbia DB 3070	Ooh–Dahdily–Dah/Eleanor (with Keely Smith) (78)	20
53	Columbia DC 604	Chili Sauce/One Mint Julep (78, export issue)	20
53	Columbia DC 609	Bigger The Figure/Honey Bones (78, export issue)	20
56	Capitol CL 14669	5 Months, 2 Weeks, 2 Days/Banana Split For My Baby (78 rpm = £12)	20
58	Capitol CL 14821	Buona Sera/Beep! Beep! (78 rpm = £12)	15
60	London HLD 9230	Ol' Man Moses (with Sam Butera's Witnesses)/Wonderland By Night	10
59	Capitol EAP1 1132	STRICTLY PRIMA (EP)	12
57	Capitol T 755	THE WILDEST (LP)	25
58	Capitol T 836	THE CALL OF THE WILDEST (LP)	20
58	Capitol T 1010	LAS VEGAS PRIMA STYLE (LP)	15
62	Ember EMB 3348	LOUIS PRIMA SWINGS (LP)	15
60s	Dot GTL 0287	HIS GREATEST HITS (LP)	12
	(see also Sam Butera's Witnesses)		

Louis PRIMA & Keely SMITH

LOUIS PRIMA & KEELY SMITH
50	Polygon P 1001	Oh Babe!/LOUIS PRIMA: Piccolina Lena (78)	10
54	Columbia SCM 5092	Take A Little Walk Around The Block/LOUIS PRIMA: Oh! Cumari (78 rpm = £10)	15
58	Capitol CL 14862	The Lip/KEELY SMITH: Foggy Day (78 rpm = £18)	5
58	Capitol CL 14948	That Old Black Magic/KEELY SMITH: You Are My Love (78 rpm = £7)	6
59	Capitol CL 14994	I've Got You Under My Skin/KEELY SMITH: Don't Take Your Love From Me	5
59	London HLD 8923	Bei Mir Bist Du Schon/I Don't Know Why (78 rpm = £22)	10
60	London HLD 9084	I'm Confessin' (That I Love You)/Night And Day	8
59	Capitol T 1160	HEY BOY! HEY GIRL! (LP)	15
60	London HA-D 2243	LOUIS AND KEELY (LP)	15
61	London HA-D 2350	ON STAGE (LP, also stereo SAH-G 6149)	each 15
	(see also Keely Smith)		

PRIMAL SCREAM
85	Creation CRE 017	All Fall Down/It Happens (foldaround p/s in poly bag)	25
86	Creation CRE 026	Crystal Crescent/Velocity Girl (p/s)	10
86	Creation CRE 026T	Crystal Crescent/Velocity Girl/Spirea X (12", p/s)	12
87	Elevation ACID 3	Gentle Tuesday/Black Star Carnival (p/s)	5
87	Elevation ACID 3T	Gentle Tuesday/Black Star Carnival/I'm Gonna Make You Mine (12", p/s)	10
87	Elevation ACID 5	Imperial/Star Fruit Surf Rider (p/s)	6
87	Elevation ACID 5T	Imperial/Star Fruit Surf Rider/So Sad About Us/Imperial (demo) (12", some in poster p/s with 'special price' sticker)	12/10
89	Creation CRELP 054	PRIMAL SCREAM (LP, with bonus 45 "Split Wide Open 1"/ "Lone Star Girl 1" [CREFRE 6, no p/s])	15
91	Creation CRELP 076	SCREAMADELICA (2 x LP)	15
97	Creation ECHO 7224	ECHO DEK (5 x 7", box set)	12
	(see also Jesus & Mary Chain, Revolving Paint Dream, P.P. & Primes, Death In Vegas)		

PRIMETTES
68	Ember EMBS 3398	LOOKING BACK WITH THE PRIMETTES AND EDDIE FLOYD (LP, 1 side each)	50
73	Windmill WMD 192	LOOKING BACK WITH THE PRIMETTES AND EDDIE FLOYD (LP, reissue)	20
	(see also Supremes, Eddie Floyd)		

PRIME-MATES
69	Action ACT 4530	Hot Tamales (Versions 1 & 2)	15

PRIME MOVERS
89	Cyanide CND 001	SINS OF THE FOREFATHERS (LP)	20

PRIME RHYME MASTERS
91	Kold Sweat KS115	You Need Discipline/To Kill A Mockingbird (12")	12

PRIMITIVES
64	Pye 7N 15721	Help Me/Let Them Tell	220
65	Pye 7N 15755	You Said/How Do You Feel	250
	(see also Mal & Primitives)		

PRIMITIVES
86	Head HEAD 010	Thru The Flowers/Across My Shoulder/Lazy/She Don't Need You (12", unreleased, white label test pressings only)	30
86	Lazy LAZY 01	Thru The Flowers/Across My Shoulder/She Don't Need You/Lazy (12", p/s)	10
86	Lazy LAZY 02	Really Stupid/We Found A Way To The Sun (p/s)	5
86	Lazy LAZY 02T	Really Stupid/We Found A Way To The Sun/Where The Wind Blows (12", p/s)	8
86	Lazy LAZY 03	Stop Killing Me/Buzz Buzz Buzz (p/s, with postcard, sleeves printed back-to-front; also a very few with badge)	5/5
87	Lazy LAZY 05	Ocean Blue/Shadow (2,000 only, given away free at London Astoria gig)	6
88	RCA PB 41761X	Crash/I'll Stick With You/Crash (Live In Studio) (10", 1,500 signed, gatefold p/s)	5

PRIMO & HOPETON
67	Rio R 139	Your Safekeep/Loving And Kind	10
68	Pama PM 753	Peace On Earth/SCHOOL BOYS: Love Is A Message	12

PRIMROSE
69	NEMS 56-4129	Just For You/Nine Till Five	25

PRIMROSE CIRCUS
70	President PT 314	P.S. Call Me Lulu/In My Mind	10

PRINCE (& REVOLUTION)
SINGLES
79	Warner Bros K 17537	I Wanna Be Your Lover/Just As Long As We're Together	10
79	Warner Bros K 17537T	I Wanna Be Your Lover/Just As Long As We're Together (12", company sleeve)	18
80	Warner Bros K 17590	Sexy Dancer/Bambi (die-cut company sleeve)	20
80	Warner Bros K 17590T	Sexy Dancer (Remix)/Bambi (12", die-cut company sleeve)	50
81	Warner Bros K 17768	Do It All Night/Head (die-cut company sleeve)	30
81	Warner Bros K 17768T	Do It All Night/Head (12", die-cut company sleeve)	60
81	Warner Bros K 17819	Gotta Stop (Messin' About)/Uptown (p/s)	60
81	Warner Bros K 17819	Gotta Stop (Messin' About)/I Wanna Be Your Lover (p/s)	60
81	Warner Bros LV 47	Gotta Stop (Messin' About)/Uptown/Head (12", stickered p/s)	100
81	Warner Bros LV 47	Gotta Stop (Messin' About)/I Wanna Be Your Lover/Head (12", stickered, colour p/s)	100
81	Warner Bros K 17866	Controversy/When You Were Mine (p/s)	25
81	Warner Bros K 17866T	Controversy/When You Were Mine (12", p/s)	40
82	Warner Bros K 17922	Let's Work/Ronnie, Talk To Russia (p/s)	40
82	Warner Bros K 17922T	Let's Work (Extended)/Ronnie, Talk To Russia (12", p/s)	100
83	Warner Bros W 9896	1999/How Come U Don't Call Me Anymore (paper labels, p/s, some with free cassette mini-album in card p/s: "1999 (Edit)"/ "Uptown"/"Controversy"/"Dirty Mind"/"Sexuality")	40/8
83	Warner Bros W 9896T	1999/How Come U Don't Call Me Anymore/D.M.S.R. (12", p/s)	10
83	Warner Bros W 9688	Little Red Corvette/Lady Cab Driver (p/s)	10
83	Warner Bros W 9688T	Little Red Corvette (Full Length Version)/Automatic/International Lover (12", stickered p/s, some with poster insert)	40/12

83	Warner Bros W 9436	Little Red Corvette/Horny Toad (poster calendar p/s) 55
83	Warner Bros W 9436	Little Red Corvette/Horny Toad (standard p/s) 40
83	Warner Bros W 9436T	Little Red Corvette (Full Length Version)/Horny Toad/D.M.S.R. (12", p/s) 15
83	Warner Bros W 9436T	Little Red Corvette (Full Length Version)/Horny Toad/D.M.S.R.
		(12", p/s, with spiral-bound calendar or poster) 85/75
84	Warner Bros W 9286C	When Doves Cry/17 Days/1999/D.M.S.R. (cassette, some with paper labels) . . . 10/8
84	Warner Bros W 9286T	When Doves Cry/17 Days//1999/D.M.S.R.
		(12", stickered shrinkwrapped double pack) 70
84	Warner Bros W 9174P	Purple Rain/God (motorbike-shaped picture disc) 40
84	Warner Bros W 9174T	Purple Rain/God (instrumental)/God (12", p/s, initially with poster) 20/8
84	Warner Bros W 9121TE	I Would Die 4 U (U.S. Remix)/Another Lonely Christmas (U.S. Remix) (12", p/s). . . 20
85	Paisley Park W 9052P	Paisley Park/She's Always In My Hair (shaped picture disc) 35
85	Paisley Park W 9052T	Paisley Park/She's Always In My Hair/Paisley Park (Remix) (12", p/s) 8
85	Paisley Park W 9052T	Paisley Park/She's Always In My Hair/Paisley Park (Remix) (12",
		mispressing with repeated 2nd track "She's Always In My Hair") 25
85	Paisley Park W 8929T	Raspberry Beret (Extended Remix)/Hello (Extended Remix) (12", p/s) 12
85	Paisley Park W 8858T	Pop Life (Extended)/Girl (12", p/s) 8
86	Paisley Park W 8751P	Kiss/Love Or Money (shaped picture disc with plinth) 30
86	Paisley Park W 8751T	Kiss (Extended)/Love Or Money (12", p/s, with poster) 15
86	Paisley Park W 8711TE	Mountains (Ext.)/Alexa De Paris (Extended) (10", white vinyl in PVC sleeve) 20
86	Paisley Park W 8711T	Mountains (Extended 9.56)/Alexa De Paris (12", p/s, with poster) 20
86	Paisley Park W 8586F	Girls And Boys (Edit)/Under The Cherry Moon//She's Always In My Hair/
		17 Days (double pack, gatefold disc) 15
86	Paisley Park W 8586P	Girls And Boys (Edit)/Under The Cherry Moon (shaped picture disc) 45
86	Paisley Park W 8586T	Girls And Boys/Under The Cherry Moon/Erotic City (12", p/s,
		with poster advertising London gigs) 18
86	Paisley Park W 8521W	Anotherloverholenyohead/I Wanna Be Your Lover
		(paper or plastic labels, poster p/s) 12
86	Paisley Park W 8521T	Anotherloverholenyohead (Extended)/I Wanna Be Your Lover (12", p/s) 10
87	Paisley Park W 8399TP	Sign O' The Times (Extended)/La La La He He Hee (Extended) (12", picture disc) . 10
87	Paisley Park W 8334W	If I Was Your Girlfriend/Shockadelica (poster p/s) 8
87	Paisley Park W 8334E	If I Was Your Girlfriend/Shockadelica (peach vinyl, PVC cover,
		with postcards & stickers) 15
87	Paisley Park W 8334T	If I Was Your Girlfriend/Shockadelica (Extended) (12", picture disc) 12
87	Paisley Park W 8289TP	U Got The Look (Long Look)/Housequake (7 min MoQuake)/
		U Got The Look (Single Cut) (12", picture disc) 8
87	Paisley Park W 8288TP	I Could Never Take The Place Of Your Man/Hot Thing (Remixed Edit)/
		Hot Thing (Extended) (12", picture disc) 15
88	Paisley Park W 7900CD	Alphabet Street (Album Version)/This Is Not Music, This Is A Trip
		(Alphabet Street) (Extended) (3" CD, with adaptor, 5" case) 10
88	Paisley Park W 7806CD	Glam Slam (Edit)/Escape (Free Yo Mind) (Edit)/Glam Slam (Remix)
		(3" CD, with adaptor, 5" case) 10
88	Paisley Park W 7745	I Wish U Heaven (Edit)/Scarlet Pussy (Edit) (poster p/s) 5
88	Paisley Park W 7745TW	I Wish U Heaven (Parts 1/2/3)/CAMILLE: Scarlet Pussy (Edit)
		(12", p/s with poster). 10
88	Paisley Park W 7745CD	I Wish U Heaven (Parts 1/2/3)/CAMILLE: Scarlet Pussy (Edit)
		(3" CD, with adaptor, 5" case) 10
89	Paisley Park W 2924TP	Batdance (LP Version)/200 Balloons (12", picture disc, PVC sleeve) 8
89	Paisley Park W 2924CDX	Batdance (LP Version)/200 Balloons (3" CD, oval card sleeve) 10
89	Paisley Park W 2814TP	Partyman (Video Mix)/Feel U Up (Long Stroke) (12", picture disc, PVC sleeve) . . . 8
89	Paisley Park W 2814CDX	Partyman (Video Mix)/Feel U Up (Long Stroke)
		(3" CD, octagonal foldout sleeve with film stills) 15
89	Paisley Park W 2814CDT	Partyman (The Purple Party Mix)/(Partyman Music Mix)/(The Video Mix)/
		Feel U Up (Short Stroke) (3" CD, card sleeve). 8
89	Paisley Park W 2757TP	The Arms Of Orion (5.03)/I Love U In Me/The Arms Of Orion (3.52)
		(12", with Sheena Easton, picture disc, PVC sleeve) 10
89	Paisley Park W 2757CDX	The Arms Of Orion (5.03)/I Love U In Me/The Arms Of Orion (3.52)
		(CD, shrink wrapped tri-fold stickered sleeve, some with sticker insert) 15/12
88	Paisley Park W 8751TP	Kiss/Love Or Money (shaped picture disc, 're-promoted' edition
		with longer, extended version of B-side & without plinth) 10

ALBUMS

83	Warner Bros 923 809-1	1999 (LP, original issue, single disc) 18
84	Warner Bros 925 110-1	PURPLE RAIN — MUSIC FROM THE MOTION PICTURE
		(LP, purple vinyl with poster) 25
86	Paisley Park WX 39P	PARADE — MUSIC FROM "UNDER THE CHERRY MOON"
		(LP, pic. disc, die-cut sleeve) 50
89	Paisley Park WX 281P	BATMAN (LP, picture disc, die-cut sleeve) 12
89	Paisley Park 927 489-2	BATMAN (CD, picture disc) 20
89	Paisley Park 925 978-2	BATMAN (CD, picture disc in 'Bat' tin with booklet) 25
94	Warners 936245793-1	BLACK ALBUM (LP, title sticker). 15
95	NPG 6103-1	EXODUS (LP, as NPG). 15
96	NPG EMI CDEMO 1102	EMANCIPATION (3-CD, as ß) 25
98	NPG BCT 9871	CRYSTAL BALL (4-CD, import only, as ß) 40

PROMOS

95	NPG 61225	Get Wild (Money Maker Radio Mix) (CD, as NPG, radio programmer's
		picture disc) 45
95	NPG 61047	Get Wild/Beautiful Girl (no p/s, as NPG) 6
96	NPG 60667	Lovesign/MARGIE COX: Standing At The Altar (no p/s, as ß) 10
96	NPG 60600	Lovesign (Radio Edit Mix)/(1-800 New Funk Version)/(The Storyboard Video Mix)
		(12", as ß, most with title sticker) 35
96	NPG 60605	Lovesign (Radio Edit Mix)/(1-800 New Funk Version)/(The Storyboard Video Mix)
		(CD, as ß) 30
01	Warners PRO 2721	THE VERY BEST OF PRINCE: (When Doves Cry/Purple Rain/Kiss/Cream/1999/
		Money Don't Matter) (CD, radio sampler) 20

(The Revolution are credited on all recordings from "Purple Rain" to "Anotherloverholenyohead")

VIV PRINCE
66	Columbia DB 7960	Light Of The Charge Brigade/Minuet For Ringo	40

(see also Pretty Things, Bunch Of Fives, Kate, Vamp, Chicago Line)

PRINCE & PRINCESS
65	Aladdin WI 609	Ready Steady Go/Take Me Serious	25

PRINCE BUSTER (& ALL STARS)
61	Starlite ST45 052	Buster's Shack (as Buster's Group)/ERIC MORRIS: Search The World	30
62	Blue Beat BB 101	My Sound That Goes Around/They Got To Go (with Torchlighters)	18
62	Blue Beat BB 116	Independence Song (with Bluebeats)/RICO & BLUEBEATS: August 1962	20
62	Blue Beat BB 133	Time Longer Than Rope/Fake King (with Voice Of The People)	30
62	Blue Beat BB 138	One Hand Washes The Other/Cowboy Comes To Town	30
63	Blue Beat BB 150	Run Man Run/Danny, Dane And Lorraine	25
63	Blue Beat BB 158	Open Up, Bartender/Enjoy It (B-side actually "Enjoy Yourself")	25
63	Blue Beat BB 162	Money/SCHOOL BOYS: Little Boy Blue	25
63	Blue Beat BB 163	King, Duke, Sir/I See Them In My Sight	30
63	Blue Beat BB 167	The Ten Commandments (with All Stars)/Buster's Welcome	20
63	Blue Beat BB 170	Madness/PRINCE BUSTER ALL STARS: Toothache	15
63	Blue Beat BB 173	Burning Creation/PRINCE BUSTER ALL STARS: Boop	30
63	Blue Beat BB 180	Three More Rivers To Cross/RAYMOND HARPER & PRINCE BUSTER ALL STARS: African Blood	20
63	Blue Beat BB 186	Fowl Thief/Remember Me	30
63	Blue Beat BB 189	Watch It Blackhead/Hello My Dear	30
63	Blue Beat BB 192	Rollin' Stone (with Charmers)/RICO & HIS BLUES BAND: This Day	30
63	Blue Beat BB 197	Window Shopping/Sodom And Gomorrah	35
63	Blue Beat BB 199	Spider And Fly/Three Blind Mice	30
63	Blue Beat BB 200	Wash All Your Troubles Away/RICO & BLUE BEATS: Soul Of Africa	18
63	Dice CC 6	They Got To Come/These Are The Times (with Voice Of The People)	12
63	Dice CC 11	Blackhead Chinaman/You Ask (I Had A Girl)	12
63	Dice CC 18	World Peace/The Lion Roars (as Prince Buster & Hazel)	12
64	Stateside SS 335	30 Pieces Of Silver/Everybody Ska	10
64	Blue Beat BB 210	Wash All Your Troubles Away/RICO & BLUE BEATS: Soul Of Africa (reissue)	38
64	Blue Beat BB 211	Bluebeat Spirit/Beggars Are No Choosers	30
64	Blue Beat BB 216	You're Mine/Tongue Will Tell	30
64	Blue Beat BB 225	Three Blind Mice/I Know	30
64	Blue Beat BB 232	Sheep On Top (song actually titled "She Pon Top")/Midnight	30
64	Blue Beat BB 234	She Loves You/Healing	40
64	Blue Beat BB 243	Jealous/Buster's Ska	30
64	Blue Beat BB 248	Thirty Pieces Of Silver/The National Dance	35
64	Blue Beat BB 254	Wings Of A Dove/MAYTALLS: Sweet Love	30
64	Blue Beat BB 262	Old Lady/Dayo Ska	30
64	Blue Beat BB 271	No Knowledge In College/In The Middle Of The Night	30
64	Blue Beat BB 274	I May Never Love You Again/Hey Little Girl	30
65	Blue Beat BB 278	Blood Pressure/Islam	90
65	Blue Beat BB 281	Blues Market/MAYTALS: Looking Down The Street	35
65	Blue Beat BB 282	Big Fight/Red Dress	30
65	Blue Beat BB 293	Agua Fumar/Long Winter (with Charmers)	40
65	Blue Beat BB 302	Ling Ting Tong/Walk Along	40
65	Blue Beat BB 307	Bonanza/Wonderful Life	30
65	Blue Beat BB 309	Here Comes The Bride (with Patsy Todd, as Jamaica's Greatest)/BUSTER'S ALLSTARS: Burkes' Law	40
65	Blue Beat BB 313	Everybody Yeah Yeah (as Jamaica's Greatest)/BUSTER'S ALLSTARS: Gun The Man Down	40
65	Blue Beat BB 314	Float Like A Butterfly/Haunted Room	40
65	Blue Beat BB 316	Sugar Pop/Feel Up (as Prince & Jamaica's Greatest)	40
65	Blue Beat BB 317	Come Home/I Thank You (as Jamaica's Greatest)	30
65	Blue Beat BB 321	My Girl/BUSTER'S ALL STARS: The Fugitive	50
65	Blue Beat BB 324	Al Capone/One Step Beyond (as Prince Buster's Allstars) (blue label or other label colours)	10/6
65	Blue Beat BB 328	Ambition/BUSTER'S ALL STARS: Ryging	30
65	Blue Beat BB 330	Rum And Coca Cola/I Love Her	25
65	Blue Beat BB 334	The Ten Commandments/BUSTER'S ALL STARS: Sting Like A Bee (reissue)	10
65	Blue Beat BB 335	Respect/BUSTER'S ALL STARS: Virginia (B-side actually "Dance Jamaica" by Val Bennett & Prince Buster's All Stars)	45
66	Blue Beat BB 338	Big Fight (Prince Buster Versus Duke Reid)/Adios, Senorita	40
66	Blue Beat BB 339	Under Arrest (But Officer)/PRINCE BUSTER'S ALLSTARS: Say Boss Man	40
66	Blue Beat BB 343	Prince Of Peace/Don't Throw Stones	90
66	Blue Beat BB 352	Day Of Light (song actually "Dayo")/It's Too Late	25
66	Blue Beat BB 355	Sunshine With My Girl/Girl Answer Your Name	30
66	Blue Beat BB 357	I Won't Let You Cry/Hard Man Fe Dead	40
66	Blue Beat BB 359	The Prophet (actually "Feel The Spirit" with Slim Smith)/BUSTER'S ALL STARS: Lion Of Judah	75
66	Blue Beat BB 362	To Be Loved/BUSTER'S ALLSTARS: Set Me Free	30
66	Rainbow RAI 107	Your Turn (Sad Song)/If You Leave Me (with Allstars)	18
67	Blue Beat BB 370	Shanty Town (Get Scanty)/BUSTER'S ALL STARS: Duppy	30
67	Blue Beat BB 373	Knock On Wood/And I Love Her	35
67	Blue Beat BB 377	Dark End Of The Street/Love Oh Love	45
67	Blue Beat BB 378	Drunkard's Psalm (Wise Man)/7 Wonders Of The World (as Prince Buster All Stars)	85
67	Blue Beat BB 382	Sit And Wonder (with His All Stars)/ROLAND ALFONSO: Sunrise In Kingston	30
67	Blue Beat BB 383	Sharing You/You'll Be Lonely On The Blue Train (as Prince Buster's Allstars; A-side actually by Prince Buster, B-side actually by Rico's Band)	30
67	Blue Beat BB 384	Take It Easy/Why Must I Cry (2nd issue, B-side actually by Hopeton Lewis)	20
67	Blue Beat BB 387	Judge Dread (Judge Four Hundred Years)/FITZROY CAMPBELL & PRINCE BUSTER ALL STARS: Waiting For My Rude Girl	25
67	Blue Beat BB 388	Dance Cleopatra/All In My Mind	60

67	Blue Beat BB 390	Soul Serenade/Too Hot.	30
67	Blue Beat BB 391	Land Of Imagination/The Appeal (B-side actually "The Barrister Appeal")	30
67	Blue Beat BB 393	Johnny Dollar/Rude Boys Rude	45
67	Blue Beat BB 395	This Gun's For Hire/Yes, Daddy	30
67	Blue Beat BB 400	All In My Mind/Judge Dread Dance (The Pardon)	30
67	Blue Beat BB 402	Vagabond/PRINCE BUSTER ALL STARS: Come Get Me	30
67	Philips BF 1552	The Ten Commandments/Don't Make Me Cry	12
67	Fab FAB 10	Shakin' Up Orange Street/Black Girl (with Allstars)	18
67	Fab FAB 11	Johnny Cool (Parts 1 & 2) (with Allstars)	20
67	Fab FAB 16	Bye Bye Baby/Human (with Allstars)	18
67	Fab FAB 25	Train To Girls Town/Give Love A Try (with Allstars)	20
67	Fab FAB 26	Going To The River (as Prince Buster & Allstars)/PRINCE BUSTER'S ALLSTARS: Julie On My Mind	20
68	Fab FAB 31	Kings Of Old (My Ancestors)/Sweet Inspiration (with Allstars)	18
68	Fab FAB 35	Try A Little Tenderness/All My Loving (with Allstars)	40
68	Fab FAB 36	The Glory Of Love/Another Sad Nite	20
68	Fab FAB 37	This Is A Hold Up/Julie On My Mind (with Allstars)	12
68	Fab FAB 38	Free Love (with Allstars)/DALTONS: All Over The World	18
68	Fab FAB 40	Rough Rider (with Allstars)/PRINCE BUSTER: 127 Orange Street (B-side actually by Prince Buster Allstars)	12
68	Fab FAB 41	Shepherd Beng Beng (with Teddy King)/TENNORS: Ride Your Donkey	12
68	Fab FAB 47	Going To Ethiopia (as Prince Buster & Allstars)/PRINCE BUSTER ALLSTARS: Shakin' Up Orange Street	15
68	Fab FAB 49	Glory Of Love/WAILERS: Mellow Mood (possibly white labels only)	100+
68	Fab FAB 56	Intensified Dirt/Don't You Know I Love You (with Allstars)	15
68	Fab FAB 57	Green Green Grass Of Home (as Prince Buster's Allstars; actually by Prince Buster & Allstars)/SOUL MAKERS: Girls Like You	12
68	Fab FAB 58	We Shall Overcome/Keep The Faith (as Prince Buster's Allstars; actually by Prince Buster & Allstars)	10
68	Fab FAB 64	Cool Stroker/It's You I Love (B-side actually by Little Roy)	18
68	Fab FAB 80	Hypocrite/New Dance (B-side actually by Little Roy)	18
68	Fab FAB 81	Wine And Grind/The Scorcher (with Allstars)	15
69	Unity UN 522	30 Pieces Of Silver/Everybody Ska (reissue)	20
69	Fab FAB 82	Dr. Rodney (Black Power)/Taxation	18
69	Fab FAB 92	Pharaoh House Crash/Ob-La-Di, Ob-La-Da	12
69	Fab FAB 93	Ob-La-Di, Ob-La-Da/Wreck A Pum Pum	8
69	Fab FAB 94	Hey Jude/Django Fever	12
69	Fab FAB 102	Black Soul/CALEDONIANS: Oh Baby (B-side actually by Claredonians)	12
69	Fab FAB 108	Wine And Grind/The Scorcher (with Allstars) (reissue)	12
69	Fab FAB 118	Bull Buck/ROLAND ALPHONSO: One Heart	12
69	Fab FAB 119	Let Her Go/Tie The Donkey's Tail	12
69	Fab FAB 122	Stand Up/Happy Reggae (with Allstars)	10
70	Fab FAB 127	Young Gifted And Black/PRINCE BUSTER'S ALLSTARS: The Rebel	10
70	Fab FAB 131	That's All/The Preaching (B-side actually titled "The Preacher")	10
70	Fab FAB 132	Ganja Plant/Creation	10
70	Fab FAB 140	Hit Me Back/Give Peace A Chance	10
70	Fab FAB 150	Big Five/Musical College	8
70	Prince Buster PB 1	Big Five/Musical College (reissue)	5
70	Prince Buster PB 2	Rat Trap/Black Organ (B-side with Allstars but actually by Ansell Collins & Prince Buster's Allstars)	8
71	Fab FAB 162	Baby Version (with Jan Fender)/Holly.	8
71	Fab FAB 176	Police Trim Rasta (with Allstars)/Smooth (B-side actually by Ansell Collins & Prince Buster Allstars)	10
71	Prince Buster PB 4	Fishey/More Fishey.	7
71	Prince Buster PB 7	I Wish Your Picture Was You/PRINCE BUSTER ALLSTARS: It Mash Up — Version (B-side actually by Dennis Alcapone)	8
71	Prince Buster PB 8	Sons Of Zion (actually by Dennis Alcapone)/ANSELL COLLINS: Short Circuit	7
71	Prince Buster PB 9	My Happiness/Human (with Allstars)	7
72	Prince Buster PB 14	Big Sister Stuff/Satta Massagana (with Allstars)	10
72	Prince Buster PB 15	Protection/Cool Operator (with Allstars)	7
72	Prince Buster PB 16	I Stand Accused/My Heart is Gone (with Allstars)	7
72	Prince Buster PB 19	Four In One Medley/Drums Drums (as Prince Buster & Allstars, B-side actually by Prince Buster Allstars)	7
72	Prince Buster PB 32	Still/Sister Big Stuff (with Allstars)	7
72	Prince Buster PB 36	South Of The Border/South Of The Border (Version) (with Allstars)	7
72	Fab FAB 36	South Of The Border/South Of The Border (Version) (with Allstars)	7
72	Prince Buster PB 47	Baldhead Pum Pum/Giver Her (with Allstars)	7
79	Blue Beat DDBB 324	Al Capone/One Step Beyond (12", p/s)	8
79	Blue Beat DDBB 334	THREE OF THE BEST (12" EP, p/s)	8
79	Blue Beat DDPB 1	Big Five/FOLK BROTHERS: Carolina/PRINCE BUSTER: Shaking Up Orange Street (12", p/s)	8
79	Blue Beat DDPB 2	PICK OF THE PUNCH (12" EP, p/s, 2 tracks each by Tennors & Prince Buster)	8
79	Blue Beat DDPB 3	NAUGHTY BUT NICE (12" EP, p/s)	8
79	Blue Beat DDPB 4	BEHIND BARS (12" EP, p/s)	8
63	Blue Beat BBLP 802	I FEEL THE SPIRIT (LP)	110
65	Blue Beat BBLP 805	SKA-LIP-SOUL (LP, with His All Stars)	100
65	Blue Beat BBLP 806	IT'S BURKE'S LAW — JAMAICA SKA EXPLOSION! (LP, as Prince Buster All Stars; 2 different sleeves, laminated plain and unlaminated 'explosion')	175
67	Blue Beat BBLP 807	WHAT A HARD MAN FE DEAD — PRINCE BUSTER SINGS FOR THE PEOPLE (LP, with Baba Brooks)	200
67	Blue Beat BBLP 808	ON TOUR (LP)	90
67	Blue Beat BBLP 809	JUDGE DREAD (LP)	90
67	Blue Beat BBLP 820	SHE WAS A ROUGH RIDER (LP)	60
68	Fab BBLP 820	SHE WAS A ROUGH RIDER (LP, reissue on Fab label)	35

68	Fab BBLP 821	WRECK A PUM PUM (LP)	35
69	Fab BBLP 822	THE OUTLAW (LP, title listed as "Queen Of The Outlaws" on disc)	75
70	Fab MS 1	FABULOUS GREATEST HITS (LP, original issue with 'West Brothers Printers' credit on rear of sleeve)	10
70	Fab MS 2	I FEEL THE SPIRIT (LP)	60
70	Fab MS 6	TUTTI FRUTTI (LP)	45
72	Melodisc MLP 12-156	SISTER BIG STUFF (LP)	45
72	Melodisc MLP 12-157	BIG FIVE (LP)	30
73	Prince Buster PB 9	ORIGINAL GOLDEN OLDIES VOLUME 1 (LP)	18
70s	Fab MS 7	THE MESSAGE DUBWISE (LP)	60

(see also Buster's Allstars, Buster's Group, Dennis Alcapone, Jim Dakota, Hortense Ellis, Heptones, Eric Morris, Terry Nelson, Schoolboys, Protegue)

PRINCE CHARLIE
| 69 | Coxsone CS 7101 | Hit And Run/Darling, There I Stand | 25 |

PRINCE FAR I
82	On-U Sound DP 1	Virgin/Danger (10")	15
79	Virgin Frontline FLX 4002	CRY TUFF DUB ENCOUNTER PART 2 (LP)	15
79	HitRun APLP 9006	DUB TO AFRICA (LP, as Prince Far I & The Arabs)	20
80	Daddy Kool DKLP 15	CRY TUFF DUB ENCOUNTER CHAPTER III (LP, as Prince Far I & The Arabs)	25
80	Pre PRE XF 3	SHOWCASE IN A SUITCASE (LP)	25
81	Pre PRE X 7	LIVITY (LP)	25

(see also Arabs)

PRINCE HAMMER
| 77 | Baby Mother HIT DD 11 | Them Must Fall/Ball Of Fire (12") | 30 |
| 78 | Hit Run HIT DD 15 | Ten Thousand Lions/North London Thing (Carry The Swing) (12") | 50 |

PRINCE HAROLD
| 66 | Mercury MF 952 | Forget About Me/Baby You've Got Me | 25 |

PRINCE JAZZBO
73	Grape GR 3047	Free From Chains/LLOYD & PATSY: Papa Do It Sweet	8
73	Techniques TE 921	Mr. Harry Skank/GLEN BROWN: Telavid Drums	8
74	Ackee ACK 532	Kick Boy Face/Version	8
74	Dip DL 5036	Penny Reel/Good Things	8
76	Third World TWLP 109	KICK BOY FACE (LP)	30
76	Black Wax WAXLP 1	NATTY PASSING THRU' (LP)	90

(see also Earl George)

PRINCE JAZZBO & I ROY
| 78 | Live & Love LAP 003 | STEP FORWARD YOUTHMAN (LP) | 25 |

PRINCE OF DARKNESS
69	Downtown DT 441	Burial Of Long Shot/MUSIC DOCTORS: Burial Of Long Shot	15
69	Downtown DT 448	Meeting Over Yonder/MUSIC DOCTORS: Ghost Rider	12
71	Downtown DT 467	Sound Of Today/MUSIC DOCTORS: Red Red Wine Version	12

PRINCE PATO EXPEDITION
| 70s | Beacon BEAS 18 | FIREBIRD (LP) | 28 |

PRINCESS
| 86 | Supreme SU 1 | PRINCESS (LP) | 12 |
| 86 | Supreme CDSU 1 | PRINCESS (CD) | 35 |

PRINCESS & SWINEHERD
| 68 | Oak RGJ 633 | PRINCESS AND THE SWINEHERD (LP, plain black sleeve) | 100 |

PRINCIPAL EDWARDS MAGIC THEATRE
69	Dandelion S 4405	Ballad Of The Big Girl Now/Lament For The Earth	10
73	Deram DM 391	Captain Lifeboy/Nothing	5
73	Deram DM 398	Weekdaze/Whizzmore Kid	15
69	Dandelion 63752	SOUNDTRACK (LP)	35
71	Dandelion DAN 8002	THE ASOMOTO RUNNING BAND (LP, gatefold sleeve)	25
74	Deram SML 1108	ROUND ONE (LP)	25

MADDY PRIOR
78	Chrysalis CHS 2232	Baggy Pants/Woman In The Wings	6
80	EMI EMI 5903	Wake Up England/Paradise (p/s, as Maddy Prior Band)	6
82	Plant Life PLRS 001	Face To Face/Half Listening (p/s, as Maddy Prior Band)	6
83	RCA/Spindrift RCA 379	Deep In The Darkest Night/Western Movies (p/s)	6
85	Making Waves SURF 108	Stookie/Incidental Music From Stookie (p/s)	6
85	Making Waves SURF 109	Deep In The Darkest Night/Western Movies (p/s, reissue)	6
78	Chrysalis CHR 1185	WOMAN IN THE WINGS (LP, with insert)	18
87	Saydisc SDL 366	A TAPESTRY OF CAROLS (LP)	20

(see also Steelye Span, Tim Hart & Maddy Prior)

PRISONERS
83	Big Beat NS 90	Hurricane/Tomorrow (She Said) (p/s)	12
84	Big Beat SW 98	ELECTRIC FIT (EP)	12
82	Own Up OWN UP U2	A TASTE OF PINK (LP)	30
83	Big Beat WIK 19	THE WISERMISERDEMELZA (LP)	25
85	Own Up OWN UP U2	A TASTE OF PINK (LP, reissue in pink sleeve on pink vinyl)	30
85	Own Up OWN UP U3	THE LAST FOURFATHERS (LP)	20
86	Countdown DOWN 2	IN FROM THE COLD (LP)	20
89	Hangman HANG 23 UP	RARE AND UNISSUED (LP)	20

(see also James Taylor Quartet)

PRISONERS/MILKSHAKES
| 86 | Empire MIC 001 | THE LAST NIGHT AT THE MIC CLUB (LP, live, 1 side each) | 18 |
| 86 | Media Burn MB 17 | THEE MILKSHAKES VS. THE PRISONERS (LP, live, 1 side each) | 18 |

(see also Milkshakes, Thee Mighty Caesars)

PRIVATE DICKS
79	Heartbeat PULSE 6	She Said So/Private Dicks (p/s)	20

PRIVATE PARTY
87	IMW 1201	Puppet Capers/Tennants Super Mix (12")	18

PRIVATE SECTOR
78	TJM TJM 8	Just Just (Wanna) Stay Free/Things Get Worse (p/s)	25

P.J. PROBY
62	Liberty LIB 55367	Try To Forget Her/There Stands The One	10
64	Decca F 11904	Hold Me/The Tips Of My Fingers	7
64	Decca F 11967	Together/Sweet And Tender Romance	7
64	Liberty LIB 10182	Somewhere/Just Like Him	6
65	Liberty LIB 10188	I Apologise/What's On Your Mind	7
65	Liberty LIB 10206	Let The Water Run Down/I Don't Want To Hear It Anymore	10
65	Liberty LIB 10215	That Means A Lot/My Prayer	12
65	Liberty LIB 10218	Maria/She Cried	6
66	Liberty LIB 10223	You've Come Back/It Ain't Necessarily So	7
66	Liberty LIB 10236	To Make A Big Man Cry/Wicked Woman	8
66	Fab FAB 2	You've Got Me Cryin'/I Need Love (some in die-cut p/s)	12/7
66	Liberty LIB 10250	I Can't Make It Alone/Sweet Summer Wine	10
67	Liberty LIB 55936	Nicki Hoeky/Good Things Are Coming My Way	15
67	Liberty LIB 55974	You Can't Come Home Again/Work With Me Annie	15
68	Liberty LBF 15046	It's Your Day Today/I Apologise Baby	7
68	Liberty LBF 15085	What's Wrong With My World/Why Baby Why	7
68	Liberty LBF 15152	The Day That Lorraine Came Down/Mery Hoppkins Never Had Days Like These (B-side features Led Zeppelin)	15
69	Liberty LBF 15245	Hanging From Your Loving Tree/Empty Bottles	15
70	Liberty LBF 15280	Today I Killed A Man/It's Too Good To Last	15
70	Liberty LBF 15386	It's Goodbye/Gift Of Love	15
72	Columbia DB 8874	We'll Meet Again/Clown Shoes	10
73	Ember EMB S 328	Put Your Head On My Shoulder/Momma Married A Preacher	7
74	Seven Sun SSUN 13	The Champ (Parts 1 & 2)	8
81	Rooster RONS 101	You've Got It All/Starting All Over Again (with Polly Brown)	5
64	Liberty LEP 2192	P. J. PROBY (EP)	18
65	Liberty LEP 2229	SOMEWHERE (EP)	18
65	Liberty LEP 2239	CHRISTMAS WITH P. J. (EP)	18
66	Liberty LEP 2251	P. J.'s HITS (EP)	25
67	Liberty LEP 2267	PROBY AGAIN (EP)	38
65	Liberty LBY 1235	I AM P. J. PROBY (LP)	30
65	Liberty LBY 1264	P. J. PROBY (LP)	30
66	Liberty LBY 1291	P. J. PROBY IN TOWN (LP)	22
67	Liberty LBY 1361	ENIGMA (LP)	30
67	Liberty LBL/LBS 83045	PHENOMENON (LP)	22
68	Liberty LBL/LBS 83087	BELIEVE IT OR NOT (LP)	30
69	Liberty LBS 83219E	THREE WEEK HERO (LP, featuring Led Zeppelin on "Jim's Blues")	40
73	Ember NR 5069	I'M YOURS (LP)	20
78	Astoria 1	ELVIS (LP; sold at theatres)	15

(see also Jett Powers, Marc Almond)

PROCESSION
68	Mercury MF 1053	Every American Citizen/Essentially Susan (p/s)	6
68	Mercury MF 1070	One Day In Every Week/Wigwam City	5
69	Mercury SMCL 20132	PROCESSION (LP)	12

PROCOL HARUM
67	Deram DM 126	A Whiter Shade Of Pale/Lime Street Blues (1st issue with darker labels)	6
67	Regal Zonophone RZ 3003	Homburg/Good Captain Clack	8
68	Regal Zonophone RZ 3007	Quite Rightly So/In The Wee Small Hours Of Sixpence	10
69	Regal Zonophone RZ 3019	A Salty Dog/Long Gone Geek	8
72	Fly Magni Fly ECHO 101	A Whiter Shade Of Pale/A Salty Dog/Homburg (p/s)	7
79	RCA LB 6	A Whiter Shade Of Pale/Noel Edmonds Introduces Record Year (Lever Brothers premium)	5
67	Regal Zono. LRZ 1001	PROCOL HARUM (LP)	45
67	Regal Zono. TA-LRZ 1001	PROCOL HARUM (reel-to-reel, mono only)	12
68	Regal Zono. (S)LRZ 1004	SHINE ON BRIGHTLY (LP, mono/stereo)	35
69	Regal Zono. SLRZ 1009	A SALTY DOG (LP)	30
70	Regal Zono. SLRZ 1014	HOME (LP, with lyric sheet)	25
71	Chrysalis ILPS 9158	BROKEN BARRICADES (LP, gatefold sleeve, first pressings have a small white "I" at the top of the label)	15/12

(see also Paramounts, Legend, Matthew Fisher, Robin Trower, Matthew Ellis, Freedom, Mick Grabham, Power Pack)

JUDD PROCTOR
61	Parlophone R 4769	Rio Grande/Plainsman	12
61	Parlophone R 4809	Palamino/Nola	12
61	Parlophone R 4841	Speakeasy/Clearway	12
62	Parlophone R 4885	The Turk/Mad	12
62	Parlophone R 4920	Backfire/It's Bluesy	12
64	Parlophone R 5126	Better Late/Boots	12
60s	Morgan MR 103P	GUITARS GALORE (LP)	45
70s	Gemini GMX 5004	GUITARS GALORE (LP, reissue)	18

MIKE PROCTOR
67	Columbia DB 8254	Mr. Commuter/Sunday, Sunday, Sunday	80

PRODIGY
91	XL XLT 17	WHAT EVIL LURKS EP (What Evil Lurks/We Gonna Rock/Android/Everybody In The Place) (12", company sleeve)	50
91	XL XLS 21	Charly/Charly (Original Mix) (p/s)	10

91	XL XLS 26	Everybody In The Place (Fairground Edit)/G-Force (Energy Flow) (p/s)	10
92	XL XLS 30	Fire (Edit)/Jericho (Original Version) (p/s)	10
92	XL XLS 35	Out Of Space/Ruff In The Jungle Bizness (Uplifting Vibes Remix) (p/s)	10
93	XL XLS 39	Wind It Up (Rewound)/We Are The Ruffest (p/s)	10
95	XL SC 1	SCIENIDE (12", white label, 500 hand-stamped promos only)	50
96	XL XLT 70LC	Firestarter/Molotov Bitch (jukebox issue, 500 copies only)	10
96	XL XLT 70P	Firestarter/Firestarter (Instrumental)/Firestarter (Empirion Mix)/Molotov Bitch (12", 'photocopied' molotov cocktail sleeve, promo only)	20
96	XL 76 XLC 76	Minefields (Radio Edit)/Minefields (Monkey Mafia Mix)/ Minefields (Headrock Beats)/Minefields (Full Length) (cassette, promo only, 50 copies with photocopied inlay)	60
96	XL XLT 76	Minefields (Radio Edit)/(Monkey Mafia Mix)/(Headrock Beats) (Full Length Version) (12", unreleased, 10 test pressings only)	300+
96	XL XLS 76CD	Minefields (Radio Edit)/(Monkey Mafia Mix)/(Headrock Beats) (Full Length Version) (CD, unreleased, advance copy only)	80
97	XL XLS 80LC	Breathe (Edit)/The Trick (jukebox issue, no p/s)	10
98	XL XLT 98	Smack My Bitch Up (Slacker Mix) (12", promo only)	20
92	XL XLLP 110	THE PRODIGY EXPERIENCE (2-LP)	18
94	XL XLLP 114	MUSIC FOR THE JILTED GENERATION (LP)	15
96	XL XLS 70CDP	FIRESTARTER (Firestarter/Charly/Everybody In The Place/Out Of Space/ Wind It Up/Firestarter/One Love/No Good/Voodoo People/Poison/Firestarter) (CD, no inlay, in-store promo only, 1000 only)	18

PROFESSIONALS

80	Virgin VS 353	Just Another Dream/Action Man (p/s)	5
80	Virgin VS 376	1-2-3/White Light White Heat/Baby I Don't Care (p/s, with giant foldout poster in stickered PVC sleeve)	5
80	Virgin VS 376	1-2-3/White Light White Heat/Baby I Don't Care (p/s, signed by Cook & Jones)	15
81	Sounds FREEBIE No. 2	Little Boys In Blue (extract)/GILLAN: I'll Rip Your Spine Out (extract) (33rpm 1-sided flexi, printed die-cut sleeve, free with *Sounds*)	5
81	Virgin VS 426	Join The Professionals/Has Anybody Got An Alibi? (gatefold p/s)	7
81	Virgin V 2220	I DIDN'T SEE IT COMING (LP)	12

(see also Sex Pistols, Greedies, Lightning Raiders, Steve Jones)

PROFESSOR LONGHAIR

65	Sue WI 397	Baby Let Me Hold Your Hand/Looka' No Hair	38
78	Harvest HAR 5154	Mess Around/Tipitina	15
60s	XX MIN 708	PROFESSOR LONGHAIR (EP)	20
72	Speakeasy 10-78	NEW ORLEANS 88 (10" LP)	48
72	Atlantic K 40402	NEW ORLEANS PIANO (LP)	32
78	Harvest SHSP 4086	LIVE ON THE QUEEN MARY (LP)	32
83	Stateside SSL 6004	LIVE ON THE QUEEN MARY (LP, reissue)	18

PROFESSOR LUDLOW & DR. SMITH

99	Fat Cat 12FAT 029	Professor's Saying Raas (12", custom sleeve)	8

PROFIL

80	CBS S CBS 8574	Hey Music Man/Jour De Chance (p/s)	10

PROFILE

65	Mercury MF 875	Haven't They Got Better Things To Do/Touch Of Your Hand	12
65	Mercury MF 981	Got To Find A Way/Don't Say Goodbye	12
69	Philips BF 1757	Politician Man/Where Is Love	6

(see also Karl Stuart & Profiles, Voice)

PROLES

79	Rock Against Racism RAR 1	Stereo Love/Thought Crime/CONDEMNED: Soldier Boys/ Endless Revolution (p/s)	30
79	Small Wonder SMALL 23	Softground/SMK (p/s)	6

PROPAGANDA

85	ZTT CTIS 101	Das Testaments Des Mabuse/The Last Word/Dr. Mabuse (cassette, "Femme Fatale" is listed but doesn't appear)	10
85	ZTT 12 ZTAS 2	Das Testaments Des Mabuse/Femme Fatale (The Woman With The Orchid)/The 9th Life (Of Dr. Mabuse) (12", white p/s)	8
85	ZTT 12 ZTAS 2 (matrix: 2A 2U)	Das Testaments Des Mabuse/Femme Fatale/The 9th Life (Of Dr. Mabuse) (12", white p/s, title sticker reads "13th Life New Mix")	15
85	ZTT 12 ZTAS 2	Das Testaments Des Mabuse (The Third Side)/Femme Fatale (The Woman With The Orchid) The Fourth Side (12", 'dark photo' p/s)	10
85	ZTT P ZTAS 8	Duel/Jewel (Rough Cut) (ZTT logo-shaped picture disc, uncut or cut)	75/10
85	ZTT DUAL 1	Duel/Jewel//Lied/The Lesson (double pack, gatefold ZTT sleeve)	8
85	ZTT 12 ZTAS 8/12 ZTAS 2	Duel (Bittersweet)/Jewel (Cut Rough) (12", p/s, shrink wrapped with "Dr. Mabuse" 12" [ZTT sleeve])	18
85	ZTT PROP 1	Bejewelled (12", 1-sided, white label, stickered title sleeve, promo only)	12
85	ZTT CTIS 108	DO WELL: The First Cut/Duel (7")/(Cut Rough)/Wonder/Bejewelled (cassette)	10
85	ZTT PZTAS 12	P-Machinery/Frozen Faces (clear vinyl, printed PVC sleeve)	5
85	ZTT 12X ZTAS 12	P-Machinery (Beta)/Complete Machinery/Frozen Faces (12", 'sofa' p/s)	10
85	ZTT 12 ZTAS 21/12 ZTAS 8	P-Machinery (Polish)/P-Machinery (Passive)/Frozen Faces (12", p/s, shrink wrapped with "Duel" 12")	18
85	ZTT 12P ZTAS 12	P-Machinery (Polish)/P Machinery (Passive)/Frozen Faces (12", p/s, clear vinyl, printed PVC sleeve)	8
85	ZTT 12X ZTAST 12	P-Machinery (Beta)//Complete Machinery/Frozen Faces//P-Machinery (Polish)/ P-Machinery (Passive)/Frozen Faces (12", clear vinyl/black vinyl double pack, gatefold PVC sleeve with poster)	30
85	ZTT CTIS 12	COMPLETE MACHINERY: Introduction/P-Machinery (Connected)/ P-Machinery (Separation)/Frozen Faces (cassette)	10
02	ZTT ZTT 180CDX	Outside World (CD, with bonus DVD, digipak, mail order only edition)	30

(see also Act, Ralph Dorper, Claudia Brücken)

PROPHET
74	UK UK 64	Have Love Will Travel/Blues In B Sharp	40

MICHAEL PROPHET
79	Grove GMDM 17	Turn Me Loose/Praise You Jah Jah (12")	15
79	Grove GMDM 25	Warn Them Jah/Don't Interfere (12")	18
82	Greensleeves GRED 72	Here Comes The Bride/MYSTIC EYES: Bring The Kuchie Come	35
80	Island ILPS 9606	SERIOUS REASONING (LP)	16

ORVAL PROPHET
63	London HLL 9729	Run Run Run/My Lois And Me	10

REX PROPHET
55	Brunswick OE 9144	CANADIAN PLOWBOY (EP)	15

PROPHETS (Jamaica)
70	Big Shot BI 554	Crystal Blue Persuasion (Parts 1 & 2)	15
70	Big Shot BI 555	Tumble Time (Parts 1 & 2)	12
70	Big Shot BI 557	Revenge Of Eastwood Version One/Version Two	12
70	Jackpot JP 712	Let's Fall In Love/Purple Moon	12
78	Grove Music GMDM 12	Give Thanks And Praise/Till I Kiss You (12")	20
79	Grove Music GMDM 4	Blessed Are The Meek (feat Trinity)/TOMMY McCOOK: Stepping High (12")	12

(see also Lloyd & Prophets, Claudette, Lloyd & Claudette, Patrick & Lloyd)

PROPHETS (U.S.)
69	Mercury MF 1097	I Got The Fever/Soul Control (DJ copy = £50)	30

(see also Creation [U.S.])

PROS & CONS
66	CBS 202341	Bend It/No Time	7

PROTEGUE (& PRINCE BUSTER'S ALL STARS)
67	Blue Beat BB 398	Foul Dance/PRINCE BUSTER'S ALL STARS: This Is It	25

PROTEX
78	Good Vibrations GOT 6	Don't Ring Me Up/(Just Want) Your Attention/Listening In (wraparound p/s)	10
79	Rough Trade GOT 1	Don't Ring Me Up/(Just Want) Your Attention/Listening In (reissue, p/s)	8
79	Polydor 2059 124	I Can't Cope/Popularity (p/s)	10
79	Polydor 2059 167	I Can Only Dream/Heartache (p/s)	10
80	Polydor 2059 245	A Place In Your Heart/Jeepster (p/s)	10

PROTOS
82	Airship AP 391	ONE DAY A NEW HORIZON (LP)	140

PROVIDENCE
73	Threshold TH 14	Fantasy Fugue/Island Of Light	5
72	Threshold THS 9	EVER SENCE THE DAWN (LP, gatefold sleeve with insert)	15

DOROTHY PROVINE
61	Warner Bros WB 53	Don't Bring Lulu/Whisper Song	5
62	Warner Bros WB 70	Crazy Words, Crazy Tune/Bye Bye Blackbird	8

PROWLER
73	Parlophone R 5986	Pale Green Hnmmmm Driving Man/Jaywick Cowboy	10

PROWLER
85	SRT SRT5KS/368	Alcatraz/So Lonely (p/s)	60

PRUDES
89	Yo Yo PRU 1	P.S. I'm Leaving/Lighthouse Keeper's Daughter (p/s, white vinyl)	5

PRUNES
70	Songbird SB 1023	Come A Little Closer/Come A Little Closer Version II	5

(see also Eric Donaldson, West Indians)

SNOOKY PRYOR
70	Flyright LP 100	SNOOKY PRYOR (LP)	18

ARTHUR PRYSOCK
65	CBS 201820	It's Too Late, Baby Too Late/My Special Prayer	15
66	CBS EP 6076	AGAIN (EP)	25
67	Verve SVLP 9176	MISTER PRYSOCK (LP)	20
78	Polydor 2383 481	DOES IT AGAIN (LP)	15

RED PRYSOCK
54	Mercury MB 3158	Blow Your Horn/Happy Feet (78)	22
57	Mercury MT 121	Teen-Age Rock/Paquino Walk (78)	30
59	Mercury AMT 1028	Chop Suey/Margie (78 rpm = £15)	18
58	Mercury MPL 6535	THE BEAT (LP)	50
58	Mercury MPL 6550	FRUIT BOOTS (LP)	45

PSEUDO EXISTORS
80	Dead Good DEAD 2	Pseudo Existence/Coming Up For Air/New Modern Warfare (rubber-stamped folded p/s, pink/white label; later red/black label & stamped white sleeve)	60/35

PSYCHEDELIC FURS
79	Epic EPC 8005	We Love You/Pulse (green, pink or orange p/s)	5
81	CBS A 1166	Dumb Waiters/Dash (1st 5,000 with playable p/s)	5
81	CBS A 13 1327	Pretty In Pink/Mack The Knife/Soap Commercial (12", shrinkwrapped with free T-shirt)	8

(see also Unwanted)

PSYCHIC PHENOMENA
97	Lowlife LOW05	THE WHOLE CIRCUMFERENCE (EP)	20

MINT VALUE £

PSYCHIC TV

82	Some Bizzare PTV 1	Just Drifting/Breakthrough (p/s) 8
82	Some Bizzare PTV 1T	Just Drifting/Just Drifting (Midnight) (12", p/s) 15
84	Temple TOPY 001	Unclean/Mirrors (12", p/s) 10
86	Temple TOPYS 009	Godstar/Godstar (BJ Mix)/Discopravity/Yes It's The B Side
		(double pack, gatefold p/s) 8
86	Temple TOPIC 009	Godstar/Godstar (California Mix) (12", picture disc) 15
86	Temple TOPYD 023	Good Vibrations/Interzone/Roman P/Hex-Sex/Godstar (Ugly Mix)/Je T'Aime
		(double pack, gatefold p/s) 6
86	Temple TOPYT 023	Roman P (Fireball Mix)/Interzone/Good Vibrations (Kundalini Mix)/Hex-Sex
		(Voodoo Mix) (12", p/s) 10
88	Temple TOPY 037	Tune In (Turn On To Thee Acide House)
		(12", p/s, as (Psychic TV/Jack The Tab) 10
88	DC DC 23	Superman/Jack The Tab (12", p/s, no artist credit on label) 20
89	Temple TOPY 048	Love, War, Riot/Eve Of Destruction (Vocoder Mixes) (12", p/s,
		including sticker) 15
94	Tribal TOPY 077CD	Tribal (Four Versions) (CD) 8
82	Some Bizzare PSY 1	FORCE THE HAND OF CHANCE (LP, with bonus LP & double-sided poster,
		featuring Marc Almond) 35
83	CBS 25737	DREAMS LESS SWEET (LP, with inner sleeve,
		some with free 12" EP [XPR 1251]) 25/20
84	Temple TOPY 003	PAGAN DAY (LP, picture disc, 999 copies). 50
84	Gramm GRAMM 23	THOSE WHO DO NOT (2-LP, 5000 copies) 30
85	Temple TOPY 004	THEMES 2 (LP) 15
85	Temple TOPY 008	THEMES 3 (LP) 15
85	Temple TOPY 010	MOUTH OF THE NIGHT (LP) 15
85	Temple TOPIC 010	MOUTH OF THE NIGHT (LP, picture disc) 20
86	Temple TOPIC 009	GODSTAR (LP, with picture disc) 15
86	Temple TOPY 014	LIVE IN PARIS (LP) 15
86	Temple TOPY 015	LIVE IN TOKYO 15
87	Temple TOPY 016	LIVE IN GLASGOW 15
87	Temple TOPY 018	LIVE IN HEAVEN (LP) 15
87	Temple TOPY 026	LIVE IN REYKJAUIK (LP) 15
87	Temple TOPY 027	LIVE EN SUISSE (LP) 15
87	Temple TOPY 028	LIVE IN TORONTO (LP). 15
87	Temple TOPY 029	LIVE IN GOTTINGEN (LP) 15
88	Temple TOPY 031	PSYCHIC TV (LP, picture disc). 15
88	Temple TOPY 032	ALBUM 10 (LP, picture disc) 15
88	Temple TOPY 038	ALLEGORY AND SELF (LP, blue vinyl) 20
88	Temple TOPY 036	LIVE AT MARDI GRAS 15
88	Temple TOPY 045	LIVE AT THEE CIRCUS 15
89	Temple TOPY 045	LIVE AT THEE RITY 15
89	Temple TOPY 046	KONDOLE / COPYCAT (LP) 15
89	Temple TOPY 047	LIVE AT THE PYRAMID NYC (LP, picture disc) 15
91	Temple TOPY 020	LIVE IN BRENGENZ (LP) 15

(see also Throbbing Gristle, Coil, Monte Cazazza, Rose McDowall)

PSYCHOPATHS

91	Elicit 12 ELIC 2	NIGHTMARES (12", no p/s) 8

PSYCHO'S MUM

89	Woronzow W 011	A SIBILANT SIN (LP, with insert) 15

PSYKYK VOLTS

79	Ellie Jay EJPS 9262	Totally Useless/Horror Story No. 5 (p/s) 50
79	MHG GHM 109	Totally Useless/Horror Story No. 5 35

PSYLONS

86	E Type ETYPE 1	The Mockery Of Decline/Clear Sky 10
87	Iron Lung IL 001	All The Things We Need (12", p/s). 15
90	Unsigned UN 001	No Choice (p/s) 8
91	Unsigned UN 002	SAND MAN EP 8

PUBLIC ENEMY

87	Def Jam 651 245-0	Rebel Without A Pause (Vocal Mix)/(Instrumental) (picture disc) 8
88	Def Jam 652 833-0	Don't Believe The Hype/Prophets Of Rage (p/s, with patch) 5
88	Def Jam 653 089-7	Night Of The Living Baseheads/Terminator X To The Edge Of Panic
		(p/s, badge pack). 5
87	Def Jam 450482-1	YO BUM RUSH THE SHOW (LP) 12

PUBLIC FOOT THE ROMAN

73	Sovereign SVNA 7259	PUBLIC FOOT THE ROMAN (LP). 30

(see also Movies)

PUBLIC IMAGE LTD (PiL)

78	Virgin VS 228	Public Image/The Cowboy Song (foldout 'newspaper' p/s) 10
79	Virgin VS 274-12	Death Disco/And No Bird Do Sing (1/2 Mix)/Death Disco Megamix
		(12", p/s, 5,000 only) 8
86	Virgin VSD 855	Home/Round//Rise/Rise (Instrumental) (double pack) 5
87	Virgin VS 988	Seattle/Selfish Rubbish (box set with 7", badge, postcard & sew-on patch) 6
88	Virgin CDT 14	This Is Not A Love Song/Blue Water/This Is Not A Love
		Song (Remixed Version)/Public Image (3" CD, card sleeve) 8
89	Virgin VSCD 1181	Disappointed/Same Old Story/Disappointed (12" Version)
		(3" CD, picture disc, card sleeve in 3" envelope-shaped plastic pouch) 8
89	Virgin VSCD 1195	Warrior (Edit)/U.S.L.S.I. (Extended Mix) (3" CD, card sleeve). 8
79	Virgin METAL 1	METAL BOX (LP, 3 x 12" with circular paper dividers & inner sheet in
		round tin) 30
90	Virgin TPAK 5	METAL BOX (CD, in round tin with insert) 20

(see also Sex Pistols, Jah Wobble, Don Letts & Jah Wobble, Vivien Goldman, Time Zone, Cowboys International)

GARY PUCKETT (& UNION GAP)

68	CBS 3365	Young Girl/I'm Losing You (as Union Gap featuring Gary Puckett)............ 5
68	CBS 3551	Lady Willpower/Daylight Stranger...................................... 5
68	CBS (S) 63342	YOUNG GIRL (LP) 32
68	CBS (S) 63429	INCREDIBLE (LP) 28
70	CBS 63794	THE NEW GARY PUCKETT AND THE UNION GAP ALBUM (LP) 22

PUDDING

67	Decca F 12603	The Magic Bus/It's Too Late... 75

TITO PUENTE

54	Seeco SV 2249	Por Tu Amor/Plaza Stomp (78, as Tito Puente & His Conjunto)............. 6
57	RCA RD 27002	LET'S CHA-CHA WITH PUENTE (LP) 15
58	RCA SF 5008	MUCHO PUENTE (LP).. 18

LEROY PULLINS

66	London HLR 10056	I'm A Nut/Knee Deep... 18
79	Pulp Music PB 1	Low Flying Aircraft/Something Just Behind My Back/So Lo (blank labels, some numbered up to 2,000 & signed, some with handmade sleeve)....... 25/20

PULP

83	Red Rhino RED 32	My Lighthouse (Remix)/Looking For Life (p/s) 50
83	Red Rhino RED 37	Everybody's Problem/There Was (p/s) 50
85	Fire BLAZE 5	Little Girl (With Blue Eyes)/Simultaneous/Blue Glow/The Will To Power (12", p/s).. 15
86	Fire BLAZE 10	Dogs Are Everywhere/The Mark Of The Devil/97 Lovers/Aborigine/ Goodnight (12", p/s) 12
87	Fire BLAZE 17	They Suffocate At Night (Edited Version)/Tunnel (Cut Up Version) (p/s) 10
87	Fire BLAZE 17T	They Suffocate At Night (Uncut Version)/Tunnel (Full Length Version) (12", p/s).. 12
87	Fire BLAZE 21T	Masters Of The Universe (Sanitised Version)/Manon/Silence (12", p/s) 12
90	Fire BLAZE 44T	My Legendary Girlfriend/Is This House?/This House Is Condemned (12", p/s)... 10
91	Fire BLAZE 51T	Countdown/Death Goes To The Disco/Countdown (Radio Edit) (12", p/s) 10
92	Gift GIF 1	O.U. (Gone Gone)/Space/O.U. (Gone Gone) (Radio Edit) (12", p/s)........... 8
92	Gift GIF 1CD	O.U. (Gone Gone) (Radio Edit)/Space/O.U. (Gone Gone) (CD)............... 15
92	Caff CAFF 17	My Legendary Girlfriend/Sickly Grin/Back In L.A. (foldover p/s with insert in poly bag, 500 only) 50
92	Fire BLAZE 44CD	My Legendary Girlfriend/Is This House?/This House Is Condemned (CD)....... 20
92	Gift GIF 3	Babies/Styloroc (Nites Of Suburbia)/Sheffield: Sex City (12", p/s) 8
92	Gift GIF 3CD	Babies/Styloroc (Nites Of Suburbia)/Sheffield: Sex City/ Sheffield: Sex City (Instrumental) (CD, card sleeve) 22
93	Gift GIF 6CD	Razzmatazz/Inside Susan: A Story In 3 Songs (Stacks/Inside Susan/ 59 Lyndhurst Grove) (CD) 15
93	Island IS 567	Lip Gloss/You're A Nightmare (p/s)..................................... 8
95	Island CIDX 613	Common People/Razzmatazz/Dogs Are Everywhere/Joyriders (CD, with sticker)... 8
96	Island ISC 574	Do You Remember The First Time/Street Lites (reissue, brown vinyl, p/s) 5
84	Red Rhino REDLP 29	IT (mini-LP) 25
94	Cherry Red CDMRED 112	IT (CD, with extra tracks; withdrawn, 1,000 only) 20
94	Island 12IS 595	THE SISTERS EP (12", p/s with print)................................... 8
94	Island ILPS 8025	HIS 'N' HERS (LP)... 15
95	Island ILPS 8041	DIFFERENT CLASS (LP, die-cut sleeve with 12 inserts)..................... 15
98	Island ILPSD 8066	THIS IS HARDCORE (2 x LP with insert) 20

PULSAR

76	Decca SKL-R 5228	POLLEN (LP) 22
77	Decca TXS 119	STRANDS OF THE FUTURE (LP).. 22

PULSE

70	Major Minor SMLP 64	PULSE (LP) 55

PUMPHOUSE GANG

77	Kitsch FAD 1	Motorcity Fantasy/Cocaine (p/s) 7

PUNCHERS

70	Punch PH 46	Sons Of Thunder (actually by Lee Perry & The Upsetters)/ Only If You Understand 22

PUNCHIN' JUDY

73	Transatlantic TRA 272	PUNCHIN' JUDY (LP) 20

PUNCTURE

77	Small Wonder SMALL 1	Mucky Pup/Can't Rock'n'Roll (p/s) 10

PUNKETTES

77	Response SR 511	Going Out Wiv A Punk/Polythene 25

PUPILS

66	Wing WL 1150	A TRIBUTE TO THE ROLLING STONES (LP) 50
69	Fontana SFL 13087	A TRIBUTE TO THE ROLLING STONES (LP, reissue) 40
	(see also Eyes)	

PUPPETS

63	Pye 7N 15556	Poison Ivy/Everybody's Talking...................................... 50
64	Pye 7N 15625	Shake With Me/Three Boys Looking For Love (existence unconfirmed)
64	Pye 7N 15634	Baby Don't Cry/Shake With Me 50

FRANK PURCELL

73	Paramount PAS 6064	JAMES BOND'S GREATEST HITS (LP).................................. 20

DANNY PURCHES

55	Columbia SCM 5183	Mama/Just One More Time.. 15
58	Columbia DB 4129	The Shrine On The Second Floor/He (78 rpm = £10)...................... 10

(BERNARD) PRETTY PURDIE
68	Direction 58-3301	Funky Donkey/Caravan	15
68	Direction 58-3628	Soul Clappin'/Blow Your Lid	10
71	Philips 6073 708	Good Livin' Good Lovin'/Day Dreaming	6
68	Direction 8-63290	SOUL DRUMS (LP)	60
71	Philips 6369 421	SOUL IS ... (LP)	25

PURE HELL
78	Golden Sphinx GSX 002	These Boots Are Made For Walking/No Rules (p/s)	20

PURE LOVE & PLEASURE
70	Stateside SSL 5026	A RECORD OF PURE LOVE AND PLEASURE (LP)	20

PURE REASON REVOLUTION
04	Poptones MC50896	Apprentice Of The Universe/Nimos & Tambos (p/s)	5
04	Poptones MC50895CD	Apprentice Of The Universe/Nimos & Tambos (CD, card p/s)	8

PURGE
69	Corn CP 101	The Mayor Of Simpleton Hall/The Knave (p/s)	150

JAMES & BOBBY PURIFY
66	Stateside SS 547	I'm Your Puppet/So Many Reasons	15
67	Stateside SS 595	Wish You Didn't Have To Go/You Can't Keep A Good Man Down	15
67	Stateside SS 2016	Shake A Tail Feather/Goodness Gracious	20
67	Stateside SS 2039	I Take What I Want/Sixteen Tons	12
67	Stateside SS 2049	Let Love Come Between Us/I Don't Want To Have To Wait	20
68	Stateside SS 2093	Do Unto Me/Everybody Needs Somebody	15
68	Bell BLL 1008	I Can't Remember/I Was Born To Lose Out	8
68	Bell BLL 1024	Help Yourself To All My Lovin'/Last Piece Of Love	8
69	Bell BLL 1043	Untie Me/We're Finally Gonna Make It	8
69	Bell BLL 1056	Let Love Come Between Us/Shake A Tail Feather	10
69	Bell BLL 1067	Do Unto Me/Wish You Didn't Have To Go	8
72	Mojo 2092 056	I'm Your Puppet/Wish You Didn't Have To Go	8
67	Stateside SL 10206	JAMES AND BOBBY PURIFY (LP)	50
67	Bell MBLL/SBLL 101	THE PURE SOUND OF THE PURIFYS (LP)	40

ALTON PURNELL
70	Dixie DIX 4	TRAVELLING LIGHT (LP)	30
(see also Bonnie Raitt)			

PURPLE ALGAE
95	Poor Person Prod. PPPR 7	ADRIFT ON A SEA OF SOUND (LP, handmade sleeve & insert, no'd, 500 only)	15

PURPLE FOX
71	Stereo Gold Award MER340	TRIBUTE TO JIMI HENDRIX (LP)	12

PURPLE GANG
67	Big T BIG 101	Granny Takes A Trip/Bootleg Whisky	12
68	Big T BIG 111	Kiss Me Goodnight Sally Green/Auntie Monica	7
68	Transatlantic	THE PURPLE GANG STRIKES (LP)	45

PURPLE HAZE
85	S.R.S. SRS 6	Hear It On The Radio (p/s)	55

PURPLE HEARTS
79	Fiction FICS 003	Millions Like Us/Beat That! (p/s)	10
79	Fiction FICS 007	Frustration/Extraordinary Sensations (p/s)	10
80	Fiction FICS 9	Jimmy/What Am I Gonna Do (p/s)	10
80	Safari SAFE 30	My Life's A Jigsaw/The Guy Who Made Her A Star/Just To Please You (initially in foldout jigsaw p/s)	12/8
82	Road Runner RR 1	Plane Crash/Scooby Doo/Gun Of Life (p/s)	12
86	UNICORN PHZ3	Friends Again/Head On Collision Time (p/s)	8
80	Fiction FIX 002/2383 568	BEAT THAT! (LP)	20
85	Razor RAZS 13	HEAD ON COLLISION TIME (LP)	12
85	Razor RAZS 19	POPISH FRENZY (LP)	12
(see also Bob Manton, Rage)			

GEOFF PURVIS
77	Fellside FE 003	THE BORDER FIDDLER (LP)	15

PUSSY
72	Deram DM 368	Feline Woman/Ska Child	20
(see also Jerusalem)			

PUSSY
69	Morgan Bluetown BT 5002	PUSSY PLAYS (LP)	350
(see also Angel Pavement, Fortes Mentum)			

PUSSYFOOT
66	Decca F 12474	Freeloader/Things That Still Remind Me	18
67	Decca F 12561	Mr Hyde/Hasty Words	22
68	Pye 7N 17520	Good Times/Till You Don't Want Me Anymore	15
(see also Rare Breed)			

PUSSY GALORE
87	Vinyl Drip SUK 001	GROOVY HATE FUCK (LP)	20
87	Product Inc. 33PROD 19	RIGHT NOW (LP)	18
89	Product INCLP 1	DIAL M FOR MOTHERFUCKER (LP)	20
(see also Jon Spencer Blues Explosion)			

ASHA PUTHLI
73	CBS 65804	ASHA PUTHLI (LP)	20
75	CBS 80978	SHE LOVES TO HEAR THE MUSIC (LP)	15
76	CBS 81443	THE DEVIL IS LOOSE (LP)	20

PUZZLE
69	Stateside SS 2146	Hey Medusa/Make The Children Happy	7
69	Stateside SSL 10285	PUZZLE (LP)	15

PVC 2
77	Zoom ZUM 2	Put You In The Picture/Pain/Deranged, Demented and Free (p/s)	15

(see also Midge Ure, Zones)

NATASHA PYNE
66	Polydor 56713	It's All In Your Head/I'm A Dreamer	8

PYRAMID
67	Deram DM 111	Summer Of Last Year/Summer Evening	45

(see also Fairport Convention, Ian Matthews)

PYRAMIDS (Jamaica)
67	President PT 161	Train Tour To Rainbow City/John Chewey	8
68	President PT 177	Wedding In Peyton Place/Girls Girls Girls	8
68	President PT 195	All Change On The Bakerloo Line/Playing Games	8
68	President PT 206	Mexican Moonlight/Mule	6
68	President PT 225	Tisko My Darling/Movement All Around	6
69	President PT 243	Do-Re-Mi/I'm Outnumbered	6
69	President PT 274	I'm A Man/Dragon Fly	8
69	Doctor Bird DB 1307	Stay With Him/Chicken Mary	20
70	Duke DU 80	Geronimo/Feel Alright	10
70	Trojan TR 7755	Feel Alright/Telstar	7
70	Trojan TR 7770	To Sir With Love/Reggae Shuffle	7
71	Trojan TR 7803	All For You/All For You Version	7
71	Creole CR 1003	Mosquito Bite/Mother's Bath	7
68	President PTL 1021	THE PYRAMIDS (LP)	40

(see also Symarip, Equals, Little Grants & Eddie, Seven Letters, Bruce Ruffin)

PYRAMIDS (U.S.)
64	London HLU 9847	Penetration/Here Comes Marsha	45

PYTHAGORAS THEOREM
70	Pye 7N 17924	Give A Damn/London Bridge	10
70	Pye 7N 17990	Our House/Free Like Me	7

PYTHON LEE JACKSON
70	Young Blood YB 1017	In A Broken Dream/Doing Fine	6
76	Young Blood YB 1077	The Blues/Cloud Nine	10
80	Young Blood YB 0089	In A Broken Dream/The Blues	6
80	Young Blood YEP 89	In A Broken Dream (mono)/In A Broken Dream (stereo)/The Blues/ Cloud Nine (EP, "Kelly Girl" Employment Agency advert on p/s)	12
74	Young Blood YB 3001	IN A BROKEN DREAM (LP, featuring Rod Stewart)	18

(see also Rod Stewart)

PYEWACKET
81	Dingles DIN 312	PYEWACKET (LP)	15
83	Familiar FAM 43	THE MAN IN THE MOON DRINKS CLARET (LP)	15

Q-BERT
97	Mo' Wax MW 084	Camel Bobsled Race/(mixes) (12")	12

(see also DJ Shadow)

Q-CHASTIC
92	Rephlex 002EP	Q-CHASTIC EP (double pack)	200

(see also Aphex Twin)

QUAD
97	Acme AC 8020LP	QUAD (LP, clear vinyl in printed clear PVC cover)	15
97	Prescription DRUG 3	QUAD (LP, 99 copies only, handmade sleeve, mail-order only)	25

(see also Sun Dial)

CHRISTINE QUAITE
62	Oriole CB 1739	Guilty Eyes/Oh My!	20
62	Oriole CB 1772	Your Nose Is Gonna Grow/Our Last Chance	20
63	Oriole CB 1845	Mister Heartache/Whisper Wonderful Words	20
63	Oriole CB 1876	In The Middle Of The Floor/Tell Me Mama	100
63	Oriole CB 1921	I Believe In Love/Here She Comes	22
64	Oriole CB 1945	Mister Stuck Up/Will You Be The Same Tomorrow	22
65	Stateside SS 435	If You've Got A Heart/So Near So Far	22
66	Stateside SS 482	Long After Tonight Is All Over/I'm Hoping (DJ copy = £100)	50

QUAKER CITY BOYS
59	London HLU 8796	Teasin'/Won't Y' Come Out, Mary Ann (78 rpm = £15)	15

QUAKERS
65	Oriole CB 1992	I'm Ready/Down The Road A Piece	150
65	Studio 36 KSP 109/110	She's Alright/Talk To Me (only 50 pressed)	450+

QUALITY DRIVEL
81	No Cure WHOOP 1	SUBLIMINAL CUTS EP (p/s)..	30

QUANDO QUANGO
84	Factory FAC 102	Atom Rock (p/s)..	6
85	Factory FAC 137	Genius/This Feeling (p/s)..	6
85	Factory FAC 137	Genius/This Feeling (12", p/s)....................................	6
85	Factory FACT 110	PIGS & BATTLESHIPS (LP)......................................	18
85	Factory FACT 110C	PIGS & BATTLESHIPS (cassette, with postcards).....................	18

QUARRY MEN
58	'P.F. Phillips Kensington'	That'll Be The Day/In Spite Of All The Danger (78 rpm shellac acetate, handwritten labels, 1 copy only, owned by Paul McCartney, worth £100,000+)	
81	'Percy Philips, Kensington' (no cat. no.)	That'll Be The Day/In Spite Of All The Danger (78rpm, private pressing reproduction of 1958 demo disc, repro Parlophone co. sleeve, 25 only)	10,000+
81	'Percy Philips, Kensington' (no cat. no.)	That'll Be The Day/In Spite Of All The Danger (45rpm, private pressing reproduction of 1958 demo disc, repro Parlophone co. sleeve, 25 only)	10,000+

(see also Beatles, Trad Grads)

JOE QUARTERMAN & FREE SOUL
73	GSF GSZ 3	So Much Trouble In My Mind (Parts 1 & 2)...........................	15
74	GSF GSZ 12	Thanks Dad Parts 1 & 2...	10
73	GSF GS 504	JOE QUARTERMAN & FREE SOUL (LP)............................	70

QUARTER NOTES
57	Parlophone R 4365	My Fantasy/Ten Minutes To Midnight (78 rpm = £10)	15

QUARTZ
77	Jet UP 36290	Sugar Rain/Street Fighting Lady/Mainline Riders	15
77	Jet UP 36317	Street Fighting Lady/Mainline Riders	12
80	Reddingtons R.R. DAN 1	Nantucket Sleighride/Wildfire (p/s, white or blue vinyl; also black vinyl)	10/5
80	Jet SJET 189	Street Fighting Lady/Mainline Riders (p/s, reissue, demos £15)	10
80	Logo GO 387	Satan's Serenade/Bloody Fool (p/s)...............................	5
80	Logo GOT 387	Satan's Serenade/Bloody Fool/Roll Over Beethoven (live) (12", p/s, blue or red vinyl).....................................	30/12
80	Sound For Industry SFI 549	Satan's Serenade (flexidisc).....................................	7
80	MCA MCA 642	Stoking The Fires Of Hell/Circles (p/s).............................	10
80	Logo MOGO 4007	LIVE QUARTZ (12" EP)..	18
81	MCA MCA 661	Stand Up And Fight/Charlie Snow (p/s)............................	18
83	Heavy Metal HEAVY 17	Tell Me Why/Streetwalker (p/s)...................................	7
77	Jet UAG 30081	QUARTZ (LP, with inner sleeve)	50
79	Jet JETLP 233	DELETED (LP, in sealed brown paper bag with insert. Reissue of 1st LP)	18
80	Reddingtons R.R. REDD 001	QUARTZ LIVE — COUNT DRACULA (LP, some in b&w 'live' sleeve)........	15/12
80	Logo MOGO 4007	LIVE QUARTZ (LP)	12
80	MCA MCF 3080	STAND UP AND FIGHT (LP, with lyric insert)........................	25
83	Heavy Metal HMRLP 9	AGAINST ALL ODDS (LP, with inner sleeve)	12
83	Heavy Metal HMRPD 9	AGAINST ALL ODDS (LP, picture disc).............................	30

(see also Black Sabbath, Copperfield, Bandy Legs)

QUATERMASS
70	Harvest SVHL 775	QUATERMASS (LP, gatefold sleeve)...............................	95
75	Harvest SHSM 2002	QUATERMASS (LP, reissue, different sleeve)	12

(see also Ian Gillan Band, Episode Six)

QUATERMASS
97	Metropolitan MM 027	The Judgement (12", no p/s)	15

QUATRAIN
69	Polydor 583 743	QUATRAIN (LP)	12

SUZI QUATRO
72	Rak RAK 134	Rolling Stone/Brain Confusion (For All The Lonely People)	20
75	Rak RAK 200	I Bit Off More Than I Could Chew/Red Hot Rosie	5
75	Rak RAK 215	I May Be Too Young/Don't Mess Around	5
75	Rak RAK 256	Roxy Roller/I'll Grow On You	5
73	Rak PSR 355	Primitive Love/Shakin' All Over (promo only)	30
78	Rak RAK 285	Stumblin' In/Stranger With You (with Chris Norman) (p/s)...............	5
79	Rak RAK 285	Stumblin' In/Stranger With You (with Chris Norman) (clear vinyl, different p/s) ...	5
79	Rak RAK 299	She's In Love With You/Space Cadets (p/s)...........................	5
86	PRT 12P 367	Wild Thing (Extended)/I Don't Want You (with Reg Presley) (12", p/s)	8
87	Rak/Golden 45 G 45 35	Can The Can/Devilgate Drive (reissue, black label)	5
87	Hackenbacker HACK 101	Am I Dreaming/Who Needs Chairs/Will You Take This Woman (only available at pantomime venues)	10
89	Teldec 247 008-7/ WEA YZ 406	Baby You're A Star/Baby You're A Star (Instrumental) (p/s, early pressings with German labels & sticker "U.K. Cat. No. YZ 406"; later WEA copies)	6/5

QUEEN
SINGLES
73	EMI EMI 2036	Keep Yourself Alive/Son And Daughter	25
74	EMI EMI 2121	Seven Seas Of Rhye/See What A Fool I've Been.......................	8
74	EMI EMI 2229	Killer Queen/Flick Of The Wrist	6
75	EMI EMI 2256	Now I'm Here/Lily Of The Valley	8
75	EMI EMI 2375	Bohemian Rhapsody/I'm In Love With My Car (p/s; beware counterfeits with 'computer-scanned' logo)......................	32
76	EMI EMI 2565	Somebody To Love/White Man (p/s, beware of counterfeit sleeves)...........	10
77	EMI EMI 2593	Tie Your Mother Down/You And I..................................	8
77	EMI EMI 2623	QUEEN'S FIRST EP: Good Old Fashioned Lover Boy/Death On Two Legs/ Tenement Funster/White Queen (As It Began) (p/s)	10
77	EMI EMI 2708	We Are The Champions/We Will Rock You (p/s)	6
78	EMI EMI 2575	Spread Your Wings/Sheer Heart Attack (p/s).........................	6
78	EMI EMI 2870	Bicycle Race/Fat Bottomed Girls (p/s)..............................	6

78	EMI EMI 2870	Bicycle Race/Fat Bottomed Girls (different p/s for export to Belgium)	250
79	EMI EMI 2910	Don't Stop Me Now/In Only Seven Days (p/s)	6
79	EMI EMI 2959	Love Of My Life (live)/Now I'm Here (live)	15
79	EMI EMI 5001	Crazy Little Thing Called Love/We Will Rock You (live) (p/s)	5
80	EMI EMI 5022	Save Me/Let Me Entertain You (live) (p/s)	5
80	EMI EMI 5076	Play The Game/A Human Body (p/s, beige label with red 'EMI' logo or white label with large black 'Queen' logo)	each 6
80	EMI EMI 5102	Another One Bites The Dust/Dragon Attack (p/s)	6
82	EMI EMI 5293	Body Language/Life Is Real (Song For Lennon) (p/s)	6
82	EMI EMI 5316	Las Palabras De Amor (The Words Of Love)/Cool Cat (p/s)	6
82	EMI EMI 5325	Backchat/Staying Power (p/s)	10
82	EMI 12EMI 5325	Backchat (Extended)/Staying Power (12", p/s)	28
84	EMI 12QUEEN 1	Radio Ga Ga (Ext. Version)/Radio Ga Ga (Instrumental)/I Go Crazy (12", p/s)	10
84	EMI QUEEN 2	I Want To Break Free (Remix)/Machines (Back To Humans) ('Freddie' p/s, gold or white lettering)	12/8
84	EMI QUEEN 2	I Want To Break Free (Remix)/Machines (Back To Humans) ('Brian', 'Roger' or 'John' p/s, each with gold lettering)	12/15/18
84	EMI 12QUEEN 2	I Want To Break Free (Extended Remix)/Machines (Back To Humans) (12", p/s, with red background with gold or black lettering)	20/12
84	EMI 12QUEEN 2	I Want To Break Free (Extended Remix)/Machines (Back To Humans) (12", p/s, with white background)	10
84	EMI QUEEN 3	It's A Hard Life/Is This The World We Created...? (p/s)	6
84	EMI QUEEN 3	It's A Hard Life/Is This The World We Created...? ('Roger Taylor' overprinted photo p/s)	20
84	EMI 12QUEEN 3	It's A Hard Life (Extended)/It's A Hard Life/Is This The World We Created...? (12")	32
84	EMI 12QUEENP 3	It's A Hard Life/Is This The World We Created...? (12", picture disc)	20
84	EMI QUEEN 4	Hammer To Fall (Edit)/Tear It Up ('live' p/s, withdrawn)	150
84	EMI QUEEN 4	Hammer To Fall (Edit)/Tear It Up (red p/s)	6
84	EMI 12 QUEEN 4	Hammer To Fall (The Headbangers Mix)/Tear It Up (12", 'live' p/s, withdrawn)	100
84	EMI 12 QUEEN 4	Hammer To Fall (The Headbangers Mix)/Tear It Up (12", red p/s)	12
84	EMI QUEEN 5	Man On The Prowl/Keep Passing The Open Windows (unreleased, white label test pressings only)	250
84	EMI QUEEN 5	Thank God It's Christmas/Man On The Prowl/Keep Passing The Open Windows (p/s)	8
84	EMI 12QUEEN 5	Thank God It's Christmas/Man On The Prowl (Extended Version)/Keep Passing The Open Windows (Extended Version) (12", p/s)	18
85	EMI QUEEN 6	One Vision (7" Mix)/Blurred Vision (p/s, some with red lyric inner sleeve)	7/5
85	EMI 12QUEEN 6	One Vision (Extended Vision)/Blurred Vision (12", p/s, some with red inner)	12/10
85	EMI 12QUEEN 6	One Vision (Extended Vision)/Blurred Vision (12", printed PVC sl. & red inner)	35
86	EMI 12QUEEN 7	A Kind Of Magic (Ext. Version)/A Dozen Red Roses For My Darling (12", p/s)	12
86	EMI 12QUEENP7	A Kind Of Magic (Extended Version)/Don't Lose Your Head (Instrumental Version) (12", picture disc)	40
86	EMI QUEEN 8	Friends Will Be Friends/Seven Seas Of Rhye (p/s)	6
86	EMI QUEEN P8	Friends Will Be Friends/Seven Seas Of Rhye (picture disc)	40
86	EMI 12QUEEN 8	Friends Will Be Friends (Extended Version)/Friends Will Be Friends (7" Version)/Seven Seas Of Rhye (12", p/s)	10
86	EMI QUEEN 9	Who Wants To Live Forever/Killer Queen (p/s)	8
86	EMI 12QUEEN 9	Who Wants To Live Forever (7" Version)/(Album Version)/Killer Queen/Who Wants To Live Forever (Piano Version) (12", p/s)	15
89	Parlophone 12QUEEN 10	I Want It All (Single Version)/Hang On In There/I Want It All (Album Version) (12", p/s)	12
89	Parlophone CDQUEEN 10	I Want It All (Album Version)/Hang On In There/I Want It All (Single Version) (CD, picture disc)	20
89	Parlophone QUEEN PD 11	Breakthru' (7" Mix)/Stealin' (shaped picture disc, 12" PVC sleeve with insert)	20
89	Parlophone QUEEN PD 11	Breakthru' (7" Mix)/Stealin' (uncut picture disc, 12" PVC sleeve with insert)	90
89	Parlophone QUEEN C11	Breakthru' (7" Mix)/Stealin' (cassette)	6
89	Parlophone 12QUEEN 11	Breakthru' (12" Version)/Breakthru' (Single Version)/Stealin' (12", p/s)	12
89	Parlophone CD QUEEN 11	Breakthru' (12" Version)/Stealin'/Breakthru' (7" Mix) (CD)	25
89	Parlophone QUEEN 12	The Invisible Man/Hijack My Heart (black vinyl, p/s)	8
89	Parlophone QUEEN X12	The Invisible Man/Hijack My Heart (clear vinyl, p/s)	12
89	Parlophone 12QUEEN 12	The Invisible Man (12" Version)/(7" Version)/Hijack My Heart (12", p/s)	12
89	Parlophone 12QUEENX12	The Invisible Man (12" Version)/The Invisible Man (7" Version)/Hijack My Heart (12", clear vinyl, PVC sleeve with insert)	20
89	Parlophone CD QUEEN 12	The Invisible Man (12" Version)/Hijack My Heart/The Invisible Man (Single Version) (CD)	30
89	Parlophone QUEEN 14	Scandal/My Life Has Been Saved (p/s)	8
89	Parlophone QUEEN P14	Scandal/My Life Has Been Saved (poster p/s)	20
89	Parlophone 12QUEEN 14	Scandal (12" Version)/Scandal (7" Version)/My Life Has Been Saved (12", p/s)	10
89	Parlophone 12QUEENS 14	Scandal (12" Version)/My Life Has Been Saved/Scandal (7" Version)/(12", p/s, 1-sided, B-side etched with group's signatures)	20
89	Parlophone CD QUEEN 14	Scandal (12" Version)/My Life Has Been Saved/Scandal (7" Version) (CD)	25
89	Parlophone QUEEN 15	The Miracle/Stone Cold Crazy (live) (p/s)	8
89	Parlophone QUEEN H15	The Miracle/Stone Cold Crazy (live) (orange hologram p/s)	15
89	Parlophone QUEEN H15	The Miracle/Stone Cold Crazy (live) (proof sleeve with negative hologram p/s)	450+
89	Parlophone 12QUEEN 15	The Miracle/Stone Cold Crazy (live)/My Melancholy Blues (live) (12", yellow p/s)	15
89	Parlophone 12QUEENP 15	The Miracle/Stone Cold Crazy (live)/My Melancholy Blues (live) (12", turquoise p/s with insert print)	18
89	Parlophone QUEENCD 15	The Miracle/Stone Cold Crazy (live)/My Melancholy Blues (live) (CD)	30
91	Parlophone QUEEN 16	Innuendo/Bijou (p/s)	6
91	Parlophone 12QUEEN 16	Innuendo (Explosive Version)/Under Pressure/Bijou (12", p/s)	8
91	Parl. 12QUEEN PD16	Innuendo (Explosive Version)/Under Pressure/Bijou (12", picture disc, PVC sleeve with insert)	20

MINT VALUE £

91	Parlophone QUEEN 17	I'm Going Slightly Mad/The Hitman (p/s)	5
91	Parlophone QUEEN PD 17	I'm Going Slightly Mad/The Hitman (shaped picture disc with insert)	20
91	Parlophone QUEEN PD 17	I'm Going Slightly Mad/The Hitman (uncut picture disc with insert)	100
91	Parlophone 12QUEENG 17	I'm Going Slightly Mad/The Hitman/Lost Opportunity (12", gatefold p/s)	15
91	Parlophone CDQUEEN 17	I'm Going Slightly Mad/The Hitman/Lost Opportunity (CD)	10
91	Parlophone 12QUEEN PD18	Headlong/All God's People/Mad The Swine (12", clear vinyl picture disc, with insert in PVC sleeve)	15
91	Parlophone CD QUEEN 18	Headlong/All God's People/Mad The Swine (CD)	10
91	Parlophone QUEEN 19	The Show Must Go On/Keep Yourself Alive (p/s)	5
91	Parlophone QUEEN C19	The Show Must Go On/Keep Yourself Alive (cassette)	25
91	Parlophone 12QUEENSG 19	The Show Must Go On/Keep Yourself Alive/Queen Talks (12", 1-sided, B-side etched with group's signatures, gatefold p/s)	18
91	Parlophone CDQUEEN 19	The Show Must Go On/Keep Yourself Alive/Queen Talks/Body Language (CD)	10
91	Parlophone CDQUEENS 19	The Show Must Go On/Now I'm Here/Fat Bottomed Girls/Las Palabras De Amor (The Words Of Love) (CD, in box with foldout poster, 10,000 only)	20
91	Parlophone QUEEN 19/20	The Show Must Go On/Bohemian Rhapsody (unissued, no p/s)	700
93	Parlophone CDR 6340	FIVE LIVE EP: Killer/Papa Was A Rolling Stone (PM Dawn Remix)/ Somebody To Love/These Are The Days Of Our Lives (as Queen featuring George Michael & Lisa Stansfield) (CD, picture disc, silver inlay)	8
95	Parlophone CDQUEENS 22	A Winter's Tale/Thank God It's Christmas/Rock In Rio Blues (CD, 'Merry Christmas' box)	8
96	Parlophone QUEEN 23	Too Much Love Will Kill You/We Will Rock You/We Are The Champions (p/s, pink vinyl)	6
96	Parlophone QUEENPD 24	Let Me Live/Fat Bottomed Girls/Bicycle Race (picture disc with poster)	6
97	Parlophone QUEEN 26	No-One But You (Only The Good Die Young)/Princes Of The Universe/ We Will Rock You (Rick Rubin 'Ruined' Remix)/ Gimme The Prize (Instrumental 'Eye' Remix) (unissued 7")	150
97	Parlophone QUEENPD 27	No-One But You (Only The Good Die Young)/We Will Rock You (Rick Rubin 'Ruined' Remix)/Tie Your Mother Down/Gimme The Prize (Instrumental 'Eye' Remix) (picture disc)	6

3" CD SINGLES

88	Parlophone QUECD 1	Seven Seas Of Rhye/See What A Fool I've Been/Funny How Love Is	12
88	Parlophone QUECD 2	Killer Queen/Flick Of The Wrist/Brighton Rock	12
88	Parlophone QUECD 3	Bohemian Rhapsody/I'm In Love With My Car/You're My Best Friend	12
88	Parlophone QUECD 4	Somebody To Love/White Man/Tie Your Mother Down	12
88	Parlophone QUECD 5	QUEEN'S FIRST EP: Good Old Fashioned Lover Boy/Death On Two Legs/ Tenement Funster/White Queen (As It Began)	12
88	Parlophone QUECD 6	We Are The Champions/We Will Rock You /Fat Bottomed Girls	12
88	Parlophone QUECD 7	Crazy Little Thing Called Love/Spread Your Wings/Flash	12
88	Parlophone QUECD 8	Another One Bites The Dust/Dragon Attack/Las Palabras De Amor	12
88	Parlophone QUECD 9	Under Pressure/Soul Brother/Body Language	12
88	Parlophone QUECD 10	Radio Ga Ga/I Go Crazy/Hammer To Fall	12
88	Parlophone QUECD 11	I Want To Break Free/Machines (Back To Humans)/It's A Hard Life	12
88	Parlophone QUECD 12	A Kind Of Magic/A Dozen Red Roses For My Darling/One Vision	12

(The above 3" CDs were all issued in card sleeves with generic plastic EMI outer packages.)

ALBUMS

78	EMI EMA 788	JAZZ (LP, gatefold sleeve with poster)	12
81	EMI EMTV 30	GREATEST HITS (LP, mispress, side 2 plays "Anne Murray's Greatest Hits")	15
85	EMI QB 1	THE COMPLETE WORKS (14-LP box set including "Complete Vision" LP of non-LP tracks, 2 booklets & map, numbered; 600 autographed)	1000+/100
86	EMI EU 3509	A KIND OF MAGIC ('Princes Of The Universe' proof sleeve; unreleased)	500
89	Band Of Joy BOJLP 001	QUEEN AT THE BEEB (LP)	15
91	Parlophone PMTV 2	GREATEST HITS 2 (2-LP, embossed gatefold sleeve)	25
91	Parlophone PCSD 115	INNUENDO (LP)	20
92	Parlophone PCSP 725	LIVE AT WEMBLEY (2-LP, gatefold sleeve)	35
92	Parlophone CDQTEL 0001	BOX OF TRIX (CD, box set, with video, book, poster, T-shirt, patch & badge)	60
92	Parlophone CQTEL 0001	BOX OF TRIX (cassette, box set, with video, book, poster, T-shirt, patch & badge)	45
95	Parlophone QUEEN BOX 20	ULTIMATE QUEEN (20 x CD set, in numbered glazed box and numbered cardboard outer box, with Freddie hologram and 2 booklets)	500

PROMOS

77	EMI SP SLP 241 A1U	We Will Rock You/We Are The Champions/Spread Your Wings (12", 1-sided)	600
78	EMI EMI 2375	Bohemian Rhapsody/I'm In Love With My Car (EMI 'Queen's Award For Export' in-house edition, blue vinyl, Queen crest label, hand-numbered, purple p/s)	3,500
78	EMI EMI 2375	Bohemian Rhapsody/I'm In Love With My Car (as above, with outer 'EMI International' carrying envelope)	3,800
78	EMI EMI 2375	Bohemian Rhapsody/I'm In Love With My Car (as above, with invites, matches, pen, ticket, menu, outer card sleeve, scarf & EMI goblets in card box)	5,000

(The blue vinyl "Bohemian Rhapsody" was limited to 200 numbered copies)

84	EMI QUEEN 1	Radio Ga Ga (Edit)/I Go Crazy ('video shoot' p/s, unreleased, proofs only)	650
84	EMI QUEENDJ 5	Man On The Prowl/Thank God It's Christmas	150
84	Flexi Ltd. (no cat. no.)	Excerpts From Their New Album 'The Works' (flexidisc sampler, p/s)	15
86	Parlophone EMCDV 2	THE HIGHLANDER SELECTION (CD Video, 50 only)	300
86	(no label or cat. no.)	A Message From Queen (cassette, 1st Fan Club Convention issue)	20
89	Flexi Ltd. (no cat. no.)	A Message From Queen (flexidisc, 4th Fan Club Convention issue)	25
89	Parlophone TEASER 1	THE TEASER TAPE (cassette, edits sampler for "The Miracle")	15
95	EMI QUEEN DJ95	Bohemian Rhapsody/I'm In Love With My Car (purple vinyl, hand numbered, p/s, 10th anniversary Fan Club Convention issue, 2,000 only)	200
95	Parlophone QUEENLHDJ 21	Heaven For Everyone (Album Version)/Heaven For Everyone (Single Version) (p/s, plain white sleeve, with poster, fold-out card & jukebox strip)	20
95	Parlophone QUEENDJ 22	A Winter's Tale/Thank God It's Christmas (jukebox issue, plain white sleeve, with jukebox strip)	10

96	Parlophone QUEENDJ 23	Too Much Love Will Kill You/We Are The Champions (jukebox issue, plain white sleeve, with jukebox strip)	10
96	Parlophone VIRGIN 1	Heaven For Everyone/Heaven For Everyone (12", white label, Virgin Radio 'Queen Day' competition prize, black 'Queen crest' p/s with handwritten details; mispressing with same track both sides, unreleased)	
96	Parlophone VIRGIN 2	Heaven For Everyone (12", 1-sided, white labels, Virgin Radio 'Queen Day' competition prize, 'Queen crest' p/s with handwritten details, 15 copies only)	600+
96	Parlophone VIRGIN 3	A Winter's Tale (12", 1-sided, white labels, Virgin Radio 'Queen Day' competition prize, 'Queen crest' p/s with handwritten details, 15 only)	600+
96	Parlophone VIRGIN 4	Mother Love (12", 1-sided, white labels, Virgin Radio 'Queen Day' competition prize, 'Queen crest' p/s with handwritten details, 15 only)	600+
96	Parlophone VIRGIN 5	Let Me Live (12", 1-sided, white labels, Virgin Radio 'Queen Day' competition prize, 'Queen crest' p/s with handwritten details, 15 only)	600+
96	Parlophone VIRGIN 6	You Don't Fool Me (12", 1-sided, white labels, Virgin Radio 'Queen Day' competition prize, 'Queen crest' p/s with handwritten details, 15 only)	600+
96	Parlophone VIRGIN 7	It's A Beautiful Day (12", 1-sided, white labels, Virgin Radio 'Queen Day' competition prize, 'Queen crest' p/s with handwritten details, 15 only)	600+
96	Parlophone VIRGIN 8	I Was Born To Love You (12", 1-sided, white labels, Virgin Radio 'Queen Day' competition prize, 'Queen crest' p/s with handwritten details, 15 only)	600+
99	EMI QUEENWL 28	Under Pressure (Remixes) (with David Bowie) (12", white label, unreleased mix, promo only)	60
99	EMI QUEEN DJ 28	Under Pressure (Rah Mix)/(Mike Spencer Mix)/The Show Must Go On (CD, card p/s, promo only)	15
73	EMI (no cat. no.)	QUEEN (LP, white label, EMI conference custom issue, die-cut sleeve, with/without outer envelope)	450/250
77	EMI (no cat. no.)	NEWS OF THE WORLD (LP, box set, with factory sample sticker, 5 photos, bio, badge & demo copy of "We Are The Champions"/ "We Will Rock You", 50 only)	500
91	Parlophone (no cat. no.)	HINTS OF INNUENDO (cassette, edits/out-takes sampler for "Innuendo")	30
91	Parlophone (no cat. no.)	EIGHT GOOD REASONS TO BUY GREATEST HITS 2 (cassette, segued excerpts)	30
91	Parlophone (no cat. no.)	A SAMPLE OF MAGIC (CD, segued excerpts from "Greatest Hits 2")	60
94	EMI CD DIG 1	DIGITAL MASTER SAMPLER (CD, picture disc)	45
97	Parlophone CDQT 1	QUEEN ROCKS (CD, Brian May interview)	75

MISPRESSINGS

75	EMI EMI 2378	Bohemian Rhapsody/I'm In Love With My Car (2nd issue, with incorrect cat. no.)	12
78	EMI EMI 2870	Bicycle Race/Fat Bottomed Girls (p/s, B-side plays Crystal Gayle's "3 O'Clock In The Morning" or Dollar track)	each 10
79	EMI EMI 2975	CLIFF RICHARD: We Don't Talk Anymore/Count Me Out (A-side plays "Bohemian Rhapsody")	12
79	EMI EMI 5001	Crazy Little Thing Called Love/We Will Rock You (live) (p/s, both sides play "We Will Rock You")	15
80	EMI EMI 5076	Play The Game/A Human Body (p/s, both sides play "A Human Body")	12
86	Parlophone RP 5452	BEATLES: Paperback Writer/Rain (picture disc, A-side plays "Friends Will Be Friends")	75

(see also Freddie Mercury, Brian May, Roger Taylor, Larry Lurex, Cross, Immortals, Hilary Hilary, Eddie Howell, Man Friday & Jive Junior)

QUEENS OF THE STONE AGE
| 98 | Roadrunner RR 8674-2 | QUEENS OF THE STONE AGE (LP) | 15 |
| 02 | Interscope 493435-2 | SONGS FOR THE DEAF (2 x LP, gatefold, red vinyl) | 18 |

QUEENSRYCHE
83	EMI America 12EA 162	Queens Of The Reich/Nightrider/Blinded/Lady Wore Black (12", p/s)	10
84	EMI America EA 183	Take Hold Of The Flame/Nightrider (p/s)	10
86	EMI America EA 22	Gonna Get Close To You/Prophecy (p/s)	10
86	EMI America EAD 22	Gonna Get Close To You/Prophecy//Queen Of The Reich (live)/ Deliverance (live) (double pack)	10
89	EMI USA 12MTG 65	Eyes Of A Stranger/Queen Of The Reich/Walk In The Shadows/ Take Hold Of The Flame (12", gatefold p/s)	12
88	EMI Manhattan 10QR 1	OVERSEEING THE OPERATION (10" EP)	10

? & THE MYSTERIANS
66	Cameo Parkway C 428	96 Tears/Midnight Hour	40
66	Cameo Parkway C 441	I Need Somebody/'8' Teen	25
67	Cameo Parkway C 467	Can't Get Enough Of You, Baby/Smokes	20
67	Cameo Parkway C 479	Girl (You Captivate Me)/Got To	20
67	Cameo Parkway C 496	Do Something To Me/Love Me Baby	20
76	London HLU 10534	96 Tears/'8' Teen	10

QUESTIONS
| 68 | Decca F 22740 | We Got Love/Something Wonderful | 25 |

QUESTIONS
| 86 | Respond KOBX 707 | Tuesday Sunshine (Jock Mix)/Tuesday Sunshine(Sass Mix)/The House That Jack Built/No One (Long Version) (12" p/s) | 8 |

TOMMY QUICKLY (& REMO FOUR)
63	Piccadilly 7N 35137	Tip Of My Tongue/Heaven Only Knows (solo)	20
63	Piccadilly 7N 35151	Kiss Me Now/No Other Love	5
64	Piccadilly 7N 35167	Prove It/Haven't You Noticed	5
64	Piccadilly 7N 35183	You Might As Well Forget Him/It's As Simple As That	5
64	Pye 7N 15708	The Wild Side Of Life/Forget The Other Guy	8
64	Pye 7N 15748	Humpty Dumpty/I'll Go Crazy	15

(see also Remo Four)

MINT VALUE £

QUICKSAND
70	Carnaby CNS 4015	Passing By/Cobblestones	8
73	Dawn DNS 1046	Time To Live/Empty Street, Empty Heart	6
74	Dawn DNLS 3056	HOME IS WHERE I BELONG (LP)	45

QUICKSILVER MESSENGER SERVICE
76	Capitol CL 15859	Gypsy Lights/Witches' Moon	5
68	Capitol (S)T 2904	QUICKSILVER MESSENGER SERVICE (LP, black label with rainbow rim)	40
69	Capitol E-(S)T 120	HAPPY TRAILS (LP)	20
70	Capitol E-ST 391	SHADY GROVE (LP)	18
70	Capitol EA-ST 498	JUST FOR LOVE (LP)	15
71	Capitol EA-ST 630	WHAT ABOUT ME? (LP)	15
72	Capitol E-SW 819	QUICKSILVER (LP)	12
72	Capitol EA-ST 11002	COMIN' THRU (LP)	12
75	Capitol E-ST 11462	SOLID SILVER (LP)	12
83	Psycho PSYCHO 10	MAIDEN OF THE CANCER MOON (2-LP)	40

(see also Dino Valenti, Nicky Hopkins)

QUICKSPACE (SUPERSPORT)
94	Love Train PUBE 04	Found A Way/Do It My Own Way (12", p/s, 1,500 only)	15
95	Kitty Kitty Corp. CHOOSY 1	Quickspace Happy Song (1)/Unique Slippy (as Quickspace Supersport, hand painted/stamped p/s, 1000 only)	6
96	Kitty Kitty Corp. CHOOSY 4	Friend/Good Timez (as Quickspace, painted wallpaper sleeve, 500 only)	6
97	Kitty Kitty Corp. CHOOSY 8	QUICKSPACE (LP, die-cut spray-painted sleeve, 1000 only)	12

QUIET FIVE
65	Parlophone R 5273	When The Morning Sun Dries The Dew/Tomorrow I'll Be Gone (some in p/s)	20/10
65	Parlophone R 5302	Honeysuckle Rose/Let's Talk It Over	8
66	Parlophone R 5421	Homeward Bound/Ain't It Funny What Some Lovin' Can Do	15
66	Parlophone R 5470	I Am Waiting/What About The Time For Me	10
67	CBS 202586	Goodnight Sleep Tight/Just For Tonight	6

(see also Kris Ife, Patrick Dane, Richard Barnes)

QUIET SUN
75	Island HELP 19	MAINSTREAM (LP)	15

(see also Phil Manzanera, Roxy Music)

QUIET WORLD
69	Dawn DNS 1001	Miss Whittington/There Is A Mountain (as Quiet World Of Lea & John)	30
70	Dawn DNS 1005	Children Of The World/Love Is Walking	30
70	Pye 7N 45005	Rest Comfortably/Gemima	12
71	Pye 7N 45074	Visitor/Sam	10
70	Dawn DNLS 3007	THE ROAD (LP)	70

(see also Steve Hackett, Genesis)

QUIK
67	Deram DM 121	Love Is A Beautiful Thing/Bert's Apple Crumble	100
67	Deram DM 139	King Of The World/My Girl	35
67	Deram DM 155	I Can't Sleep/Soul Full Of Sorrow	30
98	Klooks Kleek 60	Bert's Apple Crumble/THE SONICS: The Witch	5

(see also Meddy Evils)

QUILLER
75	BBC RESL 25	Quiller/General Direction	5

PAUL QUINCHETTE
57	Esquire 32-057	ON THE SUNNY SIDE (LP)	40

QUINCICASM
73	Saydisc SDL 249	QUINCICASM (LP)	20

ANTHONY QUINN
70	Capitol CL 15649	I Love You And You Love Me/Sometimes (I Just Can't Stand You)	5

MIKE QUINN
66	Fontana TF 761	Someone's Slipping Into My Mind/I Know What You Know	7
69	CBS 4506	Apple Pie/There's A Time	6
69	Jay Boy BOY 7	Toothbrush Nell/Fairy Cakes	5

PAUL QUINN & EDWYN COLLINS
84	Swamplands SWP 1	Pale Blue Eyes (Edited Version)/Burro (p/s)	5
84	Swamplands SWX 1	Pale Blue Eyes/Pale Blues Eyes (Western)/Burro (12", original with 'film' p/s, inner sleeve & yellow obi)	10/7

(see also Edwyn Collins, Orange Juice)

QUINTESSENCE
70	Island WIP 6075	Notting Hill Gate/Move Into The Light	7
71	Neon NE 1003	Sweet Jesus/You Never Stay The Same (some in p/s)	15/6
69	Island ILPS 9110	IN BLISSFUL COMPANY (LP, pink label)	40
70	Island ILPS 9128	QUINTESSENCE (LP, pink label)	35
70	Island ILPS 9143	DIVE DEEP (LP)	20
72	RCA SF 8273	SELF (LP)	15
72	RCA SF 8317	INDWELLER (LP)	15

(see also Kala)

QUINTET OF HOT CLUB OF FRANCE
53	Decca LF 1139	SWING FROM PARIS (10" LP)	15

(see also Django Reinhardt)

QUINTET OF THE YEAR
54	Vogue L.D.E. 087	JAZZ AT THE MASSAY HALL VOL. 3 (10" LP)	18

QUIREBOYS
90	Parlophone RPD 6248	I Don't Love You Anymore/Mayfair (Original Version) (uncut shaped picture disc)	22

(see also Wildhearts)

DARYL QUIST
63	Pye 7N 15538	Thanks To You/Keep Moving (some in p/s)	10/6
63	Pye 7N 15563	Goodbye To Love/All Through The Night	7
64	Pye 7N 15605	True To You/Above And Beyond	7
64	Pye 7N 15656	See The Funny Little Clown/When She Comes To You	7
65	Decca F 12058	Put Away Your Teardrops/Across The Street	7

QUIVER
72	Warner Bros K 16165	Green Tree/I Might Stumble	6
71	Warner Bros K 46089	QUIVER (LP)	18
72	Warner Bros K 46153	GONE IN THE MORNING (LP)	20

(see also Bridget St. John, Natural Gas, Village)

QUODLING'S DELIGHT
76	Fanfare FR 2179	AMONG THE LEAVES SO GREEN (LP)	25

QUOTATIONS (U.K.)
64	Decca F 11907	Alright Baby/Love You All Over Again	22
68	CBS 3710	Cool It/Mark Of Her Head	12
69	CBS 4378	Hello Memories/Pretend	7

(see also Fleur De Lys, Johnny B. Great, Johnny Gustafson, Merseybeats, Johnny Goodison)

QUOTATIONS (U.S.)
61	HMV POP 975	Imagination/Ala Men Say	125

QUOTING MARX
77	Full Stop PUNC 28	Opening And Closing/66 And 99	12

QUO VARDIS
(see under Vardis)

RABBI JOSEPH GORDAN
85	Bam Caruso Intl. NRICO 30	Competition/Belief In Him (large centre hole, plain beige sleeve)	15

(see also Julian Cope)

RABBIT
73	Island ILPS 9238	BROKEN ARROWS (LP)	15
74	Island ILPS 9289	DARK SALOON (LP)	15

(see also Free; Kossoff, Kirke, Tetsu & Rabbit)

RABID
82	Fallout FALL 007	BLOODY ROAD TO GLORY (EP)	5

MIKE RABIN (& DEMONS)
64	Columbia DB 7350	Head Over Heels/Leaving You (as Mike Rabin & Demons)	75
65	Polydor BM 56007	If I Were You/What Do You Do	22

OSCAR RABIN & HIS BAND
53	Polygon P 1086	Crazy Man Crazy/Forgive Me (B-side with Mel Gaynor) (78)	8

(see also David Ede Band)

JOSEPH RACAILLE
80s	Recommended RRA 16.5	6 PETITES CHANSONS (EP, clear vinyl, foldaround p/s)	6

STEVE RACE
61	Parlophone R 4808	Crosstrap/Stop Look Listen	8
63	World Records TP 285	DANCE TO THE TV THEMES (LP)	15
65	World Records TP 453	TAKE ONE (LP)	12
65	World Records (S)TP 456	LATE RACE (LP, mono/stereo)	12
66	Studio Two TWO 137	STEVE RACE (LP, stereo)	12

RACE FANS
68	Trojan TR 610	Bookie Man/UNIQUES: More Love	30

YANK RACHELL TENNESSEE JUG BUSTERS
64	'77' LA 12-23	MANDOLIN BLUES (LP)	22

RACONTEURS
XL	XLS 227	Steady As She Goes/Store Bought Bones (1,000 only, p/s)	20

(see also White Stripes)

RADAR
83	House Of Wax WAX 1	Leave Her Alone/Reach For The Sky (p/s)	22

JIMMY RADCLIFFE
65	Stateside SS 374	Long After Tonight Is Over/What I Want I Can Never Have (DJ copy = £175)	60
73	Pye International 7N 25614	Long After Tonight Is Over/What I Want I Can Never Have (reissue)	12
77	DJM DJS 10772	Long After Tonight Is Over/What I Want I Can Never Have (2nd reissue)	6

(see also Steve Karmen Big Band)

RADHA KRISHNA
71	Columbia SCX 6462	RADHA KRISHNA (LP, composed & directed by John Mayer)	40

(see also John Mayer)

RADHA KRISHNA TEMPLE (LONDON)
69	Apple APPLE 15	Hare Krishna Mantra/Prayer To The Spiritual Masters (p/s, as Radha Krishna Temple [London], some with insert)	25/8
69	Apple APPLE 15	Hare Krishna Mantra/Prayer To The Spiritual Masters (no p/s, as Radha Krishna Temple [London])	6
70	Apple APPLE 25	Govinda/Govinda Jai Jai (p/s)	35
70	Apple APPLE 25	Govinda/Govinda Jai Jai (some in company sleeve)	12/5
71	Apple SAPCOR 18	THE RADHA KRISHNA TEMPLE (LP, gatefold sleeve, some with insert)	45/40
93	Apple SAPCOR 18	THE RADHA KRISHNA TEMPLE (LP, reissue, gatefold sleeve with inner)	15
93	Apple SAPCOR 18	THE RADHA KRISHNA TEMPLE (CD)	18

RADIANTS
64	Chess CRS 8002	Voice Your Choice/If I Only Had You (DJ copy = £50)	30
68	Chess CRS 8073	Hold On/I'm Glad I'm The Loser (DJ copy = £50)	20

(see also Maurice & Mac, Caston & Majors)

RADIATORS (FROM SPACE)
77	Chiswick S 10	Television Screen/Love Detective (p/s, original issue)	5
77	Chiswick NS 19	Enemies/Psychotic Reaction (p/s)	5
78	Chiswick NS 24	Prison Bars/(Why Can't I Be A) Teenager In Love (unreleased, promo only white label in stamped white sleeve & loose printed labels)	40
79	Chiswick NS 45	Walkin' Home Alone Again/Try And Stop Me/The Hucklebuck (unreleased; white label test pressings exist with loose labels; as Radiators)	40
79	Chiswick CHIS 115	Kitty Ricketts/Ballad Of The Faithful Departed (company sleeve)	8
77	Chiswick WIK 4	TV TUBE HEART (LP)	12

(see also Pogues)

MARK RADICE
72	Paramount PARA 3024	Hey My Love/Your Love Is Like Fire	6
72	Paramount PARA 3025	New Day/Take Me To The Park	6
72	Paramount SPFA 7004	MARK RADICE (LP)	12

RADIO ACTORS
79	Charly CYS 1058	Nuclear Waste/Digital Love (p/s, reissue of Fast Breeder & Radio Actors single, 2 slightly different label designs)	5
79	DB DBS 5	Nuclear Waste/Digital Love (different p/s, 2nd reissue)	5

(see also Fast Breeder & Radio Actors, Sting, Newcastle Big Band, Police, Gilli Smyth, Inner City Unit, Steve Hillage, Sphynx)

RADIO BIRDMAN
78	Sire 6078 617	What Gives/Anglo Girl Desire	10
78	Sire 9103 332	RADIOS APPEAR (LP, with inner sleeve)	25
78	Sire SRK 6050	RADIOS APPEAR (LP, reissue)	12

RADIOHEAD
92	Parlophone TCR 6312	DRILL EP (Prove Yourself/Stupid Car/You/Thinking About You) (cassette, 3,000 only)	50
92	Parlophone 12R 6312	DRILL EP (Prove Yourself/Stupid Car/You/Thinking About You) (12", p/s, 3,000 only)	125
92	Parlophone CDR 6312	DRILL EP (Prove Yourself/Stupid Car/You/Thinking About You) (CD, 3,000 only)	200
92	Parlophone TCR 6078	Creep/Lurgee/Inside My Head/Million $ Question (cassette, 6,000 only)	15
92	Parlophone 12R 6078	Creep/Lurgee/Inside My Head/Million $ Question (12", p/s, 6,000 only)	20
92	Parlophone CDR 6078	Creep/Lurgee/Inside My Head/Million $ Question (CD, 6,000 only)	60
93	Parlophone TCR 6333	Anyone Can Play Guitar/Faithless, The Wonder Boy/Coke Babies (cassette)	5
93	Parlophone 12R 6333	Anyone Can Play Guitar/Faithless, The Wonder Boy/Coke Babies (12", p/s)	30
93	Parlophone CDR 6333	Anyone Can Play Guitar/Faithless, The Wonder Boy/Coke Babies (CD)	50
93	Parlophone 12R 6345	Pop Is Dead/Banana Co. (Acoustic)/Creep (live)/Ripcord (live) (12", g/fold p/s)	30
93	Parlophone CDR 6345	Pop Is Dead/Banana Co. (Acoustic)/Creep (live)/Ripcord (live) (CD)	50
93	Parlophone RS 6359	Creep/Yes I Am/Blow Out (Remix)/Inside My Head (live) (p/s, clear vinyl)	28
93	Parlophone 12RG 6359	U.S. LIVE EP (Creep [Acoustic KROQ]/You [live]/Vegetable [live]/Killer Cars [live]) (12", numbered gatefold p/s)	20
93	Parlophone CDR 6359	Creep/Yes I Am/Blow Out (Remix)/Inside My Head (live) (CD, digipak)	30
94	Parlophone 12R 6394	My Iron Lung/Punchdrunk Lovesick Singalong/The Trickster/Lewis (Mistreated) (12", numbered p/s)	15
94	Parlophone CDRS 6394	My Iron Lung/Punchdrunk Lovesick Singalong/Lozenge Of Love (CD)	15
94	Parlophone CDR 6394	My Iron Lung/The Trickster/Lewis (Mistreated)/Permanent Daylight/You Never Wash Up After Yourself (CD)	15
95	Parlophone 12R 6405	Planet Telex/(remixes)/High & Dry (12", limited edition, numbered p/s)	15
95	Parlophone TCR 6405	High & Dry/Planet Telex (cassette, 2/95)	6
95	Parlophone CDR 6405	Planet Telex/High & Dry/Killer Cars/Planet Telex (LFO JD Mix) (CD,2 of 2-CD set)	12
95	Parlophone CDRS 6405	High & Dry/Planet Telex/Maquiladora/Planet Telex (Hexidecimal Mix) (CD)	8
95	Parlophone CDRS 6411	Fake Plastic Trees/India Rubber/How Can I Be Sure? (1 of 2 CD set)	12
95	Parlophone CDR 6411	Fake Plastic Trees/Fake Plastic Trees (Acoustic)/Bulletproof (...I Wish I Was) (Acoustic)/Street Spirit (Fade Out) (Acoustic) (CD, 2 of 2-CD set)	10
95	Parlophone CDR 6411	Fake Plastic Trees/Fake Plastic Trees (Acoustic)/Bulletproof (...I Wish I Was) (Acoustic)/Street Spirit (Fade Out) (Acoustic) (CD, with poster)	10
95	Parlophone CDR 6415	Just/Bones (live)/Planet Telex (live)/Anyone Can Play Guitar (live) (CD, box set with 2 prints)	15
95	Parlophone 8 83115 2	The Bends/My Iron Lung (Live At Forum)/Bones (Live At Forum) (CD, for export to Ireland, slimline jewel case)	20
95	Parlophone 8 83115 2	The Bends/My Iron Lung (Live At Forum)/Bones (Live At Forum) (CD, for export to Ireland, mispressed with "Planet Telex" instead of "The Bends", slimline jewel case)	30
96	Parlophone R 6419	Street Spirit (Fade Out)/Bishop's Robes (die-cut p/s, white vinyl)	10
96	Parlophone R 6419LH	Street Spirit (Fade Out)/Bishop's Robes (jukebox issue, black vinyl)	15
96	Parlophone CDRS 6419	Street Spirit (Fade Out)/Talk Show Host/Bishop's Robes (CD, with poster)	15

97	Parlophone NODATA 01	Paranoid Android/Polyethelene (Parts 1 & 2) (blue vinyl, die-cut p/s) 15
97	Parlophone NODATALH 03	Karma Police (Album Version)/Lull (jukebox issue, black vinyl) 12
97	Parlophone 12NODATA 03	Karma Police/Meeting Up The Aisle/Climbing Up The Walls (Zero 7 Mix) (12", p/s) 12
97	Parlophone NODATALH 04	No Surprises/Palo Alto (jukebox issue, black vinyl) 12
98	Parlophone 12NODATA 04	No Surprises/Palo Alto (12", p/s) 15
93	Parlophone PCS 7360	PABLO HONEY (LP) 15
95	Parlophone PCS 7372	THE BENDS (2xLP) 15
97	Parlophone NODATA 02	OK COMPUTER (2xLP) 15
00	Parlophone LPKIDA	KID A (2xLP 10") 15
01	Parlophone LPFHEIT 45101	AMNESIAC (2xLP, 10") 15
01	Parlophone CDKIDA 4	KID A (CD, in 6"x 6" hardback book) 30
01	Parlophone 12FHEIT 45104	I MIGHT BE WRONG (mini-LP) 12
03	Parlophone 5848052	HAIL TO THE THIEF (CD, limited issue, with foldout map) 18

PROMOS

92	Parlophone 12RDJ 6078	Creep/Lurgee/Inside My Head/Million Dollar Question (12", die-cut sleeve) 100
92	Parlophone 12CDRDJ 6078	Creep (Radio Version)/Lurgee/Inside My Head/Million Dollar Question (CD) 80
93	Parlophone 12RDJ 6369	Ripcord/Prove Yourself/Faithless, The Wonderboy/ Stop Whispering (Album Version) (12", p/s) 100
93	Parlophone CDRDJ 6345	Pop Is Dead/Banana Co. (live)/Creep (live)/Ripcord (live) (CD) 75
93	Parlophone CDRDJ 6359	Creep (CD, picture disc) 50
93	Parlophone CDRDJ 6369	Stop Whispering (U.S. Version)/Prove Yourself/Lurgee (CD, promo only, card p/s & inner sleeve) 15
93	Parlophone (no cat. No.)	Stop Whispering (U.S. Version – Chris Sheldon Remix)/Creep (Acoustic)/ Pop Is Dead/Inside My Head (Live) (CD) 20
94	Parlophone (no cat. no.)	PLANET TELEX: LFO & Hexidecimal mixes (12") 25
94	Parlophone 12RSDJ 6394	My Iron Lung/Lozenge Of Love/The Trickster/Punchdrunk Lovesick Singalong (12", die-cut red or blue sleeve) 25/20
94	Parlophone 12RSDJ 6394	My Iron Lung/Lewis (Mistreated)/Permanent Daylight/You Never Wash Up After Yourself (12" die-cut red sleeve) 25/20
95	Parlophone 12RDJ 6405	CLUB MIX DJ: PLANET TELEX (Album version)/Hexadecimal Mix)/L.F.O DJ Mix)/Trashed Mix) (12") 18
95	Parlophone 12RDJ 6411	Fake Plastic Trees/India Rubber/How Can I Be Sure? (12", die-cut sleeve) 30
95	Parlophone 12RDJ 6411	Fake Plastic Trees (Edit) (Album Version) (CD) 15
95	Parlophone 12RDJ 6145	Just/Planet Telex/Killer Cars (12", die-cut sleeve) 20
95	Parlophone 12RDJ 6145	Just/Planet Telex (Karma Sun Ra Mix)Killer Cars (Mogadon Version) (12") 25
95	Parlophone CDRDJ 6415	Just (Album Version)/(Edit Version) (CD, custom sleeve) 8
95	Parlophone HIGH-1	High & Dry (1-track CD, custom sleeve) 30
95	Parlophone RHEAD US 1	JUST FOR COLLEGE: India Rubber/Maquiladora/How Can I Be Sure?/ Just (CD) 100
96	Parlophone 12RDJ 6419	Street Spirit (Fade Out)/Talk Show Host/Bishop's Robes (12", promo-only) . . . 20
96	Parlophone CDRDJ 6419	Street Spirit (Fade Out)/Talk Show Host/Bishop's Robes (CD) 20
97	EMI (no cat. no.)	Airbag (1-track Abbey Road CD-R w/mini bio and title sleeve) 20
98	Parlophone 12DATADJO3	Climbing Up The Walls (Zero 7 Mix)/(Fila Brazilia Mix) (1-sided 12", 200 only) . . . 70
98	12RDJ 6333	Anyone Can Play Guitar/Faithless, The Wonder Boy/Coke Babies (12", die-cut sleeve) 80
00	Parlophone 12KIDA 6	Idioteque (12", white label test pressing, p/s) 40
97	Parlophone 724385522925	OK COMPUTER (stickered jewel case, printed disc, mispressing plays Deep Purple's 'The Collection') 30
97	Parlophone (no cat. no.)	OK COMPUTER (cassette, in customized jiffy bag) . . . .
97	Parlophone (no cat. no.)	OK COMPUTER (promo Aiwa personal stereo, glued-in cassette, two stickers) 150
97	Parlophone CDPP 005	OK COMPUTER (CD, numbered title sleeve) 70
97	Parlophone NODATA 02	OK COMPUTER (EPK, with CD & video in polystyrene case in jiffy bag) 60
00	Parlophone CDKIDA 3	KID A (CD, card title sleeve) 15
01	Parlophone AMNESIAC 01	AMNESIAC (CD, 4-track sampler in card p/s) 15
01	Parlophone AMNESIAC 02	AMNESIAC (CD, in facsmile library book, with press release & inserts) 30
03	Parlophone 12RDJWL 6623	SKTTERBRAIN (Four Tet Mix)/REMYXOMOTOSIS (Super Collider Mix) (12", 100 only) 60
03	Parlophone LC 0299	INTERVIEW CD (p/s, 22 track promo for HAIL TO THE THIEF) 20
	(see also Headless Chickens)	

RADIO HEART

87	GFM GFMP 109	Radio Heart/Radio Heart (Instrumental) (picture disc) 10
87	GFM GFMG 109	Radio Heart/Radio Heart (Instrumental) (radio-shaped picture disc) 10
87	GFM GFMP 112	London Times/Rumour (picture disc) 5
87	GFM GFMX 112	London Times/Rumour (oblong picture disc) 6
87	NBR NBRL 1	RADIO HEART (LP, withdrawn) 12
	(see also Gary Numan)	

RADIO JAZZ

82	Formosa FORM1-12	Tired of Calling/Can't Dance For Loving You (12") 8

RADIO MOSCOW

87	Status RM 100	Hand Of Freedom (p/s) 8
91	Status RMLP 103	WORLD SERVICE (LP) 15
92	Status RMLP 104	GET A NEW LIFE (LP) 15

RADIO 9

90s	Enraptured RAPT 1031	Motorik/Fluid/Moving In Two Directions/Pianosong (10", 9 only) 15

RADIOPHONIC WORKSHOP

73	BBC RESL 13	Moonbase 3/World Of Dr. Who 20
	(see also BBC Radiophonic Workshop)	

RADIO STARS

78	Chiswick NS 36	From A Rabbit/To A Beast (6" 'hip pocket' issue, p/s) 5
	(see also John's Children, Andy Ellison, Trevor White)	

MINT VALUE £

RAELET(T)S
67	HMV POP 1591	One Hurt Deserves Another/One Room Paradise (as Raelets) 30
71	Tangerine 6121 002	Bad Water/That Goes To Show You 5
71	Tangerine 6121 003	Here I Go Again/Leave My Man (Woman) Alone 5

(see also Ray Charles, Clydie King, Merry Clayton)

GERRY RAFFERTY
| 71 | Transatlantic TRA 241 | CAN I HAVE MY MONEY BACK? (LP) . . . . 12 |

(see also Humblebums, Fifth Column)

RAG DOLLS (U.K.)
| 67 | Columbia DB 8289 | Never Had So Much Loving/Any Little Bit . . . . 10 |
| 68 | Columbia DB 8378 | My Old Man's A Groovy Old Man/They Didn't Believe Me . . . . 10 |

(see also Marionettes, Peanut, Katie Kissoon, Mac Kissoon)

RAG DOLLS (U.S.)
| 64 | Cameo Parkway P 921 | Society Girl/Ragen (with Caliente Combo) . . . . 20 |
| 65 | Stateside SS 398 | Dusty/Hey Hoagy . . . . 35 |

RAGE
80	Carrere CAR 159	Money/Thank That Woman (p/s) 8
80	Carrere CAR 159CT	Money/Thank That Woman (10", red vinyl, stickered clear sleeve) 12
81	Carrere CAR 182	Out Of Control/Double Dealer (p/s) 5
81	Carrere CAR 182CT	Out Of Control (Extended Version)/Double Dealer (12", yellow vinyl, PVC sleeve) . 15
83	Carrere CAR 304	Cry From A Hill (p/s) 10
81	Carrere CAL 124	OUT OF CONTROL (LP) 12
82	Carrere CAL 138	NICE N' DIRTY (LP) 12
83	Carrere CAL 149	RUN FOR THE NIGHT (LP) 12

(see also Nutz)

RAGE
86	Diamond RAGE 1	Looking For You/Come On Now (p/s) 5
86	Diamond RAGE 112	Looking For You/Come On Now/Great Balls Of Fire/Hallelujah I Love Her So
		(12", unissued, test pressings only) 25

(see also Case, Long Tall Shorty, Purple Hearts, Chords)

RAGE AGAINST THE MACHINE
93	Epic 658 492-6	Killing In The Name/Clear The Lane/Darkness Of Greed (12" white vinyl p/s) 10
93	Epic 659 258-6	Bullet In The Head (Remix)/Bullet In The Head (Album Version)
		Settle For Nothing (live) (12" picture disc, p/s) 8
96	Epic 663 152-7	Bulls On Parade/Hadda Be Playing On The Jukebox (red vinyl) 10

RAGGAMUFFINS
| 67 | London HLU 10134 | Four Days Of Rain/It Wasn't Happening At All. . . . . 10 |

RAGGED HEROES
| 83 | Celtic CM 013 | ANNUAL (LP) . . . . 25 |

RAGING STORMS
| 62 | London HLU 9556 | The Dribble/Hound Dog . . . . 15 |

LOU RAGLAND
| 73 | Warner Bros K 16312 | Since You Said You'd Be Mine/I Didn't Mean To Love You . . . . 50 |

RAGPICKERS
| 59 | Saga SAG 45-2906 | Fifi/Cat On A Cool Tin Roof (p/s) . . . . 7 |

(see also Bert Weedon)

RAIDER OF THE LOST DUB
| 81 | Island ILPS 9705 | RAIDERS OF THE LOST DUB (LP) (withdrawn due to legal action) . . . . 40 |

RAINBEAUS
| 60 | Vogue V 9161 | That's All I'm Asking Of You/Maybe It's Wrong (triangular centre) . . . . 160 |

(RITCHIE BLACKMORE'S) RAINBOW
74	Oyster OYR 103	Man On The Silver Mountain/Snake Charmer (as Ritchie Blackmore's Rainbow) . . 8
77	Polydor 2066 845	Kill The King (live)/Man On The Silver Mountain (live)/Mistreated (live) (p/s) 6
78	Polydor 2066 913	Long Live Rock'n'Roll/Sensitive To Light (p/s) 5
78	Polydor 2066 968	L.A. Connection/Lady Of The Lake (p/s, initially on red vinyl) 10/5
82	Polydor POSPX 421	Stone Cold/Rock Fever (12", some on blue vinyl) 10/8
83	Polydor POSP 631	Street Of Dreams/Anybody There? (p/s) 5
83	Polydor POSPP 631	Street Of Dreams/Anybody There? (picture disc, 2000 only) 20
83	Polydor POSPX 631	Street Of Dreams/Anybody There?/Power (live) (12", p/s) 10
83	Polydor POSP 654	Can't Let You Go/All Night Long (live) (p/s) 5
83	Polydor POSPP 654	Can't Let You Go/All Night Long (live) (guitar-shaped picture disc) 15
83	Polydor POSPX 654	Can't Let You Go/All Night Long (live)/Stranded (live) (12", p/s) 10
75	Oyster OYA 2001	RITCHIE BLACKMORE'S RAINBOW (LP, gatefold sleeve,
		as Ritchie Blackmore's Rainbow) 12
77	Polydor 2808 010 010	RAINBOW ON STAGE (LP, music & interview disc, with insert, promo only) 75
79	Polydor POLD 5023	DOWN TO EARTH (LP, clear vinyl, with inner sleeve) 15

(see also Ritchie Blackmore,Deep Purple, Elf, Dio, Graham Bonnet, Cozy Powell, Roger Glover, Wild Horses, Tony Carey)

CHRIS RAINBOW
81	EMI 12EMI 5215	Body Music/Girl In Collision (12", p/s) 12
81	EMI 5215-6	Body Music/Girl In Collision (p/s) 6
75	Polydor 2383 338	HOME OF THE BRAVE (LP, with lyric inner sleeve) 18
78	Polydor 2383 467	LOOKING OVER MY SHOULDER (LP, with lyric inner sleeve) 20
79	EMI EMC 3305	WHITE TRAILS (LP) 15

RAINBOW FAMILY
| 72 | President PT 375 | Travellin' Lady/My Father . . . . 35 |

RAINBOW FFOLLY
| 68 | Parlophone R 5701 | Go Girl/Drive My Car . . . . 60 |
| 67 | Parlophone PMC/PCS 7050 | SALLIES FFORTH (LP) . . . . 220 |

(see also Love Affair)

RAINBOW PEOPLE
68	Pye 7N 17582	Walk'll Do You Good/Dream Time	15
68	Pye 7N 17624	The Sailing Song/Rainbows	10
69	Pye 7N 17759	Living In A Dream World/Happy To See You Again	20

RAINBOWS
69	CBS 3995	Rainbows/Nobody But You	20
69	CBS 4568	New Day Dawning/Days And Nights	25

(see also Peeps, Martin Cure & Peeps)

RAINCOATS
79	Rough Trade ROUGH 3	THE RAINCOATS (LP, with lyric booklet)	15

(see also Slits)

RAINCHECKS
64	Solar SRP 104	Something About You/You're My Angel	18
65	R&B MRB 5002	How Are You Boy/Bye Bye Baby	35

RAINDROPS (U.K.)
59	Parlophone R 4559	Italian Style/Along Came Jones	10
60	Oriole CB 1544	Let's Make A Foursome/If I Had My Life To Live Over (78 rpm = £7)	12
60	Oriole CB 1555	Banjo Boy/Crazy Rhythm	10
61	Oriole CB 1595	Will You Love Me Tomorrow/Raindrops	12
62	Oriole CB 1707	Paintin' The Town With Teardrops/A Letter From Anne	10
67	CBS 202669	Foolman/Got To Find A Reason (credited to Raindrops '67)	10

(see also Jackie & Raindrops, Jackie Lee, Jacky, Emma Rede, Vince Hill)

RAINDROPS (U.S.)
63	London HL 9718	What A Guy/It's So Wonderful	20
63	London HL 9769	The Kind Of Boy You Can't Forget/Even Though You Can't Dance	25
64	London HL 9825	That Boy John/Hanky Panky	20
64	Fontana TF 463	The Book Of Love/I Won't Cry	20
64	London RE 1415	WHAT A GUY (EP)	110
64	London HA 8140	THE RAINDROPS (LP)	100

(see also Ellie Greenwich, Popsicles)

CLAIRE RAINE
68	Jolly JY 010	La-La-La/I Want You	8

LORRY RAINE
51	London L 899	Spin The Bottle/Who'll Take My Place When I'm Gone (78)	8
51	London L 1081	Sometime, Somewhere/Why Cry (78)	8
53	London L 1220	I've Gotta Have Love/A Wooin' We Will Go (78)	10
54	London HL 8043	You Broke My Broken Heart/I'm In Love With A Guy (78 rpm = £8)	28
55	London HL 8132	Love Me Tonight/What Would I Do (78 rpm = £10)	40

MA RAINEY
50	Jazz Collector L 16	Don't Fish My Sea/Soon This Morning (78)	10
50	Jazz Collector L 20	Jealous Hearted Blues/See See Rider Blues (78)	10
50	Jazz Collector L 35	Blues The World Forgot (Parts 1 & 2) (78)	10
50	Jazz Collector L 42	New Bo-Weavil Blues/Moonshine Blues (78)	10
50	Jazz Collector L 48	Barrel House Blues/Walking Blues (78)	10
50	Jazz Collector L 52	Misery Blues/Dead Drunk Blues (78)	10
50	Jazz Collector L 57	Morning Hour Blues/Weepin' Woman Blues (78)	10
50	Jazz Collector L 66	Moonshine Blues/Southern Blues (78)	10
51	Jazz Collector L 73	Stack O'Lee Blues/Yonder Come The Blues (78)	10
52	Jazz Collector L 78	Those Dogs Of Mine/Lucky Rock Blues (78)	10
52	Jazz Collector L 82	Honey Where Have You Been So Long/Ma Rainey's Mystery Record (78)	10
52	Jazz Collector L 87	Slave To The Blues/Oh My Babe Blues (78)	10
52	Jazz Collector L 98	Blues Oh Blues/Oh Papa Blues (78)	10
54	Jazz Collector L 107	Lawd Send Me A Man Blues/South Bound Blues (78)	10
55	Jazz Collector L 120	Gone Daddy Blues/Slow Driving Moan (78)	10
50s	Signature 908	Yonder Come The Blues/Stack O'Lee Blues (78)	10
53	London AL 3502	MA RAINEY VOLUME 1 (10" LP)	50
55	London AL 3538	MA RAINEY VOLUME 2 (10" LP)	50
56	London AL 3558	MA RAINEY VOLUME 3 (10" LP)	50
50s	Ristic LP 13	MA RAINEY (10" LP)	50
50s	Ristic LP 19	MA RAINEY (10" LP)	50
62	Riverside RL 12-108	MA RAINEY SINGS THE BLUES (LP)	25
64	Riverside RLP 8807	MOTHER OF THE BLUES (LP, gatefold sleeve with booklet)	25
70	CBS 52798	MA RAINEY AND THE CLASSIC BLUES SINGERS (LP)	15

MA RAINEY & IDA COX
60	Jazz Collector JEL 12	THE FEMALE BLUES VOL. 1 (EP)	20
64	Jazz Collector JEL 22	THE FEMALE BLUES VOL. 3 (EP, with Trixie Smith)	20

(see also Ida Cox, Tommy Ladnier)

MA RAINEY & PAPA CHARLIE JACKSON
50s	Poydras 11	Ma And Papa Poorhouse Blues/Big Feeling Blues	15

RAIN PARADE
83	Enigma BOB 4/LYN 15263	Sad Eyes Kill (3.16) (1-sided flexi with Bucketfull Of Brains mag, issue 10)	6
83	Enigma BOB 4/LYN 15263	Sad Eyes Kill (3.16) (hard vinyl white label test pressing)	12

MARVIN RAINWATER
55	MGM SP 1150	Tennessee Houn' Dog Yodel/Albino (Pink-Eyed) Stallion	65
55	MGM SP 876	Tennessee Houn' Dog Yodel/Albino (Pink-Eyed) Stallion (78)	15
56	MGM MGM 929	What Am I Supposed To Do/Why Did You Have To Go And Leave Me	30
56	MGM MGM 929	What Am I Supposed To Do/Why Did You Have To Go And Leave Me (78)	10
57	MGM MGM 961	Gonna Find Me A Bluebird/So You Think You've Got (78 rpm = £12)	30
58	MGM MGM 974	Whole Lotta Woman/Baby, Don't Go	5
58	MGM MGM 980	I Dig You Baby/Two Fools In Love (B-side with Sister Patty)	5

Marvin RAINWATER

58	MGM MGM 988	Dance Me Daddy/Because I'm A Dreamer (B-side with Sister Patty) (78 rpm = £12)	8
59	MGM MGM 1030	Half-Breed/A Song Of New Love (78 rpm = £22)	12
60	MGM MGM 1052	Nothin' Needs Nothin' (Like I Need You)/The Valley Of The Moon	20
61	London HLU 9447	Boo Hoo/I Can't Forget	100
58	MGM MGM-EP 647	MEET MARVIN RAINWATER (EP)	60
58	MGM MGM-EP 662	WHOLE LOTTA MARVIN (EP)	75
59	MGM MGM-EP 685	MARVIN RAINWATER (EP)	70
63	Ember EMB 4521	COUNTRY AND WESTERN FAVOURITES VOL. 2 (EP)	30
58	MGM MGM-D 152	SONGS BY MARVIN RAINWATER (10" LP)	100
72	Philips 6414 110	MARVIN RAINWATER GETS COUNTRY FEVER (LP)	15

(see also Connie Francis & Marvin Rainwater)

RAINY DAY
84	EMI EMI 5472	Painting Pictures/Welche Farbe Hat Der Sonnenschein (p/s)	12

RAINY DAZE
67	CBS 3200	What Do You Think/Autumn Leaves	15
67	Polydor 56731	That Acapulco Gold/In My Mind Lives A Forest	15
68	Polydor 56737	Blood Of Oblivion/Stop Sign	18
68	CBS 56731	THAT ACAPULCO GOLD (LP, unissued in U.K.)	

RAISINS
68	Major Major MM 540	Ain't That Lovin' You Baby/Stranger Things Have Happened	10
69	Major Minor MM 602	I Thank You/Don't Leave Me Like This	6
68	Major Minor MMLP 20	THE RAISINS (LP, also stereo SMLP 20)	30

(see also Coloured Raisins)

BONNIE RAITT
72	Warner Bros K 46189	GIVE IT UP (LP)	12
73	Warner Bros K 46261	TAKIN' MY TIME (LP)	12

(see also Roy Orbison, Alton Purnell)

RAKES
04	Trash Aesthetics TA 702	22 Grand Job/Something Clicked And I Fell Off The Edge (Pink vinyl, insert and fold-out sleeve. 480 only	25
04	City Rockers ROCKERS28CD	Strasbourg/Just Got Paid/Ausland Mission –Demo (CD)	12
04	City Rockers ROCKERS28	Strasbourg/Just Got Paid/Ausland Mission – Demo (p/s)	7

DON RALKE ORCHESTRA
59	Vogue V 9152	Maverick/Travellin' West (78 rpm = £15)	10
60	Warner Brothers WB 2	77 Sunset Strip (as Big Sound Of Don Ralke)/ PETE CANDOLI & HIS ORCHESTRA: 77 Sunset Strip Cha-Cha	7
60	Warner Brothers WM 8014	DANCE CAPER IN HI-FI (LP)	22
60	Warner Brothers WS 4007	YOU'VE NEVER HEARD GERSHWIN WITH BONGOS (LP)	12

TOMMY RALL, ANN MILLER, BOBBY VAN & BOB FOSSE
54	MGM SP 1079	From This Moment On/So Kiss Me Kate (by Kathryn Grayson & Howard Keel)/ Brush Up Your Shakespeare (by Keenan Wynn & James Whitmore)	6

RALLY ROUNDERS
64	Lyntone LYN 573/574	Bike Beat Part 1/Bike Beat Part 2 (actually by The Outlaws) (p/s, flexidisc)	75

(see also Outlaws, Ritchie Blackmore)

RALPH & PONYTAILS
80	Pony Tunes RATP 1	James Bond/James Bond (Different Version) (p/s)	5

BUCK RAM'S RAMROCKS
63	London HLU 9677	Benfica/Odd Man Theme	15

(see also Little Richard, Platters)

RAMA (4th STREET ORCHESTRA)
77	Rama RM 001	AH WHO SHE? GO-DEH! (LP)	60
77	Rama RM 004	(SCIENTIFIC) HIGHER RANKING DUB (LP)	80

(see also Dennis Bowell, Matumbi)

RAMASES
71	Philips 6113 001	Ballroom/Muddy Water	10
71	Philips 6113 003	Jesus Come Back/Hello Mister	7
71	Vertigo 6360 046	SPACE HYMNS (LP, foldout sleeve, swirl label, later 'spaceship' label)	50/15
75	Vertigo 6360 115	GLASS TOP COFFIN (LP, gatefold sleeve)	20

(see also 10cc, Ramases & Seleka, Ramases & Selket)

RAMASES & SELEKA
70	Major Minor MM 704	Love You/Gold Is The Ring	45

(see also Ramases)

RAMASES & SELKET
68	CBS 3717	Crazy One/Mind's Eye	120

(see also Ramases)

RAMATAM
72	Atlantic K 40415	RAMATAM (LP)	12

(see also Iron Butterfly)

EDDIE RAMBEAU
62	Stateside SS 116	Summertime Guy/Last Night Was My Last Night	12
64	Stateside SS 301	Come Closer/She's Smilin' At Me	10
65	Stateside SS 448	My Name Is Mud/I Just Need Your Love	12
66	Stateside SS 486	The Train/Yesterday's Newspapers	10
66	Stateside SS 501	I'm The Sky/I Just Need Your Love	7
66	Stateside SS 561	The Clock/If I Were You	7

(see also Marcy Jo & Eddie Rambeau)

RAMBLER
66	Pye 7N 17164	Love Minus Zero No Limit/An Bonnan Bui	7

(see also Johnny McEvoy)

RAMBLERS
63	Decca F 11775	Dodge City/Just For Chicks	40

RAMBLERS TWO
65	Pye 7N 15989	Today Is The Highway/The Mountains And The Sea	5

RAMBLETTES
65	Brunswick 05932	Thinking Of You/On Back Street	20

RAMBLING SYD RUMPO
67	Parlophone R 5638	The Ballad Of The Wogglers Moulie/Green Grow My Nadgers Oh!	10
68	Parlophone GEP 8965	RAMBLING SYD RUMPO IN CONCERT VOL. 1 (EP)	12
68	Parlophone GEP 8966	RAMBLING SYD RUMPO IN CONCERT VOL. 2 (EP)	12
70	Starline SRS 5034	THE BEST OF RAMBLING SYD RUMPO (LP)	15

(see also Kenneth Williams)

RAMBLIN' JIMMY DOLAN
51	Capitol CL 13600	Wine, Women And Pink Elephants/GENE O'QUIN: Boogie Woogie Fever (78)	10
53	Capitol CL 13982	Playin' Dominoes And Shootin' Dice/The Wheel That Does The Squeekin' (78)	10

SID RAMIN
69	CBS 70062	STILETTO (LP, soundtrack)	30

RAM JAM BAND
65	Columbia DB 7621	Shake Shake Senora/Akinla	20

(see also Geno Washington & Ram Jam Band, Ram John Holder, Ram Holder Brothers)

RAMLEH
83	Broken Flag BF V4	THE HAND OF GLORY (EP)	15
91	Shock SX 013	Slammers/Black Moby Dick (p/s, numbered, 500 only)	8
92	Dying Earth DE 003	Loser Patrol/Tracers (p/s, numbered, 500 only, 1st 30 in red sleeve)	15/8
93	Dying Earth DE 007	Say Fuck/Slackjaw (wraparound p/s, numbered, 500 only)	8
94	Format Supremacy (no cat. no.)	Welcome/Pristine Womankind (cardboard p/s, 500 only)	8
94	Freek FRR 006	HOMELESS (CD-only EP)	15
95	Broken Flag BS 78	ADIEU ALL YOU JUDGES (CD-only live EP, features Skullflower, 500 only)	20
83	Broken Flag BF V2	A RETURN TO SLAVERY (LP, with Libertarian Recordings)	40
91	Shock Records SX D14	BLOWHOLE (LP)	12

(see also Skullflower)

RAMON & CRYSTALITES
71	Songbird SB 1053	Golden Chickens/Stranger Version	18

DEE DEE RAMONE
97	Blackout BLK 5000-7	I Am Seeing UFOs (featuring Joey Ramone)/Bad Horoscope (2,500 copies only)	5

DEE DEE RAMONE & ICLC
94	Rough Trade/World Service RDT 157.1757.2	Chinese Bitch/I Don't Want To Get Involved With You/ That's What Everybody Else Does/We're A Creepy Family (CD)	10

(see also Ramones)

RAMONES
76	Sire 6078 601	Blitzkrieg Bop/Havana Affair (some with p/s)	125/10
77	Sire 6078 603	I Remember You/California Sun (live)/I Don't Wanna Walk Around With You (live) (p/s)	30
77	Sire RAM 001 (6078 606)	Sheena Is A Punk Rocker/Commando/I Don't Care (no p/s)	5
77	Sire RAM 001 (6078 606)	Sheena Is A Punk Rocker/Commando/I Don't Care (12", with or without T-shirt offer on perforated centre of numbered p/s, 12,000 only)	20/15
77	Sire 6078 607	Swallow My Pride/Pinhead/Let's Dance (live) (p/s)	12
77	Sire 6078 611	Rockaway Beach/Teenage Lobotomy/Beat On The Brat (p/s)	8
77	Sire 6078 611	Rockaway Beach/Teenage Lobotomy/Beat On The Brat (12", p/s, some with poster)	35/10
78	Sire 6078 615	Do You Wanna Dance?/It's A Long Way Back To Germany/Cretin Hop (p/s)	8
78	Sire (no cat. no.)	Questioningly/Don't Come Close/Sedated/I Just Want To Have Something To Do (some only, with spoken intros by Joey Ramone)	45/10
78	Sire SRE 1031	Don't Come Close/I Don't Want You (p/s, some on yellow vinyl)	8/5
78	Sire SRE 1031	Don't Come Close/I Don't Want You (12", p/s, yellow or red vinyl, red vinyl lacks p/s)	each 10
79	Sire SIR 4009	She's The One/I Wanna Be Sedated (p/s)	6
79	Sire SIR 4021	Rock'n'Roll High School/Rockaway Beach (live)/Sheena Is A Punk Rocker (live) (p/s)	8
80	Sire SIR 4037	Do You Remember Rock'n'Roll Radio/I Want You Around (p/s)	5
80	RSO RSO 70 (2090 512)	I Wanna Be Sedated/The Return Of Jackie And Judy (p/s)	15
80	Sire SREP 1	MELTDOWN WITH THE RAMONES: I Just Want To Have Something To Do/ Here Today Gone Tomorrow/I Wanna Be Your Boyfriend/Questioningly (EP)	15
81	Sire SIR 4051	We Want The Airwaves/You Sound LIke You're Sick (p/s)	8
81	Sire SIR 4052	She's A Sensation/All Quiet On The Eastern Front (no p/s)	8
83	Sire W 9606	Time Has Come Today/Psycho Therapy (p/s)	20
83	Sire W 9606T	Time Has Come Today/Sheena Is A Punk Rocker/Teenage Lobotomy/ Rock'n'Roll Radio (12", p/s)	25
85	Beggars Banquet BEG 128	Howling At The Moon/Chasing The Night (p/s)	6
85	Beggars Banquet BEG 128D	Howling At The Moon//Smash You/ Chasing The Night/Street Fighting Man (double pack, gatefold sleeve)	10
85	Beggars Banquet BEGTP 128	Howling At The Moon/Chasing The Night/Smash You/Street Fighting Man (12", p/s)	8
85	Beggars Banquet BEG 140	Bonzo Goes To Bitburg/Go Home Ann (p/s)	7
85	Beggars Banquet BEG 140T	Bonzo Goes To Bitburg/Go Home Ann/Daytime Dilemma (12", p/s)	10

86	Beggars Banquet BEG 157	Somebody Put Something In My Drink/Something To Believe In (p/s)	5
86	Beggars Banquet BEG 157T	Somebody Put Something In My Drink/(You) Can't Say Anything Nice/Something To Believe In (12", p/s, some with promo poster)	15/8
87	Beggars Banquet BEG 198	Real Cool Time/Life Goes On (p/s)	6
87	Beggars Banquet BEG 198T	Real Cool Time/Life Goes On/Indian Giver (12", p/s)	8
87	Beggars Banquet BEG 201	I Wanna Live/Merry Christmas (I Don't Want To Fight Tonight) (p/s)	8
87	Beggars Banquet BEG 201T	I Wanna Live/Merry Christmas (I Don't Want To Fight Tonight) (12", p/s)	10
89	Chrysalis CHS 3423	Pet Sematary/All Screwed Up (p/s)	6
92	Chrysalis CHS 3917	Poison Heart/Censorshit (p/s)	5
92	Chrysalis 0946 3 23917 66	Poison Heart/Chinese Rocks/Sheena Is A Punk Rocker (live)/Rockaway Beach (live) (12", yellow vinyl, p/s)	8
76	Sire 9103 253	RAMONES (LP, with insert)	15
77	Sire 9103 254	RAMONES LEAVE HOME (LP, with "Carbona Not Glue" or "Babysitter", both with inner sleeve)	20/12
77	Sire 9103 255	ROCKET TO RUSSIA (LP, with inner sleeve)	12
78	Sire SRK 6063	ROAD TO RUIN (LP, yellow vinyl)	15
80	Sire SRK 6077	END OF THE CENTURY (LP)	12
81	Sire SRK 3571	PLEASANT DREAMS (LP)	12
90	Beggar's Banquet (no cat. no.)	END OF THE DECADE (6 x 12" singles, box set with T-shirt, postcards & poster, 2,500 copies only)	50
91	Chrysalis CHR 1901	LOCO LIVE (LP)	15
93	Chrysalis CHR 6052	ACID EATERS (LP)	15
	(see also Paley Brothers & Ramones, Holly & Joey, Dee Dee Ramone)		

MICHEL RAMOS
60s	London DEP 95013	PLAYING THE CLASSICS (EP)	40

RAM RAM KINO
85	Temple TOPY 006	Advantage — Tantric Routines 1-4 (3.23)/(Basket Mix) (4.00)/Into The Bush (3.26)/Special (3.56) (12", p/s)	8
	(see also Crispy Ambulance)		

RAMRODS
65	United Artists UP 1113	Overdrive/Stalker	11

RAMRODS (U.S.)
61	London HLU 9282	Riders In The Sky/Zig Zag	8
61	London HLU 9355	Loch Lomond Rock/Take Me Back To My Boots And Saddle	18
61	London RE-U 1292	RIDERS IN THE SKY (EP)	100

BILL RAMSEY
62	Polydor NH 66812	Go Man Go/Rocking Mountain	12

LEE RAMSEY
96	Real Deal RD002	RD STYLE (EP)	15

RANCHERS
65	Cavern Sound IMSTL 2	An American Sailor At The Cavern/Sidetracked	20
	(see also Phil Brady & Ranchers)		

RANCID
95	Out Of Step WOOS 8 S	Time Bomb/The War's End/Blast 'Em (p/s)	6
96	Epitaph 86464-7	Ruby Soho/That's Entertainment/Disorder And Disarray (p/s)	6
98	Epitaph 1005-7	Bloodclot/Endrine/Stop (p/s)	6
98	Epitaph 1009-7	Hooligans/Cash, Culture and Violence (Bass Drop Mix)/Things to Come (Dance Hall Mix) (p/s)	6
00	Epitaph 1040-7	Let Me Go/Ben Zanotto/Dead And Fone (p/s)	6
03	Warner Brothers W 618	Fall Back Down/Killing Zone (p/s)	6
94	Epitaph 86434-1	LET'S GO (LP, 2 x 10", gatefold sleeve, white vinyl)	12

ALAN RANDALL (& SHEP'S BANJO BOYS)
70	Domino 110	The Coventry City Song/Football Football	6

ELLIOTT RANDALL
71	Polydor 2489 004	RANDALL'S ISLAND (LP)	15

FREDDY RANDALL & HIS BAND
50	Tempo A 45	Dark Night Blues/Washington And Lee Swing (78)	10
50	Tempo A 49	Riverside Blues/Jazz Club Stomp (78)	10
50	Tempo A 55	Georgia Cake Walk/Sugar Foot Strut (78)	10
58	Parlophone GEP 8715	CHICAGO JAZZ (EP)	10
58	Parlophone PMD 1046	DR JAZZ (LP)	20

TONY RANDALL & JACK KLUGMAN
72	Decca Phase Four PFS 4277	THE ODD COUPLE SINGS (LP)	20

TEDDY RANDAZZO (& DAZZLERS)
59	HMV POP 578	It's Magic/Richer Than I (78 rpm = £8)	10
60	HMV POP 806	Journey To Love/Misery	10
61	HMV POP 866	Happy Ending/But You Broke My Heart	10
61	HMV POP 925	Let The Sunshine In/Broken Bell	10
62	HMV POP 1067	Dance To The Locomotion/Cottonfields (as Teddy Randazzo & Dazzlers)	15
63	HMV POP 1119	Echoes/It Wasn't A Dream	6
63	Pye International 7N 25181	Big Wide World/Be Sure, My Love	10
62	HMV CLP 1527	JOURNEY TO LOVE (LP, also stereo CSD 1421)	60/70
63	HMV CLP 1601	TEDDY RANDAZZO TWISTS (LP, with Dazzlers)	100
	(see also Three Chuckles)		

LYNNE RANDELL
67	CBS 2847	Ciao Baby/Stranger In My Arms	225
67	CBS 2927	That's A Hoe Down/I Need You Boy	22

RAN-DELLS
63	London HLU 9760	The Martian Hop/Forgive Me Darling	30

BARBARA RANDOLPH
67	Tamla Motown TMG 628	I Got A Feelin'/You Got Me Hurtin' All Over (DJ copy = £75)	40
71	Tamla Motown TMG 788	I Got A Feelin'/You Got Me Hurtin' All Over (reissue)	15
79	Tamla Motown TMG 1133	Can I Get A Witness/You Got Me Hurtin' All Over	10

BOOTS RANDOLPH
62	London HLU 9567	Bluebird Of Happiness/Keep A Light In Your Window Tonight	5
63	London HLU 9685	Yakety Sax/I Really Don't Want To Know	5
63	London HLU 9798	Windy And Warm/Lonely Street	5
64	London HLU 9891	Hey, Mr. Sax Man/Baby Go To Sleep	5
66	London HLU 10017	Theme From A Dream/King Of The Road	5
66	London HLU 10028	These Boots Are Made For Walking/Honey In Your Heart	5
63	London RE-U 1365	THE YAKETY SAX OF BOOTS RANDOLPH (EP)	30
63	London HA-U 8106	YAKETY SAX (LP)	25
66	London HA-U 8280	MORE YAKETY SAX (LP, as Boots Randolph & His Combo)	20
67	Monument LMO/SMO 5002	HIP BOOTS (LP)	15
67	Monument LMO/SMO 5003	BOOTS WITH STRINGS (LP)	12
68	Monument LMO/SMO 5012	THE FANTASTIC BOOTS RANDOLPH (LP)	12
69	Monument LMO/SMO 5022	SAXSATIONAL (LP)	12

CHARLES RANDOLPH GREEN SOUND
69	London HLD 10283	Quintin's Theme/Number One At The Blue Whale	6

ERIC RANDOM
80	New Hormones CAT 4	LIVE IN EUROPE (cassette)	10

(see also Tiller Boys, Cabaret Voltaire, Free Agents, Pressure & Co.)

RANDOM HARVEST
82	Random Harvest RH 501	RANDOM HARVEST (LP)	12

RANDY & RAINBOWS
63	Stateside SS 214	Denise/Come Back	80

RANDY'S ALLSTARS
70	Randy's RAN 500	I'm The One, You're The One/End Us	5
70	Randy's RAN 501	Pepper Pot (act. with Count Machuki)/Same Thing (B-side actually by Gaylads)	10
70	Randy's RAN 502	Dixie/Five Cents (B-side actually "A Lover's Question" by Winston Samuels)	7
70	Randy's RAN 505	Emperor Waltz/War	10
70	Randy's RAN 506	Blue Danube Waltz/Together (B-side actually by Delroy Wilson)	8
70	Randy's RAN 507	Bridge Over Troubled Water (actually by Lyrics)/Waterfall	5
71	Explosion EX 2052	Hold On Girl (actually by Lyrics)/Hold On Girl (Version)	5

(see also Impact Allstars, Lyrics, Dave Barker, Ethiopians, Jimmy London)

RANEE & RAJ
68	Fontana TF 920	Feel Like A Clown/Rainbow Land	15
68	Fontana TF 941	Don't Tell Me I Must Go/Razor Edge	6

SUE RANEY
57	Capitol CL 14757	The Careless Years/What's The Good Word, Mr. Bluebird	6
57	Capitol CL 14792	Please Hurry Home/Don't Take My Happiness	6
58	Capitol T 964	WHEN YOUR LOVER HAS GONE (LP)	25

WAYNE RANEY (STRING BAND)
53	Parlophone DP 333	If You Never Slip Around/The Child's Side Of Life (78, export issue)	10
54	Parlophone CSMP 20	Adam/The Roosters Are Crowing (export issue) (78 rpm, export issue = £8)	25
55	Parlophone DP 413	Mama (Don't You Remember When You Were Young)/Trying To Live Without You (78, export issue)	8
50s	Parlophone DP 349	Burning Your Love Letters/Falling (78, export issue)	10
58	Parlophone GEP 8746	COUNTRY AND WESTERN (EP)	45

RANGLERS
68	Trend TRE 1007	You Never Said Goodbye/Step Down	18

ERNEST RANGLIN
62	Island WI 015	Harmonica Twist/Mitty Gritty (as Ernest Ranglin Orchestra)	35
63	Island WI 128	Exodus/ROBERT MARLEY: One Cup Of Coffee	300
66	Black Swan IEP 704	ERNEST RANGLIN & THE G.B.'s (EP, some with p/s)	180/50
64	Island ILP 909	WRANGLIN' (LP)	125
64	Island ILP 915	REFLECTIONS (LP)	100
60s	Vista Sounds	FROM KINGSTON J.A. TO MIAMI U.S.A. (LP)	25

(see also Owen Gray, Graham Bond)

MASSIMO RANIERI
71	CBS 7207	Goodbye My Love/The Sun Shining Down On Me	12

BILLY RANKIN
83	A&M AM 172	Baby Come Back/Part Of The Scenery (p/s)	6

(see also Nazareth)

KENNY RANKIN
60	Brunswick 05845	As Sure As You're Born/Teasin' Heart	8
73	Atlantic K 10275	Comin' Down/Stringman	5

RANKING DREAD
80	Art & Craft AC006	DISCO EP SHOWCASE: My Liza/Same Thing/Hard Times Leave My Life/Jah Walk Through Galilee (12" green vinyl)	15
82	Greensleeves GRED 82	Shut Me Mouth/Shut Up Shut Up (Dub Version)	20
76	Burning Sounds BS 1025	GIRLS FIESTA (LP)	22
79	Burning Sounds BS 1037	KUNTA KINTE ROOTS (LP)	25
80	Freedom Sounds FSLP 001	LOTS OF LOVING (LP)	22

MINT VALUE £

RANKING JOE
78	Greensleeves GRE10	Dub Sister Dub It/Nine Months Belly	10
78	Greensleeves GREL 2	WEAKHEART FADEAWAY (LP)	20

RANKING TREVOR AND TRINITY
78	Cha Cha CHALP 001	THREE PIECE CHICKEN AND CHIPS (LP)	25

FELA RANSOME KUTI
(see under 'K')

RAOUL & RUINED
84	Gutter Hearts GH 1	BITE BACK + BLUES (LP, fan-club only issue)	50

(see also Marc Almond)

RAPED
78	Parole KNIT 1	PRETTY PAEDOPHILES (EP)	20
78	Parole PURL 1	Cheap Night Out/Foreplay Playground (p/s, with ad sheet)	8
84	Iguana PILLAGED 1	PHILES AND SMILES (LP, official bootleg, with booklet)	20

(see also Cuddly Toys)

RAPEMAN
88	Fierce FRIGHT 031	Hated Chinee/Marmoset (p/s)	35

(see also Big Black)

JOHNNY RAPHAEL
58	Vogue V 9104	We're Only Young Once/The Lonely Road To Nowhere (78 rpm = £40)	90

RAPIERS
60s	Ilford Sound ILF 272	The Phantom Stage/Valencia	12

RAPIERS
86	Off Beat NS 112A	The Closing Theme/Still I Cry	10
83	Red Door RA 001	THE RAPIERS VOL. 1 (EP)	12
84	Twang RA 002	THE RAPIERS VOL. 2 (EP)	12
85	Twang RA 003	THE RAPIERS VOL. 3 (EP)	12
86	Twang RA 004	THE RAPIERS VOL. 4 (EP)	12
85	Off Beat WIK 40	STRAIGHT TO THE POINT (LP)	18
87	Off Beat WIK 67	1961 (LP)	18

BRIAN RAPKIN & KELVIN JONES
70s	MSR	DREAMS OF THE BEAST (LP)	20

MARIE RAPP
53	London L 1207	When A Man Loves A Woman/When I'm With You (78)	15

RARE AMBER
69	Polydor BM 56309	Malfunction Of The Engine/Blind Love	20
69	Polydor 583 046	RARE AMBER (LP)	90

RARE BIRD
70	Charisma CB 120	Sympathy/Devil's High Concern (in p/s)	10
70	Charisma CB 138	What You Want To Know/Hammerhead	7
72	Charisma CB 179	Sympathy/Devil's High Concern/What Do You Want To Know/Hammerhead (p/s)	8
73	Polydor 2058 402	Virgina/Lonely Street	5
74	Polydor 2058 471	Body And Soul/Redman	5
74	Polydor SH 1041/2	Diamonds/BARCLAY JAMES HARVEST: Negative Earth (flexi, with *Sounds*)	10/5
69	Charisma CAS 1005	RARE BIRD (LP)	25
70	Charisma CAS 1011	AS YOUR MIND FLIES BY (LP)	25
72	Polydor 2442 101	EPIC FOREST (LP & poster, some with bonus EP "Roadside Welcome"/ "Four Grey Walls"/"You're Lost" [2814 011], p/s)	35/20

(see also Fields, Fruit Machine)

RARE BREED
66	Strike JH 316	Beg, Borrow And Steal/Jeri's Theme	30

(see also Pussyfoot)

RARE EARTH
70	Tamla Motown TMG 742	Get Ready/Magic Key	20
70	T. Motown STML 11165	GET READY (LP)	20
71	T. Motown STML 11180	ECOLOGY (LP)	25
71	Rare Earth SREA 4001	ONE WORLD (LP)	12
72	Rare Earth SRESP 301	IN CONCERT (2-LP satchel sleeve)	15
73	Rare Earth SRE 3008	WILLIE REMEMBERS (LP, gatefold sleeve)	12

RASCALS
68	Atlantic 584 182	A Beautiful Morning/Rainy Day	7
68	Atlantic 584 210	People Got To Be Free/My World	7
69	Atlantic 584 255	Heaven/Baby I'm Blue	7
69	Atlantic 584 274	See/Away Away	7
69	Atlantic 584 292	Carry Me Back/Real Thing	8
70	Atlantic 584 307	Hold On/I Believe	6
70	Atlantic 2091 029	Glory, Glory/You Don't Know	6
71	CBS 7363	Love Me/Happy Song	6
71	CBS 7672	Lucky Day/Love Letter	6
68	Atlantic 587/588 098	ONCE UPON A DREAM (LP)	20
68	Atlantic 587/588 120	TIME PEACE — RASCALS' GREATEST HITS (LP)	15
69	Atlantic 588 183	FREEDOM SUITE (LP)	15
70	Atlantic 588 210	SEE (LP)	15
71	Atlantic 2400 113	SEARCH AND NEARNESS (LP)	15

(see also Young Rascals)

RENATO RASCEL
60	RCA RCA 1177	Romantica/Dimmelo Con Un Fiore	5

(EMPRESS) RASHEDA
95	Roots Music RRLP 011	HAIL H.I.M (LP)	25

(see also Royal Rasses)

RASTAFARI
73	Satril SAT8	Funky City/In The Garden	100

RASTA TWINS
(see under Aggrovators)

THE RAT & THE WHALE
80	Rewind REWIND 5	Wheels On Fire/Wheels On Fire (Long Version) (p/s)	5

(see also Alternative TV, Rat Scabies)

BASIL RATHBONE
60s	Caedmon TC 1028	EDGAR ALLAN POE (LP)	15

RATIO
70	Big Chief BC 102	Let There Be Peace In The World/Pharaoh's Walk	7

RATIONAL ANTHEM
86	Radio Humberside/HLS 001	THE NORTHERN TRAWL (LP)	50

ARMAN RATIP
70	Columbia SCX 6532	INTRODUCING THE ARMAN RATIP TRIO (LP)	80
73	Regal Zono. SLRZ 1038	THE SPY FROM ISTANBUL (LP)	40

RATS
64	Oak RGJ 145	Spoonful (1-sided, some with foldout p/s)	350/200
65	Columbia DB 7483	Spoonful/I've Got My Eyes On You Baby	12
65	Columbia DB 7607	I Gotta See My Baby Everyday/Headin' Back (To New Orleans)	80
95	Tenth Planet TP	THE RISE AND FALL OF BERNIE GRIPPLESTONE & THE SPIDERS FROM HULL (LP, gatefold sleeve, 1,000 only)	15

(see also Beat Boys, Mark Peters; the above singles do not feature Mick Ronson)

RATS
64	Oriole CB 1967	Parchman Farm/Every Day I Have The Blues	100
65	CBS 201740	Sack Of Woe/Gimme That Wine	85

RATS
74	Goodear EARLH 5003	FIRST (LP)	18

(see also World of Oz)

RATT
85	Atlantic A 9546P	Lay It Down/Got Me On The Line (shaped picture disc)	6
86	Atlantic A 9502P	You're In Love/Between The Eyes (shaped picture disc)	8

RATTLES
63	Philips BF 1277	The Stomp/Zip A Dee Doo Dah	15
64	Decca F 11873	Bye Bye Johnny/Roll Over Beethoven	20
64	Decca F 11936	Tell Me What I Can Do/Sunbeam At The Sky	15
65	Fontana TF 618	Come On And Sing/Candy To Me	15
66	Fontana TF 724	Say All Right/Love Of My Life	15
70	Decca F 23058	The Witch/Geraldine	8
64	Decca DFE 8568	TEENBEAT FROM THE STAR CLUB HAMBURG (EP)	125
64	Philips BL 7614	TWIST AT THE STAR CLUB HAMBURG (LP)	100
67	Mercury MG 1127	GREATEST HITS (LP)	28
71	Decca SKL-R 5088	THE RATTLES (LP)	22

(see also Wonderland)

CARL RAVAZZA
51	HMV B 10202	Rock, Rock, Rock/Like A Dream (78)	12

CHRIS RAVEL & RAVERS
63	Decca F 11696	I Do/Don't You Dig This Kind Of Beat	18

(see also Chris Andrews)

RAVEN
80	Neat NEAT 06	Don't Need Your Money/Wiped Out (p/s)	8
81	Neat NEAT 11	Hard Ride/Crazy World (p/s)	6
82	Neat NEAT 1512	CRASH BANG WALLOP (Crash Bang Wallop/Firepower/Run Them Down/Rock Hard) (12" EP, mauve splattered vinyl)	12
86	WEA A 9453	Gimme Some Lovin' (no p/s)	8

JON RAVEN
70s	Broadside	HARVEST (LP, with book)	15
71	Argo ZFB 29	KATE OF COALBROOKDALE (LP, as Jon & Mike Raven with Jean Ward)	150
73	Trailer LER 2083	SONGS OF A CHANGING WORLD (LP, with Nic Jones & Tony Rose, red label with insert)	25
75	Tradition TSR 019	THE BOLD NAVIGATORS: THE STORY OF ENGLAND'S CANALS IN SONG (LP, with John Kirkpatrick, Sue Harris, & Gary & Vera Aspey)	20
76	Broadside BRO 118	THE ENGLISH CANALS (LP, with John Kirkpatrick & Sue Harris)	15
81	Dingles DIN 319	REGAL SLIP (LP)	30

(see also Halliard, Black Country Three, John Kirkpatrick)

PAUL RAVEN
68	MCA MU1035	Soul Thing/We'll Go Where The World Can't	10

SIMON RAVEN
66	Piccadilly 7N 35301	I Wonder If She Remembers Me/Sea Of Love	60

RAVENS
53	Oriole CB 1148	Rock Me All Night Long/Write Me One Sweet Letter (78)	30
53	Oriole CB 1149	Begin The Beguine/Looking For My Baby (78)	30
53	Oriole CB 1258	Who'll Be The Fool?/Rough Ridin' (78)	30

MINT VALUE £

RAVENS
63   Oriole CB 1910   I Just Wanna Hear You Say/Send Me A Letter 22

RAVENS ROCK GROUP
61   Pye International 7N 25077   The Ghoul Friend/Career Girl. 20

RAVE ONS
60s Sounds Good MT 103   She's A Spoon/Keep Wrong. 90

RAVERS
69   Upsetter US 312   Badam Bam/UPSETTERS: Medical Operation 40

RAW DEAL
81   White Witch WIT 701   Out Of My Head/In The Mood (no p/s) 125
81   Neat NEAT 12   Lonewolf/Take The Sky (p/s) 7

RAW DEAL
95   Mental Disorder MAD 666   THE LEGENDARY RAW DEAL (10" LP) 12

PETER RAWES
87   Official OFFA 5   Why Should I Ask Her To Stay?/Theme From Shark/Theme From Forever
                           (with Jet Harris) (p/s) 6

(see also Jet Harris)

RAW MATERIAL
69   Evolution E 2441   Time And Illusion/Bobo's Party 50
70   Evolution E 2445   Hi There Hallelujah/Days Of The Fighting Cock 35
70   Evolution E 24495   Travelling Man (Part 1)/Part 2. 30
71   RCA Neon NE 1002   Ride On Pony/Religion 22
70   Evolution Z 1006   RAW MATERIAL (LP) 220
71   RCA Neon NE 8   TIME IS (LP) 175
(see also Shoot)

LOU RAWLS
65   Capitol CL 15398   Three O'Clock In The Morning/Nothing Really Feels The Same 10
66   Capitol CL 15465   Love Is A Hurtin' Thing/Memory Lane. 10
67   Capitol CL 15488   You Can Bring Me All Your Heartaches/A Woman Who's A Woman 15
67   Capitol CL 15499   Dead End Street/Yes It Hurts Doesn't It 15
67   Capitol CL 15507   Show Business/When Loves Goes Wrong. 25
67   Capitol CL 15515   Hard To Get Thing Called Love/(How Do You Say) I Don't Love You Anymore . . 10
67   Capitol CL 15522   Little Drummer Boy/Child With A Toy 8
68   Capitol CL 15533   My Ancestors/Evil Woman 8
68   Capitol CL 15548   You're Good For Me/Soul Serenade 10
68   Capitol CL 15560   Down Here On The Ground/I'm Satisfied 8
69   Capitol CL 15583   It's You/Sweet Charity 8
69   Capitol CL 15611   Your Good Thing (Is About To End)/Season Of The Witch. 8
70   Capitol CL 15630   You've Made Me So Very Happy/Let's Burn Down The Cornfield 6
74   Bell BLL 1390   She's Gone/Hourglass 6
63   Capitol EAP-1 20646   LOST AND LOOKIN' (EP) 50
65   Capitol T 1824   BLACK AND BLUE (LP) 25
66   Capitol (S)T 2459   LIVE (LP) 20
67   Capitol (S)T 2566   SOULIN' (LP) 22
67   Capitol (S)T 2632   CARRYIN' ON! (LP) 20
68   Capitol (S)T 2864   FEELIN' GOOD (LP). 30
69   Capitol ST 2927   YOU'RE GOOD FOR ME (LP). 20
69   Capitol E-ST 215   THE WAY IT WAS THE WAY IT IS (LP). 20
71   MGM 2315 054   NATURAL MAN (LP) 12

RAW STYLUS
93   Mo Wax MW 002   Many Ways/Many Ways (Jam Up The Vibe Mix)/Bright Lights, Big City
                           (Dark Mix) (12", die-cut stickered sleeve). 12

CLYDE RAY
57   Columbia DB 3875   Follow Me/Steady As A Rock 10
58   Columbia DB 4106   Locked In The Arms Of Love/I'm Not Afraid Anymore 8

DANNY RAY & FALCONS
70   MCA MK 5037   Scorpion/I Love You Girl 10

DIANE RAY
63   Mercury AMT 1209   Please Don't Talk To The Lifeguard/That's All I Want From You 22

FROGGIE RAY
71   Big BG 313   Uncle Charlie/Party Version. 8
71   Big BG 314   Half Moon/RUPIE EDWARDS ALL STARS: Full Moon. 7

JAMES RAY
62   Pye International 7N 25126 If You Gotta Make A Fool Of Somebody/It's Been A Drag. 20
62   Pye International 7N 25147 Itty Bitty Pieces/You Remember The Face 18

JOHNNIE RAY
53   Columbia SCM 5015   Walkin' My Baby Back Home/The Lady Drinks Champagne
                           (B-side with the Four Lads) 30
53   Columbia SCM 5033   Ma Says, Pa Says/A Full Time Job (with Doris Day) 25
53   Columbia SCM 5041   Whiskey And Gin/Tell The Lady I Said Goodbye 30
53   Columbia SCM 5074   Please Don't Talk About Me When I'm Gone/Coffee And Cigarettes
                            (B-side with the Four Lads) 35
54   Columbia SCM 5111   Nobody's Sweetheart/I Can't Escape From You 20
54   Columbia SCM 5122   She Didn't Say Nothin' At All/I'm Just A Shadow Of Myself. 20
57   Philips JK 1004   You Don't Owe Me A Thing/Look Homeward, Angel (jukebox issue) 30
57   Philips JK 1011   So Long/I Miss You So (jukebox issue) 30
57   Philips JK 1016   Yes, Tonight, Josephine/No Wedding Today (jukebox issue) 30
57   Philips JK 1025   Build Your Love (On A Strong Foundation)/Street Of Memories (jukebox issue) . 30

57	Philips JK 1026	Up Above My Head, I Hear Music On The Air/Good Evening Friends/
		Memories (with Frankie Laine, jukebox issue only) 30
57	Philips JK 1033	Pink Sweater Angel/Texas Tambourine (jukebox issue) (78 rpm = £6) 30
58	Philips PB 785	Miss Me Just A Little/Soliloquy Of A Fool (78 rpm = £6)...................... 5
58	Philips PB 808	Strollin' Girl/Plant A Little Seed (78 rpm = £6) 5
58	Philips PB 829	Lonely For A Letter/Endlessly (78 rpm = £6) 5
58	Philips PB 849	No Regrets/Up Until Now (78 rpm = £8) 5
58	Philips PB 884	What More Can I Say/You're The One Who Knows (78 rpm = £10)............. 5
59	Philips PB 901	When's Your Birthday, Baby/One Man's Love Song Is Another Man's Blues...... 5
59	Philips PB 901	When's Your Birthday, Baby/One Man's Love Song Is Another Man's Blues (78) . 12
59	Philips PB 918	Call Me Yours/Here And Now (78 rpm = £25)............................... 5
59	Philips PB 952	You're All That I Live For/I'll Never Fall In Love Again (78 rpm = £35) 5
60	Philips PB 990	When It's Springtime In The Rockies/Wagon Wheels....................... 5
60	Philips PB 1025	Before You/I'll Make You Mine 5
60	Philips PB 1047	Tell Me/Don't Leave Me Now 5
60	London HLA 9216	In The Heart Of A Fool/Let's Forget It Now................................ 5
61	Philips PB 1126	An Ordinary Couple/Cool Water 5
61	United Artists POP 902	How Many Nights How Many Days/I'll Bring Along My Banjo 5
62	London HLG 9484	I Believe (with Timi Yuro)/TIMI YURO: Smile 5
63	Brunswick 05884	Lookout Chatanooga/After My Laughter Came Tears........................ 5
69	Pye 7N 17691	Wise To The Ways Of The World/Since I Lost You Baby 5
69	Pye 7N 17760	Long And Lonely Nights/Brokenhearted Me, Evilhearted You................ 5
54	Columbia SEG 7511	JOHNNIE RAY (EP,company sleeve)...................................... 20
55	Philips BBE 12006	JOHNNIE RAY (EP) 20
57	Philips BBE 12115	WALKING AND CRYING (EP)... 22
58	Philips BBE 12192	YES, TONIGHT, JOSEPHINE (EP) 15
58	Philips BBE 12217	T.V. SERIES (EP) 15
61	Philips BBE 12460	ON THE TRAIL (EP).. 15
54	Philips BBR 8001	AT THE LONDON PALLADIUM (10" LP, red or blue sleeve) 30/20
55	Philips BBR 8062	THE VOICE OF YOUR CHOICE (10" LP).................................... 20
57	Philips BBL 7148	THE BIG BEAT (LP)... 30
58	Philips BBL 7254	AT THE DESERT INN — LAS VEGAS (LP) 20
58	Philips BBL 7264	SHOWCASE OF HITS (LP) 20
59	Philips BBL 7285	'TIL MORNING (LP, also stereo SBBL 555)................................. 15
59	Philips BBL 7348	A SINNER AM I (LP) 15
60	Philips BBL 7363	ON THE TRAIL (LP).. 15
62	Liberty LBY 1020	JOHNNIE RAY LP)... 15

(see also Four Lads, Frankie Laine & Johnnie Ray, Timi Yuro)

RICARDO RAY
| 68 | Roulette RO 501 | Nitty Gritty/Mony Mony.. 12 |

WADE RAY
| 63 | London HL 9700 | Burning Desire/Two Red Red Lips .... 18 |

RAY & COLLUNEY
| 71 | Westwood WRS 001 | TYRANTS OF ENGLAND (LP) .... 40 |

RAY & HIS COURT
| 00 | Jazzman JM 014 | Soul Freedom/RAY & HIS FAMILY: Cookie Crumbs........................... 5 |

CHRIS(TINE) RAYBURN
63	Parlophone R 5098	Slow Loving Woman/Same Old Places.................................... 10
64	Parlophone R 5144	I've Cried My Last Tear/You Forgot To Say When 10
66	Parlophone R 5422	I Wanna Be In Love Again/Another Night Alone 10
68	Music Factory CUB 2	One Way Ticket/Photograph Of Love 8
69	Pye 7N 17679	Skip A Rope/Starlight (as Christine Rayburn) 8

MARGIE RAYBURN
56	Capitol CL 14532	The Wedding Song/That's The Chance I've Got To Take 10
57	London HLU 8515	I'm Available/If You Were (78 rpm = £6) 22
58	London HLU 8648	I Would/Alright, But It Won't Be Easy (78 rpm = £12) 18

ANTHONY RAYE
| 80 | Grapevine GRP 147 | Give Me One More Chance/Hold On To What You've Got .... 10 |

SOL RAYE
| 63 | Oriole CB 1855 | Dear Michelle/I Love You Because .... 10 |
| 67 | Deram DM 154 | While I'm Here/To Be With You .... 8 |

BILLY RAYMOND
58	HMV POP 503	Making Love/I Would (78 rpm = £6)...................................... 5
58	HMV POP 526	One In Particular/Seven Daughters (78 rpm = £6).......................... 5
59	HMV POP 614	Charlie Is Their Darling/Loch Lomond 5

DANNY RAYMOND
| 71 | Big Shot BI 587 | Sister Big Stuff/BOY FRIDAY: Free Man.................................... 7 |

LEE RAYMOND with COSTELLO SISTERS
| 55 | Brunswick 05438 | Foolishly Yours/Baby Darling .... 12 |

MARK RAYMOND & CROWD
| 64 | Columbia DB 7308 | Girls/Remember Me To Julie .... 8 |

TONY RAYMOND
| 59 | Fontana H 213 | Broken-Hearted Melody/This Earth Is Mine (78 rpm = £10) .... 9 |
| 62 | Oriole CB 1777 | The Infant King/Because Of You .... 6 |

IVOR RAYMONDE & HIS ORCHESTRA
| 65 | Mercury MF 866 | Feelin' Fruggy/Grotty .... 10 |

MINT VALUE £

JULIE RAYNE
59	HMV POP 665	Waltz Me Around/Love Where Can You Be?	15
60	HMV POP 785	Bim Bam Bom/One More Time	15
61	HMV POP 868	Green With Envy Purple With Passion/My First Romance	15
63	Windsor WPS 123	Faithfully/Free To Love	12
64	Windsor WPS 128	You Can't Come Back/Straight To Your Arms	12

LISA RAYNE
65	Fontana TF 563	Don't Ever Change/It Had To Be You	10

MARTIN RAYNOR & SECRETS
65	Columbia DB 7563	Candy To Me/You're A Wonderful One	60

(see also Secrets, Simon's Secrets, Clifford T. Ward)

MIKE RAYNOR & CONDORS
67	Decca F 12605	Turn Your Head/Lazy Day	7
67	Decca F 22690	Is She A Woman Now?/My Shy Serenade	7
68	Decca F 22790	Wonderful Day/On Top Of The World	7
69	Decca F 22864	Ob-La-Di, Ob-La-Da/I'm Goin' Down (as Mike Raynor & Sky; Danish export issue)	10

RAY O VACS
50	Brunswick 04511	Sentimental Me/Once Upon A Time (78)	10

RAYS
57	London HLU 8505	Silhouettes/Daddy Cool (78 rpm = £25)	40

RAZORCUTS
86	Subway Org. SUBWAY 5	Big Pink Cake/I'll Still Be There (foldover p/s with insert, poly bag, 2,000 only)	8
86	Subway Org. SUBWAY 8	Sorry To Embarrass You/Summer In Your Heart (p/s, with insert, 2,000 only)	5
87	Sha La La BaBaBaBaBa 02	Sad Kaleidoscope/TALULAH GOSH: I Told You So (flexidisc p/s, 2,500 only)	8
80s	Caff CAFF 10	Sometimes I Worry About You/For Always/Sorry To Embarrass You/ Music From The Big Pink (foldaround p/s with insert, 500 only)	15

(see also Cinematics, Red Chair Fadeaway)

RAZORLIGHT
03	Mercury 9814044	Rip It Up/Here It Comes (numbered p/s)	8
03	Mercury 9800413	Rock 'n' Roll Lies/Action/Yeah Yeah Yeah (CD, card sleeve)	10
03	Mercury 9800414	Rock 'n' Roll Lies/In The City (some in numbered p/s)	12/8
04	Universal 9866831	Golden Touch/Dean, Take Your Time (numbered, gatefold)	6

RAZOR'S EDGE
66	Stateside SS 532	Let's Call It A Day, Girl/April	20

CHRIS REA
74	Magnet MAG 10	So Much Love/Born To Lose (no p/s)	25
79	Magnet MAGL 5028	DELTICS (LP, blue vinyl, stickered sleeve)	12

REACTA
79	Battery Operated WAC 1	Stop The World/SUS (p/s)	80

(see also Television Personalities)

REACTION
68	President PT 208	That Man/Falling In Love With You	12

REACTION
70	Columbia Blue Beat DB 119	Oh Me, Oh My/RECO: It's Love	12
70	Attack ATT 8022	You Yes You/CIMARONS: Be There	10

(see also Ezz Reco, Joe Higgs)

REACTION
78	Island WIP 6437	I Can't Resist/I Am A Case (p/s)	15

(see also Talk Talk)

AL READ
56	HMV POP 278	What Is A Home?/We Haven't Any Money	5
59	HMV POP 575	That's Life/Our Maggie's Going To Get Married	5
59	HMV 7EG 8440	SUCH A LIFE (EP)	10

PAT READER
60	Triumph RGM 1024	Ricky/Dear Daddy	50
62	Piccadilly 7N 35077	Cha Cha On The Moon/May Your Heart Stay Young Forever	50
63	Oriole CB 1903	Helpless/Lover's Lane	15

BERTICE READING
55	Parlophone R 4045	My One Sin (In Life)/Frankie And Johnnie (78)	6
55	Parlophone R 4057	Songs From "Jazz Train" Parts 1 & 2 (78, with Edric Connor)	6
55	Parlophone R 4058	Songs From "Jazz Train" Parts 3 & 4 (78)	6
55	Parlophone R 4064	Bessie Smith Blues/Everybody's Somebody's Fool (78)	6
57	Decca F 10965	No Flowers By Request/September In The Rain	12
58	Parlophone R 4462	Rock Baby Rock/It's A Boy (78 rpm = £20)	55
58	Parlophone R 4487	My Big Best Shoes/No More In Life (78 rpm = £12)	30

WILMA READING
74	Pye 7N 45380	Play It Again/Two Can Have A Party	8

REALITY FROM DREAM
75	(no label) CP 109	REALITY FROM DREAM (LP, private pressing)	130

REAL KIDS
78	Bronze BRO 54	All Kindsa Girls/Common At Noon (p/s)	8
78	Bronze BRON 509	REAL KIDS (LP)	15

REALM
66	CBS 202044	Hard Time Loving You/Certain Kind Of Girl	30

(see also Earl Preston & Realms)

REAL McCOY
67	Fontana TF 794	Show Me How You Milk A Cow/I Paid For My Laughs.	7
68	Pye 7N 17618	I Get So Excited/Somebody's Taken Maria Away	6
69	Pye 7N 17669	Quick Joey Small/Happiness Is Love	6
69	Pye 7N 17704	Round The Gum Tree/I Will	6
69	Pye 7N 17772	Gitarzan/Anytime You Need Me	6
69	Pye 7N 17850	Many The Memories/She's Different, She's Beautiful	5
70	Marble Arch MAL 1251	THIS IS THE REAL McCOY (LP)	22

(see also Tony Colton)

REAL THING
| 72 | Bell BLL 1232 | Vicious Circles Parts 1 & 2. | 5 |

(see also Chants)

REASONS
| 78 | Island WIP 6467 | Hard Day At The Office/Baby Bright Eyes (no p/s) | 30 |

REBEL
| 81 | Bridge House BHS 2 | Rocka Shocka/Drift Away (p/s) | 12 |
| 86 | Flying Pig REBS 1 | Valentino/Lonely Traveller (p/s, with free single) | 12 |

REBEL ROUSERS
| 68 | Fontana TF 973 | Should I?/As I Look | 100 |

(see also Cliff Bennett & Rebel Rousers, Soul Sounds)

REBELS (Jamaica)
| 70 | Bullet BU 440 | Nice Grind/SIDNEY ALL STARS: Nice Grind (Version) | 10 |
| 70 | Trojan TR 7779 | It's All In The Game/Easy Come | 12 |

(see also The Pioneers)

REBELS (U.K.)
| 67 | Page One POF 017 | Hard To Love You/Call Me | 20 |

REBELS
| 78 | Rigid IS REB 1029 | Suicide | 175 |

REBOUNDS
| 64 | Fontana TF 461 | Help Me/The World Is Mine | 40 |

REBS
| 58 | Capitol CL 14932 | Bunky/Renegade | 10 |

RECO
69	Downtown DT 417	Quando Quando/Reg 'A' Jeg (as Reco & Rudies)	12
69	Jackpot JP 710	Memory Of Don Drummond/THE TOBIES: Resting	15
69	Treasure Isle TI 7052	The Lion Speaks/ANDY CAPP: Pop A Top	10
69	Pama ECO 14	RECO IN REGGAE LAND (LP)	60

(see also Reaction, Don Reco, Rico Rodriguez, Father Sketto, Joe Monsano, Slim Smith, Laurel Aitken)

DON RECO
| 71 | Big Shot BI 597 | Waterloo Rock/LLOYD'S ALL STARS: Walls Soul | 12 |

(see also U Roy Junior)

EZZ RECO & LAUNCHERS
64	Columbia DB 7217	King Of Kings/Blue Beat Dance	10
64	Columbia DB 7222	Little Girl/The Bluest Beat	5
64	Columbia DB 7290	Please Come Back/At A Party	5
64	Columbia SEG 8326	JAMAICAN BLUE BEAT (EP)	20

(see also Reaction)

RECORD PLAYERS
| 78 | Wreckord WRECK 001 | DOUBLE C SIDE (EP, label also listed as Aerco AERO 1104) | 8 |
| 80 | Wreckord WRECK 002 | Give An Inch/Squirming In The Vermin By The Bonny Banks Of Clyde/67/Parasite (p/s) | 6 |

RECTIFY
| 88 | Taffcore TAFF 001 | 20TH CENTURY EP (foldout p/s) | 10 |

RED
| 83 | Jigsaw SAW 2 | RED (LP, private pressing) | 25 |

RED ALERT
80	Guardian GM-RA/B 61	BORDER GUARDS (EP)	150
82	No Future OI 5	In Britain/Screaming At The Nation/Murder Missile (p/s)	10
82	No Future OI 13	Take No Prisoners/Empire Of Crime/Sell Out (p/s)	10
83	No Future OI 20	City Invasion/Negative Reaction (p/s)	8
83	No Future OI 27	THERE'S A GUITAR BURNING (12" EP)	15
83	No Future PUNK 5	WE'VE GOT THE POWER (LP, with inner)	15

RED ALERT
| 82 | Steel City AJS7R | Run To Ground/Wild You (no p/s) | 10 |

RED BALUNE
| 78 | MCCB 001 | Capitalist Kid/Spider In Love (p/s) | 25 |

REDBEAT
| 80 | Malicious Damage MD 440 | Machines In Motion/More Or Less Cut (12", p/s) | 8 |

REDBONE
70	CBS 5061	Crazy Cajun Cakewalk Band/Night Come Down	5
70	CBS 5326	Maggie/New Blue Sermonette	6
70	CBS 64069	REDBONE (LP)	15
70	CBS 64198	POTLATCH (LP)	15
71	Epic EPC 64709	WITCH QUEEN OF NEW ORLEANS (LP)	15
72	Epic EQ 30815	MESSAGE FROM A DRUM (LP, quadraphonic)	15

MINT VALUE £

REDCAPS
63	Decca F 11716	Shout/Little Things You Do	15
63	Decca F 11789	Talkin' 'Bout You/Come On Girl	15
64	Decca F 11903	Mighty Fine Girl/Funny Things	15

REDCELL
| 92 | B12 07 | An Escape From Unpleasant Realities (12", black, red or blue vinyl) | 15 |
| 93 | B12 008 | INTERIM EP (12", no p/s) | 18 |

RED CHAIR FADEAWAY
89	Cosmic Eng. M. CTA 103	Let It Happen/Myra/Dragonfly/Grasshopper (12", p/s, 500 only)	15
89	Cosmic Eng. M. CTA 105	Mr Jones/Chimney Pots/Faraway Lights/Out Of The Grey (12", p/s, 450 only)	15
91	Tangerine MM 10	CURIOUSER AND CURIOUSER (LP, foldaround sleeve with booklet, no'd)	20
93	Aural AUR 102	MESMERISED (LP, 500 only)	12
(see also Razorcuts)			

RED CRAYOLA
| 78 | Radar ADA 22 | Wives In Orbit/Yik Yak (p/s, red vinyl) | 5 |
| 78 | Radar/Sound For Industry SFI 347 | Hurricane Fighter Plane/13TH FLOOR ELEVATORS: Reverberation (flexidisc free with *Zig Zag* magazine, issue 88) | 6 |

FREDDIE REDD
| 58 | Nixa NJL 19 | GET HAPPY (LP) | 50 |

GENE REDD & GLOBETROTTERS
| 59 | Parlophone R 4584 | Red River Valley Rock/Kentucky Home Rock | 10 |

NOEL REDDING BAND
| 75 | RCA RS 1030 | CLONAKILTY COWBOYS (LP) | 15 |
| *(see also Loving Kind, Jimi Hendrix, Fat Mattress, Lord Sutch)* | | | |

OTIS REDDING
SINGLES
64	London HLK 9833	Pain In My Heart/Something Is Worrying Me	20
64	London HLK 9876	Come To Me/Don't Leave Me This Way	20
65	Atlantic AT 4024	Mr Pitiful/That's How Strong My Love Is	15
65	Sue WI 362	Shout Bamalama/Fat Girl	30
65	Atlantic AT 4029	I've Been Loving You Too Long/Winter Wonderland (unissued, demos only)	50
65	Atlantic AT 4039	Respect/I've Been Loving You Too Long	15
65	Atlantic AT 4050	My Girl/Down In The Valley	15
66	Atlantic AT 4080	(I Can't Get No) Satisfaction/Any Ole Way	10
66	Atlantic 584 019	My Lover's Prayer/Don't Mess With Cupid	6
66	Atlantic 584 030	I Can't Turn You Loose/Just One More Day	6
66	Atlantic 584 049	Fa-Fa-Fa-Fa-Fa (Sad Song)/Good To Me	6
67	Atlantic 584 070	Try A Little Tenderness/I'm Sick Y'all	6
67	Atlantic 584 091	Respect/These Arms Of Mine	6
67	Atlantic 584 092	My Girl/Mr Pitiful	6
67	Stax 601 005	Day Tripper/Shake (dark blue labels)	10
67	Stax 601 007	Let Me Come On Home/I Love You More Than Words Can Say (dark blue labels)	10
67	Stax 601 011	Shake (live)/634-5789 (live)	10
67	Stax 601 017	The Glory Of Love/I'm Coming Home	8
67	Stax 601 027	(I Can't Get No) Satisfaction/I've Been Loving You Too Long	8
68	Stax 601 031	(Sittin' On) The Dock Of The Bay/My Sweet Lorene	8
68	Stax 601 040	The Happy Song/Open The Door	8
68	Pye International 7N 25463	She's All Right/Gama Lama	10
68	Atlantic 584 199	Hard To Handle/Amen	8
68	Atlantic 584 220	Champagne And Wine/I've Got Dreams To Remember	8
68	Atlantic 584 234	Papa's Got A Brand New Bag/Direct Me	8
69	Atlantic 584 249	A Lover's Question/You Made A Man Out Of Me	8
69	Atco 226 001	Love Man/That's How Strong My Love Is	10
69	Atco 226 002	Free Me/Higher And Higher	8
69	Evolution E 2442	She's All Right/Tuff Enuff	15
70	Atco 226 012	Look At That Girl/That's A Good Idea	6
70	Atco 2091 020	Wonderful World/Security	6
71	Atlantic 2091 062	I've Been Loving You Too Long/Try A Little Tenderness	5
71	Atlantic 2091 112	(Sittin' On) The Dock Of The Bay/Respect/Mr Pitiful (reissue)	5
72	Atlantic K 10206	White Christmas/Merry Christmas, Baby	5
66	Sue IEP 710	EARLY OTIS REDDING (EP)	100
65	Atlantic ATL 5029	THE GREAT OTIS REDDING SINGS SOUL BALLADS (LP)	50
66	Atlantic ATL 5041	OTIS BLUE: OTIS REDDING SINGS SOUL (LP)	40
66	Atlantic 587 011	THE SOUL ALBUM (LP)	25
66	Atlantic 587 035	THE GREAT OTIS REDDING SINGS SOUL BALLADS (LP, reissue)	18
66	Atlantic 587/588 036	OTIS BLUE: OTIS REDDING SINGS SOUL (LP, reissue, mono/stereo)	18
67	Atlantic 587/588 050	COMPLETE AND UNBELIEVABLE: THE OTIS REDDING DICTIONARY OF SOUL (LP)	25
67	Atlantic 587 042	PAIN IN MY HEART (LP)	20
67	Stax VOLT 418	THE HISTORY OF OTIS REDDING (LP)	20
68	Stax 589 016	OTIS REDDING IN EUROPE (LP)	20
68	Stax 230 001/231 001	THE DOCK OF THE BAY (LP)	20
68	Atlantic 587/588 113	THE IMMORTAL OTIS REDDING (LP)	20
68	Atlantic 587/588 148	OTIS REDDING AT THE WHISKEY A GO GO, LOS ANGELES (LP)	20
69	Atco 228 001	THE HISTORY OF OTIS REDDING (LP, reissue)	15
69	Atco 228 022	THE DOCK OF THE BAY (LP, reissue)	15
69	Atco 228 017	OTIS REDDING IN EUROPE (LP, reissue)	12
69	Atco 228 025	LOVE MAN (LP)	25
70	Atlantic 2464 003	REMEMBERING (LP)	18
71	Atco 2400 018	TELL THE TRUTH (LP)	18
71	Reprise K 40430	LIVE AT THE MONTEREY INTERNATIONAL POP FESTIVAL (LP, shared with Jimi Hendrix)	30
72	Atlantic K 60015	THE BEST OF OTIS REDDING (LP)	12

OTIS REDDING & CARLA THOMAS
67	Stax 601 012	Tramp/Oooh Carla, Oooh Otis (with Carla Thomas)	10
67	Stax 601 021	Knock On Wood/Let Me Be Good To You	8
68	Stax 601 033	Lovey Dovey/OTIS REDDING: New Year's Resolution	8
67	Stax 589 007	THE KING AND QUEEN OF SOUL	30

(see also Carla Thomas)

RED CHAIR FADEAWAY
90s	Waterbomb SPLAT 002	Never Remember/FUDGE: unknown track (flexi, p/s)	12

RED DIRT
70	Fontana STL 5540	RED DIRT (LP)	550+

EMMA REDE
67	Columbia DB 8136	Just Like A Man/I Gotta Be With You	30

(see also Jacky, Jackie Lee, Jackie & Raindrops, Raindrops)

TEDDY REDELL
60	London HLK 9140	Judy/Can't You See	60

MICHAEL REDGRAVE
50	Topic TRC 12	A New World Will Be Born/ALAN KANE: Me Without You (78)	8

VANESSA REDGRAVE
64	Topic STOP 111	Hanging On A Tree/Where Have All The Flowers Gone (some in title sleeve)	10/6

RED HOT CHILI PEPPERS
85	EMI America EA 205	Hollywood (Africa)/Never Mind (p/s)	10
85	EMI America 12EA 205	Hollywood (Africa) (Remix)/Hollywood (Africa) (Dub Mix)/Never Mind (12", p/s)	12
88	EMI CDP 790 869-2	ABBEY ROAD EP (CD)	8
89	EMI 12MT 70	KNOCK ME DOWN EP (12", p/s)	15
89	EMI 12MT 75	Higher Ground/Catholic Schoolgirls Rule (p/s)	10
90	EMI 12MTX 85	TASTE THE PAIN EP (12", push-out sleeve with inner)	12
90	EMI 10MTX 85	TASTE THE PAIN EP (square disc, numbered)	12
90	EMI 12MTG 88	Higher Ground/Catholic Schoolgirls Rule/None As Weird As Me (12", g/f slv.)	15
90	EMI 12MTPD 88	Higher Ground/Catholic Schoolgirls Rule/None As Weird As Me (12", picture disc, card insert)	12

RED LETTERS
70s	Burning Bing CPS 025	SACRED VOICES EP (p/s)	50

RED LIGHTS
78	Free Range PF 5	Never Wanna Leave/Seventeen (p/s)	60

RED LONDON
83	Razor RZS 105	Sten Guns In Sunderland/This Is England/Soul Train/Revolution Times (p/s)	8
84	Razor RAZ 10	THIS IS ENGLAND (LP)	40

RED LORRY, YELLOW LORRY
80s	Red Rhino RED 28	Take It All/Happy (p/s)	5

ROY REDMOND
67	Warner Bros WB 2075	Good Day Sunshine/That Old Time Feeling	20

RED ONION JAZZ BABIES
60	Collector JE 19	RED ONION JAZZ BABIES (EP)	8

(see also Louis Armstrong)

JEAN REDPATH
66	Bounty BY 6004	LOVE LILT AND LAUGHTER (LP)	20

RED RAGE
80	Flicknife FLS 203	Total Control/I Give You This (p/s)	40

RED RIVER BAND
70	Banana BA 35	I'm Gonna Use What I've Got/Shame Shame	8

REDSKINS
82	CNT CNT 007	Lev Bronstein/The Peasant Army (p/s)	25
83	CNT CNT 016	Lean On Me!/Unionize! (p/s)	7

RED SQUARES
67	Columbia DB 8160	Mountain's High/Pity Me	20
67	Columbia DB 8257	True Love Story/Lollipop	8

RED TELEVISION
71	Brecht Times	RED TELEVISION (LP, private pressing with insert)	150

REDUCERS
78	Vibes XP 1/VR 001	Things Go Wrong/We Are Normal (p/s)	50
79	Vibes VR 001	Man With A Gun/Vengeance/Can't Stop Now (p/s)	50

MIKE REDWAY
64	Oriole CB 1948	Many People/It's So Funny I Could Cry	5
65	CBS 201755	Darling Take Me Back/That's The Way Love Goes	5
65	CBS 202017	Magic Rocking Chair/When You Go	5
66	CBS 202092	One Day/Let Me Be The Someone	5
67	Deram DM 124	Have No Fear, Bond Is Here (Casino Royale)/My Poem For You	10
67	Deram DM 157	Don't Speak Of Me/Sometimes I Remember	5

(see also Rod McKuen, Typhoons, Bud Ashton)

REDWOODS
62	Columbia DB 4859	Please Mr Scientist/Where You Used To Be	20

DIZZY REECE QUINTET
56	Tempo A 140	Chorus/Basie Line	8
58	Tempo EXA 84	A VARIATION ON MONK (EP)	150
59	Tempo EXA 86	NOWHERE TO GO (EP, featuring Tubby Hayes)	150

Dizzy REECE QUINTET

59	Tempo EXA 89	ON THE SCENE (EP)	50
55	Tempo LAP 3	A NEW STAR... (10" LP)	200
57	Tempo TAP 9	PROGRESS REPORT (LP)	450
58	Esquire 32 185	ASIA MINOR (LP)	100
80s	Jasmine JASM 2013	PROGRESS REPORT (LP, reissue)	18

(see also Victor Feldman, Ronnie Scott)

CHUCK REED
57	Brunswick 05646	Whispering Heart/Another Love Has Ended (78 rpm = £7)	15
58	Columbia DB 4113	No School Tomorrow/Let's Put Our Hearts Together (78 rpm = £8)	25
62	Stateside SS 108	Just Plain Hurt/Talking No Trash	15

DEAN REED
59	Capitol CL 14986	The Search/Annabelle	10
59	Capitol CL 15030	I Kissed A Queen/A Pair Of Scissors (And A Pot Of Glue)	10

DENNY REED
61	London HLK 9274	A Teenager Feels It Too/Hot Water	18

JERRY REED
58	Capitol CL 14851	Bessie Baby/Too Young To Be Blue (78 rpm = £60)	260
69	RCA RCA 1798	Oh What A Woman/Claw	5
70	RCA RCA 2025	Georgia Sunshine/Singing '69	5
71	RCA RCA 2063	Amos Moses/The Preacher And The Bear	5
69	RCA SF 8006	ALABAMA WILD MAN (LP)	18

JIMMY REED
60	Top Rank JAR 333	Baby What You Want Me To Do/Caress Me Baby	22
60	Top Rank JAR 394	Found Love/Where Can You Be	20
60	Top Rank JAR 533	Hush-Hush/Going By The River	20
63	Stateside SS 205	Shame Shame Shame/Let's Get Together	20
64	Stateside SS 330	Shame Shame Shame/Let's Get Together (reissue)	8
66	Sue WI 4004	Odds And Ends/Going By The River Pt. II (B-side actually Pt. I)	40
67	HMV POP 1579	Two Ways To Skin A Cat/Got Nowhere To Go	20
64	Stateside SE 1016	BLUES OF JIMMY REED (EP)	40
64	Stateside SE 1026	I'M JIMMY REED (EP)	40
62	Stateside SL 10012	JIMMY REED AT CARNEGIE HALL (LP)	40
64	Stateside SL 10055	JUST JIMMY REED (LP)	40
64	Stateside SL 10069	SINGS THE BEST OF THE BLUES (LP)	40
64	Stateside SL 10086	PLAYS 12-STRING GUITAR BLUES (LP)	40
64	Stateside SL 10091	THE BOSS MAN OF THE BLUES (LP)	35
65	Fontana 688 514 ZL	THINGS AIN'T WHAT THEY USED TO BE (LP)	25
67	HMV CLP/CSD 3611	THE NEW JIMMY REED (LP)	25
68	Stateside S(S)L 10221	SOULIN' (LP)	25
69	Action ACLP 6011	DOWN IN VIRGINIA (LP)	60
69	Joy JOY(S) 111	THE LEGEND — THE MAN (LP)	15
69	Joy JOY(S) 120	AT CARNEGIE HALL (LP, reissue)	15
69	Joy JOYS 127	AT SOUL CITY (LP)	15
69	Joy JOYS 141	ROCKIN' WITH REED (LP)	15
69	Joy JOYS 151	JIMMY REED SINGS THE BEST OF THE BLUES (LP)	15
69	Joy JOYS 155	THE BEST OF JIMMY REED (LP)	15

JOE REED
71	Dawn DNS 1012	Ain't That A Shame/Follow Me	6

LES REED
62	Piccadilly 7N 35080	Theme From Dr. Finlay's Casebook/The Saint (as Les Reed Strings)	7
64	Fontana TF 455	Spanish Armada/Madrid (as Les Reed Combo)	10
70	Chapter One CH 126	Man Of Action/Madrid (as Les Reed Orchestra)	10
72	Chapter One SCH 189	Man Of Action/Lest We Forget (as Les Reed Orchestra)	6

LOU REED
72	RCA RCA 2240	Walk And Talk It/Wild Child	8
73	RCA RCA 2318	Vicious/Satellite Of Love	5
73	MGM 2006 283	I'm Waiting For The Man/Run Run Run/Candy Says (with Velvet Underground)	8
74	RCA APBO 0221	Caroline Says (Parts 1 & 2)	5
74	RCA APBO 0238	Sweet Jane/Lady Day	5
74	RCA RCA 2467	Sally Can't Dance/Ennui	5
76	RCA RCA 2666	Charley's Girl/Nowhere At All	5
78	Arista ARIST 198	Street Hassle/VELVET UNDERGROUND: I'm Waiting For The Man	
		Venus In Furs (12", p/s)	8
72	RCA SF 8281	LOU REED (LP, orange label)	12
73	RCA RS 1002	BERLIN (LP, orange label with insert)	12
75	RCA CPL 2 1101	METAL MACHINE MUSIC (2-LP, U.S. import with U.K. sticker)	30
88	RCA/HMV C 881-9	TRANSFORMER (CD, box set, 2,500, numbered, with certificate)	20

(see also Velvet Underground)

LULA REED
55	Parlophone CMSP 34	Troubles On Your Mind/Bump On A Log (export issue)	60
55	Parlophone DP 408	Troubles On Your Mind/Bump On A Log (78, export issue)	15

LULA REED & SYL JOHNSON
63	Ember EMB EP 4535	RHYTHM & BLUES BLUE BEAT STYLE (EP)	70

LULA REED & FREDDIE KING
63	Ember EMB 4536	LULA REED AND FREDDIE KING (EP)	50

(see also Freddie King)

NANCY REED
53	London L 1179	You Never Tell Me You Love Me/It's Written All Over Your Face (78)	12

OLIVER REED
61	Decca F 11390	The Wild One/Lonely For A Girl	40
62	Piccadilly 7N 35037	Sometimes/Ecstasy	22

TAWNY REED
65	Pye 7N 15935	Needle In A Haystack/I've Got A Feeling	40
66	Pye 7N 17078	You Can't Take It Away/My Heart Cries	25

VIVIEN REED
68	Direction 58-3574	I Wanna Be Free/Yours Until Tomorrow	7

WINSTON REED
72	Pama Supreme PS 365	Breakfast In Bed/RANNY WILLIAMS: Guitar Shuffle	7
73	Pama PM 863	Big Eight/RANNY WILLIAMS & CLASSICS: Big Eight – Version	7

WINSTON REEDY
83	Carousel 12CAR 48	Dim The Light/Shower Of Rain (12")	20

VALA REEGAN & VALARONS
66	Atlantic 584 009	Fireman/Living In The Past (DJ copy = £300)	200

DELLA REESE
57	London HL 7024	I Cried For You (Now It's Your Turn To Cry Over Me)/And That Reminds Me (export issue)	15
58	London HLJ 8687	You Gotta Love Everybody/I Wish (78 rpm = £10)	15
59	London HLJ 8814	Sermonette/Dreams End At Dawn (78 rpm = £12)	15
59	RCA RCA 1160	Not One Minute More/Soldier Won't You Marry Me (78 rpm = £10)	7
66	HMV POP 1553	It Was A Very Good Year/Solitary Woman	10
68	Stateside SS 2128	It Was A Very Good Year/I Had To Know My Way Around	5
72	Avco Embassy 6105 010	If It Feels Good, Do It/Good Lovin' (Makes It Right) (paper label)	10
74	People PEO 106	Who Is She And What Is She To You/If Loving You Is Wrong	6
59	London LTZ-J 15163	THE HISTORY OF THE BLUES (LP)	30
60	RCA RD 27167/SF 5057	DELLA (LP)	15
61	RCA RD 27208/SF 5091	DELLA DELLA CHA-CHA-CHA (LP)	18
62	RCA RD 27234/SF 5112	SPECIAL DELIVERY (LP)	15
63	RCA Victor RD/SF 7508	ON STAGE (LP)	15
63	RCA Victor RD/SF 7584	WALTZ WITH ME, DELLA (LP)	12
64	RCA RD/SF 7628	AT BASIN STREET EAST (LP)	12
65	RCA RD 7695	MOODY (LP)	12
65	HMV CLP 1923	C'MON AND HEAR (LP, also stereo CSD 1636)	12
66	HMV CLP/CSD 3540	I LIKE IT LIKE DAT! (LP)	12
66	HMV CLP/CSD 3573	LIVE (LP, with Bill Doggett & others)	12

TONY REESE
59	London HLJ 8987	Just About This Time Tomorrow/Lesson In Love (78 rpm = £12)	25

DEL REEVES
65	United Artists UP 1092	Girl On The Billboard/Eyes Don't Come Crying To Me	7
66	United Artists UP 1122	Women Do Funny Things To Me/My Half Of Our Past	7
66	United Artists UP 1145	Gettin' Any Feed For Your Chickens/Plain As The Tears On My Face	7

EDDIE REEVES
62	London HL 9548	Cry Baby/Talk Talk	20

JIM REEVES
78s
54	London HL 8014	Bimbo/Gipsy Heart	30
54	London HL 8030	Mexican Joe/I Could Cry (with Circle O Ranch Boys)	30
54	London HL 8055	Butterfly Love/It's Hard To Love Just One (with String Band)	30
54	London HL 8064	Echo Bonita/Then I'll Stop Loving You (with Louisiana Hayride Band)	30
54	London HL 8105	Padre Of Old San Antone/Mother Went A-Walkin'	25
55	London HL 8118	Penny Candy/I'll Follow You (with Louisiana Hayride Band)	30
55	London HL 8159	Drinking Tequila/Red-Eyed And Rowdy	35
55	London HLU 8185	Tahiti/Give Me One More Kiss	30
56	London HLU 8351	The Wilder Your Heart Beats, The Sweeter You Love/Where Does A Broken Heart Go	30
57	RCA RCA 1005	Four Walls/I Know And You Know	20
58	RCA RCA 1074	Blue Boy/Theme Of Love	25
59	RCA RCA 1144	Partners/I'm Beginning To Forget You	45
60	RCA RCA 1168	He'll Have To Go/In A Mansion Stands My Love	60

45s
54	London HL 8014	Bimbo/Gipsy Heart	210
54	London HL 8030	Mexican Joe/I Could Cry (with Circle O Ranch Boys)	210
54	London HL 8055	Butterfly Love/It's Hard To Love Just One (with String Band)	210
54	London HL 8064	Echo Bonita/Then I'll Stop Loving You (with Louisiana Hayride Band)	210
54	London HL 8105	Padre Of Old San Antone/Mother Went A-Walkin'	145
55	London HL 8118	Penny Candy/I'll Follow You (with Louisiana Hayride Band)	190
55	London HLU 8185	Tahiti/Give Me One More Kiss	190
55	London HL 8159	Drinking Tequila/Red-Eyed And Rowdy	260

(All the above 45s were issued with gold label print)
56	London HLU 8351	The Wilder Your Heart Beats, The Sweeter You Love/Where Does A Broken Heart Go	190
57	RCA RCA 1005	Four Walls/I Know And You Know	35
58	RCA RCA 1074	Blue Boy/Theme Of Love	22
59	RCA RCA 1144	Partners/I'm Beginning To Forget You (triangular or round centre)	18/12
60	RCA RCA 1168	He'll Have To Go/In A Mansion Stands My Love	7
60	RCA RCA 1197	I'm Getting Better/I Know One	7
54	London RE-P 1015	THE BIMBO BOY (EP)	90
55	London RE-P 1033	THE BIMBO VOL. 2 (EP)	90
60	RCA RD 27176	HE'LL HAVE TO GO (LP)	15
61	RCA RD 27193	THE INTIMATE JIM REEVES (LP, also stereo SF 5079)	each 15
62	London HA-U 8015	BIMBO (LP)	20

(All the above LPs were originally issued with black labels, later orange label reissues are worth around £6 each.)

MINT VALUE £

MARTHA REEVES & VANDELLAS
(see under Martha & Vandellas)

REFLECTION
68	Reflection RL 3015	THE PRESENT TENSE: SONGS OF SYDNEY CARTER (LP)	18

(see also Sounds Of Salvation)

REFLECTIONS (U.K.)
74	Purple PUR 124	Love And Affection/No More	7
75	Purple PUR 127	Moon Power/Little Star	7

REFLECTIONS (U.S.)
64	Stateside SS 294	(Just Like) Romeo & Juliet/Can't You Tell By The Look In My Eyes (DJ = £100)	60
65	Stateside SS 406	Poor Man's Son/Comin' At You	28
74	Tamla Motown TMG 907	(Just Like) Romeo & Juliet/Can't You Tell By The Look In My Eyes (reissue)	15
77	ABC ABC 4181	Like Adam And Eve/AUGUST & DENEEN: We Go Together	15
65	Stateside SE 1034	POOR MAN'S SON (EP)	100

REFUGEE
74	Charisma CAS 1087	REFUGEE (LP, with inner sleeve)	15

(see also Nice, Yes)

REGAL DEWY
78	RCA XB 1032	Love Music/Where Would I Be Without Me	8

JOAN REGAN
54	Decca F 10362	Wait For Me, Darling (with Johnston Brothers)/Two Kinds Of Tears (gold or silver lettering)	40/30
54	Decca F 10373	If I Give My Heart To You/Faded Flowers	22
54	Decca F 10397	This Ole House/Can This Be Love?	20
55	Decca F 10432	Prize Of Gold/When You're In Love	22
55	Decca F 10474	Open Up Your Heart And Let The Love In (with Rusty Regan)/If You Learn To Love Each Other	22
55	Decca F 10505	Danger! Heartbreak Ahead/Don't Be Afraid Of Love	15
55	Decca F 10521	Just Say You Love Her/Nobody Danced With Me	15
55	Decca F 10598	The Shepherd Boy/The Rose And The Flame	10
56	Decca F 10659	Love And Marriage/Cross Of Gold (Croce Di Oro)	15
56	Decca F 10710	Don't Take Me For Granted/The Boy With The Magic Guitar	5
56	Decca F 10742	Honestly/I'd Never Leave You Baby (B-side with Johnston Brothers)	5
56	Decca F 10757	Sweet Heartaches/Second Fiddle (with Ted Heath)	5
56	Decca F 10801	Gone/Make Me A Child Again	5
60	Pye 7N 15303	Must Be Santa/Will Santa Come To Shanty Town	7
61	Pye 7N 15367	We Who Are In Love/My Foolish Heart	5
61	Pye 7N 15400	Surprisin'/In The Arms Of My Love (some with p/s)	8
66	CBS 202100	Don't Talk To Me About Love/I'm No Toy (DJ copy = £85)	50
67	CBS 2657	No-One Beside Me/A Love So Fine	20
55	Decca DFE 6235	JOAN REGAN SUCCESSES (EP)	22
56	Decca DFE 6278	JOAN REGAN SUCCESSES VOL. 2 (EP)	22
54	Decca LF 1182	THE GIRL NEXT DOOR (10" LP)	70
56	Decca LK 4153	JUST JOAN (LP)	80

RUSS REGAN
59	Capitol CL 15084	Adults Only/Just The Two Of Us	10

TOMMY REGAN
64	Colpic PX 725	I'll Never Stop Loving You/This Time I'm Losing You	125

(see also Marcels)

REGENTS (U.K.)
63	Oriole CB 1912	Bye Bye Johnny/Come Along	25

(see also Buddy Britten)

REGENTS (U.K.)
66	CBS 202247	Words/Worryin' Kind	35

REGENTS (U.K.)
79	Rialto TREB 111	7 Teen (Uncensored Version)/Hole In The Heart (p/s)	6

REGENTS (U.S.)
61	Columbia DB 4666	Barbara Ann/I'm So Lonely	30
61	Columbia DB 4694	Runaround/Laura My Darling	28

REGGAE BOYS
69	Amalgamated AMG 841	Me No Born Ya/The Wicked Must Survive	20
69	Amalgamated AMG 843	The Reggae Train/Dolly House On Fire	18
69	Gas GAS 135	Ba Ba/GLEN ADAMS: Power Cut	20
69	Unity UN 530	What You Gonna Do/HEDLEY BENNETT: Hot Coffee	18
70	Bullet BU 431	Pupa Live On Eye Top/Give Me Faith	12
70	Gas GAS 122	Phrases/Give Me Faith	15
70	Upsetter US 339	Hurry Up/Thanks We Get	20
70	Pressure Beat PR 5503	Walk By Day, Fly By Night/JOE GIBBS & DESTROYERS: Unknown Tongue	20

(see also Glen Adams, Alva Lewis, Upsetters)

REGGAE STRINGS
73	Trojan TRLS 54	REGGAE STRINGS (LP)	15

(see also Horace Faith)

REGULAR FRIES
97	Fierce Panda NING 41	REGULAR FRIES: Dust It, Don't Bust It/CAMPAG VELOCET: Drencrom [Velocet Synthemesc] (p/s, 1,500 only)	18

(see Campag Velocet)

LOU REICHNER BAND
80	ESR Records S/80/CUS 733	Photograph/I Sit And Stare/The End Of The World/Out On The Streets (also listed as ESR 4, 300 only, some with insert)	50/20

AL REID
69	Blue Cat BS 161	Vietcong/MAX ROMEO: Me Want Man	28
69	Blue Cat BS 163	Darling/MAX ROMEO: It's Not The Way	28

ALTYMAN REID
72	Green Door GD 4026	A Sugar/A Sugar Part Two (with Roy Shirley)	7

(see also Roy Shirley)

CARLTON REID
66	Ska Beat JB 254	Funny/Turn On The Lights	18
69	Blue Cat BS 162	Leave Me To Cry/Warning	28

CLARENCE REID
69	Atlantic 584 290	Nobody But You Babe/Send Me Back My Money	8
69	Atlantic 584 301	I'm Gonna Tear You A New Heart/I'm A Man Of My Word	8

DUKE REID (& HIS GROUP)
60	Blue Beat BB 24	Duke's Cookies (with His Group)/JIVING JUNIORS: I Wanna Love	20
62	Blue Beat BB 119	Twelve Minutes To Go (actually by Don Drummond)/ HORTENSE ELLIS: Midnight Train	30
63	Duke DK 1002	Pink Lane Shuffle (with His Group)/LAUREL AITKEN: Low Down Dirty Girl	20
67	Master's Time MT 003	Religious Service At Bond Street Gospel Hall/Religious Service At Bond Street Gospel Hall (Continued)	10
67	Trojan TR 001	Judge Sympathy (actually by Freedom Singers & Duke Reid All Stars)/ ROLAND ALPHONSO: Never To Be Mine	45
72	Duke Reid DR 2522	Hurt Parts 1 & 2 (actually by Eagles [Jamaica])	12

(see also Chuck & Darby, Derrick Morris, Stranger)

LEYROY REID
68	Blue Cat BS 125	The Fiddler/LOVELETTES: Shook	30
68	Blue Cat BS 127	Great Surprise/TEN(N)ORS: Khaki	25

(see also Nehemiah Reed)

MARC REID
66	CBS 202244	For No One/Lonely City Blues	8
67	CBS 202581	Magic Book/My World Turns Around	8
67	CBS 2950	We Should Live Together/Sale By Auction	7

NEHEMIAH REID('S ALL STARS)
68	Island WI 3102	Family War/Give Me That Love	18
70	Hot Shot HS 03	Hot Pepper/Seawave (as Nehemiah Reid's All Stars)	10
70s	Torpedo TOR 23	Mafia/H.E.L.L. 5 (as Nehemiah Reid's All Stars)	12

(see also Leyroy Reid, Cynthia Richards)

NORVELLE REID
57	Brunswick 05725	All The Way/The World Won't End (export issue)	5

P. REID
65	Ska Beat JB 197	Redeemed/Goodbye World	18

PATTI REID
87	Fellside FE 061	PATTI REID (LP)	12

TERRY REID (& JAYWALKERS)
67	Columbia DB 8166	The Hand Don't Fit The Glove/This Time (as Terry Reid & Jaywalkers)	15
68	Columbia DB 8409	Better By Far/Fires Alive	18
69	Columbia PSRS 323	Superlungs (promo only, as "Terry Reid Is Superlungs")	20
76	ABC 4137	Oooh Baby/Brave Awakening	5
79	Capitol CL 16071	Ain't No Shadow/Bowangi	5
69	Columbia SCX 6370	TERRY REID (LP)	35
71	M. For Pleasure MFP 5220	THE MOST OF TERRY REID (LP)	12
73	Atlantic K 40340	RIVER (LP, gatefold sleeve)	12
76	ABC ABCL 5162	SEED OF MEMORY (LP)	12
79	Capitol E-ST 11857	ROGUE WAVES (LP)	12

(see also Peter Jay & Jaywalkers)

REIGN
70	Regal Zonophone RZ 3028	Line Of Least Resistance/Natural Lovin' Man	40

(see also Yardbirds, Keith Relf, Renaissance, Armageddon, Illusion)

JOHN REILLY
78	Topic 12T 359	THE BONNY GREEN TREE (LP, with booklet)	12

TOMMY REILLY & TRADESMEN
51	Hohner	Minuet/Badinerie (78)	7
63	Oriole CB 1833	Dakota/S.O.S.	6

DJANGO REINHARDT
53	Decca F 10219	Le Soir/Deccaphonie (78)	7
59	Collector JEN 6	SWING GUITARS (EP)	8
59	Collector JEN 8	IMPROVISATION (EP)	8
55	HMV 7EG 8132	DJANGO REINHARDT (EP)	8
54	Oriole/Mercury MG 10019	DJANGO (10" LP)	15
54	Vogue LDE 049	DJANGO REINHARDT VOL. 1 (10" LP)	15
54	Vogue LDE 084	DJANGO REINHARDT VOL. 2 (10" LP)	15
54	Vogue LDE 106	DJANGO REINHARDT VOL. 3 (10" LP, as Django Reinhardt Quintet)	15
54	HMV DLP 1045	DJANGO REINHARDT (10" LP)	15
54	Felsted EDL 87005	NUAGES (10" LP, as Django Reinhardt & His Rhythm)	15
59	HMV CLP 1249	DJANGO (LP)	15
60	HMV CLP 1340	THE ART OF DJANGO (LP)	15
60	HMV CLP 1389	DJANGO — THE UNFORGETTABLE (LP)	15
60s	Ember CJS 810	REQUIEM FOR A JAZZMAN (LP)	15
64	Realm RM 184	INCOMPARABLE (LP)	12
71	Xtra XTRA 1117	DJANGO REINHARDT VOL. 2 (LP)	12

(see also Quintet Of Hot Club Of France)

Joe REISMAN ORCHESTRA

JOE REISMAN ORCHESTRA
55	HMV B 10891	Bo Diddley/Bubble Boogie (78)	10
56	HMV 7M 364	Robin Hood/His Name Was Judas	5
60	Columbia DB 4553	The World Of Suzi Wong (Theme)/Melodie D'Amour	5
61	Pye International 7N 25087	The Guns Of Navarone/Yassu	5

REIVERS
59	Top Rank JAR 244	The Wee Magic Stane/The Wreck Of The John B	5
60	Top Rank JAR 283	Down In The Mines/Govan Is A Busy Place	6

REJOICE!
69	Stateside SS 8010	November Snow/Quick Draw Man	6
69	Stateside S(S)L 5009	REJOICE! (LP)	15

BOB RELF
75	Black Magic BM 101	Blowin' My Mind To Pieces/PAULA RUSSELL: Blowin' My Mind To Pieces	10

(see also Bob & Earl)

JANE RELF
71	Decca F 13231	Without A Song From You/Make My Time Pass By	25

(see also Stairway, Renaissance)

KEITH RELF
66	Columbia DB 7920	Mr. Zero/Knowing	40
66	Columbia DB 8084	Shapes In My Mind/Blue Sands	50

(see also Yardbirds, Jim McCarty, Renaissance, Reign, Together, Armageddon)

RELIGIOUS OVERDOSE
80	Glass GLASS 004	Control Addicts/25 Minutes (p/s with green label)	5

RELOAD
92	Evolution EVO 01	RELOAD EP (12", plain sleeve)	50
92	Evolution EVO 02	AUTO RELOAD EP (12", with E 621)	50
92	Evolution EVO 03	RELOAD EP (12", 1-side credited to E 621)	40
93	Infonet INF 13	AURO RELOAD EP VOLUME 2 (12", p/s)	20
93	Infonet INF 04LP	A COLLECTION OF SHORT STORIES (2-LP, some with colour booklet)	50/40
93	Infonet INF 04CD	A COLLECTION OF SHORT STORIES (CD, some with colour booklet)	40/30
95	Warp WARPLP 29	THE THEORY OF EVOLUTION (2-LP, gatefold sleeve)	20
95	Surreal Sound TAPE 2	THE BIOSPHERE (cassette, free with initial copies of *Surreal Sounds*)	15

(see also Global Communications, Link, Mystic Institute)

R.E.M.
I.R.S. SINGLES
83	I.R.S. PFP 1017	Radio Free Europe/There She Goes Again (p/s)	50
83	I.R.S. PFSX 1026	Talk About The Passion/Shaking Through/Carnival Of Sorts (Box Cars)/1,000,000 (12", p/s)	15
84	I.R.S. IRS 105	S. Central Rain (I'm Sorry)/King Of The Road (p/s)	8
84	I.R.S. IRSX 105	S. Central Rain (I'm Sorry)/Voice Of Harold/Pale Blue Eyes (12", p/s)	12
84	I.R.S. IRS 107	(Don't Go Back To) Rockville/Wolves (Lower) (p/s)	8
84	I.R.S. IRSX 107	(Don't Go Back To) Rockville/Wolves/9 - 9 (Live Version)/Gardening At Night (live) (12", p/s)	12
85	I.R.S. IRM 102	Can't Get There From Here/Bandwagon (p/s)	8
85	I.R.S. IRT 102	Can't Get There From Here (sleeve states 'Extended Mix', label states 'LP Version', but actually 3.39 edit)/Bandwagon/Burning Hell (12", p/s, some with printed banner crediting unissued tracks)	15/8
85	I.R.S. IRM 105	Wendell Gee/Crazy (p/s)	10
85	I.R.S. IRMD 105	Wendell Gee/Crazy//Ages Of You/Burning Down (double pack)	12
85	I.R.S. IRT 105	Wendell Gee/Crazy/Driver 8 (live) (12", p/s)	10
86	I.R.S. IRM 121	Fall On Me/Rotary Ten (p/s, blue, gold or silver label)	8
86	I.R.S. IRMT 121	Fall On Me/Rotary Ten/Toys In The Attic (12", p/s)	10
86	I.R.S. IRM 128	Superman/White Tornado (p/s, gold or silver label)	10
86	I.R.S. IRMT 128	Superman/White Tornado/Femme Fatale (12", p/s)	10
86	I.R.S. DIRM 128	Superman/White Tornado/Femme Fatale (CD, unissued)	
87	I.R.S. IRM 145	It's The End Of The World As We Know It (And I Feel Fine) (2.59 edit)/This One Goes Out (live) (p/s, gold or metallic blue label)	8
87	I.R.S. IRMT 145	It's The End Of The World As We Know It (And I Feel Fine)/This One Goes Out (live)/Maps And Legends (live) (12", p/s)	8
87	I.R.S. IRM 146	The One I Love/Last Date (bronze label, glossy p/s; silver label, matt p/s)	8
87	I.R.S. IRMT 146	The One I Love/Last Date/Disturbance At The Heron House (live) (12", p/s)	8
87	I.R.S. DIRM 146	The One I Love/Last Date/Disturbance At The Heron House (live) (CD)	8
88	I.R.S. DIRM 161	Finest Worksong (LP Version)/Time After Time, Etc. (live)/It's The End Of The World As We Know It (And I Feel Fine) (CD, numbered stencilled 7" box, 5,000 only)	10
91	I.R.S. DIRMT 178	The One I Love/This One Goes Out (live)/Maps And Legends (CD, with 10-page insert)	10
91	I.R.S. DIRMX 180	It's The End Of The World As We Know It (And I Feel Fine)/Radio Free Europe (Hib-Tone Version)/Last Date/White Tornado (CD, withdrawn)	8
92	I.R.S. DIRM 180	It's The End Of The World As We Know It (And I Feel Fine)/Radio Free Europe (Hib-Tone Version) (gold or silver labels, p/s, some copies have Album Version of 'Radio Free Europe')	8/5

WARNER BROS SINGLES
89	Warner Bros W 7577X	Stand/Memphis Train Blues (recycled paper p/s)	5
89	Warner Bros W 7577CD	Stand/Memphis Train Blues/(The Eleventh Untitled Song) (3" CD, card sleeve)	8
89	Warner Bros W 7577CDX	Stand/Memphis Train Blues/(The Eleventh Untitled Song) (3" CD, 'maple-leaf' pack)	12
89	Warner Bros W 2960X	Orange Crush/Ghost Riders (recycled paper p/s)	5
89	Warner Bros W 2960B	Orange Crush/Ghost Riders ('The Green Package' box set with poster)	8
89	Warner Bros W 2960CD	Orange Crush/Ghost Riders/Dark Globe (3" CD, gatefold card sleeve)	15
89	Warner Bros W 2833W	Stand/Pop Song '89 (Acoustic) (stencil die-cut p/s)	15
89	Warner Bros W 2833CD	Stand/Pop Song '89 (Acoustic)/Skin Tight (live) (3" CD, gatefold card sleeve)	15

| 89 | Warner Bros W 2833CDX | Stand/Pop Song '89 (Acoustic)/Skin Tight (live) (3" CD, black die-cut sleeve in Velcro seal envelope) .... 8 |
| 91 | Warner Bros W 0015CDX | Losing My Religion/Stand (live)/Turn You Inside-Out (live)/World Leader Pretend (live) (CD, with fold-out poster) .... 8 |

OTHER RELEASES
85	Bucketfull Of Brains BOB 5	Tighten Up (flexidisc [LYN 15742] with *Bucketfull Of Brains*) 15
85	Bucketfull Of Brains BOB 5	Tighten Up (hard vinyl test pressing, 50 only) 40
92	Lyntone BOB 32	Academy Fight Song (live)/COAL PORTERS: Watching Blue Grass Burn (p/s, free with *Bucketfull Of Brains* double issue 39/40) 8
92	Lyntone BOB 32	Academy Fight Song (live)/COAL PORTERS: Watching Blue Grass Burn (white label test pressing) 10

PROMOS
83	I.R.S. PFP 1026	Talk About The Passion/Talk About The Passion (plain sleeve, promo only) 30
88	I.R.S. WIRM(T) 161 DL	Finest Worksong (Lengthy Club Mix)/Finest Worksong (Other Mix)/Time After Time Etc. (12" in 'media' p/s) 20
92	I.R.S. CDREM 92	THE ALTERNATIVE RADIO SAMPLER (CD, 7-track promo, includes unreleased version of 'Gardening At Night') 60
92	B.O.B. BOB 32	Academy Flight Song (free with *Bucketfull Of Brains*) 20
94	Warner Bros REM 1	SAMPLER FROM THE BEST OF REM (CD, Brit Awards nomination issue) 25
95	Warner Bros SAM 1558	POP SONGS 89 — 95 (CD, 18-track sampler) 12
99	Warner Bros SAM 00132	POP SONGS 89 — 99 (CD, slimline case, promo only) 12
03	Warners PR 04359	THE BEST OF REM — IN TIME 1980-2003 (promo box set containing 18 1-trk CDs each housed in individual card sleeve in flip top box) 60

(see also Full Time Men, Syd Straw)

REMA-REMA
| 80 | 4AD BAD 5 | WHEEL IN THE ROSES: Feedback Song/Rema-Ream/Instrumental/ Fond Affections (12" EP, original pressings have blue labels) .... 12/8 |

(see also Adam & The Ants, Mass, Models, Wolfgang Press)

REMAYNS
| 85 | Bam Caruso NRIC 029 | FIRST (EP, coloured vinyl) .... 5 |

HERBIE REMINGTON
| 66 | Fontana FJL 313 | REMINGTON RIDES AGAIN (LP) .... 12 |

REMO FOUR
64	Piccadilly 7N 35175	I Wish I Could Shimmy Like My Sister Kate/Peter Gunn 20
64	Piccadilly 7N 35186	Sally Go Round The Roses/I Know A Girl 20
67	Fontana TF 787	Live Like A Lady/Sing Hallelujah 60

(see also Tommy Quickly, Johnny Sandon, Gregory Phillips, Ashton Gardner & Dyke, Mike Hurst, George Harrison)

REMOTE VIEWER
| 01 | City Centre Offices BLOCK 9 | Walsh Ambrose (plain sleeve with insert, 1000 only) .... 8 |

RENAISSANCE (U.S.)
| 68 | Polydor BM 56736 | Mary Jane (Get Off The Devil's Merry-Go-Round)/Daytime Lovers .... 35 |

RENAISSANCE (U.K.)
70	Island WIP 6079	Island/The Sea 15
78	Sire SRE 1022	Northern Lights/Opening Out (picture disc, export issue) 15
79	Sire SIR 4019	Jekyll And Hyde/Forever Changing (withdrawn) 15
69	Island ILPS 9114	RENAISSANCE (LP, pink label) 30
71	Island HELP 27	ILLUSION (LP, withdrawn, export only) 40
72	Sovereign SVNA 7253	PROLOGUE (LP) 15
73	Sovereign SVNA 7261	ASHES ARE BURNING (LP) 12

(see also Jim McCarty, Keith Relf, Jane Relf, Yardbirds, Rupert's People, Reign, Stairway)

LINE RENAUD
53	Columbia SCM 5055	April In Portugal/The Song From Moulin Rouge 7
55	Capitol CL 14230	If I Love You /Pam-Pou-De (Pam-Poo-Day) (triangular centre) 8
56	Columbia SCM 5268	Flamenco Love/To You, My Love 5
56	Columbia DB 3824	Strange/You Can't Keep Running 5

LINE RENAUD & DEAN MARTIN
| 61 | Capitol EAP1 20060 | LINE AND DINO (EP) .... 15 |

(see also Dean Martin)

RENAULTS
| 60 | Warner Bros WB 11 | Meloncolie/Stella .... 6 |

DIANE RENAY
64	Stateside SS 270	Navy Blue/Unbelievable Guy 15
64	Stateside SS 290	Kiss Me Sailor/Soft Spoken Guy 15
64	MGM MGM 1262	Watch Out Sally/Billy Blue Eyes 25
65	MGM MGM 1274	Troublemaker/I Had A Dream 25

(see also Laura Greene)

JOHN RENBOURN
65	Transatlantic TRA 135	JOHN RENBOURN (LP) 30
66	Transatlantic TRA 149	ANOTHER MONDAY (LP) 30
68	Transatlantic TRA 167	SIR JOHN ALOT OF MERRIE ENGLANDE'S MUSICK THYNGE AND YE GREENE KNIGHT (LP) 20
70	Transatlantic TRA 224	THE LADY AND THE UNICORN (LP) 20
72	Transatlantic TRA 247	FARO ANNIE (LP) 18
73	Transatlantic TRA 336	THE HERMIT (LP) 12
73	Transatlantic TRASAM 20	THE JOHN RENBOURN SAMPLER (LP) 12
73	Transatlantic TRASAM 28	SO CLEAR — THE JOHN RENBOURN SAMPLER VOL. 2 (LP) 15

(see also Pentangle, Bert Jansch & John Renbourn, Steve Tilston, Dorris Henderson)

JOHN RENBOURN & STEFAN GROSSMAN

70s	Kicking Mule SNKF 139	JOHN RENBOURN & STEFAN GROSSMAN (LP)	12
70s	Kicking Mule SNKF 161	UNDER THE VOLCANO (LP)	12

(see also Stefan Grossman)

JOHN RENBOURN'S SHIP OF FOOLS

88	Run River 009	SHIP OF FOOLS (LP)	20

DON RENDELL

55	Tempo A 108	Muskrat Ramble/Thames Walk (78, as Don Rendell Sextet) (78 rpm = £8)	25
55	Tempo A 110	You Stepped Out Of A Dream/Slow Boat To China (78, as Don Rendell Quartet)	10
55	Tempo A 112	Didn't We/Dance Of The Ooblies (78, as Don Rendell Sextet)	10
55	Tempo A 114	From This Moment On/Blow Mr. Dexter (78, as Don Rendell Quartet)	10
55	Tempo EXA 11	DON RENDELL QUARTET (EP)	50
55	Tempo EXA 12	DON RENDELL SEXTET (EP)	30
55	Tempo EXA 16	DON RENDELL SEXTET/DAMIAN ROBINSON TRIO (EP, 2 tracks each)	50
55	Tempo EXA 20	DON RENDELL QUINTET (EP)	55
57	Pye Jazz NJE 1044	DON RENDELL JAZZ SIX (EP)	30
58	Decca DFE 6501	PACKET OF BLUES (EP, as Don Rendell Jazz Six)	20
54	Decca LK 4087	JAZZ AT THE FESTIVAL HALL (LP)	70
54	Vogue LDE 050	MUSIC IN THE MAKING (10" LP)	75
55	Vogue LDE 144	DON RENDELL IN PARIS (10" LP, with Bobby Jaspa)	75
55	Tempo LAP 1	MEET DON RENDELL (10" LP)	400
56	Nixa NJL 4	TENORAMA (LP)	100
57	Nixa Jazz Today NJL 7	DON RENDELL PRESENTS THE JAZZ SIX (LP)	100
58	Decca LK 4265	PLAYTIME (LP, as Don Rendell Jazz 6)	60
62	Jazzland JLP 51	ROARIN' (LP, as Don Rendell New Jazz Quintet [with Graham Bond])	110
72	Columbia SCX 6491	SPACEWALK (LP, as Don Rendell Quintet)	120

DON RENDELL & IAN CARR QUINTET

65	Columbia 33SX 1733	SHADES OF BLUE (LP)	400
66	Columbia S(C)X 6064	DUSK FIRE (LP)	325
68	Columbia S(C)X 6214	PHASE III (LP)	180
69	Columbia S(C)X 6316	LIVE (LP)	150
69	Columbia SCX 6368	CHANGE IS (LP)	200

(see also Neil Ardley, Ian Carr, Nucleus)

DON RENDELL QUARTET/JOE HARRIOT QUARTET

57	MGM MGM-EP 615	JAZZ BRITANNIA (EP, 2 tracks each)	28

(see also Joe Harriott)

GOOGIE RENE COMBO

60	London HLY 9056	Forever/Ez-zee	18
66	Atlantic AT 4076	Smokey Joe's La La/Needing You	50
66	Atlantic 584 015	Chica-Boo/Mercy Mercy (Too Much For The Soul)	15

HENRI RENE

55	HMV 7M 308	Enchantment/Crystal Chandelier (with Hugo Winterhalter Orchestra)	6
59	London HLP 8960	La Shabla (The Shovel)/Destiny (with His Orchestra & Chorus) (78 rpm = £12)	8

RENE & HIS ALLIGATORS

66	Decca F 22324	She Broke My Heart/I Can Wait	18

RENE & RENE

65	HMV POP 1468	Chantilly Lace/I'm Not The Only One	10
67	Island WIP 6001	Loving You Could Hurt Me So Much/Little Diamonds	8

RENEGADE

80	White Witch WIT 1	LONELY ROAD (12" EP, with insert)	100

RENEGADES

66	Polydor BM 56508	Cadillac/Every Minute Of The Day	30
66	President PT 106	Thirteen Women/Walking Down The Street	90+
67	Parlophone R 5592	Take A Message/Second Thoughts	25
68	Columbia DB 8383	No Man's Land/Sugar Loaf Mountain	25

RENIA

73	Transatlantic TRA 261	FIRST OFFENDERS (LP)	18

JON RENNARD

70	Tradition TSR 003	BRIMBLEDON FAIR (LP)	12
71	Tradition TSR 010	THE PARTING GLASS (LP)	12

DON RENNIE

56	Parlophone MSP 6218	To Love, To Love Is Wonderful/One Girl — One Boy	7
56	Parlophone MSP 6237	Who Are We?/Can You Find It In Your Heart?	7

DON RENO & RED SMILEY

58	Parlophone GEP 8777	COUNTRY AND WESTERN (EP)	30
61	Melodisc MLP 12-123	HYMNS SACRED GOSPEL SONGS (LP)	15
64	Ember CW 104	SING SWEET BALLADS OF THE WEST (LP)	18

GERRY RENO

62	Decca F 11477	Don't Ever Change/What Would You Do	8
62	Decca F 11516	Who's Fooling You/Three Deadly Sins	8
63	Decca F 11774	It Only Happens In The Movies/One Lonely Guy	15

GINETTE RENO

69	Decca F 22972	Don't Let Me Be Misunderstood/Everything That I Am	8

PAUL RENO

63	Oriole CB 1872	Lonely Little Girl/Angela	10

TEDDY RENO

59	RCA RCA 1108	Ciao Ciao Bambino/Li Per Li (78)	9

the one the one you yearn for
the one you crave for the one you
hunger for the one the one that
makes you mad for it the one that
makes you crazy for it the one
that makes you dribble and drool
for it the one the one you'd sell
your soul for and the wife and
kids for and the cat and car for
the one the one that plays on the
mind at night the one spinning
round and round inside your head
the one that isn't there the one

99l

CHRIS RENSHAW & THE KEEPERS
73　Pye 7N 45285　　　Banksie (A Tribute To Gordon Banks)/National (Health) Anthem (p/s) 8

ROBERT RENTAL
78　Regular ER 102　　　Paralysis/A.C.C. (photocopied black & white foldover p/s) 30
78　Company/Regular RECO 2　Paralysis/A.C.C. (reissue, card gatefold p/s) 20
80　Mute MUTE 010　　　On Location/Double Heart (p/s) 15
79　Industrial IR 0007　　THE BRIDGE (LP, with Thomas Leer) 15
80　Rough Trade ROUGH 17　ROBERT RENTAL AND THE NORMAL (LP, 1-sided, plain red sleeve) 18
(see also Thomas Leer, Normal)

R.E.O. SPEEDWAGON
72　Epic EPC 64813　　　R.E.O. SPEEDWAGON (LP) 12
75　Epic EPC 80175　　　LOST IN A DREAM (LP) 12

REPARATA & DELRONS
65　Stateside SS 382　　Whenever A Teenager Cries/He's My Guy 25
65　Stateside SS 414　　Tommy/Momma Don't Allow 20
68　Bell BLL 1002　　　Captain Of Your Ship/Toom Toom Is A Little Boy 8
68　RCA Victor RCA 1691　I Can Hear The Rain/Always Waitin' 25
68　Bell BLL 1014　　　Saturday Night Didn't Happen/Panic (DJ copy = £60) 40
68　Bell BLL 1021　　　Weather Forecast/You Can't Change A Young Boy's Mind. 18
76　Polydor 2058 688　　Jesabee Lancer (The Belly Dancer)/We Need You 7
72　Avco 6467 250　　　ROCK AND ROLL REVOLUTION (LP) 35

REPERCUSSIONS
92　Mo' Wax MW 001　　Promise/Promise (Dub)/Field Trippin' (12", die-cut stickered sleeve). 15

THE REPLACEMENTS
86　Sire W 8727　　　　Swingin' Party/Left Of The Dial 5
86　Sire W 8679　　　　Kiss Me On The Bus/Little Mascara (p/s) 5
87　Sire W 8297　　　　Alex Chilton/Election day (p/s) 5

REQUIEM
80　Sacrificial SAC 001　Angel Of Sin/Sacrificial Wanderer (no p/s). 220

RESERVE
88　Sha La La　　　　Wherever You Go/SIDDELEYS: The Sun Slid Down/Behind The Tower
　　Ba Ba Ba-Ba Ba 006　(flexidisc, foldover p/s) 10

RESIDENTS
80　Pre PRE 009　　　THE COMMERCIAL SINGLE (p/s) 6
84　Korova KOW 36　　It's A Man's Man's Man's World/I'll Go Crazy (p/s, 5,000 only) 5
83　London RALPH 1　　INTERMISSION (12" EP) 12
79　Virgin VR 3　　　　NIBBLES (LP, 5,000 only) 12
80　Pre PRE X2　　　　THE COMMERCIAL ALBUM (LP, 5,000 only, with incorrect song order). 12

RESIDENT STYLE
84　Plunder PLUN 001　You Spend Too Much Of My Money/Lateral Movement (p/s) 5

RESISTANCE
81　Fontana KIT 1　　　Survival Kit/Big Flame (p/s) 6

RESISTANCE 77
82　Riot City RIOT 18　　NOWHERE TO PLAY (EP) 7
84　Resistance RESIST 1　You Reds/Young And Wrong (p/s). 5

RESISTORS
80　Break SMASH 1　　For Jeanie/Takeaway Love/End Of The Line (p/s) 10

RESPECT featuring PHIL OAKEY
90　Chrysalis CHS 123640　What Comes After Goodbye (Extended Mix)/Ghostdance/What Comes After
　　　　　　　　　　Goodbye (7" Version) (12", p/s). 10

JOHNNY RESTIVO
59　RCA RCA 1143　　The Shape I'm In/Ya Ya (initially with triangular centre, later round) 35/20
59　RCA RCA 1143　　The Shape I'm In/Ya Ya (78) 50
59　RCA RCA 1159　　I Like Girls/Dear Someone (78 rpm = £60) 15
60　Ember EMB S 135　Look Here Now/Sweet Sweet Lovin' 15

RESTLESS ONES
65　Herald HSR 2521　The Restless Ones/He's Everything To Me (p/s) 8

RESTRICTED HOURS
79　Stevenage (no cat. no.)　Getting Things Done/Still Living Out The Car Crash/SYNDICATE: One Way
　　　　　　　　　　Or Another/I Want To Be Somebody (white label, foldover p/s). 10
(see also Astronauts)

RETREADS
81　Eddi Osmo EO 101　Would You Listen Girl/One After 909/You Said You Knew
　　　　　　　　　　(p/s, with mini-poster insert) 55

RETURN TO FOREVER
74　Polydor 2310 283　HYMN OF GALAXY (LP) 15
(see also Chick Corea)

MARTIN REV
85　New Rose ROSE 52　CLOUDS OF GLORY (LP, red vinyl). 12
(see also Suicide)

REVELATION
80　Handshake HANDS 1　Feel It/When I Fall In Love 8

REVELATION (Jamaica)
70　Trojan TR 7727　　Suffering/MEGATONS: Crazy Elephant. 7

REVELLERS
66	Columbia DB 8093	Believe, Believe/Love Is The Greatest Thing	7
67	Spin LP 1703	REVELLERS AGAIN (LP)	35

REVELS
59	Top Rank JAR 235	Midnight Stroll/Talking To My Heart	80

REVELLS
71	CBS 7050	Mind Party/Indian Ropeman	25

DIGGER REVELL'S DENVERMEN
63	Decca F 11657	Surfside/Lisa Marie	18

REVENGE
76	Normal QS 000	Go Away/Game	12
70s	Blood CUS 614	Don't Tell Me Lies/Gimme The Good Times	10

REVENGE
78	Loony LOO 1	Our Generation/I Love Her Way (counterfeits lack ridge around label)	300
78	Loony LOO 2	We're Not Gonna Take It/Pornography (glossy p/s, counterfeits have matt sleeve, and lack ridge around label)	200

PAUL REVERE & THE RAIDERS (featuring Mark Lindsay)
61	Top Rank JAR 557	Like Long Hair/Sharon	25
65	Sue WI 344	Like Long Hair/Sharon (reissue)	15
65	CBS 202003	Steppin' Out/Blue Fox.	10
66	CBS 202027	Just Like Me/B F D R F Blues	20
66	CBS 202205	Kicks/Shake It Up	15
66	CBS 202253	Hungry/There She Goes	10
66	CBS 202411	The Great Airplane Strike/In My Community	10
67	CBS 202502	Good Thing/Undecided Man	10
67	CBS 202610	Ups And Downs/Leslie	10
67	CBS 2737	Him Or Me — What's It Gonna Be?/The Legend Of Paul Revere	10
67	CBS 2919	I Had A Dream/Upon Your Leaving	5
67	CBS 3186	Mo'reen/Oh! To Be A Man	5
68	CBS 3310	Too Much Talk/Happening '68 (featuring Mark Lindsay)	20
68	CBS 3586	Don't Take It So Hard/Observation From Flight 285 (featuring Mark Lindsay)	8
68	CBS 3757	Cinderella Sunshine/Theme From It's Happening (featuring Mark Lindsay)	5
69	CBS 4025	Mr. Sun, Mr. Moon/With You (featuring Mark Lindsay)	5
69	CBS 4260	Let Me/I Don't Know (featuring Mark Lindsay)	7
69	CBS 4504	We Gotta All Get Up Together/Frankfurt Side Street (featuring Mark Lindsay)	5
66	CBS (S)BPG 62406	JUST LIKE US (LP)	25
66	CBS (S)BPG 62797	MIDNIGHT RIDE (LP)	25
67	CBS (S)BPG 62963	GOOD THING (LP)	22
68	CBS (S)BPG 63095	REVOLUTION (LP)	22
69	CBS 63265	GOIN' TO MEMPHIS (LP, mono/stereo)	18
69	CBS 63649	HARD 'N' HEAVY (LP)	18

(see also Mark Lindsay)

REVILLOS
79	Snatzo/Dindisc DIN 1	Where's The Boy For Me/The Fiend (p/s)	6
79	Snatzo/Dindisc DIN 5	Motor Bike Beat/No Such Luck (p/s)	6
80	Snatzo/Dindisc DINZ 16	Scuba Scuba/Scuba Boy Bop (p/s)	6
80	Snatzo/Dindisc DINZ 20	Hungry For Love/Voodoo 2 (p/s, label also lists SP 703)	6
82	Superville SV 1001	She's Fallen In Love With A Monster Man/Mind Bending Cutie Doll (p/s)	6
82	Superville SV 2001	Bongo Brain/Hip City — You Were Meant For Me (p/s)	6
82	Aura AUS 135	Tell Him/Graveyard Groove (p/s)	6
83	EMI RVL 1	Bitten By A Love Bug/Cat Call	6
83	EMI 12 RVL 1	Bitten By A Love Bug (Extended Version)/Cat Call (12", p/s)	8
84	EMI RVL 2	Midnight/Z-X-7 (p/s)	5
84	EMI 12 RVL 2	Midnight (Extended Version)/Midnight (7" Version)/Z-X-7 (12", p/s)	8
80	Snatzo/Dindisc DID X 3	REV UP (LP, green or pink titles)	25
82	Superville SV 4001	ATTACK! (LP, withdrawn)	80

(see also Rezillos)

REVOLUTION
66	Piccadilly 7N 35289	Hallelujah/Shades Of Blue	55

(see also Hellions, Luther Grosvenor, Family, Traffic, Dave Mason & Cass Elliot, Spirit)

(THE) REVOLUTIONARIES
77	Sky Note SKY DD 002	Afro Rock Part 1/Afro Rock Part 2 (12")	40
77	Sky Note SKY 1002	El Bamba	20
78	Island IPR 2024	Headache/Bellyache/Toothache/Headache (12")	30
78	Ballistic FORCE 2003	FATAL DUB (12" EP)	20
75	Love LOV 01	GUN COURT DUB (LP)	40
76	Trenchtown TRELP 001	REVOLUTIONARY DUB (LP, with We The People Band)	40
78	Hawkeye HALP 001	DREAD AT THE CONTROLS (LP)	40
78	Cha Cha CHALP 002	REACTION IN DUB (LP)	35
78	Cha Cha CHALP 005	JONKANOO DUB (LP)	30
79	Burning Vibrations BV 1002	DUTCH MAN DUB (LP)	30
79	Burning Vibrations BV 1004	GREEN BAY DUB (LP)	40
79	Burning Vibrations BV 1010	BURNING DUB (LP)	30
79	Trojan TRLS 169	OUTLAW DUB (LP)	25
80	Manzie DRS LP 002	KING'S DUB (LP)	25
82	Cha Cha CHALP 014	REVIVAL (LP)	25

REVOLUTIONARY ARMY OF INFANT JESUS
87	Probe Plus PROBE 12	THE GIFT OF TEARS (LP)	40

REVOLUTIONARY BLUES BAND
70	MCA MUP(S) 402	REVOLUTIONARY BLUES BAND (LP)	18

REVOLUTIONARY CORPS OF TEENAGE JESUS VS SUICIDE
96	Creeping Bent BENT 005	FRANKIE TEARDROP EP (Frankie Teardrop [126 b.p.m.]/U.S.A. '95/	
		Frankie Teardrop [114 b.p.m.]/Womb 17) (12", p/s, 1,000 only)...............	10

(see also Suicide, Future Pilot A.KA.)

REVOLVING PAINT DREAM
84	Creation CRE 002	Flowers In The Sky/In The Afternoon (foldaround p/s in poly bag)............	25

(see also Laughing Apple, Primal Scream)

REVS
91	Vinyl Japan TASK 9	Just Ask Why/We're So Modern/Stay With Me/Julie Got A Raise (12", p/s).......	8

KIMBERLEY REW
80	Armageddon AS 004	Stomping All Over The World/Nothing's Going To Change In Your Life/	
		Fighting Someone's War (p/s)..	5
81	Armageddon AS 012	My Baby Does Her Hairdo Long/Fishing (p/s, with dB's)......................	5

(see also Soft Boys, Waves)

ROBERTA REX
68	Fontana TF 967	Joey/I Can Feel It...	6

REX (Morris) & MINORS
60	Triumph RGM 1023	Chicken Sax/Snake Eyes...	50

ALVINO REY
61	London HLD 9431	Original Mama Blues/Steel Guitar Rag...................................	10
62	London HA-D 2414	ALVINO REY'S GREATEST HITS (LP)......................................	25

LITTLE BOBBY REY & HIS BAND
60	Top Rank JAR 525	Rockin' "J" Bells/Dance Of The New Year................................	8

REYNARD
76	Pilgrim/Grapevine GRA 102	FRESH FROM THE EARTH (LP)..	40

AMBROSE REYNOLDS
83	Zulu ZULU 3	GREATEST HITS (LP)...	12

(see also Pink Military)

DEBBIE REYNOLDS
55	MGM SP 1127	Carolina In The Morning/Never Mind The Noise In The Market	
		(B-side as Debbie Reynolds' Naturals)..................................	20
56	MGM SP 1155	(Love Is) The Tender Trap/Canoodlin' Rag................................	12
57	Vogue Coral Q 72274	Tammy/French Heels..	10
58	MGM MGM 968	All Grown Up/Wall Flower..	5
58	Coral Q 72297	A Very Special Love/I Saw A Country Boy (78 rpm = £6)....................	5
58	Coral Q 72324	This Happy Feeling/Hillside In Scotland (78 rpm = £6).....................	5
58	Coral Q 72345	Hungry Eyes/Faces There Are Fairer (78 rpm = £6).......................	5
59	MGM MGM 1019	The Mating Game/Right Away (78 rpm = £11).............................	5
59	MGM MGM 1043	It Started With A Kiss/Love Is A Gamble.................................	5
60	London HLD 9028	Am I That Easy To Forget?/Ask Me To Go Steady..........................	5
60	London HLD 9128	City Lights/Just For A Touch Of Your Love...............................	5
61	London HLD 9351	Lonely People/Just A Little Girl.......................................	5
58	MGM MGM-EP 670	DEBBIE REYNOLDS (EP)...	25
58	MGM MGM-EP 671	SINGING IN THE RAIN (EP, with Gene Kelly & Donald O'Connor).............	10
59	MGM MGM-EP 694	DELIGHTFUL DEBBIE REYNOLDS (EP)...................................	15
60	MGM MGM-EP 725	FROM DEBBIE WITH LOVE (EP)..	18
59	London HA-D 2200	DEBBIE (LP, also stereo SAH-D 6051)...................................	40/50
60	London HA-D 2294	AM I THAT EASY TO FORGET? (LP, also stereo SAH-D 6106)..............	40/50
61	London HA-D 2326	FINE AND DANDY (LP)..	40
63	London HA-D/SH-D 8075	GREAT FOLK HITS (LP, mono/stereo)...................................	40/50

(see also Naturals [U.S.])

DONN REYNOLDS
58	MGM MGM 996	Blue Eyes Crying In The Rain/Bella Belinda (78 rpm = £6).................	6
58	Pye 7N 15122	Swing Low Sweet Chariot/Ramona (78 rpm = £6).........................	6
59	Pye NEP 24098	THE DONN REYNOLDS SONGBAG (EP)..................................	20

ELI REYNOLDS
70	Punch PH 37	Mr Car Man/Chiney Man...	7

JODY REYNOLDS
58	London HL 8651	Endless Sleep/Tight Capris (78 rpm = £20).............................	30

TIMMY REYNOLDS
62	Ember EMB S 133	Lullaby Of Love/JEFF MILLS: Daddy's Home.............................	12

REZILLOS
77	Sensible FAB 1	Can't Stand My Baby/I Wanna Be Your Man (p/s, 15,000 only, 5,000 no'd)....	15/10
77	Sensible FAB 2	Flying Saucer Attack/(My Baby Does) Good Sculptures (p/s, unissued)	
77	Sire 6078 612	Flying Saucer Attack/(My Baby Does) Good Sculptures (p/s)...............	10
78	Sire 6198 215	Cold Wars/William Mysterious Overture (unissued)	
78	Sire SIR 4001	Top Of The Pops/20,000 Rezillos Under The Sea (p/s)...................	8
78	Sire SIR 4008	Destination Venus/Mystery Action (p/s)...............................	6
79	Sire SIR 4014	Cold Wars (live)/Flying Saucer Attack (live)/Twist & Shout (live) (p/s)......	5
79	Sensible FAB 1 (Mark 2)	Can't Stand My Baby/I Wanna Be Your Man (reissue, new p/s,	
		run out groove reads "Come Back John Lennon").........................	7
79	Sensible FAB 1 (Mark 2)	Can't Stand My Baby/I Wanna Be Your Man (reissue, p/s, mispressing,	
		B-side plays "(My Baby Does) Good Sculptures (live)",	
		run-off groove reads "De-sire-able product?", 4,000 only).................	6
81	Sire SPC 3	Top Of The Pops/Destination Venus (cassette, flip-up box)................	7
78	Sire K 56530	CAN'T STAND THE REZILLOS (LP, with inner sleeve & postcard insert).......	25
78	Sire SRK 6069	MISSION ACCOMPLISHED ... BUT THE BEAT GOES ON (LP, live)..........	18

(see also Revillos, Shake, Jo Callis, William Mysterious)

RHABSTALLION
81	Rhab RHAB 001	Day To Day/Breadline (p/s, some with badge)	30/20

RHINOCEROS
69	Elektra EKSN 45051	You're My Girl (I Don't Want To Discuss It)/Apricot Brandy	10
69	Elektra EKSN 45058	I Will Serenade You/Belbuekul	7
70	Elektra EKSN 45080	Back Door/In A Little Room	6
70	Elektra 2101 009	Old Age/Let's Party	6
69	Elektra EKL 4030	RHINOCEROS (LP, orange label, also stereo EKS 74030)	28
69	Elektra EKL 4056	SATIN CHICKENS (LP, also stereo EKS 74056)	28
70	Elektra 2469 006	BETTER TIMES ARE COMING (LP)	18

RHODA with The SPECIAL A.K.A.
82	2-Tone CHS TT 18	The Boiler/Theme From The Boiler (p/s)	5
82	2-Tone CHS TT 1218	The Boiler/Theme From The Boiler (12", p/s)	8
	(see also Special A.K.A.)		

JAN RHODE & HIS COOL CATS
60	Qualiton Offbeat PSP 7128	Come Back Baby/So Shy	8

PAT RHODEN
66	Blue Beat BB 360	Send Your Love/Make Believe	12
68	Trojan TR 606	Woman Is Greedy/Endlessly	7
70	Pama PM 811	Maybe The Next Time/Got To See You	6
70	Pama Supreme PS 298	Do What You Gotta Do/Crying Won't Help You	6
70	Mary Lyn ML 101	Time Is Tight/MILTON & DENZIL: I Like It Like That	6
73	Pama Supreme PS 378	Out Of Time/Put A Little Rain Into My Life	6
	(see also Pat Riden, Pat & Marie, Denzil & Pat)		

WINSTON RHODEN
66	Blue Beat BB 360	Send Your Love/Make Believe	20

EMITT RHODES
71	Probe PRO 520	Fresh As A Daisy/You Take The Dark Out Of The Night	7
71	Probe PRO 529	With My Face On The Floor/Somebody Made For Me	7
71	A&M AMS 865	You're A Very Lovely Woman/Till The Day After	6
72	Probe PRO 565	Tame The Lion/Golden Child Of God	7
71	Probe SPBA 6256	EMITT RHODES (LP, gatefold sleeve)	25
71	A&M AMLS 64254	AMERICAN DREAM (LP)	30
71	Probe SPBA 6262	MIRROR (LP)	18
72	Probe SPBA 6266	FAREWELL TO PARADISE (LP)	18

TODD RHODES ORCHESTRA
55	Parlophone MSP 6171	Specks/Silver Sunset	30

RHUBARB RHUBARB
68	President PT 229	Rainmaker/Moneylender	80+

RHYTHM ACES
61	Starlite ST45 061	A Thousand Teardrops/Wherever You May Go	22
61	Starlite ST45 066	Please Don't Go Away/Oh My Darling	20
62	Blue Beat BB 134	I'll Be There/DON DRUMMOND: Dewdrops	20
62	Island WI 032	C-H-R-I-S-T-M-A-S/TOP GRANT: A Christmas Drink	18

RHYTHM & BLUES INC.
65	Fontana TF 524	Louie Louie/Honey Don't	65

RHYTHMETTES
59	Coral Q 72358	Page From The Future/I'll Be With You In Apple Blossom Time (78 rpm = £8)	10

RHYTHM FORCE
72	Tropical AL 0013	Satta Call/Satta Version	6

RHYTHM HERITAGE
76	ABC 4095	Theme From S.W.A.T./I Wouldn't Treat A Dog	5
76	ABC ABCL 5174	DISCO-FIED (LP)	12

RHYTHM KINGS
63	Vocalion POP V 9212	Blue Soul/Exotic	30

RHYTHM MAKERS
76	Polydor 2001 651	Zone/Prime Cut	8

RHYTHM OF LIFE
81	Rational RATE 6	Soon/Summertime (p/s; label also lists Rhythm RHYTHM 1)	6
82	Rational RATE 7	Uncle Sam/Portrait Of The Heart (p/s; label also lists Rhythm RHYTHM 2)	5
	(see also Josef K, Paul Haig)		

RHYTHM RULERS
70	Bullet BU 447	Second Pressure/Sammy Dead	10
	(see also Lloyd Jones, U Roy Junior, Matadors, Winston Groovy, Pat, Winston Wright)		

RIALTO
96	Jealous COUP 005	Skyscraper/DOGGER: Bitter Almonds (CD, stickered slimline green case)	12
97	EastWest EW 107 TE	Untouchable/Monday Morning 5:19 (10", p/s)	8
98	EastWest 0630 19745-2	RIALTO (CD, withdrawn)	18

RIBS
78	Aerco AERS 101	Man With No Brain/Long Time Coming (p/s)	25

RICARDO
52	Melodisc MEL 1210	Grenada (Land Of Spice)/Banana Song (78)	7

BOYD RICE & FRIENDS
90	New European BADVC 1969	MUSIC, MARTINIS AND MISANTHROPY (LP, with inner sleeve)	25
	(see also Non, Death In June, Current 93)		

MACK RICE
69	Atlantic 584 250	Love's A Mother Brother/Coal Man	8

MANDY RICE-DAVIES
64	Ember EMB 4537	MANDY (EP)	60

TIM RICE & WEBBER GROUP
69	RCA RCA 1895	Come Back Richard (Your Country Needs You)/Roll On Over The Atlantic	8

(see also Tales Of Justine, Nightshift)

BUDDY RICH
56	HMV CLP 1092	BUDDY RICH SINGS JOHNNY MERCER (LP)	12
56	Columbia Clef 33CX 10052	THE WAILING BUDDY RICH (LP)	12
57	Columbia Clef 33CX 10071	THIS ONE'S FOR BASIE (LP)	12
57	Columbia Clef 33CX 10080	BUDDY AND SWEETS (LP, with Harry 'Sweets' Edison)	15
58	HMV CLP 1185	BUDDY RICH JUST SINGS (LP)	12
59	Columbia Clef 33CX 10138	BUDDY RICH AT MIAMI (LP)	12
67	Verve VLP 9151	THAT'S RICH (LP)	12
68	Liberty LBL/LBS 83090	TAKE IT AWAY! (LP)	12

BUDDY RICH & MAX ROACH
60	Mercury MMC 14031	RICH VERSUS ROACH (LP, also stereo CMS 18021)	12

(see also Max Roach)

CHARLIE RICH
60	London HLU 9107	Lonely Weekends/Everything I Do Is Wrong	40
62	London HLS 9482	Just A Little Bit Sweet/It's Too Late	40
65	RCA RCA 1433	Too Many Teardrops/It's All Over Now	10
65	Philips BF 1432	Mohair Sam/I Washed My Hands In Muddy Water	15
67	London HLU 10104	Love Is After Me/Pass On By (silver-top label, later boxed logo label)	
		(DJ copy = £70)	30/15
69	Mercury MF 1109	Mohair Sam/I Washed My Hands In Muddy Water (reissue)	15
65	RCA RD 7719	THAT'S RICH (LP)	60
66	Philips BL 7695	THE MANY NEW SIDES OF CHARLIE RICH (LP)	20

DAVE RICH
58	RCA RCA 1092	Burn On Love Fire/City Lights (78 rpm = £12)	20
66	Polydor BM 56113	Last Two People On Earth/I Just Wanna Dance	6

JOHNNY RICH
64	Mercury MF 836	Dream On/Together	6

LEWIS RICH
66	Parlophone R 5434	I Don't Want To Hear It Anymore/Shedding Tears	15

RICHIE RICH
89	ffrr FX 113	Salsa House (Silver On Black Mix)/(Original Mix)/(Orbital Mix) (12")	15
89	ffrr FXR 156	You Used To Salsa/You Used To Hold Me (12", remix)	25

SKETTO RICH
70	Pama PM 806	Hound Dog/Black Girl	7
71	Big Shot BI 596	Know Your Friend/Know Your Friend (Version)	5

(see Buddy & Sketto, Ruddy & Sketto, Father Sketto, Owen Gray)

TONY RICH
66	Piccadilly 7N 35291	Save Your Love/Don't Mention Your Name	7
66	Piccadilly 7N 35323	It's All Up To You Now/See Saw	10

(see also Tony Sheveton)

RICHARD & GLEN
72	Duke DU 141	Boat To Progress (Parts 1 & 2)	15

RICHARD & YOUNG LIONS
66	Philips BF 1520	Open Up Your Door/Once Upon Your Smile	35

RICHARD BROTHERS
63	Island WI 060	I Need A Girl/Desperate Lover	12
63	Island WI 109	I Shall Wear A Crown/BABA BROOKS: Robin Hood	20

(see also Joe White)

CLIFF RICHARD (& DRIFTERS/SHADOWS)
78s
58	Columbia DB 4178	Move It!/Schoolboy Crush	40
58	Columbia DB 4203	High Class Baby/My Feet Hit The Ground	38
59	Columbia DB 4249	Livin' Lovin' Doll/Steady With You	110
59	Columbia DB 4290	Mean Streak/Never Mind	130
59	Columbia DB 4306	Living Doll/Apron Strings	40

(The above 78s were credited to Cliff Richard & Drifters)

59	Columbia DB 4351	Travellin' Light/Dynamite	55
60	Columbia DB 4398	A Voice In The Wilderness/Don't Be Mad At Me	90

(The above 78s were credited to Cliff Richard & Shadows)

COLUMBIA 45s
58	Columbia DB 4178	Move It!/Schoolboy Crush (green label, later black)	40/30
58	Columbia DB 4203	High Class Baby/My Feet Hit The Ground (green label, later black)	30/25
59	Columbia DB 4249	Livin' Lovin' Doll/Steady With You (green label, later black)	50/25
59	Columbia DB 4290	Mean Streak/Never Mind (green label, later black)	30/20
59	Columbia DB 4306	Living Doll/Apron Strings (green label, later black)	20/20

(The above singles were credited to Cliff Richard & Drifters)

59	Columbia DB 4351	Travellin' Light/Dynamite	10
60	Columbia DB 4398	A Voice In The Wilderness/Don't Be Mad At Me	6
60	Columbia DB 4431	Fall In Love With You/Willie And The Hand Jive	6
60	Columbia DB 4479	Please Don't Tease/Where Is My Heart	6
60	Columbia DB 4506	Nine Times Out Of Ten/Thinking Of Our Love	8

Cliff RICHARD

60	Columbia DB 4547	I Love You/"D" In Love	6
61	Columbia DB 4593	Theme For A Dream/Mumblin' Mosie	6
61	Columbia DB 4667	A Girl Like You/Now's The Time To Fall In Love	6
61	Columbia DB 4716	When The Girl In Your Arms Is The Girl In Your Heart/Got A Funny Feeling (solo)	6
62	Columbia DB 4761	The Young Ones/We Say Yeah (green label, later black)	5/7
62	Columbia DB 4828	I'm Lookin' Out The Window/Do You Want To Dance?	6
62	Columbia DB 4886	It'll Be Me/Since I Lost You	6

(The above 45s were originally green labels; later black label copies are worth at least twice the listed values unless stated.)

62	Columbia DB 4950	The Next Time/Bachelor Boy	5
63	Columbia DB 4977	Summer Holiday/Dancing Shoes	5
63	Columbia DB 7034	Lucky Lips/I Wonder	5
63	Columbia DB 7089	It's All In The Game/Your Eyes Tell It On You (solo)	5
63	Columbia DB 7150	Don't Talk To Him/Say You're Mine	5
64	Columbia DB 7203	I'm The Lonely One/Watch What You Do With My Baby	5
64	Columbia DB 7272	Constantly (solo)/True True Lovin'	5
64	Columbia DB 7305	On The Beach/A Matter Of Moments	5
64	Columbia DB 7372	The Twelfth Of Never/I'm Afraid To Go Home (solo)	5
64	Columbia DB 7420	I Could Easily Fall (In Love With You)/I'm In Love With You	5

(The above singles were credited to Cliff Richard & Shadows unless stated; the singles listed below were solo unless stated.)

64	Columbia DB 7435	This Was My Special Day/I'm Feeling Oh So Lovely (withdrawn, credited to Cliff Richard, Audrey Bayley, Joan Palethorpe & Faye Fisher)	15
65	Columbia DB 7496	The Minute You're Gone/Just Another Guy	5
65	Columbia DB 7596	On My Word/Just A Little Bit Too Late	5
65	Columbia DB 7660	The Time In Between/Look Before You Love (as Cliff Richard & Shadows)	8
65	Columbia DB 7745	Wind Me Up (Let Me Go)/The Night	5
66	Columbia DB 7866	Blue Turns To Grey/Somebody Loses (as Cliff Richard & Shadows)	5
66	Columbia DB 7968	Visions/What Would I Do (For The Love Of A Girl?)	5
66	Columbia DB 8017	Time Drags By/La La La Song (as Cliff Richard & Shadows)	5
66	Columbia DB 8094	In The Country/Finders Keepers (as Cliff Richard & Shadows)	5
66	Columbia PSRS 304	Finders Keepers (promo only, 1-sided, with spoken intro by Simon Dee)	30
67	Columbia DB 8150	It's All Over/Why Wasn't I Born Rich?	5
67	Columbia DB 8210	I'll Come Runnin'/I Get The Feelin'	10
67	Columbia DB 8245	The Day I Met Marie/Our Story Book	5
67	Columbia DB 8293	All My Love/Sweet Little Jesus Boy	5
68	Columbia DB 8376	Congratulations/High 'N' Dry	5
68	Columbia DB 8437	I'll Love You Forever Today/Girl, You'll Be A Woman Soon	10
68	Columbia DB 8476	Marianne/Mr Nice	5
68	Columbia DB 8503	Don't Forget To Catch Me/What's More (I Don't Need Her)	5
69	Columbia DB 8548	Good Times (Better Times)/Occasional Rain	5
69	Columbia DB 8581	Big Ship/She's Leaving You	10
69	Columbia DB 8615	Throw Down A Line (as Cliff & Hank)/Reflections	5
69	Columbia DB 8641	With The Eyes Of A Child/So Long	5
70	Columbia DB 8657	Joy Of Living (as Cliff & Hank)/CLIFF RICHARD: Leave My Woman Alone/ HANK MARVIN: Boogatoo	5
70	Columbia DB 8685	Goodbye Sam, Hello Samantha/You Never Can Tell	5
70	Columbia DB 8708	I Ain't Got Time Anymore/Monday Comes Too Soon	5
71	Columbia DB 8747	Sunny Honey Girl/Don't Move Away (with Olivia Newton-John)/ I Was Only Fooling Myself	10
71	Columbia DB 8774	Silvery Rain/Annabella Umbrella/Time Flies	10
71	Columbia DB 8797	Flying Machine/Pigeon	10
71	Columbia DB 8836	Sing A Song Of Freedom/A Thousand Conversations	5
72	Columbia DB 8864	Jesus/Mister Cloud	10
72	Columbia DB 8917	Living In Harmony/Empty Chairs	5
72	Columbia DB 8957	Brand New Song/The Old Accordion	8

EXPORT SINGLES

61	Columbia DC 756	Gee Whiz It's You/I Cannot Find A True Love	5
63	Columbia DC 758	What'd I Say/Blue Moon	100+
65	Columbia DC 762	Angel/Razzle Dazzle	60+

EMI SINGLES

73	EMI EMI 2012	Power To All Our Friends/Come Back Billie Joe	5
73	EMI EMI 2022	Help It Along/Tomorrow Rising/The Days Of Love/Ashes To Ashes (some in p/s).	12/6
73	EMI EMI 2088	Take Me High/Celestial Houses	5
74	EMI PSR 368	Nothing To Remind Me/The Learning (promo only)	60
74	EMI EMI 2150	(You Keep Me) Hangin' On/Love Is Here	5
75	EMI EMI 2279	It's Only Me You've Left Behind/You're The One	5
75	EMI EMI 2344	Honky Tonk Angel/(Wouldn't You Know It) Got Myself A Girl	10
76	EMI EMI 2376	Miss You Nights/Love Enough (later available with p/s in box set)	6/5
76	EMI EMI 2458	Devil Woman/Love On (Shine On)	5
76	EMI EMI 2499	I Can't Ask For Anything More Than You/Junior Cowboy	5
76	EMI EMI 2559	Hey Mr Dream Maker/No One Waits	5
77	EMI EMI 2584	My Kinda Life/Nothing Left For Me To Say	5
77	EMI EMI 2633	When Two Worlds Drift Apart/That's Why I Love You	8
78	EMI EMI 2730	Yes! He Lives/Good On The Sally Army	15
78	EMI EMI 2832	Please Remember Me/Please Don't Tease	8
78	EMI EMI 2885	Can't Take The Hurt Anymore/Needing A Friend (p/s)	8
79	EMI EMI 2920	Green Light/Imagine Love (some in p/s)	30/5
79	EMI EMI 2975	We Don't Talk Anymore/Count Me Out (p/s)	5
79	EMI EMI 2975	We Don't Talk Anymore/Count Me Out (p/s, mispress, A-side plays Queen's "Bohemian Rhapsody")	12

FLEXIDISCS & OTHER RELEASES

60	Serenade Magazine/ Rainbow (no cat. no.)	*Serenade* Presents Cliff Richard's Personal Message To You (turquoise flexidisc with magazine)	20
60s	Serenade Magazine	Cliff's Rock Party (flexidisc with magazine)	20
60s	Boyfriend Magazine	untitled flexidisc with magazine	20

60s	Rainbow Magazine	Music From America (flexidisc with magazine)	20
60s	New Spotlight	Star Souvenir Greetings (208 Radio Luxembourg flexidisc)	20
73	Spree (no cat. no.)	Good News (plain black flexidisc with spoken/sung introduction from Cliff, other side by Johnny Cash)	22
70s	Lyntone LYN 14745	The Best Of Cliff Richard And The Shadows (preview flexidisc)	8
98	Cruisin' The 50's CASB 007	Breathless/Lawdy Miss Clawdy (10" 78, p/s, with 6 inserts)	50

EPs

59	Columbia SEG 7895	SERIOUS CHARGE (soundtrack)	35
59	Columbia SEG 7903	CLIFF NO. 1 (also stereo ESG 7754)	35/45
59	Columbia SEG 7910	CLIFF NO. 2 (also stereo ESG 7769)	35/45
59	Columbia SEG 7971	EXPRESSO BONGO (soundtrack, also stereo ESG 7783)	25/40
60	Columbia SEG 7979	CLIFF SINGS NO. 1 (also stereo ESG 7788)	35/45
60	Columbia SEG 7987	CLIFF SINGS NO. 2 (also stereo ESG 7794)	35/45
60	Columbia SEG 8005	CLIFF SINGS NO. 3 (also stereo ESG 7808)	35/45
60	Columbia SEG 8021	CLIFF SINGS NO. 4 (also stereo ESG 7816)	35/45
60	Columbia SEG 8050	CLIFF'S SILVER DISCS	20
60	Columbia SEG 8065	ME AND MY SHADOWS NO. 1 (also stereo ESG 7837)	35/45
61	Columbia SEG 8071	ME AND MY SHADOWS NO. 2 (also stereo ESG 7481)	35/45
61	Columbia SEG 8078	ME AND MY SHADOWS NO. 3 (also stereo ESG 7843)	35/45
61	Columbia SEG 8105	LISTEN TO CLIFF NO. 1 (also stereo ESG 7858)	35/45
61	Columbia SEG 8119	DREAM (also stereo ESG 7867)	22/35
61	Columbia SEG 8126	LISTEN TO CLIFF NO. 2 (also stereo ESG 7870)	35/45
62	Columbia SEG 8133	CLIFF'S HIT PARADE	20
62	Columbia SEG 8151	CLIFF RICHARD	40
62	Columbia SEG 8159	HITS FROM 'THE YOUNG ONES'	18
62	Columbia SEG 8168	CLIFF RICHARD NO. 2	30

(The above EPs were originally issued with turquoise labels, later blue/black label copies are worth two-thirds these values.)

62	Columbia SEG 8203	CLIFF'S HITS	20
63	Columbia SEG 8228	TIME FOR CLIFF AND THE SHADOWS (mono)	30
63	Columbia ESG 7887	TIME FOR CLIFF AND THE SHADOWS (stereo, turquoise or blue/black)	25/35
63	Columbia SEG 8246	HOLIDAY CARNIVAL (also stereo ESG 7892)	20/30
63	Columbia SEG 8250	HITS FROM 'SUMMER HOLIDAY' (also stereo ESG 7896)	18/30
63	Columbia SEG 8263	MORE HITS FROM 'SUMMER HOLIDAY' (also stereo ESG 7898)	30/55
63	Columbia SEG 8269	CLIFF'S LUCKY LIPS	22
63	Columbia SEG 8272	LOVE SONGS (also stereo ESG 7900)	20/30
64	Columbia SEG 8290	WHEN IN FRANCE	20
64	Columbia SEG 8299	CLIFF SINGS 'DON'T TALK TO HIM'	20
64	Columbia SEG 8320	CLIFF'S PALLADIUM SUCCESSES	30
64	Columbia SEG 8338	WONDERFUL LIFE (also stereo ESG 7902)	20/30
64	Columbia SEG 8347	A FOREVER KIND OF LOVE	20
64	Columbia SEG 8354	WONDERFUL LIFE NO. 2 (also stereo ESG 7903)	20/30
64	Columbia SEG 8376	HITS FROM 'WONDERFUL LIFE' (also stereo ESG 7906)	20/30
65	Columbia SEG 8384	WHY DON'T THEY UNDERSTAND?	25
65	Columbia SEG 8395	CLIFF'S HITS FROM 'ALADDIN AND HIS WONDERFUL LAMP'	20
65	Columbia SEG 8405	LOOK IN MY EYES, MARIA	30
65	Columbia SEG 8444	ANGEL	25
65	Columbia SEG 8450	TAKE FOUR	28
66	Columbia SEG 8474	WIND ME UP	28
66	Columbia SEG 8478	HITS FROM 'WHEN IN ROME'	45
66	Columbia SEG 8488	LOVE IS FOREVER	35
66	Columbia SEG 8510	THUNDERBIRDS ARE GO! (3 tracks by Cliff & Shadows, 1 solo)	50
66	Columbia SEG 8517	LA LA LA LA LA (1 track by Bruce Welch & Hank Marvin)	35
67	Columbia SEG 8527	CINDERELLA	80
67	Columbia SEG 8533	CAROL SINGERS	30
68	Columbia SEG 8540	CONGRATULATIONS	25
77	EMI PSR 410	EVERY FACE TELLS A STORY (promo, issued to shops only)	15
77	EMI PSR 414/415	40 GOLDEN GREATS (double pack promo, issued to shops only)	15

COLUMBIA LPs

59	Columbia 33SX 1147	CLIFF (green labels, later blue/black labels)	50/30
59	Columbia 33SX 1192	CLIFF SINGS (green labels, later blue/black labels)	50/30
60	Columbia 33SX 1261	ME AND MY SHADOWS (also stereo SCX 3330)	35/55
61	Columbia 33SX 1320	LISTEN TO CLIFF! (also stereo SCX 3375)	30/65
61	Columbia 33SX 1368	21 TODAY (also stereo SCX 3409)	30/65
61	Columbia 33SX 1384	THE YOUNG ONES (soundtrack with inner, also stereo SCX 3397)	20/40
62	Columbia 33SX 1431	32 MINUTES AND 17 SECONDS WITH... (also stereo SCX 3436)	30/65

(The above LPs were originally issued with green labels, later blue/black copies are worth two-thirds the value unless stated.)

63	Columbia 33SX 1472	SUMMER HOLIDAY (soundtrack with inner sleeve, mono)	15
63	Columbia SCX 3462	SUMMER HOLIDAY (stereo, initially green labels, later blue/black)	30/20
63	Columbia SX 1512	CLIFF'S HIT ALBUM	15
63	Columbia SX 1541	WHEN IN SPAIN (also stereo SCX 3488)	20/30
64	Columbia SX 1628	WONDERFUL LIFE (soundtrack, mono, gatefold sleeve with inner sleeve)	15
64	Columbia SCX 3515	WONDERFUL LIFE (soundtrack, stereo, gatefold sleeve with inner sleeve)	25
64	Columbia SX 1676/ SCX 3522	ALADDIN AND HIS WONDERFUL LAMP (with stage cast, gatefold sleeve, mono/stereo)	18/25
65	Columbia SX 1709	CLIFF RICHARD (also stereo SCX 3546)	35/40
65	Columbia SX 1737	MORE HITS BY CLIFF (also stereo SCX 3555)	14/18
65	Columbia SX 1762	WHEN IN ROME	35
65	Columbia SX 1769	LOVE IS FOREVER (also stereo SCX 3569)	25
66	Columbia S(C)X 6039	KINDA LATIN (mono/stereo)	30/35
66	Columbia S(C)X 6079	FINDERS KEEPERS (soundtrack, with inner sleeve, mono/stereo)	15/20
67	Columbia S(C)X 6103	CINDERELLA (with stage cast)	35
67	Columbia S(C)X 6133	DON'T STOP ME NOW	30
67	Columbia S(C)X 6167	GOOD NEWS	18
67	Columbia JSX 6167	GOOD NEWS (export issue)	35
68	Columbia S(C)X 6244	CLIFF IN JAPAN (blue/black labels, later white/black labels)	30/20

68	Columbia S(C)X 6262	TWO A PENNY (blue/black labels, later white/black labels)	25/18
68	Columbia S(C)X 6282	ESTABLISHED 1958 (gatefold sleeve, half tracks by Shadows, mono/stereo)	18/15

(The above Columbia LPs were originally issued with blue/black labels; white/black copies are worth half the value unless stated)

69	Columbia S(C)X 6343	THE BEST OF CLIFF	15
69	Columbia S(C)X 6357	SINCERELY CLIFF RICHARD (mono/stereo)	25/20
70	Columbia SCX 6408	ABOUT THAT MAN (4 songs plus narration)	60
70	Columbia SCX 6435	TRACKS 'N' GROOVES	25
70	Columbia SCX 6443	HIS LAND (documentary soundtrack, with Cliff Barrows)	50
72	Columbia SCX 6519	THE BEST OF CLIFF VOLUME 2	15

EMI LPs

73	EMI EMC 3016	TAKE ME HIGH (soundtrack, some with poster)	25/15
74	EMI EMA 768	HELP IT ALONG (gatefold sleeve)	25
74	EMI EMC 3048	THE 31st OF FEBRUARY STREET	30
74	EMI TC EXSP 1601	THE MUSIC AND LIFE OF CLIFF RICHARD (6-cassette box set, music & intervews, with Brian Bennett, Olivia Newton-John, Cilla Black etc.)	25
82	EMI PSLP 350	CLIFF (promo-only sampler)	40
83	EMI EMC 1077 871/881	SILVER/ROCK'N'ROLL SILVER (2-LP, box set, with booklet)	20
87	EMI EMDB 1004	ALWAYS GUARANTEED (box set, some in embossed sleeve with free 7" "Another Christmas Day")	15/12
89	EMI CR 1	THE 30TH ANNIVERSARY PICTURE RECORD COLLECTION (2-LP, picture discs, gatefold sleeve, mail-order only)	25

OTHER LPs

63	Elstree Extra Range	SUMMER HOLIDAY (2-LP, full soundtrack recording, 80 copies only)	700+
64	Elstree Extra Range	WONDERFUL LIFE (2-LP, full soundtrack recording, 150 copies only)	700+
64	World Record Club (S)T 643	HOW WONDERFUL TO KNOW (mono/stereo)	20/25
64	EMI Regal SREG 1120	ME AND MY SHADOWS (export issue)	70
69	World R. Club STP 1051	CLIFF RICHARD	60
72	World R. Club SM 255-260	THE CLIFF RICHARD STORY (6-LP box set with booklet)	20
72	World R. Club CSM 255-260	THE CLIFF RICHARD STORY (6-cassette box set with booklet)	15
72	Readers Digest	THE BEST OF CLIFF RICHARD AND THE SHADOWS (8-LP box set)	20
80	World R. Club ALBUM 26	THE CLIFF RICHARD SONGBOOK (6-LP box set)	20

REEL-TO-REEL TAPE

64	EMI TA-SX 1628	WONDERFUL LIFE	12

(other reel-to-reel tapes may be worth up to a maximum of £12)

(see also Drifters [U.K.], Shadows, Olivia Newton-John, Sheila Walsh, Janet Jackson, Elton John, Phil Everly, Grazina)

WENDY RICHARD & DIANA BERRY

63	Decca F 11680	We Had A Dream/Keep 'Em Looking Around	15

(see also Mike Sarne)

CYNTHIA RICHARDS

69	Clandisc CLA 203	Foolish Fool/KING STITT: On The Street	15
70	Clandisc CLA 210	Conversation/DYNAMITES: Conversation Version II	12
70	Clandisc CLA 216	Can't Wait/Promises	7
70	Clandisc CLA 220	Foolish Fool/CLANCY & STITT: Dance Beat	12
71	Clandisc CLA 229	Stand By Your Man (actually by Merlene Webber)/DYNAMITES: Version 2	6
71	Big Shot BI 581	I'm Moving On/HIPPY BOYS: I'm Moving On (Version)	7
71	Escort ERT 861	Love & Unity/MAYTONES: Wah Noh Dead	7
71	G.G. GG 4528	Place In My Heart/You've Got A Friend (act. Irving [Brown] & Cynthia Richards)	8
72	Pama Supreme PS 366	Mr Postman/SKIN, FLESH AND BONES: Version	10
73	Attack ATT 8047	Aily I/REID'S ALL STARS: Aily I (Version)	6
70	Trojan TBL 123	FOOLISH FOOL (LP, actually Clancy Eccles Productions compilation)	32

(see also Bobby Aitken, Lord Comic, Sir Lord Comic)

JOHN RICHARDS

57	HMV POP 401	Let Me Be Loved/By The Fireside	7
65	Oriole CB 312	Folks Get Married In The Spring/Then I'll Be There	7
66	Polydor BM 56705	I Will Go Again To Ireland/Midnight Sky	5

JOHNNY RICHARDS

59	Esquire 32-076	THE RITES OF DIABLO (LP)	20

KEITH RICHARDS

79	Rolling Stones RSR 102	Run Rudolph Run/The Harder They Come (p/s)	15
86	Arista ARIST 678P	Jumping Jack Flash/Integrity (with Aretha Franklin) (shaped pic disc & plinth)	12
88	Virgin VS 1125	Take It So Hard/I Could Have Stood You Up (p/s)	5
88	Virgin VST 1125	Take It So Hard/I Could Have Stood You Up/It Means A Lot (12", p/s)	8
89	Virgin VS 1179	Make No Mistake (Edit)/It Means A Lot (p/s)	6
89	Virgin VST 1179	Make No Mistake (Extended Version)/(LP Version)/It Means A Lot (12", p/s)	8
88	Virgin KEITH 1234	Make No Mistake/Locked Away/Struggle/Big Enough (4 x 1-sided 7", "Talk Is Cheap" sampler box set, promo only)	75
88	Virgin 2-91047 A/B/C	TALK IS CHEAP (3 x 3" CDs in tin)	40

(see also Rolling Stones, Aranbee Pop Symphony Orchestra, Dirty Strangers, Screamin' Jay Hawkins)

LISA RICHARDS

65	Vocalion VP 9244	Mean Old World/Take A Chance (DJ copy = £75)	40

LLOYD RICHARDS

64	Port-O-Jam PJ 4004	Be Good/I Need You	25

ROY RICHARDS

66	Doctor Bird DB 1012	Contact/Maureen	20
66	Island WI 297	Green Collie/MARCIA GRIFFITHS: You No Good	25
66	Island WI 283	Double Trouble/FITSY & FREDDY: Why Did You Do It	30
66	Island WI 299	Western Standard Time/(JA) EAGLES: What An Agony	35
66	Island WI 3000	South Viet Nam/You Must Be Sorry (Vocal)	20
67	Island WI 3027	Rub-A-Dub/SHARKS: Baby Come Home	25
67	Island WI 3037	Hopeful Village Ska/DELROY WILSON: Ungrateful Baby	35

67	Island WI 3050	Port-O-Jam/DELROY WILSON: Get Ready	35
67	Studio One SO 2020	Hanky Panky/ALTON ELLIS: I Am Still In Love	40

(see also Roland Alphonso, Lord Comic, Soul Vendors, Jackie Mittoo, Derrick Morgan, Righteous Flames)

RUSTY RICHARDS
60	Top Rank JAR 297	Middle Hand Road/Golden Moon (China Night)	7

TRUDY RICHARDS
57	Capitol CL 14728	Wishbone/Hangin' Around	10
57	Capitol CL 14744	Weaker Than Wise/I Want A Big Butter And Egg Man	6
58	Capitol CL 14857	Somebody Just Like You/The Night When Love Was Born	6
57	Capitol EAP 1 1087	CRAZY IN LOVE (EP)	10
57	Capitol T 838	CRAZY IN LOVE (LP)	25

WINSTON RICHARDS
67	Rio R 124	Studio Blitz/Don't Up	15

JOE 'GROUNDHOG' RICHARDSON
69	Major Minor MM 632	Take It Off/Blues To Take It Off	8

MARK RICHARDSON
65	Stateside SS 440	Baby, I'm Sorry/Blanket Fair	8
65	Stateside SS 467	See It My Way/Think	8

RICH GYPSY
80	Splash SP 016	What Hit Me (no p/s)	25

RICH KIDS
78	EMI EMI 2738	Rich Kids/Empty Words (red vinyl, p/s)	6
78	EMI EMI 2803	Marching Men/Here Comes The Nice (p/s)	6
78	EMI EMC 3263	GHOSTS OF PRINCES IN TOWERS (LP)	18

(see also Sex Pistols, Ultravox, Spectres, Swingers, Visage)·

JONATHAN RICHMAN & MODERN LOVERS
75	United Artists UP 36006	Road Runner/It Will Stand	7
77	Beserkley BZZ 1	Road Runner (Once)/Road Runner (Twice) (p/s)	5
77	Beserkley BSERK 9	ROCK 'N' ROLL WITH THE MODERN LOVERS (LP)	12
77	Beserkley BSERK 2	JONATHAN RICHMAN AND THE MODERN LOVERS (LP)	12
77	Beserkley BSERK 12	MODERN LOVERS LIVE (LP)	12
77	Beserkley BSERK 17	BACK IN YOUR LIFE (LP)	12

RICHMOND
73	Dart ART 2008	Candy Dora/Willow Farm	5
73	Dart ART 2025	Frightened/Breakfast	5
73	Dart ART 2031	Raise Your Heads To The Wind/All I Really Need	5
74	Dart ART 2044	Peaches/Work For My Baby	5
73	Dart ARTS 65371	FRIGHTENED (LP)	20

BEN RICHMOND
63	Piccadilly 7N 35132	You Gotta Have Love/I Don't Care	7

FIONA RICHMOND
73	Raymond PR 112	FRANKLY FIONA (LP)	50

JANET RICHMOND
60	Top Rank JAR 288	You Got What It Takes/Not One Minute More	10
60	Top Rank JAR 378	June Bride/My One And Only Love	7
61	Top Rank JAR 536	Senora/I Need You	8

RICHUS FLAMES
67	Fab FAB 17	Need To Be Loved/I Am Going Home	15

(see also Righteous Flames)

RICK & KEENS
61	Mercury AMT 1150	Peanuts/I'll Be Home	75

BERESFORD RICKETTS
60	Starlite ST45 025	Cherry Baby/I Want To Know	20
60	Starlite ST45 029	Baby Baby/When I Woke Up	20
61	Starlite ST45 048	Hold Me Tight/Dream Girl (as Ricketts & Rowe)	20
62	Starlite ST45 079	I'm Going To Cry/Waiting For Me	20
62	Blue Beat BB 107	You Better Be Going/I've Been Walking (as Beresford Ricketts & Blue Beats)	22
63	Dice CC 12	Oh Jean/Rivers Of Tears (as Lauren Aitken's Group)	20
66	Blue Beat BB 350	Jailer Bring Me Water/Careless Love	22

RICO (RODRIGUEZ)
61	Blue Beat BB 56	Luke Lane Shuffle (as Rico Rodrigues & Buster's All Stars)/ BUSTER'S GROUP: Little Honey	20
62	Island WI 022	Rico Special (as Emanuel Rodrigues Orchestra; some copies may credit Reco & His Happy Orchestra)/BUNNY & SKITTER: A Little Mashin'	30
62	Planetone RC 1	London Here I Come/Midnight In Ethiopia	25
62	Planetone RC 4	Planet Rock/You Win	15
62	Planetone RC 5	Youth Boogie/Western Serenade (as Rico's Combo)	15
67	Fab FAB 12	Jingle Bells/Silent Night (with His Boys)	10
68	Pama PM 706	Soul Man/It's Not Unusual (as Reco Rodriguez)	12
68	Pama PM 715	Tender Foot Ska/Memories (as Reco Rodriguez)	15
69	Blue Cat BS 160	The Bullet/Rhythm In (as Reco Rodriguez & His Rhythm Aces)	25
69	Doctor Bird DB 1302	Baby Face (as Reco & Rudies)/RUDIES: News	25
69	Bullet BU 407	Tribute To Don Drummond/Japanese Invasion (as Rico Rodriquez)	40
71	Duke DU 96	Surprise Package (as Rico & Satch)/PETE JOHNSON: I'm Sorry	20
70s	Island IPR 2006	Ska-Wars/Ramble (12")	15
77	Island IPR 2002	Dial Africa/Dub (12")	25
78	Island IPR 2006	Ramble/Ska Wars (12")	15

RICO (Rodriguez)

79	Island IPR 2016	Take 5/Sound Check (12")	15
80	Island IPR 2030	Children Of Sanchez/You Really Got Me/Midnight In Ethiopia (12")	30
80	2-Tone CHS TT 15	Sea Cruise/Carolina (p/s, paper label)	8
82	2-Tone CHS TT 19	Jungle Music/Rasta Call (paper label, 2-Tone sleeve, with Special A.K.A.)	8
82	2-Tone CHS TT 1219	Jungle Music/Rasta Call/You/Easter Island (12", p/s, with Special A.K.A.)	12
69	Trojan TTL 12	BLOW YOUR HORN (LP, as Rico & Rudies)	35
69	Pama ECO 014	IN REGGAE LAND (LP)	120
78	Island ILPS 9485	MAN FROM WARREIKA (LP)	12
78	Ghetto Rockers PRE 1	WARREIKA DUB (LP, white label, white sleeve, beware of bootlegs)	70

(see also Special A.K.A., Reco, Andy Capp, Don Reco, Prince Buster, Pioneers, Stranger)

RICOCHET
80s	Heavy Rock HER 1	Midas Light/Off The Rails (p/s)	400

RICOTTI & ALBUQUERQUE
71	Pegasus PEG 2	FIRST WIND (LP)	20

(see also Frank Ricotti, Henry Lowther)

FRANK RICOTTI
69	CBS 52668	OUR POINT OF VIEW (LP)	30

(see also Ricotti & Albuquerque)

RICKY & THE MUTATIONS
83	Cool Ghoul COOL003	Thatcher Rap (12")	18

NELSON RIDDLE ORCHESTRA
55	Capitol CL 14241	Vera Cruz/You Won't Forget Me	5
55	Capitol CL 14262	The Pendulum Song/Brother John	5
56	Capitol CL 14510	Robin Hood/In Old Lisbon (Lisboa Antigua)	6
63	Capitol CL 15309	Supercar/The Dick Van Dyke Theme	10
66	Stateside SS 517	Batman Theme (from the T.V. series)/Nelson's Riddler	10
59	HMV GES 5792	NELSON RIDDLE PLAYS GERSHWIN (EP, stereo)	15
61	Capitol EAP4 1771	ROUTE 66 AND OTHER T.V. THEMES (EP)	10
57	Capitol T 893	C'MON . . . GET HAPPY! (LP)	12
58	Capitol ST 915	SEA OF DREAMS (LP)	12
59	Philips SBBL 565	LI'L ABNER (LP, soundtrack)	12
62	Capitol (S)T 1771	ROUTE 66 AND OTHER GREAT T.V. THEMES (LP)	15
62	MGM MGM-C 896	LOLITA (LP, soundtrack)	25
64	Stateside SL 10090	WHAT A WAY TO GO! (LP, soundtrack)	12
64	Reprise R 2021	ROBIN AND THE SEVEN HOODS (LP, soundtrack)	30
64	Reprise R 6138	GREAT MUSIC, GREAT FILMS, GREAT SOUNDS (LP)	15
66	Stateside S(S)L 10179	BATMAN (LP, TV soundtrack)	50
67	Columbia S(C)X 6155	EL DORADO (LP, soundtrack)	50

(see also Shirley Bassey)

RIDDLERS
66	Polydor BM 56716	Batman Theme/Weegie Walk	20

RIDE
89	Creation CRE 072T	Chelsea Girl EP (12")	10
90	Creation CRE 075T	Play EP (12")	8
94	Creation CRE 189T	I Don't Know Where It Comes From/Drive Blind/From Time To Time/ How Does It Feel To Feel (p/s)	8
90	Creation CRELP 074	NOWHERE (LP)	15

PAT RIDEN & BROTHER LLOYD'S ALL STARS
69	Mercury MF 1072	I Need Help/Let The Red Wine Flow (actually by Pat Rhoden)	6

(see also Pat Rhoden)

JACKIE RIDING & IMESON SOUND
66	Fab FAB 4	Don't Wanna Leave/The Wave	8

NICOLE RIEU
75	Barclay BAR 31	Live For Love/Et Bonjour A Toi L'Artiste	12

RIFF
64	Blue Beat BB 242	Oh What A Feeling/Primitive Man	20

RIFF-RAFF
73	RCA RCA 2396	Copper Kettle/You Must Be Joking	5
73	RCA SF 8351	RIFF-RAFF (LP)	20
74	RCA LPL1 5023	ORIGINAL MAN (LP)	20

RIFF RAFF
78	Chiswick SW 34	I WANNA BE A COSMONAUT (EP)	8

RIFKIN
68	Page One POF 071	Continental Hesitation/We're Not Those People Any More	60

THE RIFLES
05	Blow Up BU 029	Peace And Quiet/Breakdown (die-cut Blow Up sleeve)	10
05	Xtra Mile XMR 007	When I'm Alone/ Holiday In The Sun (p/s)	5

ELEANOR RIGBY
85	Waterloo Sunset RUSS 101	I Want To Sleep With You/At The End Of The Day (p/s, first 1,000 with condom)	12/10
87	Waterloo Sunset RUSS 103	Over And Over/Last Night In Soho (p/s)	5
87	Waterloo Sunset RUSS 103	Over And Over/Last Night In Soho/See My Friends (12", p/s)	5
87	Waterloo Sunset RUSS 104	Kiss Me Quickly It's Christmas/Mad Christmas (p/s)	5
93	Future Legend FLER 1	You Only Live Twice/Think For Yourself (p/s)	5
87	Waterloo Sunset WSR 001	CENSORSHIP (LP)	15

BRAM RIGG SET
67	Stateside SS 2020	Take The Time Be Yourself/I Can Only Give You Everything	80

DIANA RIGG
72	RCA RCA 2178	Forget Yesterday/Sentimental Journey	20

JACKIE RIGGS
56	London HLF 8244	The Great Pretender/His Gold Will Melt (78 rpm = £8)	40

RIGHTEOUS BROTHERS
63	London HL 9743	Little Latin Lupe Lu/I'm So Lonely	15
63	London HL 9814	My Babe/Fee-Fi-Fidily-I-Oh	12
65	London HL 9943	You've Lost That Lovin' Feelin'/There's A Woman	8
65	Pye International 7N 25297	Bring Your Love To Me/Try To Find Another Man	15
65	Pye International 7N 25304	Something's Got A Hold On Me/Night Owl	10
65	London HL 9962	Just Once In My Life/The Blues (withdrawn)	50+
65	London HL 9975	Hung On You/Unchained Melody	8
65	Pye International 7N 25323	Let The Good Times Roll/B Flat Blues	8
65	Pye International 7N 25334	For Your Love/My Tears Will Go Away	8
65	London HL 10011	Ebb Tide/(I Love You) For Sentimental Reasons	8
66	Pye International 7N 25358	Georgia On My Mind/My Tears Will Go Away	8
66	Verve VS 535	(You're My) Soul And Inspiration/B Side-Blues	8
66	Verve VS 537	He/He Will Break Your Heart	8
66	Sue WI 4018	You Can Have Her/Justine	30
66	London HL 10066	Just Once In My Life/The Blues (reissue)	5
66	Verve VS 542	Go Ahead And Cry/Things Didn't Go Your Way	10
66	London HL 10086	The White Cliffs Of Dover/Baby She's Mine	5
66	Verve VS 547	Island In The Sun/What Now My Love	5
67	Verve VS 554	Melancholy Music Man/Don't Give Up On Me	5
67	Verve VS 560	Stranded in The Middle Of No Place/Been So Nice	5
74	Capitol CL 15803	Dream On/Dr. Rock And Roll	7
77	Phil Spector Int'l 2010 022	You've Lost That Lovin' Feelin'/RIGHTEOUS BROTHERS BAND: Rat Race (insert)	10
65	Pye Intl. NEP 44043	THE RIGHTEOUS BROTHERS (EP)	30
66	Verve VEP 5024	SOUL AND INSPIRATION (EP)	30
66	Verve VEP 5025	THE RIGHTEOUS BROTHERS (EP, reissue)	20
65	Pye Intl. NPL 28056	SOME BLUE-EYED SOUL (LP)	40
65	London HA-U 8226	YOU'VE LOST THAT LOVIN' FEELIN' (LP)	40
65	Pye Intl. NPL 28059	RIGHT NOW! (LP)	20
65	London HA 8245	JUST ONCE IN MY LIFE (LP)	30
66	London HA 8278	BACK TO BACK (LP)	30
66	Verve (S)VLP 9131	SOUL AND INSPIRATION (LP)	30
66	Sue ILP 937	IN ACTION! (LP)	70
66	Verve (S)VLP 9140	GO AHEAD AND CRY (LP)	20
67	Verve (S)VLP 9168	SAYIN' SOMETHIN' (LP)	20
67	Verve (S)VLP 9183	THE RIGHTEOUS BROTHERS GREATEST HITS (LP)	15
68	Verve (S)VLP 9190	SOULED OUT (LP)	25
68	Verve (S)VLP 9204	THE RIGHTEOUS BROTHERS STANDARDS (LP)	15
68	Verve (S)VLP 9228	ONE FOR THE ROAD (LP)	15

(see also Bill Medley, Bobby Hatfield)

RIGHTEOUS FLAMES
67	Fab FAB 18	Gimme Some Sign Girl/Let's Go To The Dance (B-side act. by Prince Buster)	40+
67	Fab FAB 30	When A Girl Loves A Boy	40+
68	Coxsone CS 7061	You Don't Know/ROY RICHARDS & SOUL VENDORS: Summertime	20
71	High Note HS 052	Run To The Rock/GAYTONES: Run To The Rock Version	10
71	Nu Beat NB 083	Love And Emotion/Version	10

(see also Richus Flames, Alton Ellis, Flames, Soul Vendors)

RIGHTEOUS HOMES (FLAMES)
68	Coxsone CS 7049	I Was Born To Be Loved/NORMA FRAZER: Heartaches	25
68	Blue Cat BS 112	Seven Letters (actually by Winston Jarrett)/SOUL VENDORS: To Sir With Love	30

RIGHTEOUS SOULS
71	Supreme SUP 217	Mount Zion/ECCLE & NEVILL: All Over	10

RIGHTEOUS TWINS
69	Blue Cat BS 174	If I Could Hear My Master/Satan Can't Prevail	30

RIGOR MORTIS
73	Track 2094 107	Made In Japan/Hound Dog	8
73	Track 2406 106	RIGOR MORTIS SETS IN (LP)	15

(see John Entwistle, Who)

RIKKI & CUFFLINKS
79	Different HAVE 17	Nervous Breakdown/Steamin' On	5

RIKKI & THE LAST DAYS OF EARTH
77	(own label)	Oundle 29/5/77 (1-sided)	25
77	DJM DJS 10814	City Of The Damned/Victimized (p/s)	10
77	DJM DJF 20526	FOUR MINUTE WARNING (LP)	12

BILLY LEE RILEY
65	King KG 1015	I've Been Searchin'/Everybody's Twistin'	15
69	Stax STAX 120	Going Back To Memphis/Family Portrait	15
72	CBS 8182	I Got A Thing About You Baby/You Don't Love Me	6

(see also Megatons)

BOB RILEY
58	MGM MGM 977	The Midnight Line/Wanda Jean (78 rpm = £28)	60

DESMOND RILEY
69	Downtown DT 432	Tear Them/GEORGE LEE & RUDIES: Chaka Ground	15
69	Downtown DT 435	Tears On My Pillow/RUDIES: Man Pon Spot	10
69	Downtown DT 436	If I Had Wings/AUDREY: You'll Lose A Good Thing	8

69	Downtown DT 438	Out Your Fire/No Return	12
69	Downtown DT 450	Skinhead, A Message To You/MUSIC DOCTORS: Going Strong	28
69	Downtown DT 454	If I Had Wings/AUDREY: You'll Lose A Good Thing (reissue)	6

HOWARD RILEY (TRIO)
68	Opportunity CP 2499	DISCUSSIONS (LP with insert, as Howard Riley Trio)	1,000+
69	CBS 52669	ANGLE (LP)	40+
70	CBS 64077	THE DAY WILL COME (LP)	50
71	Turtle TUR 301	FLIGHT (LP, gatefold sleeve)	120
76	Incus INCUS 13	SYNOPSIS (LP, as Howard Riley Trio with Tony Oxley & Barry Guy)	100
79	Spotlite	THE OTHER SIDE (LP)	12

(see also Colosseum, Karyobin)

JEANNIE C. RILEY
69	Polydor 583 716	HARPER VALLEY P.T.A. (LP)	15
69	Polydor 583 733	YEARBOOKS AND YESTERDAYS (LP)	15
70	Polydor 583 753	THINGS GO BETTER WITH LOVE (LP)	15

JIMI/JIMMY RILEY
71	Supreme SUP 217	Mount Zion (actually by Jimi Riley & Stranger Cole)/ ECCLE & NEVIL: All Over	7
75	Dip DL 5067	Ram Goat Liver/OMAR & MARSHA PERRY: Ram Goat Dub	5

(see also Martin Riley, Sensations, Uniques)

MARTIN RILEY
69	Gas GAS 114	Walking Proud/LLOYD CHARMERS: Why Baby	10
69	Punch PH 7	Trying To Be Free/I've Got It Bad	10
70	Camel CA 53	Catch This Sound/Suspense	10
70	Escort ES 823	It Grows (actually "It's Growing")/We Had A Good Thing Going	20
71	Camel CA 77	When Will We Be Paid/WILLIE FRANCIS: He's Got The Whole World In His Hands	8

(see also Slim Smith, Slickers)

TERRY RILEY
71	CBS 64259	CHURCH OF ANTHRAX (LP, with John Cale)	18
71	CBS 64564	A RAINBOW IN CURVED AIR (LP)	18
71	CBS 64565	IN "C" (LP)	18
72	Shandar 83501/2	PERSIAN SURGERY DERVISHES (2-LP)	22

(see also John Cale)

WINSTON RILEY
73	Techniques TE 922	Woman Don't You Go Astray/Travelling Man	8

(see also Techniques)

RILEY'S ALLSTARS
71	Banana BA 343	Glory Of Love (actually "Mystic Blue" by Hugh Hendricks & Buccaneers)/ We'll Cry Together (Version)	10

(see also Bobby Davis, Techniques)

SHANE RIMMER
59	Columbia DB 4293	(Roll Along) Wagon Train/A Touch Of Pink	8
59	Columbia DB 4343	The Three Bells (Jimmy Brown Song) (as Shane Rimmer & Spinners)/ I Want To Walk You Home	8

RINGS
77	Chiswick S 14	I Wanna Be Free/Automobile (p/s)	10

(see also Maniacs, Twink)

RINGS & THINGS
68	Fontana TF 987	Strange Things Are Happening/To Me: To Me: To Me	120

RINKY DINKS
58	London HLE 8679	Early In The Morning/Now We're One (as Rinky-Dinks featuring Bobby Darin)	40
58	London HLE 8679	Early In The Morning/Now We're One (78)	42
59	London HLE 8793	Mighty Mighty Man/You're Mine (as Bobby Darin with Rinky Dinks)	30
59	London HLE 8793	Mighty Mighty Man/You're Mine (78)	50

(see also Bobby Darin)

BOBBY RIO (U.S.)
63	Stateside SS 211	Don Diddley/I Got You	20

BOBBY RIO (& REVELLES)
65	Pye 7N 15790	Boy Meets Girl/Don't Break My Heart And Run Away	50+
65	Pye 7N 15897	Everything In The Garden/When Love Was Young	45+
65	Pye 7N 15958	Value For Love/I'm Not Made Of Clay	40+
66	Piccadilly 7N 35303	Ask The Lonely/Be Lonely Little Girl (solo)	20
66	Piccadilly 7N 35337	Angelica/Lovin' You (solo)	12

RIO GRANDE
71	RCA SF 8208	RIO GRANDE (LP)	12

RIO GRANDES
66	Pyramid PYR 6001	Soldiers Take Over/Moses	15

RIOT
77	Ariola ARL 5007	ROCK CITY (LP)	12
78	Capitol E-ST 12081	NARITA (LP)	12

RIOT CLONE
82	Riot Clone RC 001	THERE'S NO GOVERNMENT LIKE NO GOVERNMENT (EP)	5
82	Riot Clone RC 002	DESTROY THE MYTH OF MUSICAL DESTRUCTION (EP)	5
84	Riot Clone RCR 004	BLOOD ON YOUR HANDS (LP)	5

RIOTS
65	Island WI 176	Telling Lies/Don't Leave Me (actually by Techniques)	32
65	Island WI 195	You Don't Know (actually by Techniques)/DON DRUMMOND & DRUMBAGO: Treasure Island	32
65	Island WI 197	I Am In Love/When You're Wrong (actually by Techniques)	30
65	Island WI 247	Yeah Yeah/BABA BROOKS: Virginia Ska	30

(see also Techniques)

RIOT SQUAD
65	Pye 7N 15752	Any Time/Jump	38
65	Pye 7N 15817	I Wanna Talk About My Baby/Gonna Make You Mine	48
65	Pye 7N 15869	Nevertheless/Not A Great Talker	45
66	Pye 7N 17041	Cry Cry Cry/How Is It Done	45
66	Pye 7N 17092	I Take It We're Through/Working Man	50+
66	Pye 7N 17130	It's Never Too Late To Forgive/Try To Realise	48
67	Pye 7N 17237	Gotta Be A First Time/Bitter Sweet Love	50

(see also Graham Bonney, Jimi Hendrix Experience, Blue Aces)

RIOT SQUAD
82	The THE 001	Total Onslaught (p/s)	7

RIOT SQUAD
82	Rondelet ROUND 23	Fuck The Tories/Civil Destruction (p/s)	6
82	Rondelet ROUND 25	Riot In The City/Religion (p/s)	5
83	Rot ASS 1	DON'T BE DENIED (EP)	6
83	Rot ASS 2	I'm OK Fuck You/In The Future/Friday Night (p/s)	6
84	Rot ASS 3	THERE AIN'T NO SOLUTION (EP)	6
84	Rot ASS 13	NO POTENTIAL THREAT (LP, with free single [ASS3], stickered sleeve)	12

RIOT SQUAD & MATUMBI
82	Extinguish EXT 004	Why Do You Make Me Wait/Paraphrase (12")	20

RIP CHORDS
63	CBS AAG 143	Here I Stand/Karen	15
63	CBS AAG 162	Gone/She Thinks I Still Care	18
64	CBS AAG 181	Hey Little Cobra/The Queen	25
64	CBS AAG 202	Three Window Coupe/Hot Rod USA	30
64	CBS BPG 62228	HEY LITTLE COBRA (LP)	80

(see also Terry Day, Terry Melcher, Bruce Johnston)

RIP CHORDS
78	Cells SELL 1	Ringing In The Streets/Music's Peace Artist/Television Television (p/s)	18

RIPCORD
89	private pressing	HARVEST HARDCORE (EP, foldout sleeve)	8

RIPLEY WAYFARERS
71	Tradition TSR 006	CHIPS AND BROWN SAUCE (LP)	15
72	Tradition TSR 013	FIVE WELLS (LP)	18
74	Tradition TSR 018	GENTLEMEN OF HIGH RENOWN (LP)	15
78	MWM MWM 1017	SONG AND DANCE TUNES (LP, as The Wayfarers)	15
85	Singabout SIN 001	DOWN THE ROAD (LP)	15

RIP 'N' LAW
71	Crab CRAB 64	In The Ghetto/Something Sweet	6

RIPPERS
68	Saga	HONESTLY (LP)	30

RIP SNORTER
79	Pye 7N 46159	Standing In A Little 'Ole/Confidentially (p/s)	8

RISING MOON
74	Theatre Projects	RISING MOON (LP)	30

RISING SONS (U.K.)
68	Pye 7N 17554	Hold Me Just A Little While Longer/Fountain Of Love	6

RISING SONS (U.S.)
65	Stateside SS 426	You're My Girl/Try To Be A Man	25

RITA
69	Major Minor MM 653	Erotica/Sexologie	20

RITA (Alston)
69	Jackpot JP 718	Love Making/NAT COLE: My Love	7

(see also Rita Alston)

RITA MITSOUKO
89	Virgin VSCD 1163	Singing In The Shower (with Sparks)/Smog/Hip Kit (3" CD)	10

(see also Sparks)

RITA & TIARAS
79	Destiny DS 1002	Gone With The Wind Is My Love/Wild Times (some with p/s) (DJ copy with p/s = £25)	10/15

JEAN RITCHIE
53	Argo ARS 1009	SONGS FROM KENTUCKY (10" LP)	20

TEX RITTER
54	Capitol CL 14175	Is There A Santa Claus?/Old Tex Kringle	5
55	Capitol CL 14277	A Whale Of A Tale/High On A Mountain Top	5
55	Capitol CL 14335	Marshal Of Wichita/September Song	5
60	Capitol EAP1-1323	DECK OF CARDS (EP)	8
52	Capitol LC 6552	COWBOY FAVOURITES (10" LP)	15
60	Capitol (S)T 1292	BLOOD ON THE SADDLE (LP)	12

MINT VALUE £

BOB RITTERBUSH
59   Top Rank JAR 118   I Wish That You Were Mine/Darling Corey (78 rpm = £7) 7

RIVALS
78   Sound On Sound SOS 100   Skateboarding In The UK/Top Of The Pops 15

RIVALS
80   Ace ACE 007   Future Rights/Flowers (p/s) 20
80   Oakwood/Ace ACE 011   Here Comes The Night/Both Sides (p/s)................................. 20

RIVAL SAVAGES
80   Savage VC 1968   Get Some (gatefold p/s) 25

HECTOR RIVERA
67   Polydor 65728   At The Party/Do It To Me... 80

ROYD RIVERS & CLIFF AUNGIER
65   Decca LK 4696   WANDERIN' (LP) 30
(see also Cliff Aungier)

BLUE RIVERS & MAROONS
67   Columbia Blue Beat DB 103 Witchcraft Man/Searching For You Baby 20
68   Spectrum SP 105   Take It Or Leave It/I've Been Pushed Around 10
68   Columbia S(C)X 6192   BLUE BEAT IN MY SOUL (LP) 50

CLIFF RIVERS
63   London HLU 9739   True Lips/Marsha.. 40
(pseudonym for Joey Castle)

DANNY RIVERS
60   Top Rank JAR 408   Hawk/I Got 35
60   Decca F 11294   Can't You Hear My Heart/I'm Waiting For Tomorrow..................... 25
61   Decca F 11357   Once Upon A Time/My Baby's Gone Away (with Alexander Combo) 40
64   Decca F 11865   There Will Never Be Anyone Else/I Don't Think You Know How I Feel 20
62   HMV POP 1000   We're Gonna Dance/Movin' In (as Danny Rivers & River Men) 50

DEEK RIVERS
62   Oriole CB 1735   One Kiss/Outsider... 20
81   Chiswick NS 71   Elvis Presley Medley/ELVIS PRESLEY:
                            Press Conference Vancouver 1957 (picture disc) 5

JOHNNY RIVERS
66   Liberty LEP 4049   MORE JOHNNY RIVERS (EP)... 22
64   Liberty LBY 3031   AT THE WHISKY A GO-GO (LP).. 22
65   Liberty LBY 3036   HERE WE A GO-GO AGAIN (LP) 22
65   Liberty LBY 3056   MEANWHILE BACK AT THE WHISKY A GO GO (LP) 20

MAVIS RIVERS
60   Capitol CL 15120   So Rare/Longing, Longing, Longing 5
63   Reprise RS 20115   Slightly Out Of Tune/Footsteps Of A Fool 5

TONY RIVERS & THE CASTAWAYS
63   Columbia DB 7135   Shake Shake Shake/Row Row Row 20
64   Columbia DB 7224   I Love The Way You Walk/I Love You 12
64   Columbia DB 7336   Life's Too Short/Tell On Me 12
65   Columbia DB 7448   She/Till We Get Home.. 12
65   Columbia DB 7536   Come Back/What To Do 12
66   Columbia DB 7971   God Only Knows/Charade 18
66   Parlophone R 5400   Nowhere Man/The Girl From New York City............................. 15
66   Immediate IM 027   Girl Don't Tell Me/The Girl From Salt Lake City 30
68   Polydor 56245   I Can Guarantee Your Love/Pantomime 6
(see also Capability Brown, Grapefruit, Harmony Grass, Senators, Sugarbeats)

RIVIERA
69   Pye 7N 17712   Baby Won't Leave Me Alone/The Love Story............................. 5

RIVIERAS
60   HMV POP 773   Blessing Of Love/Moonlight Cocktails 120

RIVIERAS
64   Pye International 7N 25237 California Sun/H B Goose Step 40

RIVINGTON PIKE
72   Decca F 13329   Wish A Little Love/I'll Be There 5

RIVINGTONS
62   Liberty LIB 55427   Papa Oom Mow Mow/Deep Water 40
63   Liberty LIB 55553   The Bird's The Word/I'm Losing My Grip 50
66   CBS 202088   Rose Growing In The Ruins/Tend To Business 50

RIVVITS
79   Alien AUX 1   Saturday Night At The Dance/Girl Next Door (p/s, with flexi). 10

FREDDIE ROACH
67   Transatlantic PR 7490   THE SOUL BOOK (LP) 15

MAX ROACH (& CLIFFORD BROWN GROUP)
55   Vogue EPV 1074   MAX ROACH AND CLIFFORD BROWN (EP).................................... 8
55   Vogue EPV 1083   MAX ROACH AND CLIFFORD BROWN (EP).................................... 8
55   Vogue EPV 1091   MAX ROACH AND CLIFFORD BROWN (EP).................................... 8
58   Emarcy ERE 1572   MAX ROACH AND CLIFFORD BROWN (EP, withdrawn) 15
55   Vogue LDE 117   MAX ROACH & CLIFFORD BROWN IN CONCERT VOL. 1 (10" LP)............... 15
55   Vogue LDE 128   MAX ROACH & CLIFFORD BROWN IN CONCERT VOL. 2 (10" LP)............... 15
58   Emarcy EJL 1282   JAZZ IN THREE-QUARTER TIME (LP)..................................... 15
59   Emarcy MMB 12005   MAX ROACH, NEWPORT (LP, by Max Roach) 15

59	Emarcy MMB 12009	THE MAX ROACH FOUR PLUS FOUR (LP, by Max Roach)	15
60	Mercury MMC 14041	I REMEMBER CLIFFORD (LP)	12
60	Mercury MMC 14054	QUIET AS IT'S KEPT (LP, by Max Roach)	12

(see also Clifford Brown, Buddy Rich)

ROAD
73	Rare Earth SRE 3006	ROAD (LP)	15

ROADHOUSE
92	Vertigo VERP 57	Hell Can Wait/Loving You/Jackson High/More Than I Want (12", picture disc)	8

ROADRUNNERS
65	Cavern Sound 2BSNL 7	PANTOMANIA (EP, with tracks by Chris Edwards & Clive Wood)	35

ROADSTER
81	Mayhem SRTS 81	Fantasy/45 MPH (p/s)	100

ROADSTERS
64	Stateside SS 293	Joy Ride/Drag	35

ROARING SIXTIES
66	Marmalade 598 001	We Love The Pirates/I'm Leaving Town	45

(see also Family)

ROBAN'S SKIFFLE GROUP
61	Storyville A45 062	Careless Love/Frankie And Johnny (some with p/s)	35/18

E.G. ROBB
63	Columbia DB 7100	Stage To Cimarron/Jezebel	15

MARTY ROBBINS
56	Philips PB 590	Long Tall Sally/Mr. Teardrop (78)	25
57	Philips PB 696	A White Sport Coat (And A Pink Carnation)/Grown-Up Tears (78)	25
57	Philips JK 1019	A White Sport Coat (And A Pink Carnation)/Grown-Up Tears (jukebox issue)	40
57	Philips PB 741	Please Don't Blame Me/Teen-Age Dream (78)	20
58	Fontana H 102	The Story Of My Life/Once-A-Week Date (78)	20
57	Philips JK 1019	A White Sport Coat (And A Pink Carnation)/Grown-Up Tears (jukebox issue)	50
58	Fontana H 128	Stairway Of Love/Just Married (78 rpm = £25)	25
58	Fontana H 150	Sittin' In A Tree House/She Was Only Seventeen (78 rpm = £30)	18
59	Fontana H 184	The Hanging Tree (from film)/The Blues Country Style (78 rpm = £35)	12
59	Fontana H 212	Cap And Gown/Last Night About This Time (78 rpm = £40)	10
59	Fontana H 229	Big Iron/Cool Water (78 rpm = £50)	10
59	Fontana H 233	El Paso/Running Gun (78 rpm = £60)	5
60	Fontana H 263	I Told My Heart/Is There Any Chance	5
60	Fontana H 270	Ballad Of The Alamo/Five Brothers (in p/s)	10
61	Fontana H 301	Don't Worry/Like All Other Times	5
61	Fontana H 324	Ghost Train/Jimmy Martinez	5
61	Fontana H 342	It's Your World/You Told Me So	5
62	CBS AAG 114	Devil Woman/April Fool's Day	5
63	CBS AAG 128	Ruby Ann/Won't You Forgive	7
63	CBS AAG 141	Cigarette And Coffee Blues/Teenager's Dad	10

EPs
59	Fontana TFE 17161	MARTY'S BIG HITS	30
59	Fontana TFE 17168	WEDDING BELLS	15
60	Fontana TFE 17167	SONG OF THE ISLANDS	15
61	Fontana TFE 17224	GUNFIGHTER	15
61	CBS AGG 20004	JUST A LITTLE SENTIMENTAL	12
61	CBS AGG 20013	JUST A LITTLE SENTIMENTAL VOL. 2	12
66	CBS AGG 20049	MARTY ROBBINS	12

LPs
59	Fontana TFL 5063	GUNFIGHTER BALLADS AND TRAIL SONGS	25
60	Fontana TFL 5086	MARTY'S GREATEST HITS	20
61	Fontana TFL 5113	MORE GUNFIGHTER BALLADS AND TRAIL SONGS (stereo STFL 541)	25
61	Fontana TFL 5145	MORE GREATEST HITS (also stereo STFL 565)	20
61	Fontana TFL 5162	JUST A LITTLE SENTIMENTAL (with Jordanaires, also stereo STFL 579)	20
62	CBS (S)BPG 62041	MARTY AFTER MIDNIGHT	20
63	CBS (S)BPG 62113	DEVIL WOMAN (mono/stereo)	15
63	CBS BPG 62131	PORTRAIT OF MARTY (mono/stereo)	15
63	CBS (S)BPG 62169	HAWAII'S CALLING ME (mono/stereo)	15
64	CBS (S)BPG 62190	THE RETURN OF THE GUNFIGHTER (mono/stereo)	15
64	CBS (S)BPG 62297	ISLAND WOMAN (mono/stereo)	15
65	CBS (S)BPG 62437	R.F.D. (mono/stereo)	15
65	CBS (S)BPG 62499	TURN THE LIGHTS DOWN LOW	15
66	CBS (S)BPG 62689	WHAT GOD HAS DONE	15
66	CBS (S)BPG 62782	THE DRIFTER	20
67	CBS (S)BPG 62962	MY KIND OF COUNTRY	25
67	CBS (S)BPG 63116	TONIGHT CARMEN	15
68	CBS 63354	CHRISTMAS WITH MARTY ROBBINS (mono/stereo)	15

(see also Jordanaires)

MEL ROBBINS
59	London HLM 8966	Save It/To Know You (initially triangular centre, later round centre)	600/320
59	London HLM 8966	Save It/To Know You (78)	150

SYLVIA ROBBINS
60	London HLJ 9118	Frankie And Johnny/Come Home	30

(see also Mickey & Sylvia)

ROBERT & REMOULDS
79	Black & White BW 1	X No. 1/Do Eyes Ever Meet? (p/s)	35

ALAN ROBERTS
70s Plant Life PLR 012   CALEDONIA (LP, with Dougie Maclean) 12
(see also Dougie MacLean)

ANDY ROBERTS
73	Elektra K 12109	Baby Baby/All Around My Grandmother's Floor 5
70	RCA SF 8086	HOME GROWN (LP) 40
71	Charisma CAS 1034	HOME GROWN (LP, reissue, different sleeve) 12
71	B&C	HOME GROWN (LP, reissue) 12
71	Pegasus PEG 5	NINA AND THE DREAM TREE (LP) 25
73	Elektra K 42139	URBAN COWBOY (LP, with insert) 15
73	Elektra K 42151	ANDY ROBERTS AND THE GREAT STAMPEDE (LP, gatefold sleeve) 15

(see also Clayton Squares, Liverpool Scene, Everyone, Plainsong)

BOB ROBERTS
70 Explosion EX 2021   Stick By Me/TOMMY McCOOK: The Designer 7

BOB ROBERTS (U.K.)
81 Solent SS 054   BREEZE FOR A BARGEMAN (LP) 15

HUGH ROBERTS
70 Explosion EX 2041   California Dreaming/One Woman (both sides actually by Lloyd Charmers) 8

J. ROBERTS
70 Bamboo BAM 30   Someday We'll Be Together/SOUND DIMENSION: Everyday People 15

JOHN ROBERTS
68	Sue WI 4042	Sockin' 1, 2, 3, 4/Sophisticated Funk 30
68	Action ACT 4511	I'll Forget You/Be My Baby.. 25

KEITH ROBERTS
72 Trailer LER 3031   PIER OF THE REALM (LP) 12

KENNY ROBERTS
57 Brunswick 05638   I'm Looking For The Bully Of The Town/Broken Teenage Heart 12

KENNY ROBERTS
65	Pye 7N 15882	Say, Do You Mean It/Since My Love Has Gone 10
66	Pye 7N 17054	Run Like The Devil/Where Goes My Heart 50

(see also Kenny Damon)

KIM ROBERTS
64 Decca F 11813   I'll Prove It/For Loving Me This Way..................................... 85

RENEE ROBERTS
62 Oriole CB 1731   I Want To Love You/Aching Heart 6

RICK ROBERTS
72 A&M AMLH 64372   WINDMILLS (LP) 12
(see also Flying Burrito Brothers)

ROCKY ROBERTS
67 Durium DRL 50026   SABATO SERA (LP)... 40

DALE ROBERTSON
60 RCA SF 5064   PRESENTS HIS ALBUM OF WESTERN CLASSICS (LP) 20

DON ROBERTSON
50	London L 629	Gamblin' Fever/On The Hudson Bay Line (78, with Lou) 10
56	Capitol CL 14575	The Happy Whistler/You're Free To Go (B-side with Lou Dinning) 7
56	Capitol CL 14629	Every Day That I Live (with Lou Dinning)/You 5
59	Capitol CL 15088	Fine Day/The Merry Men (78 rpm = £10)................................. 5

JEANNIE ROBERTSON
59	Topic 10T 52	I KEN WHERE I'M GOING (10" LP) 15
59	Topic 12T 96	JEANNIE ROBERTSON (LP, blue label, with card insert) 15
60	Collector JFS 4001	LORD DONALD (LP) 15

JIM ROBERTSON
55 MGM SPC 7   Pride Of My Heart/Walkin' And Talkin' With The Lord (export issue) 15

PAUL ROBESON
52	HMV 7P 113	Ol' Man River/I Suits Me.. 10
57	HMV DLP 1155	THE INCOMPARABLE VOICE OF PAUL ROBESON (10" LP) 12
57	HMV DLP 1165	EMPEROR OF SONG (10" LP) 15

DAVE ROBIN
65 Eyemark EMS 1003   You I Don't Want To Share/Life's Too Short............................... 6

EDE ROBIN
75 Crystal CR 7023   There Must Be A Love Somewhere/Soul Over Easy 10

RICHIE ROBIN
60 Top Rank JAR 262   Strange Dream/GERRY GRANAHAN: It Hurts 15

TINA ROBIN
57	Vogue Coral Q 72284	Over Somebody Else's Shoulder/Lady Fair (78 rpm = £10) 20
57	Vogue Coral Q 72294	Never In A Million Years/Ça C'est L'Amour (78 rpm = £10)............... 15
58	Coral Q 72309	Everyday/Believe Me (78 rpm = £12).................................... 20
58	Coral Q 72323	No School Tomorrow/Sugar Blues (78 rpm = £15) 20
62	Mercury AMT 1199	Get Out Of My Life/Why Did You Go..................................... 8

ROBIN HOODS
65 Mercury MF 865   Wait For The Dawn/Love You So... 10

ROBINS
60 Vogue V 9168   Cherry Lips/Out Of The Picture... 160

60	Vogue V 9173	Just Like That/Whole Lot Imagination 120
	(see also H.B. Barnum)	

JIMMY ROBINS
68	President PT 118	I Can't Please You/I Made It Over 150

ALVIN ROBINSON
64	Pye International 7N 25248	Something You Got/Searchin' 25
64	Red Bird RB 10010	Down Home Girl/Fever 30
66	Strike JH 307	You Brought My Heart Right Down To My Knees/Whatever You Had 25

BROTHER CLEOPHUS ROBINSON
57	Vogue EPV 1196	BROTHER CLEOPHUS ROBINSON (EP)................................ 25

DAVE ROBINSON
79	Bushays BFM 124	Ruby & Diamond (feat. Jah Thomas/Dub (12") 20

EDDIE ROBINSON
71	Ember EMB S 301	Hey Blackman Parts 1 & 2 5
70s	Myrrh MYR 1013	REFLECTIONS OF THE MAN INSIDE (LP) 15

ELZADIE ROBINSON
50	Tempo R 33	The Santa Claus Crave/St. Louis Cyclone Blues (78)...................... 10
50	Tempo R 36	Arkansas Mill Blues/Gold Mansion Blues (78, with Will Ezell)............... 10
50	Tempo R 37	Rowdy Man Blues/Going South Blues (78) 10
	(see also Will Ezell)	

FLOYD ROBINSON
59	RCA RCA 1146	Makin' Love/My Girl (initially with triangular centre, later round)............. 12/6
59	RCA RCA 1146	Makin' Love/My Girl (78).. 30+
60	RCA RCA 1179	I Believe In Love/Tattletale 7
60	RCA RD 27166	FLOYD ROBINSON (LP) 65

FREDDY ROBINSON
72	Stax 2325 085	AT THE DRIVE-IN (LP)... 18

HARRY ROBINSON
60	Top Rank JAR 325	The Skirl/Wimoweh (as Harry Robinson "String Sound") 5
61	Decca F 11319	Heavy Date/Sentimental Journey (as Harry Robinson's XV) 5
	(see also Lord Rockingham's XI)	

JACKIE ROBINSON
68	Amalgamated AMG 819	Over And Over/Woman Of Samaria...................................... 20
68	Amalgamated AMG 824	Let The Little Girl Dance/DERRICK MORGAN: I Want To Go Home 18
74	Harry J. HJ 6695	My Love For You/R.D. Livingstone: Smokey Mountains.................... 5

JACKEY ROBINSON
70	Punch PH 50	Heart Made Of Stone (actually by Jackie Bernard)/BOB TAYLOR: I May Never See My Baby Anymore 20
	(see also Jackie Robinson, Pioneers)	

JIM ROBINSON NEW ORLEANS BAND
61	Riverside RLP 369	NEW ORLEANS: THE LIVING LEGENDS (LP) 18
64	Riverside RLP 393	PLAYS SPIRITUAL AND BLUES (LP) 18

J.P. ROBINSON
72	Atlantic K 10149	George Jackson/Wall To Wall Love...................................... 10
72	Atlantic K 10209	What Can I Tell Her/Please Accept My Call 15

JUNE ROBINSON
56	Oriole CB 1319	45 Men In A Telephone Box/Oo-Shoo-Be-Doo-Be (78) 10

LLOYD ROBINSON
62	Blue Beat BB 122	Give Me A Chance/When You Walk...................................... 12
63	Blue Beat BB 159	I Need Your Love/You Told Me... 12
69	Duke DU 5	Cuss Cuss/Lavender Blue 30
70	Camel CA 41	The Worm/NEVILLE HYNES: Afro (actually by Neville Hinds).............. 12
72	Green Door GD 4028	I Can't Forget/LLOYD AND THE NOW GENERATION: I Can't Forget (Version) 5
77	Cactus CT 109	Rocky Road/Version 20
	(see also Lloyd Clarke, Lloyd Charmers, Harry J. Allstars, Matadors, Melodians)	

M. ROBINSON
64	Port-O-Jam PJ 4114	Who Are You/Follow You 20

ROSCO ROBINSON
66	Pye International 7N 25385	That's Enough/One More Time (DJ copy = £100) 60
72	Wand WN 27	That's Enough/One More Time (reissue) 15
73	Contempo C 16	We're Losing It Baby/We Got A Good Thing Going........................ 8

SUGAR CHILE ROBINSON
50	Capitol CL 13393	Christmas Boogie/Rudolph The Red Nosed Reindeer (78) 7
51	Capitol CL 13589	After School Blues/Caldonia (78) 7
51	Capitol CL 13636	Green Grass/Baby Blues (78) 7
52	Capitol CL 13796	Lazy Boy's Boogie/Whop Whop (78)..................................... 7
53	Capitol LC 6586	CAPITOL PRESENTS SUGAR CHILE ROBINSON (10" LP).................. 70

TOM ROBINSON (BAND)
75	Chebel SRT/CUS 015	GOOD TO BE GAY (EP, as Bradford Gay Liberation Front) 15
79	EMI EMI 2946	All Right All Night/Black Angel (withdrawn, demo-only) 8
	(see also Cafe Society, Phantom, Billy Karloff [& Extremes])	

ROBINSON CREW
63	Decca F 11706	Taxi (Theme From TV Series)/Stormalong 8
	(see also Lord Rockingham's XI)	

CARSON ROBISON (& HIS PLEASANT VALLEY BOYS)
53	MGM SP 1004	Lady Round The Lady/Pokeberry Promenade............................. 10

Carson ROBISON

53	MGM SP 1024	Square Dance Jitterbug/Keep On Circlin' 'Round	15
58	MGM MGM-EP 669	LIFE GETS TEEJUS (EP)	15
61	MGM MGM-EP 755	SQUARE DANCE — WITH CALLS (EP)	10
52	MGM MGM-D 101	EIGHT SQUARE DANCES (10" LP)	15

RALPH ROBLES
| 69 | London HA/SH 8385 | TAKING OVER (LP) | 20 |

NICKY ROBSON
| 80 | Scratch SCR 006 | Stars/Eye To Eye (p/s) | 20 |
| 80 | Scratch SCRT 006 | Stars (Extended)/Eye To Eye (12") | 40 |

(see also Gary Numan)

ROCAMARS
| 65 | King KG 1031 | All In Black Woman/Give Me Time | 15 |

TONY ROCCO
| 62 | Parlophone R 4886 | Stalemate/Keep A Walking | 15 |
| 62 | Parlophone R 4946 | Torture/Competition | 15 |

HARRY ROCHE CONSTELLATION
67	CBS 202653	Casino Royale/In The Pad Of The Mountain King	10
67	CBS SBPG 63013	CASINO ROYALE (LP)	35
71	Studio Two TWO 340	SPINDRIFT (LP)	20
73	Pye Intl. NSPL 41024	SPIRAL (LP)	50
73	Pye QUAD 1022	SOMETIMES (LP, quadrophonic)	25

ROCHEE & SARNOS
| 85 | Nervous NERD 018 | UNDERSTANDING SARNO (LP) | 12 |

JACKIE ROCHELLE
| 68 | Olga OLE 011 | Till The End/Grown Up Games | 5 |

ROCKABILLY PSYCHOSIS
| 84 | Big Beat WIK 18 | ROCKABILLY PSYCHOSIS AND THE GARAGE DISEASE (LP) | 12 |

DICKIE ROCK & MIAMI SHOWBAND
63	Piccadilly 7N 35154	Boys/There's Always Me	5
64	Piccadilly 7N 35202	From The Candy Store/Twenty Flight Rock	8
65	Pye 7N 15750	Round And Around/Little Baby	5
65	Pye 7N 15855	Every Step Of The Way/Rock And Roll Music	5
65	Pye 7N 17063	Come Back To Stay/Can't Make Up My Mind (p/s)	8
65	Pye NEP 24251	COME BACK TO STAY (EP)	15

ROCK AID ARMENIA
89	Life Aid Armenia ARMEN 01	Smoke On The Water/BLACK SABBATH: Paranoid (1970) (p/s)	5
89	L. A. Armenia ARMEN T01	Smoke On The Water/BLACK SABBATH: Paranoid (1970) (12", blue or white p/s)	8
89	Life Aid Armenia	Smoke On The Water (Radio Mix)/Smoke On The Water (Extended Mix)/	
	ARMENCD 01	BLACK SABBATH: Paranoid (1970) (CD)	10
90	L. A. Armenia ARMEN 002	Smoke On The Water '90 (Radio Edit)/BLACK SABBATH: Paranoid ('90) (p/s)	5

(see also Brian May, Roger Taylor, Ritchie Blackmore, Dave Gilmour, Black Sabbath, Rush, Bruce Dickinson, Ian Gillan, Free, Firm, Yes, Keith Emerson, Eighth Wonder)

ROCK-A-TEENS
| 59 | Columbia DB 4361 | Woo-Hoo/Untrue | 40 |

ROCK BROTHERS
| 56 | Parlophone MSP 6201 | Dungaree Doll/Livin' It Up (78 rpm, Parlophone R 4119 = £35) | 90 |

ROCKERS
| 59 | Oriole CB 1501 | Get Cracking/Counter Melody (78 rpm = £14) | 20 |

ROCKERS
83	CBS A 3929	We Are The Boys (Who Make All The Noise)/Rockin' On Stage (p/s)	8
83	CBS TA 3929	We Are The Boys (Who Make All The Noise) (Extended Version)/	
		Rockin' On Stage (12", p/s)	12

(see also Phil Lynott, Roy Wood, Status Quo)

ROCKET 88
| 81 | Atlantic K 50776 | ROCKET 88 (LP) | 20 |

(see also Charlie Watts, Alexis Korner, Jack Bruce, Dick Heckstall-Smith)

ROCKET FROM THE CRYPT
93	Southern Studios PUS 007	Glazed/Pressures/Cut It Loose (white label test pressing, 5-10 copies only)	30
95	Elemental ELM 32S	Born in 69/Ciao Patsy (p/s)	5
96	Elemental ELM 33S	Young Livers/Burning Army Men (p/s)	5
96	Dinked 1	Used/Lose Your Clown (in-store giveaway)	25
98	Elemental ELM 47PIC	When In Rome/Tarzan/Tiger Feet Tonight (picture disc)	7
98	Elemental ELM 48S	Lipstick/Hot Heart (p/s)	5
98	Elemental ELM 49S	Break It Up/Turkish Revenge (p/s)	5
95	Elemental ELM 27LP	HOT CHARITY (LP)	12

ROCKETS
| 60 | Philips PB 982 | Gibraltar Rock/Walkin' Home (78 rpm = £40) | 20 |
| 61 | Zodiac ZR 0010 | Warrior/Countdown | 20 |

ROCKIN' BERRIES
63	Decca F 11698	Wah Wah Wah Woo/Rockin' Berry Stomp	25
63	Decca F 11760	Itty Bitty Pieces/The Twitch	20
64	Piccadilly 7N 35197	I Didn't Mean To Hurt You/You'd Better Come Home	5
65	Piccadilly 7N 35254	You're My Girl/Brother Bill	5
65	Piccadilly 7N 35270	The Water Is Over My Head/Doesn't Time Fly	5
66	Piccadilly 7N 35304	I Could Make You Fall In Love/Land Of Love	5
66	Piccadilly 7N 35327	Midnight Mary/Money Grows On Trees	5

67	Piccadilly 7N 35373	Sometimes/Needs To Be	5
67	Piccadilly 7N 35400	Smile/Breakfast At Sam's	5
67	Pye 7N 17411	Dawn (Go Away)/She's Not Like Any Girl	5
68	Pye 7N 17519	When I Reach The Top/Pain	5
68	Pye 7N 17589	Mr. Blue/Land Of Love	5
73	Satril SAT 9	Day To Day/Big Louis' Birthday	5
74	Pye 7N 45394	Rock-A-Bye Nursery Rhyme/Long Time Ago	5
65	Piccadilly NEP 34039	I DIDN'T MEAN TO HURT YOU (EP)	35
65	Piccadilly NEP 34043	NEW FROM THE BERRIES (EP)	35
65	Piccadilly NEP 34045	HAPPY TO BE BLUE (EP)	50
64	Piccadilly NPL 38013	IN TOWN (LP)	50
65	Piccadilly NPL 38022	LIFE IS JUST A BOWL OF BERRIES (LP)	50

(see also Jefferson)

ROCKIN' DUPSEE
70s	Flyright FLY 592	ROCKIN' WITH DUPSEE (LP)	12
76	Sonnet SNTF718	DOIN' THE ZYDECO (LP)	20

ROCKIN' FOO
70	Stateside SS 2168	Rochester River/Stranger In The Attic	6
70	Stateside SSL 10303	ROCKIN' FOO (LP)	20

ROCKIN' HENRI & HAYSEEDS
63	Decca F 11700	Sally/Sweet Adeline	5

ROCKIN' HORSE
71	Philips 6006 156	The Biggest Gossip In Town/You Say	12
72	Philips 6006 200	Julian The Hooligan/Stayed Out Late Last Night	12
70	Philips 6308 075	YES IT IS (LP)	30

(see also Jimmy Campbell, 23rd Turnoff, Kirkbys, Merseys)

ROCKING HORSE
71	Camel CA 75	Running Back Home/SOUL SYNDICATE BAND: Running Back (Version)	6
72	Randy's RAN 522	Hard Time/Change Your Ways	8
73	Randy's RAN 535	I'm So Fed Up/I'm So Fed Up (Version)	5
74	Pyramid PYR 7009	New Situation/New Version	5

ROCKIN' RAMRODS
66	Polydor BM 56512	Don't Fool With Fu Manchu/Tears Melt The Stone	20

ROCKIN' REBELS
63	Stateside SS 162	Wild Weekend/Wild Weekend Cha Cha	20
63	Stateside SS 187	Rockin' Crickets/Hully Gully Rock (both sides actually by Hot-Toddys)	20

(see also Hot-Toddys)

ROCKIN' R's
59	London HL 8872	The Beat/Crazy Baby (78 rpm = £30)	50

ROCKIN' SAINTS
60	Brunswick 05843	Cheat On Me, Baby/Half And Half	100

ROCKIN' STRINGS
59	Columbia DB 4349	Red Sails In The Sunset/Autumn Leaves	7

(see also Eric Jupp)

ROCKIN' VICKERS
64	Decca F 11993	I Go Ape/Someone Like You (as Rocking Vickers)	35
66	CBS 202051	It's Alright/Stay By Me	50
66	CBS 202241	Dandy/I Don't Need Your Kind	40

(see also Sam Gopal, Motörhead)

ROCKITS
73	Mowest MW 3012	Livin' Without You/Love My Love	8

ROCK MACHINE
73	T.I.M.	THEMES (LP)	50

(see also Ugly Custard)

ROCK'N'ROLL REVIVAL SHOW
68	Decca F 12752	Midnight Train/Oh Boy (both sides featuring Tommy Bishop)	5

(see also Tommy Bishop's Ricochets)

ROCK-OLGA
60	Ember EMB S 105	Red Sails In The Sunset/My Dixieland Doll (some in p/s)	10/5

ROCKSTEADYS
67	Giant GN 2	Squeeze And Freeze/JUNIOR SMITH: I'm A Good Boy	10

ROCKSTONES
70	Trojan TR 7762	A.B.C. Reggae/BEVERLEY'S ALLSTARS: Be Yours	6
70	Summit SUM 8501	Everything Is Beautiful/BEVERLEY'S ALLSTARS: Give Up	6

(see also Gaylads)

ROCK WORKSHOP
70	CBS 5046	You To Lose/Born In The City	6
71	CBS 7252	Very Last Time/Light Is Light	5
70	CBS 64075	ROCK WORKSHOP (LP, orange label)	30
71	CBS 64394	THE VERY LAST TIME (2-LP, orange label)	40

(see also Alex Harvey)

ROCKY FELLERS
63	Stateside SS 175	Killer Joe/Lonely Treardrops	15
63	Stateside SS 212	Like The Big Guys Do/Great Big World	12
63	Pye International 7N 25225	Ching A Ling Baby/Hey Little Donkey	15

MINT VALUE £

ROCKY HORROR SHOW

75	Ode ODS 66305	Science Fiction Double Feature/Time Warp	8
74	Ode ODE 77026	THE ROCKY HORROR SHOW (LP, original US Roxy cast)	15
75	UK UKAL 1015	THE ROCKY HORROR SHOW (LP, London cast)	15
75	Ode ODE 78332	THE ROCKY HORROR PICTURE SHOW ALBUM (LP, soundtrack)	15
83	Ode OSVP 78332	THE ROCKY HORROR PICTURE SHOW ALBUM (LP, soundtrack, picture disc)	20
87	Ode OSVP 21653	THE ROCKY HORROR PICTURE SHOW ALBUM (LP, soundtrack, reissue, picture disc)	20
87	Ode ODE 9009	THE ROCKY HORROR SHOW (LP, reissue of original U.S. cast, with inner sleeve)	15
87	Ode RHVX 1	ROCKY HORROR BOX SET (4-LP box, with inserts, numbered)	30
87	Ode RHBXLP 1	ROCKY HORROR BOX SET (4-LP box, with different inserts to above)	25
90	Ode RHBXCD 1	THE ROCKY HORROR PICTURE ALBUMS (15th ANNIVERSARY) (4-CD, with booklet)	45

(see also Meat Loaf, Original Soundtracks)

GENE RODDENBERRY

76	CBS 4692	Star Trek Theme/Star Trek Philosophy	12

RODD-KEN & CAVALIERS

60	Triumph RGM 1001	Magic Wheel/Happy Valley	45

(see also Blue Men)

CLODA(GH) RODGERS

62	Decca F 11534	Believe Me I'm No Fool/End Of The Line	10
63	Decca F 11607	Sometime Kind Of Love/I See More Of Him	10
63	Decca F 11667	To Give My Love To You/I Only Live To Love You	10
64	Decca F 11812	Mister Heartache/Time	10
65	Columbia DB 7468	Wanting You/Johnny Come Home	5
66	Columbia DB 7926	Every Day Is Just The Same/You'll Come A Running	5
66	Columbia DB 8038	Stormy Weather/Lonely Room	5
69	RCA SF 8033	CLODAGH RODGERS (LP)	15
69	RCA SF 8071	MIDNIGHT CLODAGH (LP)	15
71	RCA SF 8180	RODGERS AND HART (LP)	12

EILEEN RODGERS

58	Fontana H 136	Careful, Careful/I'm Alone Because I Love You	12
58	Fontana H 156	Treasure Of Your Love/Little Bit Bluer	12
61	London HLR 9271	Sailor/Wait Till Tomorrow	15

IKE RODGERS

(see under Henry Brown)

JEAN RODGERS

65	Columbia DB 7637	Take What I Have/Baby What You Gonna Do?	6

JIMMIE RODGERS (The Blue Yodeller)

56	HMV MH 192	Blue Yodel No. 4/Waiting For A Train (78, export issue)	10
56	HMV MH 193	In The Jailhouse Now No. 2/Peach Picking Time Down In Georgia (78, export)	10
56	HMV MH 194	Blue Yodel No. 9/Jimmie The Kid (78, export issue)	10
58	HMV 7EG 8163	JIMMIE RODGERS (EP)	18
60	RCA RCX 1058	LEGENDARY JIMMIE RODGERS (EP)	15
59	RCA RD 27110	TRAIN WHISTLE BLUES (LP)	20
59	RCA RD 27138	NEVER NO MO' BLUES (JIMMIE RODGERS MEMORIAL ALBUM) (LP)	20
61	RCA RD 27203	MY ROUGH AND ROWDY WAYS (LP)	18
61	RCA RD 27241	JIMMIE THE KID (LP)	18
62	RCA RD 7505	COUNTRY MUSIC HALL OF FAME (LP)	18
63	RCA RD 7562	THE SHORT BUT BRILLIANT LIFE OF JIMMIE RODGERS (LP)	18
64	RCA RD 7644	MY TIME AIN'T LONG (LP)	18

JIMMIE RODGERS

57	Columbia DB 3986	Honeycomb/Their Hearts Were Full Of Spring (as Jimmy Rodgers)	20
57	Columbia DB 4052	Kisses Sweeter Than Wine/Better Loved You'll Never Be	10
58	Columbia DB 4078	Oh-Oh, I'm Falling In Love Again/The Long Hot Summer	10
58	Columbia DB 4130	Secretly/Make Me A Miracle (78 rpm = £6)	5
58	Columbia DB 4175	Are You Really Mine/The Wizard (78 rpm = £6)	5
58	Columbia DB 4206	Woman From Liberia/Girl In The Wood (78 rpm = £6)	5
59	Columbia DB 4235	Bimbombey/You Understand Me	5
59	Columbia DB 4281	Because You're Young/I'm Never Gonna Tell	5
59	Columbia DB 4327	Soldier, Won't You Marry Me?/Ring-A-Ling-A-Lario (78 rpm = £12)	5
59	Columbia DB 4362	Tucumcari/The Night You Became Seventeen	6
58	Columbia SEG 7770	JIMMIE RODGERS (EP)	25
58	Columbia SEG 7811	JIMMIE RODGERS SINGS (EP)	20
59	Columbia SEG 7911	JIMMIE RODGERS NO. 2 (EP)	20
58	Columbia 33SX 1082	JIMMIE RODGERS (LP)	25
58	Columbia 33SX 1097	THE NUMBER ONE BALLADS (LP)	25
59	Columbia 33SX 1144	SINGS FOLK SONGS (LP)	20
59	Columbia 33SX 1176	JIMMIE RODGERS FAVOURITES (LP)	20
59	Columbia 33SX 1206	IT'S CHRISTMAS ONCE AGAIN (LP)	20
63	London HA-D 8040	NO ONE WILL EVER KNOW (LP)	20
65	London HA-D/SH-D 8116	HONEYCOMB (LP)	20
66	Dot DLP 3710	COUNTRY MUSIC 1966 (LP)	15

RODNEY & BRUNETTES

79	London/Bomp HLZ 10574	NEW YORK BLONDES featuring MADAME X: Little GTO/Holocaust On Sunset Boulevard(no p/s)	12

(see also Blondie, Debbie Harry)

RODNEY P

97	Pussyfoot PUSSY018	TINGS IN TIME (EP)	16

RODNEY P & SKITZ
99	Ronin RDP10	Revolutionary/Dedicated (12")	8

TOMMY ROE (& ROEMANS)
63	HMV 7EG 8806	THE FOLK SINGER (EP)	20
63	HMV CLP 1614	SHEILA (LP)	40
64	HMV CLP 1704	EVERYBODY LIKES TOMMY ROE (LP)	20
65	HMV CLP 1860	BALLADS AND BEAT (LP)	25
69	Stateside S(S)L 10282	DIZZY (LP)	15

BILL ROGERS
52	Melodisc 1230	Nice Woman, Ugly Man/B.G. BARGEE: Shanto (78)	6

CE CE ROGERS
89	WEA A 8852T	Forever/Someday (12", no p/s)	20

DANE ROGERS & NU BEATS
64	Pye 7N 15621	Mary Jane/Jeanette	10

DEAN ROGERS
60	Parlophone R 4732	End Of Time (as Dean Rogers & Hi-Fi's)/Keep The Miracle Going	10
61	Parlophone R 4835	Timber/High In A Misty Sky	10

(see also Sydney James)

ERIC ROGERS
59	Decca F 11151	Joanna/Lingering Lovers (78)	7
63	Decca F 11585	The Iron Maiden/Fly-Wheel	6

JULIE ROGERS
64	Mercury MF 809	It's Magic/Without Your Love	8
64	Mercury 10023 MCE	JULIE ROGERS (EP)	20
65	Mercury 10028 MCE	THE SOUND OF JULIE (EP)	20
65	Mercury 20048 (S)MCL	THE SOUND OF JULIE (LP, mono/stereo)	20
66	Mercury 20086 (S)MCL	CONTRASTS (LP, mono/stereo)	20
67	Mercury 20100 (S)MCL	SONGS OF INSPIRATION (LP, mono/stereo)	15

KENNY ROGERS (& FIRST EDITION)
69	Reprise RSLP 6352	RUBY DON'T TAKE YOUR LOVE TO TOWN (LP)	12
70	Reprise RSLP 6385	SOMETHING'S BURNING (LP)	12

(see also First Edition)

LINCOLN ROGERS
73	Phoenix NIX 137	Let Love Come Between Us/She Looked At Me With Love	15

LYNNE ROGERS
65	RCA RCA 1479	Sometimes/I Shouldn't Care	7

MARK ROGERS & MARKSMEN
63	Parlophone R 5045	Bubble Pop/Hold It!	18

(see also Marksmen, Mark Wirtz)

PAUL ROGERS
61	HMV POP 872	Four An' Twenty Thousand Kisses/Free To Love	10
63	HMV POP 1121	Always/Joanie Don't Be Angry	10

PAULINE ROGERS
54	Columbia SCM 5106	Spinnin' The Blues/But Good	15

PIERCE ROGERS & OVERLANDERS
61	Parlophone R 4838	Do You Still Love Me?/That Someone	12

ROY ROGERS
50	HMV MH 109	Oh Dem Golden Slippers/Lucky Leather Breeches (78, export issue)	10
51	HMV BD 1267	Me And My Teddy Bear/Buffalo Billy (78)	8
51	HMV BD 1286	A Four Legged Friend/There's A Cloud In My Valley Of Sunshine (78)	8
55	HMV 7EG 8145	KING OF THE COWBOYS (EP)	22
55	HMV 7EG 8182	HAPPY TRAILS (EP)	22

ROY ROGERS & DALE EVANS
53	HMV MH 174	Hazy Mountains/You've Got A Rope Around My Heart (78, export issue)	8
54	HMV 7MC6	Old Rugged Cross/In The Garden (export issue)	8
70s	Gala Goldentone GG 2	Me And My Teddy Bear/Buffalo Billy (6", some in p/s, orange vinyl, 78rpm)	6
70s	Gala Goldentone GG 3	Happy Trails To You/A Cowboy Needs A Horse (6", some in p/s, orange vinyl, 78rpm)	6

SHORTY ROGERS & HIS ORCHESTRA
54	HMV 7EG 8044	THE WILD ONE (EP)	10
52	Capitol LC 6549	MODERN SOUNDS (10" LP, as Shorty Rogers & His Giants)	15
54	HMV DLP 1030	COOL AND CRAZY (10" LP, featuring Giants)	15
54	HMV DLP 1058	EIGHT SHORTY ROGERS' NUMBERS (10" LP)	15
56	Contemporary LDC 190	SHELLY MANNE, SHORTY ROGERS AND JIMMY GIUFFRE — THE THREE (10" LP, with Shelly Manne & Jimmy Giuffre)	18

(see also Boots Brown, Bud Shank, Shelly Manne, Jimmy Giuffre)

SIDNEY ROGERS
73	Techniques TE 923	Don't Throw Stones/Toughness	8

TIMMIE ROGERS
53	Capitol CL 13991	Nothin's Wrong With Nothin'/Oh, Yeah! (78)	7
57	London HLU 8510	Back To School Again/I've Got A Dog Who Loves Me (78 rpm = £25)	80
58	London HLU 8601	Take Me To Your Leader/Fla-Ga-La-Pa (78 rpm = £30)	100

TRACY ROGERS
65	Polydor 56029	How Love Used To Be/When I Realise	5
65	Polydor 56037	Love Story/I Remember When I Loved You (p/s)	10
66	Polydor 56077	Baby/Through Thick And Thin	25
67	Polydor 56197	Back With You Baby/In The Morning	10

MINT VALUE £

VERN ROGERS & HI-FI'S
62	Oriole CB 1785	That Ain't Right/Be Everything	10
63	Oriole CB 1826	He's New To You/Can't Complain	7
63	Oriole CB 1885	I Will/One Way Love Affair	10
63	Oriole CB 1923	Anna/Pride	7

DIANA ROGERSON
85	United Dairies UD 017	THE INEVITABLE CHRYSTAL BELLE SCRODD RECORD (LP)	30
86	United Dairies UD 021	CHRYSTAL BELLE SCRODD: BELLE DE JOUR (LP)	30
	(see also Nurse With Wound)		

ROGUES (U.K.)
67	Decca F 12718	Memories Of Missy/And You Let Her Pass By	7

ROGUES (U.S.)
65	CBS 201731	Everyday/Rogers Reef	15
	(see also Terry Day, Terry Melcher, Bruce Johnston)		

ROKES
67	RCA RCA 1587	Let's Live For Today/Ride On	20
67	RCA RCA 1646	Hold My Hand/Regency Sue	40
68	RCA RCA 1694	When The Wind Arises/The Works Of Bartholemew	55

ROKKA
80	Rock Trax RT 01	Come Back	10

CHERRY ROLAND
63	Decca F 11579	Handy Sandy/Stay As I Am	10
63	Decca F 11648	What A Guy/Just For Fun	10
	(see also Cherry Rowland)		

PAUL ROLAND
82	Aristocrat ARC 1389	Doctor Strange/Madelaine (p/s)	8
83	Aftermath AEP 12011	Blades Of Battenburg (Remix)/Captain Blood/Puppet Master/Cavalier (12", p/s)	10
85	Aftermath AEP 12012	Death Or Glory (Revamped Version)/The Great Edwardian Air Raid/Beau Brummel/The Curious Case Of Richard Fielding (12", p/s)	8
86	Aftermath AEP 12013	Gabrielle/Berlin/Sword & Sorcery (p/s)	8
86	Imaginary MIRAGE 002	Demon In A Glass Case/In The Opium Den (oversized p/s)	7
87	Bam Caruso PABL 094	Alice's House/Go Down You Murderers/Happy Families/Jumbee (demo) (p/s)	8
87	Bucketfull Of Brains BOB 14	Madhouse (Demo)/GIANT SAND: Wishing Well (flexidisc free with *Bucketfull Of Brains* magazine)	6/4
87	Bucketfull Of Brains	Madhouse (Demo)/GIANT SAND: Wishing Well (hard vinyl test pressing)	10
85	Aftermath SCOOP 2	BURNT ORCHIDS (mini LP)	12
80	Ace ACE 013	THE WEREWOLF OF LONDON (LP)	12
81	Armageddon ARM 9	THE WEREWOLF OF LONDON (Revamped Version) (LP, different sleeve)	12
	(see also Weird Strings, Midnight Rags)		

WALTER ROLAND/GEORGIA SLIM
59	Jazz Collector JEL 2	THE MALE BLUES VOL. 1 (EP)	18

ROLLER
95	Poor Person Prod.	LIFE IN THE DAY OF... (LP, handmade sleeve with insert, numbered, 500 only)	12

ROLLERS
61	London HLG 9340	Continental Walk/I Want You So	18

ROLLING STONES
DECCA SINGLES
63	Decca F 11675	Come On/I Want To Be Loved (demo copies £250)	35
63	Decca F 11742	Fortune Teller/Poison Ivy (solid centre, withdrawn, existence unconfirmed)	1,000+
63	Decca F 11764	I Wanna Be Your Man/Stones (B-side mis-spelled)	30
63	Decca F 11764	I Wanna Be Your Man/Stoned	20
64		We Were Falling In Love (EMI disc acetate, unreleased single)	800+
64	Decca F 11845	Not Fade Away/Little By Little	12
64	Decca F 11934	It's All Over Now/Good Times, Bad Times	12
64	Decca F 12014	Little Red Rooster/Off The Hook	12

(The above singles were originally issued with 'Recording First Published ...' text & 'wide' label lettering.)

65	Decca F 12104	The Last Time/Play With Fire	12
65	Decca F 12220	(I Can't Get No) Satisfaction/The Spider And The Fly	12
65	Decca F 12263	Get Off My Cloud/The Singer Not The Song	12
66	Decca F 12331	19th Nervous Breakdown/As Tears Go By	10
66	Decca F 12395	Paint It, Black/Long Long While	12

(The above singles were originally issued with a round Decca logo; later boxed-logo pressings are worth £4 each.)

66	Decca F 12497	Have You Seen Your Mother, Baby, Standing In The Shadow?/Who's Driving Your Plane	12
67	Decca F 12546	Let's Spend The Night Together/Ruby Tuesday	12
67	Decca F 12654	We Love You/Dandelion	12
68	Decca F 12782	Jumping Jack Flash/Child Of The Moon	12
69	Decca F 12952	Honky Tonk Women/You Can't Always Get What You Want (some in demo-only p/s)	60/8
71	Decca F 13195	Street Fighting Man/Surprise Surprise/Everybody Needs Somebody To Love (33rpm maxi-single)	8
71	Decca F 13203	Street Fighting Man/Surprise Surprise (jukebox edition)	22
73	Decca F 13404	Sad Day/You Can't Always Get What You Want	10
74	Decca F 13517	Paint It Black/It's All Over Now (release cancelled, demo-only)	220
75	Decca F 13584	I Don't Know Why I Love You (credited to either 'Jagger/Richard/Taylor' or 'Stevie Wonder')/Try A Little Harder	15/10
75	Decca F 13597	Out Of Time/Jiving Sister Fanny	8
76	Decca F 13635	Honky Tonk Women/Sympathy For The Devil	8

70s	Decca F 11934	It's All Over Now/Good Times, Bad Times (repressing, with stereo mix on A-side, [ZXDR instead of XDR matrix no.] boxed Decca logo)	8
87	Decca F 102	Jumping Jack Flash/Child Of The Moon (p/s, reissue)	8
87	Decca FX 102	Jumping Jack Flash/Child Of The Moon/Sympathy For The Devil (12", p/s, reissue)	12

EXPORT SINGLES

63	Decca AT 15005	I Wanna Be Your Man/Stoned	100
64	Decca AT 15006	Not Fade Away/Little By Little	100
64	Decca AT 15032	Come On/Tell Me (You're Coming Back)	140
64	Decca AT 15035	Empty Heart/Around And Around	140
65	Decca AT 15039	Time Is On My Side/Congratulations	140
65	Decca AT 15040	Little Red Rooster/Off The Hook	100
65	Decca AT 15043	(I Can't Get No) Satisfaction/The Under Assistant West Coast Promotional Man (p/s)	140
65	Decca F 12104	The Last Time/Play With Fire (with Dutch or Scandinavian p/s)	75
65	Decca F 22180	Heart Of Stone/What A Shame (some in p/s)	140/100
65	Decca F 12220	(I Can't Get No) Satisfaction/The Under Assistant West Coast Promotional Man (some with p/s)	75/30
65	Decca F 22265	Get Off My Cloud/I'm Free (some in p/s)	75/30
66	Decca F 12331	19th Nervous Breakdown/As Tears Go By (with Dutch p/s)	45
66	Decca F 12395	Paint It, Black/Long Long While (p/s)	45
67	Decca F 12546	Let's Spend The Night Together/Ruby Tuesday (p/s)	45
67	Decca F 12654	We Love You/Dandelion (p/s)	45
67	Decca F 22706	2,000 Light Years From Home/She's A Rainbow	50
68	Decca F 22825	Street Fighting Man (remix)/No Expectations (some in p/s)	45/30
69	Decca F 12952	Honky Tonk Women/You Can't Always Get What You Want (p/s)	55
71	Decca F 13126	Little Queenie/Love In Vain (some in p/s)	50/20
71	Decca F 13195	Street Fighting Man/Surprise Surprise/Everybody Needs Somebody To Love (33rpm maxi-single, p/s)	35
71	Decca F 13204	Street Fighting Man/Everybody Needs Somebody To Love (some in p/s)	35/20

SINGLES BOX SETS

80	Decca STONE 1-12	SINGLE STONES (12-single box set)	60
80	Decca BROWSE 1	SINGLE STONES (in-store, 3 x 12-single box set [STONE 1-12], with poster & badge, also available via mail-order)	150

ROLLING STONES LABEL SINGLES

71	Rolling Stones RS 19100	Brown Sugar/Bitch/Let It Rock (some in p/s)	40/6
74	Rolling Stones RS 19114	It's Only Rock 'N' Roll/Through The Lonely Nights	5
78	R. Stones 12EMI 2802	Miss You (8.26)/Faraway Eyes (12", p/s, pink vinyl)	10
81	Rolling Stones	Beast Of Burden/Everything Is Turning Gold (unreleased)	
82	Rolling Stones RSR 111	Time Is On My Side (live)/Twenty Flight Rock (live) (p/s)	5
82	Rolling Stones 12RSR 111	Time Is On My Side (live)/Twenty Flight Rock (live)/Under My Thumb (live) (12", p/s)	10
84	Rolling Stones RSR 114	She Was Hot/I Think I'm Going Mad	5
84	Rolling Stones RSRP 114	She Was Hot/I Think I'm Going Mad (shaped picture disc)	22
84	Rolling Stones SUGAR 1	Brown Sugar/Bitch (p/s, reissue)	5
84	Rolling Stones SUGARP 1	Brown Sugar/Bitch (shaped picture disc)	18
93	Rolling Stone RS LH 1	Brown Sugar/Start Me Up (jukebox issue, no p/s)	15
93	Rolling Stone ORDER LH 1	Gimme Shelter/TOM JONES: Gimme Shelter (jukebox issue, no p/s)	15

OTHER SINGLES

74	Atlantic K 19107	Brown Sugar/Happy/Rocks Off (possibly unissued)	75+
72	Sound For Industry 107	Mick Jagger Introduces 'Exile On Main Street' (flexidisc free with *NME*)	15/6

CBS SINGLES

86	CBS QA 6864	Harlem Shuffle/Had It With You (poster p/s)	6
86	CBS TA 6864	Harlem Shuffle (N.Y. Mix)/(London Mix)/Had It With You (12", p/s)	8
86	CBS QTA 6864	Harlem Shuffle (N.Y. Mix)/(London Mix)/Had It With You (12", p/s)	12
86	CBS A 7160	One Hit (To The Body)/Fight (p/s)	5
86	CBS TA 7160	One Hit (To The Body)/Fight (12", p/s)	8
89	CBS 655 193-2	Mixed Emotions (7" Version)/Mixed Emotions (Chris Kimsey's 12")/Fancyman Blues (CD, picture disc, card sleeve)	12
89	CBS 655 193-5	Mixed Emotions (7" Version)/Fancyman Blues/Tumbling Dice/Miss You (CD, picture disc, in circular tin with 'tongue' logo sticker)	30
89	CBS 655 193-6	Mixed Emotions (Chris Kimsey's 12")/Fancyman Blues (12", p/s)	8
89	CBS 655 193-6	Mixed Emotions (Chris Kimsey's 12")/Fancyman Blues/Mixed Emotions (7" Version) (12", p/s)	8
89	CBS 655 214-2	Mixed Emotions (7" Version)/Fancyman Blues/Shattered/Waiting On A Friend (CD, picture disc, in circular tin with 'tongue' logo sticker)	30
89	CBS 655 422-7	Rock And A Hard Place/Cook Cook Blues (p/s)	5
89	CBS 655 422-6	Rock And A Hard Place (Dance Mix)/Emotional Rescue/Some Girls/Rock And A Hard Place (Hard Dub Mix)/Cook Cook Blues (12", p/s)	8
89	CBS 655 422-5	Rock And A Hard Place (Michael Brauer Mix)/Rock And A Hard Place (Bonus Beats Mix)/Rock And A Hard Place (Edited 7" Version) (2nd 12", p/s)	8
89	CBS 655 422-8	Rock And A Hard Place (Dance Mix)/(Hard Dub Mix)/Cook Cook Blues (3rd 12", p/s)	8
89	CBS 655 422-2	Rock And A Hard Place (7" Version)/(Dance Mix)/(Bonus Beats Mix)/Cook Cook Blues (CD, picture disc, card sleeve)	15
89	CBS 655 422-3	Rock And A Hard Place (Dance Mix)/Cook Cook Blues/Rock And A Hard Place (Hard Dub Mix) (2nd CD)	8
89	CBS 655 448-2	Rock And A Hard Place (7" Version)/Cook Cook Blues/It's Only Rock'n'Roll (But I Like It)/Rocks Off (3rd CD, picture disc, 7" box set with poster)	25
89	CBS 655 448-5	Rock And A Hard Place (7" Version)/Cook Cook Blues/Emotional Rescue/Some Girls (CD, tongue-shaped card sleeve)	25
90	CBS 656 065-6	Almost Hear You Sigh/Beast Of Burden/Angie/Fool To Cry (12", gatefold p/s)	8
90	CBS 656 065-2	Almost Hear You Sigh/Beast Of Burden/Angie/Fool To Cry (CD, gold disc)	20
90	CBS 656 065-5	Almost Hear You Sigh/Miss You/Waiting On A Friend/Wish I'd Never Met You (CD, in tin with 'Urban Jungle' sticker)	30

90	CBS 656 122-6	Terrifying (12" Dance Remix)/Rock And A Hard Place (Dance Mix)/ Harlem Shuffle (London Mix) (12", p/s)	8
90	CBS 656 122-2	Terrifying (7" Remix Edit)/(12" Remix)/Rock And A Hard Place (7" Version)/ Harlem Shuffle (LP Version) (CD)	8
90	CBS 656 122-5	Terrifying (7" Remix Edit)/Start Me Up/Shattered/If You Can't Rock Me (2nd CD, card p/s)	8
91	CBS 656 756-6	Highwire/2,000 Light Years From Home (live)/Sympathy For The Devil (live)/ I Just Wanna Make Love To You (live) (12", gatefold p/s)	8
91	CBS 656 756-2	Highwire/2,000 Light Years From Home (live)/Sympathy For The Devil (live)/ I Just Wanna Make Love To You (live) (CD)	8
91	CBS 656 756-5	Highwire/Play With Fire (live)/Factory Girl (live) (CD)	10
91	CBS 656 892-6	Ruby Tuesday/Play With Fire (live)/You Can't Always Get What You Want (live)/Rock And A Hard Place (live) (12", p/s)	10
91	CBS 656 892-2	Ruby Tuesday/Play With Fire (live)/You Can't Always Get What You Want (live)/Undercover Of The Night (live) (CD)	10
91	CBS 656 892-5	Ruby Tuesday/Harlem Shuffle (live)/Winning Ugly (CD)	10
91	CBS 657 334-2	Sex Drive (single edit)/(Dirty Hands Mix)/(Club Version) (CD)	10

VIRGIN SINGLES

94	Virgin VS 1503	Love Is Strong/The Storm (numbered p/s, 7,000 only)	15
94	Virgin VSCDT 1503	Love Is Strong/The Storm/So Young/Love Is Strong (Bob Clearmountain Mix) (CD)	10
94	Virgin VS 1518	You Got Me Rocking/Jump On Top Of Me (numbered p/s, 7,000 only)	15
94	Virgin VST 1518	You Got Me Rocking (Perfecto Mix)/(Sexy Disco Dub Mix)/(Trance Mix) (12", p/s)	10
94	Virgin VS 1524	Out Of Tears/I'm Gonna Drive (numbered p/s, 7,000 only)	15
94	Virgin VSCDX 1524	Out Of Tears (Don Was Edit)/I'm Gonna Drive/Sparks Will Fly (Radio Clean)/ Out Of Tears (Bob Clearmountain Remix Edit) (CD, tear-shaped card p/s)	15
94	Virgin VSCDG 1524	Out Of Tears (Don Was Edit)/I'm Gonna Drive/So Young/The Storm/ Jump On Top Of Me (CD, digipak, numbered, 4,000 only, withdrawn)	400
94	Virgin VSP 1539	I Go Wild/I Go Wild (live) (picture disc)	20
96	Virgin VS 1578	Wild Horses/Tumbling Dice/Gimme Shelter (unreleased)	
96	Virgin VSCDT 1578	Wild Horses/Tumbling Dice/Gimme Shelter (CD, unreleased)	
97	Virgin VS 1653	Anybody Seen My Baby? (LP Edit)/(Soul Solution Remix Edit) (numbered picture disc, p/s, 7,500 only)	20
97	Virgin VST 1653	Anybody Seen My Baby? (Armand's Rolling Steelo Mix)/(Soul Solution Remix)/ (Bonus Roll) (12", p/s)	25
98	Virgin VSY 1667	Saint Of Me (Radio Edit)/Anyway You Look At It (picture disc)	15
98	Virgin VSTX 1667	Saint Of Me (remixes)/Anybody Seen My Baby? (remixes) (12", double pack, stickered p/s)	15
98	Virgin VSTTDT 1667	Saint Of Me (remixes)/Anybody Seen My Baby? (remixes) (12", double pack, stickered p/s)	15
98	Virgin VSY 1700	Out Of Control (Album Radio Edit)/(In Hand With Fluke Radio Edit)	10

PROMO SINGLES

83	R. Stones RSR 112 (DJ)	Let's Spend The Night Together (live)/Start Me Up (live)	20
91	CBS A 026/B 027	Highwire/Sympathy For The Devil (live) (12")	12
93	EMI ORDERLH 1	Gimme Shelter (live) (1-sided jukebox issue)	22
93	Virgin STONES 1	JUMP BACK (EP)	25
94	Virgin VSCDJ 1518	You Got Me Rocking (Original Version)/(Perfecto Mix) (CD)	15
95	Virgin VSCDJ 1539	I Go Wild (CD, 1-track)	25
95	Virgin VSCDJ 1562	Like A Rolling Stone (Edit)/(Album Version) (CD)	15
96	Virgin VSCDJ 1578	Wild Horses (Edit) (CD, 1-track)	25
97	Virgin VSCDJ 1653	Anybody Seen My Baby? (LP Edit)/(Don Was Radio Remix) (CD)	15
97	Virgin VSCDXJ 1653	Anybody Seen My Baby? (Armand's Rolling Steelo Mix)/(Soul Solution Remix) (CD)	15
98	Virgin VSCDJ 1667	Saint Of Me (Radio Edit)/(Album Version) (CD)	15
98	Virgin VSCDJX 1667	Saint Of Me (Deep Dish Grunge Garage Remix Edit) (CD, 1-track)	8
98	Virgin VSTDJ 1667	Saint Of Me (Deep Dish Grunge Garage Remix) (Part 1)/(Part 2)/ (Grunge Garage Dub)/(Rolling Dub)/Anyone Seen My Baby? (Armand's Rolling Steelo Mix)/Anybody Seen My Baby? (Bonus Roll) (12", double pack, stickered sleeve)	20
98	Virgin VSP 1700	Out Of Control (Bi-Polar At The Controls)/(Bi-Polar Outer Version) (withdrawn brown label or silver label)	55/25
98	Virgin VSTDJ 1700	Out Of Control (In Hand With Fluke)/(In Hand Full Version)/ (Bi-Polar's Fat Controller Mix)/(Bi-Polar At The Controls) (12")	15
98	Virgin VSTDDJ 1700	Out Of Control (In Hand With Fluke Instrumental)/(In Hand Full Version)/ (Bi-Polar's Fat Controller Mix)/(Bi-Polar At The Controls) (12")	15
98	Virgin VSCDJ 1700	Out Of Control (Album Radio Edit)/(Album Version) (CD)	15
98	Virgin VSCDXJ 1700	Out Of Control (In Hand With Fluke Edit)/(In Hand With Fluke Instrumental)/ (Bi-Polar At The Controls)/(Bi-Polar's Fat Controller Mix) (CD)	20
98	Virgin VSCDF 1700	Out Of Control (Album Radio Edit)/(In Hand With Fluke)/ (In Hand With Fluke Instrumental)/(Bi-Polar At The Controls) (CD)	20
98	Virgin VSCDJ 1700	Out Of Control (Album Radio Edit)/(Saber Master With Fade)/ (In Hand With Fluke Radio Edit) (CD)	20
90s	Virgin VSCDY 1838	Don't Stop (1-track CD)	18
02	Virgin VS1838	Don't Stop (Limited edition red vinyl, numbered)	12
00s	Virgin DEVIL 666	Sympathy For The Devil (Fatboy Slim Remix)/(Neptunes Remix)/ (Full Phat Remix)/(Original Version) (2x12", with press sheet)	40
02	Virgin VS1838	Don't Stop (Limited edition red vinyl, numbered)	12

EPs

64	Decca DFE 8560	THE ROLLING STONES (with unboxed or later boxed Decca logo)	30/12
64	Decca DFE 8590	FIVE BY FIVE (with unboxed or later boxed Decca logo)	30/12
65	Decca DFE 8620	GOT LIVE IF YOU WANT IT! (with unboxed or later boxed Decca logo)	30/12
83	Decca DFEX 8560	THE ROLLING STONES (12", reissue)	12
83	Decca DFEX 8590	FIVE BY FIVE (12", reissue)	12
83	Decca DFEX 8620	GOT LIVE IF YOU WANT IT (12", reissue)	12

EXPORT EPs

64	Decca SDE 7260	ROLLING STONES.	110
64	Decca SDE 7501	THE ROLLING STONES VOLUME 2	100
65	Decca SDE 7502	GOT LIVE IF YOU WANT IT!	110
65	Decca DFE 8620	GOT LIVE IF YOU WANT IT! (red label, some with yellow titles on p/s) . . . each 110
65	Decca SDE 7503	ROLLING STONES (with "Out Of Our Heads [U.K. version]" sleeve)	110

DECCA LPs

64	Decca LK 4605	ROLLING STONES (1st pressing, plays 2.52 version of "Tell Me"; Side 2 matrix: XARL 6272-1A)	600-1000
64	Decca LK 4605	ROLLING STONES (2nd pressing, plays 4.06 version of "Tell Me"; a few sleeves list "Mona", most list "I Need You, Baby" instead)	200/120
65	Decca LK 4661	ROLLING STONES NO. 2	120

(The above LPs were simultaneously pressed with both flipback and non-flipback sleeves. Values are the same.)

65	Decca LK/SKL 4733	OUT OF OUR HEADS (mono/stereo)	each 100
66	Decca TXL/TXS 101	COULD YOU WALK ON THE WATER (unreleased, proof sleeves exist)	
66	Decca LK/SKL 4786	AFTERMATH (mono/stereo)	each 100
66	Decca LK/SKL 4786	AFTERMATH (mono/stereo, front cover title is shadowed)	125/125
66	Decca LK 4786	AFTERMATH (mono, front cover title has purple shadow)	130
66	Decca TXL/TXS 101	BIG HITS (HIGH TIDE AND GREEN GRASS) (1st pressing, gatefold sleeve, with stapled 12" x 12" picture booklet, mono/stereo)	70/70
67	Decca TXL/TXS 101	BIG HITS (HIGH TIDE AND GREEN GRASS) (2nd pressing, gatefold sleeve, without booklet, mono/stereo)	30/30
67	Decca LK/SKL 4852	BETWEEN THE BUTTONS (mono/stereo)	130/100
67	Decca TXL/TXS 103	THEIR SATANIC MAJESTIES REQUEST (3-D gatefold sleeve with red inner, mono/stereo)	130/120
68	Decca LK/SKL 4955	BEGGARS BANQUET (gatefold sleeve, with Stones Decca label insert, mono/stereo)	80/60
69	Decca LK/SKL 5019	THROUGH THE PAST, DARKLY (BIG HITS VOL. 2) (octagonal gatefold sleeve, mono/stereo)	75/65
69	Decca LK 5025	LET IT BLEED (mono, red inner, with poster, some with stickered sleeve; copies without poster or sticker £40)	150/100
69	Decca SKL 5025	LET IT BLEED (stereo, blue inner, with poster, some w/ stickered sleeve; copies without poster or sticker £25)	60/40
69	Decca TXL/TXS 103	THEIR SATANIC MAJESTIES REQUEST (2nd pressing, gatefold sleeve with red inner, mono/stereo, stereo disc in stickered mono sleeve)	each 50

(The above LPs were originally issued with Decca labels with a large-print logo without a box surrounding it; later pressings with smaller print & boxed logo are worth between half the value for earlier LPs to two-thirds the value for later LPs and three-quarters for "Let It Bleed".)

70	Decca SKL 5065	GET YER YA-YA'S OUT!	18
71	Decca SKL 5084	STONE AGE.	18
71	Decca SKL 5101	GIMME SHELTER.	15
72	Decca SKL 5098	MILESTONES.	15
72	Decca SKL 5149	ROCK 'N' ROLLING STONES.	15
73	Decca SKL 5165	GOLDEN B-SIDES (unreleased, test pressings only)	600+
73	Decca SKL 5173	NO STONE UNTURNED	15

(Except where noted, the above Decca LPs were originally issued with dark blue labels & laminated sleeves; later copies are worth two-thirds the value.)

75	Decca SKL 5212	METAMORPHOSIS (dark blue label, matt sleeve)	15
70s	Decca TXS 101	BIG HITS (HIGH TIDE AND GREEN GRASS) (2nd pressing, gatefold sleeve, later issue with foldout insert & later Decca logo, stereo only)	15
75	Decca TXS 103	THEIR SATANIC MAJESTIES REQUEST (3rd pressing, 3-D matt gatefold sleeve, stereo only)	25
70s	Decca SKL 4733	OUT OF OUR HEADS (2nd pressing, light green sleeve, box Decca logo)	30
75	Decca (no cat. no.)	THE HISTORY OF THE ROLLING STONES (3-LP box set; pink label test pressings exist, no sleeves, matrices read: ZAL 12996/7, ZAL 12998/9 & ZAL 13000/1; release cancelled in favour of "Rolled Gold" 2-LP)	800+
75	Decca ROST 3/4	LIVE STONES (2-LP, compilation, pink label test pressings only, follow-up to "Rolled Gold", unreleased)	500+
83	Decca ROLL 1	THE FIRST EIGHT STUDIO ALBUMS (8-LP set, with 192-page book; wraparound card box, each LP has star printed on rear sleeve)	250

EXPORT LPs

65	Decca LK/SKL 4725	OUT OF OUR HEADS (with U.S. track listing & cover design, unboxed Decca label logo, mono/stereo, withdrawn)	150/175
66	Decca LK/SKL 4838	HAVE YOU SEEN YOUR MOTHER, LIVE (laminated sleeve & unboxed Decca label logo, mono/stereo)	125/150
67	Decca LK/SKL 4888	FLOWERS (laminated sleeve, unboxed Decca label logo)	180
70s	Decca LK/SKL 4888	FLOWERS (later pressing, laminated sleeve, boxed Decca label logo)	80
70	Decca SKL 4786	AFTERMATH (white label, black print, reportedly for export)	15
70	Decca TXS 103	THEIR SATANIC MAJESTIES REQUEST (gatefold sleeve, white label, black print, supposedly for export)	15
70	Decca SKL 5065	GET YER YA-YA'S OUT! (white label, black print, reportedly for export)	15
70s	Decca LK/SKL 4838	HAVE YOU SEEN YOUR MOTHER, LIVE (later pressing, boxed logo, laminated sleeve)	80

ROLLING STONES LABEL LPs

71	Rolling Stones COC 59100	STICKY FINGERS (zip sleeve with insert)	22
72	Rolling Stones COC 69100	EXILE ON MAIN STREET (2-LP, with inners, some with postcard inserts)	50/15
73	Rolling Stones COC 59101	GOAT'S HEAD SOUP (gatefold sleeve, with insert)	12
78	Rolling Stones CUN 39108	SOME GIRLS (LP, with uncensored inner sleeve)	15
80	Rolling Stones CUN 39111	EMOTIONAL RESCUE (LP with poster)	15
82	R. Stones CUNP 39115	STILL LIFE (AMERICAN CONCERT 1981) (LP, picture disc, a few mispressed with wrong tracks)	130/20

OTHER ALBUMS

83	R. Digest GROLA 119	THE GREAT YEARS (4-LP, box set).	35
89	ABKCO 820900-1	ROLLING STONES SINGLES COLLECTION/LONDON YEARS (4-LP set)	45

89	CBS 466 918 2	COLLECTION 1971-1989 (15-CD box set, with bonus CD, 'Collector's Edition')	130
91	Sony 468 135-9/468 135-2	FLASHPOINT/INTERVIEW 1990 (2-CD pack, shrinkwrapped with tongue logo sticker, numbered)	40
02	Virgin CDVDXX2964	FORTY LICKS (Ltd edition CD box set)	35

PROMO ALBUMS

67	Decca TXL/TXS 103	THEIR SATANIC MAJESTIES REQUEST (LP, padded silk sleeve)	1500+
69	Decca RSM. 1	PROMOTIONAL ALBUM (LP, U.K. disc in U.S. sleeve [lists RSD-1], 200 copies pressed [100 each for U.K. & U.S.], U.K. issues include a letter from Decca)	1000
86	CBS SAMP 1103	STONES ON CD — A RADIO SAMPLER (CD, poly sleeve)	200
89	CBS SAMPC 1347	SAY AHHH! (LP, promo-only compilation)	175
89	CBS (no catalogue no.)	STEEL WHEELS - THE ALBUM OF THE TOUR (box set, with LP, CD, cassette and "Terrifying" 12", European tour dates & sticker)	130
95	Virgin IVDG 2801	STRIPPED (2-CD, interview disc & album, fold-out digipak)	60
97	Virgin CDVDJ 2840	BRIDGES TO BABYLON (CD, with spoken word intros, 200 only)	70
97	Virgin IVDG 2840	BRIDGES TO BABYLON INTERVIEW (2-CD, interview disc & album, fold-out digipak)	50
97	Virgin (no catalogue no.)	BRIDGES TO BABYLON (CD in promo press box, with "Anybody Seen My Baby?" promo CD, press release, bottle opener, notebook and sheet of stamps, 200 only)	200
99	Virgin CDVDJ 2880	NO SECURITY ALBUM SAMPLER (CD, card p/s)	25
99	Virgin CDIDJ 2880	NO SECURITY (3-CD [2 interview discs], foldout digipak)	65
90s	Virgin CDVDY 2964	FORTY LICKS (CD)	45

(see also Mick Jagger, Keith Richards, Pipes Of Pan, Bill Wyman, Charlie Watts, Mick Taylor, Andrew Oldham, Bobbie Miller)

AUDLEY ROLLINS

72	Explosion EX 2062	Repatriation/HUGH ROY JUNIOR: Repatriation (Version)	10
73	Attack ATT 8060	Without You In My World/It's Flowing (actually "It's Growing")	6
73	Harry J HJ 6654	What's Your Name/NOW GENERATION: What's Your Name (Version)	6

(see also A. Boyne)

BIRD ROLLINS

72	Mojo 2092 049	Love Man From Carolina/She Needs Loving All The Time	10

(HENRY) ROLLINS BAND

91	Vinyl Solution VS 30	Let There Be Rock/Carry Me Down (12", p/s, as Henry Rollins & Hard-Ons)	18
91	Vinyl Solution VS 30CD	Let There Be Rock/Carry Me Down (CD, as Henry Rollins & Hard-Ons)	18
92	Imago 72787250187	TEARIN' (EP, poster p/s)	8
92	Imago 72787250181	TEARIN' (12" EP, poster p/s)	8
92	Imago 72787250187	TEARIN' (CD EP, poster p/s)	8
94	Imago 7432323057	LIAR (EP, poster p/s)	10
92	Quarter Stick QS 13CD	DEEP THROAT (4-CD box set, spoken-word)	45

SONNY ROLLINS

66	HMV (no cat. no.)	Alfie's Theme (1-sided promo)	20
56	Esquire EP 94	SONNY ROLLINS AND THE MODERN JAZZ QUARTET (EP)	10
57	Esquire EP 148	SONNY ROLLINS WITH THELONIUS MONK (EP)	10
58	Esquire EP 198	WAILING MISTER ROLLINS (EP)	20
60	Esquire EP 228	VALSE HOT (EP, as Sonny Rollins Plus Four)	10
61	Esquire EP 238	ROLLINS AND BROWNIE (EP, with Clifford Brown)	8
62	Esquire EP 248	SAINT THOMAS (EP)	10
56	Esquire 20-050	SONNY ROLLINS QUARTET (10" LP)	40
57	Esquire 20-080	SONNY ROLLINS QUINTET (10" LP)	25
57	Esquire 32-025	SONNY ROLLINS PLUS FOUR (LP)	35
57	Esquire 32-035	PERSPECTIVES (LP, with Modern Jazz Quartet)	40
58	Esquire 32-038	SONNY ROLLINS QUARTET (LP)	45
58	Esquire 32-045	SAXOPHONE COLOSSUS (LP, as Sonny Rollins Four)	70
58	Contemporary LAC 12118	WAY OUT WEST (LP)	20
58	Esquire 32-058	TENOR MADNESS (LP)	45
59	Esquire 32-075	SONNY ROLLINS QUINTET (LP)	30
59	Esquire 32-085	TOUR-DE-FORCE (LP)	22
59	MGM MGM-C 776	SONNY ROLLINS AND THE BIG BRASS (LP)	15
60	Contemporary SCA 5013	SONNY ROLLINS AND THE CONTEMPORARY LEADERS (LP, stereo only)	20
61	Riverside RLP 12-241	THE SOUND OF SONNY (LP)	15
62	Riverside RLP 12-258	FREEDOM SUITE (LP)	15
62	Esquire 32-155	MOVIN' OUT (LP)	35
62	RCA RD/SF 7504	THE BRIDGE (LP)	15
63	Esquire 32-175	SONNY BOY (LP)	30
63	RCA RD/SF 7524	WHAT'S NEW (LP)	15
63	RCA RD/SF 7546	OUR MAN IN JAZZ (LP)	15
64	RCA RD/SF 7593	SONNY MEETS HAWK (LP, with Coleman Hawkins)	15
64	RCA RD/SF 7626	SONNY ROLLINS & CO. (LP)	15
65	RCA RD 7670	NOW'S THE TIME (LP)	15
65	Fontana FJL 124	BLOW! (LP)	25
66	HMV CLP 1915	ROLLINS ON IMPULSE (LP)	15
66	Stateside SL 10164	SAXOPHONE COLOSSUS (LP, reissue)	12
67	RCA RD/SF 7736	STANDARD SONNY ROLLINS (LP)	15
67	HMV CLP/CSD 3529	SONNY PLAYS ALFIE (LP)	15
67	HMV CLP/CSD 3610	EAST BROADWAY RUNDOWN (LP)	15

(see also Modern Jazz Quartet, Thelonious Monk, Clifford Brown, Coleman Hawkins, Kenny Durham)

ROLL MOVEMENT

67	Go AJ 11410	I'm Out On My Own/Just One Thing	15

ROLL-UPS

80	Bridgehouse BHS 6	Blackmail/Hold On (p/s)	15
79	Bridgehouse BHLP 004	LOW DIVES FOR HIGHBALLS (LP)	25

DICK ROMAN
59	MGM MGM 1004	Party Girl/My Greatest Mistake (78 rpm = £8)	8
65	London HLU 10007	The Truth Hurts/What Good Does It Do Me	7
66	Coral Q 72485	Green Years/Ivy	6
63	Stateside SL 10023	TOUCH OF LOVE (LP)	15

LYN ROMAN
74	Brunswick BR 11	Stop, I Don't Need No Sympathy/Where Do You Go	10

MIMI ROMAN
61	Warner Bros WB 55	Johnny Will/Let It Be Me	6

MURRAY ROMAN
69	Track 613 007	YOU CAN'T BEAT PEOPLE UP AND HAVE THEM SAY I LOVE YOU (LP)	22
69	Track 613 015	A BLIND MAN'S MOVIE (LP)	18

SANDY ROMAN
66	Columbia DB 7931	Dale Anne/Home Is Where The Heart Is	5

TONY ROMAN
67	Stateside SS 2022	Shadows On A Foggy Day/Maggie	6

MAX ROMEO
68	Island WI 3104	Put Me In The Mood/My One Girl	25
68	Island WI 3111	Walk Into The Room/DAWN PENN: I'll Get You	30
68	Island WI 3124	Twelfth Of Never (actually by Pat Kelly)/VAL BENNETT: Caledonia	30
68	Unity UN 503	Wet Dream/She's But A Little Girl	8
69	Blue Cat BS 161	We Want Man/AL REID: Vietcong	28
69	Blue Cat BS 163	It's Not The Way/AL REID: Darling	28
69	Nu Beat NB 022	Blowing In The Wind/LARRY MARSHALL: Money Girl	12
69	Trojan TR 656	Sweet Chariot/Far Far Away (with Hippy Boys)	10
69	Unity UN 507	Belly Woman (actually by Derrick Morgan)/PAULETT & LOVERS: Please Stay	7
69	Unity UN 511	Twelfth Of Never (actually by Pat Kelly)/TARTONS: Solid As A Rock (actually by Tartans)	10
69	Unity UN 516	Wine Her Goosie/KING CANNON: Fire Ball	10
69	Unity UN 532	Mini-Skirt Vision/Far Far Away	5
70	Unity UN 544	Melting Pot/HIPPY BOYS: Death Rides A Horse	25
70	Unity UN 545	Clap Clap (with Hippy Boys)/Death Rides A Horse	15
70	Unity UN 547	What A Cute Man/Buy You A Rainbow	15
70	Unity UN 560	Fish In The Pot/Feel It	10
71	Bullet BU 478	Mother Oh Mother/Dreams Of Passion (actually "Judgement Rock" by Charlie Ace)	10
71	Pama Supreme PS 328	Ginal Ship/UPSETTERS: Version 2	12
71	Pama Supreme PS 306	Let The Power Fall On I/The Raid	7
71	Pama Supreme PS 318	Don't You Weep/Weeping (Version)	7
71	Punch PH 73	Chie Chie Bud/Version	7
71	Unity UN 571	Macabee (Version)/SOUL SYNDICATE: Music Book	6
71	Camel CA 66	Black Equality/Suffering	20
71	Camel CA 82	The Coming Of Jah/Watch And Pray	6
72	Camel CA 85	Rasta Bandwagon/When Jah Speaks	6
72	Camel CA 86	Public Enemy Number One/How Long Must We Wait	6
72	Big BG 334	Are You Sure/RUPIE EDWARDS ALL STARS: Are You Sure (Version)	6
72	Dynamic DYN 444	We Love America/SOUL RHYTHM: We Love Jamaica (Version)	6
72	G.G. GG 4535	Is It Really Over?/MAYTONES: Born To Be Loved	6
72	High Note Hs 058	Pray For Me (with Gaytones)/GAYTONES: Pray For Me (Version)	8
72	Pama PM 836	Wet Dream/("Bang Bang Lulu" by Lloyd Tyrell)/("Birth Control" by Lloyd Tyrell)/"Sex Education" by Classics) (maxi-single)	5
72	Pama Supreme PS 345	Pray For Me/(Version)	5
72	Pama Supreme PS 359	Are You Sure/CARL MASTERS: Va-Va-Voom	8
72	Prince Buster PB 11	River Jordan/Words Sound And Power	8
73	Dragon DRA 1028	No Joshua No/JOSHUA'S ALL STARS: No Joshua No (Version)	5
73	Magnet MA 032	Murder In The Place/(Version)	7
73	Magnet MA 032	I Woke Up In Love/(Version)	5
73	Pama PM 875	Pussy Watchman/You Are My Sunshine	5
73	Pama Supreme PS 383	Hide Away/SOUL SYNDICATE: Sweet And Gentle	5
73	Pama Supreme PS 385	Everyman Aught To Know/(Version)	6
73	Unity UN 572	Rent Crisis/Version	7
74	Ackee ACK 529	Sixpence/Eating Competition	5
75	Tropical Sound Tracs TST 107	Big Jack/Cross Over The Bridge/Please Help Me, I'm Falling	5
76	Island WIP 6305	One Step Forward/One Step Dub	10
76	Island WIP 6330	Chase The Devil/UPSETTERS FEAT. PRINCE JAZZBO: Croaking Lizard	15
69	Pama PMLP 11	A DREAM (LP)	50
71	Pama PMP 2010	LET THE POWER FALL (LP)	50
76	Island ILPS 9392	WAR INA BABYLON (LP)	18
76	Sound Trac TSL 1000	REVELATION TIME (LP)	25

(see also Max & Elaine, Maxie & Glen, Al Read, Henry & Lisa, Dennis Alcapone, George Meggie, David Isaacs)

ROMEO & EMOTIONS
67	Caltone TONE 106	Don't Want To Let You Go/I Can't Do No More	30

CHAN ROMERO
59	Columbia DB 4341	The Hippy Hippy Shake/If I Had A Way	85
60	Columbia DB 4405	My Little Ruby/I Don't Care Now	200

ROMI & JAZZ
90	Chrysalis CHSR 123545	One Love One World (Feel The Rhythm Mix)/One Love One World (Unity '90 Mix)/Love Crime (Sunrise Mix) (12", p/s)	12

RONALD & LLOYD
74	Magnet MG 042	Back In My Arms/HEPTONES: Drifting Away	8

MINT VALUE £

RONALD & RUBY
58	RCA RCA 1053	Lollipop/Fickle Baby (78 rpm = £16)	30

RONNIE RONALDE
53	Columbia SCM 5006	Song Of The Mountains/If I Were A Blackbird	10
53	Columbia SCM 5007	In A Monastery Garden/Bells Across The Meadow	10
56	Columbia SCM 5214	Ballad Of Davy Crockett/Hair Of Gold	10
56	Columbia SCM 5241	Robin Hood/Happy Trails	10
56	Columbia SCM 5262	The Yarmouth Song/Macnamara's Band	8

RONDELS
61	London HLU 9404	Back Beat No. 1/Shades Of Green	20

RONDELLS
58	London HLU 8716	Good Good/Dreamy (with Ned Jr.) (78 rpm = £60)	130

DON RONDO
56	Columbia DB 3854	Two Different Worlds/He Made You Mine	5
57	Columbia DB 3909	The Love I Never Had/Don't	5
57	London HLJ 8466	White Silver Sands/Stars Fell On Alabama	10
58	London HLJ 8567	What A Shame/Made For Each Other (78 rpm = £6)	12
58	London HLJ 8610	I've Got Bells On My Heart/School Dance (78 rpm = £6)	8
58	London HLJ 8641	Blonde Bombshell/Her Hair Was Yellow (78 rpm = £6)	10
58	London HLJ 8695	Dormi, Dormi, Dormi (Sleep, Sleep, Sleep)/In Chi Chi Chihuahua (78 rpm = £8)	5
58	London HLJ 8749	City Lights/I Could Be A Mountain (78 rpm = £8)	5
59	London HLJ 8808	Song From "The Geisha Boy"/Gretna Green (78 rpm = £8)	5
60	London HLL 9217	The King Of Holiday Island/Wanderlust	7
59	London RE-J 1154	RONDO PT. 1 (EP)	15
59	London RE-J 1155	RONDO PT. 2 (EP)	15

GENE RONDO
68	Giant GN 39	Ben Nevis/Grey Lies	12
68	Jolly JY 004	Mary, Mary/Baby, Baby	10
69	Downtown DT 422	A Lover's Question/HERBIE GRAY & RUDIES: Blue Moon	7
69	Downtown DT 431	Sentimental Reasons/Then You Can Tell Me Goodbye	7
70	Downtown DT 459	Spreading Peace/MUSIC DOCTORS: Guitar Riff	7
72	Downtown DT 490	Wanna Be Like Daddy/STUDIO SOUND: A Little More	5
72	Count Shelly CS 005	Happy Birthday Sweet Sixteen/Meditation	5
73	Magnet MA 001	Prisoner Of Love/How Many Times Girl	5
73	Magnet MA 006	Each Moments/If You Do Want Me	5
73	Magnet MA 028	Oh Sweet Africa/This Is Love	8
73	Magnet MA 035	Valley Of Tears/He'll Break Your Heart	5

(see also Gene Pancho)

RONETTES
63	London HLU 9793	Be My Baby/Tedesco And Pitman	10
64	London HLU 9826	Baby I Love You/Miss Joan And Mr Sam	10
64	London HLU 9905	(The Best Part Of) Breakin' Up/Big Red	20
64	London HLU 9922	Do I Love You?/When I Saw You	18
64	London HLU 9931	(Walking) In The Rain/How Does It Feel?	15
65	London HLU 9952	Born To Be Together/Blues For Baby	20
65	London HLU 9976	Is This What I Get For Loving You?/You Baby	28
66	London HLU 10087	I Can Hear Music/When I Saw You (withdrawn)	100
69	London HLU 10240	Be My Baby/Baby I Love You	7
69	A&M AMS 748	You Came, You Saw, You Conquered/I Can Hear Music	8
75	Phil Spector Intl. 2010 009	I'm A Woman In Love/When I Saw You	15
77	Phil Spector Intl. 2010 017	I Wonder/Walking In The Rain	18
64	London HA-U 8212	PRESENTING THE FABULOUS RONETTES FEATURING VERONICA (LP, originally on plum label, later on black label)	150/80
65	Colpix PXL 486	THE RONETTES (LP)	140
75	Phil Spector Intl. 2307 003	SING THEIR GREATEST HITS (LP)	15

(see also Ronnie Spector, Joey Dee & Starlighters)

RONNIE & DEL AIRES
64	Coral Q 72473	Drag/Wigglin' 'N' Wobblin'	30

RONNIE & HI-LITES
62	Pye International 7N 25140	I Wish That We Were Married/Twistin' And Kissin'	30

RONNIE & RAINBOWS
61	London HL 9345	Loose Ends/Sombrero	22

RONNIE & ROBYN
80	Grapevine GRP 137	As Long As You Love Me/Sidra's Theme (unissued)	

RONNIE & ROY
59	Capitol CL 15028	Big Fat Sally/Here I Am	120

RONNO
71	Vertigo 6059 029	Fourth Hour Of My Sleep/Powers Of Darkness	60

(see also Mick Ronson, Rats)

RONNY
64	Decca F 21908	Oh! My Darling Caroline/Lu La Lu	10

RONNY & THE DAYTONAS
64	Stateside SS 333	G.T.O./Hot Rod Baby	22
64	Stateside SS 367	California Bound/Hey Little Girl	20
65	Stateside SS 391	Bucket T/Little Rail Job	25
65	Stateside SS 432	Beach Boy/No Wheels	25
66	Stateside SS 484	Sandy/Sandy (Instrumental)	20

(see also Buzz & Bucky)

MICK RONSON

74	RCA APBO 0212	Love Me Tender/Only After Dark	6
74	RCA 11474 XSP	Love Me Tender/Slaughter On 10th Avenue (1-sided red or black interview flexidisc, included in press kits)	15
74	RCA LPBO 5022	Slaughter On 10th Avenue/Leave My Heart Alone	6
75	RCA RCA 2482	Billy Porter/Seven Days	6
94	Epic EPC 474742 1	HEAVEN AND HULL (LP, picture disc)	20

(see also Ronno, David Bowie, Mott The Hoople, Slaughter & The Dogs, Ian Hunter)

LINDA RONSTADT

69	Capitol E-ST 208	HOME SOWN, HOME GROWN (LP)	15
70	Capitol E-ST 407	SILK PURSE (LP)	12
72	Capitol EA-ST 635	LINDA RONSTADT (LP)	12

(see also Stone Poneys)

ROOFTOP SINGERS

63	Fontana 271 700 TF	Walk Right In/Cool Water	5
63	Fontana 680 999 TL	WALK RIGHT IN (LP)	12
66	Fontana TFL 6065	RAINY RIVER (LP)	12

(see also Tarriers)

ROOM

70	Deram SML 1073	PRE-FLIGHT (LP)	400+

ROOM

80	Box BOX 001	Motion/Waiting Room (p/s)	6
81	Box BOX 003	In Sickness And Health/Bated Breath (p/s)	5

ROOM 10

65	Decca F 12249	I Love My Love/Going Back	5

ROOM 13

82	Woronzow W 002	Murder Mystery/Need Some Dub (12", p/s)	25

(see also Bevis Frond)

MARY ROOS

72	CBS 7959	Wake Me Early In The Morning/When You're Singing (Don't Forget)	6

ROOSEVELT SINGERS

73	Sioux SI 025	Heavy Reggae/HONG GANG: Smoking Wild	10

ROOT BOYS

70	Columbia Blue Beat DB 115	Please Don't Stop The Wedding/Your Love, Your Love	8

ROOTS

78	Greensleeves GRE 7	Mash Down/Solja Man Skank	12

ROOTS & JENNY JACKSON

70	Beacon BEA 164	Save Me/If I Didn't Love You	28

ROOTS MANUVA

95	Sound Of Money SNM006	Next Type Of Motion/Raw Uncut (12")	40
99	Big Dada BD009	Juggle Tings Proper/Strange Behaviour (12")	12
99	Big Dada BD011	Motion 5000/Skiver's Guide (12")	12
01	Big Dada BD022/7	Witness (Walworth Rockers Dub)	22
99	Big Dada BD010	BRAND NEW SECOND HAND (LP)	12

ROOTS MANUVA/SKITZ

96	Ronin RDP5	Where My Mind Is At/Blessed Be The Manner/Fuck Being Polite (12")	15

ROOTS MANUVA/MC SKEME

96	Wayward AHP01	Fever/Herbman Hustling/Life's Funny (12")	50

ROOTS RADICS

79	Form BB1004	OUTERNATIONAL RIDDIM (LP)	30
82	Cha Cha CHALP 012	RADIFATION (LP)	20

RO RO

70	Parlophone R 5920	Here I Go Again/What You Gonna Do	10
72	Regal Zonophone RZ 3056	Goin' Round My Head/Down On The Road	10
73	Regal Zonophone RZ 3076	Blackbird/Feel It Coming	10
72	Regal Zono. SRZA 8510	MEET AT THE WATER (LP)	250+

(see also Ross)

GEORGE ROPER & PIPEDREAM

70s	Goldspinners GOLD 1	Manchester United/Tribute To The Fans	5

ANDY ROSE

58	London HLU 8761	Lov-A Lov-A Love/Just Young (78 rpm = £6)	25

DAVID ROSE ORCHESTRA

53	MGM SP 1009	Harlem Nocturne (with Woody Herman)/Vanessa	5
56	MGM SP 1181	Forbidden Planet/The Portuguese Washerwomen	8
60	MGM MGM 1110	Bonanza/Gloria's Theme	7
62	MGM MGM 1158	The Stripper/Ebb Tide	7
63	MGM C/CS 961	VERY BEST OF DAVID ROSE (LP)	12
65	MGM MGM-C(S) 8002	THE VELVET BEAT (LP)	12

(see also Woody Herman, Rush Adams)

DUSTY ROSE

55	London HLU 8162	The Birds And The Bees/It Makes Me So Mad (78 rpm = £20)	50
57	London RE-U 1078	COUNTRY SONGS (EP)	50

JOHNNY ROSE

60	Capitol CL 15166	Linda Lee/The Last One To Know	18

MINT VALUE £

MARGARET ROSE
57	Nestles NR 03	In The Middle Of An Island (78, 1-sided card flexi)	5

TIM ROSE
67	CBS 202631	Morning Dew/You're Slipping Away From Me	10
68	CBS 3277	I Got A Loneliness/Long Time Man	30
68	CBS 3478	I Guess It's Over/Hello Sunshine	6
68	CBS 3598	Long-Haired Boy/Looking At A Baby	6
69	CBS 4209	Roanoke/Baby You Turn Me On	6
70	CBS 2631	Morning Dew/You're Slipping Away From Me (reissue)	6
70	Capitol CL 15664	I've Gotta Get A Message To You/Ode To An Old Ball	5
67	CBS (S)BPG 63168	TIM ROSE (LP)	22
69	CBS 63636	THROUGH ROSE COLOURED GLASSES (LP)	20
71	Capitol ST 22673	LOVE — A KIND OF HATE STORY (LP)	12
74	Dawn DNLS 3062	TIM ROSE (LP)	12

TONY ROSE
70	Trailer LER 2013	YOUNG HUNTING (LP)	12
72	Trailer LER 2024	UNDER THE GREENWOOD TREE (LP)	12

ROSE GARDEN
68	Atlantic 584 163	Next Plane To London/Flower Town	7

ROSEHIPS
87	Subway Organisation SUBWAY 10	Room In Your Heart/Thrilled To Bits/Dead End (foldaround p/s with insert in poly bag)	10
87	Subway Organisation SUBWAY 10T	Room In Your Heart/Middle Of Next Week/Thrilled To Bits/So Naive/ Just Another Girl/Dead End (12", p/s)	15
87	Subway Organisation SUBWAY 16	I Shouldn't Have To Say/Loophole/Wastin' My Time/All Mine/ Sad As Sunday (p/s, with insert)	10
87	Subway Organisation SUBWAY 16T	I Shouldn't Have To Say/Loophole/Wastin' My Time/All Mine/ Sad As Sunday (12", p/s with insert)	15
88	Sweet William BILLY 001	Ask Johnny Dee/FAT TULIPS: You Opened My Eyes (33rpm flexi, p/s w/insert)	12

JIMMY ROSELLI
62	Pye International 7N 25134	The Sheik Of Araby/A Fool In Love	6
62	Pye International 7N 25156	I'm Gonna Sit Right Down And Write You A Letter/I Love You	6

ROSEMARY'S CHILDREN
86	él GPO 012	Southern Fields/Whatever Happened To Alice	12
87	Cherry Red MRED 077	KINGS AND PRINCES EP (12", p/s)	12

LEONARD ROSENMAN ORCHESTRA
57	London HA-P 2040	A TRIBUTE TO JAMES DEAN (LP)	18

ROSE OF VICTORY
83	No Future OI 24	Suffragette City/Overdrive (p/s)	12

(see also Blitz)

ROSE TATTOO
78	Carrere CAL 125	Bad Boy For Love/Tramp (p/s)	6
78	Carrere CAL 125	Bad Boy For Love/Tramp (12", p/s)	10
78	Epic EPC 9411	Rock 'N' Roll Outlaw/One Of The Boys (p/s)	5
80	Repeal PRS 2724	Release Legalise/COL PATERSON: Bong On Aussie (500 only)	40
81	Mirage PR 405	Rock 'N' Roll Is King/Sidewalk Sally (12", promo only)	12
81	Carrere CAR 200P	Rock 'N' Roll Outlaw/Remedy (picture disc)	5
81	Carrere CAR 220	Assault And Battery/Astra Wally//One Of The Boys/Manzil Madness (double pack, gatefold p/s)	5
83	Carrere CARP 263	It's Gonna Work Itself Out/Fightin' Sons (picture disc)	5
82	Albert Productions AP 854	We Can't Be Beaten/Fightin' Sons	5
82	Albert Productions AP 898	Branded/Dead Set	5
82	Albert Productions AP 1007	It's Gonna Work Itself Out/Sydney Girls	6
84	Albert Productions AP 1299	I Wish/Wild One	6
82	Albert Productions AP 1384	Freedom's Flame/Never Too Loud (p/s)	6

ROSIE (& ORIGINALS)
61	London HLU 9266	Angel Baby/Give Me Love (as Rosie & Originals)	40
61	Coral Q 72426	Lonely Blue Nights/We'll Have A Chance	40

ROSKO
70	Trojan TR 7758	Al Capone/Kaiser Bill	7
70	Philips 6009 070	Grab The Rabbit/Mohammed Ben Ali	6

(see also Emperor Rosko & Power Pack)

EMPEROR ROSKO & POWER PACK
69	Polydor 56316	Opposite Lock Parts 1 & 2	10
71	B&C CB 148	The Customs Man/Take It In Your Stride	5

(see also Rosko, Power Pack, Pleasure Garden)

FRANK ROSOLINO SEXTET
54	Capitol KC 65001	That Old Black Magic/Yo Yo	5

ROSS
74	RSO 2394 127	ROSS (LP)	12
75	RSO 2394 144	THE PIT AND THE PENDULUM (LP)	12

(see also Indian Summer, Gary Pickford-Hopkins, Ro Ro)

ANNIE ROSS
54	Esquire 10-334	Annie's Lament/Twisted (78, with Teacho Wiltshire, Art Blakey)	8
54	Esquire 10-344	Jackie/The Song Is You (78, with Quincy Jones)	10
55	Decca F 10514	Mama (He Treats Your Daughter Mean)/The Fish	12
55	Decca F 10637	I Want You To Be My Baby (with Tony Crombie)/TONY CROMBIE & HIS ORCHESTRA: Three Little Words (78 rpm = £8)	10
56	Decca F 10680	Cry Me A River/Only You	8

63	Ember EMB S 182	Bye Bye Blues/A Lot Of Livin' To Do	10
72	Columbia DB 8912	Straight On Till Morning/God Bless The Child	10
57	Pye Jazz NJE 1035	NOCTURNE FOR VOCALIST (EP)	20
50s	Esquire EP 1	WITH THE TEACHO WILTSHIRE GROUP (EP)	25
50s	Pieces Of Eight PEP 604	WITH THE TONY CROMBIE FOURTET (EP)	12
64	Transatlantic TRAEP 112	GO TO THE WALL (EP)	15
57	Nixa Jazz NJT 504	ANNIE BY CANDLELIGHT (10" LP)	125
59	Vogue LAE 12203	ANNIE ROSS (LP, with Gerry Mulligan Quintet)	60
60	Vogue LAE 12233	A GASSER (LP, with Zoot Sims)	60
63	Ember NR 5008	A HANDFULL OF SONGS (LP)	75
63	Transatlantic TRA 107	LOGUERRHYTHMS (LP)	60
65	Golden Guinea GGL 0316	ANNIE BY CANDLELIGHT (LP, reissue)	90
66	Xtra XTRA 1049	ANNIE ROSS WITH THE TONY KINSEY QUINTET (LP)	60

(see also Tony Crombie, Dave Lambert, Gerry Mulligan, Zoot Sims, Jack Parnell, Teacho Wiltshire, Art Blakey, Quincy Jones)

DAVID ROSS
| 58 | Oriole CB 1416 | Pit-A-Patter Boom Boom/Everybody's Got A Girl But Tino (as Dave Ross) | 6 |
| 58 | Oriole CB 1416 | Pit-A-Patter Boom Boom/Everybody's Got A Girl But Tino (78, as Dave Ross) | 7 |

DIANA ROSS
70	Tamla Motown TMG 743	Reach Out And Touch (Somebody's Hand)/Dark Side Of The World	5
70	Tamla Motown TMG 751	Ain't No Mountain High Enough/Can't It Wait Until Tomorrow	6
71	Tamla Motown TMG 768	Remember Me/How About You	5
71	Tamla Motown TMG 781	I'm Still Waiting/Reach Out I'll Be There	5
71	Tamla Motown TMG 792	Surrender/I'm A Winner (mono)	5
73	Tamla Motown TMSP 1131	LADY SINGS THE BLUES (2-LP, soundtrack, brown inner sleeves)	20

DIANA ROSS & MICHAEL JACKSON
78	MCA MCA 396	Ease On Down The Road/QUINCY JONES: Poppy Girls (p/s)	8
78	MCA MCAT 12-396	Ease On Down The Road (U.S. Version)/THE WIZ: Poppy Girls (12", p/s)	15
78	MCA MCAT 12-898	Ease On Down The Road (Extended Version)/THE WIZ: Poppy Girls (12", reissue, p/s)	12

(see also [Diana Ross &] Supremes, Michael Jackson, Quincy Jones)

DOCTOR (Isaiah) ROSS
66	Blue Horizon LP 1	THE FLYING EAGLE (LP, 99 copies only, with booklet)	1250
66	Xtra XTRA 1038	DOCTOR ROSS (LP, reissue of "The Flying Eagle")	50
66	Bounty BY 6020	CALL THE DOCTOR (LP)	50
72	Polydor 2460 169	LIVE AT MONTREUX (LP)	25
75	Big Bear BEAR 2	THE HARMONICA BOSS (LP)	20

ERROL ROSS
| 80 | Carrere CAR 149 | Round And Round In Circles/Reggae Music Of Today (p/s) | 6 |

GENE ROSS
| 58 | Parlophone R 4434 | Endless Sleep/The Only One (78 rpm = £10) | 25 |

JACK ROSS
| 62 | London HLD 9534 | Cinderella/Margarita | 5 |
| 62 | London HLD 9485 | Happy Jose/Sweet Georgia Brown | 5 |

JACKIE ROSS
| 64 | Pye International 7N 25259 | Selfish One/Everything But Love (DJ copy = £100) | 60 |
| 64 | Chess CRS 8003 | Jerk And Twine/New Lover(DJ copy = £70) | 40 |

JOAN ROSS
| 70 | Crab CRAB 61 | Band Of Gold/HAMMERS: Midnight Sunshine | 10 |

JOE E. ROSS
| 64 | Columbia 335X1710 | LOVE SONGS FROM A COP (LP) | 18 |

RONNIE ROSS
58	Parlophone PMC 1079	DOUBLE EVENT (LP)	75
61	Ember EMB 3323	STOMPIN' WITH (LP)	80
65	Ember FA 2023	THE SWINGIN' SOUNDS OF THE JAZZ MAKERS (LP, with Allan Ganley)	60
69	Fontana SFJL 915	CLEOPATRA'S NEEDLE (LP)	200

(see also Bill Le Sage)

SONNY ROSS
| 71 | Mojo 2093 001 | Alakazam/The Piper Must Be Paid | 10 |

SPENCER ROSS
| 60 | Philips PB 992 | Tracy's Theme/Thanksgiving Day Parade | 6 |
| 60 | London HLX 9141 | Theme Of A Lonely Evening/Bobby's Blues | 7 |

T.T. ROSS
75	Dip DL 5079	Single Girl/Funny What Love Can Do	5
76	Dip DL 5104	Last Date/I Am Sorry	5
76	Lucky LY 6000	No Charge/When I Was A Little Girl	5
76	Lucky LY 6014	Baby Why/TOUGH GANG: Part 2	5
76	Lucky LY 6017	Misty Blue/Version	5
76	House Of Eve 001	Let The World Go Away/Part 2	5
76	House Of Eve 002	Piece Of My Heart/Part 2	5
77	Lovers Rock CJ 622	I Will/I Will Dub	5

LEON ROSSELSON
70	Acorn CF 206	SONGS FOR SCEPTICAL CIRCLES	18
71	Trailer LER 3015	THE WORD IS HUGGA MUGGA CHUGGA HUMBUGGA BOOM CHIT (LP, with Roy Bailey & Martin Carthy)	15
75	Acorn CF 249	PALACES OF GOLD (LP)	18
75	Acorn CF 251	THAT'S NOT THE WAY IT'S GOT TO BE (LP, with Roy Bailey)	18

(see also Three City Four, Roy Bailey)

NITA ROSSI

65	Piccadilly 7N 35258	Every Little Day Now/Untrue Unfaithful	25
66	Piccadilly 7N 35307	Here I Go Again/Something To Give (DJ copy = £70)	40
66	Piccadilly 7N 35354	The Daddy Christmas Song/Our Love Was Meant To Be	7
67	Piccadilly 7N 35384	Misty Blue/Come Around	10

(Francis) ROSSI & (Bernard) FROST

85	Vertigo VER 17/FROS 1	Modern Romance (I Want To Fall In Love Again)/I Wonder Why (p/s)	6
85	Vertigo VERX 17/FROSX 1	Modern Romance (I Want To Fall In Love Again) (Extended Remix)/ I Wonder Why (Extended Remix) (12", p/s)	15
85	Vertigo VER 24	Jealousy/Where Are You Now? (p/s)	8
85	Vertigo VERX 24	Jealousy/Where Are You Now?/That's Alright (12", p/s)	18

(see also Status Quo, Bernie Frost, Boz Frost, Mickey Jupp, Mitchell/Coe Mysteries, Demis Roussos, Tokyo Olympics)

JOHN HENRY ROSTILL

71	Columbia DB 8794	Funny Old World/Green Apples	60

(see also Shadows)

STEVE ROSTRON

74	Sweet Folk & Country SFA 009	NO STRANGER'S FACE (LP)	30

ROTARY CONNECTION

68	Chess CRS 8072	Soul Man/Ruby Tuesday	10
69	Chess CRS 8103	The Weight/Respect	10
70	Chess CRS 8106	Want You To Know/Memory Band	10
68	Chess CRL 4538	ROTARY CONNECTION (LP)	40
69	Chess CRL(S) 4547	ALADDIN (LP)	40
69	Chess CRLS 4551	SONGS (LP)	30

DAVID LEE ROTH

86	Warner Bros W 8656P	Yankee Rose/Shy Boy (pin-up shaped picture disc)	10

(see also Van Halen)

ROTHCHILDS

66	Decca F 12411	You've Made Your Choice/It's Love	8
66	Decca F 12488	Artificial City/I Let Her Go	10

ROTORIK

01	Mosquito MSQ 018	(Sending All Processes) The Term Signal (12" EP)	8

ROUGE

78	SRT SRTSCUS 78104	Have You Seen Gene (no p/s)	75

ROUGH DIAMOND

90	Bedrock BR 1	Woman's Touch (p/s)	12

ROUGH ELEMENT

92	UAR UAR120020	The Elements/Breaking The Silence/Unbound Rage (remix) (EP)	60
94	UAR 003	Reflex Reaction/Criminal Behaviour (12")	20

ROUGH JUSTICE

80s	Rough Justice RJ 001	MILLION TO ONE (EP, p/s)	200

ROUGH RIDERS

74	Rare Earth RES 118	Hot California Beach/Do You See Me	15

ROULETTES

62	Pye 7N 15467	Hully Gully Slip 'N' Slide/La Bamba	20
63	Parlophone R 5072	Soon You'll Be Leaving Me/Tell Tale Tit	15
64	Parlophone R 5110	Bad Time/Can You Go	15
64	Parlophone R 5148	I'll Remember Tonight/You Don't Love Me	15
64	Parlophone R 5218	Stubborn Kind Of Fellow/Melody	20
65	Parlophone R 5278	I Hope He Breaks Your Heart/Find Out The Truth	15
65	Parlophone R 5382	The Long Cigarette/Junk	30
66	Parlophone R 5419	The Tracks Of My Tears/Jackpot	20
66	Oak RGJ 205	I Can't Stop (1-sided, some with p/s)	250/150
66	Parlophone R 5461	I Can't Stop/Yesterday, Today And Tomorrow	20
67	Fontana TF 822	Rhyme Boy, Rhyme/Airport People	40
67	Fontana TF 876	Help Me To Help Myself/To A Taxi Driver	20
65	Parlophone PMC 1257	STAKES AND CHIPS (LP)	300+

(see also Adam Faith, Unit 4 + 2, Argent)

ROUND ROBIN

64	London HLU 9908	Kick That Little Foot Sally Ann/Slauson Party (DJ copy = £70)	30

ROUNDTABLE

69	Jay Boy BOY 18	Saturday Gigue/Scarborough Fair	20
69	Jay Boy JSL 2	SPINNING WHEEL (LP)	35

DEMIS ROUSSOS

80	Mercury MER 25	Sorry/Love Is The Answer (p/s, A-side written by & featuring Francis Rossi/ Bernie Frost)	8

(see also Aphrodite's Child, Forminx, Rossi & Frost)

ROUTERS

62	Warner Bros WB 77	Let's Go/Mashy	10
63	Warner Bros WB 91	Make It Snappy/Half Time	10
63	Warner Bros WB 97	Stingray/Snap Happy	10
63	Warner Bros WB 108	Big Band/A Ooga	10
64	Warner Bros WB 139	Stamp And Shake/Ah Ya	10
73	Warner Bros K 16156	Let's Go/Mashy (reissue)	5
63	Warner Bros WM/WS 8126	LET'S GO! WITH THE ROUTERS (LP, features Scott Walker)	50
64	Warner Bros WM/WS 8144	PLAY 1963's GREAT INSTRUMENTALS (LP)	30
65	Warner Bros WM/WS 8162	CHARGE! (LP)	30

(see also Scott Walker)

JONATHAN ROUTH
57	Nixa NPT 19016	CANDID MIKE (10" LP)	18
62	Pye NPL 18077	CANDID CAMERA (LP)	18

ROVERS
55	Capitol CL 14283	Ichi-Bon Tami, Dachi/Why Oh-h (Why Do You Lie To Me?) (78 rpm = £95)	400

ROVING KIND
65	Decca F 12264	Ain't It True/Don't Tell Me The Time	6
66	Decca F 12381	Lies A Million/How Many Times	6

ROWAN & MARTIN
69	CBS 63490	ROWAN AND MARTIN'S LAUGH-IN (LP)	12
69	Atlantic 588 151	ROWAN AND MARTIN AT WORK (LP)	15

ROWDIES
78	Birds Nest BN 109	A.C.A.B. (All Coppers Are Bastards)/Negative Malfunction/Freeze Out	25
79	Teenage Depression TD 1/2	She's No Angel/Had Me A Real Good Time (p/s)	8

(see also Boys, Lurkers, Steve Sharp & Cleancuts)

KEITH ROWE
77	Black Swan WIP 6405	Groovy Situation/Groovy Dub	15
77	Black Swan BS 6	Groovy Situation/Groovy Dub	20
81	Seven Leaves SLD 02	Groovy Situation/Groovy Dub	15

NORMIE ROWE
66	Polydor 56132	It's Not Easy/Mary Mary	6
66	Polydor 56144	Ain't Nobody Home/Ooh La La	5
67	Polydor 56159	Going Home/I Don't Care (Just Take Me There) (some in p/s)	8/5

MAJOR ROWELY
65	Stateside SS 438	There's A Riot Going On/Do It The Right Way	20

CHERRY ROWLAND
63	Fontana TF 420	Nobody But Me/Boys	10
74	Decca F 13491	Here Is Where The Love Is/I Can Give You Back Yourself	12

(see also Cherry Roland)

JACKIE ROWLAND
72	Sioux SI 015	Indian Reservation/JUNIOR SMITH: I'm In A Dancing Mood	5
72	Sioux SI 022	Lonely Man/JOE MANSANO: The Trial Of Pama Dice	12

(see also Joe Higgs)

KEVIN ROWLAND
88	Mercury DEXYB 1412	Young Man/The Way You Look Tonight/Even When I Hold You/Walk Away (12", gatefold p/s)	8
88	Mercury ROW 112	Tonight (12" Dance Mix)/Tonight (New York Dub Mix)/Come On Eileen/Kevin Rowland's Band (12", p/s)	8

(see also Dexys Midnight Runners)

STEVE ROWLAND
67	Fontana TF 844	So Sad/I See Red	30

(see also Family Dogg)

JOHN ROWLES
68	MCA MU 1023	Hush Not A Word To Mary/The Night We Called It A Day	5
69	MCA MKPS 2001	THAT LOVIN' FEELING (LP)	15

ROX
82	Teenteeze ROX 100	HOT LOVE IN THE CITY (Hot Love In The City/Do Ya Feel Like Lovin'/Love Ya Like A Diamond (EP)	25
83	MFN 12KUT 103	KRAZY KUTZ (EP)	8

ROXY MUSIC
72	Island WIP 6144	Virginia Plain/The Numberer (initially pink labels, later orange)	each 5
73	Island WIP 6159	Pyjamarama/The Pride And The Pain	5
74	Island WIP 6173	Street Life/Hula Kula	5
74	Island WIP 6208	All I Want Is You/Your Application's Failed	5
78	Polydor/EG 2001 756	Do The Strand/Editions Of You (12", p/s)	8
79	Polydor/EGPOSPX 67	Angel Eyes (Extended 6.39)/My Little Girl (12", p/s)	8
82	E.G. ROXYX 3	More Than This/India (12", p/s)	8
86	E.G. EGOX 26	Love Is The Drug/Let's Stick Together (12", p/s, promo only)	8
79	Polydor/E.G. EGPD 001	MANIFESTO (LP, picture disc)	12
79	Polydor/E.G. EGPD 001	MANIFESTO (LP, picture disc, mispress, 1 side plays Gordon Giltrap's "Fear Of The Dark" (LP)	12
81	Polydor/E.G. EGBS 001	THE FIRST SEVEN ALBUMS (7-LP box set plus insert)	50
81	Polydor/E.G. EGBS 001	THE FIRST SEVEN ALBUMS (7-cassette box set)	35
83	E.G. 815 849-2	THE ATLANTIC YEARS 1973-1980 (CD)	18

(see also Brian Eno, Bryan Ferry, Andy Mackay, Phil Manzanera, Dumbelles, 801, Fripp & Eno)

ALVIN ROY & THE SARATOGA JAZZ BAND
61	Interdisc INT 45001	Yogi/Broken Promises	5

DEREK ROY
57	Oriole CB 1415	Derek Roy's All-Star Party (with Bob Monkhouse, Richard Murdoch, Jon Pertwee, Ted Ray & others) (78 rpm = £8)	8

(see also Jon Pertwee, Bob Monkhouse)

HUGH ROY
70	Supreme SUP 211	Double Attack/Puzzle	15
70	Explosion EX 2040	Whisper A Little Prayer (actually by Audley Rollins)/Rain A Fall (actually by Melanie)	15
70	Punch PH 34	Scandal/Son Of The Wise	12
70	Duke Reid DR 2509	Wake The Town/Big Boy And Teacher	15
70	Duke Reid DR 2510	Rule The Nation/NORA DEAN: Ay Ay Ay Ay	15

Hugh ROY

70	Duke Reid DR 2513	Wear You To The Ball (with John Holt)/EARL LINDO: The Ball	12
70	Duke Reid DR 2514	You'll Never Get Away/TOMMY McCOOK QUINTET: Rock Away	12
70	Duke Reid DR 2515	Version Galore/TOMMY McCOOK: Nehru	25
71	Duke Reid DR 2516	Testify/TOMMY McCOOK: Super Soul	12
71	Duke Reid DR 2517	Tom Drunk (with Hopeton Lewis)/TOMMY McCOOK: Wailing	12
71	Duke Reid DR 2518	True True/On The Beach	12
71	Duke Reid DR 2519	Flashing My Whip/Do It Right	15
71	Treasure Isle TI 7059	Drive Her Home (Parts 1 & 2) (with Hopeton Lewis)	15
71	Treasure Isle TI 7062	Behold/Way Back Home (with Tommy McCook)	12
71	Treasure Isle TI 7064	Everybody Bawlin'/Ain't That Loving You	15
71	Upsetter US 375	Earthquake/Suspicious Minds	18
71	Duke DU 105	Love I Tender/JOYA LANDIS: When The Lights Are Low	12
71	Duke Reid DR 2517	Tom Drunk/Wailing (as U Roy, B-side actually by Tommy McCook)	12
72	G.G. GG 4532	Way Down South/BILLY DYCE: Be My Guest	12
72	Duke DU 137	Live It Up/DENNIS BROWN: Baby Don't Do It	12
72	Jackpot JP 806	Two Ton Gulleto/Version	10
72	Dynamic DYN 448	Festival Wise/Festival Wise Part 2	8
72	Banana BA 367	Keep On Running/LARRY'S ALL STARS: (Version)	8
72	Grape GR 3026	On Top The Peak/TYPHOON ALLSTARS: Race Attack	8
72	Pama PM 835	Way Down South/BILLY DYCE: Be My Guest	12
72	Punch PH 104	Nannyscrank (title actually "Nanny Skank")/PITTSBURG ALLSTARS: Scank Version	12
72	Green Door GD 4034	Hudson Affair/KEITH HUDSON: Hot Stick (Version)	18
72	Trojan TR 7884	Hat Trick/Wet (Version)	8
73	Green Door GD 4052	King Tubby's Special/Here Come The Heartaches	12
73	Gayfeet GS 210	Hard Feeling/Regular Style	8
73	Duke DU 157	Higher The Mountain/OLD BOYS INC.: (Version)	8
73	Harry J. HJ 6651	Treasure Isle Skank/Words Of Wisdom	12
76	Soulfood SF 001	High Priest/London City Rock	15
71	Trojan TBL 161	VERSION GALORE (LP, as U Roy)	32
73	Attack ATLP 1006	U ROY (LP, as U Roy)	25

(see also U Roy, Jeff Barnes, Melodians, Delroy Wilson)

HUGH ROY JUNIOR

71	Big BG 329	Papacito/RUPIE EDWARDS: I'm Gonna Live Some Life	12
71	Supreme SUP 211	Double Attack/MURPHY'S ALL STARS: Puzzle	12
72	Ashanti ASH 405	King Of The Road/ROOSEVELT ALL STARS: (Version)	8
72	Jackpot JP 806	Two Ton Guletto/(Version)	8

I ROY

71	Moodisc MU 3509	Musical Pleasure/JO JO BENNETT: Hot Pop	15
71	Moodisc MU 3510	Heart Don't Leap (as I. Roy & Dennis Walks)/DENNIS WALKS & MUDIE'S ALLSTARS: Snow Bird	15
71	Moodisc MU 3512	Let Me Tell You Boy (with Ebony Sisters)/MUDIE'S ALLSTARS: (Version)	15
71	Moodisc HM 104	The Drifter (with Dennis Walks)/JO JO BENNETT: Snowbird	18
72	Green Door GD 4030	Hot Bomb (with Jumpers)/JUMPERS: The Bomb	12
72	Green Door GD 4044	Make Love/STAGE: Tic Toc Bill	10
73	Pyramid PYR 7001	Tip From The Prince/Fat Beef Skank	15
73	Attack ATT 8050	Space Flight/JERRY LEWIS: Burning Wire	15
73	Downtown DT 503	Blackman's Time/High Jacking	18
73	Downtown DT 519	Clapper's Tail/Live And Learn	18
73	Duke DU 156	Buck And The Preacher/PETE WESTON ALLSTARS: Preacher (Version)	12
73	Smash SMA 2337	The Magnificent Seven/Leggo Beast	12
73	Smash SMA 2338	Rose Of Sheron/Slip Out	15
73	Techniques TE 926	Pauper And The King/GREGORY ISAACS: Loving Pauper	12
73	Techniques TE 930	Monkey Fashion/Medley Mood	10
73	Ackee ACK 503	Great Great Great (with Ken Parker)/RUPIE EDWARDS ALLSTARS: (Version)	22
73	Ackee ACK 510	Sound Education/AUGUSTUS PABLO: Cinderella In Black	18
73	Harry J HJ-6655	Musical Drum Sound/NOW GENERATION: Musical Drum (Version)	12
73	Pama PM 854	Cowtown Skank/AUGUSTUS PABLO: Cowtown Skank (Version)	12
74	Atra ATRA 017	Yah Ma Ride/SWEET HARMONY: Mexican Rockin'	12
74	Ashanti ASH 412	Mood For Love (Parts 1 & 2)	12
75	Bullet BU 551	Step Right Up/ANDY'S ALLSTARS: Banjo Serenade	8
75	Lucky DL 5098	I Man Time/(Version)	12
76	Dip DL 5107	Padlock/Lock And Key (copies also exist with Lucky label)	each 10
77	Observer OB 002	Jamaican Girl/River Jordan/First Cut/Second Cut (12")	25
70s	Nationwide NW 005	Tea Pot/Tea Cup	12
79	Virgin Front Line FSL 12412	Fire In A Wire/Hill And Gully (12")	15
73	Trojan TRLS 63	PRESENTING I ROY (LP, original issue with "12 Neasden Lane" address and rough orange/white paper labels)	32
74	Trojan TRLS 71	HELL AND SORROW (LP, original issue with "12 Neasden Lane" address and rough orange/white paper labels)	28
74	Trojan TRLS 91	THE MANY MOODS OF I ROY (LP, original issue with "12 Neasden Lane" address and rough orange/white paper labels)	28
75	Grounation GROL 504	TRUTH & RIGHTS (LP)	25
76	Klik 9020	DREAD BALDHEAD (LP)	45
77	Justice JUS LP 08	CAN'T CONQUER RASTA (LP)	30
78	Third World TWS 930	THE GODFATHER (LP)	20

(see also Keith Hudson & I Roy)

LEE ROY

65	Island WI 251	Oh Ee Baby/My Loving Baby Come Back	10

LITTLE ROY

69	Crab CRAB 39	Without My Love (by Roy & Joy)/WINSTON SAMUELS: Here I Come Again	10
70	Bullet BU 445	Keep Trying/THE MATADORS: Version II	10
70	Camel CA 43	Scrooge/In The Days Of Old	12

70	Camel CA 46	You Run Come/THE LITTLE ROYS: Skank King	
		(actually "Skank Me" by Little Roy)	12
70	Camel CA 52	Fight Them/Dreadlock	12
71	Escort ERT 850	Yester-Me Yester-You Yesterday/MATADOR ALL-STARS: Yes Sir	10
71	Punch PH 75	Hard Fighter/COUNT OSSIE: Back To Africa (Version)	12

(see also Roy & Joy, Little Roys)

MAD ROY
70	Banana BA 324	Nanny (Version) (actually by Dennis Alcapone)/BIGGER D: Freedom (Version)	15
71	Banana BA 326	Home (Version) (actually by Dennis Alcapone)/SOUND DIMENSION: One Time	15
71	Banana BA 327	Universal Love/ROLAND ALPHONSO: Shelly Belly	15
71	Banana BA 328	Duppy Serenade/Sunshine (Version) (both sides actually by Dennis Alcapone)	12

(pseudonym for Leroy Wallace; see also Dennis Alcapone)

U ROY JUNIOR
72	Duke Reid DR 2520	Rock To The Beat/Love Is Not A Gamble (both actually by Dennis Alcapone)	12
72	Attack ATT 8030	This Is A Pepper (as U Roy Junior)/JOHN HOLT: Justice	12
72	Sioux SI 024	The Wedding (as U Roy Junior)/LLOYD'S ALL STARS: Buttercup	8
73	Randy's RAN 532	Froggie (as U Roy Junior)/RHYTHM RULERS: (Version)	10
73	Techniques TE 928	Aunt Kereba (as U Roy Junior)/DON RECO: Waterloo Rock	
		(B-side actually by Reco Rodriquez)	12

(see also Hugh Roy, Dennis Alcapone, Sir Harry, Shorty Perry, Heptones, Herman Chin-Loy)

ROY & ANNETTE
| 63 | R&B JB 107 | My Baby/Go Your Ways | 18 |

(see also Tommy McCook, Lester Sterling)

ROY & DUKE ALL STARS
| 68 | Blue Cat BS 113 | Pretty Blue Eyes Parts 1 & 2 | 40 |
| 68 | Blue Cat BS 117 | The Train Parts 1 & 2 | 28 |

(see also Roy Panton)

ROY & ENID
68	Coxsone CS 7063	Rocking Time/RALPH BLAKE: High Blood Pressure	25
68	Coxsone CS 7069	He'll Have To Go/CARLTON & SHOES: Love Is A Treasure	35
69	Coxsone CS 7088	Reggae For Days/SOUND DIMENSION: Holy Moses	30

(Little) ROY & JOY
| 73 | Camel CA 107 | Rainy Weather/THE DEN BROTHERS: Version | 8 |

(see also Little Roys)

ROY (Panton) & MILLIE
62	Island WI 005	We'll Meet/ROLAND ALPHONSO: Back Beat (B-side act. with City Slickers)	25
63	Island WI 050	This World/Never Say Goodbye	15
63	Island WI 090	There'll Come A Day/I Don't Want You	15
63	Blue Beat BB 154	Over And Over/I'll Go (with Prince Buster All Stars)	20
64	Black Swan WI 409	Cherry I Love You/You're The Only One	22
64	Black Swan WI 410	Oh Merna/DON DRUMMOND: Dog War Bossa Nova	22
64	Black Swan WI 427	Oh Shirley/Marie	18

(see also Roy Panton, Millie [Small])

ROY (Panton) & PATSY
| 62 | Blue Beat BB 118 | My Happy Home/In Your Arms Dear (with Hersang & His Combo) | 12 |

(see also Roy Panton)

ROY (Richards) & PAULETTE
| 63 | Island WI 067 | Have You Seen My Baby/Since You're Gone | 12 |

ROY (Panton) & YVONNE (Harrison)
| 64 | Blue Beat BB 258 | Little Girl/No More | 12 |
| 64 | Black Swan WI 436 | Two Roads/Join Together | 12 |

(see also Roy Panton)

BILLY JOE ROYAL
62	Oriole CB 1751	Never In A Hundred Years/We Haven't A Moment To Lose	15
65	CBS 201802	Down In The Boondocks/Oh! What A Night	12
65	CBS 201983	You Make Me Feel Like A Man/I've Got To Be Somebody	6
65	CBS 202009	I Knew You When/Steal Away	6
66	CBS 202052	It's A Good Time/Don't Wait Up For Me Mama	6
66	CBS 202087	Heart's Desire/Everbody's Gotta Cry (DJ copy = £75)	40
66	Atlantic 584 002	Never In A Hundred Years/We Haven't A Moment To Lose (reissue)	8
67	CBS 202548	Yo Yo/We Tried	10
67	CBS 3044	Hush/Watching From The Bandstand	8
66	CBS BPG 62590	INTRODUCING BILLY JOE ROYAL (LP)	25

BOBBY ROYAL
| 63 | HMV POP 1253 | Big Big Star/Little Word Of Love | 15 |

JAMES ROYAL (& HAWKS)
65	Parlophone R 5290	She's About A Mover/Black Cloud (as James Royal & Hawks)	25
65	Parlophone R 5383	Work Song/I Can't Stand It	35
67	CBS 202525	Call My Name/When It Comes To My Baby	20
67	CBS 2739	It's All In The Game/Green Days	7
68	CBS 2959	Take Me Like I Am/Sitting In The Station	5
68	CBS 3232	I Can't Stand It/Little Bit Of Rain	6
68	CBS 3450	Hey Little Boy/Thru' The Love	25
68	CBS 3624	A Woman Called Sorrow/Fire	20
69	CBS 3797	Time Hangs On My Mind/Anna-Lee	6
69	CBS 3915	House Of Jack/Which Way To Nowhere	10
69	CBS 4139	I've Something Bad On My Mind/She's Independent	6
69	CBS 4463	Send Out Love/I've Lost You	12
70	CBS 5032	And Soon The Darkness/I'm Going Home	6
70	Carnaby CNS 4021	Carolina/Big Heat On The Loose	6

James ROYAL (& HAWKS)

71	Carnaby 6151 002	Carolina/A Woman Called Sorrow	5
72	Carnaby 6151 006	Two Of Us/Who Are We (with Liz Christian)	5
69	CBS 63780	CALL MY NAME (LP)	30
70	Carnaby CNLS 6008	ONE WAY (LP)	40
72	Carnaby 6302 011	THE LIGHT AND SHADE OF JAMES ROYAL (LP)	40

ROBBIE ROYAL

65	Mercury MF 923	Only Me/I Don't Need You	8
65	Decca F 12097	Within My Lonely Heart/When I Found You	6

ROYAL BLUES

69	Pye 7N 17670	Mountain Of Love/Wishful Thinking	5
69	Pye 7N 17732	Mendocino/Hi-Lili Hi-Lo	5
69	Pye 7N 17769	Proud Mary/Sunny Girl Friend	5
69	Pye 7N 17847	High As A Mountain/Wildwood Flower	5

ROYALETTES

65	MGM MGM 1272	Poor Boy/Watch What Happens	20
65	MGM MGM 1279	It's Gonna Take A Miracle/Out Of Sight Out Of Mind (DJ copy = £60)	40
65	MGM MGM 1292	I Want To Meet Him/Never Again	25
66	MGM MGM 1302	You Bring Me Down/Only When You're Lonely	25
66	MGM MGM 1324	It's A Big Mistake/I Want To Meet Him	20
68	Big T BIG 106	River Of Tears/Something Wonderful	25
66	MGM MGM-C 8028	THE ELEGANT SOUND OF THE ROYALETTES (LP)	100

ROYAL GUARDSMEN

67	Stateside S(S)L 10202	SNOOPY VS THE RED BARON (LP)	18
68	London HA-P/SH-P 8351	THE RETURN OF THE RED BARON (LP)	18

ROYAL HOLIDAYS

58	London HLU 8722	Margaret/I'm Sorry (I Did You Wrong) (78 rpm = £45)	120+

ROYAL RASSES

79	12 Bakistuc 315	You Gotta Have Love (Jah Love)/Humanity (Love The Way It Should Be)/ They Know Not Jah (12")	12
79	Warrior BP 327	Royal Rasses – Aint' Nobldy Here But Me/Kingston 11 (Ghetto Rock) (12")	15
78	Ballistic UAG 30259	RASSES EXPERIENCE (LP)	12
79	Warrior WARLP 2002	HARDER NA RASS! (LP)	40

ROYAL ROCKERS

60	Top Rank JAR 326	Jet II/Swinging Mambo	18

ROYALS

64	Blue Beat BB 259	Save Mama/Out De Fire	22
68	Amalgamated AMG 831	Never See Come See/CANNONBALL BRYAN TRIO: Jumping Jack	22
69	Trojan TR 662	Pick Out Me Eye/Think You Too Bad	15
69	Duke DU 29	Never Gonna Give You Up/Don't Mix Me Up	12
73	Dip DL 5016	Promised Land/Every Jamaican Is A Rebel	6
81	Kingdom KVLP 9006	MOVING ON (LP)	20

ROYAL SHOWBAND, WATERFORD

64	HMV POP 1377	Huckle Buck/I Ran All The Way Home	6

ROYAL TEENS

58	HMV POP 454	Short Shorts/Planet Rock (78 rpm = £18)	40
59	Capitol CL 15068	Little Cricket/Believe Me	25

ROYALTONES

58	London HLJ 8744	Poor Boy/Wail! (78 rpm = £15)	20
61	London HLU 9296	Flamingo Express/Tacos	18
64	Stateside SS 309	Our Faded Love/Holy Smokes	12

ROYALTY

69	CBS 4181	That Kind Of Girl/Will You Be Staying After Sunday	6

EARL ROYCE & OLYMPICS

64	Columbia DB 7433	Que Sera Sera/I Really Do	28
65	Parlophone R 5261	Guess Things Happen That Way/Sure To Fall	25

ROY'S BOYS

64	Columbia DB 7425	Do Wah Diddy Diddy—I'm Into Something Good—I Want To Hold Your Hand/ Oh! Pretty Woman—Have I The Right?—It's All Over Now	7

LITA ROZA

51	Decca F 9731	Allentown Jail/I Wish I Knew (78)	8
51	Decca F 9785	I'm Gonna Wash That Man Right Outta My Hair/A Wonderful Guy (78)	8
52	Decca F 9955	Oakie Boogie/Raminay (78)	8
53	Decca F 10070	(How Much Is) That Doggie In The Window/Tell Me We'll Meet Again (78)	10
53	Decca F 75082	(How Much Is) That Doggie In The Window/Tell Me We'll Meet Again (export issue)	40
54	Decca F 10240	Changing Partners/Just A Dream Or Two Ago (B-side with Stargazers)	15
54	Decca F 10269	Bell Bottom Blues (with Johnston Brothers)/Make Love To Me (both with Ted Heath Orchestra)	15
54	Decca F 10277	Young At Heart/Secret Love	15
54	Decca F 10393	Call Off The Wedding/The "Mama-Doll" Song	15
55	Decca F 10427	Heartbeat/Leave Me Alone	15
55	Decca F 10431	Let Me Go, Lover!/Make Yourself Comfortable	15
55	Decca F 10479	Tomorrow/Foolishly	15
55	Decca F 10536	Two Hearts, Two Kisses (Make One Love)/Keep Me In Mind	15
55	Decca F 10541	The Man In The Raincoat/Today And Ev'ry Day	12
55	Decca F 10611	Hey There/Hernando's Hideaway	20
56	Decca F 10679	Jimmy Unknown/The Rose Tattoo	20
56	Decca F 10728	Too Young To Go Steady/You're Not Alone	8

56	Decca F 10761	No Time For Tears/But Love Me (Love But Me)	8
56	Decca F 10792	Innismore/The Last Waltz	8
56	Decca F 10830	Hey! Jealous Lover/Julie	8
57	Decca F 10861	Lucky Lips/Tears Don't Care Who Cries Them	8
57	Decca F 10884	Tonight My Heart She Is Crying/Five Oranges, Four Apples	8
63	Ember EMB S 168	Mama (He Treats Your Daughter Mean)/(He's My) Dreamboat (as Lisa Rosa)	20
57	Decca DFE 6386	LITA ROZA SELECTION (EP)	40
57	Decca DFE 6399	LITA ROZA (EP)	35
58	Decca DFE 6443	BETWEEN THE DEVIL AND THE DEEP BLUE SEA NO. 1 (EP)	35
54	Decca LF 1187	PRESENTING LITA ROZA (10" LP)	130
56	Decca LF 1243	LISTENING IN THE AFTER HOURS (10" LP)	120
57	Decca LK 4171	LOVE IS THE ANSWER (LP)	100
57	Decca LK 4218	BETWEEN THE DEVIL AND THE DEEP BLUE SEA (LP)	75
58	Pye Nixa NPL 18020	ME ON A CAROUSEL (LP, also stereo NSPL 83003)	45/50
60	Pye NPL 18047	DRINKA LITA ROZA DAY (LP)	80
64	Ember NR 5009	LOVE SONGS FOR NIGHT PEOPLE (LP)	40

(see also Stargazers, Johnston Brothers)

RPM
93	Mo' Wax MW 005	Food Of My D'Rhythm/(Version)/Take Me Out Of The Ordinary/(Version) (12", stickered sleeve)	8
94	Mo' Wax MW018	2,000/Sorti Des Ombres/(dub) (12", 3 different covers, full colour, green and purple or blue)	25/15/10

RUB-A-DUBS WITH DANDY
65	Blue Beat BB 304	Without Love/I Know	25

(see also Dandy)

RUBBER BAND
73	Youngblood YB 1052	Moonwalker/Wichita	6
69	Major Minor SMCP 5045	CREAM SONGBOOK (LP)	25
69	Major Minor SMCP 5048	HENDRIX SONGBOOK (LP)	25

RUBBER BOOTZ
67	Deram DM 134	Joy Ride/Chicano	25

JOHNNY RUBBISH
78	United Artists UP 36405	Living In NW3 4JR/Other Side (p/s)	10

RUBELLA BALLET
82	Xntrix XN 2005	The Ballet Dance/Something To Give/Unemployed/Krak Trak (p/s)	5
82	Xntrix ZN 2004	BALLET DOG (C-30 cassette with insert)	6
88	Ubiquitous DAY-GLO 6	THE BALLET'S BIRTHDAY (2-LP, box set, with book & 5 inserts)	15

RUBIN
75	MCA MU 196	You've Been Away/Baby, You're My Everything (DJ copy = £25)	15

RUBAIYATS
68	Action ACT 4516	Omar Khayam/Tomorrow	30

RUBY & GLORIA
71	Big Shot BI 583	Worried Over You/Worried Over You (Version)	8
71	Black Swan BW 1409	Talk To Me Baby/LLOYD'S ALL STARS: Talk To Me Baby (Version)	8

RUBY & ROMANTICS
63	London HLR 9679	Our Day Will Come/Moonlight And Music	15
63	London HLR 9734	My Summer Love/Sweet Love And Sweet Forgiveness	15
63	London HLR 9771	Hey There Lonely Boy/Not A Moment Too Soon	15
63	London HLR 9801	Young Wings Can Fly/Day Dreaming	15
64	London HLR 9881	Our Everlasting Love/Much Better Off Than I've Ever Been	25
64	London HLR 9916	Baby Come Home/Every Day's A Holiday	25
64	London HLR 9935	When You're Young And In Love/I Cry Alone	15
65	London HLR 9972	Your Baby Doesn't Love Me Anymore/We'll Meet Again	15
69	A&M AMS 750	Hurting Each Other/Baby I Could Be So Good At Loving You	15
63	London RE-R 1389	OUR DAY WILL COME (EP)	70+
64	London RE-R 1427	HEY THERE LONELY BOY (EP)	75
63	London HA-R 8078	OUR DAY WILL COME (LP)	85
66	London HA-R 8282	GREATEST HITS (LP)	50

(see also Danny Davis Orchestra)

RUDDY & SKETTO
71	Supreme SUP 218	Every Night/Ethiopia	8

(see also Sketto Rich)

RUDE AND DEADLY
95	Unity UNITY 002	Lightnin' and Tundra/Mash Dem Down (12")	40

RUDE ASS TINKER
90s	Deathchant DEATH 30	Imperial Break/Silk Ties (12", limited issue)	18

(see also Mu-Ziq)

RUDE BOYS
67	Island WI 3088	Rock Steady Massachusetts/Going Home	20

RUDI
78	Good Vibrations GOT 1	Big Time/Number 1 (folded p/s, 3,000 only)	20
79	Good Vibrations GOT 12	I Spy/Genuine Reply/Sometimes/Ripped In Two (p/s)	18
81	Jamming! CREATE 1	When I Was Dead/The Pressure's On (p/s)	5
82	Jamming! CREATE 3	Crimson/14 Steps (p/s)	5

RUDIES (FANATICS)
68	Blue Cat BS 107	The 7-11 Go To The Go Go Club (Parts 1 & 2)	35
68	Blue Cat BS 109	Cupid/RECO'S ALLSTARS: Wise Message	25
68	Nu Beat NB 001	Train To Vietnam/Skaville To Rainbow City	15

68	Nu Beat NB 005	Engine 59/My Girl	15
68	Fab FAB 46	I Wanna Go Home/La Mer	12
68	Fab FAB 70	Give Me The Rights/I Do Love You (as Rudies Fanatics)	12
68	Fab FAB 71	Mighty Meaty/Go (as Rudies Fanatics)	12
69	Doctor Bird DB 1301	Sin Thing/What's Your Name	15
69	Doctor Bird DB 1302	Boss Sound/RECO & RUDIES: Peace	20
69	Fab FAB 104	Brixton Market/Rudie's Joy	10
70	Pama PM 789	Give Peace A Chance/Theme From She	8
70	Trojan TR 7798	Patches/Split	10
71	Spinning Wheel SW 106	My Sweet Lord/Devil's Lead Soup	20

(see also Freddie Notes, Sonny, Binns & Rudies, Rico, Dandy, Owen & Dandy, Downtown All Stars, Desmond Riley)

RUDIMENTARY PENI

81	Outer Himalayan OH 003	RUDIMENTARY PENI (EP, A4 foldout p/s with booklet, later 14" x 7")	12/10
82	Crass 211984/2	FARCE (EP, initially in 21" x 14" foldout black & white p/s)	10/7
83	Corpus Christi CHRISTITS 6	DEATH CHURCH (LP)	14
80s	Corpus Christi	CACOPHONY (LP, with booklet)	15

(see also Magits)

RUD(D)Y (Grant) & SKETTO (Rich)

62	Dice CC 5	Summer Is Just Around The Corner/Nothing Like Time (as Ruddy & Sketto & Reco's All Stars)	18
62	Dice CC 7	Little Schoolgirl/Hush Baby (as Ruddy & Sketto & Baron Twist & His Knights)	18
62	Dice CC 10	Mr Postman/Christmas Blues (as Rudy & Sketto with Laurel's Group)	18
63	Dice CC 16	Hold The Fire/Good Morning Mr Jones	18
63	Dice CC 19	Never Set You Free/Brothers And Sisters	15
63	Blue Beat BB 198	Was It Me/Minna Don't Deceive Me	15
64	Blue Beat BB 208	Show Me The Way To Go Home/Let Me Dream	15
64	Blue Beat BB 230	Ten Thousand Miles From Home/I Need Someone (as Ruddy & Sketto)	18
64	Blue Beat BB 252	I Love You/If Only Tomorrow	20
65	Blue Beat BB 297	See What You Done/Heart's Desire (as Ruddy & Sketto)	15
65	Blue Beat BB 310	Oh Dolly/You're Mine (as Ruddy & Sketto)	18

(see also Ruddy & Sketto)

RUEFREX

80	Good Vibrations GOT 8	One By One/Cross The Line/Don't Panic (foldover p/s, 2 different designs)	each 12
83	Kabuki KAR 7	Capital Letters/April Fool (p/s)	5

RAY RUFF & CHECKMATES

64	London HLU 9889	I Took A Liking To You/A Fool Again	25

RUFFIANS

71	Banana BA 359	Room Full Of Tears (actually by Sensations)/Black Soul (actually "Black And White — Version" by Riley's Allstars)	12

(see Al Brown, Sensations)

BRUCE RUFFIN

69	Songbird SB 1002	Long About Now/Come See About Me (as Bruce Ruffin & Temptations)	18
69	Trojan TR 7704	Dry Up Your Tears/BEVERLEY'S ALLSTARS: One Way Street	8
70	Trojan TR 7737	I'm The One/Who's Gonna Be Your Man?	8
70	Trojan TR 7776	Cecelia/BEVERLEY ALL STARS: Stand Up	5
70	Summit SUM 8509	O-o-h Child/Bitterness Of Life	8
71	Summit SUM 8516	Candida/Are You Ready	5
71	Trojan TR 7814	Rain/THE PYRAMIDS: Geronimo (B-side actually by Pyramids)	8
71	Trojan TR 7814	Rain/THE PYRAMIDS: Off Limits (B-side actually by Aquarians)	8
71	Trojan TR 7832	One Big Happy Family (Parts 1 & 2)	5
72	Trojan TRM 9000	Songs Of Peace/You Are The Best/We Can Make It	18
71	Trojan TRL 23	RAIN (LP)	12

(see also Bruce Downer)

DAVID RUFFIN

69	Tamla Motown TMG 689	My Whole World Ended (The Moment You Left Me)/I've Got To Find Myself A Brand New Baby	10
69	Tamla Motown TMG 711	I've Lost Everything I've Ever Loved/We'll Have A Good Thing Going On	10
76	Tamla Motown TMG 1022	Heavy Love/Me And Rock And Roll Are Here To Stay	6
69	T. Motown (S)TML 11118	MY WHOLE WORLD ENDED (LP)	40
70	T. Motown (S)TML 11139	FEELIN' GOOD (LP)	40
73	Tamla Motown STML 11228	DAVID RUFFIN (LP)	20

(see also Temptations)

JIMMY RUFFIN

66	Tamla Motown TMG 577	What Becomes Of The Broken-Hearted?/Baby I've Got It (DJ copy = £85)	15
67	Tamla Motown TMG 593	I've Passed This Way Before/Tomorrow's Tears (DJ = £60)	15
67	Tamla Motown TMG 603	Gonna Give Her All The Love I Got/World So Wide, Nowhere To Hide (DJ copy = £50)	10
67	Tamla Motown TMG 617	Don't You Miss Me A Little Bit Baby/I Want Her Love (DJ = £40)	15
68	Tamla Motown TMG 649	I'll Say Forever My Love/Everybody Needs Love (DJ = £45)	10
68	Tamla Motown TMG 664	Don't Let Him Take Your Love From Me/Lonely Lonely Man Am I (DJ = £35)	10
69	Tamla Motown TMG 703	I've Passed This Way Before/Tomorrow's Tears	6
70	Tamla Motown TMG 726	Farewell Is A Lonely Sound/If You Let Me, I Know I Can	6
70	Tamla Motown TMG 740	I'll Say Forever My Love/Everybody Needs Love	6
70	Tamla Motown TMG 753	It's Wonderful (To Be Loved By You)/Maria (You Were The Only One)	6
71	Tamla Motown TMG 767	Let's Say Goodbye Tomorrow/Living In A world I Created For Myself	6
71	Tamla Motown TMG 784	On The Way Out (On The Way In)/Honey Come Back	8
67	T. Motown (S)TML 11048	THE JIMMY RUFFIN WAY (LP)	60
69	T. Motown (S)TML 11106	RUFF 'N' READY (LP)	45

70	T. Motown STML 11161	JIMMY RUFFIN … FOREVER (LP)	30
73	Polydor 2383 240	JIMMY RUFFIN (LP)	15
74	Sounds Superb SPR 90041	I'VE PASSED THIS WAY BEFORE (LP)	15

(see also Council Collective)

JIMMY & DAVID RUFFIN
71	Tamla Motown STML 11176	I AM MY BROTHER'S KEEPER (LP)	25

(see also David Ruffin, Temptations)

RUFFNECK
93	Represent REPREC 1	Radford(You Get Me)/You And Me (12")	18

RUFUS
74	ABC ABC 4022	You Got The Love/Rags To Rufus	5
75	ABC ABC 4038	Stop On By/Rufusized	5
75	ABC ABC 4055	Once You Get Started/Right Is Right (p/s)	5
84	Warner Bros RCKT 1	Ain't Got You/Stop On By/Don't Go To Strangers (12", with Chaka Khan)	8
75	ABC ABCL 5151	RUFUS WITH CHAKA KHAN (LP)	12

RUGBYS
69	Polydor 56781	You And I/Stay With Me	45
70	Polydor 56789	Wendegahl The Warlock/Light	20

PETE RUGOLO (& DIAMONDS)
60	Warner Bros WM 4001	BEHIND BRIGITTE BARDOT — COOL SOUNDS FROM HER HOT SCENES (LP, also stereo WS 8001)	25

(see also Diamonds, Patti Page)

RULERS
66	Rio R 105	Don't Be A Rude Boy/Be Good	15
66	Rio R 107	Copasetic/Too Late	20
67	Rio R 132	Wrong 'em Boyo/Why Don't You Change	25
67	Rio R 135	Well Covered/CARL DAWKINS: Help Time	15
67	Rio R 138	Be Mine/CARL DAWKINS: Hot And Sticky	15
69	Trojan TR 696	Got To Be Free/Situation	12

RUMBLE
70	Warner Bros WB 8011	Rich Man, Poor Man/Let Me Down	5

RUMBLERS
63	London HLD 9684	Boss/I Don't Need You No More	35
65	King KG 1021	Soulful Jerk/Hey Did A Da Da	60
63	London RE-D 1396	BOSSOUNDS (EP)	150+
63	London HA-D/SH-D 8081	BOSSOUNDS (LP, mono/stereo)	100/120

RUMPLESTILTSKIN
70	Bell BLL 1101	Squadron Leader Johnson/Rumplestiltskin	8
71	Bell BLL 1157	Wimoweh/Through My Looking Glass	8
70	Bell SBLL 130	RUMPLESTILTSKIN (LP, gatefold sleeve)	60

(see also Clem Cattini)

RUNAWAYS
76	Mercury 6167 392	Cherry Bomb/Blackmail	10
77	Mercury 6167 493	Queens Of Noise/Born To Be Bad	6
77	Mercury 6167 587	School Days/Wasted (p/s)	8
79	Cherry Red CHERRY 8	Right Now/Black Leather (p/s)	12
76	Mercury 9100 029	THE RUNAWAYS (LP, with gatefold sleeve & lyric sheet; U.S. pressing, with cat. no. SRM 1 1090, in U.K. sleeve)	15
77	Mercury 9100 032	QUEENS OF NOISE (LP, with lyric sheet)	15
77	Mercury 9100 046	LIVE IN JAPAN (LP)	12
77	Mercury 9100 099	WAITIN' FOR THE NIGHT (LP)	12
79	Cherry Red ARED 38	AND NOW … THE RUNAWAYS (LP, 1,000 copies each in yellow, red, blue & orange vinyl)	each 25
80	Cherry Red BRED 9	FLAMING SCHOOLGIRLS (LP)	15

(see also Joan Jett, Lita Ford & Ozzy Osbourne)

RUNESTAFF
85	FM VHF 5	Road To Ruin/Last Chances (p/s)	7
85	FM VHF 17	Do It!/Runestaff (no p/s)	6
85	Heavy Metal HMRLP 26	RUNESTAFF (LP)	15

RUNNING MAN
72	RCA Neon NE 11	THE RUNNING MAN (LP)	125

(see also Ray Russell Quartet, Mouse)

RUNRIG
83	Ridge RRS 103	Loch Lomond/Tuireadh Iain Ruaida (p/s)	30
84	Simple SIM 4	Dance Called America/Na H Uain A's T-Earrach (p/s)	25
84	Simple 12 SIM 4	Dance Called America/Na H Uain A's T-Earrach/Ribhinn (12", p/s)	20
84	Simple SIM 8	Skye/Hey Mandu (p/s)	15
86	Ridge RRS 006	The Work Song/This Time Of Year (p/s)	15
86	Ridge RRS 007	Alba/Worker For The Wind (p/s)	12
88	Chrysalis CHS 3284	Protect And Survive/Hearts Of Olden Glory (live) (p/s)	10
88	Chrysalis CHS 12 3284	Protect And Survive/Hearts Of Olden Glory (live)/Protect And Survive (live) (12", p/s)	12
88	Chrysalis CHSCD 3284	Protect And Survive/Hearts Of Olden Glory (live)/Protect And Survive (live) (CD)	12
89	Chrysalis CHS 3404	News From Heaven/Chi Mi'n Tir (p/s)	5
89	Chrysalis CHS 12 3404	News From Heaven/Chi Mi'n Tir/The Times They Are A'Changing (12", p/s)	8
89	Chrysalis CHS 12T 3404	News From Heaven/Chi Mi'n Tir/The Times They Are A'Changing (12", picture disc)	20
89	Chrysalis CHSCD 3404	News From Heaven/Chi Mi'n Tir/The Times They Are A'Changing (CD)	20

89	Chrysalis CHS 3451	Every River/This Time Of Year (p/s)	15
89	Chrysalis CHS 12 3451	Every River/This Time Of Year/Our Earth Was Once Green (12", p/s)	15
89	Chrysalis CHSCD 3451	Every River/This Time Of Year/Our Earth Was Once Green (CD)	15
90	Chrysalis CHSCD 3594	CAPTURE THE HEART EP: Stepping Down The Glory Road/Satellite Flood/ Harvest Moon/The Apple Came Down (10", p/s)	15
90	Chrysalis CHSCD 1235941	CAPTURE THE HEART EP: Stepping Down The Glory Road/Satellite Flood/ Harvest Moon/The Apple Came Down (12", p/s)	15
90	Chrysalis CHSCD 3594	CAPTURE THE HEART EP: Stepping Down The Glory Road/Satellite Flood/ Harvest Moon/The Apple Came Down (CD)	15
90	Chrysalis CHS 38051	Flower Of The West/Ravenscraig/Ch Mi'n Greamhradh (p/s)	10
90	Chrysalis CHSCD 3805	Flower Of The West/Ravenscraig/Ch Mi'n Greamhradh/ Harvest Moon (CD, digipak)	12
91	Chrysalis CHS 3754	HEARTHAMMER EP	8
91	Chrysalis CHSG 123754	HEARTHAMMER EP (12", gatefold p/s, with booklet)	12
91	Chrysalis CHS 123805	FLOWER OF THE WEST EP (12", numbered box set, with poster, discography & sticker)	12
93	Chrysalis CHSS 3952	Wonderful/April Come She Will (limited edition blue vinyl)	6
93	Chrysalis CHS 3975	THE GREATEST FLAME (EP, numbered postcard pack)	8
94	Chrysalis CHS P 5018	THIS TIME OF YEAR EP (12", poster/calendar sleeve)	12
78	Neptune NA 105	RUNRIG PLAY GAELIC (LP)	18
79	Ridge RR 001	THE HIGHLAND CONNECTION (LP)	15
81	Ridge RR 002	RECOVERY (LP, with inner)	20
91	Chrysalis CHR 18582	BIG WHEEL (LP, with inner)	12

RUNS
| 80 | Carrere CAR 139 | Bun In The Oven (no p/s) | 40 |

RUNT
| 71 | Bearsville K 44505 | RUNT (LP) | 15 |
| 71 | Bearsville K 44506 | RUNT — THE BALLAD OF TODD RUNDGREN (LP) | 15 |

(see also Todd Rundgren, Utopia, Nazz)

R.U.1.2.
| 78 | SRTS/78/CUS 131 | She's Gone/Purely Physical/Teenage Girl (p/s) | 20 |

RUN 229
| 80 | MM JR 7040S | Soho/Dance/In This Day And Age | 40 |

RUPERT'S PEOPLE
67	Columbia DB 8226	Reflections Of Charles Brown/Hold On	55
67	Columbia DB 8278	A Prologue To A Magic World/Dream In My Mind	70
68	Columbia DB 8362	I Can Show You/I've Got The Love	100

(see also Renaissance, Fleur-De-Lys, Gun, Sweet Feeling)

RUSH (Australia)
| 67 | Decca F 12614 | Happy/Once Again | 7 |
| 67 | Decca F 12635 | Make Mine Music/Enjoy It | 8 |

RUSH (Canada)
77	Mercury RUSH 7	Closer To The Heart/Bastille Day/Temples Of Syrinx (metallic blue or beige labels)	18/8
78	Mercury RUSH 12	Closer To The Heart/Anthem/Bastille Day/Temples Of Syrinx (12", p/s)	10
80	Mercury RADIO 7	Spirit Of Radio/The Trees (p/s)	10
80	Mercury RADIO 12	Spirit Of Radio/The Trees/Working Man (12", p/s)	10
81	Mercury VITAL 7	Vital Signs/In The Mood (p/s)	8
81	Mercury VITAL 12	Vital Signs/In The Mood/A Passage To Bangkok/Circumstances (12", p/s)	8
81	Mercury EXIT 7	Tom Sawyer (live)/A Passage To Bangkok (live) (p/s)	6
81	Mercury EXIT 12	Tom Sawyer (live)/A Passage To Bangkok (live)/Red Barchetta (live) (12", p/s)	8
81	Mercury RUSH 1	Closer To The Heart (live)/The Trees (live) (p/s)	5
82	Mercury RUSH 8	New World Man/Vital Signs (live) (p/s)	5
82	Mercury RUSH 812	New World Man/Vital Signs (live)/Freewill (live) (12", p/s)	15
82	Mercury RUSH P9	Subdivisions/Red Barchetta (live) (picture disc)	10
82	Mercury RUSH 10 PD	Countdown/New World Man (shaped picture disc)	12
82	Mercury RUSH 1012	Countdown/New World Man/Spirit Of Radio (live)/Interview Excerpts (12", p/s)	10
84	Vertigo RUSH 11	The Body Electric/The Analog Kid (p/s)	5
84	Vertigo RUSH 1110	The Body Electric/The Analog Kid/Distant Early Warning (10", p/s, red vinyl)	12
84	Vertigo RUSH 1112	The Body Electric/The Analog Kid/Distant Early Warning (12", p/s)	50
78	Mercury 9100 059	HEMISPHERES (LP, mispressing, both sides play Side 1)	50
80	Mercury 9100 071	PERMANENT WAVES (LP, with newspaper)	12
85	Vertigo VERHP 31	POWER WINDOWS (LP, picture disc, with discography on sleeve)	20

(see also McKenzie Doug & Bob, Max Webster Band)

MERRILEE RUSH & TURNABOUTS
68	Bell BLL 1013	Angel Of The Morning/Reap What You Sow	6
68	Bell BLL 1026	That Kind Of Woman/Sunshine And Roses	6
69	Bell BLL 1041	Reach Out I'll Be There/Love Street	10
68	Bell MBLL/SBLL 109	MERRILEE RUSH (LP)	20

OTIS RUSH
66	Vocalion V-P 9260	Homework/I Have To Laugh (DJ copy = £85)	60
69	Blue Horizon 57-3159	All Your Love/Double Trouble	25
68	Blue Horizon 7-63222	THIS ONE'S A GOOD UN (LP)	85
69	Atlantic 588 188	MOURNING IN THE MORNING (LP)	44
70s	Atlantic K 40495	MOURNING IN THE MORNING (LP, reissue)	15
70	Python KM 3	GROANING THE BLUES (LP)	45
76	Delmark DS 63?	COLD DAY IN HELL (LP)	20
78	Sonet SNTF756	TROUBLES, TROUBLES (LP)	15

TOM RUSH
67	Elektra EKSN 45004	Who Do You Love/On The Road Again	8
67	Elektra EKSN 45015	On The Road Again/Love's Made A Fool Of You	8
68	Elektra EKSN 45025	No Regrets/Shadow Dream Song	7
68	Elektra EKSN 45032	Something In The Way She Moves/Rockport Sunday	8
66	Xtra XTRA 5024	BLUES, SONGS & BALLADS (LP)	25
66	Xtra XTRA 5053	I GOT A MIND TO RAMBLE (LP)	25
67	Elektra EKL 308	TAKE A LITTLE WALK WITH ME (LP, also stereo EKS 7308)	35
68	Elektra EKL 4018	THE CIRCLE GAME (also stereo EKS 74018) (LP, 1st issue black 'Elektra' on red label, 2nd issue white 'Elektra' on redder label.)	25/14
69	Elektra EKL 4062	CLASSIC RUSH (LP, red label, also stereo EKS 74062)	25
70	CBS 63940	TOM RUSH (LP)	15
70	CBS 64268	WRONG END OF A RAINBOW (LP)	12
71	Elektra EKS 74062	CLASSIC RUSH (LP, reissue, 'butterfly' label)	12

JIMMY RUSHING (with ADA MOORE & BUCK CLAYTON)
57	Philips BBE 12150	CAT MEETS CHICK (EP, as Jimmy Rushing, Buck Clayton & Ada Moore)	22
57	Vanguard EPP 14003	LITTLE JIMMY ALL STAR BAND (EP)	15
57	Parlophone GEP 8597	JIMMY RUSHING (EP)	15
58	Parlophone GEP 8695	THE WAY I FEEL (EP)	15
63	Ember EMB 4523	JIMMY RUSHING (EP)	15
55	Vanguard PPT 12002	SINGS THE BLUES (10" LP)	45
57	Vanguard PPT 12016	SHOWCASE (10" LP)	40
57	Philips BBL 7105	CAT MEETS CHICK (LP, with Ada Moore & Buck Clayton)	22
57	Philips BBL 7166	THE JAZZ ODYSSEY OF JAMES RUSHING ESQ (LP, with Buck Clayton)	22
58	Vanguard PPL 11008	IF THIS AIN'T THE BLUES (LP)	18
58	Philips BBL 7252	LITTLE JIMMY RUSHING AND THE BIG BRASS (LP, also stereo SBBL 524)	20
60	Philips BBL 7360	RUSHING LULLABIES (LP)	18
61	Philips BBL 7484	THE SMITH GIRLS — BESSIE, CLARA (LP, also stereo SBBL 631)	20/25
66	Ace Of Hearts AH 119	BLUES I LOVE TO SING (LP)	15
67	Golden Guinea GGL 0384	FIVE FEET OF SOUL (LP)	12
67	Fontana FJL 405	LISTEN TO THE BLUES (LP)	15
67	HMV CLP/CSD 3632	EVERYDAY I HAVE THE BLUES (LP)	15
71	Vanguard VRS 8513	IF THIS AIN'T THE BLUES (LP, reissue)	12
72	Vanguard VRS 8518	GOING TO CHICAGO (LP)	12

(see also Count Basie, Dave Brubeck, Buck Clayton)

JIMMY RUSHING/CHAMPION JACK DUPREE
64	Ember CJS 800	TWO SHADES OF BLUE (LP, 1 side each)	30

(see also Champion Jack Dupree)

BARBARA RUSKIN
65	Piccadilly 7N 35224	Halfway To Paradise/I Can't Believe In Miracles	10
65	Piccadilly 7N 35246	You Can't Blame A Girl For Trying/No More To Fall	12
66	Piccadilly 7N 35274	Well How Does It Feel/Wishing Your Life Away	10
66	Piccadilly 7N 35296	Song Without End/Love Came Too Late	10
66	Piccadilly 7N 35328	Light Of Love/At Times Like These Mama	10
67	Parlophone R 5571	Take It Easy/Sunshowers	7
67	Parlophone R 5593	Euston Station/Hear That Telephone	7
67	Parlophone R 5642	Come Into My Arms Again/Just A Little While Longer	10
68	Parlophone R 5685	Is This Another Way/The Night Of The Spanish Tightrope Walker	5
68	President PT 217	Pawnbroker Pawnbroker/Almost	25
69	President PT 238	Gentlemen Please/24th Of July	5
69	President PT 261	Hail Love/Lady Of Leisure	5
70	President PT 280	A Little Bit Of This (And A Little Bit Of That)/Where Are We	5

RUSKORA
79	Fisher FISH1	Heaven Is Hell On Earth/Red Opera	7
80	Fisher FISH 2	Shades/Crisis	7

LONNIE RUSS
62	Fontana 267263 TF	Something Old Something New/My Wife Can't Cook	7

THANE RUSSAL (& THREE)
66	CBS 202049	Security/Your Love Is Burning Me (some with p/s)	250/125
66	CBS 202403	Drop Everything And Run/I Need You (solo)	125

ANDY RUSSELL
58	RCA RCA 1076	Seven Daughters/A Certain Smile (78 rpm = £8)	6

BOBBY RUSSELL
68	Bell BLL 1019	Dusty/I Made You This Way	6
68	Bell BLL 1034	1432 Franklin Pike Circle Hero/Let's Talk About It	6
69	Bell BLL 1050	Carlie/Ain't Society Great?	6
71	United Artists UP 35283	Saturday Morning Confusion/Little Ole Song About Love	5

BRENDA RUSSELL
79	A&M AMSP 7515	In The Thick Of It/So Good So Right (12", p/s)	10
79	A&M AMLJ 739	BRENDA RUSSELL (LP)	12

CONNIE RUSSELL
54	Capitol CL 14171	No One But You/One Arabian Night	18
54	Capitol CL 14197	Love Me/Papa's Puttin' The Pressure On	15
55	Capitol CL 14214	Foggy Night In San Francisco/This Is My Love	15
55	Capitol CL 14236	Ayuh, Ayuh/I'm Making Believe	22
55	Capitol CL 14246	Snow Dreams/Green Fire	10
55	Capitol CL 14268	Farewell, Farewell/The Magnificent Matador	10
57	Capitol CL 14676	All Of You/This Is My Love	10

DAVE RUSSELL
66	Columbia DB 7828	When I Grow Too Old To Dream/All The Tears In The World	5

(see also Dave & Diamonds)

DOROTHY RUSSELL

MINT VALUE £

| 71 | Duke Reid DR 2524 | You're The One I Love/(Version) | 6 |

JANE RUSSELL

51	London L 956	Dear Dear Dear/I Can't Get Started With You (78)	10
51	London L 969	Five Little Miles From San Berdoo/You'll Know (78)	10
53	Columbia SCM 5043	Please Do It Again/Two Sleepy People (B-side with Bob Lowery) (78 rpm = £14)	22
53	MGM MGM 662	A Little Girl From Little Rock/When Love Goes Wrong (78)	25
53	MGM MGM 664	Bye Bye Baby/Ain't There Anyone Here For Love? (78)	20
56	Capitol CL 14590	If You Wanna See Mamie Tonight/Keep Your Eyes On The Hands	10
59	MGM MGM-EP 702	JANE RUSSELL (EP)	40

JANET RUSSELL

| 88 | Harbourtown HAR 003 | GATHERING THE FRAGMENTS (LP) | 20 |

JOHN RUSSELL/RICHARD COLDMAN

| 79 | Incus INCUS 31 | HOME COOKING/GUITAR SOLOS (LP, 1 side each) | 50 |

JOHNNY RUSSELL

| 60 | MGM MGM 1074 | Lonesome Boy/Baby Won't You Tell Me So | 10 |

KEITH RUSSELL

| 65 | Piccadilly 7N 35235 | People Get Ready/Paradise | 7 |

LEON RUSSELL

| 65 | Dot DS 16771 | Everybody's Talkin' 'Bout The Young/It's Alright With Me | 10 |

(see also Asylum Choir)

PEE WEE RUSSELL & RUBY BRAFF

| 50 | Melodisc MEL 1137 | Baby Won't You Please Come Home/Dinah (78) | 7 |

RAY RUSSELL QUARTET

68	CBS Realm 52586	TURN CIRCLE (LP)	30
69	CBS Realm 52663	DRAGON HILL (LP)	30
71	RCA SF 8214	JUNE 11TH 1971 (LP)	22
71	CBS 64271	RITES AND RITUALS (LP)	35
73	Black Lion BLP 12100	SECRET ASYLUM (LP)	15

(see also Running Man, Mouse, Chopyn)

ROLAND RUSSELL

| 68 | Nu Beat NB 019 | Rhythm Hips/RHYTHM FLAMES: Deltone Special | 12 |

ROSALIND RUSSELL & EDITH ADAMS

| 55 | Brunswick 05406 | Ohio/Little Bit Of Love | 5 |

RUSSELL FAMILY

| 75 | Topic 12TS 251 | OF DOOLIN COUNTY CLARE (LP, with insert) | 12 |

RUSSIAN ROULETTE

| 84 | Red Bus RBUS 86 | Come Into My Room/Lyin' Again (p/s) | 5 |

(see also Paul King, Mungo Jerry)

CHARLIE RUSSO

| 63 | Stateside SS 165 | Preacherman/Teresa | 8 |

RUSTIKS

| 64 | Decca F 11960 | What A Memory Can Do/Hello Anne | 10 |
| 65 | Decca F 12059 | I'm Not The Loving Kind/Can't You See | 8 |

RUSTLERS

| 61 | Pye 7N 15398 | High Strung/Matter Of Who | 12 |

RUSTY & DOUG (Kershaw)

59	Oriole CB 1510	Hey Mae!/Why Don't You Love Me (78 rpm = £50+)	150
59	London HL 8972	I Like You (Like This)/Dancing Shoes (78 rpm = £30+)	30
62	Polydor NH 66970	Hey Mae!/Sweet Thing	40
62	Fontana 267 238 TF	Cajun Joe (The Ballad Of The Bayou)/Sweet Sweet Girl To Me	15

(see also Doug Kershaw)

RUSTY HARNESS

| 70 | Ember EMB S 283 | Ain't Gonna Get Married/Goodbye (some in p/s) | 10/5 |
| 73 | Ember SE 8024 | DISCOTHEQUE EXPLOSION (LP) | 12 |

RUSTY NAIL

| 60s | Hi-Fi MEP 3093 | RUSTY NAIL (EP, some in p/s) | 100/40 |

RUTH

| 67 | Columbia DB 8216 | Leaf In The Wind/Society's Child | 7 |
| 68 | Columbia DB 8386 | Cherish/Until It's Time For You To Go | 7 |

MIKE RUTHERFORD

| 80 | Charisma CB 364 | Time And Time Again/At The End Of The Day (p/s, correct B-side & label) | 5 |
| 80 | Charisma CB 364 | Time And Time Again/Overnight Job (p/s, with new label on B-side, credits & plays "Overnight Job") | 5 |

(see also Genesis, Mike & Mechanics)

RUTHLESS RAP ASSASINS

| 87 | White (Murdertone) AMC001 | We Don't Care/Kiss AMC (12") | 15 |

RUTLES

| 78 | Warner Bros K 17125 | I Must Be In Love/Cheese And Onions/With A Girl Like You (p/s) | 5 |
| 78 | Warner Bros K 17180 | Let's Be Natural/Piggy In The Middle | 6 |

(see also Dirk & Stig, Neil Innes, Monty Python, Beach Boys, Patto)

RUTS (D.C.)

| 79 | People Unite SJP 795 | In A Rut/H-Eyes (1,000 only, black-ringed label) | 25 |
| 79 | People Unite RUT 1 | In A Rut/H-Eyes (repressing) | 8 |

79	Virgin VS 271	Babylon's Burning/Society (p/s)	8
79	Virgin VS 298	Jah War/I Ain't Sofisticated (p/s)	5
80	RSO RSO 71	Babylon's Burning/XTC: Take This Town (p/s)	6
81	Virgin VS 396	Different View/Formula Eyes (p/s, as Ruts D.C.)	5
82	Bohemian BO 2	Whatever We Do/Push Yourself — Make It Work (p/s, as Ruts D.C.)	5
83	Bohemian BO 3	Weak Heart/Militant (white label, with paper insert; as Ruts D.C., promo only)	15
83	Bohemian BO 4	Stepping Bondage/Lobotomy/Rich Bitch (p/s)	12
87	Strange Fruit SFPSC 011	PEEL SESSION 14.5.79 (EP, cassette)	5
88	Virgin OVED 80	THE CRACK (LP, stickered sleeve)	15

(see also Laurel Aitken, Typhoons, Pete Zear)

BARRY RYAN (& MAJORITY)

68	MGM MGM 1423	Goodbye/I'm So Sad	10
68	MGM MGM 1442	Eloise/Love I Almost Found You (as Barry Ryan & Majority)	10
68	MGM MGM 1464	Love Is Love/I'll Be On My Way Dear	10
69	Polydor 56348	The Hunt/No Living Without Her	10
70	Polydor 56370	Magical Spiel/Caroline	10
70	Polydor 2001 035	Kitsch/Give Me A Sign	10
71	Polydor 2001 154	It Is Written/Annabella	10
72	Polydor 2001 335	From My Head To My Toes/Alimony Money Blues	10
69	MGM MGM-C(S) 8106	SINGS PAUL RYAN (LP)	35
69	Polydor 583 067	BARRY RYAN (LP)	22

(see also Paul & Barry Ryan)

CATHY RYAN

53	MGM SP 1051	Show Me The Way To Go Home/If I Had You	7

(see also Art Mooney)

KRIS RYAN (& QUESTIONS)

64	Mercury MF 818	Miss Ann/She Told Me Lies (as Kris Ryan & Questions)	10
64	Mercury MF 832	Don't Play That Song/If You Don't Come Back	12
64	Mercury MF 852	Marie Marie/I've Had Enough Of You Baby	10
65	Mercury MF 877	Tell Me How/She Belongs To Me	10
65	Mercury 10024 MCE	ON THE RIGHT TRACK (EP, as Kris Ryan & Questions)	30

MARION RYAN

57	Pye N 15105	Ding Dong Rock-A-Billy Wedding/That's Happiness (78)	6
58	Pye 7N 15121	Love Me Forever/Make The Man Love Me	6
58	Pye 7N 15130	Oh Oh, I'm Falling In Love Again/Always And Forever	6
58	Pye 7N 15138	Stairway Of Love/I Need You (78 rpm, Pye N 15157 = £8)	6
58	Pye 7N 15157	The World Goes Around And Around/Please Don't Say Goodnight	5
58	Pye 7NSR 15157	The World Goes Around And Around/Please Don't Say Goodnight (stereo)	10
59	Pye 7N 15184	Wait For Me/Jeepers Creepers (78 rpm = £10)	5
59	Pye 7N 15200	Jo-Jo The Dog-Faced Boy/Doin' What Comes Naturally (78 rpm = £10)	6
59	Pye 7N 15216	Too Much/Promise Me (78 rpm = £8)	5
60	Columbia DB 4448	Sixteen Reasons/Mangos	7
60	Columbia DB 4550	It's You That I Love/Somebody	5
62	Columbia DB 4857	No Love But Your Love/An Occasional Man (A-side with John Barry & Orch.)	6
68	Philips BF 1721	Better Use Your Head/The Seasons Change	30
57	Pye Nixa NEP 24041	THAT RYAN GIRL! (EP)	25
58	Pye NEP 24079	MARION RYAN HIT PARADE (EP)	30
59	Pye N(S)PL 18030	A LADY LOVES! (LP, mono/stereo)	60/80

(see also Ray Ellington, Gary Miller)

PAT RYAN

77	Folk Heritage FHR 094	LEA BOY'S LASSIE (LP)	15

PAUL & BARRY RYAN

65	Decca F 12260	Don't Bring Me Your Heartaches/To Remind Me Of Your Love	8
66	Decca F 12319	Have Pity On The Boy/There You Go	8
66	Decca F 12391	I Love Her/Gotta Go Out To Work	8
66	Decca F 12445	I Love How You Love Me/Baby I'm Sorry	8
66	Decca F 12494	Have You Ever Loved Somebody?/I'll Tell You Later	8
66	Decca F 12520	Missy, Missy/Rainbow Weather	8
67	Decca F 12567	Keep It Out Of Sight/Who Told You?	8
67	Decca F 12633	Claire/I'll Make It Worth Your While	8
67	MGM MGM 1354	Heartbreaker/Night Time	8
68	MGM MGM 1385	Pictures Of Today/Madrigal	8
67	Decca LK 4878	THE RYANS — TWO OF A KIND (LP)	40
68	MGM MGM-C(S) 8081	PAUL AND BARRY RYAN (LP)	35

(see also Barry Ryan)

PHIL RYAN & CRESCENTS

64	Columbia DB 7406	Mary Don't You Weep/Yes I Will	8
65	Columbia DB 7574	Gypsy Woman/Be Honest With Yourself	20

BOBBY RYDELL

59	Top Rank JAR 181	Kissin' Time/You'll Never Tame Me (78 rpm = £85)	15
59	Top Rank JAR 227	We Got Love/I Dig Girls	12
60	Columbia DB 4429	Wild One/Little Bitty Girl	8
60	Columbia DB 4471	Swingin' School/Ding-A-Ling	8
60	Columbia DB 4495	Volare/I'd Do It Again	10
60	Columbia DB 4545	Sway/Groovy Tonight	8
61	Columbia DB 4600	Good Time Baby/Cherie	8
61	Columbia DB 4651	Don't Be Afraid/That Old Black Magic	8
61	Columbia DB 4690	The Fish/The Third House	8
61	Columbia DB 4731	I Wanna Thank You/The Door To Paradise	9

Bobby RYDELL

62	Columbia DB 4785	I've Got Bonnie/Lose Her	8
62	Columbia DB 4858	I'll Never Dance Again/Gee, It's Wonderful.	8
63	Cameo Parkway C 108	Forget Him/Hey Ev'rybody (some in p/s)	15/10
60	Top Rank JKP 2059	LOVINGEST (EP)	50
63	Cameo Parkway CPE 551	SWAY WITH BOBBY RYDELL (EP)	30
63	Cameo Parkway CPE 553	BOBBY RYDELL (EP)	25
63	Summit LSE 2036	BEST OF BOBBY RYDELL (EP)	10
60	Columbia 33SX 1243	WILD ONE (LP)	60
61	Columbia 33SX 1308	SINGS AND SWINGS (LP).	22
61	Columbia 33SX 1352	SALUTES "THE GREAT ONES" (LP)	25
62	Columbia 33SX 1425	RYDELL AT THE COPA (LP)	50
62	Cameo Parkway C 1019	ALL THE HITS (LP)	20
63	Cameo Parkway C 1040	ALL THE HITS VOL. 2 (LP)	20
63	Cameo Parkway C 1043	BYE BYE BIRDIE (LP)	15
63	Cameo Parkway C 1055	WILD (WOOD) DAYS (LP)	25
65	Capitol T 2281	SOMEBODY LOVES YOU (LP)	20

(see also Chubby Checker & Bobby Rydell)

RUTH RYDELL
54	London HL 8016	On The Carousel/Someone Is Crying (78)	8

RUTHLESS RAP ASSASSINS
90	Sycopate 12SY35	Just Mellow/Here Today... Here Tomorrow (12")	8

FREDDIE RYDER
65	Mercury MF 864	To Get Your Love Back/A Little Thing Called Love	6
65	Mercury MF 879	Some Kind Of Wonderful/Slow Down	12
65	Mercury MF 935	Man Of The Moment/My Block	10
68	Columbia DB 8335	Shadows (I Can't See You)/Airport	6
68	Columbia DB 8427	Worst That Could Happen/World Of My Own	6

(see also Freddie Self, Trends)

MAL RYDER (& SPIRITS)
63	Decca F 11669	Cry Baby/Take Over (as Mal Ryder & Spirits)	20
64	Vocalion V 9219	See The Funny Little Clown/Slow Down	60
64	Piccadilly 7N 35209	Your Friend/Forget It (as Mal Ryder & Spirits)	30
65	Piccadilly 7N 35234	Lonely Room/Tell Your Friend	22

(see also Mal & Primitives)

MITCH RYDER (& DETROIT WHEELS)
66	Stateside SS 481	Jenny Take A Ride/Baby Jane	15
66	Stateside SS 498	Little Latin Lupe Lu/I Hope	15
66	Stateside SS 521	Breakout/I Need Help (DJ copy = £100)	50
66	Stateside SS 549	Devil With A Blue Dress On (Medley)/I Had It Made	15
67	Stateside SS 596	Sock It To Me Baby/I Never Had It Better	20
67	Stateside SS 2023	Too Many Fish In The Sea — Three Little Fishes/One Grain Of Sand	20
67	Stateside SS 2037	Joy/I'd Rather Go To Jail (solo)	8
67	Stateside SS 2063	What Now My Love/Blessing In Disguise (solo)	25
68	Stateside SS 2075	You Are My Sunshine/Wild Child (solo)	7
68	Stateside SS 2096	Personality/Chantilly Lace/I Make A Fool Of Myself (solo)	7
69	Dot DOT 129	Sugar Bee/I Believe (There Must Be Someone)	6
66	Stateside SE 1039	RIDIN' (EP)	50
66	Stateside S(S)L 10178	TAKE A RIDE ... (LP)	45
67	Stateside S(S)L 10189	BREAKOUT. . . !! (LP)	50
67	Stateside S(S)L 10204	SOCK IT TO ME (LP)	40
68	Stateside S(S)L 10229	WHAT NOW MY LOVE (LP, solo)	25
69	Bell MBLL/SBLL 114	ALL MITCH RYDER HITS (LP)	15

(see also Detroit)

TONY RYMOND
62	Oriole CB 1708	Handful Of Songs/She'll Have To Go	6

PARK SABLE & JUNGLE 'N' BEATS
64	Fontana TF 457	Never Be Blue/Rave On	40

JEAN SABLON
53	HMV 7M 109	The Cab/Paris You Have Not Changed	5
55	HMV 7M 272	C'est Magnifique/Sur Les Pavements Of Paris	5

SABRE
83	Neat NEAT 23	Miracle Man/On The Loose (p/s)	8

SABRES
66	Decca F 12528	Roly Poly/Will You Always Love Me?	20

(see also Peeps)

SABRES OF PARADISE
93	Sabres Of Paradise PT 001	United (Andrew Weatherall Mix) (12", p/s, actually remix of Throbbing Gristle's "United", 800 only)	25

94	Sabres Of Paradise PT 009	Smokebelch II (Entry)/(Exit) (12", red p/s)	20
94	Sabres Of Paradise PT 009R	Smokebelch II (David Holmes Mix)/(Flute Mix) (12", yellow p/s)	20
94	Sabres Of Paradise PT 014	Theme/Return Of Carter & Edge 6 (Original Mix) (12")	10
94	Sabres Of Paradise PT 014R	Theme (Underdog Vs Sabres)/(Version) (10" remix)	10
94	Warp WAP 50	Wilmot/Rumble Summons (12")	15
94	Warp 10WAP 50	WILMOT II: Wilmot Meets Lord Scruffage/Wilmot's Last Skank (10", p/s)	8
95	Warp WARP 62	Tow Truck/(mixes) (12")	10
96	Emissions SEO 11	Ysaebud (PVC sleeve, 1-sided, etched B-side, 1,000 only)	10
90s	Sabres Of Paradise 002	Internal/Internment/Internalized/The Creator Speaks (12", blue vinyl)	8
93	Warp LP 16	SABRESONIC (2-LP, with unreleased 7", 5,000 only)	20

JIMMY SACCA
| 54 | London L 8028 | You're All That I Need/Alone (78) | 15 |

(see also Hilltoppers)

SACRED ALIEN
| 81 | Greenwood GW 001 | Spiritual Planet/Energy (stickered labels, some in p/s) | 30/10 |
| 83 | Heighway Robbery SAD 001 | Legends/VIRGIN: Sittin' In Front Row (gatefold p/s) | 30 |

SACRILEGE
| 85 | C.O.T.R. GURT 4 | BEHIND THE REALMS OF MADNESS (12" EP) | 8 |

SADDAR BAZAAR
| 98 | Earworm WORM 13/WJ37 | Crystalline/ELECTROSCOPE: Circus Heights/TRANSPARENT THING: Ahh (p/s, 1,500 in hand painted sleeve, 1st 176 embossed) | 10/5 |

SADDAR BAZAAR/AMP/3RD EYE FOUNDATION
| 90s | Enraptured RAPT 4503 | Arabesque (p/s) | 5 |

SADIE'S EXPRESSION
| 69 | Plexium PXM 4 | Deep In My Heart/My Way Of Living | 7 |

BARRINGTON SADLER
| 69 | Clandisc CLA 204 | Soul Power/Rub It Down | 12 |

S. SGT. BARRY SADLER
| 66 | RCA RCA 1506 | Ballad Of The Green Berets/I'm A Lucky One | 7 |
| 66 | RCA RCA 1520 | The A Team/An Empty Glass | 5 |

JERRY SADOWITZ
| 88 | Gobshite GOBSHITE 01 | GOBSHITE (LP) | 12 |

SAFARI PARTY
| 85 | Pure & Vain 1 PAV | Hope In Hell/Not There (p/s) | 5 |

SAFARIS (& PHANTOM BAND)
| 60 | Top Rank JAR 424 | Image Of A Girl/Four Steps To Love | 100 |
| 60 | Top Rank JAR 528 | The Girl With The Story In Her Eyes/Summer Nights (with Phantom Band) | 70 |

SAFFRON SUMMERFIELD
74	Mother Earth MUM 1001	SALISBURY PLAIN (LP)	45
76	Mother Earth MUM 1202	FANCY MEETING YOU HERE (LP)	45
76	Spectator	FANCY MEETING YOU HERE (LP, reissue)	20

SA 55
| 82 | 1966 EISP 9868 | Compromise/Love Love Love Here I Come | 80 |

SAGA
| 72 | Westwood WRS 017 | SAGA (LP) | 80 |
| 73 | Westwood WRS 036 | SWEET PEG O'DERBY (LP) | 100 |

MIKE SAGAR (& CRESTERS)
| 60 | HMV POP 819 | Deep Feeling/You Know (as Mike Sagar & Cresters) | 25 |
| 61 | HMV POP 988 | The Brothers Three/Set Me Free | 18 |

(see also Cresters, Richard Harding)

SAGE
| 80 | Redball RR 032 | GOING STRONG (LP) | 45 |

SAGITTARIUS
| 67 | CBS 2867 | My World Fell Down/Libra | 20 |
| 68 | CBS 3276 | Another Time/Virgo | 25 |

(see also Bruce Johnston, Glen Campbell)

SAGRAM
| 72 | Windmill WMD 118 | POP EXPLOSION SITAR STYLE (LP) | 20 |

(see also Clem Alford, Magic Carpet)

SAHARA
| 73 | Dawn DNLS 3068 | SUNRISE (LP) | 15 |

DOUG SAHM
73	Atlantic K 10293	Is Anybody Going To San Antoine/Don't Turn Around	5
73	Atlantic K 40466	DOUG SAHM AND BAND (LP) (inc Dylan and Dr. John in his band)	18
70s	Warner Bros K 56067	GROOVERS PARADISE (LP)	12
70s	Chrysalis CHR 1249	HELL OF A SPELL (LP)	12

(see also Sir Douglas Quintet, Augie Meyers)

OLIVER SAIN (& SHIRLEY BROWN)
72	Mojo 2092 031	St. Louis Breakdown/I Ain't Gonna Tell (with Shirley Brown)	10
74	Contempo CS 2026	Bus Stop/Nightime (solo)	8
75	Contempo CS 2057	London Express/Blowing For Love (solo)	8

(see also Shirley Brown, Fontella Bass)

MINT VALUE £

ST. CHRISTOPHER

84	Bluegrass GM 001	Crystal Clear/My Fond Farewell (p/s)	10
86	Bluegrass GM 003	Go Ahead Cry/Charmelle (p/s)	8
87	Veston VOD 001	Forevermore Stars Here/Remember Me To Her/Sinking Ships (flexidisc, p/s)	6
89	Sarah SARAH 015	You Deserve More Than A Maybe/The Kind Of Girl/The Summer Of Love (foldaround p/s with poster in poly bag)	10
89	Sarah SARAH 020	All Of A Tremble/My Fortune/The Hummingbird (foldaround p/s with poster in poly bag)	7

CHERYL ST. CLAIR

66	CBS 202041	My Heart Is Not In It/We Want Love	15
66	Columbia DB 8077	What About Me/I'll Forget You Tonight	12

(see also Alison Wonder)

ISLA ST. CLAIR

81	Clare ISLA 1	THE SONG AND THE STORY (LP)	20
85	Topic 12TS 436	SCOTCH MEASURE (LP)	15

SAINT ETIENNE

90	Heavenly HVN 2	Only Love Can Break Your Heart/Only Love Can Break Your Heart (Version) (p/s)	6
90	Heavenly HVN 212	Only Love Can Break Your Heart/Only Love Can Break Your Heart (Original Version) (12", p/s)	10
90	Heavenly HVN 212R	Only Love Can Break Your Heart (A Mix Of Two Halves)/ The Official Saint Etienne World Cup Theme (12", die-cut p/s)	12
90	The Catalogue CAT 084	Only Love Can Break Your Heart (remixed by Flowered Up)/FLOWERED UP: It's On (The Posh Facker Mix) (square flexidisc with The Catalogue mag)	5/4
90	Heavenly HVN 4	Kiss And Make Up/Sky's Dead (p/s)	5
90	Heavenly HVN 412	Kiss And Make Up/Sky's Dead (12", p/s)	12
90	Heavenly HVN 412R	Kiss And Make Up (Midsummer Madness Remix)/Kiss And Make Up (Midsummer Dubness Mix) (12", p/s)	12
90	Heavenly HVN 4CD	Kiss And Make Up (7")/Kiss And Make Up (12")/Sky's Dead (CD)	15
91	Heavenly HVN 912R	Speedwell (Flying Mix)/Speedwell (Project Mix)/Nothing Can Stop Us (Instrumental)/3D Tiger (12", p/s)	8
91	Heavenly HVN 9CD	Nothing Can Stop Us/Speedwell/Nothing Can Stop Us (Instrumental) (CD)	12
92	Heavenly HVN 12CD	Only Love Can Break Your Heart/Only Love Can Break Your Heart (A Mix Of Two Halves)/Filthy (CD)	12
92	Heavenly HVN 22	Live — Paris '92 (clear flexidisc, gig freebie, 1,000 only)	10
93	Heavenly HVN 2912	Hobart Paving/Who Do You Think You Are (12", p/s, mispressed with "Hobart Paving" & "Your Head My Voice" on both sides)	15
93	Heavenly HVN 36CD	I Was Born On Christmas Day/My Christmas Prayer/Snowplough/Peterloo (CD, picture disc)	8
95	Heavenly HVN 41	XMAS '95: A Christmas Gift To You/Driving Home For Christmas/ A Message In A Bottle (CD, signed fan club edition)	75
98	Creation CRECS 279	Sylvie/(Trouser Enthusiast's Tintinnabulation Edit) (cassette)	6
03	Mantra MNT 78	Soft Like Me/Gimp Crisis (p/s, limited edition)	5
93	Heavenly HVNCDX 6	SO TOUGH/YOU NEED A MESS OF HELP TO STAND ALONE (2-CD)	20
95	Heavenly HVNLP 9CD	I LOVE TO PAINT (CD, fan club edition, 600 only)	200
95	Heavenly HVNCD 10	TOO YOUNG TO DIE (CD, with bonus CD "Too Young To Die — The Remix Album" [HVN LP 10CDR])	25
98	Fan Club SPCD 463	XMAS '98: I Don't Intend To Spend Christmas Without You/Kofi Annan (CD, fan club edition, in card sleeve)	50
98	Creation CRECD 225L	GOOD HUMOUR (CD, digipak with booklet and slipcase)	18
00	Mantra MNSTET 1	BUILT ON SAND: RARITIES 1994-1999 (CD, fan club edition)	130

(see also 50 Year Void, Sarah Cracknell, Lovecut D.B., Mike Vickers)

BARRY ST. JOHN

64	Decca F 11933	A Little Bit Of Soap/Thing Of The Past	15
64	Decca F 11975	Bread And Butter/Cry To Me	15
65	Decca F 12111	Mind How You Go/Don't You Feel Proud	15
65	Decca F 12145	Hey Boy/I've Been Crying	15
65	Columbia DB 7783	Come Away Melinda/Gotta Brand New Man	12
66	Columbia DB 7868	Everything I Touch Turns To Tears/Sounds Like My Baby (DJ copy = £100)	65
68	Major Minor MM 587	Cry Like A Baby/Long And Lonely Night	10
69	Major Minor MM 604	By The Time I Get To Phoenix/Turn On Your Light	10
69	M. Minor MMLP/SMLP 43	ACCORDING TO ST. JOHN (LP)	40

BRIDGET ST. JOHN

69	Dandelion K 4404	To B Without A Hitch/Autumn Lullaby	12
70	Warner Bros WB 8019	If You've Got Money/Yep	12
72	Polydor 2001 280	Fly High/There's A Place I Know/Suzanne (p/s)	12
72	Polydor 2001 361	Nice/Goodbye Baby Goodbye	8
73	MCA MUS 1203	Passing Thru'/The Road Was Lonely On My Own	10
69	Dandelion 63750	ASK ME NO QUESTIONS (LP, gatefold sleeve)	40
71	Dandelion DAN 8007	SONGS FOR THE GENTLE MAN (LP, gatefold sleeve, also listed as K 49007)	40
72	Dandelion 2310 193	THANK YOU FOR... (LP, gatefold sleeve)	44
74	Chrysalis CHR 1062	JUMBLE QUEEN (LP)	18

(see also Ron Geesin, Quiver)

TAMMY ST. JOHN

64	Pye 7N 15682	Boys/Hey Hey Hey Hey	10
65	Pye 7N 15762	He's The One For Me/I'm Tired Of Just Looking At You	10
65	Pye 7N 15948	Dark Shadows And Empty Hallways/I Mustn't Cry	10
66	Pye 7N 17042	Nobody Knows What's Goin' On (In My Mind But Me)/ Stay Together Young Lovers (DJ copy = £85)	50
69	Tangerine DP 0007	Concerning Love/Sound Of Love	8

(see also Trends)

ST. LOUIS JIMMY

53	Esquire 10-319	Holiday For Boogie/MEMPHIS SLIM: Harlem Bound (78)	35

ST. LOUIS UNION
66	Decca F 12318	Girl/Respect	20
66	Decca F 12386	Behind The Door/English Tea	30
66	Decca F 12508	East Side Story/Think About Me	80

SAINT ORCHESTRA
| 78 | Pye 7N 46127 | Return Of The Saint/Funko (p/s) | |

OLIVER ST. PATRICK & DIAMONDS
| 67 | Trojan TR 005 | I Want To Be Loved By You/Tulips | 12 |

CRISPIAN ST. PETERS
65	Decca F 12080	At This Moment/Goodbye, You'll Forget Me	15
65	Decca F 12207	No No No/Three Goodbyes	15
67	Decca DFE 8678	ALMOST PERSUADED (EP)	55
66	Decca LK 4805	FOLLOW ME... (LP)	58
70	Square SQA 102	SIMPLY... CRISPIAN ST. PETERS (LP)	25

KIRBY ST. ROMAIN
| 63 | Stateside SS 199 | Summer's Comin'/Miss You So | 10 |

SAINT STEVEN
| 69 | Probe SPB 1005 | OVER THE HILLS/THE BASTICH (LP) | 50 |

ST. VALENTINE'S DAY MASSACRE
| 67 | Fontana TF 883 | Brother Can You Spare A Dime/Al's Party (some with p/s) | 150/75 |

(see also Artwoods)

BUFFY SAINTE-MARIE
65	Fontana TF 574	Until It's Time For You To Go/The Flower And The Apple Tree	6
65	Fontana TF 614	The Universal Soldier/Cripple Creek	6
66	Fontana TF 695	Timeless Love/Lady Margret	6
65	Fontana TFL 6040	IT'S MY WAY! (LP)	20
65	Fontana TFL 6047	MANY A MILE (LP)	20
66	Fontana (S)TFL 6071	LITTLE WHEEL SPIN AND SPIN (LP)	20

SAINTS (Australia)
76	Power Exchange PX 242	I'm Stranded/No Time (p/s)	10
77	Power Exchange PXE 101	I'm Stranded/(STANLEY FRANK: 2 tracks) (p/s)	8
77	Harvest HAR 5123	Erotic Neurotic/One Way Street	10
77	Harvest HAR 5130	This Perfect Day/L-I-E-S	6
77	Harvest 12 HAR 5130	This Perfect Day/L-I-E-S/Do The Robot (12", with 'disclaimer' stickered p/s)	10
77	Harvest HAR 5137	1, 2, 3, 4 (River Deep, Mountain High/Lipstick On Your Collar/One Way Street/Demolition Girl) (EP, double pack, gatefold p/s)	15
77	Harvest HAR 5137	1, 2, 3, 4 (River Deep, Mountain High/Lipstick On Your Collar/One Way Street/Demolition Girl) (EP, p/s)	6
78	Harvest HAR 5148	Know Your Product/Run Down (no p/s)	7
78	Harvest HAR 5166	Security/All Times Through Paradise (p/s)	12
89	Bucketfull Of Brains BOB 26	I Dreamed Of Marie Antoinette/MOCK TURTLES: Croppies Lie Down (free with *Bucketfull Of Brains* magazine, issue 32)	6/4
77	Harvest SHSP 4065	I'M STRANDED (LP)	25
78	Harvest SHSP 4078	ETERNALLY YOURS (LP, with inner sleeve)	20
78	Harvest SHSP 4094	PREHISTORIC SOUNDS (LP)	20

SAINTS (Jamaica)
| 66 | Doctor Bird DB 1009 | Brown Eyes/BABA BROOKS & HIS BAND: King Size | 28 |
| 69 | Big Shot BI 522 | Windy Part One/Windy Part Two | 12 |

SAINTS (Jamaica)
| 73 | Count Shelley CS 043 | How Long/Feeling Good | 6 |

SAINTS (U.K.)
| 63 | Pye 7N 15548 | Wipe Out/Midgets | 25 |
| 63 | Pye 7N 15582 | Husky Team/Pigtails | 25 |

(see also Tornados, Heinz)

SAINTS (U.K.)
| 64 | MJB BEV 73/4 | SAINTS (10" LP, private pressing) | 300 |
| 64 | MJB BEVLP 127/8 | SAINTS ALIVE! (LP, private pressing) | 300 |

SAINTS JAZZ BAND
51	Decibel J 3	Old Stack O' Lee Blues/1919 March (78)	6
51	Parlophone R 3427	I Want A Girl Just Like The Girl That Married Dear Old Dad/CRANE RIVER JAZZ BAND: I'm Travelling (78 rpm = £8)	8
53	Parlophone MSP 6042	Hey Lawdy Papa/Who Walks In When I Walk Out?	8
56	Parlophone R 4240	Mahogany Hall Stomp/Stack O' Lee Blues	7
57	Parlophone R 4260	Blue Turning Grey Over You/Till We Meet Again	6
57	Parlophone R 4304	How Come You Do Me Like You Do/Willie The Weeper	6
58	Parlophone R 4417	Swingin' The Blues/I've Found A New Baby (78 rpm = £7)	6
56	Parlophone GEP 8560	SAINTS PLAY JAZZ (EP)	10
56	Parlophone GEP 8577	SAINTS JAZZ BAND (EP)	10

RUSS SAINTY (& NU NOTES)
60	Top Rank JAR 381	Happy-Go-Lucky-Me/Standing Around	15
60	Decca F 11270	Race With The Devil/Too Shy (solo)	18
61	Decca F 11325	Don't Believe Him, Donna/Your Other Love (solo)	10
62	HMV POP 1055	Keep Your Love Locked/I've Got A Girl (as Russ Sainty & Nu Notes)	10
62	HMV POP 1069	Send Me The Pillow That You Dream On/What Do You Know About That (solo)	10
63	HMV POP 1181	Unforgettable Love/The Twinkle In Your Eye (solo)	10
64	Parlophone R 5168	That's How I'm Gonna Love You/Lonesome Town (as Russ Sainty & Nu-Notes)	5
64	Columbia DB 7394	This Is My Lovely Day/Bless You, Girl (as Russ Sainty & Nu-Notes)	5

65	Columbia DB 7521	It Ain't That Easy/And Then (solo)	5
65	Columbia DB 7708	Saving My Tears (For A Rainy Day)/She (solo)	5
60s	Society SOC 1035	THE GENIUS OF LENNON AND McCARTNEY (LP)	15

(see also Nu Notes)

KYU SAKAMOTO
63	HMV POP 1171	Sukiyaki/Anoko No Namae Wa Nantenkana	8
63	HMV POP 1211	China Nights/Benkyo No Cha Cha Cha	8
64	HMV POP 1342	Rose Rose I Love You/Sayonara Tokyo	8
62	HMV CLP 1674	SUKIYAKI (LP)	100

RYUICHI SAKAMOTO
80	Island IPR 2048	Riot In Lagos/Iconic Storage (12", company sleeve)	8
82	Virgin VS 510	Bamboo Houses/Bamboo Music (p/s)	7
86	10 TEND 112	Field Work/Exhibition (double pack, gatefold p/s)	8
80	Island ILPS 9656	B-2 UNIT (LP)	18
90	Virgin VUSLP 14	BEAUTY (LP, with inner)	12

(see also David Sylvian, Yellow Magic Orchestra)

(BOB) SAKER
68	Polydor BM 56231	Still Got You/Imagination (as Bob Saker)	6
68	Parlophone R 5740	Foggy Tuesday/Ooh Nana Na (as Bob Saker)	40
69	Parlophone R 5752	Hey Joe!/Christianity	15
71	CBS 7010	What A Beautiful World/City Of The Angels	6
71	CBS 7399	Even Though We Ain't Got Money/Wild Winds Are Blowing	6

SALAMANDER
70	CBS 5102	Crystal Ball/Billy	10

(see also Onyx)

SALAMANDER
71	Youngblood SSYB 14	THE TEN COMMANDMENTS (LP, gatefold sleeve)	130

SALEM
82	Hilton FMR 056	Cold As Steel/Reach To Eternity	45

SALFORD JETS
78	WEA K 18008	Lookin' At The Squares/Dancing School (no p/s)	5
79	EMI INT 590	Manchester Boys/Last Bus (p/s)	20

SALLY & ALLEY CATS
64	Parlophone R 5183	Is It Something I Said/You Forgot To Remember	12

SALLYANGIE
69	Big T BIG 126	Two Ships/Colours Of The World	20
72	Philips 6006 259	Child Of Allah/Lady Go Lightly	20
68	Transatlantic TRA 176	CHILDREN OF THE SUN (LP, gatefold sleeve)	50
78	Transatlantic TRA 176	CHILDREN OF THE SUN (LP, reissue, different single sleeve)	20

(see also Mike Oldfield)

DOUG SALMA & HIGHLANDERS
63	Philips BF 1279	Highland Fling/The Scavenger	12

SALMONTAILS
80	Oblivion OBL 001	SALMONTAILS (LP, with Dave Pegg)	18

SALOME
69	Page One POF 137	Vivo Cantando/Amigos Amigos	7

SALSOUL STRUT
96	Records Inc. no cat. no.	Better Days/(mixes)	12

SALT
78	Grapevine GRA 111	BEYOND A SONG (LP, with insert)	18

SALT & PEPPER
61	London HLU 9338	High Noon/Come Softly To Me	15

SAL SALVADOR
55	KPL 105	SAL SALVADOR QUARTET (10" LP)	12

SALVATION
69	United Artists UP 35048	Cinderella/The Village Shuck	15
69	United Artists UAS 29062	SALVATION (LP)	25

SALVATION
83	Merciful Release MR 025	Girlsoul/Evelyn (p/s)	12
83	Merciful Release MRX 025	Girlsoul/Evelyn/Dust Up (12", p/s)	15
86	Batfish Inc. BF 103	Jessica's Crime/The Shining (p/s)	12
86	Batfish Inc. USS 104	Jessica's Crime (Extended Mix)/The Shining/Shattered Sky (12", p/s)	8

SAMMY SALVO
58	RCA RCA 1032	Oh Julie/Say Yeah (78 rpm = £20)	28
59	London HLP 8997	Afraid/Marble Heart (78 rpm = £22)	12
62	Polydor NH 66974	Billy Blue/French Poodle	8

SAM & BILL
66	Pye International 7N 25355	Fly Me To The Moon/Treat Me Right	15
67	Brunswick 05973	I Feel Like Cryin'/I'll Try	28

SAM & DAVE
66	King KG 1041	No More Pain/You Ain't No Big Thing Baby	22
66	Atlantic AT 4066	You Don't Know Like I Know/Blame Me, Don't Blame My Heart	18
66	Atlantic 584 003	Hold On I'm A Comin'/I Got Everything I Need	10
66	Atlantic 584 047	If You Got The Loving (I Got The Time)/Said I Wasn't Gonna Tell Nobody	8
67	Atlantic 584 064	You Got Me Hummin'/Sleep Good Tonight	8

67	Atlantic 584 086	You Don't Know Like I Know/Blame Me, Don't Blame My Heart (reissue) 7
67	Stax 601 004	Soothe Me/Sweet Pains (initially dark blue label, later light blue) 25/20
67	Stax 601 006	When Something Is Wrong With My Baby/A Small Portion Of Your Love
		(initially with dark blue labels, later light blue) 10/8
67	Stax 601 023	Soul Man/May I Baby 8
68	Stax 601 030	I Thank You/Wrap It Up 8
68	Atlantic 584 192	You Don't Know What You Mean To Me/This Is Your World. 7
68	Atlantic 584 211	Can't You Find Another Way/Still Is The Night 7
68	Atlantic 584 228	Everybody's Got To Believe In Somebody/If I Didn't Have A Girl Like You 6
69	Atlantic 584 237	Soul Sister, Brown Sugar/Come On In 8
69	Atlantic 584 247	You Don't Know Like I Know/Hold On I'm A Comin' 6
69	Atlantic 584 303	Ooh, Ooh, Ooh/Holdin' On 6
70	Atlantic 584 324	Baby, Baby, Don't Stop Now/I'm Not An Indian Giver. 6
66	King KGL 4001	SAM AND DAVE (LP). 60
66	Atlantic 587/588 045	HOLD ON, I'M A COMIN' (LP) 30
67	Stax 589 003	DOUBLE DYNAMITE (LP) 30
68	Stax 589 015	SOUL MEN (LP) 30
68	Major Minor MCP 5000	SAM AND DAVE (LP). 22
69	Atlantic 588 154	I THANK YOU (LP). 25
69	Atlantic 588 155	THE BEST OF SAM AND DAVE (LP) 18
69	Atlantic 587/588 181	DOUBLE TROUBLE (LP). 22
69	Atlantic 588 185	SOUL MEN (LP, reissue). 15

SAM & KITTY
80	Grapevine GRP 132	I've Got Something Good/Love Is The Greatest 15

SAM APPLE PIE
69	Decca F 22932	Tiger Man (King Of The Jungle)/Sometime Girl. 15
69	Decca LK-R/SKL-R 5005	SAM APPLE PIE (LP). 110
73	DJM DJLPS 429	EAST 17 (LP) 35

SAME
79	Wessex WEX 267	Wild About You/Movements (p/s) 70
80	Blue Print BLU 2008	Movements/Wild About You (reissue with reversed sides & blue print on p/s;
		some with no p/s). 50/40

SAM, ERV & TOM
68	Direction 58-3339	Soul Teacher/Hard To Get 10
	(see also Diplomats)	

SAM GOPAL
(see under 'G')

MIKE SAMMES & HIS SINGERS
59	Top Rank JAR 166	Upstairs And Downstairs/IVOR RAYMONDE: Mylene 5
62	Oriole CB 1738	Oh My Twisted Bach/Al Of A Twist 5
66	HMV POP 1546	Somewhere My Love/What Do I Do?. 5

SAMMY
72	Philips 6006 227	Goo Ger Woogie/Big Lovin' Woman 5
72	Philips 6308 136	SAMMY (LP). 25
	(see also Ian Gillan)	

SAMPLES
80	Sample	VENDETTA (Vendetta/ (EP). 20
84	No Future OI 14	Dead Hero/Fire Around Round/Suspicion (p/s) 12

DAVE SAMPSON & HUNTERS
60	Columbia DB 4449	Sweet Dreams/It's Lonesome 20
60	Columbia DB 4502	If You Need Me/See You Around 20
61	Columbia DB 4597	Why The Chicken?/1999. 15
61	Columbia DB 4625	Easy To Dream/That's All 15
62	Fontana H 361	Wide, Wide World/Since Sandy Moved Away (solo) 15
61	Columbia SEG 8095	DAVE (EP, also stereo ESG 7853). 125/160
	(see also Hunters [U.K.])	

TOMMY SAMPSON
58	Melodisc MEL 1411	Rockin'/Rock'n'Roll Those Big Brown Eyes (with His Strongmen) (78 = £22). . . . 25
58	Parlophone R 4458	Lazy Train/Smooth Mood (as Tommy Sampson Orchestra) (78 rpm = £12) 7

SAMSON
69	Instant INSP 004	ARE YOU SAMSON (LP). 55
	(see also Strider)	

SAMSON
78	Lightning GIL 547	Telephone/Leavin' You (p/s). 35
79	Lightning GIL 553	Mr. Rock'n'Roll/Drivin' Music (p/s) 35
79	Laser LAS 6	Mr. Rock'n'Roll (remix)/Primrose Shuffle 12
80	EMI EMI 5061	Vice Versa (Edit)/Hammerhead (p/s, withdrawn, 1,000 demos only) 45
80	Gem GEMS 34	Vice Versa (Edit)/Hammerhead (reissue, p/s, some with sticker) 8/5
80	Gem GEMS 38	Hard Times (Remix)/Angel With A Machine Gun (p/s). 5
81	RCA RCA 67	Riding With The Angels (Edit)/Little Big Man (p/s). 12
81	RCA RCA 67	Riding With The Angels (Edit)/Little Big Man (picture disc). 10
82	Polydor POSPP 471	Losing My Grip/Pyramid To The Stars (picture disc) 6
82	Polydor POSPX 471	Losing My Grip/Pyramid To The Stars/Mr. Rock'n'Roll (live)/
		Tomorrow Or Yesterday (live) (12" EP) 10
82	Polydor POSPG 519/	Life On The Run/Drivin' With ZZ!/Walking Out On You (live)/Bright Lights (live)
	SAM 1	(double pack, gatefold p/s) 7
82	Polydor SAM 2	Red Skies/Young Idea (unissued, promo only) 18
83	Polydor PODJ 554	Red Skies (DJ Edit) (1-sided promo). 12
83	Polydor POSPP 554	Red Skies/Livin', Lovin', Lyin' (picture disc) 6

83	Polydor POSPX 554	Red Skies/Livin', Lovin', Lyin'/Running Out Of Time (12", p/s)	10
84	Polydor POSP 670	Are You Ready?/Front Page News (p/s)	7
84	Polydor POSPP 670	Are You Ready?/Front Page News (picture disc)	8
84	Polydor POSPX 670	Are You Ready?/Front Page News/La Grange (12", p/s)	8
84	Polydor POSP 680	The Fight Goes On/Riding With The Angels (re-recording) (p/s)	5
84	Polydor POSPX 680	The Fight Goes On (Long Version)/Riding With The Angels (re-recording)/ Vice Versa (live) (12", p/s)	8
84	Thunderbolt THBE 1.003	Mr Rock'n'Roll/Primrose Shuffle/Telephone/Leavin' You (12", p/s)	8
86	Capitol CL 395	Vice Versa (Remix)/Losing My Grip (Remix) (p/s)	8
86	Capitol 12CLP 395	Vice Versa (Remix)/Losing My Grip (Remix) (12", picture disc)	15
87	Metal Hammer METAL 1	One Day's Heroes (as Paul Samson's Empire)/CHARIOT: Life On The Line/ HEAVY PETTIN': Heaven Sent/STRANGEWAYS: Never Gonna Lose It (EP, with/without *Metal Hammer* magazine)	6/5
79	Laser LAP 1	SURVIVORS (LP)	15
80	Gem GEMLP 108	HEAD ON (LP, 2 different mixes, A1/B1 or A2/B2 in matrix; each with insert, some with free patch)	15/12
80	Gem GEMLP 108	HEAD ON (LP, mispress with A1/B2 matrix)	20
81	Gem GEMLP 113	SHOCK TACTICS (LP, release cancelled)	
81	RCA LP 5031	SHOCK TACTICS (LP, with insert)	18
82	Polydor POLS 1077	BEFORE THE STORM (LP, initially with poster, stickered sleeve)	20/12
84	Polydor POLD 5132	DON'T GET MAD, GET EVEN (LP, with insert)	15
84	Polydor POLD 5132	DON'T GET MAD, GET EVEN (2-LP, white labels, 2 different mixes of same album, promo only)	35

(see also Bruce Dickinson, Iron Maiden, John McCoy, Tiger, Colin Towns, Thunderstick, Nicky Moore, Mammoth, Egypt)

SAM THE SHAM & THE PHARAOHS

65	MGM MGM 1269	Woolly Bully/Ain't Gonna Move	15
65	MGM MGM 1278	Ju Ju Hand/Big City Lights	10
65	MGM MGM 1285	Ring Dang Doo/Don't Try It	10
66	MGM MGM 1298	Red Hot/Long Long Way	15
66	MGM MGM 1315	Li'l Red Riding Hood/Love Me Like Before	15
66	MGM MGM 1326	The Hair On My Chinny Chin Chin/The Out Crowd	10
66	MGM MGM 1331	How Do You Catch A Girl/The Love You Left Behind	10
67	MGM MGM 1337	Oh That's Bad No That's Good/Take What You Can Get	10
67	MGM MGM 1343	Black Sheep/My Day's Gonna Come	10
68	MGM MGM 1379	Yakety Yak/Let Our Lovelight Shine	8
69	MGM MGM 1473	Woolly Bully/Ring Dang Doo	8
66	MGM MGM-EP 794	RED HOT (EP)	70
65	MGM MGM-C 1007	WOOLY BULLY (LP)	50
66	MGM MGM-C(S) 8032	LI'L RED RIDING HOOD (LP)	40
71	Atco 2400 146	SAM HARD AND HEAVY (LP, as Sam Samudio)	15

LEROY SAMUEL

72	Punch PH 113	Trying To Wreck My Life/JOHN HOLT: Pride And Joy	12

(Phillip) SAMUEL THE FIRST

71	Summit SUM 8515	Sounds Of Babylon/BEVERLEY'S ALL STARS: Second Babylon Version	10

JERRY SAMUELS

56	HMV 7M 411	Puppy Love/The Chosen Few (78 rpm = £10)	18

(see also Napoleon XIV)

WINSTON SAMUELS

64	Columbia DB 7405	You Are The One/Angela	12
64	Rio R 26	Follow/I'm So Glad	12
64	Black Swan WI 419	Luck Will Come My Way/LLOYD BREVITT: One More Time	22
64	Black Swan WI 426	You Are The One/Gloria Love (B-side actually by Beltones)	15
65	Ska Beat JB 196	Be Prepared/Jericho Wall	20
65	Ska Beat JB 213	My Bride To Be/LLOYD PREVITT: Wayward Ska	25
65	Ska Beat JB 214	Never Again/My Angel	18
66	Ska Beat JB 238	What Have I Done/Broken Hearted	25
66	Ska Beat JB 241	Ups And Downs/Come What May	20
66	Ska Beat JB 244	Time Will Tell/I'm Sorry	22
67	Island WI 3051	The Greatest/FREDDIE & FITZY: Truth Hurts	25
67	Island WI 3053	I Won't Be Discouraged/FREDDIE & FITZIE: Why Did My Little Girl Cry	25

SAMURAI

71	Greenwich GSLP 1003	SAMURAI (LP)	120+

(see also Greenslade, Web)

SAMURAI

85	Ebony EBON 25	Fires Of Hell/Dreams Of The World (no p/s)	15

SANDALS

90s	Acid Jazz JAZID 47	A Profound Gas (p/s)	10

ALEX SANDERS

70	A&M AMLS 984	A WITCH IS BORN (LP, foldout sleeve with warning sticker, withdrawn)	160

GARY SANDERS

66	Warner Bros WB 5676	Ain't No Beatle/Ain't I Good To You	12

GEORGE SANDERS

58	HMV 7EG 8395	THE GEORGE SANDERS TOUCH (EP)	15

PHARAOH SANDERS

71	Probe SPB 1019	DEAF, DUMB AND BLIND (LP)	25
70s	Impulse AS 9138	TAUHID (LP)	20
70s	Impulse AS 9199	SUMMUN BUKMUN UMYUN (LP)	25
70s	Impulse AS 9219	BLACK UNITY (LP)	25

70s	Impulse AS 9227	LIVE AT THE EAST (LP)	25
70s	Impulse AS 9229	THE BEST OF PHARAOH SANDERS (2-LP)	20
70s	Impulse 9233	WISDOM THROUGH MUSIC (LP)	20
70s	Impulse 9254	VILLAGE OF PHARAOHS (LP)	20
70s	Impulse 9261	ELEVATION (LP)	20
70s	Impulse 9280	LOVE IN US ALL (LP)	20
82	Jasmine JAS 53	THEMBI (LP)	18

PHARAOH SANDERS QUINTET
66	ESP Disk/Fontana SFJL 931	PHARAOH SANDERS QUINTET (LP)	38

RAY SANDERS
60	London HLG 7106	A World So Full Of Love/A Little Bitty Tear (export issue)	12

TOMMY SANDERSON & SANDMEN
61	Ember EMB 131	Deadline/Candelglow	11
62	Ember EMB 152	Ding Dong Rag/Piano A-Go Go	10

CHRIS SANDFORD (& CORONETS)
63	Decca F 11778	Not Too Little — Not Too Much/I'm Lookin'	5
64	Decca F 11842	You're Gonna Be My Girl/Don't Leave Me Now (with Coronets)	6
65	Fontana TF 633	I Wish They Wouldn't Always Say I Sound Like The Guy From The U.S.A. Blues/Little Man, Nobody Cares	7

GERRY SANDON
96	Twangsville TW 001	JUST GERRY (EP)	10

JOHNNY SANDON (& REMO FOUR)
63	Pye 7N 15542	Lies/On The Horizon (as Johnny Sandon & Remo Four)	15
63	Pye 7N 15559	Magic Potion/Yes (as Johnny Sandon & Remo Four)	15
64	Pye 7N 15602	Sixteen Tons/The Blizzard	10
64	Pye 7N 15665	Donna Means Heartbreak/Some Kinda Wonderful	10
64	Pye 7N 15717	The Blizzard/(I'd Be A) Legend In My Time	10
(see also Remo Four)			

SAND PEBBLES
67	Track 604 015	Love Power/Because Of Love	20
68	Toast TT 505	If You Didn't Hear Me The First Time/Flower Power	8
69	Track 604 028	Love Power/Because Of Love (reissue)	15

SANDPIPERS
66	Pye International 7N 25396	Louie Louie/Things We Said Today	5
69	A&M AMS 744	Kumbaya/Lo Mucho Que Te Quiero	6

SANDRA
86	10 TENY 78-12	(I'll Never Be) Maria Magdalena/Party Games/Little Girl (12", picture disc)	15
86	10 TEN 113-12/TENY 78-12	In The Heat Of The Night/Heatwave (Instrumental)//(I'll Never Be) Maria Magdalena/Party Games/Little Girl (12", double pack, including picture disc, gatefold PVC sleeve)	25
89	Siren SRNCD 85	Everlasting Love/Stop For A Minute/Everlasting Love (Remix)/ (I'll Never Be) Maria Magdalena (CD)	60
89	Siren SRNCD 104	Heaven Can Wait (Single Version 4.05)/(Dub Mix)/Heaven's Theme (Instrumental)/Heaven Can Wait (Extended Version) (3" CD, card sleeve)	25

SANDROSE
73	Polydor 2480 137	SANDROSE (LP)	120+

SANDS (Ireland)
70	Major Minor MM 681	Venus/Cara Mia	15

SANDS (U.K.)
67	Reaction 591 017	Mrs. Gillespie's Refrigerator/Listen To The Sky	270
(see also Others, Sundragon)			

SANDS
69	Tribune TRS 122	Dance Dance Dance/The Cheater	20
69	Tribune	SAND DOIN'S (LP)	50
(see also Tony Kenny & Sands)			

CLIVE SANDS
69	CBS 3955	Lo Mucho Que Te Quiro/Picture On The Wall	7
69	S.N.B. 55-4058	Hooked On A Feeling/Marie	7
69	S.N.B. 55-4431	Whitchi Tai Yo/In A Dream	12
69	CBS 4672	A Very Lonely Man/You Made Me What I Am	7
(see also Brothers Kane, Sarstedt Brothers, Wes Sands)			

DAVEY SANDS & ESSEX
65	Decca F 12170	Please Me Mine/All The Time	18
67	CBS 202620	Advertising Girl/Without You I'm Nothing	15

EVIE SANDS
65	Red Bird BC 118	Take Me For A Little While/Run Home To Mama (DJ copy = £85)	50
66	Cameo Parkway C 413	Picture Me Gone/It Makes Me Laugh (DJ copy = £200)	125
68	A&M AMS 736	Shadow Of The Evening/Until It's Time For You To Go	10
69	A&M AMS 748	I'll Hold Out Of My Hand/One Fine Summer Morning	10
69	A&M AMS 760	Anyway That You Want Me/I'll Never Be Alone	10
75	Capitol CL 15818	You Brought The Woman Out In Me/Early Morning Sunshine	7

JODI(E) SANDS
57	London HL 8456	With All My Heart/More Than Only Friends (as Jodi Sands)	20
57	London HL 8530	Please Don't Tell Me (Sayonara)/If You're Not Completely Satisfied (78 = £25)	20
58	Starlite ST45 005	All I Ask Of You/The Way I Love You	12
58	HMV POP 533	Someday (You'll Want Me To Want You)/Always In My Heart (78 rpm = £10)	7

MINT VALUE £

TOMMY SANDS
57	Capitol CL 14695	Teen-Age Crush/Hep Dee Hootie (Cutie Wootie) (78 rpm = £8)	25
57	Capitol CL 14724	Ring-A-Ding-A-Ding/My Love Song (78 rpm = £10)	25
57	Capitol CL 14745	Goin' Steady/Ring My 'Phone (78 rpm = £10)	25
57	Capitol CL 14781	Let Me Be Loved/Fantastically Foolish (78 rpm = £8)	15
57	Capitol CL 14811	Man, Like Wow!/A Swingin' Romance (78 rpm = £12)	15
58	Capitol CL 14834	Sing, Boy, Sing/Crazy 'Cause I Love You (78 rpm = £10)	15
58	Capitol CL 14872	Hawaiian Rock/Teen-Age Doll	25
58	Capitol CL 14889	After The Senior Prom/Big Date	20
58	Capitol CL 14925	Blue Ribbon Baby/I Love You Because (as Tommy Sands & Raiders)	32
59	Capitol CL 14971	The Worryin' Kind/Bigger Than Texas	32
59	Capitol CL 15013	Is It Ever Gonna Happen/I Ain't Gittin' Rid Of You	30
59	Capitol CL 15047	Sinner Man/Bring Me Your Love	10
59	Capitol CL 15071	That's The Way I Am/I'll Be Seeing You	10
60	Capitol CL 15109	I Gotta Have You/You Hold The Future	10
60	Capitol CL 15143	The Old Oaken Bucket/These Are The Things You Are	10
61	Capitol CL 15219	Love In A Goldfish Bowl/I Love My Baby	5
63	HMV POP 1193	Connie/Young Man's Fancy	5
63	HMV POP 1247	Only 'Cause I'm Lonely/Cinderella	5
66	Liberty LIB 55842	The Statue/Lolita (DJ copy = £85)	45
57	Capitol EAP1 848	STEADY DATE WITH TOMMY SANDS PT. 1 (EP)	50
57	Capitol EAP2 848	STEADY DATE WITH TOMMY SANDS PT. 2 (EP)	50
57	Capitol EAP3 848	STEADY DATE WITH TOMMY SANDS PT. 3 (EP)	50
57	Capitol EAP1 851	TEENAGE CRUSH (EP)	50
59	Capitol EAP1 1081	SANDS STORM PART 1 (EP)	50
59	Capitol EAP2 1081	SANDS STORM PART 2 (EP)	50
59	Capitol EAP3 1081	SANDS STORM PART 3 (EP)	50
59	Capitol EAP1 1123	THIS THING CALLED LOVE (EP)	40
57	Capitol T 848	STEADY DATE WITH TOMMY SANDS (LP)	65
58	Capitol T 929	SING, BOY, SING (soundtrack) (LP)	75
59	Capitol T 1081	SANDS STORM! (LP)	75
59	Capitol T 1123	THIS THING CALLED LOVE (LP)	40
60	Capitol (S)T 1239	WHEN I'M THINKING OF YOU (LP, mono/stereo)	25/35
61	Capitol T 1426	A DREAM WITH TOMMY SANDS (LP)	25

TONY SANDS & DRUMBEATS
60s	Studio 36 NSRS EP 1/22	Shame Shame Shame/I Got A Feeling	250

WES SANDS
63	Columbia DB 4996	There's Lots More Where This Came From/Three Cups	45

(see also Brothers Kane, Sarstedt Brothers, Clive Sands)

SANDS OF TIME
66	Pye 7N 17140	Where Did We Go Wrong/When I Look Back	10
67	Pye 7N 17236	One Day/Ev'ry Time We Say Goodbye	8

PAT SANDY
69	Attack ATT 8000	Gentle On My Mind/BIG L: Soulful	6

SANDY & TEACHERS
64	Columbia DB 7244	Listen With Mammy/Real Sweet	5

(see also Sandy Brown)

SANDY COAST
71	Polydor 2121 046	True Love/That's A Wonder	7
73	Polydor 2001 457	Blackboard Jungle Lady/Don't Get Me Wrong	7
69	Page One POLS 020	FROM THE STEREO WORKSHOP (LP)	120+
69	Page One MORS 201	SHIPWRECK (LP)	120+
73	Polydor 2310 277	STONEWALL (LP)	25

SAN FRANCISCO EARTHQUAKE
68	Mercury MF 1036	Fairy Tales Can Come True/Su Su	10

CLAUDE SANG
70	Sugar SU 105	I'm In Love Again/You'll Never Fool Me Again	6
70	Sugar SUM 1	THE WORLD OF REGGAE VOL. 1 (LP)	15

SAN REMO STRINGS
71	Tamla Motown TMG 795	Festival Time/All Turned On (DJ copy = £30)	12
72	Tamla Motown TMG 807	Reach Out, I'll Be There/Hungry For Love (DJ copy = £30)	10
73	Tamla Motown STML 11216	SAN REMO STRINGS SWING (LP)	20

BOBBY SANSOM (& GIANTS)
63	Oriole CB 1837	There's A Place/Lucille (as Bobby Sansom & Giants)	18
63	Oriole CB 1888	Where Have You Been/Do You Promise (as Bobby Sansom & Giants)	15
70	Decca F 13104	Lady One And Only/Handbags And Gladrags	5
71	Decca F 13151	I Believe In Music/The Valley Of The Shadows Of Tears	5

MONGO SANTAMARIA
63	Riverside RIF 106909	Watermelon Man/Don't Bother Me No More	15
65	CBS 201766	El Pussycat/Black Eyed Peas And Rice	25
69	Direction 58-4086	Cloud Nine/Son Of A Preacher Man	20
69	Direction 58-4430	Twenty Five Miles/El Tres	20
66	CBS SS 62123	HEY! LET'S PARTY (LP)	25
69	CBS S 233811	ALL STRUNG OUT (LP)	25
71	CBS 63904	WORKING ON A GROOVY THING (LP)	25
71	Atlantic 2400 140	MONGO'S WAY (LP)	30

SANTANA
69	CBS 4593	Persuasion/Savor	5
70	CBS 4940	Evil Ways/Jin-Go-Lo-Ba	5
70	CBS 5325	Black Magic Woman/Hope You're Feeling Better	5

69	CBS 63015	SANTANA (LP, laminated sleeve original, orange label)	18
70	CBS 63815	SANTANA (LP, non-laminated sleeve reissue, orange label)	12
70	CBS 64087	ABRAXAS (LP, orange label)	12
71	CBS 69015	SANTANA (III) (LP, gatefold sleeve, some stickered, orange label)	12
72	CBS CQ 30595	SANTANA (III) (LP, gatefold sleeve, quadrophonic)	18
72	CBS 65299	CARAVANSERAI (LP, gatefold sleeve, orange label)	12
73	CBS CQ 31610	CARAVANSERAI (LP, gatefold sleeve, quadrophonic)	18
73	CBS 69040	WELCOME (LP, embossed gatefold sleeve)	12
74	CBS CQ 32445	WELCOME (LP, embossed gatefold sleeve, quadrophonic)	15
75	CBS 66325	LOTUS (3-LP, triple-gatefold sleeve, with inners)	18
75	CBS CQ 30130	ABRAXAS (LP, gatefold sleeve, quadrophonic)	18
75	CBS Q 69081	GREATEST HITS (LP, quadrophonic)	18
75	CBS Q 69084	BORBOLETTA (LP, quadrophonic)	18
76	CBS Q 86005	AMIGOS (LP, quadrophonic)	18

CARLOS SANTANA & BUDDY MILES

72	CBS 8338	Evil Ways/Them Changes	5
83	CBS A 3359	They All Went To Mexico (with Willie Nelson)/BUDDY MILES: Mudbone (p/s)	5
72	CBS 65142	CARLOS SANTANA & BUDDY MILES LIVE (LP, gatefold sleeve)	12
73	CBS CQ 31308	CARLOS SANTANA & BUDDY MILES LIVE (LP, quadrophonic)	18

(see also Santana, Buddy Miles, Mahavishnu Orchestra, John McLaughlin, John Lee Hooker)

SANTELLS

| 66 | Sue WI 4020 | So Fine/These Are Love | 30 |

DAVID SANTO

| 68 | London HLK 10219 | Jingle Down A Hill/Rising Of Scorpio | 6 |

SANTO & JOHNNY

59	Pye International 7N 25037	Sleep Walk/All Night Diner (78 rpm, Pye N 25037 = £25)	15
60	Parlophone R 4619	Tear Drop/The Long Walk Home	10
60	Parlophone R 4644	Caravan/Summertime	10
61	Pye International 7N 25111	Theme From Come September/Hopscotch	10
61	Parlophone R 4844	Bullseye!/Twistin' Bells	10
62	Parlophone R 4865	Birmingham/The Mouse	10
62	Stateside SS 110	Spanish Harlem/Stage To Cimarron	10
64	Stateside SS 253	Three Cabelleros/Manhattan Spiritual	10
64	Stateside SS 292	In The Still Of The Night/Song For Rosemary	10
60	Parlophone GEP 8806	SANTO AND JOHNNY NO. 1 (EP)	32
60	Parlophone GEP 8813	SANTO AND JOHNNY NO. 2 (EP)	32
64	Stateside S(S)L 1008	HAWAII (LP)	20
67	Philips (S)BL 7759	PULCINELLA (LP)	15
67	Philips (S)BL 7760	MONA LISA (LP)	15

SAPODILLA PUNCH

| 69 | Mercury MF 1112 | Hold On I'm Coming/Bach To Minor | 8 |

SAPPHIRE

| 72 | SRT SRT 72226 | SAPPHIRE (LP) | 180 |

SAPPHIRE

| 82 | Sapphire Rocks SRR 001 | Jealousy (p/s) | 150 |

SAPPHIRES

63	Stateside SS 223	Where Is Johnny Now/Your True Love	60
64	Stateside SS 267	Who Do You Love/Oh So Soon	70
65	HMV POP 1441	Gotta Have Your Love/Gee Baby I'm Sorry (DJ copy = £300)	200
65	HMV POP 1461	Evil One/How Could I Say Goodbye (DJ copy = £300)	200
72	Probe PRO 556	Gotta Have Your Love/Gee Baby I'm Sorry (reissue)	15
74	Probe PRO 609	Slow Fizz/Our Love Is Everywhere	15
78	ABC 4221	Gonna Be A Big Thing/EDDIE REGAN: Playin' Hide And Seek	10

SARABAND

| 73 | Folk Heritage FHR 050 | CLOSE TO IT ALL (LP) | 25 |

SARACEN

82	Nucleus SAR 1	No More Lonely Nights/Rock Of Ages (p/s, some with patch)	8/6
83	Neat NEAT 30	We Have Arrived/Face In The Crowd (p/s)	7
82	Nucleus MPGR 492	HEROES, SAINTS AND FOOLS (LP)	15

SARAH JANE

| 66 | Pye 7N 17114 | Listen People/The World Is Round | 7 |

SARASOTA

| 96 | BIT Productions MIKE 004 | We're Gettin' Hot (1-sided 12") | 40 |
| 97 | BIT Productions MIKE 009 | Pleasure/We're Gettin' Hot (the Maximum Project Pumped Up Remix) (stickered white label 12") | 40 |

DON SARGENT

| 60 | Vogue Pop V 9160 | St. James' Infirmary/Gypsy Boots (triangular centre) | 500 |

SARI & SHALIMARS

| 68 | United Artists UP 2235 | It's So Lonely (Being Together)/You Walked Out On Me Before | 30 |

DEREK SARJEANT

61	Oak RGJ 101	FOLK SONGS SUNG BY DEREK SARJEANT (EP)	20
61	Oak RGJ 103	SONGS WE LIKE TO SING (EP, with tracks by Lisa Turner & Mick Wells)	15
61	Oak RGJ 105	FOLK SONGS SUNG BY DEREK SARJEANT VOL. 2 (EP)	15
63	Oak RGJ 117	MAN OF KENT (EP)	18

MIKE SARNE

62	Parlophone R 4974	Just For Kicks/Don't You Phone Me, I'll Phone You	6
63	Parlophone R 5010	Code Of Love/Are You Satisfied	6
63	Parlophone R 5060	Please Don't Say/Now You've Moved	5

Mike SARNE

63	Parlophone R 5090	Hello Lover Boy/Baby I'm On My Way	6
64	Parlophone R 5129	Out And About/A Place To Go	7
64	Parlophone R 5170	Love Me Please/You've Got Something (as Mike Sarne & Le Roys)	7
63	Parlophone DP 558	Just Like Eddie/Slow Twistin' Round The Totem Pole (export issue)	80
63	Parlophone GEP 8879	MIKE SARNE HIT PARADE (EP)	50
62	Parlophone PMC 1187	COME OUTSIDE (LP)	50

(see also Wendy Richards, Le Roys, Billie Davis, Rod McKuen)

SAROFEEN & SMOKE
| 71 | Pye International 7N 25556 | Susan Jane/Tomorrow | 5 |
| 71 | Pye Intl. NSPL 28153 | DO IT (LP) | 15 |

SAROLTA
| 68 | Island WIP 6035 | Open Your Hands/L.O.V.E. | 15 |

PETER SARSTEDT
68	Island WIP 6028	I Must Go On/Mary Jane	45
69	United Artists UP 2262	Morning Mountain/Step Into The Candelight (unissued)	
69	United Artists UP 35895	Frozen Orange Sea/Arethusa Loser	20
69	United Artists (S)ULP 1219	PETER SARSTEDT (LP)	20
69	United Artists UAL 29037	AS THOUGH IT WERE A MOVIE (LP)	20
71	United Artists UAS 29247	EVERY WORD YOU SAY (LP, with inner sleeve)	20

(see also Sarstedt Brothers, Brothers Kane, Peter Lincoln)

SARSTEDT BROTHERS
| 73 | Regal Zonophone RZ 3081 | Chinese Restaurant/Beloved Illusions | 7 |
| 73 | Regal Zono. SRZA 8516 | WORLDS APART TOGETHER (LP, gatefold sleeve) | 20 |

(see also Brothers Kane, Peter Sarstedt, Eden Kane, Clive Sands, Wes Sands)

SASPARELLA
| 69 | Decca F 12892 | Spooky/Come Inside | 7 |

SASSAFRAS
| 73 | Polydor 2383 245 | EXPECTING COMPANY (LP) | 15 |

SASSENACHS
| 64 | Fontana TF 518 | That Don't Worry Me/All Over You | 28 |

SATAN
| 82 | Guardian GRC 145 | Kiss Of Death/Heads Will Roll (some with p/s) | 200/50 |
| 85 | Neat NEAT 1012 | COURT IN THE ACT (LP) | 40 |

SATANIC RITES
81	Heavy Metal HEAVY 8	Live To Ride/Hit And Run (p/s)	12
85	Chub CHUBLP 001	WHICH WAY THE WIND BLOWS (LP)	25
87	Chub CHUBLP 002	NO USE CRYING (LP)	30

SATAN'S RATS
77	DJM DJS 10819	In My Love For You/Façade (p/s)	30
77	DJM DJS 10821	Year Of The Rats/Louise (p/s)	25
78	DJM DJS 10840	You Make Me Sick/Façade (p/s)	25
89	Overground OVER 01	Year Of The Rats/Louise (p/s, 600 yellow vinyl, 400 white vinyl, 25 gold vinyl, numbered test pressings)	6/7/15
89	Overground OVER 02	In My Love For You/Facade (p/s, 600 yellow vinyl, 400 white vinyl, 25 gold vinyl, numbered test pressings)	6/7/15
91	Overground OVER 14	You Make Me Sick/Louise (p/s, clear vinyl, 567 copies only)	7

YOUNG SATCH
| 70 | Black Swan BW 1401 | Bongo Bongo/BOYS: Ramba | 12 |

GIRL SATCHMO
61	Blue Beat BB 45	Satchmo's Mash Potato/Darling	20
62	Blue Beat BB 79	Twist Around Town/My New Honey (with Karl Rowe & Bluebeats)	20
63	Blue Beat BB 156	Don't Be Sad/Brother Joe (with Les Dawson Combo)	20
64	Blue Beat BB 227	Rhythm Of The New Beat/Blue Beat Chariot	20
69	Fab FAB 111	Take You For A Ride/I'm Coming Home	15
69	Trojan TR 676	Taken For A Ride/I'm Coming Home	10

(see also Pat Satchmo, Sugar & Dandy)

PAT SATCHMO
69	Punch PH 9	Hello Dolly/ERIC DONALSON: Never Get Away	12
69	Upsetter US 316	Hello Dolly/King Of The Trombone	10
70	Punch PH 24	Wonderful World/MEDITATORS: Purple Mast	12
70	Songbird SB 1039	A Handful Of Friends/CRYSTALITES: Handful — Version	10
72	Attack ATT 8024	What's Going On/LLOYD & CAREY: Tubby's In Full Swing	28

(see also Girl Satchmo, Hortense Ellis)

SATIN BELLS
68	Pye 7N 17531	Baby You're So Right For Me/When You're Ready	10
68	Pye 7N 17608	Da-Di-Da-Da/Oh No Oh Yes	5
69	Decca F 22937	I Stand Accused (Of Loving You)/Sweet Darlin'	20

(see also Three Bells)

SATIN STORM
91	Satin Storm SSP 201	Satin Storm 1999/Pleasurezone (Inst)/Buzz/Feel The Spirit (12")	30
91	Satin Storm SSHC 1	See The Light/Call In The Hardcore/Kick Up A Sound Boy/Chill Out (12", as Satin Storm Dancers)	15
92	Satin Storm DJT DAPSS 1	Let's Get Together/Free Your Mind (12", Artist not credited on labels)	40
92	Satin Storm ST 01	Sweat/Can't Wait/Can't Take No More/Tekno/Satin Storm/EBGB (12")	20
92	Satin Storm SSHC 2	What About What I Need /Drop That Bass/House Of My Dreams/Ram it (12", artist not credited on labels)	15
92	Satin Storm SSHC 3	Think I'm Going Out Of My Head/Unknown/What Do You Do? (12")	15
93	Satin Storm SSHC 4	Return Of The Blopblingers/Rough And Smooth & The Driven) (12")	10
93	Satin Storm SSHC 5	Come On, Get Together/I'm A Technician/He's On It, All Night Long (12")	10

SATISFACTION
71	Decca F 13129	Love It Is/Cold Summer	10
71	Decca F 13207	Don't Rag The Lady/Gregory Shan't	10
71	Decca SKL 5075	SATISFACTION (LP)	30+

(see also Mike Cotton Sound)

SATISFACTION
| 79 | Live & Love LAP 005 | SATISFACTION IN DUB (LP) | 40 |

SATISFIERS
| 57 | Vogue Coral Q 72247 | Where'll I Be Tomorrow Night?/Come Away, Love (78 rpm = £7) | 15 |
| 57 | Vogue Coral LVA 9068 | THE SATISFIERS (LP) | 25 |

SATTA I
| 76 | Trojan TRLS 138 | LIZZARD (LP) | 30 |

LONNIE SATTIN
56	Capitol CL 14552	Trapped (In The Web Of Love)/Your Home Can Be A Castle	8
56	Capitol CL 14638	High Steel/What Time Does The Sun Go Down?	7
57	Capitol CL 14771	I'll Never Stop Loving You/Whoo-Pie Shoo-Pie (78 rpm = £6)	7
58	Capitol CL 14831	Ring Around The Moon/My Heart's Your Home	6
60	Warner Bros WB 15	I'll Fly Away/Any More Than I	6

SATURNALIA
| 71 | Matrix TRIX 1 | MAGICAL LOVE (LP, picture disc, with booklet & ticket) | 50 |
| 73 | Matrix TRIX 1 | MAGICAL LOVE (LP, picture disc, reissue) | 15 |

(see also Horse)

SAUCERMAN
88	Fierce FRIGHT 029	Scatterbrain/Beyond Repair (12", p/s with inner, 1 side etched, 1,000 only)	8
89	Fierce FRIGHT 035	I Will Be King/Sid James Rules (withdrawn)	25
80s	Fierce	WRESTLING (12", sampler, withdrawn)	12

(see also Kray Cherubs)

LARRY SAUNDERS
| 74 | London HLU 10469 | On The Real Side/Let Me Be The Special One (DJ copy = £75) | 40 |

MAHALIA SAUNDERS
| 71 | Moodisc HME 112 | Down The Aisle/IAN ROBINSON: Three For One | 8 |
| 71 | Upsetter US 374 | Pieces Of My Heart/UPSETTERS: (Version) | 10 |

TUPPER SAUSSY
| 63 | London HAU 8127 | DISCOVER TUPPER SAUSSY (LP) | 15 |

LES SAUTERELLES
| 68 | Decca F 22824 | Heavenly Club/Dream Machine | 60 |

SAVAGE
82	Ebony EBON 10	Ain't No Fit Place/China Run	8
83	Ebony EBON 12	LOOSE 'N' LETHAL (LP)	25
85	Zebra ZEB 4	HYPERACTIVE (LP)	12

EDNA SAVAGE
55	Parlophone MSP 6175	Stars Shine In Your Eyes/A Star Is Born	8
55	Parlophone MSP 6181	Candlelight/In The Wee Small Hours Of The Morning	8
55	Parlophone MSP 6189	Arrivederci Darling/Bella Notte	8
56	Parlophone MSP 6217	Tell Me, Tell Me, Tell Me That You Love Me/Please Hurry Home	7
56	Parlophone R 4226	My Prayer/Me 'n' You 'n' The Moon	7

(see also Michael Holliday)

JOAN SAVAGE
57	Columbia DB 3929	Five Oranges, Four Apples/Bamboozled	8
57	Columbia DB 3968	With All My Heart/Love Letters In The Sand	8
57	Columbia DB 4039	Shake Me, I Rattle/Lula Rock-A-Hula	20
58	Columbia DB 4159	Hello Happiness, Goodbye Blues/Left Right Out Of My Heart	8

SAVAGE PENCIL
| 88 | Blast First FU 3LP | PRESENTS ANGEL DUST: MUSIC FOR MOVIE BIKERS (LP, picture disc, 1,000 only) | 15 |

(see also Art Attacks, Kray Cherubs)

SAVAGE RESURRECTION
| 68 | Mercury MF 1027 | Thing In E/Fox Is Sick | 40 |
| 68 | Mercury SMCL 20123 | SAVAGE RESURRECTION (LP) | 150 |

SAVAGES
| 63 | Decca DFE 8546 | EVERYBODY SURF! WITH THE SURFIN' SAVAGES (EP) | 200 |

(see also Soul Sounds, Screaming Lord Sutch, Circles, Tony Dangerfield & Thrills)

JULIAN JAY SAVARIN
70s	Lyntone LYN 3426	I Am You/Kizeesh (Corgi Books sampler)	10
73	Birth RAB 2	WAITERS ON THE DANCE (LP, some with insert)	200/135
87	Five Hours Back TOCK 002	WAITERS ON THE DANCE (LP, reissue)	20

(see also Julian's Treatment)

JIMMY SAVILE
| 62 | Decca F 11493 | Ahab The Arab/Very Unlikely | 5 |

(see also Vernons Girls)

RONNIE SAVOY
| 61 | MGM MGM 1122 | And The Heavens Cried/Big Chain | 10 |
| 61 | MGM MGM 1131 | Bewitched/It's Gotta Be love | 10 |

SAVOY BROWN (BLUES BAND)
66	Purdah 45-3503	I Tried/Can't Quit You Baby (as Savoy Brown's Blues Band)	250
67	Decca F 12702	Taste And Try, Before You Buy/Someday People (as Savoy Brown Blues Band)	20
68	Decca F 12797	Walking By Myself/Vicksburg Blues	12

MINT VALUE £

69	Decca F 12843	Train To Nowhere/Tolling Bells	20
69	Decca F 12978	I'm Tired/Stay With Me Baby	18
70	Decca F 13019	A Hard Way To Go/Waiting In The Bamboo Grove	15
70	Decca F 13098	Poor Girl/Master Hare	12
71	Decca F 13247	Tell Mama/Let It Rock	12
73	Decca F 13372	So Tired/The Saddest Feeling	7
73	Decca F 13431	Coming Down Your Way/I Can't Find You	7
67	Decca LK/SKL 4883	SHAKE DOWN (LP, mono/stereo)	70/75
68	Decca LK/SKL 4925	GETTING TO THE POINT (LP, mono/stereo)	50/55
69	Decca LK/SKL 4994	BLUE MATTER (LP, mono/stereo)	40/35
69	Decca LK/SKL 5013	A STEP FURTHER (LP, mono/stereo)	40/35
70	Decca LK/SKL 5043	RAW SIENNA (LP, mono/stereo, gatefold sleeve)	30/25
70	Decca SKL 5066	LOOKING IN (LP, gatefold sleeve)	25
71	Decca TXS 104	STREET CORNER TALKING (LP, gatefold sleeve)	22
72	Decca TXS 107	HELLBOUND TRAIN (LP, gatefold sleeve)	22
73	Decca SKL 5152	LION'S SHARE (LP)	18
73	Decca TXS 112	JACK THE TOAD (LP)	18
74	Decca SKL 5186	BOOGIE BROTHERS (LP)	15

(see also Warren Philips & The Rockets, Chris Youlden, Stone's Masonry, Jackie Lynton, Foghat)

TOM SAWYER
69	CBS 4243	Cookbook/Gates	10

(see also Unit 4 + 2)

'ACE' DINNING SAX
59	Top Rank JAR 184	Mulholland Drive/My Love (78 rpm = £15)	15

MIKE SAX & IDOLS
65	Mercury MF 886	My Little One/Come Back To Me	5

(see also Idols)

SAXON
79	Carrere SAM 109	Big Teaser/Stallions Of The Highway (12", promo only)	15
79	Carrere CAR 118	Big Teaser/Stallions Of The Highway (p/s)	10
79	Carrere CAR 129	Backs To The Wall/Militia Guard (p/s)	10
80	Carrere CAR 151	747 (Strangers In The Night)/See The Light Shining (p/s)	5
80	Carrere CAR 151	747 (Strangers In The Night)/See The Light Shining (12", p/s)	10
80	Carrere HM 5	Big Teaser/Stallions Of The Highway (p/s, reissue)	5
80	Carrere HM 6	Backs To The Wall/Militia Guard (p/s, reissue)	5
80	Carrere CAR 165	Suzie Hold On/Judgement Day (live) (p/s)	5
81	Carrere CAR 180P	And The Bands Played On/Hungry Years/Heavy Metal Thunder (picture disc)	8
81	Carrere CAR 204/ SAM 134	Never Surrender/20,000 Feet (Remix)//Bap-shoo-ap! (live)/ Street Fighting Gang (double pack)	5
83	Carrere CARP 284P	Nightmare/Midas Touch (picture disc)	10
83	Carrere CART 284	Nightmare/Midas Touch/747 (Strangers In The Night) (12", p/s, some with patch)	15/10
83	Carrere SAXON 1	The Power And The Glory/See The Light Shining (live) (poster p/s)	7
83	Carrere SAXON P 1	The Power And The Glory/See The Light Shining (live) (pic disc, 600 signed)	10/6
83	Carrere SAXON T 1	The Power And The Glory/See The Light Shining (live) (12", p/s)	8
84	Carrere CAR 323	Do It All For You/Just Let Me Rock (p/s)	5
84	Carrere CART 323	Do It All For You/Just Let Me Rock (12", p/s)	8
85	Parlophone RP 6103	Back On The Streets/Live Fast Die Young (shaped picture disc)	7
85	Parlophone 12RA 6103	Back On The Streets (Extended Version)/Back On The Streets/ Live Fast Die Young (12", p/s with poster & sticker)	8
85	Parlophone 12R 6103	Back On The Streets (Club Mix)/Back On The Streets/Live Fast Die Young (12", promo only)	15
86	Parlophone R 6112	Rock 'n' Roll Gypsy/Krakatoa (poster p/s)	5
86	Parlophone RP 6112	Rock 'n' Roll Gypsy/Krakatoa (picture disc)	7
86	EMI EMIP 5587	Rock The Nations/747/And The Bands Played On (shaped picture disc)	7
86	EMI 12EMI 5587	Rock The Nations/747/And The Bands Played On (12", clear vinyl, st'krd p/s)	4
88	EMI EMP 43	Ride Like The Wind/Red Alert (shaped picture disc)	10
88	EMI EMP 54	I Can't Wait Anymore/Broken Heroes (live) (pouch pack, with discography & poster)	7
80s	Din Disc DINSY 105	We Will Remember/Altar Of The Gods (shaped picture disc)	8
82	Carrere CAL 137	THE EAGLE HAS LANDED (LP, picture disc)	18
83	Carrere CAL 147	THE POWER AND THE GLORY (LP, picture disc)	15
84	Carrere CALP 200	CRUSADER (LP, picture disc)	15
85	Parlophone SAXONP 2	INNOCENCE IS NO EXCUSE (LP, picture disc)	18
87	EMI EMS 1163	DENIM AND LEATHER (LP, blue vinyl reissue)	15

(see also Son Of A Bitch)

AL SAXON
58	Fontana H 164	The Day The Rains Came (Le Jour Ou La Pluie Viendra)/You're The Top-Cha	8
58	Fontana H 164	The Day The Rains Came (Le Jour Ou La Pluie Viendra)/You're The Top-Cha (78)	8
59	Fontana H 188	Chattanooga Choo-Choo/Chip Off The Old Block (78 rpm = £8)	5
59	Fontana H 205	Only Sixteen/I'm All Right, Jack (78 rpm = £8)	6
59	Fontana H 222	Linda Lu/Heart Of Stone (78 rpm = £10)	6
59	Fontana H 231	Marina/Me Without You (78 rpm = £10)	6
58	Fontana TFE 17014	THOSE YOU'VE NEVER HEARD (EP)	10
59	Fontana TFE 17202	BIG DEAL (EP)	10
60	Fontana TFE 17271	THE BATTLE OF THE SEXES (EP)	10

(see also Lana Sisters, Ella Stone & Moss)

SKY 'SUNLIGHT' SAXON
87	Fierce FRIGHT 009	Dog=God (p/s, with badge, piece of shirt, sugar 'skycubes' & inserts)	20
84	Psycho PSYCHO 29	STARRY EYED (LP, some on clear vinyl)	20/12
90s	Water NOXAS 39	DRAGON SLAYER (LP, multicoloured vinyl)	12

(see also Seeds)

SKY SAXON & THE NEW SEEDS
90s Expression EXP 777-3   In Love With Life/Starry Ride/Queen/Tired Of Being Poor 6

LINDA SAXONE
64   Pye 7N 15624   Love Is A Many Splendoured Thing/The Other Side Of The Street 10
65   Polydor BM 56015   I've Got To Say No/Another Day Another Night 6
65   Polydor BM 56032   Only Last Night/Lucky Girl 6

SAXONS
63   Ace Of Clubs ACL 1173   MEET THE SAXONS (LP) 120

SAXONS
65   Decca F 12179   Saxon War Cry/Click-Ete-Clack 50
(see also Tornados)

JOHNNY SAYLES
66   Liberty LIB 12042   Deep Down In Your Heart/Anything For You 40

RAT SCABIES
84   Paradiddle Music HIT 1   Let There Be Rats/Wiped Out/Drums Drums Drums (mail-order only, no p/s) 8
(see also Damned, The Rat & The Whale, Pete Zear)

SCABS
79   Clubland Records SJP 799   Amory Building/Leave Me Alone/Don't Just Sit There/U.R.E.
     (blue/black or red/black fold out 'envelope' p/s, 2 inserts) . . . . each 40

SCAFFOLD
66   Parlophone R 5443   2 Day's Monday/3 Blind Jellyfish 8
66   Parlophone R 5548   Goodbat Nightman/A Long Strong Black Pudding 10
67   Parlophone R 5643   Thank U Very Much/Ide B The First 6
68   Parlophone R 5734   Lily The Pink/Buttons On Your Mind 6
68   Parlophone R 5679   Do You Remember?/Carry On Krow 6
68   Parlophone R 5703   1-2-3/Today 6
69   Parlophone R 5784   Charity Bubbles/Goose 6
69   Parlophone R 5812   Gin Gan Goolie/Liver Birds 8
70   Parlophone R 5847   All The Way Up/Please — Sorry 8
70   Parlophone R 5866   Busdreams/If I Could Start All Over Again 8
71   Parlophone R 5922   Do The Albert/Commercial Break 8
74   Warner Bros K 16400   Liverpool Lou/Ten Years On After Strawberry Jam 8
68   Parlophone PMC/PCS 7051   AN EVENING WITH ... — LIVE AT QUEEN ELIZABETH HALL
     (LP, black/yellow label) 22
69   Parlophone PMC/PCS 7077   L THE P (LP, black/yellow label) 20
73   Island ILPS 9234   FRESH LIVER (LP) 20
(see also McGough-McGear, Roger McGough, Mike McGear, Liverpool Scene, Grimms, John Gorman)

BOZ SCAGGS
71   CBS 7219   We Were Always Sweethearts/Painted Bells 5
71   CBS 7401   Near You/Downright Woman 5
69   Atlantic 588 205   BOZ SCAGGS (LP) 20
71   CBS 64248   MOMENTS (LP, plain orange label) 12
74   CBS S65953   SLOW DANCER (LP) 15
(see also Steve Miller Band, Steve York's Camelo Pardalis)

HARVEY SCALES & 7 SOUND
67   Atlantic 584 146   Get Down/Love It Is 10

SCAMPS
59   London HLW 8827   Petite Fleur/Naomi 12
62   Ace Of Clubs ACL 1116   TEEN DANCE AND SING ALONG PARTY (LP) 15

SCARAB
80   Inferno HEADBANGER 1   Rock Night/Wicked Woman 30
84   Pharaoh PR-001   Poltergeist/Hell On Wheels (p/s) 50

SCARECROW
78   Spilt Milk SMFM 11278   SCARECROW LIVE (LP, numbered foldout sleeve with insert;
     beware of watermarked unnumbered copies) 40

SCARLETS
64   Philips BF 1376   Let's Go/Tambourine Shake 6

CHARLES FRANCIS SCARRATT III
59   Felsted AF 113   Two Innocent Lovers/Lovemobile (78 rpm = £8) 6

SCARS
79   Fast Product FAST 8   Horrorshow/Adult-ery (p/s) 5
81   Pre PRE 014   All About You/Author Author (p/s) 7
80   Pre PRE 005   Love Song (p/s) 12
81   I.D. ID-1   Your Attention Please (gold vinyl flexidisc with *ID* magazine, issue 3) 8
81   Pre PREX 5   AUTHOR! AUTHOR! (LP) 12

SCENE
80   Inferno BEAT 2   I've Had Enough/Show 'Em Now (p/s) 12

SCENE
80   Hole In The Wall HS 1   Hey Girl/Reach The Top (p/s) 50

SCENE
83   Diamond DIA 001   Looking For A Love/Let Me Know (p/s) 8
85   Diamond DIA 003   Something That You Said/Stop-Go (p/s) 7
85   Diamond DIA 007   Good Lovin'/2 Plus 2 (some with p/s) 15/5
(see also Diplomats)

MIKE SCENE
71   Pye LBB 9050   For The Love Of Mike 7

MINT VALUE £

SCEPTERS
69   Spark SRL 1006   What's The Matter With Juliet/Something's Coming Along 40

HAL SCHAEFER ORCHESTRA & CHORUS
58   London HLT 8692   March Of The Vikings/March Of The Parisian Bakers (78 rpm= £8) 8

SCHEER
93   Son BUACD 293   Wish You Were Dead/Green Room Sex Kitten/Don't Know Why (p/s). 20

MICHAEL SCHENKER
94   EMI 724382861 1423   THE STORY OF MICHAEL SCHENKER (2-CD) 20
(see also McAuley Schenker Group, Michael Schenker Group, Scorpions, UFO)

LALO SCHIFRIN
68   Dot DOT 103   Mission: Impossible/Jim On The Move. 20
74   20th Century BTC 2150 Ape Shuffle (Theme From 'Planet Of The Apes')/Escape From Tomorrow. 25
74   Warner Bros K16333   Theme From Enter The Dragon/The Big Battle 10
76   CTI CTSP 5   Jaws Theme/Quiet Village 5
68   Dot (S)LPD 503   'MISSION: IMPOSSIBLE' — MUSIC FROM THE TV SERIES
                        (LP, TV soundtrack). 40
69   Paramount SPFL 252   MORE 'MISSION: IMPOSSIBLE' (LP, TV soundtrack) 40
70s Verve 2304 051   ROCK REQUIEM (LP) 12

SCHMETTERLINGE
77   Pye International 7N 25743 Boom Boom Boomerang/Mr Moneymaker's Music Show 10

SCHMIDT BROTHERS
90   Maison Recordings MAS1 Infinite Prowess/(Hip Shaking Instrumental Mix) (12" white label) 10
90   Maison Recordings MAS2 Whatever You Want/(Remix) (12" white label, die-cut sleeve) 10

TOBIAS SCHMIDT
96   Mosquito MSQ 06   THE FINGERPRINT EP (12", p/s) 15

ZAPPATA SCHMIDT
71   President PTLS 1041   IT'S GONNA GET YOU (LP) 40
(see also Equals)

OLIVER LINDSEY SCHMITT
72   private pressing   GRAFFENSTADDEN (LP) 40

EBERHARD SCHOENER
79   Harvest HAR 5196   Video Magic/Code Word Elvis (p/s). 8
(see also Police)

SCHOLARS
64   Stagesound SDE 29370/1 THE SCHOLARS (EP, no p/s) 15

SCHOOL BOYS
63   Blue Beat BB 162   Little Boy Blue/PRINCE BUSTER: Money. 32
63   Blue Beat BB 174   Little Dilly/The Joker (B-side actually by Prince Buster's Allstars) 32
64   Port-O-Jam PJ 4000   Dream Lover/I Want To Know 32
(see also Bill Gentles)

SCHOOLERS
69   Doctor Bird DB 1170   Ugly Man (actually by Scorchers)/Whip Cracker (actually by Vincent Gordon). . . 28

SCHOOLGIRL BITCH
78   Garage!/Aerco AERS 102 Abusing The Rules/Thinking For Yourself (no p/s) 40
78   Garage!/Aerco AERS 102 Abusing The Rules/Thinking For Yourself (spray-painted p/s) 150
78   Garage!/Aerco AERS 102 Abusing The Rules/Thinking For Yourself ('gasmask' p/s) 100
78   Garage!/Aerco AERS 102 Abusing The Rules/Thinking For Yourself ('queen' p/s) 45

SCHOOL GIRLS
63   Blue Beat BB 168   Love Another Love/Little Keithie. 15
63   Blue Beat BB 185   Live Up To Justice/Give Up 15
64   Blue Beat BB 214   Sing And Shout/Last Time 18
64   Blue Beat BB 263   Never Let You Go/BUSTER'S ALL STARS: Supercharge . . . . 50+

SCHOOL TIES
81   School Ties SCF 01   No Future 45

DON SCHROEDER
62   Philips BF 3040033   Quicksand/My Kind Of Woman 6

JOHN SCHROEDER ORCHESTRA
65   Piccadilly 7N 35240   The Fugitive Theme/Don't Break The Heart Of Kimble (some in p/s). 10/6
65   Piccadilly 7N 35253   You've Lost That Lovin' Feeling/Funny How Love Can Be. 6
66   Piccadilly 7N 35280   Ave Maria No Morro/Peter Popgunn 5
66   Piccadilly 7N 35285   Hungry For Love/Soul Destroyer. 30
65   Piccadilly 7N 35271   Agent 00 Soul/Night Rider 30
66   Piccadilly 7N 35319   On The Ball (Theme For The World)/The Britannia March 15
67   Piccadilly 7N 35362   Soul For Sale/Loving You Girl 30
69   Pye 7N 17862   The Virgin Soldiers' March/Sweet Soul Talk. 6
66   Piccadilly N(S)PL 38025 JOHN SCHROEDER'S WORKING IN THE SOULMINE (LP). 50
67   Piccadilly N(S)PL 38036 THE DOLLY CATCHER! (LP). 40
68   Marble Arch MAL 839   WORKING IN THE SOULMINE (LP, reissue). 25
71   Pye NSPL 18362   WITCHI-TAI-TO (LP). 25
72   Polydor 2460 149   TV VIBRATIONS (LP). 20
73   Polydor 2460 188   WAR AND PEACE & OTHER TELEVISION THEMES (LP) 20

IVY SCHULMAN & BOWTIES
57   London HLN 8372   Rock, Pretty Baby/BOWTIES: Ever Since I Can Remember (78 rpm = £35) . . . . . 40+

KLAUS SCHULZE
75   Caroline CA 2003   BLACK DANCE (LP) 12
(see also Tangerine Dream)

(Voices Of) WALTER SCHUMANN
54	HMV 7M 229	Haunted House/I Only Have Eyes For You	8
55	HMV 7M 323	The Man From Laramie/Let Me Hear You Whisper	8

SCHUNGE
72	Regal Zonophone RZ 3066	Misty/Joseph Demanio	7
73	Regal Zonophone RZ 3077	Ballad Of A Simple Love/Enter The Violins	7
72	Regal Zono. SLRZ 1033	BALLAD OF A SIMPLE LOVE (LP)	25

ARMANDO SCIASCIA ORCHESTRA
66	Ember EMB S 228	Theme From 'The Liars'/World Tomorrow Theme	5
66	Ember NR 5030	THE PEACH THIEF & GREAT MUSIC FROM TV SHOWS (LP)	15

SCIENCE POPTION
67	Columbia DB 8106	You've Got Me High/Back In Town	60+

SCIENTIST
69	Amalgamated AMG 848	Professor In Action/SUPERSONICS: Reflections Of Don D	28
80	JB JBLP 004	INTRODUCING (LP)	70
81	Greensleeves GREL 25	RIDS THE WORLD OF THE EVIL CURSE OF THE VAMPIRE (LP)	15
81	Starlight SLD 901	DUB LANDING (LP)	60

SCIENTIST & PRINCE JAMMY
82	Starlight SLDLP 903	DUB LANDING VOL 2 (LP)	20

SCIENTIST VERSUS PRINCE JAMMY
80	Greensleeves GRED 10	THE BIG SHOWDOWN 1980 (LP)	25

SCIENTISTS
85	Karbon KAR 007	You Only Live Twice/If It's The Last Thing I Do (p/s)	25
85	Karbon KAR 101 L	YOU GET WHAT YOU DESERVE (LP)	18
86	Karbon KAR 103 L	WEIRD LOVE (LP)	22
87	Karbon KAR 105 L	THE HUMAN JUKEBOX (LP)	22

SCIENTISTS OF SOUND
92	Bite It! BITE5	LIKE A SCIENTIST (EP)	10
94	Bite It! BITE9	Bad Boy Swing (12")	8

SCI-FI SEX STARS
86	Who Am I WM 1001 7	Rock It Miss U.S.A./Teenage Thunder (p/s)	8
86	Who Am I WM 1001	Rock It Miss U.S.A. (Death Wish IV)/Commercial Break/Teenage Thunder (Spitstyle)/Suicide (12", stickered p/s)	10

(see also Sigue Sigue Sputnik)

SCISSOR FITS
79	Dubious DUB 1/SJP 793	TAUT? TENSE? ANGULAR? AND OTHER BRITISH RAIL SANDWICHES (EP, gatefold sleeve)	8
79	Tortch TOR 005	SOON AFTER DARK (EP)	6

SCOOP
80	Sharp POINT 1	You Can Do It/Disco/My Friend Tony/Anonymity (p/s)	50

SCORCHED EARTH
85	Carrere CAR 342	Tomorrow Never Comes/Questions (promo only)	35
85	Carrere CART 342	Tomorrow Never Comes/Questions/So Long/Where Do We Go From Here (12", initially black sleeve, later red sleeve with insert)	70/60

SCORCHERS
69	Camel CA 17	Hold On Tight/THE ROYALS: 100 Lbs Of Clay	15
69	Duke DU 26	Hear Ya/VIBRATORS: Live Life	12

(see also Neville Hinds)

SCORE
66	Decca F 12527	Please Please Me/Beg Me	120+

SCORN
95	Earache SCORN 001	ELLIPSIS (5 x 12" box set)	18

SCORPION & BORIS GARDINER HAPPENING
73	Dragon DRA 1002	Deadly Sting/BORIS GARDINER HAPPENING: Boing Boing	5

SCORPIONS (Germany)
77	RCA PB 5556	He's A Woman, She's A Man/Suspender Love	8
79	Harvest HAR 5185	Is Anybody There?/Another Piece Of Meat (p/s, green vinyl, some on black vinyl)	6/7
79	Harvest HAR 5185	Is Anybody There?/Another Piece Of Meat (12", p/s)	10
79	Harvest HAR 5188	Love Drive/Coast To Coast (p/s)	6
79	Harvest 12HAR 5188	Love Drive/Coast To Coast (12", p/s)	10
79	RCA PC 9402	All Night Long/Fly To The Rainbow/Speedy's Coming/In Trance (12", p/s)	10
80	Harvest HAR 5206	Make It Real/Don't Make No Promises (p/s)	10
82	Harvest HAR 5219	No One Like You/The Zoo (p/s)	8
82	Harvest HARP 5219	No One Like You/The Zoo (picture disc)	10
84	Harvest 12HARP 5231	Big City Nights/Bad Boys Running Wild (12" picture disc, die-cut sleeve)	12
84	Harvest HAR 5225	Rock You Like A Hurricane/Coming Home (p/s)	6
85	Harvest 12HAR 5232	Still Loving You/Holiday/Big City Night (12", p/s)	8
85	Harvest 12HAR 5232	Still Loving You/Holiday/Big City Night (12", picture disc)	10
88	Harvest HARX 5240	Rhythm Of Love/We Let It Rock (box set with postcards)	8
88	Harvest HARP 5240	Rhythm Of Love/We Let It Rock (picture disc)	6
88	Harvest HARP 5242	Passion Rules The Game (die-cut picture disc)	6
91	Vertigo VER 54	Wind Of Change/Restless Nights (p/s, red vinyl)	5
91	Vertigo VERXP 54	Wind Of Change (12", etched red vinyl)	10
91	Vertigo VERXP 54	Wind Of Change/Restless Nights/Hit Between The Nights/Blackout (live) (12", picture disc)	8
91	Vertigo VERX 58	Wind Of Change (12", white vinyl, 3-D sleeve)	8
93	Mercury MERX 395	Under The Same Sun/Ship Of Fools/Partners In Crime (12", yellow vinyl)	8

MINT VALUE £

79	Harvest LP SHSP 4097	LOVE DRIVE (LP)	12
80	Harvest SHSP 4113	ANIMAL MAGNETISM (LP)	12
82	H.M. Worldwide HMILP 2	LONESOME CROW (LP, clear vinyl, reissue)	12
82	H.M. Worldwide HMIPD 2	LONESOME CROW (LP, picture disc, reissue)	15
88	Harvest SHSPP 4125	SAVAGE AMUSEMENT (LP, picture disc, with lyric sheet)	15
97	Mercury 314 534 788 2	WORLD WIDE LIVE (CD, reissue)	18

(see also Michael Schenker, Michael Schenker Group, UFO)

SCORPIONS (Jamaica)
72	Green Door GD 4019	Breaking Your Heart/IN CROWD BAND: Breaking Your Heart Version	6

(see also Bill Gentles, Lloyd Jackson)

SCORPIONS (U.K.)
61	Parlophone R 4740	(Ghost) Riders In The Sky/Torquay	20
61	Parlophone R 4768	Rockin' At The Phil/Scorpio	20

COLIN SCOT
71	United Artists UP 35216	Hey! Sandy/Nite People	5
73	Warner Bros K 16330	Call Me Mr Blue/It's Gonna Be Alright	7
71	United Artists UAG 29154	COLIN SCOT WITH FRIENDS (LP, gatefold sleeve, with Peter Hammill & Peter Gabriel)	30
73	Warner Bros K 46281	OUT OF THE BLUE (LP)	12

(see also Peter Hammill, Peter Gabriel)

WINSTON SCOTLAND
72	Green Door GD 4027	My (Girl) Little Filly/BUNNY BROWN: My Girl	7
72	Punch PH 100	Butter Cup/RONALD WILSON: I Care	7

(see also Bunny Flip, Big Youth, Bongo Les, Lennox Brown, Dennis Alcapone)

SCOTLAND WORLD CUP SQUAD
74	Polydor 2383282	SCOTLAND, SCOTLAND (LP)	12

SCOTS OF ST. JAMES
66	Go AJ 111404	Gypsy/Tic Toc	125
67	Spot JW 1	Timothy/Eiderdown Clown	200+

(see also Hopscotch, Forever More, Five Day Rain)

ANDY SCOTT
75	RCA RCA 2629	Lady Starlight/Where D'Ya Go (p/s)	12
83	Static TAK 10	Krugerrands/Face (p/s)	8
84	Static TAK 24	Let Her Dance/Suck It And See (p/s)	10
84	Static TAK 24-12	Let Her Dance (Full Version)/(Instrumental)/Suck It And See (12", p/s)	10
84	Static TAK 31	Invisible/Never Too Young (clear vinyl, stickered PVC sleeve)	12
84	Statik TAK 31-12	Invisible (Single Version)/(Instrumental)/Invisible (Extended Version)/ Never Too Young (12", clear vinyl, stickered PVC sleeve)	12

(see also Sweet, Elastic Band, Mayfield's Mule)

ARTIE SCOTT ORCHESTRA
70	Major Minor MM 670	March Of The Skinheads/Love At First Sight	10

BILLY SCOTT
58	London HLU 8565	You're The Greatest/That's Why I Was Born (78 rpm = £12)	30
60	Top Rank JAR 270	Carole/Stairway To The Stairs	6

BOBBY SCOTT
56	London HL 8254	Chain Gang/Shadrack (78 rpm = £12)	40
56	London Jazz EZ-C 19008	THE BOBBY SCOTT TRIO (EP)	10
55	London Jazz LZ-N 14001	BOBBY SCOTT TRIO (10" LP)	15

BRUCE SCOTT
65	Mercury MF 857	I Made An Angel Cry/Don't Say Goodbye To Me	25
65	MGM MGM 1291	Once A Thief Twice A Thief/So Much To Live For	7

BUNNY SCOTT
75	KLIK KLP 9004	TO LOVE SOMEBODY (LP)	15

DEREK SCOTT ORCHESTRA
63	Pye 7N 15500	Hancock's Tune/Spying Tonight	8
67	Philips BF 1568	Honey Lane/Song Without Words	5

FREDDIE SCOTT
63	Colpix PX 692	Hey Girl/The Slide	35
63	Colpix PX 709	I Got A Woman/Brand New World	35
67	London HLZ 10103	Are You Lonely For Me/Where Were You	15
67	London HLZ 10123	Cry To Me/No One Could Ever Love You	15
67	London HLZ 10139	Am I Grooving You?/Never You Mind	10
67	London HLZ 10172	He Ain't Give You None/Run Joe	10
69	Roulette RO 509	Sugar Sunday/Johnny's Hill	6
71	Jay Boy BOY 34	Just Like A Flower/Spanish Harlem	10
72	Jay Boy BOY 59	Are You Lonely For Me Baby/The Woman Of My Love	10
70s	Upfront UP 1	The Great If/Deep In The Night	10
71	Joy JOYS 215	ARE YOU LONELY FOR ME (LP)	25

HAZEL SCOTT
53	Capitol LC 6607	LATE SHOW (10" LP)	20

JACK SCOTT (& CHANTONES)
58	London HLU 8626	My True Love/Leroy (78 rpm = £20)	10
58	London HLL 8765	With Your Love/Geraldine (as Jack Scott with Chantones) (78 rpm = £40)	22
59	London HLL 8804	Goodbye Baby/Save My Soul (as Jack Scott with Chantones) (78 rpm = £50)	22
59	London HL 7069	Goodbye Baby/Save My Soul (export issue)	22
59	London HLL 8851	I Never Felt Like This/Bella (78 rpm = £60)	22
59	London HLL 8912	The Way I Walk/Midgie (triangular or round centre) (78 rpm = £80)	each 25

59	London HLL 8970	There Comes A Time/Baby Marie (triangular or round centre)	each 25
59	London HLL 8970	There Comes A Time/Baby Marie (78)	100
60	Top Rank JAR 280	What In The World's Come Over You/Baby, Baby	8
60	Top Rank JAR 375	Burning Bridges/Oh, Little One	10
60	Top Rank JAR 419	Cool Water/It Only Happened Yesterday	10
60	Top Rank JAR 524	Patsy/Old Time Religion	10
61	Top Rank JAR 547	Is There Something On Your Mind/Found A Woman	10
61	Capitol CL 15200	A Little Feeling/Now That I	10
61	Capitol CL 15216	Strange Desire/My Dream Come True	15
62	Capitol CL 15236	One Of These Days/Steps 1 And 2	15
62	Capitol CL 15261	Sad Story/I Can't Hold Your Letters In My Arms	15
63	Capitol CL 15302	Meo Myo/All I See Is Blue	15
59	London RE-I 1205	MY TRUE LOVE (EP, initially triangular centre, later round centre)	110/80
61	Top Rank JKP 3002	WHAT IN THE WORLD'S COME OVER YOU (EP)	65
61	Top Rank JKP 3011	I REMEMBER HANK WILLIAMS (EP)	50
58	London HA-L 2156	JACK SCOTT (LP)	130
60	Top Rank BUY 034	I REMEMBER HANK WILLIAMS (LP)	35
60	Top Rank 25-024	WHAT IN THE WORLD'S COME OVER YOU (LP)	75
61	Top Rank 35-109	THE SPIRIT MOVES ME (LP)	65
64	Capitol (S)T 2035	BURNING BRIDGES (LP, mono/stereo)	60/80

JANET SCOTT & JACKIE RAE

60	Fontana TFE 17203	SWEET TALK (EP, also stereo STFE 8009)	each 12
60	Fontana TFL 5102	WE LOVE LIFE! (LP, also stereo STFL 533)	each 15

(see also Jackie Rae)

JIMMY SCOTT

69	Revolution REV 002	Ob-La-Di, Ob-La-Da/Story Part 2 — Allulo & Doh	8

JOHN SCOTT

73	JSD JSD 100	JOHN SCOTT DEMONSTRATION RECORD (LP, beware, many warped)	80

JOHN SCOTT

60	Parlophone R 4697	Hi-Flutin' Boogie/Peace Pipe	5
65	Parlophone R 5380	A Study In Terror/Punjab	5
67	Polydor 56184	Rocket To The Moon Theme/The Long Duel Theme	8
68	Spark SRL 1008	Amsterdam Affair Theme/Kathleen	8

JOHNNY SCOTT QUINTET

67	Columbia S(C)X 6149	COMMUNICATION (LP)	12

JUDI SCOTT

68	Page One POF 066	Billy Sunshine/Happy Song	28

JUDY SCOTT

57	Brunswick 05687	The Game Of Love (A-One And A-Two)/With All My Heart	10
57	Brunswick 05704	Parlour Piano Theme/A Tender Word	8

JULIAN SCOTT

61	Columbia DB 4571	My Steady Date/So Tired	7

KEVIN SCOTT

59	Parlophone R 4520	Wait For Me/Love Of My Life (78 rpm = £8)	6
59	Parlophone R 4540	Ciao Ciao Bambina (Piove)/Broken-Hearted Clown	5
60	HMV POP 731	You Are Beautiful/Love Look Away	5

LINDA SCOTT

60	Columbia DB 4638	I've Told Every Little Star/Three Guesses	10
61	Columbia DB 4692	Don't Bet Money, Honey/Starlight Starbright	10
61	Columbia DB 4748	I Don't Know Why/It's All Because	10
61	Columbia DB 4829	Count Every Star/Land Of Stars	10
62	Pye International 7N 25146	Never In A Million Years/Through The Summer	15
63	London HLR 9802	Let's Fall In Love/I Know It, You Know It	15
61	Columbia 33SX 1386	STARLIGHT, STARBRIGHT (LP)	100

LINDA SCOTT

69	CBS 4528	The Composer/You Made A Fool Out Of Me	15
69	CBS 4246	First Of All/The Answer's In My Eyes	5

McBEAN SCOTT & CHAMPIONS

70	Jackpot JP 744	Top Of The World/LARRY LAWRENCE & CHAMPIONS: Everybody Reggae	8

MIKE SCOTT

65	Mercury MF 906	I Am A Rock/I'm Gonna Be Somebody Someday	6

NEIL SCOTT

61	Pye International 7N 25096	Bobby/I Haven't Found It With Another	8

NICKY SCOTT

67	Immediate IM 044	Big City/Everything's Gonna Be Alright	30
67	Immediate IM 045	Backstreet Girl/Chain Reaction	40
69	Pye 7N 17688	Honey Pie/No More Tomorrow	7

(see also Diane Ferraz & Nicky Scott)

PEGGY SCOTT

69	Polydor 56722	Every Little Bit Hurts/You Can Never Get Something For Nothing	8
79	Pinnacle PIN 73	You've Got It All/Let Me Unite You (p/s)	8

(see also Peggy Scott & Jo Jo Benson)

PEGGY SCOTT & JO JO BENSON

68	Polydor 56745	Lover's Holiday/Here With Me	10
69	Polydor 56750	Pickin' Wild Mountain Berries/Pure Love And Pleasure	8
69	Polydor 56761	Soulshake/We Were Made For Each Other	10
69	Polydor 56773	We Got Our Own Bag/I Want To Love You Babe	8

71	Atlantic 2091 066	I Thank You/Spreadin' Love	5
69	Polydor 583 731	SOULSHAKE (LP)	25
70	Polydor 583 756	LOVER'S HEAVEN (LP)	25

(see also Peggy Scott)

RAMBLIN' TOMMY SCOTT
| 54 | Parlophone CMSP 15 | Ain't Love Grand/What Do You Know — I Love Her (export issue) | 20 |

RAYMOND SCOTT
| 54 | London L 1229 | Naked City/Shadow Dance (78) | 10 |

ROBIN SCOTT
| 69 | Head HDS 4003 | The Sailor/Sound Of The Rain | 35 |
| 69 | Head HDLS 6003 | WOMAN FROM THE WARM GRASS (LP, with insert) | 150+ |

(see also Mighty Baby, M)

RONNIE SCOTT
51	Esquire 10-154	Crazy Rhythm/El Sino (78)	8
51	Esquire 10-185	Close Your Eyes/I Didn't Know What Time It Was (78, with Ronnie Ball)	8
53	Esquire 10-321	Stomping At The Savoy/Body Beautiful (78)	8
54	Esquire 10-335	Night And Day	10
56	Decca FJ 10712	Basie Talks/Flying Home (as Ronnie Scott Orchestra)	10
57	Tempo A 153	I'll Take Romance/Speak Low (as Ronnie Scott New Quintet) (78 rpm = £8)	35
55	Esquire EP 31	RONNIE SCOTT ORCHESTRA (EP)	20
55	Esquire EP 51	RONNIE SCOTT QUARTET (EP)	20
55	Esquire EP 61	RONNIE SCOTT ORCHESTRA (EP)	20
55	Esquire EP 65	RONNIE SCOTT QUINTET (EP)	10
56	Esquire EP 81	RONNIE SCOTT ORCHESTRA (EP)	20
56	Esquire EP 85	RONNIE SCOTT ORCHESTRA (EP)	25
56	Esquire EP 95	RONNIE SCOTT ORCHESTRA (EP)	18
56	Tempo EXA 45	RONNIE SCOTT BLOWS WITH THE DIZZY REECE QUARTET (EP)	80
52	Esquire 20-006	RONNIE SCOTT QUARTET (10" LP)	80
54	Esquire 32-001	THE RONNIE SCOTT JAZZ CLUB VOLUME 1 (LP)	45
54	Esquire 32-002	THE RONNIE SCOTT JAZZ CLUB VOLUME 2 (LP)	45
54	Esquire 32-003	THE RONNIE SCOTT JAZZ CLUB VOLUME 3 (LP)	45
54	Esquire 32-006	THE RONNIE SCOTT JAZZ CLUB VOLUME 4 (LP)	45
56	Decca LF 1261	AT THE ROYAL FESTIVAL HALL (10" LP)	45
57	Philips BBL 7153	PRESENTING THE RONNIE SCOTT SEXTET (LP)	70
66	Fontana TL 5332	THE NIGHT IS SCOTT AND YOU'RE SO SWINGABLE (LP)	40
69	CBS Realm Jazz 523661	LIVE AT RONNIE SCOTT'S (LP)	25
74	RCA Victor LPL1	SCOTT AT RONNIE'S (LP)	20
77	Pye NSPL 18542	SERIOUS GOLD (LP)	15

(see also Jazz Couriers, Tubby Hayes, Dizzy Reece)

SHIRLEY SCOTT
66	Transatlantic PR 7205	HIP SOUL (LP)	18
69	Atlantic 588 175	SOUL SONG (LP)	15
71	Chess 6310 109	MYSTICAL LADY (LP)	15

SIMON SCOTT (& LE ROYS)
64	Parlophone R 5164	Move It Baby/What Kind Of Woman (with Le Roys)	10
64	Parlophone R 5207	My Baby's Got Soul/Midnight (with Le Roys)	10
65	Parlophone R 5298	Tell Him I'm Not Home (as Simon Scott & All Nite Workers)/Heart Cry	18
69	Polydor 56355	Brave New World/I'm The Universe	6

(see also Le Roys)

TERRY SCOTT
62	Parlophone R 4967	My Brother/Don't Light The Fire 'Til After	20
66	Pye 7N 17093	Juanita Banana/I Like Birds	7
76	DJM DJS 665	A Bed Full Of Foreigners/Nicholas The Circus Clown (with June Whitfield)	6

TOM SCOTT
| 77 | Epic EPC 5589 | Gotcha (Theme From 'Starsky & Hutch')/Smoothin' On Down | 12 |

TOMMY SCOTT
62	Decca F 11474	Angela/Did You (as Jay & Tommy Scott)	6
64	Decca F 11839	Who Will It Be?/If It's Me That You Want	5
64	Decca F 11942	Wrap Your Troubles In Dreams/Blueberry Hill	5

TONY SCOTT
| 69 | Escort ES 805 | What Am I To Do/Bring Back That Smile | 10 |

GIL SCOTT-HERON (& BRIAN JACKSON)
73	Philips 6073 705	Lady Day And John Coltrane/When You Are Who You Are (with Pretty Purdie & The Playboys)	20
78	Arista ARIST 169	The Bottle (live)/Hello Sunday, Hello Road	8
79	Inferno HEAT 23	The Bottle (Drunken Mix)/The Bottle (Sober Mix) (with Brian Jackson)	10
79	Inferno HEAT 23-12	The Bottle (Drunken Mix)/The Bottle (Sober Mix) (12", with Brian Jackson)	15
73	Philips 6369 415	PIECES OF A MAN (LP)	40
74	RCA SF 8428	THE REVOLUTION WILL NOT BE TELEVISED (LP)	30
75	Arista ARTY 106	FIRST MINUTES OF A NEW DAY (LP)	40
76	Arista DARTY 1	IT'S YOUR WORLD (LP, with Brian Jackson)	30

MICHELLE SCOTTI
| 64 | Philips BF 1384 | Little Drummer Boy/Lonely Lonely Lonely | 6 |

SCOTT'S WASHBOARD BAND
| 60 | Columbia 33SX 1232 | HARLEM WASHBOARD (LP) | 12 |

SCOTTY (David Scott)
70	Songbird SB 1044	Sesame Street/CRYSTALITES: Version	20
71	Duke DU 106	Donkey Skank (with Tennors)/MURPHY'S ALLSTARS: Version	15
71	Songbird SB 1049	Riddle I This/Musical Chariot	12

71	Songbird SB 1051	Jam Rock Style/Jam Rock Style Version (with Crystalites) 10
71	Songbird SB 1056	Penny For Your Song/CRYSTALITES: (Version) 10
72	Songbird SB 1080	Clean Race/CRYSTALITES: Train (Version) 10
72	Harry J. HJ 6642	Skank In Bed/BONGO HERMAN: African Breakfast 8
73	Count Shelley CS 036	Salvation Train/KEN PARKER: Message To Mary 8
71	Trojan TRL 33	SCHOOLDAYS (LP)...................................... 45

(see also Lloyd Charmers, Joe White)

SCRAPING FOETUS OFF THE WHEEL
80s	Womb 12	Ramrod/Boxhead/Smut.. 20
81	Womb WOMB-OYBL-2	HOLE (LP, gatefold sleeve with lyrics, also listed as FDL 3) 40

(see also Foetus, You've Got Foetus On Your Breath, Philip & His Foetus Vibrations, Foetus Corruptus, Foetus Inc,
Foetus Uber Frisco)

SCREAMING DEAD
82	Skull DEAD 1	Valley Of The Dead/Schoolgirl Junkie (p/s) 5

DELTON SCREECHIE
81	Moa Anbessa Intl MALP 001	LIVING IN THE GHETTO (LP).................................. 25

SCRITTI POLITTI
78	St. Pancras SCRIT 1	Skank Bloc Bologna/Is And Ought Of The Western World/28.8.78
		(photocopied stapled foldout p/s, hand-stamped white labels)................ 6
79	Rough Trade RT 027T	4 A SIDES: Doubt Beat/Confidences/Bibbly O'Tek/P.A.s (12" EP) 8
79	Rough Trade	Songs To Remember/The Cassette Interview (cassette,
		with 12-page booklet & 2 photos, promo only) 10

SCROTUM POLES
79	Scrotum Poles ERECT 1	Revelation: Why Don't You Come Out Tonight?/Night Train/
		Pick The Cat's Eyes Out/Helicopter Honeymoon/Radio Tay
		(handwritten labels, 2 p/s designs, some with insert) .... each 120/100
80s	One-Tone ERECT 1	AUCHMITHY CALLING (cassette) 12

SCRUBS
86	Anubis ANU 003	Battle (p/s) 20
87	Flicknife FLS 035	Time For You (p/s).. 10

SCRUGG
68	Pye 7N 17451	I Wish I Was Five/Everyone Can See 30
68	Pye 7N 17551	Lavender Popcorn/Sandwichboard Man .... 40+
69	Pye 7N 17656	Will The Real Geraldine Please Stand Up/Only George .... 30+

(see also Floribunda Rose, John T. Kongos)

EARL SCRUGGS
72	CBS 64777	EARL SCRUGGS: HIS FAMILY AND FRIENDS
		(LP, with Byrds, Joan Baez, Bob Dylan, etc.)........................... 15

(see also Flatt & Scruggs, Byrds)

IRENE SCRUGGS
50s	Poydras 80	You've Got What I Want/My Back To The Wall....................... 8

CYRIL SCUTT & HIS BOOGIE PIANO
51	88 882	Delta Express/Steady Stomp Boogie (78)......................... 12

MR. JOHNNY SEA
60s	Fontana FJL 315	EVERYBODY'S FAVOURITE (LP)................................. 15

SEA & CAKE
95	Lissy's LIS 1	Glad You're Right/Tiger Partner/Crimson Wing (p/s, 500 only) 15
99	Hefty HEFTY 013	Window Light/JOHN McENTIRE: Setup For Bed (p/s)................... 5
95	Thrill Jockey TKCD 70951	THE BIZ (CD) 18

(see also Tortoise)

SEA-DERS
67	Decca F 22576	Thanks A Lot/Undecidedly 70
67	Decca DFE-R 8674	THE SEA-DERS (EP, export issue) .... 200+

(see also Cedars)

DAVE SEALEY
69	DJM DJS 210	Picking Up The Pieces/I Can't Go On Living Without You 6

MILT SEALEY TRIO
60s	Duc. Thompson DEP 95017	MILTON SEALEY AND KANSAS FIELDS (EP) 8

PHIL SEAMAN
68	Verve (S)VLP 9220	PHIL SEAMAN NOW ... LIVE (LP) 150
60s	Decibel BSN 103	PHIL SEAMAN STORY (LP) 40
60s	Saga OPP 102	MEETS EDDIE GOMEZ (LP) 100
74	77 Records 77 SEU 12/53	PHIL ON DRUMS (LP)...................................... 35

SEARCHERS
SINGLES
63	Pye 7N 15533	Sweets For My Sweet/It's All Been A Dream 6
63	Philips BF 1274	Sweet Nuthins/What'd I Say........................ 12
63	Pye 7N 15566	Sugar And Spice/Saints And Searchers (dark maroon or lighter pink label) ... 12/6
64	Pye 7N 15594	Needles And Pins/Saturday Night Out 5
64	Pye 7N 15630	Don't Throw Your Love Away/I Pretend I'm With You....................... 5
64	Pye 7N 15670	Someday We're Gonna Love Again/No One Else Could Love You 5
64	Pye 7N 15694	When You Walk In The Room/I'll Be Missing You 5
64	Pye 7N 15739	What Have They Done To The Rain/This Feeling Inside
		(maroon or lighter pink label) 7/5
65	Pye 7N 15794	Goodbye My Love/Till I Met You 6
65	Pye 7N 15878	He's Got No Love/So Far Away 7

65	Pye 7N 15950	When I Get Home/I'm Never Coming Back	7
65	Pye 7N 15992	Take Me For What I'm Worth/Too Many Miles (a few in export p/s)	25/7
66	Pye 7N 17094	Take It Or Leave It/Don't Hide It Away	8
66	Pye 7N 17170	Have You Ever Loved Somebody/It's Just The Way	8
67	Pye 7N 17225	Popcorn, Double Feature/Lovers	15
67	Pye 7N 17308	Western Union/I'll Cry Tomorrow	15
67	Pye 7N 17424	Secondhand Dealer/Crazy Dreams	60
68	Liberty LBF 15159	Umbrella Man/Over The Weekend	55
69	Liberty LBF 15340	Kinky Kathy Abernathy/Suzanna	65
71	RCA RCA 2057	Desdemona/The World Is Waiting For Tomorrow	15
71	RCA RCA 2139	Love Is Everywhere/And A Button	10
72	RCA RCA 2231	Sing Singer Sing/Come On Back To Me	10
72	RCA RCA 2248	Needles And Pins/When You Walk In The Room/Come On Back To Me	10
72	RCA RCA 2288	Vahevala/Madman	15
73	RCA RCA 2330	Solitaire/Spicks And Specks	6
79	Sire SIR 4029	Hearts In Her Eyes/Don't Hang On (p/s)	10
80	Sire SIR 4036	It's Too Late/This Kind Of Love Affair (p/s)	7
81	Sire SIR 4046	Love's Melody/Changing (p/s)	12
81	Sire SIR 4049	Another Night/Back To The War (p/s)	10
80s	private pressing	Don't Make Promises	10
80s	private pressing	Four Strong Winds	10

EPs

63	Pye NEP 24177	AIN'T GONNA KISS YA	12
63	Pye NEP 24183	SWEETS FOR MY SWEET (some copies with white & maroon label)	15/15
64	Pye NEP 24184	HUNGRY FOR LOVE	20
64	Pye NEP 24201	THE SEARCHERS PLAY THE SYSTEM	22
64	Pye NEP 24204	WHEN YOU WALK IN THE ROOM	20
65	Pye NEP 24218	BUMBLE BEE	20
65	Pye NEP 24222	SEARCHERS '65	30
65	Pye NEP 24228	FOUR BY FOUR	35
66	Pye NEP 24263	TAKE ME FOR WHAT I'M WORTH	110

LPs

63	Pye NPL 18086	MEET THE SEARCHERS	28
63	Pye NPL 18089	SUGAR AND SPICE	25
64	Pye NPL 18092	IT'S THE SEARCHERS	25
65	Pye NPL 18111	SOUNDS LIKE SEARCHERS	25
65	Pye NPL 18120	TAKE ME FOR WHAT I'M WORTH	40
67	Marble Arch MAL 640	SMASH HITS VOL. 1	12
67	Marble Arch MAL(S) 673	SMASH HITS VOL. 2 (mono/stereo)	12
72	RCA SF 8289	SECOND TAKE	18
79	Sire SRK 6082	SEARCHERS	15
80	Sire SRK 6086	THE SEARCHERS	12
81	Sire SRK 3523	PLAY FOR TODAY	12
83	PRT DOW 11	LOVE LIES BLEEDING (10")	12

(see also Tony Jackson & Vibrations, Chris Curtis, Pasha)

SEARS
84	Bluurg FISH 9	IF ONLY... (LP)	15

AL SEARS
52	Vogue V 2142	Berry Wells/Steady Eddie (78)	8

SEA STONE
82	Plankton 02	AGAINST THE TIDE (EP, foldout sleeve)	40
78	Plankton PKN 101	MIRRORED DREAMS (LP, with insert)	80

SEATHROUGH
70s	private pressing	LALA LAPLA (LP)	30

B.B. SEATON (HORACE SEATON)
63	Island WI 123	I'm So Glad/Tell Me	20
64	R&B JB 143	Hold On/LESTER STERLING: Peace And Love	30
72	Big BG 336	I Want Justice/RUPIE EDWARD'S ALL STARS: Justice (Version)	8
72	Bullet BU 514	I Miss My Schooldays/CONSCIOUS MINDS: School Days (Version)	5
72	Camel CA 100	Lean On Me/NOW GENERATION: Samba Pati	8
72	Pama PM 864	I Want Justice/RUPIE EDWARD'S ALL STARS: Justice (Version)	8
72	Pama Supreme PS 374	Sweet Caroline/Eleanor Rigby	5
73	Trojan TRLS 59	THE THIN LINE BETWEEN LOVE AND HATE (LP)	20

(see also Bibby, Winston & Bibby, Gaylads, Messengers)

HORACE SEATON
63	Island WI 123	I'm So Glad/Tell Me	28
64	R&B JB 143	Hold On/LESTER STERLING: Peace And Love	28

(see also Bibby, B.B. Seaton, Tommy McCook)

SEA TRAIN
68	A&M AMS 737	Let The Duchess Know/As I Lay Losing	5
69	A&M AMLS 941	SEA TRAIN (LP)	22
71	Capitol EA-ST 659	SEA TRAIN (LP)	18
72	Capitol EA-ST 829	MARBLEHEAD MESSENGER (LP, gatefold sleeve)	12
73	Warner Bros K 46222	WATCH (LP)	12

(see also Blues Project, Old & In The Way)

SEA URCHINS
87	Kvatch KVATCH 001/ Lyntone LYN 18632	Clingfilm/GROOVE FARM: Baby Blue Marine (flexidisc, 1,000 only, 500 in p/s)	15/10
87	Sha La La Ba Ba Ba Ba 5	Summershine/ORCHIDS: From This Day (flexidisc, 2,500 only, 1,000 w/p/s)	15/6
87	Sarah SARAH 001	Pristine Christine/Sullen Eyes/Everglades (foldaround p/s with 14" x 10" poster in poly bag, 1,600 only)	50+

88	Sarah SARAH 008	Solace/Please Rain Fall (foldaround p/s in poly bag)	20
89	Fierce FRIGHT 032	30.10.88 (live) (1-sided, p/s)	15
91	Cheree CHEREE 15	Please Don't Cry/Time Is All I've Seen (die-cut company sleeve)	10

JOHN SEBASTIAN
| 54 | London HL 8029 | Inca Dance/Foolish Waltz (78 rpm = £8) | 28 |
| 55 | London HL 8131 | Stranger In Paradise/Autumn Leaves | 22 |

JOHN (B.) SEBASTIAN
69	Kama Sutra 618 026	She's A Lady/The Room Nobody Lives In	6
70	Reprise RS 20902	Magical Connection/Fa-Fana-Fa	5
70	Reprise RSLP 6379	JOHN B. SEBASTIAN (LP, gatefold sleeve)	20
70	Buddah 2361 003	JOHN SEBASTIAN SONGBOOK VOLUME ONE (LP, with Lovin' Spoonful)	15
71	Reprise K 44149	THE FOUR OF US (LP, gatefold sleeve)	15

(see also Lovin' Spoonful, Even Dozen Jug Band)

SECESSION
| 80s | Siren SRN12 23 | Michael (12", p/s) | 12 |
| 88 | Siren SRNLP 11 | A DARK ENCHANTMENT (LP, with inner) | 40 |

SECOND CITY SOUND
| 65 | Decca F 12310 | Tchaikovsky One/Shadows | 8 |
| 69 | Major Minor MM 600 | The Dream Of Olwyn/A Touch Of Velvet, A Sting of Brass | 10 |

SECOND COMING
| 71 | Mercury 6338 030 | SECOND COMING (LP) | 20 |

SECOND HAND
| 68 | Polydor 583 045 | REALITY (LP, labels on early copies credit band as Moving Finger) | 100 |
| 72 | Mushroom MR 2006 | DEATH MAY BE YOUR SANTA CLAUS (LP, some copies omit "Funeral") | 100+ |

(see also Andreas Thomopoulos, Fungus, Chillum, Vulcans, Seventh Wave)

SECOND LAYER
79	Tortch-r TOR 001	FLESH AS PROPERTY (EP, white p/s, black printed labels)	25
80	Tortch TOR 006	State Of Emergency/I Need Noise/The Cutting Motion (p/s)	20
81	Tortch/Fresh FRESH 5	FLESH AS PROPERTY (EP, reissue, yellow p/s & white labels)	20
81	Cherry Red CHERRY 21	FLESH AS PROPERTY (EP, 2nd reissue, unreleased)	
82	Cherry Red BRED 14	WORLD OF RUBBER (LP, with inner)	50

(see also Outsiders, Sound)

SECRET
| 77 | Arista ARIST 142 | The Young Ones/Handel A Vandel | 25 |
| 78 | Arista ARIST 173 | Do You Really Care?/I Wanna Car Like That | 25 |

SECRET AFFAIR
79	I-Spy SEE 1	Time For Action/Soho Strut (brown p/s, black print/paper labels or black p/s, white print with plastic labels)	10/5
79	I-Spy SEE 3	Let Your Heart Dance/Sorry Wrong Number (p/s, paper label)	6
80	I-Spy SEE 5	My World/So Cool (paper labels)	6
80	I-Spy SEE 8	Sound Of Confusion/Take It Or Leave It (p/s, paper labels)	6
81	I-Spy SEE 10	Do You Know?/Dance Master (keyhole company sleeve, paper labels)	6
82	I-Spy SEE 11	Lost In The Night (Mack The Knife)/The Big Beat (p/s)	8
79	I-Spy I SPY 1	GLORY BOYS (LP, with 2 inserts)	15
80	I-Spy I SPY 2	BEHIND CLOSED DOORS (LP, with inner sleeve)	12
82	I-Spy I SPY 3	BUSINESS AS USUAL (LP, stickered sleeve)	15
90s	own label	CITY OF DREAMS (LP, handmade sleeve)	25

(see also New Hearts, Advertising, Innocents [U.K.])

SECRET KNOWLEDGE
| 90s | Sabres Of Paradise | Sugar Daddy (mixes) (12") | 10 |

SECRET OYSTER
| 74 | CBS 80489 | SEA SON (LP) | 12 |

SECRETS (U.K.)
66	CBS 202466	I Suppose/Such A Pity	30
67	CBS 202585	Infatuation/She's Dangerous	30
67	CBS 2818	I Intend To Please/I Think I Need The Cash	30

(see also Simon's Secrets, Clifford T. Ward, Martin Raynor & Secrets)

SECRETS (U.S)
| 64 | Philips BF 1298 | The Boy Next Door/Learnin' To Forget | 25 |
| 64 | Philips BF 1318 | Hey Big Boy/Other Side Of Town | 25 |

SECT
| 81 | Shoestring SHOE 1 | This is Your Life/Private Eye (p/s) | 5 |

SECTION 5
| 85 | Oi OIR 002 | WE WON'T CHANGE (LP) | 20 |
| 80s | Oi | STREET ROCK 'N' ROLL (LP) | 20 |

SECTION 25
80	Factory FAC 18	Girls Don't Count/New Noise/Up To You (tracing paper p/s)	6
81	Factory FACT 45	ALWAYS NOW (LP, in envelope/folder)	15
84	Factory FACT 90	FROM THE HIP (LP, with inner)	25

NEIL SEDAKA
59	RCA RCA 1099	The Diary/No Vacancy (78 rpm = £20)	25
59	RCA RCA 1115	I Go Ape/Moon Of Gold (78 rpm = £25)	22
59	RCA RCA 1130	You've Got To Learn Your Rhythm And Blues/Crying My Heart Out For You (78=£25)	25
59	London HLW 8961	Ring A Rockin'/Fly Don't Fly On Me (78 rpm = £120)	40

(The above RCA 45s were originally issued with triangular centres; later round-centres are worth two-thirds these values.)

59	RCA RCA 1152	Oh! Carol/One Way Ticket (triangular centre or round centre) (78 rpm = £190) . . 25/7
60	RCA RCA 1178	Stairway To Heaven/Forty Winks Away (78 rpm = £200)........................7
60	RCA RCA 1198	Run Samson Run/You Mean Everything To Me (78 rpm = £200) 7
61	RCA RCA 1220	Calendar Girl/The Same Old Fool 7
61	RCA RCA 1236	Little Devil/I Must Be Dreaming..7
61	RCA RCA 1250	Sweet Little You/I Found My World In You....................................7
61	RCA RCA 1266	Happy Birthday, Sweet Sixteen/Don't Lead Me On 7
62	RCA RCA 1282	King Of Clowns/Walk With Me..6
62	Stateside SS 105	Oh Delilah/MARVELS: Neil's Twist 15
62	RCA RCA 1298	Breaking Up Is Hard To Do/As Long As I Live................................6
62	RCA RCA 1319	Next Door To An Angel/I Belong To You......................................6
63	RCA RCA 1331	Circulate/Alice In Wonderland 6
63	RCA RCA 1343	Let's Go Steady Again/Waiting For Never 6
63	RCA RCA 1359	The Dreamer/Look Inside Your Heart 8
63	RCA RCA 1368	Bad Girl/Wait 'Til You See My Baby 18
65	RCA RCA 1475	World Through A Tear/High On A Mountain 12
59	RCA RCX 166	NEIL SEDAKA (EP) 45
60	RCA RCX 186	NEIL SEDAKA VOL. 2 (EP) 30
62	RCA RCX 212	NEIL SEDAKA VOL. 3 (EP) 30
59	RCA RD 27140	NEIL SEDAKA (LP) 90
60	RCA RD 27207/SF 5090	CIRCULATE (LP, mono/stereo) 50/60

(see also Sam Cooke, Paul Anka, 10cc)

MIKE SEDGEWICK
| 68 | Parlophone R 5694 | The Good Guys In The White Hats Never Lose/ |
| | | Woman (She's Got To Be Treated Right) ....5 |

(see also Adam Mike & Tim)

SEDUCER
83	Sticky SSR 0017	Call Your Name/Survivor 50
84	Thunderbolt THBE 1007	Indecent Exposure/Down Down/No No Baby/DTs/Wild Joker (12", p/s) 8
85	Thunderbolt THBL 016	CAUGHT IN THE ACT (LP) 15
86	Stud STUDLP 2	'EADS DOWN — SEE YOU AT THE END (LP) 15

RUDY SEEDORF
| 65 | Island WI 189 | One Million Stars/Mr. Blue ....18 |

SEEDS
66	Vocalion VN 9277	Pushin' Too Hard/Try To Understand (DJ copy = £85) 50
67	Vocalion VN 9287	Can't Seem To Make You Mine/Daisy Mae 32
88	Bam Caruso OPRA 091	Pushin' Too Hard/Greener Day 15
67	Vocalion VAN 8062	A WEB OF SOUND (LP) 60
67	Vocalion VAN/SAVN 8070	FUTURE (LP, mono/stereo) 45/60
78	Sonet SNTF 746	THE SEEDS (LEGENDARY MASTER RECORDINGS) (LP) 15
88	Strange Things STRANGEP 1	EVIL HOODOO (LP, picture disc)...................................18

(see also Sky Saxon, Ya Ho Wa 13)

SEEDS OF THE EARTH
| 75 | Contempo CS 2052 | Planting Seeds/Brother Bad...20 |
| 75 | Contempo CS 2073 | Zion Plus/Phire ....15 |

MIKE SEEGER
| 65 | Fontana TFL 6039 | MIKE SEEGER (LP)..15 |

(see also Peggy & Mike Seeger)

PEGGY SEEGER
57	Topic TRC 107	Freight Train/Cumberland Gap (78) 20
58	Topic TRC 108	Pretty Little Baby/Child Of God (78) 10
65	Decca F 12282	Pretty Little Baby/My Love And I Are One 6
57	Pye Jazz NJE 1043	ORIGINS OF SKIFFLE (EP)..20
60	Topic TOP 38	SHINE LIKE A STAR (EP) 10
61	Topic TOP 72	TROUBLED LOVE (EP)..10
61	Topic TOP 73	EARLY IN THE SPRING (EP) 10
50s	Topic 10T 9	PEGGY SEEGER (10" LP)..15
61	PRE 13005	THE BEST OF PEGGY SEEGER (LP) 15
64	Topic 12T 113	WHO'S GOING TO SHOE... (LP, with Tom Paley) 18
69	Argo (Z)DA 63	PEGGY ALONE (LP) 18
72	Argo ZFB 63	PEGGY ALONE (LP, reissue) 12
72	Argo ZFB 64	FEMALE FROLIC (LP, with Frankie Armstrong & Sandra Kerr)...............15
79	Blackthorne BR 1061	DIFFERENT THEREFORE EQUAL (LP)....................................15

(see also Al Lloyd)

PEGGY SEEGER & GUY CARAWAN
| 58 | HMV CLP 1174 | AMERICA AT PLAY (LP) ....18 |

(see also Guy Carawan)

PEGGY & MIKE SEEGER
| 68 | Argo (Z)DA 80 | PEGGY 'N' MIKE (LP) ....18 |

(see also Ewan MacColl & Peggy Seeger, Mike Seeger)

PETE SEEGER
60	Top Rank TR 5020	Careless Love/LEON BIBB: Times Are Getting Hard (p/s) 10
63	CBS AAG 187	Little Boxes/Mail Myself To You..5
58	Melodisc EPM7 78	TRIBUTE TO LEADBELLY (EP) 12
58	Topic TOP 33	PETE AND FIVE STRINGS (EP) 10
59	Topic TOP 37	HOOTENANNY NEW YORK CITY (EP, with Sonny Terry) 15
64	CBS AGG 320055	IN CONCERT (EP) 8
65	CBS EP 6065	HEALING RIVER (EP) 8
66	Ember EP 4560	D-DAY DODGERS (EP) 8
61	Philips BBL 7507	PETE SEEGER STORY SONGS (LP) 12

63	Folklore F-LAUT 1	PETE SEEGER IN CONCERT (LP)	12
63	Folklore F-LAUT 2	PETE SEEGER IN CONCERT VOL. 2 (LP)	12
64	CBS (S)BPG 62209	WE SHALL OVERCOME (LP)	15
65	Xtra XTRA 1005	SING WITH SEEGER (LP)	12
65	CBS (S)BPG 62462	I CAN SEE A NEW DAY (LP)	12
65	CBS (S)BPG 62528	STRANGERS AND COUSINS (LP)	12
66	Xtra XTRA 1016	BROADSIDES (LP)	12
66	Xtra XTRA 1034	FOLK SINGER'S GUITAR GUIDE (LP, with 16-page booklet)	12
66	Verve (S)VLP 5004	IN PERSON (LP)	12
68	Ember CW 130	PETE SEEGER (LP)	12
68	Xtra XTRA 1066	ABIYOYO AND OTHER SONGS (LP)	12

(see also Big Bill Broonzy, Sonny Terry [& Brownie McGhee], Weavers)

PETE SEEGER & BIG BILL BROONZY
| 64 | Xtra XTRA 1006 | IN CONCERT — PETE SEEGER & BIG BILL BROONZY (LP) | 20 |
| 66 | Verve Folkways VLP 5006 | IN CONCERT (LP, reissue, also ST SVLP 506) | 12/15 |

(see also Big Bill Broonzy)

SEEKERS
| 65 | Oriole CB 1935 | With A Swag On My Shoulder/Myra | 8 |
| 65 | Decca F 22167 | Chilly Winds/Kumbaya | 5 |

SEEMON & MARIJKE
| 71 | A&M AMLS 64309 | SON OF AMERICA (LP) | 30 |

SEFTONS
| 66 | CBS 202491 | I Can See Through You/Here Today | 35 |

(see also Perishers)

VIVIENNE SEGAL & HAROLD LANG
| 54 | Columbia SCM 5114 | Den Of Iniquity/BARBARA ASHLEY: That Terrific Rainbow | 7 |

BOB SEGER (SYSTEM)
68	Capitol CL 15574	Ramblin' Gamblin' Man/Tales Of Lucy Blue (as Bob Seger System)	20+
70	Capitol CL 15642	Lucifer/Big River (as Bob Seger System)	8
72	Reprise K 14208	If I Were A Carpenter/Jesse James	5
73	Reprise K 14243	Rosalie/Back In '72	5
74	Reprise K 14364	Get Out Of Denver/Long Song Comin'	5
72	Reprise K 44214	SMOKIN' O.P.'s (LP)	15

LLOYD SEIVRIGHT
| 70 | Creole CR 1001 | Mary's Boy Child/And Glory Walked Among Men | 5 |

SEIZE
| 81 | Why Not? NOT 001 | Grovelands Road/Why? (p/s) | 15 |
| 82 | Why Not? NOT 002 | EVERYBODY DIES EP (p/s) | 15 |

RICHARD SELANO
| 69 | Jolly JY 019 | All Of The Time/Broken Romance | 7 |

SELECTED FOUR
| 71 | Banana BA 351 | Selection Train/SOUND DIMENSION: Version Train | 12 |

SELECTER
79	2-Tone CHS TT 4	On My Radio/Too Much Pressure (paper label, company sleeve)	5
80	2-Tone CHS TT 8	Three Minute Hero/James Bond (no labels, silver print middle, company sleeve)	6
80	2-Tone CHS TT 8	Three Minute Hero/James Bond (paper labels, company sleeve)	5
82	Flexipop 001/SFI 566	Ready Mix Radio (1-sided clear flexidisc with *Flexipop* mag, issue 1)	8/4
80	2-Tone TT 5002	TOO MUCH PRESSURE (LP)	12

(see also Special A.K.A.)

FREDDIE SELF
| 64 | Mercury MF 839 | Don't Cry/Why Should I? | 7 |

(see also Freddie Ryder, Trends)

RONNIE SELF
| 58 | Philips PB 810 | Bop-A-Lena/Ain't I A Dog (78) | 320 |

SELF ABUSE
| 84 | Radical Change RC 5 | SOLDIER (EP) | 5 |

SELF DESTRUCT
| 91 | Retch RR 12004 | AFFRAY (12" EP) | 8 |

BROTHER JOHN SELLERS
56	Vanguard EPP 14002	BLUES AND SPIRITUALS (EP)	15
57	Columbia SEG 7740	BLUES AND SPIRITUALS (EP)	15
56	Decca DFE 6457	BROTHER JOHN SELLERS IN LONDON (EP)	15
56	Vanguard PPT 12008	BROTHER JOHN SELLERS SINGS BLUES AND FOLK SONGS (10" LP)	25
57	Vanguard PPT 12017	JACK OF DIAMONDS AND OTHER FOLK SONGS AND BLUES (10" LP)	25

PETER SELLERS (& SOPHIA LOREN)
52	Parlophone R 3785	Jakka And The Flying Saucers (An Interplanetary Fairy Tale) (both sides) (78)	15
54	HMV B 10724	Dipso-Calypso/Never Never Land (78)	12
57	Parlophone R 4337	Any Old Iron/Boiled Bananas And Carrots	7
58	Parlophone R 4491	I'm So Ashamed/A Drop Of The Hard Stuff (78 rpm = £12)	6
59	Parlophone R 4605	Puttin' On The Smile/My Old Dutch (78 rpm = £15)	6
60	Parlophone R 4702	Goodness Gracious Me! (with Sophia Loren)/Grandpa's Grave	5
61	Parlophone R 4724	Bangers And Mash (with Sophia Loren)/SOPHIA LOREN: Zoo Be Zoo Be Zoo	7
65	Parlophone R 5393	A Hard Day's Night/Help!	6
66	United Artists UP 1152	After The Fox (as Peter Sellers & Hollies)/BURT BACHARACH: The Fox-Trot	28
79	United Artists BP 335	There Are Camels Where The Taxis Used To Be/Night And Day	5
59	Parlophone GEP 8770	BEST OF SELLERS NO. 1 (EP)	8
59	Parlophone GEP 8784	BEST OF SELLERS NO. 2 (EP)	8

59	Parlophone GEP 8809	BEST OF SELLERS NO. 3 (EP)	8
59	Parlophone GEP 8822	SONGS FOR SWINGIN' SELLERS (EP, also stereo SGE 2013)	10/12
59	Parlophone GEP 8827	SONGS FOR SWINGIN' SELLERS NO. 2 (EP, also stereo SGE 2016)	10/12
61	Parlophone GEP 8832	SONGS FOR SWINGIN' SELLERS NO. 3 (EP, also stereo SGE 2019)	10/12
61	Parlophone GEP 8835	SONGS FOR SWINGIN' SELLERS NO. 4 (EP, also stereo SGE 2020)	10/12
61	Parlophone GEP 8843	PETER AND SOPHIA NO. 1 (EP, with Sophia Loren, also stereo SGE 2021)	10/12
61	Parlophone GEP 8845	PETER AND SOPHIA NO. 2 (EP, with Sophia Loren, also stereo SGE 2022)	10/15
61	Parlophone GEP 8848	PETER AND SOPHIA NO. 3 (EP, with Sophia Loren, also stereo SGE 2023)	10/15
62	Parlophone GEP 8853	TWO PETERS (EP, with Peter Ustinov, 1 side each)	10
58	Parlophone PMD 1069	THE BEST OF SELLERS (10" LP)	15
59	Parlophone PMC 1111	SONGS FOR SWINGIN' SELLERS (LP, also stereo PCS 3003)	15/25
60	Parlophone PMC 1131	PETER AND SOPHIA (LP, with Sophia Loren, also stereo PCS 3012)	20/30

(Prices for Parlophone albums are for gold on black labels. Yellow and black labels are half of these prices)

79	United Artists UAG 30266	SELLERS' MARKET (LP)	15

PETER SELLERS, SPIKE MILLIGAN & HARRY SECOMBE
64	Philips AL 3464	HOW TO WIN AN ELECTION (LP)	20

(see also Goons, Spike Milligan, Sophia Loren, Hollies, Harry Secombe, Peter Ustinov)

SELOFANE
68	CBS 3413	Girl Called Fantasy/Happiness Is Love	8
68	CBS 3700	Shingle I.A.O./Chase The Face	20

SEMA 4
79	Pollen PBM 022	4 FROM SEMA 4 (EP, 2 different coloured sleeves, 500 only, numbered)	100
79	Pollen PBM 024	UP DOWN AROUND (EP, 1,000 only)	75

ARCHIE SEMPLE
60	Columbia 33SX 1240	JAZZ FOR YOUNG LOVERS (LP)	25
62	Columbia 33SX 1450	EASY LIVING (LP)	25
63	Columbia 33SX 1580	THE TWILIGHT COMETH (LP)	18
64	77 LEU 12/6	THE CLARINET OF ARCHIE SEMPLE (LP)	25

SENATE
67	Columbia DB 8110	I Can't Stop/Ain't As Sweet As You	20
68	United Artists (S)ULP 1180	THE SENATE SOCK IT TO YOU ONE MORE TIME (LP)	40

(see also Garnet Mimms)

SENATOR BOBBY
62	Cameo Parkway P 127	Wild Thing/SENATOR EVERETT McKINLAY: Wild Thing	8

SENATORS
64	Dial DSP 7001	She's A Mod/Lot About You	50
64	Oriole CB 1957	When Day Is Done/Breakdown	35
65	CBS 201768	The Tables Are Turning/Stop Wasting Time	25

(see also Tony Rivers & Castaways)

RAY SENDIT & HIS ROCKEY TEAM
57	Felsted SD 80052	Rocket 0869/Spike's Rock	6

LOS SENORS
63	Cameo Parkway C 290	Amapola/Acapulco	5

SENSATIONAL ALEX HARVEY BAND
(see under Alex Harvey)

SENSATIONAL CREED
84	Beggars Banquet BEG 125	Nocturnal Operation/Down Periscope (p/s, reissue of Orbidöig single)	15
84	Beggars Banquet BEG 125T	Nocturnal Operation/Down Periscope/Voyage Of The Titanic (12", p/s, reissue of Orbidöig single)	25

(see also Orbidöig)

SENSATIONS (Jamaica)
67	Doctor Bird DB 1074	A Thing Called Soul/BOBBY LEE & SENSATIONS: I Was Born A Loser	25
67	Doctor Bird DB 1100	Right On Time/Lonely Lover	25
67	Doctor Bird DB 1102	Born To Love You/Lonely Lover	30
68	Duke DU 2	Those Guys/I'll Never Fall In Love	20
68	Island WI 3110	Long Time Me No See You Girl/ROY SHIRLEY: Million Dollar Baby	20
69	Camel CA 31	The Warrior (actually by Johnny Osbourne & Sensations)/JOHNNY ORGAN: Don Juan	10
70	Techniques TI 902	War Boat/Mr Blue	8
71	Duke DU 120	Remember/LARRY'S ALLSTARS: Madhouse	6
71	Duke DU 121	What Are You Doing Sunday/RUFFIANS: Sweet Dream	6

(see also Roy Shirley, Baba Dise, Winston Wright)

SENSATIONS (U.K.)
66	Decca F 12392	Look At My Baby/What A Wonderful Feeling	10
71	MCA MK 5078	Oh My Eli/Let's Get A Little Sentimental	5

SENSATIONS (featuring Yvonne) (U.S.)
61	Pye International 7N 25110	Music, Music, Music/A Part Of Me (as Sensations featuring Yvonne)	25
62	Pye International 7N 25128	Let Me In/Oh Yes I'll Be True	30

(see also Yvonne Baker)

SEONA DANCING
83	London LON 22	More To Lose (p/s)	18
83	London LONX 22	More To Lose (12", p/s)	10
83	London LON 32	Bitter Heart/Tell Her (p/s)	18
83	London LONX 32	Bitter Heart/Tell Her (12", p/s)	12

SEPTIC DEATH
85	Pusmort 0012-01D	NOW THAT I HAVE THE ATTENTION... (LP, with inner sleeve, 18 tracks)	15
88	Pusmort PUS 00703	Kichigai (p/s)	5

SEPULTURA
96	Roadrunner RR 23145	Ratamahatta/War/Slave New World (Live)/Amen/Inner Self (Live) (CD, digipak)	12
91	Roadracer RO 9328-8	ARISE (LP, picture disc)	20
94	Roadrunner RR 90000 0	CHAOS A.D. (CD, limited edition tin box; CD has embossed cover & different sleeve, Brazilian flag & 2 bonus tracks, "Policia" & "Inhuman Nature")	30

SERENADERS
59	Top Rank JAR 111	Sudden Holiday/Tango Madeira (78 rpm = £8)	6

SERENDIPITY
68	CBS 3733	Through With You/I'm Flying	90
69	CBS 4428	If I Could/Castles	60

SERENDIPITY SINGERS
64	Philips BF 1333	Don't Let The Rain Come Down (Crooked Little Man)/Freedom's Star	5

SERFS
69	Capitol E-ST 207	THE SERFS (LP)	15

WILL SERGEANT
82	WEA K 19238	Favourite Branches/RAVI SHANKAR & BILL LOVEDAY: Himalaya (p/s)	25
95	Ochre OCH 003	Cosmos/Venus In Flares (p/s, orange vinyl)	15
78	(no label or cat. no.)	WEIRD AS FISH (cassette, 7 copies only, each with a different cover)	50+
83	92 Happy Cust. HAPLP 1	THEMES FOR "GRIND" (LP)	15
	(see also Echo & Bunnymen)		

SERGIO & ESTIBALIZ
75	Epic S EPC 3187	Love Come Home/Tu Volveras	12

SERIOUS DRINKING
80s	Upright YOURS 4	Love On The Terraces/Hypocrite/Bobby Moore Was Innocent (p/s)	5

ROSITA SERRANO
51	HMV JO 226	Bibbidi-Bobbidi-Boo/Cinderella (78, export issue)	7

NANCY SESAY & MELODAIRES
81	It's War Boys S 1	C'est Fab/The Ballad Of Hong Kong/National Honk (gatefold p/s)	5
	(see also Homosexuals)		

SETTERS
70	Duke DU 65	Paint Your Wagon/Organ Man (both sides actually by Hot Rod All Stars)	10
70	Trojan TR 7738	Virgin Soldier/Brixton Reggae Festival (both actually by Hot Rod All Stars)	8

SETTLERS
67	Island ILP 947	EARLY SETTLERS (LP)	15

SEVEN AGES OF MAN
72	Rediffusion ZS 115	SEVEN AGES OF MAN (LP)	20
	(see also Madeline Bell, Gordon Beck)		

SEVEN LETTERS/SYMARIP
69	Doctor Bird DB 1189	People Get Ready/The Fit (as Seven Letters)	18
69	Doctor Bird DB 1194	Please Stay/Special Beat (as Seven Letters)	18
69	Doctor Bird DB 1195	Flour Dumpling/Equality (as Seven Letters [Symarip])	15
69	Doctor Bird DB 1206	Mama Me Want Girl/Sentry (as Seven Letters)	15
69	Doctor Bird DB 1207	Soul Crash/Throw Me Things (as Seven Letters)	18
69	Doctor Bird DB 1208	There Goes My Heart/Wish (as Seven Letters)	15
69	Doctor Bird DB 1209	Bam Bam Baji/Hold Him Joe (as Seven Letters [Symarip])	40
69	Doctor Bird DB 1306	Fung Sure/Tomorrow At Sundown (as Symarip)	18
69	Treasure Isle TI 7050	Skinhead Moonstomp/Must Catch A Train (as Symarip)	12
70	Treasure Isle TI 7054	Parson's Corner/Redeem (as Symarip)	12
70	Treasure Isle TI 7055	La Bella Jig/Holidays By The Sea (as Symarip)	10
70	Attack ATT 8013	I'm A Puppet/Vindication (as Symarip)	8
70	Trojan TBL 102	SKINHEAD MOONSTOMP (LP, as Symarip)	25
	(see also Pyramids, Equals, Laurel Aitken)		

7 SECONDS
82	Alt. Tentacles VIRUS 15	SKIN, BRAINS AND GUTS (EP, with insert)	12

SEVEN SEAS
75	Jay Boy BOY98	Super Jaws/Pat's Jam	8

SEVENTEEN
80	Vendetta VD 001	Don't Let Go/Bank Holiday Weekend (p/s)	100
	(see also Alarm)		

SEVENTH SEAL
97	Acme ACLP 8018LP	THE SEVENTH SEAL (LP)	12

SEVENTH SON
82	Rising Son FMR 067	Man In The Street/Immortal Hours (some in p/s)	75/20
84	Rising Son SRT4KS 282	Metal To The Moon/Sound And Fury (some in gatefold p/s)	60/30
87	Music Factory MF 0043	Northern Boots/The Harder You Rock (p/s)	18
89	Rising Son SRT9KLS	What More Do You Want/Sister Strange/Bitter Ashes (12", p/s)	12

SEVENTH WAVE
75	Gull GULS 14	Manifestations/Only The Beginning (Part 1)	5
	(see also Second Hand, Fungus)		

SEVENTH WAVE
89	SRT SRT9KS 2018	Tonight (p/s)	20

SEVENTH WONDER
80	Grapevine GRP 130	Captain Of My Ship/Pharaoh	10

SEVERED HEAD
83	Plastic Canvas PC 002	Heavy Metal/Killin' The Kidz (p/s)	35

MINT VALUE £

SEVERINE
71	CBS 7230	Chance In Time/Nothing Bad Can Be This Good.	8
71	Philips 6009 135	Un Banc, Un Arbre, Une Rue/Viens.	5
71	Philips 6009 151	La La Melodie/Je Ferme Les Yeux, Je Compte Dix	5

DAVID SEVILLE & HIS ORCHESTRA (& THE CHIPMUNKS)
57	London HLU 8359	Armen's Theme/Carousel In Rome (initially gold label print, later silver)	18/10
57	London RE-U 1085	DAVID SEVILLE & HIS ORCHESTRA (EP)	20
59	London RE-U 1219	WITCH DOCTOR AND FRIENDS (EP)	20
59	London HA-U 2153	THE WITCH DOCTOR PRESENTS DAVID SEVILLE AND HIS FRIENDS (LP)	28
64	Liberty LBY 1218	THE CHIPMUNKS SING THE BEATLES (LP)	12
(see also Alfi & Harry)			

ALEC SEWARD
56	Vogue LDE 165	CITY BLUES (10" LP)	40

SEX AIDS
83	Riot City RIOT 23	BACK ON THE PISS AGAIN (EP)	5
(see also Vice Squad)			

SEX BEATLES
79	Charly CYS 1061	Well You Never/Fatal Fascination (p/s)	5

SEXHURT
98	Dobbstown BOB 23	A ROMANTIC EVENING WITH BIG RED STRAPS (LP, with free straps)	12

SEX PISTOLS
76	EMI 401	Anarchy In The U.K (4.01 longer version)/No Fun (Abbey Road 2-sided acetate, only 3 confirmed)	6,000+
76	EMI	Anarchy In The U.K. (3.36 version) (1-sided Abbey Road acetate).	4,000+
76	EMI EMI 2566	Anarchy In The U.K./I Wanna Be Me (black p/s, with Chris Thomas production credit on B-side).	90
76	EMI EMI 2566	Anarchy In The U.K./I Wanna Be Me ('Demo Record Not For Resale'. Black p/s, Chris Thomas credit on both sides and with information slip)	225
76	EMI EMI 2566	Anarchy In The U.K./I Wanna Be Me (Dave Goodman production credit on B-side)	25
76/77		God Save The Queen/No Feelings (double sided 7" acetate on LTS – few copies pressed and used by Malcolm McLaren to get gigs and record deal)	6,000+
77	A&M AMS 7284	God Save The Queen/No Feelings (withdrawn, some in brown envelope with press release)	7,500+/7,000+
77	Virgin VS 181	God Save The Queen/Did You No Wrong (p/s)	8
77	Virgin VS 181	God Save The Queen/Did You No Wrong (plain blue no Queen's head sample sleeve – one known copy, Jamie Reid autograph added later)	1,500
77	Virgin VS 184	Pretty Vacant/No Fun (p/s)	8
77	Virgin VS 184	Pretty Vacant/No Fun (p/s with push-out centre).	30
77	Virgin VS 191	Holidays In The Sun/Satellite (withdrawn p/s)	15
77	Virgin/Lyntone LYN 3261	Lentilmas — A Seasonal Offering To You From Virgin Records (flexidisc, Xmas freebie to journalists; some with Xmas card)	1500/450
78	Virgin VS 220	No-One Is Innocent (A Punk Prayer By Ronald Biggs)/ SID VICIOUS: My Way (p/s)	6
78		SID VICIOUS: My Way (1-sided Pye Studios acetate)	700+
78	Virgin VS 220	No-One Is Innocent (mispress, plays Motors track)/SID VICIOUS: My Way (p/s).	35
78	Virgin VS 22012	The Biggest Blow (A Punk Prayer By Ronald Biggs)/(Interview)/SID VICIOUS: My Way (12", p/s [matrix: VS 22012A3], some without interview [VS 22012 A1]).	20/10
79	Virgin VS 240	Something Else/Friggin' In The Riggin' (p/s)	8
79	Virgin VS 240	Something Else/Friggin' In The Riggin' (p/s, black & white labels)	12
79	Virgin VS 290	The Great Rock 'n' Roll Swindle/Rock Around The Clock (vocals by Tenpole Tudor) (withdrawn 'American Express' p/s)	5
79	Virgin VS 290	The Great Rock 'n' Roll Swindle (mispressing with 'lawyers' telephone conversation' track)/Rock Around The Clock ('American Express' p/s)	40
80	Virgin VS 339	(I'm Not Your) Stepping Stone/Pistols Propaganda (p/s, mispressing, B-side plays "Substitute")	25
80	Virgin VS 339	(I'm Not Your) Stepping Stone/Pistols Propaganda (p/s, mispressing, B-side plays Gillan track "No Laughing In Heaven")	30
80	Virgin SEX 1	PISTOLS PACK (6 x 7" in p/s; all in plastic wallet)	40
81	Virgin VS 443	Who Killed Bambi?/Rock Around The Clock (by Tenpole Tudor & Pistols, p/s)	10
85	Chaos DICK 1	Submission/No Feelings (p/s, 5,000 only, blue, pink or yellow vinyl)	7/15/5
85	Chaos SUB 1	Submission (12", 1-sided test pressing, die-cut sleeve, label has big red 'A')	20
85	Chaos	Pretty Vacant (unreleased, 20 copies only)	50
85	Chaos CARTEL 1	Submission (12", 1-track promo, withdrawn).	60
86	Archive 4 TOF 104	THE ORIGINAL SEX PISTOLS LIVE (4-track 12", p/s, 5,000 only)	8
86	Archive 4 TOF 104	THE ORIGINAL SEX PISTOLS LIVE (4-track 12", p/s, blue vinyl)	15
88	Virgin CDT 3	Anarchy In The U.K./No Fun/EMI (3" CD, card sleeve)	18
88	Virgin CDT 37	God Save The Queen/Did You No Wrong/Don't Give Me No Lip Child (3" CD, gatefold card sleeve)	15
88	Spiral Scratch SCRATCH 4	Pretty Vacant (Demo)/I Wanna Be Me (Demo) (with *Spiral Scratch* magazine, issue 4, B-side actually plays "Seventeen")	10/4
96	Virgin VUSCDJ 113	Pretty Vacant (live) (CD, promo only, card sleeve)	20
77	Virgin V 2086/SPOTS 001	NEVER MIND THE BOLLOCKS, HERE'S THE SEX PISTOLS (LP, pink rear sleeve, with no track listing, with poster & 1-sided single, "Submission" [VDJ 24], shrink wrapped with orange or green-stickered versions extremely rare)	600/150
77	Virgin V 2086	NEVER MIND THE BOLLOCKS, HERE'S THE SEX PISTOLS (LP, with track listing, no shrink wrap)	20
78	Virgin V 2086	NEVER MIND THE BOLLOCKS, HERE'S THE SEX PISTOLS (LP, pink rear sleeve with no track listing)	25
78	Virgin VP 2086	NEVER MIND THE BOLLOCKS, HERE'S THE SEX PISTOLS (LP, picture disc)	40
79	Virgin VD 2510	THE GREAT ROCK 'N' ROLL SWINDLE (2-LP, including "Watcha Gonna Do About It", with paper insert)	30

79	Virgin VD 2510	THE GREAT ROCK 'N' ROLL SWINDLE (2-LP, "I Wanna Be Me" and "Who Killed Bambi?" replace "Watcha Gonna Do About It", with spoken overdubs on "God Save The Queen Symphony")	20
80	Factory FACT 30	THE HEYDAY (gold interview cassette in satin pouch with Xmas card)	50
81	Factory FACT 30	THE HEYDAY (cassette, in vinyl pouch without Xmas card)	25
86	Virgin CDV 2086	NEVER MIND THE BOLLOCKS, HERE'S THE SEX PISTOLS (CD, mispressing, plays country music titles)	20

(see also Public Image Ltd, Professionals, Rich Kids, Steve Jones, Cash Pussies, Spectres (UK), Swingers)

SEXY GIRLS
69	Fab FAB 100	Pom-Pom Song/LITTLE JOE & BUSTER'S ALLSTARS: Hy There (B-side actually by Melltones)	15
69	Dice CC 100	Pom-Pom Song/LITTLE JOE & BUSTER'S ALLSTARS: Hy There (B-side actually by Melltones) (reissue)	15

DENNY SEYTON & SABRES
64	Mercury MF 800	Tricky Dicky/Baby What You Want Me To Do	20
64	Mercury MF 814	Short Fat Fanny/Give Me Back My Heart	22
64	Mercury MF 824	The Way You Look Tonight/Hands Off	22
65	Parlophone R 5363	Just A Kiss/In The Flowers By The Trees (as Denny Seyton Group)	30
65	Wing WL 1032	IT'S THE GEAR (14 HITS) (LP)	45

TONY SHABAZZ
79	Ethnic Fight FT DD 4436	Mr Fitzy/RUDDIE MOWATT: Public Enemy (12")	60

SHACK
88	Ghetto GTG B 1	Emergency/Liberation (p/s)	10
88	Ghetto GTG T 1	Emergency/Liberation/Faith (12", p/s)	20
88	Ghetto GTG CD 1	Emergency/Liberation/Faith/What's It Like (CD)	15
89	Ghetto GTG B 2	High Rise Low Life/Who Killed Clayton Square? (p/s)	5
89	Ghetto GTG T 2	High Rise Low Life/Who Killed Clayton Square?/High Rise Low Life (Bert Hardy Mix) (12", p/s)	8
90	Ghetto GTG B 11	I Know You Well/I Feel No Way (p/s)	5
90	Ghetto GTG 11T	I Know You Well (Extended Mix)/I Feel No Way/(If You Want It Mix) (12", p/s)	8
90	Ghetto GTG CD 11	I Know You Well (7" Version)/(If You Want It Mix)Feel No Way/(Ext. Mix) (CD)	8
88	Ghetto GHETT 1	ZILCH (LP, distributed by Epic, or later independent issue)	12/15
88	Ghetto GHETT D 1	ZILCH (CD)	18

(see also Pale Fountains)

SHADE JOEY & NIGHTOWLS
64	Parlophone R 5180	Bluebirds Over The Mountain/That's When I Need You Baby	85

SHADER
81	Piston Broke REDASH 1	Bad News Blues (no p/s)	100

SHADES (U.S.)
58	London HLX 8713	Sun Glasses (with Knott Sisters)/KNOTT SISTERS: Undivided Attention	45
58	London HLX 8713	Sun Glasses (with Knott Sisters)/KNOTT SISTERS: Undivided Attention (78)	15

SHADES
62	Starlite ST45 074	Weird Walk/Joe's Shuffle	22

SHADES (Jamaica)
69	Gas GAS 119	Never Gonna Give You Up/Let Me Remind You (both actually by Techniques)	12

(see also Techniques)

SHADES OF BLUE (U.K.)
65	Parlophone R 5270	Voodoo Blues/Luceanne	48
65	Pye 7N 15988	Where Did All The Good Times Go/I Ain't No Use	12

(see also Toby Twirl)

SHADES OF BLUE (U.S.)
66	Sue WI 4022	Oh! How Happy/Little Orphan Boy	35

SHADES OF JOY
69	Fontana STL 5498	SHADES OF JOY (LP)	25

JOHNNY SHADOW (& DANNY GAVIN)
63	Pye 7N 15506	Golli Golli/I'm Coming Home To You (with Danny Gavin) (some in p/s)	15/7
63	Pye 7N 15529	Golli Guitar/Week (with Danny Gavin)	7
65	Parlophone R 5286	Kiss Me Now/What Colour Is The Wind	7
65	Parlophone R 5308	Atom Bomb Song Part 3/Talented Man	7

(see also Ivy League)

SHADOWFAX
79	BFD SFX 100	Really Into You (p/s)	50
80	Risky Discs RISK 1	The Russians Are Coming/Calling The Shots	8

SHADOWS (U.S.)
58	HMV POP 563	Jungle Fever/Under Stars Of Love (78 rpm = £65)	100

SHADOWS (U.K.)
SINGLES
59	Columbia DB 4387	Saturday Dance/Lonesome Fella (78 rpm = £200)	50
60	Columbia DB 4484	Apache/Quartermaster's Stores (green label, later black)	10/18
60	Columbia DB 4530	Man Of Mystery/The Stranger	7
61	Columbia DB 4580	F.B.I./Midnight	7
61	Columbia DB 4637	The Frightened City/Back Home	7
61	Columbia DB 4698	Kon-Tiki/36-24-36	7
61	Columbia DB 4726	The Savage/Peace Pipe	7
62	Columbia DB 4790	Wonderful Land/Stars Fell On Stockton	7
62	Columbia DB 4870	Guitar Tango/What A Lovely Tune	7

(The above singles were originally issued with green labels; later black label copies are worth £12-£15 unless otherwise stated.)

62	Columbia DB 4948	Dance On!/All Day	5
63	Columbia DB 4984	Foot Tapper/The Breeze And I	5
63	Columbia DB 7047	Atlantis/I Want You To Want Me	5
63	Columbia DB 7106	Shindig/It's Been A Blue Day	6
63	Columbia DB 7163	Geronimo/Shazam	5
64	Columbia DB 7231	Theme For Young Lovers/This Hammer	5
64	Columbia DB 7261	The Rise And Fall Of Flingel Bunt/It's A Man's World	5
64	Columbia DB 7261	The Rise And Fall Of Flingel Bunt/It's A Man's World (mispressing with A-side on both sides)	12
64	Columbia DB 7342	Rhythm 'n' Greens/The Miracle	6
64	Columbia DB 7416	Genie With The Light Brown Lamp/Little Princess	6
65	Columbia DB 7476	Mary Anne/Chu-Chi	8
65	Columbia DB 7588	Stingray/Alice In Sunderland (in export p/s)	20
65	Columbia DB 7650	Don't Make My Baby Blue/My Grandfather's Clock (in export p/s)	20
65	Columbia DB 7769	The War Lord/I Wish I Could Shimmy Like My Sister Arthur	8
66	Columbia DB 7853	I Met A Girl/Late Night Set	8
66	Columbia DB 7952	A Place In The Sun/Will You Be There	8
66	Columbia DB 8034	The Dreams I Dream/Scotch On The Socks ('B' label demos worth £50)	30
67	Columbia PSR 305	Thunderbirds Are Go (1-sided advance promo)	65
67	Columbia DB 8170	Maroc 7/Bombay Duck	7
67	Columbia PSR 308	Maroc 7 (1-sided demo with spoken-word intro)	60
67	Columbia PSR 310	Chelsea Boot/Jigsaw (demo only)	80
67	Columbia DB 8264	Tomorrow's Cancelled/Somewhere	12
68	Columbia DB 8326	Running Out Of World/HANK MARVIN: London's Not Too Far	12
68	Columbia DB 8372	Dear Old Mrs. Bell/Trying To Forget The One You Love	12
69	Columbia DB 8628	Slaughter On Tenth Avenue/HANK MARVIN: Midnight Cowboy	15

EPs

61	Columbia SEG 8061	THE SHADOWS (also stereo ESG 7834)	12/30
61	Columbia SEG 8094	THE SHADOWS TO THE FORE	12
62	Columbia SEG 8135	SPOTLIGHT ON THE SHADOWS	15
62	Columbia SEG 8148	THE SHADOWS NO. 2 (only some sleeves list "No. 2")	15
62	Columbia SEG 8166	THE SHADOWS NO. 3	15
62	Columbia SEG 8171	WONDERFUL LAND OF THE SHADOWS	15

(The above EPs were originally issued with turquoise labels; later blue/black label copies are worth two-thirds the values listed.)

62	Columbia SEG 8193	THE BOYS (mono)	12
62	Columbia ESG 7881	THE BOYS (stereo, turquoise labels, later black/blue labels)	40/35
63	Columbia SEG 8218	OUT OF THE SHADOWS (mono)	15
63	Columbia ESG 7883	OUT OF THE SHADOWS (stereo, turquoise or black/blue labels)	40/35
63	Columbia SEG 8233	DANCE ON WITH THE SHADOWS	18
63	Columbia SEG 8249	OUT OF THE SHADOWS NO. 2 (also stereo ESG 7895)	18/35
63	Columbia SEG 8268	FOOT TAPPING WITH THE SHADOWS	18
63	Columbia SEG 8278	LOS SHADOWS (2 different sleeves)	18
63	Columbia SEG 8286	SHINDIG WITH THE SHADOWS	20
64	Columbia SEG 8321	THOSE BRILLIANT SHADOWS	20
64	Columbia SEG 8342	DANCE WITH THE SHADOWS	20
64	Columbia SEG 8362	RHYTHM AND GREENS (also stereo ESG 7904)	18/35
64	Columbia SEG 8375	DANCE WITH THE SHADOWS NO. 2	20
65	Columbia SEG 8396	THEMES FROM "ALADDIN AND HIS WONDERFUL LAMP"	20
65	Columbia SEG 8408	DANCE WITH THE SHADOWS NO. 3	22
65	Columbia SEG 8445	ALICE IN SUNDERLAND	22
65	Columbia SEG 8459	THE SOUND OF THE SHADOWS	25
66	Columbia SEG 8473	THE SOUND OF THE SHADOWS NO. 2	25
66	Columbia SEG 8494	THE SOUND OF THE SHADOWS NO. 3	25
66	Columbia SEG 8500	THOSE TALENTED SHADOWS	22
66	Columbia SEG 8510	THUNDERBIRDS ARE GO! (with Cliff Richard)	65
67	Columbia SEG 8528	THE SHADOWS ON STAGE AND SCREEN	35

LPs

| 61 | Columbia 33SX 1374 | THE SHADOWS (also stereo SCX 3414) | 20/40 |
| 62 | Columbia 33SX 1458 | OUT OF THE SHADOWS (also stereo SCX 3449) | 20/30 |

(The above LPs were originally issued with green labels; later blue/black label copies are worth two-thirds the values listed.)

63	Columbia 33SX 1522	GREATEST HITS (stereo SCX 1522)	15
64	Columbia 33SX 1619	DANCE WITH THE SHADOWS (also stereo SCX 3511)	20/22
65	Columbia 33SX 1736	THE SOUND OF THE SHADOWS (also stereo SCX 3554)	20/22
65	Columbia 33SX 1791	MORE HITS! (stereo SCX 3578)	15
66	Columbia 33SX/SCX 6041	SHADOW MUSIC	15
67	Columbia S(C)X 6148	JIGSAW	18
67	Columbia S(C)X 6199	FROM HANK, BRUCE, BRIAN AND JOHN	18
68	Columbia S(C)X 6282	ESTABLISHED 1958 (half by Cliff Richard, mono/stereo)	18/15

(The above LPs were originally issued with blue/black labels; later silver/black label copies are worth half the values listed.)

70	Columbia SCX 6420	SHADES OF ROCK	18
72	World Records ALBUM 72	THE SHADOWS (6-LP box set)	30
73	EMI EMA 762	ROCKIN' WITH CURLY LEADS	15
75	EMI EMC 3066	SPECS APPEAL	12
77	EMI EMTV 3	TWENTY GOLDEN GREATS (mispressing, side 2 plays Pink Floyd's "Animals")	12

(see also Cliff Richard, Drifters, Five Chestnuts, Hank Marvin, Marvin Welch & Farrar, Bruce Welch, John Henry Rostill, Brian Bennett, Jet Harris, Tony Meehan, Vipers Skiffle Group, Marty Wilde, Krew Kats, Interns, Strangers, Wasp, MacArthur Park, Thunder Company, Alan Hawkshaw)

SHADOWS OF KNIGHT
66	Atlantic AT 4085	Gloria/Dark Side	30
66	Atlantic 584 021	Oh Yeah/Light Bulb Blues	20
66	Atlantic 584 045	Bad Little Woman/Gospel Zone	20
67	Atlantic 584 136	Someone Like Me/Three For Love	20
69	Buddah 201 024	Shake/From Way Out To Way Under	25
79	Radar ADA 11	GLORIA (LP)	20

SHADROCKS
67	Island WI 3061	Go Go Special/Count Down	12
68	Jay Boy BOY 2	There Is/Jigsaw	6

SHADY
98	Narcotic Candy BBQ 41 TT	Narcotic Candy/Micro Bodi Dot Con (10", p/s)	8
98	Narcotic Candy BBQ 41 CD	Narcotic Candy/Micro Bodi Dot Con (CD)	8

(see also Mercury Rev)

SHADY BARD
05	Private Pressing	Torch Song/Bobby/Memory Tree (CD-R in PVC sleeve, sold at gigs)	20
06	Static Caravan Van 108	Treeology EP (CD, hand wrapped in brown paper and string, 100 only)	30

DOREEN SHAFFER
69	Unity UN 536	No Matter What/Walk Through This World	8
69	Unity UN 538	How Much Is That Doggy In The Window/As Long As He Needs Me	6

(see also Bob Marley/Wailers, Lloyd Clarke, Doreen & Jackie)

JOHN SHAFT
72	Downtown DT 488	Forever Music/BLOSSOM JOHNSON: The Boy I Love	6

SHAFTESBURY
80	O.K. SRT CUS 025	Hit Man	5
80	O.K. OKA 001	THE LULL BEFORE THE STORM (LP, with insert)	20
81	O.K. OKA 002	WE ARE THE BOYS (LP)	15

BOBBY SHAFTO
62	Parlophone R 4870	Over And Over/I Want My Bed	8
62	Parlophone R 4958	Feel So Blue/I Haven't Got A Girl	8
64	Parlophone R 5130	She's My Girl/Wonderful You	8
64	Parlophone R 5167	Love, Love, Love (Don't Let Me Down)/I Don't Love You Anymore	8
64	Parlophone R 5184	Who Wouldn't Love A Girl Like That/I Remember	8
65	Parlophone R 5252	How Could You Do A Thing Like That To Me/Baby Then	8
66	Parlophone R 5403	Lonely Is As Lonely Does/The Same Old Room	15
66	Parlophone R 5481	A Little Like You/See Me Cry	8

SHAG NASTY
79	Shag Nasty SN 1	No Bullshit Just Rock 'n' Roll/Looking For A Love? (p/s)	30

SHAGRAT
90	Shagrat ORC 001	Amanda/Peppermint Flickstick (p/s, 500 only, some autographed)	6/10
91	Shagrat ENT 001	NOTHING EXCEEDS LIKE EXCESS (mini LP, as Steve Took's Shagrat, numbered, 400 only)	12

(see also Tyrannosaurus Rex, Pink Fairies, Larry Wallis, Tools You Can Trust)

SHAKE
79	Sire SIR 4016	Culture Shock/Dream On	10
79	Sire SIR 4016-10	Culture Shock/Glass House/Dream On/(But) Not Mine (10", p/s)	12

(see also Rezillos, Jo Callis, TV 21)

SHAKEOUTS
65	Columbia DB 7613	Every Little Once In A While/Well Who's That	50

SHAKERS (U.K.)
63	Polydor NH 52158	Money/Memphis Tennessee	20
63	Polydor NH 52213	Hippy Hippy Shake/Dr. Feelgood	20
63	Polydor NH 66991	Hippy Hippy Shake/Dr. Feelgood	20
63	Polydor NH 52258	Money/Hippy Hippy Shake	20
63	Polydor NH 52272	Whole Lotta Lovin'/I Can Tell	20
63	Polydor 237 139	LET'S DO THE SLOP, TWIST, MADISON, HULLY GULLY WITH THE SHAKERS (LP)	60

(see also Kingsize Taylor & Dominoes)

SHAKERS (U.S.)
73	Probe PRO 582	One Wonderful Moment/Love, Love, Love	6
74	ABC ABC 4018	One Wonderful Moment/Love, Love, Love (reissue)	5

JOHN & JOAN SHAKESPEARE
69	Decca F 12896	Number One Theme/Fade Out (some with p/s)	30/10

CHRIS SHAKESPEARE GLOBE SHOW
69	Page One POF 113	Ob-La-Di, Ob-La-Da/Tin Soldier	18

(see also Globe Show)

SHAKESPEARES
68	RCA Victor RCA 1695	Something To Believe In/Burning My Fingers	40

(see also Fynn McCool)

SHAKEY JAKE
69	Liberty LBL 83217E	FURTHER ON UP THE ROAD (LP)	35

SHAKEY VICK
69	Pye N(S)PL 18276	LITTLE WOMAN, YOU'RE SO SWEET (LP)	18

SAM SHAM
69	Blue Cat BS 157	Drumbago's Dead/SPARTERS: Song Of The Year	15

SHAME
67	MGM MGM 1349	Don't Go Away Little Girl/Dreams Don't Bother Me (125 with picture insert) . .	90/70

(see also Shy Limbs, King Crimson, Gods, Emerson Lake & Palmer)

SHAMEN
86	One Big Guitar OBG 003T	THEY MAY BE RIGHT ... BUT THEY'RE CERTAINLY WRONG (12" EP)	15
86	Skipping Kitten	WAYWARD WEDNESDAY IN MAY AFFAIR ("Four Letter Girl"/"Stay In Bed")	
	(no cat. no.)	(33rpm 1-sided flexidisc, with insert, free with *Skipping Kitten* fanzine)	5
89	Moksha SOMA 6CD	You, Me And Everything (Evil Edit)/Reraptyouare (Evil Edit)/	
		Ed's Bonus Beats (CD, no inlay)	8

(see also Alone Again Or, Stretchheads)

SHAMES
66	CBS 202344	Sugar And Spice/Ben Franklin's Almanac	25
66	CBS 202450	I Wanna Meet You/We Could Be Happy	15
67	CBS 2704	Mr Unreliable/Georgia.	12
67	CBS 2929	It Could Be We're In Love/I Was Lonely When.	22
68	CBS 3820	Greenburg, Glickstein, Charles, David, Smith And Jones/Warm.	12

(see also Isaac Guillory)

SHAM 69
77	Step Forward SF 4	I Don't Wanna/Ulster/Red London (black & white photo p/s).	15
77	Step Forward SF 412	I Don't Wanna/Ulster/Red London (12", black & white photo p/s).	12
77	Polydor (no cat. no.)	Song Of The Streets/Fanx (1-sided concert freebie, red brick-wall label;	
		white label copies are counterfeits)	25
78	Polydor 2058 966	Borstal Breakout/Hey Little Rich Boy (p/s)	12
78	Polydor 2059 023	Angels With Dirty Faces/The Cockney Kids Are Innocent (p/s).	8
78	Polydor 2059 050	If The Kids Are United/Sunday Morning Nightmare (p/s)	8
78		What Have We Got? (1-sided gig only 45, 500 only)	25
79	Step Forward SF 412	I Don't Wanna/Red London/Ulster (12" reissue, yellow p/s).	8
79	Step Forward SF 4	I Don't Wanna/Red London (reissue, p/s).	5
79		Hersham Boys/Day Tripper (original 'Pye Studios' acetate for 'Hersham'	
		single, release withdrawn as unable to clear copyright)	250
79	Polydor POSP 64	Hersham Boys/I Don't Wanna/Tell Us The Truth (live) (p/s)	5
79	Polydor POSPX 64	Hersham Boys/I Don't Wanna (live)/Rip Off (live)/I'm A Man, I'm A Boy (live)/	
		Tell Us The Truth (live) (12", p/s).	8
79	Polydor POSP 82	You're A Better Man Than I/Give A Dog A Bone (p/s)	5
87	Legacy LGY 70	Ban The Gun/Ban The Gun (withdrawn)	15
79	Polydor POLD 5025	THE ADVENTURES OF THE HERSHAM BOYS (LP, with 12" EP [2812 045],	
		stickered sleeve)	12
80	Polydor 2383 596	THE FIRST, THE BEST AND THE LAST (LP, with live EP [RIOT 1/2816 028])	12

(see also Jimmy Edwards)

SHAMROCKS
65	Polydor BM 56503	La La La La La/And I Need You	8

WINSTON SHAN(D)
69	Bullet BU 399	Throw Me Corn/Darling Remember (B-side actually by Pat Edwards)	8
69	Bullet BU 411	Matilda (as Wilston Shan)/HARMONIANS: Come To Me	8
70	Moodisc MU 3505	I'll Run Away/Time Is The Master	7
72	Camel CA 88	Audrey (as Winston Shan)/So Nice (as Winston Shan)	6

DAVE SHAND & HIS ROCKIN' RHYTHM
56	Oriole CB 1321	Rockin' The Boat/LIZZIE BORDEN: You Can't Chop Your Poppa Up In	
		Massachusetts (actually by Derek Nimmo) (78)	10

SHANE & SHANE GANG
64	Pye 7N 15662	Whistle Stop/Who Wrote That Song	15

SHANES
65	Columbia DB 7601	I Don't Want Your Love/New Orleans	55

SHANGAANS
65	Columbia DB 7551	Genzene (What Have I Done)/Yeh Girl	10
65	Columbia Studio 2 TWO 109	JUNGLE DRUMS (LP)	18

SHANGRI-LAS
64	Red Bird RB 10008	Remember (Walking In The Sand)/It's Easier To Cry.	10
64	Red Bird RB 10014	Leader Of The Pack/What Is Love?.	10
65	Red Bird RB 10018	Give Him A Great Big Kiss/Twist And Shout	15
65	Red Bird RB 10025	Out In The Streets/The Boy	15
65	Red Bird RB 10030	Give Us Your Blessings/Heaven Only Knows	15
65	Red Bird RB 10036	Right Now And Not Later/Train From Kansas City	20
66	Red Bird RB 10043	I Can Never Go Home Anymore/Bulldog	12
66	Red Bird RB 10048	Long Live Our Love/Sophisticated Boom Boom	15
66	Red Bird RB 10053	He Cried/Dressed In Black	15
66	Red Bird RB 10068	Past, Present, And Future/Paradise	20
67	Mercury MF 962	The Sweet Sound Of Summer/I'll Never Learn.	10
67	Mercury MF 979	Take The Time/Footsteps On The Roof	10
65	Red Bird RB 40 002	THE SHANGRI-LAS (EP).	75
66	Red Bird RB 40 004	I CAN NEVER GO HOME ANYMORE (EP, unreleased)	
65	Red Bird RB 20 101	THE SHANGRI-LAS — LEADER OF THE PACK (LP).	60
66	Mercury MCL 20096	GOLDEN HITS OF THE SHANGRI-LAS (LP).	15

BUD SHANK
56	Vogue V 2376	Royal Garden Blues/It Had To Be You (with Bill Perkins Quintet)	5
56	Vogue V 2383	When Your Lover Has Gone/There's A Small Hotel	
		(with Bob Brookmeyer).	5
56	Vogue V 2385	Shank's Pranks/Left Bank (with Shorty Rogers Quintet)	5
59	Vogue LAE 12248	LATIN CONTRASTS (LP)	20

(see also Shorty Rogers)

MINT VALUE £

ANANDA SHANKAR

69	Reprise RSLP 6398	ANANDA SHANKAR (JUMPING JACK FLASH) (LP)	100
60s	EMI	ANANDA SHANKAR AND HIS MUSIC (LP)	60
71	Reprise K 44092	ANANDA SHANKAR (LP, reissue)	35

RAVI SHANKAR

66	Fontana TF 712	Song From The Hills/Dhun	5
72	Apple APPLE 37	Joi Bangla/Oh Bhaugowan/Raga Mishri-Jhinjhoti (p/s)	20
74	Dark Horse AMS 7133	I Am Missing You/Lust (as Shankar Family & Friends)	5
59	Vogue VA 160156	INDIA'S MASTER MUSICIAN (LP)	20
62	HMV ASD 463	MUSIC OF INDIA (LP)	15
63	Melodisc MLP 12-151	THE EXCITING MUSIC OF RAVI SHANKAR (LP)	15
65	Fontana TF 5253	INDIA'S MASTER MUSICIAN (LP, reissue)	15
66	Fontana TL 5285	PORTRAIT OF GENIUS (LP)	15
66	Fontana TL 5357	SOUND OF THE SITAR (LP)	15
67	Fontana TL 5424	IN NEW YORK (LP)	15
71	Mushroom 300 MR 8	FOUR RAGA MOODS (2-LP)	35
73	Apple SAPDO 1002	IN CONCERT — 1972 (2-LP, with Ali Akbar Khan, gatefold sleeve)	120
74	Dark Horse AMLH 22002	SHANKAR FAMILY & FRIENDS (LP)	15
76	Dark Horse AMLH 22007	RAVI SHANKAR'S MUSIC FESTIVAL FROM INDIA (LP)	20
96	Apple SAPDO 1002	IN CONCERT — 1972 (2-LP, reissue)	18
96	Apple SAPDO 1002	IN CONCERT — 1972 (CD)	18

(see also Ali Akbar Khan, Will Sergeant)

BILL SHANKLY

70s	Technical TECLP 001A	SHANKS ON SOCCER (2-LP)	30

DEAN SHANNON

60	HMV POP 820	Blinded With Love/Jezebel	25
62	HMV POP 1103	Ubangi Stomp/Blowing Wild	35

DEL SHANNON

SINGLES

61	London HLX 9317	Runaway/Jody	7
61	London HLX 9317	Runaway/Jody (mispressed B-side, plays "The Snake" by Maximillian)	30
61	London HLX 9402	Hats Off To Larry/Don't Gild The Lily, Lily	7
61	London HLX 9462	So Long Baby/The Answer To Everything	7
62	London HLX 9515	Hey! Little Girl/You Never Talked About Me	7
62	London HLX 9587	Cry Myself To Sleep/I'm Gonna Move On	7
62	London HLX 9609	The Swiss Maid/Ginny In The Mirror	5
63	London HLX 9653	Little Town Flirt/The Wamboo	7
63	London HLX 9710	Two Kinds Of Teardrops/Kelly	7
63	London HLX 9761	Two Silhouettes/My Wild One	7
63	London HLU 9800	Sue's Gonna Be Mine/Since She's Gone	7
64	London HLU 9858	That's The Way Love Is/Time Of The Day	7
64	Stateside SS 269	Mary Jane/Stains On My Letter	10
64	Stateside SS 317	Handy Man/Give Her Lots Of Lovin'	10
64	Stateside SS 349	Do You Want To Dance/This Is All I Have To Give	10
65	Stateside SS 395	Stranger In Town/Over You	10
65	Stateside SS 430	Break Up/Why Don't You Tell Him	10
65	Stateside SS 452	Move It On Over/She Still Remembers Tony	15
66	Stateside SS 494	I Can't Believe My Ears/I Wish I Wasn't Me Tonight	15
66	Liberty LIB 55866	The Big Hurt/I Got It Bad	12
66	Liberty LIB 55889	For A Little While/Hey Little Star	15
67	Liberty LIB 55939	She/What Makes You Run	15
67	Liberty LIB 10277	Mind Over Matter/Led Along	12
67	Liberty LBF 15020	Runaway '67/Show Me	12
68	Liberty LBF 15061	Thinkin' It Over/Runnin' On Back	15
68	Liberty LBF 15079	Gemini/Magical Musical Box	35
69	Stateside SS 8025	Comin' Back To Me/Sweet Mary Lou	12
70	Stateside SS 8040	Sister Isabelle/Colorado Rain	12

EPs

62	London RE-X 1332	RUNAWAY WITH DEL SHANNON	25
63	London RE-X 1346	DEL SHANNON NO. 2	25
63	London RE-X 1383	DEL'S OWN FAVOURITES	30
63	London RE-X 1387	FROM DEL TO YOU	35
65	Stateside SE 1029	DEL SHANNON'S HITS	35
67	Liberty LEP 2272	THE NEW DEL SHANNON	50

LPs

61	London HA-X 2402	RUNAWAY WITH DEL SHANNON	50
63	London HA-X 8071	HATS OFF TO DEL SHANNON	40
63	London HA-X 8091	LITTLE TOWN FLIRT	45
65	Stateside SL 10115	HANDY MAN	40
65	Stateside SL 10130	DEL SHANNON SINGS HANK WILLIAMS	40
65	Stateside SL 10140	ONE THOUSAND SIX HUNDRED AND SIXTY-ONE SECONDS WITH DEL SHANNON	40
66	Liberty (S)LBY 1320	THIS IS MY BAG (mono/stereo)	25/30
66	Liberty (S)LBY 1335	TOTAL COMMITMENT (mono/stereo)	25/30
68	Liberty LBL/LBS 83114E	THE FURTHER ADVENTURES OF CHARLES WESTOVER	55
73	United Artists UAS 29474	LIVE IN ENGLAND	18

(see also Maximillian)

LINDA SHANNON

59	Parlophone R 4603	Goodbye Charlie/If You Only Knew	5

MIKE SHANNON & STRANGERS

(see under Strangers)

SHAPE OF THE RAIN
71	RCA Neon NE 1001	Woman/Wasting My Time	7
71	RCA RCA 2129	My Friend John/Yes	5
71	RCA Neon NE 7	RILEY, RILEY, WOOD & WAGGETT (LP, gatefold sleeve)	50

SHAPES
79	Sofa SEAT 1/FRR 004	THE SHAPES (WOT'S FOR LUNCH, MUM?) (EP, no p/s, with insert)	22
79	Good Vibrations GOT 13	Blast Off/Airline Disasters (p/s)	15

SHAPES & SIZES
66	Decca F 12441	A Little Lovin' Somethin'/Rain On My Face	7

HELEN SHAPIRO
SINGLES
61	Columbia DB 4782	Tell Me What He Said/I Apologise	8
63	Columbia DB 4966	Queen For Tonight/Daddy Couldn't Get Me One Of Those	30
63	Columbia DB 7026	Woe Is Me/I Walked Right In	5
63	Columbia DB 7072	Not Responsible/No Trespassing	5
63	Columbia DB 7130	Look Who It Is/Walking In My Dreams	10
64	Columbia DB 7190	Fever/Ole Father Time	25
64	Columbia DB 7266	Look Over Your Shoulder/You Won't Come Home	10
64	Columbia DB 7340	Shop Around/He Knows How To Love Me	100
64	Columbia DB 7395	I Wish I'd Never Loved You/I Was Only Kidding	10
65	Columbia DB 7517	Tomorrow Is Another Day/It's So Funny I Could Cry	10
65	Columbia DB 7587	Here In Your Arms/Only Once	10
65	Columbia DB 7690	Something Wonderful/Just A Line	10
66	Columbia DB 7810	Forget About The Bad Things/Wait A Little Longer	10
66	Columbia DB 8073	In My Calendar/Empty House	10
67	Columbia DB 8148	Make Me Belong To You/The Way Of The World	10
67	Columbia DB 8256	She Needs Company/Stop And You Will Become Aware (DJ copy = £175)	125
68	Pye 7N 17600	You'll Get Me Loving You/Silly Boy (I Love You)	10
69	Pye 7N 17714	Today Has Been Cancelled/Face The Music	10
69	Pye 7N 17785	You've Guessed/Take Me For A While	10
70	Pye 7N 17893	Take Down A Note Miss Smith/Couldn't You See	10
70	Pye 7N 17975	Waiting On The Shores Of Nowhere/A Glass Of Wine	10

EPs
61	Columbia SEG 8128	HELEN (mono, 'smiling' or 'cross-armed' sleeve)	each 15
61	Columbia ESG 7872	HELEN (stereo, 'smiling' or 'cross-armed' sleeve)	each 20
61	Columbia SEG 8136	HELEN'S HIT PARADE	15
62	Columbia SEG 8170	A TEENAGER SINGS THE BLUES (also stereo ESG 7880)	20/25
62	Columbia SEG 8174	MORE HITS FROM HELEN	15
62	Columbia SEG 8209	EVEN MORE HITS FROM HELEN	18
63	Columbia SEG 8229	'TOPS' WITH ME NO. 1 (also stereo ESG 7888)	20/30
63	Columbia SEG 8243	'TOPS' WITH ME NO. 2 (also stereo ESG 7891)	20/30

LPs
62	Columbia 33SX 1397	'TOPS' WITH ME (also stereo SCX 3428)	20/40
63	Columbia 33SX 1494	HELEN'S SIXTEEN (also stereo SCX 3470)	35/60
63	Columbia 33SX 1561	HELEN IN NASHVILLE	30
64	Columbia 33SX 1661	HELEN HITS OUT (also stereo SCX 3533)	35/60
65	EMI Encore! ENC 209	12 HITS AND A MISS HELEN SHAPIRO	20
74	Columbia SCX 6565	THE VERY BEST OF HELEN SHAPIRO	12
	(see also Ella Stone & Moss)		

SHARADES
64	Decca F 11811	Dumb Head/Boy Trouble	75+
	(see also Ladybirds, Breakaways)		

BILLY SHA RAE
71	Action ACT 4602	Do It/Crying Clown	15

(BILLY) SHARI
58	Decca F 11069	Going Home For Christmas/Count Every Star (as Shari)	5
68	United Artists UP 2235	It's So Lonely Being Together/You Walked Out On Me Before	5

SHARKS
68	RCA RCA 1776	Goodbye Lorene/Funkology	10
	(see also Marcisa & Jeff, Roy Richards)		

SHARKS
73	Island ILPS 9233	FIRST WATER (LP, 'pink rim palm tree' label with inner sleeve)	15
74	Island ILPS 9271	JAB IT IN YORE EYE (LP, 'palm tree' label with inner sleeve)	15
	(see also Chris Spedding, Andy Fraser Band)		

RALPH SHARON
53	Decca LF 1107	SPRING FEVER (10" LP)	12
53	Decca LF 1138	AUTUMN LEAVES (10" LP)	20
53	Lyragon AF 1	COCKTAIL TIME (10" LP)	15
	(see also Tony Bennett)		

BOBBY SHARP & OTHERS
65	Stateside SS 404	Blues For Mr. Charlie (Parts 1 & 2)	
		(with Paul Sindap, Joe Lee Wilson & Little Butler)	15

DEE DEE SHARP
62	Columbia DB 4818	Mashed Potato Time/Set My Heart At Ease	20
62	Columbia DB 4874	Gravy (For My Mashed Potatoes)/Baby Cakes	20
62	Cameo Parkway C 230	Ride/Night	40
63	Cameo Parkway C 244	Do The Bird/Lover Boy	20
63	Cameo Parkway C 260	Rock Me In The Cradle Of Love/You'll Never Be Mine	20
63	Cameo Parkway C 274	Wild/Why Doncha Ask Me	20
65	Cameo Parkway C 375	I Really Love You/Standing In The Need Of Love (DJ copy = £125)	80

65	Cameo Parkway C 382	It's A Funny Situation/There Ain't Nothing I Wouldn't Do (demo-only)	150
66	Atlantic 584 056	My Best Friend's Man/Bye Bye Baby	18
69	Action ACT 4522	What Kind Of Lady/You're Gonna Miss Me	40
79	London HA-U 8514	CAMEO PARKWAY SESSIONS (LP)	25

(see also Chubby Checker & Dee Dee Sharp)

STEVE SHARP & THE CLEANCUTS
| 80 | Happy Face MM 122 | We Are The Mods/He Wants To Be A Mod | 125 |

(see also Rowdies)

RAY SHARPE
| 59 | London HLW 8932 | Linda Lu/Red Sails In The Sunset (triangular or round centre) (78 rpm = £30) | 50/40 |
| 63 | United Artists UP 1032 | Hey Little Girl/Day You Left Me | 15 |

ROCKY SHARPE & THE REPLAYS
| 82 | Chiswick DICE 9 | Heart/Mary (Won't You Marry Me) (withdrawn, approx. 100 only) | 10 |

SHARPEES
66	Stateside SS 495	Tired Of Being Lonely/Just To Please You (DJ copy = £125)	70
73	President PT 389	Do The 45/Make Up Your Mind	15
73	President PT 399	Tired Of Being Lonely/Just To Please You (reissue)	15

SHARPS
| 57 | Vogue V 9086 | Lock My Heart/Love Is Here To Stay (78 rpm = £120) | 750 |
| 58 | Vogue V 9096 | Shufflin'/What Will I Gain (78 rpm = £120) | 750 |

(see also Thurston Harris)

S-HATERS
| 81 | Outer Himmilayan OHR 02 | Death Of A Vampire/Research (p/s) | 6 |

SHAVERS, GETZ, COLE, NORVO, BELLSON, MILLER, etc
| 52 | Vogue V 2104 | Charlie Got Rhythm Parts 1 & 2 (78) | 10 |

ADRIAN SHAW
| 96 | Woronzow W0027 | TEA FOR THE HYDRA (LP, 299 copies only, in hand-finished sleeves) | 15 |

(see also Hawkwind, Bevis Frond)

ARTIE SHAW
| 54 | MGM EPC 3 | ARTIE SHAW (EP, export issue) | 5 |

MARLENA SHAW
67	Chess CRS 8054	Mercy Mercy Mercy/Go Away Little Boy	15
73	United Artists UP 35517	Last Tango In Paris/Save The Children	5
76	United Artists UP 36125	It's Better Than Walking Out/Be For Real	10

NINA SHAW
| 68 | CBS 3239 | Woven In My Soul/Love So Fine | 7 |
| 69 | CBS 4227 | One Fine Day/Somewhere In The World | 10 |

RICKY SHAW
| 62 | London HLU 9606 | No Love But Your Love/Be Still, Be Still, My Own | 8 |

ROLAND SHAW ORCHESTRA
54	Decca F 10407	No One But You (with Kim Bennett)/The High And The Mighty	8
55	Decca F 10449	Softly, Softly (with Kim Bennett)/A Trumpeter's Lullaby	8
50s	Decca F 10758	Trails End/You're Only Young Once	8
64	Decca DFE 8573	RIDERS IN THE SKY (EP)	10
66	Decca DFE 8657	THE IPCRESS FILE (EP, with the Ivor Raymond Orchestra)	8
66	Decca DFE 8670	I SPY (EP)	10
65	Decca LK 4730	JAMES BOND IN ACTION (LP)	25
66	Decca LK 4765	THEMES FOR SECRET AGENTS (LP, mono)	22
66	Phase 4 Stereo PFS 4094	THEMES FOR SECRET AGENTS (LP, stereo)	22
67	Phase 4 Stereo PFS 4125	MORE JAMES BOND IN ACTION (LP)	22
60s	London BSP	DIAMONDS ARE FOREVER (LP, gatefold sleeve)	22

SANDIE SHAW
SINGLES
64	Pye 7N 15671	As Long As You're Happy Baby/Ya-Ya-Da-Da	30
64	Pye 7N 15704	(There's) Always Something There To Remind Me/Don't You Know	5
64	Pye 7N 15743	I'd Be Far Better Off Without You/Girl Don't Come	5
65	Pye 7N 15783	I'll Stop At Nothing/You Can't Blame Him	5
65	Pye 7N 15841	Long Live Love/I've Heard About Him	5
65	Pye 7N 15940	Message Understood/Don't You Count On It	5
65	Pye 7N 15987	How Can You Tell/If Ever You Need Me	5
65	Pye 7N 17036	Tomorrow/Hurting You	8
66	Pye 7N 17163	Run/Long Walk Home	8
66	Pye 7N 17212	Think Sometimes About Me/Hide All Emotion	5
67	Pye 7N 17239	I Don't Need Anything/Keep In Touch	5
67	Pye 7N 17272	Puppet On A String/Tell The Boys (pink label, later blue)	5/6
67	Pye 7N 17346	Tonight In Tokyo/You've Been Seeing Her Again	5
67	Pye 7N 17378	You've Not Changed/Make Me Cry	5
68	Pye 7N 17441	Today/London (pink label, later blue)	each 6
68	Pye 7N 17504	Don't Run Away/Stop	10
82	Virgin VS 484	Anyone Who Had A Heart/Anyone Who Had A Heart (Instrumental) (p/s)	12
84	Rough Trade RTT 130	Hand In Glove/I Don't Owe You Anything/Jeanne (12", p/s, with The Smiths)	8

EPs
64	Pye NEP 24208	(THERE'S) ALWAYS SOMETHING THERE TO REMIND ME	20
65	Pye NEP 24220	LONG LIVE LOVE	20
65	Pye NEP 24232	TALK ABOUT LOVE	20
65	Pye NEP 24234	SANDIE	20
66	Pye NEP 24236	MESSAGE UNDERSTOOD	20
66	Pye NEP 24247	TOMORROW	25

MINT VALUE £

66	Pye NEP 24254	NOTHING COMES EASY.	22
66	Pye NEP 24264	RUN WITH SANDIE SHAW	22
67	Pye NEP 24271	SANDIE SHAW IN FRENCH	40
67	Pye NEP 24273	SANDIE SHAW IN ITALIAN.	40
67	Pye NEP 24281	TELL THE BOYS	25

LPs

65	Pye NPL 18110	SANDIE SHAW.	25
65	Pye NPL 18122	ME.	25
67	Pye N(S)PL 18182	PUPPET ON A STRING	22
67	Pye N(S)PL 18205	LOVE ME, PLEASE LOVE ME	22
68	Pye N(S)PL 18232	THE SANDIE SHAW SUPPLEMENT.	22
69	Pye N(S)PL 18323	REVIEWING THE SITUATION	35

THOMAS SHAW
72	Xtra XTRA 1132	THOMAS SHAW (LP).	15

TIMMY SHAW & STERNPHONES
64	Pye International 7N 25239	Gonna Send You Back To Georgia/I'm A Lonely Guy	30

TREVOR SHAW
81	CMS PR 26	WHEELS IN MOTION (LP).	20

DOROTHY SHAY
53	Capitol LC 6618	THE PARK AVENUE HILLBILLIE (10" LP).	12

SHE
85	Neat NEAT 50	Never Surrender/Breaking Away (p/s).	5
85	Neat NEAT 5012	Never Surrender/Breaking Away/On My Way (12", p/s)	8

LEE SHEARIN
50	London L 695	Give A Broken Heart A Chance To Cry/I Need You (78)	8

GEORGE SHEARING (QUINTET)
51	Decca LF 1036	THE NEARNESS OF YOU (10" LP, as George Shearing Trio).	12
52	MGM MGM-D 103	YOU'RE HEARING GEORGE SHEARING (10" LP).	12
53	MGM MGM-D 118	I HEAR MUSIC (10" LP)	12
54	MGM MGM-D 129	TOUCH OF GENIUS (10" LP).	12
56	Vogue LDE 188	THE VERY FIRST SESSION (10" LP).	12
56	Capitol LC 6803	THE SHEARING SPELL (10" LP).	12
59	Capitol T/ST 1275	LATIN AFFAIR (LP)	12
	(see also Peggy Lee)		

SHEDS
85	John Wayne's S/bags 1	BIMBO EP (cassette, shrink wrapped with free packet of tomato seeds)	7
	(see also Super 8)		

SHED SEVEN
94	Polydor YORKX 1	Mark/Casino Girl/Mobile 10 (12", p/s)	12
94	Polydor YORKX 2	Dolphin/Immobilise/Dolphin (Remix) (12", p/s)	8
96	Polydor 576 214-7	Going For Gold/Making Waves (withdrawn 'nude' gatefold p/s, some without disc).	18/8
96	Polydor 5762147	Going For Gold/Making Waves (gold vinyl, numbered sleeve)	5
96	Polydor 5765967	BULLY BOY (EP, orange vinyl, gatefold sleeve, numbered).	5

BOBBY SHEEN
66	Capitol CL 15455	Dr. Love/Sweet, Sweet Love (DJ copies = £175)	125
72	Capitol CL 15713	Dr. Love/Sweet, Sweet Love (reissue).	20
	(see also Bob B. Soxx & Blue Jeans)		

SHEEP (U.K.)
73	Myrrh MYR 1000	SHEEP (LP, with insert)	25
	(see also Lonesome Stone)		

SHEEP (U.S.)
66	Stateside SS 493	Hide And Seek/Twelve Months Later.	30
69	Stateside SS 2147	Hide And Seek/HAWKS: The Grissle.	15

IREEN SHEER
70	Bell BLL 1129	Hey Pleasure Man/You Walked Away	5
71	Parlophone R 5930	Many Rivers/Is It Me	5
74	Polydor 2041 533	Bye Bye I Love You/Roseberry Avenue	6

SHEER KHAN
84	SRT 4KS 140	Last Generation/Lady's Dance (p/s)	70
85	Mill	QUIET ENOUGH FOR LOVE (LP).	30

SHEFFIELDS
64	Pye 7N 15600	It Must Be Love/Say Girl.	50
64	Pye 7N 15627	I Got My Mojo Working/Hey Hey Lover Boy.	70
65	Pye 7N 15767	Bag's Groove (Skat Walking)/Plenty Of Love.	75

SHEIKS (U.K.)
66	Parlophone R 5500	Missing You/Tell Me Bird	8

SHEIKS (U.S.)
59	London HLW 9012	Très Chic/Little French Doll (78 rpm = £30)	15

SHEILA & JENNY
64	Ember EMB S 3202	When The Boy's Happy/Please Don't Break Her Heart (some in p/s).	10/6

ERNIE SHELBY
73	Mojo 2093 026	Bend Over Backwards/Punish Me.	5

ALLEN SHELDON
70	Plexium PXM 14	Mirror Of My Mind/Old Windmill Tree	20

DOUG SHELDON
61	Decca F 11368	The Book Of Love/Play Me The Blues	10
61	Decca F 11398	Runaround Sue/Come With Me	10
61	Decca F 11416	Your Ma Said You Cried In Your Sleep/You're Only Fooling Yourself	10
62	Decca F 11433	My Kingdom For A Girl/You Never Had It So Good	10
62	Decca F 11463	A Big Big Baby/If You'd Be Mine	10
62	Decca F 11514	Lollipops And Roses/One Way To Say Goodbye	10
62	Decca F 11529	Live Now Pay Later/Me	7
63	Decca F 11564	I Saw Linda Yesterday/My Billy	8
63	Decca F 11654	Let's Make A Habit Of This/I Was Alone	8
63	Decca F 11790	Mickey's Monkey/Falling In Love With Love	10
65	Sue WI 332	Take It Like A Man/Lonely Boy	18
65	Pye 7N 17011	It's Because Of You/How Can I Tell Her?	7
63	Decca DFE 8527	HERE I STAND (EP)	75

SANDI SHELDON
76	Epic EPC 4186	You're Gonna Make Me Love You/Baby You're Mine	18

SHELL
66	Columbia DB 8082	Goodbye Little Girl/Little Bit Of Lovin'	12

SHELLEY
64	Pye 7N 15711	I Will Be Wishing/Why Don't You Say You Love Me	12
65	Pye 7N 15773	Stairway To A Star/I Heard A Whisper	8
65	Pye 7N 15913	Where Has Your Smile Gone/Paradise	8

LIZ SHELLEY
65	Brunswick 05940	Make Me Your Baby/You Made Me Hurt	10
66	Brunswick 05953	No More Love/I Can't Find You	10

PETE SHELLEY
82	Lyntone 10952/53	Qu'est-Ce Que C'est, Qu'est Que Ça (Dub)/ANIMAL MAGNET: More (hard vinyl test pressing, numbered, some with info sheet/letter)	15/12
80	Groovy STP 2	SKY YEN (mini-LP)	12

(see also Buzzcocks, Free Agents, Tiller Boys)

SHELLS
61	London HLU 9288	Baby, Oh Baby/Angel Eyes	55
62	London HLU 9644	It's A Happy Holiday/Deep In My Heart	40

ALAN SHELLY & MANU DIBANGO'S BROTHERS
69	Philips BF 1709	Lady Black Wife/Give Me Time	12

ANNE SHELTON
54	HMV B 10732	Juke Box Rag/Love Him So Much I Could Scream (78)	8
53	HMV 7M 164	Answer Me (Mutterlein)/The Bridge Of Sighs	12
54	HMV 7M 186	The Book/Why Does It Have To Be Me	12
54	HMV 7M 197	Cross Over The Bridge/(O Baby Mine) I Get So Lonely	12
54	HMV 7M 240	Goodnight, Well It's Time To Go/If I Give My Heart To You	12
54	HMV 7M 279	My Gypsy Heart/Teach Me Tonight	12
57	Philips JK 1012	Absent Friends/Seven Ages Of Man (jukebox issue)	15
58	Philips PB 779	Until They Sail/Ha! Ha! Ha!	7
58	Philips PB 815	The Girl He Left Behind/Sail Along, Silv'ry Moon	7
58	Philips PB 852	Volare/Do You Love Me Like You Kiss Me? (78 rpm = £8)	7
58	Philips PB 878	Hurry Home/I.T.A.L.Y. (I Trust And Love You) (78 rpm = £8)	7
59	Philips PB 920	Just Love Me/Could I Love You More	6
59	Philips PB 956	Now Hear This!/To Love And Be Loved	6
59	Philips PB 969	The Village Of St. Bernadette/You're Not Living In Vain (78 rpm = £12)	6
60	Philips PB 994	The Angels' Lullaby/Where Can I Go	6
60	Philips PB 1042	Papa Loves Mama/Come Back Again	6
61	Philips PB 1096	Sailor/A Souvenir Of Ireland (some with p/s)	8/5

EPs
50s	London BEP 6043	ANNE SHELTON WITH ORCHESTRAL ACCOMPANIMENT (export issue)	10
56	Decca DFE 6321	FOUR STANDARDS	8
56	Philips BBE 12090	ANNE SHELTON	8
58	Philips BBE 12169	THE SHELTON SOUND	8
58	Philips BBE 12205	ITALIAN TOUCH	8
58	Philips BBE 12218	ANNE SHELTON	8
59	Philips BBE 12292	JUST LOVE ME	8
60	Philips BBE 12344	SONGS OF FAITH	8
60	Philips BBE 12347	MY YIDDISHE MOMMA (also stereo SBBE 9003)	10/8
61	Philips BBE 12430	FAVOURITES	8
62	Philips BBE 12526	SPRING FEVER	8

LPs
52	Decca LF 1023	FAVOURITES (10")	30
53	Decca LF 1106	FAVOURITES VOL. 2 (10")	30
57	Philips BBL 7188	THE SHELTON SOUND	22
59	Philips BBL 7291	SONGS FROM THE HEART	20
60	Philips BBL 7393	ANNE SHELTON SHOWCASE	22
62	Philips BBL 7541	A SOUVENIR OF IRELAND (also stereo SBBL 664)	15/20

ROSCOE SHELTON
65	Sue WI 354	Strain On My Heart/Question (A- & B-side labels reversed)	40

CAROL SHELYNE
65	Liberty LIB 55794	The Girl With The Horn Rim Glasses/Boys Do Make Passes At Girls Who Wear Glasses	7

DEANNA SHENDEREY
65	Decca F 12090	Comin' Home Baby/I've Got That Feeling	8

SHENLEY (Duffas) & ANNETTE
61   Blue Beat BB 72   Million Dollar Baby/The First Time I Met You 15

SHENLEY (Duffas) & HYACINTH (Brown)
66   Rio R 80   The World Is On A Wheel/ROY & CORNELL: Salvation 15
(see also Baba Brooks)

SHENLEY (Duffas) & (Little) LUNAN
65   Rio R 52   Something On Your Mind/The Rain Came Tumbling Down 12
(see also Shenley Duffas)

SHEP & LIMELITES
61   Pye International 7N 25090   Daddy's Home/This I Know 110
61   Pye International 7N 25112   Ready For Your Love/You'll Be Sorry 100

JEAN SHEPARD
56   Capitol EAP 1030   SONGS OF A LOVE AFFAIR NO. 1 (EP) 10
56   Capitol EAP2 728   SONGS OF A LOVE AFFAIR NO. 2 (EP) 10
60   Capitol T 1253   THIS IS JEAN SHEPARD (LP) 12
63   Capitol ST 1922   THE BEST OF (LP). 12
64   Capitol ST 2187   LIGHTHEARTED AND BLUE (LP). 15

BILLY SHEPHARD
59   Felstad AF 117   You Call Everybody Darling/Somebody Stole My Gal. 5

PAULINE SHEPHERD
57   Columbia DB 4010   Love Me To Pieces/Just Between You And Me 12

SHEPHERD BOYS (& GIRLS)
56   Columbia SCM 5282   Little Girls And Little Boys/Teenage Love (Shepherd Boys & Girls) (78 = £6) 8
56   Columbia DB 3816   Summer Sweetheart/Song For A Summer Night 6

SHEPHERD/SHEPPARD SISTERS
57   HMV POP 411   Alone (Why Must I Be Alone)/Congratulations To Someone 10
58   Mercury 7MT 196   Gettin' Ready For Freddy/Best Thing There Is (Is Love) (Sheppard Sisters) 15
58   Mercury 7MT 218   Eating Pizza/A Boy And A Girl (as Sheppard Sisters) (78 rpm = £7) 10
58   Mercury AMT 1005   Dancing Baby/Is It A Crime? (78 rpm = £7) 7
63   London HLK 9681   Don't Mention My Name/What Makes Little Girls Cry 20
63   London HLK 9758   Talk Is Cheap/Greatest Lover. 15

TOM SHEPLEY'S BAND
78   Tradition TSR 031   HOW DO YOU DO? (LP) 15

ARCHIE SHEPP
66   HMV CLP/CSD 3524   FOUR FOR TRANE (LP) 20
66   HMV CLP/CSD 3561   ON THIS NIGHT (LP). 20
67   HMV CLP/CSD 3600   LIVE IN SAN FRANCISCO (LP) 15
67   Polydor 623 235   ARCHIE SHEPP AND THE NEW YORK CONTEMPORARY FIVE (LP) 12
67   Fontana 681 014 ZL   RUFUS (LP, with John Tchicai) 12
68   Impulse MIPL/SIPL 508   MAMA TOO TIGHT (LP) 12
68   Polydor 623 267   NEW YORK CONTEMPORARY FIVE VOL. 2 (LP). 12
69   Impulse MILP/SIPL 512   THE MAGIC OF JU-JU (LP) 12
69   Impulse MIPL/SIPL 516   THE WAY AHEAD (LP) 12
69   Atlantic 583 732   ONE FOR THE TRANE (LP) 12
69   Impulse SIPL 520   THREE FOR A QUARTER, ONE FOR A DIME (LP). 12
(see also John Coltrane)

SHEPPARDS
71   Jay Boy BOY 30   How Do You Like It/Stubborn Heart 40

SHEPPERTON FLAMES
69   Deram DM 257   Take Me For What I Am/Goodbye 45
(see also Mike Berry)

SHERE KHAN
69   Tepee TPR 1007   Little Louise/No Reason. .... 100+

SHERIDAN
70   Gemini GMS 001   Follow Me Follow/When Love Breaks Your Heart 15
(see also Sheridan-Price, Mike Sheridan & Night Riders, Mike Sheridan's Lot)

DANI SHERIDAN
66   Planet PLF 106   Guess I'm Dumb/Songs Of Love 35

MIKE SHERIDAN & NIGHT RIDERS
63   Columbia DB 7141   Tell Me What'cha Gonna Do/No Other Guy 30
63   Columbia DB 7183   Please Mr. Postman/In Love. 30
64   Columbia DB 7302   What A Sweet Thing That Was/Fabulous 20
65   Columbia DB 7462   Here I Stand/Lonely Weekends 20
(see also Roy Wood, Idle Race, Mike Sheridan's Lot, Nightriders, Sheridan-Price, Sight & Sound)

MIKE SHERIDAN'S LOT
65   Columbia DB 7677   Take My Hand/Make Them Understand 28
66   Columbia DB 7798   Don't Turn Your Back On Me, Babe/Stop, Look, Listen 20
(see also Roy Wood, Idle Race, Mike Sheridan & Night Riders, Nightriders, Sheridan-Price, Sight & Sound)

TONY SHERIDAN & THE BEAT BROTHERS
64   Polydor NH 52315   Jambalaya/Will You Still Love Me Tomorrow (with The Beat Brothers) 10
64   Polydor NH 52927   Skinny Minny/You'd Better Move On (with The Beat Brothers)................. 10
(see also Bobby Patrick Big Six, Beat Brothers, Pete Best Four)

TONY SHERIDAN & THE BEATLES
(see under The Beatles)

SHERIDAN-PRICE
70	Gemini GMS 009	Sometimes I Wonder (as Sheridan & Rick Price)/SHERIDAN: Lightning Never Strikes Twice	25
70	Gemini GME 1002	THIS IS TO CERTIFY THAT... (LP, gatefold sleeve)	20

(see also Rick Price, Mike Sheridan & Nightriders, Mike Sheridan's Lot, Idle Race, Sight & Sound, Sheridan)

ROGER SHERLOCK
78	Inchecronin INC 7419	MEMORIES OF SLIGO (LP)	12

ALLAN SHERMAN
63	Warner Bros WB 106	Hello Muddah Hello Faddah/Rat Fink	5
64	Warner Bros WEP 6148	YOUR MOTHER'S HERE TO STAY (EP)	12

BIM SHERMAN
78	Yard Internationa YI 1001	What Sweet You So/U BLACK: Pot A Bubble (12")	15
79	Hit Run DD6/7	Down In Jamtown (with Jah Lion)/Version (12")	40
79	Hit Run HIT DD 11	Love Only Jah (with Jah Buzz)/Version (12")	45

JOE SHERMAN
58	Fontana H 129	Miraculous Music Box/Make Me Laugh (78 rpm = £6)	6
58	Fontana H 147	Buttermilk/Please Don't Say Goodnight (78 rpm = £6)	6

SHE ROCKERS
88	Music Of Life NOTE014	Give It A Rest (12")	8

BILLY SHERRILL
61	Mercury AMT 1131	Like Making Love/Rules Of The Game	6

SHERRYS
62	London HLW 9625	Pop Pop Pop-Pie/Your Hand In Mine	25
63	London HL 9686	Let's Stomp Again/Slop Time	22
63	London RE 1363	DO THE POPEYE (EP)	110

SHERWOOD
86	Sherwood SRT6KL 901	RIDING THE RAINBOW (12" EP)	50

BOBBY SHERWOOD
55	Vogue Coral Q 72097	The Kentuckian Song/Far Away Places	6

HOLLY SHERWOOD
71	Bell BLL 1180	Day By Day/Great Golden Day	6

ROBERTA SHERWOOD
56	Brunswick 05572	Lazy River/This Train	10
57	Brunswick 05654	Tears Don't Care Who Cries Them/You're Nobody Till Somebody Loves You	7
57	Brunswick 05670	Mary Lou/What Does It Matter	7
63	Stateside SS 154	You Always Hurt The One You Love/In San Francisco	6
63	Stateside SL 10039	ON STAGE (LP)	18

TONY SHERWOOD TRIO
60s	Zodiac ZR 010	Piano Boogie Twist/Tom Dooley	15

SHERWOODS
61	Pye International 7N 25097	Nanette/El Scorpion	10

SHERWOODS
64	Solar SRP 105	Memories/Some Other Time	8

SHE TRINITY
66	Columbia DB 7874	He Fought The Law/The Union Station Blues	15
66	Columbia DB 7943	Have I Sinned/Wild Flower	8
66	Columbia DB 7959	Wild Flower/The Man Who Took The Valise Off The Floor Of Grand Central Station At Noon	12
66	Columbia DB 7992	Yellow Submarine/Promise Me You'll Never Cry	15
67	CBS 2819	Across The Street/Over And Over Again	7
70	President PT 283	Hair/Climb That Tree	40

(see also Shotgun Express, Beryl Marsden, Gilded Cage)

SHEVELLES
63	Oriole CB 1915	Ooh Poo Pa Doo/Like I Love You	20

SHEVELLS
64	United Artists UP 1059	I Could Conquer The World/How Would You Like Me To Love You	30
65	United Artists UP 1076	Walking On The Edge Of The World/Not So Close	20
65	United Artists UP 1081	Watermelon Man/Taking Over Your Life	20
66	United Artists UP 1125	Come On Home/I Gotta Travel All Over	45
68	Polydor 56239	Big City Lights/Coffee Song	15

(see also Mike Stevens & Shevells)

TONY SHEVETON
62	Oriole CB 1705	Lullaby Of Love/I Have A Feeling	18
62	Oriole CB 1726	Lonely Heart/Foolish Doubts	18
62	Oriole CB 1766	Hey Little Girl/Kissing Date	25
63	Oriole CB 1788	Runaround Sue Is Getting Married/I Love The Girl Next Door	25
63	Oriole CB 1895	Million Drums/Dance With Me	15
64	Oriole CB 1975	Excuses/Is It Me, Is It You?	18

(see also Tony Rich)

SHIDE & ACORN
73	private pressing	UNDER THE TREE (LP)	200+
94	Acme AC 8006LP	UNDER THE TREE (LP, reissue, 500 only, numbered)	15

(see also Jeremy Cahill)

SHIELA
71	Nu Beat NB 079	Only Heaven Knows/GRANT & RICHARDS: Freedom Psalm	7

TREVOR SHIELD
69	Trojan TR 664	The Moon Is Playing Tricks On Me/KING CANNON: Soul Special	12
69	Trojan TR 665	Please/JAY BOYS: Splendour Splash	12
72	Ashanti ASH 407	Rough Road/JAY BOYS: Rough The Road	6

(see also Beltones, Trevor)

SHIELDS
58	London HLD 8706	You Cheated/That's The Way It's Gonna Be (78 rpm = £20)	40

KEITH SHIELDS
67	Decca F 12572	Hey Gyp (Dig The Slowness)/Deep Inside Your Mind	60
67	Decca F 12609	The Wonder Of You/Run, Run, Run	20
67	Decca F 12666	So Hard Livin' Without You/Baby Do You Love Me	20

(see also Marty Wilde [& Wildcats])

PETER SHILTON & RAY CLEMENCE
80	Polydor POSP 206	Side By Side/We're Gonna Win Again (p/s)	6

PETER SHILTON & JON SAMMELS
73	Sports Talk ST 102	SIMON SMITH INTERVIEWS.... 1973 (LP)	20

YASUKI SHIMIZU
88	Benelux Crammed MTM 12	MUSIC FOR COMMERCIALS (LP)	12

SHINDIGS
65	Parlophone R 5316	One Little Letter/What You Gonna Do	35
65	Parlophone R 5377	A Little While Back/Why Say Goodbye	35

SHINDOGS
67	Fontana TF 790	Who Do You Think You Are/Yes, I'm Going Home	12

(see also Delaney & Bonnie, James Burton)

JOHNNY SHINES
69	Blue Horizon 7-63212	LAST NIGHT'S DREAM (LP, with Otis Spann, mono or stereo)	90
74	Xtra XTRA 1142	COUNTRY BLUES (LP)	25

DON SHINN (& THE SOUL AGENTS)
66	Polydor BM 56075	A Minor Explosion/Pits Of Darkness (with The Soul Agents)	60
69	Columbia S(C)X 6319	TEMPLES WITH PROPHETS (LP)	50
69	Columbia SCX 6355	DEPARTURES (LP)	50

(see also The Soul Agents)

SHINS
04	Sub Pop SP644	So Says I/When I Goose Step (1,000 only, picture disc)	7
02	Sub Pop SP550	OH INVERTED WORLD (LP)	12

SHIP
72	Elektra K 42122	THE SHIP — A CONTEMPORARY FOLK JOURNEY (LP, gatefold sleeve)	25

SHIRALEE
67	Fontana TF 855	I'll Stay By Your Side/Penny Wren	20

SHIRELLES
SINGLES
58	Brunswick 05746	I Met Him On A Sunday/I Want You To Be My Boyfriend (78 rpm = £45)	60+
60	London HL 9233	Tonight's The Night/The Dance Is Over	20
60	Top Rank JAR 540	Will You Love Me Tomorrow/Boys	10
61	Top Rank JAR 549	Dedicated To The One I Love/Look-A-Here Baby	20
61	Top Rank JAR 567	Mama Said/Blue Holiday	15
61	Top Rank JAR 578	What A Sweet Thing That Was/A Thing Of The Past	12
61	Top Rank JAR 590	Big John/Twenty One	15
62	Top Rank JAR 601	Baby It's You/The Things I Want To Hear	20
62	HMV POP 1019	Soldier Boy/Love Is A Swingin' Thing	12
62	Stateside SS 119	Welcome Home Baby/Mama Here Comes The Bride	12
62	Stateside SS 129	Stop The Music/It's Love That Really Counts	15
63	Stateside SS 152	Everybody Loves A Lover/I Don't Think So	12
63	Stateside SS 181	Foolish Little Girl/Not For All The Money In The World	15
63	Stateside SS 213	Don't Say Goodnight And Mean Goodbye/I Didn't Mean To Hurt You	15
63	Stateside SS 232	What Does A Girl Do/Don't Let It Happen To Us	15
63	Pye International 7N 25229	It's A Mad, Mad, Mad, Mad World/31 Flavours	15
64	Pye International 7N 25233	Tonight's You're Gonna Fall In Love With Me/20th Century Rock And Roll	15
64	Pye International 7N 25240	Sha La La/His Lips Get In The Way	12
64	Pye International 7N 25279	Maybe Tonight/Lost Love	15
65	Pye International 7N 25288	Are You Still My Baby/I Saw A Tear	12
66	Pye International 7N 25386	Shades Of Blue/When The Boys Talk About The Girls	12
67	Pye International 7N 25425	Too Much Of A Good Thing/Bright Shiny Colours	20
69	Mercury MF 1093	There's A Storm Going On In My Heart/Call Me (If You Want Me)	20
75	Pye Disco Demand DDs 115	Last Minute Miracle/March	15
61	Top Rank JKP 3012	THE SHIRELLES SOUND FEATURING "WILL YOU LOVE ME TOMORROW" (EP)	90
61	Top Rank 35-115	THE SHIRELLES SING — TO TRUMPET AND STRINGS (LP)	80
62	Stateside SL 10006	BABY IT'S YOU (LP)	70
63	Stateside SL 10041	THE SHIRELLES' HITS (LP)	60
70	Wand WNS 4	ETERNALLY SOUL (LP, with King Curtis)	20
71	Wand WCS 1001	TONIGHT'S THE NIGHT (LP)	20
72	RCA Victor SF 8237	HAPPY AND IN LOVE (LP)	15
72	RCA Victor SF 8279	THE SHIRELLES (LP)	15
72	Wand WCS 1009	REMEMBER WHEN VOL. 1 (LP)	20
72	Wand WCS 1010	REMEMBER WHEN VOL. 2 (LP)	20

(see also Shirley & Shirelles, Shirley Alston)

SHIRLEY
74	London HLA 10477	I Hear Those Church Bells Ringing/Chapel Of Love/I Do Love You	7

DON SHIRLEY
56	London HA-A 2003	PIANO PERSPECTIVES (LP)	12
56	London HA-A 2004	TONAL EXPRESSIONS (LP)	12
62	London HAA 2448	DROWN IN MY OWN TEARS (LP, also stereo [SAHA 6238])	12

ROY SHIRLEY
66	Ska Beat JB 253	Paradise/Calling	20
66	Doctor Bird DB 1068	Hold Them/Be Good	25
67	Doctor Bird DB 1079	I'm A Winner/Sleeping Beauty	20
67	Doctor Bird DB 1088	Prophet/What To Do	20
67	Doctor Bird DB 1093	Musical Field/LEE PERRY & DYNAMITES: Trial And Crosses	35
67	Doctor Bird DB 1108	Thank You/Touch Them	18
67	Caltone CAL 101	Get On The Ball/JOHNNY MOORE: Sound And Soul	25
67	Island WI 3070	People Rock Steady/I'm Trying To Find A Home (actually by Uniques)	30
67	Island WI 3071	Musical War/Soul Voice	20
67	Island WI 3120	Girlie/GLEN ADAMS: She's So Fine	35
68	Doctor Bird DB 1165	Hush A Bye/Musical Dinner	15
68	Doctor Bird DB 1168	Dance The Reggae/The Agreement	20
68	Giant GN 32	Dance Hall Arena/The Musical Train	12
68	Giant GN 33	Warming Up The Scene/GLEN ADAMS: Lonely Girl	15
68	Island WI 3098	Thank You/Touch Them	18
68	Island WI 3108	Move All Day/Rollin' Rollin'	18
68	Island WI 3110	Million Dollar Baby/SENSATIONS: Long Time No See You Girl	18
68	Island WI 3118	Good Is Better Than Bad/Fantastic Lover	18
68	Island WI 3119	Facts Of Life/Lead Us Not Into Temptation (as Roy Shirley & Uniques; B-side actually by Roy Shirley & Slim Smith)	18
68	Island WI 3125	If I Did Know/Good Ambition	18
68	Amalgamated AMG 815	The World Needs Love/Dance The A	12
68	Fab FAB 54	Think About The Future/Golden Festival	10
69	Duke DU 18	Life/I Like Your Smile	8
71	Nu Beat NB 090	Hold Them One/Two Three Four	5
72	Punch PH 103	Don't Be A Loser/Jamaican Girl	6
72	Punch PH 108	A Sugar/ALTYMAN REID: A Sugar (Version)	6
75	R&JJ 001	Heart Breaking Jepsey/(Version)	5
80s	Shirley SHIRLEY 1	For Everyone/Version (p/s)	5

(see also Val Bennett, Glen Adams, Shirley & Charmers, Sensations, Denzil, Errol & His Group, Ronsig, Stranger & Glady, Untouchables)

SUSAN SHIRLEY
68	Mercury MF 1038	Sun Shines Out Of Your Shoes/Tomorrow Today	5
69	Mercury MF 1087	Too Many Tears/Boy From Boston Massachusetts USA	5
70	Philips 6006 037	Really Into Somethin'/My Friend The Clown	30
71	Columbia DB 8835	Jealous Guy/Oh Yoko	6
72	Columbia DB 8937	The Other Side Of Me/Imagine	5

SHIRLEY & CHARMERS
72	Bullet BU 502	Rum Rhythm/LLOYD CHARMERS: Rhythm (Version)	6

(see also Roy Shirley)

SHIRLEY & LEE
56	Vogue V 9059	Let The Good Times Roll/Do You Mean To Hurt Me So (78 rpm = £45)	150
57	Vogue V 9063	I Feel Good/Now That It's Over (78 rpm = £45)	100
57	Vogue V 9067	That's What I Wanna Do/When I Saw You (78 rpm = £55)	95
57	Vogue V 9072	Rock All Nite/Don't You Know I Love You (78 rpm = £55)	120
57	Vogue V 9084	Rockin' With The Clock/The Flirt (78 rpm = £55)	130
57	Vogue V 9088	I Want To Dance/Marry Me (78 rpm = £55)	80
57	Vogue V 9094	Feel So Good/You'd Be Thinking Of Me (78 rpm = £55)	80
58	Vogue V 9103	I'll Thrill You/Love No One But You (78 rpm = £55)	85
58	Vogue V 9118	Everybody's Rockin'/Don't Leave Me Here To Cry (78 rpm = £75)	115
59	Vogue V 9129	All I Want To Do Is Cry/Come On And Have Your Fun (78 rpm = 55)	80
59	Vogue V 9135	A Little Word/That's What I'll Do (78 rpm = £55)	80
59	Vogue V 9137	I'll Do It/Lee's Dream (78 rpm = £55)	80

(The above 45s were originally issued with triangular centres; later round-centre issues are worth two-thirds of these values.)

59	Vogue V 9156	True Love/When Day Is Done (78 rpm = £65)	80

(Later Vocalion pressings of the above singles are worth two-thirds the values listed.)

60	London HLI 9186	I've Been Loved Before/Like You Used To Do	25
60	London HLI 9209	Let The Good Times Roll/Keep Loving Me	20
65	Island WI 257	Let The Good Times Roll/I'm Gone	20
57	Vogue VE 1-70101	ROCK 'N' ROLL (EP, triangular centre, later round)	300/220
60	Vogue VE 1-70145	SHIRLEY AND LEE (EP)	250
71	Jay Boy JSX 2005	LET THE GOOD TIMES ROLL (LP)	20

SHIRLEY & RUDE BOYS
67	Blue Beat BB 375	Gently Set Me Free/BUSTER'S ALL STARS: Rock Steady	100+

SHIRLEY & SHIRELLES
69	Bell BLL 1049	Look What You've Done To My Heart/A Most Unusual Boy	15
69	Bell BLL 1065	Plaything/Looking Glass	6
72	Bell BLL 1251	Look What You've Done To My Heart/A Most Unusual Boy (reissue)	8

(see also Shirelles)

SHIRTS
78	Harvest HAR 5170	Lonely Android/Running Through The Night (p/s)	5

SHIVA
82	Heavy Metal HEAVY 13	Rock Lives On/Sympathy For The Devil (p/s)	20
82	Heavy Metal HEAVY 16	Angel Of Mons/Stranger Lands (p/s)	10
82	Heavy Metal HMRLP 6	FIREDANCE (LP)	25

MINT VALUE £

BUNNY SHIVEL
| 67 | Capitol CL 15487 | You'll Never Find A Love Like Mine/The Slide | 20 |

JOYCE SHOCK
58	Philips PB 780	Pit A Patter Boom Boom/Bells In My Heart (78).	9
58	Philips PB 824	Take Your Foot From The Door!/I've Got Bells On My Heart (78 rpm = £8)	10
58	Philips PB 872	Hoopa Hoola/You're Not Losing A Daughter, Mama (78 rpm = £6)	10
59	Philips PB 934	Personality/I Can't Love You Anymore (78 rpm = £6)	10
59	Philips PB 957	Cry, Baby, Cry/Dear Diary (78 rpm = £6)	10

SHOCK ABSORBERS
| 69 | Major Minor SMCP 5028 | GUITAR PARTY (LP) | 20 |

SHOCK HEADED PETERS
| 84 | él EL 1 | I, Blood Brother Be/Truth Has Come (p/s) | 7 |
(see also Lemon Kittens, Underneath, Karl Blake, Sol Invictus)

SHOCKING BLUE
69	Olga OLE 015	Send Me A Postcard/Harley Davidson (demo only).	60
69	Penny Farthing PEN 702	Venus/Hot Sand.	5
70	Penny Farthing PEN 713	Mighty Joe/Wild Wind.	5
70	Penny Farthing PEN 721	Never Marry A Railroad Man/Roll Engine Roll	5
70	Penny Farthing PEN 744	Sally Was A Good Old Girl/Long And Lonesome Road	5
70	Penny Farthing PELS 500	SHOCKING BLUE AT HOME (LP).	30
70	Penny Farthing PELS 510	SCORPIO'S DANCE (LP)	30

SHOES
| 67 | Polydor 56739 | Farewell In The Rain/What In The World Is Love. | 12 |

SHOGUN
86	Attack ATA 913	High In The Sky/When The Lights Go Down (p/s).	30
87	Jet JET 12049	Cloak And Dagger/Too Late For The Hunter/Tokyo Girl (12", p/s, red vinyl)	8
86	Attack ATA 006	SHOGUN (LP)	75

TROY SHONDELL
61	London HLG 9432	This Time/Girl After Girl	10
62	Liberty LIB 55398	Island In The Sky/Tears From An Angel	15
63	London HL 9668	I Got A Woman/Some People Never Learn	15
64	London HAY 8128	MANY SIDES OF TROY SHONDELL (LP)	90

SHONDELLS
| 64 | Ember EMB S 191 | My Love/Don't Cry My Soldier Boy | 45 |

SHOOT
| 73 | EMI EMI 2026 | On The Frontier/Ships And Sails. | 5 |
| 72 | EMI EMA 73 | ON THE FRONTIER (LP). | 18 |
(see also Yardbirds, Raw Material)

SHOOTER
| 78 | EMI Intl. INS 3020 | SHOOTER (LP) | 12 |

SHOOTING PARTY
| 88 | Lisson DOLER 9 | Safe In The Arms Of Love (Phil's Extra Beat Update)/Safe In The Arms Of Love (Hot Power Mix) (12", p/s) | 12 |

SHOP ASSISTANTS
85	Subway Organisation SUBWAY 1	All Day Long/All That Ever Mattered/It's Up To You/Switzerland (red foldaround hand-coloured p/s in poly bag, later blue).	12/6
90	Avalanche AGAP 001C	Here It Comes/I'd Rather Be With You//You Trip Me Up/The Other One (with 33rpm Flexi Records flexidisc).	5
90	Avalanche AGAP 001B	Here It Comes/Look Out/I'd Rather Be With You/Adrenalin (12", box set with flexidisc, badge, postcard & lyric sheet, 1st 200 numbered)	8/5
(see also Buba & Shop Assistants)

DINAH SHORE
53	HMV 7M 119	Keep It A Secret/Bella Musica	15
53	HMV 7M 139	Sweet Thing/Three-Cornered Tune	15
54	HMV 7M 183	Changing Partners/Think	15
54	HMV 7M 221	This Must Be The Place/Come Back To My Arms	15
54	HMV 7M 236	Three Coins In The Fountain/Pakistan	15
54	HMV 7M 250	If I Give My Heart To You/Let Me Know.	15
56	HMV 7M 352	Love And Marriage/Compare (78 rpm = £8)	10
57	RCA RCA 1003	The Cattle Call/Promises, Promises (Skip Redwine).	7
58	RCA RCA 1054	Thirteen Men/I'll Never Say "Never Again" Again	15
58	RCA RD 27072	HOLDING HANDS AT MIDNIGHT (LP)	25
59	Capitol (S)T 1247	DINAH, YES INDEED! (LP)	18
60	Fontana Fortune Z 4026	BUTTONS AND BOWS (LP)	15
60	Capitol (S)T 1296	SOMEBODY LOVES ME (LP)	15
60	Capitol (S)T 1354	DINAH SINGS SOME BLUES WITH RED (LP, with Red Norvo)	15
(see also Doris Day)

BRIAN SHORT
| 71 | Transatlantic TRA 245 | ANYTHING FOR A LAUGH (LP, gatefold sleeve) | 20 |
(see also Black Cat Bones)

J.D. SHORT
| 73 | Sonet SNTF 648 | THE LEGACY OF THE BLUES VOL. 8 (LP). | 12 |

KEVIN SHORT
| 79 | EMI INT 574 | Punk Strut/Short Cut (no p/s, demos only) | 30 |

SHORT KUTS with Eddie Harrison
| 68 | United Artists UP 2233 | Your Eyes May Shine/Letting The Tears Tumbling Down. | 30 |

SHORTWAVE (BAND)
75	RCA Victor SF 8400	SHORTWAVE BAND (LP, with lyric sheet)	12
77	Crescent/Avada ARS 111	GREATEST HATS (LP)	20
79	Pye 2CN 111	SHORTWAVE (LP)	12

SHORTY (THE PRESIDENT)
73	Ackee ACK 509	Aquarius Pressure/Halfway Tree Pressure (as Shorty The President)	10
73	Ackee ACK 517	Jelly-Belly-Nelly/Message Of Love (as Shorty)	6

(see also Shorty Perry)

SHORTY & THEM
64	Fontana TF 460	Pills Or Love's Labours Lost/Live Laugh And Love	35

SHOTGUN EXPRESS
66	Columbia DB 8025	I Could Feel The Whole World Turn Round/Curtains	50
67	Columbia DB 8178	Funny 'Cos Neither Could I/Indian Thing	55
83	See For Miles CYM 2	I Could Feel The Whole World Turn Round/Curtains/ Funny 'Cos Neither Could I/Indian Thing (10", p/s)	15

(see also Rod Stewart, Peter Bardens, Spencer Davis, Brian Auger, She Trinity, Beryl Marsden, Fleetwood Mac)

SHOTS
65	Columbia DB 7713	Keep A Hold Of What You've Got/She's A Liar	40

(see also Smoke)

SHOUT
72	Explosion 2058	Life Is Rough/Life Is Rough – Version	5

SHOUTS
64	React EA 001	She Was My Baby/That's The Way It's Gonna Be	45

(see also Gene Vincent)

SHOWBIZ KIDS
80s	Top Secret CON 1	She Goes To Finos/I Don't Want To Discuss That (p/s)	35

(see also Toy Dolls)

SHOW BOYS
69	Gas GAS 129	People Are Wondering/Long Time	10

SHOWMEN
62	London HLP 9481	It Will Stand/Country Fool	70
62	London HLP 9571	The Wrong Girl/I Love You Can't You See	150
69	Pama PM 767	Action/What Would It Take	15

(see also Norman Johnson, General Johnson, Chairmen Of The Board)

SHOWSTOPPERS
68	Beacon 3-100	Ain't Nothing But A House Party/What Can A Man Do (red swirly label)	15
68	Beacon 3-106	Shake Your Mini/Heartbreaker	40
68	MGM MGM 1436	Eeny Meeny/How Easy Your Heart Forgets Me	15
69	Beacon BEA 110	Don't Leave Me Standing In The Rain/Do You Need My Love	10
69	Beacon BEA 130	Just A Little Bit Of Lovin'/School Prom	15
69	Beacon BEA 100	Ain't Nothing But A House Party/What Can A Man Do (reissue, yellow label)	10
70	Beacon BEA 100	Ain't Nothing But A House Party/What Can A Man Do (reissue, green label)	8
71	Beacon BEA 3-182	Actions Speak Louder Than Words/ Pick Up Your Smile	20

SHOWTIMERS
64	HMV POP 1328	You Must Be Joking/Don't Say Goodbye	10

SHOX
80	Axis AXIS 4	No Turning Back/Lying Here (p/s)	15
80	Beggars Banquet BEG 33	No Turning Back/Lying Here (p/s, reissue)	8

MARK SHREEVE
83	Uniton U 021	ASSASSIN (LP)	15

SHUBERT
68	Fontana TF 942	Until The Rains Come/Let Your Love Go	20

SHUDDER TO THINK
90s	Dischord	Vacation Brain (p/s, with insert)	12

MORT SHUMAN
59	Decca F 11184	Turn Me Loose/I'm A Man (78 rpm = £25)	50
66	Fontana TF 685	Cry A Little/She Ain't Nothing But A Little Child	8
67	Immediate IM 048	Monday Monday/Little Children	16

SHUSHA
71	Tangent TGS 108	PERSIAN LOVE SONGS AND MYSTIC CHANTS (LP)	20
72	Tangent TGS 114	SONGS OF LONG TIME LOVERS (LP)	15
74	United Artists UAS 29575	SHUSHA (LP)	12
74	United Artists UAS 29684	THIS IS THE DAY (LP)	12
75	United Artists UAS 29879	BEFORE THE DELUGE (LP)	12
78	Tangent TGS 138	FROM EAST TO WEST (LP)	12
83	Linnet LIN 1	DURABLE FIRE: SONGS BY BRITISH POETS (LP)	12

SHUTDOWNS
63	Colpix PX 11016	Four In The Floor/Beach Buggy	40

SHY
74	Deram DM417	Disney Girls (1957)/The Time That I Love You The Most	7

SHY
87	RCA PT 41180	Break Down The Walls/Under Fire/Young Heart (12", gatefold p/s)	5
83	Ebony EBON 15	ONCE BITTEN TWICE SHY (LP)	20

SHY LIMBS
69	CBS 4190	Reputation/Love	100
69	CBS 4624	Lady In Black/Trick Or Two	75+

(see also Shame)

SHY ONES
63	Oriole CB 1848	Nightcap/Carry Me Back	20
64	Oriole CB 1924	La Route/Susanna	18

(see also Spotnicks)

SHYSTER
68	Polydor 56202	Tick Tock/That's A Hoe Down	200

(see also Fleur-De-Lys)

SHYWOLF
82	MRS SW 001	Lucretia/California Jam (p/s)	40

LEROY SIBBLES & ROCKY ELLIS
68	Studio One SO 2042	Love Me Girl/WRIGGLERS: Reel Up	30
79	Warrior Records WAR 133	Ras-Tafari/MYSTIC EYES: Forward With Love/(Dub)	30

(see also John Holt, King Rocky)

DUDLEY SIBLEY
67	Coxsone CS 7010	Run Boy Run/Message Of Old (B-side actually by Joe Higgs & Ken Boothe)	35
67	Island WI 3034	Gun Man/Monkey Speaks His Mind (B-side actually by Dinsdell Thorpe)	40

(see also Delroy & Sporty, King Sporty, Mr. Foundation)

SIDDELEYS
86	Sha La La Ba Ba Ba 006	Wherever You Go/RESERVE: The Sun Slid Down (flexidisc with fanzines, p/s)	10/8
87	Medium Cool MC 005	What Went Wrong This Time? (p/s)	18
88	Sombrero THREE	Sunshine Thuggery/Are You Still Evil When You're Sleeping/Falling Off My Feet Again (12", p/s)	18

SIDEKICKS
66	RCA RCA 1538	Suspicions/Up On The Roof	15

ANN SIDNEY
65	HMV POP 1411	The Boy In The Woolly Sweater/Lonely Doll	5

SIDNEY, GEORGE & JACKIE
71	Summit SUM 8528	Lady Of My Complexion/No Sad Song	5
72	Summit SUM 8535	Story Book Children/Gorgeous Marvellous	5
74	Attack ATT 8064	At The Club/Reggae Fever	30

(see also Pioneers)

PAUL SIEBEL
70	Elektra EKSN 45085	Bride 1945/Miss Cherry Lane	5
70	Elektra EKS 74064	WOODSMOKE AND ORANGES (LP)	22
71	Elektra EKS 74081	JACK-KNIFE GYPSY (LP)	22

SIEGE
85	Siege THM 1	Goddess Of Fire (no p/s)	18

SIEGEL-SCHWALL BAND
68	Vanguard SVRL 19044	SHAKE (LP)	15

CHRIS SIEVEY
79	Rabid TOSH 109	Baiser/Last (p/s)	10
79	Razz RAZZXEP 1	BAISER (33rpm EP, 2 tracks each by Sievey & Freshies, handwritten labels)	35
80	Razz RAZZ 4	My Tape's Gone/Moon Midsummer (some with *True Life Revealing Confessions Of Romance And Love* fanzine)	10/6
81	Razz RAZZ 5	Hey/FRESHIES: We're Like You (p/s)	6
82	Razz RAZZ 8	RED INDIAN MUSIC (EP)	8
82	Razz RAZZ 9	Skip The Flight/Jim Baiser ("Baiser"/"Last" with new labels & sleeve)	8

(see also Freshies, Going Red?)

LABI SIFFRE
70	Pye Intl. NSPL 28135	LABI SIFFRE (LP)	20
71	Pye Intl. NSPL 28147	THE SINGER AND THE SONG (LP, gatefold sleeve)	20
72	Pye Intl. NSPL 28163	CRYING, LAUGHING, LOVING, LYING (LP, gatefold sleeve with lyric insert)	15
75	EMI EMC 3065	REMEMBER MY SONG (LP)	125
98	EMI/Mr. Bongo MRBLP 011	REMEMBER MY SONG (LP, reissue)	12

RON SIG
71	Camel CA 58	1970's/(Version)	6
71	Camel CA 59	You Girl/ROY SHIRLEY & SLIM SMITH: Facts Of Life	8

SIGHT & SOUND
68	Fontana TF 927	Ebenezer/Our Love (Is In The Pocket)	30
68	Fontana TF 982	Alley Alley/Little Jack Monday	15

(see also Jefferson, Sheridan & Price, Mike Sheridan)

BUNNY SIGLER
67	Cameo Parkway P 153	Let The Good Times Roll — Feel So Good/There's No Love Left (DJ copy = £85)	40
73	Epic S EPC 1177	Tossin' And Turnin'/Picture Us	5
76	London HLU 10518	Let The Good Times Roll/Girl Don't Make Me Wait	15

SIGNS
66	Decca F 12522	Ain't You Got A Heart/My Baby Comes To Me	8

SIGUE SIGUE SPUTNIK
86	Parlophone 12 SSS 1	Love Missile F1-11 (Bangkok Remix)/(Dance Mix)/Hack Attack (Dub Mix) (12", p/s, 'German' or 'Spanish' obi sleeve bands)	each 10
86	Parlophone 12 SSSX 1	Love Missile F1-11 (Trailer Mix): Love Missile F1-11 (Video Mix)/Love Missile F1-11 & Actuality Sound/Hack-Attack (12", p/s, with 6 poster inserts)	12
88	Parlophone 12 SSSW 3	Success (Extended)/(Seven Inch) Frankenstein Cha-Cha-Cha (Extended) (12", 'Pete Waterman' p/s, withdrawn)	30
88	Parlophone CD SSS 3	Success (Seven Inch) Frankenstein Cha-Cha-Cha/Last Temptation Of Sputnik (CD)	12

89	Parlophone CD SSS 4	Albinoni Vs Star Wars (Part 1 – 7" Version)/(Part 1 – Extended Version)/	
		(Part 2 – Extended Version) (Bonus Beats) (CD)	12
89	Parlophone CD SSS 5	Dancerama (7" Mix)/(12" Extended)/(Album Mix Extended) (CD)	15
86	Parlophone PCSS 7305	FLAUNT IT (LP, box set with insert)	12

(see also Bizet Boys, Sci Fi Sex Stars, Generation X, Sisters Of Mercy)

SIGUR RóS

99	Fat Cat 12FAT 036	Svefn-G-Englar (12" EP, custom sleeve 2,000 only)	25
99	Fat Cat CD FAT 036	Svefn-G-Englar (CD, 2000 only)	20
00	Fat Cat 12FAT 039	NY BATTERY (mini-LP, 2,000 only)	30
00	Fat Cat CATCD FAT 039	NY BATTERY (CD, mini-Album, 2,000 only)	20
00	Fat Cat FATLP 11	AGAETIS BYRJUN (2-LP)	20
03	Fat Cat FATLP 22	() (LP)	12
03	FAT KAT FATPK 01 A	Interactive Press Kit for () Album (2 x CD in DVD case)	20
05	EMI 3384632	TAKK (LP, special book edition)	15

SILENT ECLIPSE

92	White (Mendoza) MEN018	How Many Miles Back To London/MCs (12")	40
92	Mendoza MEN018	How Many Miles Back To London/Mcs (12")	15
93	Monroe RLP001	THE DAMNED (EP)	20

SILENT MAJORITY

71	Hot Wax HWX 110	Frightened Girl/Colours Of My Love	8

SILENT MOVIES

79	ESR Records ESR 1	Ain't No Van Gough/What Did Ya Say? (p/s)	40

SILENT NOISE

79	Silent Noise/Easy ER 02	I've Been Hurt (Too Many Times Before)/Heart To Heart	75

SILHOUETTES (Jamaica)

69	Sound System SSR 103	In Times Like These (act. by Lloyd Jackson & Groovers)/In Times Like These	6

SILHOUETTES (U.S.)

58	Parlophone R 4407	Get A Job/I Am Lonely (78 rpm = £50)	88
58	Parlophone R 4425	Headin' For The Poorhouse/Miss Thing (78 rpm £75)	150

SILICON TEENS

79	Mute MUTE 003	Memphis Tennessee/Let's Dance (p/s, some with poster)	5/10

ERIC SILK (& His Southern Jazz Band)

56	Esquire EP 70	AND HIS SOUTHERN JAZZ BAND (EP)	10
56	Esquire EP 100	AND HIS SOUTHERN JAZZ BAND (EP)	10
57	Esquire EP 110	AND HIS SOUTHERN JAZZ BAND (EP)	10
57	Esquire EP 128	AND HIS SOUTHERN JAZZ BAND (EP)	10
57	Esquire EP 150	AND HIS SOUTHERN JAZZ BAND (EP)	10
57	Esquire 20-065	SOUTHERN JAZZ (LP)	18
58	Esquire 20-095	THE SILKEN TOUCH (LP)	18
67	Polydor 582 002	OFF THE CUFF (LP)	15

SILKIE

65	Fontana TF 556	Blood Red River/Close The Door Gently	6
65	Fontana TF 603	You've Got To Hide Your Love Away/City Winds	8
66	Fontana TF 659	Keys To My Soul/Leave Me To Cry	6
66	Fontana TF 709	Born To Be With You/So Sorry Now	6
65	Fontana TL 5256	THE SILKIE SING THE SONGS OF BOB DYLAN (LP)	20

JUDEE SILL

72	Asylum SYLA 8751	JUDEE SILL (LP, gatefold sleeve)	12
73	Asylum SYL 9006	HEART FOOD (LP)	12

SILLY SISTERS

76	Chrysalis CHR 1101	SILLY SISTERS (LP, with lyric insert)	12

(see also Steeleye Span, Maddy Prior, June Tabor)

SILVER (Jamaica)

68	Jolly JY 006	Baby Oh Yeah/Rock Steady Is Here To Stay (as Silver & Magnets)	12
68	Jolly JY 012	Things/Sweet Lovin'	12
68	Jolly JY 017	I Need A Girl/Lost And Found	8
70	Columbia Blue Beat DB 117	Love Me Forever/Sugar, Sugar (B-side as Silver & Noreen)	5
71	Fab FAB 163	Change Has Got To Come/Magnet Stomp (as Silver & Magnets)	6

SILVER (U.S.)

76	Arista ARIST 79	Musician (It's Not An Easy Life)/Right On Time	6
76	Arista ARTY 144	SILVER (LP, U.S. disc & inner [AL 4076] in U.K. sleeve)	12

(see also Grateful Dead)

ANDEE SILVER

64	HMV POP 1297	Too Young To Go Steady/Sleeping Beauty	10
64	HMV POP 1344	The Boy I Used To Know/What Do You Do	10
66	Fontana TF 666	Only Your Love Can Save Me/Window Shopping	20
69	Decca F 22872	Go Now/You're Just What I Was Looking For Today	8
69	Decca F 22953	With A Little Love/Te Quiero (unreleased)	
70	Decca F 23071	Love Me/You're Breaking My Heart (export issue)	10
70	Decca SKL-R 5059	A HANDFUL OF SILVER (LP)	45

EDDIE SILVER

58	Parlophone R 4439	Seven Steps To Love/Put A Ring On Her Finger (78 rpm = £10)	15
58	Parlophone R 4483	Rockin' Robin/The Ways Of A Woman In Love (78 rpm = £15)	20

HORACE SILVER QUINTET/TRIO

54	Vogue LDE 065	THE HORACE SILVER TRIO (10" LP)	15

MINT VALUE £

69	Blue Note BST 84277	SERENADE TO A SOUL SISTER (LP)	15

LORRAINE SILVER
65	Pye 7N 15922	Lost Summer Love/I'll Know You'll Be There (DJ copy = £125)	75
66	Pye 7N 17055	The Happy Faces/When The Love Light Starts Shining Thru His Eyes	40

SILVER APPLES
90s	Enraptured RAPT 4507	Fractal Flow/Love Fingers (p/s)	5

SILVER BIRCH
73	Brayford BRO 2	SILVER BIRCH (LP, private pressing)	150+

SILVER BULLET
89	Tam Tam TTT008	Bring Forth The Guillotine (12")	10

SILVER BYKE
68	London HLZ 10200	Who Needs Tomorrow/I've Got Time	12

SILVER EAGLE
67	MGM MGM 1345	Theodore/True As A Brand New Lie	20

SILVERGINGER 5
01	Infernal INFERNAL 13CD/X	BLACK LEATHER MOJO (2-CD, in stickered leather-effect slipcase, 5000 only)	25

(see also Ginger, Super$hit666, Wildhearts)

SILVERHEAD
72	Purple PUR 104	Ace Supreme/Oh No No No	7
72	Purple PUR 110	Rolling With My Baby/In Your Eyes	7
73	Purple TPSA 7506	SILVERHEAD (LP)	20
73	Purple TPSA 7511	SIXTEEN AND SAVAGED (LP)	20

(see also Michael Des Barres, Blondie)

SILVER MOUNTAIN
83	Road Runner RR 9884	SHAKIN' BRAINS (LP)	15

SILVERS
66	Polydor BM 56094	What A Way To Start A Day/Blue Blue Eyes	7

PHIL SILVERS
57	Fontana Fortune Z 4040	BUGLE CALLS FOR BIG BAND (LP)	15

SILVER SISTERS
60	Parlophone R 4669	Waiting For The Stars To Shine/When A Boy Meets A Girl	10

DOOLEY SILVERSPOON
76	Seville SEV 1022	Game Players/Believe In Me	15

SILVERSTARS
69	Trojan TR 646	Old Man Say/Promises	12

SILVER STARS STEEL BAND
63	Island ILP 904	THE SILVER STARS STEEL BAND (LP)	18

(see also Clancy Eccles)

SHEL SILVERSTEIN
73	CBS 65452	FREAKIN' AT THE FREAKER'S BALL (LP, with Dr. Hook)	12

(see also Dr. Hook)

SILVERTONES
66	Doctor Bird DB 1028	True Confession (with Duke Reid)/TOMMY McCOOK & SUPERSONICS: More Love	28
66	Doctor Bird DB 1041	It's Real (with Lynn Tait & Boys)/LYNN TAIT & BOYS: Storm Warning	28
66	Rymska RA 105	True Confession/GRANVILLE WILLIAMS ORCHESTRA: Honky Tonk Ska	30
67	Treasure Isle TI 7020	Cool Down/TOMMY McCOOK & SUPERSONICS: Shadow Of Your Smile	18
68	Treasure Isle TI 7027	In The Midnight Hour/TOMMY McCOOK & SUPERSONICS: Soul For Sale	15
68	Treasure Isle TI 7039	Old Man River/TOMMY McCOOK & SUPERSONICS: Our Man Flint	15
68	Treasure Isle TI 7042	Slow And Easy/TOMMY McCOOK & SUPERSONICS: Moving	15
69	Trojan TR 7705	Intensified Change/Marie	12
71	Clandisc CLA 234	Tear Drops Will Fall/DYNAMITES: Tear Drops — Version	6
73	Techniques TE 924	That's When It Hurts/I'll Take You Home	6
71	Trojan TRLS 69	SILVER BULLETS (LP)	35

(see also Valentines, Tommy McCook, Vincent Gordon, Alton Ellis, Carl Bryon, Charmers)

SILVERWING
80	Mayhem SILVER 1	Rock'n'Roll Are Four-Letter Words/High Class Woman	7
82	Mayhem SILV 02	Sittin' Pretty/Teenage Love (p/s)	8
82	Mayhem SILV 212	Sittin' Pretty/Teenage Love/Flashbomb Fever/Rock'n'Roll Mayhem (12")	10
82	Mayhem SILV 3	That's Entertainment/Flashbomb Fever (poster p/s)	5
83	Bullet BULP 1	ALIVE AND KICKING (LP)	15

(see also Pet Hate, Big Amongst Sheep)

VICTOR SILVESTER & HIS ROCK 'N' ROLL RHYTHM
57	Columbia DB 3888	Rockin' Rhythm Roll/Society Rock	10
57	Columbia DB 3907	Alligator Roll/Off Beat Rock	10

VICTOR SILVESTER ORCHESTRA
62	Columbia	World Cup Cha Cha Cha Santiago	10
66	Columbia DB 7900	The World Cup Waltz/The World Cup Cha Cha Cha	30

SIMBA
71	Fire FIR 100	Louie Louie/Movin'	5

SIMIAN
02	Source SOUR 067	Never Be Alone/(Simian Mobile Disco Remix) (p/s)	5
03	Source SOUR 069	La Breeze/(Brian Eno Remix) (p/s)	5

BEVERLEY SIMMON(D)S
68	Pama PM 716	Mr. Pitiful/That's How Strong My Love Is	10
73	Pama Supreme PS 380	You're Mine/What A Guy (as Beverley Simmonds)	8
69	Pama PMLP/PMSP 9	REMEMBER OTIS (LP)	20

(see also Little Beverly)

(JUMPIN') GENE SIMMONS
64	London HLU 9913	Haunted House/Hey, Hey Little Girl	20
64	London HLU 9933	The Jump/The Dodo	20

GENE SIMMONS
79	Casablanca CAN 134	Radioactive/When You Wish Upon A Star (p/s, red vinyl with mask, picture label, some mispressed with black/red vinyl)	20/40
79	Casablanca CAN 134	Radioactive/When You Wish Upon A Star (p/s, black vinyl)	12

(see also Kiss)

JEFF SIMMONS
69	Straight STS 1057	LUCILLE HAS MESSED UP MY MIND (LP)	60

(see also Frank Zappa)

LITTLE MAC SIMMONS
66	Outasite OSEP 1	BLUES FROM CHICAGO (EP, 99 copies only)	200

(Zoot) SIMMS & (Lloyd) ROBINSON
62	Blue Beat BB 143	White Christmas/Searching	10

JASON SIMMS & MUSIC THROUGH SIX
68	Domain D 5	It's Got To Be Mellow/MUSIC THROUGH SIX: Floppy Ears	15

(see also Music Through Six)

ZOOT SIMMS (Jamaica)
63	Blue Beat BB 183	Press Along/PRINCE BUSTER ALLSTARS: 100 Ton Megaton (B-side actually "Mighty As A Rose" by Raymond Harper)	18
63	Blue Beat BB 193	Golden Pen/ERIC MORRIS: So You Shot Reds	22
64	Port-O-Jam PJ 4007	Please Don't Do It/Don't Do It (as Simms & [Lloyd] Robinson)	28
68	Blue Cat BS 118	Bye Bye Baby/AL & THRILLERS: Heart For Sale	60+
69	Coxsone CS 7095	Tit For Tat/We Can Talk It Over (as Simms & Elmond)	30

SEIJA SIMOLA
78	Sonet SON 2145	Give Love A Chance/Little Smile (p/s)	12

SIMON
67	RCA Victor RCA 1609	I Like The Way/Little Tin Soldier	5
68	RCA Victor RCA 1668	Dream Seller/Sweet Reflections Of You	5
69	Plum PLS 002	Mrs Lillyco/There's No More You	25

JOE SIMON
66	London HLU 10057	Teenager's Prayer/Long Hot Summer	28
67	Monument MON 1004	My Special Prayer/Travelin' Man	10
68	Monument MON 1010	Nine Pound Steel/The Girl's Alright With Me	20
68	Monument MON 1014	No Sad Songs/Come On And Get It	10
68	Monument MON 1019	You Keep Me Hangin' On/What Makes A Man Feel Good	7
68	Monument MON 1025	Message From Maria/I Worry About You	7
69	Monument MON 1029	Looking Back/Standing In The Safety Zone	7
69	Monument MON 1032	The Chokin' Kind/Come On And Get It	7
70	Monument MON 1042	Moon Walk (Parts 1 & 2)	5
70	Monument MON 1049	Yours Love/I Gotta Whole Lot Of Lovin'	7
70	Monument MON 1051	That's The Way I Want Our Love/When	15
71	Polydor 2066 066	Your Time To Cry/I Love You More (Than Anything)	8
74	Mojo 2093 030	Step By Step/Talk Don't Bother Me	6
67	Monument LMO/SMO 5005	SIMON PURE SOUL (LP)	20
68	Monument LMO/SMO 5017	NO SAD SONGS (LP)	20
69	Monument LMO/SMO 5026	SIMON SINGS (LP)	20
70	Monument LMO/SMO 5030	THE CHOKIN' KIND (LP)	20
70	Monument LMO/SMO 5033	BETTER THAN EVER (LP)	20
71	Mojo 2918 001	THE SOUNDS OF SIMON (LP)	20
72	Mojo 2918 003	DROWNING IN THE SEA OF LOVE (LP)	20

PAUL SIMON
65	CBS 201797	I Am A Rock/Leaves That Are Green	25
73	CBS 1545	Kodachrome (withdrawn)	15+
65	CBS (S) 62579	THE PAUL SIMON SONGBOOK (LP, mono/stereo)	32/42
72	CBS CQ 30750/Q 69007	PAUL SIMON (LP, quadrophonic)	20
74	CBS CQ 32280/Q 69035	THERE GOES RHYMIN' SIMON (LP, quadrophonic)	18
75	CBS Q 86001	STILL CRAZY AFTER ALL THESE YEARS (LP, quadrophonic)	18

(see also Simon & Garfunkel, Jerry Landis, Tom & Jerry)

TONY SIMON
67	Track 604 012	Gimme A Little Sign/Never Too Much To Love	20

SIMON & GARFUNKEL
SINGLES
65	CBS 201977	The Sound Of Silence/We've Got A Groovy Thing Goin'	8
66	CBS 202045	Homeward Bound/Leaves That Are Green	8
66	CBS 202303	I Am A Rock/Flowers Never Bend With The Rainfall	8
66	CBS 202285	The Dangling Conversation/The Big Bright Green Pleasure Machine	15
66	CBS 202378	A Hazy Shade Of Winter/For Emily, Whenever I May Find Her	7
67	CBS 202608	At The Zoo/The 59th Street Bridge Song (Feelin' Groovy)	10
67	CBS 2911	Fakin' It/You Don't Know Where Your Interest Lies	20
68	CBS Special Prods. WB 73	The Sound Of Silence/GEORGIE FAME: By The Time I Get To Phoenix (p/s)	5

SIMON & GARFUNKEL

68	CBS Special Prods. WB 728	The 59th Street Bridge Song (Feelin' Groovy)/TREMELOES:	
		Here Comes My Baby (p/s, mail-order only with Pepsi Cola tokens)	7
69	CBS 4162	The Boxer/Baby Driver (p/s)	7
65	CBS EP 6053	WEDNESDAY MORNING 3AM (EP)	20
66	CBS EP 6074	I AM A ROCK (EP)	20
67	CBS EP 6360	FEELING GROOVY (EP)	20
68	CBS EP 6400	MRS ROBINSON (EP)	15
66	CBS (S)BPG 62690	THE SOUNDS OF SILENCE (LP, mono/stereo)	18/22
66	CBS (S)BPG 62860	PARSLEY, SAGE, ROSEMARY AND THYME (LP, mono/stereo)	15/20

(The above LPs were originally issued with flipback sleeves & textured orange labels.)

67	Allegro ALL 836	SIMON AND GARFUNKEL (LP)	30
68	CBS (S) 70042	THE GRADUATE (LP, soundtrack, blue label, mono/stereo)	18/15
68	CBS (S) 63370	WEDNESDAY MORNING 3AM (LP, flipback sleeve,	
		textured orange label, mono/stereo)	18/15
72	CBS CQ 30995	BRIDGE OVER TROUBLED WATER (LP, quadrophonic)	18

(see also Paul Simon, Art Garfunkel, Tom & Jerry)

NINA SIMONE
SINGLES

59	Parlophone R 4583	I Loves You Porgy/Love Me Or Leave Me	35
59	Pye International 7N 25029	Solitaire/Chilly Winds Don't Blow (78 rpm = £10)	7
63	Colpix PX 200	You Can Have Him/Return Home	8
64	Colpix PX 799	Exactly Like You/The Other Woman	8
65	Philips BF 1388	Don't Let Me Be Misunderstood/Monster	8
65	Philips BF 1415	I Put A Spell On You/Gimme Some	10
66	Philips BF 1465	Either Way I Lose/Break Down And Let It Out	15
61	Parlophone GEP 8844	MY BABY JUST CARES FOR ME (EP)	50
62	Parlophone GEP 8864	INTIMATE NINA SIMONE (EP)	25
64	Colpix PXE 303	FINE AND MELLOW (EP)	15
66	Colpix PXE 306	JUST SAY I LOVE HIM (EP)	15
66	Colpix PXE 307	I LOVE TO LOVE (EP)	15
65	Philips BE 12585	DON'T LET ME BE MISUNDERSTOOD (EP)	12
65	Philips BE 12589	STRANGE FRUIT (EP)	12
61	Pye Intl. NPL 28014	AT THE TOWN HALL (LP)	18
62	Pye Jazz NJL 36	FORBIDDEN FRUIT (LP)	18
64	Colpix PXL 419	FORBIDDEN FRUIT (LP, reissue)	15
64	Colpix PXL 421	NINA AT THE VILLAGE GATE (LP)	22
65	Colpix PXL 465	FOLKSY NINA (LP)	22
65	Fontana SFJL 954	TELL ME MORE (LP)	15
65	Philips BL 7662	BROADWAY . . . BLUES . . . BALLADS (LP)	15
65	Philips BL 7671	I PUT A SPELL ON YOU (LP)	18
65	Philips BL 7678	IN CONCERT (LP)	15
66	Philips BL 7683	PASTEL BLUES (LP)	15
66	Philips (S)BL 7722	LET IT ALL OUT (LP)	15
66	Philips (S)BL 7726	WILD IS THE WIND (LP)	15
67	Philips (S)BL 7764	HIGH PRIESTESS OF SOUL (LP)	15
67	RCA RD/SF 7883	SINGS THE BLUES (LP)	15
68	RCA RD/SF 7967	SILK AND SOUL (LP)	15
69	RCA RD/SF 7979	NUFF SAID! (LP)	12

SUGAR SIMONE

66	Rainbow RAI 103	Is It Because/I Want To Know	20
67	Rainbow RAI 115	I Love My Baby/I'll Keep You Satisfied	12
67	Sue WI 4029	Suddenly/King Without A Throne	40
67	Go AJ 11409	It's Alright/Take It Easy	28
68	CBS 3250	The Vow/Spinning Wheel	18
69	Doctor Bird DB 1192	Black Is Gold/The Invitation	22
69	Doctor Bird DB 1193	The Squeeze Is On/Tell Me	22
69	Doctor Bird DB 1201	Come And Try/Don't Listen To What They Say	12
69	Fab FAB 106	Boom Biddy Boom/RUDIES: What Can I Do	8
69	Fab FAB 107	I Need A Witness/Johnny Dollar	10
69	Upfront UPF 1	Turns On The Heatwave/Crying Blues	7
70	Beacon BEA 156	Keep On Trying/Only The Lonely	7
70	Beacon BEA 174	Why Can't I Touch You/Gotta Get It Off My Mind	7

(see also Sugar & Dandy, Les Foster, Larry Foster & Soul Explosion, Lance Hannibal)

SIMON PLUG & GRIMES

70	Deram DM 296	Is This A Dream?/I'm Going Home	12
70	President PT 310	Way In, Way Out/Long Long Summer	5
71	President PT 354	Pull Together/I'll Keep Smiling	5

SIMON'S SECRETS

68	CBS 3406	Naughty Boy/Sympathy	30
68	CBS 3856	I Know What Her Name Is/Keeping My Head Above Water	30

(see also Secrets, Clifford T. Ward, Martin Raynor & Secrets)

SIMON SISTERS

64	London HLR 9893	Winkin', Blinkin' And Nod/So Glad I'm Here	18
65	London HLR 9984	Cuddlebug/No One To Talk My Trouble To	15

NIC SIMPER'S FANDANGO

83	Paro PAR 0S4	Just Another Day (In The Life Of A Fool)/Wish I'd Never Woke Up	6
79	Gull GULP 1033	SLIPSTREAMING (LP)	20

(see also Deep Purple, Warhorse)

SIMPLE IMAGE

70	Carnaby CNS 4013	Spinning Spinning Spinning/Shy Boy	15

SIMPLE MINDS
79	Zoom ZUM 10	Life In A Day/Special View (p/s)	5
79	Zoom ZUM 11	Chelsea Girl/Garden Of Hate (p/s)	5
80	Arista ARIST 325	Changeling/Premonition (live) (p/s)	5
80	Arista ARIST 372	I Travel/New Warm Skin (p/s, with blue vinyl flexidisc: "Kaleidoscope"/"Film Theme Dub")	8
81	Arista ARIST 394	Celebrate/Changeling (p/s)	5
81	Virgin VS 451	Sweat In Bullet/20th Century Promised Land (non-gatefold p/s)	12
89	Virgin SMBXC 1	STREET FIGHTING YEARS (box set w/ interview cassettes & songbook, no'd)	18

(see also Johnny & Self Abusers)

SIMPLICITY PEOPLE
73	Grape GR 3062	Murderer/BIG YOUTH: The Killer	12
73	Harry J HJ 6649	Time Is Getting Harder/HARRY J ALLSTARS: Time Is Getting Harder	6

SIMPLY RED
85	The Hit HOT 001	Every Bit Of Me (with *The Hit* magazine)	10
85	Lyntone LYN 15914	Something's Burning/10,000 MANIACS: Grey Victory (33rpm 1-sided clear flexidisc free with *Jamming!* magazine, issue 29)	12/8
85	Elektra EKR 9P	Money's Too Tight (To Mention)/Open Up The Red Box (picture disc)	7
85	Elektra EKR 19TX	Come To My Aid (Survival Mix)/Granma's Hands/Come To My Aid (Heavy Dub Mix)/Valentine (12", p/s)	8
85	Elektra EKR 29P	Holding Back The Years/I Won't Feel Bad (shaped picture disc)	10
85	Elektra EKR 29T	Holding Back The Years (Extended)/I Won't Feel Bad/Drowning In My Own Tears (12", p/s)	8
86	WEA YZ 63R	Jericho/Jericho The Musical (red vinyl in clear PVC sleeve)	6
86	WEA YZ 75B	Open Up The Red Box (Remix)/Look At You Now (foldout box p/s)	6
86	WEA YZ 75F	Open Up The Red Box (Remix)/Look At You Now//Holding Back The Years/I Won't Feel Bad (shrinkwrapped double pack)	5
86	WEA YZ 75TF	Open Up The Red Box (Remix)/Look At You Now (live)/Heaven The Movie (live)//Holding Back The Years (Extended)/Drowning In My Own Tears/Picture Book In Dub (12", double pack)	8
87	WEA YZ 103F	The Right Thing/There's A Light//Holding Back The Years/Drowning In My Own Tears (double pack)	6
87	WEA YZ 161TW	Ev'ry Time We Say Goodbye/Ev'ry Time We Say Goodbye (live in studio)/Love For Sale (live in studio) (12", envelope pack with sheet music & 4 postcards)	8
89	WEA YZ 349TE	It's Only Love (Valentine Mix)/Turn It Up/I'm Gonna Lose You (10", numbered stitched cardboard die-cut sleeve)	8
85	Elektra EKT 27P	PICTURE BOOK (LP, picture disc, die-cut sleeve)	15

(see also Frantic Elevators)

BILL SIMPSON
64	Piccadilly 7N 35179	I Love You For Sentimental Reasons/My Love Is Like A Red Red Rose (p/s)	8

DANNY SIMPSON
69	Trojan TR 653	Outa Sight/JOHN HOLT: I Want You Closer	12

DUDLEY SIMPSON ORCHESTRA
78	BBC RESL 58	Blake's 7/The Federation March (p/s)	8

HOKE SIMPSON
58	HMV POP 442	I Finally Found You/Gi-Gi	8

JEANETTE SIMPSON
67	Giant GN 16	Rain/Whatcha Gonna Do About It	12
68	Giant GN 29	My Baby Just Cares For Me/Don't Let Me Cry No More (with Superboys)	12
68	Giant GN 35	Through Loving You/Send Me Some Lovin' (with Missions)	10

LEO SIMPSON
65	Blue Beat BB 351	I Love Her So/Good To Be Seen (as Leo Simmo)	18
73	Pyramid PYR 7004	Waxy Doodle/Go Away	6

(see also Lionel Simpson)

LIONEL SIMPSON
65	Ska Beat JB 205	Tell Me What You Want/Love Is A Game	20
65	Ska Beat JB 221	Red River Valley/Eight People	15
66	Ska Beat JB 233	Give Over/Never Before	20

(see also Leo Simpson)

MARTIN SIMPSON
76	Trailer LER 2099	GOLDEN VANITY (LP)	12

RED SIMPSON
66	Capitol ST 2468	ROLL TRUCK ROLL (LP)	12

VALERIE SIMPSON
72	Tamla Motown STML 11194	EXPOSED (LP)	15

(see also Ashford & Simpson)

CHUCK SIMS
58	London HLR 8577	Little Pigeon/Life Isn't Long Enough (78 rpm = £55)	350

FRANKIE LEE SIMS
71	Specialty SPE 5009	Married Woman Blues/Lucy Mae Blues	5
71	Specialty SNTF 5004	LUCY MAE BLUES (LP)	15

JOAN SIMS
63	Parlophone R 5021	Oh Not Again Ken/Hurry Up Gran	6
67	CBS 202635	Sweet Lovely Whatsisname/The Lass With The Delicate Hair	6

KELLY SIMS
60	Top Rank JAR 321	Betrayed By Love/A Girl In Love	6

MINT VALUE £

ZOOT SIMS

51	Esquire 10-107	Yellow Duck/Boot It Zoot (78)	6
57	Esquire EP 183	ZOOT! (EP)	20
57	Esquire EP 204	ZOOT'S CASE (EP)	20
52	Esquire 20-002	ZOOT SIMS QUARTET/QUINTET (10" LP)	40
53	Esquire 20-010	ZOOT SIMS ALLSTARS (10" LP)	20
53	Esquire 20-018	ZOOT SIMS QUARTET/QUINTET (10" LP)	20
54	Vogue LDE 056	ZOOT SIMS GOES TO TOWN (10" LP)	200
55	Esquire 20-040	ZOOT SIMS QUARTET/QUINTET (10" LP)	60
50s	Esquire 32-040	ZOOT SIMS SEPTET (LP)	30
58	HMV CLP 1165	GEORGE HANDY COMPOSITIONS (LP)	18
58	HMV CLP 1188	PLAYS FOUR ALTOS (LP)	40
61	Vogue LAE 12309	CHOICE (LP)	20
61	Fontana TFL 5176	ZOOT AT RONNIE SCOTT'S (LP)	150
62	Fontana (S)TFL 588	ZOOT AT RONNIE SCOTT'S (LP, reissue)	100
62	Fontana 886 151 TY	SOLO FOR ZOOT (LP, also mono [680 982 TL], £20)	50
65	Fontana FJL 123	COOKIN'! (LP)	150
60s	Xtra XTRA 5001	TROTTING! (LP)	15

(see also Sims-Wheeler Vintage Jazz Band)

SIMS TWINS/VALENTINOS

68	Soul City SCM 001	THE VALENTINOS/THE SIMS TWINS (LP, 1 side each)	60

SIMS-WHEELER VINTAGE JAZZ BAND

60	Polydor NH 66638	Never On A Sunday/Ma Curly Headed Baby	5

(see also Zoot Sims)

FRANK SINATRA

59	Capitol CL 14997	Time After Time/French Foreign Legion (78)	6
59	Capitol CL 15006	To Love And Be Loved/No-One Ever Tells You (78)	8
59	Capitol CL 15052	High Hopes/All My Tomorrows (78)	12
59	Capitol CL 15086	Talk To Me/They Came To Cordura (78)	15
53	Columbia SCM 5052	Birth Of The Blues/Why Try To Change Me Now?	40
53	Columbia SCM 5060	You Do Something To Me/Lover	40
53	Columbia SCM 5076	Santa Claus Is Comin' To Town/My Girl	40
54	Capitol CL 14064	Young-At-Heart/Take A Chance	20
54	Capitol CL 14120	Three Coins In The Fountain/I Could Have Told You	25
54	Capitol CL 14174	White Christmas/The Christmas Waltz	25
54	Capitol CL 14188	When I Stop Loving You/It Worries Me	18
55	Capitol CL 14221	Someone To Watch Over Me/The Gal That Got Away	18
55	Capitol CL 14238	Melody Of Love/I'm Gonna Live Till I Die	18
55	Columbia SCM 5167	S'posin'/How Deep Is The Ocean	30
55	Capitol CL 14240	You, My Love/Just One Of Those Things	18
55	Capitol CL 14270	Don't Change Your Mind About Me/Why Should I Cry Over You	18
55	Capitol CL 14292	Two Hearts, Two Kisses (Make One Love)/From The Bottom To The Top	18
55	Capitol CL 14296	Learnin' The Blues/If I Had Three Wishes	18
55	Capitol CL 14326	Not As A Stranger/How Could You Do A Thing Like That To Me	18
55	Capitol CL 14352	My Funny Valentine/I Get A Kick Out Of You	15
55	Capitol CL 14360	It Never Entered My Mind/In The Wee Small Hours Of The Morning	15
55	Capitol CL 14373	Fairy Tale/Same Old Saturday Night	15

(The above Capitol 45s were originally issued with triangular centres; later round-centre copies are worth half these values.)

56	Capitol CL 14503	Love And Marriage/Look To Your Heart	8
56	Capitol CL 14511	(Love Is) A Tender Trap/Weep They Will	7
56	Capitol CL 14564	You'll Get Yours/Flowers Mean Forgiveness	6
56	Capitol CL 14584	Five Hundred Guys/(How Little It Matters) How Little We Know	5
56	Capitol CL 14607	"Johnny Concho" Theme (Wait For Me)/Hey! Jealous Lover	5
56	Capitol CL 14620	The Impatient Years/Our Town	5
56	Capitol CL 14644	Who Wants To Be A Millionaire? (with Celeste Holm)/Mind If I Make Love To You?	6
56	Capitol CL 14646	You're Sensational/You Forgot All The Words	5
57	Capitol CL 14696	Can I Steal A Little Love?/Your Love For Me	5
57	Capitol CL 14719	So Long, My Love/Crazy Love	5
57	Capitol CL 14750	Something Wonderful Happens In Summer/You're Cheatin' Yourself	5
57	Capitol CL 14800	All The Way/Chicago	5
57	Capitol CL 14804	Mistletoe And Holly/Jingle Bells	5
58	Capitol CL 14819	Witchcraft/Tell Her You Love Her	6
58	Capitol CL 14863	Nothing In Common/How Are Ya Fixed For Love (with Keely Smith)	5
58	Capitol CL 14904	The Song From "Kings Go Forth" (Monique)/The Same Old Song And Dance	5
58	Fontana H 140	If I Forget You/I'm A Fool To Want You	10
58	Capitol CL 14956	Mr. Success/Sleep Warm	5
59	Capitol CL 14997	Time After Time/French Foreign Legion	5
59	Capitol CL 15006	To Love And Be Loved/No-One Ever Tells You	5
59	Capitol CL 15052	High Hopes/All My Tomorrows	5
59	Capitol CL 15086	Talk To Me/They Came To Cordura	5
60	Capitol CL 15116	It's Nice To Go Trav'ling/Brazil	5
60	Capitol CL 15135	River, Stay 'Way From My Door/It's Over, It's Over, It's Over	5
60	Capitol CL 15150	Nice 'n' Easy/This Was My Love	5
60	Capitol CL 15168	Ol' MacDonald/You'll Always Be The One I Love	5

EPs

54	HMV 7EG 8004	TOMMY DORSEY & HIS ORCHESTRA (plain sleeve, 2 tracks with Sinatra)	10
54	HMV 7EG 8070	FRANK SINATRA (plain sleeve)	8
54	Capitol EAP1-488	SONGS FOR YOUNG LOVERS NO. 1	8
55	HMV 7EG 8128	MOONLIGHT SINATRA	12
55	Columbia SEG 7565	FRANK SINATRA (plain sleeve)	10
55	Columbia SEG 7582	SINATRA SERENADE (plain sleeve)	10
55	Columbia SEG 7597	FRANKIE'S FAVOURITES (plain sleeve)	10
55	Capitol EAP 2-488	SONGS FOR YOUNG LOVERS NO. 2	8
55	Capitol EAP 1-571	SONGS FROM "YOUNG AT HEART"	8

56	Capitol EAP 1-590	MELODY OF LOVE	8
56	Capitol EAP 1-629	SESSION WITH SINATRA	8
56	Capitol EAP 1025	OUR TOWN	8
56	Capitol EAP 2-488	YOUNG AT HEART	8
60	Fontana TFE 17273	'BYE BABY	8
61	Capitol SEP1-221	NO ONE CARES (stereo)	8
61	Capitol SEP2-1221	NO ONE CARES NO. 2 (stereo)	8
61	Capitol SEP3-1221	NO ONE CARES NO. 3 (stereo)	8

CAPITOL LPs

54	Capitol LC 6654	SONGS FOR YOUNG LOVERS (10")	30
54	Capitol LC 6689	SWING EASY (10") Decca Pressing/EMI·	30
55	Capitol LC 6702	IN THE WEE SMALL HOURS VOL. 1 (10")	25
55	Capitol LC 6705	IN THE WEE SMALL HOURS VOL. 2 (10")	25

(The above LPs were originally pressed by Decca. Subsequent pressings were by EMI, and are worth 40% less)

56	Capitol LCT 6106	SONGS FOR SWINGIN' LOVERS	15
56	Capitol LCT 6111	FRANK SINATRA CONDUCTS TONE POEMS OF COLOUR	18
57	Capitol LCT 6123	THIS IS SINATRA	15
57	Capitol LCT 6130	CLOSE TO YOU	15
57	Capitol LCT 6135	A SWINGIN' AFFAIR	15
57	Capitol LCT 6144	A JOLLY CHRISTMAS FROM FRANK SINATRA	15
58	Capitol (S)LCT 6152	WHERE ARE YOU? (mono/stereo)	15
58	Capitol LCT 6155	THIS IS SINATRA VOL. 2	15
58	Capitol (S)LCT 6168	FRANK SINATRA SINGS FOR ONLY THE LONELY (mono/stereo)	15
59	Capitol (S)LCT 6179	COME DANCE WITH ME	15
59	Capitol LCT 6181	LOOK TO YOUR HEART	15
59	Capitol (S)LCT 6185	NO ONE CARES	15
60	Capitol W 587	SWING EASY	15
61	Capitol W(S) 1417	NICE'N'EASY (mono/stereo)	15
61	Capitol W(S) 1491	SINATRA'S SWINGIN' SESSION! (mono/stereo)	15
62	Capitol W(S) 1594	COME SWING WITH ME! (mono/stereo)	15
62	Capitol W(S) 1676	POINT OF NO RETURN (mono/stereo)	15
62	Capitol T 20389	LONDON BY NIGHT	15
62	Capitol W(S) 1538	ALL THE WAY (mono/stereo)	15
63	Capitol W(S) 1729	SINATRA SINGS ... OF LOVE AND THINGS! (mono/stereo)	15
63	Capitol W 1/2/3-1762	THE GREAT YEARS (3-LP)	20
63	Capitol W 1825	FRANK SINATRA SINGS RODGERS AND HART	15
64	Capitol T 20577	MY FUNNY VALENTINE	15
65	Capitol W 20652	SINGING AND SWINGING	15
65	Capitol (S)T 1919	TELL HER YOU LOVE HER	15
65	Capitol T 20734	THE CONNOISSEUR'S SINATRA	15
66	Capitol T 20757	SINATRA FOR THE SOPHISTICATED	12
67	Capitol (S)T 2700	THE MOVIE SONGS	12
85	Capitol SINATRA 20	FRANK SINATRA: THE CAPITOL YEARS (20-LP, box set)	80+
90	Capitol C1-94777	THE CAPITOL YEARS (5-LP, box set)	25

PHILIPS/FONTANA LPs

54	Philips BBR 8003	SING AND DANCE WITH FRANK SINATRA (10")	30
55	Philips BBR 8038	FABULOUS FRANK (10")	25
55	Philips BBR 8040	YOUNG AT HEART (10", with Doris Day)	25
57	Philips BBR 8114	CHRISTMAS DREAMING (10")	30
57	Philips BBL 7137	DORIS AND FRANK (6 tracks each by Doris Day & Frank Sinatra)	25
57	Philips BBL 7168	FRANKIE	20
57	Philips BBL 7180	THAT OLD FEELING	20
58	Fontana TFL 5000	THE VOICE	25
58	Fontana TFL 5006	ADVENTURES OF THE HEART	20
58	Fontana TFL 5030	THE FRANK SINATRA STORY	18
59	Fontana TFL 5048	PUT YOUR DREAMS AWAY	25
59	Fontana TFL 5054	THE BROADWAY KICK	20
60	Fontana TFL 5074	LOVE IS A KICK	18
60	Fontana TFL 5082	COME BACK TO SORRENTO	18
60	Fontana TFL 5107	REFLECTIONS	15
61	Fontana TFL 5138	SINATRA SOUVENIR	15
61	Fontana SET 303	SINATRA PLUS (2-LP)	18

REPRISE LPs

61	Reprise R 1001	RING-A-DING-DING!	15
61	Reprise R(9) 1002	SINATRA SWINGS (mono/stereo)	12
62	Reprise R(9) 1003	I REMEMBER TOMMY... (die-cut gatefold sleeve, mono/stereo)	12
62	Reprise R(9) 1004	SINATRA AND STRINGS (mono/stereo)	12
62	Reprise R(9) 1005	SINATRA AND SWINGIN' BRASS (mono/stereo)	15
62	Reprise R(9) 1006	SINATRA SINGS GREAT SONGS FROM GREAT BRITAIN (mono/stereo)	30/45
66	Reprise R(9) 1018	MOONLIGHT SINATRA	15
66	Reprise R(S)LP 1019	IN CONCERT: SINATRA AT 'THE SANDS' (2-LP, with Count Basie)	18
70	Reprise R(S)LP 1031	WATERTOWN	15

OTHER LPs

56	HMV DLP 1123	IT'S D-LOVELY (with Tommy Dorsey Orchestra)	25
58	RCA RD 27069	FRANKIE AND TOMMY (with Tommy Dorsey Orchestra)	20
69	World Records SM 137-142	THE SINATRA TOUCH (6-LP, box set, mail-order only)	30
81	World Records ALBUM 47	THE SINATRA TOUCH (4-LP, box set, mail-order only)	20
83	Mobile Fidelity SC 1	THE SINATRA COLLECTION (16-LPs in silver box, with *Swing Easy* LP unavailable elsewhere)	300+

(see also Nancy Sinatra, Count Basie, Tommy Dorsey, Dean Martin, Doris Day)

FRANK & NANCY SINATRA

67	Reprise REP 30082	SOMETHING STUPID (EP)	10
69	Reprise R(S)LP 1026	THE SINATRA FAMILY WISH YOU A HAPPY CHRISTMAS (LP)	20

MINT VALUE £

NANCY SINATRA

61	Reprise RS 20017	Cuff Links And Tie Clips/Not Just Your Friend (with p/s)	15/10
62	Reprise RS 20045	To Know Him Is To Love Him/Like I Do	12
63	Reprise RS 20144	I See The Moon/Put Your Head On My Shoulder	10
64	Reprise RS 20335	True Love/The Answer To Everything	8
65	Reprise RS 20407	So Long Babe/If He'd Loved Me	10
66	Reprise RS 20432	These Boots Are Made For Walkin'/The City Never Sleeps At Night	5
66	Reprise REP 30069	RUN FOR YOUR LIFE (EP)	18
66	Reprise REP 30072	I MOVE AROUND (EP)	18
67	Reprise REP 30080	SORRY 'BOUT THAT (EP)	18
67	Reprise REP 30086	NASHVILLE NANCY (EP)	15
66	Reprise R 6202	BOOTS (LP)	15
66	Reprise R 6207	HOW DOES THAT GRAB YOU? (LP)	15
66	Reprise R(S)LP 6221	NANCY IN LONDON (LP)	15
67	Reprise RLP 6239	SUGAR (LP)	15
67	Reprise R(S)LP 6251	COUNTRY, MY WAY (LP)	15
68	Reprise R(S)LP 6277	MOVIN' WITH NANCY (LP)	15
69	Reprise RSLP 6333	NANCY (LP)	15
72	RCA DPS 2037	THIS IS NANCY SINATRA (LP)	12
73	RCA SF 8331	WOMAN (LP)	12

(see also Elvis Presley)

NANCY SINATRA & LEE HAZLEWOOD

67	Reprise RS 20629	Lady Bird/Sand	6
67	Reprise RS 23215	Some Velvet Morning/Tony Rome	6
71	Reprise K 14093	Did You Ever?/Back On The Road Again	5
67	Reprise REP 30083	JACKSON (EP)	15
68	Reprise R(S)LP 6273	NANCY & LEE (LP)	15
72	RCA Victor SF 8240	DID YOU EVER? (LP)	15

(see also Lee Hazlewood, Frank Sinatra)

BETTY SINCLAIR

70	Torpedo TOR 19	Why Why Why/HOT ROD ALL STARS: Fistful Of Dollars	12

JIMMY SINCLAIR & TRENTON SPENCE ORCHESTRA

61	Blue Beat BB 47	Verona/To Prove My Love	10

STEPHEN SINCLAIR

62	HMV POP 1066	Mister Sandman/Part Lights	6

WINSTON SINCLAIR

69	Nu Beat NB 026	Another Heartache/Come On Little Girl	8

(see also Harmonisers)

SINDECUT

92	VST 1326DJ	Won't Change/Panic Stricken!!/Crack Business	8
87	BAAD BD666	SINDECUTS KICKIN' IT (EP)	20
88	BAAD BD 777	CAN'T GET ENOUGH (EP)	14
90	Virgin V2635	CHANGING THE SCENERY (LP)	15

SINDELFINGEN

73	Medway	ODGIPIG (LP, private pressing, with insert)	550
90	Cenotaph CEN 111	ODGIPIG/TRIANGLE (2-LP, reissue with live album, 300 only)	25

SINEWAVE

72	Chapter One SCH 172	Clochemerle/Star Trek	10

PETE SINFIELD

73	Manticore K 43501	STILL (LP, textured gatefold sleeve)	18

(see also Emerson Lake & Palmer, King Crimson, Greg Lake)

SINGAROUND

69	G. Guinea GSGL 10436	SINGAROUND (LP)	15

RAY SINGER

64	Ember EMB S 187	Tell Me Now/I'm Comin' Home	7
64	Ember EMB S 199	It's Gotta Be/Hey, Who?	7
65	Ember EMB S 215	I'm The Richest Man Alive/Pretty Little Rambling Rose (some in p/s)	12/7
65	Fontana TF 621	You'll Come Crying To Me/Who Can I Talk To About You	7
67	Ember EMB S 231	What's Done Has Been Done/Won't It Be Fine	55+
60s	Ember NR	RAY SINGER (LP)	30

(see also Nirvana [U.K.])

SUSAN SINGER

62	Oriole CB 1703	Gee It's Great To Be Young/Hello First Love	15
62	Oriole CB 1741	Bobby's Loving Touch/Johnny Summertime	70
62	Oriole CB 1778	Love Me With All Your Heart/Autumn Leaves	15
63	Oriole CB 1802	Lock Your Heart Away/Answer To A Prayer	15
63	Oriole CB 1882	I Know/That Old Feeling	15

(see also Susan Holiday)

SINGING BELLES

60	Top Rank JAR 350	The Empty Mailbox/Someone Loves You, Joe	10

SINGING DOGS

57	Pye NEP 24029	SINGING DOGS (EP)	25

SINGING POSTMAN

64	Ralph Tuck Promotions Ltd. BEV EP 153	Come Along A Me/Moind Yer Hid Boy/Hev Yew Gotta Loight Boy/ Miss From Diss (EP)	12
66	Parlophone GEP 8956	FIRST DELIVERY (EP)	10
72	Starline SRS 5063	THE BEST OF (LP)	15

SINGING PRINCIPAL

73	Action ACT 4608	Thank You Baby/Women's Lib	60

SINGING REINDEER
60	Capitol CL 15124	The Happy Birthday Song/I Wanna Be An Easter Bunny 5

(see also "Dancer, Prancer & Nervous")

MARGIE SINGLETON
60	Melodisc 45-1544	Angel Hands/The Eyes Of Love. 15
62	Mercury AMT 1197	Magic Star/Only Your Shadow Knows 20
68	Fontana TL 5456	SINGS COUNTRY WITH SOUL (LP)....................................... 18

SINISTER DUCKS
83	Situation 2 SIT 25	Suicide: March Of The Sinister Ducks/
		Homicide: Old Gangsters Never (foldout p/s) 10

(see also Bauhaus)

EARL SINK(S)
61	Warner Bros WB 38	Look For Me, I'll Be There/Super Market (as Earl Sink) 15
61	Warner Bros WB 51	Superstitious/Little Suzie Parker....................................... 20
63	Capitol CL 15310	Looking For Love/Raining On My Side Of Town (as Earl Sinks) 15

(see also Crickets, Sinx Mitchell)

SINNER
79	Whitetower AMC 705	Need Your Love/Beggar/God's In His Heaven (foldout p/s) 75

SINNERMAN & SARA
68	MGM MGM-C(S) 8099	SINNERMAN AND SARA (LP).. 20

SINNERS
63	Columbia DB 7158	I Can't Stand It/If You Leave Me Now 7
64	Columbia DB 7295	It's So Exciting/Leave Him 8

(see also Linda Laine & Sinners)

SINS OF THE FLESH
90s	Plastic Head 014	In The Image Of Torture (12", p/s)..................................... 10

SIOUXSIE & BANSHEES
78	Polydor 2059 052	Hong Kong Garden/Voices (10,000 only in gatefold p/s; beige plastic,
		silver plastic, red plastic or red paper label) .... each 25
78	Polydor 2059 052	Hong Kong Garden/Voices (p/s) 5
79	Polydor POSP 9	The Staircase (Mystery)/20th Century Boy (p/s) 6
79	Polydor POSP 59	Playground Twist/Pull To Bits (p/s, some with red paper label) 5/4
79	Polydor 2059 151	Mittageisen (Metal Postcard)/Love In A Void (p/s)......................... 7
80	Polydor 2059 249	Christine/Eve White, Eve Black (with Nigel Gray credit on B-side, p/s) 5
80	Polydor POSPX 205	Israel (Extended)/Red Over White (Extended) (12", a few with
		'Made In England' credit, most with 'Made In France' credit) 10/8
82	Polydor POSPG 450	Fireworks/Coal Mind (gatefold p/s)..................................... 6
82	Polydor POSP 510	Slowdive/Cannibal Roses (p/s, red paper label) 5
83	Wonderland SHEG 4	Dear Prudence/Tattoo (foldout p/s)..................................... 6
83	Fan Club FILE 1	Head Cut/Running Town (freebie, p/s) 30
84	Wonderland SHEX 6	Swimming Horses/Let Go/The Humming Wires (12", p/s with poster) 8
85	Wonderland SHE 7	Dazzle/I Promise (p/s).. 8
85	Wonderland SHE 8	Overground/Placebo Effect (p/s)....................................... 8
85	Wonderland SHE 9	Cities In Dust/An Execution (poster p/s) 6
85	Wonderland SHEX 9	Cities In Dust/An Execution/Quarterdrawing Of The Dog (12", p/s,
		'banned' picture label) 8
86	Wonderland SHEDP 10	Candyman/Lullaby (with free 2nd single, gatefold p/s, 2,000 only)........... 8
87	Wonderland SHEG 11	This Wheel's On Fire/Shooting Sun/Sleepwalking (On The High Wire)/
		She's Cracked (numbered double pack, gatefold p/s) 10
88	Spiral Scratch SCRATCH 2	An Interview With... (free with *Spiral Scratch* mag, 5,000 only) 6/4
88	Wonderland SHE 14	Peek A Boo/False Face (gatefold pop-up p/s) 7
88	Wonderland SHECD 15	Killing Jar/Something Wicked (This Way Comes) (CD). 12
88	Wonderland SHE 16	The Last Beat Of My Heart (numbered, gilded p/s) 5
88	Wonderland SHECD 16	The Last Beat Of My Heart (CD) 8
78	Polydor POLD 5009	THE SCREAM (LP, with inner sleeve; some with labels reversed)........... 12/10
87	Wonderland SHELP 4	THROUGH THE LOOKING GLASS (LP, mispressing, 1 side plays
		Jimi Hendrix's "War Heroes") 25

(see also Creatures, Cure, Glove)

SIR ALEC & HIS BOYS
67	Deram DM 116	I'm A Believer/Green Green Grass Of Home 7

SIR ALICK & PHRASER
82	Recommended/Black	In Search Of The Perfect Baby/PROLIFIKURDS: Nursery Crymes
	Noise 7 NO 5	(printed p/s in PVC sleeve or standard p/s)............................. 10

(see also Homosexuals)

SIR BEANZ OBE
99	Mapache Chet002	MARS ATTACKS (EP) 15
01	SFDB 005	HIEROGLYPHIC AUDIO VISUAL (EP) 8

SIR (Clancy) COLLINS BAND
68	Collins Downbeat CR 005	Sock It Softly (with Bob Stackie)/LESTER STERLING, SIR COLLINS & BAND:
		Three Wise Men... 35
68	Collins Downbeat CR 0011	Collins And The Boys/Bob Stackie In Soho (both with Bob Stackie) 30
68	Collins Downbeat CR 0017	Soul Feelings/SIR COLLINS: Hello Stella.................................. 35
69	Duke DU 46	Black Panther/I Want To Be Loved 20
69	Duke DU 47	Black Diamonds (with Diamonds)/DIAMONDS: I Remember 15
69	Duke DU 55	Brother Moses/Funny Familiar Feeling (both with Earthquakes) 15

(see also Bob Stackie, Earthquakes, Collins Band, Owen Gray)

SIRCONICAL
99	Twisted Nerve TN 004	CATALOGUE OF ERRORS EP: Frail/Moondance/Bimbo Quick
		(wraparound p/s)... 8

SIR COXSONE SOUND

SIR COXSONE SOUND
75	Safari SFA 100	KING OF DUB ROCK (LP)	35
76	Regal RLP 001	KING OF DUB ROCK PART 2 (LP)	20

SIR D's GROUP
61	Blue Beat BB 66	Hey Diddle Diddle (with K. Brown)/Pocket Money (with Mossman & Zeddze)	25

(see also Kent Brown & Rainbows)

SIR DOUGLAS QUINTET
65	London HLU 9964	She's About A Mover/We'll Take Our Last Walk Tonight	12
65	London HLU 9982	The Tracker/Blue Norther	10
65	London HLU 10001	The Story Of John Hardy/In Time	8
66	London HLU 10019	The Rains Came/Bacon Fat	8
69	Mercury MF 1079	Mendocino/I Wanna Be Your Mama Again	10
69	Mercury MF 1129	Dynamite Woman/Too Many Dociled Minds	8
65	London HA-U 8311	THE SIR DOUGLAS QUINTET (LP)	50
69	Mercury SMCL 20160	MENDOCINO (LP)	25
69	Mercury SMCL 20186	TOGETHER AFTER FIVE (LP)	25

SIREN
71	Dandelion DAN 7002	Strange Locomotion/I'm All Aching (label also lists K 19004)	6
69	Dandelion 63755	SIREN (LP)	22
71	Dandelion DAN 8001	STRANGE LOCOMOTION (LP, gatefold sleeve, label also lists K 49001)	25

(see also Kevin Coyne, Clague)

SIR GIBBS
68	Amalgamated AMG 822	People Grudgeful/Pan Ya Machet (both sides actually by Pioneers)	20

SIR HARRY
71	Duke DU 127	Last Call/ORGAN D: Hot Organ	10
72	Duke DU 136	Apples To Apples/DRUM BEAT ALL STARS: Good Life	10
72	Bullet BU 519	Mr. Parker's Daughter/U.ROY: On Top Of The Peak	8
72	Downtown DT 493	Meet The Boss/Musical Light	12
73	Downtown DT 504	Apollo 17 (with Cables)/Uptown Rock	12

(see also Barbara Jones)

SIR HENRY (& HIS BUTLERS)
68	Columbia DB 8351	Camp/Pretty Style (as Sir Henry & His Butlers)	8
68	Columbia DB 8497	The Rolo Sensation (Camp)/Pretty Style (reissue, as Sir Henry & His Butlers)	10
70	Columbia DB 8740	Annie Got A Date/Like A Rose	5

SIR HORATIO
82	Rock Steady/666 Mix 1T	Abracadubra/Sommadub (12", plain sleeve)	15

(see also A Certain Ratio)

SIR LORD COMIC
67	Doctor Bird DB 1070	The Great Wuga Wuga (with Cowboys)/THREE TOPS: Feel So Lonesome	42
70	Pressure Beat PR 5507	Jack Of My Trade/CYNTHIA RICHARDS: United We Stand	25

(see also Lord Comic)

SIRUS
91	White 002	THE ONE AND ONLY (EP)	30

SIR WASHINGTON
69	Star ST 1	Apollo 12/When You Kiss Me	12
70	Big Chief BC 100	Apollo 13/Space	10

SISTER
70	Camel CA 55	Feel It/MAYTONES: Serious	8
73	Camel CA 106	Every Day Is The Same Kind Of Thing/Sweat Of Your Brow	5

(see also Paulette & Gee, Ebony Sisters)

SISTERHOOD
86	Merciful Release SIS 010	Giving Ground (RSV)/Giving Ground (AV) (p/s)	5

(see also Sisters Of Mercy, James Ray & Performance)

SISTER SLEDGE
73	Atlantic K 10375	Mama Never Told Me/Neither One Of Us	15
75	Atlantic K 10551	Love Don't You Go Through No Changes On Me/Don't You Miss Me	20
75	Atlantic K 10683	Love Has Found Me/Love Ain't Easy	5
77	Cotillion K 10876	Cream Of The Crop/Love Ain't Easy	5

SISTERS LOVE
70	A&M AMS 772	Forget It, I've Got It/Eye To Eye	8
70	A&M AMS 808	The Bigger Your Love/Piece Of My Heart	10
72	Tamla Motown TMG 828	Mr. Fix It Man/You've Got To Make Your Choice	8
73	Mowest MW 3009	I'm Learning To Trust My Man/Try It You'll Like It	20
75	Tamla Motown TMG 1002	I'm Learning To Trust My Man/Try It You'll Like It (reissue)	10

SISTERS OF MERCY
80	Merciful Release MR 7	The Damage Done/Watch/Home Of The Hitmen (p/s, 1,000 only; beware of counterfeits without 'MR 7' matrix number)	200+
82	CNT CNT 002	Body Electric/Adrenochrome (p/s)	85
82	Merciful Release MR 015	Alice/Floorshow (white background p/s)	30
83	Merciful Release MR 019	Anaconda/Phantom (p/s)	5
83	Merciful Release MR 021	Alice/Floorshow/1969/Phantom (12", p/s)	8
83	Merciful Release MR 023	THE REPTILE HOUSE (12" EP, with lyric sheet)	10
83	Merciful Release MR 027	Temple Of Love/Heartland (p/s)	5
83	Merciful Release MRX 027	Temple Of Love (Extended)/Heartland/Gimme Shelter (12", without bardcode on p/s)	8
84	Merciful Release MR 029	Body And Soul/Train (p/s)	8
84	Merciful Release MR 029T	Body And Soul/Body Electric/Train/Afterhours (12", p/s)	10
84	Merciful Release/WEA	ALICE/TEMPLE OF LOVE/REPTILE HOUSE/BODY AND SOUL (4 x 12" box set, promo only)	150

84	Merciful Release MR 033	Walk Away/Poison Door (p/s, some with flexidisc "Long Train" [SAM 218]).... 15/8
84	Merciful Release MR 033T	Walk Away/Poison Door/On The Wire (12", p/s, with flexi "Long Train")....... 15/8
85	Merciful Release MR 335	No Time To Cry/Blood Money (p/s) 8
85	Merciful Release MR 035T	No Time To Cry/Blood Money/Bury Me Deep (12", p/s) 10
87	Merciful Release MR 39	This Corrosion/Torch (box set, with 3 postcards, 5,000 only) 10
87	Merciful Release MR 39CD	This Corrosion (11.15)/Torch/Colours (CD, black disc, gatefold card sleeve with gauze inner, some without 'WEA' logo on back sleeve)............ 10
88	Merciful Release MR 43C	Dominion/Untitled/Sandstorm/Ozymandias (cassette in presentation box)....... 6
88	Merciful Release MR 43TB	Dominion (Extended)/Untitled/Sandstorm/Emma (12", box set with poster) 8
88	Merciful Release MR 43CD	Dominion (Extended)/Untitled/Sandstorm/Ozymandias (3" CD, black disc with adaptor, 5" case)................................... 8
88	Merciful Release MR 44CD	Lucretia My Reflection (Extended 9.52)/Long Train (1984) (3" CD, with adaptor, 5" case) 8
90	Merciful Release MR 47CDX	More/More (Extended)/You Could Be The One (CD, 12" foldout p/s) 8
90	Merciful Release MR 51TX	Doctor Jeep (Extended)/Burn (live)/Amphetamine Logic (live) (12", p/s, 6,000 only) 8
85	Merciful Release MR 337L	FIRST AND LAST AND ALWAYS (LP, gatefold sleeve, beware of copies with faked autographs!) 18
87	Merciful Release MR 441L	FLOODLAND (LP, numbered sleeve with lyric sheet) 12
	(see also Mission, Sisterhood, Ghost Dance, Dead Or Alive)	

SITUATION
| 66 | CBS 202392 | Situation Now/Time... 20 |

SIVUCA
| 74 | Vanguard VSD 79337 | SIVUCA (LP)... 12 |

SIX OF ONE
| 64 | Mercury MF 812 | He's The One You Love/I Love My Little Girl .... 10 |

SIXPENCE
| 67 | London HLJ 10124 | You're The Love/What To Do .... 6 |

EARL SIXTEEN
79	Sufferers Heights SUFF 007	African Tribesman/MIKEY DREAD: Yoruba Dub (12")....................... 20
81	DATC DCD 004	MR D.J./GILLY BUCHANAN: Ghetto Youths/DATC MUSIC STABLE : Dub (12")... 25
81	Dread At The Controls DATCLP003	REGGAE SOUND (LP).. 40

SIX TEENS
| 56 | London HLU 8345 | A Casual Look/Teen Age Promise (78 rpm = £110) .... 350+ |

SIXTH COMM
87	Eyas Media EYAS 002	CONTENT WITH BLOOD/TURN OF THE WHEEL (LP, embossed, textured sleeve, 2,000 only) 20
87	Eyas Media EYAS 005	TASTE FOR FLESH (1st 2,000 in laminated, full-cover sleeve)............. 18/12
88	Eyas Media EYAS 006	FRUITS OF YGGDRASIL (LP, limited issue, 669 copies only) 25
90	Eyas Media EYAS 013	ASYLUM (LP) 15
90	Eyas Media EYAS 071	COMING OF SEVEN (LP) 12

64 SPOONS
| 78 | Bushbaby | LADIES DON'T HAVE WILLIES (EP) .... 10 |

SIZE SEVEN GROUP
65	Mercury MF 845	Where Do We Go From Here/Till I Die................................ 8
65	Mercury MF 854	In Time/Walking Proud 8
65	Mercury MF 896	It's Got To Be Love/I Met Her In The Rain 6

SKA CHAMPIONS
| 65 | Blue Beat BB 305 | My Tears/Yesterday's Dreams .... 20 |

SKA CITY ROCKERS
| 80 | Inferno BEAT 1 | Time Is Tight/Roadrunner/You Don't Know Like I Know (p/s) .... 6 |
| 80 | Inferno BEAT 1 | Time Is Tight/Roadrunner/You Don't Know Like I Know (12", p/s) .... 10 |

SKA-DOWS
80	Cheapskate CHEAP 1	Apache/The Tune That Time Forgot (p/s).............................. 7
80	Cheapskate CHEAP 4	Telstar/Yes Yes Yes (p/s) 8
81	Cheapskate CHEAP 25	Yes Yes Yes/Twice (p/s) 8
81	Penthouse PENT 7	Ska's On 45/Rhapsody In Buh (plain stickered sleeve) 6
81	Penthouse PENT 127	Ska's On 45/The Ska-Dows Live (Let's Twist Again/Everybody Knows It's Shocking/Aye-Ho — Kinky Reggae) (12", p/s)........................... 12
81	Cheapskate CHEAP 36	Ska's On 45/Rhapsody In Buh (p/s, reissue) 6
81	Cheapskate CHEAPT 36	Ska's On 45/The Ska-Dows Live (Let's Twist Again/Everybody Knows It's Shocking/Aye-Ho — Kinky Reggae) (12", p/s, reissue)................... 8
82	Cheapskate CHEAP 41	We Gotta Get Out Of This Place/Ska'd For Life........................ 5
82	Cheapskate SKATE 3	SKA'D FOR LIFE (LP) 15

SKA KINGS
| 64 | Atlantic AT 4003 | Jamaica Ska (actually by Keith Lynn & Ken Lazarus, & Byron Lee/Dragonaires)/ Oil In My Lamp (actually by Eric Morris with Byron Lee & Dragonaires) .... 20 |
| 65 | Parlophone R 5338 | Bimbo/Ska'ville .... 8 |

SKATALITES (Jamaica)
65	Island WI 161	Trip To Mars/DOTTIE & BONNIE: Bunch Of Roses 35
65	Island WI 164	Good News/OWEN & LEON: The Fits Is On Me........................... 25
65	Island WI 168	Guns Of Navarone (actually by Roland Alphonso & Studio One Orchestra)/ Marcus Garvey (actually "Where's Marcus Garvey" by Bongoman Byfield) 8
65	Island WI 175	Dragon Weapon/DESMOND DEKKER & FOUR ACES: It Was Only A Dream 25
65	Island WI 191	Dr. Kildare/Sucu Sucu .... 60+
65	Island WI 207	Ball O' Fire/LINVAL SPENCER: Can't Go On 20
65	Island WI 226	Dick Tracy/RITA & SOULETTES: One More Chance .... 60+

SKATALITES (Jamaica)

65	Island WI 228	Beardman Ska/BONNIE & RITA: Bless You 20
65	Island WI 244	Lucky Seven/JUSTIN HINDS & DOMINOES: Never Too Young 25
66	Island WI 260	Independent Anniversary Ska (I Should Have Known Better)/
		WAILERS: Jumbie Jamboree.. 80
65	Ska Beat JB 177	Latin Goes Ska/LORD TANAMO: Night Food Ska 35
65	Ska Beat JB 178	Silver Dollar/My Business 20
65	Ska Beat JB 182	Street Corner/DREAMLETS: Really Now 30
65	Ska Beat JB 206	Timothy/KING SCRATCH & DYNAMITES: Gumma 40
73	Trojan Maxi TRM 9008	Guns Of Navarone/Bonanza Ska/Napolean Solo..................... 5
67	Studio One SOL 9006	SKA AUTHENTIC (LP)... 130

(see also Justin Hinds, Deltas, Four Aces, Maytals, Jackie Opel, Joe White, Jackie Mittoo)

SKATALITES (U.K.)
68	Decca F 12743	Don't Knock It/I Know... 6
69	Spark SRL 1034	'Cos You're The One I Love/Please Let Me Hide 8

SKAVENGERS
80	Identity Discs ID 001	Party Girls/Go To Pieces/Happy 10

SK'BOO
70s	Cuecumber CUE 1001	It's A Hard Road/Music Is Life/Talking Pictures/God's Peace In Mind........... 5

(see also Them)

BOBBY SKEL
64	London HLU 9942	Kiss And Run/Say It Now 18

SKELETAL FAMILY
83	Luggage RRP 00724	Trees/Just A Friend (foldout p/s)............................... 12

(see also Ghost Dance)

SKELETON CREW
87	B BS 1	BOOGIE-WOOGIE, SKIFFLE & BLUES (12" EP, p/s) 15
88	B BS 2	House Of The Rising Sun/Hurricane Janine (white label promo only) 15

(see also King Earl Boogie Band, Manfred Mann's Earth Band)

SKEPTIK
84	Zenon	RETURN TO HELL (12" EP) 8

SKEPTIX
82	Zenon SKEP 001	Routine Machine/Curfew (p/s) 5
83	Zenon SKEP 002	Scarred For Life/Born To Lose/Peaceforce (p/s) 5
83	Zenon SKEP 003	RETURN TO HELL (EP)... 5

SKERNE
81	Guardian GRC 81	BETTER LATE THAN NEVER (LP, private pressing) 15

FATHER SKETTO
73	Pama PM 877	Big Nine/RECO'S GROUP: Old Lady............................... 5

(see also Sketto Rich, Ruddy & Sketto)

SKIDDY & DETROIT
72	Grape GR 3030	The Exile Song/BUNNY GALE: In The Burning Sun Joh-Ho 8

ALAN SKIDMORE (QUINTET)
69	Deram Nova SDN 11	ONCE UPON A TIME (LP)....................................... 150
71	Philips 6308 041	T.C.B. (LP) 130

(see also John Mayall's Bluesbreakers, Brian Bennett, Centipede)

JIMMY SKIDMORE
72	DJM DJSL 026	SKID MARKS (LP).. 50

SKID ROW (Ireland)
70	Song 003	Saturday Morning Man (Irish pressing) 25
70	CBS 4893	Sandie's Gone (Parts 1 & 2)................................... 15
71	CBS 7181	Night Of The Warm Witch/Mr. Deluxe 10
70	CBS 63965	SKID (LP, orange label, red & blue sleeve)....................... 55
71	CBS 64411	34 HOURS (LP, orange label) 50

(see also Gary Moore, Thin Lizzy, Peggy's Leg, UFO)

SKID ROW (U.S.)
89	Atlantic A 8935P	Youth Gone Wild/Rattlesnake Shake (Live) (guitar-shaped picture disc)........ 8

SKIDS
78	No Bad NB 1	Charles/Reasons/Test Tube Babies (p/s) 10
78	Virgin VS 227	Sweet Suburbia/Open Sound (p/s, white vinyl) 5
78	Virgin VS 232-12	WIDE OPEN (12" EP, red vinyl) 5
79	Virgin VS 262	Masquerade/Out Of Town//Another Emotion/Aftermath Dub (double pack)....... 5
79	Virgin VS 306	Working For The Yankee Dollar/Vanguard's Crusage//All The Young Dudes/
		Hymns From A Haunted Ballroom (double pack) 5
92	Virgin VSCDT 1411	THE SKIDS VS THE RUTS EP (EP, shared with The Ruts) 10
79	Smash Hits HIT 002	The Olympian/XTC: Ten Feet Tall (33rpm red flexi with *Smash Hits* mag) 6/4
79	Virgin V 2116	SCARED TO DANCE (LP, blue vinyl, withdrawn) 40
79	Virgin V 2138	DAYS IN EUROPA (LP, with insert, 1st pressing with withdrawn cover featuring
		German 'gothic' lettering & 1936 Olympics picture) 12
80	Virgin V 2174	THE ABSOLUTE GAME (LP, with free LP "Strength Through Joy"
		[VDJ 33]).. 12

(see also Big Country)

BJORN SKIFS
78	EMI EMI 2785	When The Night Comes/Don't Stop Now 6
81	EMI EMI 5172	Haunted By A Dream/Fangad I En Drom 8

SKILLETS
70	Pantonic PAN 6303	BOTH SIDES NOW (LP) 15

SKIN
80s	Product Inc. 12 PROD 6	Girl Come Out/(Version) (12", p/s)	8
80s	Product Inc. 12 PROD 3	One Thousand Years (12", p/s)	8
80s	Product Inc. 33 PROD 11	SHAME, HUMILITY, REVENGE (LP, with inner)	12

SKIN ALLEY
70	CBS 5045	Tell Me/Better Be Blind	10
72	Transatlantic BIG 506	You Got Me Danglin'/Skin Valley Serenade	8
72	Transatlantic BIG 511	In The Midnight Hour/Broken Eggs	8
69	CBS 63847	SKIN ALLEY (LP)	50
70	CBS 64140	TO PAGHAM AND BEYOND (LP)	30
72	Transatlantic TRA 260	TWO QUID DEAL (LP, with inner sleeve & poster)	35
73	Transatlantic TRA 273	SKIN TIGHT (LP)	22

SKIN DEEP
85	Enemy ENEMY 1	FOOTBALL VIOLENCE (EP)	40

SKIN, FLESH & BONES
74	Pyramid PYR 7014	Butter Te Fish/Bammie And Fish	5

(see also Vincent Gordon, Cynthia Richards)

JIMMIE SKINNER
59	Mercury AMT 1030	Walkin' My Blues Away/Dark Hollow (78 rpm = £15)	15
59	Mercury AMT 1062	John Wesley Hardin/Misery Loves Company	10
60	Mercury AMT 1088	Riverboat Gambler/Married To A Friend	5
60	Mercury AMT 1117	Reasons To Live/I'm A Lot More Lonesome Now	5
64	London RE-B 1421	KENTUCKY COLONEL VOL. 1 (EP)	15
64	London RE-B 1422	KENTUCKY COLONEL VOL. 2 (EP)	15
64	London RE-B 1423	KENTUCKY COLONEL VOL. 3 (EP)	15

JIMMIE SKINNER/GEORGE JONES
59	Mercury ZEP 10012	COUNTRY AND WESTERN (EP, 2 tracks each)	45

SKI PATROL
80	Clever Metal VIN 1	Everything Is Temporary/Silent Screams (p/s)	10
80	Malicious Damage MD 2	Agent Orange/Driving (p/s, with insert)	12
81	Malicious Damage MD 3	Cut/Faith In Transition (p/s)	10

(see also Wall)

SKIP & FLIP
59	Top Rank JAR 156	It Was I/Lunch Hour (78 rpm = £22)	10
59	Top Rank JAR 248	Fancy Nancy/It Could Be	15
60	Top Rank JAR 358	Cherry Pie/(I'll Quit) Cryin' Over You	10

(see also Gary Paxton, Skip Battin, Hollywood Argyles)

SKIP BIFFERTY
67	RCA Victor RCA 1621	On Love/Cover Girl	35
67	RCA Victor RCA 1648	Happy Land/Reason To Live	35
68	RCA Victor RCA 1720	Man In Black/Mr. Money Man	50
68	RCA Victor RD/SF 7941	SKIP BIFFERTY (LP, black label, later orange)	90/45

(see also Chosen Few, Heavy Jelly, Griffin, Graham Bell, Arc, Bell & Arc, Every Which Way, Loving Awareness)

SKITZ
98	Ronin RDP8	Fingerprints Of The Gods (12")	12

SKREWDRIVER
77	Chiswick S 11	You're So Dumb/Better Off Crazy (orange or green p/s)	45
77	Chiswick NS 18	Anti-Social/19th Nervous Breakdown (p/s)	30
78	Chiswick NS 28	Streetfight/Unbeliever (unissued, Trident label)	300
80	TJM TJM 4	Built Up, Knocked Down/A Case Of Pride/Breakout (p/s)	25
82	Skrewdriver SKREW 1T	BACK WITH A BANG (12", p/s)	40
83	White Noise WN 1	White Power/Smash The I.R.A./Shove The Dove (p/s)	45
83	White Noise WN 2	Voice Of Britain/Sick Society (p/s)	35
77	Chiswick CH 3	ALL SKREWED UP (mini-LP, 12-track, 45rpm, 3 different colour sleeves)	50
77	Chiswick WIK 3	ALL SKREWED UP (LP, 15-track, 33rpm, unissued in U.K.; German-only)	100

SKROTEEZ
82	Skroteez SPILL 1	OVERSPILL (EP)	20

SKULLFLOWER
86	Broken Flag BF V9	BIRTHDEATH (12" EP)	30
89	Shock SX 001	(I Live) In The Bottomless Pit/Bo Diddley's Shitpump (foldaround p/s in poly bag, 500 only, 75 copies in 'burns victim' sleeve)	20/12
90	Toe Jam	Rotten Sun/Spook Rise (p/s, numbered, 500 only)	8
92	Dying Artefact DE 002	Bad Alchemy/Blues For H.M. (p/s in poly bag, numbered, 500 only)	8
94	Freak Records RR 001	White Fang 2/Glassy Essence (wraparound sleeve, stamped label)	7
89	Shock SX 008	XAMAN (LP)	12
89	Broken Flag BFV 10	FORM DESTROYER (LP)	20

(see also Ramleh)

SKULLS
89	Snake Skin SS 001	Graveyard Signal/Idols And Dolls (p/s, 300 only)	10

SKULLSNAPS
73	GSF GSZ 7	My Hang Up Is You/It's A New Day	40

SKUNKS
78	Eel Pie EPS 001	Good From The Bad/Back Street Fightin' (2,000 only, die-cut 'swirl' sleeve)	12

(see also Craze, Hard Corps)

SKY
68	United Artists UP 2234	Air-O-Plane Ride/Weather Forecast	5
69	Decca F 12971	On Our Way/The Singer Is Singing His Song	5

(see also Knack)

SKY
71	RCA RCA 2070	Goodie Two Shoes/Make It On Time (as U.S. Sky)	5
71	RCA SF 8168	DON'T HOLD BACK (LP, as U.S. Sky)	12

PATRICK SKY
65	Vanguard VSD 79179	PATRICK SKY (LP)	20
70	Vanguard SVRL 19054	A HARVEST OF GENTLE CLANG (LP)	20

SKYBIRD
74	Holyground HGS 118	SUMMER OF '73 (LP, 250 copies only)	60

SKY BLUES
67	Centaur CPC 1003	PLAYERS AT EASE: COVENTRY CITY (LP)	12

SKYLINERS
59	London HLB 8829	Since I Don't Have You/One Night, One Night (78 rpm = £70+)	225
59	London HLU 8924	This I Swear/Tomorrow (78 rpm = £70+)	80
59	London HLU 8971	It Happened Today/Lonely Way (78 rpm = £80+)	75
60	Polydor NH 66951	Pennies From Heaven/I'll Be Seeing You	15
61	Pye International 7N 25091	I'll Close My Eyes/The Door Is Still Open	18

SKYSOUNDS
66	Anglo TPMA 101/102	Two Timer/No Matter Where I Wander (private pressing)	5

FREDDIE SLACK (& Orchestra)
50	Capitol 13340	Whatever Happened To Ol' Jack?/Is I Gotta Practice, Ma? (78)	8
50	Capitol 13379	Be-Bop Boogie/On The Road To Mandolin (78)	7
51	Capitol LC 6529	FREDDIE SLACK'S BOOGIE WOOGIE (10" LP)	35

(see also Ella Mae Morse & Freddie Slack)

SLACK ALICE
74	Fontana 6007 038	Motorcycle/Ridin' The Wind	5
74	Philips 6308 214	SLACK ALICE (LP)	18

(see also Sandra Alfred, Sandra Barry)

SLADE
SINGLES
69	Fontana TF 1056	Wild Winds Are Blowing/One Way Hotel (credited to *The* Slade)	150
70	Fontana TF 1079	Shape Of Things To Come/C'mon C'mon	150
70	Polydor 2058 054	Know Who You Are/Dapple Rose	150
71	Polydor 2058 112	Get Down With It/Do You Want Me/The Gospel According To Rasputin (with writing credit: Holder/Hill/Lea/Powell/Penniman; some copies repressed as "Get Down And Get With It")	8
72	Polydor 2058 195	Look What You Dun/Candidate	7
72	Polydor 2058 231	Tak Me Bak 'Ome/Wonderin'	7
73	Polydor 2058 377	Skweeze Me Pleeze Me/Kill 'Em At The Hot Club Tonite	6
73	Polydor 2058 407	My Friend Stan/My Town	6
74	Polydor 2058 453	Everyday/Good Time Gals	6
74	Polydor 2058 453	Everyday/Good Time Gals (mispressed with Hollies' "The Air That I Breathe" on A-side)	6
75	Polydor 2058 547	How Does It Feel?/So Far So Good (p/s)	8
75	Polydor 2058 663	In For A Penny/Can You Just Imagine (some in p/s)	8/6
76	Polydor 2058 716	Nobody's Fool/L.A. Jinx	6
77	Barn 2014 105	Gypsy Roadhog/Forest Full Of Needles	7
77	Barn 2014 106	Burning In The Heat Of Love/Ready Steady Kids	18
77	Barn 2014 114	My Baby Left Me; That's Alright/O.H.M.S. (p/s)	6
78	Barn 2014 121	Give Us A Goal/Daddio	8
78	Barn 2014 127	Rock'n'Roll Bolero/It's Alright By Me	15
79	Barn BARN 002	Ginny Ginny/Dizzy Mama (yellow vinyl only, some with sticker)	10/8
79	Barn BARN 010	Sign Of The Times/Not Tonight Josephine	15
79	Barn BARN 011	Okey Cokey/My Baby's Got It	10
80	RSO RSO 051	Okey Cokey/My Baby's Got It (withdrawn reissue, existence unconfirmed)	
80	S.O.T.B. SUPER 45 3	SIX OF THE BEST — NIGHT STARVATION (12" EP, die-cut sleeve)	15
80	Cheapskate CHEAP 5	ALIVE AT READING '80 (EP, die-cut sleeve)	7
80	Cheapskate CHEAP 11	Merry Xmas Everybody/Okey Cokey/Get Down And Get With It (as Slade & Reading Choir, some in die-cut p/s)	8/5
80	Polydor 2058 422	Merry Xmas Everybody/Don't Blame Me (reissue, green background, 'holly leaf' design, colour group photo p/s)	5
81	Cheapskate CHEAP 16	We'll Bring The House Down/Hold On To Your Hats (p/s)	7
81	Cheapskate CHEAP 21	Wheels Ain't Comin' Down/Not Tonight Josephine (p/s)	7
81	Cheapskate CHEAP 24	Knuckle Sandwich Nancy/I'm Mad (p/s)	10
81	RCA	Tak Me Bak 'Ome/Gudbuy T'Jane) (12" EP, p/s)	10
82	RCA RCA 191	Ruby Red/Funk Punk And Junk (p/s)	10
82	RCA RCAD 191	Ruby Red/Funk Punk And Junk//Rock And Roll Preacher (live)/ Take Me Bak 'Ome (live) (double pack, gatefold p/s)	5
82	RCA RCA 291	(And Now The Waltz) C'est La Vie/Merry Xmas Everybody (p/s)	5
82	Speed SPEED 201	Okey Cokey/Get Down And Get With It (no p/s)	8
82	Speed SPEEDP 201	Okey Cokey/Get Down And Get With It (picture disc)	5
83	RCA RCA 373	My Oh My/Merry Xmas Everybody (live)/Keep Your Hands Off My Power Supply (3-track edition, p/s)	7
83	RCA RCA 373	My Oh My/Merry Xmas Everybody (live)/Keep Your Hands Off My Power Supply (12", p/s)	8
83	RCA RCA 385	Run Runaway/Two Track Stereo One Track Mind (p/s)	6
84	RCA RCAT 455	All Join Hands/My Oh My/Here's To... (The New Year)/ Merry Xmas (Live & Kickin') (12", stickered p/s)	8
85	RCA PB 40027	Myzterious Mizster Jones/Mama Nature Is A Rocker (p/s)	7
85	RCA PB 40027	Myzterious Mizster Jones/Mama Nature Is A Rocker (picture disc, PVC sleeve)	10
85	RCA PT 40028	Myzterious Mizster Jones (Extended Version)/Mama Nature Is A Rocker/ My Oh My (Piano And Vocal Version) (12", p/s)	8
85	Polydor POSPX 780	Merry Xmas Everybody/Don't Blame Me (12", p/s)	12

85	RCA PB 40449/PB 40549	Do You Believe In Miracles/My Oh My (Swing Version)//Santa Claus Is Coming To Town/Auld Lang Syne/You'll Never Walk Alone (double pack, gatefold PVC sleeve, 2nd 45 without p/s)	30
85	RCA PT 40450D (PT 40450/PT 40550)	Do You Believe In Miracles/My Oh My (Swing Version)/Time To Rock/ Santa Claus Is Coming To Town/Auld Lang Syne/You'll Never Walk Alone (12", 'Slade Xmas' double pack, separate sleeves in gatefold PVC cover)	20
87	RCA PB 41147D	Still The Same/Gotta Go Home//The Roaring Silence/Don't Talk To Me About Love (21st anniversary double pack, gatefold p/s)	10
88	Cheapskate BOYZ 3	Let's Dance (1988 Remix)/Standing On The Corner (p/s)	7
88	Counterpoint CDEP 12 C	How Does It Feel/Far Far Away//(WIZZARD: 2 tracks) (CD)	10
80s	Polydor 2058 422	Merry Xmas Everybody/Don't Blame Me (export p/s from various artist box set, green background, 4 individual photos)	25
80s	SLADE 1	An Interview With Slade (picture disc, 2,000 only, PVC sleeve)	10
91	Polydor PZ 189	Universe/Red Hot/Gypsy Roadhog/Merry Xmas Everybody (12", stickered p/s)	8
81	Polydor POSP 399	CUM ON FEEL THE NOIZE (EP)	6
81	Polydor POSPX 399	CUM ON FEEL THE NOIZE (Cum On Feel The Noize/Coz I Luv You/Tak Me Back 'Ome/Gudbye T'Jane)	6

FLEXIDISCS

72	Polydor/Sound For Industry SFI 122	The Whole World's Going Crazee/MIKE HUGG: Bonnie Charlie (33rpm free with *Music Scene* magazine)	18/8
73	Lyntone LYN 2645	Slade Talk To *Melanie* Readers (with *Melanie* magazine)	15/8
74	Lyntone LYN 2797	Slade exclusive to all *19* readers (with *19* magazine)	15/8
75	Lyntone LYN 3156/7	Far Far Away/Thanks For The Memory (with Smith's Crisps offer)	8
75	Fan Club LYN 2645/2797	Slade talk to *Melanie* readers/Slade talk to *19* readers	10

PROMOS etc.

72	Polydor 2814 008	Hear Me Calling/Get Down With It (33rpm sampler for "Slade Alive", 500 only)	125
74	Polydor 2058 492	The Bangin' Man/She Did It To Me (export p/s)	25
75	Polydor 2058 585	Thanks For The Memory (with altered lyrics)/Raining In My Champagne	25
77	Barn 2014 105	Gypsy Roadhog/Forest Full Of Needles (mono, DJ copy)	25
80	S.O.T.B. SUPER 3	Night Starvation/When I'm Dancing I Ain't Fightin'	45

ALBUMS

70	Polydor 2383 026	PLAY IT LOUD (LP)	15
72	Polydor 2383 101	SLADE ALIVE (LP, gatefold sleeve)	12
73	Polydor 2383 261	OLD NEW BORROWED AND BLUE (LP, gatefold sleeve)	12
73	Polydor 2442 119	SLADEST (LP)	12
74	Polydor 2442 126	SLADE IN FLAME (LP, gatefold sleeve)	12
76	Polydor 2383 377	NOBODY'S FOOLS (LP, with inner sleeve)	12
77	Barn 2314 103	WHATEVER HAPPENED TO SLADE (LP, with lyric sheet)	20
78	Barn 2314 106	SLADE ALIVE VOLUME 2 (LP)	20
79	Barn NARB 003	RETURN TO BASE (LP)	30

(see also Ambrose Slade, Steve Brett, 'N Betweens, Vendors, Dummies, Jimmy Lea, Gary Holton, China Dolls, Clout, Gang Of Angels, Metal Gurus)

PRENTIS SLADE
61	Parlophone R 4850	I Can Tell/Looking For A Friend	6

SLADE BROTHERS
66	Pye 7N 17080	Peace In My Mind/Life's Great Race	70

SLAM CREEPERS
68	Olga OLE 009	Saturday/Hold It Baby	12
73	Sonet SON 2003	We Are Happy People/Yansbro Memories	5

SLANES
65	Blue Beat BB 300	It Takes Time/LIGES: Have Mercy Baby (B-side actually by Frank Cosmo)	20

IVOR SLANEY ORCHESTRA
64	HMV POP 1347	High Wire/Sacramento	8
66	Columbia DB 8020	Long Weekend/Eleven Up (as Slaney Strings)	8

SLAPP HAPPY
74	Virgin VS 105	Casablanca Moon/Slow Moon's Rose	12
75	Virgin VS 124	Johnny's Dead/Mr. Rainbow (p/s)	12
83	Half Cat HC 001	Everybody's Slimmin' (Even Men And Women!)/Blue-Eyed Villain (p/s)	12
72	Polydor 2310 204	SORT OF (LP, with insert)	125
74	Virgin V 2014	SLAPP HAPPY (LP)	18
74	Virgin V 2024	DESPERATE STRAIGHTS (LP, with Henry Cow)	18
86	Recommended RRS 5	SORT OF (LP, reissue)	15

(see also Henry Cow, Peter Blegvad, Anthony Moore, Art Bears)

SLAUGHTER (& THE DOGS)
77	Rabid TOSH 101	Cranked Up Really High/The Bitch (p/s, blue, later cream plastic labels)	12
77	Rabid TOSH 101	Cranked Up Really High/The Bitch (p/s, repressings with b&w paper label)	10
77	Decca FR 13723	Where Have All The Boot Boys Gone/You're A Bore (paper label)	8
77	Decca LF 13723	Where Have All The Boot Boys Gone/You're A Bore (12", p/s, 10,000 only)	12
77	Decca FR 13743	Dame To Blame/Johnny T	12
78	Decca F 13758	Quick Joey Small/Come On Back (promo with self sealing 'spit proof' sticker on PVC sleeve)	75
78	Decca FR 13758	Quick Joey Small/Come On Back (with Mick Ronson)	6
79	TJM TJM 3	It's Alright/Edgar Allen Poe/Twist & Turn/UFO (12", p/s)	12
79	DJM DJS 10927	You're Ready Now/Runaway (p/s)	6
80	Decca FR	Where Have All The Boot Boys Gone (reissue, p/s)	10
80	DJM DJS 10936	East Side Of Town/One By One (p/s, as Slaughter)	6
80	DJM DJS 10945	I'm The One/What's Wrong Boy? (live)/Hell In New York (p/s, as Slaughter)	5
82	Thrush THRUSH 1	HALF ALIVE (12" EP)	10
88	Damaged Goods FNARR 1	Where Have All The Boot Boys Gone/You're A Bore/Johnny T. (p/s, 1,000 only: 500 on green vinyl, 500 on red vinyl)	each 15
78	Decca SKL 5292	DO IT DOG STYLE (LP)	30

78	Rabid HAT 23	LIVE SLAUGHTER RABID DOGS (LP, plain white sleeve with large sticker)	12
80	DJM DJF 20566	BITE BACK (LP, as Slaughter)	12
89	Damaged Goods FNARRLP 2	DO IT DOG STYLE (LP, reissue, 1,000-only, multi-coloured vinyl, numbered, with 2 multi-coloured stickers)	12

(see also Studio Sweethearts, Ed Banger)

SLAUGHTER JOE
| 85 | Creation CRE 019 | I'll Follow You Down/Napalm Girl (foldaround p/s in poly bag) | 5 |
| 87 | Kaleidoscope S. KLSLP 003 | ALL AROUND MY HOBBY HORSE'S HEAD (LP) | 12 |

(see also Television Personalities, Missing Scientists)

SLAVE
| 84 | Cotillion BT 6955 | Just A Touch Of Love/Wait For Me (12") | 10 |
| 77 | Cotillion K 50358 | SLAVE (LP) | 15 |

MARTIN SLAVIN & HIS GANG
| 60 | Oriole CB 1587 | Rock-A-Charleston/The Charleston's Gonna Rock The Hop | 8 |

(see also Martinas & His Music)

SLAYER
84	Roadrunner RR 2444 2	HAUNTING THE CHAPEL (12" EP)	15
87	London LON 133	Criminally Insane/Aggressive Perfector (Remix) ('cross' p/s, some on red vinyl with patch)	30
87	London LONX 133	Criminally Insane/Postmortem/Aggressive Perfector (Remix) (12", red vinyl, no p/s)	25
89	Roadrunner RR 2444 2	Haunting The Chapel/Chemical Warfare/Captor Of Sin (CD, reissue)	15
87	Enigma 720151	LIVE UNDEAD (LP, picture disc)	20
87	London LONPP 34	REIGN IN BLOOD (LP, picture disc)	20
03	Universal B 00001519-02	SOUNDTRACK TO THE APOCALYPSE (4-CD set in 'ammo box' with backstage laminate, flag, bonus DVD in 'blood pack' and booklet)	40
03	Universal B 00001619-02	SOUNDTRACK TO THE APOCALYPSE (3-CD/1-DVD set in triple gatefold sleeve)	25

F. SLEDGE
| 67 | Blue Beat BB 386 | Red Eye Girl/Try To Love Again (actually by "Go On Girl"/"Giving You A Try Girl" by Freddie McKay & Buster's Group) | 40 |

PERCY SLEDGE
66	Atlantic 584 001	When A Man Loves A Woman/Love Me Like You Mean It	8
66	Atlantic 584 034	Warm And Tender Love/Sugar Puddin'	8
66	Atlantic 584 055	Heart Of A Child/My Adorable One	15
67	Atlantic 584 071	It Tears Me Up/Oh, How Happy	10
67	Atlantic 584 080	Baby, Help Me/You've Lost That Something Wonderful	15
67	Atlantic 584 108	Out Of Left Field/It Can't Be Stopped	8
67	Atlantic 584 140	Pledging My Love/You Don't Miss Your Water	8
68	Atlantic 584 177	Take Time To Know Her/It's All Wrong But It's Alright	8
68	Atlantic 584 225	Come Softly To Me/You're All Around Me	8
69	Atlantic 584 264	Any Day Now/The Angels Listened In	10
69	Atlantic 584 286	Kind Woman/Woman Of The Night	6
69	Atlantic 584 300	True Love Travels On A Gravel Road/Faithful And True	6
72	Atlantic K 10144	Rainbow Road/Standing on The Mountain	8
72	Atlantic K 10165	Baby, Help Me/Warm And Tender Love/Take Time To Know Her	8
74	Capricorn 2089 009	I'll Be Your Everything/Walkin' In The Sun	6
67	Atlantic 587/588 048	WARM AND TENDER SOUL (LP)	30
67	Atlantic 587/588 081	THE PERCY SLEDGE WAY (LP)	25
68	Atlantic 587/588 105	WHEN A MAN LOVES A WOMAN (LP)	28
69	Atlantic 587/588 153	THE BEST OF PERCY SLEDGE (LP)	15

SLEDGEHAMMER
79	Slammer SRTS79CUS 395	Sledgehammer/Feel Good (some with p/s)	20/10
80	Slammer CELL 2	Living In Dreams/Fantasia (p/s)	10
80s	Slammer MRSB 2	In The Middle Of The Night	10
80	Valiant STRONG 1	Sledgehammer/Feel Good (p/s, reissue)	10
80	Valiant ROUND 2	Sledgehammer/Feel Good (p/s, 2nd reissue)	6
85	Illuminated ILL 33	In The Queue/Oxford City (shaped picture disc)	25
83	Illuminated JAMS 32	BLOOD ON THEIR HANDS (LP, some with bonus 12")	30/25

SLEEPWALKERS
| 59 | Parlophone R 4580 | Sleep Walk/Golden Mile | 15 |

SLEEPY
| 68 | CBS 3592 | Love's Immortal Fire/Is It Really The Same | 25 |
| 68 | CBS 3838 | Rosie Can't Fly/Mrs. Bailey's Barbecue And Grill | 28 |

(see also Grapefruit, Fynn McCool)

SLENDER PLENTY
| 67 | Polydor BM 56189 | Silver Tree Top School For Boys/I've Lost A Friend And Found A Lover | 22 |

SLENDER THREAD
| 80 | Rock MHMS 193 | I See The Light/Where Is The Beat | 80 |

JIMI SLEVIN
| 82 | Claddagh CCF 7 | FREEFLIGHT (LP) | 25 |

(see also Peggy's Leg)

RICKY SLICK
| 72 | Dynamic DYN 449 | Family Man/Family Man (Version) | 5 |

SLICKERS
68	Blue Cat BS 133	Wala Wala/LESTER STERLING: Super Special	25
68	Blue Cat BS 134	Nana (actually by George Dekker)/MARTIN RILEY: I May Never See My Baby Anymore	25
69	Blue Cat BS 154	Frying Pan/RARFIELD WILLIAMS: Code It	35

69	Amalgamated AMG 852	Man Beware/Matty Matty	10
69	Amalgamated AMG 866	Money Reaper/Man Beware	10
70	Bullet BU 449	Coolie Girl/BIGGIE: Bawling Baby	6
70	Trojan TR 7718	Run Fattie/Hoola Bulla (song actually "Bulla Man")	8
71	G.G. GG 4524	Oh My Baby/WINSTON WRIGHT: Change Of Love (Version)	6
71	Punch PH 59	Johnny Too Bad/Johnny Too Bad (Version)	6
71	Dynamic DYN 406	Johnny Too Bad/ROLAND ALFONSO: Saucy Horde (act. by Roland Alphonso)	8
71	Dynamic DYN 419	You Can't Win/Don't Fight The Law	6
72	Explosion EX 2061	Bounce Me Johnny/Bounce Me (Version) (actually "Say You")	6

(see also G.G. Allstars, Clancy Eccles, Viceroys)

SLIM & FREEDOM SINGERS
| 70 | Banana BA 304 | Do Dang Do (actually by Leroy Sibbles)/ | |
| | | JACKIE MITTOO & SOUND DIMENSION: Hot Milk | 25 |

SLIME
| 78 | Toadstool GOOD 1 | Controversial/Loony (p/s) | 8 |

(see also Johnny Moped)

SLIPKNOT
| 00 | Roadrunner RR 8655-6 | SLIPKNOT (LP, picture disc) | 15 |

SLITS
79	Island WIP 6505	Typical Girls/I Heard It Through The Grapevine (p/s)	10
79	Island 12 WIP 6505	Typical Girls (Brink Style)/I Heard It Through The Grapevine/	
		Liebe And Romanze (12", p/s)	10
80	Rough Trade RT 039/Y Y 1	In The Beginning There Was Rhythm/POP GROUP:	
		Where There's A Will There's A Way (p/s)	5
79	Island ILPS 9573	CUT (LP, with inner sleeve)	18
80	Rough Trade/Y Y 3	BOOTLEG RETROSPECTIVE (LP, plain sleeve)	30
81	CBS 85269	THE RETURN OF THE GIANT SLITS (LP, some with bonus 45	
		"American Radio Interview"/"Face Dub" [XPS 125])	22/18
80	CBS	Man Next Door/ Same Human (12", p/s)	15
81	CBS A1498	Earthbeat Begin Again Rhythm (7", p/s)	8

(see also Raincoats)

P.F. SLOAN
65	RCA Victor RCA 1482	Sins Of The Family/This Mornin'	15
67	RCA Victor RCA 1623	Sunflower Sunflower/The Man Behind The Red Balloon	10
72	Epic EPC 65179	RAISED ON RECORDS (LP)	22
80s	Big Beat WIK 73	SONGS OF OTHER TIMES (LP, some tracks as Grass Roots)	25

(see also Grass Roots, Fantastic Baggys, Willie & Wheels)

SAMMI SLOAN
| 68 | Columbia DB 8480 | Yes I Would/Be His Girl | 20 |

SLOWBONE
| 74 | Rare Earth RES 119 | Get What You're Given/Oh Man | 6 |

(see also Roll Ups)

SLOWBURNER
| 89 | Burn BURN LP 001 | AN EMOTIONAL BUSINESS (LP) | 12 |

SLR CREW
| 88 | SLR XPR1536 | Bass Drum/Life's A Bitch (12") | 35 |

SL TROOPERS
88	Global Rhythm GR001	Debut (Unarmed And Dangerous) (12")	30
89	Music Of Life NOTE32	Movement (12")	14
90	Kold Sweat KS101	Knowledge/Put Your Brain In Gear (12")	8
91	Kold Sweat KSEP201	SYSTEMATIC TERROR (EP)	10

SLUSH
| 78 | Ember EMB 5367 | White Christmas/Rich Man (no p/s) | 70 |

SLY & THE FAMILY STONE
(see under Sly [& Family] Stone)

SMACK
| 78 | Asprin 001 | Edward Fox/Came Again (p/s, original issue) | 5 |

JOAN SMALL
56	Parlophone MSP 6219	Change Of Heart/Come Next Spring	6
56	Parlophone R 4211	Love Is A Stranger/Autumn Concerto	6
57	Parlophone R 4269	Gonna Get Along Without You Now/You Can't Say I Love You To A	
		Rock & Roll Tune (78 rpm = £6)	15
58	Parlophone R 4431	Afraid/How Many Times (Can I Fall In Love) (78 rpm = £10)	6
60	Parlophone R 4622	The Big Hurt/Ask Me To Go Steady	10

KAREN SMALL
| 66 | Vocalion V 9281 | To Get You Back Again/That's Why I Cry | 30 |

MILLIE SMALL
(see under Millie)

SMALL FACES
SINGLES
65	Decca F 12208	Whatcha Gonna Do About It?/What's A Matter, Baby?	15
65	Decca F 12276	I've Got Mine/It's Too Late	25
66	Decca F 12317	Sha-La-La-La-Lee/Grow Your Own	10
66	Decca F 12393	Hey Girl/Almost Grown	15
66	Decca F 12470	All Or Nothing/Understanding (curved or boxed Decca logo)	12
66	Decca F 12500	My Mind's Eye (alternate demo mix, matrix no. ends T1-1C)/	
		I Can't Dance With You (withdrawn)	35

66	Decca F 12500	My Mind's Eye (matrix no. ends T2-1C)/I Can't Dance With You	8
67	Decca F 12565	I Can't Make It/Just Passing.	20
67	Decca F 12619	Patterns/E Too D (some with export p/s).	140/70
67	Immediate AS 1	Small Faces (1-sided sampler for "Small Faces", promo only)	100
67	Immediate IM 050	Here Comes The Nice/Talk To You	10
67	Immediate IM 057	Itchycoo Park/I'm Only Dreaming	10
67	Immediate IM 062	Tin Soldier/I Feel Much Better (some in p/s).	70/15
68	Immediate IM 064	Lazy Sunday/Rollin' Over	10
68	Immediate IM 069	The Universal/Donkey Rides, A Penny A Glass (lilac label, later pink)	12/8
69	Immediate IM 077	Afterglow (Of Your Love)/Wham Bam, Thank You Mam (demos [& perhaps some copies] have demo version of B-side).	60/10
75	Immediate IM 064	Lazy Sunday/Rollin' Over (p/s, reissue with white label)	8
80	Virgin VS 367	Tin Soldier/Tin Soldier (live)/Rene.	6
86	Archive 4 TOF 103	Itchycoo Park/Lazy Sunday/Sha-La-La-La-Lee/Here Comes The Nice (12", p/s)	10
88	Castle Comms. Special Edition CD 3-9	THE SMALL FACES (Itchycoo Park/Lazy Sunday/All Or Nothing (live)/ Autumn Stone) (3" CD EP, with adaptor, 5" case, 5,000 only)	10

LPs

66	Decca LK 4790	SMALL FACES (original red label)	140
67	Decca LK 4879	FROM THE BEGINNING (original red label)	150
67	Immediate IMLP/IMSP 008	SMALL FACES (mono/stereo).	160/170
68	Immediate IMLP/IMSP 012	OGDENS' NUT GONE FLAKE (lilac label, circular foldout sleeve, mono/stereo).	130/100
68	Immediate IMLP/IMSP 012	OGDENS' NUT GONE FLAKE (pink label, circular foldout sleeve, m/s).	90/60
69	Decca LK 4790	SMALL FACES (boxed Decca label)	40
69	Decca LK 4879	FROM THE BEGINNING (boxed Decca label).	20
69	Immediate IMLP/IMSP 022	IN MEMORIAM (export issue [German copies more common, £60]).	150
69	Immediate IMAL 01/02	THE AUTUMN STONE (2-LP, gatefold sleeve)	40
75	Immediate/NEMS IML 1001	OGDENS' NUT GONE FLAKE (reissue, round sleeve, white label)	20
76	NEMS AML 1008	MAGIC MOMENTS.	15
77	Immediate/NEMS IML 2001	OGDENS' NUT GONE FLAKE (reissue, square sleeve).	15
77	Decca ROOTS 5	ROCK ROOTS — THE DECCA SINGLES	15
78	Charly CR 300005	OGDENS' NUT GONE FLAKE (export release, square sleeve).	15
78	Charly CR 300025	THE SMALL FACES — LIVE U.K. 1969 (export release)	15
80	Virgin/Immediate V 2166	SMALL FACES: BIG HITS (gatefold sleeve)	15
80	Virgin/Immediate V 2178	FOR YOUR DELIGHT, THE DARLINGS OF WAPPING WHARF LAUNDERETTE	25
97	Castle CLA 016	OGDENS' NUT GONE FLAKE (reissue, round sleeve with obi)	15
91	Castle CLACT 016	OGDENS' NUT GONE FLAKE (CD, in round tin box with beer mats & booklet)	60

(see also Faces, Steve Marriott, Humble Pie, Jimmy Winston & His Reflections, Winston's Fumbs, Billy Nicholls, Kenney Jones)

SMALL ADS

81	Bronze BRO 115	Small Ads/Motorway Madness (p/s)	7
81	Bronze BRO 125	HP Man/Radio Love (p/s)	7
81	Bronze BRO 135	Friday Nite Cowboy/I Wanna Fly Concorde (p/s).	7

SMALL HOURS

80	Automatic K 17708	The Kid/Business In Town/Midnight To Six/End Of The Night (p/s)	30
80	Automatic K 17708X	The Kid/Business In Town/Midnight To Six/End Of The Night (10", p/s).	20

SMALL WORLD

81	Whaam! WHAAM 003	Love Is Dead/Liberty (p/s)	100
83	Valid VC 001	First Impressions/Stupidity Street/Tomorrow Never Comes (p/s)	100

SMART

82	Complex CPX 001	This Time (p/s).	35

SMART ALEC

79	B&C BCS 20	Scooter Boys/Soho (p/s)	100

LEROY SMART

77	Conflict COND 2001	Jahovia/Dub (12")	20
77	Conflict COLPD 2001	BALLISTIC AFFAIR (LP)	20
77	Dread Hot DHLP 1001	DREAD HOT IN AFRICA (LP)	30
78	Dread Hot DHLP 1004	IMPRESSIONS (LP)	20
78	Burning Sounds BS 1009	PROPAGANDA (LP).	25

LEROY SMART & BIG YOUTH

79	Dub Vendor DVD 01	Pride And Ambition (original style)/'78 Style (12")	60+

SMASHING PUMPKINS

91	Hut	I Am One (1-sided blue flexidisc)	80
91	Caroline SMASH 1	Siva/Rhinoceros (no p/s, promo only)	80
91	Hut HUTT 6	Siva/Window Paine (12", p/s, 5,000)	30
92	Hut HUTT 10	LULL EP (Rhinoceros/Blue/Slunk/Bye June [Demo]) (12", p/s)	10
92	Hut CDHUT 10	LULL EP (Rhinoceros/Blue/Slunk/Bye June [Demo]) (CD)	8
92	Hut HUTC 017	PEEL SESSIONS: Siva/A Girl Named Sandoz/Smiley (cassette EP)	5
92	Hut HUTT 017	PEEL SESSIONS: Siva/A Girl Named Sandoz/Smiley (12" EP, p/s)	12
92	Hut HUTEN 018	I Am One/Terrapin (live)/Bullet Train To Osaka (10", p/s, 6,000 only)	20
92	Hut HUTT 18	I Am One/Plume/Starla (12", p/s)	12
93	Sup Pop SP 90	Tristessa/La Dolly Vita/Honeyspider (12", 5,000 only)	35
93	Hut HUT 31	Cherub Rock/Purr Snickety (p/s, clear vinyl, numbered, 5,000 only)	20
93	Hut HUTT 31	Cherub Rock/Pissant/French Movie Theme/(Star Spangled Banner) (12", p/s, last track uncredited)	8
93	Hut HUT 37	Today/Apathy's Last Kiss (p/s, red vinyl, 5,000 only)	10
93	Hut HUTT 37	Today/Hello Kitty Kat/Obscured (12", p/s)	8
94	Hut HUT 43	Smile (Disarm/Siamese Dream) (stickered p/s, purple vinyl)	10
94	Hut HUTL 48	Rocket/Never Let Me Down (box set, salmon pink vinyl, 1,500 only)	40
93	Hut HUTTDJ 73	Zero (12", promo only)	12

94	Hut SPBOX 1	SIAMESE SINGLES (Rocket/Never Let Me Down//Cherub Rock/Purr Snickety/ Today/Apathy's Last Kiss/Smile [Disarm/Siamese Dream]) (4 x 7" box set, black vinyl, 6,000 only)	75
94	Hut HUTLPX 2	GISH (LP, with inner)	12
95	Hut HUTDLP 30	MELLON COLLIE AND THE INFINITE SADNESS (3 x LP, 12 page booklet, numbered)	60
96	Hut HUTLP 41	PISCES ISCARIOT (LP, yellow vinyl)	18
96	Hut	THE AEROPLANE FLIES HIGH (5 x CD single box set with handle, lock & booklet)	50

ROY SMECK
54	Brunswick LA 8649	SONGS OF THE RANGE (10" LP)	15

PHILIP LLOYD SMEE & DONATO CINICOLO III
71	Deroy PLS 1	DAS LUNE/SYNTHI-A (LP, private pressing, handmade sleeve, 2 copies only)	400

SMILEY
72	Philips 6006 206	Penelope/I Know What I Want	5

(see also Creation)

BRETT SMILEY
74	Anchor ANC 70	Va Va Va Voom/Space Age (p/s)	5

K. SMILEY
72	Pressure Beat PB 5514	Tipatone/Do It To Me	8

SMILIN' JOE
54	London HL 8106	A.B.C.'s Parts 1 & 2 (78)	100

SMIRKS
78	Besmirkly BZZ17	OK UK/Streets (p/s)	8

SMITH
69	Stateside-Dunhill SS 8028	Baby It's You/I Don't Believe	6
70	Stateside-Dunhill SS 8042	Take A Look Around/Mojalesky Ridge	6
70	Stateside-Dunhill SS 8055	What Am I Gonna Do/Born In Boston	6
69	Stateside-Dunhill SSL 5016	A GROUP CALLED SMITH (LP)	15
70	Stateside-Dunhill SSL 5031	MINUS-PLUS (LP)	15

SMITH (U.K.)
81	Rarn RARNS 1	Here Comes My Baby/Just Another Line/Too Late (p/s)	70

ADAM (Eric) SMITH
62	Island WI 057	I Wonder Why/My Prayer	20

ALEXANDER MURRAY SMITH & BLACK O'TOWN SYNCOPATORS
63	Decca F 11604	"Steptoe And Son" Theme/Ragtime Tuba	6

A.S.A.P. (Adrian Smith & Project)
89	EMI 12 EMPD 107	Silver And Gold/Blood Brothers (12", silver & gold vinyl)	10
90	EMI EMPD 131	Down The Wire (Crossed Line Mix)/When She's Gone (shaped picture disc)	7

(see also Iron Maiden, Urchin)

ARTHUR 'GUITAR BOOGIE' SMITH (& HIS CRACKERJACKS)
50	MGM MGM 254	Mule Train/ROY LEAR & BETTY SMITH: Dime A Dozen (78)	6
50	MGM MGM 329	Guitar Boogie/Be Bop Rag (78)	6
51	MGM MGM 363	Mandolin Boogie/The Memphis Blues (78)	8
52	MGM MGM 484	Alabama Jubilee/Fiddle-Faddle (78, with Crackerjacks)	8
52	MGM MGM 518	Guitar And Piano Boogie/Banjo Buster (78)	10
52	MGM MGM 555	Express Train Boogie/River Rag (78)	10
53	MGM SP 1008	Guitar Boogie/Be Bop Rag	30
53	MGM SP 1021	Five String Banjo Boogie/South (78 rpm, MGM 599 = £8)	18
53	MGM SP 1039	Express Train Boogie/River Rag	20
53	MGM MGM 630	Recitation Sonny Smith: In Memory Of Hank Williams/HANK WILLIAMS & HIS DRIFTING COWBOYS: I Saw The Light (78)	8
53	MGM MGM 660	Big Mountain Shuffle/KEN CURTIS: The Call Of The Faraway Hills (78)	6
53	MGM MGM 695	Three D Boogie/He Went That-A-Way (78)	6
54	MGM SP 1096	Oh, Baby Mine, I Get So Lonely/Outboard (78 rpm = £10)	18
54	MGM SP 1110	Redheaded Stranger/Texas Hop (78 rpm, MGM 779 = £10	20
54	MGM MGM 3011	Guitar Boogie/Boomerang (78)	10
55	MGM SP 1122	Hi Lo Boogie/Truck Stop Grill (78 rpm, MGM 805 = £10	5
54	MGM MGM-EP 510	ARTHUR 'GUITAR BOOGIE' SMITH AND HIS CRACKERJACKS (EP)	20
54	MGM MGM EPC 5	ARTHUR 'GUITAR BOOGIE' SMITH (EP, export issue)	20
59	MGM MGM-EP 695	ARTHUR 'GUITAR BOOGIE' SMITH AND HIS CRACKERJACKS (EP)	20
63	Stateside SE 1005	MISTER GUITAR (EP)	20
53	MGM MGM-D 111	FINGERS ON FIRE (10" LP)	28
54	MGM MGM-D 131	FOOLISH QUESTIONS (10" LP)	28

BARRY SMITH
74	People PEO 114	Hold On To It (Parts 1 & 2)	20

BEASLEY SMITH & HIS ORCHESTRA
56	London HLD 8235	Goodnight, Sweet Dreams/Parisian Rag	25
56	London HLD 8273	My Foolish Heart/Old Spinning Wheel	25

BESSIE SMITH
51	Columbia DB 2796	Empty Bed Blues (Parts 1 & 2) (78)	8
58	Philips BBE 12202	EMPRESS OF THE BLUES (EP)	18
59	Philips BBE 12231	EMPRESS OF THE BLUES NO. 2 (EP)	18
59	Philips BBE 12233	EMPRESS OF THE BLUES NO. 3 (EP)	18
60	Philips BBE 12360	BESSIE SMITH (EP)	15
55	Philips BBL 7019	THE BESSIE SMITH STORY VOLUME 1 (LP, with Louis Armstrong)	25
55	Philips BBL 7020	THE BESSIE SMITH STORY VOLUME 2 (LP)	25

MINT VALUE £

55	Philips BBL 7042	THE BESSIE SMITH STORY VOLUME 3 (LP)	25
55	Philips BBL 7049	THE BESSIE SMITH STORY VOLUME 4 (LP)	25
62	Philips BBL 7513	BESSIE'S BLUES 1923-1924 (LP)	30
66	CBS BPG 62377	THE BESSIE SMITH STORY VOLUME 1 (LP)	12
66	CBS BPG 62378	THE BESSIE SMITH STORY VOLUME 2 (LP)	12
66	CBS BPG 62379	THE BESSIE SMITH STORY VOLUME 3 (LP)	12
66	CBS BPG 62380	THE BESSIE SMITH STORY VOLUME 4 (LP)	12
71	CBS 66258	THE WORLD'S GREATEST BLUES SINGER (2-LP, some with booklet)	20/15
71	CBS 66262	ANY WOMAN'S BLUES (2-LP)	15
71	CBS 66273	EMPTY BED BLUES (2-LP)	15
72	CBS 66264	THE EMPRESS (2-LP)	15
73	CBS 67232	NOBODY'S BLUES BUT MINE (2-LP)	15

BETTY SMITH QUINTET

57	Tempo A 163	Sweet Georgia Brown/Little White Lies (78 rpm = £9)	20
58	Decca F 10986	Hand Jive/Bewitched (as Betty Smith Group) (78 rpm = £7)	8
58	Decca F 11031	Will The Angels Play Their Harps For Me/Betty's Blues (78 rpm = £7)	8
58	Decca F 11071	Begin The Beguine/Song Of The Boulevards (78 rpm = £10)	5
59	Decca F 11124	Song Of India/Stormy Weather (78 rpm = £12)	5
57	Tempo EXA 74	BETTY SMITH QUINTET (EP)	15
57	Decca DFE 6446	BETTY SMITH QUINTET (EP)	15

(see also Betty Smith Skiffle Group) (see Jeff Rowena)

BETTY SMITH SKIFFLE GROUP

57	Tempo A 162	There's A Blue Ridge Round My Heart, Virginia/Double Shuffle (78 rpm = £8)	15

(see also Betty Smith Quintet)

BUSTER SMITH

61	London Jazz LTZ-K 15206	THE LEGENDARY BUSTER SMITH (LP)	12

CARL SMITH

52	Columbia DB 3077	Let's Live A Little/Me And My Broken Heart (78)	6
53	Columbia DC 608	Our Honeymoon/Sing Her A Love Song (78, export issue)	6
56	Philips PB 572	Loose Talk/More Than Anything Else In The World (78)	7
59	Philips PB 943	Ten Thousand Drums/The Tall, Tall Gentlemen (78 rpm = £15)	10
60	Philips BBL 7437	THE CARL SMITH TOUCH (LP)	15

CLARA SMITH

69	VJM VLP 15	CLARA SMITH VOLUME 1 (LP)	15
69	VJM VLP 16	CLARA SMITH VOLUME 2 (LP)	15
69	VJM VLP 17	CLARA SMITH VOLUME 3 (LP)	15

CLARA SMITH & FLETCHER HENDERSON

61	Philips BBE 12491	BLUES BY CLARA SMITH 1926-1928 (EP)	15

(see also Fletcher Henderson)

CONNIE SMITH

66	RCA Victor RD 7785	CUTE AND COUNTRY (LP)	15
71	RCA LSA 3042	WHERE IS MY CASTLE (LP)	12
73	RCA LSA 3150	IT AIN'T LOVE (LP)	12

DAVE SMITH & ASTRONAUTS

67	C'mbia Blue Beat DB 104	A Lover Like You/Cup Of Love	12

DAVE SMITH & JUDY DINNING

83	Rubber RUB 043	WAITING FOR THE CHANGE (LP)	20

DICK SMITH BAND

79	Smile SR 012	Body Heat/Motorway Madness (p/s)	75
80	Hol-O-Gram HOL 001	Way Of The World/Giving The Game Away (some with p/s)	45/25

EDDIE SMITH

55	Parlophone MSP 6186	Silver Star Stomp/Stumbling (as Eddie Smith & Chiefs)	15
60	Top Rank JAR 285	Upturn/Border Beat (as Eddie Smith & Hornets)	25

EDGEWOOD SMITH & FABULOUS TAILFEATHERS

67	Sue WI 4037	Ain't That Lovin'/Yeah	45

EFFIE SMITH

66	Sue WI 4010	Dial That Telephone Parts 1 & 2	25

ELLIOTT SMITH

98	Domino RUG 074	Ballad Of Big Nothing/Some Song (p/s)	6
98	Dreamworks DRMS 22347	Waltz No. 2/Our Thing (p/s)	8
99	Dreamworks DRMS 7	Baby Britain/Waltz No. 1 (p/s)	6
98	Domino REWIGLP 001	ELLIOTT SMITH (LP)	50
98	Domino REWIGLP 002	ROMAN CANDLE (LP)	50
98	Domino REWIGLP	EITHER/OR (LP)	50

ELSON SMITH

61	Fontana H 291	Flip Flop/Are You Ready For That	25

ERNIE SMITH

71	Duke DU 119	Bend Down/Heaven Help Us All	6
71	Horse HOSS 6	Sunday Morning/One Three	5
73	London SHS 8442	ERNIE SMITH (LP)	12

ETHEL SMITH

55	Brunswick 05470	Hernando's Hideaway/Lemon Merengue	8

(LITTLE) GEORGE (HARMONICA) SMITH

65	Blue Horizon 45-1002	Blues In The Dark/Telephone Blues (as Little George Smith)	80
70	Blue Horizon 57-3170	Someday You're Gonna Learn/Before You Do Your Thing (as George Smith)	18
69	Liberty LBL/LBS 83218E	BLUES WITH FEELING — A TRIBUTE TO LITTLE WALTER (LP, with Chicago Blues Band)	45
70	Blue Horizon 7-63856	NO TIME TO JIVE (LP)	120
71	Deram SML 1082	ARKANSAS TRAP (LP)	60

(see also Bacon Fat)

GLORIA SMITH

59	London HLU 8903	Playmates/Don't Take Your Love From Me (78 rpm = £10)	15

GORDON SMITH

69	Blue Horizon 57-3156	Too Long/Funk Pedal	20
69	Blue Horizon 7-63211	LONG OVERDUE (LP)	75

(see also Kevin Coyne)

HAROLD SMITH'S MAJESTIC CHOIR

69	Chess CRS 8100	We Can All Walk A Little Bit Prouder/Why Am I Treated So Bad	8

HARVEY SMITH

75	Hankerchief Hanky 3	True Love/ End Of The World (p/s)	7

HUEY 'PIANO' SMITH & THE CLOWNS

58	Columbia DB 4138	Don't You Just Know It/High Blood Pressure (78 rpm = £40)	75
60	Top Rank JAR 282	Don't You Just Know Kokomo/FRANKIE FORD: Cheatin' Woman	25
62	Top Rank JAR 614	Pop-Eye/Scald-Dog (as Huey Smith)	10
65	Sue WI 364	If It Ain't One Thing It's Another/Tu-Ber-Cu-Lucas And The Sinus Blues	25
65	Sue WI 380	Rockin' Pneumonia And The Boogie Woogie Flu (Parts 1 & 2)	25
78	Chiswick NS 43	Rockin' Pneumonia And The Boogie Woogie Flu (unissued)	
65	Sue ILP 917	ROCKIN' PNEUMONIA AND THE BOOGIE WOOGIE FLU (LP, titled "Havin' A Good Time" on labels)	40

(see also Frankie Ford, Lee Allen, Bobby Marchan, Robert Parker)

HURRICANE SMITH

72	Columbia SCX 6510	DON'T LET IT DIE (LP)	15

IAN SMITH & INNER MIND

71	Bullet BU 490	Devil Woman/Nenn Street Rub	6

(see also Smithy All Stars)

JENNIE SMITH

59	Philips PB 924	Huggin' My Pillow (Sweet Side)/Huggin' My Pillow (Sweet Beat Side) (78 = £18)	5

JIMMY SMITH

SINGLES

62	HMV POP 1025	Walk On The Wild Side Parts 1 & 2	12
65	Verve VS 509	Hobo Flats Parts 1 & 2	7
65	Verve VS 521	Who's Afraid Of Virginia Woolf Parts 1 & 2	7
65	Verve VS 523	The Cat/Basin Street Blues	20
65	Verve VS 531	The Organ Grinder's Swing/I'll Close My Eyes	6
66	Verve VS 534	Slow Theme From "Where The Spies Are" Parts 1 & 2	6
66	Verve VS 536	Got My Mojo Working Parts 1 & 2	8
66	Verve VS 540	I'm Your Hoochie-Coochie Man Parts 1 & 2	7
67	Verve VS 551	Cat In A Tree Parts 1 & 2	8
67	Verve VS 562	Mickey Mouse Parts 1 & 2	8

EPs

64	Verve VEP 5008	WALK ON THE WILD SIDE	8
64	Verve VEP 5017	A COOL YULE WITH...	8
65	Verve VEP 5021	CREEPER	8
65	Verve VEP 5016	PLAYS THE BLUES	8
65	Verve VEP 5022	SWINGING WITH THE INCREDIBLE JIMMY SMITH	8

LPs

62	Verve CLP 1596/CSD 1462	BASHIN' THE UNPREDICTABLE (Verve label with HMV number)	15
63	Verve (S)VLP 9039	HOBO FLATS	15
64	Verve VLP 9057	ANY NUMBER CAN WIN	15
64	Verve VLP 9068	WHO'S AFRAID OF VIRGINIA WOOLF	15
64	Verve (S)VLP 9079	THE CAT	30
65	Verve (S)VLP 9093	MONSTER	20
66	Verve (S)VLP 9108	ORGAN GRINDER SWING	15
66	Liberty (S)VLP 9123	GOT MY MOJO WORKING	15
66	Verve (S)VLP 9142	HOOCHIE COOCHIE MAN	15
67	Verve (S)VLP 9159	PETER & THE WOLF	15
67	Verve (S)VLP 9160	THE DYNAMIC DUO (with Wes Montgomery)	15
67	Verve (S)VLP 9182	RESPECT	20
68	Verve (S)VLP 9218	STAY LOOSE	15
68	Verve (S)VLP 9227	LIVIN' IT UP	15
68	Verve (S)VLP 9231	CHRISTMAS COOKIN'	15
69	Verve (S)VLP 9241	FURTHER ADVENTURES OF JIMMY AND WES (with Wes Montgomery)	15
71	Verve 2304 020	I'M GON' GIT MYSELF TOGETHER	15
71	Verve 2304 021	OTHER SIDE	12
71	Verve 2304 033	THE BEST OF JIMMY SMITH	12
72	Verve 2304 044	THE BEST OF JIMMY SMITH VOL. 2	12
73	Decca SKL 5146	AT THE LOWERY ORGAN	12
74	Verve 2304 167	PORTUGUESE SOUL	18

(see also Kenny Burrell)

JOEY SMITH & BABA BROOKS BAND

64	R&B JB 131	Maybe Once/Tell Me You're Mine	25

MINT VALUE £

JOHNNY SMITH & STAN GETZ
52	Vogue V 2137	Tabou/Moonlight In Vermont (78)	7

(see also Stan Getz)

JUDI SMITH
65	Decca F 12132	Leaves Come Tumbling Down/Come My Way	20

JUNIOR SMITH
67	Giant GN 1	Cool Down Your Temper/I'm Groovin'.	8
68	Giant GN 18	I'm Gonna Leave You Girl/I Love You, I Love You	8
68	Giant GN 25	Come Cure Me/I Want Your Lovin'.	8
68	Gas GAS 132	Gimme Little/Trip To War Land	12
69	Crystal CR 7002	Put On The Pressure/I Don't Know	6
72	Sioux SI 019	Saturday Child/JUMBO STERLING: Hot Dog	8
72	Sioux SI 023	You Don't Know/JUMBO STERLING: My Sugar Ain't Sweet	6

(see also Stranger Cole, Derrick Morgan, Rocksteadys)

KATHY SMITH
70	Polydor 2310 081	SOME SONGS I'VE SAVED (LP)	25

KEELY SMITH (& LOUIS PRIMA)
57	Capitol CL 14717	Hurt Me/High School Affair	8
57	Capitol CL 14739	Young And In Love/You Better Go Now	8
57	Capitol CL 14754	Good Behaviour/You'll Never Know	8
57	Capitol CL 14803	Autumn Leaves/I Keep Forgetting (78 rpm = £7)	7
58	Capitol CL 14862	Foggy Day/The Lip (B-side with Louis Prima)	6
58	Capitol CL 14948	That Old Black Magic (with Louis Prima)/You Are My Love (78 rpm = £18)	6
59	Capitol CL 14994	I've Got You Under My Skin (with Louis Prima)/Don't Take Your Love From Me	6
59	London HLD 8984	If I Knew I'd Find You (I'd Climb The Highest Mountain)/Don't Let The Stars Get In Your Eyes (78 rpm = £28)	12
60	London HLD 9240	Here In My Heart/Close.	8
64	Reprise R 20346	You're Breaking My Heart/Crazy	6
61	London RE-D 1269	YOU LOVERS (EP)	30
65	Capitol EAP 1-20629	IT'S MAGIC (EP)	12
65	Reprise R 30042	JOHN LENNON, PAUL McCARTNEY SONGBOOK VOL. 1 (EP)	12
65	Reprise R 30045	THE SUCCESS OF KEELY SMITH (EP)	10
65	Reprise R 30046	JOHN LENNON, PAUL McCARTNEY SONGBOOK VOL. 2 (EP)	12
66	Reprise R 30053	SOMEBODY LOVES ME (EP)	10
66	Reprise R 30062	I'VE GOT THE WORLD ON A STRING (EP)	10
58	Capitol (S)T 914	I WISH YOU LOVE (LP, mono/stereo)	15
59	Capitol T 1073	POLITELY (LP)	14
59	Capitol T 1145	SWINGIN' PRETTY (LP)	14
59	Capitol T 1160	HEY BOY! HEY GIRL! (LP, soundtrack, with Louis Prima)	20
64	Reprise R 6086	LITTLE GIRL BLUE, LITTLE GIRL NEW (LP)	12
65	Reprise R 6132	THE INTIMATE SMITH (LP)	12
65	Reprise R 6142	THE JOHN LENNON-PAUL McCARTNEY SONGBOOK (LP)	12
65	Reprise R 5012	YOU'RE BREAKING MY HEART (LP)	12
66	Reprise R 6175	THAT OLD BLACK MAGIC (LP)	12

(see also Louis Prima, Frank Sinatra)

LONNIE LISTON SMITH (& THE COSMIC ECHOES)
75	RCA RCA 2568	Expansions (Parts 1 & 2) (& Cosmic Echoes)	10
76	RCA RCA 2668	Chance For Peace/Sunset	5
76	RCA RCA 2727	Get Down Everybody/Inner Beauty	5
79	RCA PB 9450	Expansions/A Chance For Peace	6
79	RCA PC 9450	Expansions/A Chance For Peace (12", reissue)	15
75	RCA SF 8434	EXPANSIONS (LP, with Cosmic Echoes)	10
76	RCA SF 8461	VISIONS OF A NEW WORLD (LP)	20
76	RCA RS 1053	REFLECTIONS OF A GOLDEN DREAM (LP, with Cosmic Echoes)	20
77	RCA PL 11822	RENAISSANCE (LP, with Cosmic Echoes)	20

LONNIE SMITH
67	CBS 63146	FINGER LICKIN' GOOD (LP).	25
70s	Blue Note BST 84290	THINK (LP).	25
70s	Blue Note BST 84313	TURNING POINT (LP)	25
70s	Blue Note BST 84326	MOVE YOUR HAND (LP).	28
70s	Blue Note BST 84351	DRIVES (LP).	25

LORENZO SMITH
66	Outasite 45-503	(Too Much) Firewater/Count Down (99 copies only)	100

LOU SMITH
60	Top Rank JAR 520	Cruel Love/Close To My Heart	10

MARTHA SMITH
65	Pye 7N 15778	As I Watch You Walk Away/It Always Seems Like Summer	20
65	Pye 7N 15860	Love Means Nothing To You/The Song Is Love	7

MARVIN SMITH
66	Coral Q 72486	Time Stopped/Have More Time (DJ copy = £125)	50
74	Contempo CS 2034	Let The Good Times Roll/Ain't That A Shame	5

MEL SMITH
81	Mercury MEL 1	Mel Smith's Greatest Hits/Richard & Joey (p/s, with Roger Taylor)	15

MELODY SMITH
71	CBS CBS 7561	You Never Hear A Teardrop Fall/Rastus Ravel.	10

MICHAEL SMITH
82	Island ILPS 9717	MI CYAAN BELIEVE IT (LP)	12

MICK SMITH
76	Midas MFHR 078	SOMEBODY NOBODY KNOWS (LP)	35
77	Alida Star AS 771	WORDS AND MUSIC (LP)	30
79	Repercussion RR 1000	RAINDANCE (LP, as Mike Smith)	25

MIKE SMITH
85	Proto ENA 130	Medley (7" version)/Bits And Pieces (in p/s)	7
85	Proto ENAT 130	Medley (12" version)/Glad All Over (12", p/s)	12
90	Mooncrest MOON 1010	You Gotta Play Rock'N'Roll/Operator	6

(see also Dave Clark 5, Smith & D'Abo)

O.C. (OCIE) SMITH
57	London HLA 8480	Lighthouse/Too Many (as Ocie Smith) (78 rpm = £20)	80
68	CBS 3343	The Son Of Hickory Holler's Tramp/On A Clear Day You Can See Forever	6
70	CBS 5203	Baby I Need Your Loving/San Francisco Is A Lonely Town	8
68	CBS (S) 63147	THE DYNAMIC O.C. SMITH (LP)	20
68	CBS (S) 63362	HICKORY HOLLER REVISITED (LP)	15
69	CBS 63805	AT HOME (LP)	25

(see also Art Mooney)

OTELLO SMITH & TOBAGO BAD BOYS
67	Direction 58-3082	My Home Town/Trouble	5
68	Direction 8-63242	THE BIG ONES GO SKA (LP)	40

PATTI SMITH (GROUP)
76	Arista ARIST 47	Gloria (In Excelsis Deo) (Edit)/My Generation (p/s)	5
77	Arista ARIST 12135	Gloria (In Excelsis Deo)/My Generation (live) (12", Rough Trade copies in brown paper bag with titles in felt pen)	10/7
78	Arista ARIST 181	Because The Night/God Speed (p/s)	10
78	Sire 6078 614	Hey Joe (Version)/Piss Factory (p/s)	15
78	Arista ARIST 197	Privilege (Set Me Free)/Ask The Angels (p/s)	5
78	Arista ARIST 12197	Privilege (Set Me Free)/Ask The Angels/25th Floor (Live Version)/Babelfield (12", p/s)	10
79	Arista ARIST 264	Frederick/Fire Of Unknown Origin (p/s)	5
79	Arista ARIST 281	Dancing Barefoot/5-4-3-2-1 (live) (p/s)	5
79	Arista ARIST 291	So You Want To Be A Rock'n'Roll Star/Frederick (live) (p/s)	5
88	Fierce FRIGHT 017	Brian Jones/Stockinged Feet/Jesus Christ (1-sided, white label)	15
75	Arista ARTY 122	HORSES (LP, blue label)	12
76	Arista SPARTY 1001	RADIO ETHIOPIA (LP, as Patti Smith Group, with lyric insert)	12
78	Arista SPARTY 1043	EASTER (LP, as Patti Smith Group, with lyric insert)	12
79	Arista SPARTY 1086	WAVE (LP, as Patti Smith Group, with lyric insert)	12

PAUL SMITH
65	Columbia DB 7636	Piccadilly Paper Boy/Yakety Yak	7

PETER SMITH
70s	Pilgrim JLPS 148P	FAITH, FOLK & CLARITY (LP, with Kinfolk)	18
70s	Galliard GAL 4016P	FAITH, FOLK & FESTIVITY (LP)	12

RAY SMITH
60	London HL 9051	Rockin' Little Angel/That's All Right	75

ROY SMITH (Jamaica)
70	Grape GR 3013	See Through Craze/TERRY CARL & DERRICK: I'm The One	12
70	Jackpot JP 723	The Wedding/Air Balloon	8

ROY SMITH (& THE STARGAZERS) (U.K.)
55	Decca F 10529	Red Roses (For My Lady Fair)/The Devil's In Your Eyes	5
55	Decca F 10644	He/Glengarry (solo)	5

(see also Stargazers)

SLIM SMITH (& THE UNIQUES)
66	Island WI 3023	I've Got Your Number/The New Boss	35
67	Coxsone CS 7016	Hip Hug/FREEDOM SINGERS: I Want Money	30
67	Coxsone CS 7034	Rougher Yet/I'll Never Let Go	50+
67	Coxsone CS 7009	Mercy Mercy/JACKIE MITTOO: Baba Boom	30
68	Trojan TR 619	Watch This Sound/Out Of Love (as Slim Smith & Uniques)	25
69	Unity UN 504	Everybody Needs Love/JUNIOR SMITH: Come Back Girl	10
69	Unity UN 508	For Once In My Life/Burning Desire	7
69	Unity UN 510	Zip A Dee Doo Dah/On Broadway	7
69	Unity UN 513	Let It Be Me/Love Makes Me Do Foolish Things (both with Paulette)	7
69	Unity UN 515	Somebody To Love/Confusion	7
69	Unity UN 520	Slip Away/Spanish Harlem	10
69	Unity UN 524	Sunny Side Of The Sea/A Place In The Sun	10
69	Unity UN 527	Blessed Are The Meek/Conversation	10
69	Unity UN 537	Keep That Light Shining On Me/Build My World Around You	7
69	Unity UN 539	Love Me Tender/This Feeling	7
69	Unity UN 542	Honey/There's A Light	7
69	Jackpot JP 703	If It Don't Work Out/Love Power	7
69	Gas GAS 132	The Vow (& Doreen Shaeffer)/JAMES NEPHEW: Why Don't You Say	5
70	Gas GAS 150	What Kind Of Life/MARTIN RILEY: It's All In The Game	7
70	Unity UN 570	Jenny/The Race	7
71	Supreme SUP 219	Stay/You're My Everything	7
71	Pama Supreme PS 334	Send Me Some Loving/I'm Lost	7
71	Camel CA 81	Spanish Harlem/Slip Away	8
71	Escort ERT 851	My Love Come True/This Feeling	6
71	Escort ERT 852	Life Keeps Turning/My Girl	6
71	Escort ERT 859	My Girl/RECO: Plus One	10
71	Jackpot JP 779	Keep Walking/Will You Still Love Me Tomorrow	7
72	Jackpot JP 786	I Need Your Loving/You've Got What It Takes	7
72	Jackpot JP 788	Take Me Back/Where Do I Turn	6

72	Jackpot JP 789	Rain From The Skies/You're No Good	8
72	Jackpot JP 798	Closer Together/Blinded By Love	6
72	Jackpot JP 799	Turning Point/Money Lover	6
72	Dynamic DYN 428	Just A Dream/Send Me Some Loving	6
72	Pama PM 850	The Time Has Come/RECO & HIS BAND: (Version)	6
72	Pama Supreme PS 373	A Place In The Sun/Stranger On The Shore	6
72	Camel CA 89	Take Me Back/Where Do I Turn	6
72	Explosion EX 2074	The Time Has Come/Blessed Is The Man	6
73	Explosion EX 2078	Stand Up And Fight/The Sunny Side Of The Sea	8
73	Green Door GD 4058	Let Me Love You/If It Don't Work Out	8
73	Bullet BU 523	A Place In The Sun/Burning Fire	6
69	Pama ECO 9	EVERYBODY NEEDS LOVE (LP)	40
72	Trojan TBL 186	JUST A DREAM (LP)	22
73	Trojan TBL 198	GREATEST HITS (LP)	18
70s	Lord Koos KLP 1	SLIM SMITH (LP)	18

(see also Wonder Boy, Pioneers, Uniques, Roy Shirley, Ron Sig, Dakota Jim, Dennis Alcapone, David Isaacs, John Holt, Heptones, Melodians, Count Ossie, Winston Williams)

SOMETHIN' SMITH & THE REDHEADS

58	Fontana H 112	I'm Gonna Wrap Up All My Heartaches/Ev'ry Night At Nine O'Clock (78)	6
58	Fontana H 154	I Don't Want To Set The World On Fire/You Made Me Love You (78 rpm = £6)	10
58	Fontana TFR 6005	PUT THE BLAME ON ME (10" LP)	18

TAB SMITH & HIS ORCHESTRA

53	Vogue V 2172	Ace High/Deejay Special (78)	8
54	Vogue V 2203	Down Beat/Boogie Joogie (78)	8
54	Vogue V 2282	Cuban Boogie/Red Hot And Blue (78)	8
55	Vogue V 2299	All My Life/Seven Up (78)	8
56	Vogue V 2410	Jump Time/Rock City (78 rpm = £8)	15
56	Vogue V 2416	My Mother's Eyes/These Foolish Things (78)	8
59	London HLM 8801	Smoke Gets In Your Eyes/My Happiness Cha-Cha (78 rpm = £15)	10

TERRY SMITH

| 69 | Philips (S)BL 7871 | FALL OUT (LP) | 150 |
| 77 | Lambert LAM 002 | TERRY SMITH AND TONY LEE TRIO (LP) | 22 |

(see also If)

TRIXIE SMITH

51	Tempo R 42	Black Bottom Stomp/He Likes It Slow (78)	25
52	Vocalion V 1006	Freight Train Blues/Trixie's Blues (78)	30
52	Vocalion V 1017	My Daddy Rocks Me (Parts 1 & 2) (78)	30
53	Jazz Collector L 102	The World's Jazz Crazy And So Am I/Railroad Blues (78)	12
50s	Poydras 101	TRIXIE SMITH (10" EP, 45 rpm)	15
50s	Ristic 12	TRIXIE SMITH (10" EP, 45 rpm)	15
50s	Audubon AAE	TRIXIE SMITH (10" LP)	30

TRIXIE SMITH/MA RAINEY

| 64 | Jazz Collector JEL 22 | FEMALE BLUES VOL. 3 (EP, 2 tracks each) | 15 |

TRULY SMITH

66	Decca F 12373	My Smile Is Just A Frown Turned Upside Down/Love Is Me, Love Is You	18
66	Decca F 12415	I Love Him/Buttermilk Hill	5
66	Decca F 12489	You Are The Love Of My Life/The Merry Go Round Is Slowing	5
67	Decca F 12554	Windows And Doors/Take A Broken Heart	5
67	Decca F 12645	I Wanna Go Back There Again/Window Cleaner	20
67	Decca F 12700	The Boy From Chelsea/Little Man With A Stick	5
68	MGM MGM 1431	This Is The First Time/Taking Time Off	6

VERDELLE SMITH

66	Capitol CL 15234	In My Room/Like A Man	18
66	Capitol CL 15456	Tar And Cement/A Piece Of The Sky	18
66	Capitol CL 15481	I Don't Need Anything/If You Can't Say Anything Nice	12
67	Capitol CL 15516	There's So Much Love Around Me/Baby Baby	12

WARREN SMITH

60	London HL 7101	I Don't Believe I'll Fall In Love/Cave-In (export issue)	40
61	London HLG 7110	Odds And Ends/A Whole Lot Of Nothin' (export issue)	40
64	Liberty LIB 55699	Blue Smoke/Judge And Jury	15

WAYNE SMITH

81	Black Joy DH 815	Life Is A Moment In Space/Ain't No Me Without You (12")	20
85	Greensleeves GRED 169	Under Me Sleng Teng/MICHAEL BUCKLEY: Dance Gate (12")	12
85	Greensleeves GRED 177	Sleng Teng Mix Down Remix/PAD ANTHONY: Cry For Me (12")	20
81	Black Joy BHLP 2005	YOUTHMAN SKANKING (LP)	40

WHISPERING SMITH

| 72 | Blue Horizon 2431 015 | OVER EASY (LP) | 125 |

WHISTLING JACK SMITH

67	Deram DM 112	I Was Kaiser Bill's Batman/The British Grin And Bear	5
68	Decca F 12741	Havah Nagilah/RUDI BENNETT: I'm So Proud	5
67	Deram DML 1009	AROUND THE WORLD WITH WHISTLING JACK SMITH (LP)	15

(see also Rudi Bennett)

WILLIE 'THE LION' SMITH

| 72 | Polydor 2460 156 | PORK AD BEANS (LP) | 12 |

SMITH & D'ABO

| 76 | CBS 81583 | SMITH & D'ABO (LP) | 12 |

(see also Manfred Mann, Dave Clark Five, Band Of Angels, Mike Smith)

SMITH BROTHERS (U.S.)

| 78 | Grapevine GRP 109 | There Can Be A Better Way/Payback's A Drag | 10 |

SMITHFIELD MARKET

73	Gloucester GLS 0435	LONDON IN 1665 (LP, private pressing, gatefold sleeve)	800
74	Globe/Gloucester GLS 0443	AFTER SHAKESPEARE (LP, private pressing, die-cut sleeve, with insert)	700

SMITH & MIGHTY

88	Three Stripes SAM114R	Walk On (12")	10
00	Studio !K7 !K700lp	BASS IS MATERIAL (LP)	15

SMITH, PERKINS & SMITH

72	Island ILPS 9198	SMITH, PERKINS & SMITH (LP)	15

THE SMITHS
SINGLES

83	Rough Trade RT 131	Hand In Glove/Handsome Devil (p/s, original pressing with Manchester address on rear sleeve; later issue with London address)	18/12
83	Rough Trade RT 131	Hand In Glove/Handsome Devil (p/s, additional later issue with no address)	25
83	Rough Trade RT 131	Hand In Glove/Handsome Devil (later pressing with misprinted blue/negative p/s)	1000+
83	Rough Trade RT 136	This Charming Man/Jeane (Rough Trade 'tower' or plain logo on p/s)	10
83	Rough Trade RTT 136	This Charming Man (Manchester)/This Charming Man (London)/Accept Yourself/Wonderful Woman (12", p/s)	15
83	Rough Trade RTT 136	This Charming Man (Manchester)/This Charming Man (London)/Accept Yourself/Wonderful Woman (12", p/s, later pressing with band title on sleeve)	30
83	Rough Trade RTT 136NY	This Charming Man (New York Vocal)/This Charming Man (New York Instrumental) (12", p/s)	15
83	Rough Trade RTT 136NY	This Charming Man (New York Vocal)/This Charming Man (New York Instrumental) 12", p/s, later pressing with band title on sleeve)	50
84	Rough Trade RT 146	What Difference Does It Make?/Back To The Old House ('Morrissey' or 'Terence Stamp' p/s)	8/10
84	Rough Trade RTT 146	What Difference Does It Make?/Back To The Old House/These Things Take Time (12", Morrissey or Terence Stamp p/s)	8
84	Rough Trade RTT 146	What Difference Does It Make?/Back To The Old House/These Things Take Time ('Terence Stamp' p/s, later pressing with band title on sleeve)	15
84	Rough Trade RT 156	Heaven Knows I'm Miserable Now/Suffer Little Children (p/s)	5
84	Rough Trade RTT 156	Heaven Knows I'm Miserable Now/Girl Afraid/Suffer Little Children (12", p/s)	8
84	Rough Trade RT 166	William, It Was Really Nothing/Please Please Please Let Me Get What I Want (original issue with 'man on bed' p/s)	8
84	Rough Trade RTT 166	William, It Was Really Nothing/How Soon Is Now?/Please Please Please Let Me Get What I Want (12", original with green 'man on bed' p/s)	8
85	Rough Trade RT 176	How Soon Is Now?/Well I Wonder	5
85	Rough Trade RTT 176	How Soon Is Now?/Well I Wonder/Oscillate Wildly (12", p/s)	8
85	Rough Trade RT 181	Shakespeare's Sister/What She Said (p/s)	5
85	Rough Trade RTT 181	Shakespeare's Sister/What She Said/Stretch Out And Wait (12", p/s & inner)	8
85	Rough Trade RT 186	Meat Is Murder/Nowhere Fast/Stretch Out And Wait (live EP, unissued, test pressings only)	1000+
85	Rough Trade RT 186	Meat Is Murder/Nowhere Fast/Stretch Out And Wait (Live EP, unissued, Mayking test pressings)	800+
85	Rough Trade RT 186	Meat Is Murder/William It Was Really Nothing/Nowhere Fast/Stretch Out And Wait/Miserable Lie (live 12" EP, unissued, test pressings only)	1000+
85	Rough Trade RT 186	That Joke Isn't Funny Anymore/Meat Is Murder (live) (p/s)	5
85	Rough Trade RTT 186	That Joke Isn't Funny Anymore/Nowhere Fast (live)/Stretch Out And Wait (live)/Shakespeare's Sister (live)/Meat Is Murder (live) (12", p/s)	8
85	Rough Trade RT 191	The Boy With The Thorn In His Side/Asleep (p/s)	5
86	Rough Trade RT 192	Bigmouth Strikes Again/Money Changes Everything (p/s)	5
86	Rough Trade RT 193	Panic/Vicar In A Tutu (p/s, with 'Hang The DJ' stickers)	10
86	Rough Trade RTT 193	Panic/Vicar In A Tutu/The Draize Train (12", p/s, with 'Hang The DJ' stickers)	15
86	Rough Trade RT 194C	Ask/Cemetry Gates/Golden Lights (cassette with picture inlay)	12
87	Rough Trade RT 195	Shoplifters Of The World Unite/Half A Person/London (12", p/s, mispressing, A-side plays "You Just Haven't Earned It Yet Baby", some in carrier bag)	70/50
87	Rough Trade RTT 195	Shoplifters Of The World Unite/Half A Person/London (12", p/s, in carrier bag)	30
87	Rough Trade RT 196	Sheila Take A Bow/Is It Really So Strange (p/s)	5
87	Rough Trade RT 197	Girlfriend In A Coma/Work Is A Four Letter Word (grey p/s)	5
87	Rough Trade RT 197	girfriend In A Coma/Work Is A Four Letter Word (mispressed green p/s, incorrectly shows additional 12" track 'I Keep Mine Hidden' on reverse of sleeve)	200
87	Rough Trade RTT 197	Girlfriend In A Coma/Work Is A Four Letter Word/I Keep Mine Hidden (12", rare grey p/s)	35
87	Rough Trade RTT 197C	Girlfriend In A Coma/Work Is A Four Letter Word/I Keep Mine Hidden (cassette with picture inlay)	12
87	Rough Trade RT 198	I Started Something I Couldn't Finish/Pretty Girls Make Graves (Troy Tate demo) (p/s)	5
87	Rough Trade RT 198C	I Started Something I Couldn't Finish/Pretty Girls Make Graves/Some Girls Are Bigger Than Others/What's The World (live) (cassette)	12
87	Rough Trade RT 200	Last Night I Dreamt Somebody Loved Me/Rusholme Ruffians (John Peel version) (p/s)	5
87	Rough Trade RTT 200CD	Last Night I Dreamt Somebody Loved Me/Rusholme Ruffians (John Peel version)/Nowhere Fast (John Peel version)/William, It Was Really Nothing (John Peel Version) (CD)	20
87	Rough Trade RT 166	William, It Was Really Nothing/How Soon Is Now? (reissue, 'Billie Whitelaw' p/s)	25
87	Rough Trade RTT 166	William, It Was Really Nothing/How Soon Is Now?/Please Please Please Let Me Get What I Want (12", reissue, 'Billie Whitelaw' p/s)	40
88	Spiral Scratch SCRATCH 3	An Interview With The Smiths (with Spiral Scratch magazine, issue 3)	5
93	WEA YZ001	This Charming Man/Jeane (p/s WEA reissue)	5
93	WEA YZ002	How Soon Is Now (p/s WEA reissue)	5
93	WEA YZ003	There Is A Light That Never Goes Out (p/s, WEA reissue)	15

THE SMITHS

PROMOS & WHITE LABELS

83	N/A	Pack of 3 (Rough Trade promo cassette, promoting Hand In Glove and tracks by two other bands)	50
83	Rough Trade RT 136	Reel Around The Fountain/Jeane (unissued, white label test pressings only)	550
83	Rough Trade RTT 136	This Charming Man (one-sided white label test pressing)	100
83	Rough Trade RTT13NY	This Charming Man (Manchester)/This Charming Man (London)/Accept Yourself/Wonderful Woman (12" white label test pressing)	150
84	Rough Trade RT146	What Difference Does It Make?/Back To The Old House (white label promo)	30
84	Rough Trade RTT146	What Difference Does It Make?/Back To The Old House/These Things Take Time (12" white label test pressing)	40
84	Rough Trade RT 61 DJ	Still Ill/You've Got Everything Now	25
84	Rough Trade ROUGH 61	THE SMITHS (white label promo)	30
84	Rough Trade RT131	Hand In Glove (one-sided white label 1984 test pressing)	250
84	Rough Trade RT131	Hand In Glove/Handsome Devil (white label test pressing for 1984 repressing)	200
84	Rough Trade RT131	Hand In Glove/Handsome Devil (Mayking white label test pressing for 1984 repressing)	200
84	Rough Trade ROUGH76	HATFUL OF HOLLOW (white label promo, with incorrect sleeve, no black dot appears between 'Accept Yourself' and Girl Afraid' on reverse of sleeve)	40
85	Rough Trade RTT 171	Barbarism Begins At Home (12", 1-sided white label test pressing)	50
85	Rough Trade RTT 171	Barbarism Begins At Home (Edited Version)/Barbarism Begins At Home (12", 2-sided, p/s)	50
85	Rough Trade RTT 171	Barbarism Begins At Home (12", 1-sided promo, p/s)	50
85	Rough Trade RTT 176	How Soon Is Now/Oscillate Wildly (white label test pressing with Oscillate Wildly instead of Well I Wonder on the B-side)	400
85	Rough Trade RT 186	That Joke Isn't Funny Anymore/Meat Is Murder (live) (Mayking test pressing)	35
86	Rough Trade ROUGH 96	THE QUEEN IS DEAD (Mayking test pressing)	50
86	Rough Trade RTT 193	Panic/Vicar In A Tutu/The Draize Train (12" white label test pressing with promo posters)	50
87	Rough Trade RTT 195	You Just Haven't Earned It Yet Baby/Half A Person/London (12", white label test pressing)	500
87	Rough Trade RT 198	I Started Something I Couldn't Finish/Pretty Girls Make Graves (Troy Tate demo) (Mayking test pressing)	50
87	Rough Trade RT166-B	How Soon Is Now (1-sided white label test pressing for B-side of reissued William, It Was Really Nothing 7")	250
88	Rough Trade ROUGH 126	RANK (white label promo, in mispressed sleeve, no cover star or title on sleeve, just states 'The Smiths')	50

CD SINGLE REISSUES

88	Rough Trade RTT 146CD	What Difference Does It Make?/Back To The Old House/These Things Take Time.	20
88	Rough Trade RTT 156CD	Heaven Knows I'm Miserable Now/Girl Afraid/Suffer Little Children.	20
88	Rough Trade RTT 166CD	William, It Was Really Nothing/How Soon Is Now?/Please, Please, Please Let Me Get What I Want	30
88	Rough Trade RTT 171CD	Barbarism Begins At Home/Shakespeare's Sister/Stretch Out And Wait	33
88	Rough Trade RTT 191CD	The Boy With The Thorn In His Side/Rubber Ring/Asleep	20
88	Rough Trade RTT 193CD	Panic/Vicar In A Tutu/The Draize Train	25
88	Rough Trade RTT 194CD	Ask/Cemetery Gates/Golden Lights	15
88	Rough Trade RTT 215CD	The Headmaster Ritual/Nowhere Fast (live)/Stretch Out And Wait (live)/Meat Is Murder (live)	40
93	WEA YZ0003CD1	There Is A Light That Never Goes Out/Hand In Glove (live)/Some Girls Are Bigger Than Others (live) Money Changes Everything (CD1, WEA reissue)	10
93	WEA YZ0003CD2	There Is A Light That Never Goes Out/Hand In Glove (Sandy Shaw)/I Don't Owe You Anything (Sandy Shaw)/Jeane (Sandy Shaw) (CD2, WEA Reissue)	10

ALBUMS

84	Rough Trade ROUGH 76	HATFUL OF HOLLOW (LP, original gatefold issue, with incorrect sleeve, no black dot appears between 'Accept Yourself' and 'Girl Afraid' on reverse of sleeve)	20
85	Rough Trade ROUGHCD 81	MEAT IS MURDER (CD, original issue)	18
86	Rough Trade ROUGHCD 61	THE SMITHS (CD, original issue)	18
86	Rough Trade ROUGHCD 96	THE QUEEN IS DEAD (CD, original issue)	18
87	Rough Trade ROUGH 101	THE WORLD WON'T LISTEN (LP, original issue, with inner)	18
87	Rough Trade ROUGHCD 101	THE WORLD WON'T LISTEN (CD, original issue)	18
87	Rough Trade ROUGHCD 106	STRANGEWAYS HERE WE COME (CD, original issue)	18
87	Rough Trade RT 225	LOUDER THAN BOMBS (2-LP, gatefold sleeve)	20
87	Rough Trade ROUGH CD 225	LOUDER THAN BOMBS (CD)	20
88	R. Trade ROUGH CD 76	HATFUL OF HOLLOW (CD, original sleeve)	18
88	R. Trade ROUGH 126	RANK (LP, gatefold sleeve, with inner, ltd. edition with poster and cover sticker denoting amended catalogue number)	30
88	R. Trade ROUGH 126D	RANK (DAT)	50

10" REISSUE ALBUMS

93	WEA SMITHS 1	THE SMITHS (2-LP)	12
93	WEA SMITHS 2	HATFUL OF HOLLOW (2-LP)	12
93	WEA SMITHS 3	MEAT IS MURDER (2-LP)	12
93	WEA SMITHS 4	THE QUEEN IS DEAD (2-LP)	12
93	WEA SMITHS 5	THE WORLD WON'T LISTEN (2-LP)	12
93	WEA SMITHS 6	STRANGEWAYS HERE WE COME (2-LP)	12
93	WEA SMITHS 7	RANK (2-LP)	12

(see also Morrissey, Sandie Shaw, The The, Electronic)

SMITHY ALL STARS

71	Hillcrest HCT 3	Witchfinder General/Deserted	5

(see also Ian Smith & Inner Mind)

SMOG

95	City Slang EFAD 49517	A Hit/Wine Stained Lips (p/s, yellow vinyl)	15

SMOKE

67	Columbia DB 8115	My Friend Jack/We Can Take It	35
67	Columbia DB 8252	If The Weather's Sunny/I Would If I Could, But I Can't	35
67	Island WIP 6023	It Could Be Wonderful/Have Some More Tea	55
68	Island WIP 6031	Utterly Simple/Sydney Gill (unreleased)	
70	Revolution Pop REVP 1002	Dreams Of Dreams/My Birth	20
71	Pageant SAM 101	Ride Ride Ride/Guy Fawkes	12
72	Regal Zonophone RZ 3071	Sugar Man/That's What I Want	25
74	Decca FR 13484	Shagalagalu/Gimme Good Loving	5
74	Decca FR 13514	My Lullaby/Looking High	6
70s	Gull	IT'S SMOKE TIME (LP, reissue of German-only LP)	25
88	M. Blue Town MBT 5001	MY FRIEND JACK (LP)	20

(see also Shots)

SMOKESTACK LIGHTNIN'
69	Bell MBLL/SBLL 116	OFF THE WALL (LP)	20

SMOKEY BABE
62	'77' LA 12-12	SMOKEY BABE AND HIS FRIENDS (LP)	25

SMOKEY CIRCLES
70	Carnaby CNLS 6006	THE SMOKEY CIRCLES ALBUM (LP)	40

SMOKIE & HIS SISTER
67	CBS 202605	Creators Of Rain/In Dreams Of Silent Seas	5

SMOKIN' ROADIE
83	Zone To Zone ZON 3	Midnight/Ripp Off (p/s)	32

SMOKEY SMOTHERS
69	Polydor 623 239	THE DRIVING BLUES (LP)	30

DES SMYTH & COLLEGEMEN
65	Pye 7N 15867	The Pillow That Whispers/Lonely Streets	5
65	Pye 7N 15996	Wedding Bells/All For The Love Of A Girl	5

GILLI SMYTH & MOTHER GONG
78	Charly CRL 5007	MOTHER (LP, with insert)	15

(see also Gong)

DONALD SMYTHE
71	Punch PH 83	Where Love Goes/HURRICANES: You Can Run	40

GLORIA SMYTHE
60	Vogue V 9159	I'll Be Over After A While/Gee Baby Ain't I Good To You	10

SNAFU
74	WWA WWS 007	Dixie Queen/Monday Morning	5
74	WWA WWA 003	SNAFU (LP, gatefold sleeve)	15
74	WWA WWA 013	SITUATION NORMAL (LP)	15

(see also Whitesnake, Freedom)

SNAKEBITE
83	Astor ASTOR 1	Blow You Away/Thin Ice (no p/s)	25

SNAKES
76	Dynamite DYR45006	Teenage Head/Lights Out (p/s)	7

(see also The Motors)

SNAPE
73	Transatlantic TRA 269	ACCIDENTALLY BORN IN NEW ORLEANS (LP)	25

(see also Alexis Korner)

SNAPPERS
59	Top Rank JAR 167	Big Bill/If There Were (78 rpm = £50)	18

SNAPPERS
67	CBS 2719	Upside Down Inside Out/Memories	12

SNATCH
78	Lightning LIG 502	Stanley/I.R.T. (p/s)	10
78	Lightning LIG 505	All I Want/When I'm Bored ('foil' p/s)	10
80	Fetish FET 004	Shopping For Clothes/Joey/Red Army (12", die-cut p/s)	8

(see also Johnny Thunders, Judy Nylon)

SND
99	City Centre Offices BLOCK 4	Medley Systems/(Locked Grooves) (1000 only)	12

SNEAKY PETES
60	Decca F 11199	Savage (Parts 1 & 2)	10

SNEEKERS
64	Columbia DB 7385	I Just Can't Get To Sleep/Bald Headed Woman	130+

LEN SNIDER
63	London HLU 9790	Everyone Knows/I'll Be Coming Home Tonight	7

SNIFF 'N' THE TEARS
79	Chiswick NS 40	Driver's Seat (cancelled, test pressings only)	15

SNIVELLING SHITS
77	Ghetto Rockers PRE 2	Terminal Stupid/I Can't Come (p/s, first pressing of 500, paper labels/black print)	60
77	Ghetto Rockers PRE 2	Terminal Stupid/I Can't Come (p/s, 2nd pressing, plastic labels/juke box centre)	25
89	Damaged Goods FNARR 4	Isgodaman?/Terminal Stupid/I Can't Come (p/s)	20
89	Dam. Goods FNARR4B	Isgodaman?/Terminal Stupid/I Can't Come (box set with badge & inserts, pink vinyl in stamped plain white sleeve)	25
90	Dam. Goods FNARR LP 3	I CAN'T COME (LP, brown vinyl)	12

(see also Doctor Dark)

SNOBS
64	Decca F 11867	Buckle Shoe Stomp/Stand And Deliver	25

SNOOKY & MOODY
66	Blue Horizon 45-1003	Snooky And Moody's Blues/Telephone Blues (99 copies only)	135

HANK SNOW (& RAINBOW RANCH BOYS)
52	HMV B 10284	My Two Timin' Woman/The Rhumba Boogie (78)	8
52	HMV B 10354	Lady's Man/I Went To Your Wedding (78)	8
53	HMV JO 424	The Alphabet/My Religion's Not Old Fashioned (But It's Real Genuine) (78 export issue)	7
54	HMV 7MC 7	Why Do You Punish Me (For Loving You)/When Mexican Joe Meets Jole Blon (with Rainbow Ranch Boys) (export issue)	18
54	HMV 7MC 15	Spanish Fire Ball/Between Fire And Water (with Rainbow Ranch Boys) (export issue)	18
54	HMV 7MC 24	My Arabian Baby/I Don't Hurt Anymore (with Rainbow Ranch Boys) (export issue)	18
54	HMV 7MC 25	My Religion's Not Old-Fashioned (But It's Real Genuine)/The Alphabet (with Rainbow Ranch Boys) (export issue)	18
54	HMV 7MC 31	Yellow Roses/Would You Mind (with Rainbow Ranch Boys) (export issue)	18
59	RCA RCA 1151	Old Shep/The Last Ride (78 rpm = £12)	10
61	RCA RCA 1248	Poor Little Jimmie/Beggar To A King	5
58	RCA RCX 116	COUNTRY GUITAR NO. 4 (EP)	12
59	RCA RCX 142	COUNTRY GUITAR NO. 7 (EP)	15
63	RCA RCX 7125	WHEN TRAGEDY STRUCK (EP)	12
64	RCA RCX 7154	THAT COUNTRY GENTLEMAN (EP)	15
59	RCA RD 27115	WHEN TRAGEDY STRUCK (LP)	15
62	RCA Camden CDN 164	SOUTHERN CANNONBALL (LP)	12
63	RCA Camden CDN 5102	THE ONE AND ONLY HANK SNOW (LP)	12
63	RCA RD/SF 7579	RAILROAD MAN (LP)	12

(see also Chet Atkins)

SNOWBOY
90s	Acid Jazz AJTEN 1	Theme From The New Avengers/(Mixes) (12")	8
90s	Acid Jazz JAZIDLP 146	THE MANY FACES OF SNOWBOY (2-LP)	20

SNOW PATROL
98	Jeepster JPR7004	Little Hide/Sticky Teenage Twin (1,000 only, p/s)	25
98	Jeepster JPRLP004	SONGS FOR POLAR BEARS (LP)	18

SNOWBOY & NOEL McKOY
90s	Acid Jazz JAZID 42T	Lucky Fellow (12", p/s)	12

BILL SNYDER & HIS (MAGIC PIANO &) ORCHESTRA
54	London REP 1011	BEWITCHED (EP)	12
51	London H-APB 1004	BEWITCHED (10" LP)	15
54	Brunswick LA 8667	THE STARLIT HOUR (10" LP)	12
57	Brunswick LAT 8200	CAFE RENDEZVOUS (LP)	12
58	Brunswick LAT 8254	SWEET AND LOVELY (LP)	12

RON SNYDER
63	Parlophone R 4993	Oh My Twisted Bach/Narcissus	6

ERROL SOBERS
70	Beacon BEA 159	Sugar Shaker/You're In Love	15

(see also Bobby Bridger)

SOCIALITES
64	Warner Bros WB 148	Jive Jimmy/You're Losing Your Touch	45

SOCIAL SECURITY
78	Heartbeat PULSE 1	I Don't Want My Heart To Rule My Head/Stella's Got A Fella/Cider/Choc Ice (p/s)	15

SOCIETIE
67	Deram DM 162	Bird Has Flown/Breaking Down	60

SOCRATES
72	Deram DM 362	Eating Momma's Cookin'/Dearest Agnes	12

SODS
79	Tap TAP 1	Moby Grape/Negative Positive (p/s)	30
79	Stortbeat SB 5	No Pictures Of Us/Plaything (p/s)	30
79	Step Forward SFLP 3	MINUTES TO GO (LP)	20

SOFT BOYS
77	Raw RAW 5	GIVE IT TO THE SOFT BOYS (EP, acetate with withdrawn track, "Vyrna Knowl Is A Headbanger" in place of "Ventilator")	200
77	Raw RAW 5	GIVE IT TO THE SOFT BOYS (EP)	20
78	Radar ADA 8	(I Want To Be An) Anglepoise Lamp/Fat Man's Son (p/s)	8
79	Raw RAW 37	GIVE IT TO THE SOFT BOYS (EP, unreleased reissue)	
79	Raw RAW 41	Where Are The Prawns (unreleased)	
80	Armageddon AEP 002	NEAR THE SOFT BOYS (EP)	8
80	Armageddon AS 005	I Wanna Destroy You/I'm An Old Pervert (Disco) (p/s)	8
81	Armageddon AS 029	Only The Stones Remain/The Asking Tree (p/s)	8
82	Bucketfull Of Brains BOB 1	Love Poisoning/When I Was A Kid (p/s, with/without *Bucketfull Of Brains* magazine)	15/12
83	Midnight Music DING 4	He's A Reptile/Song No. 4 (p/s, 2 different designs)	8
87	Bucketfull Of Brains BOB 17	Deck Of Cards/ROBYN HITCHCOCK & PETER BUCK: Flesh No. 1 (flexidisc with *Bucketfull Of Brains* magazine, issue 23)	6/4
89	Overground OVER 4	The Face Of Death/The Yodelling Hoover (p/s, 600 yellow vinyl, 400 white vinyl, 15 gold test pressings)	6/6/15
85	Delorean SOFT 1P	WADING THROUGH A VENTILATOR (12" EP, picture disc)	10
79	Two Crabs CLAW 1001	A CAN OF BEES (LP, original issue, black & white labels)	20

80	Aura AUL 709	A CAN OF BEES (LP, reissue)	12
80	Armageddon ARM 1	UNDERWATER MOONLIGHT (LP)	12
82	Armageddon BYE 1	TWO HALVES FOR THE PRICE OF ONE (LP)	12
83	M. Music CHIME 0002	INVISIBLE HITS (LP)	12
84	Two Crabs CLAW 1001	A CAN OF BEES (LP, 2nd reissue, black & red labels)	12

(see also Robyn Hitchcock, Kimberley Rew)

SOFT CELL
80	Big Frock ABF 1	MUTANT MOMENTS (EP, plain p/s with postcard; beware of counterfeits without postcard & in wraparound p/s!)	60
81	Some Bizzare HARD 1	A Man Can Get Lost/Memorabilia (p/s, 10,000 only)	10
81	Some Bizzare HARD 12	Memorabilia (Extended)/Persuasion (Extended) (12", p/s)	10
81	Some Bizzare BZS 212	Tainted Love/Where Did Our Love Go/Tainted Dub/Memorabilia (12", p/s, limited edition with 4 tracks)	10
81	Some Bizzare No Cat. No.	Metro Mr. X/B-MOVIE: Remembrance Day (white label test pressing)	60
81	Lyntone LYN 10410	Metro Mr. X/B-MOVIE: Remembrance Day (red or green flexidisc, with/without *Flexipop* magazine, issue 12)	8/6
81	Some Bizzare BZS 612	Bedsitter/Facility Girls (12", p/s)	8
82	Some Bizzare BZS 912	Torch/Insecure Me (12", p/s)	8
82	Some Bizzare CELBX 1	THE 12" SINGLES (6 x 12" box set, with booklet)	50
83	Some Bizzare BZS 17	Numbers/Memorabilia (live) (foldout card p/s)	7
83	Some Bizzare BZS 2020	Soul Inside/You Only Live Twice//Loving You — Hating Me/ Her Imagination (double pack)	8
83	Lyntone (no cat. no.)	Say Hello, Wave Goodbye (live) (flexidisc, blue vinyl, fan club issue, 500 only)	18
84	Lyntone (no cat. no.)	Ghostrider (live '83) (flexidisc, blue, black or green vinyl, fan club issue)	15
84	Some Bizzare BZSR 2212	Down In The Subway (Remix)/Disease And Desire/Born To Lose (12", p/s)	18
91	Some Bizzare SOFCP 1	Say Hello, Wave Goodbye — '91/Numbers/Torch (Original Extended Version) (CD, picture disc)	8
91	Some Bizzare SOFCP 2	Tainted Love—Where Did Our Love Go/Loving You — Hating Me/ Where The Heart Is (CD, in different colours of leather pouch)	10
91	Some Bizzare (no cat. no.)	Megamix '91 (12", promo only, custom p/s)	12

(see also Marc Almond, Marc & Mambas, Anne Hogan)

SOFTIES
| 77 | Charly CYS 1036 | Suicide Pilot/C.I. Angel (p/s) | 5 |

(see also Captain Sensible)

MICK SOFTLEY
65	Immediate IM 014	I'm So Confused/She's My Girl	35
67	CBS 202469	Am I The Red One/That's Not My Kind Of Love	65+
70	CBS 5130	Can You Hear Me Now/Time Machine	7
71	CBS 7337	Goin' Down The Road/Gypsy	7
72	CBS 8269	Lady Willow/From The Land Of The Crab	7
65	Columbia 33SX 1781	SONGS FOR SWINGIN' SURVIVORS (LP)	100+
70	CBS 64098	SUNRISE (LP, gatefold sleeve)	35
71	CBS 64395	STREET SINGER (LP)	30
72	CBS 64841	ANY MOTHER DOESN'T GRUMBLE (LP)	35

SOFT MACHINE
67	Polydor 56151	Love Makes Sweet Music/Reelin' Feelin' Squeelin'	130
78	Harvest HAR 5155	Soft Space (Parts 1 & 2) (p/s)	8
69	Probe SPB 1002	THE SOFT MACHINE VOLUME TWO (LP)	35
70	CBS 66246	THIRD (2-LP)	25
71	CBS 64280	FOURTH (LP)	20
72	CBS 64806	FIFTH (LP)	18
73	CBS 68214	SIX (2-LP)	12
73	CBS 65799	SEVEN (LP, gatefold sleeve)	12
75	Harvest SHSP 404	BUNDLES (LP, with inner sleeve)	12
76	Harvest SHSP 4056	SOFTS (LP)	12
77	Harvest SHTW 800	TRIPLE ECHO (3-LP, box set, with colour booklet)	45
78	Harvest SHSP 4083	ALIVE & WELL (LP)	12

(see also Robert Wyatt, Kevin Ayers, Hugh Hopper, Elton Dean, Daevid Allen, Matching Mole, 'Igginbottom, Lyn Dobson)

SOFT PEDALLING
| 70 | Decca F 23034 | It's So Nice/Rolling On Home | 5 |

SOFT SHOE
| 78 | Aardvark AARD 1 | FOR THOSE ALONE (LP, with insert) | 100 |

SOHEP
| 81 | Merciful Release MR 3 | So Much Fun/You Could Be So Nice Dear (p/s) | 10 |

SOHO SKIFFLE GROUP
57	Melodisc 1403	Give Me A Big Fat Woman/The Midnight Special (78)	18
57	Melodisc 1421	Frankie And Johnny/Streamline Train (78)	18
57	Melodisc EMP 7 72	SOHO SKIFFLE GROUP (EP)	85

MARTIAL SOLAL
| 63 | RCA Victor RD/SF 7614 | AT NEWPORT '63 (LP) | 12 |

SOLAR PLEXUS
| 73 | Polydor 2383 222 | SOLAR PLEXUS (LP) | 30 |

SOLDIER
| 82 | Heavy Metal HEAVY 12 | Sheralee/Force (p/s, some with postcard) | 35/25 |

SOLENT
| 73 | Decca F 13375 | My World Fell Down/The Sound Of Summer's Over | 10 |

SOLID GOLD CADILLAC
| 73 | RCA SF 8311 | SOLID GOLD CADILLAC (LP) | 25 |
| 73 | RCA SF 8365 | BRAIN DAMAGE (LP) | 18 |

(see also Chris Spedding, Mike Westbrook)

SOLID N MIND
90	Liberty Grooves LIB001	An Original Break (12")...	20

SOLID ROCK BAND
78	Chapel Lane RWA 1	FOOTPRINTS ON THE WATER (LP, gatefold sleeve)........................	15

SOLID SENDERS
(see under Wilko Johnson)

SOL INVICTUS
90	Cerne 004	Abbatoirs Of Love/CURRENT 93: This Ain't The Summer Of Love (live in Japan, gig freebie, 93 only with insert & gig ticket [200 without insert])).....	60/25
91	Shock SX 016	See The Dove Fall/Somewhere In Europe (numbered foldover p/s in poly bag, 1,000 only)	15
91	World Serpent WS7 002	Looking For Europe (1-sided, etched B-side, foldover sleeve in poly bag, 963 only).	15
00	Tursa 026	Eve (picture disc, 1,000 only)..	20
01	Tursa 029	HILL OF CROSSES (LP, 1,000 only, signed)............................	20
02	Tursa 030	THRONES (LP, 1,000 only, signed)...................................	12
02	Tursa 014	THE BLADE (LP, 1,000 only, signed).................................	12
89	SVL SVL 009	IN THE JAWS OF THE SERPENT (LP, with insert).....................	20
90	Tursa 001	TREES IN WINTER (LP)	30
90	Tursa 002	LEX TALIONIS (CD, special edit in leather wallet).....................	30
91	Tursa 003	KILLING TIDE (LP)..	25
91	Tursa 003	KILLING TIDE (CD, special edit in felt bag)............................	20

(see also Current 93, Death In June, Nurse With Wound, Karl Blake, Shock Headed Peters)

SOLITAIRES
58	London HLM 8745	Walking Along/Please Kiss This Letter (78 rpm = £55)..................	150

SOLSTICE
82	private pressing	MORNING LIGHT (cassette EP)......................................	10
83	Roke RO 001C	New Life/Peace For The New Age (cassette)	6
84	Equinox EQRLP 001	SILENT DANCE (LP, gatefold sleeve)	25

SOLUTION
72	Decca SKL-R 5124	SOLUTION (LP)	18

SOME CHICKEN
77	Raw RAW 7	New Religion/Blood On The Wall (p/s)	20
78	Raw RAW 13	Arabian Daze/No. 7	15
78	Raw RAW 13	Arabian Daze/No. 7 (purple vinyl)	120
78	Raw RAWT 13	Arabian Daze/No. 7 (12")	8

SOMEONE'S BAND
70	Deram DM 313	Story/Give It To You	15
70	Deram SML 1068	SOMEONE'S BAND (LP)..	150+

GORDON SOMERS & HIS GROUP
64	Top Ten TPSX 101	THE SOUND OF THE BEATLES (EP).................................	8

SOMETHING HAPPENS!
86	Prophet PRS 002	TWO CHANCES (EP, p/s)	8

ELKE SOMMER
61	Columbia DB 4688	Be Not Notty/The Faithful Hussar	5

JOANIE SOMMERS
60	Warner Bros WB 23	Be My Love/Why Don't You Do Right?................................	6
61	Warner Bros WB 31	Ruby Duby Du/Bob White	6
61	Warner Bros WB 44	One Boy/I'll Never Be Free..	6
62	Warner Bros WB 71	Johnny Get Angry/Summer Place..................................	6
62	Warner Bros WB 78	Passing Strangers/When The Boys Get Together....................	6
63	Warner Bros WB 85	Goodbye Joey/Bobby's Hobbies...................................	6
63	Warner Bros WB 105	Little Girl Bad/Wishing Well.......................................	7
65	Warner Bros WB 150	If You Love Him/I Think I'm Gonna Cry..............................	15
60	Warner Bros WEP 6013	POSITIVELY THE MOST (EP, also stereo WSEP 2013).................	15/18
61	Warner Bros WEP 6047	THE VOICE OF THE SIXTIES (EP, also stereo WSEP 2047)............	15/18
64	Warner Bros W(S)EP 6121	JOHNNY GET ANGRY No. 1 (EP, mono/stereo)......................	15/18
64	Warner Bros W(S)EP 6123	JOHNNY GET ANGRY No. 2 (EP, mono/stereo)......................	15/18
61	Warner Bros WM 4045	THE VOICE OF THE 60s (LP, also stereo WS 8045)..................	25/28
62	Warner Bros WM 4062	FOR THOSE WHO THINK YOUNG (LP, also stereo WS 8062).........	25/28
63	Warner Bros WM 8107	JOHNNY GET ANGRY (LP, also stereo WS 8107).....................	30/32
64	Warner Bros WM 8119	LET'S TALK ABOUT LOVE (LP, also stereo WS 8119)................	20/22

(see also Ed Byrnes)

SONGSTERS
54	London HL 8100	Bahama Buggy Ride/It Isn't Right (78 rpm = £10)......................	15

SON HOUSE
60s	Saydisc Roots SL 504	THE VOCAL INTENSITY OF SON HOUSE (LP)..........................	40
66	CBS (S)BPG 62604	THE LEGENDARY FATHER OF FOLK BLUES (LP)	40
70	Liberty LBS 83391	JOHN THE REVELATOR (LP)...	40

SON HOUSE/J.D. SHORT
69	Xtra XTRA 1080	DELTA BLUES (LP)	35

SONIA
79	D Roy DRDD 18	Ooh Baby Baby/Back Street Dub (12")................................	12

SONIC ASSASSINS
81	Flicknife FLEP 101	SONIC ASSASSINS (12" EP, p/s)......................................	8

(see also Hawkwind)

SONIC BOOM

90	Silvertone SONIC 1	Octaves/Tremeloes (10", orange vinyl PVC sleeve, mail-order only)	18
91	Silvertone SONIC 2	(I Love You) To The Moon And Back/Capo Waltz (live) (gig freebie in black die-cut sleeve, promo only, 33rpm, p/s later available separately)	12/8
90	Silvertone ORE ZLP 506	SPECTRUM (LP, gatefold rotatable plastic disc sleeve with inner)	25

(see also Spacemen 3, Spectrum)

SONIC YOUTH

86	Blast First BFFP 3	Flower/Halloween (12", p/s, some on yellow vinyl)	22/14
86	Blast First BFFP 3	Flower/Rewolf (12", p/s, censored version)	25
86	Blast First BFFP 3(B)	(Savage Pencil etch)/Halloween II (12", p/s, A-side engraved, 1st 100 signed)	40/20
86	Blast First BFFP 3X	Flower/Halloween/Satan Supermix (12", unreleased)	
86	Blast First BFFP 7	Starpower (edit)/Bubblegum (p/s, some with badge & poster)	12/4
88	Fierce FRIGHT 015/016	Stick Me Donna Magick Momma/Making The Nature Scene (live) (p/s, 2 x 1-sided 7" with etched B-sides)	25
88	Fierce FRIGHT 015/016	Stick Me Donna Magick Momma/Making The Nature Scene (live) (p/s, single disc reissue)	15
88	Catalogue CAT 064	Teenage Riot (square flexidisc sewn into *The Catalogue* magazine)	15/8
89	Blast First BFFP 46	Touch Me I'm Sick/MUDHONEY: Halloween (12", p/s)	18
89	Blast First BFFP 48	Providence (stereo)/Providence (mono) (promo only)	5
90	Geffen GEF 81	KOOL THING EP: Kool Thing/That's All I Know (p/s)	8
92	Geffen DGCT 11	100% (10" EP, orange vinyl)	10
92	Geffen DGCT 11	100% (10" EP, black vinyl promo)	40
92	Geffen DGCT 11	100% (12" EP, promo only, white label)	50
92	Geffen DGCTD 11	100% (CD EP, digipak)	10
92	Geffen GFST 26	YOUTH AGAINST FASCISM: Purr/The Destroyed Room/YAF (12" EP)	12
92	Geffen GFSTD 26	YOUTH AGAINST FASCISM: Purr/The Destroyed Room/YAF (CD EP)	8
92	Geffen Z-19664 DJ	Personality Crisis/Dirty Boots (DJ promo only)	8
93	Blast First BFFP 26 T	MASTER DIK (12" EP, with inner)	8
94	Geffen GFSV 72	Bull In The Heather/Razor Blade/Doctor's Orders (10", silver vinyl, no'd p/s)	10
83	Neutral NEUTRAL 9	CONFUSION IS SEX (LP)	20
85	Blast First BFFP 1	BAD MOON RISING (LP, with lyric insert)	12
85	NOT NOT 1/BUT 2	WALLS HAVE EARS (2-LP, 2,000 copies only, numbered)	50
87	Blast First CHAT 1	SISTER INTERVIEW DISC (LP)	18
88	Blast First BFFP 34	DAYDREAM NATION (2-LP, 1st 1,000 with signed poster)	25
94	Geffen DGC 24632	EXPERIMENTAL JET SET, TRASH & NO STAR (LP, blue vinyl)	20

(see also Ciccone Youth, Mudhoney)

SONLIGHT ORCHESTRA

70s	Myrrh MYR 1036	PLAYS LOVE & OTHER GREATS (LP)	18

SONNY

71	Ackee ACK 127	Love And Peace/LARRY & ALVIN: Throw Me Corn	10

SONNY (& SONNY'S GROUP)

65	Atlantic AT 4038	Laugh At Me/Tony (as Sonny & Sonny's Group)	6
65	Atlantic AT 4060	The Revolution Kind/Georgia And John Quetzal (as Sonny & Sonny's Group)	8
67	Atlantic 584 131	I Told My Love To Go Away/Misty Roses (solo)	5

(see also Sonny & Cher)

SONNY (Burke) & YVONNE

64	Island WI 134	Life Without Fun/SONNY BURKE GROUP: Mount Vesuvius	25

(see also Sonny Burke)

SONNY & CHER

64	Reprise R 20309	Baby Don't Go/Walkin' The Quetzal	8
65	Atlantic AT 4035	I Got You Babe/It's Gonna Rain	5
65	Atlantic AT 4047	But You're Mine/Hello	5
65	Vocalion VL 9247	The Letter/Spring Fever (B-side by 'Sonny & Cher (Instrumental)')	15
66	Atlantic AT 4069	What Now My Love/I Look For You	6
66	Atlantic 584 018	Have I Stayed Too Long/Leave Me Be	5
66	Atlantic 584 040	Little Man/Monday	5
66	Atlantic 584 057	Living For You/Turn Around	6
67	Atlantic 584 078	The Beat Goes On/Love Don't Come	8
67	Atlantic 584 110	Podunk/Beautiful Story	5
67	Atlantic 584 129	It's The Little Things/Plastic Man	5
68	Atlantic 584 162	Good Combination/You And Me	10
68	Atlantic 584 168	Circus/SONNY BONO: I Would Marry You Today	5
68	Atlantic 584 215	You Gotta Have A Thing Of Your Own/I Got You Babe	5
65	Reprise R 30056	CAESAR AND CLEO (EP, 2 tracks each by Sonny & Cher, Caesar & Cleo)	20
64	Atlantic ATL/STL 5036	LOOK AT US (LP, mono/stereo)	15/18
66	Atlantic 587 006	THE WONDROUS WORLD OF SONNY AND CHER (LP)	15
67	Atlantic 587/588 052	IN CASE YOU'RE IN LOVE (LP)	15

(see also Caesar & Cleo, Cher, Sonny, Date With Soul)

SONNY & DAFFODILS

63	Ember EMB EP 4538	SONNY & DAFFODILS (EP)	65

SON OF A BITCH

96	Hengest SOABCDS 1	Treacherous Times/Victim You (CD, stickered jewel case)	10

(see also Saxon)

SON OF NOISE

91	Music Of Life NOTE53	Son Of Noise/Ill Justice (12")	15
91	Kold Sweat KS117	Master Of Menace/Milk In The Chocolate (12")	12
93	Little Rascool LR001	Crazy Mad Flow/Retrocide 93 (12")	10
92	Kold Sweat KSEP207	NEGATIVE FORCES/THE MIGHTY SON/THE MISSION (EP)	12
92	Kold Sweat KSLP03	THE MIGHTY SON OF NOISE (LP)	16

MINT VALUE £

SONS & LOVERS
67	Camp 602 002	Matters/Peaceful Is The River	6
68	Beacon 3-101	Help Me (I'm On Top Of The World)/Feel Alright	5
68	Beacon 3-107	Happiness Is Love/Things You Do	5

SONS OF ALBATROSS
75	Decca FR 13605	Africa/Ha-ri-ah	35

SONS OF DEMENTED CHILDREN
87	Hatter MAD 003	Spoof Dealer/Busking (p/s, with insert)	18

SONS OF FRED
65	Columbia DB 7605	Sweet Love/I'll Be There	110
65	Parlophone R 5391	I, I, I (Want Your Lovin')/She Only Wants A Friend	72
66	Parlophone R 5415	Baby What Do You Want Me To Do/You Told Me	140

(see also Odyssey)

SONS OF JAH
79	Natty Congo PFULP 3502	BURNING BLACK (LP)	25
82	Natty Congo NCLP 001	UNIVERSAL MESSAGE (LP)	15

SONS OF MAN
67	Oak RGJ 612	SONS OF MAN (EP, no p/s)	400+

(see also Aubrey Small)

SONS OF MOSES
75	MCA MCA 169	Soul Symphony/Fatback	10

SONS OF PILTDOWN MEN
63	Pye International 7N 25206	Mad Goose/Be A Party	15

SONS OF PIONEERS
54	HMV 7EG 8069	SONS OF THE PIONEERS (EP)	12
57	RCA RD 27016	FAVOURITE COWBOY SONGS (LP)	15

SONS OF SOUL
66	Doctor Bird DB 1037	Yeah Yeah Baby/So Ashamed	18

SONSONG
76	Zebra ZM 5761	SONSONG (LP)	30

SOPHOMORES
60s	Seeco CELP 451	THE SOPHOMORES (LP)	30

SORROWS
65	Piccadilly 7N 35219	I Don't Wanna Be Free/Come With Me	35
65	Piccadilly 7N 35230	Baby/Teenage Letter	35
65	Piccadilly 7N 35260	Take A Heart/We Should Get Along Fine	15
66	Piccadilly 7N 35277	You've Got What I Want/No, No, No (a few with export p/s)	30/15
66	Piccadilly 7N 35309	Let The Live Live/Don't Sing No Sad Songs For Me	35
66	Piccadilly 7N 35336	Let Me In/How Love Used To Be	35
67	Piccadilly 7N 35385	Pink, Purple, Yellow And Red/My Gal	100
66	Piccadilly N(S)PL 38023	TAKE A HEART (LP, mono/stereo)	160/260

(see also Don Fardon)

SORT SOL
81	4AD AD 101	Marble Station/Misguided (p/s)	8

S.O.U.L. (Sounds Of Unity & Love)
72	Pye Intl. NSPL 28162	CAN YOU FEEL IT (LP)	35
70s	Pye Intl.	WHAT IS IT (LP)	65

HORATIO SOUL
68	Island WI 3132	Ten White Horses/Angela (Sweet Sweet)	8
69	Crystal CR 7006	Nobody's Gonna Sleep Tonight/Turn Around Baby	6

JIMMY SOUL
62	Stateside SS 103	Twistin' Matilda/I Can't Hold Out Any Longer	8
63	Stateside SS 178	If You Wanna Be Happy/Don't Release Me	18
64	Stateside SS 274	I Hate You Baby/Change Partners	10
64	Stateside SE 1010	IF YOU WANNA BE HAPPY (EP)	40

SHARON SOUL
65	Stateside SS 411	How Can I Get To You/Don't Say Goodbye Love (DJ copy = £150)	100

SOUL AGENTS
64	Pye 7N 15660	I Just Wanna Make Love To You/Mean Woman Blues	40
64	Pye 7N 15707	Seventh Son/Let's Make It Pretty Baby	70
65	Pye 7N 15768	Don't Break It Up/Gospel Train	65

(see also Loot, Don Shinn, Hookfoot)

SOUL AGENTS (Jamaica)
67	Coxsone CS 7007	Get Ready It's Rocksteady/BOB & BELTONES: Smile Like An Angel (B-side actually by Bop & Beltones)	15
67	Coxsone CS 7018	For Your Education/SUMMERTAIRES: Tell Me	40
67	Coxsone CS 7027	Lecture/SOUL BOYS: Blood Pressure	25

SOUL BOYS
66	Rio R120	Rudie Get Wise/JACKIE OPEL: I Don't Want Her	45
67	Island WI 3052	Blood Pressure/RITA MARLEY: Come To Me	40

(see also Soul Agents [Jamaica])

SOUL BROTHERS
65	Mercury MF 916	Gotta Get A Good Thing Going/Good Lovin' Never Hurt	20
65	Decca F 12116	I Keep Ringing My Baby/I Can't Take It	18
65	Parlophone R 5321	I Can't Believe It/You Don't Want To Know	15
66	Ska Beat JB 259	Bugaloo/I'll Come Back	50

SOUL BROTHERS (Jamaica)

65	Ska Beat JB 226	Train To Skaville/WAILERS: I Made A Mistake	45
66	Rio R 118	Crawfish/RITA MARLEY: You Lied	30
66	Rio R 121	Mr T.N.T/MARCIA GRIFFITHS: Mr Everything	25
66	Island WI 282	Green Moon/E Gal OK	20
66	Island WI 294	Ska-Bostello/DON DRUMMOND: Looking Through The Window	25
66	Island WI 296	Sound One/MARTINE: Grandfather's Clock (B-side actually by Emille Straker & Merrymen or Martinis)	20
66	Island WI 3013	More & More/DELROY WILSON: Dancing Mood	22
66	Island WI 3016	Mr Flint/Too Young To Love (B-side actually by Freddie McGregor)	30
67	Island WI 3036	Sound Pressure/ETHIOPIANS: For You	30
67	Island WI 3039	Hi-Life/DELROY WILSON: Close To Me	20
67	Coxsone CS 7001	Take Ten/HUGH GODFREY: Deh Pon Dem	25
67	Coxsone CS 7020	Hey Windell/KEN BOOTHE: Home Home Home	25
67	Coxsone CS 7024	One Stop/TENNORS: Pressure And Slide	20
67	Studio One SO 2006	Hot And Cold/TERMITES: Mercy Mr. Percy	22
67	Studio One SO 2016	Honeypot/VICEROYS: Lose And Gain	20
70	Pressure Beat PR 5506	Pussy Catch A Fire (actually by Soul Twins)/DESTROYERS: Follow This Beat (B-side actually "Secret Weapon" by Ansell Collins)	15
67	Coxsone CSL 8001	HOT SHOT SKA (LP)	90
67	Coxsone CSL 8002	CARIB SOUL (LP)	95

(see also Earl Van Dyke & Soul Brothers, Soul Twins, Lee Perry, Tony Gregory, Ethiopians, Itals, Hortense & Delroy, Gaylads, Jennors, Derrick Morgan, Summertaires, Delroy Wilson)

SOUL BROTHERS SIX

67	Atlantic 584 118	Some Kind Of Wonderful/I'll Be Loving You	50
69	Atlantic 584 164	Some Kind Of Wonderful/Somebody Else Is Loving My Baby	10
72	Atlantic K 10204	Some Kind Of Wonderful/Check Yourself	6
74	Atlantic K 10471	Thank You For Loving Me/Somebody Else Is Loving My Baby	10

SOUL CATS

69	Camel CA 23	Keep It Moving/Your Sweet Love	10
69	Gas GAS 109	Choo Choo Train/The Load (actually "Swinging For Joy" by Count Ossie Band)	10
71	Hillcrest HCT 2	Reggay Got Soul (actually by Carl Bryan)/Land Of Love	8
70s	Junior JR 103	Reggay Got Soul (actually by Carl Bryan)/Land Of Love (reissue)	8

SOUL CHILDREN

69	Stax STAX 137	The Sweeter He Is Parts 1 & 2	6
71	Stax 2025 050	Give Me One Good Reason/Bring It Here	6
72	Stax 2025 102	Hearsay/Don't Take My Sunshine	6
74	Stax STXS 2006	Love Makes It Right/Love Makes It Right (mono)	6
72	Stax 2325 076	GENESIS (LP)	15
74	Stax STX 1005	FRICTION (LP)	15

SOUL CITY

62	Cameo Parkway P 103	Everybody Dance Now/Who Knows (DJ copy = £125)	70

SOUL CITY EXECUTIVES

69	Soul City SC 109	Happy Chatter/Falling In Love	10

SOUL CLAN

68	Atlantic 584 202	Soul Meeting/That's How It Feels (some in p/s)	12/8

(see also Solomon Burke, Arthur Conley, Don Covay, Ben E. King, Joe Tex)

SOUL DEFENDERS

71	Banana BA 354	Way Back Home/SOUL REBELS: Stand For Your Rights	18
72	Ackee ACK 147	Sound Almighty/COUNT OSSIE: Meditation	12

(see also Eric Donaldson, Carey Johnson)

SOUL DIRECTIONS

70	Attack ATT 8011	Su Su Su/Better Herring	10

GEORGE SOULE

75	United Artists UP 35771	Get Involved/Everybody's Got A Song To Sing	8

SOULETTES

65	Ska Beat JB 204	Opportunity/DIZZY JOHNNY & STUDIO 1 ORCHESTRA: Sudden Destruction	28
70	Upsetter US 337	Let It Be/UPSETTERS: Big Dog	18
71	Jackpot JP 766	My Desire/Bring It Up	12
71	Jackpot JP 767	All Of Your Loving/LLOYD CLARKE: Love Me	12
73	Attack ATT 8044	This World/Same Thing	5

(see also Rita Marley, Ken Boothe, Roland Alphonso, Uniques)

SOUL DESTROYERS

00	Stark Relaity STARK008	Blow Your Top Pt. 1/Blow Your Top Pt. 2	12

SOUL EXPLOSION

69	Downtown DT 455	Let's Try It Again/Gumpton Rock	6
70	J-DAN JDN 4405	My Mother's Eyes/Gum Pot	7

SOUL FLAMES

68	Nu Beat NB 020	Mini Really Fit Dem/Soul Train	9

SOUL GENERATION

79	Grapevine GRP 131	Hold On/The Lonely Sea	15
73	Sticky SBL 135	BEYOND BODY AND SOUL (LP)	28

SOULFUL STRINGS

67	Chess CRS 8068	Burning Spear/Within You, Without You	30
69	Chess CRS 8094	I Wish It Would Rain/Listen Here	20
69	Chess CRLS 4534	GROOVIN' WITH THE SOULFUL STRINGS (LP)	30

SOUL KINGS

69	Blue Cat BS 169	The Magnificent Seven/RUPIE EDWARDS: Long Lost Love	30

MINT VALUE £

SOUL LEADERS
67 Rio R 134   Pour On The Sauce/Beauty Is Only Skin Deep 18

SOULMATES (Jamaica)
69 Amalgamated AMG 836   Them A Laugh And A Ki Ki/The Hippys Are Here (B-side actually by
  Hippy Boys)... 30
69 Amalgamated AMG 842   On The Move/Jump It Up (B-side actually by Viceroys) 25
69 Camel CA 33   Beware Of Bad Dogs/Short Cut (actually by Glen Adams)................... 12
70 Unity UN 555   Ten Cent/DOREEN SHAFFER: Stay With Me Forever 10

SOULMATES (U.K.)
65 Parlophone R 5334   Too Late To Say You're Sorry/Your Love 75
66 Parlophone R 5407   Bring Your Love Back Home (with Jet Set)/When Love Is Gone 10
66 Parlophone R 5506   Mood Melancholy/Sayin' Something.............................. 8
67 Parlophone R 5601   Is That You?/Time's Run Out 7
(see also Liza Strike)

SOUL MERCHANTS
67 President PT 166   Whole Lot Of Lovin'/Stormy Weather 5

SOUL PARTNERS
69 Pama PM 766   Walk On Judge/Lose The One You Love 15

SOUL PEOPLE
68 Island WIP 6040   Hummin'/Soul Drink 20

SOUL PROPRIETORS
65 Concord CON STD 74   All/Lonely Separation (private pressing) .... 300+

SOUL REBELS
72 Banana BA 374   Listen And Observe/What's Love 45
(see also Soul Defenders)

SOUL RHYTHMS
69 Bullet BU 404   Work Boy Work/CECIL THOMAS: Girl Lonesome Fever................... 12
69 High Note HS 013   National Lottery/Round Seven................................. 12
69 Gas GAS 113   Soul Call/Musical Gate 10
(see also Hippy Boys, Max Romeo)

SOUL RUNNERS
67 Polydor 56732   Grits 'n' Cornbread/Spreading Honey......................... 20

SOUL SEARCHERS
74 Sussex SXX 2   Blow Your Whistle (Parts 1 & 2) 6
74 Sussex LPSX 4   SALT OF THE EARTH (LP)................................... 20

SOUL SISTERS (U.S.)
64 Sue WI 312   I Can't Stand It/Blueberry Hill 40
64 Sue WI 336   Loop De Loop/Long Gone 50
65 London HLC 9970   Foolish Dreamer/Good Time Tonight (DJ copy = £100) 60
72 United Artists UP 35388   Good Time Tonight/Some Soul Food 10
64 Sue ILP 913   THE SOUL SISTERS (LP)..................................... 150

SOUL SISTERS (Jamaica)
69 Amalgamated AMG 839   Wreck A Buddy/VERSATILES: Push It In 18
(see also Dennis Brown)

SOUL SOUNDS
67 Columbia S(C)X 6158   SOUL SURVIVAL (LP) 25
(see also Savages, Rebel Rousers)

SOUL STIRRERS
69 Duke DU 25   Come See About Me/LLOYD CHARMERS: 5 To 5 12
(see also Sam Cooke)

SOUL SURVIVORS
67 Stateside SS 2057   Expressway To Your Heart/Hey Gyp......................... 25
68 Stateside SS 2094   Explosion (In Your Soul)/Dathon's Theme 15
69 Atlantic 584 275   Mama Soul/Tell Daddy 30

SOUL SYNDICATE
72 Green Door GD 4021   Riot (actually by Johnny Moore & Soul Syndicate)/Smoke Without Fire
  (actually by Keith Hudson).................................... 15
(see also Rockin' Horse)

SOUL TONES
70 Pama PM 790   Dancing Time/BUNNY BARRETT: Love Locked Out 15

SOUL TWINS (Jamaica)
70 High Note HS 043   Little Suzie/Cherrie 8
72 Clandisc CLA 238   Don't Call Me Nigga/DYNAMITES: Joe Louis.......................... 6

SOUL TWINS (U.S.)
77 Grapevine GRP 101   Quick Change Artist/Give The Man A Chance 15

SOUL VENDORS
67 Coxsone CS 7028   You Troubled Me/BOP & BELTONES: Love 25
67 Coxsone CS 7029   Fat Fish/MARCIA GRIFFITHS: Call To Me......................... 50
67 Studio One SO 2018   Rocking Sweet Pea/JOE HIGGS: Change Of Plans................... 45
67 Studio One SO 2022   Cool Shade/RICHARD ACE: I Need You 25
67 Studio One SO 2028   Just A Little Bit Of Soul/ALTON ELLIS: I Am Just A Guy 22
67 Studio One SO 2031   Take Me/DELROY WILSON: I'm Not A King 25
67 Studio One SO 2032   Pe Da Pa/ERNEST WILSON: Money Worries 25
67 Studio One SO 2034   Hot Rod/GAYLADS: Africa (We Want To Go) 25
67 Studio One SO 2035   Pupa Lick/ETHIOPIANS: Leave My Business Alone 30
68 Studio One SO 2038   Psychedelic Rock/Gaylads: I'm Free 30

68	Studio One SO 2043	Chinese Chicken/JACKIE MITTOO: Put It On.	25
68	Studio One SO 2044	Happy Ogan (actually titled "Happy Organ")/INVADERS: Soulful Music	25
68	Studio One SO 2048	Evening Time/RIGHTEOUS FLAMES: Ease Up	25
68	Studio One SO 2058	Frozen Soul/ERNEST WILSON: If I Were A Carpenter.	25
68	Studio One SO 2066	Soul Joint/Soul Limbo	25
68	Coxsone CS 7037	Grooving Steady/ROY RICHARDS: Warm And Tender Ska	25
68	Coxsone CS 7038	Whipping The Prince (actually by Ed Hangle & Alton Ellis)/ HEPTONES: If You Knew	18
68	Coxsone CS 7048	Last Waltz/HAMLINS: Sentimental Reasons	20
68	Coxsone CS 7057	Real Rock/AL CAMPBELL: Don't Run Away	40+
68	Coxsone CS 7071	West Of The Sun/ALTON ELLIS: A Fool	25
69	Coxsone CS 7084	Sixth Figure/DENZIL LAING: Man Payaba	25
69	Studio One SO 2070	Captain Cojoe/JACKIE MITTOO: Drum Song.	25
67	Coxsone CSL 8010	ON TOUR (LP)	120+

(see also Dobby Dobson)

SOUND
79	Tortch TOR 003	PHYSICAL WORLD (EP)	18
80	Korova KOW 10	Heyday/Brute Force (p/s)	5
81	Korova KOW 21	Sense Of Purpose/Point Of No Return (p/s).	5
79	Tortch TOR 008	THE SOUND (LP, possibly unissued)	
80	Korova KODE 2	JEOPARDY (LP, with inner)	12
85	Statik STAB 1	SHOCK OF DAYLIGHT (mini-LP)	12

(see also Outsiders, Second Layer)

SOUND BARRIER
| 68 | Beacon BEA 109 | She Always Comes Back To Me/Groovin' Slow | 55 |

SOUND CEREMONY
89	Celestial Sound SRT 8KF	You're Breaking My Heart (p/s)	10
79	Celestial Sound RWG 001	GUITAR STAR (LP)	20
79	Celestial Sound RWG 002	RON WARREN GANDERTON & SOUND CEREMONY (LP)	20
81	Celestial Sound RWG 003	PRECIOUS AS ENGLAND (LP).	20

SOUND DIMENSION
69	Coxsone CS 7083	Scorcia/CECIL & JACKIE: Breaking Up (B-side actually "Hold Me Baby" by Basil Daley).	22
69	Coxsone CS 7085	Soul Trombone (Suffering Stink)/LARRY & ALVIN: Your Cheating Heart	22
69	Coxsone CS 7090	Soulful Strut/Breaking Up	25
69	Coxsone CS 7093	More Scorcha/LENNIE HIBBERT: Village Soul.	25
69	Coxsone CS 7097	Time Is Tight/BARRY LLEWELLYN: Sad Song.	22
69	Bamboo BAM 5	Doctor Sappa Too/Soul Eruption (B-side actually by Roy Richards & Sound Dimension)	15
69	Bamboo BAM 7	Baby Face/GLADIATORS: Anywhere	12
69	Bamboo BAM 9	Jamaica Rag/C. MARSHALL: I Need Your Loving	12
69	Bamboo BAM 13	Whoopee/NORMA FRAZER: Working (B-side actually by Marcia Griffiths)	15
69	Bamboo BAM 14	Black Onion/Bitter Blood	12
70	Bamboo BAM 18	Poison Ivy/Botheration (Version).	10
70	Bamboo BAM 50	Money Maker/BURNING SPEAR: Door Peeper	45
70	Banana BA 313	In The Summertime/In The Summertime (Version)	25
70	Banana BA 338	My Sweet Lord (Instrumental)/DENNIS BROWN: Silky (B-side actually by Monty Alexander & Cyclones)	12
70	Supreme SUP 202	More Games/MR. FOUNDATION: Maga Dog (actually by Invaders).	10
72	Ackee ACK 149	Solas/GLADIATORS: Sonia	10

(see also Brentford Road Allstars, Jackie Mittoo, Bob Andy, Horace Andy, John Holt, Larry Marshall, Irving Brown, Heptones, Freedom Singers, Winston Francis, Jerry Jones, Ethiopians, Cables, Alton Ellis, Gladiators, Ken Boothe, Soul Vendors)

SOUNDGARDEN
90	A&M AMX 560	Hands All Over/Come Together/Heretic/Big Dumb Sex (10", foldout pack)	8
90	A&M AMY 574	Loud Love/Big Dumb Sex/Get On The Snake/Fresh Deadly Roses (12", etched, stickered p/s)	8
92	A&M AMY 102	Outshined/I Can't Give You Anything/Homicidal Suicidal (12", p/s, limited ed.)	8
92	A&M AMY 723	Rusty Cage/Touch Me/Show Me (12", poster p/s, 5000 only).	12
96	A&M 5818457	Burden In My Hand/Karaoke (p/s, white vinyl, numbered, 5000 only).	15
94	A&M 540215-1	SUPERUNKNOWN (2 x LP, clear or blue vinyl, stickered, 2 lyric sheets)	18

SOUND OF JIMMY NICOL
| 65 | Decca F 12107 | Clementine/Bim Bam | 20 |

(see also Jimmy Nicol)

SOUND NETWORK
| 65 | Mercury MF 944 | Watching/How About Now | 30 |

SOUNDS AROUND
| 66 | Piccadilly 7N 35345 | What Does She Do?/Sad Subject | 20 |
| 67 | Piccadilly 7N 35396 | Red White And You/One Of Two | 25 |

(see also Peter & Wolves, John Pantry, Norman Conquest, Factory)

SOUNDS COMBINE
| 71 | Escort ERT 862 | African Museum/African Museum (Version). | 8 |

SOUNDS GALACTIC
| 70 | Phase 4 Stereo PFS 4208 | AN ASTRONOMICAL ODYSSEY (LP) | 15 |

SOUNDS INCORPORATED
61	Parlophone R 4815	Mogambo/Emily.	15
62	Decca F 11540	Sounds Like Locomotion/Taboo	8
63	Decca F 11590	Stop/Go	8
63	Decca F 11723	Order Of The Keys/Keep Moving.	25
64	Columbia DB 7239	The Spartans/Detroit.	6
64	Columbia DB 7321	Spanish Harlem/Rinky Dink.	6

64	Columbia DB 7404	William Tell/Bullets	6
65	Columbia DB 7545	Time For You/Hall Of The Mountain King	7
65	Columbia DB 7676	My Little Red Book/Justice Neddi	7
65	Columbia DB 7737	On The Brink/I'm Comin' Thru	30
67	Polydor 56209	How Do You Feel/Dead As You Go	7
69	Decca 22883	Warmth Of The Sun/Apollo (export)	6
64	Columbia SEG 8360	TOP GEAR (EP)	28
64	Columbia 33SX 1659	SOUNDS INCORPORATED (LP, also stereo SCX 3531)	28/32
65	EMI Regal SREG 1071	RINKY DINK (LP, export issue)	22
66	Studio Two TWO 144	SOUNDS INCORPORATED (LP)	18

(see also Tony Newman)

SOUND SIXTY-SIX
| 66 | Decca F 12323 | Flight 4864/The Bouncer | 8 |

SOUNDS NICE
69	Parlophone R 5797	Love At First Sight/Love You Too ('featuring Tim Mycroft')	6
69	Parlophone R 5821	Sleepless Night/Continental Exchange ('featuring Tim Mycroft')	6
69	Parlophone PMC/PCS 7089	LOVE AT FIRST SIGHT (LP)	22

(see also Third Ear Band, Chris Spedding, Clem Cattini Ork)

SOUNDS OF JOHNNY HAWKSWORTH
| 66 | Columbia DB 8059 | Goal/"Goal — World Cup 1966" Theme | 15 |

(see also Johnny Hawksworth)

SOUNDS OF LES AND BARRY
| 65 | Fontana TF 657 | Looie Girl/She Who Needs Me | 6 |

SOUNDS OF MODIFICATION
| 68 | Stateside SL/SSL 10262 | SOUNDS OF MODIFICATION (LP) | 15 |

SOUNDS OF SALVATION
| 74 | Reflection RL 310 | SOUNDS OF SALVATION (LP, with booklet) | 90 |

(see also Reflection)

SOUNDS OF ZION
| 60s | Tabernacle TEP 1 | HOME TO GLORY (EP) | 8 |

SOUNDS ORCHESTRAL
66	Piccadilly 7N 35284	Thunderball/Mr Kiss Kiss Bang Bang	10
65	Piccadilly 7N 35248	Moonglow/Scarlatti Potion No. 9	7
65	Pye NPL 38016	THUNDERBALL — SOUNDS ORCHESTRAL MEET JAMES BOND (LP, some in gatefold sleeve)	20/30

SOUNDS PROGRESSIVE
| 70 | Eyemark EMCL 1009S | KID JENSEN INTRODUCES SOUNDS PROGRESSIVE (LP) | 25 |

SOUNDS SENSATIONAL
| 67 | HMV POP 1584 | Love In The Open Air/Night Cry | 15 |

SOUND STAGE ORCHESTRA
| 76 | BBC RESL 30 | Grandstand/Rugby Special | 6 |

SOUND SYSTEM
| 65 | Island WI 258 | You Don't Know Like I Do/Take Me Serious | 15 |

(see also Owen Gray)

EPIC SOUNDTRACKS
| 81 | Rough Trade RT 084 | Popular, Classical: Jelly Babies/A 3-Acre Floor/Pop In Packets (p/s) | 5 |

(see also Swell Maps, Thurston Moore Kim Gordon & Epic Soundtracks)

SOUND VISION
| 70s | Key KL 007 | IN CONCERT (LP, featuring Judy MacKenzie) | 25 |

SOUP DRAGONS
86	Popshop 001/ Lyntone LYN 16674	If You Were The Only Girl In The World/LEGEND: Talk Open (33rpm flexi with *Pure Popcorn* fanzine, later with *The Legend* fanzine)	8/6/5
86	Subway Organisation SUBWAY 2	THE SUN IS IN THE SKY (EP, unreleased, 1,000 only, foldaround p/s in poly bag)	15
86	Subway Organisation SUBWAY 4	Whole Wide World/I Know Everything (with insert in poly bag, orange or blue foldaround p/s)	5
86	Raw TV Products RTV 1	Hang Ten!/Slow Things Down (p/s, blue or red vinyl)	5
86	Raw TV Products RTV 2	Head Gone Astray/Girl In The World/So Sad I Feel (PVC sleeve, with poster)	10
89	Raw TV Products	DEEP TRASH (cassette, withdrawn)	15
90	Raw TV SOUPLP 2	LOVEGOD (LP, with foiled sleeve & lyric sheet)	12

(see also BMX Bandits, Future Pilot A.K.A.)

SOUP GREENS
| 65 | Stateside SS 457 | That's Too Bad/Like A Rolling Stone | 50 |

SOUPHERBS
| 65 | Oak RGJ 601 | SOUPHERBS (LP) | 220+ |

HARRY SOUTH ORCHESTRA
| 75 | EMI EMI 2252 | The Sweeney (TV Theme) (Parts 1 & 2) | 20 |
| 67 | Mercury 20081 MCL | PRESENTING HARRY SOUTH (LP) | 25 |

JOE SOUTH
62	Oriole CB 1752	Masquerade/I'm Sorry For You	10
63	MGM MGM 1206	Same Old Song/Standing Invitation	7
65	MGM MGM 1267	Concrete Jungle/Last One To Know	7
65	HMV POP 1474	I Want To Be Somebody/Deep Inside Me	7
68	Capitol CL 15535	Birds Of A Feather/It Got Away	5
69	Capitol CL 15568	Don't Throw Your Love To The Wind/Redneck	5
69	Capitol CL 15579	Games People Play/Mirror Of Your Mind	5

69	Capitol CL 15608	Don't It Make You Want To Go Home/Heart's Desire	15
70	Capitol CL 15666	Hush/Party People	5
69	Capitol E-(S)T 108	INTROSPECT (LP)	15
70	Capitol ST 21548	WALK A MILE IN MY SHOES (LP)	12

SOUTH COAST SKA STARS
| 80 | Safari SAFE 27 | South Coast Rumble/Head On (p/s) | 8 |

(see also Ray Fenwick)

JERI SOUTHERN
51	London L 1070	I'm In Love Again/You're The Cause Of It All (78)	10
54	Brunswick 05343	Remind Me/Little Boy Grown Tall	12
55	Brunswick 05367	The Man That Got Away/Speak Softly To Me	12
55	Brunswick 05490	An Occasional Man/It's D'Lovely	12
56	Brunswick 05529	Where Walks My True Love?/Don't Explain	10
57	Brunswick 05665	Fire Down Below/Smoke Gets In Your Eyes (78 rpm = £8)	7
57	Brunswick 05709	Scarlet Ribbons (For Her Hair)/Would I	6
57	Brunswick 05722	Bells Are Ringing/Just In Time	6
58	Brunswick 05737	I Waited So Long/The Mystery Of Love (78 rpm = £8)	6
59	Capitol CL 15054	Run/Don't Look At Me That Way	6
59	Brunswick OE 9438	CARESSES (EP)	15
59	Columbia SEG 7935	RIDIN' HIGH (EP)	15
55	Brunswick LA 8699	WARM (10" LP)	28
56	Brunswick LAT 8100	THE SOUTHERN STYLE (LP)	22
57	Brunswick LAT 8209	JERI GENTLY JUMPS (LP)	22
58	Columbia 33SX 1110	SOUTHERN BREEZE (LP)	15
58	Columbia 33SX 1134	COFFEE, CIGARETTES AND MEMORIES (LP)	15
59	Columbia 33SX 1155	JERI SOUTHERN MEETS JOHNNY SMITH (LP)	15
59	Capitol (S)T 1173	JERI SOUTHERN MEETS COLE PORTER (LP, mono/stereo)	12
60	Capitol (S)T 1278	AT THE CRESCENDO (LP, mono/stereo)	12

JOHNNY SOUTHERN & HIS WESTERN RHYTHM KINGS
| 57 | Melodisc MEL 1413 | We Will Make Love/Crazy Heart (78 rpm = £6) | 10 |
| 57 | Melodisc MEL 1434 | She's Long, She's Tall/Lonesome Whistle (78 rpm = £6) | 10 |

SOUTHERN COMFORT
71	Harvest HAR 5035	Willie Urricane/Berkshire Berk	10
71	Harvest HAR 5047	Morning Has Broken/Cosmic Jig	10
71	Harvest SHSP 4012	FROG CITY (LP)	12
72	Harvest SHSP 799	SOUTHERN COMFORT (LP)	18
72	Harvest SHSP 4021	STIR DON'T SHAKE (LP)	12

(see also Matthews Southern Comfort)

SOUTHERN SOUND
| 66 | Columbia DB 7982 | Just The Same As You/I Don't Wanna Go | 350+ |

SOUTHERN TONES
| 58 | Jazz Collector JEN 10 | WAITING FOR THE LORD (EP) | 10 |

SOUTHLANDERS
55	Parlophone MSP 6182	Ain't That A Shame/Have You Ever Been Lonely (78 rpm, R 4069 = £7)	20
56	Parlophone MSP 6236	Hush-A-Bye Rock/The Wedding Of The Lucky Black Cat (78 rpm, R4171 = £7)	20
57	Decca F 10946	Alone/Swedish Polka	6
57	Decca F 10958	Peanuts/I Never Dreamed	7
58	Decca F 10982	Put A Light In The Window/Penny Loafers And Bobby Socks (78 rpm = £10)	10
58	Decca F 11014	Down Deep/Wishing For Your Love (78 rpm = £6)	5
58	Decca F 11032	I Wanna Jive Tonight/Torero (78 rpm = £7)	15
58	Decca F 11067	The Mole In A Hole/Choo-Choo-Choo-Choo Cha-Cha-Cha (tri-centre, repressings have solid centre) (78 rpm = £10)	8/5
58	Decca DFE 6508	THE SOUTHLANDERS NUMBER ONE (EP)	30

SOUTHSIDE JOHNNY & THE ASBURY DUKES
| 77 | Epic EPC 5230 | Little Girl So Fine/I Ain't Got The Fever (withdrawn) | 20 |

SOUTH SIDE MOVEMENT
| 73 | Pye International 7N 25615 | I Been Watchin' You/Have A Little Mercy | 8 |

SOUTHWEST F.O.B.
| 68 | Stax STAX 107 | Smell Of Incense/Green Skies | 20 |

SOUTHWIND
| 70 | Harvest HAR 5019 | Boogie Woogie Country Girl/Honky Tonkin' | 5 |

PHIL SOUTHWOOD
| 61 | QRS 1-462 | D's Dilemma/Sister Sadie (some in p/s) | 20/12 |

SOVEREIGNS
| 66 | King KG 1050 | Bring Me Home Love/That's The Way Love Is | 18 |

RED SOVINE
56	Brunswick 05513	Why Baby Why? (with Webb Pierce)/Sixteen Tons (78 rpm = £18)	35
62	Top Rank JKP 3015	COUNTRY MUSIC (EP)	20
66	London HA-B 8288	GIDDY-UP GO (LP)	15
67	London HA-B 8343	I DIDN'T JUMP THE FENCE (LP)	15
69	London HA-B 8379	TELL MAUDE I SLIPPED (LP)	15

(see also Webb Pierce)

THE SOWELL RADICS
| 81 | Attack TACK 24 | Caution/Bali-Hi Special (12") | 40 |
| 81 | Attack TACK 27 | Fight Fight Fight/Aces Rock (12") | 40 |

MINT VALUE £

BOB B. SOXX & THE BLUE JEANS

63	London HLU 9646	Zip-A-Dee-Doo-Dah/Flip And Nitty.	18
63	London HLU 9694	Why Do Lovers Break Each Other's Heart?/Dr Kaplan's Office.	25
63	London HLU 9754	Not Too Young To Get Married/Annette	20
69	London HLU 10243	Zip-A-Dee-Doo-Dah/Why Do Lovers Break Each Other's Heart?.	5
63	London HA-U 8121	ZIP-A-DEE-DOO-DAH (LP)	135
75	Phil Spector Intl. 2307 004	BOB B. SOXX & THE BLUE JEANS (LP)	35

(see also Darlene Love, Bobby Sheen, Blossoms, Crystals, Phil Spector)

SPACE
79	Pye NSPH 28725	JUST BLUE (LP, picture disc)	20

(see also Madeline Bell)

SPACE
90	Space LP 1	SPACE (LP)	50
90	Space CD 1	SPACE (CD, beware of counterfeits).	40

(see also J.A.M.S., KLF, Timelords, Disco 2000)

SPACE
93	Hug HUG 1T	If It's Real/Lookin'/I'm Free (12", p/s with free 'fortune fish').	30
95	Home Recordings 12HOMEX 1	Money Remixes By Consolidated: Money (Lost In Space Remix)/(Still Lost In Space/Safe Bass Mix)/(Space Club Mix)/(Instrumental) (12", p/s, yellow vinyl).	8
96	Gut CDGUT 1	Neighbourhood (Radio Edit)/Turn Me On To Spiders/Rejects/ Neighbourhood (Live It Club Mix) (CD).	10

SPACE ART
77	Arista AHAL 8001	SPACE ART (LP)	15

SPACEMEN
59	Top Rank JAR 228	The Clouds/The Lonely Jet Pilot	10

SPACEMEN 3
86	Glass GLAEP 105	Walkin' With Jesus (Sound Of Confusion)/Rollercoaster/Feel So Good (12" maxi-single, p/s, some with numbered insert)	75/60
87	Glass GLAEP 108	Transparent Radiation/Ecstasy Symphony/Transparent Radiation (Flashback)/Things'll Never Be The Same/Starship (12" maxi-single, p/s).	50
88	Glass GLASS 12054	Take Me To The Other Side/Soul 1/That's Just Fine (12", p/s).	35
88	Cheree CHEREE 5	Extract From An Evening Of Contemporary Sitar Music (flexi, p/s, with *Cheree* fanzine).	6
88	Fire BLAZE 29S	Revolution/Che (die-cut company sleeve).	5
88	Fire BLAZE 29T	Revolution/Che/May The Circle Be Unbroken (12").	8
88	Fire BLAZE 29CD	Revolution/Che/May The Circle Be Unbroken (3" CD).	8
89	Fire THREEBIE 3	Revolution/Suicide/Repeater/Love Intro Theme (Xtacy) (12", mail-order only, numbered p/s).	25
89	Sniffin' Rock SR 008	When Tomorrow Hits (some with *Sniffin' Rock* magazine)	15/10
89	Fire BLAZE 36S	Hypnotized/Just To See You Smile (Honey Pt 2) (die-cut company sleeve).	5
89	Fire BLAZE 36T	Hypnotized/Just To See You Smile (Honey Pt 2)/The World Is Dying (12", with poster).	10
89	Fire BLAZE 36CD	Hypnotized/Just To See You Smile (Honey Pt 2)/The World Is Dying (3" CD, with adaptor, 5" case).	10
91	Fire BLAZE 41	Big City (Edit)/Drive (p/s).	5
91	Fire BLAZE 41TR	Big City (Remix)/I Love You (Remix) (12", unissued, white label promo, 50 only).	50
91	Catalogue CAT 089	I Love You//Sometimes (2 x flexis, with *The Catalogue* magazine)	10
86	Glass GLALP 018	SOUND OF CONFUSION (LP)	25
87	Glass GLALP 026	THE PERFECT PRESCRIPTION (LP, gold/silver or bronze/silver sleeve).	25
88	Glass GLALP 030	PERFORMANCE (LP)	20
88	Glass GLACD 030	PERFORMANCE (CD)	18

(see also Sonic Boom, Spiritualized, Darkside, Spectrum)

SPACEPIMP
95	Clear CLR 415	The Pimp/Spacechace/K9 Law (12", p/s, some on clear vinyl)	25/20

SPAGHETTI HEAD
75	RCA RCA 2513	Big Noise From Winnetka/Funky Axe	20

(see also Clem Cattini Ork, Tornados)

SPAGHETTI JUNCTION
72	Columbia DB 8935	Work's Nice — If You Can Get It/Step Right Up	25

(see also Hank Marvin)

SPANIELS
60	Joy JOYS 197	THE SPANIELS (LP)	20

MUGGSY SPANIER & DIXIELAND/RAGTIME BAND
56	Tempo A 36	Tin Roof Blues/Muskrat Rumble	6

(see also Sidney Bechet)

SPANISH BOYS
65	Blue Beat BB 331	I Am Alone/BUSTER'S ALL STARS: Vera Cruz	50

SPANISHTONIANS
67	Pyramid PYR 6005	Kisses/ROLAND ALPHONSO: Women Of The World	22
67	Pyramid PYR 6009	Suffer Me Not/ROLAND ALPHONSO: Guantanamera Ska	22
67	Pyramid PYR 6018	Rudie Gets Plenty/ROLAND ALPHONSO: Sock It To Me	22

SPANISHTOWN SKABEATS
65	Blue Beat BB 315	Oh My Baby (actually by Charmers)/Stop That Train	200+
65	Blue Beat BB 320	King Solomon/BUSTER'S ALLSTARS: Devil's Daffodil.	60

SPANKY & OUR GANG
67	Mercury MF 982	Sunday Will Never Be The Same/Distance.	15
67	Mercury MF 999	Making Every Minute Count/If You Could Only Be Me	8
67	Mercury MF 1010	Lazy Day/It Ain't Necessarily Byrd Avenue	8
68	Mercury MF 1018	Sunday Mornin'/Echoes	8

68	Mercury MF 1023	Like To Get To Know You/Three Ways From Tomorrow	12
68	Mercury MF 1052	Give A Damn/The Swingin' Gate	10
69	Mercury MF 1123	And She's Mine/Leopard Skin Phone	7
75	Epic S EPC 3850	I Won't Brand You/When I Wanna	7
67	Mercury 20114 (S)MCL	SPANKY AND OUR GANG (LP)	35
68	Mercury 20121 SCML	LIKE TO GET TO KNOW YOU (LP)	30
69	Mercury 20150 SCML	ANYTHING YOU CHOOSE/WITHOUT RHYME OR REASON (LP)	30

(see also Mama & Papas)

OTIS SPANN

64	Decca F 11972	Stirs Me Up/Keep Your Hand Out Of My Pocket	18
68	Blue Horizon 57-3142	Bloody Murder/Can't Do Me No Good	15
69	Blue Horizon 57-3155	Walkin'/Temperature Is Rising (with Fleetwood Mac)	20
64	Decca LK 4615	THE BLUES OF OTIS SPANN (LP)	70
64	Storyville SLP 157	GOOD MORNING MR. BLUES (LP)	35
64	Storyville SLP 168	PIANO BLUES (LP, with Memphis Slim)	35
65	Decca LK 4661	BLUES NOW (LP)	40
66	Stateside SL 10169	THE BLUES NEVER DIE (LP)	40
67	HMV CLP/CSD 3609	BLUES ARE WHERE IT'S AT (LP)	40
67	Storyville 670 157	PORTRAITS IN BLUES VOL. 3 (LP, reissue of SLP 157)	18
67	Polydor 545 030	NOBODY KNOWS MY TROUBLES (LP)	40
67	Bounty BY 6037	NOBODY KNOWS MY TROUBLES (LP)	30
68	Stateside (S)SL 10255	BOTTOM OF THE BLUES (LP)	40
69	Chess CRLS 4556	FATHERS AND SONS (LP)	25
69	Blue Horizon 7-63217	BIGGEST THING SINCE COLOSSUS (LP, with Fleetwood Mac)	100
69	Deram DML/SML 1036	CRACKED SPANNER HEAD (LP)	60
69	Python KM 4	RAISED IN MISSISSIPPI (LP, 99 copies only, with Robert Jnr. Lockwood)	60
70	Vanguard VSD 6514	CRYIN' TIME (LP)	18

(see also Fleetwood Mac, Memphis Slim, Johnny Shines, Lonnie Johnson)

SPANNER THRU MA BEATBOX

| 87 | Earthly Delights EARTH 3 | SPANNER THRU MA BEATBOX (LP) | 15 |

SPARKERS

| 69 | Blue Cat BS 155 | Dig It Up/DELROY WILSON: This Life Makes Me Wonder | 50 |

(see also Samuel Edwards)

LOU SPARKES

| 69 | Gayfeet GS 203 | By The Time I Get To Phoenix/Lover Boy | 8 |
| 70 | Gayfeet GS 208 | We Will Make Love/ROLAND ALPHONSO: Sticker | 8 |

(see also Eric Boswell)

SPARKS

72	Bearsville K 15505	Wonder Girl/(No More) Mr. Nice Guy	15
74	Bearsville K 15516	Girl From Germany/Beaver O'Lindy (brown or white label)	10
74	Island WIP 6211	Never Turn Your Back On Mother Earth/Alabamy Right (p/s)	10
75	Island WIP 6221	Something For The Girl With Everything/Marry Me (title sleeve)	6
75	Island WIP 6236	Get In The Swing/Profile (title sleeve)	6
75	Island WIP 6239	Looks, Looks, Looks/Pineapple (title sleeve)	6
75	Island WIP 6249	Looks, Looks, Looks/Pineapple (DJ copy in promo p/s)	15
76	Island WIP 6282	I Want To Hold Your Hand/England (withdrawn after 1 day)	15
76	Island WIP 6357	I Like Girls/England	5
77	Island WIP 6282	I Want To Hold Your Hand/Under The Table With Her (promo only)	25
77	Island WIP 6193	This Town Ain't Big Enough For The Both Of Us/Barbecutie (reissue, orange sunset label)	25
79	Virgin VS 244	The No. 1 Song In Heaven/The No. 1 Song In Heaven (Version) (p/s, green vinyl)	8
79	Virgin VS 244-12	The No. 1 Song In Heaven/The No. 1 Song In Heaven (Long Version) (12", p/s, blue or red vinyl)	10
79	Virgin VS 270-12	Beat The Clock/Beat The Clock (Long Version) (12", black, blue, orange, yellow or pink vinyl, picture disc label, die-cut p/s) each	10
79	Virgin VS 289-12	Tryouts For The Human Race/Tryouts For The Human Race (Long Version) (12", die-cut p/s, orange, yellow, blue or green vinyl, picture disc label) each	10
79	Island WIP 6532	This Town Ain't Big Enough For The Both Of Us/Looks, Looks, Looks	7
80	Virgin VS 343-12	Young Girls (Disco Version)/Young Girls (Long Version)/Just Because You Love Me (12", p/s)	10
81	Why Fi WHYT 1	Tips For Teens/Don't Shoot Me (12", p/s)	10
83	Atlantic A 9866	Cool Places/Sports (no p/s)	5
85	London LONX 69	Change/This Town Ain't Big Enough For Both Of Us (Acoustic Version) (12", p/s)	8
85	Epic A 6671	Armies Of The Night/EVELYN KING: Give It Up (p/s)	5
85	Epic TA 6671	Armies Of The Night/EVELYN KING: Give It Up (12", p/s)	12
86	Consolidated TOON T2	Music That You Can Dance To (UK Extended Club Version)/Fingertips (Extended Club Version) (12", p/s)	8
87	Consolidated TOON T4	Rosebud (Extended Club Mix)/Theme For Rosebud (Cinematic Mix)/Rosebud (FM Mix) (12", p/s)	8
88	Carrere CART 427	So Important (Extremely Important Mix)/(Incredibly Important Mix)/(Single Version) (12", p/s)	8
93	Finiflex FF 1004	National Crime Awareness Week (13 Minutes In Heaven)/National Crime Awareness Week (Perkins Playtime) (12", p/s)	18
93	Finiflex FFCD 1004	National Crime Awareness Week (Psycho Cut)/National Crime Awareness Week (Highly Strung Hoedown)/National Crime Awareness Week (Complete Psycho)/National Crime Awareness Week (13 Minutes In Heaven) (CD)	30
94	Logic 7432 134461	When Do I Get To Sing My Way/(mixes) (12", doublepack, p/s)	15
94	Logic 74321 24302-2	Excerpts From Gratuitous Sax & Senseless Violins (CD, picture disc, gatefold card p/s, promo only)	50
97	Roadrunner RR 2262-6	The No. 1 Song In Heaven (Tin Tin Out Mix)/part 2/(Heavenly Dub) (with Jimmy Somerville) (12", die-cut sleeve)	10

99	Winney CD IFPI LAE 1	The Cute Candidate/This Town Ain't Big Enough For The Both Of Us (1920 Archival Recording)/The Winney Empire/The Cute Candidate On TV/The Race For President (CD, fan club only issue)	10
00	Recognition CDREC 14	The Calm Before The Storm (Radio Edit)/The Calm Before The Storm/It's Educational (CD, unreleased)	15
76	Bearsville K 85505	TWO ORIGINALS OF SPARKS (2-LP, gatefold sleeve with 12-page booklet)	18
79	Virgin V 2115	NO. 1 IN HEAVEN (LP, yellow vinyl with lyric inner sleeve)	12

(see also Les Rita Mitsouko, Adrian Musey, Trevor White)

L. SPARKS

72	Big Shot BI 601	You Don't Care/TONY'S ALL STARS: Must Care (Version)	6
72	Pama PM 833	You Don't Care/TONY'S ALL STARS: Must Care (Version)	6

(see also Lloyd Parks, Termites)

SPARKY AND THE INNER CITIZENS

76	Contempo CS2102	Golden Gate Get Down (Short Version) Golden Gate Get Down (Long Version)	10

CANDY SPARLING

62	Piccadilly 7N 35046	When's He Gonna Kiss Me?/Lonely For You	10
63	Piccadilly 7N 35096	Can You Keep A Secret/Charm Bracelet	10

SPARROW (Jamaica)

60	Kalypso XX 10	Carnival Boycott/Gloria (with Lord Melody)	6
60	Kalypso XX 17	The Sack/Round And Around	5
60s	Melodisc CAL 15	Leading Calypsonians/Love Is Everywhere	6
60s	Melodisc CAL 17	Clara Honey Bunch/Family Sized Cokes	5
60s	Melodisc CAL 18	Goaty/I Confess	5

(see also Mighty Sparrow, King Sparrow)

SPARROW (U.S.)

66	CBS 202342	Tomorrow's Ship/Isn't It Strange	70

(see also Steppenwolf)

JACK SPARROW

66	Doctor Bird DB 1005	Ice Water/ROLAND ALPHONSO: Ska-Culation	45
66	Doctor Bird DB 1027	More Ice Water/ROLAND ALPHONSO: Miss Ska-Culation	45

SPARTA

81	Suspect SUS 1	Fast Lane/Fighting To Be Free (some in p/s)	50/18
81	Suspect SUS 2	Angel Of Death/Tonight (wraparound p/s)	15

(see also Ethiopians))

SPARTANS

62	Stateside SS 117	Can You Waddle? (Parts 1 & 2)	8

SPAZZTIC BLUR

87	Earache MOSH 5	BEFO DA AWBUM (LP)	15

ROGER RUSKIN SPEAR

71	United Artists UP 35221	REBEL TROUSER: Trouser Freak/Trouser Press/Release Me/Drop Out (EP)	5
72	United Artists UAG 29381	ELECTRIC SHOCKS (LP)	20
74	United Artists UAS 29508	UNUSUAL (LP)	20

(see also Bonzo Dog [Doo Dah] Band)

SPEAR OF DESTINY

83	Epic SPEAR 13-1	Flying Scotsman (Extended)/Africa/The Man Who Tunes The Drums (12", p/s, with poster, some autographed)	10
83	Epic WA 3372	The Wheel/The Hop (picture disc)	5
83	Epic DA 3372	The Wheel/The Hop//Grapes Of Wrath (live)/The Preacher (live) (double pack)	6
84	Epic DA 4068	Prisoner Of Love/Rosie//Rainmaker (live)/Don't Turn Away (live) (double pack)	6
86	Dale DALE 2	BOTTOM DRAWER (EP, p/s, white label, 500 only, numbered)	6

(see also Theatre Of Hate, Pack)

BRITNEY SPEARS

00	Jive BRITNEY no cat. no.	OOPS!... I DID IT AGAIN (CD, with promo-only 24pp book, "It's Britney")	40

SPECIAL DUTIES

81	Charnel H. SARCOPHAGI 2	Violent Society/Colchester Council (wraparound p/s)	15
82	Rondelet ROUND 15	VIOLENT SOCIETY (EP)	7
82	Rondelet ROUND 20	POLICE STATE (EP)	7
82	Rondelet ROUND 24	Bullshit Crass/You're Doing Yourself No Good (p/s)	7
83	Expulsion OUT 1	Punk Rocker/Too Much Talking (p/s)	7
82	Rondelet ABOUT 9	77 IN 82 (LP)	12

SPECIALS (THE SPECIAL A.K.A.)

79	2-Tone TT 1/TT 2	Gangsters (as The Special A.K.A.)/THE SELECTER: The Selecter (paper label, some in stamped plain white sleeve; matrix numbers TT1-3 & TT2-1)	20/15
79	2-Tone TT 1/TT 2	Gangsters (as The Special A.K.A.)/THE SELECTER: The Selecter (paper label, die-cut 2-Tone sleeve, 2nd issue with Chrysalis CHS TT 1/2 matrix no.)	6
79	2-Tone CHS TT 5	Message To You Rudy/Nite Klub (paper label, company sleeve, as The Specials featuring Rico)	6
80	2-Tone CHS TT 7	THE SPECIAL A.K.A. LIVE (EP, p/s, paper label)	6
80	2-Tone CHS TT 11	Rat Race/Rude Boys Outa Jail (company sleeve, paper label, as The Specials)	6
80	2-Tone CHS TT 13	Stereotype/International Jet Set (company sleeve, paper label, as The Specials)	6
80	2-Tone CHS TT 16	Do Nothing/Maggie's Farm (p/s, paper label, as The Specials)	6
81	2-Tone CHS TT 17	Ghost Town/Why/Friday Night Saturday Morning (paper labels p/s)	6
81	2-Tone CHS TT 1217	Ghost Town (6.02 Extended Version)/Why/Friday Night, Saturday Morning (12", p/s)	10
82	2-Tone CHS TT 23	War Crimes (The Crime Is Still The Same)/War Crimes (p/s)	5
82	2-Tone CHS TT 1023	War Crimes (The Crime Is Still The Same)/War Crimes (The Crime Is Still The Same) (Version) (10", p/s, as The Special A.K.A.)	7
83	2-Tone CHS TPTT 25	Racist Friend/Bright Lights	5

83	2-Tone CHS TPTT 25	Racist Friend/Bright Lights (picture disc, as The Special A.K.A.) 6
84	2-Tone CHS TT 26	Nelson Mandela/Break Down The Door (p/s) 5
84	2-Tone CHS TT 1226	Nelson Mandela/Break Down The Door (12", p/s) 8
84	2-Tone CHS TT 27	What I Like Most About You Is Your Girlfriend/Can't Get A Break//War Crimes
		(The Crime Is Still The Same)/(Version) (double pack, as The Special A.K.A.) 8
84	2-Tone CHS TPTT 27	What I Like Most About You Is Your Girlfriend/Can't Get A Break (picture disc) 6
84	2-Tone CHS TT 1227	What I Like Most About You Is Your Girlfriend/Can't Get A Break
		(12", poster p/s with free single) 10
86	Strange Fruit SFPS 018	THE PEEL SESSIONS (EP) 10
79	2-Tone TT 5001	SPECIALS (LP) 15
80	2-Tone CDL TT 5001	MORE SPECIALS (LP, some with poster & bonus 7": Roddy Radiation &
		The Specials' "Braggin' And Tryin' Not To Lie"/Judge Roughneck's
		"Rude Buoys Outa Jail" [TT 999]) 25/15

(see also Colourfield, Selecter, Rhoda, Rico)

SPECIMEN
| 83 | London LON 24 | Returning From A Journey/Kiss Kiss Bang Bang (bat-shaped disc) . . . . 10 |
| 80s | Trust TRUE T 001 | Sharp Teeth (12", p/s) . . . . 8 |

SPECKLED RED
60s	Storyville SEP 384	STORYVILLE BLUES ANTHOLOGY VOL. 4 (EP) 18
63	Esquire 32-190	THE DIRTY DOZENS (LP) 35
66	Storyville DL 601	THE DIRTY DOZENS (LP, reissue) 12
71	VJM LC 11	OH RED (LP) 20

PHIL SPECTOR
63	London HA-U 8141	A CHRISTMAS GIFT FOR YOU (LP, various artists, Spector as producer;
		plum label, later black label) 70/25
72	Apple APCOR 24	PHIL SPECTOR'S CHRISTMAS ALBUM (LP, reissue of London HA-U 8141) 30
74	Warner Bros K 59010	PHIL SPECTOR'S CHRISTMAS ALBUM (LP, 2nd reissue, with poster) 18
76	Phil Spector Intl. 2307 008	RARE MASTERS VOL. 1 (LP, various artists, Spector as producer) 35
76	Phil Spector Intl. 2307 009	RARE MASTERS VOL. 2 (LP, various artists, Spector as producer) 35
80	Phil Spector Intl. 2307 015	PHIL SPECTOR '74/'79 (LP, various artists, Spector as producer) 25
81	Phil Spector Intl. WOS 001	WALL OF SOUND (9-LP box set, various artists, Spector as producer) 130

(see also Ronettes, Crystals, Darlene Love, Bob B. Soxx & Blue Jeans, Teddy Bears)

RONNIE SPECTOR
71	Apple APPLE 33	Try Some, Buy Some/Tandoori Chicken (initially with p/s) 35/12
77	Epic EPC 5185	Say Goodbye To Hollywood/Baby Please Don't Go (with E Street Band) 12
81	Red Shadow LP 002	SIREN (LP) 20

(see also Ronettes)

SPECTRES
66	Piccadilly 7N 35339	I (Who Have Nothing)/Neighbour, Neighbour 350
66	Piccadilly 7N 35352	Hurdy Gurdy Man/Laticia 300
67	Piccadilly 7N 35368	We Ain't Got Nothin' Yet/I Want It (beware bootlegs) 275

(Demos are more common and worth £50 less than stock copies)
(see also Traffic Jam, Status Quo)

SPECTRES
| 80 | Direct Hit DH 1 | This Strange Effect/Getting Away With Murder (p/s) . . . . 7 |
| 81 | Demon D 1002 | Stories/Things (p/s) . . . . 5 |

(see also Rich Kids, Swingers)

SPECTRES (Ireland)
| 65 | Lloyd Sound UED QU 1 | The Facts Of Life/Whirlpool . . . . 280+ |

SPECTRUM
65	Columbia DB 7742	Little Girl/Asking You 6
67	RCA RCA 1589	Samantha's Mine/Saturday's Child 5
67	RCA RCA 1619	Portobello Road/Comes The Dawn 8
67	RCA RCA 1651	Headin' For A Heatwave/I Wanna Be Happy With You 5
68	RCA RCA 1700	London Bridge Is Coming Down/Tables And Chairs 6
68	RCA RCA 1753	Little Red Boat By The River/Forget Me Not 5
68	RCA RCA 1775	Ob-La-Di, Ob-La-Da/Music Soothes The Savage Beast 6
69	RCA RCA 1853	Free/The Tale Of Wally Toft 5
69	RCA RCA 1883	Glory/Nodnol 5
70	RCA RCA 1976	Portobello Road/Comes The Dawn (reissue) 6
71	Parlophone R 5908	I'll Be Gone/Launching Place — Pt II 6
69	RCA Intl. INTS 118	THE LIGHT IS DARK ENOUGH (LP) 40

SPECTRUM
| 87 | Phoenix Modernist THE 1 | All Or Nothing (Contemporary Version)/All Or Nothing (Traditional Version) |
| | | (12", p/s with 2 inserts & free 7", distributed by Nine Mile & Cartel) . . . . 8 |

(see also Steve Marriott, Chris Farlowe, P.P. Arnold, Creation)

SPECTRUM
92	Beechwood TT 015e	Taste The Ozone/MOONSHAKE: Night Tripper 5
94	Silvertone	Soul Kiss Glide Divine/STEREOLAB: Tone Burst (demo)/Tempter (demo)
		(unrel., with colour photocopied wraparound p/s, 25 test pressings only) . . . . 150+

(see also Spacemen 3, Sonic Boom)

CHRIS SPEDDING
70	Harvest HAR 5013	Rock'n'Roll Band/BATTERED ORNAMENTS: Goodbye We Loved You (Madly) . . . 12
75	Island WIP 6225	My Bucket's Got A Hole In It/I Can't Boogie 8
75	RAK RAK 210	Motor Bikin'/Working For The Union 5
76	RAK RAK 246	Pogo Dancing/Pose (p/s) 6
77	RAK RAK 261	Get Outa My Pagoda/Hey Miss Betty 5
70	Harvest SHSP 4004	BACKWOOD PROGRESSION (LP) 40
72	Harvest SHSP 4017	THE ONLY LICK I KNOW (LP) 40

(see also Sharks, Nucleus, Sounds Nice, Panhandle, Solid Gold Cadillac, Matthew Ellis, Vibrators, Battered Ornaments, IOFR)

MINT VALUE £

SPEED
78   It IT 1   Big City/All Day And All The Night (some in p/s) 40/15
(see also Cobra, Tearjerkers)

SPEED (Jamaica)
71   Bullet BU 477   There's A Train/Blue Moon 7

SPEEDBALL(S)
80   No Pap/Dirty Dick DD 1/2   No Survivors/Is Somebody There? (miscredited as 'Speedballs' on label,
        some in withdrawn printed die-cut sleeve) 60/25

SPEEDOMETERS
78   Mascot NICE 1   Disgrace/Work (p/s) 5
78   Mascot NICE 2   Liverpool Ladies (p/s) 5

SPEEDY J
94   Warp WAP 46   Pepper (The Hot Mix)/Beam Me Up (The Pegasus Mix) (12") 8

DAVEY SPEIRS
69   Beltona LBA/LBS 61   A MAN OF CONSTANT SORROW (LP) 15

SPELLBINDERS
66   CBS 202453   Help Me (Get Myself Back Together)/Danny Boy (DJ copy = £85) 40
67   CBS 202622   Chain Reaction/For You (DJ copy = £75) 40
67   CBS 2776   Since I Don't Have You/I Believe 12
69   Direction 58-3970   Help Me/Chain Reaction 20

BENNY SPELLMAN
62   London HLP 9570   Lipstick Traces/Fortune Teller 50

BARRINGTON SPENCE
75   Grounation GRO 2009   For The Rest Of My Life/Version 5

JOHNNY SPENCE
61   Parlophone R 4736   Wheels/First Romance 6
68   Verve (S)VLP 9222   WHY NOT? (LP, as Johnnie Spence Big Band) 15

DON SPENCER
62   HMV POP 1087   Fireball/I'm All Alone Again (blue or black labels) 12
63   HMV POP 1186   Busy Doing Nothing/The Joker 5
63   HMV POP 1205   Worried Mind/Give Give Give A Little 5
64   HMV POP 1306   Pride Is Such A Little Word/For Love (with Le Roys) 5
(see also Le Roys)

DON SPENCER/XL5
63   HMV 7EG 8802   FIREBALL AND OTHER TITLES (EP, 2 tracks each) 40

JEREMY SPENCER (Band)
70   Reprise RS 27002   Linda/Teenage Darling 5
79   Atlantic K 11363   Travelling/Cool Breeze (as Jeremy Spencer Band) 5
70   Reprise RSLP 9002   JEREMY SPENCER (LP) 40
71   Reprise K 44105   JEREMY SPENCER (LP, reissue) 20
73   CBS 65387   JEREMY SPENCER AND THE CHILDREN OF GOD (LP) 12
(see also Fleetwood Mac)

JO SPENCER
71   Dynamic DYN 415   Bed Of Roses/Forgive Me 5

SPENCER & THE SAINTS
68   Tabernacle TS 1005   Something Within/When You Get To Heaven 15

SONNY SPENCER
59   Parlophone R 4611   Oh Boy/Gilee 22

JON SPENCER BLUES EXPLOSION
94   Matador OLE 077   Afro/Relax Her (p/s) 5
91   Hut HUTLP 3   THE JON SPENCER BLUES EXPLOSION (LP) 12
(see also Pussy Galore)

BRINDLEY D. SPENDER
68   Domain D 8   The Company I Keep/On A Day Like Today 7

SPERMICIDE
79   No Wonder NOW 3   Femme Prothèse/Belgique (p/s with lyrics) 20

SPHERES
78   Sphere   FESTIVAL AND SUNS (LP, with insert) 25
(see also Jimmy Winston)

SPHERICAL OBJECTS
78   Object Music OM 01   The Kill/The Knot (p/s) 5
78   Object Music OM 04   Seventies Romance/Sweet Tooth (p/s) 5
78   Object Music PBJ 001   PAST & PARCEL (LP) 12
79   Object Music OBJ 004   ELLIPTICAL OPTIMISM (LP) 12
(see also Alternomen Unlimited, Noyes Brothers)

SPHYNKTA
83   Sultanic SUL 666   In The Shade Of The Gods/Jesus Bless My Upside-Down Cross
        (p/s, red vinyl, with 'devil' tattoo) 60
83   Sultanic SUL 999   Death And Violence/Ritual Slaughter (Of Your Daughter) (p/s, red vinyl) 40
84   Sultanic SUL 000   Spike Up My Sphynkta/No Pain No Gain (unissued) .... 100+

SPHYNX
78   Charisma CDS 4011   XITINTODAY (LP, some with booklet) 15/25
(see also Inner City Unit, Gong, Radio Actors)

SPICE (U.K.)
68   United Artists UP 2246   What About The Music?/In Love .... 180+
(see also Uriah Heep, Godz, Toe-Fat)

SPICE GIRLS

96	Virgin VSLH 1588	Wannabe/Bumper To Bumper (jukebox issue, large centre hole) 5
96	Virgin VSCXD 1588	Wannabe (Radio Edit)/Wannabe (Dave Way Alternative Mix)/Wannabe (Dub Slam)/Wannabe (Instrumental) (CD, fold-out postcard inlay, stickered case) 15

(see also Geri Halliwell)

GEORGE SPICER

74	Topic 12T 235	BLACKBERRY FOLD (LP) 15

SPIDELLS

66	Sue WI 4019	Find Out What's Happening/That'll Make My Heart Break 30

SPIDER

66	Decca F 12430	The Comedown Song/Blow Ya Mind 25

SPIDER

80	Alien ALIEN 14	Children Of The Street/Down 'N' Out (some in p/s) 35/8
80	Alien ALIEN 16	College Luv/Born To Be Wild (some in p/s) 35/8

SPIDER-MAN

73	Buddah 2318 075	FROM BEYOND THE GRAVE (LP) 12

SPIDERS

66	Philips BF 1531	Sad Sunset/Hey Boy 50

SPIDERS (U.S.)

54	London HL 8086	I'm Slippin' In/I'm Searching (78) 70

SPIDERS FROM MARS

76	Pye NSPL 18479	SPIDERS FROM MARS (LP) 15

(see also David Bowie, Mick Ronson)

BERND SPIER

65	Oriole CB 1987	A Million And One Times/My Mistake 5

SPILL

92	Virgin VS 1141	Don't Wanna Know About Evil (7" Wireless Road Mix)/(Saspelofiska Dub Mix) (p/s) 10
92	Virgin VST 1141	Don't Wanna Know About Evil (Tumble Mix)/(Rumble Mix)/ (Danny's Moto Mix)/(The Groovy Beats Mix) (12", p/s) 12
92	Virgin VSCDT 1141	Don't Wanna Know About Evil (Tumble Mix)/(Rumble Mix)/ (7" Wireless Road Mix)/(Saspelofiska Dub Mix) (CD) 8

(see also Beth Orton)

ARTHUR SPINK BAND

68	Beltona BL 2766	Beatles Och Aye/Harry Lauder Medley 5

SPINNERS

66	Fontana TE17468	THE SINGING CITY (EP) 10

(see also Liverpool Spinners, Shane Rimmer)

SPINNERS (U.S.)

61	Columbia DB 4693	That's What Girls Are Made For/Heebie Jeebies (DJ copy = £250) 200
65	Tamla Motown TMG 514	Sweet Thing/How Can I? (demos with 'Spinners' or 'Detroit Spinners' credit) 300/250
65	Tamla Motown TMG 514	Sweet Thing/How Can I? (stock copies credited to 'Spinners'). 200

(see also Detroit Spinners)

SPINNING WHEEL

79	private pressing	JACOB'S FLEECE (LP). 20

(see also Dragonsfire)

SPIRALS

58	Capitol CL 14958	The Rockin' Cow/Everybody Knows 15

SPIRAL SKY

93	Acme AC 8002LP	SPIRAL SKY (LP, numbered & sealed with insert, 500 only) 15

(see also Sun Dial, Ohr Musik)

SPIRAL STAIRCASE

68	CBS 3507	Baby What I Mean/Makin' Your Mind Up 25
69	CBS 4187	More Today Than Yesterday/Broken Hearted Man (DJ copy = £85) 50
69	CBS 4524	No One For Me To Turn To/Sweet Little Thing 25

SPIRAL TRIBE

92	Big Life BLRT 79	Breach The Peace/Do ET/Seven/23 Minute Warning (12", p/s) 25
92	Big Life BLRT 85	Forward The Revolution/World Traveller Adventurer/Ragga Boom/ Track 13 (criminal drug) (12", p/s). 25
92	Big Life BLRR 85	Forward The Revolution (The Youth Remix) (1-sided, etched 12") 15
93	Butterfly BFLT 04	Sirius 23/Earthworm/Going All The Way/Predator (12", p/s, as Spiral Tribe Sound System) 20
93	Butterfly BFL LP 6	TECNO TERRA (2-LP). 140

SPIRIT

68	CBS 3523	Uncle Jack/Mechanical World 12
69	CBS 3880	I Got A Line On You/She Smiles 6
69	CBS 4511	Dark Eyed Woman/Ice. 5
69	CBS 4565	Dark Eyed Woman/New Dope In Town 12
70	CBS 4773	1984/Sweet Stella Baby 10
70	CBS 5149	Animal Zoo/Red Light Roll On. 6
78	Sound For Industry SFI 326	Midnight Train/Potatoland Theme (flexidisc free with *Dark Star* magazine). 6
68	CBS 63278	SPIRIT (LP, orange label) 25
68	CBS 63523	THE FAMILY THAT PLAYS TOGETHER (LP, orange label) 18
69	CBS 63729	CLEAR (LP, orange label). 22
71	Epic EPC 64191	THE TWELVE DREAMS OF DR. SARDONICUS (LP, g/fold sleeve, yellow label) .. 15

| 72 | Epic EPC 64507 | FEED-BACK (LP, yellow label) | 12 |
| 81 | Beggars Banquet BEGA 23 | POTATOLAND (LP, with cartoon book) | 12 |

(see also Kapt. Kopter & Fabulous Twirlybirds, Jo Jo Gunne)

SPIRIT OF JOHN MORGAN

69	Carnaby CNS 4005	Ride On/Along Came John	8
71	RCA RCA 2085	Floating Opera Show/Never Let Go	6
69	Carnaby CNLS 6002	THE SPIRIT OF JOHN MORGAN (LP)	60
70	Carnaby CNLS 6007	AGE MACHINE (LP)	65
71	Carnaby 6437 503	THE SPIRIT OF JOHN MORGAN (LP, reissue)	25

(see also John Morgan)

SPIRIT OF MEMPHIS QUARTET

| 58 | Parlophone PMD 1070 | NEGRO SPIRITUALS (10" LP) | 25 |
| 65 | Vogue LAE 1033 | NEGRO SPIRITUALS (LP, reissue) | 15 |

SPIRIT OF PLAY

| 88 | Release KIDS 1988 | Children In Need/Children In Need (Instrumental) (with Paul McCartney) (some in p/s) | 50/10 |

SPIRIT OF PROGRESS

| 71 | Philips 6006089 | Om Pa Pa/It's A Beautiful Day | 25 |

SPIRITUALIZED

90	Dedicated ZB 43783	Anyway That You Want Me/Step Into The Breeze (p/s)	10
90	Dedicated ZT 43784	Anyway That You Want Me (Extended)/Step Into The Breeze 1 & 2 (12", p/s)	15
90	Dedicated ZT 43780	Anyway That You Want Me (Remix)/Step Into The Breeze 1 & 2 (12", p/s)	25
90	Dedicated ZD 43784	Anyway That You Want Me/Step Into The Breeze 1 & 2 (CD)	15
91	Fierce FRIGHT 053	Feel So Sad/I Want You (gig freebie, no p/s, stamped plain white sleeve with date & venue details)	30
91	Dedicated SPIRT 001T	Feel So Sad (Rhapsodies)/(Glides And Chimes) (12", p/s)	10
91	Dedicated SPIRT 001CD	Feel So Sad (Rhapsodies)/(Glides And Chimes) (CD)	8
91	Dedicated SPIRT 002	Run/I Want You (p/s, some with luminous sleeve & clear luminous vinyl)	8/6
91	Dedicated SPIRT 002T	Run/Luminescence (Stay With Me)/I Want You/Effervescent (Chimes) (12", some with luminous sleeve)	15/10
91	Dedicated SPIRT 002CD/ ZD 44846	Run/Luminescence (Stay With Me)/I Want You/ Effervescent (Chimes) (CD)	15
91	Dedicated SPIRT 003	Why Don't You Smile Now? (Edit)/Sway (clear vinyl, p/s)	6
91	Dedicated SPIRT 003 CD	Why Don't You Smile Now? (Edit)/Sway/Why Don't You Smile Now? (CD, front cover has "Smile/Sway")	8
91	Dedicated SPIRT 004	I Want You/You Know It's True (Instrumental)/100 Bars (Flashback) (p/s, mail-order with *NME* coupon only)	15
92	Dedicated SPIRT 004CD	I Want You/You Know It's True (Instrumental)/100 Bars (Flashback) (CD, no p/s, mail-order with *NME* coupon only)	15
92	Dedicated DEDCD 004	LAZER GUIDED MELODIES (CD EP, 4-track sampler of album)	12
92	Dedicated SPIRT 005	Medication/Smiles (p/s, red vinyl, 3000 only)	6
92	Dedicated SPIRT 005T	Medication/Angel Sigh/Feel So Sad (12", p/s, with poster, 3000 only)	10
93	Dedicated SPIRT 006	Smiles (Live)/100 Bars (A Cappella) (7" flexidisc, fan-club only)	20
93	Greenpeace GR'NP'CE 001	Good Dope, Good Fun/MERCURY REV: 'Boys Peel Out (Live)' (gig 7", with booklet)	15
93	Dedicated SPIRT 007	ELECTRIC MAINLINE EP (Good Times/Lay Back In The Sun) (p/s, on yellow vinyl)	5
93	Dedicated SPIRT 007CD	ELECTRIC MAINLINE EP (Good Times/Lay Back In The Sun/ Electric Mainline) (CD)	8
94	Dedicated SPIRT 009	Let It Flow/Don't Go/Stay With Me/Don't Go/Stay With Me (The Individual) (10", p/s)	8
95	Dedicated 7432 13 11782	Lay Back In The Sun/The Slide Song/Spread Your Wings/ Lay Back In The Sun (CD)	15
96	Dedicated SPIRT 101T	Pure Phase Tones For DJs (12")	15
97	Dedicated SPIRT 011CD	Broken Heart (Instrumental) (CD, available via *NME*, 500 only)	35
98	Dedicated SPIRT 014T	I Think I'm In Love/(Chemical Brothers Vocal Mix)/(Chemical Brothers Inst.)	6
98	Dedicated SPIRT 014DJ	I Think I'm In Love/(Chemical Brothers Vocal Mix)/(Chemical Brothers Inst.) (12", DJ promo, 200 only)	20
98	Dedicated SPIRT 015DJ	Come Together (Death In Vegas Mix)/(Two Lone Swordsmen Mix) (12" promo, p/s)	8
92	Dedicated DEDLP 004S	LAZER GUIDED MELODIES (LP, ltd. ed. with/without bonus 7" single 'Anyway That You Want Me'/'Why Don't You Smile Now?' [CWNN 7001])	25/20
93	Dedicated no cat. no.	SUMMER EUROPEAN 93 BOX (3-CD promo set, with ribbon and insert)	70
93	Dedicated DEDLP 008	FUCKED UP INSIDE (LP, mail-order only)	40
93	Dedicated DEDCD 008	FUCKED UP INSIDE (CD, mail-order only)	35
93	Dedicated DEDLP 017	PURE PHASE (2-LP, 45rpm)	40
97	Dedicated DEDLP 034	LADIES AND GENTLEMEN WE ARE FLOATING IN SPACE (2-LP, limited issue)	30
97	Dedicated DEDCD 034S	LADIES AND GENTLEMEN WE ARE FLOATING IN SPACE (12 x 3" CDs, in blister packs in card box w/insert, 1000 only, 200 w/clear plastic backs)	60/40
97	Dedicated DEDCD 034P	LADIES AND GENTLEMEN WE ARE FLOATING IN SPACE (CD, 'Elvis version', given to Mercury Music Prize personnel, 50 copies only)	35
01	Dedicated OPM 001 CD	LET IT COME DOWN: RADIO INTERVIEW (CD, Jason Pierce speaks to Stuart Maconie plus 7 tracks)	30

(see also Spacemen 3)

SPIROGYRA

72	Pegasus PGS 3	Dangerous Dave/Captain's Log	12
71	B&C CAS 1042	ST. RADIGUND'S (LP, with lyric inner)	80
72	Pegasus PEG 13	OLD BOOT WINE (LP)	80+
73	Polydor 2001-419	I Hear You're Going Nowhere/Old Boot Wine	35
73	Polydor 2310 246	BELLS, BOOTS AND SHAMBLES (LP)	200+

SPITFIRE (& BLACKFIRE BARMIES)

| 82 | Carrere CAR 253 | So You Want To Be A Rock'n'Roll Star/Spitfire Boogie | 50 |

SPITFIRE BOYS
77	RK RK 1001	British Refugee/Mein Kampf (push-out centre)	75
77	RK RK 1001	British Refugee/Mein Kampf (reissue, solid centre, p/s)	60
83	RK RK 1001	British Refugee/Mein Kampf (2nd reissue to cash in on Frankie Goes To Hollywood's success, p/s, no solid centre)	75

(see also Frankie Goes To Hollywood)

SPITZBROOK
79	Ace SPIT 1	Stranger/Looking At You (p/s)	60

VICTORIA SPIVEY
60	Fontana TFE 17264	TREASURES OF NORTH AMERICAN NEGRO MUSIC NO. 5 (EP)	15
56	HMV 7EG 8190	VICTORIA SPIVEY (EP)	20
65	Xtra XTRA 1022	VICTORIA SPIVEY (LP)	25

SPIZZ (OIL/ENERGI)
79	Rough Trade RTSO 1	6000 Crazy/1989/Fibre (p/s)	5
79	Rough Trade RTSO 2	Cold City/Red And Black/Solarisation (Shun)/Platform 3 (as Spizz Oil) (p/s)	5
79	Rough Trade RTSO 3	Soldier Soldier/Virginia Plain (as Spizz Energi) (p/s)	6
79	Rough Trade RTSO 4	Where's Captain Kirk?/Amnesia (as Spizz Energi) (p/s)	6

S.P.K. (SEPPUKU/SURGICAL PENIS KLINIK)
80	Industrial IR 0011	MEAT PROCESSING SECTION (Mekano/Slogun) (p/s, labels list "Slogan"/"Factory", with insert, as Surgical Penis Klinik)	20
83	Side Effekts SER 003	Dekompositiones (12", p/s, as Seppuku)	15
81	Side Effekts SER 01	INFORMATION OVERLOAD UNIT (LP, 1st 1,000 with booklet & poster)	30/20
83	Walter Ulbright WULP 002	AUTO-DA-FE (LP)	18
84	WEA WX 10	MACHINE AGE VOODOO (LP)	12
86	Sterile SRC 4	LIVE AT THE CRYPT (cassette)	12
80s	Side Effekts SER 002	LEICHENSCHREI (LP)	15

SPLINTER
74	Dark Horse AMS 7135	Costafine Town/Elly May	5
75	Dark Horse AMS 5501	Drink All Day/Haven't Got Time (withdrawn)	12
75	Dark Horse AMS 5502	China Light/Drink All Day	8
75	Dark Horse AMS 5503	Which Way Will I Get Home/Green Bus Line	8
76	Dark Horse AMS 5506	Half Way There/What Is It (If You Never Ever Tried It Yourself)	8
77	Dark Horse K 17009	Round And Round/I'll Bend For You	7
77	Dark Horse K 17116	New York City (Who Am I)/Baby Love	7
78	Barn BARN 4	Danger Zone/Swear To God	8
76	Dark Horse DH 2	SPLINTER (LP, promo only, plain white sleeve)	130

(see also Elastic Oz Band)

SPLIT BEAVER
81	Heavy Metal HEAVY 7	Savage/Hound Of Hell (some with p/s)	18/5
82	Heavy Metal HMRLP 3	WHEN HELL WON'T HAVE YOU (LP, silver or red label)	18/15

SPLIT ENZ
76	Chrysalis CHS 2120	Late Last Night/Walking Down The Road (p/s)	5
77	Chrysalis CHS 2131	Another Great Divide/Stranger Than Fiction (p/s)	5
77	Chrysalis CHS 2170	My Mistake/Crosswords (p/s)	5
77	Chrysalis CHS 2170-12	My Mistake/Crosswords/The Woman Who Loves You (12", p/s)	8
79	Illegal ILS 19	I See Red/Give It A Whirl/Hermit McDermitt (p/s)	5
80	A&M AMLH 64822	TRUE COLOURS (LP, laser etched)	12

(see also Crowded House, Tim Finn)

SPLIT IMAGE
82	Heroes ER 01	Now That We've Parted	25

SPLIT KNEE LOONS
81	Avatar AAA 111	THE SPECIAL COLLECTORS EP (p/s, brown vinyl, some with badge)	8/6

(see also Gillan, Bernie Tormé, John McCoy,Colin Towns)

SPLIT SCREENS
78	Rok ROK III/IV	Just Don't Try/JUST FRANK: You (die-cut company sleeve)	10

SPLODGENESSABOUNDS
80	Deram ROLF 1	Two Little Boys/Horse/Sox/Butterfly (p/s, some with 'Splodge' boomerang)	15/7
81	Deram BUM 3	COWPUNK MEDLUM (EP, p/s, with free flexi [BUMF 3])	8

SPOILERS
72	London HLU 10399	Turbo Rock/Sad Man's Land	10

SPOILT BRATZ
88	Spoilt Bratz SB 1	SPOILT BRATZ: (Not So) Hot/You Talk Too Much/I Could Die/She's A Drag (cassette, private issue, 200 only)	35
88	Spoilt Bratz SB 2	GASOLINE & SUICIDE: Sex Doll, Love Cramp/Going Down Again/Stuck In A Rut/Crawling On Broken Glass (cassette, private issue, 200 only)	35
89	Spoilt Bratz BRAT 3	BE MY GUEST: Pain Reliever/Past Times/Ignorance (cassette, private issue)	35

(see also Terrorvision)

SPOKESMEN
65	Brunswick 05941	The Dawn Of Correction/For You Babe	12
65	Brunswick 05948	It Ain't Fair/Have Courage Be Careful	12
66	Brunswick 05950	Michelle/Better Days Are Yet To Come	8
66	Brunswick 05958	Today's The Day/Enchanté	8

SPONTANEOUS COMBUSTION
71	Harvest HAR 5046	Lonely Singer/200 Lives/Leaving	15
72	Harvest HAR 5060	Gay Time Night/Spaceship	10
73	Harvest HAR 5066	Sabre Dance/Part 2	8
72	Harvest SHVL 801	SPONTANEOUS COMBUSTION (LP)	60
72	Harvest SHVL 805	TRIAD (LP, with 3 inserts)	45

(see also Time)

SPONTANEOUS MUSIC ENSEMBLE

SPONTANEOUS MUSIC ENSEMBLE
66	Eyemark EMP L1002	CHALLENGE (LP)	200
68	Island ILP 979	KARYOBIN ... ARE THE IMAGINARY BIRDS SAID TO LIVE IN PARADISE (LP, pink label)	120
69	Marmalade 608 008	SPONTANEOUS MUSIC ENSEMBLE (LP)	50
71	Tangent TNGS 107	SOURCE FROM AND TOWARDS (LP)	30
72	Marmalade 2384 009	SPONTANEOUS MUSIC ENSEMBLE (LP, reissue)	25
73	Emanem 303	FACE TO FACE (LP)	30
73	Tangent TNGS 118	SO WHAT DO YOU THINK (LP)	20
77	Incus INCUS 24	BIOSYSTEM (LP)	50

(see also Howard Riley Trio)

SPOOKY TOOTH
67	Island WIP 6022	Sunshine Help Me/Weird	20
68	Island WIP 6037	Love Really Changed Me/Luger's Grove	15
68	Island WIP 6046	The Weight/Do Right People	10
69	Island WIP 6048	Nobody There At All/ART: Room With A View (unissued, white labels only)	40
69	Island WIP 6060	Son Of Your Father/I've Got Enough Heartache	7
73	Island WIP 6168	All Sewn Up/As Long As The World Keeps Turning	6
68	Island ILP 980/ILPS 9080	IT'S ALL ABOUT (LP, pink or palm tree label)	60/25
69	Island ILPS 9098	SPOOKY TWO (LP, pink label)	45
69	Island ILPS 9107	CEREMONY (LP, with Pierre Henry, pink label, gatefold sleeve)	30
70	Island ILPS 9117	THE LAST PUFF (LP, pink label)	25
73	Island ILPS 9227	YOU BROKE MY HEART SO I BUSTED YOUR JAW (LP, pink rim label)	15
73	Island ILPS 9255	WITNESS (LP, pink rim label)	15
74	Good Ear EARL 2001	THE MIRROR (LP)	12
74	Island ILPS 9292	THE MIRROR (LP, export issue)	18

(see also Gary Wright, V.I.P.s, Art, Luther Grosvenor, Hellions, Revolution, State Of Mickey & Tommy, Mike Harrison, Foreigner)

SPORTS
78	Stiff LAST 5	WHO LISTENS TO THE RADIO EP: Who Listens To The Radio/Step By Step/ So Obvious/Suspicious (originals have 'koala photo' p/s)	8
79	Sire SIR 6001	Who Listens To The Radio/Hit Single ('fireplace' p/s)	5
80	Sire SRUK 6001	WHO LISTENS TO THE RADIO (LP)	15

SPOTLIGHTERS
59	Vogue Pop V 9130	Please Be My Girlfriend/Whisper (with Bob Thompson & His Band)	500
59	Vogue Pop V 9130	Please Be My Girlfriend/Whisper (with Bob Thompson & His Band) (78)	130

SPOTLIGHTS
66	Philips BF 1485	Batman And Robin/Day Flower	20

SPOTNICKS
62	Oriole CB 1724	Orange Blossom Special/The Spotnicks Theme	10
62	Oriole CB 1755	Galloping Guitars/The Rocket Man	10
63	Oriole CB 1790	Hava Nagila/High Flyin' Scotsman	10
63	Oriole CB 1818	Just Listen To My Heart/Pony Express	10
63	Oriole CB 1844	Valentina/Save The Last Dance For Me/No Yaga Daga Blues	10
63	Oriole CB 1886	Anna/The Sailor's Hornpipe	12
64	Oriole CB 1953	Lovesick Blues/The Space Creatures	15
64	Oriole CB 1981	Donner Wetter/Shamus O'Toole	15
63	Oriole EP 7075	ON THE AIR (EP)	22
64	Oriole EP 7078	SPOTNICKS IN PARIS (EP)	22
64	Oriole EP 7079	SPOTNICKS AT THE OLYMPIA PARIS (EP)	22
63	Oriole PS 40036	OUT-A SPACE: THE SPOTNICKS IN LONDON (LP, also stereo SPS 40037)	32/42
64	Oriole PS 40054	THE SPOTNICKS IN SPAIN (LP)	30
65	Oriole PS 40064	THE SPOTNICKS IN BERLIN (LP)	35
81	Air CHM 1171	THE VERY BEST OF THE SPOTNICKS (LP)	12

(see also Bob Lander & Spotnicks, Shy Ones)

JACK SPRATT & LEROY SIBBLES & HEPTONES
69	Coxsone CS 7100	Give Me Your Love/LARRY & ALVIN: Magic Moments	32

SPREADEAGLE
72	Charisma CAS 1055	THE PIECE OF PAPER (LP)	12

SPREDTHICK
78	An Actual ACT 003	SPREDTHICK (LP, with insert)	18

SPRIGUNS (OF TOLGUS)
76	Decca F 13676	Nothing Else To Do/Lord Lovell	8
77	Decca F 13739	White Witch/Time Will Pass	8
74	private pressing	ROWDY DOWDY DAY (cassette, as Spriguns Of Tolgus)	50
75	Alida Star C'tage ASC7755	JACK WITH A FEATHER (LP, as Spriguns Of Tolgus)	750+
76	Decca SKL 5262	REVEL WEIRD & WILD (LP, with lyric insert)	110
77	Decca SKL 5286	TIME WILL PASS (LP, with lyric insert)	110
92	Kissing Spell KSLP 002	ROWDY DOWDY DAY (LP, reissue)	15

(see also Mandy Morton Band, Terra Cotta)

SPRING
71	RCA Neon NE 6	SPRING (LP, foldout sleeve)	140+

SPRINGBOARD
69	Polydor 545007	SPRINGBOARD (LP)	50+

DUSTY SPRINGFIELD
SINGLES
63	Philips BF 1292	I Only Want To Be With You/Once Upon A Time	8
64	Philips BF 1313	Stay Awhile/Something Special	8
64	Philips BF 1348	I Just Don't Know What To Do With Myself/My Colouring Book	8
64	Philips BF 1369	Losing You/Summer Is Over	8
64	Philips BF 1381	Oh Holy Child/SPRINGFIELDS: Jingle Bells (with p/s)	6

65	Philips BF 1396	Your Hurtin' Kinda Love/Don't Say It Baby	6
65	Philips BF 1418	In The Middle Of Nowhere/Baby Don't You Know	5
65	Philips BF 1430	Some Of Your Lovin'/I'll Love You For A While	5
66	Philips BF 1466	Little By Little/If It Hadn't Been For You	5
66	Philips BF 1482	You Don't Have To Say You Love Me/Every Ounce Of Strength	5
66	Philips BF 1502	Goin' Back/I'm Gonna Leave You	5
66	Philips BF 1510	All I See Is You/Go Ahead On (with p/s)	8
67	Philips BF 1553	I'll Try Anything/The Corrupt Ones	8
67	Philips BF 1577	Give Me Time/The Look Of Love	8
67	Philips BF 1608	What's It Gonna Be/Small Town Girl	30
68	Philips BF 1682	I Close My Eyes And Count To Ten/No Stranger Am I	5
68	Philips BF 1706	I Will Come To You/The Colour Of Your Eyes	5
68	Philips BF 1730	Son Of A Preacher Man/Just A Little Lovin'	15
69	Philips BF 1811	Am I The Same Girl/Earthbound Gypsy	15
69	Philips BF 1826	Brand New Me/Bad Case Of The Blues	7
70	Philips BF 1835	Morning Please Don't Come (with Tom Springfield)/TOM SPRINGFIELD: Charley	7
70	Philips 6006 045	How Can I Be Sure/Spooky	15
72	Philips 6006 214	Yesterday When I Was Young/I Start Counting	6
73	Philips 6006 295	Who Gets Your Love/Of All The Things	6
74	Philips 6006 325	Learn To Say Goodbye/Easy Evil	6
74	Philips 6006 350	What's It Gonna Be/Bring Him Back	15
75	Philips 6006 446	Yesterday When I Was Young/The Look Of Love	7
78	Mercury DUSTY 1	A Love Like Yours (Don't Come Knocking Every Day)/Hollywood Movie Girls	5
78	Mercury DUSTY 002	That's The Kind Of Love I've Got For You/Sandra	5
79	Mercury DUSTY 003	I'm Coming Home Again/Save Me Save Me	5
79	Mercury DUSTY 4	Baby Blue/Get Yourself To Love (p/s)	6
79	Mercury DUSTY 412	Baby Blue (Disco Version)/Baby Blue (7" Version) (12")	10

EPs

64	Philips BE 12560	I ONLY WANT TO BE WITH YOU	15
64	Philips BE 12564	DUSTY	15
65	Philips BE 12572	DUSTY IN NEW YORK	30
65	Philips BE 12579	MADEMOISELLE DUSTY	30
68	Philips BE 12605	IF YOU GO AWAY	20
68	Philips 6850 751	STAR DUSTY (Audio Club Of Great Britain release)	12
82	Philips CUT 111	CLASSIC CUTS	8

LPs

64	Philips (S)BL 7594	A GIRL CALLED DUSTY (mono/stereo)	22/30
65	Philips (S)RBL 1002	EVERYTHING'S COMING UP DUSTY (gatefold sleeve with booklet, mono/stereo)	25/30
66	Philips (S)BL 7737	GOLDEN HITS	15
67	Philips (S)BL 7820	WHERE AM I GOING?	22
68	World Record Club ST 848	DUSTY SPRINGFIELD	15
68	Philips (S)BL 7864	DUSTY... DEFINITELY	18
69	Wing WL 1211	STAY AWHILE	15
69	Philips SBL 7889	DUSTY IN MEMPHIS	30
70	Philips SBL 7927	FROM DUSTY... WITH LOVE	22
71	Philips 6382 016	THIS IS DUSTY SPRINGFIELD	18
71	Audio Club/G.B. 6850 002	STAR DUSTY	15
71	Audio Club/G.B. 6856 020	SHEER MAGIC	40
72	Philips 6308 117	SEE ALL HER FACES	15
73	Philips 6382 063	THIS IS DUSTY SPRINGFIELD VOL. 2 — MAGIC GARDEN	15
73	Philips 6308 152	CAMEO	15
75	Philips 6382 105	SINGS BURT BACHARACH AND CAROLE KING	15
94	Philips 522 254-2	THE LEGEND OF DUSTY SPRINGFIELD (4-CD boxed set, 2,000 only)	40+

(see also Lana Sisters, Springfields, Tom Springfield, Pet Shop Boys)

RICK SPRINGFIELD
72	Capitol EA-ST 80001	BEGINNINGS (LP)	10

TOM SPRINGFIELD (& HIS) ORCHESTRA
69	Philips BF 1759	Theme From From The Troubleshooters/Homage To Spewdley Parsons (with p/s)	6
69	Decca LK/SKL 5003	LOVE'S PHILOSOPHY BY... (LP, featuring Dusty Springfield)	25

(see also Springfields, Dusty Springfield)

SPRINGFIELD PARK
68	CBS 3775	Never An Everyday Thing/I Can See The Sun Shine	5

SPRINGFIELDS
61	Philips PB 1145	Dear John/I Done What They Told Me To	6
61	Philips PB 1168	Breakaway/Good News	5
61	Philips PB 1178	Bambino/Star Of Hope (with p/s)	8
62	Philips PB 1241	Silver Threads And Golden Needles/Aunt Rhody	5
62	Philips 326 536 BF	Swahili Papa/Gotta Travel On	8
61	Philips BBE 12476	THE SPRINGFIELDS (EP, also stereo SBBE 9068)	15/22
62	Lyntone P125E	CHRISTMAS WITH THE SPRINGFIELDS (EP, mail-order via *Woman's Own*)	8
62	Philips 433 622 BE	KINDA FOLKSY (EP)	15
63	Philips 433 623 BE	KINDA FOLKSY No. 2 (EP)	15
63	Philips 433 624 BE	KINDA FOLKSY No. 3 (EP)	15
63	Philips BBE 12538	HIT SOUNDS (EP)	10
63	Philips 433 643 BE	FOLK SONGS FROM THE HILLS (EP)	10
62	Philips BBL 7551/SBBL 674	KINDA FOLKSY (LP, mono/stereo)	15/20
63	Philips 632 304 BL	FOLK SONGS FROM THE HILLS (LP)	18
64	Philips BET 606	THE SPRINGFIELDS STORY (2-LP)	20
69	Fontana SFL 13098	THE SPRINGFIELDS SING AGAIN (LP)	18

(see also Dusty Springfield, Lana Sisters, Tom Springfield, Mike Hurst)

SPRINGFIELDS

88	Sarah SARAH 010	Sunflower/Clown/Are We Gonna Be Alright? (foldaround p/s with 14" x 10" poster in polyester bag; yellow p/s, later orange p/s)	25/18
91	Sarah SARAH 040	Wonder (p/s, with insert)	7

BRUCE SPRINGSTEEN

SINGLES

75	CBS A 3661	Born To Run/Meeting Across The River	5
76	CBS A 3940	Tenth Avenue Freeze-Out/She's The One	12
78	CBS A 6424	Prove It All Night/Factory	15
78	CBS A 6532	Badlands/Something In The Night	12
78	CBS A 6720	Promised Land/Streets Of Fire	45
80	CBS A 9309	Hungry Heart/Held Up Without A Gun (p/s, blue or black lettering)	40/30
80	CBS A 9568	Sherry Darling/Be True (p/s)	25
81	CBS A 1179	The River/Independence Day (p/s)	10
81	CBS A 13-1179	The River/Born To Run/Rosalita (12", p/s, some sleeves credit 'East Street Band')	15/10
81	CBS A 1557	Cadillac Ranch/Wreck On The Highway (p/s)	25
82	CBS A 2794	Atlantic City/Mansion On The Hill (p/s)	40
82	CBS A 2969	Open All Night/The Big Pay Back (p/s)	25
84	CBS WA 4436	Dancing In The Dark/Pink Cadillac (Cadillac-shaped picture disc)	30
84	CBS A 4662	Cover Me/Jersey Girl (live) (poster p/s)	10
84	CBS WA 4662	Cover Me/Jersey Girl (live) (Bruce-shaped picture disc with plinth, withdrawn)	25
84	CBS DA 4662/A 4436	Cover Me/Jersey Girl (live)//Dancing In The Dark/Pink Cadillac (shrinkwrapped double pack, both 45s in p/s)	12
84	CBS DA 4662/A 7077	Cover Me/Jersey Girl (live)//Born To Run/Meeting Across The River (shrinkwrapped double pack, no p/s on 2nd 45)	12
84	CBS QTA 4662	Cover Me (Undercover Mix)/Cover Me (Dub)/Shut Out The Light/ Dancing In The Dark (Dub)/Jersey Girl (live) (12", p/s)	8
84	CBS A 6561	I'm Going Down/Janey, Don't You Lose Heart (p/s)	7
85	CBS A 7077	Born To Run/Meeting Across The River (reissue, blue p/s, withdrawn)	25
85	CBS A 6342	I'm On Fire/Born In The U.S.A. (p/s, with competition postcard)	10
85	CBS WA 6342	I'm On Fire/Born In The U.S.A. (p/s, flag-shaped picture disc)	25
85	CBS TA 6342	I'm On Fire/Rosalita/Born In The U.S.A. (Freedom Mix)/Johnny Bye Bye (12", p/s)	10
85	CBS QTA 6375	Glory Days/Stand On It/Sherry Darling/Racing In The Street (12", poster p/s)	8
85	CBS BRUCE 1	BORN IN THE U.S.A. — THE 12" COLLECTION (4 x 12" & 7", box with poster)	40
86	CBS 650 193-0	War (live)/Merry Xmas Baby (live)//My Home Town (live)/Santa Claus Is Coming To Town (live) (shrinkwrapped double pack, both 45s in p/s)	12
86	CBS 650 193-7	War/Merry Xmas Baby (live) (p/s)	5
86	CBS 650 193-6	War/Merry Xmas Baby (live)/Incident On 57th Street (live) (12", poster p/s)	10
87	CBS 650 381-7	Fire (live)/For You (live) (p/s)	6
87	CBS 650 381-6	Fire (live)/For You (live)/Born To Run (live)/No Surrender (live)/ 10th Avenue (live) Freeze-Out (12", p/s)	15
87	CBS BRUCE B2	Born To Run/Spirit In The Night//Johnny 99/Because The Night (double pack box set)	10
87	CBS BRUCE BP 2	Born To Run (live)/Johnny 99 (live) (p/s, badge pack)	5
87	CBS BRUCE C2	Born To Run (live)/Spirit In The Night (live)/Johnny 99 (live)/Seeds (live) (CD, card sleeve with gauze inner)	10
87	CBS 651 141-0	Brilliant Disguise/Lucky Man (gatefold p/s, with discography)	10
87	CBS 651 141-6	Brilliant Disguise/Lucky Man (12", p/s, with poster)	12
87	CBS 651 295-7	Tunnel Of Love/Two For The Road (p/s)	5
87	CBS 651 295-0	Tunnel Of Love/Two For The Road (postcard-shaped picture disc)	15
87	CBS 651 295-8	Tunnel Of Love/Two For The Road/Santa Claus Is Coming To Town (12", p/s with poster)	10
87	CBS 651 295-2	Tunnel Of Love/Santa Claus Is Coming To Town (live)/Two For The Road (CD, card sleeve)	45
88	CBS BRUCE 3	Tougher Than The Rest/Tougher Than The Rest (live) (p/s, with patch)	6
88	CBS BRUCE C3	Tougher Than The Rest/Roulette/Be True (Live)/Born To Run (New Live) (CD, card sleeve)	10
88	CBS BRUCE Q4	Spare Parts/Cover Me (live)/Spare Parts (live)/I'm On Fire (live) (12", different p/s)	15
88	CBS BRUCE C4	Spare Parts/Pink Cadillac/Spare Parts (live)/Chimes Of Freedom (live) (CD, card sleeve)	12
88	CBS BRUCE B4	Spare Parts/Pink Cadillac/Spare Parts (live)/Chimes Of Freedom (live) (CD, BRUCE C4 disc in silver tin)	25
92	Sony 658 138-5	57 Channels (And Nothin' On)/Stand On It/Janey, Don't You Lose Heart (CD, picture disc, digipak)	22
92	Columbia 657 890-8	Better Days/Tougher Than The Rest/Part Man Part Monkey (12" picture disc)	10
94	Columbia 660 065-8	Streets Of Philadelphia/If I Should Fall Behind/Growing Up/Big Muddy (12", picture disc)	12

LPs

73	CBS 65480	GREETINGS FROM ASBURY PARK, N.J. (cutaway gatefold sleeve, orange label)	12
74	CBS 65780	THE WILD, THE INNOCENT AND THE E STREET SHUFFLE (orange label, yellow lettering on sleeve; with "Ashbury" mis-spelling on label)	12
75	CBS 69170	BORN TO RUN (with "*John* Landau" misprint on rear sleeve)	12
79	CBS 66353	BRUCE SPRINGSTEEN (3-LP, box set)	22
84	CBS 11-86304	BORN IN THE U.S.A. (picture disc)	30
87	CBS 460 270-0	TUNNEL OF LOVE (picture disc)	15
87	CBS CDCBS 460 270-9	TUNNEL OF LOVE (CD, picture disc)	20
92	Sony 471 423-0	HUMAN TOUCH (picture disc)	15
92	Sony 471 424-0	LUCKY TOWN (picture disc)	15

(see also Nils Lofgren, Roy Orbison)

SPRINGTIME

78	Sonet SON 2143	Mrs Caroline Robinson/Honey Bye Bye (p/s)	6

SPROG & WIDGIT
72   Diddley Do DIDLP 02   32 ENGLISH FOLK SONGS IN THE SILLY TRADITION (2-LP, gatefold sleeve). . . . 18

SPRONG & NYAH SHUFFLE
69   Grape GR 3001   Moonwalk/Think 25

BILLY SPROUD & ROCK 'N' ROLL SIX
57   Columbia DB 3893   Rock Mr. Piper/If You're So Smart (How Come You Ain't Rich) (78 rpm = £15) . . . 45

SPROUTS
58   RCA RCA 1031   Teen Billy Baby/Goodbye, She's Gone (78 rpm = £28) 50

SPUD
75   Philips 9108 002   A SILK PURSE (LP). 12
75   Philips 9108 003   A HAPPY HANDFUL (LP) 12
77   Sonet SNTF 742   SMOKING IN THE BOG (LP, with lyric sheet). 12

SPUD AND THE FABS
80   Whitetower AMC 706   Your Place Or Mine (p/s). 25

THE SPUNKY ONION
74   Contempo CS2006   Cookie Man (Part 1)/Cookie Man (part 2) 15

WILD JIMMY SPURRILL
60s XX MIN 717   NOBLE 'THIN MAN' WATTS AND WILD JIMMY SPURRILL (EP) 18
(see also Noble 'Thin Man' Watts, Guitar Crusher)

SPURS
88   Outback OUT 1   Soldier (p/s) 12

SPYROGYRA
79   Infinity (no cat. no.)   MORNING DANCE (LP, picture disc, in-house issue, top-flap
                                   poly sleeve, 50 copies). 50

SPYS
79   No Bad NB 3   The Young Ones/Heavy Scene (p/s) 5

SQUAD
79   Squad SQS 1   Red Alert/£8 A Week (some in die cut p/s) 40/20

SQUADRONAIRES
54   Decca F 10248   Coach Call Boogie/Donegal Cradle Song. 12
54   Decca F 10274   Wolf On The Prowl/Mudhopper 12
57   Columbia DB 3882   Rock And Roll Boogie/Right Now, Right Now (78 rpm = £8) 18
53   Decca LF 1141   CONTRASTS IN JAZZ (10" LP) 18

LESTER SQUARE & THE SQUARE DEAL SURFS
84   Thin Sliced TSR 4T   The Plug (12", p/s). 8
(see also Monochrome Set)

SQUEEZE
77   BTM SBT 107   Take Me I'm Yours/No, Disco Kid, No (unreleased)
77   Deptford Fun City DFC 01   PACKET OF THREE (EP, red & blue photo p/s) 6
77   Deptford Fun City DFC 01   PACKET OF THREE (12" EP, plain pink die-cut sleeve, 500 only). 10
78   A&M AMSP 7335   Take Me I'm Yours/Night Nurse (12", p/s). 5
78   A&M AMS 7360   Bang Bang/All Fed Up (p/s, green vinyl) 5
78   A&M AMS 7398   Goodbye Girl/Saints Alive (3-D p/s) 5
79   A&M AMS 7426   Cool For Cats/Model (p/s, brilliant pink vinyl, 5,000 only) 6
79   A&M AMS 7426   Cool For Cats/Model (p/s, red vinyl, 1,000 only) 8
79   A&M AMSP 7426   Cool For Cats/Model (12", p/s, pale pink vinyl) 10
79   A&M AMS 7495   Christmas Day/Going Crazy (p/s, white vinyl) 5
79   A&M AMS 7507   Another Nail In My Heart/Pretty Thing (p/s, clear vinyl) 5
80   Lyntone LYN 7010/1   Wrong Way (green vinyl flexidisc, free with Smash Hits) 6/4
81   A&M AMS 8147   Tempted/Yap Yap Yap (p/s, with free U.S. 5" single "Another Nail In
                                   My Heart"/"If I Didn't Love You", p/s, shrinkwrapped) 5
81   A&M AMS 8166   Labelled With Love/Squabs On Forty Five (withdrawn p/s) 15

SQUIBBY & REFLECTIONS
68   Direction 58-3453   Ragamuffin/For A Little While 6
68   Direction 58-3606   Loving You Has Made My Life Worthwhile/Better Off Without You 5
69   Direction 58-4073   You Got It/Come Back To Me 8

SQUIBS
81   Oily SLICK 1   On The Line (plain sleeve, with insert) 25
81   Oily SLICK 3   Parades/Out On The Town (p/s). 20

BILLY SQUIER
82   Capitol CL 261   Emotions In Motion/Catch 22 (p/s) 12
82   Capitol CL 261   Emotions In Motion/Catch 22 (picture disc). 15
84   Capitol SQD 1   Rock Me Tonite/Can't Get Next To You//She's A Runner/Listen To The Heart
                                   (double pack). 6
86   Capitol CL 433   Love Is The Hero/Learn How To Live (live) (p/s) 7
86   Capitol 12CL 433   Love Is The Hero (extended version with Freddie Mercury intro)/
                                   Learn How To Live (live) (12", p/s) 55
(see also Freddie Mercury, Roger Taylor)

SQUIRE
79   Rok ROK I/II   Get Ready To Go/COMING SHORTLY: Doing The Flail (company sleeve) 30
79   I-Spy SEE 2   Walking Down The King's Road/It's A Mod Mod Mod
                                   Mod World (company sleeve) 7
79   I-Spy SEE 4   The Face Of Youth Today/I Know A Girl (keyhole company sleeve,
                                   paper or plastic labels) 4/6
80   Stage One STAGE 2   My Mind Goes Round In Circles/Does Stephanie Know? (p/s) 6
82   Hi-Lo HI 001   No Time Tomorrow/Don't Cry To Me (p/s) 5

MINT VALUE £

82	Hi-Lo HI 002	Girl On A Train/Every Trick In The Book (p/s)	5
83	Hi-Lo HIT 003	Every Trick In The Book/Every Trick In The Book (Elastic Mix) (12", p/s)	8
83	Hi-Lo HI 004	Jesamine/When I Try, I Lie (p/s)	10
84	Hi-Lo HI 005/SFC 2	The Young Idea/It's Getting Better (Squire Fan Club issue)	10
85	Hi-Lo LOX 1	Does Stephanie Know? (flexidisc)	12
94	Detour DR 020	The Place I Used To Live/Make Love To You/Over You (p/s, 900 only, 50 on white vinyl: 2nd pressing of 250 copies, white labels & purple print: 3rd pressing, 588 copies on clear splattered vinyl)	10/5/5/5
83	Hi-Lo LO 01	HITS FROM 3,000 YEARS AGO (LP)	18
83	Hi-Lo LO 02	GET SMART (LP, with poster)	15
85	Hi-Lo LO 03	THE SINGLES ALBUM (LP)	15

(see also Anthony Meynell)

CHRIS SQUIRE
75	Atlantic K 50203	FISH OUT OF WATER (LP, with inner sleeve & poster)	12

(see also Yes)

JOHN SQUIRE
02	North Country Records NC001	Joe Louis/Home Sweet Home (p/s)	5
04	North Country Records NC003	Room in Brooklyn/Nighthawks (picture disc)	5
04	North Country Records NC004	Lighthouse & Buildings (CD promo, unique p/s, withdrawn single)	8

(see also Stone Roses)

DOROTHY SQUIRES
57	Pye NEP 24036	DOROTHY SQUIRES (EP)	10
58	Pye Nixa NPL 18015	SINGS BILLY REID (LP)	18
67	Ace Of Clubs SCL-R 1230	THIS IS MY LIFE (LP)	12
68	Marble Arch MAL(S) 1211	REFLECTIONS (LP, mono/stereo)	each 12

ROSEMARY SQUIRES
56	Decca F 10685	Band Of Gold/Where You Are	7
58	HMV POP 462	Happy Is The Bride/Give Me The Simple Life	7
58	HMV POP 541	There Goes My Lover/Please Be Kind	7
64	HMV POP 1288	Bluesette/Nothing's Changed	7
56	MGM MGM-EP 640	MY LOVE IS A WANDERER (EP)	20
60	HMV 7EG 8588	ROSEMARY (EP)	20
63	HMV CLP 1669	EVERYTHINGS COMING UP ROSY (LP, mono/stereo [CSD 1508])	30/40
65	HMV CLP 1832	SOMETHING TO REMEMBER ME BY (LP, mono/stereo [CSD 1586])	30/40

(see also Streamliners & Joanne)

S.R.C.
69	Capitol CL 15576	Black Sheep/Morning Mood	20
87	Bam Caruso OPRA 063	Black Sheep/BRAIN: Nightmares In Red (jukebox issue, die-cut company sleeve)	5
69	Capitol (S)T 2991	S.R.C. (LP)	45
69	Capitol E-(S)T 134	MILESTONES (LP)	45
70	Capitol E-(S)T 273	TRAVELLER'S TALE (LP)	46

STACCATOS
61	Parlophone R 4828	Main Line/Topaz	15

STACCATOS
68	Fontana TF 966	Butchers And Bakers/Imitations Of Love	28

STACCATOS (U.S.)
66	Capitol CL 15478	Let's Run Away/Face To Face (With Love)	7
67	Capitol CL 15505	Half Past Midnight/Weatherman	7

CLARENCE STACEY
59	Pye International 7N 25025	Just Your Love/Lonely Guy (78 rpm = £15)	35

GWEN STACEY
65	RCA RCX 7166	INTRODUCING GWEN STACEY (EP)	150

BOB STACKIE
68	Collins Downbeat CR 009	Grab It Hold It Feel It (with Sir Collins Band)/DAN SIMMONDS: Way Out Sound	40

(see also Sir Collins [Band], Owen Gray)

STACKRIDGE
71	MCA MKS 5065	Dora, The Female Explorer/Everyman	5
72	MCA MKS 5103	Anyone For Tennis?/Amazingly Agnes	5
71	MCA MDKS 8002	STACKRIDGE (LP, gatefold sleeve)	25
72	MCA MKPS 2025	FRIENDLINESS (LP)	18
74	MCA MCG 3501	THE MAN IN THE BOWLER HAT (LP, gatefold sleeve)	15
76	MCA MCF 2747	DO THE STANLEY (LP)	12
76	Rocket ROLL 3	MR. MICK (LP)	12

STACKWADDY
70	Dandelion S 5119	Roadrunner/Kentucky	12
72	Dandelion 2001 331	You Really Got Me/Willie The Pimp	10
71	Dandelion DAN 8003	STACKWADDY (LP, gatefold sleeve with inner sleeve; also listed as K 49003)	70
72	Dandelion 2310 231	BUGGER OFF! (LP)	75

STADIUM DOGS
77	Audiogenic A 17	Easy Beat/Android Rocker/Media Withdrawal (die-cut p/s)	10

JO STAFFORD
58	Philips PB 812	Sweet Little Darlin'/Star Of Love (78)	6
53	Columbia SCM 5011	Star Of Hope/Somebody	18
53	Columbia SCM 5012	It Is No Secret/He Bought My Soul At Calvary	20
53	Columbia SCM 5013	You Belong To Me/Jambalaya (On The Bayou)	40

53	Columbia SCM 5026	Keep It A Secret/Once To Every Heart	22
53	Columbia SCM 5046	Something To Remember You By/Blue Moon	15
53	Columbia SCM 5064	September In The Rain/JO STAFFORD & FRANKIE LAINE: Chow, Willy	30
57	Philips JK 1003	On London Bridge/Perfect Love (jukebox issue)	20
58	Philips PB 818	With A Little Bit Of Luck/Wouldn't It Be Loverly	7
58	Philips PB 876	Hibiscus/How Can We Say Goodbye (78 rpm = £8)	7
59	Philips PB 898	My Heart Is From Missouri/It Won't Be Easy	5
59	Philips PB 935	Pine Top's Boogie Woogie/All Yours (78 rpm = £15)	10
60	Philips PB 991	It Is No Secret/He Bought My Soul At Calvary (reissue)	6
60	Philips PB 1034	Candy/Indoor Sport	5

EPs

54	Columbia SEG 7516	WITH NELSON EDDY (plain sleeve)	10
54	Columbia SEG 7548	SHOW SONGS (plain sleeve)	10
55	Philips BBE 12014	JO STAFFORD No. 1	12
57	Philips BBE 12138	JO STAFFORD No. 2	12
57	Philips BBE 12141	JO STAFFORD WITH THE ART VAN DAMME QUINTET	12
58	Philips BBE 12214	T.V. SERIES	12
60	Capitol EAP 20049	THE JO STAFFORD TOUCH	12
61	Capitol EAP 20154	SIMPLE MELODY	12
61	Philips BBE 12459	JO + JAZZ	12

LPs

50	Capitol LC 6500	AMERICAN FOLK SONGS (10")	18
51	Capitol LC 6515	KISS ME KATE (10", with Gordon MacRae)	15
53	Capitol LC 6575	CAPITOL PRESENTS JO STAFFORD (10")	30
53	Capitol LC 6611	SUNDAY EVENING SONGS (10", with Gordon MacRae)	20
54	Capitol LC 6635	CAPITOL PRESENTS JO STAFFORD, VOL. 2 (10")	30
54	Columbia 33S 1024	AS YOU DESIRE ME (10")	30
54	Philips BBR 8011	MY HEART'S IN THE HIGHLANDS (10")	20
56	Philips BBR 8076	THE VOICE OF YOUR CHOICE (10")	22
56	Philips BBL 7100	HAPPY HOLIDAY (soundtrack)	18
57	Philips BBL 7169	ONCE OVER LIGHTLY	15
57	Philips BBL 7187	SKI TRAILS	15
58	Philips BBL 7243	SWINGIN' DOWN BROADWAY	15
59	Philips BBL 7290	I'LL BE SEEING YOU	15
59	Philips BBL 7327	BALLAD OF THE BLUES	15
60	Philips BBL 7395	JO STAFFORD SHOWCASE	18
61	Philips BBL 7428	JO + JAZZ (also stereo SBBL 595)	each 15
62	Capitol (S)T 1653	AMERICAN FOLK SONGS (reissue, mono/stereo)	each 12
62	Capitol (S)T 1696	WHISPERING HOPE (with Gordon MacRae)	12

(see also Jonathan & Darlene Edwards, Gordon MacRae, Tommy Dorsey)

JO STAFFORD & FRANKIE LAINE

53	Columbia SCM 5014	Settin' The Woods On Fire/Piece A-Puddin'	28
55	Philips BBR 8075	FLOATIN' DOWN TO COTTON TOWN (10" LP)	40

(see also Frankie Laine)

TERRY STAFFORD

63	Stateside SS 225	Heartache On The Way/You Left Me Here To Cry	15
64	London HLU 9871	Suspicion/Judy	10
64	London HLU 9902	Playing With Fire/I'll Touch A Star	10
64	London HLU 9923	Follow The Rainbow/Are You A Fool Like Me	10
64	London RE-U 1436	SUSPICION (EP)	70
64	London HA-U 8200	SUSPICION (LP)	70

STAGEFRIGHT

85	STN STN 1	Strangers In The Night/Heartless/Rock City (no p/s)	150

STAIFFI & HIS MUSTAFAS

60	Pye International 7N 25057	Mustafa Cha Cha Cha/Zoubida	5

STAINED GLASS

74	Sweet Folk & C. SFA 019	OPEN ROAD (LP)	90

CHRIS STAINTON & GLEN TURNER

76	Decca SKL-R 5259	TUNDRA (LP)	15

(see also Made In Sheffield, Joe Cocker, Grease Band)

STAIRS

92	Imaginary MIRAGE 029	Weed Bus (12", unissued, test pressings only, proof p/s)	40

STAIRSTEPS

71	Buddah 2011 092	Stay Close To Me/I Made A Mistake	15
75	Dark Horse AMS 5505	From Us To You/Time (some in USA p/s)	18/10
76	Dark Horse AMS 5507	Pasado/Throwin' Stones Atcha	10
71	Buddah 2359 021	STEP BY STEP BY STEP (LP)	28
71	Buddah 2365 015	STAY CLOSE TO ME (LP)	28
72	Buddah 2365 016	THE STAIRSTEPS (LP)	28
76	Dark Horse AMLH 22004	2ND RESSURECTION (LP)	30

(see also Five Stairsteps)

STAIRWAY

88	New World NWCD 168	MOONSTONE (CD)	18

(see also Jane Relf, Yardbirds, Renaissance)

STAKKA AND SKYNET

00	Underfire UDFR 016	Knight Lore/Global Report (12")	10
01	Underfire UDFRLPS 04	CLOCKWORK SAMPLER EP: Decoy/Side Effects (Kemal and Rob Data remix)/ 9000 series/Side Effects (Teebee remix) (2 x 12", stickered, die-cut sleeve)	20
01	Underfire UDRFRLP 04	CLOCKWORK (LP, 5 discs)	40

MINT VALUE £

STAKKER
(see under Humanoid)

STAMFORD BRIDGE
70	Penny Farthing PEN 715	Peter Osgood/Stamford Bridge	12

TERRY STAMP
75	A&M AMLH 68329	FAT STICKS (LP, with lyric insert)	15

(see also Third World War)

STAMPEDE
82	Polydor POSP 507	Days Of Wine And Roses/Photographs (p/s)	12
82	Polydor POSP 507	Photographs/Days Of Wine And Roses (A-side switched, no p/s)	35
82	Polydor POSPX 507	Days Of Wine And Roses/Movin' On/Photographs/Missing You (12", p/s)	30
83	Polydor POSP 592	The Other Side/The Runner (p/s)	10
82	Polydor ROCK 1	OFFICIAL BOOTLEG (LP)	20
83	Polydor POLS 1083	HURRICANE TOWN (LP)	15

STAMPEDERS
72	Stateside SS 2202	Monday Morning Choo Choo/Then Came The White Man	5
72	Regal Zonophone RZ 3069	Johnny Lightning/Today's The Beginning Of The Rest Of Your Life	6
73	Regal Zonophone RZ 3079	Oh My Lady/No Destination	6
72	Regal Zono. SLRZ 1032	THE STAMPEDERS (LP)	25
74	Regal Zono. SLRZ 1039	FROM THE FIRE (LP)	25

JOE STAMPLEY
73	Dot DOT 145	Soul Song/Not Too Long Ago	10

JEAN STANBACK
69	Deep Soul DS 9101	I Still Love You/If I Ever Needed Love	50

STANDELLS
64	Liberty LIB 55722	I'll Go Crazy/Help Yourself	35
66	Capitol CL 15446	Dirty Water/Rari	45
65	Liberty LBY 1243	THE STANDELLS IN PERSON AT P.J.'s (LP)	55

JOHNNY STANDLEY
56	Capitol EAP 1020	IT'S IN THE BOOK (EP)	10

STANDS
00s	Echo ECS 142	When This River Rolls Over You/She Speaks Of These Things (autographed p/s, 1000 only)	8

ARNOLD STANG
59	Fontana H 226	Where Ya' Calling From, Charlie/Ivy Will Cling (78 rpm = £6)	7

IVAN STANG
97	XXX X-DAY 23	EMBRACE YOUR NORTH TIBETAN HERITAGE! (LP, 1-sided, with ranting insert)	20

PAUL STANLEY
79	Casablanca CAN 140	Hold Me Touch Me/Goodbye (p/s)	6
79	Casablanca CAN 140	Hold Me Touch Me/Goodbye (p/s, purple vinyl with mask & picture label, most with mispressed B-side: "Love In Chains")	20

(see also Kiss)

PETE STANLEY & WIZZ JONES
65	Columbia DB 7776	The Ballad Of Hollis Brown/Riff Minor	15
66	Columbia SX 6083	SIXTEEN TONS OF BLUEGRASS (LP)	100

(see also Wizz Jones)

PETE STANLEY & ROGER KNOWLES
70s	Xtra TRANS 1146	PICKING AND SINGING (LP)	35

STANLEY BROTHERS
61	Melodisc MLP 12-118	MOUNTAIN SONG FAVOURITES (LP)	12
61	Melodisc MLP 12-122	SACRED SONGS FROM THE HILLS (LP)	12

ROY STANNARD ORCHESTRA
87	SS SS 100	The Peanut Vendor/'Swingin' ' The Blues	5

LISA STANSFIELD
81	Devil DEV 2	Your Alibis/Thought Police (p/s)	5

VIV(IAN) STANSHALL
70	Liberty LBF 15309	Labio-Dental Fricative/Paper Round (with Sean Head Show Band featuring Eric Clapton)	30
71	Fly BUG 4	Suspicion (with Gargantuan Chums)/Blind Date (with biG GRunt)	12
74	Warner Bros K 16424	Lakonga/Baba Tunde	7
76	Harvest HAR 5114	Young Ones/Are You Havin' Any Fun/Question	20
80	Charisma CB 373	Terry Keeps His Clips On/King Cripple (p/s)	6
81	Charisma CB 382	Calypso To Colapso/Smoke Signals At Night (p/s)	5
74	Warner Bros K 56052	MEN OPENING UMBRELLAS AHEAD (LP, with inner)	60
78	Charisma CAS 1139	SIR HENRY AT RAWLINSON END (LP, soundtrack, with insert)	18
81	Charisma CAS 1153	TEDDY BOYS DON'T KNIT (LP)	25

(see also Bonzo Dog [Doo Dah] Band, Grimms)

STAPLE SINGERS
64	Riverside 106902 RIF	Hammer And Nails/Glory Land	10
67	Columbia DB 8292	For What It's Worth/Are You Sure?	30
69	Soul City SC 117	For What It's Worth/Are You Sure? (reissue)	20
69	Stax STAX 118	I See It/The Ghetto	6
71	Stax 2025 019	Heavy Makes You Happy/Love Is Plentiful	6
72	Stax 2025 068	Respect Yourself/You're Gonna Make Me Cry	6
72	Stax 2025 110	I'll Take You There/Just Another Soldier	6
62	Riverside REP 3220	THE SAVIOUR IS BORN (EP)	15

63	Stateside SL 10015	SWING LOW (LP)	30
63	Riverside RLP 3501	HAMMER AND NAILS (LP)	25
65	Fontana 688 515 ZL	UNCLOUDY DAY (LP)	20
66	Columbia SX 6023	FREEDOM HIGHWAY (LP)	20
69	Stax (S)XATS 1004	SOUL FOLK IN ACTION (LP)	15
69	Stax SXATS 1018	WE'LL GET OVER (LP)	15
71	Stax 2362 005	THE STAPLE SINGERS (LP)	15
71	Stax 2362 011	SOUL FOLK IN ACTION (LP, reissue)	15
72	Stax STX 1001	CITY IN THE SKY (LP)	15
72	Stax 2325 069	BEALTITUDE/RESPECT YOURSELF (LP)	15

CYRIL STAPLETON & HIS ORCHESTRA

54	Decca F 10293	Long Distance Love/There'll Be No Teardrops Tonight	8
55	Decca F 10456	Tango Mambo/Mexican Madness	8
55	Decca F 10470	Fanfare Boogie/Time After Time	10
55	Decca F 10488	Elephant Tango/Gabrielle	12
55	Decca F 10559	Blue Star (The "Medic" Theme) (with Julie Dawn)/Honey Babe (with Gordon Langhorn)	18
56	Decca F 10703	The Italian Theme/Come Next Spring	10
56	Decca F 10735	The Happy Whistler (with Desmond Lane)/Tiger Tango	8
56	Decca F 10793	Highway Patrol/Maids Of Madrid	10
57	Decca F 10883	Rock, Fiddle, Rock/Chantez, Chantez	7
57	Decca F 10912	Forgotten Dreams/It's Not For Me To Say	6
58	Decca F 10979	Monday Blues (Parts 1 & 2)	8
66	Pye 7N 17040	The Theme From The Power Game/'Lil (some in p/s)	7
67	Pye 7N 17397	No That's Me Over Here/The Flower Girls	6
68	Pye 7N 17629	The Forsyte Saga/The Lonely Sea And The Sky (in p/s)	7
69	Pye 7N 17807	Department S (Theme)/W. Somerset Maugham TV Theme (some in p/s)	20/10
54	Decca DFE 6288	PRESENTING CYRIL STAPLETON (EP)	10
54	Decca DFE 6340	PRESENTING CYRIL STAPLETON NO. 2 (EP)	10
67	Pye NEP 24272	A COUNTESS FROM HONG KONG (EP)	10
62	Ace Of Clubs ACL 1114	COME TWISTIN' (LP)	20

(see also Gordon Langhorn, Desmond Lane)

STEVEN STAPLETON & DAVID TIBET

91	United Dairies UD 037	THE SADNESS OF THINGS/THE GRAVE AND BEAUTIFUL NAME OF SADNESS (LP, one side each)	35

(see also Current 93, Nurse With Wound, Tibet & Stapleton)

STA-PREST

80	Avatar AAA 103	Schooldays/Tomorrow (p/s)	75

BUDDY STARCHER

64	London RE-B 1424	BUDDY STARCHER AND HIS MOUNTAIN GUITAR VOL. 1 (EP)	20
64	London RE-B 1425	BUDDY STARCHER AND HIS MOUNTAIN GUITAR VOL. 2 (EP)	20
64	London RE-B 1426	BUDDY STARCHER AND HIS MOUNTAIN GUITAR VOL. 3 (EP)	20

STARFIGHTERS

80	Motor City MCR 105	I'm Falling/Heaven And Hell (some in p/s)	40/7
81	Jive JIV 003	Alley Cat Blues/Don't Touch Me (p/s)	7
81	Jive JIVET 003	Alley Cat Blues/Don't Touch Me (12", p/s)	15
81	Jive JIVET 6	Power Crazy/I Want You (p/s)	6
81	Jive JIVET 6	Power Crazy/I Want You/Get Out While You Can (12", p/s)	8
81	Jive HOP 200	STARFIGHTERS (LP, with inner)	22
82	Jive HOP 200	POWER CRAZY (LP)	10
82	Jive HOP 205	IN FLIGHT MOVIE (LP)	12

STARGAZERS

53	Beltona BL 2594	White Heather For Luck/Rothesay Bay (78)	6
53	Decca F 10047	Broken Wings/Make It Soon (78)	14
54	Decca F 10213	I See The Moon/Eh Cumpari	25
54	Decca F 10259	The Happy Wanderer/Till We Two Are One	20
54	Decca F 10379	365 Kisses/I Need You Now	10
54	Decca F 10412	Rose Of The Wildwood/Come The Morning	10
55	Decca F 10437	Somebody/(My Baby Don't Love Me) No More (& Sonny Farrar Banjo Band)	15
55	Decca F 10523	The Crazy Otto Rag/Hey, Mr. Banjo	12
55	Decca F 10569	At The Steamboat River Ball/I Love You A Mountain (with Sonny Farrar Banjo Band)	8
55	Decca F 10594	Close The Door/I've Got Four Big Brothers	15
55	Decca F 10626	Twenty Tiny Fingers/An Old Beer Bottle	15
55	Decca F 10668	(Love Is) The Tender Trap/When The Swallows Say Goodbye	8
56	Decca F 10696	Zambesi/When The Swallows Say Goodbye	12
56	Decca F 10731	Hot Diggity (Dog Ziggity Boom)/Rockin' And Rollin'	12
56	Decca F 10775	She Loves To Rock/John Jacob Jingleheimer Smith	12
57	Decca F 10867	You Won't Be Around/Mangos	7
57	Decca F 10898	Honky Tonk Song/Golly!	7
56	Decca DFE 6341	THE STARGAZERS (EP)	28
56	Decca DFE 6362	ROCKIN' AND ROLLIN' (EP)	25
54	Decca LF 1186	PRESENTING THE STARGAZERS (10" LP)	40
59	Decca LK 4309	SOUTH OF THE BORDER (LP)	35

(see also Roy Smith & Stargazers, Lita Roza, Dickie Valentine)

STARJETS

78	Epic S EPC 6902	Here She Comes Again/Watch Out	15
79	Epic S EPC 6968	It Really Doesn't Matter/Schooldays	12
79	Epic S EPC 7123	Run With The Pack/Watch Out	10
79	Epic S EPC 6968/7123	It Really Doesn't Matter/Schooldays//Run With The Pack/Watch Out (double pack, die-cut sleeves, promo only)	25
79	Epic S EPC 7417	Ten Years/One More Word (p/s)	10

79	Epic S EPC 7417	Ten Years/One More Word (Manchester gig issue, stamped white labels)	20
79	Epic S EPC 7770	War Stories/Do The Push (p/s)	15
79	Epic S EPC 7986	Schooldays/What A Life (p/s)	25
80	Epic S EPC 8276	Shiraleo/Standby 19 (p/s)	10
79	Epic EPC 83534	GOD BLESS STARJETS (LP)	25

STARLIGHTERS
| 50 | Capitol CL 13263 | Rag Mop/If Not Bad (78) | 6 |

STARLINGS
| 80s | Ruffin A-M 029 | NEW BLOOD (EP) | 8 |

STARLITES
73	Downtown DT 502	You're A Wanted Man/G.G. ALL STARS: Back To Dubwise	7
74	Big Shot BI 629	Mama Dee Part One/Mama Dee Part Two	8
75	Bullet BU 554	Healing In The Barnyard/G.G. ALL STARS: Version	6
	(see also Bellfield)		

CINDY STARR
68	C'mbia Blue Beat DB 107	Pain Of Love/Hippy Ska (as Cindy Starr & Rude Boys)	18
68	C'mbia Blue Beat DB 110	The Way I Do/Sad Movies (Make Me Cry) (as Cindy Starr & Mopeds)	15
	(see also Mopeds, Teardrops)		

EDWIN STARR
66	Polydor BM 56702	Stop Her On Sight (S.O.S.)/I Have Faith In You (demos £500+)	25
66	Polydor BM 56717	Headline News/Harlem	20
67	Polydor BM 56726	It's My Turn Now/Girls Are Getting Prettier	25
68	Polydor BM 56753	Stop Her On Sight (S.O.S.)/Headline News (reissue)	10
67	Tamla Motown TMG 630	I Want My Baby Back/Gonna Keep On Tryin' Till I Win (DJ copy = £50)	25
68	Tamla Motown TMG 646	I Am The Man For You Baby/My Weakness Is You (DJ copy = £85)	35
68	Tamla Motown TMG 672	25 Miles/Mighty Good Lovin' (DJ copy = £45)	10
69	Tamla Motown TMG 692	Way Over There/If My Heart Could Tell The Story (DJ copy = £50)	20
69	Tamla Motown TMG 720	Oh How Happy/O, O, O, Baby (demos only, unissued, with Blinky)	300
70	Tamla Motown TMG 725	Time/Running Back And Forth	20
70	Tamla Motown TMG 754	War/He Who Picks A Rose	8
71	Tamla Motown TMG 764	Stop The War Now!/Gonna Keep On Tryin' Till I Win	8
71	Tamla Motown TMG 790	Agent Double 0 Soul/Back Street (DJ copy = £40)	10
72	Tamla Motown TMG 810	Funky Music Sho' Nuff Turns Me On/Cloud Nine	8
73	Tamla Motown TMG 875	Love The Lonely People's Prayer/You've Got My Soul On Fire	20
73	Tamla Motown TMG 930	Ain't It Hell Up In Harlem/Who's Right Or Wrong	8
75	Bradleys BRAD 7520	Stay With Me/I'll Never Forget You	15
75	Bradleys BRAD 7531	Pain/Party	10
76	GTO GT 65	Accident/Eavesdropper	8
70s	Tamla Motown TMG 905	Stop Her On Sight/Headline News (reissue)	6
70s	Tamla Motown TMG 1028	Time/Running Back And Forth (reissue)	10
69	T. Motown (S)TML 11094	SOUL MASTER (LP)	50
69	T. Motown (S)TML 11115	25 MILES (LP)	30
70	T. Motown (S)TML 11131	JUST WE TWO (LP, as Edwin Starr & Blinky)	25
70	Tamla Motown STML 11171	WAR AND PEACE (LP)	18
72	Tamla Motown STML 11199	INVOLVED (LP)	15
72	Tamla Motown STML 11209	THE HITS OF EDWIN STARR (LP)	15
74	Tamla Motown STML 11260	HELL UP IN HARLEM (LP, soundtrack)	15
	(see also Blinky & Edwin Starr, Holidays)		

FRANK STARR
| 62 | London HLU 9545 | Little Bitty Feeling/Lost In A Dream | 12 |

FREDDIE STARR & MIDNIGHTERS
63	Decca F 11663	Who Told You?/Peter Gunn Locomotion	30
63	Decca F 11786	It's Shaking Time/Baby Blue	32
64	Decca F 12009	Never Cry On Someone's Shoulder/Just Keep On Dreaming	45
71	A&M AMS 838	Naomi/Free To Carry On (solo)	5
78	PVK PVK 004	FREDDIE STARR (LP)	12
	(see also Howie Casey & Seniors)		

JIMMY STARR
| 58 | London HL 8731 | It's Only Make Believe/Ooh Crazy (78 rpm = £20) | 30 |

KAY STARR
51	Vogue V 9009	Ain't Misbehavin'/Good For Nothin' Joe (78)	6
51	Vogue V 9010	Them There Eyes/What Is This Thing Called Love? (78)	6
54	Capitol CL 14151	Am I A Toy Or A Treasure?/Fortune In Dreams	20
54	Capitol CL 14167	Fool, Fool, Fool/Allez-Vous En.	20
55	HMV 7M 300	If Anyone Finds This, I Love You/Turn Right	15
55	HMV 7M 307	Foolishly Yours/For Better Or Worse	12
55	HMV 7M 315	Where, What Or When?/Good And Lonesome	12
56	HMV 7M 371	Rock And Roll Waltz/I've Changed My Mind 1,000 Times	20
56	HMV 7M 420	Second Fiddle/Love Ain't Right	12
57	HMV POP 345	A Little Loneliness/Touch And Go	8
57	HMV POP 357	Jamie Boy/The Things I Never Had	8
58	RCA RCA 1065	Stroll Me/Rockin' Chair (78 rpm = £6)	6
60	Capitol CL 15105	Riders In The Sky/Night Train	5
60	Capitol CL 15137	Wheel Of Fortune/If You Love Me (Really Love Me)	6

EPs
55	Vogue EPV 1014	KAY STARR	12
56	HMV 7EG 8165	WHAT A STAR IS KAY	10
56	HMV 7EG 8184	KAY STARR'S AGAIN	10
60	Top Rank JKP 2042	HEAVENLY KAY STARR	12
60	Capitol EAP1 1254	MOVING	10

60	Capitol EAP2 1254	MOVING PT. 2	10
60	Capitol EAP3 1254	MOVING PT. 3	12
61	Capitol EAP 1-20063	WHEEL OF FORTUNE	15
62	Capitol EAP 1-20210	WELL I ASK YOU	10

LPs

53	Capitol LC 6574	CAPITOL PRESENTS KAY STARR (10")	20
54	Capitol LC 6630	THE KAY STARR STYLE (10")	20
56	Capitol LC 6835	THE HITS OF KAY STARR (10")	20
57	Capitol T 580	IN A BLUE MOOD	20
57	London HA-U 2039	SWINGING WITH THE STARR	20
58	RCA RD 27056	BLUE STARR	18
60	Capitol (S)T 1254	MOVIN'!	12
60	Capitol (S)T 1303	LOSERS, WEEPERS	12
60	Capitol (S)T 1374	MOVIN' ON BROADWAY	12
61	Capitol T 1358	ONE MORE TIME	12
61	Capitol (S)T 1438	JAZZ SINGER	12
62	Capitol T 1468	ALL STARR HITS!	12
62	Capitol (S)T 1681	I CRY BY NIGHT	12
63	Capitol (S)T 1795	JUST PLAIN COUNTRY	12
64	Capitol (S)T 2106	THE FABULOUS FAVOURITES	12

MAXINE STARR

63	London HLU 9712	Wishing Star/Sailor Boy	8

RANDY STARR

57	London HL 8443	After School/Heaven High (Man So Low) (78 rpm = £15)	40
58	Felsted AF 106	Pink Lemonade/Count On Me (78 rpm = £10)	15
60	Top Rank JAR 264	Workin' On The Santa Fe/You're Growing Up	7

RINGO STARR

71	Apple R 5898	It Don't Come Easy/Early 1970 (p/s, B-side with Ringo or George Harrison production credit)	6/5
72	Apple R 5944	Back Off Boogaloo/Blindman (p/s, blue label)	6
73	Apple R 5992	Photograph/Down And Out (p/s)	6
74	Apple R 5995	You're Sixteen/Devil Woman (p/s)	5
74	Apple R 6000	Only You/Call Me (p/s)	5
75	Apple R 6004	Snookeroo/Oo-wee	12
76	Apple R 6011	Oh My My/No No Song	20
76	Polydor 2001 694	A Dose Of Rock 'N' Roll/Cryin'	10
76	Polydor 2001 695	You Don't Know Me At All/Cryin' (unissued in U.K., Europe only)	
76	Polydor 2001 699	Hey Baby/Lady Gaye	10
77	Polydor 2001 734	Drowning In The Sea Of Love/Just A Dream	100
78	Polydor 2001 782	Lipstick Traces/Old Time Relovin' (unissued in U.K., Europe only)	
78	Polydor 2001 795	Tonight/Heart On My Sleeve	100
72	R.O.R. ROR 2001	Steel (1-sided promo-only interview disc for 'Ringo Or Robin' reception at Liberty's department store; available for 1 week only p/s)	2000
74	Parlophone PSR 374	Interview By Bob Mercer With Ringo For The Salesmen And Uxbridge Road/Only You (promo only)	1500
70s	Apple R 5944	Back Off Boogaloo/Blindman (green apple label)	250
70s	Parlophone R 5995	You're Sixteen/Devil Woman (p/s)	25
84	Apple G45 13	It Don't Come Easy/Back Off Boogaloo (P/s EMI Golden 45s series)	35
99	Mercury 546 668-2	I Wanna Be Santa Claus (CD)	25
70	Apple PCS 7101	SENTIMENTAL JOURNEY (LP)	20
70	Apple TD-PCS 7101	SENTIMENTAL JOURNEY (reel-to-reel tape, jewel case)	25
70	Apple PAS 10002	BEAUCOUPS OF BLUES (LP, gatefold sleeve)	20
78	Polydor 2480 429	SCOUSE THE MOUSE (LP, with Adam Faith, Donald Pleasance etc.; some w/stickered sleeve & printed [not photocopied] competition insert)	110/50
78	Polydor 3194 429	SCOUSE THE MOUSE (cassette)	40
90	EMI EMS 1375	RINGO STARR & HIS ALL STARR BAND (LP)	30
00	Eagle Records EEECDO11	THE ANTHOLOGY...SO FAR (3xCD in slip case)	30

(see also Beatles, Harry Nilsson, Billy Connolly & Chris Tummings, Traveling Wilburys)

STELLA STARR

67	Piccadilly 7N 35366	Bring Him Back/Say It (DJ copy = £100)	75

TONY STARR

64	Decca F 11847	I'll Take A Rocket To The Moon/Next Train Leaving	60

STARR BOUNDS

75	Horse HOSS 95	Heavenly (parts 1 & 2)	8

STARSAILOR

00s	Chrysalis CHS 5123	Fever/Coming Down/Love Is Here (gatefold p/s)	8
00s	Chrysalis CHS 5125	Good Souls/The Way Young Lovers Do (p/s, with fold-out picture insert)	6
00s	Chrysalis CHS 5130	Alcoholic/Let It Shine (p/s)	6
00s	Chrysalis CHSDJ 5136	Poor Misguided Fool (Soulsavers Remix)/(Single Version) (promo-only, die-cut sleeve)	10

STARS OF HEAVEN

85	Hotwire HWS 853	Clothes Of Pride/All About You (beige or black label, some with p/s)	8/6

STAR SPANGLES

02	Capitol R 6593	Which Of The Two Of Us Is Gonna Burn This House Down/Stain Glass Shoes (p/s)	10

STARTIME KIDS

59	Fontana H 182	The Railroad Song/I Don't Want To Walk Without You, Baby (78 rpm = £6)	6

STATE OF MICKEY & TOMMY

67	Mercury MF 996	With Love From One To Five/I Know What I Will Do	100
67	Mercury MF 1009	Frisco Bay/Nobody Knows Where You've Been	70

(see also Spooky Tooth, Nero & Gladiators, Foreigner)

STATESMEN
63	Studio Republic	FIVE PLUS ONE (LP, private pressing)	110

STATE STREET SWINGERS/CHICAGO BLACK SWANS
73	Collectors Items 003	STATE STREET SWINGERS (LP)	12

STATE TROOPER
85	Neat 5212	SHE GOT THE LOOK (12" EP)	10

(see also Michael Schenker Group)

STATIC
67	Page One POF 039	When You Went Away/Let Me Tell You	10

STATIC
81	Eeyo EEYO 1	Voice On The Line/Stealin' (no p/s, 1,000 only)	10

(see also White Lightning)

STATIC
City Centre Offices BLOCK 013	Headphones (plain sleeve with inserts, 1000 copies)	8
City Centre Offices BLOCK 016	TURN ON SWITCH OFF (12" EP)	8
City Centre Offices BLOCK 021	GHOST BOY (Feat. Ronald Lippok) (12" EP, custom sleeve)	8

STATION SKIFFLE GROUP
57	Esquire 10-503	Don't You Rock Me Daddy-O/Hugged My Honey (78)	15
57	Esquire 10-516	Steamboat Bill/Titanic (78)	22
58	Esquire EP 161	STATION SKIFFLE GROUP (EP)	65

(see also Jimmy Miller)

STATION 360
84	SRT STA 360	Optimist	30

STATLER BROTHERS
65	CBS 201796	Flowers On The Wall/Bill Christian	5
66	CBS BPG 62713	FLOWERS ON THE WALL (LP)	15

(see also Johnny Cash)

CANDI STATON
69	Capitol CL 15601	I'd Rather Be An Old Man's Sweetheart/For You	8
69	Capitol CL 15620	Heart On A String/I'm Just A Prisoner	8
70	Capitol CL 15646	Sweet Feeling/Evidence	8
70	Capitol CL 15658	Stand By Your Man/How Can I Put Out The Flame (When You Keep The Fire Burning)	8
75	United Artists UP 35823	Love Chain/I'm Gonna Hold On	6
70	Capitol ST 21631	I'M JUST A PRISONER (LP)	30

DAKOTA STATON
55	Capitol CL 14314	Don't Leave Me Now/A Little You	12
55	Capitol CL 14339	I Never Dreamt/Abracadabra	12
59	Capitol EAP1 1054	THE DYNAMIC DAKOTA STATON (EP)	7
59	Capitol EAP2 1054	THE DYNAMIC DAKOTA STATON (EP)	7
59	Capitol EAP3 1054	THE DYNAMIC DAKOTA STATON (EP)	7
58	Capitol T 876	THE LATE, LATE SHOW (LP)	15
59	Capitol (S)T 1054	THE DYNAMIC DAKOTA STATON (LP)	5
59	Capitol T 1170	CRAZY HE CALLS ME (LP)	15
60	Capitol (S)T 1325	MORE THAN THE MOOD (LP)	15
60	Capitol (S)T 1387	BALLADS AND THE BLUES (LP)	15
61	Capitol (S)T 1241	TIME TO SWING (LP)	12
62	Capitol (S)T 1597	'ROUND MIDNIGHT (LP)	12
62	Capitol (S)T 1649	DAKOTA AT STORYVILLE (LP)	12

STATUES
60	London HLG 9192	Blue Velvet/Keep The Hall Burning	45

STATUS QUO
PYE SINGLES
68	Pye 7N 17449	Pictures Of Matchstick Men/Gentleman Joe's Sidewalk Café (some with '75c Minimum' on B-side label credit)	15
68	Pye 7N 17497	Black Veils Of Melancholy/To Be Free	20
68	Pye 7N 17581	Ice In The Sun/When My Mind Is Not Live	8
68	Pye 7N 17650	Technicolor Dreams/Paradise Flat (withdrawn, demos more common, £300)	1000
69	Pye 7N 17665	Make Me Stay A Bit Longer/Aunt Nellie	22
69	Pye 7N 17728	Are You Growing Tired Of My Love/So Ends Another Life	22
69	Pye 7N 17825	The Price Of Love/Little Miss Nothing	22
70	Pye 7N 17907	Down The Dustpipe/Face Without A Soul (black, blue or reissue Precision labels)	5/5/5
70	Pye 7N 17998	In My Chair/Gerdundula (some with p/s)	45/8
71	Pye 7N 45077	Tune To The Music/Good Thinking	20
73	Pye 7N 45229	Mean Girl/Everything (blue labels)	5
73	Pye 7N 45253	Gerdundula/Lakky Lady (red label)	5
77	Pye BD 103	Down The Dustpipe/Mean Girl/In My Chair/Gerdundula (12", generic sleeve, reissued on PRT)	8
78	Pye 7N 46103	Pictures of Matchstick Men/Ice In The Sun (red labels, reissued on PRT)	each 5
79	Pye Flashbacks FBS 2	Pictures Of Matchstick Men/Down The Dustpipe (yellow vinyl, p/s)	6
79	Pye Flashbacks FBS 2	Pictures Of Matchstick Men/Down The Dustpipe (black vinyl, no p/s, reissued on PRT)	5
79	Pye 7P 103	In My Chair/Gerdundula (p/s)	5
79	Pye QUO 1/SFI 434	In My Chair (flexi, concert freebie, with *Record Mirror* Quo special)	10

VERTIGO SINGLES

72	Vertigo 6059 071	Paper Plane/Softer Ride (swirl label, solid centre)	6
73	Vertigo 6059 085	Caroline/Joanne (with B-side miscredited to Lancaster)	5
74	Vertigo 6059 101	Break The Rules/Lonely Night (mispressed, B-side labels on both sides)	7
76	Vertigo 6059 153	Wild Side Of Life/All Through The Night (brown plastic labels)	6
77	Vertigo 6059 184	Rockin' All Over The World/Ring Of A Change (p/s, some with small poster)	15/5
78	Vertigo QUO 2	Accident Prone/Let Me Fly (p/s)	5
82	Vertigo QUO 9	Jealousy/Calling The Shots (unreleased in U.K.; Irish promos only)	150+
82	Vertigo QUOP 10	Caroline (Live At The NEC)/Dirty Water (live) (picture disc)	5
83	Vertigo QUOP 14	Marguerita Time/Resurrection (picture disc)	8
83	Vertigo QUO 1414	Marguerita Time/Resurrection//Caroline/Joanne (double pack, stickered gatefold p/s)	10
84	Vertigo QUO 15	Too Close To The Ground/I Wonder Why (release cancelled)	
85	Vertigo QUO 17	Naughty Girl (actually "Dreamin' ") (unreleased)	
86	Vertigo QUOPD 18	Rollin' Home/Lonely ('Q'-shaped picture disc)	8
86	Vertigo QUOPD 18	Rollin' Home/Lonely (uncut picture disc)	150
86	Vertigo QUODP 19	Red Sky/Don't Give It Up//Rockin' All Over The World/Whatever You Want (double pack, gatefold p/s)	6
86	Vertigo QUOPB 191	Red Sky/Don't Give It Up/The Milton Keynes Medley (12", 'Wembley Souvenir Pack', poster p/s)	15
86	Vertigo QUO 20	In The Army Now/Heartburn (stickered p/s, with sew-on patch, shrinkwrapped)	10
86	Vertigo QUOPD 20	In The Army Now/Heartburn (picture disc)	15
86	Vertigo QUODP 20	In The Army Now/Heartburn//Marguerita Time/ What You're Proposing (double pack, gatefold p/s)	6
86	Vertigo QUO 2012	In The Army Now (Military Mix)/Heartburn/Late Last Night (12", stickered p/s, with poster)	8
86	Vertigo QUOP 21	Dreamin'/Long-Legged Girls (p/s, with foldout poster/calendar)	6
88	Vertigo QUOCD 22	Ain't Complaining (Extended)/That's Alright/Lean Machine/ In The Army Now (Remix) (CD, card sleeve)	15
88	Vertigo QUOCD 23	Who Gets The Love? (Extended)/Hallowe'en/The Reason For Goodbye/ The Wanderer (Sharon The Nag Mix) (CD, card sleeve)	25
88	Vertigo QUACD 1	Running All Over The World (Extended)/Magic/Whatever You Want (CD, card sleeve)	20
88	Vertigo QUO 2512	Burning Bridges (On And Off And On Again) (Extended Version)/ Whatever You Want/Marguerita Time (12", mispressing also including 7" edit)	10
88	Vertigo QUOCD 25	Burning Bridges (On And Off And On Again) (Extended Version)/ Whatever You Want/Marguerita Time (CD)	15
89	Vertigo 080 322-2	Ain't Complaining (Extended)/That's Alright/Lean Machine/ In The Army Now (Remix)/Ain't Complaining (Video) (CD Video)	20
89	Vertigo 080 630-2	Burning Bridges (On And Off And On Again) (Extended Version)/ Whatever You Want (Extended Version)/Marguerita Time/ Who Gets The Love?/Burning Bridges (Video) (CD Video)	25
89	Vertigo QUOCD 26	Not At All/Everytime I Think Of You/Gone Thru The Slips (CD)	10
89	Vertigo QUOCD 27	Little Dreamer/Rotten To The Bone/Doing It All For You (CD)	10
90	Vertigo QUO 2812	The Anniversary Waltz/The Power Of Rock/Perfect Remedy (12", p/s, mispress, B-side plays "Little Lady" (live) & exclusive "Paper Plane" re-recording)	45
90	Vertigo QUO 2812	The Anniversary Waltz/The Power Of Rock/Perfect Remedy (12", p/s, mispress, A-side plays "The Power Of Rock [Full Version]")	45
91	Vertigo QUO 31	Fakin' The Blues (Edit)/Heavy Daze (p/s, swirl label, release cancelled, approximately 25 copies only)	400+
91	Vertigo QUO 3112	Fakin' The Blues (Edit)/Fakin' The Blues (Album Version)/Heavy Daze/ Better Times (12", swirl label, p/s, cancelled, approx. 25 copies only)	300+
91	Vertigo QUOCD 31	Fakin' The Blues (Edit)/Fakin' The Blues (Album Version)/Heavy Daze/Better Times (CD, unissued, 2,000 later sent out by fan club, no inlay)	40
92	Vertigo QUO 3212	Rock 'Til You Drop/Medley/Forty-Five Hundred Times (12", p/s, mispressing, omits "Forty-Five Hundred Times")	15
92	Vertigo QUOCD 32	Rock 'Til You Drop/Medley/Forty-Five Hundred Times (CD in no'd guitar-shaped case)	12

OTHER SINGLES

75	Lyntone LYN 3154/5	Down Down/Break The Rules (Smiths Crisps flexidisc, a few with 'Smiths' p/s)	15/6
80s	Lyntone QUO 1-4	Interview picture discs (4-single pack)	20
92	Polydor QUODD 33	Roadhouse Medley (Anniversary Waltz Part 25) (Radio Edit)/(Extended)/ Don't Drive My Car (Live) (CD, numbered 4-fold digipak, 2nd CD card template)	10
94	Polydor QUO 34	I Didn't Mean It/Whatever You Want (p/s, blue vinyl)	5
94	Polydor QUODD 34	I Didn't Mean It (Acoustic Version)/(Hooligan Version)/Survival/She Knew Too Much (CD, numbered digipak, 2nd CD card template)	10
94	Polydor QUODD 35	Sherri Don't Fail Me Now (Extended)/Tossin' And Turnin'/Down To You (CD, numbered digipak, 2nd CD card template)	8
94	Polydor QUODD 36	Restless (LP Version)/And I Do/Democracy (CD, no'd digipak, 2nd CD card template)	8
95	PolyGram TV 576262 7	Fun Fun Fun (with The Beach Boys)/Mortified (numbered picture disc)	5
96	PolyGram TV 5759447	All Around My Hat (with Maddy Prior)/I'll Never Get Over You (numbered picture disc)	6
99	From The Makers Of... FTMOCD1	FAKIN' THE BLUES (MILLENNIUM EDITION) (CD, fanclub mail order-only edition, hand-no'd exclusive p/s, contains unreleased Vertigo CD [QUOCD 31])	50
00	PolyGram PSPCD464	NIGHT & DAY (CD EP, 4-track sampler, mail order-only via tokens from The Mail On Sunday, insufficient pressed to meet demand)	25

PROMO-ONLY SINGLES

68	Pye 7N 17449	Pictures Of Matchstick Men/Gentleman Joe's Sidewalk Café (75c Minimum) ('A' label)	60
68	Pye 7N 17497	Black Veils Of Melancholy/To Be Free ('A' label)	70
68	Pye 7N 17581	Ice In The Sun/When My Mind Is Not Live ('A' label)	60
68	Pye 7N 17650	Technicolor Dreams/Paradise Flat('A' label)	400
69	Pye 7N 17665	Make Me Stay A Bit Longer/Aunt Nellie ('A' label)	70

MINT VALUE £

69	Pye 7N 17728	Are You Growing Tired Of My Love/So Ends Another Life ('A' label)	70
69	Pye 7N 17825	The Price Of Love/Little Miss Nothing ('A' label)	70
70	Pye 7N 17907	Down The Dustpipe/Face Without A Soul ('A' label)	60
70	Pye 7N 17998	In My Chair/Gerdundula ('A' label)	60
71	Pye 7N 45077	Tune To The Music/Good Thinking ('A' label)	60
72	Phonogram DJ 005	Roadhouse Blues/BLACK SABBATH: Children Of The Grave (100 copies only)	375
72	Vertigo 6059 071	Paper Plane/Softer Ride ('A' label)	45
73	Pye 7N 45229	Mean Girl/Everything ('A' label)	50
73	Pye 7N 45253	Gerdundula/Lakky Lady ('A' label)	40
75	Lyntone LYN 3154	Down Down (Smiths Crisps 1-sided gold flexidisc test pressing, plays "Bye Bye Baby" by Bay City Rollers)	25
75	Lyntone LYN 3155	Break The Rules (Smiths Crisps 1-sided gold flexidisc test pressing, plays "Bye Bye Baby" by Bay City Rollers)	25
79	Pye 7P 103	In My Chair/Gerdundula ('A' label)	20
81	Vertigo QUO JB 6	Rock 'N' Roll/Hold You Back (jukebox issue, B-side at 33rpm)	10
86	Vertigo QUODJ 2112	Dreamin' (Wet Mix)/Long-Legged Girls/The Quo Xmas Cake Mix (12")	15
88	Vertigo QUOLP 99	Ain't Complaining (12" promo, 1-sided)	30
88	Vertigo QUODJ 2212	Ain't Complaining (Extended)/That's Alright/Lean Machine (12")	10
88	Vertigo QUODJ 25	Burning Bridges (On & Off & On Again)/Burning Bridges (On & Off & On Again)	12
90	Vertigo (no cat. no.)	The Power Of Rock (Album Version)/(Single Edit)/Perfect Remedy (12" white label)	50+

LPs
68	Pye N(S)PL 18220	PICTURESQUE MATCHSTICKABLE MESSAGES (mono/stereo)	90/70
69	Pye N(S)PL 18301	SPARE PARTS (blue label, mono/stereo)	90/70
69	Marble Arch MAL(S) 1193	STATUS QUO-TATIONS (mono/stereo, most stereo copies exported)	30/50
70	Pye NSPL 18344	MA KELLY'S GREASY SPOON (very early copies with poster)	50/15
71	Pye NSPL 18371	DOG OF TWO HEAD (gatefold sleeve, blue labels, reissued with red, black or PRT "Piccadilly Circus" labels)	each 15
72	Vertigo 6360 082	PILEDRIVER (swirl label, gatefold sleeve)	25
73	Vertigo 6360 098	HELLO! (spaceship label, with inner sleeve & poster)	15
74	Vertigo 9102 001	QUO (with poster/lyric sheet; also Record Club issue [ACB 00217])	15/25
75	Vertigo 9102 002	ON THE LEVEL (gatefold sleeve, with inner sleeve)	12
76	Vertigo 9102 006	BLUE FOR YOU (gatefold sleeve, with inner sleeve)	12
77	Pye FILD 005	THE FILE SERIES (2-LP, single sleeve with inner sleeves; repressed on Precision)	20
79	Pye NPSL 18607	JUST FOR THE RECORD (red vinyl)	15
79	Pye FILD 005	THE FILE SERIES (2-LP, reissue with different sleeve, inners; repressed on PRT)	18
82	Phonogram PRO BX 1	FROM THE MAKERS OF... (3-LP, with inserts in round metal tin, some numbered)	20/18
82	Phonogram PRO BX 1	FROM THE MAKERS OF... (3-LP, with inserts in round metal tin, mispressing – record 3 plays side 5 twice)	25
82	Phonogram PRO BX 1	FROM THE MAKERS OF... (3-LP, with inserts in round metal tin, mispressing – record 1 side 2 plays Siouxsie & The Banshees' "Melt (12" Mix)")	25
82	Phonogram PRO LP 1	FROM THE MAKERS OF... (3-LP, with inserts in cardboard box)	15
83	Vertigo VERH 10	BACK TO BACK (in-store promo copies with poster insert)	18
85	PRT Flashbacks FBLP 8082	NANANA	15
88	PRT PYX 4007	FROM THE BEGINNING (picture disc)	25
90	Essential! ESBLP 136	THE EARLY WORKS (5-LP box set with book)	30
91	Baktabak LINT 5003	INTROSPECTIVE (clear vinyl, 4 Pye-era tracks & interview)	20
92	Polydor 517 367-1	LIVE ALIVE QUO (with inner sleeve)	20
94	Polydor 523 607-1	THIRSTY WORK (with inner sleeve)	22

CASSETTES
81	Vertigo 7215 038	THE MUSIC OF STATUS QUO VOLUME 1: 1972-1974 (cassette-only compilation)	25
82	Phonogram PRO MC 1	FROM THE MAKERS OF... (2 cassettes with inserts in 7" box)	15
98	Readers Digest RDC1831-4	THE COMPLETE STATUS QUO (4 cassettes & book, mail-order only)	35

CDs
83	Vertigo 800 035-2	1+9+8+2	40
83	Vertigo 800 053-2	NEVER TOO LATE	40
83	Vertigo 814 66-2	BACK TO BACK	30
85	PRT CDNSP 773	THE BEST OF STATUS QUO (THE EARLY YEARS)	18
86	PRT CDMP 8834	MA KELLY'S GREASY SPOON	18
86	PRT CDMP 8837	DOG OF TWO HEAD	18
89	Vertigo 842 098-2	PERFECT REMEDY (two different inlay designs)	each 30
91	Vertigo 848 087-2	WHATEVER YOU WANT & JUST SUPPOSIN'	50
91	Vertigo 848 090-2	IF YOU CAN'T STAND THE HEAT & 1+9+8+2	25
98	Readers Digest RDCD1831-4	THE COMPLETE STATUS QUO (4-CD, mail-order only)	60
01	From The Makers Of ... FTMOCD2	FTMO LIVE! NO.1 (fanclub mail-order only, soundchecks & interviews)	50
02	Time Life TL SQC 069 827-2	THE ULTIMATE COLLECTION (4-CD, mail-order only)	45
03	From The Makers Of ... FTMO LIVE 2-1/2 [matrix]	FTMO LIVE! NO.2 (2-CD, fanclub mail-order only)	25

PROMO-ONLY ALBUMS & ALBUM SAMPLERS
82	Phonogram PRO BX 1	FROM THE MAKERS OF... (3-LP, 20 copies in bronze tin for in-house use)	300+
86	Vertigo MADDOX 18	IN THE ARMY NOW (LP, 4-track sampler, includes unreleased version of "Dreamin'")	75
88	Vertigo QUOLP 99	AIN'T COMPLAINING (LP, 4-track one-sided sampler)	25
88	Vertigo	AIN'T COMPLAINING (box set containing LP sampler [QUOLP 99], cassette, 1-track video, photo & press sheet)	100
88	Music & Media MM 1221	INTERVIEW (LP, uncut test pressing for unreleased saw-shaped picture disc)	50
89	Vertigo 842 077-9	LITTLE DREAMER (CD, card p/s, 4-track sampler for PERFECT REMEDY album)	50

90	Phonogram (no cat. no.)	ROCKING ALL OVER THE YEARS SNIPPETS (cassette, titles inlay) 20
90	Vertigo 846 797-2	ROCKING ALL OVER THE YEARS (CD, in Butlin's party pack containing "Kiss Me Quo" baseball cap, stick of Status Quo rock, and selection of party poppers, streamers, whistle, trumpet, silver Quo balloons & pack of condoms, all with "Anniversary Waltz" stickers in custom carrier bag) 75
97	PolyGram TV QUO 5-2	WHATEVER YOU WANT – THE VERY BEST OF STATUS QUO (CD, 5-track sampler different to above, no p/s, withdrawn) 25
99	Eagle (no cat. no.)	UNDER THE INFLUENCE (CD-R, titles inlay in slimline jewel case) 25
00	Universal QUO 2	FAMOUS IN THE LAST CENTURY (CD, 3-track sampler, no p/s) 15
01	Vertigo QUOBOX1	ROCKERS ROLLIN': QUO IN TIME 1972-2000 (CD, 10-track sampler, double card p/s) 20
01	Universal 5892162	ROCKERS ROLLIN': QUO IN TIME 1972-2000 (set of 4 CD-Rs with title inserts) 50+
02	Universal (no cat. no.)	HEAVY TRAFFIC (CD-R, titles insert, 13- or 14-track version) . . . . each 18+
02	Universal (no cat. no.)	5 TRACKS TAKEN FROM THE FORTHCOMING ALBUM "HEAVY TRAFFIC" (CD-R, titles insert) . . . . 18+
02	Sanctuary CMRCD 490	SWEDISH RADIO SESSIONS (CD-R, titles insert, commercial release cancelled) 50
03	Universal RIF1	RIFFS (CD, full album promo, p/s, slimline jewel case) 18

(see also Spectres, Traffic Jam, Rossi & Frost, Bob Young, Andy Bown, Alan Lancaster's Bombers, Partners In Crime, Party Boys, Rockers, John Du Cann, Manchester United Football Squad, Marietta, Stretch, Jimmy Sweep)

STAVELY MAKEPEACE
69	Pyramid PYR 6072	(I Want To Love You Like A) Mad Dog/Greasy Haired Woman 5
70	Pyramid PYR 6082	Tarzan Harvey/Reggae Denny (unissued, test pressings exist) 6

(see also Lieutenant Pigeon, Shel Naylor)

STAVERTON BRIDGE
70s	Saydisc SDL 266	STAVERTON BRIDGE (LP, with lyrics) 35

MARY STAVIN & GEORGE BEST
70s	Lifestyle LEG 22	IT TAKES TWO TO SHAPE UP (LP) 12

STEAK CATS
93	April 10 Records TEN1	The Steak Song/Dead Real Soon/Fluffy's Lament/My Name Is Miguel (12") 8

STEAM
69	Fontana TF 1058	Na Na Hey Hey Kiss Him Goodbye/It's The Magic In You Girl 8

STEAMHAMMER
69	CBS 4141	Junior's Wailing/Windmill. 25
69	CBS 4496	Autumn Song/Blues For Passing People 18
71	Reflection HRS 9	Junior's Wailing/You'll Never Know 7
68	CBS (S) 63611	STEAMHAMMER (LP) 48
70	CBS (S) 63694	STEAMHAMMER MK. II (LP). 45
70	B&C CAS 1024	MOUNTAINS (LP). 30
70	Reflection REFL 1	STEAMHAMMER (LP, reissue, different sleeve). 32
71	Reflection REFL 12	STEAMHAMMER MK. II (LP, reissue) 25

(see also Armageddon)

STEAM-SHOVEL
68	Trojan/Big Bear TR 635	Rudi, The Red Nosed Reindeer/White Christmas 7
68	Decca F 22863	Rudi, The Red Nosed Reindeer/White Christmas (export issue) 12

(see also Locomotive)

STEEL
81	Neat NEAT 14	Rock Out/All Systems Go (p/s) 10

BETTE ANNE STEELE
55	Capitol CL 14315	Barricade/Give Me A Little Kiss Will Ya, Huh? 8

DAVY STEELE
83	Bracken BKN 1001	LONG TIME GETTING THERE (LP) 12

DORIS STEELE
59	Oriole CB 1468	Why Must I?/Never Again (78 rpm = £10) 10

JAN STEELE & JOHN CAGE
76	Obscure OBS 5	VOICES AND INSTRUMENTS (LP). 12

SONDRA & JON STEELE
55	Parlophone MSP 6166	I'm Crazy With Love/Fill My Heart With Happiness 8

TOMMY STEELE (& THE STEELMEN)
58	Weekend Mail (no cat. no.)	THE TRUTH ABOUT ME (6" in envelope, mail-order only) (78) 22
56	Decca F 10795	Rock With The Caveman/Rock Around The Town (with The Steelmen) 35
56	Decca F 10808	Doomsday Rock/Elevator Rock. 30
56	Decca F 10819	Singing The Blues/Rebel Rock (with The Steelmen). 20
57	Decca F 10849	Knee Deep In The Blues/Teenage Party (with The Steelmen) 15
57	Decca F 10877	Butterfingers/Cannibal Pot. 8
57	Decca F 10896	Shiralee/Grandad's Rock 12
57	Decca F 10923	Water Water/A Handful Of Songs 7
57	Decca F 10941	Hey You!/Plant A Kiss 6
58	Decca F 10976	Happy Guitar/Princess 6
58	Decca F 10991	Nairobi/Neon Sign. 6
58	Decca F 11026	It's All Happening/What Do You Do (78 rpm = £7). 5
58	Decca F 11041	The Only Man On The Island/I Puts The Lightie On 6
58	Decca F 11072	Come On Let's Go/Put A Ring On Her Finger (78 rpm = £8) 10
58	Decca F 11089	A Lovely Night/Marriage Type Love 5
59	Decca F 11117	Hiawatha/The Trial (78 rpm = £8) 6
59	Decca F 11152	Tallahassee Lassie/Give! Give! Give! (78 rpm = £8) 10
59	Decca F 11162	You Were Mine/Young Ideas (78 rpm = £15). 5
59	Decca F 11177	Little White Bull/Singing Time (in p/s) (78 rpm = £25) 6

(The above 45s were originally issued with triangular centres; later round-centre copies are worth two-thirds of the values listed.)

Tommy STEELE

EPs

56	Decca DFE 6388	YOUNG LOVE	25
56	Decca DFE 6389	SINGING THE BLUES	20
57	Decca DFE 6398	THE TOMMY STEELE STORY NO. 1	20
57	Decca DFE 6424	THE TOMMY STEELE STORY NO. 2	20
57	Decca F 10915	ALL STAR HIT PARADE NO. 2 (with other artists)	12

(The above EPs were originally issued with triangular centres; later round-centre reissues are worth two-thirds the values listed.)

58	Decca DFE 6472	THE DUKE WORE JEANS	12
58	Decca DFE 6551	C'MON LET'S GO	15
59	Decca DFE 6592	SWEET GEORGIA BROWN	15
59	Decca DFE 6607	TOMMY THE TOREADOR	10
60	Decca DFE 6660	WHAT A MOUTH	12

LPs

57	Decca LF 1287	THE TOMMY STEELE STAGE SHOW (10")	25
57	Decca LF 1288	THE TOMMY STEELE STORY (10")	22
58	Decca LF 1308	THE DUKE WORE JEANS (10", soundtrack)	20
60	Decca LK 4351	GET HAPPY WITH TOMMY	18
67	RCA Victor RB/SB 6735	HALF A SIXPENCE (soundtrack, gatefold sleeve)	12

STEELERS

70	Direction 58-4675	Get It From The Bottom/I'm Sorry	7

STEELEYE SPAN

71	B&C CB 164	Rave On/Reels/Female Drummer (p/s)	7
72	Pegasus PGS 6	JIGS AND REELS (maxi-single, some with p/s)	10/6
72	Chrysalis CHS 2005	John Barleycorn/Bride's Favourite/Tansey's Fancy	5
70	RCA SF 8113	HARK! THE VILLAGE WAIT (LP, with insert)	30
71	United Artists UAG 29160	HARK! THE VILLAGE WAIT (LP, reissue)	12
71	B&C CAS 1029	PLEASE TO SEE THE KING (LP, initially in 'hessian' textured sleeve)	18/12
72	Charisma CS 5	INDIVIDUALLY AND COLLECTIVELY (LP)	15
72	Pegasus PEG 9	TEN MAN MOP, OR MR. RESERVOIR BUTLER RIDES AGAIN (LP, gatefold sleeve, initially with 8-page booklet)	20/12
72	Chrysalis CHR 1008	BELOW THE SALT (LP, gatefold sleeve, green label)	12
73	Charisma CS 12	ALMANACK (LP)	12
73	Chrysalis CHR 1046	PARCEL OF ROGUES (LP, gatefold sleeve, with lyric insert)	12
74	Mooncrest CREST 8	PLEASE TO SEE THE KING (LP, reissue)	12
74	Chrysalis CHR 1053	NOW WE ARE SIX (LP, with lyric inner sleeve, green label)	12
74	Mooncrest CREST 9	TEN MAN MOP, OR MR. RESERVOIR BUTLER RIDES AGAIN (LP, initially in gatefold sleeve, later single)	20/12
75	Chrysalis CHR 1091	ALL AROUND MY HAT (LP, with lyric insert)	12

(see also Maddy Prior, Tim Hart & Maddy Prior, Gay & Terry Woods, Ashley Hutchings, Fairport Convention, Martin Carthy, Silly Sisters, Bob Johnson & Pete Knight)

STEEL MILL

71	Penny Farthing PEN 770	Green Eyed God/Zang Will	8
72	Penny Farthing PEN 783	Get On The Line/Summer's Child	18
75	Penny Farthing PEN 894	Green Eyed God/Zang Will (reissue)	6
71	Penny Farthing PELS 549	GREEN EYED GOD (LP)	150

STEEL PULSE

77	Anchor ANC 1046	Nyah Luv/Luv Nyah	5

STEELY DAN

72	Probe PRO 562	Dallas/Sail The Waterway	5
73	Probe PRO 577	Do It Again/Fire In The Hole	5
73	Probe PRO 587	Reelin' In The Years/Only A Fool	5
73	Probe PRO 602	Show Biz Kids/Razor Boy	5
73	Probe PRO 606	My Old School/Pearl Of The Quarter	5
74	Probe PRO 622	Rikki Don't Lose That Number/Any Major Dude Will Tell You	5
79	ABC ABC 4241	Rikki Don't Lose That Number/Any Major Dude Will Tell You (p/s, reissue, yellow vinyl)	5
73	Probe SPB 1062	CAN'T BUY A THRILL (LP, original)	12
73	Probe SPD 1079	COUNTDOWN TO ECSTASY (LP, original)	12
80s	MCA 203 16009	GAUCHO (LP, audiophile pressing)	12
82	MCA MCF 3165	GOLD (LP, with free EP [MSAMT 21])	12

(see also Donald Fagen)

WOUT STEENHUIS

65	Columbia DB 7722	Desert Island/Teran Boelan	6
66	Columbia DB 8027	Nivram/Bay Of Paradise	6
64	Columbia 33SX 1585	SURFIN' WITH STEENHUIS (LP)	12

STEEPLECHASE

71	Polydor 2489 001	LADY BRIGHT (LP)	20

(see also Dean Parrish)

STEERPIKE

68	(no label credit) ADM 417	STEERPIKE (LP, private pressing)	550

BILL STEGMEYER & HIS ORCHESTRA

54	London HL 8078	On The Waterfront (From The Film)/We Just Couldn't Say Good-Bye	35

LOU STEIN

57	London HLZ 8419	Almost Paradise/Soft Sands	22
58	Mercury 7MT 226	Who Slammed The Door/Got A Match?	8

JIM STEINMAN

81	Epic EPCA 13-1236	Rock And Roll Dreams Come Through/Love And Death And An American Guitar/The Storm (12", p/s, blue vinyl)	8
81	Epic EPCA 1561	Lost Boys And Golden Girls/Left In The Dark (p/s)	5
81	Epic EPCA 1707	Dance In My Pants/Dance In My Pants (unissued, promo only)	5

MINT VALUE £

| 84 | MCA MCA 889 | Tonight Is What It Means To Be Young/Hold That Snake (p/s) | 5 |
| 81 | Epic EPC 11-84361 | BAD FOR GOOD (LP, picture disc) | 12 |

(see also Meat Loaf)

STEINWAYS
| 85 | Kent TOWN 106 | You've Been Leading Me On/JOHNNY CASWELL: You Don't Love Me No More | 15 |

STELLA
| 82 | President PT 504 | Si Tu Aimes Ma Musique/If You Do Like My Music (p/s) | 7 |

STELLASTARR
| 00s | 2220 TWENTY-7 S001 | Somewhere Across Forever/No Weather (p/s, 1000 only) | 15 |
| 00s | 2220 TWENTY-CDS 001 | Somewhere Across Forever/No Weather/School Ya (CD, 1000 only) | 15 |

STAN STENNETT
| 60s | Audio JDT 1 | STYLE (EP) | 8 |

MALCOLM STENT
| 70s | Starline SWL 2002 | GO AND PLAY UP YOUR OWN END (LP) | 15 |

STEP
80	Epic/Direction S DIR 8733	Love Letter/Land Of 1,000 Dances (p/s)	5
80	Epic/Direction S DIR 8944	Let Me Be The One/634 5789 (p/s)	5
80	Epic/Direction S DIR 9311	Tears That I Cry/Shake (p/s)	5
81	Epic EPC A 1291	Chain Gang/In The House (p/s)	5

STEPASIDE
| 80 | Gale GALELP 01 | SIT DOWN AND RELAPSE (LP) | 20 |

MIKE STEPHEN
| 63 | Decca F11702 | It's Over/Too Many Late Nights | 7 |

EWAN STEPHENS
| 71 | Decca F 13219 | Queen Of The Good Times/We Can Give It A Try | 5 |
| 72 | Decca F 13299 | Brother, Surely We Can Work It Out/Long, Long Summer | 5 |

(see also Turquoise)

LEIGH STEPHENS
| 69 | Philips SBL 7897 | RED WEATHER (LP) | 40 |
| 71 | Charisma CAS 1040 | AND A CAST OF THOUSANDS (LP) | 30 |

(see also Blue Cheer)

STEPPENWOLF
68	RCA RCA 1679	Sookie Sookie/Take What You Need	10
68	RCA RCA 1735	Born To Be Wild/Everybody's Next One	10
68	Stateside-Dunhill SS 8003	Magic Carpet Ride/Sookie Sookie	10
69	Stateside-Dunhill SS 8013	Rock Me/Jupiter Child	7
69	Stateside-Dunhill SS 8017	Born To Be Wild/Everybody's Next One (reissue)	6
69	Stateside-Dunhill SS 8027	Magic Carpet Ride/Sookie Sookie (reissue)	6
70	Stateside-Dunhill SS 8035	Monster/Move Over	6
70	Stateside-Dunhill SS 8038	The Pusher/Your Wall's Too High	6
70	Stateside-Dunhill SS 8049	Hey Lawdy Mama/Twisted	6
70	Stateside-Dunhill SS 8056	Screaming Night Hog/Spiritual Fantasy	5
70	Probe PRO 510	Who Needs Ya/Earschplittenloudenboomer	5
71	Probe PRO 525	Snowblind Friend/Hippo Stomp	5
71	Probe PRO 534	Ride With Me/For Madmen Only	6
71	Probe PRO 544	For Ladies Only/Sparkle Eyes	6
68	RCA RD/SF 7974	STEPPENWOLF (LP, initially white sleeve, later silver sleeve)	35/25
68	Stateside (S)SL 5003	STEPPENWOLF THE SECOND (LP)	20
69	Stateside (S)SL 5011	AT YOUR BIRTHDAY PARTY (LP)	15
69	Stateside (S)SL 5015	EARLY STEPPENWOLF (LP)	15
69	Stateside (S)SL 10276	CANDY (LP, soundtrack, 2 tracks by Steppenwolf, 1 track by Byrds)	30
70	Stateside-Dunhill SSL 5020	STEPPENWOLF (reissue)	15
70	Stateside-Dunhill SSL 5021	MONSTER (LP, gatefold sleeve)	15
70	Stateside-Dunhill SSL 5029	STEPPENWOLF 'LIVE' (2-LP, gatefold sleeve)	15
70	Probe SPBA 6254	STEPPENWOLF 7 (LP)	15
71	Probe SPBA 6260	FOR LADIES ONLY (LP)	15
71	Probe SPBA 1033	GOLD (LP)	15
72	Probe SPBA 1059	REST IN PEACE (LP)	12

(see also Sparrow, John Kay)

STEPPES
| 79 | South Circular SGS 108 | The Beat Drill/FIFTY FANTASTICS: God's Got Religion (p/s, white label) | 10 |

(see also Fifty Fantastics, Disco Zombies)

STEPPES
| 87 | Help HELPF 101 | History Hates No Man/BEVIS FROND: African Violets (flexi) | 8¶ |

STEPPING TALK
| 79 | Eustone/Rough Trade TO1 | Alice In Sunderland/Health And Safety/Common Problems/John Turtles (p/s, with stamped inner) | 6 |

STEPTOE & SON
(see under Wilfred Brambell & Harry H. Corbett)

STEREOLAB
SINGLES
91	Duophonic DS 45-01	SUPER 45: The Light That Will Cease To Fail/Au Grand Jour/Brittle/Au Grand Jour! (10" EP, with insert, mail-order, sold at gigs and some record shops 40 with hand-painted p/s, in poly bag)	150/100
91	Duophonic DS 45-01	SUPER 45: The Light That Will Cease To Fail/Au Grand Jour/Brittle/Au Grand Jour! (25 test pressings, 10" cut into 12" discs)	150
91	Too Pure PURE 4	SUPER ELECTRIC: Super Electric/High Expectation/The Way Will Be Opening/Contact (10" EP, with red and yellow sleeve, with insert)	8

91	Duophonic DS 45-02	STUNNING DEBUT ALBUM: Doubt/Clanger (20 black test pressings withdrawn due to pressing fault/warping, different cut of both tracks) 100
91	Duophonic DS 45-02	STUNNING DEBUT ALBUM: Doubt/Clanger (p/s, mail-order, sold at gigs and some record shops gatefold p/s with insert in poly bag; multi coloured vinyl, unknown quantity but probably over 200) 150
91	Duophonic DS 45-02	STUNNING DEBUT ALBUM: Doubt/Clanger (p/s, mail-order, gigs and some record shops, gatefold p/s with insert in poly bag; 985 copies on clear vinyl) . . . 50
92	Duophonic DS 45-04	Harmonium/Farfisa (p/s, mail-order, gigs and some record shops 1,306 copies on transparent amber vinyl, with insert & fluorescent sticker) 30
93	Duophonic DS45-05/06	SHIMMIES IN SUPER 8 (2 x 7", green and white vinyl, foldout sleeve with inserts) 30
92	Too Pure PURE 14	Low Fi/Varoom!/Laissez-Faire/Elektro (He Held The World In His Iron Grip) (10", p/s, clear vinyl, 2,000 only, numbered) 30
93	Sub Pop SP107/283	Lo Boob Oscillator/Tempter (clear vinyl, p/s with US/German address on back cover) 20/15
93	Spacewatch FLX 2107	Ronco Symphony (demo)/Seeming And The Meaning (demo)/ SUBMARINER: Lyricist Downer (clear vinyl flexi comes with *Spacewatch* fanzine in sleeve) 18
93	Duophonic D-UHF-D 01	Jenny Ondioline/Fruition/Golden Ball/French Disko (10", p/s) 10
93	Duophonic D-UHF-D 01	Jenny Ondioline (Part 1)/Golden Ball (Studio) (10", factory custom pressings; 5 copies on multicoloured vinyl; 25 on 'thin' clear vinyl, 3 on 'thick' clear vinyl, later endorsed & signed by band; no p/s) 200/80
93	Duophonic D-UHF-CD 01	Jenny Ondioline/Fruition/Golden Ball/French Disko (CD) 12
93	Clawfist 20	CRUMB DUCK (10" EP, shared with Nurse With Wound; 37 with hand-drawn p/s (Gain/Sadier only) and 1,450 regular p/s) 100/20
93	Duophonic D-UHF-D 03	French Disko/Jenny Ondioline ('teaser' single, p/s, 1,500 only, some with hand printed sleeves, others with regular printed sleeves) 25/15
93	Duophonic D-UHF-D 01P	French Disko/Jenny Ondioline (CD, 1,000 only, hand-made p/s) 15
94	Duophonic D-UHF-D 04S	Ping Pong/Moogie Wonderland (p/s, 2,150 on pink vinyl, 3,322 on green, some on black) 10/10/3
94	Duophonic D-UHF-D 04T	Ping Pong/Moogie Wonderland (10", p/s) 7
94	Silvertone (no cat. no)	Tone Burst (demo)/Tempter (demo)/SPECTRUM: Soul Kiss Glide Divine (unreleased, with colour photocopied wraparound p/s, 25 test pressings only) . . . . 150+
94	Duophonic D-UHF-07	Wow And Flutter/Heavy Denim (3,000 only with hand-painted p/s) 12
95	Wurlitzer Jukebox WJ 3	The Eclipse/Yes Sir! I Can Moogie/CAT'S MIAOW: Shoot The Moon (flexidisc, 1,000 only with insert and info sheet) 15
95	Duophonic Super 45s DS 45-10	Long Hair Of Death/YO LA TENGO: Evanescent Psychic Pez Drop (gig single, fluorescent yellow vinyl, plain white stickered card sleeve, 3,000 only) 10
95	Flying Nun STEREO 1	French Disko/Super Electric (CD, also listed as B 8595, promo only) 15
95	Duophonic STEREO 2	John Cage Bubblegum/Revox (CD, also listed as B 8595, promo only) 10
96	Duophonic D-UHF-D 10S	Cybele's Reverie/Brigitte (p/s, with insert) 5
96	Duophonic D-UHF-D 10	Cybele's Reverie/Les Yper Yper Sound/Brigitte/Young Lungs(10", p/s, 2,000 only, (25 black vinyl test pressing and 102 cut into 12" disc = £25) 10
96	Lissy's LISS 15	You Used To Call Me Sadness/FUXA: Skyhigh (p/s, 400 on white vinyl, 1,500 on black) 20/8
96	Duophonic D-UHF-D 12	Speedy Car/TORTOISE: Yaus (gig freebie, blue vinyl, p/s, 3,000 only) 10
96	Duophonic D-UHF-D 12	Speedy Car/TORTOISE: Yaus (orange vinyl export issue, p/s, 3,000 only) 20
96	Duophonic D-UHF-D 14S	Fluorescences/Pinball (p/s) 5
96	Duophonic D-UHF-D 14	Fluorescences/Pinball/You Used To Call Me Sadness/Soop Groove (12", p/s) 8
96	Duophonic D-UHF-D 15	Metronomic Underground (Wagon Christ Mix)/Percolations (12", plain red sleeve, 2,500 only) 15
97	Duophonic DS 4517	Splitting The Atom (Parts 1 & 2) (with Sonic Boom/Monkey Brain (p/s, 2,500 only) 10
97	Duophonic D-UHF-D 18	Iron Man/The Incredible He Woman (red vinyl, p/s, gig single, 2,000 only) 5
97	Duophonic Super 45s DS 3311	Simple Headphone Mind/NURSE WITH WOUND: Trippin' With The Birds (12", 5,000 copies, 1,000 copies on yellow vinyl, in sealed foil sleeve = £25) 10
97	Duophonic Super 45s CD 3311	Simple Headphone Mind/NURSE WITH WOUND: Trippin' With The Birds (CD, sealed foil sleeve, 1,000 only) 30
98	Duophonic D-UHF-D 19	Refractions In The Plastic Pulse/Contronatura (12", die-cut stickered sleeve, yellow or black vinyl) 6/10
99	Duophonic D-UHF-D24	THE UNDERGROUND IS COMING: The Super-It/Monkey Jelly/ Fried Monkey Eggs (Instrumental)/Fried Monkey Eggs (Vocal) (p/s) 10
01	Duophonic D-UHF 026	Captain Easychord (12") 10

ALBUMS

90	Too Pure PURE 19	SPACE AGE BACHELOR PAD MUSIC (LP) 15
92	Too Pure PURELP 11	PENG! (LP) 15
93	Duophonic D-UHF-D 02	TRANSIENT RANDOM NOISE-BURSTS WITH ANNOUNCEMENTS (2-LP, with inner sleeves, poor playing-quality gold vinyl, with stickered sleeve, 1,500 only, numbered) 50
95	Duophonic D-UHF-D 05X	MARS AUDIAC QUINTET (2-LP, gatefold sleeve, 1st 1,000 copies with bonus coloured vinyl single "Klang Tone"/"Ulan Bator" [D-UHF-06]) 50
95	Duophonic D-UHF-D 08	MUSIC FOR THE AMORPHOUS BODY STUDY CENTRE (40 black vinyl test pressings 10" sides cut into 12" discs) 75
95	Duophonic D-UHF-D 08	MUSIC FOR THE AMORPHOUS BODY STUDY CENTRE (10" LP, 3,000 only, insert) 30
95	Duophonic D-UHF-CD 08	MUSIC FOR THE AMORPHOUS BODY STUDY CENTRE (CD, first issue with white cover & "1st edition" printed on disc available at Charles Long art exhibition; reissue has yellow sleeve) 35/20
95	Duophonic D-UHF LP 09	REFRIED ECTOPLASM – SWITCHED ON VOL 2 (LP, orange vinyl, card insert) . . 20
96	United Dairies UD 059	CRUMB DUCK (LP, shared with Nurse With Wound (2 extra tracks, reissue of Clawfist EP, 50 copies on pink vinyl, 500 on fluorescent green vinyl) 60/40
96	Duophonic UHF D-UHF-D11	EMPEROR TOMATO KETCHUP (2-LP, yellow glitter vinyl, gatefold sleeve) 60

(see also McCarthy, Spectrum, Mouse On Mars, Clear Spot)

STEREOLAB & BRIGITTE FONTAINE
90s	Duophonic Super 45s DS 45-25	Caliméro/MONADE: Cache Cache (white vinyl, p/s)	8

STEREOPHONICS
96	V2 SPH 1	Looks Like Chaplin/More Life In A Tramp's Vest (p/s, 500 only)	70
96	V2 SPHD 1	Looks Like Chaplin/More Life In A Tramp's Vest/Raymond's Shops (CD)	40
96	V2 SPH 2	Local Boy In The Photograph/Too Many Sandwiches (p/s, 2,000 only)	15
97	V2 SPH 4	More Life In A Tramp's Vest/Raymond's Shop (p/s)	12
97	V2 VVR 500 0448	A Thousand Trees/Home To Me/Looks Like Chaplin/Summertime (CD, digipak)	15
99	V2 VVR 500 6777	Pick A Part That's New/Nice To Be Out (Demo) (p/s)	8
01	V2 VVR 501 6247	Have A Nice Day/Surprise (p/s)	6
01	V2 VVR 501 5937	Mr Writer/Maritime Belle Vue In Kiel (embossed p/s)	5
02	V2 VVR 501 9177	Vegas 2 Times/(Live Version) (p/s)	5
03	V2 VVR 502 1897	Maybe Tomorrow/Have Wheels, Will Travel (p/s)	5
99	V2 no catalogue number	PERFORMANCE AND COCKTAILS (7 x 10" box set, with booklet and CD, promo mail order only)	70
97	V2 VVR 1000 431	WORD GETS AROUND (LP, gatefold sleeve)	12
97	Banana VVR 1000431	WORD GETS AROUND (LP, with bonus 12")	30
01	V2 no cat. no.	THE SINGLES (10-track CD-R, paper p/s)	20

STEREOS
61	MGM MGM 1143	I Really Love You/Please Come Back To Me	42
61	MGM MGM 1149	The Big Knock/Sweet Water	30
66	MGM MGM 1328	Sweet Water/The Big Knock (reissue)	5

STEREOTYPES
79	Hinterland/SRT no cat. no.	THE STEREOTYPES EP (no p/s)	250

STEREOTYPES
80	Art Theft AT 001	Calling All The Shots/Lovers Of The Future (p/s)	8

DEAN STERLING & TEENBEATS
61	Pye 7N 15345	Send Me A Girl/Lost Love	10

FITZROY STERLING
68	Gas GAS 102	Got To Play It Cool/Jezebel	12
70	Bullet BU 422	That's Alright/Queen Of Hearts	8
70	Bullet BU 438	Freedom Street/FITZROY ALL STARS: Freedom Street Version	8
71	Escort ERT 858	Girl Tell Me What To Do/Be Careful	8
71	Pama PM 820	My Sweet Lord/Darling That's Right	5

LESTER STERLING (& HIS GROUP)
63	Island WI 121	Clean The City/Long Walk Home (B-side actually by Charmers)	20
63	R&B JB 111	Air Raid Shelter/ROY & ANNETTE: I Mean It	25
63	R&B JB 115	Gravy Cool/WINSTON & BIBBY: Lover Lover Man	35
64	R&B JB 143	Peace And Love/HORACE SEATON: Hold On	15
64	R&B JB 150	Hot Cargo/MAYTALS: Marching On	20
64	R&B JB 155	Baskin' Hop (as Lester Sterling & His Group)/MAYTALS: Shining Light	20
64	R&B JB 172	Indian Summer (as Lester Sterling & His Group)/ STRANGER & PATSY: I'll Forgive You	20
66	Doctor Bird DB 1057	Inez (with Tommy McCook & Supersonics)/GLORIA CRAWFORD: Sad Movies	25
67	Doctor Bird DB 1107	Soul Voyage/ALVA LEWIS: Revelation	30
67	Collins Downbeat CR 001	Sir Collins Special/Lester Sterling '67	30
68	Coxsone CS 7080	Affrickaan Beat/PARAGONS: My Satisfaction	45+
68	Blue Cat BS 116	Zigaloo/Wiser Than Solomon	25
68	Unity UN 502	Bangarang (with Stranger Cole)/STRANGER COLE: If We Should Ever Meet	8
69	Unity UN 505	Reggae On Broadway/CLIQUE: Love Can Be Wonderful	6
69	Unity UN 509	Spoogy/TOMMY McCOOK: Monkey Fiddle	8
69	Unity UN 512	Regina/Bright As A Rose	7
69	Unity UN 517	1,000 Tons Of Megaton/KING CANNON: Five Card Stud	10
69	Unity UN 518	Man About Town/Man At The Door	8
69	Unity UN 531	Lonesome Feeling/Bright As A Rose	6
69	Big Shot BI 507	Forest Gate Rock/RAVING RAVERS: Rock Rock And Cry	8
69	Gas GAS 103	Reggae In The Wind/SOUL SET: Try Me One More Time (B-side actually by Stranger & Gladdy)	6
70	Unity UN 562	Slip Up/DAVE BARKER: On Broadway	10
71	Nu Beat NB 095	Iron Side Part 1/COXSON'S ALL STARS: Iron Side Part 2	8
71	Smash SMA 2321	Sir Collins Special/Version (actually "Heart Of The Knight" by Gaytones)	8
72	Ashanti ASH 409	Iron Side Part 1/COXSON'S ALL STARS: Iron Side Part 2	6
72	Ashanti ASH 410	War Is Not The Answer/COXSON'S ALL STARS: Version	6
69	Pama SECO 15	BANGARANG (LP)	55

(see also Mister Versatile, Bobby Aitken, Eric Morris, Sir Collins Band, Slickers, Uniques)

NINA STERN
65	Pye 7N 15823	Take It From Me/Please Come Back To Me	8

STEROID KIDDIES
70s	Steroid/Grundinga SK 001	THE KIDDIES EP	55

STEROID MAXIMUS
90s	Big Cat ABB 28	QUILOMBO (LP)	20

STEROIDS
78	Radar ADA 11	In The Colonies/Sha La La Loo Ley (p/s)	6

STEVE 'N' BONNIE
72	Young Blood YB 1033	Brief Encounter/Don't/Lady	6
72	Young Blood SSYB 16	BRIEF ENCOUNTER (LP)	18

STEVE & EYDIE
(see under Eydie Gorme & Steve Lawrence)

STEVE & STEVIE
68	Toast TLP 2	STEVE AND STEVIE (LP)	25

(see also Tin Tin, Fut)

APRIL STEVENS
53	Parlophone MSP 6060	C'est Si Bon/Soft Warm Lips	12
54	Parlophone MSP 6088	How Could Red Riding Hood (Have Been...)/You Said You'd Do It	12
67	MGM MGM 1366	Falling In Love Again/Wanting You (DJ copy = £200)	100
76	MGM 2006 586	Wanting You/Falling In Love Again (reissue)	5

(see also Nino Tempo & April Stevens)

CAT STEVENS
66	Deram DM 102	I Love My Dog/Portobello Road	7
66	Deram DM 110	Matthew And Son/Granny	7
67	Deram DM 118	I'm Gonna Get Me A Gun/School Is Out	7
67	Deram DM 140	Bad Night/Laughing Apple	7
67	Deram DM 156	Kitty/Blackness Of The Night	7
68	Deram DM 178	Lovely City/Image Of Hell	7
68	Deram DM 211	Here Comes My Wife/It's A Supa (Dupa) Life	7
69	Deram DM 260	Where Are You/The View From The Top	7
70	Island WIP 6086	Lady D'Arbanville/Time/Fill My Eyes (some in p/s)	8/5
67	Deram DML/SML 1004	MATTHEW AND SON (LP)	25
67	Deram DML/SML 1018	NEW MASTERS (LP)	22
67	Deram	CATS AND DOGS (LP, unreleased, test pressings only)	30
70	Island ILPS 9118	MONA BONE JAKON (LP, pink label)	75
70	Island ILPS 9135	TEA FOR THE TILLERMAN (LP, gatefold sleeve, pink label)	20
71	Island ILPS 9154	TEASER AND THE FIRECAT (LP, pink label)	20

CHUCK STEVENS
57	Columbia DB 3883	Take A Walk/The Way I Do	8
57	Columbia DB 3938	My London/Couldn't Care More	7

CONNIE STEVENS
60	Warner Bros WB 3	Sixteen Reasons (with Don Ralke)/Little Sister (with Buddy Cole Trio)	10
60	Warner Bros WB 17	Too Young To Go Steady/A Little Kiss Is A Kiss, Is A Kiss	10
60	Warner Bros WB 25	Apollo/Why Do I Cry For Joey	10
61	Warner Bros WB 41	And This Is Mine/Make-Believe Lover	10
61	Warner Bros WB 47	The Greenwood Tree/If You Don't, Somebody Else Will	5
62	Warner Bros WB 63	Why'd You Wanna Make Me Cry/Just One Kiss	15
62	Warner Bros WB 73	Mr. Songwriter/I Couldn't Say No	10
64	Warner Bros WB 128	They're Jealous Of Me/A Girl Never Knows	10
60	Warner Bros WEP 6007	CONNIE STEVENS AS CRICKET (EP, also stereo WSEP 2007)	15/20
63	Warners WEP/WSE 6105	CONNIE STEVENS AS CRICKET NO. 2 (EP, mono/stereo)	15/20
63	Warners WEP/WSE 6112	CONNIE STEVENS AS CRICKET NO. 3 (EP, mono/stereo)	15/20
62	Warner Bros WM 4061	CONNIE (LP, also stereo WS 8061)	20/25
63	Warner Bros WM/WS 8111	THE HANK WILLIAMS SONG BOOK (LP)	15

(see also Edward Byrnes)

DODIE STEVENS
59	London HLD 8834	Pink Shoe Laces/Coming Of Age (78 rpm = £20)	20
60	London HLD 9174	No/A-Tisket A-Tasket	10
61	London HLD 9280	Yes, I'm Lonesome Tonight/Too Young	10
63	London HLP 9672	Don't Send Me Roses/Daddy Couldn't Get Me One Of Those	10
64	Liberty LIB 83	I Wore Out Our Record/You Don't Have To Prove A Thing	8

JOHNNY STEVENS & BLUE BEATS
64	Blue Beat BB 229	Shame/Ball And Chain	18

JOHNNY STEVENS & LES DAWSON SYNDICATE
62	Melodisc M 1586	Last Chicken In The Shop/Oh Yeah (some in p/s)	10

KIRK STEVENS
57	Decca F 10863	Once/This Silver Madonna	8

MEIC STEVENS
65	Decca F 12174	Did I Dream/I Saw A Field (as Mike Stevens)	40+
70	Warner Bros WB 8007	Ballad Of Old Joe Blind/Blue Sleep	15
70	Wren WSP 2005	Nid Oes Un Gwydr Ffenestr/Rhywbeth Gwell I Ddod	40
68	Wren WRE 1048	MIKE STEVENS (EP, p/s)	50
68	Wren WRE 1053	RHIF 2 (EP, p/s)	50
69	Wren WRE 1073	MWG (EP, p/s)	50
70	Newyddion Da ND1	MEIC STEVENS (EP, p/s)	100
70	Sain SAIN 004	Y Brawd Houdini (EP, p/s)	50
71	Wren WRE 1107	Byw Yn Y Wlad (EP, p/s)	50
71	Sain SAIN 13	Diolch Yn Fawr (EP, p/s)	50
70	Warner Brothers WS 3005	OUTLANDER (LP, with insert)	150+
72	Wren WRL 536	GWYMON (LP)	300
77	Sain SAIN 1065	GOG (LP)	120
79	Tic Toc no cat. no.	CANAEON CYNNAR (LP, private pressing)	220
82	Sain SAIN 1239	NOS DU NOS DA (LP)	50
83	Sain SAIN 1312	LAPIS LAZULI (LP)	50
97	Tenth Planet TP 028	GHOST TOWN (LP, gatefold sleeve, numbered, 1000 only)	12

(Please note, this is not Mike Stevens who made 45's with the Shevells! See also Gary Farr)

MICK STEVENS
71	Deroy (no cat. no.)	SEE THE MORNING (LP, private pressing)	160
75	Deroy (no cat. no.)	NO SAVAGE WORD (LP, private pressing)	110

MIKE STEVENS (& SHEVELLS)
65	Decca F 12174	Did I Dream/I Saw A Field (solo)	6
66	Pye 7N 17243	Cathy's Clown/Go-Go Train (as Mike Stevens & Shevells)	15
68	Polydor 56269	Guaranteed To Drive You Wild/Hog-Tied (as Mike Stevens & Shevells)	6

(see also Shevells)

MORT STEVENS & HIS ORCHESTRA
70	Capitol CL 15655	"Hawaii Five-O" Theme/McGarrett's Theme	5

RAY STEVENS
58	Capitol CL 14881	Chickie-Chickie Wah Wah/Crying Goodbye	15
61	Mercury AMT 1158	Jeremiah Peabody's Polyunsaturated Quick Dissolving Fast Acting Pleasant Tasting Green And Purple Pills/Teen Years	6
62	Mercury AMT 1184	Ahab The Arab/It's Been So Long	12
63	Mercury AMT 1207	Harry The Hairy Ape/Little Stone Statue	6
66	London HLU 10027	Devil May Care/Make A Few Memories	6
68	Monument MON 1022	Mr. Businessman/Face The Music	6
71	Mercury 6052 072	Bubble Gum The Bubble Dancer/Jeremiah Peabody's Polyunsaturated Quick Dissolving Fast Acting Pleasant Tasting Green And Purple Pills	6

RICKY STEVENS
61	Columbia DB 4739	I Cried For You/I Am	7
62	Columbia DB 4778	Forever/Now, It's All Over	7
63	Columbia DB 4981	My Mother's Eyes/I'll Get By	7
62	Columbia SEG 8172	I CRIED FOR YOU (EP)	65

ROY STEVENS
66	London HLU 10016	Party People/ABC	10

SHAKIN' STEVENS (& SUNSETS)
70	Parlophone R 5860	Spirit Of Woodstock/Down On The Farm	55
72	Polydor 2058 213	Sweet Little Rock'n'Roller/White Lightning	38
74	Emerald MD 1176	Honey Honey/Holey Moley 2001	32
76	Mooncrest MOON 51	Jungle Rock/Girl In Red	18
77	Track 2094 134	Never/You Always Hurt The One You Love	15
77	Track 2094 136	Somebody Touched Me/Way Down Yonder In New Orleans (some in p/s)	20/8
78	Track 2094 141	Justine/Wait And See	20
78	Epic SEPC 6567	Treat Her Right/I Don't Want No Other Baby	15
79	Epic SEPC 6845	Endless Sleep/Fire	15
79	Epic SEPC 7235	Spooky/I Don't Want No Other Baby	15
80	Epic SEPC 8090	Hot Dog/Apron Strings (p/s)	15
80	Epic SEPC 8573	Hey Mae/I Guess I Was A Fool (in p/s)	8
80	Epic SEPC 8778	Solid As A Rock/Generation X (p/s)	5
80	Epic SEPC 9064	Shooting Gallery/Make It Right Tonight (p/s)	10
81	Battle Of The Bands BOB 2	Jungle Rock/Girl In Red (p/s, reissue, as Shakin' Stevens & Sunsets)	5
81	Mint CHEW 51	No Other Baby/Manhattan Melodrama (p/s)	5
81	Epic A 1643	It's Raining/You And I Were Meant To Be (picture disc)	5
81	Solid Gold SGR 107	Shaky Sings Elvis (Parts 1 & 2) (medley) (p/s)	5
82	Epic EPCA 1742	Oh Julie/I'm Knocking (poster p/s)	5
82	Epic EPCA 2656	Give Me Your Heart Tonight/Thinkin' Of You (p/s, with poster)	5
82	Epic EPCA 2656	Give Me Your Heart Tonight/Thinkin' Of You (picture disc)	5
82	Everest/Premier EV 1000	Tiger/Sweet Little Sixteen/Give Me A Break (picture disc)	5
83	Epic WA 3565	It's Late/It's Good For You Baby (feet-shaped picture disc)	8
83	Epic WA 3774	Cry Just A Little Bit/Love Me Tonight (picture disc)	5
83	Kelloggs KELL 1	Oh Julie/ABBA: I Have A Dream (free with Kelloggs' 'Rice Krispies')	5
84	Epic A 4291	A Love Waiting For You/As Long As I Have You (live) (poster p/s)	5
84	Epic QA 4677	A Letter To You/Come Back And Love Me (p/s, with free post bag game)	5
84	Epic DA 4882	Teardrops/You Shake Me Up//Shakin' Stevens Party Mix (Parts 1 & 2) (double pack)	8
85	Epic GA 6072	Breakin' Up My Heart/I'll Give You My Heart (gatefold pop-up p/s)	5
86	Epic SHAKY 2	Because I Love You/Tell Me One More Time (2 picture sleeves, sealed together on edge with sticker, with autograph)	8
87	Epic SHAKY P5	What Do You Want To Make Those Eyes At Me For/You're Evil (picture disc)	5
89	Epic SHAKY C10	Love Attack/Love Attack (Extended Version)/As Long As I Have You (live) (CD, card sleeve)	8
81	Magnum Force MFEP 001	Memphis Earthquake/You Mostest Girl/Evil Hearted Ada/My Bucket's Got A Hole In It (EP, p/s)	8
82	Magnum Force MFEP 007	Frantic/Ready Teddy/Tear It Up/Monkey's Uncle (EP, p/s)	8
83	Magnum Force MFEP 010	Justine/Jungle Rock/Story Of The Rockers/My Baby Died (EP, p/s)	8
83	Epic 40-2620	GREATEST ORIGINAL HITS (EP, cassette)	12
70	Parlophone PCS 7112	A LEGEND (LP)	55
71	CBS 52901	I'M NO J.D. (LP)	45
72	Contour 2870 152	ROCKIN' AND SHAKIN' (LP)	15
73	Emerald GES 1121	SHAKIN' STEVENS AND THE SUNSETS (LP)	18
78	Track 2406 011	SHAKIN' STEVENS (LP)	15
80	Epic EPC 84547	MARIE MARIE (LP, withdrawn)	18
81	Epic EPC 10027	SHAKY (LP, feet-shaped picture disc)	12
83	Epic BX 86301	THE BOP WON'T STOP (LP & cassette, box set, with Shaky autograph book)	18

TERRI STEVENS
59	Felsted AF 112	My Wish Tonight/All Alone	10
59	Felsted AF 126	Adonis/Vieni, Vieni	8

VIRGINIA STEVENS
77	Mulligan LUN A 332	TIOCFAIDH AN SAMHRADH — TRADITIONAL SONGS FROM THE WEST OF IRELAND (LP, with booklet)	15

RICHARD STEVENSEN
70	Pye NSPL 18358	GATES OF ME (LP)	15

MICKEY STEVENSON
72	Ember EMBS 320	Here I Am/Joe Poor Loves Daphne Elizabeth Richard	6
72	Ember NR 5063	HERE I AM (LP)	30

STEVIE'S BUZZ
96	Nice no cat. no.	Autumn Stone/P.P. & THE PRIMES: Understanding (promo only, large centre)	8

(see also P.P. Arnold, Buzzcocks, Primal Scream)

MINT VALUE £

AL STEWART

66	Decca F 12467	The Elf/Turn To Earth	125+
67	CBS 3034	Bedsitter Images/Swiss Cottage Manoeuvres	10
70	CBS 4843	Electric Los Angeles Sunset/My Enemies Have Sweet Voices	8
70	CBS 5351	The News From Spain/Elvaston Place	7
72	CBS 7763	You Don't Even Know Me/I'm Falling	6
72	CBS 7992	Amsterdam/Songs Out Of Clay	6
73	CBS SCBS 1971	Terminal Eyes/Last Day Of June 1934	10
67	CBS (S)BPG 63087	BEDSITTER IMAGES (LP)	85
69	CBS (S) 63460	LOVE CHRONICLES (LP, gatefold sleeve)	25
70	CBS 63848	ZERO SHE FLIES (LP, gatefold sleeve)	25
70	CBS 64023	FIRST ALBUM (BEDSITTER IMAGES) (LP, remixed reissue, different track listing)	18
72	CBS 64739	ORANGE (LP)	15
73	CBS 65726	PAST, PRESENT AND FUTURE (LP, gatefold sleeve)	12
75	CBS 80477	MODERN TIMES (LP)	12

(see also Jimmy Page)

BILLY STEWART

62	Pye International 7N 25164	Reap What You Sow/Fat Boy	25
63	Pye International 7N 25222	Strange Feeling/Sugar And Spice	25
65	Chess CRS 8009	I Do Love You/Keep Loving	15
65	Chess CRS 8017	Sitting In The Park/Once Again	15
66	Chess CRS 8028	Because I Love You/Mountains Of Love	20
66	Chess CRS 8038	Love Me/Why Am I Lonely	15
66	Chess CRS 8040	Summertime/To Love To Love	15
66	Chess CRS 8045	Secret Love/Look Back And Smile	20
66	Chess CRS 8050	Ole Man River/Every Day I Have The Blues	20
67	Chess CRS 8067	Cross My Heart/Why (Do I Love You So)	15
69	Chess CRS 8092	Summertime/I Do Love You	10
72	Chess 6145 017	Sitting In The Park/Summertime	8
65	Chess CRE 6010	IN CROWD (EP, with Ramsey Lewis Trio, et al)	40
67	Chess CRE 6024	I DO LOVE YOU (EP)	50
66	Chess CRL 4523	UNBELIEVABLE (LP)	40
72	Chess 6310 125	GOLDEN DECADE (LP)	15

BOB STEWART

55	MGM SP 1114	It's A Woman's World/I Went Out Of My Way	6

DAVID A. STEWART

92	Anxious ZT 43046	LILY WAS HERE (12", with 2 Orb mixes, featuring Candy Dulfer, p/s)	8

(see also Eurythmics, Longdancer, Stewart & Harrison)

DAVIE STEWART

78	Topic 12T 293	DAVIE STEWART (LP, with insert)	12

DELANO STEWART

68	Doctor Bird DB 1138	That's Life/Tell Me Baby	25
68	High Note HS 004	Let's Have Some Fun/Dance With Me	12
69	High Note HS 014	Rocking Sensation/GAYTONES: One Look	15
70	High Note HS 027	Got To Come Back/Don't Believe In Him	8
70	High Note HS 034	Hallelujah/I Wish It Could Last	7
70	High Hote HS 039	Wherever I Lay My Hat/Don't Believe Him (B-side actually by Gladstone Anderson & Gaytones)	12
70	High Note HS 041	Stay A Little Bit Longer/Stay A Little Bit Longer (Version II) (B-side actually by Gladstone Anderson & Gaytones)	12
70	Trojan TBL 138	STAY A LITTLE BIT LONGER (LP)	28

(see also Winston Stewart, Gaylads, Patsy Todd)

GRAHAM STEWART SEVEN

59	Tempo EXA 91	GRAHAM STEWART SEVEN (EP)	10

JAMES STEWART

65	Brunswick 05938	The Legend Of Shenandoah/CHARLES 'BUD' DANT CHORUS: We're Ridin' Out Tonight	12

JAMES STEWART & HENRY FONDA

70	Stateside SS 2179	Rolling Stone/Theme From Cheyenne Social Club	8

JOHN STEWART

69	Capitol E-(S)T 203	CALIFORNIA BLOODLINES (LP)	12

(see also Kingston Trio, Cumberland Three)

JOHNNY STEWART

58	HMV POP 480	Wishing For Your Love/Promise Me	7

PAUL STEWART (MOVEMENT)

66	Philips BF 1513	Queen Boadicea/Talkin'	7
67	Decca F 12577	Saturday Morning Man/Too Too Good (as Paul Stewart Movement)	12

(see also Hamilton & [Hamilton] Movement)

RAPHAEL STEWART & HOT TOPS

71	Punch PH 71	Put Your Sweet Lips/JUSTINS: Stand By Me	10

ROD STEWART

SINGLES

64	Decca F 11996	Good Morning Little Schoolgirl/I'm Gonna Move To The Outskirts Of Town	120
65	Columbia DB 7766	The Day Will Come/Why Does It Go On?	110
66	Columbia DB 7892	Shake/I Just Got Some	120
68	Immediate IM 060	Little Miss Understood/So Much To Say	90
70	Vertigo 6086 002	It's All Over Now/Jo's Lament	15
73	Mercury 6052 371	Oh No Not My Baby/Jodie (tartan sleeve)	6

76	Mercury 6160 006	Maggie May/You Wear It Well/Twistin' The Night Away (p/s)	5
77	Mercury 6160 007	Mandolin Wind/Girl From The North Country/Sweet Little Rock'N'Roller.	5
76	Mercury 6167 327	It's All Over Now/Handbags And Gladrags	7
77	Riva RIVA 1	You're Insane/You're Insane (DJ copy, 500 only)	20
77	Riva RIVA 3	Tonight's The Night/The First Cut Is The Deepest (withdrawn B-side)	10
78	Riva RIVA 9	Sailing/Stone Cold Sober (p/s)	5
78	Riva RIVA 9	Sailing/Stone Cold Sober(HMS Ark Royal Commemorative issue, blue vinyl, p/s)	150
78	Riva RIVA 15	Ole Ola/Que Sera Sera — I'd Walk A Million Miles For One Of Your Goals (p/s)	5
80	Riva RIVA 23	If Lovin' You Is Wrong/Last Summer (p/s)	5
80	Virgin VS 366	Little Miss Understood/So Much To Say (p/s, reissue)	5
80	Riva W 7929TP	Excerpts From "Foolish Behaviour" (flexidisc free with London Evening News)	10/6
81	Riva RIVA 29M	Oh God I Wish I Was Home Tonight/Somebody Special (cassette)	5
82	Riva RIVA 35	How Long/Jealous (p/s, with free sticker)	5
82	Decca F 11996	Good Morning Little Schoolgirl/I'm Gonna Move To The Outskirts Of Town (reissue)	8
82	Immediate IM 060	Little Miss Understood/So Much To Say (reissue, p/s)	5
83	Warner Bros W 9440P	Sweet Surrender/Ghetto Blaster (picture disc)	7
83	Warner Bros W 96564T	Baby Jane/Ready Now/If Lovin' You Is Wrong (12", p/s, with poster)	10
84	Warner Bros SAM 194	Infatuation (1-sided picture disc in wallet with interview cassette)	15
86	Warner Bros W 8668TP	Love Touch/Heart Is On The Line/Hard Lesson To Learn (12", picture disc)	10
86	Warner Bros W 8625TE	Every Beat Of My Heart (Tartan Mix)/Trouble/Some Guys Have All The Luck/ I Don't Want To Talk About It (live) (12", p/s with poster)	10
88	Warner Bros WX 152TP	Lost In You (Extended Remix)/Lost In You (Fade)/Almost Illegal (12", pic disc)	10
89	Warner Bros W 2686P	This Old Heart Of Mine/Ain't Love A Bitch/Tonight I'm Yours (Don't Hurt Me) (with Ronald Isley, shaped picture disc)	10
89	Warner Bros W 2647TG	Downtown Train/Stay With Me/Cindy Incidentally/To Love Somebody (12", gatefold p/s)	10
89	Warner Bros W 7729 TP	My Heart Can't Tell You No/The Wild Horse/Passion (12", p/s)	8
91	Warner Bros W 0030 TP	The Motown Song/Sweet Soul Music/Try A Little Tenderness (12", p/s)	10
91	Warner Bros W 0059 TE	Broken Arrow/The Killing Of Georgie Parts 1 & 2/I Was Only Joking (10", p/s)	8
70s	Mercury BRAUN 3	MAGGIE MAY (EP, freebie)	6

LPs

70	Vertigo VO 4	AN OLD RAINCOAT WON'T EVER LET YOU DOWN (gatefold sleeve, swirl label)	20
70	Vertigo 6360 500	GASOLINE ALLEY (gatefold sleeve, swirl label)	18
71	Mercury 6338 063	EVERY PICTURE TELLS A STORY (black label, with poster)	30
72	Mercury 6499 153	NEVER A DULL MOMENT (gatefold sleeve)	15
73	Mercury 6499 484	SING IT AGAIN, ROD.	12
75	Riva RVLP 4	ATLANTIC CROSSING (gatefold sleeve, blue vinyl/orange vinyl)	25
76	Mercury 6672 013	THE VINTAGE YEARS	12
76	Philips SON 001	RECORDED HIGHLIGHTS & ACTION REPLAYS	12
78	St. Michael 21020 102	REASON TO BELIEVE (only available in Marks & Spencer)	30
80	Phonogram IMP 117 2188/ 3014	MAGGIE MAY (only available in Marks & Spencer)	15
84	Warner Bros 9250 951	CAMOUFLAGE (with bonus 1-sided picture disc "Infatuation" in wallet with interview tape [SAM 194])	35

(see also Jeff Beck, Shotgun Express, Faces, Python Lee Jackson, Long John Baldry, Ted Wood)

ROMAN STEWART

72	Songbird SB 1075	Changing Times (with Dave)/CRYSTALITES: Changing Times Version	12
73	Downtown DT 518	Try Me/BIG YOUTH: Rhythm Style	12
73	Techniques TE 932	Tonight I'm Staying Here (& Tennors)/Lady Love (& Tennors)	8
75	Camel CA 2002	Wolverton Mountain/PITTERSON ALL STARS: Version	5

SANDY STEWART

58	London HLE 8683	A Certain Smile/Kiss Me Richard (78 rpm = £15)	15
63	Pye International 7N 25176	My Colouring Book/I Heard You Cried Last Night	6

SONNY STEWART & HIS SKIFFLE KINGS

57	Philips PB 719	The Northern Line/Black Jack (78)	22
57	Philips PB 773	Let Me Lie/Mama Don't Allow It (78)	22

TINGA STEWART

71	Songbird SB 1048	Hear That Train/CRYSTALITES: Hear That Train — Version	7
72	Tropical AL 0018	A Brand New Me/BROWNS ALL STARS: Nice Version	6
74	Dragon DRA 1025	The Message/Dub	12

WINSTON STEWART

64	R&B JB 147	But I Do/MAYTALS: Four Seasons	35
64	Port-O-Jam PJ 4002	All Of My Life/How Many Times	30

(see also Andy & Clyde, Gaylads, Delano Stewart, Winston & Tonettes)

WYNN STEWART

60	London HL 7087	Wishful Thinking/Uncle Tom Got Caught (export issue)	30

(Dave) STEWART & HARRISON

70	Multicord MULT SH 1	GIRL (EP)	15

(see also Longdancer, Eurythmics, David A. Stewart)

REX STEWART'S LONDON FIVE

55	Tempo EXA 8	REX STEWART'S LONDON FIVE (EP)	8

STICKERS

71	Bullet BU 492	One Night Of Sin/Sin (Version) (both sides actually by Jackie Brown)	5

(see also Jackie Brown)

STICK SHIFTS

80	Chiswick CHIS 118	Automobile/Parramatta Road (3 different p/s)	12

MINT VALUE £

ARBEE STIDHAM
70s	Mainstream MSL 1011	A TIME FOR BLUES (LP)	12

STIFF LITTLE FINGERS
78	Rigid Digits SRD-1	Suspect Device/Wasted Life (hand-made p/s, 500 only, red label with catalogue number on right-hand side)	80
78	Rigid Digits SRD-1	Suspect Device/Wasted Life (re-pressing, different machine-cut p/s, various colour labels/yellow labels)	18
78	Rough Trade RT 004	78 R.P.M./Alternative Ulster (p/s, A & B-sides reversed)	10
78	Rough Trade RT 004	Alternative Ulster/78 R.P.M. (p/s)	5
78	Rough Trade RT 006	Suspect Device/Wasted Life (reissue)	8
79	Rough Trade RT 015	Gotta Getaway/Bloody Sunday (p/s)	5
81	SLFDJ1	Just Fade Away/Go For It (DJ promo)	10
82	Chrysalis CHSDJ 2580	Listen/Two Guitars Clash (p/s, jukebox issue)	10
82	Chrysalis/Melody Maker [no cat. no.]	Excerpts From Now Then/IGGY POP: Excerpts From Zombie Birdhouse (flexidisc, free with *Melody Maker*)	6/4
89	Virgin SLFDJ1	St. Patrix, The Wild Rover/Johnny Was (DJ promo, unreleased as 7")	12
91	Essential ESSX 2007	Beirut Moon/Stand Up And Shout/Interview With Jake Burns (CD, limited edition)	30
02	EMI Gold 7243 5 38560 21	LIVE IN ABERDEEN (CD)	35
	(see also Billy Karloff & Extremes)		

STIFFS
79	Dork UR 1	Standard English/S.C. Rip/Brookside Riot Squad (die-cut sleeve)	25
79	Dork UR 2	Inside Out/Kids On the Street (die cut sleeve or later Zonophone Z3, p/s)	20
80	Zonophone Z 14	Volume Control/Nothing To Lose (p/s)	10
80	Stiff BUT 86	Goodbye My Love/Magic Roundabout (p/s)	10
85	Dork UR 7(12)	The Young Guitars/Yer Under Attack (12", red or blue p/s)	10/8

STILETTOS
80	Ariola ARO 200	This Is The Way/Who Can It Be (p/s)	20

STILL COOL
79	Hit Run HITDD 22	Insane Love/Stereo Version '79 (12")	25

STILL LIFE
68	Columbia DB 8345	What Did We Miss/My Kingdom Cannot Lose	50
71	Vertigo 6360 026	STILL LIFE (LP, gatefold sleeve, swirl label)	150
	(see also Jon, Titus Groan)		

STEPHEN STILLS
71	Atlantic 2091 046	Love The One You're With/To A Flame	5
71	Atlantic 2091 069	Sit Yourself Down/We Are Not Helpless	5
71	Atlantic 2091 117	Change Partners/Relaxing Town	5
71	Atlantic 2091 141	Marianne/Nothing To Do But Today	5
70	Atlantic 2401 004	STEPHEN STILLS (LP)	15
71	Atlantic 2401 013	STEPHEN STILLS 2 (LP, gatefold sleeve)	12
73	Atlantic K 40440	DOWN THE ROAD (LP)	12
	(see also Buffalo Springfield, Al Kooper Mike Bloomfield & Stephen Stills, Crosby Stills Nash & Young, Manassas, Stills-Young Band)		

STILLWATER TRIO
70s	Sharon 330	LIFE'S RAILROAD (LP)	18

STILLS-YOUNG BAND
76	Reprise K 14446	Long May You Run/12-8 Blues	5
76	Reprise K 14482	Like A Hurricane (edit)/Hold Back The Tears	5
76	Reprise K 54081	LONG MAY YOU RUN (LP)	12
	(see also Stephen Stills, Manassas, Neil Young, Buffalo Springfield, Crosby Stills Nash & Young)		

STING
87	A&M AMCD 410	We'll Be Together (Extended Mix 5.54)/(Previous Version 4.28)/Conversation With A Dog/We'll Be Together (Instrumental Version) (3" CD, with adaptor in plastic tray in gatefold card sleeve)	10
87	A&M AMCD 431	Englishman In New York/Ghost In The Strand (Instrumental)/Bring On The Night-When The World Is Running Down (live) (CD)	10
88	A&M AMCD 439	Fragile/Fragile (Portuguese Version)/Fragilidad/Mariposa Libre (CD)	8
88	A&M AMCD 911	COMPACT HITS (CD EP)	8
88	A&M AMCD 458	They Dance Alone (Gueca Solo) (with Eric Clapton & Mark Knopfler)/Ellas Damzon Solas (Gueca Solo)/St. Estamos Juntos (CD)	8
88	A&M AMCDR 580	Englishman In New York/Englishman In New York (Ben Liebrand Mix)/If You Love Somebody Set Them Free (Jellybean Dance Mix) (CD, picture disc)	8
85	A&M DREAMP 1	THE DREAM OF THE BLUE TURTLES (LP, picture disc, die-cut sl., with insert)	12
91	A&M 397 171-2	ACOUSTIC LIVE IN NEWCASTLE (CD, box set with book)	20
	(see also Police, Last Exit, [Fast Breeder &] Radio Actors, Newcastle Big Band)		

STINGERS
72	Upsetter US 395	Preacher Man/UPSETTERS: Version	12

STINGRAY (TV series)
(see under Century 21)

STING-RAYS
82	Rocket XPRES 78	Radiator Rock/Slap Bass Boogie (die-cut sleeve)	8
82	Big Beat SW 82	Dinosaurs/Math Of Trend/Another Cup Of Coffee/You're Gonna Miss Me (white label test pressing, 100 Club gig freebie, 80 only)	20
83	Big Beat SW 82	Dinosaurs/Math Of Trend/Another Cup Of Coffee/You're Gonna Miss Me (p/s)	5
84	Big Beat NS 95	Escalator/Loose Lip Synch Ship/Escalator (Instrumental) (p/s)	5
85	Big Beat NS 109	Don't Break Down/Don't Break Down (Version) (p/s)	5
85	Media Burn MB 2/ Lyntone LYN 16436	Bonus Track/I Want My Woman/Flash On You (33 rpm, red vinyl flexidisc with *The Sting-Rays Story* magazine)	5
86	Kaleidoscope Sound 102	BEHIND THE BEYOND (12" EP)	5

83	Big beat WIKM 16	DINOSAURS (LP).	12
84	Media Burn MB 1	LIVE RETALIATION (LP, white or black vinyl).	each 12
87	K'scope Sound KSLP 1	CRYPTIC AND COFFEE TIME (LP).	12
88	Media Burn MB 18	GOODBYE TO ALL THAT — LIVE VOL. 2 (LP, red or black vinyl).	each 12

STINKY TOYS
| 77 | Polydor 2056 630 | Boozy Creed/Driver Blues (p/s). | 15 |
| 77 | Polydor 2393 174 | STINKY TOYS (LP). | 25 |

(PETER) LEE STIRLING (& BRUISERS)
63	Columbia DB 4992	My Heart Commands Me/Welcome Stranger (as Lee Stirling & Bruisers).	7
63	Parlophone R 5063	I Could If I Wanted To/Right From The Start (as Lee Stirling & Bruisers).	7
64	Parlophone R 5112	Now That I've Found You/I Believe (as Peter Lee Stirling & Bruisers).	7
64	Parlophone R 5158	Sad, Lonely And Blue/I'm Looking For Someone To Love (as Peter Lee Stirling & Bruisers).	7
64	Parlophone R 5198	Everything Will Be Alright/You'll Be Mine (as Peter Lee Stirling & Bruisers).	7
66	Decca F 12433	The Sweet And Tender Hold Of Your Love/Everybody Needs A Someone.	7
66	Decca F 12535	Oh What A Fool/I'm Sportin' A New Baby.	7
67	Decca F 12628	You Don't Live Twice/8.35 On The Dot.	25
67	Decca F 12674	Goodbye Thimblemill Lane/Hey Conductor.	6
69	MCA MU 1093	Big Sam/Mr. Average Man.	6
70	MCA MK 5027	Goodbye Summer Girl/Judas In Blue.	5

(see also Bruisers, Hungry Wolf)

GARY STITES
59	London HLL 8881	Lonely For You/Shine That Ring (78 rpm = £20).	25
59	London HLL 9003	Starry Eyed/Without Your Love (78 rpm = £25).	20
60	London HLL 9082	Lawdy, Miss Clawdy/Don't Wanna Say Goodbye.	25

KING STITT
69	Clandisc CLA 200	Who Yea/DYNAMITES: Mr Midnight.	12
69	Clandisc CLA 202	Vigerton Two/On The Street.	12
69	Clandisc CLA 203	On The Street/CYNTHIA RICHARDS: Foolish Fool.	15
69	Clandisc CLA 206	The Ugly One/CLANCY ECCLES: Dance Beat.	12
70	Clandisc CLA 207	Herbsman Shuffle (with Andy [Capp])/HIGGS & WILSON: Don't Mind Me.	12
70	Clandisc CLA 223	King Of Kings/DYNAMITES: Reggaedelic.	12
71	Clandisc CLA 235	Merry Rhythm/CLANCY ECCLES: John Crow Skank.	6
71	Banana BA 332	Back Out Version/VEGETABLES: Holly Rhythm.	12
71	Banana BA 334	Rhyming Time/Reality.	12

(see also Kurass)

SONNY STITT
53	Esquire 20-013	SONNY STITT-BUD POWELL QUARTET (10" LP).	20
58	Esquire 32-049	S.P.J. JAZZ (LP, with Bud Powell & J.J. Johnson).	18
58	Columbia Clef 33CX 10114	NEW YORK JAZZ (LP).	18
59	Esquire 32-078	STITT'S BITS (LP).	18
59	HMV CLP 1280	ONLY THE BLUES (LP).	15
60	HMV CLP 1363	PERSONAL APPEARANCE (LP).	12
60	HMV CLP 1384	SONNY STITT WITH THE OSCAR PETERSON TRIO (LP).	12
61	HMV CLP 1420/CSD 1341	BLOWS THE BLUES (LP, mono/stereo).	12/15
67	Marble Arch MAL 753	SONNY STITT (LP).	15

(see also Oscar Peterson, J.J. Johnson)

ALAN STIVELL
72	Philips 6414 406	RENAISSANCE OF THE CELTIC HARP (LP).	12
73	Fontana 6399 005	A L'OLYMPIA (LP).	12
74	Fontana 6399 008	REFLECTIONS (LP).	12
74	Philips 6325 304	FROM CELTIC ROOTS (LP).	12
75	Fontana 9299 547	STIVELL (LP).	12

STOCKER, GREENWOOD & FRIENDS
| 79 | Changes CR1400 | BILLY + NINE (LP). | 25 |

(see also Slack Alice)

STOCKHOLM MONSTERS
81	Factory FAC 41	Fairytales/Death Is Slowly (p/s).	15
82	Factory FAC 58	Happy Ever After/Soft Babies (p/s).	15
84	Factory FAC 107	All At Once (p/s).	15

STOCKINGTOPS
| 68 | Toast TT 500 | You're Never Gonna Get My Lovin'/You Don't Know What Love Is All About. | 15 |
| 68 | CBS 3407 | I Don't Ever Wanna Be Kicked By You/The World We Live In Is A Lonely Place. | 7 |

(see also Sue & Sunny, Sue & Sunshine, Myrtelles)

STOCKTON'S WING
| 78 | Tara 2004 | STOCKTON'S WING (LP). | 12 |

STOICS
| 68 | RCA RCA 1745 | Earth, Fire, Air And Water/Search Of The Sea. | 28 |

STOKES
| 65 | London HLU 9955 | Whipped Cream/Pie Crust. | 12 |

SIMON STOKES & NIGHTHAWKS
| 70 | Elektra EKSN 45082 | Voodoo Woman/Can't Stop Now. | 10 |

RHET STOLLER (& HIS ECHOES)
60	Decca F 11271	Walk Don't Run/All Rhet.	15
60	Decca F 11302	Chariot/Night Theme.	10
63	Decca F 11738	Countdown/Over The Steppes (as Rhet Stoller & His Echoes).	10
64	Melodisc MEL 1595	Beat That/Treble Gold + One.	18
64	Windsor PS 119	Caravan/Short Cut.	18

Rhet STOLLER

64	Windsor PS 130	Ricochet/Knockout	18
66	Columbia DB 8013	Uncrowned King/Surf Ride (unissued, demos only)	20
69	Mosaic MOSAIC 1	SUNSHINE ANYTIME (EP, as Rhet Stoller & Music)	10
67	Coronet EC 101	THE INCREDIBLE RHET STOLLER (LP)	32

JACKIE STOLLINGS (& NASHVILLE BOYS)
| 62 | Starlite ST45 092 | Footsteps Of A Fool/And Then I Knew (B-side with Nashville Boys) | 6 |

MORRIS STOLOFF (& COLUMBIA PICTURES ORCHESTRA)
56	Brunswick 05553	Moonglow/Theme From "Picnic"	7
56	Brunswick 05597	Theme From "The Solid Gold Cadillac"/Sweet Sue Just You	5
57	Brunswick 05666	Theme From "Fire Down Below"/Theme From "Full Of Life"	5

STOMPERS
| 62 | Fontana H 385 | Quarter To Four Stomp (Surf Stompin')/Foolish One | 30 |

ALEXANDER STONE
| 70 | Gemini GMS 003 | I Try To Make You Good/Man In A Suitcase | 5 |

CLIFFIE STONE & HIS ORCHESTRA
55	Capitol CL 14330	Barracuda/The Popcorn Song (with Billy Strange & Speedy West)	110
55	Capitol CL 14330	Barracuda/The Popcorn Song (with Billy Strange & Speedy West) (78)	28
56	Capitol CL 14666	Jingle Bells/Rudolph The Red Nosed Reindeer	5
58	Capitol CL 14928	Near You/Nobody's Darlin' But Mine	5
59	Capitol CL 14996	Blood On The Saddle/Cool Water	5
59	Capitol T 1080	THE PARTY'S ON ME (LP)	15

(see also Jeanne Gayle, Billy Strange)

ELLA STONE & MOSS
| 70s | Phoenix SNIX 128 | The Prophet/Now Or Never | 6 |

(see also Helen Shapiro, Al Saxon)

GEORGE STONE
| 65 | Stateside SS 479 | Hole In The Wall/My Beat | 15 |

KIRBY STONE QUARTET/FOUR
56	Vogue Coral Q 72129	Honey Hush/Lassus Trombone (78 rpm = £10)	15
59	Philips PB 903	That "I Had A Dream, Dear" Rock/Sweet Nothings (78 rpm = £10)	5
63	Warner Bros WB 102	The Great Escape (March)/Fancy Dan	5
63	Warner Bros WB 118	Washington Guitar/Blue Guitar	5
59	London HA-A 2164	MAN, I FLIPPED WHEN I HEARD THE KIRBY STONE FOUR (LP)	15

MARK STONE
| 58 | London HLR 8543 | Ever Since I Met Lucy/The Stroll (78 rpm = £40) | 85 |

SLY (& FAMILY) STONE
68	Columbia DB 8369	Dance To The Music/Let Me Hear It From You (DJ copy = £150)	100
68	Direction 58-3568	Dance To The Music/Let Me Hear It From You (reissue)	8
68	Direction 58-3707	M'Lady/Life	8
69	Direction 58-3938	Everyday People/Sing A Simple Song	8
69	Direction 58-4279	Stand!/I Want To Take You Higher	8
69	Direction 58-4471	Hot Fun In The Summertime/Fun	8
70	Direction 58-4782	Thank You (Falettinme Be Mice Elf Agin)/Everybody Is A Star	8
70	CBS 5054	I Want To Take You Higher/You Can Make It If You Try	6
71	Epic EPC 7632	Family Affair/Luv 'n' Haight	5
72	Epic EPC 7810	Running Away/Brave And Strong	5
73	Epic EPC 1655	If You Want Me To Stay/Thankful & Thoughtful	5
74	Epic EPC 2530	Time For Livin'/Small Talk (as Sly Stone)	5
75	Epic EPC 2882	Loose Booty/Can't Strain My Brain (as Sly Stone)	5
74	CBS SEPC 3048	Dance To The Music/Stand/Ride The Rhythm/Colour Me True (promo-only)	8
68	Direction 8-63412	DANCE TO THE MUSIC (LP)	20
68	Direction 8-63461	M'LADY (LP)	20
69	Direction 8-63655	STAND! (LP, CBS sleeve with Direction label)	20
70	Epic EPC 69002	GREATEST HITS (LP, gatefold sleeve)	12
72	Epic EPC 64613	THERE'S A RIOT GOING ON (LP, gatefold sleeve, with free EP/newspaper)	15
73	CBS Q 69002	GREATEST HITS (LP, quadrophonic, gatefold sleeve)	15
73	Epic EPC 69039	FRESH (LP, gatefold sleeve)	12
74	Epic EPC 69070	SMALL TALK (LP)	12
75	Epic EPC 22004	HIGH ENERGY (2-LP, gatefold sleeve)	15
75	Epic EPC 69165	HIGH ON YOU (LP, as Sly Stone)	12

(see also Rosie Banks)

STONE ANGEL
| 75 | SSLP 04 | STONE ANGEL (LP, private pressing) | 180 |
| 94 | Acme AC 8008 LP | STONE ANGEL (LP, reissue, 500 only) | 15 |

(see also Ken Saul))

STONEFIELD TRAMP
| 74 | Acorn/Tramp CF 247 | DREAMING | 135 |

(see also Terry Friend, Rob Van Spyk)

STONE GRAPHICS
| 68 | Parlophone R 5735 | A Tale Of Long Ago/Travelling Man | 12 |

STONEGROUND
71	Warner Bros K 16126	You Must Be One Of Us/It Takes A Lot To Laugh	5
71	Warner Bros K 46087	STONEGROUND (LP)	15
71	Warner Bros K 53999	FAMILY ALBUM (LP)	15

STONEGROUND BAND
| 70s | Nut | SUNSTRUCK!! (LP, stickered sleeve) | 30 |

HARRY STONEHAM & JOHNNY EYDEN
67	Tepee TPRLP 100	TWO GUYS TO FOLLOW (LP, mono [70s reissues credited to Harry Stoneham £15])	25

STONEHENGE MEN
62	HMV POP 981	Big Feet/Pinto	45

STONEHOUSE
71	RCA SF 8197	STONEHOUSE CREEK (LP)	80

E.V. STONEMAN
63	London HA-B/SH-B 8089	E.V. STONEMAN AND THE STONEMAN FAMILY (LP)	12

STONEPILLOW
69	Phase 4 Stereo PFS 4163	ELEAZAR'S CIRCUS (LP)	10

STONE PONEYS
67	Capitol CL 15523	A Different Drum/I've Got To Know	10

(see also Linda Ronstadt)

STONE ROSES
SINGLES
85	Thin Line THIN 001	So Young/Tell Me (12", p/s, 1,200 only; beware of counterfeits!)	120
87	Black/Revolver 12 REV 36	Sally Cinnamon/Here It Comes/All Across The Sand (12", 'Printed In England' on rear p/s & no barcode, "All Across The Sands" listed on label; different mixes of 2 tracks to later reissue – increasingly difficult to find original)	30
88	Silvertone ORE 1	Elephant Stone/The Hardest Thing In The World (catalogue number in black print on rear of p/s)	8
88	Silvertone ORET1	Elephant Stone (4.48)/Elephant Stone (7" Version) (3.00)/Full Fathom Five/The Hardest Thing In The World (12", p/s, cat. no. in black print on rear of p/s) (unique recording of Full Fathom Five on original pressing)	20
89	Silvertone ORE 2	Made Of Stone/Going Down (p/s, cat. no. in black print on rear of p/s)	7
89	Silvertone ORET 2	Made Of Stone/Going Down/Guernica (12", p/s, catalogue number in black print on rear of p/s)	20
89	Silvertone ORE 6	She Bangs The Drums/Standing Here (p/s)	5
89	Silvertone ORET 6	She Bangs The Drums/Mersey Paradise/Standing Here (12", p/s)	8
89	Silvertone OREX 6	She Bangs The Drums/Standing Here (p/s, with postcard, 3,000 only)	8
89	Silvertone OREZ 6	She Bangs The Drums/Mersey Paradise/Standing Here (12", p/s, with colour print (I Wanna Be Adored cover), 5,000 only)	12
89	Silvertone ORE 13	What The World Is Waiting For/Fools Gold 4.15 (paper label, with postcard stickered p/s credits "What The World Is Waiting For")	6
89	Silvertone ORE 13	Fools Gold 4.15/What The World Is Waiting For (repressing, p/s credits "Fools Gold")	5
89	Silvertone ORET 13	What The World Is Waiting For/Fools Gold 9.23 (12", stickered p/s credits "What The World Is Waiting For", with print)	10
89	Silvertone ORECD 13	Fools Gold 9.23/What The World Is Waiting For/Fools Gold 4.15 (CD, inlay credits "What The World Is Waiting For")	8
89	Black/Revolver 12 REV 36	Sally Cinnamon/Here It Comes/All Across The Sand (12", 'Printed in W Germany' on rear p/s – barcode)	10
89	Black/Revolver REV 36	Sally Cinnamon/Here It Comes (p/s)	5
90	Silvertone ORE 1	Elephant Stone (7" Version)/The Hardest Thing In The World (catalogue number in red print on rear of p/s)	5
90	Silvertone ORE 2	Made Of Stone/Going Down (p/s, cat. no. in blue print on rear of p/s)	5
90	Fierce FRIGHT 044	SPIKE ISLAND EP (fan interviews, P.A. announcements & fireworks, with cigarette, badge, bag of grass & banana sweet)	15
90	Silvertone OREZ 13	Fools Gold (The Top Won Mix!)/(The Bottom Won Mix!) (12")	18
90	Silvertone OREZCD 13	Fools Gold (The Top Won Mix!)/(The Bottom Won Mix!) (Gold CD)	12
90	Silvertone ORE 17	One Love/Something's Burning (p/s, with postcard)	5
90	Silvertone OREZ 17	One Love/Something's Burning (12", p/s, with print)	5
91	Silvertone ORE 31	I Wanna Be Adored (3.28)/Where Angels Play (p/s)	5
91	Silvertone ORET 31	I Wanna Be Adored (4.52)/Where Angels Play/Sally Cinnamon (Live at the Hacienda) (12", p/s)	8
91	Silvertone OREZ 31	I Wanna Be Adored (4.52)/Where Angels Play/Sally Cinnamon (Live at the Hacienda) (12", stickered p/s with print)	30
92	Silvertone ORE 35	Waterfall (7" Version 3.31)/One Love (7" Version 3.40) (p/s)	5
92	Silvertone OREZT 35	Waterfall (12" Version 5.23)/One Love (Adrian Sherwood 12" Version 7.10) (12", p/s, with print)	20
92	Silvertone ORE 40	I Am The Resurrection (Pan And Scan Radio Version)/I Am The Resurrection (Highly Resurrected Dub) (p/s)	5
92	Silvertone ORET 40	I Am The Resurrection (Extended 19:9 Ratio Club Mix)/(Original LP Version)/Fools Gold (Bottom Won Mix) (12", some with print)	40+/10
93	Silvertone ORECD 37	So Young/Tell Me (CD, from "CD Singles Collection")	12
92	Silvertone SRBX 2	12" SINGLES COLLECTION (10 x 12" singles box set, 1,000 only)	150+
92	Silvertone SRBX 1	CD SINGLES COLLECTION (8 x CD singles box set, 1,000 only)	75+
94	Geffen GFST 84	Love Spreads/Your Star Will Shine/Breakout/Groove Harder (12" p/s)	10
95	Geffen GFST 87	Ten Storey Love Song/Moses/Ride On (12", stickered/numbered p/s)	10
95	Silvertone ORE T 71	Fools Gold '95 (Tall Paul Remix)/Original 9.53/(Cricklewood Ballroom Mix) (12", p/s)	8
95	Geffen GFST 22060	Begging You(Album Version)/(Chic Mix)/(Cox's Ultimatum Mix)/(Stone Corporation Vox) (12" p/s with art print)	10
99	Jive Electro 052390	Fools Gold '99 (Grooverider's Mix)/She Bangs The Drums (Kelly Reverb Kiss My Arse Mix)/Fools Gold (Rabbit In The Moon's Message To Majors Mix) (12", p/s)	8

PROMOS
85	Thin Line THIN 001	So Young/Tell Me (12", promo (pale) pink label test pressing, 100 only) (in Cartel sleeve with press pack)	150+ / 250-300+
89	Silvertone ORE DJ 6	She Bangs The Drums (7", promo)	10
89	Silvertone ORE DJ T 13	Fools Gold 9.53/What The World Is Waiting For (12" promo, B-side white label)	18

MINT VALUE £

89	Silvertone ORE DJ 13	Fools Gold 4.15/ What The World Is Waiting For (7", promo)	10
90	Silvertone ORE DJ T 17	One Love/Something's Burning (12", promo, B-side white label)	10
90	Silvertone ORE DJ 17	One Love (7" edit) /Something's Burning (7", edit) (7", promo)	10
90	Silvertone ORE DJ CD 17	One Love /Something's Burning (CD promo, p/s)	8
92	Silvertone ORE T DJ 34	Waterfall (12" Version 5.23)/One Love (Adrian Sherwood 12" Version 7.10) (12" promo)	15
94	Geffen STONEPRO1	Love Spreads (Radio Edit, Album version) (CD promo, no p/s) (mastered at Nimbus/Mayking)	10/20
95	Silvertone OREDJ 71	Fools Gold (The Tall Paul Remix)/Fools Gold 9.23/ Fools Gold (Cricklewood Ballroom Mix) (12")	10
95	Geffen WGFSX 22060	Begging You (Album Version)/(Chic Mix)/(Stone Corporation Vox)/ (Young American Primitive Remix) (12", no p/s, some with press sheet)	15/10
95	Geffen WGFST 22060	Begging You (Album Version)/(Cox's Ultimatum Mix)/(Overworld Mix)/ (Lakota Mix) (12", no p/s)	10
95	Geffen WGFTD 22060	Begging You (Radio Edit)/(Chic Mix) (CD, b&w p/s)	8

ALBUMS

89	Silvertone ORE LP 502	THE STONE ROSES (LP, original pressing, embossed sleeve with gold lettering)	18
89	Silvertone ORE LP 502	THE STONE ROSES (LP, original pressing, gold lettering)	12
91	Silvertone OREZ LP 502	THE STONE ROSES (2-LP, reissue, numbered gatefold sleeve with silver lettering)	15
91	Silvertone OREZ CD 502	THE STONE ROSES (CD, reissue, numbered with silver lettering)	18
92	Silvertone ORE LP 521	TURNS INTO STONE (LP, original pressing)	15
94	Geffen GEF 24503	SECOND COMING (2-LP, original pressing, gatefold)	12
95	Silvertone ORE LP 535	THE COMPLETE STONE ROSES (2-LP)	15
95	Silvertone OREZ CD 535	THE COMPLETE STONE ROSES (2-CD, includes two rare tracks)	18
96	Garage Flower GARAGE LP 1	GARAGE FLOWER (LP, few with print)	15/30
99	Geffen/Simply Vinyl SVLP 111	SECOND COMING (2-LP, limited edition, gatefold, heavy duty 180gm vinyl)	15
99	Silvertone 0591242	THE STONE ROSES – 10th Anniversary Edition (2-CD ltd edition in slipcase, enhanced with videos, booklet & sleeve notes)	20
00	Silvertone 9260151	THE REMIXES (2-LP)	15
02	Silvertone 9260382	THE VERY BEST OF THE STONE ROSES (CD Ltd Edn, stickered slipcase, includes 4 postcards, remastered tracks)	15
02	Silvertone 9260371	THE VERY BEST OF THE STONE ROSES (2-LP)	15

(see also Ian Brown, John Squire)

STONE'S MASONRY

66	Purdah 45-3504	Flapjacks/Hot Rock (99 copies only)	200+

(see also Action, Mighty Baby, Savoy Brown)

STONE TEMPLE PILOTS

93	Atlantic A 5759 T	Sex Type Thing/Wicked Garden/Plush (12", p/s)	10
94	Atlantic A 7192 X	Interstate Love Song/Lounge Fly (purple vinyl)	7

STONE THE CROWS

70	Polydor 2066 060	Mad Dogs & Englishmen/Sad Mary	5
72	Polydor 2058 301	Good Time Girl/On The Highway	5
70	Polydor 2425 017	STONE THE CROWS (LP)	25
70	Polydor 2425 042	ODE TO JOHN LAW (LP)	25
71	Polydor 2425 701	TEENAGE LICKS (LP)	20
72	Polydor 2391 043	ONTINUOUS PERFORMANCE (LP)	18

(see also White Trash, Maggie Bell)

STONEY & MEAT LOAF

71	Rare Earth RES 103	What You See Is What You Get/The Way You Do The Things You Do	12
79	Prodigal PROD 10	What You See Is What You Get/The Way You Do The Things You Do (reissue)	8
72	Rare Earth SRE 3005	STONEY AND MEAT LOAF (LP)	25
79	Prodigal PDL 2010	MEAT LOAF (FEATURING STONEY & MEAT LOAF) (LP, revised reissue of "Stoney And Meat Loaf" with different tracks)	15
86	Motown ZL 72217	MEAT LOAF (FEATURING STONEY & MEAT LOAF) (LP, 2nd reissue)	12

(see also Meat Loaf)

STOOGES

89	Spiral Scratch SCRATCH 5	She Creatures Of Hollywood Hills/Untitled (as Iggy & Stooges, free with *Spiral Scratch* magazine, issue 5)	6/4
69	Elektra EKS 74051	THE STOOGES (LP, orange label)	70
70	Elektra EKS 74071	FUN HOUSE (LP, orange label)	70
70	Elektra 2410 009	FUN HOUSE (LP, reissue, red label)	20
73	CBS 65586	RAW POWER (LP, as Iggy & Stooges, plain orange label, with inner sleeve)	15
77	Elektra K 42032	THE STOOGES (LP, reissue, 'butterfly' label)	15
77	Elektra K 42051	FUN HOUSE (LP, reissue, 'butterfly' label)	15

(see also Iggy Pop)

STOP

80	Elite CAB 101	I Can Feel It/Iauwata (12")	12

STOPOUTS

78	Skeleton LYN 5912	Strange Thoughts/Just For You And Me (p/s)	15

STOREY SISTERS

58	London HLU 8571	Bad Motorcycle/Sweet Daddy (78 rpm = £40)	100

STORM/CUTMASTER SWIFT

91	White SOLID001	Playing The Field/Live In Spain (12")	18

BILLY STORM
59	Philips PB 916	I've Come Of Age/This Is Always (78 rpm = £12)	15
60	London HLK 9236	Sure As You're Born/In The Chapel In The Moonlight	12

DANNY STORM (& STROLLERS)
62	Piccadilly 7N 35025	Honest I Do/Sad But True (some in p/s)	15/10
62	Piccadilly 7N 35053	Just You/I Told You So	10
62	Piccadilly 7N 35091	I Just Can't Fool My Heart/Thinking Of You	10
63	Piccadilly 7N 35143	Say You Do/Let The Sunshine In (as Danny Storm & Strollers)	10

GALE STORM
56	London HLD 8222	I Hear You Knocking/Never Leave Me	45
56	London HLD 8232	Memories Are Made Of This/A Teen-Age Prayer (78 rpm = £7)	40
56	London HLD 8283	Ivory Tower/I Ain't Gonna Worry (78 rpm = £7)	45
56	London HLD 8286	Why Do Fools Fall In Love/I Walk Alone (78 rpm = £7)	40
56	London HL 7008	Why Do Fools Fall In Love/I Walk Alone (export issue)	20
56	London HLD 8311	Don't Be That Way (Please Listen To Me)/Tell Me Why (78 rpm = £8)	35
56	London HLD 8329	A Heart Without A Sweetheart/Now Is The Hour (78 rpm = £12)	22
57	London HLD 8393	Lucky Lips/On Treasure Island (78 rpm = £12)	35
57	London HLD 8413	Orange Blossoms/My Heart Belongs To You (78 rpm = £10)	20
57	London HLD 8424	Dark Moon/A Little Too Late	20
58	London HLD 8570	Love Theme From "Farewell To Arms"/I Get That Feeling (78 rpm = £12)	10
58	London HLD 8632	You/Angry (78 rpm = £15)	15
56	London HB-D 1056	PRESENTING GALE STORM (10" LP)	65
58	London HA-D 2104	SENTIMENTAL ME (LP)	50

RORY STORM & HURRICANES
63	Oriole CB 1858	Dr. Feelgood/I Can Tell	35
64	Parlophone R 5197	America/Since You Broke My Heart	20
(see also Keef Hartley, Paddy Klaus & Gibson)			

STORM BUGS
80	Storm Bugs	STORM BUGS (EP, white label, foldout insert, plain white sleeve)	5

ROBB STORME (& WHISPERS)
60	Decca F 11282	1000, 900 And When/I Don't Need Your Love Anymore	12
61	Decca F 11313	Music/Five Minutes More (as Robb Storme & Whispers)	7
61	Decca F 11364	Near You/Lonely Town (as Robb Storme & Whispers)	7
61	Decca F 11388	Transistor Sister/Earth Angel	12
62	Decca F 11432	Pretty Hair And Angel Eyes/A Mile Of Broken Hearts	10
63	Pye 7N 15515	Sixteen Years Ago Tonight/Surprise Surprise	7
63	Piccadilly 7N 35133	Happens Ev'ryday/Surprise Surprise	6
63	Piccadilly 7N 35160	To Know Her Is To Love Her/Bu Bop A Lu Bop A Lie	6
65	Pye 7N 15819	Love Is Strange/Shy Guy	6
65	Columbia DB 7756	Where Is My Girl?/Double Oh Seven (as Robb Storme & Whispers)	8
66	Columbia DB 7993	Here Today/Don't Cry (as Robb Storme Group)	15
62	Decca DFE 6700	WHEELS (EP)	110

STORMER
78	Ring O' 2017 113	My Home Town/Shake It Baby (some in promo p/s)	70/40

STORMTROOPER
78	Solent SS 047	I'm A Mess/It's Not Me (some in stamped plain sleeve with insert)	30/12

STORMTROOPER
80	Heartbeat BEAT 1	Pride Before A Fall/Still Comin' Home (p/s)	25

STORYTELLER
71	CBS 7182	Remarkable/Laugh That Came Too Soon	5
70	Transatlantic TRA 220	STORYTELLER (LP)	25
71	Transatlantic TRA 232	MORE PAGES (LP)	25
(see also Johnny Neal & Starliners, Terry Durham, Other Two, Andy Bown)			

STORYTELLER
85	Storyteller ZELSP 438	Mystery Girl (p/s)	50

BABE STOVALL
76	Southern Sound SD 203	THE BABE STOVALL STORY (LP)	12

STOWAWAYS
79	Supermusic SUP 27	I Wanna Be Me/My Friends/You'll Tie Me Down (p/s)	25

STP 23
89	Wau! Mr. Modo WMS 001R	Let Jimi Take Over/Let Jimi Take Over (Remix By Youth) (12", p/s)	10

STRAFE FÜR REBELLION
80s	Touch TO 6	SANTA MARIA (LP, with inner)	15

STRAIGHT EIGHT
78	Eel Pie EPS 003	Modern Times/Tell Me If You Wanna Bleed (p/s)	10
79	Warner Bros K 18049	Spread It Around/It Ain't Easy/Oh No (p/s)	5
80	Logo DEAL 1	I'm Sorry/Satisfied (p/s)	6
80	Logo DEAL 2	Tombstone/On The Rebound (p/s)	5
82	Logo GO 416	Tomorrow/Faded Stars/You Are What You Are (some with p/s)	10/8
79	Eel Pie EPRP 001	NO NOISE FROM HERE (LP)	12
80	Logo LOGO 1032	STRAIGHT TO THE HEART (LP)	12
80	Logo FLUSH 1	SHUFFLE'N'CUT (LP)	12

STRAIGHT UP
80	Rok XX/XIX	One Out All Out/JUSTIN CASE: T.V. (die-cut company sleeve)	10

EMILLE STRAKER & HIS MERRYMEN
(see under Merrymen)

PETER STRAKER

69	Polydor 56345	Breakfast In Bed/The Right To Cry	5
69	Polydor 56362	I Never Thought I'd Fall In Love/Birdie Told Me	5
70	Polydor 2058 039	Carousel/It's A New Day	5
77	EMI EMI 2700	Ragtime Piano Joe/Saddest Clown	10
78	EMI EMI 2758	Jackie/I've Been To Hell And Back	12
77	EMI EMC 3204	THIS ONE'S ON ME (LP)	15

BILLY STRANGE (& CHALLENGERS)

61	London HLG 9321	Where Your Arms Used To Be/Sadness Done Come	10
64	Vocalion V-N 9228	The James Bond Theme/007 Theme	15
64	Vocalion V-N 9231	Goldfinger/"Munsters" Theme	18
66	Vocalion V-N 9257	Thunderball/"Ninth Man" Theme	12
66	Vocalion V-N 9259	Get Smart/Run Spy, Run	15
67	Vocalion V-N 9289	"A Few Dollars More" Theme/You Only Live Twice	10
63	Vocalion VA/SVN 8022	12-STRING GUITAR (LP)	18
64	Vocalion VAN 8026	MR GUITAR (LP)	18
64	Vocalion VAN/SAVN 8032	THE JAMES BOND THEME (LP)	22
65	Vocalion VAN/SAVN 8038	GOLDFINGER (LP)	22
65	Vocalion VAN/SAVN 8042	ENGLISH HITS OF '65 (LP)	15
65	Vocalion VAN/SAVN 8045	STRANGE PLAYS THE HITS (LP)	15
66	Vocalion VAN/SAVN 8050	FOLK-ROCK HITS (LP)	15
66	London HA-F/SH-F 8274	THE FUNKY 12 STRING GUITAR (LP, as Billy Strange & Transients)	12
66	Vocalion VAN/SAVN 8065	BILLY STRANGE & THE CHALLENGERS (LP)	15
70	London ZGL 104	GREAT WESTERN THEMES (LP)	12

(see also Cliffie Stone)

GILES STRANGE

66	Stateside SS 570	Watch The People Dance/You're Goin' Up To The Bottom	55

STEVE STRANGE

82	Palace PALACE 1	In The Year 2525/Strange Connexions (white label, unreleased)	50
82	Palace PALACE 1	In The Year 2525/Strange Connexions (p/s, available separately)	30

(see also Visage)

STRANGE CRUISE

86	EMI 12EMI 5549	Rebel Blue Rocker/Love Addiction (12", p/s)	10
86	EMI EMC 3513	STRANGE CRUISE (LP)	18

STRANGE DAYS

75	Retreat RTS 263	Monday Morning/Joe Soap	5
75	Retreat RTL 6005	NINE PARTS TO THE WIND (LP)	15

STRANGE FRUIT

71	Village Thing VTSX 1001	Cut Across Shorty/Shake That Thing	12

STRANGELOVE

92	Sermon SERT 001	Visionary/Front/Chances/Snakes (12", p/s, 1,000 only)	20
93	Sermon SERT 002	Hysteria/Unknown/My Dark Walls/Sea (12", some in p/s)	10/8
93	Sermon SERT 002CD	Hysteria/Unknown/My Dark Walls/Sea (CD)	15
93	R. T. Singles Club 45REV 18	Zoo'd Out/Circles (p/s)	12
94	Food 12FOOD 49	Time For The Rest Of Your Life/Motorpsycho Nitemare/It's So Easy (12", p/s)	8
94	Food CDFOOD 49	Time For The Rest Of Your Life/Motorpsycho Nitemare/It's So Easy (CD)	8
94	M. Tongue MOTHER 1F	All Because Of You/MY LIFE STORY: "Under The Ice" (flexidisc)	8
95	Food FOODDJ 62	World Outside (live)/Hysteria Unknown (live) (gig freebie, some with jukebox centre)	6
96	Food FOODLP 15	LOVE AND OTHER DEMONS (LP, with 12 page booklet)	12

STRANGELOVES

65	Stateside SS 446	I Want Candy/It's About My Baby	22
65	Immediate IM 007	Cara-Lin/Roll On Mississippi	25
66	London HLZ 10020	Night Time/Rhythm Of Love	30
66	London HLZ 10063	Hand Jive/I Gotta Dance	10
69	London HLZ 10238	Honey Do/I Wanna Do It	10

(see also Beach-Nuts)

STRANGE MOVEMENTS

79	Good Vibrations GOT 5	Dancing In The Ghetto/Amuse Yourself (foldout p/s)	25

STRANGER (Cole)

63	Blue Beat BB 165	Rough And Tough (with Duke Reid Band)/DUKE REID BAND: The Mood I Am In	20
63	Blue Beat BB 195	Miss Reamer/RICO & HIS BLUES BAND: Blues From The Hills	20

(see also Stranger Cole)

STRANGER (Cole) & GLADY (Anderson)

67	Island WI 3128	Love Me Today/Over Again	45
68	Amalgamated AMG 806	Seeing Is Knowing/ROY SHIRLEY: Music Is The Key	25
71	Clandisc CLA 230	Tomorrow (as Stranger & Gladdy)/DYNAMITES: Tomorrow Version	7
71	Supreme SUP 227	My Application (as Stranger & Gladdy)/TADDY & DIAMONDS: Oh No, My Baby	7
73	Count Shelley CS 015	Don't Give Up The Fight (as Stranger & Gladdy)/TIDALS: Stand Firm	5
73	Dragon DRA 1014	Conqueror/Conqueror (Instrumental Version)	5

(see also Stranger Cole, Gladdy & Followers, Gladstone Anderson, Gladdy & Stranger, Charlie Kelly)

STRANGER (Cole) & HORTENSE (Ellis)

74	Count Shelley CS 049	Mocking Bird/Corra Bella Baby	6

STRANGER (Cole) & KEN (Boothe)

63	R&B JB 120	Thick In Love/All Your Friends	28

(see also Stranger Cole, Ken Boothe)

STRANGER (Cole) & PATSY (Todd)

63	Blue Beat BB 171	When I Call Your Name/Take My Heart (with Duke Reid All Stars)	12
63	Island WI 113	Senor And Senorita/DON DRUMMOND: Snowboy	30
64	Island WI 141	Oh Oh I Need You/DON DRUMMOND: J.F.K.'s Memory	35

64	Island WI 144	Tom, Dick And Harry/We Two, Happy People	15
64	Island WI 152	Yeah Yeah Baby/BABA BROOKS: Boat Ride	25
64	Island WI 160	Miss B/Thing Come To Those Who Wait	15
65	Black Swan WI 462	Hey Little Girl/CORNELL CAMBELL: Make Hay	30
66	Rio R 81	Give Me One More Chance/Fire In Cornfield	12
66	Doctor Bird DB 1050	Give Me The Right/Tonight	25
67	Doctor Bird DB 1084	Tell It To Me/Your Photograph	25
67	Doctor Bird DB 1087	Down The Trainlines/Sing And Pray	40
69	Escort ES 807	My Love/SWEET CONFUSION: Windsor Castle	15
69	Escort ES 811	Why Did You/Do You Remember	8

(see also Stranger Cole, Patsy)

STRANGERS (with Mike Shannon)

64	Philips BF 1335	One And One Is Two/Time And The River (as Strangers with Mike Shannon)	35
64	Philips BF 1378	Do You Or Don't You/What Can I Do	8

(see also Shadows)

STRANGERS

67	Pye 7N 17240	Look Out (Here Comes Tomorrow)/Mary Mary	18
67	Pye 7N 17351	You Didn't Have To Be So Nice/Daytime Turns To Night	10
68	Pye 7N 17585	I'm On An Island/Step Inside	7

STRANGE STONE

77	own label DER 1399	STRANGE STONE (LP, private pressing, numbered sleeve with insert, 255 only)	500

STRANGER THAN FICTION

80s	Ellie Jay EJSP 9301	Into The Void/Darkness (p/s)	25

STRANGEWAYS

78	Real ARE 2	Show Her You Care/You're On Your Own (p/s)	125
79	Real ARE 7	All The Sounds Of Fear/Wasting Time (p/s)	125

(see also Ada Wilson)

STRANGLERS

SINGLES

77	United Artists UP 36211	(Get A) Grip (On Yourself)/London Lady (card/paper p/s)	5/4
77	United Artists UP 36248	Peaches/Go Buddy Go ('group' p/s with 'blackmail' lettering, withdrawn)	600
77	United Artists UP 36248	Peaches/Go Buddy Go ('peach' p/s)	6
77	United Artists UP 36277	Something Better Change/Straighten Out (p/s)	6
77	United Artists UP 36300	No More Heroes/In The Shadows (p/s, 'wreath' label)	6
80	United Artists 12-BP 344	Bear Cage (Extended)/Shah Shah A Go Go (Extended) (12", p/s or company sleeve)	12/8
81	Liberty BP 383	Thrown Away/Top Secret (p/s)	5
81	Liberty BP 393	Just Like Nothing On Earth/Maninwhite (p/s)	7
82	Epic EPCA A-2893	The European Female/Savage Breast (p/s, yellow vinyl)	5
82	Epic EPCA 11-2893	The European Female/Savage Breast (picture disc)	5
84	Epic A 4738	Skin Deep/Here And There ('skin-feel' p/s, with 'Skin Deep' tattoo, 10,000 only)	6
84	Epic EPC GA 4921	No Mercy/In One Door//Hot Club (Riot Mix)/Head On The Line (double pack)	8
84	Epic WA 4921	No Mercy/In One Door (ear-shaped picture disc)	7
86	Epic 650 055-0	Nice In Nice/Since You Went Away (shaped picture disc)	6
86	Epic SOLAR P1	Always The Sun/Norman Normal (shaped picture disc)	5
86	Epic SOLAR D1	Always The Sun/Norman Normal//Nice In Nice/Since You Went Away (double pack, shrinkwrapped & stickered)	6
86	Epic HUGE P1	Big In America/Dry Day (shaped picture disc)	5
86	Epic HUGE D1	Big In America/Dry Day//Always The Sun/Norman Normal (double pack, shrinkwrapped & stickered)	5
87	Epic SHEIK P1	Shakin' Like A Leaf/Hit Man (shaped picture disc)	7
88	Epic VICE 1	All Day And All Of The Night/¡Viva Vlad! ('Monica Coughlan' p/s, withdrawn sold via fan club)	6
88	Epic VICE P1	All Day And All Of The Night/¡Viva Vlad! (shaped picture disc)	7
88	Epic CDVICE 1	All Day And All Of The Night (Jeff Remix)/¡Viva Vlad!/Who Wants The World (live)/Strange Little Girl (live) (CD, card sleeve, 5,000 only)	10
89	Liberty EMR 84	Grip '89 — (Get A) Grip (On Yourself)/Waltzinblack (p/s, red vinyl with poster in gatefold PVC wallet, 5,000 only)	5
89	Liberty CDEM 84	Grip '89 (Gripping Stuff 12" Mix)/Grip '89 (Single Mix)/Waltzinblack/Tomorrow Was The Hereafter (CD)	10
90	Epic TEARS Q1	96 Tears/Instead Of This (in embossed stickered tin)	5
90	Epic TEARS P1	96 Tears/Instead Of This/Poisonality (CD, picture disc)	8

ALBUMS

77	United Artists UAG 30045	STRANGLERS IV — RATTUS NORVEGICUS (LP, 10,000 with 7" "Choosey Susie"/"Peasant In The Big Shitty" (Live At The Nashville, 12/76) [FREE 3, orange p/s,"What Do You Expect..." in run-off groove], some with sticker)	20/12
78	United Artists UAK 30222	BLACK AND WHITE (LP, 75,000 with white vinyl 7" "Walk On By"/"Tits"/"Mean To Me" [FREE 9, black die-cut sleeve & card insert], some mispressed on blue or beige vinyl)	65/12
79	United Artists UAG 30262	THE RAVEN (LP, 20,000 with 3-D cover, cartoon on inner sleeve)	20
82	Liberty LBG 30353	THE COLLECTION '77-82 (LP, withdrawn logo sleeve)	25
82	Liberty LBG 30353	THE COLLECTION '77-82 (LP, Stranglers' own concept sleeve, unissued)	
83	Epic EPC 25237	FELINE (LP, with bonus 1-sided 7" "Aural Sculpture" [XPS 167])	12
86	Epic EPC 26648	DREAMTIME (LP, picture disc)	12

FREEBIES, PROMOS & MISCELLANEOUS

75	Safari (no. cat no)	My Young Dreams/Wasted (existence unconfirmed)	150
77	United Artists FREE 4	Peaches (radio version)/Go Buddy Go (promo only, some with p/s)	600/125
77	United Artists UP 36262	Mony Mony/Mean To Me (p/s, as Celia And The Mutations)	7
77	United Artists UP 36277	Something Better Change/Straighten Out	25
77	United Artists FREE 8	No More Heroes (1-sided radio edit, promo only)	70

77	United Artists UP 36300	No More Heroes (1-sided, misprinted "No More Stheroes")	25
77	United Artists UP 36300	No More Heroes/In The Shadows (p/s, stamped, misprinted "No More Stheroes")	25
78	United Artists UP 36429	Walk On By (Promo Edit)/Old Codger/Tank	25
79	United Artists UA STR 1 DJ	Don't Bring Harry/HUGH CORNWELL: Wired (45rpm, promo only)	20
79	United Artists (no cat. no.)	Two Sunspots (unreleased)	30
80	Stranglers Info Service SIS 001	Tomorrow Was The Hereafter/Bring On The Nubiles (Cocktail Version) (numbered p/s, label has "Nublies")	8
82	SIS/Liberty FREE 3	Peasant In The Big Shitty (Live At The Nashville, 12/76)/Choosey Susie (fan club reissue, black p/s, with "Ello 'Elen" in run-off groove)	5
82	Epic EPC A2893	The European Female (In Celebration Of)/(Promo Edit)	10
82	Liberty BP 410	La Folie (Promo Edit)/Waltzinblack	10
82	SIS/Liberty UP 36350	5 Minutes/Rok It To The Moon (reissue)	5
82	SIS/Liberty UP 36429	Walk On By/Old Codger/Tank (reissue, 33rpm)	5
82	SIS/Liberty FREE 18	Mony Mony/Mean To Me (reissue, as Celia & the Mutations)	5
83	Epic/S.I.S. XPS 167	Aural Sculpture (reissue, 1-sided)	5
91	Stranglers Info S. SIS 004	New Day Today (flexidisc with *Strangled* fan magazine, issue 32)	5

MISPRESSINGS

78	United Artists UP 36248	Peaches/Go Buddy Go (p/s, mispressing, B-side plays Buzzcocks' "Oh Shit")	60
78	United Artists FREE 9	Walk On By/Mean To Me/Tits (EP [free with LP U.A. UAK 30222], mispressing, black die-cut sleeve & card insert, blue/clear or pink/clear vinyl)	30/15
78	United Artists UP 36379	Nice 'N' Sleazy/Shut Up (p/s, mispressing, B-side plays tracks by other artist)	30
81	Liberty BP 393	Just Like Nothing On Earth/Maninwhite (p/s, mispressing, plays A-side both sides)	20
82	United Artists BP 407	Golden Brown/Love 30 (B-side plays "Everybody Salsa")	20
79	United Artists UAG 30262	THE RAVEN (LP, mispressing, 2nd side plays country & western [B-side matrix: UAK 30263])	25

(see also Jean-Jacques Burnel [& Dave Greenfield], Celia & Mutations, A Marriage Of Convenience, Fools Dance)

STRAPS

80	Donut DONUT 1	Just Can't Take Anymore/New Age (p/s)	6
82	Donut DONUT 3	Brixton/No Liquor (p/s)	8
83	Cyclops CYC 2	THE STRAPS ALBUM (LP)	15

(see also Public Image Ltd.)

STRATEGY

| 82 | Ebony EBON 7 | Technical Overflow/Astral Planes (some in p/s) | 60/50 |

STRATE JACKET

| 70s | Wessex | You're A Hit (stamped plain sleeve) | 12 |

STRATUS

| 85 | Steel Trax STEEL 31001 | THROWING SHAPES (LP) | 18 |

(see also Grand Prix, Uriah Heep, Iron Maiden, Praying Mantis)

STRAWBERRY ALARM CLOCK

67	Pye International 7N 25436	Incense And Peppermints/The Birdman Of Alkatrash	20
68	Pye International 7N 25446	Tomorrow/Birds In My Tree	15
68	Pye International 7N 25456	Sit With The Guru/Pretty Song From Psych-Out	15
69	MCA MU 1080	Good Morning Starshine/Me And The Township	8
68	Pye Intl. N(S)PL 28106	INCENSE AND PEPPERMINTS (LP)	50

STRAWBERRY CHILDREN

| 67 | Liberty LBF 15012 | Love Years Coming/One Stands Here | 30 |

(see also Jim Webb)

STRAWBERRY JAM

| 69 | Pye 7N 17711 | Per-Son-Al-Ly/This Is To A Girl | 25 |

STRAWBERRY PARK

| 82 | Sonet 2245 | Summer Is A Coming/Beach Party (some in p/s) | 7/6 |

STRAWBERRY SWITCHBLADE

83	92 Happy Customers HAP 1	Trees And Flowers/Go Away (p/s)	10
83	92 Happy Cust. HAPT 1	Trees And Flowers/Go Away/Trees And Flowers (Just Music) (12", p/s)	10
85	Korova KOW 38TP	Since Yesterday/By The Sea/Sunday Mornings (12", picture disc)	8
85	Korova KOW 39	Let Her Go/Beautiful End (shaped picture disc)	7
85	Korova KOW 42	Jolene/Being Cold (strawberry-shaped picture disc)	8
85	Korova/Flexi FLX 388-1	Strawberry Switchblade LP sampler (clear vinyl square flexidisc sewn into gatefold booklet; cat. no. only visible in run-off groove)	6
85	Korova KODE 11	STRAWBERRY SWITCHBLADE (LP, with bonus 7" "Trees And Flowers", initially mispressed with some tracks playing twice & others out of order)	15/10

(see also Poems, Rose McDowall)

STRAWBS

68	A&M AMS 725	Oh How She Changed/Or Am I Dreaming	7
68	A&M AMS 738	The Man Who Called Himself Jesus/Poor Jimmy Wilson	8
70	A&M AMS 791	Forever/Another Day	8
71	A&M AMS 837	Witchwood/Keep The Devil Outside/We'll Meet Again Sometime (live) (withdrawn)	10
71	A&M AMS 874	Benedictus/Keep The Devil Outside	6
73	A&M AMS 7047	Part Of The Union/Will You Go (p/s)	5
69	private pressing	STRAWBERRY MUSIC SAMPLER NO. 1 (LP, publisher's sampler, 100 only)	500
69	A&M AMLS 936	STRAWBS (LP; disc inserted in middle or at edge of sleeve)	35/18
70	A&M AMLS 970	DRAGONFLY (LP, with lyric insert, mustard label)	30
70	A&M AMLS 994	JUST A COLLECTION OF ANTIQUES AND CURIOS (LP, gatefold sleeve, mustard label; 2 different rear sleeves)	18
71	A&M AMLH 64304	FROM THE WITCHWOOD (LP, gatefold sleeve)	15
72	A&M AMLH 68078	GRAVE NEW WORLD (LP, triple gatefold sleeve, with 12-page booklet)	15
73	A&M AMLH 68144	BURSTING AT THE SEAMS (LP, with inner sleeve)	12
73	Hallmark SHM 813	ALL OUR OWN WORK (LP, with Sandy Denny)	12

(see also Dave Cousins, Sandy Denny, Fire, Foggy, Monks, Davey & Morris, Hudson-Ford)

STRAY

72	Big T BIG 141	Our Song/Mama's Coming Home	5
70	Transatlantic TRA 216	STRAY (LP, die-cut sleeve)	38
71	Transatlantic TRA 233	SUICIDE (LP)	35
72	Transatlantic TRA 248	SATURDAY MORNING PICTURES (LP, gatefold sleeve)	18
73	Transatlantic TRA 268	MUDANZAS (LP, gatefold sleeve)	18
74	Transatlantic TRA 281	MOVE IT (LP, die-cut sleeve with inner)	12
75	Transatlantic TRA 3066	TRACKS (LP)	15
75	Dawn DNLS 3066	STAND UP AND BE COUNTED (LP)	15
76	Pye NSPL 18482	HOUDINI (LP)	15
76	Pye NSPL 18512	HEARTS OF FIRE (LP)	15

STRAY CATS

81	Arista CSCAT 2	Rock This Town/Can't Hurry Love (cassette, flip-top case)	6
81	Arista SCAT 4	You Don't Believe Me/Cross That Bridge (p/s)	5
81	Arista SCAT 5	Little Miss Prissy/Sweet Love On My Mind (live)/Something Else (live) (p/s)	7
83	Arista SCAT 123	Stray Cat Strut/Built For Speed/Sweet Love On My Mind (live)/ Drink That Bottle Down (live) (12", p/s, reissue)	8
83	Arista SCAPD 6	(She's Sexy) And 17/Lookin' Better Every Beer (shaped picture disc)	10
83	Arista SCAT 126	(She's Sexy) And 17/Lookin' Better Every Beer/Cruisin'/Lucky Charm (12", p/s)	8
83	Arista SCAT 7	Rebels Rule/Lookin' Through My Back Door (p/s, with stickers)	6
83	Arista SCAT 127	Rebels Rule/Lookin' Through My Back Door/Look At That Cadillac (12", p/s)	8
89	EMI USA MT 62	Bring It Back Again/Runaway Boys (live) (p/s)	5
89	EMI USA MTS 62	Bring It Back Again/Runaway Boys (live) (p/s, with 3 postcards)	5
89	EMI USA 12MTP 67	Gina/Two Of A Kind (p/s)	5
92	Pump 907 047-0	Elvis On Velvet (Radio Edit)/Lust'n'Love (p/s)	5

STRAY DOG

| 74 | Manticore K 43506 | STRAY DOG (LP) | 18 |
| 74 | Manticore K 53504 | WHILE YOU'RE DOWN THERE (LP) | 12 |

(see also Emerson Lake & Palmer)

STREAMLINERS & JOANNE

| 61 | Columbia DB 4689 | Frankfurter Sandwiches/Pachalafaka | 5 |
| 62 | Columbia DB 4808 | Everybody's Doin' The Twist/Do Something | 5 |

(see also Rosemary Squires)

STREET

| 69 | London HLU 10275 | Apollo... Amen/Why Concern Yourself | 5 |

DANNY STREET

63	Phillips BF 1250	Only Love Can Break A Heart/ Cold Cold Winter	6
65	Philips BF 1387	Don't Go To Him/As It's Meant To Be	5
60s	Domino DO 114	Melanie/Birds An' Bees An' Things	5
71	London HLU 10342	My Little Guy/You Blew It	6

GARY STREET & FAIRWAYS

| 68 | Domain D 2 | Flipperty Flop/Hold Me Closer | 15 |

(see also Fairways)

JOHN STREET & INMATES OF NO. 12

| 67 | Deram DM 147 | Keep A Little Love/My Kind Of Luck | 7 |

JUDY STREET

| 78 | Grapevine GRP 106 | What/You Turn Me On | 15 |

STREETFIGHTER (U.K.)

| 81 | Streetfighter 749 | STREETFIGHTER (12" EP) | 25 |

STREETFIGHTER

| 82 | J.R. JR 7049S | CRAZY DREAM (EP) | 35 |

STREET LEGAL

| 84 | Weird Brothers SLW 1 | Rollin' On/Mississippi Moonshine (p/s) | 150 |

STREET PEOPLE

| 70 | Stateside SS 2163 | Jennifer Tomkins/All Night Long | 8 |

STREET PEOPLE

| 79 | Ellie Jay Special Pressing EJSP 9276 | PERSONAL VALUES EP (500 only, p/s) | 75 |

STREETS

| 04 | 679 071 | Fit But You Know It/FUTUREHEADS: Fit But You Know It (10", die-cut p/s, 150 only) | 8 |

STREETWALKERS

74	Reprise K 54017	STREETWALKERS (LP, with lyric sheet)	15
75	Vertigo 6360 123	DOWNTOWN FLIER (LP)	12
77	Vertigo 9102 012	VICIOUS BUT FAIR (LP)	12
76	Vertigo 9102 010	RED CARD (LP, red vinyl with inner sleeve, numbered)	12

(see also Family)

BARBRA STREISAND

SINGLES

62	CBS AAG 130	My Colouring Book/Lover Come Back To Me	6
63	CBS AAG 179	Happy Days Are Here Again/Down With Love	6
64	CBS AAG 223	People/Draw Me A Circle	6
64	CBS AAG 233	Funny Girl/I Am A Woman	6
64	CBS 201543	People/I Am A Woman You Are Man (p/s)	12
65	CBS 201754	People/Funny Girl	6
65	CBS 202025	Second Hand Rose/He Touched Me	5
66	CBS 202417	Sleep In Heavenly Peace (Silent Night)/Gounod's "Ave Maria" (p/s)	7
70	CBS 5321	Stoney End/I'll Be Home	6

Barbra STREISAND

79	CBS 12 7714	The Main Event/Fight/Instrumental (12" picture label)	8
79	CBS 13 8000	No More Tears (with Donna Summer)/Wet (12", p/s)	7
81	CBS S CBS 9517	What Kind Of Fool/Make It Like A Memory (with Barry Gibb)	5
83	CBS A 4125	No Matter What Happens (Studio Version)/ No Matter What Happens (Original Soundtrack Version) (p/s)	5
84	CBS TA 4754	Left In The Dark/Here We Are At LastWoman In Love/Guilty Memory (12", p/s, withdrawn)	50
85	CBS A 4994	Make No Mistake, He's Mine (with Kim Carnes)/Clear Sailing (p/s)	5
85	CBS A 4994	Make No Mistake, He's Mine (with Kim Carnes)/Clear Sailing// Memory/Evergreen (p/s, shrinkwrapped double pack)	8
86	CBS DA 6988	Send In The Clowns/Being Alive/Somewhere/Not While I'm Around (p/s, shrinkwrapped double pack)	10
89	CBS CP BARB 3	All I Ask Of You (from "The Phantom Of The Opera")/Somewhere/ Memory/Send In The Clowns (CD, picture disc, 2,000 only)	15
89	CBS BARB QT 3	All I Ask Of You/On My Way To You/Make No Mistake, He's Mine (with Kim Carnes)/Since I Fell For You (12", p/s with poster, 3,000 only)	8
89	CBS BARB C4	We're Not Makin' Love Anymore/Wet/No More Tears (Enough Is Enough) (with Donna Summer) (CD, picture disc)	8

EPs

63	CBS AGG 320042	LOVER COME BACK TO ME	15
63	CBS AGG 320054	BARBRA STREISAND	10
64	CBS EP 6048	EN FRANÇAIS	12
65	CBS EP 6068	MY MAN	12
66	CBS EP 6150	SECOND HAND ROSE	10

LPs

64	Capitol (S)W 2059	FUNNY GIRL (original cast recording, mono/stereo)	12
66	CBS (S)BPG 62784	HAROLD SINGS ARLEN (WITH FRIEND) (mono/stereo)	12
71	CBS CQ 30378	STONEY END (quadrophonic)	12
71	CBS CQ 30792	BARBRA JOAN STREISAND (quadrophonic)	12
73	CBS SQ 30992	FUNNY GIRL (soundtrack, quadrophonic)	12
73	CBS CQ 31760	LIVE CONCERT AT THE FORUM (quadrophonic)	12
77	CBS 66349	BARBRA STREISAND DELUXE BOX SET ("Greatest Hits Volume 1"/ "Stoney End"/"Streisand Superman")	25
79	CBS 66349	BARBRA STREISAND: 3-RECORD BOX SET ("Greatest Hits Volume 1", "Volume 2" & "Wet")	25
88	CBS 651379 6	NUTS (soundtrack)	15
91	Columbia 468734 2	JUST FOR THE RECORD (4-CD box set with 92-page booklet)	45
94	Columbia 4775 992	BARBRA — THE CONCERT (2-CD)	12
94	Columbia XPCD 147	THE EVENT OF THE DECADE, A RETROSPECTIVE (2-CD, promo only)	80+

'TEXAS' BILL STRENGTH

55	Capitol CL 14357	Cry, Cry, Cry/The Yellow Rose Of Texas (78 rpm = £8)	18

STRESS

85	Adventures In Reality ARR 14	THE BIG WHEEL (LP, with insert)	40

STRETCH

75	Anchor ANCL 2014	ELASTIQUE (LP)	15
76	Anchor ANCL 2016	YOU CAN'T BEAT YOUR BRAIN FOR ENTERTAINMENT (LP)	12
77	Anchor ANCL 2023	LIFE BLOOD (LP)	18
78	Hot Wax HW 1	FORGET THE PAST (LP)	25

(see also Elmer Gantry, Kirby, Status Quo, Clifford Davis, Legs, Curved Air)

WILLIAM R. STRICKLAND

69	Deram DML/SML 1041	WILLIAM R. STRICKLAND IS ONLY THE NAME (LP)	18

PETE STRIDE & JOHN PLAIN

80	Beggars Banquet BEGA 17	NEW GUITARS IN TOWN (LP, with inner sleeve)	12

(see also Lurkers)

STRIDER

73	GM GMS 002	Higher And Higher/Ain't Got No Love	5
74	GM GMS 023	Seems So Easy/Arthur Hydrogen	5
73	GM GML 1002	EXPOSED (LP)	18
74	GM GML 1012	MISUNDERSTANDING (LP)	15

(see also Samson)

STRIFE

77	Outlaw OUT 1	School/Go/Feel So Good (p/s)	10
75	Chrysalis 1063	RUSH (LP)	12
78	Gull 1029	BACK TO THUNDER (LP, some on green vinyl)	18/15

LIZA STRIKE

68	Parlophone R 5725	All's Quiet On West 23rd/Mr Daddy-Man	8

(see also Liza & Jet Set, Soulmates, Vice Versa)

STRIKERS & CHILDREN OF SELSTON BAGTHORPE PRIMARY SCHOOL CHOIR

78	Eagle EGL 003	Good Old Charlie/Forest Fire	8

STRING-A-LONGS

61	London HLU 9278	Wheels/Am I Asking Too Much	5
61	London HLU 9354	Panic Button/Brass Buttons	7
61	London HLU 9394	Should I/Take A Minute	6
61	London HLU 9452	Scottie/Ming Bird	10
62	London HLD 9535	Sunday/Twistwatch	10
62	London HLD 9588	Spinning My Wheels/My Blue Heaven	10
63	London HLD 9652	Mathilda/Replica	10

61	London RE-U 1322	THE STRING-A-LONGS (EP)	40
63	London RE-D 1350	THE STRING-A-LONGS (EP)	40
63	London RE-D 1398	STRINGALONG WITH THE STRING-A-LONGS (EP)	35
63	London HA-D/SH-D 8054	THE STRING-A-LONGS (LP, mono/stereo)	50/60
69	London HAU/SHU 8371	WIDE WORLD HITS (LP)	40

STRING CHEESE
| 72 | RCA SF 8222 | STRING CHEESE (LP) | 20 |

STRING DRIVEN THING
70	Concord CON 7	Another Night/Say What You Like	15
72	Charisma CB 195	Eddie/Hooked On The Road	5
70	Concord CON 1001	STRING DRIVEN THING (LP)	140+
72	Charisma CAS 1062	STRING DRIVEN THING (LP, pink label)	25
73	Charisma CAS 1070	THE MACHINE THAT CRIED (LP, pink label, gatefold sleeve)	18
74	Charisma CAS 1097	PLEASE MIND YOUR HEAD (LP, with lyric sheet)	15
76	Charisma CAS 1112	KEEP YOUR 'AND ON IT (LP)	15

STRIPES OF GLORY
| 62 | Vogue V 9194 | The Denial/O' Send The Fire | 18 |

SYLVIA STRIPLIN
| 86 | Music Of Love MOLS 8 | Give Me Your Love/Give Me Your Love (Version) (12") | 25 |

STROKES
01	Rough Trade RTRADES 010	The Modern Age/Last Night (p/s, 2000 only)	30
01	Rough Trade RTRADESCD 010	The Modern Age/Last Night/Barely Legal (CD, card sleeve)	10
01	Rough Trade RTRADES 023	Hard To Explain/New York City Cops (p/s, 2000 only)	8
01	Rough Trade RTRADESCD 0041	Last Nite/When It Started (CD, withdrawn)	8
02	Rough Trade RTRADES 063	Someday/Alone Together/Is This It (p/s, yellow vinyl)	12

STROLLERS
| 58 | Vogue V 9113 | Jumping With Symphony Sid/Swinging Yellow Rose Of Texas (78 rpm = £22) | 35 |
| 58 | Vogue V 9124 | Little Bitty Pretty One/Flute Cha-Lypso (78 rpm = £38) | 35 |

STROLLERS
| 61 | London HLL 9336 | Come On Over/There's No One But You | 50 |

BARRETT STRONG
| 60 | London HLU 9088 | Money (That's What I Want)/Oh I Apologise | 175 |
| 76 | Capitol CL 15864 | Man Up In The Sky/Gonna Make It Right | 40 |

CHAD STUART & JEREMY CLYDE
(see under Chad & Jeremy)

GLEN STUART
| 60s | Honey Hit TB 126 | Make Me An Angel/Walking To Heaven (some with p/s) | 10/6 |

GLEN STUART & CLANSMEN
| 59 | Pye 7N 15232 | Weepy Willow/Della Darling (78 rpm = £7) | 5 |

KARL STUART & PROFILES
| 65 | Mercury MF 870 | Love Of My Eyes/Not A Girl In A Million | 5 |
| 65 | Mercury MF 875 | Haven't They Got Better Things To Do/The Touch Of Your Hand | 5 |
(see also Profile, Voice)

MIKE STUART SPAN
(see under 'M')

NAT STUCKEY
67	Pye International 7N 25403	Sweet Thang/Paralyze My Mind	6
69	RCA RCA 1833	Loving You/Joe And Mabel's 12th Street Bar And Grill	5
69	RCA RCA 1890	Cut Across Shorty/Understand, Little Man	5

STUD
| 70 | Deram SML-R 1084 | STUD (LP) | 50 |
(see also Taste, Family, Blossom Toes, Eric Burdon & Animals)

STUDS
| 92 | Rehouse REH 1 | Forwards and Backwards/Indecisive Gunslinger | 6 |
| 93 | Rehouse REH 1-12 | Seige under Water/Blood Thong | 6 |

STUDIO ONE ALLSTARS
| 67 | Island WI 3038 | Sherry (actually by Bumps Oakley)/Out Of My Mind (actually by Soul Junior) | 25 |

STUDIO SIX
66	Polydor 56131	When I See My Baby/Don't Tell Lies	10
67	Polydor 56162	Bless My Soul (I've Been And Gone And Done It)/People Say	10
67	Polydor 56189	Times Were When/I Can't Sleep	10
67	Polydor 56219	Strawberry Window/Falling Leaves	35
69	Polydor 56361	Bless My Soul/People Say	10

STUDIO SWEETHEARTS
| 79 | DJM DJS 10915 | I Believe/It Isn't Me (p/s) | 20 |
(see also Cult, Slaughter & Dogs)

STUKAS
| 77 | Sonet SON 2134 | I Like Sport/I'll Send You A Postcard/Dead Lazy (p/s) | 8 |
| 77 | Chiswick NS 21 | Klean Living Kids/Oh Little Girl (p/s) | 10 |

STUMP
| 88 | Ensign CHEN 9 | A FIERCE PANCAKE (LP, with inner lyric sleeve) | 12 |

STUPIDS
| 85 | Children Of Rev. COR 3 | VIOLENT NUN (EP, some mispressed) | 6 |

STYLE COUNCIL

83	Polydor TSCX 2	Money-Go-Round/ Money-Go-Round (Dance Mix) (12", white label, promo)	8
85	Polydor TSDJ 8	Walls Come Tumbling Down! (censored)/The Whole Point II/Blood Sports (12", no p/s, promo only)	8
85	Polydor TSCG 9	Come To Milton Keynes/(When You) Call Me (alternate gatefold p/s)	5
85	Polydor TSC DP 10	The Lodgers (re-recorded)/You're The Best Thing (live)/Big Boss Groove (live)/ You're The Best Thing/Long Hot Summer (stickered, shrinkwrapped double pack)	5
86	Polydor CINE 1/CINEC 1	Have You Ever Had It Blue/Mr. Cool's Dream//Have You Ever Had It Blue/ Uncut Version/With Everything To Lose (live in London) (p/s, with free cassette & insert in printed PVC sleeve)	6
87	Polydor TSCSX 14	Wanted/Cost Of Loving (Instrumental)/Cost Of Loving (Vocal) (12", p/s)	8
87	Polydor TSCCD 14	Wanted/Cost Of Loving (Instrumental)/Cost Of Loving (Vocal) (CD, card p/s)	10
87	Polydor TSCCD 101	CAFE BLUE (CD EP, card sleeve)	10
87	Polydor TSCEP 2	THE BIRDS & THE B's (EP, p/s)	5
87	Polydor TSCCD 102	THE BIRDS & THE B's (CD EP, card sleeve)	10
87	Polydor TSCEP 3	MICK TALBOT IS AGENT '88 (EP, p/s)	5
88	Polydor TSCCD 15	Life At A Top People's Health Farm (7" Version)/Spank! (Life At A Top People's Health Club)/Sweet Loving Ways/Life At A Top People's Health Farm (Um & Argh Mix) (CD, card sleeve)	10
88	Polydor TSCCD 16	1-2-3-4 EP: How She Threw It All Away/Love The First Time/ Long Hot Summer (Tom Mix)/I Do Like To Be B-Side The A-Side (CD)	8
88	Polydor 080 400-2	1-2-3-4 EP: How She Threw It All Away/Love The First Time/ Long Hot Summer (Tom Mix)/How She Threw It All Away (Video) (CD Video)	12
88	Polydor 080 336-2	Have You Ever Had It Blue (Uncut Version)/Mr. Cool's Dream/With Everything To Lose (live in London)/Have You Ever Had It Blue (Video) (CD Video)	12
88	Polydor 080 206-2	Long Hot Summer (Extended Version)/Party Chambers/The Paris Match/ Le Depart/Long Hot Summer (Video) (CD Video)	12
88	Polydor 080 560-2	Life At A Top People's Health Farm (Extended Remix)/Spank! (Life At A Top People's Health Club)/Sweet Loving Ways/Life At A Top People's Health Farm (7" Version) (Video) (CD Video)	12
89	Polydor TSCB 17	Promised Land (Juan Atkins Mix)/Can You Still Love Me (stickered box set, with numbered 7" & poster)	5
89	Polydor TSC XS 17	Promised Land (Joe Smooth's Alternate Club Mix)/Can You Still Love Me (Club Vocal)/Can You Still Love Me (12 O'clock Dub) (12", orange p/s)	8
89	Polydor TSCCD 17	The Promised Land (Longer Version Juan Atkins Mix)/(Pianopella)/ Can You Still Love Me? (Dub)/(Vocal) (CD)	8
89	Polydor TSCD 17	The Promised Land (Radio Edit)/The Promised Land (Longer Version)/ Can You Still Love Me? (Vocal)/Can You Still Love Me? (Dub) (CD)	8
89	Polydor LHSCD 1	Long Hot Summer '89 Mix/Everybody's On The Run (Version One)/ Everybody's On The Run (Version Two) (CD)	8
84	Lyntone LYN 15344/45	It Just Came To Pieces In My Hands (Coventry)/Speak Like A Child (London) (33rpm fan club flexidisc)	10
87	Polydor COST 2	Angel/Heaven's Above (12", promo only)	10
87	Polydor TSCLP 4	THE COST OF LOVING (LP, single disc)	12
87	Polydor 831 443-2	THE COST OF LOVING (CD)	15
88	Polydor TSCIN 1	INTERVIEW WITH THE STYLE COUNCIL (LP, promo only)	40
98	Polydor TSCLP 6 (/2)	MODERNISM: A NEW DECADE (LP or 2 x 12", both in p/s, promo only)	each 90

(see also Council Collective, Paul Weller, Jam, Merton Parkas, King Truman)

STYLOS
64	Liberty LBS 10173	Head Over Heels/Bye Bye, Baby, Bye Bye	120

POLY STYRENE
80	United Artists BP 370	Talk In Toytown/Sub Tropical (p/s)	5
80	United Artists UAG 30320	TRANSLUCENCE (LP, with lyric inner)	12

(see also X-Ray Spex, Mari Elliott)

STYX
75	RCA RCA 2518	Lady/Children Of The Land	5
78	A&M AMS 7388	Blue Collar Man/Superstars (12", coloured vinyl)	8
79	A&M AMS 7446	Renegade/Sing For The Day (p/s, red vinyl)	5
81	A&M AMS 8102	The Best Of Times/Light (p/s, laser etched)	5
81	A&M AMS 8118	Too Much Time On My Hands/Queen Of Spades (p/s, coloured vinyl)	5
83	A&M AM 120	Don't Let It End/Rockin' The Paradise (shaped picture disc)	6
78	A&M AMLH 64724	PIECES OF EIGHT (LP, translucent vinyl)	12

SUBHUMANS
81	Spiderleg SDL 3	Religious Wars/Love Is.../Work Experience/It's Gonna Get Worse (p/s)	8
82	Spiderleg SPIDL 5	Big City/Reason For Existence/Cancer/Peroxide (p/s)	7

SUBMARINER
93	Spacewatch FLX 2107	Lyricist Downer/Seeming And The Meaning (demo)/STEREOLAB: Ronco Symphony (demo) (clear vinyl flexi with paper strip insert)	25

SUBMARINES
87	Head HEAD 4	Grey Skies Blue/I Saw The Children (p/s)	6

SUBS
78	Stiff OFF 1	Gimme Your Heart/Party Clothes (p/s)	5

(see also Larry Wallis)

SUBSTITUTE
79	Ignition IR 2	The One/Look Sharp (some in p/s)	35/20

(see also Vibrators)

SUB SUB
90s	Ten Records Ltd. TENX 373	Space Face/Ecto-Jam-Sub (12", die-cut sleeve)	45
90s	Robs Records 12ROB 07	Coast/Inside Of This/Past/Inside Out (12", p/s)	12
90s	Robs Records 7ROB 9	Ain't No Love/Parkside Mix (p/s)	5
90s	Robs Records 12ROB 9	Ain't No Love (Original Mix)/(Parkside Mix)/(Parkside Raw Dub) (12", die-cut p/s)	8

90s	Robs Records 12ROB 09R	Ain't No Love (On The Floor)/(On The House)/(On Yer Face) (12", die-cut p/s)	8
90s	Robs Records CDROB 9	Ain't No Love (Radio Edit)/(Original Mix)/(Parkside Mix)/(On The House Mix) (CD)	10
90s	Robs Records 7ROB 19	Respect (Radio Edit)/(Dasliva-McCready Mix)	8
90s	Robs Records 12ROB 19	Respect (Original Mix)/(Dasliva-McCready Mix)/(Dasliva's Acid Dub) (12", p/s)	8
90s	Robs Records CDROB 19	Respect (Edit)/(Original Mix)/(Dasliva-McCready Mix)/(Dasliva's Acid Dub)/(Primetime Mix) (CD)	8
90s	Robs Records 12ROB 29	Angel (Original Mix)/(Primetime Mix)/Senna/Southern Trees (Instrumental) (12", p/s)	8
90s	Robs Records 12ROB 29X	Angel (Primetime Dub)/(Deep Love Mix)/(Deep Love Instrumental)/(Pegasus Retro Mix) (12", p/s)	8
90s	Robs Records CDROB 29	Angel (Original Edit)/(Deep Love Mix)/(Primetime Mix)/Southern Trees (Inst.) (CD)	8
90s	Robs Records 12ROB 39	Southern Trees/Jaggernath/Northern Trees (12", p/s)	8
90s	Robs Records CDROB 39	Southern Trees (7" Mix)/Jaggernath/Northern Trees (CD)	10
90s	Robs Records 12ROB 51	Smoking Beagles/Crunch/(Instrumental Version) (12", custom stickered p/s)	8
90s	Robs Records 12ROB 53	This Time I'm Not Wrong/Heads Will Roll (Instrumental Demo)/Firesuite (12", p/s)	8
90s	Robs Records CDROB 53	This Time I'm Not Wrong (Edit)/This Time I'm Not Wrong/Heads Will Roll (Instrumental Demo)/Firesuite (CD)	8
90s	Robs Records CDROB 30	FULL FATHOM FIVE (CD)	18

(see also Doves)

SUBTERRANEANS

87	Mother MUM 6	Slum/Maxi Joy (p/s)	5
87	Mother 12MUM 6	Slum/Maxi Joy/Head For The Light (12", p/s)	8

SUBURBAN STUDS

77	Pogo POG 001/LYN 44845	No Faith/Questions (no p/s, 'with horns' version)	15
77	Pogo POG 001/LYN 44845	No Faith/Questions (p/s)	6
78	Pogo POG 002	I Hate School/Young Power (p/s)	6
78	Pogo POW 001	SLAM (LP)	20

SUBWAYS

03	Bus Stop BS0502	No Heart, No Soul/We Get Around/Young For Eternity (live) (CD)	35
04	Private Pressing	DEMO (CD, sold at gigs, p/s)	60
04	Transgressive 58241H1	I Am/I Want To Hear What You Gotta Say/You Got Me (500 only, p/s)	25
05	Infectious WEA384	Oh Yeah/I Am Young (white vinyl, p/s)	8

SUBWAY SECT

78	Braik BRS 01	Nobody's Scared/Don't Split It (p/s)	12
79	Rough Trade RT 007	Ambition/A Different Story (initially in yellow text p/s, later orange text p/s)	7/6

(see also Vic Godard [& Subway Sect])

NIKKI SUDDEN

81	Rather GEAR 11	Back To The Start/Ringing On My Train (p/s)	5
82	Abstract ABS 009	Channel Steamer/Chelsea Embankment (p/s)	5
80s	Rather RATHER 10	BEAU GESTE (cassette, with insert)	12
85	Hotwire HWLP 8504	THE LAST BANDITS IN THE WORLD (LP)	12

(see also Swell Maps, Last Bandits, Jeremy Gluck)

(A) SUDDEN SWAY

80	Chant CHANT 1	Jane's Third Party/Don't Go (p/s, as A Sudden Sway)	15
80	own label	Jane's Third Party/Don't Go (cassette, as A Sudden Sway)	8
81	Chant CHANT 2/EJSP 9692	TO YOU, WITH REGARD (12" EP, with insert)	20
84	Chant CHANT 3	The Traffic Tax Scheme (12" with badge & inserts in folder)	12
86	WEA BYN 8B	Spacemate (2 x 12" box set with stickers, info sheets, 2 booklets & poster)	12
87	Strange Fruit SFPSC 005	PEEL SESSION 16.11.83 (EP, cassette)	5

SUE & MARY

62	Decca F 11517	Traitor In Disguise/I Love You	6

SUE & SUNNY

65	Columbia DB 7748	Every Ounce Of Strength/So Remember	10
67	Columbia DB 8099	You Can't By-Pass Love/I Like Your Style	20
68	CBS 3874	Little Black Book/The Show Must Go On	15
68	Island WIP 6043	Set Me Free/NIRVANA ORCHESTRA: City Of The South	10
69	CBS 4567	Let Us Break Bread/Stop Messing About With My Heart	7
70	CBS 4757	You Devil, Cotton-Eyed Joe/Night In The City	7
70	Deram DM 318	Ain't That Telling You People/Didn't I Blow Your Mind	10
71	Deram DM 328	Freedom/Break Up	10
71	Reflection HRS 10	Let Us Break Bread Together/Michael From Mountains	6
72	Deram DM 355	I'm Gonna Make You Love Me/High On The Thought Of You	8
70	CBS 63740	SUE AND SUNNY (LP)	25
70	Reflection REFL 4	SUE AND SUNNY (LP)	30

(see also Sue & Sunshine, Myrtelles, Stockingtops, Brotherhood Of Man)

SUE & SUNSHINE

64	Columbia DB 7409	A Little Love/If You See Me Crying	8
65	Columbia DB 7533	We're In Love/Don't Look Behind	7

(see also Sue & Sunny, Myrtelles, Stockingtops)

SUEDE

91	RML RML 001	Be My God/Art (12", unissued, 250+ white label copies only, no p/s; counterfeits have off-white labels)	100
92	Nude NUD 1 S	The Drowners (Radio Edit)/To The Birds (p/s, 1,000 copies only)	25
92	Nude NUD 1 CD	The Drowners (Radio Edit)/To The Birds/My Insatiable One (CD, promo only)	8
92	Nude NUD 3 T	Metal Mickey/Where Pigs Don't Fly/He's Dead (12", test pressing, plain sleeve)	30
93	Nude SUEDE 1	My Insatiable One (clear flexidisc, fan club/gig freebie)	20
94	Nude NUD 10 S	We Are The Pigs/Killing Of A Flash Boy (numbered gatefold p/s)	5
94	Nude NUD 11 T	The Wild Ones/Eno's Introducing The Band/Asda Town (12", photo insert, p/s)	15
94	Nude NUD 11 CD 2	The Wild Ones/Eno's Introducing The Band/Asda Town (CD)	5
94	Nude NUD 9 T	Stay Together/The Living Dead/My Dark Star (12", numbered gatefold p/s)	20

MINT VALUE £

95	Nude NUD 12 CD 2	New Generation/Animal Nitrate (live)/The Wild Ones (live)/	
		Pantomime Horse (live) (CD, digipak)	15
96	Nude NUD 21S	Trash/Europe Is Our Playground (p/s, mail order only)	12
97	Nude SIS 1 CD	LIVE (CD EP, 6-track fan club-only issue)	20
97	Nude NUD 24 S	Saturday Night/Beautiful Ones (double pack, p/s, mail-order only)	10
97	Nude NUD 30 CD 2	Film Star (live)/Rent (live)/Saturday Night (live) (CD, featuring Neil Tennant)	8
98	Nude SIS 2 CD	IMPLEMENT YEAH! (CD EP, fan club-only issue)	12
98	Nude SUEDE 1 CDF	ON FILM (CD EP, 6-track, promo only)	15
99	Nude NUD 667043	ELECTRICITY EP (minidisc, withdrawn)	15
99	Nude INT 1 CD	HEAD MUSING (CD, 2-track interview, promo only)	15
93	Nude NUDE 1LP	SUEDE (LP, with inner sleeve; some with carrier bag from	
		Chain With No Name stores)	20/15
02	fan club	OBSESSIONS (2-CD, with DVD, fan club issue, in numbered box)	20
02	fan club	POSITIVITY (2-CD, with DVD, fan club issue, in numbered box)	20
	(see also Elastica)		

SUGAR (Simone) & DANDY (Livingstone)

63	Carnival CV 7006	One Man Went To Mow/Cryin'	8
64	Carnival CV 7009	Oh Dear What Can The Matter Be/Tra La La	8
64	Carnival CV 7015	What A Life/Time And Tide	8
64	Carnival CV 7016	I'm Not Crying Now/Blues Got A Hold On Me	8
65	Carnival CV 7023	Let's Ska/Only Heaven Knows	8
65	Carnival CV 7024	I'm Into Something Good/Crazy For You	8
65	Carnival CV 7027	Think Of The Good Times/Girl Come See	8
65	Carnival CV 7029	I Want To Be Your Lover/I Don't Know What I'm Going To Do Now	7
66	Blue Beat BB 367	Meditation (as Jetliners)/GIRL SATCHMO & JET LINERS: Nature Of Love	18
67	Page One POF 044	Let's Ska/Only Heaven Knows	8
64	Carnival CX 1000	THE SKA'S THE LIMIT (LP)	40
67	Page One FOR 006	THE SKA'S THE LIMIT (LP, reissue)	20
	(see also Sugar Simone)		

SUGAR & PEE WEE

58	Vogue Pop V 9112	One, Two, Let's Rock/Just A Few Little Words (78 rpm = £170)	750

SUGAR & SPICE

69	London HLU 10259	Cruel War/Not To Return	6

SUGAR BEARS

72	Philips 6073 812	You Are The One/Someone Like You	5

SUGARBEATS

66	Polydor BM 56069	I Just Stand Here/The Ballad Of Ole Betsy	20
66	Polydor BM 56120	Alice Designs/Sunny Day Girl	18
	(see also Tony Rivers & Castaways)		

SUGARCUBES

87	One Little Indian 7z TP 7	Birthday/Birthday (Icelandic) (p/s)	7
87	One Little Indian 12 TP 7	Birthday/Birthday (Icelandic)/Cat (Icelandic) (12", p/s)	12
87	One Little Indian 7TP 7CD	Birthday/Motorcrash/Cat (Icelandic)/Birthday (Icelandic) (CD)	10
87	One Little Indian L12 TP 9	Cold Sweat (Remix)/Birthday (Original Demo Version)/	
		Dragon (Icelandic)/Traitor (Icelandic) (12", p/s, 5,000 only)	8
87	One Little Indian 7TP 9CD	Cold Sweat/Dragon (Icelandic)/Traitor (Icelandic)/Revolution (CD)	8
88	One Little Indian 10 TP 10	Deus (Remix)/Luftgitar (Icelandic) (with Johnny Triumph/	
		Organic Prankster (10", p/s)	7
88	One Little Indian 7TP 10CD	Deus/Organic Prankster/Luftgitar (12" Version)/Night Of Steel (CD)	18
88	One Little Indian 12TP 11L	BIRTHDAY CHRISTMAS MIX (12" EP, double groove, with Jesus & Mary Chain)	12
88	One L. Indian 12TP 11CDL	BIRTHDAY CHRISTMAS MIX (CD EP, with Jesus & Mary Chain)	8
89	House Of Dolls HOD 010	Dark Disco/HOST: Homelands/MURRUMBRIDGE WHALERS: Giving Away To	
		Trains/SHARK TABOO: Tinsel Town (live) (no p/s, with House Of Dolls mag)	6/4
90	One Little Indian TP BOX 2	7.8 (8 x 7" box set)	25
90	One Little Indian TP BOX 1	12.11 (11 x 12" box set)	40
90	One Little Indian TP BOX 3	CD.6 (6 x CD box set)	45
88	One Little Indian DTPLP 5	LIFE'S TOO GOOD (DAT)	20
89	One Little Indian	HERE TODAY, TOMORROW NEXT WEEK! (LP, silver vinyl, gatefold sleeve	
	TPLP 15SP	with sticker & inner)	20
89	One Little Indian TPLP 15L	SYKURMOLARNIR ILLUR ARFUR! (LP, as Sykurmolarnir, gatefold sleeve)	15
	(see also Björk, Kukl, Ornamental)		

SUGAR LOAF

70	RCA INTS 1113	SOUL STURRING (LP)	60

SUGARLOAF

70	Liberty LBF 15401	Green-Eyed Lady/West Of Tomorrow	12
71	Liberty LBS 83415	SUGARLOAF (LP)	15
74	United Artists UAS 29165	SPACESHIP EARTH (LP)	12
75	Polydor 2310 394	DON'T CALL US, WE'LL CALL YOU (LP, with Jerry Corbetto)	15

SUGAR MINOTT

79	Warrior WAR 124	Never Too Young/DON CARLOS: Hey Little Girl (12")	20
79	United Artists UAG 30310	GIVE THE PEOPLE (LP)	20
79	Island ILPS 9591	BLACK ROOTS (LP)	20

SUGARPLUMS

70	Fab FAB 160	Red River Reggae/Too Much	7

SUGAR SHOPPE

68	Capitol CL 15555	Skip-A-Long Sam/Let The Truth Come Out	20

SUICIDAL TENDENCIES

87	Virgin VS 967-12	Possessed To Skate/Human Guinea Pig/Two Wrongs Don't Make A Right	
		(12", picture disc)	12
88	Virgin VST 1039	Institutionalised/War Inside My Head/Cyco (12", p/s)	15
88	Virgin V 2551	HOW WILL I LAUGH TOMORROW WHEN I CAN'T EVEN SMILE TODAY? (LP)	15

SUICIDE

77	Sound For Industry SFI 323	Johnny/(Real Kids track) (flexidisc via *Circuit* magazine)	8
78	Red Star/Bronze BRO 57	Cheree/I Remember (p/s)	10
78	Red Star/Bronze 12 BRO 57	Cheree/I Remember (12", 'limited edition', p/s)	12
79	Island WIP 6543	Dream Baby Dream/Radiation (p/s)	6
79	Island 12 WIP 6543	Dream Baby Dream (Long Version)/Radiation (12", p/s)	20
86	Demon D 1046	Cheree/I Remember (promo only)	5
89	Chapter 22 12CHAP 36	Rain Of Ruin/Surrender (12")	10
89	Chapter 22 12CHAP 42	SUICIDE (12", unissued)	
77	Red Star/Bronze BRON 508	SUICIDE (LP)	12
78	Red Star FRANKIE 1	24 MINUTES OVER BRUSSELS (LP, official bootleg, 1,000 only, no p/s)	30
80	Ze/Island ILPS 7007	SUICIDE: ALAN VEGA/MARTIN REV (LP, with printed inner sleeve)	14
89	Contempo CONTE 148	HALF ALIVE (LP, clear vinyl, 1,000 only)	12
98	Blast First BFFP 133 1/2	SUICIDE (2-LP)	18
99	Blast First BFFP 162	FIRST REHEARSAL TAPES (2-LP)	15
	(see also Alan Vega, Martin Rev)		

SUICIDE TWINS

86	Lick LICLP 9	SILVER MISSILES AND NIGHTINGALES (LP)	15
	(see also Hanoi Rocks)		

BIG JIM SULLIVAN

61	Decca F 11387	You Don't Know What You've Got/Hot Hiss Of Steam (as Big Jim Sullivan Combo)	12
65	Mercury MF 928	She Walks Through The Fair/Don't Know What I'm Doing (as Jim Sullivan Sound)	25
73	MAM MAM 100	Out Of The Question/Alone Again	6
67	Mercury SML 30001	SITAR BEAT (LP)	40
	(see also Maureeny Wishfull, Brian Bennett, Tiger)		

MAXINE SULLIVAN

54	Parlophone MSP 6086	Boogie Woogie Maxine/Piper In The Glen (with Vic Ash) (78 rpm = £8)	15

PHIL SULLIVAN with LONZO & OSCAR'S PEAPICKERS

59	Melodisc MEL 1512	Love Never Dies/Luckiest Man In Town	5

YMA SUMAC

52	Capitol CL 13746	Suray Surita/Zana (78)	7
52	Capitol CL 13766	Wimoweh/Babalu (78)	7
54	Capitol CL 14094	Ripui (Farewell)/Llulla Mak'ta (Andean Don Juan) (78)	7
55	Parlophone DP 324	La Benita/A Ti Solita Tequiero (export 78)	7
55	Parlophone DP 334	Amor Indo/Un Amor (export 78)	7
55	Capitol EAP1 564	YMA SUMAC MAMBO (EP)	15
55	Capitol EAP2 564	YMA SUMAC MAMBO (EP)	15
57	Capitol EAP1 770	LEGEND OF JIVARO PT. 1 (EP)	15
57	Capitol EAP2 770	LEGEND OF JIVARO PT. 2 (EP)	15
57	Capitol EAP3 770	LEGEND OF JIVARO PT. 3 (EP)	15
53	Capitol LC 6522	VOICE OF THE XTABAY (10" LP)	40
54	Capitol LC 6609	LEGEND OF THE SUN VIRGIN (10" LP)	30
59	Capitol T 1169	FUEGO DEL ANDE (LP)	30
64	Regal REG 2007	VOICE OF THE XTABAY (LP)	20
72	London HLU/SHU 8431	MIRACLES (LP)	25

HUBERT SUMLIN

65	Blue Horizon 45-1000	Across The Board/Sumlin Boogie (99 copies only)	110
	(see also Howlin' Wolf)		

DONNA SUMMER

74	People PEO 115	The Hostage/Let's Work Together Now	15
79	Casablanca SANL 151	Hot Stuff/Journey To The Centre Of Your Heart (12", red vinyl)	15
84	Casablanca FEEL 12	I Feel Love/I Feel Love (Version) (12")	12
87	WEA U 8237P	Dinner With Gershwin (Parts 1 & 2) (12", picture disc)	8
89	WEA U 7780P	This Time I Know It's For Real/Whatever Your Heart Desires (shaped pic disc)	5
89	WEA U 7567CD	I Don't Wanna Get Hurt/Dinner With Gershwin/I Don't Wanna Get Hurt (Instrumental) (3" CD)	8
89	WEA U 7494	Love's About To Change My Heart (Extended Remix)/Love's About To Change My Heart (Instrumental)/Jeremy (3" CD)	8
89	WEA U 7361	When Love Takes Over You (Extended Remix)/When Love Takes Over You (Instrumental)/Bad Reputation (3" CD)	8
	(see also Donna Gaines, John Barry)		

SUMMERHILL

69	Polydor 583 746	SUMMERHILL (LP)	35

ANDY SUMMERS & ROBERT FRIPP

82	A&M (no cat. no.)	Hardy Country/Stultified/Yellow Leader/I Advance Masked (clear flexidisc)	6
	(see also Police, King Crimson)		

BOB(BY) SUMMERS

59	Capitol CL 15063	Rattle Rhythm/Excitement (as Bob Summers)	15
60	Capitol CL 15130	Little Brown Jug/Twelfth Street Rag (as Bobby Summers)	8

SUMMER SET

66	Columbia DB 8004	Farmer's Daughter/Papa-Oom-Mow-Mow	35
66	Columbia DB 8004	Farmer's Daughter/What Are You Gonna Do (2nd issue with different B-side)	30
67	Columbia DB 8215	Overnight Changes/It's A Dream	70
	(see also Candy Choir)		

SUMMERTAIRES

66	Ska Beat JB 258	My Heart Cries Out/SOUL BROTHERS: James Bond Girl	40
	(see also Jackie Mittoo, Soul Agents)		

MINT VALUE £

SUMMER WINE
72	Philips 6006 217	Why Do Fools Fall In Love/Ode To Steel Guitar	5
72	Philips 6006 238	Take A Load Off Your Feet/ Sound Of Summer's Over	5

(see also Tony Rivers, John Perry)

SUN
78	Capitol EMC 3262	LIVE ON DREAM ON (LP)	12

SUN ALSO RISES
70	Village Thing VTS 2	THE SUN ALSO RISES (LP)	20

SUN & MOON
88	Geffen GEF 39	The Speed Of Life/Death Of Imagination (p/s)	5
88	Geffen GEF 39T	The Speed Of Life/Death Of Imagination/The Boy Who Sees Everything/ I Love You, You Bastard (12", p/s)	8
89	Midnight DONG 44CD	ALIVE; NOT DEAD (CD EP)	15
89	Geffen 9241 882	THE SUN AND THE MOON (CD)	25

(see also Chameleons)

SUNDAE TIMES
68	President PT 203	Baby Don't Cry/Aba-Aba	5
68	President PT 219	Jack Boy/I Don't Want Nobody	5
70	President PT 285	Live Today/Take Me Higher Baby	5
70	Joy JOYS 159	US COLOURED KIDS (LP)	20

SUNDANCE
73	Decca F 13423	Coming Down/Eagles	5
73	Decca F 13461	Stand By/Willie The Gambler	5
74	Decca F 13494	Loving You/Can You Feel It	5
73	Decca TXS 111	RAIN STEAM SPEED (LP, with insert)	18
74	Decca SKL 5183	CHUFFER (LP)	18

SUNDAY AFTERNOONS
70s	Longman	SUNDAY AFTERNOONS (LP)	90

SUNDAYS
89	Rough Trade RTX 218	Can't Be Sure/I Kicked A Boy (export issue, brown p/s)	6
89	Rough Trade RTTX 218	Can't Be Sure/I Kicked A Boy/Don't Tell Your Mother (12", export issue, brown p/s)	10
89	Rough Trade RTT 218CD	Can't Be Sure/I Kicked A Boy/Don't Tell Your Mother (3" CD, card sleeve)	8
90	Catalogue CAT 076	I Won (square flexidisc with *The Catalogue* magazine)	10
97	Parlophone CDR 6475	Summertime/Nothing Sweet/Gone (CD)	8
90	Rough Trade ROUGH 148P	READING, WRITING AND ARITHMETIC (LP, picture disc, stickered sleeve)	20

SUNDAY SING TRIO
70s	Sharon SHLP 1221	ONE OF THESE DAYS (LP)	15

SUN DIAL
90	UFO 45 001T	Exploding In Your Mind/Otherside/Slow Motion (12", 1-sided, p/s)	10
91	Tangerine TANGERINE 111	Exploding In Your Mind (Colour Mix)/Otherside/Slow Motion (12", unreleased, 80 white label test pressings only)	30
91	UFO PF 2	Fireball/Only A Northern Song ('Pre-Flight' 7", promo only)	20
91	UFO UFO 45002 T	OVERSPILL EP (12", orange vinyl)	10
92	UFO UFO 45008 T	FAZER EP (12")	10
90	Tangerine MM 07	OTHER WAY OUT (LP, with insert, some signed in silver ink)	20/30
91	UFO UFO 1LP	OTHER WAY OUT (LP, reissue in gatefold sleeve)	12
92	UFO UFO 8	REFLECTER (LP, clear vinyl)	15
94	Acme AC 8001	RETURN JOURNEY (LP, official bootleg; 200 promos with inserts, 500 numbered commercial copies)	20/12
95	Acme AC 8011LP	ACID YANTRA (LP, gatefold sleeve)	12

(see also Modern Art, Spiral Sky, Quad)

SUNDOWNERS
63	Piccadilly 7N 35142	Baby Baby/House Of The Rising Sun	6
64	Piccadilly 7N 35162	Come On In/Shot Of Rhythm And Blues	6
65	Parlophone R 5243	Where Am I/Gonna Make The Future Bright	6
68	Columbia DB 8339	Dr. J. Wallace-Brown/Love Is In The Air	6
68	Spark SRL 1016	Gloria The Bosom Show/Don't Look Back	6

SUNDOWN PLAYBOYS
72	Apple APPLE 44	Saturday Nite Special/Valse De Soleil Couche (some in p/s)	30/10
72	Apple APPLE 44	Saturday Nite Special/Valse De Soleil Couche (10", 78rpm, pink-patterned die-cut sleeve)	225

SUNDRAGON
68	MGM MGM 1380	Green Tambourine/I Need All The Friends I Can Get	5
68	MGM MGM 1391	Blueberry Blue/Far Away Mountain	20
68	MGM MGM 1458	Five White Horses/Look At The Sun	20
68	MGM MGM-C(S) 8090	GREEN TAMBOURINE (LP)	70

(see also Sands, Others)

SUNFIGHTER
76	EMI EMI 2493	Drag Race Queen/Riding On Your Star	12
76	EMI EMI 2553	Such A Lovely Night/Don't Get Me Wrong	10

(see also Chris Rainbow)

SUNFOREST
70	Deram Nova (S)DN 7	SOUND OF SUNFOREST (LP, mono/stereo)	each 110

SUNNY & HI-JUMPERS
65	Carnival CV 7022	Tarry Till You're Better/Dance Til You're Better	6
65	Carnival CV 7025	Going To Damascus/Sweet Potatoes	6

SUNNY & THE SUNGLOWS/SUNLINERS
63	London HL 9792	Talk To Me (as Sunny & the Sunglows)/Every Week, Every Month, Every Year (as Sunny & the Sunliners)	25

SUNNYLAND SLIM
65	'77' LA 12-23	CHICAGO BLUES SESSION (LP, with Little Brother Montgomery)	35
65	Storyville SLP 169	I DONE YOU WRONG (LP)	25
68	Storyville 670 169	PORTRAITS IN BLUES (LP, reissue of SLP 169)	20
69	Liberty LBS 83237	SLIM'S GOT THIS THING GOIN' ON (LP)	25
69	Blue Horizon 7-63213	MIDNIGHT JUMP (LP)	65
74	Sonet SNTF 671	THE LEGACY OF THE BLUES VOL. II (LP)	12

SUNNYSIDERS
55	London HL 8135	Hey! Mr. Banjo/Zoom, Zoom, Zoom.	50
55	London HL 8160	Oh Me Oh My Oh/(Let's Gather Round) The Parlour Piano	30
55	London HLU 8180	Banjo Woogie/She Didn't Even Say Goodbye	30
55	London HLU 8202	I Love You Fair Dinkum/Stay On The Sunny Side	25
56	London HLU 8246	Doesn't He Love Me/Humdinger (78 rpm = £6)	30

SUNN0))) (correct spelling!)
04	Anti-Mosh (no. cat. No.)	Candlewolf Of The Golden Chalice (12")	20

SUN RA ARKESTRA
74	Decca F 13542	Don't Go/Can We Change.	30
82	Y 1 RA	NUCLEAR WAR (12" EP)	35
69	Fontana STL 5514	HELIOCENTRIC WORLDS VOL. 1 (LP)	40
69	Fontana STL 5499	HELIOCENTRIC WORLDS VOL. 2 (LP)	40
60s	Sonet 23 SPL	JAZZ BY SUN RA (LP)	30
71	Black Lion BLP 30103	PICTURES OF INFINITY — IN CONCERT (LP)	20
71	Byg 529 341	THE SOLAR MYTH APPROACH VOL. 2 (LP)	25
	Polydor 2460 106	PICTURES OF INFINITY (LP)	25
78	Affinity AFF 10	S-M APPROACH (LP, with Solar-Myth Ark).	15
79	Cobra COB 37001	FATE IN A PLEASANT MOOD (LP)	18
	Y Y 19	STRANGE CELESTIAL ROAD (LP)	15
	Recommended 11 RRA	NIGHTS DE LA FONDATION MAEGHT VOL. 1 (LP, with insert)	15

SUN RA & MYTH SCIENCE ARKESTRA
90	Blast First BFFP 60	SUN RA & MYTH SCIENCE ARKESTRA (3 x 10", box set, with insert)	35

SUNRAYS
65	Capitol CL 15416	I Live For The Sun/Bye, Baby, Bye	12
66	Capitol CL 15433	Andrea/You Don't Phase Me	12

SUNRISE
76	Grapevine GRA 105	BEFORE MY EYES (LP)	30

SUNSET BOYS
79	Gimp GIM 1234	Wreck My Bed/Tutti Frutti/Copy Cat (Blues)/Wreck My Bed (Hippy Version) (p/s).	5
	(see also Maxim's Trash)		

SUN SET
67	Polydor BM 56193	East Baby/You Can Ride My Rainbow	10

SUNSETS
61	Ember EMB S 125	Cry Of The Wild Goose/Manhunt.	15

SUNSHINE
72	Warner Brothers K 46169	SUNSHINE (LP)	12
	(see also Pretty Things)		

MONTY SUNSHINE
61	Columbia SEG 8059	MONTY (EP)	8
61	Columbia SEG 8127	SUNSHINE (EP)	8
63	London RE-R 1368	GONNA BUILD A MOUNTAIN (EP, with His Band)	8
63	London HAR 8037	MONTY SUNSHINE AND HIS BAND (LP, also stereo [SHR 8037])	each 12
64	London HAR 8158	BLACK MOONLIGHT & SUNSHINE (LP, also stereo [SHR 8158])	each 12
	(see also Lonnie Donegan)		

MR. SUNSHINE
56	MGM SP 1160	Along The China Coast/MRS. SUNSHINE: Two Car Garage.	7

SUNSHINE COMPANY
67	Liberty LBF 15008	Happy/Blue May	10
67	Liberty LBF 15034	Back On The Street Again/A Year Of Janie's Time	8
68	Liberty LBF 15060	Look Here Comes The Sun/It's Sunday	7
68	Liberty LBF 15149	On A Beautiful Day/To Put Up With You	8
68	Liberty LBL/LBS 83120	THE SUNSHINE COMPANY (LP)	30
69	Liberty LBL/LBS 83159	SUNSHINE AND SHADOWS (LP)	30

SUNSPOTS
63	Decca F 11672	Paella/Vancouver.	7

SUNSTROKE
78	Hot Stuff HS 004	SUNSTROKE (EP)	5

SUNTREADER
73	Island HELP 13	ZIN ZIN (LP)	12

SUPERBOYS
68	Giant GN 22	Ain't That A Shame/Do It Right Now	8
68	Giant GN 31	You're Hurtin' Me/Funky Soul	8
	(see also Dandy & Superboys, Little Sal)		

SUPERCHUNK
93	Domino RUG 9	Ribbon/Who Needs Light (p/s).	6

SUPER 8

95	García POUM 001	Billy The Kid/It Doesn't Matter/How Can I Understand The Flies? ('hairloss' p/s, 500 only, 37 sold, 35 returned for refund, the rest believed burned)	25

(see also Sheds)

SUPER FURRY ANIMALS

95	SFAP1	Frisbee (12" promo, 1-sided, unreleased intended debut single. Own label)	28
96	Creation CRE 222	Hometown Unicorn/Don't Be A Fool Billy (p/s)	12
96	Creation CRESCD 231	God! Show Me Magic/Death By Melody/Dim Bendith (CD, picture disc)	8
96	Creation CRESCD 235	Something For The Weekend/Waiting To Happen/Arnofio (Glo In The Dark) (CD)	8
96	Creation CRESCD 235	Something 4 The Weekend/Waiting To Happen (p/s)	9
96	Creation CRE 247	The Man Don't Give A Fuck (p/s, 1-sided, blue vinyl)	15
96	Creation CRE 247 T	The Man Don't Give A Fuck/(Howard Marks Mix)/(Wishmountain Mix)/ (Darren Price Mix) (12", p/s)	20
96	Creation CRESCD 247	The Man Don't Give A Fuck/(Howard Marks Mix)/(Wishmountain Mix) (CD, picture disc)	20
96	Creation CTP 229	The Man Don't Give A Fuck/Dim Brys Dim Chwys (12" 1-sided promo)	14
96	Debiel SS 01	(Nid) Hon Yw'r Gan Sy'n Mynd I Achub Yr Laith (1-sided gig freebie)	12
97	Creation CRE 275	Play It Cool/Pass The Time (fold out poster sleeve)	8
97	Creation CRE 283	Demons/Hit And Run (fold out poster sleeve)	8
98	Creation CRE 288	Ice Hockey Hair/Smokin' (stickered p/s, limited edition)	10
99	Creation CTP 323X	Wherever I Lay My Phone (That's My Home) (12" promo, p/s)	10
00	Placid Casual PLC02	Ysbediau Heulog/Charge (White vinyl in pvc sleeve, 3000 only)	7
03	Epic 6739067	Golden Retriever/Summer Snow/Blue Fruit (picture disc, limited edition, numbered, stickered poly sleeve)	12
04	Placid Casual PLC08EP	Slow Life/Motherfokker/Lost Control (CD promo, 'floppy disc' sleeve)	8
95	Ankst ANKST 057	LLANFAIRPWLLGWYNGYLLGOGERYCHWYRNDROBWLLANTYSILIO-GOGOGOCHYNYGOFOD (IN SPACE) (EP) (1st issue/2nd issue, same cat. no)	15/10
95	Ankst ANKST 057	LLANFAIRPWLLGWYNGYLLGOGERYCHWYRNDROBWLLANTYSILIO-GOGOGOCHYNYGOFOD (IN SPACE) (EP) (CD, 1st issue/2nd issue, same cat no)	20/18
95	Ankst ANKST 62	MOOG DROOG EP (EP, 1st issue/2nd issue, same cat. no, p/s)	15/10
95	Ankst ANKST 62	MOOG DROOG EP (CD, 1st issue/2nd issue, same cat. no)	20/18
96	Creation CRELP 190	FUZZY LOGIC (LP, with insert)	20
97	Creation CRELP 214	RADIATOR (2 x LP)	18
98	Creation CRECD 229 L	OUT SPACED (CD, rubber pack [black, green yellow])	18
99	Creation CRELP 242	GUERRILLA (LP, gatefold, pop up sleeve)	12
00	Placid Casual PLC03LP	MWNG (LP, ltd white vinyl, p/s, PVC sleeve, 2000 copies)	15
03	Epic 5123751	PHANTOM POWER (2 x LP etched vinyl with insert) packaging. 3000 copies) (Price for sealed/opened)	15
04	Placid Casual PLo7CD	PHANTOM PHORCE (2 x LP ltd version with bonus 'Slow Life' EP disc, fold-out packaging. 3000 copies) (Price for sealed/opened)	35/25
05	Epic 5176711	SONGBOOK – THE SINGLES VOLUME ONE (2 x 12" pop up gatefold sleeve)	20

SUPERGRASS

94	Backbeat (no cat. no.)	Caught By The Fuzz/Strange Ones (hand-stamped labels, 1,000 only, later re-pressed)	22
94	Backbeat (no cat. no.)	Mansize Rooster/Sitting Up Straight (luminous green vinyl, printed green cardboard or plain die-cut sleeve, 500 only)	25/15
94	Backbeat (no cat. no.)	Mansize Rooster/Sitting Up Straight (marbled green vinyl, plain sleeve)	8
94	Parlophone R 6396	Caught By The Fuzz/Strange Ones (p/s, reissue)	15
94	Parlophone 12R 6396DJ	Caught By The Fuzz/Strange Ones (12", p/s, promo only)	12
94	Parlophone CDR 6396	Caught By The Fuzz/Strange Ones/Caught By The Fuzz (Acoustic) (CD)	10
95	Parlophone R 6402	Mansize Rooster/Sitting Up Straight (p/s, red vinyl)	10
95	Parlophone CDR 6402	Mansize Rooster/Sitting Up Straight/Odd (CD)	8
95	Parlophone RS 6410	Lenny/Wait For The Sun (p/s, light blue vinyl)	7
95	Parlophone GRASS 2	Sofa (Of My Lethargy) (Radio Edit)/(Album Version) (CD, promo only, card p/s)	8
96	Parlophone R 6428	Going Out/Melanie Davis (p/s, burgundy vinyl)	7
97	Parlophone R 6461	Richard III/Nothing More's Gonna Get In My Way (p/s, yellow vinyl)	7
97	Parlophone R 6469	Sun Hits The Sky/Some Girls Are Bigger Than Others (numbered p/s, white vinyl)	7
97	Parlophone 12RDJ 6469	Sun Hits The Sky (Bentley Rhythm Ace Sun Hits The Sky Mix) (12", no p/s, promo only)	12
99	EMI CDIN 125	INTERVIEW (CD, tri-fold digipak, promo only)	15
99	Parlophone R 6531	Mary/(Live Version) (p/s, silver vinyl)	7
02	Parlophone R 6583	Never Done Nothing Like That Before (1-sided, stamped white label, die-cut black sleeve with barcode sticker, 1,500 only)	10
97	Parlophone GRASS 9497	THE SINGLES 1994-1997 (8 x 7" black vinyl, 'grass'-covered box set, with signed & numbered insert, promo only)	60
95	Parlophone PCSX 7373	I SHOULD COCO (LP, with inner & bonus single "Stone Free"/"Odd?" [PCSS 7373])	30

(see also Jennifers)

SUPERMATIX

81	MC 4	BAD TIMING EP (p/s)	6

SUPER$HIT666

00	Infernal INFERNAL003LP	SUPER$HIT666 (10" LP, with inner sleeve, purple or black vinyl)	10

(see also Backyard Babies, Hellacopters, Wildhearts)

SUPERSISTER

72	Polydor 2001 379	No Tree Will Grow/She Was Naked	12
71	Dandelion 2310 146	TO THE HIGHEST BIDDER (LP, gatefold sleeve)	25
71	Polydor 2419 030	SUPER STARSHINE 3 (LP)	20
72	Polydor 2419 061	PRESENT FROM NANCY (LP)	15
73	Polydor 2480 153	PUDDING & YESTERDAY (LP)	25
73	Polydor 2925 021	ISKANDER (LP, gatefold sleeve with lyric sheet)	12

SUPERSONICS

53	London L 1197	New Guitar Boogie Shuffle/The Sheik Of Araby (78)	15
54	London HL 8022	Cherokee/Linger Awhile (B-side with Arlene James) (78)	15

SUPERTONES
70	Banana BA 312	Freedom Blues/First Time I Met You	12

(see also Jackie Mittoo)

SUPPORTERS
70	RCA 1972	Sing Your Own Team/On The Ball	30

(DIANA ROSS &) SUPREMES
SINGLES
64	Stateside SS 257	When The Lovelight Starts Shining Thru' His Eyes/ Standing At The Crossroads Of Love (DJ copy = £100)	50
64	Stateside SS 327	Where Did Our Love Go/He Means The World To Me (DJ copy = £100)	10
64	Stateside SS 350	Baby Love/Ask Any Girl (DJ copy = £100)	10
65	Stateside SS 376	Come See About Me/(You're Gone But) Always In My Heart (DJ copy = £100)	15
65	Tamla Motown TMG 501	Stop! In The Name Of Love/I'm In Love Again (DJ copy = £100)	15
65	Tamla Motown TMG 516	Back In My Arms Again/Whisper You Love Me Boy (DJ copy = £85)	20
65	Tamla Motown TMG 527	Nothing But Heartaches/He Holds His Own (DJ copy = £85)	18
65	Tamla Motown TMG 543	I Hear A Symphony/Who Could Ever Doubt My Love (DJ copy = £75)	15
66	Tamla Motown TMG 548	My World Is Empty Without You/Everything Is Good About You (DJ copy = £75)	15
66	Tamla Motown TMG 560	Love Is Like An Itching In My Heart/He's All I Got (DJ copy = £150)	40
66	Tamla Motown TMG 575	You Can't Hurry Love/Put Yourself In My Place (DJ copy = £70)	10
66	Tamla Motown TMG 585	You Keep Me Hangin' On/Remove This Doubt (DJ copy = £60)	10
67	Tamla Motown TMG 597	Love Is Here And Now You're Gone/There's No Stopping Us Now (DJ copy = £70)	10
67	Tamla Motown TMG 607	The Happening/All I Know About You (DJ copy = £75)	10

(The singles listed above are credited to Supremes.)

67	Tamla Motown TMG 616	Reflections/Going Down For The Third Time (DJ copy = £60)	10
67	Tamla Motown TMG 632	In And Out Of Love/I Guess I'll Always Love You (DJ copy = £40)	8
68	Tamla Motown TMG 650	Forever Came Today/Time Changes Things (DJ copy = £40)	8
68	Tamla Motown TMG 662	Some Things You Never Get Used To/You've Been So Wonderful To Me (DJ = £40)	8
68	Tamla Motown TMG 677	Love Child/Will This Be The Day? (DJ copy = £40)	8
68	Tamla Motown PSRS 317	Love Child (special Royal Command Performance promo sent to journalists with Ken East 'talking invite' as edit of Love Child plays in the background)	40+
69	Tamla Motown TMG 695	I'm Living In Shame/I'm So Glad I Got Somebody (Like You Around) (DJ copy = £40)	8
69	Tamla Motown TMG 704	No Matter What Sign You Are/The Young Folks (DJ copy = £40)	8
69	Tamla Motown TMG 721	Someday We'll Be Together/He's My Sunny Boy (DJ copy = £35)	8

(The singles listed above are credited to Diana Ross & Supremes.)

70	Tamla Motown TMG 735	Up The Ladder To The Roof/Bill, When Are You Coming Back (DJ copy = £30)	6
70	Tamla Motown TMG 747	Everybody's Got The Right To Love/But I Love You More (DJ copy = £25)	6
71	Tamla Motown TMG 760	Stoned Love/Shine On Me (DJ copy = £30)	6
71	Tamla Motown TMG 782	Nathan Jones/Happy (Is A Bumpy Road) (DJ copy = £30)	6

(The singles listed above are credited to Supremes and do not feature Diana Ross.)

EPs
65	Tamla Motown TME 2008	THE SUPREMES HITS (originally with flipback sleeve & push-out centre)	30/20
66	Tamla Motown TME 2011	SHAKE	65

LPs
64	Stateside SL 10109	MEET THE SUPREMES	38
65	Tamla Motown TML 11002	WITH LOVE — FROM US TO YOU	45
65	Tamla Motown TML 11012	WE REMEMBER SAM COOKE	50
65	Tamla Motown TML 11018	THE SUPREMES SING COUNTRY, WESTERN AND POP	50
65	Tamla Motown TML 11020	MORE HITS BY THE SUPREMES	20
66	T. Motown (S)TML 11026	THE SUPREMES AT THE COPA	25
66	T. Motown (S)TML 11028	I HEAR A SYMPHONY	25
66	T. Motown (S)TML 11039	SUPREMES A-GO GO	25
67	T. Motown (S)TML 11047	THE SUPREMES SING MOTOWN	25
67	T. Motown (S)TML 11054	THE SUPREMES SING RODGERS AND HART	25

(The LPs listed above are credited to Supremes.)

68	T. Motown (S)TML 11063	GREATEST HITS (original pressing with flipback laminated sleeve)	15
68	T. Motown (S)TML 11070	'LIVE' AT LONDON'S TALK OF THE TOWN	20
68	T. Motown (S)TML 11073	REFLECTIONS	20
69	T. Motown (S)TML 11088	SING & PERFORM FUNNY GIRL (mono/stereo)	20/15
69	T. Motown (S)TML 11095	LOVE CHILD (mono/stereo)	20/15
69	T. Motown (S)TML 11114	LET THE SUNSHINE IN (mono/stereo)	20/15
70	T. Motown (S)TML 11137	CREAM OF THE CROP (mono/stereo)	20/15
70	Tamla Motown STML 11157	RIGHT ON (as Supremes)	15
71	Tamla Motown STML 11189	TOUCH (LP, as Supremes)	15
73	T. Motown STML 11222	PRODUCED AND ARRANGED BY JIMMY WEBB (LP, as Supremes)	15

(The LPs listed above are credited to Diana Ross & Supremes unless otherwise stated. All the albums listed above were originally issued with flipback sleeves; later pressings are worth two-thirds these values.)

SUPREMES & FOUR TOPS
71	Tamla Motown TMG 777	River Deep, Mountain High/It's Gotta Be A Miracle (This Thing Called Love)	8
71	Tamla Motown TMG 793	You Gotta Have Love In Your Heart/I'm Glad About It	8
71	T. Motown STML 11179	THE SUPREMES AND THE FOUR TOPS — MAGNIFICENT 7 (LP)	15

DIANA ROSS & THE SUPREMES & THE TEMPTATIONS
69	Tamla Motown TMG 685	I'm Gonna Make You Love Me/A Place In The Sun	6
69	Tamla Motown TMG 709	I Second That Emotion/The Way You Do The Things You Do	6
70	Tamla Motown TMG 730	Why (Must We Fall In Love)/Uptight (Everything Is Alright)	6
69	T. Motown (S)TML 11096	DIANA ROSS & THE SUPREMES JOIN THE TEMPTATIONS (LP)	15
69	T. Motown (S)TML 11110	THE ORIGINAL SOUNDTRACK FROM TCB (LP, gatefold laminated sleeve)	15
70	T. Motown STML 11122	TOGETHER (LP, flipback sleeve)	15

(see also Primettes, Diana Ross, Temptations, Four Tops, Florence Ballard)

ADAM SURF & PEBBLE BEACH BAND
76	Paladin PAL 3	Fun Fun Fun/Blue Surf	8

MINT VALUE £

SURFARIS
63	London HLD 9751	Wipe Out/Surfer Joe	15
63	Brunswick 05894	Waikiki Run/Point Panic	15
64	Brunswick 05902	Scatter Shield/Bat Man	15
66	Dot DS 26756	Wipe Out/Surfer Joe (reissue)	6
63	London RE-D 1405	WIPE OUT (EP)	70
63	London HA-D 8110	WIPE OUT (LP)	60
63	Brunswick LAT/STA 8561	THE SURFARIS PLAY (LP, mono/stereo)	45/55
64	Brunswick LAT/STA 8567	HIT CITY '64 (LP, mono/stereo)	45/55
64	Brunswick LAT 8582	FUN CITY (LP)	55
65	Brunswick LAT 8605	HIT CITY '65 (LP)	55
65	Brunswick LAT 8631	IT AIN'T ME BABE (LP, also stereo STA 8631)	5/60
66	Dot DLP 3535	WIPE OUT (LP, reissue)	25
76	MCA MCF 2761	SURFERS RULE (LP)	15
77	MCA Coral CDL 8050	GONE WITH THE WAVE (LP)	15
87	MCA MCL 1842	WIPE OUT – THE SINGLES ALBUM 1963-1967 (LP, withdrawn)	20

SURFERS
59	Vogue V 9147	Mambo Jambo/ALAN KALANI: A Touch Of Pink	18

LES SURFS
64	RCA RCA 1432	Just For The Boy/Stop	10
65	RCA RCA 1461	Go Your Way/Chained To A Memory	7
67	Fontana TF 832	When I Tell You (That I Love You)/I Want To Be Free	6

SURGEONS
79	Surgery S-100	Sid Never Did It/Breaking Rocks On Ricker's Island	50

SURGICAL SUPPORTS
81	Industrious Youth CONSTRUCT 2	WITHDRAWN FOR DISPOSAL EP	30

JOHN SURMAN (Trio)
69	Deram DM 224	Obeah Wedding/Can't Stop The Carnival	40
68	Deram DML/SML 1030	JOHN SURMAN (LP)	75
69	Deram DML-R/SML-R 1045	HOW MANY CLOUDS CAN YOU SEE? (LP)	100
70	Futura GER 12	ALORS! (LP)	40
71	Dawn DNLS 3006	THE TRIO (LP)	60
71	Dawn DNLS 3018	WHERE FORTUNE SMILES (LP, with insert, with John McLaughlin, Karl Berger, Stu Martin & Dave Holland)	40
71	Dawn DNLS 3022	CONFLAGRATION (LP)	40
71	Deram SML 1094	TALES OF THE ALGONQUIN (LP, with John Warren)	100
72	Island HELP 10	WESTERING HOME (LP)	20
73	Island ILPS 9237	MORNING GLORY (LP)	20

(see also Morning Glory, Trio, Mike Westbrook, John McLaughlin, Alan Skidmore/Mike Osborne/John Surman)

SURPLUS STOCK
79	Outatune OUT 7911	Spiv/Vips (p/s)	7

SURPRISES
79	Dead Dog DEAD 01	Jeremy Thorpe Is Innocent/Flying Attack/Little Sir Echo (p/s)	50

SURVIVORS
65	Rio R 55	Take Charge/Ska-Ology	10
65	Rio R 70	Rawhide Ska/OWEN GRAY: Girl I Want You	10

SURVIVORS
79	Capitol PSR 436	Pamela Jean/After The Game (Credits the Beach Boys on p/s, Survivors on disc)	10

(see also The Beach Boys)

SUSIE
71	Decca F 13217	I Feel The Earth Move/We Are All The Same	8

SUSSED
80	Graduate GRAD 7	I've Got Me A Parka/Myself, Myself And I Repeated (p/s, paper labels; later reissued [1986] with silver labels)	6
81	Shoestring LACE 002	I Like You/Tango/The Perv (p/s)	10

(SCREAMING) LORD SUTCH (& THE SAVAGES)
61	HMV POP 953	Till The Following Night/Good Golly Miss Molly	22
63	Decca F 11598	Jack The Ripper/Don't You Just Know It	18
63	Decca F 11747	I'm A Hog For You/Monster In Black Tights	22
64	Oriole CB 1944	She's Fallen In Love With A Monster Man/Bye Bye Baby	50
64	Oriole CB 1962	Dracula's Daughter/Come Back Baby	50
65	CBS 201767	The Train Kept A-Rollin'/Honey Hush (as Lord Sutch)	50
66	CBS 202080	The Cheat/Black And Hairy	50
70	Atlantic 584 321	'Cause I Love You/Thumping Beat	12
70	Atlantic 2091 006	'Cause I Love You/Thumping Beat (reissue)	6
70	Atlantic 2091 017	Election Fever/Rock The Election	10
72	Atlantic K 10221	Gotta Keep A-Rockin'/Flashing Lights/Hands Of Jack The Ripper	10
76	SRT SRTS 76361	Monster Ball/Rang-Tang-A-Lang	5
76	SRT SRTS 76375	I Drink To Your Health Marie (Parts 1 & 2)	5
77	Decca F 13697	Jack The Ripper/I'm A Hog For You	5
81	Ridgemount RMR 45 010	LOONABILLY (EP, p/s, with bonus "Loon Party" single)	6
70	Atlantic 2400 008	LORD SUTCH AND HIS HEAVY FRIENDS (LP)	30
72	Atlantic K 40313	HANDS OF JACK THE RIPPER (LP, as Lord Sutch & Heavy Friends)	30
81	Ace MAD 1	THE METEORS MEET SCREAMING LORD SUTCH (mini-LP, one side each, stickered cartoon print on plain grey card sleeve, 1,000 only)	125

(see also Savages, Meteors, Led Zeppelin, Cliff Bennett & Rebel Rousers, Circles, Nero & Gladiators, Neil Christian & Crusaders)

GLEN SUTTON
(see under Murray Kellum)

RALPH SUTTON
53	Lyragon LF 2	STRIDE PIANO (10" LP)	12

(see also Tony Parenti)

SUZANNE
77	Ring O' 2017 108	Born On Hallowe'en/Like No One Else (some in promo p/s)	25/12
78	Ring O' 2017 111	You Really Got A Hold On Me/You Could Be Right This Time	10
78	Ring O' 2320 105	SUZANNE (LP, unreleased)	

SUZI & BIG DEE IRWIN
66	Polydor BM 65715	Ain't That Lovin' You Baby/I Can't Get Over You	15

(see also Big Dee Irwin)

SUZY & THE RED STRIPES
77	A&M AMS 7461	Seaside Woman/B-side To The Seaside (yellow vinyl, die-cut p/s)	12
79	A&M AMSP 7461	Seaside Woman/B-side To The Seaside (yellow vinyl, die-cut p/s, in box set with badge & 10 'saucy' mini-postcards)	40
80	A&M AMS 7548	Seaside Woman/B-side To The Seaside (reissue, cartoon p/s, as Linda McCartney alias Suzy & Red Stripes)	10
80	A&M AMSP 7548	Seaside Woman/B-side To The Seaside (12", as Linda McCartney alias Suzy & Red Stripes)	12
86	EMI EMI 5572	Seaside Woman/B-side To The Seaside (p/s)	6
86	EMI 12EMI 5572	Seaside Woman/B-side To The Seaside (12", p/s)	10

(see also Paul McCartney [& Wings])

SVANTE
68	United Artists UP 2224	Baby I Need Your Lovin'/Just One Word From You	7

SVENSK
67	Page One POF 036	Dream Magazine/Getting Old	25
67	Page One POF 050	You/All I Have To Do Is Dream	18

(see also Jason Paul)

SWALLOWS
56	Vogue EPV 1113	RHYTHM AND BLUES (EP, 2 tracks by Dominoes)	300

SWALLOWS with SONNY THOMPSON
52	Vogue V 2136	Roll, Roll Pretty Baby/It Ain't The Meat (78)	40

(see also Sonny Thompson & His Rhythm & Blues Band)

SWAMP DOGG
74	Island USA 002	Did I Come Back Too Soon/I Wouldn't Leave Here	5
72	Mojo 2916 014	TOTAL DESTRUCTION TO YOUR MIND (LP)	15

(see also Jerry Williams, Brooks & Jerry)

BILLY SWAN
75	Monument MNT 80615	I CAN HELP (LP)	15
75	CBS 69162	ROCK & ROLL MOON (LP)	12
76	Monument MNT 81387	BILLY SWAN (LP)	12

SWAN ARCADE
73	Trailer LER 2032	SWAN ARCADE (LP)	20
84	Fellside FE 037	TOGETHER FOREVER (LP)	20

SWANEE RIVER BOYS
54	Parlophone CMSP 7	Do You Believe/Gloryland Boogie (export issue)	15
54	Parlophone DP 385	Was He Quiet Or Did He Cry/I Have Desire (78, export issue)	12

BETTYE SWANN
67	CBS 2942	Make Me Yours/I Will Not Cry (DJ copy = £100, demos in p/s = £150)	60
69	Capitol CL 15586	Don't Touch Me/(My Heart Is) Closed For The Season	60
72	Atlantic K 10174	Victim Of A Foolish Heart/Cold Day In Hell	25
72	Atlantic K 10273	Today I Started Loving You Again/I'd Rather Go Blind	8
73	Mojo 2092 059	Make Me Yours/I Will Not Cry (reissue)	10
75	Atlantic K 10622	Doing It For The One I Love/All The Way In Or All The Way Out	6
75	Contempo CS 9019	Make Me Yours/I Will Not Cry (reissue)	8
76	Atlantic K 10851	Heading In The Right Direction/Be Strong Enough To Hold On	10

(see also Sam Dees & Bettye Swann)

RUTH SWANN
75	Spark SRL 1124	Tainted Love/Boy, You'd Better Move On	8

SWANS
63	Stateside SS 224	He's Mine/You Better Be A Good Girl Now	35
64	Cameo Parkway C 302	The Boy With The Beatle Hair/Please Hurry Home	30

SWANS
86	K.422/Some Bizzare KDE 312	A Screw (Holy Money)/Blackmail/A Screw (12", p/s)	8
88	Product Inc. PROD 23	Love Will Tear Us Apart/Trust Me (red vinyl, 750 only, p/s)	12
88	Product Inc. 12PROD 23	Love Will Tear Us Apart (Red Version)/Trust Me/Love Will Tear Us Apart (black version)/Our Love Lies (12", black vinyl, p/s)	20
80s	Product Inc. 12PROD 16	New Mind/Damn You To Hell/I'll Swallow You (12", p/s)	8
84	K.422/Some Bizzare KCC 1	COP (LP, with inner)	30
85	Zensor NDO 3	FILTH (LP)	30
86	K. 422/Some Bizzare KCC 2	GREED (LP, with inner)	15
86	K. 422/Some Bizzare KCC 3	HOLY MONEY (LP)	15
86	no label BURN ONE	PUBLIC CASTRATION IS A GOOD IDEA (2-LP)	20
95	Young God YGLP 004	BODY TO BODY, JOB TO JOB (LP)	20
89	MCA MCG 6047	THE BURNING WORLD (LP, with insert)	12
95	Young God YGLP 005B	LOVE OF LIFE (LP, in box)	25

MINT VALUE £

BERNICE SWANSON
65	Chess CRS 8008	Lying Awake/Baby I'm Yours (DJ copy = £70)	40

DAVE SWARBRICK
67	Bounty BYI 6030	RAGS, REELS AND AIRS (LP, with Martin Carthy & Diz Disley)	50
67	Polydor Special 236 514	RAGS, REELS AND AIRS (LP, reissue, with Martin Carthy & Diz Disley)	30
76	Transatlantic TRA 337	SWARBRICK (LP)	15
77	Transatlantic TRA 341	SWARBRICK 2 (LP)	15
78	Sonet SNTF 763	LIFT THE LID AND LISTEN (LP)	15
78	Sonet SNTF 764	THE CEILIDH ALBUM (LP, as Dave Swarbrick & Friends)	15
81	Logo LOGO 1029	SMIDDYBURN (LP)	15

(see also Martin Carthy & Dave Swarbrick, Fairport Convention,Young Tradition, Vashti Bunyan, Ian Campbell)

DAVE SWARBRICK & SIMON NICOL
81	White Bear WBR 001	LIVE AT THE WHITE BEAR (LP)	20
83	Woodworm WR 006	CLOSE TO THE WIND (LP)	15

(see also Dave Swarbrick, Fairport Convention, Young Tradition)

SWARBRIGG (PLUS TWO)
75	MCA MCA 179	That's What Friends Are For/Love Is	6

ROSALYN SWEAT & PARAGONS
73	Duke DU 160	Blackbird Singing/Always	8
74	Horse HRLP 703	BLACKBIRD SINGING (LP)	15

(see also Paragons)

SWE-DANES
60	Warner Bros WB 7	Scandinavian Shuffle/Hot Toddy	6
60	Warner Bros WB 22	Swe-Dane Shuffle/At A Georgia Camp Meeting	6
61	Warner Bros WEP 6017	THE SWE-DANES (EP; also stereo SWEP 2017)	20/25

(see also Alice Babbs)

SWEDEN THROUGH THE AGES
86	Snappy SW 001	IT HELPS TO CRY EP (12", p/s)	12

(see also Billy MacKenzie)

SWEDISH MODERN JAZZ GROUP
61	Tempo TAP 31	SAX APPEAL (LP)	220

SWEENEY'S MEN
67	Pye 7N 17312	Old Maid In The Garrett/Derby Ram	10
68	Pye 7N 17459	Waxies Dargle/Old Woman In Cotton	10
69	Transatlantic TRASP 19	Sullivan's John/Rattlin' Roarin' Willy	8
68	Transatlantic TRA 170	SWEENEY'S MEN (LP)	70
69	Transatlantic TRA 200	THE TRACKS OF SWEENEY (LP)	80
76	Transatlantic TRASAM 37	SWEENEY'S MEN (LP, reissue)	20
77	Transatlantic TRASAM 40	THE TRACKS OF SWEENEY (LP, reissue)	18

(see also Gay & Terry Woods, Dr. Strangely Strange)

JIM SWEENY
58	Philips PB 811	The Midnight Hour/Till The Right One Comes Along (78 rpm = £8)	15

JIMMY SWEEP
81	Tamarin TAM 3	London Town/Bridgetown Girls (written, produced by & feat. Alan Lancaster)	10
82	PRT 7P 233	London Town/Bridgetown Girls (reissue)	8

(see also Status Quo)

SWEET
SINGLES
68	Fontana TF 958	Slow Motion/It's Lonely Out There	450+
69	Parlophone R 5803	The Lollipop Man/Time	100
70	Parlophone R 5826	All You'll Ever Get From Me/The Juicer	40
70	Parlophone R 5848	Get On The Line/Mr. McGallagher	70
71	RCA RCA 2051	Funny Funny/You're Not Wrong For Loving Me	12
71	RCA RCA 2087	Co Co/Done Me Wrong, All Right	5
71	Parlophone R 5902	All You'll Ever Get From Me/The Juicer (reissue)	15
71	RCA RCA 2121	Alexander Graham Bell/Spotlight	5
73	RCA RCA 2403	Ballroom Blitz/Rock & Roll Disgrace (mispressed at wrong speed, 49rpm; matrix: 2403-A-1E)	15
74	RCA RCA 2480	Turn It Down/Someone Else Will	5
75	RCA RCA 2578	Action/Sweet FA	5
76	RCA RCA 2541	The Lies In Your Eyes/Cockroach	5
76	RCA RCA 2748	Lost Angels/Funk It Up	5
77	RCA PB 5011	Fever Of Love/A Distinct Lack Of Ancient	6
77	RCA PB 5046	Stairway To The Stars/Why Don't You Do It To Me	8
78	Polydor POSP 5	California Nights/Show Me The Way (unreleased)	
79	Polydor POSP 36	Call Me/Why Don't You	7
79	Polydor POSP 73	Big Apple Waltz/Why Don't You	35
80	RCA PE 5226	Fox On The Run/Hellraiser/Ballroom Blitz/Blockbuster (EP, p/s)	15
80	Polydor POSP 131	Give That Lady Some Respect/Tall Girls	7
80	Polydor POSP 160	Sixties Man/Tall Girls	5
80	Polydor POSP 160	Sixties Man/Oh Yeah	15
80	Polydor POSP 160	Sixties Man/Oh Yeah (mispressing, B-side plays "Tall Girls")	20
81	RCA GOLD 524	Blockbuster/Hellraiser (pink 'Golden Groove' p/s)	8
81	RCA GOLD 551	Ballroom Blitz/Wig Wam Bam (pink 'Golden Groove' p/s)	8
84	Anagram ANA 27	The Sixteens/Action (p/s)	10
84	Anagram ANA 28	It's The Sweetest Mix/Fox On The Run (p/s)	5
84	Anagram 12 ANA 28	It's The Sweetest Mix/Fox On The Run (12" p/s; matrix no. 12 ANA 28 AI)	8
84	Anagram 12 ANA 28	It's The Sweetest Mix/Fox On The Run (12" p/s; matrix no. 12 ANA 28.A)	10
85	Anagram ANA 29	Sweet 2th — The Wig Wam-Willy Mix/The Teen Action Mix (p/s)	10
85	Anagram ANA 29	Sweet 2th — The Wig Wam-Willy Mix/The Teen Action Mix (12", p/s)	10
89	RCA PB 43337	Wig Wam Bam/Little Willy (p/s)	15

LPs
71	MFP MFP 5248	GIMME DAT DING (1 side each by Sweet & Pipkins)	12
71	RCA SF 8288	FUNNY HOW SWEET CO-CO CAN BE	25
74	RCA LPL 15039	SWEET FANNY ADAMS	12
76	RCA RS 1036	GIVE US A WINK	12
77	RCA PL 25072	OFF THE RECORD (with inner sleeve)	15
78	RCA Camden CDS 1168	THE SWEET	12
79	Polydor POLD 5022	CUT ABOVE THE REST (with inner sleeve)	15
70s	RCA LPL 15080	DESOLATION BOULEVARD (LP, gatefold sleeve)	15
70s	RCA SF 8316	THE SWEET'S BIGGEST HITS (LP)	12
80	Polydor POLS 1021	WATER'S EDGE	18
82	Polydor 2311 1179	IDENTITY CRISIS	22
84	Anagram GRAM 16	SWEET SIXTEEN (LP)	15
84	Anagram P GRAM 16	SWEET SIXTEEN (LP, picture disc)	30

(see also Brian Connolly, Mayfield's Mule, Elastic Band, Andy Scott)

SWEET AROMA
73	Rhino RNO 113	Happiness/Rock Reggae (demos or stock copies)	5

SWEET CHARIOT
69	MCA MK 5010	Heavenly Road/Wish I Were A Child	8
73	Columbia DB 8999	When I'm A Kid/Mozart '73	8
70s	T.O.G. SCEP 001	Angelina/Young At Heart/America	8
72	De Wolfe DWLP 3230	SWEET CHARIOT & FRIENDS (LP, library issue only)	40

SWEET CHARLES
88	Urban URB 15	Yes It's You/LYN COLLINS: Rock Me Again And Again And Again (die-cut sleeve)	5
88	Urban URBX 15	Yes It's You/LYN COLLINS: Rock Me Again And Again And Again/ Think About It (12", die-cut sleeve)	10
88	Urban URBLP 9	FOR SWEET PEOPLE FROM SWEET CHARLES (LP)	15

SWEET CONFUSION
69	Escort ES 809	Elizabeth Serenade/Don At Rest	8
69	Escort ES 812	Hotter Scorcher/Conquer Lion	8

(see also Stranger & Patsy)

SWEET CORPORALS
59	Top Rank JAR 217	The Same Old Army/Warm And Willing	5

SWEET DREAMS
74	Bradleys BRADL 1008	WE'LL BE YOUR MUSIC (LP)	15

(see also Polly Brown, Jimmy Thomas)

SWEET FEELING
67	Columbia DB 8195	All So Long Ago/Charles Brown	150

(see also Rupert's People)

SWEETHEARTS
65	Blue Beat BB 389	Sit Down And Cry (actually with Clinton & Rufus)/ PRINCE BUSTER: Ghost Dance	70

HARRY SWEETING
68	Coxsone CSL 8012	FROM JAMAICA WITH LOVE (LP)	100+

SWEET INSPIRATIONS
67	Atlantic 584 117	Why (Am I Treated So Bad)/I Don't Want To Go On Without You	8
67	Atlantic 584 132	Let It Be Me/When Something Is Wrong With My Baby	8
68	Atlantic 584 167	Sweet Inspiration/I'm Blue	8
68	Atlantic 584 233	What The World Needs Now Is Love/You Really Didn't Mean It	8
69	Atlantic 584 241	Sweet Inspiration/I'm Blue	6
69	Atlantic 584 279	Sweets For My Sweet/Get A Little Older	6
70	Atlantic 584 312	(Gotta Find) A Brand New Lover (Parts 1 & 2)	6
71	Atlantic 2091 073	Evidence/Change Me Not	6
68	Atlantic 587/588 090	THE SWEET INSPIRATIONS (LP)	20
69	Atlantic 587/588 137	WHAT THE WORLD NEEDS NOW IS LOVE (LP)	20
69	Atlantic 587/588 194	SWEETS FOR MY SWEET (LP)	20
70	Atlantic 2465 003	SWEET SWEET SOUL (LP)	20

(see also Cissy Houston)

SWEET JESUS
91	Chapter 22 CHAP 63	Cat Thing/Honey Loving Honey/Peach/Baby Blue (12" EP, unreleased, 25 test pressings only)	10

SWEET LITTLE BUNTY
75	Ackee ACK 540	I (Who Have Nothing)/Oh Me Oh My	6

SWEET PAIN
71	United Artists UP 35268	Timber Gibbs/Chain Up The Devil	5
69	Mercury 20146 SMCL	SWEET PAIN (LP)	55

SWEET PLUM
69	Middle Earth MDS 103	Lazy Day/Let No Man Steal Your Thyme	25
70	Middle Earth MDS 105	Set The Wheels In Motion/Catch A Cloud	25

SWEET SAVAGE
81	Park PRK 1001	Take No Prisoners/Killing TIme (p/s, red and yellow label)	200
80s	Crashed CAR 48	Straight Through The Heart/Teaser (no p/s)	150
80s	private pressing	The Raid/Prosecutors Of Greed (possibly unreleased)	50+

SWEETSHOP
68	Parlophone R 5707	Barefoot And Tiptoe/Lead The Way	20

(see also Mark Wirtz)

MINT VALUE £

SWEET SLAG
71 President PTLS 1042   TRACKING WITH CLOSE-UPS (LP)......................................80+

SWEET THUNDER
78 Fantasy FTC 158   Everybody's Singin' Love Songs/Joyful Noise 5

SWEET THURSDAY
69 Polydor 2310 051   SWEET THURSDAY (LP)..20
(see also Nicky Hopkins, Mark-Almond)

SWEGAS
70 Trend 6099 001   What You Gonna Do/There Is Nothing In It 8
71 Trend 6480 002   CHILD OF LIGHT (LP, gatefold sleeve) 22

SWELL MAPS
78 Rather GEAR ONE   Read About Seymour/Ripped And Torn/Black Velvet (p/s)....................15
79 Rough Trade RT 010/   Read About Seymour/Ripped And Torn/Black Velvet (p/s,
    Rather GEAR ONE MK. 2   reissue, different back sleeve)..7
79 R. Trade RT 012/GEAR 3   Dresden Style/Mystery Track/Ammunition Train/Full Moon (Dub) (p/s) 7
79 R. Trade RT 021/GEAR 6   Real Shocks/English Verse/Monlogues (p/s, 2 different colours) 8
79 R. Trade RT 036/GEAR 7   Let's Build A Car/Big Maz In The Country/...Then Poland (p/s)...............7
81 Rough Trade RT 012/   Dresden Style (new vocal)/Ammunition Train/Full Moon (Dub) (p/s,
    Rather GEAR 3   reissue, different back sleeve)..7
79 Rough Trade ROUGH 2/   A TRIP TO MARINEVILLE (LP, with inner sleeve, some with bonus EP in
    Rather TROY 1   die-cut sleeve [Rather GEAR FIVE])..............................20/15
80 Rough Trade ROUGH 15   SWELL MAPS IN 'JANE FROM OCCUPIED EUROPE' (LP)...................12
81 Rough Trade ROUGH 21   WHATEVER HAPPENS NEXT... (2-LP) 18
84 Rough Trade ROUGH 41   SWELL MAPS IN 'COLLISION TIME' (LP) 12
(see also Cult Figures, Nikki Sudden, Steve Treatment, Phones Sportsman Band, Epic Soundtracks, Metrophase, Last Bandits)

ANTHONY SWETE
69 RCA RCA 1905   Backfield in Motion/Soul Deep 8

JONATHAN SWIFT
71 CBS 64412   INTROVERT (LP, nude cover)..12
72 CBS 64751   SONGS (LP, with lyric insert)..12

TUFTY SWIFT
77 Free Reed FRR 017   HOW TO MAKE A BAKEWELL TART (LP, with booklet) 25
85 Shark SHARK 04   YOU'LL NEVER DIE FOR LOVE (LP, private pressing) 15

ALAN SWIMMER & DEE DAVIDSON
70s Fab FAB 242   Take Me Back To Jamaica/Thousands Of Children......................5

STEVE SWINDELLS
74 RCA LPL1 5057   MESSAGES (LP, with insert) 12
(see also Hawkwind)

SWINDLEFOLK
68 Deroy   A-ROVIN' (LP, private pressing)..75
69 Deroy   SWINDLED (LP, private pressing) 75

SWINGERS
67 Blue Beat BB 379   Simpleton/FRANCIS: Warn The People ....60+

SWINGERS
60 Vogue V 9158   Love Makes The World Go Round/Jackie............................20

SWINGERS
81 Magnet MAG 202   Be My Baby/Swinging...5
(see also Spectres, Rich Kids)

SWINGING BLUE JEANS
63 HMV POP 1170   It's Too Late Now/Think Of Me..12
63 HMV POP 1206   Do You Know/Angie 15
63 HMV POP 1242   Hippy Hippy Shake/Now I Must Go 6
64 HMV POP 1273   Good Golly Miss Molly/Shakin' Feelin' 6
64 HMV POP 1304   You're No Good/Don't You Worry About Me 5
64 HMV POP 1327   Promise You'll Tell Her/It's So Right 7
64 HMV POP 1375   It Isn't There/One Of These Days 7
65 HMV POP 1409   Make Me Know You're Mine/I've Got A Girl 7
65 HMV POP 1477   Crazy 'Bout My Baby/Good Lovin' 10
66 HMV POP 1501   Don't Make Me Over/What Can I Do Today...............................10
66 HMV POP 1533   Sandy/I'm Gonna Have You 10
66 HMV POP 1564   Rumours, Gossip, Words Untrue/Now The Summer's Gone 12
67 HMV POP 1596   Tremblin'/Something's Coming Along 18
67 HMV POP 1605   Don't Go Out Into The Rain/One Woman Man 12
64 HMV 7EG 8850   SHAKE WITH THE SWINGING BLUE JEANS (EP) 55
64 HMV 7EG 8868   YOU'RE NO GOOD MISS MOLLY (EP) 50
64 HMV CLP 1802   BLUE JEANS A' SWINGING (LP, also stereo CSD 1570) 75/100
64 Regal SREG 1073   TUTTI FRUTTI (LP, export issue) 55
67 MFP MFP 1163   SWINGING BLUE JEANS (LP, reissue of HMV CLP 1802) 15
74 Dart BULL 1001   BRAND NEW AND FADED (LP) 18
(see also Ray Ennis & Blue Jeans, Blue Jeans, Escorts, Terry Sylvester)

SWINGING CATS
80 Two Tone CHS TT 14   Mantovani/Away (p/s)..5

SWINGIN' MEDALLIONS
66 Philips BF 1500   Double Shot Of My Baby's Love/Here It Comes Again......................8
66 Philips BF 1515   She Drives Me Out Of My Mind/You Gotta Have Faith 10

SWINGING SOUL MACHINE
69 Polydor 56760   Spooky's Day Off/Nobody Wants You...................................15
(see also Machine)

SWING OUT SISTER
88	Mercury 080 122-2	Breakout/Fooled By A Smile/Communion/Surrender (12" Version)/ Breakout (Video) (CD Video)	8

(see also Teresa Del Fuego)

SWS
88	DTI MAC2	Boys From The Bec/Our Rhymes Are Fly (12")	20
90	Cue TCUE003	Overture/Empirical Expansions/Info Nation/Leaf In The Wind	30

SYD & JOE
72	Bullet BU 498	Three Combine/I'm The Nearest To Your Heart	5

SYDNEY (Crooks) ALL STARS
70	Bullet BU 436	The Return Of Batman/In Action	10
70	Bullet BU 437	Outer Space/Full Moon	10

(see also Pioneers, Junior English, Sammy Morgan)

ERIC SYKES & HATTIE JACQUES
62	Decca F 11512	Doctor Kildare/Bedtime Story	5

(see also Eric & Hattie, Goons)

JOHN SYKES
82	MCA MCA 792	Please Don't Leave Me/(Instrumental) (with Phil Lynott, some in p/s)	35/10

(see also Thin Lizzy, Phil Lynott, Tygers Of Pan Tang, Whitesnake)

ROOSEVELT SYKES
50	Jazz Collector L 40	Three, Six And Nine/We Can Sell That Thing (78)	12
56	Vogue V 2389	Fine And Brown/Too Hot To Hold (78 rpm = £30)	75
56	Vogue V 2393	Walkin' This Boogie/Security Blues (78 rpm = £30)	75
66	Delmark DJB 2	BACK TO THE BLUES (EP)	30
59	Encore ENC 183	BIG MAN OF THE BLUES (LP)	18
61	Columbia 33SX 1343	FACE TO FACE WITH THE BLUES (LP)	30
62	Columbia 33SX 1422	THE HONEYDRIPPER (LP, with Alexis Korner)	65
65	Bluesville BVLP 1006	THE RETURN OF ROOSEVELT SYKES (LP)	30
67	'77' 77LEU 12-50	BLUES FROM BAR ROOMS (LP)	18
67	Riverside RLP 8819	MR SYKES' BLUES 1929-1932 (LP)	25
67	Ember EMB 3391	ROOSEVELT SYKES SINGS THE BLUES (LP)	18
71	Barclay 920 294	THE HONEYDRIPPERS' DUKE'S MIXTURE (LP)	12
70s	Delmark DL 607	HARD DRIVIN' BLUES (LP, blue label)	12

(see also Robert Pete Williams)

SYKO & CARIBS
64	Blue Beat BB 213	Do The Dog/Jenny	15
64	Blue Beat BB 223	Big Boy/Sugar Baby	15

SYLTE SISTERS
63	London HLU 9753	Summer Magic/Well It's Summertime	12

SYLVAIN SYLVAIN
80	RCA PB 9500	Every Boy And Every Girl/Emily	5

(see also New York Dolls)

SYLVAN
65	Columbia DB 7674	We Don't Belong/Life's Colours Have Gone	18

FOSTER SYLVERS
73	MGM 2006 292	Misdemeanour/So Close	6

C. SYLVESTER & PLANETS
64	Blue Beat BB 206	Going South/LITTLE JOYCE: Oh Daddy	12

ROLAND SYLVESTER
64	Carnival CV 7018	Grandfather's Clock/SANDRA MURRAY: Nervous	6

TERRY SYLVESTER
74	Polydor 2383 394	I BELIEVE (LP, with insert)	12

(see also Escorts, Swinging Blue Jeans, Hollies)

SYLVIA
67	Fontana TF 884	Make Me A Woman/Without Your Love	7
68	Fontana TF 932	Down Hill/A Few Sweet Moments Of Love	8

SYLVIA (U.S.)
68	Soul City SC 103	I Can't Help It/It's A Good Life	15
75	London HLU 10415	Pillow Talk/My Thing	7

DAVID SYLVIAN
84	Virgin VSY 633	Red Guitar/Forbidden Colours (Version) (picture disc)	5
84	Virgin VS 700	The Ink In The Well (Remix)/Weathered Wall (Instrumental) (poster p/s)	5
84	Virgin VS 700-12	The Ink In The Well/Weathered Wall (Instrumental) (12", poster p/s)	8
84	Virgin VS 717	Pulling Punches (7" Mix)/Backwaters (Remix) (p/s, with 3 postcards)	5
84	Virgin VSY 717	Pulling Punches (7" Mix)/Backwaters (Remix) (picture disc)	7
84	Virgin VS 717-12	Pulling Punches (Extended Mix)/Backwaters (Remix) (12", p/s, & 3 postcards)	10
85	Virgin VS 835-12	WORDS WITH THE SHAMAN (12" EP, p/s)	10
85	Virgin VSS 815	Taking The Veil/Answered Prayers (rectangular picture disc, stickered PVC sleeve)	7
86	Virgin VS 895	Silver Moon/Gone To Earth (p/s)	5
86	Virgin VSP 895	Silver Moon/Gone To Earth (gatefold p/s)	6
88	Virgin CDT 23	Words With The Shaman: Part 1 — Ancient Evening/Part 2 — Incantation/ Part 3 — Awakening (Songs From The Tree Tops) (3" CD, gatefold card p/s)	12
89	Virgin VSCD 1221	Pop Song/A Brief Conversation Ending In Divorce/ The Stigma Of Childhood (Kin) (3" CD, card sleeve)	25
89	Virgin VSCDX 1221	Pop Song/A Brief Conversation Ending In Divorce/ The Stigma Of Childhood (Kin) (CD, presentation card pack, with discography)	50
85	Virgin SYL 1	ALCHEMY (Cassette)	12

89	Virgin DSCD 1	WEATHERBOX (5-CD box set, with poster & booklet) 150
98	Virgin CDIVDJ 2876	DEAD BEES ON A CAKE - PROMOTIONAL INTERVIEW CD (CD, card p/s,
		promo only)... 20
04	Townsend SOUNDLPSS 1	BLEMISH (LP, gatefold sleeve, featuring Derek Bailey, 2,000 only)............ 18

(See also Japan)

DAVID SYLVIAN & ROBERT FRIPP

| 93 | Virgin VSC 1462 | Jean The Birdman/Earthbound/Endgame (cassette, in slipcase) .... 12 |
| 94 | Virgin DAMAGE 1 | DAMAGE (gold CD in silver-coloured box) .... 25 |

DAVID SYLVIAN & RYUICHI SAKAMOTO

82	Virgin VS 510	Bamboo Houses (7" Mix)/Bamboo Music (7" Mix) (some with gatefold p/s)..... 5/4
83	Virgin VSY 601	Forbidden Colours/RYUICHI SAKAMOTO: The Seed And The Sower
88	Virgin CDT 18	Forbidden Colours/Bamboo Houses/Bamboo Music (3" CD, card sleeve)....... 15
92	Virgin VUSCD 57	Heartbeat (Tainal Kalki II)/Nuages (cassette, card slipcase) 10
92	Virgin VUSDG 57	Heartbeat (Tainai Kaiki II)/Nuages/Forbidden Colours/Heartbeat I
		(CD box set, with postcards) 12

(see also Japan, Yellow Magic Orchestra)

SYLVIN & GLENROY

| 70 | Torpedo TOR 25 | What You Gonna Do 'Bout It/KEN JONES: Sad Mood. .... 6 |

SYMARIP

(see under Seven Letters/Symarip, see also Pyramids)

SYMBOL

| 79 | Art & Craft AC 001 | Motherless Children/RANKING CARETAKER: Take It Away (12")............. 50 |
| 79 | Kebra Nagast KH 04 | Black Man's Word/Mr. Oppressor (12")................................. 15 |

SYMBOLS

65	Columbia DB 7459	One Fine Girl/Don't Go.. 10
65	Columbia DB 7664	You're My Girl/Why Do Fools Fall In Love 10
66	President PT 104	See You In September/To Make You Smile Again 6
66	President PT 113	Canadian Sunset/The Gentle Art Of Loving............................. 6
67	President PT 128	You'd Better Get Used To Missing Her/Hideaway 5
67	President PT 144	Bye Bye Baby/The Things You Do To Me............................... 6
67	President PT 173	(The Best Part Of) Breaking Up/Again 8
68	President PT 190	Lovely Way To Say Goodnight/Pretty City 15
68	President PT 216	Do I Love You/Schoolgirl 18
75	Crystal CR 7021	Canadian Sunset (Instrumental)/Canadian Sunset (Vocal Recording) 6
68	President PTL 1018	THE BEST PART OF THE SYMBOLS (LP) 35

(see also Johnny Milton & Condors)

SYMON & PI

| 68 | Parlophone R 5662 | Sha La La La Lee/Baby Baby....................................... 22 |
| 68 | Parlophone R 5719 | Got To See The Sunrise/Love Is Happening To Me..................... 10 |

SYMPHONICS

| 73 | Polydor 2058 341 | Heaven Must Have Sent You/Using Me............................... 15 |

SYMPHONIC SLAM

| 76 | A&M AMLH 69023 | SYMPHONIC SLAM (LP).. 80 |

PAT SYMS

| 64 | Oriole CB 1971 | It's Got To Be You Or No One/Lost .... 6 |

SYLVIA SYMS

| 58 | Brunswick 05744 | I Could Have Danced All Night/Be Good (To Me)........................ 6 |
| 58 | Brunswick 05771 | The Night They Invented Champagne/The Nature Of Things................. 5 |

SYN

| 67 | Deram DM 130 | Created By Clive/Grounded .... 110 |
| 67 | Deram DM 145 | 14-Hour Technicolour Dream/Flowerman............................. 85 |

(see also Syndicats, Yes, Peter Banks)

SYNCHROJAK

| 95 | Ferox FER 014 | SYNCHROJAK (12" EP, plain sleeve) .... 8 |
| 95 | Ferox FER 108 | PHAZE 11 (12" EP, plain sleeve) .... 8 |

SYNCHROMESH

| 80 | Rok ROK XI/XII | October Friday/E.F. BAND: Another Day Gone (company die-cut sleeve) .... 40 |

SYNCOPATORS

| 61 | Decca F 11359 | Everything Stops For Tea/If I Had A Talking Picture Of You............... 7 |

SYNDICATE

| 79 | Stevenage/Rock Against Racism | One Way Or Another/I Want To Be Somebody/RESTRICTED HOURS: Getting Things Done/Still Living Out The Car Crash (white label, foldover p/s).......... 12 |

(see also Astronauts)

SYNDICATE OF SOUND

66	Stateside SS 523	Little Girl/You.. 35
66	Stateside SS 538	Rumours/The Upper Hand 18
66	Stateside S(S)L 10185	LITTLE GIRL (LP) 60

SYNDICATS

64	Columbia DB 7238	Maybellene/True To Me.. 200
65	Columbia DB 7441	Howlin' For My Baby/What To Do 225
65	Columbia DB 7686	On The Horizon/Crawdaddy Simone (demos more common, £420) .... 750+

(see also Peter Banks, Ray Fenwick, Syn, Tomorrow, Yes)

SYNANTHESIA

| 69 | RCA SF 8058 | SYNANTHESIA (LP)... 200 |

SYREETA

(see under Syreeta Wright)

SYRUP
70   Amity OTS 501   Gentlemen Joe's Sidewalk Café/Love Is Love 5

SYSTEM
77   Tash   THE OTHER SIDE OF TIME (LP, 250 copies only) 110

SYZYGY
85   Taptag TAP 3   LADY IN GREY (mini-LP) 20
     (see also Blackthorn)

GABOR SZABO
86   Mercury 6167 780   Keep Smilin'. 5
66   HMV CLP 3614   JAZZ RAGA (LP) 50
67   Impulse MILP 506   THE SORCERER (LP, mono) 30

ERROL T. & ROOSEVELT ALL STARS
72   Ashanti ASH 406   Jamaica Born And Bred/Version 7

T. & UNKNOWN
80   Carrere CAR 142   My Generation/Woodstock Rock (p/s) 15

TABLE
77   Virgin VS 176   Do The Standing Still/Magical Melon Of The Tropics (p/s) 8
78   Chiswick NS 28   Sex Cells/The Road Of Lyfe (p/s) 7

TABLE TOPPERS
62   Starlite ST45 069   Rocking Mountain Dew/My Wild Irish Rose Rock 20

CHARLIE TABOR
63   Island WI 061   Blue Atlantic/Red Lion Madison 18

JUNE TABOR
86   Strange Fruit SFPS 015   THE PEEL SESSIONS (12" EP) 15
76   Topic 12TS 298   AIRS AND GRACES (LP) 12
77   Topic 12TS 360   ASHES AND DIAMONDS (LP) 12
     (see also Silly Sisters)

SAM TACIT
59   Decca F 11168   Skippy/Happy Little Caterpillar 6

TAD & MALL FRY
62   London HLU 9542   Checkered Continental Pants/Pretty Blue Jean Baby 15

TADPOLES
69   High Note HS 032   Rasta/Like Dirt 8

TAGES
66   Columbia DB 8019   Crazy 'Bout My Baby/In My Dreams 12
66   HMV POP 1515   So Many Girls/I'm Mad 55
67   Parlophone R 5640   Treat Me Like A Lady/Wanting 12
68   Parlophone R 5702   There's A Blind Man Playin' Fiddle In The Street/Like A Woman 15
68   MGM MGM 1443   Halcyon Days/I Read You Like An Open Book 12
     (see also Blond)

BLIND JOE TAGGART
52   Tempo R 55   Religion Is Something Within You/Mother's Love (78) 20
55   Jazz Collector L 129   Religion Is Something Within You/Mother's Love (78, reissue) 15

TAGMEMICS
80   Index INDEX 003   Chimneys/(Do The) Big Baby/Take Your Brain Out For A Walk (p/s, with insert) . . 10
     (see also Art Attacks)

JACQUELINE TAIEB
68   Fontana TF 952   Tonight I'm Going Home/7 A.M. . . . . 80+

LYN(N) TAIT(T) (& THE JETS)
66   Doctor Bird DB 1006   Vilma's Jump Up (as Lyn Taitt & The Comets)/GLEN MILLER &
                                   HONEYBOY MARTIN: Dad Is Home 25
66   Doctor Bird DB 1047   Spanish Eyes (with Tommy McCook)/STRANGER & HORTENSE: Loving Wine . . 25
67   Island WI 3066   Something Stupid/Blue Tuesday (as Lyn Tait & the Jets) 30
67   Island WI 3075   I Don't Want To Make You Cry/Nice Time (as Lyn Tait & the Jets) 30
68   Island WI 3139   Napoleon Solo/Pressure And Slide (as Lyn Taitt & the Jets) 40
68   Amalgamated AMG 810   El Casino Royale/Dee's Special (as Lyn Taitt & the Jets) 20
68   Pama PM 723   Soul Food/Music Flames (as Lyn Tait & the Jets) 30
68   Island ILP 969   SOUNDS ROCK STEADY (LP, as Lyn Taitt & the Jets) 110
68   Big Shot BBTL 4002   GLAD SOUNDS (LP, as Lyn Taitt & the Jets) 60
     (see also Justin Hines, Mike Thompson Jnr, ALton Ellis, Ken Boothe, Baba Brooks)

TAJ MAHAL
     (see under 'M')

TAKE FIVE
60s   D.S.C.A (no cat. no.)   MY GIRL (EP, oversized p/s; Dundee Students Charity Appeal record) 40

MINT VALUE £

TAKE IT
80s	Fresh Hold TRI	Man Made World/Taking Sides/How It Is (p/s)	40
80	Fresh Hold FHR 1	Twenty Lines/Armchairs/Friends And Relations (foldout p/s with insert)	20

'TAKERS
64	Pye 7N 15690	If You Don't Come Back/Think	20
(see also Undertakers, Jackie Lomax)			

TAKE THAT
91	Dance U.K. DUK 2	Do What U Like/Waiting Around (p/s)	15
91	Dance U.K. CADUK 2	Do What U Like/Waiting Around (cassette)	10
91	Dance U.K. 12DUK 2	Do What U Like (Club Mix)/Do What U Like (Radio Mix)/Waiting Around (12", p/s; most with wrong tracks listed on sleeve)	25
91	RCA PB 45085	Promises/Do What U Like (p/s)	5
91	RCA PB 45085P	Promises/Do What U Like (poster p/s)	8
91	RCA PT 45086	Promises (12" Mix)/Do What U Like (12" Mix) (12", p/s)	10
92	RCA PB 45257	Once You've Tasted Love/Guess Who Tasted Love (p/s)	5
92	RCA PB 45265	Once You've Tasted Love/Guess Who Tasted Love (spined p/s with pull-out hexagonal pop-up calendar)	15
92	RCA PK 45257	Once You've Tasted Love/Guess Who Tasted Love (cassette with stencil)	8
92	RCA PB 45258	Once You've Tasted Love (Aural Mix)/Guess Who Tasted Love (Guess Who Mix)/Once You've Tasted Love (Radio Version) (12" picture disc, with insert)	18
92	RCA 74321 10100 7	It Only Takes A Minute/Satisfied (p/s, with Mark & Robbie prints)	15
92	RCA 74321 10101 7	It Only Takes A Minute/It Only Takes A Minute (Royal Rave Mix) (different p/s, with Jason & Howard prints & paper frame)	8
92	RCA 74321 10814 7	I Found Heaven (7" Radio Mix)/(Mr. F's Garage Mix) (poster p/s)	10
92	RCA 74321 10813 7B	I Found Heaven (7" Radio Mix)/I'm Out (picture disc)	10
92	RCA 74321 11600 7	A Million Love Songs/A Million Love Songs (The Lovers Mix) (p/s, with tattoos)	10
92	RCA 74321 112313 1	Could It Be Magic (Deep In Rapino's Club Mix)/Take That Club Megamix/Could It Be Magic (Mr F Mix) (12", poster p/s)	8
93	RCA 74321 13311 7	Why Can't I Wake Up With You (Radio Edit)/Promises (live)/Clap Your Hands (live) (EP)	5
95	RCA (no cat. no.)	Every Guy (CD, unreleased, 1-track promo only)	18
93	RCA 74321 16926-1	EVERYTHING CHANGES (LP, picture disc)	12
(see also Robbie Williams)			

TALBOT BROTHERS
59	Melodisc MEL 1507	Bloodshot Eyes/She's Got Freckles	15
60s	Melodisc CAL 20	Bloodshot Eyes/She's Got Freckles (reissue)	6

ZIGGY TALENT
55	Brunswick 05506	Cheek To Cheek (Cha Cha)/Bozooki Blues	7

TALES OF JUSTINE
67	HMV POP 1614	Albert/Monday Morning (some in p/s)	160/80
97	Tenth Planet TP 034	PETALS FROM A SUNFLOWER (LP, gatefold sleeve, numbered, 1,000 only)	15
(see also Tim Rice)			

TALION
89	Major WADES 1	KILLING THE WORLD (LP)	12

TALISKER
75	Caroline CA 1513	DREAMING OF GLENISLA (LP)	15

TALISMAN
73	Argo AFW 110	Stepping Stones/Dr Jazz	5
72	Argo ZFB 33	PRIMROSE DREAMS (LP)	15
73	Argo ZDA 161	STEPPING STONES (LP)	15

TALISMEN
65	Stateside SS 408	Masters Of War/Casting My Spell	50

TALKING HEADS
77	Sire 6078 604	Love Goes To Building On Fire/New Feeling (p/s)	7
77	Sire SAM 87	Love Goes To Building On Fire/New Feeling (limited edition, some in p/s)	12/10
77	Sire 6078 610	Psycho Killer/I Wish You Wouldn't Say That (p/s)	8
77	Sire 6078 610	Psycho Killer/Psycho Killer (Acoustic)/I Wish You Wouldn't Say That (12", p/s)	12
78	Sire 6078 620	Pulled Up/Don't Worry About The Government (p/s)	7
79	Sire SIR 4004	Take Me To The River/Found A Job (p/s)	7
79	Sire SIR 4004/SAM 87	Take Me To The River/Found A Job/Love Goes To Building On Fire/Psycho Killer (double pack, gatefold p/s)	15
79	Sire SIR 4027	Life During Wartime (live version)/Electric Guitar (p/s)	12
79	WEA SPC 9	Take Me To The River/Psycho Killer (cassette)	5
80	Sire SIR 4033	I Zimbra/Paper (p/s)	7
80	Sire SIR 4040	Cities/Cities (live) (p/s)	7
80	Sire SIR 4040T	Cities/Cities (live)/Artists Only (live) (12", p/s)	10
80	Sire SIR 4048	Once In A Lifetime/Seen And Not Seen (p/s)	5
80	Sire SIR 4050	Houses In Motion (Special Re-Mixed Version)/Air (p/s)	8
84	Sire W 9451T/SAM 176	This Must Be The Place (Full Version)/Moon Rocks//Slippery People (Remix)/Making Flippy Floppy (Remix) (12", p/s, double pack)	15
84	EMI 12EMI 5504	Slippery People (live version)/This Must Be The Place (Naïve Melody) (12", p/s)	10
84	EMI 12EMI 5509	Girlfriend Is Better/Once In A Lifetime (12", p/s)	10
85	EMI 12EMI 5520	Lady Don't Mind (Extended Mix)/Give Me Back My Name (12", p/s)	10
85	EMI 12EMID 5520	Lady Don't Mind/Give Me Back My Name//Slippery People (live)/This Must Be The Place (Naive Melody) (live) (12", p/s, double pack)	12
85	EMI EMIP 5530	Road To Nowhere/Television Man (picture disc)	6
85	EMI 12 EMID 5530/ 12 EMI 5504	Road To Nowhere/Television Man (Extended)//Slippery People (Long Live Version)/Naive Melody (live) (12", stickered double pack)	10
86	EMI 12EMI 5567	Wild Wild Life (Extended Mix)/People Like Us (12", p/s)	8
87	EMI EM 1	Radio Head (LP version)/Hey Now (p/s)	6

87	EMI EMD 1	Radio Head/Hey Now (Movie Version)//Radio Head (Movie Version)/ Radio Head (Extended Remix) (double pack, gatefold p/s)	8
88	EMI EM 68	Blind/Bill (p/s)	5
88	EMI CDEM 68	Blind (Vocal Mix)/Blind/Bill (CD)	15
88	EMI 10 EM 53	Nothing But Flowers/Mommy Daddy You And I/Ruby Dear (10", p/s)	10
88	EMI CDEM 53	Nothing But Flowers/Ruby Dear (Bush Mix)/Mommy Daddy You And I/Facts Of Life (CD)	12
92	EMI EM 250	Lifetime Piling Up/Love For Sale (p/s)	5
92	EMI CDEMS 250	Lifetime Piling Up/Road To Nowhere/Love For Sale/Lady Don't Mind (CD)	10
79	Sire K 56707	FEAR OF MUSIC (LP, with free single "Psycho Killer"/"New Feeling" [SAM 108])	15
83	EMI 9237711	SPEAKING IN TONGUES (LP, clear vinyl in special cover)	18

TALK TALK

82	EMI EMI 5265	Mirror Man/Strike Up The Band (p/s)	8
82	EMI 12EMI 5314	Today (Extended)/It's So Serious (12", p/s)	10
82	EMI EMI 5352	Talk Talk (Remix)/Mirror Man (p/s)	5
82	EMI EMIP 5352	Talk Talk (Remix)/Mirror Man (picture disc)	6
82	EMI EMIP 5352	Talk Talk (Extended)/Talk Talk (BBC Version) (12", p/s)	15
83	EMI 12EMI 5373	My Foolish Friend (Extended)/Call In The Nightboys/My Foolish Friend (12", p/s)	8
84	EMI EMI 5433	Such A Shame/Again Again Again (p/s)	5
84	EMI 12EMI 5433	Such A Shame (Extended)/Such A Shame/Again, A Game... Again (12", p/s)	8
84	EMI EMID 5433	THE TALK TALK DEMOS (double pack, poster p/s [EMI 5433 & PSR 467])	12
84	EMI EMI 5443	It's My Life (Extended)/Does Caroline Know?/It's My Life (12", p/s)	15
84	EMI 12EMI 5480	Dum Dum Girl (Extended)/Such A Shame (Dub)/Without You (Extended)/ Dum Dum Girl (U.S. Mix) (12", p/s)	12
86	EMI EMI 5540	Life's What You Make it/It's Getting Late In The Evening (p/s)	5
86	EMI 12EMID 5540	Life's What You Make It (Extended)/It's Getting Late In The Evening/ It's My Life/Does Caroline Know? (12", p/s, double pack)	20
86	EMI 12EMIX 5540	Life's What You Make It (Extended Dance Mix)/Life Is What You Make It (Early Mix)/It's Getting Late In The Evening (12", p/s)	8
86	EMI EMIP 5551	Living In Another World/For What It's Worth (shaped picture disc)	12
88	Parlophone CDR 6189	I Believe In You/John Cope/Eden (Edited Version) (CD)	12
90	Parlophone R 6254	It's My Life/Rennee (live)	6
90	Parlophone CDR 6264	Life's What You Make it/(live)/Tomorrow Started (live) (CD)	8
91	Verve TALKD 1	After The Flood/Myrrhman (CD, picture disc in 3-CD box)	15
91	Verve TALKD 2	New Grass/Stump (CD, picture disc)	10
91	Verve TALKD 3	Ascension Day/5.09 (CD, picture disc)	10
91	Verve TALKD1/2/3	After The Flood/Myrrhman//New Grass/Stump/Ascension Day/5.09 (3-CD, in die-cut box)	40
88	Parlophone PC50105	SPIRIT OF EDEN (LP)	12

(see also Reaction)

TOM TALL

55	London HL 8150	Are You Mine/Boom Boom Boomerang (as Ginny Wright & Tom Tall)	38
55	London HLU 8216	Give Me A Chance/Remembering You (78 prm = £10)	50
56	London HLU 8231	Underway/Goldie Jo Malone (78 rpm = £15)	50
57	London HLU 8429	Don't You Know/If You Know What I Know (with Ruckus Taylor) (78 rpm = £22)	40
55	London RE-U 1035	COUNTRY SONGS VOL. 2 (EP, as Tom Tall & Ginny Wright)	45

(see also Ginny Wright)

TALL BOYS

82	Big Beat NS 79	Island Of Lost Souls/Another Half Hour Till Sunrise (p/s)	6
84	Big Beat NED 8	WEDNESDAY ADDAM'S BOYFRIEND (12" EP)	8
85	Big Beat NST 107	Final Kick/Interceptor/Dragster/Action Woman (12" EP)	8
86	Big Beat NST 114	Brand New Gun/Last House On The Left/Took A Long Time (12" EP)	8

(see also Meteors)

TALMY/STONE BAND

62	Decca F 11543	Madison Time/Madison Time (A-side with Alan Freeman)	6
62	Ace Of Clubs ACL 1134	ROSES ARE RED & OTHER HITS OF 1962 (LP)	18

TALULAH GOSH

86	53rd & 3rd AGARR 4	Beatnik Boy/My Best Friend (p/s)	8
86	53rd & 3rd AGARR 5	Steaming Train/Just A Dream (p/s)	5
86	53rd & 3rd AGARR 4/5T	Beatnik Boy/My Best Friend/Steaming Train/Just A Dream (12", p/s)	8
86	Sha La La 002/LYN 18147	WHO NEEDS THE BLOODY CARTEL ANYWAY (EP, p/s, flexidisc)	8
87	53rd & 3rd AGARR 8	Talulah Gosh/Don't Go Away (p/s)	5
87	53rd & 3rd AGARR 8T	Talulah Gosh/Don't Go Away (12", p/s)	8
88	53rd & 3rd AGARR 14	Bringing Up Baby/The Girl With The Strawberry Hair (p/s)	6
88	53rd & 3rd AGARR 14T	Bringing Up Baby/I Can't Get No Satisfaction, Thank God/The Girl With The Strawberry Hair/Do You Remember?/Sunny Inside (12", p/s)	8
88	53rd & 3rd AGARR 16	Testcard Girl (p/s)	5
87	53rd & 3rd AGAS 004	ROCK LEGENDS VOL. 69 (LP, clear vinyl)	15
91	Sarah 064	THEY'VE SCOFFED THE LOT (LP)	12

TAMANGOES

79	Grapevine GRP 122	I Really Love You/You've Been Gone So Long (withdrawn)	25

JAMES TAMLIN

65	Columbia DB 7438	Is There Time/Main Line Central Station	10
65	Columbia DB 7577	Yes I Have/Now There Are Two	7

TAMLINS

79	Deb Music DEB 007	Still Water/AUGUSTUS PABLO: Spirit Of Umoja (12")	20

TAMPA RED

50	Jazz Collector L 58	Easy Rider Blues/Come On Mama Do That Dance (78)	15
52	HMV JO 301	Pretty Baby Blues/Since Baby's Been Gone (78, export issue)	40
50s	Square M 2	Moot It Boy/She Rocks Me (With One Steady Roll) (78)	40
64	RCA RCX 7160	R & B VOL. 3 (EP)	25

MINT VALUE £

60s	Memory TR 1	TAMPA RED (LP)	35

TAMPA RED/GEORGIA TOM
59	Jazz Collector JEL 3	THE MALE BLUES VOLUME 2 (EP)	20

TAMS
63	Stateside SS 146	Untie Me/Disillusioned	25
63	HMV POP 1254	What Kind Of Fool Do You Think I Am/Laugh It Off	25
64	HMV POP 1298	It's All Right, You're Just In Love/You Lied To Your Daddy	18
64	HMV POP 1331	Hey Girl Don't Bother Me/Take Away (DJ copy = £200)	150
65	HMV POP 1464	Concrete Jungle/Till The End Of Time	16
69	Stateside SS 2123	Be Young, Be Foolish, Be Happy/That Same Old Song	15
70	Capitol CL 15650	Too Much Foolin' Around/How Long Love	15
71	Probe PRO 532	Hey Girl Don't Bother Me/Take Away (Reissue)	6
75	ABC ABC 4020	Hey Girl Don't Bother Me/Be Young, Be Foolish, Be Happy	8
68	Stateside (S)SL 10258	A LITTLE MORE SOUL (LP)	48
70	Stateside SSL 10304	BE YOUNG, BE FOOLISH, BE HAPPY (LP)	32
74	Probe SPB 1044	THE BEST OF THE TAMS (LP)	15
74	ABC ABCL 5118	THE BEST OF THE TAMS (LP, reissue)	12

JOCK TAMSON'S BAIRNS
(see under 'J')

TANAMO
63	Island WI 108	Come Down/I Am Holding On (actually by Lord Tanamo)	30

TANDOORI CASSETTE
83	IKA IKA 001	Angel Talk/Third World Brief Case (p/s, 5,000 only)	15

(see also Nazareth, Alex Harvey, Tear Gas, Stone The Crows)

SHARON TANDY
65	Mercury MF 898	Love Makes The World Go Round/By My Side	25
65	Pye 7N 15806	Now That You've Gone/Hurtin' Me	20
65	Pye 7N 15939	I've Found Love/Perhaps Not Forever	10
67	Atlantic 584 098	Toe Hold/I Can't Get Over It	20
67	Atlantic 584 124	Stay With Me/Hold On	35
67	Atlantic 584 137	Our Day Will Come/Look And Find	22
68	Atlantic 584 166	Fool On The Hill/For No One	22
68	Atlantic 584 181	Love Is Not A Simple Affair/Hurry Hurry Choo-Choo	20
68	Atlantic 584 194	You've Gotta Believe It/Border Town	20
68	Atlantic 584 214	The Way She Looks At You/He'll Hurt Me	20
68	Atlantic 584 219	Hold On/Daughter Of The Sun	40+
69	Atlantic 584 242	Gotta Get Enough Time/Somebody Speaks Your Name	20

(see also Fleur-De-Lys, Tony & Tandy)

NORMA TANEGA
66	Stateside SS 496	Walkin' My Cat Named Dog/I'm In The Sky	10
66	Stateside SS 537	Bread/Waves	7
66	Stateside S(S)L 10182	WALKIN' MY CAT NAMED DOG (LP)	30

TANGERINE DREAM
74	Virgin PR 214	Phaedra (Edit)/Mysterious Semblance At The Strand Of Nightmares (promo)	30
76	Virgin VDJ 17	Stratosfear/The Big Sleep In Search Of Hades (promo only)	25
77	MCA PSR 413	Betrayal (Sorceror Theme)/Search (promo only)	25
77	Virgin VS 199	Encore/Hobo March	5
81	Virgin VS 444	Chronozon/Network 23 (p/s)	8
84	Jive Electro P 74	Warsaw In The Sun/Polish Dance (map-shaped picture disc)	20
84	Jive Electro T 74	Warsaw In The Sun (Parts 1 & 2)/Polish Dance/Rare Bird (12", p/s)	15
85	Jive JIVE 101	Streethawk/Tear Garden (p/s)	15
85	Jive Electro T 101	STREETHAWK (12" EP)	20
87	Jive Electro T 143	Tyger/Tyger (7" Version)/21st Century Common Man II (12", p/s)	8
89	Private 663 747	ORANGES DON'T DANCE (CD EP, promo only)	20
74	Polydor Super 2383 297	ATEM (LP)	15
75	Polydor Super 2383 314	ALPHA CENTAURI (LP)	15
79	Virgin V 2111	FORCE MAJEURE (LP, clear vinyl)	15
80	Virgin VBOX 2	TANGERINE DREAM '70-80 (4-LP box set)	25
80	Virgin TCVX 2	TANGERINE DREAM '70-80 (4-cassette box set)	25
81	Virgin V 2212	EXIT (LP, 1st 1,000 with poster)	12
84	MCA MCF 3233	FIRESTARTER (LP, soundtrack)	12
84	Jive HIP 22	POLAND — THE WARSAW CONCERT (2-LP, gatefold sleeve, with inners)	15
84	Jive Electro HIPX 22	POLAND — THE WARSAW CONCERT (2-LP, picture disc)	25
85	Heavy Metal HMI PD 29	FLASHPOINT (LP, soundtrack, picture disc)	25
85	Heavy Metal HMXD 29	FLASHPOINT (CD, soundtrack; playable CD [most copies faulty])	50
86	Jive Electro TANG 1	IN THE BEGINNING (6-LP box set, with booklet)	25
87	Jive HIP 26	LE PARC (LP)	12
87	Jive CHIP 26	LE PARC (CD, U.K. pressing [most copies pressed in Europe])	18
90	Virgin TD AK 11	TANGERINE DREAM (3-CD, 'Collector's Edition' box set)	25

(see also Edgar Froese, Klaus Schulze)

TANGERINE PEEL
67	United Artists UP 1193	Every Christian Lion-Hearted Man Will Show You/Trapped	28
68	CBS 3402	Solid Gold Mountain/Light Across The River	8
68	CBS 3676	Talking To No One/Wishing Tree	8
69	MGM MGM 1470	Never Say Never Again/A Thousand Miles Away	12
69	MGM MGM 1487	Play Me A Sad Song And I'll Dance/Wish You Could Be Here With Me	7
70	RCA RCA 1936	Move Into My World/In Between	6
70	RCA RCA 1990	Soft Delights/Thinking Of Me	6
70	RCA RCA 2036	What Am I To Do?/Don't Let Me Be Misunderstood	6
70	RCA LSA 3002	SOFT DELIGHTS (LP)	25

TANK

81	Kamaflage KAM 1	Don't Walk Away/Shellshock/Hammer On (p/s, some with cover mounted patch) 7/5
82	Kamaflage KAM 3	Turn Your Head Around/Steppin' On A Landmine (p/s). 15
82	Kamaflage KAM 7	Crazy Horses/Filth Bitch Boogie (p/s). 5
82	Kamaflage KAP 1	(He Fell In Love With A) Stormtrooper/Blood Guts And Beer (picture disc) 7
83	MFN KUT 101	ECHOES OF A DISTANT BATTLE (EP) 8
82	Kamaflage KAMLP 1	FILTH HOUNDS OF HADES (LP, 1st pressing, with black & yellow sleeve) 15
82	Kamaflage KAMLP 1	FILTH HOUNDS OF HADES (LP, 2nd pressing, with bonus p/s 7" "Don't Walk Away (live)"/"The Snake" [KAM F1]) 12
83	Music For Nations MFN 3P	THIS MEANS WAR (LP, picture disc). 20
80s	Kamaflage KAMLP 3	POWER OF THE HUNTER (LP) 12
	(see also Damned, UK)	

TANNAHILL WEAVERS

76	Plant Life PLR 001	ARE YE SLEEPING MAGGIE? (LP, with lyric insert) 12
78	Plant Life PLR 010	THE OLD WOMAN'S DANCE (LP) 12

HOLLY TANNEN & PETE COOPER

79	Plant Life PLR 015	FROSTY MORNING (LP). 12

PHIL TANNER

68	EDF SSLP 1005	PHIL TANNER (LP, with lyric book) 25

TANTONES

57	Vogue V 9085	So Afraid/Tell Me (78 rpm = £175) 850

TANTRUM

80	Ovation OV 1247	RATHER BE ROCKIN' (LP) 12

TANZ DER YOUTH

78	Radar ADA 19	I'm Sorry, I'm Sorry/Delay (p/s) 5
	(see also Brian James, Damned)	

TAO JONES INDEX

97	RCA 512541	Pallas Athena (live)/V-2 Schneider (live) (12", p/s) 12
	(see also David Bowie)	

TAPESTRY

67	London HLZ 10138	Carnaby Street/Taming Of The Shrew. 18
68	NEMS 56-3679	Like The Sun/Florence 15
69	NEMS 5639-64	Heart & Soul/Who Wants Happiness. 30

DEMETRISS TAPP

64	Coral Q 72470	Lipstick Paint A Smile On Me/If You Find Love 40

TARANTULA

70	A&M AMLS 959	TARANTULA (LP) 15

JIMMY TARBUCK

65	Immediate IM 018	Someday/(We're) Wastin' Time 12
67	Philips	Stewball/When My Little Girl Is Smiling (p/s). 8

TARHEEL SLIM & LITTLE ANN

65	Sue WI 390	You Make Me Feel So Good/Got To Keep On Lovin' You 40

DAVE TARRIDA

99	Mosquito MSQ 013	PLAYING THE GAME (12" EP) 10

TARRIERS

56	London HLN 8340	Cindy, Oh Cindy/Only If You Praise The Lord (gold or silver label lettering, as Vince Martin & Tarriers) 25/15
57	Columbia DB 3891	The Banana Boat Song/No Hidin Place 6
57	Columbia DB 3961	Tom Dooley/Everybody Loves Saturday Night 6
57	Columbia DB 4025	Dunya/Quinto (My Little Pony). 5
58	Columbia DB 4148	I Know Where I'm Going/Acres Of Clams. 5
58	London HLU 8600	Lonesome Traveller/East Virginia (78 rpm = £8) 12
60	London RET 1236	HARD TRAVELIN' VOLUME 1 (EP) 8
60	London RET 1237	HARD TRAVELIN' VOLUME 2 (EP) 8
57	Columbia 33S 1115	THE TARRIERS (10" LP). 20
	(see also Vince Martin, Rooftop Singers)	

TARTAN HORDE

75	United Artists UP 35891	Bay City Rollers, We Love You/Rollers Theme 12
	(see also Nick Lowe, Rat Scabies, Roogalator)•	

TARTANS

67	Island WI 3058	Dance All Night/What Can I Do 20
68	Caltone TONE 115	Awake The Town (with Lynn Taitt's Band)/LYNN TAITT & JETS: The Brush . . . . 40+
68	Caltone TONE 117	Coming On Strong/It's Alright (with Tommy McCook's Band). 18
71	Escort ERT 843	A Day Will Come/ROBI'S All STARS: Version 8
	(see also Devon & Tartans, Kaddo Strings, Max Romeo, Derrick Morgan)	

TASAVALLAN PRESIDENTTI

73	Sonet SNTF 636	LAMBERTLAND (LP). 25
74	Sonet SNTF 658	MILKY WAY MOSES (LP, with insert) 25

TASKFORCE

00	White(Lowlife)grafpromo1	Graf Da Bus Up (1-Sided 12") 60
00	White(Lowlife) (no cat no)	Wha Blow (1-Sided 12") 60
02	White (no cat no)	Graf Da Bus Up/Wha Blow (12") 25
00	Lowlife LOW10	VOICE OF THE GREAT OUTDOORS (EP) 18
01	Rehab RHB001	A LIFE WITHOUT INSTRUCTIONS (EP). 15
99	K'Boro KBR1005	NEW MIC ORDER (EP) 60

MINT VALUE £

TASSELS
59	London HL 8885	To A Soldier Boy/The Boy For Me (78 rpm = £40)	100
59	Top Rank JAR 229	To A Young Lover/My Guy And I	30

TASTE
68	Major Minor MM 560	Blister On The Moon/Born On The Wrong Side Of Time	18
69	Polydor 56313	Born On The Wrong Side Of Time/Same Old Story	7
70	Major Minor MM 718	Born On The Wrong Side Of Time/Blister On The Moon	7
69	Polydor 583 042	TASTE (LP)	35
70	Polydor 583 083	ON THE BOARDS (LP)	25
71	Polydor 2310 082	LIVE TASTE (LP)	15
72	Polydor 2383 120	TASTE — LIVE AT THE ISLE OF WIGHT (LP)	15

(see also Rory Gallagher, Stud)

TASTE OF HONEY
69	Rim RIM 19	8.05/Charleston	5

BUDDY TATE
58	Felsted FAJ 7004	SWINGING LIKE TATE (LP)	30

HOWARD TATE
66	Verve VS 541	Ain't Nobody Home/How Come My Bulldog Won't Bark	15
67	Verve VS 549	Look At Granny Run Run/Half A Man	20
67	Verve VS 552	Get It While You Can/Glad I Knew Better	15
67	Verve VS 555	Baby I Love You/How Blue Can You Get	25
67	Verve VS 556	I Learned It All The Hard Way/Part Time Love	15
68	Verve VS 565	Stop/Shoot 'Em All Down	15
68	Verve VS 571	Night Owl/Every Day I Have The Blues	20
70	Major Minor MM 696	My Soul's Got A Hole In It/It's Too Late	8
67	Verve (S)VLP 9179	GET IT WHILE YOU CAN (LP)	50

PHIL TATE ORCHESTRA
58	Oriole CB 1438	Dream Lover/Zing, Went The Strings Of My Heart	5
59	Oriole CB 1514	Countdown (Jive)/Green Turtle	5
60	Oriole CB 1539	Falling In Love Again/Dancing On The Ceiling	5
60	Oriole CB 1568	Moulin Rouge Waltz/I Won't Dance (78)	10
61	Oriole CB 1601	Are You Lonesome Tonight/Whispering Tango (78 = £12)	6
63	Oriole CB 1832	Hi-Lili, Hi-Lo/Theme From 'Dr. Kildare'	5
63	Oriole CB 1878	Devils Horn (Twist)/Hitch Hike (Twist)	5
62	Oriole EP 7060	TUNES FOR TWISTERS (EP)	10

TOMMY TATE
66	Columbia DB 8046	Big Blue Diamonds/A Lover's Reward	85

TATTY OLLITY
70s	Tatty TR 101	Punktuation	10

ART TATUM
51	Melodisc MEL 1157	Fine And Dandy/Ja Da (78)	6
54	Vogue EPV 1008	ART TATUM (EP)	8
55	Columbia SEG 7540	ART TATUM (EP)	8
50s	Melodisc EPM7 108	ART TATUM TRIO (EP)	8
55	Columbia Clef SEB 10003	ART TATUM (EP)	10
56	Columbia Clef SEB 10027	TATUM-CARTER-BELLSON TRIO (EP, with Benny Carter & Louis Bellson)	8
57	Columbia Clef SEB 10062	TATUM-CARTER-BELLSON TRIO (EP, with Benny Carter & Louis Bellson)	8
57	Philips BBE 12136	UNFORGETTABLE ART (EP)	8
57	Vogue EPV 1212	ART TATUM (EP)	8
58	Columbia Clef SEB 10084	ART TATUM AT HOLLYWOOD BOWL (EP)	8
58	Columbia Clef SEB 10101	ART TATUM — BUDDY DE FRANCO QUARTET (EP)	8
59	Columbia Clef SEB 10116	DELICATE TOUCH OF ART TATUM (EP)	8
60	Fontana TFE 17235	ART TATUM NO. 1 (EP)	8
60	Fontana TFE 17236	ART TATUM NO. 2 (EP)	8
60	Fontana TFE 17237	ART TATUM NO. 3 (EP)	8
60	HMV 7EG 8604	THE GREATEST PIANO OF THEM ALL (EP)	8
60	HMV 7EG 8619	ART TATUM — BUDDY DE FRANCO QUARTET (EP)	8
61	HMV 7EG 8684	INCOMPARABLE MUSIC OF ART TATUM (EP)	8
62	Ember EMB 4502	MEMORIES OF ART TATUM (EP)	8
51	Capitol LC 6524	ART TATUM (10" LP)	15
53	Capitol LC 6625	OUT OF NOWHERE (10" LP)	25
54	Vogue LDE 081	ART TATUM "JUST JAZZ" (10" LP)	20
55	Vogue Coral LRA 10011	THE ART TATUM TRIO (10" LP)	15
55	Columbia Clef 33CX 10005	THE GENIUS OF ART TATUM (LP)	12
55	Capitol LC 6638	ART TATUM ENCORES (10" LP)	15
56	Columbia Clef 33CX 10053	THE GENIUS OF ART TATUM (NO. 2) (LP)	12
57	Columbia Clef 33C 9033	THE GENIUS OF ART TATUM (NO. 3) (10" LP)	15
57	Columbia Clef 33C 9039	PRESENTING THE ART TATUM TRIO (10" LP)	15
57	Vogue Coral LVA 9047	HERE'S ART TATUM (LP)	12
58	Columbia Clef 33CX 10115	ART TATUM (LP)	12
59	Columbia Clef 33CX 10137	ART TATUM-BEN WEBSTER QUARTET (LP)	25
60	Top Rank 35/067	ART TATUM DISCOVERIES (LP)	12
61	Brunswick LAT 8358	THE ART OF TATUM (LP)	12
61	Ember EMB 3314	MEMORIES OF ART TATUM (LP)	12
61	Ember EMB 3326	MEMORIES OF ART TATUM VOL. 2 (LP)	12
64	Xtra XTRA 1007	ART TATUM (LP)	12
67	Fontana FJL 904	ART (LP)	15

BERNIE TAUPIN
71	DJM DJLPS 415	TAUPIN (LP)	15

TAVARES
77	Capitol E-ST 11628	LOVE STORM (LP)	12

JOHN TAVENER

70	Apple SAPCOR 15	THE WHALE (LP, gatefold sleeve)	60
71	Apple SAPCOR 20	CELTIC REQUIEM (LP, gatefold sleeve, with insert & 'Apple' inner sleeve)	120
77	Ring O' 2320 104	THE WHALE (LP, reissue, different single sleeve)	45
92	Apple SAPCOR 15	THE WHALE (LP, 2nd reissue, gatefold sleeve with inner sleeve)	25
92	Apple SAPCOR 15	THE WHALE (CD)	25
93	Apple SAPCOR 20	CELTIC REQUIEM (LP, reissue, gatefold sleeve with inner sleeve)	25
93	Apple SAPCOR 20	CELTIC REQUIEM (CD)	25

TAVERNERS

69	Saga EROS 8146	SELDOM SOBER (LP)	20
73	Trailer LER 2080	BLOWING SANDS (LP, red label)	18
74	Folk Heritage FHR 062	TIMES OF OLD ENGLAND (LP)	25
78	Folk Heritage FHR 101	SAME OLD FRIENDS (LP, with insert)	12

TAW FOLK

75	Sentinel SENS 1030	DEVONSHIRE CREAM AND CIDER (LP)	12

CYRIL TAWNEY

69	Polydor 236 577	THE OUTLANDISH KNIGHT (LP)	25
70	Argo ZFB 4	SINGS CHILDREN'S SONGS FROM DEVON AND CORNWALL (LP)	25
70	Argo ZFB 9	A MAYFLOWER GARLAND (LP)	25
72	Argo ZFB 28	TAWNEY IN PORT (LP)	12
73	Argo ZFB 87	I WILL GIVE MY LOVE (LP)	12

ALLAN TAYLOR

71	Liberty LBF 15447	Sometimes/Song For Kathy	6
73	United Artists UP 35541	My Father's Room/Always You	6
71	Liberty LBS 83483	SOMETIMES (LP, gatefold sleeve)	25
72	United Artists UAS 29275	THE LADY (LP)	20
73	United Artists UAG 29468	THE AMERICAN ALBUM (LP, gatefold sleeve)	15

(see also Fairport Convention)

AUSTIN TAYLOR

60	Top Rank JAR 511	Push Push/A Heart That's True	15

BILLY TAYLOR (TRIO)

57	Esquire EP 115	BILLY TAYLOR (EP)	15
57	Esquire EP 169	BILLY TAYLOR TRIO (EP)	20
54	Felsted EDL 87009	JAZZ AT STORYVILLE (10" LP)	35
54	Esquire 20-053	AT THE TOWN HALL 1954 (LP)	30
54	Esquire 32-010	A TOUCH OF TAYLOR (LP)	30
57	HMV DLP 1181	MY FAIR LADY LOVES JAZZ (10" LP)	20
60	Vogue LAE 12192	TAYLOR MADE PIANO (LP)	20

BOBBY TAYLOR

64	Columbia DB 7282	Temptation/Mod Bod	10

BOBBY TAYLOR (& VANCOUVERS)

68	Tamla Motown TMG 654	Does Your Mama Know About Me/Fading Away (with Vancouvers)	50
73	Epic EPC 1720	I Can't Quit Your Love/Queen Of The Ghetto (solo)	8
69	T. Motown (S)TML 11093	BOBBY TAYLOR AND THE VANCOUVERS (LP)	75
70	T. Motown (S)TML 11125	TAYLOR MADE SOUL (LP, solo)	100

BRYAN TAYLOR

61	Piccadilly 7N 35018	The Donkey's Tale/Let It Snow On Christmas Day	40

CECIL TAYLOR JAZZ UNIT

60s	Fontana SFJL 926	NEFERTITI, THE BEAUTIFUL ONE HAS COME (LP)	20

CECIL TAYLOR QUARTET

60	Contemporary LAC 12216	LOOKING AHEAD! (LP)	20

CHIP TAYLOR

62	Warner Bros WB 82	Here I Am/I Love You But I Know	6
73	Buddah 2011 151	Angel Of The Morning/Swear To God, Your Honor	5
73	Buddah 2318 074	GASOLINE (LP)	12
74	Warner Bros K 56032	CHIP TAYLOR'S LAST CHANCE (LP)	12

(see also Wes Voigt)

DREW TAYLOR

60s	One Up OU 2175	DREW'S BREW (LP)	12

DUFFY TAYLOR BLUES

69	Page One POF 130	You Wrecked My Life/I'll Be There	8

EDDIE TAYLOR

65	Big Bear BEAR 6	READY FOR EDDIE (LP)	12

ELIZABETH TAYLOR

63	Colpix PXL 459	IN LONDON (LP, TV soundtrack, music by John Barry, mono/stereo)	40/50

(see also John Barry)

FELICE TAYLOR

67	President PT 120	It May Be Winter Outside/BOB KEENE ORCHESTRA: Winter Again	10
67	President PT 133	I'm Under The Influence/BOB KEENE ORCHESTRA: Love Theme	10
67	President PT 155	I Feel Love Comin' On/BOB KEENE ORCHESTRA: Comin' On Again	10
68	President PT 193	Captured By Your Love/I Can Feel Your Love (Coming Down On Me)	15
68	President PT 220	Suree-Surrender/All I Want To Do Is Love You	10

(Original President issues have an horizontal artist credit. Re-issues have a vertical credit)

GEOFF TAYLOR

55	Esquire EP 55	GEOFF TAYLOR SEXTET (EP)	10
57	Esquire EP 105	GEOFF TAYLOR ALL STARS (EP)	10

MINT VALUE £

GLORIA TAYLOR
70	Polydor BM 56788	You Gotta Pay The Price/Loving You And Being Loved By You	15

HOUND DOG TAYLOR
66	Outasite 45-504	Christine/Alley Music (99 copies only)	80

JAMES TAYLOR
70	Apple APPLE 32	Carolina In My Mind/Something's Wrong	12
68	Apple (S)APCOR 3	JAMES TAYLOR (LP, gatefold sleeve, black inner, orange cover lettering, mono/stereo)	70/50
70	Apple SAPCOR 3	JAMES TAYLOR (LP, 2nd issue, gatefold sleeve, 'Apple' inner sleeve, black cover lettering)	35
70	Warner Bros WS 1843	SWEET BABY JAMES (LP, orange label, later green label)	each 18
71	Warner Bros WS 2561	MUD SLIDE SLIM AND THE BLUE HORIZON (LP, g/fold sleeve, green label)	18
72	Warner Bros K 46043	SWEET BABY JAMES (LP, reissue, green label)	12
72	Warner Bros K 46085	MUD SLIDE SLIM AND THE BLUE HORIZON (LP, reissue, gatefold sleeve, green label)	12
73	Warner Bros K 46185	ONE MAN DOG (LP, green label, with insert & stickered sleeve)	12
91	Apple SAPCOR 3	JAMES TAYLOR (LP, reissue, gatefold sleeve)	18
91	Apple SAPCOR 3	JAMES TAYLOR (CD)	18

JAMES TAYLOR QUARTET
87	Re-Elect President FORD 1	Blow Up/One Mint Julep (p/s)	8
88	Urban URB 24	Starsky And Hutch Theme/(Version)	5
88	Urban URBX 24	Starsky And Hutch Theme/(Version) (12")	8
92	Big Life JTQ 7 PROMO 1	Absolution (live) (gig freebie, plain black sleeve with postcard, 1 side etched)	5
90s	Big Life	Hope And Pray (p/s)	5
90s	Acid Jazz JAZID 124S	Whole Lotta Love (white label, withdrawn)	100
90s	Acid Jazz JAZID 124T	Whole Lotta Love (12" EP, company sleeve)	25
90s	Acid Jazz JAZID 139	Creation (10", p/s, some mispressed with Hungarian porn music on A-side)	75/15
90s	Acid Jazz JTQ 1	Europa (Extended)/Redneck (12", company sleeve)	40
87	Re-Elect Pres. REAGAN 2	MISSION: IMPOSSIBLE (mini-LP, 45rpm)	12
87	Re-Elect Pres. KENNEDY 1	THE MONEY SPYDER (LP)	12
90s	Acid Jazz JAZID 110	EXTENDED PLAY (12" EP)	10
95	Acid Jazz JAZIDLP 115L	IN THE HANDS OF THE INEVITABLE (LP, with bonus 2-track 12")	12
90s	Acid Jazz AJXLP 117	THE PENTHOUSE SUITE (LP)	12

(see also Prisoners, Daggermen, New Jersey Kings)

JEREMY TAYLOR
62	Decca F 11502	Ag. Pleeze Daddy/Jo'burg Talking Blues	5
68	Fontana TF 962	Red Velvet Steering Wheel/Nasty Spider	5
66	Decca LK 4731	ALWAYS SOMETHING NEW (LP)	30
68	Fontana (S)TL 5475	HIS SONGS (LP)	15
69	Fontana (S)TL 5523	MORE OF HIS SONGS (LP)	15
72	Galliard GAL 4018	PIECE OF GROUND (LP)	20

JOHN TAYLOR
71	Turtle TUR 301	PAUSE AND THINK AGAIN (LP)	120+

JOHNNIE TAYLOR
67	Stax 601 003	Ain't That Lovin' You/Outside Love	30/20
68	Stax STAX 106	Who's Makin' Love/I'm Trying	8
69	Stax STAX 114	Take Care Of Your Homework/Hold On This Time	8
69	Stax STAX 122	(I Wanna) Testify/I Had To Fight With Love	10
69	Stax STAX 129	I Could Never Be President/It's Amazing	8
70	Stax STAX 141	Love Bones/Separation Line	8
70	Stax STAX 150	Steal Away/Friday Night	20
70	Stax STAX 156	I Am Somebody (Parts 1 & 2)	8
71	Stax 2025 021	Jody's Got Your Girl And Gone/A Fool Like Me	8
73	Stax 2025 083	Standing In For Jody/Shackin' Up	8
73	Stax 2025 194	I Believe In Love/Love Depression	8
75	Stax STXS 2021	It's September/Just One Moment	8
75	Stax STXS 2025	Friday Night/I Ain't Particular	10
76	CBS 4886	Disco Lady/Somebody's Gettin' It (blue vinyl)	8
67	Stax 589 008	WANTED, ONE SOUL SINGER (LP)	50
69	Stax (S)XATS 1006	WHO'S MAKING LOVE (LP)	30
69	Stax 228 008	LOOKING FOR JOHNNIE TAYLOR (LP)	25
69	Stax SXATS 1024	THE J.T. PHILOSOPHY CONTINUES (LP)	25
70	Soul City SCB 2	ROOTS OF JOHNNIE TAYLOR (LP)	75
71	Stax 2363 009	WHO'S MAKING LOVE (LP, reissue)	12
71	Stax 2362 015	GREATEST HITS (LP)	12
74	Stax STXH 5003	SUPER TAYLOR (LP)	15
75	Stax STS 3014	TAYLORED IN SILK (LP)	15
76	CBS 81201	EARGASM	12
78	CBS 82776	EVER READY (LP)	12

(LITTLE) JOHNNY TAYLOR
65	Vocalion V 9234	Part Time Love/Somewhere Down The Line (DJ copy = £75)	45
66	Vocalion VP 9264	One More Chance/Looking At The Future	30
72	Mojo 2092 033	Everybody Knows About My Good Thing (Parts 1 & 2)	8
72	Mojo 2092 044	It's My Fault Darling/There's Something On Your Mind	8
65	Vocalion VA-F 8031	LITTLE JOHNNY TAYLOR (LP)	100
72	Mojo 2916 015	EVERYBODY KNOWS ABOUT MY GOOD THING (LP)	30
73	Contempo COLP 1003	OPEN HOUSE AT MY HOUSE (LP)	15
74	Contempo CLP 502	SUPER TAYLORS (LP, with Ted Taylor)	15

JOSEPH TAYLOR
72	Leader LEA 4050	UNTO BRIGG FAIR (LP, gatefold sleeve with booklet)	20

KINGSIZE TAYLOR (& DOMINOS)

64	Polydor NH 66990	Memphis Tennessee/Money (reissue of Shakers single)	20
64	Polydor NH 66991	Hippy Hippy Shake/Dr. Feelgood (reissue of Shakers single)	20
64	Decca F 11874	Stupidity/Bad Boy	40
64	Decca F 11935	Somebody's Always Trying/Looking For My Baby (solo)	40
65	Polydor BM 56152	Thinkin'/Let Me Love You	30
63	Polydor EPH21 628	TWIST AND SHAKE (EP, manufactured in Germany)	100
64	Decca DFE 8569	TEENBEAT 2 — FROM THE STAR CLUB, HAMBURG (EP)	120

(see also Shakers, Paddy Klaus & Gibson)

KO KO TAYLOR

66	Chess CRS 8035	Wang Dang Doodle/Blues Heaven (DJ copy = £50)	25
72	Chess 6145 018	Violent Love/The Egg Or The Hen/Wang Dang Doodle	8

LIVINGSTON TAYLOR

70	Warner Bros WS 3006	LIVINGSTONE TAYLOR (LP)	12

MICK TAYLOR

65	CBS 201770	London Town/Hoboin'	25+

MICK TAYLOR

79	CBS 82600	MICK TAYLOR (LP, with inner sleeve)	12
90	Maze 084 649	STRANGER IN THIS TOWN (LP)	12

(see also Rolling Stones, Gods, Institute Of Formal Research)

MIKE TAYLOR

65	Columbia SX 6042	PENDULUM (LP)	275+
66	Columbia SX 6137	TRIO (LP)	300+

(see also Jack Bruce)

MONTANA TAYLOR

52	Vocalion V 1011	Indiana Avenue Stomp/ROMEO NELSON: Head Rag Hop (78)	6

NEVILLE TAYLOR (& CUTTERS)

58	Parlophone R 4447	House Of Bamboo/Mercy, Mercy, Percy (solo) (78 rpm = £20)	40
58	Parlophone R 4476	Tears On My Pillow/I Don't Want To Set The World On Fire (solo) (78 rpm = £12)	20
58	Parlophone R 4493	A Baby Lay Sleeping/The Miracle Of Christmas (solo) (78 rpm = £10)	12
59	Parlophone R 4524	Crazy Little Daisy/The First Words Of Love (solo) (78 rpm = £15)	30
60	Oriole CB 1546	Dance With Dolly/Free Passes (78 rpm = £20+)	30
60	Embassy WB 373	It Ain't Necessarily So/BOBBIE BRITTON: Woman Is A Sometime Love (78 rpm = £6)	6
60s	Honey Hit TB 127	Joshua Fit The Battle Of Jericho/It's Me, It's Me, It's Me, My Love (some p/s)	12/6

(see also Hal Munro, Bobbie Britton)

PEGGY TAYLOR

60	Top Rank JAR 421	(Won't You Come Home) Bill Bailey/So Similar	7

R. DEAN TAYLOR

68	Tamla Motown TMG 656	Gotta See Jane/Don't Fool Around	8
71	Tamla Motown TMG 763	Indiana Wants Me/Love's Your Name	8
71	Tamla Motown TMG 786	Ain't It A Sad Thing/Backstreet (unissued)	
71	Rare Earth RES 101	Ain't It A Sad Thing/Backstreet (has TMG 786 matrix in run-out groove)	15
74	Tamla Motown TMG 896	There's A Ghost In My House/Let's Go Somewhere	8
71	Tamla Motown STML 11185	INDIANA WANTS ME (LP)	25

ROD TAYLOR

78	Little Lute HITDD 311	Jah Should Come Now/Africa Be Free/PRINCE HAMMER: Maccabee Bible (12")	30
78	Hit Run APLP 9031	IF JAH SHOULD COME DOWN NOW (LP)	50
80	Greensleeves GREL 17	WHERE IS YOUR LOVE MANKIND? (LP, green vinyl)	22

ROD TAYLOR & MIKEY DREAD & KING TUBBY

79	Sufferers Heights SUFF 006	Behold Him/Parrot Jungle/His Majesty/Dread All The Way (12")	30

ROGER TAYLOR

77	EMI EMI 2679	I Wanna Testify/Turn On The TV (demo copies £80)	60
81	EMI EMI 5157	Future Management/Laugh Or Cry (p/s)	20
81	EMI EMI 5200	My Country (Edit)/Fun In Space (p/s)	40
84	EMI EMI 5478	Man On Fire/Killing Time (p/s)	12
84	EMI 12 EMI 5478	Man On Fire (Extended)/Killing Time (12", p/s)	60
84	EMI EMI 5490	Strange Frontier/I Cry For You (Remix) (p/s)	15
84	EMI 12 EMI 5490	Strange Frontier (Extended)/I Cry For You (Extended Remix)/Two Sharp Pencils (Get Bad) (12", p/s)	45
94	Parlophone R 6379	Nazis 1994/Nazis 1994 (Version) (red vinyl, numbered p/s)	5
94	Parlophone 12RC 6379	Nazis 1994 (Single Version)/(Radio Mix)/(Makita Mix — Extended)/(Big Science Mix) (12", clear vinyl, with numbered insert in PVC sleeve)	8
94	Parlophone CDR 6379	Nazis 1994 (Single Version)/(Radio Mix)/(Kick Mix)/(Schindler's Mix — Extended)/(Makita Mix — Extended)/(Big Science Mix) (CD)	8
94	Parlophone NAZIS 1	Nazis 1994 (Radio Mix)/Nazis 1944 (Kick Mix) (12", black vinyl, p/s, promo only)	40
94	Parlophone NAZIS 3	Nazis 1994 (Radio Mix)/(Kick Mix)/(Big Science Mix)/(Makita Mix) (12", black vinyl, p/s, promo only)	40
94	Parlophone NAZIS 4	Nazis 1994 (Schindler's Mix)/(Big Science Mix)/(Makita Mix — Extended) (12", black vinyl, p/s, promo only)	40
94	Parlophone 12RDJ 6379	Nazis 1994 (Schindler's Mix)/(Big Science Mix)/(Makita Mix — Extended) (12", white label DJ promo)	180
94	Parlophone R 6389	Foreign Sand (Single Version)/You Had To Be There (as Roger Taylor & Yoshiki) (blue vinyl, numbered p/s)	6
94	Parlophone 12R 6389	Foreign Sand (Single Version)/(Album Version)/You Had To Be There/Final Destination (as Roger Taylor & Yoshiki) (12", picture disc, with no'd insert)	8
94	Parlophone R 6399	Happiness/Ride The Wild Wind (live) (green vinyl, numbered p/s)	6
94	Parlophone 12R 6399	Happiness/Dear Mr. Murdoch/Everybody Hurts Sometime (live)/Old Friends (live) (12", picture disc, with numbered insert)	8

Roger TAYLOR

94	Parlophone CDPCS 157	Happiness/Dear Mr. Murdoch/Everybody Hurts Sometime (live)/ Old Friends (live) (CD, numbered)	25
81	EMI EMC 3369	FUN IN SPACE (LP)	15
84	EMI RTA 1	STRANGE FRONTIER (LP)	15
93	Parlophone PCSD 157	HAPPINESS? (LP, some numbered)	40

(see also Queen, Cross, Hilary Hilary, Ian Hunter, Fox, Kansas, Camy Todorow, Mel Smith, Billy Squier)

ROSEMARY TAYLOR
75	JD 2009	TAYLORMAID (LP, private pressing with insert)	200

(see also Great Saturday Night Swindle)

SAM ('THE MAN') TAYLOR
54	MGM SP 1106	Please Be Kind/This Can't Be Love (as Sam 'The Man' Taylor & Cat Men)	30
56	MGM MGM-EP 531	SAM TAYLOR ORCHESTRA (EP)	38

(see also Claude Cloud)

TED TAYLOR FOUR
58	Oriole CB 1464	Son Of Honky Tonk/Farrago (78 rpm = £10)	12
60	Oriole CB 1573	M.1./You Are My Sunshine	12
61	Oriole CB 1574	Fried Onions/Yellow Rock Of Texas	12
61	Oriole CB 1628	Cat's Eyes/Canyon	8
61	Oriole CB 1630	Flyover/Haunted Pad	15
62	Oriole CB 1713	Jericho/Everytime We Say Goodbye	15
62	Oriole CB 1767	Surfrider/Talent Spot	20

VERNON TAYLOR
59	London HLS 8905	Today Is A Blue Day/Breeze (unreleased)	
60	London HLS 9025	Mystery Train/Sweet And Easy To Love	80

VIC TAYLOR
67	Treasure Isle TI 7021	Heartaches/When It Comes To Loving You I'm Alright (B-side actually "Loving Pauper" by Dobby Dobson)	18
71	Trojan TRLS 38	DOES IT HIS WAY (LP)	20

(see also Tommy McCook)

VINCE TAYLOR (& HIS PLAYBOYS)
58	Parlophone R 4505	Right Behind You Baby/I Like Love (solo) (78 rpm = £45)	60
59	Parlophone R 4539	Brand New Cadillac/Pledging My Love	50
60	Palette PG 9001	I'll Be Your Hero/Jet Black Machine	25
61	Palette PG 9020	Move Over Tiger/What'cha Gonna Do	25
76	Chiswick (N)S 2	Brand New Cadillac/Pledging My Love (no p/s)	5
97	Cruisin' 50 CASB 006	Brand New Cadillac/Right Behind You Baby (78, 300 only)	10

WALTER TAYLOR
50s	Poydras 2	Thirty-Eight And Plus/Diamond Ring Blues	8

TAYLOR MAIDS
55	Capitol CL 14322	Po-Go Stick/Theme From "I Am A Camera" (Why Do I)	12

T-BONES
64	Columbia DB 7401	How Many More Times/I'm A Lover Not A Fighter	45
65	Columbia DB 7489	Won't You Give Him (One More Chance)/Hamish's Express Relief	40

(see also Gary Farr & T-Bones, Kevin Westlake)

T. CONNECTION
77	T.K. XC 9109	Do What You Wanna Do/Got To See My Baby (12")	10

TEA
74	Vertigo 6147 006	Good Times/Judy	5
75	Philips 6305 238	TEA (LP)	15
75	Philips 9118 001	THE SHIP (LP)	15

TEA & SYMPHONY
69	Harvest HAR 5005	Boredom/Armchair Theatre	20
69	Harvest SHVL 761	AN ASYLUM FOR THE MUSICALLY INSANE (LP, gatefold sleeve)	140
70	Harvest SHVL 785	JO SAGO (LP)	250

TEACHO & HIS STUDENTS
58	Felsted AF 104	Rock-et/Stop (78 rpm = £60)	60

TEA COMPANY
68	Mercury SMCL 20127	COME AND HAVE SOME TEA WITH THE TEA COMPANY (LP)	30

ANTHONY TEAGUE
62	Decca F 11548	Like I Don't Love You/My Guardian Angel	7

TEAM DOKUS
94	Tenth Planet TP 007	TEAM DOKUS (LP, numbered, 500 only)	15

TEA PARTY
94	Chrysalis CHR 6072	SPLENDOR SOILS (LP)	12
95	Chrysalis CHR 6108	THE EDGES OF TWILIGHT (LP)	12

TEARDROP EXPLODES
79	Zoo CAGE 003	Sleeping Gas/Camera Camera/Kirkby Workers' Dream Fades (red or blue p/s)	12/10
79	Zoo CAGE 005	Bouncing Babies/All I Am Is Loving You (p/s)	10
80	Zoo CAGE 008	Treason (It's Just A Story)/Read It In Books (some in blue & green p/s)	10/6
80	Mercury TEAR 1	When I Dream/Kilimanjaro (p/s)	5
80	Vertigo TEAR 2	Reward/Strange House In The Snow (p/s)	8
81	Mercury TEAR 312	Treason (It's Just A Story) (Remix)/Traison (C'est Juste Une Histoire)/ Use Me (12", p/s)	10
81	Mercury TEAR 4	Ha Ha I'm Drowning/Poppies In The Field (some in withdrawn p/s)	30/5
81	Mercury TEAR 44	Ha Ha I'm Drowning/Poppies In The Field/Bouncing Babies/ Read It In Books (double pack, gatefold p/s)	8

81	Mercury TEAR 44	Ha Ha I'm Drowning/Poppies In The Field/Bouncing Babies/	
		Read It In Books (double pack, withdrawn gatefold p/s)	20
81	Mercury TEAR 5	Passionate Friend/Christ Versus Warhol (p/s)	8
81	Mercury TEAR 512	Passionate Friend/Christ Versus Warhol (12")	8
81	Mercury TEAR 6	Colours Fly Away/Window Shopping For A New Crown Of Thorns (p/s & insert)	8
81	Mercury TEAR 612	Colours Fly Away/East Of The Equator/Window Shopping (12", p/s)	8
82	Mercury TEAR 7	Tiny Children/Rachael Built A Steamboat (p/s)	5
82	Mercury TEAR 7G	Tiny Children/Rachael Built A Steamboat (gatefold p/s)	5
82	Mercury TEAR 712	Tiny Children/Rachael Built A Steamboat/Sleeping Gas (live) (12", p/s)	8
83	Mercury TEAR 88	You Disappear From View/Suffocate//Ouch Monkey's/Soft Enough For You/	
		The In-Psychlopedia (double pack, gatefold p/s)	8
89	Fontana DROP 112	Serious Danger/Sleeping Gas/Seven Views Of Jerusalem (p/s)	8
90	Fontana DROT 2	Count To Ten And Run For Cover/Reward/Poppies/	
		Just Like Leila Khaled Said (12", p/s)	8
90	Fontana DROCD 2	Count To Ten And Run For Cover/Reward/Poppies/Just Like Leila Khaled Said (CD)	8
80	Mercury 6359 035	KILIMANJARO (LP, original issue, 'group photo' on cover & inner sleeve)	18
81	Mercury 6359056	WILDER (LP)	12
90	Mercury 8424391	EVERYBODY WANTS TO SHAG THE TEARDROP EXPLODES (LP, with inner)	15

(see also Julian Cope, Rabbi Joseph Gordan, Lori & Chameleons)

TEARDROPS (Jamaica)

71	Ackee ACK 126	Let Me Be Free/CINDY STARR: Sentimental Girl	7
71	Big Shot BI 582	Two In One/LAURIE'S ALL STARS: Rock-A-Boogie	7

TEARDROPS

78	Bent BIGB 3	IN AND OUT OF FASHION (12" EP, foldout p/s in poly bag)	18
79	TJM TJM 9	Seeing Double/Teardrops And Heartaches (p/s)	20
80s	Illuminated JAMS 2	FINAL VINYL (LP)	15

TEAR GAS

70	Famous SFMA 5751	PIGGY GO-GETTER (LP)	50
71	Regal Zono. SLRZ 1021	TEAR GAS (LP)	100

(see also Alex Harvey, Tandoori Cassette)

TEARJERKERS

80	Back Door DOOR 1	Murder Mystery/Heart On The Line (die cut p/s with insert)	5
81	Good Vibrations GOT 9	Love Affair/Bus Stop (p/s)	5

(see also Speed)

TEARS FOR FEARS

81	Mercury IDEA 1	Suffer The Children/Wino (p/s, original issue with light labels)	8
81	Mercury IDEA 12	Suffer The Children (Remix)/Wino/Suffer The Children (Instrumental) (12", p/s)	10
82	Mercury IDEA 212	Pale Shelter (You Don't Give Me Love) (Extended)/Pale Shelter/	
		The Prisoner (12", original p/s)	8
82	Mercury IDEA 33	Mad World/Mad World (World Remix) (p/s)	5
82	Mercury IDEA 33	Mad World/Mad World (World Remix)//Suffer The Children/	
		Ideas As Opiates (double pack)	10
82	Mercury IDEA 4	Change/The Conflict (poster p/s)	7
82	Mercury IDEA 4	Change/The Conflict (withdrawn 'fishing net' sleeve)	150
83	Mercury IDEA R/B 5	Pale Shelter/We Are Broken (p/s, red or blue vinyl) each	5
83	Mercury IDEAG 5	Pale Shelter/We Are Broken (p/s, translucent green vinyl)	7
83	Mercury IDEAP 5	Pale Shelter/We Are Broken (picture disc)	12
83	Mercury IDEA 512	Pale Shelter/We Are Broken (12", p/s)	10
83	Mercury IDEA 6	(The) Way You Are/The Marauders (rumours of poster issue remain unconfirmed)	5
83	Mercury IDEAS 6	(The) Way You Are/The Marauders//Change (Live)/Start Of The Breakdown	
		(live) (shrink wrapped double pack)	8
84	Mercury IDEA 7	Mother's Talk/Empire Building (clear vinyl picture disc)	5
84	Mercury IDEA 7	Mother's Talk/Empire Building (green vinyl, p/s, with window sticker)	8
84	Mercury IDEA 12	Mother's Talk (Beat Of The Drum Mix)/Empire Building (12", p/s)	8
85	fan club ANTAR 4502	Mother's Talk/Interview	18
85	Mercury IDEC 8	Shout/The Big Chair (calendar pack with 6 cards)	7
85	Mercury IDEA 99	Everybody Wants To Rule The World/Pharaohs//Everybody Wants To Rule	
		The World (Urban Mix)/Interview (double pack)	8
85	Mercury IDEA 910	Everybody Wants To Rule The World/Pharaohs (10", p/s)	7
85	Mercury RACE 112	Everybody Wants To Run The World/(Running Version) (12", p/s)	12
85	Mercury IDEAP 10	Head Over Heels (Remix)/When In Love With A Blind Man (poster p/s)	5
85	Mercury IDEP 10	Head Over Heels (Remix)/When In Love With A Blind Man	
		(clover-shaped picture disc)	8
85	Mercury IDEA 11	I Believe/Sea Song (p/s, sealed with set of postcards, withdrawn)	8
85	Mercury IDEA 1111	I Believe (A Soulful Re-Recording)/Sea Song//I Believe (Original Version)/	
		Shout (Dub Version) (double pack, gatefold p/s)	5
85	Mercury IDEP 10	Head Over Heels/When In Love With A Blind Man (poster p/s)	8
89	Fontana IDCDL 12	Sowing The Seeds Of Love (Full Version)/Tears Roll Down/Shout (U.S. Remix)	
		(3" CD, red/yellow plastic sunflower pack)	15
89	Fontana IDSUN 13	Woman In Chains/Always In The Past/My Life In The Suicide Ranks/	
		Woman In Chains (Instrumental) (3" CD, gold card 'sun' pack)	15
88	Mercury 080 032-2	Everybody Wants To Rule The World/The Marauders/When In Love With A Blind	
		Man/Pharaohs/Everybody Wants To Rule The World (Video) (CD Video)	15
88	Mercury 080 064-2	Shout/Everybody Wants To Rule The World (Urban Mix)/Shout (U.S.A. Mix)/	
		Shout (Video) (CD Video)	15
88	Mercury 080 062-2	Head Over Heels/Sea Song/The Working Hour/Mother's Talk (U.S.A.)/	
		Head Over Heels (Video) (CD Video)	15
88	Mercury 080 068-2	I Believe (A Soulful Re-Recording)/Start Of The Breakdown/	
		Ideas As Opiates/Change/I Believe (Video) (CD Video)	12
89	Fontana IDPT 12	Sowing The Seeds Of Love/Tears Roll Down/Shout (US Remix) (12" picture disc,	
		PVC sleeve)	10
89	Fontana 081 376-2	Sowing The Seeds Of Love (Full Version)/Tears Roll Down/	
		Shout (U.S. Remix)/Sowing The Seeds Of Love (Video) (CD Video)	10

89	Fontana IDEAB 13	Woman In Chains/Always In The Past (p/s, with badges)	6
89	Fontana IDSUN 13	Woman In Chains/(Instrumental Version)/Always In The Past (3" CD, in sun-shaped pack)	10
90	Fontana IDPOS 14	Advice For The Young At Heart/Johnny Panic And The Bible Of Dreams (poster p/s)	6
90	Fontana IDCDS 14	Advice For The Young At Heart/Johnny Panic And The Bible Of Dreams/Music For Tables (CD)	10
92	Fontana IDEAP 16	Woman In Chains/Always In The Past/Woman In Chains (Instrumental) (12" picture disc, numbered, with poster)	8
95	Mercury FFFCJ 1	Raoul And The Kings Of Spain/God's Mistake/Falling Down/Secrets (CD, sampler, promo only, card sleeve, withdrawn)	18
92	Mercury PROMO BOX	TEARS ROLL DOWN (box set, with CD, promo-only cassette & press release)	60
93	Mercury	THE ELEMENTAL INTERVIEW (CD, promo only)	18

(see also Graduate)

TEARS ON THE CONSOLE

| 75 | Holyground HG 120 | TEARS ON THE CONSOLE (LP, with booklet, 120 demo copies only) | 125 |
| 90 | Magic Mixture MM 3 | TEARS ON THE CONSOLE (LP, reissue, 425 only, with insert) | 12 |

(Band's name is actually Chick Shannon & Last Exit)

TEASER

| 89 | LTW 9KS 2049 | Here Tonight (p/s) | 20 |

TEA SET

| 66 | King KG 1048 | Join The Tea Set/Ready Steady Go! | 20 |

TEA SET

78	Waldo's Beat Series 003	CUPS AND SAUCERS (EP, with stapled lyric book sleeve)	8
79	Waldo's Beat PS 006	Parry Thomas/Tri-X Pan (gatefold p/s with poster 'mystery' envelope)	8
80	Demon D 1009	South Pacific/The Preacher (foldout p/s with inserts)	8

TECHNIQUES (Jamaica)

65	Island WI 231	Little Did You Know/DON DRUMMOND: Cool Smoke	25
67	Treasure Isle TI 7019	Queen Majesty/Fighting For The Right	35
67	Treasure Isle TI 7026	Love Is Not A Gamble/Bad-Minded People	25
68	Treasure Isle TI 7031	My Girl/Drink Wine (with Tommy McCook & Supersonics)	25
68	Treasure Isle TI 7038	Devoted/Bless You (with Tommy McCook & Supersonics)	25
68	Treasure Isle TI 7040	It's You I Love/Travelling Man (with Tommy McCook & Supersonics)	60
68	Duke DU 1	I Wish It Would Rain/There Comes A Time	60
69	Duke DU 6	A Man Of My Word/The Time Has Come	18
69	Duke DU 22	What Am I To Do/You're My Everything	15
69	Duke DU 60	Where Were You/Just One Smile	12
69	Camel CA 10	Who You Gonna Run To/Hi There (B-side act. "Look Who's Back" by Carl Bryan)	12
69	Camel CA 19	Everywhere Everyone/Find Yourself Another Fool	25
67	Treasure Isle TI 7001	You Don't Care (with Tommy McCook & Supersonics Band)/ TOMMY McCOOK & SUPERSONICS BAND: Down On Bond Street	25
70	Treasure Isle TI 7054	He Who Keepeth His Mouth/One Day (act. by Johnny Osborne & Sensations)	15
70	Techniques TE 904	Lonely Man/I Feel Alive	10
70	Techniques TE 906	Feel A Little Better (actually by Techniques Allstars)/You'll Get Left	10
70	Big Shot BI 536	He Who Keepeth His Mouth/One Day (act. by Johnny Osborne & Sensations)	12
71	Banana BA 350	Since I Lost You/RILEY'S ALLSTARS: Version	15

(see also Techniques All Stars, Riots, Tommy McCook, Mighty Avengers, Gaylads, Rad Bryan)

TECHNIQUES (U.S.)

| 58 | Columbia DB 4072 | Hey! Little Girl/In A Round About Way (78 rpm = £30) | 90+ |

TECHNIQUES ALL STARS

70	Big Shot BI 543	Come Back Darling/Move Over (actually by Johnny Osborne & Sensations)	12
70	Big Shot BI 545	Elfrego Bacca (actually by Dave Barker)/TECHNIQUES: Iron Joe (B-side actually by Techniques All Stars)	10
70	Techniques TE 900	Something Tender/CANNONBALL: Bewitch	8
70	Trojan TR 7728	El Dora/TECHNIQUES: If It's Not True (B-side actually by Techniques All Stars)	8

(see also Dennis Alcapone, Ansell Collins)

TEDDIE & THE TIGERS

| 67 | Spin SP 2004 | Hold On I'm Comin'/First Love Never Dies | 25 |

TEDDY

| 71 | Upsetter US 353 | Elusion/UPSETTERS: Big John Wayne | 15 |

TEDDY & THE CONQUERORS

| 71 | High Note HS 053 | Homebound/GAYTONES: Homebound Chapter 3 | 8 |

TEDDY & THE FRAT GIRLS

| 85 | Alternative Tentacles VIRUS 19 | I Wanna Be A Man/I Owe It All To The Girls/Clubnite/ Alophen Baby/The Eggman Don't Cometh (p/s) | 5 |

TEDDY & PEARL

(see under Teddy Johnson & Pearl Carr)

TEDDY & THE TWILIGHTS

| 63 | Stateside SS 167 | I'm Just Your Clown/Bikini Bimbo | 18 |

TEDDY BEARS

58	London HL 8733	To Know Him Is To Love Him/Don't You Worry, My Little Pet (78 rpm = £15)	12
59	London HLP 8836	I Don't Need You Anymore/Oh Why (78 rpm = £18)	25
59	London HLP 8889	You Said Goodbye/If You Only Knew (78 rpm = £20+)	35
59	London HA-P 2183	THE TEDDY BEARS SING! (LP)	250

(see also Phil Spector, Carol Connors)

WILLIE TEE

| 67 | Atlantic 584 116 | Thank You John/Walking Up A One-Way Street | 40 |
| 71 | Mojo 2092 025 | Walking Up A One-Way Street/Thank You John/Teasin' You | 15 |

TEEGARDEN & VAN WINKLE
69	Atco 228028	BUT ANYHOW (LP) 15

TEENAGE FANCLUB
90	Paperhouse PAPER 003	Everything Flows/Primary Education/Speeeder (1,500 only, die-cut p/s) 8
90	Paperhouse PAPER 005	The Ballad Of John And Yoko (p/s, 1-sided, 5,000 only, 2nd side engraved) 6
91	Creation CRESCD 105	Star Sign/(Demo Version)/Heavy Metal 6/Like A Virgin (CD, card sleeve) 12
91	Creation CRESCD 111	The Concept/What You Do To Me (Demo) (CD, card sleeve) 10
95	Creation CRESCD 216	HAVE LOST IT EP (CD, digipak) 8
03	Creation POOLS 5	Did I Say/The Cabbage (p/s, 500 only) 5
91	Creation CRELP 096	THE KING (LP, available for 1 week only, sprayed plain sleeve) 20
91	Creation CRECD 096	THE KING (CD, available for 1 week only, sprayed plain sleeve) 20

(see also Boy Hairdressers, BMX Bandits, Clouds, Eugenius)

TEENAGE FILMSTARS
79	Clockwork COR 002	(There's A) Cloud Over Liverpool/Sometimes Good Guys
		Don't Follow Trends (1st 150 with foldout p/s) 100/25
80	Wessex WEX 275	The Odd Man Out/I Apologise 25
80	Blueprint BLU 2013	The Odd Man Out/I Apologise (reissue, p/s) 20
80	Fab Listening FL 1	I Helped Patrick McGoohan Escape/We're Not Sorry (p/s) 15

(see also Television Personalities, Times, O Level)

TEENAGERS
57	RCA RCX 102	THE TEENAGERS (EP) 60

TEENAGERS featuring FRANKIE LYMON
(see under Frankie Lymon)

TEENBEATS
79	Safari SAFE 17	I Can't Control Myself/I Never Win (p/s) 15
79	Safari SAFE 19	Strength Of The Nation/I'm Gone Tomorrow (some with p/s) 20/8

TEEN BEATS (U.S.)
60	Top Rank JAR 342	The Slop Beat/Califf Boogie (featuring Don Rivers & Califfs) 15

TEEN QUEENS
65	R&B MRB 5000	Eddie My Love/Just Goofed 20

TEEN STARLETS
61	Top Rank JAR 583	The Children's Picnic Song/Theme From 'Spinster' 5

TEE SET
70	Major Minor MM 666	Ma Belle Amie/Angels Coming 7
70	Columbia DB 8375	Mr Music Man/In My House 5
70s	Waldo's 3	CUPS AND SAUCERS EP (foldout sleeve) 8
70	Columbia SCX 6419	MA BELLE AMIE (LP) 15

TEESIDE FETTLER
74	Tradition TSR 016	RING OF IRON (LP) 15
75	Tradition TSR 021	TRAVELLING THE TEES (LP) 15

TEETH
79	Soho SH 8	Say Hello To Suzy/Human Bondage (p/s) 5

JOHN TEJADA
98	Ferox 030	SONIC LIFE EP (12", plain sleeve) 8

TELEGRAMS
78	Creole CR 163	Oh Baby Please/Hey Baby 5

(See also Steve Allan, Alan Carvell, Carvells, Five Sapphires)

TELESCOPES
87	private cassette	THE TREE 'ATES EP (demo cassette) 10
88	Cheree CHEREE 1	Forever Close Your Eyes/LOOP: Soundhead (33rpm flexi, p/s, 1,000 only) 6
89	Cheree CHEREE 2	Kick The Wall/This Is The Last Of What's Coming Now (p/s, with insert,
		1,000 only, light grey/blue p/s) 5
89	Cheree CHEREE 2	Kick The Wall/This Is The Last Of What's Coming Now
		(numbered re-pressing, 500 only, red wraparound p/s) 8

TELEVISION
77	Elektra K 12252	Marquee Moon Parts 1 & 2 5
78	Elektra K 12287	Foxhole/Careful (12", red vinyl) 8
79	Ork/WEA NYC 1T	Little Johnny Jewel Parts 1 & 2/Little Johnny Jewel (live) (12", p/s) 8

(see also Neon Boys)

TELEVISION PERSONALITIES
78	Teen '78 SRTS/CUS/77/089	14th Floor/Oxford Street W1 (p/s, various different sleeve designs) 50/35
78	Kings Road LYN 5976/7	WHERE'S BILL GRUNDY NOW? (EP, hand-stamped label, 2,000 only) 25
78	Kings Road LYN 5976/7	WHERE'S BILL GRUNDY NOW? (EP, white labels, various sleeves) 12
79	Rough Trade RT 033	WHERE'S BILL GRUNDY NOW? (EP, reissue, different p/s, printed labels) 10
80	Rough Trade RT 051	Smashing Time/King & Country (p/s) 15
81	Rough Trade RT 063	I Know Where Syd Barrett Lives/Arthur The Gardener (p/s) 12
82	Whaam! WHAAM 4	Three Wishes/Geoffrey Ingram/And Don't The Kids Just Love It
		(p/s, 2 different sleeve designs, 2,000 only) 15
82	Creation Artefact 002/	Biff Bang Pow!/A Picture Of Dorian Gray (1-sided flexidisc,
	Lyntone LYN 13546	some with *Communication Blur* fanzine) 25/18
83	Rough Trade RT 109	A Sense Of Belonging/Paradise Estate (p/s) 12
86	Dreamworld DREAM 4	How I Learnt To Love The Bomb/Then God Snaps His Fingers/
		Now You're Just Being Ridiculous (12", p/s, 3,700 only) 14
86	Dreamworld DREAM 10	How I Learnt To Love The Bomb/Grocer's Daughter/
		Girl Called Charity (7", reissue, p/s, 1,000 only) 15
87	Dreamworld DREAM 13(T)	Privilege/Me And My Desires (unreleased)
89	Overground OVER 03	14th Floor/Oxford Street W1 (numbered p/s,
		600 yellow vinyl, 400 white vinyl; 1,000 black vinyl) 6/7/4

89	Caff CAFF 5	I Still Believe In Magic/Respectable (p/s, some in poly bag, 500 only) 35/25
90	Overground OVER 13	I Know Where Syd Barrett Lives/Arthur The Gardener (reissue, p/s, 2000 only) 6
90	Overground OVER 15	Silly Girl (unissued, 100 test pressings only) 18
92	Seminal Twang TWANG 15	We Will Be Your Gurus/Miro/An Exhibition By Jane/Love Is Better Than War (p/s) . . 7
81	Rough Trade ROUGH 24	AND DON'T THE KIDS JUST LOVE IT (LP, 1st 1,000 with insert) 50/35
81	Whaam! WHAAM 3	MUMMY YOU'RE NOT WATCHING ME (LP, 3,500 only, 1st 1,000 with insert) . . 50/35
82	Whaam! BIG 5	THEY COULD HAVE BEEN BIGGER THAN THE BEATLES (LP, 2,500 only,
		hand-painted sleeve) 35
83	Whaam! BIG 10	TURN ON ... TUNE IN (LP, unreleased)
84	Dreamworld HWDS 001	I KNOW WHERE DAN TREACY LIVES (live at Forum 20/9/84)
		(cassette only, fan club issue) 35
85	Illuminated JAMS 37	THE PAINTED WORD (LP) 25
86	Dreamworld BIG DREAM 2	THEY COULD HAVE BEEN BIGGER THAN THE BEATLES
		(LP, reissue with insert) 20
86	Dreamworld BIG DREAM 4	MUMMY YOU'RE NOT WATCHING ME (LP, reissue with insert) 20
87	Dreamworld BIG DREAM 6	PRIVILEGE (LP, unreleased)

(see also Teenage Filmstars, Times, O Level, Missing Scientists, Reacta, Dry Rib, Slaughter, Gifted Children)

TELEX
78	Sire SIR 4006	Twist A Saint-Tropez/Le Fond De L'Air (p/s). 5
79	Sire SIR 4017	Moskow Diskow/Twist A Saint-Tropez (p/s) 6
79	Sire SIR 4017T	Moskow Diskow (Disco Version)/Twist A Saint-Tropez (Disco Version) (12") 10
79	Sire SIR 4020	Rock Around The Clock/Moskow Diskow 5
79	Sire SIR 4020T	Rock Around The Clock (Extended Version)/Moskow Diskow (Disco Version) (12"). 8
80	Sire SIR 4039	Eurovision (English Version)/Eurovision (French Version) (p/s) 5
80	Sire SIR 4043	Getting Old (New Mix)/Tropical (p/s). 6
80	Sire SIR 4047	Soul Waves/Soul Waves (instrumental) (p/s) 6
80	Sire SIR 4047T	Soul Waves (Extended)/Dance To The Music (Remix)/
		Colonel Olrick (12"). 12
82	Interdisc IN 2	L'amour Toujours/Cloche Et Sifflets (p/s). 5
79	Sire SRK 6072	LOOKING FOR ST. TROPEZ (LP, with lyric inner sleeve) 15
82	Interdisc INTO 1	BIRDS AND BEES (LP) 20

TELHAM TINKERS
| 84 | Eron ERON 031 | HOT IN ALICE SPRINGS (LP, with insert) . . . . 12 |

TELLERS
| 74 | Pyramid PYR 7011 | No Work, No Pay/Version. . . . . 6 |
| 74 | Dragon DRA 1031 | Ta It Deh/Hit Dib. . . . . 6 |

TELSTARS
| 62 | Oriole CB 1754 | I Went A' Walkin'/A Rose And A Thorn . . . . 15 |

TEMPERANCE SEVEN
61	Argo EAF 14	THE TEMPERANCE SEVEN INCH RECORD (EP). 12
61	Argo RG 11	THE TEMPERANCE SEVEN PLUS ONE (LP) 20
61	Parlophone PMC 1152	THE TEMPERANCE SEVEN 1961 (LP, also stereo PCS 3021) 22

(see also Ted Wood)

TEMPEST
| 73 | Bronze ILPS 9220 | TEMPEST (LP, foldover cover with lyric inner sleeve) . . . . 30 |
| 74 | Bronze ILPS 9267 | LIVING IN FEAR (LP, die-cut cover with inner sleeve) . . . . 25 |

(see also Colosseum)

TEMPEST
85	Magnet PEST 1	Always The Same/Love In The Wintertime (p/s) 50
85	Magnet 10PEST 1	Always The Same/The Physical Act (10"). 25
85	Magnet PEST 2	Bluebelle/I Want To Live (p/s) 50
85	Magnet 10PEST 2	Bluebelle/I Want To Live (10") 25
86	Magnet LAZY 1	Lazy Sunday/You've Always Got Something To Say (p/s) 15
86	Magnet PEST 3	Didn't We Have A Nice Time?/The Physical Act 50

BOBBY TEMPEST
| 59 | Decca F 11125 | Love Or Leave/Don't Leave Me (78 rpm = £10) . . . . 12 |

BOB TEMPLE
| 57 | Parlophone R 4264 | Come Back, Come Back/Vim Vam Vamoose (78 rpm = £10) . . . . 120 |

GERRY TEMPLE
61	HMV POP 823	No More Tomorrows/So Nice To Walk You Home 40
61	HMV POP 939	Seventeen Come Sunday/Tell You What I'll Do 38
63	HMV POP 1114	Angel Face/Since You Went Away. 45
68	RCA Victor RCA 1670	Lovin' Up A Storm/Everything I Do is Wrong. 15

RICHARD TEMPLE
| 70 | Jay Boy BOY 31 | That Beatin' Rhythm/Could It Be (DJ copy = £30). . . . . 15 |

SHIRLEY TEMPLE
| 59 | Top Rank JAR 139 | On The Good Ship Lollipop/Animal Crackers In My Soup (78 rpm = £25) . . . . 8 |
| 59 | Top Rank JKR 8003 | I REMEMBER (EP). . . . . 20 |

TEMPLEAIRES
| 60s | Vogue V 2421 | He Spoke/What Will Heaven Have In Store For Me . . . . 20 |

TEMPLE OF THE DOG
92	A&M AM 0091	Hunger Strike/All Night Thing (picture disc) 15
92	A&M AMY 0091	Hunger Strike/Your Saviour/All Night Thing (12", p/s, with poster). 15
92	A&M AMCD 0091	Hunger Strike/Your Saviour/All Night Thing (CD, digipak) 20
91	A&M 395350-1	TEMPLE OF THE DOG (LP) 30

(see also Pearl Jam)

TEMPLE ROW
| 72 | Polydor 2058254 | King & Queen/One Of A Million Faces | 50 |

NINO TEMPO
57	London HLU 8387	Tempo's Tempo/June's Blues (as Nino Tempo & His Band) (78 rpm = £80).	320
75	A&M AMS 7190	Come See Me Round Midnight/High On Music (as Nino Tempo & 5th Avenue).	5
58	London HB-U 1075	ROCK 'N' ROLL BEACH PARTY (10" LP)	300

(see also Nino Tempo & April Stevens, April Stevens)

NINO TEMPO & APRIL STEVENS
62	London HLK 9580	Sweet And Lovely/TOP NOTES: Twist And Shout	15
63	London HLK 9782	Deep Purple/I've Been Carrying A Torch For You So Long That I Burned A Great Big Hole In My Heart.	10
64	London HLK 9829	Whispering/Tweedle Dee	7
64	London HLK 9859	Stardust/1-45	8
64	London HLK 9890	Tea For Two/I'm Confessin' (That I Love You)	8
66	London HLU 10084	All Strung Out/I Can't Go On Living Baby Without You	12
67	Atlantic 584 048	Coldest Night Of The Year/Ooh La La (as April Stevens & Nino Tempo)	8
67	London HLU 10106	The Habit Of Lovin' You Baby/You'll Be Needing Me Baby	12
67	London HLU 10130	My Old Flame/Wings Of Love	8
68	Atlantic 584 151	Deep Purple/Sweet And Lovely	6
68	London HLU 10209	Ooh Poo Pah Doo/Let It Be Me	7
69	London HLU 10245	All Strung Out/My Old Flame	15
69	Bell BLL 1087	Sea Of Love/On The Dock Of The Bay/Twilight Time	6
73	A&M AMS 7075	Put It Where You Want It/I Can't Get Over You Baby.	8
64	London RE-K 1412	DEEP PURPLE (EP).	22
64	London HA-K 8168	NINO TEMPO AND APRIL STEVENS — DEEP PURPLE (LP)	50
64	Atlantic (S)AL 5006	SING THE GREAT SONGS (LP, mono/stereo)	35/45
67	London HA-U/SH-U 8314	ALL STRUNG OUT (LP)	40

(see also Nino Tempo, April Stevens)

TEMPOS
| 59 | Pye International 7N 25026 | See You In September/Bless You My Love (78 rpm = £80). | 100 |

TEMPREES
72	Stax 2025 147	Explain To Her Mama/Dedicated To The One I Love	8
74	Stax STS 2027	At Last/I'll Live Her Life	8
72	Stax 2325 083	LOVE MEN (LP)	30
74	Stax STX 1040	THREE (LP)	30

TEMPTATIONS
| 60 | Top Rank JAR 384 | Barbara/Someday | 40 |

TEMPTATIONS
SINGLES
64	Stateside SS 278	The Way You Do The Things You Do/Just Let Me Know (DJ copy = £120)	50
64	Stateside SS 319	I'll Be In Trouble/The Girl's Alright With Me (DJ copy = £120).	60
64	Stateside SS 348	Why You Wanna Make Me Blue/Baby Baby I Need You (DJ copy = £200)	100
65	Stateside SS 378	My Girl/(Talking 'Bout) Nobody But My Baby (DJ copy = £150).	40
65	Tamla Motown TMG 504	It's Growing/What Love Has Joined Together (DJ copy £100).	40
65	Tamla Motown TMG 526	Since I Lost My Baby/You've Got To Earn It (DJ copy = £100)	40
65	Tamla Motown TMG 541	My Baby/Don't Look Back (DJ copy = £100)	40
66	Tamla Motown TMG 557	Get Ready/Fading Away (DJ copy = £100)	30
66	Tamla Motown TMG 565	Ain't Too Proud To Beg/You'll Lose A Precious Love (spelt "Previous") (DJ = £130)	20
66	Tamla Motown TMG 578	Beauty Is Only Skin Deep/You're Not An Ordinary Girl (DJ copy = £130)	20
66	Tamla Motown TMG 587	(I Know) I'm Losing You/Little Miss Sweetness (DJ copy = £80)	15
67	Tamla Motown TMG 610	All I Need/Sorry Is A Sorry Word (DJ copy = £60)	20
67	Tamla Motown TMG 620	You're My Everything/I've Been Good To You (DJ copy = £50)	15
67	Tamla Motown TMG 633	(Loneliness Made Me Realise) It's You That I Need/I Want A Love I Can See (DJ £85)	45
68	Tamla Motown TMG 641	I Wish It Would Rain/I Truly, Truly Believe (DJ copy = £30)	15
68	Tamla Motown TMG 658	I Could Never Love Another (After Loving You)/Gonna Give Her All The Love I've Got (DJ copy = £30)	15
68	Tamla Motown TMG 671	Why Did You Leave Me Darling/How Can I Forget (DJ copy = £30).	15
69	Tamla Motown TMG 688	Get Ready/My Girl (DJ copy = £30)	8
69	Tamla Motown TMG 699	Ain't Too Proud To Beg/Fading Away (DJ copy = £25)	8
69	Tamla Motown TMG 707	Cloud Nine/Why Did She Have To Leave Me (Why Did She Have To Go) (DJ = £25)	8
69	Tamla Motown TMG 716	Runaway Child, Running Wild/I Need Your Lovin'.	10
70	Tamla Motown TMG 722	I Can't Get Next To You/Running Away (Ain't Gonna Help You)	8
70	Tamla Motown TMG 741	Psychedelic Shack/That's The Way Love Is.	6
70	Tamla Motown TMG 749	Ball Of Confusion (That's What The World Is Today)/It's Summer	6
71	Tamla Motown TMG 773	Just My Imagination (Running Away With Me)/You Make Your Own Heaven And Hell Right Here On Earth	6
71	Tamla Motown TMG 783	It's Summer/Unite The World (Ungena Za Ulimwengu).	6
72	Tamla Motown TMG 800	Superstar/Gonna Keep Tryin' Till I Win Your Love	8
72	Tamla Motown TMG 808	Take A Look Around/Smooth Sailing (From Now On).	6
72	Tamla Motown TMG 832	Smiling Faces Sometimes/Mother Nature	8
73	Tamla Motown TMG 839	Papa Was A Rolling Stone (Parts 1 & 2).	6

EPs
| 65 | Tamla Motown TME 2004 | THE TEMPTATIONS. | 50 |
| 66 | Tamla Motown TME 2010 | IT'S THE TEMPTATIONS. | 40 |

LPs
65	Tamla Motown TML 11009	MEET THE TEMPTATIONS	200
65	Tamla Motown TML 11016	SING SMOKEY.	60
66	T. Motown (S)TML 11023	THE TEMPTIN' TEMPTATIONS (mono/stereo).	50/60
66	T. Motown (S)TML 11035	GETTIN' READY (mono/stereo).	50/55

67	T. Motown (S)TML 11042	GREATEST HITS	20
67	T. Motown (S)TML 11053	THE TEMPTATIONS LIVE!	30
67	T. Motown (S)TML 11057	WITH A LOT O'SOUL	40
68	T. Motown (S)TML 11068	IN A MELLOW MOOD	40
68	T. Motown (S)TML 11079	THE TEMPTATIONS WISH IT COULD RAIN	40
69	T. Motown (S)TML 11104	THE TEMPTATIONS LIVE AT THE COPA	25
69	T. Motown (S)TML 11109	CLOUD NINE	30
70	T. Motown (S)TML 11133	PUZZLE PEOPLE	30
70	T. Motown (S)TML 11141	'LIVE' AT LONDON'S TALK OF THE TOWN	20
70	Tamla Motown STML 11147	PSYCHEDELIC SHACK	30
70	Tamla Motown STML 11170	GREATEST HITS Vol. 2	15
71	Tamla Motown STML 11184	THE SKY'S THE LIMIT	20
72	Tamla Motown STML 11202	SOLID ROCK	15
72	Tamla Motown STML 11218	ALL DIRECTIONS	15
73	Tamla Motown STML 11229	MASTERPIECE	15

(see also David Ruffin, Eddie Kendricks, Diana Ross)

TEMPUS FUGIT
69	Philips BF 1802	Come Alive/Emphasis On Love	38

(see also Jensens)

TEN BENSON
98	Sweet SWEE 010	The Claw (p/s)	5

10cc
72	UK UK 22	Johnny Don't Do It/4% Of Something	6
74	UK UK 57	The Worst Band In The World/18 Carat Man Of Means	6
73	UK UKAL 1005	10cc (LP)	12
80s	Mercury HS 9102 500	THE ORIGINAL SOUNDTRACK (LP, half-speed master)	12
80s	Mercury HS 9102 504	GREATEST HITS (LP, half-speed master)	12
95	Avex AVEXLP	MIRROR MIRROR (LP)	12

(see also Godley & Creme, Graham Gouldman, Mindbenders, Mockingbirds, Hotlegs, Whirlwinds, Tristar Airbus, Yellow Bellow Room Boom, Nick Mason & Rick Fenn, Frabjoy & Runcible Spoon, Manchester Mob, Ramases)

TENDER TONES
69	Crab CRAB 38	Devil Woman/Nobody Cares	8

TEN FEET
66	RCA RCA 1544	Got Everything But Love/Factory Worker	30
67	CBS 3045	Shot On Sight/Losing Game	40

TEN FEET FIVE
65	Fontana TF 578	Baby's Back In Town/Send Me No More Lovin'	40

(see also Troggs)

TEN FOOT BONELESS
88	Fierce FRIGHT 027	Powerslide/Duane Peters Is God (12", yellow or white p/s, with inner)	12

(see also Pooh Sticks)

TENNENT & MORRISON
72	Polydor 2383 152	TENNENT & MORRISON (LP, with insert)	120

(see also Joe Soap)

TENNESSEE JAY BIRDS
51	London L 1007	Sticks And Stones/Trouble Trouble (78)	10

TENNIS SHOES
78	Bonaparte BONE 3	(Do The) Medium Wave/Rolf Is Stranger Than Richard/So Large (p/s)	8

TEN(N)ORS
68	Doctor Bird DB 1152	Massy Massa/CLIVE ALLSTARS: San Sebastian	25
68	Doctor Bird DB 1175	Sufferer (Make It)/Little Things	25
68	Island WI 3133	Ride Your Donkey/I've Got To Get You Off My Mind	8
68	Island WI 3140	Copy Me Donkey (as Tenors)/The Stage (B-side actually by Ronnie Davis)	30
68	Island WI 3156	Grampa/ROMEO STEWART: While I Was Walking	22
68	Blue Cat BS 127	Khaki/LEYROY REID: Great Surprise (Pound Get A Blow)	18
68	Big Shot BI 501	Reggae Girl/CLIVE ALLSTARS: Donkey Trot	18
68	Fab FAB 41	Ride Your Donkey/I've Got To Get You Off My Mind	12
68	Fab FAB 50	Let Go Yah Donkey/ROMEO STEWART: While I Was Walking	12
69	Big Shot BI 514	You're No Good/Do The Reggae	15
69	Big Shot BI 517	Another Scorcher/My Baby	15
69	Duke Reid DR 2502	Hopeful Village/TOMMY McCOOK: The Village	10
69	Bullet BU 406	Greatest Scorcher/Making Love	10
69	Crab CRAB 26	Baff Boom/Feel Bad	12
69	Crab CRAB 29	True Brothers/Sign Of The Time	6
69	Crab CRAB 36	I Want Everything/Cherry	8
73	Explosion EX 2079	Weather Report/Weather Report — Version	8
73	Pyramid PYR 7000	Money Never Built A Mountain/My World	5

(see also Jennors, Prince Buster, Soul Brothers)

TENPOLE TUDOR
80	Korova KOW 4	Real Fun/What's In A Word (p/s)	5

(see also Sex Pistols)

10,000 MANIACS
84	Reflex RE 1	My Mother The War (Remix)/Planned Obsolescence/National Education Week (12", p/s)	20
84	Press P 2010	HUMAN CONFLICT 5 (12" EP, gatefold p/s)	30
85	Lyntone LYN 15914	Grey Victory/SIMPLY RED: Something's Burning (33rpm 1-sided clear flexidisc free with *Jamming!* magazine, issue 29)	12/8
84	Press P 3001 LP	SECRETS OF THE I-CHING (LP, with insert; later re-pressed in different 'Chinese Chicken' sleeve, some with insert)	25/15

TEN WHEEL DRIVE (with GENYA RAVAN)

71	Polydor 2066 034	Mornin' Much Better/Stay With Me	5
69	Polydor 583 577	CONSTRUCTION NO. 1 (LP)	15
70	Polydor 2425 002	BRIEF REPLIES (LP, with Genya Ravan)	15
71	Polydor 2425 065	PECULIAR FRIENDS (LP, with Genya Ravan)	15

(see also Goldie [& Gingerbreads])

TEN YEARS AFTER

68	Deram DM 176	Portable People/The Sounds	15
68	Deram DM 221	Hear Me Calling/I'm Going Home	8
71	Deram XDR 48532	She Lies In The Morning/Sweet Little Sixteen (demo only)	15
72	Chrysalis/Philips 6155 006	One Of These Days/Baby Won't You Let Me Rock 'n' Roll You	5
89	Chrysalis CHS 3477	Highway Of Love/Rock 'n' Roll Music To The World (p/s)	5
67	Deram DML/SML 1015	TEN YEARS AFTER (LP, mono/stereo)	50/40
68	Deram DML/SML 1023	UNDEAD (LP, mono/stereo)	40/30
69	Deram DML/SML 1029	STONEDHENGE (LP, gatefold sleeve, mono/stereo)	40/30
69	Deram DML/SML 1052	SSSSH! (LP, gatefold sleeve, mono/stereo)	25
70	Deram DML/SML 1065	CRICKLEWOOD GREEN (LP, gatefold sleeve, initially with Alvin Lee poster, mono/stereo)	28/20
71	Deram SML 1078	WATT (LP, gatefold sleeve)	18
71	Chrysalis CHR 1001	A SPACE IN TIME (LP)	18
72	Deram SML 1096	ALVIN LEE AND COMPANY (LP)	12
72	Chysalis CHR 1009	ROCK & ROLL MUSIC TO THE WORLD (gatefold sleeve)	12

(see also Alvin Lee, Chick Churchill)

TERMINAL

80s	Cargo CRS 0081	Hold On (some in p/s)	100/50

TERMITES

65	Oriole CB 1989	Tell Me/I Found My Place	30
65	CBS 201761	Every Day Every Day/No-One In The Whole Wide World	10

TERMITES (Jamaica)

67	Studio One SO 2006	Mercy Mr. Percy/SOUL BROTHERS: Hot And Cold	30
67	Studio One SO 2029	It Takes Two To Make Love/Beach Boy	25
67	Coxsone CS 7008	Sign Up/DELROY WILSON: Troubled Man	25
67	Coxsone CS 7025	Do It Right Now/SUMMERTAIRES: Stay (B-side actually by Gaylads)	25
68	Studio One SO 2040	Mr D.J. (actually by Delroy Wilson)/Tripe Girl (actually by Heptones)	30
68	Coxsone CS 7039	Mama Didn't Know/I Made A Mistake	100+
68	Pama PM 729	Push It Up/Two Of A Kind (B-side act. by Clancy Eccles & Cynthia Richards)	12
68	Pama PM 738	Show Me The Way/What Can I Do	20
69	Nu Beat NB 017	Push Push/Girls (actually by Hi Tones)	12
67	Studio One SOL 9003	DO THE ROCK STEADY (LP)	100

(see also L. Sparks, Ken Boothe, Upsetters)

PETE TERRACE

67	Pye International 7N 25427	At The Party/No! No! No!	25
67	Pye International 7N 25440	Shotgun Boo-Ga-Loo/I'm Gonna Make It	40
67	Pye Intl. NPL 28102	BOOGALOO (LP)	50

TERRA COTTA

78	Terra Cotta TC 001	To Be Near You (p/s, with insert)	20

(see also Spriguns)

TERRAIN

83	Terrain Musak TS 001	Who's To Blame?/Vacation (no p/s)	150

TERRAPLANE

85	Epic 26439	BLACK AND WHITE (LP)	15
87	Epic 460157 1	MOVING TARGET (LP)	12

(see also Thunder, Nuthin' Fancy)

LLOYD TERRELL

68	Island WI 3158	My Argument (as Lloyd & Johnny Melody)/JOHNNY MELODY: Foey Man (B-side actually by George Dekker)	60+
68	Pama PM 710	Bang Bang Lulu/MRS MILLER: I Never Knew	5
68	Pama PM 740	How Come (actually by Lee Perry)/MRS MILLER: Oh My Lover	10
69	Pama PM 752	Lulu Returns/MRS MILLER: I Feel The Music	10
69	Nu Beat NB 023	Mr Rhya/After Dark	5
70	Pama PM 792	Birth Control/VAL BENNET: Return To Peace	5
70	Bullet BU 434	Exposure/Baby Huey	7
71	Escort ERT 855	One Woman/CHARMERS: What Should I Do (act. by Dave Barker & Charmers)	7
73	Pama PM 863	Big Eight/JUNIOR BYLES: Auntie Lu Lu	7

(see also Charmers, Lloyd Charmers, Lloyd & Johnny, Lloyd & Ken, Lloydie & Lowbites)

TAMMI TERRELL

66	Tamla Motown TMG 561	Come On And See Me/Baby Don'tcha Worry (DJ copy = £150)	100
69	T. Motown (S)TML 11103	THE IRRESISTIBLE TAMMI TERRELL (LP)	85

(see also Marvin Gaye & Tammi Terrell)

TAMMI TERRELL/CHUCK JACKSON

69	Marble Arch MAL 1110	THE EARLY SHOW (LP)	20

(see also Chuck Jackson)

TERRI & TERRORS

79	Fresh FRESH 4	Laugh At Me/Laugh At Me (Again) (folded p/s)	5

TERRORVISION

90	(own label)	TERRORVISION: Brand New Toy/Human Error/Pain Reliever/The Pilgrims Rest (cassette, private issue)	20
91	(own label)	PUMP ACTION SUNSHINE: Urban Space Crime/My House/Jason (cassette, private issue)	20

91	(own label)	TERRORVISION: Blackbird/American TV/Pain Reliever/Human Being (cassette, private issue)	20
92	Total Vegas 12VEGAS 1	THRIVE EP (12" EP)	12
92	Total Vegas CDVEGAS 1	THRIVE EP (CD EP)	20
92	Total Vegas CDVEGAS 2	My House/Coming Up/Tea Dance (CD)	20
93	Total Vegas CDATVR 1	Problem Solved/Corpse Fly/We Are The Roadcrew/Sailing Home (CD)	25
93	Total Vegas CDPVEGAS 3	American TV/Psycho Killer/Hole For A Soul (CD)	15
92	Total Vegas ATVRLP 1	FORMALDEHYDE (LP, 14 tracks, green vinyl, 500 only, stickered sleeve)	30+
92	Total Vegas ATVRCD 1	FORMALDEHYDE (CD, 14 tracks, 1,000 only)	15+
93	Total Vegas VEGASLPS 1	FORMALDEHYDE (reissue LP, 12 tracks, 1,000 copies with 12-page booklet, stickered sleeve & lyric inner)	20+
93	Total Vegas BOOT 1	LIVE AT THE DON VALLEY STADIUM (CD, picture disc, 250 promo copies only)	30+
	(see also Spoilt Bratz)		

TERRY
66	Fontana TF 751	Spilt Milk/The Way That I Remember Him	7

CLARK TERRY (& BOB BROOKMEYER)
61	Riverside RLP 12-246	DUKE WITH A DIFFERENCE (LP)	12
65	Fontana TL 5265	TONIGHT (LP, with Bob Brookmeyer)	12
66	Fontana TL 5290	POWER OF POSITIVE SWINGING (LP, with Bob Brookmeyer)	12
66	Fontana TL 5373	MUMBLES (LP)	12
67	Fontana (S)TL 5394	GINGERBREAD MEN (LP, with Bob Brookmeyer)	12
68	Impulse MIPL/SIPL 507	IT'S WHAT'S HAPPENIN' (LP)	12
	(see also Coleman Hawkins)		

DEWEY TERRY
73	Tumbleweed TW 3502	CHIEF (LP)	20
	(see also Don & Dewey, Don Harris, Harvey Mandel)		

GORDON TERRY
57	London REA 1098	COUNTRY CLAMBAKE (EP)	30

PAT TERRY (GROUP)
70s	Myrrh MYR 1031	PAT TERRY GROUP (LP)	18

SONNY TERRY (TRIO)
53	Parlophone MSP 6017	Hootin' Blues/TOMMY REILLY: Bop! Goes The Weasel (78rpm, R 3598 = £8)	35
55	Vogue V 2326	Fox Chase/John Henry (78)	8
56	Vogue EPV 1095	SONNY TERRY (EP)	50
55	Vogue LDE 137	FOLK BLUES (10" LP)	40
55	Vogue LDE 165	CITY BLUES (10" LP)	40
58	Melodisc MLP 516	WHOOPIN' THE BLUES (10" LP)	45
58	Topic 10T 30	HARMONICA BLUES (10" LP)	45
65	Topic 12T 30	HARMONICA BLUES (12" LP, reissue)	25
66	Xtra XTRA 5025	SONNY'S STORY (LP)	22
67	Capitol T 20906	WHOOPIN' THE BLUES (LP, reissue)	12
69	Ember CW 136	BLIND SONNY TERRY & WOODY GUTHRIE (LP)	15
69	Xtra XTRA 1064	SONNY TERRY (LP)	18
70	Xtra XTRA 1099	BLUES FROM EVERYWHERE (LP)	18
71	Xtra XTRA 1110	ON THE ROAD (LP, with J.C. Burris)	18
	(see also Woody Guthrie)		

SONNY TERRY & BROWNIE McGHEE
60	Columbia DB 4433	Talking Harmonica Blues/Rockin' And Whoopin'	35
64	Oriole CB 1946	Dissatisfied Woman/SONNY TERRY: Goin' Down Slow	20
50s	Melodisc EPM7 83	ME AND SONNY (EP)	35
58	Pye Jazz NJE 1060	THE BLUEST (EP)	20
59	Pye Jazz NJE 1073	SONNY TERRY & BROWNIE McGHEE & CHRIS BARBER'S JAZZ BAND (EP)	20
59	Pye Jazz NJE 1074	TERRY AND McGHEE IN LONDON PT. 1 (EP)	25
59	Topic TOP 37	HOOTENANNY NEW YORK CITY (EP, with Pete Seeger)	25
61	Top Rank JKP 3007	WORK-PLAY-FAITH-FUN-SONGS (EP)	25
64	Ember EP 4562	SONNY TERRY AND BROWNIE McGHEE (EP)	30
64	Topic TOP 121	R AND B FROM S AND B (EP)	25
64	Realm REP 4002	PAWNSHOP BLUES (EP)	25
64	Vocalion EPV 1274	SONNY TERRY AND BROWNIE McGHEE (EP)	30
65	Vocalion EPV 1279	I SHALL NOT BE MOVED (EP)	30
58	Topic 12T 29	BROWNIE McGHEE AND SONNY TERRY (LP)	30
58	Pye Nixa Jazz NJT 515	SONNY, BROWNIE AND CHRIS (10" LP, with Chris Barber)	45
58	Pye Nixa Jazz NJL 18	SONNY TERRY AND BROWNIE McGHEE IN LONDON (LP)	30
58	London Jazz LTZ-C 15144	BACK COUNTRY BLUES (LP)	50
60	Columbia 33SX 1223	BLUES IS MY COMPANION (LP)	50
61	World Record Club 7379	SONNY TERRY AND BROWNIE McGHEE (LP)	20
61	Vogue LAE 12247	BLUES IS A STORY (LP, also stereo SEA 5014)	30/40
63	Vogue LAE 12266	DOWN SOUTH SUMMIT MEETIN' (LP)	25
63	CBS 52165	BACK COUNTRY BLUES (LP)	25
64	Xtra XTRA 1004	BIG BILL BROONZY/SONNY TERRY/BROWNIE McGHEE (LP)	30
64	Vogue LAE 552	BROWNIE McGHEE AND SONNY TERRY (LP)	30
64	Realm RM 165	BACK COUNTRY BLUES (LP)	18
64	Stateside SL 10076	BLUES HOOT (LP, some tracks by Lightnin' Hopkins)	40
64	Fontana 688 006ZL	LIVIN' WITH THE BLUES (LP)	22
65	Society SOC 1015	BROWNIE & SONNY SING AND PLAY (LP)	12
66	Philips BL 7675	AT THE BUNK HOUSE (LP)	20
66	Verve (S)VLP 5010	GUITAR HIGHWAY (LP, mono/stereo)	20/25
66	Fontana TL 5289	HOMETOWN BLUES (LP)	20
67	Ace Of Hearts (Z)AHT 182	HOMETOWN BLUES (LP, reissue)	12
69	Capitol T 20906	WHOOPIN' THE BLUES (LP)	16
69	Stateside SSL 10291	LONG WAY FROM HOME (LP)	15
69	Marble Arch MAL 843	SONNY TERRY AND BROWNIE McGHEE IN LONDON (LP)	12

| 70 | Fontana SFJL 979 | WHERE THE BLUES BEGAN (LP) | 15 |
| 73 | Mainstream MSL 1019 | HOMETOWN BLUES (LP, gatefold sleeve) | 12 |

(see also Brownie McGhee, Chris Barber, Pete Seeger, Big Bill Broonzy, Lightnin' Hopkins, Big Joe Turner)

TERRY & JERRY
| 65 | R&B MRB 5009 | People Are Doing It Every Day/Mama Julie | 22 |

TERRY, CARL & DERRICK
| 69 | Grape GR 3012 | True Love/ROY SMITH: Another Saturday Night | 8 |

TERRY SISTERS
| 57 | Parlophone R 4364 | It's The Same Old Jazz/Broken Promises (78 rpm = £8) | 12 |
| 58 | Parlophone R 4509 | Sweet Thing (Tell Me That You Love Me)/You Forgot To Remember (78 rpm = £8) | 10 |

TERRY-THOMAS ESQUIRE
56	Decca F 10804	A Sweet Old Fashioned Boy (with Rock 'N' Roll Rotters)/Lay Down Your Arms	18
56	Decca F 10804	A Sweet Old Fashioned Boy/Lay Down Your Arms (78)	6
61	Decca LK 4398	STRICTLY T-T (LP)	45

TESCO BOMBERS
| 82 | Y Y14 | Hernando's Hideaway/Break The Ice At Parties/Girl From Ipanema (p/s) | 5 |

(see also Homosexuals)

TEST DEPARTMENT
83	Some Bizzare TEST 112	Compulsion/Pulsations (12", p/s)	10
87	Some Bizzare 12MOP 13	Victory (12", p/s)	10
80s	Media City CMC 1	Gododdin (12", p/s, Welsh gig freebie with Brith Gof)	10
90	Mop MOP 5T	Jihad/(Desert Mix)/(Oil Mix) (12", p/s)	12
93	Mop MOP 8T	Bang On It/(Tao Systems Mix)/(TC Ruff House Remix) (12", die-cut p/s)	10
82	Test TEST ONE	HISTORY (cassette, with booklet in plastic bag)	15
80s	Pleasantly Surprised PS 5	ECSTASY UNDER DURESS (cassette, in bag with inserts, 2 editions)	20/15
84	Test TEST 33	BEATING THE RETREAT (LP, box set)	12
90s	Mop MOP 3	A GOOD NIGHT OUT (LP)	12

JACK TETER TRIO
50	London L 501	Johnson Rag/ Back Of The Yards (78)	8
50	London L 689	Kansas City Kitty/Just A Little Nightcap (78)	6
51	London L 997	Here Comes My Ball And Chain/There's A Little White Horse (78)	8

TETRACK
| 78 | Greensleeves GRE 8 | Only Jah Knows/ROCKERS ALL STARS: Jah Jah Dub | 20 |
| 78 | Rockers APD 2 | Love And Unity/JAH LEVE & JAH BULL: Two The Hard Way/JUNIOR DAN: Jah Foundation (12") | 30 |

ALAN TEW ORCHESTRA
76	Epic EPC 4676	The Sweeney/The Prowler	15
67	Decca Phase 4 PFS 4120	THIS IS MY SCENE (LP)	35
72	CBS 64665	LET'S FLY (LP)	30

JOE TEX
65	Atlantic AT 4015	Hold What You've Got/Fresh Out Of Tears	20
65	Atlantic AT 4021	You Better Get It/You Got What It Takes	18
65	Sue WI 370	Yum Yum Yum/You Little Baby Face Thing	25
65	Atlantic AT 4027	A Woman Can Change A Man/Don't Let Your Left Hand Know	12
65	Atlantic AT 4045	I Want To (Do Everything For You)/Funny Bone	15
65	Atlantic AT 4058	A Sweet Woman Like You/Close Your Door	15
66	Atlantic AT 4081	The Love You Save/If Sugar Was As Sweet As You	12
66	Atlantic 584 016	S.Y.S.L.J.F.M. (Letter Song)/I'm A Man	10
66	Atlantic 584 035	You Better Believe It/I Believe I'm Gonna Make It	29
67	Atlantic 584 068	Papa Was Too/The Truest Woman In The World	8
67	Atlantic 584 096	Hold What You've Got/A Sweet Woman Like You	8
67	Atlantic 584 102	Show Me/Woman Sees A Hard Time (When Her Man Is Gone)	15
67	Atlantic 584 119	Woman Like That, Yeah/I'm Going And Get It	8
67	Atlantic 584 144	Skinny Legs And All/Watch The One (That Brings The Bad News)	8
68	Atlantic 584 171	Men Are Getting Scarce/You're Gonna Thank Me Woman	8
68	Atlantic 584 212	Go Home And Do It/Keep The One You Got	8
69	Atlantic 584 296	We Can't Sit Down Now/It Ain't Sanitary	8
70	Atlantic 584 318	You're Alright Ray Charles/Everything Happens On Time	8
71	Mercury 6052 067	I Knew Him/Bad Feet	6
72	Mercury 6052 111	Give The Baby Anything/Takin' A Chance	6
72	Mercury 6052 129	I Got 'Cha/Mother Prayer	6
72	Mercury 6052 156	You Said A Bad Word/It Ain't Gonna Work Baby	6
65	Atlantic ATL 5043	THE NEW BOSS (LP)	75
66	Atlantic ATL 587 009	THE LOVE YOU SAVE (LP)	40
67	Atlantic 587 053	I'VE GOT TO DO A LITTLE BETTER (LP)	30
67	Atlantic 587/588 059	THE NEW BOSS (LP, reissue)	22
67	London HA-U 8334	THE BEST OF JOE TEX (LP)	55
67	Atlantic 587/588 079	GREATEST HITS (LP)	20
68	Atlantic 587/588 104	LIVE AND LIVELY (LP)	30
68	Atlantic 587/588 118	SOUL COUNTRY (LP)	25
69	Atlantic 587/588 130	YOU BETTER GET IT (LP)	25
69	Atlantic 588 193	BUYING A BOOK (LP)	18
72	Atlantic K 40239	FROM THE ROOTS CAME THE RAPPER (LP)	12
72	Mercury 6338 093	I GOTCHA (LP)	12

(see also Soul Clan)

TEXANS
| 64 | Columbia DB 7242 | Being With You/Wondrous Look Of Love | 5 |

TEXTONES
| 87 | Enigma 3268-1 | CEDAR CREEK (LP) | 15 |

TEXTOR SINGERS
54	Capitol CL 14211	Sobbin' Women/Remember Me 12

RUDY THACKER & STRINGBEANS
62	Starlite ST45 087	The Ballad Of Johnny Horton/Tomorrow Is My Last Day 20

JAKE THACKRAY
67	Columbia SCX 6178	LAST WILL AND TESTAMENT (LP)....................................... 20
69	Columbia SCX 6345	JAKE'S PROGRESS (LP)... 12
71	Note NTS 105	LIVE PERFORMANCE (LP).. 12
72	Columbia SCX 6506	BANTAM COCK (LP).. 12

THAMESIDERS/DAVY GRAHAM
63	Decca DFE 8538	FROM A LONDON HOOTENANNY (EP, 2 tracks each) 40

(see also Davy Graham)

SISTER ROSETTA THARPE
52	Brunswick 04989	Cain't No Grave Hold My Body Down/Ain't No Room In Church For Liars (78)... 15
57	Mercury MT 126	When The Saints Go Marching In/Cain't No Grave Hold My Body Down (78) 10
57	Mercury MT 185	Up Above My Head There's Music In The Air/
		Jericho (Joshua Fit The Battle Of Jericho) (78)........................... 15
60	MGM MGM 1072	If I Can Help Somebody/Take My Hand, Precious Lord 8
58	Brunswick OE 9284	GOSPEL SONGS No. 2 (EP).. 18
62	Mercury ZEP 10127	GOSPEL SINGER (EP, with Sally Jenkins Singers)......................... 18
64	Mercury 10000MCE	SISTER ROSETTA THARPE (EP)... 18
62	MGM MGM-EP 746	SISTER ROSETTA THARPE (EP)... 18
57	Mercury MPL 6529	GOSPEL TRAIN (LP).. 35
59	Brunswick LAT 8290	GOSPEL TRAIN (LP).. 22
61	Mercury MMC 14057	THE GOSPEL TRUTH (LP) 20

(see also Little Richard)

SISTER ROSETTA THARPE & SISTER MARIE KNIGHT
51	Brunswick 04851	Didn't It Rain/SISTER ROSETTA THARPE: Two Little Fishes And Five
		Loaves Of Bread (78, with Sam Price Trio) 15

(see also Marie Knight, Rev. Kelsey, Sammy Price)

THAT PETROL EMOTION
85	Pink PINKY 4	Keen/A Great Depression On A Slum Night (p/s) 5

(see also Undertones)

T.H.C. ROLLER
94	Poor Person Prod. PPPR 4	CHAPTER IN THE LIFE OF T.H.C. ROLLER (LP, handmade sleeve
		with insert & king-size rolling papers, numbered, 500 only) 20
94	Poor Person Prod.	THIS MUST BE THE JOINT (LP, 500 only)................................ 70

THEATRE OF HATE
80	S.S. SS 3	Original Sin/Legion (p/s)... 10
81	Burning Rome BRR 1	Rebel Without A Brain/My Own Invention (p/s, mispress with
		2 B-side labels)... 8
81	Burning Rome BRR 1	Rebel Without A Brain/My Own Invention (p/s)............................ 6
82	Burning Rome BRRT 4	Eastworld/Assegai (12").. 8
85	Bliss TOH 1EP	The Wake/Love Is A Ghost/Poppies/Legion (EP, 33rpm,
		with T-shirt in stickered pack, some sealed).......................... 10/5
81	S.S. SSSSS 1P	HE WHO DARES WINS — LIVE AT THE WAREHOUSE, LEEDS
		(LP, white labels, some copies autographed) 12
81	Straight Music TOH 1	LIVE AT THE LYCEUM (cassette).. 12

(see also Pack, Spear Of Destiny, Senate, Cult, Crisis)

THEAUDIENCE
97	Mercury AUD 1	I Got The Wherewithal/Je Suis Content (red vinyl, limited edition)............ 18

THEE
65	Decca F 12163	Each And Every Day/There You Go!..................................... 40

THEE MIGHTY CAESARS
80s	Swag SWG 001	She's Just Fifteen Years Old/The Swag (1-sided flexidisc) 6
88	Crypt LP 014	ENGLISH PUNK ROCK EXPLOSION (LP)................................. 12

(see also Milkshakes, Prisoners, Billy Childish)

BOB THEIL
82	Private (no cat. no.)	SO FAR (LP, private pressing)... 180

LLANS THELWELL & HIS CELESTIALS
66	Island WI 262	Choo Choo Ska/Busty Brown: Lonely 20

THEM
64	Decca F 11973	Don't Start Crying Now/One Two Brown Eyes............................. 60
64	Decca F 12018	Baby Please Don't Go/Gloria 10
65	Decca F 12094	Here Comes The Night/All For Myself................................... 10
65	Decca F 12175	One More Time/How Long Baby?....................................... 10
65	Decca F 12215	(It Won't Hurt) Half As Much/I'm Gonna Dress In Black 10
65	Decca F 12281	Mystic Eyes/If You And I Could Be As Two 10
66	Decca F 12355	Call My Name/Bring 'Em On In 10
66	Decca F 12403	Richard Cory/Don't You Know?.. 12
67	Major Minor MM 509	Gloria/Friday's Child 20
67	Major Minor MM 513	The Story Of Them (Parts 1 & 2) 25
73	Deram DM 394	Gloria/Baby Please Don't Go (reissue).................................. 7
65	Decca DFE 8612	THEM (EP).. 125
65	Decca DFE 8612	THEM (EP, export-only 'band-on-ladder' p/s)........................... 500
65	Decca LK 4700	(THE ANGRY YOUNG) THEM (LP, orig. label, some with flipback sleeve) 110/70
66	Decca LK 4751	THEM AGAIN (LP, original label, some with flipback sleeve) 110/70
70	Decca LK 4700	(THE ANGRY YOUNG) THEM (LP, re-pressing, red label,
		boxed Decca logo) 20

70	Decca LK 4751	THEM AGAIN (LP, re-pressing, red label, boxed Decca logo) 20
70	Decca (S)PA 86	THE WORLD OF THEM (LP, original issue) 20
78	Sonet SNTF 738	BELFAST GYPSIES (LP, features Them without Van Morrison). 25

(see also Van Morrison, Trader Horne, Taste, Sk'boo, Belfast Gypsies, Moses K. & Prophets, Peter Barden, Jackie McCauley)

THEME MACHINE
| 81 | BBC RESL 104 | Themes Ain't What They Used To Be/Lost In A World Of Dreams............. 5 |

THERAPY
| 72 | CBS 69017 | ALMANAC (LP) .... 12 |
| 73 | Indigo IRS 5124 | ONE NIGHT STAND (LP, private pressing) .... 15 |

THERAPY?
89	demo cassette	THIRTY SECONDS OF SILENCE (cassette, 100 only) 15
90	demo cassette	MEAT ABSTRACT (cassette sold at gigs, 150 only) 15
90	Multifuckingnational MFN 1	Meat Abstract/Punishment Kisses (p/s, labels on wrong sides, 1,000 only) 30
92	A&M (no cat. no.)	TEETHGRINDER (12", double pack, white labels in presentation pack)........ 30
92	A&M THX 1	Have A Merry Fucking Christmas: Teenage Kicks/With Or Without You (Xmas gig freebie).. 18
92	Wiiija WIJ 11	PLEASURE DEATH (mini-LP, 10 white labels) .... 75+

THERMOMETERS
| 80 | Fokker FEP 100 | 20th Century Girl/Newtown Refugees/Stole Your Drugs (some in oversized p/s)... 20/15 |

THE SHOVE
| 81 | Shove Off Records | ROUGH AND READY EP (some with p/s) .... 25/15 |

THE THE
80	4AD AD 10	Controversial Subject/Black And White (p/s)............................. 30
81	Some Bizzare BZS 4	Cold Spell Ahead/Hot Ice (p/s).. 25
82	Epic EPC A 13-2787	Uncertain Smile/Three Orange Kisses From Kazan/ Waitin' For The Upturn (12", yellow vinyl, p/s)........................ 12
83	Epic A 3710	This Is The Day/Mental Healing Process//Absolute Liberation/ Leap Into The Wind (double pack, gatefold p/s) 6
83	Melody Maker [no cat. no.]	Dumb As Death's Head/SINES: Jonathon (flexidisc with *Melody Maker*)........ 5
86	Epic PS 215	Sweet Bird Of Truth (Radio Edit) (1-sided, promo only)................... 5
86	Epic TRUTH D2	Heartland/Born In The New S.A./Flesh And Bones//Perfect/ Fruit Of The Heart (12", p/s, double pack) 8
86	Epic TRUTH Q3	Infected/Infected (Energy Mix)/Disturbed (12", uncensored 'wank' p/s)........ 12
86	Epic TRUTH T3	Infected/Infected (Energy Mix)/Disturbed/Soul Mining (Remix)/ Sinking Feeling (12", p/s, double pack, with sticker) 10
87	Epic TENSE 1	Slow Train To Dawn/Harbour Lights (p/s, with 2 car stickers)............. 5
82	private cassette	PORNOGRAPHY OF DESPAIR (LP, unreleased, cassettes exist)
83	Epic EPC 25525	SOUL MINING (LP, with inner sleeve, initially with 12" single "Perfect"/"Soup Of Mixed Emotions"/"Fruit Of The Heart") 15
86	Epic EPC 26770	INFECTED (LP, with poster & inner, 1st 25,000 with 'torture' sleeve)....... 18/12
02	Sony 5079022	LONDON TOWN (5-CD box set)... 30

(see also Matt Johnson, Gadgets)

THEY MUST BE RUSSIANS
| 80s | no label | UNTITLED EP (mail-order only, wraparound sleeve with insert) .... 10 |

(see also Joe 9T & Thunderbirds)

THICK PIGEON
| 80s | Factory FACT 85 | TOO CRAZY COWBOYS (LP).. 40 |

THIEVES
| 79 | Arista ARIGV 226 | 400 Dragons/Headlights (green vinyl).................................... 5 |

(see also Fairport Convention)

THIEVES LIKE US
| 80 | Earlobe ELS 1 | Mind Made/Strike Out (p/s)... 8 |

THIGHPAULSANDRA
| 01 | World Serpent ESKATON 27 | Michel Publicity Window/Paralysed (p/s) .... 5 |

(see also Coil)

THIN END OF THE WEDGE
| 81 | Jungle JR 051S | Lights Are On Green/I'm Not Dead Yet (some in p/s)...................... 30/6 |

(see also Damascus)

THING
| 85 | Grimm GRIM1 | I'm Beautiful, Because She's Blind/Gamma! Gamma! Hey! (brown vinyl) .... 6 |

THINGS
| 80 | Imperial IP 4301 | Pieces Of You/Lost Love (p/s) .... 10 |
| 88 | Epitaph E 86402 | THINGS (LP).. 12 |

(see also Buzzcocks)

THIN ICE
| 88 | Blag It SJP 858 | Freedom Road (p/s) .... 40 |

THIN LIZZY
SINGLES
70	Parlophone DIP 513	The Farmer/I Need You (Irish only, as Thin Lizzie)..................... 1,000+
71	Decca F 13208	NEW DAY (EP, 33rpm, some without p/s)............................. 275/125
72	Decca F 13355	Whiskey In The Jar/Black Boys On The Corner 8
72	Decca F 13355	Whiskey In The Jar/Black Boys On The Corner (demos in p/s)............. 30
73	Decca F 13402	Randolph's Tango/Broken Dreams (2 versions of A-side: matrices ZDR 53384 & ZCPDR 53312)........................... each 15
73	Decca F 13467	The Rocker/Here I Go Again (demos £25) 5
74	Decca F 13507	Little Darlin'/Buffalo Gal.. 8

74	Vertigo 6059 111	Philomena/Sha La La	8
75	Vertigo 6059 124	Rosalie/Half Caste	6
75	Vertigo 6059 129	Wild One/For Those Who Love To Die	8
76	Vertigo 6059 150	Jailbreak/Running Back (p/s)	25
77	Vertigo 6059 177	Dancing In The Moonlight/Bad Reputation (p/s)	10
78	Decca F 13748	Whiskey In The Jar/Vagabond Of The Western World/Sitamoia (p/s)	6
79	Vertigo LIZZY 3	Waiting For An Alibi/With Love (p/s, some with cartoon lyric sheet)	8/5
79	Decca THIN 1	Things Ain't Working Out Down At The Farm/The Rocker (10,000 with p/s)	8
79	Vertigo LIZZY 5	Sarah/Got To Give Up (3 different p/s designs)	each 5
70s	Vertigo DJ 016	It's Only Money/JANNE SCHAFFER: Dr Abraham (promo only, no p/s)	200
80	Vertigo LIZZY 7 701	Killer On The Loose/Don't Play Around//Got To Give It Up (live)/ Chinatown (live) (double pack)	8
81	Lyntone LYN 10138/9	Song For Jimmy/GRAHAM BONNET: Night Games/POLECATS: We Say Yeah/ WAY OF THE WEST: Monkey Love (orange vinyl flexidisc with *Flexipop*, issue 10)	10
82	Vertigo LIZZY 10	Hollywood (Down On Your Luck) (10", p/s, 1-sided, existence unconfirmed)	
82	Vertigo LIZZY PD 10	Hollywood (Down On Your Luck)/Pressure Will Blow (picture disc)	6
83	Vertigo LIZZY 1111/22	Cold Sweat/Bad Habits//Angel Of Death (live)/Don't Believe A Word (live) (double pack)	8
83	Vertigo LIZZY 1112	Cold Sweat/Bad Habits/Angel Of Death (live)/Don't Believe A Word (live) (12", p/s)	8
83	Vertigo LIZZY 1212	Thunder And Lightning/Still In Love With You (live) (12", p/s, some with poster)	12
83	Vertigo LIZZY 13	The Sun Goes Down/Baby Please Don't Go (p/s)	5
83	Vertigo LIZZY 1312	The Sun Goes Down (Remix)/The Sun Goes Down/Baby Please Don't Go (12", p/s)	10

LPs

71	Decca SKL 5082	THIN LIZZY (dark blue label, early copies laminated sleeve/later matt)	40/30
72	Decca TXS 108	SHADES OF A BLUE ORPHANAGE (gatefold sleeve, dark blue label)	30
73	Decca SKL 5170	VAGABONDS OF THE WESTERN WORLD (dark blue label, some with insert)	25/18
76	Decca SKL 5249	REMEMBERING	12
83	Vertigo VERL 3	THUNDER AND LIGHTNING (with free 12")	20
83	Vertigo	LIFE — LIVE (2-LP, gatefold sleeve, with inners)	15

(see also Phil Lynott, Wild Horses, Phenomena, Eric Bell Band, Funky Junction, Greedies, John Sykes, Gary Moore)

THIRD & FOURTH GENERATION
| 72 | Punch PH 91 | Rudies Medley (actually by Peter Tosh & Soulmates)/Rude Boy — Version | 10 |

(see also Peter Tosh)

THIRD DIMENSION
| 70 | Unity UN 566 | Peace And Love/Peace And Love — Version | 6 |

THIRD EAR BAND
69	Harvest SHVL 756	ALCHEMY (LP)	40
70	Harvest SHSP 773	THIRD EAR BAND: ELEMENTS (LP)	35
72	Harvest SHSP 4019	MUSIC FROM MACBETH (LP)	20
76	Harvest SHSM 2007	EXPERIENCES (LP)	15

(see also High Tide, Sounds Nice)

THIRD EYE BAND
| 82 | Scarlet Quest 01 | Pass Myself/May The Circle Remain Unbroken (p/s) | 80 |

THIRD QUADRANT
| 82 | Rock Cottage (no cat. no.) | SEEING YOURSELF AS YOU REALLY ARE (LP, private pressing, wraparound sleeve with handwritten insert, blank white label) | 40 |
| 88 | own label | LAYERED (private cassette, 500 only) | 12 |

THIRD RAIL
| 67 | Columbia DB 8274 | Run, Run, Run/No Return | 25 |

THIRD WORLD ALL STARS
| 75 | Third World TWLP 103 | REBEL ROCK (LP) | 25 |

THIRD WORLD WAR
71	Fly BUG 7	Ascension Day/Teddy Teeth Goes Sailing (p/s)	8
71	Fly BUG 11	A Little Bit Of Urban Rock/Working Class Man	6
71	Fly FLY 4	THIRD WORLD WAR (LP)	30
72	Track 2406 108	THIRD WORLD WAR II (LP)	70

(see also Terry Stamp)

THIRTEEN SENSES
02	Private Pressing	NO OTHER LIFE IS ATTRACTIVE EP (CD)	35
04	Vertigo 9816335	Thru The Glass/No Other Life Is Attractive (1,500 only p/s)	8
04	Vertigo 9816335	Thru The Glass/No Other Life Is Attractive (CD, 1,500 only)	8
03	Private Pressing	NO OTHER LIFE IS ATTRACTIVE (CD)	25

13TH FLOOR ELEVATORS
78	Radar/Sound For Industry SFI 347	Reverberation/RED CRAYOLA: Hurricane Fighter Plane (flexidisc free with *Zig Zag* magazine, No. 88)	8/6
78	Radar ADA 13	You're Gonna Miss Me/Tried To Hide (green vinyl)	6
78	Radar RAD 13	THE PSYCHEDELIC SOUNDS OF ... (LP)	15
79	Radar RAD 15	EASTER EVERYWHERE (LP)	15

(see also Roky Erickson, Red Crayola)

31ST OF FEBRUARY
| 69 | Vanguard (S)VRL 19045 | THE 31ST OF FEBRUARY (LP) | 18 |

35mm DREAMS
| 81 | More Than This ASA 100 | More Than This/The Bearer (foldout p/s) | 5 |
| 81 | More Than This ASA 200 | Fasten Your Safety Belts/Corstorphine/Instamatic Dance (p/s) | 5 |

39 LYON ST
(see under Associates)

32ND TURN-OFF
69	Jay Boy JSL 1	32ND TURN OFF (LP)	40+

(see also Equals)

THIS DRIFTIN'S GOTTA STOP
70s	private pressing	THIS DRIFTIN'S GOTTA STOP (LP)	15

THIS HEAT
80	Piano THIS 1201	Health And Efficiency/Graphic/Varispeed (12", p/s with insert)	12
79	Piano THIS 1	THIS HEAT (LP)	15
81	Rough Trade ROUGH 26	DECEIT (LP, original)	15

THIS MORTAL COIL
83	4AD AD 310	Song To The Siren/16 Days (Reprise) (p/s)	5
83	4AD BAD 310	16 Days/Gathering Dust/Song To The Siren/16 Days (reprise) (12", p/s)	8
84	4AD AD 410	Kangaroo/It'll End In Tears (p/s, 2 different designs & label colours, 2,500 of each)	each 5
86	4AD BAD 608	Come Here My Love/Drugs (10", p/s with inner sleeve)	10
91	4AD TMC 1CD	Extracts From "Blood": Late Night/You And Your Sister/I Come And Stand At Every Door/With Tomorrow (CD, card sleeve, promo only)	20
80s	4AD DAD 1005	BLOOD (2-LP, with inners)	18

(see also Cocteau Twins, Modern English, Cindytalk)

THIS 'N' THAT
66	Mercury MF 938	Someday/Loving You	18
67	Strike JH 310	Get Down With It/I Care About You	8

(see also Cleo)

B.J. THOMAS
66	Hickory 45-1395	Never Tell/Billy & Sue	15
66	Pye International 7N 25374	Mama/Wendy	10
68	Pye International 7N 25467	The Eyes Of A New York Woman/I May Never Get To Heaven	6
69	Pye International 7N 25487	It's Only Love/You Don't Love Me Anymore (The Train Song)	5
69	Wand WN 1	Raindrops Keep Falling On My Head/Never Had It So Good	5
70	Wand WN 5	I Just Can't Help Believing/Send My Picture To Scranton, PA	5
72	Wand WN 24	Rock And Roll Lullaby/Are We Losing Touch? (feat. Duane Eddy)	5

CARLA THOMAS
61	London HLK 9310	Gee Whiz/For You	25
61	London HLK 9359	A Love Of My Own/Promises	22
62	London HLK 9618	I'll Bring It On Home To You/I Can't Take It	22
64	Atlantic AT 4005	I've Got No Time To Lose/A Boy Named Tom	20
66	Atlantic AT 4074	Comfort Me/I'm For You	15
66	Atlantic 584 011	Let Me Be Good To You/Another Night Without My Man	8
66	Atlantic 584 042	B-A-B-Y/What Have You Got To Offer Me	8
67	Stax 601 002	Something Good (Is Going To Happen To You)/It's Starting To Grow	8
67	Stax 601 008	When Tomorrow Comes/Unchanging Love (dark blue label, later light blue)	15/8
68	Stax 601 032	Pick Up The Pieces/Separation	10
68	Stax STAX 103	Where Do I Go/I've Fallen In Love	8
69	Stax STAX 112	I Like What You're Doing To Me/Strung Out	8
69	Stax STAX 131	Unyielding/I've Fallen In Love	6
72	Stax 2025 082	Love Means/You've Got A Cushion To Fall On	6
91	Kent 6T 7	I'll Never Stop Loving/Prophets Band/Peaches Baby	40
67	Stax 589 004	CARLA THOMAS (LP)	40
67	Stax 589 012	THE QUEEN ALONE (LP)	35
69	Stax SXATS 1019	MEMPHIS QUEEN (LP)	60
71	Stax 2363 004	MEMPHIS QUEEN (LP, reissue)	15
72	Stax 2362 023	LOVE MEANS... (LP)	15

(see also Otis Redding & Carla Thomas)

CHARLIE THOMAS (& DRIFTERS)
74	EMI International INT 502	Midsummer Night In Harlem/Lonely Drifter Don't Cry (with Drifters)	12
75	EMI International INT 506	I'm Gonna Take You Home/Run, Run, Roadrunner	10

CLAUDETTE THOMAS
68	Caltone TONE 116	Roses Are Red My Love/YVONNE HARRISON: Near To You	30

CREEPY JOHN THOMAS
69	RCA RCA 1912	Ride A Rainbow/Moon And Eyes Song	12
69	RCA SF 8061	CREEPY JOHN THOMAS (LP)	80

(see also Paul Kossoff, Edgar Broughton Band)

DAVID THOMAS & THE PEDESTRIANS
83	Recommended REDT 7	Didn't Have A (Very) Good Time (1-sided picture disc free with label's quarterly magazine)	8
84	Rough Trade ROUGH 30	THE SOUND OF THE SAND (LP)	12
85	Rough Trade ROUGH 80	MORE PLACES FOREVER (LP)	12

(see also Pere Ubu)

DON THOMAS
76	DJM DJS 10670	Come On Train Parts 1 & 2 (DJ copy in p/s = £30)	15

DYLAN THOMAS
60s	Caedmon TC 0997	UNDER MILK WOOD VOL. 2 (LP)	15

ETTA THOMAS
74	Santa Ponsa PNS 14	Just Ask Me/99 Ways	10

GENE THOMAS
64	United Artists UP 1047	Baby's Gone/Stand By Love	20

HERSAL THOMAS
50	Parlophone R 3261	Suitcase Blues/Hersal Blues (78)	70

MINT VALUE £

IRMA THOMAS

64	Liberty LIB 66013	Breakaway/Wish Someone Would Care	28
64	Liberty LIB 66041	Anyone Who Knows What Love Is (Will Understand)/Time Is On My Side	30
65	Liberty LIB 66080	He's My Guy/True True Love	28
65	Liberty LIB 66095	Some Things You Never Get Used To/You Don't Miss A Good Thing (Until It's Gone)	25
65	Sue WI 372	Don't Mess With My Man/Set Me Free	50
65	Liberty LIB 66106	I'm Gonna Cry Till My Tears Run Dry/ Nobody Wants To Hear Nobody's Troubles	25
66	Liberty LIB 66137	Take A Look/What Are You Trying To Do (DJ copy = £125)	75
66	Liberty LIB 66178	It's A Man's-Woman's World	20
72	Atlantic K 10167	Full Time Woman/She's Taking My Part	6
72	United Artists UP 35402	Time Is On My Side/Anyone Who Knows What Love Is (Will Understand) (reissue)	8
65	Liberty LEP 4035	TIME IS ON MY SIDE (EP)	85
68	Minit MLL/MLS 40004E	TAKE A LOOK (LP)	75
76	Island HELP 29	LIVE (LP)	15

JAMO THOMAS & HIS PARTY BROTHERS ORCHESTRA

66	Polydor BM 56709	I Spy (For The FBI)/Snake Hip Mama	15
69	Polydor 56755	I Spy (For The FBI)/Snake Hip Mama (reissue)	8
69	Chess CRS 8098	I'll Be Your Fool/Jamo Soul	20
71	Mojo 2092 013	I Spy (For The FBI)/Snake Hip Mama (2nd reissue)	8

JIMMY THOMAS

69	Parlophone R 5773	The Beautiful Night/Above A Whisper (withdrawn; DJ copy = £150)	250
69	Spark SRL 1035	(We Ain't Looking For) No Trouble/Springtime	6
70	Spark SRL 1040	White Dove/You Don't Have To Say Goodbye	6
72	Jay Boy BOY 67	Where There's A Will/Just Tryin' To Please You	6
	(see also Sweet Dreams)		

KID THOMAS

70s	JSP 4503	Rockin' This Joint Tonight/Cozy Lounge Blues	5

KID THOMAS/EMANUEL BAND

64	'77' LA 12/26	VICTORY WALK (LP, with Barry Martyn's Band)	30

LEON THOMAS

73	Philips 6369 417	BLUES & SOULFUL TRUTH (LP)	20

NICKY THOMAS

70	Amalgamated AMG 863	Danzella/JOE GIBBS ALLSTARS: Kingstonians Reggae	25
70	Trojan TR 7750	Love Of The Common People/DESTROYERS: Compass	5
70	Trojan TR 7796	God Bless The Children/Red Eye	7
71	Trojan TR 7807	If I Had A Hammer/Lonely Feelin'	7
71	Trojan TR 7830	Tell It Like It Is/B.B.C.	5
70	Trojan TBL 143	LOVE OF THE COMMON PEOPLE (LP)	12
	(see also Joe Gibbs)		

PETER THOMAS SOUND ORCHESTRA

70	Polydor 2418 074	CHARIOTS OF THE GODS (LP)	35

RAMBLIN' THOMAS

52	Tempo R 51	Jug Head Blues/Hard Dallas Blues (78)	20
	(see also Blind Blake, Blind Lemon Jefferson)		

RUDY THOMAS

83	Mobiliser MMLP 34	VERY BEST OF (LP)	15

RUFUS THOMAS

63	London HLK 9799	Walking The Dog/Fine And Mellow	25
64	London HLK 9850	Can Your Monkey Do The Dog/I Want To Get Married	20
64	London HLK 9884	Somebody Stole My Dog/I Want To Be Loved	20
64	Atlantic AT 4009	Jump Back/All Night Worker	20
66	Atlantic 584 029	Willy Nilly/Sho' Gonna Mess Him Up	10
67	Atlantic 584 089	Jump Back/Walking The Dog	8
67	Stax 601 013	Greasy Spoon/Sophisticated Sissy	10
67	Stax 601 028	Down Ta My House/Steady Holding On	10
68	Stax 601 037	The Memphis Train/I Think I Made A Boo-Boo	20
68	Stax STAX 105	Funky Mississippi/So Hard To Get Along With	6
71	Stax 2025 060	The Breakdown (Parts 1 & 2)	6
71	Stax 2025 080	Do The Funky Penguin (Parts 1 & 2)	6
64	Atlantic AET 6001	DO THE DOG (EP)	60
65	Atlantic AET 6011	JUMP BACK WITH RUFUS (EP)	70
64	London HA-K 8183	WALKING THE DOG (LP)	95
70	Stax SXATS 1033	FUNKY CHICKEN (LP)	35
71	Stax 2363 001	FUNKY CHICKEN (LP, reissue)	15
71	Stax 2362 010	DOING THE PUSH AND PULL LIVE AT P.J.'s (LP)	25
72	Stax 2362 028	DID YOU HEAR ME? (LP)	22
74	Stax STX 1004	CROWN PRINCE OF DANCE (LP)	30

TIMMY THOMAS

73	Mojo 2027 012	Why Can't We Live Together/Funky Me	8
77	T.K. XB 9052	The Magician/Don't Put It Down	5
73	Mojo 2956 002	WHY CAN'T WE LIVE TOGETHER (LP)	30

VAUGHAN THOMAS

70	Page One POF 167	Need You Girl/Come Together	6
70	Page One POF 178	Is This What I Get For Loving You/Since You've Been Mine	6
72	Jam JAL 101	VAUGHAN THOMAS (LP)	20

WAYNE THOMAS

67	Coral Q 72491	I've Never Known A Lady/My Life's Gonna Change	6

ANDREAS THOMOPOULOS
70	Mushroom 100 MR 1	SONGS OF THE STREET (LP)	80
71	Mushroom 150 MR 4	BORN OUT OF THE TEARS OF THE SUN (LP)	50

(see also Secondhand)

BARBARA THOMPSON
74	Explosion EX 2087	Single Girl/DANDY & COUNT PRINCE MILLER: Version	5

BOBBY THOMPSON
69	Columbia Blue Beat DB 113	That's How Strong My Love Is/Trouble In Town	6
69	Jolly JY 001	That's How Strong My Love Is/Trouble In The Town	12

(see also Dandy)

CHERYLE THOMPSON
64	Stateside SS 291	Teardrops/Black Night	12

CHRIS THOMPSON
73	Village Thing VTS 21	CHRIS THOMPSON (LP)	25

EDDIE THOMPSON
55	Jazz Today JTE 101	THE FABULOUS EDDIE THOMPSON (EP)	50
57	Nixa NJE 1030	PIANO MOODS VOLUME 6 (EP)	50
60	Ember EMB 3303	PIANO MOODS (LP)	100
60	Tempo TAP 24	HIS MASTER'S JAZZ (LP)	250
60s	77 LEU 12/39	BY MYSELF (LP)	42

ERIC THOMPSON
68	CBS EP 6398	THE MAGIC ROUNDABOUT NO. 1 (EP)	8
68	CBS EP 6399	THE MAGIC ROUNDABOUT NO. 2 (EP)	8

HANK THOMPSON (& BRAZOS VALLEY BOYS)
53	Capitol CL 13977	The Wild Side Of Life/Rub-A-Dub-Dub (78)	6
54	Capitol CL 14161	Honky-Tonk Girl/Wake-Up Irene (78)	6
56	Capitol CL 14517	Honey, Honey Bee Ball/Don't Take It Out On Me (78 rpm = £8)	12
56	Capitol CL 14668	I'm Not Mad, Just Hurt/The Blackboard Of My Heart	12
58	Capitol CL 14869	Li'l Liza Jane/How Do You Hold A Memory (78 rpm = £8)	12
58	Capitol CL 14945	Gathering Flowers/Squaws Along The Yukon	8
58	Capitol CL 14961	I've Run Out Of Tomorrows/You're Going Back To Your Old Ways Again	8
60	Capitol CL 15114	A Six Pack To Go/What Made Her Change	28
56	Capitol EAP 1028	SONGS OF THE BRAZO VALLEY NO. 1 (EP)	15
57	Capitol EAP1-826	HANK (EP)	15
59	Capitol EAP1-1111	FAVOURITE WALTZES (EP)	15
57	Capitol T 729	HANK THOMPSON'S ALL-TIME HITS (LP)	20
58	Capitol T 975	DANCE RANCH (LP)	20
61	Capitol (S)T 1246	SONGS FOR ROUNDERS (LP)	20
61	Capitol (S)T 1469	THIS BROKEN HEART OF MINE (LP)	20
62	Capitol (S)T 1632	AT THE GOLDEN NUGGET (LP)	15
65	Capitol T 2089	GOLDEN COUNTRY HITS (LP)	12
66	Capitol T 2274	BREAKING IN ANOTHER HEART (LP)	12
68	Capitol T 2826	JUST AN OLD FLAME (LP)	12

JACKIE THOMPSON
69	Direction 58-4521	Bad Women A Dime A Dozen/Games People Play	10

JOHNNY THOMPSON & ONE-EYED JACKS
65	Ember EMB S 206	For Us There'll Be No Tomorrow/Soul Chant (some in p/s)	12/6

KAY THOMPSON
56	London HLA 8268	Eloise/Just One Of Those Things (78 rpm = £10)	40

LINVAL THOMPSON
75	Faith FA 010	Girl You Got To Run/Run Come Feel	5
75	Faith FA 018	Jah Redder Than Red/Version	8
79	Greensleeves GRED 12	I Never Run And Hide/Natty Dread Style (12")	20
79	Greensleeves GRED 24	One More Chance/Long Time Me Nah Rub You In A Dance (12")	15
78	Burning Sounds BSD 1014	LOVE IS THE QUESTION (LP)	25
78	Burning Sounds BS 1027	ROCKING VIBRATION (LP)	20
79	Burning Sounds BS 1035	I LOVE JAH (LP)	20

LUCKY THOMPSON
56	Vogue V 2388	But Not For Me/East Of The Sun	12

MIKE THOMPSON Jnr.
67	Island WI 3090	Rocksteady Wedding/Flower Pot Bloomers (both with Lyn Taitt & Jets)	25

MOLLIE THOMPSON
66	Asteroid JH 101	SONG NOTES SINGS FROM WORLDS AFAR (LP, private pressing)	30

OWEN THOMPSON
72	Camel CA 103	Must I Be Blue/Version	8

PETER THOMPSON & NTH DEGREE
65	Fontana TF 656	For Me It's All Over/The Way You Used To Do	8

RICHARD THOMPSON
72	Island ILPS 9197	HENRY THE HUMAN FLY (LP, 'pink rim palm tree' label)	12

RICHARD & LINDA THOMPSON
74	Island WIP 6186	I Want To See The Bright Lights Tonight/When I Get To The Border	5
75	Island WIP 6220	Hokey Pokey/I'll Regret It All In The Morning	5
73	Island ILPS 9266	I WANT TO SEE THE BRIGHT LIGHTS TONIGHT (LP)	15
74	Island ILPS 9305	HOKEY POKEY (LP, 'palm tree' label with lyric insert)	15
75	Island ILPS 9348	POUR DOWN LIKE SILVER (LP, 'palm tree' label with lyrics)	12

Richard & Linda THOMPSON

75	Island	OFFICIAL LIVE TOUR 1975 (LP, unreleased, test pressings unconfirmed) .... 100+
76	Island ICD 8	GUITAR/VOCAL (2-LP, gatefold sleeve) 20
78	Chrysalis CHR 1177	FIRST LIGHT (LP) 12

(see also Fairport Convention, Richard Thompson, Sandy Denny, Marc Ellington, Nick Drake, Bunch, Gary Farr, Paul McNeill & Linda Peters)

ROY THOMPSON
67	Columbia DB 8108	Sookie Sookie/Love You Say 30

SIR CHARLES THOMPSON
53	Vogue LDE 032	SIR CHARLES THOMPSON'S ALL STARS WITH CHARLIE PARKER (10" LP)... 20
56	Vanguard PPT 12011	AND HIS BAND FEATURING COLEMAN HAWKINS (10" LP) 15

SONNY THOMPSON & HIS RHYTHM & BLUES BAND
52	Vogue V 2143	Real, Real Fine (Parts 1 & 2) (78)..................................... 42
53	Esquire 10-320	House Full Of Blues/Creepin' (78)..................................... 42
53	Esquire 10-339	Screamin' Boogie/The Fish (78).. 45
60	Starlite ST45 008	Screamin' Boogie/The Fish 250
56	Parlophone GEP 8562	SONNY THOMPSON INSTRUMENTALS (EP, as Sonny Thompson Orchestra) ... 60

(see also Claude Cloud & Thunderclaps, Swallows)

SUE THOMPSON
54	Mercury MB 3133	I'm Not That Kind Of Girl/I Long To Tell You (78)........................ 8
61	Polydor NH 66967	Sad Movies/Throwing Kisses... 15
62	Polydor NH 66973	Norman/Never Love Again 15
62	Polydor NH 66976	Two Of A Kind/It Has To Be Me 8
62	Polydor NH 66979	Have A Good Time/If The Boy Only Knew 8
63	Polydor NH 66987	What's Wrong Bill/I Need A Harbour..................................... 8
62	Fontana 267 244TF	James (Hold The Ladder Steady)/My Hero................................ 10
63	Fontana 267 262TF	Willie Can/Too Much In Love 10
64	Hickory 45-1240	Big Daddy/I'd Like To Know You Better 10
64	Hickory 45-1255	Bad Boy/Toys.. 10
65	Hickory 45-1284	Paper Tiger/Mama Don't Cry At My Wedding............................. 15
65	Hickory 45-1328	It's Break Up Time/Afraid 20
65	Hickory 45-1340	Just Kiss Me/Sweet Hunk Of Misery.................................... 20
65	Hickory 45-1359	I'm Looking For A World/Walkin' My Baby 6
65	Hickory 45-1381	What Should I Do/After The Heartache................................... 10
67	London HLE 10142	Ferris Wheel/Don't Forget To Cry 5
65	Hickory LPE 1507	INTRODUCING KRIS JENSEN AND SUE THOMPSON (EP, 2 tracks each) 18
64	Hickory LPM 102	PAPER TIGER (LP) 28

(see also Kris Jensen)

SUE THOMPSON & BOB LUMAN
63	Polydor NH 66989	I Like Your Kind Of Love/Too Hot To Dance............................. 15
63	Hickory 45-1221	I Like Your Kind Of Love/Too Hot To Dance (reissue)..................... 7

(see also Bob Luman)

GUNILLA THORN
63	HMV POP 1239	Merry-Go-Round/Go On Then 85

TRACEY THORN
82	Cherry Red CHERRY 53	Plain Sailing/Goodbye Joe (p/s) 5

(see also Marine Girls, Everything But The Girl, Grab Grab The Haddock)

DAVID THORNE
62	Stateside SS 141	The Alley Cat Song/The Moon Was Yellow............................... 6
63	Stateside SS 190	One More Fool, One More Broken Heart/Don't Let It Get Away.............. 7
64	Stateside SE 1020	WHAT WILL I TELL MY HEART (EP)....................................... 20
63	Stateside SL 10036	THE ALLEY CAT SONGSTER (LP)... 35

KEN THORNE ORCHESTRA
63	HMV POP 1176	"The Legion's Last Patrol" Film Theme/Kisses In The Night.................. 5
68	United Artists ULP 1201	INSPECTOR CLOUSEAU (LP, soundtrack)................................. 30
69	Stateside S(S)L 10271	THE TOUCHABLES (LP, with Nirvana, Wynder K. Frog, et al.) 45

WOODY THORNE
62	Vogue Pop V 9202	Sadie Lou/Teenagers In Love.. 400

CLAUDE THORNHILL & HIS ORCHESTRA
54	London HL 8042	Pussy-Footin'/Adios (78 rpm = £8) 40
54	London RE-P 1009	CLAUDE THORNHILL GOES MODERN (EP)................................. 20
54	London H-ABP 1019	CLAUDE THORNHILL GOES MODERN (10" LP) 25
54	London H-ABP 1021	DREAM MUSIC (10" LP) 25

EDDIE THORNTON OUTFIT
69	Instant IN 003	Baby Be My Gal/SONNY BURKE OUTFIT: All You........................ 12

WILLIE MAE 'BIG MAMA' THORNTON
54	Vogue V 2284	Hound Dog/Mischievous Boogie (78) (as Willie Mae 'Big Mama' Thornton)..... 120
65	Sue WI 345	Tom Cat/Monkey In The Barn (as Willie Mae Thornton) 250
69	Mercury SMCL 20176	STRONGER THAN DIRT (LP) 40
78	Vanguard VPC 40001	MAMA'S PRIDE (LP) 25

GEORGE THOROGOOD & DESTROYERS
79	Sonet SON 2183	SO MUCH TROUBLE (EP) 5
77	Sonet SNTF 760	GEORGE THOROGOOD AND THE DESTROYERS (LP) 12

BILLY THORPE & AZTECS
65	Parlophone R 5381	Twilight Time/Over The Rainbow. 7

THOR'S HAMMER
66	Parlophone DP 565	Once/A Memory (export issue)	150
66	Parlophone DP 567	If You Knew/Love Enough (export issue)	185
66	Parlophone CGEP 62	THOR'S HAMMER (EP, export issue, gatefold p/s, with bonus 45 "If You Knew"/"Love Enough" [CGEP 62])	900+

LINDA THORSON
68	Ember EMB S 257	Here I Am/Better Than Losing You (p/s)	50/30

THOSE HELICOPTERS
80	State Of The Art STATE 1	Shark/Eskimo (p/s)	6
81	Lavender LAVENDER 001	Dr. Janov/Technical Smack (p/s)	5

THOSE NAUGHTY LUMPS
79	Zoo CAGE 002	Iggy Pop's Jacket/Pure And Innocent (foldout p/s)	6
80	Open Eye OP-EP 1002	DOWN AT THE ZOO (EP)	6

THOUGHTS
66	Planet PLF 118	All Night Stand/Memory Of Your Love	90

(see also Tiffany [& Thoughts], Paul Dean & Soul Savages)

THOUGHTS & WORDS
69	Liberty LBF 15187	Morning Sky/Give Me A Reason	8
69	Liberty LBL 83224	THOUGHTS & WORDS (LP)	15

THOUGHTS OF DES COX
69	Morgan MR 4S	Isn't It Nice/It's All Very Strange	10

THRASHER WONDERS
50s	Melodisc MEL 1106	Charity/GOSPEL KEYS: Motherless Child (78)	6
50s	Melodisc MEL 1190	Blind Old Barnabas/Jesus I Love You (78)	6

THREADBARE CONSORT
80s	private pressing	WEARING THIN (LP)	15

THREADS
86	Unicorn PHZ 2	Step Back/UNDERGROUND ARROWS: Backbeat Of Life (p/s)	10

THREADS OF LIFE
72	Alco ALC 530	THREADS OF LIFE (LP, actually by Alco)	425

THREATS
82	Rondelet ROUND 22	GO TO HELL (EP)	6
82	Rondelet ROUND 29	Politicians & Ministers/Writing's On The Wall/Deep End Depression (p/s)	5
82	Rondelet ROUND 1229	POLITICIANS & MINISTERS (12" EP)	8

THREE BARRY SISTERS
59	Decca F 11099	Little Boy Blue/My Sweetie's Coming To Call (78 rpm = £8)	10
59	Decca F 11118	Tall Paul/Till Then (78 rpm = £8)	12
59	Decca F 11141	Jo Jo — The Dog Faced Boy/I-Aye Ove-Lay Oo-Yay (78 rpm = £8)	10
60	Decca F 11201	Spoilsport/Bonnie Prince Charlie (78 rpm = £12)	8

(see also Barry Sisters)

THREE BELLS
60	Pye 7N 15252	Steady Date/In Between (Wishing I Was Sweet Sixteen)	8
64	Columbia DB 7399	Softly In The Night/He Doesn't Love Me	10
65	Columbia DB 7570	Someone To Love/Over And Over Again	10
66	Columbia DB 7980	Cry No More/He Doesn't Want You	15

(see also Satin Bells)

THREE CAPS
66	Atlantic 584 043	I Got To Handle It/Zig-Zagging	18
69	Atlantic 584 251	Cool Jerk/Hello Stranger	18
71	Atlantic 2091 105	Cool Jerk/Hello Stranger (reissue)	8
66	Atlantic 587/588 019	DANCE THE COOL JERK (LP)	45

(see also Capitols)

THREE CHUCKLES
55	HMV 7M 292	Runaround/At Last You Understand (78 rpm = £30)	40
56	HMV 7M 333	Still Thinking Of You/Times Two I Love You (78 rpm = £35)	35
57	HMV POP 292	We're Gonna Rock Tonight/Want You Give Me A Chance (78 rpm = £40)	100

(see also Teddy Randazzo)

THREE CITY FOUR
65	Decca LK 4705	THREE CITY FOUR (LP)	140
67	CBS 63039	SMOKE AND DUST WHERE THE HEART SHOULD HAVE BEEN (LP)	90

(see also Martin Carthy, Leon Rosselson)

THREE COINS
70	Sugar SU 106	Come And Do The Right Thing/It's So Long	6

3 COLOURS RED
96	Fierce Panda NING 17	This Is My Hollywood	6
99	Creation CRE 313	This Is My Time/Paranoid People (Demo) (numbered p/s, mail-order only)	6

THREE DEGREES
65	Stateside SS 413	Gee Baby I'm Sorry/Do What You're Supposed To Do	50
65	Stateside SS 459	Close Your Eyes/Gotta Draw The Line (DJ copy = £100)	60
71	Mojo 2092 001	Maybe/There's So Much Love Around Me	6
71	Mojo 2092 002	You're The One/Rose Garden	6
71	Mojo 2092 009	There's So Much Love Around Me/Maybe (reissue)	6
71	Mojo 2092 009	There's So Much Love Around Me/Yours (different B-side)	6
75	Pye International 7N 25671	Sugar On Sunday/Maybe	6
71	Mojo 2916 002	THE THREE DEGREES (LP)	30

MINT VALUE £

THREE DOG NIGHT
69	Stateside-Dunhill SS 8008	Nobody/It's For You	6
70	Stateside-Dunhill SS 8052	Mama Told Me Not To Come/Rock And Roll Widow	5
69	Stateside-Dun. (S)SL 5006	THREE DOG NIGHT (LP)	18
69	Stateside-Dun. (S)SL 5013	SUITABLE FOR FRAMING (LP)	15
70	Stateside-Dunhill SSL 5023	CAPTURED LIVE AT THE FORUM (LP)	12
70	Probe SPBA 6251	IT AIN'T EASY (LP)	12

(see also Danny Hutton)

THREE DOLLS
57	MGM MGM 958	The Living End/The Octopus Song	10

THREE GOOD REASONS
65	Mercury MF 883	Build Your Love/Don't Leave Me Now	8
65	Mercury MF 899	Nowhere Man/Wire Wheels	15
65	Mercury MF 929	The Moment Of Truth/Funny Kind Of Loving	7

THREE JOHNS
82	CNT CNT 003	English White Boy Engineer/Secret Agent (p/s)	8
83	CNT CNT 011	Pink Headed Bug/Lucy In The Rain (p/s)	7
83	CNT CNT 013	Men Like Monkeys/Two Minute Ape!/Windolene/ Marx's Wife/Paris 1941 (12", p/s)	8

THREE KAYES (SISTERS)
56	HMV 7M 401	Ivory Tower/Mister Cuckoo (Sing Your Song)	30
56	HMV POP 251	Lay Down Your Arms/First Row Balcony (as Three Kaye Sisters)	25

(see also Kaye Sisters, Frankie Vaughan)

THREE MAN ARMY
72	Pegasus PGS 1	What's Your Name/Travellin'	6
74	Reprise K 14292	Polecat Woman/Take Me Down From The Mountain	5
71	Pegasus PEG 3	A THIRD OF A LIFETIME (LP)	45
73	Reprise K 44254	THREE MAN ARMY (LP)	30
74	Reprise K 54015	THREE MAN ARMY TWO (LP)	30

(see also Gun, Baker Gurvitz Army, Andy Newman)

THREE PEOPLE
66	Decca F 12473	Have You Ever Been There/Good Times	6
66	Decca F 12514	Suspicions/Easy Man To Find	6
67	Decca F 12581	Got To Find A Reason/Simple Thing Would Be For You To Start Loving Me	6

(see also John Bromley)

THREE PIECES
75	Fantasy FTC 116	I Need You Girl/Short'nin' Bread	15

THREE PROFESSORS
56	Columbia DB 3845	Yew Stept Owt Offa Dreme/Vulgar Boatman Rock (78 rpm = £6)	5

THREE QUARTERS
65	Columbia DB 7467	People Will Talk/Love Come A-Tricklin' Down	15
65	Columbia DB 7576	The Pleasure Girls/Little People	6

THREE'S A CROWD
66	Fontana TF 673	Look Around The Corner/Living In A Dream	18

(see also Embers, Writing On The Wall)

THREE TOPS
67	Doctor Bird DB 1101	Miserable Friday/This World Has A Feeling	20
67	Studio One SO 2023	Moving To Progress/Love And Inspiration	22
67	Trojan TR 003	It's Raining/Sound Of Music	40+
67	Treasure Isle TI 7008	Do It Right/You Should Have Known	20
68	Coxsone CS 7033	A Man Of Chances/HORTENSE ELLIS: A Groovy Kind Of Love	40
68	Coxsone CS 7051	Great Train In '68/You Should Have Known	20
73	Bullet BU 527	Take Time Out/Just Like A Log	12

(see also Dion Cameron & Three Tops, Sir Lord Comic, King Rocky)

THREE WISE MEN
83	Virgin VS 642	Thanks For Christmas/Countdown To Christmas Partytime (p/s)	10

(see also XTC)

THREE WISE MEN
86	Rhythm King LEFT7T	Refresh Yourself (12")	8

THRILLERS
68	Blue Cat BS 128	The Last Dance/DELTA CATS: Unworthy Baby	20

(see also Phil Pratt)

PERCY 'THRILLS' THRILLINGTON
77	Regal Zono. EMI 2594	Uncle Albert — Admiral Halsey/Eat At Home	100
77	Regal Zono. EMC 3175	THRILLINGTON (LP, with inner sleeve)	125
77	Regal Zono. TC-EMC 3175	THRILLINGTON (cassette)	40

(see also Paul McCartney)

THRILLS
66	Capitol CL 15469	No One/What Can Go Wrong (DJ copy = £200)	100
79	Grapevine GRP 126	Show The World Where It's At/What Can Go Wrong	10

THRILLS
02	Virgin 5468857	Santa Cruz (You're Not That Fat)/Deckchairs And Cigarettes (p/s, white vinyl)	10
02	Virgin VSCDT 1842	Santa Cruz (You're Not That Fat)/Deckchairs And Cigarettes/ Your Love is Like Las Vegas/Plans (CD)	10
03	Virgin VS 1862	Santa Cruz/Don't Play It Cool (p/s, purple vinyl)	5

03	Virgin Virgin VS 1842	One Horse Town/Don't Play It Cool (yellow vinyl, p/s)	5
03	Virgin VS 1852	Big Sur/Your Love Is Like Las Vegas (blue vinyl, p/s)	8
03	Virgin VSDJ 1855	Last Night I Dreamt That Somebody Loved Me (1-sided gig issue, p/s, 500 only)	
100			
03	Virgin V 2974	SO MUCH FOR THE CITY (LP)	12

THROBBING GRISTLE
78	Industrial IR 0003	United/Zyklon B Zombie (p/s)	10
78	Industrial IR 0003/U	United/Zyklon B Zombie (p/s, white or clear vinyl, 1,000 only of each)	20
80	Industrial IR 0003	United/Zyklon B Zombie (longer version) (p/s, reissue, 'Memorial Issue' scratched in matrix)	12
80	Industrial IR 0013	Subhuman/Something Came Over Me (in polythene camouflage bag)	15
80	Industrial IR 0015	Adrenalin/Distant Dreams (Part Two) (in polythene camouflage bag)	15
81	Fetish FET 006	Discipline (live, Berlin)/Discipline (live, Manchester) (12", p/s)	25
76	Industrial IR 0001	BEST OF VOLUME II (private cassette, 500 copies only)	50+
77	Industrial IR 0002	SECOND ANNUAL REPORT (LP, 785 only, white heavy duty sleeve, with questionnaire, xerox strip & 2 stickers)	90
78	Industrial IR 0004	D.O.A. THE THIRD AND FINAL REPORT (LP, 1st 1,000 with calendar & p'card)	30/15
78	Fetish FET 2001	SECOND ANNUAL REPORT (LP, 2,000 only, T.G. 'lightning flash' sleeve, with questionnaire & insert)	25
79	Fetish FET 2001	SECOND ANNUAL REPORT (LP, reissue, glossy sleeve with inserts)	15
79	Industrial IR 0004	D.O.A. THE THIRD AND FINAL REPORT (LP, re-pressing, 1,000 only, banded as 16 equal length tracks)	20
79	Industrial IR 0008	20 JAZZ FUNK GREATS (LP, 5,000 only, 1st 2,000 with b&w poster)	30/15
80	Industrial IR 0009	HEATHEN EARTH (LP, gatefold sleeve, 785 on blue vinyl)	80/18
81	Fetish FET 2001	SECOND ANNUAL REPORT (LP, backwards version, 1st 2,000 in T.G. 'flash' sleeve, later in black & white sleeve)	25/15
81	Fetish FX 1	A BOXED SET (5-LP box set with 28-page booklet & badge, 5,000 only)	125
82	Death 01	MUSIC FROM THE DEATH FACTORY, MAY '79 (LP, 50 only)	250+
82	Power Focus 001	ASSUME POWER FOCUS (LP, 500 only, numbered)	60
82	T.G. 33033	LIVE AT THE DEATH FACTORY, MAY '79 (LP, reissue picture disc, 1,355 only)	40
82	Walter Ulbricht 001	JOURNEY THROUGH THE BODY (LP, 1,000 only)	30
82	Karnage/Illuminated KILL 1	THEE PSYCHICK SACRIFICE (2-LP)	25
84	Illuminated JAMS 35	IN THE SHADOW OF THE SUN (LP, soundtrack)	18
84	Illuminated JAMS 39	THE INDUSTRIAL RECORDS STORY 1976-1981 (LP)	30
84	Casual Abandon CAS 1J	ONCE UPON A TIME (LP)	25
84	Mental Decay 01-1	SPECIAL TREATMENT (LP)	25
80s	Sprut 001	VERY FRIENDLY — THE FIRST ANNUAL REPORT OF T.G. (LP)	25
80s	Industrial IRC 1-IRC 24	24 HOURS (box set of cassettes with total of 24 hours playing time; every set is unique)	150-200

(see also Psychic TV, Coil, Sabres Of Paradise)

THROWING MUSES
89	4AD BADD 903	Dizzy/Santa Claus/Mania (live)/Downtown (live) (10", gatefold p/s)	10
93	4AD CADD 2013	RED HEAVEN (LP, with free live Kristin Hersh LP)	15
93	4AD CADD 2013CD	RED HEAVEN (CD, with free live Kristin Hersh CD)	20

(see also Belly, Kristin Hersh)

THUNDER
89	EMI EMS 11	She's So Fine/Girl's Going Out Of Her Head (p/s, with free patch)	5
90	EMI EMPD 126	Dirty Love/Fired Up (logo-shaped picture disc with insert in PVC sleeve)	10
90	EMI EMPD 126	Dirty Love/Fired Up (uncut picture disc with insert in PVC sleeve)	15
90	EMI EMS 137	Back Street Symphony/No Way Out Of The Wilderness (box set with postcards, some also with badge)	each 6
90	EMI 12 EMPD 137	Back Street Symphony/No Way Out Of The Wilderness/An Englishman On Holiday (live) (12", picture disc with insert in PVC sleeve)	8

(see also Terraplane, Nuthin' Fancy)

JOHNNY THUNDER
63	Stateside SS 149	Loop De Loop/Don't Be Ashamed	10
63	Stateside SS 168	Rock-A-Bye My Darling/The Rosy Dance	10
63	Stateside SS 200	Jailer, Bring Me Water/Outlaw	15
63	Stateside SS 229	Hey Child/Everybody Likes To Dance With Johnny	10
64	Stateside SS 337	More, More, More Love, Love, Love/Shout It To The World	10
65	Stateside SS 370	Send Her To Me/Everybody Likes To Dance With Johnny	20
65	Stateside SS 454	Dear John I'm Going To Leave You/Suzie-Q	10
65	Stateside SS 476	Everybody Do The Sloopy/Beautiful	10
66	Stateside SS 499	My Prayer/A Broken Heart	10
63	Stateside SL 10029	LOOP DE LOOP (LP)	75

JOHNNY THUNDER & RUBY WINTERS
| 67 | Stateside SS 2005 | Make Love To Me/Teach Me Tonight | 15 |

MARGO THUNDER
| 75 | Capitol CL 15808 | Expressway To Your Heart/Hush Up Your Mouth | 10 |

THUNDERBIRDS
| 66 | Polydor 56710 | Your Ma Said You Cried (In Your Sleep Last Night)/Before It's Too Late | 50 |

(see also Chris Farlowe & Thunderbirds)

THUNDERBIRDS (Australia)
| 61 | Oriole CB 1610 | Wild Weekend/Rat Race | 20 |
| 61 | Oriole CB 1625 | New Orleans Beat/Delilah Jones | 20 |

THUNDERBIRDS (T.V.)
(see under Barry Gray)

THUNDERBIRDS (U.S.)
| 55 | London HL 8146 | Ayuh, Ayuh/Blueberries (78 rpm = £25) | 100 |

(see also Bert Convy & Thunderbirds, Midnighters)

THUNDERBOLTS
62   Decca F 11522   Fugitive/Feelin' In A Mood 15

THUNDERBOYS
80   Recent EJSP 9339   Fashion/Someone Like You (p/s). 40

THUNDERCLAP NEWMAN
70   Track 2094 001   Accidents/I See It All. 5
70   Track 2094 002   Wild Country/Hollywood. 5
70   Track 2094 003   The Reason/Stormy Petrel 5
79   Track 2095 002   Wild Country/Hollywood (reissue, p/s) 8
70   Track 2406 003   HOLLYWOOD DREAM (LP) 30
(see also Stone The Crows, One In A Million, Paul McCartney & Wings, Speedy Keen, Andy Newman)

THUNDER COMPANY
70   Columbia DB 8706   Ridin' On The Gravy Train (5.03)/Bubble Drum 38
70   Columbia DB 8706   Ridin' On The Gravy Train (2.35 Edit)/Bubble Drum (demo only) 48
(see also Brian Bennett, Shadows)

THUNDERMUG
73   London HLZ 10411   Africa/Will They Ever 6
72   Axe AXS 502   STRIKES (LP). 15

JOHNNY THUNDERS (& THE HEARTBREAKERS)
78   Real ARE 1   Dead Or Alive/Downtown (p/s). 15
78   Real ARE 3   You Can't Put Your Arms Around A Memory (Edit)/Hurtin' (p/s) 12
78   Real ARE 3T   You Can't Put Your Arms Around A Memory/Hurtin'
                           (12", p/s, blue or pink vinyl, die-cut company sleeve) 12
83   Jungle JUNG 5   VINTAGE '77 (12" EP) 12
84   Jungle JUNG 14P   Get Off The Phone/All By Myself (picture disc). 10
84   Jungle JUNG 14T   GET OFF THE PHONE EP (12") 8
85   Jungle JUNG 18T   CHINESE ROCKS (12" EP). 8
85   Jungle JUNG 23P   Crawfish/Tie Me Up (with Patti Palladin, picture disc) 8
87   Jungle JUNG 33T   QUE SERA SERA (12" EP) 8
77   Real RAL 1   SO ALONE (LP, with inner sleeve). 12
(see also New York Dolls, Heartbreakers)

THUNDERSTICK
83   Thunderbolt THBE 1002   FEEL LIKE ROCK'N'ROLL (12" EP, p/s, some with patch) 12/8
83   Thunderbolt THBL 008   BEAUTY AND THE BEASTS (LP). 12
(see also Samson, Gillan)

THUNDERTHIGHS
74   Philips 6006 386   Central Park Arrest/Sally Wants A Dress (p/s) 12

THUNDERTRAIN
77   Jelly JPLP 1   TEENAGE SUICIDE (LP) 12

THURSDAY'S CHILDREN
66   Piccadilly 7N 35276   Just You/You Don't Believe Me 20
66   Piccadilly 7N 35306   Crawfish/Come Softly To Me 10
(see also Phil Cordell)

THYRDS
64   Oak RGJ 133   Hide 'N' Seek/I've Got My Mojo Working 245
64   Decca F 12010   Hide 'N' Seek/No Time Like The Present 60

TIARAS
63   Warner Bros WB 92   You Told Me/I'm Gonna Forget You. 18

TIBET & STAPLETON
96   United Dairies UDOR 1   MUSICALISCHE KÜRBS HÜTTE (LP, clear vinyl, with insert) 25
(see also Current 93, Steven Stapleton & David Tibet)

TICH & QUACKERS
65   Oriole CB 1980   Santa Bring Me Ringo/Santa's Got Such A Terrible Cold 8

TICKAWINDA
75   Pennine PSS 153   ROSEMARY LANE (LP). 300

KATHRYN TICKELL
84   Saydisc SDL 343   ON KIELDER SIDE (LP) 12

TICKETS
79   Bridgehouse BHS 3   I'll Be Your Pin Up/Guess I Have To Sit Alone (p/s). 6
(see also Wasted Youth)

TICKLE
67   Regal Zonophone RZ 3004   Subway (Smokey Pokey World)/Good Evening. 340
(see also Junior's Eyes, Outsider, Bunch Of Fives)

TICKLERS
52   Melodisc MEL 1214   Don't Fence Her In/Glamour Gal (78) 8
53   Motta's 13   Four Days Love/Healing In The Balm Yard (78) 6

TIDAL WAVE
69   Decca F 22973   With Tears In My Eyes/We Wanna Know 10
69   Storm PD 9616   Spider Spider/Crazy Horse. 175

TIDBITS
71   Fly BUG 12   Jean Harlow/Vietnam/Six O'Clock Blues 6

PETER TIERNEY & NIGHTHAWKS
65   Fontana TF 547   Oh How I Need You/That's Too Bad 10

ROY TIERNEY
61   Philips BF 1159   Cupid/The Lonely One (some in p/s) 18/8
61   Philips BF 1194   Just Out Of Reach (Of My Two Empty Arms)/Casanova. 10

TIERNEY'S FUGITIVES
65 Decca F 12247   Did You Want To Run Away?/Morning Mist 20

TIFFANIES
67 Chess CRS 8059   It's Got To Be A Great Song/He's Good For Me (DJ copy = £140) 75

TIFFANY (with THOUGHTS)
65 Parlophone R 5311   I Know/Am I Dreaming 12
66 Parlophone R 5439   Find Out What's Happening/Baby Don't Look Down (as Tiffany with Thoughts) . 40
(see also Thoughts)

TIFFANY SHADE
68 Fontana (S)TL 5469   TIFFANY SHADE (LP) 75

JIMMY & LOUISE TIG
69 Deep Soul DS 9105   A Love That Never Grows Cold/Who Can I Turn To 40

TIGER
75 United Artists UP 35848   I Am An Animal/Stop That Machine. 5
76 Retreat RTL 6006   TIGER (LP, with inner sleeve) 15
76 EMI EMC3153   GOIN' DOWN LAUGHING (LP) 12
(see also Hackensack, Samson, Brinsley Schwarz, Big Jim Sullivan)

TIGER (Jamaica)
70 New Beat NB 052   Soul Of Africa/Dallas Texas 7
70 New Beat NB 064   Musical Scorcher/Three Dogs Night 7
71 Camel CA 70   Guilty/United We Stand 7
71 New Beat NB 075   African Beat/Black Man Land 7
71 New Beat NB 088   Have You Ever Been Hurt/Our Day Will Come 7

TIGER LILY
75 Gull GULS 12   Monkey Jive/Ain't Misbehavin' 8
77 Gull GULS 54   Monkey Jive/Ain't Misbehavin' (reissue, p/s) 15/5
80 Dead Good DEAD 11   Monkey Jive/Ain't Misbehavin' (2nd reissue, different p/s) 5
(see also Ultravox)

TIGERMOTH
84 Rogue FMSL 2006   TIGERMOTH (LP). 15

TIGERS
69 Polydor 56339   Rain Falls On The Lonely/Smile For Me 8

TIGERS
80s Strike KIK 1   Kidding Stops/Big Expense, Small Income (p/s) 8

TIGHT LIKE THAT
72 Village Thing VTS 12   HOKUM (LP). 22

TIGHTS
78 Cherry Red CHERRY 1   Bad Hearts/It/Cracked (p/s) 20
78 Cherry Red CHERRY 2   Howard Hughes/China's Eternal (p/s) 8
78 Ch. Red CSP-CHERRY 2   Howard Hughes/China's Eternal (cassette) 6

TIKKI, TAKI, SUZI, LIES
70 UPC UPC 102   Welcome To My House/I Believe In Love 6
70 UPC UPC 109   Ba-Da-Da-Dum/Dream Stealer 25

TILLER BOYS
79 New Hormones ORG 3   Big Noise From The Jungle/Slaves And Pyramids/What Me Worry? (p/s) 6
(see also Buzzcocks, Pete Shelley, Eric Random)

TILLERMEN
71 Duke DU 109   Be Loving To Me/Judgement Rock 7
(see also Greyhound)

MEL TILLIS
67 London HLR 10141   Life Turned Her That Way/If I Could Only Start Over 7
68 London HA-R 8345   MR. MEL (LP) 22

BERTHA TILLMAN
62 Oriole CB 1746   Oh, My Angel/Lovin' Time 75

JOHNNY TILLOTSON
59 London HLA 8930   True True Happiness/Love Is Blind (78 rpm £50). 50
60 London HLA 9048   Why Do I Love You So/Never Let Me Go 30
60 London HLA 9101   Earth Angel/Pledging My Love 30
60 London HLA 9231   Poetry In Motion/Princess, Princess. 8
61 London HLA 9275   Jimmy's Girl/His True Love Said Goodbye. 10
61 London HLA 9412   Without You/Cutie Pie. 18
62 London HLA 9514   Dreamy Eyes/Much Beyond Compare 6
62 London HLA 9550   It Keeps Right On A-Hurtin'/She Gave Sweet Love To Me 10
62 London HLA 9598   Send Me The Pillow You Dream On/What'll I Do 6
62 London HLA 9642   I Can't Help It/I'm So Lonesome I Could Cry 6
63 London HLA 9695   Out Of My Mind/Judy, Judy, Judy 10
63 London HLA 9811   Funny How Time Slips Away/A Very Good Year For Girls 10
63 MGM MGM 1214   Talk Back Trembling Lips/Another You. 10
63 MGM MGM 1225   Worried Guy/Please Don't Go Away 6
63 MGM MGM 1235   I'm Watching My Watch/I Rise, I Fall 6
64 MGM MGM 1247   Suffering From A Heartache/Worry. 6
64 MGM MGM 1252   She Understands Me/Tomorrow 10
64 MGM MGM 1266   Angel/Little Boy. 7
65 MGM MGM 1275   Then I'll Count Again/One's Yours, One's Mine. 6
65 MGM MGM 1281   Heartaches By The Number/Your Memory Comes Along. 6
65 MGM MGM 1290   Our World/My Gidget 7
66 MGM MGM 1300   Hello Enemy/I Never Loved You Anyway 6

MINT VALUE £

66	MGM MGM 1311	Me Myself And I/Country Boy, Country Boy	6
66	MGM MGM 1319	No Love At All/What Am I Gonna Do	6
68	MGM MGM 1393	Cabaret/If I Were A Rich Man	6
69	London HLU 10281	Tears On My Pillow/Remember When	5
62	London RE-A 1345	JOHNNY TILLOTSON (EP)	40
63	London RE-A 1388	J.T. (EP)	50
63	MGM MGM-EP 788	JOHNNY TILLOTSON (EP)	35
64	MGM MGM-EP 790	JOHNNY TILLOTSON'S HIT PARADE (EP)	35
61	London HA-A 2431	JOHNNY TILLOTSON'S BEST (LP)	100
62	London HA-A 8019	IT KEEPS RIGHT ON A-HURTIN' (LP)	70
64	MGM MGM-C 972	ALONE WITH YOU (LP)	30
65	MGM C/CS 1002	SHE UNDERSTANDS ME (LP)	30
65	MGM MGM-C(S) 8005	JOHNNY TILLOTSON SINGS OUR WORLD (LP)	25
66	MGM MGM-C(S) 8025	NO LOVE AT ALL (LP)	25

TILSLEY ORCHESTRA

66	Fontana TF 783	"Thunderbirds" Theme/Theme From "The Power Game"	20
67	Polydor 56150	Mr. Aitch Theme/Cotton Reed	8
67	Fontana (S)TL 5411	TOP T.V. THEMES (LP)	25
69	Fontana SFL 13139	TOP T.V. THEMES (LP, reissue)	12

(see also Electric Banana)

STEVE TILSTON

71	Village Thing VTS 5	AN ACOUSTIC CONFUSION (LP)	25
72	Transatlantic TRA 252	COLLECTION (LP, gatefold sleeve)	15
77	Cornucopia CR 1	SONGS FROM THE DRESS REHEARSAL (LP, with Rupert Hine/John Renbourn)	20
83	TM PROP 4	IN FOR A PENNY IN FOR A POUND (LP, with Peter Bardens)	12

TIMBER

71	Elektra K 12022	Bring America Home/Splinters From Timber	6
72	Elektra K 12042	Outlaw/Song For Two Signs	6
71	Elektra K 42093	BRING AMERICA HOME (LP)	15

TIME

| 65 | Pye 7N 17019 | Take A Bit Of Notice/Every Now And Then | 50 |
| 66 | Pye 7N 17146 | The First Time I Saw The Sunshine/Annabel | 20 |

TIME

| 75 | B.U.K. BULP 2005 | TIME (LP) | 45 |

(see also Spontaneous Combustion)

T.I.M.E. (Trust In Men Everywhere)

68	Liberty LBL/LBS 83144	T.I.M.E. (LP)	65
69	Liberty LBF 15082	Take Me Along/Make It Alright	10
69	Liberty LBL/LBS 83232	SMOOTH BALL (LP)	90

TIMEBOX

67	Piccadilly 7N 35369	I'll Always Love You/Save Your Love	50
67	Piccadilly 7N 35379	Soul Sauce/I Wish I Could Jerk Like My Uncle Cyril	50
67	Deram DM 153	Walking Through The Streets Of My Mind/Don't Make Promises	20
68	Deram DM 194	Beggin'/A Woman That's Waiting	30
68	Deram DM 219	Girl Don't Make Me Wait/Gone Is The Sad Man	30
69	Deram DM 246	Baked Jam Roll In Your Eye/Poor Little Heartbreaker	22
69	Deram DM 271	Yellow Van/You've Got The Chance	18

(see also Bo Street Runners, [Mike] Patto, V.I.Ps)

TIME CODE

| 86 | Jive LOUT 1 | Village House Stomp/Louie Louie (12") | 8 |

TIMELORDS

88	KLF 003GG	Gary In The Tardis (Radio)/(Minimal) (white label promo, 500 only)	15
88	KLF 003GG	Gary In The Tardis (Radio)/(Minimal) (12", p/s)	10
88	KLF 003P	Doctorin' The Tardis (Radio)/(Minimal) (car-shaped picture disc)	15
88	KLF 003R	Doctorin' The Tardis (Radio)/Doctorin' The Tardis (Minimal)/ Gary Glitter Joins The JAMs (12", 4,000 only, most in stickered black die-cut sleeve, some in full 'Gary Glitter' p/s)	30/8
88	KLF TCD 003	Doctorin' The Tardis (12" mix)/What Time Is Love? (KLF original) (CD)	10
88	KLF CD 003	Doctorin' The Tardis (Radio)/Doctorin' The Tardis (Minimal)/Doctorin' The Tardis (Club Mix)/Doctorin' The Tardis (Video) (CD Video)	30

(see also KLF, Disco 2000, JAMs, Bill Drummond, Orb, Space)

TIMES

65	EMI 7ES 24	Ooh Wee/Shepherd Blues/Suzie/Running And Hiding (EP, demo only)	65
66	Columbia DB 7804	Think About The Times/Tomorrow Night	25
66	Columbia DB 7904	(She Can't Replace) The Love We Knew/Reconciled	35

TIMES

81	Whaam! WHAAM 2	Red With Purple Flashes/Biff! Bang! Pow! (p/s)	35
82	Art Pop POP 50	Here Come The Holidays (Voici Les Vacances)/Three Cheers For The Sun (A-side as Joni Dee & Times, p/s, some with 'Times' sticker)	15/10
83	Art Pop POP 49	I Helped Patrick McGoohan Escape/The Theme From "Danger Man" (p/s)	12
84	Art Pop POP 46	Boys Brigade/Power Is Forever (p/s)	7
84	Art Pop POP 45	Blue Fire/Where The Blue Begins (p/s)	6
85	Unicorn PHZ 1	London Boys/(Where To Go) When The Sun Goes Down (p/s)	5
90	Caff CAFF 13	Extase/BIFF BANG POW!: Sleep (p/s, with insert)	20
85	Art Pop 43DOZ	BOYS ABOUT TOWN (EP)	10
81	Whaam! BIG 1	POP GOES ART (LP, hand-sprayed sleeve)	35
82	Art Pop ART 20	POP GOES ART! (LP, reissue, hand-sprayed sleeve, some with magazine cuttings taped to plain white cover)	25/20
83	Art Pop ART 19	THIS IS LONDON (LP, white label w/ blue print or black label w/ white print)	18/15

83	Art Pop No. 1	I HELPED PATRICK McGOOHAN ESCAPE (mini-LP)	18
84	Art Pop ART 17	HELLO EUROPE (LP, purple or blue sleeve)	12
85	Art Pop ARTPOP 2	BLUE PERIOD (mini-LP, grey or blue sleeve)	12/10
86	Art Pop ART 16	UP AGAINST IT (LP)	12
86	Art Pop ART 15	ENJOY! (LP, gatefold sleeve)	12
90	Art Pop ART 20	POP GOES ART (LP, 'hand-painted' picture disc reissue, signed)	15
93	Creation CRELP 137	ALTERNATIVE COMMERCIAL CROSSOVER (LP, with inner)	12

(see also Television Personalities, Teenage Filmstars, O Level, Biff Bang Pow!, L'Orange Mechanik)

TIME UK
83	Red Bus TIM 123	The Cabaret/Remember Days (gatefold p/s)	10

(see also the Jam)

TIMES
89	Creation CRE 071 T	Manchester (12", p/s)	10

(see also Television Personalities, Teenage Filmstars, O Level, Biff Bang Pow!, L'Orange Mechanik)

TIME ZONE
88	Virgin CDT 29	World Destruction (12" A)/(12" B)/(12" Instrumental Blast) (featuring John Lydon & Afrika Bambaataa) (3" CD, gatefold card p/s)	8

(see also Public Image Ltd., Sex Pistols)

BOBBY TIMMONS
61	Riverside RLP 334	SOUL TIME (LP, with Art Blakey, also stereo [RLP 9334])	15

SALLY TIMMS & DRIFTING COWGIRLS
87	T.I.M. 12 MOT 6	This House Is A House Of Trouble! (Extended) (with Marc Almond)/The Anchor Of Love/Heavenly Gates (12", p/s)	10

(see also Marc Almond, Mekons)

TIMON
68	Pye 7N 17451	Bitter Thoughts Of Little Jane/Ramblin' Boy	100
70	Threshold TH 3	And Now She Says She's Young/I'm Just A Travelling Man	8

(see also Tymon Dogg)

TIMONEERS
76	WHM WHM 1919	ROASTED LIVE (LP)	20

AL TIMOTHY & HIS BAND
55	Decca F 10558	Gruntin' Blues/You Mad Man!	10

TIM TAM & TURN ONS
67	Island WIP 6007	Wait A Minute/Ophelia	40

TINA & MEXICANS
68	Pye 7N 17525	One Love Two/Longing To Hold You	6

TINDERSTICKS
92	Tippy Toe 1	Patchwork/Milky Teeth (p/s, hand-coloured inner sleeve & insert; 1,000 only, numbered in positive or negative figures [from -500 to 500])	45
93	Tippy Toe/Ché TIPPY-CHE 2	Marbles/Joe Stumble/For Those.../Benn (10", p/s, stickered PVC sleeve, innersleeve & insert, 2,000 only)	20
93	Rough Trade 45rev16	A Marriage Made In Heaven/A Marriage Made In Heaven (Instrumental) ('singles club' release, p/s, 5,000 only)	20
93	Domino RUG 006	UNWIRED EP: Feeling Relatively Good/Rotweilers And Mace/She/Kooks (EP, numbered p/s; 1 copy in 10 with 'Domino' stamp, 1,500 only)	20
93	This Way Up WAY 1811	City Sickness/Untitled/The Bullring (p/s, 1,500 only)	8
93	This Way Up WAY 1899	City Sickness/Untitled/The Bullring (CD)	15
93	Clawfist XPIG 21	We Have All The Time In The World/GALLON DRUNK: Known Not Wanted ('singles club' release, p/s, 1,400 only)	25
93	Tippy Toe 003	LIVE IN BERLIN: Raindrops/Tyed (in stamped brown paper bag, mail-order/tour release, 1,500 only)	20
94	This Way Up WAY 2899	Kathleen/Summat Moon/Sweet, Sweet Man/E Type Joe (CD)	15
95	Sub Pop SP 297	THE SMOOTH SOUND OF TINDERSTICKS: Here/Harry's Dilemma (p/s, 3,000 only)	10
93	This Way Up	TINDERSTICKS (1st album) (LP)	25
94	This Way Up	TINDERSTICKS (2nd album) (LP)	25
94	This Way Up WAY 3288	LIVE IN AMSTERDAM (10" LP, brown sleeve)	20
94	This Way Up WAY 3299	LIVE IN AMSTERDAM (CD, numbered brown paper sleeve)	25
95	This Way Up	THE BLOOMSBURY THEATRE 12/3/95 (LP)	50

PROMOS
93	This Way Up WAY 1755	FIRST ALBUM SAMPLER (CD, card sleeve with 'dancer' postage stamp sticker, 1000 only)	20
94	This Way Up WAY 3999	TINDERSTICKS (CD, card sleeve, 300 in brown paper envelope hand-sealed with red wax)	20
94	This Way Up WAY 4099	SECOND ALBUM SAMPLER (CD, jewel case, 1,500 only)	18
95	This Way Up WAY 4522	Travelling Light/Waiting 'Round You/I've Been Loving You Too Long (10", unreleased, 25 white label test pressings only)	30
96	This Way Up WAY 5655	Petites Gouttes D'Eau/Ma Soeur (CD, sampler, 2,000 only)	10
97	This Way Up WAY 6299	CURTAINS (CD, card sleeve in stamped 5" box with booklet, biography, 1,800 only; 100 copies with 6 black & white photos)	30/20
97	Chop 'Em Out (no cat. no.)	AN INTERVIEW WITH DAVE AND DICKON (CD-R, generic inlay, 20 copies only)	18

(see also Asphalt Ribbons)

TINGA (Stewart) & ERNIE (Wilson)
69	Explosion EX 2009	She's Gone/Old Old Song	8

TINGHA & TUCKER
(see under Century 21)

TINKERBELL'S FAIRYDUST

TINKERBELL'S FAIRYDUST
67	Decca F 12705	Lazy Day/In My Magic Garden	35
68	Decca F 12778	Twenty Ten/Walking My Baby	35
69	Decca F 12865	Sheila's Back In Town/Follow Me Follow	40
69	Decca LK/SKL 5028	TINKERBELL'S FAIRYDUST (LP, unreleased; finished copies or test pressings in sleeve)	1,200/700

TINKERS
69	Fontana SFJL 935	TIL THE WILD BIRDS (LP)	18
72	Argo ZFB 35	SPRING RAIN (LP)	20

BABS TINO
62	London HLR 9589	Forgive Me/If I Didn't Love You So Much	20
63	London RE-R 1377	FORGIVE ME (EP)	75

TIN PAN SKIFFLE GROUP
57	Nestles NR 06	Poor Howard (1-sided card flexi 78)	10

MICK TINSLEY
67	Decca F 12544	Let It Be Me/How're You Gonna Tell Me	6

(see also Hedgehoppers Anonymous)

TINTERN ABBEY
67	Deram DM 164	Beeside/Vacuum Cleaner	1000+

TIN TIN
69	Polydor 56332	Only Ladies Play Croquet/He Wants To Be A Star	7
70	Polydor 2058 023	Toast And Marmalade For Tea/Manhattan Woman	10
70	Polydor 2058 076	Come On Over Again/Back To Winona	7
71	Polydor 2001 146	Shana/Rocky Mountain	5
71	Polydor 2058 114	Is That The Way/Swans On The Canal	6
72	Polydor 2058 232	Toast And Marmalade For Tea/Cavalry's Coming/Ships On The Starboard	5
72	Polydor 2058 238	Talking Turkey/Cavalry's Coming	5
69	Polydor 2384 011	TIN TIN (LP)	18
72	Polydor 2382 080	ASTRAL TAXI (LP)	15

(see also Steve & Stevie)

TINY ALICE
72	Kama Sutra 2013 043	Doctor Jazz/The Chocolate Dandies Of 1932/15¢ Hamburger Mama	5
72	Kama Sutra 2319 015	TINY ALICE (LP)	12

TINY TIM
68	Reprise RS 20760	Bring Back Those Rockabye Baby Days	7
68	Reprise RS 23258	Tiptoe Through The Tulips/I Got You Babe	6
68	Reprise RS 20769	Hello Hello/The Other Side	20
69	Reprise RS 20802	Great Balls Of Fire/As Time Goes By	6
69	Reprise RS 20845	Mickey The Monkey/Neighbourhood Children	6
71	Reprise RS 27004	There Will Always Be An England/Bless 'Em All/It's A Long Way To Tipperary/Have You Seen My Little Sue (78 rpm with union jack/plain label = £10)	5
72	Wand WN 33	Am I Just Another Pretty Face/Movies	5
74	Polydor 2058 485	Happy Wanderer/My Nose Always Gets In The Way	5
68	Reprise RSLP 6292	GOD BLESS TINY TIM (LP)	30
69	Reprise RSLP 6323	TINY TIM'S SECOND ALBUM (LP)	30
69	Reprise RSLP 6351	FOR ALL MY LITTLE FRIENDS (LP)	20

DIMITRI TIOMKIN
54	Vogue Coral Q 2016	The High And The Mighty/Dial M For Murder	15

TINY TOPSY (& CHARMS)
58	Parlophone R 4397	Come On, Come On, Come On/A Ring Around My Finger (with Charms)	110
58	Parlophone R 4397	Come On, Come On, Come On/A Ring Around My Finger (with Charms) (78)	30
58	Parlophone R 4427	You Shocked Me/Waterproof Eyes (solo) (78 = £25)	75
61	Pye International 7N 25104	After Marriage Blues/Working On Me Baby (solo)	30

KEITH TIPPETT
69	Polydor 2384 004	YOU ARE HERE, I AM THERE (LP)	80
71	Vertigo 6360 024	DEDICATED TO YOU BUT YOU WEREN'T LISTENING (LP, gatefold sleeve, swirl label)	75
72	RCA SF 8290	BLUEPRINT (LP)	75
76	Steam SJ 104	TNT (LP, with Stan Tracey)	15
77	Vinyl VS 101	WARM SPIRITS, COOL SPIRITS (LP)	12
78	Ogun OGD 003/4	FRAMES (2-LP)	22

(see also Centipede, Ovary Lodge, Nicra)

JULIE TIPPETTS
76	Utopia UTS 601	SUNSET GLOW (LP)	25

(see also Julie Driscoll, Brian Auger, Centipede, Keith Tippett, Elton Dean, Ninesense, Mark Charig)

TIPPIE & THE CLOVERS
63	Stateside SS 160	My Heart Said/Bossa Nova Baby	25

LESTER TIPTON
80	Grapevine GRP 138	This Won't Change/MASQUERADERS: How	40

TIP TOPS
63	Cameo Parkway P 868	He's Braggin'/Oo-Kook-A-Boo	40

TÍR NA NOG
71	Chrysalis ILPS 9153	TÍR NA NOG (LP)	20
72	Chrysalis CHR 1006	A TEAR AND A SMILE (LP)	18
73	Chrysalis CHR 1047	STRONG IN THE SUN (LP)	15

TITANIC
72	CBS 7278	Sante Fe/Half Breed	5
72	CBS 8185	Rain 2,000/Blond	20
73	CBS 1670	Richmond Express/Heia Valenga	5
71	CBS 64104	TITANIC (LP)	18
72	CBS 64791	SEA WOLF (LP)	15
73	CBS 65661	EAGLE ROCK (LP)	12

TITANS
58	London HLU 8609	Don't You Just Know It/Can It Be (78 rpm = £30)	90

TITUS GROAN
70	Dawn DNX 2503	Open The Door Homer/Woman Of The World/Liverpool (p/s)	20
70	Dawn DNLS 3012	TITUS GROAN (LP, gatefold sleeve)	55

CAL TJADER
65	Verve VS 529	Soul Sauce/Naked City Theme (DJ copy = £100)	50
58	Vocalion LAE 556	RITMO CALIENTE (LP, as Cal Tjader Quintet)	20
62	HMV/Verve CLP 1587	IN A LATIN BAG (LP, as Cal Tjader Sextet, also stereo [CSD 1454])	15
65	Vocalion LAE-F 599	GREATEST HITS (LP)	15
65	Verve (S)VLP 9136	SOUL BIRD: WHIFFENPOOF (LP)	15
68	Verve (S)VLP 9192	THE BEST OF CAL TJADER (LP)	15
68	Verve (S)VLP 9215	HIP VIBRATIONS (LP)	15
69	Fontana STL 5527	SOLAR HEAT (LP)	12

TNT
84	Neat NEAT 39	Back On The Road/Rockin' The Night (p/s)	8

TOAD
72	RCA Victor SF 8241	TOAD (LP)	100+

TOAD THE WET SPROCKET
79	Sprockets BRS 004	Pete's Punk Song/Feel It (fold out p/s)	40
80	Sprockets BRS 008	Reaching For The Sky/One Glass Of Whiskey (foldout stapled p/s)	70

RUTH TOBI
69	Concord CON 002	Lazy/That's When I Cry	5

AMON TOBIN
94	Ninja Tune Zen 48	SUPERMODIFIED (2 x LP)	20

TOBRUK
83	Neat NEAT 32	Wild On The Run/The Show Must Go On (p/s)	7
85	Parlophone 12R 6093	Falling/Like Lightning/Under The Gun (12", p/s)	8
85	Parlophone R 6101	On The Rebound/Poor Girl (p/s)	10
88	FM WKFMLP 105	PLEASURE AND PAIN (LP)	15

TOBY JUG
69	private pressing	GREASY QUIFF (LP, with insert)	225

TOBY JUG
71	Decca F 13173	Breakaway Man/Brotherhood	5

TOBY TWIRL
68	Decca F 12728	Harry Faversham/Back In Time	30
68	Decca F 12804	Toffee Apple Sunday/Romeo And Juliet 1968	75
69	Decca F 12867	Movin' In/Utopia Daydream	20
	(see also Shades Of Blue)		

TODAY'S WITNESS
72	Emblem TDR 345	TODAY'S WITNESS (LP)	35

ART & DOTTY TODD
58	London HLB 8620	Chanson D'Amour (Song Of Love)/Along The Trail With You (78 rpm = £8)	20
59	London HLN 8838	Straight As An Arrow/Stand There, Mountain (78 rpm = £15)	20

DIANE TODD
58	Decca F 10993	It's A Wonderful Thing To Be Loved/You Are My Favourite Dream (78 rpm = £8)	8

EILEEN TODD
54	London HL 8010	Paradise/Ill Wind (78)	6

GARY TODD & ROGER TURNER
79	Incus INCUS 79	SUNDAY BEST (LP)	50

NICK TODD
57	London HLD 8500	Plaything/The Honey Song (78 rpm = £12)	50
58	London HLD 8537	At The Hop/I Do (78 rpm = £8)	18
59	London HLD 8902	Tiger/Twice As Nice (78 rpm = £20)	30

PATSY TODD
76	Doctor Bird DB 1086	Pitta Patta Rocky Steady (with Count Ossie)/COUNT OSSIE: Nyah Bongo	20
68	High Note HS 007	Fire In Your Wire/AL & VIBRATORS: Move Up Calypso	8
69	High Note HS 012	We Were Lovers/Give Me A Chance (B-side with Delano Stewart)	8
	(see also Patsy, Stranger & Patsy, Derrick & Patsy)		

SHARKEY TODD & MONSTERS
59	Parlophone R 4536	Cool Gool/The Horror Show (78 rpm = £20)	22
	(see also Wally Whyton, Vipers [Skiffle Group])		

WILF TODD & HIS MUSIC
66	Oak WT 101	WILF TODD AND HIS MUSIC (LP)	15

WILF TODD COMBO
64	Blue Beat BB 240	He Took Her Away/Have You Ever Been Lonely	12

MINT VALUE £

CAMY TODOROW
85	Virgin VS 816	Bursting At The Seams/Don't Stop It, I Like It (with Roger Taylor) (p/s)	30
85	Virgin VS 816-12	Bursting At The Seams (Backroom Version)/Bursting At The Seams (Instrumental)/Don't Stop It, I Like It (12", p/s, with Roger Taylor)	50

(see also Roger Taylor)

TOE-FAT
70	Parlophone R 5829	Working Nights/Bad Side Of The Moon	20
72	Chapter One SCH 175	Brand New Band/Can't Live Without You	15
70	Parlophone PCS 7097	TOE-FAT (LP)	60
70	Regal Zono. SLRZ 1015	TOE-FAT TWO (LP)	55

(see also Cliff Bennett, Uriah Heep, Glass Menagerie)

TOGETHER
68	Columbia DB 8491	Henry's Coming Home/Love Mum And Dad	60

(see also Keith Relf)

TOGETHER
69	Aurora 4278	Memories Of Melinda/Good Morning World	8

TOGGERY FIVE
64	Parlophone R 5175	Bye Bye Bird/I'm Gonna Jump	45
65	Parlophone R 5249	I'd Much Rather Be With The Boys/It's So Easy	40

TOKENS
61	Parlophone R 4790	Tonight I Fell In Love/I Love My Baby	30
61	RCA RCA 1263	The Lion Sleeps Tonight/Tina	6
62	RCA RCA 1279	B'wa Nina (Pretty Girl)/Weeping River	7
62	RCA RCA 1313	I'll Do My Crying Tomorrow/Dream Angel Goodnight	12
62	RCA RCA 1322	Wishing/A Bird Flies Out Of Sight	6
64	Fontana TF 500	He's In Town/Oh Kathy	10
66	Fontana TF 683	I Hear Trumpets Blow/I Could See Me Dancing With You	7
67	Stateside SS 598	Green Plant/Saloogy	8
67	Warner Bros WB 5900	Portrait Of My Love/She Comes And Goes	6
67	Warner Bros WB 7056	It's A Happening World/How Nice?	6
68	Warner Bros WB 7169	Till/Poor Man	6
70	Buddah 2011 011	Don't Worry Baby/Some People Sleep	6
62	RCA RD 27256/SF 5128	THE LION SLEEPS TONIGHT (LP, mono/stereo)	55/75
62	RCA RD 7535	WE THE TOKENS SING FOLK (LP)	30
70	Buddah 2359 007	THE TOKENS (LP)	20

(see also U.S. Double Quartet, We Ugly Dogs)

TOKYO BLADE
83	Powerstation OHM 2	Powergame/Death On Main Street (p/s)	8
85	Powerstation LEG 1T	THE CAVE SESSIONS (12" EP)	15
85	Tokyo Blade TBR 1	BLACKHEARTS AND JADED SPADES (LP, gatefold sleeve)	15

TOKYO OLYMPICS
83	Ritz 031	Shot By Love (Part 1)/(Part 2) (p/s)	5
83	Ritz 12 031	Shot By Love (Part 1)/(Part 2) (12", p/s)	8
83	Ritz 050	Radio (Turns Her On)/(Mix Version) (p/s)	5
83	Ritz 12 050	Radio (Turns Her On)/(Mix Version) (12", p/s)	8
83	Polydor 2078 143	One Step From Paradise/Paradise Disco Mix (p/s, Ireland-only)	5
82	Polydor 2908 046	RADIO (LP, Ireland-only, produced by Francis Rossi & Bernie Frost)	12

(see also Rossi & Frost)

TOKYO ROSE
83	Guardian GRC 270	Dry Your Eyes/This Is Tokyo Rose (p/s)	100

ISRAEL 'POPPER STOPPER' TOLBERT
70	Stax STAX 157	Big Leg Woman/I Got Love	7
71	Stax 2362 020	POPPER STOPPER (LP)	18

TOLL
86	Broken Flag BF V7	CHRIST KNOWS (LP, featuring Tim Gane)	20

(see also Ramleh, McCarthy)

GARY DALE TOLLETT & THE CRICKETS
01	Rollercoaster RRCT 1001	Go Boy Go/Gone (78, 250 only)	10

TOM & JERRIO
65	HMV POP 1435	Boo-Ga-Loo/Boomerang	28

TOM & JERRY (cartoon characters)
58	MGM MGM-EP 688	JOHANN MOUSE (EP)	15

TOM & JERRY
59	Gala GSP 806	Baby Talk/PAUL SHELDON: Thank You Pretty Baby (picture labels)	45
63	Pye International 7N 25202	I'm Lonesome/Looking At You	95

(see also Simon & Garfunkel)

TOM & MICK
69	Olga OLE 014	Somebody's Taken Maria Away/Pandemonium	8

TOM CATS
61	Starlite ST45 054	Tom Tom Cat/Big Brother	25

TOMCATS
97	Essex ESSEX 1018LP	THE TOMCATS (LP, with bonus 7": "Seventh Son"/"Walking"/"You Gotta Help"/"Looking For My Baby" by Second Thoughts [10187])	12

(see also July)

TOMITA
77	RCA Red Seal RL1 1919	THE TOMITA PLANETS SUITE (LP, withdrawn after 1 day)	20

LEE TOMLIN
66   CBS 202455   Sweet Sweet Lovin'/Save Me 25

ALBERT TOMLINSON
68   Giant GN 28   Don't Wait For Me/LLOYD EVANS: Losing You 40

ROY TOMLINSON
68   Coxsone CS 7056   I Stand For I/MARTIN: I Second That Emotion (actually by Martin Riley) 38

TOMMY (Cowan)
72   Dynamic DYN 433   Geraldine/Reverend Leroy 5
(see also Jamaicans)

TOMMY (McCook) & UPSETTERS
69   Trojan TR 7717   Lock Jaw (actually by Dave Barker)/YARDBROOMS: My Desire 15
(see also Tommy McCook, Upsetters)

TOMORROW
67   Parlophone R 5597   My White Bicycle/Claramont Lake 50
67   Parlophone R 5627   Revolution/Three Jolly Little Dwarfs 55
69   Parlophone R 5813   My White Bicycle/Claramont Lake (reissue) 40
68   Parlophone PMC/PCS 7042 TOMORROW (LP, yellow/black label; mono/stereo) 150/125
76   Harvest SHSP 2010   TOMORROW (LP, reissue) 15
(see also Keith West, Steve Howe, Twink, Four + One, In Crowd, Syndicats, Aquarian Age, Fairies, Bodast)

TOMORROW COME SOME DAY
69   SNB 97   TOMORROW COME SOME DAY (LP) 400
(see also Ithaca, Friends, Agincourt, Alice Through The Looking Glass, BBC Radiophonic Workshop/Peter Howell)

TOMORROW'S CHILDREN
70   Plexium PXM 17   You're My Baby/Maybe Today 5
71   Plexium PXM 25   Sing A Song/Don't Believe 5
71   Plexium PXM 26   Keep A Little Love In Your Life/My Way Of Living 5

TOMORROW'S CHILDREN (Jamaica)
67   Island WI 3073   Bang Bang Rock Steady/Rain Rock Steady (some w/same label on both sides) . 18

TOMPALL & GLASER BROTHERS
68   MGM MGM-C 8082   THROUGH THE EYES OF LOVE (LP) 25

TONE DEAF & THE IDIOTS
80s Lyntone BLI 1/Angel BL 12 Why Does Politics Turn Men Into Toads/Repatriate The National Front (flexi) . . . 10
(see also Idiots)

ELEANOR TONER
65   Decca F 12119   All Cried Out/A Hundred Guitars 8
65   Decca F 12192   Will You Still Love Me Tomorrow/Between The Window And The Phone 15
66   Decca F 12454   Black Rose/Time To Spare Darling 5

TONES ON TAIL
82   4AD BAD 203   A Bigger Splash/Means Of Escape/Copper/Instrumental (12", p/s) 10
(see also Bauhaus, Love & Rockets)

TONETTES
62   Island WI 064   Love That Is Real/Pretty Baby 12
(see also Marlene Webber, Lyrics, Don Drummond)

OSCAR TONEY JR.
67   Stateside SS 2033   For Your Precious Love/Ain't That True Love 28
67   Stateside SS 2046   Turn On Your Love Light/Any Day Now 20
67   Stateside SS 2061   You Can Lead Your Woman To The Altar/Unlucky Guy 20
68   Bell BLL 1003   Without Love There Is Nothing/Love That Never Grows Cold 10
68   Bell BLL 1011   No Sad Songs/Never Get Enough Of Your Love 10
69   Bell BLL 1057   Down In Texas/Just For You 10
72   Capricorn K 17505   Thank You, Honey Chile/I Do What You Wish 6
73   Contempo C 6   Kentucky Bluebird/Everything I Own 6
73   Contempo CS2075   Chicken Heads/Everybody's Needed 15
74   Contempo CS 2002   Is It Because I'm Black/Make It Easy On Yourself 10
75   Contempo CS 2043   I've Been Loving You Too Long/For Your Precious Love 6
67   Stateside (S)SL 10211 FOR YOUR PRECIOUS LOVE (LP) 60

TONGUE & GROOVE
69   Fontana STL 5528   TONGUE & GROOVE (LP) 38
(see also Charlatans)

TONIGHT
78   TDS 1   Drummerman/Stroll On By (p/s) 8
78   TDS 2   Money, That's Your Problem/No Sympathy (p/s) 5
78   TDS 4   Wheels/I Can Play Faster Than You Can (p/s) 5
78   TDS 5   Jealousy Kills/Second Hand Man 5
(see also Andy Arthurs, Celia & Mutations)

TERRY TONIK
80   Posh TOFF 1   Just A Little Mod/Smashed And Blocked
                        (some with die-cut p/s, a few also with promo A4 booklet) 110/70/30

TONTO
74   Polydor 2383 308   IT'S ABOUT TIME (LP) 12
(see also Tonto's Expanding Head Band)

TONTON (MACOUTE)
72   RCA 2190   Summer Of Our Love/Greyhound Lady (as Tonton) 12
71   RCA Neon NE 4   TONTON MACOUTE (LP) 55

TONTO'S EXPANDING HEAD BAND
71   Atlantic 2400 150   ZERO TIME (LP, gatefold sleeve) 25
(see also Tonto)

TONY & CHAMPIONS

TONY & CHAMPIONS
70   Duke DU 90   Eye For An Eye/CHAMPIONS: Broke My Heart — Version 6
      (see also Errol & Champions, Domino Johnson)

TONY & DENNIS
67   Trojan TR 002   Folk Song/TOMMY McCOOK & SUPERSONICS: Starry Night 35

TONY & GRADUATES
60s   Hit HIT 13   The Statue 50

TONY & HIPPY BOYS
69   Gas GAS 121   Janet/HARMONIANS: Believe Me 20

TONY & HOWARD with DICTATORS
65   Oriole CB 307   Just In Case/Walk Right Out Of The Blues. 25

TONY & HOWIE
72   Banana BA 371   Fun It Up/Fun Version. 15

TONY & JOE
58   London HLN 8694   The Freeze/Gonna Get A Little Kissin' Tonight (78 rpm = £20) 40

TONY (Tomas) & LOUISE
62   Island WI 059   Ups And Downs/TONY TOMAS: Brixton Lewisham 12
      (see also Tony Washington)

TONY & TANDY
69   Atlantic 584 262   Two Can Make It Together/The Bitter And The Sweet (with Fleur De Lys) 25
71   Atlantic 2091 075   Two Can Make It Together/Look And Find 8
      (see also Sharon Tandy, Fleur De Lys)

TONY & TYRONE
70   Ember EMBS 290   Everyday Fun/Whip Your Loving On Me (p/s) 5

TONY, CARO & JOHN
72   private pressing   ALL ON THE FIRST DAY (LP, with insert) 300

TONY'S ALLSTARS
72   Green Door GD 4041   Rub Up A Daughter/DENNIS ALCAPONE: Daughter Version 8
72   Bullet BU 509   Dub Up A Daughter (as Prince Tony's Allstars)/
                                DENNIS ALCAPONE: Daughter Version 8
72   Big Shot BI 601   Must Care/L. SPARKS: You Don't Care. 6
73   Downtown DT 508   You Don't Say/DENNIS ALCAPONE: Version. 8

TONY'S DEFENDERS
66   Columbia DB 7850   Yes I Do/It's Easy To Say Hello 25
66   Columbia DB 7996   Since I Lost You Baby/Waiting For A Call From You 25
      (see also Mike Stuart Span)

TOO FUNK
95   Ferox FER 008   THE RETURN OF TOO FUNK (12" EP) 15
95   Ferox FER 011   STORM THE FUNK (12" EP, plain sleeve) 8
96   Ferox FER 024   HOTEL IBIS (12" EP). 8

TOOLS
81   Oily SLICK 2   Gotta Make Some Money Somehow/TV Eyes (p/s) 8

STEVE TOOK
      (see under Shagrat)

TOOMORROW
70   RCA RCA 1978   You're My Baby Now/Goin' Back (in custom RCA sleeve) 60
70   Decca F 13070   I Could Never Live Without Your Love/Roll Like A River 60
70   RCA LSA 3008   TOOMORROW (LP, soundtrack, with insert) 125
      (see also Olivia Newton-John)

TOO MUCH
78   Lightning GIL 513   Who You Wanna Be/Another Time Another Place (some in p/s). 25/8
78   Lightning GIL 552   Lick Me One More Time//Be Mine/It's Only For Me (p/s) 25

DAVID TOOP
75   Obscure OBS 48   NEW AND REDISCOVERED MUSICAL INSTRUMENTS
                                (LP, with Max Eastley & Brian Eno) 25
70s   Quartz   WOUNDS (LP, with Paul Burwell) 25
      (see also Brian Eno)

TOOTS (Actually LEE PERRY)
70   Upsetter US 327   Do You Like It/UPSETTERS: Touch Of Fire 12

TOOTS & THE MAYTALS
      (see under Maytals)

TOP NOTES
      (see under Nino Tempo & April Stevens)

TOPO D. BILL
70   Charisma CB 116   Witchi Tai To/Jam (some in p/s) 10/7
      (see also Bonzo Dog [Doo Dah] Band, Roger Ruskin Spear)

TOPO GIGIO
      (see under Century 21)

TOPPERS
57   Brunswick 05678   Stash Pandowski (She's Not Very Much Good For Pretty)/Pots And Pans 6

TOP SECRET
81   Cheapskate CHEAP 35   She's So Ugly/I Love Me (no p/s) 5

TINY TOPSY
      (see under Tiny)

TOP TOPHAM

69	Blue Horizon 57-3167	Christmas Cracker/Cracking Up Over Christmas	22
70	Blue Horizon 7-63857	ASCENSION HEIGHTS (LP)	100

(see also Fox, Yardbirds)

TORA TORA

80	Mancunian Metal TT 5000	Red Sun Setting/Highway (Shooting Like A Bullet) (p/s)	15
80	Tora TT 5001	Don't Want To Let You Go/Sorry I Broke Your Heart	40

STEVE TORCH

70s	Redball RR 005	Live In Fear/Smoke Your Own (p/s)	5

(BERNIE) TORMÉ (BAND)

78	Jet JET 126	I'm Not Ready/Free (p/s, as Bernie Tormé Band, orange or black vinyl)	6/5
79	Jet JET 137	Weekend/Secret Service/All Night/Instant Impact (as Bernie Tormé Band, p/s)	5
70s	Peter Collins PC 1	The Hunter/Soul Sister	8
80	Island WIP 6586	The Beat/I Want/Bony Maronie (p/s, pink vinyl, promos on black vinyl)	8
81	Fresh FRESH 7	All Day And All Of The Night/What's Next (p/s, also listed as Parole PURL 5)	12
82	Kamaflage KAMLP 2	TURN OUT THE LIGHTS (LP, white vinyl)	12

(see also Gillan, Split Knee Loons, Girl)

MEL TORME (& MEL-TONES)

SINGLES

56	Vogue Coral Q 72150	Mountain Greenery/Jeepers Creepers	10
56	Vogue Coral Q 72159	Blue Moon/That Old Black Magic	5
56	Vogue Coral Q 72185	Love Is Here To Stay/Goody Goody	5
56	London HLN 8305	Lulu's Back In Town/The Lady Is A Tramp	10
56	London HLN 8322	Lullaby Of Birdland/I Love To Watch The Moonlight	10
56	Vogue Coral Q 72202	All Of You/It Don't Mean A Thing	5
56	Decca F 10800	Walkin' Shoes/The Cuckoo In The Clock (with Ted Heath & His Music)	5
56	Decca F 10809	Waltz For Young Lovers/I Don't Want To Walk Without You	5
57	Vogue Coral Q 72217	My Rosemarie/How (as Mel Torme & Mel-Tones)	5
60	Philips PB 1045	The White Cliffs Of Dover/I've Got A Lovely Bunch Of Coconuts	5
61	HMV POP 859	Blue Moon/The Moon Song	5
61	MGM MGM 1144	The Christmas Song/Shine On Your Shoes	6
62	London HLK 9643	Comin' Home Baby/Right Now (DJ copy = £75)	40
64	Verve VS 505	Yes Indeed/Her Face	5
56	Decca DFE 6384	WALKIN' SHOES (EP)	10
56	MGM MGM-EP 562	VOICE IN VELVET (EP)	10
57	MGM MGM-EP 591	VOICE IN VELVET NO. 2 (EP)	10
58	London Jazz EZ-N 19027	MEL TORME SINGS FRED ASTAIRE PT. 1 (EP)	10
58	London Jazz EZ-N 19028	MEL TORME SINGS FRED ASTAIRE PT. 2 (EP)	10
58	London Jazz EZ-N 19029	MEL TORME SINGS FRED ASTAIRE PT. 3 (EP)	10
58	Philips BBE 12181	TORME MEETS THE BRITISH (EP)	10
59	Coral FEP 2026	MEL TORME SINGS AT THE CRESCENDO PT. 1 (EP)	10
59	Coral FEP 2027	MEL TORME SINGS AT THE CRESCENDO PT. 2 (EP)	10
59	Coral FEP 2028	MEL TORME SINGS AT THE CRESCENDO PT. 3 (EP)	10
59	Parlophone GEP 8790	FOR SWINGERS (EP)	10
63	London REK 1372	MAGIC OF MEL (EP)	10

LPs

55	Vogue Coral LVA 9004	MEL TORME AT THE CRESCENDO	20
56	Vogue Coral LVA 9032	MUSICAL SOUNDS ARE THE BEST SONGS	20
56	London Jazz LTZ-N 15009	MEL TORME AND THE MARTY PAICH "DEK-TETTE"	15
56	London HA-N 2016	IT'S A BLUE WORLD	15
57	London Jazz LTZ-N 15076	MEL TORME SINGS FRED ASTAIRE	15
57	Philips BBL 7205	TORME MEETS THE BRITISH	30
58	HMV CLP 1238	MEL TORME	15
59	Parlophone PMC 1096	GENE NORMAN PRESENTS MEL TORME AT THE CRESCENDO	15
60	Parlophone PMC 1114	SONGS FOR ANY TASTE	15
60	HMV CLP 1315	OLÉ TORMÉ (with Billy May)	15
60	HMV CLP 1382	BACK IN TOWN (with Mel-Tones)	15
60	HMV CLP 1405/CSD 1330	SWINGS SCHUBERT ALLEY (with Marty Paich Orch., mono/stereo)	each 15
61	HMV CLP 1449/CSD 1349	SWINGIN' ON THE MOON (mono/stereo)	each 15
62	HMV CLP 1584/CSD 1442	MY KIND OF MUSIC (mono/stereo)	each 15
63	London HA-K/SH-K 8021	MEL TORME AT THE RED HILL (with Jimmy Wisner Trio, mono/stereo)	each 15
63	London HA-K 8065	COMIN' HOME BABY	15
63	Verve (S)VLP 9027	I DIG THE DUKE, I DIG THE COUNT (mono/stereo)	each 12
64	Atlantic ATL/SAL 5005	SUNDAY IN NEW YORK (mono/stereo)	each 12
70	Capitol ST 21585	RAINDROPS KEEP FALLIN' ON MY HEAD (LP)	12

TORNADOS

62	Decca F 11449	Love And Fury/Popeye Twist	15
62	Decca F 11494	Telstar/Jungle Fever	5
63	Decca F 11562	Globetrotter/Locomotion With Me (some B-sides credit "Locomotion With You")	5
63	Decca F 11606	Robot/Life On Venus	5
63	Decca F 11662	The Ice Cream Man/Theme From "The Scales Of Justice"	5
63	Decca F 11745	Dragonfly/Hymn For Teenagers	10
64	Decca F 11838	Joystick/Hot Pot	10
64	Decca F 11889	Monte Carlo/Blue Blue Beat	15
64	Decca F 11946	Exodus/Blackpool Rock	15
65	Columbia DB 7455	Granada/Ragunboneman	20
65	Columbia DB 7589	Early Bird/Stompin' Through The Rye (as Tornados '65)	20
65	Columbia DB 7687	Stingray/Aqua Marina	45
66	Columbia DB 7856	Pop-Art Goes Mozart/Too Much In Love To Hear	35
66	Columbia DB 7984	Is That A Ship I Hear/Do You Come Here Often	45
62	Decca DFE 8510	THE SOUNDS OF THE TORNADOS (EP)	22
62	Decca DFE 8511	TELSTAR (EP)	22
63	Decca DFE 8521	MORE SOUNDS FROM THE TORNADOS (EP)	30

63	Decca DFE 8533	TORNADO ROCK (EP)	40
63	Decca LK 4552	AWAY FROM IT ALL (LP)	65
72	Decca SPA 253	THE WORLD OF THE TORNADOS (LP)	15
76	Decca REM 4	REMEMBERING...THE TORNADOS (LP)	12

(see also Heinz, Billy Fury, Clem Cattini Ork, Saints, Original Tornados, Roger LaVern & Microns, Saxons, George Bellamy, Gemini, Roger La Vern & Microns)

TO ROCOCO ROT
| 98 | Fat Cat 12FAT 007 | She Understands The Dynamics (12", custom sleeve) | 8 |

MITCHELL TOROK
54	London HL 8004	Caribbean/Weep Away (with Louisiana Hayride Band) (tri or round centre)	40/20
54	London HL 8048	Hootchy Kootchy Henry (From Hawaii)/Gigolo (78 rpm = £6)	50
54	London HL 8083	The Haunting Waterfall/Dancerette (with Louisiana Hayride Band) (78 rpm = £6)	50
55	Brunswick 05423	The World Keeps Turning Around/A Peasant's Guitar (78 rpm = £6)	18
56	Brunswick 05586	When Mexico Gave Up The Rhumba/I Wish I Was A Little Bit Younger	18
56	Brunswick 05626	Red Light, Green Light (with Tulane Sisters)/Havana Huddle (78 rpm = £6)	18
57	Brunswick 05642	Drink Up And Go Home/Take This Heart (78 rpm = £6)	15
57	Brunswick 05657	Pledge Of Love/What's Behind That Strange Door (78 rpm = £8)	15
57	Brunswick 05718	Two Words (True Love)/You're Tempting Me (with Anita Kerr Quartet) (78 = £10)	10
60	London HLW 9130	Pink Chiffon/What You Don't Know (Won't Hurt You)	12
54	London RE-P 1014	LOUISIANA HAYRIDE (EP, with Louisiana Hayride Band)	60
60	London HA-W 2279	CARIBBEAN (LP)	70

TORPEDO (& THE CARIBBEANS)
| 55 | Parlophone MP 143 | Montego Bay/Lazy Jane (export 78) | 10 |
| 56 | Parlophone MP 148 | Pretty Woman/War Man Power Man (export 78) | 10 |

MICHELLE TORR
| 66 | Fontana TF 676 | Only Tears Are Left For Me/I Love That Man | 15 |
| 77 | Sonet SON 2104 | I'm Just A Simple Country Girl From France/Une Petite Française (p/s) | 5 |

GEORGE TORRENCE & NATURALS
| 68 | London HLZ 10181 | Lickin' Stick/So Long Goodbye | 12 |
| 71 | Jay Boy BOY 48 | Lickin' Stick/So Long Goodbye (reissue) | 6 |

EMILIANA TORRINI
01	Fat Cat 281 TP 7	E1 (Grain Remix)/(Process Remix) (p/s)	8
01	Fat Cat 282 TP 7	E2 (Mice Parade Remix)/(VVM Remix)/(Mum Remix) (p/s)	7
01	Fat Cat 283 TP 7	E3 (Professor Ludlow & Dr Smith Remix)/(Stromba Remix) (p/s)	8
01	Fat Cat 284 TP 7	E4 (Antenna Farm Remix)/(Motion Remix) (p/s)	8
01	Fat Cat 285 TP 7	E5 (Lucky Kitchen Remix)/(Team Doyobi Remix) (p/s)	8
01	Fat Cat 286 TP 7	E6 (Foehn Remix)/(Chasm Remix) (p/s)	8
01	Fat Cat 287 TP 7	E7 (Immense Remix)/(Fonn Remix) (p/s)	8
01	Fat Cat 281 TP 7	E8 (Di Lacuna Remix)/(Transient Waves Remix) (p/s)	8

CLAIRE TORRY
67	Fontana TF 852	The Music Attracts Me/It Takes One To Make The Other Cry (as Claire Terry)	6
67	Fontana TF 878	Unsure Feelings/The End Of A Lifetime (as Claire Terry)	6
69	Decca F 12945	Love For Living/Love Tomorrow, Love Today (as Clare Torry)	6

TORTOISE
96	Duophonic D-UHF-D 12	Yaus/STEREOLAB: Speedy Car (gig freebie, blue vinyl, p/s, 3,000 only)	20
96	Duophonic D-UHF-D 12	Yaus/STEREOLAB: Speedy Car (orange vinyl export issue, p/s, 3,000 only)	20
96	City Slang EFA 04971	RHYTHMS, RESOLUTIONS & CLUSTERS (LP, clear vinyl)	20
	Duophonic Super 45s DS 33 09	Gamera/Cliff Dweller Society (12", 1500 on red vinyl, 1500 on clear vinyl, 1500 on black vinyl, 1000 on fluorescent yellow vinyl)	25/25/25/30

(see also Sea & Cake)

TORTURE
| 81 | Wildebeest WILD 1 | Last Post/Lucky/Finding My Way Home | 50 |

PETER TOSH
69	Unity UN 525	The Return Of Al Capone/LENNEX BROWN: O Club (B-side actually by Lennon Brown)	15
69	Unity UN 529	Sun Valley (as Peter Touch)/HE(A)DLEY BENNETT: Drums Of Fu Manchu	15
71	Bullet BU 486	Maga Dog/THIRD & FOURTH GENERATION: Bull Dog	12
72	Pressure Beat PR 5509	Them A Fe Get A Beatin' (as Peter Touch)/THIRD & FOURTH GENERATION: Version	18
79	Rolling Stones RSR 103	I'm The Toughest/Toughest Version (p/s)	5
79	Rolling Stones RSR 104	Buck In Hamm Palace/The Day The Dollar Die	5
78	Rolling Stones COC 39109	BUSH DOCTOR (LP, with inner sleeve and 'scratch & sniff' sticker)	10

(see also Peter Touch, Bob Marley & Wailers, Cat & Nicky Campbell, Glen Adams)

TOTAL CHAOS
| 83 | Volume VOL 1 | There Are No Russians In Afghanistan/Primitive Feeling/Revolution Part 10 (p/s) | 6 |
| 83 | Volume VOL 2 | Factory Man/Brixton Prison/She Don't Care/Die (p/s) | 7 |

TOTALLY OUTTA HAND BAND
| 78 | Kilgaron KIL 1 | Teenage Revolution/Too Much Trouble By Far (p/s) | 8 |

TOTNAMITES
| 61 | Oriole CB 1615 | Danny Boy/Tip Top Tottenham Hotspur | 10 |

TOTO
78	CBS S 11-6784	Hold The Line/Takin' It Back (picture disc)	6
82	CBS A 11-2079	Rosanna/It's A Feeling (picture disc)	6
82	CBS A 11-2510	Africa/We Made It (Africa-shaped picture disc)	10
83	CBS A 11-3392	I Won't Hold You Back/Afraid Of Love (picture disc)	6
88	CBS 651 607-2	Pamela/Stay Away/Africa/Rosanna (CD, card sleeve)	8
89	CBS 654 569-3	SOLID GOLD (Pamela/Africa/Hold The Line) (3" CD EP, gatefold card sleeve)	4
84	Polydor 822 8237-7	DUNE (LP, soundtrack, 1 track by Brian Eno)	15

TINA TOTT
| 69 | Pye 7N 17823 | Take Away The Emptiness Too/Burning In The Background Of My Mind........ 45 |

TOTTENHAM HOTSPUR F.C.
| 81 | Towerbeu SHELF 1 | Ossie's Dream (Spurs Are On Their Way To Wembley)/Glory, Glory Tottenham Hotspur (12", blue vinyl)...................... 10 |
| 67 | Columbia SEG 8532 | THE SPURS GO MARCHING ON: SINGALONG SPURS (EP) .... 20 |

(see also Terry Venables)

TOUCH
| 69 | Deram DM 243 | Miss Teach/We Feel Fine .... 18 |
| 69 | Deram DML/SML 1033 | THIS IS TOUCH (LP, some with poster)........................... 120/65 |

TOUCH
80	Ariola ARO 209	When The Spirit Moves You/My Life Depends On You (p/s)............. 5
80	Ariola ARO 243	Don't You Know What Love Is/My Life Depends On You (some in p/s)....... 20/6
80	Ariola ARO 250	Love Don't Fail Me Now (p/s)................................... 6
80	Ariola ARL 5036	TOUCH (LP) 12

TOUCH
| 88 | Touch T7:45 | Departing Platform 5/Touch Ritual (Radio Cut-Up) (p/s)............... 5 |

PETER TOUCH
65	Island WI 211	Hoot Nanny Hoot (actually by Peter Tosh & Wailers)/ BOB MARLEY: Do You Remember (actually Peter Tosh & Wailers) 100
65	Island WI 215	Shame And Scandal (with Wailers)/WAILERS: The Jerk.................. 60
67	Island WI 3042	I Am The Toughest (actually by Peter Tosh & Wailers)/ MARCIA GRIFFITHS: No Faith 60
69	Jackpot JP 706	The Crimson Pirate/Moon Duck................................. 12

(see also Peter Tosh, Bop & The Beltone, Glen Adams)

TOURS
79	Tours T 1	Language School/Foreign Girls (paper p/s).................... 15
79	Tours T 1	Language School/Foreign Girls (printed PVC sleeve) 12
79	Virgin VS 307	Tourist Information/You Knew (p/s)............................ 6

AL TOUSAN
| 61 | London HLU 9291 | Naomi/Indinna (some copies miscredited to 'Al Pousan') .... 10 |

(see also Allen Toussaint)

ALLEN TOUSSAINT
69	Soul City SC 119	We The People/Tequila 20
72	Reprise K 14200	Soul Sister/She Once Belonged To Me 6
72	Reprise K 44202	LIFE, LOVE AND FAITH (LP) 22
75	Reprise K 54021	SOUTHERN NIGHTS (LP) 12

(see also Al Tousan)

CALINE & OLIVER TOUSSAINT
| 78 | Epic S EPC 6334 | The Gardens Of Monaco/Les Jardins De Monaco...................... 12 |

ROBERTA TOVEY
| 65 | Polydor BM 56021 | Who's Who/Not So Old (some in p/s)............................. 45/25 |

TOWER OF POWER
72	Reprise K 16190	Down To The Night Club/You Got To Funkifize 5
73	Reprise K 16278	So Very Hard To Go/Clean Slate 8
73	Reprise K 16211	You're Still A Young Man/Skating On Thin Ice 8
74	Reprise K 16389	Don't Change Horses/Time Will Tell 5
75	Reprise K 16543	It's Not The Crime/Only So Much Time On The Ground................. 8
73	Reprise K 46223	TOWER OF POWER (LP) 15
74	Reprise K 46282	BACK TO OAKLAND (LP)..................................... 15
75	Reprise K 56093	URBAN RENEWAL (LP) 15

TOWERS OF LONDON
| 05 | TVT TOL1 | On A Noose/All You Want Me For (white vinyl, signed p/s) .... 8 |

JOHNNY TOWERS
| 62 | Philips 326554 BF | The Lonely Man Theme/There's No Place Like Rome.................. 8 |
| 63 | Philips 326570 BF | This Kind Of Love/My First Romance............................ 7 |

COLIN TOWNS
78	Virgin VS 204	Full Circle (Main Theme)/Olivia (p/s)........................... 10
80	MCA MCA 643	Breakdown/Working Man (p/s)................................. 15
78	Virgin V 2093	FULL CIRCLE (LP, soundtrack) 12

(see also Gillan, Samson, Split Knee Loons)

TOWNSEL SISTERS
| 60 | Polydor NH 66954 | Will I Ever/I Know .... 12 |

DEVIN TOWNSEND
| 98 | USG/East West USG 1028-4 | Christeen/Wild Colonial Boy/Night (CD, withdrawn)..................... 10 |

(see also Wildhearts)

ED TOWNSEND
58	Capitol CL 14867	For Your Love/Over And Over Again............................. 10
58	Capitol CL 14927	When I Grow Too Old To Dream/You Are My Everything 10
59	Capitol CL 14976	Richer Than I/Getting By Without You 7
59	Capitol CL 15020	Don't Ever Leave Me/Lover Come Back To Me 7
59	Capitol CL 15072	This Little Love Of Mine/Hold On 7
60	Capitol CL 15141	Don't Get Around Much Anymore/Do Nothin' Till You Hear............. 7
60	Warner Bros WB 21	Stay With Me (A Little While Longer)/I Love Everything About You 40
59	Capitol EAP1 1091	ED TOWNSEND (EP)... 20
59	Capitol T 1140	NEW IN TOWN (LP) 25
76	Curtom K 56180	NOW (LP).. 20

JOHN TOWNSEND
70s	Sweet Folk All SFA 002	NO MUCKING ABOUT (LP)	18

PETE TOWNSHEND
80	Atco K 11486	Let My Love Open The Door/Classified/Greyhound Girl (p/s, with sticker)	5
82	Atco K 11751P	Uniforms/Dance It All Away (picture disc)	5
82	Atco K 11751PT	Uniforms/Dance It All Away (12", picture disc)	8
82	Eva-Tone 623827XS	My Generation/Pinball Wizard (U.S. square flexidisc sewn into U.K. copies of Richard Barnes' *Maximum R&B* book; with/without book)	20/8
89	Virgin VSCD 1198	A Friend is A Friend (3.30)/Man Machines (Extended Mix)/Real World (Can You Really Dance?)/A Friend is A Friend (Album Version 4.45) (3" CD, card p/s)	10
89	Virgin VSCD 1209	I Won't Run Anymore/A Fool Says/Dig (Original Demo Version Recorded November 1987) (3" CD, card sleeve)	10
72	Track 2408 201	WHO CAME FIRST (LP, gatefold sleeve with poster)	20

(see also The Who, Meher Baba, Billy Nicholls, Angie, Elton John)

PETE TOWNSHEND & RONNIE LANE
77	Polydor 2058 944	Street In The City/RONNIE LANE: Annie (limited issue)	20
77	Polydor 2058 944	Street In The City/RONNIE LANE: Annie (12", p/s)	12
77	Polydor 2442 147	ROUGH MIX (LP, gatefold sleeve)	15

(see also Who, Ronnie Lane)

TOYAN
81	Greensleeves GREL 20	HOW THE WEST WAS WON (LP)	25
83	Vista STLP 1023	MURDER (LP, as Toyan with Tippa Lee)	45

TOY DOLLS
81	GBH SSM 005	Tommy Kowey's Car/She Goes To Finos (500 only)	60
81	GRC GRC 104	Tommy Kowey's Car/She's A Working Ticket/Everybody Jitterbug/Teenager In Love/I've Got Asthma (yellow paper p/s, with insert)	60
82	Zonophone Z 31	Everybody Jitterbug/(She's A) Working Ticket (p/s)	30
83	Volume VOL 3	Nellie The Elephant/Dig That Groove Baby (p/s)	12
83	Volume VOL 5	Cheerio And Toodle Pip/H.O. (p/s)	8
83	Volume VOL 7	Alfie From The Bronx/Hanky Panky (p/s)	8
84	Volume VOL 10	We're Mad/Deirdre's A Slag (p/s)	6
84	Volume VOLT 10	We're Mad/Deirdre's A Slag/Rupert The Bear (12", p/s)	10
85	Volume VOL 12	She Goes To Fino's/Spiders In The Dressing Room (p/s)	5
85	Volume VOL 17	James Bond (Lives Down Our Street)/Olga... I cannot! (p/s)	8
85	Volume VOLT 17	James Bond (Lives Down Our Street)/Olga... I cannot! / Griefsville (12", p/s)	8
86	Volume VOL 21	Geordie's Gone To Jail/Idle Gossip (p/s)	8
84	Volume VOLP 1	DIG THAT GROOVE, BABY (LP)	15
85	Volume VOLP 2	A FAR OUT DISC (LP)	12

(see also Showbiz Kids)

TOY DOLLS (U.S.)
63	London HLN 9647	Little Tin Soldier/Fly Away	25

TOYS
79	SRT SRTS/79/CUS 345	My Mind Wanders/The Girl On My Wall/Toytime/I'd Do Anything For You (p/s)	10
79	Toy TOYS 2	STILL DANCING (EP, hand-stamped white label, foldaround p/s)	20

TOYS
80	Red Bus RBUS 54	Go To The Police/Breakdown	50

TOYS (U.S.)
65	Stateside SS 460	A Lover's Concerto/This Night	8
66	Stateside SS 483	Attack/See How They Run	12
66	Stateside SS 502	May My Heart Be Cast Into Stone/On Backstreet	20
66	Stateside SS 519	Silver Spoon/Can't Get Enough Of You Baby	22
66	Stateside SS 539	Baby Toys/Happy Birthday Broken Heart	10
67	Philips BF 1563	Ciao Baby/I Got Carried Away	20
67	Philips BF 1581	My Love Sonata/I Close My Eyes	15
69	Bell BLL 1053	A Lover's Concerto/Baby Toys	7
66	Stateside (S)SL 10175	THE TOYS SING "A LOVER'S CONCERTO" AND "ATTACK" (LP, mono/stereo)	40/45

TOYSHOP
69	Polydor 56317	Say Goodbye To Yesterday/Send My Love To Lucy	18

TRACE
74	Vertigo 6360 852	TRACE (LP)	15
75	Vertigo 6413 080	BIRDS (LP)	18

(see also Curved Air)

AL TRACE & HIS LITTLE TRACERS
53	MGM MGM 693	Mocking Bird Boogie/You're Only A Part-Time Sweetheart (78)	6

TRACE FAMILY TRIO
54	Parlophone DP 381	I'll Be No Stranger There/I've Got A Longing To Go (78, export issue)	8

TRACER
83	Mouse Hole TRA 1	CHANNELLED AGGRESSION EP (p/s)	125

MARK TRACEY
62	Parlophone R 4944	Caravan Of Lonely Men/Never Ending (with John Barry & His Orchestra)	10

STAN TRACEY
58	Vogue LA 160130	STAN TRACEY SHOWCASE (LP)	70
59	Vogue LA 160155	LITTLE KLUNK (LP, as Stan Tracey Trio)	130
65	Columbia 33SX 1774	JAZZ SUITE (LP, as Stan Tracey Quartet, also stereo SCX 3589)	75
66	Columbia S(C)X 6051	ALICE IN JAZZLAND (LP, as Stan Tracey Big Band)	40
67	Columbia S(C)X 6124	STAN TRACEY... IN PERSON (LP)	40
68	Columbia S(C)X 6205	WITH LOVE FROM JAZZ (LP)	50

69	Ace Of Clubs ACL 1259	LITTLE KLUNK (LP, reissue) 35
69	Columbia S(C)X 6320	WE LOVE YOU MADLY (LP, as Stan Tracey Big Brass) 50
69	Columbia SCX 6358	THE LATIN AMERICAN CAPER (LP, with Big Brass & Woodwind) 40
70	Columbia SCX 6385	FREE AN' ONE (LP, as Stan Tracey Quartet) 70
70	Columbia SCX 6413	SEVEN AGES OF MAN (LP, as Stan Tracey Big Band) 35
72	Columbia SCX 6485	PERSPECTIVES (LP as Stan Tracey Trio). 40

(see also New Departures Quartet, Mike Osborne, Neil Ardley, Laurie Johnson)

ZEN TRACEY
62	Decca F 11492	Shamrocker (Phil The Fluter's Ball)/Two By Two 6

TRACK
66	Columbia DB 7987	Why Do Fools Fall In Love?/Cry To Me. 18

TRACK 4
82	Track 4 TR4 001	Mr Charisma (p/s, with insert) 100

TRACTOR
72	Dandelion 2001 282	Stone Glory/Marie/As You Say. 18
78	UK UK 93	Roll The Dice/Vicious Circle. 8
81	Cargo CRS 002	No More Rock & Roll/Northern City 10
81	Roach RR 2	Average Man's Hero/Big Big Boy (p/s) 5
72	Dandelion 2310 217	TRACTOR (LP). 100

(see also Way We Live)

TRACY
66	Columbia DB 7802	Don't Hold It Against Me/These Four Walls 12

TRACY
69	Columbia DB 8569	Life's Like That/Let Me Love You. 7
69	Columbia DB 8637	Follow Me/A City Called Soul. 12
71	Columbia DB 8750	Rock Me In The Cradle/Strange Love 10

GRANT TRACY & SUNSETS
61	Ember EMB S 126	Say When/Please Baby Please 18
61	Ember EMB S 130	Pretend/Love Me 18
62	Ember EMB S 148	The Great Matchmaker/Tears Came Rolling Down 18
62	Ember EMB S 155	Taming Tigers/The Painted Smile 18
63	Decca F 11741	Everybody Shake/Turn The Lights Down, Jenny. 18
64	Ember EMB 3352	TEENBEAT (LP) 70

(see also Pete Dello, Honeybus)

WENDALL TRACY
58	London HLM 8664	Who's To Know/Corrigidor Rock (78 rpm = £8) 30

TRADER HORNE
69	Pye 7N 17846	Morning Way/Sheena 20
70	Dawn DNS 1003	Here Comes The Rain/Goodbye Mercy Kelly. 15
70	Dawn DNLS 3004	MORNING WAY (LP, with photo & insert) 75

(see also Them, Fairport Convention, Jackie McAuley)

TRADEWINDS
59	RCA RCA 1141	Crossroads/Furry Murray (78 rpm = £25) 20

TRADE WINDS
65	Red Bird RB 10020	New York Is A Lonely Town/Club Seventeen 20
66	Kama Sutra KAS 202	Mind Excursion/Little Susan's Dreaming 15

TRAD GRADS
61	Decca F 11403	Runnin' Shoes/Rag-Day Jazz-Band Ball. 7

(see also Quarry Men)

TRADITION
77	Venture VNLP 8877	MOVIN' ON (LP) 15
77	Venture CUT 6	IN DUB (LP) 45
78	RCA PL 25169	TELL YOUR FRIENDS ABOUT DUB (LP) 20
78	RAC PL 25186	ALTERNATIVE ROUTES (LP) 30

TRAFFIC
67	Island WIP 6002	Paper Sun/Giving To You (some in p/s). 18/7
67	Island WIP 6017	Hole In My Shoe/Smiling Phases (some in p/s) 15/7
67	Island WIP 6025	Here We Go Round The Mulberry Bush/Coloured Rain (1st 100,000 in p/s) 15/7
68	Island WIP 6030	No Face, No Name, No Number/Roamin' In The Gloamin' With 40,000 Headmen . . 10
68	Island WIP 6041	You Can All Join In/Withering Tree (unissued in U.K.)
68	Island WIP 6041	Feelin' Alright/Withering Tree. 10
68	Island WIP 6050	Medicated Goo/Shanghai Noodle Factory 7
74	Island WIP 6207	Walking In The Wind/Walking In The Wind (Instrumental) 7
78	Island IEP 7	HOLE IN MY SHOE (EP, picture disc) 10
67	Island ILP 961/ILPS 9061	MR FANTASY (LP, gatefold sleeve, 1st pressing
		pink label with black 'circle' logo, mono/stereo) 125/75
68	Island ILPS 9081T	TRAFFIC (LP, gatefold sleeve with stapled-in booklet;
		pink label with black 'circle' logo, or pink rim label with 'palm tree' logo) 45/18
69	Island ILP(S) 9097	LAST EXIT (LP, pink label with black 'circle' logo,
		or pink rim label with 'palm tree' logo) 50/20
69	Island ILP(S) 9112	THE BEST OF TRAFFIC (LP, 1st pressings have pink "I" label, subsequent
		pressings have pink rim label with 'palm tree' logo) 15/12
70	Island ILPS 9081	MR. FANTASY (LP, 2nd pressing, pink rim label with 'palm tree' logo) 15
70	Island ILPS 9116	JOHN BARLEYCORN MUST DIE (LP, gatefold sleeve, 1st pressings have
		pink "I" label). 25
71	Island ILPS 9142	LIVE — NOVEMBER '70 (LP, unreleased, test pressing unconfirmed) . . . . 75+

(see also Spencer Davis Group, Stevie Winwood, Revolution, Hellions, Dave Mason, Gordon Jackson)

MINT VALUE £

TRAFFIC JAM
67 Piccadilly 7N 35386   Almost But Not Quite There/Wait Just A Minute 300
(Demos are more common and worth £50 less than stock copies)
(see also Status Quo, Spectres)

TRAGICIAN
79 Look LKSP 6411   The Wild The Scared And The Timid/Traces Of Impact (numbered gatefold p/s) . 35

PHIL TRAINER
73 BASF 05 19573-5   Beautiful Jim/No No No (p/s) 5
73 BASF BAG 22 29107-3   PHIL TRAINER (LP) 20
(see also Trees)

TRAIN SET
80s Play Hard DEC 11   She's Gone (12", p/s) 35
80s Play Hard DEC 17   Hold On (12", p/s) 35

TRAITOR'S GATE
85 Bullet BOLT 12   DEVIL TAKES THE HIGH ROAD (EP) 8

TRAITS
67 Pye International 7N 25404   Harlem Shuffle/Strange Lips (Start Ole Memories) 30
(see also Roy Head)

ALAN TRAJAN
69 MCA MK 5002   Speak To Me, Clarissa/This Might Be My Last Number 15
69 MCA MKPS 2000   FIRM ROOTS (LP) 100

TRAMLINE
68 Island ILPS 9088   SOMEWHERE DOWN THE LINE (LP, pink label) 90
69 Island ILPS 9095   MOVES OF VEGETABLE CENTURIES (LP, pink label) 80
(see also Whitesnake)

BOBBY LEE TRAMMELL
64 Sue WI 326   New Dance In France/Carolyn 40

TRAMMY (Ron Wilson)
72 Techniques TE 920   Horns Of Paradise/TECHNIQUES ALL STARS: Grass Root 8

TRAMP
69 Young Blood SBY 4   Vietnam Rose/Each Day 12
74 Spark SRL 1107   Put A Record On/You've Gotta Move 8
69 Music Man SMLS 603   TRAMP (LP) 120
73 Spark Replay SRLM 2001   TRAMP (LP, reissue) 50
74 Spark SRLP 112   PUT A RECORD ON (LP) 50
(see also Dave Kelly, Jo-Ann Kelly, Brunning Hall Sunflower Blues Band, Fleetwood Mac)

TRAMWAY
80s Sarah SRH 43   Maritime City/Boathouse/Star (p/s, with insert) 7

TRANSATLANTICS
65 Fontana TF 593   Many Things From Your Window/I Tried To Forget 30
65 Fontana TF 638   Stand Up And Fight Like A Man/But I Know. 15
65 Mercury MF 948   Don't Fight It/Look Before You Leap. 45
65 King KG 1033   Run For Your Life/It's All Over. 15
66 King KG 1040   Louie Go Home/Find Yourself Another Guy. 20

TRANSCRIPT CARRIERS
93 Transcript Carriers TC998   THE HAEMORRHOID FRY UP (EP) 18

TRANSIENT WAVES
98 Fat Cat 12FAT 011   Born With A Body And Fucked In The Heads/(2 Lone Swordsmen Mix)/
    (Skye [Stasis] Mix) (12", custom embossed sleeve) 10

TRANSMITTERS
78 Ebony EYE 11   Party/0.5 Alive (p/s) 5
78 Ebony EYE 12   Nowhere Train/Uninvited Guest/Persons Unknown (die-cut p/s). 5
79 Step Forward SF 1212   The Ugly Man/The One That Won The War/Free Trade/Curious (12", p/s) 8
70s Eccentric EX 2 C50   I JAX DUB (cassette) 12
78 Ebony EBY 1002   24 HOURS (LP) 15
81 Heartbeat MB 4   AND WE CALL THIS LEISURE TIME (LP) 12

TRANSPARENT ILLUSION
81 Vortex VEX 001/002   Vortex/Nuclear Release (p/s) 20
82 Vortex VEX 5   Guilty Rich Men (p/s) 10
81 Vortex VEX 3   STILL HUMAN (LP) 35
82 Vortex VEX 4   CHAGRIN RECEIVER (LP) 20

TRANSPORTER
70s Mother Truck MT 1   Kids On The Run/Intoxicating 6

TRAPEZE
69 Threshold TH 2   Send Me No More Letters/Another Day 10
72 Threshold TH 11   Coast To Coast/Your Love Is Alright. 10
75 Warner Bros K 16606   Sunny Side Of The Street/Monkey 10
79 Aura AUS 114   Don't Ask Me How I Know/Take Good Care (p/s). 15
80 Aura AUS 116   Running Away/Don't Break My Heart (p/s). 15
69 Threshold THS 2   TRAPEZE (LP) 30
70 Threshold THS 4   MEDUSA (LP) 35
73 Threshold THS 8   YOU ARE THE MUSIC ... WE'RE JUST THE BAND (LP) 18
74 Warner Bros K 56064   HOT WIRE (LP) 15
74 Threshold THS 11   THE FINAL SWING (LP) 12
79 Aura AUL 708   HOLD ON (LP) 15
81 Aura AUL 717   LIVE IN TEXAS ... DEAD ARMADILLOS (LP) 15
(see also Finders Keepers, Montanas, Deep Purple, Glenn Hughes, Judas Priest, Whitesnake)

TRASH

69	Apple APPLE 6	Road To Nowhere/Illusions (initial copies as White Trash, later Trash)......	200/50
69	Apple APPLE 17	Golden Slumbers – Carry That Weight/Trash Can...........................	18

(see also Poets, Pathfinders)

TRASHCAN SINATRAS

89	Go! Discs GODX 34	Obscurity Knocks/The Best Man's Fall/Drunken Chorus/Who's He? (12", p/s)...	12
89	Go! Discs GODCD 34	Obscurity Knocks/The Best Man's Fall/Drunken Chorus/Who's He? (CD).......	12
90	Go! Discs GOD 41	Only Tongue/Useless Begins With You/Tonight You Belong To Me (p/s)......	6
90	Go! Discs GODX 41	Only Tongue/Useless Begins With You/Tonight You Belong To Me (12", p/s)...	10
90	Go! Discs GOD 46	Circling The Circumference/My Mistake (p/s)...........................	8
90	Go! Discs GODX 46	Circling The Circumference/My Mistake/White Horses (12", p/s)...........	12
93	Go! Discs GODX 98	Hayfever/Say/Kangaroo Court/Skin Diving (12", p/s).....................	8
93	Go! Discs GODCD 98	Hayfever/Say/Kangaroo Court/Skin Diving (CD, in box)...................	12
93	Go! Discs GOD 100	I've Seen Everything/Houseproud/I'm The One Who Fainted (p/s)...........	6
96	Go! Discs GOD 151	How Can I Apply?/Save Me (p/s).......................................	6
90	Go! Discs 828 2011	CAKE (LP)...	15

TRASHMEN

64	Stateside SS 255	Surfin' Bird/King Of The Surf..	40
64	Stateside SS 276	Bird Dance Beat/A-Bone..	45

TRAVELING WILBURYS

88	Warner Bros W 7732W	Handle With Care/Margarita (gatefold p/s with sticker, some sealed)........	10/8
88	Warner Bros W 7732TE	Handle With Care (Extended)/Margarita (10", p/s).......................	10
88	Warner Bros W 7732T	Handle With Care (Extended)/Margarita (12", p/s).......................	10
88	Warner Bros W 7732CD	Handle With Care (LP Version)/Margarita/Handle With Care (Extended Version) (3" CD, with adaptor, 5" case)...................	12
89	Warner Bros W 7637TW	End Of The Line (Extended)/Congratulations (12", p/s, with/without sheet of stickers)........................	15/10
89	Warner Bros W 7637CD	End Of The Line (Extended Version)/Congratulations (3" CD, gatefold card p/s in PVC sleeve)........................	15
90	Warner Bros W 9773T	Nobody's Child/DAVE STEWART: Lumière/RINGO STARR: With A Little Help From My Friends (12", p/s).....................	12
90	Warner Bros W 9773CD	Nobody's Child/DAVE STEWART: Lumière/RINGO STARR: With A Little Help From My Friends (CD)....................	12
90	Warner Bros W 9523	She's My Baby/New Blue Moon (Instrumental Version) (p/s)...............	6
90	Warner Bros W 9523T	She's My Baby (LP Version)/New Blue Moon (Instrumental Version)/ Runaway (12", p/s)...	12
90	Warner Bros W 9523CD	She's My Baby (LP Version)/New Blue Moon (Instrumental Version)/ Runaway (CD)..	12
91	Warner Bros W 0019	Wilbury Twist/New Blue Moon (Instrumental) (p/s)....................	6
91	Warner Bros W 0018W	Wilbury Twist/New Blue Moon (Instrumental) (card p/s with 4 postcards).......	15
91	Warner Bros W 0019T	Wilbury Twist/New Blue Moon (Instrumental)/Cool Dry Place (12", p/s).........	12
91	Warner Bros W 0019CD	Wilbury Twist/New Blue Moon (Instrumental)/Cool Dry Place (CD, silver or black print)..	12
88	Warner Bros WX 224W	VOLUME ONE (LP, some with stickered sleeve & sticker inserts)............	45
88	Warner Bros WX 224CD	VOLUME ONE (CD)...	45
90	Warner Bros WX 7799-2 324-2	VOLUME THREE (CD)...	40

(see also George Harrison, Bob Dylan, Roy Orbison, Jeff Lynne, Tom Petty)

TRAVELLERS

77	Paradise PDS 001	Jah Give Us The World (feat. U Brown)/Girl I Left Behind (12")...............	15

TRAVELLING FOLK

70s	Cuchulainn CCHS 1017	TRAVELLING FOLK (LP)...	15

PAT TRAVERS

76	Polydor SFI 221/2814 040	Makes No Difference (1-sided flexidisc, promo only, black & white p/s)........	15

(see also Nicko McBrain)

TRAVIS

73	A&M AMLS 68120	SHINE ON ME (LP)...	45

(see also Paul Travis)

TRAVIS

96	Red Telephone Box PHONE 001	All I Want Do Is Rock/Line Is Fine/Funny Thing (10", numbered, stickered p/s, 750 only)..	50
97	Independiente ISOM 1S	U16 Girls/Hazy Shades/Good Time Girls (p/s)............................	6
97	Independiente ISOM 3S	All I Want Do Is Rock/Blue On A Black Weekend (p/s).....................	12
97	Independiente ISOM 5S	Tied To The 90s/Me Beside You (p/s)...................................	7
97	Independiente GOODT 1	The Line Is Fine/All I Want To Do Is Rock/More Than Us/ Tied To The 90s (12", promo only)...................................	10
00	Independiente ISOM 45455	Coming Around/Coming Around (Version) (juke box promo)................	7
99	Independiente ISM 4946249	THE MAN WHO (CD, with bonus CD [Driftwood/Slide Show/More Than Us])....	20

MERLE TRAVIS

53	Capitol CL45 13985	Gamblers Guitar/Shut Up And Drink Your Beer (78 rpm = £8)................	40
54	Capitol CL 14051	Green Cheese/Re-Enlistment Blues (78)................................	8
54	Capitol CL 14110	Jolie Fille (Pretty Girl)/I Can't Afford The Coffee (78).....................	8
56	Capitol EAP1 032	MERLE TRAVIS GUITAR (EP)...	20
57	Capitol EAP2 650	MERLE TRAVIS GUITAR NO. 2 (EP).....................................	18
59	Capitol EAP1 891	BACK HOME (EP)...	15
63	Capitol EAP1 1391	WALKIN' THE STRINGS (EP)..	15
57	Capitol T 891	BACK HOME (LP)..	30
63	Capitol (S)T 1664	TRAVIS! (LP)..	20
65	Capitol T 2102	MERLE TRAVIS & JOE MAPHIS (LP).....................................	20

(see also Brown's Ferry Four)

MINT VALUE £

PAUL TRAVIS
75 A&M AMLS 68290   RETURN OF THE NATIVE (LP, with lyric inner) 20
(see also Travis)

TRAVIS & BOB
59 Pye International 7N 25018 Tell Him No/We're Too Young (78 rpm = £10)......................... 15
61 Mercury AMT 1142   Baby Stay Close To Me/Give Your Love To Me 7

TRAX FOUR
66 Ace Of Clubs S/ACL 1216   WINGDING PARTY!!! (LP, mono/stereo)........................... 40

JACK TRAYLOR & STEELWIND
73 Grunt FTR 0194   CHILD OF NATURE (LP) 20

TREASURE BOY
67 Trojan TR 010   Love Is A Treasure (actually by Freddie McKay)/
    TOMMY McCOOK: Zazuka 25

TREBLETONES
61 Butlin CP 2424   Butlin Holiday/Butlin Holiday.. 8
63 Oriole CB 1838   In Real Life/Dream Of A Lifetime 12

TREDEGAR
86 Aries CEP 0001   Duma/The Jester (p/s).. 75
86 Aries CEP LP 001   TREDEGAR (LP, gatefold sleeve, embossed) 12
(see also Budgie)

HERBERT BEERBOHM TREE
65 OMY 69   KEEP THOSE DOGS AWAY (EP) 25

TREEBOUND STORY
86 Fon ELM 1   I REMEMBER EP (12", p/s)... 8

TREES
70 CBS 5078   Nothing Special/Epitaph.. 18
70 CBS 63837   THE GARDEN OF JANE DELAWNEY (LP) 120
71 CBS 64168   ON THE SHORE (LP)... 120
87 Decal LIK 12   ON THE SHORE (LP, reissue)...................................... 18
87 Decal LIK 15   THE GARDEN OF JANE DELAWNEY (LP, reissue) 18
(see also Casablanca, Juliet Lawson, Trainer)

TREETOPS
67 Parlophone R 5628   Don't Worry Baby/I Remember 15
68 Parlophone R 5669   California My Way/Carry On Living................................... 12
70 Columbia DB 8727   Mississippi Valley/Man Is A Man 7
71 Columbia DB 8799   Without The One You Love/So Here I Go Again 15

TREKKAS
65 Planet PLF 105   Please Go/I Put A Spell On You..................................... 80

TREMBLING BLUE STARS
96 Shinkansen SHINKANSEN 1 Abba On The Jukebox/She's Always There (p/s, 1,000 only)................ 10

TREMELOES
66 Decca F 12423   Blessed/The Right Time 18
66 CBS 202242   Good Day Sunshine/What A State I'm In 8
67 CBS 202519   Here Comes My Baby/Gentlemen Of Pleasure 5
67 CBS 2723   Silence Is Golden/Let Your Hair Hang Down (p/s).................... 6
67 CBS 2930   Even The Bad Times Are Good/Jenny's Alright (p/s) 6
67 CBS 3043   Be Mine/Suddenly Winter.. 5
68 CBS 3234   Suddenly You Love Me/As You Are................................... 5
68 CBS 2889   Helule Helule/Girl From Nowhere 5
68 CBS 3680   My Little Lady/All The World To Me................................... 5
68 CBS 3873   I Shall Be Released/I Miss My Baby 5
69 CBS 4065   Hello World/Up Down All Around 5
69 CBS 4582   (Call Me) Number One/Instant Whip 5
68 CBS Special Products   Here Comes My Baby/SIMON & GARFUNKEL: The 59th Street
    WB 728   Bridge Song (p/s, mail-order only with Pepsi Cola tokens) 6
73 Epic EPC 1399   Ride On/Hands Off 5
73 CBS 1139   Here Comes My Baby/Silence Is Golden (p/s, 'Hall Of Fame Hits' series) 5
84 Meteor MTS 002   Silence Is Golden (Acappella version)/The Last Word 5
68 CBS EP 6402   MY LITTLE LADY (EP)... 18
67 CBS (S)BPG 63017   HERE COME THE TREMELOES (LP)................................ 22
68 CBS (S)BPG 63138   THE TREMELOES: CHIP, RICK, ALAN AND DAVE (LP)................ 22
69 CBS 63547   THE TREMELOES 'LIVE' IN CABARET (LP).......................... 18
70 CBS 64242   MASTER (LP)... 15
(see also Brian Poole & Tremeloes, Trems, Chip Hawkes)

TREMORS
80s Redball RR 0002   Modern World/Smashed Reality (p/s) 5

TREMS
73 Epic EPC 1660   Make It Break It/Movin' On.. 5
(see also Tremeloes)

TREND
67 Page One POF 004   Boyfriends And Girlfriends/Shoot On Sight............................ 35

TREND
70 Trendy TREND 1   Teenage Crush/Cool Johnny (some with press sheet) 50/40

TREND
80 MCA MCA 583   Polly And Wendy/Family Way (p/s) 20
80 MCA MCA 629   This Dance Hall Must Have A Back Way Out/Fiction, Love & Romance (p/s) 15

TRENDS

MINT VALUE £

TRENDS
63	Piccadilly 7N 35171	All My Loving/Sweet Little Miss Love	15
64	Pye 7N 15644	You're A Wonderful One/The Way You Do The Things You Do	20

(see also Tammy St. John, Freddie Self, Freddie Ryder)

TRENDSETTERS
64	Silver Phoenix 1001	You Don't Care/My Heart Goes	60

TRENDSETTERS
60s	Oak RGJ 999	AT THE HOTEL DE FRANCE (EP)	25

TRENDSETTERS LTD
64	Parlophone R 5118	In A Big Way/Lucky Date	15
64	Parlophone R 5161	Hello Josephine/Move On Over	18
64	Parlophone R 5191	Go Away/Lollipops And Roses	12
65	Parlophone R 5324	You Sure Got A Funny Way Of Showing Your Love/I'm Coming Home	10

(see also King Crimson, Giles Giles & Fripp, Brain)

CHARLES TRENET
58	Columbia SEG 7819	BOUM! (EP)	8

TRENIERS
58	Coral Q 72319	Ooh-La-La/Pennies From Heaven (78 rpm = £12)	45
58	Fontana H 137	Go! Go! Go!/Get Out Of The Car (featuring Don Hill, Alto Sax) (78 rpm = £30)	100
59	London HLD 8858	When Your Hair Has Turned To Silver/Never, Never (78 rpm = £35)	45

JACKIE TRENT
61	Oriole CB 1711	Pick Up The Pieces/In Your Heart	10
62	Oriole CB 1749	The One Who Really Loves You/Your Conscience Or Your Heart	50
63	Piccadilly 7N 35121	Melancholy Me/So Did I	5
64	Piccadilly 7N 35165	If You Love Me/Only One Such As You	25
64	Pye 7N 15692	Somewhere In The World/I Heard Somebody Say	5
64	Pye 7N 15742	Don't Stand In My Way/How Soon	5
65	Pye 7N 15776	Where Are You Now (My Love)/On The Other Side Of The Tracks	5
65	Pye 7N 15865	When Summertime Is Over/To Show I Love Him	5
65	Pye 7N 15949	It's All In The Way You Look At Life/Time After Time	6
66	Pye 7N 17047	You Baby/Send Her Away	30
66	Pye 7N 17082	Love Is Me Love Is You/This Time	6
66	Pye 7N 17158	If You Ever Leave Me/There Goes My Love, There Goes My Life	6
67	Pye 7N 17249	Open Your Heart/Love Can Give	15
67	Pye 7N 17323	Your Love Is Everywhere/It's Not Easy Loving You	6
67	Pye 7N 17415	That's Your/Stop Me And Buy One	6
67	Pye 7N 17437	Bye Bye Love (German Version)/Alles Okay (Send Her Away)	6
69	Pye 7N 17693	I'll Be There/Close To You	5
78	Casino Classics CC 4	You Baby/Send Her Away/FAMILY AFFAIR: Love Hustle	6
65	Pye NEP 4225	WHERE ARE YOU NOW (EP)	15
65	Pye NPL 18125	THE MAGIC OF JACKIE TRENT (LP)	18
67	Pye NPL 18173	ONCE MORE WITH FEELING (LP)	15
67	Pye NPL 18201	STOP ME AND BUY ONE (LP)	18

TRESPASS
79	Trial CASE 1	One Of These Days/Bloody Moon (p/s)	20
80	Trial CASE 2	Jealousy/Live It Up! (p/s)	15
81	Trial CASE 3	Bright Lights/The Duel/Man And Machine (p/s)	15

TREVOR (Shield)
64	Blue Beat BB 228	Down In Virginia/Hey Little Schoolgirl (with Caribs)	15
68	Blue Cat BS 129	Tender Arms (with Joe White & Glen Brown)/DERMOTT LYNCH: Something Is Worrying Me	20
68	Blue Cat BS 130	Pretty Girl (with Joe White & Glen Brown)/DERMOTT LYNCH: You Went Away	20
69	Blue Cat BS 153	Everyday Is Like A Holiday/Have You Time (by Trevor & Maytones)	35

TREVOR & KEITH
70	Punch PH 41	The Ark/MINNA BOYS: False Reador (actually titled "Got To Move")	7

(see also Carl Bryan)

T. REX
(see under Marc Bolan /T. Rex; see also Tyrannosaurus Rex)

TRIARCHY
79	SRT/79/CUS 599	Save The Khan/Juliet's Tomb (some in p/s, 1,000 only)	80/30
79	Direct NEON 1	Save The Khan/Juliet's Tomb (reissue, p/s)	35
80	Direct NEON 2	Metal Messiah/Sweet Alcohol/Hell Hound On My Trail (some in p/s)	70/30

TRIBAN
69	Cambrian CSP 707	Leaving On A Jet Plane/Night In The City	6
71	Decca F 13115	Black Paper Roses/One Way Mirror	5
69	Cambrian MCT 592	TRIBAN (LP)	20
72	Cambrian	RAINMAKER (LP)	18

TRIBE (U.K.)
66	Planet PLF 108	The Gamma Goochie/I'm Leavin'	70
67	RCA RCA 1592	Love Is A Beautiful Thing/Steel Guitar	20

TRIBE (U.S.)
66	Polydor 56510	Dancin' To The Beat Of My Heart/Woofin'	40

TRIBE
73	Probe PRO 597	Koke Parts 1 & 2	5

TONY TRIBE
69	Downtown DT 419	Red Red Wine/RECO & RUDIES: Blues	5
69	Downtown DT 439	Gonna Give You All The Love/HERBIE GREY: Why Wait	7

MINT VALUE £

TRIBESMAN
79	Boa BOA 102-12	Finsbury Park/The Tribe (12")	20
79	Boa BOA 001	STREET LEVEL (LP)	20

TRIBUTE
73	Jam JAM 48	Bobby Charlton/City Summer	12

TRICKY DISCO
91	Warp WAP 11	HOUSEFLY EP (12")	10

TRI-CORE
92	Underground UNR 001T	BELFAST SAYS EP (12")	80

TRIDENT
84	SRT TRI 1	Destiny/Power Of The Trident	50

(see also Filthy Rich)

TRIFFIDS
65	Fontana TL 5231	THE TRIFFIDS ARE REALLY FOLK (LP)	12

TRIFLE
69	United Artists UP 2270	All Together Now/Got My Thing	7
70	Dawn DNS 1008	Old-Fashioned Prayer Meeting/Dirty Old Town	6
71	Dawn DNLS 3017	FIRST MEETING (LP)	60

(see also George Bean)

PANDIT KANWAR SAIN TRIKHA
71	Mushroom 100 MR 7	THREE SITAR PIECES (LP)	45

TRILOGY
71	Mercury 6338 034	I'M BEGINNING TO FEEL IT (LP)	15

TRINIDAD ALL STARS
56	Parlophone DP 524	Trouble In Arima/Stone Cold Dead In De Market (78, export issue)	12

TRINIDAD STEEL BAND
51	Melodisc 1185	Caroline/Six String Calypso (78)	8
52	Vogue V 9017	Mango Walk/Take Me (78)	10
52	Vogue V 9018	Ramadin/Johnny (78)	10

TRINITY
77	Burning Sounds BS 011	Natty Tired To Carry Load/Dubwise	10
77	Magnum DERD 1003	UPTOWN GIRL (LP)	40

TRINITY HOUSE
77	Profile GMOR 146	FLASHBACK THROUGH HISTORY (LP, private pressing, with insert)	40

TRIO
70	Dawn DNLS 3006	TRIO (2-LP, with poster)	70
71	Dawn DNLS 3022	CONFLAGRATION (LP, with poster)	60
76	Dawn DNLS 3072	LIVE AT WOODSTOCK TOWN HALL (LP, with Stu Martin)	18

(see also John Surnam)

TRIPLETS
69	President PT 245	When Lovers Say Goodbye/You Won't See Me Leaving	10

TRIPPERS
66	Pye International 7N 25388	Dance With Me/Keep A-Knockin'	20

TRISHA
65	CBS 201800	The Darkness Of My Night/Confusion	7

TRISTAR AIRBUS
72	RCA RCA 2170	Travellin' Man/Willie Morgan On The Wing	10

(see also Wimple Winch, 10cc, Hotlegs)

TRIUMVIRAT
74	Harvest SHSP 4030	ILLUSION ON A DOUBLE DIMPLE (LP)	12
75	Harvest SHSP 4048	SPARTACUS (LP)	12

TRIXIE'S BIG RED MOTORBIKE
82	Chew CH 9271	A Splash Of Red/Invisible Boyfriend (white label, stapled foldover p/s)	15
83	Lobby Ludd (no cat. no.)	TRIXIE'S BIG RED MOTORBIKE (EP, plain sleeve with stapled strip)	12
84	Lobby Ludd L 100001	Norman And Narcissus/In Timbuktu (p/s)	10
84	Lobby Ludd L 100002	A Splash Of Red/Invisible Boyfriend (reissue, different p/s)	10
84	Lobby Ludd L 100003	TRIXIE'S BIG RED MOTORBIKE (EP, reissue, stapled p/s)	10
84	Nathan NAT 001	That's The End Of That/CLIVE PIG & LEE VALLEY: As Soon As She's Gone (33rpm flexi & sweet with Wally's Dog fanzine)	6/4

TRIXONS
69	Major Minor MM 665	Just Another Song/Sunny Side Sam	20

MARCUS TRO
65	Ember EMB S 203	Tell Me/What's The Matter Little Girl (some in p/s)	12/7
65	Ember EMB 3365	INTRODUCING MARCUS TRO (LP)	35

TROGGS
SINGLES
66	CBS 202038	Lost Girl/The Yella In Me	45
66	Fontana TF 689	Wild Thing/From Home	8
66	Fontana TF 717	With A Girl Like You/I Want You	7
66	Page One POF 001	I Can't Control Myself/Gonna Make You	7
66	Page One POF 010	Any Way That You Want Me/6-5-4-3-2-1	7
67	Page One POF 015	Give It To Me/You're Lyin'	7
67	Page One POF 022	My Lady/Girl In Black (withdrawn)	45
67	Page One POF 022	Night Of The Long Grass/Girl In Black	7
67	Page One POF 030	Hi Hi Hazel/As I Ride By	8

67	Page One POF 040	Love Is All Around/When Will The Rain Come	7
68	Page One POF 056	Little Girl/Maybe The Madman?	7
68	Page One POF 064	Surprise Surprise/Marbles And Some Gum?	8
68	Page One POF 082	You Can Cry If You Want To/There's Something About You	8
68	Page One POF 092	Hip Hip Hooray/Say Darlin'!	7
69	Page One POF 114	Evil Woman/Sweet Madeline	7
69	Page One POF 126	Wild Thing/I Can't Control Myself	7
70	Page One POF 164	Easy Lovin'/Give Me Something	7
70	Page One POF 171	Lover/Come Now	7
70	Page One POF 182	The Raver/You	7
71	DJM DJM 248	Lazy Weekend/Let's Pull Together	7
72	Jam JAM 25	Wild Thing/With A Girl Like You/Love Is All Around	5
72	Pye 7N 45147	Everything's Funny/Feels Like A Woman	7
73	Pye 7N 45244	Listen To The Man/Queen Of Sorrow	7
73	Pye 7N 45295	Strange Movies/I'm On Fire	8
75	Penny Farthing PEN 861	Good Vibrations/Push It Up To Me	6
75	Penny Farthing PEN 884	Wild Thing (Reggae Version)/Jenny Come Down	6
75	Penny Farthing PEN 889	Summertime/Jenny Come Down	6
75	Penny Farthing PEN 901	(I Can't Get No) Satisfaction/Memphis, Tennessee	6
76	Penny Farthing PEN 919	I'll Buy You An Island/Supergirl	5
77	Penny Farthing PEN 929	Feeling For Love/Summertime	5
78	Raw RAW 25	Just A Little Too Much/The True Troggs Tapes (p/s)	6
67	Page One POE 001	TROGGS TOPS (EP)	22
67	Page One POE 002	TROGGS TOPS VOLUME TWO (EP)	40
67	Page One	TRACK A TROGG (EP, unreleased)	
81	DJM DJS 6	TROGGS TAPES (EP, double pack)	10
LPs			
66	Fontana (S)TL 5355	FROM NOWHERE — THE TROGGS (LP, mono/stereo)	35/45
66	Page One POL 001	TROGGLODYNAMITE (LP)	50
67	Page One FOR 001	THE BEST OF THE TROGGS (LP)	30
67	Page One POL(S) 003	CELLOPHANE (LP, mono/stereo)	50/65
68	Page One POL 1	THE TROGGS ON TOUR (LP, export issue)	150+
68	Page One FOR 007	THE BEST OF THE TROGGS VOLUME TWO (LP)	35
68	Page One POL(S) 012	MIXED BAG (LP)	110
69	Page One POS 602	TROGGLOMANIA (LP)	40
70	DJM Silverline DJML 009	CONTRASTS (LP, original issue)	22

(see also Reg Presley, Chris Britton, Ronnie Bond, Ten Feet Five)

CHUCK TROIS & AMAZING MAZE
68	Action ACT 4517	Call On You/Woodsman	15

TROJAN
88	GI GILP 444	THE MARCH IS ON (LP)	18

TROJANS
58	Decca F 11065	Man I'm Gonna Be/Make It Up	20
58	Decca F 11065	Man I'm Gonna Be/Make It Up (78)	15

TROLL BROTHERS
73	SRT SRT 73316	You Turn Me On/Turn Out The Lights (p/s)	10

TROMBONES UNLIMITED
66	Liberty LIB 55874	Daydream/The Phoenix Love Theme (Senza Fine)	5
66	Liberty LBY 1350	YOU'RE GONNA HEAR FROM ME (LP)	12

TRONICS
61	Fontana H 348	Cantina/Pickin' & Stompin'	18

TRONICS
78	Tronics T 001	Suzie (actually "Suzie's Vibrator")/Favourite Girls (plain sleeve with inserts)	8
79	Tronics T 002	Time Off/Goodbye (p/s)	8
81	Alien ALIEN 18	Shark Fucks/Time Off (p/s, with insert)	6
81	Lyntone	Love Backed By Force/(tracks by Dancing Did & Instant Automatons, flexidisc with *Chainsaw* fanzine, issue 12)	5
83	Red Rhino RED 3	Wild Cat Rock/Tonight (p/s)	5
82	Press PRESS 1	TRANZISTER SISTER (12" EP)	8
81	Alien BALIEN 3	LOVE BACKED BY FORCE (LP)	25

(see also Les Zarjaz)

TROOPERS
57	Vogue V 9087	Get Out/My Resolution (78 rpm = £190)	700+

TROOPS OF TOMORROW
82	Troops TROOPS 1	TROOPS OF TOMORROW (12" EP)	8

(see also Vibrators, Fallen Angels)

TROPIC SHADOWS
72	Big Shot BI 603	Our Anniversary/Anniversary (Version)	6

ARCHIBALD TROTT
64	Black Swan WI 407	Get Together/Just Because	18

(see also Baba Brooks)

TROUBADORS/TROUBADOUR SINGERS
57	London HLR 8469	Fascination/Midnight In Athens	8
58	London HLR 8541	The Lights Of Paris/The Flaming Rose	8
58	London RE-R 1135	THE TROUBADORS (EP)	8
58	London HA-R 2095	THE TROUBADORS IN SPAIN (LP)	12

(see also Jane Morgan)

TROUBLE
88	Justice JTT002	I Get Hype/I Guess It's Dope(12")	40

BOBBY TROUP
55	Capitol CL 14219	Julie Is Her Name/Instead Of You	12
54	Capitol LC 6660	BOBBY TROUP (10" LP)	22

BOB TROW QUARTET
54	London HL 8082	Soft Squeeze Baby/I Went Along For The Ride (78 rpm = £10)	45

ROBIN TROWER
78	Chrysalis CHS 2247	It's For You/My Love/In City Dreams (p/s, red vinyl)	5
81	Chrysalis CHS 2497	What It Is/Into Money (p/s, clear vinyl)	5
73	Chrysalis CHR 1039	TWICE REMOVED FROM YESTERDAY (LP)	12
74	Chrysalis CHR 1057	BRIDGE OF SIGHS (LP)	12
75	Chrysalis CHR 1073	FOR EARTH BELOW (LP)	12

(see also Paramounts, Procol Harum)

TROY & T-BIRDS
61	London HL 9476	Twistle/Take Ten	15

DORIS TROY
63	London HLK 9749	Just One Look/Bossa Nova Blues	30
64	Atlantic AT 4011	What'cha Gonna Do About It/Tomorrow Is Another Day	20
65	Atlantic AT 4020	Please Little Angel/One More Chance	15
65	Atlantic AT 4032	Heartaches/You'd Better Stop	15
65	Cameo Parkway C 101	I'll Do Anything (He Wants Me To)/But I Love Him (DJ copy = £200)	130
68	Atlantic 584 148	Just One Look/What'cha Gonna Do About It	10
68	Toast TT 507	I'll Do Anything (Anything He Wants Me To)/Heartaches	15
70	Apple APPLE 24	Ain't That Cute/Vaya Con Dios (some with p/s)	22/10
70	Apple APPLE 28	Jacob's Ladder/Get Back	12
71	Mojo 2092 011	I'll Do Anything (He Wants Me To)/But I Love Him (reissue)	15
73	Mojo 2092 062	Baby I Love You/To My Father's House	6
74	People PEO 112	Stretchin' Out/Don't Tell Your Mama	6
65	Atlantic AET 6007	WATCHA GONNA DO ABOUT IT (EP)	75
70	Apple SAPCOR 13	DORIS TROY (LP)	48
73	Mojo 2956 001	THE RAINBOW TESTAMENT (LP, with Gospel Truth)	32
74	Polydor 2464 001	JUST ONE LOOK (LP)	18
74	People PLEO 12	STRETCHING OUT (LP)	20
92	Apple SAPCOR 13	DORIS TROY (LP, reissue, gatefold sleeve with bonus 12" [SAPCOR 132])	12

WILLIAM TRUCKAWAY
69	Reprise RS 20842	Bluegreens On The Wing/Besides Yourself	12
71	Reprise K 44165	BREAKAWAY (LP, with lyric insert)	18

TRUE STYLE
91	Liberty Grooves LIB002	CODES OF CONDUCT (EP)	30

TRUFFLE
81	Chesnut NUT 6	Round Tower (p/s)	150

TRUTH
65	Pye 7N 15923	Baby Don't You Know/Come On Home	18
65	Pye 7N 15998	Who's Wrong/She's A Roller	25
66	Pye 7N 17035	Girl/Jailer Bring Me Water	12
66	Pye 7N 17095	I Go To Sleep/Baby You've Got It	40
66	Deram DM 105	Jingle Jangle/Hey Gyp (Dig The Slowness)	100
67	Decca F 12582	Walk Away Renee/Fly Away Bird	20
68	Decca F 22764	Seuno/Old Ma Brown	35

TRUTH
83	WEA TRUTH 1F	Confusion/Me And My Girl//Love A Go Go/From The Heart (p/s, double pack)	8
84	IRS IRS 115	Exception Of Love/If You Ever Find Love (p/s)	5

TRUTH & BEAUTY
74	Rak RAK 181	Tuff Little Surfer Boy/Touch-a Touch-a Touch Me	15

TRUTH OF TRUTHS
71	Oak OR 1001	TRUTH OF TRUTHS (LP)	25

TRUX
82	Trux TRX 01	Bad Luck (no p/s)	200

TRYDAN
80	Sain SAIN 77S	Mods A Rocers/Di-Waith, Di-'Fynedd	5

TANIA TSANAKLIDOU
78	EMI EMI 2797	Charlie Chaplin (English)/Charlie Chaplin (Greek)	12

TSD
96	Avex AVEXCD 21	Heart & Soul (Hyper Go Go 7" Edit)/Heart & Soul (Strike 12")/Heart & Soul (Hyper Go Go 12")/Heart & Soul (Dyme Brothers 12")/Heart & Soul (Johnny Versace 12") (CD)	12
96	Avex AVEXT 34	Baby I Love You (Divine Bootleg Remix)/Baby I Love You (Daniele Davoli Remix)/Baby I Love You (Radio Edit) (12", p/s)	10
96	Avex AVEXCD 34	Baby I Love You (7" Edit)/Baby I Love You (Divine Bootleg)/Baby I Love You (Daniele Davoli Remix)/The Chris Rogers Interview (CD)	12

(see also STEPS)

T.S.O.L.
81	Frontier FLP 1004	DANCE WITH ME (LP)	18
82	Alt. Tentacles VIRUS 10	WEATHERED STATUES (EP)	6

T2
70	Decca SKL 5050	IT'LL ALL WORK OUT IN BOOMLAND (LP)	60
97	Essex 1019LP	T2 (LP)	12

(see also Flies, Cross & Ross)

ERNEST TUBB (& HIS TEXAS TROUBADORS)

51	Brunswick 04783	Rose Of The Mountains/Kentucky Waltz (with Red Foley) (78)	10
52	Brunswick 04933	Walking The Floor Over You/Somebody's Stolen My Honey (78)	10
56	Brunswick 05527	Thirty Days/Answer The Phone (triangular centre) (78 rpm = £12)	40
56	Brunswick 05587	So Doggone Lonesome/If I Never Have Anything Else (78 rpm = £10)	20
50s	Decca BM 31214	What Am I Living For/Goodbye Sunshine, Hello Blues (export issue)	15
55	Brunswick OE 9148	COUNTRY DOUBLE DATE (EP)	20
58	Brunswick OE 9372	THE DADDY OF 'EM ALL PT. 1 (EP)	20
58	Brunswick OE 9373	THE DADDY OF 'EM ALL PT. 2 (EP)	20
58	Brunswick OE 9374	THE DADDY OF 'EM ALL PT. 3 (EP)	20
56	Brunswick LA 8736	JIMMIE RODGERS SONGS (10" LP)	40
57	Brunswick LAT 8161	FAVOURITES (LP)	20
58	Brunswick LAT 8260	THE DADDY OF 'EM ALL (LP)	20
59	Brunswick LAT 8292	THE IMPORTANCE OF BEING ERNEST (LP)	20
60	Brunswick LAT 8313	THE ERNEST TUBB STORY VOLUME ONE (LP)	15
60	Brunswick LAT 8314	THE ERNEST TUBB STORY VOLUME TWO (LP)	15
60	Brunswick LAT 8349	THE ERNEST TUBB RECORD SHOP (LP)	18
66	Brunswick LAT 8627	MY PICK OF THE HITS (LP)	18

(see also Red Foley & Ernest Tubb)

JUSTIN TUBB

54	Brunswick 05302	Somebody Ughed Over You/Something Called The Blues (78)	8
67	RCA Victor RCA 1585	But Wait There's More/The Second Thing I'm Gonna Do	6
64	RCA RCX 7133	JUSTIN TUBB (EP)	30
63	Ember CW 100	STAR OF THE GRAND OLE OPRY (LP, pink & grey labels)	12
64	Ember CW 110	THE MODERN COUNTRY MUSIC SOUND OF JUSTIN TUBB (LP, pink & grey labels)	12

TUBES

79	A&M AMS 7423	Prime Time (promo box of 7 different coloured vinyl editions & picture disc)	30

TUBEWAY ARMY

78	Beggars Banquet BEG 5	That's Too Bad/Oh! I Didn't Say (p/s)	8
78	Beggars Banquet BEG 8	Bombers/O.D. Receiver/Blue Eyes (p/s)	8
79	Beggars Banquet BEG 17T	Down In The Park/Do You Need The Service?/I Nearly Married A Human 2 (12", p/s)	20
79	Banquet Banquet BEG 18P	Are "Friends" Electric?/We Are So Fragile (picture disc, with insert)	10
79	Banquet Banquet SPC 4	Are "Friends" Electric?/We Are So Fragile (cassette in cigarette-pack style box)	8
79	Beggars Banquet BACK 2	That's Too Bad/Oh! Didn't I Say/Bombers/Blue Eyes/O.D. Receiver (double pack, gatefold p/s)	5
79	Beggars Banquet BACK 2	That's Too Bad/Oh! Didn't I Say/Bombers/Blue Eyes/O.D. Receiver (double pack, gatefold p/s, mispressed 2nd disc omits "O.D. Receiver")	15
83	Beggars Banquet BEG 92E	TUBEWAY ARMY VOL. 1 (12" EP, with "That's Too Bad [Alternate Mix]", yellow vinyl)	10
85	Beggars Banquet BEG 123E	1978-1979 VOL. 2 (12", blue vinyl, p/s)	10
85	Beggars Banquet BEG 124E	1978-1979 VOL. 3 (12", red vinyl, p/s)	10
78	Beggars Banquet BEGA 4	TUBEWAY ARMY (LP, blue vinyl, g/fold stickered sleeve, some w/ badge)	60/50
79	Beggars Banquet BEGA 7	REPLICAS (LP, with large black & white poster)	20
85	B. Banquet BEGC 7879	TUBEWAY ARMY 1978/1979 (cassette only)	12

(see also Gary Numan, Paul Gardiner)

BESSIE TUCKER

55	HMV 7EG 8085	BLUES BY BESSIE (EP)	20

BILLY JOE TUCKER

61	London HLD 9455	Boogie Woogie Bill/Mail Train	50

ORRIN TUCKER

50	London L 556	I Need Lovin'/Everybody Loves My Baby (78)	6

SOPHIE TUCKER

54	Mercury MG 20035	MY DREAM (LP)	14
54	Mercury MG 20046	CABARET DAYS (LP)	14
54	Mercury MPL 6000	LATEST AND GREATEST SPICY SAUCY SONGS (LP)	12
56	Mercury MPL 6503	CABARET DAYS (LP, reissue)	12
57	Brunswick LAT 8144	THE GREAT SOPHIE TUCKER (LP)	12
57	Mercury MPL 6513	BIGGER AND BETTER THAN EVER (LP)	12

TOMMY TUCKER

64	Pye International 7N 25238	Hi-Heel Sneakers/I Don't Want 'Cha	25
64	Pye International 7N 25246	Long Tall Shorty/Mo' Shorty	25
64	London HLU 9932	Oh! What A Feeling/Wine Bottles	40
69	Chess CRS 8086	Hi-Heel Sneakers/I Don't Want 'Cha (reissue)	15
64	Pye Intl. NEP 44027	HI HEEL SNEAKERS (EP)	50

WINSTON TUCKER

73	Explosion EX 2083	I'm A Believer/You'll Be Mine	5

(see also Winston Groovy)

TUCKY BUZZARD

71	Capitol CL 15687	She's A Striker/Heartbreaker	5
73	Purple PUR 113	Gold Medallions/Fast Bluesy Woman	7
77	Purple PUR 134	Gold Medallions/Superboy Rock 'N' Roller '73	7
73	Purple TPSA 7510	ALRIGHT ON THE NIGHT (LP)	22
73	Purple TPSA 7512	BUZZARD (LP)	22

(see also End)

TUDOR LODGE

71	Vertigo 6059 044	The Lady's Changing Home/Back To The Good Times We Had	20
71	Vertigo 6360 043	TUDOR LODGE (LP, foldout textured sleeve, swirl label)	350

TUDOR MINSTRELS

TUDOR MINSTRELS
66 Decca F 12536   Love In The Open Air/A Theme From "The Family Way" 22

TUDORS
83 Stiff BUY 172   Tied Up With Joe Cool/Cry Baby Cry (p/s) 7

TUESDAY'S CHILDREN
66 Columbia DB 7978   When You Walk In The Sand/High And Drifting 20
66 Columbia DB 8018   High On A Hill/Summer Leaves Me With A Sigh 22
67 King KG 1051   A Strange Light From The East/That'll Be The Day 30
67 Pye 7N 17406   Baby's Gone/Guess I'm Losin' You 15
68 Pye 7N 17474   In The Valley Of The Shadow Of Love/Ain't You Got A Heart 10
68 Mercury MF 1063   She/Bright-Eyed Apples 12
(see also Warm Sounds)

T.U.F.F.
80s SONO 001   We've Got A Hot One (Speed Mix) (unreleased, white label promos only) 10
(see also Hard Corps)

TONY TUFF
79 Niagra NIADD 101   Ease Up Oppressor/JAH THOMAS: Answet The Phone (12") 10
79 King Sounds GMDM 26   You Wrong/TOMMY McCOOK: Sensimena (12") 25
80 Art & Craft 003   Look Ya/TONY TUFF & JAH STITCH: Rumours Of War (12") 40

TUFF GONG ALLSTARS
72 Punch PH 114   You Should Have Known Better (actually by The Wailing Souls)/Known Better .. 12
(see also Wailing Souls)

TULIPS
74 Explosion EX 2091   Mocking Bird/DES ALL STARS: Version 7

LEE TULLY
57 London HL 8363   Around The World With Elwood Pretzel (Parts 1 & 2) (gold or silver print) .. 100/60
57 London HL 8363   Around The World With Elwood Pretzel (Parts 1 & 2) (78) 20

TUNDRA
70s Greenwich Village GVR 208   THE KENTISH SONGSTER (LP) 12
78 Sweet Folk & C. SFA 078   A KENTISH GARLAND (LP, gatefold sleeve) 20

TUNE ROCKERS
58 London HLT 8717   The Green Mosquito/Warm Up (78 rpm = £15) 35

TUNEWEAVERS
57 London HL 8503   Happy Happy Birthday Baby/PAUL GAYTEN: Yo, Yo, Walk (78 rpm = £50) 180
(see also Paul Gayten)

TUNJI with CHRIS McGREGOR
60s Jika 001   Ko Gbele Oko/Lisabi Egba 8

TUNNEL RUNNERS
80 Sonic International SI 4282   Plastic Land/Drug (numbered p/s) 80

PADDY TUNNEY
65 Topic 12T 139   A WILD BEES NEST (LP, blue label) 12
66 Topic 12T 153   IRELAND HER OWN (LP, with Arthur Kearney, Frank Kelly & Joe Tunney,
    blue label) 12
66 Topic 12T 165   THE IRISH EDGE (LP, blue label, later reissued) 15/12

TUNNG
04 Static Caravan VAN 72   Tales From Black/Pool Beneath The Pond (500 only) 35
05 Static Caravan VAN 73   Maypole Song/Suprize Me 44 (100 lathe cut only, p/s) 60
05 Nowhere Fast SLOW03   Magpie Bites/The Bonnie Black Hare (1000 only hand numbered
    poster sleeve) 8
05 Static Caravan VAN 94   Tunng Vs Dollboy Vs Dollboy Vs Tunng (1000 only, 200 with art sleeve) 5/7
05 Static Caravan VAN 88   MOTHER'S DAUGHTERS AND OTHER SONGS (LP, 300 only – withdrawn) 60

TURBO
80 Cargo CRS 004   STALLION (EP, p/s) 100
82 Turbo CUS 1261   Charged For Glory/Race For The Dawn 8

TURGID TOOL
01 Stand STAND 11   Terror In A Turgid Tool/Stand Up For England (pop-up p/s) 8

TURIN BRAKES
99 Anvil ANV 027   THE DOOR EP (CD) 25
99 Source SOURV 008   THE STATE OF THINGS EP: Boss/Balham To Brooklyn/All Away/State Of
    Things (doublepack) 15
99 Source SOUR 008   THE STATE OF THINGS EP: Boss/Balham To Brooklyn/All Away/State Of
    Things (CD) 12

BRUCE TURNER
54 Columbia SCMC 9   Falling Leaves/I Wished On The Moon (export issue) 5
60 Melodisc MEL 1551   Nuages/My Guy's Come Back 5
60s CRD 1000   Jamaica Jump/Big Noise From Winetka 5
62 Storyville SXP 2025   BRUCE TURNER AND HIS JUMP BAND (EP) 8
63 Philips 433 627 BE   JUMPING FOR JOY NO. 1 (EP) 8
63 Philips 433 627 BE   JUMPING FOR JOY NO. 2 (EP) 8
63 77 EP/EU 1   LIVING JAZZ (EP) 10
64 Philips BL 7590   GOING PLACES (LP) 12

DENNIS TURNER
62 London HL 9537   Lover Please/How Many Times 25

GORDON TURNER
70 Charisma CAS 1009   MEDITATION (LP) 30

IKE TURNER

72	United Artists UP 35411	Lawdy Miss Clawdy/Tacks In My Shoes/Soppin' Molasses (with Family Vibes) . . .	6
84	Fleetville FV 303	New Breed Part 1/New Breed Part 2	5
60s	Ember EMB 3395	IKE TURNER ROCKS THE BLUES (LP)	40
72	United Artists UAG 29362	BLUES ROOTS (LP)	18
75	DJM DJSLM 2010	FUNKY MULE (LP).	15

(see also Ike & Tina Turner)

IKE & TINA TURNER

SINGLES

60	London HLU 9226	A Fool In Love/The Way You Love Me	25
61	London HLU 9451	It's Gonna Work Out Fine/Won't You Forgive Me	25
64	Sue WI 306	Gonna Work Out Fine/Won't You Forgive Me (reissue)	30
64	Sue WI 322	The Argument/Poor Fool	40
64	Sue WI 350	I Can't Believe What You Say/My Baby Now	40
65	Warner Bros WB 153	Finger Poppin'/Ooh Poo Pah Doo	25
65	Sue WI 376	Please, Please, Please/Am I A Fool In Love	40
66	London HLU 10046	River Deep — Mountain High/I'll Keep You Happy	8
66	Warner Bros WB 5753	Tell Her I'm Not Home/Finger Poppin'.	15
66	HMV POP 1544	Anything You Wasn't Born With/Beauty Is Just Skin Deep	30
66	London HLU 10083	A Love Like Yours (Don't Come Knockin' Every Day)/Hold On Baby	15
66	Stateside SS 551	Goodbye, So Long/Hurt Is All You Gave Me.	15
66	Warner Bros WB 5766	Somebody (Somewhere) Needs You/(I'll Do Anything) Just To Be With You	
		(DJ copy = £120)	85
67	HMV POP 1583	I'm Hooked/Dust My Broom (DJ copy = £100)	50
67	London HLU 10155	I'll Never Need More Than This/Save The Last Dance For Me	15
68	London HLU 10189	So Fine/So Blue Over You	10
68	London HLU 10217	We Need An Understanding/It Sho' Ain't Me	15
69	London HLU 10242	River Deep — Mountain High/Save The Last Dance For Me	5
69	Minit MLF 11016	I'm Gonna Do All I Can/You've Got Too Many Ties That Bind	10
69	London HLU 10267	I'll Never Need More Than This/A Love Like Yours	8
69	Liberty LBF 15223	Crazy 'Bout You Baby/I've Been Lovin' You Too Long	10
70	Liberty LBF 15303	Come Together/Honky Tonky Women.	6
70	A&M AMS 783	Make 'Em Wait/Everyday I Have To Cry	12
70	Harvest HAR 5018	The Hunter/Bold Soul Sister	15
70	Liberty LBF 15367	I Want To Take You Higher/Contact High	5
71	Liberty LBF 15432	Proud Mary/Funkier Than A Mosquito's Tweeter.	5
71	A&M AMS 829	River Deep — Mountain High/Oh Baby.	6
71	United Artists UP 35245	Ooh Poo Pah Doo/I Wanna Jump	5
72	United Artists UP 35373	Feel Good/Outrageous	5

EPs

64	Sue IEP 706	THE SOUL OF IKE AND TINA TURNER.	200
65	Warner Bros WEP 619	THE IKE AND TINA TURNER SHOW	50
66	Warner Bros WEP 620	SOMEBODY NEEDS YOU	85
83	Sue ENS 1	SUE SESSIONS	12

LPs

65	Warner Bros WM 8170	THE IKE AND TINA TURNER SHOW	45
65	London HA-C 8248	THE GREATEST HITS OF IKE & TINA TURNER	60
66	Ember EMB 3368	THE IKE AND TINA TURNER REVUE	38
66	Warner Bros W 1579	THE IKE AND TINA TURNER SHOW	38
66	London HA-U/SH-U 8298	RIVER DEEP MOUNTAIN HIGH	50
67	Warner Bros WB 5904	THE IKE AND TINA TURNER SHOW VOL. 2.	35
69	London HA-U/SH-U 8370	SO FINE (with Fontella Bass).	35
69	Liberty LBS 83241	OUTTA SEASON	22
69	Minit MLS 40014	IN PERSON	25
69	Warner Bros ES 1810	GREATEST HITS	20
70	Liberty LBS 83350	COME TOGETHER.	20
70	Harvest SHSP 4001	THE HUNTER	90
71	Liberty LBS 83455	WORKIN' TOGETHER	20
71	Liberty LBS 83468/9	LIVE IN PARIS	15
71	Capitol E-ST 571	HER MAN...HIS WOMAN	15
71	United Artists UAD 60005/6	WHAT YOU HEAR IS WHAT YOU GET	15
72	United Artists UAG 29256	NUFF SAID.	15
73	Mojo 2916 020	PEACHES (with tracks by Ikettes).	15

(see also Ike Turner, Tina Turner, Ikettes)

JESSE LEE TURNER

59	London HLL 8785	The Little Space Girl/Shake, Baby, Shake (78 rpm = £30).	55
60	London HLP 9108	I'm The Little Space Girl's Father/Valley Of Lost Soldiers	20
60	Top Rank JAR 303	That's My Girl/Teenage Misery.	18
60	Top Rank JAR 516	Do I Worry (Yes I Do)/All Right, Be That Way.	15
62	Vogue V 9201	The Voice Changing Song/All You Gotta Do Is Ask	15

(BIG) JOE TURNER

51	Parlophone DP 265	Roll 'Em Pete/Goin' Away Blues (with Pete Johnson) (78, export only)	60
56	London HLE 8301	Corrine Corrina/Morning, Noon And Night (triangular or round centre)	375/90
56	London HLE 8301	Corrine Corrina/Morning, Noon And Night (78)	40
56	London HLE 8332	Boogie Woogie Country Girl/The Chicken And The Hawk (78 rpm = £45)	750
57	London HLE 8357	Lipstick, Powder And Paint/Rock A While (gold label print, later silver)	425/290
57	London HLE 8357	Lipstick, Powder And Paint/Rock A While (78)	40
60	London HLE 9059	Honey Hush/Tomorrow Night.	55
60	London HLK 9119	My Little Honey Dripper/Chains Of Love	55
65	Atlantic AT 4026	Midnight Cannonball/Baby I Still Want You	20
56	London REE 1047	THE KING AND QUEEN OF R&B (EP, 2 tracks by Ruth Brown).	200
57	London REE 1111	PRESENTING JOE TURNER (EP, initially tri-centre, later round centre)	240/150
57	London Jazz LTZ-K 15053	BOSS OF THE BLUES (LP, also stereo SAH-K 6019).	80/100
59	London HA-E 2173	ROCKIN' THE BLUES (LP)	120

(Big) Joe TURNER

60	London Jazz LTZ-K 15205	BIG JOE RIDES AGAIN (LP, also stereo SAH-K 6123)	75/90
60	London HA-E 2231	BIG JOE IS HERE (LP)	80
64	Realm RM 207	JOE TURNER SINGS THE BLUES VOL. 1 (LP)	20
64	Realm RM 229	JOE TURNER SINGS THE BLUES VOL. 2 (LP)	20
65	CBS 52229	JOE TURNER SINGS THE BLUES VOL. 2 (LP, reissue)	15
65	Fontana 688 802 ZL	JUMPIN' THE BLUES (LP)	28
67	Atlantic Special 590 006	BOSS OF THE BLUES (LP)	20
68	Stateside (S)SL 10226	SINGING THE BLUES (LP)	25
70	Philips SBL 7911	THE REAL BOSS OF THE BLUES (LP)	15
74	Atlantic K 40525	HIS GREATEST RECORDINGS (LP)	12

(see also Pete Johnson, Meade Lux Lewis, Pete Johnson, Albert Ammons, Sonny Terry & Brownie McGhee)

JOE TURNER/RUTH BROWN

56	London REE 1047	KING AND QUEEN OF R&B (EP, 2 tracks each)	230

(see also Ruth Brown, Big Joe Turner)

JOE TURNER & PETE JOHNSON GROUP

56	Emarcy ERE 1500	JOE TURNER & PETE JOHNSON GROUP (EP)	45

(see also Pete Johnson, Big Joe Turner)

MEL TURNER (& Bandits)

61	Melodisc MEL 1580	Let Me Hold Your Hand/I'll Be With You In Apple Blossom Time (with Bandits)	20
62	Columbia DB 4791	Daddy Cool/Swing Low Sweet Chariot (with Bandits)	20
63	Columbia DB 4963	Don't Cry/I Need	10
63	Columbia DB 7076	I Can't Stand Up Alone/Doing The Ton (with Mohicans)	10
63	Carnival CV 7003	Mohican Crawl/White Christmas	10
66	Island WI 276	Welcome Home Little Darlin'/C'est L'Amour	40

NIK TURNER

(see under Inner City Unit, Sphynx, Hawkwind)

PRECIOUS CLARENCE TURNER

67	Saga SOC 1041	BOOGIE WOOGIE EXPLOSIONS (LP)	12

SAMMY TURNER

59	London HLX 8918	Lavender Blue (Dilly, Dilly)/Sweet Annie Laurie (78 rpm = £10)	18
59	London HLX 8963	Always/Symphony (78 rpm = £10)	15
60	London HLX 9062	Paradise/I'd Be A Fool Again	15
62	London HLX 9488	Raincoat In The River/Falling	20
60	London HA-X 2246	LAVENDER BLUE MOODS (LP)	90

SIMON TURNER

73	UK UKAL 1003	SIMON TURNER (LP)	15

SPYDER TURNER

67	MGM MGM 1332	Stand By Me/You're Good Enough For Me	40
74	Kwanza K 19502	Since I Don't Have You/Happy Days	10

TINA TURNER

78	United Artists UP 36513	Sometimes When We Touch/Earthquakes And Hurricanes	5
82	Virgin VS 500	Ball Of Confusion/Ball Of Confusion (Instrumental) (with B.E.F.) (p/s)	8
83	Capitol 12CLP 316	Let's Stay Together/I Wrote A Letter (12", picture disc)	8
84	Capitol CLP 325	Help/Rock'n'Roll Widow (picture disc)	7
84	Capitol CLP 338	Better Be Good To Me/When I Was Young (picture disc)	7
84	Capitol CL 343	Private Dancer/Nutbush City Limits (p/s)	7
85	Capitol CLP 364	We Don't Need Another Hero/(Instrumental) (picture disc)	7
86	Capitol CLP 338	Break Every Rule/Girls (picture disc)	5
86	Capitol CLX 430	Two People/Havin' A Party (p/s, with poster)	5
87	Capitol CLD 439	What You Get Is What You See/Tina Turner Montage (box set)	5
87	Capitol 7CLD 439	What You See Is What You Get/Take Me To The River//Tina Turner Montage Mix (Parts 1 & 2) (double pack)	5
87	Capitol CLP 452	Break Every Rule/Girls (picture disc)	5
87	Capitol 12 CLP 459	Paradise Is Here/The Midnight Hour (12", picture disc)	8
90	Capitol CLPD 593	Be Tender With Me Baby/Be Tender With Me Baby (live) (picture disc)	5
91	10 FLX 2007-1	A Change Is Gonna Come (Excerpt) (with B.E.F.) (flexidisc, p/s, from "Music Of Quality And Distinction Vol 2", promo only)	5
85	Capitol TINAP 1	PRIVATE DANCER (LP, picture disc)	18

(see also Ike & Tina Turner, Eric Clapton)

TITUS TURNER

60	London HLU 9024	We Told You Not To Marry/Taking Care Of Business	25
61	Oriole CB 1611	Pony Train/Bla Bla Cha Cha Cha	20
61	Parlophone R 4746	Sound-Off/Me And My Lonely Telephone	25
61	Blue Beat BB 32	Miss Rubberneck Jones/Way Down Yonder	18

ZEB TURNER

51	Vogue V 9002	Chew Tobacco Rag/No More Nothin' (78)	20

TURNING POINT

77	Gull GULP 1022	CREATURES OF THE NIGHT (LP)	20
78	Gull GULP 1027	SILENT PROMISE (LP)	15

TURNING SHRINES

86	Temple TOPY 7	FACE OF ANOTHER (12" EP)	8

TURNSTYLE

68	Pye 7N 17653	Riding A Wave/Trot	300

TURQUOISE

68	Decca F 12756	53 Summer Street/Tales Of Flossie Fillett	35
68	Decca F 12842	Woodstock/Saynia	35

(see also Ewan Stephens)

STANLEY TURRENTINE
66	Fontana TL 5300	TIGER TAIL (LP)	12
72	Polydor 2383 111	FLIPPED — FLIPPED OUT (LP)	12
72	CTI CTL 2	SUGAR (LP)	12
73	CTI CTL 8	CHERRY (LP, with Milt Jackson)	12

(see also Milt Jackson & Stanley Turrentine)

TURTLES
65	Pye International 7N 25320	It Ain't Me Babe/Almost There	12
66	Pye International 7N 25341	Let Me Be/Your Ma Said You Cried (In Your Sleep Last Night)	15
66	Immediate IM 031	You Baby/Wanderin' Kind	20
66	London HLU 10095	Can I Get To Know You Better/Like The Seasons	10
67	London HLU 10115	Happy Together/We'll Meet Again	7
67	Pye International 7N 25421	Let Me Be/Almost There	8
67	London HLU 10135	She'd Rather Be With Me/The Walking Song	7
67	London HLU 10153	You Know What I Mean/Rugs Of Woods And Flowers	8
67	London HLU 10168	She's My Girl/Chicken Little Was Right	12
68	London HLU 10184	Sound Asleep/Umbassa The Dragon	10
68	London HLU 10207	The Story Of Rock And Roll/Can't You Hear The Cows	10
68	London HLU 10223	Elenore/Surfer Dan	7
69	London HLU 10251	You Showed Me/Buzz-Saw	8
69	London HLU 10279	You Don't Have To Walk In The Rain/Come Over	10
69	London HLU 10291	Love In The City/Bachelor Mother	7
67	Pye Intl. NEP 44089	IT AIN'T ME BABE (EP)	55
67	London HA-U 8330	HAPPY TOGETHER (LP)	45
68	London HA-U/SH-U 8376	THE TURTLES PRESENT THE BATTLE OF THE BANDS (LP)	48

(see also Flo & Eddie)

JANE TURZY
53	Brunswick 05186	Call Me Up/I've Got A Letter (both with Grady Martin & Slewfoot Five) (78)	8

(see also Grady Martin)

RITA TUSHINGHAM & LYNN REDGRAVE
68	Stateside SS 2081	Smashing Time/Waiting For My Friend	15

TUSKAN RAIDERS
95	Clear CLR 410(X)	Bantha Trax (12", p/s, some on clear vinyl)	40/25

(see also µ-Ziq)

TU-TONES
51	London L 1079	Oh You Million Dollar Doll/Don't Fence Me In (78, as Lee Monti's Tu-Tones)	8
59	London HLW 8904	Still In Love WIth You/Saccharin Sally (78 rpm = £25)	125

TUTTI'S TRUMPETS
(see under Camarata)

WESLEY & MARILYN TUTTLE
55	Capitol CL 14291	Jim, Johnny And Jonas/Say You Do	10

TUXEDOMOON
80	Pre PRE 10	Dark Companion/59 To One (p/s)	5
82	Crepuscule TWI 055	Ninotchka (12", p/s)	8
88	Cramboy CBOY 8080	Time To Lose (12", p/s)	8

T.V. & TRIBESMEN
66	Pye International 7N 25375	Barefootin'/Fat Man	30

T.V. PERSONALITIES
(see under Television Personalities)

T.V. PRODUCT
79	Limited Edition TAKE 3	Nowhere's Safe/Jumping Off Walls/PRAMS: Me/Modern Man (folded p/s)	12

(see also Mission)

TV 21
80	Powbeat AAARGH! 1	Playing With Fire/Shattered By It All (foldout p/s)	12
80	Powbeat AAARGH! 2	Ambition/Ticking Away/This Is Zero (foldout p/s)	15
81	Demon D 1004	On The Run/End Of A Dream (p/s)	8
82	Decca	All Join Hands/A Journey Up The Zambezi (And Back) (p/s)	8

(see also DNV, Shake)

SHANIA TWAIN
95	Mercury MERCD 433	Any Man Of Mine/Raining On Our Love/God Ain't Gonna Getcha For That/Still Under The Weather (CD)	12
99	Mercury 562 264 2	Man! I Feel Like A Woman (Original Version) (CD, digipak, with lyrics, withdrawn)	12
99	NMC PILOT 54	ON THE WAY (CD, withdrawn)	18

TWELFTH NIGHT
73	Acorn CF 239	TWELFTH NIGHT (EP)	8

TWELFTH NIGHT
80	Twelfth Night TN 001	THE FIRST 7" ALBUM ("The Cunning Man"/"Für Helene") (p/s)	30
80s	Revolution REV 009	Eleanor Rigby/East Of Eden (p/s)	7
86	Virgin/Charisma CB 424	Shame/Blue Powder Monkey (p/s)	5
86	Virgin/Charisma CBY 424	Shame/Blue Powder Monkey (picture disc)	8
86	Virgin/Charisma CB 424-12	Shame (Full Mix)/Shame (7")/Blue Powder Monkey (12", p/s)	8
86	Virgin/Charisma CBY 424-12	Shame (Full Mix)/Shame (7")/Blue Powder Monkey (12", picture disc)	10
86	Virgin/Charisma CB 425-12	Take A Look (Album Version)/Take A Look (Part 4)/Blondon Fair (Extended) (12", p/s)	8
80	Twelfth Night TN 001	TWELFTH NIGHT (cassette)	15
81	Twelfth Night TN 002	LIVE AT THE TARGET (LP)	12
84	Music For Nations MFN 36	ART & ILLUSION (mini-LP)	10
86	Charisma CASG 1174	X (LP, fold-out cover)	12

MINT VALUE £

20th CENTURY FOX ORCHESTRA
65	Stateside SS422	Those Magnificent Men In Their Flying Machines/Arizona 10

(see also Ron Goodwin)

25 RIFLES
79	25 Rifles TFR 1	World War 3/Revolution Blues/Hey Little/Dance 'Bout Now (12") 15

23 JEWELS
79	Temporary TEMP 1	You Don't Know Me/Playing Bogart (white labels, plain sleeve with photocopied insert) 10
80	Temporary TEMP 2	WELTSCHMERZ A GO-GO! (EP, white label) 8

23RD TURNOFF
67	Deram DM 150	Michael Angelo/Leave Me Here 50

(see also Kirkbys, Jimmy Campbell, Rockin' Horse)

23 SKIDOO
81	Pineapple PULP 23	Ethics/Another Baby's Face (p/s) 8
81	Fetish FE 10	Last Words/Version (promo only) 12
81	Fetish FE 11	The Gospel Comes To New Guinea/Last Words (12", p/s) 10
82	Fetish FP 20	Tearing Up The Plans/Just Like Everybody/Gregouka (12", p/s) 10
85	Illuminated ILL 2812	Coup/Version (In The Palace) (12", p/s) 8
82	Fetish FM 2008	SEVEN SONGS (mini-LP) 12

(see also Current 93)

22:20S
90s	own label 2201	Such A Fool/Baby, You're Not In Love (1,000 only, die-cut sleeve) 15

TWICE AS MUCH
66	Immediate IM 033	Sittin' On A Fence/Baby I Want You 15
66	Immediate IM 036	Step Out Of Line/Simplified 12
66	Immediate IM 039	True Story/You're So Good 18
67	Immediate IM 042	Crystal Ball/Why Don't They All Go Away And Leave Me Alone 18
66	Immediate IMLP/IMSP 007	OWN UP (LP) 35
69	Immediate IMCP 013	THAT'S ALL (LP) 35

TWIGGY
67	Ember EMB S 239	Beautiful Dreams/I Need Your Hand In Mine (some in p/s) 25/15
67	Ember EMB S 244	When I Think Of You/Over And Over (some in p/s) 25/15
71	Bell BLL 1158	Zoo Do Zoo Song/Little Pleasure Acre (as Twiggy & Friends) 5
72	Columbia DB 8853	A Room In Bloomsbury (with Chistopher Gable)/You Are My Lucky Star/ All I Do Is Dream 5
76	Mercury 6007 100	Here I Go Again/In Love Together (p/s) 5
78	Mercury 6007 175	Falling Angel/Virginia 5
72	Ember SE 8012	TWIGGY & THE GIRLFRIENDS (LP) 22
72	Columbia SCXA 9251	THE BOYFRIEND (LP, soundtrack, with Christopher Plummer) 15

TWIGGY & ANNIE
66	Columbia DB 7799	Some Do, Some Don't/With Open Arms 6

TWILIGHTS (Australia)
66	Columbia DB 8065	Needle In A Haystack/I Don't Know Where The Wind Will Blow Me 20
67	Columbia DB 8125	What's Wrong With The Way I Live/It's Dark 15
68	Columbia DB 8396	Cathy, Come Home/The Way They Play 18

TWILIGHTS (U.S.)
65	London HLU 9992	Take What I Got/She's There 18

TWILIGHT ZONERZ
79	ZIP/Dining Out ZERO ZERO 1	ZERO ZERO ONE (EP, various silk-screened in red & hand-coloured p/s, signed & numbered) 15
80	ZIP/Dining Out ZIP 002	Brighton Rock/Diversion (p/s) 6

(see also Occult Chemistry)

TWINK (& FAIRIES)
78	Chiswick SWT 26	Do It '77/Psychedelic Punkeroo/Enter The Diamonds (12", p/s, with Fairies) 12
86	Twink TWK 2	SPACE LOVER (EP) 12
90	Twink 12TWK 5	PSYCHEDELIC PUNKEROO (12" EP) 8
70	Polydor 2343 032	THINK PINK (LP, with some insert) 120/80
70	Polydor 2343 032	THINK PINK (LP, red vinyl with insert) 300
90	Twink TWKLP 1	MR RAINBOW (LP) 12
91	Twink LP 2	ODDS & BEGINNINGS (LP, with insert, numbered & signed, some on red vinyl, 1,500 only) 10/15

(see also Pretty Things, Pink Fairies, Fairies, Tomorrow, Aquarian Age, Rings, Mick Farren, Magic Muscle)

TWINKLE (Ripley)
64	Decca F 12013	Terry/The Boy Of My Dreams 6
65	Decca F 12076	Golden Lights/Ain't Nobody Home But Me 10
65	Decca F 12139	Tommy/So Sad 10
65	Decca F 12219	Poor Old Johnny/I Need Your Hand In Mine 10
65	Decca F 12305	The End Of The World/Take Me To The Dance 10
66	Decca F 12464	What Am I Doing Here With You?/Now I Have You 12
69	Instant IN 005	Micky/Darby And Joan 10
74	Bradleys BRAD 7418	Days/Caroline (as Twinkle Ripley) 7
82	EMI 5278	I'm A Believer/For Sale (p/s) 5
65	Decca DFE 8621	TWINKLE — A LONELY SINGING DOLL (EP) . . . . 60+

(see also Bill & Coo, Silkie Davis)

TWINKLE & HOT ROD ALL STARS
70	Torpedo TOR 3	Jook Jook/Graduate 5

TWINKLE BROTHERS

70	Jackpot JP 731	Shu Be Du/All My Enemies Beware	8
70	Jackpot JP 740	Miss World/Take What You've Got	8
70	Jackpot JP 741	Sweet Young Thing/Grandma	8
71	Jackpot JP 768	Do Your Own Thing/BOY WONDER: They Talk About Love	8
71	Green Door GD 4007	Miss Labba Labba/The Best Is Yet To Come	10
71	Big Shot BI 593	You Took Me By Suprise/You Took Me By Surprise — Version (both sides actually by Tony Brevitt)	12
71	Big Shot BI 600	It's Not Who You Know/I Need Someone	8
71	Tropical AL 002	Love Sweet Love/HERON ATTAR: Poor Man's Life	5
72	Sioux SI 003	Happy Song/Little Caesar	5
73	Camel CA 106	Room Full All Full/Version	7
73	Magnet MG 033	Mother And Wife/Version	5
73	Pama PM 876	Push It Inna/Village Ram	7
75	Faith FA 007	Friends/No Big Thing	5
75	Faith FA 022	Mother And Wife/GENE RONDO: Impossible Dream	6
75	Grounation GROL 506	RASTA PON TOP (LP)	35
78	Front Line FCL 5001	LOVE (10" LP)	12

(see also Busty Brown, Sammy Jones)

TWINS

73	Downtown DT 511	Rastafari Ruler/TYRONE TAYLOR: Yesterday	8

TWINSET

67	Decca F 12629	Tremblin'/Sneakin' Up On You	15

TWIN-TONES

58	RCA RCA 1040	Jo Ann/Before You Go (78 rpm = £25)	55

TWIN TUNES QUINTET

58	RCA RCA 1046	The Love Nest/Baby Lover (78 rpm = £10)	18

TWIST

79	Polydor 2059 156	This Is Your Life/Life's A Commercial Break (p/s)	10
79	Polydor POSP 84	Ads/Rebound	10
79	Polydor 2383 552	THIS IS YOUR LIFE (LP)	20

TWIST

91	East West YZ 586	The Fat Lady Sings/Heavy Duty (p/s)	5

TWISTED ACE

81	Heavy Metal HEAVY 9	Firebird/I Won't Surrender (some in p/s)	10/5

TWISTED SISTER

82	Secret SHH 137-12	RUFF CUTS (12" EP, p/s)	12
83	Atlantic A 9827P	The Kids Are Back/Shoot 'Em Down (shaped picture disc)	8
86	Atlantic A 9478D	Leader Of The Pack/I Wanna Rock (p/s, with free single)	5
86	Atlantic A 9478P	Leader Of The Pack/I Wanna Rock (shaped picture disc)	6
85	Atlantic 781 275-1P	COME OUT AND PLAY (LP, picture disc)	12

TWISTERS

60	Capitol CL 15167	Turn The Page/Dancing Little Clown	8
62	Aral/Windsor PSA 106	Peppermint Twist Time/Silly Chilli	12+

CONWAY TWITTY

78s

57	Mercury MT 173	Shake It Up/Maybe Baby	50
58	MGM MGM 992	It's Only Make Believe/I'll Try	6
59	MGM MGM 1003	The Story Of My Love/Make Me Know You're Mine	15
59	MGM MGM 1016	Hey Little Lucy! (Don'tcha Put No Lipstick On)/When I'm Not With You	25
59	MGM MGM 1029	Mona Lisa/Heavenly	35
59	MGM MGM 1047	Rosaleena/Halfway To Heaven	50

45s

58	MGM MGM 992	It's Only Make Believe/I'll Try	10
59	MGM MGM 1003	The Story Of My Love/Make Me Know You're Mine	10
59	MGM MGM 1016	Hey Little Lucy! (Don'tcha Put No Lipstick On)/ When I'm Not With You	10
59	MGM MGM 1029	Mona Lisa/Heavenly	7
59	MGM MGM 1047	Rosaleena/Halfway To Heaven	10
60	MGM MGM 1056	Lonely Blue Boy/My One And Only You	10
60	MGM MGM 1066	What Am I Living For/The Hurt In My Heart	8
60	MGM MGM 1082	Is A Blue Bird Blue/She's Mine	10
60	MGM MGM 1095	What A Dream/Tell Me One More Time	8
60	MGM MGM 1108	Whole Lotta Shakin' Goin' On/The Flame	12
61	MGM MGM 1118	C'est Si Bon/Don't You Dare Let Me Down	8
61	MGM MGM 1129	The Next Kiss/Man Alone	8
61	MGM MGM 1137	It's Drivin' Me Wild/Sweet Sorry	10
62	MGM MGM 1152	Tower Of Tears/Portrait Of A Fool	12
62	MGM MGM 1170	Comfy An' Cozy/Unchained Melody	10
62	MGM MGM 1187	I Hope I Think I Wish/The Pick Up	12
63	MGM MGM 1201	Handy Man/Little Piece Of My Heart	12
63	MGM MGM 1209	She Ain't No Angel/Got My Mojo Workin'	12
63	HMV POP 1258	Go On And Cry/She Loves Me	8
68	MGM MGM 1404	It's Only Make Believe/Mona Lisa	5
70	MCA MU 1120	That's When She Started To Stop Loving You/I'll Get Over Losing You	5
70	MCA MU 1132	Hello Darlin'/Girl At The Bar	5
72	MCA MMU 1149	Lead Me On/One's On The Way/You're Looking At Country (with Loretta Lynn)	5
72	MCA MMU 1150	I Can't See Me Without You/I Wonder What She'll Think About Me Leaving/After The Fire Is Gone	5
72	MCA MU 1169	I Can't Stop Loving You/Since She's Not With The One She Loves	5
73	MCA MU 1223	You've Never Been This Far Before/You Make It Hard	5
75	MCA MCA 180	As Soon As I Hang Up The Phone/A Lifetime Before (with Loretta Lynn)	5

MINT VALUE £

75	MCA MCA 197	I See The Want To In Your Eyes/The Girl From Tupelo	5
75	MCA MCA 211	Don't Cry Joni/Touch The Hand	5

EPs

58	MGM MGM-EP 684	IT'S ONLY MAKE BELIEVE	65
59	MGM MGM-EP 698	HEY LITTLE LUCY	65
60	MGM MGM-EP 719	SATURDAY NIGHT WITH CONWAY TWITTY	65
60	Mercury ZEP 10069	I NEED YOUR LOVIN'	150+
60	MGM MGM-EP 738	IS A BLUEBIRD BLUE?	65
61	MGM MGM-EP 752	THE ROCK 'N' ROLL STORY	80

LPs

59	MGM MGM-C 781	CONWAY TWITTY SINGS	90
60	MGM MGM-C 801	SATURDAY NIGHT WITH CONWAY TWITTY	90
60	MGM MGM-C 829	LONELY BLUE BOY	90
63	MGM MGM-C 950	R AND B '63	70
68	MCA MUP(S) 342	HERE'S CONWAY TWITTY (AND HIS LONELY BLUE BOYS)	18
68	MGM C/CS 8100	THE ROCK AND ROLL STORY	50
69	MCA MUPS 363	NEXT IN LINE	18
69	MCA MUPS 386	DARLING, YOU KNOW I WOULDN'T LIE	12
70	MCA MUP(S) 404	I LOVE YOU MORE TODAY	12
70	MCA MUP(S) 412	TO SEE MY ANGEL CRY	12
71	MCA MUPS 426	FIFTEEN YEARS AGO	12
71	MCA MUPS 429	WE ONLY MAKE BELIEVE (with Loretta Lynn)	12
72	MCA MUPS 443	I WONDER WHAT SHE'LL THINK ABOUT ME LEAVING	12
74	MCA MCF 2547	LOUISANA WOMAN/MISSISSIPPI MAN (with Loretta Lynn)	12
74	MCA MCF 2557	YOU'VE NEVER BEEN THIS FAR BEFORE	12

(see also Loretta Lynn)

TWO & A HALF

66	CBS 202248	Midnight Swim/Faith	10
66	CBS 202404	Questions/In Harmony	8
67	CBS 202526	The Walls Are High/Love You	8
67	Decca F 22672	Suburban Early Morning Station/Just Couldn't Believe My Ears	15
67	Decca F 22715	I Don't Need To Tell You/Christmas Will Be Round Again	18

TWO FOR THE ROAD

70s	Pastiche BJ 2929	TWO FOR THE ROAD (LP)	20

TWO KINGS

65	Island WI 240	Rolling Stone/SUFFERER: Tomorrow Morning (B-side act. by Frank Cosmo)	18
65	Island WI 249	Hit You Let You Feel It/Honey I Love You (both sides actually by Fugitives)	18

TWO MAN SOUND

78	Miracle M12	Que Tal America/Brazil O Brazil (12")	8

TWO MUCH

67	Fontana TF 858	Wonderland Of Love/Mister Money	7
68	Fontana TF 900	It's A Hip Hip Hippy World/Stay In My World	10

TWO-NINETEEN (2.19) SKIFFLE GROUP

57	Esquire 10-497	Freight Train Blues/Railroad Bill (78)	15
57	Esquire 10-502	I'm A-Lookin' For A Home/When The Saints Go Marching In (78)	15
57	Esquire 10-509	In The Valley/Tom Dooley (78)	15
57	Esquire 10-512	Where Can I Go?/Roll The Union On (78)	20
57	Esquire 10-515	This Little Light Of Mine/Union Maid (78)	20
57	Esquire EP 126	TWO-NINETEEN SKIFFLE GROUP (EP)	40
57	Esquire EP 146	TWO-NINETEEN SKIFFLE GROUP (EP)	55
58	Esquire EP 176	TWO-NINETEEN SKIFFLE GROUP (EP)	55
58	Esquire EP 196	TWO-NINETEEN SKIFFLE GROUP (EP)	60

TWO OF CLUBS

64	Columbia DB 7371	The Angels Must Have Made You/True Love Is Here	20

TWO OF EACH

67	Decca F 12626	Every Single Day/I'm Glad I Got You	8
68	Pye 7N 17555	The Summer Of Our Love/Saturday Morning	7

2.3

78	Fast Products FAST 2	Where To Now?/All Time Low (p/s)	15

2 THE TOP

89	Rhyme & Reason 12RNR2	The Rhythm I Give Em (12")	18
90	President PT12590	Score To Settle/The Matter At Hand (12")	20

TWO PEOPLE

86	Polydor	Mouth Of An Angel (p/s)	20
80s	Polydor	This Is The Shirt (p/s)	10

TWO SPARKS

72	Moodisc HM 113	Run Away Girl/When We Were Young	8

(see also Carl Bryan, Winston Wright)

TWO TIMES DEF

92	White(Mendoza)MEN016	First And Last (12")	60

TY

98	Wayward W0002	I.A.A.D. (EP)	12

ARLYNE TYE

59	London HLL 8825	The Universe/Who Is The One (78 rpm = £20)	25

TYGERS OF PAN TANG

79	Neat NEAT 03	Don't Touch Me There/Burning Up/Bad Times (p/s)	12
80	MCA MCA 582	Don't Touch Me There/Burning Up/Bad Times (p/s, reissue)	10
80	MCA MCA 612	Rock'n'Roll Man/All Right On The Night/Wild Man (p/s)	5
80	MCA MCA 634	Suzie Smiled/Tush (p/s)	5
80	MCA MCA 644	Euthanasia/Straight As A Die (p/s)	5
81	MCA MCA 672	Hellbound/Bad Times//Bad Times/Don't Take Nothin' ('The Audition Tapes' double pack)	6
81	MCA MCA 692	The Story So Far/Silver And Gold/All Or Nothing (p/s)	5
81	MCA MCA 723	Don't Stop By/Slave To Freedom (p/s)	5
81	MCA MCAT 723	Don't Stop By/Slave To Freedom (12", p/s)	12
81	MCA MCA 755	Love Don't Stay/Paradise Drive (p/s)	8
81	MCA MCA 759	Do It Good/Slip Away (no p/s)	30
81	MCA MCA 769	Love Potion No. 9/The Stormlands (p/s)	5
81	MCA MCAP 769	Love Potion No. 9/The Stormlands (picture disc)	5
82	MCA MCA 777	Rendezvous/Life Of Crime (white vinyl, p/s)	6
82	MCA MCA 777	Rendezvous/Life Of Crime (red or blue vinyl, p/s)	5
82	MCA MCA 777	Rendezvous/Life Of Crime (p/s or poster p/s)	4/5
82	MCA MCA 790	Paris By Air/Love's A Lie (poster p/s or standard p/s with earring)	5/10
82	MCA MCA 798	Making Tracks/What You Saying (p/s)	5
82	MCA MCAT 798	Making Tracks (Extended Remix)/What You Saying (12", p/s)	10
80	MCA MCF 3075	WILD CAT (LP, with lyric insert)	12
81	MCA MCF 3104	SPELLBOUND (LP, with poster)	12
81	MCA MCF 3123	CRAZY NIGHTS (LP, stickered sleeve, insert, initially with bonus 12")	22/12
85	MFN MFN 50	THE WRECK AGE (LP, lyric sleeve)	12
86	Neat 1037	FIRST KILL (LP, with inner)	12
	(see also John Sykes)		

TYLA GANG

76	Stiff BUY 4	Styrofoam/Texas Chainsaw Massacre Boogie (die-cut printed sleeve)	5
78	Beserkley BSERK 16	MOONPROOF (LP, yellow vinyl, with insert)	12
	(see also Ducks Deluxe)		

BIG 'T' TYLER

57	Vogue V 9079	King Kong/Sadie Green (78 rpm = £70)	200+

JIMMY TYLER & HIS ORCHESTRA

56	Parlophone MSP 6215	Fool 'Em Devil/Stardust	18

(Alvin) RED TYLER & GYROS

60	Top Rank JAR 306	Junk Village/Happy Sax	15

TERRY TYLER

61	Pye International 7N 25119	A Thousand Feet Below/Answer Me	10

TOBY TYLER

64	Emidisc no cat. no.	The Road I'm On (Gloria)/Blowin' In The Wind (acetate, 1 copy only)	3000
64	Emidisc no cat. no.	The Road I'm On (Gloria) (acetate 1 copy only)	1750
89	Archive Jive TOBY 1	The Road I'm On (Gloria) (mail-order issue, numbered p/s, 1-sided, 1,500 only)	15
93	Zinc Alloy ZAR CDS 9005	Blowin' In The Wind/The Road I'm On (Gloria)/Blowin' In The Wind (Take No. 6) (CD)	10
93	Zinc Alloy ZAR CD 9006	THE MAXIMUM SOUND SESSION (CD)	22
	(see also Marc Bolan)		

T. TEXAS TYLER

59	Parlophone GEP 8788	COUNTRY ROUND-UP (EP)	30
67	London HA-B 8322	MAN WITH A MILLION FRIENDS (LP)	25

TYMES

63	Cameo Parkway P 871	So Much In Love/Roscoe James McClain	15
63	Cameo Parkway P 884	Wonderful Wonderful/Come With Me To The Sea (some in p/s)	25/15
64	Cameo Parkway P 891	Somewhere/View From My Window	15
64	Cameo Parkway P 908	To Each His Own/Wonderland Of Love	15
64	Cameo Parkway P 919	The Magic Of Our Summer Love/With All My Heart	15
64	Cameo Parkway P 924	Here She Comes/Malibu (DJ copy = £200)	120
69	Direction 58-3903	People/The Love of Ivy	6
69	Direction 58-4450	If You Love Me Baby/Find My Way	10
71	CBS 7250	Someone To Watch Over Me/She's Gone (featuring George Williams)	6
63	Cameo Parkway P 7032	SO MUCH IN LOVE (LP)	70
69	Direction 8-63558	PEOPLE (LP, mono or stereo)	25
78	London HAU 8516	CAMEO PARKWAY SESSIONS (LP)	25

ROB TYNER & HOT RODS

77	Island WIP 6418	'Till The Night Is Gone (Let's Rock)/Flipside Rock (p/s)	5
	(see also MC 5, Eddie & Hot Rods)		

TYPHOONS

63	Embassy WB 589	Surf City/I Want To Stay Here	10
65	Embassy WB 677	Tired Of Waiting For You/Baby Please Don't Go	10
65	Embassy WT 1115	Hard Day's Night/And I Love Her/I Should Have Known Better/ Tell Me Why (EP)	15
65	Embassy WT 2006	Ticket To Ride/Here Comes The Night/I'll Be There/I Can't Explain (EP)	20
	(see also Bud Ashton, Ray Pilgrim, Mike Redway, Starlings)		

TYPHOONS

81	Bohemian BO 1	Telstar/In Fae A Brothin' (p/s)	5
	(see also Ruts)		

TYRANNOSAURUS REX

68	Regal Zonophone RZ 3008	Debora/Child Star (with promo only p/s, some with insert)	400/450
68	Regal Zonophone RZ 3008	Debora/Child Star (demo copy as above, but without promo only p/s)	120
68	Regal Zonophone RZ 3008	Debora/Child Star	35
68	Regal Zonophone RZ 3011	One Inch Rock/Salamanda Palaganda (promo only p/s, some with insert)	375/425
68	Regal Zonophone RZ 3011	One Inch Rock/Salamanda Palaganda	40
69	Regal Zonophone RZ 3016	Pewter Suitor/Warlord Of The Royal Crocodiles	90
69	Regal Zonophone RZ 3022	King Of The Rumbling Spires/Do You Remember (with promo only p/s)	450
69	Regal Zonophone RZ 3022	King Of The Rumbling Spires/Do You Remember (demo, without promo only p/s)	120
69	Regal Zonophone RZ 3022	King Of The Rumbling Spires/Do You Remember	45
70	Regal Zonophone RZ 3025	By The Light Of A Magical Moon/Find A Little Wood	45
72	Magni Fly ECHO 102	Debora/One Inch Rock/The Woodland Bop/The Seal Of Seasons (p/s)	5
82	Old Gold OG 9234	Debora/One Inch Rock (1,000 mispressed with "Beltane Walk" on B-side)	5
91	Tyrannosaurus Rex TYR 1	Sleepy Maurice/1968 Radio Promos (Tyrannosaurus Rex Appreciation Society release, 2,000 only, p/s with card insert)	8
68	Regal Zonophone LRZ 1003	MY PEOPLE WERE FAIR AND HAD SKY IN THEIR HAIR BUT NOW THEY'RE CONTENT TO WEAR STARS ON THEIR BROWS (LP, mono, with lyric sheet & manuscript)	85/45
68	Regal Zonophone SLRZ 1003	MY PEOPLE WERE FAIR AND HAD SKY IN THEIR HAIR BUT NOW THEY'RE CONTENT TO WEAR STARS ON THEIR BROWS (LP, stereo, with lyric sheet & manuscript)	40/20
68	Regal Zonophone TA-LRZ 1003	MY PEOPLE WERE FAIR AND HAD SKY IN THEIR HAIR BUT NOW THEY'RE CONTENT TO WEAR STARS ON THEIR BROWS (reel-to-reel tape, mono)	35
68	Regal Zonophone (S)LRZ 1005	PROPHETS, SEERS AND SAGES, THE ANGELS OF THE AGES (LP, with lyric sheet, textured sleeve, mono/stereo)	65/35
69	R. Zonophone (S)LRZ 1007	UNICORN (LP, gatefold sleeve, original with blue label; mono/stereo)	85/50
70	R. Zonophone (S)LRZ 1007	UNICORN (LP, gatefold sleeve, later issue with red label; mono/stereo)	60/30
70	R. Zonophone SLRZ 1013	A BEARD OF STARS (LP, some with lyric sheet)	60/30

(see also Marc Bolan/T. Rex, John's Children, Dib Cochran & Earwigs, Shagrat)

LLOYD TYRELL
(see under Lloyd Terrell)

TYSONDOG

83	Neat NEAT 33	Eat The Rich/Dead Meat (p/s)	7
85	Neat NEAT 46	Shoot To Kill/Hammerhead (p/s)	6
85	Neat NEAT 4612	Shoot To Kill/Hammerhead/Changeling/Back To The Bullet (12", p/s)	15
86	Neat NEAT 56	School's Out/Don't Let The Bastards Grind You Down (p/s)	8
86	Neat NEAT 1031	CRIMES OF INSANITY (LP, with inner)	18

TYTAN

82	Kamaflage KAM 6	Blind Men And Fools/The Ballad Of Edward Case (p/s)	18
82	Kamaflage KAMA 6	Blind Men And Fools/The Ballad Of Edward Case (12", p/s)	20
85	Metal Masters METALP 105	ROUGH JUSTICE (LP)	18

JUDIE TZUKE

78	Rocket ROKN 541	For You/Sukarita	5
78	Rocket XPRES 2	For You/Sukarita (reissue, p/s)	5
79	Rocket XPRES 17	Stay With Me Till Dawn/New Friends Again (p/s)	7
85	Legacy LGY 22	I'll Be The One/Falling (p/s, with postcards)	5

(see also Tzuke & Paxo, Zookie)

TZUKE & PAXO

76	Good Earth GD 12	These Are The Laws/It's Only Fantasies	15

U BLACK

78	Hit Run HIT 621	Wicked Are To Blame/Dub (12")	20
77	Third World TWS 926	WESTBOUND THING A SWING (LP)	40

U BROWN

77	Klik KLP 9018	SATTA DREAD (LP)	30
77	Third World TWS 909	LONDON ROCK (LP)	30
78	Live & Love LALP 002	REVELATION TIME (LP)	30

UBX

80	Crazy Plane SP 002	Crazy Today/Mister Fix It (p/s)	150

U.F.O.

70	Beacon BEA 161	Shake It About/Evil	25
70	Beacon BEA 165	Come Away Melinda/Unidentified Flying Object	20
70	Beacon BEA 172	Boogie For George/Treacle People (some with postcard)	18/25
71	Beacon BEA 181	Prince Kajuku/The Coming Of Prince Kajuku	15
73	Chrysalis CHS 2024	Give Her The Gun/Sweet Little Thing (unreleased in U.K.)	
74	Chrysalis CHS 2040	Doctor Doctor/Lipstick Traces	12
75	Chrysalis CHS 2072	Shoot Shoot/Love Lost Love (unissued)	
77	Chrysalis CHS 2146	Alone Again Or/Electric Phase	10
77	Chrysalis CHS 2178	Gettin' Ready/Lights Out (unissued)	
78	Chrysalis CHS 2241	Only You Can Rock Me/Cherry/Rock Bottom (p/s, some red vinyl, with frisbee offer)	6/8

79	Chrysalis CHS 2287	Doctor Doctor (live)/On With The Action (live)/Try Me (p/s, clear or mauve vinyl) 6/10
79	Chrysalis CHS 2318	Shoot Shoot (live)/Only You Can Rock Me (live)/I'm A Loser (live) (p/s, clear vinyl) 6
79	Chrysalis CHS 2321	Shoot Shoot (Edit)/Only You Can Rock Me (Edit) (promo) 8
79	Chrysalis CHS 2399	Young Blood/Lights Out (p/s, red vinyl) 6
80	Chrysalis CHS 2454	Couldn't Get It Right/Hot 'n' Ready (live) (p/s, clear vinyl) 6
81	Chrysalis CHS 2482	Lonely Heart/Long Gone (p/s, clear vinyl with patch) 5
81	Chrysalis CHS 2576	Let It Rain/Heel Of A Stranger/You'll Get Love (p/s, clear vinyl) 5
81	Chrysalis CHS 12 2576	Let It Rain/Heel Of A Stranger/You'll Get Love (12", p/s) 8
81	Chrysalis UFO DJ 1	Call My Name (one-sided, promo only) 10
82	Chrysalis CHSP 2607	Back Into My Life/The Writer (picture disc) 7
83	Lyntone LYN 12821	Blinded By A Lie (edit)/Diesel In The Dust (edit)/When It's Time To Rock (edit) (flexidisc with/without *Metal Fury* magazine, issue 12) 15/10
83	Chrysalis CHS 2672	When It's Time To Rock/Everybody Knows (p/s, with patch) 5
83	Chrysalis CHSP 2672	When It's Time To Rock/Everybody Knows/Push It's Love (picture disc) 6
85	Chrysalis UFOP 1	This Time/The Chase (shaped picture disc) 8
92	Essential ESS T 2009	One Of Those Nights/Ain't Life Sweet/Long Gone (1991 Version) (12", p/s) 10
92	Essential ESS X 2009	One Of Those Nights/She's The One/Long Gone (1991 Version) (CD) 12
70	Beacon BEAS 12	U.F.O. 1 (LP) 30
72	Beacon BEAS 19	U.F.O. 2 — FLYING (ONE HOUR SPACE ROCK) (LP, some with inner lyric sleeve) 22/30
74	Chrysalis CHS 1059	PHENOMENON (LP, misprinted green label, matt sleeve, also on cassette) 18
77	Chrysalis CHR 1127	LIGHTS OUT (LP) 14
78	Chrysalis CDL 1182	OBSESSION (LP, with poster) 18
80	Chrysalis CDL 1239	NO PLACE TO RUN (LP, in six sleeve variations: green, blue, yellow, purple, turquoise, black) (value for separate albums £7.50 each) .... set 55
82	Chrysalis CHR 1360	MECHANIX (LP, with poster) 12
82	AKP 2	LIVE IN JAPAN 1971 (LP, picture disc) 12
92	Essential ESS LP 178	HIGH STAKES AND DANGEROUS MEN (LP) 12
97	Zoom Club ZCR CD 1	ON WITH THE ACTION — THE ROUNDHOUSE LIVE, 1976 (CD, in tin with bonus track) 18

(see also Michael Schenker Group)

LESLIE UGGAMS
58	Columbia DB 4160	The Ice Cream Man/I'm Old Enough 5
59	Philips PB 954	One More Sunrise (Morgen)/The Eyes Of God 5
59	Philips PB 999	The Carefree Years/Lullaby Of The Leaves 5
60	Philips PB 1063	Inherit The Wind/Love Is Like A Violin 5
61	Philips PB 1124	Sixteen Going On Seventeen/My Favourite Things 5
60	Philips BBL 7370	THE EYES OF GOD (LP) 12

UGLY CUSTARD
70	Kaleidoscope KAL 100	UGLY CUSTARD (LP) 60

(see also Hungry Wolf, Alan Parker, Rock Machine)

UGLYS
65	Pye 7N 15858	Wake Up My Mind/Ugly Blues 50
65	Pye 7N 15968	It's Alright/A Friend 30
66	Pye 7N 17027	A Good Idea/A Quiet Explosion 50
66	Pye 7N 17178	End Of The Season/Can't Recall Her Name 50
67	CBS 2933	And The Squire Blew His Horn/Real Good Girl 50
69	MGM MGM 1465	I See The Light/Mary Cilento (6 demo copies only, pink/silver labels) ...... 1500+

(see also Steve Gibbons, Balls, Lemon Tree, Move, Trevor Burton)

UK
88	Chain Reaction	UK (LP) 12

(see also Business, Tank)

U.K. BONDS
65	Polydor BM 56061	The World Is Watching Us/I Said Goodbye To The Blues 7
66	Polydor BM 56112	Anything You Do Is Alright/The Last Thing I Ever Do 18

U.K. DECAY
79	Plastic PLAS 001	U.K. Decay/Car Crash/PNEUMONIA: Exhibition/Coming Attack (folded p/s) ... 18
81	Plastic PLAS 002	BLACK EP (p/s, reissue has slightly different p/s) 6/5
81	Fresh FRESH 26	Unexpected Guest/Dresden (foldout p/s) 6
81	Fresh FRESH 33	Sexual/Twist In The Tale (poster p/s) 5
82	C. Christi CHRIST ITS 1	Rising From The Dread/Testament/Werewolf/Jerusalem Over (The White Cliffs Of Dover) (12", p/s with insert) 8

(see also Pneumonia)

U.K.s
64	HMV POP 1310	Ever Faithful, Ever True/Your Love Is All I Want 20
64	HMV POP 1357	I Will Never Let You Go/I Know 20

U.K. SUBS
78	City NIK 5	C.I.D./Live In A Car/B.I.C. (p/s, clear, red, blue, green or orange vinyl; also black vinyl) 7/5
79	Gem GEMS 5	Stranglehold/World War/Rockers (p/s, red vinyl) 5
79	Gem GEMS 10	Tomorrow's Girls/Scum Of The Earth/Telephone Numbers (p/s, blue vinyl) 6
79	Gem GEMS 14	She's Not There/Kicks/Victims/The Same Thing (p/s, green vinyl) 5
80	Gem GEMS 30	Teenage/Left For Dead/New York State Police (p/s, pink or orange vinyl) 4/5
82	Ramkup CAC 2	Party In Paris (1-sided fan club single, no p/s, 500 only) 25
83	Fall Out FALL 017	Another Typical City (p/s) 5
83	Fall Out FALL 12017	Another Typical City (12" p/s) 8
81	Gem GEMEP 45	KEEP RUNNIN' EP (Keep Runnin' [Till You Burn]/Ice Age/ Perfect Girl/Party In Paris [French Version]) 8
82	Abstract ABS 012	SHAKE UP THE CITY (EP, red vinyl) 7

84	Gem FALL 12024	SPELL EP (12")	10
79	Gem GEMLP 100	ANOTHER KIND OF BLUES (LP, blue vinyl, with inner sleeve)	12
80	Gem GEMLP 106	BRAND NEW AGE (LP, clear vinyl, with insert)	12
80	Gem GEMLP 111	CRASH COURSE LIVE (LP, purple vinyl, 15,000 w/export 12" [GEMEP 1])	15/10
81	Gem GEMLP 112	DIMINISHED RESPONSIBILITY (LP, red vinyl with inner sleeve)	12
82	Abstract AABT 300	RECORDED '79-'81 (LP, blue vinyl with free stencil)	12
83	Scarlett FALLLP 018	FLOOD OF LIES (LP)	12

(see also Urban Dogs)

ANYAOGU UKONU & HIS AFRO-CALYPSOIANS
56	London HA-U 2019	AFRO U.S.A (LP)	30

JAMES 'BLOOD' ULMER
81	Rough Trade RT 045	Are You Glad To Be In America?/T.V. Blues (p/s)	5

ULTERIOR MOTIVES
79	Motive Music MMR 1	Another Lover (p/s)	30

ULTIMATE SPINACH
68	MGM MGM-C(S) 8071	ULTIMATE SPINACH (LP)	55
68	MGM MGM-C(S) 8094	BEHOLD AND SEE (LP)	65

ULTRA HIGH FREQUENCY
74	Pye International 7N 25628	We're On The Right Track/We're On The Right Track (version)	15

ULTRAFUNK
74	Contempo CS 2001	Living In The City/Who Is He And What Is He To You	6
74	Contempo CS 2023	Freddy Mack/Kung Fu Man	6
75	Contempo CS 2020	Sweet F.A./Use Me	7
76	Contempo CX 14	Gotham City Boogie/Sunrise	7
76	Contempo CX 14	Gotham City Boogie/Sunrise (12")	8
77	Contempo CS 2071	Sting Your Jaws (Parts 1 & 2)	5
75	Contempo CLP 509	ULTRAFUNK (LP)	25

ULTRA VIOLENT
83	Riot City RIOT 25	CRIME FOR REVENGE (EP)	5

ULTRA VIVID SCENE
89	4AD BAD 906	Mercy Seat/Codeine/H Like In Heaven/Mercy Seat (LP Version) (12", uncut p/s [most copies die-cut])	22
89	4AD AD 908	Something To Eat/H Like In Heaven (freebie, 1,000 only)	10
90	4AD AD 0016	Special One/Kind Of Drag	7
90	4AD UVS 1	Staring At The Sun/Three Stars (12", promo only)	10
92	4AD UVS 2	Medicating Angels/Mirror To Mirror (12", promo only)	10

ULTRAVOX
77	Island WIP 6375	Dangerous Rhythm/My Sex (initially no p/s, later with p/s)	5/8
77	Island WIP 6392	Young Savage/Slip Away (p/s)	10
77	Island WIP 6404	Rockwrock/Hiroshima Mon Amour (p/s)	5
77	Island IEP 8	RETRO (EP, 33rpm)	6
78	Island WIP 6454	Slow Motion/Dislocation (p/s)	5
78	Island 12WIP 6454	Slow Motion/Dislocation (12", p/s, translucent vinyl)	8
78	Island WIP 6459	Quiet Men/Cross Fade (p/s)	7
78	Island 12WIP 6459	Quiet Men/Cross Fade (12", p/s, white vinyl)	8
80	Chrysalis CHS 2441	Sleepwalk/Waiting (p/s, clear vinyl)	6
80	Chrysalis CHS 2481	Vienna/Passionate Reply (p/s, clear vinyl)	6
80	Chrysalis CHS 2457	Passing Strangers/Face To Face (p/s, clear vinyl)	5
81	Fan Club	The Voice (live)	5
86	Chrysalis UV 5	All Fall Down/Dreams (p/s, with free single)	5
77	Island ILPS 9449	ULTRAVOX (LP, gatefold sleeve)	12
77	Island ILPS 9505	HA! HA! HA! (LP, with 7" Quirks/Modern Love [WIP 6417] & inner sleeve)	12
82	Chrysalis PCDL 1394	QUARTET (LP, marbled picture disc)	12

(see also Tiger Lily, John Foxx, Midge Ure, Helden)

UMPS & DUMPS
80	Topic 12TS 416	THE MOON'S IN A FIT (LP)	15

UNANIMOUS DECISION
91	Kold Sweat KS109	Make A Living (12")	8
92	Kold Sweat KSEP211	RAP SINGS THE BLUES (EP)	14
93	Kold Sweat KSMEP 301X	IT AIN'T CLEVER (DOUBLE PACK EP)	8

UNCLE DOG
72	Signpost SG 4253	OLD HAT (LP)	40+

(see also Carol Grimes)

UNCOMMUNITY
85	Black Dwarf BDBG 1	Brutality Of Fact/Wall Of Sleep (Soundtrack)/The Price Of Your Entry Is Sin (card sleeve, 525 only, numbered, hand-painted labels, with insert)	25

(see also McCarthy)

UNCOOL DANCEBAND
79	Polydor PB 30	Let Me Be Your Boyfriend/Heads I Win (no p/s)	100
81	Polydor POSP 253	Jacqueline/No. 17 (no p/s)	20

UNDEAD
82	Riot City RIOT 7	It's Corruption/Undead (p/s)	7
82	Riot City RIOT 15	VIOLENT VISIONS (EP)	6
84	City 006	KILLING OF REALITY (LP, lyric insert)	25

UNDERDOGS
83	Riot City RIOT 26	EAST OF DACHAU (EP)	10

UNDERGROUND
69	Major Minor SMCP 5014	BEAT PARTY (LP)	25

(see also Madeline Bell)

UNDERGROUNDS
72	High Note HS 061	Skavito/Savito	12

UNDERGROUND SET
70	Pantonic PAN 6302	UNDERGROUND SET (LP)	40+

UNDERGROUND SUNSHINE
69	Fontana TF 1049	Birthday/All I Want Is You	10

UNDERGROUND WITH STYLE
92	UAR UAR001	Lyrics Of A Gangster/Unbound Rage/Words Of Reality (EP)	25

UNDERNEATH
86	él GPO 17	THE IMP OF THE PERVERSE (EP)	6
86	él GPO 17T	THE IMP OF THE PERVERSE (12" EP)	8
86	él ACME 9	LUNATIC DAWN OF THE DISMANTLER (LP)	12

(see also Karl Blake, Shock Headed Peters, Lemon Kittens)

UNDERTAKERS
63	Pye 7N 15543	Everybody Loves A Lover/Mashed Potatoes	20
63	Pye 7N 15562	What About Us/Money	20
64	Pye 7N 15607	Just A Little Bit/Stupidity	20

(see also 'Takers, Jackie Lomax)

UNDER THE SUN
79	Redball RR 010	UNDER THE SUN (LP)	60

UNDERTONES
78	Good Vibrations GOT 4	TEENAGE KICKS (EP, white poster p/s; apparently pink later)	50/70+
78	Sire SIR 4007	TEENAGE KICKS (EP, reissue)	7
79	Sire SIR 4015	Jimmy Jimmy/Mars Bars (green vinyl, printed PVC sleeve & insert; also p/s)	5/4
79	Sire SIR 4022	Here Comes The Summer/One Way Love/Top Twenty (p/s)	5
79	Sire SIR 4024	You've Got My Number (Why Don't You Use It!)/Let's Talk About Girls (p/s)	5
79	no label	CRACKS 90 MANAGEMENT EP: Teenage Kicks/Get Over You/Jimmy Jimmy/ Here Comes The Summer (promo-only, numbered with typed insert, 250 only)	60
80	Sire SIR 4038	My Perfect Cousin/Hard Luck (Again) (p/s)	5
81	Ardeck 12 ARDS 6	My Perfect Cousin/Hard Luck (Again)/Don't Wanna See (You Again) (12", p/s)	8
81	Ardeck ARDS 9	Julie Ocean/Kiss In The Dark (p/s)	5
83	Ardeck ARDS 11	The Love Parade/Like That (p/s)	5
83	Ardeck 12 ARDS 11	The Love Parade/Like That/You're Welcome/Crises Of Mine/ Family Entertainment (12", p/s)	10
83	Ardeck ARDS 12	Got To Have You Back/Turning Blue (p/s)	8
83	Ardeck ARDS 13	Chains Of Love/Window Shopping For New Clothes (p/s)	10
94	Dojo TONES 1	TEENAGE KICKS (EP, 2nd reissue, green vinyl, no'd poster p/s, 2,000 only)	6
79	Sire SRK 6071	UNDERTONES (LP, black & white cover, without "Teenage Kicks" & "Get Over You" & different version of "Here Comes The Summer" to reissue)	12
80	Sire SRK 6088	HYPNOTISED (LP, with cardboard mobile)	12
83	Ardeck ARD 104	THE SIN OF PRIDE (LP, mispressing with different tracks: "Bittersweet" & "Stand So Close")	40
94	Dojo DOJOLP 192	HYPNOTISED (10" LP, numbered, 500 only)	12
94	Dojo DOJOLP 193	POSITIVE TOUCH (10" LP, numbered, 500 only)	12
94	Dojo DOJOLP 194	THE SIN OF PRIDE (10" LP, numbered, 500 only)	12

(see also Feargal Sharkey, That Petrol Emotion)

UNDERWORLD
92	Tomato PLUM 2001	Mother Earth/Mother Earth (FM Mix)/The Hump/ The Hump (Groove Without A Doubt Mix) (12", p/s)	60
93	Boys Own BOIX 13	Mmm... Skyscraper I Love You/Mmm... Skyscraper I Love You (Telegraph 6.11.92)/Mmm... Skyscraper I Love You (Jam Scraper) (12", p/s)	25
93	Boys Own BOIXCD 13	Mmm... Skyscraper I Love You/Mmm... Skyscraper I Love You (Telegraph 6.11.92)/Mmm... Skyscraper I Love You (Jam Scraper) (CD)	25
93	Boys Own Collect 002	Rez/Cowgirl (12", company sleeve)	10
93	Boys Own Collect 002P	Rez/Cowgirl (12", glossy pink sleeve, pink vinyl, white label)	30
94	Junior Boys Own JB 017	Spikee/Dogman Go Woof (12", p/s)	10

(see also Lemon Interrupt)

UNDISPUTED TRUTH
71	Tamla Motown TMG 776	Save My Love For A Rainy Day/Since I Lost You	25
71	Parlophone TMG 776	Save My Love For A Rainy Day/Since I Lost You (mispress on Parlophone)	50
71	Tamla Motown TMG 789	Smiling Faces Sometimes/You Got The Love I Need	15
72	Tamla Motown TMG 818	Superstar/Ain't No Sun Since You've Been Gone	10
74	Tamla Motown TMG 897	Help Yourself/What It Is	8
76	Warner Bros K 16804	You + Me = Love Parts 1 & 2	8
76	Warner Bros K 16804	You + Me = Love Parts 1 & 2 (12")	15
72	T. Motown STMA 8004	FACE TO FACE WITH THE TRUTH (LP)	25
72	T. Motown STML 11197	THE UNDISPUTED TRUTH (LP)	25
73	T. Motown STML 11240	THE LAW OF THE LAND (LP)	20
75	T. Motown STML 11277	DOWN TO EARTH (LP)	20
75	T. Motown STMA 8023	COSMIC TRUTH (LP)	20
75	T. Motown STML 12009	HIGHER THAN HIGH (LP)	20

UNDIVIDED ATTENTION
99	Hairy Parents no matrix	A Change To The Scheduled Programme/Missed Treatment (12")	15

UNEXPLORED BEATS
95	Unexplored Beats UXB 001	Skool Beats/Inner Life (12")	30

(see also Black Dog)

UNICORN
70	Hollick & Taylor HT 1258	Going Home/Another World	30

UNICORN
71	Transatlantic BIG 138	P.F. Sloan/Going Back Home	6
72	Transatlantic BIG 509	Cosmic Kid/All We Really Want To Do	6
71	Transatlantic TRA 238	UPHILL ALL THE WAY (LP)	18
74	Charisma CAS 1092	BLUE PINE TREES (LP)	12

UNIFICS
68	London HLR 10231	Court Of Love/Which One Should I Choose	12

UNION GAP
(see under Gary Puckett & Union Gap)

UNIQUES
80	Charly CTD 121	You Don't Miss Your Water/It's All Over Now/All These Things	5

UNIQUES (featuring Joe Stampley) (U.S)
65	Pye International 7N 25303	Not Too Long Ago/Fast Way Of Living (DJ copy = £130)	85
66	Pye Intl. NPL 28094	UNIQUELY YOURS (LP)	110

UNIQUES (Jamaica)
67	Collins Downbeat CR 002	Dry The Water/I'm A Fool For You	40
67	Island WI 3070	People Rock Steady/I'm Trying To Find A Home (credited to Roy Shirley)	40
67	Island WI 3084	Gypsy Woman/KEN ROSS: Wall Flower	22
67	Island WI 3086	Let Me Go Girl/SOULETTES: Dum Dum	25
68	Island WI 3087	Never Let Me Go/HENRY III: Won't Go Away	22
68	Island WI 3106	Speak No Evil/GLAN ADAMS: That New Girl	25
68	Island WI 3107	Lesson Of Love/DELROY WILSON: Til I Die	22
68	Island WI 3114	Build My World Around You/LLOYD CLARKE: I'll Never Change	70+
68	Island WI 3117	Give Me Some More Of Your Loving/VAL BENNETT: Lovell's Special	22
68	Island WI 3122	My Conversation/SLIM SMITH: Love One Another	25
68	Island WI 3123	The Beatitude/KEITH BLAKE: Time On The River (actually "Time & The River")	40
68	Island WI 3145	Girl Of My Dreams/LESTER STERLING: Tribute To King Scratch	70+
68	Trojan TR 619	Watch This Sound/Out Of Love	15
68	Trojan TR 645	A-Yuh/Just A Mirage	15
68	Blue Cat BS 126	Girls Like Dirt/GLEN ADAMS: She Is Leaving	15
69	Gas GAS 117	Too Proud To Beg/Love And Devotion	12
69	Nu Beat NB 034	Crimson And Clover/What A Situation	10
69	Nu Beat NB 037	I'll Make You Love Me/Lover's Prayer	30
69	Unity UN 527	The Beatitude/My Conversation	10
69	Trojan TRL 15	ABSOLUTELY THE UNIQUES (LP)	110

(see also Slim Smith, Melodians, Lloyd Charmers, Tommy McCook)

UNIQUES
72	Trojan TR 7852	Mother And Child Reunion/Corner Hop	6
72	Trojan TR 7866	Lonely For Your Love/LIONS DEN: Chick-A-Bow	6

(see also Pioneers)

UNITED SONS OF AMERICA
71	Mercury 6338 036	GREETINGS FROM THE U.S. OF A. (LP)	15

UNITED STATES DOUBLE QUARTET
67	Stateside SS 590	Life Is Groovy/Split	18+
67	BT Puppy BTS 45524	Life Is Groovy/Split (reissue)	12

(see also Tokens, Kirby Stone 4)

UNITED STATES OF AMERICA
68	CBS 3745	Garden Of Earthly Delights/Love Song For The Dead Che	20
68	CBS (S) 63340	UNITED STATES OF AMERICA (LP, mono/stereo)	40

UNITED STATES OF EXISTENCE
87	Bam Caruso OPRA 081	Gone/PAUL ROLAND: Madam Guillotine (jukebox issue, company sleeve)	5

UNIT 4 + 2
64	Decca F 11821	The Green Fields/Swing Down Chariot	15
64	Decca F 11994	Sorrow And Pain/The Lonely Valley	12
65	Decca F 12144	(You've) Never Been In Love Like This Before/Tell Somebody You Know	8
65	Decca F 12211	Hark/Stop Wasting Your Time	7
65	Decca F 12299	You've Got To Be Cruel To Be Kind/I Won't Let You Down	7
66	Decca F 12333	Baby Never Say Goodbye/Rainy Day	12
66	Decca F 12398	For A Moment/Fables	12
66	Decca F 12509	I Was Only Playing Games/I've Seen The Light	10
67	Fontana TF 834	Too Fast, Too Slow/Booby Trap	15
67	Fontana TF 840	Butterfly/A Place To Go	12
67	Fontana TF 891	Loving Takes A Little Understanding/Would You Believe What I Say? (as Unit)	25
68	Fontana TF 931	You Ain't Goin' Nowhere/So You Want To Be A Blues Player	12
69	Fontana TF 990	I Will/3.30	40
65	Decca DFE 8619	UNIT 4 + 2 (EP)	60
65	Decca LK 4697	UNIT 4 + 2 — FIRST ALBUM (LP)	65
69	Fontana SFL 13123	UNIT 4 + 2 (LP)	60

(see also Roulettes, Tom Sawyer, Capability Brown, Argent)

UNIVERSAL INDICATOR
92	Rephlex TB-303	1-BLUE (12")	25
92	Rephlex TR-606	2-RED (12")	25
93	Rephlex MC-202	3-YELLOW (12")	20
95	Rephlex SH-101	4-GREEN (7", 10" + 12" in bag, all green vinyl)	40

(see also Kosmik Kommando)

UNIVERSALS

UNIVERSALS
67	Page One POF 032	I Can't Find You/Hey You	100
67	Page One POF 049	Green Veined Orchid/While The Cat's Away	28

(see also Chris Lamb & Universals, Gidian, Lace, Gary Walker & Rain, Plastic Penny)

U.N.K.L.E.
97	Mo' Wax MW 069L	Berry Meditation (mixes) (12", clear etched vinyl promo, sealed/unsealed poly sleeve)	40/25
99	Mo' Wax MW 108CD 1	Be There/(Underdog Mixes) (CD, 1 of 2-CD set, card sleeve)	10
99	Mo' Wax MW 108CD 2	Be There/Knock/Rabbit In Your Headlights (CD, 2 of 2-CD set, card sleeve)	12
95·	Mo' Wax MW 028	THE TIME HAS COME EP (2 x 12" EP, picture disc, later black vinyl)	15/20
94	Mo' Wax MWCD 028	THE TIME HAS COME EP (CD, picture disc, stickered card sleeve)	8
98	Mo' Wax MW 085CDX	PSYENCE FICTION (CD, gatefold card sleeve)	25

(see also DJ Shadow)

UNKNOWN ARTIST
57	Woodbine Cigarettes	Big Beat (78, same track on both sides)	15
50s	Capstan Cigarettes	Capstan Go (1-sided flexi 78, promo)	15
50s	Capstan Cigarettes	Cha Cha (1-sided 78, promo)	15
50s	Strand Cigarettes	You're Never Alone With A Strand (78, p/s, same track on both sides)	35
66	Major MAJ 1	Roarin' 'N' Scorin'/The Toast Of Merseyside (p/s)	25

UNKNOWNS
66	London HLU 10082	Melody For An Unknown Girl/Peith's Song	7

UNLEASHED
03	Century Media 77544-0	...AND WE SHALL TRIUMPH IN VICTORY (Numbered box set with 6 picture disc LPs and booklet, 2000 only)	75

UNLIMITED TOUCH
83	Prelude PRL 25294	YES, WE'RE READY (LP)	12

UNTAMED
64	Decca F 12045	So Long/Just Wait	50
65	Parlophone R 5258	Once Upon A Time/I'm Asking You	95
65	Stateside SS 431	I'll Go Crazy/My Baby Is Gone	55
66	Planet PLF 103	It's Not True/Gimme Gimme Some Shade	70

(see also Lindsay Muir's Untamed)

UNTAMED YOUTH
79	Hardcore HAR 001	Untamed Youth/Runnin' Wild (p/s, 1,000 only)	15

UNTOUCHABLES
80	Fried Egg EGG 2	Keep On Walking/Keep Your Distance (p/s)	5

UNTOUCHABLES (Jamaica)
68	Blue Cat BS 137	Prisoner In Love/EDWARD RAPHAEL: True Love	30
68	Trojan TR 613	Tighten Up/ROY SHIRLEY: Good Ambition	28
70	Upsetter US 345	Same Thing All Over/UPSETTERS: It's Over	20
70	Upsetter US 350	Knock On Wood/UPSETTERS: Tight Spot	20
71	Bullet BU 460	Can't Reach You/CARL DAWKINS: Natural Woman	10
73	Bread BR 1113	Pay For The Wicked/Pay For The Wicked – Version (actually titled "Pray For The Wicked')	10

(see also Inspirations, Dave Barker, Leroy Reid)

UNWANTED
77	Raw RAW 6	Withdrawal/1978/Bleak Outlook (p/s)	35
77	Raw RAWT 6	Withdrawal/1978/Bleak Outlook (12", reissue)	20
78	Raw RAW 15	Secret Police/These Boots Are Made For Walking (p/s)	20
78	Raw RAW 30	Memory Man/Guns Of Love (unissued)	

(see also Psychedelic Furs)

STANLEY UNWIN
61	Pye NPL 18062	ROTATEY DISKERS WITH UNWIN (LP)	20

UPBEATS
58	London HLU 8688	Just Like In The Movies/My Foolish Heart (78 rpm = £12)	25
59	Pye International 7N 25016	You're The One I Care For/Keep Cool Crazy Heart (78 rpm = £6)	12
59	Pye International 7N 25028	Teenie Weenie Bikini/Satin Shoes (78 rpm = £15)	12

PHIL UPCHURCH COMBO
61	HMV POP 899	You Can't Sit Down Parts 1 & 2	30
66	Sue WI 4005	You Can't Sit Down Parts 1 & 2 (reissue)	25
66	Sue WI 4017	Nothing But Soul/Evad	40
72	Blue Thumb ILPS 9219	DARKNESS, DARKNESS (LP)	20

ROBERT UPCHURCH
74	Phil. Intl. PIR 2652	The Devil Made Me Do It/Glad You're Mine	10
70s	Phil. Intl 82168 4ZP 2000	The Devil Made Me Do It/You're The Reason Why (12")	8

UPCOMING WILLOWS
65	Island WI 182	Jonestown Special/SHENLEY DUFFAS: La La La	30
65	Island WI 184	Red China/SHENLEY DUFFAS: You Are Mine	30

(see also Shenley Duffas)

UPFRONT RUDIES
92	Krazy Fly Recz RUDIE 9	REAL SKILLS (EP)	20

UPP
75	Epic EPC 80625	UPP (LP)	15

(see also Clark-Hutchinson)

UPROAR

82	Beat The System RAW 1	Rebel Youth/No More War/Fallen Angel/Victims (p/s)	7
83	Lightbeat RAW 2	DIE FOR ME (EP)	7
83	Volume VOL 9	NOTHING CAN STOP YOU (EP)	5
80s	Beat The System BTSLP 1	AND THE LORD SAID LET THERE BE UPROAR (LP)	25

UPSETTERS

65	Island WI 223	Country Girl/Strange Country (both sides actually by Ossie & Upsetters)	32
65	Rio R 70	Walk Down The Aisle/So Bad	18
66	Doctor Bird DB 1034	Wildcat/I Love You So	25
(see also Ossie & Upsetters, Dave Barker)			

UPSETTERS

69	Duke DU 11	Eight For Eight/Stand By Me (B-side actually by Inspirations)	30
69	Camel CA 13	Taste Of Killing/My Mob	30
69	Punch PH 18	Return Of The Ugly/I've Caught You	18
69	Punch PH 19	Dry Acid/REGGAE BOYS: Selassie	40
69	Punch PH 21	Clint Eastwood/Lennox Mood	8
69	Upsetter US 300	Eight For Eight/You Know What I Mean (B-side actually by Inspirations)	15
69	Upsetter US 301	Return Of Django/Dollar In The Teeth	5
69	Upsetter US 303	Ten To Twelve/LEE PERRY: People Funny Fi True	18
69	Upsetter US 307	Night Doctor/TERMITES: I'll Be Waiting	18
69	Upsetter US 309	Kiddyo/Endlessly (both sides actually by Silvertones)	15
69	Upsetter US 310	A Dangerous Man From MI5/WEST INDIANS: Oh Lord	15
69	Upsetter US 313	Live Injection/BLEECHERS: Everything For Fun	8
69	Upsetter US 315	Cold Sweat/Pound Get A Blow (B-side actually by Bleechers)	15
70	Upsetter US 317	Vampire/BLEECHERS: Check Him Out	15
70	Upsetter US 318	Soulful I/MILTON HENRY: Bread And Butter	15
70	Upsetter US 321	Drugs And Poison/Stranger On The Shore	15
70	Upsetter US 325	Kill Them All/Soul Walk	15
70	Upsetter US 326	Bronco/One More	18
70	Upsetter US 332	Na Na Hey Hey/Pick Folk Kinkyest	20
70	Upsetter US 333	Granny Show/Version	20
70	Upsetter US 334	Fire Fire/Jumper	15
70	Upsetter US 335	The Pillow/Grooving	15
70	Upsetter US 336	Self Control/The Pill	18
70	Upsetter US 338	Fresh Up/Toothaches	15
70	Upsetter US 342	Dreamland/BOB MARLEY: Version Of Cup	45
70	Upsetter US 343	Sipreano/Ferry Boat	20
70	Upsetter US 346	Bigger Joke/Return Of The Vampire	15
70	Upsetter US 349	Upsetting Station (actually plays "Did Your Grave" by Bob Marley & Wailers)/UPSETTERS: Justice (Instrumental)	38
70	Upsetter US 352	Heart And Soul/Zig Zag	18
70	Spinning Wheel SW 100	Haunted House/Double Wheel	30
70	Spinning Wheel SW 101	The Miser/CHUCK JUNIOR: Do It Madly	25
70	Spinning Wheel SW 102	The Chokin' Kind/CHUCK JUNIOR: Penny Wise	25
70	Spinning Wheel SW 103	Land Of Kinks/O'NEIL HALL: This Man	25
70	Trojan TR 7748	Family Man/Mellow Mood	12
70	Trojan TR 7749	Capo/Mama Look	15
70	Punch PH 27	The Result/Feel The Spirit	40
71	Bullet BU 461	All Combine Parts 1 & 2	10
71	Bullet BU 499	Beat Down Babylon/JUNIOR BYLES: Version	18
71	Upsetter US 353	Illusion/Big John Wayne (as Upsetters & King Teddy)	18
71	Upsetter US 361	Capasetic (actually "Copasetic" by Lord Comic)/All Africans (actually "Don't Cross The Nation" by Little Roy)	20
71	Upsetter US 365	Earthquake/JUNIOR BYLES: Palace Called Africa	15
71	Upsetter US 370	Dark Moon/DAVID ISAACS: You'll Be Sorry	15
72	Upsetter US 385	French Connection/Version	15
72	Upsetter US 387	Festival Da Da/JUNIOR BYLES: Version	15
72	Upsetter US 393	Crummy People/BIG YOUTH: Moving — Version	15
72	Upsetter US 394	Water Pump Parts 1 & 2	15
72	Randy's RAN 523	Nebuchadnezzer/JUNIOR BYLES: King Of Babylon	10
72	Punch PH 109	Hail To Power/JUNIOR BYLES: Pharaoh Hiding	10
73	Upsetter US 396	Puss Sea Hole/WINSTON GROOVY: Want To Be Loved	15
73	Upsetter US 397	Jungle Lion/Freak Out Skank	20
73	Upsetter US 398	Cow Thief Skank (with Charlie Ace)/7 3/4 Skank	20
73	Downtown DT 499	Black Ipa/Ipa Skank	18
73	Downtown DT 506	Sunshine Showdown/Sunshine Version	18
73	Downtown DT 512	Tighten Up Skank/Mid-East Rock	15
73	Downtown DT 513	Sucky Skank/Yucky Skank	18
74	Count Shelly CS 052	San-San/OSBOURNE GRAHAM: Baby Don't Go	8
74	Dip DL 5031	Enter The Dragon/JOY WHITE: Lady Lady	12
74	Dip DL 5032	Rebels Train/Rebels Dub	8
75	Dip DL 5054	Cane River Rock/Riverside Rock	12
75	Dip DL 5056	I Man Free/King Burnett: Version	12
75	Dip DL 5073	Key Card/Domino Game	8
78	Island IPR 2010	Close Together/Dreadlocks In The Moonlight (12" as UPSETTERS REVIEW featuring JUNIOR MURVIN)	20
69	Pama Special PSP 1014	CLINT EASTWOOD (LP)	75
69	Trojan TTL 13	THE UPSETTER (LP)	15
69	Trojan TRL 19	THE RETURN OF DJANGO (LP)	20
70	Trojan TTL 28	SCRATCH THE UPSETTER AGAIN (LP)	12
70	Trojan TBL 119	THE GOOD, THE BAD AND THE UPSETTERS (LP)	30
70	Trojan TBL 125	EASTWOOD RIDES AGAIN (LP)	35
70	Pama SECO 24	THE MANY MOODS OF THE UPSETTERS (LP)	65

74	Trojan TRLS 70	DOUBLE SEVEN (LP)	35
75	DIP DLPD 6002	RETURN OF THE WAX (LP, white-label only, plain sleeve)	45
76	Island ILPS 9417	SUPER APE (LP)	15

(see also Lee Perry, Ossie & Upsetters, Hippy Boys, Bob Marley/Wailers, Family Man, Tommy McCook, Max Romeo, Melodians, Lord Creator, Dennis Alcapone)

UPSETTING BROTHERS
| 71 | Supreme SUP 229 | Not You Baby/DREAD LOCK ALL-STARS: Baby (Version) | 12 |

UPTOWNERS
| 64 | London HLU 9877 | If'n/Search Is Over | 12 |

URBAN CLEARWAY
| 70 | Torpedo TOR 21 | Open Up Wide Parts 1 & 2 | 6 |

URBAN DISTURBANCE
| 79 | Rok ROK V/VI | Wild Boys In Cortinas/V.I.P.s: Can't Let You Go (die-cut sleeve) | 25 |

URBAN DOGS
82	Fallout FALL 008	New Barbarians/Speed Kills/Cocaine (p/s)	5
82	Fallout FALL 011	Limo Life/Warhead (p/s)	5
88	Fallout FALL LP 12	URBAN DOGS (LP)	12

(see Hanoi Rocks, U.K. Subs, Vibrators)

URCHIN
| 77 | DJM DJS 10776 | Black Leather Fantasy/Rock & Roll Woman (in promo p/s) | 325 |
| 78 | DJM DJS 10850 | She's A Roller/Long Time No Woman (in promo p/s) | 325 |

(see also A.S.A.P., Iron Maiden)

URCHINS
| 66 | Polydor BM 56145 | I Made Her That Way/Twas On A Night Like This | 6 |

URIAH HEEP
70	Vertigo 6059 037	Lady In Black/Simon The Bullet Freak (unissued in U.K.)	
71	Bronze WIP 6111	Look At Yourself/Simon The Bullet Freak	7
72	Bronze WIP 6126	The Wizard/Gypsy	6
72	Bronze WIP 6140	Easy Livin'/Why	6
73	Bronze BRO 7	Stealin'/Sunshine	6
74	Bronze BRO 10	Something Or Nothing/What Can I Do	5
75	Bronze BRO 17	Prima Donna/Shout It Out	5
76	Bronze BRO 27	One Way Or Another/Misty Eyes	5
76	Bronze BRODJ 1	One Way Or Another/Misty Eyes (promo only p/s, 750 copies)	20
77	Bronze BRO 37	Wise Man/Crime Of Passion	5
77	Bronze BRO 47	Free Me/Masquerade (p/s)	6
78	Bronze BRO 62	Come Back To Me/Cheater	5
82	Bronze BRO 143	THE ABOMINOG JUNIOR (EP, p/s)	6
83	Bronze BROP 166	Lonely Nights/Weekend Warriors (picture disc)	8
83	Bronze BROG 168	Stay On Top/Playing For Time//Gypsy/Easy Livin'/Sweet Lorraine/Stealin' (double pack, gatefold p/s)	7
85	Portrait WA 6103	Rockerama/Back Stage Girl (shaped picture disc)	10
88	Legacy LGYT 65	Easy Livin' (live)/Corina (live)/Gypsy (live) (12", red vinyl)	8
88	Castle Comms. CD3-16	URIAH HEEP (CD EP, 5,000 only)	10
70	Vertigo 6360 006	VERY 'EAVY... VERY 'UMBLE (LP, gatefold sleeve, swirl label)	45
71	Vertigo 6360 028	SALISBURY (LP, gatefold sleeve, swirl label)	40
71	Bronze ILPS 9142	VERY 'EAVY... VERY 'UMBLE (LP, reissue)	15
71	Bronze ILPS 9152	SALISBURY (LP, reissue)	15
71	Bronze ILPS 9169	LOOK AT YOURSELF (LP, 'mirror' sleeve)	20
89	Legacy LLP 120	RAGING SILENCE (LP, picture disc)	12

(see also Gods, Head Machine, Natural Gas, Spice, King Crimson, John Lawton, Grand Prix, Stratus)

URUSEI YATSURA
95	Modern Ind. MIR 001	Pampered Adolescent/BLISTERS: A Dull Thought In Itself (burgundy vinyl, p/s, 500 only)	20
95	Ché CHÉ 38	Siamese/Lo-Fi (orange & grey vinyl, p/s)	8
95	Love Train PUBE 08	Kernel/Teendream (p/s, 1,000 only)	8

US
| 70s | Jeff Wayne Music SD 015 | You're OK With Us/Tomorrow (p/s, promo for Johnson Wax) | 10 |

(see also David Essex, Randells)

U.S. DOUBLE QUARTET
(see United States Double Quartet)

USELESS UNICORN
| 74 | Horny HORN 11 | RUBBER HORN (LP, gatefold sleeve, with pop-up horn) | 15 |

USERS
77	Raw RAW 1	Sick Of You/(I'm) In Love With Today (p/s, some numbered on rear)	15/10
77	Raw RAWT 1	Sick Of You/(I'm) In Love With Today (12", no p/s)	15
78	Warped WARP 1	Warped 45: Kicks In Style/Dead On Arrival (p/s, 5,000 only, numbered sleeve, some un-numbered)	18

US FOLK
| 65 | Eyemark EMS 1001 | Funny Old World/Dives | 6 |

U.S. SKY
(see under Sky)

U.S. T-BONES
65	Liberty LIB 55836	No Matter What Shape/Feelin' Fine	12
66	Liberty LIB 55867	Sippin'n'Chippin'/Moment Of Softness	15
66	Liberty LIB 55951	The Proper Thing To Do/Tee-Hee-Hee	15

MINT VALUE £

PETER USTINOV
53   Parlophone MSP 6012   Mock Mozart (with Anthony Hopkins, Harpsichord)/Phoney Folk-Lore 7
(see also Peter Sellers)

UTOPIA (Germany)
73   United Artists UAG 29438   UTOPIA (LP) 25
(see also Amon Düül II)

UTOPIA (U.S.)
77   Bearsville K 55514   RA (LP, with lyric inner & pyramid insert) 12
82   Epic EPC 25207   UTOPIA (LP, with free 5-track EP) 12

U2
SINGLES: IRISH PRESSINGS

79	CBS 7951	U2: THREE (Out Of Control/Stories For The Boys/Boy-Girl) (p/s, black vinyl) (CBS 'Sunburst Label' with UK TM NoB81 809) on label (First Pressing))	350
79	CBS 7951	U2: THREE (Out Of Control/Stories For The Boys/Boy-Girl) (p/s, black vinyl)	60
80	CBS 7951	U2: THREE (Out Of Control/Stories For The Boys/Boy-Girl) (p/s, white vinyl)	400
80	CBS 7951	U2: THREE (Out Of Control/Stories For The Boys/Boy-Girl) (p/s, orange vinyl)	160
80	CBS 7951	U2: THREE (Out Of Control/Stories For The Boys/Boy-Girl) (p/s, yellow vinyl)	120
80	CBS 7951	U2: THREE (Out Of Control/Stories For The Boys/Boy-Girl) (p/s, brown vinyl mispressing, fewer than 50 copies exist)	1200
81	CBS 12-7951	U2: THREE (12" EP, with numbered sticker, orange CBS sleeve, 1,000 only)	1500
81	CBS 12-7951	U2: THREE (12" EP, reissue, die-cut CBS sleeve)	90
81	CBS 12-7951	U2: THREE (12" EP, 2nd reissue, plain black sleeve, slightly different labels)	50
85	CBS 40-7951	U2: THREE (cassette, reissue)	50
80	CBS 8306	Another Day/Twilight (Demo Version) (p/s, yellow vinyl)	160
80	CBS 8306	Another Day/Twilight (Demo Version) (p/s, orange vinyl)	200
80	CBS 8306	Another Day/Twilight (Demo Version) (p/s, white vinyl)	225
80	CBS 8306	Another Day/Twilight (Demo Version) (p/s, black vinyl, initially with postcard designed by Bono)	550/75
80	CBS 8687	11 O'Clock Tick Tock/Touch (p/s, yellow vinyl)	80
80	CBS 9065	I Will Follow/Boy-Girl (live) (p/s, yellow vinyl)	80
80	CBS 9065	I Will Follow/Boy-Girl (live) (p/s, orange vinyl)	150
80	CBS 9065	I Will Follow/Boy-Girl (live) (p/s, white vinyl)	225
80	CBS 9065	I Will Follow/Boy-Girl (live) (p/s, brown vinyl, fewer than 50 copies)	1200
82	CBS PAC 1	4 U2 PLAY (4 x 7", each in p/s, black vinyl)	200
82	CBS PAC 1	4 U2 PLAY (4 x 7", each in p/s, yellow vinyl)	500
82	CBS PAC 1	4 U2 PLAY (4 x 7", each in p/s, orange or white vinyl)	650/1200
80s	CBS PAC 2	PAC 2 (4 x 7" with p/s in plastic wallet)	65
80s	CBS PAC 3	PAC 3 (4 x 7" with p/s in plastic wallet)	65

SINGLES: UK PRESSINGS

80	Island WIP 6601	11 O'Clock Tick Tock/Touch (p/s)	40
80	Island WIP 6630	A Day Without Me/Things To Make And Do (p/s)	40
80	Island WIP 6656	I Will Follow/Boy-Girl (live) (p/s)	40
81	Island WIP 6679	Fire/J. Swallo (p/s)	20
81	Island UWIP 6679	Fire/J. Swallo/11 O'Clock Tick Tock (live)/The Ocean (live)/Cry (live)/ The Electric Co. (live) (double pack, single p/s)	28
81	Island WIP 6733	Gloria/I Will Follow (live) (p/s)	25
82	Island WIP 6770	A Celebration/Trash, Trampoline And The Party Girl (p/s)	45
83	Island WIP 6848	New Year's Day/Treasure (Whatever Happened To Pete The Chop) (p/s)	10
83	Island WIP 6848	New Year's Day/Treasure (Whatever Happened To Pete The Chop) (p/s, mispressing, B-side plays Martha Reeves, Motown label)	125
83	Island UWIP 6848	New Year's Day/Treasure (Whatever Happened To Pete The Chop)// Fire (live)/I Threw A Brick Through A Window (live)/A Day Without Me (live) (double pack, single p/s, black inners)	25
83	Island 12WIP 6848	New Year's Day/Treasure (Whatever Happened To Pete The Chop)/ Fire (live)/I Threw A Brick Through A Window/A Day Without Me (12", p/s)	18
83	Island IS 109	Two Hearts Beat As One/Endless Deep (p/s)	10
83	Island ISD 109	Two Hearts Beat As One/Endless Deep//New Year's Day (U.S.A. Remix)/ Two Hearts Beat As One (U.S.A. Remix) (p/s, double pack)	28
83	Island 12IS 109	Two Hearts Beat As One (Club Mix)/New Year's Day/ Two Hearts Beat As One (U.S Remix) (12", p/s)	20
84	Island IS 202	Pride (In The Name Of Love)/Boomerang 2 (Vocal) (p/s)	10
84	Island ISP 202	Pride (In The Name Of Love)/Boomerang 2 (Vocal) (picture disc)	50
84	Island ISD 202	Pride (In The Name Of Love)/4th Of July//Boomerang I (Instrumental)/ Boomerang 2 (Vocal) (double pack, gatefold p/s)	20
84	Island CIS 202	Pride (In The Name Of Love)/Boomerang I/4th Of July/Boomerang 2/ A Celebration (cassette)	30
84	Island 12IS 202	Pride (In The Name Of Love)/4th Of July/Boomerang 2 (12",white p/s)	15
84	Island 12ISX 202	Pride (In The Name Of Love)/Boomerang I/Boomerang 2/ 11 O'Clock Tick Tock/Touch (Full Length Version) (12", blue p/s)	40
85	Island ISD 220	The Unforgettable Fire/A Sort Of Homecoming (live)/Love Comes Tumbling/ Sixty Seconds In Kingdom Come/The Three Sunrises (double pack, gatefold p/s)	20
85	Island ISP 220	The Unforgettable Fire/A Sort Of Homecoming (live) (logo-shaped pic disc)	60
85	Island 12IS 220	The Three Sunrises/The Unforgettable Fire/A Sort Of Homecoming (live)/ Love Comes Tumbling/Bass Trap (12", p/s)	15
87	Island IS 319	With Or Without You/Walk To The Water/Luminous Times (Hold Onto Love) (p/s)	8
87	Island CIS 319	With Or Without You/Luminous Times (Hold Onto Love)/ Walk To The Water (cassette)	9
87	Island 12IS 319	With Or Without You/Luminous Times (Hold Onto Love)/ Walk To The Water (12", p/s)	15
87	Island CID 319	With Or Without You/Luminous Times (Hold Onto Love)/ Walk To The Water (CD, gatefold card p/s)	25
87	Island IS 328	I Still Haven't Found What I'm Looking For/Spanish Eyes/Deep In The Heart (p/s)	8

87	Island CIS 328	I Still Haven't Found What I'm Looking For/Spanish Eyes/ Deep In The Heart (cassette)	9
87	Island 12IS 328	I Still Haven't Found What I'm Looking For/Spanish Eyes/ Deep In The Heart (12", p/s)	15
87	Island IS 340	Where The Streets Have No Name/Silver And Gold/The Sweetest Thing (p/s, paper label)	10
87	Island CIS 340	Where The Streets Have No Name/Race Against Time/Silver And Gold/ The Sweetest Thing (cassette)	9
87	Island 12IS 340	Where The Streets Have No Name/Race Against Time/Silver And Gold/ The Sweetest Thing (12", p/s with "Silver And Gold" lyric insert)	40
87	Island CID 340	Where The Streets Have No Name (edit)/Race Against Time/Silver And Gold/ The Sweetest Thing (CD, gatefold p/s)	25
88	Island IS 400	Desire/Hallelujah Here She Comes (non-gatefold p/s)	7
88	Island ISG 400	Desire/Hallelujah Here She Comes (gatefold p/s)	6
88	Island CIDP 400	Desire/Hallelujah Here She Comes/Desire (Hollywood Remix) (CD, picture disc)	35
88	Island IS 402	Angel Of Harlem/A Room At The Heartbreak Hotel (p/s)	6
88	Island CIDP 402	Angel Of Harlem (Remix)/A Room At The Heartbreak Hotel/Love Rescue Me (Live At "Smile Jamaica" Concert London Oct '88) (CD, picture disc)	25
88	Island CIDX 402	Angel Of Harlem (Remix)/A Room At The Heartbreak Hotel/Love Rescue Me (live) (3" CD, long box, U.S. import with stickered U.K. matrix number)	35
88	Island U2 PK 1	THE JOSHUA TREE SINGLES (4 x 7"s in PVC wallet with 'obi' band)	55
89	Island IS 411	When Love Comes To Town/Dancing Barefoot (p/s)	6
89	Island CIDP 411	When Love Comes To Town/Dancing Barefoot/When Love Comes To Town (Live From The Kingdom Mix) (with BB King)/God Part II (The Hard Metal Dance Mix) (CD, picture disc)	25
89	Island CIDX 411	When Love Comes To Town/Dancing Barefoot/When Love Comes To Town (Live From The Kingdom Mix) (with Little Richard)/God Part II (The Hard Metal Dance Mix) (as U2 with B.B. King) (3" CD, long box, U.S. import with stickered U.K. matrix number)	35
89	Island 422	All I Want Is You/Unchained Melody (p/s)	6
89	Island ISB 422	All I Want Is You (Edit)/Unchained Melody (in numbered tin box)	30
89	Island CIS 422	All I Want Is You (Edit)/Unchained Melody (cassette)	10
89	Island 12IS 422	All I Want Is You (Full Version)/Unchained Melody/Everlasting Love (12", p/s)	15
89	Island 12 ISB 422	All I Want Is You (Full Version)/Unchained Melody/Everlasting Love (12", p/s, box set with 4 prints)	25
89	Island CIDP 422	All I Want Is You (4.14)/Unchained Melody/Everlasting Love/ All I Want Is You (Full Version) (CD, picture disc)	35
91	Island IS 500	The Fly/Alex Descends Into Hell For A Bottle Of Milk (p/s)	6
91	Island IS 509	Mysterious Ways/Mysterious Ways (Solar Plexus Club Mix) (p/s)	6
91	Island 12IS 509	Mysterious Ways (4.04)/(Solar Plexus Extended Club Mix 7.01)/ (Apollo 440 Magic Hour Remix)/(Tabla Motown Remix)/ (Solar Plexus Club Mix) (12", p/s, withdrawn)	22
92	Island IS 515	One/Satellite Of Love (p/s)	6
92	Island IS 525	Even Better Than The Real Thing/Salomé (p/s)	6
92	Island 12IS 525	Even Better Than The Real Thing/Salomé/Where Did It All Go Wrong/ Lady With The Spinning Head (UVI) (Extended Dance Mix) (12", with giant "Zoo TV" poster)	35
92	Island REAL U2	Even Better Than The Real Thing (Perfecto Mix)/(Trance Mix)/ (Sexy Dub Mix) (12", title sleeve)	12
92	Island CREAL 2	Even Better Than The Real Thing (Perfecto Mix)/(Sexy Dub Mix)/ (Apollo 440 Stealth Sonic Remix)/(V16 Exit Wound Remix) (A440 Vs. U2 Instrumental Remix) (CD)	12
92	Island IS 550	Who's Gonna Ride Your Wild Horses (Temple Bar Edit)/Paint It Black (p/s)	7
92	Island CIDX 550	Who's Gonna Ride Your Wild Horses (Temple Bar Edit)/Paint It Black/Salomé (Zooromancer Remix)/Can't Help Falling In Love (Triple Peaks Remix) (CD, picture disc, tri-fold digipak with 4 prints, some sealed)	50/40
93	Island IS 578	Stay (Faraway, So Close!)/I've Got You Under My Skin (p/s)	8
	Island CID 578	Stay (Faraway, So Close!)/I've Got You Under My Skin (as Frank Sinatra & Bono)/Lemon (Bad Yard Club)/Lemon (Perfecto Mix) (CD, 'The Swing Format')	25
93	Island CIDX 578	Stay (Faraway, So Close!)/Slow Dancing/Bullet The Blue Sky (live)/ Love Is Blindness (live) (CD, 'The Live Format', foldout digipak)	25
95	Atlantic A 7131	Hold Me, Thrill Me, Kiss Me, Kill Me/ELLIOTT GOLDENTHAL: Themes From Batman Forever (p/s, red vinyl)	12
95	Atlantic A 7131	Hold Me, Thrill Me, Kiss Me, Kill Me/ELLIOTT GOLDENTHAL: Themes From Batman Forever (p/s, red vinyl, B-side miscredited to U2)	23
93	Island CID 578	Stay (Faraway, So Close!)/I've Got You Under My Skin (as Frank Sinatra & Bono)/Lemon (Bad Yard Club)/Lemon (Perfecto Mix) (CD, 'The Swing Format')	25
97	Island ISD(X) 649 D(J)	Discothèque (Howie B Hairy B Mix)/Discothèque (Hexidecimal Mix)/ Discothèque (DM Deep Extended Club Mix)/Discothèque (DM Deep Beats Mix)/ Discothèque (DM Tec Radio Mix)/Discothèque (DM Deep Instrumental Mix)/ Discothèque (Single Version)/Discothèque (David Holmes Mix) (3 x 12" in silver title sleeve with pink, orange & blue inners; with barcode & front sticker)	20
97	Island CID 649	Discothèque/Holy Joe (Garage Mix)/Holy Joe (Guilty Mix) (CD, jewel case, withdrawn)	55
97	Island 12IS 684	Mofo (Mother's Mix)/Mofo (House Flavour Mix)/Mofo (Romin Mix)/Mofo (Phunk Force Mix)/Mofo (Black Hole Dub) (12", die-cut p/s, 2,000 only)	20
01	Island CIDX 780	Elevation (Tomb Raider Mix)/Last Night On Earth (Live)/Don't Take Your Guns To Town (CD, blue/silver poster pack, colour reversed top to bottom, withdrawn)	75

DVD SINGLES

01	Island CIDV 780	Elevation (Tomb Raider Mix)/Elevation (Tomb Raider Mix [video])/ (excerpts from MTV's "Making Of The U2 Video")	15
01	Island CIDV 788	Walk On (Single Version)/(4 x 30 second clips from Elevation 2001 — U2 Live from Boston)	15

PROMO-ONLY SINGLES

80	Island WIP 6601	11 O'Clock Tick Tock/Touch (p/s, 'A' label)	75
80	Island WIP 6630	A Day Without Me/Things To Make And Do (p/s, 'A' label)	75
80	Island WIP 6656 DJ	I Will Follow (Special Edited DJ Version) (1-sided, company sleeve)	90
81	WIP 6679	Fire (Radio Edit) (1-sided, p/s)	75
81	WIP 6733	Gloria (Radio Edit) (1-sided, p/s)	75
84	Island U2 2	Wire/Bad/The Unforgettable Fire (12", black die-cut sleeve)	80
87	Island ISJ 319	With Or Without You/Walk To The Water (jukebox issue, large centre hole)	18
87	Island ISJ 328	I Still Haven't Found What I'm Looking For/Spanish Eyes (jukebox issue, solid centre or large centre hole)	90/18
87	Island ISJB 340	Where The Streets Have No Name/Silver And Gold (jukebox issue, large centre hole)	18
88	Island 12ISX 400	Desire (9.23 Hollywood Remix) (12", 1-sided, custom black p/s, 800 only)	50
88	Island U2V 7	EXCERPTS FROM RATTLE AND HUM (In God's Country [live]/Hawkmoon 269/Bad [live]/God Part II/With Or Without You [live]) (CD, card gatefold sleeve)	125
88	Island IS 319	With Or Without You/Luminous Times (Hold Onto Love)/Walk To The Water/With Or Without You (Video) (CD Video, withdrawn, less than 100 copies)	750
89	Island 12 ISX 411	U2 3D DANCE MIXES: When Love Comes To Town (Live From The Kingdom Dance Mix)/God Part II (Hard Metal Dance Club Mix)/Desire (Hollywood Remix 5.23) (12" EP, custom sleeve)	60
90	Island RHB 1	Night And Day (Twilight Remix)/Steel String Mix) (12", p/s, numbered, 4,000 copies only)	90
91	Island U2-3	OCTOBER 1991: I Will Follow/Pride (In The Name Of Love)/God Part II/Where The Streets Have No Name) (CD EP, 250 only)	600
91	Island IS 500B	Alex Descends Into Hell (test pressings only, pink handwritten label, no p/s)	150
92	Island 12 IS 515B	Lady With The Spinning Head (UVI)/Satellite Of Love (12", test pressings only, with press release, white label)	180
92	Island 12IS 550DJ	Salomé (Zooromancer Remix 8.02)/Can't Help Falling In Love (Mystery Train Dub 8.20) (12", black die-cut sleeve, 1,000 only)	125
92	Island REAL 1	Even Better Than The Real Thing (The Perfecto Mix)/Even Better Than The Real Thing (Trance Mix)/Even Better Than The Real Thing (Sexy Dub Mix) (12", black die-cut sleeve with title sticker)	40
92	Island REAL 2DJ	Even Better Than The Real Thing (The Perfecto Mix-Radio Edit) (2-sided radio promo, some with p/s)	50/40
93	Island NUMJB 1	Numb (2-sided jukebox issue, large centre hole)	30
93	Island NUMCD 1	Numb (CD, 1-track, with lyric inner, 250 only)	120
93	Island 12LEM DJ 1	Lemon (Bad Yard Club)/(Momo Beats)/(Version Dub)/(Serious Def Dub)/(Perfecto Mix)/(Trance Mix) (12", double pack, p/s, 1,000 only, numbered with press sheets; discs sometimes sold individually - without outer sleeve @ £25 each)	135
93	Island LEMCD 1	Lemon (Radio Edit) (CD, 1-track, with lyric inner)	50
95	Island 12 MELON 1	MELON (Salomé [Zooromancer Remix]/Numb [Bad Yard Club Mix]/Numb [The Soul Assassins Mix]/Numb [Gimme Some More Dignity Mix]) (12" EP, 800 only)	45
95	Atlantic A 7131	Hold Me, Thrill Me, Kiss Me, Kill Me/Themes From Batman Forever (black vinyl, jukebox issue, large centre hole)	20
95	Atlantic A 7131	Hold Me, Thrill Me, Kiss Me, Kill Me/Themes From Batman Forever (red vinyl, some with B-side miscredited to U2)	18/12
96	Island PRECD 1	U2 PREVIOUSLY: Lemon/Mysterious Ways/One/Desire/I Still Haven't Found What I'm Looking For (CD, card sleeve)	40
97	Island ISJB 649	Discothèque/Holy Joe (Garage Mix) (jukebox issue, large centre hole)	15
97	Island ISD(X) 649 D(J)	Discothèque (Howie B Hairy B Mix)/Discothèque (Hexidecimal Mix)//Discothèque (DM Deep Extended Club Mix)/Discothèque (DM Deep Beats Mix)//Discothèque (DM Tec Radio Mix)/Discothèque (DM Deep Instrumental Mix)//Discothèque (Single Version)/Discothèque (David Holmes Mix) (3 x 12" in silver title sleeve with pink, orange & blue inners; no barcode or front sticker)	50
97	Island DISCO 1	Discothèque (Radio Edit) (CD, 1-track, jewel case)	18
97	Island DISCO 2	Discothèque (Radio Edit)/Discothèque (Album Version) (CD, jewel case)	40
97	Island no cat. no.	Discothèque (Hexidecimal Remix — Radio Edit) (CD-R, 1-track, jewel case)	160
97	Island ISJB 658	Staring At The Sun/North And South Of The River (jukebox issue, large centre hole)	15
97	Island 12IS 658DJ	Staring At The Sun (Monster Truck Mix)/Staring At The Sun (Lab Rat Mix)/Staring At The Sun (Sad Bastard's Mix) (12", p/s)	35
97	Island ISJB 664	Last Night On Earth (Single Mix)/Last Night On Earth (First Night In Hell Remix) (jukebox issue, large centre hole)	15
97	Island 12IS 664DJ	Last Night On Earth (First Night In Hell Remix)/Happiness Is A Warm Gun (The Gun Mix)/Pop Muzik (Pop Mart Mix)/Happiness Is A Warm Gun (The Danny Sabre Mix) (12", p/s)	40
97	Island MUZIK 1	Pop Muzik (Pop Mart Mix — Radio Edit) (CD, 1-track, picture disc, jewel case, 250 only)	70
97	Island ISJB 673	Please/Where The Streets Have No Name (live) (jukebox issue, large centre hole)	18
97	Island CIDDJ 673	Please/Please (Call Out Hook) (CD)	40
97	Island PLEASE CD 1	Please (Single Edit)/Please (Single Version) (CD, plain disc with handwritten title, jewel case, no inlay, less than 50 pressed)	180
97	Island PLEASE CD 1	Please (Single Edit)/Please (Single Version) (CD, 2-track, yellow graphics on disc, jewel case)	28
97	Island ISJB 684	If God Will Send His Angels (Single Vesion)/Sunday Bloody Sunday (live from Sarajevo) (jukebox issue, large centre hole)	18
97	Island 12MOFO 1	Mofo (Phunk Force Mix)/Mofo (Black Hole Dub)/Mofo (Romin Remix) (12", orange label, orange & silver die-cut title sleeve)	45
97	Island 12MOFO 2	Mofo (Mother's Mix)/Mofo (House Flavor Mix) (12", pink label, pink & silver die-cut title sleeve, 250 only)	60
97	Island 12MOFO 3	Mofo (Explicit Mix) (12", 1-sided, stamped white label, plain black die-cut sleeve, 200 only)	150

97	Island 12MOFO 3	Mofo (Explicit Mix)/Mofo (Explicit Mix) (12", 2-sided misspressing [same track both sides], stamped white label, plain black die-cut sleeve) 225
97	Island MOFOCD 1	Mofo (Album Version) (CD, 1-track, card sleeve, export issue [to Mexico]) 165
97	Island MOFOCD 2	Mofo (Phunk Force Mix) (CD, 1-track, jewel case, export issue [to Mexico]) 165
98	Island SWEET CD 1	Sweetest Thing (CD, 1-track) 18
98	Island CIDDJ 727	Sweetest Thing/Twilight (Live)/An Cat Dubh (Live)/Stories For Boys Out Of Control (Live) (CD, die-cut sleeve) 90
99	Columbia XPCD 1206	BONO & WYCLEF JEAN: New Day (Edit)/New Edit (Version) (CD, card sleeve) . . 18
00	Island GROUND CD 1	The Ground Beneath Her Feet/The Million Dollar Hotel Movie Trailer (CD-ROM, card sleeve, blue die-cut slipcase) 50
00	Island 12 BEAUT 1	Beautiful Day (Quincey & Sonance Mix) (1-sided 12", in black die-cut title sleeve) 45
01	Island BEAUT CD1	Beautiful Day (1-track promo, CD jewel case) 18
01	Island ISJB770	Stuck In A Moment You Can't Get Out Of/Big Girls Are Best (UK jukebox promo 7" with large centre) 30
01	Island STUCK CD 1	Stuck In A Moment You Can't Get Out Of (1-track CD, picture sleeve jewel case) 18
01	Island 12 ELE 1	Elevation (Escalation Mix)/Elevation (Influx Mix) (12", red custom p/s, 250 only) 35
01	Island ELE CD 2	Elevation (Tomb Raider Mix) (1-track CD, Lara Croft sleeve, withdrawn) 50
01	Island 12 ELE 2	Elevation (Paul Vandyk Remix)/Elevation (The Vandit Club Mix) (12", blue custom p/s, 250 only, exclusive mixes) 45
01	Island ELE CD 2	Elevation (Tomb Raider Mix) (1-track CD,group sleeve) 15
01	Island WALKCD 1	Walk On (Single Version) (1-track CD, brown sleeve, jewel case, withdrawn) 40
01	Island WALKCD 2	Walk On (Single Version)/Walk On (Video Version) (CD, blue sleeve, jewel case) . . 18
02	Island STORM CD 1	Electrical Storm (William Orbit Mix)/Electrical Storm (Radio Edit) (CD) 18
02	Island CID 808	Electrical Storm (William Orbit Mix)/New York (Nice Mix)/New York (Nasty Mix)/ Bad (Live)/Where The Streets Have No Name (2-CD + DVD set in limited issue collectors' wallet, mail-order only) 60
	Island NEWCD U2 13	NEW SONGS AND MIXES FROM THE BEST OF 1990-2000 (CD sampler, black . . . . inner sleeve, silver outer sleeve) 55
03	Island HANDSCD 1	The Hands That Built America (promo only 1-track CD, card sleeve) 25
03	Island 12 Sun U2	Staring At The Sun (Brothers In Rhythm Club Mix)/Staring At The Sun (Brothers In Rhythm Ambient Mix) (12", black die-cut custom sleeve) 35
02	Island 12REMIX U2 13	U2 REMIXES FROM THE 1990S (2 x 12" sampler, black inner sleeves, silver outer sleeve) 35
04	Island U2PRO1	Vertigo (1-track promo in jewel case) 12
04	Island U2PRO2	Vertigo (Jacknife Lee 7" mix) (7" vinyl promo, picture sleeve, matt/gloss finish) . . 90
04	Island 10IS878DJ	Vertigo (Jacknife Lee 7" mix)/Vertigo (Jacknife Lee 10" mix) 10" vinyl p/s 50
04	Island 12IS878DJ	Vertigo (Jacknife Lee 10" mix)/Vertigo (Jacknife Lee 12" mix) 12" vinyl p/s 30
04	Island CID878/X878/V878	Vertigo (CD1, CD2 & DVD set in wallet issued by U2.Com) 60
05	Island 12IS886	Vertigo (Redanka Power Mix)/Vertino (Trent Reznor Mix) 12", promo p/s) 30
05	Island (no cat no)	Vertigo (Trent Reznor mix) 1 track CDR with title cover in PVC sleeve) 60
05	Island U2PRO4	Sometimes You Can't Make It On Your Own (Radio edit 99bpm)/Sometimes You Can't Make It On Your Own (Radio Edit 96bpm) (CD in jewel case) 12
05	Island CID886/X/V	Sometimes You Can't Make It On Your Own (CD1, CD2 & DVD set in wallet, issued by U2.com) 25
05	Island CIDDJ890	City Of Blinding Lights (Radio Edit) (1 track CD promo, jewel case) 12
05	Island 12IS890DJ	City Of Blinding Lights (Phones P.D.A in N.Y.C Remix/City Of Blinding Lights (Paradise Soul Vocal Mix)/All Because Of You (Killahurtz Fly Mix) 12", p/s) 30
05	Island CID890/X/V	City Of Blinding Lights (CD1, CD2 & DVD set in wallet via U2.com) 25
05	Island CIDDJ906	All Because Of You (Single Mix) (1-track CD promo, jewel case) 15
05	Island CID906/X/V	All Because Of You (CD1, CD2 & DVD set in wallet via u2.com) 25
05	Island PRO5	Vertigo/Cry/The Electric Co/Beautiful Day/All Because Of You (CD, clear case) 100

ALBUMS

80	Island ICT 9646	BOY ('1+1' cassette) 40
81	Island ICT 9680	OCTOBER ('1+1' cassette, in plastic case or 'cigarette pack' card box) 40
83	Island PILPS 9733	WAR (LP, picture disc, beware of counterfeits with ILPS cat. no.) 85
83	Island ICT 9733	WAR ('1+1' cassette) 40
85	Island CID 112	WAR (LP, pink cover lettering) 140
85	Island CID 110	BOY (CD, with title rear sleeve; no bar code) 110
85	Island CID 111	OCTOBER (CD, with title rear sleeve; no bar code) 110
85	Island CID 113	UNDER A BLOOD RED SKY (CD, with picture rear sleeve; no bar code) 110
85	Island CID 102	THE UNFORGETTABLE FIRE (CD, no bar code) 110
91	Island U2-8	ACHTUNG BABY (LP, with 10 art prints) 60
93	Island U2-9	ZOOROPA (LP) 45
95	Island MELONCD 1	MELON (REMIXES FOR PROPAGANDA) (CD, 9-track compilation, card sleeve, fan club issue, 20,000 only; some sealed with *Propaganda* No. 21) 60/35
97	Island U2 10	POP (2-LP, gatefold sleeve) 25
98	Island U2 11	THE BEST OF 1980-1990 (2-LP, gatefold sleeve) 75
00	Island U2 12	ALL THAT YOU CAN'T LEAVE BEHIND (LP, with booklet) 25
02	Island U2 13	THE BEST OF 1990-2000 (2 x LP, gatefold) 25
04	Island U2 14	HOW TO DISMANTLE AN ATOMIC BOMB (LP, with booklet) 20
04	Island CIDXU214	HOW TO DISMANTLE AN ATOMIC BOMB (CD & DVD set in numbered slipcase) . . 18

PROMO-ONLY ALBUMS

83	Island U2 1	UNDER A BLOOD RED SKY — A DIALOGUE WITH U2 LIVE (LP, custom sleeve, with cue sheet, numbered, 1,000 only) 90
87	Island U2-6	THE JOSHUA TREE (CD, LP & cassette in black/gold 'pizza' box set) 285
87	Island U2 6-1 — U2 6-5	THE JOSHUA TREE COLLECTION Red Hill Mining Town/Where The Streets Have No Name/Trip Through Your Wires/Running To Stand Still//I Still Haven't Found What I'm Looking For/One Tree Hill//Exit/Mothers Of The Disappeared//In God's Country/Bullet The Blue Sky (5 x 7" set, in black box, 250 only) 700

(The above singles sell for around £20-£25 individually, except for U2 6-2, £35)

87	Island U2 6-1 — U2 6-5	THE JOSHUA TREE COLLECTION (5 x 7" black box set, with U2 6-1 mispressed with Red Hill Mining Town both sides, less than 50 copies)	1800
87	Island U2CLP 1	THE U2 TALKIE: A CONVERSATION WITH LARRY, BONO, ADAM & THE EDGE (LP, music & interview with Dave Fanning for "The Joshua Tree")	65
87	Island U2CC 1	THE U2 TALKIE (cassette)	35
87	Island BOU2 1	CASSETTE SAMPLER (cassette, 17-track instore BEST OF compilation)	55
88	Island U2-7	RATTLE AND HUM (CD, LP & cassette in flight case with leather tag, 250 only)	2100
89	Island U2 2D1	U2 2 DATE (LP, 8-track hits compilation)	40
91	Island U2-8	ACHTUNG BABY (CD, cassette in 'User's Kit', including map/poster, torch, key ring, spanner & screwdriver in printed green nylon kit bag)	1200
91	Island CIDDJ U2-8	ACHTUNG (graphics CD, in jewel case marked "promo only — not for sale")	120
97	Island CID U2 10	POP (CD, in large cube-shaped picture box set, with prismatic pen & custom notepad)	325
97	Island POP 1	U2 TALK POP (CD, interview with Dave Fanning, card sleeve)	50
97	Island POP 2	U2 TALK POP (CD, interview with Dave Fanning, card sleeve, same tracks as POP 1)	50
97	Island POP 3	U2 TALK POP (CD, interview with Dave Fanning, card sleeve, same track as POP 1)	50
98	Island CIDDU211	THE BEST OF THE 'B' SIDES 1980-1990 (2-CD, discs marked 'A' and 'B', in card sleeves with gold slipcase)	80
98	Island BXU2 11	THE 'BEST OF' COLLECTION 1980-1990 (14 x 7" singles, 2-CDs, 16-page booklet, in gold box, 2,000 copies only)	450
00	Island MDH CD1	THE MILLION DOLLAR HOTEL (CD, card sleeve)	40
00	Island CID U212	ALL THAT YOU CAN'T LEAVE BEHIND (promo pack, with 1-track CD "Beautiful Day" [BEAUT CD 1] in blue picture slipcase, booklet, window sticker, video tape, "Playback" invitation, in laminated picture bag with rope handles; some with signed print)	600/200
00	Island (no cat. no)	THE DAVE FANNING INTERVIEW (CD-R, dated 4.10.00, in white card sleeve, plastic outer sleeve)	80
00	Island (no cat. no)	ALBUM INTERVIEW (CD-R, dated 25.10.00, in white card sleeve, plastic outer sleeve)	80
01	no cat. no.	CD FREE WITH SUNDAY TIMES NEWSPAPER (5 tracks + 2 video tracks)	12/15
02	Island CIDDJ U2 13	THE BEST OF THE B-SIDES OF 1990-2000 (2-CD set card sleeves in card wallet)	60
02	Island BX U2 13	THE BEST OF COLLECTION 1990-2000 (15 x 7", with 2 CDs & 16-page booklet in silver fliptop card box)	350
02	Island REMIXCD U2 13	REMIXES FROM THE 90s (CD, 5-track album sampler in card sleeve, silver card wallet)	45
04	Island U2PRO3	HOW TO DISMANTLE AN ATOMIC BOMB – INTERVIEW (CD, jewel case)	75
05	Island U1COMV1	U2 COMMUNICATION (CD & DVD fan club issue)	50

(see also Bono & Gavin Friday, The Edge, Adam Clayton & Larry Mullen, Passengers)

VACELS
65	Pye International 7N 25330	Can You Please Crawl Out Your Window/I'm Just A Poor Boy	25

VAGABONDS
63	Island ILP 916	PRESENTING THE FABULOUS VAGABONDS (LP)	110

(see also Jimmy James & Vagabonds, Jamaica's Own Vagabonds)

VAGINA DENTATA ORGAN
80s	WSNS 004	Cold Meat: Sex Star I/II (12", picture disc)	40
87	Temple TOPY 012	MUSIC FOR HASHASINS (LP)	50
80s	Cold Meat	EROS AND THANATOS (LP)	70

VAGRANTS
66	Fontana TF 703	I Can't Make A Friend/Young Blues	60

VALADIERS
63	Oriole CBA 1809	I Found A Girl/You'll Be Sorry Someday (DJ copy = £1000)	900

RICKY VALANCE
60	Columbia DB 4493	Tell Laura I Love Her/Once Upon A Time	10
60	Columbia DB 4543	Movin' Away/Lipstick On Your Lips	12
61	Columbia DB 4586	Jimmy's Girl/Only The Young	12
61	Columbia DB 4592	Why Can't We/Fisherboy	12
61	Columbia DB 4680	Bobby/I Want To Fall In Love	15
61	Columbia DB 4725	I Never Had A Chance/It's Not True	12
62	Columbia DB 4787	Try To Forget Her/At Times Like These	12
62	Columbia DB 4864	Don't Play No. 9/Till The Final Curtain Falls	15
65	Decca F 12129	Six Boys/Face The Crowd	15
76	Valley VLY 001	RICKY VALANCE (EP, no p/s)	25

(see also Jason Merryweather)

VAL & V's

67	CBS 2780	Do It Again A Little Bit Slower/For A Rainy Day	15
67	CBS 2956	I Like The Way/With This Theme	15
68	CBS 3316	This Little Girl/Dreamer	12

RITCHIE VALENS

58	Pye International 7N 25000	Come On Let's Go/Dooby Dooby Wah (78 rpm = £160)	200
59	London HL 8803	Donna/La Bamba (78 rpm = £110)	30
59	London HL 7068	Donna/La Bamba (export issue)	30
59	London HL 8886	That's My Little Suzie/Bluebirds Over The Mountains (tri or round centre)	40/25
59	London HL 8886	That's My Little Suzie/Bluebirds Over The Mountains (78)	200
62	London HL 9494	La Bamba/Ooh, My Head	20
59	London RE 1232	RITCHIE VALENS (EP, initially triangular centre, later round centre)	180/120
61	London HA 2390	RITCHIE (LP)	130
64	London HA 8196	HIS GREATEST HITS (LP)	70
67	President PTL 1001	I REMEMBER RITCHIE VALENS (LP)	25
79	London HA-R 8535	RITCHIE VALENS (LP)	15

CATERINA VALENTE

60	Polydor NH 66816	Malaguena/Secret Love	5
60	Decca LK 4350	RENDEZVOUS WITH CATERINA (LP)	12
60	Polydor LPHM 46.065	COSMOPOLITAN LADY (LP)	12
61	Polydor LPHM 46.310	CATERINA CHERIE (LP)	12

DINO VALENTI

68	CBS 65715	DINO (LP)	55

(see also Quicksilver Messenger Service)

BILLY VALENTINE

55	Capitol CL 14320	It's A Sin/Your Love Has Got Me (Reelin' And Rockin') (78 rpm = £8)	65

DICKIE VALENTINE (& STARGAZERS)

78s

52	Melodisc P 210	Lorelei/Never (from 'Golden Girl')	7
59	Pye Nixa N 15192	Venus/Where? (In The Old Home Town)	10
59	Pye N 15202	A Teenager In Love/My Favourite Song	10
59	Pye N 15221	One More Sunrise (Morgen)/You Touch My Hand	6

45s

54	Decca F 10346	Endless/I Could Have Told You	40
54	Decca F 10394	The Finger Of Suspicion (with Stargazers)/Who's Afraid (Not I, Not I, Not I)	35
54	Decca F 10415	Mister Sandman/Runaround	45
55	Decca F 10430	A Blossom Fell/I Want You All To Myself (Just You)	20
55	Decca F 10484	Ma Cherie Amie/Lucky Waltz	18
55	Decca F 10493	I Wonder/You Too Can Be A Dreamer	18
55	Decca F 10517	Hello Mrs. Jones (Is Mary There?)/Lazy Gondolier	15
55	Decca F 10549	No Such Luck/The Engagement Waltz	15
55	Decca F 10628	Christmas Alphabet/Where Are You Tonight?	35
55	Decca F 10645	The Old Pi-Anna Rag/First Love	18
55	Decca F 10667	Dreams Can Tell A Lie/Song Of The Trees	10
56	Decca F 10714	The Voice/The Best Way To Hold A Girl	10
56	Decca F 10753	My Impossible Castle/When You Came Along	10
56	Decca F 10766	Day Dreams/Give Me A Carriage With Eight White Horses	8
56	Decca F 10798	Christmas Island/The Hand Of Friendship	10
56	Decca F 10820	Dickie Valentine's Rock 'N' Roll Party Medley (Parts 1 & 2)	10
57	Decca F 10874	Chapel Of The Roses/My Empty Arms	8
57	Decca F 10906	Puttin' On The Style/Three Sides To Every Story	8
57	Decca F 10949	Long Before I Knew You/Just In Time	8
57	Decca F 10950	Snowbound For Christmas/Convicted	8
58	Decca F 11005	Love Me Again/King Of Dixieland	8
58	Decca F 11020	In My Life/Come To My Arms	6
58	Decca F 11066	Take Me In Your Arms/An Old-Fashioned Song	6
59	Pye Nixa 7N 15192	Venus/Where? (In The Old Home Town)	8
59	Pye 7N 15202	A Teenager In Love/My Favourite Song	7
59	Pye 7N 15221	One More Sunrise (Morgen)/You Touch My Hand	5

EPs

55	Decca DFE 6236	SWING ALONG WITH DICKIE VALENTINE	15
56	Decca DFE 6279	PRESENTING DICKIE VALENTINE	15
56	Decca DFE 6363	ONLY FOR YOU	15
57	Decca DFE 6427	DICKIE GOES DIXIE	12
57	Decca DFE 6429	STANDARDS	12
58	Decca DFE 6529	WITH VOCAL REFRAIN BY DICKIE VALENTINE	12
59	Decca DFE 6549	BELONGING TO SOMEONE	10
59	Pye NPL 24120	DICKIE VALENTINE HIT PARADE	10

LPs

54	Decca LF 1163	PRESENTING DICKIE VALENTINE (10")	30
55	Decca LF 1211	HERE IS DICKIE VALENTINE (10")	25
56	Decca LF 1257	OVER MY SHOULDER (10")	25
58	Decca LK 4269	WITH VOCAL REFRAIN BY...	20
61	Ace Of Clubs ACL 1082	DICKIE	12
67	Philips BL 7831	AT THE TALK OF THE TOWN	12

JACK VALENTINE

55	MGM SPC 8	Dressing Up My Heart/Song Of The Bandit (export issue)	18

VALENTINES (Jamaica)

67	Doctor Bird DB 1065	Blam Blam Fever/BABA BROOKS: The Scratch	40

VALENTINES (U.S.)

60	Ember EMB S 123	Hey Ruby/That's How I Feel	80

MINT VALUE £

VALENTINO
75	Gaiee GAE 101	I Was Born This Way/Liberation	15

ANNA VALENTINO
57	London HLD 8421	Calypso Joe/You're Mine (78 rpm = £20)	30

DANNY VALENTINO
59	MGM MGM 1049	Stampede/(You Gotta Be A) Music Man	38
60	MGM MGM 1067	Biology/A Million Tears	18
60	MGM MGM 1109	Pictures/Till The End Of Forever	15

MARK VALENTINO
63	Stateside SS 148	The Push And Kick/Walking Alone	25
63	Stateside SS 186	Do It/Hey You're Looking Good	15
63	Stateside SS 233	Jivin' At The Drive In/Part Time Job	25

VALENTINOS
68	Soul City SC 106	It's All Over Now/Tired Of Livin' In The Country	25
68	Stateside SS 2137	Tired Of Being Nobody/The Death Of Love	15
71	Polydor 2058 090	Don't Raise Up Your Hands In Anger/Stand Up And Be Counted	8
68	Soul City SCM 001	THE VALENTINOS/THE SIMS TWINS (LP, with Sims Twins)	70

(see also Bobby Womack)

VALERIE (The Rock 'N' Roll Youngster)
56	Columbia DB 3832	Tonight You Belong To Me/The Man Who Owns The Sunshine	20

DANA VALERY
64	Decca F 11881	This Is My Prayer/Would I Love You Again (Tien Va Pas)	5
64	Decca F 11977	I Wake Up Crying/Never Let Go	6

JOE VALINO (& GOSPELAIRES)
57	HMV POP 283	The Garden Of Eden/Caravan	20
58	London HLT 8705	God's Little Acre/I'm Happy With What I've Got (with Gospelaires)	15
58	London HLT 8705	God's Little Acre/I'm Happy With What I've Got (78, with Gospelaires)	12
60	Columbia DB 4406	Hidden Persuasion/Back To Your Eyes	5

VALKYRIES
64	Parlophone R 5123	Rip It Up/What's Your Name?	38

DIORIS VALLADARES ORCHESTRA
64	Island IEP 703	AUTHENTIC MERINGUE (EP)	12
64	Island ILP 910	LET'S GO LATIN (LP, withdrawn)	30+

MARCOS VALLE
68	Verve	SAMBA '68 (LP)	18

RUDY VALLEE
54	HMV 7MC 8	The Whiffenpoof Song/Taps (export issue)	8

VALLEY OF ACHOR
75	Dovetail DOVE 18	A DOOR OF HOPE (LP, gatefold sleeve)	20

(see also Achor, Wine Of Lebanon)

FRANKIE VALLI
66	Philips BF 1467	(You're Gonna) Hurt Yourself/VALLI BOYS: Night Hawk	20
66	Philips BF 1512	You're Ready Now/Cry For Me	20
66	Philips BF 1529	The Proud One/Ivy	10
67	Philips BF 1556	Beggin'/Dody	7
67	Philips BF 1580	Can't Take My Eyes Off You/The Trouble With Me	7
67	Philips BF 1603	I Make A Fool Of Myself/September Rain	7
68	Philips BF 1634	To Give (The Reason I Live)/Watch Where You Walk	7
69	Philips BF 1795	The Girl I'll Never Know/A Face Without A Name	6
70	Philips 320 226 BF	You're Ready Now/Cry For Me (reissue)	10
74	Private Stock PVT 1	My Eyes Adored You/Watch You Walk	5
67	Philips (S)BL 7814	SOLO (LP)	25
69	Philips SBL 7856	TIMELESS (LP)	20
75	Mowest MWS 7007	INSIDE YOU (LP)	12
77	Private Stock PVLP 1029	LADY PUT THE LIGHT OUT (LP, withdrawn)	35

FRANKIE VALLI & THE FOUR SEASONS
71	Warner Bros K 16107	Whatever You Say/Sleeping Man (withdrawn, 300 only)	32
72	Tamla Motown TMG 819	You're A Song/Sun Country	10
72	Mowest MW 3002	The Night/When The Morning Comes	50
73	Mowest MW 3003	Walk On, Don't Look Back/Touch The Rainchild	10
75	Mowest MW 3024	The Night/When The Morning Comes (reissue)	10
72	Mowest MWSA 5501	CHAMELEON (LP)	20

(see also Four Seasons, Wonder Who)

JUNE VALLI
53	HMV B 10568	Crying In The Chapel/Love Every Moment You Live (78)	6
53	HMV JO 324	Why Don't You Believe Me/A Shoulder To Weep On (78, export issue)	6
54	HMV 7M 245	I Understand (Just How You Feel)/Old Shoes And A Bag Of Rice	12
54	HMV 7M 259	Tell Me, Tell Me/Boy Wanted	12
55	HMV 7M 284	Wrong, Wrong, Wrong/Ole Pappy Time	12
56	HMV 7M 347	Por Favor (Please)/The Things They Say	12
59	Mercury AMT 1034	The Answer To A Maiden's Prayer/In His Arms	7
59	Mercury AMT 1048	An Anonymous Letter/Bygones	7
60	Mercury AMT 1091	Apple Green/Oh! Why	6
61	Mercury AMT 1130	I Guess Things Happen That Way/Tell Him For Me	5

VALUES
66	Ember EMB S 211	Return To Me/That's The Way (some with p/s)	80/50

VALVES
77	Zoom ZUM 1	Robot Love/For Adolfs Only (p/s)	18
77	Zoom ZUM 3	Tarzan Of The Kings Road/Ain't No Surf In Portobello (p/s)	15
79	Albion DEL 3	I Don't Mean Nothing At All/Linda Vindalco (p/s)	8

VAMP
68	Atlantic 584 213	Floatin'/Thinkin' Too Much	55
69	Atlantic 584 263	Green Pea/Wake Up And Tell Me (withdrawn)	130+

(see also Sam Gopal, Viv Prince, Clark-Hutchinson)

VAMPIRES
59	Parlophone R 4599	Swinging Ghosts/Clap Trap	15

VAMPIRES
68	Pye 7N 17553	Do You Wanna Dance/My Girl	15

ILA VAN
74	Pye Intl. DDS 108	Can't Help Loving Dat Man/I've Got The Feeling	10

PAUL VANCE
66	Pye International 7N 25387	Dommage, Dommage/Sexy	6

HARRY VANDA
69	Polydor 56357	I Love Marie/Gonna Make It	7

(see also Easybeats)

VAN DER GRAAF GENERATOR
69	Polydor 56758	People You Were Going To/Firebrand	250
70	Charisma CB 122	Refugees/The Boat Of Millions Of Years	45
72	Charisma CB 175	Theme One/W (some with p/s)	25/5
76	Charisma CB 297	Wondering/Meurglys III	8
76	Charisma PRO 002	Wondering (Song)/Wondering (Heroics) (promo only)	25
70	Charisma CAS 1007	THE LEAST WE CAN DO IS WAVE TO EACH OTHER (LP, pink label, original mix, matrices read: CAS 1007 A/B, gatefold sleeve, some with poster)	60/35
70	Charisma CAS 1007	THE LEAST WE CAN DO IS WAVE TO EACH OTHER (LP, pink label, remix, matrices read: CAS 1007 A+G/B+G, gatefold sleeve; some with poster)	45/20
70	Charisma CAS 1027	H TO HE, WHO AM THE ONLY ONE (LP, pink label, gatefold sleeve)	30
71	Charisma CAS 1051	PAWN HEARTS (LP, gatefold sleeve, pink label, some with insert)	30/15
72	Charisma CS 2	1968-71 (LP, pink label)	15
75	Charisma CAS 1109	GODBLUFF (LP, with inner sleeve)	12

(see also Peter Hammill, Long Hello, Juicy Lucy, Misunderstood)

MAMIE VAN DOREN
58	Capitol CL 14850	Something To Dream About/I Fell In Love (promos in p/s) (78 rpm = £6)	30/25

EARL VAN DYKE (& SOUL BROTHERS)
64	Stateside SS 357	Soul Stomp/Hot 'N' Tot (DJ copy = £200)	140
65	Tamla Motown TMG 506	All For You/Too Many Fish In The Sea (as Earl Van Dyke & Soul Brothers) (DJ copy = £200)	130
70	Tamla Motown TMG 759	Six By Six/All For You (matt black label, later shiny)	10
72	Tamla Motown TMG 814	I Can't Help Myself/How Sweet It Is (To Be Loved By You) (& Soul Brothers)	10
65	Tamla Motown TML 11014	THAT MOTOWN SOUND (LP)	175

GULLIVER VAN DYKE
69	Vogue VRS 7034	Set Me Free/The Day Has Gone	6

LEROY VAN DYKE
61	Mercury AMT 1166	Walk On By/My World Is Caving In	6
62	Mercury AMT 1173	Big Man In A Big House/Faded Love	6
62	Mercury AMT 1183	I Sat Back And Let It Happen/A Broken Promise	7
65	Warner Bros WB 5650	It's All Over Now Baby Blue/Just A State Of Mind	7
66	Warner Bros WB 5807	You Couldn't Get My Love Back/Fool Such As I	7
67	Warner Bros WB 5777	Almost Persuaded/Less Of Me	7
62	Mercury MMC 14101	WALK ON BY (LP)	50
63	Mercury MMC 14118	MOVIN' VAN DYKE (LP)	50

VANDYKE & THE BAMBIS
64	Piccadilly 7N 35180	Doin' The Mod/All I Want Is You	45

VAN DYKE PARKS
(see under 'P')

VAN DYKES
66	Stateside SS 504	No Man Is An Island/I Won't Hold It Against You	25
66	Stateside SS 530	I've Gotta Go On Without You/What Will I Do	30

LON & DERREK VAN EATON
73	Apple APPLE 46	Warm Woman/More Than Words (some in p/s)	55/22
75	A&M AMS 7157	Wildfire/Music Lover	5
75	A&M AMS 7178	Dancing In The Dark/All You're Hungry For Is Love	5
73	Apple SAPCOR 25	BROTHER (LP, gatefold sleeve, some with insert)	65/45

NICK VAN EEDE
78	Barn 201 4128	Rock'n'Roll Fool/Ounce Of Sense	6
79	Barn BARN 003	All Or Nothing/Hold On To Your Heart	7
79	Barn BARN 008	I Only Want/Dicing	7

(see also Drivers)

VANGELIS
75	RCA RS 1025	HEAVEN AND HELL (gatefold sleeve)	12
76	Polydor 2489 113	L'APOCALYPSE DES ANIMAUX (LP, TV soundtrack)	18
83	Polydor BOX 1	CHARIOTS OF FIRE (LP, soundtrack, box set)	12
89	Polydor VGPK 1	THEMES (LP, 'display pack')	12

(see also Aphrodite's Child, Forminx, Cosmic Baby, Jon & Vangelis)

VAN HALEN

MINT VALUE £

VAN HALEN
78	Warner Bros K 17107	You Really Got Me/Atomic Punk	5
78	Warner Bros K 17162	Runnin' With The Devil/Eruption.	5
79	Warner Bros K 17371	Dance The Night Away/Outta Love Again.	7
79	Warner Bros K 17371P	Dance The Night Away/Outta Love Again (picture disc).	10
80	Warner Bros K 17645	And The Cradle Will Rock/Everybody Wants Some (p/s)	5
85	Warner Bros W 9199T	Hot For Teacher/Little Dreamer/Hear About It Later (12", p/s)	8
86	Warner Bros W 8740P	Why Can't This Be Love/Get Up (shaped picture disc with plinth, stickered PVC sleeve).	10
86	Warner Bros W 8642P	Dreams/Inside (car-shaped picture disc with stand, stickered PVC sleeve)	12
88	Warner Bros W 7816TW	When It's Love/Apolitical Blues (12", silver foldout p/s).	8
88	Warner Bros W 7816TP	When It's Love/Apolitical Blues (12", picture disc).	8

(see also David Lee Roth, Sammy Hagar)

CHERRY VANILLA
77	RCA PB 5053	The Punk/Foxy Bitch (title sleeve).	8
78	RCA PL 25122	BAD GIRL (LP).	12
79	RCA PL 25217	VENUS DE VINYL (LP)	15

VANILLA FUDGE
67	Atlantic 584 123	You Keep Me Hanging On/Take Me For A Little While	6
67	Atlantic 584 139	(Illusions Of My Childhood) Eleanor Rigby (Parts 1 & 2)	7
68	Atlantic 584 179	Where Is My Mind?/The Look Of Love	12
69	Atlantic 584 257	Shotgun/Good Good Lovin'.	6
69	Atlantic 584 276	Some Velvet Morning/Thoughts	12
67	Atlantic 587/588 086	VANILLA FUDGE (LP, red & plum label)	25
68	Atlantic 587/588 100	THE BEAT GOES ON (LP)	22
68	Atlantic 587/588 110	RENAISSANCE (LP)	22
69	Atco 228 020	NEAR THE BEGINNING (LP)	18
70	Atco 228 029	ROCK 'N' ROLL (LP)	18

(see also Beck Bogert & Appice, Cactus)

VANITY FARE
68	Page One POF 075	I Live For The Sun/On The Other Side Of Life	7
68	Page One POF 100	Summer Morning/Betty Carter.	7
69	Page One POF 117	Highway Of Dreams/Waiting For The Downfall	7
69	Page One POF 142	Early In The Morning/You Made Me Love You	7
69	Page One POF 158	Hitchin' A Ride/Man Child.	7
69	Page One POLS 010	THE SUN, THE WIND AND OTHER THINGS (LP)	38

(see also Avengers)

BILL VAN LOO
01	City Centre Offices BLOCK 12	Tones (For Sarah) (plain sleeve with inserts, 1,000 only).	8

TEDDY VANN (ORCHESTRA)
60	London HLU 9097	Cindy/I'm Waiting	25
61	Philips PB 1160	The Lonely Crowd/I Was Born To Love You.	6
78	Capitol CL 16012	Theme From 'Coloured Man'/Intro To 'Coloured Man' (as Teddy Vann Orchestra)	5

ORNELLA VANONI
67	Decca F 22703	Only Two Can Play/Can I?	10

DAVE VAN RONK
65	Stateside SL 10153	INSIDE (LP)	15

ROB VAN SPYK
70s	private pressing	FOLLOW THE SUN (LP)	30

(see also Stonefield Tramp)

TOWNES VAN ZANDT
99	Exile EX 7013	Riding The Range/Dirty Old Town (p/s, 2000 only)	6
69	RCA SF 8040	OUR MOTHER THE MOUNTAIN (LP)	20
73	United Artists UAS 29442	THE LATE GREAT TOWNES VAN ZANDT (LP, gatefold sleeve)	30
87	Heartland HLD 003	AT MY WINDOW (LP)	15
01	Charly SNAB 903 CD	TEXAS TROUBADOUR (4-CD, book-style box set)	35

VAPORS
79	United Artists BP 321	Prisoners/Sunstroke (p/s)	5

PETER VARDAS
59	Top Rank JAR 173	He Threw A Stone/Checkerboard Love (78 rpm = £6)	8

VARDIS
79	Redball RR 017	100 MPH (EP).	120

VARIATIONS
65	Immediate IM 019	The Man With All The Toys/She'll Know I'm Sorry	18
69	Major Minor MM 638	Crimson And Clover/She Couldn't Dance	10

VARIATIONS (U.S.)
75	UK USA 10	Sayin' It And Doin' It Pts I & II	8

VARICOSE VEINS
78	Warped WARP 1	INCREDIBLE (EP, mail-order only, 200 only, beware of counterfeits)	60

(see also Orange Disaster)

PAUL VARNEY
91	PWL PWLT 201	If Only I Knew (On The Buses Piano Edit)/If Only I Knew (Hurley's House Mix)/If Only I Knew (Silk's Answer)/If Only I Knew (Maurice's Underground Mix) (12", p/s).	10
91	PWL PWCD 201	If Only I Knew (7" Version)/If Only I Knew (12" Version)/If Only I Knew (Dub)/If Only I Knew (On The Buses Piano Edit) (CD)	10

SYLVIE VARTAN
65	RCA Victor RCA 1490	One More Day/I Made My Choice	70
65	RCA Victor RCA 1495	Another Heart/Think About You	12
79	RCA PB 1578	I Don't Want The Night To End/Distant Shores (p/s, coloured vinyl)	6
65	RCA Victor RCX 7165	SYLVIE VARTAN (EP)	100

VARUKERS
81	Tempest/Inferno HELL 1	Protest And Survive/No Scapegoat (p/s)	6
83	Riot City RIOT 27	Die For Your Government/All Systems Fail (p/s)	7
83	Riot City RIOT 29	Led To The Slaughter/The End Is Nigh (p/s)	7
82	Tempest/Inferno HELL 4	DON'T WANNA BE A VICTIM (EP)	6
83	Riot City RIOT 31	ANOTHER RELIGION ANOTHER WAR (12" EP)	10
84	Rot ASS 16	MASSACRED MILLIONS (12" EP)	12
84	Attack ATTACK 001	PREPARE FOR THE ATTACK (LP)	15

VASELINES
87	53rd & 3rd AGARR 10	Son Of A Gun/Rory Rides Away/You Think You're A Man (12", die-cut sleeve)	20
88	53rd & 3rd AGARR 17	Dying For It/Molly's Lips (p/s)	10
88	53rd & 3rd AGARR 17T	Dying For It/Molly's Lips/Teenage Superstars/Jesus Wants Me For A Sunbeam (12", p/s)	12
88	53rd & 3rd AGARR 17CD	Dying For It/Molly's Lips/Teenage Superstars/Jesus Wants Me For A Sunbeam (CD)	12
90	53rd & 3rd AGAS 7	DUM DUM (LP)	15

(see also Pastels, BMX Bandits)

VASHTI
65	Decca F 12157	Some Things Just Stick In Your Mind/I Want To Be Alone	35
66	Columbia DB 7917	Train Song/Love Song	25

(see also Vashti Bunyan)

CLAUDE VASORI
99	Jazzman JM 010	Tic-Splash/VINCENT GEMINIANI: Ophis Le Serpentaire	5

RAY VASQUEZ
61	Starlite ST45-055	Nothing Ever Changes My Love For You/Easy To Love	6
61	Starlite STEP 17	IN THE STILL OF THE NIGHT (EP)	10

DENNY VAUGHAN
53	Parlophone R 3657	Forevermore/Take It Off (with Nancy Reed) (78)	6

(see also Nancy Reed)

FRANKIE VAUGHAN
59	Philips PB 896	Honey Bunny Baby/The Lady Is A Square (78)	8
59	Philips PB 913	Come Softly To Me/Say Something Sweet To Your Sweetheart (with Kaye Sisters)(78)	10
59	Philips PB 930	The Heart Of A Man/Sometime Somewhere (78)	10
59	Philips PB 931	Walkin' Tall/I Ain't Gonna Lead This Life (78)	10
57	Rainbow/Weekend 14140	The Truth About Me (78, 5", mail-order only, some with mailer)	10/15
53	HMV 7M 167	Istanbul (Not Constantinople)/Cloud Lucky Seven	10
54	HMV 7M 182	The Cuff Of My Shirt/Heartless	10
54	HMV 7M 252	My Son, My Son/Cinnamon Sinner (Selling Lollipop Lies)	10
54	HMV 7M 270	Happy Days And Lonely Nights/Danger Signs	10
55	HMV 7M 298	Too Many Heartaches/Unsuspecting Heart	10
57	Philips JK 1002	Garden Of Eden/Priscilla (jukebox issue)	25
57	Philips JK 1014	What's Behind That Strange Door/Cold, Cold Shower (jukebox issue)	25
57	Philips JK 1022	These Dangerous Years/Isn't This A Lovely Evening (jukebox issue)	20
57	Philips JK 1030	Gotta Have Something In The Bank, Frank/Single (with Kaye Sisters, jukebox issue)	18
57	Philips JK 1035	Kisses Sweeter Than Wine/Rock-A-Chicka (jukebox issue)	15
57	Philips PB 775	Kisses Sweeter Than Wine/Rock-A-Chicka	22
58	Philips PB 793	We're Not Alone/Can't Get Along Without You	5
58	Philips PB 825	Kewpie Doll/So Many Women	5
58	Philips PB 834	Wonderful Things/Judy	5
58	Philips PB 865	Am I Wasting My Time On You/So Happy In Love	5
59	Philips PB 423	Give Me The Moonlight, Give Me The Girl/Happy Go Lucky	5
59	Philips PB 895	That's My Doll/Love Is The Sweetest Thing	5
59	Philips PB 896	Honey Bunny Baby/The Lady Is A Square	8
59	Philips PB 913	Come Softly To Me/Say Something Sweet To Your Sweetheart (& Kaye Sisters)	5
59	Philips PB 930	The Heart Of A Man/Sometime Somewhere	5
59	Philips PB 931	Walkin' Tall/I Ain't Gonna Lead This Life	5
56	Philips BBE 12022	FRANKIE VAUGHAN (EP)	12
57	HMV 7EG 8245	MISTER ELEGANT (EP)	12
57	Woman's Own P 117 2E	SWINGIN' (EP)	8
57	Philips BBE 12111	FRANKIE VAUGHAN (EP)	10
59	Philips BBE 12299	HEART OF A MAN (EP)	10
61	Philips BBE 12484	LET ME SING AND I'M HAPPY (EP, also in stereo SBBE 9071)	15
61	Philips BBE 12485	LET ME SING AND I'M HAPPY NO. 2 (EP, also in stereo SBBE 9072)	15
61	Philips BBE 12486	LET ME SING AND I'M HAPPY NO. 3 (EP, also in stereo SBBE 9073)	15
57	Philips BBL 7198	HAPPY GO LUCKY (LP)	18
58	Philips BBL 7233	THE FRANKIE VAUGHAN SHOWCASE (LP)	18
59	Philips BBL 7330	AT THE LONDON PALLADIUM (LP, also on stereo SBBL 511)	15
61	Philips BBL 7482	LET ME SING — AND I'M HAPPY! (LP, also stereo SBL 629)	15
61	Philips BBL 7490	WARM FEELING (LP, also stereo SBBL 645)	15

(see also Kaye Sisters, Alma Cogan & Frankie Vaughan, Marilyn Monroe)

ROY VAUGHAN BOOGIE TRIO
50	Jazz Parade B 3	Oval Boogie/Rumble Boogie (78)	8

Sarah VAUGHAN

SARAH VAUGHAN

50	MGM MGM 331	Tenderly/I'll Wait And Pray (78)	6
51	MGM MGM 388	I'm Gonna Sit Right Down And Write Myself A Letter/I'm Thru With Love (78)	6
55	Mercury MB 3205	My Funny Valentine/How Important Can It Be (78)	6
55	Philips PB 455	Summertime/I Cried For You (78)	6
57	Mercury MT 151	Poor Butterfly/Whatever Lola Wants (Lola Gets) (78)	6
57	Mercury MT 176	Band Of Angels/Please Mr Brown (78)	6
58	Mercury 7MT 198	My Darling, My Darling/Bewitched (78 rpm = £6)	10
58	Mercury 7MT 212	Padre/Spin Little Bottle (78 rpm = £6)	10
58	Mercury 7MT 222	Too Much, Too Soon/What's So Bad About It (78 rpm = £8)	10
59	Mercury AMT 1010	Everything I Do/I Ain't Hurtin' (78 rpm = £8)	8
59	Mercury AMT 1029	Cool Baby/Are You Certain? (78 rpm = £12)	10
59	Mercury AMT 1044	Careless/Separate Ways	7
59	Mercury AMT 1057	Broken-Hearted Melody/Misty (78 rpm = £20)	10
59	Mercury AMT 1080	You're My Baby/Eternally	6
59	Mercury AMT 1087	Don't Look At Me That Way/Sweet Affections	6
60	Columbia DB 4491	Ooh! What A Day/My Dear Little Sweetheart	10
60	Columbia DB 4511	If I Were A Bell/Teach Me Tonight (with Count Basie & Joe Williams)	5
60	Columbia DB 4542	Serenata/Let's	5
63	Columbia DB 4990	My Favourite Things/Great Day	5
69	Mercury AMT 1107	The Boy From Ipanema/The Fever (p/s)	5

EPs

56	London RE-U 1065	SARAH VAUGHAN SINGS (with John Kirby's Orchestra)	15
57	Emarcy YEP 9507	SARAH VAUGHAN	12
57	Mercury MEP 9511	SARAH VAUGHAN HIT PARADE	12
57	Mercury MEP 9519	SARAH VAUGHAN HIT PARADE NO. 2	12
59	Mercury ZEP 10011	SONGS FROM SARAH	12
59	Mercury ZEP 10030	AFTER HOURS AT THE LONDON HOUSE	12
59	Mercury ZEP 10041	SARAH WITH FEELING	12
59	Mercury ZEP 10101	NO COUNT SARAH	12
60	Mercury ZEP 10054	SMOOTH SARAH	12
60	Mercury ZEP 10087	LIVE FOR LOVE (also stereo SEZ 19006)	each 15
62	Mercury ZEP 10115	NO COUNT BLUES (also stereo SEZ 19023)	each 15

LPs

55	Oriole/Mercury MG 26005	IMAGES (10")	25
55	Mercury MG 25188	THE DIVINE SARAH	15
56	London HB-U 1049	SARAH VAUGHAN SINGS (10", with John Kirby & His Orchestra)	25
56	Emarcy EJL 100	IN THE LAND OF HI FI (10")	20
56	Philips BBL 7082	SARAH VAUGHAN	15
56	Mercury MPT 7503	MAKE YOURSELF COMFORTABLE (10")	20
57	Mercury MPT 7518	IMAGES (10", reissue)	15
57	Emarcy EJL 1258	SASSY	15
57	Mercury MPL 6522	SINGS GREAT SONGS FROM HIT SHOWS PART 1	15
57	Philips BBL 7165	LINGER AWHILE	15
57	Mercury MPL 6523	SINGS GREAT SONGS FROM HIT SHOWS PART 2	15
57	Mercury MPL 6525	SINGS GEORGE GERSHWIN VOL. 1	15
57	Mercury MPL 6527	SINGS GEORGE GERSHWIN VOL. 2	15
58	Mercury MPL 6532	WONDERFUL SARAH	15
58	Emarcy EJL 1273	SWINGIN' EASY	15
58	Mercury MPL 6540	IN ROMANTIC MOOD	15
58	Mercury MPL 6542	AT MISTER KELLY'S	15
59	Mercury CMS 18011	SINGS GEORGE GERSHWIN VOL. 1 (stereo reissue of MPL 6525)	15
59	Mercury CMS 18012	SINGS GEORGE GERSHWIN VOL. 2 (stereo reissue of MPL 6527)	15
59	Mercury MMC 14001	AFTER HOURS AT THE LONDON HOUSE	15
59	Mercury MMC 14011	VAUGHAN AND VIOLINS (also stereo CMS 18003)	each 15
60	Mercury MMC 14021	NO COUNT SARAH	15
60	Mercury MMC 14024	GREAT SONGS FROM HIT SHOWS PART 1 (reissue of MPT 6522)	12
60	Mercury CMS 18019	GREAT SONGS FROM HIT SHOWS PART 1 (stereo reissue of MPT 6522)	12
60	Mercury MMC 14026	GREAT SONGS FROM HIT SHOWS PART 2 (reissue of MPT 6523)	12
60	Mercury CMS 18023	GREAT SONGS FROM HIT SHOWS PART 2 (stereo reissue of MPT 6523)	12
60	Columbia 33SX 1252	DREAMY (also stereo SCX 3324)	each 15
61	Mercury MMC 14059	CLOSE TO YOU (also stereo CMS 18040)	each 15
62	Columbia 33SX 1340	THE DIVINE ONE (also stereo SCX 3390)	each 15
62	Columbia 33SX 1360	COUNT BASIE — SARAH VAUGHAN (also stereo SCX 3403)	each 15
64	Mercury 20011 (S)MCL	SASSY SWINGS THE TIVOLI (also stereo)	each 15
65	Mercury 20042 (S)MCL	MY HEART SINGS (also stereo)	each 15

SARAH VAUGHAN & BILLY ECKSTINE

57	Mercury MT 164	Passing Strangers/The Door Is Open (78)	7
59	Mercury AMT 1020	Alexander's Ragtime Band/No Limit (78 rpm = £12)	7
59	Mercury AMT 1071	Passing Strangers/SARAH VAUGHAN: Smooth Operator	8
56	MGM MGM-EP 561	DEDICATED TO YOU (EP)	10
59	MGM MGM-EP 690	BILLY ECKSTINE AND SARAH VAUGHAN (EP)	10
59	Mercury 10025 MCE	PASSING STRANGERS (EP)	10
60	Mercury 10027 MCE	TOGETHER AGAIN (EP)	10
61	Mercury ZEP 10108	BEST OF BERLIN VOL. 1 (EP, also stereo SEZ 19016)	10/12
58	Mercury MPL 6530	THE BEST OF IRVING BERLIN (LP)	18
	(see also Billy Eckstine)		

BILLY VAUGHN (& HIS ORCHESTRA)

55	London HL 8112	Melody Of Love/Joy Ride (gold label print)	5
55	London HLD 8205	The Shifting Whispering Sands (Parts 1 & 2) (with Ken Nordine) (gold print)	5
56	London HLD 8238	Theme From 'The Threepenny Opera'/I'd Give A Million Tomorrows (gold label print, later with silver label print)	5
56	London HLD 8319	When The Lilac Blooms Again/Autumn Concerto (gold print, later silver)	5
56	London HLD 8342	Petticoats From Portugal/La La Colette (gold print, later silver)	5

57	London HLD 8417	The Ship That Never Sailed/Little Boy Blue (with Ken Nordine) 5
57	London HLD 8511	Johnny Tremain/Naughty Annetta (as Billy Vaughn's Orchestra & Chorus) 5
57	London HLD 8522	Raunchy/Sail Along Silvery Moon 5
58	London HLD 8612	Tumbling Tumbleweeds/Trying (78 rpm = £6) 5
58	London HLD 8680	Sail Along Silvery Moon/The Singing Hills (78 rpm = £6) 5
58	London HLD 8703	La Paloma/Here Is My Love (78 rpm = £6) 5
58	London HLD 8772	Cimarron (Roll On)/You're My Baby Doll (78 rpm = £8+) 5
59	London HLD 8797	Blue Hawaii/Tico Tico (78 rpm = £8+) 5
59	London HLD 8859	Your Cheatin' Heart/Lights Out (78 rpm = £8+) 5
59	London HLD 8920	All Nite Long/Blues Stay Away From Me (78 rpm = £8+) 5
59	London HLD 8952	Morgen (One More Sunrise)/Sweet Leilani (78 rpm = £8+) 5
59	London HLD 8996	(It's No) Sin/After Hours (78 rpm = £8+) 5
56	London HB-D 1048	MELODIES OF LOVE (10" LP) 20
57	London HA-D 2025	THE GOLDEN INSTRUMENTALS (LP, also stereo SAH-D 6018) . . . . each 15
57	London HA-D 2045	SWEET MUSIC AND MEMORIES (LP) 12
58	London HA-D 2072	INSTRUMENTAL SOUVENIRS (LP) 12
58	London HA-D 2090	MELODIES IN GOLD (LP) 12
58	London HA-D 2120	SAIL ALONG SILVERY MOON (LP, also stereo SAH-D 6037) . . . . each 12
58	London HA-D 2129	PLAYS THE MILLION SELLERS (LP, also stereo SAH-D 6003) . . . . each 12
59	London HA-D 2151	LA PALOMA (LP, also stereo SAH-D 6009) . . . . each 12
59	London HA-D 2178	BILLY VAUGHN PLAYS (LP) 12
59	London HA-D 2195	CHRISTMAS CAROLS (LP) 12
59	London HA-D 2201	BLUE HAWAII (LP) 12
60	London HA-D 2209	GOLDEN HITS (LP, also stereo SAH-D 6056) . . . . each 12
60	London HA-D 2241	GOLDEN SAXOPHONES (LP, also stereo SAH-D 6070) . . . . each 12
60	London HA-D 2251	MUSIC FOR THE GOLDEN HOURS (LP, also stereo SAH-D 6075) . . . . each 12
60	London HA-D 2256	A SUMMER PLACE (LP, also stereo SAH-D 6080) . . . . each 12
60	London HA-D 2278	LINGER AWHILE (LP, also stereo SAH-D 6096) . . . . each 12
60	London HA-D 2292	LOOK FOR A STAR (also stereo SAH-D 6104) . . . . each 12
61	London HA-D 2304	GREAT GOLDEN HITS (also stereo SAH-D 6114) . . . . each 12
61	London HA-D 2324	HIT PARADE (also stereo SAH-D 6127) . . . . each 12

(see also Hilltoppers, Ken Nordine)

MORRIS VAUGHN

69	Fontana TF 1031	My Love Keeps Growing/Make It Look Good 25

VAZZ

85	CRV 5401	Breath/Violent Silence (in folder & bag with postcards & inserts) 5

V.D.U.'s

79	Thin Sliced	Don't Cry For Me/Little White Lie/Holiday Romances (p/s) 6

(see also Boys Wonder)

CHUCK VEDDER

59	London HL 8951	Spanky Boy/Arriba 30
59	London HL 8951	Spanky Boy/Arriba (78) 20

BOBBY VEE
SINGLES

60	London HLG 9179	Devil Or Angel/Since I Met You, Baby 25
61	London HLG 9255	Rubber Ball/Everyday 8
61	London HLG 9316	More Than I Can Say/Stayin' In 7
61	London HLG 9389	How Many Tears/Baby Face 8
61	London HLG 9438	Take Good Care Of My Baby/Bashful Bob 6
61	London HLG 7111	Take Good Care Of My Baby/Bashful Bob (export issue) 30
61	London HLG 9459	Love's Made A Fool Of You/Susie-Q 15
61	London HLG 9470	Run To Him/Walkin' With My Angel 6
62	Liberty LIB 55388	Run To Him/Walkin' With My Angel (reissue) 8
62	Liberty LIB 55419	Please Don't Ask About Barbara/I Can't Say Goodbye 7
62	Liberty LIB 55451	Sharing You/At A Time Like This 6
62	Liberty LIB 10046	A Forever Kind Of Love/Remember Me, Huh? 7
63	Liberty LIB 10069	The Night Has A Thousand Eyes/Tenderly Yours 6
63	Liberty LIB 55530	Bobby Tomorrow/Charms 6
63	Liberty LIB 10124	Stranger In Your Arms/Yesterday And You 6
64	Liberty LIB 10141	She's Sorry/Buddy's Song 10
64	Liberty LIB 55700	Hickory, Dick And Doc/I Wish You Were Mine Again 10
65	Liberty LIB 10197	Keep On Trying/Cross My Heart 8
65	Liberty LIB 10213	True Love Never Runs Smooth/Hey Little Girl 8
65	Liberty LIB 55828	Run Like The Devil/Take A Look Around Me 20
66	Liberty LIB 55877	Look At Me Girl/Save A Love 8
67	Liberty LIB 10272	Like You've Never Known Before/Growing Pains 8
67	Liberty LIB 15016	Come Back When You Grow Up/Let The Four Winds Blow 6
67	Liberty LIB 15042	Beautiful People/I May Be Gone 6
68	Liberty LBF 15058	Maybe Just Today/You're A Big Girl Now 6
68	Liberty LBF 15096	Medley, My Girl - Hey Girl/Take Good Care Of My Baby 6
68	Liberty LBF 15134	Do What You Gotta' Do/Thank You 6
69	Liberty LBF 15178	(I'm Into Looking For) Someone To Love Me/Sunrise Highway 6
69	Liberty LBF 15234	I'm Gonna Make It Up To You/Let's Call It A Day 8
69	Liberty LBF 15305	Electric Trains And You/In And Out Of Love 8

EPs

61	London RE-G 1278	BOBBY VEE NO. 1. 35
61	London RE-G 1299	BOBBY VEE NO. 2. 35
61	London RE-G 1308	BOBBY VEE NO. 3. 35
61	London RE-G 1323	BOBBY VEE NO. 4. 40
61	London RE-G 1324	HITS OF THE ROCKIN' 50's 40
62	Liberty LEP 2053	SINCERELY 25
63	Liberty LEP 2084	JUST FOR FUN (2 tracks by Bobby Vee, 2 by Crickets) 28

63	Liberty LEP 2089	A FOREVER KIND OF LOVE	25
63	Liberty (S)LEP 2102	BOBBY VEE'S BIGGEST HITS (mono/stereo)	25/35
63	Liberty (S)LEP 2116	BOBBY VEE MEETS THE CRICKETS (mono/stereo)	25/35
64	Liberty LEP 2149	BOBBY VEE MEETS THE CRICKETS VOL. 2	30
64	Liberty LEP 2181	NEW SOUNDS	40
65	Liberty LEP 2212	BOBBY VEE MEETS THE VENTURES (with Ventures)	30

LPs

61	London HA-G 2320	BOBBY VEE SINGS YOUR FAVOURITES	60
61	London HA-G 2352	BOBBY VEE (also stereo SAH-G 6152)	55/60
61	London HA-G 2374	WITH STRINGS AND THINGS (also stereo SAH-G 6174)	55/60
61	London HA-G 2406	SINGS HITS OF THE ROCKIN' 50s (also stereo, SAH-G 6206)	50/55
61	London HA-G 2428	TAKE GOOD CARE OF MY BABY (also stereo, SAH-G 6224)	50/55
61	Liberty (S)LBY 1004	TAKE GOOD CARE OF MY BABY (reissue)	30
62	Liberty (S)LBY 1084	BOBBY VEE RECORDING SESSION (mono/stereo)	30/32
62	Liberty (S)LBY 1086	BOBBY VEE MEETS THE CRICKETS (mono/stereo)	18/20
62	Liberty (S)LBY 1112	BOBBY VEE'S GOLDEN GREATS (mono/stereo)	30/32
63	Liberty (S)LBY 1139	THE NIGHT HAS A THOUSAND EYES (mono/stereo)	30/32
63	Liberty (S)LBY 1147	BOBBY VEE MEETS THE VENTURES (with Ventures)	30/32
63	Liberty (S)LBY 1188	I REMEMBER BUDDY HOLLY (mono/stereo)	30/32
65	Liberty (S)LBY 1263	BOBBY VEE LIVE! ON TOUR (mono/stereo)	22/25
67	Liberty (S)LBY 1341	LOOK AT ME GIRL	25
68	Liberty LBL/LBS 83112E	JUST TODAY	22
69	Liberty LBL/LBS 83130E	DO WHAT YOU GOTTA DO	15

(see also Crickets, Ventures)

V8
| 85 | Music Factory MF 104 | Lonely Days | 12 |

ALAN VEGA
81	Celluloid WIP 6744	Jukebox Babe/Lonely (p/s)	6
81	Celluloid 12WIP 6744	Jukebox Babe/Lonely (12", p/s)	12
88	Sniffin' Rock SR 009	Wacko Warrior/(track by African Headcharge) (with *Sniffin' Rock* fanzine No. 12)	8
81	Ze/Island ILPS 9692	COLLISION DRIVE (LP)	12

(see also Suicide, Future Pilot AKA Alan Vega)

VEHICLE
| 71 | Deram DM 342 | Mr. Organ Grinder/Cloudy Day | 5 |

VEIN
(see under Intra Vein)

VEINS
| 80 | Redball RR 3 | Complete Control Rock 'n' Roll/Champagne | 25 |

VEJTABLES
| 65 | Pye International 7N 25339 | I Still Love You/Anything | 35 |

MARTHA VELEZ
69	London HLK 10266	It Takes A Lot To Laugh/Come Here Sweet Man	12
69	London HLK 10280	Tell Mama/Swamp Man	15
72	Blue Horizon 2096 010	Boogie Kitchen/Two Bridges	20
69	London HA-K/SH-K 8395	FIENDS AND ANGELS (LP)	40
70	Blue Horizon 7-63867	FIENDS AND ANGELS AGAIN (LP)	75
76	Sire 9103 252	ESCAPE FROM BABYLON (LP)	18

CAETANO VELOSO
| 71 | Famous SFM 1002 | CAETANO VELOSO (LP) | 12 |

VELOURS
| 67 | | I'm Gonna Change/Don't Pity Me | 75 |
| 77 | MGM 2006 603 | I'm Gonna Change/Don't Pity Me | 20 |

(see also Fantastics)

VELVELETTES
64	Stateside SS 361	Needle In A Haystack/Should I Tell Them?	60
65	Stateside SS 387	He Was Really Sayin' Something/Throw A Farewell Kiss	75
65	Tamla Motown TMG 521	Lonely Lonely Girl Am I/I'm The Exception To The Rule	130
66	Tamla Motown TMG 580	These Things Will Keep Me Loving You/Since You've Been Loving Me	30
66	Tamla Motown TMG 595	He Was Really Sayin' Something/Needle In A Haystack	20
67	Tamla Motown TMG 595	He Was Really Sayin' Something/Needle In A Haystack (later pressing)	15
71	Tamla Motown TMG 780	These Things Will Keep Me Loving You/Since You've Been Loving Me (reissue)	10
72	Tamla Motown TMG 806	Needle In A Haystack/I'm The Exception To The Rule	8

VELVET HUSH
| 68 | Oak RGJ 648 | Broken Heart/Lover Please | 210+ |

(see also Factory [Oak label])

VELVET LOVE
| 75 | Alaska ALA 1010 | Symphony Of Dreams/Ridin' High | 8 |

VELVET OPERA
69	CBS 4189	Anna Dance Square/Don't You Realize	10
70	CBS 4802	Black Jack Davy/Statesboro' Blues	10
70	Spark SRL 1045	She Keeps Giving Me These Feelings/There's A Hole In My Pocket	7
69	CBS 63692	RIDE A HUSTLER'S DREAM (LP)	60

(see also Elmer Gantry's Velvet Opera, Stretch, Hudson-Ford, Johnny Joyce)

VELVETS
61	London HLU 9328	That Lucky Old Sun/Time And Time Again	25
61	London HLU 9372	Tonight (Could Be The Night)/Spring Fever	30
61	London HLU 9444	Laugh/Lana	30
61	London RE-U 1297	VELVETS (EP)	165

VEL-VETS
74   Disco Demand DDS 109   I Got To Find Me Somebody/What Now My Love 15

VELVETTES
64   Mercury MF 802   He's The One I Want/That Little Boy Of Mine (some in p/s) 25/18

VELVETT FOGG
69   Pye 7N 17673   Telstar '69/Owed To The Dip 10
69   Pye NSPL 18272   VELVETT FOGG (LP, laminated sleeve; beware of non-laminated counterfeits) . . 90
(see also Ghost)

VELVET UNDERGROUND
71	Atlantic 2091 008	Who Loves The Sun/Sweet Jane.	18
73	MGM 2006 283	I'm Waiting For The Man/Run Run Run/Candy Says	
		(as Lou Reed & Velvet Underground).	8
73	Atlantic K 10339	Sweet Jane/Rock And Roll (as Velvet Underground featuring Lou Reed).	8
82	Polydor POSPX 603	Heroin/Venus In Furs/I'm Waiting For The Man/Run Run Run (12", p/s).	8
88	Old Gold OG 4049	I'm Waiting For The Man/Heroin (12", no p/s)	8
88	Old Gold OG 4051	Venus In Furs/All Tomorrow's Parties (12", no p/s).	8
67	Verve (S)VLP 9184	THE VELVET UNDERGROUND AND NICO (LP, single sleeve,	
		'non-banana' cover, mono/stereo)	110/85
68	Verve 2315 056	THE VELVET UNDERGROUND AND NICO (LP, UK pressing in	
		stickered US peelable banana gatefold censored sleeve, stereo).	110
68	Verve (S)VLP 9201	WHITE LIGHT WHITE HEAT (LP, 'skull' sleeve, mono/stereo).	110/75
69	MGM MGM-CS 8108	THE VELVET UNDERGROUND (LP, 'Val Valentin mix', flapped sleeve, with	
		horizontal split of Lou Reed picture on rear sleeve).	100
71	Atlantic 2400 111	LOADED (LP).	18
71	MGM 2315 056	THE VELVET UNDERGROUND AND NICO (LP, reissue, gatefold sleeve).	18
71	MGM Select 2353 022	THE VELVET UNDERGROUND (LP, reissue, gatefold sleeve)	18
71	MGM Select 2353 024	WHITE LIGHT WHITE HEAT (LP, reissue)	18
72	MGM Select 2683 006	ANDY WARHOL'S VELVET UNDERGROUND (2-LP)	22
72	Atlantic K 30022	LIVE AT MAX'S KANSAS CITY (LP).	12
73	Polydor 2383 180	SQUEEZE (LP).	12
84	Polydor SPELP 73	WHITE LIGHT WHITE HEAT (LP, reissue, different sleeve).	12
86	Polydor VUBOX 1	THE VELVET UNDERGROUND BOX SET (5-LP box set, with booklet).	40
87	Mercury 6641 900	1969 VOL. 1 (2-LP)	15
88	HMV C88 1-15	THE VELVET UNDERGROUND AND NICO (LP or CD box set, with booklet,	
		1500 only). . . . . each	25

(see also Lou Reed, Nico, John Cale)

TERRY VENABLES
74   Decca F 13500   What Do You Want To Make Those Eyes At Me For?/Lucy 6
(see also Tottenham Hotspur F.C.)

VENDORS
64   Domino Studios   Don't Leave Me Now/Twilight Time/Take Your Time/Peace Pipe
     (no cat. no.)   (acetate, private pressing, 12 copies only) . . . . 500+
(see also 'N Betweens, Slade)

VENGERS
63   Oriole CB 1879   Shake And Clap/Shakedown 20

VENOM
81	Neat NEAT 08	In League With Satan/Live Like An Angel, Die Like An Devil (p/s)	20
82	Neat NEAT 13	Bloodlust/In Nomine Satanas (p/s)	20
82	Neat NEAT 13	Bloodlust/In Nomine Satanas (purple vinyl).	75
83	Neat NEAT 27	Die Hard/Acid Queen (p/s, some with poster).	20/15
83	Megaforce LOM 1/NEAT 27	Die Hard/Acid Queen (picture disc, export issue, 1,000 only)	25
84	Neat NEAT 38	Warhead/Lady Lust (p/s)	10
84	Neat NEATP 38	Warhead/Lady Lust (p/s, mauve vinyl).	20
84	Neat NEAT 3812	Warhead/Lady Lust/Gates Of Hell (12", p/s).	15
85	Neat NEATP 43	Manitou/Woman (picture disc).	15
85	Neat NEATSHAPE 43	Manitou/Woman (shaped picture disc)	18
85	Neat NEATC 43	Manitou/Woman/Dead Of Night/Dutch Radio Interview (cassette).	18
85	Neat NEAT 4312	Manitou/Woman/Dead Of Night (12", p/s).	18
85	Neat NEATS 47	Nightmare/Satanarchist (shaped picture disc)	25
85	Neat NEAT 4712	Nightmare/Satanarchist/F.O.A.D./Warhead (live) (12", 'face' p/s).	20
85	Neat NEAT 4712	Nightmare/Satanarchist/F.O.A.D./Warhead (live) (12", p/s, withdrawn)	25
85	Neat NEATSP 4712	Nightmare/Satanarchist/F.O.A.D./Warhead (live) (12", picture disc, withdrawn) . .	40
85	Neat 5312	HELL AT HAMMERSMITH EP (Witching Hour/Teacher's Pet/Poison)	
		(12", 10,000 only).	20
81	Neat 1002	WELCOME TO HELL (LP, 1st issue, with poster and lyric insert)	20
82	Neat 1005	BLACK METAL (LP, 1st issue, textured sleeve, with poster, some on	
		coloured vinyl).	30/20
82	Neat NEAT 1005	BLACK METAL (LP, green marbled vinyl).	400
83	Neat NEATP 1002	WELCOME TO HELL (LP, reissue, purple vinyl).	50
84	Neat 1015	AT WAR WITH SATAN (LP, textured sleeve, 1st 19,000 with poster)	20/15
85	Neat NEATP 1005	BLACK METAL (LP, reissue, picture disc)	40
85	Neat NEATP 1015	AT WAR WITH SATAN (LP, picture disc).	40
85	Neat NEATP 1024	POSSESSED (LP, picture disc)	20
85	Neat NEAT 1024	POSSESSED (LP, blue vinyl)	20
86	Demon APKPD 12	OBSCENE MATERIAL (LP, picture disc)	20
86	Raw Power RAWLP 001	FROM HELL TO THE UNKNOWN (2-LP)	25
86	A.P. APK 12	OFFICIAL BOOTLEG (LP, picture disc).	15
89	Under One Flag FLAG 36P	PRIME EVIL (LP, numbered picture disc, stickered clear sleeve)	20

CAROL VENTURA
65   Stateside SS 466   Please Somebody Help Me/The Old Lady Of Threadneedle Street 20
65   Stateside SL 10146   CAROL! (LP) 22
66   Stateside S(S)L 10180   I LOVE TO SING (LP) 22

Charlie VENTURA

CHARLIE VENTURA
55	Vogue Coral Q 72048	I Love You/Intermezzo	7

DAVE VENTURA
64	Mercury MF 805	The Hurt Stays In The Heart/Is A Redbird Red?	8
64	Mercury MF 827	I Forgot What It Was Like/I'll Never Love Again	7

TOBY VENTURA
63	Decca F 11581	If My Heart Were A Storybook/Vagabond	40

VENTURES
SINGLES
60	Top Rank JAR 417	Walk Don't Run/Home	10
60	London HLG 9232	Perfidia/No Trespassing	10
61	London HLG 9292	Ram-Bunk-Shush/Lonely Heart	10
61	London HLG 9344	Lullaby Of The Leaves/Ginchy	8
61	London HLG 9411	Theme From 'Silver City'/Bluer Than Blue	10
61	London HLG 9465	Blue Moon/Wailin'	15
61	London HLG 7113	Lady Of Spain/Blue Moon (export issue)	30
62	Liberty LIB 60	Lolita Ya-Ya/Lucille	8
62	Liberty LIB 67	The 2,000 Pound Bee Parts 1 & 2	12
63	Liberty LIB 68	El Cumbanchero/Skip To M'Limbo	8
63	Liberty LIB 78	The Ninth Wave/Damaged Goods	10
64	Liberty LIB 91	Journey To The Stars/Walkin' With Pluto	10
64	Liberty LIB 96	Walk Don't Run '64/The Cruel Sea	12
64	Liberty LIB 10142	Penetration/Solar Race	8
65	Liberty LIB 300	Slaughter On Tenth Avenue/Rap City	8
65	Liberty LIB 303	Diamond Head/Lonely Girl	10
65	Liberty LIB 306	The Swingin' Creeper/Pedal Pusher	8
65	Liberty LIB 308	The Stranger/Bird Rockers	8
65	Liberty LIB 10219	Sleigh Ride/White Christmas	8
66	Liberty LIB 316	Secret Agent Man/007-11	8
67	Liberty LIB 10266	Theme From The Wild Angels/High And Dry	8
67	Liberty LIB 55967	Strawberry Fields Forever/Endless Dream	8
68	Liberty LBF 15075	Flights Of Fantasy/Pandora's Box	15
70	Liberty LBF 15221	Hawaii Five-O — Theme/Higher Than Thou	15
71	United Artists UP 36316	Theme From 'Shaft'/Tight Fit	6
72	United Artists UP 35326	Joy/Cherries Jubilee	5
73	United Artists UP 35574	Skylab/Little People	7
77	United Artists UP 36223	Starsky And Hutch/Charlie's Angels	5

EPs
61	London REG 1279	THE VENTURES	25
61	London REG 1283	THE VENTURES (export issue)	30
61	London REG 1288	RAM-BUNK-SHUSH!	30
62	London REG 1326	ANOTHER SMASH	30
62	London REG 1328	COLOURFUL VENTURES	25
62	Liberty LEP 2058	TWIST WITH THE VENTURES	20
62	Liberty LEP 2131	SMASH HITS	20
63	Liberty LEP 2104	THE VENTURES PLAY TELSTAR AND LONELY BULL	25
64	Liberty LEP 2174	THE VENTURES PLAY COUNTRY GREATS	25
65	Liberty LEP 2212	BOBBY VEE MEETS THE VENTURES (with Bobby Vee)	35
66	Liberty LEP 2250	SECRET AGENT MEN	35

ORIGINAL LPs
61	London HA-G 2340	THE VENTURES (also stereo SAH-G 6143)	40/55
61	London HA-G 2376	ANOTHER SMASH (also stereo SAH-G 6176)	30/45
61	London HA-G 2409	THE COLOURFUL VENTURES (also stereo SAH-G 6209)	30/45
62	Liberty LBY 1002	WALK DON'T RUN	25
62	London HA-G 2429	TWIST WITH THE VENTURES (also stereo SAH-G 6225)	30/45
62	Liberty LBY 1072	TWIST PARTY	25
63	Liberty (S)LBY 1110	GOING TO THE VENTURES DANCE PARTY! (mono/stereo)	25/35
63	Liberty (S)LBY 1147	BOBBY VEE MEETS THE VENTURES (with Bobby Vee)	35/45
63	Liberty (S)LBY 1150	SURFING (mono/stereo)	22/30
64	Liberty (S)LBY 1169	LET'S GO! (mono/stereo)	18/25
64	Liberty (S)LBY 1189	THE VENTURES IN SPACE (mono/stereo)	22/30
65	Liberty (S)LBY 1228	WALK DON'T RUN — VOL. 2 (mono/stereo)	22/30
65	Liberty (S)LBY 1252	KNOCK ME OUT (mono/stereo)	20/22
65	Liberty (S)LBY 1270	ON STAGE (mono/stereo)	20/22
66	Liberty (S)LBY 1274	VENTURES A-GO GO (mono/stereo)	18/22
66	Liberty (S)LBY 1285	THE VENTURES' CHRISTMAS ALBUM (mono/stereo)	22/30
66	Liberty (S)LBY 1297	WHERE THE ACTION IS! (mono/stereo)	18/22
66	Liberty (S)LBY 1323	GO WITH THE VENTURES (mono/stereo)	18/22
67	Liberty (S)LBY 1345	GUITAR FREAKOUT (mono/stereo)	18/22
67	Liberty (S)LBY 1372	SUPER PSYCHEDELICS (mono/stereo)	18/22
67	Liberty (S)LBY 1375	THE BEST OF THE VENTURES (mono/stereo)	18/22
68	Liberty LBL/LBS 83046E	GOLDEN GREATS (mono/stereo)	18/22
68	Liberty LBL/LBS 83085E	GREAT PERFORMANCES VOL. 1	18
68	Liberty LBL/LBS 83092E	$1,000,000 WEEKEND	18
68	Liberty LBL/LBS 83124E	LONELY BULL	15
68	Liberty LBX 2	VENTURES SAMPLER	15
68	Liberty LBL/LBS 83138E	FLIGHTS OF FANTASY	15
69	Liberty LBL/LBS 83164E	THE HORSE	15
69	Liberty LBL/LBS 83193E	UNDERGROUND FIRE	15
70	Liberty LBL/LBS 83289	SWAMP ROCK (mono/stereo)	15/12
71	United Artists UAS 29249	BEST OF POP SOUNDS (export issue)	15
72	United Artists UAS 29280	THEME FROM 'SHAFT'	12
72	United Artists UAS 29340	THE VENTURES PLAY THE CLASSICS — "JOY" (omits "One Fine Day", stickered sleeve)	12

73	United Artists UAD 60051/2	LEGENDARY MASTER S (2 x LP)	15

REISSUE LPs

68	Liberty LBL/LBS 83015E	ON STAGE (stereo)	15
68	Liberty LBL/LBS 83033E	SUPER PSYCHEDELICS (stereo)	15
68	Liberty LBL/LBS 83089E	GUITAR FREAKOUT (stereo)	15
68	Liberty LBL/LBS 83116E	I LIKE IT LIKE THAT (reissue of "A-Go Go", different sleeve, stereo)	15
68	Liberty LBL/LBS 83123E	WALK DON'T RUN (different sleeve, stereo)	15
68	Liberty LBL/LBS 83125E	LET'S GO! (different sleeve, stereo)	15
68	Liberty LBL/LBS 83126E	OUT OF LIMITS (reissue of "In Space", different sleeve, stereo)	15
68	Liberty LBL/LBS 83127E	KNOCK ME OUT (different sleeve, stereo)	15

(see also New Ventures, Bobby Vee, Trini Lopez)

VENUS & RAZORBLADES

77	Spark SRL 1153	I Wanna Be Where The Boys Are/Dogfood (numbered p/s)	8
78	Spark SRL 1159	Workin' Girl/Midnight	8

BILLY VERA

68	Atlantic 584 196	With Pen In Hand/Good Morning Blues	8

BILLY VERA & JUDY CLAY

68	Atlantic 584 164	Storybook Children/Really Together	6
69	Atlantic 584 293	Reaching For The Moon/Tell It Like It Is	6
68	Atlantic 588 158	THE STORYBOOK CHILDREN (LP)	22

(see also Judy Clay)

JOHN VERITY BAND

74	Probe SPB 1087	JOHN VERITY BAND (LP)	12

(see also Argent)

TIM VERLANDER

72	Midas MR 007	TIM VERLANDER (LP, with booklet)	35

VERMILION

78	Illegal ILM 0010	Angry Young Women/Nymphomania/Wild Boys (p/s)	15
79	Illegal ILS 0015	I Like Motorcycles/The Letter (p/s)	8

(see also Menace)

VERN & ALVIN

69	Blue Cat BS 167	Everybody Reggae/Another Fool	25
69	Big Shot BI 525	Old Man Dead/G.G. RHYTHM SECTION: Reggae Me	15

(see also Maytones)

VERN & SON

71	G.G. GG 4523	Little Boy Blue/TYPHOON ALL STARS: Little Boy Blue — Version	6

(see also Maytones)

LARRY VERNE

60	London HLN 9194	Mr. Custer/Okeefenokee Two Step	5
61	London HLN 9263	Mr. Livingstone/Roller Coaster	5

LYN VERNON

60	Top Rank JAR 323	Woodchoppers Ball/Caravan	7

MIKE VERNON

72	Blue Horizon 2096 007	Let's Try It Again/Little Southern Country Girl	25
71	Blue Horizon 2931 003	BRING IT BACK HOME (LP, textured sleeve with insert)	125

VERNONS GIRLS

58	Parlophone R 4497	Lost And Found/White Bucks And Saddle Shoes (78 rpm = £6)	25
59	Parlophone R 4532	Jealous Heart/Now Is The Month Of Maying (78 rpm = £10)	20
59	Parlophone R 4596	Don't Look Now But/Who Are They To Say?	20
60	Parlophone R 4624	We Like Boys/Boy Meets Girl	18
60	Parlophone R 4654	Madison Time (with Jimmy Saville)/The Oo-We	15
61	Parlophone R 4734	Ten Little Lonely Boys/Anniversary Song	12
61	Parlophone R 4832	Let's Get Together/No Message	12
62	Decca F 11450	Lover Please/You Know What I Mean	6
62	Decca F 11495	The Loco-motion/Don't Wanna Go	8
62	Decca F 11549	Funny All Over/See For Yourself	7
63	Decca F 11629	Do The Bird/I'm Gonna Let My Hair Down	8
63	Decca F 11685	He'll Never Come Back/Stay-At-Home	7
63	Decca F 11781	Tomorrow Is Another Day/Why Why Why	10
64	Decca F 11807	We Love The Beatles/Hey Lover Boy	15
64	Decca F 11887	Only You Can Do It/Stupid Little Girl	10
64	Decca F 12021	It's A Sin To Tell A Lie/Don't Say Goodbye	5
62	Decca DFE 8506	THE VERNONS GIRLS (EP)	45
58	Parlophone PMC 1052	THE VERNONS GIRLS (LP)	85

(see also Krimson Kake, Wilde Three, Jimmy Saville, Lee Francis, Samantha Jones, Breakaways)

LILI VERONA

54	HMV 7MC 13	Massa Johnny/Hoggin' In The Cocoa (export issue)	15
56	Melodisc MEL 1383	French Lesson/Pica Now (78, with Gulf Stream Calypso Boys)	10
59	HMV DLP 1202	JAMAICA SINGS (10" LP)	22

VERSATILE NEWTS

80	Shanghai No. 2	Newtrition/Blimp (p/s, stamped white label)	25

(see also Felt)

VERSATILES

68	Island WI 3142	Teardrops Falling/Someone To Love	22
68	Amalgamated AMG 802	Just Can't Win/LEADERS: Sometimes I Sit Down Down And Cry	22
68	Crab CRAB 1	Children Get Ready/Someone To Love	10
69	Big Shot BI 520	Worries A Yard/VAL BENNETT: Hound Dog Special	8
69	Crab CRAB 5	Spread Your Bed/Worries A Yard	8
69	Amalgamated AMG 854	Lu Lu Bell/Long Long Time	8
70	New Beat NB 060	Pick My Pocket/FREEDOM SINGERS: Freedom	8

MINT VALUE £

71	Nu Beat NB 076	Give To Me/TIGER: With Hot	7
74	Dip DL 5039	Cutting Razor/UPSETTERS: Black Belt Jones	8

(see also Pioneers, Soul Sisters)

VERUKAS
(see under Varukers)

VERVE
92	Hut HUT 12	All In The Mind/One Way To Go (p/s)	5
92	Hut HUTT 12	All In The Mind/Man Called Sun/One Way To Go (12" promo, white label)	25
92	Hut HUT 16	She's A Superstar (Edit)/Feel (p/s)	7
92	Hut HUTEN 21	GRAVITY GRAVE EP (Gravity Grave [Edit]/Endless Life/ She's A Superstar [Live at Clapham Grand]) (10", p/s)	10
92	Hut HUTT 16	She's A Superstar/Feel (12" promo, white label)	18
92	Strange Fruit SFPMA 214	HUT — THE PEEL SESSIONS (10", p/s)	7
92	Strange Fruit SFMCD 214	HUT — THE PEEL SESSIONS (CD)	8
93	Hut HUTUS 1/YARDCD 1	THE VERVE EP (Gravity Grave [Edit]/A Man Called Sun/She's A Superstar [Edit]/Endless Life/Feel) (CD, export issue to U.S., 3,000 issued in U.K.)	8
93	Hut HUTEN 29	Blue/Twilight/Where The Geese Go/No Come Down (10", p/s)	12
93	Hut HUTCD 29	Blue/Twilight/Where The Geese Go/No Come Down (CD)	8
93	Hut HUT 35	Slide Away/Make It 'Til Monday (pink vinyl, p/s)	6
93	(no label) FLEXI 1	Make It 'Til Monday (Glastonbury '93) (clear vinyl stickered flexi with magazine)	35
95	Hut HUT 54	This Is Music/Let The Damage Begin (purple vinyl, p/s)	8
95	Hut HUT 55	On Your Own/I See The Door (green vinyl, p/s)	8
95	Hut HUT 55	On Your Own/I See The Door (green vinyl, p/s, mispressing, B-side plays 'Friends' by Daryll-Ann)	15
97	Hut HUTTR 82	Bitter Sweet Symphony (James Lavelle Remix)/(James Lavelle Instrumental Remix) (12", stickered plain die-cut sleeve, promo only)	15
97	Hut HUTTP 82	Bitter Sweet Symphony (Extended Version)/(M.S.G. Mix)/(Instrumental) (12", plain die-cut sleeve, promo only)	8
97	Hut HUT 88	The Drugs Don't Work (Radio Edit)/(Demo Version)/Three Steps/The Crab (12", p/s, 5000 only)	8
97	Hut HUTLH 92	Lucky Man/Never Wanna See You Cry (jukebox issue)	7
97	Hut HUTT 92	Lucky Man/Never Wanna See You Cry/MSG/The Longest Day (12", p/s)	8
98	Hut HUTTX 100	Sonnet/Stamped/So Sister/Echo Bass (12", title sleeve)	12
97	Hut HUTLPX 45	URBAN HYMNS (2-LP)	18
97	Hut HUTLPX 45	URBAN HYMNS (2-LP, with inner sleeves, printed outer mailer, 5,000 only)	30
97	Hut CDPHUT 45	URBAN HYMNS (CD, ribbon-tied black gatefold sleeve, promo only)	40
93	Jolly Roger JOLLY ROGER 2	VOYAGER 1 (LP, official bootleg, blue vinyl, 1,000 only)	70

VETS
79	SRT SRTS 79	Flies/Contrix (no p/s)	120

V FOR VENDETTA
(see under David J.)

VHF
80	Lion PAW 1	Heart Of Stone	75

VIBRATIONS
61	Pye International 7N 25107	The Watusi/Wallflower	25
64	London HLK 9875	My Girl Sloopy/Daddy Woo Woo	20
66	Columbia DB 7895	Canadian Sunset/The Story Of A Starry Night	25
67	Columbia DB 8175	Pick Me/You Better Beware	30
67	Columbia DB 8318	Talkin' 'Bout Love/One Mint Julep	25
68	Direction 58-3511	Love In Them There Hills/Remember The Rain	15
67	Columbia SX 6106	NEW VIBRATIONS (LP)	75
69	Direction 8-63644	GREATEST HITS (LP)	45
72	RCA SF 8254	THE VIBRATIONS (LP)	30

(see also Jayhawks)

VIBRATORS
76	RAK RAK 245	We Vibrate/Whips And Furs	10
76	RAK RAK 246	Pogo Dancing/The Pose (as Vibrators with Chris Spedding)	10
77	RAK RAK 253	Bad Times/No Heart (unreleased, two acetates exist; £150)	
77	Epic EPC 5302	Baby Baby/Into The Future (p/s)	5
77	Epic EPC 5565	London Girls/Stiff Little Fingers (live) (p/s)	5
78	Epic EPC 6393	Judy Says (Knock You On The Head)/Pure Mania (p/s)	5
80	Rat Race RAT 2	Gimme Some Lovin'/Power Cry (live) (p/s, in slightly different colours)	5
80	Rat Race RAT 4	Disco In Mosco/Take A Chance (p/s, with various coloured writing)	5
77	Epic EPC 82097	PURE MANIA (LP)	15
78	Epic EPC 82495	V2 (LP, with inner lyric sleeve)	15

(see also Boyfriends, Chris Spedding, Nazis Against Fascism, Substitute, Troops Of Tomorrow, Urban Dogs)

VIBRATORS (Jamaica)
66	Doctor Bird DB 1036	Sloop John B/Amour	18

(see also Al & Vibrators, Wilbert Francis & Vibrators)

VICE CREEMS
78	Tiger GRRRR 1	Won't You Be My Girl?/01-01-212 (gatefold p/s)	30
79	Zig Zag ZZ22 001	Danger Love/Like A Tiger (p/s)	22

VICEROYS
67	Island WI 3095	Lip And Tongue/DAWN PENN: When Am I Gonna Be Free	42
67	Coxsone CS 7031	Magadown/RICHARD ACE: Don't Let The Sun Catch You Crying	35
67	Studio One SO 2016	Lose And Gain (as Voiceroys)/SOUL BROTHERS: Honey Pot	30
67	Studio One SO 2025	Shake Up/NORMA FRAZER: Telling Me Lies	30
68	Studio One SO 2064	Last Night/Ya Ho	25
68	Blue Cat BS 121	Fat Fish/OCTAVES: You're Gonna Lose	35
69	Studio One SO 2077	Things A-Come To Bump/LYRICS: Old Man Say	25

69	Punch PH 3	Jump In A Fire/Give To Get (as Voiceroys)	15
69	Crab CRAB 12	Work It/You Mean So Much To Me (B-side actually by Paragons)	30
69	Crab CRAB 27	Death A-Come (actually by Lloyd Robinson)/MATADOR ALLSTARS: The Sword	8
73	Harry J. HJ 6658	Chucky (Parts 1 & 2)	5
74	Harry J. HJ 6669	Wheel & Jig (Parts 1 & 2)	5
82	Trojan TRLS 206	WE MUST UNITE (LP)	45
83	Csa CSLP 5	BRETHEREN AND SISTREN (LP)	50

(see also Richard Ace, Interns [Jamaica], Derrick Morgan, Vincent Gordon, Hub)

VICEROYS (U.K.)
70	Bullet BU 441	Chariot Coming/SYDNEY ALLSTARS: Stackata	10
70	Bullet BU 444	Power Control/SLICKERS: Dip Dip	10
70	Bullet BU 450	Come On Over/SYDNEY ALLSTARS: Version	10
70	Bullet BU 453	Fancy Clothes/BIGGIE: Jack And Jill	10
71	Bullet BU 470	Rebel Nyah/Feel The Spirit	10

VICE SQUAD
80	Riot City RIOT 1	Last Rockers/Living On Dreams/Latex Love (p/s, with poster)	8
81	Riot City RIOT 2	Resurrection/Young Blood/Hurricane (p/s)	6
82	Riot City RIOT 12 1/2	SINGLES (12" EP)	8
82	Zonophone Z 26	Out Of Reach/Sterile/Out Of Reach (p/s)	5
82	Zonophone Z 30	Rock 'n' Roll Massacre/Stand Strong And Proud/Tomorrow	5
80s	Vice Squad Fan Club	EVIL (EP, flexidisc)	12

(see also Sex Aids)

VICE VERSA
| 80 | Neutron NT 001/PX 1092 | MUSIC 4 (EP, poster p/s) | 10 |

(see also Liza Strike)

VICIOUS PINK (PHENOMENA)
82	Mobile Suit Corp. CORP 1	My Private Tokyo/Promises (p/s)	5
82	Mobile Suit Corp. CORP 12	My Private Tokyo (Long Version)/(Remix)/Promises (12", p/s)	8
83	Warehouse WARE 1T	Je T'Aime (Moi Non Plus) (12" Disco Version)/In The Swim (12", p/s)	8

(see also Soft Cell)

MIKE VICKERS (ORCHESTRA)
65	Columbia DB 7657	On The Brink/The Puff Adder (as Mike Vickers & Orchestra)	40
66	Columbia DB 7825	Eleventy One/The Inkling	15
66	Columbia DB 7906	Morgan — A Suitable Case For Treatment/Gorilla Of My Dreams (as Mike Vickers Orchestra)	15
67	Columbia DB 8171	Air On A G-String/Proper Charles (as Mike Vickers Orchestra)	8
67	Columbia DB 8281	Captain Scarlet And The Mysterons/Kettle Of Fish	25
90s	Emidisc EMIDISC 101	On The Brink/SAINT ETIENNE: Emidisc Theme (promo only)	7
68	Columbia S(C)X 6180	I WISH I WERE A GROUP AGAIN (LP)	40+

(see also Manfred Mann, Baker Street Philharmonic)

SUE VICKERS
| 72 | Threshold TH 8 | Loving You The Way I Do/Take Me With You | 5 |

MACK VICKERY
| 60 | Top Rank JAR 420 | Fantasy/Hawaiian Stroll | 12 |

VICKY
67	Philips BF 1565	Colours Of Love (Love Is Blue)/Who Can Tell	12
67	Philips BF 1599	Sunshine Boy/Tell Me	10
68	Philips BF 1631	Dance With Me Until Tomorrow/Give Me Your Hand	10

(see also Vicky Leandros)

VICKY & JERRY
| 60 | HMV POP 715 | Don't Cry/A Year Ago Tonight | 20 |

VICTIM
78	Good Vibrations GOT 2	Strange Things By Night/Mixed Up World (wraparound p/s)	10
79	TJM TJM 13	THE VICTIM (EP, unreleased)	
79	TJM TJM 14	Why Are Fire Engines Red/I Need You (p/s)	25
80	TJM TJM 15	The Teen Age/Junior Criminals/Hung On To Yourself (p/s)	25
80	Illuminated ILL 1	The Teen Age/Junior Criminals/Hung On To Yourself (p/s, reissue)	15

VICTIMIZE
| 79 | I.M.E. IME 1 | Baby Buyer/Hi Rising Failure (folded p/s) | 70 |
| 80 | I.M.E. IME 2 | Wh?r? Did Th? Mon?y Go (p/s) | 80 |

VICTIMS OF CHANCE
| 70 | Stable SLE 8004 | VICTIMS OF CHANCE (LP) | 60+ |

VICTIMS OF CIRCUMSTANCE
| 80s | Double Vision DV 1 | Very Little Glory/OPPOSITION: Wires (p/s) | 10 |

VICTIMS OF PLEASURE
| 80 | P.A.M. VOP 1 | When You're Young/If I Was/Sporting Pastimes (p/s) | 10 |

VICTIMS OF VICTIMISATION
| 87 | Death DEAD 2 | Kill Or Be Killed/As A Doornail (p/s) | 18 |

TONY VICTOR
62	Decca F 11459	Dear One/There Was A Time	28
63	Decca F 11626	Thinking Of You/Hokey Cokey	12
63	Decca F 11708	In The Still Of The Night/Money	12

VICTORIA
71	Atlantic 2091 084	Tule's Blues/Helplessly Hoping	6
71	Atlantic 2400 176	VICTORIA (LP)	30
71	Mojo 2466 008	SECRET OF THE BLOOM (LP)	45

VICTORIANS
64   Liberty LIB 55693   Oh What A Night For Love/Happy Birthday Blue........................... 20

VICTORS
65   Oriole CB 1984   Take This Old Hammer/Answer's No 10

VICTORS
69   High Note HS 019   Reggae Buddy/Easy Squeeze 12
71   Escort ERT 846   Me A Tell Yuh/LLOYD'S ALL-STARS: More Echo............................ 8

VIDELS
60   London HLI 9153   Mister Lonely/I'll Forget You 80

VIGILANTES
61   Pye International 7N 25082   Eclipse/Man In Space 20

(PAUL) VIGRASS
68   RCA RCA 1755   New Man/Curly 7
69   RCA RCA 1800   Suzie/Funky Piano Joe (as Vigrass) 6
69   RCA RCA 1857   Free Lorry Ride/Flying 6
70   RCA RCA 1911   Stop/Like It Never Was 6

VIKINGS
63   Island WI 035   Maggie Don't Leave Me/Henchmen (both actually with Victor Wong).......... 20
63   Island WI 065   Hallelujah/Helpin' Ages (actually by Maytals) 12
63   Island WI 075   Six And Seven Books Of Moses/Zacions (actually by Maytals)............. 12
63   Island WI 101   Never Grow Old/Irene (actually by Maytals) (some with p/s) 25/20
63   Island WI 107   Just Got To Be/You Make Me Do (actually by Maytals)...................... 20
63   Island WI 117   Fever/Cheer Up (actually by Maytals)................................... 20
64   Island WI 167   Daddy/It's You (actually by Maytals).................................. 20
64   Black Swan WI 423   Down By The Riverside/This Way 20
64   Black Swan WI 428   Treat Me Bad/Sitting On Top 25
64   Black Swan WI 430   Come Into My Parlour/I Am In Love 20
     (see also Maytals, Flames [Jamaica], Bonnie & Skitto)

VIKINGS
66   Alp 595 011   Bad News Feeling/What Can I Do 25

VILENESS
90   Noisome STENCH 3   March Of The Vile/Sex Is Vile (12", vile-scented p/s) 10

VILLAGE
69   Head HDS 4002   Man In The Moon/Long Time Coming...................................... 50
     (see also Peter Bardens, Quiver)

VILLAGE IDIOTS
66   Piccadilly 7N 35282   Laughing Policeman/I Know An Old Lady 6

VILLAGERS/PARCEL OF ROGUES
73   Deroy (no cat. no.)   PARCEL OF FOLK (LP, private pressing, with insert)................... 70+

VILLAGE SOUL CHOIR
70   Direction 58-4969   Catwalk/Country Walk.. 8

VILLAGE STOMPERS
63   Columbia DB 7123   Washington Square/Turkish Delight 8

CATERINA VILLALBA
60   Ember EMB S 104   Quando La Luna/Amore Fantastico (p/s) 6

JOE VINA
59   Top Rank JAR 251   Marina/That's Alright... 5

RAE VINCE & VINCENTS
64   Piccadilly 7N 35211   One Fine Day/Little Girl, I'm Sad 6

GENE VINCENT (& BLUE CAPS)
78s
56   Capitol CL 14599   Be-Bop-A-Lula/Woman Love 15
56   Capitol CL 14628   Race With The Devil/Gonna Back Up, Baby.............................. 25
56   Capitol CL 14637   Bluejean Bop/Who Slapped John?...................................... 15
57   Capitol CL 14681   Jumps, Giggles And Shouts/Wedding Bells (Are Breaking Up That
                              Old Gang Of Mine) 30
57   Capitol CL 14693   Crazy Legs/Important Words 30
57   Capitol CL 14722   Bi-I-Bickey-Bi, Bo-Bo-Go/Five Days, Five Days....................... 30
57   Capitol CL 14763   Lotta Lovin'/Wear My Ring... 25
57   Capitol CL 14808   Dance To The Bop/I Got It 25
58   Capitol CL 14830   Walkin' Home From School/I Got A Baby............................... 45
59   Capitol CL 15053   Right Now/The Night Is So Lonely 180
     (The above 78s are credited to Gene Vincent & Blue Caps)
45s
56   Capitol CL 14599   Be-Bop-A-Lula/Woman Love 40
56   Capitol CL 14628   Race With The Devil/Gonna Back Up, Baby............................. 100
56   Capitol CL 14637   Bluejean Bop/Who Slapped John?...................................... 65
57   Capitol CL 14681   Jumps, Giggles And Shouts/Wedding Bells (Are Breaking Up That
                              Old Gang Of Mine) (promo copy in p/s) 150
57   Capitol CL 14681   Jumps, Giggles And Shouts/Wedding Bells (Are Breaking Up That
                              Old Gang Of Mine) .... 75+
57   Capitol CL 14693   Crazy Legs/Important Words (in promo p/s) 75
57   Capitol CL 14693   Crazy Legs/Important Words 50
57   Capitol CL 14722   Bi-I-Bickey-Bi, Bo-Bo-Go/Five Days, Five Days (in p/s) 150
57   Capitol CL 14722   Bi-I-Bickey-Bi, Bo-Bo-Go/Five Days, Five Days....................... 75
57   Capitol CL 14763   Lotta Lovin'/Wear My Ring... 50
57   Capitol CL 14808   Dance To The Bop/I Got It 55

58	Capitol CL 14830	Walkin' Home From School/I Got A Baby (in p/s)	70
58	Capitol CL 14830	Walkin' Home From School/I Got A Baby	40
58	Capitol CL 14868	Baby Blue/True To You	40
58	Capitol CL 14908	Rocky Road Blues/Yes I Love You, Baby	40
58	Capitol CL 14935	Git It/Little Lover	40
59	Capitol CL 14974	Say Mama/Be Bop Boogie Boy	30
59	Capitol CL 15000	Who's Pushin' Your Swing/Over The Rainbow	22
59	Capitol CL 15035	Summertime/Frankie And Johnnie	20
59	Capitol CL 15053	Right Now/The Night Is So Lonely	22
59	Capitol CL 15099	Wild Cat/Right Here On Earth	15
60	Capitol CL 15115	My Heart/I've Got To Get You Yet	20

(The above singles are credited to Gene Vincent & Blue Caps. Later 45s were solo, unless otherwise stated.)

60	Capitol CL 15136	Pistol Packin' Mama (as Gene Vincent & Beat Boys)/Weeping Willow	15
60	Capitol CL 15169	Anna-Annabelle/Ac-Cent-Tchu-Ate The Positive	15
61	Capitol CL 15179	Maybe/Jezebel	15
61	Capitol CL 15185	If You Want My Lovin'/Mister Loneliness	15
61	Capitol CL 15202	She She Little Sheila/Hot Dollar	15
61	Capitol CL 15215	I'm Going Home (To See My Baby)/Love Of A Man	15
61	Capitol CL 15231	Unchained Melody/Brand New Beat (with The Blue Caps)	15
62	Capitol CL 15243	Lucky Star/Baby Don't Believe Him (with Dave Burgess Band)	18
62	Capitol CL 15264	Be-Bop-A-Lula/The King Of Fools (with Charles Blackwell Orchestra)	18
63	Capitol CL 15290	Held For Questioning/You're Still In My Heart (with Charles Blackwell Orchestra)	18
63	Capitol CL 15307	Rip It Up/High Blood Pressure (unissued, demo copies only)	250+
63	Capitol CL 15307	Crazy Beat/High Blood Pressure	40
63	Columbia DB 7174	Temptation Baby/Where Have You Been All My Life	20
64	Columbia DB 7218	Humpity Dumpity/A Love 'Em And Leave 'Em Kinda Guy	20
64	Columbia DB 7293	La-Den-Da Den-Da-Da/The Beginning Of The End	20
64	Columbia DB 7343	Private Detective/You Are My Sunshine (as Gene Vincent & Shouts)	20
66	London HLH 10079	Bird Doggin'/Ain't That Too Much	40
66	London HLH 10099	Lonely Street/I've Got My Eyes On You	35
68	Capitol CL 15546	Be-Bop-A-Lula/Say Mama	15
69	Dandelion S 4596	Be-Bop-A-Lula '69/Ruby Baby	12
70	Dandelion S 4974	White Lightning/Scarlet Ribbons (For Her Hair)	15
71	Kama Sutra 2013 018	The Day The World Turned Blue/High On Life (some with large centre)	10
73	Spark SRL 1091	Story Of The Rockers/Pickin' Poppies (push-out or solid centre)	10
74	BBC BEEB 001	Roll Over Beethoven/Say Mama/Be-Bop-A-Lula '71 (push-out or solid centre)	7
77	Capitol CL 15906	Say Mama/Lotta Lovin'/Race With The Devil	5
81	Capitol CL 203	She She Little Sheila/Say Mama/Dance To The Bop (p/s)	5
87	Nighttracks SFNT 001	Nighttracks (Distant Drums/Be-Bop-A-Lula) (p/s, promo only with insert)	10

EPs

58	Capitol EAP 1-985	HOT ROD GANG	85
59	Capitol EAP 1-1059	A GENE VINCENT RECORD DATE	75
60	Capitol EAP 3-1059	A GENE VINCENT RECORD DATE PART 3	85
61	Capitol EAP 1-20173	IF YOU WANT MY LOVIN'	85
62	Capitol EAP 1-20354	RACE WITH THE DEVIL	80
63	Capitol EAP 1-20461	TRUE TO YOU	90
64	Capitol EAP 1-20453	THE CRAZY BEAT OF GENE VINCENT NO. 1	85
64	Capitol EAP 2-20453	THE CRAZY BEAT OF GENE VINCENT NO. 2	85
64	Capitol EAP 3-20453	THE CRAZY BEAT OF GENE VINCENT NO. 3	85
69	EMIdisc (no cat. no.)	LIVE & ROCKIN'! (fan club issue, mail-order, 99 only)	250
79	Rollin' Danny RD 1	RAINY DAY SUNSHINE (L.A. 1969 demos, 500 only)	12
81	Magnum Force MFEP 003	RAINY DAY SUNSHINE (reissue)	8

LPs

56	Capitol T 764	BLUEJEAN BOP! (originally with turquoise labels; later rainbow)	130/85
57	Capitol T 811	GENE VINCENT AND THE BLUECAPS (turquoise or rainbow labels)	130/85
58	Capitol T 970	GENE VINCENT ROCKS! & THE BLUECAPS ROLL (originally with turquoise labels, later rainbow labels)	130/85
59	Capitol T 1059	A GENE VINCENT RECORD DATE	80
59	Capitol T 1207	SOUNDS LIKE GENE VINCENT	80
60	Capitol (S)T 1342	CRAZY TIMES! (mono/stereo)	70/110
63	Capitol T 20453	THE CRAZY BEAT OF GENE VINCENT	70
64	Columbia 33SX 1646	SHAKIN' UP A STORM (as Gene Vincent & The Shouts)	80
65	Music F. Pleasure MFP 1053	CRAZY TIMES (reissue)	15
67	London HA-H 8333	GENE VINCENT	55

(The Capitol compilations listed above may exist with later label designs. These would be worth half the values listed.)

67	Capitol T 20957	THE BEST OF GENE VINCENT ('rainbow' label; reissue with pink label £12)	20
68	Capitol ST 21144	THE BEST OF GENE VINCENT VOL. 2 ('rainbow' label; reissue with pink label £12)	22
70	Dandelion 63754	I'M BACK AND I'M PROUD (gatefold sleeve)	35
71	Kama Sutra 2316 005	THE DAY THE WORLD TURNED BLUE	30
71	Kama Sutra 2316 009	IF YOU COULD ONLY SEE ME TODAY	30
87	Charly BOX 108	GENE VINCENT: THE CAPITOL YEARS '56-'63 (10-LP box set with 36-page booklet; later remastered and reissued with slimmer box, 1989)	70
90	EMI CDGV 1	THE GENE VINCENT BOX SET (Complete Capitol & Columbia Recordings, 1956-64) (6-CD set)	50

RORY VINCENT

| 73 | Columbia SCXA 9254 | SINGS THE MUSIC OF WLODEK GULGOWSKI (LP) | 15 |

CAROLE VINCI

| 78 | EMI EMI 2801 | Vivre/Souffire Et Sourire | 12 |

JOEY VINE

| 65 | Immediate IM 017 | Down And Out/The Out Of Towner | 22 |

MINT VALUE £

VINEGAR JOE
72	Island WIP 6125	Never Met A Dog/Speed Queen Of Ventura	5
72	Island WIP 6148	Rock'n'Roll Gypsies/So Long	5
73	Island WIP 6174	Black Smoke From The Calumet/Long Way Round	5
72	Island ILPS 9183	VINEGAR JOE (LP)	25
72	Island ILPS 9214	ROCK 'N ROLL GYPSIES (LP, gatefold sleeve)	20
73	Island ILPS 9262	SIX STAR GENERAL (LP, gatefold sleeve)	20

(see also Dada, Robert Palmer, Elkie Brooks)

VINES
01	RexRec REKD 195	Factory/Ain't No Room/Drown The Baptists (p/s, 500 only)	20
03	Heavenly NR 72435 5378477	Fuck The World/Fuck The World (white vinyl, title sleeve, 300 only)	10

EDDIE 'MR. CLEANHEAD' VINSON
51	Vogue V 2023	Queen Bee Blues/Jump And Grunt (78)	32
64	Riverside RLP 3302	BACK DOOR BLUES (LP)	40
72	Philips 6369 406	THE ORIGINAL CLEANHEAD (LP)	18

(see also Wynonie Harris)

V. VINSTRICK & J.J. ALLSTARS
68	Doctor Bird DB 1167	Love Is Not A Game/CINDERELLA: The Way I See You	20

BOBBY VINTON
61	Fontana H 307	Little Lonely One/Corrine Corrina	12
62	London HLU 9592	I Love You The Way You Are/CHUCK & JOHNNY: You Are My Girl	12
62	Columbia DB 4878	Roses Are Red/You And I	5
62	Columbia DB 4900	Rain Rain Go Away/Over Over	5
63	Columbia DB 4961	Trouble Is My Middle Name/Let's Kiss And Make Up	5
63	Columbia DB 7015	Over The Mountain/Faded Pictures	5
63	Columbia DB 7052	Blue On Blue/Those Little Things	5
63	Columbia DB 7110	Blue Velvet/Is There A Place	15
63	Columbia DB 7179	There! I've Said It Again/The Girl With The Bow In Her Hair	5
64	Columbia DB 7240	My Heart Belongs To Only You/Warm And Tender	5
64	Columbia DB 7303	Tell Me Why/Remembering	5
64	Columbia DB 7348	Clinging Vine/Imagination Is A Magic Dream	5
64	Columbia DB 7422	Mr Lonely/The Bell That Couldn't Jingle	15
62	Columbia SEG 8212	YOUNG IN HEART (EP)	18
64	Columbia SEG 8363	SONGS OF CHRISTMAS (EP)	18
63	Columbia 33SX 1517	SINGS THE BIG ONES (LP)	18
63	Columbia 33SX 1566	BLUE ON BLUE (LP)	18

MATT VINYL
77	Housewife's Choice	Useless Tasks (p/s)	8

VIOLATORS
82	No Future OI 9	Gangland/Fugitive (p/s, with insert)	10
82	No Future OI 19	Summer Of '81/Live Fast Die Young (p/s)	8
83	Future FS 2	Life On The Red Line/Crossing The Sangsara (p/s)	6

VIOLENTS
63	HMV POP 1130	Alpen Ros/Ghia	18

VIOLENT THIMBLE
67	Polydor 56217	Gentle People Parts 1 & 2	10

VIPERS (SKIFFLE GROUP)
56	Parlophone R 4238	Ain't You Glad/Pick A Bale Of Cotton	20
57	Parlophone R 4261	Don't You Rock Me Daddy-O/10,000 Years Ago	20
57	Parlophone R 4286	Jim Dandy/Hi Liley, Liley Lo	20
57	Parlophone R 4289	The Cumberland Gap/Maggie May	20
57	Parlophone R 4308	Streamline Train/Railroad Steam Boat	18
57	Parlophone R 4351	Homing Bird/Pay Me My Money Down	18
57	Parlophone R 4371	Skiffle Party Medley Parts 1 & 2	18
58	Parlophone R 4393	Baby Why?/No Other Baby (as Vipers) (78 rpm = £8)	25
58	Parlophone R 4435	Make Ready For Love/Nothing Will Ever Change (My Love For You) (as Vipers) (78=£8)	15
58	Parlophone R 4484	Summertime Blues/Liverpool Blues (as Vipers) (78 rpm = £25)	35
57	Parlophone GEP 8615	SKIFFLE MUSIC VOL. 1 (EP)	20
57	Parlophone GEP 8626	SKIFFLE MUSIC VOL. 2 (EP)	25
57	Parlophone GEP 8655	SKIFFLING ALONG WITH THE VIPERS (EP)	30
57	Parlophone PMD 1050	COFFEE BAR SESSION (10" LP)	50+

(see also Jet Harris & Tony Meehan, Shadows, Wally Whyton, Sharkey Todd & Monsters)

VIPERS
78	Mulligan LUNS 718	I've Got You/No Such Thing (p/s)	10

VIPPS
66	CBS 202031	Wintertime/Anyone	40

(see also VIPS)

VIPS
64	RCA RCA 1427	Don't Keep Shouting At Me/She's So Good	80
66	Island WI 3003	I Wanna Be Free/Don't Let It Go	40
67	Island WIP 6005	Straight Down To The Bottom/In A Dream	60

(see also Vipps, Art, Spooky Tooth, Felder's Orioles, Timebox, Patto, Baron & His Pounding Piano, Keith Emerson)

V.I.P.s
78	Bust SOL 3	MUSIC FOR FUNSTERS (EP)	20
79	Rok ROK V/VI	Can't Let You Go/URBAN DISTURBANCE: Wild Boys In Cortinas	25
80	Gem GEMS 43	I Need Somebody To Love (Could It Be You?)/One More Chance// Stuttgart Special/Who Knows/Janine (double pack, stickered p/s)	10

(see also Mood Six, Jed Dmochowski)

VIRGIL BROTHERS
69	Parlophone R 5787	Temptation 'Bout To Get Me/Look Away	20
69	Parlophone R 5802	Good Love/When You Walk Away	6

VIRGINIANS
63	Pye International 7N 25175	Limbo Baby/Greenback Dollar	10

VIRGINIA TREE
75	Minstrel 0001	FRESH OUT (LP)	35

(see also Shirley Kent, Ghost)

VIRGINIA WOLF
86	Atlantic A 9459	Waiting For Your Love/Take A Chance (p/s)	10

VIRGINIA WOLVES
66	Stateside SS 563	Stay/B.L.T. (DJ copy = £85)	45

VIRGIN PRUNES
81	Baby BABY 001	TWENTY TENS (EP)	8
81	Rough Trade RT 072	In The Greylight/War/Moments Of Mine (Despite Straight Lines) (1st issue in blue p/s with insert, later in black p/s without insert)	6/4
81	Rough Trade RT 090	A New Form Of Beauty Part Two: Come To Daddy/Sweet Home Under White Clouds/Sad World (10", p/s, 33rpm)	7
81	Rough Trade RT 091T	A New Form Of Beauty Part Three: The Beast (Seven Bastard Suck)/ The Slow Children (Abbagal)/Brain Damage/No Birds To Fly (12", p/s)	8
81	Rough Trade RT 089-091	A NEW FORM OF BEAUTY (7"/10"/12" box set)	22
82	Rough Trade RT 106	Pagan Lovesong/Dave-id Is Dead (p/s)	5
82	Rough Trade 12 RT 106	Pagan Lovesong (Vibe Akimbo)/Pagan Lovesong/Dave-id Is Dead (12", p/s)	8
87	Baby BABY 011	HERESIE (10", double pack, gatefold p/s, 1st 1,000 on clear vinyl)	10/7

(see also Gavin Friday, Bono & Gavin Friday)

VIRGIN SLEEP
67	Deram DM 146	Love/Halliford House	45
68	Deram DM 173	Secret/Comes A Time	45

VIRTUE
85	Other OTH 1	We Stand To Fight (p/s)	20

VIRTUES (Jamaica)
65	Island WI 196	Your Wife And Mother/Amen (actually with Ambassadors)	15
68	Doctor Bird DB 1164	High Tide/RUPIE EDWARDS & VIRTUES: Burning Love	25

(see also Lloyd & Devon)

VIRTUES (U.S.)
59	HMV POP 621	Guitar Boogie Shuffle/Guitar In Orbit	22
59	HMV POP 637	Flippin' In/Shufflin' Along (78 rpm = £20)	22

FRANK VIRTUOSO ROCKETS
56	Melodisc MEL 1386	Rollin' And A-Rockin'/Rock — Good Bye Mambo (78)	25
56	Melodisc MEL 1393	Toodle-Oo Kangaroo/Hop-Skip-Jump Mambo (78)	15
58	Melodisc MEL 1386	Rollin' And A-Rockin'/Rock — Good Bye Mambo (red label, tri centre, export issue)	30
58	Melodisc MEL 1386	Rollin' And Rockin'/Toodle-Oo Kangaroo (green label, round centre)	15

VISAGE
79	Radar ADA 48	Tar/Frequency 7 (p/s)	10
81	Polydor POSPX 194	Fade To Grey/The Steps (12", p/s)	15
81	Polydor POSPX 236	Mind Of A Toy (Dance Mix)/We Move (Dance Mix)/Frequency 7 (Dance Mix) (12", p/s)	10
82	Polydor POSPP 441	Night Train/I'm Still Searching (picture disc)	5
82	Polydor POSPP 523	Pleasure Boys/The Anvil (picture disc)	7
82	Polydor POSPX 523	Pleasure Boys (Dance Mix)/The Anvil (Dance Mix) (12", 800 only)	12
82	Polydor POSPV 523	Der Amboss (12", 1-sided, stickered plain black sleeve & labels, promo only)	12
88	Polydor 080 012-2	Mind Of A Toy/We Move (Dance Mix)/Frequency 7 (Dance Mix)/ Mind Of A Toy (Video) (CD Video)	15
83	Polydor VIS 1	FADE TO GREY (DANCE MIX PROMO) (LP, stamped white sleeve, promo only)	20

(see also Rich Kids, Steve Strange, Strange Cruise, Midge Ure, Ultravox)

TONY VISCONTI
79	Regal Zonophone RZ 3089	I Remember Brooklyn/Sitting In A Field Of Heather	15

(see also Dib Cochran & Earwigs)

VISCOUNTS
60	Pye 7N 15249	That's All Right/Rockin' Little Angel	8
60	Pye NEP 24132	VISCOUNTS' HIT PARADE (EP)	25

(see also Gordon Mills)

VISCOUNTS (U.S.)
59	Top Rank JAR 254	Harlem Nocturne/Dig	22
60	Top Rank JAR 388	The Touch (Le Grisbi)/Chug-A-Lug	20
60	Top Rank JAR 502	Night Train/Summertime	18
65	Stateside SS 468	Harlem Nocturne/Dig (reissue)	15
61	Top Rank JKP 3005	VISCOUNTS ROCK (EP)	100

VISIONS
69	Grape GR 3009	Captain Hook/The Girl	40

(see also King Horror)

VISITORS
78	NRG SRTS/NRG 002	Take It Or Leave It/No Compromise	30

VISITORS
79	Deep Heat DEEP ONE	Electric Heat/Moth/One Line (p/s)	8
80	Departure RAPTURE 1	Empty Rooms/The Orcadian Visitors (foldover p/s)	7

VISITORS
87 Sha La La   Goldmining/MAGIC SHOP: It's True (flexidisc, p/s,
      BA BA BA BA BA 8   free with *Simply Thrilled* & other fanzines) 10/7

VITAL FORCE
87 Buce BUCE 1   Roll The Dice/Poor Little Rich Boy (no p/s) 25

AMOR VIVI
70 Big Shot BI 534   Dirty Dog/Round And Round The Moon 8

VIVIENNE
57 HMV 7EG 8290   VIVIENNE (EP) 8

VIXEN
88 EMI MTPD 48   Edge Of A Broken Heart/Charmed Life (shaped picture disc) 7
88 EMI MTL 1028   VIXEN (LP, early copies play extra track "Charmed Life", withdrawn) 12

VLADO & ISOLDA
84 Ariola 106 500   Ciao Amore (English)/Ciao Amore (Croatian) 10

VOGUES (U.K.)
66 Columbia DB 7985 Younger Girl/Lies. 18
(see also Llan)

VOGUES (U.S.)
65 London HLU 9996   You're The One/Some Words. 18
66 London HLU 10014 Five O'Clock World/Nothing To Offer You 18
66 King KG 1035   Magic Town/Humpty Dumpty 22
68 Reprise RS 20766 My Special Angel/I Keep It Hid. 6
68 Reprise RS 20686 Turn Around Look At Me/Then. 6
69 Reprise RS 20788 Till/I Will 6
69 London HLG 10247 Five O'Clock World/You're The One 15
69 Reprise RS 20820 Earth Angel/P.S. I Love You 6
69 Reprise RS 23366 No, Not Much/You Were Too Good To Me 6
69 Reprise RS 20844 Green Fields/Easy To Say 5
66 King KGL 4003   MEET THE VOGUES (LP) 50
66 King KGL 4006   FIVE O'CLOCK WORLD (LP) 40
69 Reprise RSLP 6314 TURN AROUND, LOOK AT ME (LP) 25
69 Reprise RSLP 6326 TILL (LP) 18

VOICE
66 Mercury MF 905   Train To Disaster/Truth . . . . 200+
(see also Karl Stuart & Profile, Profile, Miller Anderson)

VOICE OF PROGRESS
82 Negus Roots NERLP 003 MINI BUS DRIVER (LP) 40

VOICEROYS
(see under Viceroys)

VOICES
56 Beltona BL 2667   Rock And Roll Hit Parade Medley (Parts 1 & 2) (78 rpm = £12) 18

VOICES IN LATIN
68 Morgan MR 104P   VOICES IN LATIN (LP). 60

VOICES OF EAST HARLEM
70 Elektra 2101 013   Right On Be Free/Gotta Be A Change — Oh Yeah. 8
70 Elektra 2101 018   No No No/Music In The Air. 8
70 Elektra 2469 007   RIGHT ON BE FREE (LP) 25

VOIDS
66 Polydor BM 56073 Come On Out/I'm In A Fix. 80

CRISTIAN VOGEL
94 Ferox FER 004   NARCO SYNTHESIS EP (12", plain sleeve) 25
94 Mosquito MSQ 01 WE EQUATE MACHINES WITH FUNKINESS EP (12", custom sleeve) 25
95 Mosquito MSQ 03 ARTISTS IN CHARGE OF EXPERT SYSTEMS EP (12", custom sleeve) 20
95 Solid SOL 002   DEFUNKT EP (12", three untitled tracks) 20
96 Solid SOL 004   The Visit/Spoke/Small Dogs (12") 30
(see also Blue Arsed Fly)

WES VOIGHT
59 Parlophone R 4586 I'm Movin' In/I'm Ready To Go Steady 130
(see also Chip Taylor)

VOIZ
77 Pilgrim/Grapevine GRA 110 BOANERGES (LP, with insert) 15

HOWARD VOKES COUNTRY BOYS
62 Starlite STEP 27   HOWARD VOKES COUNTRY BOYS (EP) 20
63 Starlite STEP 37   MOUNTAIN GUITAR (EP) 20
67 Starlite GRK 508   HOWARD VOKES COUNTRY BOYS
                   (EP; reissue, with sleeve sticker over original catalogue number) 12

VOLCANOS
61 Philips PB 1098   Ruby Duby Du/Redhead 20
61 Philips PB 1113   Tightrope/Great Imposter 20
62 Philips PB 1246   Polaris/Scotch Mist 20
60 Philips BBE 12432 THE VOLCANOS (EP) 100

VOLTZ
82 Airship   KNIGHT'S FALL (LP) . . . . 70+

VOLUMES
62 Fontana 270 109TF I Love You/Dreams 120
63 London HL 9733   Sandra/Teenage Paradise. 75

VOLUNTEERS
63   Parlophone R 5088   Farther Along/Little David 8
(see also Karol Keyes)

VON BONDIES
03   Must Destroy   Tell Me What You See (1-sided, p/s) 15
      DESTROYER 2

VONTASTICS
66   Chess CRS 8043   Day Tripper/My Baby.. 30
67   Stateside SS 2002   Lady Love/When My Baby Comes Back Home 60

VON TRAP FAMILY
80   Woronzow W 001   Brand New Thrill/Dreaming/No Reflexes (p/s, 500 only)...................... 18
(see also Bevis Frond)

VOOMINS
65   Polydor 56001   If You Don't Come Back/March Of The Voomins............................ 18

VOXPOPPERS
58   Mercury 7MT 202   The Last Drag/Wishing For Your Love (78 rpm = £20) .... 30+
58   Mercury MEP 9533   VOXPOPPERS (EP)... 165

VOYAGER
85   Fighting Cock   Run Away Heart/Don't Hold Back (p/s)...................................... 15

V2
78   Bent SMALL BENT 1   Speed Freak/Nothing To Do/That's It (800 only, later reissued on red vinyl) 15
79   TJM TJM 1   Man In The Box/When The World Isn't There (12", p/s) 20
79   TJM TJM 6   Is Anybody Out There? (unissued)
70s   Groove   Gee Whiz It's You/Face In The Crowd (p/s, stamped white labels) 30

VULCANS
73   Trojan TRLS 53   STAR TREK (LP) 25

VULCAN'S HAMMER
73   Brown BVH 1   TRUE HEARTS AND SOUND BOTTOMS (LP, with insert).................. 300+

VULTURES
79   Rubber Connection SP 522   Time Let's Go/Is This A Man (p/s, with insert & sticker)...................... 6

VULTURES
88   Narodnik NRK 006T   Good Thing/You're Not Scared/What I Say/Jack The Ripper (12", p/s)........... 7

V/VM
01   V/VM VVMT 147   SNOOKER LOOPY (SCREWED BACK BY V/VM) (8 x 7", unboxed set; red,
      yellow, green, brown, blue, pink, black, & white vinyl, poly inners with
      wraparound paper p/s; 147 sets only) 30

V/VM & THIRD EYE FOUNDATION
97   Fat Cat 12FAT 006   Lumberjack WLTM/Female Pig Herder/Looks Unimportant Poss Romance/
      Will Travel North West/There's No End In Sight
      (12", custom 'bullet hole' sleeve) 10

WACKERS
63   Oriole CB 1902   I Wonder Why/Why Can't It Happen To Me............................... 20
64   Piccadilly 7N 35195   Love Or Money/Hooka Tooka.. 12
64   Piccadilly 7N 35210   The Girl Who Wanted Fame/You're Forgetting 12

ADAM WADE
60   Top Rank JAR 296   Tell Her For Me/Don't Cry My Love 7
60   Top Rank JAR 370   Ruby/Too Far 7
63   Columbia DB 4891   Don't Let Me Cross Over/Rain From The Skies............................ 50
60   HMV 7EG 8620   AND THEN CAME ADAM (EP) 18
64   Columbia SEG 8316   FOUR FILM SONGS (EP) 18
61   HMV CLP 1451   ADAM AND EVENING (LP) 30

CLIFF WADE
69   Morgan Bluetown BT 1S   You've Never Been To My House/Sister 18

JOHNNY WADE
60   HMV POP 757   Funny Thing/Shadow Love 8

WELLINGTON WADE
63   Oriole CB 1857   Let's Turkey Trot/It Ain't Necessarily So................................. 22
(see also Ian & Zodiacs)

ADRIAN WAGNER
74   Atlantic K 50082   DISTANCES BETWEEN US (LP, with Robert Calvert) 20
78   Charisma CAS 1135   THE LAST INCA (LP, with booklet) 12
(see also Robert Calvert)

ROBERT WAGNER
57   London HLU 8491   Almost Eighteen/So Young 10

MINT VALUE £

CHUCK WAGON
79	A&M AMS 7450	Rock 'n' Roll Won't Go Away/The Spy In My Face (p/s, black or purple vinyl) .	10/15

(see also Dickies)

PORTER WAGONER
67	RCA Victor RCA 1586	The Cold Hard Facts Of Life/You Can't Make A Heel Toe The Mark	6
64	RCA Victor RCX 7157	A LITTLE SLICE OF LIFE (EP)	15
64	RCA Victor RCX 7158	Y'ALL COME (EP)	15
64	RCA Victor RD 7693	THE BLUE GRASS STORY (LP)	20
65	RCA Camden CDN 5128	AN OLD LOG CABIN FOR SALE (LP)	12

WAH! (HEAT)
81	Inevitable INEV 001	Better Scream/Joe (wraparound p/s in poly bag)	5
81	Inevitable INEV 004	Seven Minutes To Midnight/Don't Step On The Cracks (p/s, different colour sleeves)	5

(see also Faction))

WAILERS (Jamaica)
(see under Bob Marley)

WAILERS (U.S.)
59	London HL 8958	Tall Cool One/Road-Runner (78 rpm = £12)	28
59	London HL 8994	Mau-Mau/Dirty Robber (tri centre, later round) (78 rpm = £110)	150/75
64	London HL 9892	Tall Cool One/Road-Runner (reissue)	6

WAILING COCKS
78	Bird's Nest BN 116	Rockin' Youth/Stand Up For Peace	5
78	Bird's Nest BN 121	Listen To The Wailing Cocks/Listen To The Wailing Cocks	5

WAILING SOULS
70	Banana BA 305	Row Fisherman Row/Thou Shalt Not Steal	18
70	Banana BA 307	Back Out/Pack Your Things	18
71	Banana BA 335	Walk Walk Walk/KING SPORTY: Love Me — Version (B-side actually by Denis Alcapone)	30
71	Green Door GD 4014	Harbour Shark/Harbour Shark — Version	25
76	Conflict 301	Black Out/Dub	10
81	Cha Cha CHAD 51	Grabbing And Running/Dub	20
82	Greensleeves GRED 111	They Don't Know Jah/Sticky Stay (12")	30
82	Upfront UPF 001	Take We Back (feat Ranking Trevor)/RANKING TREVOR: Yard Oh (12")	15

(see also Denis Alcapone, Tuff Gong All Stars)

WAILING WAILERS
(see under Bob Marley & Wailers)

CHERRY WAINER
58	Pye 7N 15161	Itchy Twitchy Feeling/Cerveza (78 rpm = £6)	10
58	Pye 7N 15170	Valencia/Blue Cha Cha (78 rpm = £6)	8
59	Pye 7N 15197	The Happy Organ/Spanish Marching Song (78 rpm = £6)	8
59	Pye 7N 15217	The Song Of Lotus Lee/Iced Coffee (78 rpm = £6)	5
59	Top Rank JAR 253	I'll Walk The Line/Saturday Night In Tia Juana	7
60	Columbia DB 4528	Happy Like A Bell (Ding Dong)/Money (That's What I Want)	25
63	Honey Hit TB 128	Sleepwalk/Red River Rock (with Red Price Combo, some with p/s)	10/5
59	Pye NEP 24099	CHERRY WAINER (EP)	25
60	Top Rank BUY 042	WALTZES IN SPRINGTIME (LP)	20

(see also Red Price Combo)

PHIL WAINMAN
65	Columbia DB 7615	Hear Me A Drummer Man/Hear His Drums	12
68	Fontana TF 978	Going Going Gone/Hey Paradiddle	6

LOUDON WAINWRIGHT III
71	Atlantic 2400 103	ALBUM I (LP)	18
72	Atlantic K 40107	ALBUM I (LP, reissue)	12
72	Atlantic K 40272	ALBUM II (LP)	15

WAITING FOR THE SUN
78	Profile GMOR 167	WAITING FOR THE SUN (LP, private pressing)	50

(see also After The Fire)

TOM WAITS
79	Asylum K 12347	Somewhere/Red Shoes By The Drugstore	5
86	Island ISD 260	In The Neighbourhood/Singapore//Tango Till They're Sore/Rain Dogs (double pack, p/s)	5
73	Asylum SYM 9007	CLOSING TIME (LP, with insert)	22
74	Asylum SYM 9012	THE HEART OF SATURDAY NIGHT (LP)	18
75	Asylum SYSP 903	NIGHTHAWKS AT THE DINER (2-LP, gatefold sleeve)	20
76	Asylum K 53030	CLOSING TIME (LP, reissue)	12
76	Asylum K 53035	THE HEART OF SATURDAY NIGHT (LP, 'door' label)	12
77	Asylum K 53050	SMALL CHANGE (LP, 'sky' label)	12
77	Asylum K 53068	FOREIGN AFFAIRS (LP, with inner sleeve)	12
79	Asylum K 53088	BLUE VALENTINE (LP, gatefold sleeve)	12
80	Asylum K 52252	HEARTATTACK AND VINE (LP, with inner sleeve)	12
81	Elektra K 52316	BOUNCED CHEQUES (LP)	12
86	WEA 960 321-1	THE ASYLUM YEARS (2-LP, gatefold sleeve)	15

(see also Roy Orbison)

WAKE
69	Pye 7N 17813	Angelina/So Happy	15
70	Carnaby CNS 4010	Live Today Little Girl/Days Of Emptiness	15
70	Carnaby CNS 4014	Boys In The Band/To Make You Happy	12
70	Carnaby CNS 4016	Noah/To Make You Happy	12
71	Carnaby 6151 001	Linda/Got My Eyes On You	12
70	Carnaby CNLS 6005	23.59 (LP)	100

WAKE

82	Scan SCN 01	On Our Honeymoon/Give Up (p/s in bag)	20
84	Scan 45/Factory FAC 88	Talk About The Past/Everybody Works So Hard (p/s)	7
84	Scan 45/Factory FAC 8812	Talk About The Past/Everybody Works So Hard (12", p/s)	12
87	Factory FAC12 178	Something No-one Else Can Bring/ Gruesome Castle	12
89	Sarah SARAH 21	Crush The Flowers/Carbrain (p/s)	7
90s	Sarah SARAH 48	Major John/Lousy Pop Group (p/s)	7
83	Factory FACT 60	HARMONY (LP)	25
91	Factory FACT 130	HERE COMES EVERYBODY (LP)	20
90s	Sarah SARAH 602	MAKE IT LOUD (LP)	15
90s	Sarah SARAH 618	TIDAL WAVE OF HYPE (LP)	15

JIMMY WAKELY

56	Vogue Coral Q 72125	Are You Mine? (with Ruth Ross)/Yellow Roses	15
56	Brunswick 05542	Are You Satisfied? (with Gloria Wood)/Mississippi Dreamboat	15
56	Brunswick 05563	Folsom Prison Blues/That's What The Lord Can Do	15
57	Brunswick LAT 8179	SANTA FE TRAIL (LP)	20

(see also Karen Chandler, Bob Hope, Margaret Whiting)

RICK WAKEMAN (Band)

73	A&M AMS 7061	Catherine/Anne	5
75	A&M AMS 7206	Love's Dream/Orpheus' Song	6
75	A&M/Lyntone LYN 3176/7	Wagner's Dream/Love's Dream/Count Your Blessings	
		(with 2 tracks by Roger Daltrey, flexidisc free with *19* magazine)	10/5
79	A&M AMS 7435	Birdman Of Alcatraz (Theme From 'My Son My Son')/Falcons De Neige (p/s)	5
79	A&M AMS 7436	Animal Showdown/Sea Horses (p/s)	5
79	A&M AMSP 7436	Animal Showdown/Sea Horses (picture disc, in PVC sleeve)	6
79	A&M AMS 7497	Swan Lager/Woolly Willy Tango	5
80	A&M AMS 7510	I'm So Straight I'm A Weirdo/Do You Believe In Fairies? (p/s)	5
80	WEA K 18354	The Spider/Danielle (some with p/s, 2,000 only)	8/4
71	Polydor 2460 135	PIANO VIBRATIONS (LP, with John Schroeder Orchestra)	15
74	A&M QU-84361	THE SIX WIVES OF HENRY VIII (LP, gatefold sleeve, quadrophonic mix)	18
75	A&M AMLH 64546	LISZTOMANIA (LP, soundtrack, with Roger Daltrey)	12
89	A&M RWCD 20	RICK WAKEMAN: 20TH ANNIVERSARY (4-CD box set, 1,000 only)	80

(see also Strawbs, Yes, Dib Cochran & Earwigs, Steve Howe, Jon Anderson)

HOWARD WALES
(see under Jerry Garcia)

WALHAM GREEN EAST WAPPING CARPET CLEANING
RODENT & BOGGIT EXTERMINATING ASSOCIATION

68	Columbia DB 8426	Sorry Mr. Green/Death Of A Kind	60+

ANNA WALKER & CROWNETTES

69	Pama PM 768	You Don't Know/Billy Joe	8

BILLY WALKER (U.S.)

60	Philips PB 1001	Forever/Changed My Mind	6
66	London HLU 10060	Million And One/Close To Linda	6

BOOTS WALKER

69	London HLP 10265	No One Knows/Geraldine	12+

CLINT WALKER

60	Warner Bros WEP 6006	INSPIRATION (EP, also stereo WSEP 2006)	12/18

DAVID WALKER

68	RCA RCA 1664	Ring The Changes/Keep A Little Love	40+

(see also Paradox)

GARY WALKER (& RAIN)

66	CBS 202036	You Don't Love Me/Get It Right	20
66	CBS 202081	Twinkie-Lee/She Makes Me Feel Better	7
68	Polydor 56237	Spooky/I Can't Stand To Lose You (as Gary Walker & Rain)	15
69	Philips BF 1740	Come In You'll Get Pneumonia/Francis (as Gary Walker & Rain)	55
74	United Artists UP 35742	Hello How Are You/Fran	5
66	CBS EPS 5742	HERE'S GARY (EP)	35

(see also Walker Brothers, Paul & Ritchie & Cryin' Shames, Badfinger, Universals)

JACKIE WALKER

58	London HLP 8588	Oh Lonesome Me/Only Teenagers Allowed (78 rpm = £60)	250

JERRY JEFF WALKER

68	Atlantic 584 200	Mr Bojangles/Round And Round	7
68	Atco 228 006	MR BOJANGLES (LP)	20
71	Atlantic 2466 007	BEIN' FREE (LP)	18

JIMMY WALKER

53	Lyragon J 706	A Fine Romance/Hallelujah (78)	6

JOHN WALKER

67	Philips BF 1593	Anabella/You Don't Understand Me	8
67	Philips BF 1612	If I Promise/I See Love In You	5
68	Philips BF 1655	I'll Be Your Baby Tonight/Open The Door Homer	5
68	Philips BF 1676	Kentucky Woman/I Cried All The Way Home	5
68	Philips BF 1724	Woman/A Dream	5
69	Philips BF 1758	Yesterday's Sunshine/Little One	5
69	Carnaby CNS 4004	Everywhere Under The Sun/Traces Of Tomorrow	5
70	Carnaby CNS 4009	True Grit/Sun Comes Up	5
70	Carnaby CNS 4012	Cottonfields/Jamie	5
70	Carnaby CNS 4017	Over And Over Again/Sun Comes Up	5
67	Philips (S)BL 7829	IF YOU GO AWAY (LP)	32
69	Carnaby CNLS 6001	THIS IS JOHN WALKER (LP)	32

(see also Walker Brothers, John & Scott Walker, Johnny & Judy)

John & Scott WALKER

MINT VALUE £

JOHN & SCOTT WALKER
66	Philips BE 12597	SOLO JOHN — SOLO SCOTT (EP, 2 tracks each)	12

(see also Walker Brothers, Scott Walker, John Walker, Scott Engel)

JUNIOR WALKER & ALL STARS
65	Tamla Motown TMG 509	Shotgun/Hot'Cha (DJ copy = £100)	45
65	Tamla Motown TMG 520	Do The Boomerang/Tune Up (DJ copy = £150)	60
65	Tamla Motown TMG 529	Shake And Fingerpop/Cleo's Back (DJ copy = £85)	40
66	Tamla Motown TMG 550	Cleo's Mood/Baby You Know It Ain't Right (DJ copy = £85)	40
66	Tamla Motown TMG 559	Road Runner/Shoot Your Shot (DJ copy = £100)	15
66	Tamla Motown TMG 571	How Sweet It Is (To Be Loved By You)/Nothing But Soul	15
67	Tamla Motown TMG 571	How Sweet It Is (To Be Loved By You)/Nothing But Soul (later pressing)	7
66	Tamla Motown TMG 586	Money (That's What I Want) Parts 1& 2 (DJ copy = £60)	22
67	Tamla Motown TMG 596	Pucker Up Buttercup/Any Way You Wanna (DJ copy = £65)	25
68	Tamla Motown TMG 637	Come See About Me/Sweet Soul (DJ copy = £75)	15
68	Tamla Motown TMG 667	Hip City Parts 1 & 2 (DJ copy = £40)	20
69	Tamla Motown TMG 682	Home Cookin'/Mutiny (DJ copy = £35)	15
69	Tamla Motown TMG 691	Road Runner/Shotgun (DJ copy = £30)	8
69	Tamla Motown TMG 712	What Does It Take (To Win Your Love)/Brainwasher (DJ copy £30)	8
70	Tamla Motown TMG 727	These Eyes/I've Got To Find A Way To Win Maria Back (DJ copy = £30)	10
70	Tamla Motown TMG 750	Do You See My Love (For You Growing)/Groove And Move (DJ copy = £28)	8
72	Tamla Motown TMG 824	Walk In The Night/Right On Brothers And Sisters/Gotta Hold On To This Feeling (maxi-single)	8
73	Tamla Motown TMG 840	Take Me Girl, I'm Ready/I Don't Want To Do Wrong	8
73	Tamla Motown TMG 857	Way Back Home (Vocal)/Way Back Home (Instrumental)	10
73	Tamla Motown TMG 857	Way Back Home (Vocal)/Way Back Home (Instrumental)/Country Boy (reissue)	20
73	Tamla Motown TMG 872	Wholly Holy/Peace And Understanding Is Hard To Find	6
74	Tamla Motown TMG 889	Don't Blame The Children/Soul Clappin'	6
74	Tamla Motown TMG 894	Gotta Hold On To This Feeling/I Ain't Going Nowhere (DJ copy = £25)	10
76	Tamla Motown TMG 1027	I'm So Glad/Dancin' Like They Do On Soul Train (as Jr. Walker)	8
66	Tamla Motown TME 2013	SHAKE AND FINGERPOP (EP)	52
65	Tamla Motown TML 11017	SHOTGUN (LP)	65
66	T. Motown (S)TML 11029	SOUL SESSION (LP, mono/stereo)	45/60
66	T. Motown (S)TML 11038	ROAD RUNNER (LP, mono/stereo)	40/45
69	T. Motown (S)TML 11097	HOME COOKIN' (LP)	35
69	T. Motown (S)TML 11120	JUNIOR WALKER'S GREATEST HITS (LP, original with flipback sleeve)	20
70	T. Motown (S)TML 11140	THESE EYES (LP)	30
70	T. Motown STML 11152	LIVE (LP)	25
70	T. Motown STML 11167	A GASSSSSSSSSS! (LP)	25
72	T. Motown STML 11198	RAINBOW FUNK (LP)	20
72	T. Motown STML 11211	MOODY JR. (LP)	20
73	T. Motown STML 11234	PEACE AND UNDERSTANDING IS HARD TO FIND (LP)	15
75	T. Motown STML 11274	JR. WALKER AND THE ALL STARS (LP)	15
76	T. Motown STML 12018	HOT SHOT (by Jr. Walker)	15
76	T. Motown STML 12033	SAX APPEAL (by Jr. Walker)	15
76	Motown STML 12048	WHOPPER BOPPER SHOW STOPPER (by Jr. Walker)	15

KARL WALKER & ALLSTARS
66	Rymska RA 103	One Minute To Zero/Don't Come Back (both sides actually featuring Tommy McCook & Supersonics)	35

(see also Kent Walker, Ernel Braham)

KENT WALKER
68	Fab FAB 53	When You Going To Show Me How/Come Yah Come Yah	8

(see also Karl Walker, Ernel Braham)

ROB WALKER
71	Upsetter US 366	Run Up Your Mouth (actually by Stranger Cole)/UPSETTERS: Mouth Version	15
71	Jackpot JP 761	Hear My Heart/Puppet On A String	15

(see also Stranger Cole, Tommy McCook)

RONNIE WALKER
69	Stateside SS 2151	It's A Good Feeling/Precious	30
75	Polydor 2006 578	Magic's In The Air/They Can't Say Hello	8

SCOTT WALKER
67	Philips BF 1628	Jackie/The Plague	10
68	Philips BF 1662	Joanna/Always Coming Back To You	8
69	Philips BF 1793	Lights of Cincinnati/Two Weeks Since You've Gone	6
71	Philips 6006 168	I Still See You/My Way Home	6
73	Philips 6006 311	The Me I Never Knew/This Way Mary	5
73	CBS 1795	A Woman Left Lonely/Where Love Has Died	5
74	CBS 2521	Delta Dawn/We Had It All	5
67	Philips MCP 1006	GREAT SCOTT (cassette EP)	15
67	Philips (S)BL 7816	SCOTT (LP, mono/stereo)	18/22
68	Philips BL 7840	SCOTT 2 (LP, mono, originally with signed portrait)	25/15
68	Philips SBL 7840	SCOTT 2 (LP, stereo, originally with signed portrait)	35/20
68	Ember EMB LP 3393	LOOKING BACK WITH SCOTT WALKER (LP, mono or stereo)	25
69	Philips SBL 7882	SCOTT 3 (LP, gatefold sleeve)	35
69	Philips SBL 7900	SCOTT WALKER SINGS SONGS FROM HIS TV SERIES (LP)	18
69	Philips SBL 7910	THE BEST OF SCOTT WALKER VOL. 1 (LP)	18
69	Philips SBL 7913	SCOTT 4 (LP)	45
70	Philips 6308 035	'TIL THE BAND COMES IN (LP)	50
72	Philips 6382 007	THIS IS... SCOTT WALKER (LP)	20
72	Philips 6308 127	THE MOVIEGOER (LP)	40
73	Philips 6308 148	ANY DAY NOW (LP)	40
73	CBS 65725	STRETCH (LP)	25
73	Philips 6850 013	THE ROMANTIC SCOTT WALKER (LP, Audio Club issue)	35
73	Philips 6856 022	TERRIFIC (LP, Audio Club issue, reissue of "Scott 2" with different tracks)	40

1266   Rare Record Price Guide 2008

73	Philips 6382 052	THIS IS SCOTT WALKER VOL. 2 (LP)	12
74	CBS 80254	WE HAD IT ALL (LP)	20
76	Philips 6625 017	SPOTLIGHT ON SCOTT WALKER (2-LP)	18
81	Zoo ZOO 2	FIRE ESCAPE IN THE SKY — THE GODLIKE GENIUS OF SCOTT WALKER (LP)	18
81	Philips 6359 090	SINGS JACQUES BREL (LP)	12

(see also Scott Engel, Scott Engel & John Stewart, John & Scott Walker, Walker Brothers, Routers)

SLYFORD WALKER
| 80 | Art & Craft ACD002 | I Love You (feat. Jah Stitch)/Version (12") | 20 |

(see also Glen Brown)

STEWART WALKER
| 98 | Mosquito MSQ 012 | ARTIFICIAL MUSIC FOR ARTIFICIAL PEOPLE (12" EP) | 15 |

T-BONE WALKER
54	London HL 8087	The Hustle Is On/Baby Broke My Heart (78)	40
65	Liberty LIB 12018	Party Girl/Here In The Dark	20
63	London REP 1404	TRAVELLIN' BLUES (EP)	100
54	Capitol LC 6681	CLASSICS IN JAZZ (10" LP)	80
63	Capitol T 1958	T-BONE WALKER (LP)	50
65	MFP MFP 1043	THE BLUES OF T-BONE WALKER (LP)	20
65	Liberty LBY 4047	SINGS THE BLUES (LP)	60
66	Liberty LBY 3057	SINGING THE BLUES (LP)	65
68	MCA MUPS 331	THE TRUTH (LP)	30
68	Stateside S(S)L 10223	STORMY MONDAY BLUES (LP)	45
69	Stateside S(S)L 10265	FUNKY TOWN (LP)	40
73	Reprise K 94001	VERY RARE (2-LP)	20
74	Atlantic K 40131	T-BONE BLUES (LP)	15

WENDY WALKER
| 63 | Decca F 11573 | Window Shopping/Ain't A Boy In The World | 8 |
| 63 | Decca F 11671 | Boys Will Be Happy/Casanova | 8 |

WALKER BROTHERS
65	Philips BF 1401	Pretty Girls Everywhere/Doin' The Jerk	12
65	Philips BF 1409	Love Her/The Seventh Dawn	8
65	Philips BF 1428	Make It Easy On Yourself/But I Do	6
65	Philips BF 1454	My Ship Is Coming In/You're All Around Me	6
66	Philips BF 1473	The Sun Ain't Gonna Shine Anymore/After The Lights Go Out	6
66	Philips BF 1497	(Baby) You Don't Have To Tell Me/My Love Is Growing	6
66	Philips BF 1514	Another Tear Falls/The Saddest Night In The World	7
66	Philips BF 1537	Deadlier Than The Male/Archangel	7
67	Philips BF 1548	Stay With Me Baby/Turn Out The Moon	7
67	Philips BF 1576	Walking In The Rain/Baby Make It The Last Time	7
76	GTO GT 42	No Regrets/Remember Me	5
76	GTO GT 67	Lines/First Day	5
77	GTO GT 78	We're All Alone/Have You Seen My Baby	5
66	Philips BE 12596	I NEED YOU (EP)	15
67	Philips BE 12603	THE WALKER BROTHERS (EP, existence unconfirmed)	
67	Philips MCP 1004	THE HITS OF THE WALKER BROTHERS & DUSTY SPRINGFIELD (cassette EP)	12
65	Philips BL 7691	TAKE IT EASY WITH THE WALKER BROTHERS (LP)	18
66	Philips (S)BL 7732	PORTRAIT (LP, with photo insert, mono/stereo)	20/30
67	Philips (S)BL 7770	IMAGES (LP)	20
67	Philips DBL 002	THE WALKER BROTHERS STORY (2-LP)	20
68	Wing WL 1188	THE FABULOUS WALKER BROTHERS (LP)	15
75	GTO GTLP 007	NO REGRETS (LP)	12

(see also Scott Walker, Scott Engel, John Walker, John & Scott Walker, Gary Walker [& Rain], Routers)

WALKIE TALKIES
| 79 | Sire SIR 4023 | Rich And Nasty/Summer In Russia (p/s) | 6 |

(see also Pauline Murray & Invisible Girls, Mission)

WALKING FLOORS
| 80s | My Death Telephone TEL 1 | No Next Time/Removal (foldover p/s) | 8 |

DENNIS WALKS
68	Amalgamated AMG 816	Having A Party/GROOVERS: Day By Day	20
68	Blue Cat BS 144	Belly Lick/DRUMBAGO & BLENDERS: The Game Song	22
69	Bullet BU 402	Heart Don't Leap/CLARENDONIANS: I Am Sorry	12
69	Bullet BU 408	Love Of My Life/Under The Shady Tree	12
71	Moodisc HM 101	Time Will Tell/Under The Shady Tree	7
74	Magnet MG 062	Don't Play That Song/Version	6

(see also I Roy)

SHELTON WALKS
| 73 | Bullet BU 550 | No Money No Friend/BOB MAC ALL STARS: Money Dub | 6 |
| 74 | Dip DL 5026 | One Of Us Will Weep/KING EDWARDS ALL STARS: Version | 6 |

WALL
| 79 | Small Wonder SMALL 13 | New Way/Suckers/Uniforms (p/s) | 5 |
| 80 | Fresh FRESHLP 2 | PERSONAL TROUBLES AND PUBLIC ISSUES (LP) | 15 |

(see also Ski Patrol)

MAX WALL
51	Polygon P 1028	Take It Easy/Me And My Tune (78)	6
73	York YR 203	The Fiddley Foodle Bird/Story Of The Fiddley Foodle Bird	5
75	DJM DJS 10352	Why Should I Care/Devil Bomb	5
77	Stiff BUY 12	England's Glory/Dream Tobacco (p/s)	5

REM WALL & HIS GREEN VALLEY BOYS
| 60 | Top Rank JAR 324 | Heartsick And Blue/One More Time | 8 |

MINT VALUE £

ERROL WALLACE
| 69 | Escort ES 817 | Bandit/ASTON BORROT: Family Man Mood (actually by Aston "Family Man" Barrett) | 12 |

GIG WALLACE & HIS ORCHESTRA
| 60 | Philips PB 981 | Rockin' On The Railroad/Show Me The Way To Go Home (78 rpm = £15) | 10 |

IAN WALLACE
| 61 | Parlophone R 4726 | I Can't Do My Bally Bottom Button Up/In Other Words | 6 |

JERRY WALLACE
54	Polygon P 1133	Dixieanna/Runnin' After Love (78)	10
58	London HL 8719	With This Ring/How The Time Flies (78 rpm = £15)	35
58	London HL 7062	With This Ring/How The Time Flies (export issue)	15
59	London HLH 8943	Primrose Lane/By Your Side (78 rpm = £15)	12
60	London HLH 9040	Little Coco Palm/Mission Bell Blues	10
60	London HLH 9110	You're Singing Our Love Song To Somebody Else/King Of The Mountain	10
60	London HLH 9177	Swingin' Down The Lane/Teardrop In The Rain	8
61	London HLH 9264	There She Goes/Angel On My Shoulder	8
61	London HLH 9363	Life's A Holiday/I Can See An Angel	8
62	London HLH 9630	Shutters And Boards/Am I That Easy To Forget	8
64	London HLH 9914	Even The Bad Times Are Good/In The Misty Moonlight	8
65	Mercury MF 853	Time/Rainbow	8

SIPPIE WALLACE
| 67 | Storyville 671 198 | SIPPIE WALLACE SINGS THE BLUES (LP) | 25 |

WALLACE BROTHERS
64	Sue WI 334	Precious Words/You're Mine	40
65	Sue WI 355	Lover's Prayer/Love Me Like I Love You	40
67	Sue WI 4036	I'll Step Aside/Hold My Heart For A While	40
67	Sue ILP 950	SOUL CONNECTION (LP)	250

WALLACE COLLECTION
69	Parlophone R 5764	Daydream/Baby I Don't Mind	10
69	Parlophone R 5793	Fly Me To The Earth/Love	20
70	Parlophone R 5844	Serenade/Walk On Out	10
69	Parlophone PMC/PCS 7076	LAUGHING CAVALIER (LP)	18
70	Parlophone PCS 7099	WALLACE COLLECTION (LP)	15

'FATS' WALLER (& HIS RHYTHM)
51	HMV JO 205	It's A Sin To Tell A Lie/Come Down To Earth My Angel (78, export issue)	6
51	London L 1032	Cow Cow Boogie/TEDDY WEATHERFOOD: Sugar Foot Stomp (78)	6
52	HMV JO 291	I'm On A See-Saw/As Long As The World Goes 'Round (78, export issue)	6
53	HMV 7M 128	My Very Good Friend The Milkman/Shortnin' Bread	7
53	HMV 7M 157	A Good Man Is Hard To Find/The Girl I Left Behind Me	7
53	HMV 7M 142	Honey Hush/You've Been Reading My Mail	7
54	HMV 7M 208	You've Been Taking Lessons In Love/I've Got A New Lease Of Life	7
54	HMV 7M 244	By The Light Of The Silvery Moon/Romance A La Mode (with Deep River Boys)	7
60	RCA RCA 1189	Dinah/When Somebody Thinks You're Wonderful	5
59	RCA RCX 1053	YOUR FEET'S TOO BIG (EP)	10
53	London AL 3507	REDISCOVERED FATSSOLOS (10" LP)	20
53	HMV DLP 1008	FAVOURITES (10" LP)	15
53	HMV DLP 1017	PLAYS AND SINGS (10" LP)	15
54	HMV DLP 1056	RHYTHM AND ROMANCE WITH FATS WALLER (10" LP)	15
54	London AL 3521	FATS AT THE ORGAN (10" LP)	15
54	London AL 3522	JIVIN' WITH FATS (10" LP)	15
55	HMV DLP 1082	FUN WITH FATS (10" LP)	15
55	HMV CLP 1036	THOMAS "FATS" WALLER NO. 1 (LP)	12
55	HMV CLP 1042	THOMAS "FATS" WALLER NO. 2 (LP)	12
56	HMV DLP 1111	YOUNG FATS WALLER (10" LP)	15
56	HMV DLP 1118	FAVOURITES NO. 2 (10" LP)	15
57	HMV DLP 1138	SPREADIN' RHYTHM AROUND (10" LP)	15
57	RCA RD 27047	FATS 1935-1937 (LP)	15
58	RCA RC 24004	FATS 1938-1942 (10" LP)	15
59	RCA Camden CDN 131	THE REAL FATS WALLER (LP)	12
60	RCA RD 27185	HANDFUL OF KEYS (LP)	12

(see also Louisiana Sugar Babies, Deep River Boys, James P. Johnson)

GORDON (WALLER)
68	Columbia DB 8337	Rosecrans Boulevard/Red, Cream And Velvet	12
68	Columbia DB 8440	Every Day/Because Of A Woman	10
68	Columbia DB 8518	Weeping Annaleah/The Seventh Hour	10
69	Bell BLL 1059	I Was A Boy When You Needed A Man/Lady In The Window	6
70	Bell BLL 1106	You're Gonna Hurt Yourself/Sunshine	6
72	Vertigo 6360 069	GORDON (LP, as Gordon, single sleeve, swirl label)	250

(see also Peter & Gordon)

GEORGE WALLINGTON
| 50s | Columbia CLEF33C9035 | THE WORK SHOP OF GEORGE WALLINGTON TRIO (10" LP) | 60 |
| 57 | Esquire 32-132 | NEW YORK SCENE (LP) | 70 |

BOB WALLIS & HIS STORYVILLE JAZZMEN
57	77 EP 10	NEW ORLEANS JAM SESSION VOLUME 1 (EP)	15
60	Pye Jazz NJE 1079	BOB WALLIS STORYVILLE JAZZMEN (EP)	10
60	Pye Jazz NJE 1085	BOB WALLIS PLAYS (EP)	12
62	Storyville SEP 368	BOB WALLIS STORYVILLE JAZZMEN (EP)	10
59	77 Records 77LE 12/2	THE RAVING SOUNDS OF BOB WALLIS (LP)	30
60	Top Rank BUY 023	EVERYBODY LOVES SATURDAY NIGHT (LP)	20
61	Pye Jazz NJL 27	OLE MAN RIVER (LP)	25
61	Pye Jazz NJL 30	TRAVELLIN' BLUES (LP)	25
62	Pye Jazz NJL 41	THE WALLIS COLLECTION (LP)	15

Rare Record Price Guide 2008

BOB WALLIS & SANDY BROWN
62   Pye Jazz 7NJ 2060   Oh Didn't It Rain/In A Little Spanish Town 6

LARRY WALLIS
77   Stiff BUY 22   Police Car/On Parole (with p/s or die-cut company sleeve) 7/5
   (see also Pink Fairies, Subs, Deviants, Shagrat, Peter Wyngarde)

WALL OF SLEEP
95   Woronzow WOO 24   WALL OF SLEEP (LP, with insert) 12

WALL OF VOODOO
82   Illegal ILS 31   On Interstate 15/There's Nothing On This Side 5
83   Illuminated ILS 0036   Mexican Radio/Call Of The West (p/s) 5

WALLY BROTHERS
74   Explosion EX 2090   The Man Who Sold The World/Version 5

WALRUS
70   Deram DM 308   Who Can I Trust?/Tomorrow Never Comes 18
71   Deram DM 323   Never Let My Body Touch Ground/Why? 20
71   Deram SML 1072   WALRUS (LP) 60

JAMES WALSH GYPSY BAND
79   RCA PB 11403   Cuz It's You Girl/Bring Yourself Together (DJ copy = £150) 100

SHEILA WALSH & CLIFF RICHARD
83   DJM SHEIL 100   Drifting/It's Lonely When The Lights Go Out (picture disc) 6
83   DJM SHEILT 100   Drifting/It's Lonely When The Lights Go Out (12", picture disc) 8
83   DJM DJF 20581   DRIFTING (LP, with inner sleeve, as Sheila Walsh) 12
   (see also Cliff Richard)

BURT WALTERS
68   Trojan TR 636   Honey Love/KING CANNONBALL BRYAN: Thunderstorm 15
   (see also Lee 'Scratch' Perry)

DAVE WALTON
66   CBS 202057   Love Ain't What It Used To Be/Tell Me A Lie 8
66   CBS 202098   Every Window In The City/I've Left The Troubled Ground 15
67   CBS 202508   After You There Can Be Nothing/Can I Get It From You 30
   (see also The First Gear)

RON WALTON
76   Gull GULS40   Soul Disco/ Always Be The One 15

TRAVIS WAMMACK
65   Atlantic AT 4017   Scratchy/Fire Fly (DJ copy = £100) 45
72   United Artists UP 35412 Whatever Turns You On/Slip Away 6
73   United Artists UP 35468 So Good/Darling, You're All That I Need 6

WANDERER
59   Top Rank JAR 183   The Happy Hobo/True True Happiness 6

WANDERERS
81   Polydor POSP 239   Ready To Snap/Beyond The Law 25
81   Polydor POSP 284   The Times They Are A'Changin'/Little Bit Frightening 6
81   Polydor POLS 1028   ONLY LOVERS LEFT (LP) 15
   (see also Lords Of The New Church, Stiv Bators, Dead Boys)

WANDERERS (Jamaica)
69   Trojan TR 7721   Wiggle Waggle/Jaga Jaga War 8

WANDERERS (U.S.)
60   MGM MGM 1102   I Could Make You Mine/I Need You More 45
61   MGM MGM 1169   As Time Goes By/There Is No Greater Love 28
64   United Artists UP 1020   Run Run Senorita/After He Breaks Your Heart 30
   (see also Ray Pollard)

WANGLERS
79   Matchbox Classics MC 5   KICKIN' OUT FOR THE COAST (EP, white label,
                              yellow or red stickered foldover p/s) 10

DEXTER WANSEL
77   Phil. Intl ZS8 3616   Disco Lights/Ode Infinitum (no p/s) 18
78   Phil. Intl. PIR 6255   All Night Long/What The World Is Coming To 10
86   Streetwave SWAVE 9   Life On Mars (Parts 1 & 2) (12", p/s) 8
78   Phil. Intl. PIR 82786   VOYAGER (LP) 20
80s CBS   LIFE ON MARS (LP) 25

WAR
71   Liberty LBF 15443   Sun Oh Son/Lonely Feelin' 6
71   United Artists UP 35281 All Day Music/Get Down 6
72   United Artists UP 35327 Slippin' Into Darkness/Nappy Head 5
73   United Artists UP 35469 The World Is A Ghetto/Four Cornered Room 5
73   United Artists UP 35521 The Cisco Kid/Beetles In The Bag 5
73   United Artists UP 35576 Gypsy Man/Deliver The Word 5
74   United Artists UP 35623 Me And Baby Brother/In Your Eyes 5
71   Liberty LBG 83478   WAR (LP) 30
72   United Artists UAS 29269 ALL DAY MUSIC (LP) 15
73   United Artists UAS 29400 THE WORLD IS A GHETTO (LP) 12
73   United Artists UAG 29521 DELIVER THE WORD (LP) 12
75   United Artists UAG 29843 WHY CAN'T WE BE FRIENDS (LP) 12
   (see also Eric Burdon & War)

BILL WARD
90   Chameleon 0174910   WARD ONE: ALONG THE WAY (LP, with innersleeve) 12
   (see also Black Sabbath)

Billy WARD

BILLY WARD & HIS DOMINOES
53	Parlophone R 3789	Don't Thank Me/Rags To Riches (78)	40
54	Parlophone MSP 6112	Three Coins In The Fountain/Lonesome Road (78 rpm = £35)	175
56	Brunswick 05599	St. Therese Of The Roses/Home Is Where You Hang Your Heart (78 rpm = £6)	55
57	Brunswick 05656	Evermore/Half A Love (Is Better Than None) (78 rpm = £8)	30
57	London HLU 8465	Stardust/Lucinda (78 rpm = £6)	25
57	London HLU 8502	Deep Purple/Do It Again (78 rpm = £6)	25
58	London HLU 8634	Jennie Lee/Music, Maestro, Please (78 rpm = £20)	35
59	London HLU 8883	Please Don't Say 'No'/Behave, Hula Girl (78 rpm = £20)	20
58	London REU 1114	BILLY WARD & HIS DOMINOES (EP)	190
58	Parlophone PMD 1061	BILLY WARD & HIS DOMINOES FEATURING CLYDE McPHATTER (10" LP)	700
58	London HA-U 2116	YOURS FOREVER (LP)	60

(see also Dominoes, Clyde McPhatter, Jackie Wilson)

CHRISTINE WARD
66	Decca F 12339	The Face Of Empty Me/Girl I Used To Know	18

CLARA WARD & HER SINGERS
65	Stateside SS 474	Gonna Build A Mountain/God Bless The Child	10

CLIFFORD T. WARD
72	Dandelion 2001 327	Carrie/Sidetrack	12
72	Dandelion 2001 382	Coathanger/Rayne	8
73	Charisma CB 212	Wherewithal/Thinking Of Something To Do	6
74	Charisma CB 233	Jayne/Maybe I'm Right	6
75	Charisma CB 248	Jigsaw Girl/Cellophane	6
75	Philips 6006 490	No More Rock'n'Roll/Gandalf	6
76	Philips 6006 542	Ocean Of Love/Tomorrow Night	6
77	Mercury 6007 132	Up In The World/Not Waving, Drowning (Revisited)	6
77	Mercury 6007 149	I Got Lost Tonight/Detriment (p/s)	7
77	Mercury LUV 1	Someone I Know/If I Had Known (gatefold p/s)	8
80	WEA K 18294	Convertible/Taking The Long Way Round	7
81	WEA K 18426	The Best Is Yet To Come/Lost Again	7
81	WEA K 18486	Contrary/Climate Of Her Favour	7
84	Philips 880 550 7	Messenger/Where Do Angels Really Come From (p/s)	8
86	Tembo TML 114	Cricket/Computer	10
86	Tembo TML 123	Sometime Next Year/Turbo (p/s)	8
72	Dandelion 2310 216	SINGER SONGWRITER (LP)	15
73	Charisma CAS 1006	HOME THOUGHTS (LP)	12
75	Charisma CAS 1098	ESCALATOR (LP)	12
75	Philips 9109 500	NO MORE ROCK'N'ROLL (LP)	12
75	Philips 9109 216	WAVES (LP)	12

(see also Secrets, Simon's Secrets, Martin Raynor & Secrets)

DALE WARD
64	London HLD 9835	Oh Julie/Letter From Sherry	20

HEDLEY WARD TRIO
55	Melodisc MEL 1344	Rock Around The Clock/Who Dat Up There (78)	12
56	Melodisc MEL 1352	Who's Sorry Now/Big Ears (78)	10
56	Melodisc MEL 1387	Steamboat Rock/My Baby's Got Such Lovin' Ways (78)	25

ROBIN WARD
63	London HLD 9821	Wonderful Summer/Dream Boy	20

TERRY WARD with BUMBLIES
65	Fontana TF 558	Gotta Tell/When I Come To You	8

SHEELAGH WARDE
59	Top Rank JAR 131	Let Mr. Maguire Sit Down/The Golden Jubilee (78 rpm = £7)	7

WARDENS
70s	SNO PEAS TIC 001	Lust Like This/Do So Well (with insert)	20

WARD SINGERS
56	London Jazz EZ-C 19024	THE FAMOUS WARD SINGERS (EP)	20
56	London Jazz LZ-C 14013	THE FAMOUS WARD SINGERS (10" LP)	25

WARDS OF COURT
67	Deram DM 127	All Night Girl/How Could Say One Thing	40

LEON WARE
77	Motown STML 12050	MUSICAL MASSAGE (LP)	30

WARHORSE
71	Vertigo 6059 027	St. Louis/No Chance	18
70	Vertigo 6360 015	WARHORSE (LP, swirl label, gatefold sleeve)	75
72	Vertigo 6360 066	RED SEA (LP, swirl label, gatefold sleeve)	100

(see also Deep Purple, Nic Simper's Fandango)

FRED WARING & HIS PENNSYLVANIANS
59	Capitol CL 14981	Dry Bones/Way Back Home	5
55	Brunswick OE 9194	THE BALLAD OF DAVY CROCKETT (EP)	12
51	Brunswick LAT 8011	LISTENING TIME (LP)	12
53	Brunswick LA 8625	WALT DISNEY FILM SONGS (10" LP)	15
54	Brunswick LA 8651	A SONG OF EASTER (10" LP)	12
54	Brunswick LA 8678	SONGS OF INSPIRATION (10" LP)	12
54	Brunswick LA 8693	'TWAS THE NIGHT BEFORE CHRISTMAS (10" LP)	12
55	Brunswick LA 8704	HARMONIZIN' THE OLD SONGS (10" LP)	12
55	Brunswick LAT 8068	FOR LISTENING ONLY (LP)	12

RAY WARLEIGH
69	Philips (S)BL 7881	RAY WARLEIGH'S FIRST ALBUM (LP)	25

(see also John Mayall's Blues Breakers, Alexis Korner)

OZZIE WARLOCK & WIZARDS
59	HMV POP 635	Juke Box Fury/Wow!.	15

(see also Tony Osborne)

WARM
78	Warm 2001	It's The Kooler/Teenage Space Queen (p/s)	5
78	Warm SMS 001/2001/S	THE DEMO TAPES (EP, double pack)	8
78	Warm WARM 2003	Floosie/Chewing Gum Sue/Bye Bye It's Blues/Sometimes (p/s)	5

JOHNNY WARMAN
78	Ring O' 2017 112	Head On Collision/London's Burning/Mind Games (some in p/s)	20/10

WARM DUST
71	Trend 6099 002	It's A Beautiful Day/Worm Dance.	15
70	Trend TNLS 700	AND IT CAME TO PASS (2-LP).	50
71	Trend 6480 001	PEACE FOR OUR TIME (LP)	50

WARM GOLD
60s	Hurls 008	A TASTE OF CORNWALL (EP)	25

WARM JETS
78	Bridgehouse BHS 1	Sticky Jack/Shell Shock (p/s, some with sides reversed & small extra labels)	8
79	RSO RSO 47	Big City Boys/Mr Natural (p/s)	5

WARM SENSATION
69	Columbia DB 8568	I'll Be Proud Of You/The Clown	20

(see also Ivy League)

WARM SOUNDS
67	Immediate IM 058	Sticks And Stones/Angeline	20
67	Deram DM 120	Birds And Bees/Doo-Dah	12
68	Deram DM 174	Nite Is A-Comin'/Smeta Mergaty	35

(see also Denny Gerrard, Tuesday's Children, Open Road)

HERB & BETTY WARNER
59	Felsted AF 114	Slowly/'BUGS' BOWER GROUP: Slowly (78 rpm = £6)	7

JACK WARNER
71	President PT 360	You Have Got The Gear/Somebody Asked Me.	7
68	MFP MFP 1278	YER CAN'T 'ELP LAUGHIN' (LP)	12

JACK WARNER with TOMMY REILLY
58	Oriole CB 1426	An Ordinary Copper/On The Way Up (78 rpm = £6)	7

FLORENCE WARNER
73	Epic EPC 1626	For No Good Reason/Remember	6
75	Epic EPC 3817	Anyway I Love You/Dreamer	6
73	Epic EPC 80077	FLORENCE WARNER (LP)	18

GALE WARNING
56	Pye N 15061	Heartbreak Hotel/Met Rock (78)	12
56	Oriole CB 1349	Rock Those Crazy Skins/I Need Your Love (78)	12

WARP NINE
75	Stax STXS 2030	Theme From 'Star Trek'/Para Song One	5

FRAN WARREN
52	MGM MGM 548	What Is This Thing Called Love/One For The Wonder (78)	5
59	MGM MGM 1008	Shame/As Long As You Believe Me	10

GUY WARREN OF GHANA
59	Brunswick 05791	Monkies And Butterflies/An African's Prayer (with Rod Saunders)	6
59	Brunswick 05791	Monkies And Butterflies/An African's Prayer (with Rod Saunders) (78)	7
57	Brunswick LAJ 8237	AFRICA SPEAKS - AMERICA ANSWERS (LP)	35
64	Clumbia 33SX 1584	EMERGENT DRUMS (LP)	100
69	Columbia SCX 6340	AFRO-JAZZ (LP, as Guy Warren Of Ghana)	50
72	Regal Zono. SLRZ 1031	THE AFRICAN SOUNDS OF GUY WARREN OF GHANA (LP)	50+

SHORTY WARRENT & HIS WESTERN RANGE
52	London L 1125	I Thought She Was Local/You're Breaking The Only Heart (That Truly Loves You) (78)	12

WARRIOR
72	Eden LP 27	INVASION! (LP, private pressing, plain white sleeve & label, some handwritten, 100 only)	160

WARRIÖR
80	Rambert RAM ONE	Don't Let It Show/The Lord's Prayer/Silver Lady (10", p/s)	100
80	Goodwood GM 12326	TROUBLE MAKER (LP).	150

WARRIOR
80	Rainbow RSL 132	LET BATTLE COMMENCE (LP, private pressing, 500 only)	90

WARRIOR
82	Neat NEAT 20	Dead When It Comes To Love/Kansas City/Stab In The Back (some in die-cut p/s)	15/10
84	Warrior WOO 2	Breakout/Dragon Slayer/Take Your Chance (paper sleeve)	55
83	Warrior WOO 1	FOR EUROPE ONLY (mini-LP).	20

WARRIORS
64	Decca F 11926	Don't Make Me Blue/You Came Along	30+

(see also Hans Christian, Jon Anderson)

WARSAW PAKT
78	Island PAKT 1	Safe And Warm/Sick And Tired (a few with p/s)	30/18
77	Island ILPS 9515	NEEDLE TIME (LP, numbered stamped mailer p/s, with insert)	20
79	Stuff Central	SEE YOU IN COURT (cassette only)	20

DEE DEE WARWICK

65	Mercury MF 860	Do It With All Your Heart/Happiness	40
65	Mercury MF 867	We're Doin' Fine/You Don't Know	30
65	Mercury MF 890	Gotta Get Hold Of Myself/Another Lonely Saturday	45
66	Mercury MF 909	A Lover's Chant/Worth Every Tear I Cry	200
65	Mercury MF 937	I Want To Be With You/Alfie	15
65	Mercury MF 953	Yours Till Tomorrow/I'm Gonna Make You Love Me	15
67	Mercury MF 974	When Love Slips Away/House Of Gold	40
68	Mercury MF 1061	I'll Be Better Off (Without You)/Monday, Monday	25
69	Mercury MF 1084	Foolish Heart/Thank God	8
69	Mercury MF 1125	That's Not Love/It's Not Fair	10
70	Atlantic 2091 011	She Didn't Know (She Kept On Talking)/Make Love To Me	8
70	Atlantic 2091 037	If This Was The Last Song/I'm Only Human	6
71	Atlantic 2091 057	Cold Night In Georgia/Searching	6
71	Atlantic 2091 092	Suspicious Minds/I'm Glad I'm A Woman	15
75	Private Stock PVT 13	Get Out Of My Life/Funny How Places Change	20
66	Mercury 10036 MCE	WE'RE DOING FINE (EP)	70
71	Atco	TURNIN' AROUND (LP)	30

DIONNE WARWICK
SINGLES

63	Stateside SS 157	Don't Make Me Over/I Smiled Yesterday	30
63	Stateside SS 191	This Empty Place/Wishin' And Hopin'	25
63	Pye International 7N 25223	Please Let Him Love Me/Make The Music Play (reissue)	6
64	Pye International 7N 25234	Anyone Who Had A Heart/The Love Of A Boy	6
64	Pye International 7N 25241	Walk On By/Anytime Of Day	6
64	Pye International 7N 25256	You'll Never Get To Heaven/A House Is Not A Home	6
64	Pye International 7N 25265	Reach Out For Me/How Many Days Of Sadness	6
65	Pye International 7N 25290	You Can Have Him/Don't Say I Didn't Tell You	5
65	Pye International 7N 25302	Who Can I Turn To/That's Not The Answer	5
65	Pye International 7N 25310	(Here I Go Again) Looking With My Eyes/Only The Strong, Only The Brave	5
65	Pye International 7N 25316	Here I Am/They Long To Be Close To You	5
65	Pye International 7N 25338	Are You There (With Another Girl)/If I Ever Make You Cry	5
66	Pye International 7N 25357	In Between The Heartaches/Long Day, Short Night	5
66	Pye International 7N 25368	A Message To Michael/Here Where There Is Love	6
66	Pye International 7N 25378	Trains And Boats And Planes/Don't Go Breaking My Heart	5
66	Pye International 7N 25395	Another Night/Go With Love	5
67	Pye International 7N 25424	Alfie/The Beginning Of Loneliness	5
67	Pye International 7N 25428	The Windows Of The World/Walk Little Dolly	5
67	Pye International 7N 25435	I Say A Little Prayer/Window Wishin'	5
68	Pye International 7N 25445	(Theme From) The Valley Of The Dolls/Zip-A-Dee-Doo-Dah	5
68	Pye International 7N 25457	Do You Know The Way To San Jose?/Let Me Be Lonely	5
68	Pye International 7N 25474	Who Is Gonna Love Me?/(There's) Always Something There To Remind Me	5
75	Warner Bros WB 16530	Take It From Me/Sure Thing	5
75	Warner Bros K 16595	Move Me No Mountain/We'll Burn Our Bridges Behind Us	8

EPs

64	Pye Intl. NEP 44024	IT'S LOVE THAT REALLY COUNTS	15
64	Pye Intl. NEP 44026	DON'T MAKE ME OVER	12
65	Pye Intl. NEP 44039	WISHIN' AND HOPIN'	12
65	Pye Intl. NEP 44044	DIONNE	12
65	Pye Intl. NEP 44046	FOREVER MY LOVE	12
65	Pye Intl. NEP 44049	WHO CAN I TURN TO?	12
66	Pye Intl. NEP 44051	HERE I AM	12
66	Pye Intl. NEP 44067	MESSAGE TO MICHAEL	15
66	Pye Intl. NEP 44073	WINDOW WISHIN'	15
66	Pye Intl. NEP 44077	I JUST DON'T KNOW WHAT TO DO WITH MYSELF	15
67	Pye Intl. NEP 44083	I LOVE PARIS	15
68	Pye Intl. NEP 44090	DO YOU KNOW THE WAY TO SAN JOSE?	15

LPs

64	Pye Intl. NPL 28037	PRESENTING DIONNE WARWICK	20
64	Pye Intl. NPL 28046	MAKE WAY FOR DIONNE WARWICK	18
65	Pye Intl. NPL 28055	THE SENSITIVE SOUND OF DIONNE WARWICK	18
66	Pye Intl. NPL 28071	HERE I AM	18
66	Pye Intl. NPL 28076	DIONNE WARWICK IN PARIS	18
67	Pye Intl. NPL 28096	HERE WHERE THERE IS LOVE	18
68	Pye Intl. N(S)PL 28114	VALLEY OF THE DOLLS	18

WASHBOARD RHYTHM KINGS

56	HMV 7EG 8101	WASHBOARD RHYTHM KINGS (EP)	22

WASHBOARD SAM

72	RCA RD 8274	FEELING LOWDOWN (LP, with Big Bill Broonzy & Memphis Slim)	25

(see also Big Bill Broonzy, Memphis Slim)

ALBERT WASHINGTON & KINGS

67	President PT 137	Doggin' Me Around/A Woman Is A Funny Thing	10
68	President PT 182	I'm The Man/These Arms Of Mine	50
68	President PT 227	Woman Love/Bring It On Up	10
69	President PT 242	Turn On The Bright Lights/Lonely Mountain	10
73	President PT 391	Rome, GA/Telling All Your Friends	10

BABY WASHINGTON

64	Sue WI 302	That's How Heartaches Are Made/Doodlin'	85
64	Sue WI 321	I Can't Wait Until I See My Baby/Who's Gonna Take Care Of Me	100
65	London HLC 9987	Only Those In Love/Ballad Of Bobby Dawn	25
68	United Artists UP 2247	Get A Hold Of Yourself/Hurt So Bad	60
69	Atlantic 584 299	I Don't Know/I Can't Afford To Lose Him	15
70	Atlantic 584 316	Breakfast In Bed/What Becomes Of A Broken Heart	12

73	People PEO 105	Just Can't Get You Out Of My Mind/You're Just A Dream	10
74	People PEO 107	I've Got To Break Away/Can't Get Over You	10
66	London HA-C 8260	THAT'S HOW HEARTACHES ARE MADE (LP)	100
66	London HA-C 8292	ONLY THOSE IN LOVE (LP)	85
68	United Artists SULP 1217	WITH YOU IN MIND (LP)	100

(see also Baby Washington/Wilbert Harrison)

BABY WASHINGTON & DON GARDNER

73	People PEO 101	Forever/Baby Let Me Get Close To You	8
74	People PLEO 13	LAY A LITTLE LOVIN' ON ME (LP)	40

(see also Don Gardner & Dee Dee Ford)

BABY WASHINGTON/WILBERT HARRISON

71	Joy JOYS 191	BATTLE OF THE GIANTS (LP)	18

DINAH WASHINGTON

52	Oriole CB 1130	Mad About The Boy/I Can't Face The Music (78)	20
54	Oriole CB 1266	My Man's An Undertaker/Since My Man Has Gone And Went (78)	18
54	Oriole CB 1279	Fat Daddy/TV Is The Thing (78)	18
54	Mercury MB 3132	Until Sunrise/Am I Blue (78)	10
54	Mercury MB 3160	Dream/I Don't Hurt Anymore (78)	12
55	Mercury MB 3188	Teach Me Tonight/Wishing Well (78)	6
55	Mercury MB 3207	That's All I Want From You/You Stay On My Mind (78)	6
56	Mercury MT 124	Cat On A Hot Tin Roof/The First Time (78)	15
59	Mercury AMT 1051	What A Diff'rence A Day Made/Come On Home	10
59	Mercury AMT 1069	Unforgettable/Nothing In The World	7
60	Mercury AMT 1105	This Bitter Earth/I Understand	7
60	Mercury AMT 1119	Love Walked In/I'm In Heaven Tonight	7
61	Mercury AMT 1125	We Have Love/Looking Back	7
61	Mercury AMT 1162	September In The Rain/Wake The Town And Tell The People	8
62	Mercury AMT 1170	Tears And Laughter/If I Should Lose You	6
62	Mercury AMT 1176	Dream/Such A Night	7
63	Columbia DB 7049	Soulville/Let Me Be The First To Know	25
56	Emarcy EJT 501	AFTER HOURS WITH MISS D. (10" LP)	38
57	Emarcy EJL 1255	DINAH! (LP)	28
57	Mercury MPL 6519	SINGS THE BEST IN BLUES (LP)	18
59	Top Rank RX 3006	THE BLUES (LP, with Betty Roche)	18
60	Mercury MMC 14030	WHAT A DIFF'RENCE A DAY MADE (LP)	18
60	Mercury MMC 14048	THE UNFORGETTABLE DINAH WASHINGTON (LP)	18
61	Mercury MMC 14063	I CONCENTRATE ON YOU (LP, also stereo CMS 18043)	18/20
61	Mercury MMC 14107	SEPTEMBER IN THE RAIN (LP)	15
62	Mercury MMC 14085	FOR LONELY LOVERS (LP)	15
62	Mercury MMC 14099	TEARS AND LAUGHTER (LP)	15
65	Fontana FJL 125	DINAH! (LP)	12

(see also Brook Benton & Dinah Washington)

ELLA WASHINGTON

69	Monument MON 1030	He Called Me Baby/You're Gonna Cry, Cry, Cry	22

GENO WASHINGTON & RAM JAM BAND

66	Piccadilly 7N 35312	Water/Understanding	8
66	Piccadilly 7N 35329	Hi! Hi! Hazel/Beach Bash	8
66	Piccadilly 7N 35346	Que Sera Sera/All I Need	10
66	Piccadilly 7N 35359	Michael/Hold On To My Love	10
67	Piccadilly 7N 35392	She Shot A Hole In My Soul/I've Been Hurt By Love	12
67	Piccadilly 7N 35403	Tell It Like It Is/Girl I Want To Marry	8
67	Pye 7N 17425	Different Strokes/You Got Me Hummin'	7
68	Pye 7N 17570	I Can't Quit Her/Put Out The Fire Baby	7
68	Pye 7N 17649	I Can't Let You Go/Bring It To Me Baby	10
69	Pye 7N 17745	My Little Chickadee/Seven Eleven	7
71	Pye 7N 45019	Alison Please/Each And Every Part Me	7
71	Pye 7N 45085	Feeling So Good/Would You Believe My Little Chickadee	6
66	Piccadilly NEP 34054	HI (EP)	25
68	Pye NEP 24293	DIFFERENT STROKES (EP)	25
68	Pye NEP 24302	SMALL PACKAGE OF HIPSTERS (EP)	30
66	Piccadilly NPL 38026	HAND CLAPPIN', FOOT STOMPIN', FUNKY-BUTT . . . LIVE! (LP)	25
67	Piccadilly N(S)PL 38032	HIPSTERS, FLIPSTERS, FINGER-POPPIN' DADDIES! (LP)	25
68	Piccadilly N(S)PL 38029	SHAKE A TAIL FEATHER! (LP)	25
68	Pye N(S)PL 18219	LIVE! — RUNNING WILD (LP)	25

(see also Ram Jam Band, Ram John Holder, Ram Holder Brothers, Dave Greenslade)

GEORGE E. WASHINGTON

64	Fontana TF 510	Spare A Thought For Me/Words Of Love	5

GROVER WASHINGTON JR.

73	Kudu KUS 4001	Inner City Blues/Ain't No Sunshine	6
72	Kudu KUL 1	INNER CITY BLUES (LP)	12

JERRY WASHINGTON

75	Contempo CS 2040	Right Here Is Where You Belong/In My Life I Haved Loved	8
75	Contempo CLP 517	RIGHT HERE IS WHERE YOU BELONG (LP)	20

KENNETH WASHINGTON (& CHRIS BARBER BAND)

67	CBS 202494	If I Had A Ticket/They Kicked Him Out Of Heaven (with Chris Barber & T-Bones)	10
67	CBS 202592	Gimme That Old Time Religion (with Chris Barber Band)/ Just A Closer Walk With Thee	5

(see also Chris Barber)

NORMAN T. WASHINGTON

68	Pama PM 730	Same Thing All Over/You've Been Cheating	8
68	Pama PM 741	Tip Toe/Don't Hang Around	10
69	Punch PH 11	Oh Happy Day/Spinning	7
70	Gas GAS 159	It's Christmas Time Again/If I Could See You.	8
70	Punch PH 26	Sweeter Than Honey/1,000 Pearls.	7
70	Punch PH 31	Last Goodbye/Mother's Pride	7

SHERI WASHINGTON & BAND

57	Vogue V 9070	I Got Plenty/Ain't I Talkin' To You Baby (78 rpm = £150).	550

SISTER ERNESTINE B. WASHINGTON

50	Melodisc MEL 1101	God's Amazing Grace/Where Could I Go But To The Lord (78).	10
55	Melodisc EPM 7-52	SISTER ERNESTINE B. WASHINGTON (EP).	20

TONY WASHINGTON (& HIS D.C.s)

63	React EA 002	Crying Man/Please Mr. DJ	20
63	Island WI 068	Something Gotta Be Done/TONY & LOUISE: I Have Said.	20
64	Sue WI 327	Show Me How (To Milk A Cow)/Boof Ska	25
64	Fontana TF 478	Surely You Love Me/Man To Man	15
65	Black Swan WI 459	But I Do/Night Train (as Tony Washington & His D.C.s)	25
65	Black Swan WI 460	Dilly Dilly/Night Train (as Tony Washington & His D.C.s)	25

(see also Tony & Louise)

WASHINGTON D.C.s

64	Ember EMB S 190	Kisses Sweeter Than Wine/Where Did You Go	15
66	CBS 202226	32nd Floor/Whole Lot More	15
67	CBS 202464	Seek And Find/I Love Gerald Chevin The Great (some in p/s)	60/30
69	Domain D 9	I've Done It All Wrong/Anytime	30

(see also Dave Clark Five, Freedom)

WASP

75	EMI EMI 2253	Melissa/Little Miss Bristol	25

(see also Brian Bennett, Shadows)

W.A.S.P.

84	Music For Nations PKUT 109	Animal (Fuck Like A Beast)/Show No Mercy (shaped picture disc, pig's head or codpiece designs)	each 20
84	M. F. Nations 12KUT 109	Animal (Fuck Like A Beast)/Show No Mercy (12", gold, white, clear or red vinyl, U.K. issue pressed in France)	35/15/20/12
84	Capitol CLP 336	I Wanna Be Somebody/Tormentor (Ragewars) (p/s)	5
84	Capitol 12 CLP 336	I Wanna Be Somebody/Tormentor (Ragewars) (12", picture disc).	10
84	Capitol CL 344	Schooldaze/Paint It Black (poster p/s)	5
84	Capitol 12 CL 344	Schooldaze/Paint It Black (12", p/s)	8
85	Capitol CLP 374	Blind In Texas/Savage (shaped picture disc).	7
86	Capitol CLD 388	Wild Child/Mississippi Queen//On Your Knees/Hellion (double pack).	5
86	Capitol 12CL 388	Wild Child/Mississippi Queen (12", p/s)	8
86	Capitol CLP 432	9.5 N.A.S.T.Y./Easy Living (shaped picture disc)	6
87	Capitol CL 469	I Don't Need No Doctor/Widowmaker (live) (p/s, blood pack)	5
87	Capitol CLB 469	I Don't Need No Doctor/Widowmaker (live) (p/s, with repro backstage pass)	5
89	Capitol CLP 521	Mean Man/Locomotive Breath (shaped picture disc)	5
89	Capitol CLPD 534	The Real Me/The Lake Of Fools (shaped picture disc)	5
89	Capitol CLPD 546	Forever Free (Eagle Edit)/L.O.V.E. Machine (Live '89) (die-cut pic. disc)	6

WASPS

77	4-Play FOUR 001	Teenage Treats/She Made More Magic (p/s)	25
77	NEMS NES 115	Can't Wait 'Til '78/MEAN STREET: Bunch Of Stiffs (p/s).	18
78	RCA PB 5137	Rubber Cars/This Time (p/s)	12

WASTE

86	Morterhate MORT 21	NOT JUST SOMETHING TO BE SUNG (EP, foldout p/s)	20

WASTED YOUTH

80	Bridge House BHS 5	Jealousy/Baby (p/s, clear vinyl).	5
82	Bridge House BHFNEE 1	Caveman (1-sided, limited issue)	8
80	Bridge House BHLP006	WILD AND WANDERING (LP)	12
82	Bridge House BHLP007	THE BEGINNING OF THE END (LP)	12

WASTELAND

79	Ellie Jay/Disaster EJSP 9261	WANT NOT EP (p/s, 2,000 only).	50
80	Invicta INV 014	Friends, Romans, Countrymen/Leave Me Alone (p/s, 1,000 only)	35

WATCH COMMITTEE

68	Philips BF 1695	Throw Another Penny In The Well/Now I Think The Other Way.	5

WATERFALL

76	Bob FRR 001	FLIGHT OF THE DAY (LP, private pressing).	50+
79	Avada AVA 104	THREE BIRDS (LP, with insert)	25
81	Gun Dog GUN 003LP	BENEATH THE STARS (LP, private pressing)	25

WATER FOR A THIRSTY LAND

74	MRA P 100	WATER FOR A THIRSTY LAND (LP, with insert)	22

WATER INTO WINE BAND

73	Myrrh MYR 1004	HILL CLIMBING FOR BEGINNERS (LP, brown or white cover, with insert)	250/150
76	CJT 002	HARVEST TIME (LP, private pressing)	200

WATER PISTOLS

76	State STATE 38	Gimme That Punk Junk/Soft Punk (p/s, with insert)	10

WATERPROOF CANDLE

68	RCA RCA 1717	Electrically Heated Child/Saturday Morning Repentance	15

ETHEL WATERS

66	World Record Club T 949	ETHEL WATERS (LP)	12

(see also Ida Cox)

MUDDY WATERS

53	Vogue V 2101	Walkin' Blues/Rollin' Stone Blues (78)	70
54	Vogue V 2273	Hello Little Girl/Long Distance Call (78)	70
55	Vogue V 2372	Honey Bee/Too Young To Know (78)	70
65	Chess CRS 8001	My John The Conquer Root/Short Dress Woman	20
65	Chess CRS 8019	I Got A Rich Man's Woman/My Dog Can't Bark	15
69	Chess CRS 8083	Let's Spend The Night Together/I'm A Man	15
69	Python PKM 04	Country Boy/All Night Long (99 copies only)	85
55	Vogue EPV 1046	MUDDY WATERS WITH LITTLE WALTER (EP)	175
56	London RU-E 1060	MISSISSIPPI BLUES (EP)	175
63	Pye Intl. NEP 44010	MUDDY WATERS (EP)	38
65	Chess CRE 6006	I'M READY (EP)	55
66	Chess CRE 6022	THE REAL FOLK BLUES VOL. 4 (EP)	45
59	London Jazz LJZ-M 15152	THE BEST OF MUDDY WATERS (LP)	80
61	Pye Jazz NJL 34	AT NEWPORT (LP)	55
64	Pye Intl. NPL 28038	MUDDY WATERS — FOLK SINGER (LP)	45
64	Pye Intl. NPL 28040	THE BEST OF MUDDY WATERS (LP)	100
64	Pye Intl. NPL 28048	MUDDY SINGS BIG BILL (LP)	45
65	Chess CRL 4513	AT NEWPORT (LP, reissue)	35
66	Chess CRL 4515	THE REAL FOLK BLUES (LP)	40
67	Chess CRL 4525	MUDDY, BRASS AND THE BLUES (LP)	38
67	Chess CRL 4529	SUPER BLUES (LP, with Little Walter & Bo Diddley)	28
68	Chess CRL 4537	THE SUPER SUPER BLUES BAND (LP, with Howlin' Wolf & Bo Diddley)	50
68	Bounty BY 6031	DOWN ON STOVALL'S PLANTATION (LP)	30
69	Chess CRL 4542	ELECTRIC MUD (LP)	25
69	Chess CRL 4553	AFTER THE RAIN (LP)	30
69	Chess CRL 4556	FATHERS AND SONS (LP)	30
69	Polydor 236 574	BLUES MAN (LP)	20
69	Python PLP 12	MUDDY WATERS (LP, 99 copies only)	48
69	Python PLP 18	MUDDY WATERS VOLUME 2 (LP, 99 copies only)	48
69	Python PLP 19	MUDDY WATERS VOLUME 3 (LP, 99 copies only)	48
70	Syndicate Chapter SC 001/2	BACK IN THE EARLY DAYS (2-LP)	35
70	Syndicate Chapter SC 002	GOOD NEWS (LP)	30
70	Sunnyland KS 100	VINTAGE MUDDY WATERS (LP, gatefold sleeve with inserts, 99 copies only)	45
71	Chess 6671 001	McKINLEY MORGANFIELD AKA MUDDY WATERS (LP)	20
72	Black Bear LP 901	RARE LIVE RECORDINGS VOL. 1 (LP)	25
72	Black Bear LP 902	RARE LIVE RECORDINGS VOL. 2 (LP)	25
72	Black Bear LP 903	RARE LIVE RECORDINGS VOL. 3 (LP)	25
72	Chess 6310 121	THE LONDON SESSIONS (LP)	15
74	Chess 6310 129	CAN'T GET NO GRINDIN' (LP)	15
77	Blue Sky SKY 81853	HARD AGAIN (LP)	15

(see also Little Walter, Howlin' Wolf, Bo Diddley, Luther 'Georgia Boy Snake' Johnson)

ROGER WATERS

84	Harvest HAR 5228	5.01 AM (The Pros And Cons Of Hitch-Hiking)/4.30 AM (Apparently They Were Travelling Abroad) (p/s)	5
84	Harvest 12HAR 5228	5.01 AM (The Pros And Cons Of Hitch-Hiking)/4.30 AM (Apparently They Were Travelling Abroad)/4.33 AM (Running Shoes) (12", p/s)	8
84	Harvest HAR 5230	5.06 AM (Every Stranger's Eyes)/4.39 AM (For The First Time Today) (p/s)	15
87	EMI EM 6	Radio Waves/Going To Live In L.A. (Demo) (p/s)	6
87	EMI CDEM 6	Radio Waves (Remix)/Going To Live In L.A. (Demo)/Radio Waves (7" Version) (CD)	10
87	EMI EM 20	Sunset Strip/Money (live) (unissued; Europe-only)	
87	EMI EM 37	The Tide Is Turning (After Live Aid)/Money ('live') (p/s)	6
87	EMI CDEM 37	The Tide Is Turning (After Live Aid)/Money ('live')/Get Back To Radio (Demo Recording) (CD)	10
90	Mercury 878 147-2	PIECES FROM THE WALL: Another Brick In The Wall Part 2 (Edit)/Young Lust (Edit)/Run Like Hell/In The Flesh? (CD, promo only)	20
92	Columbia 658 139 9	What God Wants Part I (Video Edit)/What God Wants Part I (Album Version)/What God Wants Part III (CD, box set with prints)	12
70	Harvest SHSP 4008	MUSIC FROM THE FILM "THE BODY" (LP, with Ron Geesin, green labels, with Waters/Geesin photos)	30
70	Harvest SHSP 4008	MUSIC FROM THE FILM "THE BODY" (LP, with Ron Geesin, black labels)	12
87	EMI KAOS DJ 1	RADIO KAOS (LP, 'banded' radio promo, custom sleeve)	25

(see also Pink Floyd, Ron Geesin)

LAL & MIKE WATERSON

73	Trailer LER 2076	BRIGHT PHOEBUS (LP, yellow label)	22

WATERSONS

65	Topic 12T 125	NEW VOICES (LP, blue label, with Harry Boardman & Maureen Craik)	18
65	Topic 12T 136	FROST AND FIRE (LP, blue label)	18
66	Topic 12T 142	WATERSONS (LP, blue label)	18
66	Topic 12T 167	A YORKSHIRE GARLAND (LP, blue label)	18
60s	Topic TS 346	THE WATERSONS SOUND (LP)	15

LOVELACE WATKINS

67	Fontana TF 879	I Apologise Baby/You Can't Stop Love	10
72	Uni UNLS 119	LOVE IS (LP)	15
72	York FYK 404	LOVE MAKES THE WORLD GO ROUND (LP)	15

DILYS WATLING

64	Philips BF 1305	Don't Say You Love Me/Now's The Time	6
65	Philips BF 1393	I'm Over You/Act Like A Lady	6
69	Pye 7N 17791	Have Another Dream On Me/Sweet Darlin'	6

DOC WATSON

64	Fontana TFL 6045	DOC WATSON (LP)	25
65	Fontana TFL 6055	DOC WATSON & SON (LP)	25
72	Vanguard VSD 9/10	ON STAGE (2-LP)	20

EARL WATSON
61   Ember EMB S 129   Nightmare/That Old Black Magic 10

JOHN L. WATSON (& HUMMELFLUGS)
64   Pye 7N 15746   Looking For Love/Dance With You 7
65   Piccadilly 7N 35233   Standing By/I'll Make It Worth Your While 8
70   Deram DM-R 285   A Mother's Love/Might As Well Be Gone (solo). 10
70   Deram SML 1061   WHITE HOT BLUE BLACK (LP) 35
(see also Web)

JOHNNY WATSON & KAMPAI KINGS
60   Oriole CB 1532   Moshi, Moshi, Anone!/ABDULLA & HIS LITTLE BAND:
                         Fatima's Theme (78 rpm = £30) 5

JOHNNY 'GUITAR' WATSON
76   Fantasy FTC 124   I Don't Need A Lone Ranger/You Can Stay But The Noise Must Go 8
(see also Larry Williams & Johnny 'Guitar' Watson)

PAULA WATSON
63   Oriole 45-CV1785   Love Me Forever/Tell All The World About You 15

ROGER WATSON
74   Tradition TSR 017   THE PICK AND THE MALT SHOVEL (LP) 15

WAH WAH WATSON
76   CBS 81582   ELEMENTARY (LP) 12

BEN WATT
81   Cherry Red CHERRY 25   Cant/Aubade/Tower Of Silence (p/s) 8
82   Cherry Red 12CHERRY 36   SUMMER INTO WINTER (12" EP, with Robert Wyatt, p/s). 10
(see also Everything But The Girl)

LU WATTERS & AND HIS YERBA BUENA JAZZ BAND
55   Vogue EPV 1053   LU WATTERS (EP). 8
56   Vogue EPV 1130   LU WATTERS JAZZ BAND (EP). 8
52   Vogue LDE 009   LU WATTERS AND HIS JAZZ BAND (10" LP). 18
55   Columbia Clef 33C 9004   LU WATTERS AND HIS YERBA BUENA JAZZ BAND (10" LP) 15
56   London HB-U 1061   LU WATTERS – 1947 (10" LP) 15
57   Columbia Clef 33C 9036   DIXIELAND JAMBOREE (10" LP). 15

WATTS 103RD STREET RHYTHM BAND
(see under Charles Wright & Watts 103rd Street Rhythm Band)

CHARLIE WATTS
93   Continuum CDCTUM 103   My Ship/You Got To Me Head (CD) 12
86   CBS 450 253-1   LIVE AT FULHAM TOWN HALL (LP, as Charlie Watts & His Orchestra,
                         with insert). 15
91   UFO UFO 2 LP   FROM ONE CHARLIE (10" LP, box set with book & Charlie Parker photo,
                         some signed) 30/20
(see also Rolling Stones, People Band, Rocket 88)

NOBLE 'THIN MAN' WATTS (& HIS BAND)
57   London HLU 8627   Hard Times (The Slop)/Midnight Flight (with His Rhythm Sparks) 75
57   London HLU 8627   Hard Times (The Slop)/Midnight Flight (with His Rhythm Sparks) (78). 20
64   Sue WI 347   Noble's Theme/JUNE BATEMAN: I Don't Wanna. 60
60s   XX MIN 717   NOBLE 'THIN MAN' WATTS AND WILD JIMMY SPURRILL (EP). 30
79   Flybright 547   BLAST OFF (LP, mono). 20
(see also Wild Jimmy Spurrill)

WATUSI WARRIORS
59   London HL 8866   Wa-Chi-Bam-Ba/Kalahari (78 rpm = £8) 15

WAVELENGTH
82   Ariola ARO 290   Rio/Beach Party. 7

NANCY WAYBURN
65   Warner Bros WB 5646   The World Goes On Without Me/Listen To My Heart. 20

WAYFARERS
61   Decca F 11370   Whistle Down The Wind/Think Of A Stranger 8
70s   MWM 1017   SONGS & DANCE TUNES (LP) 15

WAYGOOD ELLIS
67   Polydor 56729   I Like What I'm Trying To Do/Hey Lover 40
(see also Fleur-De-Lys)

ALVIS WAYNE
63   Starlite ST45 104   Don't Mean Maybe, Baby/I'd Rather Be With You . . . . 600+

ARTIE WAYNE
52   London L 1164   Rachel/Tonight Or Never (78). 15

BOBBY WAYNE
51   London L 924   When The Wind Was Green/Buffalo Billy (78) 12
51   London L 968   Immaculate Mother/Mother At Your Feet Is Kneeling (78) 10
51   London L 972   Runnin' Around/Always You (78). 12
51   London L 973   Wild Card/Let Me In (78) 12
51   London L 1077   I Am Free/How Long Is Forever (78) 12
51   London L 1078   If You Turn Me Down/Let's Make Up Your Mind (78) 12
55   Mercury MB 3151   They Were Doin' The Mambo/A String Of Broken Hearts (78) 8
(see also Teresa Brewer)

BOBBY WAYNE
65   Pye International 7N 25315   Ballad Of A Teenage Queen/River Man. 10

CARL WAYNE (& VIKINGS)
64	Pye 7N 15702	What's A Matter Baby/Your Loving Ways (as Carl Wayne & Vikings)	45
65	Pye 7N 15824	This Is Love/You Could Be Fun (as Carl Wayne & Vikings)	35
70	RCA RCA 2032	Maybe God's Got Something Up His Sleeve/Rosanna	6
72	RCA RCA 2177	Imagine/Sunday Kind Of Love	5
72	RCA RCA 2257	Take My Hands For A While/Sweet Seasons	5
73	Pye 7N 45290	You're A Star/Bluebird	5
75	Polydor 2058 527	Way Back In The Fifties/Candy (You Know That I'm In Love With You)	6
77	Target TGT 125	A Little Give, A Little Take/Home Lovin' Man	6
77	DJM DJS Weeken 10797	Hi Summer/My Girl And Me	6
72	RCA SF 8239	CARL WAYNE (LP)	20

(see also Move, Ace Kefford Stand, Cheetahs, Acid Gallery, Keith Powell [& Valets])

CHRIS WAYNE & ECHOES
60	Decca F 11231	Lonely/Counting Girls	15

JEFF WAYNE
69	Columbia S(C)X 6330	TWO CITIES (LP, soundtrack)	35

(see also Ran-Dells)

JERRY WAYNE
60	Vogue V 9169	Half-Hearted Love/Ten Thousand Miles	25

JOHN WAYNE
73	RCA PL 13484	AMERICA, WHY I LOVE HER (LP)	15

PAT WAYNE (& BEACHCOMBERS)
63	Columbia DB 7121	Go Back To Daddy/Jambalaya	20
63	Columbia DB 7182	Roll Over Beethoven/Is It Love?	20
64	Columbia DB 7262	Bye Bye Johnny/Strictly For The Birds	20
64	Columbia DB 7417	Brand New Man/Nobody's Child	18
65	Columbia DB 7603	Come Dance With Me/I Don't Want To Cry (solo)	10
65	Columbia DB 7739	My Friend/Tomorrow Mine (solo)	8
66	Columbia DB 7944	The Night Is Over/Hombre (solo)	10

RICK(Y) WAYNE (& OFF-BEATS)
60	Triumph RGM 1009	Chick A'Roo/Don't Pick On Me (with Fabulous Flee-Rakkers)	45
60	Pye 7N 15289	Make Way Baby/Goodness Knows (as Ricky Wayne & Off-Beats)	40
65	Oriole CB 306	Say You're Gonna Be My Own/It's A Crying Shame (as Rick Wayne)	15
65	CBS 201764	In My Imagination/Don't Ever Share Your Love (as Rick Wayne)	10

(see also [Fabulous] Flee-Rekkers)

TERRY WAYNE
57	Columbia DB 4002	Matchbox/Your True Love (78 rpm = £7)	25
57	Columbia DB 4035	Plaything/Slim Jim Tie (78 rpm = £8)	25
58	Columbia DB 4067	All Mama's Children/Forgive Me (78 rpm = £8)	25
58	Columbia DB 4112	Oh! Lonesome Me/There's Only One You (78 rpm = £12)	20
58	Columbia DB 4205	Little Brother/Where My Baby Goes (78 rpm = £15)	18
59	Columbia DB 4312	Brooklyn Bridge/She's Mine	20
58	Columbia SEG 7758	TERRIFIC (EP)	100

THOMAS WAYNE
59	London HLU 8846	Tragedy/Saturday Date (78 rpm = £20)	38
59	London HL 7075	Tragedy/Saturday Date (export issue)	20

WAYS & MEANS
66	Columbia DB 7907	Little Deuce Coupe/The Little Old Lady From Pasadena	25
66	Pye 7N 17217	Sea Of Faces/Make The Radio A Little Louder	22
68	Trend TRE 1005	Breaking Up A Dream/She	55

WAY WE LIVE
71	Dandelion DAN 8004	A CANDLE FOR JUDITH (LP, gatefold sleeve, also listed as K 49004)	130

(see also Tractor, Beau)

WBI RED NINJA
90	Red Ninja SRT90LS 2532	Danger Zone/This Mike's For Hire/Bad Testament (12")	20
91	Red Ninja RN002	HELLZ A PLACE I KNOW (EP)	12

WEAPON
80	Weapon WEAP 1	It's A Mad Mad World/Set The Stage Alight (p/s)	30
81	Virgin WEAPONE	It's A Mad Mad World/Set The Stage Alight (12", p/s, reissue)	40

(see also Headbangers, Wildfire)

WEASELSNOUT
72	Weaselsnout WUS 140	UNSUNG LIES (LP, private pressing)	165

WEATHER
69	Philips BF 1734	Look In My Eyes/Running Forward	30+
69	Philips BF 1819	Jamboree Special/Two Peculiar People	6

ALFIE WEATHERBY
58	Columbia DC 729	49 Juke Boxes/Why Am I Crying? (78, export issue)	25

WEATHER REPORT
71	CBS 64521	WEATHER REPORT (LP)	12
72	CBS 64943	I SING THE BODY ELECTRIC (LP)	12
73	CBS 65532	SWEETNIGHTER (LP)	12
74	CBS 80027	MYSTERIOUS TRAVELLER (LP)	12

(see also Joe Zawinul)

DENNIS WEAVER
77	DJM DJS 10758	Devil In My Arms/Flat Bed Truck (p/s, promo)	8
75	DJM DJF 20479	McCLOUD COUNTRY (LP)	12

MINT VALUE £

WEAVERS
59	Top Rank JAR 120	Wild Goose Grasses/Meet The Johnson Boys	6
57	Vanguard PPL 11006	AT THE CARNEGIE HALL (LP)	15
57	Vanguard PPL 11011	ON TOUR (LP)	15
59	Top Rank RX 3008	AT HOME (LP)	15
61	Brunswick LAT 8357	BEST OF THE WEAVERS (LP)	15
62	Fontana TFL 6011	WEAVERS' ALMANAC (LP)	15

(see also Pete Seeger)

JANE WEAVER v DOVES
98	Manchester MANC 9	Seven Day Smile/ANDY VOTEL & JANE WEAVER: Gutter Girl (p/s)	8
98	Manchester MANCCD 9	Seven Day Smile/ANDY VOTEL & JANE WEAVER: Gutter Girl/JANE WEAVER: You're Not The Only Person That I Used To Know (CD)	10

(see also Doves)

WEB
68	Deram DM 201	Hatton Mill Morning/Conscience	30
68	Deram DM 217	Baby Won't You Leave Me Alone/McVernon Street	30
69	Deram DM 253	Monday To Friday/Harold Dubbleyew	30
68	Deram SML 1025	FULLY INTERLOCKING (LP)	90
70	Deram SML 1058	THERAPHOSA BLONDI (LP)	90
70	Polydor 2383 024	I SPIDER (LP)	140+

(see also John L. Watson [& Hummelflugs], Samurai, Greenslade)

WEB
96	Fat Cat 12FAT 001	EVA EP (12", plain sleeve)	20

DEAN WEBB
59	Parlophone R 4549	Warm Your Heart/Hey Miss Fannie	50
59	Parlophone R 4587	The Rough And The Smooth/Streamline Baby	50

DON WEBB
60	Coral Q 72385	Little Ditty Baby/I'll Be Back Home	90+

GEORGE WEBB DIXIELANDERS
56	Decca DFE 6351	AND HIS DIXIELANDERS (EP)	15
50s	Melodisc EPM7 70	THE GEORGE WEBB DIXIELANDERS (EP)	10

JANET WEBB
71	Polydor 2058-131	I Cried For You/Mama (p/s)	10

JILLA WEBB
56	MGM SP 1180	You Gotta Love Me Now/What Do You Think It Does To Me?	10

JIM(MY) WEBB
68	CBS 3672	I Keep It Hid/I Need You (as Jim Webb)	25
71	Reprise RS 20978	P.F. Sloan/Psalm One-Five-O	10
73	Reprise K 14279	Campo De Encino/Once In The Morning	5
68	CBS (S) 63335	JIM WEBB SINGS JIM WEBB (LP, as Jim Webb)	30
71	Reprise RSLP 6421	WORDS AND MUSIC (LP, with insert)	22
71	Reprise K 44101	WORDS AND MUSIC (LP, reissue)	15
72	Reprise K 44134	AND SO ON (LP)	18
72	Reprise K 44173	LETTERS (LP)	18
74	Asylum SYL 9014	LAND'S END (LP, with inner sleeve)	20
77	Atlantic K 50370	EL MIRAGE (LP, with inner sleeve)	15

(see also Strawberry Children, Glen Campbell)

JOHNNY WEBB
56	Columbia DB 3805	Dig/Glendora	10
57	Columbia DB 3904	The Song Of The Moonlight/Give Me More	8
60s	Melodisc MEL 1617	Travelin' Man/Hold Back The Town (some with p/s)	12/6

(see also June Laverick)

PETA WEBB
73	Topic 12TS 223	I HAVE WANDERED IN EXILE (LP, blue label)	35

(see also Oak)

PETA WEBB & PETE COOPER
86	Heart	HEART IS TRUE (LP)	15

ROGER WEBB (& HIS TRIO)
67	RCA 1599	A Man And His Woman/The Spiderman	10
71	Columbia DB 8803	Strange Report/Summer Fancy	12
82	Chandos SBR 102	The Gentle Touch/Arthur's Theme	6
84	Chips CH 104	Hammer House Of Horror/Cover Theme (p/s)	12
64	Parlophone PMC 1233	JOHN, PAUL AND ALL THAT JAZZ (LP)	12

SKEETER WEBB
55	Parlophone CMSP 32	Was It A Bad Dream/Your Secret's Not A Secret Anymore (export issue)	15

SONNY WEBB & CASCADES
64	Oriole CB 1873	You've Got Everything/Border Of The Blues	40
64	Polydor NH 52158	You've Got Everything/Border Of The Blues (reissue)	12

MARLENE WEBBER
70	Bamboo BAM 33	My Baby/BRENTFORD ALLSTARS: You Gonna Hold Me (Version)	15
71	Ackee ACK 120	Natengula/Natengula-Kera (as Merlin Webber)	8
71	Ackee ACK 122	Cumbaya/Hail-Hi Freedom (as Merlin Webber)	8
71	Smash SMA 2322	Hard Life/COLLINS ALL STARS: Version Life (as Merlene Webber)	10
71	Trojan TR 7815	Stand By Your Man/CLANCY ECCLES: Credit Squeeze	8

(see also Webber Sisters, Tonettes)

WEBBER SISTERS
67	Island WI 3109	My World/ALVA LEWIS: Lonely Still	60

(see also Delroy Wilson)

WEBS
68	London HLU 10188	This Thing Called Love/Tomorrow	20

WEBSPINNERS
73	Buddah 2011 150	Spider Man — Theme/Goin' 'Cross Town	6

BEN WEBSTER
55	Columbia CLEF 33CX 10014	MUSIC FOR LOVERS (LP)	20
59	HMV CLP 1336	BEN WEBSTER AND ASSOCIATES (LP)	25
65	Fontana FJL 126	INTIMATE! (LP)	25
69	Ember CJS 822	BEN WEBSTER AT EASE (LP)	15
70	Fontana FJL 316	BIG BEN TIME (LP)	20
72	Philips 6308 101	WEBSTER'S DICTIONARY (LP)	25

CHASE WEBSTER
64	Hickory 45-1283	Life Can Have Meaning/Where Is Your Heart	6

DEENA WEBSTER
68	Parlophone R 5699	You're Losing/Wish You Were Here	10
68	Parlophone R 5721	Your Heart Is Free Just Like The Wind/Queen Merka And Me	8
68	Parlophone R 5738	Scarborough Fair/The Water Is Wide	7
69	Parlophone R 5798	Joey/It's Alright With Me	6
68	Parlophone PMC/PCS 7052	TUESDAY'S CHILD (LP)	35

WEDDING PRESENT
85	Reception REC 001	Go Out And Get 'Em Boy/(The Moment Before) Everything's Spoiled Again (p/s, 500 only, a few with poster & badge)	30/20
85	City Slang CSL 001	Go Out And Get 'Em Boy/(The Moment Before) Everything's Spoiled Again (reissue, different foldout p/s, 1,000 only)	10
86	Reception REC 002	Once More/At The Edge Of The Sea (p/s, 3,500 only)	8
86	Reception REC 002/12	DON'T TRY AND STOP ME MOTHER (12" EP, combines REC 001 & 002)	8
86	Reception REC 003	This Boy Can Wait/You Should Always Keep In Touch With Your Friends (p/s, matrix numbers: 003 A2 & 003 B1)	6
86	Reception REC 003	This Boy Can Wait/You Should Always Keep In Touch With Your Friends (p/s, mispress both sides play B-side, matrix numbers: 003 A1 & 003 A2)	5
86	Reception REC 003/12	This Boy Can Wait (Extended)/You Should Always Keep In Touch With Your Friends/Living And Learning (12", p/s)	8
87	Reception REC 005	My Favourite Dress/Every Mother's Son/Never Said (p/s, white vinyl, 3,000 only, 2,000 of which free with GEORGE BEST LP)	6
87	Reception	A Million Miles/What Did Your Last Servant Die Of? (DJ promo, 200 only)	8
87	Reception REC 006/C	Anyone Can Make A Mistake/All About Eve/Getting Nowhere Fast (cassette, shrinkwrapped with badge)	5
88	Reception REC 010X	Davni Chasy/Katrusya (promo only)	6
88	House Of Dolls HOD 004	Unfaithful (Peel Session)/TRUDY: Living On A Moon/HUNTERS CLUB: Little Sister/CLAYTOWN TROUPE: Real Life (free with *House Of Dolls* mag)	5
89	M'night Music DONG 39 CD	Pourquoi Es Tu Devenue Si Rasionable? (CD, unreleased)	
89	RCA	Davni Chasy/Katrusya (promo only)	10
90	RCA PB 43403	Brassneck/Don't Talk, Just Kiss (custom hand-painted p/s, 3,000 only)	6
92	RCA PB 45185	Blue Eyes/Cattle And Cane (p/s)	8
92	RCA PB 45183	Go Go Dancer/Don't Cry No Tears (p/s)	5
92	RCA PB 45181	Three/Think That It Might (p/s)	5
92	RCA PB 45311	Silver Shorts/Falling (p/s)	5
92	RCA PB 45313	Come Play With Me/Pleasant Valley Sunday (p/s)	5
87	Reception LEEDS 1	GEORGE BEST (LP, 2,000 only with white vinyl 7": My Favourite Dress/ Every Mother's Son/Never Said [REC 005] & inner sleeve; later with bonus black vinyl 7" or 12" edition)	12/10
88	Reception LEEDS 2	TOMMY (LP, 1,000 signed by band, with poster & inner sleeve)	15

WEDGEWOODS
64	Pye 7N 15642	September In The Rain/Gone Gone Away	12
65	Pye 7N 15846	Peace/Summer Love	10

FRED WEDLOCK
70s	Trans VTS 20	FROLLICKS (LP)	30

BUDDY WEED & HIS ORCHESTRA
57	Vogue V 9075	The Kent Song/For Love (78 rpm = £8)	25

BERT WEEDON
56	Parlophone MSP 6242	The Boy With The Magic Guitar/Flannel-Foot (78 rpm = £10)	18
57	Parlophone R 4256	Theme From ITV's '$64,000 Question'/Twilight Time	18
57	Parlophone R 4315	The Jolly Gigolo/Soho Fair	18
57	Parlophone R 4381	Play That Big Guitar/Quiet, Quiet, Ssh! (78 rpm = £7)	12
58	Parlophone R 4446	Big Note Blues/Rippling Tango (78 rpm = £10)	12
59	Saga SAG 2906	Fifi/Cat On A Hot Tin Roof (as Bert Weedon & Rag Pickers)	18
59	Top Rank JAR 117	Guitar Boogie Shuffle/Bert's Boogie (78 rpm = £10)	7
59	Top Rank JAR 121	Sing Little Birdie/The Lady Is A Tramp	5
59	Top Rank JAR 122	Petite Fleur/My Happiness	5
59	Top Rank JAR 123	Charmaine/It's Time To Say Goodnight	5
59	Top Rank JAR 136	Teenage Guitar/Blue Guitar	6
59	Top Rank JAR 210	Jealousy/Tango, Tango (78 rpm = £10)	5
59	Top Rank JAR 211	Stardust/Summertime (78 rpm = £10)	5
59	Top Rank JAR 221	Nashville Boogie/King Size Guitar (78 rpm = £15)	6
60	Top Rank JAR 300	Big Beat Boogie/Theme From 'A Summer Place' (some with p/s)	8/5
60	Top Rank JAR 360	Twelfth Street Rag/Querida	6
60	Top Rank JAR 415	Apache/Lonely Guitar	8
60	Top Rank JAR 517	Sorry Robbie/Easy Beat	7
61	Top Rank JAR 537	Ginchy/Yearning	7
61	Top Rank JAR 559	Mr. Guitar/Eclipse	8
56	Esquire EP 56	WAXING THE WINNERS (EP)	25

MINT VALUE £

59	Selmer Amplifiers	DEMONSTRATION RECORD WITH DAVID GELL (EP, with mailer)	10/20
61	Top Rank JKP 3008	WEEDON WINNERS (EP)	15
64	HMV 7EG 8856	GUITAR MAN (EP)	15
60	Top Rank BUY 026	KINGSIZE GUITAR (LP)	35
61	Top Rank 35/101	HONKY TONK GUITAR (LP)	30

(see also George Chisholm, Craig Douglas, Ragpickers)

WEEDS
| 86 | In Tape IT 34 | China Doll/Crazy Face (p/s) | 12 |

WEE THREE
| 73 | People PEO 104 | Get On Board/Get On Board (Instrumental) | 8 |

WEE WILLIE & WINNERS
| 74 | Action ACT 4624 | Get Some/A Plan For The Man | 20 |
| 74 | People PEO 116 | I Don't Know What You Got But I Know What I Need (Parts 1 & 2) | 8 |

WEEZER
94	Geffen GFS 85	Undone: The Sweater Song/Mykel And Carli/Susanne/Holiday (p/s)	15
94	Geffen GFSCD 85	Undone: The Sweater Song/Mykel And Carli/Susanne/Holiday (CD)	18
95	Geffen GFS 88	Buddy Holly/Jamie (p/s)	12
95	Geffen GFSV 95	Say It Ain't So (Remix)/No One Else (Live & Acoustic)/Jamie (10", p/s)	12
95	Geffen GEF 24629	WEEZER (LP)	18

WE FIVE
65	Pye International 7N 25314	You Were On My Mind/Small World	12
66	Pye International 7N 25346	Let's Get Together/Cast Your Fate To The Wind	18
66	Pye Intl. NEP 44056	LET'S GET TOGETHER (EP)	60
65	Pye Intl. NPL 28067	YOU WERE ON MY MIND (LP)	50

WE 4
| 67 | HMV POP 1603 | Pretty Flowers/I'll Make You A Miracle | 5 |
| 69 | Major Minor MM 593 | Candy Floss Man/Perry Park | 6 |

FRANN WEIGLE
| 50 | London L 551 | Rockin' Chair/My Diary Of Broken Dreams (78) | 8 |

BRUCIE WEIL
| 53 | London L 1203 | Little Boy Blues/God Bless Us All (78) | 8 |

BOB WEIR
| 72 | Warner Bros WB 7611 | One More Saturday Night/Cassidy | 5 |
| 72 | Warner Bros K 46165 | ACE (LP) | 15 |

(see also Grateful Dead, Kingfish, Bobby & Midnites)

FRANK WEIR & HIS ORCHESTRA
| 55 | Decca LF 1208 | PRESENTING FRANK WEIR AND HIS SAXOPHONE (10" LP) | 12 |

(see also Bill Darnell, Vera Lynn, Janie Marden)

NORRIS WEIR (& JAMAICANS)
70	Duke DU 85	Hard On Me (with Jamaicans)/TOMMY COWAN & JAMAICANS: Please Stop The Wedding	6
74	Dragon DRA 1030	Reggay Revolution/Version	5
75	Horse HOSS 81	Dr. Honey/Honey Dub	5

(see also Jamaicans)

WEIRD STRINGS
| 80 | Velvet Moon VM 1 | Oscar Mobile/Ancient Square (foldover p/s) | 10 |
| 80 | Ace ACE 009 | Criminal Cage/Mi££ionaire (p/s) | 8 |

(see also Paul Roland, Midnight Rags)

FRANK WEISS
| 71 | Stax 2362 011 | WEISS TO MEMPHIS (LP) | 12 |

BRUCE WELCH
| 74 | EMI EMI 2141 | Please Mr. Please/Song Of Yesterday | 50 |

(see also Marvin, Welch & Farrar; Shadows, Cliff Richard)

ELIZABETH WELCH
| 80 | Industrial IR 002 | Stormy Weather/Ya're Blase (p/s) | 10 |

HONEE WELCH
| 69 | London HLU 10288 | I'm Gonna Try/It's My Girl | 7 |

KEN & MITZIE WELCH
| 62 | London RE-R 1275 | A PIANO, ICE BOX AND BED (EP) | 12 |

LENNY WELCH
60	London HLA 9094	You Don't Know Me/I Need Someone	8
62	London HLA 9601	Taste Of Honey/Old Cathedral	8
63	London HLA 9810	Since I Fell For You/Are You Sincere	8
64	London HLA 9880	Ebb Tide/Congratulations Baby	8
64	London HLR 9910	If You See My Love/Father Sebastian	8
65	London HLR 9981	Darling Take Me Back/Time After Time	12
65	London HLR 9991	Two Different Worlds/I Was There	10
65	London HLR 10010	Run To My Lovin' Arms/Coronet Blue	30
66	London HLR 10031	Rags To Riches/I Want You To Worry	15
66	London HA-R/SH-R 8267	TWO DIFFERENT WORLDS (LP)	30
66	London HA-R 8290	RAGS TO RICHES (LP)	25

TIM WELCH
| 60 | Columbia DB 4529 | Weak In The Knees/A Boy And A Girl In Love | 7 |

WELD OF LIQUOR
| 95 | Weld Record WELD 05 | We Are The Weld/For Manze's Sake (vinegar-scented p/s) | 10 |

1976, Anarchy/No Fun acetate, £6000+.

1977, the famed A&M God Save The Queen, £7,000+.

1976, more affordable Pistols demo, £225.

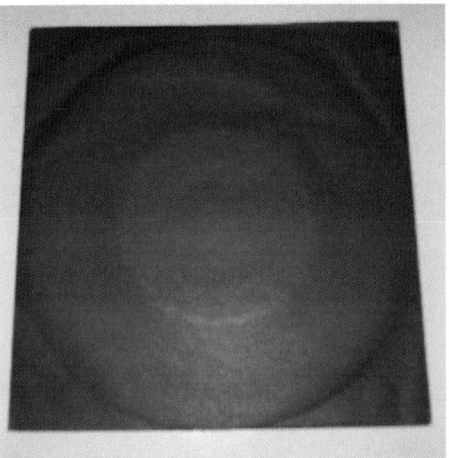

1977, Pistols sample with no 'Queen's head, £1,500.

1977, 999 promo playing at 78rpm, £200+.

1981, cheeky CRASS Our Wedding flexi. £200+.

Rare Record Price Guide 2008

1980, mega-rare withdrawn Lambrettas p/s, £500.

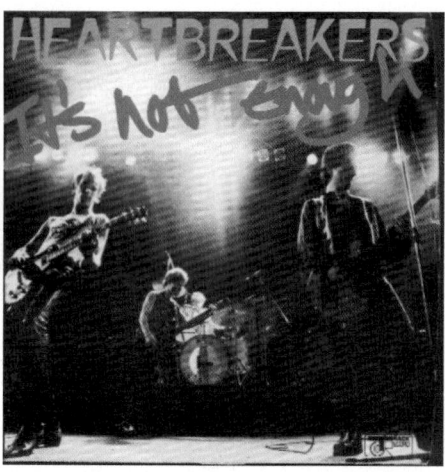

1977, withdrawn Heartbreakers single with p/s, £250.

1977, unissued pre-peroxide Billy Idol, Gen X p/s, £500.

1977, Those Damned Hot Rods on Damned LP, £220.

1977, withdrawn XTC Science Friction 7", £2,500+.

1978, side 2 of debut Joy Division EP, £800.

1963, Bob Marley's first single as Robert Marley, £270.

1967, Bob Marley undercover as Summertairs, £90.

1966, Millie Small EP on Island, £55.

1966, Ska compilation LP with amazing cover, £200.

1963, Lee Perry, B-side of Old For New 7", £45.

1967, The Wailers' I Stand Predominate, £250.

1969, Derrick Morgan LP on the Doctor Bird label, £120.

1967, Heptones LP, on the Studio One label, £100+.

1982, £18 will buy this Eloy picture disc.

1970, *Black Cat Bones* LP, £80.

1979, Iron Maiden, *Soundhouse Tapes* EP, £100.

1979, Samson's Mr. Rock & Roll 7", £35.

1983, misprinted blue/negative sleeve, £1000+.

1985, unissued test of Smiths *Meat Is Murder* EP, £800+

1985, label from first Stone Roses 12" single, £120.

2002, 1-sided Oasis My Generation promo is worth £30.

1988, collectable DAT from Kylie, £100

1992, withdrawn toe-sucking Madonna picture disc, £2000.

Rare Record Price Guide 2008

1993, rare Hip Hop: Blade, Clear The Way, £50.

1993 Braintax, *Fat Head* EP, £50.

1994, Hip Hop: Guttersnypes, *Trails Of Life* EP, £18.

2001, Jehst, The Trilogy Remix 12", £55.

1987, Jus Bad's Freestyle/Proud 12", £60.

1988, Trouble's I Get Hype 12", £40.

Rare Record Price Guide 2008

1996, Feeder debut *Two Colours* single on CD, £50.

2002, Libertines debut 7", What A Waster, £30.

1990, p/s of Manic's free magazine flexi, £60.

2005, label from White Stripes rare *Satan* LP promo, £150.

2005, Tunng's Maypole Song etched 7" is worth £60.

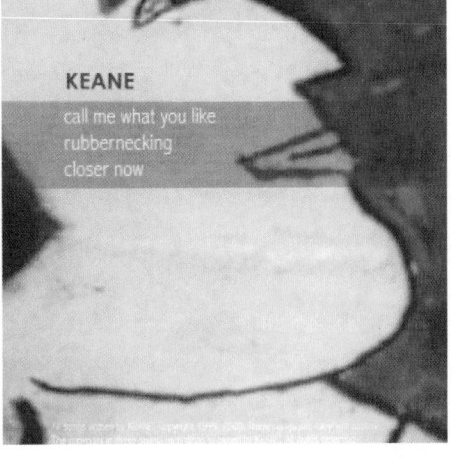

2000, only 500 of first Keane CD single pressed, £100+.

Rare Record Price Guide 2008

1968, Fonda cover on this classic soundtrack LP, £100.

1970, features The Strawberry Alarm Clock, £90.

1960, soundtrack LP from *Wagon Train* TV show, £25.

1960, *Let's Make Love* soundtrack EP in stereo, £55.

1971, rare and collectable library music LP, £150.

1974, Marc Duval library music LP, £60.

Rare Record Price Guide 2008

WELFARE STATE
78   Look LKLP 6347   WELFARE STATE SONGS (LP, with insert) 60

LAWRENCE WELK ORCHESTRA
56	Vogue Coral Q 72140	Chain Gang/The Poor People Of Paris	7
56	Vogue Coral Q 72141	The 'Threepenny Opera' Theme/Rock And Roll Waltz	7
57	Vogue Coral Q 72233	Pizzicato Waltz/Whispering Heart	6
57	Vogue Coral Q 72256	Around The World In 80 Days/Ten Little Trees	7
61	London HLD 9261	Calcutta (Nicolette)/Melodie D'Amour.................................	7
64	Dot DS 16697	The 'Addams Family' Theme/Apples And Bananas........................	20

PAUL WELLER ('Modfather')
SINGLES
91	Freedom High FHP 1	Into Tomorrow/Here's A New Thing (p/s, with or without 'Paul Weller Movement' on label)	25
91	Freedom High FHPC 1	Into Tomorrow/Here's A New Thing (cassette)........................	14
91	Freedom High FHPT 1	Into Tomorrow/Here's A New Thing/That Spiritual Feeling/ Into Tomorrow (8-Track Demo) (12", p/s)	30
91	Freedom High FHPCD 1	Into Tomorrow/Here's A New Thing/That Spiritual Feeling/ Into Tomorrow (8-Track Demo) (CD)	70
92	Go! Discs GOD 86	Uh Huh Oh Yeh/Fly On The Wall (paper or plastic labels, p/s)........	8
92	Go! Discs GODX 86	Uh Huh Oh Yeh/Arrival Time/Fly On The Wall/Always There To Fool You (12", p/s)	12
92	Go! Discs GODCD 86	Uh Huh Oh Yeh/Fly On The Wall/Arrival Time/Always There To Fool You (CD, digipak)	14
92	Go! Discs GOD 91	Above The Clouds/Everything Has A Price To Pay (paper or plastic labels, p/s)	7
92	Go! Discs GODX 91	Above The Clouds/Everything Has A Price To Pay/All Year Round (live)/ Feeling Alright (12", p/s)...	10
92	Go! Discs GODCD 91	Above The Clouds/Everything Has A Price To Pay/All Year Round (live)/ Feeling Alright (CD, digipak)	14
93	Go! Discs GOD 102	Sunflower/Bull-Rush — Magic Bus (p/s)	7
93	Go! Discs GODX 102	Sunflower/Kosmos SXDub 2,000/Bull-Rush — Magic Bus (live)/ That Spiritual Feeling (New Mix) (12", p/s)........................	10
93	Go! Discs GODCD 102	Sunflower/Kosmos SXDub 2,000/Bull-Rush — Magic Bus (live)/ That Spiritual Feeling (New Mix) (CD, digipak)	14
93	Go! Discs GOD 104	Wild Wood/Ends Of The Earth (p/s)	6
93	Go! Discs GODT 104	Wild Wood/Ends Of The Earth (10", p/s, with poster)...............	12
93	Go! Discs GODCD 104	Wild Wood/Ends Of The Earth (CD, sealed with 5 postcards)	16
94	Go! Discs GOD 107	THE WEAVER EP (The Weaver/This Is No Time/Another New Day/Ohio [live]) (p/s)	6
94	Go! Discs GODT 107	THE WEAVER EP (10", numbered sticker on p/s)	12
94	Go! Discs GODCD 107	THE WEAVER EP (The Weaver/This Is No TIme/ Another New Day/Ohio [live]) (CD, digipak)	14
94	Go! Discs GOD 111	Hung Up/Foot Of The Mountain (live from Royal Albert Hall 23.11.93)/ The Loved/Kosmos (Lynch Mob Bonus Beats) (p/s)...................	6
94	Go! Discs GODX 111	Hung Up/Foot Of The Mountain (live from Royal Albert Hall 23.11.93)/ The Loved/Kosmos (Lynch Mob Bonus Beats) (12", p/s)..............	10
94	Go! Discs GODCD 111	Hung Up/Foot Of The Mountain (live from Royal Albert Hall 23.11.93)/ The Loved/Kosmos (Lynch Mob Bonus Beats) (CD, digipak)	12
94	Go! Discs GOD 121	Out Of The Sinking/Sunflower (Lynch Mob Dub)/Sexy Sadie (p/s)	6
94	Go! Discs GODCD 121	Out Of The Sinking/Sunflower (Lynch Mob Dub)/Sexy Sadie (CD)	10
95	Go! Discs GODCD 127	THE CHANGING MAN EP (CD, digipak)	12

ALBUMS
92	Go! Discs 828343-1	PAUL WELLER (LP, gatefold with booklet)...........................	25
93	Go! Discs 828513-1	WILD WOOD (LP, gatefold with poster)	25
95	Go! Discs 850 070-7	STANLEY ROAD (LP, 6 x 7" in box set with booklet)	28
95	Go! Discs 828 620-2	STANLEY ROAD (CD, 12" box set with booklet)	22
01	Independiente ISOM26LP	DAYS OF SPEED (2 x LP, gatefold, numbered)	30
03	Universal 635271	FLY ON THE WALL (3 x LP with inserts)	18
04	V2 VVR 1026901	STUDIO 150 (LP, 2000 only)	18

PROMOS & FREEBIES
92	Go! Discs	Kosmos (12")...	22
93	no label (WELLER+ F1)	The Loved (blank clear 1-sided flexi free with *The Big Issue* mag)	14/6
93	Go! Discs PWBCD 1	Wild Wood (The Sheared Wood Remix) (CD, no inlay)...............	16
94	Go! Discs PN PCD 2	Sexy Sadie (1-track CD, available via mail order with 1st 500 copies of "Highlights & Hang-Ups" video)	20
94	PNME1	Shadow Of The Sun (Live)/Sunflower (Lynch Mob Dub)/Wild Wood (Sheared Wood) (7" given away with *NME*)	8
95	Go! Discs PW-G-CD 1	Into Tomorrow/Wild Wood/Out Of The Sinking (CD, free with *The Guardian Guide* magazine)......................................	6
95	Go! Discs SPLINT 1	Walk On Gilded Splinters (12", 1-sided white label)	65
95	Go! Discs LYNCH 1	Whirlpools End (Lynch Mob Mix) (12", 1-sided white label, stamped 1-sided white label, 500 only)	65
96	Go! Discs LYNCH1	Peacock Suit/Eye Of The Storm (CD)	12
97	Island ISJB 666	Brushed/Shoot The Dove (jukebox issue)	8
97	Island	Heavy Soul (1-sided)...	55
99	Island 12 IS 734DJ	Wild Wood (Sheared Wood Remix) (12", 1 sided white label)	18
00	Island WELLERCD 1	HELIOCENTRIC SAMPLER (CD EP, with *The Daily Telegraph*, card sleeve)	10
00	Island SWEEPCD 1	Sweetpea, My Sweetpea (1-track CD, card sleeve)	10
89	EMI Mus. Pub. CDWELLER 3	THE SONGS OF PAUL WELLER 1982-1988 (CD, 10-track sampler)	110
95	Go! Discs (no cat. no.)	CD SAMPLER (CD, given away in queue for London 100 Club gig, 200 only) ...	45
96	Go! Discs PWRT 1	PEACOCK SUIT (CD, 7-track picture disc)	28
97	Island PAUL-CD 1	WILD WOOD TO HEAVY SOUL (CD, 8-track sampler).................	35
97	Southern Songs WELLER 1	PAUL WELLER (LP, white label, live at Hayward Gallery)............	65
97	Island PW ICD 1	HEAVY SOUL (CD, promo-only interview, card sleeve or jewel case)	20/28
97	Island PW ICD 1	HEAVY SOUL (box set, including CD "Paul Weller Interview", EPK, 5 cards & insert)	45
97	Island KINGS 1	KINGS ROAD (CD sampler, 350 only)	45

Paul WELLER

98	Island CLASSICD 1	MODERN CLASSICS (CD, 5-track sampler, card sleeve, promo only) 28
99	Island INTCD 3	IN CONVERSATION (CD, interview, gatefold card p/s, promo only) 32
01	Independiente PROMO	DAYS OF SPEED SELECTIONS (3-CD, card sleeves, promo only) 45
03	Universal FLY1	A SELECTION FROM FLY ON THE WALL (CD, card sleeve) 20
03	Universal CUFF1	BUTTON DOWN (LP, Weller and Kate Moss 'negative' sleeve) 45

(see also Jam, Style Council)

ORSON WELLES
| 59 | Top Rank TR 5001 | The Courtroom Scene From The Film 'Compulsion' (both sides) (some in p/s) . . 12/7 |

(see also Manowar)

NICK WELLINGS & SECTION
| 77 | The Label TLR 011 | You Better Move On/Punk Funk . . . . 6 |

BOBBY WELLINS
| 78 | Vortex VS1 | LIVE JUBILATION (LP) . . . . 40 |
| 78 | Vortex VS2 | DREAMS ARE FREE (LP) . . . . 40 |

BOBBY WELLS
| 68 | Beacon 3-102 | Let's Copp A Groove/Recipe For Love (yellow/white/green label). . . . . 30/20/15 |
| 79 | Grapevine GRP 124 | Be's That Way Sometimes/Recipe For Love . . . . 10 |

HOUSTON WELLS (& MARKSMEN)
62	Parlophone R 4955	This Song Is Just For You/Paradise 12
62	Parlophone R 4980	Shutters And Boards/North Wind 12
63	Parlophone R 5031	Only The Heartaches/Can't Stop Pretending 10
63	Parlophone R 5069	Blowing Wild (The Ballad Of Black Gold)/Crazy Dreams 12
64	Parlophone R 5099	Anna Marie/Moon Watch Over My Baby 12
64	Parlophone R 5141	Galway Bay/Livin' Alone (as Houston Wells & Outlaws) 12
65	Parlophone R 5226	Blue Of The Night/Coming Home (solo) 7
68	CBS 3572	Teach Me Little Children/Does My Ring Hurt Your Finger 6
63	Parlophone GEP 8878	JUST FOR YOU (EP) 50
64	Parlophone GEP 8914	RAMONA (EP) 70
64	Parlophone PMC 1215	WESTERN STYLE (LP) 50

(see also Marksmen, Outlaws)

JEAN WELLS
| 71 | Mojo 2092 023 | After Loving You/Puttin' The Best On The Outside. . . . . 10 |
| 70 | Sonet SNTF 606 | WORLD! HERE COMES JEAN WELLS (LP) . . . . 50 |

JOHNNY WELLS
| 59 | Columbia DB 4377 | Lonely Moon/The One And Only One . . . . 18 |
| 67 | Parlophone R 5559 | Guess I'm Dumb/Wondering Why . . . . 18 |

JUNIOR WELLS
66	Delmark DS 9612	Hoodoo Man Blues (blue label) 30
66	Delmark DS 628	Southside Blues Jam (blue label) 20
68	Mercury MF 1056	Girl You Lit My Fire/It's A Man Down There 15
66	Delmark DJB 1	BLUES WITH A BEAT (EP) 35
60s	XX MIN 715	JUNIOR WELLS (EP). 22
68	Fontana (S)TFL 6084	IT'S MY LIFE BABY (LP). 35
68	Vanguard SVRL 19011	COMING AT YOU (LP, also stereo, VSD 79262) 30
68	Vanguard SVRL 19028	IT'S MY LIFE BABY (LP, reissue) 20
68	Mercury SMCL 20130	YOU'RE TUFF ENOUGH (LP). 40
71	Delmark DS 628	SOUTHSIDE BLUES JAM (LP) 20
75	Delmark DS 635	JUNIOR WELLS ON TAP (LP) 20

(see also Buddy Guy)

KITTY WELLS
64	Brunswick 05920	I Gave My Wedding Dress Away/I've Thought Of Leaving You 7
55	Brunswick OE 9149	KITTY SINGS (EP). 25
61	Brunswick LAT 8361	KITTY'S CHOICE (LP) 25
64	Brunswick LAT 8575	QUEEN OF COUNTRY MUSIC (LP) 20
65	Brunswick LAT 8601	ESPECIALLY FOR YOU (LP). 20
65	Brunswick LAT 8621	LONESOME SAD AND BLUE (LP) 20
66	Brunswick LAT/STA 8646	SINGS SONGS MADE FAMOUS BY JIM REEVES (LP, mono/stereo) 18/22
66	Brunswick LAT 8659	COUNTRY ALL THE WAY (LP, mono/stereo) 18/22
67	Brunswick LAT 8683	LOVE MAKES THE WORLD GO ROUND (LP) 15

MARY WELLS
62	Oriole CBA 1762	You Beat Me To The Punch/Old Love 75
63	Oriole CBA 1796	Two Lovers/Operator 75
63	Oriole CBA 1829	Laughing Boy/Two Wrongs Don't Make A Right 75
63	Oriole CBA 1847	Your Old Standby/What Love Has Joined Together 75
63	Stateside SS 242	You Lost The Sweetest Boy/What's Easy For Two Is So Hard For One 30
64	Stateside SS 288	My Guy/Oh Little Boy 12
64	Stateside SS 316	Once Upon A Time (with Marvin Gaye)/What's The Matter With You, Baby 40
65	Stateside SS 372	Ain't It The Truth/Stop Takin' Me For Granted 25
65	Stateside SS 396	Use Your Head/Everlovin' Boy 25
65	Stateside SS 415	Never Never Leave Me/Why Don't You Let Yourself Go 25
65	Stateside SS 439	He's A Lover/I'm Learnin'. 25
65	Stateside SS 463	Me Without You/I'm Sorry. 25
68	Stateside SS 2111	The Doctor/Two Lovers' History 20
66	Atlantic AT 4067	Dear Lover/Can't You See (You're Losing Me). 45
66	Atlantic 584 054	Me And My Baby/Such A Sweet Thing 15
67	Atlantic 584 104	Hey You Set My Soul On Fire/Coming Home 15
70	Direction 58-4816	Dig The Way I Feel/Love Shooting Bandit 15
72	Atlantic K 10254	Dear Lover/Can't You See (You're Losing Me) (reissue) 10
65	Tamla Motown TME 2007	MARY WELLS (EP) 100
63	Oriole PS 40045	TWO LOVERS (LP) 150

63	Oriole PS 40051	BYE BYE BABY (LP)	150
64	Stateside SL 10095	SINGS MY GUY (LP)	80
65	Stateside SL 10133	MARY WELLS (LP)	80
65	Tamla Motown TML 11006	MY BABY JUST CARES FOR ME (LP)	70
66	Stateside S(S)L 10171	LOVE SONGS TO THE BEATLES (LP)	45
66	Tamla Motown TML 11032	GREATEST HITS (LP)	50
68	Stateside S(S)L 10266	SERVIN' UP SOME SOUL (LP)	40
68	Atlantic 587 049	THE TWO SIDES OF MARY WELLS (LP)	30
69	T. Motown (S)TML 11102	VINTAGE STOCK (LP, unissued)	
70	Regal Starline SRS 5040	MY GUY (LP)	15

(see also Marvin Gaye)

ALEX WELSH & DIXIELANDERS

55	Decca F 10538	I'll Build A Stairway To Paradise/Eccentric	5
55	Decca F 10557	Blues My Naughtie Sweetie Gives To Me/Shoe Shiner's Blues	5
55	Decca F 10607	As Long As I Live/New Orleans Stomp	10
55	Decca F 10651	Sugar/Smiles	5
55	Decca F 10652	What Can I Say After I Say I'm Sorry/Hard-Hearted Hannah	5
61	Columbia DB 4686	Tansy/Memphis March	6
55	Decca DFE 6254	DIXIELANDERS AT THE RFH (EP)	10
55	Decca DFE 6283	AND HIS DIXIELAND BAND (EP)	15
55	Decca DFE 6315	MUSIC FROM PETE KELLY (EP)	15
62	Columbia SEG 8143	WELSH WAILS (EP)	15
66	Strike JHE 201	ALEX WELSH ENTERTAINS (EP)	15
58	Nixa NJT 516	THE MELROSE FOLIO (LP)	15
59	Columbia 33SX 1219	MUSIC OF THE MAUVE DECADE (LP)	15
61	Columbia 33SX 1322	IT'S RIGHT HERE FOR YOU (LP)	15
62	Columbia 33SX 1429	ECHOES OF CHICAGO (LP)	15
66	Strike JHL 102	STRIKE ONE (LP)	15
68	Columbia SX 6213	AT HOME WITH... (LP)	15
69	Columbia SX 6333	AND HIS BAND '69 (LP)	15
70	Columbia SCX 6376	DIXIELAND PARTY (LP)	15
71	Polydor 2460-123	TRIBUTE TO LOUIS ARMSTRONG VOL. 1 (LP)	15
71	Polydor 2460-124	TRIBUTE TO LOUIS ARMSTRONG VOL. 2 (LP)	15
71	Polydor 2460-125	TRIBUTE TO LOUIS ARMSTRONG VOL. 3 (LP)	15

DANNY WELTON

60	Coral Q 72409	Boogie Woogie/To Each His Own	8

WENDY & LEMMY

82	Bronze BRO 151	Stand By Your Man/No Class/Masterplan (p/s)	7

(see also Motörhead)

WE'RE TIRED

77	Deadline DEADS 8	My Life's On The Line/Against All Odds (p/s)	20
77	Deadline DEADS 11	Guide Me Through Hell/Time Is Against Me (p/s)	25
78	Deadline DEADS 15	Over The Edge/Anal Retentive (p/s, as We're Tired & We're Proud)	8
77	Deadline DEADLP 2	FIND THE PRICE IN TIME (LP)	50

WERLWINDS

61	Columbia DB 4650	Winding It Up/Dig Deep	20

HOWARD WERTH & MOONBEAMS

74	Charisma CB 225	Lucinda/Johan	5
75	Charisma CAS 11004	KING BRILLIANT (LP, with inner sleeve)	12

(see also Audience)

BRIAN WESKE

62	Oriole CB 1723	In The Midst Of The Crowd/All Mine Alone	10
62	Oriole CB 1776	24 Hours In A Day/Where Does The Clown Go	10

FRED WESLEY & J.B.s

73	Polydor 2066 322	Doing It To Death/Everybody Got Soul (with J.B.s)	12
74	Mojo 2093 025	J.B. Shout/Back Stabbers (with J.B.s)	10
80	RSO RSO 67	Houseparty/I Make Music (solo)	10
80	RSO RSO 67	Houseparty/I Make Music (12", solo)	18
74	Polydor 2391 125	DAMN RIGHT, I AM SOMEBODY (LP, with J.B.s)	50
74	Polydor 2391 161	BREAKIN' BREAD (LP, with J.B.s)	30

(see also James Brown, J.B.s)

WES MINSTER FIVE

64	Carnival CV 7017	Shakin' The Blues/Railroad Blues	12
65	Carnival CV 7019	Sticks And Stones/Mickey's Monkey	18

(see also Maynell Wilson, Dave Greenslade)

FRANK WESS

64	Fontana TL 5291	THE AWARD WINNER (LP)	12

ADAM 'BATMAN' WEST

76	Target TGT 111	Batman And Robin/The Story Of Batman	7

DODIE WEST

64	Decca F 12046	Goin' Out Of My Head/Is He Feeling Blue	15
65	Piccadilly 7N 35239	In The Deep Of The Night/Rovin' Boy (some in p/s)	30/20
65	Piccadilly 7N 35261	Thinking Of You/And Love Will Come	8
66	Piccadilly 7N 35287	Make The World Go Away/Who Does He Think He Is	8
68	Philips BF 1698	Living In Limbo/Birdie Told Me	7

Keith WEST

KEITH WEST
67	Parlophone R 5623	Excerpt From "A Teenage Opera"/MARK WIRTZ ORCHESTRA: Theme From "A Teenage Opera"	7
67	Parlophone R 5651	Sam (From "A Teenage Opera')/MARK WIRTZ'S MOOD MOSAIC: Thimble Full Of Puzzles (promos in art sleeve)	20/8
68	Parlophone R 5713	On A Saturday/The Kid Was A Killer	55
72	Parlophone R 5957	Excerpt From "A Teenage Opera"/Sam (From "A Teenage Opera")	7
73	Deram DM 402	Riding For A Fall/Days About To Rain	7
74	Deram DM 410	Havin' Someone/Know There's No Livin' Without You	7

(see also Tomorrow, Four + One, In Crowd, Mark Wirtz)

LESLIE WEST('S MOUNTAIN)
69	Bell BLL 1078	Dreams Of Milk And Honey/Wheels On Fire (as Leslie West's Mountain)	20
69	Bell SBLL 126	MOUNTAIN (LP, as Leslie West's Mountain)	20
75	RCA RS 1009	THE GREAT FATSBY (LP)	15
76	Phantom PHS 701	THE LESLIE WEST BAND (LP)	12

(see also Jolliver Arkansas, Mountain, West Bruce & Laing)

MAE WEST
67	Stateside SS 2021	Twist And Shout/Day Tripper	18
73	MGM 2006 203	Great Balls Of Fire/Men	10
56	Brunswick LAT 8082	THE FABULOUS MAE WEST (LP)	50
67	Stateside (S)SL 10197	WAY OUT WEST (LP)	30
73	Polydor 2315 207	GREAT BALLS OF FIRE (LP)	18

SPEEDY WEST & JIMMY BRYANT
55	Capitol EAP1 520	TWO GUITARS COUNTRY STYLE PT. 1 (EP)	30
55	Capitol EAP2 520	TWO GUITARS COUNTRY STYLE PT. 2 (EP)	30
53	Capitol LC 6619	CAPITOL PRESENTS SPEEDY WEST & JIMMY BRYANT (10" LP)	40
55	Capitol LC 6694	TWO GUITARS COUNTRY STYLE (10" LP)	40

TABBY WEST
58	Capitol CL 14861	All That I Want/If You Promise Not To Tell	7

MIKE WESTBROOK (CONCERT BAND)
69	Deram DM 234	A Life Of Its Own/Can't Get It Out Of My Mind	22
70	Deram DM 286	Requiem/Hooray	22
70	Deram DM 311	Magic Garden/Original Peter (with Norma Winstone)	30
67	Deram DML 1013	CELEBRATION (LP, as Mike Westbrook Concert Band)	120
68	Deram DML/SML 1031	RELEASE (LP)	70
69	Deram SML 1047	MARCHING SONG VOL. 1 (LP)	70
69	Deram SML 1048	MARCHING SONG VOL. 2 (LP)	70
70	Deram SML 1069	LOVE SONGS (LP, as Mike Westbrook Concert Band with Norma Winstone)	80
71	RCA SER 5612	TYGER: A CELEBRATION OF WILLIAM BLAKE (LP, with insert)	100
72	RCA Neon NE 10	MIKE WESTBROOK'S METROPOLIS (LP, gatefold sleeve)	60
72	Cadillac SGC 1001	LIVE (LP, private pressing)	30
75	RCA SF 8433	CITADEL/ROOM 315 (2-LP, with John Surman)	30
75	Transatlantic TRA 323	LOVE/DREAM & VARIATIONS (LP)	25
76	Transatlantic TRA 312	PLAYS FOR THE RECORD (LP)	20
78	Original ORA 001	GOOSE SAUCE (LP)	20
78	Original ORA 002	PIANO (LP)	20
79	RCA PL 25252	MAMA CHICAGO (LP)	20
80	Original ORA 203	WESTBROOK BLAKE (LP)	30
82	Original ORA 309	THE CORTEGE (LP)	30
83	Westbrook LWN 1	A LITTLE WESTBROOK MUSIC (LP)	35
88	Venture VEB 13	LONDON BRIDGE IS BROKEN DOWN (LP)	15

(see also Solid Gold Cadillac, John Surman, Norma Winstone)

WEST, BRUCE & LAING
73	RSO 2090 113	Dirty Shoes/Backfire	6
73	CBS 65314	WHY DONTCHA (LP)	12
73	RSO 2394 107	WHATEVER TURNS YOU ON (LP)	12
74	RSO 2394 128	LIVE 'N' KICKIN' (LP)	12

(see also Jack Bruce, Leslie West, Mountain)

WEST COAST CONSORTIUM
67	Pye 7N 17352	Some Other Someday/Looking Back	18
68	Pye 7N 17482	Colour Sergeant Lillywhite/Lady From Baltimore	40

(see also Consortium)

WEST COAST DELEGATION
67	Deram DM 113	Reach The Top/Mr. Personality Man	18

WEST COAST KNACK
67	Capitol CL 15497	I'm Aware/Time Waits For No One	15

WEST COAST POP ART EXPERIMENTAL BAND
68	Reprise RSLP 6298	A CHILD'S GUIDE TO GOOD AND EVIL (LP)	100

JOHNNY WESTERN
60	Philips PB 1030	The Ballad Of Paladin/The Guns Of Rio Muerto (B-side with Richard Boone)	7

WESTERNAIRES ORCHESTRA with CURLY WILLIAMS
57	Brunswick 05692	Walking Alone In A Crowd/Sweet Talk (Won Her Loving Heart)	6

WEST FIVE
65	HMV POP 1396	Congratulations/She Mine	35
65	HMV POP 1428	Someone Ain't Right/Just Like Romeo And Juliet	25
66	HMV POP 1513	If It Don't Work Out/Back To Square One	10

(see also Ferris Wheel)

WEST INDIANS
68	Doctor Bird DB 1121	Right On Time/Hokey Pokey	25
68	Doctor Bird DB 1127	Falling In Love/I Mean It	25
69	Camel CA 16	Strange Whisperings/CARL DAWKINS: Hard To Handle	15
71	Dynamic DYN 413	Never Gonna Give You Up/REBELLIOUS SUBJECTS: Never Give Up	10

(see also Prunes, Kilowatts, Upsetters)

CLIVE WESTLAKE
68	Fontana TF 940	199 Days/From The Beginning To The End	6

JILL WESTLAKE
58	Columbia DB 4132	Sharin'/Over And Over Again (78 rpm = £10)	12

KEVIN WESTLAKE & GARY FARR
68	Marmalade 598 007	Everyday/Green	15

(see also Gary Farr & T-Bones, T-Bones, Blossom Toes, B.B. Blunder)

WESTMORELITES
70	Clandisc CLA 217	Zion/CLANCY ECCLES & DYNAMITES: Revival	8

(see also Minstrels)

GLEN WESTON
68	Columbia DB 8328	With This Ring/Liane	5

KIM WESTON
64	Stateside SS 359	A Little More Love/Go Ahead And Laugh (DJ copy = £150)	85
65	Tamla Motown TMG 511	I'm Still Loving You/Just Loving You (DJ copy = £225)	120
65	Tamla Motown TMG 538	Take Me In Your Arms (Rock Me A Little While)/Don't Compare Me With Her (DJ copy = £125)	80
66	Tamla Motown TMG 554	Helpless/A Love Like Yours (DJ copy = £175)	80
67	MGM MGM 1338	I Got What You Need/Someone Like You (DJ copy = £50)	30
67	MGM MGM 1357	That's Groovy/Land Of Tomorrow (DJ copy = £50)	30
68	MGM MGM 1382	Nobody/You're Just The Kind Of Guy (DJ copy = £85)	50
69	Major Minor MM 619	From Both Sides Now/We Try Harder	6
70	Major Minor MM 683	Danger, Heartbreak Dead Ahead/I'll Be Thinking	10
75	Tamla Motown TMG 1000	Do Like I Do/MARVELETTES: Finders Keepers, Losers Weepers	100
65	Tamla Motown TME 2005	KIM WESTON (EP)	150
66	Tamla Motown TME 2015	ROCK ME A LITTLE WHILE (EP)	350
67	MGM MGM-C(S) 8055	FOR THE FIRST TIME (LP)	75
71	Stax 2362 021	KIM KIM KIM (LP)	40

(see also Johnny Nash & Kim Weston, Marvin Gaye & Kim Weston)

PETE WESTON
70	Gas GAS 146	Something Sweet/BIM & BAM: Love Letters	8
70	Punch PH 28	In The Mood (& His Band)/Slide Mongoose (actually "Sly Mongoose")	8

(see also I Roy)

WEST ONE
88	Que Q 9	California '69/Eurotrash (gig freebie, white label)	12

WEST POINT SUPERNATURAL
67	Reaction 591 013	Time Will Tell/Night Train	18

WESTSIDE
74	People PEO 111	Running In And Out Of My Life/Highway Demon	5

WESTWIND
70	Penny Farthing PEN 737	Love Is A Funny Sort Of Thing/Breakout	8
70	Penny Farthing PELS 505	LOVE IS (LP)	120

WE THE PEOPLE
66	London HLH 10089	He Doesn't Go About It Right/You Burn Me Up And Down	110

WE THREE TRIO
65	London HLA 9966	Baby The Rain Must Fall/Shine For Me	7
67	Fontana TL 5308	THE WE THREE TRIO (LP)	18

WET WET WET
86	Lyntone/Jamming!	I Can Give You Everything/FLOOR: Hold On (flexidisc free with *Jamming!* magazine)	8
87	Precious JWLS 4	Sweet Little Mystery/Don't Let Me Be Lonely Tonight (shaped picture disc)	8
88	Precious 080274-2	Angel Eyes/I Don't Believe/Wishing I Was Lucky/Angel Eyes (video) (CD, some are golden)	15

WE UGLY DOGS
67	BT Puppy BTS 45537	First Spring Rain/Poor Man	10

(see also Tokens, U.S. Double Quartet)

W. GIMMICS
65	Polydor EPH 27 125	HOT RODS (EP, manufactured in Europe)	60

WHALE FEATHERS
71	Blue Horizon 2431 009	WHALE FEATHERS (LP)	65

WHALES
68	CBS 3766	Come Down Little Bird/Beachcomber	12
69	CBS 4126	Tell It To The Rain/Girl, Hey Girl	8

WHAM!
82	Innervision IVL A 2442	Wham Rap! (Enjoy What You Do) (Special Club Remix)/(Special U.S. Mix) (p/s, 1st pressing, paper label, songwriting credit: "Panos/Ridgeley")	7
83	Innervision IVL A 2442	Wham Rap! (Enjoy What You Do) (Special Club Remix)/(Special U.S. Mix) (reissue, red & blue title p/s)	5
82	Innervision IVL A 13-2442	Wham Rap! (Enjoy What You Do) (Special Club Remix)/(Special U.S. Mix) (12", paper label, p/s, "Panos/Ridgeley" or "Michael/Ridgeley" songwriting credit)	12/7

WHAM!

82	Innervision IVL A 13-2442	Wham Rap! (Enjoy What You Do) (Social Mix)/(Unsocial Mix) (12", initially in p/s, later in plain black die-cut sleeve) 15/7
82	Innervision IVL A 2442	Wham Rap! (Enjoy What You Do) (Special Club Remix)/(Special U.S. Mix) (12", reissue, red & blue title p/s) 12
83	Innervision IVL A 13-2766	Young Guns (Go For It)/Going For It (12", p/s) 10
83	Innervision IVL A 3143	Bad Boys/Bad Boys (Instrumental) (poster p/s) 8
83	Innervision IVL WA 3143	Bad Boys/Bad Boys (Instrumental) (picture disc) 12
83	Innervision IVL WA 3613	Club Tropicana/Blue (Armed With Love) (picture disc) 15
84	Epic TA 4440	Wake Me Up Before You Go-Go/Wake Me Up (Instrumental)/ A Ray Of Sunshine (12", poster p/s) 15
84	Epic QA/WA 4743	Freedom/Freedom (Instrumental) (George Michael- or Andrew Ridgeley- shaped picture disc in wallet, PVC gatefold sleeve; each or as set) 18/30
85	Epic QTA 4949	Everything She Wants (U.S. Remix)/Last Christmas (The Pudding Mix) (12", reissue, A-sides reversed, some w/ stickered p/s & free calendar) 15/7
85	Epic WTA 6716	I'm Your Man (Extended Stimulation)/Do It Right (Instrumental)/ I'm Your Man (A Capella) (12", picture disc) 10
89	Epic 654 915-3	Wake Me Up Before You Go-Go/Freedom/The Edge Of Heaven (3" CD, 'Solid Gold Classics' series) 15
83	Epic (no cat. no.)	Bad Boys/(track by other artist) (no p/s, free with 'KP Crisps' offer) 7
84	Epic KELL 4	Club Tropicana/HERBIE HANCOCK: Rock It (no p/s, promo only, free with 'Rice Krispies' offer) 7
84	Epic (no cat. no.)	Merry Xmas From Wham (fan club Christmas single, no p/s) 10
86	Epic WHAM 2	THE FINAL (2-LP box, gold vinyl picture discs, with sealed T-shirt, calendar, pencil, note-pad and no'd certificate) 55
84	Innervision CDIVL 25328	FANTASTIC (CD) 45
84	Epic CDEPC 86311	MAKE IT BIG (CD) 45

(see also George Michael, Pepsi & Shirley)

PEETIE WHEATSTRAW
69	Matchbox SDR 191	THE DEVIL'S SON IN LAW (LP) 25
69	Matchbox SDR 192	THE HIGH SHERIFF FROM HELL (LP) 25

BILLY ED WHEELER
64	London HLR 9920	On The Outside (Lookin' In)/The Right Foot In His World 8
65	London HLR 9950	Ode To The Little Brown Shack Out Back/Sister Sara 8
65	London HAR/SHR 8221	MEMORIES OF AMERICA (LP) 18

KENNY WHEELER & JOHN DANKWORTH ORCHESTRA
68	Fontana STL 5494	WINDMILL TILTER (LP) 150
70s	Incus 10	SONG FOR SOMEONE (LP) 80

(see also Johnny Dankworth, Elton Dean)

WHEELS
65	Columbia DB 7682	Gloria/Don't You Know 140
66	Columbia DB 7827	Bad Little Woman/Road Block (mispressing, demos & a few issues play "Call My Name" on B-side) 140
66	Columbia DB 7827	Bad Little Woman/Road Block 350
66	Columbia DB 7981	Kicks/Call My Name 140

(see also James Brothers, Demick & Armstrong)

WHEELS OF TIME
67	Spin SP 62008	1984/So Long (some in company sleeves) 60/50

WHERE FORTUNE SMILES
(see under John Surman)

WHICHWHAT
69	Beacon BEA 127	Gimme Gimme Good Lovin'/Wonderland Of Love 25
69	Beacon BEA 131	Why Do Lovers Break Each Other's Heart/When I See Her Smile 6
69	Beacon BEA 133	In The Year 2525/Parting 10
69	Beacon BEA 144	I Wanna Be Free/It's All Over Again 18
70	Beacon BEA 169	Vietnam Rose/Shame And Solution 6
70	Beacon BEAS 14	WHICHWHAT'S FIRST (LP) 50

WHIP
71	Mother MOT 6	Julie Ivory Towers/MUFF & BANKHOUSE ASSEMBLY: Funky Shoot Out 10

WHIRLWIND
78	Chiswick NS 25	Hang Loose/Together Forever (p/s) 10
78	Chiswick NS 42	I Only Wish (That I'd Been Told)/Ducktails (unissued)
78	Chiswick CHIS 103	I Only Wish (That I'd Been Told)/Ducktails (p/s) 10
79	Chiswick CHIS 117	You Got Class/Losing To You (unissued in U.K.; France-only)
80	Chiswick CHIS 122	Heaven Knows/Cruisin' Around (p/s) 10
80	Chiswick CHIS 127	Stayin' Out All Night/Running Wild (unissued; p/s only)
80	Chiswick PSR 447	Midnight Blue/Honey Hush/Such A Fool/Stayin' Out All Night (promo only) 8
78	Chiswick CH 4	BLOWIN' UP A STORM (10" mini-LP) 12
78	Chiswick WIK 7	BLOWIN' UP A STORM (LP, with 2 extra tracks) 15
80	Chiswick CWK 3012	MIDNIGHT BLUE (LP) 15

WHIRLWINDS
64	HMV POP 1301	Look At Me/Baby Not Like You 60

(see also Mockingbirds, Graham Gouldman, 10cc)

NANCY WHISKEY (& HER SKIFFLERS)
57	Oriole CB 1394	He's Solid Gone/Ella Speed (as Nancy Whiskey & Her Skifflers) (78 rpm = £12) . 22
58	Oriole CB 1452	Hillside In Scotland/I Know Where I'm Goin' (78 rpm = £12) 18
59	Oriole CB 1485	The Old Grey Goose/Johnny Blue (78 rpm = £12) 15
65	Fontana TF 612	Bowling Green/I'm Leaving Today 8
67	CBS 3090	Freight Train/The Game 8
57	Topic 7T 10	NANCY WHISKEY SINGS (7" LP) 35
57	Oriole MG 10018	THE INTOXICATING MISS WHISKEY (10" LP, with Chas McDevitt Skiffle Group) 30

(see also Chas McDevitt Skiffle Group)

WHISPERS
71	Mojo 2916 003	THE WHISPERS (LP)	35
74	Contempo CRM 106	THE WHISPERS (LP)	18
74	Janus 9104 400	WHISPERS GETTIN' LOUDER (LP)	18

WHISTLER
71	Deram SML 1083	HO-HUM (LP)	30

WHISTLING WILLIE
68	Duke DU 8	Penny Reel/Soul Tonic	5

(see also Neville, Neville Willoughby)

DAVE WHITAKER
65	CBS BPG 62532	MUSIC TO SPY BY (LP)	22

SHARON WHITCOMB & FRED
72	RA RALP 6011	SPICE OF LIFE (LP)	20

IAN WHITCOMB
65	Capitol CL 15382	This Sporting Life/Fizz	6
65	Capitol CL 15395	You Turn Me On/Poor But Honest	10
65	Capitol CL 15418	N-N-Nervous!/The End	6
66	Capitol CL 15431	Good Hard Rock/High Blood Pressure	6
66	Stateside SS 573	Where Did Robinson Crusoe Go With Friday/Poor Little Bird	6
72	Ember EMBS 324	You Turn Me On/This Sporting Life (mono)	12
73	Ember NR 5065	YOU TURN ME ON (LP, with Jimmy Page & John Paul Jones)	50

BARRY WHITE
67	President PT 139	All In The Run Of A Day/Don't Take Your Love From Me	25

BERGEN WHITE
76	Private Stock PVT 69	Duke Of Earl/She Won't Let You Down	7

BRIAN WHITE & MAGNA JAZZ BAND
62	HMV CLP 1534	BRIAN WHITE AND THE MAGNA JAZZ BAND (LP)	125

(see also Magna Jazz Band)

BUKKA WHITE
66	Fontana 688 804 ZL	SKY SONGS (LP, with Big Willie)	38
66	CBS Realm 52629	BUKKA WHITE (LP)	50
69	Blue Horizon 7-63229	MEMPHIS HOT SHOTS (LP)	80
69	Sonet SNTF 609	THE LEGACY OF THE BLUES VOL. 1 (LP, with insert)	15

CHRIS WHITE
76	Charisma CB 272	Spanish Wine/She's Only Dancing	7
76	Charisma CB 282	Natural Rhythm/Another Little Miracle	6
76	Charisma CB 294	Don't Look Down/Summertime Summertime	6
77	Charisma CB 303	Don't Worry Baby/Child Of The Sun	12
76	Charisma CAS 1118	MOUTH MUSIC (LP)	22

(see also Joyce's Angels)

DANNY WHITE
67	Sue WI 4031	Keep My Woman Home/I'm Dedicating My Life	75
74	MCA MU 155	Cracked Up Over You/Taking Inventory	10

DUKE WHITE
63	Island WI 084	It's Over/Forever	15
64	Black Swan WI 442	Be Wise/BABA BROOKS: Musical Workshop	28
65	Black Swan WI 444	Sow Good Seeds/BABA BROOKS BAND: Bus Strike	28

ED WHITE
61	Pye 7N SR15320	Coral Reef/Tropical Blue (stereo only)	15

GEORGIA WHITE
54	Vocalion V 1038	Was I Drunk?/Moonshine Blues (78)	20

IAN WHITE
70	private pressing	IAN WHITE (LP)	20

JAY WHITE
56	London RE-F 1045	FAR-AWAY PLACES VOL. 1 (EP)	12

JEANETTE WHITE
69	A&M AMS 761	Music/No Sunshine (yellow DJ copy or brown label = £75) (silver label)	20

JOE WHITE
64	R&B JB 137	Sinners (as Joe White & Maytals)/ROLAND ALPHONSO: King Solomon	32
64	Ska Beat JB 180	Punch You Down (with Chuck)/TOMMY McCOOK: Cotton Tree	42
64	Island WI 145	When Are You Young/Wanna Go Home	15
64	Island WI 159	Hog In A Co Co/SKATALITES: Sandy Gully	30
64	Island WI 166	Downtown Girl/RICHARD BROS.: You Are My Sunshine (B-side is actually "Cool Smoke" by Don Drummond)	30
65	Island WI 201	Low-Minded People (as Chuck & Joe White)/Irene	15
66	Doctor Bird DB 1001	Every Night (with Chuck)/BABA BROOKS & HIS BAND: First Session	30
66	Doctor Bird DB 1024	My Love For You/SAMMY ISMAY & BABA BROOKS BAND: Cocktails For Two	25
66	Doctor Bird DB 1043	So Close (as Joe White & Della)/BABA BROOKS & HIS BAND: Eighth Games	25
67	Doctor Bird DB 1069	Rudies All Around/Bad Man	30
67	Doctor Bird DB 1080	Lonely Nights/I Need You	20
67	Doctor Bird DB 1090	I Need A Woman/Hot Hops	15
68	Blue Cat BS 108	Way Of Life (actually by Lyn Tait & Jets)/I'm So Proud	45
68	Blue Cat BS 119	Try A Little Tenderness/LYN TAITT & CARL BRYAN: Tender Arms	25
68	Blue Cat BS 130	Pretty Girl/DERMOTT LYNCH: You Went Away	25
69	Sugar ESS 102	My Guiding Star/If I Needed Someone	12
70	Sugar SU 103	Yesterday/I Am Free	12
70	Trojan TR 7742	So Much Love/Maybe Now	5

Joe WHITE

70	Trojan TR 7768	I'm Going To Get There/RUPIE EDWARDS ALLSTARS: Kinky Funky Reggae	10
70	Big BG 301	This Is The Time/The Other Day	8
71	Big BG 309	Baby I Care/Ain't Misbehavin'	5
72	Songbird SB 1072	Trinity/SCOTTY: Monkey Drop	12
72	Dynamic DYN 440	Kenyatta/RECORDING BAND: Version	15
73	Gayfeet GS 202	If It Don't Work Out/BABA BROOKS BAND: Ki Salaboca	12
73	Harry J. HJ 6648	Joe White (Mrs. Jones)/Joe White (Mrs. Jones) – Version (song actually titled "Me And Mrs Jones")	5
77	Ultra PFU 1002	Give And Take (On Both Sides)/Roots Dub	5
70s	Magnet MGT 006	SINCE THE OTHER DAY (LP)	20

(see also Chuck, Rue Lloyd)

JOSH WHITE

50	Jazz Parade B 10	I Want You And I Need You/One Meat Ball (78)	10
50	Jazz Parade B 11	The Blind Man Stood On The Road And Cried/St. James Infirmary (78)	10
50	Jazz Parade B 12	Got A Head Like A Rock/No. 12 Train (78)	10
50	London L 739	Take A Gal Like You/Wanderings (78)	10
50	London L 810	Like A Natural Man/The Foggy, Foggy Dew (78)	10
50	London L 828	I'm Gonna Move To The Outskirts Of Town/Hard Time Blues (78)	10
50	London L 907	T.B. Blues/Molly Malone (78)	10
50	Melodisc MEL 8008	Mean Mistreatin' Woman/Baby Baby (12" 78)	10
51	Melodisc MEL 1145	Fare Thee Well/Outskirts Of Town (78)	10
51	Melodisc MEL 1146	House I Live In/When I Lay Down (78)	10
51	Melodisc MEL 1155	Dupree/Miss Otis Regrets (78)	10
51	Vogue B 10	I Want You And I Need You/One Meat Ball (78)	10
51	London L 1028	On Top Of Old Smoky/Black Girl (with Bill Hill's Orchestra & Stargazers) (78)	10
51	London L 1138	Barbara Allen/The Lass With The Delicate Air (78)	6
52	London L 1142	Lonesome Road/He Never Said A Mumblin' Word (78)	8
52	London L 1143	Call Me Darling/I Want You, I Need You (78)	15
52	London L 1144	Waltzing Landing/Apples, Peaches And Cherries (78)	15
52	London L 1161	Free And Equal Blues (Parts 1 & 2) (78)	15
54	London L 907	T.B. Blues/Molly Malone (78, silver label reissue)	10
57	Pye NJE 1057	BLUES AND... PART 1 (EP)	10
57	Pye NJE 1058	BLUES AND... PART 2 (EP)	10
57	Pye NJE 1059	BLUES AND... PART 3 (EP)	10
57	HMV 7EG 8465	THE JOSH WHITE STORIES (EP)	12
58	Mercury YEP 9504	SOUTHERN BLUES (EP)	12
64	Storyville SEP 388	STORYVILLE BLUES ANTHOLOGY VOL. 8 (EP)	12
64	Mercury 10006 MCE	JOSH WHITE (EP)	15
51	London H-APB 1005	A JOSH WHITE PROGRAM (10" LP)	20
52	Brunswick LA 8562	BALLADS AND BLUES (10" LP)	20
54	Brunswick LA 8653	BALLADS AND BLUES VOL. 2 (10" LP)	20
54	London H-APB 1032	JOSH WHITE SINGS — VOL. 2 (10" LP)	20
54	Mercury MG 25014	SONGS BY JOSH WHITE (10" LP)	20
55	London H-APB 1038	JOSH COMES A-VISITIN' (10" LP)	20
56	Nixa Jazz Today NJL 2	BLUES AND... (LP)	20
58	HMV CLP 1159	JOSH WHITE STORIES VOLUME 1 (LP)	15
58	HMV CLP 1175	JOSH WHITE STORIES VOLUME 2 (LP)	15
62	Storyville SLP 123	JOHN HENRY, BALLADS, BLUES AND OTHER SONGS (LP)	15
62	Mercury MMC 14102	AT THE TOWN HALL (LP)	15
62	HMV CLP 1588	JOSH WHITE LIVE! (LP)	15
62	Golden Guinea GGL 0160	EMPTY BED BLUES (LP)	20
62	Golden Guinea GGL 0205	CHAIN GANG SONGS, SPIRITUALS AND BLUES (LP)	12
64	Mercury 20039 MCL	THE BEGINNING (LP)	18
64	Ace Of Hearts AH 65	JOSH WHITE (LP)	12
65	Mercury 20067 MCL	I'M ON MY OWN WAY (LP)	15
65	Saga SOC 988	JOSH WHITE AND CARL SANDBURG (LP)	12
60s	Storyville SLP 175	BLUES SINGER AND BALLADEER (LP)	12

(see also Teddy Moss/Josh White)

JOSH & BEVERLEY WHITE

64	Realm REP 4003	BEVERLEY & JOSH WHITE JNR (EP)	12

K.C. WHITE

72	Dynamic DYN 434	Man No Dead/Man No Dead — Version	8
73	Green Door GD 4056	First Cut Is The Deepest/No Good Girl	10
73	Technique TE 929	Anywhere But Nowhere/Bush In Session	10

KITTY WHITE

51	Brunswick 04726	Paradise/You're Tired Of Me (78)	8
51	Capitol CL 13549	I'm Playing With Fire/It Pays To Advertise (78)	8
54	London HL 8102	Jesse James/Scratch My Back (B-side with Dave Howard)	75
54	London HL 8102	Jesse James/Scratch My Back (78, B-side with Dave Howard)	20

LENNY WHITE

75	Atlantic K 50213	VENUSIAN SUMMER (LP)	12
79	Elektra K 12328	Lady Madonna/12 Bars From Mars	5
81	Elektra K 12500	Kid Stuff/Slipaway	5
83	Elektra ED 4921	My Turn To Love You (Special Mix)/(Dub Version) (12")	12

LOUISA JANE WHITE

69	Philips BF 1810	When The Battle Is Over/Blue Ribbons	10
70	Philips BF 1834	How Does It Feel/Truth In My Tears	6

SHEILA WHITE

66	CBS 202465	Misfit/Switch Off The Night	7

STEVE WHITE & GARY WALLACE

90s	Acid Jazz JAZID 20T	Never Stop (12", company sleeve)	35

(see also Style Council)

TAM WHITE
67	Decca F 12711	World Without You/Someone You Should Know (unreleased)	
68	Decca F 12723	Dancing Out Of My Heart/I'll Stay Loving You	10
68	Decca F 12849	Waiting Till The Night Comes Around/Girl Watcher	10
69	Deram DM 261	That Old Sweet Roll/Don't Make Promises	25
70	Middle Earth MDS 104	Lewis Carroll/Future Thoughts	50
70	Middle Earth MDLS 304	TAM WHITE (LP)	45

(see also Buzz, Boston Dexters)

TERRY WHITE & TERRIERS
59	Decca F 11133	Rock Around The Mailbags/Blackout (78 rpm = £40)	80

THOMAS WHITE
79	Hit Run HD 12	Ivory Girl/KEITH FRANCIS: Prejudice Country (12")	50

TONY JOE WHITE
68	Monument MON 1024	Soul Francisco/Whompt Out On You	8
69	Monument MON 1031	Polk Salad Annie/Aspen Colorado	15
69	Monument MON 1036	Willie And Laura Mae Jones/Baby Scratch My Back	10
68	Monument LMO/SMO 5027	BLACK AND WHITE (LP)	22
70	Monument LMO/SMO 5035	TONY JOE WHITE CONTINUED (LP)	22
70	Monument SMO 5043	TONY JOE (LP)	22
71	Warner Bros WS 1900	TONY JOE WHITE (LP)	18
71	Warner Bros K 46068	TONY JOE WHITE (LP, reissue)	12
72	Warner Bros K 46147	THE TRAIN I'M ON (LP)	15
73	Warner Bros K 46229	HOME-MADE ICE CREAM (LP)	18
73	Warner Bros K 56149	THE BEST OF TONY JOE WHITE (LP)	12

TREVOR WHITE
76	Island WIP 6291	Crazy Kids/Movin' In The Right Direction (with p/s)	10

(see also Sparks, Radio Stars)

WHITE DUCK
72	Uni UN 541	Billy Goat/Really	8
73	Uni UN 555	Honey, You'll Be Alright/Carry Love	8
72	Uni UNLS 123	WHITE DUCK (LP)	20
73	Uni UNLS 129	IN SEASON (LP)	20

WHITE ELEPHANT
70s	White Elephant RIOCH 1	CITY WALLS (LP, with other artists)	12

RICK WHITEFIELD
71	Horse HOSS 10	Hey Mama/Ride Baby Ride	6

WHITEFIRE
78	Whitefire 98DB 001	SUZANNE (EP)	40

WHITE HART
79	Tradition TSR 033	IN SEARCH OF REWARD (LP)	60

WHITE HEAT
79	Valium VAL 01	Nervous Breakdown/Sammy Sez (gatefold p/s)	35
80	Valium VAL 02	Finished With The Fashions/Ordinary Joe (p/s, with insert)	22
81	Valium VAL 03	City Beat/It's No Use (Young Ones) (p/s)	15
82	Valium VALP 101	IN THE ZERO HOUR (LP)	20

WHITE HEAT
84	Rock Shop RSR 007	WHITE HEAT (LP)	20

WHITEHOUSE
01	SLA-003	Cruise (Force The Truth)/Instrumental Version (12")	20
02	SLA-004	Wriggle Like A Fucking Eel/Instrumental Version (12")	18
80	Come Org. WDC 881004	BIRTHDEATH EXPERIENCE (LP)	100
80	Come Org. WDC 881005	TOTAL SEX (LP)	100
80	Come Org. WDC 881007	ERECTOR (LP, different coloured vinyls)	100
81	Come Org. WDC 881010	DEDICATED TO PETER KÜRTEN, SADIST AND MASS SLAYER (LP, some on coloured vinyl, some in custom sleeve)	100
81	Come Org. WDC	GREAT WHITE DEATH (LP)	100
81	Come Org. WDC 881013	BÜCHENWALD (LP)	100
81	Come Org. WDC 881017	NEW BRITAIN (LP, with insert)	125
80s	Come Org. WDC 881027	PSYCHOPATHIA SEXUALIS (LP, clear or black vinyl)	100
80s	Come Org. WDC 883033	RIGHT TO KILL — DEDICATED TO DENNIS ANDREW NEILSEN (LP, & inserts)	100
80s	Come Org. WDC	150 MURDEROUS PASSIONS (LP, with Nurse With Wound)	75
80s	United Dairies UD 009	150 MURDEROUS PASSIONS (LP, with Nurse With Wound, reissue)	40
80s	United Dairies UD 009	150 MURDEROUS PASSIONS (LP, with Nurse With Wound, export issue, sealed in black vinyl)	125

(Many of the above LPs were issued in customised white card sleeves & were later available in a generic 'Peter Kürten' sleeve, originally used for the 2nd pressing of the 'Peter Kürten' LP. This latter design was also used for counterfeits. There may also be various coloured vinyl variations of the above LPs, worth around the same value.)

81	Come Org. WDC 881020	LIVE ACTION 1 (cassette)	20
80s	Come Org. WDC 881022	LIVE ACTION 2 (cassette)	20
80s	Come Org. WDC 883044	RADIO INTERVIEWS/LIVE ACTION USA VOL. 1 (cassette)	12
80s	Come Org. WDC 883046	LIVE ACTION 13 USA VOL. III (cassette)	12
80s	Come Org. WDC 883047	LIVE ACTION 14 USA VOL. IV (cassette)	12
80s	Come Org. WDC 883048	LIVE ACTION 15/LIVE ACTION 16 USA VOL. V (cassette)	12
80s	Come Org. WDC 883049	LIVE ACTION 20 USA VOL VI (cassette)	12
80s	Come Org. WDC 883050	LIVE ACTION 22/LIVE ACTION 23 (cassette)	12
80s	Come Org. WDC 883052	USA REHEARSAL (cassette)	12
80s	Come Org. WDC 883053	LIVE ACTION 24/LIVE ACTION 25 (cassette)	12

MINT VALUE £

80s	Come Org. WDC 883055	LIVE ACTION 26 (cassette)... 12
80s	Susan Lawley 1	CREAM OF THE SECOND COMING (2-LP).................................. 45
91	Susan Lawley SL 002	THANK YOUR LUCKY STARS (LP) 30
92	Susan Lawley SL 003	TWICE IS NOT ENOUGH (LP).. 30

(see also Come, Nurse With Wound, New Order, Skullflower, Konstruktivits)

WHITE LIGHTNING

| 84 | Wild Party PP 1000 | This Poison Fountain/Hypocrite (no p/s, 1,000 only) .... 40 |
| 90 | Workshop JOB LP 2 | AS MIDNIGHT APPROACHES (LP, with inner)............................. 15 |

(see also Static)

WHITE NOISE

75	Virgin VDJ 2	An Extract From White Noise 2 (promo only) 5
69	Island ILPS 9099	AN ELECTRIC STORM (LP, pink label) 55
75	Virgin V 2032	WHITE NOISE 2 (LP)... 15

(see also BBC Radiophonic Workshop)

WHITE ON BLACK

| 74 | Saydisc SDL 251 | WHITE ON BLACK (LP) .... 40 |

WHITE PLAINS

| 70 | Deram SML 1067 | WHITE PLAINS (LP) .... 20 |
| 71 | Deram SML 1092 | WHEN YOU ARE A KING (LP) .... 20 |

(see also Edison Lighthouse, David & Jonathan, Kestrels, Brotherhood Of Man, Peter's Faces, Carter-Lewis & Southerners, Ivy League)

WHITESNAKE

78	EMI International INEP 751	SNAKEBITE (EP, white vinyl, p/s; later black vinyl with no p/s)........... each 10
78	EMI International INT 568	Lie Down/Don't Mess With Me... 5
79	EMI International INT 578	The Time Is Right For Love/Come On (live).............................. 5
80	United Artists BP 352	Fool For Your Loving/Mean Business/
		Don't Mess With Me (some in luminous p/s).......................... 8/5
82	Liberty BPP 416	Here I Go Again/Bloody Luxury (picture disc)........................... 10
82	Liberty BP 418	Love An' Affection/Victim Of Love (withdrawn) 35
83	Liberty BPP 420	Guilty Of Love/Gambler (shaped picture disc) 10
84	Liberty BPP 423	Standing In The Shadows/All Or Nothing (US Mix) (picture disc)........... 6
87	EMI EMIW 5606	Still Of The Night/Here I Go Again (p/s, white vinyl with poster)........... 8
87	EMI 12 EMIP 5606	Still Of The Night/Here I Go Again/You're Gonna Break My Heart Again
		(12", picture disc) 10
87	EMI EMP 3	Is This Love/Standing In The Shadows '87/Need Your Love So Bad '87
		(shaped picture disc, all mispressed with 2 tracks,
		some with 3rd track on bonus white label 7")....................... 10/6
87	EMI 12EMW 3	Is This Love/Standing In The Shadows '87/Need Your Love So Bad '87/
		Still Of The Night (CD, card sleeve) 8
87	EMI CDEM 3	Is This Love/Standing In The Shadows '87/Need Your Love So Bad '87
		(12", p/s, white vinyl) 8
87	EMI 10EMI 35	Here I Go Again '87 (US remix)/Guilty Of Love (10", p/s, white vinyl)........ 8
88	EMI 12EMP 23	Give Me All Your Love/Fool For Your Loving/Don't Break My Heart Again
		(12", picture disc) 8
90	EMI EMPD 128	The Deeper The Love/Judgement Day (picture disc, with insert) 5
90	EMI EMPD 150	Now You're Gone (Remix)/Wings Of The Storm
		(shaped picture disc with plinth).................................... 7
78	EMI Intl. INS 3022	TROUBLE (LP, grey or pink inner sleeve)......................... each 12
82	Liberty LBGP 30354	SAINTS AN' SINNERS (LP, picture disc)............................... 15
84	Liberty LBGP 240 000 0	SLIDE IT IN (LP, picture disc, U.S. mixes) 15
87	EMI EMCP 3528	WHITESNAKE 1987 (LP, picture disc)................................. 15
89	EMI EMCDJ 1013	SLIP OF THE TONGUE (LP, with track by track interview, promo only) 25

(see also David Coverdale, Deep Purple, Rainbow, Roger Glover, Bernie Marsden, Jon Lord, Phenomena, Cozy Powell, Young & Moody Band, Company, Snafu, Bogdon, Forcefield, Gogmagog, Tramline, National Health)

WHITE SPIRIT

80	Neat NEAT 05	Back To The Grind/Cheetah (p/s) 10
81	MCA MCA 638	Midnight Chaser/Suffragettes (p/s).................................. 35
81	MCA MCA 652	High Upon High/No Reprieve/Arthur Guitar 15
80	MCA MCF 3079	WHITE SPIRIT (LP, with lyric insert) 18

(see also Gillan, Iron Maiden)

WHITE SS

| 78 | White SS CIA 72 | Mercy Killing/I'm Not One (live) (p/s) .... 25 |

WHITE STRIPES

01	XL XLS 139	Hotel Yorba (Live At The Hotel Yorba)/Rated X (p/s, 4000 only).............. 5
02	XL XLS 142	Fell In Love With A Girl/I Just Don't Know What To Do With Myself (p/s, 5000 only).. 5
02	XL XLS 142 CD/2	Fell In Love With A Girl/Let's Shake Hands/Lafayette Blues/Fell In Love With
		A Girl (Live)/Lovesick (Live At The Forum)/I Just Don't Know What To Do With
		Myself/Fell In Love With A Girl (Video) (2-CD) 10
02	XL XLS 148	Dead Leaves And The Dirty Ground/Stop Breaking Down (Live) (p/s, 5000 only).. 5
02	XL/MOJO no cat. no.	Red Death At 6:14 (1-sided, promo only, red vinyl, numbered label, 3000 only,
		mail order only via *Mojo* magazine, with letter)...................... 40
02	XL XLS 162	Merry Christmas From The White Stripes: Candy Cane Children/The Reading
		Of The Story Of The Magi/The Singing Of Silent Night (1000 only, p/s) 20
03	XL XLS 166	I Just Don't Know What To Do With Myself/Who's To Say (p/s) 6
03	XL XLS 166 DVD	I Just Don't Know What To Do With Myself/Lafayette Blues (Live)/Black Math
		(Live) (CD) 15
02	XL (no cat. no)	Fell In Love With A Girl/Let's Shake Hands/Lafayette Blues (printed CD-R, promo) . 10
03	XL (no cat. no)	I Just Don't Know What To Do With Myself/Who's To Say/Lafayette Blues (Live
		On Radio 1 Evening Session)/I'm Finding It Harder To Be A Gentleman (Live On
		The John Peel Show) (promo CD)................................... 10
03	XL LP 162 DJ	Seven Nation Army — Elephant Sampler/In The Cold, Cold Night (p/s).......... 8

03	XL no cat. no.	Seven Nation Army (1-sided 12" promo, stamped white label, no p/s) 45
04	XL XLS 181	There's No Home For You Here/I Fought Piranhas/Let's Build A Home
		(die-cut sleeve) 5
05	XL (no. cat. no)	Blue Orchid (Michel Gondry Remix)/Blue Orchid (Jim Jarmusch Remix)
		(12" remix, 2000 only, sold on tour, p/s) 20
05	XL XLS 218	My Doorbell/Same Boy You've Always Known (live) (red vinyl, p/s) 12
03	XL XLLP 162	ELEPHANT (2-LP, custom sleeve, 500 only). 80
05	XL XLLP 191 P	GET BEHIND ME SATAN (2 x LP, 300 only worldwide, promo, different p/s) 150
05	XL (no. cat. no)	DENIAL TWIST (10 x printed/stickered CDs in different artwork card wallets.
		One given away at each night of UK autumn tour.
		Each CD blank – 10 downloads were available online only) . . . . set 225

(see also Raconteurs)

WHITE TRASH
69	Apple APPLE 6	Road To Nowhere/Illusions (early copies as White Trash, later Trash) 200/30

(see also Trash, Poets, Stone The Crows)

WHITE ZOMBIE
89	Caroline CAROL 1457	God Of Thunder/Love Razor/Disaster Blaster 2 (12", withdrawn) 15

(see also Rob Zombie)

JUNE WHITFIELD
53	Philips PB 137	Seven Lonely Days/Dancing With Someone (78) 5
53	Philips PB 195	Diamonds Are A Girl's Best Friend/Bye Bye Baby (78). 5

(see also Terry Scott)

WILBUR WHITFIELD
57	Vogue V 9078	P.B. Baby/The One I Love (78 rpm = £150) 700

(see also Little Wilbur & Pleasers)

LEONARD WHITING
65	Pye 7N 15943	Piper/That's What Mama Says 40

MARGARET WHITING
55	Capitol CL 14213	My Own True Love (Tara's Theme)/Can This Be Love (triangular centre) 18
55	Capitol CL 14242	Heat Wave/Come Rain Or Shine (triangular centre) 18
55	Capitol CL 14307	Stowaway/All I Want Is All There Is And Then Some (triangular centre) 18
55	Capitol CL 14348	A Man/Mama's Pearls (triangular centre) 18
55	Capitol CL 14375	Lover, Lover/I Kiss You A Million Times (triangular centre) 18
56	Capitol CL 14527	I Love A Mystery/Bidin' My Time 10
56	Capitol CL 14591	Old Enough/Day In — Day Out 8
57	Capitol CL 14685	The Money Tree/Maybe I Love Him 8
57	London HLD 8451	Kill Me With Kisses/Speak For Yourself, John (78 rpm = £12) 25
58	London HLD 8562	I Can't Help (If I'm Still In Love With You)/That's Why I Was Born (78 rpm = £15) . . 20
58	London HLD 8662	Hot Spell/I'm So Lonesome I Could Cry (78 rpm = £15) 20
66	London HLD 10078	Nothing Lasts Forever/The Wheel Of Hurt 15
67	London HLD 10114	Just Like A Man/The World Inside Your Arms 8
68	London HLU 10196	Faithfully/Am I Losing You 6
68	London HLU 10227	Maybe Just Once More/Can't Get You Out Of My Mind 6
53	Capitol LC 6585	CAPITOL PRESENTS MARGARET WHITING (10" LP). 30
56	Capitol LC 6811	MARGARET WHITING (10" LP) 30
58	London HA-D 2109	GOIN' PLACES (LP). 30
61	HMV CLP 1418/CSD 1339	SINGS THE JEROME KERN SONGBOOK VOL. ONE (LP, mono/stereo) 15/18
61	HMV CLP 1419/CSD 1340	SINGS THE JEROME KERN SONGBOOK VOL. TWO (LP, mono/stereo) 15/18
61	London HA-D 2321	JUST A DREAM (LP) 25
67	London HA-U/SH-U 8317	THE WHEEL OF HURT (LP) 18
67	London HA-U 8332	MAGGIE ISN'T MARGARET ANYMORE (LP) 18

(see also Jimmy Wakely, Bob Hope, Dean Martin)

RAY WHITLEY
65	HMV POP 1473	I've Been Hurt/There Is One Boy (DJ copy = £250) 150

BOBBY WHITLOCK
72	CBS 65109	BOBBY WHITLOCK (LP). 18
73	CBS 65301	RAW VELVET (LP). 15

(see also Derek & Dominoes)

SLIM WHITMAN
78s
58	London HLP 8590	A Very Precious Love/Careless Hands 12
58	London HLP 8642	Candy Kisses/Tormented 10
58	London HLP 8708	Wherever You Are/At The End Of Nowhere 15
59	London HLP 8835	I Never See Maggie Alone/The Letter Edged In Black. 25

SINGLES
54	London L 1149	Indian Love Call/China Doll 30
54	London HL 1149	Indian Love Call/China Doll (re-pressing with different prefix) 18
54	London L 1214	There's A Rainbow In Every Teardrop/Danny Boy. 25
54	London HL 1214	There's A Rainbow In Every Teardrop/Danny Boy (re-pressing) 20
54	London L 1226	North Wind/Darlin' Don't Cry 30
54	London HL 1226	North Wind/Darlin' Don't Cry (re-pressing with different prefix) 25
54	London HL 8018	Stairway To Heaven/Lord, Help Me To Be As Thou 50
54	London HL 8039	Secret Love/Why 25
54	London HL 8061	Rose Marie/We Stood At The Altar 15
54	London HL 8080	Beautiful Dreamer/Ride Away 20
54	London HL 8091	The Singing Hills/I Hate To See You Cry. 20
55	London HL 8125	When I Grow Too Old To Dream/Cattle Call 20
55	London HL 8141	Haunted Hungry Heart/Roll On, Silvery Moon 20
55	London HLU 8167	I'll Never Stop Loving You/I'll Never Take You Back Again 20

55	London HLU 8196	Song Of The Wild/You Have My Heart	20
56	London HLU 8230	Tumbling Tumbleweeds/Tell Me.	20
56	London HLU 8252	I'm A Fool/My Heart Is Broken In Three	20
56	London HLU 8287	Serenade/I Talk To The Waves.	20
56	London HLU 8327	Dear Mary/Whiffenpoof Song.	20
56	London HLU 8350	I'm Casting My Lasso Towards The Sky/There's A Love Knot In My Lariat	15
57	London HLP 8403	I'll Take You Home Again Kathleen/Careless Love	18

(The above singles were originally issued with gold label print & tri-centres; later round-centre and/or silver label print copies are worth half these values.)

57	London HLP 8416	Curtain Of Tears/Smoke Signals (silver label print)	12
57	London HLP 8420	Gone/An Amateur In Love (gold label print).	25
57	London HLP 8434	Many Times/Warm, Warm Lips	12
57	London HLP 8459	Lovesick Blues/Forever	12
57	London HLP 8518	Unchain My Heart/Hush-A-Bye	12
58	London HLP 8590	A Very Precious Love/Careless Hands	12
58	London HLP 8642	Candy Kisses/Tormented	12
58	London HLP 8708	Wherever You Are/At The End Of Nowhere	10
59	London HLP 8835	I Never See Maggie Alone/The Letter Edged In Black.	8
59	London HLP 8896	What Kind Of God (Do You Think You Are)/A Tree In The Meadow (unissued)	
60	London HLP 9103	Roll, River, Roll/Twilla Lee	6
61	London HLP 9302	Vaya Con Dios/Ramona	6
64	Liberty LIB 66040	I'll Hold You In My Heart/No Other Arms, No Other Lips	5
65	Liberty LIB 66103	Reminiscing/Mansion On The Hill	5
65	Liberty LIB 12013	Remember Me (I'm The One Who Loves You)/Virginia	5
65	Liberty LIB 12020	More Than Yesterday/Broken Down Merry-Go-Round	5
66	Liberty LIB 66181	A Travelin' Man/I Remember You	5
66	Liberty LIB 66212	One Dream/Jerry	5
67	Liberty LIB 66226	What's The World A-Comin' To/You Bring Out The Best In Me	5
68	Liberty LBF 15066	Cool Water/Down In The Valley	5
69	Liberty LBF 15198	My Happiness/Rose Marie	5
69	Liberty LBF 15220	Stranger On The Shore/Star Of Hope	5
70	Liberty LBF 15394	My Heart Has A Mind Of Its Own/How Could I Not Love You.	5
70	Liberty LBF 15430	Snowbird/How Could I Not Love You	5

EPs

54	London RE-P 1006	SLIM WHITMAN AND HIS SINGING GUITAR (at least 8 different colour sleeves, with matt or gloss finish & various label designs)	12/18
55	London RE-P 1042	SONG OF THE WILD.	15
56	London RE-P 1064	SLIM WHITMAN VOL. 2 PT. 1.	15
56	London RE-P 1070	SLIM WHITMAN VOL. 2 PT. 2.	15
57	London RE-P 1100	SLIM WHITMAN VOL. 2 PT. 3.	15
59	London RE-P 1199	SLIM WHITMAN SINGS (triangular silver-top centre, later round)	15/10
60	London RE-P 1258	SLIM WHITMAN SINGS No. 2.	15
63	London RE-P 1360	THE WAYWARD WIND	15
64	Liberty LEP 4018	IRISH LOVE SONGS THE SLIM WHITMAN WAY	12
65	Liberty LEP 4027	SLIM WHITMAN SINGS MORE IRISH SONGS	12
66	Liberty LEP 4046	A SATISFIED MIND	15

LPs

54	London H-APB 1015	SLIM WHITMAN & HIS SINGING GUITAR (10", gold or silver label print)	55/35
56	London HA-U 2015	SLIM WHITMAN & HIS SINGING GUITAR VOL. 2.	40
59	London HA-P 2139	SLIM WHITMAN SINGS.	28
59	London HA-P 2199	SLIM WHITMAN SINGS VOL. 2	28
60	London HA-P 2343	SLIM WHITMAN	28
61	London HA-P 2392	JUST CALL ME LONESOME	28
62	London HA-P 2443	SLIM WHITMAN SINGS VOL. 3 (also stereo SAH-P 6232)	28/30
62	London HA-P 8013	SLIM WHITMAN SINGS VOL. 4	22
63	London HA-P 8059	HEART SONGS AND LOVE SONGS	22
63	London HA-P 8093	I'M A LONELY WANDERER.	22
64	Liberty LBY 3032	YODELING	15
65	Liberty LBY 3034	COUNTRY SONGS, CITY HITS.	15

MARVA WHITNEY

70	Polydor 2001 036	This Girl's In Love With You/He's The One	30
72	Mojo 2092 041	Daddy Don't Know About The Sugar Bear/We Need More.	20
69	Polydor 583 767	IT'S MY THING (LP).	150

(see also James Brown)

JAKI WHITREN

73	Epic EPC 65645	RAW BUT TENDER (LP, with insert)	40

TIM WHITSETT

64	Sue WI 318	Macks By The Tracks/Shine.	40

TIM WHITSETT/STICKS HERMAN

60s	Range JRE 7002	RHYTHM & BLUES (EP).	30

PAUL WHITSUN JONES & WALLAS EATON & HOLLAND

65	Oriole CB 1991	Shake It Baby/Instant Marriage	12

WHITSUNTIDE EASTER

77	Pilgrim/Grapevine GRA 109	NEXT TIME YOU PLAY A WRONG NOTE...MAKE IT A SHORT ONE (LP, gatefold sleeve)	100

ROGER WHITTAKER (& COMPANIONS)

62	Fontana H 358	The Charge Of The Light Brigade/Keep It A Secret.	5
62	Fontana 267 217TF	Steel Men/After The Laughter	5
63	Fontana 267 258TF	Butterfly/Times Is Tough	5
63	Fontana TF 393	The Sinner/Settle Down (as Rog Whittaker & Companions)	5
64	Fontana TF 437	Mud Puddle/Acre Of Wheat (as Rog Whittaker & His Companions)	5

(see also Hank & Mellowmen)

TOMMY WHITTLE (& HIS QUARTET)

55	Esquire EP 37	TOMMY WHITTLE QUINTET (EP).	15
56	Esquire EP 37	TOMMY WHITTLE QUINTET (EP).	20
58	HMV 7EG 8325	TOMMY WHITTLE QUARTET (EP).	40
54	Esquire 20-028	WAXING WITH WHITTLE (LP).	30
55	Esquire 20-048	TOMMY WHITTLE QUINTET (LP).	50
56	Esquire 20-061	SPOTLIGHTING TOMMY WHITTLE (LP).	75
56	Esquire 20-068	LULLABY & RHYTHM (LP).	125
60	Tempo TAP 27	NEW HORIZONS (LP).	200+
60s	Ember EMB 3305	EASY LISTENING (LP).	75

WHIZZ KIDS

79	Dead Good DEAD SIX	P.A.Y.E./99% Proof/National Assistance/Cheek To Cheek (p/s, with insert)	20
80	Ovation OVS 1213	Suspect No. 1/Coma Life (ps)	10

THE WHO
SINGLES

65	Brunswick 05926	I Can't Explain/Bald Headed Woman	25
65	Brunswick 05935	Anyway Anyhow Anywhere/Daddy Rolling Stone	30
65	Brunswick 05944	My Generation/Shout And Shimmy	20
66	Brunswick 05951	Circles/Instant Party Mixture (unreleased)	
66	Reaction 591 001	Substitute/Circles (temporarily withdrawn)	40
66	Reaction 591 001	Substitute/Instant Party (temporarily withdrawn)	35
66	Brunswick 05956	The Kids Are Alright/The Ox (existence unconfirmed)	
66	Brunswick 05956	A Legal Matter/Instant Party	40
66	Reaction 591 001	Substitute/WHO ORCHESTRA: Waltz For A Pig (B-side actually by Graham Bond Organisation)	20
66	Brunswick 05965	The Kids Are Alright/The Ox	45
66	Brunswick 05968	La-La-La-Lies/The Good's Gone	40
66	Reaction 591 004	I'm A Boy/In The City	8
66	Reaction 591 010	Happy Jack/I've Been Away	8
67	Track 604 002	Pictures Of Lily/Doctor, Doctor	8
67	Track 604 006	The Last Time/Under My Thumb	55
67	Track 604 011	I Can See For Miles/Someone's Coming	8
68	Track 604 023	Dogs/Call Me Lightning	15
68	Track 604 024	Magic Bus/Dr. Jekyll And Mr Hyde	8
69	Track 604 027	Pinball Wizard/Dogs Part Two	8
70	Track 604 036	The Seeker/Here For More	8
70	Track 2094 002	Summertime Blues/Heaven And Hell	8
70	Track 2094 004	See Me, Feel Me/Overture From 'Tommy' (withdrawn)	20
71	Track 2094 009	Won't Get Fooled Again/Don't Know Myself (p/s, large centre/with middle)	30/40
73	Track 2094 115	5.15/Water	7
75	Polydor 2001 561	Overture/See Me Feel Me/Listening To You (from "Tommy" soundtrack, p/s)	6
76	Polydor 2058 803	Substitute/I'm A Boy/Pictures Of Lily (12", company sleeve)	8
79	Polydor WHO 2	Long Live Rock/I'm The Face/My Wife (withdrawn, blank run-off groove)	6
80	Polydor WHO 3	5.15/I'm One (p/s)	6
82	Polydor WHOP 6	Athena/A Man Is A Man (picture disc)	6
82	Polydor WHOPX 6	Athena/A Man Is A Man/Won't Get Fooled Again (12", picture disc)	8
82	Polydor WHOPX 6	Athena/A Man Is A Man/Won't Get Fooled Again (12", picture disc, mispressing, plays "Why Did I Fall For That")	15
89	Polydor POCD 907	My Generation/Substitute/Baba O'Riley/Behind Blue Eyes (CD, card sleeve)	10
89	Polydor POCD 917	Won't Get Fooled Again (Extended Version)/Bony Maronie/Dancing In The Street/Mary-Anne With The Shaky Hand (CD, card sleeve)	15

EXPORT SINGLES

66	Brunswick 05956	A Legal Matter/Instant Party (with Scandinavian p/s)	120
68	Decca AD 1001	My Generation/Shout And Shimmy (some in p/s)	145/95
68	Decca AD 1002	A Legal Matter/Instant Party	80
72	Track 2094 102	Join Together/Baby Don't You Do It (p/s, for Spain)	20

PROMO SINGLES

69	Track PRO 1	The Acid Queen/We're Not Gonna Take It (existence unconfirmed)	
69	Track PRO 2	Go To The Mirror!/Sally Simpson	60
69	Track PRO 3	I'm Free/1921	60
69	Track PRO 4	Christmas/Overture	60

EP

66	Reaction 592 001	READY STEADY WHO	75
70	Track 2252 001	EXCERPTS FROM "TOMMY" (33rpm)	20
83	Reaction WHO 7	READY STEADY WHO (reissue)	15

LPs

65	Brunswick LAT 8616	MY GENERATION	180
66	Reaction 593 002	A QUICK ONE	90
67	Track 612 002	THE WHO SELL OUT (mono, 500 with stickered sleeve & poster)	375/60
67	Track 613 002	THE WHO SELL OUT (stereo, 500 with stickered sleeve & poster)	375/60
68	Track 612/613 006	DIRECT HITS (mono/stereo)	30/22
69	Track 613 013/014	TOMMY (2-LP, fold-out glossy gatefold sleeve, with numbered 12-page booklet)	110
70	Track 2406 001	LIVE AT LEEDS (foldout sleeve with 12 inserts including poster; blue or red print on sleeve)	32
70	Track 2407 008	BACKTRACK 8: A QUICK ONE (mono budget reissue)	18
70	Track 2407 009	BACKTRACK 9: SELL OUT (stereo budget reissue)	12
70	Track 2407 014	BACKTRACK 14: THE OX	22
70	Track 2856 001	WHO DID IT? (mail-order only, withdrawn)	440
71	Track 2408 102	WHO'S NEXT	15
71	Track 2406 006	MEATY, BEATY, BIG AND BOUNCY (gatefold sleeve)	12
71	Track 2406 006	MEATY, BEATY, BIG AND BOUNCY (gatefold sleeve, mispressed, plays "The Seeker" instead of "Magic Bus")	20
72	Track 2406 007	TOMMY PART ONE	12

72	Track 2406 008	TOMMY PART TWO.. 12
73	Track 2657 013	QUADROPHENIA (2-LP, original with 22-page photo booklet, matt labels) 20
74	Track 2406 116	ODDS AND SODS (cut-away braille sleeve, with poster & lyric sheet)......... 15
75	Polydor 2490 129	THE WHO BY NUMBERS 15
80	Virgin V 2179	MY GENERATION (reissue) 18
81	Polydor 2675 216	PHASES (9-LP box set, stickered cover) 100

(see also High Numbers, Pete Townshend, Roger Daltrey, John Entwistle, Keith Moon, Kenney Jones, Graham Bond Organisation, Rigor Mortis, McEnroe & Cash)

WALLY WHYTON (& VIPERS)
59	Parlophone R 4585	Don't Tell Me Your Troubles/It's All Over You 7
60	Parlophone R 4630	All Over This World/Got Me A Girl... 5
60	Parlophone (no mono no.)	WILLUM AND ME (EP, stereo/mono) 18/15
60	Pye 7N 15304	It's A Rat Race/Marriage Of Convenience/95% Of Me Loves You
		(with Sally Miles)/You're Going To Be Caught (as Wally Whyton & Vipers)....... 6
61	Piccadilly 7N 35089	Little Red Pony/Christmas Land 6
68	Fontana TF 960	Gentle On My Mind/Ballad Of The Bol Weevil 5
69	Fontana TF 994	Wichita Lineman/Leave Them A Flower 5
69	Fontana TF 1030	Jig Alone/Out On The Road 5
68	Fontana STL 5476	IT'S ME, MUM (LP) 12
70	Fontana STL 5535	LEAVE THEM A FLOWER (LP) 12

(see also Vipers, Sharkey Todd & Monsters)

WICHITA FALL
| 69 | Liberty LBS 83208 | LIFE IS BUT A DREAM (LP) .... 12 |

WICHITA TRAIN WHISTLE
| 68 | Dot DOT 111 | Don't Cry Now/Tapioca Tundra (unissued) |
| 68 | Dot (S)LPD 516 | MICHAEL NESMITH PRESENTS THE WICHITA TRAIN WHISTLE SINGS (LP) .... 40 |

(see also Michael Nesmith)

WIDOWMAKER
76	Jet JET 766	On The Road/Pin A Rose On Me 7
76	Jet JET 767	When I Met You/Pin A Rose On Me 5
76	Jet JET 782	Pin A Rose On Me/On The Road 5
76	Jet 2310 432	WIDOWMAKER (LP) 15
77	United Artists UAG 30038	TOO LATE TO CRY (LP, gatefold sleeve) 12

(see also Luther Grosvenor, Steve Ellis, Huw Lloyd Langton)

WIGGANS
| 61 | Blue Beat BB 29 | Rock Baby/Let's Sing The Blues... 22 |

PERCY WIGGINS
| 67 | Atlantic 584 113 | Book Of Memories/Can't Find Nobody .... 10 |

SPENCER WIGGINS
| 67 | Stateside SS 2024 | Uptight Good Woman/Anything You Do Is Alright.......................... 20 |
| 70 | Pama PM 794 | I'm A Poor Man's Son/That's How Much I Love You .... 15 |

WIKKYD VIKKER
| 83 | Boogie FUR 0235 | Black Of The Night/Release (no p/s)..................................... 120 |

WILBURN BROTHERS
59	Brunswick 05799	That Silver-Haired Daddy Of Mine/A Boy's Faithful Friend (78 rpm = £6)........ 10
59	Brunswick LAT 8291	SIDE BY SIDE (LP) 20
61	Brunswick LAT 8501	CITY LIMITS (LP) 18
62	Brunswick LAT 8507	FOLK SONGS (LP) 15
67	Brunswick LAT 8686	COOL COUNTRY (LP)... 15

WILD & WANDERING
| 86 | Iguana VYK 14 | 2,000 LIGHT ALES FROM HOME (12" EP, with insert) .... 25 |

(see also Pop Will Eat Itself)

WILD ANGELS
68	Major Minor MM 569	Nervous Breakdown/Watch The Wheels Go Round 25
69	B&C CB 114	Buzz Buzz/Please Don't Touch 12
70	B&C CB 123	Sally-Ann/Wrong Number, Try Again 12
71	B&C CB 145	Three Nights A Week/Time To Kill 8
72	Decca F 13308	Jo-Jo Ann/My Way 7
72	Decca F 13356	Beauty School Dropout/Midnight Rider 7
73	Decca F 13374	Running Bear/Sussin'.. 6
73	Decca F 13412	Greased Lightning/Born To Hand-Jive/Beauty School Dropout 6
73	Decca F 13456	Clap Your Hands And Stamp Your Feet/Wild Angels Rock'n'Roll 5
70	B&C BCM 101	LIVE AT THE REVOLUTION (LP) 18
70	B&C BCM 102	RED HOT'N'ROCKIN' (LP) 18
72	Decca SKL 5134	OUT AT LAST (LP).. 12

WILD BUNCH
| 84 | Ariwa ARILP 15 | THE WILD BUNCH (LP)... 20 |

WILDCATS
| 59 | London HLT 8787 | Gazachstahagen/Billy's Cha Cha (78 rpm = £12)......................... 22 |

JACK WILDE
| 69 | Elektra EKSN 45068 | Apple Pie Mother And The Flag/Ballad Of Baby Browning .... 6 |
| 70 | Capitol ST 22545 | THE JACK WILD ALBUM (LP) .... 12 |

KIM WILDE
83	Rak 12 RAK 365	Dancing In The Dark (Extended)/Dancing In The Dark (Instrumental)
		(12", p/s, with poster) 10
84	MCA KIMP 1	The Second Time/Lovers On A Beach (picture disc) 12
84	MCA KIMP 2	The Touch/Shangri-La (shaped picture disc) 10
85	MCA KIMP 3	Rage To Love/Putty In Your Hands (shaped picture disc) 10

88	MCA KIM X7	Hey Mister Heartache (Kilowatt Remix)/Hey Mister Heartache/	
		Tell Me Where You Are (12", p/s)	8
88	MCA DKIM 7	Hey Mister Heartache (Extended)/Tell Me Where You Are/	
		You Keep Me Hangin' On/Another Step (Closer To You) (Extended Version)	
		(CD, 4th track w/Junior)	12
88	MCA KIMB 8	You Came/Stone (box set)	5
88	MCA DKIM 8	You Came (Extended)/You Came (7" Version)/Stone (5" CD, unreleased)	
88	MCA DIM 8	You Came (Extended)/You Came (7" Version)/Stone (3" CD)	12
88	MCA DKIM 9	Never Trust A Stranger (Extended Version)/You Came (Pettibone Mix)/	
		Wotcha Gonna Do? (CD)	12
88	MCA KIMB 10	Four Letter Word/She Hasn't Got Time For You ('88) (numbered box set)	5
89	MCA DKIMT 11	Love In The Natural Way (7" Version)/You'll Be The One Who'll Lose/	
		Love In The Natural Way (Extended Version) (CD, picture disc)	12

MARTY WILDE (& WILDCATS)
78s

57	Philips PB 750	Honeycomb/Wild Cat (as Marty Wilde & Wildcats)	15
58	Philips PB 781	Love Bug Crawl/Afraid Of Love	35
58	Philips PB 804	Sing, Boy, Sing/Oh-Oh, I'm Falling In Love Again (with Wildcats)	20
58	Philips PB 835	Endless Sleep/Her Hair Was Yellow (as Marty Wilde & Wildcats)	10
58	Philips PB 850	My Lucky Love/Misery's Child (as Marty Wilde & Wildcats)	12
58	Philips PB 875	No One Knows/The Fire Of Love	18
59	Philips PB 902	Donna/Love-a, Love-a, Love-a	25
59	Philips PB 926	A Teenager In Love/Danny	30
59	Philips PB 959	Sea Of Love/Teenage Tears	40
59	Philips PB 972	It's Been Nice/Bad Boy	55
60	Philips PB 1002	Johnny Rocco/My Heart And I	90

SINGLES

57	Philips JK 1028	Honeycomb/Wild Cat (as Marty Wilde & Wildcats) (jukebox issue)	60
58	Philips PB 804	Sing, Boy, Sing/Oh-Oh, I'm Falling In Love Again (with Wildcats)	45
58	Philips PB 835	Endless Sleep/Her Hair Was Yellow (as Marty Wilde & Wildcats)	15
58	Philips PB 850	My Lucky Love/Misery's Child (as Marty Wilde & Wildcats)	12
58	Philips PB 875	No One Knows/The Fire Of Love	15
59	Philips PB 902	Donna/Love-a, Love-a, Love-a	10
59	Philips PB 926	A Teenager In Love/Danny	10
59	Philips PB 959	Sea Of Love/Teenage Tears	10
59	Philips PB 972	It's Been Nice/Bad Boy	10
60	Philips PB 1002	Johnny Rocco/My Heart And I	12
60	Philips PB 1022	The Fight/Johnny At The Crossroads	12
60	Philips PB 1037	I Wanna Be Loved By You/Angry	8
60	Philips PB 1078	Little Girl/Your Seventeenth Spring	7
61	Philips PB 1101	Rubber Ball/Like Makin' Love	7
61	Philips PB 1121	When Does It Get To Be Love/Your Loving Touch	7
61	Philips PB 1161	Hide And Seek/Crazy Dream	7
61	Philips PB 1191	Tomorrow's Clown/The Hellions	7
61	Philips PB 1206	Come Running/Ev'ryone	12
62	Philips PB 1240	Jezebel/Don't Run Away	8
62	Philips 326 546BF	Ever Since You Said Goodbye/Send Me The Pillow You Dream On	7
63	Columbia DB 4980	Lonely Avenue/Brand New Love	8
63	Philips 326 579BF	No! Dance With Me/Little Miss Happiness	7
63	Columbia DB 7145	Save Your Love For Me/Bless My Broken Heart	8
64	Columbia DB 7198	When Day Is Done/I Can't Help The Way I Feel	8
64	Columbia DB 7285	Kiss Me/My, What A Woman	8
64	Decca F 11979	The Mexican Boy/Your Kind Of Love	8
66	Philips PB 1490	I've Got So Used To Loving You/The Beginning Of The End	6
68	Philips BF 1632	By The Time I Get To Phoenix/Shutters And Boards	6
68	Philips BF 1669	Abergavenny/Alice In Blue	5
69	Philips BF 1753	All The Love I Have/Any Day	5
69	Philips BF 1783	Endless Sleep/Donna	5
69	Philips BF 1815	Shelley/Jump On The Train (with Deke Leonard)	5
70	Philips BF 1839	No Trams To Lime Street/Prelude To Old Age	5
71	Philips 6006 126	Busker/It's So Real	5

EPs

57	Philips BBE 12164	PRESENTING MARTY WILDE	65
58	Philips BBE 12200	MORE OF MARTY	50
59	Philips BBE 12327	SEA OF LOVE	50
60	Philips BBE 12385	VERSATILE MR. WILDE	55
60	Philips BBE 12422	MARTY WILDE FAVOURITES	50
62	Philips BBE 12517	COME RUNNING	45
63	Philips BE 433 638	MARTY	45

LPs

59	Philips BBL 7342	WILDE ABOUT MARTY	60
60	Philips BBL 7380	MARTY WILDE SHOWCASE	60
60	Philips BBL 7385	THE VERSATILE MR. WILDE (also stereo SBBL 570)	55/65
69	Philips SBL 7877	DIVERSIONS	18
70	Philips 6308 010	ROCK 'N' ROLL	12

(see also Wilde Three, Brian Bennett, Shadows, Keith Shields, Capricorn, Deke Leonard)

WILDER BROTHERS

57	HMV POP 365	I Want You/Teenage Angel	250
57	HMV POP 365	I Want You/Teenage Angel (78)	60

WILDERNESS ROAD

74	Dawn DNLS 3057	WILDERNESS ROAD (LP, unissued)	

MINT VALUE £

WILDE THREE
65	Decca F 12131	Since You've Gone/Just As Long	70
65	Decca F 12232	I Cried/Well Who's That?	65

(see also Marty Wilde, Justin Hayward, Vernons Girls)

WILDFIRE
84	Mausoleum GUTS 8405	Jerusalem/Fight Fire With Fire (p/s)	5
83	Mausoleum SKUL 8307	BRUTE FORCE AND IGNORANCE (LP)	25
83	Mausoleum SKUL 8338	SUMMER LIGHTNING (LP, with insert)	15

(see also Weapon)

WILDHEARTS
SINGLES
92	East West YZ 669T	MONDO AKIMBO A-GO-GO (12" EP, with inner sleeve)	25
92	East West YZ 669TX	MONDO AKIMBO A-GO-GO (12" EP, white vinyl, with inner sleeve, advance copies with artwork postcard & press sheet)	40/35
92	East West YZ 669CD	MONDO AKIMBO A-GO-GO (CD EP)	40
93	East West YZ 773	Greetings From Shitsville/The Bullshit Goes On (p/s, brown vinyl, with insert)	12
93	East West YZ 784CD	TV EP: TV Tan/Show A Little Emotion/Dangerlust/Down On London (CD)	8
94	East West YZ 794	Caffeine Bomb/Girlfriend Clothes (p/s, green vinyl, with insert)	5
94	East West YZ 794CD	Caffeine Bomb/Girlfriend Clothes/Shut Your Fucking Mouth And Use Your Fucking Brain/And The Bullshit Goes On (CD, digipak)	12
94	East West YZ 828TE	Suckerpunch/Beautiful Thing You/Two-Way Idiot Mirror/29 x The Pain (10", p/s, 1-sided, etched)	12
94	East West YZ 828CD	Suckerpunch/Beautiful Thing You/Two-Way Idiot Mirror/29 x The Pain (CD)	8
94	East West YZ 874TEX	If Life Is Like A Lovebank I Want An Overdraft/Geordie In Wonderland/ Hate The World Day/Fire Up (10", gatefold sleeve with banknote)	10
94	East West YZ 874CDX	If Life Is Like A Lovebank I Want An Overdraft/Geordie In Wonderland/ Hate The World Day/Fire Up (CD, 'wallet' pack with banknote)	8
95	East West YZ 923TEX	I Wanna Go Where The People Go/Shandy Bang/Can't Do Right For Doing Wrong/Give The Girl A Gun (10", p/s)	10
95	East West YZ 976TEX	Just In Lust/Mindslide/Friend For Five Minutes/S.I.N (In Sin) (10", p/s)	10
95	Round WILD1CDX	Sick Of Drugs/Underkill/Bad Time To Be Having A Bad Time/Skychaser High (CD, with grass-growing mat, title sticker, mispressing, plays Tony Christie)	15
97	Mushroom MUSH 6CD	Anthem/So Good To Be Back Home/Time To Let You Go (CD, mispressing, plays country music)	12
02	Round SMALP048	Vanilla Radio/Better Than Cable (picture disc, stickered PVC sleeve, 1500 only)	8

ALBUMS
92	East West 4509-91202-1	DON'T BE HAPPY... JUST WORRY (LP, as 2 x 12", with inner sleeves)	25
92	East West 4509-91202-2	DON'T BE HAPPY... JUST WORRY (2-CD, with bonus disc containing "Anti-Dance Mixes" of "Mondo Akimbo A-Go Go" tracks)	25
93	East West 4509-93287-1	EARTH VS THE WiLDHEARTS (LP, with exclusive uncredited track)	20
93	East West 4509-93201-2	EARTH VS THE WiLDHEARTS (CD, first issue with "93" rear artwork, without "Caffeine Bomb")	18
94	East West 4509-99039-2	FISHING FOR LUCKIES (CD, 6-track mini-album, fan club/mail-order only)	40
95	East West 0630-10404-1	P.H.U.Q. (LP, gatefold sleeve)	15
95	East West 0630-10437-2	P.H.U.Q. (CD, stickered felt case, unique inlay)	15
95	East West 0630-12850-1	FISHING FOR MORE LUCKIES (LP, reissue, with 3 extra tracks "Underkill", "Saddened" & "I Wanna Go Where The People Go [Early Version]", unreleased, most copies destroyed)	100
95	East West 0630-12850-4	FISHING FOR MORE LUCKIES (cassette, reissue, with 3 extra tracks, unreleased, most copies destroyed)	35

(CD copies of "Fishing For MORE Luckies" [0630-12850-2] were NOT destroyed and cut-outs were later made available at mid-price)

96	Round 0630-14888-1	FISHING FOR LUCKIES (2-LP, reissue, gatefold, Side 3 exclusive to vinyl)	18
97	Mushroom MUSH13LP	ENDLESS, NAMELESS (LP, inner sleeve)	15
98	Kuro Neko KNEKLP3	ANARCHIC AIRWAVES – THE WiLDHEARTS AT THE BBC (2-LP, 200 mail-order copies only – 1000 copies made but 800 destroyed)	25
98	Kuro Neko KNEK3L	ANARCHIC AIRWAVES – THE WiLDHEARTS AT THE BBC (CD in square stickered metal tin, no insert, 1000 copies only)	15
99	Kuro Neko KNEK3LTD	ANARCHIC AIRWAVES – THE WiLDHEARTS AT THE BBC (2-CD, with bonus disc "THE REST OF READING")	20
98	Kuro Neko KNEK4LB	LANDMINES & PANTOMIMES – THE LAST OF THE WiLDHEARTS...? (CD in square stickered metal tin in card box with insert, 1000 copies only)	30
03	Gut GUTLP25	THE WiLDHEARTS MUST BE DESTROYED (LP, gatefold sleeve)	12

(see also Backyard Babies, Chasers, Energetic Krusher, Ginger, Honeycrack, Jellys, Quireboys, SilverGinger 5, Super$hit666, Devin Townsend, Yo-Yo's)

WILD HONEY
72	Mam MAM 97	He's My Sugar/People Of The Universe	8
72	Mam MAM 154	Baby Don't You Know Anymore/He's My Sugar (featuring Tina Charles)	8

(see also Tina Charles)

WILD HORSES
79	EMI International INTS 599	Criminal Tendencies/The Rapist (p/s)	5
80	EMI EMI 5047	Face Down/Dealer (p/s)	5
80	EMI EMI 5078	Fly Away/Blackmail (p/s, white vinyl; black vinyl demos £15)	6
80	EMI 12EMI 5078	Fly Away/Blackmail (12", p/s, white vinyl)	8
81	EMI EMI 5149	I'll Give You Love/Rocky Mountain Way (p/s)	5
81	EMI EMI 5149	I'll Give You Love/Rocky Mountain Way//The Kid/On A Saturday Night (double pack, gatefold p/s)	5
81	EMI EMI 5199	Everlasting Love/The Axe (no p/s)	5
80	EMI EMC 3326	WILD HORSES (LP, with inner sleeve)	12
81	EMI EMC 3368	STAND YOUR GROUND (LP, with inner sleeve)	15

(see also Thin Lizzy, Motörhead, Rainbow, Dio)

WILD MAGNOLIAS
75	Barclay BAR 30	Smoke My Peace Pipe/Handa Wanda	8

75	Barclay BAR 34	They Call Us Wild/Jumalaka Boom Boom	8
75	Barclay 80 529	THE WILD MAGNOLIAS 1 (LP, gatefold sleeve)	25
75	Barclay 90 033	THEY CALL US WILD (LP, gatefold sleeve)	25

WILD OATS
| 63 | Oak RGJ 117 | WILD OATS (EP) | 750+ |

WILD ONES
| 64 | Fontana TF 468 | Bowie Man/Purple Pill Eater | 60 |
| 65 | United Artsts ULP 1119 | THE ARTHUR SOUND (LP) | 40 |

WILD SILK
68	Polydor 56256	Poor Man/Stop Crying	6
69	Columbia DB 8534	(Visions In A) Plaster Sky/Toymaker	22
69	Columbia DB 8611	Help Me/Crimson And Gold	10

WILD SWANS
82	Zoo CAGE 009	The Revolutionary Spirit/God Forbid (unissued, stamped white label)	12
82	Zoo CAGE 009	The Revolutionary Spirit/God Forbid (12", p/s)	10
82	Zoo CAGE 009	The Revolutionary Spirit/God Forbid (12", p/s, with 'The Lament Of Icarus' painting in top right of front sleeve, withdrawn)	15

(see also Lotus Eaters, Care)

WILD THING
69	Elektra EKSN 45076	Old Lady/Next To Me	6
70	Elektra EKS 74059	PARTYIN' (LP)	18
71	Elektra 2410 003	PARTYIN' (LP, reissue)	12

WILD TURKEY
72	Chrysalis CHS 2004	Good Old Days/Life Is A Symphony	5
72	Chrysalis CHR 1002	BATTLE HYMN (LP, gatefold sleeve)	18
73	Chrysalis CHR 1010	TURKEY (LP)	18

(see also Babe Ruth, Jethro Tull, Man, Gary Pickford-Hopkins, Whitesnake)

WILD UNCERTAINTY
| 66 | Planet PLF 120 | Man With Money/Broken Truth | 75 |

WILD WALLY
| 70 | Concord CON 1003 | I GO APE (LP) | 18 |

WILDWEEDS
| 67 | Chess CRS 8065 | It Was Fun While It Lasted/Sorrow's Anthem | 12 |

WILD WILL'S BLUE WASHBOARD BOYS
| 71 | Flyright LP 4701 | BABY YUM YUM (LP) | 12 |

WILFRED & MILLICENT
| 65 | Island WI 190 | The Vow/I'll Never Believe In You | 12 |

(see also Jackie [Edwards] & Millie [Small])

MIKE WILHELM
| 76 | Zigzag/United Artists ZZ 1 | MIKE WILHELM (LP, sold via *Zigzag* magazine) | 45 |

(see also Charlatans, Flamin' Groovies)

ROBERT WILKINS
| 60s | Piedmont PLP 13162 | REV ROBERT WILKINS (LP) | 20 |

ROGER WILKINS
| 70 | Spokane SPL 1002 | BEFORE THE REVERENCE (LP) | 40 |

WILLETT FAMILY
| 62 | Topic 12T 84 | THE ROVING JOURNEYMAN (LP, blue label with booklet) | 20 |

AL WILLIAMS
| 80 | Grapevine GRP 136 | I Am Nothing/Brand New Love | 30 |

ANDY WILLIAMS
56	London HLA 8284	Walk Hand In Hand/Not Any More	30
56	London HLA 8315	Canadian Sunset/High Upon A Mountain (gold or silver label print)	40/25
56	London HL 7013	Canadian Sunset/High Upon A Mountain (export issue)	20
56	London HLA 8360	Baby Doll (From The Film)/Since I've Found My Baby (gold or silver print)	40/25
57	London HLA 8399	Butterfly/It Doesn't Take Very Long	22
57	London HLA 8437	I Like Your Kind Of Love/Stop Teasin' Me	18
57	London HLA 8487	Lips Of Wine/Straight From My Heart	18
58	London HLA 8587	Are You Sincere/Be Mine Tonight	15
58	London HL 7034	Are You Sincere/Be Mine Tonight (export issue)	10
58	London HLA 8710	Promise Me, Love/Your Hand, Your Heart, Your Love	12
59	London HLA 8784	Hawaiian Wedding Song/House Of Bamboo	8
59	London HLA 8957	Lonely Street/Summer Love (78 rpm = £10)	7
59	London HLA 9018	The Village Of St. Bernadette/I'm So Lonesome I Could Cry (78 rpm = £20)	6
60	London HLA 9099	Wake Me When It's Over/We Have A Date	6
60	London HLA 9241	Don't Go To Strangers/You Don't Want My Love	6
61	London HLA 9348	The Bilbao Song/How Wonderful To Know	6
67	CBS CBS 2675	Music To Watch Girls By/The Face I Love	5
57	London RE-A 1088	ANDY WILLIAMS' BIG HITS (EP)	18
57	London RE-A 1102	ANDY WILLIAMS' BIG HITS No. 2 (EP)	22
63	London RE-A 1394	ANDY WILLIAMS' BEST (EP)	12
57	London HA-A 2054	ANDY WILLIAMS SINGS STEVE ALLEN (LP)	40
58	London HA-A 2113	ANDY WILLIAMS SINGS RODGERS AND HAMMERSTEIN (LP)	40
59	London HA-A 2203	TWO TIME WINNERS (LP)	40
60	London HA-A 2238	LONELY STREET (LP)	22
62	London HA-A 8005	ANDY WILLIAMS' BEST (LP)	15
63	London HA-A 8090	UNDER PARIS SKIES (LP)	22
73	CBS CQ 30797	YOU'VE GOT A FRIEND (LP, quadrophonic)	12
73	CBS CQ 31303/Q 64869	LOVE THEME FROM "THE GODFATHER" (LP, quadrophonic)	12

AUDREY WILLIAMS

56	MGM SP 1179	Ain't Nothing Gonna Be All Right No How/Livin' It Up And Havin' A Ball (78 = £8) .	25

(see also Hank Williams)

BIG JOE WILLIAMS

57	Jazz Collector JEN 3	A MAN SINGS THE BLUES (EP)	18
57	Jazz Collector JEN 4	A MAN SINGS THE BLUES VOLUME 2 (EP).	15
67	Delmark DJB 4	ON THE HIGHWAY (EP)	15
60s	XX MIN 700	BIG JOE WILLIAMS (EP)	18
63	Esquire 32-191	BLUES ON HIGHWAY 51 (LP).	40
63	'77' LA 12-19	PINEY WOODS BLUES (LP).	30
64	CBS BPG 63813	CLASSIC DELTA BLUES (LP).	20
64	Storyville SLP 158	PORTRAITS IN BLUES VOLUME 4 (LP)	20
64	Storyville SLP 163	PORTRAITS IN BLUES VOLUME 7 (LP)	20
65	Fontana 688 800 ZL	TOUGH TIMES (LP).	25
66	Xtra XTRA 1033	BIG JOE WILLIAMS (LP).	30
66	Bounty BY 6018	BACK TO THE COUNTRY (LP).	40
66	Society SOC 1020	BIG JOE, SONNY, BROWNIE, LIGHTNIN' (LP, with Lightnin' Hopkins, Sonny Terry & Brownie McGhee)	15
69	Storyville 618 011	DON'T YOU LEAVE ME HERE (LP)	22
69	Liberty LBL/LBS 83207	HAND ME DOWN MY OLD WALKING STICK (LP)	22
69	Xtra XTRA 5059	LIVE AT FOLK CITY (LP).	15
70	RCA Intl. INTS 1087	CRAWLIN' KING SNAKE (LP).	18
72	Delmark DS 627	NINE STRING GUITAR (LP)	15

(see also Poor Joe Williams)

BILLY WILLIAMS (QUARTET)

78s

54	Vogue Coral Q 2012	Sh'Boom/Whenever Wherever	15
54	Vogue Coral Q 2039	The Honeydripper/Love Me (as Billy Williams Quartet)	18
56	Vogue Coral Q 72149	A Crazy Little Palace/Cry Baby (as Billy Williams Quartet)	8
56	Vogue Coral Q 72180	Pray/You'll Reach Your Star	8
57	Vogue Coral Q 72222	Follow Me/Shame, Shame, Shame (as Billy Williams Quartet)	18
58	Coral Q 72303	Don't Let Go/Baby, Baby (as Billy Williams Quartet)	6
58	Coral Q 72316	Steppin' Out Tonight/There I've Said It Again (as Billy Williams Quartet)	8
58	Coral Q 72331	I'll Get By/It's Prayin' Time	8
59	Coral Q 72359	Nola/Tied To The Strings Of Your Heart	12
59	Coral Q 72369	Goodnight Irene/Red Hot Love	20
59	Coral Q 72377	Telephone Conversation/Go To Sleep, Go To Sleep, Go To Sleep (with Barbara McNair)	15

SINGLES

54	Vogue Coral Q 2039	The Honeydripper/Love Me (as Billy Williams Quartet)	50
56	Vogue Coral Q 72149	A Crazy Little Palace/Cry Baby (as Billy Williams Quartet)	50
56	Vogue Coral Q 72180	Pray/You'll Reach Your Star	18
57	Vogue Coral Q 72222	Follow Me/Shame, Shame, Shame (as Billy Williams Quartet)	30
57	Vogue Coral Q 72241	Butterfly/The Pied Piper	30
57	Vogue Coral Q 72266	I'm Gonna Sit Right Down And Write A Letter/Date With The Blues	20
57	Vogue Coral Q 72295	Got A Date With An Angel/The Lord Will Understand	40
58	Coral Q 72303	Don't Let Go/Baby, Baby (as Billy Williams Quartet)	40
58	Coral Q 72316	Steppin' Out Tonight/There I've Said It Again (as Billy Williams Quartet)	50
58	Coral Q 72331	I'll Get By/It's Prayin' Time	20
59	Coral Q 72359	Nola/Tied To The Strings Of Your Heart	10
59	Coral Q 72369	Goodnight Irene/Red Hot Love	30
59	Coral Q 72377	Telephone Conversation/Go To Sleep, Go To Sleep, Go To Sleep (with Barbara McNair)	25
60	Coral Q 72402	I Cried For You/Lover Of All Lovers	18
60	Coral Q 72414	Begin The Beguine/For You	8

LPs

58	Coral LVA 9092	BILLY WILLIAMS	100
60	Coral LVA 9120	HALF SWEET HALF BEAT	40
61	Coral LVA 9139	THE BILLY WILLIAMS REVUE	30

(see also Barbara McNair)

BOBBY WILLIAMS

68	Action ACT 4509	Baby I Need Your Love/Try It Again	40
73	Contempo C 17	Let's Jam/You're My Baby	15

CHRIS WILLIAMS & HIS MONSTERS

59	Columbia DB 4383	The Monster/The Eton Boating Song	35
60	Triumph RGM 1003	Kicking Around/Midnight Rocker (unissued; white label demo copies only)	250+

CINDY WILLIAMS

67	Parlophone R 5648	They Talk About Us/Did He Call Today Mama	8

CLARENCE WILLIAMS (& HIS WASHBOARD BAND)

54	Columbia SCM 5134	High Society/Left All Alone With The Blues (78 rpm, DB 3513 = £6)	15
58	Fontana TFE 17053	TREASURE OF NORTH AMERICAN MUSIC VOLUME 3 (EP)	15
59	Parlophone GEP 8733	CLARENCE WILLIAMS' WASHBOARD BAND (EP)	15
64	Jazz Collector JEL 18	JAZZ ORIGINATORS (EP).	12
54	London AL 3526	CLARENCE WILLIAMS AND HIS ORCHESTRA (10" LP).	20
55	Columbia 33S 1067	BACK ROOM SPECIAL (10" LP).	20
57	London AL 3561	CLARENCE WILLIAMS AND HIS ORCHESTRA VOL. 2 (10" LP)	20
60	Fontana TFL 5087	SIDNEY BECHET MEMORIAL (LP)	15
62	Philips BBL 7521	CLARENCE WILLIAMS VOL. 1: 1927-1935 (LP)	15

CLIVE WILLIAMS

70s	Rock Steady Rev. REVR 6	Take Good Care Of My Baby/RICO: In Loving Memory Of Don Drummond	12

COOTIE WILLIAMS

67	Transatlantic (no. cat. no)	SOLID GOLD TRUMPET OF 67 (LP)	10

DAN WILLIAMS & HIS ORCHESTRA

55	London CAY 110	Donkey City/SHAW PARK CALYPSO BAND: Take Her To Jamaica (78 rpm = £6)	10

DANNY WILLIAMS

59	HMV POP 624	Tall A Tree/I Look At You	10
59	HMV POP 655	So High — So Low/My Own True Love	10
59	HMV POP 703	Youthful Years/It Doesn't Matter	10
60	HMV POP 803	A Million To One/Call Me A Dreamer	8
61	HMV POP 839	We Will Never Be As Young As This Again/Passing Breeze	7
61	HMV POP 885	The Miracle Of You/Lonely	7
61	HMV POP 932	Moon River/A Weaver Of Dreams (repressings with black label, £5)	5
62	HMV POP 968	Jeannie/It Might As Well Be Spring/Unchain My Heart	7
62	HMV POP 1002	The Wonderful World Of The Young/A Kind Of Loving	6
62	HMV POP 1035	Tears/Tiara Tahiti	7
63	HMV POP 1112	My Own True Love/Who Can Say?	8
63	HMV POP 1150	More/Rhapsody	6
63	HMV POP 1172	The Wild Wind/Once Upon A Time	8
63	HMV POP 1203	A Day Without You/Secret Love	6
63	HMV POP 1236	How Do You Keep From Crying?/Now The Day Is Over	6
63	HMV POP 1263	White On White/After You	8
64	HMV POP 1305	Today/Lonely In A Crowd	6
64	HMV POP 1325	The Seventh Dawn/The World Around Me	6
64	HMV POP 1372	Forget Her, Forget Her/Lollipops And Roses	30
65	HMV POP 1388	The Roundabout Of Love/I Wanna Be Around	5
65	HMV POP 1410	Go Away/Masquerade	15
65	HMV POP 1455	Lovely Is She/Gone And Forgotten	5
65	HMV POP 1487	And So We Meet Again/Violets For Your Furs	5
66	HMV POP 1506	I've Got To Find That Girl Again/Throw A Little Lovin' My Way	30
67	Deram DM 149	Never My Love/Whose Little Girl Are You (with inverted matrix, later re-pressed with matrix correct way up)	12/6
62	HMV 7EG 8748	HITS OF DANNY WILLIAMS (EP)	12
62	HMV 7EG 8763	DANNY WILLIAMS SWINGS WITH TONY OSBORNE (EP)	12
63	HMV 7EG 8800	"THE DAYS OF WINE AND ROSES" AND OTHER FILM FAVOURITES (EP)	12
61	HMV CLP 1458/CSD 1369	DANNY (LP, mono/stereo)	25/30
61	HMV CLP 1521	MOON RIVER AND OTHER TITLES (LP)	25
62	HMV CLP 1605/CSD 1471	SWINGING FOR YOU (LP, mono/stereo)	22/30
66	HMV CLP/CSD 3523	ONLY LOVE (LP)	30
66	Woman's Privilege AZ 3	ROMANCE WITH DANNY WILLIAMS (LP, mail-order via *Woman* magazine)	15
67	Deram DML 1017	DANNY WILLIAMS (LP)	18

DEL WILLIAMS

72	Grape GR 3027	Searching For Your Love/G.G. ALL STARS: Searching (Version)	5

DELROY WILLIAMS

71	Trojan TR 7813	Down In The Boondocks/Baby Make It	7

GEORGE WILLIAMS

69	Bullet BU 405	No Business Of Yours/Mast It Up (actually titled "Mash It Up")	10

GEORGE WILLIAMS & HIS ORCHESTRA

55	Vogue Coral Q 72053	The Rompin' Stomper/Knock-Out Choo-Choo	8
56	HMV DLP 1140	RHYTHM WAS HIS BUSINESS (10" LP)	15
56	HMV DLP 1140	RHYTHM WAS HIS BUSINESS (LP)	15

GRANVILLE WILLIAMS ORCHESTRA

67	Island WI 3062	Hi-Life/More	12
67	Island ILP 971	HI-LIFE (LP)	60

(see also Silvertones)

HANK WILLIAMS (& HIS DRIFTING COWBOYS)

78s

50	MGM MGM 269	Lovesick Blues/Wedding Bells	10
51	MGM MGM 381	Moanin' The Blues/The Blues Come Around	10
51	MGM MGM 405	Dear John/Fly Trouble	10
51	MGM MGM 454	Hey, Good Lookin'/Howlin' At The Moon	10
51	MGM MGM 459	Cold, Cold Heart/I'm A Long Gone Daddy	10
52	MGM MGM 471	I Can't Help It (If I'm Still In Love With You)/Baby, We're Really In Love	10
52	MGM MGM 483	Why Don't You Love Me/I'd Still Want You	10
52	MGM MGM 505	Honky-Tonk Blues/I'm Sorry For You, My Friend	10
52	MGM MGM 527	Long Gone Lonesome Blues/Half As Much	10
52	MGM MGM 553	Nobody's Lonesome For Me/Mind Your Own Business	10
52	MGM MGM 566	Jambalaya (On The Bayou)/Settin' The Woods On Fire	10
53	MGM MGM 585	I'll Never Get Out Of This World Alive/I Could Never Be Ashamed Of You (as Hank Williams & His Drifting Cowboys)	10
53	MGM MGM 609	Kaw-Liga/Take These Chains From My Heart (& His Drifting Cowboys)	10
53	MGM MGM 630	I Saw The Light/ARTHUR 'GUITAR BOOGIE' SMITH: Recitation Sonny Smith: In Memory Of Hank Williams	10
53	MGM MGM 652	Ramblin' Man/I Won't Be Home No More	10
53	MGM MGM 666	My Bucket's Got A Hole In It/Let's Turn Back The Years	10
53	MGM MGM 678	Window Shopping/You Win Again	10
54	MGM MGM 704	Weary Blues (From Waitin')/I Can't Escape From You	10
54	MGM MGM 733	There'll Be No Teardrops Tonight/Crazy Heart	10
54	MGM MGM 768	I'm Satisfied With You/I Ain't Got Nothin' But Time	10
55	MGM MGM 799	I'm Gonna Sing/California Zephyr	12
56	MGM MGM 889	The First Fall Of Snow/Someday You'll Call My Name (withdrawn)	
56	MGM MGM 896	Your Cheatin' Heart/A Teardrop On A Rose	12
56	MGM MGM 921	There's No Room In My Heart (For The Blues)/I Wish I Had A Nickel	12

Hank WILLIAMS

56	MGM MGM 931	Blue Love (In My Heart)/Singing Waterfall	15
57	MGM MGM 942	Low Down Blues/My Sweet Love Ain't Around	15
57	MGM MGM 957	Rootie Tootie/Lonesome Whistle	15
57	MGM MGM 966	Leave Me Alone With The Blues/With Tears In My Eyes	15

SINGLES

53	MGM SP 1016	I'll Never Get Out Of This World Alive/I Could Never Be Ashamed Of You (as Hank Williams & His Drifting Cowboys)	55
53	MGM SP 1034	Kaw-Liga/Take These Chains From My Heart (& His Drifting Cowboys)	50
53	MGM SP 1049	Ramblin' Man/I Won't Be Home No More	45
53	MGM SP 1048	My Bucket's Got A Hole In It/Let's Turn Back The Years	45
54	MGM SP 1067	Weary Blues (From Waitin')/I Can't Escape From You	45
54	MGM SP 1085	There'll Be No Teardrops Tonight/Crazy Heart	45
54	MGM SP 1102	I'm Satisfied With You/I Ain't Got Nothin' But Time	45
56	MGM SP 1163	The First Fall Of Snow/Someday You'll Call My Name (unreleased)	
56	MGM MGM 921	There's No Room In My Heart (For The Blues)/I Wish I Had A Nickel	35
56	MGM MGM 931	Blue Love (In My Heart)/Singing Waterfall	35
57	MGM MGM 942	Low Down Blues/My Sweet Love Ain't Around	35
57	MGM MGM 957	Rootie Tootie/Lonesome Whistle	35
57	MGM MGM 966	Leave Me Alone With The Blues/With Tears In My Eyes	30
66	MGM MGM 1309	You Win Again/I'm So Lonesome I Could Cry	15
66	MGM MGM 1322	Kaw-Liga/Let's Turn Back The Years	10

EPs

54	MGM MGM-EP 512	HANK WILLIAMS AND HIS DRIFTING COWBOYS (company sleeve)	25
54	MGM EPC 7	HANK WILLIAMS (export issue)	30
55	MGM MGM-EP 551	JUST WAITIN' (as Luke The Drifter, company sleeve, later p/s)	20/30
56	MGM MGM-EP 569	I SAW THE LIGHT (No. 1) (company sleeve, later p/s)	15/20
57	MGM MGM-EP 582	HONKY TONKIN'	22
57	MGM MGM-EP 608	I SAW THE LIGHT (No. 2)	22
57	MGM MGM-EP 614	HONKY TONK BLUES	22
58	MGM MGM-EP 639	SONGS FOR A BROKEN HEART (No. 1)	22
58	MGM MGM-EP 649	SONGS FOR A BROKEN HEART (No. 2)	22
58	MGM MGM-EP 675	HANK'S LAMENTS	22
60	MGM MGM-EP 710	THE UNFORGETTABLE HANK WILLIAMS	22
60	MGM MGM-EP 726	THE UNFORGETTABLE HANK WILLIAMS (No. 2)	22
60	MGM MGM-EP 732	THE UNFORGETTABLE HANK WILLIAMS (No. 3)	22
61	MGM MGM-EP 757	HANK WILLIAMS FAVOURITES	22
63	MGM MGM-EP 770	THE AUTHENTIC SOUND OF THE COUNTRY HITS	22

LPs

52	MGM MGM-D 105	HANK WILLIAMS SINGS (10, company sleeve, later p/s)	40/55
53	MGM MGM-D 119	HANK WILLIAMS AS LUKE THE DRIFTER (10", company sleeve, later p/s)	35/45
55	MGM MGM-D 137	HANK WILLIAMS MEMORIAL ALBUM (10")	38
56	MGM MGM-D 144	MOANIN' THE BLUES (10")	45
58	MGM MGM-D 150	SING ME A BLUE SONG (10")	45
58	MGM MGM-D 154	THE IMMORTAL HANK WILLIAMS (10")	45
59	MGM MGM-C 784	THE UNFORGETTABLE HANK WILLIAMS	25
60	MGM MGM-C 811	THE LONESOME SOUND OF HANK WILLIAMS	30
60	MGM MGM-C 834	WAIT FOR THE LIGHT TO SHINE	20
62	MGM MGM-C 893	ON STAGE	20
63	MGM MGM-C 956	THE SPIRIT OF HANK WILLIAMS	20
66	MGM MGM-C 8019	MAY YOU NEVER BE ALONE	18
66	MGM MGM-C 8020	IN MEMORY OF HANK WILLIAMS	18
66	MGM MGM-C 8021	I'M BLUE INSIDE	20
66	MGM MGM-C 8022	LUKE THE DRIFTER	18
66	MGM MGM-C 8023	THE MANY MOODS OF HANK WILLIAMS	18
67	MGM MGM-C(S) 8031	THE LEGEND LIVES ANEW	15
67	MGM MGM-C(S) 8038	MORE HANK WILLIAMS AND STRINGS	15
67	MGM MGM-C 8040	LOVE SONGS, COMEDY AND HYMNS	20
68	MGM MGM-C(S) 8057	I WON'T BE HOME NO MORE	12
68	MGM MGM-C(S) 8075	HANK WILLIAMS AND STRINGS VOL. 3	12
70	MGM MGM-CS 8114	THE ESSENTIAL HANK WILLIAMS	12
74	MGM 2683 046	ON STAGE VOLUMES 1 & 2 (2-LP)	12
76	MGM 2353 128	LIVE AT THE GRAND OL' OPRY	12
79	World Records SM 551-556	THE LEGENDARY HANK WILLIAMS (6-LP box set)	25

(see also Audrey Williams)

HANK WILLIAMS & HANK WILLIAMS Jr.

| 65 | MGM MGM-C 1008 | SINGING TOGETHER (LP) | 20 |

HANK WILLIAMS Jr.

63	MGM MGM 1223	Long Gone Lonesome Blues/Doesn't Anybody Know My Name	6
63	MGM MGM 1242	Goin' Steady With The Blues/Guess What, That's Right, She's Gone	5
64	MGM MGM 1254	Endless Sleep/My Bucket's Got A Hole In It	5
65	MGM MGM 1276	Mule Skinner Blues/I Went To All That Trouble	5
66	MGM MGM 1294	You're Ruinin' My Life/Pecos Jail	5
66	MGM MGM 1299	Cold Cold Heart/Is It That Fun To Heart Someone	5
66	MGM MGM 1316	Standing In The Shadows/It's Written All Over Your Face	5
64	MGM MGM-C 996	YOUR CHEATIN' HEART (LP)	15
67	MGM MGM-C(S) 8049	MY OWN WAY (LP)	15
70	MGM MGM-CS 8116	LIVE AT COBO HALL, DETROIT (LP)	15

(see also Connie Francis)

JABBO WILLIAMS

| 50 | Jazz Collector L 51 | Jab Blues/Pratt City (78) | 8 |

JEANETTE WILLIAMS

| 69 | Action ACT 4534 | Stuff/You Gotta Come Through | 20 |
| 70 | Action ACT 4557 | Hound Dog/I Can Feel A Heartbreak | 20 |

(LITTLE) JERRY WILLIAMS
65	Cameo Parkway C 100	Baby You're My Everything/Just What Do You Plan To Do About It (DJ copy = £120) 85
74	Pye Disco Demand DDS 102	If You Ask Me/Yvonne (as Jerry Williams) 12

(see also Swamp Dogg, Brooks & Jerry)

JIMMY WILLIAMS
65	Atlantic AT 4042	Walking On Air/I'm So Lost 25

JOE WILLIAMS
59	Columbia SCD 2116	Party Blues Parts 1 & 2 5
60	Columbia DB 4560	Somebody/One Is A Lonesome Number. 5
58	Columbia SEG 7810	JOE WILLIAMS WITH COUNT BASIE (EP) 15
59	Columbia SEG 7984	BALLADS AND BLUES COLUMBIA (EP) 10
59	Columbia/Clef SEB 10110	GROOVY JOE WILLIAMS (EP). 10
60	Columbia SEG 8001	EVERYDAY I HAVE THE BLUES (EP) 12
60	Columbia SEG 8016	JOE SINGS THE BLUES (EP). 12
56	London HB-C 1065	JOE WILLIAMS SINGS (10" LP) 25
57	HMV CLP 1109	THE GREATEST (LP). 20
58	Columbia 33SX 1087	A MAN AIN'T SUPPOSED TO CRY (LP) 20
60	Columbia 33SX 1229	JOE WILLIAMS SINGS ABOUT YOU (LP, also stereo SCX 3308) 12/15
60	Columbia 33SX 1253	THAT KIND OF WOMAN (LP, also stereo SCX 3325) 12/15
61	Columbia SX 1392	TOGETHER (LP, with Harry "Sweets" Edison, also stereo SCX3421) 15

(see also Count Basie)

JOHN WILLIAMS
67	Columbia DB 8128	She's That Kind Of Woman/My Ways Are Set 12
67	Columbia DB 8251	Flowers In Your Hair/Can't Find Time For Anything Now. 10
67	Columbia SX 6169	JOHN WILLIAMS (LP) 110

(see also Maureeny Wishfull)

JOHN WILLIAMS
84	Island IS 155	Paul McCartney's Theme From The Honorary Consul/Clara's Theme (p/s) 12

JOHN WILLIAMS ORCHESTRA (U.S.)
66	Stateside S(S)L 10187	HOW TO STEAL A MILLION (LP, soundtrack) 45
83	MCA MCA 70000	E.T. — THE EXTRA TERRESTRIAL (LP, soundtrack, box set with booklet & poster) 40
83	MCA CAC 70000	E.T. — THE EXTRA TERRESTRIAL (cassette, soundtrack, box set with booklet & poster) 20

JOHNNY WILLIAMS
73	Epic S EPC 1547	Put It In Motion/It's So Wonderful 10
73	Contempo C 20	Just A Little Misunderstanding/Your Love Controls My Mind 15
74	Polydor 2001 596	You're Something Kinda Mellow/You Make Me Want To Last Forever 15

KENNETH WILLIAMS
63	Decca DFE 8548	EXTRACTS FROM PIECES OF EIGHT AND ONE OVER THE EIGHT (EP) 10
66	Decca DFE 8671	KENNETH WILLIAMS IN SEASON (EP). 10
67	Decca LK 4856	ON PLEASURE BENT (LP) 18
70	Regal Starline SRS 5034	THE BEST OF RAMBLING SYD RUMPO (LP). 12
70	Decca PA/SPA 64	THE WORLD OF KENNETH WILLIAMS (LP, mono/stereo) 15

(see also Rambling Syd Rumpo, Tony Hancock)

LARRY WILLIAMS
57	London HLN 8472	Short Fat Fannie/High School Dance (78 rpm = £8) 50
58	London HLN 8532	Bony Moronie/You Bug Me Baby (78 rpm = £8). 30
58	London HLU 8604	Dizzy Miss Lizzy/Slow Down (78rpm = £25) 40
59	London HLU 8844	She Said "Yeah"/Bad Boy (78 rpm = £30). 30
60	London HLU 8911	I Can't Stop Loving You/Steal A Little Kiss (78 rpm = £50). 30
60	London HLM 9053	Baby, Baby/Get Ready 30
65	Sue WI 371	Strange/Call On Me 40
65	Sue WI 381	Turn On Your Lovelight/Dizzy Miss Lizzy 40
68	MGM MGM 1447	Shake Your Body Girl/Love, I Can't Seem To Find It. 20
59	London RE-U 1213	LARRY WILLIAMS (EP). 125
65	Sue ILP 922	LARRY WILLIAMS ON STAGE (LP) 80
70s	Specialty SNTF 5025	SLOW DOWN (LP). 20

LARRY WILLIAMS & JOHNNY 'GUITAR' WATSON
65	Decca F 12151	Sweet Little Baby/Slow Down 20
67	Columbia DB 8140	Mercy, Mercy, Mercy/A Quitter Never Wins (DJ copy = £175) 75
76	Epic EPC 4421	Too Late/Two For The Price Of One 20
65	Decca LK 4691	THE LARRY WILLIAMS SHOW (LP, with Stormsville Shakers) 80

(see also Johnny 'Guitar' Watson, Philip Goodhand-Tait [& Stormville Shakers])

LEONA WILLIAMS
74	Fountain FB 303	LEONA WILLIAMS AND HER DIXIE BAND (LP) 12

LEW WILLIAMS
50s	London (no cat. no.)	Cat Talk (1-sided, orange label demo-only) 50

LLOYD WILLIAMS
66	Doctor Bird DB 1051	Sad World/TOMMY McCOOK'S BAND: A Little Bit Of Heaven. 30
68	Treasure Isle TI 7029	Funky Beat/Goodbye Baby 22
68	Doctor Bird DB 1135	Wonderful World (with Tommy McCook)/TOMMY McCOOK SUPERSONICS: Mad Mad World 28
70	Bamboo BAM 41	I'm In Love With You/Little Girl 18

LORETTA WILLIAMS
66	Atlantic 584 032	Baby Cakes/I'm Missing You 40

MINT VALUE £

LUCINDA WILLIAMS
89	Rough Trade 130	LUCINDA WILLIAMS (LP, with inner lyric bag)	12

LUTHER WILLIAMS ORCHESTRA
61	Limbo XL 101	Early In The Morning/Little Vilma	5
61	Melodisc MLP 12-125	TROPICAL RHYTHMS OF JAMAICA (LP)	15

MARY LOU WILLIAMS
53	London L 1174	Laughing Rag/Rag Of Rags (78)	6
54	Felsted ED 82011	Autumn In New York/En Ce Tempa-La (78)	6
64	Sue WI 311	Chuck-a-Lunk Jug (Parts 1 & 2)	25
55	Vogue EPV 1042	DON CARLOS MEETS MARY LOU WILLIAMS (EP)	12
56	Parlophone GEP 8567	AT THE PIANO (EP)	10
56	Columbia SEG 7608	MARY LOU WILLIAMS (EP)	12
55	Esquire EP 66	MARY LOU WILLIAMS QUARTET (EP)	12
53	Vogue LDE 022	PLAYS IN LONDON (10" LP)	22
54	Esquire 20-026	PIANO PANORAMA (10" LP)	22
55	Felsted EDL 87012	IN PARIS (10" LP)	22

MASON WILLIAMS
68	Warner Bros WB 7190	Classical Gas/Long Time Blues	8

MAURICE WILLIAMS (& ZODIACS)
60	Top Rank JAR 526	Stay/Do You Believe (as Maurice Williams & Zodiacs)	22
61	Top Rank JAR 550	I Remember/Always	18
61	Top Rank JAR 563	Come Along/Do I	30
61	Top Rank JKP 3006	STAY WITH MAURICE WILLIAMS & THE ZODIACS (EP)	175

(see also Gladiolas)

MIKE WILLIAMS
66	Atlantic 584 027	Lonely Soldier/If This Isn't Love	20

MOON WILLIAMS
73	DJM DJS10283	Forever Kind Of Love/All For YoU	300

OTIS WILLIAMS & HIS CHARMS
55	Parlophone CMSP 36	Ivory Tower/In Paradise (export issue)	325
56	Parlophone MSP 6239	Ivory Tower/In Paradise (78 rpm, R 4175 = £15)	500
56	Parlophone R 4210	One Night Only/It's All Over (78 rpm = £25)	375
57	Parlophone R 4293	Walkin' After Midnight/I'm Waiting Just For You (78 rpm = £55)	500
58	Parlophone R 4495	The Secret/Don't Wake Up The Kids (78 rpm = £75)	80
62	Parlophone R 4860	The Secret/Two Hearts	65

(see also Charms)

PAT WILLIAMS ORCHESTRA
74	Capitol CL 15797	Police Story Theme/Magician Theme	6

PAUL WILLIAMS
73	Sonet SNTF 654	DELTA BLUES SINGER (LP)	15

PAUL WILLIAMS
74	A&M AMS 7125	That's What Friends Are For/Born To Fly	8
74	A&M AMLS 63653	PHANTOM OF THE PARADISE (LP, soundtrack)	20

PAUL WILLIAMS
70s	Parry Music Library PML 168 AQUARIUS (LP)		18

PAUL WILLIAMS BIG ROLL BAND/SET
64	Columbia DB 7421	Gin House/Rockin' Chair (as Paul Williams Big Roll Band)	22
65	Columbia DB 7768	The Many Faces Of Love/Jumpback (as Paul Williams & Zoot Money Band)	25
68	Decca F 12844	My Sly Sadie/Stop The Wedding (as Paul Williams Set)	15

(see also Zoot Money's Big Roll Band, John Mayall's Bluesbreakers, Alan Price [Set], Juicy Lucy)

PAULINE WILLIAMS
73	Explosion EX 2084	My Island/My Island (Version)	5

POOR JOE WILLIAMS
60	Collector JEN 3	A MAN SINGS THE BLUES (EP)	18
60	Collector JEN 4	A MAN SINGS THE BLUES VOL. 2 (EP)	18

(see also Big Joe Williams)

RANNY/RONNY WILLIAMS
69	Bullet BU 426	Summer Place (with Hippy Boys)/Big Boy	10
69	Gas GAS 120	Throw Me Corn (as Ronny Williams)/HIPPY BOYS: Temptation	10
69	Unity UN 526	Ambitious Beggar/Pepper Seed	16
70	Punch PH 32	Smile/Musical I.D.	10

(see also Winston Reed)

RITA WILLIAMS
58	Oriole CB 1417	Looking For Someone To Love/Love Me Forever (78 rpm = £8)	12

ROBBIE WILLIAMS
98	Chrysalis CDCHSS 5080	Let Me Entertain You/Full Monty Medley: Make Me Smile (Come Up And See Me/You Can Leave Your Hat On/Land Of A 1000 Dances)/I Wouldn't Normally Do This Kind Of Thing)/I Am The Resurrection (CD)	8

PROMOS
96	RCA FREELX 1	Freedom '96 (Radio Edit)/Freedom '96 (Full Length Version) (jukebox issue)	8
96	RCA PROPERDJ 1	Freedom '96 (Radio Edit)/Freedom '96 (Full Length Version) (CD, test pressing, no text on disc)	20
97	Chrysalis CHSLH 5055	Old Before I Die/Making Plans For Nigel (jukebox issue)	8
97	Chrysalis CDCHSDJ 5055	Old Before I Die (CD, withdrawn, different sleeve)	15
97	Chrysalis CHSLH 5063	Lazy Days/Teenage Millionaire (jukebox issue)	8
97	Chrysalis CHSLH 5068	South Of The Border/Cheap Love Song (jukebox issue)	8
97	Chrysalis 12CHSDJ 5068	South Of The Border (remixes) (12", stickered black sleeve)	10

97	Chrysalis 12CHSDJS 5068	South Of The Border (remixes) (12", stickered white sleeve) 10
97	Chrysalis CDCHSDJ 5072	Angels (Edit) (CD) 8
98	Chrysalis 12CHSDJD 5080	Let Me Entertain You (remixes) (12", double-pack)......................... 15
98	Chrysalis/HMV HMV 78	Millennium/ROYAL ALBERT HALL ORCHESTRA: Nimrod, Enigma Variations
		Op. 36 (78rpm, promo only, 1,000 only, numbered p/s) 40
99	Chrysalis CHSLH 5107	Strong/Antmusic (jukebox issue) 8
99	Chrysalis CDCHSLH 5112	It's Only Us/She's The One (jukebox issue)................................. 8
00	Chrysalis CDCHSLH 5118	Rock DJ/She's The One (jukebox issue) 8
00	EMI CDLIC 173	United/United (Apollo 440 Remix)/CD-ROM Interview
		(CD, Pepsi freebie, card sleeve) 8
97	Chrysalis RWEPK 01	THE EPK CD (interview and excerpts from LIFE THRU A LENS).............. 25
98	Chrysalis CDPP 080	I'VE BEEN EXPECTING YOU (metal case with album CD, interview disc in
		digipak, EPK video in p/s, gold press release and photos) 200

(see also Take That)

ROBERT PETE WILLIAMS
63	'77' LA 12-17	THOSE PRISON BLUES (LP) 30
70s	Blues Beacon 1932 101ST	SUGAR FARM (LP) 22
72	Saydisc AMS 2002	ROBERT PETE WILLIAMS (LP) 20
73	Sonet SNTF 649	LEGACY OF THE BLUES (LP) 15

ROBERT PETE WILLIAMS/ROOSEVELT SYKES
| 67 | '77' LEU 12-50 | BLUES FROM THE BOTTOM (LP) .... 20 |

(see also Roosevelt Sykes)

ROBERT WILLIAMS
| 90 | Blast First FU8 | CHROME, FIRE AND SMOKE (2-LP, picture disc, 1000 only)............... 28 |

ROGER WILLIAMS
55	London HLU 8214	Autumn Leaves/Take Care 12
56	London HLU 8341	Two Different Worlds (with Jane Morgan)/I'll Always Walk With You 12
57	London HLU 8379	Anastasia/A Serenade For Joy 10
57	London HLR 8422	Almost Paradise/For The First Time I've Fallen In Love..................... 7
57	London HLR 8516	Till/Big Town 7
58	London HLR 8572	Arrivederci Roma/The Sentimental Touch 6
58	London HLR 8643	Indiscreet/Young And Warm And Wonderful 6
58	London HLR 8690	Near You/The Merry Widow Waltz 6
58	London HLR 8758	The World Outside (Warsaw Concerto)/Piano Concerto No. 1 (Tchaikovsky) 5
59	London HLR 8820	The Key To The Kingdom/Dearer Than Dear 5
59	London HLR 8857	Mockin' Bird Hill/Memories Are Made Of This (78 rpm = £8) 6
59	London HLR 8986	Mary's Boy Child/O Mio Babbino Caro (Oh! My Beloved Father) (78 rpm = £12).. 6
57	London HA-R 2057	SONGS OF THE FABULOUS FIFTIES VOL. 1 (LP)........................... 12
57	London HA-R 2058	SONGS OF THE FABULOUS FIFTIES VOL. 2 (LP)........................... 12
58	London HA-R 2089	THE BOY NEXT DOOR (LP) 12
58	London HA-R 2096	SONGS OF THE FABULOUS FORTIES VOL. 1 (LP, stereo SAH-R 6035)..... 12
58	London HA-R 2097	SONGS OF THE FABULOUS FORTIES VOL. 2 (LP, stereo SAH-R 6036)..... 12

(see also Jane Morgan)

SAM WILLIAMS
| 78 | Grapevine GRP 116 | Love Slipped Thru' My Fingers/TOWANDA BARNES: You Don't Mean It .... 25 |

SMITTY WILLIAMS
| 62 | MGM MGM 1167 | The Cure/Oh Seymour .... 7 |

SONNY WILLIAMS
| 59 | London HLD 8931 | Bye Bye Baby Goodbye/Lucky Linda (78 rpm = £20) .... 40 |

SYLVIAN WILLIAMS
| 69 | Big Shot BI 532 | Sweeter Than Honey/Son Of Reggae .... 35 |
| 69 | Big Shot BI 533 | This Old Man/When Morning Comes .... 7 |

TEX WILLIAMS
54	Brunswick 05327	River Of No Return/Dawn In The Meadow 12
54	Brunswick 05341	This Ole House (with Rex Allen)/They Were Doin' The Mambo.............. 12
55	Brunswick 05393	Money/If You'd Believe Me 12
56	Brunswick 05516	Be Sure You're Right (And Then Go Ahead)/Old Betsy 7
57	Brunswick 05684	Talkin' To The Blues/Every Night (with Anita Kerr Singers)................. 12
60	Top Rank JAR 330	The Keeper Of Boothill/Bummin' Around................................. 10
55	Brunswick OE 9147	ALL THE GREATS (EP)... 15
61	Capitol (S)T 1463	SMOKE, SMOKE, SMOKE! (LP).. 18

(see also Roberta Lee, Rex Allen)

TONY WILLIAMS
61	Reprise RS 20019	Sleepless Nights/Mandolino Mandolino 10
61	Reprise RS 20030	My Prayer/Miracle 10
63	Philips BF 1282	How Come/When I Had You 100
60	Mercury MMC 14027	A GIRL IS A GIRL IS A GIRL (LP).. 40
61	Reprise R 6001/	SINGS HIS GREATEST HITS (LP, mono/stereo) 20/30
	ST R9 6006	

(see also Platters, Linda Hayes)

TONY WILLIAMS' LIFETIME
69	Polydor 583 574	EMERGENCY! (2-LP, gatefold sleeve)................................... 30
70	Polydor 2425 019	TURN IT OVER (LP).. 22
71	Polydor 2425 065	EGO (LP) 15

(see also Lifetime, John McLaughlin)

WILLY WILLIAMS
| 81 | Black Roots BR 017 | Come Mek We Rally/YABBY YOU: Thirty Pieces Of Silver (12") .... 45 |

MINT VALUE £

WINSTON WILLIAMS
70	Jackpot JP 733	D.J.'s Choice/SLIM SMITH: Can't Do Without It	
		(B-side actually titled "Lesson/Story Of Love" by Uniques)	12
70	Jackpot JP 743	The People's Choice/BOBBY JAMES: Let Me Go Girl	12
71	Jackpot JP 757	Love Version/SLIM SMITH: Ball Of Confusion	12

BOBBY WILLIAMSON
54	HMV 7MC 26	Sh-Boom/Love March (export issue)	20

CLAUDE WILLIAMSON
54	Capitol KC 65003	All God's Chillun Got Rhythm/Woody 'N' You	7

DUDLEY WILLIAMSON
67	Doctor Bird DB 1117	Coming On The Scene/Anything You Want	35

(see also Dudley & Attractions)

MARK WILLIAMSON
70s	Myrrh MYR 1154	MISSING IN ACTION (LP)	15

ROBIN WILLIAMSON
72	Island HELP 2	MYRRH (LP)	18
78	Criminal STEAL 4	AMERICAN STONEHENGE (LP)	12

(see also Incredible String Band, Vashti Bunyan)

SONNY BOY WILLIAMSON (I)/BIG BILL BROONZY
65	RCA Victor RD 7685	BIG BILL BROONZY/SONNY BOY WILLIAMSON (LP)	60

SONNY BOY WILLIAMSON (I)
69	Matchbox SDR 169	SONNY BOY AND HIS PALS (LP)	25
70	RCA Intl. INTS 1088	BLUEBIRD BLUES (LP)	15

SONNY BOY WILLIAMSON (II)
63	Pye International 7N 25191	Help Me/Bye Bye Bird	20
64	Pye International 7N 25268	Lonesome Cabin/The Goat	20
65	Sue WI 365	No Nights By Myself/Boppin' With Sonny Boy	40
66	Chess CRS 8030	Bring It On Home/Down Child	20
66	Blue Horizon 45-1008	From The Bottom/Empty Bedroom	80
64	Pye Intl. NEP 44037	SONNY BOY WILLIAMSON (EP)	25
65	Chess CRE 6001	HELP ME (EP)	35
66	Chess CRE 6013	IN MEMORIAM (EP)	35
66	Chess CRE 6018	REAL FOLK BLUES VOL. 2 (EP)	30
64	Pye Intl. NPL 28036	DOWN AND OUT BLUES (LP)	50
64	Storyville SLP 158	PORTRAITS IN BLUES, VOL. 4 (LP)	35
65	Chess CRL 4510	IN MEMORIAM (LP)	45
66	Storyville SLP 170	THE BLUES OF SONNY BOY WILLIAMSON (LP)	30
66	Fontana 670 158	PORTRAITS IN BLUES, VOL. 4 (LP, reissue)	22
67	Storyville 671 170	THE BLUES OF SONNY BOY WILLIAMSON (LP, reissue)	25
68	Marmalade 607/608 004	DON'T SEND ME NO FLOWERS (LP, with Brian Auger & Jimmy Page)	65
74	Rarity RLP 1	THE LAST SESSIONS — 1963 (LP)	25

(see also Ottilie Patterson)

SONNY BOY WILLIAMSON (II) & YARDBIRDS
65	Fontana TL 5277	SONNY BOY WILLIAMSON & THE YARDBIRDS (LP)	160
68	Fontana SFJL 960	SONNY BOY WILLIAMSON & THE YARDBIRDS (LP, reissue, different sleeve)	30
71	Philips 6435 011	SONNY BOY WILLIAMSON & THE YARDBIRDS (LP, 2nd reissue)	15

(see also Yardbirds, Brian Auger)

STU WILLIAMSON
56	London Jazz LZ-N 14030	SAPPHIRE (10" LP)	20

WILLIE (Francis) & LLOYD (Lindsay)
71	Camel CA 80	Marcus Is Alive/GLADIATORS: Freedom Train	12

(see also Willie Francis)

WILLIE & WHEELS
77	ABC ABC 4184	Skateboard Craze/Do What You Did (p/s)	15

(see also P.F. Sloan, Grass Roots, Fantastic Baggys')

FOY WILLING & RIDERS OF THE PURPLE SAGE
59	Columbia SEG 7834	COWBOY NUMBER 1 (EP)	10
59	Columbia SEG 7855	COWBOY NUMBER 2 (EP)	10

DORIS WILLINGHAM
69	Jay Boy BOY 1	You Can't Do That/Lost Again	20

CHUCK WILLIS
57	London HLE 8444	C.C. Rider/Ease The Pain (78 rpm = £35)	80
57	London HLE 8489	That Train Has Gone/Love Me Cherry (78 rpm = £30)	75
58	London HLE 8595	Betty And Dupree/My Crying Eyes (78 rpm = £30)	75
58	London HLE 8635	What Am I Living For/Hang Up My Rock And Roll Shoes (78 rpm = £35)	50
58	London HL 7039	What Am I Living For/Hang Up My Rock And Roll Shoes (export issue)	30
59	London HLE 8818	My Life/Thunder And Lightning (78 rpm = £45)	45
59	Fontana TFE 17138	CHUCK WILLIS WAILS (EP)	275
65	Atlantic ATL 5003	I REMEMBER CHUCK WILLIS (LP)	85
69	Atlantic 588 145	I REMEMBER CHUCK WILLIS (LP, reissue)	22

DOUG WILLIS
97	Z Records ZEDD 12029	Get Your Own (12")	10

HAL WILLIS
68	President PT 197	The Lumberjack/Klondike Mike	12

LLOYD WILLIS
70	Pressure Beat PR 5502	Mad Rooster (Parts 1 & 2)/As Far As I Can See	
		(actually "The Wicked Must Survive" by Reggae Boys)	15
70	Unity UN 543	Ivan Hitler The Conqueror/The Splice	18

(see also Dynamic Gang, Urie Aldridge)

RALPH WILLIS
54	Esquire 10-370	Lazy Woman Blues/Goodbye Blues (78)	20
54	Esquire 10-380	Old Home Blues/Salty Dog (78)	20
61	Esquire EP 241	RALPH WILLIS (EP)	40

SLIM WILLIS
65	R&B MRB 5004	Running Around/No Feeling For You	28

TIMMY WILLIS
72	United Artists UP 35352	Mr. Soul Satisfaction/I'm Wondering	10
73	Epic EPC 1309	Give Me A Little Sign/Don't Want To Set Me Free	15

WILLIS BROTHERS
67	London HLB 10132	Bob/Show Her Lots Of Gold	8
65	London HAB 8235	GIVE ME FORTY ACRES (LP)	15
66	London HAB 8295	THE WILD SIDE OF LIFE (LP)	15

NEVILLE WILLOUGHBY
72	Duke DU 140	Wheel And Tun Me/Hey Mama	5

(see also Neville, Whistling Willie)

WILLOWS
56	London HLU 8290	Church Bells May Ring/Baby Tell Me (78 rpm = £140)	750

(see also Tony Middleton)

BOB WILLS & HIS TEXAS PLAYBOYS
51	MGM MGM 455	'Tater Pie/Ida Red Likes The Boogie (78)	10
53	MGM MGM 613	Snatchin' And Grabbin'/I Want To Be Wanted (78)	10

BOB WILLS with TOMMY DUNCAN
60	London HL 7102	Heart To Heart Talk/What's The Matter With The Mill (export issue)	20

MICK WILLS
88	Woronzow WOO 9	FERN HILL (LP)	18
97	Acme AC 8013LP	THE MAGIC GARDEN (LP, foldover gatefold sleeve in poly bag)	12

VIOLA WILLS
68	President PT 108	Lost Without The Love Of My Guy/I Got Love	15
68	President PT 150	Together Forever/Don't Kiss Me Hello And Mean Goodbye	15
68	President PT 152	I've Got To Have All Of You/Night Scene	8
68	President PT 154	You're Out Of My Mind/Any Time	20
74	Goodear EAR 103	Run To The Nearest Exit/Day In The Life Of A Woman	10
74	Goodear EARLH 5002	SOFT CENTRES (LP)	15

WILMER & DUKES
68	Action ACT 4500	Give Me One More Chance/Get It	20

ADA WILSON
79	Ellie Jay EJSP 9288	In The Quiet Of My Room/I'm In Control Here (p/s)	12
80	Barn BARN 012	In The Quiet Of My Room/I'm In Control Here (reissue, no p/s)	6

(see also Strangeways)

AL WILSON
68	Liberty LBF 15044	Do What You Gotta Do/Now I Know What Love Is	30
68	Liberty LBF 15121	The Snake/Who Could Be Lovin' You	45
69	Liberty LBF 15236	Shake Me Wake Me/I Stand Accused	8
69	Liberty LBF 15257	Lodi/By The Time I Get To Phoenix	8
75	Bell BLL 1436	The Snake/Willoughby Brook	10
69	Liberty LBS 83173	SEARCHING FOR THE DOLPHINS (LP)	25
74	Bell BELLS 247	LA LA PEACE SONG (LP)	20

BRIAN WILSON
66	Capitol CL 15438	Caroline, No/Summer Means New Love	30
88	Sire W 7814 CD	Love And Mercy (LP Version)/One For The Boys (LP Version)/ He Couldn't Get His Poor Old Body To Move (3" CD)	15
88	Sire W 7787 CD	Night Time (LP Version)/One For The Boys/Being With The One You Love (3" CD)	15
88	Sire W 7814 B	LOVE AND MERCY (7" box set, with interview and postcards, limited edition)	50
98	Giant/Mojo 74321 58760 2	INTERVIEW/IMAGINATION (promo CD, with Peter Buck)	40
04	Nonesuch 7559 79869 7	Wonderful/Wind Chimes (three different coloured vinyl – blue, yellow,green)	15
04	Nonesuch 7559 79885 7	Good Vibrations/Our Prayer/Good Vibrations (live) (p/s) (limited edition)	8
05	Nonesuch 7559 79895 7	Our Prayer (Freeform Reform) (10" 1-sided clear vinyl in clear plastic sleeve)	10

(see also Beach Boys, Date With Soul, American Spring)

BRIAN WILSON & MIKE LOVE
67	Capitol CL 15513	Gettin' Hungry/Devoted To You (as Brian Wilson & Mike Love)	25

CARL WILSON
81	Caribou CRB 84840	CARL WILSON (LP, with lyric insert)	15
82	Caribou CRB 25225	YOUNGBLOOD (LP, with lyric insert)	15

(see also Beach Boys)

CLIVE WILSON
64	R&B JB 144	Mango Tree/Midnight In Chicago	22

DELROY WILSON
63	Island WI 097	Naughty People/I Shall Not Remove	25
63	Island WI 103	One, Two, Three/Back Biter	20
63	Island WI 116	You Bend My Love/Can't You See	20
63	R&B JB 108	Lion Of Judah/Joe Liges	30
63	R&B JB 128	Prince Pharoah/Don't Believe Him	30
63	R&B JB 132	Squeeze Your Toe/Sugar Pie	28
64	Black Swan WI 405	Spit In The Sky/Voodoo Man	25
64	Black Swan WI 420	Goodbye/Treat Me Good	20
64	R&B JB 148	Lover Mouth/Every Mouth Must Be Fed	25

MINT VALUE £

64	R&B JB 168	Sammy Dead/CYNTHIA & ARCHIE: Every Beat	20
65	Island WI 205	Pick Up The Pieces/Oppression	18
66	Doctor Bird DB 1022	Give Me A Chance/(It's) Impossible	25
66	Island WI 3013	Dancing Mood/SOUL BROTHERS: More And More	30
67	Island WI 3033	Riding For A Fall/Got To Change Your Ways	25
67	Island WI 3037	Ungrateful Baby/ROY RICHARDS: Hopeful Village Ska	25
67	Island WI 3039	Close To Me/SOUL BROTHERS: Hi-Life	25
67	Island WI 3050	Get Ready/ROY RICHARDS: Port-O-Jam	30
67	Studio One SO 2009	Won't You Come Home Baby/PETER & HORTENSE: I've Been Lonely	30+
67	Studio One SO 2014	Mother Word/HEPTONES: Fat Girl	20
67	Studio One SO 2019	Never Conquer/Run For Your Life	25
67	Studio One SO 2031	I'm Not A King/HEPTONES: Take Me (B-side actually by Soul Vendors)	35
68	Island WI 3099	This Old Heart Of Mine/GLEN ADAMS: Grab A Girl	42
68	Island WI 3127	Once Upon A Time/I Want To Love You (B-side actually with Stranger Cole)	25
68	Coxsone CS 7064	True Believer/MARSHALL WILLIAMS: College Girl	25
68	Studio One SO 2040	Mr. D.J./HEPTONES: Tripe Girl	60+
68	Studio One SO 2046	Rain From The Skies/How Can I Love Someone	25
68	Studio One SO 2057	Feel Good All Over/I Like The Way You Walk	25
69	Studio One SO 2074	Easy Snappin'/WEBBER SISTERS: Come On	25
69	High Note HS 011	Put Yourself In My Place/It Hurts	12
69	High Note HS 015	I'm The One Who Loves You/AFROTONES: If I'm In A Corner	12
69	High Note HS 022	Your Number One/I've Tried My Best	20
69	High Note HS 028	Good To Me/What Do You Want Me To Do	12
69	Camel CA 15	Sad Mood (actually by Ken Parker)/STRANGER COLE: Give It To Me	12
70	Trojan TR 7740	Show Me The Way/BEVERLEY'S ALLSTARS: Version	10
70	Trojan TR 7769	Gave You My Love/BEVERLEY'S ALLSTARS: Version	10
70	Summit SUM 8503	Got To Get Away/BEVERLEY'S ALLSTARS: Version	8
70	Joe JRS 11	Don't Play That Song (with Reaction)/BOSS ALL STARS: Just One Look	8
70	Unity UN 559	Drink Wine, Everybody/Someone To Call My Own	6
71	Smash SMA 2317	I Am Trying/COLLINS ALLSTARS: Version	6
71	Smash SMA 2318	Satisfaction/Satisfaction Version (B-side with Alton Ellis)	7
71	Smash SMA 2323	What It Was/LLOYD CLARKE: Chicken Thief	7
71	Jackpot JP 763	Better Must Come/BUNNY LEE'S ALLSTARS: Better Must Come — Version	10
71	Jackpot JP 769	Cool Operator/I'm Yours	10
71	Jackpot JP 770	Try Again/AGGROVATORS: Try Again — Version	10
71	Jackpot JP 780	Keep Your Love Strong/Nice To Be Near	10
71	Jackpot JP 781	Peace And Love/JEFF BARNES: Who's Your Brother	12
71	Banana BA 333	Just Because Of You/I Love You Madly	10
72	Banana BA 367	You Keep On Running (& U Roy)/LARRY'S ALL STARS: Running Version	15
72	Bullet BU 520	Hear Come The Heartaches (actually "Here Come The Heartaches")/You'll Be Sorry	8
72	Jackpot JP 792	Who Cares/HUGH ROY JUNIOR: Who Cares — Version	10
72	Jackpot JP 795	The Same Old Song/Stay By Me	10
72	Jackpot JP 804	Cheer Up/Loving You	10
72	Spur SP 2	Adis Ababa/KEITH HUDSON: Rudie Hot Stuff	50+
73	Downtown DT 501	Pretty Girl/JOE GIBBS & PROFESSIONALS: Face Girl	8
73	Grape GR 3038	Can I Change My Mind/Just Because	10
73	Green Door GD 4060	Ain't That Peculiar/What Is Man	8
73	Smash SMA 2336	Trying To Wreck My Life/Live And Learn	10
74	Faith FA 006	Love Got Me Doing Things/PHIL PRATT ALL STARS: Version	5
74	Harry J. HJ 6667	What Will Happen To The Youth Of Today/Baby Don't Do It	5
75	Fab FAB 266	Dancing Mood/Version	12
64	R&B JBL 1112	I SHALL NOT REMOVE (LP)	200
68	Coxsone CSL 8016	GOOD ALL OVER (LP)	100+
72	Trojan TRLS 44	BETTER MUST COME (LP)	32
73	Big Shot BILP 102	CAPTIVITY (LP)	40

(see also Hortense & Delroy, Joe Liges, Roy Richards, Soul Brothers, Dennis Alcapone, Stranger Cole, Uniques, Soul Vendors)

DENNIS WILSON (& RUMBO)

70	Stateside SS 2184	Sound Of Free/Lady (as Dennis Wilson & Rumbo)	70
77	Caribou CRB 5663	River Song/Farewell My Friend	15
77	Caribou CRB 81672	PACIFIC OCEAN BLUE (LP, gatefold sleeve, some on blue vinyl)	75/80

(see also Beach Boys)

DOYLE WILSON with JIMMY LACEY & BAND

58	Vogue Pop V 9117	Hey-Hey/You're The One For Me (78 rpm = £150)	600

EDDIE WILSON

62	Oriole CB 1780	Dankeschoen-Bitteschoen-Wiederschoen/Rheinlaender Waltz	7

EDDIE WILSON

69	Action ACT 4536	Shing-A-Ling Stroll/Don't Kick The Teenager Around	25
70	Action ACT 4555	Get Out On The Street/Must Be Love	20

EDITH WILSON

60s	Fountain FB 302	1921-1922 WITH JOHNNY DUNN'S JAZZHOUNDS (LP)	15

ERNEST ('SOUL') WILSON

67	Studio One SO 2032	Money Worries/SOUL VENDORS: Pe Da Pa	28
68	Studio One SO 2058	If I Were A Carpenter/SOUL VENDORS: Frozen Soul	42
68	Coxsone CS 7044	Storybook Children (as Ernest 'Soul' Wilson)/LITTLE FREDDIE: After Laughter (B-side actually by Freddie McGregor)	28
68	Coxsone CS 7059	Undying Love/SOUL VENDORS: Tropic Isle	28
69	Amalgamated AMG 837	Private Number/GLEN ADAMS: She's So Fine	20
69	Crab CRAB 9	Private Number/Another Chance	12
69	Crab CRAB 17	Freedom Train/STRANGER COLE: You Should Never Have To Come	12
69	Crab CRAB 21	Just Once In My Life (with Freddy)/GLEN ADAMS: Mighty Organ	20
76	Fab FAB 280	Storybook Children/SOUND DIMENSION: Version	10

(see also Tinga & Ernest)

ERNEST WILSON & FREDDY (McGregor)
70	Crab CRAB 45	Sentimental Man/It's A Lie	8
70	Unity UN 564	Love Makes The World Go Round/Love (Version Instrumental)	8
71	Gas GAS 168	What You Gonna Do About It/DOBBY DOBSON: Halfway To Paradise	8
71	Jackpot JP 765	Let Them Talk/The Truth Hurts	6

FRANK WILSON
79	Tamla Motown TMG 1170	Do I Love You (Indeed I Do)/Sweeter As The Days Go By (DJ copy in p/s £125)	75

FRANK WILSON & CAVALIERS
64	Fontana TF 505	Last Kiss/That's How Much I Love You	18

GADDY WILSON
60	Philips PB 980	Nothin'At Night/I'll Never Be Myself Again (78)	12

GARLAND WILSON
53	HMV 7M 122	Just You, Just Me/Sweet Georgia Brown	6

JACK WILSON QUARTET
64	London HA-K/SH-K 8170	THE JACK WILSON QUARTET (LP, featuring Roy Ayers)	20
66	Vocalion LAE-L 603	RAMBLIN' (LP)	20

(see also Roy Ayers)

JACKIE WILSON
78s
57	Vogue Coral Q 72290	Reet Petite/By The Light Of The Silvery Moon	10
57	Coral Q 72290	Reet Petite/By The Light Of The Silvery Moon (2nd pressing)	10
58	Coral Q 72306	To Be Loved/Come Back To Me	10
58	Coral Q 72332	I'm Wanderin'/As Long As I Live	18
58	Coral Q 72338	We Have Love/Singing A Song	18
58	Coral Q 72347	Lonely Teardrops/In The Blue Of The Evening	40
59	Coral Q 72366	That's Why/Love Is All	40
59	Coral Q 72372	I'll Be Satisfied/Ask	50
59	Coral Q 72380	You Better Know It/Never Go Away	75
59	Coral Q 72384	Talk That Talk/Only You, Only Me	80

45s
57	Vogue Coral Q 72290	Reet Petite/By The Light Of The Silvery Moon	25
57	Coral Q 72290	Reet Petite/By The Light Of The Silvery Moon (2nd pressing)	15
58	Coral Q 72306	To Be Loved/Come Back To Me	25
58	Coral Q 72332	I'm Wanderin'/As Long As I Live	25
58	Coral Q 72338	We Have Love/Singing A Song	22
58	Coral Q 72347	Lonely Teardrops/In The Blue Of The Evening	25
59	Coral Q 72366	That's Why/Love Is All	20
59	Coral Q 72366	That's Why/Love Is All (mispressing, B-side plays "You Better Know It")	18
59	Coral Q 72372	I'll Be Satisfied/Ask	18
59	Coral Q 72380	You Better Know It/Never Go Away	18
59	Coral Q 72384	Talk That Talk/Only You, Only Me	18
60	Coral Q 72393	Doggin' Around/The Magic Of Love	18
60	Coral Q 72407	A Woman, A Lover, A Friend/(You Were Made For) All My Love	15
60	Coral Q 72412	Alone At Last/Am I The Man	15
61	Coral Q 72421	The Tear Of The Year/My Empty Arms (withdrawn B-side, demos only)	65
61	Coral Q 72424	The Tear Of The Year/Your One And Only Love	15
61	Coral Q 72430	Please Tell Me Why/(So Many) Cute Little Girls	15
61	Coral Q 72434	I'm Comin' On Back To You/Lonely Life	15
61	Coral Q 72439	You Don't Know What It Means/Years From Now	15
61	Coral Q 72444	The Way I Am/My Heart Belongs To Only You	15
62	Coral Q 72450	The Greatest Hurt/There'll Be No Next Time	15
62	Coral Q 72453	Sing (And Tell The Blues So Long)/I Found Love (B-side with Linda Hopkins)	15
62	Coral Q 72454	I Just Can't Help It/My Tale Of Woe	15
63	Coral Q 72460	Baby Workout/What Good Am I Without You	15
63	Coral Q 72464	Shake A Hand/Say I Do (as Jackie Wilson & Linda Hopkins)	15
63	Coral Q 72465	Shake! Shake! Shake!/He's A Fool	15
63	Coral Q 72467	Baby Get It/The New Breed	15
64	Coral Q 72474	Big Boss Line/Be My Girl	15
64	Coral Q 72476	Squeeze Her — Tease Her (But Love Her)/Give Me Back My Heart	15
65	Coral Q 72480	Yes Indeel/When The Saints Go Marching In (with Linda Hopkins)	18
65	Coral Q 72481	No Pity (In The Naked City)/I'm So Lonely (DJ copy = £45)	20
65	Coral Q 72482	I Believe I'll Love On/Lonely Teardrops	15
66	Coral Q 72484	To Make A Big Man Cry/Be My Love (DJ copy = £45)	20
66	Coral Q 72487	Whispers/The Fairest Of Them All)DJ copy = £85)	40
67	Coral Q 72493	(Your Love Keeps Lifting Me) Higher And Higher/I'm The One To Do It (DJ = £85)	20
67	Coral Q 72496	Since You Showed Me How To Be Happy/The Who-Who Song (DJ copy = £75)	30
68	MCA MU 1014	For Your Precious Love/Uptight (Everything's Alright) (with Count Basie)	10
68	Decca AD 1008	For Your Precious Love/Uptight (Everything's Alright) (export issue)	25
69	MCA Soul Bag BAG 2	(Your Love Keeps Lifting Me) Higher And Higher/Whispers (Gettin' Louder)	10
69	MCA Soul Bag BAG 7	Since You Showed Me How To Be Happy/Chain Gang	10
69	MCA MU 1104	Since You Showed Me How To Be Happy/The Who-Who Song (reissue)	10
69	MCA MU 1105	Helpless/Do It The Right Way	10
70	MCA MU 1131	(Your Love Keeps Lifting Me) Higher And Higher/Whispers (Gettin' Louder) (reissue)	8
72	MCA MU 1160	I Get The Sweetest Feeling/Soul Galore	8
73	Brunswick BR 3	Beautiful Day/What'cha Gonna Do About Love	20
75	Brunswick BR 18	I Get The Sweetest Feeling/(Your Love Keeps Lifting Me) Higher And Higher	6
75	Brunswick BR 23	Whispers (Gettin' Louder)/Reet Petite	6
75	Brunswick BR 28	Don't Burn No Bridges/Don't Burn No Bridges (Instrumental) (with Chi-Lites)	6
70s	Brunswick BR 43	It Only Happens When I Look At You/Just As Soon As The Feeling's Over	75

Jackie WILSON

EPs

59	Coral FEP 2016	JACKIE WILSON (triangular or round centre)......................	100/70
60	Coral FEP 2043	THE DYNAMIC JACKIE WILSON (triangular or round centre)	100/70

LPs

58	Coral LVA 9087	HE'S SO FINE	160
59	Coral LVA 9108	LONELY TEARDROPS	160
60	Coral LVA 9121	SO MUCH	110
60	Coral LVA 9130	JACKIE SINGS THE BLUES..	125
60	Coral LVA 9135	MY GOLDEN FAVOURITES...	90
61	Coral LVA 9144	A WOMAN, A LOVER, A FRIEND	115
61	Coral LVA 9148	YOU AIN'T HEARD NOTHIN' YET...................................	85
62	Coral LVA 9151	BY SPECIAL REQUEST (also stereo SVL 3018)	75/90
62	Coral LVA 9202	BODY AND SOUL	65
63	Coral LVA/SVL 9209	JACKIE (mono/stereo)...	70/80
63	Coral LVA/SVL 9214	THE WORLD'S GREATEST MELODIES (mono/stereo)...................	55/65
66	Coral LVA 9231	SPOTLIGHT ON JACKIE WILSON	70
66	Coral LVA/SVL 9232	SOUL GALORE (mono/stereo).....................................	70/80
67	Coral LVA 9235	WHISPERS..	75
68	MCA MUP(S) 304	HIGHER AND HIGHER	20
68	MCA MUP(S) 333	TWO MUCH (with Count Basie & His Orchestra).....................	20
69	MCA MUPS 361	I GET THE SWEETEST FEELING...................................	20
70	MCA MUPS 405	DO YOUR THING	25
73	Brunswick BRLS 3001	YOU GOT ME WALKIN'...	25
73	Brunswick BRLS 3004	GREATEST HITS	15
75	Brunswick BRLS 3016	THE VERY BEST OF JACKIE WILSON	15

(see also Billy Ward & Dominoes, Clyde McPhatter, Count Basie, Chi-Lites, Linda Hopkins)

JACKIE WILSON/CLYDE McPHATTER

62	Ember JBS 705	Tenderly/CLYDE McPHATTER: Harbour Lights	250
62	Ember NR 5001	MEET BILLY WARD & THE DOMINOES (LP, 1 side each)................	200

(see also Clyde McPhatter)

JOE WILSON

71	Pye International 7N 25550	Sweetness/When A Man Cries..........................	6

LALA WILSON

(see under Alexander Jackson & Turnkeys)

MARTY WILSON & STRAT-O-LITES

58	Brunswick 05750	Hey! Eula/Hedge-Hopper (78 rpm = £6)	18

MAYNELL WILSON (actually Wilson Maynell) & WESTMINSTER FIVE

64	Carnival CV 7014	Hey Hey Johnny/Baby	8
67	CBM CBM 001	Motown Feeling/Mean Ole World.................................	7

(see also Wes[t]minster Five)

MURRY WILSON

67	Capitol CL 15525	Plumber's Tune/Love Won't Wait.................................	8
67	Capitol (S)T 2819	THE MANY MOODS OF MURRY WILSON (LP).........................	25

(see also Beach Boys)

NANCY WILSON

64	Capitol CL 15343	The Best Is Yet To Come/Never Let Me Go	5
64	Capitol CL 15352	(You Don't Know) How Glad I Am/Never Less Than Yesterday	7
65	Capitol CL 15378	Don't Come Running Back To Me/Love Has Many Faces.............	10
65	Capitol CL 15412	Where Does That Leave Me/Gentle Is My Love	20
66	Capitol CL 15443	Power Of Love/Rain Sometimes	12
66	Capitol CL 15466	You've Got Your Troubles/Uptight (Everything's Alright)...........	20
67	Capitol CL 15508	Don't Look Over Your Shoulder/Mercy, Mercy, Mercy.............	15
68	Capitol CL 15536	You Don't Know Me/Ode To Billie Joe	10
68	Capitol CL 15547	Face It Girl It's Over/The End Of Our Love (DJ copy = £85)........	55
75	Capitol CL 15810	You're Right As Rain/There'll Always Be Forever	5
62	Capitol EAP1 20604	SECOND TIME AROUND (EP)	10
64	Capitol EAP4 2082	TODAY, TOMORROW, FOREVER (EP).............................	10
62	Capitol (S)T 1767	HELLO YOUNG LOVERS (LP, mono/stereo)................. each	15
63	Capitol (S)T 1828	BROADWAY — MY LOVE (LP, mono/stereo)................ each	15
63	Capitol (S)T 1934	HOLLYWOOD — MY WAY (LP, mono/stereo) .... each	15
63	Capitol (S)T 2012	YESTERDAY'S LOVE SONGS (LP, mono/stereo) .... each	15
64	Capitol (S)T 2082	TODAY, TOMORROW, FOREVER (LP).............................	15
65	Capitol (S)T 2136	THE NANCY WILSON SHOW (LP)	15
65	Capitol (S)T 2155	HOW GLAD I AM (LP)	15
65	Capitol (S)T 2321	TODAY— MY WAY (LP)..	15
65	Capitol (S)T 2351	GENTLE IS MY LOVE (LP)	15
66	Capitol (S)T 2433	FROM BROADWAY WITH LOVE (LP)	15
66	Capitol (S)T 2495	A TOUCH OF TODAY (LP).......................................	30
66	Capitol (S)T 2555	TENDER LOVING CARE (LP)....................................	12
67	Capitol (S)T 2634	NANCY — NATURALLY (LP)	12

NANCY WILSON & CANNONBALL ADDERLEY

63	Capitol EAP4 1657	NANCY WILSON & CANNONBALL ADDERLEY (EP)...................	8
62	Capitol (S)T 1657	NANCY WILSON & CANNONBALL ADDERLEY (LP, mono/stereo)........	12/15

(see also Cannonball Adderley)

PEANUTS WILSON

58	Coral Q 72302	Cast Iron Arm/You've Got Love (78 rpm = £155)	500
76	MCA MCA 240	Cast Iron Arm/DON WOODY: Barking Up The Wrong Tree............	6

PHIL WILSON

87	Creation CRE 036D	Waiting For A Change/Even Now/Down In The Valley/Love In Vain (double pack)	5
89	Caff CAFF 3	Better Days/You Won't Speak (p/s, with insert, handwritten label)............	12

(see also June Brides)

REUBEN WILSON
74	People PEO 109	I'll Take You There/Cisco Kid	6
76	Chess 6078 700	Got To Get Your Own Parts 1 & 2	12
73	People PLEO 01	CISCO KID (LP)	15
74	People PLEO 20	THE SWEET LIFE (LP)	15

RON WILSON
68	Island WI 3112	Dread Saras/DAVID BROWN: All My Life	28

(see also Winston Scotland, Douglas Brothers)

SHARK WILSON & BASEMENT HEATERS
71	Ashanti ASH 400	Make It Reggae/Version	12

SMILEY WILSON
60	London HLG 9066	Running Bear/Long As Little Birds Fly	30

TONY WILSON
69	Bell BLL 1081	Baby, I Love, Love I Love You/Come Back To My Lonely World	6
76	Bearsville K 55513	I LIKE YOUR STYLE (LP)	12

(see also Hot Chocolate)

TREVOR WILSON
65	Ska Beat JB 207	You Couldn't Believe/You Told Me You Care	15

GABY WILTON & CHARLIE ACE
72	Bullet BU 511	Babylon Falling/CHARLIE ACE: Make It Love	8

JOHNNY WILTSHIRE & HIS TREBLETONES
59	Oriole CB 1494	If The Shoe Fits/Cha Cha Choo Choo (78 rpm = £30)	45

TEACHO WILTSHIRE
57	Oriole CB 1376	Coffee Break/Shut-Eye (78)	12

(see also Annie Ross)

WIMPLE WINCH
66	Fontana TF 686	What's Been Done/I Really Love You	200+
66	Fontana TF 718	Save My Soul/Everybody's Worried 'Bout Tomorrow	300+
67	Fontana TF 781	Rumble On Mersey Square South/Typical British Workmanship	200+
67	Fontana TF 781	Rumble On Mersey Square South/Typical British Workmanship (mispressing, B-side plays "Atmospheres")	400+

(see also Just Four Men, Four Just Men, Pacific Drift, Tristar Airbus)

LEM WINCHESTER & BENNY GOLSON
59	Esquire 32-142	WINCHESTER SPECIAL (LP)	25
61	Esquire 32-172	ANOTHER OPUS (LP)	12

KAI WINDING
65	Verve VS 512	Comin' Home Baby/More	15
55	London LTZ-N 15003	K AND J.J. (LP, with J.J. Johnson Quintet)	15
59	Philips SBBL 515	TROMBONES (LP)	18
61	Parlophone PMC 1138	SLIDE RULE (LP, with J.J. Johnson Quintet)	20
63	Verve VLP 9049	SOUL SURFIN' (LP)	30

(see also Dizzy Gillespie, J.J. Johnson Quintet)

WIND IN THE WILLOWS
68	Capitol CL 15561	Moments Spent/Friendly Lion	20
68	Capitol ST 2956	WIND IN THE WILLOWS (LP)	25

(see also Debbie Harry, Blondie)

WINDMILL
69	MCA MU 1090	Big Bertha/Hey, Drummer Man	5
70	MCA MK 5024	Such Sweet Sorrow/I Can Fly	10
70	MCA MK 5045	Wilbur's Thing/Two's Company, Three's A Crowd	5

WINDOWS
78	Skeleton SKL 008	Re-Arrange/Over Dub (p/s)	7
81	Skeleton SKULP 2	UPPERS ON DOWNERS (LP, with inserts)	12

(see also Mutants)

BARBARA WINDSOR
62	HMV 45POP 1104	I'm Not That Sort Of Girl/It Has Better Be A Wonderful Life (with Harry Fowler & Kenny Lynch)	6
63	HMV POP 1128	Sparrows Can't Sing/On Mother Kelly's Doorstep	6
67	Parlophone R 5629	Don't Dig Twiggy/Swinging London	8
70	UPC UPC 101	When I Was A Child/What A Right Carry On	5
72	Decca F 13323	Grin And Bare It/Cheeky Sorta' Bird	5

WINDY & CARL
95	Enraptured RAPT 4501	Emerald/Fragments Of Time And Space (500 in hand-painted p/s, 300 in tracing paper sleeve)	12/10
96	Enraptured RAPT 4509	Christmas Song/GRIMBLE GRUMBLE: Odyssey And Oracle (no'd p/s, coloured vinyl, 350 only)	20

WINDY CORNER
73	Deroy DER 977	THE HOUSE AT WINDY CORNER (LP, private pressing)	300+

WINE OF LEBANON
76	Dovetail DOVE 46	WINE OF LEBANON (LP)	25

(see also Achor)

WINGS
(see under Paul McCartney & Wings)

WINGS OVER JORDAN
51	Vogue V 303	Deep River/Old Ship Of Zion (78)	10

MINT VALUE £

GODFREY WINN
67   Decca F12713   Loveshade/I Pass 5

PETE WINSLOW & KING SIZE BRASS
73   BBC 103S   GIRL ON THE TESTCARD (LP) 15

WINSTON
60s   Holyground   WINSTON SINGS (EP) 10

WINSTON (Richards) & BIBBIE (Seaton)
63   R&B JB 115   Lover Man/LESTER STIRLING: Gravy Cool 28

WINSTON (Francis) & CECIL (Locke)
70   Banana BA 306   United We Stand/SOUND DIMENSION: Sweet Message 15

WINSTON & ERROL
71   Punch PH 74   There Is A Land/Goodnight My Love 6

WINSTON & FAY
64   Blue Beat BB 272   Fay Is Gone (Winston & Errol)/MONARCHS: Sauce And Tea 22

WINSTON & GEORGE
66   Pyramid PYR 6002   Denham Town/Keep The Pressure On 15

WINSTON (Groovy) & PAT (Rhoden)
68   Trojan TR 605   Pony Ride/Baby You Send Me 8
71   Bullet BU 475   The Same Thing For Breakfast/Sweeter Than Honey 8
(see also Winston Tucker)

WINSTON & ROY
62   Blue Beat BB 80   Babylon Gone/COUNT OSSIE ON AFRICAN DRUMS: First Gone 25

WINSTON & RUPERT
70   Bullet BU 425   Come By Here/Somebody 10
70   Moodisc HM 106   Musically Beat/Let Me Tell You Girl 10
(see also Eternals)

WINSTON (Richards) & TONETTES
65   Ska Beat JB 225   You Make Me Cry/CHECKMATES: Invisible Ska 25

JIMMY WINSTON (& HIS REFLECTIONS)
66   Decca F 12410   Sorry She's Mine/It's Not What You Do (But The Way That You Do It) 250
76   Nems NEMS 12   Sun In The Morning/Just Wanna Smile (solo) 8
(see also Small Faces, Winston's Fumbs, Spheres)

ERIC WINSTONE (& HIS) ORCHESTRA
52   Nixa NY 7743   I Don't Care/Slow Train Blues (78) 6
64   Pye 7N 15603   "Dr. Who" Theme/Pony Express 18
73   Avenue AVINT 1005   PLAYS 007 (LP) 20

NORMA WINSTONE
72   Argo ZDA 148   EDGE OF TIME (LP) . . . . 120+
(see also Mike Westbrook, Michael Garrick)

WINSTONS
69   Pye International 7N 25493   Colour im Father/Amen, Brother 20
69   Pye International 7N 25500   Love Of The Common People/Wheel Of Fortune 7

WINSTONS & M-SQUAD
71   Green Door GD 4003   Carroll Street/Carroll Street — Version (B-side act. by Ansel Collins/M-Squad) . . . 6

WINSTON'S FUMBS
67   RCA RCA 1612   Real Crazy Apartment/Snow White 400
(see also Small Faces, Jimmy Winston & His Reflections, Yes, Spheres, Federals)

EDGAR WINTER (GROUP)
70   CBS 64083   ENTRANCE (LP, as Edgar Winter) 18
71   CBS 64298   EDGAR WINTER'S WHITE TRASH (LP) 15
72   CBS 67244   ROAD WORK (2-LP) 18
73   CBS EQ 31584/Q 65074   THEY ONLY COME OUT AT NIGHT (LP, quadrophonic) 12

JOHNNY WINTER
69   CBS 4386   I'm Yours And I'm Hers/I'll Drown In My Tears 6
69   Liberty LBF 15219   Rollin' And Tumblin'/Bad Luck And Trouble 7
70   CBS 4794   Johnny B. Goode/I'm Not Sure 6
70   CBS 5358   Rock 'N' Roll Hoochie Koo/21st Century Man 5
71   CBS 7227   Jumping Jack Flash/Good Morning Little School Girl 5
69   CBS 63619   JOHNNY WINTER (LP) 30
69   Liberty LBL/LBS 83240E   THE PROGRESSIVE BLUES EXPERIMENT (LP) 25
70   CBS 66231   SECOND WINTER (2-LP, 3-sides) 25
70   Buddah 2359 011   FIRST WINTER (LP) 20
70   CBS 64117   JOHNNY WINTER AND... (LP) 15
71   CBS 64289   JOHNNY WINTER AND... LIVE (LP) 15
73   CBS 65484   STILL ALIVE AND WELL (LP) 12
74   CBS CQ 32188/Q 65484   STILL ALIVE AND WELL (LP, quadrophonic) 15
(see also Johnny & Jammers)

HUGO WINTERHALTER ORCHESTRA
53   HMV 7M 120   Tic Tac Toe/Hesitation 5
54   HMV 7M 273   Land Of Dreams/Song Of The Barefoot Contessa 5
56   HMV POP 241   Canadian Sunset/This Is Real (with Eddie Haywood) 5

DON WINTERS
60   Brunswick 05827   Someday Baby/That's All I Need 15

JONATHAN WINTERS
61   HMV CLP 1482   HERE'S JONATHAN (LP) 20

LIZ WINTERS & BOB CORT SKIFFLE GROUP
57	Decca F 10878	Freight Train/Love Is Strange (78 rpm = £10)	20
57	Decca F 10899	Maggie May/Jessamine (78 rpm = £10)	20
57	Decca DFE 6409	LIZ WINTERS AND BOB CORT (EP)	25

(see also Bob Cort Skiffle Group)

LOIS WINTERS
56	London HLD 8266	Japanese Farewell Song/JAN GARBER & HIS ORCHESTRA: My Dear (78 rpm = £8)	35

MIKE & BERNIE WINTERS
57	Parlophone R 4384	How Do You Do?/Does My Baby?	6
66	CBS 202458	That Man Batman/Insky Spinsky Spider (with p/s)	8

RON WINTERS
63	Colpix PX 11022	Snow Girl/In The Middle Of The Morning	25

RUBY WINTERS
68	Stateside SS 2090	I Want Action/Better (DJ copy = £150)	100
79	Creole CR 171	Baby Lay Down/Lovin' Me Is A Full Time Job	5
79	Creole CR 174	Back To Love/I've Been Waiting For You All My Life	5

WYOMA WINTERS
54	HMV 7M 222	Where Can I Go Without You?/Won't You Give A Repeat Performance	7
54	HMV 7M 260	Toy Balloon/Shish Kebab	7

STEVIE WINWOOD
77	Island WIP 6394	Time Is Running Out/Penultimate Zone (12", pre-release sleeve)	10
80	Island IPR 2040	While You See A Chance/Vacant Chair (12", pre-release sleeve)	8
80	Island WIP 6655	While You See A Chance/Vacant Chair (p/s)	5
81	Island WIP 6747	There's A River/Two Way Stretch (p/s)	5
86	Island IS 294	Freedom Overspill/Spanish Dancer (p/s, with bonus cassette of LP highlights & interview [SW 2])	6
86	Island 12 ISD 294	Freedom Overspill (Liberty Mix)/(LP Version)/Spanish Dancer (12", stickered g/fold p/s & t/p 7" "Low Spark Of High-Heeled Boys"/"Gimme Some Lovin' ")	10
88	Virgin VST 1085	Roll With It (12" Mix)/The Morning Side/Roll With It (7" Version) (12", gatefold p/s)	8
91	Virgin VSCDX 1317	I Will Be Here/Don't You Know What The Night Can Do (live)/In The Night Of Day (CD, velvet box with family tree and print)	8
86	Island SWCLP 1	A CONVERSATION WITH (LP, promo interview on BACK IN THE HIGH LIFE LP)	12
87	Island SWWLP 1	IN CONVERSATION (LP, promo interview on CHRONICLES LP)	12
87	Island SW 1/2/3	BACK IN THE HIGH LIFE (3 x 7" set, each in p/s, promo only)	20
87	Island	CHRONICLES (5 x 7" box set, promo, 500 only)	30

(see also Winwood Kabaka Amoa, Anglos, Spencer Davis Group, Traffic, Blind Faith)

WINWOOD/KABAKA/AMAO
73	Island HELP 14	AIYE-KETA THIRD WORLD (LP)	15

(see also Stevie Winwood)

WIPEOUT
82	M&L MNL 2/ACE 37	Baby Please Don't Go/Two-O-Five/Crawdaddy/Should A' Known Better (p/s)	15
83	Out OUT 1A/B1	NO SWEAT (LP)	15

WIPEOUT
90s	Deluxe DELUX 002	Snowflake/Confusion Bee (12")	10

WIPERS
84	Psycho PSYCHO 22	IS THIS REAL? (LP, with lyric insert)	12
84	Psycho PSYCHO 23	YOUTH OF AMERICA (LP)	12

WIRE
77	Harvest HAR 5144	Mannequin/Feeling Called Love/12XU (p/s)	12
78	Harvest HAR 5151	I Am The Fly/Ex-Lion Tamer (p/s)	12
78	Harvest HAR 5161	Dot Dash/Options R (p/s)	10
79	Harvest HAR 5172	Outdoor Miner/Practice Makes Perfect (p/s, some on white vinyl)	8/5
79	Harvest HAR 5187	A Question Of Degree/Former Airline (p/s)	7
79	Harvest HAR 5192	Map Ref 41° N 93° W/Go Ahead (p/s)	10
79	Harvest SPSLP 299	154 (12", p/s, white label sampler with insert & press release; beware of counterfeits)	30
81	Rough Trade RT 079	Our Swimmer/Midnight Bahnhof Cafe (p/s)	7
83	Rough Trade RTT 123	Crazy About Love/Second Length (Our Swimmer)/Catapult 30 (12", p/s, 2 different sleeve colours)	each 10
88	Mute MUTE 67	Kidney Bingos/Pieta (p/s)	6
89	Mute MUTE 87	Eardrum Buzz/The Offer (p/s, clear vinyl, withdrawn)	12
89	Mute CDMUTE 98	IN VIVO (CD EP)	8
77	Harvest SHSP 4076	PINK FLAG (LP, with lyric inner)	20
78	Harvest SHSP 4093	CHAIRS MISSING (LP, 1st 10,000 with lilac lyric inner sleeve)	20
79	Harvest SHSP 4105	154 (LP, with inner lyric sleeve & bonus 7" EP: "Song 2"/ "Get Down [Parts I & II]"/"Let's Panic"/"Later"/ "Small Electric Piece" [PSR 444, no p/s])	20
84	Rough Trade ROUGH 29	DOCUMENT AND EYEWITNESS (LP, with free 12" EP [ROUGH 2912])	20
84	Rough Trade COPY 004	DOCUMENT AND EYEWITNESS (cassette, in special box)	15
84	Rough Trade COPY 004	DOCUMENT AND EYEWITNESS (cassette with bonus 12" EP tracks)	12
86	Pink PINKY 7	PLAY POP (mini-LP)	10
87	Mute STUMM 42	THE IDEAL COPY (LP, with inner)	12
89	Mute STUMM 66	IBTABA (IT'S BEGINNING TO AND BACK AGAIN) (LP, with 4 postcards & signed print)	18

(see also Cupol, Colin Newman)

MARK WIRTZ (ORCHESTRA & CHORUS)

68	Parlophone R 5668	(He's Our Dear Old) Weatherman (From "A Teenage Opera")/Possum's Dance	22
68	Parlophone R 5683	Mrs. Raven/Knickerbocker Glory.	12
69	CBS 4306	My Daddie Is A Baddie/I Love You Because.	6
69	CBS 4539	Caroline/Goody, Goody, Goody.	6
64	World Record Club T 452	TEN AGAIN (LP, by Belle Gonzalez & Russ Loader, Wirtz as producer)	35

(see also Mood Mosaic, Keith West, Sweet Shop, Philwit & Pegasus, Mark Rogers & Marksmen, Belle Gonzalez,
Russ Loader, Zion De Gallier, Elmer Hockett's Hurdy Gurdy, Steve Flynn, Fickle Finger, Matchmaker)

WISDOM

76	Crystal CR 026	Nefertiti/What-Cha-Gonna-Du-About You	8

NORMAN WISDOM

56	Columbia SCM 5222	Two Rivers/Boy Meets Girl (with Ruby Murray)	18
57	Columbia DB 3864	Up In The World/Me And My Imagination	12
57	Columbia DB 3903	The Wisdom Of A Fool/Happy Ending	10
59	Top Rank JAR 246	Follow A Star/Give Me A Night In June	5
61	Columbia SCD 2160	Narcissus (The Laughing Record)/I Don't 'Arf Love You (with Joyce Grenfell)	5
69	CBS 4569	Where Do I Go From Here?/Just Like The Day	5
56	Columbia SEG 7612	NORMAN WISDOM (EP)	15
57	Columbia SEG 7687	NORMAN AND RUBY (EP, with Ruby Murray)	15
58	Columbia SEG 7856	NORMAN WISDOM (EP)	15
59	Top Rank JKP 2052	FOLLOW A STAR (EP)	12
58	Columbia 33SX 1085	NORMAN WISDOM IN "WHERE'S CHARLEY?" (LP)	15
67	Wing WL 1216	I WOULD LIKE TO PUT ON RECORD (LP)	15

(see also Ruby Murray)

WISE BLOOD

85	Wise 1-12	Motorslug/Death Rape 2000 (12", p/s)	12
86	Wise 2-12	Someone Drowned In My Pool/Stumbo (12", p/s)	12
91	Wise 003	DISHDIRT (LP, with sticker)	15
91	Big Cut 030X	PEDAL TO THE METAL (mini-LP)	12

(see also Foetus)

WISE BOYS

60	Parlophone R 4693	Why, Why, Why/My Fortune	10

WISE GUYS

60	Top Rank JAR 271	(Little Girl) Big Noise/As Long As I Have You	12

MAC WISEMAN

55	London HLD 8174	The Kentuckian Song/Wabash Cannon Ball (78 rpm = £15).	65
56	London HLD 8226	My Little Home In Tennessee/I Haven't Got The Right To Love You	65
56	London HLD 8226	My Little Home In Tennessee/I Haven't Got The Right To Love You (78)	20
56	London HLD 8259	Fireball Mail/When The Roses Bloom Again (78 rpm = £30)	65
57	London HLD 8412	Step It Up And Go/Sundown (78 rpm = £50)	400
59	London HL 7084	Jimmy Brown The Newsboy/I've Got No Use For Woman (export issue)	40
56	London RE-D 1056	SONGS FROM THE HILLS (EP)	35
58	London RE-D 1147	SONGS FROM THE HILLS VOL. 2 (EP)	35
60	London RE-D 1242	SONGS FROM THE HILLS VOL. 3 (EP)	35
56	London HB-D 1052	SONGS FROM THE HILLS (10" LP)	65
60	London HA-D 2217	GREAT FOLK BALLADS (LP).	40

TREVOR WISHART

78	private pressing	RED BIRD: A POLITICAL PRISONER'S DREAM (LP, with insert)	20
79	private pressing	BEACH SINGULARITY AND MENAGERIE (LP, with insert)	20

WISHBONE ASH

70	MCA MK 5061	Blind Eye/Queen Of Torture	6
72	MCA MKS 5097	No Easy Road/Blowin' Free	6
73	MCA MUS 1210	So Many Things To Say/Rock'n'Roll Widow	5
74	MCA MCA 165	Hometown/Persephone	5
75	MCA MCA 176	Silver Shoes/Persephone	6
76	MCA/SFI 263	Outward Bound/Runaway/Mother Of Pearl/You Rescue Me (flexidisc, with/without "New England" tour programme)	12/5
77	MCA MCA 291	Phoenix/Blowin' Free/Jail Bait (p/s)	5
78	MCA MCA 392	You See Red/Bad Weather Blues (live) (p/s)	5
79	MCA MCA 518	Come On/Fast Johnny (p/s)	5
80	MCA MCA 549	Living Proof/Jail Bait (live) (p/s)	5
80	MCA MCA 577	Helpless (live)/Blowin' Free (live) (p/s)	5
81	MCA MCA 695	Underground/My Mind Is Made Up (p/s)	5
81	MCA MCA 726	Get Ready/Kicks On The Street (p/s, some with patch)	8/5
70	MCA MKPS 2014	WISHBONE ASH (LP, gatefold sleeve, black label)	25
71	MCA MDKS 8004	PILGRIMAGE (LP, gatefold sleeve, black label)	20
72	MCA MDKS 8006	ARGUS (LP, gatefold sleeve, black label).	18
73	MCA MDKS 8011	WISHBONE FOUR (LP, gatefold sleeve, black label, with poster & lyrics)	15

(Red/brown, red/yellow & red/pink label copies of the above LPs also exist, and are worth the same values.)

74	MCA MCSP 254	LIVE DATES (2-LP, gatefold sleeve)	15
74	MCA MCG 2585	THERE'S THE RUB (LP)	12
78	MCA MCG 3528	NO SMOKE WITHOUT FIRE (LP, with stickered sleeve & inner, with bonus live single "Come In From The Rain"/"Lorelei" [PSR 431])	12
80	MCA MCG 4012	LIVE DATES II (LP, gatefold sleeve, with live bonus LP)	15
82	AVM ASH 1	TWIN BARRELS BURNING (LP).	12
85	Neat NEAT 1027	RAW TO THE BONE (LP)	20

(see also Home)

WISHFUL THINKING

66	Decca F 12438	Turning Round/V.I.P.	20
66	Decca F 12499	Step By Step/Looking Around	7
67	Decca F 12598	Count To Ten/Hang Around Girl	8
67	Decca F 12627	Peanuts/Cherry Cherry	12

67	Decca F 22673	Meet The Sun/Easier Said Than Loving You	10
68	Decca F 22742	Alone/Vegetables (export issue)	10
68	Decca F 12760	It's So Easy/I Want You Girl	15
72	B&C CB 169	Lu La Le Lu/We're Gonna Change All This	7
72	B&C CB 184	Clear White Light/Hiroshima	10
67	Decca SKL 4900	LIVE VOL. 1 (LP)	50
71	Charisma CAS 1038	HIROSHIMA (LP)	25

WISHING STONES

86	Head HEAD 2	Beat Girl/Two Steps Take Me Back (p/s)	6
87	Head HEAD 6	New Ways/House Is Not A Home (p/s)	5
87	Head HEAD 612	New Ways/Wildwood/Hold Up/A House Is Not A Home (12", p/s)	8

(see also The Loft)

WITCHES BREW

80s	Pussy PU 016	Angeline (p/s)	20

WITCHFINDER GENERAL

81	Heavy Metal HEAVY 6	Burning A Sinner/Satan's Children (p/s)	30
82	Heavy Metal 12HM 17	Soviet Invasion/Rabies/R.I.P. (live) (12", p/s)	35
83	Heavy Metal HEAVY 21	Music/Last Chance (p/s)	12
83	Heavy Metal HMPD 21	Music/Last Chance (picture disc)	8
82	Heavy Metal HMRLP 8	DEATH PENALTY (LP, red, blue or clear vinyl, with inner)	25
82	Heavy Metal HMRPD 8	DEATH PENALTY (LP, picture disc)	18
83	Heavy Metal HMRLP 13	FRIENDS OF HELL (LP, red, silver or clear vinyl)	18
83	Heavy Metal HMRPD 13	FRIENDS OF HELL (LP, picture disc)	15

WITCHFYNDE

79	Rondelet ROUND 1	Give 'Em Hell/Getting' Heavy (p/s)	6
80	Rondelet ROUND 4	In The Stars/Wake Up Screaming (p/s)	5
83	Expulsion OUT 3	I'd Rather Go Wild/Cry Wolf (p/s)	20
80	Rondelet ABOUT 1	GIVE 'EM HELL (LP)	25
80	Rondelet ABOUT 2	STAGE FRIGHT (LP)	12
83	Expulsion EXIT 5	CLOAK AND DAGGER (LP)	12
83	Expulsion PEXIT 5	CLOAK AND DAGGER (LP, picture disc)	18
84	Mausoleum SKULL 8352	LORDS OF SIN (LP, gatefold sleeve, with bonus 12" [Cloak & Dagger/ I'd Rather Go Wild/Moon Magic/Give 'Em Hell])	12

BILL WITHERS

71	A&M AMS 845	Everybody's Talkin'/Harlem	6
71	A&M AMS 858	Ain't No Sunshine/Harlem	6
72	A&M AMS 7004	Lean On Me/Better Off Dead	6
72	A&M AMS 7038	Use Me/Let Me In Your Life	6
73	A&M AMS 7055	Kissing My Love/I Don't Know	6
73	A&M AMS 7068	Look What I Found/The Lady Is Waiting	6
73	A&M AMS 7080	Ain't No Sunshine/Harlem/Grandma's Hands	6
72	A&M AMLH 68107	STILL BILL (LP)	20
71	A&M AMLS 65002	JUST AS I AM (LP)	15
73	A&M AMLD 3001	LIVE AT CARNEGIE HALL (2-LP)	15
74	A&M AMLH 68230	'JUSTMENTS	15

JIMMY WITHERSPOON

78s

54	Parlophone R 3914	It/Highway To Happiness	20
54	Parlophone R 3951	Oh Boy/I Done Told You	20
54	Vogue V 2261	Failing By Degrees/New Orleans Woman	20
54	Vogue V 2295	Who's Been Jivin' With You/Rain, Rain, Rain	20
56	Vogue V 2060	Big Fine Girl/No Rollin' Blues	20
56	Vogue V 2356	Jump, Children/Take Me Back Baby	20

SINGLES

54	Parlophone MSP 6125	It/Highway To Happiness	100
54	Parlophone MSP 6142	Oh Boy/I Done Told You	100
56	Vogue V 2060	Big Fine Girl/No Rollin' Blues	75
62	Vogue V 2420	When The Lights Go Out/All That's Good	75
64	Stateside SS 304	Evenin'/Money Is Getting Cheaper	15
64	Stateside SS 325	I Will Never Marry/I'm Coming Down With The Blues	15
64	Stateside SS 362	You're Next/Happy Blues	15
65	Stateside SS 429	Come Walk With Me/Oh How I Love You	15
65	Stateside SS 461	Love Me Right/Make My Heart Smile Again	15
66	Stateside SS 503	If There Wasn't Any You/I Never Thought I'd See The Day	15
66	Verve VS 538	It's All Over But The Crying/If I Could Have You Back Again	8
67	Verve VS 553	Past Forty Blues/My Baby's Quit Me	6
71	Probe PRO 526	Handbags And Gladrags/It's Time To Live	5
75	Capitol CL 15828	Fool's Paradise/Reflections	5

EPs

61	Vogue EPV 1269	JIMMY WITHERSPOON AT MONTEREY	35
61	Vogue EPV 1270	JIMMY WITHERSPOON AT MONTEREY No. 2	35
64	Vocalion EPVH 1278	JIMMY WITHERSPOON	25
65	Vocalion EPVH 1284	OUTSKIRTS OF TOWN	25
66	Vocalion VEH 170158	FEELING THE SPIRIT VOL. 1	25
66	Vocalion VEH 170159	FEELING THE SPIRIT VOL. 2	25

LPs

59	London Jazz LTZ-K 15150	NEW ORLEANS BLUES (with Wilbur de Paris)	42
60	Vogue LAE 12218	SINGIN' THE BLUES	42
61	Vogue LAE 12253	AT THE RENAISSANCE (with Gerry Mulligan)	38
64	Society SOC 968	SINGS THE BLUES	15
64	Stateside SL 10088	EVENIN' BLUES	45

Jimmy WITHERSPOON

65	Stateside SL 10105	BLUES AROUND THE CLOCK	48
65	Fontana 688 005 ZL	THERE'S GOOD ROCKIN' TONIGHT	38
65	Stateside SL 10114	SOME OF MY BEST FRIENDS ARE BLUES	48
65	Stateside SL 10139	BLUE SPOON	40
65	Vogue VRL 3005	JIMMY WITHERSPOON IN PERSON	35
66	Ember EMB 3369	JIMMY WITHERSPOON	30
67	Fontana (S)TL 5382	'SPOON SINGS AND SWINGS	45
67	Verve (S)VLP 9156	BLUE POINT OF VIEW	25
67	Transatlantic PR 7300	EVENIN' BLUES (reissue)	18
68	Transatlantic PR 7356	SOME OF MY BEST FRIENDS ARE THE BLUES (reissue)	18
68	Stateside (S)SL 10232	LIVE	30
68	Verve (S)VLP 9181	BLUES IS NOW (with Brother Jack McDuff)	22
68	Verve (S)VLP 9216	SPOONFUL OF SOUL	22
68	Transatlantic PR 7418	SPOON IN LONDON	25
68	Transatlantic PR 7475	BLUES FOR EASY LIVERS	20
69	Stateside SSL 10289	THE BLUES SINGER	25
69	Ember CJS 820	SINGS THE BLUES AT THE RENAISSANCE (reissue, with Gerry Mulligan)	12
69	Polydor Intl. 623 256	BACK DOOR BLUES	25
71	Probe SPB 1031	HANDBAGS AND GLADRAGS	18

(see also Eric Burdon & Jimmy Witherspoon, Brother Jack McDuff)

JIMMY WITHERSPOON/HELEN HUMES
| 60 | Vogue EPV 1198 | RHYTHM AND BLUES CONCERT (EP, 2 tracks each) | 80 |

(see also Helen Humes)

BITTER WITHY
| 69 | Nevis NEVIS R005 | SAMPLER (LP) | 20 |

WITNESSES
| 60s | Herald ELR 1076 | THE WITNESSES (EP) | 100 |

WIZARD'S CONVENTION
| 76 | RCA RS 1085 | WIZARD'S CONVENTION (LP, with insert) | 15 |

(see also Deep Purple, Roger Glover, Jon Lord, David Coverdale, Ray Fenwick,Tony Ashton, Glenn Hughes, ELP, Hardin & York)

WIZZARD
| 73 | Harvest SHSP 4025 | WIZZARD BREW (LP, with lyric insert) | 12 |
| 74 | Warner Bros K 56029 | INTRODUCING EDDY AND THE FALCONS (LP, gatefold sleeve with poster) | 12 |

(see also Roy Wood, Balls, Idle Race, Grunt Futtock)

WKGB
| 79 | Fetish FET 002 | Non-Stop/Ultra Marine (p/s) | 5 |

(DARRYL WAY'S) WOLF
73	Deram DM 378	Wolf/Spring Fever	8
73	Deram DM 395	A Bunch Of Fives/Five In The Morning	8
73	Deram DM 401	Two Sisters/Go Down	8
73	Deram SDL 14	CANIS LUPUS (LP, as Darryl Way's Wolf, gatefold sleeve)	22
73	Deram SML 1104	SATURATION POINT (LP, as Darryl Way's Wolf)	22
74	Deram SML 1116	NIGHT MUSIC (LP)	20

(see also Curved Air, King Crimson, Marillion)

WOLF
| 81 | Gremlin GREM 73 | See Them Running/Creatures Of The Night (no p/s) | 70 |

WOLF
| 82 | Chrysalis CHS 2592 | Head Contact/Rock'n'Roll (p/s, clear vinyl, some with sticker) | 15/6 |
| 84 | Mausoleum 8323 | EDGE OF THE WORLD (LP) | 15 |

RICHARD WOLFE & HIS ORCHESTRA
| 60 | London HLR 9143 | Banjo Boy/Voila | 6 |

WOLFETONES
| 65 | Fontana STL 5244 | THE FOGGY DEW (LP) | 12 |

WOLFGANG PRESS
| 83 | 4AD (no cat. no.) | Kings Of Soul (Crowned Mix)/(De-Throned Mix)/(7" Mix) (12", same both sides, promo only, 50 copies pressed) | 15 |

(see also Mass, Models)

WOLFMAN
| 04 | Rough Trade RTRADS177 | For Lovers/Back From The Dead (with Pete Doherty, p/s) | 8 |

WOLFRILLA
| 71 | Concord CON 015 | Song For Jimi/Come Tomorrow | 7 |

WOOLLY WOLSTENHOLME
| 80 | Polydor 2374 165 | MAESTOSO (LP) | 12 |

(see also Barclay James Harvest)

WOLVES
64	Pye 7N 15676	Journey Into Dreams/What Do You Mean	18
64	Pye 7N 15733	Now/This Year Next Year	25
65	Pye 7N 17013	At The Club/Distant Dreams	35
66	Parlophone R 5511	Lust For Life/My Baby Loves Them	60+

BOBBY WOMACK
68	Minit MLF 11001	Broadway Walk/Somebody Special	15
68	Minit MLF 11005	What Is This?/What You Gonna Do	20
68	Minit MLF 11010	Fly Me To The Moon/Take Me	10
69	Minit MLF 11012	California Dreamin'/Baby You Oughta Think It Over	15
72	United Artists UP 35339	That's The Way I Feel About 'Cha/Come, L'Amore	7
72	United Artists UP 35375	Woman's Gotta Have It/If You Don't Want My Love	5

73	United Artists UP 35456	I Can Understand It/Harry Hippie (some in p/s) 10/8
73	United Artists UP 35512	Across 110th Street/Hang On In There (as Bobby Womack & Peace) 10
73	United Artists UP 35565	Nobody Wants You When You're Down And Out/
		I'm Through Trying To Prove My Love For You 6
74	Jay Boy BOY 75	What Is This?/I Wonder 15
75	United Artists UP 35859	Check It Out/Interlude No. 2 6
76	United Artists UP 36042	Where There's A Will There's A Way/Everything's Gonna Be Alright 6
76	United Artists UP 36098	Daylight/Trust Me 10
79	Arista ARIST 284	How Could You Break My Heart/I Honestly Love You 20
82	Tamla Motown TMG1267	So Many Sides of You/ Just My Imagination (7", p/s) 60
87	Arista RIS 17	How Could You Break My Heart/Give It Up (p/s) 20
87	Arista RIST 17	How Could You Break My Heart/Give It Up/Mr. D.J. Don't Stop The Music (12", p/s) . 15
72	United Artists UAS 29365	UNDERSTANDING (LP) 15
73	United Artists UAS 29451	ACROSS 110th STREET (LP, soundtrack, with J.J. Johnson) 25
73	United Artists UAS 29306	COMMUNICATION (LP) 15
73	United Artists UAG 29456	FACTS OF LIFE (LP) 15
74	United Artists UAS 29574	LOOKIN' FOR A LOVE AGAIN (LP) 15
75	United Artists UAG 29715	I CAN'T UNDERSTAND IT (LP) 15
79	Arista ARTY 165	ROADS OF LIFE (LP) 20

(see also Valentinos, Ted Wood)

WOMB

69	Dot DLP 25933	WOMB (LP) 25
70	Dot DLP 25959	OVERDUB (LP) 30

WOMENFOLK

64	RCA RCA 1439	Turn Around/One Man's Hand 8
65	RCA RCA 1465	My Heart Tells Me To Believe/The Way I Feel 6
66	RCA Victor RCA 1522	The Last Thing On My Mind/Meditation 7
64	RCA LSP 2919/SF 7671	NEVER UNDERESTIMATE THE POWER OF WOMENFOLK (LP) 20
65	RCA RD 7704	AT THE HUNGRY I (LP) 18

ALISON WONDER

70	Columbia DB 8667	Once More With Feeling/Black Paper Roses 10

(see also Cheryl St. Clair)

GIRL WONDER

66	Doctor Bird DB 1015	Mommy Out Of The Light/Cutting Wood 18

(LITTLE) STEVIE WONDER

SINGLES

63	Oriole CBA 1853	Fingertips (Parts 1 & 2) (DJ copy = £85) 40
63	Stateside SS 238	Workout, Stevie, Workout/Monkey Talk (DJ copy = £85) 50
64	Stateside SS 285	Castles In The Sand/Thank You (For Loving Me All The Way) (DJ copy = £100) .. 60
64	Stateside SS 323	Hey, Harmonica Man/This Little Girl (DJ copy = £85) 50

(The above singles were credited to Little Stevie Wonder.)

65	Tamla Motown TMG 505	Kiss Me Baby/Tears In Vain (DJ copy = £100) 60
65	Tamla Motown TMG 532	High-Heel Sneakers/Music Talk (DJ copy = £100) 50
66	Tamla Motown TMG 545	Uptight (Everything's Alright)/Purple Raindrops (DJ copy = £150) 20
66	Tamla Motown TMG 558	Nothing's Too Good For My Baby/With A Child's Heart (DJ copy = £150) 40
66	Tamla Motown TMG 570	Blowin' In The Wind/Ain't That Asking For Trouble (DJ copy = £75) 25
66	Tamla Motown TMG 588	A Place In The Sun/Sylvia (DJ copy = £50) 20
67	Tamla Motown TMG 602	Travelin' Man/Hey Love (DJ copy = £50) 15
67	Tamla Motown TMG 613	I Was Made To Love Her/Hold Me (DJ copy = £40) 8
67	Tamla Motown TMG 626	I'm Wondering/Every Time I See You I Go Wild (DJ copy = £40) 15
68	Tamla Motown TMG 653	Shoo-Be-Doo-Be-Doo-Da-Day/Why Don't You Lead Me To Love (DJ copy = £30) . 8
68	Tamla Motown TMG 666	You Met Your Match/My Girl (DJ copy = £35) 15
68	Tamla Motown TMG 679	For Once In My Life/Angie Girl (DJ Copy = £30) 6
69	Tamla Motown TMG 690	My Cherie Amour/I Don't Know Why I Love You (DJ copy = £25) 6
69	Tamla Motown TMG 717	Yester-Me, Yester-You, Yesterday/I'd Be A Fool Right Now (DJ copy = £25) 6
70	Tamla Motown TMG 731	Never Had A Dream Come True/Somebody Knows, Somebody Cares (DJ = £25). 6
70	Tamla Motown TMG 744	Signed, Sealed, Delivered, I'm Yours/I'm More Than Happy (I'm Satisfied)
		(DJ copy = £25) 6
70	Tamla Motown TMG 757	Heaven Help Us All/I Gotta Have A Song (DJ copy = £20) 6
71	Tamla Motown TMG 772	We Can Work It Out/Don't Wonder Why (some in p/s) (DJ copy = £25) 30/6
71	Tamla Motown TMG 779	Never Dreamed You'd Leave In Summer/If You Really Love Me (DJ copy = £25) . 8
72	Tamla Motown TMG 798	If You Really Love Me/Think Of Me As Your Soldier 5
64	Stateside SE 1014	I CALL IT PRETTY MUSIC BUT THE OLD PEOPLE CALL IT THE BLUES (EP) .. 150
65	Tamla Motown TME 2006	LITTLE STEVIE WONDER (EP) 100
63	Oriole PS 40049	TRIBUTE TO UNCLE RAY (LP) 250
63	Oriole PS 40050	THE TWELVE-YEAR-OLD GENIUS — LIVE (LP) 200
64	Stateside SL 10078	THE JAZZ SOUL OF LITTLE STEVIE WONDER (LP) 175

(The above EPs and LPs were credited to Little Stevie Wonder.)

65	Stateside SL 10108	HEY, HARMONICA MAN (LP) 200
66	T. Motown (S)TML 11036	UPTIGHT (EVERYTHING'S ALRIGHT) (LP, mono/stereo) 50
67	T. Motown (S)TML 11045	DOWN TO EARTH (LP, mono/stereo) 50
68	T. Motown (S)TML 11059	I WAS MADE TO LOVE HER (LP) 40
68	T. Motown (S)TML 11075	GREATEST HITS (LP) 18
68	T. Motown (S)TML 11085	SOMEDAY AT CHRISTMAS (LP) 60
69	T. Motown (S)TML 11098	FOR ONCE IN MY LIFE (LP) 25
69	T. Motown (S)TML 11128	MY CHERIE AMOUR (LP) 20
70	T. Motown STML 11150	STEVIE WONDER 'LIVE' (LP) 15
70	T. Motown STML 11164	'LIVE' AT THE TALK OF THE TOWN (LP) 15
70	T. Motown STML 11169	SIGNED, SEALED AND DELIVERED (LP) 15
71	T. Motown STML 11183	WHERE I'M COMING FROM (LP) 18

(The above albums originally came with flipback sleeves; see also Diana Ross, Dionne Warwick, Gary Byrd)

WONDER BOY
69	Jackpot JP 703	Sweeten My Coffee (actually by Slim Smith)/MISTER MILLER: Cherry Pink	12
69	Jackpot JP 705	Love Power (actually by Slim Smith)/PAT KELLY: Since You Are Gone	12
71	Jackpot JP 764	Just For A Day/He Ain't Heavy	8
71	Concord CON 015	Just For A Day/He Ain't Heavy	5

(see also Slim Smith, Pat Kelly)

WONDER BOY
75	Ackee ACK 546	Pressure Parts 1 & 2	6

WONDERLAND
68	Polydor 56539	Poochy/Moscow	12

ALICE WONDERLAND
63	London HLU 9783	He's Mine/Cha Linde	25

WONDER STUFF
87	Far Out GONE ONE	It's Not True.../A Wonderful Day/Like A Merry-Go-Round/Down Here (EP, p/s)	30
87	Far Out GONE 002	Unbearable/Ten Trenches Deep (some with p/s)	10/5
87	Far Out GO BIG 002	Unbearable/Ten Trenches Deep/I Am A Monster/Frank (12", p/s)	8
88	Polydor GONE 3	Give Give Give Me More More More/A Song Without An End (p/s)	6
88	Polydor GONECD 3	Give Give Give Me More More More/A Song Without An End/ Meaner Than Mean/Sell The Free World (CD)	10
88	Polydor 080 582-2	Give Give Give Me More More More (video)/A Song Without An End/ Meaner Than Mean/Sell The Free World (CD Video)	10
88	Polydor GONECD 4	A Wish Away/Jealousy/Happy-Sad/Goodbye Fatman (CD)	10
88	Polydor GONECD 5	It's Yer Money I'm After Baby/Astley In The Noose/Ooh, She Said/ Rave From The Grave (CD)	10
89	Polydor GONE 6	Who Wants To Be The Disco King?/(same) (promo only, with dayglo p/s)	12
89	House Of Dolls HOD 011	Who Wants To Be The Disco King? (King Of Disco Megamix)/PRUDES: Christmas/SANDKINGS: Colourblind/WORLD MUSIC: Stop Playing With My Heart (no p/s, free with *House Of Dolls* magazine)	6/4
87	Far Out	A HANDFUL OF SONGS (private cassette)	20
87	Polydor	A HANDFUL OF SONGS (cassette, promo only, different to above)	15
88	Polydor GONECD 1	THE EIGHT-LEGGED GROOVE MACHINE (CD, mispressed with "Wish Away" printed on front cover)	30

(see also Vic Reeves)

WONDERWHEEL
(see under Gary Wright)

WONDER WHO
65	Philips BF 1440	Don't Think Twice, It's Alright/Sassy	12
66	Philips BF 1504	On The Good Ship Lollipop/You're Nobody Till Somebody Loves You	10
67	Philips BF 1600	Lonesome Road/FOUR SEASONS: Around And Around	20

(see also Four Seasons, Frankie Valli)

ROYCE WONG
65	Blue Beat BB 301	Everything's Gonna Be Alright/Hang Your Head And Cry	20

WONKY ALICE
92	Pomona POM 004	SIRIUS EP (12", p/s)	12

ANITA WOOD
62	London HLS 9585	I'll Wait Forever/I Can't Show You How I Feel	22
64	Sue WI 328	Dream Baby/This Happened Before	40

BOBBY WOOD
64	Pye International 7N 25264	I'm A Fool For Loving You/My Heart Went Boing! Boing! Boing!	12

BRENTON WOOD
67	Philips BF 1579	Oogum Boogum Song/I Like The Way You Love Me	8
67	Liberty LBF 15021	Gimme Little Sign/I Think You Got Your Fools Mixed Up	15
68	Liberty LBF 15065	Baby You Got It/Catch You On The Rebound	8
68	Liberty LBF 15103	Some Got It, Some Don't/Me And You	8
70	Pye International 7N 25522	Great Big Bundle Of Love/Can You Dig It	15
71	United Artists UP 35266	Gimme Little Sign/I Think You Got Your Fools Mixed Up (reissue)	6
73	Epic EPC 1383	Another Saturday Night/Attempted Love	6
67	Liberty LBL/LBS 83088E	GIMME A LITTLE SIGN (LP)	40

CHUCK WOOD
67	Big T BIG 104	Seven Days Too Long/Soul Shing-A-Ling	25
68	Big T BIG 107	I've Got My Lovelight Shining/Baby You Win	15
71	Mojo 2092 010	Seven Days Too Long/Soul Shing A Ling (reissue)	10
75	Pye Disco Demand DDS 111	Seven Days Too Long/Wigan's Chosen Few (some in p/s)	15/10

DEL WOOD
54	London HL 8036	Ragtime Annie/Backroom Polka (78 rpm = £6)	50
54	London RE-P 1007	RAGTIME PIANO (EP)	15
57	RCA RD 27011	DOWN YONDER (LP)	12

GLORIA WOOD
53	Capitol CL 13947	Hey, Bell Boy/Anybody Hurt? (78)	8

RONNIE WOOD
74	Warner Bros K 16463	I Can Feel The Fire/Breathe On Me (as Ron Wood)	10
75	Warner Bros K 16618	If You Don't Want Me Love/I've Got A Feeling	9
76	Warner Bros K 16679	Big Bayou/Sweet Baby Mine	12
79	CBS 7785	Seven Days/Come To Realise	7
92	Continuum 12210-2	Show Me/Breathe On Me (CD, with Ronnie Wood print, signed & numbered, in black card case tied with ribbon, 600 only)	45

74	Warner Bros K 56065	I'VE GOT MY OWN ALBUM TO DO (LP, with insert)	15
75	Warner Bros K 56145	NOW LOOK (LP)	12
76	Atlantic K 50308	MAHONEY'S LAST STAND (LP, soundtrack, with Ronnie Lane)	15
79	CBS 83337	GIMME SOME NECK (LP, with inner sleeve)	12
81	CBS 85227	1234 (LP) (with inner sleeve)	12

(see also Faces, Rolling Stones, Jeff Beck, Ted Wood)

ROY WOOD

72	Harvest HAR 5048	When Gran'ma Plays The Banjo/Wake Up	7
75	Jet JET 754	Oh What A Shame/Bengal Jig (cartoon p/s)	5
75	Jet JET 761	Look Thru' The Eyes Of A Fool/Strider (some copies miscredited as "Looking Thru' The Eyes Of A Fool")	6/5
76	Jet JET 785	Any Old Time Will Do/The Rain Came Down On Everything	5
77	Warner Bros K 16961	The Stroll/Jubilee (p/s, by Wizzo Band)	5
77	Warner Bros K 17028	I Never Believed In Love/Inside My Life (as Roy Wood & Annie Haslam)	7
78	Warner Bros K 17094	Dancin' At The Rainbow's End/Waiting At This Door (p/s, as Wizzo Band)	5
78	Warner Bros K 17248	Keep Your Hands On The Wheel/Giant Footsteps	6
79	Automatic K 17459P	(We're) On The Road Again/Saxmaniacs (picture disc)	5
76	Harvest SHDW 408	THE ROY WOOD STORY (2-LP)	12
82	Speed SPEED 1000	THE SINGLES (LP, initially without "I Wish It Could Be Christmas Everyday")	12

(see also Wizzard, Gerry Levine & Avengers, Mike Sheridan, Danny King['s Mayfair Set], Move, ELO, Renaissance [UK], Rockers, Birds)

TED WOOD

76	Penny Farthing PEN 891	Am I Blue/Shine (B-side features Rod Stewart, Ronnie Wood, Gary Glitter & Bobby Womack)	8

(see also Temperance Seven)

WOODEN HORSE

72	York SYK 526	Pick Up The Pieces/Wake Me In The Morning	20
73	York SYK 543	Wooden Horses/Typewriter And Guitar	20
72	York FYK 403	WOODEN HORSE (LP)	200
73	York FYK 413	WOODEN HORSE II (LP, withdrawn, some with sleeve)	800/500

(see also Fox)

WOODEN O & GUESTS

69	Middle Earth MDLS 301	A HANDFUL OF PLEASANT DELITES (LP)	95

(see also 'Middle Earth Sampler' in Various Artists section)

KEN WOODMAN & HIS PICCADILLY BRASS

66	Strike JLH 101	THAT'S NICE (LP)	25

WOODPECKERS

64	Decca F 11835	The Woodpecker/You Can't Sit Down	8
65	Oriole CB 311	Hey Little Girl/What's Your Name	22

STANLEY WOODRUFF & U.S. TRIO

77	Grapevine GP 102	What Took You So Long/Now Is Forever	10

CAROL WOODS

72	Ember NR 5059	OUT OF THE WOODS (LP)	12

CORA WOODS

56	Parlophone DP 505	Rocks In Your Head/I Don't Want To Cry (export 78)	10

DANNY WOODS

72	Invictus INV 532	Everybody's Tippin'/Roller Coaster	8

DONALD WOODS & EARL PALMER BAND

58	Vogue V 9107	Memories Of An Angel/That Much Of Your Love (78 rpm = £150)	650

GAY & TERRY WOODS

77	Polydor 2058 810	Save The Last Dance For Me/One More Time	6
78	Rockburgh ROCS 202	We Can Work This One Out/Piece Of Summer (p/s)	5
75	Polydor 2383 322	BACKWOODS (LP)	55
76	Polydor 2383 375	THE TIME IS RIGHT (LP, with lyric insert)	45
76	Polydor 2383 406	RENOWNED (LP, with lyric insert)	45
78	Rockburgh ROC 104	TENDER HOOKS (LP, with lyric insert)	15

(see also Woods Band, Gay Woods, Steeleye Span, Sweeney's Men)

NICK WOODS

62	London HLU 9621	Ballad Of Billy Budd/Don't Let Me Down	8

PHIL WOODS

55	Esquire 20-055	NEW JAZZ QUINTET (10" LP)	25

WOODS BAND

71	Greenwich GSLP 1004	THE WOODS BAND (LP, gatefold sleeve)	90
77	Rockburgh CREST 29	THE WOODS BAND (LP, reissue in different sleeve)	15

(see also Gay & Terry Woods)

MAGGIE WOODWARD

59	Vogue V 9148	Ali Bama/Zulu Warrior (78 rpm = £20)	15

WOODY KERN

69	Pye 7N 17672	Biography/Tell You I'm Gone (demo)	110
69	Pye NSPL 18273	THE AWFUL DISCLOSURES OF MARIA MONK (LP)	40

BRIAN WOOLEY

58	Esquire EP 170	BRIAN WOOLEY'S JAZZMEN (EP)	10
58	Esquire EP 190	WILD 'N WOOLEY (EP)	12

MINT VALUE £

SHEB WOOLEY

51	MGM MGM 439	Hoot Owl Boogie/Country Kisses (78)	18
54	MGM MGM 757	Panama Pete/Blue Guitar (78)	12
55	MGM SP 1130	38-24-35/I Flipped (78 rpm, MGM 824 = £12)	25
55	MGM SPC 5	Hill Billy Mambo/I Go Outa My Mind (export issue)	30
58	MGM MGM 981	The Purple People Eater/I Can't Believe You're Mine	25
58	MGM MGM 981	The Purple People Eater/Recipe For Love (2nd pressing, different B-side)	15
58	MGM MGM 981	The Purple People Eater/I Can't Believe You're Mine (78)	8
58	MGM MGM 997	Santa And The Purple People Eater/Star Of Love) (78 rpm = £20)	12
59	MGM MGM 1017	Sweet Chile/More	10
60	MGM MGM 1081	Luke The Spook/My Only Treasure	15
61	MGM MGM 1132	The Wayward Wind/Bars Across The Windows	10
61	MGM MGM 1147	That's My Pa/Meet Mr. Lonely	12
62	MGM MGM 1162	Laughing The Blues/Somebody Please	12
65	MGM MGM 1257	Hootenanny Hoot/Old Joe Rag	6
65	MGM MGM 1263	Blue Guitar/Natchez Landing	5
56	MGM MGM-EP 540	JEST PLAIN, WILD AND WOOLEY (EP)	40
61	MGM MGM-C 859	SONGS FROM THE DAY OF RAWHIDE (LP)	25
62	MGM MGM-C 903	THAT'S MY MA AND THAT'S MY PA (LP)	25
63	MGM MGM-C 945	SPOOFING THE BIG ONES! (LP)	20
63	MGM MGM-C 955	TALES OF 'HOW THE WEST WAS WON' (LP)	20

(see also Ben Colder)

CHARLIE WOOLFE

| 68 | NEMS 56-3675 | Dance Dance Dance/Home | 12 |

(see also At Last The 1958 Rock & Roll Show)

WOOLIES

| 67 | RCA RCA 1602 | Who Do You Love?/Hey Girl | 45 |

WOOLLY FISH

| 70 | Plexium PXM 16 | Way You Like It/Sound Of Thick | 10 |

BRENDA WOOTTON

71	Sentinel SENS 1006	PASTIES & CREAM (LP, with John The Fish)	18
73	Sentinel SENS 1016	CROWDY CRAWN (LP, with Richard Gendall)	18
74	Sentinel SENS 1021	NO SONG TO SING? (LP, with Robert Bartlett, private pressing with lyric inner sleeve)	15
76	Sentinel SENS 1031	STARRY-GAZEY PIE (LP, with Robert Bartlett)	15

WORD

| 83 | Word WORD 001 | Colour It!/Recurring | 5 |

WORDBUG

91	Boss Tuneage BOSSTAGE6	LOSING IT ALL (LP, also listed as Home 4, with insert)	18
94	Boss Tunage BOSTAGE 021	Locked In (p/s)	8
94	Boss Tunage BOSTAGE 023	Died Waiting (p/s, blue vinyl, with insert)	7

WORK

| 81 | Woof WOOF 2 | I Hate America/Fingers & Toes/Duty (p/s, clear vinyl) | 5 |
| 82 | Recommended | SLOW CRIMES (LP, with insert) | 12 |

(see also Art Bears)

JIMMY WORK

56	London HLD 8270	When She Said "You All"/There's Only One You (78 rpm = £20)	75
56	London HLD 8308	You've Gotta Heart Like A Merry-Go-Round/Blind Heart (78 rpm = £20)	60
55	London RE-D 1039	COUNTRY SONGS — WORK STYLE (EP)	60

WORKFORCE

| 80s | WF WF 1 | The Right To Work/Holy Moses (p/s) | 5 |

WORKS

| 72 | London HLU 10360 | Orange Medley (Music Inspired By "A Clockwork Orange")/Sweet Charity | 5 |

WORLD

| 70 | Liberty LBF 15402 | Angelina/Come Out Into The Open | 7 |
| 70 | Liberty LBG 83419 | LUCKY PLANET (LP, gatefold sleeve) | 40 |

(see also Neil Innes, Bonzo Dog [Doo-Dah] Band)

WORLD COLUMN

| 76 | Capitol CL 15852 | So Is The Sun/It's Not Right | 10 |
| 76 | Capitol CL 15852 | So Is The Sun/It's Not Right (with Cleethorpes Anniversary sticker) | 30 |

WORLD OF OZ

68	Deram DM 187	The Muffin Man/Peter's Birthday (Black And White Rainbows)	15
68	Deram DM 205	King Croesus/Jack	15
69	Deram DM 233	Willow's Harp/Like A Tear	20
69	Deram DML/SML 1034	THE WORLD OF OZ (LP)	60

(see also David Kubinec)

WORLD OF TWIST

90	Circa YR 55	The Storm/She's A Rainbow (p/s)	5
91	Circa YR 72	Sweets/This Too Shall All Pass Away (p/s)	5
92	Caff CAFF 16	The Sausage/Skidding Into Love/Space Rockit (p/s, with insert)	8

BIMBI WORRICK

| 69 | Polydor 56321 | Long Time Comin'/Tomorrow Is My Day | 8 |

WORRYING KYNDE

| 67 | Piccadilly 7N 35370 | Call Out The Name/Got The Blame | 55 |

WORTH

| 70 | CBS 5309 | Shoot 'Em Up Baby/Take The World In Your Hands | 5 |

JOHNNY WORTH
57	Columbia DB 3962	Let's Go/Just Because	6

MARION WORTH
60	London HL 7089	Are You Willing, Willie/This Heart Of Mine (export issue)	25
60	London HL 7097	That's My Kind Of Love/I Lost Johnny (export issue)	25

STAN WORTH ORCHESTRA
63	London HLU 9703	Roman Holiday/Wiggle Wobble Walkers	10

WRANGLERS
64	Parlophone R 5163	Liza Jane/It Just Won't Work	65

(see also Kenny Bernard, Kenny & Wranglers)

LINK WRAY (& HIS RAY MEN)
58	London HLA 8623	Rumble/The Swag (as Link Wray & His Ray Men) (78 rpm = £25)	45
63	Stateside SS 217	Jack The Ripper/The Black Widow	30
64	Stateside SS 256	The Sweeper/Weekend	20
65	Stateside SS 397	Good Rockin' Tonight/I'll Do Anything For You	22
71	Polydor 2066 120	Fire And Brimstone/Jukebox Mama	6
73	Polydor 2066 320	Lawdy Miss Clawdy/Shine The Light	6
73	Virgin VS 103	I'm So Glad, I'm So Proud/Shawnee Tribe	6
76	Virgin VS 142	I Know You're Leaving Me Now/Quicksand	6
64	Stateside SE 1015	MR. GUITAR (EP, sleeve credits *Link Ray*)	110
71	Polydor 2489 029	LINK WRAY (LP)	25
71	Union Pacific UP 002	THERE'S GOOD ROCKIN' TONIGHT (LP)	25
73	Virgin V 2006	BEANS & FATBACK (LP)	15
73	Polydor 2391 063	BE WHAT YOU WANT TO (LP)	12
74	Polydor 2391 128	THE LINK WRAY RUMBLE (LP)	12

(see also Robert Gordon with Link Wray)

RAY WRAY QUARTET
62	Salvo SLO 1808	When Your Lover Has Gone/A Song Is Born	25

WRECKERS
64	Granta GR 7EP 1010	THE WRECKERS' SOUND (EP)	100

JENNY WREN
66	Fontana TF 672	Chasing My Dreams All Over Town/A Thought Of You	100
66	Fontana TF 772	The Merry-Go-Round (Is Slowing You Down)/Take A Walk Bobby	15

BIG JOHN WRENCHER
75	Big Bear BB 4	BIG JOHN'S BOOGIE (LP)	12

WRIGGLERS
68	Giant GN 26	The Cooler/You Cannot Know	50
68	Blue Cat BS 106	Get Right/If I Did Look	25

(see also Wrigglers)

BETTY WRIGHT
68	Atlantic 584 216	Girls Can't Do What The Guys Do/Sweet Lovin' Daddy	15
72	Atlantic K 10143	Clean Up Woman/I'll Love You Forever	8
72	Atlantic K 10190	Is It You Girl/Cryin' In My Sleep	6
75	RCA RCA 2548	Where Is The Love/My Baby Ain't My Baby Any More	6
72	Atlantic K 40364	I LOVE THE WAY YOU LOVE (LP)	15

CHARLES WRIGHT & WATTS 103rd STREET RHYTHM BAND
69	Warner Bros WB 7250	Do Your Thing/A Dance, A Kiss And A Song	8
69	Warner Bros WB 7298	Till You Get Enough/Light My Fire	8
70	Warner Bros WB 7365	Love Land/Sorry Charlie	8
70	Warner Bros WB 7417	Express Yourself/Living On Borrowed Time	20
72	Jay Boy BOY 71	Spreadin' Honey/Charley (as Watts 103rd Street Rhythm Band)	10
70s	Warner Bros	EXPRESS YOURSELF (LP)	30

DALE WRIGHT
58	London HLD 8573	She's Neat/Say That You Care (as Dale Wright & Rock-Its) (78 rpm = £65)	220
59	Pye International 7N 25022	That's Show Biz/That's My Gal (as Dale Wright & Wright Guys) (78 rpm = £80)	100

EARL WRIGHT
75	Capitol CL 15825	Thumb A Ride/Like A Rolling Stone	10

GARY WRIGHT('S WONDERWHEEL)
71	A&M AMLS 2004	EXTRACTIONS (LP)	15
72	A&M AMLS 64296	FOOTPRINT (LP)	15
72	A&M AMLH 64362	RING OF CHANGES (LP, as Wright's Wonderwheel; unissued, test pressings only)	50

(see also Spooky Tooth, Magic Christians, Thomas F. Browne)

GINNY WRIGHT (& TOM TALL)
55	London HL 8119	Indian Moon/Your Eyes Feasted Upon Her (solo)	55
55	London HL 8119	Indian Moon/Your Eyes Feasted Upon Her (solo) (78)	15
55	London HL 8150	Are You Mine?/Boom Boom Boomerang (with Tom Tall)	40
55	London RE-U 1035	COUNTRY SONGS VOL. 2 (EP, with Tom Tall)	45

(see also T. Tommy Cutrer & Ginny Wright, Tom Tall)

IAN WRIGHT
93	M&G MAGCD 45	Do The Right Thing (7" Version)/(Rollo – 2-1 Up Mix)/(Second To None Mix)/ (Rollo Dub Mix)/(Air Max Mix)/(Rollo 1-0 Down Mix) (CD, slimline case)	8

(see also Pet Shop Boys)

MILTON WRIGHT & TERRA SHIRMA STRINGS
77	Grapevine GRP 103	I Belong To You/The Gallop	15

NAT WRIGHT
59	HMV POP 629	Anything/For You My Love	75

OTIS WRIGHT

69	High Note HS 033	Man Of Galilee/Take Up The Cross	6
67	Doctor Bird DLM 5005	PEACE PERFECT PEACE (LP)	35+
67	Doctor Bird DLM 5006	IT WILL SOON BE DONE (LP)	35+
68	High Notes BSL5003	SACRED SONGS (LP)	30
60s	Coxsone TLP 1001	OVER IN GLORYLAND (LP)	40+
73	Tabernacle BSLP 5021	SOUL STIRRING GOSPEL SONGS (LP)	30

O.V. WRIGHT

65	Vocalion VP 9249	You're Gonna Make Me Cry/Monkey Dog	30
66	Vocalion VP 9255	Poor Boy/I'm In Your Corner	30
66	Vocalion VP 9272	Gone For Good/How Long Baby	25
67	London HLZ 10137	8 Men 4 Women/Fed Up With The Blues	20
68	Sue WI 4043	What About You/What Did You Tell This Girl Of Mine	50
68	Action ACT 4505	Oh Baby Mine/Working Your Game	30
69	Action ACT 4527	I Want Everyone To Know/I'm Gonna Forget About You	25
65	Vocalion VEP 170165	CAN'T FIND TRUE LOVE (EP)	150
68	Island ILP 975	8 MEN, 4 WOMEN (LP)	125

OWEN WRIGHT

| 70 | Banana BA 310 | Wala Wala (actually by Burning Spear)/JERRY & FREEDOM SINGERS: Got To Be Sure (B-side actually by Horace Andy) | 15 |

RICK WRIGHT

| 78 | Harvest SHVL 818 | WET DREAM (LP, gatefold stickered sleeve) | 12 |
| | (see also Pink Floyd, Zee) | | |

RITA WRIGHT

| 68 | Tamla Motown TMG 643 | I Can't Give Back The Love I Feel For You/Something On My Mind (DJ = £40) | 25 |
| 71 | Tamla Motown TMG 791 | I Can't Give Back The Love I Feel For You/Something On My Mind (reissue) | 8 |

RITA WRIGHT

| 78 | Jet UP 36382 | Love Is All You Need/Touch Me, Take Me | 48 |

RUBEN WRIGHT

| 66 | Capitol CL 15460 | Hey Girl/I'm Walking Out On You (DJ copy = £75) | 40 |

RUBY WRIGHT

53	Parlophone MSP 6025	Till I Waltz Again With You/When I Gave You My Love (with Charlie Gore)	35
54	Parlophone MSP 6073	Bimbo/Boy, You Got Yourself A Gal	35
54	Parlophone MSP 6133	Santa's Little Sleigh Bells/Toodle-oo To You	22
55	Parlophone MSP 6150	What Have They Told You?/I Had The Funniest Feeling	25
56	Parlophone MSP 6209	I Fall In Love With You Ev'ry Day/Do You Believe?	25
59	Parlophone R 4556	Three Stars/I Only Have One Lifetime	12
59	Parlophone R 4556	Three Stars/I Only Have One Lifetime (78)	30
59	Parlophone R 4589	You're Just A Flower From An Old Bouquet/Sweet Night Of Love	10
59	Parlophone GEP 8785	THE THREE STARS GIRL (EP)	60

SAMUEL E. WRIGHT

| 73 | Paramount PARA 3035 | There's Something Funny Going On/300 Pounds Of Hunger | 15 |

STEVE WRIGHT

| 59 | London HLW 8991 | Wild, Wild, Woman/Love You (78 rpm = £125) | 250 |

SYREETA WRIGHT

| 72 | Mowest MWS 7001 | SYREETA (LP) | 20 |

WINSTON WRIGHT

69	Doctor Bird DB 1308	Five Miles High/CARL DAWKINS: Only Girl	25
69	Camel CA 32	Power Pack/TWO SPARKS: Throwing Stones	15
69	Explosion EX 2003	Barefoot Brigade/Slippery	15
69	Trojan TR 7701	Moonlight (Lover) Groover/SENSATIONS: Everyday Is Just A Holiday	12
69	Trojan TR 7715	Moon Invader (with Tommy McCook)/RADCLIFF RUFFIN: You Got To Love Me	18
70	Trojan TR 7775	Meshwire (with Tommy McCook)/BARONS: Darling Please Return	18
70	Explosion EX 2011	Flight 404/LLOYD & ROBIN: Gawling Come Down (B-side actually "Higher Than The Highest Mountain" by Monty Morris)	20
70	Explosion EX 2015	Funny Girl/Funny Girl Version II	20
70	Duke DU 62	Poppy Cock (with J.J. All Stars)/CARL DAWKINS: This World And Me (B-side actually "Satisfaction")	20
70	Bamboo BAM 60	Reggae Feet/DON DRUMMOND: Royal Flush (B-side act. titled "The Rocket")	30
70	High Note HS 040	Soul Pressure/Seed You Sow (with Gaytones)	12
70	Moodisc MU 3501	Musically Red (with Maudie's Allstars; actually also with Count Sticky)/RHYTHM RULERS: Bratah	10
70	G.G. GG 4504	It's Been A Long Time/PAULETTE & GEE: Feel It More And More	8
70	Techniques TE 907	Top Secret/Crazy Rhythm	10
71	Upsetter US 378	Example (with 3rd & 4th Generation)/UPSETTER: Version	15
71	Duke DU 111	Silhouettes/That Did It	10
71	Camel CA 71	Silhouettes/That Did It	12
	(see also Ethiopians, John Holt, J.J. Allstars, Slickers)		

ZACHARIAH WRIGHT

| 70s | Bamboo BAM 403 | Lumumba Limbo/Green, Red and Gold | 10 |

BERNARD WRIGLEY

| 74 | Topic 12TS 241 | ROUGH AND WRIGLEY (LP) | 12 |
| 76 | Transatlantic TRA 327 | SONGS, STORIES AND ELEPHANTS (LP) | 12 |

WRIGLEYS

| 69 | Page One POF 118 | A Little Bit/Come Down Little Bird | 10 |

WRIT

| 66 | Decca F 12385 | Did You Ever Have To Make Up Your Mind/Solid Golden Teardrops | 10 |

WRITING ON THE WALL
69	Middle Earth MDS 101	Child On A Crossing/Lucifer Corpus	40
73	Pye 7N 45251	Man Of Renown/Buffalo	20
69	Middle Earth MDLS 303	THE POWER OF THE PICTS (LP)	200
95	Pie & Mash PAM 003	RARITIES FROM THE MIDDLE EARTH (LP, 500 copies only)	12
95	Tenth Planet TP 017	CRACKS IN THE ILLUSION OF LIFE (LP, gatefold sleeve)	12
96	Tenth Planet TP 018	BURGHLEY ROAD (LP, 1,000 copies only)	12

(see also 'Middle Earth Sampler' in Various Artists; Three's A Crowd)

W12 SPOTS
70s	Shepherds Bush SB 1	Sid Never Did/COSMIC PUNKS: 99 Years	12

WUGGERY
98	Wuggery WUG 1	Wuggery Muggery/Wugwats Weekend (p/s)	8

WURZEL
87	GWR GWR 4	Bess/People Say I'm Crazy (p/s)	8
87	GWR GWT 4	Bess/People Say I'm Crazy/Midnight In London/E.S.P. (12", p/s)	15

(see also Motörhead)

WURZELS
77	EMI EMI 2686	One For The Bristol City/Cheddar Cheese (p/s)	6
05	Rough Trade RTRADS302	Remember Me/I Am A Cider Drinker (British Sea Power) (7" ltd ed. 1,966 copies)	10

(see also British Sea Power)

JOHNNY WYATT
68	President PT 109	This Thing Called Love/To Whom It May Concern (horizontal/vertical artist credit)	100/25

ROBERT WYATT
74	Virgin VS 114	I'm A Believer/Memories	5
77	Virgin VS 115	Yesterday Man/Sonia	6
70	CBS 64189	THE END OF AN EAR (LP)	30
74	Virgin V 2017	ROCK BOTTOM (LP)	15
75	Virgin V 2034	RUTH IS STRANGER THAN RICHARD (LP)	12
82	Rough Trade ROUGH 35	NOTHING CAN STOP US (LP, early pressing without "Shipbuilding")	12

(see also Soft Machine, Matching Mole, Centipede, Ben Watt)

RICHARD ('POPCORN') WYLIE
63	Columbia DB 7012	Brand New Man/So Much Love In My Heart (as Richard Wylie)	45
77	Grapevine GRP 100	Rosemary What Happened (Parts 1 & 2) (as Richard 'Popcorn' Wylie)	18

BILL WYMAN
74	Rolling Stones RS 19112	Monkey Grip Glue/What A Blow	6
74	Rolling Stones RS 19115	White Lightning/Pussy	7
76	Rolling Stones RS 19119	A Quarter To Three/Soul Satisfying	5
76	Rolling Stones RS 19120	Apache Woman/Soul Satisfying	8
81	A&M AMS 8144	(Si Si) Ju Suis Un Rock Star/Rio De Janeiro	6
81	Polydor POSP 259	Tenderness (Maria Muldaur)/Noche De Amor	7
81	Polydor POSP 297	Green Ice Theme/Cloudhoppers (p/s)	12
74	Rolling Stones COC 59102	MONKEY GRIP (LP)	18
76	Rolling Stones COC 59105	STONE ALONE (LP)	18
81	A&M AMLSP 68540	BILL WYMAN (LP, picture disc)	15
81	Polydor POLS 11031	GREEN ICE (LP, soundtrack)	15
83	Ripple (no cat. no.)	DIGITAL DREAMS (LP, soundtrack, promo only)	100

(see also Rolling Stones, End)

WYNDER K. FROG
66	Island WI 280	Turn On Your Lovelight/Zooming	30
66	Island WI 3011	Sunshine Superman/Blues For A Frog	30
67	Island WIP 6006	Green Door/Dancing Frog	40
67	Island WIP 6014	I Am A Man/Shook Shimmy & Shake	50
68	Island WIP 6044	Jumping Jack Flash/Baldy	30
67	Island ILP 944/ILPS 9044	SUNSHINE SUPERFROG (LP, white label, mono/stereo)	60/100
68	Island ILP 982/ILPS 9082	OUT OF THE FRYING PAN (LP, pink label)	50

(see also Keef Hartley Band, Miller Anderson, Fair Weather, Grease Band)

MARTYN WYNDHAM-READ
70	Trailer LER 2009	NED KELLY AND THAT GANG (LP, white label, later 'highway' label)	18/12
71	Trailer LER 2028	MARTYN WYNDHAM-READ (LP)	15
73	Argo ZFB 82	HARRY THE HAWKER IS DEAD (LP)	25
75	Trailer LER 2092	MAYPOLES TO MISTLETOE (LP)	12
77	Broadside BRO 128	ENGLISH SPORTING BALLADS (LP, 1 side by High Level Ranters, 2000 only)	20

(see also A.L. Lloyd)

PETER WYNGARDE
70	RCA Victor RCA 1967	La Ronde De L'Amour/The Way I Cry Over You	30
70	RCA Victor PW 1	"Commits" Rape/The Way I Cry Over You (LP sampler, promo only)	45
70	RCA Victor SF 8087	PETER WYNGARDE (LP, gatefold sleeve)	80

(see also Larry Wallis, Tyrannosaurus Rex)

ALBERT WYNN CREOLE JAZZ
52	Vocalion V 1018	Down By The Levee/Parkway Stomp (78)	6

SANDY WYNNS
65	Fontana TF 550	Touch Of Venus/Lovers' Quarrel	250

MARK WYNTER
60	Decca F 11263	Image Of A Girl/Glory Of Love	8
60	Decca F 11279	Kickin' Up The Leaves/That's What I Thought	8
61	Decca F 11323	Dream Girl/Two Little Girls	8
61	Decca F 11354	Exclusively Yours/Warm And Willing	8
61	Decca F 11380	Girl For Ev'ry Day/The Best Time For Love	10

MINT VALUE £

62	Decca F 11434	Heaven's Plan/In Your Heart.	12
62	Decca F 11467	Angel Talk/I Love Her Still	15
62	Pye 7N 15466	Venus In Blue Jeans/Please Come Back To Me.	6
62	Pye 7N 15492	Go Away Little Girl/That Kinda Talk	5
63	Pye 7N 15511	Aladdin's Lamp/It Can Happen Any Day.	6
63	Pye 7N 15525	Shy Girl/Because Of You	6
63	Pye 7N 15554	Running To You/Don't Cry	8
63	Pye 7N 15577	It's Almost Tomorrow/Music To Midnight	6
64	Pye 7N 15595	The Boy You're Kissin'/I Learned A Lot From You	6
64	Pye 7N 15626	Only You/It's Love You Want	6
64	Pye 7N 15658	Answer Me/I Wish You Everything	6
64	Pye 7N 15686	Love Hurts/Can't Help Forgiving You	6
64	Pye 7N 15716	Forever And A Day/And I Love Her	6
65	Pye 7N 15771	Can I Get To Know You Better/Am I Living A Dream.	8
65	Pye 7N 15861	Someday You'll Want Me To Want You/Here Comes Summer	6
60	Decca DFE 6674	MARK TIME (EP)	30
63	Pye NEP 24176	IT'S MARK TIME (EP)	20
64	Pye NEP 24185	WYNTER TIME (EP).	20
61	Decca LK 4409	THE WARMTH OF WYNTER (LP)	35
64	Golden Guinea GGL 0250	MARK WYNTER (LP).	15
65	Ace Of Clubs ACL 1141	MARK WYNTER (LP).	30
67	Marble Arch MAL 647	MARK WYNTER (LP).	12

(see also Joe Brown & Mark Wynter)

GAIL WYNTERS
| 67 | London HLE 10144 | Snap Your Fingers/Find Myself A New Love | 12 |

JOHNNY X & THE SINGIN' SWINGIN' EIGHT
| 63 | Fontana TF 408 | Lemonade/Come Closer Melinda. | 12 |

X-CALIBURS
| 65 | CBS 201805 | We Will Love/Swing That Chariot | 8 |
| 65 | Mercury MF 941 | You'll Find Out/That's What Happens (possibly as Xcalibres). | 8 |

X-CELLS
| 81 | Snotty Snail NEL COL 4 | Freedom Man/SCHIZOID: Nowhere To Go (p/s) | 12 |

X-CERTS
| 78 | Zama | Feeling The Groove (p/s) | 15 |
| 81 | Recreational PLAY 1 | Together/Untogether (p/s, with lyric insert) | 6 |

X-DREAMYSTS
78	Good Vibrations GOT 5	Right Way Home/Dance Away Love (p/s)	18
79	Polydor 2059 129	Bad News/Money Talks (p/s)	10
80	Polydor 2059 235	I Don't Wanna Go/Silly Games (p/s)	10
80	Polydor 2059 252	Stay The Way You Are/Race Against Time (p/s)	10

X-E-CUTORS
| 80 | Rok ROK 13/14 | Too Far To Look Inside My Head/X-FILMS: After My Blood (die-cut co. sleeve) | 10 |

XERO
83	Brickyard XERO 1	Oh Baby/Hold On (2-track issue, p/s)	22
83	Brickyard XERO 1	Oh Baby/Hold On/Lone Wolf (3-track limited issue, p/s)	15
83	Brickyard XERO 1T	Oh Baby/Hold On/Lone Wolf (12", plain card sleeve with sticker, withdrawn)	20
83	Brickyard XERO 1T	Oh Baby/Hold On/Killer Frog (12", reissue)	10

(see also Bruce Dickinson, Iron Maiden)

XILES
| 65 | Xiles XIL 004 | Our Love Will Never End/The Only People In This World. | 20 |

XIT
72	Rare Earth RES 107	I Was Raised/End	5
73	Rare Earth RES 111	Reservation Of Education/Young Warrior	5
72	Rare Earth SREA 4002	PLIGHT OF THE RED MAN (LP)	18

XL5
| 63 | HMV POP 1148 | XL5 (Zero G)/Caviare. | 20 |
| 63 | HMV 7EG 8802 | FIREBALL AND OTHER TITLES (EP, 2 tracks by Don Spencer) | 50 |

XL5's
| 80 | Fourplay FOUR 004 | Fireball/Misirlou. | 8 |

X-MAL DEUTSCHLAND
| 83 | 4AD AD 311 | Incubus Succubus II/Vito (p/s, some with "Vito" listed as A-side) | 20/7 |

X-MEN
| 84 | Creation CRE 006 | Do The Ghost/Talk (foldaround p/s in bag, orange/blue or yellow/green p/s) | 5 |
| 85 | Creation CRE 013 | Spiral Girl/Bad Girl (foldaround p/s in polyester bag) | 5 |

X-O-DUS

79	Factory FAC 11	English Black Boys/See Them A-Come (12", dark-grey textured p/s, later light grey p/s) 8

XPOZEZ

80s	Fight FIGHT 1	SYSTEMS KILL (EP) 6
82	Red Rhino RED 15	1,000 Marching Feet/Terminal Case (p/s) 5
83	Sexual Phonograph SPH 2	(Be My) New York Doll/It's All Been Done Before (p/s) 5

X-RAYS

59	London HLR 8805	Chinchilla/Out Of Control (78 rpm = £40) 40

X-RAY SPEX

77	Virgin VS 189	Oh Bondage, Up Yours/I Am A Cliche (some in p/s) 18/5
77	Virgin VS 189-12	Oh Bondage, Up Yours/I Am A Cliche (12", company sleeve) 15
78	EMI International INT 553	The Day The World Turned Day-Glo/Lama Poseur (p/s, 15,000 orange vinyl) 8/5
78	EMI International INT 563	Identity/Let's Submerge (p/s, initially on pink vinyl) 8/5
78	EMI International INT 573	Germ Free Adolescents/Age (p/s) 7
79	EMI International INT 583	Highly Inflammable/Warrior In Woolworths (p/s, initially on red vinyl) 10/7
78	EMI Intl. INS 3023	GERM FREE ADOLESCENTS (LP, with lyric inner sleeve) 18
90s	EMI Intl. INS 3023	GERM FREE ADOLESCENTS (LP, orange vinyl reissue) 12
(see also Poly Styrene, Essential Logic)		

XS DISCHARGE

80	G. Marxist COMMINIQUE 3	Across The Border/Frustration (p/s)..................................... 15
80	Groucho Marxist WH 3	Life's A Wank (p/s) 20

XS ENERGY

78	World WRECK 1	Eighteen/Jenny's Alright/Horrorscope! (numbered foldover yellow or green p/s, stamped white labels) 15
79	Dead Good DEAD 1	Eighteen/Jenny's Alright/Horrorscope! (reissue, 'National Souvenir Issue', different foldover p/s, stamped white labels)........................... 10
79	Dead Good DEAD 1	Eighteen/Jenny's Alright/Horrorscope! (stamped white sleeve & yellow printed labels) 8
79	Dead Good DEAD 3	Use You/Imaginary (p/s) 7

XTC

77	Virgin VS 188	Science Friction/She's So Square (unreleased, in picture sleeve) .... 2500+
77	Virgin VS 188	Science Friction/She's So Square (unreleased, no picture sleeve).......... 80
77	Virgin VS 188-12	3D EP (12" version of the above, p/s)................................... 10
78	Virgin VS 201	Statue Of Liberty/Hang On To The Night (p/s) 6
78	Virgin VS 209	This Is Pop?/Heatwave (p/s) 6
79	Virgin VS 259	Life Begins At The Hop/Homo Safari (30,000 clear vinyl, PVC sleeve & insert) 6
79	Virgin VS 282	Making Plans For Nigel/Bushman President (Homo Safari Series No. 2)/ Pulsing, Pulsing (initially with game-board p/s with playing pieces).......... 6/4
79	Smash Hits HIT 002	Ten Feet Tall/SKIDS: The Olympian (33rpm red flexidisc with Smash Hits) 8/5
80	Virgin VS 365	Generals And Majors/Don't Lose Your Temper//Smokeless Zone/ The Somnambulist (double pack) 6
81	Virgin VS 372	Towers Of London/Set Myself On Fire (live)//Battery Brides (live)/ Scissor Man (double pack) 6
81	RSO RSO 71	Take This Town/RUTS: Babylon's Burning (p/s) 6
81	Virgin VS 384	Sgt. Rock (Is Going To Help Me)/Generals And Majors (1st 20,000 in poster p/s, with stickered PVC sleeve) 6/4
82	Lyntone LYN 11032	Looking For Footprints (flexidisc free with Flexipop magazine, issue 16; on red, blue, green or yellow vinyl) 8/5
82	Virgin VS 490	No Thugs In Our House/Chain Of Command/Limelight/ Over Rusty Water (9" die-cut gatefold p/s)................................ 8
87	Virgin CDEP 3	Dear God/Homo Safari/Bushman President/Egyptian Solution/ Mantis On Parole/Frost Circus/Procession Toward Learning Land (CD, gatefold card sleeve) 10
88	Virgin CDT 9	Senses Working Overtime/Egyptian Solution (Homo Safari Series No. 3)/ Blame The Weather/Tissue Tigers (The Arguers) (3" CD, card sleeve)......... 8
89	Virgin VSCD 1158	Mayor Of Simpleton/Ella Guru/Living In A Haunted Heart/ The Good Things (3" CD, gatefold card sleeve) 12
89	Virgin VSCD 1177	King For A Day (7" Version)/King For A Day (12" Version)/ My Paint Heroes (Home Demo)/Skeletons (Home Demo) (3" CD, 'crown' pack) 12
92	Virgin VS 1426	Wrapped In Grey (p/s, withdrawn, 2,000 only) 70
92	Virgin VSCDT 1426	WRAPPED IN GREY (CD EP, withdrawn, 2,000 only) 100
78	Virgin V 2095	WHITE MUSIC (LP, with black inner sleeve)............................... 12
78	Virgin V 2108	GO 2 (LP, with insert, 1st 15,000 with bonus 12" EP: "Go +") 15
79	Virgin V 2129	DRUMS AND WIRES (LP, with gatefold insert, 1st 15,000 with free 7": "Chain Of Command"/"Limelight" [VDJ 30]) 12
80	Virgin V 2173	BLACK SEA (LP, with green paper outer sleeve & lyric insert)............... 12
84	Virgin V 2251	WAXWORKS (LP, with bonus LP, "Beeswax")............................. 14
84	Virgin V 2325	THE BIG EXPRESS (LP, circular sleeve & lyric inner)....................... 12
88	Virgin CDVT 2581	ORANGES AND LEMONS (LP, as 3-CD single box set) 12
(see also Mr Partridge, Barry Andrews, Three Wise Men, Dukes Of Stratosphere, Colonel, Spys)		

XTRAVERTS

78	Spike SRTS SP 001	Blank Generation/A-Lad-In-Sane...120
78	Rising Sun RS 1	Police State/PLASTIC PEOPLE: Demolition (p/s, multi-coloured vinyl) 60
81	Xtraverts XTRA 001	Speed/1984 (white labels, 'photo' or 'no photo' foldout poster p/s) 35/40

YABBY U/YABBY YOU/YABBY YOUTH
78	Prophets PHTS 2337	King Pharaoh Plague On The Land/Babylon Kingdom Fall (12")	30
79	Grove Music GMDM 18	Babylon A Fall/TONY TUFF - Falling Babylon (12")	40
79	Grove Music GMDM 24	Lady Lady/Stop Your Quarelling (12", B-side with Tommy McCook)	30
76	Lucky PD LPYU	RAM-A-DAM (LP) (with two different sleeves)	each 100
77	Grove Music GMLP 001	DELIVER ME FROM MY ENEMIES (LP, credited to The Yabby You Vibration on sleeve)	60
77	Grove Music GMLP 004	BEWARE DUB (LP)	80
78	Nationwide PRO 001	CHANT DOWN BABYLON KINGDOM (LP)	60
78	Rama PD LP	YU RAM-A-DAM (LP)	50
80	Grove / Island ILPS 9615	JAH JAH WAY (LP)	30
82	WLN WNLP001	YABBY YOU MEETS SLY 'N' ROBBIE (LP, with Tommy McCook)	25

YACHTS
77	Stiff BUY 19	Suffice To Say/Freedom Is A Heavy Wine (p/s)	6
78	Radar ADA 23	Look Back In Love (Not In Anger)/I Can't Stay Long (p/s, blue vinyl)	8
79	Radar RAD 19	THE YACHTS (LP, with live 7" "Suffice To Say"/"On And On" [SAM 98, p/s])	12

(see also Big In Japan)

YADS
92	Fairfields YAD 2	Yippee For Shtonk/It's There, You Mong (p/s)	7

YA HO WA 13
83	Psycho PSYCHO 2	GOLDEN SUNRISE (LP, 319 copies only, different coloured vinyls, some on black vinyl without sleeve)	60

(see also Seeds)

YAKS
65	Decca F 12115	Yakety Yak/Back In '57	22

YANA
56	HMV POP 252	Climb Up The Wall/If You Don't Love Me	18
57	HMV POP 340	Mr. Wonderful/Too Close For Comfort	15
58	HMV POP 481	I Need You/I Miss You Mama (78 rpm = £8)	12
58	HMV POP 546	Papa And Mama/In The Morning	12

YANCEY
79	Octane WS 302	Standing Waiting/Woman (no p/s)	20
79	Hammer HS 302	Standing Waiting/Woman (reissue)	8

JIMMY YANCEY
54	HMV 7EG 8062	JIMMY YANCEY (EP)	20
55	HMV 7EG 8083	JIMMY YANCEY (EP)	20
58	Vogue EPV 1203	YANCEY'S PIANO (EP)	20
54	London AL 3525	JIMMY YANCEY — A LOST RECORDING DATE (10" LP)	25
56	Vogue LDE 166	JAZZ IMMORTALS VOLUME 2 (10" LP)	30
68	Atlantic 590 018	LOWDOWN DIRTY BLUES (LP)	15

MAMA YANCEY/DON EWELL
57	Tempo LAP 7	MAMA YANCEY-DON EWELL (10" LP)	30

(see also Don Ewell)

ZALMAN YANOVSKY
67	Kama Sutra KAS 209	As Long As You're Here/Ereh Er'uoy Sa Gnol Sa (unreleased)	
67	Pye International 7N 25438	As Long As You're Here/Ereh Er'uoy Sa Gnol Sa	8
71	Kama Sutra 2316 003	ALIVE AND WELL IN ARGENTINA (LP)	18

(see also Mugwumps, Lovin' Spoonful)

YARDBIRDS
64	Columbia DB 7283	I Wish You Would/A Certain Girl	25
64	Columbia DB 7391	Good Morning Little Schoolgirl/I Ain't Got You	25
65	Columbia DB 7499	For Your Love/Got To Hurry	10
65	Columbia DB 7594	Heart Full Of Soul/Steeled Blues	8
65	Columbia DB 7706	Evil Hearted You/Still I'm Sad (some copies with A-side miscredited to "Samwell-Smith & McCartney")	5
66	Columbia DB 7848	Shapes Of Things/You're A Better Man Than I	6
66	Columbia DB 7848	Shapes Of Things/Still I'm Sad (mispressing)	45
66	Columbia DB 7928	Over, Under, Sideways, Down/Jeff's Boogie	20
66	Columbia DB 8024	Happenings Ten Years Time Ago/Psycho Daisies	35
67	Columbia DB 8165	Little Games/Puzzles	30
68	Columbia DB 8368	Goodnight Sweet Josephine/Think About It (unreleased; EMIdisc acetates only)	200+
64	Columbia SEG 8421	FIVE YARDBIRDS (EP)	90
67	Columbia SEG 8521	OVER UNDER SIDEWAYS DOWN (EP)	160
64	Columbia 33SX 1677	FIVE LIVE YARDBIRDS (LP, 1st pressing, blue/black label, flipback sleeve)	120
69	Columbia 33SX 1677	FIVE LIVE YARDBIRDS (LP, 2nd pressing, black/silver label, flipback sleeve)	22
60s	Columbia TA SX 6063	FIVE LIVE YARDBIRDS (reel-to-reel tape)	20
66	Columbia SCXC 28	HAVING A RAVE UP WITH THE YARDBIRDS (LP, export issue)	125
66	Columbia S(C)X 6063	THE YARDBIRDS (LP, 1st pressing, blue/black label, flipback sleeve, mono/stereo)	35/40
69	Columbia S(C)X 6063	THE YARDBIRDS (LP, 2nd pressing, black/silver label, flipback sleeve)	18

70	Columbia S(C)X 6063	THE YARDBIRDS (LP, 3rd pressing, black/silver label, non-flipback sleeve; some sleeves misprinted without front cover illustration)	18/15
84	Charly BOX 104	SHAPES OF THINGS (LP, box set)	30

(see also Eric Clapton, Jeff Beck, Jimmy Page, Keith Relf, Reign, Stairway, Sonny Boy Williamson & Yardbirds, Shoot)

PER YARROH
88	HMV PY 1	Laughing Inside/Laughing Inside (p/s, promo only; actually by Roy Harper)	7

(see also Roy Harper)

TOM YATES
67	CBS BPG 63094	SECOND CITY SPIRITUAL (LP, as Thomas Yates)	65
72	President PTLS 1053	LOVE COMES WELL ARMED (LP, with booklet)	30
77	Satril SATL 4007	SONG OF THE SHIMMERING WAY (LP, with insert)	25

Y BLEW
67	Qualiton QSP 7001	Maes 'B'/Beth Sy'n Dod Rhyngom Ni (p/s)	10

YEAH YEAH YEAHS
01	Wichita WEBB 029T	YEAH YEAH YEAHS EP: Bang/Mystery Girl/Art Star/Miles Away/Our Time (12", p/s)	10

YEAR ONE
69	Major Minor MM 660	Eli's Comin'/Will You Be Staying After Sunday	10

YEH YEH
85	Berlin BRS 001	You Will Pay/7 Bells (1st pressing in grey p/s)	5

YELLO
81	Do It DUN 11	Bimbo/I.T. Splash (p/s)	6
82	Do It DUN 13	Bostich/She's Got A Gun (Instrumental) (p/s)	5
82	Do It DUNIT 13	Bostich/Downtown Samba/She's Got A Gun/Daily Disco (12", p/s)	10
82	Do It DUN 18	She's Got A Gun/Glue Head (p/s)	5
82	Do It DUNIT 18	She's Got A Gun/The Evening's Young/There Is No Reason (12", p/s)	8
82	Do It DUN 23	Pinball Cha Cha/Smile On You (p/s)	5
82	Do It DUNIT 23	Pinball Cha Cha/Smile On You (12", p/s)	5
83	Stiff PBUY 176	I Love You/Rubber West (3-D picture disc, with glasses)	5
83	Stiff BUY 191	Lost Again/Base For Alec (p/s)	6
83	Stiff DBUY 191	Lost Again/Base For Alec//Let Me Cry/She's Got A Gun (double pack)	6
85	Elektra EKR 17T	Desire/Oh Yeah (Indian Summer "Stella Suite Part 2"/Oh Yeah/ XS (First Ever Version) (12", double pack, some sealed)	15/12
86	Mercury MERDP 218	Goldrush/She's Got A Gun (live at Palladium N.Y.)/I Love You/ Desire (double pack, unreleased)	
86	Mercury MERXD 218	Goldrush/Goldrush II/She's Got A Gun (live)//Pinball Cha-Cha/ Vicious Games (12", double pack)	8
87	Mercury MERXR 253	The Rhythm Divine (Version Two)/Dr. Van Steiner (Instrumental)/The Rhythm Divine (Original 7" Version) (12", p/s, as Yello featuring Billy MacKenzie)	30
87	Mercury YELCD 1	The Race (13.22)/La Habanera (CD, individually silk-screened card sleeve, various colours)	8
87	Mercury 080 528-2	The Race (Extended Version)/Another Race (Magician's Version)/ The Race (Video) (CD Video)	10
88	Mercury 080 644-2	Tied Up In Red (Video)/Wall St. Bongo/Third Of June (CD Video)	10
83	Stiff BUYIT 176	I Love You (Extended)/Swing/Bostich (12", p/s)	8
83	Stiff BUYIT 191	Lost Again/Base For Alec/No More Words/Pumping Velvet (12", p/s)	8
89	Mercury 080 832-2	Third Of June/Alhambra/Otto Di Cantania/Of Course I'm Lying (Video) (CD Video)	10
83	Stiff SEEZ 48	YOU GOTTA SAY YES TO ANOTHER EXCESS (LP, with bonus white label 12": "I Love You"/"Lost Again"/"You Gotta Say To Another Excess [remix]"/"Pumping Velvet")	15
87	Mercury MERH 100	ONE SECOND (LP, with bonus 12" in p/s: "Call It Love (Trego Snare Version 2)"/"Santiago [live at Roxy New York]")	15
88	Mercury 836 778-1	FLAG (LP, HMV competition issue, 100 only)	70
95	Urban 527 728-2	HANDS ON YELLO: THE UPDATES (2-CD, withdrawn)	30

(see also Associates)

YELLOTONE
03	Ai AI 004	GREEN MAYO EP (12", p/s)	8

YELLOW
70	CBS 4869	Roll It Down The Hill/Living A Lie	28

YELLOW BALLOON
67	Stateside SS 2008	Yellow Balloon/Noollab Wolley	22
68	Stateside SS 2124	Stained Glass Window/Can't Get Enough Of Your Love	18

YELLOW BELLOW ROOM BOOM
68	CBS 3205	Seeing Things Green/Easy Life	20

(see also 10cc, Frabjoy & Runcible Spoon)

YELLOW MAGIC ORCHESTRA
79	A&M AMSP 7447	Tong Poo/Cosmic Surfin' (12", p/s, yellow vinyl)	10
80	A&M JAPAN 2	Nice Age/Rydeen (p/s, yellow vinyl)	7
80	A&M AMS 7502	Computer Game/Firecracker/Technopolis (yellow vinyl, PVC sleeve)	7
80	A&M AMS 7559	Behind The Mask/Yellow Magic (p/s, yellow vinyl)	7
82	Alfa ALF 2145	Rydeen/Absolute Ego Dance (white vinyl, stickered sleeve)	5
80	A&M LH 68516	MULTIPLIES (LP, yellow vinyl)	12

(see also Ruichi Sakamoto)

YELLOW PAGES
68	Page One POF 090	Here Comes Jane/Ring-A-Ding	30

(see also Mirage)

MINT VALUE £

YELLOW PAYGES
70	UNI UNS 516	Follow The Bouncing Ball/Little Woman	8
71	UNI UNS 534	Birds Of A Feather/Lady Friend	5

YELLOW 6
90s	Enraptured RAPTLP 36	OVERTONE (2-LP, clear vinyl, numbered, handprinted sleeve, 300 only)	20

YELLOWSTONE & VOICE
72	Regal Zono. SRZA 8511	YELLOWSTONE & VOICE (LP)	20

YEMM & YEMEN
66	Columbia DB 8022	Black Is The Night/Do Blondes Really Have More Fun?	35+

YES
69	Atlantic 584 280	Sweetness/Something's Coming	40
69	Atlantic 584 298	Looking Around/Everydays (unconfirmed demos)	150+
70	Atlantic 584 323	Time And A Word/The Prophet	100
70	Atlantic 2091 004	Sweet Dreams/Dear Father	35
71	Atlantic 2814 003	I've Seen All Good People (a) Your Move/Starship Trooper (a) Life Seeker (promo only)	75
72	6-A1/-B1	Siberian Khatru/And You And I (white label promo)	50
74	Atlantic K 10407	Roundabout/And You And I	5
77	Atlantic K 10985	Going For The One/Parallels (unconfirmed)	60+
77	Atlantic K 10985T	Going For The One (Extended)/Parallels (12", unconfirmed)	40+
83	Atco B 9817P	Owner Of A Lonely Heart/Our Song (blue, black or grey shaped picture disc)	8
83	Atco B 9817C	Owner Of A Lonely Heart/Our Song (cassette)	20
70s	Lyntone LYN 2535	Interview/Five Songs (flexidisc or vinyl, some with 80-page Yes songbook)	70/35
69	Atlantic 588 190	YES (LP, red/plum label with lyric insert)	40
70	Atlantic 2400 006	TIME AND A WORD (LP, red/plum label, with lyric insert)	30
71	Atlantic 2400 101	THE YES ALBUM (LP, red/plum label, gatefold sleeve)	25
71	Atlantic 2401 019	FRAGILE (LP, red/plum label, gatefold sleeve with booklet)	30
72	Atlantic K 50012	CLOSE TO THE EDGE (LP, textured sleeve, with lyric insert)	12
77	Atlantic DSK 50379	GOING FOR THE ONE (LP, as 3 x 12" singles, promo only)	100+
80	Atlantic K 50842	CLASSIC YES (LP, with bonus 7" "Roundabout"/"Your Move" [SAM 141])	15
80	Atlantic K 50842	CLASSIC YES (LP, promo, with different sleeve)	30+

(see also Jon Anderson, Hans Christian, Syn, Syndicats, Winston's Fumbs, Warriors, Federals, Peter Banks, Flash, Asia, Rick Wakeman, Steve Howe, Refugee, Chris Squire)

YETTIES
69	Acorn CF 203	FIFTY STONE OF LOVELINESS (LP)	15
60s	Argo ZBF 38	DORSET IS BEAUTIFUL (LP)	20
60s	Argo ZBF 86	ALL AT SEA (LP)	20
60s	Argo ZDA 168	OF YETMINSTER (LP)	20

JOHN YLVISAKER
68	Avantgarde AV 107	COOL LIVIN' (LP)	60

YOBS
77	NEMS NES 114	Run Rudolph Run/The Worm Song (p/s)	7
78	Yob YOB 79	Silent Night/Stille Nacht (p/s)	7
81	Safari YULE 1	Rub-A-Dum-Dum/Another Christmas (p/s)	7
82	Fresh FRESH 41	Yobs On 45/The Ballad Of Warrington (p/s)	7
80	Safari RUDE 1	CHRISTMAS ALBUM (LP)	12

(see also Boys)

MAHARISHI MAHESH YOGI
67	Liberty LBS 83075E	MAHARISHI MAHESH YOGI (LP)	20

YOLANDA
60	Triumph RGM 1007	With This Kiss/Don't Tell Me Not To Love You	35

(see also Kenny Graham & His Satellites)

YO LA TENGO
95	Duophonic Super 45s DS 45-10	Evanescent Psychic Pez Drop/STEREOLAB: Long Hair Of Death (gig single, fluorescent yellow vinyl, plain white stickered card sleeve, 3,000 only)	20
96	Earworm WORM 4	Blue — Green Arrow/Watching The Sun Set On Johnny Carson (2,000 only, 100 in handmade p/s)	12/8

NOLA YORK
64	HMV POP 1326	I Don't Understand/Here I Stand	5
66	Philips BF 1527	A Whole Lotta Lovin'/You Just Didn't Wanna Know	5
67	Philips BF 1558	I Can Hear You Calling/Clown Face	6
67	Philips BF 1582	Photographs/He's Looking At Her	5
67	Philips BF 1606	There's So Much Love All Around Me/Sleeping Boutique	5
68	Philips BF 1714	Ciao Baby/We'll Get To Heaven	6

(see also Bow Bells)

PETE YORK PERCUSSION BAND
73	Decca TXS 109	PERCUSSION BAND (LP, with Ian Paice, gatefold sleeve)	40

(see also Spencer Davis Group, Hardin & York, Deep Purple)

RUSTY YORK
58	Parlophone R 4398	Peggy Sue/Shake 'Em Up Baby (unissued, demos only)	1,000+

(see also Bonnie Lou & Rusty York)

STEVE YORK'S CAMELO PARDALIS
73	Virgin V 2003	MANOR LIVE (LP)	15

(see also Elkie Brooks, Boz Scaggs, Lol Coxhill, Graham Bond, Mike Patto)

YORK BROTHERS
54	Parlophone CMSP 5	Why Don't You Open The Door?/You're My Every Dream Come True (export issue)	25
54	Parlophone CMSP 22	Strange Town/Three O'Clock Blues (export issue)	25
58	Parlophone GEP 8736	COUNTRY AND WESTERN (EP)	40
58	Parlophone GEP 8753	COUNTRY AND WESTERN NO. 2 (EP)	40

YOU & I
73	Grape GR 3055	Morning Has Broken/Don't Take Love For A Game	5

YOU KNOW WHO GROUP
65	London HLR 9947	Roses Are Red My Love/Playboy	18

CHRIS YOULDEN
73	Deram DM 377	Nowhere Road/Standing On The Corner	12
73	Deram SML 1099	NOWHERE ROAD (LP)	32
74	Deram SML 1112	CITY CHILD (LP)	32

(see also Savoy Brown)

BARRY YOUNG
65	Dot DS 16756	One Has My Name (The Other Has My Heart)/Show Me The Way	15

BILLY YOUNG
72	Atlantic K 10277	The Sloopy/Same Old Thing Again	10
72	Jay Boy BOY 55	I'm Available/Sweet Woman	10

BILLY YOUNG/LIZZIE MILES
56	HMV 7EG 8178	THE BLUES THEY SANG (EP, with Jelly Roll Morton)	30

BOB YOUNG
86	Making Waves SURF 115	Mean Girl/Living On An Island (p/s)	8
86	Making Waves SPRAY 104	IN QUO COUNTRY (LP)	15

(see also Status Quo, Young & Moody Band)

BRETT YOUNG (& GHOST SQUAD)
63	Pye 7N 15578	Guess What/It Just Happened	10
64	Pye 7N 15641	Never Again/You Can't Fool Me (as Brett Young & Ghost Squad)	10

COLIN YOUNG
71	Trend 6099 005	Anytime At All/You're No Good	8

DARREN YOUNG
63	Parlophone R 4919	My Tears Will Turn To Laughter/I've Just Fallen For Someone	25

(see also Johnny Gentle)

DESI YOUNG
70	Pressure Beat PB 5504	News Flash/JOE GIBBS & DESTROYERS: News Flash – Version	18

FARON YOUNG
55	Capitol CL 14336	Live Fast, Love Hard, Die Young/Forgive Me, Dear (78 rpm = £10)	35
56	Capitol CL 14574	If You Ain't Lovin' (You Ain't Livin')/All Right (78 rpm = £10)	25
56	Capitol CL 14655	I've Got 5 Dollars And It's Saturday Night/You're Still Mine (78 rpm = £10)	28
57	Capitol CL 14735	The Shrine Of St. Cecilia/He Was There (78 rpm = £10)	12
57	Capitol CL 14762	Love Has Finally Come My Way/Moonlight Mountain (78 rpm = £10)	10
57	Capitol CL 14793	Honey Stop! (And Think Of Me)/Vacation's Over (78 rpm = £12)	15
58	Capitol CL 14822	Snowball/The Locket (78 rpm = £12)	10
58	Capitol CL 14860	I Can't Dance/Rosalie (Is Gonna Get Married)	15
58	Capitol CL 14891	Every Time I'm Kissing You/Alone With You	10
58	Capitol CL 14930	I Hate Myself/That's The Way I Feel	7
59	Capitol CL 14975	Last Night At A Party/A Long Time Ago	15
59	Capitol CL 15004	That's The Way It's Gotta Be/We're Talking It Over	7
59	Capitol CL 15050	I Hear You Talkin'/Country Girl	28
57	Capitol EAP1 778	SWEETHEARTS OR STRANGERS PT. 1 (EP, with Country Deputies)	15
57	Capitol EAP2 778	SWEETHEARTS OR STRANGERS PT. 2 (EP, with Country Deputies)	15
58	Capitol EAP3 778	SWEETHEARTS OR STRANGERS PT. 3 (EP, with Country Deputies)	15
63	Capitol EAP1 1549	HELLO WALLS	15
58	Capitol T 1004	OBJECTS OF MY AFFECTION (LP)	22
59	Capitol T 1096	THIS IS FARON YOUNG (LP)	22
64	Mercury 20026MCL	STORY SONGS FOR COUNTRY FOLK (LP)	15
64	Mercury 20025MCL	COUNTRY DANCE FAVOURITES (LP)	15

GEORGIE YOUNG & ROCKIN' BOCS
58	London HLU 8748	Nine More Miles/The Sneak (78 rpm = £15)	15

HARRY YOUNG
65	Dot DS 16756	Show Me The Way/One Has My Name	10

JIMMY YOUNG
54	Decca F 10232	A Baby Cried/Remember Me	20
54	Decca F 10406	Give Me Your Word/Lonely Nightingale	18
55	Decca F 10444	These Are The Things We'll Share/Don't Go To Strangers	12
55	Decca F 10483	If Anyone Finds This, I Love You/The Sand And The Sea	12
55	Decca F 10502	Unchained Melody/Help Me Forget	22
55	Decca F 10597	The Man From Laramie/No Arms Can Ever Hold You	22
55	Decca F 10640	Someone On Your Mind/I Look At You	15
56	Decca F 10694	Chain Gang/Capri In May	15
56	Decca F 10736	Rich Man, Poor Man/The Wayward Wind	12
56	Decca F 10774	More/I'm Gonna Steal You Away	12
57	Decca F 10842	Lovin' Baby/My Faith, My Hope, My Love	8
57	Decca F 10875	Round And Round/Walkin' After Midnight	8
57	Decca F 10925	Man On Fire/Love In The Afternoon	7
57	Decca F 10948	Deep Blue Sea/Harbour Of Desire	7
55	Pye NEP 24004	JIMMY YOUNG SINGS (EP)	18
56	Decca DFE 6277	PRESENTING JIMMY YOUNG (EP)	18

Jimmy YOUNG

57	Decca DFE 6404	JIMMY YOUNG (EP)	18
55	Decca LF 1200	PRESENTING JIMMY YOUNG (10" LP)	35
57	Decca LK 4219	THE NIGHT IS YOUNG (LP)	25
58	Columbia 33SX 1102	YOU (LP)	15

JOE E. YOUNG & TONIKS
68	Toast TT 502	Life Time Of Lovin'/Flower In My Hand	25
69	Toast TT 514	Good Day Sunshine/Life Time Of Lovin'	20
68	Toast (S)TLP 1	SOUL BUSTER! (LP)	40

JOHNNY YOUNG
67	Decca F 22548	Step Back/Cara Lyn (as Johnny Young & Kompany)	8
67	Decca F 22636	Lady/Good Evening Girl	6
68	RCA RCA 1826	Always Thinking Of You/Dreaming Country (as Johnny Young Four)	6

JOHNNY YOUNG
70	Blue Horizon 7-63852	FAT MANDOLIN (LP)	80

KAREN YOUNG
65	Mercury MF 943	I'm Yours, You're Mine/Are You Kidding	8
65	Pye 7N 15956	We'll Start The Party Again/Wonderful Summer	8
68	Major Minor MM 584	Too Much Of A Good Thing/You Better Sit Down	50
69	M. Minor MMLP/SMLP 66	SINGS NOBODY'S CHILD AND 13 OTHER GREAT SONGS (LP)	25

KATHY YOUNG & INNOCENTS
61	Top Rank JAR 534	A Thousand Stars/Eddie My Darling	40
61	Top Rank JAR 554	Happy Birthday Blues/Someone To Love	30

(see also Innocents)

LEON YOUNG STRINGS
64	Pye 7N 15646	This Boy/Glad All Over	50

LESTER YOUNG (QUINTET)
56	Vogue V 2362	New Lester Leaps In/She's Funny That Way	6
56	Vogue V 2384	You're Driving Me Crazy/East Of The Sun	6
56	Vogue EPV 1127	LESTER YOUNG (EP)	10
53	Mercury MG 25015	KANSAS CITY 7/THE LESTER YOUNG QUARTET (LP, 1 side each)	15
55	Felsted EDL 87014	BATTLE OF THE SAXES (10" LP)	15
55	Columbia Clef 33C 9001	LESTER YOUNG WITH THE OSCAR PETERSON TRIO (10" LP)	15
56	Columbia Clef 33C 9015	LESTER YOUNG (10" LP)	15
56	Columbia Clef 33CX 10031	THE PRESIDENT, LESTER YOUNG (LP)	15
56	Columbia Clef 33CX 10054	THE JAZZ GIANTS '56 (LP)	15
57	Columbia Clef 33CX 10070	PRES (LP)	15
58	London Jazz LTZ-C 15132	BLUE LESTER (LP)	15
59	HMV CLP 1302	PRES AND TEDDY (LP, with Teddy Wilson)	12
59	Fontana TFL 5064	LESTER YOUNG MEMORIAL ALBUM VOL. 1 (LP, with Count Basie)	12
60	Fontana TFL 5065	LESTER YOUNG MEMORIAL ALBUM VOL. 2 (LP, with Count Basie)	15
62	Stateside SL 10002	LESTER YOUNG & KANSAS CITY 5 (LP)	12
65	Fontana TL 5260	PREZ (LP)	12
66	Fontana FJL 128	LESTER YOUNG LEAPS AGAIN (LP)	12

(see also Count Basie, Coleman Hawkins & Lester Young, Oscar Peterson)

LESTER YOUNG & CHARLIE PARKER, ET AL.
50	Melodisc 8003	JAZZ AT THE PHILHARMONIC, VOL. 2: BLUES FOR NORMAN, PARTS 1 & 2 (12" 78)	10

LLOYD YOUNG
72	Bullet BU 500	Bread And Butter/SHALIMAR ALLSTARS: Version	8
72	Duke DU 135	Soup/J.J. ALLSTARS: Version	12
72	Green Door GD 4037	Shalimar Special/G. MAHTANI ALLSTARS: Version	8
72	Techniques TE 917	High Explosion/ANSELL COLLINS: Version	8

(see also Carey & Lloyd)

MIGHTY JOE YOUNG
72	Sonet SNTF 633	THE LEGACY OF THE BLUES VOL. 4 (LP)	15
72	Delmark DS 629	BLUES WITH A TOUCH OF SOUL (LP, blue label)	20

NEIL YOUNG
69	Reprise RS 23405	The Loner/Everybody Knows This Is Nowhere	20
70	Reprise RS 20861	Oh Lonesome Me (Long Version)/Sugar Mountain	12
70	Reprise RS 23462	Down By The River (edit)/Cinnamon Girl (alternate mix)	7
70	Reprise RS 20958	Only Love Can Break Your Heart/Birds	6
71	Reprise RS 23488	When You Dance I Can Really Love/After The Goldrush	6
72	Reprise K 14167	Old Man/The Needle And The Damage Done	6
73	Reprise SAM 15	Don't Be Denied/Love In Mind/Last Dance (p/s, 1-sided, promo only sampler for TIME FADES AWAY LP)	20
74	Reprise K 14350	Southern Man/Till The Morning Comes/After The Goldrush/Heart Of Gold (special sleeve)	5
76	Reprise K 14431	Don't Cry No Tears/Stupid Girl	6
93	Reprise PRO 808	The Needle And The Damage Done (from UNPLUGGED)/Love Is A Rose (from DECADE (CD, promo only)	8
93	Columbia XPCD 308	My Back Pages/All Along The Watchtower/Knocking On Heaven's Door (CD, promo only)	8
93	Geffen NYCD 1	LUCKY THIRTEEN ALBUM SAMPLER (Ain't It The Truth/Depression Blues/This Note's For You) (CD, promo only)	15
69	Reprise RSLP 6317	NEIL YOUNG (LP, with/without name on front of sleeve)	35/50
69	Reprise RSLP 6349	EVERYBODY KNOWS THIS IS NOWHERE (LP)	30
70	Reprise RSLP 6383	AFTER THE GOLDRUSH (LP, gatefold sleeve with lyric insert)	25
71	Reprise K 44059	NEIL YOUNG (LP, reissue)	12
71	Reprise K 44073	EVERYBODY KNOWS THIS IS NOWHERE (LP, reissue)	12
71	Reprise K 44088	AFTER THE GOLDRUSH (LP, reissue, gatefold sleeve with lyric insert)	12

72	Reprise K 54005	HARVEST (LP, thick cardboard gatefold sleeve with insert)	15
72	Reprise K 64015	JOURNEY THROUGH THE PAST (2-LP, soundtrack, fold-out sleeve & inners)	20
73	Reprise K 54010	TIME FADES AWAY (LP, with lyric insert)	15
74	Reprise K 54014	ON THE BEACH (LP, with inner sleeve)	25
75	Reprise K 54040	TONIGHT'S THE NIGHT (LP, gatefold sleeve with inner sleeve & insert)	15
75	Reprise K 54057	ZUMA (LP, with inner sleeve & lyric insert)	15
77	Reprise K 54088	AMERICAN STARS AND BARS (LP, with inner sleeve)	12
79	Reprise K 54105	RUST NEVER SLEEPS (LP, with inner sleeve & lyric insert)	12
79	Reprise K 64041	LIVE RUST (2-LP, with inner sleeves)	18
80	Reprise K 54109	HAWKS & DOVES (LP, with inner sleeve)	12
85	Geffen GEF 26377	OLD WAYS (LP)	12

(see also Buffalo Springfield, Crosby Stills Nash & Young, Stills-Young Band, Crazy Horse)

RALPH YOUNG
55	Brunswick 05466	The Man From Laramie/The Bible Tells Me So	18
55	Brunswick 05500	Bring Me A Bluebird/A Room In Paris	12
56	Brunswick 05605	The Legend Of Wyatt Earp/Do You Know?	12

(see also Jack Pleis)

ROGER YOUNG
66	Columbia DB 7869	Sweet, Sweet Morning/Whatcha Gonna Give Me?	40
66	Columbia DB 8092	No Address/It's Been Nice	230+

ROBERT YOUNG
71	CBS 7350	Rosemary Blue/When Time Began	6

ROY YOUNG (BAND)
59	Fontana H 200	Just Keep It Up/Big Fat Mama (78 rpm = £10)	25
59	Fontana H 215	Hey Little Girl/Just Ask Your Heart (78 rpm = £15)	20
60	Fontana H 237	I Hardly Know Me/Gilee	20
60	Fontana H 247	Taboo/I'm In Love	15
61	Fontana H 290	You Were Meant For Me/Plenty Of Love (as Roy Young & Hunters)	18
61	Ember EMB S 128	Four And Twenty Thousand Kisses/Late Last Evening	12
70	RCA SF 8161	ROY YOUNG BAND (LP)	18

SUSANNAH YOUNG
67	Philips BF 1559	Lazy Afternoon/Here's That Rainy Day	5
67	Philips BL 7728	SWEETEST SOUNDS (LP)	12

TOMMIE YOUNG
73	Contempo C 12	Everybody's Got A Little Devil In Their Soul/Do You Still Feel The Same Way	10
73	Contempo C 23	She Don't Have To See You/That's All Part Of Loving Him	10
74	Contempo CLP 501	DO YOU STILL FEEL THE SAME WAY (LP)	75

VICKI YOUNG
54	Capitol CL 14144	Riot In Cell Block Number Nine/Honey Love (78)	8
55	Capitol CL 14228	Hearts Of Stone/Tweedlee Dee (triangular centre) (78 rpm = £10)	8
55	Capitol CL 14281	Live Fast, Love Hard, Die Young/Zoom, Zoom, Zoom(triangular centre)(78 = £10)	25
56	Capitol CL 14528	Steel Guitar/Bye Bye For Just A While (78 rpm = £10)	12
56	Capitol CL 14653	Spanish Main/Tell Me In Your Own Sweet Way (with Joe 'Fingers' Carr)(78 = £10)	12
56	Capitol EAP1 593	VICKI YOUNG (EP)	40

(see also Joe 'Fingers' Carr)

YOUNG AL CAPONE
71	Green Door GD 4012	Girl Called Clover/Girl Called Clover (Version)	8

YOUNG & MOODY (BAND)
77	Magnet MAG 87	Chicago Blue/Warm Winds	5
79	Fabulous JC 1	The Devil Went Down To Georgia/You Can't Catch Me	5
79	Fabulous JC 3	All The Good Friends/Playing Your Game (p/s)	5
81	Bronze BRO 120	These Eyes/I Won't Let Go (p/s)	5
81	Bronze BRO 130	Don't Do That/How Can I Help You Tonight (p/s, featuring Lemmy and Linda & Coleen Nolan)	5
77	Magnet MAG 5015	YOUNG AND MOODY (LP, with lyric insert, as Young & Moody)	12

(see also Bob Young, Whitesnake, Snafu, Cozy Powell, Motörhead, Nolan Sisters)

YOUNG BLOOD
68	Pye 7N 17495	Green Light/Don't Leave Me In The Dark	20
68	Pye 7N 17588	Just How Loud/Masquerade	15
68	Pye 7N 17627	Bang-Shang-A-Lang/I Can't Stop	15
69	Pye 7N 17696	The Continuing Story Of Bungalow Bill/I Will	15

(see also Cozy Powell, Ace Kefford Stand, Big Bertha)

YOUNG BLOOD
84	Landslide LAND 1	FIRST BLOOD (12" EP, p/s)	18

YOUNGBLOODS
69	RCA RCA 1821	Darkness, Darkness/On Sir Francis Drake	8
69	RCA RCA 1877	Get Together/Beautiful	8
69	RCA SF 8026	ELEPHANT MOUNTAIN (LP)	20
70	Warner Bros WS 1878	ROCK FESTIVAL (LP)	15
70	RCA LSA 3012	THE BEST OF THE YOUNGBLOODS (LP)	12
71	Warner Bros K 46100	RIDE THE WIND (LP)	15
72	RCA Victor SF 8218	SUNLIGHT (LP)	15

YOUNG BUCKS
77	Blueport BLU 1	Get Your Feet Back On The Ground/Cold, Cold Morning (p/s)	6

YOUNG DISCIPLES
90	Talkin' Loud TLKX 2	Get Yourself Together/Young Disciples Theme (12", p/s)	8

YOUNGFOLK
68	President PT 136	Lonely Girl/Joey	20

MINT VALUE £

YOUNG FOLK
72   Midas MR 001   RIBBLE VALLEY DREAM (LP) 30

YOUNG FREDDIE
70   Camel CA 38   Drink And Gamble/LENNOX BROWN & HUE ROY: King Of The Road 10
(see also Freddie McGregor)

YOUNG GROWLER & CALYPSO RHYTHM KINGS
66   Columbia DB 7870   Amy The Sunbather/Sweet Trinidad 7
66   Columbia DB 7958   "V" For Victory/Be Nice To Women (some in 'Test Match' p/s)............... 12/7
66   Columbia SEG 8502   V FOR VICTORY (EP) 12

YOUNG-HOLT TRIO
67   Coral Q 72489   Wack Wack/This Little Light Of Mine (DJ copy = £75) 40

YOUNG-HOLT UNLIMITED
69   MCA MU 1053   Soulful Strut/Country Slicker Joe 10
72   MCA MU 1159   Just Ain't No Love/Love Makes A Woman 10
73   Contempo COLP-R 1004   PLAYS SUPERFLY (LP)... 40
69   MCA MUP(S) 368   SOULFUL STRUT (LP) 30
(see also Ramsey Lewis Trio)

YOUNG IDEA
66   Columbia DB 7961   The World's Been Good To Me/It Can't Be.............................. 10
66   Columbia DB 8067   Gotta Get Out Of The Mess I'm In/Games Men Play 8
67   Columbia DB 8132   Peculiar Situation/Just Look At The Rain............................... 8
67   Columbia DB 8205   With A Little Help From My Friends/Colours Of Darkness 8
67   Columbia DB 8284   Mister Lovin' Luggage Man/Room With A View......................... 8

YOUNG JESSIE
58   London HLE 8544   Shuffle In The Gravel/Make Believe (78 rpm = £50)..................... 300

YOUNG MARBLE GIANTS
80   Rough Trade RT 043   Final Day/Radio Silents/Cakewalking/(uncredited 4th track) (p/s)............ 6
81   Rough Trade RT 059   TESTCARD (EP) 6
(see also Jah Scouse)

YOUNG MC
88   Delicious Vinyl BRW 120   KNOW HOW (12", EP).. 20

YOUNG ONES
63   Decca F 11705   How Do I Tell You/Baby That's It 5

YOUNG ONES
78   Virgin VS 205   Rock 'N' Roll Radio/Little Bit Of Loving (p/s)............................. 6

YOUNG RASCALS
65   Atlantic AT 4059   I Ain't Gonna Eat My Heart Out Anymore/Slow Down..................... 12
66   Atlantic AT 4082   Good Lovin'/Mustang Sally 10
66   Atlantic 584 024   You Better Run/Love Is A Beautiful Thing 15
66   Atlantic 584 050   Come On Up/What Is The Reason...................................... 15
66   Atlantic 584 067   Too Many Fish In The Sea/No Love To Give 10
67   Atlantic 584 081   I've Been Lonely Too Long/If You Knew................................. 15
67   Atlantic 584 085   I Ain't Gonna Eat My Heart Out Anymore/Good Lovin'.................... 8
67   Atlantic 584 111   Groovin'/Sueno 10
67   Atlantic 584 128   A Girl Like You/It's Love.. 10
67   Atlantic 584 138   How Can I Be Sure/I Don't Love You Anymore 6
68   Atlantic 584 161   It's Wonderful/Of Course 10
66   Atlantic 587/588 012   THE YOUNG RASCALS (LP) 25
67   Atlantic 587/588 060   COLLECTIONS (LP) 18
67   Atlantic 587/588 074   GROOVIN' (LP) 25
(see also Rascals, Joey Dee & Starlighters)

YOUNG SATCH
70   Black Swan BW 1401   Bonga Bonga Bonga/HI-TALS: Ram Buck 10

YOUNG SISTERS
62   London HLU 9610   Casanova Brown/My Guy.. 20

YOUNG SOULS
69   Amalgamated AMG 844   Why Did You Leave/Main A Wail 18

YOUNG TRADITION
74   Argo AFW 115   The Shepherd's Hymn/The Boar's Head Carol 6
68   Transatlantic TRAEP 164   CHICKEN ON A RAFT (EP)... 25
66   Transatlantic TRA 142   THE YOUNG TRADITION (LP) 25
67   Transatlantic TRA 155   SO CHEERFULLY ROUND (LP) 20
68   Transatlantic TRA 172   GALLERIES (LP, with Dave Swarbrick)................................. 22
68   Transatlantic TRASAM 13   THE YOUNG TRADITION SAMPLER (LP)................................ 15
(see also Dave Swarbrick, Peter Bellamy)

YOUNG TURKS
66   CBS 202353   Duel At Diablo/Our Lady From Maxim's 12

YOUNG WORLD SINGERS
64   Brunswick 05916   Ringo For President/A Boy Like That 6

YOUR FAVOURITE HORSE
00s   Endorphin ENDORLP 010   EVERYDAY MAGIC (LP, orange vinyl)................................. 12

YOUTH
66   Polydor 56121   As Long As There Is Your Love/Your One And Only Love 15

YOUTH
69   Deram DM 226   Meadow Of My Love/Love Me Or Leave Me 15

JOHNNY YOUTH
69	Grape GR 3002	Darling It Won't/HIP CITY BOYS: Moon Train.	10

YOUTH VALLEY CHORALE
63	London HLU 9818	Do You Hear What I Hear/Little Bell	5

YOU'VE GOT FOETUS ON YOUR BREATH
81	Self Immolation WOMB 07	Wash It All Off/333 (p/s)	20
80s	Self Immolation	Tell Me, What Is The Bane Of Your Life?	20
81	Self Imm. WOMB OYBL-1	DEAF (LP)	35
81	Self Imm. WOMB OYBL-2	ACHE (LP)	30

(see also Foetus etc., Philip & His Foetus Vibrations, Scraping Foetus Off The Wheel)

LES YPER SOUND
67	Fontana TF 880	Too Fortiche/Psyche Rock	40
69	Philips TFE 8004	MASS FOR THE PRESENT TIME (LP)	80

YR HWNTWS
82	Loco LOCO 1001	YR HWNTWS (LP)	80

Y TRWYNAU COCH
70s	Record. Sqwar RSROC 1	WASTOD AR Y TU FAS (BANANAS) (EP, around 1,000 only)	50
78	Recordian Sqwar RSROC 002	Merched Dan 15 (I Often Think Of Girls Under 15)/Byw Ar Arian Fy Rhieni/Mynd I'r Capel Mewn Levis/Ail Ddechre (around 1,000 only)	50
80s	Record. Coch OCHR 2198	RHEDEG RHAG Y TORPIDOS (LP)	30

JOHNNY YUKON
60	Top Rank JAR 347	Made To Be Loved/Magnolia	7

YUNGUN/MR THING
03	White (Janomi) JACKIT0001	STRAIGHT JACK IT (EP)	15

TIMI YURO
61	London HLG 9403	Hurt/I Apologise	15
62	London HLG 9484	Smile/I Believe (B-side with Johnnie Ray)	15
62	Liberty LIB 55410	Let Me Call You Sweetheart/Satan Never Sleeps	12
62	Liberty LIB 55469	What's A-Matter Baby (Is It Hurting You)/Thirteenth Hour	20
63	Liberty LIB 55519	The Love Of A Boy/I Ain't Gonna Cry No More	30
63	Liberty LIB 55587	Make The World Go Away/Look Down	12
64	Liberty LIB 10177	Hurt/Be Anything (But Be Mine)	10
64	Mercury MF 826	If/I'm Afraid The Masquerade Is Over	20
65	Mercury MF 848	You Can Have Him/Could This Be Magic	12
65	Mercury MF 859	Get Out Of My Life/Can't Stop Running Away	50
65	Mercury MF 903	Once A Day/Pretend	7
65	Mercury MF 949	Turn The World Around The Other Way/Just A Ribbon	7
66	Mercury MF 978	Cuttin' In/Why Not Now	8
68	Liberty LBF 15092	Something Bad On My Mind/Wrong	10
68	Liberty LIB 15142	I Must Have Been Out Of My Mind/Interlude	25
68	Liberty LIB 15182	It'll Never Be Over For Me/As Long As There Is You	500
65	Liberty LEP 2214	TIMI YURO: SOUL! (EP)	30
66	Liberty LEP 2253	MAKE THE WORLD GO AWAY (EP)	75
62	London HA-G 2415	TIMI YURO (LP)	75
62	Liberty LBY 1042	SOUL! (LP)	35
63	Liberty (S)LBY 1154	WHAT'S A-MATTER BABY (LP)	25/30
64	Liberty LBY 1192	MAKE THE WORLD GO AWAY (LP)	25
64	Mercury 20032 MCL	THE AMAZING YURO (LP)	22
65	Liberty LBY 1247	HURT (LP)	30
66	Liberty (S)LBY 1275	LET ME CALL YOU SWEETHEART (LP)	22/30
66	Liberty (S)LBY 1290	THE BEST OF TIMI YURO (LP)	20
68	Liberty LBL/LBS 83115	GREAT PERFORMANCES (LP)	15
68	Liberty LBL/LBS 83128	TIMI IN THE BEGINNING (LP)	20
69	Liberty LBS 83198E	SOMETHING BAD ON MY MIND (LP)	75
69	Mercury SMWL 21010	TALENTED TIMI (LP)	18

(see also Johnnie Ray)

AFFIE YUSUF
93	Ferox FER 001	ACID WAVES 1 (12" EP, plain sleeve)	12
93	Ferox FER 003	ACID WAVES 2 (12" EP, plain sleeve)	12

(HELMUT) ZACHARIAS
64	Polydor NH 52341	Tokyo Melody/Teatime In Tokyo	5
65	Polydor 236 809	PLAYS THE HITS OF THE BEATLES (LP)	12

JOHN ZACHERLE
58	London HLU 8599	Dinner With Drac Part 1/Dinner With Drac — Conclusion (78 rpm = £30)	30

(see also Dave Appell & Applejacks)

ZAFTIG MADEL
84	Shine SHTUP 3	Dori Duz/Curvy 'N' Creamy (p/s)	6

MINT VALUE £

ZAGER & EVANS
69	RCA SF 8056	2525 (LP)	28

ZAKARRIAS
71	Deram SML 1091	ZAKARRIAS (LP)	300+

ALEX ZANETIS
71	Moodisc HM 102	Guilty/JOLLY BOYS: Do Fe Do	5

TOMMY ZANG
59	HMV POP 611	Break The Chain/I'll Put A String On Your Finger	10
62	Polydor NH 66955	I'm Gonna Slip You Offa My Mind/Every Hour, Every Day	10
62	Polydor NH 66957	Hey, Good Lookin'/With Love (For You)	20
62	Polydor NH 66960	Take These Chains From My Heart/Truly, Truly	10
62	Polydor NH 66977	I Can't Hold Your Letters (In My Arms)/She's Getting Married	10
62	Polydor NH 66980	Just Call My Name/I Love You Because	10

WILLY ZANGO
74	DJM DJS 312	Hot Rod/The Voice Of Melody	7

ZAPP
80	Warner K 17712T	More Bounce To The Ounce/Brand New Player (12")	8

FRANK ZAPPA/MOTHERS OF INVENTION
SINGLES
66	Verve VS 545	It Can't Happen Here/How Could I Be Such A Fool (as Mothers Of Invention)	42
67	Verve VS 557	Big Leg Emma/Why Don't You Do Me Right (as Mothers Of Invention)	42
71	Reprise K 14100	Tears Began To Fall/Junier Mintz Boogie (as Mothers Of Invention)	38
71	United Artists UP 35319	What Will This Evening Bring Me This Morning?/Daddy, Daddy, Daddy	38
74	Discreet K 19201	Cosmic Debris/Uncle Remus	8
74	Discreet K 19202	Don't Eat The Yellow Snow/Camarillo Brillo	8
79	CBS 7261	Dancin' Fool/Baby Snakes	8
80	CBS 7950	Joe's Garage/Catholic Girls	6
80	CBS 7950	Joe's Garage/BOB DYLAN: When You Gonna Wake Up (mispressing)	30
80	CBS 8652	I Don't Wanna Get Drafted/Ancient Armaments (p/s)	6
81	CBS A 1622	You Are What You Is/Harder Than Your Husband (p/s)	6
81	CBS A 12-1622	You Are What You Is/Pink Napkins/Harder Than Your Husband/ Soup 'N Old Clothes (12", picture disc)	15
81	CBS XPS 147	Shut Up 'N' Play Yer Guitar/Variation On The C. Santana Secret (p/s, issued free with "Ship Arriving Too Late To Save A Drowning Witch" LP)	6
82	CBS A 2412	Valley Girl/Teenage Prostitute (p/s)	6
84	EMI EMI 5499	Baby Take Your Teeth Out/Stevie's Spanking (p/s)	8
93	Zappa Records 12 FRANK 102	Valley Girl/You Are What You Is (12", p/s)	8
91	Zappa Records 12 FRANK 101	Stairway To Heaven/Bolero (12", p/s)	8

LPs: VERVE ORIGINALS
66	Verve (S)VLP 9154	FREAK OUT! (as Mothers Of Invention, mono/stereo, single disc)	55/45
67	Verve (S)VLP 9174	ABSOLUTELY FREE (as Mothers Of Invention, mono/stereo)	40/30
68	Verve (S)VLP 9199	WE'RE ONLY IN IT FOR THE MONEY (as Mothers Of Invention, gatefold sleeve, mono/stereo)	45/30
68	Verve (S)VLP 9223	LUMPY GRAVY (gatefold sleeve, mono/stereo)	45/35
69	Verve (S)VLP 9237	CRUISING WITH RUBEN AND THE JETS (as Mothers Of Invention, mono/stereo)	45/35
69	Verve (S)VLP 9239	MOTHERMANIA — THE BEST OF THE MOTHERS (as Mothers Of Invention, mono/stereo)	35/25

LPs: VERVE REISSUES
71	Verve/Polydor 2683 004	FREAK OUT (2-LP)	30
72	Verve/Polydor 2317 034	WE'RE ONLY IN IT FOR THE MONEY (gatefold sleeve)	25
72	Verve/Polydor 2317 035	ABSOLUTELY FREE (gatefold sleeve)	25
72	Verve/Polydor 2317 046	LUMPY GRAVY (gatefold sleeve)	25
72	Verve/Polydor 2317 047	MOTHERMANIA — THE BEST OF THE MOTHERS	30
73	Verve/Polydor 2352 017	MOTHERMANIA — THE BEST OF THE MOTHERS (2nd reissue)	30
73	Verve/Polydor 2317 069	CRUISIN' WITH RUBEN AND THE JETS (gatefold sleeve)	35
75	Verve/Polydor 2352 057	ROCK FLASHBACKS (LP)	15

LPs: ORIGINAL REPRISE/WARNERS/DISCREET ISSUES
70	Reprise RSLP 6356	HOT RATS (1st pressing, pink, gold & green 'riverboat' label, gatefold sleeve)	35
70	Reprise RSLP 6356	HOT RATS (2nd pressing, tan 'riverboat' label, gatefold sleeve)	22
70	Reprise RSLP 6370	BURNT WEENY SANDWICH (as Mothers Of Invention, 1st pressing, pink, gold & green 'riverboat' label, gatefold sleeve)	22
70	Reprise RSLP 2028	WEASELS RIPPED MY FLESH (as Mothers Of Invention, tan 'riverboat' label)	22
70	Reprise RSLP 2030	CHUNGA'S REVENGE (tan 'riverboat' label, green or red gatefold sleeve)	30/22
71	Reprise K 44150	FILLMORE EAST, JUNE 1971 (as Mothers Of Invention)	22
72	Reprise K 44179	JUST ANOTHER BAND FROM L.A. (as Mothers Of Invention, gatefold sleeve)	22
72	Reprise K 44203	WAKA/JAWAKA (Hot Rats)	18
72	Reprise K 44209	THE GRAND WAZOO (gatefold sleeve)	18
73	DiscReet K 41000	OVER-NITE SENSATION (as Mothers Of Invention, gatefold sleeve)	18
74	DiscReet K 69201	ROXY AND ELSEWHERE (2-LP, as Mothers Of Invention, gatefold sleeve)	20
74	DiscReet K 49201	APOSTROPHE (') (no lyric insert)	18
75	DiscReet K 59207	ONE SIZE FITS ALL (as Mothers Of Invention, gatefold sleeve)	18

(First pressings of the above LPs were issued without Warner Bros logo on label or sleeve; copies with Warners logos are post-1975 pressings worth £6-£8 each.)

76	Warner Bros K 56298	ZOOT ALLURES (LP)	12
77	DiscReet K 69204	ZAPPA IN NEW YORK (LIVE) (2-LP, with & without reference to "Punky's Whips")	25
77	DiscReet K 69204	ZAPPA IN NEW YORK (LIVE) (2-LP, "Punky's Whips" listed on sleeve but not on label or LP)	25

Rare Record Price Guide 2008

77	DiscReet K 69204	ZAPPA IN NEW YORK (LIVE) (2-LP, plays "Punky's Whips", listed on sleeve but not on label)	55
78	DiscReet K 59210	STUDIO TAN	12
78	DiscReet K 59211	SLEEP DIRT	12
78	DiscReet K 59212	ORCHESTRAL FAVORITES	12

LPs: REPRISE

71	Reprise K 44078	HOT RATS (tan 'riverboat' label, gatefold sleeve)	15
71	Reprise K 44083	BURNT WEENY SANDWICH (tan 'riverboat' label)	15
71	Reprise K 44019	WEASELS RIPPED MY FLESH (tan 'riverboat' label)	20
71	Reprise K 44020	CHUNGA'S REVENGE (tan 'riverboat' label, gatefold sleeve)	20

(The above LPs were issued without Warner Bros logo on label or sleeve; post-1975 pressings with logos are worth £6-£8 each.)

OTHER LPs

69	Transatlantic TRA 197	UNCLE MEAT (2-LP, as Mothers Of Invention)	30
71	United Artists UDF 50003	200 MOTELS (2-LP, with booklet & poster, as Frank Zappa & Mothers Of Invention)	50
79	CBS 88339	SHEIK YERBOUTI (2-LP, gatefold sleeve printed with lyrics)	18
79	CBS 86101	JOE'S GARAGE ACT 1 (gatefold sleeve, lyric insert)	12
79	CBS 88475	JOE'S GARAGE ACTS 2 & 3 (2-LP, gatefold sleeve, lyric insert)	18
81	CBS 88560	YOU ARE WHAT YOU IS (2-LP, gatefold sleeve, lyric insert)	18
81	CBS 88516	TINSELTOWN REBELLION (2-LP, gatefold sleeve with lyrics)	18
81	CBS 66368	SHUT UP 'N' PLAY YER GUITAR (3-LP box set, with inner sleeves)	30
82	CBS 85804	SHIP ARRIVING TOO LATE TO SAVE A DROWNING WITCH (with bonus 7" "Shut Up 'N' Play Yer Guitar"/"Variation On The C. Santana Secret" [XPS 147])	15
83	CBS 25251	THE MAN FROM UTOPIA	12
84	EMI EL 2701531	BOULEZ CONDUCTS ZAPPA: 'THE PERFECT STRANGER'	12
84	EMI no cat. no.	FRANCESCO ZAPPA (with inner sleeve)	15
84	EMI 2402943	THING-FISH (3-LP, box set, with libretto)	35
86	EMI EN 352	JAZZ FROM HELL	15
86	EMI EC 3507	FRANK ZAPPA MEETS THE MOTHERS OF PREVENTION (European version)	12
95	Simply Vinyl SLVP 0024	WEASELS RIPPED MY FLESH (180 gm vinyl)	12
95	Simply Vinyl SLVP 0025	BURNT WEENY SANDWICH (gatefold sleeve, 180 gm vinyl)	12

LPs: EMI REISSUES

84	EMI EMC 3500	THE MAN FROM UTOPIA	12
84	EMI EMC 3501	SHIP ARRIVING TOO LATE TO SAVE A DROWNING WITCH (with inner sleeve)	15
84	EMI FZAP1	JOE'S GARAGE ACTS 1, 2 & 3 (3-LP, box set, inner sleeves only, with libretti)	30
84	EMI E5 0021	TINSELTOWN REBELLION (2-LP, gatefold sleeve, printed with lyrics)	18
84	EMI no cat. no.	SHEIK YERBOUTI (2-LP, gatefold sleeve, printed with lyrics)	18
84	EMI no cat. no.	SHUT UP 'N' PLAY YER GUITAR (3-LP box set, with inner sleeves)	30
84	EMI EN 2402343	THEM OR US (2-LP, gatefold sleeve, printed with lyrics)	18

LPs: ZAPPA

84	Zappa Records ZAPPA 1	FREAK OUT (2-LP, gatefold sleeve, some in single sleeve £35)	18
80s	Zappa Records ZAPPA 5	LONDON SYMPHONY ORCHESTRA VOLUME II	12
88	Zappa Records ZAPPA 6	GUITAR (2-LP, gatefold sleeve)	18
88	Zappa Records ZAPPA 7	YOU CAN'T DO THAT ON STAGE ANY MORE SAMPLER (2-LP, gatefold sleeve)	18
88	Zappa Records ZAPPA 14	BROADWAY THE HARD WAY (gatefold sleeve with inner sleeve)	15
90	Zappa Records ZAPPA 30	THEM OR US (2-LP, gatefold sleeve, printed with lyrics)	15
90	Zappa Records ZAPPA 20	JOE'S GARAGE ACTS 1, 2 & 3 (3-LP, box set, original sleeves, with libretti)	30
91	Zappa Records ZAPPA 28	SHEIK YERBOUTI (2-LP, gatefold sleeve without lyrics)	18
91	Zappa Records ZAPPA 35	BURNT WEENY SANDWICH (gatefold sleeve)	12
91	Zappa Records ZAPPA 37	ZAPPA IN NEW YORK (LIVE) (2-LP, plays "Punky's Whips", listed on label, but not on sleeve)	18
91	Zappa Records ZAPPA 42	SHIP ARRIVING TOO LATE TO SAVE A DROWNING WITCH	12
92	Zappa Records ZAPPA 39	ROXY AND ELSEWHERE (2-LP, as Mothers Of Invention, gatefold lyric sleeve)	15

(see also Flo & Eddie, Jeff Simmons, Wild Man Fischer, Captain Beefheart, John Lennon, Geronimo Black)

ZAP POW

72	Harry J HJ 6650	Lottery Spin/Lottery Spin — Version	7
73	Trojan TR 7741	This Is Reggae Music/Break Down The Barriers	7
73	Blue Mountain BM 1027	This Is Reggae Music/Break Down The Barriers	6
74	Island WIP 6181	This Is Reggae Music/Break Down The Barriers	6

LES ZARJAZ

85	Creation CRE 014	One Charming Nyte/My Baby Owns A Fallout Zone (foldover p/s, poly bag)	8
86	Kaleid. Sound KS 104	INTER BLOCK ROCK (12" EP)	7

(see also Tronics)

LENA ZAVARONI

74	Philips 6006 367	Ma (He's Making Eyes At Me)/Rock-A-Bye Your Baby With A Dixie Melody	5
74	Philips 6006 391	(You've Got) Personality/Schools Out	7
74	Philips 6308 201	MA! HE'S MAKING EYES AT ME (LP)	15

JOE ZAWINUL

71	Atlantic 2400 151	ZAWINUL (LP)	12

(see also Weather Report)

PETE ZEAR

80	(no label) matrix: 22-1	Tomorrow's World/Fast Food (stamped white label, with insert, numbered)	10

(see also Ruts, Rat Scabies)

ZEE

84	Harvest HAR 5277	Confusion/Eyes Of A Gypsy (p/s)	8
84	Harvest HAR 125277	Confusion (Extended Mix)/Eyes Of A Gypsy (Dub) (12", p/s)	10
84	Harvest SHSP 2401 018	IDENTITY (LP, with inner sleeve)	15
84	Harvest SHSP 2401 018	IDENTITY (cassette, with extra track)	15

(see also Rick Wright)

ZEITGEIST

80	Enchaine ENC 1	Shake-Rake/Sniper (p/s)	6
82	Jamming CREATE 4	Stop (p/s)	5

ZENITH

86	ZENITH 5001	Heavy Heavy Heart (p/s)	100

SI ZENTNER ORCHESTRA

62	Liberty LIB 55374	(Up A) Lazy River/Shufflin' Blues	5
64	Liberty LIB 10169	The James Bond Theme/Bond's 007 Theme	5
63	Liberty LBY 1164	RHYTHM PLUS BLUES (LP)	25

ZEPHYR

70	Probe SPB 1006	ZEPHYR (LP)	45

(see also Tommy Bolin)

ZEPHYRS

63	Decca F 11647	What's All That About/Oriental Dream	35
64	Columbia DB 7199	I Can Tell/Sweet Little Baby	30
64	Columbia DB 7324	A Little Bit Of Soap/No Message	30
64	Columbia DB 7410	Wonder What I'm Gonna Do/Let Me Love You Baby	30
65	Columbia DB 7481	She's Lost You/There's Something About You	30
65	Columbia DB 7571	I Just Can't Take It/She Laughed	30

ZERO

75	BEEB 014	Angels Theme/Truckin'	5

EARL ZERO

78	Studio 16 WE 401	Rough And Tough/PRINCE JAZZBO: Suffer Must Live (12")	25
79	Sufferers Height SUF004	Please Officer/Pablo – Moonlight City (12")	35
79	Greensleeves GRED 23	City Of The Wicked/Rightous Works (12")	30

ZERO FIVE

65	Columbia DB 7751	Dusty/Just Like A Girl	8

ZEROS

77	Small Wonder SMALL 2	Hungry/Radio Fun	20
79	Rok ROK XV/XVI	What's Wrong With A Pop Group/ACTION REPLAY: Decisions (die-cut co. sleeve)	20

021

81	UK UK 201	Pop Song (p/s)	120

ZERO ZERO SEVEN

80s	Scanlite BOND 1	Message From Bond/James Bond Theme (p/s)	5

ZERO 7

00	Ultimate Dilemma UDR	EP VOL. 1 (12")	18
00	Ultimate Dilemma UDR 040	EP VOL. 2 (12")	18

ZERO ZERO SEVEN BAND

65	Marble Arch MAL 590	JAMES BOND THRILLERS (LP)	12

MONICA ZETTERLUND

58	Columbia DB 4246	There's No You/Don't Be That Way	8
59	Columbia SEG 8015	SWEDISH SWEET (EP)	60
58	Columbia 33CSX 20	SWEDISH SENSATION (LP, export only)	65

Z'EV

82	Fetish FE 13	Wipeout!/Element L. (p/s)	10
88	Coercion COERCIONLP 001	THE INVISIBLE MAN (LP)	30

ZIMM & DEE DEE

71	Green Door GD 4006	You've Got A Friend (actually by Winston Francis & Donna Hinds)/GROOVERS: Cheep	7

(see also Winston Francis)

TUCKER ZIMMERMAN

69	Regal Zonophone RZ 3020	The Red Wind/Moondog	6
69	Regal Zono. (S)LRZ 1010	TEN SONGS BY TUCKER ZIMMERMAN (LP)	25
72	Village Thing VTS 13	TUCKER ZIMMERMANN (LP)	25

ZIOR

71	Nepentha 6129 002	Za Za Za Zilda/She's A Bad Bad Woman	18
71	Nepentha 6129 003	Cat's Eyes/I Really Do	18
71	Nepentha 6437 005	ZIOR (LP, gatefold sleeve)	65

(see also Monument, Cardboard Orchestra)

ZIPPERS

64	Hickory 45-1252	My Sailor Boy/Pretend You're Still Mine	10

ZIPS

79	Black Gold ZIPS1	Take Me Down/Don't Be Pushed Around/I'm In Love Over and Over (500 only with A4 insert)	100

ZIPZ

80	Voyage VOY 14	As I Pass You By/Tonight (p/s)	8

ZODIAC

68	Elektra EKL 4009	COSMIC SOUNDS (LP, also stereo EKS 74009)	30

ZODIAC MINDWARP AND THE LOVE REACTION
87	Mercury WARP 3	Prime Mover/Laughing In The Face Of Death/Hangover From Hell	
		(12", limited issue, black vinyl sleeve)	8
87	Mercury ZODR 212A	Backseat Education/Whore Of Babylon/Lager Woman From Hell/Messin' With	
		My Best Friend's Girl (12", rubber sleeve)	8

ZODIAC MOTEL
87	Swordfish SWF 004	Sunshine Miner/Crescendo (p/s)	8
87	Swordfish ZOMO 1	Sunshine Miner/Crescendo/Inside My Mind/Sugarblood (12", p/s)	8
87	Swordfish ZOMO 2	Crystal Injection/I Can Only Give You Everything/Destiny Ranch/	
		Stephanie Blue (12", p/s)	8
87	Swordfish SWFLP 001	THE STORY OF ROLAND FLAGG (LP)	12

ZODIACS
57	Oriole CB 1383	Why Don't They Understand/The Game Of Love (78)	18
58	Oriole CB 1432	The Yum-Yum Song/Secrets (78 rpm = £10)	6

ZAC ZOLAR & ELECTRIC BANANA
84	Butt FUN 5	Take Me Home/James Marshall	5

(see also Pretty Things, Phil May, Fenmen, Electric Banana)

ROB ZOMBIE
98	Geffen GFS 22367	Dragular/Halloween (picture disc)	5
98	Geffen GFS 22367	Dragular/Dragular (remix) (picture disc)	5

(see also White Zombie)

ZOMBIES
64	Decca F 11940	She's Not There/You Make Me Feel Good	10
64	Decca F 12004	Leave Me Be/Woman	10
65	Decca F 12072	Tell Her No/What More Can I Do	10
65	Decca F 12125	She's Coming Home/I Must Move	12
65	Decca F 12225	Whenever You're Ready/I Love You	12
65	Decca F 12296	Is This The Dream/Don't Go Away	12
66	Decca F 12322	Remember You/Just Out Of Reach	15
66	Decca F 12426	Indication/How We Were Before	15
66	Decca F 12495	Gotta Get A Hold Of Myself/The Way I Feel Inside	15
67	Decca F 12584	Goin' Out Of My Head/She Does Everything For Me	15
68	Decca F 12798	I Love You/The Way I Feel Inside	15
67	CBS 2960	Friends Of Mine/Beechwood Park	40
67	CBS 3087	Care Of Cell 44/Maybe After He's Gone	40
68	CBS 3380	Time Of The Season/I'll Call You Mine	40
65	Decca DFE 8598	THE ZOMBIES (EP)	110
65	Decca LK 4679	BEGIN HERE (LP)	250
65	RCA RD 7791	BUNNY LAKE IS MISSING (LP, soundtrack)	60
68	CBS (S)BPG 63280	ODESSEY AND ORACLE (LP, mono/stereo)	220/250
70	Decca SPA 95	THE WORLD OF THE ZOMBIES (LP)	20
73	Epic EPC 65728	TIME OF THE ZOMBIES (2-LP)	30

(see also Unit Four Plus Two, Argent, Neil MacArthur, Colin Blunstone)

ZONES
78	Zoom ZUM 4	Stuck With You/No Angels (p/s)	5
78	Arista ARTIST 205	Sign Of The Times/Away From It All	5

(see also PVC 2)

ZOO
70	Major Minor SMLP 74	ZOO (LP)	30
71	Barclay 521172	ZOO (LP)	30

ZOOKIE
77	DJM DJS 10796	Judie Judie Hold On/I Couldn't Be You	8
78	DJM DJS 10866	Bubbles/Don't Rock Me	8

(see also Judie Tzuke, Tzuke & Paxo)

ZOOT ALORS
79	Decca FR 13874	Send Me A Postcard/It's A Crime (possibly promo only)	80

ZORN
01	City Centre Offices	Eckerman (plain sleeve with inserts, 1000 only)	10
	BLOCK 11		

ZORRO
79	Bridgehouse BHEP 1	'Arrods Don't Sell 'Em/Soldier Boy/Starflight (some with p/s)	60/25

ZORRO FIVE
70	Decca F 23042	Reggae Shhh!/Reggae Meadowlands	5

ZOSKIA
84	All The Madmen MAD 8	Rape/Thank You (p/s)	5
85	Temple TOPY 005	Be Like Me (12", p/s, transparent vinyl)	12
86	All The Madmen MADT 8	Rape/Black Action (12", p/s)	6

ZOSKIA MEETS SUGARDOG
84	Temple TOPYS 021	J.G. / That's Heavy Baby	10

ZOUNDS
81	Crass 4219844/3	Can't Cheat Karma/War/Subvert (gatefold paper p/s, with poster)	8
81	Rough Trade RT 069	Demystification/Great White Hunter (p/s)	8
82	Rough Trade RT 094	Dancing/True Love (p/s)	8
82	Not So Brave NSB 001	LA VACHE QUI RIT (EP, with poster)	8
82	Rough Trade RT 098	More Trouble Coming Every Day/Knife (p/s)	8
80s	Recommended RR 14.15	Menáge (12.59) (1-sided, other side printed, foldout sleeve in PVC sleeve)	8
84	Rough Trade ROUGH 31	THE CURSE OF ZOUNDS (LP)	12

ZOVIET-FRANCE

ZOVIET-FRANCE
82	Red Rhino RED 12	ZOVIET-FRANCE (12" EP, printed hessian sleeve)	60
83	Red Rhink RED 23	NORSCHE (LP)	40
84	Red Rhink RED 40	MOHNOMISCHE (LP)	40
84	Red Rhino REDLP 45	ELSTRE (LP)	40

ZUIDERZEE
66	CBS 202062	(You're My) Soul And Inspiration/Please Don't Call Me	6
66	CBS 202235	Peace Of Mind/Provocative Child	8

TAPPA ZUKIE
73	Count Shelly CSLP 04	MAN A WARRIOR (LP)	45
76	Stars (No. Cat. No.)	TAPPA ZUKIE IN DUB (LP)	100
76	KLIK 9022	M.P.L.A. (LP)	12

ZULU
77	Big Bear BB9	Red Red Libanon/Okavanga Swamp (12")	15

ZUM ZEAUX
70s	Black Pig PUG1	WOLF AT THE DOOR (LP)	35

ZUTONS
02	Deltasonic DKTCD 007	Devil's Deal/Six Foot Man/Zutonkhamuun (CD)	35
03	Deltasonic DLT011	Creepin' An A Crawlin'/Rumblin' Ramblin' (p/s, with sticker)	8

ZYGOAT
74	Polydor 2058 124	Catching A Thief/Letitia's Song	5
74	Polydor 2383 270	ELECTROPHON (LP)	15

ZZEBRA
74	Polydor 2058 446	Zardoz/Amusofi	18
75	Polydor 2058 579	Mr. J/Put The Light On Me	5
74	Polydor 2383 296	ZZEBRA (LP)	12
75	Polydor 2383 326	PANIC (LP, with insert)	12

(see also John McCoy, Gillan)

ZZ TOP
72	London HLU 10376	Francene/Down Brownie	18
74	London HLU 10458	Beer Drinkers And Hell Raisers/La Grange	12
75	London HLU 10475	La Grange/Just Got Paid	18
75	London HLU 10495	Tush/Blue Jean Blues	12
76	London HLU 10538	It's Only Love/Asleep In The Desert	10
77	London HLU 10547	Arrested For Driving While Blind/Neighbour, Neighbour	15
77	London HLU 10547	Arrested For Driving While Blind/Neighbour, Neighbour (mispressing, B-side plays Ray Charles' "I Can See Clearly Now")	18
79	Warner Bros K 17647	Cheap Sunglasses/Esther Be The One	8
80	Warner Bros K 17576	I Thank You/A Fool For Your Stockings (p/s)	8
83	Warner Bros W 9693T	Gimme All Your Lovin'/If I Could Only Flag Her Down (car-shaped picture disc)	15
84	Warner Bros W 9334T	T.V. Dinners (Full Length)/Cheap Sunglasses//Legs (Metal Mix)/ A Fool For Your Stockings (12" double pack)	10
84	Warner Bros W 9576T	Sharp Dressed Man/I Got The Fix/La Grange (12", p/s, some shrinkwrapped with sticker)	8
85	Warner Bros W 2001F	Sleeping Bag/Party On The Patio//Sharp Dressed Man/I Got The Fix (p/s, sealed, stickered double pack)	10
85	Warner Bros W 2001P	Sleeping Bag/Party On The Patio ('sphinx'-shaped picture disc)	10
85	Warner Bros W 2001P	Sleeping Bag/Party On The Patio (shaped pic-disc, part 1 of interlocking set)	25
85	Warner Bros W 2001DP	Sleeping Bag/Party On The Patio ('sleeping bag'-shaped picture disc)	10
86	Warner Bros W 2002BP	Stages/Hi-Fi Mama (shaped pic-disc, part 2 of interlocking set)	8
86	Warner Bros W 2003FP	Rough Boy/Delirious (shaped pic-disc, part 3 of interlocking set, some shrinkwrapped with bonus 12")	30/20
86	Warner Bros W 2003T	Rough Boy/Delirious/Legs (12", p/s with poster)	8
72	London SH-U 8433	RIO GRANDE MUD (LP, original issue)	20
73	London SH-U 8459	TRES HOMBRES (LP, original issue)	20
75	London SH-U 8482	FANDANGO! (LP, original issue)	15
76	London LDU 1	TEJAS (LP, original foldout sleeve)	15
83	Warner Bros W 3774	ELIMINATOR (LP, with bonus stickered p/s 12" "Legs [Metal Mix]")	18
85	Warner Bros W 3774P	ELIMINATOR (LP, picture disc)	12
87	Warner Bros 925 661-2	ZZ TOP'S FIRST ALBUM/RIO GRANDE MUD/TRES HOMBRES/ FANDANGO/TEJAS/EL LOCO (3-CD set of 1st 6 LPs, with booklet)	35

Various Artists

VARIOUS ARTISTS EPs 50s/60s
(alphabetical by title)

A

56	Decca F 10752	ALL STAR HIT PARADE (Dickie Valentine/Joan Regan/Winifred Atwell/ Dave King/Lita Roza/David Whitfield)	12
57	Decca F 10915	ALL STAR HIT PARADE No. 2 (Johnston Bros/Bill Cotton/Jimmy Young/ Max Bygraves/Beverley Sisters/Tommy Steele)	12
63	Pye NEP 24168	ALL STAR HIT PARADE (Kenny Ball/Chris Barber Jazz Band/Joe Brown/ Lonnie Donegan Skiffle Group/Mary Wynter)	12
64	Pye NEP 24172	ALL STAR HIT PARADE VOL. 2 (Joe Brown/Petula Clark/Julie Grant/ Benny Hill/Mark Wynter)	12
64	Decca DFE 8571	AMERICAN COUNTRY JUBILEE NO. 1 (Ray Phillips/Audrey Inman/ Marvin McCullough/Billy Parker)	12
58	Pye Nixa NEP 24096	ARCHERS – EVERYDAY STORY OF BRITISH COUNTRY FOLK	10

B

63	Concert Hall BPC 712	BEAT TIME (Timebeats/Charlie Young/Heartbeats)	20
63	Concert Hall BPC 717	THE BIG BEAT (Bob Miller & Millermen/Al Saxon/Roy Young/Duffy Power)	20
65	Embassy WT 2008	THE BIG FOUR (Jaybirds/Redd Wayne/Les Carle/Joan Baxter)	10
65	Embassy WT 2011	THE BIG FOUR (Jaybirds/Terry Brandon/Les Carle/Typhoons)	10
66	Fontana TF 17469	THE BIG FOUR (Dave Dee Dozy Beaky Mick & Tich/Spencer Davis Group/ Mindbenders/Pretty Things)	12
56	Philips BBE 12021	THE BIG FOUR (Roy Hamilton/Frankie Laine/Mitch Miller Orchestra/ Something Smith & Redheads)	15
56	Philips BBE 12040	THE BIG FOUR NO. 2 (Mindy Carson/Don Cherry/Frankie Laine/Jo Stafford)	15
56	Philips BBE 12088	THE BIG FOUR NO. 3 (Shirley Bassey/Ronnie Carroll/David Hughes/ Anne Shelton)	12
56	Philips BBE 12091	THE BIG FOUR NO. 4 (Rosemary Clooney/Doris Day/Four Lads/Frankie Laine)	15
57	Philips BBE 12114	THE BIG FOUR NO. 5 (Shirley Bassey/Ronnie Carroll/Anne Shelton/ Frankie Vaughan)	12
57	Philips BBE 12139	THE BIG FOUR NO. 6 (Shirley Bassey/Ronnie Carroll/Kaye Sisters/ Frankie Vaughan)	12
57	Philips BBE 12145	THE BIG FOUR NO. 7 (Tony Bennett/Doris Day/Guy Mitchell/Johnnie Ray)	15
57	Philips BBE 12158	THE BIG FOUR NO. 8 (Shirley Bassey/Robert Earl/Kaye Sisters/Steve Martin)	12
58	Philips BBE 12165	THE BIG FOUR NO. 9 (Robert Earl/Anne Shelton/Joyce Shock/ Frankie Vaughan & Kaye Sisters)	12
58	Philips BBE 12190	THE BIG FOUR NO. 10 (Jimmy Lloyd/Robert Earl/Kaye Sisters/Anne Shelton)	12
59	Philips BBE 12288	THE BIG FOUR NO. 11 (Shirley Bassey/Kaye Sisters/Frankie Vaughan/ Marty Wilde)	12
59	Philips BBE 12336	THE BIG FOUR NO. 12 (Frankie Laine/G. Mitchell/Johnnie Ray/Leslie Uggams)	15
66	Philips BBE 12593	THE BIG FOUR (Roger Miller/Four Seasons/Dusty Springfield/Walker Bros)	12
64	Fontana TFE 18010	BLOWIN' IN THE WIND (withdrawn; Bob Dylan/Joan Baez/Pete Seeger)	100
59	Fontana TFE 17081	THE BLUES (Danny Barker/Jimmy Giuffre/Jo Jones/Pee Wee Russell)	10
61	Pieces Of 8 PEP 605	THE BLUES (Big Bill Broonzy/Josh White)	12
64	Pye Intl. NEP 44029	THE BLUES VOL. 1 PT. 1 (John Lee Hooker/Muddy Waters/Sonny Boy Williamson/Jimmy Witherspoon)	35
64	Pye Intl. NEP 44035	THE BLUES VOL. 1 PT. 2 (Howling Wolf/Buddy Guy/Little Walter/Muddy Waters)	35
66	Chess CRE 6011	THE BLUES VOL. 2 PT. 1 (Otis Rush/Chuck Berry/John Lee Hooker/ Little Walter)	40
64	Pye Intl. NEP 44038	BLUES FESTIVAL (Sugar Pie De Santo/Willie Dixon/Sonny Boy Williamson/ Howlin' Wolf)	30
63	Columbia SEG 8226	BLUES ON PARADE NO. 1 (Jimmy Cotton/Brownie McGhee/ Roosevelt Sykes/Sonny Terry)	25
56	HMV 7EG 8178	THE BLUES THEY SANG (Lizzie Miles/Billy Young & Jelly Roll Morton)	25
61	Pye NEP 24142	BYE BYE BIRDIE (Brook Brothers/Patti Brook/Joe Brown/Jimmy Justice/ Kids/Viscounts)	15
61	RCA RCX 205	BREAKFAST AT TIFFANY'S (Henry Mancini)	15
61	Philips BBE 12472	BYE BYE BIRDIE NO. 1 (original cast; Marty Wilde et al.; stereo SBBE 9064)	12/15
61	Philips BBE 12473	BYE BYE BIRDIE NO. 2 (original cast; Marty Wilde et al.; stereo SBBE 9065)	12/15
61	Philips BBE 12474	BYE BYE BIRDIE NO. 3 (original cast; Marty Wilde et al.; stereo SBBE 9066)	12/15
61	Philips BBE 12475	BYE BYE BIRDIE NO. 4 (original cast; Marty Wilde et al.; stereo SBBE 9067)	12/15

C

63	Cameo Parkway CPE 552	CAMEO BIG FOUR (Bobby Rydell/Chubby Checker/Dovells/Orlons)	30
60	Top Rank JKP 2055	COUNTRY AND WESTERN EXPRESS VOL. 1 (Bill Alex Dixie Drifters/ Jenny Herrill/Elmer Snodgrass/Musical Pioneers)	10
60	Top Rank JKP 2056	COUNTRY AND WESTERN EXPRESS VOL. 2 (Jack Chambers & Rainbow Boys/Ralph Hodge & Hodges Brothers Band)	10
60	Top Rank JKP 2063	COUNTRY AND WESTERN EXPRESS VOL. 4 (Claude Gray/Eddie Noack)	22
60	Top Rank JKP 2065	COUNTRY AND WESTERN EXPRESS VOL. 6 (Tony Douglas/James O'Gwynn)	22
63	CBS AGG 20033	COUNTRY AND WESTERN HITS VOL. 1 (Carl Butler/Lester Flatt & Earl Scruggs/Lefty Frizzell/Stonewall Jackson/Ray Price)	10
64	CBS AGG 20041	COUNTRY AND WESTERN HITS VOL. 2 (Johnny Cash/Lester Flatt & Earl Scruggs/Lefty Frizzell/Marty Robbins)	12

65	Hickory LPE 1505	COUNTRY AND WESTERN SHOWCASE VOL. 2 (Roy Acuff/Wilma Lee/ Stoney Cooper) 10
57	Philips BBE 12149	COUNTRY AND WESTERN SPECTACULAR (George Morgan/Ray Price/ Mel Tillis/Marty Robbins) 12
59	Mercury ZEP 10038	COUNTRY AND WESTERN TRAIL BLAZERS NO. 1 (Connie Hall/ James O'Gwynn/Jimmy Skinner/Charlie Walker) 12
60	Mercury ZEP 10052	COUNTRY AND WESTERN TRAIL BLAZERS NO. 2 (Bill Clifton & Dixie Mountain Boys/George Jones) 12
60	Mercury ZEP 10080	COUNTRY AND WESTERN TRAIL BLAZERS NO. 3 (James O'Gwynn/ Connie Hall) 12
60s	Heritage 105	THE COUNTRY BLUES (99 only) 80
58	RCA RCX 107	COUNTRY GUITAR VOL. 1 (Bonnie, Jim Edward & Maxine Brown/ Hank Locklin/Jim Reeves/Hank Snow) 12
58	RCA RCX 110	COUNTRY GUITAR VOL. 2 (Skeeter Davis/Don Gibson/Jim Reeves/Hank Snow) . 15
59	RCA RCX 127	COUNTRY GUITAR VOL. 5 (Eddy Arnold/Browns/Skeeter Davis/ Johnny & Jack/Hank Snow/Porter Wagoner) 12
59	RCA RCX 141	COUNTRY GUITAR VOL. 6 (Hank Locklin/Eddy Arnold/Browns/Hank Snow/ Porter Wagoner/Johnny & Jack) 12
59	RCA RCX 147	COUNTRY GUITAR VOL. 8 (Browns/Don Gibson/Hawkshaw Hawkins/ Johnny & Jack/Jim Reeves) 12
59	RCA RCX 159	COUNTRY GUITAR VOL. 9 (Hank Locklin/Gail Davis/Skeeter Davis/Jimmy Driftwood/Jim Reeves) 15
59	RCA RCX 176	COUNTRY GUITAR VOL. 10 (Hank Locklin/Skeeter Davis/Hawkshaw Hawkins/Johnny & Jack/Sons Of The Pioneers/Hank Snow) 15
59	RCA RCX 177	COUNTRY GUITAR VOL. 11 (Browns/Eddy Arnold/Jack Clement/Hank Snow) . . . 12
60	RCA RCX 185	COUNTRY GUITAR VOL. 12 (Eddy Arnold/Hawkshaw Hawkins/Jim Reeves/ Hank Snow/Porter Wagoner) 12
62	RCA RCX 7105	COUNTRY GUITAR VOL. 16 (Bill Monroe & Blue Grass Boys/Monroe Bros) 15
63	Decca DFE 8522	COUNTRY JUBILEE VOL. 1 (Sonny Miller/Ray Phillips/Ott Stephens/ Sonny Williams) 10
63	Decca DFE 8523	COUNTRY JUBILEE VOL. 2 (Kendall Hayes/Margie Laffery/ Lonesome Pine Fiddlers/Marvin McCullough) 10

D

60s	XX MIN 706	DARK MUDDY BOTTOM (Jimmy Slim/Good Jelly Bess/Lightning Leon/ Little Red Walters/Willie B.) 22
50s	Poydras 102	DEPRESSION BLUES 28
63	Decca DFE 8520	DISCS-A-GO GO (Karl Denver/Billy Fury/Jet Harris/Vernons Girls) 60
60s	Jan & Dil JR 450	DOWN HOME BLUES — SIXTIES STYLE (Lightning Leon/Jerry McCain/ Little Red Walters) 30
60s	XX MIN 709	DOWNHOME HARP (Kid Thomas/Eddie Hope/Jerry McCain) 15
59	Fontana TFE 17146	DRUMBEAT (Lana Sisters/Adam Faith/Bob Miller & Millermen/ Sylvia Sands/Roy Young) 45

E

65	Edinburgh S.C. ESC 02	EDINBURGH STUDENTS CHARITIES APPEAL (33rpm, die-cut paper p/s; Athenians/Avengers/Ray & Archie Fisher/Lynn & Kathy) 50
66	Edinburgh S.C. ESC 03	EDINBURGH STUDENTS CHARITIES APPEAL (33rpm, Athenians/Gear System/Old Bailey's Jazz Advocates) 60
67	Philips P 160E	EXQUISITE FORM (freebie; Dave Dee, Dozy, Beaky, Mick & Tich/Herd/ Walker Brothers/Dusty Springfield) 18

F

59	Jazz Collector JEL 12	THE FEMALE BLUES VOL. 1 (Ida Cox/Ma Rainey) 18
60	Jazz Collector JEL 14	THE FEMALE BLUES VOL. 2 (Bertha Henderson/Rosa Henderson) 18
64	Jazz Collector JEL 22	THE FEMALE BLUES VOL. 3 (Ma Rainey/Trixie Smith) 18
64	Pye Intl. NEP 44030	FESTIVAL OF THE BLUES NO. 1 (Willie Dixon/Buddy Guy/Muddy Waters/ Sonny Boy Williamson) 22
58	Parlophone GEP 8694	FLUTE COCKTAIL (Bill Doggett/Johnny Pate Quartet) 10
63	Ember EMB EP 4530	FOOL BRITANNIA (Peter Sellers/Dan Massey/Anthony Newley/Joan Collins/ Maureen Lipton) 12
57	Philips BBE 12140	FOUR GREAT MOVIE THEMES (Vic Damone/Hi-Lo's/Frankie Laine/Jerry Vale) . 12
63	Decca DFE 8538	FROM A LONDON HOOTENANNY (Davy Graham/Thamesiders) 15

G

59	MGM MGM-EP 703	GIRLS AND MORE GIRLS (June Allyson/Ava Gardner/Judy Garland/ Kathryn Grayson) 10
67	Down with the Game 202	GOD DON'T LIKE IT (99 only) 35
67	Down with the Game 203	GOD DON'T LIKE IT VOLUME 2 (99 only) 35
60s	XX MIN 707	GOING TO CALIFORNIA (Little Sonny Willis/Eddie Williams) 15
59	Philips BBE 12318	GREAT COUNTRY AND WESTERN HITS (Johnny Cash/Johnny Horton/ Stonewall Jackson/Carl Smith) 15
66	Pye Intl. NEP 45054	THE GREATEST ON STAGE (Maxine Brown/Chuck Jackson/Shirelles/ Dionne Warwick) 25
63	London RE-U 1393	GROUP OF GOODIES (Marcie Blane/Kokomo/Bill Black's Combo/ Ernie Maresca) 50
59	Mercury ZEP 10010	GROUPS GALORE (Del Vikings/Mark IV/Diamonds/Hi-Liters) 160
56	Philips BBE 12077	GUYS AND DOLLS (Frankie Laine/Rosemary Clooney/Jo Stafford/Jerry Vale) . . . 12

H

64	Hickory LPE 1500	HICKORY SHOWCASE VOL. 1 (Roy Acuff/Wilma Lee/Stoney Cooper) 10
57	Capitol EAP1 852	HIT CALYPSOS (Andrews Sisters/Nat 'King' Cole/Stan Kenton/ Lord Flea Calypsonians) 10
65	Pye NEP 24213	THE HITMAKERS NO. 1 (Searchers/Kenny Ball Jazzmen/Dixie Cups/ Dionne Warwick) 15

65	Pye NEP 24214	THE HITMAKERS NO. 2 (Honeycombs/Tony Jackson/Kinks/Shangri-La's) 25
65	Pye NEP 24215	THE HITMAKERS NO. 3 (Chuck Berry/Julie Grant/Rockin' Berries/ Sandie Shaw) 18
66	Pye NEP 24241	THE HITMAKERS VOL. 1 (Ivy League/Tommy Quickly/Sandie Shaw/ Sounds Orchestral) 12
66	Pye NEP 24242	THE HITMAKERS VOL. 2 (Chuck Berry/Kinks/Sue Thompson/Shangri-La's) 30
66	Pye NEP 24243	THE HITMAKERS VOL. 3 (Kinks/Lancastrians/Rockin' Berries/Searchers) 15
66	Piccadilly NEP 34100	THE HITMAKERS (Petula Clark/Kenny Ball/Anita Harris/Honeycombs) 10
66	Pye Intl. NEP 44065	HITMAKERS INTERNATIONAL (Fontella Bass/James Brown/Petula Clark/ Lovin' Spoonful) 25
56	Mercury MEP 9003	HIT PARADE VOL. 1 (Georgia Gibbs/Platters/Crew Cuts/Patti Page) 20
56	Mercury MEP 9510	HIT PARADE VOL. 2 (Sarah Vaughan/Ralph Marterie/Patti Page/Crew Cuts) 20
57	Brunswick OE 9340	HIT PARADE (Rex Allen/Peggy Lee/Jeri Southern/Victor Young Orchestra) 10
58	Brunswick OE 9450	HIT PARADE NO. 2 (Carmen Cavallaro/Four Aces/Grandpa Jones/ Jack Pleis & His Orchestra) 12
65	Decca DFE 8648	HITS VOL. 1 (Chris Andrews/Fortunes/Hedgehoppers Anonymous/ Jonathan King) 10
65	Decca DFE 8649	HITS VOL. 2 (Lulu/Chris Andrews/Marianne Faithfull/Fortunes) 12
65	Decca DFE 8653	HITS VOL. 3 (Pinkerton's Assorted Colours/St. Louis Union/Mexicans/ Paul & Barry Ryan) 15
66	Decca DFE 8662	HITS VOL. 4 (Dave Berry/Val Doonican/Joy Marshall/Crispian St. Peters) 12
66	Decca DFE 8663	HITS VOL. 5 (Animals/Los Bravos/Alan Price Set/Small Faces) 15
66	Decca DFE 8667	HITS VOL. 6 (Jonathan King/Lulu/Alan Price Set/Small Faces) 15
67	Decca DFE 8675	HITS VOL. 7 (Ronnie Aldrich/Val Doonican/Bachelors/Small Faces) 15
62	Mercury ZEP 10133	HITSVILLE! (Brook Benton/Crew Cuts/Phil Philips/Diamonds) 35
59	Coral FEP 2034	HITSVILLE VOL. 1 (Buddy Holly/McGuire Sisters/Betty Madigan/Billy Williams) . 70
59	Coral FEP 2035	HITSVILLE VOL. 2 (Lennon Sisters/Art Lund/Teresa Brewer/Jackie Wilson) 50
65	Tamla Motown TME 2001	HITSVILLE U.S.A. NO. 1 (Marvin Gaye/Brenda Holloway/Carolyn Crawford/ Eddie Holland) . . . . 200+
66	Post War Blues 100	HOBOS AND DRIFTERS 50

I

65	Chess CRE 6010	IN CROWD (Radiants/Ramsey Lewis Trio/Little Milton/Billy Stewart) 45
56	Mercury MEP 9503	ITEMS FROM GUYS AND DOLLS (Richard Hayes/Kitty Kallen/Frankie Laine/ David Le Winter) 12
62	Pye Jazz NJE 1083	IT'S TRAD, DAD — FILM SOUNDTRACK (Bob Wallis/Kenny Ball & His Jazzmen) 15

J

| 67 | Natchez NEP-701 | THE JUG BANDS VOLUME 1 . . . . 15 |
| 64 | Columbia SEG 8337 | JUST FOR YOU (Peter & Gordon/Freddie & Dreamers) . . . . 18 |

K

63	Lyntone LYN 347/348	KEELE RAG RECORD (flexidisc; Rhythm Unlimited & Halettes/Keele Quintet) . . 18
64	Lyntone LYN 508/509	KEELE RAG RECORD NO. 2 (flexidisc; Escorts/Lance Harvey & Kingpins/ Keele Row; some in die-cut sleeve) 35/30
65	Lyntone LYN 765/766	KEELE RAG RECORD (flexidisc; Bob Wilson/Changing Times/ Lance Harvey & Kingpins/Incas) 45
56	London RE-E 1047	THE KING AND QUEEN OF R&B (Ruth Brown/Joe Turner) 220
61	RCA Victor RCX 203	KINGS OF THE BLUES VOL. 2 (Jazz Gillum/Big Maceo/Washboard Sam/ Sonny Boy Williamson) 20
61	RCA Victor RCX 204	KINGS OF THE BLUES VOL. 3 (Arthur Big Boy Crudup/Furry Lewis/ Poor Joe Williams) 25
59	Top Rank 45-TR 5004	KING SIZE (maxi-single; Craig Douglas/Sheila Buxton/Bert Weedon) 15
60	Warner Bros WEP 6010	KOOKIE STARS OF SEVENTY SEVEN SUNSET STRIP (Joannie Sommers/Eddie Byrne/Connie Stevens) 15

L

66	Holyground HG 111	THE LAST THING ON MY MIND (EP, 99 copies only) 60
59	Top Rank JKR 8008	LET'S GO NO. 1 (Jimmy Lee/Johnny Hines/Treetoppers) 30
59	Top Rank JKR 8012	LET'S GO NO. 2 (Johnny Hines/Billy Mack/Victors/Ted & Ray) 30
60	Philips BBE 12414/ SBBE 9031	LET'S MAKE LOVE — FILM SOUNDTRACK (Yves Montand/Marilyn Monroe/ Frankie Vaughan; mono/stereo) 65/80
63	Embassy WEP 1104	LIVERPOOL BEAT (Typhoons/Mike Redway/Ray Pilgrim/Bobby Stevens) 10
57	London RE-D 1075	LONDON HIT PARADE NO. 1 (Tab Hunter/Hilltoppers/Pat Boone/ Fontane Sisters) 25
57	London RE-P 1096	LONDON HIT PARADE NO. 2 (Fats Domino/Slim Whitman/Ken Copeland/ Roy Brown) 100
58	London RE-D 1097	LONDON HIT PARADE NO. 3 (Pat Boone/Gale Storm/Tab Hunter/Jim Lowe) 30
58	London RE-D 1130	LONDON HIT PARADE NO. 4 (Pat Boone/Nick Todd/ Bonnie Guitar/Hilltoppers) 30
58	London RE-D 1136	LONDON TOPPERS NO. 2 (export issue; Pat Boone/Nick Todd/Tab Hunter/ Jim Lowe) 30
58	London RE-P 1137	LONDON TOPPERS NO. 3 (export issue; Slim Whitman/Fats Domino/ Ricky Nelson/Ernie Freeman) 80
58	London RE-D 1145	LONDON HIT PARADE NO. 5 (Pat Boone/Fontane Sisters/Frank De Rosa) 25

M

59	Jazz Collector JEL 2	THE MALE BLUES VOL. 1 (Georgia Slim/Walter Roland) 25
59	Jazz Collector JEL 4	THE MALE BLUES VOL. 3 (Blind Blake/Ramblin' Thomas) 25
59	Jazz Collector JEL 5	THE MALE BLUES VOL. 4 (Tall Tom/Pinewood Tom) 25
59	Jazz Collector JEL 8	THE MALE BLUES VOL. 5 (Blind Lemon Jefferson/Buddy Boy Hawkins) 25
60	Jazz Collector JEL 10	THE MALE BLUES VOL. 6 (Hound Head Henry/Frankie Jaxon) 25
60	Jazz Collector JEL 13	THE MALE BLUES VOL. 7 (Blind Lemon Jefferson/Ed Bell) 25
61	Jazz Collector JEL 24	THE MALE BLUES VOL. 8 (Blind Lemon Jefferson/Leadbelly) 25

MINT VALUE

67	Piccadilly NEP 34100	MAXWELL HOUSE PRESENTS HITMAKERS (Kenny Ball/Petula Clark/Honeycombs/Anita Harris) 1
57	Decca DFE 6408	MERRY CHRISTMAS (Dave King/Mantovani Orchestra/Dickie Valentine/ David Whitfield) 1
60	MGM MGM-EP 749	MGM EVERGREENS (Billy Eckstine/Tommy Edwards/Lennie Hayton/ Sam 'The Man' Taylor & Catmen) 1
69	Middle Earth MDE 201	MIDDLE EARTH SAMPLER (WRITING ON THE WALL: Aries/WOODEN O: Overture/ARCADIUM: Poor Lady) (promo only, 33rpm, no p/s) 10
64	RCA RCX 7159	MONTH'S BEST FROM THE COUNTRY AND WEST (Eddy Arnold/Bobby Bare/George Hamilton IV/Connie Smith) 1
64	RCA RCX 7162	MONTH'S BEST FROM THE COUNTRY AND WEST VOL. 2 (Skeeter Davis/Bobby Bare/Don Gibson/Jim Reeves/Hank Snow) 1
64	RCA RCX 7171	MONTH'S BEST FROM THE COUNTRY AND WEST VOL. 3 (Eddy Arnold/Archie Campbell/Porter Wagoner/Dottie West) 1
65	RCA RCX 7172	MONTH'S BEST FROM THE COUNTRY AND WEST VOL. 4 (Bobby Bare/Jim Edward Brown/Willie Nelson/Connie Smith) 1
65	RCA RCX 7178	MONTH'S BEST FROM THE COUNTRY AND WEST VOL. 5 (Bobby Bare/Norma Jean/Porter Wagoner/Connie Smith) 10
65	RCA RCX 7181	MONTH'S BEST FROM THE COUNTRY AND WEST VOL. 6 (Don Gibson/ Bobby Bare/Carl Belew/George Hamilton IV/Hank Locklin/Dottie West) 1
67	RCA RCX 7186	MONTH'S BEST FROM THE COUNTRY AND WEST VOL. 7 (Waylon Jennings/ Stu Phillips/Connie Smith/Dottie West) 10
60s	Jan & Dil TR 451	MORE DOWN HOME BLUES (Good Jelly Boss/Juke Boy Bonner/ Papa Lightfoot/Snooky Prior) 3
60	Philips BBE 12348	MOST HAPPY FELLA HITS (Doris Day/Four Lads/Frankie Laine/Jo Stafford) 1
64	Stateside SE 1021	MOVIE MUSIC (John Barry/Artie Butler/Eddie Heywood/Bill Ramal Combo)..... 2
60s	Mercury YARD 002	MUSIC FOR 5 AM (promo for Yardley; Hollies & others) 1

N

56	Vogue EPV 1106	NEGRO SPIRITUALS (Original Five Blind Boys/Sensational Nightingales) 2
64	Vocalion EPVP 1271	NEGRO SPIRITUALS (Dixie Hummingbirds/Sensational Nightingales) 2
64	Vocalion EPVP 1276	NEGRO SPIRITUALS (Five Blind Boys/Spirits Of Memphis) 2
66	Tamla Motown TME 2014	NEW FACES FROM HITSVILLE (Jimmy Ruffin/Chris Clark & Lewis Sisters/ Tammi Terrell/Monitors) 250
57	Pye NEP 24052	NIXA HIT PARADE NO. 1 (Gary Miller/Pet Clark/Lonnie Donegan/John Frazer).. 1
58	Pye NEP 24064	NIXA HIT PARADE NO. 2 (Pearl Carr & Teddy Johnson/Petula Clark/ Lonnie Donegan Skiffle Group/Colin Hicks & Cabin Boys) 2
58	Pye NEP 24071	NIXA HIT PARADE NO. 3 (Marion Ryan/Gary Miller/Lonnie Donegan/ Edmund Hockridge) 1
58	Pye NEP 24078	NIXA HIT PARADE NO. 4 (Marion Ryan/Pet Clark/Joe Henderson/Gary Miller) ... 1
58	Pye NEP 24082	NIXA HIT PARADE NO. 5 (Petula Clark/Lonnie Donegan Skiffle Group/ Marion Ryan/Bill Shepherd Orchestra) 1
58	Pye NEP 24090	NIXA HIT PARADE NO. 6 (Lita Roza/Petula Clark/Lonnie Donegan Skiffle Group/Joe Henderson) 1
59	Pye NEP 24100	NIXA HIT PARADE NO. 7 (Lita Roza/Petula Clark/Lonnie Donegan Skiffle Group/Edmund Hockridge) 1

O

65	Columbia SEG 8413	ON THE SCENE (Downliners Sect/Animals/Cherokees/Cheynes/ Georgie Fame/Yardbirds) 100
63	MGM MGM-EP 787	ORIGINAL HITS (Tommy Edwards/Johnny Ferguson/Jimmy Jones/ Conway Twitty) 45
63	London RE-K 1390	THE ORIGINAL HITS (Drifters/Ritchie Barrett/Coasters/Ben E. King).......... 65
65	Atlantic AET 6006	ORIGINAL HITS VOL. 2 (Barbara Lewis/Coasters/Solomon Burke/Drifters)..... 55
62	Ember EMB 4522	ORIGINAL RHYTHM AND BLUES HITS (Jesse Belvin/Ray Charles/ Linda Hayes/Jimmy McCracklin/Johnny Moore Blazers) 75
55	Pye Jazz NJE 1043	ORIGINS OF SKIFFLE (Isla Cameron/Guy Carawan/Peggy Seeger) 20
57	Columbia SEG 7669	OUR CHOICE (Eddie Calvert/Michael Holliday/Ruby Murray) 12
68	Apple (no cat. no.)	OUR FIRST FOUR (4 x 7" in presentation pack, including "Hey Jude" [R 5722] & "Those Were The Days" by Mary Hopkin [APPLE 2], "Sour Milk Sea" by Jackie Lomax [APPLE 3] & "Thingumybob" by Black Dyke Mills Band [APPLE 4]; each mounted in PVC pocket on printed dayglo card insert, in 10" x 12" card or plastic outer box) 750/1,000

P

55	Decca DFE 6147	PARADE OF STARS (Joan Regan/Edmundo Ros & Stargazers/ Dickie Valentine/Stargazers) 12
58	Pye NSEP 85000	POPS GO STEREO (Marion Ryan/Tony Osborne Orch./Bill Shepherd Orch.) 15

R

67	Action ACT 002 EP	RAG GOES MAD AT THE MOJO (33rpm; Joe Cocker's Blues Band/ Tangerine Ayr Band/Pitiful Souls/Delroy Good Good Band; in conjunction with Sheffield University rag magazine Twikker)............... 85
56	Vogue EPV 1113	RHYTHM AND BLUES (Dominoes/Swallows).......................... 300
60s	Range JRE 7002	RHYTHM AND BLUES (Sticks Herman/Tim Whitsett) 15
60s	Range JRE 7006	RHYTHM AND BLUES (Harry Lewis/Tommy Wills) 15
63	Stateside SE 1008	RHYTHM AND BLUES (Jimmy Reed/John Lee Hooker) 35
64	Stateside SE 1009	R&B CHARTMAKERS (Martha/Vandellas/Miracles/Marvin Gaye/Marvelettes) ... 110
64	Stateside SE 1018	R&B CHARTMAKERS NO. 2 (Miracles/Kim Weston/Supremes/Marvelettes) 110
64	Stateside SE 1022	R&B CHARTMAKERS NO. 3 (Marvin Gaye/Darnells/Eddie Holland/ Martha & Vandellas) 150
64	Stateside SE 1025	R&B CHARTMAKERS NO. 4 (Supremes/Eddie Holland/Temptations/ Contours)...................... 100
60	Vogue EPV 1198	RHYTHM AND BLUES CONCERT (Helen Humes/Jimmy Witherspoon) 80
64	Pye Intl. NEP 44021	RHYTHM AND BLUES SHOWCASE VOL. 1 (Don & Bob/Dale Hawkins/ Clarence Henry/Larry Williams) 35

64	Pye Intl. NEP 44022	RHYTHM AND BLUES SHOWCASE VOL. 2 (Jimmy McCracklin/ Muddy Waters/Little Walter/Howlin' Wolf) 35
57	Vogue VE 170111	ROCK AND ROLL (Mister Google Eyes August/Louis Jones Rock & Roll Band/Walter Price Rock & Roll Band/Clarence Gatemouth Brown) 160
62	Capitol EAP1 20197	ROUND-UP (Tommy Collins/Farmer Boys/Ferlin Husky/Texas Bill Strength)..... 15
60	Top Rank JKP 2060	RUSHING FOR PERCUSSION (Preston Epps/Sandy Nelson) 20

S

60s	S.A.U.C.C. PR 5462	ST. ANDREWS UNIVERSITY CHARITIES CAMPAIGN (20th Century Sounds/ Steve Hall & Roosters/Black Ring; no p/s) 35
64	Lyntone LYN 738/739	SHEFFIELD UNIVERSITY RAG RECORD (flexidisc; Vantennas/Dave Allen Band/ Addy Street Five/Los Caribos; die-cut sleeve) 40
55	Columbia SEG 7528	SHOUT FOR JOY (Pete Johnson/Albert Ammons/Meade Lux Lewis).......... 30
63	London RE-P 1403	SINGING THE BLUES (Ernie K-Doe/Showmen/Jesse Hill/Chris Kenner) 110
58	Decca DFE 6485	SIX FIVE SPECIAL (Jackie Dennis/Joan Regan/Diane Todd/Dickie Valentine).... 40
66	Lyntone LYN 995	THE SOUND OF THE STARS (flexidisc with *Disc And Music Echo*; with/without mag & envelope/stamp)........................ 20/10
65	Keele Rag/Lyntone LYN 951/952	SOUNDS OF SAVILE (flexidisc; Hipster Image/London Apprentices/ Tom & Brennie; some in die-cut title sleeve) 80/50
55	Decca DFE 6147	STAR PARADE (Stargazers/Edmundo Ros Orchestra/Joan Regan & Squadronaires/Dickie Valentine) 12
60s	208 Radio Luxembourg	STAR SOUVENIR GREETINGS (flexidisc)........................ 15
60	Mercury ZEP 10088	SURPRISE PACKAGE (Ben Hewitt/Diamonds)........................ 120
59	Top Rank JKR 8007	SWEET BEAT (Lee Allen Band/Fred Parris/Cindy Mann/Mellokings) 50

T

63	Oriole EP 7080	TAKE SIX (Mark Peters' Silhouettes/Ian & Zodiacs/Faron's Flamingos/Earl Preston & T.T.s/Rory Storm & Hurricanes/Sonny Wade & Cascades).......... 70
59	Mercury ZEP 10015	TEAR IT UP (Boyd Bennett Orchestra/Red Prysock/Hi-Liters)............... 160
57	Mercury MEP 9522	TEEN-AGE ROCK (Red Prysock/Rusty Draper/Chuck Miller/Crew Cuts) 135
58	RCA RCX 111	TEENAGE TOPS (Ray Peterson/Jimmy Dell/Marlin Greene/ Barry De Vorzon).. 45
64	Ember EMB 4540	TEEN SCENE '64 (Dave Clark Five/Ray Singer/Washington D.C.s)............ 50
60	Heritage RE 102	THAT CONWAY ROCK (with Walter Hawkins & William Moore, 99 copies only) 50
58	Brunswick OE 9425	THEY SOLD A MILLION NO. 9 (Bobby Helms/Four Aces/Jerry Lewis/ Kitty Kallen) 25
59	Brunswick OE 9426	THEY SOLD A MILLION NO. 10 (Andrews Sisters/Four Aces/Ink Spots/ Mills Brothers).. 12
59	Brunswick OE 9427	THEY SOLD A MILLION NO. 11 (Ink Spots/Louis Jordan & His Tympany Five/ Mills Brothers/Weavers)..................................... 20
59	Brunswick OE 9431	THEY SOLD A MILLION NO. 15 (Four Aces/Bill Haley & His Comets).......... 25
60s	Argo EAF 66	THROUGH THE LOOKING GLASS (SCENES FROM) (soundtrack) 10
57	Decca DFE 6411	TOPS IN POPS NO. 1 (Beverley Sisters/Bob Cort Skiffle Group/Terry Dene/ Tommy Steele) 20
58	Decca DFE 6467	TOPS IN POPS NO. 3 (Jackie Dennis/D. King/Southlanders/David Whitfield) ... 18
59	Decca DFE 6583	TOPS IN POPS NO. 7 (Beverley Sisters/Ted Heath & His Music/ Lord Rockingham's XI/Tommy Steele) 15
63	Stateside SE 1004	TOP TEEN DANCES (Johnnie Morisette/Huey 'Piano' Smith & Clowns/ Al Brown's Tunetoppers/Spartans) 30
57	Parlophone R 4356	TOP TEN SPECIAL (Jim Dale/King Brothers/Vipers Skiffle Group) 15
67	Pye NEP 24276	TOP T.V. THEMES (Cyril Stapleton/Ron Grainer Orchestra/Barry Gray Orchestra/Eliminators/Johnny Keating & Z Men) 15
60	Fontana TFE 17265	TREASURES OF NORTH AMERICAN NEGRO MUSIC VOL. 6 (Reverend J.C. Burnett/Reverend J.M. Gates/Reverend W. Mosley) 15
65	Century 21 MA 105	T.V. CENTURY 21 THEMES (David Graham/Sylvia Anderson/Peter Dyneley/ Barry Gray Orchestra/Gary Miller/Eric Winstone Orchestra) 15
64	Decca DFE 8585	T.V. THEMES (Andrew Oldham Orchestra/Ted Heath Music/ Ron Grainer Music/Cyril Stapleton Orchestra) 40
66	Pye NEP 24244	T.V. THEMES 1966 (Laurie Johnson Orchestra/John Schroeder Orchestra/ Cyril Stapleton Orchestra) 12
62	Starlite STEP 31	TWIST OFF (Wayne Farmer/Medallions/Charles Perrywell/Piano Slim/ Teenbeats/Dellos) 200
62	Starlite STEP 29	TWIST ON (Mighty Trojans/Dee Dee Gaudet/Dixie Lee/ Percy & The Rocking Aces) 170

V

65	Vogue VRE 5002	VOGUE SURPRISE PARTIE (Petula Clark/Jean Jacques Debout/ Francoise Hardy/Michel Paje) 15

W

69	Apple CT 1	WALLS ICE CREAM PRESENTS (Mary Hopkin/Iveys/Jackie Lomax/ James Taylor; with/without p/s) 40/12
65	Liberty LEP 4036	WE SING THE BLUES (Jesse Hill/Ernie K. Doe/Aaron Neville/Benny Spellman) .. 60
64	Fontana TFE 18009	WITH GOD ON OUR SIDE (withdrawn; Bob Dylan/Joan Baez/Pete Seeger)..... 100
66	Chess CRE 6009	WITH THE BLUES (Eddie Boyd Blues Combo/Buddy Guy) 35

Y

64	Fontana TFE 18011	YE PLAYBOYS AND PLAYGIRLS (withdrawn; Bob Dylan/Joan Baez/ Pete Seeger) 100
68	Chess CRE 6026	YOUR CHESS REQUESTS (Fontella Bass/Tony Clarke/Mitty Collier/ Billy Stewart) 60
57	Mercury MEP 9525	YOUR CHOICE (Hal Mooney Orchestra/Chuck Miller/Sarah Vaughan/ Florian Zabach) 20
58	Mercury MEP 9532	YOUR CHOICE NO. 2 (Ralph Marterie Orchestra/Patti Page/ Platters/Myoshi Umeki)...................................... 15

MINT VALUE

UNTITLED EPS

60s	Coxsone SCE 1	(no p/s, 33rpm; Gaylads/Hugh Godfrey/Glen & Dave/Roy Richards/Cables/Richard Ace)	7
63	Embassy WEP 1086	(p/s; Mike Redway/Bud Ashton Group/Rory Pilgrim)	1
69	De Wolfe	(Lemon Dips, et al.)	3

VARIOUS ARTISTS SINGLES & EPs
70s/80s/90s/00s
(alphabetical by title)

A

90	Metro Music DWM-1	ABSLOM DAAK — DALEK KILLER (Mark Ayres/Dominic Glynn/The Slaves Of Kane) (square flexi, with/without *Doctor Who Magazine*)	8/
96	Sticky STICKY 19	ACOUSTICKY (Hood/Boyracer et al.)	1
97	Ferox FER 028	FURTHER ADVENTURES IN TECHNO SOUL (12" sampler; Dan Curtin/The Invisibles et al.)	1
98	Twisted Nerve TN 003	ALL OAR NOTHING (10", p/s; Badly Drawn Boy/Mum & Dad/Dakota Oak/Sirconical/Andy Votel)	3
56	Decca F 10752	ALL STAR HIT PARADE (EP, credited to the Lord's Taverners)	1
57	Decca F 10915	ALL STAR HIT PARADE NO. 2 (EP, credited to the Lord's Taverners)	
85	Lyntone LYN 16705	ALTERNATIVE TOP OF THE POPS (flexidisc, spoken word)	
84	Relegated	ARISTOCRAP (p/s; Pulex Irritans/Seventh Plague/Vendetta)	1
95	Sticky STICKY 16	AROUND THE WORLD WITH STICKY RECORDS (Rory Commodore [a.k.a. Tindersticks]/Boy Racer/Heck/Cornershop, picture disc, 700 only)	1

B

83	Secret SHH 138	BACK ON THE STREET (p/s; Skin Disease/Angela Rippon's Bum/Venom/Strike/East End Badoes)	1
92	Rhythmic Tech. ART 1	NORT ROUTE (12")	2
87	Other OTH 6	BATTLEAXE (p/s; Black Riders/Holosade/Kes/Teacher's Pet)	3
78	Good Vibrations GOT 7	BATTLE OF THE BANDS (double pack, no'd p/s; Idiots/Rudi/Outcasts/Spider)	1
95	Ka-boom KA-BOOM 1	BIG BOLLOCKED BONFIRE BLOW-UP (Hood, et al.)	1
80	Vinyl Drip DRIP 001	BLACKPOOL ROX (p/s; Membranes/Section 25/Syntax/Kenneth Turner Set)	
79	Skeleton SKL 002	THE BLANK TAPES VOL. 1 (folded p/s; Attempted Moustache/Junk Act/Geisha Girls/Zorkie Twins)	
81	Secret SHH 126	BOLLOCKS TO CHRISTMAS (p/s; Business/4-Skins/Gonads/Max Splodge)	30
97	Fisheye FISH 2	BREAKING THE PLASTIC HYMEN: VINYL VIRGINS & LOW FI WHORES (2 x 7", Hood et al.)	
80s	Secret	BRITANNIA WAIVES THE RULES (12", p/s; Exploited/Chron Gen/Infa Riot)	1
94	Fierce Panda NING 04	BUILT TO BLAST (double pack, p/s; Green Day/Flying Medallions/Fabric/Understand/China Drum/Joeyfat)	
80	Crass 421984/5	BULLSHIT DETECTOR (12", p/s; A.P.F. Brigade/Alternative/Amebix/Clockwork Criminals/Counter Attack/Crass/Frenzy Battalion/Fuck The CIA/Icon/Reputations In Jeopardy/Sceptics/Sinyx/Speakers/Andy T.)	2

C

95	Orange ORANGE 001	CARMIHOOD (Hood/Carmine)	8
98	Twisted Nerve TNXMS 1	CHRISTMAS STOCKING FILLER (Badly Drawn Boy/Dakota Oak/Sirconical/Mum & Dad/Elbow) (green vinyl in green wraparound sleeve or red vinyl in red sl.)	60
98	Twisted Nerve TNXM 025	CHRISTMAS STOCKING FILLER 2 (10", p/s; Andy Votel/D.O.T./Lost Children's Desk/Misty Dixon/Cherrystones)	10
95	Spangle SPANG 001	CLUB SPANGLE EP (p/s; Marion et al.)	6
97	SKAM 0161	COMPILATION (CD, Skam & V/VM artists)	18
80s	No Future	A COUNTRY FIT FOR HEROES (12", p/s)	12
80s	No Future	A COUNTRY FIT FOR HEROES VOL. 2 (12", p/s)	20
94	Fierce Panda NING 02	CRAZED AND CONFUSED (p/s; Supergrass/Ash et al.)	30
80	Clancrest FLX 135	CUP TRIUMPHS: EXCERPTS FROM FA CUP FINALS (gold flexi in card folder)	10

D

71	Dandelion DS 7001	DANDELION (die-cut sleeve; Principal Edwards Magic Theatre/Stackwaddy/Siren/The Way We Live)	15
86	BBC ZRSL 193	DOCTOR WHO (cassette, holographic inlay; Dominic Glynn/Mankind/BBC Radiophonic Workshop)	8
86	BBC 12RXL 193	DOCTOR WHO (12", holographic p/s; Dominic Glynn/Mankind/BBC Radiophonic Workshop)	12
87	BBC RESL 193	DOCTOR WHO (p/s, reissue; Dominic Glynn/Mankind)	5

E

79	Fast Products FAST 9B	EARCOM 2 (12", p/s; Joy Division/Thursdays/Basczax)	12
79	Fast Products FAST 9C	EARCOM 3 (double pack, gatefold p/s with colour postcard insert; D.A.F./Middle Class/Noh Mercy/Stupid Babies)	5
97	Fat Cat 12FAT 003	8. 8.5, 9 (12", custom sleeve)	10
99	Lowlife LOW8	EASTER ISLAND (EP)	25
78	Stiff FREEBIE 2	EXCERPTS FROM STIFF'S GREATEST HITS (promo only sampler, 33rpm)	8
96	Mo' Wax MWEX 001-010	EXCURSIONS (10 x 12", box set; the Prunes/IO/Olde Scottish/David Caron/DJ Solo & DJ Aura/Midnight Funk Assoc./Stasis/Solo feat. JT/Twig Bud/DJ Shadow)	40
99	AI AI 001	EXPERIMENTS IN COLOUR (12"; Normal/Cell/Fil)	20

F

78	Factory FAC 2	A FACTORY SAMPLE (double pack, p/s, in plastic bag, with 5 stickers; Joy Division/Cabaret Voltaire/Durutti Column/John Dowie; beware of counterfeits) 100/75
81	Pax PAX 1	5 MILES TO MIDNIGHT (12", p/s; Brothers/Doormen/I Scream/Mortuary In Wax) . . 8
95	555 5X555	5x555 (5x7" box set; Boyracer/Mike Nichols And His Excellency/Amy Linton & Stewart Anderson/Father/Hood) 30
91	Fontana FONT 1	THE FONTANA SINGLES BOX SET VOLUME 1 — HITS AND RARITIES (12-single box set, with 12 inserts) 30
91	Fontana FONT 2	THE FONTANA SINGLES BOX SET VOLUME 2 — HITS AND RARITIES (12-single box set, with 12 inserts) 30
95	Malpractice MAL 03	FORCED INDIGNATION (1000 only; Hood/Hem) 5
79	Heartbeat PULSE 4	4 ALTERNATIVES (p/s; 48 Hours/Joe Public/Numbers/X-Certs) 15
80	Con (no cat. no.)	THE FOUR EPs (cassette; Mark Perry et al.) 15
92	Kerrang! K/EMI 1	4 PLAY (with issue 397 of Kerrang!) 5
96	Ché CHE 059	4 TRACK 3 BAND TOUR EP (p/s, Mogwai/Urusei Yatsura/Backwater, 50 only) . . . 25
94	Fierce Panda NING 05	FROM GREER TO ETERNITY (double pack, p/s; Lush/Ivy/Solar Race// Splendora/Jale/Fuzzy) 8
96	Mosquito MSQ 05	FRESH AS YOU FUCKIN' LIKE (12"; Paul Hannah/Russ Gabriel/Steve Patton/ Cristian Vogel/Si Begg) 25

G

72	Chess 6145 011	GENESIS — THE BEGINNINGS OF ROCK 10
83	Mouth MOUTH 1	G-FORCE (Shady Deal/Dead Loss/Blythe Rocket/Egypt) 20
70	Village Thing VTSX 1000	THE GREAT WHITE DAP (Wizz Jones/Sun Also Rises/Ian A. Anderson/ Pigsty Hill Light Orchestra) 20

H

80	Groucho Marxist COMMUNIQUE 2	HA! HA! FUNNY POLIS (PAISLEY ROCKS AGAINST RACISM) (p/s; Defiant Pose/Fegs/Urban Enemies/XS Discharge) 20
71	Abreaction ABR 001	HART ROCK (Brass Alley/Yellow/Trilogy/Lucas Tyson) (no p/s) 30
90s	Sub Pop	HELTER SHELTER (box set, 4 x 7", Elastica/Gene) 12
89	Hometown Atrocities 1	THE HOMETOWN ATROCITIES EP (wraparound p/s, either 'glossy', or 'kylie'; Headless Chickens/Jackson Penis/Beaver Patrol/Mad At The Sun) 150/200
88	House Of Dolls HOD 002	HOUSE OF DOLLS (no p/s; Cardiacs/Orange Cartest/In Two A Circle/ Decadent Few; free with House Of Dolls magazine) 7/5
88	House Of Dolls HOD 004	HOUSE OF DOLLS (no p/s; Wedding Present/Trudy/Hunters Club/ Claytown Troupe; free with House Of Dolls magazine) 7/5
89	House Of Dolls HOD 009	HOUSE OF DOLLS (no p/s; Pop Will Eat Itself/Wild Poppies/Blow Up/ Godspeed; free with House Of Dolls magazine) 7/5
89	House Of Dolls HOD 010	HOUSE OF DOLLS (no p/s; Sugarcubes/Host/Murrumbidgee Whalers/ Shark Taboo; free with House Of Dolls magazine) 7/5
89	House Of Dolls HOD 011	HOUSE OF DOLLS (no p/s; Wonder Stuff/Prudes/Sandkings/World Of Music; free with House Of Dolls magazine) 7/5
75	Solid Sender SEP 100	HOUSTON JUMP (James Widemouth Brown & His Orchestra/Henry Hayes Four Kings & Carl Campbell/Goree Carter & Hepcats) 10

I

97	B. Banquet Random 2.2	I DIE, YOU DIE (12", green vinyl promo, die-cut sleeve, 1200 only; Greenhaus/ Mike Dearborn/Dave Clarke) 10
78	Radar SAM 88	INTERNATIONAL ARTISTS (13th Floor Elevators/Red Crayola/ Lost & Found/Golden Dawn; Red Crayola Hope & Anchor gig freebie with Howdy From Texas The Lone Star State magazine) 12/8
83	Future FUTURE 1	THE INVISIBLE FRAME (p/s, Blitz/And Also The Trees & others) 7

J

| 93 | Mo' Wax MW 010 | JAZZ HIP JAP SAMPLER (12", stickered sleeve; Monday Michiru/Jeff Brown & 331/3; Magic Ware) . . . . 15 |
| 98 | Fierce Panda NING 63 | THE JOY OF PLECS (2 x 7"; Cay/Chicks/Max Tractor/The Monsoon Bassoon/ The Samurai Seven/Fantasmagroover) (wraparound p/s, with insert) . . . . 8 |

L

79	Decca FR 13864	THE LONDON BOYS (p/s; David Bowie/Small Faces/Birds/Dobie Gray) 7
73	Ronco MR EP 001	LONG LIVE ROCK (no p/s; Billy Fury/Eugene Wallace/Wishful Thinking) 15
87	Barracuda Blue 12UTA 9	LUNACY IS LEGEND (12", p/s; Times/Necessitarians/Nikki Sudden) 8

M

71	Track 2094 011	MAXI TRACK RECORD (John's Children/Crazy World Of Arthur Brown/ Thunderclap Newman/Jimi Hendrix; withdrawn blue sleeve crediting Pete Townshend as producer) 125
71	Track 2094 011	MAXI TRACK RECORD (John's Children/Crazy World Of Arthur Brown/ Thunderclap Newman/Jimi Hendrix; red & white sleeve with press pack, also maroon & gold sleeve without press pack) 60/10
86	MM Vinyl Conflict 1	MELODY MAKER EP (with magazine) 5
97	Begg. Banquet Random 2.1	METAL (12", red vinyl promo, die-cut sleeve, 1200 only; Robert Armani) 10
85	Davy Lamp DL 1	MINERS BENEFIT (numbered plain white sleeve; Newtown Neurotics/ Respect/Real By Real/Austin's Shirts) 6
97	V/VM VVMT4	MISSINGTOE & WHINE (EP, 500 only) 15
99	Twisted Nerve TN 009	MODERN MUSIC FOR MOTORCYCLES (10" EP, some on yellow vinyl; Dakota Oak/Alfie/Sirconical & Andy Votel/Mum & Dad/Badly Drawn Boy) 20/10
99	Twisted Nerve TNC 009	MODERN MUSIC FOR MOTORCYCLES (cassette; Dakota Oak/Alfie/Sirconical & Andy Votel/Mum & Dad/Badly Drawn Boy) 15
95	Fierce Panda NING 15	MORTAL WOMBAT (double pack, p/s; Super Furry Animals/Baby Bird/ Panda/Mexican Pets/Harvey's Rabbit/Spare Snare) 8
75	Happy Time HT12	MUSIC FROM THUNDERBIRDS AND DOCTOR WHO (p/s) 7
80	EMI 12EMI 5074	MUTHA'S PRIDE (12", p/s; Wildfire/Quartz/White Spirit/Baby Jane) 20

N

98	Lowlife LOW6	98 Series Vol. 1 (EP) 30
98	Lowlife LOW7	98 Series Vol. 2 (EP) 25
80	Neutron NT 003	1980! THE FIRST FIFTEEN MINUTES EP (gatefold p/s with inserts; Vice Versa/Clock DVA/I'm So Hollow/Stunt Kites).......................... 15
87	NME	NME HAT TRICK (Sonic Youth/Sly & Robbie et al.)......................... 7

O

95	Enraptured RAPT 4503	OMBRES (p/s; Amp/Third Eye Foundation/Saddar Bazaar) 6
82	Neat NEAT 25	ONE TAKE NO DUBS (12", p/s; Black Rose/Hellanbach/Alien/Avenger)........ 12

P

90s	Fierce Panda NING 12CD	PANDEMONIUM (Easyworld, et al.) (250 only)............................ 10
80s	A&M A&M PARTY 1/2/3/4/5/6	THE PARTY PARTY PACK (6 x 7", with picture sleeves, in PVC outer sleeve; Sting/Pauline Black/Dave Edmunds/Midge Ure/Modern Romance/Bad Manners/ Chas & Dave/Bananarama/Elvis Costello/Bad Manners/Altered Images)........ 50
97	V/VM VVMT4	PRIVILEGED FRAMES FOR REFERENCE (12" EP, p/s, 450 only) 20
88	Bam Caruso BRAV 092	PSYCHE-OUT (Smoke) (flexi, given away with Music Week)................. 15

R

93	Raptor RAP 1	RAPTOR PRESENTS . . . (12", p/s, 500 only; Ash/Buttlip/Marrow Bone/Fat) 40
82	Recommended RR-8.9	RECOMMENDED RECORDS SAMPLER (Peter Blegvad/Homosexuals/Faust/ R. Stevie Moore; 1-sided, clear vinyl, with PVC cover) 10
78	Virgin VR 08 10274/ SHOL 2550	RECORD MIRROR (no p/s; Tangerine Dream/XTC/Motors/U-Roy; with 2nd EP "The State Disco Party" & Record Mirror magazine) 7
91	Ptolemaic Terrascope POT 8	RED FLIPPER (no p/s, Nurse With Wound/The Underworlde/ Caravan Of Dreams).. 15
91	Epic HOT 1	RED HOT & DANCE (4 x 12" promo box set with insert, sticker and condom) ... 18
94	Fierce Panda NING 03	RETURN TO SPLENDOUR (double pack in foldover p/s with insert in poly bag, 1,000 only; Bluetones et al.) 15
77	Rollercoaster RRCEP 00002	ROCKABILLY HOP (test pressings only) 15
83	Consett Music Project RD 1	ROCK AND DOLE (Obnoxious Tartus/Decade Waltz/Task Force/Hot Banana).... 25
92	Melody Maker MMI	ROLLERCOASTER EP (CD, Blur/Jesus & Mary Chain/Dinosaur Jr./ My Bloody Valentine; 2,000 only) 10
80	Energy NRG 1	ROOM TO MOVE (p/s; Big Self/Outcasts/Shock Treatment/Vipers)............ 7

S

95	Atol ATOL 02	S4C MAKES ME WANT TO SMOKE CRACK VOL. 1 (500 only, Catatonia et al.) .. 25
81	Springtime RARA 1001	THE SECRET POLICEMAN'S OTHER BALL (Sting/Phil Collins/Bob Geldof) (10", promo only sampler)... 15
94	Fierce Panda/ Damaged Goods NING 01	SHAGGING IN THE STREETS (double pack, wraparound p/s in poly bag, 1,000 only; S*M*A*S*H/Blessed Ethel/Mantaray/Done Lying Down/ These Animal Men/Action Painting!) 15
93	Duophonic DS 45-05/06	SHIMMIES IN SUPER 8 (double pack, 1 disc green vinyl, other white vinyl, numbered in poly bag, 800 with tri-foldout p/s, 400 also with sticker & 2 inserts; Stereolab/Huggy Bear/Darlin'/Colm) .... each 35
95	Enraptured RAPT 4502	SILVER APPLES TRIBUTE (10", 12 in hand-drawn sleeve; Windy & Carl/Scaredycat/Third Eye Foundation/Flowchart/Sabine 25/10
80	Sleep 'N' Eat	SLEEP 'N' EAT (includes Originators) 6
80s	Smash Hits	SMASH HITS INTERVIEW PACK (4 flexidiscs in envelope sleeve; Duran Duran/Spandau Ballet/Boy George/Frankie Goes To Hollywood) 10
86	Broken Flag BF F1	THE SOFT VOLCANO ERUPTS (flexidisc; Controlled Bleeding/Kehamas Curse/ Uncommunity/Nails Of Christ/Cananes/Ramleh).......................... 10
73	Sounds (SH 0999)	SOUNDS PRESENTS FROM POLYDOR'S 'THE GUITAR ALBUM' (flexidisc with Sounds magazine; Eric Clapton & others)..................... 8/6
79	Groucho Marxist WH 1	SPECTACULAR COMMODITY (p/s; Mental Errors/Mod Cons/ Poems/Sneex/XS Discharge) 10
01	Simba SIM 014-2	SPLIT (Hundred Reasons/Garrison) 15
58	Decca F 11043	STAR BAND HIT PARADE (EP, credited to the Lord's Taverners) 6
70s	Stiff BUY 1-10	STIFF BOX SET NO. 1 (10 x 7" box set) 35
70s	Stiff BUY 11-20	STIFF BOX SET NO. 2 (10 x 7" box set) 35
88	Underground (no cat no)	STRUM + DRUM (Wedding Present & others) (cassette with Underground magazine, issue 13) 8/6
83	Sue ENS 3	SUE SOUL SISTERS.. 10
83	Sue ENS 4	SUE SOUL BROTHERS... 10
83	Sue ENS 6	SUE INSTRUMENTALS.. 10

T

90s	Enraptured RAPT 4513	TERRASCOPE/TERRASTOCK (Bevis Frond/Damon & Naomi/Flying Saucer Attack/Silver Apples) 12
83	White Noise WN 3	THIS IS WHITE NOISE (p/s; Skrewdriver/Brutal Attack/Die Hards/A.B.H.) ... 35
02	Warner Bros 50466 13441	TOP-DECK SKA 45'S BOX (8 x 7"s, coloured vinyl in cardboard box)........ 25
82	Total Noise TOT 1	TOTAL NOISE # 1 (Business/Blitz/Dead Generation/Gonads) 10
95	Ankst CD 061	TRISKAIDEKAPHILIA (CD, Super Furry Animals/Catatonia et al.).............. 15

U

86	Underground 7	UNDERGROUND RHYTHM AND NOISE (cassette with Underground issue 7).... 8/6
80s	Fierce FRIGHT/SFTRI 38	AN UNHOLY MONTAGE (200 only [100 U.K./100 U.S.], coloured vinyl with numbered insert)...................................... 25
98	Wurlitzer JUKEBOX 37	UNITED IN THE HATRED OF (676 only, 176 in embossed sleeve) 10/5
96	V/VM VVMT1	UPLINK DATA TRANSMISSIONS (12" EP, with 'data sheets', 250 only) 25

W

98	B.Banquet Random 2.3	WARRIORS (12", blue vinyl promo, die-cut sleeve, 1200 only; Dave Angel/ Liberator DJs/Steve Stoll) 8

98	B.Banquet Random 2.4	WE ARE GLASS (12", clear vinyl promo, die-cut sleeve, 1200 only; Claude Young/ Alex Hazzard/Peter Lazonby)	8
80	Fuck Off FEP 001	WEIRD NOISE (p/s, white labels; Danny & Dressmakers/The Door & The Window/Instant Automatons/012/Sell-Outs)	10
82	Bluurg FISH 1	WESSEX '82 (Subhumans/Pagans/Organized Chaos/The Heads)	6
75	Solid Sender SEP 101	WEST SIDE CHICAGO	10
77	MPL MPL 1	WE'VE MOVED! (Wings/Gene Vincent/Frank Sinatra et al., promo only excerpts sampler, some with press pack)	175/125
84	Rather/Seventeen GEAR 17	WHAT A NICE WAY TO TURN SEVENTEEN NO. 2 (p/s; Swell Maps & others; with magazine)	12
78	Spider SP 04 EP	WREXHAM IS THE NAME (Wrexham supporters/Arfon Griffiths et al.)	10

Y

| 80s | Wonderful World Of WOW 1 | YOU ARE NOT ALONE (p/s, with insert; Oi Polloi/Hex/Stalag 17/Symbol Of Freedom) | 8 |

UNTITLED EPs & SINGLES

73	Buddah 2011 164	(Shangri-La's/Tradewinds/Ad Libs)	12
87	Metal Hammer METAL 1	(Paul Samson's Empire/Chariot/Heavy Pettin'/Strangeways; some with *Metal Hammer* magazine)	6/4
94	Kennel Club VTDOG 10	(Strangelove/Tindersticks/God Machine/Breed (10", numbered, 1,500 only, free with *Purr* magazine issue 2)	10/8
89	The Catalogue CAT 074	THE SHAMEN: Purple Haze/SLEEPING DOGS WAKE: This Little Piggy/SUGARCUBES: Cindy/KITCHENS OF DISTINCTION: Margaret's Injection/HAM: Voulez Vous (square flexidisc with *The Catalogue* magazine)	5/4
98	Fat Cat 12FAT 008	REMIXES (12", custom sleeve; remixes of Fat Cat 12FAT 003 by Autechre et al.)	12
94	Kennel Club VTDOG 10	TINDERSTICKS: Girl On Death Row/STRANGELOVE: Wolf's Story/ GOD MACHINE: The Devil Song/BREED: Diamonds Are Forever (10", numbered p/s, free with *Purrs* magazine, issue 2, 1,500 only)	10/8
96	SKAM MASK 1	UNTITLED (12", custom sleeve, 100 only; Freeform/Funkstorung/ Boards Of Canada/Jega)	150
97	SKAM MASK 2	UNTITLED (12", custom sleeve, 350 only; Hellinterface/Funkstorung/Bola/ Jega/Intron)	75
98	Mosquito MSQ 012.5	(10"; Si Begg/Blue Arsed Fly)	15

VARIOUS ARTISTS LPs & COMPILATIONS
(alphabetical by title)
A

70	ATP 102	THE ABBEY TAVERN	20
88	Woronzow WOO 6	ACID JAM (with insert)	20
69	Action ACLP 6005	ACTION PACKED SOUL	60
70s	Jem JEM	A DEAL A DAY	25
96	Ferox FERLP 1	ADVENTURES IN TECHNO SOUL (2-LP; Too Funk/Paul Hannah/ Carl Craig et al.)	20
85	United Dairies UD 012	AN AFFLICTED MAN'S MUSICA BOX (3 different editions, 1st in gatefold sleeve)	75/30/30
75	Leader LEE 4056	A FINE HUNTING DAY — SONGS OF THE HOLME VALLEY BEAGLES (with book)	15
70	Pama PMP 2004	AFRICAN MELODY	45
71	Trojan TBL 166	AFRICA'S BLOOD (Lee Perry, et al.) (orange/white label)	25
70s	Contempo 2870 311	AFRO ROCK FESTIVAL	15
70	Atlantic 2464 013	THE AGE OF ATLANTIC	15
66	Stateside SL 10172	AN ALBUM FULL OF SOUL	50
69	Key KL 002	ALIVE!	20
84	Creation CRELP 001	ALIVE IN THE LIVING ROOM	12
70	Talisman STAL 5013	ALL FOLK TOGETHER	20
84	Whaam! BIG 8	ALL FOR ART... AND ART FOR ALL	30
71	Utd. Artists UDX 201/202	ALL GOOD CLEAN FUN (2-LP)	20
83	Neat NEAT 102A/B	ALL HELL LET LOOSE	20
61	Blue Beat BBLP 801	ALL STARS — JAMAICAN BLUES	300
70	Speciality SPE 6609	ALL THE BLUES ALL THE TIME	22
62	Golden Guinea GGL 0162	ALL THE HITS BY ALL THE STARS	12
58	Pye Nixa NJT 509	ALL THE WINNERS (10")	20
76	Riva RVLP 2	ALL THIS AND WORLD WAR TWO (2-LP, box set with booklet)	15
58	Parlophone PMD 1064	ALL TIME COUNTRY AND WESTERN HITS (10")	30
73	Polydor 2460 186	AMERICAN BLUES LEGENDS '73	15
63	Polydor LPHM 46 397	AMERICAN FOLK BLUES FESTIVAL (also stereo SLPHM 237 597)	18/22
70s	Rare Records 2	AMERICAN FOLK BLUES FESTIVAL 1962	18
64	Fontana TL 5204	AMERICAN FOLK BLUES FESTIVAL 1963	22
65	Fontana TL 5225	AMERICAN FOLK BLUES FESTIVAL 1964	22
66	Fontana TL 5286	AMERICAN FOLK BLUES FESTIVAL 1965	22
66	Fontana (S)TL 5389	AMERICAN FOLK BLUES FESTIVAL 1966 (mono/stereo)	22/35
70	CBS 63912	AMERICAN FOLK BLUES FESTIVAL 1969	15
80s	Pleasantly Surprised PS 2	THE ANGELS ARE COMING (2-cassette, with booklet)	25
83	No Future MPUNK 8	ANGELS WITH DIRTY FACES	12
60s	'77' 77LA 12/13	ANGOLA PRISON SPIRITUALS	18
80	Polydor EYETV 1	ANOTHER FEAST OF IRISH FOLK	12
69	Immediate IMAL 03/04	ANTHOLOGY OF BRITISH BLUES VOLUME 1 (2-LP, gatefold sleeve)	28
69	Immediate IMAL 05/06	ANTHOLOGY OF BRITISH BLUES VOLUME 2 (2-LP, gatefold sleeve)	28

64	London HA-K/SH-K 8174	APOLLO SATURDAY NIGHT (mono/stereo)	60/75
93	Art ART 2CD	APPLIED RHYMIC TECHNOLOGY (CD)	30
93	Art ART 4CD	APPLIED RHYMIC TECHNOLOGY (CD)	20
80s	Ram RAMLP 001	THE ART OF SOLVING PROBLEMS (with poster & insert)	18
74	Ashanti SHAN 106	ASHANTI SHOWCASE	15
69	Atco 228 021	ATCO BLOCKBUSTERS	15
69	Atlantic 587/588 180	ATLANTIC BLOCKBUSTERS	15
65	Atlantic ATL 5020	ATLANTIC DISCOTHEQUE	45
60s	Atlantic AP 2	ATLANTIC IS SOUL	18
60s	Atlantic AC 3	ATLANTICLASSICS	30
67	Pye NPL 18198	AT LAST THE 1948 SHOW	15
90	Dover/PWL CCD 19	A TON OF HITS — THE HIT FACTORY VOL. 4 (2-CD)	25
64	Decca LK 4597	AT THE CAVERN	70
63	London HA-R 8133	AT THE HOOTENANNY — VOLUME 3	15
70	Beacon SBEAB 9	AUTHENTIC CHICAGO BLUES	22
72	Windmill WMD 124	AUTHENTIC CHICAGO BLUES	18
66	RCA RD 7776	AUTHENTIC COWBOYS & THEIR WESTERN FOLKSONGS	12
57	London WB 91034	AUTHENTIC CARIBBEAN CALYPSOS (10" LP)	30
64	Stateside SL 10107	AUTHENTIC SKA	70
64	Stateside SL 10068	AUTHENTIC R & B	50
79	Heartbeat HB 1	AVON CALLING — THE BRISTOL COMPILATION (with poster)	25
80	K-Tel NE 1100	AXE ATTACK (early copies with demo of Iron Maiden's "Running Free")	12
85	Steeltrax JCI 7102	AXE ATTACK (LP)	30
80s	Flaccid FLAC 1	AYLESBURY GOES FLACCID	18
74	Deroy DER 1052	AYRSHIRE FOLK (LP, private pressing)	20

B

70	Track 2407 001	BACKTRACK ONE	12
70	Track 2407 002	BACKTRACK TWO	12
70	Track 2407 006	BACKTRACK SIX	25
70	Track 2407 007	BACKTRACK SEVEN	12
54	London AL 3535	BACKWOODS BLUES (10")	65
73	Incus INCUS 11	BALANCE (Ian Brighton, et al.)	70
62	Fontana 688 200 ZL	BALLIN'	18
79	JSP 1005	BANDERA ROCKABILLIES	15
68	Pama PMLP 4	BANG BANG LULU	28
60	Melodisc 12-115	BANJO BREAKDOWN	15
64	Storyville 670 155	BARRELHOUSE BLUES AND BOOGIE-WOOGIE VOLUME 1	18
65	Storyville 670 183	BARRELHOUSE BLUES AND BOOGIE-WOOGIE VOLUME 2	18
65	Storyville SLP 213	BARRELHOUSE BLUES AND BOOGIE-WOOGIE VOL. 3	18
59	Fontana TFR 6018	BARRELHOUSE, BOOGIE WOOGIE AND BLUES (10")	25
58	Vogue Coral LRA 10022	BARRELHOUSE PIANO (10" LP)	25
59	Vogue Coral LRA 10023	BARRELHOUSE PIANO VOLUME 2 (10" LP)	28
83	London CAVE 1	THE BATCAVE — YOUNG LIMBS AND NUMB HYMNS	12
71	Trojan TBL 167	BATTLE AXE	40
52	Capitol LC 6510	BATTLE OF THE BANDS (10" LP)	15
71	B&C BCM 103	BATTLE OF THE BANDS VOL. 1	18
64	Melodisc MLP 12-192	BATTLE OF THE GIANTS	20
53	MGM MGM-D 115	A BATTLE OF JAZZ: HOT VERSUS COOL (10")	28
71	BBC REC 118	BBC's FOLK ON TWO PRESENTS NORTHUMBRIAN FOLK	18
69	Beacon BEAB 1	BEACON BRINGS IT TO YOU	18
71	Revival RVS 1004	BEALE STREET MESS AROUND	12
84	Well Suspect SUSS 1	THE BEAT GENERATION AND THE ANGRY YOUNG MEN	20
86	Mercury WILD 1	BEAT RUNS WILD (Wet Wet Wet et al.)	25
87	Pink PINKY 15	BEAUTY (McCarthy et al.)	12
80s	Porrit's Hill PHEW 2	BECKET HOUSE	12
77	Impulse IS/BED/123	BEDROCK — ALTOGETHER BEDROCK LP (private pressing)	12
68	Elektra EUK 262	BEGIN HERE (also stereo EUKS 7262)	20
78	Rip Off ROLP 1	BELFAST ROCKS	45
71	Delmark DS 622	BELL'S BLUES HARP	15
68	Bell MBLL 102	BELL'S CELLAR OF SOUL VOLUME 1	40
69	Bell MBLL 107	BELL'S CELLAR OF SOUL VOLUME 2	40
69	Bell MBLL 117	BELL'S CELLAR OF SOUL VOLUME 3	40
69	Bell MBLL/SBLL 111	THE BEST FROM BELL	20
69	Bell MBLL/SBLL 124	THE BEST FROM BELL VOLUME 2	20
78	Stiff ODD 2	BE STIFF (TOUR '78 OFFICIAL RELEASE) (promo only)	12
78	Stiff DEAL 1	BE STIFF ROUTE '78 (with 16-page booklet & biographies, etc.)	12
70s	Storyville 671 188	THE BEST OF THE BLUES	18
67	United Artists LAS 29021	THE BEST OF BOND (mono)	15
69	United Artists UAS 29021	THE BEST OF BOND (stereo)	15
65	Xtra XTRA 1031	THE BEST OF BRITISH FOLK	15
69	Pama SECO 18	THE BEST OF CAMEL	40
72	Paramount SPFL 286	BEST OF FILM MUSIC	15
76	Epic EPC 81224	THE BEST OF OKEH VOL. I	15
76	Epic EPC 81532	THE BEST OF OKEH VOL. II	15
69	President PTL 1016	THE BEST OF PRESIDENT VOLUME 1	15
69	President PTL 1036	THE BEST OF PRESIDENT VOLUME 2	15
67	Xtra XTRA 1053	BEST OF SCOTTISH FOLK	12
83	Statik STATLP 14	THE BEST OF YOUR SECRET'S SAFE WITH US	15
73	Attack ATLP 1011	BIG BAMBOO	30
60	Fontana TFL 5080	THE BIG BEAT!	55
64	London HA-B 8199	THE BIG 'D' JAMBOREE	25
78	Giorno GPS	BIG EGO	20
69	Fontana SFXL 55	THE BIG FOLK	15
69	Minit MLL/MLS 40007E	THE BIG ONE	22

71	Wand WCS 1005	BIG SIXTEEN GOLDEN OLDIES	12
64	Capitol ST 2146	BIG SOUNDS OF THE DRAGS Vol 2	30
72	CBS 64844	THE BIG SUR FESTIVAL	15
70	Pama SECO 32	BIRTH CONTROL	28
70	Matchbox SDX 207/8	BLACK DIAMOND EXPRESS TO HELL (2-LP)	25
60	Columbia 33SX 1244	BLACKPOOL NIGHTS	35
58	HMV CLP 1167	BLACK SLACKS AND BOBBY SOCKS	230
70	Ember SE 8009	BLACK SOUL EXPLOSION	18
70	CBS 52796	BLACK WHITES AND BLUES	20
83	Quiet QLP 3	BLOOD ON THE ROQ! (withdrawn)	15
68	Coxsone CSP 1	BLUE BEAT SPECIAL	35
66	RCA Victor RD 7786	BLUEBIRD BLUES	28
63	Stateside SL 10021	THE BLUEGRASS HALL OF FAME	15
65	London HA-B 8227	BLUEGRASS HALL OF FAME VOL. 2	18
64	London HA-B 8118	BLUEGRASS SPECTACULAR	12
62	Columbia 33SX 1417	THE BLUES	55
64	Pye Intl. NPL 28030	BLUES VOL. 1	22
64	Pye Intl. NPL 28035	BLUES VOL. 2	22
64	Pye Intl. NPL 28045	BLUES VOL. 3	22
64	Chess CRL 4003	BLUES VOL. 4	30
65	Chess CRL 4512	BLUES VOL. 5	30
68	Immediate IMLP 014	BLUES ANYTIME VOL. 1	25
68	Immediate IMCP 015	BLUES ANYTIME VOL. 2	25
68	Immediate IMLP 019	BLUES ANYTIME VOL. 3	25
70	Xtra XTRA 1105	THE BLUES ARE ALIVE AND WELL	12
65	Fontana TFL 6048	THE BLUES AT NEWPORT 1964 PART 1	25
69	Saga FID 2165	BLUES AT SUNRISE	25
66	London HA-S 8265	THE BLUES CAME DOWN FROM MEMPHIS	80
73	Flyright LP 504	BLUES CAME TO CHAPEL HILL	15
65	Storyville SLP 176	BLUESCENE USA: VOLUME 1 — CHICAGO	22
65	Storyville SLP 177	BLUESCENE USA: VOLUME 2 — LOUISIANA BLUES	22
65	Storyville SLP 181	BLUESCENE USA: VOLUME 3 — BLUES ALL AROUND MY BED	22
67	Storyville SLP 180	BLUESCENE USA: VOLUME 4 — MISSISSIPPI BLUES	22
71	Python PLP-KM 17	BLUES — CHICAGO STYLE (LP)	35
60	Philips BBL 7369	BLUES FELL THIS MORNING	55
73	Polydor 2383 257	BLUES FOR MR. CRUMP	25
72	Transatlantic TRASAM 25	BLUES FOR YOUR POCKET	15
69	Chess CRLS 4558	BLUES FROM BIG BILL'S COPACABANA	35
69	Python PLP 6	BLUES FROM CHICAGO (99 copies only)	42
70	Python PLP 9	BLUES FROM CHICAGO VOL. 2 (99 copies only)	42
71	Python PLP 15	BLUES FROM CHICAGO VOL. 3 (99 copies only)	40
60s	Heritage 1004	BLUES FROM MAXWELL STREET (99 copies only)	100
71	Pye Intl. NPL 28142	BLUES FROM THE BAYOU	25
72	Saydisc SDM 226	BLUES FROM THE DELTA	22
71	Python PLP 21	BLUES FROM THE WINDY CITY (99 copies only)	45
77	Flyright LP 4713	BLUES FROM THE WINDY CITY	15
80	Kicking Mule SNKF 159	BLUES GUITAR WORKSHOP	15
63	Stateside SL 10076	BLUES HOOT	30
57	Pye Nixa NJL 8	(ALAN LOMAX PRESENTS) BLUES IN THE MISSISSIPPI NIGHT	20
60s	Sunflower (no cat. no.)	BLUES IS MY COMPANION (99 copies only)	42
60s	Sunflower (no cat. no.)	BLUES KEEP FALLING (99 copies only)	42
64	Joy JOYS 177	BLUES JAM	12
69	Blue Horizon 7-66227	BLUES JAM AT CHESS (2-LP)	55
69	Immediate IMLP 024	BLUES LEFTOVERS	15
67	Saydisc Match. SDM 142	BLUES LIKE SHOWERS OF RAIN	90
68	Saydisc Match. SDM 167	BLUES LIKE SHOWERS OF RAIN VOLUME 2	90
65	Decca LK 4681	BLUES NOW	45
72	Blues Obscurities BOV 1	BLUES OBSCURITIES VOL. 1: SOUTHERN BLUES/DARK MUDDY BOTTOM (plain cover with photocopied inserts)	30
72	Blues Obscurities BOV 2	BLUES OBSCURITIES VOL. 2: LONESOME HARMONICA	30
72	Blues Obscurities BOV 3	BLUES OBSCURITIES VOL. 3: WEST COAST BLUES	30
72	Blues Obscurities BOV 4	BLUES OBSCURITIES VOL. 4: ONE RAINY MORNING	30
72	Blues Obscurities BOV 5	BLUES OBSCURITIES VOL. 5: SOMETHING'S GONE WRONG	30
72	Blues Obscurities BOV 6	BLUES OBSCURITIES VOL. 6: COMING BACK HOME	30
72	Blues Obscurities BOV 7	BLUES OBSCURITIES VOL. 7	30
72	Blues Obscurities BOV 8	BLUES OBSCURITIES VOL. 8	30
72	Blues Obscurities BOV 9	BLUES OBSCURITIES VOL. 9	30
72	Blues Obscurities BOV 10	BLUES OBSCURITIES VOL. 10	30
74	London HA-U 8454	BLUES OBSCURITIES VOL. 1: DARK MUDDY BOTTOM (reissue)	18
74	London HA-U 8455	BLUES OBSCURITIES VOL. 2: LONESOME HARMONICA (reissue)	18
74	London HA-U 8456	BLUES OBSCURITIES VOL. 3: STRETCHIN' OUT	18
69	Mercury SMXL 77	BLUES PACKAGE '69	18
69	Highway 51 H 102	BLUES PEOPLE	50
68	Matchbox SDR 146	BLUES PIANO	15
72	Atlantic K 40404	BLUES PIANO — CHICAGO PLUS	22
68	Kokomo K 1001	A BLUES POTPOURRI (99 copies only)	55
71	Rarities (Tony's Records)	BLUES RARITIES VOL. 1 (2-LP)	25
69	Atlantic Special 590 019	THE BLUES ROLL ON (reissue of "Southern Folk Heritage: The Blues Roll On")	12
69	Poppy PYM 11001	BLUES ROOTS VOLUME ONE	25
66	Decca LK 4748	BLUES SOUTHSIDE CHICAGO	55
71	Python PLP 16	BLUES TODAY — SOUTHERN STYLE (99 copies only)	40
71	Polydor 2675 007	BOMBERS	15
65	Topic 12T 128	BONNY LASS COME O'ER THE BURN	12
73	Storyville SLP 229	BOOGIE WOOGIE BOYS	15
70s	Milestone MLP 2009	BOOGIE WOOGIE RARITIES	15

VARIOUS ARTISTS LPs & COMPILATIONS

60s	Storyville 670184	BOOGIE WOOGIE TRIO	15
55	London AL 3544	BOOGIE WOOGIE WITH THE BLUES (10")	50
69	Pama SECO 17	BOSS REGGAE	80
74	Eron 002	BOTH SIDES OF THE DOWNS (with insert)	25
80	Aardvark STEAL 2	BOUQUET OF STEEL (blue vinyl with 27-page booklet)	15
91	BBC CD 844	BRINGING IT ALL BACK HOME (2-CD, with booklet)	25
87	GWR GBS 1	BRISTOL CUSTOM BIKE SHOW 1986 (some with poster)	15/12
81	Bristol Recorder BR 002	THE BRISTOL RECORDER VOL. 2 (with magazine booklet)	15
93	EMI CD 502046	BRITISH BEAT BEFORE THE BEATLES 1955/56 (CD)	18
93	EMI CD 502047	BRITISH BEAT BEFORE THE BEATLES 1957 (CD)	18
93	EMI CD 502048	BRITISH BEAT BEFORE THE BEATLES 1958 (CD)	18
93	EMI CD 502049	BRITISH BEAT BEFORE THE BEATLES 1959 (CD)	18
93	EMI CD 502050	BRITISH BEAT BEFORE THE BEATLES 1960 (CD)	18
93	EMI CD 502051	BRITISH BEAT BEFORE THE BEATLES 1961 (CD)	18
93	EMI CD 502052	BRITISH BEAT BEFORE THE BEATLES 1962 (CD)	18
68	Island ILP 966/ILPS 9066	BRITISH BLUE-EYED SOUL	75
67	Tamla Motown TML 11055	BRITISH MOTOWN CHARTBUSTERS (mono, flipback sleeve)	25
69	T. Motown STML 11055	BRITISH MOTOWN CHARTBUSTERS (stereo reissue, flipback sleeve)	18
68	T. Motown (S)TML 11082	BRITISH MOTOWN CHARTBUSTERS VOL. 2 (original, flipback sleeve)	18
93	Hammer (no cat. no)	BRITISH OI! — WORKING CLASS ANTHEMS	12
70	Trojan TBL 106	BRIXTON CAT	35
64	Decca LK 4598	BRUM BEAT	100
64	Dial DLP 1	BRUM BEAT	75
79	Big Bear BRUM 1	BRUM BEAT — LIVE AT THE BARREL ORGAN (2-LP, with inserts)	20
80	MCA MCF 3074	BRUTE FORCE	20
70	Buddah 2349 008	BUDDAH IN MIND	12
72	Flyright LP 106	BULL CITY BLUES	12
66	Decca LK 4734	BUMPER BUNDLE 16 HITS	25
77	Stiff SEEZ 2	A BUNCH OF STIFF RECORDS	12
79	Cherry Red ARED 2	BUSINESS UNUSUAL (with *Zig Zag* small labels catalogue)	15
81	Autumn AU 2	BUSTED AT OZ	20
84	Dambusters DAM 003	BUTTONS AND BOWS VOLUME 1 (2-LP)	30
84	Dambusters DAM 006	BUTTONS AND BOWS VOLUME 2 (2-LP)	30

C

56	Columbia 33S 1083	CABARET NIGHT IN PARIS (10" LP)	15
57	Columbia 33S 1099	CABARET NIGHT IN PARIS No. 4 (10" LP)	15
57	Columbia 33S 1105	CABARET NIGHT IN PARIS No. 5 (10" LP)	15
87	MCA MCLD 622	CALIFORNIA DREAMIN' (2-LP)	18
50s	Melodisc MLP 507	CALYPSO CARNIVAL (10" LP)	18
72	Topic 12TS 219	CANNY NEWCASSEL (with booklet, blue label)	20
67	Bounty BY 6035	CAN'T KEEP FROM CRYING (TOPICAL BLUES ON THE DEATH OF PRESIDENT KENNEDY)	25
78	Capitol CAPS 1025	CAPITOL SOUL CASINO	12
50s	Parlophone CPMD 13	CARIBBEAN CALYPSO (10" LP)	25
71	Trojan TBL 171	CARIBBEAN DANCE FESTIVAL (wraparound paper sleeve)	10
73	Flyright LP 505	CAROLINA COUNTRY BLUES	15
81	Secret SEC 2	CARRY ON OI!	12
73	Nottingham Festival FEST 2	CASTLE ROCK	100
65	Capitol T2340	CAT BALLOU AND OTHER MOTION PICTURE SONGS (Frankie De Vol/Nat 'King' Cole/Stubby Kaye)	15
78	Nice NICE 1	CATCH A WAVE (2 x 10", gatefold sleeve)	30
77	CBS 82401	CBS ROCKABILLY CLASSICS VOL. 1	12
78	CBS 82993	CBS ROCKABILLY CLASSICS VOL. 2	12
79	CBS 83911	CBS ROCKABILLY CLASSICS VOL. 3	12
86	NME 022	C-86 (LP, promo-only for cassette, 500 pressed)	12
90	Cerne CERNE 001/002/003	THE CERNE BOX SET (3-LP box set; Nurse With Wound/Current 93/Sol Invictus; with 3 inserts)	125
80	Quality QP 32/80	CHAMPIONS AGAIN: HIGHLIGHTS OF 1979-80 SEASON	20
71	Chess 6671 102	CHARLIE PARKER MEMORIAL CONCERT	12
60s	Columbia	CHARTBUSTERS USA	40
73	Checker 6445 150	CHESS GOLDEN DECADE VOL. 1: THE EARLY 50s	12
73	Checker 6445 151	CHESS GOLDEN DECADE VOL. 2: 1956 TAKE IT EASY GREASY	12
73	Checker 6445 152	CHESS GOLDEN DECADE VOL. 3: 1957 DIMESTORE PONYTAIL	12
74	Chess 6445 153	CHESS GOLDEN DECADE VOL. 4: 1958-1959 BOOK OF LOVE	12
74	Chess 6445 154	CHESS GOLDEN DECADE VOL. 5: 1959-1961 GOOD MORNING LITTLE SCHOOLGIRL	12
74	Chess 6445 202	CHESS GOLDEN DECADE VOL. 6: 1961-1962 TALKIN' TRASH	12
74	Chess 6445 203	CHESS GOLDEN DECADE VOL. 7: 1963-1965 HIGH HEEL SNEAKERS (gatefold sleeve)	15
74	Chess 6445 204	CHESS GOLDEN DECADE VOL. 8: 1965-1966 THE IN CROWD	12
78	Chess 9124 213	CHESS ROCKABILLIES	12
64	Chess CRL 4004	CHESS STORY VOL. 1	50
65	Chess CRL 4516	CHESS STORY VOL. 2	50
72	Delmark DL 624	CHICAGO AIN'T NOTHING BUT A BLUES BAND	12
71	Vanguard VSD 79217	CHICAGO BLUES VOLUME 2	12
66	Fontana TFL 6068	CHICAGO/THE BLUES/TODAY	22
66	Fontana TFL 6069	CHICAGO/THE BLUES/TODAY VOLUME 2	22
66	Fontana TFL 6070	CHICAGO/THE BLUES/TODAY VOLUME 3	22
69	Vanguard SVRL 19020	CHICAGO/THE BLUES/TODAY VOLUME 1	25
69	Vanguard SVRL 19021	CHICAGO/THE BLUES/TODAY VOLUME 2	25
69	Vanguard SVRL 19022	CHICAGO/THE BLUES/TODAY VOLUME 3	20
68	Sunflower ET 1401	THE CHICAGO HOUSE BANDS (99 copies only)	40
69	Kokomo K 1005	CHICAGO SESSIONS VOLUME 1 (99 copies only)	50
70	Flyright LP 4700	CHICKEN STUFF	15

80	Relics LSD 1	CHOCOLATE SOUP FOR DIABETICS VOL. 1	15
81	Relics ACID 1	CHOCOLATE SOUP FOR DIABETICS VOL. 2 (gatefold sleeve)	15
83	Relics CSFD 3	CHOCOLATE SOUP FOR DIABETICS VOL. 3	12
84	MCA CHUNK 1	CHUNKS OF FUNK	20
58	Philips BBR 8112	CHRISTMAS (10")	15
73	United Artists UDX 205/6	CHRISTMAS AT THE PATTI (2 x 10", gatefold sleeve)	18
68	Chess CRLS 4541	CHRISTMAS DEDICATION	22
81	Ze/Island ILPS 7017	A CHRISTMAS RECORD (LP, initially white vinyl, then black)	each 12
63	London HA-U 8141	A CHRISTMAS GIFT FOR YOU (plum label, later black label)	80/25
78	Incus INCUS 33	CIRCADIAN RHYTHM	50
72	Specialty SNTF 5015	CITY BLUES	12
80s	White Elephant RIOCH 1	CITY WALLS — A SOUTHAMPTON COMPILATION (with insert)	12
70	Charisma CAS 1008	CLASSICAL HEADS	12
55	London AL 3559	CLASSIC JAZZ PIANO (10")	25
69	Atlantic 587 167	CLASSIC RHYTHM AND BLUES	12
70s	Waldo's DS 005	CLEANING UP THE MUSIC BIZ	12
85	Pusmort 0012-02	CLEANSE THE BACTERIA	20
72	Pegasus PS 1	CLOGS (FOLK SAMPLER) (with insert)	12
90s	Distronics ITCD 3	THE CLOSING PARTY — IN THE CITY LIVE UNSIGNED (CD)	50
72	Pegasus PS 2	CLUB FOLK VOLUME ONE	18
72	Pegasus PS 3	CLUB FOLK VOLUME TWO	18
70	Trojan TTL 54	CLUB ROCK STEADY	25
68	W.I.R.L. ILP 965	CLUB ROCK STEADY '68	45
67	W.I.R.L. ILP 948	CLUB SKA '67	20
67	W.I.R.L. ILP 956	CLUB SKA '67 VOL. 2	35
70	Trojan TTL 48	CLUB SKA VOLUME ONE	20
70	Trojan TTL 51	CLUB SKA VOLUME TWO (Existence unconfirmed)	30
68	Island ILP 964	CLUB SOUL	50+
67	Elektra EUK 253	A COLD WIND BLOWS	15
65	Tamla Motown TML 11001	A COLLECTION OF 16 TAMLA MOTOWN HITS	55
67	Tamla Motown TML 11043	A COLLECTION OF 16 ORIGINAL BIG HITS VOL. 4	38
67	Tamla Motown TML 11050	A COLLECTION OF 16 ORIGINAL BIG HITS VOL. 5	32
68	T. Motown (S)TML 11074	A COLLECTION OF 16 ORIGINAL BIG HITS VOL. 6	28
69	T. Motown (S)TML 11092	A COLLECTION OF 16 ORIGINAL BIG HITS VOL. 7 — THE MOTOWN SOUND	28
70	T. Motown (S)TML 11130	A COLLECTION OF 16 ORIGINAL BIG HITS VOL. 8	20
75	Chicago 202	COLLECTORS BLUES SERIES VOL. 1	22
75	Chicago 205	COLLECTORS BLUES SERIES VOL. 2	22
75	Chicago 210	COLLECTORS BLUES SERIES VOL. 3	22
75	Chicago 212	COLLECTORS BLUES SERIES VOL. 4	22
75	Chicago 213	COLLECTORS BLUES SERIES VOL. 5	22
54	London AL 3514	COLLECTORS' ITEMS VOLUME ONE (10")	18
54	London AL 3533	COLLECTORS' ITEMS VOLUME TWO (10")	18
56	London AL 3550	COLLECTORS' ITEMS VOLUME THREE (10")	18
86	Color Disc COLORS 4	COLOR SUPPLEMENT (400 only)	15
93	2-Tone CHR TT 5013	THE COMPACT 2-TONE STORY (4-CD, box set with book)	35
76	Incus INCUS 21	COMPANY 1	45
77	Incus INCUS 29	COMPANY 6	45
77	Incus INCUS 30	COMPANY 7	45
72	Apple STCX 3385	THE CONCERT FOR BANGLA DESH (3-LP box set, with booklet)	22
70	Transatlantic TRASAM 14	THE CONTEMPORARY GUITAR SAMPLER	12
70	Transatlantic TRASAM 15	CONTEMPORARY GUITAR SAMPLER VOL. 2	12
64	Decca LK 4664	CONVERSATION WITH THE BLUES	70
57	Tempo TAP 10	COOL MUSIC FOR A HOT NIGHT – MOOD MUSIC IN THE MODERN MANNER	130
72	Wicksteed WCKLP 02	CORBY CATCHMENT AREA (private pressing)	200+
78	ABC ABCL 5247	COTTON PICKIN' ROCK	12
80s	Third Mind TMLP 09	COULD YOU WALK ON THE WATER	15
64	London HA-B 8145	COUNTRY & WESTERN GOLDEN HIT PARADE VOL. 1	18
64	London HA-B 8146	COUNTRY & WESTERN GOLDEN HIT PARADE VOL. 2	18
60	Philips BBL 7410	COUNTRY AND WESTERN REQUESTS	12
62	Philips BBL 7552	COUNTRY AND WESTERN REQUESTS VOL. 2	12
63	Mercury 20015 MCL	COUNTRY AND WESTERN ROUND UP	12
60	Storyville SLP 129	THE COUNTRY BLUES	20
73	Specialty SNTF 5014	COUNTRY BLUES	15
60s	Saydisc Roots RL 334	COUNTRY BLUES OBSCURITIES VOLUME 1	20
66	Stateside SL 10170	COUNTRY COUSINS	18
56	Brunswick LA 8729	COUNTRY FAVOURITES VOL. ONE (10")	30
65	London HA-B 8243	COUNTRY GUITAR HALL OF FAME	15
64	London HA-B 8198	THE COUNTRY MUSIC FESTIVAL	12
66	London HA-B 8263	COUNTRY MUSIC FESTIVAL VOL. 2	12
66	London HA-B 8287	COUNTRY MUSIC FESTIVAL VOL. 3	12
63	Stateside SL 10017	THE COUNTRY MUSIC HALL OF FAME	18
63	London HA-B 8076	COUNTRY MUSIC HALL OF FAME VOL. 1	15
63	London HA-B 8077	COUNTRY MUSIC HALL OF FAME VOL. 2	15
64	London HA-B 8156	COUNTRY MUSIC HALL OF FAME VOL. 3	15
64	London HA-B 8157	COUNTRY MUSIC HALL OF FAME VOL. 4	15
65	London HA-B 8216	COUNTRY MUSIC HALL OF FAME VOL. 5	12
65	London HA-B 8217	COUNTRY MUSIC HALL OF FAME VOL. 6	12
66	London HA-B 8283	COUNTRY MUSIC HALL OF FAME VOL. 7	12
66	London HA-B 8284	COUNTRY MUSIC HALL OF FAME VOL. 8	12
67	London HA-B 8328	COUNTRY MUSIC HALL OF FAME VOL. 9	12
67	London HA-B 8329	COUNTRY MUSIC HALL OF FAME VOL. 10	12
68	London HA-B 8354	COUNTRY MUSIC HALL OF FAME VOL. 11	12
68	London HA-B 8355	COUNTRY MUSIC HALL OF FAME VOL. 12	12
65	London HA-B 8206	THE COUNTRY MUSIC MEMORIAL ALBUM	12
62	Stateside SL 10003	COUNTRY MUSIC SPECTACULAR	15

63	Starlite STLP 15	COUNTRY MUSIC U.S.A. (reissued as GRK 605) 15/12
64	London HA-B 8185	COUNTRY MUSIC U.S.A. 15
65	London HA-B 8224	COUNTRY MUSIC WHO'S WHO. 15
59	Capitol T 1179	THE COUNTRY'S BEST 12
69	Pama ECO 2	CRAB — GREATEST HITS 60
80	Rabid/Absurd LAST 1	THE CRAP STOPS HERE 25
87	Supreme CDSU 1	THE CREAM OF SUPREME (CD) 25
60	Fontana TFL 5103	THE CREAM OF 'TAKE IT FROM HERE' (also stereo SFL 534) 12
60s	Saydisc Roots RL 332	CREAM OF THE CROP 12
74	Eron 005	CRYPTADIA 15

D

68	H. Note/B. Shot BSLP 5002	DANCING DOWN ORANGE STREET. 85
76	Dark Horse DH 1 (DHSAM 1)	DARK HORSE RECORDS '76 (promo only sampler, stickered sleeve & inner) . . . 40
86	EMI EQ 5003	DAVE CLARK'S TIME (2-LP, with brochure and lyric inner, some with
		hologram) 30/25
71	Dawn DNLB 3024	DAWN TAKEAWAY CONCERT 12
79	Dead Good DEAD 4	DEAD GOOD'S DEAD GOODS (unissued)
78	Virgin VD 2508	DEAD ON ARRIVAL (glow-in-the-dark vinyl with poster) 15
66	Highway 51 H 100	DECADE OF THE BLUES — THE 1950's (99 copies only) 60
66	Highway 51 H 104	DECADE OF THE BLUES — THE 1950's VOLUME 2 (99 copies only) 50
88	Hard Caw CAW2	RAINING HARD ON SNOW. 12
54	Decca LF 1160	DECCA SHOWCASE VOL. 3 (10") 15
55	Decca LF 1265	DECCA SHOWCASE VOL. 5 (10") 18
65	London HA-B 8249	DECK OF CARDS 12
71	United Artists UAS 29153	DEEPER INTO THE VAULTS. 12
70	Polydor 2673 001	DEEP OVERGROUND POP. 15
70	Stax SXATS 1037	THE DEEP SOUL OF STAX. 22
71	Flyright LP 102	DEEP SOUTH COUNTRY BLUES 18
93	Beggars Banquet BBQLP399	DEAFENING DIVINITIES VOL. 2. 12
86	Decal LIK 9	DERAM DAYZE 15
68	Deram SML 1027	THE DERAM GOLDEN POPS SAMPLER. 80
67	Island ILP 955	DERRICK HARRIOTT'S ROCK (SKA) STEADY PARTY 200
72	Trojan TTL 54	DERRICK HARRIOTT'S ROCKSTEADY PARTY (reissue – unconfirmed) 50
85	Yangki 01	DEVASTATE TO LIBERATE 15
89	Blast First BFDJ 1	DEVIL'S JUKEBOX (10 x 7" in numbered box, with booklet, 3,000 only) 20
79	Topic 12TS 349	DEVON TRADITION — AN ANTHOLOGY FROM TRADITIONAL SINGERS . . . 15
73	London ZGU 131	DIMENSION DOLLS. 15
70	Mercury 6641 006	DIMENSION OF MIRACLES 15
80	DinDisc DONE 1	DINDISC 1980 (with free 20"x 20" game) 12
74	DIP DLP 5026	D.I.P. PRESENTS THE UPSETTER (Lee Perry et al.) 70
69	Minit MLL/MLS 40005	DIRT BLUES. 32
70	BBC REC 65M	DISC A DAWN 25
57	RCA RC 2400	DISCTIONARY OF JAZZ (10") 12
67	Island ILP 943	DOCTOR SOUL 80
82	BBC 2-LP-22001	DOCTOR WHO COLLECTOR'S EDITION (2-LP, with poster) 30
80s	Pleasantly Surprised PS 12	DOCUMENT (cassette) 18
70	Python PLP	DOWNHOME BLUES (99 copies only) 45
70	Python PLP 14	DOWNHOME BLUES VOLUME 2 (99 copies only). 45
71	Python PLP 22	DOWNHOME BLUES VOLUME 3 (99 copies only). 45
71	Flyright LP 4703	DOWN IN HOGAN'S ALLEY 15
67	Down With The Game 200	DOWN WITH THE GAME VOLUME 1 (99 copies only) 50
67	Down With The Game 201	DOWN WITH THE GAME VOLUME 2 (99 copies only) 50
68	Down With The Game 203	DOWN WITH THE GAME VOLUME 3 (99 copies only) 50
68	Down With The Game 204	DOWN WITH THE GAME VOLUME 4 (99 copies only) 50
68	Down With The Game 205	DOWN WITH THE GAME VOLUME 5 (99 copies only) 50
68	Down With The Game 206	DOWN WITH THE GAME VOLUME 6 (99 copies only) 50
67	Island ILP 954	DR. KITCH 30
82	Beggars Banquet BEGA 35	DR. RHINO AND MR HYDE. 12
85	Capitol EG 26 0573 1-4	DREAM BABIES 15
80s	Pleasantly Surprised PS 6	DREAMS AND DESIRES (cassette, in bag) 15
72	Ember EMB 3413	A DROP OF THE HARD STUFF 12
59	Parlophone PMC 1101	DRUMBEAT (Adam Faith et al.) 60
60	Columbia SCX 3359	DRUM NIGHT AT BIRDLAND 12
68	Island ILP 976	THE DUKE AND THE PEACOCK 80
69	Trojan TTL 8	DUKE REID'S GOLDEN HITS. 40
67	Island ILP 958	DUKE REID'S ROCK STEADY 210
70	Trojan TTL 53	DUKE REID'S ROCK STEADY (reissue, existence unconfirmed) 30
69	BBC REC 35S	DUNGEON FOLK. 12
88	Big Beat WIK 74	DUNHILL FOLK ROCK VOL 1 – IS IT ANY WONDER. 18
73	Dragon HELP 9	DYNAMIC SOUNDS OF JAMAICA VOL. 1. 15

E

70	Matchbox SDR 199	EARLY BLUES VOLUME 1: SKOODLE-UM-SKOO. 20
70	Matchbox SDR 206	EARLY FOLK BLUES VOLUME 2: HOMETOWN SKIFFLE. 20
70	Middle Earth MDLS 20	EARTHED. 45
80	Dead Good GOOD 1	EAST (with inner & stickered sleeve) 25
73	Southern Sound SD 200	EAST VERNON BLUES. 30
63	Decca LK 4546	EDINBURGH FOLK FESTIVAL VOLUME 1 25
63	Decca LK 4563	EDINBURGH FOLK FESTIVAL VOLUME 2 25
55	Philips BBR 8046	EIGHT EVERGREENS (10") 15
75	Island/Transatlantic	ELECTRIC MUSE — THE STORY OF FOLK INTO ROCK
	FOLK 1001	(4-LP box set with booklet) 45
85	Push PUSH 001	ELEGANCE, CHARM AND DEADLY DANGER 25
80s	Master BBSLP 007	ELEMENTALS 20

83	Extract XX 001	THE ELEPHANT TABLE ALBUM (2-LP)	18
57	Philips BBR 8115	ELLA, LENA, BILLIE AND SARAH (10")	15
71	Island IDLP 1	EL PEA (pink rim label)	15
83	Psycho PSYCHO 1	ENDLESS JOURNEY VOL. 1 (numbered)	22
83	Psycho PSYCHO 3	ENDLESS JOURNEY VOL. 2 (numbered)	18
83	Psycho PSYCHO 19	ENDLESS JOURNEY VOL. 3 (numbered)	18
76	Topic 12T 296	ENGLISH COUNTRY MUSIC	15
88	MEK MEK 006	THE ENGLISH REBELS (with insert)	20
01	Ai AILP 002	ESTATE (CD, in stamped sleeve)	20
89	Gee Street GEE A 002	ETERNITY PROJECT ONE	20
89	Gee Street GEE ACD 002	ETERNITY PROJECT ONE (CD)	25
67	Speciality SPE 6601	EVERY DAY I HAVE THE BLUES	18
72	Blue Horizon 2683 007	THE EXCELLO STORY (2-LP)	80
68	Amal. AMGLP 2002	EXPLOSIVE ROCKSTEADY	70

F

67	Elektra EUK 259	FANTASTIC FOLK	12
64	Topic 12T 110	FAREWELL NANCY (blue label)	15
76	Lightning LIP 2	FAREWELL TO THE ROXY (2-LP)	18
76	Polydor 2475 605	A FEAST OF IRISH FOLK	12
68	Zeus CF 201	FESTIVAL AT TOWERSEY	50
63	Pye Intl. NPL 28033	FESTIVAL OF THE BLUES	28
67	Marble Arch MAL 724	FESTIVAL OF THE BLUES (reissue)	12
61	Melodisc 12-116	FIDDLIN' COUNTRY STYLE	12
60s	Melodisc MS 4	15 OLDIES BUT GOODIES	18
65	Sue ILP 920	50 MINUTES & 24 SECONDS OF RECORDED DYNAMITE!	80
85	L.A.Y.L.A.H. LAY 10	THE FIGHT IS ON (Nurse With Wound, Organum, et al.)	30
72	Warner Bros K 66013	FILLMORE: THE LAST DAYS (3-LP box set with poster & booklet)	30
72	CBS 63816	FILLMORE WEST	12
65	London HA-B 8205	FINGERS ON FIRE	15
60	HMV CLP 1358/CSD 1298	FINGS AIN'T WOT THEY USED TO BE	30
64	London HA-B 8117	FIRE ON THE STRINGS	15
69	Music Man	FIREPOINT — A COLLECTION OF FOLK BLUES	120
73	Spark SRLM 2003	FIREPOINT — A COLLECTION OF FOLK BLUES (reissue)	40
71	CBS 66311	THE FIRST GREAT ROCK FESTIVALS OF THE 70s: ISLE OF WIGHT AND ATLANTA (3-LP)	35
58	Esquire 20-091	THE FIRST MODERNS (10")	20
57	Esquire 20-089	THE FIRST NATIONAL SKIFFLE CONTEST (10")	80
56	Mercury MPT 7512	FIRST ROCK 'N' ROLL PARTY (10")	130
89	Confection LC 7871	FLAIR: THE OTHER WORLD OF BRITISH FOOTBALL (2-LP)	20
75	Chrysalis CHR 1081	FLASH FEARLESS V THE ZORG WOMEN PARTS 5 & 6 (Alice Cooper, Elkie Brooks, et al.)	15
80s	Alt. Tentacles VIRUS 22	FLEX YOUR HEAD	15
64	Blue Beat BBLP 803	FLY FLYING SKA	300+
69	Atlantic 588 184	FLYING HIGH (record club edition)	15
76	Flams/Wounded WR 1068	FOLK AT THE CHEQUERS (private pressing)	15
64	Ember NR 5015	FOLK BLUES SONG FEST	20
66	Waverley ZLP 2067	FOLK FAVOURITES	12
69	World Rec. Club ST 890	FOLK FESTIVAL	20
76	Transatlantic TRA 324	FOLK FESTIVAL (2-LP)	20
60	Top Rank 35/070	FOLK FESTIVAL AT NEWPORT 1959 VOLUME 1	15
60	Top Rank 35/071	FOLK FESTIVAL AT NEWPORT 1959 VOLUME 2	15
60	Top Rank 35/072	FOLK FESTIVAL AT NEWPORT 1959 VOLUME 3	15
62	Fontana TFL 6000	FOLK FESTIVAL AT NEWPORT (VOL. 1)	15
62	Fontana TFL 6004	FOLK FESTIVAL AT NEWPORT (VOL. 2)	15
62	Fontana TFL 6009	FOLK FESTIVAL AT NEWPORT (VOL. 4)	15
63	Pye Intl. NPL 28033	FOLK FESTIVAL OF THE BLUES	20
73	Counterpoint CPT 3994	FOLK FROM McTAVISH'S KITCHENS	30
73	Windmill WMD	FOLK HERITAGE	30
82	Fuck Off (no cat. no.)	FOLK IN HELL (cassette)	15
73	Nottingham Festival FEST 1	FOLK NOTTINGHAM STYLE	200
65	Decca LK 4783	FOLK NOW	20
70	BBC REC 955	FOLK ON FRIDAY	18
71	Talisman STAL 5019	FOLK PHILOSOPHY	20
63	Golden Guinea GGL 0265	THE FOLK SCENE	15
66	Folkscene SSP 001	FOLK SCENE (LP, private pressing)	100
61	Topic 12T 157	THE FOLK SONGS OF BRITAIN — SONGS OF COURTSHIP	18
61	Topic 12T 158	THE FOLK SONGS OF BRITAIN VOL. 2 — SONGS OF SEDUCTION	18
61	Topic 12T 159	THE FOLK SONGS OF BRITAIN VOL. 3 — JACK OF ALL TRADES	18
61	Topic 12T 160	THE FOLK SONGS OF BRITAIN VOL. 4 — CHILD BALLADS 1	18
61	Topic 12T 161	THE FOLK SONGS OF BRITAIN VOL. 5 — CHILD BALLADS 2	18
61	Topic 12T 194	THE FOLK SONGS OF BRITAIN VOL. 6 — SAILORMEN AND SERVINGMAIDS	18
61	Topic 12T 195	THE FOLK SONGS OF BRITAIN VOL. 7 — FAIR GAME AND FOUL	18
61	Topic 12T 196	THE FOLK SONGS OF BRITAIN VOL. 8 — A SOLDIER'S LIFE FOR ME	18
61	Topic 12T 197	THE FOLK SONGS OF BRITAIN VOL. 9 — SONGS OF CEREMONY	18
61	Topic 12T 198	THE FOLK SONGS OF BRITAIN VOL. 10 — SONGS OF ANIMAL	18

(Each of the above 10 LPs came with blue labels and a booklet.)

69	Topic	THE FOLK SONGS OF BRITAIN VOLS. 1-10 (10 x LP box set)	100
61	Topic TPS 201	TOPIC SAMPLER No. 6 — FOLK SONGS	12
57	HMV DLP 1143	FOLK SONG TODAY (SONGS AND BALLADS OF ENGLAND AND SCOTLAND) (10")	25
65	HMV CLP 1910	FOLKSOUND OF BRITAIN	18
71	Nicro K 220971	FOLK UPSTAIRS	80
63	Ember CEL 902	FOOL BRITANNIA	15
65	Decca LK 4695	FOURTEEN — THE LORD'S TAVERNERS' ALBUM	35

89	él (no cat. no)	4-2-4 FOOTBALL CLASSICS	15
79	Pickwick PLD 8013	40 FOLK FAVOURITES (2-LP, limited edition)	18
70	Bamboo BLP 205	FREEDOM SOUNDS	50
81	Fresh FRESHLP 8	A FRESH SELECTION	12
72	Trojan TRL 51	FROM BAM BAM TO CHERRY OH BABY	20
80	Disques/Crepescule TWI 007	FROM BRUSSELS WITH LOVE (cassette, in pouch with booklet)	20
80	Disques Du Crepuscule IPCD 72001	FROM BRUSSELS WITH LOVE (CD)	50
70	Liberty LBS 83321	FROM THE BAYOU	18
70	Liberty LBS 83278	FROM THE VAULTS	18
83	New European BADVC 666	FROM TORTURE TO CONSCIENCE (with insert)	80
71	Cutty Wren	FROST LANE	50
89	Sub Pop DAMP 104	FUCK ME, I'M RICH!	15
89	Unrest UNREST 14	FULL FORCE VOL. 3	15
70	Trojan TBL 137	FUNKY CHICKEN	18
87	Urban	(JAMES BROWN'S) FUNKY PEOPLE VOL. 1	12
87	Urban URBLP 14	(JAMES BROWN'S) FUNKY PEOPLE VOL. 2	12
70	Bamboo BLP 206	FUNKY REGGAE	40
82	Come Org. WDC 881021	FÜR ILSE KOCH (some on red vinyl; beware of bootlegs)	120/75
98	Ferox FER CD 4	FURTHER ADVENTURES IN TECHNO SOUL (CD)	18
70	Ember	FUTURE STAR EXPLOSION	12

G

69	Pama ECO 4	GAS — GREATEST HITS	70
66	Doctor Bird DLM 5001	GAYFEET	130
00	Ai AILP 001	GEMOTE (CD)	20
55	HMV DLP 1039	GENE NORMAN PRESENTS JUST JAZZ (10")	20
72	Chess 6641 047	GENESIS — THE BEGINNINGS OF ROCK (4-LP box set with booklet)	50
73	Chess 6641 125	GENESIS — MEMPHIS TO CHICAGO (4-LP box set with booklet)	50
75	Chess 6641 174	GENESIS — SWEET HOME CHICAGO (4-LP box set with booklet)	50
69	Kokomo K 1004	GEORGIA GUITARS 1927-1938 (99 copies only)	55
67	Coxsone CSL 8007	GET READY ROCK STEADY	120+
60s	Riverside RLP 12-106	GIANTS OF BOOGIE WOOGIE	15
69	Pama SECO 20	A GIFT FROM PAMA	40
71	Wand WCS 1003	THE GIRLS WITH SOUL	12
80s	Sarah	GLASS ARCADE (The Field Mice/The Sea Urchins, et al.)	20
72	Revelation REV 1/2/3	GLASTONBURY FAYRE REVELATIONS — A MUSICAL ANTHOLOGY (3-LP, poster sleeve with booklets, pyramid & printed polythene bag)	100
66	Columbia SX 6062	GO!	85
80s	Touch & Go TG 11	GOD'S FAVOURITE DOG	20
95	Lissy's LISS 5	GODZ IS NOT A PUT ON (500 only, in hand-pressed sleeve; some with free 7")	30/20
72	Flyright LP 103	GOIN' AWAY WALKING	15
70	Python LP 1	GOIN' BACK TO CHICAGO (99 copies only)	42
70	Warner Bros WS 1874	GOING HOME	12
60s	Heritage 1003	GOING TO CALIFORNIA (99 copies only)	70
68	Decca LK 4931	GOIN' UP THE COUNTRY	15
69	Oliver & Boyd SBN 05 002118/9	THE GOLDEN BIRD (2-LP)	30
64	Columbia 33SX 1664	GOLDEN GOODIES VOL. 1	55
64	Columbia 33SX 1672	GOLDEN GOODIES VOL. 2	55
69	Roulette RCP 1000	GOLDEN GOODIES VOL. 1	25
69	Roulette RCP 1001	GOLDEN GOODIES VOL. 2	25
59	Philips BBL 7331	GOLDEN HITS	18
60	Philips BBL 7422	GOLDEN HITS VOL. 2	15
61	Philips BBL 7581	GOLDEN HITS VOL. 3	18
57	Capitol T 830	THE GOLD RECORD (blue label)	15
88	53rd & 3rd AGAS 3	GOOD FEELINGS	15
75	Eron 004	GOOD FOLK OF KENT (with insert)	40
65	Atlantic ATL 5004	GOOD OLD FIFTIES	50
68	Elek. EUK 260/EUKS 7260	GOOD TIME MUSIC (U.K. version of "What's Shakin' ", gold or red label)	40/30
72	CBS 67234	GOSPEL SOUND (2-LP)	20
59	Brunswick LAT 8290	GOSPEL TRAIN	20
64	London HA-B 8172	GRAND OLE OPRY SPECTACULAR VOL. 1	18
64	London HA-B 8173	GRAND OLE OPRY SPECTACULAR VOL. 2	18
86	BBC REB 609	GRANGE HILL — THE ALBUM	18
73	Greasy Truckers GT 4997	GREASY TRUCKERS — LIVE AT DINGWALLS DANCE HALL (2-LP with insert)	20
73	United Artists UDX 203/4	GREASY TRUCKERS PARTY (2-LP, gatefold sleeve)	25
72	Vanguard VSD 25/26	GREAT BLUESMEN (2-LP)	18
54	London AL 3530	THE GREAT BLUES SINGERS (10")	45
60s	Riverside RLP 12-121	THE GREAT BLUES SINGERS	25
70	Trojan TBL 111	GREATER JAMAICA	25
75	Brunswick BRLS 3006	GREATEST HITS	15
64	Stateside SL 10075	THE GREATEST GOSPEL SONGS OF OUR TIME	20
67	Doctor Bird DLM 5009	GREATEST JAMAICAN BEAT	150
66	Pye Intl. NPL 28052	THE GREATEST ON STAGE	12
65	RCA RD/SF 7755	GREAT MOMENTS IN JAZZ — NEWPORT JAZZ FESTIVAL 1964	12
70	Transatlantic TRASAM 17	GREAT SCOTS SAMPLER	20
70	Transatlantic TRASAM 21	GREAT SCOTS SAMPLER VOL. 2	20
54	HMV DLP 1054	GREAT TRUMPET SOLOISTS (10")	25
85	Crashed METALPS 107	GREEN METAL	30
71	Bamboo BDLP 215	GROOVING WITH BAMBOO	40+
69	Direction 8-63452	GROOVY BABY	30

63	Realm RM 149	GROUP BEAT '63	40
63	London HA-U 8086	GROUP OF GOODIES	50
64	World Record Club TP 444	GROUP '64	20
78	Virgin VCL 5001	GUILLOTINE (10" mini-LP, with inner sleeve)	18
60s	Storyville SLP 166	GUITAR BLUES	22
73	Transatlantic TRA 271	GUITAR WORKSHOP (2-LP)	20
71	Sunnyland KS 102	GULF COAST BLUES (99 copies only)	40
69	Trojan TTL 16	GUNS OF NAVARONE	12
69	Liberty LBX 3	GUTBUCKET	20
68	Island ILP 977	GUY STEVENS' TESTAMENT OF ROCK AND ROLL	40
71	Wand WCS 1002	THE GUYS WITH SOUL	20

H

58	Oriole MG 20033	HAIL VARIETY!	12
70	Probe PSS 1	HANDLE WITH CARE	12
88	HandMade (no cat. no.)	HANDMADE FILMS MUSIC — THE 10th ANNIVERSARY (CD, promo only)	100
85	Anagram GRAM 23	HANG 11 (MUTANT SURF PUNKS)	20
68	Immediate IMLYIN 2	HAPPY TO BE PART OF THE INDUSTRY OF HUMAN HAPPINESS	25
88	BPM BPLP2	HARDCORE ONE (LP)	30
77	VJM VLP 40	HARD LUCK BLUES	15
74	Decca DPA 3009/10	HARD UP HEROES 1963-68 (2-LP, gatefold sleeve)	25
57	London TKL 93119	HARLEM CONGREGATION	30
56	London AL 3553	HARLEM PIANO ROLL (10")	20
72	Carnival 2941 001	HARPIN' ON IT	12
71	Harvest SHSS 3	HARVEST BAG	12
69	Harvest SPSLP 118	HARVEST SAMPLER OF THE INITIAL FOUR JUNE RELEASES (promo only)	80
63	Reprise R 50001	HAVE YOURSELF A MERRY LITTLE CHRISTMAS	15
71	Sunnyland KS 101	HAVIN' A GOOD TIME — CHICAGO BLUES ANTHOLOGY (99 copies only)	45
66	Polydor 582 701	HEADLINE NEWS	15
71	Vertigo 6360 045	HEADS TOGETHER, FIRST ROUND (gatefold sleeve, swirl label)	20
94	Mo' Wax MWLP 026	HEADZ: A SOUNDTRACK OF EXPERIMENTAL BEATHEAD JAMS (3-LP)	25
96	Mo' Wax MW 061LP	HEADZ VOLUME 2A (4-LP)	25
90	Imaginary ILLUSION 016	HEAVEN AND HELL VOLUME 1: A TRIBUTE TO THE VELVET UNDERGROUND	70
81	Heavy Metal HMR LP 1	HEAVY METAL HEROES	30
82	Heavy Metal HMR LP 7	HEAVY METAL HEROES VOLUME 2	25
84	Heavy Metal HMR LP 24	HEAVY METAL RECORDS (blue, clear & white vinyl, round sleeve)	15
68	Trojan TRL 6	HERE COMES THE DUKE	30
65	Pye NPL 18121	HERE COME THE GIRLS	15
85	Rock 'N' Dole RDR 2	HEROES	15
80s	Temps Modernes LTMV:XI	HEURES SANS SOLEIL	25
69	Pama PSP 1002	HEY BOY HEY GIRL	38
58	Capitol T 926	HI-FI DRUMS	12
58	Melodisc MLP 518	HIGHLIFE: AUTHENTIC WEST AFRICAN MUSIC VOL. 1 (10")	12
58	Melodisc MLP 519	HIGHLIFE: AUTHENTIC WEST AFRICAN MUSIC VOL. 2 (10")	12
59	Parlophone PMD 1085	HIGHWAY TO HEAVEN (10")	18
52	Capitol LC 6508	THE HISTORY OF JAZZ — THE SOLID SOUTH	20
52	Capitol LC 6527	THE HISTORY OF JAZZ — THIS MODERN AGE	12
68	Atlantic 587 094	HISTORY OF RHYTHM AND BLUES — VOL. 1, THE ROOTS 1947-52	18
68	Atlantic 587 095	HISTORY OF RHYTHM AND BLUES — VOL. 2, THE GOLDEN YEARS 1953-55	18
68	Atlantic 587 096	HISTORY OF RHYTHM AND BLUES — VOL. 3, ROCK 'N' ROLL 1956-57	18
68	Atlantic 587 097	HISTORY OF RHYTHM AND BLUES — VOL. 4, THE BIG BEAT 1958-60	18
68	Atlantic 587 140	HISTORY OF RHYTHM AND BLUES — VOL. 5	18
68	Atlantic 587 141	HISTORY OF RHYTHM AND BLUES — VOL. 6	18
69	Bamboo BDLP 203	HISTORY OF SKA VOLUME ONE	60+
87	Stylus/PWL SMD 740	HIT FACTORY — THE BEST OF STOCK, AITKEN & WATERMAN VOL. 1 (CD)	25
87	Fanfare/PWL HFCD 4	HIT FACTORY — THE BEST OF STOCK, AITKEN & WATERMAN VOL. 2 (CD, with exclusive mix of Kylie Minogue's "I Should Be So Lucky", etc)	30
64	Pye NPL 18108	THE HITMAKERS	20
65	Pye NPL 18115	THE HITMAKERS VOL. 2	20
65	Pye NPL 18116	THE HITMAKERS VOL. 3	20
66	Pye NPL 18144	THE HITMAKERS VOL. 4	20
57	Pye Nixa NPT 19015	HIT PARADE OF 1956 (10")	22
59	Pye Nixa NPT 19032	HIT PARADE OF 1958	15
66	Marble Arch MAL 650	HITS FROM THE IVY LEAGUE, THE ROCKIN' BERRIES & THE SORROWS	12
77	Stiff FIST 1	HITS — GREATEST STIFFS (with 7", Max Wall's "England's Glory" [BUY 12])	12
65	Tamla Motown TML 11019	HITSVILLE U.S.A.	110
67	Stax 589 005	HIT THE ROAD STAX	25
81	United Dairies UD 05	HOISTING THE BLACK FLAG	35
55	Philips BBR 8048	HOLLYWOOD DANCE DATE (10")	12
62	Golden Guinea GGL 0129	HONEY HIT PARADE	12
74	Melodisc 12-216	HONEYS	35
52	Capitol LC 6544	HONKY TONK PIANO (10")	15
60s	Riverside RLP 8806	HONKY TONK TRAIN (with booklet)	22
65	Summit ATL 4150	HOOTENANNY AT THE BARGE	15
64	Stateside SL 10079	HOOTENANNY AT THE TROUBADOUR	18
63	Decca LK 4544	HOOTENANNY IN LONDON	20
63	Fontana 688 009ZL	HOOTENANNY SATURDAY NIGHT	20
64	Waverley ZLP 2025	HOOT'NANNY SHOW VOLUME 1	20
64	Waverley ZLP 2032	HOOT'NANNY SHOW VOLUME 2	20
71	Pama PMP 2006	HOT NUMBERS	40
71	Pama PMP 2009	HOT NUMBERS VOLUME TWO	30+
77	WEA M 100	HOT PLATTER CORDON BLEU (available via *Melody Maker*)	20
70	Trojan TBL 128	HOT SHOTS OF REGGAE	15
72	Hot Wax SHW 5008	HOT WAX GREATEST HITS	15
69	Track 613 016	THE HOUSE THAT TRACK BUILT (gatefold sleeve)	35
69	Blue Horizon PR 45/46	HOW BLUE CAN WE GET (2-LP, gatefold sleeve with insert)	35

I

69	Liberty LBL/LBS 83252	I ASKED FOR WATER ... AND SHE GAVE ME GASOLINE	60
80	TJM TJM 11	IDENTITY PARADE	12
88	Bam Caruso MARX 085	ILLUSIONS FROM THE CRACKLING VOID.	15
90s	Dig The Fuzz DIG 013	ILLUSIONS OF ALICE IN WONDERLAND (650 only, with booklet)	20
69	Immediate IMLYIN 1	IMMEDIATE LETS YOU IN.	15
86	Food BITE 4	IMMINENT VOL. 4	12
67	Parlophone PMC 7024	I'M SORRY, I'LL READ THAT AGAIN	18
70	Highway 51 H-104	I'M YOUR COUNTRY MAN (99 copies only)	40
77	United Artists UAS 30101	IMPERIAL ROCKABILLIES	12
79	United Artists UAS 30173	IMPERIAL ROCKABILLIES VOL. 2.	12
80	United Artists UAS 30312	IMPERIAL ROCKABILLIES VOL. 3.	12
66	CBS/Denson Shoes	THE IN CROWD (shoe offer compilation)	25
69	Trojan TTL 15	INDEPENDENT JAMAICA	12
67	Fontana TL 5426	INDIAN MUSIC	12
79	Object Music OBJ 002	INDISCRETE MUSIC — DUBIOUS COLLABORATION (500 only).	15
84	Illuminated JAMS 39	THE INDUSTRIAL RECORDS STORY 1976-1981	20
84	United Dairies UD 015	IN FRACTURED SILENCE.	35
95	RCA 74321 315501	IN FROM THE STORM — THE MUSIC OF JIMI HENDRIX (LP, picture disc)	15
69	T. Motown (S)TML 11124	IN LOVING MEMORY (TRIBUTE TO MRS LOUCYE G. WAKEFIELD)	75
70	Blue Horizon PR 37	IN OUR OWN WAY (OLDIES BUT GOODIES)	35
70	Ember EMB 34111	IN REGGAE TIME	15
66	Ember FA 2034	IRELAND'S GREATEST SOUNDS: FIVE TOP GROUPS FROM BELFAST'S MARITIME CLUB	75
64	Decca LK 4633	IRISH FOLK NIGHT	15
63	Topic 12T 86	THE IRON MUSE (blue label with lyric insert)	15
79	Rationale RATE 8	IRRATIONALE (cassette, in bag with booklet)	20
61	Oriole MG 20046	IT'S ALL HAPPENING HERE	35
64	Philips BL 7609	IT'S ALL OVER TOWN.	20
63	Pye Golden Guinea GGL 0249	IT'S DANCE TIME	18
88	Bam Caruso MARX 100	IT'S ONLY A PASSING PHASE	15
84	Sain 002	IT'S UNHEARD OF.	150

J

69	Amalgamated CSP 3	JACKPOT OF HITS	35
68	Blue Cat BCL 1	JAMAICAN MEMORIES.	100
64	Atlantic 587 075	JAMAICA SKA (colour 'Dancers' sleeve)	50
67	Atlantic 587 075	JAMAICA SKA (reissue, orange sleeve)	30
68	Flyright LP 3502	JAMBALAYA ON THE BAYOU — VOLUME 1	20
69	Flyright LP 3503	JAMBALAYA ON THE BAYOU — VOLUME 2	20
72	Utd. Artists UAS 60027/8	THE JAMES BOND COLLECTION (2-LP, with booklet)	25
72	Rolling Stones COC 39100	JAMMING WITH EDWARD	15
55	Columbia Clef 33CX 10008	JAM SESSION	12
61	HMV/Utd Artists CSD 1381	JAZZ ALIVE — A NIGHT AT THE HALF NOTE	12
56	Tempo TAP 5	JAZZ AT THE FLAMINGO	80+
55	Columbia 33CX 10078	JAZZ AT THE PHILHARMONIC, 1955 VOL. 1	12
55	Columbia 33CX 10079	JAZZ AT THE PHILHARMONIC, 1955 VOL. 2	12
68	Columbia SLJS 1	JAZZ EXPLOSION	12
72	Decca ECS 2114	JAZZ IN BRITAIN 1968-1969.	25
62	Parlophone PMC 1195	JAZZ IN THE MAKING.	12
84	Streetsounds MUSIC 1	JAZZ JUICE	30
85	Streetsounds SOUND 1	JAZZ JUICE (reissue)	25
86	Streetsounds SOUND 4	JAZZ JUICE 2.	20
86	Streetsounds SOUND 5	JAZZ JUICE 3.	20
86	Streetsounds SOUND 6	JAZZ JUICE 4.	20
87	Streetsounds SOUND 8	JAZZ JUICE 5.	18
87	Streetsounds SOUND 9	JAZZ JUICE 6.	18
88	Streetsounds SOUND 10	JAZZ JUICE 7.	18
88	Streetsounds SOUND 11	JAZZ JUICE 8.	15
88	Streetsounds SOUND 12	JAZZ JUICE 9.	15
57	London AL 3562	JAZZ OF THE ROARING TWENTIES VOL. 2 (10")	12
58	Philips BBL 7184	JAZZ OMNIBUS	12
63	VJM LC 6	JAZZ PANORAMA OF THE SIXTIES	12
58	Vogue LAE 12097	JAZZ PIANISTS GALORE	12
57	London AL 3565	JAZZ PIANO RARITIES (10")	15
55	Columbia Clef 33C 9007	JAZZ SCENE (10").	15
55	Columbia Clef 33C 9008	JAZZ SCENE VOL. 2 (10")	15
62	Parlophone PMC 1177	JAZZ SOUNDS OF THE 20s VOL. 4: BLUES SINGERS & ACCOMPANISTS	15
56	Vogue LAE 12038	JAZZ WEST COAST	12
57	Vogue LAE 12061	JAZZ WEST COAST VOLUME 2.	12
58	Vogue LAE 12115	JAZZ WEST COAST VOLUME 3.	12
61	Vogue LAE 12235	JAZZ WEST COAST VOLUME 5.	12
77	Decca DPA 3035/3036	THE JOE MEEK STORY (2-LP).	35
60	Top Rank 35/064	JOHN HAMMOND'S SPIRITUALS TO SWING VOLUME 1	15
60	Top Rank 35/065	JOHN HAMMOND'S SPIRITUALS TO SWING VOLUME 2	15
72	Vanguard VRS 8523/4	JOHN HAMMOND'S SPIRITUALS TO SWING: LEGENDARY CARNEGIE HALL CONCERTS OF 1938/9 (2-LP)	18
69	BBC REC 52S	JOHN PEEL PRESENTS TOP GEAR	30
70	BBC REC 68M	JOHN PEEL'S ARCHIVE THINGS	15
60	HMV CLP 1327	A JUG OF PUNCH (also issued as XLP 50003)	35
67	Ace Of Hearts AH 163	JUGS AND WASHBOARDS	15
67	RCA Victor RD 7893	JUGS WASHBOARDS AND KAZOOS	15
70s	Eric's ERICS 008	JUKEBOX AT ERIC'S	15
62	Embassy WLP 6052	JUKE BOX FAVOURITES	12

76	RCA RS 1066	JUMPING AT THE GO GO	18
77	Policy Wheel PW 459-1	JUMPING ON THE HILL	12
64	R&B JBL 1111	JUMP JAMAICA WAY	250
69	RCA Intl. INT 1014	JUST A LITTLE BIT OF SOUL	22
79	Kick KK 1	JUST FOR KICKS	35

K

59	Capitol T 1057	K.C. IN THE 30's	20
72	Joy JOYS 223	KEEP THE FAITH VOL. 1	15
72	Joy JOYS 224	KEEP THE FAITH VOL. 2	15
72	Joy JOYS 225	KEEP THE FAITH VOL. 3	15
56	Vogue LAE 12028	KENTON'S SIDEMEN (Don Rendell, et al.)	60
81	White Witch	KENT ROCKS (200 only)	180
71	Jay Boy JSX 2009	KERBSIDE ENTERTAINERS	12
54	HMV DLP 1048	KEYBOARD KINGS OF JAZZ (10")	25
72	Key	KEY COLLECTION (with insert)	15
70	Trojan TBL 140	KING SIZE REGGAE	20
77	Chrysalis CHR 1137	THE KING OF ELFLAND'S DAUGHTER	20
68	Polydor 623 273	KINGS OF RHYTHM AND BLUES	15
60s	Gryphon 13159	KINGS OF THE TWELVE STRING GUITAR	20
71	Flyright LP 101	KINGS OF THE TWELVE STRING GUITAR (reissue)	15
60s	Saydisc Roots RL 333	KINGS OF MEMPHIS TOWN 1927-1930	18
94	Mercury 522 476-1	KISS MY ASS (red, white or blue vinyl)	12
86	Ten DIX 28	KNIGHTS & EMERALDS	15
86	Ten XID 11	KNIGHTS & EMERALDS	15

L

79	The Label TRLP 002S	THE LABEL SOFA ('translumar defractor' 3D picture disc, stickered PVC sleeve)	35
79	Cherry Red ARED 4	LABELS UNLIMITED	12
83	Fetish FR 2011	THE LAST TESTAMENT (with inner, stickered sleeve)	18
87	Other OTH 10	LAST WARRIOR	18
68	Island ILP 986	LEAPING WITH MR LEE (by Bunny Lee All Stars)	195
80	Atra ATRA LP 1003	THE LEGENDS (Augustus Pablo et al.)	12
03	Ai AILP 004	LEISURE (100 copies only)	15
99	Jazzman 1	LE JAZZBEAT!	15
66	Blue Horizon LP 2	LET ME TELL YOU ABOUT THE BLUES	900
63	Polydor SLPHM 237 622	LET'S DO THE TWIST, HULLY GULLY, SLOP, SURF, LOCOMOTION, MONKEY	30
66	Neshoba N 11	LET'S GO DOWN SOUTH (99 copies only)	55
58	Brunswick LAT 8271	LET'S HAVE A PARTY	25
73	Bell DUBL 9002/3	LET THE GOOD TIMES ROLL	15
81	Alt. Tentacles VIRUS 4	LET THEM EAT JELLYBEANS (with lyric poster)	20
74	Sonet SNTX 1	LEGACY OF THE BLUES SAMPLER	12
80s	Third Mind/Abstract	LIFE AT THE TOP	25
81	WEA K 58412	LIFE IN THE EUROPEAN THEATRE	12
68	Transatlantic TRASAM 2	LISTEN HERE!	15
81	NEMS NEL 6020	LIVE AND HEAVY	12
80	BUN 01	LIVE AT BUNJIES (gatefold sleeve with insert)	30
74	Key KL 021	LIVE AT SPREE	20
77	NEMS NEL 6013	LIVE AT THE VORTEX	15
65	Fontana TL 5240	LIVE AT THE WHISKEY A-GO-GO	35
68	Big Shot BBTL 4000	LIVE IT UP	75
64	Embassy WLP 6065	LIVERPOOL BEAT	15
65	Ember NR 5028	LIVERPOOL TODAY — LIVE AT THE CAVERN	35
64	CBS Realm RM 209	LIVIN' WITH THE BLUES	18
70	Trojan TBL 135	LOCH NESS MONSTER	20
87	4AD CAD 703D	LONELY IS AN EYESORE (cardboard pack with book)	30
87	4AD CADX 703	LONELY IS AN EYESORE (CD, LP & cassette, in wooden box with etching, screen print & video, 100 only)	1000+
81	Plant Life PLR 032	LOVELY IN THE DANCES: SONGS OF SYDNEY CARTER	15
71	Count Shelly SSLP 03	LOOK BEFORE YOU LEAP	18
91	Holyground HG 121	LOOSE ROUTES (2-LP, gatefold foldover sleeve)	30
65	Storyville 616002	LOUISIANA PRISON BLUES	15
69	Pama PSP 1001	A LOVELY DOZEN	30

M

76	Cornish Legend CLM 1	MADE IN CORNWALL (with insert)	25
58	Pye Nixa Jazz NJL 13	(LEONARD FEATHER PRESENTS) MAD THAD	12
79	Object Music OBJ 003	A MANCHESTER COLLECTION	25
88	Bop BC V001	MANCHESTER, NORTH OF ENGLAND (white labels only)	12
70	Trojan TBL 129	MAN FROM CAROLINA	20
53	Brunswick LA 8567	MAN WITH A HORN (10" LP)	12
70	CBS 52798	MA RAINEY AND THE CLASSIC BLUES SINGERS	20
69	Marmalade 643 314	MARMALADE — 100% PROOF	18
72	Village Thing VTSAM 16	MATCHBOX DAYS	25
68	President PTL 1002	MAR-V-LUS SOUND OF R&B AND SOUL MUSIC	40
60s	Wudwink ISMF 107	MARY'S FOLK	200
78	CBS 82670	MAX'S KANSAS CITY	12
66	CBS Special Prod. WSR 853	McDONALDS ALL-STAR FAVOURITES	12
69	Liberty LBL/LBS 83190	ME AND THE DEVIL	50
78	Topic 12T 376	MELODEON GREATS — A COLLECTION OF MELODEON MASTERPIECES	15
69	Atco 228 023	MEMPHIS GOLD	15
64	London HA 8129	MEMORIES ARE MADE OF HITS VOL. 1	32
64	London HA 8130	MEMORIES ARE MADE OF HITS VOL. 2	32
64	London HA 8131	MEMORIES ARE MADE OF HITS VOL. 3	32

64	London HA 8138	MEMORIES ARE MADE OF HITS VOL. 4	32
64	London HA 8148	MEMORIES ARE MADE OF HITS VOL. 5	32
64	London HA 8171	MEMORIES ARE MADE OF HITS VOL. 6	32
64	London HA 8189	MEMORIES ARE MADE OF HITS VOL. 7	32
65	London HA 8213	MEMORIES ARE MADE OF HITS VOL. 8	32
54	Vogue Coral LVC 10008	MERRY CHRISTMAS (10")	20
69	T. Motown (S)TML 11126	MERRY CHRISTMAS FROM MOTOWN (mono/stereo)	25
67	Capitol T 9030	MERRY CHRISTMAS TO YOU	15
85	Neat NEAT 1014	METAL BATTLE	15
80	BBC REH 397	METAL EXPLOSION	30
82	Ebony EBON 1	METAL FATIGUE	15
80	EMI EMC 3318	METAL FOR MUTHAS	25
80	EMI EMC 3337	METAL FOR MUTHAS VOL. 2	15
82	Ebony EBON 8	METAL MANIAXE	15
87	Other OTH 9	METAL WARRIOR	50
60	RCA/Camden CDN 122	METRONOME ALL STARS	12
80	MGM 2315 394	THE MGM ROCKABILLY COLLECTION	12
56	Nixa Jazz Today NJL 3	MIDNIGHT AT NIXA	12
66	Atlantic 587 021	MIDNIGHT SOUL	20
69	Storyville 616 009	MIDNIGHT SPECIAL	15
62	Brunswick LAT 8401	MIDNIGHT JAMBOREE (also stereo STA 3061)	12
56	London AL 3554	MIDWESTERN JAZZ (10")	15
66	Xtra XTRA 1047	THE MIKE RAVEN BLUES SHOW	22
69	Transatlantic TRASAM 5	THE MIKE RAVEN BLUES SAMPLER	22
72	Polydor	MILL VALLEY JAM SESSION	12
60	Coral LVA 9126	MILLION-AIRS	18
80	Pipe PIPE 2	MINIATURES (with poster insert, 500 only)	15
80	Pipe PIPE 2	MINIATURES (cassette with mini-booklet insert, 100 only)	30
71	Trojan TBL 174	MISS LABBA LABBA REGGAE	28
60	Top Rank BUY 028	MR. BLUE	30
60s	Bounty BY 6025	MODERN CHICAGO BLUES	35
69	London HAB 8380	MODERN COUNTRY HITS OF TODAY VOL. 1	12
69	London HAB 8381	MODERN COUNTRY HITS OF TODAY VOL. 2	12
53	Capitol LC 6561	MODERN IDIOM (10")	15
55	HMV DLP 1022	MODERN JAZZ PIANO (10")	15
56	Tempo TAP 2	MODERN JAZZ SCENE 1956	60+
53	Esquire 20-011	MODERN MIXTURE VOLUME ONE (10")	20
79	Bridge House BHLP 003	MODS MAYDAY '79 (original issue)	20
80	Polydor 2488810	MONSTERS OF ROCK	15
73	Stax STX 1029	MONTREUX FESTIVAL 1973	12
70	Trojan TTL 31	MOONLIGHT GROOVER	20
80	Danceville	THE MOONLIGHT TAPES	12
70	Liberty LBS 83377	MORE FROM THE VAULTS	12
62	HMV CLP 1583	MORE OF YOUR FAVOURITE TV AND RADIO THEMES	15
68	Marble Arch MAL 813	MORE RHYTHM AND BLUES	12
65	private pressing	MORE SINGING AT THE COUNT HOUSE	30
72	Island HELP 5	MORRIS ON (black label with pink 'i')	18
80	Conventional CON 013	MOTHER OF A PUNK (cassette)	12
86	Iguana VYK LP 11	MOTOR CITY 9 (with booklet)	15
65	Tamla Motown TML 11007	THE MOTORTOWN REVUE LIVE	110
66	Tamla Motown TML 11027	THE MOTORTOWN REVUE IN PARIS	100
70	T. Motown (S)TML 11127	THE MOTORTOWN REVUE LIVE	20
69	T. Motown (S)TML 11121	MOTOWN CHARTBUSTERS VOL. 3 (original with flipback sleeve)	15
70	T. Motown STML 11162	MOTOWN CHARTBUSTERS VOL. 4 (original with flipback sleeve)	15
74	T. Motown STML 11270	MOTOWN CHARTBUSTERS VOL. 9 (green vinyl)	12
72	Tamla Motown STMA 8005	MOTOWN DISCO CLASSICS VOL. 2	15
66	Tamla Motown TML 11030	MOTOWN MAGIC	50
68	Tamla Motown TML 11064	MOTOWN MEMORIES (flipback sleeve)	60
68	Tamla Motown TML 11077	MOTOWN MEMORIES VOL. 2	60
70	T. Motown STML 11143	MOTOWN MEMORIES VOL. 3	60
72	Tamla Motown STML 11200	MOTOWN MEMORIES	15
80	Tamla Motown ZL 72032	MOTOWN MOD CLASSICS VOL. 1	15
80	Tamla Motown STML 12133	MOTOWN MOD CLASSICS VOL. 2	15
72	Tamla Motown TMSP 1130	THE MOTOWN STORY (5-LP box set)	25
83	Tamla Motown TMSP 6019	THE MOTOWN STORY — THE FIRST 25 YEARS (box set)	20
77	Mountain PSLP 200	MOUNTAIN ROCKS INTO '77 (Mountain label sampler, promo only)	20
53	London AL 3503	MUGGY, TESCH AND THE CHICAGOANS (10")	15
57	Pye NJL 11	MURDERER'S HOME	15
71	Mushroom 100 MR 16	THE MUSHROOM FOLK SAMPLER	35
57	Brunswick LAT 8201	MUSIC FOR THE BOYFRIEND — HE REALLY DIGS ROCK'N'ROLL	70
57	Brunswick LAT 8202	MUSIC FOR THE BOYFRIEND — HE REALLY DIGS JAZZ	15
57	Brunswick LAT 8205	MUSIC FOR THE BOYFRIEND — THE FEMININE TOUCH	15
67	Argo RG 533	MUSIC FROM THE FAR NORTH (with foldout inner)	15
73	Charisma CADS 101	MUSIC FROM FREE CREEK (2-LP)	20
54	Decca LF 1224	MUSIC OF AFRICA — BEST RECORDINGS OF 1953 (10")	12
54	Decca LF 1084	MUSIC OF AFRICA — TANGAKA (10")	12
54	Decca LF 1172	MUSIC OF AFRICA — CONGO SONGS & DANCES (10")	12
54	Decca LF 1173	MUSIC OF AFRICA — UGANDA PROTECTORATE (10")	12
70	Disques Vogue VRLS 3043	LA MUSIQUE PROGRESSIVE	12
81	Ze ISSP 4001	MUTANT DISCO (3 x 12" box set, numbered, 2,000 only)	12
77	EMI NUT 4	MY GENERATION	12

N

73	Enterprise ESAM 100	THE NAME OF THE GAME	15
71	Eden LP 43	NAPTON FOLK CLUB (private pressing, 100 only)	35

62	London HA-B 8003	NASHVILLE SATURDAY NIGHT	18
63	London HA-B 8028	NASHVILLE STEEL GUITAR	18
69	Bamboo BLP 201	NATURAL REGGAE VOLUME ONE	50+
70	Bamboo BLP 204	NATURAL REGGAE VOLUME TWO	60+
81	4AD CAD 117	NATURES MORTES — STILL LIVES (export issue)	60
85	Musique Brut BRV 002	NECROPOLIS, AMPHIBIANS AND REPTILES: THE MUSIC OF ADOLF WOLFLI	20
70s	Bounty BY 6012	NEGRO FOLKLORE FROM TEXAS STATE PRISON	22
57	Vogue LAE 12033	NEGRO SPIRITUALS	25
61	World Records LH 12	NEGRO SPIRITUALS	15
87	Broken Flag BF V8	NEVER SAY WHEN	40
72	Atlantic K 20024	THE NEW AGE OF ATLANTIC	15
80	Logo MOGO 4011	NEW ELECTRIC WARRIORS	20
53	London AL 3509	NEW ORLEANS HORNS (10")	15
56	London AL 3557	NEW ORLEANS HORNS VOLUME 2 (10")	15
67	Ace Of Hearts AH 140	NEW ORLEANS MEMORIES	12
74	Flyright LP 4708	NEW ORLEANS R&B VOLUME 1	15
74	Flyright LP 4709	NEW ORLEANS R&B VOLUME 2	15
60s	'77' 77LA 12/16	NEW ORLEANS TODAY	18
60s	'77' 77LA 12/29	NEW ORLEANS TODAY VOL. 2	18
65	Fontana TFL 6038	NEWPORT BROADSIDE — TOPICAL SONGS AT THE NEWPORT FOLK FESTIVAL 1963	25
65	Fontana TFL 6041	NEWPORT FOLK FESTIVAL EVENING CONCERT VOL. 1	25
65	Fontana TFL 6050	NEWPORT FOLK FESTIVAL VOL. 1	12
57	Philips BBL 7147	NEWPORT JAZZ FESTIVAL	12
57	Philips BBL 7152	NEWPORT JAZZ FESTIVAL	12
58	London Jazz LTZ C15155	NEWPORT SPIRITUAL STARS	22
03	Ai AILP 005	NEW TOWN (2-LP, 1500 copies only)	15
77	Vertigo 6300 902	NEW WAVE	15
72	Flyright LP 4706	NEW YORK CITY BLUES	15
55	London AL 3541	NEW YORK JAZZ OF THE ROARING TWENTIES (10")	15
72	Flyright LP 4707	NEW YORK RHYTHM AND BLUES	15
69	Island IWP(S) 6	NICE ENOUGH TO EAT (pink label)	12
57	Vanguard PPL 11004	A NIGHT AT THE APOLLO	15
69	Blue Horizon 7-63210	THE 1968 MEMPHIS COUNTRY BLUES FESTIVAL	50
83	DEL 306	19th CAMBRIDGE FOLK FESTIVAL VOLUME 1	20
81	NMX	NMX: LIVE AT SHEFFIELD (cassette)	20
68	Spark SRLM 107	NO INTRODUCTION	20
69	Trojan TTL 14	NO MORE HEARTACHES	20
70	Polydor 545 017	NON STOP SOUL	30
69	Regal Starline SRS 5013	NO ONE'S GONNA CHANGE OUR WORLD	18
64	Concert Hall AM 2339	NORTHUMBRIAN MINSTRELS	25
60	Fontana TFL 5123	NOTHIN' BUT THE BLUES (gatefold sleeve)	22
71	CBS 66278	NOTHING BUT THE BLUES (2-LP, Blue Horizon pressings may also exist (£75))	35
82	See For Miles CM 112	NOT JUST BEAT MUSIC, 1965-70	15
79	Giorno GPS	THE NOVA CONVENTION	20
70	Decca Nova SPA 72	NOVA SAMPLER	15
70s	Warm PFLP 201	NOVA-VAGA	15
79	A&M AMLE 68505	NO WAVE ('pizza' picture disc)	15
79	A&M AMLE 68505	NO WAVE (orange, mauve or blue vinyl)	each 12
69	Pama ECO 6	NU BEAT — GREATEST HITS	40
73	Elektra K 62012	NUGGETS (Original Artyfacts From The First Psychedelic Era 1965-1968) (2-LP, gatefold sleeve)	40
86	Numa NUMA 1004	NUMA RECORDS YEAR 1 (with bonus Italian 12" "My Dying Machine")	15
86	Numa NUMAC 1004	NUMA RECORDS YEAR 1 (cassette)	12
90s	NWOBHM CD 002	NWOBHM — VOLUME 2 (CD)	30
90s	NWOBHM CD 003	NWOBHM — VOLUME 3 (CD)	30

O

69	Liberty LBS 83234	OAKLAND BLUES	22
80	Object Music OBJ 006	OBJECTIVITY	15
79	Rok ROK LP 001	ODD BODS, MODS AND SODS	75
58	Parlophone PMC 1072	OH BOY!	60
78	Raw RAWLP 2	OH NO IT'S MORE FROM RAW (Users/Killjoys et al.)	20
72	Music F. Pleasure MFP 1416	OH! WHAT A CARRY ON	15
98	MPO IRL 01	OH YEAH (CD, 'Heineken Rock Awards' issue free with *Hot Press* magazine, with Neil Hannon/Ash et al.)	18
80	EMI ZIT 1	OI! — THE ALBUM (initially mail-order only from *Sounds* magazine)	30
87	Link LP 23	OI! GLORIOUS OI!	12
84	Syndicate SYNLP 4	OI! OF SEX	12
83	Secret SEC 5	OI! OI! THAT'S YER LOT	15
75	Super Beeb BELP 004	OLD GREY WHISTLE TEST	12
64	Stateside SL 10094	OLDIES R & B	60
60	Parlophone PMC 1127	OLD TIME MUSIC HALL	15
69	Transatlantic XTRA 1076	O LIVERPOOL WE LOVE YOU (Stan Kelly/Bill Shankley/ Jimmy Tarbuck et al.)	40
68	Big Shot BBTL 4001	ONCE MORE	60+
69	Marmalade 643 314	100% PROOF	12
86	Stateside/EMI SSL 6002	ONE MINIT AT A TIME	18
73	Charisma CLASS 3	ONE MORE CHANCE	12
63	Columbia 33SX 1536	ONE NIGHT STAND	40
63	Stateside SL 10065	ON STAGE LIVE!	70
69	Atco 228 009/010	ON STAGE — LIVE (2-LP)	25
73	Xtra XTRA 1133	ON THE ROAD AGAIN	70
64	Columbia 33SX 1662	ON THE SCENE	100
63	Stateside SL 10024	OPRY TIME IN TENNESSEE	18

VARIOUS ARTISTS LPs & COMPILATIONS

65	Allegro ALL 778	ROY ORBISON SINGS (some tracks by Jerry Lee Lewis, Tommy Roe; black or blue label)	12
65	Ember FA 2005	ROY ORBISON AND OTHERS (with 4 tracks by Orbison)	12
67	Polydor 236 216	ORIGINAL AMERICAN FOLK BLUES FESTIVAL	15
64	Rio RLP 1	THE ORIGINAL COOL JAMAICAN SKA	130+
70	Mercury SMCL 20182	ORIGINAL GOLDEN HITS OF THE GREAT BLUES SINGERS	15
73	Prince Buster PB 10	ORIGINAL GOLDEN OLDIES VOLUME 2	12
70	Mercury SMCL 20183	ORIGINAL GOLDEN RHYTHM AND BLUES HITS VOLUME 1	20
60	London HA-G 2308	THE ORIGINAL HITS	50
61	London HA-G 2339	THE ORIGINAL HITS VOL. 2	50
63	Golden Guinea GGL 0240	THE ORIGINAL HOOTENANNY	15
67	Ember SPE 6602	THE ORIGINAL SOUND OF DETROIT	18
68	United Artists ULP 1182	ORIGINAL SOUNDTRACKS OF HITS MUSIC	15
64	Vocalion VA 8017	ORIGINAL SURFIN' HITS	65
52	Vogue LDE 006	ORIGINATORS OF MODERN JAZZ (10")	15
75	Trailer LET SAM 2087	OUR FOLK MUSIC HERITAGE	12
62	London HA-U 2404	OUR SIGNIFICANT HITS	70
65	Ace Of Hearts AH 72	OUT CAME THE BLUES	18
67	Ace Of Hearts AH 158	OUT CAME THE BLUES VOLUME 2	18

P

64	Golden Guinea GGL 0268	PACKAGE TOUR	22
65	Blue Beat BBLP 804	PAIN IN MY BELLY	250
55	London HA-A 2001	THE PAJAMA GAME	15
67	Island ILP 945	PAKISTANI SOUL SESSION	60
61	Parlophone PMC 1134	PARADE OF THE POPS	15
57	HMV DLP 1076	PARIS TU N'A PAS CHANGÉ	12
85	LIL LP2	PARKSIDE STEELWORKS	60
68	Studio One SOL 9009	PARTY TIME IN JAMAICA	120
66	Decca LK 4824	PENTHOUSE MAGAZINE PRESENTS THE BEDSIDE BOND	40
83	Psycho PSYCHO 6	THE PERFUMED GARDEN	20
84	Psycho PSYCHO 15	THE PERFUMED GARDEN II	20
81	Cherry Red BRED 15	PERSPECTIVES AND DISTORTION (gatefold sleeve)	15
86	Streetsounds PHST 1986	THE PHILADELPHIA YEARS (14-LP box set)	30
75	Warner Bros K 59010	PHIL SPECTOR'S CHRISTMAS ALBUM (2nd reissue, some with poster)	18/15
80	Phil Spector Intl. 2307 015	PHIL SPECTOR '74/'79	25
67	Riverside RLP 8809	PIANO BLUES 1927-1933	20
56	Vogue Coral LVA 9069	PIANO JAZZ — BARRELHOUSE AND BOOGIE WOOGIE	12
70s	Horse HRLP 704	PICK HITS	12
72	Flyright LP 104	PIEDMONT BLUES	15
82	Cherry Red PZRED 41	PILLOWS AND PRAYERS (picture disc in printed PVC sleeve)	12
60	HMV CLP 1362/XLP 50004	A PINCH OF SALT — BRITISH SEA SONGS OLD AND NEW	20
53	London AL 3506	PIONEERS OF BOOGIE WOOGIE (10")	40
54	London AL 3537	PIONEERS OF BOOGIE WOOGIE VOLUME TWO (10")	40
73	Trojan TBL 203	PIPELINE	15
80	Incus INCUS 37	PISA 1980: IMPROVISOR'S SYMPOSIUM	50
81	K-Tel NE 1134	THE PLATINUM ALBUM	12
70s	Flyright LP 4711	PLAY MY JUKEBOX	12
81	P. Surprised KLARK 002	PLEASANTLY SURPRISED — AN HOUR OF ELOQUENT SOUNDS (cassette)	20
71	Argo ZPR 264/5	POETRY AND JAZZ IN CONCERT 250	15
56	Mercury MPT	POP PARADE VOL. 1 (10")	18
56	Mercury MPT	POP PARADE VOL. 2 (10")	18
57	Mercury MPT 7519	POP PARADE VOL. 3 (10")	18
57	Mercury MPT 7523	POP PARADE VOL. 4 (10")	18
57	Mercury MPT 7525	POP PARADE VOL. 5 (10")	30
70	Polydor 2682 001	POP PARTY	12
68	Polydor 236 517/8/9	POP PARTY! (3-LP in box)	40
79	Target TARG1	POP POP POP	12
91	Shock SX 012	THE PORTABLE ALTAMONT (CD)	20
83	Fall Out FALL 032	POSH HITS VOL. 1	12
65	Post War Blues PWB 1	POST WAR BLUES: CHICAGO (99 copies only)	42
66	Post War Blues PWB 2	POST WAR BLUES: MEMPHIS ON DOWN (99 copies only)	42
67	Post War Blues PWB 3	POST WAR BLUES: EASTERN AND GULF COAST STATES (99 copies only)	42
68	Post War Blues PWB 4	POST WAR BLUES: TEXAS (99 copies only)	42
68	Post War Blues PWB 5	POST WAR BLUES: DETROIT (99 copies only)	42
60s	Post War Blues PWB 6	POST WAR BLUES: WEST COAST (99 copies only)	42
60s	Post War Blues PWB 7	POST WAR BLUES: THE DEEP SOUTH (99 copies only)	42
69	Python PWBC 1	POST WAR COLLECTOR SERIES VOL. 1 (99 copies only)	42
63	Stateside SL 10046	PREACHIN' THE BLUES	35
80	4AD BAD 11	PRESAGES (mini-LP, green/pink or brown sleeve)	15/20
79	Preseli PRE 001	PRESELI FOLK (private pressing with insert)	30
70	Kokomo K 1006	PRE-WAR TEXAS BLUES (99 copies only)	45
60s	Jazz Collector JGN 1001	PRIMITIVE PIANO	20
87	A&M AMA 3906	PRINCE'S TRUST 10TH ANNIVERSARY BIRTHDAY PARTY (2-LP, some stickered, with Paul McCartney 7": "Long Tall Sally"/"I Saw Her Standing There" [p/s, FREE 21])	40/25
63	London HA-B 8062	PRISONERS' SONGS	20
70	Lyntone LYN 2745	PRIVATE EYE'S GOLDEN YEARS OF SOUND 1964-70	20
02	Ai AILP 003	PRODUCE (300 only)	18
90	United Dairies UD 134	PSILOTRIPITAKA (3-LP [UD 01, 03 & 04], with bonus LP "Registered Nurse" [UD 00], 1,000 only, some possibly in leather bag)	400/125
90	United Dairies UD 134CD	PSILOTRIPITAKA (3-CD [UD 01, 03 & 04], with bonus CD "Registered Nurse" [UD 00CD], 1,000 only, 30 in 'leather bondage bag')	400/60
91	Delerium DELP 005	PSYCHEDELIC SAUNA (2-LP, 500 numbered on multi-coloured vinyl)	18
65	Sue ILP 919	PURE BLUES VOLUME ONE	70
83	Guardian GRC 2162	PURE OVERKILL	18

73	Purple TPSS 1	PURPLE PEOPLE	15
85	Color Disc COLORS 2	PURPLE TWILIGHT (400 only)	20
68	Island ILP 978	PUT IT ON, IT'S ROCK STEADY	25
71	Pye PSA 6	PYE SALES SAMPLER (sampler for Pye & Dawn releases; 99 copies only, with release sheet)	20

Q

68	Stateside S(S)L 10209	A QUARTET OF SOUL	40
70	Trojan TBL 136	QUEEN OF THE WORLD	20
59	Vogue LAE 12031	THE QUINTET OF THE YEAR	15

R

54	London AL 3515	RAGTIME PIANO ROLL (10")	15
54	London AL 3523	RAGTIME PIANO ROLL VOLUME 2 (10")	15
55	London AL 3542	RAGTIME PIANO ROLL VOLUME 3 (10")	15
57	London AL 3563	RAGTIME PIANO ROLL VOLUME 4 (10")	15
81	Island ILPS 9705	RAIDERS OF THE LOST DUB (LP, withdrawn)	12
76	Phil Spector Intl. 2307 008	RARE MASTERS VOL. 1	30
76	Phil Spector Intl. 2307 009	RARE MASTERS VOL. 2	30
78	Polydor 2482 274	RARE TRACKS	12
69	United Artists (S)UX 1214	RAVE	25
74	Mooncrest CREST 17	RAVE ON	12
73	Attack ATLP 1012	RAVE ON BROTHER	35
67	Ace Of Clubs ACL 1220	RAW BLUES (also stereo SCL 1220)	18
77	Raw RAWLP 1	RAW DEAL (black & white sleeve & red/blue label)	15
61	Pye NPL 18069	RAZZAMATAZZ AND ALL THAT JAZZ	30
83	Mean MNLP 82	READING ROCK VOL. 1 (2-LP)	20
64	Decca LK 4577	READY, STEADY, GO!	40
68	Pama PMLP 3	READY STEADY GO ROCKSTEADY	40+
64	Decca LK 4634	READY, STEADY, WIN	75
65	Stateside SL 10112	THE REAL R & B	45
80s	Recloose Org. LOOSE 12	R.O. (RECLOOSE ORGANISATION) (picture disc with insert)	20
82	Recommended 104	RECOMMENDED SAMPLER	15
79	Destiny DS 10001	THE RECORD COLLECTOR	20
81	Recorder BR 003	RECORDER THREE	20
70	CBS 52797	RECORDING THE BLUES	22
65	Red Bird RB 20-102	RED BIRD GOLDIES	65
81	WEA K 58344	RED HOT ROCKABILLIES (with inner sleeve)	12
70	Trojan TBL 115	REGGAE FLIGHT 404	12
68	Big Shot BIL 3000	REGGAE GIRL	100
69	Pama ECO 3	REGGAE HITS '69 VOL. 1	25
69	Pama ECO 11	REGGAE HITS VOL. 2	25
69	Pama PTP 1001	REGGAE HIT THE TOWN	25
68	Studio One SOL 9007	REGGAE IN THE GRASS	95
71	Trojan TBL 181	REGGAE JAMAICA	15
71	Trojan TBL 193	REGGAE JAMAICA VOL. 2	18
71	Bamboo BDLP 208	REGGAEMATIC SOUNDS	70
70	Trojan TBL 144	REGGAE MOVEMENT	20
70	Trojan TBL 130	REGGAE REGGAE REGGAE	12
69	Coxsone CSP 2	REGGAE SPECIAL	30
70	Trojan TBL 151	REGGAE STEADY GO	18
68	Coxsone CSL 8017	REGGAE TIME	85+
72	Ashanti ANB 201	REGGAE TIME	15
71	Pama PMP 2012	REGGAE TO REGGAE	32
69	Pama PSP 1004	REGGAE TO UK WITH LOVE	50
80s	Ré 0101	RE RECORDS QUARTERLY VOL. No. 1 (with book)	15
64	Decca LK 4616	RHYTHM AND BLUES	80
67	Marble Arch MAL 726	RHYTHM AND BLUES	12
64	Golden Guinea GGL 0280	RHYTHM AND BLUES VOL	20
64	Golden Guinea GGL 0351	RHYTHM AND BLUES VOL. 2	12
69	Liberty LBL 83216	RHYTHM AND BLUES VOLUME 1: END OF AN ERA	30
70	Liberty LBL 83328	RHYTHM AND BLUES VOLUME 2: SWEET 'N' GREASY	22
64	Golden Guinea GGL 0293	RHYTHM AND BLUES ALL STARS	12
69	Minit MLL/MLS 40008E	RHYTHM AND BLUES CLASSICS	30
69	Minit MLL/MLS 40009E	RHYTHM AND BLUES CLASSICS VOL. 2	30
63	CBS Realm RM 101	R&B GREATS VOLUME 1	22
64	CBS Realm RM 175	R&B GREATS VOLUME 2	22
64	Mercury MCL 20019	RHYTHM AND BLUES PARTY	62
76	Philips 6436 028	RHYTHM AND BLUES PARTY (reissue)	15
89	Performance PFP 1004	RHYTHM OF THE RAIN — 16 HITS OF THE 60s	12
73	Tamla Motown STML 11232	RIC TIC RELICS	20
68	Coxsone CSL 8015	RIDE ME DONKEY	80+
69	Trojan TTL 18	RIDE YOUR DONKEY	12
86	SMP/Inferno SINLP 3	THE RIGHT TRACK	12
03	Dig The Fuzz DIG048	RIOT OF THE AMPHETAMINE GENERATION (400 copies only, with booklet)	40
55	Vogue Coral LRA 10023	RIVERBOAT JAZZ (10" LP)	15
71	London SHU 8245	RIVERTOWN BLUES	22
61	London HA-A 2338	ROCK-A-HITS	95
57	London HB-C 1067	ROCK 'N' ROLL (10")	110
59	London HA-E 2180	ROCK AND ROLL FOREVER	95
60	HMV DLP 1204	ROCKET ALONG — NEW BALLADS ON OLD LINES (10")	18
70s	Flynight FLY 662	ROCKIN' ACCORDION	12
58	Decca LF 1300	ROCKIN' AT THE '2 I'S' (10")	60
59	London HA-E 2167	ROCKIN' TOGETHER	80
63	Philips BL 7583	ROCKING GUITARS (LP)	30

69	Decca LK 5002	ROCK STEADY	18
69	Pama PMLP 7	ROCKSTEADY COOL	45
68	Coxsone CSL 8013	ROCKSTEADY COXSONE STYLE	130
80	Guardian GRC 80	ROKSNAX	50
68	Atlantic Special 590 019	ROOTS OF THE BLUES	15
82	Guardian GRC 130	ROXCALIBUR	70
77	Harvest SHSP 4069	THE ROXY LONDON W.C.2 (JAN - APR 77) (with inner bag)	12
94	Mo' Wax MWLP 003	ROYALTIES OVERDUE (2-LP, coloured vinyl)	60
84	Bam Caruso KIRI 024	RUBBLE 1: THE PSYCHEDELIC SNARL (with 8-page insert; first 2000 with inner sleeve and lightshow labels)	20
86	Bam Caruso KIRI 025	RUBBLE 2: POP-SIKE PIPE DREAMS (with inner sleeve)	20
86	Bam Caruso KIRI 026	RUBBLE 3: NIGHTMARES IN WONDERLAND (with inner sleeve)	20
88	Bam Caruso RUBBLE CD 2	RUBBLE 3: NIGHTMARES IN WONDERLAND (CD)	18
86	Bam Caruso KIRI 027	RUBBLE 4: THE 49 MINUTE TECHNICOLOUR DREAM (some with 4-page insert; first 2000 with inner sleeve and lightshow labels)	20
86	Bam Caruso KIRI 044	RUBBLE 5: THE ELECTRIC CRAYON SET (with inner sleeve)	15
86	Bam Caruso KIRI 049	RUBBLE 6: THE CLOUDS HAVE GROOVY FACES (with inner sleeve)	15
88	Bam Caruso KIRI 083	RUBBLE 7: PICTURES IN THE SKY (with inner sleeve)	15
91	Bam Caruso KIRI 051	RUBBLE 8: ALL THE COLOURS OF DARKNESS	15
85	Bam Caruso KIRI 065	RUBBLE 9: FROM THE HOUSE OF LORDS (1000 copies only)	18
91	Bam Caruso KIRI 079	RUBBLE 9: PLASTIC WILDERNESS	15
88	Bam Caruso KIRI 098	RUBBLE 10: PROFESSOR JORDAN'S MAGIC SOUND SHOW (with inner sleeve)	15
86	Bam Caruso KIRI 069	RUBBLE 11: ADVENTURES IN THE MIST (with inner sleeve)	20
86	Bam Caruso KIRI 070	RUBBLE 12: STAIRCASE TO NOWHERE (with inner sleeve)	20
89	Bam Caruso KIRI 102	RUBBLE 13: FREAK BEAT FANTOMS	20
88	Bam Caruso KIRI 106	RUBBLE 14: THE MAGIC ROCKING HORSE (with inner sleeve)	20
91	Bam Caruso KIRI 084	RUBBLE 15: 5000 SECONDS OVER TOYLAND	20
91	Bam Caruso KIRI 096	RUBBLE 16: GLASS ORCHID AFTERMATH	15
91	Bam Caruso KIRI 099	RUBBLE 17: A TRIP IN A PAINTED WORLD	20
92	Bam Caruso KIRI 101	RUBBLE 18: RAINBOW THYME WINDERS (unreleased, 25 test pressings only)	200
92	Bam Caruso KIRI 109	RUBBLE 19: EIDERDOWN MINDFOG (unreleased, 25 test pressings only)	200
90s	Bam Caruso KIRI 110	RUBBLE 20: THRICE UPON A TIME — NOTHING IS REAL (unreleased)	
92	Forty NME 40 LP	RUBY TRAX (3-LP, box set)	75
92	Forty NME 40 CD	RUBY TRAX (3-CD)	60
81	Naive NAIVE 2	RUPERT PREACHING AT A PICNIC (handmade sleeve)	25
69	Xtra XTRA 1035	RURAL BLUES (2-LP)	25
69	Liberty LBL 83213	RURAL BLUES VOLUME 1: GOIN' UP THE COUNTRY	25
69	Liberty LBL 83214	RURAL BLUES VOLUME 2: SATURDAY NIGHT FUNCTION	25
70	Liberty LBL 83329	RURAL BLUES VOLUME 3: DOWN HOME STOMP	25

S

70	Transworld SPLP 101	SAMANTHA PROMOTIONS (orange cover, private pressing, a few with poster)	500
70	Transworld SPLP 102	SAMANTHA PROMOTIONS (purple cover, private pressing, a few with poster)	500
60	Parlophone PMC 1130	SATURDAY CLUB	50
64	Decca LK 4583	SATURDAY CLUB	40
67	Atlantic Special 590 007	SATURDAY NIGHT AT THE APOLLO (reissue of "Apollo Saturday Night")	22
63	Brunswick LAT/STA 8520	SATURDAY NIGHT AT THE GRAND OLE OPRY	15
70	CBS 52799	SAVANNAH SYNCOPATORS	15
81	Suspect SU S3	SCENE OF THE CRIME	75
65	Columbia 33SX 1730	SCENE '65	150
74	Polydor 2383 282 A	SCOTLAND SCOTLAND (Scottish World Cup Squad/Rod Stewart/Dennis Law)	15
69	Bamboo BDLP 202	A SCORCHA FROM BAMBOO	40+
68	CBS 63288	SCREENING THE BLUES	25
95	Blue Eyed Dog VTDOG 12	SEARCH AND DISOBEY (2-LP, 10")	25
81	Airship AP 342	SEASIDE ROCK (2-LP, with insert)	20
81	Come Org. WDC 881008	THE SECOND COMING (various coloured vinyls)	30
84	Davies LP-D2 VOR 8	A SECRET LIVERPOOL (1-sided cardboard sleeve or 2-sided normal sleeve)	25/20
87	Cherry Red BRED 74	SEEDS I: POP (TV Personalities/Marine Girls, et al.)	30
87	Cherry Red BRED 76	SEEDS II: ART (Punishment Of Luxury/Nightingales, et al.)	15
68	Elektra EUK 261	SELECT ELEKTRA (also stereo EUKS 7261)	30
80	Kathedral KATH 1	SENT FROM COVENTRY (with booklet)	15
88	Sarah SARAH 587	SHADOW FACTORY (The Sea Urchins/14 Iced Bears, et al.)	18
68	Atlantic 587 109	SHAKE, RATTLE AND ROCK	25
74	Topic 12TS 234	SEA SHANTIES	15
78	GVR 201	THE SHANTY MEN	18
74	Eron 003	SHEPWAY FOLK (with insert)	30
78	Virgin VCL 5003	SHORT CIRCUIT — LIVE AT THE ELECTRIC CIRCUS (10"; orange, yellow, blue or black vinyl)	70/40/12/7
78	Virgin VCL 5003	SHORT CIRCUIT — LIVE AT THE ELECTRIC CIRCUS (10"; black vinyl with free John Dowie EP [VED 1004])	12
90	Horaces HRH 101	SHRINE — THE RAREST SOUL LABEL	12
87	ABC NOSE 15	SICK SICK SICK	12
76	Topic 12TS 281	THE SILVER BOW — SHETLAND FOLK FIDDLING VOL. 1	15
66	Chess CRL 4519	SING A SONG OF SOUL	40
57	RCA Camden CDN 147	SINGIN' THE BLUES	12
79	Sire SMP 1	THE SIRE MACHINE TURNS YOU UP	12
57	Parlophone PMC 1047	SIX-FIVE SPECIAL	50
76	BBC REB 252	SIX-FIVE SPECIAL	12
71	Pama PMP 2015	16 DYNAMIC REGGAE HITS	30
66	Island ILP 930	SKA AT THE JAMAICA PLAYBOY CLUB (gatefold sleeve)	200
67	Coxsone CSL 8003	SKA-A-GO-GO	90
66	Doctor Bird DLM 5000	SKA-BOO-DA-BA	150
67	Studio One SOL 9000	SKA TO ROCKSTEADY	100

60s	Page One FOR 006	SKA'S THE LIMIT.	15
68	Ace Of Clubs ACL 1250	SKIFFLE.	35
80s	Kent KENT 052	SMART! 16 IMMACULATE CUTS TAILORED FOR STYLE.	12
81	RSB 1	THE SNOOPIES ALBUM (THE LAST REMAINS OF A RICHMOND VENUE) (numbered, with booklet, 1,000 only)	20
67	Polydor 583 064	SOCK IT TO 'EM	20
60s	Solar	THE SOLAR BOX SET	40
70s	United Artists LBR 1007	SOLD ON SOUL.	15
71	Bamboo BDLP 212	SOLID GOLD	50
66	Atlantic ATL 5048	SOLID GOLD SOUL.	22
67	Atlantic 587 058	SOLID GOLD SOUL VOL. 2	22
75	Disco Demand DDLP 5002	SOLID SOUL SENSATIONS	18
81	Some Bizzare BZLP 1	THE SOME BIZZARE ALBUM.	12
72	South. Preservation SPR 1	SOME COLD RAINY DAY	25
75	Flyright LP 114	SOME COLD RAINY DAY (reissue)	15
65	Lestar LLP 101	SOME FOLK IN LEICESTER (private pressing)	20
58	Decca LK 4292	SOMETHING NEW FROM AFRICA.	18
70	Pama PMP 2003	SOMETHING SWEET FROM THE LADY	45
60	Topic 12001	SONGS AGAINST THE BOMB	12
72	Argo ZDA 147	SONGS AND MUSIC OF THE REDCOATS	15
77	Topic 12T 317	SONGS & SOUTHERN BREEZES — COUNTRY SINGERS FROM HAMPSHIRE & SUSSEX	15
77	private pressing	SONGS AT A SUSSEX FEAST	12
79	EMI NUT 18	SONGS LENNON AND McCARTNEY GAVE AWAY.	12
67	Fontana STL 5436	SONGS OF GRIEF AND GLORY.	12
69	Liberty LBX 4	SON OF GUTBUCKET.	20
76	Harvest SHSM 2012	SON OF MORRIS ON	50
83	Syndicate SYNLP 3	SON OF OI!	15
72	Probe SPB 1061	SOUL BIBLE.	15
69	Direction (S)PR 28	SOUL DIRECTION	25
69	Page One POS 608	SOULED AGAIN.	20
69	Polydor 584 163	SOUL FEVER.	20
60s	Minit MLL 40011E	SOUL FOOD.	40
69	Soul City SCB 1	SOUL FROM THE CITY.	45
70	Specialty SPE 6606	SOUL FROM THE VAULTS	15
74	Trojan TRL 65	SOULFUL REGGAE.	12
70	Polydor 583 757	SOUL GOLD.	18
72	Avco 6467 251	SOUL — IN THE BEGINNING —	12
68	Trojan TRL 3	SOUL OF JAMAICA.	35
68	Polydor Special 236 213	SOUL PARTY	20
69	Pama PMLP 8	SOUL SAUCE FROM PAMA	20+
69	Polydor 236 554	SOUL SELLER.	18
70s	United Artists UAL 229018	SOUL SENSATION.	15
66	Stateside SL 10186	SOUL SIXTEEN	45
66	Sue ILP 934	SOUL '66	75
67	CBS BPG 62965	SOUL SOUNDS	40
67	HMV CLP 3617	SOUL SOUNDS OF THE 60s	45
67	Stateside SL 10203	SOUL SUPPLY	50
86	SMP/Inferno SIMLP 4	SOUL TIME.	12
65	Pye Intl. NPL 28061	THE SOUND OF BACHARACH	20
95	EMI EMI 8322 801	THE SOUND GALLERY.	20
58	Fontana TFL 5025	THE SOUND OF JAZZ.	15
68	President PTL 1008	THE SOUND OF SOUL	30
72	United Artists UAS 29215	SOUND OF THE CITY.	12
79	Grapevine GRAL 1001	SOUND OF THE GRAPEVINE.	20
64	Stateside SL 10077	THE SOUND OF THE R&B HITS	75
69	Joy JOY 125	SOUNDS LIKE SKA.	12
70	Sentinel SENS 1001	SOUNDS LIKE WEST CORNWALL	20
78	Sonet SNTF 806	SOUTHEND ROCK	12
69	London HAK 8405	SOUTHERN COMFORT.	30
83	Spectrum ASPEC 001	SOUTHERN COMFORT.	75
80s	Spectrum ASPEC 003	SOUTHERN COMFORT 3	50
60s	Saydisc Roots RL 328	SOUTHERN SANCTIFIED SINGERS	15
61	London Jazz LTZ-K 15209	SOUTHERN FOLK HERITAGE VOLUME 1: SOUNDS OF THE SOUTH	20
61	London Jazz LTZ-K 15210	SOUTHERN FOLK HERITAGE VOLUME 2: BLUE RIDGE MOUNTAIN MUSIC.	20
61	London Jazz LTZ-K 15211	SOUTHERN FOLK HERITAGE VOLUME 3: ROOTS OF THE BLUES	20
61	London Jazz LTZ-K 15209	SOUTHERN FOLK HERITAGE VOLUME 7: THE BLUES ROLL ON	20
54	London AL 3529	SOUTHSIDE CHICAGO JAZZ (10")	18
71	Python PLP 10	SOUTHSIDE CHICAGO (99 copies only).	40
70	CBS Special Prod. WSR 932	SPARKLING COLOUR (multicoloured vinyl)	12
58	Tempo TAP 17	SPEAK LOW — MORE MUSIC IN THE MODERN MANNER	100+
73	Tempo TMP 9001	SPIN A MAGIC TUNE.	20
57	Pye Nixa NPT 19019	SPIN WITH THE STARS — SELECTION NO. 2 (10")	18
57	Pye Nixa NPT 19021	SPIN WITH THE STARS — SELECTION NO. 3 (10")	18
65	Fontana TL 5243	SPIRITUAL AND GOSPEL FESTIVAL	20
59	Top Rank 35/064	SPIRITUALS TO SWING VOLUME 1	15
59	Top Rank 35/065	SPIRITUALS TO SWING VOLUME 2	15
82	WEA K 58415	A SPLASH OF COLOUR.	15
62	Liberty LBY 1001	THE STARS OF LIBERTY	30
57	Decca LF 1299	STARS OF THE 6.5 SPECIAL (10")	50
84	Broken Flag BF V5	STATEMENT.	40
84	Pleasantly Surprised PS 3	STATE OF AFFAIRS (cassette, in poly bag with foldout booklet & insert)	20
85	Statik POL 274	STATIK COMPILATION ONE (2-LP)	20
04	Ai AILP 006	STATION (2-LP, clear vinyl, 1000 copies only)	15

69	Stax XATS 1007	STAX SOUL EXPLOSION	18
70s	Stax STXH 5004	THE STAX STORY (VOL. 1)	20
70s	Stax STXH 5005	THE STAX STORY (VOL. 1)	15
67	Stax 589 010	THE STAX/VOLT SHOW VOL. 1	20
67	Stax 589 011	THE STAX/VOLT SHOW VOL. 2	20
78	Stiff GET 1	STIFFS LIVE STIFFS	12
60	Topic 10T 59	STILL I LOVE HIM	12
84	ABC ABCLP 3	STOMPING AT THE KLUB FOOT VOL. 1	12
84	ABC ABCLP 4	STOMPING AT THE KLUB FOOT VOL. 2	12
69	CBS 66218	THE STORY OF THE BLUES (2-LP)	20
70	CBS 66232	THE STORY OF THE BLUES VOLUME 2 (2-LP)	20
94	Tenth Planet TP 010	THE STORY OF OAK RECORDS	25
94	Wooden Hill WHCD 007	THE STORY OF OAK RECORDS (CD)	18
70	Pama PMP 2002	STRAIGHTEN UP	20
71	Pama PMP 2007	STRAIGHTEN UP VOLUME TWO	20
71	Pama PMP 2014	STRAIGHTEN UP VOLUME THREE	20
72	Pama PMP 2017	STRAIGHTEN UP VOLUME FOUR	15
77	Beggars Banquet BEGA 1	STREETS	15
80s	Streetsounds	STREETSOUND ELECTRO (box set)	70
83	Streetsounds ELCST 1	STREETSOUND ELECTRO 1	18
83	Streetsounds ELCST 2	STREETSOUND ELECTRO 2	18
84	Streetsounds ELCST 3	STREETSOUND ELECTRO 3	18
84	Streetsounds ELCST 4	STREETSOUND ELECTRO 4	18
79	Open Eye OE LP 501	STREET TO STREET – A LIVERPOOL ALBUM	20
81	Open Eye OE LP 502	STREET TO STREET – A LIVERPOOL ALBUM VOL. 2	12
81	Decca SKIN 1	STRENGTH THROUGH OI!	50
85	Wonderful World WOWLP 3	STRENGTH THROUGH OI! (reissue)	20
80s	Private Pressing CFCEPI	STUFF THE NEIGHBOURS, PLAY IT LOUD (p/s, in poly bag, with fanzine)	12
86	Sub Pop SP 0010	SUB POP 100	20
81	Chick CHR 001	SUBWAY (clear vinyl)	15
80s	INST-4	SUCK	12
98	Sorted SRLP 04	SUCTION PRINTS (handpainted or wraparound sleeve)	35/15
65	Sue ILP 919	SUE SAMPLER RECORD FOR CLUBS (promo, no sleeve, typed labels with detail sheet)	120
65	London HA-C 8239	THE SUE STORY	55
65	Sue ILP 925	THE SUE STORY!	60
69	United Artists UAS 29028	THE SUE STORY (reissue)	20
66	Sue ILP 933	THE SUE STORY VOL. 2	60
66	Sue ILP 938	THE SUE STORY VOL. 3	60
76	Giorno GPS	SUGAR, ALCOHOL & MEAT	20
82	CBS 22139	SUMMER MEANS FUN (2-LP)	20
75	Island ISS 1	SUMMER '75 (promo-only sampler)	15
66	Reprise R 5031	THE SUMMIT	50
86	Sun/Charly BOX 105	SUN RECORDS: THE BLUES YEARS (9-LP box with booklet)	60
81	Sunset Gun	SUNSET GUN (cassette with *Sunset Gun* fanzine)	15
68	Ember NR 5038	SUNSTROKE	20
73	Philips 6369 416	SUPER BLACK BLUES	18
69	Blue Horizon (S)PR 31	SUPER DUPER BLUES	25
70	Polydor 2485 002	SUPERGROUPS	12
70	Polydor 2485 003	SUPERGROUPS VOL. 2	12
68	Pye Intl. NPL 28107	SUPER SOUL	25
74	People PLEO 24	SUPER SWEET SOUL	15
64	Vocalion VA 8018	SURF BATTLE	60
86	Capitol EMS 1180	SURF CITY/DRAG CITY	22
88	Decal LIK 39	SURFERS STOMP	22
71	Blue Horizon 7-66263	SWAMP BLUES (2-LP)	75
68	Stateside S(S)L 10243	SWEET SOUL SOUNDS	50
68	Coxsone CSL 8018	SWING EASY	125
68	Saga FID 2136	SWINGING SAGA	15
58	Tempo TAP 21	SWINGIN' THE BLUES	25
93	Tenth Planet TP 002	SYDE TRYPS ONE (numbered, 500 only, with insert)	25
93	Tenth Planet TP 004	SYDE TRYPS TWO ... FROM THERE TO UNCERTAINTY (numbered, 500 only, with insert)	25
93	Tenth Planet TP 006	SYDE TRYPS THREE (numbered, 500 only, with insert)	25
94	Tenth Planet TP 008	SYDE TRYPS FOUR (numbered, 500 only, with insert)	25
96	Tenth Planet TP 024	SYDE TRYPS SIX (numbered, gatefold sleeve, 1,000 only)	18

T

72	Rubber RUB 001	TAKE OFF YOUR HEAD AND LISTEN	15
71	A&M Mayfair AMLB 51029	TAKE ONE	12
86	Subway Org. SUBORG 001	TAKE THE SUBWAY TO YOUR SUBURB (mini-LP, red or yellow sleeve)	12
78	Grapevine GRAL 1000	TALK OF THE GRAPEVINE	25
65	London HA-B 8250	THE TALL 12	12
67	London HA-B 8315	THE TALL 12 VOL. 2	12
80	Fuck Off (no cat. no)	TAPEZINE 2 (cassette)	15
58	Capitol T 1009	TEENAGE ROCK (turquoise or 'rainbow' label)	55/50
63	Stateside SL 10020	TENNESSEE GUITAR	20
56	Nixa Jazz Today NJL 4	TENORAMA	100
77	Talisman STAL 1051	10 YEARS ON – THE UNIVERSAL FOLK CENTRE (LP)	20
70s	Fountain FV 205	TEXAS BLUES	18
69	Highway 51 H 103	TEXAS-LOUISIANA BLUES (99 copies only)	60
62	Ace Of Clubs ACL 1108	THANK YOUR LUCKY STARS	25
63	Golden Guinea GGL 0190	THANK YOUR LUCKY STARS	15
63	Decca LK 4554	THANK YOUR LUCKY STARS VOLUME 2	35
72	Dandelion 2485 021	THERE IS SOME FUN GOING FORWARD (with poster)	18

69	Action ACLP 6009	THESE KIND OF BLUES VOL. 1	100
82	MCA MCA 6111	THE THING	20
81	TTFTC 001	THE THING FROM THE CRYPT (I NEARLY DIED LAUGHING)	15
57	Tempo TAP 11	THIRD BRITISH FESTIVAL OF JAZZ	15
80s	Come Org. WDC 881021	33 FÜR ILSE KOCH (some on red vinyl)	70
68	Minit MLL/MLS 40002	THIRTY-THREE MINITS OF BLUES AND SOUL	45
83	2-Tone CHR TT 5007	THIS ARE 2-TONE (with free poster, green or pink sleeve)	15
64	Island ILP 910	THIS IS BLUE BEAT (unreleased, white labels unconfirmed)	200+
69	Island IWP 5	THIS IS THE BLUES	25
69	Chess CRL 4540	THIS IS CHESS	30
72	Peg PS 2	THIS IS FOLK VOL. 1	12
72	Peg PS 3	THIS IS FOLK VOL. 2	12
76	Loma/Warners K 56265	THIS IS LOMA VOL. 1	20
76	Loma/Warners K 56266	THIS IS LOMA VOL. 2	20
76	Loma/Warners K 56267	THIS IS LOMA VOL. 3	20
76	Loma/Warners K 56268	THIS IS LOMA VOL. 4	20
76	Loma/Warners K 56269	THIS IS LOMA VOL. 5	20
76	Loma/Warners K 56270	THIS IS LOMA VOL. 6	20
63	Oriole PS 40047	THIS IS MERSEYBEAT VOL. 1	70
63	Oriole PS 40048	THIS IS MERSEYBEAT VOL. 2	70
80	Grapevine GRAL 1002	THIS IS NORTHERN SOUL	30
69	Pama PSP 1003	THIS IS REGGAE	20
71	Pama PMP 2005	THIS IS REGGAE VOLUME TWO	15
71	Pama PMP 2008	THIS IS REGGAE VOLUME THREE	15
72	Pama PMP 2016	THIS IS REGGAE VOLUME FOUR	15
60s	Island IWP 3	THIS IS SUE!	30
60	Philips BBL 7356	THIS WONDERFUL WORLD OF JAZZ	12
63	RCA RD/SF 7608	THE THREE GREAT GUYS (Paul Anka, Sam Cooke & Neil Sedaka)	30
70	Saydisc Matchbox SDR182	THOSE CAKEWALKIN' BABIES FROM HOME	22
66	Allegro ALL 807	THUNDERBALL AND OTHER SECRET AGENT THEMES	15
69	Trojan TTL 7	TIGHTEN UP VOLUME TWO (pink Island label with different track listing & sleeve)	40+
69	Parlophone PMC 7072	THAT TODDLIN' TOWN — CHICAGO (1926-1928)	12
71	CBS SPR 52	TOGETHER!	12
92	Too Pure SFRLP 119	TOO PURE — THE PEEL SESSIONS (LP, limited issue, custom sleeve)	35
64	Ember FA 2018	TOPS OF THE POPS	12
64	Golden Guinea GGL 0277	TOP 10 HITS, ORIGINAL ARTISTS	15
63	Golden Guinea GGL 0196	TOP TV THEMES	15
70	Marble Arch MALS 1359	TOP TV SOUNDTRACK THEMES	15
72	Studio 2 TWO 391	TOP TV THEMES AND COMMERCIALS	30
82	Zoo ZOO 4	TO THE SHORES OF LAKE PLACID (gatefold sleeve with 4-page booklet)	18
64	Topic TPS 114	TOPIC SAMPLER NO. 1 — FOLK SONGS (blue label)	20
66	Topic TPS 145	TOPIC SAMPLER NO. 2 — FOLK SONGS (blue label)	20
66	Topic TPS 166	TOPIC SAMPLER NO. 3 — MEN AT WORK (blue label)	20
66	Topic TPS 168	TOPIC SAMPLER NO. 4 — FROM ERIN'S GREEN SHORE (blue label)	20
66	Topic TPS 205	TOPIC SAMPLER No. 7 — SEA SONGS & SHANTIES (blue label)	20
72	Topic TPSS 221	TOPIC SAMPLER NO. 8 — ENGLISH GARLAND (blue label)	20
56	Tempo TAP 4	TOP TRUMPETS	12
90s	Acid Jazz JAZIDLP 13	TOTALLY WIRED	15
90s	Acid Jazz JAZIDLP 16	TOTALLY WIRED VOLUME TWO	15
90s	Acid Jazz JAZIDLP 22	TOTALLY WIRED VOLUME THREE	15
90s	Acid Jazz JAZIDLP 103	TOTALLY WIRED SWEDEN	15
55	Decca LK 4088	TRADITIONAL JAZZ AT THE ROYAL FESTIVAL HALL	15
55	Decca LK 4100	TRADITIONAL JAZZ AT THE ROYAL FESTIVAL HALL VOL. 2	15
77	Free Reed FRRD 021/022	THE TRANSPORTS (2-LP, with book)	60
76	Eron 006	TRAVELLING FOLK (with insert)	25
70	RCA Intl. INTS 1175	TRAVELLING THIS LONESOME ROAD	12
61	'77' LA 12-2	A TREASURY OF FIELD RECORDINGS VOLUME 1	30
61	'77' LA 12-3	A TREASURY OF FIELD RECORDINGS VOLUME 2	30
61	Embassy WLP 6041	TRIBUTE TO CLIFF	15
60	Embassy WLP 6034	TRIBUTE TO ELVIS	15
64	Columbia 33SX 1635	TRIBUTE TO MICHAEL HOLLIDAY	25
72	CBS 64861	A TRIBUTE TO WOODY GUTHRIE PART 1 (gatefold sleeve)	12
69	Key KL 003	A TRIBUTE TO YOUTH PRAISE	40
80	Skeleton SKL LP 1	A TRIP TO THE DENTIST (with insert)	15
61	Parlophone PMC 1139	TRIPLE TREAT	20
80	Skeleton SKLLP 1	A TRIP TO THE DENTIST (with insert)	30
50s	Esquire 32-036	TROMBONE BY THREE	12
71	Revival RVS 1007	TROUBLE IN MIND... (GEORGIA BLUES)	15
67	Riverside RLP 8802	TUB JUG WASHBOARD BANDS	15
74	Melodisc 12-193	12 BIG HITS	15
74	Melodisc 12-217	12 CARAT GOLD	20
60s	Envoy VOY 9159	12 STRING STORY	12
63	Fontana 688 0082L	12 STRING GUITAR: THE FOLK SINGERS	15
66	London HA-F/SH-F 8285	THE TWELVE-STRING STORY — GUITAR SOLOS	18
79	Polydor POLS 1006	20 OF ANOTHER KIND	20
83	VCL VCLP 007	21ST ANNIVERSARY INSTRUMENTAL ALBUM	12
65	Ember EMB 3359	25 YEARS OF RHYTHM & BLUES HITS	45
89	WEA 241 690-1	TWIST & SHOUT — 12 ATLANTIC TRACKS PRODUCED BY PHIL SPECTOR (gatefold sleeve)	25
63	Philips BL 7578	TWIST AT THE STAR-CLUB, HAMBURG	70

U-V

68	BBC REC 28M	ULSTER'S FLOWERY VALE	20
69	Island ILP 993/ILPS 9093	THE UNFOLDING OF THE BOOK OF LIFE VOL. 1	18

70s	Flyright FLY 577	UNISSUED CHICAGO BLUES	12
72	Nevis NEV R 007	UNITY CREATES STRENGTH.	25
69	Pama ECO 7	UNITY'S GREATEST	40
88	Unicorn PHZA 17	UNSUNG HEROES (red vinyl)	15
80	Safari UPP 1	UPPERS ON THE SOUTH DOWNS (original issue without Purple Hearts)	12
68	Atlantic 588 122	UPTOWN SOUL	20
88	Urban URBLP 15	URBAN ACID	15
77	Specialty SNTF 5023	URBAN BLUES	12
69	Liberty LBL 83215	URBAN BLUES VOLUME 1: BLUES UPTOWN.	25
70	Liberty LBL 83327	URBAN BLUES VOLUME 2: NEW ORLEANS BOUNCE	22
80	Pungent PUN 1	URBAN DEVELOPMENT (cassette, with/without *Fumes* fanzine).	20/12
72	Village Thing VTSAM 15	US	12
50s	Audubon AAM	VAUDEVILLE (10").	20
70	VJM VLP 30	VAUDEVILLE BLUES.	15
78	Attrix RB 03	VAULTAGE '78 (TWO SIDES OF BRIGHTON)	
		(originally hand-screened sleeve, later with insert)	20/15
71	Trojan TBL 175	VERSION GALORE VERSION TWO.	12
73	Trojan TBL 200	VERSION GALORE VERSION THREE.	12
72	Trojan TBL 182	VERSION TO VERSION.	12
73	Trojan TBL 206	VERSION TO VERSION VOLUME THREE.	12
70	Vertigo 6499 407/8	VERTIGO ANNUAL 1970 (2-LP, set no.: 6657 001).	30
87	BB BBLP 02	VINYL FRONTIER	12
55	Philips BBR 8071	VISIT TO JAZZLAND (10")	12
55	Philips	VISIT TO JAZZLAND NO. 2 (10")	12
56	Philips BBR 8098	VISIT TO JAZZLAND NO. 3 (10")	12

W

70s	Object Music OBJ 007	WAITING ROOM.	15
62	Columbia 33SX 1385	WAKEY WAKEY.	25
85	Psycho PSYCHO 35	THE WAKING DREAM.	15
64	Pye Intl. NPL 28041	WALKING BY MYSELF	40
64	Pye Intl. NPL 28044	WALKING THE BLUES	35
81	Phil Spector Intl. WOS 001	WALL OF SOUND (9-LP box set).	120
78	CBS WOW 100	THE WAR OF THE WORLDS (boxed 2-LP, book & poster).	18
63	Ace Of Hearts AH 55	WASHBOARD RHYTHM	15
70s	Polydor 218 006	WAY INTO THE 70'S	12
78	Bridgehouse BHLP 001	A WEEKEND AT THE BRIDGEHOUSE E16 (with bonus 12" EP)	30
57	Rainbow Records	WEEKEND FILM STAR RECORD ALBUM (5 x 8" flexi 78s,	
		mail order from *Weekend* magazine)	75
85	Music For Nations MFN 49	WELCOME TO THE METAL ZONE (2-LP)	18
59	Coral LVA 9096	WE LIKE GIRLS	25
59	Coral LVA 9098	WE LIKE GUYS	25
63	London HA-P 8061	WE SING THE BLUES.	80
65	Liberty LBY 3051	WE SING THE BLUES	60
65	Sue ILP 921	WE SING THE BLUES!	75
72	Syndicate Chapter SC 005	WE THREE KINGS.	15
70	Trojan TTL 34	WHAT AM I TO DO.	20
68	Elektra EKS 7304	WHAT'S SHAKIN' (reissue of "Good Time Music")	15
80	S & T	WHERE THE HELL IS LEICESTER? (with bonus single & booklet).	25
86	Sunrise A40 111M	WHERE WOULD YOU RATHER BE TONIGHT?	25
83	Kamera KAM 14	THE WHIP (with insert)	25
79	London Bomp DHS-Z 3	WHO PUT THE BOMP? (2-LP, gatefold sleeve)	20
70	Trojan TBL 131	WHO YOU GONNA RUN TO	50
72	private pressing	WHOLLY GRAIL	25
74	Topic 12TS 227	WILD HILLS O'WANNIE — THE SMALL PIPES OF NORTHUMBRIA	12
61	Philips BBL 7430	WINNERS OF DOWNBEAT'S INTERNATIONAL CRITICS' POLL 1960	12
66	Dot DLP 3535	WIPE OUT	25
76	RCA RS 1085	WIZARD'S CONVENTION (with insert)	12
82	Womad WOMAD 001	WOMAD: RAINDROPS CLATTERING ON BANANA LEAVES	15
67	RCA Victor RD 7840	WOMEN OF THE BLUES	20
81	Stiff FREEB 3	WONDERFUL TIME OUT THERE (Xmas freebie)	12
81	Glass GLASS 010	THE WONDERFUL WORLD OF GLASS	15
87	Black Crow CRO 217 A	WOODY LIVES: A TRIBUTE TO WOODY GUTHRIE	15
96	Magna Carta MA 9010/2	WORKING MAN	15
63	London HA-P 8099	A WORLD OF BLUES	40
69	Decca (S)PA-R 14	THE WORLD OF BLUES POWER	12
70	Decca (S)PA 63	THE WORLD OF BLUES POWER VOL. 2	12
73	Decca SPA 263	THE WORLD OF BLUES POWER VOL. 3	18
69	Pama SECO 19	A WORLD OF BULLET	50
71	Decca SPA 156	WORLD OF CONTEMPORARY FOLK	12
71	Argo SPA-A 132	THE WORLD OF FOLK	20
73	Argo SPA-A 307	THE WORLD OF FOLK VOLUME 2	20
78	Yuk NE 1023	THE WORLD'S WORST RECORD SHOW (multi-coloured vinyl)	20
69	Decca (S)PA 34	WOWIE ZOWIE! — THE WORLD OF PROGRESSIVE MUSIC	15

Y-Z

70s	P. Spec. Intl. PSI 2307 007	YESTERDAY'S HITS TODAY	12
	Cathexis/Pleasantly	YOU BET WE'VE GOT SOMETHING AGAINST YOU	50
	Surprised PS 014		
69	Island IWPS 2	YOU CAN ALL JOIN IN (pink label)	15
70	Trojan TBL 142	YOU CAN'T WINE	15
69	Trojan TTL 9	YOU LEFT ME STANDING	25
69	Young Blood SBYB 1	YOUNGBLOOD VOL. 1	15
78	Stiff DEAL 1	YOU'RE EITHER ON THE TRAIN OR OFF THE TRAIN	
		(promo only, with booklet)	12

62	HMV CLP 1565	YOUR FAVOURITE TV AND RADIO THEMES	15
63	HMV CLP 1676	YOUR FAVOURITE TV AND RADIO THEMES (VOL. 3)	15
63	HMV CLP 1762	YOUR FAVOURITE TV AND RADIO THEMES (VOL. 4)	15
66	HMV CLP 3521	YOUR FAVOURITE TV AND RADIO THEMES (VOL. 5)	15
71	Bamboo BDLP 211	YOUR JAMAICAN GIRL	70
82	Statik STATLP 7	YOUR SECRET'S SAFE WITH US (2-LP)	20
84	Zulu ZULU 6	THE ZULU COMPILATION	20

FILM & TV SOUNDTRACK LPs
(alphabetical by title, composers/artists in brackets)

(N.B. Only the first issues of soundtracks by the Beatles and Elvis Presley are listed below:
for later repressings see their individual entries.)

A

73	United Artists UAS 29451	ACROSS 110TH STREET (J.J. Johnson & Bobby Womack).	30
70	Paramount SPFL 260	THE ADVENTURERS (Antonio Carlos Jobim)	12
62	RCA RD 7512	ADVISE AND CONSENT (Jerry Fielding)	15
64	Parlophone PMC 1230	A HARD DAY'S NIGHT (Beatles) (1st pressing, with "The Parlophone Co. Ltd" label rim copy & "Sold In The UK..." text; mono, with mid-sized "mono" lettering on front cover)	40
64	Parlophone PCS 3058	A HARD DAY'S NIGHT (Beatles) (1st pressing, with "The Parlophone Co. Ltd" label rim copy & "Sold In The UK..." text; stereo, with mid-sized "stereo" lettering on front cover)	100
67	United Artists (S)ULP 1172	AFRICA ADDIO (Riz Ortolani/Jimmy Roselli)	20
66	United Artists (S)ULP 1151	AFTER THE FOX (Burt Bacharach/Hollies)	35
60	Philips BBL 7429	THE ALAMO (also stereo SBBL 599) (Dimitri Tiomkin)	12/15
56	Nixa NPT 19010	ALEXANDER THE GREAT (Mario Nascimbene) (10"; beware of counterfeits). . .	150
69	MGM CS 8112	ALFRED THE GREAT (Ray Leppard).	150
72	Warner Bros K 56009	ALICE'S ADVENTURES IN WONDERLAND (John Barry) (gatefold sleeve)	15
79	20th Century T 593	ALIEN (Jerry Goldsmith)	20
61	Fontana (S)TFL 591	ALL NIGHT LONG (mono/stereo, Dave Brubeck/Johnny Dankworth, et al.) . . .	25/35
71	Buddah 2318 034	ALL THE RIGHT NOISES (Melanie)	15
65	Reprise R 6151	AMERICANIZATION OF EMILY (Johnny Mandel)	20
65	RCA RD 7732	THE AMOROUS ADVENTURES OF MOLL FLANDERS (John Addison)	35
57	Brunswick LAT 8175	ANASTASIA (Alfred Newman)	15
60	Philips SBBL 514	ANATOMY OF A MURDER (Duke Ellington)	15
76	BBC REB 236	ANGELS AND 15 OTHER BBC TV THEMES (Alan Parker, et al.)	15
72	Polydor 2383 109	ANTONY AND CLEOPATRA (John Scott) (foldout sleeve)	35
60	London HA-T 2287	THE APARTMENT (Adolph Deutsch).	15
79	Elektra K 62025	APOCALYPSE NOW (2-LP, music & dialogue).	20
69	CBS 70054	APRIL FOOLS (Marvin Hamlisch)	15
58	London HA-D 2078	APRIL LOVE (Pat Boone/Shirley Jones/Lionel Newman Orchestra)	12
66	RCA Victor RD 7817	ARABESQUE (Henry Mancini)	15
66	Fontana FJL 135	L'ASCENSEUR POUR L'ECHAFAUD/FEMME DISPARAISSANTE (Miles Davis/Art Blakey [1 side each])	50
54	HMV DLPC 1	AS LONG AS THEY'RE HAPPY (Jack Buchanan) (10")	50
87	Illegal ILP 017	ATHENS, GA. — INSIDE/OUT (R.E.M.)	12
67	Pye NPL 18198	AT LAST THE 1948 SHOW (TV soundtrack).	25
67	Marble Arch MAL 695	THE AVENGERS AND OTHER FAVOURITES (Laurie Johnson)	35

B

66	Fontana TL 5306	BABY, THE RAIN MUST FALL (Elmer Bernstein).	40
62	Pye Intl. NPL 28020	BARABBAS (Mario Nascimbene)	18
68	Stateside (S)SL 10260	BARBARELLA (Bob Crewe/Charles Fox)	100
67	London HA-D 8337	BAREFOOT IN THE PARK (Neal Hefti)	30
75	Warner Bros K 56189	BARRY LYNDON (Leonard Rosenman).	18
66	Stateside S(S)L 10179	BATMAN (Nelson Riddle) (TV show music)	50
89	W.B./Paisley Park WX 281P	BATMAN (Prince) (picture disc, die-cut sleeve).	12
89	W.B./Paisley Park 925 978-2	BATMAN (Prince) (CD, picture disc in 'Bat' tin with booklet).	25
69	United Artists UAS 29019	BATTLE OF BRITAIN (Ron Goodwin)	12
66	Warner Bros W 1617	BATTLE OF THE BULGE (Benjamin Frankel)	25
60	Columbia 33SX 1225	BEAT GIRL (John Barry/Adam Faith)	50
57	London HAP 2056	BEAU JAMES (Joseph Lilley)	30
64	RCA Victor RD 7679	BECKET (dialogue only).	15
68	Decca LK/SKL 4923	BEDAZZLED (Peter Cook/Dudley Moore).	100
70	Island ILPS 9140	BE GLAD FOR THE SONG HAS NO ENDING (Incredible String Band).	15
60	Capitol W/SW 1435	BELLS ARE RINGING (André Previn) (mono/stereo)	15/18
73	Ronco RR 2006	THE BELSTONE FOX (Laurie Johnson) (gatefold sleeve)	15
60	MGM MGM-C(S) 802	BEN HUR (Miklos Rozsa) (box set with hardback book; mono/stereo)	15/20
70	Stateside SSL 10311	BEYOND THE VALLEY OF THE DOLLS (Stu Phillips/Strawberry Alarm Clock). . .	90
66	Stateside S(S)L 10188	THE BIBLE (Toshiro Mayuzumi)	15
59	London HA-T 2142	THE BIG COUNTRY (Jerome Moross) ('sun' cover)	15
61	HMV CSD 1408	THE BIG COUNTRY (Jerome Moross) ('cast' cover)	12
68	MGM MGM-C(S) 8066	BIGGEST BUNDLE OF THEM ALL (Riz Ortolani/Eric Burdon)	20
86	MCA MCF 3328	BIGGLES (Stanislas/Deep Purple/Motley Crue et al.)	18
69	United Artists (S)ULP 1228	THE BIG GUNDOWN (Ennio Morricone)	20
67	United Artists (S)ULP 1183	BILLION DOLLAR BRAIN (Richard Rodney Bennett)	40
73	Polydor 2490 117	BLACK CAESAR (James Brown)	50
79	Pickwick SHM 3017	THE BLACK HOLE (John Barry)	12
62	Stateside SL 10026	BLACK NATIVITY (Alex Bradford)	20
72	Pye NSPL 18376	BLOOMFIELD.	35
66	MGM MGM-C(S) 8039	BLOW-UP (Herbie Hancock/Yardbirds).	80
68	Dot (S)LPD 508	BLUE (Manos Hadjidakis).	30

61	RCA RD 27238/SF 5115	BLUE HAWAII (Elvis Presley) (black/silver label, mono/stereo) 25/40
66	RCA RD 7795	BOEING BOEING (Neal Hefti). 30
69	MCA MUPS 360	BOOM! (John Barry/Georgie Fame) 50
68	Warner Bros W 1742	BONNIE AND CLYDE (Charles Strouse) 20
66	MGM MGM-C(S) 8010	BORN FREE (John Barry/Matt Monro,1st pressing) 20
70	Paramount SPFL 263	BORSALINO (Claude Bolling) 15
58	RCA RD 27054	BOTH ENDS OF THE CANDLE (Gogi Grant) 15
57	Brunswick LAT 8193	BOY ON A DOLPHIN (Hugo Friedhoffer). 40
79	A&M AMLH 64731	THE BOYS FROM BRAZIL (Jerry Goldsmith/Elaine Paige) 15
77	United Artists UAG 30097	A BRIDGE TOO FAR (John Addison) (gatefold sleeve) 12
80	MCA MCF 2013	BUCK ROGERS IN THE 25th CENTURY (Stu Phillips) 12
71	Capitol E-SW 621	THE BUGALOOS (LP). 18
72	Bell BELLS 209	THE BURGLARS (Ennio Morricone) 30
66	RCA RD 7791	BUNNY LAKE IS MISSING (Paul Glass/Zombies) 60
65	Liberty LBY 1246	BURKE'S LAW (Herschel/Burke/Gilbert) (TV series music) 15
63	RCA Victor RD/SF 7580	BYE BYE BIRDIE (musical) (Charles Strouse; mono/stereo) 18/20

C

56	Philips BBR 8104	CALAMITY JANE (Doris Day/Howard Keel) (10"). 18
66	RCA Victor RD/SF 7820	CALIFORNIA HOLIDAY (Elvis Presley) (black/red dot labels, mono/stereo) . . . 25/40
69	Stateside (S)SL 10276	CANDY (Dave Grusin/Steppenwolf, et al.) 20
69	MCA MUPS 380	CAN HIERONYMUS MERKIN EVER FORGET MERCY HUMPPE
		AND FIND TRUE HAPPINESS? (Anthony Newley) 15
64	Philips SBL 7634	CAPTAIN FROM CASTILE (Robert Farnon) 12
60	Delyse DL 3057/DLS 6057	CAPTAIN HORATIO HORNBLOWER (Robert Farnon) (mono/stereo). 60/75
86	Virgin V 2401	CAPTIVE (The Edge et al.) 12
64	MGM MGM-C 984	THE CARPETBAGGERS (Elmer Bernstein) 12
64	London HA-A/SH-A 8219	THE CARPETBAGGERS (Elmer Bernstein) 15
67	RCA Victor RD/SF 7874	CASINO ROYALE (Burt Bacharach/Herb Alpert/Dusty Springfield)
		(mono/stereo) 50/60
66	United Artists (S)ULP 1140	CAST A GIANT SHADOW (Elmer Bernstein/Vince Hill) 18
71	Polydor 2383 035	CATCH MY SOUL (P.J. Proby/P.P. Arnold, et al.) 15
65	Columbia SX 1756	CATCH US IF YOU CAN (Dave Clark Five) . . . . 50+
62	Fontana TFL 5170/STFL 585	CHANNEL THRILL: THE T.V. THRILLER THEMES (Johnny Gregory) 12/15
62	Warner Bros WS 8177	THE CHAPMAN REPORT (Leonard Rosenman) 15
63	RCA SF 7620	CHARADE (Henry Mancini) 30
63	MGM MGM-C 969	THE CHARGE IS MURDER (John Green) 20
68	United Artists SULP 1189	THE CHARGE OF THE LIGHT BRIGADE (John Addison/Manfred Mann) . . . 25
83	Polydor BOX 1	CHARIOTS OF FIRE (Vangelis) (box set) 12
66	CBS (S)BPG 62665	THE CHASE (John Barry) (mono/stereo). 30/40
69	Polydor 583 736	CHE! (Lalo Schifrin) 15
67	Fontana TL 5417	CHIMES AT MIDNIGHT (Angelo Lavagnino) 30
74	ABC ABCL 5068	CHINATOWN (Jerry Goldsmith) 20
68	United Artists (S)ULP 1200	CHITTY CHITTY BANG BANG (Sherman Brothers) (gatefold sleeve) 15
68	RCA Victor RD/SF 7917	CLAMBAKE (Elvis Presley) (black/red dot labels, mono/stereo) 20/30
01	Trunk SOUP 001LP	THE CLANGERS (Vernon Elliot) (TV soundtrack, with knitted sleeve, 26 only). . . 60
74	Buddah BDLP 4010	CLAUDINE (Curtis Mayfield/Gladys Knight). 15
63	Stateside S(S)SL 10044	CLEOPATRA (Alex North). 15
72	Warner Bros K 46127	A CLOCKWORK ORANGE (Walter Carlos). 12
65	Fontana (S)TL 5259	THE COLLECTOR (Maurice Jarre). 25
78	MGM 2315 398	COMA (Jerry Goldsmith) 15
67	MGM MGM-C(S) 8058	THE COMEDIANS (Laurence Rosenthal) 15
72	Pye NSPL 18389	CONCERTO FOR HARRY — SOMETHING TO HIDE (Roy Budd) 35
75	Polydor 2383 350	CONFESSIONS OF A POP PERFORMER (Three's A Crowd/Ed Welch). 30
71	Philips 6332 033	CONTINENTAL CIRCUS (Gong) 40
62	Parlophone PMC 1194	THE COOL MIKADO (John Barry Seven/Frankie Howerd, et al.) 80
67	Brunswick AXA 4544	COUNTESS FROM HONG KONG (Charles Chaplin) (with booklet) 15
70	Capitol E-ST 640	CROMWELL (Frank Cordell) 15
70	Word WST 5550	THE CROSS & THE SWITCHBLADE (Ralph Carmichael) 25
77	EMI EMA 782	CROSS OF IRON (Ernest Gold) (gatefold sleeve) 20
80	CBS 70182	CRUISING (John Hiatt/Willy DeVille/Germs). 12
73	Buddah 2318 091	CURTIS IN CHICAGO (Curtis Mayfield/Impressions/Jerry Butler,
		Gene Chandler, Leroy Hutson) (TV soundtrack, gatefold sleeve) 18
68	Stateside (S)SL 10222	CUSTER OF THE WEST (Bernardo Segall) 50

D

81	2-Tone CHR TT 5004	DANCE CRAZE (with poster) 20
62	Fontana TFL 5184	DANGEROUS FRIENDSHIPS (Art Blakey, et. al.). 18
70	RCA SF 8138	DARLIN' LILI (Henry Mancini) (gatefold sleeve). 15
63	MGM MGM-C 952	DAVID AND LISA (Mark Lawrence/Victor Feldman All Stars) 15
74	Phase 4 Stereo PFS 4339	THE DAY OF THE LOCUST (John Barry) 20
67	Stateside (S)SL 10217	THE DAY THE FISH CAME OUT (Mikis Theodorakis) 15
68	Stateside (S)SL 10263	DEADFALL (John Barry/Shirley Bassey) 35
73	Columbia SCX 6550	DEAF SMITH AND JOHNNY EARS (Daniele Patucchi) 35
74	CBS 80546	DEATH WISH (Herbie Hancock). 20
68	Stateside (S)SL 10259	DECLINE AND FALL... OF A BIRDWATCHER (Ron Goodwin) 100
55	MGM MGM-C 755	DEEP IN MY HEART (Howard Keel/Vic Damone, et al.). 12
58	London HA-D 2111	DESIRE UNDER THE ELMS (Elmer Bernstein) 25
63	Colpix PXL 440	DIAMOND HEAD (John Williams) 35
76	Pye Intl. NSPL 28219	DIAMOND MERCENARIES (Georges Garvarentz) 15
76	Bradley BRADS 8002	DIAMONDS (Roy Budd) 20
71	United Artists UAS 29216	DIAMONDS ARE FOREVER (John Barry/Shirley Bassey) 20
59	Top Rank RX 3016	THE DIARY OF ANNE FRANK (Alfred Newman) 30
83	Ripple (no cat. no.)	DIGITAL DREAMS (Bill Wyman) (promo only) 100
68	MGM MGM-C(S) 8048	DIRTY DOZEN (Frank de Vol/Trini Lopez) (yellow label). 18

67	Stateside S(S)L 10214	DOCTOR DOLITTLE (Lionel Newman) (foldout sleeve) 20
62	Columbia 33SX 1446	DON'T KNOCK THE TWIST (Chubby Checker/Gene Chandler, et al.) 25
67	RCA Victor RD/SF 7892	DOUBLE TROUBLE (Elvis Presley) (black/red dot labels, mono/stereo)...... 20/30
67	CBS S 63189	DR. FAUSTUS (Mario Nascimbene)................................... 75
65	United Artists (S)ULP 1097	DOCTOR NO (Monty Norman) (mono/stereo)........................ 30/35
69	Capitol EST 672	THE DOUBLE DECKERS (TV soundtrack) 25
87	Crammed MTM 14	DOWN BY LAW (John Lurie).. 15
74	Studio Two TWO 500	DRACULA (HAMMER PRESENTS...) (Christopher Lee) (gatefold sleeve) 15
70	President PTLS 1068	DRAKE'S DREAM (Paul Jones)...................................... 20
59	Parlophone PMCL 1101	DRUMBEAT (Adam Faith/John Barry Seven, et al.)...................... 60
60	HMV CLP 1352/CSD 1296	DRUM CRAZY (THE GENE KRUPA STORY) (Leith Stevens) (mono/stereo) ... 12/15
66	United Artists (S)ULP 1141	DUEL AT DIABLO (Neal Hefti)...................................... 20
58	Decca LF 1308	THE DUKE WORE JEANS (Tommy Steele) (10")......................... 20
84	Polydor 422 8237-7	DUNE (Toto, 1 track by Brian Eno) 15

E

75	MCA MCF 2580	EARTHQUAKE (John Williams)...................................... 15
69	Stateside-Dunhill SSL 5018	EASY RIDER (Steppenwolf/Jimi Hendrix/Byrds, et al.).................... 15
58	HMV DLP 1088	EDDIE FOY AND THE SEVEN LITTLE FOYS (10", Bob Hope/James Cagney) 30
54	Brunswick LAT 8040	THE EGYPTIAN (Alfred Newman) 40
61	MGM MGM-C 876	EL CID (Miklos Rosza) (also stereo [CS 6048]).................... 12/15
67	Columbia S(C)X 6155	EL DORADO (Nelson Riddle)....................................... 50
63	Colpix PXL 459	ELIZABETH TAYLOR IN LONDON (John Barry) (mono/stereo)........... 30/40
69	RCA Victor RD 8011	ELVIS ("TV Special", mono)....................................... 15
74	Warner Bros K 56084	EMMANUELLE (Pierre Bachelet).................................... 15
76	Warner Bros K 56231	EMMANUELLE 2 (Francis Lai) 15
57	Vogue Coral LVA 9063	END AS A MAN (Kenyon Hopkins) 30
74	DJM DJLPS 431	ENGLAND MADE ME (John Scott) 12
74	Warner Bros K 46275	ENTER THE DRAGON (Lalo Schifrin) 35
84	Alt. Ten. VIRUS 30	ERASERHEAD (Fats Waller/Peter Ivers/et al.) (with insert) 20
76	EMI EMC 3148	ESCAPE FROM THE DARK (Ron Goodwin)............................ 15
74	Blast U 828	ESCAPE OF THE CHRIST KNOWS WHAT (Stanislaw Varga)............... 12
82	MCA MCFP 3160	E.T. (THE EXTRA TERRESTRIAL) (John Williams) (picture disc) 15
83	MCA MCA 70000	E.T. — THE EXTRA TERRESTRIAL
		(John Williams) (box set, with booklet & poster)....................... 40
83	MCA CAC 70000	E.T. — THE EXTRA TERRESTRIAL
		(John Williams) (cassette, box set, with booklet & poster) 20
67	Brunswick LAT 8678	AN EVENING WITH BORIS KARLOFF AND FRIENDS.................... 30
60	RCA RD 27210	EXODUS (Ernest Gold) (also stereo SF 5093) 12
74	Warner Bros K 56071	THE EXORCIST (Jack Nitzsche, et al.) 12
71	Ember NR 5057	EXPERIENCE — THE ORIGINAL SOUNDTRACK (Jimi Hendrix) (g/fold sleeve) .. 12
72	Deram SML 1095	EXTREEMS (Tony Klinger & Michael Lyons) 25

F

57	Capitol LCT 6139	A FACE IN THE CROWD (Tom Glazer) (10")............................ 20
64	CBS (S)BPG 62277	FALL OF THE ROMAN EMPIRE (Dimitri Tiomkin) 20
67	Decca LK/SKL 4847	THE FAMILY WAY (Paul McCartney/George Martin) (mono/stereo) 100
60	Top Rank 30/003/4/5	FANTASIA (various classical pieces) (3-LP, with book) 30
58	Capitol LCT 6162	A FAREWELL TO ARMS (Mario Nascimbene) 15
67	MGM MGM-C(S) 8053	FAR FROM THE MADDING CROWD (Richard Rodney Bennett) 20
68	London HA-U/SH-U 8358	THE FASTEST GUITAR ALIVE (Roy Orbison) 30
67	Stateside S(S)L 10213	FATHOM (Johnny Dankworth)...................................... 45
73	Pye NSPL 18398	FEAR IS THE KEY (Roy Budd)...................................... 85
70	United Artists UAS 29118	FELLINI-SATYRICON (Nino Rota) 20
65	Columbia 33SX 1693	FERRY CROSS THE MERSEY (Gerry & Pacemakers/Cilla Black/Fourmost)
		(also stereo SCX 3544) 40/45
63	CBS SBPG 62148	55 DAYS AT PEKING (Dimitri Tiomkin/Andy Williams) 18
66	Columbia S(C)X 6079	FINDERS KEEPERS (Cliff Richard) (with inner sleeve, mono/stereo) 15/20
68	Warner Bros WF(S) 2550	FINIAN'S RAINBOW (Fred Astaire/Petula Clark et al.)................... 25
57	Brunswick LAT 8194	FIRE DOWN BELOW (Arthur Benjamin)............................... 40
84	MCA MCF 3233	FIRESTARTER (Tangerine Dream).................................. 12
78	United Artists UAS 30181	F-I-S-T (Bill Conti) 12
67	RCA Victor RD/SF 7875	A FISTFUL OF DOLLARS (Ennio Morricone) 20
68	RCA Victor RD 7994	A FISTFUL OF DOLLARS/FOR A FEW DOLLARS MORE/
		THE GOOD, THE BAD AND THE UGLY (Hugo Montenegro)................ 12
72	United Artists UAS 29345	A FISTFUL OF DYNAMITE (Ennio Morricone) 40
71	CBS 70091	FIVE EASY PIECES (Tammy Wynette, et al.) 12
59	London SH-U 6044	THE FIVE PENNIES (Danny Kaye, et al.) (gatefold sleeve)................ 12
65	RCA Victor RD 7723	FLAMING STAR AND SUMMER KISSES (Elvis Presley)
		(mono only, black labels, later orange).......................... 100/500+
85	Heavy Metal HMI PD 29	FLASHPOINT (Tangerine Dream) (picture disc) 20
85	Heavy Metal HMXD 29	FLASHPOINT (Tangerine Dream) (CD, playable [most copies faulty]) 50
68	Stateside SSL 10253	A FLEA IN HER EAR (Bronislau Kaper) 12
71	Decca SKL 5093	FLIGHT OF THE DOVES (Roy Budd/Dana)............................ 12
61	Golden Guinea GGL 0092	THE FLINTSTONES (TV soundtrack)................................. 15
62	Brunswick LAT 8392	FLOWER DRUM SONG (Nancy Kwan, et al.) (also stereo STA 3054)...... 12/18
64	Ace Of Clubs ACL 1166	FLYING CLIPPER (Riz Ortolani).................................... 15
63	MGM MGM-C/CS 6068	FOLLOW THE BOYS (Connie Francis) (mono/stereo) 18/20
62	MGM MGM-C 882	THE 4 HORSEMEN OF THE APOCALYPSE (André Previn) 12
59	RCA RB 16158	FOR THE FIRST TIME (Mario Lanza)................................. 12
65	Ember NR 5029	FOUR IN THE MORNING (John Barry) (mono)......................... 30
74	T. Motown STML 11269	FOXY BROWN (Willie Hutch) 15
66	RCA Victor RD/SF 7793	FRANKIE AND JOHNNY (Elvis Presley) (black/red dot labels, mono/stereo) .. 40/60
64	Fontana TL 5208	FREEDOM ROAD (Madeleine Bell, et al.) (TV production) 15
71	Paramount SPFL 269	FRIENDS (Elton John) 12

MINT VALUE £

72	Fantasy FAN 9406	FRITZ THE CAT (Bo Diddley/Billie Holiday, et al.)	35
63	United Artists (S)ULP 1052	FROM RUSSIA WITH LOVE (John Barry/Matt Monroe) (mono/stereo)	30/40
60	London HA-T 2257	THE FUGITIVE KIND (Kenyon Hopkins)	30
67	RCA RD 7860	FUNERAL IN BERLIN (Konrad Elfers/Puppets)	25
63	RCA Victor RD/SF 7609	FUN IN ACAPULCO (Elvis Presley) (black/silver label, mono/stereo)	20/45

G

65	Liberty (S)LBY 1261	GENGHIS KHAN (Dusan Radic) (mono/stereo)	20
56	Vogue Coral LVA 9003	GENTLEMEN MARRY BRUNETTES (Robert Farnon)	35
53	MGM MGM-D 116	GENTLEMEN PREFER BLONDES (Marilyn Monroe, et al.) (10")	100
65	Mercury 20061 MCL	GENTLE RAIN (Luis Bonfa & Deodato)	15
98	Stella STELP 2	GET CHISHOLM! (David Beaumont, et al.)	12
70	RCA SF 8137	GETTING STRAIGHT (Ronald Stein)	15
57	Capitol LCT 6122	GIANT (Dimitri Tiomkin)	15
60	RCA RD 27192/SF 5078	G.I. BLUES (Elvis Presley) (black/silver label, mono/stereo)	18/45
66	MGM MGM-C(S) 8034	GIRL FROM U.N.C.L.E. (Jerry Goldsmith & Teddy Randazzo)	50
65	RCA Victor RD/SF 7714	GIRL HAPPY (Elvis Presley) (black/red dot labels, mono/stereo)	18/40
68	Polydor 583 714	GIRL ON A MOTORCYCLE (Les Reed)	40
63	RCA Victor RD/SF 7534	GIRLS! GIRLS! GIRLS! (Elvis Presley) (black/silver labels, mono/stereo)	20/45
66	United Artists SULP 1120	THE GLORY GUYS (Riz Ortolani)	30
72	Paramount SPFA 7003	THE GODFATHER (Nino Rota) (gatefold sleeve)	20
75	ABC ABCL 5128	THE GODFATHER — PART 2 (Nino Rota) (gatefold sleeve)	20
58	London HA-T 2125	GOD'S LITTLE ACRE (Elmer Bernstein)	30
72	Mother MO 4001	GOLD (MC5/David McWilliams, et al.)	35
74	Philips 9299 225	GOLD (Elmer Bernstein)	15
73	United Artists UAS 29576	THE GOLDEN VOYAGE OF SINBAD (Miklos Rozsa)	18
64	United Artists (S)ULP 1076	GOLDFINGER (John Barry/Shirley Bassey) (mono/stereo)	22/28
67	MGM CS 8056	GONE WITH THE WIND (Max Steiner)	15
64	Decca LK 4673	GONKS GO BEAT (Lulu/Nashville Teens/Graham Bond, et al.)	150
68	United Artists (S)ULP 1197	THE GOOD, THE BAD AND THE UGLY (Ennio Morricone)	20
61	HMV CSD 1386	GOODBYE AGAIN (Georges Auric)	12
65	Stateside SL 10126	GOODBYE CHARLIE (André Previn)	12
69	Warner Bros W(S) 1786	GOODBYE COLUMBUS (Charles Fox/Association)	20
70	DJM DJLPS 408	GOODBYE GEMINI (Christopher Gunning/Peddlers/Jackie Lee)	60
68	CBS (S) 70042	THE GRADUATE (Simon & Garfunkel) (original issue, blue label, laminated sleeve, mono/stereo)	15/12
66	MGM MGM-CS 8037	GRAND PRIX (Maurice Jarre)	15
53	HMV ALP 1071	THE GREAT CARUSO (Mario Lanza)	12
63	United Artists (S)ULP 1041	THE GREAT ESCAPE (Elmer Bernstein) (mono/stereo)	20
77	Arista SPARTY 1013	THE GREATEST (Michael Masser/George Benson)	12
65	United Artists SULP 1093	THE GREATEST STORY EVER TOLD (Alfred Newman)	15
65	RCA RD 7759	THE GREAT RACE (Henry Mancini)	30
71	Pye NSPL 18373	GREAT SONGS AND THEMES FROM GREAT FILMS (Roy Budd)	50
75	MCA MCF 2707	THE GREAT WALDO PEPPER (Henry Mancini)	15
68	United Artists SULP 1220	GREAT WESTERN FILM THEMES (Various Artists)	15
81	Polydor POLS 11031	GREEN ICE (Bill Wyman)	15
70	Polydor 2384 021	GROUPIE GIRL (Opal Butterfly/English Rose, et al.)	20
67	RCA RD/SF 7899	GUNN (Henry Mancini)	20
61	Philips BBL 7500	THE GUNS OF NAVARONE (Dimitri Tiomkin/Mitch Miller) (also stereo SBBL 646)	12/15
69	RCA SF 8025	THE GURU (Ustad Vilayet Khan)	12

H

65	United Artists SULP 1106	THE HALLELUJAH TRAIL (Elmer Bernstein)	15
75	Contour 2870 437	THE HANGED MAN (Bullet) (TV soundtrack)	60
68	United Artists SULP 1204	HANG 'EM HIGH (Dominic Frontiere) (stereo/mono)	15/12
69	United Artists SULP 1231	HANNIBAL BROOKS (Francis Lai)	40
70	United Artists UAS 29084	THE HAPPY ENDING (Michel Legrand)	20
56	Philips BBL 7100	HAPPY HOLIDAY (Jo Stafford)	15
65	RCA Victor RD/SF 7767	HAREM HOLIDAY (Elvis Presley) (black/red dot labels, mono/stereo)	20/30
65	Warner Bros W 1599	HARLOW (Neal Hefti)	30
66	United Artists (S)ULP 1154	HAWAII (Elmer Bernstein)	15
80s	PRT/Chips CHILP 1	HAWK THE SLAYER (Harry Robertson) (gatefold sleeve)	15
68	RCA RD/SF 8051	HEAD (Monkees) (mono/stereo)	80/55
73	Fantasy FT 516	HEAVY TRAFFIC (Chuck Berry/Sergio Mendes/et al.)	15
72	Reprise K 44168	THE HEIST (Quincy Jones/Little Richard)	35
74	Tamla Motown STML 11260	HELL UP IN HARLEM (Edwin Starr)	15
65	Parlophone PMC 1255	HELP! (Beatles) (1st pressing, with "The Gramophone Co. Ltd" & "Sold In The UK…" label text; mono, with "mono" in outline type on front cover)	40
65	Parlophone PCS 3071	HELP! (Beatles) (1st pressing, with "The Gramophone Co. Ltd" & "Sold In The UK…" label text; stereo, with "stereo" in outline type on front cover)	70
67	United Artists (S)ULP 1186	HERE WE GO ROUND THE MULBERRY BUSH (Spencer Davis/Traffic/Andy Ellison) (mono/stereo)	35/30
59	Capitol T 1160	HEY BOY! HEY GIRL! (Louis Prima/Keely Smith, et al.)	20
62	Columbia 33SX 1421	HEY, LET'S TWIST (Joey Dee, et al.)	20
83	A&R FILM 001	HIGH ROAD TO CHINA (John Barry)	15
70	Columbia SCX 6443	HIS LAND (Cliff Richard/Cliff Barrows)	20
67	United Artists ULP 1161	THE HONEY POT (John Addison)	15
59	London HA-T 2197	THE HORSE SOLDIERS (David Buttolph)	25
59	Philips BBL 7292	HOUSEBOAT (George Duning)	20
62	MGM MGM-C 915/CS 6061	HOW THE WEST WAS WON (Alfred Newman/Debbie Reynolds)	12
87	Silva Screen FILM 041	HOW TO GET AHEAD IN ADVERTISING/WITHNAIL & I	20
87	Silva Screen FILMCD 041	HOW TO GET AHEAD IN ADVERTISING/WITHNAIL & I (CD)	18
65	United Artists (S)ULP 1098	HOW TO MURDER YOUR WIFE (Neal Hefti)	35

68	CBS (S)BPG 63276	HOW TO SAVE A MARRIAGE AND RUIN YOUR LIFE (Michel Legrand/Ray Conniff)	18
72	Atlantic K 40371	HOW TO STEAL A DIAMOND IN FOUR UNEASY LESSONS (Quincy Jones)	18
66	Stateside S(S)L 10187	HOW TO STEAL A MILLION (John Williams)	45
61	Golden Guinea GGL 0069	HUCKLEBERRY HOUND (TV soundtrack)	12
67	RCA Victor RD/SF 7877	HURRY SUNDOWN (Hugo Montenegro)	28

I

69	MGM MGM-C(S) 8101	ICE STATION ZEBRA (Michel Legrand)	20
70	United Artists UAS 29044	IF IT'S TUESDAY THIS MUST BE BELGIUM (Walter Scharf)	15
67	Brunswick LAT/STA 8689	I'LL NEVER FORGET WHAT'S 'ISNAME (Francis Lai)	40
65	United Artists ULP 1105	I'LL TAKE SWEDEN (Bob Hope/Frankie Avalon, et al.)	15
68	RCA Victor RD/SF 7931	IN COLD BLOOD (Quincy Jones)	45
65	RCA RD 7707	IN HARM'S WAY (Jerry Goldsmith)	25
67	Stateside S(S)L 10207	IN LIKE FLINT (Jerry Goldsmith)	50
63	Colpix PXL 459	IN LONDON (TV soundtrack) (Elizabeth Taylor/John Barry, mono)	30
68	United Artists ULP 1201	INSPECTOR CLOUSEAU (Ken Thorne)	20
69	RCA Victor RD/SF 7990	INTERLUDE (Georges Delarue/Timi Yuro)	15
62	Colpix PXL 427	THE INTERNS (Leith Stevens)	20
67	United Artists (S)ULP 1181	IN THE HEAT OF THE NIGHT (Quincy Jones/Ray Charles)	25
65	CBS BPG 62530	THE IPCRESS FILE (John Barry) (mono only)	50
84	Illuminated JAMS 35	IN THE SHADOW OF THE SUN (Throbbing Gristle)	18
63	United Artists SULP 1051	IRMA LA DOUCE (Andre Previn)	12
66	CBS (S)BPG 62843	IS PARIS BURNING? (Maurice Jarre)	25
69	Paramount SPFL 256	THE ITALIAN JOB (Quincy Jones/Matt Monro)	100
63	RCA Victor RD/SF 7565	IT HAPPENED AT THE WORLD'S FAIR (Elvis Presley) (black/silver label, mono/stereo)	20/45
63	Columbia 33SX 1533	IT'S ALL HAPPENING (Tommy Steele/Shane Fenton, et al.) (also stereo SCX 3486)	15/22
63	United Artists (S)ULP 1053	IT'S A MAD MAD MAD MAD WORLD (Ernest Gold)	20
62	Columbia 33SX 1412	IT'S TRAD, DAD! (Helen Shapiro/Gene Vincent, et al.)	25
65	Decca LK 4677	I'VE GOTTA HORSE (Billy Fury/Bachelors, et al.)	50
71	CBS 70083	I WALK THE LINE (Johnny Cash)	15
59	London LTZ-T 15160	I WANT TO LIVE (Johnny Mandel)	20

J

72	United Artists UAD 60027/8	THE JAMES BOND COLLECTION (John Barry) (2-LP, with booklet)	25
57	Capitol LCT 6140	THE JAMES DEAN STORY (Leith Stevens)	25
54	Brunswick LA 8671	JAZZ THEMES FROM "THE WILD ONE" (Leith Stevens) (10")	30
62	HMV CLP 1582	JESSICA (Mario Nascimbene)	15
77	Pye NSPH 28504	JESUS OF NAZARETH (Maurice Jarre) (gatefold sleeve)	15
73	Reprise K 64017	JIMI HENDRIX — SOUNDTRACK RECORDINGS FROM THE FILM (2-LP)	18
68	Stateside (S)SL 10264	JOANNA (Rod McKuen/Mike Sarne)	15
71	Mercury 6338 029	JOE (Bobby Scott/Jenny Butler)	20
64	United Artists ULP 1060	JOHNNY COOL (Billy May/Sammy Davis Jr.)	25
72	Reprise K 64015	JOURNEY THROUGH THE PAST (Neil Young) (2-LP, fold-out cover with inner sleeves)	20
77	Polydor/EG 2302 079	JUBILEE (Adam & Ants/Brian Eno, et al.)	12
61	HMV CLP 1545	JUDGMENT AT NUREMBURG (Ernest Gold)	20
66	RCA RD 7788	JUDITH (Sol Kaplan)	12
67	Fontana (S)TL 5317	JULIET OF THE SPIRITS (Nino Rota)	30
63	Decca LK 4524	JUST FOR FUN (Tornados/Karl Denver, et al.)	40
64	Decca LK 4620	JUST FOR YOU (Applejacks/Merseybeats, et al.)	40
70	Monument LMO/SMO 5031	JUSTINE (Jerry Goldsmith)	15

K

71	MGM 2315 019	KELLY'S HEROES (Lalo Schifrin/Mike Curb)	25
66	United Artists (S)ULP 1139	KHARTOUM (Frank Cordell)	40
72	Polydor 2383 102	KIDNAPPED (Roy Budd/Mary Hopkin)	25
58	RCA RD 27088	KING CREOLE (Elvis Presley) (black/silver labels)	50
76	Reprise K 54090	KING KONG (John Barry) (with poster)	15
61	MGM MGM-CS 6043	KING OF KINGS (Miklos Rozsa)	20
58	Capitol LCT 6165	KINGS GO FORTH (Elmer Bernstein)	15
66	Fontana (S)TL 5302	KING RAT (John Barry)	20
64	RCA Victor RD/SF 7645	KISSIN' COUSINS (Elvis Presley) (black/red dot labels, mono/stereo)	18/40
54	MGM MGM-C 753	KISS ME KATE (Howard Keel, et al.)	20
65	United Artists ULP 1104	THE KNACK (AND HOW TO GET IT) (John Barry)	
54	Brunswick LA 8668	KNOCK ON WOOD (Danny Kaye) (10")	
69	Stateside (S)SL 10277	KRAKATOA: EAST OF JAVA (Frank De Vol)	
74	Warner Bros K 46271	KUNG FU (TV soundtrack) (with inner sleeve) (Jim Helms)	

L

61	RCA RD 27202	LA DOLCE VITA (Nino Rota) (gatefold sleeve)	45
63	Ace Of Hearts AH 70	THE LADY AND THE TRAMP (Peggy Lee)	20
69	Stateside S(S)L 10267	LADY IN CEMENT (Hugo Montenegro)	20
73	Tamla Motown TMSP 1131	LADY SINGS THE BLUES (Diana Ross) (2-LP, with brown inner sleeve)	25
71	United Artists UAS 29120	THE LANDLORD (Al Kooper)	20
72	MGM 2315 072	THE LAST RUN (Jerry Goldsmith/Steve Lawrence)	35/30
73	United Artists UAS 29440	LAST TANGO IN PARIS (Gato Barbieri)	12
71	Probe SPB 1027	THE LAST VALLEY (John Barry) (some with insert)	25
63	Pye Intl. NPL 28023	LAWRENCE OF ARABIA (Maurice Jarre) (also NSPC 93001 str	15
85	United Artists 86002	LEGEND (Jerry Goldsmith)	18
71	M. F. Pleasure MFP 50034	THE LEGEND OF FRENCHIE KING (Francis Lai)	30
74	Warner Bros K 56085	THE LEGEND OF THE 7 GOLDEN VAMPIRES (James Bernard/Peter Cushing)	
64	Stateside S(S)L 10058	THE LEOPARD (Nino Rota)	

MINT VALUE £

70	Apple PXS 1	LET IT BE (Beatles) (box set, 1st pressing, dark green label, red Apple logo on LP rear sleeve & white inner, with *Get Back* book housed in black card tray ['PXS 1' not listed on package])	175
70	Apple PCS 7096	LET IT BE (Beatles) (2nd pressing, green Apple logo on rear sleeve, plain white inner)	15
60	Philips BBL 7414/SBBL 592	LET'S MAKE LOVE (Marilyn Monroe/Yves Montand/Frankie Vaughan)	60/75
79	Warner Bros K 56751	LIFE OF BRIAN (Monty Python) (with inner sleeve)	12
59	Philips SBBL 565	LI'L ABNER (Nelson Riddle)	12
64	Columbia SX 1626	LILIES OF THE FIELD (Jerry Goldsmith)	20
81	RK RKLP 5005	LION OF THE DESERT (Maurice Jarre)	12
69	CBS 70049	THE LION IN WINTER (John Barry)	20
66	MGM MGM-CS 8029	THE LIQUIDATOR (Lalo Schifrin/Shirley Bassey)	50
71	CBS 70087	LITTLE FAUSS AND BIG HALSY (Johnny Cash)	15
73	United Artists UAS 29475	LIVE AND LET DIE (George Martin/Wings) (gatefold sleeve)	25
87	Warner Bros 925 616-1	THE LIVING DAYLIGHTS (John Barry)	12
76	MGM 2315 376	LOGAN'S RUN (Jerry Goldsmith)	25
62	MGM MGM-C 896	LOLITA (Nelson Riddle)	25
67	Polydor 583 014	LONG DUEL (Patrick John Scott/Vince Hill)	20
63	Stateside S(S)L 10045	THE LONGEST DAY (dialogue only)	20
83	CES CES 1001	THE LONG GOOD FRIDAY (Francis Monkman) (numbered sleeve with insert, black label print, 2,000 only)	50
83	CES CES 1001	THE LONG GOOD FRIDAY (Francis Monkman) (re-pressing, with insert, blue label print, 500 only)	50
84	CES CES 1001	THE LONG GOOD FRIDAY (Francis Monkman) (3rd pressing, with insert, blue label print, 5,000 only)	40
89	Silva Screen FILM 020	THE LONG GOOD FRIDAY (Francis Monkman) (reissue)	20
89	Silva Screen FILM 020	THE LONG GOOD FRIDAY (Francis Monkman) (CD)	25
65	MGM C/CS 6079	LOOKING FOR LOVE (Connie Francis)	18
70	CBS 70073	LOOT (Keith Mansfield/Steve Ellis)	60
65	Colpix PXL 521	LORD JIM (Bronislau Kaper)	20
69	Uni UNLS 103	LOST MAN (Quincy Jones)	25
70	CBS 70067	LOVE CIRCLE (Ennio Morricone)	60
57	RCA RC 24001	LOVING YOU (Elvis Presley) (10", silver spot label)	110

M

73	Tamla Motown STMA 8003	THE MACK (Willie Hutch)	15
69	RCA Victor SF 8017	MACKENNA'S GOLD (Quincy Jones/Jose Feliciano)	15
69	Warner Bros WS 1805	THE MADWOMAN OF CHAILLOT (Michael Lewis)	30
70	Pye Intl. NSPL 28133	THE MAGIC CHRISTIAN (Ken Thorne/Badfinger, et al.)	30
54	Brunswick LAT 8045	MAGNIFICENT OBSESSION (Frank Skinner)	30
65	MGM MGM-C 995	THE MAGNIFICENT SHOWMAN (Dimitri Tiomkin)	25
76	Atlantic K 50308	MAHONEY'S LAST STAND (Ronnie Lane & Ron Wood)	18
63	Ace Of Clubs ACL 1135	MAIGRET (Ron Grainer) (TV series music)	15
66	CBS SBPG 62525	MAJOR DUNDEE (Daniele Amfitheatrof/Mitch Miller)	15
67	United Artists SULP 1155	A MAN AND A WOMAN (Francis Lai)	18
66	Brunswick LAT/STA 8651	A MAN COULD GET KILLED (Bert Kaempfert)	15
67	RCA RB 6712/3	A MAN FOR ALL SEASONS (2-LP, dialogue only)	20
59	Top Rank 35/043	MAN FROM INTERPOL (Tony Crombie) (TV series music)	25
66	RCA Victor RD 7758	THE MAN FROM U.N.C.L.E. (Hugo Montenegro)	40
64	Stateside S(S)L 10087	MAN IN THE MIDDLE (Lionel Bart & John Barry)	30
56	Brunswick LAT 8101	THE MAN WITH THE GOLDEN ARM (Elmer Bernstein)	25
74	United Artists UAS 29671	THE MAN WITH THE GOLDEN GUN (John Barry/Lulu)	15
63	Stateside S(S)L 10048	MARILYN (Marilyn Monroe) (mono/stereo)	40/50
72	MCA MUPS 441	MARY QUEEN OF SCOTS (John Barry)	25
70	United Artists UAS 29122	MASTER OF THE ISLANDS (Henry Mancini)	18
69	Philips SBL 7876	MAYERLING (Francis Lai)	30
64	United Artists SULP 1059	McLINTOCK (Frank De Vol)	40
80	Polydor POLD 5034	McVICAR (Roger Daltrey) (some on clear vinyl)	25/18
71	Polydor 2383 043	MELODY (Bee Gees, Richard Hewson, et al.)	12
69	CBS 70061	ME, NATALIE (Henry Mancini/Rod McKuen)	12
57	London HA-P 2076	MEN IN WAR (Elmer Bernstein)	15
58	Capitol T 1016	MERRY ANDREW (Danny Kaye)	15
69	Bell BELL 6053	MERRY CHRISTMAS (David Frost/Billy Taylor)	40
5	MGM MGM-C(S) 8001	MICKEY ONE (Stan Getz & Eddie Sauter) (with booklet, mono/stereo)	20/25
	United Artists UAS 29043	MIDNIGHT COWBOY (John Barry/Nilsson/Elephant's Memory) (orange/pink label)	12
	Mercury 20072 (S)MCL	"MIRAGE" (Quincy Jones)	30
	MV CLP 1481	THE MISFITS (Alex North)	25
66	(S)LPD 503	MISSION: IMPOSSIBLE — MUSIC FROM THE TV SERIES (Lalo Schifrin)	40
70	ury 25181	MISS SADIE THOMPSON (George Duning) (10")	30
80	na TL 5347	MODESTY BLAISE (Johnny Dankworth)	50
69	ount SPFL 259	THE MOLLY MAGUIRES (Henry Mancini)	15
79	B 384	MONKEY (Godiego) (TV soundtrack)	25
69	Uni nt SPFL 255	MONTE CARLO OR BUST! (Ron Goodwin)	45
	Colu sts UAG 30247	MOONRAKER (John Barry/Shirley Bassey)	12
70s	Columbi CX 6346	MORE (Pink Floyd) (laminated flipback sleeve, 'couple facing west' photo on green-tinted rear sleeve)	35
70s	Columbia S X 6346	MORE (Pink Floyd) (laminated non-flipback sleeve, 'couple facing west' photo on black-tinted rear sleeve)	25
	6346	MORE (Pink Floyd) (laminated non-flipback sleeve, 'couple facing east' photo on black-tinted rear sleeve)	35
72	Ember NR 5061	MORE EXPERIENCE (Jimi Hendrix)	12
69	Paramount SPFL 152	MORE 'MISSION: IMPOSSIBLE' (Lalo Schifrin)	40
60	MGM MGM-C(S) 957	MORE MUSIC FROM BEN-HUR (Miklos Rozsa)	15/20

66	RCA Victor RD 7832	MORE MUSIC FROM 'THE MAN FROM U.N.C.L.E.' (Hugo Montenegro) 45
62	MGM	MORE MUSIC FROM 'MUTINY ON THE BOUNTY' (Bronislau Kaper) 20
68	MGM CS8063	MORE THAN A MIRACLE (Piero Piccioni) 15
65	Columbia S(C)X 6303	MRS BROWN YOU'VE GOT A LOVELY DAUGHTER (Hermans Hermits,
		mono or stereo, some with manuscript) 25/30
77	Pye NSPH 19	MUPPET SHOW VOL. 1 (TV soundtrack) (gatefold sleeve) 12
78	Pye NSPH 21	MUPPET SHOW VOL. 2 (TV soundtrack) 12
67	RCA RD 7847	MURDERERS' ROW (Lalo Schifrin) 75
72	Harvest SHSP 4019	MUSIC FROM MACBETH (Third Ear Band) 20
80	Unicorn Kachana KPM 7009	MUSIC FROM THE AVENGERS, THE NEW AVENGERS
		AND THE PROFESSIONALS
		(Laurie Johnson/London Studio Orchestra) (gatefold sleeve) 25
70	Harvest SHSP 4008	MUSIC FROM THE BODY (Ron Geesin & Roger Waters) (black labels) 12
70	Harvest SHSP 4008	MUSIC FROM THE BODY (Ron Geesin & Roger Waters)
		(photos/green labels) 22
62	MGM MGM-CS 6060	MUTINY ON THE BOUNTY (Bronislau Kaper) 20
85	Cloud Nine CN 4002	MYSTERIOUS ISLAND (Bernard Herrman) 25

N

70	United Artists UAS 29108	NED KELLY (Shel Silverstein/Mick Jagger/Waylon Jennings) 35
72	Bell BELLS 202	NICHOLAS AND ALEXANDRA (Richard Rodney Bennet) 15
67	RCA RD 7848	NIGHT OF THE GENERALS (Maurice Jarre) 40
65	MGM MGM-C 994	NIGHT OF THE IGUANA (Benjamin Frankel) 15
69	United Artists (S)ULP 1235	THE NIGHT THEY RAIDED MINSKY'S (Charles Strouse) 20
62	Decca LK 4527	NINE HOURS TO RAMA (Malcolm Arnold) 100
68	Dot (S)LPD 507	NO WAY TO TREAT A LADY (American Breed) 30

O

72	Harvest SHSP 4020	OBSCURED BY CLOUDS (Pink Floyd) (rounded sleeve) 20
76	Phase 4 Stereo PF5 4381	OBSESSION (Bernard Herrman) 15
83	A&M AMLX 64967	OCTOPUSSY (John Barry/Rita Coolidge) 12
83	A&M 394 967-2	OCTOPUSSY (John Barry) (CD, withdrawn) 75
68	Dot (S)LPD 514	THE ODD COUPLE (Neal Hefti) 30
60	London HA-T 2220	ODDS AGAINST TOMORROW (John Lewis) 12
75	MCA MCF 2591	ODESSA FILE (Andrew Lloyd Webber/Perry Como) 12
64	Stateside S(S)L 10056	OF LOVE AND DESIRE (Ronald Stein) 12
69	Paramount SPFL 251	OH! WHAT A LOVELY WAR (Alfred Ralston, et al.) (gatefold sleeve) 15
70	Starline SRS 5019	OLIVER IN THE OVERWORLD (Freddie Garrity) 20
73	Warner Bros K 46227	O LUCKY MAN! (Alan Price) (gatefold sleeve) 18
57	Brunswick LAT 8226	OMAR KHAYYAM/THE MOUNTAIN (Victor Young/Daniele Amfitheatrof) 30
75	Fantasy FTA 3004	ONE FLEW OVER THE CUCKOO'S NEST (Jack Nitzsche) (gatefold sleeve) 15
69	United Artists UAS 29020	ON HER MAJESTY'S SECRET SERVICE (John Barry) (foldout sleeve) 40
59	Columbia 33SX 1208	ON THE BEACH (Ernest Gold) 12
70	Fontana SFJL 950	ORFEU NEGRO (BLACK ORPHEUS) (Luis Bonfa/Antonio Carlos Jobim) 15
69	RCA SF 8014	OTLEY (Stanley Myers/Don Partridge) 25
66	Stateside S(S)L 10174	OUR MAN FLINT (Jerry Goldsmith) 50
76	Warner Bros K 56286	THE OUTLAW JOSEY WALES (Jerry Fielding) 25

P

58	Philips BBL 7197	THE PAJAMA GAME (Doris Day, et al.) 15
63	Warner Bros WM 8141	PALM SPRINGS WEEKEND (Frank Perkins) 20
74	EMI EMC 3020	PAPILLON (Jerry Goldsmith) 15
66	RCA Victor RD/SF 7810	PARADISE, HAWAIIAN STYLE (Elvis Presley)
		(black/red dot labels, mono/stereo) 25/40
61	HMV CLP 1499	PARIS BLUES (Duke Ellington) 15
61	Warner Bros WS 8044	PARRISH (Max Steiner/George Creely) 20
70	Stateside SSL 10302	PATTON (Jerry Goldsmith) 15
65	Mercury 20063 SML	THE PAWNBROKER (Quincy Jones) 25
66	Philips (S)BL 7782	THE PEKING MEDALLION (Georges Garvarentz/Dusty Springfield) 30
67	Ember NR 5040	THE PENTHOUSE (John Hawksworth) 40
71	Pye NSPL 18365	PERCY (Kinks) 35
70	Warner Bros WS 2554	PERFORMANCE (Mick Jagger/Jack Nitzsche/Randy Newman, et al.) 30
71	CBS 64816	THE PERSUADERS (John Barry) 15
59	RCA RD 27123/SF 5033	PETER GUNN (Henry Mancini) 15
55	Philips BBL 7059	PETE KELLY'S BLUES (Sammy Cahn, Matty Matlock, et al.) 12
61	Ace Of Hearts AH 26	PETE KELLY'S BLUES (Peggy Lee, Ella Fitzgerald) 12
79	Gem GEM 102	PHANTASM (Fred Myrow & Malcolm Seagrave) 20
62	United Artists ULP 1016	PHAEDRA (Mikis Theodorakis) 12
56	Brunswick LAT 8120	PICNIC (George Duning) 25
68	Philips SBL 7858	PLAYTIME (Jacques Tati, Yan Tatore, Leo Petit) 35
70	Paramount SPFL 258	POOKIE (Fred Karlin/Sandpipers) 15
57	Capitol LCT 6141	THE PRIDE AND THE PASSION (Georges Antheil) 15
69	Stateside (S)SL 10278	THE PRIME OF MISS JEAN BRODIE (Rod McKuen/Mike Redway) 15
86	Bam Caruso WEBA 066	THE PRISONER (Ron Grainer, et al.) (fan club issue, gatefold sleeve
		with inner sleeve, booklet, membership form, map & poster) 35
66	HMV CLP/CSD 3623	PRIVILEGE (Paul Jones & Mike Leander) 18
69	RCA SF 8072	THE PRODUCERS (John Morris) 15
69	United Artists UAS 29005	A PROFESSIONAL GUN (Ennio Morricone) 40
67	RCA Victor RD/SF 7876	THE PROFESSIONALS (Maurice Jarre) 50
60	Contemporary LAC 12293	THE PROPER TIME (Shelly Manne) 15
62	Stateside S(S)L 10248	PRUDENCE AND THE PILL (Bernard Ebbinghouse) 25
75	Unicorn RHS 336	PSYCHO (Bernard Herrmann) 20

Q

71	Sonet SNTF 622	QUIET DAYS IN CLICHY (Country Joe McDonald)	20
66	CBS (S)BPG 62869	THE QUILLER MEMORANDUM (John Barry/Matt Monro) (mono/stereo)	20/25

R

88	Silva Screen FILM 033	THE RAGGEDY RAWNEY (Michael Kamen)	12
71	Reprise K 44159	RAINBOW BRIDGE (Jimi Hendrix) (matt gatefold sleeve, 'steamboat' label)	15
75	Dart ARTS 65376	RANSOM (Jerry Goldsmith)	50
60	London HAD 2288	THE RAT RACE (Sam Butera & The Witnesses)	25
67	United Artists (S)ULP 1184	RED AND BLUE (Vanessa Redgrave)	40
72	Paramount SPFL 275	THE RED TENT (Ennio Morricone)	20
70	CBS 70068	THE REIVERS (John Williams)	12
76	United Artists UAS 30007	THE RETURN OF A MAN CALLED HORSE (Laurence Rosenthal)	12
75	RCA Red Seal RS 1010	THE RETURN OF THE PINK PANTHER (Henry Mancini)	18
69	United Artists ULP 1226	REVOLUTION (Quicksilver Messenger Service/Steve Miller, et al.)	20
70	United Artists UAS 29137	RIDER IN THE RAIN (Francis Lai)	20
68	MGM MGM-C(S) 8079	THE RISE AND FALL OF THE THIRD REICH (Lalo Schifrin)	28
53	Brunswick LA 8578	ROAD TO BALI (Bob Hope, Bing Crosby) (10")	30
62	Decca LKR 4427	THE ROAD TO HONG KONG (Robert Farnon/Bob Hope & Bing Crosby)	12
67	Decca LK/SKL 4892	ROBBERY (Johnny Keating/Jackie Lee)	30
64	Reprise R 2021	ROBIN AND THE SEVEN HOODS (Nelson Riddle)	30
61	RCA RD 27233	ROCCO AND HIS BROTHERS (Nino Rota)	20
57	Mercury MPT 7527	ROCK ALL NIGHT (Platters, Norah Hayes, et al.) (10")	175
67	Polydor 583 013	JULES VERNE'S ROCKET TO THE MOON (John Scott)	150
57	Brunswick LAT 8162	ROCK, PRETTY BABY (Henry Mancini/Rod McKuen)	100
87	Ode RHVX 1	ROCKY HORROR BOX SET (Richard O'Brien) (4-LP box, with inserts, numbered)	30
87	Ode RHBXLP 1	ROCKY HORROR BOX SET (Richard O'Brien) (4-LP box, with different inserts to above)	25
75	Ode ODE 78332	THE ROCKY HORROR PICTURE SHOW (Richard O'Brien) (Original Soundtrack)	15
83	Ode OSVP 78332	THE ROCKY HORROR PICTURE SHOW ALBUM (picture disc)	20
86	Ode ODE 21653	THE ROCKY HORROR PICTURE SHOW ALBUM (reissue)	12
87	Ode OSVP 21653	THE ROCKY HORROR PICTURE SHOW ALBUM (reissue, picture disc)	20
90	Ode RHBXCD 1	THE ROCKY HORROR PICTURE SHOW — 15TH ANNIVERSARY (Richard O'Brien, et al.) (4-CD box)	45
75	United Artists UAS 29865	ROLLERBALL (Andre Previn)	15
77	MCA MCF 2813	ROLLERCOASTER (Lalo Schifrin/Sparks)	12
68	Dot (S)LPD 519	ROSEMARY'S BABY (Kryzstophe Komeda)	35
65	Parlophone PMC 1262	ROTTEN TO THE CORE (New Jazz Voices)	20
64	RCA Victor RD/SF 7678	ROUSTABOUT (Elvis Presley) (black/red dot labels, mono/stereo)	16/40
64	Capitol (S)T 1771	ROUTE 66 AND OTHER GREAT T.V. THEMES (Nelson Riddle) (TV show)	15
66	United Artists ULP 1147	THE RUSSIANS ARE COMING THE RUSSIANS ARE COMING (Johnny Mandel)	15
71	MGM 2315 028	RYAN'S DAUGHTER (Maurice Jarre) (gatefold sleeve)	12

S

72	RCA SF 8211	SACCO AND VANZETTI (Ennio Morricone/Joan Baez)	12
53	Brunswick LA 8604	SALOMÉ (George Duning) (10")	50
68	United Artists SULP 1202	SALT AND PEPPER (Johnny Dankworth/Sammy Davis Jr)	15
67	Stateside S(S)L 10198	THE SAND PEBBLES (Jerry Goldsmith)	15
65	Mercury MCL 20065	THE SANDPIPER (Johnny Mandel)	20
68	United Artists (S)ULP 1190	THE SCALPHUNTERS (Elmer Bernstein)	15
78	Polydor 2480 429	SCOUSE THE MOUSE (Ringo Starr/Adam Faith, et al.) (some w/stickered sleeve & printed [not photocopied] competition insert)	110/30
78	Polydor 3194 429	SCOUSE THE MOUSE (Ringo Starr/Adam Faith, et al.) (cassette)	40
70	CBS 70077	SCROOGE (Leslie Bricusse) (musical, gatefold sleeve)	12
80	EMI EMC 3340	THE SEA WOLVES (Roy Budd/Matt Monroe)	18
62	Reprise R 2013	SERGEANTS 3 (Billy May)	30
73	Paramount SPFL 296	SERPICO (Mikis Theodorakis)	25
64	United Artists ULP 1072	THE 7th DAWN (Riz Ortolani)	15
74	United Artists UAS 29763	THE SEVENTH VOYAGE OF SINBAD (Bernard Hermann)	25
71	Stax 2659 007	SHAFT — ORIGINAL SOUNDTRACK (Isaac Hayes) (2-LP, gatefold sleeve)	22
73	Probe SPB 1077	SHAFT IN AFRICA (Johnny Pate/Four Tops)	40
74	ABC ABCL 5035	SHAFT IN AFRICA (Johnny Pate/Four Tops) (reissue)	35
72	MGM 2315 115	SHAFT'S BIG SCORE! (Gordon Parks/O.C. Smith/Isaac Hayes)	35
66	CBS BPG 62755	SHAKESPEARE WALLAH (Satyajit Ray)	15
68	Philips SBL 7867	SHALAKO (Robert Farnon)	15
80	Warner Bros K 56827	THE SHINING (Bela Bartok et al.)	15
69	MGM MGM-CS 8103	SHOES OF THE FISHERMAN (Alex North)	12
70	Stateside SSL 10307	THE SICILIAN CLAN (Ennio Morricone)	20
72	MCA MUPS 458	SILENT RUNNING (Pete Schikele/Joan Baez)	20
66	RCA RD 7792	THE SILENCERS (Elmer Bernstein/Vikki Carr)	45
58	MGM MGM-C 760	SILK STOCKINGS (Fred Astaire)	12
58	Capitol T 929	SING, BOY, SING (Tommy Sands)	75
56	MGM D 140	SINGIN' IN THE RAIN/EASTER PARADE (Gene Kelly/Judy Garland) (10")	12
66	MGM MGM-C(S) 8011	THE SINGING NUN (Debbie Reynolds)	15
78	Charisma CAS 1139	SIR HENRY AT RAWLINSON END (Vivian Stanshall) (with insert)	18
64	United Artists ULP 1071	633 SQUADRON (Ron Goodwin)	25
69	RCA SF 8010	SKIDOO (Nilsson)	20
74	Polydor 2442 126	SLADE IN FLAME (Slade)	12
73	Polydor 2391 084	SLAUGHTER'S BIG RIP-OFF (James Brown)	50
66	Mercury MCL 20080	THE SLENDER THREAD (Quincy Jones)	20
73	CBS 70127	SLEUTH (John Addison)	12
69	NEMS 6-70059	THE SMASHING BIRD I USED TO KNOW (Bobby Richards)	20
68	Stateside S(S)L 10224	SMASHING TIME (John Addison)	30

73	PRT FBLP 8085	SMIKE	15
56	Pye Disneyland DPL 39003	SNOW WHITE AND THE SEVEN DWARFS (Disney Orchestra)	30
61	Philips BBL 7504	SNOW WHITE AND THE THREE STOOGES (Harry Harris)	12
70	Pye NSPL 18348	SOLDIER BLUE AND OTHER THEMES (Roy Budd)	40
60	London HA-T 2221	SOLOMON AND SHEBA (Mario Nascimbene)	75
59	Capitol LCT 6180	SOME CAME RUNNING (Elmer Bernstein)	30
59	London HA-T 2176	SOME LIKE IT HOT (Marilyn Monroe) (also stereo SAH-T 6040)	90/100
83	Liberty UASP 30226	SOME LIKE IT HOT (Marilyn Monroe) (picture disc)	15
67	RCA RD 7845	SONGS FROM THE SWINGER (Marty Paich/Ann-Margret)	30
74	Rapple/RCA APL1-0220	SON OF DRACULA (Ringo Starr/Harry Nilsson, fold-out sleeve)	15
65	CBS (S)BPG 62558	THE SONS OF KATIE ELDER (Elmer Bernstein/Johnny Cash)	30/40
73	CBS 70123	SOUNDER (Taj Mahal)	15
69	RCA Victor SF 8024	THE SOUTHERN STAR (Matt Monro/Georges Garvarentz)	20
58	London HA-D 2079	SPANISH AFFAIR (Daniele Amfitheatrof)	50
76	Atlantic K 56248	SPARKLE (Curtis Mayfield/Aretha Franklin)	12
61	Brunswick LAT 8363	SPARTACUS (Alex North) (gatefold sleeve)	25
68	RCA Victor RD/SF 7957	SPEEDWAY (Elvis Presley/Nancy Sinatra) (black/red dot labels, mono/stereo)	60/40
53	Capitol CCL 7505	SPELLBOUND/THE RED HOUSE (Miklos Rosza) (10")	25
66	RCA RD 7787	THE SPY WHO CAME IN FROM THE COLD (Sol Kaplan)	20
77	United Artists UAG 30098	THE SPY WHO LOVED ME (Marvin Hamlisch/Carly Simon) (gatefold sleeve)	12
68	CBS 62919	THE SPY WITH THE COLD NOSE (Riz Ortolani)	35
66	Fontana TL 5354	STAGECOACH (Jerry Goldsmith)	30
55	Philips BBL 7007	A STAR IS BORN (Judy Garland)	15
79	CBS 70174	STAR TREK — THE MOTION PICTURE (Jerry Goldsmith)	15
77	20th C. BTD 541	STAR WARS (John Williams) (2-LP, with insert)	18
69	CBS 70062	STILETTO (Sid Ramin)	30
52	Capitol LC 6542	A STREET CAR NAMED DESIRE (Alex North) (10")	50
61	MGM MGM-C 864	THE SUBTERRANEANS (André Previn)	15
63	Columbia 33SX 1472	SUMMER HOLIDAY (Cliff Richard) (with inner sleeve, mono)	15
63	Columbia SCX 3462	SUMMER HOLIDAY (Cliff Richard) (stereo, with inner sleeve, initially with green labels, later with blue/black labels)	30/20
71	Warner Bros K 46098	SUMMER OF '42 (Michel Legrand)	12
57	London HA-R 2077	THE SUN ALSO RISES (Hugo Friedhofer)	25
70	Avco Embassy 6466 002	SUNFLOWER (Henry Mancini)	18
55	HMV DLP 1104	SUN VALLEY SERENADE (Glenn Miller)	15
62	Golden Guinea GGL 0106	SUPERCAR — FLIGHT OF FANCY (Barry Gray/Edwin Astley)	50
72	Buddah 2318 065	SUPERFLY (Curtis Mayfield) (gatefold sleeve)	20
73	Buddah 2318 087	SUPER FLY T.N.T. (Osibisa)	15
64	Stateside SL 10089	SURF PARTY (Astronauts, Routers, et al.)	50
79	EMI EMC 3222	SUSPIRIA (Goblin)	40
69	MCA MUCS 133	SWEET CHARITY (Shirley MacLaine, et al.)	25
57	Brunswick LAT 8195	SWEET SMELL OF SUCCESS (Elmer Bernstein)	25
68	Stateside S(S)L 10250	THE SWEET RIDE (Pete Rugolo/Dusty Springfield)	15
68	CBS 70043	THE SWIMMER (Marvin Hamlisch)	25
65	MGM MGM-C 8012	THE SWINGIN' SET (Dave Clark Five/Animals, et al.)	30
66	Mercury 20057 SMCL	SYLVIA (David Raksin)	15

T

70	Pye NSPL 18353	TAKE A GIRL LIKE YOU (Stanley Myers/Foundations)	30
73	EMI EMC 3016	TAKE ME HIGH (Cliff Richard) (some with poster)	25/15
67	RCA RB 6711	THE TAMING OF THE SHREW (dialogue only) (with insert)	15
57	Vogue Coral LVA 9070	TAMMY/INTERLUDE (Frank Skinner/Debbie Reynolds) (1 film per side)	30
63	United Artists ULP 1025	TARAS BULBA (Franz Waxman)	25
76	Arista ARTY 132	TAXI DRIVER (Bernard Herrman)	30
69	T. Motown (S)TML 11110	T.C.B. (Supremes/Temptations, et al.) (laminated gatefold sleeve)	15
58	London HA-D 2074-5	THE TEN COMMANDMENTS (Elmer Bernstein) (2-LP)	30
71	RCA Victor SF 8162	THAT'S THE WAY IT IS (Elvis Presley) (glossy or matt sleeve)	15/12
75	CBS 80575	THAT'S THE WAY OF THE WORLD (Earth, Wind & Fire)	12
79	Arista SPART 1088	THAT SUMMER (Boomtown Rats/Elvis Costello et al.) (yellow vinyl, g/fold sl.)	12
63	Parlophone PMC 1197	THAT WAS THE WEEK THAT WAS (Millicent Martin, et al.) (also stereo PCS 3040)	15
59	Coral LVA 9102	THEMES FROM HORROR MOVIES (Dick Jacobs)	25
70	United Artists UAS 29128	THEY CALL ME MISTER TIBBS (Quincy Jones)	60
69	Philips SBL 7898	THEY CAME TO ROB LAS VEGAS (Georges Gavarentz)	70
70	Stateside SSL 10305	THEY SHOOT HORSES, DON'T THEY? (John Green)	15
73	Elektra K 46239	THE THIEF WHO CAME TO DINNER (Henry Mancini)	18
82	MCA MCF 3148	THE THING (Ennio Morricone)	15
66	Verve VLP 9147	THIS PROPERTY IS CONDEMNED (Kenyon Hopkins)	35
68	United Artists SULP 1218	THE THOMAS CROWN AFFAIR (Michel Legrand/Noel Harrison)	35
68	Sunset SLS 50519	THE THOMAS CROWN AFFAIR (Michel Legrand, reissue)	20
65	Stateside SL 10136	THOSE MAGNIFICENT MEN IN THEIR FLYING MACHINES (Ron Goodwin)	30
54	Capitol LC 6665	THREE SAILORS AND A GIRL (Gordon MacRae, et al.) (10")	15
61	Golden Guinea GGL 0065	THREE WORLDS OF GULLIVER (Bernard Herrmann)	20
85	Cloud Nine CN 4003	THREE WORLDS OF GULLIVER (Bernard Herrmann) (reissue)	15
65	United Artists (S)ULP 1110	THUNDERBALL (John Barry) (mono/stereo)	each 22
67	United Artists (S)ULP 1159	THUNDERBIRDS ARE GO! (Barry Gray/Cliff Richard & Shadows) (mono/stereo)	80/100
69	Polydor 583 717	TILL DEATH DO US PART (Wilfred Burns)	15
72	RCA SF 8253	TIME FOR LOVING (Michel Legrand/Dusty Springfield, et al.)	12
63	MGM MGM-C 934	TO KILL A MOCKINGBIRD (Elmer Bernstein)	15
64	United Artists SULP 1062	TOM JONES (John Addison)	15
59	MGM MGM-C 772	TOM THUMB (Russ Tamblyn)	15
68	Instant INLP 002	TONITE LET'S ALL MAKE LOVE IN LONDON (Pink Floyd/Chris Farlowe, et al.)	100
70	RCA LSA 3008	TOOMORROW (with insert)	75

MINT VALUE

67	Fontana (S)TL 5446	TO SIR, WITH LOVE (Ron Grainer/Lulu/Mindbenders)	3
69	Stateside S(S)L 10271	THE TOUCHABLES (Ken Thorne/Nirvana/Wynder K. Frog, et al.)	3
74	Stax STXH 5001	TOUGH GUYS (Isaac Hayes)	12
75	Warner Bros K 56102	THE TOWERING INFERNO (John Williams)	12
66	Polydor 582 004	THE TRAP (Ron Goodwin)	3
60	Pye Nonesuch PPLD 206	THE TRIAL OF LADY CHATTERLEY (drama/documentary)	12
67	United Artists ULP 1176	TRIPLE CROSS (Georges Garvarentz/Tony Allen)	25
82	CBS 70223	TRON (Wendy Carlos/Journey)	15
73	T. Motown STML 11225	TROUBLE MAN (Marvin Gaye)	20
74	Stax STXD 4001/2	TRUCK TURNER (Isaac Hayes) (2-LP)	18
70	Capitol E-ST 263	TRUE GRIT (Elmer Bernstein/Glen Campbell)	20
61	Fontana TFL 5110	T.V. WESTERN THEMES (also stereo STFL 538) (Johnny Gregory)	10/12
69	Polydor 583 728	TWISTED NERVE/LES BICYCLETTES DE BELSIZE (Les Reed/Barry Mason, Bernard Herrman)	100
69	Columbia S(C)X 6330	TWO CITIES (Jeff Wayne)	35
67	RCA RD/SF 7891	TWO FOR THE ROAD (Henry Mancini)	20
63	United Artists ULP 1027	TWO FOR THE SEESAW (André Previn)	15
71	United Artists UDF 50003	200 MOTELS (Frank Zappa) (2-LP, with booklet & poster)	50
70	MCA MKPS 2013	TWO MULES FOR SISTER SARA (Ennio Morricone)	30
62	Columbia 33SX 1482	TWO TICKETS TO PARIS (Joey Dee)	20

U

05	Trunk JBHO10LP	UFO	30
60	London HA-T 2258	THE UNFORGIVEN (Dimitri Tiomkin)	18
68	Fontana (S)TL 5460	UP THE JUNCTION (Manfred Mann)	40
70	Fontana 6852 005	UP THE JUNCTION (Manfred Mann) (reissue)	12
69	Stax (S)XATS 1005	UPTIGHT (Booker T & MGs)	15

V

73	Philips 6303 075	THE VALACHI PAPERS (Riz Ortolani)	25
68	Stateside (S)SL 10228	VALLEY OF THE DOLLS (André Previn/John Williams)	30
71	London SH-U 8420	VANISHING POINT (Delaney & Bonnie/Sam & Dave, et al.)	35
82	MGM 2315 437	VICTOR, VICTORIA (Henry Mancini)	15
63	Colpix PXL 516	THE VICTORS (Sol Kaplan/Frank Sinatra)	20
59	RCA SF 5092	VICTORY AT SEA (Richard Rogers)	12
85	Parlophone BOND 1	A VIEW TO A KILL (John Barry/Duran Duran)	12
58	London HAT 2118	THE VIKINGS (Mario Nascimbene)	40
68	Dot (S)LPD 515	VILLA RIDES (Maurice Jarre)	15
63	MGM MGM-C 951/CS 6074	THE VIPs (Miklos Rozsa)	20
66	United Artists (S)ULP 1126	VIVA MARIA! (Georges Delerue) (mono/stereo)	30/40
67	United Artists (S)ULP 1185	VIVRE POUR VIVRE (LIFE FOR LIFE) (Francis Lai)	18

W

60	Mercury MMC 14033	WAGON TRAIN (Stanley Wilson, et al.)	25
62	MGM MGM-C 891	WALK ON THE WILD SIDE (Elmer Bernstein)	20
66	Brunswick STA 8636	THE WAR LORD (Jerome Moross)	35
85	London YEAR 2	WATER	12
78	Satril SATL 4009	THE WATER MARGIN (Godiego) (TV soundtrack)	12
67	United Artists ULP 1173	THE WAY WEST (Bromislaw Kaper/Serendipity Singers)	12
67	Virtuoso TPLS 13010	WELLES RAISES KANE (Bernard Herrman)	30
64	Piccadilly N(S)PL 38011	WHAT A CRAZY WORLD (Joe Brown/Susan Maughan/Marty Wilde; mono/stereo)	22/40
64	Golden Guinea GGL 0272	WHAT A CRAZY WORLD (Joe Brown/Susan Maughan/Marty Wilde) (reissue)	12
64	Stateside SL 10090	WHAT A WAY TO GO! (Nelson Riddle)	12
66	RCA SF 7818	WHAT DID YOU DO IN THE WAR, DADDY? (Henry Mancini)	20
65	United Artists ULP 1096	WHAT'S NEW PUSSYCAT? (Burt Bacharach/Tom Jones/Manfred Mann, et al.)	20
66	MGM MGM-C(S) 8006	WHEN THE BOYS MEET THE GIRLS (Connie Francis/Herman's Hermits) (mono/stereo)	15/18
69	MGM MGM-C(S) 8102	WHERE EAGLES DARE (Ron Goodwin)	12
69	Paramount SPFL 254	WHERE'S JACK? (Elmer Bernstein/Mary Hopkin)	12
66	United Artists (S)ULP 1166	WHIPLASH WILLIE (André Previn)	15
67	United Artists (S)ULP 1168	THE WHISPERERS (John Barry)	30
67	Warner Bros W 1656	WHO'S AFRAID OF VIRGINIA WOOLF? (Alex North)	25
98	Trunk BARKED 4	THE WICKER MAN (Giovanni) (with inserts, some red vinyl)	50/30
57	London HA-N 2023	WILD BILL HICKOCK AND JINGLES ON THE SANTA FE TRAIL (TV s/track)	18
69	Warner Bros WS 1814	THE WILD BUNCH (Jerry Fielding) (red label original)	50
71	Warner Bros K 46035	THE WILD BUNCH (Jerry Fielding) (reissue)	15
78	A&M AMLH 64730	THE WILD GEESE (Roy Budd/Joan Armatrading)	20
68	Capitol (S)T 5099	WILD IN THE STREETS (Les Baxter/Gurus) (original issue, black label, rainbow rim)	18
71	MGM 2315 062	WILD ROVERS (Jerry Goldsmith)	20
83	Chrysalis CHR 1453	WILD STYLE (various artists)	20
71	Paramount SPFL 274	WILLY WONKA AND THE CHOCOLATE FACTORY (Leslie Bricusse)	20
75	Arista ARTY 111	THE WIND AND THE LION (Jerry Goldsmith)	15
87	Filmtrax MOMENT 110	WITHNAIL AND I (David Dundas)	25
78	MCA MCSP 287	THE WIZ (Diana Ross/Michael Jackson, et al.) (gatefold sleeve with booklet & poster)	15
57	MGM MGM-C 757	THE WIZARD OF OZ (Judy Garland, et al.)	40
67	Capitol (S)T 2800	WOMAN TIMES SEVEN (Riz Ortolani)	20
64	Columbia SX 1628	WONDERFUL LIFE (Cliff Richard) (gatefold sleeve with inner, also stereo SCX 3515)	15/25
63	Elstree Extra Range	SUMMER HOLIDAY (2-LP, full soundtrack recording, 80 copies only)	350
64	Elstree Extra Range	WONDERFUL LIFE (2-LP, full soundtrack recording, 150 copies only)	350
68	Apple (S)APCOR 1	WONDERWALL MUSIC (George Harrison) (with insert & black inner sleeve, mono/stereo)	250/60

70	Atlantic 2663 001	WOODSTOCK (Jimi Hendrix/Who/Joe Cocker, et al.) (3-LP in foldout sleeve with inners)	20
60	RCA RD 27198	THE WORLD OF SUZIE WONG (George Duning)	15
57	Brunswick LAT 8174	WRITTEN ON THE WIND/FOUR GIRLS IN TOWN (Frank Skinner)	25

Y

65	MGM MGM-C 997	THE YELLOW ROLLS-ROYCE (Riz Ortolani)	15
69	Apple PMC 7070	YELLOW SUBMARINE (Beatles) (1st pressing, laminated flipback sleeve with red lines above & below rear liner note & black inner; with "Sold In The UK..." label text; mono)	175
69	Apple PCS 7070	YELLOW SUBMARINE (Beatles) (1st pressing, laminated flipback sleeve with red lines above & below rear liner note & black inner; with "Sold In The UK..." label text; stereo)	60
79	Warwick WW 5075	YESTERDAY'S HERO	20
61	Golden Guinea GGL 0081	YOGI BEAR TV SERIES (TV soundtrack)	12
69	CBS (S) 70045	YOU ARE WHAT YOU EAT (Tiny Tim/Electric Flag, et al.)	12
71	Ember NR 5055	YOU CAN'T HAVE EVERYTHING (Joe Parnello/Bobby Scott)	12
79	MCA MCF 2804	YOUNGBLOOD (War)	15
66	Philips (S)BL 7792	YOUNG GIRLS OF ROCHEFORT (Michel Legrand)	25
57	Brunswick LAT 8252	THE YOUNG LIONS (Hugo Friedhofer)	35
61	Columbia 33SX 1384	THE YOUNG ONES (Cliff Richard) (with inner sleeve, also stereo SCX 3397)	20/40
67	United Artists (S)ULP 1171	YOU ONLY LIVE TWICE (John Barry/Nancy Sinatra)	20
65	MGM MGM-CS 6081	YOUR CHEATIN' HEART (Hank Williams Jr.)	18
67	Kama Sutra KLP 402	YOU'RE A BIG BOY NOW (Lovin' Spoonful)	32

Z

70	MGM MGM CS 8120	ZABRISKIE POINT (Pink Floyd/Jerry Garcia/Kaleidoscope, et al.)	20
71	Probe SPB 1026	ZACHARIAH (Country Joe & Fish/James Gang, et al.)	12
69	Philips 600-287	ZITA	50
64	Ember NR 5012	ZULU (John Barry) (yellow/orange label, flipback sleeve)	25
65	Stateside SL10127	ZORBA THE GREEK (Nikis Theodoratis)	12

ORIGINAL STAGE SHOW & RADIO CAST RECORDING LPs
(alphabetical by title)

A

60	Columbia SX 1211	ALADDIN (Bob Monkhouse)	25
64	Columbia SX 1676	ALADDIN AND HIS WONDERFUL LAMP (g/fold sleeve, also stereo SCX 3522)	18/22
70	Argo ZTA 501-2	ALICE IN WONDERLAND (2-LP, Jane Asher)	20
71	RCA SER 5618	AMBASSADOR (Howard Keel)	20
82	Key LP 4	ANDY CAPP (Alan Price)	15
70	CBS 70053	ANNE OF GREEN GABLES	15
50	Brunswick LAT 8002	ANNIE GET YOUR GUN	12
58	Capitol LCT 6150	ANNIE GET YOUR GUN	12
70	CBS 70052	ANN VERONICA (Arthur Lowe)	15
69	Studio Two TWO 233	ARCADIANS	12

B

66	Columbia S(C)X 6009	BABES IN THE WOOD (mono/stereo) (Frank Ifield)	20/22
69	RCA Intl. INT 1037	BANDWAGON	12
59	Decca SKL 4136	BELLE — OR THE BALLAD OF DOCTOR CRIPPEN	20
58	Philips BBL 7201	BELLS ARE RINGING (Judy Holliday)	12
64	Capitol (S)W 2191	BEN FRANKLIN IN PARIS	12
65	Parlophone PMC 1238	BEYOND OUR KEN	20
61	Parlophone PMC 1145	BEYOND THE FRINGE (Peter Cook etc.)	15
74	CBS 70133	BILLY (gatefold sleeve, with lyric sheet)	15
62	HMV CLP 1569/CSD 1441	BLITZ! (mono/stereo)	15/18
54	HMV DLP 1078	THE BOYFRIEND (10")	12
63	Decca LK 4564	THE BOYS FROM SYRACUSE (Bob Monkhouse)	15
63	Parlophone PMC 1190	BRIDGE ON THE RIVER WYE (also stereo PCS 3036)	20/25
56	HMV CLP 1064	BUCCANEER (Kenneth Williams)	40
61	Philips ABL 3383	BYE BYE BIRDIE — LONDON CAST (Marty Wilde) (also stereo SABL 205)	20/22
61	HMV CSD 1366	BYE BYE BIRDIE (Studio cast including Sid James)	50

C

66	Columbia KOS 3040	CABARET	12
69	CBS (S)BRG 70039	CABARET (Judi Dench)	12
64	Melodisc MLP 12-146	CALYPSO CARNIVAL	15
64	HMV CLP 1756/CSD 1559	CAMELOT	12
60s	Encore	CAN CAN	40
64	Decca LK/SKL 4596	THE CANTERBURY TALES	12
65	Pye N(S)PL 18408	THE CARD	40
71	Polydor 2383 035	CATCH MY SOUL — THE ROCK-OTHELLO	12
66	CBS (S)BPG 62627	CHARLIE GIRL	15
58	Decca LK 4303	CINDERELLA (Tommy Steele)	25
67	Columbia S(C)X 6103	CINDERELLA (Cliff Richard/Shadows)	35
64	Decca LK 4559	CINDY-ELLA (Cleo Laine)	12
66	Decca LK/SKL 4810	COME SPY WITH ME (Barbara Windsor)	22
56	HMV CLP 1082	CRANKS (Anthony Newley)	50
60	HMV CLP 1375	NEW CRANKS (Bernard Cribbins)	50
59	HMV CLP 1298	THE CROOKED MILE	15

MINT VALUE £

D

Year	Label	Title	Value
75	Warner Bros K 56186	DAD'S ARMY	12
70	CBS 70063	DAMES AT SEA	20
57	HMV CLP 1108	DAMN YANKEES	12
65	Decca LK/SKL 4675	DIVORCE ME, DARLING	12
62	Decca LK 4413/SKL 4145	DO RE MI	12
61	RCA RD 27228/SF 5107	DO RE MI	12
82	Geffen GEF 85578	DREAMGIRLS (gatefold sleeve, with insert)	12

E

78	Astoria AST 1	ELVIS (P.J. Proby/Shakin' Stevens/Tim Whitnall) (sold at performances of "Elvis" show, laminated sleeve)	30
78	MCA MOG 3527	EVITA (silver sleeve)	12
58	Pye NPL 18016	EXPRESSO BONGO (Millicent Martin)	18

F

60	MGM MGM-C 871	THE FANTASTICS	12
60	Decca SKL 4092	FINGS AIN'T WOT THEY USED TO BE	15
64	Reprise F(S) 2015	FINIAN'S RAINBOW — REPRISE REPERTORY THEATRE PRESENTS (mono/stereo)	15/18
59	Capitol SW 1321	FIORELLO!	12
60	HMV CSD 1305	FLOWER DRUM SONG	12
60	HMV CLP 1366	FOLLOW THAT GIRL (Susan Hampshire)	15
63	Ember CEL 902	FOOL BRITANNIA (Studio Cast: Peter Sellers/Anthony Newley/Joan Collins)	20
66	Parlophone PMC 7014	FOUR DEGREES OVER	12
57	Oriole MG 20016	FREE AS AIR	15
64	Parlophone PCS 3065	FUNNY GAME POLITICS	15
64	Capitol (S)W 2059	FUNNY GIRL (Original Broadway Cast) (mono/stereo)	12
63	HMV CLP 1685	A FUNNY THING HAPPENED ON THE WAY TO THE FORUM (Frankie Howerd)	20

G

72	Bell BELLS 203	GODSPELL (David Essex)	12
64	Capitol (S)W 2124	GOLDEN BOY (Sammy Davis Jr.)	12
71	Columbia SCXA 9252	GONE WITH THE WIND (gatefold sleeve)	12
57	HMV CLP 1103	GRAB ME A GONDOLA	12
53	Brunswick LAT 8022	GUYS AND DOLLS	12
64	Reprise F(S) 2016	GUYS AND DOLLS — REPRISE REPERTORY THEATRE PRESENTS	15/18
70s	RCA Red Seal SER 5686	GYPSY (gatefold sleeve)	12

H

68	RCA RD/SF 7959	HAIR (Broadway)	12
69	Polydor 583 043	HAIR (London)	12
63	Decca LK/SKL 4521	HALF-A-SIXPENCE	12
70s	Groovy STP 3	HANGAHAIR	12
57	Oriole MG 20014	HARMONY CLOSE (Bernard Cribbins)	25
65	RCA Victor RD/SF 7768	HELLO, DOLLY! (with insert)	12
64	Pye NPL 18100/NSPL 83022	HIGH SPIRITS	20
60	Fontana TFL 5104	HITS FROM THE GANG SHOWS!	12
70	CBS BRG 70027	HOUDINI — MAN OF MAGIC	15
63	RCA RD/SF 7564	HOW TO SUCCEED IN BUSINESS WITHOUT REALLY TRYING	15

I

68	RCA Victor RD/SF 7938	I DO! I DO!	15
64	Oriole PS 40062	INSTANT MARRIAGE	30
76	EMI EMC 3139	IRENE	12

J

68	CBS 66207	JACQUES BREL IS ALIVE AND WELL AND LIVING IN PARIS (2-LP)	15
75	MCA MCF 2726	JEEVES	50
74	RSO 2394 141	JOHN, PAUL, GEORGE, RINGO AND BERT (with London cast)	15
58	Decca LK 4352	JOHNNY THE PRIEST	100
83	TER S1044	JOHNNY THE PRIEST (Limited Edition reissue)	25
66	HMV CLP/CSD 3591	JORROCKS	15
56	Philips	JOYCE GRENFELL REQUESTS THE PLEASURE	15

K

| 53 | Brunswick LAT 8026 | THE KING AND I | 12 |
| 64 | Reprise F(S) 2017 | KISS ME KATE — REPRISE REPERTORY THEATRE PRESENTS | 12/15 |

L

60	Capitol SW 1240	LITTLE MARY SUNSHINE	12
64	Pye NSPL 83023	LITTLE ME	12
59	Decca LK 4320	LOCK UP YOUR DAUGHTERS	12
73	Reflection RL 306	LONESOME STONE	22

M

64	Decca LK/SKL 4643	MAGGIE MAY (mono/stereo)	15/18
72	Columbia SCX 6504	MAID OF THE MOUNTAINS	12
60	HMV CLP 1333	MAKE ME AN OFFER (Daniel Massey)	20
60s	CBS (S) 70051	MAME	12
68	London HA-R/SH-R 8362	MAN OF LA MANCHA	12
59	HMV CLP 1275	MARIGOLD	12
61	Oriole MG 20054	MINE FAIR SADIE	20
60	HMV CLP 1365	THE MOST HAPPY FELLA!	12
68	CBS 70048	MR. & MRS.	15

57	Brunswick LAT 8184	MR. WONDERFUL	12
50s	Capitol W 990	THE MUSIC MAN	15

N

72	Ace Of Clubs ACL 1238	A NIGHT OF MUSIC HALL	15
63	Decca LK/SKL 4576	NO STRINGS	20

O

63	Decca LK/SKL 4542	OH! WHAT A LOVELY WAR	12
50	Brunswick LAT 8001	OKLAHOMA	12
60	Decca LK 4359	OLIVER! (also stereo SKL 4105)	15
60	World Record Club TP 151	OLIVER! (mono/stereo) (cast includes Steve Marriot)	12
61	HMV CLP 1459/CSD 1370	OLIVER! (mono/stereo) (Alma Cogan)	30/35
60	London HA-T 2286	ONCE UPON A MATTRESS	12
80	Warner Bros K 56850	ONE MO' TIME	12
61	Decca LK 4393/SKL 4133	ONE OVER THE EIGHT (mono/stereo) (Kenneth Williams)	25/30
61	Decca LK 4395/SKL 4134	ON THE BRIGHTER SIDE	15
67	CBS	ON THE LEVEL	12
63	CBS 60005	ON THE TOWN	30
65	Parlophone PCS 3066	OUR MAN CRICHTON (Kennet Moore)	20

P

65	CBS BPG 62598	PASSION FLOWER HOTEL (mono only)	30
65	Ace Of Clubs ACL 1112	PERCHANCE TO DREAM	15
63	Parlophone PMC 1198	PETER COOK PRESENTS THE ESTABLISHMENT	20
65	RCA RD 7722	PETER PAN	12
69	Philips SBL 7916	PHIL THE FLUTER	20
74	Fontana SFL 13190	PHIL THE FLUTER	12
59	Decca LK 4337	PIECES OF EIGHT (Kenneth Williams)	20
59	Decca SKL 4084	PIECES OF EIGHT (stereo) (Kenneth Williams)	25
77	MCA MCF 2826	THE POINT (Mickey Dolenz)	12
60	Melodisc MLP 12-117	PREACHIN', PRAYIN', SINGIN' AND SHOUTIN' GOSPEL	15
64	London HA-U/SH-U 8201	THE PRINCE AND THE PAUPER	15
78	EMI EMC 3233	PRIVATES ON PARADE	20
69	United Artists UAS 29075	PROMISES, PROMISES	15

R

75	UK UKAL 1015	THE ROCKY HORROR SHOW (London Cast)	15
74	Ode ODE 77026	THE ROCKY HORROR SHOW (U.S. Roxy Cast)	15

S

56	Oriole MG 20004	SALAD DAYS	12
58	Pye NPL 18011	SHARE MY LETTUCE (Kenneth Williams)	30
60s	Philips 632 303 BL	SPACE IS SO STARTLING	20
61	Decca LK 4408/SKL 4142	STOP THE WORLD I WANT TO GET OFF (Anthony Newley)	12
67	Wing WL 1172	SUMMER SONG	20
67	CBS (S)BRG 70035	SWEET CHARITY	15

T

60	Fontana TFL 5103	TAKE IT FROM HERE (excerpts from radio show, also stereo STFL 534)	25/30
60	Capitol SW 1492	TENDERLOIN	12
63	Parlophone PMC 1197	THAT WAS THE WEEK THAT WAS (also stereo PCS 3040)	15
67	World Record Club SH 849	THOROUGHLY MODERN MILLIE	15
72	Decca SKL 5137	TOM BROWNE'S SCHOOLDAYS	15
69	Columbia S(C)X 6330	TWO CITIES (Jeff Wayne)	25
66	United Artists (S)ULP 1116	TWANG! (Lionel Bart)	30

V

63	Decca LK/SKL 4536	VIRTUE IN DANGER	12

W

64	Decca LK/SKL 4610	WAIT A MINIM	15
	HMV DLP 1097	WATER GYPSIES (10") (Dora Bryan)	25
65	HMV CLP 1834/CSD 1587	THE WAYWARD WAY	35
54	Parlophone PMD 1011	WEDDING IN PARIS (10")	20
61	HMV CLP 1467	WILDEST DREAMS	15
56	HMV DLP 1125	WILD GROWS THE HEATHER (10")	20

Y

68	RCA SB 6792	THE YOUNG VISITORS	15
67	MGM MGM-C(S) 8045	YOU'RE A GOOD MAN, CHARLIE BROWN	12

SPORT RECORDINGS

87	BBC Radio Derby	BACK TO THE TOP (cassette, limited edition)	20
77	Quality QP 23/77	BATTLE OF THE GIANTS: 1977 FA CUP FINAL — MANCHESTER UNITED V LIVERPOOL	15
78	Quality QP 26/78	BOBBY'S DAZZLERS: 1978 FA CUP FINAL — IPSWICH V ARSENAL	15
71	Quality QP 8/71	CHELSEA KINGS OF EUROPE: 1971 EUROPEAN CUP WINNERS CUP FINAL — CHELSEA V REAL MADRID	20
70	Quality QP 4/70	CHELSEA'S CUP:1970 FA CUP FINAL — CHELSEA V LEEDS	20
85	BBC Radio Derby	THE DERBY COUNTY STORY (double cassette, in numbered foldout case)	20
73	Quality QP 12/73	EUROPEAN CUP: THE MATCH 1968 — MANCHESTER UNITED V BENFICA	30

MINT VALUE £

78	Quality QP 25/78	FABULOUS FOREST: 1978 LEAGUE CUP FINAL — FOREST V LIVERPOOL, WEMBLEY AND OLD TRAFFORD REPLAY	15
79	Quality QP 28/79	FOREST ARE MAGIC: 1979 LEAGUE CUP FINAL — FOREST V SOUTHAMPTON	15
80	Quality QP 33/80	FOREST'S EURO DOUBLE: 1979 EUROPEAN CUP FINAL V MALMÖ/1980 EUROPEAN CUP FINAL V HAMBURG	12
84	Quality HM 2	THE FRIENDLY FINAL: EVERTON V LIVERPOOL MILK CUP 1984	15
75	Quality QP 17/75	HAIL TO THE HAMMERS: 1975 FA CUP FINAL — WEST HAM V FULHAM	15
80	Quality QP 31/80	HAMMERS HEROES: 1980 FA CUP FINAL OFFICIAL SOUVENIR	15
81	Quality QP 34/81	LEAGUE CUP FINAL 1981: WEMBLEY HIGHLIGHTS AND THE REPLAY: LIVERPOOL V WEST HAM	15
76	Quality QP 18/76	LEAGUE CUP FINAL 1976: MANCHESTER CITY V NEWCASTLE UNITED	15
72	Quality QP 9/72	LEAGUE CUP FINAL 1972: CHELSEA V STOKE CITY	20
74	Quality QP 15/74	LIVERPOOL'S CUP: 1974 FA CUP FINAL — LIVERPOOL V NEWCASTLE	15
82	Quality QP 38/82	LIVERPOOL'S 1982 LEAGUE CUP DOUBLE: LIVERPOOL V SPURS	15
78	Quality QP 27/78	LIVERPOOL, THE LEGEND OF EUROPE: 1978 EUROPEAN CUP FINAL — LIVERPOOL V BRUGES	12
79	Quality QP 29/79	MATCH OF THE CENTURY: 1979 FA CUP FINAL — ARSENAL V MANCHESTER UNITED	15
71	Quality QP 7/71	1971 FA CUP FINAL: ARSENAL V LIVERPOOL	15
71	Quality QP 6/71	1971 LEAGUE CUP FINAL: SPURS V ASTON VILLA	20
72	BBC REC 122M	1972 FA CUP FINAL: LEEDS V ARSENAL	15
69	Quality QP 37/81	1969 FA CUP FINAL: MANCHESTER CITY V LEICESTER CITY	15
69	Quality QP 2/69	1969 HOME INTERNATIONAL TOURNAMENT: ENGLAND V SCOTLAND	15
73	Quality QP 15/74	SUNDERLAND'S CUP: 1973 FA CUP FINAL — SUNDERLAND V LEEDS	20
76	Quality QP 19/76	SUPER SAINTS: 1976 FA CUP FINAL — SOUTHAMPTON V MANCHESTER UNITED	15
81	Quality Products QP 36/81	VILLA THE CHAMPIONS: HIGHLIGHTS OF 1980-81 SEASON	12
77	Quality QP 22/77	VILLA'S HAT TRICK: ASTON VILLA V EVERTON 1977 LEAGUE CUP FINAL REPLAY	15
81	Quality QP 37/81	VIVA EL KOP: THE STORY OF LIVERPOOL'S 1981 EUROPEAN CUP VICTORY	12
75	Quality QP 16/75	VIVA THE VILLA: 1975 FOOTBALL LEAGUE CUP FINAL	15
76	Quality QP 21/76	WE'VE KOPPED THE CUP: 1976 UEFA CUP FINAL — LIVERPOOL V BRUGES	12
80	Quality QP 30/80	WOLVES CUP: 1980 FOOTBALL LEAGUE CUP	15
74	Quality QP 14/74	WONDERFUL WOLVES: 1974 LEAGUE CUP FINAL — WOLVERHAMPTON WANDERERS V MANCHESTER CITY	20
66	Centaur CPC 1234	WORLD CUP '66	40
81	Quality QP 35/81	YEAR OF THE COCKEREL: 1981 CENTENARY CUP FINAL	15

MUSIC LIBRARY LPS

Still comparatively little is known about the mysterious and often forgotten sub-genre of music known as "library", or rather non-commercial music pressed just for use in film, TV and radio. Since the mid 90s collecting interest has peaked, dropped away and is now well on the rise again, as are prices for some of the rarer and more important pieces. Collectors also seem to favour early recordings by famous artists such as Jimmy Page or Tubby Hayes.

Original pressing numbers and distribution still remain mysterious, most people guestimate that 500 to 1,000 copies for each library pressing is about the average, especially as we move towards the mid 70s. Older and larger music companies, such as De Wolfe, originally issued recordings on 10" (throughout the late 60s) in incredibly short runs maybe only 200 to 300 copies, and if these recordings proved commercially successful, they were re-pressed later on 12".

Obviously, the original smaller pressings are more desirable. But still pressing numbers and habits remain shrouded in mystery. It has to be noted that many international and desirable labels distributed their library recordings in the UK and these do turn up from time to time. However, we only list original UK pressings in this price guide.

This year we have expanded and reorganised this small library section and listed LPs alphabetically by Library company. Also, it's worth noting that, for libraries such as Chappell and Conroy, not all LPs have titles - they simply list the artist names and track titles. In these cases we have just put down the LP catalogue numbers. This whole section should expand further over the next few years as more information slowly comes to light, especially about some of the rarer 10" jazz and experimental pressings of the mid 1960s period.

One final note; all library records are still the property of the library companies that issued them and they can, at any time, ask for them back. This is all a little unlikely, but you have been warned.

AMPHONIC
| 73 | AMPSLP1001 | Moodsetter/Pacesetter | 20 |

APOLLO SOUNDS
| 71 | APP 5012 | Robin Jones - DENGA (blue label) | 40 |
| 71 | APP 5016 | Robin Jones - EL MAJA (blue label) | 20 |

BOSWORTH
66	BLP 102	ELECTRONIC MUSIC (10")	40
67	BLP 104	ATONAL JAZZ STRUCTURES (10")	25
68	BLP 108	JAZZ DRAMATICS (10")	20
69	BLP 109	MODERN RHYTHM (10")	20
70	BLP 116	INDUSTRIAL ROCK (10")	15
70	BLP 118	MODERN DRAMATICS (10")	25
70	BLP 120	HARD AND FAST (10")	25
71	BLP 121	MISCELLANEA (10")	25
72	BLP 126	RHYTHMIC MOODS (10")	15
73	BLP 130	KEYBOARD PLUS	20
74	BLP 135	RHYTHM AT RANDOM	40
75	BLP 141	AMERICA '76	50
75	BLP 142	LET'S GO SOLO	15
75	BLP 143	MUSICAL COCKTAIL	20

CHAPPELL

70	CIS 5001	BIG BAND SOUNDS VOL. 1	12
70	CIS 5003	INDUSTRIAL SOUNDS VOL. 2	25
70	CIS 5007	LIGHT ATMOSPHERE VOL. 2	40
70	CIS 5008	MUSIC FOR DRAMA VOL. 1 (John Barry etc)	30
70	CIS 5009	MUSIC FOR DRAMA VOL. 2	25
70	CIS 5013	DANCE MUSIC VOLUME 1 (Night Club)	25
70	CIS 5023	JAZZ (SMALL GROUP) (John Barry etc)	30
70	CIS 5024	MUSIC FOR DRAMA VOL. 3 (Robert Farnon)	30
75	CIS 5047	POP SOUNDS	40
70	672-677	672-677	25
70	678-682	678-682	20
71	1040	1040	15
72	LPC 1045	Lee Mason	100
72	LPC 1051	Lee Mason	75
72	LPC 1052	Mark Duval	60
72	LPC 1053	Pop Sounds	30
73	LPC 1055	Electronic Music	25
73	LPC 1056	Cacavas / Hawksworth - Mark Duval	50
73	LPC 1058	Mark Duval	50
73	LPC 1059	Lee Mason	75
73	LPC 1060	Robert Farnon	20
73	LPC 1063	Roger Webb	30
73	LPC 1065	Rhythm'n'Brass - Mark Duval	100
73	LPC 1068	Dave Holland	30
73	LPC 1069	Light And Bright - Mark Duval	40
74	LPC 1070	Mark Duval	60
74	LPC 1711	Mark Duval	30
74	LPC 1075	Mark Duval	20
74	LPC 1076	Mark Duval	120
74	LPC 1077	Mark Duval	40

CONROY

70	BMLP070	BMLP070	15
70	BMLP071	BMLP071	20
70	BMLP072	Electronic Percussion Points	40
70	BMLP074	Theme And Variation	20
70	BMLP080	Electroscope	30
71	BMLP089	BMLP089	20
72	BMLP090	BMLP090	25
72	BMLP092	London's Underground	75
73	BMLP093	BMLP093	80
73	BMLP097	BMLP097	30
74	BMLP101	Happy Moog	25
74	BMLP103	Clap Trap	25
74	BMLP114	Soft Sounds	30
75	BMLP115	Londons Underground 2	20
75	BMLP117	Sounds And Percussion	20
75	BMLP123	Electronic Sounds	30
75	BMLP124	Dramatic Tempi	75
75	BMLP128	Chromozones	35
75	BMLP131	On The Road	40
75	BMLP132	Sounds Funky	20
75	BMLP143	Feelings	300

CONROY EUROBEATS SERIES

73	EURO 1	Silly Synthesisers	15
73	EURO 2	Ethnic / India	40
73	EURO 3	Modern Baroque	20
73	EURO 4	Romantic Backgrounds	50
73	EURO 5	Dramatic Backgrounds	50
73	EURO 10	World At Work	50
73	EURO 11	Colla Voce	65

DE WOLFE

All original issues have Blue and white "Standard Bearer" labels. Later issues with red labels are worth approx half the original value. 12" pressings of original 10" LP's are worth approx half.

65	DW LP2949	Band 8 (10")	40
65	DW LP2950	High Speed Jazz (10")	20
65	DW/LP2966	Mind On The Run (10")	50
66	DW/LP2968	Journey Into Sound (10")	40
66	DW LP2973	Abstractions Of The Industrial North (10")	75
66	DW LP2974	The Wild One (10") - features Jimmy Page	60
67	DW/LP2975	Town Beat (10")	20
67	DW/LP3022	Checkpoint (10")	20
67	DW/LP3040	Electric Banana (10")	100
67	DW/LP3066	Don't Lose Your Cool (10")	30
68	DW/LP3069	More Electric Banana (10")	80
68	DW/LP3088	Quietly With Johann (10")	20
69	DW/LP3114	Who's Gonna Buy? The Lemon Dips (10")	75
66	DW LP3115	Caribbean Sound (10")	20
69	DW/LP3123	Even More Electric Banana (10")	40
69	DW/LP3135	Electroshake Vol. 2 (10")	25

MINT VALUE £

69	DW/LP3136	Pop Sounds By The Cool (10").. 40
70	DW/LP3154	Heavy Gravy (10")... 25
71	DW/LP3182	Vocal Patterns.. 25
71	DW/LP3212	Moonshade.. 30
71	DW LP3214	Anglo Amercan Jazz... 100
71	DW/LP3220	Afro-Rock.. 75
71	DW/LP3224	Little Bossa.. 25
71	DW/LP3227	Vocal Shades And Tones.. 150
72	DW/LP3243	Hogan, The Hawk And Dirty John Crown................................ 40
73	DW/LP3285	Big Beat... 60
74	DW/LP3318	Hard Hitter.. 40
75	DW/LP3324	Bite Hard.. 40
75	DW/LP3328	Rhythmes.. 60
76	DW/LP3347	A Rose For Dracula... 25

DE WOLFE "In Editions" Series
| 76 | Timing 12 | Conversations Between East And West.................................. 45 |
| 76 | Timing 14 | Cradle Of Time.. 30 |

HARMONIC
| 68 | CBL618 | FONTEYNS FOLK JAZZ (10")... 30 |
| 69 | CBL621 | MORE BEAT (10").. 20 |

KPM
66	KPM/ACW1	Music For Your Movies.. 20
69	KPM1021	Light Jazz Feeling.. 30
69	KPM1029	Colours In Rhythm.. 30
69	KPM1037	Flamboyant Themes.. 20
69	KPM1038	Flamboyant Themes 2.. 25
69	KPM1042	Jazz Graphics/Spy Set.. 25
69	KPM1044	The Big Beat... 100
69	KPM1046	Sounds In Percussion.. 20
69	KPM1049	Chorus And Orchestra... 100
69	KPM1054	Native Africa... 25
70	KPM1055	Dramatic Background... 30
70	KPM1059	Gentle Sounds 3... 20
69	KPM1061	Impact And Action.. 20
69	KPM1063	Contemporary Colour... 20
70	KPM1067	The Big Beat - Volume 2.. 75
70	KPM1070	Bugaloo In Brazil... 40
70	KPM1071	The Brazillian Suite... 40
71	KPM1076	Speed And Excitement.. 35
72	KPM1079	Beat Industrial... 30
72	KPM1084	Mediterranean Intrigue... 40
71	KPM1085	Electronic Music.. 40
71	KPM1086	Music For A Young Generation.. 50
71	KPM1087	Technical Viewpoint.. 50
71	KPM1088	Bass Guitar And Percussion - Volume 1................................. 40
71	KPM1089	Bass Guitar And Percussion - Volume 2................................. 30
71	KPM1090	Bass Guitar And Percussion - Volume 3................................. 30
71	KPM1091	Vibraphone Jazz Quartet... 20
71	KPM1094	Accent on Percussion/Construction In Jazz.............................. 30
71	KPM1095	Theme Suites /Mustang... 40
71	KPM1100	The Big Screen... 20
72	KPM1102	Electrosound... 30
72	KPM1103	Electromusic... 25
72	KPM1104	Electrosonic... 25
72	KPM1111	Brass Plus Moog... 20
72	KPM1119	Look On The Bright Side.. 15
72	KPM1122	Move With The Times... 25
72	KPM1123	Friendly Faces... 20
72	KPM1124	Big Business... 35
73	KPM1126	Summer Songbirds... 40
73	KPM1128	Counterpoint In Rhythm.. 40
73	KPM1130	Afro Rock.. 75
73	KPM1131	Trendsetters... 25
74	KPM1137	Great Expectations.. 30
74	KPM1138	Gathering Crowds.. 20
74	KPM1161	Industry Volume 1.. 20
74	KPM1163	Rock Spectrum... 20
74	KPM1165	Jazz Inclination.. 30
74	KPM1166	Piano Vibrartions... 30
74	KPM1167	Outdoor Life... 15
74	KPM1168	Drama... 20
74	KPM1170	Sounds Of The Time.. 20
74	KPM1171	Impact... 20
74	KPM1171	Visual Impact.. 15
74	KPM1177	Hot Wax... 20
77	KPM1178	Caricatures.. 15
77	KPM1183	Middle East Suite.. 15
77	KPM1191	Landscapes.. 15
77	KPM1192	The Road Forward.. 20
77	KPM1196	Rock On... 30
77	KPM1214	Pulse Of The City.. 15

PEER INTERNATIONAL

70	PIL9006	My Thing	60
71	PIL9009	Big Hammer	40
72	PIL9013	Mindbender	150
73	PIL9023	Reggae For Real	75
74	PIL9026	Solar Flares	60
74	PIL9027	Electric Bazaar	40
75	PIL9028	Scoop!	25
76	PIL9029	5+4	25
77	PIL9037	Hit Man	25
77	PIL9038	Hangover	40
78	PIL9039	Lost Star	40

PROGRAMME MUSIC
All later re-badged and re-sleeved as JW Media records. Prices remain the same.

75	PM8	On The Side Of Angels	35
75	PM11	Music To Varnish Owls By	20
75	PM18	Ad-Version Therapy!	20

REGENCY LINE

75	RL1001	Light Background Vol. 1	15
75	RL1002	Themes	15
75	RL1003	Rock	15
75	RL1004	Rock	15
75	RL1008	Synthesiser Spots	15
76	RL1013	Dramatic Moods	20
76	RL1019	The Detectives	25

STANDARD

	ESL 103	Solo Guitar (Michael Chapman)	40
	ESL 104	Electronic Music	100

STUDIO G

70	LPSG1001	Beat Group	120
70	LPSG1002	Big Jazz & Big Beat	40
70	LPSG1008	Dramatic And Horror	20
80	LPSG4004	Abstract	15

STUDIO ONE

71	SO7	MAURICE POP	15
73	SO14	PIERRE LAVIN POP BAND	30

SYLVESTER

67	SMC/LP501	Jazz Waves (10")	15
67	SMC/LP502	Voices In The Wind (10")	35
67	SMC/LP505	And So On (10")	15
70	SMC/LP525	Jazz For Action	40
71	SMC/LP527	Blue Cylinder	30
71	SMC/LP529	Ultra Pop-Op	40

THEMES

74	TIM1012	Synthesizer And Percussion	25
74	TIM1013	Breath Of Danger	40
74	TIM1015	Mystery Movie	20
75	TIM1018	The All American Powerhouse	20
76	TIM1021	The Voice Of Soul	40
76	TIM1022	The Sound Of Soul	50
76	TIM1024	Drama Suite - Part 1	125
76	TIM1025	The Drama Suite - Part II	125
76	TIM1025	Things To Come	40

A

ABBA: Rarities (42); & D (144); D (158); R (184); R (212); F (217); F (6); D (265)
ABBEY ROAD: F & D (223)
ABC: I (263)
ABSURD LABEL: D (255)
ACE RECORDS: F (256)
AC/DC: D (91); I, D, F, (197); R & I (222)
ACID JAZZ: F (290)
ACID MOTHERS TEMPLE: F & D (261)
DAVID ACKLES: F & D (237)
A CERTAIN RATIO: I & D (188)
ACT: I (294)
ACTORS WHO SING F (306)
THE ACTION: F & D (94)
ADAM & THE ANTS: F & D (114); D (256); F & D (311)
BRYAN ADAMS: F & D (148)
HASIL ADKINS: F (277)
THE ADVERTS: F & D (113)
AEROSMITH: F & D (119); R (173)
AEROVONS: F (282)
A-HA: F & D (80); F & D (116)
JAN AKKERMAN: F (219)
THE ALARM: F & D (84); R (253)
THE ALBION BAND: I & D (174)
ARTHUR ALEXANDER: F & D (66)
ALL ABOUT EVE: F & D (113)
THE ALLMAN BROTHERS: R (122)
ALL SAINTS: R & D (227)
ALL TOMORROW'S PARTIES: R (250)
MARC ALMOND/SOFT CELL: F & D (103); F & D (223); F & D (224); F & D(225); I (266). See also SOFT CELL.
ALTERED IMAGES: F & D (129)
ALTERNATIVE TV: F & D (211)
AMAZING BLONDEL: I & D (191)
AMBIENT MUSIC: F & D (178)
AMEN: I & D (266)
AMON DUUL II: F & D (167)
TORI AMOS: F & D (176); I & D (243)
GERRY ANDERSON: F & D (167); F & D (168); F & D (173)
IAN ANDERSON: F (264); I(293)
THE ANIMALS: D (76); I & D (183); F & D (184); F (256). See also ERIC BURDON.
PAUL ANKA: F & D (155)
ANTHRAX: F & D (101); I (247)
AOR: F (234)
APPLE LABEL: D (46); D & I (108); D(152)
ARAB STRAP: I & D (247)
JOAN ARMATRADING: F & D (158)
THE ART OF NOISE & ZTT: D (110); I (238)
PP ARNOLD: I (295)
THE ARTWOODS: I & D (153)
ASH: I & D (196)
ASIA: F & D (192); Geoff Downes: I. See also JOHN WETTON.
THE ASSOCIATES: F & R (252) See also BILLY MacKENZIE.
THE ASSOCIATION: F & D (118)
'AS TIME GOES BY': F (237); F (238); F (239); F (240)
RICK ASTLEY: & D (115)
ATLANTIC JAZZ: D (270)
ATOMIC ROOSTER & D (104)
BRIAN AUGER: F (257)
AUCTIONS: F(218); F (221); F (230); F (239); F (291) See also BONHAM'S, CHRISTIE'S and SOTHEBY'S.

AUSTRALASIAN GARAGE ROCK: F (287)
AUTUMN RECORDS: D (210)
'THE AVENGERS' & D (171)
DAVID AXELROD & D (254); I (265)
KEVIN AYERS: I & D (154); I (229)
ROY AYERS: F (290)
AZTEC CAMERA: I & D (244)

B

BABES IN TOYLAND: I & D (190)
BABYBIRD: I (267)
BURT BACHARACH: R (196); I (323)
'BACKTRACK' LABEL & D (101)
BAD COMPANY: F (277)
BAD SEEDS: I (315)
BADFINGER & D (109); R (256)
BADLY DRAWN BOY: I & D (246)
DANNY BAKER: F (176)
LAVERN BAKER & D (61)
ED BALL: I & D (194)
HANK BALLARD: F (284)
BAMBOO LABEL: F (303)
BANANARAMA & D (38); D(101)
THE BAND & US/UK D (48); R (254); I (317) See also ROBBIE ROBERTSON.
THE BANGLES & D (91)
PETER BANKS: I & D (169)
BARCLAY JAMES HARVEST & D (111); R & D (240); F (276); I (321)
BASTA LABEL: F (230)
BBC RADIOPHONIC WORKSHOP: F (255)
BRIGITTE BARDOT: D (188)
SYD BARRETT & Pink Floyd: D (104); F (258); F (271) See also PINK FLOYD.
GARY BARLOW: R (205). See also TAKE THAT.
THE BARRON KNIGHTS & D (64)
JOHN BARRY: F & D 1957-64 (182); D (262)
SHIRLEY BASSEY: R (185); F & D (222)
BATH FESTIVAL R & F (259)
'BATMAN' & Related: D (217)
BAUHAUS & D (98); R (246)
BBC RADIO SESSIONS: I (113); I & R (149); I & R (169)
THE BEACH BOYS: D (40); D (65); D (80); I (133); D (141); R (201); F (224); R (229); F (248); I (259); R (262); F (270); F (300). See also MIKE LOVE, BRIAN WILSON.
THE BEASTIE BOYS & D (232); D (245)
THE BEATLES: D (38); F & D (41); F (44); D (45); F; I (50); D (62); D (70); D (83); R (92); F (94); R (94); F (98); I (108); D (112); D/R (115); D (122); F (128); R (132); D (140); D (146); D (151); F (158); F (166); D (170); D (175); D (176); I (177); D(178); D (181); D (182); D (183); R (184); F (187); I & D (193); F, R, (195); I & D (196); R (197); R (200); F (206); R (207); R (208); F (211); F (212); F (215); R & I (219); I (227); D (230); F (233); F (235); F (236); F (241); F & I & R (242); R (243); F(250); R (253); F (254); R (256); F (267); F (268); F (270); F (278); F(283); F(284); F (292); F (308). See also GEORGE HARRISON, JOHN LENNON, PAUL McCARTNEY, RINGO STARR.
BEATS INTERNATIONAL & D (136) See also THE HOUSEMARTINS.

THE BEAU BRUMMELS & UK/US D (75)
THE BEAUTIFUL SOUTH & D (136); I & D (240).
 See also THE HOUSEMARTINS.
BE-BOP DELUXE & Bill Nelson: D (220)
BECK: I & D (224); I (280); DFG (325)
THE BEE GEES: F & D (85); F & D (100)
MADELINE BELL: I (321)
BELLE & SEBASTIAN & D (237); I & D (322)
PAT BENATAR: F (313)
ARIEL BENDER: I (207)
BOYD BENNETT: F (278)
CLIFF BENNETT & THE REBEL ROUSERS:
 F & D (49); F & D (265)
CHUCK BERRY: D (53); R (124);
 R & D (150); F (276)
DAVE BERRY & D (48)
RICHARD BERRY & D (173)
PETE BEST: I & D (193)
THE BETA BAND & D (239)
THE BETTERDAYS: I & D (143)
THE BEVIS FROND & D (116); I (174)
THE B-52s & D (132); I (228); D (271)
THE BIG BOPPER & D (116)
BIG BROTHER & THE HOLDING COMPANY
 & Big Brother/Janis Joplin: D (88).
 See also JANIS JOPLIN.
BIG COUNTRY & D (130); I (163); F (271);
 F (276)
THE BIG THREE & D (83)
THE BIRDS: F & D (239).
 See also THE CREATION, QUIET MELON,
RONNIE WOOD.
JANE BIRKIN I (282)
THE BIRTHDAY PARTY & BOYS NEXT DOOR
 & D (151); I (240).
 See also NICK CAVE.
BJORK & Sugarcubes:
 D (175); D (234); I (276).
 See also THE SUGARCUBES.
CILLA BLACK: I & D (51); I & D (217)
TONY BLACKBURN: I (280)
THE BLACK CROWES & D (169)
BLACK DOG: I (285)
BLACK FLAG: I & D (184).
 See also HENRY ROLLINS.
RITCHIE BLACKMORE: I & D (228).
 See also DEEP PURPLE.
CHARLES BLACKWELL: I & D (228)
OTIS BLACKWELL: F (277)
BLACK SABBATH & D (74); R (246); I (314).
 See also TONY MARTIN, OZZY
OSBOURNE.
BLAXPLOITATION: R (226); R (260)
BLIND FAITH & D (118).
 See also ERIC CLAPTON.
'BLINDS & SHUTTERS': R (131)
BLONDIE: D (66); F & D (241); D (266)
BLODWYN PIG: I & D (200)
THE BLOW MONKEYS: I & D (183)
BLUE BEAT LABEL & D (192)
BLUE CHEER & D (197)
BLUE HORIZON LABEL: D (55); D (67);
 F (324); F (325).
BLUE OYSTER CULT: I (293)
BLUES: F & D (155); F (293)
THE BLUETONES: I & D (200)
COLIN BLUNSTONE: I & D (226).
 See also THE ZOMBIES.
BLUR & D (179); I & R & D (211); F (224);
 R & D (242)
CURT BOETTCHER & US: D (229)

MARC BOLAN/TYRANNOSAURUS REX/T.REX:
 D (36); D (54); D (64); D (84); D (95);
 F & D (77); F (127); F (128); F & D (144);
 R (179); F (190); F & D (191); R (207);
 I (210); F & D (217); F (257); I (277);
 F (324).
 See also MICKEY FINN, JOHN'S CHILDREN.
GRAHAM BOND & D (38)
'JAMES BOND': F & D (158);
 CD Reissues (286)
BONHAM'S ROCK MEMORABILIA AUCTIONS:
 F (183)
BON JOVI & D (93); D (111)
BONNIE PRINCE BILLY: F & D & I (295)
BONZO DOG BAND & D (100); I (258);
 I (320)
BOOKER T. & THE MGs: R & D (231)
THE BOO RADLEYS: I & D (192)
BOOTLEGS: F (149); F (240); F (252); F (273)
BOSTON & D (234)
DAVID BOWIE: D(43); F (48); D (63); F (75);
 D (85); F & D (90); F (109); F (97);
 F (103); F (116); D (118); R (123);
 F (126); F & D (131); F (137); F & D
 (141); F & D (147); F & D (153); F (159);
 I & R (165); F & D (172); D (185);
 R (190); R (197); F (207); D (208);
 R (215); F (222); F (226); F (227);
 F (243); F & D (249); F (251); F (254);
 F (259) F (278); R (283); F (286); F
(299). See also TIN MACHINE.
JOE BOYD: I & D (122)
BOY GEORGE: I (240); I (277).
 See also CULTURE CLUB.
BOYZONE & D (250)
KIRK BRANDON: I (191)
BRAZILIAN COLLECTABLES: F
BREAD: I & D (219)
THE BREEDERS: F & I (275)
BRITAIN'S RAREST RECORDS (232)
BRITISH COMEDY & D (236)
BRITISH INVASION & US D (114)
BRITISH ROCK'N'ROLL: I & D (161)
BRITISH SEA POWER I & D (302)
BRITPOP NOW (194)
BRITPOP THEN (195)
BRONSKI BEAT & D (72)
ELKIE BROOKS: I & D (177)
BROS & D (109)
EDGAR BROUGHTON: I (321)
ARTHUR BROWN: I & D (129); F (169)
IAN BROWN: I (315)
JAMES BROWN & D (40); D (60); F & D (214);
 F & D (215); F & D (216); D & F (217)
JOE BROWN & D (138)
PETE BROWN & D (114); I (270); I (321)
RUTH BROWN & D (65)
JACKSON BROWNE & D (102); I (220)
DENNY BRUCE: I (223)
BRUMBEAT F & D (180)
BUBBLEGUM MUSIC & D (74)
JEFF BUCKLEY & D (284)
TIM BUCKLEY & D (103)
BUFFALO SPRINGFIELD & D (142)
 See also CS&N, CSN&Y, NEIL YOUNG.
ERIC BURDON & Animals: D (183);
 Solo: D (184); I (209).
 See also THE ANIMALS.
LEROY BURGESS: F (277)
SONNY BURGESS: I & D (153)
SOLOMON BURKE & D (69); I (276)

The Beatles In America ★ Dylan and the 'Bromberg sessions' Meconubilti Special ★ Hendrix ★ Tommy on SACD ★ Earl Slick Act ★ Slash on Guns N' Roses ★ Nurse With Wound ★ Gary Crowley McGough & McGear ★ 2004 Album Preview ★ New Vinyl Chart

SOLD! The £1,240 Iron Maiden 45

RECORD COLLECTOR

FEBRUARY 2004 Issue 294 £3.30

20 LPs THAT SHOOK THE WORLD

THE BRITISH R&B EXPLOSION

EDWYN COLLINS: I (157); F & D (193); F & D (194)
GLENDA COLLINS: F & D (225)
PHIL COLLINS & D (87); F (257).
 See also GENESIS.
COLOSSEUM & D (164)
COME & D (163)
BRITISH COMEDY RECORDS: F (71)
WORLDWIDE COMEDY RECORDS: F (310)
THE COMMUNARDS & D (102)
COMPACT DISCS: F (93); F (87); F (88);
 F (89); F (90); F (94); D (104); F (105);
 F (106); F (107); F (108); D (109);
 D (110); F (152); F (223)
CONFLICT: F (270)
BRIAN CONNOLLY: F & D (212).
 See also THE SWEET.
CONVENTIONS: F (110)
RUSS CONWAY: R (195)
RY COODER & D (59)
SAM COOKE & D (44); D (243)
ALICE COOPER & D (97); R (238); I (267)
JULIAN COPE: I (267)
THE CORAL: I (283); F (290)
CORNERSHOP: I & D (225)
HUGH CORNWELL: I (168); I (304).
 See also THE STRANGLERS.
THE CORRS & D (239)
ELVIS COSTELLO: F (49); D (91); R (171);
 I & D (193); I & D (194)
COUGARS, BARONS, NERO & GLADIATORS & D (72)
COUNTRY JOE & FISH: F & D (83); R (204);
 I & D (227); I (301)
COUNTRY MUSIC: F(141); F (144); F (168)
COUNTRY ROCK SPECIAL: F & D (166)
JAYNE COUNTY: I & D (197)
COVER VERSIONS (209)
GRAHAM COXON: I (279)
KEVIN COYNE: I (275)
CRADLE OF FILTH: I & D (234)
CRAMPS & D (78)
CRASS: I (300)
RANDY CRAWFORD & D (54)
CREAM: F & D (101) R (217); I, F & D (218);
 F & I (310).
 See also ERIC CLAPTON.

CREATION RECORDS: I (310)
THE CREATION: I, F & D (191); F & I (299).
 See also THE BIRDS.
THE CREATURES: I & D (240).
 See also SIOUXSIE & THE BANSHEES.
CREEDENCE CLEARWATER REVIVAL:
 F & D (98); F (269)
CRICKETS: F & D (128); I (306).
DAVID CROSBY: I (116); I (265).
 See also CS&N, CSN&Y.
CROSBY, STILLS & NASH & D (41).
 See also DAVID CROSBY.
CROSBY, STILLS, NASH & YOUNG & D (115);
 R (200); D (303).
 See also DAVID CROSBY, NEIL YOUNG.
SHERYL CROW & D (215)
CROWDED HOUSE & D (154).
 See also NEIL FINN.
GARY CROWLEY: I (294)
CRUSHED BUTLER: F (226)
THE CULT & D (94); I & D (182); I (264)
CULTURE CLUB & D (53); I & D (231).
 See also BOY GEORGE.
THE CURE & D (61); F (106); F & D (167);
 F & D (168); F & D (169); R (187);
 F (252); F (282); I (293)
CURVED AIR & D (102)

D

DAKOTAS, EAGLES, HUNTERS & D (67)
DICK DALE & D (203)
ROGER DALTREY: I (239). See also THE WHO.
THE DAMNED: F & D (81); F & D (82);
 I (198); I (265); I & F (325)
DANCE: F (239)
DANDELION LABEL & Listing (149)
TONY DANGERFIELD: I & D (241)
DANGER MAN/THE PRISONER: D (162)
DANNY & THE JUNIORS: F & I (314)
TERENCE TRENT D'ARBY & D (106); F (282)
BOBBY DARIN & D (149); R (197)
DARK & D (172)
THE DARKNESS: I (290); F (295)
SHAUN DAVEY: I (182)
DAVE DAVIES: I (270)
BILLIE DAVIS: I & D (233)
MILES DAVIS: F (219); R & D (225); D (266);
 R (283)
THE SPENCER DAVIS GROUP: I & D (198)
DAWN OF THE REPLICANTS: I & D (237)
DANIELLE DAX & THE LEMON KITTENS:
 I & D (123)
DORIS DAY: F & D (148); R (192)
CHRIS DE BURGH & D (86); I (266)
DEACON BLUE & D (130);
RICKY ROSS: I (262)
DEAD OR ALIVE & D (150); I (180)
JAMES DEAN: F (270)
ROGER DEAN: F(267)
DEATH IN VEGAS: I & D (278)
DECCA LABEL: I (167)
DAVE DEE, DOZY, BEAKY, MICK, TICH & D (41)
DECAL LABEL: I (114)
DECEPTIVE LABEL: F (222)
KIKI DEE: I & D (197); I (317)
DEEP PURPLE: D (67); R (191); F (222);
 I (227); F (247); D (272); F & D (305).
 See also RITCHIE BLACKMORE,
 EPISODE SIX, GLENN HUGHES.
DEEP SOUL: F (252)
DEF JAM: R (251)
DEF LEPPARD: F & D (100); I (171); I (325)

THE G.T.O.s/PAMELA DE BARRES: I & D (123)
GUIDED BY VOICES I (296)
GUNS N' ROSES & D (118); D (148); I (294)
ARLO GUTHRIE & D (107)

H

STEVE HACKETT: I (272)
MERLE HAGGARD & D, R (196)
LUKE HAINES: I (264)
NORMAN HAINES & D (169)
HAIRCUT 100: I & D (170)
BILL HALEY & D (38); R & D (139); I & D (176)
TERRY HALL: I & D (182).
See also THE FUN BOY THREE.
HALL & OATES: I & D (170)
HAMBURG SCENE: R (240)
PETER HAMMILL / VAN DER GRAAF GENERATOR:
D (83); I (166); I (261)
LIONEL HAMPTON: F (279)
MARTIN HANNET: F (311)
HANOI ROCKS: F & D (141)
HAPPY MONDAYS: F & D (131)
HAPSHASH & THE COLOURED COAT:
I (299)
HARDCORE: See under U.S. Hardcore.
HARD ROCK CAFE MEMORABILIA (178)
FRANCOISE HARDY: I, F & D (310)
STEVE HARLEY & COCKNEY REBEL
& D (136); I (155)
ROY HARPER & D (95); R (185); I (321)
EMMYLOU HARRIS: I & D (149); I (240)
JET HARRIS & TONY MEEHAN & D (74)
WEE WILLIE HARRIS: I & D (164)
GEORGE HARRISON: D (104); R (208);
F (260); F (269).
See also THE BEATLES.
HARVEST LABEL: F (139); F & D (140);
R (240); F (321); F (322)
ALEX HARVEY: F & D (107) F (307)
JANCIS HARVEY: F & D (319)
PJ HARVEY & D (188); D (229); D (257).
JULIANA HATFIELD: I & D (188)
RICHIE HAVENS: F (276)
RONNIE HAWKINS: I & D (89)
HAWKWIND & D (70); F & D (157);
I & D (162); R (189); F (202); F (273)
ISAAC HAYES & I (264)
TUBBY HAYES: F (300)
JUSTIN HAYWARD: I (282)
LEE HAZLEWOOD: I & D (246)
JEFF HEALEY: I (255)
HEART & D (145)
HEAVY METAL: F & D (114); F (184);
F (203); F (204); F (205)
HEFNER: I & D (245)
RICHARD HELL: I & D (215).
See also TELEVISION.
JIMI HENDRIX: D (50); F & D (85); D (86);
D (121); R (124); F & D (133);
F & D (134); D & R (140); I (153);
D (162); I (166); D (171); R (176);
F (179); F (188); R (196); F 1967 (209);
I & R (214); R (215); R (219); F (228);
F & D (248); F (255); R (263); F (295); F
(303). See also NOEL REDDING.
DON HENLEY: I (313)
KEN HENSLEY & D (179)
HERE AND NOW TOURS & I (293)
HERMAN'S HERMITS & D (91)
NICK HEYWARD / HAIRCUT 100:
I & D (170); I (270)
HI LABEL & Singles Listing (112)

HIGH LLAMAS & D (286)
CHRIS HILLMAN: I (230).
See also THE BYRDS, THE FLYING
BURRITO BROTHERS.
EDDIE HINTON F (325)
HIP-HOP: F (246)
HOLE & D (191)
THE HOLLIES: D (71); I & D (109);
I & D (110); I & D (111); F (260); I (323)
MARK HOLLIS: I (221).
See also TALK TALK.
BUDDY HOLLY: F (56); D (88); D (101);
D (114); F (147); F (205); F (234); D (267)
HOLLYWOOD STARS: F (254)
THE HONEYBUS & D (111)
THE HONEYCOMBS & D (193)
HOOD & I (271)
MARY HOPKIN: I & D (108)
NICKY HOPKINS: F & D (183)
BRUCE HORNSBY: I (165)
HORSLIPS: I (255)
HOT CHOCOLATE & D (57)
HOT ROD: D (191)
THE HOUSE OF LOVE & D (127).
See also GUY CHADWICK.
THE HOUSEMARTINS & D (136).
See also BEATS INTERNATIONAL,
THE BEAUTIFUL SOUTH.
WHITNEY HOUSTON & D (163)
HOWLIN' WOLF & D (78)
GLENN HUGHES: I (237).
See also DEEP PURPLE.
THE HUMAN LEAGUE: I & D (187); I (264)
IAN HUNTER: I & D (213); I (264).
See also MOTT THE HOOPLE.
HUSKER DU: I & D (158)
ASHLEY HUTCHINGS: I (267)
HMV: R (112)

I

IBIZA: F (242)
ICARUS (211)
THE IDLE RACE & D (181)
IDLEWILD: I & D (249); I & D (277)
BILLY IDOL & IDOL/GEN X: D (97); I (273)
See also GENERATION X.

IMMEDIATE LABEL: F (250)
THE INCREDIBLE STRING BAND
  & Solo: D (93); R (214)
THE IN CROWD: R (263)
INDEPENDENT LABELS: F (64); F (125); D (209);
  D (210). See also BASTA, DECEPTIVE,
  DRUNKEN FISH, EARWORM, FACTORY,
  FIERCE PANDA, KOKOPOP, NEW ROSE/
  FAN CLUB, ROUGH TRADE, SKAM, SST,
  SUB POP, TJM, WURLITZER JUKEBOX,
  ZOOM & COLLECTABLE INDIE SINGLES
  series.
THE INDIGO GIRLS & D (193)
INDUSTRIAL MUSIC: F & D (185)
NEIL INNES: I & D (183)
INSPIRAL CARPETS: I & D (129)
INSTRUMENTALS: F & D (64)
INSTRUMENTAL GROUPS: F (67); F(72)
INSURING YOUR COLLECTION: F (166)
INTERNATIONAL ARTISTS LABEL: D (110)
INTERNET COLLECTING: F (246)
INVICTUS / HOT WAX LABELS: D (242)
INXS & D (114)
IQ & D (162)
IRON MAIDEN & D (98); D (135); I & D (206);
  R (257); R (272); I & D (289)
ISLAND LABEL: D (*) (60); F & D (Pt. 1) (201);
  D (Pt 2) (202); D (Pt 3), (203); D (Pt 4),
  D (204); D (205); D (206); D (207); D (208)
THE ISLEY BROTHERS: F & D (165)
IT BITES & D (129)

J

JANET JACKSON & D (189)
JAZZMAN RECORDS
  & Gerald Short: I (259)
JOE JACKSON & D (83)
MAHALIA JACKSON: D (268)
MICHAEL JACKSON: D (62); F & D (99);
  D (191); D (192); R (194); F (235)
MILLIE JACKSON: I (303)
TONY JACKSON & D (172)
CHRIS JAGGER: I & D (174)
JAH WOBBLE: I & D (228)
THE JAM & D (47); D (90); I (154);
  F (157); F (210); F (322).
  See also THE STYLE COUNCIL,
  PAUL WELLER.
JAMAICAN SOUND SYSTEMS: I (289)
JAMES & D (137); F & I (224)
ELMORE JAMES: R & D (161); R (174)
ETTA JAMES & D (58); D(200)
THE J.A.M.s / THE KLF: I & D (140)
BERT JANSCH: F & D (171); F & D (173);
  F (235); F (251)
CHAS JANKEL: I (297)
JAPAN & D (36); I & D (298)
JAPANESE UNDERGROUND: F (250)
JEAN-MICHEL JARRE & D (134); F (220)
JASON & THE SCORCHERS: I & D (166)
JEFFERSON AIRPLANE/STARSHIP:
  F & D (91); F & D (92); R (159);
  F & D (211); I (234)
WAYLON JENNINGS: I & D (189)
THE JESUS & MARY CHAIN & D (116)
JESUS JONES & D (141)
JETHRO TULL & D (86); R (108); I & D (151);
  R (199); R (214); R (229); F (258)
JJ72: F & D & I (265)
BILLY JOEL & D (70)
JOHN'S CHILDREN & D (58).
  See also MARC BOLAN.

JOHN THE POSTMAN: I & D (230)
ELTON JOHN: D (77); F (111); F (219);
  F & D (220); F & D (221); F & D (222);
  F (250); I (267).
BOB JOHNSTON F (296)
ROBERT JOHNSON & D (246)
BRIAN JONES: F (119).
  See also THE ROLLING STONES.
GLORIA JONES: I (324)
HOWARD JONES & D (69); F (192)
JANIE JONES: I & D (166)
JOHN PAUL JONES: I (221); I (241).
  See also LED ZEPPELIN.
TOM JONES: F (132); F & D (133); I (293)
WIZZ JONES: I (300)
JANIS JOPLIN & Big Brother/Joplin: D (88);
  R (175); F & I (213).
  See also BIG BROTHER &
  THE HOLDING COMPANY.
THE JORDANAIRES: I & D (169)
JOURNEY & D (235); I (315)
JOY DIVISION: F (112); D & R (221);
  R & I (238).
  See also NEW ORDER.
JUDAS PRIEST: D (310)
JUKEBOXES: F (186)
JULY: I & D (190)

K

(UK) KALEIDOSCOPE & D (125); I (206)
(US) KALEIDOSCOPE & D (109)
EDEN KANE & D (102)
KANSAS: D (313)
KATRINA AND THE WAVES & I (219)
NIGEL KENNEDY: I (205)
NIK KERSHAW: F (68)
CHAKA KHAN / RUFUS & D (68)
KID CREOLE: I (276)
KID KOALA: I (293)
JOHNNY KIDD & PIRATES & D (36);
  I & D (135); F & D (206)
KILLING JOKE & I (305)
KING BISCUIT FLOWER HOUR (225)
KING RECORDS: F & D (274)
ALBERT KING: F (274)
B.B. KING & D (52); R (265); F (274)
BEN E. KING: I & D (93)
CAROLE KING: F, D & I (239)
FREDDIE KING: F (274)
KING CRIMSON & D (101); I (148);
  R (264); F (274); I (317).
  See also IAN McDONALD, JOHN WETTON.
THE KINGPINS (188)
THE KINKS: F (62); D (73); D (99);
  I & D (169); I (183); I (200);
  F & D + F & D (246); F (260)
KATHY KIRBY I & D (288)
KISS: F & D (146); F & D (147); I (204);
  I (252)
THE KLF: I & D (140)
GLADYS KNIGHT: I (288)
MARK KNOPFLER: I & D (173); I (302).
  See also DIRE STRAITS.
KOKOPOP LABEL & Listing (163)
ALEXIS KORNER & D (58)
AL KOOPER: F (157); F & D (157);
  F & D (158); I (319)
KORN & D (248)
ALEXIS KORNER: F (324)
LEO KOTTKE & D (204)
KRAFTWERK & D (137); I (170); F (290)
BILLY J. KRAMER & D (73)

STEVIE NICKS: Solo & D (156)
NICO & D (98). See also
 THE VELVET UNDERGROUND.
HARRY NILSSON: I & D (199); R (253)
999: I & D (235)
NINJA TUNE: D & I (255)
NIRVANA (UK) & D (96); I (172)
NIRVANA (US) & D (150); F (159); D (170);
 F (178); F (210); D (236); F (296)
 See also FOO FIGHTERS.
THE NITS: I (318)
JACK NITSZCHE: F(254)
THE NITTY GRITTY DIRT BAND & D (174)
THE NOLANS & D (139)
NORTHERN SOUL: F & D (145); D (206);
 F & I (222); F (240); F (297)
NORTON RECORDS: F (283)
NOW! COMPILATIONS: R (239)
TED NUGENT: I (269)
'NUGGETS' COMPILATIONS (84)
GARY NUMAN / TUBEWAY ARMY: D & I (76);
 F & D (133); F & D (134); I (200);
 F (218); I (259)
NURSE WITH WOUND: I (294)
NWOBHM F (296)
MICHAEL NYMAN: I (281)
LAURA NYRO F (306)

O

OAK RECORDS & D (150)
OASIS & D (185); D (202); I (210); R & D (218);
 F (223); F (242); F & D (248)
OASIS: F (200)
OCEAN COLOUR SCENE: I & D (203)
PHIL OCHS: F & D (81)
SINEAD O'CONNOR & D (138)
OFFSPRING & D (262)
OI!: F & D (177)
OKEH: F & D (199)
MIKE OLDFIELD & D (128); F (206); F (226);
 R (252); I (264)
'THE OLD GREY WHISTLE TEST' ARCHIVES
 (177); I (265); F (290)
O.M.D. & D (143); I (230); I (263)
ONE HIT WONDERS: F & D (197)

THE 101ERS: I (311)
THE ONLY ONES & D (117); I & F (186)
YOKO ONO: I & D (154)
THE OPEN MIND & D (288)
ORANGE JUICE: I (157); & D (193); R (225).
 See also EDWYN COLLINS.
THE ORB: I & D (168)
ROY ORBISON & D (43); F & D (117); I (136);
 F (158); R (192); F & D (208); R (262)
GENESIS P-ORRIDGE: I & D (237).
 See also THROBBING GRISTLE.
BETH ORTON: I & D (279)
OZZY OSBOURNE & D (115); I & D (240);
 R (263); I (280).
 See also BLACK SABBATH.
OSCARS: F (283)
JIMMY OSMOND: I (261)
JOHN OTWAY: I & D (190)
THE OUTLAWS & D (36)
OVERGROUND LABEL: I & D (189)
OVERSEAS RELEASES: F (68)
OZRIC TENTACLES: R (175); I & D (260)

P

JIMMY PAGE: D & R (163); I (184);
 R & D (191); R & D (225); F (319).
 See also LED ZEPPELIN.
ROBERT PALMER & D (102); I (279)
MAY PANG: I (311)
VANESSA PARADIS: F (300)
PARADISE GARAGE & F (252)
THE PARAMOUNTS:
 See under PROCOL HARUM.
PARLIAMENT & D (163)
CHARLIE PARKER: R (258)
GRAHAM PARKER: F (266); I (313)
LARRY PARNES & D (122)
ALAN PARSONS I F & D (307)
GRAM PARSONS & D (166); F (181)
DOLLY PARTON & D (66)
PATTO & D (132)
PAVEMENT: I & D (218)
PAVLOV'S DOG & D (262)
PEARL JAM & D (163)
JOHN PEEL: I (146); I (147); I (148); I (281);
 I (305); I (306); I (307); D (318)
PENETRATION: I & D (169)
THE PENGUINS & D (202)
DAN PENN & SPOONER OLDHAM: I (244)
PENTANGLE & D (173)
PERE UBU & D (119); I (206)
CARL PERKINS & D (73); F (76); F & D (223)
LEE 'SCRATCH' PERRY: F (249); R (268);
 I (289)
JEAN-JACQUES PERREY: I & D (214)
PETER & GORDON & D (107)
GILLES PETERSON: I (295)
PET SHOP BOYS: F & D (89); D (110);
 D (126); R (142); R (151); D (171);
 R (243); F (251); F (262); I (273)
PHILADELPHIA INTERNATIONAL: F (282)
LOUIS PHILIPPE: I (312)
ANTHONY PHILLIPS: D (156).
 See also GENESIS.
SAM PHILLIPS: I (253)
PHILLIPS ROCK & POP MEMORABILIA
 AUCTIONS: F (91); F (98); F (106);
 F (110); F (118); F (122); F (131);
 F (134); F (143); F (159); F (164)
PIANO MAGIC & D (273)
WILSON PICKETT & D (48)
PICTURE DISCS (189)

FEARGAL SHARKEY / THE UNDERTONES & D (77)
SANDIE SHAW & D (57); I (184)
SHRED! F (295)
THE SHIRELLES & D (52)
SHRINE RECORDS & D (254)
JANE SIBERRY: I & D (211)
SIGUE SIGUE SPUTNIK & D (206); F (260)
SIGUR ROS: F, I & D (319)
JUDEE SILL: F (324)
SIMON & GARFUNKEL: F & D (36); F (204);
R (266). See also PAUL SIMON.
PAUL SIMON: D (248).
See also SIMON & GARFUNKEL.
NINA SIMONE: F (286)
SIMPLE MINDS & D (60); F & D (83); F (96);
D (128); I & D (186); I (298)
SIMPLY RED & D (121); D (196)
FRANK SINATRA: D (51); D (90); R & D (137);
D (138); F (227); D (276)
SINGER VS SONG: D (257)
SINGER/SONGWRITER: I & D (318)
SINGLES: F (103)
SIOUXSIE & THE BANSHEES & D (65);
D (108); R (188); I & D (306).
See also THE CREATURES.
THE SISTERS OF MERCY & D (99)
SKA, ROCKSTEADY & REGGAE: F & D (182);
F (183); F (307)
RICKY SKAGGS: I & D (150)
SKAM LABEL & D (230)
SKIFFLE: R (234)
SLADE & D (58); I (212); I (242)
SLASH: I (258). See also GUNS 'N ROSES
SLAYER & I (251)
PERCY SLEDGE & D (92)
EARL SLICK: I (294)
SLIPKNOT: F (248); F, I & D (258); I (266);
R (272)
THE SLITS & D (139); I (217)
SLY & THE FAMILY STONE & D (164)
THE SMALL FACES & K. Jones: I & D (158);
D (197); R (214)
S*M*A*S*H & D (179)
THE SMASHING PUMPKINS & D (220)
CURT SMITH: I (225).
See also TEARS FOR FEARS
ELLIOTT SMITH: I (257)
PATTI SMITH & D (204)
THE SMITHS & D (73); D (96); D (104);
I & D (159); R (172); I (176); D (204);
D (266); F (286); F (311).
See also MORRISSEY.
SMOG & D (251)
SOFT CELL & D (*) (43); D (103); I (278).
See also MARC ALMOND.
SOFT MACHINE: F (186).
See also ROBERT WYATT, KEVIN AYERS.
SOLESIDES RECORDS: I & D (257); R (258)
SONIC YOUTH & D (115); I (323)
SONNY & CHER & D (42); F & D (226)
SOTHEBY'S ROCK MEMORABILIA
AUCTIONS: F (42); F (62); F (74); F (73);
F (86); F (97); F (111); F (122); F (131);
F (134); F (159); F (170); F (183)
SOUL: F (105); F & D (145); F (249)
SOUL BROTHER: F (266)
SOUNDS INCORPORATED: F (288)
SOUNDTRACKS: F & D (188); F (226); F (273);
I (291); F (302). See also ROCK ON FILM.
SOUND BURGER: F (279)
THE SOUND: I (271)
THE SOUP DRAGONS & D (133)

THE SOUTHLANDERS: F (261)
SPACE: I & D (223)
SPACEMEN 3: F (285)
SPANDAU BALLET & D (45)
SPARKLEHORSE & D (264)
SPARKS & D (61); I & D (183); I (254); I (287).
SPEAR OF DESTINY / THEATRE OF HATE:
D (102). See also KIRK BRANDON
BRITNEY SPEARS & D (252)
SPECIALTY LABEL: D (225)
PHIL SPECTOR & D (*) (61); D (*) (62);
D (*) (63); F & D (159); F (313)
RONNIE SPECTOR: I & D (234)
CHRIS SPEDDING & D (198)
SPEKTACLE MAGAZINE: I(265)
'SKIP' SPENCE: F (242)
THE JON SPENCER BLUES EXPLOSION:
I & D (248).
See also PUSSY GALORE.
THE SPICE GIRLS & D (213); R (217);
F & D (226)
SPIRIT & D (127); F (211)
SPIRITUALIZED: I & D (268)
SPOCK'S BEARD: I (243)
SPOOKY TOOTH: D (82)
THE SPOTNICKS & D (66)
BUFFALO SPRINGFIELD: R (263)
DUSTY SPRINGFIELD & D (103); R (200);
D (237); R (254); F (279)
BRUCE SPRINGSTEEN: F (60); F & D (71);
D (82); R (89); F & D (99); F & D
(106); F & D (121); F (164); I (211);
F & R (232); I (234); F (283)
SQUEEZE & D (40); I & D (145); F (220);
D (221); I (263)
SST LABEL: F(164)
THE STANDELLS & D (141)
VIVIAN STANSHALL: I & D(189)
ALVIN STARDUST & D (60)
EDWIN STARR: F (286)
RINGO STARR & D (132); I (191); I (232);
I (285). See also THE BEATLES.
STARTING YOUR COLLECTION: F (146); F (147)
STATE OF THE MARKET: F (228); F (229)
STATIC CARAVAN: F (264)
STATUS QUO: F & D (89); F & D (90); F & D
(175); I & D (176); R & I (268); I (278);
(317).
STAX LABEL: F & D (72); F & D (73); R (174)
STEELEYE SPAN & D (225)
STEELY DAN & D (117); I & F (259)
STEPS & I (270)
STEREOLAB & D (174); F (259)
THE STEREOPHONICS & D (243)
CAT STEVENS: I (313)
SHAKIN' STEVENS & D (81); I (311)
AL STEWART: I & D (114); I (263); I (320)
ROD STEWART: I & D (116); I (280)
STIFF LITTLE FINGERS & D (152); I (293)
STING & D (166). See also THE POLICE.
MIKE STOLLER: F (286)
THE STONE ROSES & D (126); I & D (222);
F (303)
STONE THE CROWS: I (282)
THE STOOGES & D (115).
See also IGGY POP.
STORIES BEHIND THE SONGS (130)
RORY STORM & HURRICANES & D (99)
STORYTELLER: I & D (222)
STRANGELOVE: I & D (218)

THE STRANGLERS & D (75); F (111); D (265); D (270). See also J.J. BURNEL, HUGH CORNWELL.
THE STRAWBS & D (177)
BARBRA STREISAND & D (218)
STRING CHEESE INCIDENT & I (306)
STRONTIUM 90: F (218)
JOE STRUMMER: I (252). See also CLASH, 101ers
MARTY STUART: I & D (166)
STUDIO ONE LABEL: F (297)
THE STYLE COUNCIL & D (71); R (232).
See also THE JAM, PAUL WELLER.
STYX: I & D (312)
SUB POP LABEL & D (159)
SUE: D (203); D (204)
SUEDE: F & D (164); I & D (206)
SUGAR: I & D (158)
THE SUGARCUBES & D (118); I (227).
See also BJORK.
SUGAR HILL RECORDS: F & D (244)
SUICIDE: I & D (225)
BIG JIM SULLIVAN: I (320)
SUN LABEL: D (54); R (76); R (92); R (95); F (108); F, R & D (185); 7" reissues (271).
SUN RA: R (258)
SUNSHINE POP & D (217)
SUPER FURRY ANIMALS: I & D (238)
SUPERGRASS & D (191)
SUPERTRAMP: I (236)
THE SUPREMES:
See under DIANA ROSS & SUPREMES.
SURF: F & D (190); F & D (192); R (204); F (288)
SURVIVOR: I (323)
SCREAMING LORD SUTCH & D (50); I & D (241)
STUART SUTCLIFFE: F (205)
BILLY SWAN: I & D (184)
THE SWEENEY: R (266)
THE SWEET & D (66).
See also BRIAN CONNOLLY.
SWELL MAPS: I & D (149)
SWING OUT SISTER & I (301)
THE SWINGING BLUE JEANS & D (40)
DAVID SYLVIAN: I & D (128); Pt 2 (129); F (260). See also JAPAN.

TAKE THAT & D (168). See also GARY BARLOW & ROBBIE WILLIAMS
TALES OF JUSTINE: F (222)
TALKING HEADS & D (88).
See also DAVID BYRNE.
TALK TALK & D (148).
See also MARK HOLLIS.
SHEL TALMY: F (55); D (56)
TAMLA MOTOWN: See under MOTOWN.
SHARON TANDY: I (296)
TANGERINE DREAM & D (117); I (183)
HOWARD TATE: I (298)
JAMES TAYLOR: I (295)
JOHNNY TAYLOR: F (252)
MIKE TAYLOR: F & D (309)
THE TEARDROP EXPLODES & D (87)
TEARS FOR FEARS & D (70); D (124); I (262).
See also CURT SMITH
TEENAGE FANCLUB & D (167); I (282)
TELEVISION & D (148).
See also RICHARD HELL.
THE TELEVISION PERSONALITIES & TVP's:
D (142)
THE TEMPTATIONS: I & D (150); I (260)
10CC: F & D 1964-72 (55); F & D (56); I & D (190)
10,000 MANIACS & D (159)
TEN YEARS AFTER: I & D (221)
TERRORVISION & D (190)
TEXAS & D (247)
THAMES TV RECORD SALE: F (162)
THE THE & D (120); I (168); I (275)
THEATRE OF HATE/SPEAR OF DESTINY:
D (102).
See also KIRK BRANDON.
THEM: F & D (89); Van Morrison: D (149)
THERAPY? & D (181)
THIEVERY CORPORATION: I & D (312)
THIN LIZZY & D (99); F (268); I (303).
See also GARY MOORE.
THE THIRTEENTH FLOOR ELEVATORS /
ROKY ERICKSON & D (147)
THIS HEAT & D (230)
RUFUS THOMAS: I & D (194)
RICHARD THOMPSON: I (283); I (321)
THE THOMPSON TWINS & D (58)
GEORGE THOROGOOD: I (301)
THRASH METAL: F (269)
THE THRILLS: I (289)
THROBBING GRISTLE & D (98); R (282).
See also GENESIS P-ORRIDGE.
THUNDER & D (142)
THUNDERCLAP NEWMAN: I (323)
'THUNDERBIRDS' & D (167)
JOHNNY THUNDERS & THE NEW YORK
DOLLS & D (143); F (183); F (261)
TANITA TIKARAM & D (127)
'TIL TUESDAY: I & D (170)
TIN MACHINE & D (131).
See also DAVID BOWIE.
TINDERSTICKS & D (175); I & D (231)
TINTERN ABBEY: F (284)
TINY TIM: F & D (210)
TJM RECORDS: D (126)
TOMORROW: I & D (187)
TOP 20 COLLECTABLE ARTISTS: F (158); F (245)
TOP 100 COLLECTABLE CDs (104)
TOP 100 RAREST RECORDS (304)
TOP 100 UK AUCTION ITEMS (100)

TOP 100 UK EPs (101)
TOP 100 UK LPs (102)
TOP 100 UK SINGLES (100)
TOP 100 RAREST UK RECORDS (232)
TOP 200 ALBUMS OF THE 20TH CENTURY (245)
TOP 500 COLLECTABLE ARTISTS: 1996 (201);
  1997 (213); 1998 (225); 1999 (237);
  2000 (248)
TOP 1000 RARE RECORDS (77)
TOP OF THE POPS: F (173)
TOWERING INFERNO: I & D (194)
THE TORNADOS: I & D (211) Short Take (278).
  See also JOE MEEK.
TOTO & I (292)
ALLEN TOUSSAINT: F (256)
PETE TOWNSHEND: D (108); I & R (245).
  See also THE WHO.
T'PAU & D (104)
GRANT TRACY & SUNSETS: I & D (210)
STAN TRACY & I (272)
TRAFFIC & D (63); F (299)
TRANSVISION VAMP & D (119)
THE TRASHMEN: F, I & D (227)
TRAVIS & D (249)
THE TREMELOES & D (47)
T. REX: See under MARC BOLAN.
TRIUMPH LABEL: F (186)
THE TROGGS & D (46); R (273)
TROJAN RECORDS: F (251); F & D(287)
ROBIN TROWER: I & D(185); I (266)
THE TUBES & I (305)
TUBEWAY ARMY: See under GARY NUMAN.
MOE TUCKER: I & D (151).
  See also THE VELVET UNDERGROUND.
BIG JOE TURNER & D (241)
IKE & TINA TURNER & D (64)
SHANIA TWAIN & D (248)
2-TONE LABEL: D (122); D (123); R (171);
  F, I & D (300)
TWIGGY: I & D (219)
TWINKLE & D (178)
CONWAY TWITTY: R (82); F & D (168)
TYRANNOSAURUS REX:
  See under MARC BOLAN.

U

U2 & D (51); D (85); D (103); F & D (107);
  F & R (112); F & D (127); R (145);
  D (161); D (162); F (174); D (193);
  R & D (211); F (234); F & D (241);
  D (257); F (301)(326)
UB40 & D (78)
UFO & D (259)
ULTRAVOX / JOHN FOXX: D (39)
THE UNDERTONES / FEARGAL SHARKEY:
  D (77); I (169); F (292)
UNIT FOUR PLUS TWO & D (71)
UNIVERSAL: F (268)
MIDGE URE: I (267)
URIAH HEEP & D (126); I (258)
U.S. HARDCORE: Overview Pt 1 (156);
  Overview Pt 2 & Top 100 7" Singles (157)

V

RICKY VALANCE & D (212)
RICHIE VALENS & D (76)
VAN DER GRAAF GENERATOR &
  PETER HAMMILL & D (83); F (255)
TOWNES VAN ZANDT & D (270)
VANGELIS & D (217)
THE VAPORS: F (210)
COLIN VEARNCOMBE: I (241)
THE VELVELETTES: I (308)

THE VELVET UNDERGROUND & D (49);
  R (120); R (194); F (233); F (265);
  F (310). See also JOHN CALE, NICO,
  LOU REED, MOE TUCKER.
VENOM & I (250); F (321)
THE VENTURES & D (48)
MIKE VERNON & D (72); D (73); I (324)
VERTIGO LABEL: F (79); F (123); Pt 2 (124);
  F (314); F (315)
THE VERVE: F & D (219)
THE VIBRATORS & D (239)
VIDEO: I & F (144); F (150)
VIETNAM: F (275)
VILLAGE THING LABEL & D (169)
GENE VINCENT: F & D (70); R (103);
  I & D (213); D (247)
THE VIOLENT FEMMES: I & D (180)
TONY VISCONTI & D (78)
VOICE OF THE BEEHIVE & D (119)
VOLUME CD MAGAZINE: F (165)

W

TOM WAITS & D (236)
RICK WAKEMAN: I & D (196); I (292)
JUNIOR WALKER: F & D (198)
SCOTT WALKER & D (127)
THE WALKER BROTHERS & D (47)
WAR & D (196)
CLIFFORD T. WARD & D (246)
WAR OF THE WORLDS: F & D (312)
WARP RECORDS: F (244)
DIONNE WARWICK & D (41); I (281)
GENO WASHINGTON: I & D (253)
WAS (NOT WAS) & D (157); I (215)
W.A.S.P. & D (120)
THE WATERBOYS/MIKE SCOTT: D (142); I (226)
PETE WATERMAN: R (256)
ROGER WATERS & D (132); I (317).
  See also PINK FLOYD.
CHARLIE WATTS: D (253).
  See also ROLLING STONES.
ANDY WEATHERALL & D (257)
JIMMY WEBB: I & D (174); I (311)
THE WEDDING PRESENT & D (117);
  I & D (162); I (266)
BERT WEEDON & D (60); I (249)
PAUL WELLER: I (154); R (157); D (182);
  I (289); F (322).
  See also THE JAM, THE STYLE COUNCIL.
KIM WESTON: I (319)
WET WET WET & D (108)
JOHN WETTON: I (244).
  See also ASIA, KING CRIMSON.
WHAM! & D (74); D (92); Short Take (220).
  See also GEORGE MICHAEL.
THE WHAT FOUR & D (239)
SNOWY WHITE: I (195)
THE WHITE STRIPES & D (291)
PETER WHITEHEAD: I (184)
WHITESNAKE & D (56); R (181)
SLIM WHITMAN & D (172)
THE WHO: F & D (53); D (66); D (76); R (79);
  D (84); R (126); F (164); F (165);
  R (179); I & D (181); I (192); R (203);
  F (211); F (215); F & D (228);
  F & D (229); F & D (230); F & D (241);
  R (246); R (255); R (263); F (268);
  F (277). See also ROGER DALTREY,
  PETE TOWNSHEND.
JANE WIEDLIN & SOLO / GO-GO's: D (111)
KIM WILDE & D (99); I & D (169); I (307)
MARTY WILDE & I (275)

THE WILDE FLOWERS (186)
THE WILDHEARTS: I & D (195)
WILD TURKEY: I & D (200)
THE WILD, WILD KLUBS: F (239)
ANDY WILLIAMS & I (251)
HANK WILLIAMS & D (125)
LARRY WILLIAMS & D (133)
ROBBIE WILLIAMS: D (245); R (256);
   F (262); F (305).
   See also TAKE THAT.
BRIAN WILSON: I (185); F (303); I (310)
JACKIE WILSON & D (56)
WINGS: See under PAUL McCARTNEY.
STEVE WINWOOD & D (121); R (189).
   See also BLIND FAITH, THE SPENCER
   DAVIS GROUP.
WIRE & D (100)
MARK WIRTZ & D (188)
WISHBONE ASH & D (186)
WIZZARD: See under ROY WOOD.
BOBBY WOMACK & D (77)
STEVIE WONDER: D (47); D (82)
THE WONDER STUFF & D (124); I (258)
'WONDERWALL': I (233)
RONNIE WOOD: F (228).
   See also THE BIRDS, THE CREATION,
   THE ROLLING STONES.
ROY WOOD / WIZZARD & D (80);
   I & F (179); I & D (180).
   See also THE MOVE.
LINK WRAY & D (85); I (168)
WRECKLESS ERIC & I (305)
RICK WRIGHT & SOLO: D (132);
   I & D (206). See also PINK FLOYD.
WRITING ON THE WALL & D (201)
WURLITZER JUKEBOX LABEL & D (227)
ROBERT WYATT & D (80); I (154);
REISSUES DISCUSSED (264)
BILL WYMAN: I (231); I (261).
   See also THE ROLLING STONES.
PETER WYNGARDE: I & D (206)

X
XOTIC MIND LABEL: F (196)
X-RAY SPEX & D (123); I (197)
XTC & D (135); I & D (209); F (261); I (272);
   I (318)

Y
THE YARDBIRDS: D & R (68); D (134);
   D (152); I & R (215).
   See also ERIC CLAPTON.
YAZOO / ALISON MOYET & D (67)
YES & D (98); R (221); F & I (249); F (269).
   See also PETER BANKS, TOMORROW.
NEIL YOUNG: F & D (143); F & D (144);
   F & D (145); F (176); F & D (192); R(200);
   I & D (203); F (253); F (272); I (278).
   See also BUFFALO SPRINGFIELD, CSN&Y.
PAUL YOUNG & D (50)

Z
FRANK ZAPPA & THE MOTHERS OF
   INVENTION: F & D (61); D (93);
   F & D (118); D (165); D (171); D (177);
   D (191); R (199); R (205); F (251); R (266)
THE ZOMBIES & D (50).
   See also COLIN BLUNSTONE.
ZOOM LABEL: D (74)
Z.T.T. LABEL: F & D (110); F & D (111);
   F & D (112); F (301)
ZZ TOP & D (103

BRITISH PSYCHEDELIA GUIDE
This series of collectable British psychedelic
records ran in alphabetical order:

231   Accent – Dantalian's Chariot
232   David – The Fut
233   Elmer Gantry's Velvet Opera – The Hush
234   Icarus – Junior's Eyes
235   Kaleidoscope – Lyons & Malone
236   Neil MacArthur – Mellow Candle
237   Mighty Baby – Motivation
238   The Move – Now
239   Octopus – Owl
240   Pandamonium – Pregnant Insomnia
241   The Pretty Things – The Rokes
242   The Rolling Stones
243   Rupert's People – The Searchers
244   Secondhand – Skip Bifferty
245   Sleepy – Soft Machine
246   Sons Of Man – The Sweet
247   Sweet Feeling – Tinkerbell's Fairydust
248   Tintern Abbey – Traffic
249   The Troggs – The 23rd Turnoff
250   Twink – Vamp
251   Van Der Graaf Generator
252   Velvet Hush – Walham Green
253   Gary Walker – White Trash
254   The Who
255   Wild Silk – Mark Wirtz
256   World Of Oz – Writing On The Wall
257   Yardbirds
258   Yes
259   The Zombies
260   "Chocolate Soup For Diabetics"
       compilations
261   "Perfumed Garden" compilations
262   "Rubble" & "Circus Days" compilations
263   "Rubble" compilations
264   Nuggets 2
265   Acid Drops, Space Dust, etc
266   Psych Comps A–E
267   See For Miles
268   Psych Comps E–H
269   Psych Comps H–M
270   Psych Comps Pa–Ps
271   Psych Comps Sa–We

Sleeve Type A: coloured wavy lines with small box on front (left), large box on reverse (right).

Sleeve Type B: coloured wavy lines without box on front (left), with large box on reverse (right).

Sleeve Type C: multicoloured shapes on front (left) and LP details on reverse (right).

Green sleeve Type 1: straight cut at top (left) and "6/- to 50/- record tokens" on reverse (right).

Green sleeve Type 1B: wavy cut at top (left) and "6/- to 50/- record tokens" on reverse (right).

Green sleeve Type 2: rectangular box on front (left), "6/- to 50/- record tokens" on reverse (right).

Green sleeve Type 3: wavy cut at top (left) and "Fran The Fan" advert on reverse (right).

Green sleeve Type 4: wavy cut at top (left) and "Morphy-Richards offer" advert on reverse (right).

Green sleeve Type 5: straight cut at top (left), "Fran The Fan, Dear Miss Brown" ad. on reverse (right).

Green sleeve Type 6: top wavy cut, front rectangular box (left), "6/- to 50/-" on reverse (right).

Green sleeve Type 7: wavy cut at top (left) and "Big M" advert on reverse (right).

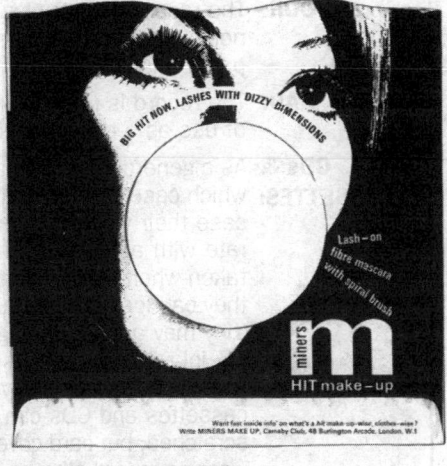

Green sleeve Type 8: wavy cut at top (left) and "Hit make-up" advert on revesre (right).

RECORD COLLECTOR'S
GRADING SYSTEM

In order to assist everyone who buys and sells rare discs, *Record Collector* magazine has originated a set of standards for the condition of second-hand records, cassettes and CDs. Anyone buying or selling records through the magazine must use our conditions to state what amount of wear and tear the disc, its sleeve and/or contents have been subject to. The seven standard condition categories, and a description of what each one means, are listed below:

MINT: The record itself is in brand new condition with no surface marks or deterioration in sound quality. The cover and any extra items such as the lyric sheet, booklet or poster are in perfect condition. Records advertised as Sealed or Unplayed should be Mint.

EXCELLENT: The record shows some signs of having been played, but there is very little lessening in sound quality. The cover and packaging might have slight wear and/or creasing.

VERY GOOD: The record has obviously been played many times, but displays no major deterioration in sound quality, despite noticeable surface marks and the occasional light scratch. Normal wear and tear on the cover or extra items, without any major defects, is acceptable.

GOOD: The record has been played so much that the sound quality has noticeably deteriorated, perhaps with some distortion and mild scratches. The cover and contents suffer from folding, scuffing of edges, spine splits, discoloration, etc.

FAIR: The record is still just playable but has not been cared for properly and displays considerable surface noise; it may even jump. The cover and contents will be torn, stained and/or defaced.

POOR: The record will not play properly due to scratches, bad surface noise, etc. The cover and contents will be badly damaged or partly missing.

BAD: The record is unplayable or might even be broken, and is only of use as a collection-filler.

CDs & CASSETTES: As a general rule, CDs and cassettes either play perfectly — in which case they are in Mint condition — or they don't, in which case their value is minimal. Cassette tape is liable to deteriorate with age, even if it remains unplayed, so care should be taken when buying old tapes. CDs are difficult to grade visually: they can look perfect but actually be faulty, while in other cases they may appear damaged but still play perfectly. Cassette and CD inlays and booklets should be graded in the same way as record covers and sleeves. In general, the plastic containers for cassettes and CDs can easily be replaced if they are broken or scratched, but card covers and digipaks are subject to the same wear as record sleeves.

RECORD COLLECTOR'S
GRADING READY RECKONER

This Ready Reckoner will help you work out the value of a record in any condition. For example, if you see a disc which is valued at £10 in Mint condition, but which you consider to be in only Very Good condition, then you can consult the Ready Reckoner and find out the appropriate price for the record — in this case, £5. As very few collectors are interested in records in Poor or Bad condition, we consider that any disc worth less than £10 in Mint condition is effectively worthless in Poor or Bad condition.

MINT	EX	VG	Good	Fair	Poor	Bad
1,000	800	500	300	150	80	25
500	400	250	150	75	40	12
300	240	150	90	45	25	8
250	200	125	75	38	20	6
200	160	100	60	30	15	5
150	120	75	45	25	13	4
125	100	60	38	18	12	3
100	80	50	30	15	8	2.50
75	60	35	22	10	6	2
50	40	25	15	8	4	1.50
40	32	20	12	6	3	1
30	25	15	9	4.50	2.50	—
25	20	12	7.50	3.50	2	—
22	18	11	6.50	3	1.75	—
20	16	10	6	2.50	1.50	—
15	12	8	4.50	2	1	—
12	10	6	3.50	1.75	0.75	—
10	8	5	3	1.50	—	—
8	6	4	2.50	1	—	—
7	5	3.50	2	0.75	—	—
6	4.50	3	1.75	—	—	—
5	4	2.50	1.50	—	—	—
4	3.25	2	1.25	—	—	—
3	2.50	1.50	1	—	—	—
2	1.75	1	—	—	—	—

NOTES

NOTES

NOTES